2023 Higher Education Directory®

Published by

Higher Education Publications, Inc.

Edited by

Mary Pat Rodenhouse

Reston, Virginia

2023

2023 Edition

Copyright © 2022 by
Higher Education Publications, Inc.
7245 Arlington Boulevard, Suite 319
Falls Church, VA 22042
(888) 349-7715
(571) 313-0478
FAX (571) 313-0526
Email: info@hepinc.com
Internet address: www.hepinc.com

Carnegie classification codes with permission from
The Carnegie Foundation for the Advancement of Teaching.

Internet addresses (URL's) were originally drawn from lists maintained by Washington and Lee University and the University of North Carolina-Chapel Hill and through the annual survey sent out by Higher Education Publications, Inc.

Printed in the United States of America

ISBN-13: 978-0-914927-00-6
ISSN 0736-0797
Library of Congress Catalogue Card Number: 83-641119
Library of Congress Cataloging-in Publication Data

HEP. . . Higher Education Directory®
    Falls Church, VA; Higher Education Publications.
    V.: 28cm
    Annual
    Began with issue for 1983.

    A directory of accredited postsecondary, degree-granting institutions in the U.S., its possessions and territories accredited by regional, national, professional and specialized agencies recognized as accrediting bodies by the U.S. Secretary of Education and the Council for Higher Education Accreditation (CHEA) which honors recognition provided by the former Council on Postsecondary Accreditation (COPA)/Commission on Recognition of Postsecondary Accreditation (CORPA)
    Description based on 2023.
    Cover title: 2023 Higher Education Directory®
    Spine title: 2023 Higher Education Directory® Forty-first Edition

    ISSN 0736-0797 = The Higher Education Directory®.

 1. Education, Higher—United States—Directories.
 2. Recognized accrediting agencies and associations—United States—Directories.
 3. Acronyms, explanatory notes and symbols—United States—Directories.
 4. Institution changes (additions, deletions, mergers and name changes)—United States—Directories.
 5. Administrative officers, titles and title codes—United States—Directories.
 6. United States Department of Education offices, statewide agencies for higher education and educational associations (and consortia)—United States—Directories.
 7. Religious affiliation by denomination.
 8. Carnegie classification codes.
 9. Statistics.
10. Universities and colleges—United States—Directories.
11. College administrators alphabetical listing, phone numbers—United States—Directories.
12. Regional, national, professional and specialized accreditation alphabetical listing—United States—Directories.
13. Institutional FICE & Unit ID Number listing—United States—Directories.
14. Institutional alphabetical listing—United States—Directories.
 I. Higher Education Publications, Inc.
 II. Title: Higher Education Directory®.

L901.E34 378.73-dc19 83-641119 AACR 2 MARC-S

Table of Contents

Dedication and Acknowledgments

This 41st edition of the Higher Education Directory is again dedicated to Frederick F. Hafner, who founded Higher Education Publications, Inc. on September 26, 1982. He steadfastly shepherded it from the print to the digital age with fairness, integrity and pride. Mr. Hafner passed away on December 25, 2020 and is missed by the many who knew and loved him.

Forty years ago, Higher Education Publications, Inc. was formed to produce a directory to succeed the Department of Education's *Education Directory: Colleges and Universities*.

Our thanks to the thousands of people who have supplied us the necessary data contained in the directory. We are most appreciative of the many subscribers who have supported us in our efforts to bring you the most accurate and current information available. And, a special thanks to all of you who suggest im-provements to our directory.

The accuracy and completeness of the contents of the 2022 edition was assured by a group of editors, updating and proofing specialists including Mary Pat Rodenhouse, Jodi Mondragon, Emmy Brown, Jackie Hafner, and Doris Jean. Barbara Herrman handled our typesetting. Mark Schreiber managed the HigherEd Direct update system and the database.

You may be familiar with our website, but if you have not yet visited it, I encourage you to go to www. hepinc.com. The site features the latest news on higher education, accreditations and administrative changes along with many helpful resources. Also, please visit our LinkedIn and Facebook pages. We strive to continue to meet the goals we established for ourselves forty years ago—to provide you with the most authoritative, timely and accurate information on the higher education community.

Reston, Virginia

Foreword

The 2023 edition of the *Higher Education Directory®* contains listings of accredited, degree-granting institutions of postsecondary education in the United States and its territories.

Criteria for Listing in this Directory

To be listed in this Directory, an institution must meet the following guidelines:

(1) They are degree-granting (legally authorized to offer and are offering a program of college-level studies leading toward a degree[1]);

(2) They have submitted the information required for listing; and

(3) They meet one of the following criteria for listing:

    A. The institution is accredited at the college level by an accrediting agency that is recognized by the U.S. Secretary of Education;

    B. The institution holds pre-accredited status with an accrediting agency recognized by the U.S. Secretary of Education whose recognition includes the pre-accreditation status;

    C. The institution is accredited at the college level by an accrediting agency recognized by the Council for Higher Education Accreditation (CHEA).

"College level" means a postsecondary associate, baccalaureate, post-baccalaureate, or rabbinical education program.

Verification of Accreditations

Verification of each accreditation for all institutions was done by comparing the accreditation against the current Directory (and updated lists) for each respective regional, national, professional and specialized association or agency, along with telephone calls to numerous accrediting associations whenever there was a question of accuracy. Over 20,000 accreditations were verified through September 2022.

The reader is reminded that many institutions have programs which may not be recognized by a professional or specialized association, but are considered fine programs. The institutions may or may not have sought such recognition.

General Organization of the Directory

Our approach to the organization of the material is to make the desired information readable and easy to find. There are four indexes which are cross-referenced to the main institutional listing.

A. Prologue
    1. Accrediting agencies with addresses. Regional accrediting commissions are listed alphabetically while national, professional and specialized bodies are listed alphabetically under headings showing their specialties.
    2. Acronyms used in the Directory for accrediting bodies are listed alphabetically.
    3. Explanatory notes and symbols.
    4. U.S. postal abbreviations of states.
    5. Institution changes.
    6. Administrative officers' description and job codes.
    7. U.S. Department of Education offices.
    8. Statewide agencies of higher education.
    9. Higher education associations.
    10. Consortia of institutions of higher education.
    11. Association name index.
    12. Religious affiliation by denomination.
    13. Carnegie classification codes.
    14. Statistical data.

B. College and university listings by state with institutional characteristics and administrative officers.
    1. Institution Name. If an * appears before the institution's name, it is a part of a system. A line between institutions separates two systems.
    2. Alpha Code. The first institution listed on a page is coded (A), the second (B), etc. The Administrators' index is also coded to enable the reader to locate the desired institution quickly.
    3. Address.
    4. County.
    5. FICE Identification. This was the Federal Interagency Commission on Education number originally assigned by the Department of Education. We continue to use the term FICE. However, the Department of Education in their Office of Student Financial Assistance uses OPEID, Office of Postsecondary Education Identification. OPEID consists of the first six digits of the FICE plus two more digits indicating branch campuses. Numbers beginning with 66 are for accredited institutions for which we cannot locate a FICE or OPEID number. These are identification numbers only.
    6. Telephone Number.
    7. Unit ID Number. A unique number developed by the National Center for Education Statistics (NCES) for the Education Department's IPEDS Reports.
    8. Carnegie Classification Code. (see page **xlviii**)
    9. Main FAX Number.
    10. School Calendar.
    11. URL (Universal Resource Locator).
    12. Date Established.
    13. Annual Tuition & Fees for 2020-21 school year.
    14. Fall 2020 Enrollment. Head count (not FTE) in degree programs as reported on the latest IPEDS survey.
    15. Type of Student Body.
    16. Affiliation or Control.
    17. IRS Status.
    18. Highest Degree Offered.
    19. Accreditation (see page **vi**). **N.B. Institutional accreditation is in bold face.**
    20. Administrative and academic officers with job classification code (see page **xxvi** for descriptions).
    21. Non-system branch campuses. The names of these campuses are in italic type and their listings are shortened. Non-system branch campuses are listed if they are identified by the parent institutions' accrediting organization as a branch campus.

C. Index of administrators is an alphabetical listing of all the administrators with their most direct phone number and E-mail address. The page and reference letter indicate the page on which the administrator's institution listing begins.

D. Index of regional, national, professional and specialized accreditation alphabetically by state. This index standardizes and simplifies reviewing of the 151 accrediting classifications.

E. FICE number index. Numeric listing of FICE number and school.

F. Alphabetic index of institutions.

---

[1]The *Higher Education Directory®* lists degree-granting institutions approved by regional, national, professional or specialized accrediting agencies.

Accrediting Agencies

The following regional, national, professional and specialized accrediting agencies are recognized by the U.S. Secretary of Education or the Council for Higher Education Accreditation (CHEA). The U.S. Department of Education (USDE) dates specified are the date of initial listing as a U.S. Department of Education recognized agency, the date of the U.S. Secretary's most recent grant of renewed recognition based on the last full review of the agency by the National Advisory Committee on Institutional Quality and Integrity, and the date of the agency's next scheduled review for renewal of recognition.[1]   The Council for Higher Education (CHEA) date reflects initial recognition by CHEA.

Regional Accrediting Bodies

Delaware, District of Columbia, Maryland, New Jersey, New York, Pennsylvania, Puerto Rico, Virgin Islands and throughout the U.S.

Middle States Commission on Higher Education   M
   USDE: 1952/2017/2023   CHEA: 2013
1007 North Orange Street, 4th Floor, MB #166
Wilmington, DE 19801
(267) 284-5026
Heather Perfetti, President
E-mail: info@msche.org
URL: www.msche.org

Connecticut, Maine, Massachusetts, New Hampshire, Rhode Island, Vermont

New England Commission of Higher Education   EH
   USDE: 1952/2018/2023   CHEA: 2013
301 Edgewater Place, Suite 210
Wakefield, MA 01880
(781) 425-7785 Fax (781) 425-1001
Lawrence Schall, President
E-mail: info@neche.org
URL: www.neche.org

Arizona, Arkansas, Colorado, Illinois, Indiana, Iowa, Kansas, Michigan, Minnesota, Missouri, Nebraska, New Mexico, North Dakota, Ohio, Oklahoma, South Dakota, West Virginia, Wisconsin, Wyoming and throughout the U.S.

Higher Learning Commission   HLC
   USDE: 1952/2017/2023   CHEA: 2015
230 South LaSalle Street, Suite 7-500
Chicago, IL 60604-1411
(800) 621-7440 Fax (312) 263-7462
Barbara Gellman-Danley, President
E-mail: info@hlcommission.org
URL: www.hlcommission.org

Alaska, Idaho, Montana, Nevada, Oregon, Utah, Washington and throughout the U.S.

Northwest Commission on Colleges and Universities NW
   USDE: 1952/2018/2023   CHEA: 2019
8060 165th Avenue, NE, Suite 200
Redmond, WA 98052
(425) 558-4224 Fax (205) 525-9848
Sonny Ramaswamy, President
E-mail: info@nwccu.org
URL: www.nwccu.org

Alabama, Florida, Georgia, Kentucky, Louisiana, Mississippi, North Carolina, South Carolina, Tennessee, Texas, Virginia

Commission on Colleges
Southern Association of Colleges and Schools   SC
   USDE: 1952/2019/2022   CHEA: 2015
1866 Southern Lane
Decatur, GA 30033-4097
(404) 679-4500 Fax (404) 679-4558
Belle S. Wheelan, President
E-mail: questions@sacscoc.org
URL: www.sacscoc.org

California, Hawaii, American Samoa, Guam, Commonwealth of the Northern Marianas, Federated States of Micronesia, Republic of the Marshall Islands, Republic of Palau and throughout the U.S.

Senior College and University Commission
Western Association of Schools and Colleges   WC
   USDE: 1952/2018/2023   CHEA: 2014
1080 Marina Village Pkwy, Suite 500
Alameda, CA 94501
(510) 748-9001 Fax (510) 748-9797
Jamienne Studley, President
E-mail: wasc@wscuc.org
URL: www.wscuc.org

Accrediting Commission for Community and Junior Colleges
Western Association of Schools and Colleges   WJ
   USDE: 1952/2019/2024   CHEA: 2016
331 J Street, Suite 200
Sacramento, CA 95814
(415) 506-0234 Fax (415) 506-0238
Mac Powell, President
E-mail: accjc@accjc.org
URL: www.accjc.org

[1]U.S. Department of Education, Nationally Recognized Accrediting Agencies, www2.ed.gov/admins/finaid/accred/accreditation.html.

National, Professional and Specialized Accrediting Bodies

Acupuncture

Accreditation Commission for Acupuncture and Herbal Medicine (ACAHM)
USDE: 1988/2021/2024
8941 Aztec Drive, Suite 2
Eden Praire, MN 55347
(952) 212-2434   Fax (952) 657-7068
Mark S. McKenzie, Executive Director
E-mail: info@acahm.org
URL: www.acahm.org

First-professional master's degree, professional master's level certificate and diploma programs and professional post-graduate doctoral programs in acupuncture and herbal medicine, and free-standing institutions that offer such programs **ACUP**

Allied Health

Accrediting Bureau of Health Education Schools (ABHES)
USDE: 1969/2021/2026
6116 Executive Boulevard, Suite 730
North Bethesda, MD 20852
(301) 291-7550
India Y. Tips, Executive Director
E-mail: info@abhes.org
URL: www.abhes.org

Institutions specializing in allied health education **ABHES**
Specialized programs for
Medical assistant **MAAB**
Medical laboratory technician **MLTAB**
Surgical technologist **SURTEC**

Commission on Accreditation of Allied Health Education Programs (CAAHEP)
CHEA: 2001
9355 113th Street N, #7709
Seminole, FL 33775
(727) 210-2350   Fax (727) 210-2354
Gina Scarboro, Executive Director
E-mail: mail@caahep.org
URL: www.caahep.org

The Commission on Accreditation of Allied Health Education Programs (CAAHEP) is recognized as an accrediting agency for accreditation of education for the allied health occupations. In carrying out its accreditation activities, CAAHEP cooperates with the Committees on Accreditation sponsored by various allied health and medical specialty organizations. CAAHEP is the coordinating agency for accreditation of education for the following allied health occupations:
Advanced cardiovascular sonography **ACS**
Anesthesia technologist **AT**
Anesthesiologist assistant **AA**
Art therapist **ACATE**
Assistive technology practitioner **ATECH**
Blood bank technology **BBT**
Cardiovascular technologist **CVT**
Clinical researcher **CR**
Cytotechnologist **CYTO**
Diagnostic medical sonographer **DMS**
Emergency medical technician-paramedic **EMT**
Exercise science **EXSC**
Kinesiotherapy **KIN**
Lactation consultant **LC**
Medical assistant **MAC**
Medical illustrator **MIL**
Neurodiagnostic technologist **NDT**
Orthotist/prosthetist **OPE**
Perfusionist **PERF**
Polysomnographic technologist **POLYT**
Recreation therapist **CARTE**

Surgical assistant **SURGA**
Surgical technologist **SURGT**

Anesthesia Technology

Commission on Accreditation of Allied Health Education Programs (see listing under Allied Health)
Committee on Accreditation for Anesthesia Technology Education
(612) 836-3311
Marc McGaffic, Chair
E-mail: coaatechchair@gmail.com

Programs for anesthesia technology **AT**

Anesthesiologist Assistant

Commission on Accreditation of Allied Health Education Programs (see listing under Allied Health)
Accreditation Review Committee for the Anesthesiologist Assistant
(612) 836-3311
Jennifer Anderson Warwick, Executive Director
E-mail: arc-aa@arc-aa.org

Post-baccalaureate programs for anesthesiologist assistant **AA**

Art

Commission on Accreditation
National Association of Schools of Art and Design (NASAD)
USDE: 1966/2018/2023
11250 Roger Bacon Drive, Suite 21
Reston, VA 20190
(703) 437-0700   Fax (703) 437-6312
Karen P. Moynahan, Executive Director
E-mail: info@arts-accredit.org
URL: nasad.arts-accredit.org

Institutions and departments within institutions offering degree and non-degree granting programs in art/design and art/design-related programs **ART**

Art Therapy

Commission on Accreditation of Allied Health Education Programs (see listing under Allied Health)
Accreditation Council for Art Therapy Education (ACATE)
4875 Eisenhower Avenue, Suite 240
Alexandria, VA 22304
(724) 830-1140
Ron Hunt, Coordinator
E-mail: acatecouncil@gmail.com

Programs for the art therapist **ACATE**

Assistive Technology

Commission on Accreditation of Allied Health Education Programs (see listing under Allied Health)
Committee on Accreditation for Rehabilitation Engineering and Assistive Technology Education (CoA-RATE)
2025 M Street NW, Suite 800
Washington, DC 20036
(202) 367-1121
Andrea Van Hook, Executive Director
E-mail: execoffice@resna.org

Programs for the assistive technology practitioner **ATECH**

Athletic Training

Commission on Accreditation of Athletic Training Education (CAATE)
CHEA: 2014
2001 K Street NW, 3rd Floor North

Washington, DC 20006
(512) 733-9700
Dale West, Executive Director
E-mail: support@caate.net
URL: www.caate.net

Programs for athletic training **CAATE**

Audiology

Accreditation Commission for Audiology Education
CHEA: 2012
11480 Commerce Park Drive, Suite 220
Reston, VA 20191
(703) 226-1056   Fax (703) 790-8631
Andrew Stafford, Director of Professional Standards and Credentialing
E-mail: info@acaeaccred.org
URL: www.acaeaccred.org

Programs leading to the Doctor of Audiology degree **ACAE**

Council on Academic Accreditation in Audiology and Speech Language Pathology
American Speech-Language-Hearing Association (ASHA)
USDE: 1967/2021/2026   CHEA: 2003
2200 Research Boulevard, #310
Rockville, MD 20850-3289
(301) 296-5700   Fax (301) 296-8570
Kimberlee Moore, Director of Accreditation
E-mail: accreditation@asha.org
URL: caa.asha.org

Doctoral degree programs in audiology **AUD**

Aviation

Aviation Accreditation Board International
CHEA: 2013
115 South 8th Street, Suite 102
Opelika, AL 36801
(334) 748-9359   Fax (334) 748-9360
Guy Smith, President
E-mail: ceci@aabi.aero
URL: www.aabi.aero

Non-engineering programs for aviation **AAB**

Behavior Analysis

Accreditation Board
Association for Behavior Analysis International
CHEA: 2021
550 W. Centre Avenue
Portage, MI 49024
(269) 402-9310
Jenna Mrljak, ABAI Education Manager
E-mail: abaiaccreditation@abainternational.org
URL: https://accreditation.abainternational.org

Programs in behavior analysis **ABAI**

Bible College Education

Commission on Accreditation
Association for Biblical Higher Education (ABHE)
USDE: 1952/2017/2022   CHEA: 2001
5850 T. G. Lee Boulevard, Suite 130
Orlando, FL 32822
(407) 207-0808   Fax (407) 207-0840
Lisa Beatty, Director, Commission on Accreditation
E-mail: coa@abhe.org
URL: www.abhe.org

Bible colleges and programs offering undergraduate and graduate programs **BI**

Blood Bank Technology

Commission on Accreditation of Allied Health Education Programs (see listing under Allied Health)
AABB
Committee on Accreditation of Specialists in Blood Bank Technology/Transfusion Medicine

4550 Montgomery Avenue, Suite 700 North Tower
Bethesda, MD 20814
(301) 215-6540
Melanie Sloan, Senior Director of Accreditation and Quality
E-mail: accreditation@aabb.org

Programs for blood bank technologist **BBT**

Business

Accrediting Council for Independent Colleges and Schools (ACICS)
   USDE: 1956/2016/2021
1350 Eye Street NW, Suite 560
Washington, DC 20005
(202) 336-6780   Fax (202) 789-1747
Michelle Edwards, President/CEO
E-mail: info@acics.org
URL: www.acics.org

Institutions offering certificates/diplomas, associate, baccalaureate and master's degree programs to educate students for professional, technical, or occupational careers **ACICS**

ACICS is no longer a U.S. Department of Education recognized accrediting agency, the Department will provisionally certify accredited institutions for 18 months to allow institutions time to seek recognition from another accrediting agency.

Accreditation Council for Business Schools and Programs (ACBSP)
   CHEA: 2001
11520 West 119th Street
Overland Park, KS 66213
(913) 339-9356   Fax (913) 339-6226
Jeffrey Alderman, President/CEO
E-mail: info@acbsp.org
URL: www.acbsp.org

Business administration, management, accounting and related business fields **ACBSP**

International Accreditation Council for Business Education
   CHEA: 2011
11960 Quivira Road, Suite 300
Overland, KS 66213
(913) 631-3009   Fax (913) 631-9154
Phyllis Okrepkie, President
E-mail: iacbe@iacbe.org
URL: www.iacbe.org

Undergraduate and graduate level business programs in institutions that grant associates, bachelor's and/or graduate degrees **IACBE**

Cardiac Sonography

Commission on Accreditation of Allied Health Education Programs (see listing under Allied Health)
Committee on Accreditation for Advanced Cardiovascular Sonography (COA-ACS)
2530 Meridian Parkway, Suite 450
Durham, NC 27713
Mary Alice Dilday
(919) 465-9020
E-mail: coaacs@gmail.com

Programs for advanced cardiovascular sonography **ACS**

Cardiovascular Technology

Commission on Accreditation of Allied Health Education Programs (see listing under Allied Health)
Joint Review Committee on Education in Cardiovascular Technology (JRC-CVT)
1449 Hill Street
Whitinsville, MA 01588-1032
(978) 456-5594

Jackie Long-Goding, Executive Director
E-mail: office@jrccvt.org
URL: www.jrccvt.org

Programs for cardiovascular technology **CVT**

Chiropractic

The Council on Chiropractic Education (CCE)
   USDE: 1974/2022/2027   CHEA: 2005
10105 E. Via Linda, Suite 103 PMB 3642
Scottsdale, AZ 85258
(480) 443-8877
Craig S. Little, President
E-mail: cce@cce-usa.org
URL: www.cce-usa.org

Programs leading to and institutions offering the Doctorate of Chiropractic (D.C.) degree **CHIRO**

Christian Studies Education

Accreditation Commission
Transnational Association of Christian Colleges and Schools (TRACS)
   USDE: 1991/2021/2026   CHEA: 2001
15935 Forest Road
Forest, VA 24551
(434) 525-9539
Timothy Eaton, President
E-mail: info@tracs.org
URL: www.tracs.org

Christian liberal arts institutions which offer certificates/diplomas and associate, baccalaureate and graduate degrees **TRACS**

Clinical Laboratory Sciences

National Accrediting Agency for Clinical Laboratory Sciences (NAACLS)
   CHEA: 2002
5600 North River Road, Suite 720
Rosemont, IL 60018
(773) 714-8880   Fax (773) 714-8886
Marissa James, Chief Executive Officer
E-mail: info@naacls.org
URL: www.naacls.org

Programs for:
   cytogenetic technologist **CGTECH**
   diagnostic molecular scientist **DMOLS**
   histologic technician/technologist **HT**
   medical laboratory scientist **MLS**
   medical laboratory technician **MLTAD**
   pathologists' assistant **PA**

Clinical Pastoral Education

Accreditation Commission
Association for Clinical Pastoral Education, Inc. (ACPEI)
   USDE: 1969/2017/2022
120 West Trinity Place
WeWork, Floor 4
Decatur, GA 30030
(404) 320-1472   Fax (404) 320-0849
Trace Haythorn, Executive Director/CEO
E-mail: acpe@acpe.edu
URL: www.acpe.edu

Basic, advanced and supervisory clinical pastoral education programs **PAST**

Clinical Research

Commission on Accreditation of Allied Health Education Programs (see listing under Allied Health)
Committee on Accreditation of Academic Programs in Clinical Research (CAAPCR)
(734) 604-1989
Stephen A. Sonstein, Chair
E-mail: ssonstein@gmail.com

Academic programs in clinical research **CR**

Construction Education

American Council for Construction Education (ACCE)
   CHEA: 2001
300 Decker Drive
Irving, TX 75062
(972) 600-8800
Steve Nellis, President/CEO
E-mail: acce@acce-hq.org
URL: www.acce-hq.org

Associate, baccalaureate and master's degree programs **CONST**

Continuing Education

Accrediting Council for Continuing Education and Training (ACCET)
   USDE: 1978/2019/2024
1722 N Street NW
Washington, DC 20036
(202) 955-1113
Res Helfer, Executive Director
E-mail: info@accet.org
URL: www.accet.org

Institutions offering noncollegiate continuing education and institutions offering occupational associate degree programs **CNCE**

Cosmetology

National Accrediting Commission of Career Arts and Sciences (NACCAS)
   USDE: 1970/2021/2026
3015 Colvin Street
Alexandria, VA 22314
(703) 600-7600   Fax (703) 379-2200
Darin M. Wallace, Executive Director
E-mail: webinfo@naccas.org
URL: www.naccas.org

Postsecondary schools and departments of cosmetology arts and sciences and massage therapy **COSME**

Counseling and Related Educational Programs

Council for Accreditation of Counseling and Related Educational Programs (CACREP)
   CHEA: 2002
500 Montgomery Street, Suite 350
Alexandria, VA 22314
(703) 535-5990
M. Sylvia Fernandez, President and CEO
E-mail: cacrep@cacrep.org
URL: www.cacrep.org

Programs in counseling and its specialties **CACREP**

Masters in Psychology and Counseling Accrediation Council
   CHEA: 2021
595 New Loudon Road, #265
Latham, New York 12110
(518) 764-7581
Pat O'Connor, Executive Director
E-mail: mpcaced@gmail.com
URL: http://mpcacaccreditation.org

Programs in counseling and psychological services **MPCAC**

Culinary Arts

Accrediting Commission
American Culinary Federation
   CHEA: 2004
6816 Southpoint Pkwy, Suite 400
Jacksonville, FL 33216

(904) 824-4468   Fax (904) 940-0741
Heidi Cramb, Executive Director
E-mail: acf@acfchefs.net
URL: www.acfchefs.org

Programs in culinary arts which award certificates, diplomas or associate degrees and bachelor degree programs in culinary management **ACFEI**

Cytotechnology

Commission on Accreditation of Allied Health Education Programs (see listing under Allied Health)
Cytotechnology Programs Review Committee
American Society of Cytopathology
100 West 10th Street, Suite 605
Wilmington, DE 19801
(302) 543-6583   Fax (302) 543-6597
Elizabeth Jenkins, Executive Director
E-mail: asc@cytopathology.org
URL: www.cytopathology.org

Programs for the cytotechnologist **CYTO**

Dance

Commission on Accreditation
National Association of Schools of Dance (NASD)
   USDE: 1983/2019/2024
11250 Roger Bacon Drive, Suite 21
Reston, VA 20190
(703) 437-0700   Fax (703) 437-6312
Karen P. Moynahan, Executive Director
E-mail: info@arts-accredit.org
URL: nasd.arts-accredit.org

Institutions and departments within institutions offering degree and non-degree-granting programs in dance and dance-related disciplines **DANCE**

Dental and Dental Auxiliary Programs

Commission on Dental Accreditation
American Dental Association (ADA)
   USDE: 1952/2017/2022
211 East Chicago Avenue, Suite 1900
Chicago, IL 60611
(800) 621-6108   Fax (312) 440-2915
Sherin Tooks, Director
E-mail: tookss@ada.org
URL: www.ada.org/coda

Programs leading to:
   D.D.S. or D.M.D. degree, advanced general
      dentistry and specialty programs **DENT**
   Dental hygiene **DH**
   Dental assisting **DA**
   Dental laboratory technology **DT**
   Dental therapy **DTH**

Diagnostic Medical Sonography

Commission on Accreditation of Allied Health Education Programs (see listing under Allied Health)
Joint Review Committee on Education in Diagnostic Medical Sonography
6021 University Boulevard, Suite 500
Ellicot City, MD 21043-6090
(443) 973-3251   Fax (866) 738-3444
Gerry Magat, Executive Director
E-mail: mail@jrcdms.org
URL: www.jrcdms.org

Programs for the diagnostic medical sonographer **DMS**

Dietetics

Accreditation Council for Education in Nutrition and Dietetics
Academy of Nutrition and Dietetics
   USDE: 1974/2017/2023

120 South Riverside Plaza, Suite 2190
Chicago, IL 60606-6995
(312) 899-0040   Fax (312) 899-4817
Rayane AbuSabha, Executive Director
E-mail: acend@eatright.org
URL: www.eatrightpro.org/acend

Graduate programs in nutrition and dietetics **DIET**
Coordinated programs in dietetics **DIETC**
Didactic programs **DIETD**
Post-baccalaureate internships **DIETI**
Dietetic technician programs **DIETT**

Distance Education and Training

Distance Education Accrediting Commission
   USDE: 1959/2022/2027   CHEA: 2001
1101 17th Street NW, Suite 808
Washington, DC 20036
(202) 234-5100
Leah K. Matthews, Executive Director
E-mail: info@deac.org
URL: www.deac.org

Distance education institutions including associate, baccalaureate, master's, and doctoral degree-granting programs primarily through the distance learning method **DEAC** (formerly DETC)

Emergency Medical Services

Commission on Accreditation for Allied Health Programs (see listing under Allied Health)
Committee on Accreditation of Educational Programs for the Emergency Medical Services Professions
8301 Lakeview Parkway, Suite 111-312
Rowlett, TX 75088
(214) 703-8445   Fax (214) 703-8992
George Hatch Jr., Executive Director
E-mail: george@coaemsp.org
URL: www.coaemsp.org

Programs for the emergency medical technician-paramedic **EMT**

English Language

Commission on English Language Program Accreditation (CEA)
   USDE: 2003/2022/2027
1001 North Fairfax Drive, Suite 630
Alexandria, VA 22314
(703) 665-3400   Fax (703) 519-2071
Heidi Vellenga, Executive Director
E-mail: info@cea-accredit.org
URL: www.cea-accredit.org

English language programs **CEA**

Exercise Sciences

Commission on Accreditation of Allied Health Education Programs (see listing under Allied Health)
Committee on Accreditation for the Exercise Sciences
401 W. Michigan Street
Indianapolis, IN 46202
(317) 777-1135   Fax (317) 634-7817
William Coale, Director
E-mail: wcoale@acsm.org
URL: www.coaes.org

Programs for exercise science and related departments **EXSC**

Family and Consumer Sciences

Council for Accreditation
American Association of Family and Consumer Sciences (AAFCS)
   CHEA: 2001
107 S. West Street, #816
Alexandria, VA 22314

(703) 706-4600   Fax (703) 636-7648
Nancy Bock, Executive Director
E-mail: accreditation@aafcs.org
URL: www.aafcs.org

Baccalaureate programs in family and consumer sciences **AAFCS**

Fire and Emergency

International Fire Service Accreditation Congress
   CHEA: 2011
1723 West Tyler Avenue
Oklahoma State University
Stillwater, OK 74078
(405) 744-8303   Fax (405) 744-7377
Eldonna Sadler, Interim Manager/Operations Coordinator
E-mail: admin@ifsac.org
URL: www.ifsac.org

Fire and emergency related programs **IFSAC**

Forensic Science

Forensic Science Educational Program Accreditation Commission
American Academy of Forensic Sciences (AAFS)
   CHEA: 2012
410 North 21st Street
Colorado Springs, CO 80904
(719) 636-1100   Fax (719) 636-1993
Nancy J. Jackson, FEPAC Accreditation and Outreach Coordinator
E-mail: info@aafs.org
URL: www.aafs.org

Bachelor or master's degree programs in forensic science **FEPAC**

Funeral Service Education

Committee on Accreditation
American Board of Funeral Service Education (ABFSE)
   USDE: 1972/2021/2026   CHEA: 2001
992 Mantua Pike, Suite 108
Woodbury Heights, NJ 08097
(816) 233-3747   Fax (856) 579-7354
Robert C. Smith III, Executive Director
E-mail: exdir@abfse.org
URL: www.abfse.org

Institutions and programs awarding diplomas, associate and bachelor's degrees in funeral service or mortuary science **FUSER**

Health Informatics and Information Management

Commission on Accreditation for Health Informatics and Information Management Education (CAHIIM)
   CHEA: 2012
200 East Randolph Street, Suite 5100
Chicago, IL 60601
(312) 235-3255
Angela Kennedy, Chief Executive Officer
E-mail: info@cahiim.org
URL: www.cahiim.org

Associate and baccalaureate degree programs in health information management and master's degree programs in health informatics and health information management **CAHIIM**

Healthcare Management

Commission on Accreditation of Healthcare Management Education (CAHME)
   CHEA: 2003
PO Box 911

Spring House, PA 19477
(301) 298-1820
Anthony Stanowski, President and CEO
E-mail: info@cahme.org
URL: www.cahme.org

Graduate programs in healthcare management **HSA**

Hospitality Management

Accreditation Commission for Programs in Hospitality Management
    CHEA: 2022
PO Box 400
Oxford, MD 21654
(410) 226-5527
Dorothy Fenwick, Executive Director
E-mail: info@acpha-commission.org
URL: www.acpha-cahm.org

Hospitality administration/management programs **ACPHA**

Human Services

Council for Standards in Human Services Education (CSHSE)
    CHEA: 2014
3337 Duke Street
Alexandria, VA 22314
(571) 257-3959
Yvonne Chase, President
E-mail: info@cshse.org
URL: www.cshse.org

Human services educational programs **CSHSE**

Industrial Technology

The Association of Technology, Management, and Applied Engineering
    CHEA: 2002
6207 Route 30, Suite 1027
Greensburg, PA 15601
(919) 635-8335   Fax (919) 779-5642
Amy Good, Managing Director of Accreditation
E-mail: accreditation@atmae.org
URL: www.atmae.org

Technology, applied technology, engineering technology and technology-related programs at the associate, baccalaureate and master's degree level **NAIT**

Interior Design

Council for Interior Design Accreditation (CIDA)
    CHEA: 2013
206 Cesar E. Chavez Avenue SW, Suite 350
Grand Rapids, MI 49503-4014
(616) 458-0400   Fax (616) 458-0460
Holly Mattson, Executive Director
E-mail: info@accredit-id.org
URL: www.accredit-id.org

Professional degree level programs (master's and baccalaureate degrees) **CIDA**

Jewish Studies

Association of Institutions of Jewish Studies (AIJS)
    USDE: 2015/2021/2026
500 West Kennedy Boulevard
Lakewood, NJ 08701
(732) 363-7330   Fax (732) 415-8198
Shia Lowinger, Interim Executive Director
E-mail: info@theaijs.com
URL: theaijs.com

Postsecondary institutions of Jewish or Classical Torah Studies **AIJS**

Journalism and Mass Communications

Accrediting Committee
Accrediting Council on Education in Journalism and Mass Communications (ACEJMC)
    CHEA: 2002
2101 Knight Hall, 7765 Alumni Drive
College Park, MD 20742
(301) 405-1527
Patricia Thompson, Executive Director
E-mail: patt@umd.edu
URL: www.acejmc.org

Units within institutions offering professional baccalaureate and master's degree programs in journalism and mass communications **JOUR**

Kinesiotherapy

Commission on Accreditation of Allied Health Education Programs (see listing under Allied Health)
Committee on Accreditation of Education Programs for Kinesiotherapy
Kareesa Keys, Administrative Officer
E-mail: kinesiotherapy.ao@gmail.com

Kinesiotherapy programs **KIN**

Lactation Education

Commission on Accreditation of Allied Health Education Programs (see listing under Allied Health)
Lactation Education Accreditation and Approval Review Committee (LEAARC)
110 Horizon Drive, Suite 210
Raleigh, NC 27615
(984) 500-5902
Jackie Long-Goding, Executive Director
E-mail: office@LEAARC.org
URL: www.leaarc.org

Landscape Architecture

Landscape Architectural Accreditation Board
American Society of Landscape Architects (ASLA)
    CHEA: 2003
636 Eye Street, NW
Washington, DC 20001-3736
(202) 898-2444   Fax (202) 898-1185
Kristopher Pritchard, Director Accreditation and Education
E-mail: info@asla.org
URL: www.asla.org

Baccalaureate and master's programs leading to the first professional degree **LSAR**

Law

Council of the Section of Legal Education and Admissions to the Bar
American Bar Association (ABA)
    USDE: 1952/2021/2026
321 North Clark Street, 19th Floor
Chicago, IL 60654-7598
(312) 988-6738   Fax (312) 988-5681
William E. Adams, Managing Director of Accreditation and Legal Education
E-mail: legaled@americanbar.org
URL: www.americanbar.org/groups/legal_education

Programs in legal education; professional schools of law **LAW**

Library and Information Studies

Committee on Accreditation
American Library Association (ALA)
    CHEA: 2013

225 North Michigan Avenue, Suite 1300
Chicago, IL 60611-2795
(312) 280-2432   Fax (312) 280-2433
Karen O'Brien, Director of Accreditation
E-mail: accred@ala.org
URL: www.ala.org/accreditation

Master's programs in library and information studies **LIB**

Marriage and Family Therapy

Commission on Accreditation for Marriage and Family Therapy Education
American Association for Marriage and Family Therapy (AAMFT)
    CHEA: 2003
112 South Alfred Street
Alexandria, VA 22314-3061
(703) 253-0448   Fax (703) 253-0508
Jill Fogolin, Director of Accreditation
E-mail: coa@aamft.org
URL: www.coamfte.org

Clinical training programs at the master's, doctorate and post-graduate levels **MFCD**

Massage Therapy

Commission on Massage Therapy Accreditation
    USDE: 2002/2021/2023
900 Commonwealth Place, Suite 200-331
Virginia Beach, VA 23464
(202) 888-6790   Fax (202) 888-6787
Dawn Hogue, Executive Director
E-mail: info@comta.org
URL: www.comta.org

Institutions that award postsecondary certificates, diplomas, and associate degrees in the practice of massage therapy, bodywork, aesthetics/esthetics and skin care **COMTA**

Medical Assistant Education

(see listing under Allied Health)
Accrediting Bureau of Health Education Schools (ABHES)

Medical assistant programs **MAAB**

Commission on Accreditation of Allied Health Education Programs (see listing under Allied Health)
Medical Assisting Education Review Board
2020 North California Avenue, #213 Suite 7
Chicago, IL 60647
(312) 392-0155
Sarah R. Marino, Executive Director
E-mail: maerb@maerb.org
URL: www.maerb.org

One and two year medical assistant programs **MAC**

Medical Illustrator Education

Commission on Accreditation of Allied Health Education Programs (see listing under Allied Health)
Accreditation Review Committee for the Medical Illustrator
Shelley Wall, Chair, ARC-MI
E-mail: swall@utoronto.ca

Programs for medical illustrator **MIL**

Medical Laboratory Science Education

(see listing under Clinical Laboratory Sciences)
National Accrediting Agency for Clinical Laboratory Sciences (NAACLS)

Programs for medical laboratory scientist **MLS**

Medical Laboratory Technician Education

(see listing under Allied Health)
Accrediting Bureau of Health Education Schools (ABHES)

Schools and programs for the medical laboratory technician **MLTAB**

(see listing under Clinical Laboratory Sciences)
National Accrediting Agency for Clinical Laboratory Sciences (NAACLS)

Programs for medical laboratory technician **MLTAD**

Medical Physics

Commission on Accreditation of Medical Physics Education Programs, Inc.
 CHEA: 2017
1631 Prince Street
Alexandria, VA 22314
(571) 298-1239   Fax (571) 298-1301
Michael McNitt-Gray, President
E-mail: campep_admin@campep.org
URL: www.campep.org

Medical physics programs **CAMPEP**

Medicine

Liaison Committee on Medical Education (LCME)
 USDE: 1952/2018/2023
The LCME is administered in odd-numbered years, beginning each July 1, by:
American Medical Association (AMA)
330 North Wabash Avenue, Suite 39300
Chicago, IL 60611
(312) 464-4933
Barbara Barzansky, LCME Co-Secretary
E-mail: barbara.barzansky@ama-assn.org
URL: www.lcme.org

The LCME is administered in even-numbered years, beginning each July 1, by:
Association of American Medical Colleges (AAMC)
655 K Street NW, Suite 100
Washington, DC 20001-2399
(202) 826-0596
Veronica Catanese, LCME Co-Secretary
E-mail: vcatanese@aamc.org
URL: www.aamc.org

Programs leading to the M.D. degree **MED**

Midwifery Education

Midwifery Education Accreditation Council (MEAC)
 USDE: 2001/2021/2026
850 Mt. Pleasant Avenue
Ann Arbor, MI 48103
(360) 466-2080   Fax (480) 907-2936
Shailushi Ritchie, Interim Director of Operations
E-mail: info@meacschools.org
URL: www.meacschools.org

Accreditation of direct-entry midwifery educational institutions and programs conferring degrees and certificates **MEAC**

Montessori Teacher Education

Montessori Accreditation Council for Teacher Education (MACTE)
 USDE: 1995/2021/2026
420 Park Street
Charlottesville, VA 22902
(434) 202-7793
Rebecca Pelton, President
E-mail: info@macte.org
URL: www.macte.org

Montessori teacher-education programs and institutions **MACTE**

Music

Commission on Accreditation
National Association of Schools of Music (NASM)
 USDE: 1952/2019/2024
11250 Roger Bacon Drive, Suite 21
Reston, VA 20190
(703) 437-0700   Fax (703) 437-6312
Karen P. Moynahan, Executive Director
E-mail: info@arts-accredit.org
URL: nasm.arts-accredit.org

Institutions and departments within institutions offering degree and non-degree-granting programs in music and music-related disciplines **MUS**

Naturopathic Medical Education

Council on Naturopathic Medical Education (CNME)
 USDE: 2003/2021/2026
PO Box 178
Great Barrington, MA 01230
(413) 528-8877   Fax (413) 528-8880
Daniel Seitz, Executive Director
E-mail: council@cnme.org
URL: www.cnme.org

Naturopathic doctoral education programs **NATUR**

Neurodiagnostic Technology

Commission on Accreditation of Allied Health Education Programs (see listing under Allied Health)
Committee on Accreditation for Education in Neurodiagnostic Technology
1449 Hill Street
Whitinsville, MA 01588
(978) 338-6300   Fax (978) 832-2638
Jackie Long-Goding, Executive Director
E-mail: office@coa-ndt.org
URL: www.coa-ndt.org

Programs for the electroneurodiagnostic technologist **NDT**

Nuclear Medicine Technology

Joint Review Committee on Educational Programs in Nuclear Medicine Technology
 CHEA: 2013
820 West Danforth Road, #B1
Edmund, OK 73003
(405) 285-0546   Fax (405) 285-0579
Jan Winn, Executive Director
E-mail: mail@jrcnmt.org
URL: www.jrcnmt.org

Programs for the nuclear medicine technologist **NMT**

Nurse Anesthetists

Council on Accreditation of Nurse Anesthesia Educational Programs
 USDE: 1955/2018/2023   CHEA: 2011
10275 West Higgins Road, Suite 906
Rosemont, IL 60018-5603
(224) 275-9130
Francis Gerbasi, Chief Executive Officer
E-mail: accreditation@coacrna.org
URL: www.coacrna.org

Nurse anesthesia educational institutions and programs at the post-master's certificate, master's and doctoral degree levels **ANEST**

Nurse-Midwifery

Accreditation Commission for Midwifery Education
 USDE: 1982/2018/2023
8403 Colesville Road, Suite 1230

Silver Spring, MD 20910
(240) 485-1803   Fax (240) 485-1818
Angela Smith, Executive Director
E-mail: acme@acnm.org
URL: www.midwife.org/accreditation

Pre-certification, basic certificate and master's degree nurse-midwifery educational programs **MIDWF**

Nursing

Commission on Collegiate Nursing Education (CCNE)
 USDE: 2000/2018/2023
655 K Street NW, Suite 750
Washington, DC 20001
(202) 887-6791   Fax (202) 887-8476
Jennifer Butlin, Executive Director
E-mail: jbutlin@ccneaccreditation.org
URL: www.aacnnursing.org/ccne

Baccalaureate and higher degree nursing education **NURSE**

Accreditation Commission for Education in Nursing
 USDE: 1952/2018/2023   CHEA: 2011
3390 Peachtree Road NE, Suite 1400
Atlanta, GA 30326
(404) 975-5000   Fax (404) 975-5020
Marsal P. Stoll, CEO
E-mail: info@acenursing.org
URL: www.acenursing.org

Programs in:
 Practical nursing (certificate) **PNUR**
 Diploma nurse education **DNUR**
 Associate degree **ADNUR**
 Baccalaureate and higher degree nurse education **NUR**

National League for Nursing
Commission for Nurse Education Accreditation
 USDE: 2021/2026
2600 Virginia Avenue NW, Eighth Floor
Washington, DC 20037
(202) 909-2487
Teresa Shellenbarger, Executive Director
E-mail: tshellenbarger@nln.org
URL: cnea.nln.org

Programs for nursing education **CNEA**

Nurse Practitioner

National Nurse Practitioner Residency and Fellowship Training Consortium
 USDE: 2022/2026
625 Main Street
Middletown, CT 06457
(202) 780-9651
Kerry Bamrick, Executive Director
Email: info@nppostgradtraining.com
URL: nppostgradtraining.com

Nurse practitioner residency and fellowship training programs **NNPR**

Occupational Education

Council on Occupational Education (COE)
 USDE: 1969/2021/2024
7840 Roswell Road, Bldg 300, Suite 325
Atlanta, GA 30350
(770) 396-3898   Fax (770) 396-3790
Gary Puckett, President/Executive Director
E-mail: info@council.org
URL: www.council.org

Occupational/vocational institutions that grant certificates or diplomas and the applied associate degree in specific career and technical education **COE**

Occupational Therapy

Accreditation Council for Occupational Therapy Education
American Occupational Therapy Association
　USDE: 1952/2017/2022　　CHEA: 2013
6116 Executive Boulevard, Suite 200
North Bethesda, MD 20852-4929
(301) 652-6611
Teresa Brininger, Director of Accreditation
E-mail: accred@aota.org
URL: www.acoteonline.org

Occupational therapy programs **OT**
Occupational therapy assistant programs **OTA**

Opticianry

Commission on Opticianry Accreditation
　CHEA: 2010
PO Box 592
Canton, NY 13617
(703) 468-0566
Debra White, Director of Accreditation
E-mail: director@COAccreditation.com
URL: www.coaccreditation.com

Two-year opticianry degree programs **OPD**

Optometry

Accreditation Council on Optometric Education
American Optometric Association (AOA)
　USDE: 1952/2018/2023　　CHEA: 2012
243 North Lindbergh Boulevard
St. Louis, MO 63141
(314) 991-4100　Fax (314) 991-4101
Stephanie Puljak, ACOE Director
E-mail: accredit@aoa.org
URL: www.theacoe.org

Programs in:
　First professional **OPT**
　Optometric residency **OPTR**
　Optometric technology **OPTT**

Orthotic and Prosthetic Education

Commission on Accreditation of Allied Health Education Programs (see listing under Allied Health)
National Commission on Orthotic and Prosthetic Education (NCOPE)
330 John Carlyle Street, Suite 200
Alexandria, VA 22314
(703) 836-7114　Fax (703) 890-2425
Robin C. Seabrook, Executive Director
E-mail: info@ncope.org
URL: www.ncope.org

Programs for orthotic and prosthetic education **OPE**

Osteopathic Medicine

Commission on Osteopathic College Accreditation
American Osteopathic Association
　USDE: 1952/2021/2026
Department of Education
142 East Ontario Street
Chicago, IL 60611-2864
(312) 202-8124　Fax (312) 202-8200
Jed Brinton, Secretary, COCA
E-mail: predoc@osteopathic.org
URL: www.osteopathic.org/accreditation

Programs leading to and institutions offering the D.O. (Doctor of Osteopathy/Osteopathic Medicine) degree **OSTEO**

Perfusion

Commission on Accreditation of Allied Health Education Programs (see listing under Allied Health)
Accreditation Committee - Perfusion Education (AC-PE)

519 West Ridge Road
Littleton, CO 80120
(303) 794-6283
E-mail: office@ac-pe.org
URL: www.ac-pe.org

Programs for the perfusionist **PERF**

Pharmacy

Accreditation Council for Pharmacy Education (ACPE)
　USDE: 1952/2017/2022　　CHEA: 2004
190 South LaSalle Street, Suite 3000
Chicago, IL 60603
(312) 664-3575　Fax (866) 228-2631
Janet P. Engle, Executive Director
E-mail: info@acpe-accredit.org
URL: www.acpe-accredit.org

Professional degree programs in pharmacy **PHAR**

Physical Therapy

Commission on Accreditation in Physical Therapy Education
American Physical Therapy Association (APTA)
　USDE: 1977/2018/2023　　CHEA: 2012
3030 Potomac Avenue, Suite 100
Alexandria, VA 22305
(703) 706-3245　Fax (703) 684-7343
Mary Romanello, Director of Accreditation
E-mail: accreditation@apta.org
URL: www.capteonline.org

Professional programs for the physical therapist **PTA**
Programs for the physical therapist assistant **PTAA**

Physician Assistant

Accreditation Review Commission on Education for the Physician Assistant (ARC-PA)
　CHEA: 2004
3325 Paddocks Pkwy, Suite 345
Suwanee, GA 30024
(770) 476-1224　Fax (470) 253-8721
Sharon Luke, Executive Director
E-mail: accreditationservices@arc-pa.org
URL: www.arc-pa.org

Programs for the physician assistant **ARCPA**

Planning (City and Regional)

Planning Accreditation Board
　CHEA: 2013
2334 West Lawrence Avenue, Suite 209
Chicago, IL 60625
(773) 334-7200
Jesmarie Johnson, Executive Director
E-mail: jjohnson@planningaccreditationboard.org
URL: www.planningaccreditationboard.org

Bachelor and master's level programs in planning **PLNG**

Podiatry

Council on Podiatric Medical Education
American Podiatric Medical Association (APMA)
　USDE: 1952/2022/2027　　CHEA: 2004
9312 Old Georgetown Road
Bethesda, MD 20814-1621
(301) 581-9200　Fax (301) 571-4903
Heather Stagliano, Director
E-mail: cpmestaff@cpme.org
URL: www.cpme.org

Colleges and programs of podiatric medicine, including first professional and doctorate degree programs **POD**

Polysomnographic Technology

Commission on Accreditation of Allied Health Education Programs (see listing under Allied Health)
Committee on Accreditation for Polysomnographic Technologist Education
1711 Frank Avenue
New Bern, NC 28560
(252) 626-3238
Karen Monarchy Rowe, Executive Director
E-mail: karenmonarchy@suddenlink.net

Programs for polysomnographic technology **POLYT**

Psychology

Psychological Clinical Science Accreditation System (PCSAS)
　CHEA: 2012
Dept of Psychological and Brain Sciences
Indiana University
1101 East 10th Street
Bloomington, IN 47405
(479) 301-8008
Joe Steinmetz, Executive Director
E-mail: jsteinmetz@pcsas.org
URL: www.pcsas.org

Psychological clinical science doctoral training programs **PCSAS**

Commission on Accreditation
American Psychological Association (APA)
　USDE: 1970/2021/2026　　CHEA: 2013
750 First Street NE
Washington, DC 20002-4242
(202) 336-5979　Fax (202) 336-5978
Jacqueline Remondet Wall, Director, Office of Program Consultation and Accreditation
E-mail: apaaccred@apa.org
URL: www.apa.org/ed/accreditation

Doctoral programs in:
　Clinical psychology **CLPSY**
　Counseling psychology **COPSY**
　Combined professional-scientific psychology **PSPSY**
　School psychology **SCPSY**
　Doctoral internship program in health service psychology **IPSY**
　Post-doctoral residency in health service psychology **PDPSY**

Public Affairs and Administration

Commission on Peer Review and Accreditation
Network of Schools of Public Policy, Affairs and Administration (NASPAA)
　CHEA: 2004
1029 Vermont Avenue, NW, Suite 1100
Washington, DC 20005
(202) 628-8965　Fax (202) 626-4978
Martha Bohrt, Chief Accreditation Officer
E-mail: copra@naspaa.org
URL: www.naspaa.org

Master's degree programs in public affairs, public policy and administration **SPAA**

Public Health

Council on Education for Public Health (CEPH)
　USDE: 1974/2019/2024
1010 Wayne Avenue, Suite 220
Silver Spring, MD 20910-5600
(202) 789-1050
Laura Rasar King, Executive Director

E-mail: lking@ceph.org
URL: www.ceph.org

Baccalaureate and graduate level programs in schools of public health and public health programs outside of schools of public health **PH**

Rabbinical and Talmudic Education

Accreditation Commission
Association of Advanced Rabbinical and Talmudic Schools (AARTS)
   USDE: 1974/2018/2023   CHEA: 2011
2329 Nostrand Avenue, Suite M-200
Brooklyn, NY 11210
(212) 363-1991   Fax (212) 533-5335
Bernard Fryshman, Interim Executive Director
E-mail: office@aarts-schools.org

Advanced rabbinical and Talmudic schools **RABN**

Radiologic Technology

Joint Review Committee on Education in Radiologic Technology
   USDE: 1957/2022/2027   CHEA: 2004
20 North Wacker Drive, Suite 2850
Chicago, IL 60606-3182
(312) 704-5300   Fax (312) 704-5304
Leslie F. Winter, Chief Executive Officer
E-mail: mail@jrcert.org
URL: www.jrcert.org

Programs for:
   Magnetic resonance **RADMAG**
   Medical dosimetry **RADDOS**
   Radiographer **RAD**
   Radiation therapist technologist **RTT**

Recreation, Park and Leisure Studies

Council on Accreditation of Parks, Recreation, Tourism and Related Professions
   CHEA: 2003
1401 Marvin Road NE, Suite 307 #172
Lacey, WA 98516
(360) 205-2096   Fax (360) 453-7893
Shelley Dahle, COAPRT Programs Manager
E-mail: coaprt@accreditationcouncil.org
URL: www.accreditationcouncil.org

Baccalaureate degree programs in recreation, park resources and leisure studies **CAPRT**

Recreation Therapy

Commission on Accreditation of Allied Health Education Programs (see listing under Allied Health)
Committee on Accreditation of Recreational Therapy Education (CARTE)
Indiana University
School of Public Health
1025 East 7th Street, Suite 111
Bloomington, IN 47405
(812) 856-3683
Jared Allsop, Chair
E-mail: jallsop@indiana.edu

Recreational therapy education programs **CARTE**

Respiratory Care

Commission on Accreditation for Respiratory Care (CoARC)
   CHEA: 2012
264 Precision Boulevard
Telford, TN 37690
(817) 283-2835   Fax (817) 354-8519
Thomas Smalling, CEO
E-mail: tom@coarc.com
URL: www.coarc.com

Degree programs in respiratory care **COARC**

Certificate programs in polysomnography
COARCP

School Psychology

National Association of School Psychologists (NASP)
   CHEA: 2022
4340 East West Highway, Suite 402
Bethesda, MD 20814
(301) 657-0270   Fax (301) 657-0275
Kathleen Minke, Executive Director
E-mail: kminke@naspweb.org
URL: naspaonline.org

Programs in school psychology **NASP**

Social Work

Commission on Accreditation
Council on Social Work Education (CSWE)
   CHEA: 2003
333 John Carlyle Street, Suite 400
Alexandria, VA 22314
(703) 683-8080   Fax (703) 683-8099
Darla Spence Coffey, President/CEO
E-mail: info@cswe.org
URL: www.cswe.org

Baccalaureate and master's degree programs **SW**

Speech-Language Pathology

Council on Academic Accreditation in Audiology and Speech Language Pathology
American Speech-Language-Hearing Association (ASHA)
   USDE: 1967/2021/2026   CHEA: 2003
2200 Research Boulevard, #310
Rockville, MD 20850-3289
(301) 296-5700   Fax (301) 296-8570
Kimberlee Moore, Director of Accreditation
E-mail: accreditation@asha.org
URL: caa.asha.org

Master's in speech-language pathology **SP**

Sports Management

Commission on Sports Management Accreditation
   CHEA: 2018
2236 Water Blossom Lane
Fort Collins, CO 80526
(202) 329-1189
Heather Alderman, Executive Director
E-mail: cosma@cosmaweb.org
URL: www.cosmaweb.org

Sports management degree programs **COSMA**

Surgical Assisting and Technology

(see listing under Allied Health)
Accrediting Bureau of Health Education Schools (ABHES)

Surgical technologist programs **SURTEC**

Commission on Accreditation of Allied Health Education Programs (see listing under Allied Health)
Accreditation Review Council on Education in Surgical Technology and Surgical Assisting
19751 East Mainstreet, Suite 339
Parker, CO 80138
(303) 694-9262
Ron Kruzel, Executive Director
E-mail: info@arcstsa.org
URL: www.arcstsa.org

Programs for the surgical assistant **SURGA**
Programs for the surgical technologist **SURGT**

Teacher Education

Association for Advancing Quality in Educator Preparation
   CHEA: 2021
173 Milkweed Drive
Lake Frederick, VA 22630
(301) 276-5106
Mark LaCelle-Peterson, President & CEO
E-mail: aaqep@aaqep.org
URL: aaqep.org

Programs that prepare professional educators **AAQEP**

Council for the Accreditation of Educator Preparation
   CHEA: 2014
1140 19th Street NW, Suite 400
Washington, DC 20036
(202) 223-0077   Fax (202) 296-6620
Christopher Koch, President
E-mail: caep@caepnet.org
URL: caepnet.org

Educator preparation programs **CAEP**
NCATE Educator preparation program **CAEPN**
TEAC Education preparation program **CAEPT**

National Association for the Education of Young Children
   CHEA: 2021
1401 H Street NW, Suite 600
Washington, DC 20005
(202) 232-8777   Fax (202) 328-1846
Michelle Kang, Chief Executive Officer
E-mail: info@naeyc.org
URL: https://www.naeyc.org/accreditation

Degree programs in early childhood education **NAEYC**

Theatre

Commission on Accreditation
National Association of Schools of Theatre (NAST)
   USDE: 1982/2019/2024
11250 Roger Bacon Drive, Suite 21
Reston, VA 20190
(703) 437-0700   Fax (703) 437-6312
Karen P. Moynahan, Executive Director
E-mail: info@arts-accredit.org
URL: nast.arts-accredit.org

Institutions and departments within institutions offering degree granting and non-degree-granting programs in theatre and theatre-related disciplines **THEA**

Theology

The Commission on Accrediting
The Association of Theological Schools (ATS)
   USDE: 1952/2021/2026   CHEA: 2012
10 Summit Park Drive
Pittsburgh, PA 15275-1110
(412) 788-6505   Fax (412) 788-6510
Frank Yamada, Executive Director
E-mail: yamada@ats.edu
URL: www.ats.edu

Freestanding schools, as well as schools or programs affiliated with larger institutions, offering graduate professional education for ministry and graduate study of theology **THEOL**

Trade and Technical Education

Accrediting Commission of Career Schools and Colleges (ACCSC)
   USDE: 1967/2021/2026
2101 Wilson Boulevard, Suite 302
Arlington, VA 22201
(703) 247-4212   Fax (703) 247-4533

Michale McComis, Executive Director
E-mail: info@accsc.org
URL: www.accsc.org

Private, postsecondary degree-granting and non-degree-granting institutions that are predominantly organized to educate students for trade, occupational or technical careers **ACCSC**

Veterinary Medicine

Council on Education
American Veterinary Medical Association (AVMA)
USDE: 1952/2021/2026   CHEA: 2012
1931 North Meacham Road, Suite 100
Schaumburg, IL 60173
(800) 248-2862   Fax (847) 925-1329
Karen Martens Brandt, Director Education and Research
E-mail: kbrandt@avma.org
URL: www.avma.org

Colleges of veterinary medicine offering programs leading to a D.V.M./D.M.V. professional degree **VET**

Other

New York State Board of Regents
Commission of Education
USDE: 1952/2018/2023
State Education Department
The University of the State of New York
89 Washington Avenue, Room 110 EB
Albany, NY 12234
(518) 474-5844   Fax (518) 473-4909
Betty A. Rosa, Commissioner of Education
E-mail: commissioner@nysed.edu
URL: www.nysed.gov

Degree-granting institutions of higher education in New York that designate the agency as their sole or primary nationally recognized accrediting agency for purposes of establishing eligibility to participate in Higher Education Act programs **NY**

Accrediting Agencies Recognized for their Pre-accreditation Categories[1]

Under the terms of the Higher Education Act and other Federal legislation providing funding assistance to postsecondary education, an institution or program is eligible to apply for participation in certain Federal programs if, in addition to meeting other statutory requirements, it is accredited by a nationally recognized accrediting agency—or if it is an institution with respect to which the U.S. Secretary of Education has determined that there is satisfactory assurance the institution or program will meet the accreditation standards of such agency or association within a reasonable time. An institution or program may establish satisfactory assurance of accreditation by acquiring pre-accreditation status with a nationally recognized accrediting agency which has been recognized by the U.S. Secretary of Education for the award of such status. According to the Criteria for Nationally Recognized Accrediting Agencies, if an accrediting agency has developed a pre-accreditation status, it must demonstrate that it applies criteria and follows procedures that are appropriately related to those used to award accreditation status. The criteria for recognition also requires an agency's standards for pre-accreditation to permit an institution or program to hold pre-accreditation no more than five years.

The following is a list of accrediting agencies recognized by the U.S. Secretary of Education for their pre-accreditation categories and the categories which are recognized.

Regional Institution Accrediting Bodies

Middle States Commission on Higher Education: *Candidate for Accreditation*

New England Commission of Higher Education: *Candidate for Accreditation*

Higher Learning Commission: *Candidate for Accreditation*

Northwest Commission on Colleges and Universities: *Candidate for Accreditation*

Southern Association of Colleges and Schools
Commission on Colleges: *Candidate for Accreditation*

Western Association of Schools and Colleges
Accrediting Commission for Community and Junior Colleges: *Candidate for Accreditation*

Western Association of Schools and Colleges
Senior College and University Commission: *Candidate for Accreditation*

National, Institutional and Specialized Accrediting Bodies

Academy of Nutrition and Dietetics
Accreditation Council for Education in Nutrition and Dietetics: *Pre-accreditation*

Accreditation Commission for Acupuncture and Oriental Medicine: *Pre-accreditation, Candidate for Accreditation*

Accreditation Commission for Midwifery Education: *Pre-accreditation*

Accreditation Council for Pharmacy Education: *Candidate, Pre-candidate*

American Optometric Association
Accreditation Council on Optometric Education: *Preliminary Approval* (for professional degree programs); *Candidacy Pending* (for optometric residency programs in Veterans Administration facilities)

American Osteopathic Association
Commission on Osteopathic College Accreditation: *Provisional Accreditation*

American Physical Therapy Association
Commission on Accreditation in Physical Therapy Education: *Candidate for Accreditation*

American Podiatric Medical Association
Council on Podiatric Medical Education: *Candidate for Accreditation*

American Psychological Association
Commission on Accreditation: *Preaccreditation (doctoral internship and postdoctoral residency programs only)*

American Speech-Language-Hearing Association
Council on Academic Accreditation in Audiology and Speech Language Pathology: *Candidate for Accreditation*

American Veterinary Medical Association
Council on Education: *Reasonable Assurance of Accreditation*

Association for Biblical Higher Education
Commission on Accreditation: *Candidate for Accreditation*

Association of Advanced Rabbinical and Talmudic Schools
Accreditation Commission: *Correspondent, Candidate for Accreditation*

The Association of Theological Schools
The Commission on Accrediting: *Candidate for Accredited Membership*

Council on Education for Public Health: *Pre-accreditation*

Council on Naturopathic Medical Education: *Pre-accreditation*

Council on Occupational Education: *Candidate for Accreditation*

Midwifery Education Accreditation Council: *Pre-accreditation*

National League for Nursing
Commission for Nurse Education Accreditation: *Pre-accreditation*

Transnational Association of Christian Colleges and Schools
Accreditation Commission: *Candidate for Accreditation*

---

[1]U.S. Department of Education, Nationally Recognized Accrediting Agencies and Associations, www2.ed.gov/admins/finaid/accred/accreditation_pg8.html.

Abbreviations, Explanatory Notes and Symbols

Abbreviations

Listed below are the abbreviations used in this Directory for the recognized regional accrediting commissions and the recognized national, professional and specialized accrediting bodies. Addresses for these associations can be found under our listing of Accrediting Agencies beginning on page viii.

The recognized regional accrediting commissions are indicated throughout this Directory by the following abbreviations:

EH New England Commission of Higher Education

HLC Higher Learning Commission, North Central Association

M Middle States Commission on Higher Education

NW Northwest Commission on Colleges and Universities

SC Southern Association of Colleges and Schools, Commission on Colleges

WC Western Association of Schools and Colleges, Senior College and University Commission

WJ Western Association of Schools and Colleges, The Accrediting Commission for Community and Junior Colleges

National, professional and specialized accrediting agencies and associations are listed below. Wherever possible, degree levels are shown by the following symbols: (C) diploma/certificate; (A) associate; (B) baccalaureate; (M) master's; (S) beyond master's but less than doctorate; (FP) first professional; (D) doctorate.

AA Commission on Accreditation of Allied Health Education Programs: anesthesiologist assistant (M)

AAB Aviation Accreditation Board International: aviation (A,B,M,D)

AAFCS American Association of Family and Consumer Sciences: family and consumer sciences (B)

AAQEP Association for Advancing Quality in Educator Preparation: professional educators (C,B,M)

ABAI Association for Behavior Analysis International Accreditation Board: behavior analysis (M,D)

ABHES Accrediting Bureau of Health Education Schools: allied health (C,A, B,M)

ACAE Accreditation Commission for Audiology Education: audiology (D)

ACATE Commission on Accreditation of Allied Health Education Programs: art therapy (M)

ACBSP Accreditation Council for Business Schools and Programs: business administration, management, accounting and related business fields (A,B,M,D)

ACCSC Accrediting Commission of Career Schools and Colleges: occupational, trade and technical education (C,A,B,M)

ACFEI American Culinary Federation, Inc.: culinary arts and culinary management (C,A,B)

ACICS Accrediting Council for Independent Colleges and Schools: business and business-related programs (C,A,B,M)

ACPHA Accreditation Commission for Programs in Hospitality Administration: hospitality administration/management (A,B)

ACS Commission on Accreditation of Allied Health Education Programs: advanced cardiovascular sonography (C)

ACUP Accreditation Commission for Acupuncture and Herbal Medicine: acupuncture (C,M,D)

ADNUR Accreditation Commission for Education in Nursing: nursing (A)

AIJS Association of Institutions of Jewish Studies: Jewish studies (C,A,B)

ANEST Council on Accreditation of Nurse Anesthesia Educational Programs: nurse anesthesia (C,M,D)

ARCPA Accreditation Review Commission on Education for the Physician Assistant: physician assisting programs (A,B,M)

ART National Association of Schools of Art and Design: art and design (C, A,B,M,D)

AT Commission on Accreditation of Allied Health Education Programs: anesthesia technology (A)

ATECH Commission on Accreditation of Allied Health Education Programs: assistive technology (C,M)

AUD American Speech-Language-Hearing Association: audiology (D)

BBT Commission on Accreditation of Allied Health Education Programs: blood bank technology (C,M)

BI Association for Biblical Higher Education: bible college education (C, A,B,M,FP,D)

CAATE Commission on Accreditation of Athletic Training Education: athletic training (B,M,D)

CACREP Council for Accreditation of Counseling & Related Education programs: counseling and its specialties (M,D)

CAEP Council for the Accreditation of Educator Preparation: teacher education (B,M,D)

CAEPN Council for the Accreditation of Educator Preparation: teacher education (B,M,D)

CAEPT Council for the Accreditation of Educator Preparation: teacher education (B,M,D)

CAHIIM Commission on Accreditation for Health Informatics and Information Management Education: health information management and health informatics (A,B,M)

CAMPEP Commission on Accreditation of Medical Physics Education Programs, Inc.: medical physics (C,M,D)

CAPRT Council on Accreditation of Parks, Recreation, Tourism and Related Professions: recreation, park resources, and leisure studies (B)

CARTE Commission on Accreditation of Recreational Therapy Education: recreational therapy (B,M)

CEA Commission on English Language Program Accreditation: english language (C)

CGTECH National Accrediting Agency for Clinical Laboratory Sciences: cytogenetic technologist (B)

CHIRO Council on Chiropractic Education: chiropractic education (FP,D)

CIDA Council for Interior Design Accreditation: interior design (B,M)

CLPSY American Psychological Association: clinical psychology (D)

CNCE Accrediting Council for Continuing Education and Training: continuing education (C,A)

CNEA Commission for Nurse Education Accreditation: nursing (C,A,B,M,D)

COARC Commission on Accreditation for Respiratory Care: respiratory care (A,B,M)

COARCP   Commission on Accreditation for Respiratory Care: polysomnography (C)

COE   Council on Occupational Education: occupational, trade, and technical education (C,A)

COMTA   Commission on Massage Therapy Accreditation: massage therapy, bodywork, aesthetics/esthetics and skin care (C,A)

CONST   American Council for Construction Education: construction education (A,B,M)

COPSY   American Psychological Association: counseling psychology (D)

COSMA   Commission on Sports Management: sports management (B,M,D)

COSME   National Accrediting Commission of Career Arts and Sciences: cosmetology and massage therapy (C)

CR   Commission on Accreditation of Allied Health Education Programs: clinical researcher (C,A,M)

CSHSE   Council for Standards in Human Services Education: human services (A,B,M)

CVT   Commission on Accreditation of Allied Health Education Programs: cardiovascular technology (C,A,B)

CYTO   Commission on Accreditation of Allied Health Education Programs: cytotechnology (C,B,M)

DA   American Dental Association: dental assisting (C,A)

DANCE   National Association of Schools of Dance: dance (C,A,B,M,D)

DEAC   Distance Education and Accrediting Commission: home study schools (A,B,M,D)

DENT   American Dental Association: dentistry (FP,D)

DH   American Dental Association: dental hygiene (C,A,B,M)

DIET   Academy of Nutrition and Dietetics: nutrition and dietetics (M)

DIETC   Academy of Nutrition and Dietetics: coordinated dietetics programs (B,M,D)

DIETD   Academy of Nutrition and Dietetics: didactic dietetics programs (B,M)

DIETI   Academy of Nutrition and Dietetics: dietetic post-baccalaureate internships

DIETT   Academy of Nutrition and Dietetics: dietetic technician (A)

DMOLS   National Accrediting Agency for Clinical Laboratory Sciences: diagnostic molecular scientist (C,B,M)

DMS   Commission on Accreditation of Allied Health Education Programs: diagnostic medical sonography (C,A,B,M)

DNUR   Accreditation Commission for Education in Nursing: nursing (C)

DT   American Dental Association: dental laboratory technology (C,A)

DTH   American Dental Association: dental therapy (A)

EMT   Commission on Accreditation of Allied Health Education Programs: emergency medical technician-paramedic (C,A,B)

EXSC   Commission on Accreditation of Allied Health Education Programs: exercise science (C,A,B,M)

FEPAC   American Academy of Forensic Sciences: forensic science (B,M)

FUSER   American Board of Funeral Service Education: funeral service education (C,A,B)

HSA   Commission on Accreditation of Healthcare Management Education: healthcare management (M)

HT   National Accrediting Agency for Clinical Laboratory Sciences: histologic technology (C,A,B)

IACBE   International Accreditation Council for Business Education: business programs, accounting and business related (A,B,M,D)

IFSAC   International Fire Service Accreditation Congress Degree Assembly: fire and emergency related programs (A,B,M)

IPSY   American Psychological Association: doctoral internships in health service psychology

JOUR   Accrediting Council on Education for Journalism and Mass Communications: journalism and mass communications (B,M)

KIN   Commission on Accreditation of Allied Health Education Programs: kinesiotherapy (B)

LAW   American Bar Association: law (FP,D)

LC   Commission on Accreditation of Allied Health Programs: lactation consultant (C,A,B,M)

LIB   American Library Association: library and information studies (M)

LSAR   American Society for Landscape Architects: landscape architecture (B,M)

MAAB   Accrediting Bureau of Health Education Schools: medical assisting (C,A)

MAC   Commission on Accreditation of Allied Health Education Programs: medical assisting (C,A)

MACTE   Montessori Accreditation Council for Teacher Education: Montessori teacher education (C)

MEAC   Midwifery Education Accreditation Council: midwifery education (C, A,B,M,D)

MED   Liaison Committee on Medical Education: medicine (FP,D)

MFCD   American Association for Marriage and Family Therapy: marriage and family therapy (M,D)

MIDWF   Accreditation Commission for Midwifery Education: nurse midwifery (C,M,D)

MIL   Commission on Accreditation of Allied Health Education Programs: medical illustrator (B,M)

MLS   National Accrediting Agency for Clinical Laboratory Sciences: medical laboratory scientist (C,B)

MLTAB   Accrediting Bureau of Health Education Schools: medical laboratory technician (C,A)

MLTAD   National Accrediting Agency for Clinical Laboratory Sciences: medical laboratory technician (C,A)

MPCAC   Masters in Psychology and Counseling Accreditation Council: counseling and psychology (M)

MUS   National Association of Schools of Music: music (C,A,B,M,D)

NAEYC   National Association for the Education of Young Children: early childhood education (A,B,M)

NAIT   The Association of Technology, Management, and Applied Engineering: technology, applied technology, engineering technology and technology-related programs (A,B,M)

NASP   National Association of School Psychologists: school psychology (S,D)

NATUR Council on Naturopathic Medical Education: naturopathic medical education (FP,D)

NDT Commission on Accreditation of Allied Health Education Programs: neurodiagnostic technology (C,A)

NMT Joint Review Committee on Educational Programs in Nuclear Medicine Technology: nuclear medicine technology (C,A,B,M)

NNPR National Nurse Practitioner Residency and Fellowship Training Consortium: nurse practitioner residency and fellowship training

NUR Accreditation Commission for Education in Nursing: nursing (B,M,D)

NURSE Commission on Collegiate Nursing Education: nursing (C,B,M,D)

NY New York State Board of Regents:
Degree-granting institutions of higher education in New York that designate the agency as their sole or primary nationally recognized accrediting agency for purposes of establishing elibility to participate in Higher Education Act programs

OPD Commission on Opticianry Accreditation: opticianry (A)

OPE Commission on Accreditation of Allied Health Education Programs: orthotics and prosthetics (C,B,M)

OPT American Optometric Association: optometry (FP,D)

OPTR American Optometric Association: optometric residency programs

OPTT American Optometric Association: optometric technician (C)

OSTEO American Osteopathic Association, Office of Osteopathic Education: osteopathic medicine (FP,D)

OT American Occupational Therapy Association: occupational therapy (M,D)

OTA American Occupational Therapy Association: occupational therapy assistant (A,B)

PA National Accrediting Agency for Clinical Laboratory Sciences: pathologist's assistant (C,M)

PAST Association for Clinical Pastoral Education: clinical pastoral education

PCSAS Psychological Clinical Science Accreditation System: psychological clinical science (D)

PDPSY American Psychological Association: post-doctorate residency in health service psychology

PERF Commission on Accreditation of Allied Health Education Programs: perfusionist (C,B,M)

PH Council on Education for Public Health: public health (B,M,D)

PHAR Accreditation Council for Pharmacy Education: pharmacy (FP,D)

PLNG Planning Accreditation Board: certified planning (B,M)

PNUR Accreditation Commission for Education in Nursing: practical nursing (C)

POD American Podiatric Medical Association: podiatry (FP,D)

POLYT Commission on Accreditation of Allied Health Education Programs: polysomnographic technologist education (C,A)

PSPSY American Psychological Association: combined professional-scientific psychology (D)

PTA American Physical Therapy Association: physical therapy (D)

PTAA American Physical Therapy Association: physical therapy assistant (A)

RABN Association of Advanced Rabbinical and Talmudic Schools: rabbinical and Talmudic education (A,B,M,D)

RAD Joint Review Committee on Education in Radiologic Technology: radiography (C,A,B)

RADDOS Joint Review Committee on Education in Radiologic Technology: medical dosimetry (C,B,M)

RADMAG Joint Review Committee on Education in Radiologic Technology: magnetic resonance (C,A,B)

RTT Joint Review Committee on Education in Radiologic Technology: radiation therapy (C,A,B,M)

SCPSY American Psychological Association: school psychology (D)

SP American Speech-Language-Hearing Association: speech-language pathology (M)

SPAA Network of Schools of Public Policy, Affairs and Administration: public affairs and administration (M)

SURGA Commission on Accreditation of Allied Health Education Programs: surgical assistant (C,A)

SURGT Commission on Accreditation of Allied Health Education Programs: surgical technology (C,A)

SURTEC Accrediting Bureau of Health Education Schools: surgical technology (C,A)

SW Council on Social Work Education: social work (B,M)

THEA National Association of Schools of Theatre: theatre (C,A,B,M,D)

THEOL Association of Theological Schools: theology (M,FP,D)

TRACS Transnational Association of Christian Colleges and Schools: christian studies education (C,A,B,M,D)

VET American Veterinary Medical Association: veterinary medicine (FP,D)

Explanatory Notes and Symbols

Associate degree: includes junior colleges, community colleges, technical institutes, and schools offering at least a two-year program of college-level studies, either leading to an associate degree wholly or principally creditable toward a baccalaureate degree.

Baccalaureate: includes those institutions offering programs of studies leading to the customary bachelor of arts or bachelor of science degrees.

First professional degree: includes those institutions that offer the academic requirements for selected professions based on programs that require at least two academic years of previous college work for entrance and a total of at least six years of college work for completion.

Master's: includes those institutions offering the customary first graduate degree, master of arts or master of science degree in the liberal arts and sciences, or the next degree in the same field after the first professional degree.

Specialist/beyond master's but less than doctorate: includes those institutions offering "postgraduate pre-doctoral degrees".

Graduate non-degree granting: includes institutions offering work beyond the bachelor's level but not conferring degrees. In some instances the degrees are conferred by cooperating institutions.

Doctorate: includes those institutions offering a Ph.D. or its equivalent in any field.

Postdoctoral research only: includes institutions operating solely for the purpose of research at the postdoctoral level.

First Talmudic/Rabbinic degree: undergraduate degree granted by accredited Rabbinical schools. The schools in New York "using this designation do not imply that the 'First Talmudic/Rabbinic Degree' is equivalent to any secular academic degree recognized by the Board of Regents".*

Second Talmudic/Rabbinic degree: graduate degree granted by accredited Rabbinical schools. The schools in New York "using this designation do not imply that the 'Second Talmudic/Rabbinic Degree' is equivalent to any secular academic degree recognized by the Board of Regents".*

Special 5yr Faith Based: undergraduate degree granted by accredited faith-based school that requires 5 years of study to complete.

_____

*The University of the State of New York, The State Education Department, Albany, New York, letter August 17, 1983.

Symbols

* The institution is part of a system.

Used preceding any of the acronyms for the accrediting agencies the following symbols indicate that:

\# The accrediting agency has stated publicly that the institution or program is preliminary or provisionally accredited, accredited with some reservations, or approved on probation.

@ The institution or program has attained a pre-accredited status.

& The institution is covered under the regional accreditation of the parent institution.

U.S. Postal Abbreviation of States and Territories

Alabama	AL
Alaska	AK
American Samoa	AS
Arizona	AZ
Arkansas	AR
California	CA
Colorado	CO
Connecticut	CT
Delaware	DE
District of Columbia	DC
Florida	FL
Georgia	GA
Guam	GU
Hawaii	HI
Idaho	ID
Illinois	IL
Indiana	IN
Iowa	IA
Kansas	KS
Kentucky	KY
Louisiana	LA
Maine	ME
Maryland	MD
Marshall Islands	MH
Massachusetts	MA
Michigan	MI
Micronesia	FM
Minnesota	MN
Mississippi	MS
Missouri	MO
Montana	MT
Nebraska	NE
Nevada	NV
New Hampshire	NH
New Jersey	NJ
New Mexico	NM
New York	NY
North Carolina	NC
North Dakota	ND
Northern Marianas	MP
Ohio	OH
Oklahoma	OK
Oregon	OR
Palau	PW
Pennsylvania	PA
Puerto Rico	PR
Rhode Island	RI
South Carolina	SC
South Dakota	SD
Tennessee	TN
Texas	TX
Utah	UT
Vermont	VT
Virgin Islands	VI
Virginia	VA
Washington	WA
West Virginia	WV
Wisconsin	WI
Wyoming	WY

Institution Changes

FICE/ID Number

Institutions and Offices Added

California

Antiochian House of Studies	667432
Career Care Institute	037974
Central Coast College	026023
Contra Costa Medical Career College	042749
Integrity College of Health	041816
Minerva University	667427
Premiere Career College	031258
Rhombus University	667430

District of Columbia

Career Technical Institute	031043

Florida

Florida Education Institute	036276
FVI School of Nursing and Technology	042063
Genesis University	667431
Med Academy	042447
Westfield Business School	667425

Georgia

Atlanta Institute of Music and Media	031045

Louisiana

Infinity College	042454

New Jersey

Keser Torah-Mayan Hatalmud	041803
Mosdos Yaakov V'Yisroel	667434
Seminary Bnos Chaim	042712
Yeshiva Gedola Tiferes Yaakov Yitzchok	042801
Yeshiva Gedola Tiferes Yerachmiel	042738
Yeshiva Ohr Zechariah	042796
Yeshivas Emek Hatorah	042703

New York

Arnot Ogden Medical Center	006435
Bais Medrash of Dexter Park	042846
Congregation YMH	667428
Eisek HaTorah D'Rachmistrivka	667435
Yeshiva Aish Torah Dushinsky	667429
Yeshiva and Kolel Bais Medrash Elyon	026229
Yeshiva of Ocean	042766
Yeshivat Hechal Shemuel	042785

North Carolina

Watts School of Nursing	006483

Ohio

Athena Career Academy	041922
Hondros College of Business	667426
Ohio Institute of Allied Health	035833

FICE/ID Number

Oklahoma

ATA College	040603

Utah

Noorda College of Osteopathic Medicine	667433

Institutions and Offices Dropped

Alaska

Charter College	770822
(Duplicate listing of Charter College FICE # 25769)	

Arizona

Ottawa University Phoenix, AZ	666066
(Closed)	
University of Phoenix Southern Arizona Campus	770236
(Closed)	

Arkansas

University of Arkansas System eVersity	667336
(No longer accredited by DEAC)	

California

American Conservatory Theater	020992
(Closed)	
Chicago School of Professional Psychology-Anaheim Campus	770492
(No longer considered a branch campus)	
Ezra University	667316
(No longer accredited by BI)	
FIDM/Fashion Institute of Design and Merchandising-Orange County	666004
(Closed)	
Hawthorn University	667358
(Closed)	
Marymount California University	010474
(Closed)	
Mayfield College	041156
(No longer degree granting)	
San Francisco Art Institute	003948
(Closed)	
The Broad Center for the Management of School Systems	667228
(No longer accredited by WC)	
University of Phoenix Bay Area Campus	770193
(Closed)	
Western State University College of Law	010832
(No longer considered a branch campus)	

Colorado

CollegeAmerica Colorado Springs	666293
(Closed)	
Colorado Northwestern Community College Craig	770039
(No longer considered a branch campus)	

FICE/ID Number

Florida

Florida Career College *(No longer degree granting)*	666025
Florida Career College *(No longer degree granting)*	770613
Florida Career College *(No longer degree granting)*	770679
Florida Career College *(No longer degree granting)*	770682
Med-Life Institute-Naples *(No longer degree granting)*	667220
Sarasota University *(No longer accredited by DEAC)*	667337
Universal Career School *(Closed)*	038563
University of Phoenix Central Florida Main Campus *(Closed)*	770932
University of Phoenix North Florida Campus *(Closed)*	770197
University of Phoenix South Florida Main Campus *(Closed)*	770237

Georgia

University of Phoenix Atlanta Campus *(Closed)*	770200

Illinois

Coyne College *(Closed)*	007549
Lincoln College *(Closed)*	001709
Pacific College of Health and Science *(No longer considered a branch campus)*	666615
Spoon River College-Macomb Campus *(No longer considered a branch campus)*	770097
University of Phoenix Chicago Campus *(Closed)*	770205

Kansas

Butler Community College *(No longer considered a branch campus)*	770256
Butler of Andover *(No longer considered a branch campus)*	770253
Butler of Council Grove *(No longer considered a branch campus)*	770254
Butler of Marion *(No longer considered a branch campus)*	770255
Butler of McConnell *(No longer considered a branch campus)*	770257
Wichita Technical Institute *(No longer degree granting)*	010503

Kentucky

Daymar College-Bowling Green *(Closed)*	666439

Louisiana

Baton Rouge School of Computers *(No longer accredited by ACCSC)*	021975

Maryland

Stratford University Baltimore Campus *(Closed)*	770616

FICE/ID Number

Michigan

Career Quest Learning Center *(Closed)*	039153
University of Detroit Mercy Corktown Campus *(No longer considered a branch campus)*	770291
University of Detroit Mercy School of Law *(No longer considered a branch campus)*	770292

Minnesota

Hennepin Technical College *(No longer considered a branch campus)*	770299

Missouri

Missouri University of Science & Technology Global-St. Louis *(No longer considered a branch campus)*	770323
Saint Louis College of Health Careers-Fenton Campus *(No longer degree granting)*	666274

New Jersey

Brookdale Community College Freehold Campus *(No longer considered a branch campus)*	770125
Eastern International College-Belleville Campus *(Closed)*	770580
University of Phoenix Jersey City Campus *(Closed)*	770218
Westminster Choir College *(No longer considered a branch campus)*	770128

New York

Long Island University - LIU Brentwood *(No longer considered a branch campus)*	666076
Mesivta Torah Vodaath Seminary *(No longer recognized by AIJS)*	007264
Pacific College of Health and Science *(No longer considered a branch campus)*	666139

North Carolina

Hosanna Bible College *(No longer accredited by TRACS)*	667373
University of Phoenix Charlotte Campus *(Closed)*	770216

Ohio

Remington College Cleveland Campus *(No longer degree granting)*	007777
Southern State Community College Fayette Campus *(Closed)*	770362
Zane State College *(No longer considered a branch campus)*	770365

Oklahoma

Platt College *(No longer degree granting)*	770585

Oregon

Birthingway College of Midwifery *(Closed)*	036683

Institution Changes

FICE/ID Number

FICE/ID Number

Name Changes

Arizona

from: Arizona College 031150
  to: Arizona College of Nursing

from: West Coast Ultrasound Institute 770550
  to: Triad Education

California

from: American Graduate University 666982
  to: Patten University

from: Claremont Lincoln Univeristy 667215
  to: Claremont Lincoln University

from: College of Exercise Science, International Sports 042434
  Sciences Association, LLC
  to: Lional University

from: Emperor's College of Traditional Oriental 026090
  Medicine
  to: Emperor's College

from: Humboldt State University 001149
  to: California State Polytechnic University-Humboldt

from: Northwestern Polytechnic University 666759
  to: San Francisco Bay University

from: Reach Institute for School Leadership 667313
  to: Reach University

from: The Santa Barbara and Ventura Colleges of Law 667229
  to: The Colleges of Law

from: West Coast Ultrasound Institute 036393
  to: Triad Education

from: West Coast Ultrasound Institute 770942
  to: Triad Education

Colorado

from: Otero Junior College 001362
  to: Otero College

from: Pikes Peak Community College 008896
  to: Pikes Peak State College

from: Spartan College 007297
  to: Spartan College of Aeronautics and Technology

from: Trinidad State Junior College 001368
  to: Trinidad State College

from: Trinidad State Junior College San Luis Valley 770047
  Campus
  to: Trinidad State College San Luis Valley Campus

Connecticut

from: Hartford Seminary 001387
  to: Hartford International University for Religion and
  Peace

from: Paier College of Art 007459
  to: Paier College

Florida

from: College of Business and Technology 030716
  to: CBT Technology Institute

from: Naaleh College 667347
  to: Woodmont College

Georgia

from: Miller-Motte Technical College 770710
  to: Miller-Motte College

from: Miller-Motte Technical College 770711
  to: Miller-Motte College

from: Miller-Motte Technical College 770844
  to: Miller-Motte College

Illinois

from: UIC John Marshall Law School 001698
  to: University of Illinois Chicago School of Law

Iowa

from: Morningside College 001879
  to: Morningside University

Kansas

from: Grantham University 004283
  to: University of Arkansas - Grantham

from: Kansas State University Polytechnic, College of 004611
  Technology and Aviation
  to: Kansas State University Salina Aerospace and
  Technology Campus

Louisiana

from: Louisiana College 002007
  to: Louisiana Christian University

from: Northwest Louisiana Technical College 005469
  Shreveport Campus
  to: Northwest Louisiana Technical Community
  College Shreveport Campus

Michigan

from: Compass College of Cinematic Arts 041633
  to: Compass College of Film and Media

Minnesota

from: American Academy of Acupuncture and Oriental 038333
  Medicine
  to: American Academy of Health and Wellness

from: Hibbing Community College, A Technical and 002355
  Community College
  to: Minnesota North College

from: Itasca Community College 002356
  to: Minnesota North College - Itasca

from: Mesabi Range College 004009
  to: Minnesota North College - Mesabi Range Virginia

from: Mesabi Range College Eveleth 770300
  to: Minnesota North College - Mesabi Range Eveleth

from: Rainy River Community College 006775
  to: Minnesota North College - Rainy River

from: Vermilion Community College 002350
  to: Minnesota North College - Vermilion

Missouri

from: Saint Louis College of Health Careers-South 023405
  Taylor
  to: Saint Louis College of Health Careers

Montana

from: Yellowstone Christian College 667254
  to: Montana Christian College

Nebraska

from: Mid-Plains Community College North Platte - 770338
  North Campus
  to: Mid-Plains Community College North Platte

Institution Changes

FICE/ID Number

New Jersey

from: Union County College   002643
   to: Union College

New Mexico

from: New Mexico State University at Carlsbad   002659
   to: Southeast New Mexico College

New York

from: Dominican College of Blauvelt   002713
   to: Dominican University New York

from: Houghton College   002734
   to: Houghton University

from: Iona College   002737
   to: Iona University

from: Maria College of Albany   002763
   to: Maria College

from: Medaille College   002777
   to: Medaille University

from: Medaille College Rochester Campus   770140
   to: Medaille University Rochester Campus

from: Memorial College of Nursing   012203
   to: St. Peter's Hospital College of Nursing

from: Molloy College   002775
   to: Molloy University

from: Nyack College   002790
   to: Alliance University

from: Roberts Wesleyan College   002805
   to: Roberts Wesleyan University

from: Schenectady County Community College   006785
   to: SUNY Schenectady County Community College

from: St. John Fisher College   002821
   to: St. John Fisher University

from: Touro College Executive Offices   667405
   to: Touro University - Executive Offices

from: Touro College Flatbush   770146
   to: Touro University - Flatbush

from: Touro College Harlem   770989
   to: Touro University - Harlem

from: Touro College Jacob D. Fuchsberg Law Center   770148
   to: Touro University - Long Island

from: Touro College Kew Gardens Hills   770992
   to: Touro University - Kew Gardens Hills

from: Touro College Main Campus   010142
   to: Touro University - Main Campus

from: Touro College of Dental Medicine   770991
   to: Touro University, Touro College of Dental
      Medicine - Westchester New York

from: Touro College of Osteopathic Medicine -   770990
      Middletown Campus
   to: Touro University - Middletown Campus

from: Utica College   002883
   to: Utica University

from: Yeshiva Gedolah Ohr Yisrael   667077
   to: Yeshiva Ohr Yisrael

North Carolina

from: Miller-Motte Technical College   030632
   to: Miller-Motte College

Ohio

from: American Winds College of Aeronaautics   667401
   to: American Winds College of Aeronautics

from: Ohio Valley College of Technology   023014
   to: East Ohio College

Oklahoma

from: Platt College   023068
   to: Miller-Motte College

Pennsylvania

from: Bloomsburg University of Pennsylvania   003315
   to: Commonwealth University of Pennsylvania

from: California University of Pennsylvania   003316
   to: Pennsylvania Western University

from: Harrisburg Area Community College Lancaster   770157
      Campus
   to: HACC Lancaster Campus

from: Harrisburg Area Community College Lebanon   770158
      Campus
   to: HACC Lebanon Campus

from: Harrisburg Area Community College York   770159
      Campus
   to: HACC York Campus

from: Moravian College   003301
   to: Moravian University

from: Triangle Tech   770586
   to: Triangle Tech, Sunbury

Puerto Rico

from: Universidad Ana G. Mendez Online Campus   667292
   to: Ana G. Mendez University

South Carolina

from: Converse College   003431
   to: Converse University

from: Miller-Motte Technical College   666256
   to: Miller-Motte College

from: Miller-Motte Technical College   770778
   to: Miller-Motte College

Tennessee

from: Daymar College   666492
   to: Hussian College Clarksville

from: Miller-Motte Technical College   770781
   to: Miller-Motte College

Utah

from: Ameritech College of Healthcare   022708
   to: Joyce University of Nursing and Health Sciences

from: Dixie State University   003671
   to: Utah Tech University

Virginia

from: Bluefield College   003703
   to: Bluefield University

from: Dabney S. Lancaster Community College   004996
   to: Mountain Gateway Community College

from: IGlobal University   667105
   to: Washington University of Science & Technology

from: Lord Fairfax Community College   008659
   to: Laurel Ridge Community College

from: Patrick Henry Community College   003751
   to: Patrick & Henry Community College

Washington

from: Community Colleges of Spokane District 17   010784
   to: Community Colleges of Spokane

	FICE/ID Number
from: Edmonds Community College	005001
to: Edmonds College	
from: Gather 4 Him Bible College	667359
to: Pacific Northwest Christian College	

Wisconsin

from: College of Menominee Nation Oneida Campus	770424
to: College of Menominee Nation	

Codes and Descriptions of Administrative Officers

We have modified the Manpower Codes used in the *Higher Education Directory* to better reflect the organizational structures of colleges and universities. Codes are now grouped by major organizational division—Executive, Academic, External Affairs, Fiscal Affairs, Institutional Affairs, Information Technology, and Student Affairs. Some codes have been redefined and several have been added. New and modified codes are marked by an asterisk (*).

Executive

(01) **Chief Executive Officer (President/Chancellor)** - Directs all affairs and operations of a higher education institution.

(02) **Chief Executive Officer Within a System (President/Chancellor)** - Directs all affairs and operations of a campus or an institution which is part of a university-wide system.

(03) **Executive Vice President** - Responsible for all or most functions and operations of an institution under the direction of the Chief Executive Officer.

(100) **Chief of Staff** - Senior non-secretarial staff assistant to the President/Chancellor. Manages administration and operations of the Office of the President.

(00)* **Chairman of the Board** - Directs the operations of the institution's Board of Directors.

(101) **Secretary of the Institution/Board of Governors** - Responsible for liaison between the Board and the institution. Maintains governance and official Board records.

(125)* **President/Chancellor Emeritus** - A past chief executive currently holding an advisory or honorary position at the institution.

(17) **Chief of Health Care Professions** - Senior administrator of academic health care programs, hospitals, clinic or affiliated healthcare programs.

(12) **Director of Branch Campus** - Official who is in charge of a branch campus.

(04) **Administrative Assistant to the President** - Senior administrative assistant to the Chief Executive Officer.

(41) **Athletic Director** - Manages intramural and intercollegiate programs including employment, scheduling, promotion, maintenance and related functions.

Academic Affairs

(05) **Chief Academic Officer** - Directs the academic program of the institution. Typically includes academic planning, teaching, research, extensions and coordination of interdepartmental affairs. May include Provost.

(20) **Associate Academic Officer** - Responsible for many of the functions and operations under the direction of the Chief Academic Officer.

(08) **Chief Library Officer** - Directs the activities of all institutional libraries.

Dean or Director. Serves as the principal administrator for the institutional program indicated:

(47) **Agriculture**
(76) **Allied Health Sciences**
(48) **Architecture/Interior Design**
(49) **Art and Sciences**
(50) **Business**
(77) **Computer and Information Science**
(51) **Continuing Education**
(78) **Cooperative Education**
(52) **Dentistry**
(53) **Education**
(54) **Engineering**
(55) **Evening/Adult Programs**
(56) **Extension**
(59) **Family and Consumer Sciences**
(57) **Fine Arts**
(97) **General Studies**
(80) **Government/Public Affairs**
(58) **Graduate Programs**
(92) **Honors Program**
(79) **Humanities**
(60) **Journalism/Communications**

(61) **Law**
(62) **Library Services**
(81) **Mathematics/Sciences**
(63) **Medicine**
(64) **Music**
(65) **Natural Resources**
(66) **Nursing**
(75) **Occupational Education**
(106) **Online Education/E-learning**
(67) **Pharmacy**
(68) **Physical Education**
(82) **Political Science/International Affairs**
(107) **Professional Programs**
(69) **Public Health**
(83) **Social and Behavioral Sciences**
(70) **Social Work**
(87) **Summer Session/School**
(72) **Technology**
(73) **Theology**
(74) **Veterinary Medicine**
(94) **Women's Studies**

External Affairs

(111)* **Director of Institutional Advancement** - Responsible for the comprehensive plan to ensure ongoing growth in public awareness of an institution and its strategic goals.

(30) **Director of Development** - Organizes and directs programs connected with the fund raising activities of the institution. May include Advancement.

(110)* **Associate Advancement/Development Officer** - Assists and supports the Chief Advancement/Development Officer.

(29) **Director of Alumni Relations** - Coordinates alumni activities between the institution and the alumni.

(44) **Director Annual Giving** - Operates the annual giving from all supporters of the institutions.

(112)* **Director Planned Giving/Major Gifts** - Identifies, cultivates and solicits planned and major gifts for ongoing financial support.

(102) **Director of Foundation/Corporate Relations** - Directs institution's efforts in the area of soliciting grants and gifts from foundations and corporations.

(26) **Chief Public Relations/Marketing/Communications Officer** - Directs public relations program. May include alumni relations, publication, marketing and development.

(27) **Associate Public Relations/Marketing/Communications Officer** - Assists and reports to the Chief Public Relations/Marketing/Communications Officer.

(31) **Chief Community Relations Officer** - Directs the educational (usually non-credit), cultural and recreational services to the community.

(103) **Director of Workforce Development** - Directs the institution's efforts in course development and instruction for students and the community in skills necessary to gain employment.

Fiscal Affairs

(10) **Chief Financial/Business Officer** - Directs business and financial affairs including accounting, purchasing, investments, auxiliary enterprises and related business matters.

(21) **Associate Financial/Business Officer** - Assists and reports to the Chief Business Officer. May include Controller.

(45) **Chief Institutional Planning Officer** - Directs the long-range planning and the allocation of the institution's resources.

(115)* **Chief Investment Officer** - Responsible for the oversight of the endowment and other financial assets of the college.

(25) **Chief Contract and Grants Administrator** - Conducts administrative activities in connection with contracts and grants.

(109) **Chief Auxiliary Services Officer** - Responsible for management and operations of college support services including food service, bookstore, vending, student union, and printing.

(114)* **Chief Budget Administrator** - Responsible for preparation and management of institutional budgets.

(113)* **Bursar** - Responsible for the overall operations of student financial services including billing, receivables and cashiering functions.

(96) **Director of Purchasing** - Coordinates purchasing of goods and services.

(116)* **Audit Officer** - Responsible for independent assessment of the effectiveness of internal administrative accounting controls and helps ensure conformance with managerial policies.

(40) **Director of Bookstore** - Responsible for the operation of the bookstore including purchasing, advertising, sales, employment, inventory and related functions.

Institutional Affairs

(11) **Chief of Operations/Administration** - Responsible for administrative functions that are generally non-academic and non-financial.

(117)* **Chief Risk Management Officer** - Responsible for the oversight of the college's risk management programs including emergency and crisis response management, operational risk, technology and cyber risks, insurance and facility vulnerability, and threat assessment.

(15) **Chief Human Resources Officer** - Administers the institution's personnel policies and programs for staff or faculty and staff.

(16) **Associate Human Resources Officer** - Assists and reports to the Chief Human Resources Officer.

(118)* **Director Employee Benefits** - Manages the college's compensation and benefit programs, policies and procedures.

(09) **Director of Institutional Research** - Conducts research and studies on the institution including design of studies, data collection, analysis and reporting.

(46) **Chief Research Officer** - Initiates and directs research in using the facilities and personnel in new areas of academic and scientific exploration.

(108) **Director of Institutional Assessment** - Facilitates and directs institution-wide assessment activities for academic programs and non-academic departments.

(22) **Director of Affirmative Action/Equal Opportunity** - Responsible for the institution's program relating to affirmative action and equal opportunity.

(28) **Director of Diversity** - Responsible for the institution's diversity programs.

(43) **Director of Legal Services (General Counsel)** - Salaried staff person responsible for advising on legal rights, obligations and related matters.

(19) **Director of Security/Safety** - Manages campus police. Responsible for security programs, training, traffic and parking regulations.

(18) **Chief Facilities/Physical Plant Officer** - Responsible for the construction, rehabilitation and maintenance of buildings and grounds.

(86) **Director of Government Relations** - Coordinates institution's relations with local, state, and federal government.

Information Technology (IT)

(13) **Chief Information Technology Officer (CIO)** - Responsible for oversight of IT infrastructure and support, computation and communication infrastructure and services, and administrative information systems across the institution.

(14) **Associate Information Technology Officer** - Assists and reports to the Chief Information Officer.

(24) **Director of Educational Media** - Responsible for audio-visual services and multi-media learning devices.

(90) **Director of Academic Computing** - Responsible for operation and coordination of the institution's various academic computer facilities and labs.

(91) **Director of Administrative Computing** - Responsible for operation of the institution's administrative computing facility.

(105) **Director of Web Services** - Directs the development, operations and content of the institution's web sites.

(119)* **Director of IT Security** - Responsible for technology security in order to protect information and prevent unauthorized access.

(120)* **Director of Online/E-learning Platform** - Coordinates all aspects of institution's online learning platforms.

Student Affairs

(32) **Chief Student Affairs/Student Life Officer** - Responsible for the direction of student life programs including counseling and testing, housing, placement, student union, relationships with student organizations and related functions.

(35) **Associate Student Affairs/Student Life Officer** - Assists Chief Student Life Officer in the non-academic student life activities.

(84) **Director of Enrollment Management** - Plans, develops, and implements strategies to sustain enrollment. Supervises administration of all admissions and financial aid operations.

(07) **Director of Admissions** - Responsible for the recruitment, selection and admission of students.

(123)* **Director of Graduate Admissions** - Responsible for the recruitment, selection and admission of graduate students.

(06) **Registrar** - Responsible for student registration, scheduling of classes, examinations and classroom facilities, student records and related matters.

(37) **Director of Student Financial Aid** - Directs the administration of all forms of student aid.

(39) **Director Resident Life/Student Housing** - Manages student housing operations.

(36) **Director of Student Placement** - Directs the operation of the student placement office to provide career counseling and job placement services to undergraduates, graduates and alumni.

(38) **Director of Student Counseling** - Directs non-academic counseling and testing for students including referral to outside agencies.

(121)* **Director of Student Success/Academic Advising** - assists students in the development and ongoing achievement of their educational goals through academic support and planning.

(124)* **Director of Student Retention** - Develops and evaluates programs and initiatives to improve student retention, engagement and transition.

(89) **Director of First Year Experience** - Works with academic and students affairs to facilitate freshman engagement, learning, transition and integration into the college community.

(93) **Director of Minority Education/Students** - Develops and supports the overall success of students, particularly those from underrepresented minority groups.

(23) **Director of Health Services** - Directs the operation of clinics, medical staff and other programs which provide institutional health services.

(42) **Chaplain/Director Campus Ministry** - Plans, directs the pastoral ministry and religious activities.

(85) **Director of Foreign Students** - Directs student life activities solely concerned with foreign students.

(104) **Director of Study Abroad** - Coordinates and advises students and faculty on academic studies conducted internationally.

(33) **Dean of Men** - Directs student life activities solely concerned with male students.

(34) **Dean of Women** - Directs student life activities solely concerned with female students.

(122)* **Director of Greek Life** - Responsible for all aspects of fraternity and sorority life on campus.

Other

(88) **Use this code for those titles that do not fit the above positions.**

United States Department of Education Offices

Dr. Miguel Cardona **(A)**
Secretary of Education
United States Department of Education
400 Maryland Avenue, SW
Washington, DC 20202
(202) 401-2000
URL: www.ed.gov

Mr. James Kvaal **(B)**
Under Secretary of Education
Office of the Under Secretary
United States Department of Education
400 Maryland Avenue, SW
Room 7E307
Washington, DC 20202
(202) 453-7333
URL: sites.ed.gov/ous/

Annmarie Weisman **(C)**
Dpty Asst Secretary for Policy/Planning/
Innovation
Office of Postsecondary Education
United States Department of Education
400 Maryland Avenue, SW
Room 293-01
Washington, DC 20202
(202) 453-6914
E-MAIL: annmarie.weisman@ed.gov
URL: www2.ed.gov/about/offices/list/ope/ppi.
html

George Alan Smith Ed.D. **(D)**
Executive Director
National Advisory Committee on
Institutional Quality & Integrity
Office of Postsecondary Education
United States Department of Education
400 Maryland Avenue, SW
Room 271-03
Washington, DC 20202
(202) 453-7757
E-MAIL: george.alan.smith@ed.gov
URL: https://sites.ed.gov/naciqi

Herman Bounds Jr., Ed.S. **(E)**
Director
Accreditation Group
Office of Post Secondary Education
U.S. Department of Education
400 Maryland Avenue, SW
Room 270-01
Washington, DC 20202
(202) 453-6128
E-MAIL: herman.bounds@ed.gov
URL: www.ed.gov/accreditation?src=rn

Ms. Peggy Carr **(F)**
Commissioner
National Center for Education Statistics
550 12th Street, SW
Room 4061
Washington, DC 20202
(202) 245-6168
E-MAIL: peggy.carr@ed.gov
URL: www.nces.ed.gov

Statewide Agencies of Higher Education

ALABAMA

Alabama Commission on Higher Education **(G)**
PO Box 302000
Montgomery, AL 36130-2000
(334) 242-1998
Dr. Jim Purcell
Executive Director
E-MAIL: jim.purcell@ache.edu
URL: www.ache.edu

Alabama Community College System **(H)**
PO Box 302130
Montgomery, AL 36130-2130
(334) 293-4524
FAX: (334) 293-4504
Jimmy H. Baker
Chancellor
E-MAIL: jimmy.baker@accs.edu
URL: www.accs.edu

ALASKA

Alaska Commission on Postsecondary Education **(I)**
PO Box 110505
Juneau, AK 99811-0505
(907) 465-6740
FAX: (907) 465-5316
Ms. Sana Efird
Executive Director
E-MAIL: eed.acpe-execdirector@alaska.gov
URL: www.acpe.alaska.gov

ARIZONA

Arizona Board of Regents **(J)**
2700 North Central Avenue
Suite 400
Phoenix, AZ 85004
(602) 229-2505
FAX: (602) 229-2555
Mr. John Arnold
Executive Director
E-MAIL: john.arnold@azregents.edu
URL: www.azregents.edu

Arizona Board of Regents Arizona Commission for Postsecondary Education **(K)**
2700 North Central Avenue
Suite 400
Phoenix, AZ 85004
(602) 229-2500
FAX: (602) 229-2555
Daniel Helm
Interim Executive Director
E-MAIL: acpe@azhighered.gov
URL: highered.az.gov

ARKANSAS

Arkansas Division of Higher Education **(L)**
101 East Capitol Avenue
Suite 300
Little Rock, AR 72201
(501) 371-2000
Dr. Maria Markham
Director
E-MAIL: maria.markham@adhe.edu
URL: www.adhe.edu

CALIFORNIA

California Community Colleges Chancellor's Office **(M)**
1102 Q Street
Suite 4400
Sacramento, CA 95811
(916) 445-8752
Dr. Daisy Gonzales
Interim Chancellor
E-MAIL: info@cccco.edu
URL: www.cccco.edu

COLORADO

Colorado Department of Higher Education **(N)**
1600 Broadway
Suite 2200
Denver, CO 80202
(303) 862-3001
FAX: (303) 996-1329
Dr. Angie Paccione
Executive Director
E-MAIL: questions@dhe.state.co.us
URL: highered.colorado.gov

Colorado Community College System **(O)**
9101 East Lowry Boulevard
Denver, CO 80230-6011
(720) 858-2424
FAX: (303) 620-4043
Joseph Garcia
Chancellor
E-MAIL: chancellor@cccs.edu
URL: www.cccs.edu

CONNECTICUT

Board of Regents for Higher Education Connecticut State Colleges & Universities **(P)**
61 Woodland Street
Hartford, CT 06105
(860) 723-0011
Terrence Cheng
President
E-MAIL: tcheng@commnet.edu
URL: www.ct.edu/regents/

Office of Higher Education **(Q)**
450 Columbus Boulevard
Suite 707
Hartford, CT 06103
(860) 947-1801
Mr. Timothy D. Larson
Executive Director
E-MAIL: timothy.d.larson@ct.gov
URL: www.ctohe.org

DELAWARE

Delaware Department of Education Higher Education Office **(R)**
401 Federal Street
Dover, DE 19901
(302) 735-4120
FAX: (302) 739-5894
Shana Payne
Director
E-MAIL: dheo@doe.k12.de.us
URL: www.delawarestudentsuccess.org

Delaware Technical Community College **(S)**
PO Box 897
Dover, DE 19903
(302) 857-1667
Dr. Mark T. Brainard
President
E-MAIL: brainard@dtcc.edu
URL: www.dtcc.edu

DISTRICT OF COLUMBIA

Office of the State Superintendent of Education Government of the District of Columbia **(T)**
1050 First Street, NE
Washington, DC 20002
(202) 272-6436
Dr. Christina Grant
State Superintendent of Education
E-MAIL: christina.grant@dc.gov
URL: www.osse.dc.gov

District of Columbia Higher Education Licensure Commission **(U)**
1050 1st Street, NE
5th Floor
Washington, DC 20002
(202) 481-3951
FAX: (202) 741-0229
Mrs. Angela Lee
Executive Director
E-MAIL: osse.elcmail@dc.gov
URL: helc.osse.dc.gov

FLORIDA

Board of Governors State University System of Florida **(V)**
325 West Gaines Street
Suite 1614
Tallahassee, FL 32399-0400
(850) 245-0466
FAX: (850) 245-9685
Mr. Marshall M. Criser III
Chancellor
E-MAIL: chancellor@flbog.edu
URL: www.flbog.edu

Florida Department of Education Division of Florida Colleges **(W)**
325 West Gaines Street
Suite 1244 Turlington Building
Tallahassee, FL 32399
(850) 245-0407
Ms. Kathryn S. Hebda
Chancellor
E-MAIL: chancellorfcs@fldoe.org
URL: www.fldoe.org/schools/higher-ed/fl-college-system/

GEORGIA

Board of Regents of the University System of Georgia **(X)**
270 Washington Street, SW
Atlanta, GA 30334
(404) 962-3049
Dr. Sunny Purdue
Chancellor
E-MAIL: chancellor@usg.edu
URL: www.usg.edu/regents/

HAWAII

University of Hawaii Board of Regents **(Y)**
2444 Dole Street
Bachman Hall, Room 209
Honolulu, HI 96822
(808) 956-8213
FAX: (808) 956-5156
Mr. Randy Moore
Chair
E-MAIL: bor@hawaii.edu
URL: www.hawaii.edu/offices/bor/

IDAHO

Idaho State Board of Education **(Z)**
PO Box 83720
Boise, ID 83720-0037
(208) 332-1571
FAX: (208) 334-2632
Mr. Matt Freeman
Executive Director
E-MAIL: matt.freeman@osbe.idaho.gov
URL: www.boardofed.idaho.gov

ILLINOIS

Illinois Board of Higher Education (A)
1 N. Old State Capitol Plaza
Suite 333
Springfield, IL 62701-1377
(217) 782-2551
Fax: (888) 261-2881
Ms. Ginger Ostro
Executive Director
E-mail: chase@ibhe.org
URL: www.ibhe.org

Illinois Community College Board (B)
401 East Capitol Avenue
Springfield, IL 62701
(217) 785-0123
Fax: (217) 524-4981
Dr. Brian Durham
Executive Director
E-mail: brian.durham@illinois.gov
URL: www2.iccb.org/iccb/

INDIANA

Indiana Commission for Higher (C)
Education
101 West Ohio Street
Suite 300
Indianapolis, IN 46204
(317) 232-1020
Fax: (317) 464-4410
Mr. Chris Lowery
Commissioner for Higher Education
E-mail: clowery@che.in.gov
URL: www.in.gov/che/

IOWA

Board of Regents, State of Iowa (D)
11260 Aurora Avenue
Urbandale, IA 50322-7905
(515) 281-3934
Fax: (515) 281-6420
Mr. Mark J. Braun
Executive Director
E-mail: mark.braun@iowaregents.edu
URL: www.iowaregents.edu

Iowa College Student Aid (E)
Commission
475 SW 5th Street
Suite D
Des Moines, IA 50309
(515) 725-3410
Fax: (515) 725-3401
Dr. Mark Wiederspan
Executive Director
E-mail: mark.wiederspan@iowa.gov
URL: www.iowacollegeaid.gov

Iowa Department of Education (F)
Division of Community Colleges and
Workforce Preparation
400 East 14th Street
Des Moines, IA 50319-0146
(515) 281-8260
Jeremy Varner
Administrator
E-mail: jeremy.varner@iowa.gov
URL: www.educateiowa.gov

KANSAS

Kansas Board of Regents (G)
1000 SW Jackson Street
Suite 520
Topeka, KS 66612-1368
(785) 430-4240
Fax: (785) 430-4233
Dr. Blake Flanders
President and CEO
E-mail: bflanders@ksbor.org
URL: www.kansasregents.org

Kansas Legislative Research (H)
Department
Room 68 West, State Capitol Building
300 SW 10th Avenue
Topeka, KS 66612-1504
(785) 296-3181
Ms. Jessa Farmer
Senior Research Analyst
E-mail: kslegres@klrd.ks.gov
URL: www.kslegresearch.org

KENTUCKY

Kentucky Council on Postsecondary (I)
Education
100 Airport Road
Third Floor
Frankfort, KY 40601
(502) 892-3001 or (502) 573-1555
Fax: (502) 573-1535
Dr. Aaron Thompson
President
E-mail: aaron.thompson@ky.gov
URL: cpe.ky.gov

Kentucky Community & Technical (J)
College System
300 North Main Street
Versailles, KY 40383
(859) 256-3248
Fax: (859) 256-3116
Dr. Paul Czarapata
President
E-mail: paul.czarapata@kctcs.edu
URL: www.kctcs.edu

LOUISIANA

Louisiana Board of Regents (K)
1201 N. Third Street
Suite 6-200
Baton Rouge, LA 70802
(225) 342-4253
Dr. Kim Hunter Reed
Commissioner of Higher Education
E-mail: emily.skaikay@laregents.edu
URL: regents.la.gov

Louisiana Department of Education (L)
PO Box 94064
Baton Rouge, LA 70804-9064
(225) 342-3607
Fax: (225) 342-7316
Dr. Cade Brumley
State Superintendent of Education
E-mail: cade.brumley@la.gov
URL: www.louisianabelieves.com

MAINE

Maine Department of Education (M)
Higher Education and Educator Support
Services
23 State House Station
Augusta, ME 04333-0023
(207) 624-6620
Fax: (207) 624-6700
Ms. Pender Makin
Commissioner of Education
E-mail: commish.doe@maine.gov
URL: www.maine.gov/doe/

MARYLAND

Maryland Higher Education (N)
Commission
6 North Liberty Street, 10th Floor
Baltimore, MD 21201
(410) 767-3300
Fax: (410) 332-0250
Dr. James D. Fielder
Secretary of Higher Education
E-mail: james.fielder@maryland.gov
URL: www.mhec.maryland.gov

MASSACHUSETTS

Massachusetts Department of (O)
Higher Education
One Ashburton Place
Room 1401
Boston, MA 02108
(617) 994-6901
Fax: (617) 727-6656
Mr. Carlos Santiago
Commissioner
E-mail: commissioner@dhe.mass.edu
URL: www.mass.edu

MICHIGAN

Michigan Department of Labor and (P)
Economic Opportunity, Proprietary/Post
Secondary Schools
201 N. Washington Square
Lansing, MI 48913
(517) 930-9135
Vern Westendorf
State Administrative Manager
E-mail: westendorfv@michigan.gov
URL: www.michigan.gov/pss

Michigan Workforce Development (Q)
201 North Washington Square
Victor Office Center, 3rd Floor
Lansing, MI 48913
(517) 335-5858
Fax: (517) 241-9810
URL: www.michigan.gov/wda

MINNESOTA

Minnesota Office of Higher (R)
Education
1450 Energy Park Drive
Suite 350
St. Paul, MN 55108-5227
(651) 642-0567
Fax: (651) 642-0675
Mr. Dennis W. Olson Jr.
Commissioner
E-mail: info.ohe@state.mn.us
URL: www.ohe.state.mn.us

Minnesota State Colleges and (S)
Universities
30 7th Street East
Suite 350
St. Paul, MN 55101-7804
(651) 201-1638
Dr. Devinder Malhotra
Chancellor
E-mail: chancellor@minnstate.edu
URL: www.minnstate.edu

MISSISSIPPI

Mississippi Board of Trustees of (T)
State Institutions of Higher Learning
3825 Ridgewood Road
Jackson, MS 39211
(601) 432-6198
Dr. Alfred Rankins Jr.
Commissioner of Higher Education
E-mail: commissioner@ihl.state.ms.us
URL: www.mississippi.edu/ihl/

Mississippi Community College (U)
Board
3825 Ridgewood Drive
Jackson, MS 39211
(601) 432-6734
Mr. Kell Smith
Executive Director
E-mail: ksmith@mccb.edu
URL: www.mccb.edu

MISSOURI

Coordinating Board for Higher (V)
Education Missouri Department of Higher
Education
PO Box 1469
Jefferson City, MO 65101
(573) 751-1876
Mr. Leroy Wade
Interim Commissioner of Higher Education
E-mail: info@dhewd.mo.gov
URL: dhewd.mo.gov/cbhe/

MONTANA

Office of the Commissioner of (W)
Higher Education
PO Box 203201
Helena, MT 59620-3201
(406) 449-9125
Fax: (406) 449-9171
Mr. Clayton Christian
Commissioner
E-mail: cchristian@montana.edu
URL: www.mus.edu/che

NEBRASKA

Nebraska's Coordinating (X)
Commission for Postsecondary
Education
PO Box 95005
Lincoln, NE 68509-5005
(402) 471-2847
Dr. Michael Baumgartner
Executive Director
E-mail: mike.baumgartner@nebraska.gov
URL: ccpe.nebraska.gov

NEW HAMPSHIRE

New Hampshire Department of (Y)
Education Division of Educator Support
and Higher Education Higher Education
Commission
101 Pleasant Street
Concord, NH 03301
(603) 271-3494
Mr. Stephen Appleby
Director
E-mail: stephen.m.appleby@doe.nh.gov
URL: www.education.nh.gov/who-we-are/
higher-education-commission

Community College System of New (Z)
Hampshire
26 College Drive
Concord, NH 03301
(603) 230-3501
Dr. Mark Rubinstein
Chancellor
E-mail: mrubinstein@ccsnh.edu
URL: www.ccsnh.edu

NEW JERSEY

State of New Jersey Office of the (a)
Secretary of Higher Education
1 John Fitch Plaza, 10th Floor
PO Box 542
Trenton, NJ 08625-0542
(609) 292-8052
Fax: (609) 292-7225
Brian K. Bridges PhD
Secretary of Higher Education
E-mail: brian.bridges@oshe.nj.gov
URL: nj.gov/highereducation/

NEW MEXICO

New Mexico Higher Education (b)
Department
2044 Galisteo Street
Suite 4
Santa Fe, NM 87505
(505) 476-8400
Ms. Stephanie Rodriguez
Cabinet Secretary
E-mail: exec.admin@state.nm.us
URL: www.hed.state.nm.us

NEW YORK

New York State Education (c)
Department
89 Washington Avenue
Room 111
Albany, NY 12234
(518) 474-3852
Dr. Betty A. Rosa
Commissioner
E-mail: commissioner@nysed.gov
URL: www.nysed.gov

Community Colleges and the (d)
Education Pipeline
The State University of New York
353 Broadway, Room T9
Albany, NY 12246
(518) 320-1276
Johanna Duncan-Poitier
Senior Vice Chancellor
E-mail: johanna.duncan-poitier@suny.edu
URL: www.suny.edu/powerofsuny/
educationpipeline/

New York State Education (e)
Department Office of Higher Education
89 Washington Avenue
Room 975
Albany, NY 12234
(518) 486-3633
Mr. William Murphy
Deputy Commissioner
E-mail: hedepcom@nysed.gov
URL: highered.nysed.gov

NORTH CAROLINA

The University of North Carolina (f)
System
140 Friday Center Drive
Chapel Hill, NC 27517
(919) 962-4622
Mr. Peter Hans
President
E-mail: president@northcarolina.edu
URL: www.northcarolina.edu

Statewide Agencies of Higher Education

North Carolina Community Colleges (A)
200 West Jones Street
Raleigh, NC 27603
(919) 807-6950
Mr. William S. Carver
Interim President
E-MAIL: bcarver@nccommunitycolleges.edu
URL: www.nccommunitycolleges.edu

NORTH DAKOTA

North Dakota State Board of Higher (B)
Education
600 East Boulevard Avenue, Dept 215
State Capitol, 10th Floor
Bismarck, ND 58505-0230
(701) 328-2960
FAX: (701) 328-2961
Mr. Nick Hacker
Board Chair
E-MAIL: nicholas.hacker@ndus.edu
URL: www.ndus.edu/board

OHIO

Ohio Department of Higher (C)
Education
25 South Front Street
Columbus, OH 43215
(614) 466-6000
Mr. Randy Gardner
Chancellor
E-MAIL: chancellor@highered.ohio.gov
URL: www.ohiohighered.org

OKLAHOMA

Oklahoma State Regents for Higher (D)
Education
655 Research Parkway
Suite 200
Oklahoma City, OK 73104
(405) 225-9100
FAX: (405) 225-9235
Ms. Allison D. Garrett
Chancellor
E-MAIL: chancellorgarrett@osrhe.edu
URL: www.okhighered.org

OREGON

Higher Education Coordinating (E)
Commission
3225 25th Street SE
Salem, OR 97302
(971) 273-9222
Mr. Ben Cannon
Executive Director
E-MAIL: info.hecc@hecc.oregon.gov
URL: www.oregon.gov/HigherEd

Oregon Higher Education (F)
Coordinating Commission Office of
Community Colleges and Workforce
Development
3225 25th Street SE
Salem, OR 97302
(503) 947-2428
Donna Lewelling
Director
E-MAIL: donna.j.lewelling@hecc.oregon.gov
URL: www.oregon.gov/highered/about/
pages/office-ccwd.aspx

PENNSYLVANIA

Pennsylvania Department of (G)
Education Office of Postsecondary and
Higher Education
333 Market Street
12th Floor
Harrisburg, PA 17126-0333
(717) 787-4313
FAX: (717) 772-3622
Tanya I. Garcia Ph.D.
Deputy Secretary and Commissioner
E-MAIL: tagarcia@pa.gov
URL: www.education.pa.gov/postsecondary-
adult/pages/default.aspx

Pennsylvania Department of (H)
Education Liaison to Postsecondary and
Higher Education Institutions
333 Market Street
12th Floor
Harrisburg, PA 17126-0333
(717) 783-6786
FAX: (717) 772-3622
Ms. Lynette Kuhn
Division Chief - Higher Education, Access &
Equity
E-MAIL: lykuhn@pa.gov
URL: www.education.pa.gov

RHODE ISLAND

Rhode Island Office of the (I)
Postsecondary Commissioner
560 Jefferson Boulevard
Suite 200
Warwick, RI 02886
(401) 736-1100
Dr. Shannon Gilkey
Commissioner on Postsecondary Education
E-MAIL: media@riopc.edu
URL: riopc.edu

Community College of Rhode Island (J)
400 East Avenue
Warwick, RI 02886
(401) 825-2188
FAX: (401) 825-2166
Dr. Meghan Hughes
President
E-MAIL: meghanhughes@ccri.edu
URL: www.ccri.edu

SOUTH CAROLINA

South Carolina Commission on (K)
Higher Education
1122 Lady Street
Suite 400
Columbia, SC 29201
(803) 737-2155
Dr. Rusty L. Monhollon
President and Executive Director
E-MAIL: rmonhollon@che.sc.gov
URL: www.che.sc.gov

South Carolina State Board for (L)
Technical and Comprehensive Education
111 Executive Center Drive
Columbia, SC 29210
(803) 896-5320
Dr. Tim Hardee
System President
E-MAIL: andrewsl@sctechsystem.edu
URL: www.sctechsystem.edu

SOUTH DAKOTA

South Dakota Board of Regents (M)
306 East Capitol Avenue
Suite 200
Pierre, SD 57501
(605) 773-3455
FAX: (605) 773-5320
Brian L. Maher
Executive Director and Chief Executive
Officer
E-MAIL: info@sdbor.edu
URL: sdbor.edu

South Dakota Department of (N)
Education
Office of the Secretary
800 Governors Drive
Pierre, SD 57501-2235
(605) 773-5669
FAX: (605) 773-6139
Ms. Tiffany Sanderson
Secretary of Education
E-MAIL: doe@state.sd.us
URL: doe.sd.gov

TENNESSEE

Tennessee Higher Education (O)
Commission
312 Rosa Parks Avenue
9th Floor
Nashville, TN 37243
(615) 741-7562
Dr. Emily House
Executive Director
E-MAIL: emily.house@tn.gov
URL: https:www.tn.gov/thec

Tennessee Board of Regents (P)
1 Bridgestone Park
Nashville, TN 37214
(615) 365-1505
Dr. Jothany L. Reed
Vice Chancellor for Academic Affairs
E-MAIL: jothany.reed@tbr.edu
URL: www.tbr.edu/board/tennessee-board-
regents

University of Tennessee Board of (Q)
Trustees
UT Tower - Suite 1235
400 W. Summit Hill Drive
Knoxville, TN 37902
(865) 974-8886
Ms. Cynthia Moore
Secretary/Special Counsel to the Board of
Trustees
E-MAIL: cynthia.moore@tennessee.edu
URL: trustees.tennessee.edu

TEXAS

Texas Higher Education (R)
Coordinating Board
PO Box 12788
Austin, TX 78711-2788
(512) 427-6101
FAX: (512) 427-6127
Harrison Keller
Commissioner of Higher Education
E-MAIL: commissioner@highered.texas.gov
URL: www.highered.texas.gov

Texas Higher Education (S)
Coordinating Board Division of College
Readiness and Success
PO Box 12788
Austin, TX 78711-2788
(512) 427-6247
FAX: (512) 427-6127
Jerel Booker J.D.
Assistant Commissioner
E-MAIL: jerel.booker@highered.texas.gov
URL: www.highered.texas.gov

UTAH

Utah System of Higher Education (T)
State Board of Regents
60 South 400 West
Salt Lake City, UT 84101-1284
(801) 646-4756
Mr. David Woolstenhulme
Commissioner of Higher Education
E-MAIL: dwoolstenhulme@ushe.edu
URL: www.ushe.edu

VERMONT

Vermont Agency of Education (U)
1 National Life Drive
Davis 5
Montpelier, VT 05620-2501
(802) 828-1130
FAX: (802) 828-6430
Mr. Brad James
Education Finance Manager
E-MAIL: brad.james@vermont.gov
URL: www.education.vermont.gov

VIRGINIA

State Council of Higher Education (V)
for Virginia
101 North 14th Street
James Monroe Building, 10th Floor
Richmond, VA 23219
(804) 225-2600
Mr. Peter Blake
Director
E-MAIL: peterblake@schev.edu
URL: www.schev.edu

Virginia's Community Colleges (W)
300 Arboretum Place
Suite 200
Richmond, VA 23236
(804) 819-4972
Sharon Morrissey
Interim Chancellor
E-MAIL: smorrissey@vccs.edu
URL: www.vccs.edu

WASHINGTON

Washington Student Achievement (X)
Council
P.O. Box 43430
Olympia, WA 98504
(360) 753-7800
Mr. Michael P. Meotti
Executive Director
E-MAIL: info@wsac.wa.gov
URL: www.wsac.wa.gov

Washington State Board for (Y)
Community and Technical Colleges
PO Box 42495
Olympia, WA 98504-2495
(360) 704-4355
FAX: (360) 704-4415
Paul Francis
Executive Director
E-MAIL: pfrancis@sbctc.edu
URL: www.sbctc.edu

WEST VIRGINIA

West Virginia Higher Education (Z)
Policy Commission
1018 Kanawha Boulevard, East
Suite 700
Charleston, WV 25301-2800
(304) 558-0699
FAX: (304) 558-1011
Dr. Sarah Armstrong Tucker
Chancellor
E-MAIL: sarah.tucker@wvhepc.edu
URL: https://www.wvhepc.edu

WISCONSIN

State of Wisconsin Higher (a)
Educational Aids Board
PO Box 7885
Madison, WI 53707-7885
(608) 267-2206
FAX: (608) 267-2808
Dr. Connie Hutchison
Executive Secretary
E-MAIL: connie.hutchinson@wi.gov
URL: heab.wi.gov

Wisconsin Technical College System (b)
PO Box 7874
Madison, WI 53707-7874
(608) 267-9066
Dr. Morna K. Foy
President
E-MAIL: president@wtcsystem.edu
URL: www.wtcsystem.edu

WYOMING

Wyoming Community College (c)
Commission
2300 Capitol Avenue
5th Floor, Suite B
Cheyenne, WY 82002
(307) 777-7763
Dr. Sandy Caldwell
Executive Director
E-MAIL: sandra.caldwell@wyo.gov
URL: communitycolleges.wy.edu

AMERICAN SAMOA

Board of Higher Education (d)
(American Samoa) American Samoa
Community College
PO Box 2609
Pago Pago, AS 96799
(684) 699-9155
E-MAIL: info@amsamoa.edu
URL: www.amsamoa.edu

FEDERATED STATES OF MICRONESIA

Board of Regents College of (e)
Micronesia-FSM
PO Box 159
Kolonia Pohnpei, FM 96941
(691) 320-2480
Suzanne L. Gallen
Chairwoman
E-MAIL: national@comfsm.fm
URL: www.comfsm.fm

PUERTO RICO

Puerto Rico Council on Education (A)
PO Box 9023271
San Juan, PR 00902-3271
(787) 722-2121, ext. 3800
Mr. Edward Moreno Alonso
Chairman Board of Education
URL: www.ce.pr.gov

Higher Education Associations

AACSB International (A)
777 South Harbour Island Boulevard
Suite 750
Tampa, FL 33602-5730
(813) 769-6500
Ms. Caryn L. Beck-Dudley
President and Chief Executive Officer
E-MAIL: mediarelations@aacsb.edu
URL: www.aacsb.edu

AASA, The School Superintendents (B)
Association
1615 Duke Street
Alexandria, VA 22314
(703) 528-0700
FAX: (703) 841-1543
Dr. Daniel A. Domenech
Executive Director
E-MAIL: ddomenech@aasa.org
URL: www.aasa.org

AAUW (C)
1310 L Street, NW
Suite 1000
Washington, DC 20005
(202) 785-7700
Gloria Blackwell
Chief Executive Officer
E-MAIL: executive@aauw.org
URL: www.aauw.org

ABET (D)
415 North Charles Street
Baltimore, MD 21201
(410) 347-7700
Michael K. J. Milligan PhD,PE,CAE
Executive Director and CEO
E-MAIL: comms@abet.org
URL: www.abet.org

Academy of Legal Studies in (E)
Business
Western Carolina University
College of Business
Forsyth Hall
Cullowhee, NC 28723
(513) 255-6950
Mr. Daniel Herron
Executive Secretary
E-MAIL: herron3653@gmail.com
URL: www.alsb.org

Academy of Nutrition and Dietetics (F)
Accreditation Council for Education in
Nutrition and Dietetics (ACEND)
120 South Riverside Plaza
Suite 2190
Chicago, IL 60606-6995
(312) 899-0040, ext. 5400
FAX: (312) 899-4817
Dr. Rayane AbuSabha
Executive Director
E-MAIL: acend@eatright.org
URL: www.eatrightpro.org/acend

Accreditation Commission for (G)
Acupuncture and Herbal Medicine
(ACAHM)
8941 Aztec Drive
Suite 2
Eden Prairie, MN 55347
(952) 212-2434
Mr. Mark McKenzie
Executive Director
E-MAIL: mark.mckenzie@acahm.org
URL: www.acahm.org

Accreditation Commission for (H)
Education in Nursing (ACEN)
3390 Peachtree Road, NE
Suite 1400
Atlanta, GA 30326
(404) 975-5000
Dr. Marsal Stoll
CEO
E-MAIL: mstoll@acenursing.org
URL: www.acenursing.org

Accreditation Commission for (I)
Midwifery Education (ACME)
8403 Colesville Road
Suite 1230
Silver Spring, MD 20910
(240) 485-1800
Angela Smith
Executive Director
E-MAIL: asmith@acnm.org
URL: www.midwife.org/Accreditation

Accreditation Committee - Perfusion (J)
Education
6663 South Sycamore Street
Littleton, CO 80120
(303) 794-6283
Ms. Theresa Sisneros
Executive Director
E-MAIL: office@ac-pe.org
URL: www.ac-pe.org

Accreditation Council for Business (K)
Schools and Programs
11520 West 119th Street
Overland Park, KS 66213
(913) 339-9356
Mr. Jeffrey Alderman
President & CEO
E-MAIL: info@acbsp.org
URL: www.acbsp.org

Accreditation Council for Pharmacy (L)
Education
190 S. LaSalle Street
Suite 300
Chicago, IL 60603
(312) 664-3575
FAX: (866) 228-2631
Janet P. Engle, PharmD PhD (Hon)
Executive Director
E-MAIL: jengle@acpe-accredit.org
URL: www.acpe-accredit.org

Accreditation Review Commission (M)
on Education for the Physician Assistant
(ARC-PA)
3325 Paddocks Parkway
Suite 345
Suwanee, GA 30024
(770) 476-1224
FAX: (470) 253-8271
Ms. Sharon Luke
Executive Director
E-MAIL: sharonluke@arc-pa.org
URL: www.arc-pa.org

Accreditation Review Committee for (N)
the Anesthesiologist Assistant
(612) 836-3311
Ms. Jennifer Anderson Warwick
Executive Director
E-MAIL: arc-aa@arc-aa.org
URL: https://caahep-public-site-5be3d9.webflow.io/
committees-on-accreditation/anesthesiologist-assistant

Accreditation Review Committee for (O)
Medical Illustration
University of Toronto
312 Health Sciences Complex
3359 Mississauga Road North
Mississauga, ON L5L 1CS
(905) 569-4265
Dr. Shelley Wall
ARC-MI Chair
E-MAIL: s.wall@utoronto.ca
URL: https://caahep-public-site-5be3d9.webflow.io/
committees-on-accreditation/medical-illustration

Accreditation Review Council on (P)
Education in Surgical Technology and
Surgical Assisting
19751 E. Main Street
Suite 339
Parker, CO 80138
(303) 694-9262
Mr. Ron Kruzel
Executive Director
E-MAIL: info@arcstsa.org
URL: www.arcstsa.org

Accrediting Bureau of Health (Q)
Education Schools (ABHES)
6116 Executive Boulevard
Suite 730
North Bethesda, MD 20852
(703) 917-9503
India Y. Tips
Executive Director
E-MAIL: itips@abhes.org
URL: www.abhes.org

Accrediting Commission for (R)
Community and Junior Colleges Western
Association of Schools and Colleges
331 J Street
Suite 200
Sacramento, CA 95814
(415) 506-0234
Dr. Mac Powell
President
E-MAIL: accjc@accjc.org
URL: accjc.org

Accrediting Commission of Career (S)
Schools and Colleges
2101 Wilson Boulevard
Suite 302
Arlington, VA 22201
(703) 247-4212
FAX: (703) 247-4533
Dr. Michale McComis
Executive Director
E-MAIL: mccomis@accsc.org
URL: www.accsc.org

Accrediting Council for Continuing (T)
Education & Training (ACCET)
1722 N Street, NW
Washington, DC 20036
(202) 955-1113
Mr. Res Helfer
Executive Director
E-MAIL: info@accet.org
URL: www.accet.org

Accrediting Council for Independent (U)
Colleges and Schools
1350 Eye Street, NW
Suite 560
Washington, DC 20005
(202) 336-6780
FAX: (202) 789-1747
Ms. Michelle Edwards
President & CEO
E-MAIL: medwards@acics.org
URL: www.acics.org

Accrediting Council on Education in (V)
Journalism and Mass Communications
University of Maryland
2101 Knight Hall
7765 Alumni Drive
College Park, MD 20742
(301) 405-1527
Patricia Thompson
ACEJMC Executive Director
E-MAIL: patt@umd.edu
URL: www.acejmc.org

ACPE: The Standard in Spiritual (W)
Care & Education
WeWork, Floor 4
120 West Trinity Place
Decatur, GA 30030
(678) 636-6217
Trace Haythorn Ph.D
Executive Director/CEO
E-MAIL: trace.haythorn@acpe.edu
URL: www.acpe.edu

ACT, Inc. (X)
500 ACT Drive
Box 168
Iowa City, IA 52243-0168
(319) 337-1000
Ms. Janet Godwin
Chief Executive Officer
URL: www.act.org

AEF: The Association of National (Y)
Advertisers (ANA) Educational
Foundation
155 E. 44th Street
4th Floor
New York, NY 10017
(212) 986-8060
Mr. Gordon McLean
President
E-MAIL: gm@aef.com
URL: aef.com

American Academy for Liberal (Z)
Education (AALE)
Washington, DC 20016
(202) 389-6550
Mary Ann Powers
Executive Director
E-MAIL: aaleinfo@aale.org
URL: www.aale.org

American Anthropological (a)
Association
2300 Clarendon Boulevard
Suite 1301
Arlington, VA 22201
(703) 528-1902
FAX: (703) 528-3546
Dr. Edward Liebow
Executive Director
E-MAIL: eliebow@americananthro.org
URL: www.americananthro.org

American Association for Adult and (b)
Continuing Education (AAACE)
2900 Delk Road
Suite 700, PMB 321
Marietta, GA 30067
(678) 498-2644
FAX: (404) 393-9506
Laura Danze
Managing Director
E-MAIL: lauradanze@aaace.org
URL: www.aaace.org

American Association for (c)
Employment in Education
PO Box 510
Sycamore, IL 60178
(614) 485-1111
Mr. Tim Neubert
Executive Director
E-MAIL: execdir@aaee.org
URL: www.aaee.org

American Association for Marriage (d)
and Family Therapy Commission on
Accreditation for Marriage and Family
Therapy Education
112 South Alfred Street
Alexandria, VA 22314
(703) 253-0448
FAX: (703) 253-0508
Ms. Jill Fogolin
Director of Accreditation
E-MAIL: jfogolin@aamft.org
URL: www.coamfte.org

American Association for Women in (e)
Community Colleges (AAWCC)
PO Box 175
Lansdowne, PA 19050
Dr. Monique Umphrey
President
E-MAIL: info@aawccnatl.org
URL: www.aawccnatl.org

American Association of Colleges for (f)
Teacher Education
1602 L Street, NW
Suite 601
Washington, DC 20036
(202) 478-4505
Dr. Lynn M. Gangone
President & Chief Executive Officer
E-MAIL: lgangone@aacte.org
URL: www.aacte.org

American Association of Colleges of (g)
Nursing
655 K Street, NW
Suite 750
Washington, DC 20001-2399
(202) 463-6930
FAX: (202) 785-8320
Dr. Deborah Trautman
President & Chief Executive Officer
E-MAIL: dtrautman@aacnnursing.org
URL: www.aacnnursing.org

American Association of Colleges of (h)
Osteopathic Medicine
7700 Old Georgetown Road
Suite 250
Bethesda, MD 20814
(301) 968-4100
FAX: (301) 968-4101
Dr. Robert Cain DO
President and CEO
E-MAIL: president@aacom.org
URL: www.aacom.org

American Association of Collegiate (i)
Registrars and Admissions Officers
(AACRAO)
1108 16th Street, NW
Suite 400
Washington, DC 20036
(202) 293-9161
FAX: (202) 872-8857
Ms. Melanie Gottlieb
Executive Director
E-MAIL: gottliebm@aacrao.org
URL: www.aacrao.org

American Association of Community (j)
Colleges
1 Dupont Circle, NW
Suite 700
Washington, DC 20036
(202) 728-0200, ext. 235
FAX: (202) 833-2467
Dr. Walter G. Bumphus
President/CEO
E-MAIL: wbumphus@aacc.nche.edu
URL: www.aacc.nche.edu

American Association of Family and (A)
Consumer Sciences (AAFCS)
107 S. West Street, #816
Alexandria, VA 22314
(703) 706-4600
Fax: (703) 636-7648
Nancy Bock
Executive Director
E-mail: staff@aafcs.org
URL: www.aafcs.org

American Association of Medical (B)
Assistants
20 North Wacker Drive
Suite 1575
Chicago, IL 60606
(312) 899-1500
Fax: (312) 899-1259
Mr. Donald A. Balasa J.D., MBA
Chief Executive Officer
E-mail: dbalasa@aama-ntl.org
URL: aama-ntl.org

American Association of Physics (C)
Teachers
One Physics Ellipse
College Park, MD 20740-3845
(301) 209-3311
Fax: (301) 209-0845
Dr. Beth A. Cunningham
Executive Officer
E-mail: eo@aapt.org
URL: www.aapt.org

American Association of Presidents (D)
of Independent Colleges and Universities
PO Box 7070
Provo, UT 84602-7070
(801) 422-4648
Mr. Joshua Figueira
Executive Director
E-mail: director@aapicu.org
URL: www.aapicu.org

American Association of State (E)
Colleges and Universities
1717 Rhode Island Avenue, NW
Suite 700
Washington, DC 20036
(202) 293-7070
Fax: (202) 296-5819
Dr. Mildred Garcia
President
E-mail: presg@aascu.org
URL: www.aascu.org

American Association of Teachers (F)
of Slavic and East European Languages
University of Southern California
3501 Trousdale Parkway
THH 255L
Los Angeles, CA 90089-4353
(213) 740-2734
Dr. Elizabeth Durst
Executive Director
E-mail: aatseel@usc.edu
URL: www.aatseel.org

American Association of University (G)
Professors
555 New Jersey Avenue, NW
6th Floor
Washington, DC 20001
(202) 737-5900
Fax: (202) 737-5526
Dr. Julie Schmid
Executive Director
E-mail: aaup@aaup.org
URL: www.aaup.org

American Bar Association Section (H)
of Legal Education and Admissions to
the Bar
321 North Clark Street
19th Floor
Chicago, IL 60654
(312) 988-6746
Mr. William E. Adams
Managing Director Accreditation & Legal
Education
E-mail: legaled@americanbar.org
URL: www.americanbar.org/groups/
legal_education

American Board of Funeral Service (I)
Education Committee on Accreditation
992 Mantua Pike
Suite 108
Woodbury Heights, NJ 08097
(816) 233-3747
Fax: (856) 579-7354
Robert C. Smith III
Executive Director
E-mail: exdir@abfse.org
URL: www.abfse.org

American Catholic Philosophical (J)
Association
University of St. Thomas
Center for Thomistic Studies
3800 Montrose Boulevard
Houston, TX 77006
(713) 942-3483
Fax: (713) 525-6964
Dr. Brian Carl
Secretary
E-mail: acpa@stthom.edu
URL: www.acpaweb.org

American Chemical Society (K)
Approval Program Office
1155 Sixteenth Street, NW
Washington, DC 20036
(202) 872-4589
Fax: (202) 872-6066
E-mail: cpt@acs.org
URL: www.acs.org/acsapprovalprogram

American College of Nurse-Midwives (L)
8403 Colesville Road
Suite 1230
Silver Spring, MD 20910
(240) 485-1800
Fax: (240) 485-1818
Ms. Katrina Holland
Chief Executive Officer
E-mail: info@acnm.org
URL: www.midwife.org

American College Personnel (M)
Association (ACPA)
1 Dupont Circle, NW
Suite 300
Washington, DC 20036-1188
(202) 835-2272
Fax: (202) 827-0601
Mr. Chris Moody
Executive Director
E-mail: info@acpa.nche.edu
URL: www.myacpa.org

American Collegiate Retailing (N)
Association
Montclair State University
Department of Marketing, SB 592A
1 Normal Avenue
Montclair, NJ 07043
(973) 655-7935
Dr. Patrali Chatterjee
President
E-mail: chatterjeep@montclair.edu
URL: www.acraretail.org

American Conference of Academic (O)
Deans (ACAD)
14460 Falls of Neuse Road
Suite 149-279
Raleigh, NC 27614
(202) 281-5115
Ms. Laura A. Best
Executive Director
E-mail: info@acad.org
URL: www.acad.org

American Council for Construction (P)
Education
300 Decker Drive
Suite 330
Irving, TX 75062
(972) 600-8800
Mr. Steve Nellis
President/CEO
E-mail: steve.nellis@acce-hq.org
URL: www.acce-hq.org

American Council of Trustees and (Q)
Alumni
1730 M Street, NW
Suite 600
Washington, DC 20036-4525
(202) 467-6787
Dr. Michael B. Poliakoff
President & CEO
E-mail: info@goacta.org
URL: www.goacta.org

American Council on Education (R)
1 Dupont Circle, NW
Washington, DC 20036
(202) 939-9300
Ted Mitchell
President
E-mail: president@acenet.edu
URL: www.acenet.edu

American Counseling Association (S)
P.O. 31110
Alexandria, VA 22310-9998
(800) 347-6647, ext. 231
Fax: (800) 473-2329
Mr. Shawn E. Boynes
Chief Executive Officer
E-mail: sboynes@counseling.org
URL: www.counseling.org

American Culinary Federation (T)
Education Foundation Accrediting
Commission
6816 Southpoint Parkway
Suite 400
Jacksonville, FL 32216
(904) 824-4468
Fax: (904) 940-0741
Director of Education & Programs
E-mail: acf@acfchefs.net
URL: www.acfchefs.org

American Educational Research (U)
Association
1430 K Street, NW
Suite 1200
Washington, DC 20005
(202) 238-3200
Fax: (202) 238-3250
Dr. Felice J. Levine
Executive Director
E-mail: flevine@aera.net
URL: www.aera.net

American Forensic Association (V)
PO Box 67021
Chestnut Hill, MA 02467-0001
Dr. Jarrod Atchison
President
E-mail: atchisrj@wayne.edu
URL: www.americanforensicassoc.org

American Institute of Architecture (W)
Students
1735 New York Avenue, NW
3rd Floor
Washington, DC 20006
(202) 808-0075
Mr. Larry H. Hoffer
Executive Director
E-mail: mailbox@aias.org
URL: www.aias.org

American Library Association Office (X)
for Accreditation
225 N. Michigan Avenue
Suite 1300
Chicago, IL 60601
(312) 280-2434
Karen O'Brien
Director, Office for Accreditation
E-mail: accred@ala.org
URL: www.ala.org/accreditation

American Mathematical Association (Y)
of Two Year Colleges
Southwest Tennessee Community College
5983 Macon Cove
Memphis, TN 38134
(901) 333-5643
Anne Dudley
Executive Director
E-mail: adudley@amatyc.org
URL: www.amatyc.org

American Occupational Therapy (Z)
Association Accreditation Council for
Occupational Therapy Education
(ACOTE)
6116 Executive Boulevard
Suite 200
North Bethesda, MD 20852-4929
(301) 652-6611 Ext. 2981
Fax: (240) 762-5140
Dr. Teresa Brininger
Director of Accreditation
E-mail: accred@aota.org
URL: acoteonline.com

American Optometric Association (a)
Accreditation Council on Optometric
Education
243 North Lindbergh Boulevard
Floor 1
St. Louis, MO 63141
(314) 991-4100
Fax: (314) 991-4101
Director
E-mail: accredit@aoa.org
URL: www.theacoe.org

American Osteopathic Association (b)
Commission on Osteopathic College
Accreditation
142 East Ontario Street
Chicago, IL 60611-2864
(312) 202-8124
Jed Brinton JD
Secretary
E-mail: jbrinton@osteopathic.org
URL: osteopathic.org/accreditation

American Physical Therapy (c)
Association
3030 Potomac Avenue
Suite 100
Alexandria, VA 22305-3085
(703) 684-2782
Mr. Justin Moore
Chief Executive Officer
E-mail: dorisellmore@apta.org
URL: www.apta.org

American Political Science (d)
Association
1527 New Hampshire Avenue, NW
Washington, DC 20036
(202) 483-2512
Fax: (202) 483-2657
Dr. Steven Rathgeb Smith
Executive Director
E-mail: apsa@apsanet.org
URL: www.apsanet.org

American Psychological Association (e)
Office of Program Consultation &
Accreditation
750 First Street, NE
Washington, DC 20002-4242
(202) 336-5979
Fax: (202) 336-5978
Dr. Jacqueline Remondet Wall
Director
E-mail: apaaccred@apa.org
URL: accreditation.apa.org

American Real Estate and Urban (f)
Economics Association
c/o Travelink
404 BNA Drive, Suite 650
Nashville, TN 37217
(800) 242-0528
Fax: (615) 367-0012
Shelley Riggs
Administrative Manager
E-mail: areuea@travelink.com
URL: www.areuea.org

American Society for Engineering (g)
Education
1818 N Street, NW
Suite 600
Washington, DC 20036
(202) 331-3545
Fax: (202) 265-8504
Dr. Norman L. Fortenberry
Executive Director
E-mail: n.fortenberry@asee.org
URL: www.asee.org

American Society for Microbiology (h)
1752 N Street, NW
Washington, DC 20036
(202) 737-3600
Ms. Irene Hulede
Director, Education
E-mail: ihulede@asmusa.org
URL: www.asm.org

American Society for Microbiology (i)
Subcommittee on Postgraduate
Educational Programs
1752 N Street, NW
Washington, DC 20036-2804
(202) 942-9281
Ms. Sue Williams
Program Coordinator
E-mail: certification@asmusa.org
URL: www.asm.org/fellowships/cpep/

Higher Education Associations

American Speech-Language-Hearing (A) Association (ASHA)
2200 Research Boulevard
Rockville, MD 20850
(301) 296-5700
Ms. Vicki R. Deal-Williams
Chief Executive Officer
URL: www.asha.org

American Student Government (B) Association
412 NW 16th Avenue
Suite 4
Gainesville, FL 32601-4203
(352) 373-6907
Fax: (352) 373-8120
Mr. Butch Oxendine Jr.
Executive Director
E-MAIL: butch@asgaonline.com
URL: www.asgahome.org

American Veterinary Medical (C) Association
1931 North Meacham Road
Suite 100
Schaumburg, IL 60173
(800) 248-2862
Fax: (847) 925-1329
Dr. Karen Martens Brandt
Director Education and Research
E-MAIL: kbrandt@avma.org
URL: www.avma.org

APPA-Leadership in Educational (D) Facilities
PO Box 29
Alexandria, VA 22313-0029
(703) 684-1446
E. Lander Medlin
President & CEO
E-MAIL: lander@appa.org
URL: www.appa.org

Association for Advancement of (E) Blood/ Biotherapies Committee on Accreditation of Specialist in Blood Bank Tech/Transfusion Medicine
4550 Montgomery Avenue, Suite 700 North Tower
Bethesda, MD 20814
(301) 215-6540
Ms. Melanie Sloan
Senior Director Accreditation and Quality
E-MAIL: msloan@aabb.org
URL: caahep-public-site-5be3d9.webflow.io/committees-accreditation/specialist-in-blood-bank-technology-transfusion-medicine

Association for Asian Studies 825 (F)
Victors Way, Suite 310
Ann Arbor, MI 48108
(734) 665-2490
Ms. Hilary Finchum-Sung Executive
Director
E-MAIL: hvfinchum@asianstudies.org
URL: www.asianstudies.org

Association for Biblical Higher (G) Education Commission on Accreditation
5850 T.G. Lee Boulevard
Suite 130
Orlando, FL 32822
(407) 207-0808
Fax: (407) 207-0840
Dr. Lisa L. Beatty
Executive Director, Commission on
Accreditation
E-MAIL: lisa.beatty@abhe.org
URL: https://www.abhe.org/accreditation/

Association for Business (H) Communication
P.O. Box 304
Natural Bridge Sta, VA 24579-0304
Dr. Kathryn Rybka
Interim Executive Director
E-MAIL: interim.exec.director@businesscommunication.org
URL: www.businesscommunication.org

Association for Business Simulation (I) and Experiential Learning
Lander Universisty
College of Business
320 Stanley Avenue
Greenwood, SC 29649
(864) 388-8232
Dr. Mick Fekula
VP & Executive Director
E-MAIL: mfekula@lander.edu
URL: www.absel.org

Association for Chaplaincy and (J) Spiritual Life in Higher Education
(203) 432-8751
Maytal Saltiel
President
E-MAIL: maytal.saltiel@yale.edu
URL: www.acslhe.org

Association for Collaborative (K) Leadership (ACL)
1502 W. Broadway
Suite 102
Madison, WI 53713
(608) 571-7096
E-MAIL: admin@national-acl.org
URL: www.national-acl.org

Association for Continuing Higher (L) Education
400 West 1st Street
Chico, CA 95929
(530) 898-5808
Dr. Tina Marie Coolidge
President
E-MAIL: admin@acheinc.org
URL: www.acheinc.org

Association for Education and (M) Rehabilitation of the Blind and Visually Impaired AER Accreditation Program
5680 King Centre Drive
Suite 600
Alexandria, VA 22315
(703) 671-4500
Mr. Lee Sonnenberg
Executive Director
E-MAIL: accreditation@aerbvi.org
URL: www.aerbvi.org

Association for Education in (N) Journalism and Mass Communication
234 Outlet Pointe Boulevard
Suite A
Columbia, SC 29210-5667
(803) 798-0271
Fax: (803) 772-3509
Ms. Amanda Caldwell
Executive Director
E-MAIL: amanda@aejmc.org
URL: www.aejmc.org

Association for General and Liberal (O) Studies
428 5th Street
Columbus, IN 47201
(812) 376-7468
Ms. Joyce Lucke
Executive Director
E-MAIL: execdir@agls.org
URL: www.agls.org

Association for Information Systems (P)
PO Box 2712
Atlanta, GA 30301-2712
(404) 413-7445
Mr. Matthew Nelson
Associate Executive Director
E-MAIL: matt@aisnet.org
URL: aisnet.org

Association for Institutional (Q) Research
1563 Capital Circle, SE
Suite 1012
Tallahassee, FL 32301
(850) 385-4155
Fax: (850) 385-5180
Dr. Christine M. Keller
Executive Director & CEO
E-MAIL: ckeller@airweb.org
URL: www.airweb.org

Association for Library and (R) Information Science Education (ALISE)
4 Lan Drive
Suite 310
Westford, MA 01886
(978) 674-6190
Fax: (978) 250-1117
Ms. Cambria Happ
Executive Director
E-MAIL: office@alise.org
URL: www.alise.org

Association for Prevention Teaching (S) and Research
1001 Connecticut Avenue, NW
Suite 610
Washington, DC 20036
(202) 463-0550
Fax: (202) 463-0555
Ms. Allison L. Lewis
Executive Director
E-MAIL: all@aptrweb.org
URL: www.aptrweb.org

Association for the Study of Higher (T) Education (ASHE)
9450 SW Gemini Drive
PMB 88737
Beaverton, OR 97008
(202) 660-4106
Dr. Jason P. Guilbeau
Executive Director
E-MAIL: office@ashe.ws
URL: www.ashe.ws

Association for Theatre in Higher (U) Education (ATHE)
PO Box 922
Santa Cruz, CA 95061
(628) 222-4088
Ms. Aimee Zygmonski
Executive Director
E-MAIL: info@athe.org
URL: www.athe.org

Association of Advanced Rabbinical (V) and Talmudic Schools Accreditation Commission
2329 Nostrand Avenue
Suite M200
Brooklyn, NY 11210
(212) 363-1991
Fax: (212) 533-5335
Dr. Bernard Fryshman
Interim Executive Director
E-MAIL: office@aarts-schools.org

Association of American Colleges & (W) Universities
1818 R Street, NW
Washington, DC 20009
(202) 387-3760
Dr. Lynn Pasquerella
President
E-MAIL: commish@aacu.org
URL: www.aacu.org

Association of American Law (X) Schools
1614 20th Street, NW
Washington, DC 20009-1001
(202) 296-8851
Fax: (202) 296-8869
Ms. Judith Areen
Executive Director
E-MAIL: info@aals.org
URL: www.aals.org

Association of American Medical (Y) Colleges
655 K Street, NW
Suite 100
Washington, DC 20001-2399
(202) 828-0460
Dr. David J. Skorton
President and CEO
E-MAIL: fcoley@aamc.org
URL: www.aamc.org

Association of American (Z) Universities
1200 New York Avenue, NW
Suite 550
Washington, DC 20005
(202) 408-7500
Dr. Barbara R. Snyder
President
E-MAIL: leah.norton@aau.edu
URL: www.aau.edu

Association of Catholic Colleges and (a) Universities
1 Dupont Circle, NW
Suite 650
Washington, DC 20036
(202) 457-0650
Rev. Dennis H. Holtschneider C.M.,Ph.D.
President
E-MAIL: accu@accunet.org
URL: www.accunet.org

Association of College and (b) University Housing Officers-International
1445 Summit Street
Columbus, OH 43201-2105
(614) 292-0099
Fax: (614) 292-3205
Ms. Mary DeNiro
CEO/Executive Director
E-MAIL: office@acuho-i.org
URL: www.acuho-i.org

Association of College Unions (c) International (ACUI)
One City Centre, Suite 200
120 West Seventh Street
Bloomington, IN 47404-3839
(812) 245-2284
Dr. John Taylor
Chief Executive Officer
E-MAIL: acui@acui.org
URL: www.acui.org

Association of Collegiate (d) Conference and Events Directors-International (ACCED-I)
1001-A East Harmony Road
#516
Fort Collins, CO 80525
(970) 449-4960, ext. 4
Ms. Karen Nedbal
Executive Director
E-MAIL: karen@acced-i.org
URL: www.acced-i.org

Association of Collegiate Schools of (e) Architecture
611 Pennsylvania Avenue, SE
Suite 514
Washington, DC 20003
(202) 785-2324
Michael Monti Ph.D.
Executive Director
E-MAIL: mmonti@acsa-arch.org
URL: www.acsa-arch.org

Association of Collegiate Schools of (f) Planning
c/o Donna Dodd, Executive Director
2910 Kerry Forest Parkway, D4-206
Tallahassee, FL 32309
(850) 385-2054
Laxmi Ramasubramanian
President
E-MAIL: presidentsoffice@acsp.org
URL: www.acsp.org

Association of Community College (g) Trustees
1101 17th Street NW
Suite 300
Washington, DC 20036
(202) 775-4450
Jee Hang Lee
President and CEO
E-MAIL: jhee@acct.org
URL: www.acct.org

Association of Departments of (h) English
85 Broad Street
Suite 500
New York, NY 10004-2434
(646) 576-5136
Mr. Stephen Olsen
Interim Director
E-MAIL: solsen@mla.org
URL: ade.mla.org

Association of Departments of (i) Foreign Languages
85 Broad Street
Suite 500
New York, NY 10004-2434
(646) 576-5153
Fax: (646) 576-5160
Dr. Lydia B. Tang
Associate Director
E-MAIL: ltang@mla.org
URL: www.adfl.mla.org

Association of Governing Boards of (j) Universities and Colleges
1133 20th Street, NW
Suite 300
Washington, DC 20036
(202) 296-8400
Mr. Henry V. Stoever
President and CEO
E-MAIL: jpez-berlin@agb.org
URL: www.agb.org

**Association of Graduate Liberal (A)
Studies Programs**
c/o Rice University
6100 Main Street, MS-550
Houston, TX 77005
(713) 348-6118
Mr. Christopher Pastore
President
E-MAIL: cpastore@sas.upenn.edu
URL: www.aglsp.org

**Association of International (B)
Education Administrators-AIEA**
811 Ninth Street
Suite 215
Durham, NC 27705
(919) 893-4980
Dr. Darla K. Deardorff
Executive Director
E-MAIL: info@aieaworld.org
URL: www.aieaworld.org

**Association of Jesuit Colleges and (C)
Universities**
1 Dupont Circle, NW
Suite 405
Washington, DC 20036
(202) 862-9893
Rev. Michael J. Garanzini S.J.
President
E-MAIL: info@ajcunet.edu
URL: www.ajcunet.edu

**Association of Military Colleges and (D)
Schools of the United States**
Arnold, MD
(703) 272-8406
Col. Ray Rottman
Executive Director
E-MAIL: amcsus1@gmail.com
URL: www.amcsus.org

**Association of Performing Arts (E)
Professionals**
919 18th Street, NW
Suite 650
Washington, DC 20006
(202) 833-2787
FAX: (202) 833-1543
Ms. Lisa Richards Toney
President and CEO
E-MAIL: executiveoffice@apap365.org
URL: www.apap365.org

Association of Practical Theology (F)
,
(303) 765-3139
Kathrine Turpin
President
E-MAIL: kturpin@iliff.edu
URL: www.practicaltheology.org

**Association of Presbyterian (G)
Colleges and Universities**
c/o Agnes Scott College
Box 1102
141 E. College Avenue
Decatur, GA 30030
(470) 443-1948
Mr. Jeff Arnold
Executive Director
E-MAIL: jeff.arnold@presbyteriancolleges.org
URL: www.presbyteriancolleges.org

**Association of Public and Land- (H)
Grant Universities**
1220 L Street, NW
Suite 1000
Washington, DC 20005
(202) 478-6040
FAX: (202) 478-6046
Mr. Mark Becker
President
E-MAIL: presidentbecker@aplu.org
URL: www.aplu.org

Association of Research Libraries (I)
21 Dupont Circle, NW
Suite 800
Washington, DC 20036
(202) 296-2296
FAX: (202) 872-0884
Mary Lee Kennedy
Executive Director
E-MAIL: mkennedy@arl.org
URL: arl.org

**Association of Schools Advancing (J)
Health Professions**
122 C Street, NW
Suite 200
Washington, DC 20001-2109
(202) 237-6481
Mr. John Colbert
Executive Director
E-MAIL: john@asahp.org
URL: www.asahp.org

**Association of Specialized and (K)
Professional Accreditors**
3023 N. Clark Street
#317
Chicago, IL 60657
(773) 857-7900
Mr. Joseph Vibert
Executive Director
E-MAIL: jvibert@aspa-usa.org
URL: aspa-usa.org

Association of Teacher Educators (L)
PO Box 793
Manassas, VA 20113
(703) 659-1708
Alisa Chapman
Executive Director
E-MAIL: achapman@ate1.org
URL: www.ate1.org

**The Association of Technology, (M)
Management, and Applied Engineering
(ATMAE)**
6207 Route 30
Suite 1027
Greensburg, PA 15601
(919) 635-8335
Ms. Amy Good
Managing Director of Accreditation
E-MAIL: accreditation@atmae.org
URL: www.atmae.org

**Association of Theological Schools (N)
The Commission on Accrediting**
10 Summit Park Drive
Pittsburgh, PA 15275-1110
(412) 788-6505
FAX: (412) 788-6510
Dr. Frank M. Yamada
Executive Director
E-MAIL: yamada@ats.edu
URL: www.ats.edu

Association of University Presses (O)
1412 Broadway
Suite 2135
New York, NY 10018
(212) 989-1010
FAX: (212) 989-0275
Peter M. Berkery Jr.
Executive Director
E-MAIL: pberkery@aupresses.org
URL: www.aupresses.org

**Association of University Programs (P)
in Health Administration**
1730 Rhode Island Avenue, NW
Suite 810
Washington, DC 20036
(202) 763-7283
Daniel Gentry Ph.D., MHA
President & CEO
E-MAIL: aupha@aupha.org
URL: www.aupha.org

**Association of University Research (Q)
Parks**
9070 South Rita Road
Suite 1750
Tucson, AZ 85747
(520) 529-2521
Ms. Vickie Palmer
Chief Executive Officer
E-MAIL: vickiepalmer@aurp.net
URL: www.aurp.net

**Aviation Accreditation Board (R)
International**
115 S. 8th Street
Suite 102
Opelika, AL 36801
(334) 748-9359
FAX: (334) 748-9360
Guy Smith Ph.D.
President
E-MAIL: victoria@aabi.aero
URL: www.aabi.aero

Big Ten Academic Alliance (S)
1819 South Neil Street
Suite D
Champaign, IL 61820-7271
(217) 244-9849
FAX: (217) 244-7127
Ms. Kara McKinn
Coordinator Communications
E-MAIL: info@btaa.org
URL: www.btaa.org

Broadcast Education Association (T)
1 M Street, SE
Washington, DC 20003
(202) 602-0584
Ms. Heather Birks
Executive Director
E-MAIL: heather@beaweb.org
URL: www.beaweb.org

**Career Education Colleges & (U)
Universities**
1530 Wilson Boulevard
Suite 1050
Arlington, VA 22209
(571) 970-3941
FAX: (866) 363-2181
Dr. Jason Altmire
President and CEO
E-MAIL: president@career.org
URL: www.career.org

**Carnegie Foundation for the (V)
Advancement of Teaching**
51 Vista Lane
Stanford, CA 94305
(650) 566-5100
FAX: (650) 326-0278
Dr. Timothy Knowles
President
URL: www.carnegiefoundation.org

**College and University Professional (W)
Association for Human Resources
(CUPA-HR)**
1811 Commons Point Drive
Knoxville, TN 37932
(877) 287-2474
FAX: (865) 637-7674
Dr. Andy Brantley
President & Chief Executive Officer
E-MAIL: memberservice@cupahr.org
URL: https://www.cupahr.org

College Art Association (X)
50 Broadway
21st Floor
New York, NY 10004
(212) 691-1051
FAX: (212) 627-2381
Ms. Meme Omogbai
Executive Director
E-MAIL: info@collegeart.org
URL: www.collegeart.org

The College Board (Y)
250 Vesey Street
New York, NY 10281
(212) 713-8000
Mr. Jeremy Singer
President
URL: www.collegeboard.org

College English Association (Z)
112 North Shore Boulevard
Anderson, IN 46011
(765) 644-7591
Mr. Scott Borders
Executive Director
E-MAIL: cea.english@gmail.com
URL: cea-web.org

College Media Association (a)
355 Lexington Avenue
15th Floor
New York, NY 10017
(212) 297-2195
Ms. Marla Schrager
Interim Executive Director
E-MAIL: mschrager@kellencompany.com
URL: www.collegemedia.org

**Columbia Scholastic Press (b)
Association**
Columbia University
90 Morningside Drive
Suite B01
New York, NY 10027
(212) 854-9400
Mr. Edmund J. Sullivan
Executive Director
E-MAIL: cspa@columbia.edu
URL: www.cspa.columbia.edu

**Commission on Accreditation for (c)
Health Informatics and Information
Management Education (CAHIIM)**
200 E. Randolph Street
Suite 5100
Chicago, IL 60601
(312) 235-3255
Dr. Angela Kennedy
Chief Executive Officer
E-MAIL: info@cahiim.org
URL: www.cahiim.org

**Commission on Accreditation of (d)
Allied Health Education Programs**
9355 - 113th Street N. #7709
Seminole, FL 33775
(727) 210-2350
FAX: (727) 210-2354
Gina Scarboro DBA, CAA.
Executive Director
E-MAIL: mail@caahep.org
URL: www.caahep.org

**Commission on Accreditation of (e)
Healthcare Management Education
(CAHME)**
PO Box 911
Spring House, PA 19477
(301) 298-1825
Dr. Anthony Stanowski
President & CEO
E-MAIL: astanowski@cahme.org
URL: cahme.org

**Commission on Collegiate Nursing (f)
Education (CCNE)**
655 K Street NW
Suite 750
Washington, DC 20001
(202) 887-6791
FAX: (202) 887-8476
Dr. Jennifer Butlin
Executive Director
E-MAIL: jbutlin@ccneaccreditation.org
URL: www.ccneaccreditation.org

Commission on Dental Accreditation (g)
211 East Chicago Avenue
Suite 1900
Chicago, IL 60611
(312) 440-4653
Dr. Sherin Tooks
Director
E-MAIL: tookss@ada.org
URL: ada.org/en/coda

**Commission on English Language (h)
Program Accreditation (CEA)**
1001 North Fairfax Street
Suite 630
Alexandria, VA 22314
(703) 665-3400
Dr. Heidi E. Vellenga
Executive Director
E-MAIL: hvellenga@cea-accredit.org
URL: www.cea-accredit.org

**The Commission on Independent (i)
Colleges and Universities (CICU) in New
York**
17 Elk Street
Albany, NY 12207
(518) 436-4781
Ms. Lola W. Brabham
President
E-MAIL: info@cicu.org
URL: www.cicu.org

**Commission on Massage Therapy (j)
Accreditation**
900 Commonwealth Place
Suite 200-331
Virginia Beach, VA 23464
(202) 888-6790
FAX: (202) 888-6787
Ms. Dawn Hogue
Executive Director
E-MAIL: dhogue@comta.org
URL: www.comta.org

**Commission on Opticianry (k)
Accreditation**
PO Box 592
Canton, NY 13617
(703) 468-0566
Mrs. Debra White
Director of Accreditation
E-MAIL: director@coaccreditation.com
URL: www.coaccreditation.com

Higher Education Associations

Committee on Accreditation for Education in Neurodiagnostic Technology (A)
1449 Hill Street
Whitinsville, MA 01588
(978) 338-6300
Fax: (978) 832-2638
Dr. Jackie Long-Goding PhD,RRTNPS
Executive Director
E-mail: office@coa-ndt.org
URL: www.coa-ndt.org

Committee on Accreditation of Education Programs for Kinesiotherapy (CoA-KT) (B)
(601) 266-5371
Ms. Kareesa Keys
Administrative Officer
E-mail: kinesiotherapy.ao@gmail.com URL: https://caahep-public-site-5be3d9.cwebflow.io/ommittees-on-accreditation/kinesiotherapy

Committee on Accreditation for the Exercise Sciences (C)
401 West Michigan Street
Indianapolis, IN 46202
(317) 777-1135
Fax: (317) 634-7817
Mr. William Coale
Director
E-mail: wcoale@coaes.org
URL: www.coaes.org

Committee on Accreditation for Polysomnographic Technologist Education (D)
1711 Frank Avenue
New Bern, NC 28560
(252) 626-3238
Ms. Karen Monarchy Rowe
Executive Director
E-mail: karenmonarchy@gmail.com
URL: https://caahep-public-site-5be3d9.webflow.io/committees-on-accreditation/polysomnographic-technology

Committee on Accreditation of Educational Programs for the Emergency Medical Services Professions (E)
8301 Lakeview Parkway
Suite 111-312
Rowlett, TX 75088
(214) 703-8445, ext. 112
Fax: (214) 703-8992
Dr. George W. Hatch Jr.
Executive Director
E-mail: george@coaemsp.org
URL: www.coaemsp.org

Conference on College Composition and Communication (F)
111 West Kenyon Road
Urbana, IL 61801-1096
(877) 369-6283
Dr. David F. Green
Secretary
E-mail: cccc@ncte.org
URL: cccc.ncte.org

Council for Accreditation of Counseling and Related Educational Programs (CACREP) (G)
500 Montgomery Street
Suite 350
Alexandria, VA 22314
(703) 535-5990
Dr. M. Sylvia Fernandez
President and CEO
E-mail: cacrep@cacrep.org
URL: www.cacrep.org

Council for Adult and Experiential Learning (H)
10 W. Market Street
Suite 1100
Indianapolis, IN 46204
(312) 499-2600
Ms. Jeannie McCarron
Senior Director, Member Engagemenet
E-mail: jmcarron@cael.org
URL: www.cael.org

Council for Advancement and Support of Education (I)
1201 Eye Street, NW
Suite 300
Washington, DC 20005
(202) 328-2273
Fax: (202) 387-4973
Ms. Sue Cunningham
President and CEO
E-mail: president@case.org
URL: www.case.org

Council for Agricultural Science and Technology (CAST) (J)
4420 West Lincoln Way
Ames, IA 50014-3447
(515) 292-2125
Mr. Kent G. Schescke
Executive Vice President & CEO
E-mail: cast@cast-science.org
URL: www.cast-science.org

Council for Aid to Education (K)
1732 1st Avenue
#21535
New York, NY 10128
(212) 661-5800
Dr. Robert Yayac
President & CEO
E-mail: info@cae.org
URL: www.cae.org

Council for Christian Colleges & Universities (L)
321 8th Street, NE
Washington, DC 20002-6107
(202) 546-8713
Shirley V. Hoogstra J.D.
President
E-mail: council@cccu.org
URL: www.cccu.org

Council for Economic Education (M)
122 East 42nd Street
Suite 1012
New York, NY 10168
(212) 827-3600
Fax: (212) 827-3610
Ms. Nan Morrison
President and CEO
E-mail: njmorrison@councilforeconed.org
URL: www.councilforeconed.org

Council for Higher Education Accreditation (N)
1 Dupont Circle, NW
Suite 510
Washington, DC 20036
(202) 955-6126
Fax: (202) 915-0818
Dr. Cynthia Jackson-Hammond
President
E-mail: chea@chea.org
URL: chea.org

Council for Interior Design Accreditation (CIDA) (formerly FIDER) (O)
206 Cesar E. Chavez Avenue, SW
Suite 350
Grand Rapids, MI 49503-4014
(248) 875-6705
Ms. Holly Mattson
Executive Director
E-mail: info@accredit-id.org
URL: www.accredit-id.org

Council for Research in Music Education University of Illinois at Urbana-Champaign School of Music (P)
1114 W. Nevada Street
M/C 056
Urbana, IL 61801
(217) 244-6310
Dr. Janet R. Barrett
Editor
E-mail: janetbar@illinois.edu
URL: bcrme.press.illinois.edu

Council for the Accreditation of Educator Preparation (Q)
1140 19th Street, NW
Suite 400
Washington, DC 20036
(202) 223-0077
Mr. Christopher Koch
President
E-mail: caep@caepnet.org
URL: www.caepnet.org

Council for the Advancement of Standards in Higher Education (R)
2598 E. Sunrise Boulevard
Suite 2014
Fort Lauderdale, FL 33304
(800) 889-7270
Ms. Doreen Murner
Executive Director
E-mail: executive_director@cas.edu
URL: www.cas.edu

Council of Colleges of Acupuncture and Herbal Medicine (CCAHM) (S)
9615 E. County Line Road
Suite B-584
Centennial, CO 80112
(410) 464-6040
Ms. Roberta Herman MBA, CAE
Executive Director
E-mail: rherman@ccahm.org
URL: ccahm.org

Council of Colleges of Arts & Sciences (T)
1935 County Road B2 W
Suite 165
Rockville, MD 55113
(952) 641-3037
Amber Elaine Cox MSW
Executive Director
E-mail: connect@ccas.net
URL: www.ccas.net

Council of Graduate Schools (U)
1 Dupont Circle, NW
Suite 230
Washington, DC 20036-1146
(202) 223-3791
Fax: (202) 331-7157
Dr. Suzanne Ortega
President
E-mail: president@cgs.nche.edu
URL: www.cgsnet.org

Council of Independent Colleges (V)
1 Dupont Circle, NW
Suite 320
Washington, DC 20036-1142
(202) 466-7230
Dr. Marjorie Hass
President
E-mail: cic@cic.edu
URL: www.cic.edu

The Council of Writing Program Administrators (W)
(765) 973-8637
Dr. Kelly Blewett
Secretary
E-mail: cwpasecretary@gmail.com
URL: www.wpacouncil.org

Council on Academic Accreditation in Audiology and Speech-Language Pathology American Speech-Language-Hearing Association (X)
2200 Research Boulevard #310
Rockville, MD 20850
(301) 296-5796
Ms. Kimberlee Moore
Chief Accreditation Officer
E-mail: accreditation@asha.org
URL: https://caa.asha.org/

Council on Accreditation of Nurse Anesthesia Educational Programs (COA) (Y)
10275 W. Higgins Road
Suite 906
Rosemont, IL 60018-5603
(224) 275-9130
Francis Gerbasi Ph.D., CRN
Chief Executive Officer
E-mail: fgerbasi@coacrna.org
URL: www.coacrna.org

Council on Accreditation for Two-Year Colleges (Z)
200 South 14th Street
Parsons, KS 67357
(620) 820-1223
Fax: (620) 421-0921
Dr. Barbara Jones
Executive Director
E-mail: meganf@labette.edu
URL: www.catyc.com

Council on Accreditation of Parks, Recreation, Tourism and Related Professions (COAPRT) (a)
1401 Marvin Road NE
Suite 307, #172
Lacey, WA 98516
(360) 205-2096
Shelley Dahle
Program Manager
E-mail: copart@accreditationcouncil.org
URL: www.accreditationcouncil.org

Council on Chiropractic Education (b)
10105 E. Via Linda
Suite 103, PMB 3642
Scottsdale, AZ 85258
(480) 443-8877
Craig S. Little Ed.D.
President
E-mail: cce@cce-usa.org
URL: www.cce-usa.org

Council on Education for Public Health (c)
1010 Wayne Avenue
Suite 220
Silver Spring, MD 20910
(202) 789-1050
Dr. Laura Rasar King
Executive Director
E-mail: lking@ceph.org
URL: www.ceph.org

Council on Governmental Relations (d)
1200 New York Avenue, NW
Suite 460
Washington, DC 20005
(202) 289-6655
Fax: (202) 289-6698
Ms. Wendy Streitz
President
E-mail: wstreitz@cogr.edu
URL: www.cogr.edu

Council on Higher Education Solutions for Adults (CHESA) (e)
303 W. Burleson Street
Marshall, TX 75670
(903) 472-2762
Fax: (903) 471-8675
Dr. Tracy Andrus Sr.
President/CEO
E-mail: tandrus26@gmail.com

Council on Naturopathic Medical Education (f)
PO Box 178
Great Barrington, MA 01230
(413) 528-8877
Dr. Daniel Seitz J.D., Ed.D
Executive Director
E-mail: danseitz@cnme.org
URL: www.cnme.org

Council on Occupational Education (g)
7840 Roswell Road
Building 300, Suite 325
Atlanta, GA 30350
(800) 917-2081
Fax: (770) 396-3790
Dr. Gary Puckett
President/Executive Director
E-mail: gary.puckett@council.org
URL: www.council.org

Council on Podiatric Medical Education (h)
9312 Old Georgetown Road
Bethesda, MD 20814
(301) 581-9200
Fax: (301) 571-4903
Dr. Heather M. Stagliano
Executive Director
E-mail: hstagliano@cpme.org
URL: cpme.org

Council on Social Work Education (i)
333 John Carlyle Street
Suite 400
Alexandria, VA 22314
(703) 519-2048
Dr. Tanya Smith Brice
VP of Education
E-mail: tbrice@cswe.org
URL: www.cswe.org

Council on Undergraduate Research (j)
267 Kentlands Boulevard #4021
Gaithersburg, MD 20878
(202) 783-4810
Mrs. Lindsay L. Currie
Executive Officer
E-mail: lcurrie@cur.org
URL: www.cur.org

CSAB, Inc. (k)
417 Terrace Way
Towson, MD 21204-3725
(410) 339-5456
Ms. Liz Glazer
Executive Director
E-mail: lglazer@csab.org
URL: www.csab.org

Cultural Vistas (A)
1250 H Street, NW
Suite 300
Washington, DC 20005
(212) 497-3500
Ms. Jennifer Clinton
President & CEO
E-MAIL: info@culturalvistas.org
URL: www.culturalvistas.org

Cytotechnology Programs Review (B)
Committee (CPRC) American Council of
Cytopathology
100 W. 10th Street, Suite 605
Wilmington, DE 19801
(302) 543-6583, ext 102
Ms. Sandra Hitchens
CPRC Coordinator
E-MAIL: shitchens@cytopathology.org
URL: https://caahep-public-site-5be3d9.webflow.io/
committees-on-accreditation/cytotechnology

Decision Sciences Institute (C)
University of Houston
C.T. Bauer College of Business
4250 Martin Luther King Blvd
Room 325A
Houston, TX 77204-6021
(713) 743-4815
Ms. Vivian Landrum
Executive Director
E-MAIL: info@decisionsciences.org
URL: decisionsciences.org

Distance Education Accrediting (D)
Commission
1101 17th Street, NW
Suite 808
Washington, DC 20036
(202) 234-5100
Dr. Leah K. Matthews
Executive Director
E-MAIL: info@deac.org
URL: www.deac.org

Education Commission of the States (E)
700 Broadway
Suite 810
Denver, CO 80203-3442
(303) 299-3600
Mr. Jeremy Anderson
President
E-MAIL: ecs@ecs.org
URL: www.ecs.org

Education Development Center (F)
300 Fifth Avenue
Suite 2010
Waltham, MA 02451
(617) 969-7100
FAX: (617) 969-5979
Mr. David Offensend
President and CEO
E-MAIL: contact@edc.org
URL: www.edc.org

EDUCAUSE (G)
4845 Pearl East Circle
Suite 118, PMB 43761
Boulder, CO 80301-6112
(303) 449-4430
FAX: (303) 440-0461
John O'Brien Ph.D.
President and CEO
E-MAIL: info@educause.edu
URL: www.educause.edu

Financial Management Association (H)
International
University of South Florida
Muma College of Business
4202 East Fowler Avenue, BSN 3403
Tampa, FL 33620-5500
(833) 946-4512
FAX: (813) 974-3318
Ms. Michelle Lui
Executive Director
E-MAIL: fma@coba.usf.edu
URL: www.fma.org

Friends Association for Higher (I)
Education
1501 Cherry Street
Philadelphia, PA 19102
(215) 241-7116
E-MAIL: fahe@quaker.org
URL: www.quakerfahe.com

The Gerontological Society of (J)
America
1220 L Street, NW
Suite 901
Washington, DC 20005-4001
(202) 587-2821
Mr. James Appleby
CEO
E-MAIL: membership@geron.org
URL: www.geron.org

H. Wiley Hitchcock Institute for (K)
Studies in American Music
Brooklyn College, CUNY
2900 Bedford Avenue
Brooklyn, NY 11210-2889
(718) 951-5655
Stephanie Jensen-Moulton
Director
E-MAIL: hisam@brooklyn.cuny.edu
URL: www.hisam.org

HEATH Resource Center at the (L)
National Youth Transitions Center The
George Washington University Graduate
School of Education & Human
Development
2134 G Street, NW
Suite 308
Washington, DC 20052-0001
E-MAIL: askheath@gwu.edu
URL: www.heath.gwu.edu

Higher Education Resource (M)
Services (HERS)
1901 East Asbury Avenue
Suite 220
Denver, CO 80208
(303) 871-6866
FAX: (303) 871-6766
Dr. Gloria Thomas
President
E-MAIL: gthomas@hersnetwork.org
URL: www.hersnetwork.org

Higher Learning Commission (N)
230 South LaSalle Street
Suite 7-500
Chicago, IL 60604-1411
(312) 263-0456 / (800) 621-7440
FAX: (312) 263-7462
Dr. Barbara Gellman-Danley
President
E-MAIL: info@hlcommission.org
URL: hlcommission.org

Hispanic Association of Colleges (O)
and Universities
4801 NW Loop 410
Suite 701
San Antonio, TX 78229
(210) 692-3805
FAX: (210) 692-0823
Dr. Antonio R. Flores
President and CEO
E-MAIL: hacu@hacu.net
URL: www.hacu.net

IACLEA (International Association of (P)
Campus Law Enforcement
Administrators)
520 S. Walnut Street
Box 2388
Bloomington, IN 47402-2388
(855) 442-2532
Mr. Paul M. Cell
Executive Director
E-MAIL: pcell@iaclea.org
URL: www.iaclea.org

The Institute for Higher Education (Q)
Policy
1825 K Street, NW
Suite 720
Washington, DC 20006
(202) 861-8223
FAX: (202) 861-9307
Mamie Voight
President
E-MAIL: mvoight@ihep.org
URL: www.ihep.org

Institute of International Education (R)
Council for International Exchange of
Scholars
1400 K Street, NW
Suite 700
Washington, DC 20005
(202) 686-4000
FAX: (202) 686-4029
E-MAIL: scholars@iie.org
URL: www.cies.org

International Accreditation Council (S)
for Business Education
11960 Quivira Road
Suite 300
Overland Park, KS 66213
(913) 631-3009
FAX: (913) 631-9154
Dr. Pat Hafford
President
E-MAIL: phafford@iacbe.org
URL: www.iacbe.org

International Association of Baptist (T)
Colleges and Universities
Dallas Baptist University
3000 Mountain Creek Parkway
Dallas, TX 75211
(214) 333-5186
Mrs. Ashley Hill
Executive Director
E-MAIL: ashleyhill@baptistschools.org
URL: www.baptistschools.org

International Communication (U)
Association
1500 21st Street, NW
Washington, DC 20036
(202) 955-1444
Ms. Laura Sawyer
Executive Director
E-MAIL: lsawyer@icahdq.org
URL: www.icahdq.org

International Council on Education (V)
for Teaching
5201 University Boulevard
PLG 301
Laredo, TX 78041
(956) 326-2420
FAX: (956) 326-2419
James O'Meara
President
E-MAIL: president@icet4u.org
URL: www.icet4u.org

International Fire Service (W)
Accreditation Congress
1723 W. Tyler Avenue
Stillwater, OK 74078
(405) 744-8303
FAX: (405) 744-7377
Director
E-MAIL: admin@ifsac.org
URL: ifsac.org

Joint Review Committee on (X)
Education in Cardiovascular Technology
(JRC-CVT)
1449 Hill Street
Whitinsville, MA 01588-1032
(978) 456-5594
Ms. Jackie Long-Goding
Executive Director
E-MAIL: office@jrccvt.org
URL: www.jrccvt.org

Joint Review Committee on (Y)
Education in Diagnostic Medical
Sonography
6021 University Boulevard
Suite 500
Ellicott City, MD 21043
(443) 973-3251
Mr. Gerry Magat MS
Executive Director
E-MAIL: mail@jrcdms.org
URL: www.jrcdms.org

Joint Review Committee on (Z)
Education in Radiologic Technology
20 North Wacker Drive
Suite 2850
Chicago, IL 60606-3182
(312) 704-5300
Leslie F. Winter
Chief Executive Officer
E-MAIL: lwinter@jrcert.org
URL: www.jrcert.org

Joint Review Committee on (a)
Educational Programs in Nuclear
Medicine Technology
820 West Danforth Road
Suite B1
Edmond, OK 73003
(405) 285-0546
Ms. Jan M. Winn
Executive Director
E-MAIL: mail@jrcnmt.org
URL: jrcnmt.org

Journalism Association of (b)
Community Colleges
c/o CNPA Services, Inc.
2701 K Street
Sacramento, CA 95816-5131
(916) 288-6021
FAX: (916) 288-6002
Mr. Joe Wirt
Administrator
E-MAIL: joe@cnpa.com
URL: jaccorline.org

Landscape Architectural (c)
Accreditation Board of the American
Society of Landscape Architects
636 Eye Street, NW
Washington, DC 20001-3736
(202) 216-2359
FAX: (202) 898-1185
Mr. Kristopher Pritchard
Accreditation & Education Director
E-MAIL: kpritchard@asla.org
URL: asla.org/laab

Laspau - Latin American (d)
Scholarship Programs of American
Universities
25 Mount Auburn Street
Suite 200
Cambridge, MA 02138-6095
(617) 495-5255
Ms. Angelica Natera
Executive Director
E-MAIL: angelica_natera@harvard.edu
URL: www.laspau.harvard.edu

Law School Admission Council (e)
662 Penn Street
Newtown, PA 18940
(215) 968-1162
Ms. Kellye Testy
President and CEO
E-MAIL: fwilliams@lsac.org
URL: www.lsac.org

Liaison Committee on Medical (f)
Education (LCME) American Medical
Association
330 North Wabash Avenue
Suite 39300
Chicago, IL 60611-5885
(312) 464-4933
Barbara Barzansky Ph.D.,MHPE
LCME Co-Secretary
E-MAIL: barbara.barzansky@ama-assn.org
URL: www.lcme.org

Linguistic Society of America (g)
522 21st Street, NW
Suite 120
Washington, DC 20006-5012
(202) 835-1714
FAX: (202) 835-1717
Ms. Katha Kissman
Interim Executive Director
E-MAIL: kkissman@lsadc.org
URL: www.linguisticsociety.org

Literacy Research Association, Inc. (h)
PO Box 3105
LaGrange, GA 30241
(706) 443-1334
FAX: (706) 883-8215
Mr. VJ Mayor
Executive Director
E-MAIL: vjmayor@asginfo.net
URL: www.LiteracyResearchAssociation.org

Lutheran Educational Conference of (i)
North America
5915 S. Remington Place
Suite 100
Sioux Falls, SD 57108
(605) 271-9894
Mr. Kenneth Gaschk
E-MAIL: ken.gaschk@cuw.edu
URL: www.lutherancolleges.org

Medical Assisting Education Review (j)
Board
2020 N Carolina Avenue
#213, Suite 7
Chicago, IL 60647
(312) 392-0155
Mr. Jim Hardman
Assistant Director, MAERB
E-MAIL: jhardman@maerb.org
URL: www.maerb.org

Higher Education Associations

Middle States Commission on (A)
Higher Education
1007 North Orange Street
4th Floor, MB #166
Wilmington, DE 19801
(267) 284-5026
Dr. Heather F. Perfetti
President
E-MAIL: president@msche.org
URL: www.msche.org

Midwest Association of Colleges (B)
and Employers
938 E. Georgia Street
Suite100
Indianapolis, IN 46202
(866) 606-1316
E-MAIL: admin@mwace.org
URL: www.mwace.org

Midwestern Higher Education (C)
Compact (MHEC)
105 Fifth Avenue South
Suite 450
Minneapolis, MN 55401
(612) 677-2777
FAX: (612) 767-3353
Ms. Susan G. Heegaard
President
E-MAIL: susanh@mhec.org
URL: www.mhec.org

Midwifery Education Accreditation (D)
Council (MEAC)
6417 Penn Ave S
Ste 8 ipmb 1075
Minneapolis, MN 55423-1196
(360) 466-2080
Amari Fauna
Director of Accreditation
E-MAIL: info@meacschools.org
URL: www.meacschools.org

Modern Language Association (E)
85 Broad Street
Suite 500
New York, NY 10004-2434
(646) 576-5000
Dr. Paula M. Krebs
Executive Director
E-MAIL: pkrebs@mla.org
URL: mla.org

Montessori Accreditation Council for (F)
Teacher Education (MACTE)
420 Park Street
Charlottesville, VA 22902
(434) 202-7793
Dr. Rebecca Pelton
President
E-MAIL: rebecca@macte.org
URL: www.macte.org

NACADA: The Global Community (G)
for Academic Advising
Kansas State University
2323 Anderson Avenue
Suite 225
Manhattan, KS 66502-2912
(785) 532-5717
FAX: (785) 532-7732
Dr. Melinda Anderson
Executive Director
E-MAIL: nacada@ksu.edu
URL: www.nacada.ksu.edu

NACAS (H)
435 Merchant Walk Square
Suite 300-139
Charlottesville, VA 22902
(434) 245-8425
FAX: (434) 245-8453
Mr. Matt Marcial
CEO
E-MAIL: matt.marcial@nacas.org
URL: www.nacas.org

NASPA-Student Affairs (I)
Administrators in Higher Education
111 K Street, NE
10th Floor
Washington, DC 20002-4409
(202) 265-7500
Dr. Kevin Kruger
President
E-MAIL: office@naspa.org
URL: www.naspa.org

The National Academy of Education (J)
500 5th Street, NW
Washington, DC 20001
(202) 334-2341
Mr. Gregory White
Executive Director
E-MAIL: info@naeducation.org
URL: www.naeducation.org

National Academy of Kinesiology (K)
2001 Juniper Drive
Mahomet, IL 61853
Ms. Kim Scott
Business Manager
E-MAIL: staff@nationalacademyofkinesiology.
org
URL: nationalacademyofkinesiology.org

National Accrediting Agency for (L)
Clinical Laboratory Sciences
5600 North River Road
Suite 720
Rosemont, IL 60018
(773) 714-8880
FAX: (773) 714-8886
Marisa James
CEO
E-MAIL: marisajames@naacls.org
URL: www.naacls.org

National Accrediting Commission of (M)
Career Arts & Sciences
3015 Colvin Street
Alexandria, VA 22314
(703) 600-7600
Mr. Darren Wallace
Executive Director
E-MAIL: dwallace@naccas.org
URL: www.naccas.org

National Association for College (N)
Admission Counseling
1050 North Highland Street
Suite 400
Arlington, VA 22201
(703) 836-2222
FAX: (703) 243-9375
Angel B. Perez
Chief Executive Officer
E-MAIL: ceo@nacacnet.org
URL: www.nacacnet.org

National Association for Equal (O)
Opportunity in Higher Education
600 Maryland Avenue SW
Suite 800E
Washington, DC 20024
(202) 552-3300
Lezli Baskerville Esquire
President & CEO
E-MAIL: lbaskerville@nafeo.org
URL: www.nafeoonation.org

National Association for the Legal (P)
Support of Alternative Schools
18520 N.W. 67th Avenue #188
Miami, FL 33015
(800) 456-7784
Mrs. Chau Trinh
Institutional Representative
E-MAIL: educate@nalsas.org
URL: www.nalsas.org

National Association for Practical (Q)
Nurse Education and Service, Inc.
2071 N. Bechtle Avenue
PMB 307
Springfield, OH 45504
(703) 933-1003
FAX: (703) 940-4089
Ann Bauer LPN
President
E-MAIL: president@napnes.org
URL: www.napnes.org

National Association of Agricultural (R)
Educators
One Paragon Centre
2525 Harrodsburg Road
Suite 200
Lexington, KY 40504-3358
(859) 967-2892
Alissa Smith
Chief Executive Officer
E-MAIL: asmith.naae@uky.edu
URL: www.naae.org

National Association of College and (S)
University Attorneys
1 Dupont Circle, NW
Suite 620
Washington, DC 20036
(202) 833-8390
Ona Alston Dosunmu
President & CEO
E-MAIL: oad@nacua.org
URL: www.nacua.org

National Association of College and (T)
University Business Officers
1110 Vermont Avenue, NW
Suite 800
Washington, DC 20005
(202) 861-2500
Lynne C. Schaeffer
Interim President and CEO
E-MAIL: lynne.schaefer@nacubo.org
URL: nacubo.org

National Association of College & (U)
University Food Services
1515 Turf Lane
Suite 100
East Lansing, MI 48823
(517) 332-2494
FAX: (517) 332-8144
E-MAIL: membership@nacufs.org
URL: www.nacufs.org

National Association of College (V)
Stores
500 East Lorain Street
Oberlin, OH 44074
(440) 775-7777
FAX: (440) 775-4769
Mr. Ed Schlichenmayer
Chief Executive Officer
E-MAIL: info@nacs.org
URL: www.nacs.org

National Association of College (W)
Wind and Percussion Instructors
Station 6670
Montevallo, AL 35115
(940) 898-2588
Ms. Danielle Woolery
President
E-MAIL: dwoolery@twu.edu
URL: www.nacwpi.org

National Association of Colleges (X)
and Employers
62 Highland Avenue
Bethlehem, PA 18017-9481
(610) 868-1421
FAX: (610) 868-0208
Mr. Shawn VanDerziel
Executive Director
E-MAIL: svanderziel@nacedweb.org
URL: www.naceweb.org

National Association of Correctional (Y)
Education Standards and Accreditation
(NACESA)
303 W. Burleson Street
Marshall, TX 75670
(903) 472-2762
FAX: (903) 471-8675
Dr. Tracy L. Andrus Sr.
E-MAIL: tandrus26@gmail.com

National Association of Educational (Z)
Procurement
7918 Jones Branch Drive
Suite 300
McLean, VA 22102-3345
(443) 281-9901
Ms. Krista Ferrell
Executive Director
E-MAIL: kferrell@naepnet.org
URL: www.naepnet.org

National Association of Independent (a)
Colleges and Universities
1025 Connecticut Avenue, NW
Suite 700
Washington, DC 20036-5405
(202) 785-8866
FAX: (202) 835-0003
Dr. Barbara Mistick
President
E-MAIL: geninfo@naicu.edu
URL: naicu.edu

National Association of Schools of (b)
Art and Design
11250 Roger Bacon Drive
Suite 21
Reston, VA 20190
(703) 437-0700
FAX: (703) 437-6312
Karen P. Moynahan
Executive Director
E-MAIL: info@arts-accredit.org
URL: nasad.arts-accredit.org

National Association of Schools of (c)
Dance
11250 Roger Bacon Drive
Suite 21
Reston, VA 20190
(703) 437-0700
FAX: (703) 437-6312
Karen P. Moynahan
Executive Director
E-MAIL: info@arts-accredit.org
URL: nasd.arts-accredit.org

National Association of Schools of (d)
Music
11250 Roger Bacon Drive
Suite 21
Reston, VA 20190
(703) 437-0700
FAX: (703) 437-6312
Karen P. Moynahan
Executive Director
E-MAIL: info@arts-accredit.org
URL: nasm.arts-accredit.org

National Association of Schools of (e)
Theatre
11250 Roger Bacon Drive
Suite 21
Reston, VA 20190
(703) 437-0700
FAX: (703) 437-6312
Karen P. Moynahan
Executive Director
E-MAIL: info@arts-accredit.org
URL: nast.arts-accredit.org

National Association of State (f)
Directors of Teacher Education and
Certification
1629 K Street, NW
Suite 300
Washington, DC 20006
(202) 204-2208
Dr. Phillip S. Rogers
Executive Director
E-MAIL: philrogers@nasdtec.org
URL: www.nasdtec.net

National Association of Student (g)
Financial Aid Administrators
1801 Pennsylvania Avenue, NW
Suite 850
Washington, DC 20006-3606
(202) 785-0453
FAX: (202) 785-1487
Mr. Justin Draeger
President
E-MAIL: info@nasfaa.org
URL: www.nasfaa.org

National Association of System (h)
Heads
3300 Metzerott Road
Adelphi, MD 20783
(301) 445-2780
Rebecca Martin
Executive Director
E-MAIL: rmartin@nash-dc.org
URL: www.nashonline.org

National Catholic Educational (i)
Association
407 Bicksler Square SE
Leesburg, VA 20175-3773
(571) 257-0010
FAX: (703) 243-0025
Mr. Lincoln Snyder
President/CEO
E-MAIL: lsnyder@ncea.org
URL: www.ncea.org

National Coalition for Campus (j)
Children's Centers
188 Front Street
Suite 116-104
Franklin, TN 37064
(615) 614-3723
Ms. Tonya Palla
Executive Director
E-MAIL: tonyap@campuschildren.org
URL: www.campuschildren.org

National Collegiate Athletic Association (A)
PO Box 6222
Indianapolis, IN 46206-6222
(317) 917-6222
Mr. Tom Paskus
Principal Academic Research Scientist
E-MAIL: research@ncaa.org
URL: www.ncaa.org

National Commission on Orthotic and Prosthetic Education (NCOPE) (B)
330 John Carlyle Street
Suite 200
Alexandria, VA 22314
(703) 836-7114 x 225
FAX: (703) 890-2425
Ms. Robin Seabrook
Executive Director
E-MAIL: rseabrook@ncope.org
URL: www.ncope.org

National Communication Association (C)
1765 N Street, NW
Washington, DC 20036
(202) 464-4622
FAX: (202) 464-4600
Dr. Shari Miles-Cohen
Executive Director
E-MAIL: smiles-cohen@natcom.org
URL: www.natcom.org

National Council for Continuing Education and Training (D)
9526 Argyle Forest Boulevard
Suite B2-322
Jacksonville, FL 32222
(904) 466-9466
Mr. Ed Harper
Executive Director
E-MAIL: nccet@nccet.org
URL: www.nccet.org

National Council of Instructional Administrators (NCIA) Dept of Educational Administration (E)
141 Teachers College Hall
PO Box 880360
University of Nebraska - Lincoln
Lincoln, NE 68588-0360
(402) 472-3726
FAX: (402) 472-4300
Katherine Wesley
Executive Director
E-MAIL: kwesley4@unl.edu
URL: cehs.unl.edu/ncia/

National Council of University Research Administrators (F)
1015 18th Street, NW
Suite 901
Washington, DC 20036
(202) 466-3894
FAX: (202) 223-5573
Kathleen M. Larmett
Executive Director
E-MAIL: larmett@ncura.edu
URL: www.ncura.edu

National Education Association (G)
1201 16th Street, NW
Suite 810
Washington, DC 20036
(202) 833-4000
FAX: (202) 822-7974
Ms. Kim A. Anderson
Executive Director
E-MAIL: mboyd@nea.org
URL: www.nea.org/he

National Forensic Association (H)
University of Wisconsin-Eau Claire
Hibbard Humanities Hall 256
124 Garfied Avenue
Eau Claire, WI 54701
(7180 836-3305
Ms. Karen Morris
President
E-MAIL: morriskr@uwec.edu
URL: sites.google.com/site/
    nationalforensicsassociation/

National Institute for Learning Outcomes Assessment (I)
University of Illinois at Urbana-Champaign
CRC, 51 Gerty Drive, Room 127
Champaign, IL 61820
(217) 244-2155
Dr. Gianina Baker
Acting Director
E-MAIL: baker44@illinois.edu
URL: www.learningoutcomeassessment.org

National League for Nursing (J)
The Watergate Building, 8th Floor
2600 Virginia Avenue, NW
Washington, DC 20037
(800) 669-1656
Dr. Beverly Malone
President & Chief Executive Officer
E-MAIL: oceo@nln.org
URL: www.nln.org

National Rural Education Association (K)
615 McCallie Avenue
Hunter Hall 311-B
Chattanooga, TN 37403
(423) 425-4539
Dr. Allen Pratt
Executive Director
E-MAIL: allen-pratt@utc.edu
URL: www.nrea.net

National Society for Experiential Education (L)
c/o Talley Management Group, Inc.
19 Mantua Road
Mt. Royal, NJ 08061
(856) 423-3427
FAX: (856) 423-3420
Haley Brust
Executive Director
E-MAIL: nsee@talley.com
URL: www.nsee.org

National Writing Project (M)
2120 University Avenue
University of California
Berkeley, CA 94704
(510) 679-2424
Elyse Eidman-Aadahl
Executive Director
E-MAIL: nwp@nwp.org
URL: www.nwp.org

Network of Schools of Public Policy, Affairs, and Administration (N)
1029 Vermont Avenue, NW
Suite 1100
Washington, DC 20005
(202) 628-8965
Ms. Angel Wright-Lanier
Executive Director
E-MAIL: naspaa@naspaa.org
URL: www.naspaa.org

New England Commission of Higher Education (NECHE) (O)
301 Edgewater Place
Suite 210
Wakefield, MA 01880
(781) 425-7785
FAX: (781) 425-1001
Dr. Lawrence M. Schall
President
E-MAIL: info@neche.org
URL: www.neche.org

New England Board of Higher Education (P)
45 Temple Place
Boston, MA 02111
(617) 533-9519
Dr. Michael K. Thomas
President and CEO
E-MAIL: presidentsoffice@nebhe.org
URL: www.nebhe.org

North American Association of Summer Sessions (Q)
North Carolina State University
2016 Harris Hall
Campus Box 7302
Raleigh, NC 27695-7302
(919) 515-2261
Dr. Lowell Davis
President
E-MAIL: naass@naass.org
URL: www.naass.org

Northwest Commission on Colleges and Universities (R)
8060 165th Avenue, NE
Suite 100
Redmond, WA 98052
(425) 558-4224
FAX: (205) 525-9848
Dr. Sonny Ramaswamy
President
E-MAIL: sonny@nwccu.org
URL: www.nwccu.org

Planning Accreditation Board (S)
2334 W. Lawrence Avenue
Suite 209
Chicago, IL 60625
(773) 334-7200
Ms. Jesmarie Soto Johnson
Executive Director
E-MAIL: jjohnson@
    planningaccreditationboard.org
URL: www.planningaccreditationboard.org

Quality Education for Minorities (QEM) Network (T)
1818 N Street, NW
Suite 350
Washington, DC 20036
(202) 659-1818
Dr. Erin Lynch
President
E-MAIL: elynch@qem.org
URL: www.qem.org

Society for College and University Planning (U)
1330 Eisenhower Place
Ann Arbor, MI 48108
(734) 669-3270
Mike Moss CAE
President
E-MAIL: mike.moss@scup.org
URL: www.scup.org

Society for Slovene Studies (V)
148 Russell Street #3
Worcester, MA 01609
Ms. Kristina Helena Reardon
Secretary
E-MAIL: kristina.reardon@gmail.com
URL: www.slovenestudies.com

The Society for the Future of Higher Education (W)
c/o Western Kentucky University
1906 College Heights Boulevard #8020
Bowling Green, KY 42101-1041
(270) 745-2907
Ms. Vivienne Felix
Executive Director
E-MAIL: society@sfhe.org
URL: sfhe.us

Society of American Foresters (X)
2121 K Street, NW
Suite 315
Washington, DC 20037
(866) 897-8720
FAX: (202) 938-3911
Mr. Terry Baker
Chief Executive Officer
E-MAIL: landreani@safnet.org
URL: www.eforester.org

Society of Professors of Education (Y)
University of West Georgia
College of Education
Dept of LAI
1601 Maple Street
Carrollton, GA 30118-5160
(678) 839-6132
Dr. Robert C. Morris
Secretary-Treasurer
E-MAIL: rmorris@westga.edu
URL: societyofprofessorsofeducation.com

Southeastern Universities Research Association (Z)
1201 New York Avenue, NW
Suite 430
Washington, DC 20005
(202) 408-7872
FAX: (202) 408-8250
Mr. Sean J. Hearne
President & CEO
URL: www.sura.org

Southern Association for College Student Affairs (a)
Clemson University
211B Grantt Circle
Clemson, SC 29634-0707
(864) 656-5100
Dr. Tony W. Cawthon
Executive Director
E-MAIL: cawthon@clemson.edu
URL: www.sacsa.org

Southern Association of Colleges and Schools Commission on Colleges (b)
1866 Southern Lane
Decatur, GA 30033-4097
(404) 679-4512
Dr. Belle S. Wheelan
President
E-MAIL: bwheelan@sacscoc.org
URL: sacscoc.org

Southern States Communication Association (c)
University of Tennessee at Knoxville
293 Communications Building
1345 Circle Park Drive
Knoxville, TN 37996-0324
(423) 425-4633
FAX: (423) 756-5559
Mr. John Haas
Executive Director
E-MAIL: jhaas1@utk.edu
URL: www.ssca.net

State Higher Education Executive Officers Association (d)
3035 Center Green Drive
Suite 100
Boulder, CO 80301-2205
(303) 541-1600
FAX: (303) 541-1639
Dr. Robert Anderson
President
E-MAIL: randerson@sheeo.org
URL: www.sheeo.org

Tennessee Independent Colleges and Universities Association (e)
555 Marriott Drive
Suite 315
Nashville, TN 37214
(615) 242-6400
Dr. Claude O. Pressnell Jr.
President
E-MAIL: pressnell@ticua.org
URL: www.ticua.org

Transnational Association of Christian Colleges and Schools (TRACS) (f)
15935 Forest Road
Forest, VA 24551
(434) 525-9539
Dr. Timothy W. Eaton
President
E-MAIL: info@tracs.org
URL: www.tracs.org

The Tuition Exchange (g)
3 Bethesda Metro Center
Suite 700
Bethesda, MD 20814
(301) 941-1827
FAX: (301) 657-9776
Mr. Robert D. Shorb
Executive Director/CEO
E-MAIL: rshorb@tuitionexchange.org
URL: www.tuitionexchange.org

UNCF (h)
1805 7th Street NW
4th Floor
Washington, DC 20001
(800) 331-2244
Dr. Michael Lomax
President & CEO
E-MAIL: lori.bonnette@uncf.org
URL: www.uncf.org

University Aviation Association (i)
8092 Memphis Avenue
Suite 132
Memphis, TN 38053
(901) 563-0505
Ms. Dawn E. Vinson
Executive Director
E-MAIL: hello@uaa.aero
URL: www.uaa.aero

University Film and Video Association (j)
960 War Eagle Drive S
Colorado Springs, CO 80919
(646) 498-1182
Ms. Christina Lane
President
E-MAIL: home@ufva.org
URL: www.ufva.org

Higher Education Associations

University Photographers'   (A)
Association of America
P.O. Box 433
Clalfon, NJ 07830-0433
(908) 335-0157
Mr. Glenn Carpenter
UPAA President
E-MAIL: carpenter@morainevalley.edu
URL: www.upaa.org

University Professional &   (B)
Continuing Education Association
(UPCEA)
One Dupont Circle, NW
Suite 450
Washington, DC 20036
(202) 659-3130
Dr. Robert Hansen
CEO
E-MAIL: rhansen@upcea.edu
URL: upcea.edu

University Risk Management and   (C)
Insurance Association, Inc.
PO Box 1027
Bloomington, IN 47402
(812) 727-7130
FAX: (812) 727-7129
Ms. Jenny Whittington
Executive Director
E-MAIL: urmia@urmia.org
URL: www.urmia.org

Urban Affairs Association   (D)
c/o Urban Studies Program
University of Wisconsin-Milwaukee
PO Box 413
Milwaukee, WI 53201-0413
(414) 208-4589
Dr. Margaret Wilder
UAA Executive Director
E-MAIL: info@uaamail.org
URL: www.urbanaffairsassociation.org

WASC Senior College and University   (E)
Commission
1080 Marina Village Parkway
Suite 500
Alameda, CA 94501
(510) 748-9001
FAX: (510) 748-9797
Ms. Jamienne S. Studley
President
E-MAIL: kmatarrese@wscuc.org
URL: https://www.wscuc.org/

Western Interstate Commission for   (F)
Higher Education
3035 Center Green Drive
Suite 200
Boulder, CO 80301-2204
(303) 541-0201
Dr. Demaree K. Michelau
President
E-MAIL: dmichelau@wiche.edu
URL: www.wiche.edu

Consortia of Institutions of Higher Education

Alabama Association of (A)
Independent Colleges and Universities
4266 Lomac Street
Montgomery, AL 36106
(334) 356-2220
Fax: (334) 356-2202
Paul M. Hankins
President
E-mail: hankinsp@knology.net
URL: www.aaicu.net

Arkansas' Independent Colleges and (B)
Universities
PO Box 300
Little Rock, AR 72203
(501) 378-0843
Fax: (501) 374-1523
Mr. Andy Goodman
President
E-mail: agoodman@arkindcolleges.org
URL: www.arkindcolleges.org

Associated Colleges of the Midwest (C)
180 N. Michigan Avenue
Suite 2020
Chicago, IL 60601
(312) 263-5000
Ms. Sonya Malunda
President
E-mail: smalunda@acm.edu
URL: www.acm.edu

Association of Independent (D)
California Colleges and Universities
1121 L Street
Suite 802
Sacramento, CA 95814
(916) 446-7626
Ms. Kristen F. Soares
President
E-mail: aiccu@aiccu.edu
URL: www.aiccu.edu

Association of Independent (E)
Colleges and Universities in
Massachusetts
5 Brighton Street
Belmont, MA 02478
(617) 742-5147
Mr. Rob McCarron
President
E-mail: rob.mccarron@aicum.org
URL: www.aicum.org

Association of Independent Colleges (F)
and Universities of Ohio
41 South High Street
Suite 1690
Columbus, OH 43215
(614) 228-2196
Fax: (614) 228-8406
Mr. C. Todd Jones
President & General Counsel
E-mail: tjones@aicuo.edu
URL: www.aicuo.edu

Association of Independent (G)
Colleges and Universities of
Pennsylvania
101 North Front Street
Harrisburg, PA 17101-1404
(717) 232-8649
Fax: (717) 233-8574
Thomas P. Foley J.D.
President
E-mail: foley@aicup.org
URL: www.aicup.org

Association of Independent (H)
Colleges and Universities of Rhode
Island
50 Park Row West
Suite 100
Providence, RI 02903
(401) 272-8270
Mr. Daniel Egan
President
E-mail: degan@aicuri.org
URL: www.aicuri.org

Association of Independent Colleges (I)
of Art & Design
236 Hope Street
Providence, RI 02906
(401) 270-5991
Fax: (401) 270-5993
Ms. Deborah Obalil
President & Executive Director
E-mail: deborah@aicad.org
URL: aicad.org

Association of Independent (J)
Kentucky Colleges and Universities
c/o Harrod & Associates
2 HMB Circle
Frankfort, KY 40601
(502) 695-5007
Dr. OJ Oleka
President
E-mail: info@aikcu.org
URL: www.aikcu.org

Association of Vermont Independent (K)
Colleges
PO Box 254
Montpelier, VT 05601
(802) 828-8826
Susan Stitely
President
E-mail: sstitely@vermont-icolleges.org
URL: vermont-icolleges.org

Atlanta Regional Council for Higher (L)
Education
141 E. College Avenue
Box 1084
Decatur, GA 30030
(404) 471-6422
Ms. Tracey Brantley
Executive Director
E-mail: tbrantley@atlantahighered.org
URL: www.atlantahighered.org

Boston Theological Interreligious (M)
Consortium
PO Box 391069
Cambridge, MA 02139
(207) 370-5275
Stephanie Edwards PhD
Executive Director
E-mail: btioffice@bostontheological.org
URL: www.bostontheological.org

CCUMC (Consortium of College & (N)
University Media Centers)
201 E. Main Street
Suite 1405
Lexington, KY 40507
(859) 514-9185
Kristy Howard
Executive Director
E-mail: ccumc@ccumc.org
URL: ccumc.org

Central Pennsylvania Consortium (O)
c/o Franklin & Marshall College
PO Box 3003
Lancaster, PA 17604-3003
(717) 358-4282
Fax: (717) 358-4455
Ms. Kathryn Missildine
Executive Assistant
E-mail: kathy.missildine@fandm.edu
URL: www.centralpennsylvaniaconsortium.
  org

CHESLA, Connecticut Higher (P)
Education Supplemental Loan Authority
10 Columbus Boulevard
7th Floor
Hartford, CT 06106-1978
(860) 761-8453
Ms. Jeanette W. Weldon
Executive Director
E-mail: jweldon@chesla.org
URL: www.chesla.org

Christian College Consortium (Q)
1020 Hesli Hill Court
Shoreview, MN 55126-1408
(651) 336-6371
Dr. James H. Barnes III
President
E-mail: j-barnes@bethel.edu
URL: ccconsortium.org

Community College Futures (R)
Assembly
Bellwether College Consortium
Alamo Colleges District
2222 N. Alamo Street
San Antonio, TX 78215
(210) 485-0836
Ms. Rose Martinez
E-mail: martinez1702@alamo.edu
URL: www.bellwethercollegeconsortium.com

Community Colleges for Iowa (S)
855 East Court Avenue
Des Moines, IA 50309
(515) 282-4692
Ms. Emily Shields
Executive Director
E-mail: ejshields@ccforiowa.org
URL: ccforiowa.org

The Consortium for Graduate Study (T)
in Management
229 Chesterfield Business Parkway
Chesterfield, MO 63005
(636) 681-5553
Fax: (636) 681-5499
Mr. Peter J. Aranda III
Executive Director and CEO
E-mail: arandap@cgsm.org
URL: www.cgsm.org

Consortium of Universities of the (U)
Washington Metropolitan Area
1020 19th Street, NW
Suite 500
Washington, DC 20036
(202) 331-8080
Dr. Andrew Flagel
President & CEO
E-mail: aflagel@consortium.org
URL: www.consortium.org

Consortium on Financing Higher (V)
Education
1 Main Street
Suite 1210
Cambridge, MA 02142
(617) 253-5030
Ms. Janet L. Rapelye
President
E-mail: cofhe-info@mit.edu
URL: web.mit.edu/cofhe/

Cooperating Raleigh Colleges (W)
William Peace University
15 E. Peace Street
Raleigh, NC 27604
(919) 346-6169
Ms. Maura DiColla
Director
E-mail: director@crcraleighcolleges.org
URL: www.crcraleighcolleges.org

Council of Independent Colleges in (X)
Virginia
PO Box 1005
Bedford, VA 24523
(540) 586-0606
Fax: (540) 586-2630
Mr. Robert B. Lambeth Jr.
President
E-mail: lambeth@cicv.org
URL: www.cicv.org

Council of Presidents (Y)
410 Eleventh Avenue SE
Suite 101
Olympia, WA 98501
(360) 292-4100
Mr. Ruben Flores
Interim Executive Director
E-mail: rflores@councilofpresidents.org
URL: www.councilofpresidents.org

Federation of Independent Illinois (Z)
Colleges and Universities
1123 South Second Street
Springfield, IL 62704
(217) 789-1400
Mr. David W. Tretter
President
E-mail: davetretter@federationedu.com
URL: www.federationedu.org

Five College Consortium (a)
97 Spring Street
Amherst, MA 01002
(413) 542-4009
Fax: (413) 542-4028
Dr. Sarah K. A. Pfatteicher
Executive Director
E-mail: fciexecdirector@fivecolleges.edu
URL: www.fivecolleges.edu

Georgia Independent College (b)
Association
50 Hurt Plaza SE
Suite 655
Atlanta, GA 30303
(404) 233-5433
Ms. Jenna Colvin
President
E-mail: jcolvin@georgacolleges.org
URL: www.georgiacolleges.org

Graduate Theological Foundation (c)
751 S. Orange Avenue
Sarasota, FL 34236
(800) 423-5983
Fax: (405) 653-9435
Paul J. Kirbas DMin, PhD
President
E-mail: provost@gtfeducation.org
URL: www.gtfeducation.org

Great Lakes Colleges Association (d)
535 West William
Suite 301
Ann Arbor, MI 48103
(734) 661-2350
Fax: (734) 661-2349
Dr. Michael (Mickey) McDonald
President
E-mail: mickey@glca.org
URL: www.glca.org

Greater Cincinnati Collegiate (e)
Connection
Union Institute & University
2090 Florence Avenue
Cincinnati, OH 45206
(513) 487-1163
Ms. Janet Piccirillo
Executive Director
E-mail: janet.piccirillo@myunion.edu
URL: www.gccollegiateconnection.org

Hartford Consortium for Higher (f)
Education
349 Main Street
2nd Floor
East Hartford, CT 06108
(860) 929-3009
Mr. Greg Haddad
Coordinator of Operations & External
Relations
E-mail: ghaddad@hartfordconsortium.org
URL: www.hartfordconsortium.org

Higher Education Consortium of (g)
Metropolitan St. Louis
734 West Port Plaza
Suite 273
St. Louis, MO 63146
(314) 985-8833
Fax: (314) 985-8835
Ms. Cassandra M. Pinkston
Chief Executive Officer
E-mail: cpinkston@hecstl.org
URL: www.hecstl.org

Higher Education Data Sharing (h)
(HEDS) Consortium
Wabash College
Trippet Hall
410 West Wabash Avenue
Crawfordsville, IN 47933
(765) 361-6331
Charles Blaich
Director
E-mail: kmcdorman@hedsconsortium.org
URL: www.hedsconsortium.org

Independent Colleges and (i)
Universities of Missouri
PO Box 1865
Jefferson City, MO 65102-1865
(573) 635-9160
Fax: (573) 635-6258
Mr. William A. Gamble
Executive Director
E-mail: bill@molobby.com
URL:
  independentcollegesanduniversitiesofmo.
  com

Independent Colleges and (j)
Universities of New Jersey
142 West State Street
Trenton, NJ 08608
(609) 218-5026
Fax: (609) 498-0055
Steve Reynolds
President and CEO
E-mail: sreynolds@njcolleges.org
URL: www.njcolleges.org

Independent Colleges and (k)
Universities of Texas, Inc.
1303 San Antonio Street
Suite 820
Austin, TX 78701
(512) 472-9522
Dr. Steven Johnson
President
E-mail: steven.johnson@icut.org
URL: icut.org

Consortia of Institutions of Higher Education

Independent Colleges of Indiana (A)
30 S. Meridian Street
Suite 800
Indianapolis, IN 46204
(317) 236-6090
Kurt D. Dykstra
President and CEO
E-MAIL: ksmith@icindiana.org
URL: www.icindiana.org

Independent Colleges of (B)
Washington
600 Stewart Street
Suite 600
Seattle, WA 98101
(206) 623-4494
Terri Standish-Kuon Ph.D.
President & CEO
E-MAIL: info@icwashington.org
URL: www.icwashington.org

Inter-University Consortium for (C)
Political and Social Research (ICPSR)
The University of Michigan
Institute for Social Research
PO Box 1248
Ann Arbor, MI 48106-1248
(734) 615-8400
Dr. Margaret Levenstein
Director
E-MAIL: maggiel@umich.edu
URL: www.icpsr.umich.edu

Inter-University Council of Ohio (D)
(IUC)
10 West Broad Street
Suite 450
Columbus, OH 43215
(614) 464-1266
FAX: (614) 464-9281
Mr. Bruce Johnson
President
E-MAIL: johnson.3287@osu.edu
URL: www.iuc-ohio.org

Iowa Association of Independent (E)
Colleges and Universities
3775 EP True Parkway #253
West Des Moines, IA 50265
(515) 282-3175
Mr. Gary Steinke
President
E-MAIL: president@iaicu.org
URL: www.iowaprivatecolleges.org

Kansas Independent College (F)
Association
700 South Kansas Avenue
Suite 622
Topeka, KS 66603
(785) 235-9877
Mr. Matthew E. Lindsey
President
E-MAIL: matt@kscolleges.org
URL: www.kscolleges.org

Lehigh Valley Association of (G)
Independent Colleges
1309 Main Street
Bethlehem, PA 18018
(610) 625-7888
Diane Dimitroff
Executive Director
E-MAIL: dimitroffd@lvaic.org
URL: www.lvaic.org

Louisiana Association of (H)
Independent Colleges and Universities
PO Box 3332
Baton Rouge, LA 70821
(225) 389-9885
Dr. Eric Turner
President & CEO
E-MAIL: turner@laicu.org
URL: www.laicu.org

Maryland Independent College and (I)
University Association
140 South Street
Annapolis, MD 21401
(410) 269-0306
Ms. Sara Fidler
President
E-MAIL: sfidler@micua.org
URL: www.micua.org

Massachusetts Education & Career (J)
Opportunities Inc
18 Chestnut Street
Suite 210
Worcester, MA 01608
(508) 754-6829
FAX: (508) 797-0069
Mr. Mark Bilotta
CEO
E-MAIL: mbilotta@massedco.org
URL: www.massedco.org

Michigan Independent Colleges & (K)
Universities
120 N. Washington Square
Suite 950
Lansing, MI 48933
(517) 372-9160
Robert LeFevre
President
E-MAIL: rlefevre@micolleges.org
URL: www.micolleges.org

National Student Exchange (L)
2613 Northridge Parkway
Suite 106
Ames, IA 50010
(515) 450-5529
Dr. Debra Sanborn
President
E-MAIL: info@nse.org
URL: nse.org

New England Faculty Development (M)
Consortium
108 Bromfeld Road
Somerville, MA 02144
(617) 627-4007
Annie Soisson Ed.D
President
E-MAIL: annie.soisson@tufts.edu
URL: www.nefdc.org

New Hampshire College & (N)
University Council
2 Pillsbury Street
Suite 302
Concord, NH 03301
(603) 225-4199
Dr. Debby Scire
President and CEO
E-MAIL: scire@compactnh.org
URL: www.nhcuc.org

New Jersey Association of State (O)
Colleges and Universities
150 West State Street
Trenton, NJ 08608
(609) 989-1100
Mr. Eugene Lepore
Executive Director
E-MAIL: elepore@njascu.org
URL: www.njascu.org

New Jersey Council of County (P)
Colleges
330 West State Street
Trenton, NJ 08618
(609) 392-3434
Dr. Aaron Fichtner
President
E-MAIL: afichtner@njccc.org
URL: www.njccc.org

North Carolina Independent (Q)
Colleges and Universities
530 North Blount Street
Raleigh, NC 27604
(919) 832-5817
FAX: (919) 833-0794
Dr. A. Hope Williams
President
E-MAIL: williams@ncicu.org
URL: www.ncicu.org

North Dakota Independent College (R)
Fund
University of Mary
7500 University Drive
Bismarck, ND 58504
(701) 355-8329
Mr. Paul Keeney
Executive Director
E-MAIL: plkeeney@umary.edu

Northeast Consortium of Colleges (S)
and Universities in Massachusetts
(NECCUM)
c/o Office of the President
Northern Essex Community College
100 Elliott Street
Haverhill, MA 01830
(978) 556-3719
Ms. Michelle Sunday
E-MAIL: msunday@necc.mass.edu
URL: uml.edu/registrar/policies-and-
procedures/neccum.aspx

Oak Ridge Associated Universities (T)
MS-22
PO Box 117
Oak Ridge, TN 37831-0117
(865) 576-3300
FAX: (865) 576-3816
Mr. Andy Page
President and CEO
E-MAIL: andy.page@orau.org
URL: www.orau.org

Oregon Alliance of Independent (U)
Colleges & Universities
8215 SW Tualatin Sherwood Road
Suite 200
Tualatin, OR 97062
(503) 342-0004
Mr. Brent Wilder
President
E-MAIL: info@oaicu.org
URL: oaicu.org

Pennsylvania's State System of (V)
Higher Education Foundation, Inc.
100 Noble Boulevard
Suite 10 #1014
Carlisle, PA 17013
FAX: (717) 720-7082
Ms. Cynthia Pritchard
President/CEO
E-MAIL: cpritchard@thepafoundation.org
URL: www.thepafoundation.org

Pittsburgh Council on Higher (W)
Education
201 Wood Street
Pittsburgh, PA 15222
(412) 657-8105
Ms. Karina Chavez
Executive Director
E-MAIL: kchavez@pointpark.edu
URL: pche-pa.org

Quad-Cities Graduate Study Center (X)
WIU - QC Campus
3300 River Drive
Moline, IL 61265
(309) 762-9481, x62274
Shirley Moore
E-MAIL: shirley@gradcenter.org
URL: www.gradcenter.org

Second Nature (Y)
186 Alewife Brook Pkwy
#1182
Cambridge, MA 02138
(617) 722-0036
FAX: (617) 259-1734
Dr. Timothy Carter
President
E-MAIL: info@secondnature.org
URL: www.secondnature.org

South Carolina Independent (Z)
Colleges & Universities, Inc.
PO Box 12007
Columbia, SC 29211
(803) 799-7122
FAX: (803) 254-7504
Dr. Jeffrey Perez
President & CEO
E-MAIL: jeff@scicu.org
URL: www.scicu.org

South Metropolitan Higher (a)
Education Consortium
202 S. Halsted Street
Chicago Heights, IL 60411
(708) 709-3764
Ms. Allessandra Kummelehne
Executive Director
E-MAIL: akummelehne@prairiestate.edu
URL: southmetroed.org

Southern Regional Education Board (b)
592 Tenth Street, NW
Atlanta, GA 30318-5776
(404) 875-9211
FAX: (404) 872-1477
Dr. Stephen L. Pruitt
President
E-MAIL: stephen.pruitt@sreb.org
URL: www.sreb.org

Strategic Ohio Council for Higher (c)
Education (SOCHE)
3155 Research Boulevard
Suite 204
Dayton, OH 45420
(937) 258-8890
FAX: (937) 258-8899
Dr. Cassie Barlow
President
E-MAIL: cassie.barlow@soche.org
URL: www.soche.org

Texas International Education (d)
Consortium
611 West 14th Street
Austin, TX 78701
(512) 477-9283
FAX: (512) 600-6065
Robin Lerner
President & CEO
E-MAIL: info@tiec.org
URL: www.tiec.org

Tuition Plan Consortium/Private (e)
College 529 Plan
(314) 727-0900
Mr. Robert Cole
President & CEO
E-MAIL: robert@pc529.com
URL: www.privatecollege529.com

The Virginia College Fund (f)
1015 E. Main Street
Richmond, VA 23219
(804) 355-3271
FAX: (804) 355-3271
Mr. Carthan F. Currin III
President
E-MAIL: office@thevcf.org
URL: www.thevcf.org

Virginia Tidewater Consortium for (g)
Higher Education
4900 Powhatan Avenue
Norfolk, VA 23529-0293
(757) 683-3183
FAX: (757) 683-4515
Dr. Lawrence G. Dotolo
President
E-MAIL: lgdotolo@aol.com
URL: www.vtc.odu.edu

Washington Theological Consortium (h)
415 Michigan Avenue, NE
Suite 105
Washington, DC 20017
(202) 832-2675
FAX: (202) 526-0818
Dr. Larry Golemon
Executive Director
E-MAIL: wtc@washtheocon.org
URL: washtheocon.org

West Virginia Independent Colleges (i)
& Universities
c/o Three Point Strategies, LLC
PO Box 7058
Charleston, WV 25356
(304) 814-9348
Mr. Ben Beakes
Executive Director
E-MAIL: wvicu@wvicu.org
URL: www.wvicu.org

Wisconsin Association of (j)
Independent Colleges and Universities
122 West Washington Avenue
Suite 700
Madison, WI 53703-2723
(608) 256-7761
FAX: (608) 256-7065
Liza Simon
Interim President & CEO
E-MAIL: mail@waicu.org
URL: www.waicu.org

The Work Colleges Consortium   (A)
CPO 2163
Berea, KY 40404
(859) 985-3156
Ms. Robin Taffler
Executive Director
E-MAIL: info@workcolleges.org
URL: www.workcolleges.org

NAME INDEX

US Department of Education Offices, Statewide Agencies of Higher Education, Higher Education Associations, Consortia of Institutions of Higher Education

Institutions By Religious Affiliation

African Methodist Episcopal
Allen University ... SC
Edward Waters College ... FL
Jackson Theological Seminary ... AR
Paul Quinn College ... TX
Payne Theological Seminary ... OH
Shorter College ... AR
Wilberforce University ... OH

African Methodist Episcopal Zion Church
Clinton College ... SC
Hood Theological Seminary ... NC
Livingstone College ... NC

American Baptist
Alderson Broaddus University ... WV
Bacone College ... OK
Berkeley School of Theology ... CA
Eastern University ... PA
Franklin College of Indiana ... IN
Judson University ... IL
Linfield University ... OR
Northern Seminary ... IL
Ottawa University ... KS
University of Sioux Falls ... SD

Assemblies Of God Church
Ascent College ... VA
Assemblies of God Theological Seminary ... MO
Bridges Christian College ... LA
Evangel University ... MO
Global University ... MO
Lumbee River Christian College ... NC
North Central University ... MN
Northpoint Bible College ... MA
Northwest University ... WA
Southeastern University ... FL
Southwestern Assemblies of God University ... TX
Trinity Bible College & Graduate School ... ND
University of Valley Forge ... PA
Vanguard University of Southern California ... CA

Baptist
American Baptist College ... TN
Arkansas Baptist College ... AR
Arlington Baptist University ... TX
Baptist Bible College ... MO
Baptist Missionary Association Theological Seminary ... TX
Baptist University of the Americas ... TX
Baylor University ... TX
Bethel University ... MN
Bluefield University ... VA
Boston Baptist College ... MA
Brewton-Parker College ... GA
Campbell University ... NC
Campbellsville University ... KY
Cedarville University ... OH
Central Baptist College ... AR
Central Baptist Theological Seminary ... KS
Central Baptist Theological Seminary of Minneapolis ... MN
Chowan University ... NC
Clarks Summit University ... PA
Dallas Baptist University ... TX
East Texas Baptist University ... TX
Gardner-Webb University ... NC
Hardin-Simmons University ... TX
Howard Payne University ... TX
Huntsville Bible College ... AL
International Baptist College and Seminary ... AZ
Jacksonville College ... TX
Maple Springs Baptist Bible College & Seminary ... MD
Missouri Baptist University ... MO
Morris College ... SC
Oakland City University ... IN
Samford University ... AL
Selma University ... AL
Shaw University ... NC
Shorter University ... GA
Simmons College of Kentucky ... KY
Southeastern Baptist College ... MS
The Crown College of the Bible ... TN
The John Leland Center for Theological Studies ... VA
Trinity Baptist College ... FL
Truett McConnell University ... GA
University of the Cumberlands ... KY
Veritas Baptist College ... IN
Virginia Beach Theological Seminary ... VA
Virginia Union University ... VA
West Coast Baptist College ... CA

Brethren Church
Ashland University ... OH

Christian Church (Disciples Of Christ)
Barton College ... NC
Bethany College ... WV
Bushnell University ... OR
Chapman University ... CA
Christian Theological Seminary ... IN
Columbia College ... MO
Culver-Stockton College ... MO
Eureka College ... IL
Jarvis Christian College ... TX
Lexington Theological Seminary ... KY
Midway University ... KY
Phillips Theological Seminary ... OK
Texas Christian University ... TX
Transylvania University ... KY
University of Lynchburg ... VA
William Woods University ... MO

Christian Churches And Churches of Christ
Boise Bible College ... ID
Central Christian College of the Bible ... MO
Dallas Christian College ... TX
Great Lakes Christian College ... MI
Johnson University ... TN
Kentucky Christian University ... KY
Lincoln Christian University ... IL
Manhattan Christian College ... KS
Point University ... GA

Christian Methodist Episcopal
Lane College ... TN
Miles College ... AL
Texas College ... TX

Christian Reformed Church
Calvin Theological Seminary ... MI
Calvin University ... MI
Dordt University ... IA

Church Of Christ
Pepperdine University ... CA

Church Of God
Anderson University ... IN
Lee University ... TN
Mid-America Christian University ... OK
Pentecostal Theological Seminary ... TN
The University of Findlay ... OH
Universidad Teologica Del Caribe ... PR
Warner Pacific University ... OR
Warner University ... FL

Church of God in Christ
All Saints Bible College ... TN

Church of New Jerusalem
Bryn Athyn College of the New Church ... PA

Church Of The Brethren
Bethany Theological Seminary ... IN
Bridgewater College ... VA
Manchester University ... IN
McPherson College ... KS

Church Of The Nazarene
Eastern Nazarene College ... MA
MidAmerica Nazarene University ... KS
Mount Vernon Nazarene University ... OH
Nazarene Bible College ... CO
Nazarene Theological Seminary ... MO
Northwest Nazarene University ... ID
Olivet Nazarene University ... IL
Point Loma Nazarene University ... CA
Southern Nazarene University ... OK
Trevecca Nazarene University ... TN

Churches Of Christ
Abilene Christian University ... TX
Amridge University ... AL
Crowley's Ridge College ... AR
Faulkner University ... AL
Freed-Hardeman University ... TN
Harding University Main Campus ... AR
Heritage Christian University ... AL
Lipscomb University ... TN
Lubbock Christian University ... TX
Mid-Atlantic Christian University ... NC
Southwestern Christian College ... TX
York College ... NE

Cumberland Presbyterian
Bethel University ... TN
Memphis Theological Seminary ... TN

Evangelical Covenant Church Of America
North Park University ... IL

Evangelical Free Church Of America
Trinity International University ... IL

Evangelical Lutheran Church In America
Augsburg University ... MN
Augustana College ... IL
Augustana University ... SD
Bethany College ... KS
California Lutheran University ... CA
Capital University ... OH
Carthage College ... WI
Concordia College ... MN
Finlandia University ... MI
Gettysburg College ... PA
Grand View University ... IA
Gustavus Adolphus College ... MN
Lenoir-Rhyne University ... NC
Luther College ... IA
Luther Seminary ... MN
Lutheran School of Theology at Chicago ... IL
Midland University ... NE
Muhlenberg College ... PA
Newberry College ... SC
Pacific Lutheran University ... WA
Roanoke College ... VA
St. Olaf College ... MN
Susquehanna University ... PA
Texas Lutheran University ... TX
Thiel College ... PA
United Lutheran Seminary ... PA
Wartburg College ... IA
Wartburg Theological Seminary ... IA
Wittenberg University ... OH

Evangelical Lutheran Synod
Bethany Lutheran College ... MN

Free Methodist
Central Christian College of Kansas ... KS
Greenville University ... IL
Seattle Pacific University ... WA
Spring Arbor University ... MI

Free Will Baptist
California Christian College ... CA
Randall University ... OK
Southeastern Free Will Baptist College ... NC
Welch College ... TN

Friends
Earlham College and Earlham School of Religion ... IN
George Fox University ... OR
Guilford College ... NC
Malone University ... OH
William Penn University ... IA
Wilmington College ... OH

Greek Orthodox
Hellenic College-Holy Cross Greek Orthodox School of Theology ... MA

Interdenominational
Athens College of Ministry ... GA
Bethany Global University ... MN
Christian Witness Theological Seminary ... CA
Denver Seminary ... CO
Evangelical Seminary of Puerto Rico ... PR
Faith International University ... WA
God's Bible School and College ... OH
Haven University ... CA
Interdenominational Theological Center ... GA
Kentucky Mountain Bible College ... KY
Messiah University ... PA
Oak Hills Christian College ... MN
Palm Beach Atlantic University ... FL
Phoenix Seminary ... AZ
Rocky Mountain College ... MT
South Florida Bible College ... FL
The King's University ... TX
Union Bible College ... IN
Wesley Biblical Seminary ... MS

Jewish
Academy for Jewish Religion ... NY
Academy for Jewish Religion, California ... CA
Bais Medrash Ateres Shlomo ... NY
Hebrew Union College-Jewish Institute of Religion ... NY
Mechon L'Hoyroa ... NY
New York Medical College ... NY
Reconstructionist Rabbinical College ... PA
Women's Institute of Torah Seminary ... MD

Latter-day Saints
Brigham Young University ... UT
Brigham Young University Hawaii ... HI
Brigham Young University-Idaho ... ID
Ensign College ... UT

Lutheran
Valparaiso University ... IN

Lutheran Church - Missouri Synod
Concordia Seminary ... MO
Concordia Theological Seminary ... IN
Concordia University ... NE
Concordia University Chicago ... IL
Concordia University Irvine ... CA
Concordia University Texas ... TX
Concordia University Wisconsin ... WI
Concordia University, St. Paul ... MN

Mennonite Brethren Church
Fresno Pacific University ... CA
Tabor College ... KS

Mennonite Church
Anabaptist Mennonite Biblical Seminary ... IN
Bethel College ... KS
Bluffton University ... OH
Eastern Mennonite University ... VA
Goshen College ... IN
Grace College and Seminary ... IN
Hesston College ... KS
Rosedale Bible College ... OH

Missionary Church
Bethel University ... IN

Moravian Church
Moravian University ... PA
Salem College ... NC

Multiple Protestant Denominations
Huston-Tillotson University ... TX
LeMoyne-Owen College ... TN
Paine College ... GA

Non-denominational
Belmont University ... TN
California Victor University ... CA
Carolina College of Biblical Studies ... NC
Cedar Crest College ... PA
China Evangelical Seminary North America ... CA
Georgetown College ... KY
Grace University ... CA
Grove City College ... PA
Heartland Christian College ... MO
Montreat College ... NC
North American University ... TX
Pacific Bible College ... OR
Patrick Henry College ... VA
Providence Christian College ... CA
Regional Christian University ... TX
Sattler College ... MA
Shepherds Theological Seminary ... NC
Southern Bible Institute and College ... TX
The Bible Seminary ... TX
University of Fort Lauderdale ... FL
Washington Theological Seminary ... VA
Washington University of Virginia ... VA
Williamson College ... TN

North American Baptist
Sioux Falls Seminary ... SD

Original Free Will Baptist Church
University of Mount Olive ... NC

Other Protestant
Beulah Heights University ... GA
Manna University ... NC
Ohio Christian University ... OH

Pentecostal Church of God
Messenger College ... TX
Universidad Pentecostal Mizpa ... PR

Pentecostal Holiness Church
Emmanuel College .... GA
Southwestern Christian University .... OK

Pentecostal/Charismatic Non-Denominational
Urshan College and Urshan Graduate School of Theology .... MO

Presbyterian
Sterling College .... KS
Whitworth University .... WA

Presbyterian Church (U.S.A.)
Agnes Scott College .... GA
Austin College .... TX
Austin Presbyterian Theological Seminary .... TX
Belhaven University .... MS
Blackburn College IL
Bloomfield College .... NJ
Buena Vista University .... IA
Carroll University .... WI
Columbia Theological Seminary .... GA
Davis & Elkins College .... WV
Eckerd College .... FL
Grace Mission University .... CA
Hampden-Sydney College .... VA
Hanover College .... IN
Hastings College .... NE
King University .... TN
Lees-McRae College .... NC
Louisville Presbyterian Theological Seminary .... KY
Lyon College .... AR
Macalester College .... MN
Mary Baldwin University .... VA
McCormick Theological Seminary IL
Millikin University IL
Missouri Valley College .... MO
Monmouth College IL
Muskingum University .... OH
Pittsburgh Theological Seminary .... PA
Presbyterian College .... SC
Princeton Theological Seminary .... NJ
Queens University of Charlotte .... NC
Rhodes College .... TN
Schreiner University .... TX
Stillman College .... AL
Tusculum University .... TN
Union Presbyterian Seminary .... VA
University of Dubuque .... IA
University of Jamestown .... ND
University of Pikeville .... KY
University of the Ozarks .... AR
Warren Wilson College .... NC
Waynesburg University .... PA
Westminster College .... PA
William Peace University .... NC
Wilson College .... PA

Presbyterian Church In America
Covenant College .... GA
Covenant Theological Seminary .... MO
Presbyterian Theological Seminary in America .... CA
Reformed University .... GA
Virginia Christian University .... VA

Protestant Episcopal
Bexley Seabury IL
Church Divinity School of the Pacific .... CA
General Theological Seminary .... NY
Nashotah House .... WI
Saint Augustine's University .... NC
Seminary of the Southwest .... TX
Sewanee: The University of the South .... TN
Trinity Episcopal School for Ministry .... PA
Virginia Theological Seminary .... VA
Voorhees College .... SC

Reformed Church In America
Central College .... IA
Hope College .... MI
New Brunswick Theological Seminary .... NJ
Northwestern College .... IA
Western Theological Seminary .... MI

Reformed Episcopal Church
Reformed Episcopal Seminary .... PA

Reformed Presbyterian Church
Evangelia University .... CA
Geneva College .... PA
Reformed Presbyterian Theological Seminary .... PA

Roman Catholic
Alvernia University .... PA
Anna Maria College .... MA
Aquinas College .... MI
Aquinas College .... TN
Aquinas Institute of Theology .... MO
Assumption College for Sisters .... NJ
Assumption University .... MA
Athenaeum of Ohio .... OH
Augustine Institute .... CO
Ave Maria School of Law .... FL
Avila University .... MO
Barry University .... FL
Belmont Abbey College .... NC
Benedictine College .... KS
Benedictine University IL
Boston College .... MA
Brescia University .... KY
Briar Cliff University .... IA
Cabrini University .... PA
Caldwell University .... NJ
Calumet College of Saint Joseph .... IN
Canisius College .... NY
Cardinal Stritch University .... WI
Carlow University .... PA
Carroll College .... MT
Catholic Theological Union IL
Chestnut Hill College .... PA
Christendom College .... VA
Christian Brothers University .... TN
Clarke University .... IA
College of Our Lady of the Elms .... MA
College of Saint Benedict .... MN
College of Saint Mary .... NE
College of the Holy Cross .... MA
Conception Seminary College .... MO
Creighton University .... NE
DePaul University IL
DeSales University .... PA
Divine Word College .... IA
Dominican School of Philosophy and Theology .... CA
Dominican University IL
Donnelly College .... KS
Duquesne University .... PA
Edgewood College .... WI
Emmanuel College .... MA
Fairfield University .... CT
Felician University .... NJ
Fontbonne University .... MO
Franciscan Missionaries of Our Lady University .... LA
Franciscan University of Steubenville .... OH
Gannon University .... PA
Georgetown University .... DC
Georgian Court University .... NJ
Gonzaga University .... WA
Gwynedd Mercy University .... PA
Holy Apostles College and Seminary .... CT
Holy Cross College .... IN
Holy Family University .... PA
Immaculata University .... PA
John Carroll University .... OH
Kenrick-Glennon Seminary, Kenrick School of Theology .... MO
King's College .... PA
La Roche University .... PA
La Salle University .... PA
Laboure College .... MA
Lewis University IL
Loras College .... IA
Lourdes University .... OH
Loyola Marymount University .... CA
Loyola University Chicago IL
Loyola University Maryland .... MD
Loyola University New Orleans .... LA
Madonna University .... MI
Magdalen College of the Liberal Arts .... NH
Marian University .... IN
Marian University .... WI
Marquette University .... WI
Marymount University .... VA
Marywood University .... PA
Mercy College of Health Sciences .... IA
Mercy College of Ohio .... OH
Mercyhurst University .... PA
Merrimack College .... MA
Misericordia University .... PA
Mount Angel Abbey & Seminary .... OR
Mount Carmel College of Nursing .... OH
Mount Marty University .... SD
Mount Mary University .... WI
Mount Mercy University .... IA
Mount Saint Mary's University .... CA
Mount St. Joseph University .... OH
Mount St. Mary's University .... MD
Neumann University .... PA
Newman University .... KS
Niagara University .... NY
Notre Dame College .... OH
Notre Dame of Maryland University .... MD
Notre Dame Seminary, Graduate School of Theology .... LA
Oblate School of Theology .... TX
Ohio Dominican University .... OH
Our Lady of the Lake University .... TX
Pontifical College Josephinum .... OH
Pontifical Faculty of the Immaculate Conception at the Dominican House of Studies .... DC
Pontifical John Paul II Institute for Studies on Marriage and Family .... DC
Pope St. John XXIII National Seminary .... MA
Presentation College .... SD
Providence College .... RI
Quincy University IL
Regis University .... CO
Rivier University .... NH
Rockhurst University .... MO
Rosemont College .... PA
Sacred Heart Major Seminary .... MI
Sacred Heart Seminary and School of Theology .... WI
Saint Anselm College .... NH
Saint Anthony College of Nursing IL
Saint Bernard's School of Theology & Ministry .... NY
Saint Charles Borromeo Seminary .... PA
Saint Elizabeth University .... NJ
Saint Francis Medical Center College of Nursing IL
Saint Francis University .... PA
Saint Gregory the Great Seminary .... NE
Saint John's Seminary .... CA
Saint John's Seminary .... MA
Saint John's University .... MN
Saint Joseph Seminary College .... LA
Saint Joseph's College of Maine .... ME
Saint Joseph's Seminary .... NY
Saint Joseph's University .... PA
Saint Leo University .... FL
Saint Louis University .... MO
Saint Martin's University .... WA
Saint Mary Seminary and Graduate School of Theology .... OH
Saint Mary's College .... IN
Saint Mary's College of California .... CA
Saint Mary's Seminary and University .... MD
Saint Mary's University of Minnesota .... MN
Saint Mary-of-the-Woods College .... IN
Saint Meinrad School of Theology .... IN
Saint Michael's College .... VT
Saint Norbert College .... WI
Saint Patrick's Seminary & University .... CA
Saint Peter's University .... NJ
Saint Vincent College .... PA
Saint Vincent Seminary .... PA
Saint Xavier University IL
Salve Regina University .... RI
Seattle University .... WA
Seton Hall University .... NJ
Seton Hill University .... PA
Siena Heights University .... MI
Spring Hill College .... AL
SS. Cyril and Methodius Seminary .... MI
St. Ambrose University .... IA
St. Bonaventure University .... NY
St. Catherine University .... MN
St. John Vianney College Seminary .... FL
St. John Vianney Theological Seminary .... CO
St. John's University .... NY
St. Joseph School of Nursing .... NH
St. Mary's University .... TX
St. Thomas University .... FL
St. Vincent De Paul Regional Seminary .... FL
Stonehill College .... MA
The Catholic University of America .... DC
The College of Saint Scholastica .... MN
The Pontifical Catholic University of Puerto Rico .... PR
The University of Scranton .... PA
Thomas More University .... KY
Trinity Washington University .... DC
Universidad Central de Bayamon .... PR
University of Dallas .... TX
University of Dayton .... OH
University of Detroit Mercy .... MI
University of Holy Cross .... LA
University of Mary .... ND
University of Notre Dame .... IN
University of Providence .... MT
University of Saint Francis .... IN
University of Saint Joseph .... CT
University of Saint Mary .... KS
University of Saint Mary of the Lake-Mundelein Seminary IL
University of Saint Thomas .... MN
University of San Diego .... CA
University of San Francisco .... CA
University of St. Francis IL
University of St. Thomas .... TX
University of the Incarnate Word .... TX
University of the Sacred Heart .... PR
Ursuline College .... OH
Villanova University .... PA
Viterbo University .... WI
Walsh University .... OH
Wheeling University .... WV
Wyoming Catholic College .... WY
Xavier University .... OH
Xavier University of Louisiana .... LA

Russian Orthodox
Holy Trinity Orthodox Seminary .... NY

Seventh-day Adventist
AdventHealth University .... FL
Andrews University .... MI
Kettering College .... OH
La Sierra University .... CA
Loma Linda University .... CA
Oakwood University .... AL
Pacific Union College .... CA
Southern Adventist University .... TN
Southwestern Adventist University .... TX
Union College .... NE
Universidad Adventista de las Antillas .... PR
Walla Walla University .... WA
Washington Adventist University .... MD

Southern Baptist
B.H. Carroll Theological Institute .... TX
Blue Mountain College .... MS
California Baptist University .... CA
Carson-Newman University .... TN
Charleston Southern University .... SC
Clear Creek Baptist Bible College .... KY
Gateway Seminary .... CA
Hannibal-LaGrange University .... MO
Houston Baptist University .... TX
Louisiana Christian University .... LA
Midwestern Baptist Theological Seminary .... MO
Mississippi College .... MS
New Orleans Baptist Theological Seminary .... LA
North Greenville University .... SC
Oklahoma Baptist University .... OK
Ouachita Baptist University .... AR
Southeastern Baptist Theological Seminary .... NC
Southwest Baptist University .... MO
Southwestern Baptist Theological Seminary .... TX
The Baptist College of Florida .... FL
The Southern Baptist Theological Seminary .... KY
Union University .... TN
University of Mary Hardin-Baylor .... TX
University of Mobile .... AL
Wayland Baptist University .... TX
William Carey University .... MS
Williams Baptist University .... AR
Wingate University .... NC

The Christian And Missionary Alliance
Alliance University .... NY
Crown College .... MN
Simpson University .... CA
Toccoa Falls College .... GA

Unification Church
Unification Theological Seminary .... NY

Unitarian Universalist
Meadville Lombard Theological School IL
Starr King School for the Ministry .... CA

United Brethren Church
Huntington University .... IN

United Church Of Christ
Catawba College .... NC
Chicago Theological Seminary IL
Doane University .... NE
Eden Theological Seminary .... MO
Elmhurst University IL
Heidelberg University .... OH
Lakeland University .... WI
Lancaster Theological Seminary .... PA
Northland College .... WI
Piedmont University .... GA
The Defiance College .... OH
Tougaloo College .... MS
United Theological Seminary of the Twin Cities .... MN

United Methodist
Adrian College .... MI
Albion College .... MI
Albright College .... PA
Allegheny College .... PA
American University .... DC
Andrew College .... GA
Baker University .... KS
Bennett College .... NC

Bethune Cookman University	FL	Ohio Northern University	OH
Birmingham-Southern College	AL	Ohio Wesleyan University	OH
Brevard College	NC	Oklahoma City University	OK
Centenary College of Louisiana	LA	Otterbein University	OH
Central Methodist University	MO	Pfeiffer University	NC
Claflin University	SC	Philander Smith College	AR
Claremont School of Theology	CA	Randolph-Macon College	VA
Clark Atlanta University	GA	Reinhardt University	GA
Columbia College	SC	Rust College	MS
Cornell College	IA	Saint Paul School of Theology	KS
Dakota Wesleyan University	SD	Shenandoah University	VA
DePauw University	IN	Simpson College	IA
Dillard University	LA	Southwestern College	KS
Emory & Henry College	VA	Southwestern University	TX
Emory University	GA	Spartanburg Methodist College	SC
Ferrum College	VA	Tennessee Wesleyan University	TN
Florida Southern College	FL	Texas Wesleyan University	TX
Garrett-Evangelical Theological Seminary	IL	Union College	KY
Greensboro College	NC	United Theological Seminary	OH
Hamline University	MN	University of Evansville	IN
Hendrix College	AR	University of Indianapolis	IN
High Point University	NC	Virginia Wesleyan University	VA
Huntingdon College	AL	Wesley Theological Seminary	DC
Iliff School of Theology	CO	Wesleyan College	GA
Iowa Wesleyan University	IA	West Virginia Wesleyan College	WV
Kansas Wesleyan University	KS	Wiley College	TX
Kentucky Wesleyan College	KY	Wofford College	SC
LaGrange College	GA	Young Harris College	GA
Lebanon Valley College	PA		
Lindsey Wilson College	KY	**Wesleyan Church**	
Louisburg College	NC	Allegheny Wesleyan College	OH
Lycoming College	PA	Houghton University	NY
McKendree University	IL	Indiana Wesleyan University	IN
McMurry University	TX	Oklahoma Wesleyan University	OK
Methodist Theological School in Ohio	OH	Southern Wesleyan University	SC
Methodist University	NC		
Millsaps College	MS	**Wisconsin Evangelical Lutheran Synod**	
Morningside University	IA	Martin Luther College	MN
Nebraska Wesleyan University	NE		
North Carolina Wesleyan College	NC		
North Central College	IL		

Carnegie Classification Code Definitions*

The *Higher Education Directory®* lists the updated 2021 Carnegie Classifications. Due to space limitation, the *Higher Education Directory®* only lists the basic classification—which was substantially revised in 2018. These new codes are listed below:

Associate's Colleges: Institutions at which the highest level degree awarded is an associate's degree. The institutions are sorted into nine categories based on the intersection of two factors: disciplinary focus (transfer, career & technical or mixed) and dominant student type (traditional, nontraditional or mixed). Excludes Special Focus Institutions and Tribal Colleges.

Assoc/HT-High Trad: Associate's Colleges: High Transfer-High Traditional
Assoc/HT-Mix Trad/Non: Associate's Colleges: High Transfer-Mixed Traditional/Nontraditional
Assoc/HT-High Non: Associate's Colleges: High Transfer-High Nontraditional
Assoc/MT-VT-High Trad: Associate's Colleges: Mixed Transfer/Career & Technical-High Traditional
Assoc/MT-VT-Mix Trad/Non: Associate's Colleges: Mixed Transfer/Career & Technical-Mixed Traditional/Nontraditional
Assoc/MT-VT-High Non: Associate's Colleges: Mixed Transfer/Career & Technical-High Nontraditional
Assoc/HVT-High Trad: Associate's Colleges: High Career & Technical-High Traditional
Assoc/HVT-Mix Trad/Non: Associate's Colleges: High Career & Technical-Mixed Traditional/Nontraditional
Assoc/HVT-High Non: Associate's Colleges: High Career & Technical-High Nontraditional

Baccalaureate/Associate's Colleges. Includes four-year colleges (by virtue of having at least one baccalaureate degree program) that conferred more than 50 percent of degrees at the associate's level. Excludes Special Focus Institutions, Tribal Colleges, and institutions that have sufficient masterÖs or doctoral degrees to fall into those categories.

Bac/Assoc-Assoc Dom: Baccalaureate/Associate's Colleges: Associate's Dominant
Bac/Assoc-Mixed: Baccalaureate/Associate's Colleges: Mixed Baccalaureate/Associate's

Baccalaureate Colleges. Includes institutions where baccalaureate or higher degrees represent at least 50 percent of all degrees but where fewer than 50 master's degrees or 20 doctoral degrees were awarded during the update year. (Some institutions above the master's degree threshold are also included; see Methodology) Excludes Special Focus Institutions and Tribal Colleges.

Bac-A&S: Baccalaureate Colleges: Arts & Sciences Focus
Bac-Diverse: Baccalaureate Colleges: Diverse Fields

Master's Colleges and Universities. Generally includes institutions that awarded at least 50 master's degrees and fewer than 20 doctoral degrees during the update year (with occasional exceptions; see Methodology). Excludes Special Focus Institutions and Tribal Colleges.

Masters/L: Master's Colleges & Universities: Larger Programs
Masters/M: Master's Colleges & Universities: Medium Programs
Masters/S: Master's Colleges & Universities: Small Programs

Doctoral Universities. Includes institutions that awarded at least 20 research/scholarship doctoral degrees during the update year (this does not include professional practice doctoral-level degrees, such as the JD, MD, PharmD, DPT, etc.). Excludes Special Focus Institutions and Tribal Colleges.

DU-Highest: Doctoral Universities: Very High Research Activity
DU-Higher: Doctoral Universities: High Research Activity
DU-Mod: Doctoral/Professional Universities: Moderate Research Activity

Special Focus Institutions, Two-year. Institutions where a high concentration of degrees is in a single field or set of related fields. Excludes Tribal Colleges.

Spec 2-yr-Health: Special Focus Two-Year: Health Professions
Spec 2-yr-Tech: Special Focus Two-Year: Technical Professions
Spec 2-yr-A&S: Special Focus Two-Year: Arts & Design
Spec 2-yr-Other: Special Focus Two-Year: Other Fields

Special Focus Institutions, Four-year. Institutions where a high concentration of degrees is in a single field or set of related fields. Excludes Tribal Colleges.

Spec-4-yr-Faith: Special Focus Four-Year: Faith-Related Institutions
Spec-4-yr-Med: Special Focus Four-Year: Medical Schools & Centers
Spec-4-yr-Other Health: Special Focus Four-Year: Other Health Professions Schools
Spec-4-yr-Eng: Special Focus Four-Year: Engineering Schools
Spec-4-yr-Other Tech: Special Focus Four-Year: Other Technology-Related Schools
Spec-4-yr-Bus: Special Focus Four-Year: Business & Management Schools
Spec-4-yr-Arts: Special Focus Four-Year: Arts, Music & Design Schools
Spec-4-yr-Law: Special Focus Four-Year: Law Schools
Spec-4-yr-Other: Special Focus Four-Year: Other Special Focus Institutions

Tribal Colleges. Colleges and universities that are members of the American Indian Higher Education Consortium, as identified in IPEDS Institutional Characteristics.

Tribal: Tribal Colleges

---

*All data provided by Carnegie Classification of Institutions of Higher Education by The American Council on Education. For more detailed information, please visit https://carnegieclassifications.acenet.edu. Basic classification methodology can be found at https://carnegieclassifications.acenet.edu/classification_descriptions/basic.php.

Statistics

Institutions of Higher Education by Control, Level and State

STATE	TWO YEAR PRIVATE	TWO YEAR PUBLIC	FOUR YEAR PRIVATE	FOUR YEAR PUBLIC	TOTAL PRIVATE	TOTAL PUBLIC	SYSTEM OFFICE	GRAND TOTAL
AL	2	24	18	15	20	39	2	61
AK	2	0	4	3	6	3	1	10
AZ	5	19	27	4	32	23	1	56
AR	3	22	16	11	19	33	2	54
CA	45	103	264	50	309	153	28	490
CO	12	6	20	23	32	29	2	63
CT	0	12	18	7	18	19	1	38
DE	1	0	2	3	3	3	0	6
DC	2	0	17	3	19	3	0	22
FL	33	0	79	40	112	40	1	153
GA	8	23	42	26	50	49	1	100
HI	2	6	5	4	7	10	2	19
ID	0	3	7	5	7	8	0	15
IL	10	47	80	12	90	59	6	155
IN	6	1	43	15	49	16	2	67
IA	0	18	38	3	38	21	3	62
KS	0	25	23	9	23	34	0	57
KY	2	16	31	8	33	24	1	58
LA	5	16	14	17	19	33	4	56
ME	1	7	14	7	15	14	2	31
MD	1	16	21	16	22	32	1	55
MA	2	16	70	14	72	30	2	104
MI	2	23	42	21	44	44	1	89
MN	4	25	40	12	44	37	3	84
MS	0	15	10	9	10	24	0	34
MO	7	17	61	13	68	30	3	101
MT	5	5	8	6	13	11	1	25
NE	6	7	15	7	21	14	2	37
NV	3	1	2	6	5	7	1	13
NH	1	7	10	4	11	11	2	24
NJ	5	18	46	13	51	31	0	82
NM	0	13	9	8	9	21	0	30
NY	24	36	194	44	218	80	6	304
NC	1	58	51	17	52	75	2	129
ND	1	4	7	7	8	11	1	20
OH	18	17	73	22	91	39	0	130
OK	5	12	14	15	19	27	0	46
OR	2	17	23	8	25	25	0	50
PA	34	17	111	16	145	33	1	179
RI	0	1	9	3	9	4	0	13
SC	2	18	25	15	27	33	0	60
SD	0	4	11	7	11	11	1	23
TN	9	13	48	10	57	23	2	82
TX	23	40	81	69	104	109	8	221
UT	1	1	14	7	15	8	1	24
VT	1	1	10	4	11	5	1	17
VA	9	24	56	17	65	41	1	107
WA	3	4	23	35	26	39	2	67
WV	5	8	12	11	17	19	2	38
WI	1	16	30	13	31	29	2	62
WY	1	4	1	4	2	8	0	10
AS	0	0	0	1	0	1	0	1
GU	0	1	1	1	1	2	0	3
MH	0	1	0	0	0	1	0	1
MP	0	0	0	1	0	1	0	1
PR	3	0	40	14	43	14	3	60
FM	0	1	0	0	0	1	0	1
PW	0	1	0	0	0	1	0	1
VI	0	0	0	1	0	1	0	1
Total	**318**	**810**	**1930**	**736**	**2248**	**1546**	**108**	**3902**

Figures do not include 660 additional branch campuses.

50 Largest Universities by Fall 2020 Enrollment

Institution	Enrollment
1. Western Governors University	147866
2. Southern New Hampshire University	134345
3. Grand Canyon University	103427
4. Liberty University	93349
5. Arizona State University	74795
6. University of Central Florida	71881
7. Texas A & M University	70418
8. The Ohio State University Main Campus	61369
9. Florida International University	58836
10. University of Maryland Global Campus	58526
11. University of Florida	53372
12. New York University	52775
13. University of Illinois Urbana-Champaign	52679
14. University of Minnesota	52017
15. University of South Florida	50626
16. University of Texas at Austin	50476
17. Rutgers University - New Brunswick	50411
18. American Public University System	50047
19. Michigan State University	49695
20. Walden University	49695
21. University of Washington	48149
22. The University of Texas at Arlington	48072
23. University of Michigan-Ann Arbor	47907
24. University of Houston	47090
25. Purdue University Main Campus	46655
26. University of Southern California	46287
27. University of Arizona	45601
28. University of Wisconsin-Madison	44640
29. University of California-Los Angeles	44589
30. Brigham Young University-Idaho	44481
31. University of the People	43722
32. Florida State University	43569
33. Indiana University	43064
34. University of California-Berkeley	42327
35. California State University-Fullerton	42051
36. Kennesaw State University	41181
37. University of North Texas	40953
38. Utah Valley University	40936
39. University of Cincinnati Main Campus	40826
40. University of Maryland College Park	40709
41. California State University-Northridge	40381
42. Texas Tech University	40322
43. California State University-Long Beach	40069
44. University of California-San Diego	39576
45. University of Georgia	39147
46. University of California-Davis	39074
47. Capella University	38930
48. George Mason University	38541
49. The University of Alabama	37840
50. Texas State University	37812

Institutions by Control and Tuition Range

Tuition	Public*	Private	Total
0 - 1,000	79	750	829
1,001 - 2,000	129	1	130
2,001 - 4,000	267	17	284
4,001 - 6,000	422	38	460
6,001 - 8,000	219	66	285
8,001 - 10,000	208	77	285
Over 10,000	222	1299	1521
Total	**1546**	**2248**	**3794**

* Figures for Public Institutions are In-State Tuitions

Universities, Colleges and Schools

by State*

*Includes the District of Columbia and, separately, U.S. Service Schools, American Samoa, Federated States of Micronesia, Guam, Marshall Islands, Northern Marianas, Palau, Puerto Rico, and Virgin Islands.

ALABAMA

Alabama Agricultural and Mechanical University (A)

4900 Meridian Street, Normal AL 35762-1357
County: Madison FICE Identification: 001002
Unit ID: 100654
Telephone: (256) 372-5230 Carnegie Class: Masters/L
FAX Number: (256) 372-5244 Calendar System: Semester
URL: www.aamu.edu
Established: 1875 Annual Undergrad Tuition & Fees (In-State): $10,024
Enrollment: 5,977 Coed
Affiliation or Control: State IRS Status: 501(c)3
Highest Offering: Doctorate
Accreditation: SC, AAFCS, CAEP, DIETD, PLNG, SP, SW

01 President Dr. Daniel K. WIMS
03 Executive VP/COO Vacant
05 Interim Provost/VP Academic Affairs Dr. Lena WALTON
10 Vice President Business & Finance Vacant
111 VP Mktg/Comm/Advancement Mr. Jamal ALI
32 Vice President Student Affairs Dr. Braque TALLEY
46 Interim VP Inst Rsrch/Spons Pgms Dr. Daniel WIMS
114 AVP Budget & Planning Mr. Gregory JACKSON
84 AVP of Enrollment Mgmt Vacant
13 Int Chief Information Officer Ms. Kylie NASH
21 AVP Finance/Comptroller Ms. Courtney DAVIS
15 Interim Director Human Resources Ms. Cheryl JOHNSON
18 Dir Facilities and Admin Services Mr. Brian SHIPP
06 Registrar Ms. Brenda K. WILLIAMS
30 Interim Director of Development Ms. Kim DAVIS
41 Director of Athletics Mr. Bryan HICKS
35 Director of Student Activities Ms. Diann ANDERSON
37 Director of Financial Aid Mr. Darryl JACKSON
23 Dir Student Health & Counseling Mrs. Carlquista SLAY
36 Dir Career Development Services Ms. Yvette CLAYTON
09 Dir Institutional Research Dr. James WALKE
26 Director Marketing & PR Mr. Jerome SAINTJONES
39 Dir of Residential Housing Ms. Karla MILLER
19 Chief of Police Mr. Montrez PAYTON
08 Director Learning Resources Center Dr. Annie PAYTON
96 Director of Purchasing Mr. Jeffrey ROBINSON
58 Dean Graduate School/AVP Acad Affs Dr. John JONES
47 Dean Col Agricultural/Life/Nat Sci Dr. Lloyd WALKER
53 Dean College of Education Dr. Samantha STRAHAN
54 Dean College of Engineering Dr. Zhengtao DENG
50 Dean Col of Business/Pub Affs Dr. Charles RICHARDSON
04 Sr Executive Assistant to President Ms. Freddie A. GAMBLES
102 Dir Foundation/Corporate Relations Mr. Jamal ALI
29 Director Alumni Relations Mrs. Sandra STUBBS
43 Dir Legal Services/General Counsel Ms. Roslyn CREWS
45 Chief Institutional Planning Mr. Jamal ALI
07 Director of Admissions Mr. Dwayne GREEN
86 Director Government Relations Ms. Roslyn CREWS

Alabama College of Osteopathic Medicine (B)

445 Health Sciences Boulevard, Dothan AL 36303
County: Houston Identification: 667138
Unit ID: 483975
Telephone: (334) 699-2266 Carnegie Class: Spec-4-yr-Med
FAX Number: N/A Calendar System: Semester
URL: www.acom.edu
Established: 2011 Annual Graduate Tuition & Fees: N/A
Enrollment: 705 Coed
Affiliation or Control: Independent Non-Profit IRS Status: 501(c)3
Highest Offering: First Professional Degree; No Undergraduates
Accreditation: OSTEO

01 President Rick SUTTON
05 Dean/CAO James C. JONES
10 Chief Financial Officer Derek MILLER
09 VP of Institutional Effectiveness Carmen LEWIS
32 Assoc Dean Student Services Phillip REYNOLDS
84 Exec Dir Enrollment Management Tara RYALS
06 Registrar Yasmine HILL
07 Dir of Admissions & Enrollment Linda GOODSON
37 Director Student Financial Aid Travis COBB
29 Director Alumni Affairs Audrey BAWCUM
26 Dir of Communications & Marketing Sarah SENN
19 Director Security/Safety MaryAnn MAY
102 Director Foundation/Corporate Rels Amy BUNTING
08 Chief Library Officer Lisa ENNIS
15 Chief Human Resources Officer Kevin BROYLES
25 Chief Contract and Grants Administr Audrey VASAUSKAS

*Alabama Community College System (C)

135 South Union Street, Montgomery AL 36104-4340
County: Montgomery Identification: 667303
Telephone: (334) 293-4500 Carnegie Class: N/A
FAX Number: (334) 293-4504
URL: www.accs.cc

01 Chancellor Mr. Jimmy H. BAKER
05 VC Instruction/Research/Development Dr. Vicky OHLSON
10 VC Admin/Financial Services Mr. Bryan HELMS
32 VC Student Success Mr. Olivier CHARLES
100 Chief of Staff & VC SDSA Ms. Susan Y. PRICE
15 Director Human Resources Ms. Nikita T. PAYNE

*Bevill State Community College (D)

1411 Indiana Avenue, Jasper AL 35501
County: Walker FICE Identification: 005733
Unit ID: 102429
Telephone: (205) 387-0511 Carnegie Class: Assoc/HVT-Mix Trad/Non
FAX Number: (205) 387-5192 Calendar System: Semester
URL: www.bscc.edu
Established: 1965 Annual Undergrad Tuition & Fees (In-State): $5,214
Enrollment: 3,204 Coed
Affiliation or Control: State IRS Status: 501(c)3
Highest Offering: Associate Degree
Accreditation: SC, ADNUR, EMT, PNUR, SURGT

02 President Dr. Joel HAGOOD
05 VP Instructional/Student Services Dr. Leslie HARTLEY
26 Dir of Public Relations/Enroll Mgmt Ms. Tana COLLINS-ALLRED
10 Vice Pres Administration/Finance Mr. John SKALNIK
32 Dean of Students Ms. Melissa STOWE
15 Director of Human Resources Ms. Mary KINARD
18 Director of Facilities & Security Mr. Randy STULTS
121 Dean of Student Success/Athletics Mr. Max WEAVER
76 Director of Health Sciences Ms. Reitha CABANISS
103 Dean Workforce Solutions/Econ Dev Mr. Al MOORE
25 Dir IE/Research & Grants Dr. Russell HOWTON

*Bishop State Community College (E)

351 N Broad Street, Mobile AL 36603-5898
County: Mobile FICE Identification: 001030
Unit ID: 102030
Telephone: (251) 405-7000 Carnegie Class: Assoc/HVT-Mix Trad/Non
FAX Number: N/A Calendar System: Semester
URL: www.bishop.edu
Established: 1965 Annual Undergrad Tuition & Fees (In-State): $4,860
Enrollment: 2,176 Coed
Affiliation or Control: State IRS Status: 501(c)3
Highest Offering: Associate Degree
Accreditation: SC, ACBSP, ACFEI, ADNUR, CAHIIM, PNUR, #PTAA

02 President Dr. Reggie SYKES
03 Executive Vice President Dr. Lawrence BRANDYBURG
05 Dean of Instruction Mr. Roderick MCSWAIN
76 Dean of Health Sciences Dr. Dolly HORTON
103 Dean of Workforce Development Vacant
32 Chief Student Affairs Officer Dr. Katheryne PAVEY
10 Dean of Business/Finance Mrs. Lois GWINN
20 Associate Academic Dean Mr. Theodore LABAY
20 Associate Dean of Instruction Dr. Andrea AGNEW
06 Registrar Mr. Philip URBANEK
15 Director of Human Resources Mrs. Kenya PARRISH-ONUKWULI
111 Director Institutional Advancement Mrs. Sherrica HUNT
18 Director of Physical Plant Mr. Kenneth HOLDER
26 Director of Public Relations Ms. Courtney STEELE
09 Dir of Institutional Research Mr. Claude BUMPERS
37 Mgr Student Fin Aid/Veterans Svcs Dr. Gail BEGGS
13 Chief Info Technology Officer Mr. Lee THRASHER
19 Director Security/Safety Chief Lloyd WASHINGTON
41 Athletic Director Mr. Trenton EAGER

*Calhoun Community College (F)

PO Box 2216, Decatur AL 35609-2216
County: Limestone FICE Identification: 001013
Unit ID: 101514
Telephone: (256) 306-2500 Carnegie Class: Assoc/MT-VT-Mix Trad/Non
FAX Number: (256) 306-2877 Calendar System: Semester
URL: www.calhoun.edu
Established: 1963 Annual Undergrad Tuition & Fees (In-State): $4,940
Enrollment: 8,278 Coed
Affiliation or Control: State IRS Status: 501(c)3
Highest Offering: Associate Degree
Accreditation: SC, ADNUR, DA, DH, EMT, MLTAD, NAEYC, PNUR, PTAA, SURGT

02 President Dr. Jimmy HODGES
05 VP Academic Affairs Vacant
32 Vice President of Student Services Dr. Patricia WILSON
10 Dean of Business & Finance Mr. Jason MORGAN
07 Director Admiss/Records/Registrar Ms. Alanna THOMPSON
08 Director of Library Services Mr. James LOYD
13 Director Information Systems Mr. Nathan TYLER
26 Director of PR & CETV Mr. Wes TORAIN
12 Dean of Research Park Campus Mr. Mark BRANON
18 Exec Director of Physical Plant Mr. Bruce CAUSEY
09 Dean Planning/Research & Grants Dr. Debra HENDERSHOT
103 Director Workforce Solutions Vacant
76 Dean Health Sciences Mr. Bret MCGILL
81 Dean Math/Natural Sciences Mr. Rodney ALFORD
79 Dean Humanities & Social Sciences Dr. Donna ESTILL
15 Director Human Resources & Payroll Mrs. Kim GAINES
19 Director Public Safety Mr. Kevin DAVENPORT
36 Director of Career Services & Co-op Mrs. Kelli MORRIS
37 Director Student Financial Aid Mrs. Janett SPENCER
04 Secretary to President Ms. Belinda NOE
41 Athletic Director Dr. Nancy KEENUM

27 Asst Director of PR & CETV Ms. Sherika ATTIPOE
51 Director of Adult Education Ms. Wendy ROBERTS
72 Dean of Technologies Mr. John HOLLEY
50 Dean of Business and CIS Ms. Cynthia BUCHHEIT
30 Director of Development Ms. Johnette DAVIS
124 Director Advising and Retention Dr. Ellie MEYER
96 Director of Purchasing Ms. Vanessa LOONEY

*Central Alabama Community College (G)

1675 Cherokee Road, Alexander City AL 35010
County: Tallapoosa FICE Identification: 001007
Unit ID: 100760
Telephone: (256) 234-6346 Carnegie Class: Assoc/MT-VT-Mix Trad/Non
FAX Number: (256) 234-0384 Calendar System: Semester
URL: www.cacc.edu
Established: 1963 Annual Undergrad Tuition & Fees (In-State): $4,930
Enrollment: 1,546 Coed
Affiliation or Control: State IRS Status: 501(c)3
Highest Offering: Associate Degree
Accreditation: SC, ADNUR

02 President Mr. Jeff LYNN
10 Dean of Financial Services Ms. Lisa SAWYER
05 Dean of Academic Programs Dr. Bryan JOHNSON
32 Dean of Students Ms. Jerri CARROLL
09 Assoc Dean of Inst Effect/Compl Ms. Cindy ENTREKIN
76 Health Science Program Admin Dr. Jennifer STEELE
08 Librarian Ms. Denita OLIVER
06 Records Manager Vacant
26 Public Relations Officer Mr. Brett PRITCHARD
37 Director Student Financial Aid Ms. Stephanie MILLER
04 Administrative Asst to President Ms. Lisa FORNWALT
15 Exec Director of Human Resources Ms. Tina SHAW
103 Dean Workforce/Econ Development Mr. Michael BARNETTE
13 Director of Information Systems Mr. Tyler GRAY

*Chattahoochee Valley Community College (H)

2602 College Drive, Phenix City AL 36869-7960
County: Russell FICE Identification: 012182
Unit ID: 101028
Telephone: (334) 291-4900 Carnegie Class: Assoc/MT-VT-High Trad
FAX Number: (334) 291-4944 Calendar System: Semester
URL: www.cv.edu
Established: 1973 Annual Undergrad Tuition & Fees (In-State): $4,920
Enrollment: 1,399 Coed
Affiliation or Control: State IRS Status: 501(c)3
Highest Offering: Associate Degree
Accreditation: SC, ADNUR, MAAB, PNUR

02 President Ms. Jacqueline SCREWS
05 Dean of Instruction Vacant
04 Administrative Asst to President Ms. Terrah BOISCLAIR
32 Dean of Students and Campus Service Dr. Sherri TAYLOR
10 Dean of Financial Affairs Mr. Dexter JACKSON
15 Director of Human Resources Ms. Robin JONES
45 Director of Strategic Initiatives Dr. RoseMary WATKINS
103 Assoc Dean of Workforce Development Dr. Beth MULLIN
35 Assoc Dean of Student Development Mrs. Vickie WILLIAMS
41 Director of Athletics Mr. Benjamin HICKS
07 Director of Admissions/Registrar Ms. Sanquita ALEXANDER
37 Executive Director of Financial Aid Ms. Melissa CREASY
13 Director of Information Systems Mr. Warner TAYLOR
26 Marketing & Media Coordinator Ms. Myya ROBINSON
60 Chair of English and Communication Ms. Samantha VANCE
57 Chair of Fine Arts Dr. William BYRD
50 Chair of Business and Computer Info Ms. Sheila LARKIN
66 Chair of Health Sciences Dr. Bridgett JACKSON
81 Chair of Mathematics Ms. Shawn JUNGHANS
81 Chair of Science Ms. Merry CUERVO
72 Director of Applied Technology Mr. Clint LANGLEY
19 Director of Public Safety Mr. Kenneth HARRISON
51 Director of Adult Education Dr. Darren DEAN
08 Director Learning Resources Center Ms. Elizabeth BRADSHER
18 Director of Plant Operations Mr. Scot CRAIG

*Coastal Alabama Community College (I)

1900 Highway 31 S, Bay Minette AL 36507-2698
County: Baldwin FICE Identification: 001060
Unit ID: 101161
Telephone: (251) 580-2100 Carnegie Class: Assoc/MT-VT-High Trad
FAX Number: (251) 580-2253 Calendar System: Semester
URL: www.coastalalabama.edu
Established: 1965 Annual Undergrad Tuition & Fees (In-State): $4,860
Enrollment: 6,653 Coed
Affiliation or Control: State IRS Status: 501(c)3
Highest Offering: Associate Degree
Accreditation: SC, ACFEI, ADNUR, DA, EMT, PNUR, SURGT

01 President Dr. Craig POUNCEY
10 Chief Financial Officer Ms. Jessica DAVIS
103 Dean Workforce Development Dr. Josh DUPLANTIS
32 Dean Student Services Mr. Vinson BRADLEY
05 Dean Academic Instruction Ms. Mary Beth LANCASTER
102 Dean External Funding Dr. Melinda BYRD-MURPHY

13	Dean Information Technology	Vacant
66	Dean Nursing & Allied Health	Dr. Tiffany SCARBOROUGH
75	Dean Career/Tech Education	Ms. Linda GRANT
18	Dean Operations & Maintenance	Vacant
106	Director Center for Teach/Learning	Ms. Ann STRICKLAND
37	Director Financial Aid	Ms. Gail BEGGS
19	Chief of College Police	Mr. Jonathan DAVIDSON
15	Exec Director Human Resources	Ms. Michelle BUGOS
04	Admin Assistant to the President	Ms. Joni LAMBERT
06	Registrar	Ms. Robin SESSIONS
09	Director Inst Effectiveness	Ms. Lindsay HUTCHERSON
26	Chief Public Relations Officer	Ms. Sara DAVIS
41	Athletic Director	Mr. Daniel HEAD
84	Director Enrollment Mgmt	Ms. Beth BRYARS

*Enterprise State Community College (A)

PO Box 1300, Enterprise AL 36331-1300
County: Coffee FICE Identification: 001015
Unit ID: 101143
Telephone: (334) 347-2623 Carnegie Class: Assoc/HT-Mix Trad/Non
FAX Number: (334) 393-6223 Calendar System: Semester
URL: www.escc.edu
Established: 1963 Annual Undergrad Tuition & Fees (In-State): $4,960
Enrollment: 1,808 Coed
Affiliation or Control: State IRS Status: 501(c)3
Highest Offering: Associate Degree
Accreditation: **SC**

02	Chief Executive Officer/President	Mr. Daniel LONG
05	Exec Vice Pres/Dean of Instruction	Vacant
32	Dean of Students	Ms. Kassie MATHIS
10	Dir of Financial Services	Ms. Paula HELMS
37	Director of Financial Aid	Ms. Laticia DUBOSE
26	Dir Marketing & Media Relations	Ms. Cassidy GIBBS
04	Administrative Asst to President	Ms. Jennifer ADAMS
06	Registrar	Ms. Jennifer OLSEN
102	Dir Foundation/Community Relations	Ms. Chellye STUMP
103	Dir Workforce Devel & Adult Educ	Ms. Leigh SHIVER
13	Director of Information Technology	Mr. Jason TRULL
15	Human Resources Coordinator	Ms. Jessica SOLOMON
18	Plant Supervisor	Mr. Michael HELMS
121	Director Counseling/Student Success	Ms. Dava FOSTER
108	Director Inst Effectiveness & Plng	Mr. Andrew DAVIS
19	Campus Police Chief	Mr. Jeff SPENCE
88	Aviation Division Director	Col. Stanley SMITH
121	Director of Student Support Service	Mr. Michael HARRISON
31	Instructional Res & Cmty Educ Dir	Ms. Ann KELLEY-SPENCE
41	Athletic Director	Mr. Jermaine WILLIAMS

*Gadsden State Community College (B)

1001 George Wallace Dr, PO Box 227,
Gadsden AL 35902-0227
County: Etowah FICE Identification: 001017
Unit ID: 101240
Telephone: (256) 549-8200 Carnegie Class: Assoc/HVT-High Trad
FAX Number: N/A Calendar System: Semester
URL: www.gadsdenstate.edu
Established: 1925 Annual Undergrad Tuition & Fees (In-State): $3,936
Enrollment: 3,993 Coed
Affiliation or Control: State IRS Status: 501(c)3
Highest Offering: Associate Degree
Accreditation: **SC**, ADNUR, DMS, EMT, MLTAD, PNUR, RAD

02	President	Dr. Kathy MURPHY
03	Executive Vice President	Dr. Tera SIMMONS
10	Dean Financial/Administrative Svcs	Dr. Kevin MCFRY
32	Dean Student Services	Dr. Janekia MITCHELL
72	Dean Tech Educ/Workforce Devel	Mr. Alan SMITH
76	Dean Health Sciences	Dr. Kenneth KIRKLAND
05	Dean of Academic Programs/Services	Dr. Farrah HAYES
108	Dean of Institutional Effectiveness	Ms. Pam JOHNSON
51	Director of Adult Education	Mr. Matthew BURTTRAM
26	Director Public Relations/Marketing	Ms. Jackie EDMONDSON
18	Director Physical Plant	Mr. Stewart DAVIS
21	Director of Financial Services	Ms. Jacqueline CLARK
15	Director Human Resources	Mr. Kevin WILLOUGHBY
41	Athletic Director	Mr. Garrett B. LEWIS
35	Assoc Dean Student Services	Ms. Kelley PEARCE
37	Director of Financial Aid	Mr. Ian FREYBERG
06	Registrar	Ms. Laura SWANN
13	Chief Information Officer	Mr. Alan WALLACE

*George C. Wallace Community College - Dothan (C)

1141 Wallace Drive, Dothan AL 36303-9234
County: Dale FICE Identification: 001018
Unit ID: 101286
Telephone: (334) 983-3521 Carnegie Class: Assoc/HVT-High Trad
FAX Number: (334) 983-6066 Calendar System: Semester
URL: www.wallace.edu
Established: 1947 Annual Undergrad Tuition & Fees (In-State): $4,800
Enrollment: 3,681 Coed
Affiliation or Control: State IRS Status: 501(c)3
Highest Offering: Associate Degree
Accreditation: **SC**, ADNUR, COARC, EMT, MAC, PNUR, PTAA, RAD, SURGT

02	President	Dr. Linda C. YOUNG
30	VP/Dean Institutional Svcs/Cmty Dev	Dr. Ashli WILKINS
32	Act Dean Student Affs/Sparks Campus	Mr. Mickey BAKER
05	Dean of Instructional Affairs	Ms. Leslie REEDER
10	Dean of Business Affairs	Mr. Marc NICHOLAS
07	Director Admissions/Registrar	Mr. Keith SAULSBERRY
08	Dir Learning Resources Ctrs System	Mr. A. P. HOFFMAN
37	Director of Financial Aid	Mr. Anthony JOUVENAS
13	Director ITS	Mr. Patrick ADKINSON
15	Director of Human Resources	Ms. Brooke STRICKLAND
09	Dir Institutional Effectiveness	Ms. Mandy SESSIONS
40	Bookstore Manager	Mr. Jeremy JAMES
21	Director of Accounting & Finance	Ms. Heather JOHNSON-WALKER
26	Dir Public Relations & Marketing	Ms. Taylor WHEELER
41	Athletic Director	Mr. Mackey SASSER

*George Corley Wallace State Community College - Selma (D)

PO Box 2530, 3000 Earl Goodwin Pkwy,
Selma AL 36702-2530
County: Dallas FICE Identification: 005699
Unit ID: 101301
Telephone: (334) 876-9227 Carnegie Class: Assoc/MT-VT-Mix Trad/Non
FAX Number: (334) 876-9250 Calendar System: Semester
URL: www.wccs.edu
Established: 1963 Annual Undergrad Tuition & Fees (In-State): $4,560
Enrollment: 1,316 Coed
Affiliation or Control: State IRS Status: 501(c)3
Highest Offering: Associate Degree
Accreditation: **SC**, ACBSP, ADNUR, PNUR

02	President	Dr. James M. MITCHELL
05	Dean of Instruction	Dr. Tammie BRIGGS
103	Asst Dean Workforce Development	Mr. Raji GOURDINE
10	Dean of Business & Finance	Vacant
32	Dean of Students/Exec to President	Dr. Donitha GRIFFIN
08	Librarian	Vacant
76	Director of Health Sciences	Dr. Pearlie MILLER
37	Financial Aid Director	Ms. Anessa KIDD
07	Director of Admissions/Counselor	Mr. Lonzy CLIFTON
09	Asst Dean of Institutional Effect	Mrs. Veronica BROWN
26	Director of Community Relations	Dr. Glenn KING
19	Public Safety Coordinator	Mr. Charles DYSART
41	Athletic Director	Mr. Marcus HANNAH
18	Director of Facilities & Safety	Mr. Keith JACKSON
15	Human Resources Coordinator	Ms. Colleen DIXON

*J.F. Drake State Community and Technical College (E)

3421 Meridian Street N, Huntsville AL 35811-1584
County: Madison FICE Identification: 005260
Unit ID: 101462
Telephone: (256) 539-8161 Carnegie Class: Assoc/HVT-Mix Trad/Non
FAX Number: (256) 539-6439 Calendar System: Semester
URL: www.drakestate.edu
Established: 1961 Annual Undergrad Tuition & Fees (In-State): $4,830
Enrollment: 825 Coed
Affiliation or Control: State IRS Status: 501(c)3
Highest Offering: Associate Degree
Accreditation: **SC**, PNUR

02	President	Dr. Patricia SIMS
05	Dean of Instruction	Dr. Carolyn HENDERSON
10	Director of Fiscal Affairs	Mr. Akeem ALEXANDER
103	Director of Workforce Development	Dr. Karen RAY
07	Director of Admissions/Registrar	Vacant
15	Human Resource Specialist	Mrs. Katie CHANCE
13	Coordinator of IT Services	Mr. Glenn HARBIN
08	Director of Library Services	Ms. Carla CLIFT
37	Director Student Financial Aid	Ms. Jennifer O'LINGER
26	Director of Public Relations	Mr. Mark MOORE
121	Student Success Specialist	Ms. Tiffany GREEN
108	Dir of Institutional Effectiveness	Ms. Lesley SHOTTS
32	Dean of Student Services	Dr. Nicole BELL
18	Director of Operations	Mr. Bruce BULLUCK
04	Admin Assistant to the President	Ms. Terell JACKSON
36	Coordinator of Placement	Ms. Karen RAY

*J.F. Ingram State Technical College (F)

PO Box 220350, Deatsville AL 36022-0350
County: Elmore FICE Identification: 030025
Unit ID: 101471
Telephone: (334) 285-5177 Carnegie Class: Not Classified
FAX Number: (334) 285-5328 Calendar System: Semester
URL: www.istc.edu
Established: 1965 Annual Undergrad Tuition & Fees (In-State): $5,472
Enrollment: 399 Coed
Affiliation or Control: State IRS Status: 501(c)3
Highest Offering: Associate Degree
Accreditation: **COE**

02	President	Mrs. Annette FUNDERBURK
05	Dean of Instruction	Dr. William YOUNG
11	Dean of Administration	Dr. Brannon LENTZ
32	Dean of Students/Support Svcs	Mrs. Rosie EDWARDS

20	Associate Dean of Instruction	Dr. Julliana PROBST
35	Student Services Director	Dr. Craig SHORE
15	Human Resources Coordinator	Ms. Andrea RICHARDSON
88	Re-Entry/Counseling Programs Coord	Mr. Rick VEST
10	Business Office Director	Mrs. Amelia FOX
04	Administrative Asst to President	Mrs. Samantha ROSE

*Jefferson State Community College (G)

2601 Carson Road, Birmingham AL 35215-3098
County: Jefferson FICE Identification: 001022
Unit ID: 101505
Telephone: (205) 853-1200 Carnegie Class: Assoc/HVT-Mix Trad/Non
FAX Number: (205) 853-8505 Calendar System: Semester
URL: www.jeffersonstate.edu
Established: 1963 Annual Undergrad Tuition & Fees (In-State): $5,850
Enrollment: 8,526 Coed
Affiliation or Control: State IRS Status: 501(c)3
Highest Offering: Associate Degree
Accreditation: **SC**, ACBSP, ACFEI, ADNUR, #COARC, CONST, EMT, FUSER, MLTAD, NAEYC, PTAA, RAD

02	President	Mr. Keith A. BROWN
32	Vice President for Student Affairs	Vacant
05	VP for Academic Affairs	Ms. Danielle COBURN
10	Chief Financial Officer	Mr. David MORRIS
97	Assoc Dean Transf Gen Stds Shelby	Ms. Liesl W. HARRIS
97	Assoc Dn Transf Gen Stds Jefferson	Ms. Kristin R. HENDERSON
106	Assoc Dean Distance/Dev Education	Mr. Alan B. DAVIS
103	Dir Center for Workforce Education	Ms. Leah M. BIGBEE
13	Chief Information Officer	Mr. Colin EUBANKS
37	Assoc Director Financial Aid	Ms. Morgan CHANDLER
18	Director Maintenance	Mr. Perry HARRIS
08	Director of Learning Resources	Ms. Barbara GOSS
36	Director Career/Learning Services	Dr. Tamara PAYNE
84	Associate Dean Enrollment Services	Mr. Adam GOODMAN
15	Director Human Resources	Mrs. Debbie BOONE
26	Director Media Relations	Mr. David BOBO
96	Purchasing Coordinator	Ms. Ann CIMALORE
19	Interim Director Safety & Security	Mr. Ronphael KENNEDY
09	Dean Institutional Effectiveness	Ms. Amanda E. KIN
04	Administrative Asst to President	Ms. Janie STARNES
25	Director Resource Development	Ms. Kelli CREAMER
86	Assoc Dean Economic Development	Mr. Guin ROBINSON
20	Dean of Instruction	Mr. Brian GORDON
72	Assoc Dean for Technical Programs	Vacant
76	Assoc Dean of Health-Related Pgms	Dr. Vanessa LEBLANC
51	Director Adult Education	Ms. Tierra WRIGHT
88	Director of Articulation	Mr. Barry GRAVES

*Lawson State Community College (H)

3060 Wilson Road, SW, Birmingham AL 35221-1798
County: Jefferson FICE Identification: 001059
Unit ID: 101569
Telephone: (205) 925-2515 Carnegie Class: Assoc/MT-VT-High Trad
FAX Number: (205) 925-3716 Calendar System: Semester
URL: www.lawsonstate.edu
Established: 1949 Annual Undergrad Tuition & Fees (In-State): $4,860
Enrollment: 2,823 Coed
Affiliation or Control: State IRS Status: 501(c)3
Highest Offering: Associate Degree
Accreditation: **SC**, ACBSP, ADNUR, DA, PNUR

02	President	Dr. Cynthia T. ANTHONY
05	Vice Pres of Instructional Services	Dr. Bruce CRAWFORD
10	Vice Pres Admin & Fiscal Services	Mrs. Sharon CREWS
32	Dean of Students	Vacant
117	Dir Fin Services/Risk Assessment	Dr. Craig D. LAWRENCE
20	Academic Dean	Dr. Sherri DAVIS
21	Director of Accounting	Ms. Monique SILAS
50	Assoc Dean Business/Info Tech	Dr. Alice MILTON
49	Assoc Dean Lib Arts/Col Trans Pgms	Dr. Karl PRUITT
76	Assoc Dean of Health Professions	Dr. Sherika DERICO
75	Dean of Career Tech & Workforce Dev	Dr. Joye JONES
35	Dean of Student Life	Vacant
07	Dir of Admissions/Enrollment Mgmt	Mr. Dorian WALUYN
08	Librarian	Ms. Julie KENNEDY
37	Director Student Financial Aid	Ms. Cassandra HOLLINS
15	Director of Human Resources	Ms. Elma BELL
26	Director of Public Relations	Mrs. Geri ALBRIGHT
18	Director of Facilities	Vacant
19	Director Safety/Security	Mr. James BLANTON
13	Director Information Mgmt Systems	Mr. James MANKOWICH
41	Athletic Director	Dr. Eric AGEE
06	Registrar	Ms. Lori CHISEM
38	Coordinator Student Counseling	Dr. Renee HERNDON
09	Coordinator of Data Management	Mrs. Jamie GLASS
106	Dir Online Education/E-learning	Dr. Kesha JAMES
25	Director of Title III	Dr. Myrtes D. GREEN
103	Asst Dean Workforce Development	Mr. Tommy HOBBS
88	Assist Dean Career Tech Programs	Ms. Nancy WILSON

*Lurleen B. Wallace Community College (I)

PO Drawer 1418, 1000 Dannelly Blvd,
Andalusia AL 36420-1224
County: Covington FICE Identification: 008988
Unit ID: 101602
Telephone: (334) 222-6591 Carnegie Class: Assoc/MT-VT-Mix Trad/Non
FAX Number: (334) 881-2300 Calendar System: Semester

URL: www.lbwcc.edu
Established: 1969 Annual Undergrad Tuition & Fees (In-State): $4,860
Enrollment: 1,666 Coed
Affiliation or Control: State IRS Status: 501(c)3
Highest Offering: Associate Degree
Accreditation: SC, ADNUR, DMS, EMT, PTAA

02 President ... Dr. Brock KELLEY
04 Administrative Asst to President ... Ms. Cindy GREEN
10 Chief Financial Officer ... Ms. Lisa CARNLEY
05 Dean of Instruction ... Dr. Shannon LEVITZKE
32 Dean of Student Affairs ... Mr. Jason JESSIE
12 Dean of the Greenville Campus ... Ms. Peige JOSEY
103 Dir Workforce Development ... Mr. Chad SUTTON
111 Director Institutional Advancement ... Ms. Chrissie DUFFY
09 Assoc Dean Inst Effect & Quality ... Dr. Kristina ANDERSON
15 Assoc Director Human Resources ... Ms. Ashley WILLIAMSON
18 Dir College Facilities/Maintenance ... Mr. Tim JONES
07 Director Admissions & Records ... Ms. Jan RILEY
41 Athletic Director ... Mr. Steve HELMS
08 Director of Learning Resources ... Mr. Hugh CARTER
37 Director of Financial Aid ... Ms. Donna BASS
26 Public Info Officer/Dir Marketing ... Ms. Maggie JONES

*Marion Military Institute (A)

1101 Washington Street, Marion AL 36756-3213
County: Perry FICE Identification: 001026
Unit ID: 101648
Telephone: (800) 664-1842 Carnegie Class: Assoc/HT-High Trad
FAX Number: (334) 683-2380 Calendar System: Semester
URL: www.marionmilitary.edu
Established: 1842 Annual Undergrad Tuition & Fees (In-State): $9,418
Enrollment: 401 Coed
Affiliation or Control: State IRS Status: 501(c)3
Highest Offering: Associate Degree
Accreditation: SC

02 President ... Col. David J. MOLLAHAN
10 Comptroller ... Mrs. Jada L. HARRISON
05 Chief Academic Officer ... Mr. David IVEY
32 VP Student Affairs/Commandant ... Col. Ed PASSMORE
111 VP for Institutional Advancement ... Mrs. Suzanne MCKEE
41 Director of Athletics ... Dr. Michelle IVEY
84 Director of Enrollment Management ... Mrs. Brittany CRAWFORD
29 Director of Alumni and Comm Affairs ... Mrs. Dawn CURTIS
88 ROTC Professor of Military Science ... MG. Juan MARTINEZ
09 Director of Institutional Research ... Mr. Logan LOGAN
06 Registrar ... Vacant
15 Dir Human Resources/Compliance ... Ms. Carmon P. FIELDS
37 Director of Financial Aid ... Ms. Jacqueline WILSON
08 Director Service Academy Program ... LTC. Thomas BOWEN
18 Director of Facilities ... SCPO. Robert D. SUMLIN
17 Director of Health Services ... Mrs. Rene SUMLIN
20 Chief Instructional Officer ... Mrs. Camie JONES

*Northeast Alabama Community College (B)

PO Box 159, 138 Alabama Highway 35,
Rainsville AL 35986-0159
County: DeKalb/Jackson FICE Identification: 001031
Unit ID: 101897
Telephone: (256) 638-4418 Carnegie Class: Assoc/MT-VT-Mix Trad/Non
FAX Number: (256) 638-3052 Calendar System: Semester
URL: www.nacc.edu
Established: 1963 Annual Undergrad Tuition & Fees (In-State): $4,860
Enrollment: 2,530 Coed
Affiliation or Control: State IRS Status: 501(c)3
Highest Offering: Associate Degree
Accreditation: SC, ADNUR, EMT, PNUR

02 President ... Dr. J. David CAMPBELL
05 Dean of Instruction ... Mr. Chad GORHAM
20 Associate Dean of Instruction ... Mrs. Barbara KILGORE
32 Dean of Student Services ... Ms. Sherie GRACE
10 Dean of Admin Services ... Mr. Rodney BONE
37 Director of Financial Aid ... Mr. Kip WILLIAMSON
103 Dir Workforce Devel/Skills Training ... Mr. Kerry WRIGHT
26 Director of Promotions & Marketing ... Mrs. Meg NIPPERS
45 Dir Inst Planning & Assessment ... Ms. Olivia DODD
18 Chief Facilities/Physical Plant ... Mr. Kent JONES
06 Registrar/Chief Bus Ofcr/Dir Purch ... Mr. Rodney BONE
30 Development Director ... Ms. Heather RICE
19 Director of Police/Security ... Mr. Van MCALPIN
04 Executive Asst to President ... Ms. Brenda STRINGER
08 Dir Learning Resource Ctr/Library ... Mrs. Julia EVERETT
15 Human Resources Director ... Mrs. Lynde MANN
29 Event Planning/Alumni Relations ... Mrs. Chasley BROWN
72 Director of Educational Technology ... Mrs. Patricia FALK
41 Athletic Director ... Mrs. Barbara KILGORE

*Northwest - Shoals Community College (C)

800 George Wallace Boulevard,
Muscle Shoals AL 35661-3205
County: Colbert FICE Identification: 005697
Unit ID: 101736
Telephone: (256) 331-5200 Carnegie Class: Assoc/HVT-Mix Trad/Non
FAX Number: (256) 331-5222 Calendar System: Semester
URL: www.nwscc.edu
Established: 1963 Annual Undergrad Tuition & Fees (In-State): $4,831
Enrollment: 3,360 Coed
Affiliation or Control: State IRS Status: 501(c)3
Highest Offering: Associate Degree
Accreditation: SC, ADNUR, EMT, MAC, PNUR

02 President ... Dr. Jeff GOODWIN
103 Dean of WF Devel/IE/Advancement ... Mr. John MCINTOSH
05 Dean Academic Affairs ... Dr. Timmy JAMES
84 Executive Director of Enrollment ... Mr. Carl COLLINS
37 Executive Director of Financial Aid ... Ms. Lisa LILLEY
32 Dean of Students ... Dr. Crystal REED
10 Controller ... Ms. Kim GILBREATH
15 Dir of Human Resources/Payroll ... Ms. Tia STONE
13 Director of Management Info Systems ... Vacant
76 Assoc Dean Health Studies ... Vacant
55 Exec Dir Adult Educ/WF Strategies ... Ms. Tara BRANSCOME
04 Administrative Asst to President ... Ms. Teresa HARRISON
26 Public Information Officer ... Mr. Trent RANDOLPH
35 Exec Director of Student Services ... Ms. Brittany JONES
108 Asst Dean WF Devel/IE/Advancement ... Ms. Leslie TOMLINSON
10 Dean of Finance/CFO ... Ms. Dawnelle ROBINSON
09 Director of Institutional Research ... Ms. Angie STONE
106 Executive Director of Distance Educ ... Ms. April COOKSON
18 Executive Director of Facilities ... Mr. Dillard MCCOWN
111 Director of Advancement ... Ms. Katie SMITH
06 Asst Dir Enrollment Mgmt/Registrar ... Ms. MaLea MILSTEAD

*Reid State Technical College (D)

PO Box 588, 100 Hwy 83, Evergreen AL 36401-0588
County: Conecuh FICE Identification: 005692
Unit ID: 101994
Telephone: (251) 578-1313 Carnegie Class: Assoc/HVT-High Trad
FAX Number: (251) 578-5355 Calendar System: Semester
URL: www.rstc.edu
Established: 1966 Annual Undergrad Tuition & Fees (In-State): $4,920
Enrollment: 279 Coed
Affiliation or Control: State IRS Status: 501(c)3
Highest Offering: Associate Degree
Accreditation: COE

01 President ... Dr. Coretta BOYKIN
108 Asst Dean of Institutional Effect ... Dr. Serena BROWN
10 Director of Accounting ... Ms. Jenelle SMITH
18 Director of Facilities ... Ms. Jenelle SMITH
37 Director of Financial Aid ... Ms. Christy GOODWIN
15 Director of Human Resources ... Ms. Brenda JACKSON
05 Director of Instructional Services ... Ms. Shirley JOHNSON
07 Admissions/Records Clerk ... Ms. Natalie RAY
41 Athletic Director ... Mr. David COLE
40 Bookstore Manager ... Ms. Laushaun WATSON
19 Campus Police Officer ... Mr. James WILKINS
36 Career Coach ... Ms. Evalen THOMAS
07 Coordinator of Recruitment ... Ms. Melissa STALLWORTH
09 DE Coord/Research Analyst ... Ms. Latrisa SIMPKINS
103 Director of Workforce Development ... Mr. David COLE
32 Director of Student Services ... Vacant
114 Fiscal Accountant ... Mr. Dustin BUSH
88 Instructional Support Services ... Ms. Clarinda MIXON
08 Librarian ... Vacant
14 Network/Server Administrator ... Mr. Charles HIGDON
06 Registrar ... Ms. Vickie NICHOLSON
118 Payroll Accounting Clerk ... Ms. Sharon NORTH

*Shelton State Community College (E)

9500 Old Greensboro Road, Tuscaloosa AL 35405-8522
County: Tuscaloosa FICE Identification: 005691
Unit ID: 102067
Telephone: (205) 391-2211 Carnegie Class: Assoc/HVT-Mix Trad/Non
FAX Number: (205) 391-2426 Calendar System: Semester
URL: www.sheltonstate.edu
Established: 1953 Annual Undergrad Tuition & Fees (In-State): $4,560
Enrollment: 3,743 Coed
Affiliation or Control: State IRS Status: 501(c)3
Highest Offering: Associate Degree
Accreditation: SC, ADNUR, CAHIIM, COARC, PNUR

02 President ... Dr. Chris COX
04 Executive Asst to the President ... Ms. Channing H. MARLOWE
15 Dean of Human Resources ... Mr. Kevin DAVIS
31 Dean of Community Relations ... Mr. Joe EATMON
32 Dean of Student Services ... Mrs. Amanda HARBISON
05 Dean of Instruction ... Dr. Michael GREEN
103 Dean of Workforce & Econ Devel ... Dr. Jonathan KOH
12 Dean Fredd Campus/Title III ... Dr. Anika LODREE
21 Comptroller Business Services ... Mrs. Michelle BASS
75 Assoc Dean of Technical Services ... Mr. Grant COCKRELL
20 Assoc Dean of Acad Services ... Vacant
76 Assoc Dean of Health Services ... Dr. Andrea BOWDEN-EVANS
13 Assoc Dean of Info Tech Services ... Mr. Claude LAKE
35 Assoc Dean of Student Success ... Vacant
07 Director of Admissions/Registrar ... Mrs. Fannie BATES-REESE
08 Head Librarian ... Ms. Kelly GRIFFITHS
55 Director Adult Education ... Ms. Kristen BOBO
09 Dir Institutional Effective/Rsrch ... Dr. Louis SHEDD
26 Dir of Media Communication ... Vacant
106 Director of eLearning ... Dr. Christine WILSON
41 Athletic Director ... Ms. Cara CROSSLIN
88 Director of Advising ... Ms. Sophia EVERETT
30 Director of Development ... Mrs. Shannon CHANDLER
25 Director of Grants ... Dr. Margaret PURCELL
103 Director of Workforce Development ... Mrs. Nicole DUBOSE
37 Director of Financial Aid ... Ms. Nicole ELAM
04 Administrative Asst to President ... Mrs. Ann H. TINSLEY

*Snead State Community College (F)

PO Box 734, Boaz AL 35957-0734
County: Marshall FICE Identification: 001038
Unit ID: 102076
Telephone: (256) 593-5120 Carnegie Class: Assoc/HT-High Non
FAX Number: N/A Calendar System: Semester
URL: www.snead.edu
Established: 1898 Annual Undergrad Tuition & Fees (In-State): $5,344
Enrollment: 2,006 Coed
Affiliation or Control: State IRS Status: Exempt
Highest Offering: Associate Degree
Accreditation: SC, ADNUR

02 President ... Dr. Joe WHITMORE
32 Vice President for Student Services ... Mr. Jason CANNON
10 Interim Chief Financial Officer ... Ms. Tina SIMONS
13 Acting Chief IT Officer ... Mr. Don RODEN
26 Director of Marketing/PR ... Ms. Shelley SMITH
05 Vice President for Academic Affairs ... Mr. Vann SCOTT
103 Director Workforce Development ... Ms. Teresa WALKER
09 Director of IE/IR ... Ms. Janna BONDS
106 Associate Dean Online Learning ... Mr. Michael GIBSON
81 Science Division Director ... Ms. Deborah RHODEN
79 Humanities/Languages Div Director ... Dr. Cynthia DENHAM
83 Social Sc/Business/Off Adm Div Dir ... Dr. Meredith JACKSON
81 Mathematics Division Director ... Dr. Cheri COLVIN
57 Fine Arts Division Director ... Dr. Barbara HUDSON
76 Director of Health Sciences ... Dr. Lisa BROCK
41 Athletic Director ... Mr. Mark RICHARD
08 Head Librarian ... Mr. John MILLER
15 Director of Human Resources ... Ms. Amanda GUNNELS
18 Director of Physical Plant ... Mr. Steve WILLIAMS
07 Director of Admissions/Recruitment ... Ms. Tristin CALLAHAN
19 Director Security/Safety ... Mr. Paul GORE
29 Director Alumni Relations ... Ms. Shelley SMITH
102 Foundation Coordinator ... Ms. Kelli CONLEY
37 Director of Financial Aid ... Ms. Amanda GENTRY
88 Coordinator of Testing/Secondary Ed ... Ms. Tonya SHIELDS

*Southern Union State Community College (G)

PO Box 1000, Wadley AL 36276-1000
County: Randolph FICE Identification: 001040
Unit ID: 251260
Telephone: (256) 395-2211 Carnegie Class: Assoc/MT-VT-High Trad
FAX Number: (256) 395-2215 Calendar System: Semester
URL: www.suscc.edu
Established: 1922 Annual Undergrad Tuition & Fees (In-State): $4,860
Enrollment: 3,950 Coed
Affiliation or Control: State IRS Status: 501(c)3
Highest Offering: Associate Degree
Accreditation: SC, ADNUR, EMT, PNUR, PTAA, RAD, SURGT

02 President ... Mr. Todd SHACKETT
05 Dean of Academics ... Dr. Linda NORTH
32 Dean Student Development ... Mr. Gary BRANCH
35 Associate Dean of Students ... Ms. Derika GRIFFIN
20 Assoc Dean of Instruction ... Mr. Steve SPRATLIN
72 Dean of Technical Educ/Wrkfce Dev ... Dr. Darin BALDWIN
06 Registrar ... Ms. Amber LOVELACE
10 VP of Financial & Admin Services ... Mr. Ben JORDAN
04 Assistant to the President ... Ms. Alison OSBORN
09 Assoc Dean of Inst Research ... Mr. Eddie PIGG
13 Director of MIS ... Vacant
15 Director of Human Resources ... Ms. Sandra HUGHLEY
31 Director of Media Relations ... Ms. Shondae BROWN
37 Director Student Financial Aid ... Ms. Melissa TODD
45 Assoc Dean of Inst Effectiveness ... Ms. Robin BROWN
19 Chief of Campus Police ... Mr. Jimmy HOLMES
84 Director Enrollment Management ... Dr. Christopher FRANKLIN

*Trenholm State Community College (H)

PO Box 10048, Montgomery AL 36108
County: Montgomery FICE Identification: 005734
Unit ID: 102313
Telephone: (334) 420-4200 Carnegie Class: Assoc/HVT-High Trad
FAX Number: (334) 420-4206 Calendar System: Semester
URL: www.trenholmstate.edu
Established: 1963 Annual Undergrad Tuition & Fees (In-State): $4,770
Enrollment: 1,526 Coed
Affiliation or Control: State IRS Status: Exempt
Highest Offering: Associate Degree
Accreditation: SC, ACFEI, #COARC, DA, DMS, MAC, PNUR, RAD

02 Acting President ... Dr. Kemba CHAMBERS
10 Dean of Finance/Admin Svcs ... Vacant
05 Exec VP of Instructional Services ... Vacant
30 Dean of Development ... Dr. Suresh C. KAUSHIK
32 Dean of Students ... Ms. Theresa MAYS
20 Dean of Instruction ... Dr. Nakia ROBINSON
103 Dean of Workforce Development ... Mr. Danny PERRY
76 Associate Dean of Health Svcs ... Dr. Tracie CARTER
13 Director of IT ... Vacant

09 Dir of Institutional Effectiveness ..... Dr. Mimi JOHNSON
18 Director Physical Plant ..... Mr. Robert ALLEN
37 Director Student Financial Aid ..... Ms. Betty EDWARDS
06 Registrar ..... Dr. Tennie S. MCBRYDE
84 Director of Enrollment Management ..... Ms. Valerie ALLEN-PORTERFIELD
08 Head Librarian ..... Mr. Paul BLACKMON
26 Public Information Officer ..... Ms. Angela HURST
15 Director of Human Resources ..... Dr. Pam ROLLINS
51 Dir Title III/Marketing/Cont Educ ..... Ms. Carol WILLIAMS
36 Coordinator Job Placement ..... Ms. Shawanda WALKER
04 Administrative Asst to President ..... Mrs. Shearese G. GRANT

*Wallace State Community College - Hanceville (A)

PO Box 2000, 801 Main Street, NW,
Hanceville AL 35077-2000

County: Cullman — FICE Identification: 007871
Unit ID: 101295
Telephone: (256) 352-8000 — Carnegie Class: Assoc/HVT-High Trad
FAX Number: (256) 352-8228 — Calendar System: Semester
URL: www.wallacestate.edu
Established: 1966 — Annual Undergrad Tuition & Fees (In-State): $4,860
Enrollment: 4,763 — Coed
Affiliation or Control: State — IRS Status: 501(c)3
Highest Offering: Associate Degree
Accreditation: SC, ACBSP, ACFEI, ADNUR, CAHIIM, COARC, DA, DH, DMS, EMT, MAC, MLTAD, NAEYC, OTA, PNUR, POLYT, PTAA, RAD

02 President ..... Dr. Vicki KAROLEWICS
10 Dean of Finance & Admin Svcs ..... Mary H. INGRAM
05 Dean of Academic Affairs ..... Dr. Beth BOWNES-JOHNSON
72 Dean of Applied Technologies ..... Wes RAKESTRAW
76 VP for Lrng/Dean Health Sciences ..... Lisa GERMAN
32 Vice President for Students ..... Vacant
121 Director of Advising ..... Whit RICE
109 Auxiliary Director ..... Mark BOLIN
08 Head Librarian ..... Lisa HULLETT
37 Director of Financial Aid ..... Becky GRAVES
55 Extended Day Program Director ..... Wayne MANORD
15 Director of Human Resources ..... Alyce FLANIGAN
111 VP for Advancement and Innovation ..... Suzanne HARBIN
18 Director of Physical Plant ..... Billy ROSE
26 Director Communications/Marketing ..... Kristen HOLMES
06 Registrar ..... Jennifer TWITTY
09 Dir of Research/Planning/Assessment ..... Mattie HUDSON
103 Director Workforce Development ..... Jamie BLACKMON
13 Chief Information Officer ..... Matthew MCFALL
41 Athletic Director ..... Paul BAILEY
19 Director Security/Safety ..... Tyler RODEN

Alabama State University (B)

915 S Jackson Street, Montgomery AL 36101-0271

County: Montgomery — FICE Identification: 001005
Unit ID: 100724
Telephone: (334) 229-4100 — Carnegie Class: DU-Mod
FAX Number: (334) 834-6861 — Calendar System: Semester
URL: www.alasu.edu
Established: 1867 — Annual Undergrad Tuition & Fees (In-State): $11,068
Enrollment: 4,072 — Coed
Affiliation or Control: State — IRS Status: 501(c)3
Highest Offering: Doctorate
Accreditation: SC, ACBSP, ART, CACREP, CAEP, CAHIIM, MUS, OPE, OT, PTA, SW, THEA

01 President ..... Dr. Quinton T. ROSS, JR.
05 Provost/Vice Pres Academic Affs ..... Dr. Carl PETTIS
10 Vice Pres Business & Finance ..... Mr. William HOPPER
13 Int Vice Pres Technology Services ..... Ms. Sonya SATTERFIELD
26 VP Marketing and Strategic Comm ..... Ms. Lois RUSSELL
111 VP for Institutional Advancement ..... Vacant
15 Director Human Resources ..... Mr. Derrick CARR
20 Assoc Provost Academic Affairs ..... Dr. Kennedy WEKESA
32 VP Student Affairs/ Enrollment Mgmt ..... Dr. Derrick BREWSTER
18 Vice Pres Facilities Mgt/Operations ..... Mr. Donald DOTSON
45 Assoc Vice Pres Inst Effectiveness ..... Dr. Christine THOMAS
35 Int Asst Vice Pres Student Affairs ..... Dr. Rakesha HINES
21 Comptroller/AVP Business & Fin ..... Mrs. Alondrea J. PRITCHETT
108 Dir Acad Planning & Evaluation ..... Vacant
09 Director Institutional Research ..... Dr. Bryn BAKOYEMA
88 Coord Quality Enhancement Planning ..... Dr. Rolanda HORN
08 Dean Libraries/Learning Resource ..... Dr. Janice FRANKLIN
07 Director Admissions/Recruitment ..... Mr. Freddie WILLIAMS
37 Assoc VP Student Affs/Financial Aid ..... Mr. Kelvin FRANCOIS
36 Director Career Services ..... Dr. Sabrina CROWDER
50 Dean College Business Admin ..... Dr. Kamal HINGORANI
89 Dean University College ..... Dr. Evelyn HODGE
53 Dean College of Education ..... Dr. Nicole STRANGE-MARTIN
64 Dean Visual & Performing Arts ..... Dr. Wendy COLEMAN
58 Dean Graduate Studies ..... Dr. Caterina BRISTOL
81 Dean College of Sci Math & Tech ..... Dr. Audrey NAPIER
49 Dean Liberal Arts/Social Sci ..... Dr. Kathaleen AMENDE
76 Dean College Health Sciences ..... Dr. Charlene PORTEE
51 Director Continuing Education ..... Mrs. Mia WILLIAMS
29 Director Alumni Relations ..... Mr. Cromwell HANDY
23 Sr Director Health Services ..... Dr. Joyce LLOYD-DAVIS
19 Depty Director of Public Safety ..... Mr. Kevin KENDRICK
38 Dir Counseling & Development Svcs ..... Mr. Chris JOHNS
39 Dir Housing/Residential Life ..... Ms. Rakesia HINES
41 Director of Athletics ..... Dr. Jason CABLE
25 Director Research & Sponsored Pgms ..... Mr. Pernell JENKINS
96 Director of Procurement ..... Ms. Patricia THOMAS
101 Board Liaison ..... Mrs. Danielle KENNEDY-JONES
106 Dir Online Education/E-learning ..... Dr. Patrice GLENN-JONES
43 General Counsel ..... Mr. Kenneth THOMAS
06 Registrar ..... Ms. Marie MCNEAR
27 Chief Public Relations/Marketing ..... Mr. Kenneth MULLINAX
28 Int Dir of Diversity/Intl Affairs ..... Dr. Rakesha HINES
100 Chief of Staff ..... Dr. Kevin A. ROLLE
84 Director Enrollment Management ..... Mr. Freddie WILLIAMS

Amridge University (C)

1200 Taylor Road, Montgomery AL 36117-3553

County: Montgomery — FICE Identification: 025034
Unit ID: 100690
Telephone: (800) 351-4040 — Carnegie Class: Masters/S
FAX Number: (334) 387-3878 — Calendar System: Semester
URL: www.amridgeuniversity.edu
Established: 1967 — Annual Undergrad Tuition & Fees: $6,950
Enrollment: 775 — Coed
Affiliation or Control: Churches Of Christ — IRS Status: 501(c)3
Highest Offering: Doctorate
Accreditation: SC

01 President ..... Dr. Michael C. TURNER
05 Academic Vice President/Dean ..... Dr. Lee TAYLOR
32 VP of Student Affairs & Technology ..... Dr. Laina T. COSTANZA
06 Registrar ..... Mrs. Elaine P. TARENCE
08 Director Learning Resources ..... Vacant
10 Controller ..... Dr. Anita L. CROSBY
113 Bursar ..... Mrs. B. P. TURNER
37 Financial Aid Director ..... Ms. Starr PEACOCK
13 System Admin Network Operations ..... Mr. Jack TEMPLE
18 Maintenance ..... Mr. Robert SHIRLEY
24 Coordinator of Network Opers ..... Mr. Thomas PATTERSON
38 Director of Student Counseling ..... Vacant
73 Chair School of Theology ..... Dr. Rodney CLOUD
50 Chair Col of Business & Ldrshp ..... Dr. Kenyetta MCCURTY
97 Dean of College of General Studies ..... Vacant
15 Human Resources Coordinator ..... Mrs. Patsy MORETZ
08 Head Librarian ..... Mr. Terence SHERIDAN
84 Enrollment Coordinator ..... Mr. Brooks HOUSLEY

Athens State University (D)

300 N Beaty Street, Athens AL 35611-1902

County: Limestone — FICE Identification: 001008
Unit ID: 100812
Telephone: (256) 233-8100 — Carnegie Class: Bac-Diverse
FAX Number: (256) 216-3324 — Calendar System: Semester
URL: www.athens.edu
Established: 1822 — Annual Undergrad Tuition & Fees (In-State): N/A
Enrollment: 2,867 — Coed
Affiliation or Control: State — IRS Status: 501(c)3
Highest Offering: Master's
Accreditation: SC, ACBSP, CAEP, CAEPN

01 President ..... Dr. Philip K. WAY
05 Provost/VP for Academic Affairs ..... Dr. Catherine WEHLBURG
88 Senior Executive to the President ..... Vacant
32 VP Enroll/Student Support Svcs ..... Ms. Sarah MCABEE
84 Asst VP for Enrollment Mgmt ..... Dr. Rick BARTH
10 Vice President Financial Affairs ..... Mr. Mike MCCOY
21 Business Manager/Asst VP Finance ..... Mr. Jonathan CRAFT
111 Vice Pres for University Advance ..... Dr. Keith FERGUSON
103 VP Corporate & Community Relations ..... Dr. Kim LAFEVOR
08 Director of Libraries ..... Vacant
50 Dean College of Business ..... Mr. Gary VALCANA
53 Dean College of Education ..... Dr. Lee VARTANIAN
49 Dean College of Arts & Sciences ..... Vacant
36 Dir of Career Development Center ..... Dr. Michael RADDEN
37 Dir of Student Financial Services ..... Mr. Mitchell BAZZEL
06 Registrar ..... Ms. Tracy RABY
07 Chief of Records ..... Ms. Teresa SUIT
29 Dir Alumni Affairs/Major Gifts ..... Ms. Rachel O'SULLIVAN
30 AVP University Development ..... Mr. David BROWN
26 Director of Printing & Public Rels ..... Mr. Chris LATHAM
09 Director of Institutional Research ..... Vacant
18 Director of Physical Plant ..... Mr. Kerry WARREN
15 Director of Human Resources ..... Mr. Jeff POWERS
51 Director of Ctr for Lifelong Lrng ..... Mr. Andrew DOLLAR
121 Sr Director of Student Success Ctr ..... Mr. Derrek SMITH
28 Dir Student Inclusion Initiatives ..... Mr. Richard COLLIE
04 Administrative Asst to President ..... Vacant
101 Secretary of the Institution/Board ..... Mrs. Jackie GOOCH
13 Chief Info Technology Officer ..... Ms. Belinda KRIGEL
19 Chief of Security/Safety ..... Mr. Jerry CRABTREE

Auburn University (E)

Auburn AL 36849

County: Lee — FICE Identification: 001009
Unit ID: 100858
Telephone: (334) 844-4000 — Carnegie Class: DU-Highest
FAX Number: N/A — Calendar System: Semester
URL: www.auburn.edu
Established: 1856 — Annual Undergrad Tuition & Fees (In-State): $11,796
Enrollment: 30,737 — Coed
Affiliation or Control: State — IRS Status: 501(c)3
Highest Offering: Doctorate
Accreditation: SC, AAB, ACPHA, ART, AUD, CACREP, CAEP, CEA, CIDA, CLPSY, CONST, COPSY, DIETD, @DIETI, IPSY, JOUR, LSAR, MFCD, MUS, NAEYC, NURSE, PHAR, PLNG, SP, SPAA, SW, THEA, VET

01 President ..... Dr. Christopher B. ROBERTS
03 Executive Vice President ..... Lt Gen. Ronald L. BURGESS
05 Interim Provost/VP Academic Affairs ..... Dr. Vini NATHAN
29 VP Alumni Affairs ..... Ms. Gretchen R. VANVALKENBURG
10 VP Business & Finance & CFO ..... Ms. Kelli D. SHOMAKER
111 Senior VP for Advancement ..... Mr. John MORRIS
32 Senior VP Student Affairs ..... Dr. Bobby R. WOODARD
84 Vice Pres Enrollment Services ..... Dr. Joffery GAYMON
46 Vice Pres Research ..... Dr. James WEYHENMEYER
101 Secretary to Board of Trustees ..... Mr. Jon G. WAGGONER
43 General Counsel ..... Ms. Jaime S. HAMMER
13 VP & Chief Information Officer ..... Mr. James O'CONNOR
78 Dir AL Cooperative Extension Sys ..... Dr. Mike PHILLIPS
41 Director of Athletics ..... Mr. C. Allen GREENE
86 Exec Director Governmental Affairs ..... Mr. Jared WHITE
26 Exec Director Public Affairs ..... Dr. Jennifer ADAMS
116 AVP Internal Audit/Compl & Privacy ..... Mr. M. Kevin ROBINSON
19 Exec Director Risk Mgmt & Safety ..... Mr. Chris O'GWYNN
27 Assistant VP Univ Comm & Mktg ..... Mr. Mike CLARDY, JR.
88 Univ Ombudsperson ..... Mr. Kevin COONROD
20 Associate Provost Faculty Affairs ..... Dr. Emmett WINN
20 Associate Provost Acad Effectivenes ..... Dr. Norman GODWIN
88 Asst VP Strat Initiatives & Comm ..... Ms. Julie HUFF
28 Assoc Prov/VP Inclus & Diversity . Dr. Taffye BENSON-CLAYTON
25 Assistant VP Research ..... Ms. Martha M. TAYLOR
35 Associate VP Student Affairs ..... Dr. Lady D. COX
39 Assoc VP Campus Living ..... Dr. Bryan RUSH
121 Director of University Advising ..... Dr. Ruthanna SPIERS
31 VP University Outreach ..... Dr. Royrickers COOK
85 Asst Provost Intl Programs ..... Dr. Andrew R. GILLESPIE
18 Associate VP Facilities ..... Mr. Daniel P. KING
15 Associate VP Human Resources ..... Ms. Karla S. MCCORMICK
21 Assoc VP Financial Svcs/Controller ..... Ms. Amy K. DOUGLAS
96 Dir Procurement & Business Svcs ..... Ms. Missty KENNEDY
37 Exec Dir Student Financial Svcs ..... Mr. Michael C. REYNOLDS
22 Director Affirmative Action/EEO ..... Ms. Kelley G. TAYLOR
108 Director Academic Assessment ..... Dr. Katie BOYD
09 Director Institutional Research ..... Dr. Matthew CAMPBELL
88 Director University Writing ..... Dr. Christopher BASGIER
120 Director Teaching & Learning Center ..... Dr. Asim ALI
88 Exec Dir Performing Arts Center ..... Mr. Christopher J. HEACOX
39 Dir Univ Housing/Residence Life ..... Mt. Nyerere TRYMAN
36 Acting Director Career Center ..... Dr. Jaime MILLER
38 Director Student Counseling Svcs ..... Dr. Doug HANKES
117 Director Security/Safety ..... Mr. Kelvin KING
40 Director University Bookstore ..... Ms. Catherine LEE
06 University Registrar ..... Ms. Karen BATTYE
47 Dean Agriculture & Dir AAES ..... Dr. Paul M. PATTERSON
48 Acting Dean Architecture/Design ..... Dr. Karen L. ROGERS
50 Dean Business ..... Dr. Annette L. RANFT
53 Dean Education ..... Dr. Jeffrey T. FAIRBROTHER
54 Dean Engineering ..... Vacant
65 Dean Forestry/Wildlife Sci ..... Dr. Janaki R. ALAVALAPATI
59 Dean Human Sciences ..... Dr. Susan G. HUBBARD
49 Interim Dean Liberal Arts ..... Dr. Ana FRANCO-WATKINS
66 Dean Nursing ..... Dr. Gregg NEWSCHWANDER
67 Interim Dean Pharmacy ..... Dr. Daniel W. SURRY
81 Dean Sciences & Mathematics ..... Dr. Nicholas J. GIORDANO
74 Dean Veterinary Medicine ..... Dr. Calvin M. JOHNSON
58 Dean Graduate School ..... Dr. George FLOWERS
08 Dean University Libraries ..... Dr. Shali L. ZHANG
04 Administrative Asst to President ..... Ms. Janie A. BOLES
07 Assoc Director of Admissions ..... Ms. Allison SAGGUS
104 Director of Auburn Abroad ..... Ms. Deborah WEISS
30 Associate VP of Development ..... Ms. Tara JONES
44 Director of Annual Giving ..... Mr. Ryan A. KING
114 Asst VP Budgets & Business Opers ..... Mr. Bryan ELMORE

Auburn University at Montgomery (F)

PO Box 244024, Montgomery AL 36124-4023

County: Montgomery — FICE Identification: 008310
Unit ID: 100830
Telephone: (334) 244-3000 — Carnegie Class: Masters/L
FAX Number: (334) 244-3762 — Calendar System: Semester
URL: www.aum.edu
Established: 1967 — Annual Undergrad Tuition & Fees (In-State): $8,860
Enrollment: 5,212 — Coed
Affiliation or Control: State — IRS Status: 501(c)3
Highest Offering: Doctorate
Accreditation: SC, CACREP, CAEP, MLS, NURSE, SPAA, @SW

01 Chancellor ..... Dr. Carl A. STOCKTON
05 Provost/Sr Vice Chancellor ..... Dr. Mrinal VARMA
10 Vice Chanc Financial & Admin Svcs ..... Mr. Scott PARSONS
58 Assoc Provost Grad Studies/Faculty ..... Dr. Matthew RAGLAND
20 Assoc Provost Undergraduate Studies ..... Dr. Joy CLARK
84 Assoc Provost Enrollment ..... Dr. Sameer PANDE
41 Athletic Director ..... Ms. Jessie ROSA
85 Director of Global Initiatives ..... Mr. Ayush TANEJA
15 Chief HR Officer ..... Ms. Leslie MEADOWS
08 Dean of Library ..... Mr. Phill JOHNSON
07 Director of Admissions/Recruiting ..... Mr. Ronnie MCKINNEY
37 Sr Director of Financial Aid ..... Mr. Anthony RICHEY
109 Chief Campus Services Officer ..... Mr. Daryl MORRIS
39 Dir Housing & Residence Life ..... Ms. Iyisha HAMPTON
13 Chief Information Officer ..... Mr. Tobias MENSE
32 Dean of Students ..... Dr. Leon HIGDON
19 Director of Police Operations ..... Ms. Brenda MITCHELL

06 Registrar ... Ms. Holly BENSON
36 Director Career Development ... Mr. Bradley ROBBINS
26 Director of Communications ... Mr. Troy JOHNSON
25 Mgr Research Compl/Spons Programs ... Ms. Debra TOMBLIN
50 Dean of College of Business ... Dr. Ross DICKENS
53 Dean of College of Education ... Dr. Sheila AUSTIN
83 Dean Col Liberal Arts/Social Sci ... Dr. Andrew MCMICHAEL
66 Dean of Nursing/Health Sci ... Dr. Jean LEUNER
23 Dir of Counseling and Health Svcs ... Ms. Greta CHAMBLESS
81 Dean College of Sciences ... Dr. Douglas LEAMAN
04 Executive Admin Asst to Chancellor ... Ms. Robin FORESTER
88 Special Asst/Collab Part/Dist Educ ... Dr. Shanta VARMA
29 Dir of Alumni Relations ... Ms. Valerie RANKIN
22 Director Disability Services ... Ms. Tamara MASSEY-GARRETT

Birmingham-Southern College (A)

900 Arkadelphia Road, Birmingham AL 35254-0001
County: Jefferson — FICE Identification: 001012
Unit ID: 100937
Telephone: (205) 226-4600 — Carnegie Class: Bac-A&S
FAX Number: (205) 226-4627 — Calendar System: 4/1/4
URL: www.bsc.edu
Established: 1856 — Annual Undergrad Tuition & Fees: $18,900
Enrollment: 1,129 — Coed
Affiliation or Control: United Methodist — IRS Status: 501(c)3
Highest Offering: Baccalaureate
Accreditation: SC, MUS

01 President ... Mr. Daniel COLEMAN
05 Interim Provost ... Dr. Tim SMITH
10 Int VP Finance/CFO ... Mr. Lane ESTES
11 VP Administration/Chief Oper Ofcr ... Mr. Lane ESTES
111 VP Advancement and Communications ... Ms. Virginia G. LOFTIN
13 VP Information Technology ... Mr. Anthony HAMBEY
32 VP Student Development ... Dr. David EBERHARDT
84 VP Enrollment Management ... Mr. Trent GILBERT
20 Interim Assistant Provost ... Dr. Laura STULTZ
20 Assistant Provost ... Ms. Martha Ann STEVENSON
06 Registrar ... Ms. Amy SMITH
42 Chaplain ... Rev. Julie HOLLY
29 Director Alumni Engagement ... Ms. Dana PORTER
23 Director of Health Services ... Ms. Yvette SPENCER
26 Director of Communications ... Ms. Amy ABEYTA
08 Director of the Library ... Ms. Tiffany NORRIS
18 Director of Facilities & Events ... Mr. Travis PRINCE
15 Assoc VP/Director Human Resources ... Vacant
38 Director of Counseling ... Ms. Cara BLAKES
41 Athletic Director ... Ms. Kyndall WATERS
19 Chief of Campus Police ... Mr. Jeff HARRIS
110 Director Advancement Services ... Ms. Kimberly BURNETT
28 Dir Student Diversity & Inclusion ... Vacant
68 Dir Physical Fitness & Recreation ... Mr. Mike ROBINSON
88 Director of Leadership Studies ... Dr. Kent ANDERSEN
88 Director of Service Learning ... Ms. Kristin HARPER
104 Assoc Dir of International Programs ... Ms. Anne LEDVINA
40 Bookstore Manager ... Ms. Melissa FOSTER
96 Purchasing Manager ... Mr. Tim WILDING
30 Director Development ... Ms. Kimberly WOLFE
44 Director Development-Annual Giving ... Ms. Mercedes BUCHANAN
112 Director Donor Relations ... Ms. Jalete NELMS
25 Director Grants & Special Projects ... Dr. Joe CHANDLER
39 Associate Dean of Students ... Mr. David MILLER
04 Assistant to the President ... Ms. Ame JOHNSEY
07 Director of Admissions ... Ms. Amanda HARDIE
100 Chief of Staff ... Ms. Marvelouse GUERRIER
36 Director Student Placement ... Vacant
122 Asst Dir Stdnt Involve/Greek Life ... Ms. Stephanie SCHROEDER
37 Director Student Financial Aid ... Ms. Traci VEYL

Columbia Southern University (B)

21982 University Lane, Orange Beach AL 36561-3845
County: Baldwin — FICE Identification: 041215
Unit ID: 450933
Telephone: (251) 981-3771 — Carnegie Class: Masters/L
FAX Number: (251) 981-3815 — Calendar System: Other
URL: www.columbiasouthern.edu
Established: 1993 — Annual Undergrad Tuition & Fees: $5,775
Enrollment: 18,533 — Coed
Affiliation or Control: Proprietary — IRS Status: Proprietary
Highest Offering: Doctorate
Accreditation: @SC, DEAC

01 President ... Dr. Ken STYRON
05 Provost and Chief Academic Officer ... Dr. Janell GIBSON
100 Chief of Staff ... Mrs. Chelsea HOFFMAN
26 Chief Marketing Officer ... Mr. Dale LEATHERWOOD
13 Chief Information Officer ... Mr. Scott OSWALD
10 Chief Financial Officer ... Mr. Pat TROUP
88 VP Business Development/Mil Init ... Mr. Rick COOPER
20 Vice Provost Academic Affairs ... Dr. Misti KILL
49 Dean Col Arts & Sciences/Asst Prov ... Dr. Sonya ROGERS
117 Dean College Safety/Emergency Svc ... Dr. Misti KILL
50 Dean College of Business/Asst Prov ... Dr. Elwin JONES
111 VP of University Relations ... Mrs. Caroline WALTERS
88 Assistant Provost Special Programs ... Dr. Joe MANJONE
88 Vice Prov Inst Effect/Plng/Compl ... Dr. Khalilah BURTON
88 Assoc VP of Business Intelligence ... Mr. Ed WITHERINGTON
14 Assoc VP of Information Technology ... Mr. Charles MIMS
32 Vice Provost of Student Affairs ... Dr. Lee BARNETT
21 Associate VP of Finance ... Mr. Craig TAYLOR
88 Assist Provost Strategic Academic ... Mrs. Dayna FULLER
20 Dean Faculty Devel Svcs & Support ... Dr. John WILLEY
08 Dean of Library ... Ms. Jennifer STEINFORD
88 Associate Dean College of Safety/Em ... Dr. Tamara MOURAS
24 Dir of Instructional Design & Tech ... Mr. Tom HEITMAN
29 Dir of Community & Alumni Relations ... Mrs. Vicki BARNES
40 Director of Bookstore Operations ... Mr. David BARNES
09 Dir of Inst Research & Assessment ... Mrs. Cherea SCHELLHASE
06 Registrar ... Mrs. Rachel FARRIS
37 Director of Financial Aid ... Mrs. Marie WILLIAMS
86 Dir of State Auth & TIX Coordinator ... Mrs. Alexis HARRIS
07 Director of Admissions ... Mrs. Cindy CHIRIBAO
35 Director of Student Support Center ... Mr. Justin BOYKIN
88 Director of Success Center ... Mrs. Wendy TROUP
88 Dir Student Resolution and Conflict ... Mr. Austin HANES
121 Director of Academic Advising ... Mrs. Jacqueline BEVERLY
88 Director of Military Outreach ... Dr. Ernie ROSADO
88 Director of Veteran Initiatives ... Mr. Andrew ROMAN
16 Director of Human Resources ... Mrs. Jennifer MURRAY
108 Dir Acad Assessment & Data Analysis ... Dr. John HOPE
88 Asst Prov Curriculum Planning & Acc ... Ms. Sonya KOPP
88 Director of Corporate Outreach ... Ms. Sherri TWITTY
102 Director of Corporate Relations ... Mr. Tony ATCHLEY
51 Director of Continuing Education ... Ms. Mimi HENNING
88 Program Manager Vietnam ... Mr. Quang TRONG TRAN
113 Director of Student Accounts ... Mr. Aaron COLLINS
114 Int Dir of Administrative Operation ... Ms. Erica GRANT
36 Director of Career Services ... Mr. Keith CULLEN
88 Director of Academic Supp Services ... Mrs. Rachel IVERSON
18 Director of Maintenance ... Mr. Blain SNYDER
04 Manager Office of the CEO ... Mrs. Tara COLLINS
19 Manager Security and Reception ... Mr. Mike JOHNS
91 Director of Technical Support ... Mrs. Pam GOUGH
88 Director of Software Development ... Mr. Jamie BARROWS
88 Director of Network Operations ... Mr. Jamie ANDREWS

Edward Via College of Osteopathic Medicine-Auburn Campus (C)

910 S. Donahue Drive, Auburn AL 36832
Telephone: (334) 442-4000 — Identification: 770965
Accreditation: &OSTEO

† Branch campus of Edward Via College of Osteopathic Medicine, Blacksburg, VA

Faulkner University (D)

5345 Atlanta Highway, Montgomery AL 36109-3398
County: Montgomery — FICE Identification: 001003
Unit ID: 101189
Telephone: (334) 272-5820 — Carnegie Class: Masters/L
FAX Number: (334) 386-7107 — Calendar System: Semester
URL: www.faulkner.edu
Established: 1942 — Annual Undergrad Tuition & Fees: $22,990
Enrollment: 2,961 — Coed
Affiliation or Control: Churches Of Christ — IRS Status: 501(c)3
Highest Offering: Doctorate
Accreditation: SC, #ARCPA, CAEP, IACBE, LAW, @PTA, SP, THEOL

01 President ... Mr. Mitch HENRY
00 Chancellor ... Dr. Billy D. HILYER
05 Vice President Academic Affairs ... Dr. Dave RAMPERSAD
10 Vice President Financial Services ... Mr. Joseph VICKERY
32 Interim VP Student Services ... Ms. Candace CAIN
84 Vice President Enrollment Mgmt ... Mr. Mark HUNT
15 Vice President Human Resources ... Mrs. Renee DAVIS-KEPHART
111 Vice President Advancement ... Dr. John TYSON
43 General Counsel ... Dr. Gerald JONES
61 Dean Jones School of Law ... Dr. Charles CAMPBELL
49 Dean College Arts & Sciences ... Dr. Jeffrey ARRINGTON
50 Dean College Business/Exec Educ ... Dr. Dave KHADANGA
73 Dean College of Biblical Studies ... Dr. Todd BRENNEMAN
53 Dean College of Education ... Dr. Leslie COWELL
76 Dean College of Health Sciences ... Dr. Leah FULLMAN
21 Associate Vice President of Finance ... Mr. Jamie HORN
110 Assoc Vice President Advancement ... Mr. Billy CAMP
61 Assoc Dean Academics Jones Law ... Dr. Michael DEBOER
06 Registrar ... Mr. Don REYNOLDS
37 Director Student Financial Aid ... Ms. Linda PYNES
12 Director Mobile Center ... Dr. Chris COKER
12 Director Birmingham Center ... Vacant
12 Director Huntsville Center ... Mr. Bryan COLLINS
41 Athletic Director ... Mr. Hal WYNN
08 Director of Libraries ... Mrs. Angela MOORE
26 Director of University Marketing ... Mr. Patrick GREGORY
07 Director of Admissions ... Mr. Mike HORN
121 Director Student Success ... Mrs. Michelle OTWELL
92 Director of Honors Program ... Dr. Andrew JACOBS
35 Interim Dean of Students ... Mrs. Keri HARTLEY
36 Director Career Services ... Mrs. Marie OTTINGER
38 Director Counseling Center ... Mrs. Michelle BOND
04 Exec Assistant to the President ... Mrs. Beverly TOLLIVER
19 Director Security/Safety ... Mr. David FOWLER
39 Director Student Housing ... Mrs. Keri HARTLEY
106 Director Faulkner University Online ... Mrs. Tiffany CANTRELL
09 Director of Institutional Research ... Mrs. Breanna YARBROUGH
29 Director Alumni Affairs ... Mr. Joey WIGINTON

Fortis Institute (E)

100 London Parkway Suite 150, Birmingham AL 35211
County: Jefferson — Identification: 666683
Unit ID: 455628
Telephone: (205) 940-7800 — Carnegie Class: Spec 2-yr-Health
FAX Number: (205) 942-6708 — Calendar System: Other
URL: www.fortisinstitute.edu
Established: 2008 — Annual Undergrad Tuition & Fees: $13,649
Enrollment: 551 — Coed
Affiliation or Control: Proprietary — IRS Status: Proprietary
Highest Offering: Associate Degree
Accreditation: ABHES, DH, MLTAD

01 Campus President ... Mr. Khaled SAKALLA
05 Academic Dean ... Ms. Patricia A. CUNNINGHAM
37 Director of Financial Aid ... Ms. Angela MCFADDEN
06 Senior Registrar ... Vacant
07 Director of Admissions ... Ms. Jesse JOHNSON

Heritage Christian University (F)

PO Box HCU, Florence AL 35630-0050
County: Lauderdale — FICE Identification: 021997
Unit ID: 101453
Telephone: (256) 766-6610 — Carnegie Class: Spec-4-yr-Faith
FAX Number: (256) 767-7887 — Calendar System: Semester
URL: www.hcu.edu
Established: 1968 — Annual Undergrad Tuition & Fees: $11,532
Enrollment: 110 — Coed
Affiliation or Control: Churches Of Christ — IRS Status: 501(c)3
Highest Offering: Master's
Accreditation: BI

01 President ... Dr. Kirk BROTHERS
05 VP of Academic Affairs/Dean ... Dr. Michael D. JACKSON
10 Sr Vice Pres Administration ... Mr. Pat MOON
111 Vice President of Advancement ... Mr. Robert YOUNGBLOOD
32 Vice Pres Student Services ... Mr. Travis HARMON
110 Assoc VP of Advancement ... Mr. J.T HARRISON
33 Dean of Men ... Dr. Ed GALLAGHER
34 Dean of Women ... Dr. Rosemary SNODGRASS
58 Director of Graduate Programs ... Dr. Jeremy BARRIER
06 Registrar ... Mr. Nathan B. DAILY
08 Librarian ... Miss Jamie S. COX
78 Director of Field Education ... Mr. Brad MCKINNON
07 Director of Admissions ... Mrs. Rebecca HARRISON
106 Director Distance Learning ... Ms. Autumn RICHARDSON
09 Dir of Institutional Effectiveness ... Mr. Monte TATOM
13 Web Communications and Tech Manager ... Mr. Justin CONNOLLY
26 Director Marketing & Events ... Ms. Brittany VANDER MAAS
37 Director of Financial Aid ... Mrs. Mechelle THOMPSON

Herzing University (G)

280 W Valley Avenue, Birmingham AL 35209-4816
Telephone: (205) 916-2800 — FICE Identification: 010193
Accreditation: &HLC, EMT

† Regional accreditation is carried under the parent institution in Madison, WI.

Huntingdon College (H)

1500 East Fairview Avenue, Montgomery AL 36106-2148
County: Montgomery — FICE Identification: 001019
Unit ID: 101435
Telephone: (334) 833-4497 — Carnegie Class: Bac-Diverse
FAX Number: (334) 833-4347 — Calendar System: Semester
URL: www.huntingdon.edu
Established: 1854 — Annual Undergrad Tuition & Fees: $27,900
Enrollment: 920 — Coed
Affiliation or Control: United Methodist — IRS Status: 501(c)3
Highest Offering: Master's
Accreditation: SC, MUS

01 President ... Rev. J. Cameron WEST
10 Treasurer & SVP for IE/Plng & Admin ... Mr. Jay A. DORMAN
30 SVP for Student & Inst Development ... Mr. Anthony J. LEIGH
05 Chief Academic Officer ... Dr. Thomas PERRIN
07 VP for Admission ... Ms. Stephanie HICKS
09 VP Inst Research & Accreditation ... Dr. Sidney J. STUBBS
13 VP for Technology ... Dr. Anneliese H. SPAETH
26 VP Communications & Marketing ... Ms. Suellen S. OFE
117 VP Risk Management ... Dr. Christopher CLARK
20 Associate Dean of Faculty ... Dr. Sarah C. SOURS
04 Exec Asst to President/Corp Secy ... Ms. Sandra B. KELSER
19 Chief of Security ... Mr. Michael S. WARD
06 Registrar ... Ms. Maryann M. BECK
21 AVP Finance Svcs & Reporting ... Ms. Belinda G. DUETT
41 Director of Athletics ... Mr. Eric LEVANDA
08 Director Houghton Memorial Library ... Mr. Eric A. KIDWELL
121 Dir Staton Ctr for Lrng Enrichment ... Dr. Lisa OLENIK DORMAN
18 VP Auxiliary Services ... Ms. Laura DUNCAN
37 Director of Financial Aid ... Ms. Brittany DAVIS
36 Dir of Center for Career & Vocation ... Ms. Sherry Leigh FARQUHAR
38 Director of Counseling Services ... Dr. Latonya GRAHAM
35 Director of Student Activities ... Mr. Joe THOMAS
42 Chaplain ... Rev. Rhett BUTLER
40 Bookstore Manager ... Ms. Nancy JACKSON
23 Director of Institutional Health ... Ms. Nyree CONVILLE
28 Dir Diversity and Equity Inclusion ... Dr. Chris CLARK

Huntsville Bible College (I)

906 Oakwood Avenue NW, Huntsville AL 35811-1632
County: Madison — FICE Identification: 038943
Unit ID: 449348
Telephone: (256) 469-7536 — Carnegie Class: Spec-4-yr-Faith
FAX Number: (256) 469-7549 — Calendar System: Semester

URL: https://huntsvillebiblecollege.org/
Established: 1986 Annual Undergrad Tuition & Fees: $4,560
Enrollment: 114 Coed
Affiliation or Control: Baptist IRS Status: 501(c)3
Highest Offering: Doctorate
Accreditation: BI

01 President .... Dr. John L. CLAY
05 Dean of Academics/Instruction .... Rev. Chantaye KNOTTS
07 Admissions Officer .... Ms. Vernita CHANDLER
10 Chief Financial Officer .... Ms. Jacqueline ROBINSON
111 Advancement Officer .... Ms. Eloise MCNEALEY
58 Dean of Graduate Studies .... Dr. Mitchell WALKER
20 Dean of Distant Learning .... Rev. Trevor CRENSHAW
32 Director of Student Services .... Ms. Linda FLETCHER
08 Director of Library Media .... Ms. Victoria RICHARDSON
08 Librarian .... Ms. Carla CLIFT
37 Financial Aid Ofcr/Title IX Coord .... Ms. Doris LACEY
04 Administrative Assistant .... Ms. Cindy SMITH

Jacksonville State University (A)

700 Pelham Road N, Jacksonville AL 36265-1602
County: Calhoun FICE Identification: 001020
Unit ID: 101480
Telephone: (256) 782-5881 Carnegie Class: Masters/L
FAX Number: (256) 782-5888 Calendar System: Semester
URL: www.jsu.edu
Established: 1883 Annual Undergrad Tuition & Fees (In-State): $11,120
Enrollment: 9,238 Coed
Affiliation or Control: State IRS Status: 501(c)3
Highest Offering: Doctorate
Accreditation: SC, AAFCS, ABAI, ART, CAATE, CACREP, CAEP, #COARC, DIETD, #JOUR, MUS, NAIT, NURSE, SPAA, SW, THEA

01 President .... Dr. Don C. KILLINGSWORTH
05 Provost/Sr VP Academic Affairs .... Dr. Christie SHELTON
10 Sr VP Finance & Administration .... Dr. Arlitha WILLIAMS-HARMON
111 VP for University Advancement .... Dr. Emily MESSER
32 VP Student Affairs .... Mr. Terry CASEY
84 VP for Enrollment Management .... Dr. Emily W. MESSER
121 Vice Provost Student Success .... Dr. Tim KING
13 VP Information Technology .... Mr. Vinson HOUSTON
116 Chief Internal Auditor .... Mr. Nelson CLARK
15 Director Human Resources .... Ms. Allison CASEY
43 Legal Counsel .... Mr. Greg HARLEY
41 Director Athletics .... Mr. Greg SEITZ
20 Vice Provost .... Vacant
57 Dean School of Arts & Hum .... Dr. Staci L. STONE
81 Dean School of Science .... Dr. Timothy LINDBLOM
76 Dean School Health Prof & Wellness ... Dr. Tracey D. MATTHEWS
53 Dean School of Education .... Dr. Kimberly WHITE
50 Int Dean Sch of Business & Industry ..... Dr. Brent CUNNINGHAM
83 Dean School Human Svc & Soc Science .... Dr. Mary NEWTON
08 Dean Library Services .... Mr. John-Bauer GRAHAM
88 Associate Vice Provost .... Ms. Lisa M. WILLIAMS
06 Registrar .... Ms. Emily WHITE
21 University Controller .... Vacant
109 Assoc VP Business & Aux Svcs .... Dr. Kevin HOULT
30 Exec Dir University Development .... Mr. William NASH
39 Director Residence Life .... Ms. Rochelle SMITH
39 Dir Univ Housing Operations .... Ms. Brooke LYON
85 Dir International Programs .... Ms. Chandni KHADKA
09 Sr Dir Inst Research/Effectiveness .... Ms. Kim PRESSON
29 Director of Alumni Relations .... Ms. Kaci OGLE
37 Director Financial Aid .... Ms. Charlotte COLE
18 Dir Capital Planning/Facilities .... Mr. David THOMPSON
36 Career Development Coordinator .... Ms. Rebecca E. TURNER
88 Dir Disability Resources .... Dr. Sean CREECH
96 Procurement/Fixed Assets .... Ms. Denise HUNT
26 Chief Marketing/Comm Officer .... Mr. Tim GARNER
19 Director Public Safety .... Mr. Michael BARTON
22 Dir Com Standards & Title IX .... Ms. Jasmine NUNEZ
04 Admin Assistant to the President ...... Ms. Catherine H. CHAPPELL
106 Director Online Education/E-learnin .... Mr. Chris CASEY
07 Director of Admissions .... Ms. Lauren FINDLEY
105 University Webmaster .... Mr. Chris NEWSOME
28 Director of Diversity .... Ms. Charlcie P. VANN
86 Chief External Officer .... Ms. Leigha CAUTHEN

Miles College (B)

5500 Myron Massey Boulevard, Fairfield AL 35064-2621
County: Jefferson FICE Identification: 001028
Unit ID: 101675
Telephone: (205) 929-1000 Carnegie Class: Bac-Diverse
FAX Number: (205) 929-1453 Calendar System: Semester
URL: www.miles.edu
Established: 1898 Annual Undergrad Tuition & Fees: $12,714
Enrollment: 1,440 Coed
Affiliation or Control: Christian Methodist Episcopal IRS Status: 501(c)3
Highest Offering: Baccalaureate
Accreditation: SC, ACBSP, CAEP, SW

01 President .... Ms. Bobbie KNIGHT
05 Provost/Sr VP Academic Affairs .... Dr. Jarralynne AGEE
10 Sr VP Finance/Business Admin .... Ms. Diana KNIGHTON
111 VP Institutional Advancement .... Mr. Arthur J. BRIGATI
42 Dean of Chapel/VP Stdnt Life/Engage .... Rev. Larry BATIE
84 VP Enrollment Mgmt/Chief Innov Ofcr .. Mr. Michael A. JOHNSON
32 Dean of Students/Alumni Affairs .... Mr. Charles STALLWORTH
100 Chief of Staff .... Mr. Kenneth COACHMAN
06 College Registrar .... Vacant
41 Athletic Director .... Mr. Reginald RUFFIN
106 Dean of Online Education .... Dr. Vidal ADADEVOH
15 Director Human Resources .... Vacant
18 Director Building Operations .... Mr. Richard WILLIS
37 Asst Director Financial Aid .... Ms. Nakia BELSER

Oakwood University (C)

7000 Adventist Boulevard, NW, Huntsville AL 35896-0003
County: Madison FICE Identification: 001033
Unit ID: 101912
Telephone: (256) 726-7000 Carnegie Class: Bac-A&S
FAX Number: N/A Calendar System: Semester
URL: www.oakwood.edu
Established: 1896 Annual Undergrad Tuition & Fees: $19,990
Enrollment: 1,374 Coed
Affiliation or Control: Seventh-day Adventist IRS Status: 501(c)3
Highest Offering: Master's
Accreditation: SC, ACBSP, CAEPN, DIETD, DIETI, NUR, SW, THEOL

01 President/CEO .... Dr. Leslie POLLARD
05 Interim Provost .... Dr. James MBYIRUKIRA
10 Vice President Financial Admin .... Ms. Sabrina COTTON
32 VP Student Life & Mission .... Dr. David RICHARDSON
46 VP QAResearch & Faculty Development .... Dr. Prudence L. POLLARD
84 VP Enrollment Svcs/Retention .... Dr. Karen BENN MARSHALL
111 Exec Dir Advancement/Development .... Mrs. Cheri WILSON
20 Asst VP Academic Administration .... Vacant
21 Asst VP Financial Admin/Controller .... Mrs. Gail CALDWELL
35 Asst VP Student Life & Mission .... Ms. Adrienne MATTHEWS
13 Chief Info Technology Officer (CIO) .... Vacant
15 Int Exec Dir of Empl Svcs/Human Res .... Mrs. Sylvia GERMANY
25 Contracts .... Ms. Cheryl SULLIVAN
26 Director Public Relations .... Vacant
07 Director Recruitment & Admissions .... Mr. Lewis JONES
37 Director Financial Aid .... Mrs. Julain GUNN CLARKE
06 Registrar .... Ms. Traci MOORE
39 Residence Life Coordinator-Men .... Mr. Woodrow VAUGHN
39 Resident Life Coordinator-Women .... Ms. Linda ANDERSON
08 Director Library Services .... Mrs. Heather RODRIGUEZ JAMES
18 Director Physical Plant .... Mr. Handel FRASER
19 Director Security .... Mr. Melvin HARRIS
38 Dir Counseling & Health Services .... Vacant
51 Dir Adult & Continuing Education ..... Mrs. Ellengold GOODRIDGE
121 Dean for Student Success .... Vacant
50 Dean Business & Info Systems .... Dr. Theodore BROWN
53 Dean Education .... Dr. James MBYIRUKIRA
76 Chair Allied Health .... Dr. Andrew YOUNG
88 Chair English & Foreign Languages .... Dr. Benson PRIGG
64 Chair Music .... Dr. Jason FERDINAND
81 Chair Biological Sciences .... Dr. Elaine VANTERPOOL
88 Dean Chemistry .... Vacant
66 Chair Nursing .... Dr. Dorothy FORDE
68 Chair Health & Human Sciences .... Dr. Andrew YOUNG
70 Chair Social Work .... Dr. Shalunda SHERROD
73 Dean Religion & Theology .... Dr. R Clifford JONES
77 Chair Math & Computer Science .... Dr. Lisa JAMES
82 Chair History & Political Science .... Dr. Samuel LONDON
83 Chair Psychology .... Dr. Martin HODNETT
60 Chair Communication .... Dr. Rennae ELLIOTT

Remington College, Mobile Campus (D)

4368 Downtowner Loop South, Mobile AL 36609
County: Mobile FICE Identification: 026055
Unit ID: 366535
Telephone: (251) 343-8200 Carnegie Class: Assoc/HVT-Mix Trad/Non
FAX Number: (251) 343-0577 Calendar System: Quarter
URL: www.remingtoncollege.edu
Established: 1986 Annual Undergrad Tuition & Fees: $17,148
Enrollment: 248 Coed
Affiliation or Control: Independent Non-Profit IRS Status: 501(c)3
Highest Offering: Associate Degree
Accreditation: ACCSC

01 Director of Campus Administration .... Tekia ROCKER
05 Dean .... Tekia ROCKER
07 Director of Admissions .... Tasha CARTER
06 Registrar/Retention .... Don SCHERMERHORN
32 Student Success Coordinator .... Jayne HARRIS

Samford University (E)

800 Lakeshore Drive, Birmingham AL 35229-0001
County: Jefferson FICE Identification: 001036
Unit ID: 102049
Telephone: (205) 726-2011 Carnegie Class: DU-Mod
FAX Number: (205) 726-2171 Calendar System: Semester
URL: www.samford.edu
Established: 1841 Annual Undergrad Tuition & Fees: $34,198
Enrollment: 5,729 Coed
Affiliation or Control: Baptist IRS Status: 501(c)3
Highest Offering: Doctorate
Accreditation: SC, ANEST, #ARCPA, @AUD, CAEP, CIDA, DIETD, DIETI, LAW, MUS, NURSE, PHAR, PTA, SP, SW, THEA, THEOL

01 President .... Dr. Beck A. TAYLOR
125 President Emeritus .... Dr. Andrew WESTMORELAND
100 Chief of Staff .... Dr. Michael D. MORGAN
43 General Counsel .... Mr. W. Clark WATSON
41 Athletic Director .... Mr. Martin NEWTON
04 Exec Assistant to the President .... Ms. Darlene KUHN
05 Provost .... Dr. Michael HARDIN
28 Associate Provost .... Dr. Denise GREGORY
108 Sr Associate Provost .... Dr. Marci S. JOHNS
06 Registrar .... Mr. Jeremy DIXON
88 Asst Provost Faculty Success .... Dr. P J HUGHES
25 Chief Contract/Grants Administrator .... Ms. Linnea MINNEMA
08 Dean of University Library .... Dr. Kimmetha D. HERNDON
76 Dean of Health Professions .... Dr. Alan JUNG
49 Dean Howard College Arts/Sciences .... Mr. Tim HALL
50 Dean Brock School of Business .... Dr. Chad M. CARSON
88 Director of University Fellows .... Dr. Todd KRULAK
73 Dean Beeson School of Divinity .... Dr. Douglas A. SWEENEY
104 Director Global Engagement .... Ms. Lauren DOSS
53 Dean OB School of Education .... Dr. Anna MCEWAN
61 Dean Cumberland School of Law .... Mr. Blake HUDSON
57 Int Dean School of the Arts .... Mr. Larry THOMPSON
66 Dean School of Nursing .... Dr. Melondia R. CARTER
69 Int Dean of Public Health .... Dr. Melissa LUMPKIN
67 Dean School of Pharmacy .... Dr. Michael A. CROUCH
111 VP for Univ Advancement .... Dr. Betsy B. HOLLOWAY
26 Asst VP Marketing & PR .... Ms. Jessica BLACK
105 Asst VP Creative & Web .... Mr. Todd COTTON
27 Executive Dir Broadcast Media .... Mr. Brad RADICE
30 Asst VP Univ Adv & Exec Dir Devel .... Mr. Douglas WILSON
112 Director Gift and Estate Planning .... Mr. Gene HOWARD
110 Sr Dir of Philanthropic Engagement .... Ms. Rhonda WHITE
88 Director Parent Programs .... Ms. Julie BOYD
29 Exec Director Alumni Programs .... Ms. Casey RAMEY
10 VP Finance/Business/Strategy .... Mr. Colin M. COYNE
109 Director of Business Services .... Mr. Wade WALKER
115 Sr AVP Business & Financial Affairs .... Ms. Lisa IMBRAGULIO
15 Asst VP & Dir of Human Resources .... Mr. Joel WINDHAM
18 Assoc VP Operations .... Mr. Jeff POLECHEK
19 Director Public Safety .... Dr. Tommy TAYLOR
21 Controller .... Mr. Mike DARWIN
13 Chief Information Officer .... Ms. Debi WHITCOMB
90 Director Learning Applications .... Mr. Chad OWENS
114 Dir of Budget & Financial Planning .... Mr. Matt DEFORE
09 Director of Institutional Research .... Mr. Toner EVANS
18 Director Operations .... Ms. Allison BRYMER
88 Dir Strat & Appl Analysis .... Dr. Randolph HORN
32 Vice President for Student Affairs .... Dr. Phil KIMREY
124 Asst VP for Student Development .... Ms. April ROBINSON
38 Director Student Counseling .... Mr. Richard YOAKUM
84 VP for Enrollment Mgmt .... Mr. Jason BLACK
39 Asst VP Campus & Residential Life .... Ms. Lauren M. TAYLOR
22 Director of Diversity Access .... Mr. David PRESLEY
37 Dir of Student Financial Services .... Mr. Lane M. SMITH
36 Dir Career Development .... Ms. Dora DITCHFIELD

Selma University (F)

1501 Lapsley Street, Selma AL 36701-5232
County: Dallas FICE Identification: 001037
Unit ID: 102058
Telephone: (334) 872-2533 Carnegie Class: Not Classified
FAX Number: (334) 872-7746 Calendar System: Semester
URL: www.selmauniversity.edu
Established: 1878 Annual Undergrad Tuition & Fees: N/A
Enrollment: N/A Coed
Affiliation or Control: Baptist IRS Status: 501(c)3
Highest Offering: Master's
Accreditation: #BI

01 President .... Dr. Stanford ANGION
05 Chief Academic Officer .... Dr. Cheryl WASHINGTON
32 Vice Pres Student Affairs .... Vacant
10 Int Chief Financial Officer .... Uletor NIX
06 Registrar .... Ms. Marion HARRIS
100 Chief of Staff/Compliance Officer .... Mr. James E. BURRELL

South University (G)

5355 Vaughn Road, Montgomery AL 36116-1120
Telephone: (334) 395-8800 FICE Identification: 004463
Accreditation: &SC, ACBSP, MAC, NURSE, PTAA

† Regional accreditation is carried under the parent institution in Savannah, GA.

Spring Hill College (H)

4000 Dauphin Street, Mobile AL 36608-1791
County: Mobile FICE Identification: 001041
Unit ID: 102234
Telephone: (251) 380-4000 Carnegie Class: Bac-Diverse
FAX Number: (251) 460-2182 Calendar System: Semester
URL: www.shc.edu
Established: 1830 Annual Undergrad Tuition & Fees: $41,868
Enrollment: 1,191 Coed
Affiliation or Control: Roman Catholic IRS Status: 501(c)3
Highest Offering: Master's
Accreditation: SC, NURSE

01 President .... Dr. Joseph LEE
10 Vice President Finance/Accounting .... Dr. Kenneth ENGLAND
30 VP Alumni Relations/Development .... Dr. Racheal BANKS
32 Vice Pres Student Affairs .... Mr. Kevin ABEL

13	Director of IT	Mr. Christopher HUGHES
20	Associate Provost	Vacant
21	Treasury Manager	Ms. Heidi BUTLER
37	Director of Financial Aid	Ms. Rebecca ROBINSON
06	Registrar	Ms. Linnea BATTLES
121	Director Student Advising Services	Mr. Michael COZART
29	Director of Alumni Relations	Vacant
15	Director of Personnel	Ms. Lisa ROBINSON
07	Director of Admissions	Mr. Jacon JONES
19	Director of Public Safety/Security	Mr. Kevin ANDERSON
38	Director of Counseling Services	Ms. Chiara JOHNSON
42	Director of Campus Ministry	Ms. Colleen LEE
41	Director Athletics & Recreation	Mr. Joseph NILAND, JR.
31	Dir Foley Community Service Center	Ms. Jennifer IRIZARRY
26	Dir Communications/Instl Marketing	Ms. Tyloria CRENSHAW
27	Communications Officer	Mr. Fletcher DEVERY
36	Director of Career Services	Ms. Jordan COCKRELL
40	Bookstore Manager	Vacant
08	Director of Library	Mr. Bret HEIM
39	Dir Resident Life/Student Housing	Mr. Nathan MCQUINN
44	Director Annual Giving	Vacant
03	Executive Vice President	Dr. Kenneth ENGLAND
04	Admin Assistant to the President	Ms. Laura ALLSUP

Stillman College (A)

3601 Stillman Boulevard, Tuscaloosa AL 35401
County: Tuscaloosa — FICE Identification: 001044
Unit ID: 102270
Telephone: (205) 366-8817 — Carnegie Class: Bac-Diverse
FAX Number: N/A — Calendar System: Semester
URL: www.stillman.edu
Established: 1876 — Annual Undergrad Tuition & Fees: $11,322
Enrollment: 712 — Coed
Affiliation or Control: Presbyterian Church (U.S.A.) — IRS Status: 501(c)3
Highest Offering: Baccalaureate
Accreditation: SC, CAEPN, IACBE

01	President	Dr. Cynthia WARRICK
03	Executive Vice President	Mr. Derrick C. GILMORE
05	Provost/VP Academic Affairs	Dr. Mark MCCORMICK
10	Chief Financial Officer	Mr. Chavis PAULK
108	VP Institutional Effectiveness	Dr. Victoria BOMAN
111	VP Institutional Advancement	Ms. Luanne BAKER
32	Vice President for Students Affairs	Rev. Tyshawn GARDNER
31	Director Community Relations	Mr. Mason BONNER
13	Director of Info Tech	Vacant
26	VP Strategic Initiatives	Mrs. RaSheda WORKMAN
29	Director Alumni Affairs	Ms. Jean WILSON-SYKES
18	Senior Director Campus Services	Mr. Phillip CUNNINGHAM
53	Dean of Education	Dr. James GRAY
49	Dean of Arts & Sciences	Dr. Norman GOLAR
50	Dean School of Business	Mr. Isaac MCCOY
08	Dean of Library	Ms. Evelyn KING
37	Director of Financial Aid	Mr. Kenneth WILSON
23	Dir Student Development/Health Svcs	Vacant
13	Director of Info Technology	Mr. Michael HUBBARD
85	Director of Intl Student Affairs	Mr. Kyris BROWN
19	Chief of Campus Police	Ms. Carla LONGMIRE
41	Athletic Director	Mr. Kenyon ALSTON
15	Director Human Resources	Ms. LaKeya GOINS
42	College Chaplain	Dr. Joseph SCRIVNER
101	Board Liaison	Ms. RaSheda WORKMAN
04	Executive Asst to President	Ms. Markedia WELLS
35	Dean of Student Life	Mr. Marcus KENNEDY
06	Registrar	Mrs. Greta EUBANKS
106	Director of Online Education	Ms. Kristi GARRETT
30	Director of Development	Mr. Tyler DAVIDSON
124	Dean of Retention and Placement	Ms. Tasha WASHINGTON
84	Director Enrollment Management	Mrs. Valarie WILSON

Talladega College (B)

627 W. Battle Street, Talladega AL 35160-2354
County: Talladega — FICE Identification: 001046
Unit ID: 102298
Telephone: (256) 761-6212 — Carnegie Class: Bac-Diverse
FAX Number: (256) 761-8680 — Calendar System: Semester
URL: www.talladega.edu
Established: 1867 — Annual Undergrad Tuition & Fees: $13,866
Enrollment: 1,156 — Coed
Affiliation or Control: Independent Non-Profit — IRS Status: 501(c)3
Highest Offering: Master's
Accreditation: SC, SW

01	President	Dr. Billy C. HAWKINS
05	Provost/VP for Academic Affairs	Dr. Lisa LONG
10	VP Finance & Administration/CFO	Vacant
32	Vice President Student Affairs	Dr. Jeffery BURGIN
111	VP Institutional Advancement	Dr. Kristie KENNEY
18	Director Facilities Management	Mr. Thomas GANCHUK
37	Director Financial Aid	Ms. Amanda HEADEN
07	Director of Admissions	Mr. Joel SWAN
09	Int Director Institutional Research	Dr. Syed RAZA
35	Interim VP Student Affairs	Mr. Michael BROWN
41	Athletic Director	Mr. Kevin HEROD
08	Librarian/Director	Vacant
13	Interim IT Director	Ms. Norda THREATT
36	Director of Career Placement	Ms. Sherissa GAITOR
19	Chief Campus Police	Ms. Shajuana DENNARD
50	Dean Div Administration & Business	Dr. Jonathan ELIMIMIAN
79	Dean Div Humanities/Fine Arts	Dr. Angela WALKER
81	Dean Div of Natural Sci/Math	Dr. Alison BROWN

83	Dean Div EWJ Social Sciences/Educ	Dr. Rebecca MCKAY
21	Senior Associate Vice President	Mr. Bruce SMITH
23	Health Services on Campus	Ms. Stanmetrica CURRY
25	Title III Coor/Grants Administrator	Dr. Charles SMITH
29	Director Alumni Relations	Mr. Anthony JONES
06	Registrar	Ms. Barbra SMITH
38	Director Office of Counseling/ADA	Mr. Michael BROWN
104	Director Study Abroad	Vacant
15	Human Resources Manager	Mrs. Brenda RHODEN
26	Director of Public Relations	Ms. Pasiley BOSTON
39	Director of Housing and Residence	Ms. Candace GARRETT
124	Director of Special Events/Protocol	Mr. Anthony JONES
04	Admin Assistant to the President	Mrs. Nadine BALLARD

Troy University (C)

University Avenue, Troy AL 36082-0001
County: Pike — FICE Identification: 001047
Unit ID: 102368
Telephone: (334) 670-3100 — Carnegie Class: Masters/L
FAX Number: (334) 670-3774 — Calendar System: Semester
URL: www.troy.edu
Established: 1887 — Annual Undergrad Tuition & Fees (In-State): $8,908
Enrollment: 16,497 — Coed
Affiliation or Control: State — IRS Status: 501(c)3
Highest Offering: Doctorate
Accreditation: SC, ACBSP, ADNUR, CAATE, CACREP, CAEP, COSMA, MUS, NUR, SW

01	Chancellor	Dr. Jack HAWKINS, JR.
05	Sr Vice Chanc for Academic Affairs	Dr. Lance TATUM
32	Sr Vice Chanc Student Svcs/Admin	Mr. Sohail AGBOATWALA
111	Int SVC Advancement/Economic Dev	Dr. John SCHMIDT
10	Sr VC for Fin Affs & Online Educ	Dr. James BOOKOUT
15	Assoc VC for Human Resources	MS. Ashley ENGLISH
12	Vice Chancellor Troy Dothan	Dr. Don JEFFREY
12	Vice Chancellor Troy Phenix City	Dr. Dionne ROSSER-MIMS
12	Vice Chanc Troy Montgomery	Mr. Ray WHITE
35	Assoc Dean of Student Svcs Dothan	Ms. Sandra HENRY
20	Asst Dean of Academics	Vacant
53	Assoc Dean Col of Education	Dr. Fred FIGLIANO
49	CAS Campus Coordinator Montgomery	Mr. Martin OLLIFF
49	CAS Campus Coordinator Dothan	Dr. Robert VILARDI
30	Assoc Vice Chanc for Development	Ms. Rebecca WATSON
37	Assoc VC for Financial Aid	Ms. Angela JOHNSON
20	Associate Provost for Academics	Dr. Lee VARDAMAN
26	Chief Marketing Officer	Ms. Samantha JOHNSON
21	Assoc Vice Chanc/Controller	Ms. Tara DONALDSON
06	Registrar	Ms. Vickie MILES
84	Assoc VC for Enrollment Management	Mr. Buddy STARLING
08	Dean Library Services	Dr. Chris SHAFFER
13	Chief Technology Officer	Dr. Greg PRICE
27	Director University Relations	Mr. Matthew CLOWER
29	Director Alumni Affairs	Ms. Faith W. WARD
36	Coordinator Career Services	Ms. Lauren COLE
18	Director Facilities/Physical Plant	Vacant
60	Interim Director of Journalism	Dr. Amanda DIGGS
04	Exec Assistant to the Chancellor	Mr. Tom DAVIS
38	University Counselor	Ms. Fran SCHEEL
123	Director of Graduate Admissions	Vacant
88	Associate Controller	Ms. Brenda JOHNS
09	Senior Director of IRPE	Mr. Ronnie CREEL
86	Director of Governmental Relations	Mr. Marcus PARAMORE
44	Director of Annual Giving	Ms. Meredith WELCH
25	Director Sponsored Programs	Ms. Judy FULMER
08	Int Dir of Library Svcs Troy Dothan	Mr. Martin OLLIFF
08	Dir of Lib Svcs Troy Montgomery	Mr. Jeff SIMPSON
20	Dean Undergrad Pgms/Assoc Provost	Dr. Hal FULMER
35	Dean of Student Svcs Troy Campus	Mr. Herbert REEVES
49	Dean Arts & Sciences	Dr. Steven TAYLOR
50	Dean Business	Dr. Judson EDWARDS
53	Dean Education	Dr. Kerry PALMER
58	Assoc Provost/Dean Graduate Pgms	Dr. Mary TEMPLETON
76	Dean Health/Human Services	Dr. John GARNER
57	Dean Communication/Fine Arts	Dr. Larry BLOCHER
35	Assoc Dean Student Svcs Troy Mont	Dr. James SMITH
39	Director Student Housing	Mr. Herbert REEVES
41	Sr Vice Chanc for Athletics	Mr. Brent JONES
85	Assoc Dean Intl Student Services	Ms. Maria FRIGGE
105	Director Web Services	Mr. John LESTER
108	Director Institutional Assessment	Ms. Wendy BROYLES
19	Chief of University Police	Mr. George BEAUDRY
104	Study Abroad Coordinator	Ms. Sarah MCKENZIE
96	Director of Procurement & Asset Mgt	Ms. April JOHNSON

Tuskegee University (D)

1200 W. Montgomery Road, Tuskegee Inst. AL 36088
County: Macon — FICE Identification: 001050
Unit ID: 102377
Telephone: (334) 727-8011 — Carnegie Class: Masters/M
FAX Number: (334) 727-5276 — Calendar System: Semester
URL: www.tuskegee.edu
Established: 1881 — Annual Undergrad Tuition & Fees: $22,614
Enrollment: 2,747 — Coed
Affiliation or Control: Independent Non-Profit — IRS Status: 501(c)3
Highest Offering: Doctorate
Accreditation: SC, CAEPN, CONST, DIETD, NUR, OT, SW, #VET

01	President	Dr. Charlotte P. MORRIS
05	Provost/SVP Academic Affairs	Vacant
10	Exec Vice Pres Finance/CFO	Ms. Kimberly LEWIS

46	Vice Pres Research/Dean Grad Stdnts	Dr. Shaik JEELANI
18	Vice Pres Facilities/Construction	Vacant
32	Vice Pres Student Affairs	Vacant
15	Chief Human Resources Officer	Ms. Cassandra TARVER-ROSS
43	VP External Affairs/General Counsel	Vacant
26	Sr Dir Comm/Public Rels/Mktg	Mr. Michael TULLIER
101	Exec Asst to Pres/Secy to the Board	Mrs. Chandra CHAMBLISS
13	Chief Information Officer	Ms. Bernice GREEN
114	Asst Vice Pres Budget & Planning	Vacant
20	Asst Provost	Dr. Tamara FLOYD-SMITH
47	Dean of CAENS	Dr. Walter A. HILL
09	AVP Institutional Research	Dr. Kellei BISHOP -SAMUELS
53	Dean School of Education	Dr. Carlton E. MORRIS
50	Dean Col Business/Info Sciences	Dr. Kia KOONG
54	Dean College of Engineering	Dr. Heshmat AGLAN
66	Dean Sch Nursing/Allied Health	Dr. Constance HENDRICKS
35	Dean of Student Life	Ms. Tameka ANGOLA HARPER
42	Dean of the Chapel	Dr. Gregory S. GRAY
08	Director of Library Services	Mrs. Juanita ROBERTS
30	Director of Development	Ms. Krystal FLOYD
29	Alumni Affairs Director	Ms. Kimberly HOLLAND
102	Dir Corp/Foundation Relations	Vacant
51	Int Assoc Prov Cont Educ/Extension	Dr. Ntam BAHARANYI
36	Asst Career Development/Placement	Ms. Chantel BOYD
113	Asst Bursar	Ms. Stacie HENDERSON
37	Director of Financial Aid	Mr. Advergus D. JAMES, JR.
18	Project Mgr Sodexho/Physical Plant	Mr. Tony WARD
91	Director of Applications Support	Ms. Jamie REYNOLDS
06	Registrar	Dr. Elaine BROMFIELD
96	Director of Purchasing	Ms. Cassandra PARKER
48	Interim Dean School of Architecture	Mr. Roderick FLUKER
74	Dean College of Veterinary Medicine	Dr. Rubye PERRY
49	Dean College of Arts and Sciences	Dr. Channapatana PRAKASH
88	Dean National Center Bioethics	Dr. Reuben WARREN
07	Director of Admissions	Vacant
100	Chief of Staff	Dr. Shirley FRIAR
104	Director Study Abroad	Dr. Rhonda COLLIER
11	Chief of Operations	Dr. Charles SMITH
19	Director Security/Safety	Chief Patrick MARDIS
38	Coordinator Student Counseling	Mrs. Ardelia M. LUNN
39	Director Housing & Residence Life	Mr. William SAMUEL, SR.
41	Athletic Director	Mr. Willie SLATER

United States Sports Academy (E)

One Academy Drive, Daphne AL 36526-7055
County: Baldwin — FICE Identification: 021706
Unit ID: 102395
Telephone: (251) 626-3303 — Carnegie Class: Spec-4-yr-Other
FAX Number: (251) 621-2527 — Calendar System: Semester
URL: www.ussa.edu
Established: 1972 — Annual Undergrad Tuition & Fees: N/A
Enrollment: 338 — Coed
Affiliation or Control: Independent Non-Profit — IRS Status: 501(c)3
Highest Offering: Doctorate
Accreditation: SC, ACBSP

01	President & CEO	Dr. Thomas J. ROSANDICH
05	Provost	Dr. Tomi WAHLSTROM
10	Director of Admin & Finance	Ms. Tania DAVIS
26	Director of Communications	Mr. Eric MANN
88	Chair of Sports Management	Dr. Brandon SPRADLEY
58	Director of Doctoral Studies	Dr. Fred CROMARTIE
88	Chair of Sports Coaching	Dr. Roch KING
20	Dean of Undergraduate Studies	Dr. Vandy PACETTI-DONELSON
68	Actg Dir of Sports Exercise Science	Mr. Robert HERRON
06	Registrar	Ms. Ashley BARNES
18	Building and Grounds	Mr. Ed SWANN
13	Chief Info Technology Officer	Mr. Anthony FRANKLIN
105	Web Master	Mr. Corey BLAKE
15	Human Resources Generalist	Ms. Brandy CORNIE
37	Financial Aid Counselor	Ms. Autumn JORDAN
120	Senior Instructional Designer	Ms. Holly PARK

*University of Alabama System Office (F)

500 University Boulevard East, Tuscaloosa AL 35401
County: Tuscaloosa — FICE Identification: 008004
Unit ID: 100733
Telephone: (205) 348-5861 — Carnegie Class: N/A
FAX Number: (205) 348-9788
URL: www.uasystem.ua.edu

01	Chancellor	Mr. Finis E. ST. JOHN, IV
43	General Counsel/Sr Vice Chancellor	Mr. Sid J. TRANT
05	Sr VC Academic/Student Affairs	Dr. Tonjanita JOHNSON
10	SVC Finance/Administration	Dr. Dana S. KEITH
26	Director of System Communications	Mrs. Lynn L. COLE
86	Sr Vice Chanc for External Affairs	Mr. Clay M. RYAN
15	Asst Vice Chanc for Human Resources	Mr. Jon GARNER
86	Director of External Affairs	Mr. Charlie M. TAYLOR
19	Director of System Security	Mr. Steve ANDERSON
101	Secretary of the Board of Trustees	Mr. Mark D. FOLEY
116	Chief Audit/Compliance Officer	Mr. Chip BIVINS

*The University of Alabama (G)

801 University Boulevard, Tuscaloosa AL 35487
County: Tuscaloosa — FICE Identification: 001051
Unit ID: 100751
Telephone: (205) 348-6010 — Carnegie Class: DU-Highest
FAX Number: N/A — Calendar System: Semester
URL: www.ua.edu

Established: 1831 Annual Undergrad Tuition & Fees (In-State): $11,620
Enrollment: 37,840 Coed
Affiliation or Control: State IRS Status: 501(c)3
Highest Offering: Doctorate
Accreditation: SC, ART, CAATE, CACREP, CAEPN, CEA, CIDA, CLPSY, DANCE, DIETC, DIETD, JOUR, LAW, LIB, MUS, NAEYC, NURSE, SP, SPAA, SW, THEA

02 President .... Dr. Stuart R. BELL
100 Chief Administrative Officer .... Mr. Chad TINDOL
05 Executive Vice President & Provost .... Dr. James DALTON
28 VP for Diversity/Equity & Inclusion .... Dr. G. Christine TAYLOR
10 Vice Pres for Financial Affairs .... Mr. Matt FAJACK
111 Vice Pres for Advancement .... Mr. Robert 'Bob' PIERCE
32 Interim Vice Pres for Student Life .... Dr. Steven HOOD
88 Vice Pres for Community Affairs .... Dr. Samory T. PRUITT
26 VP Strategic Communications .... Mr. Ryan BRADLEY
46 Vice President for Research .... Dr. Russell J. MUMPER
13 Vice Provost/Chief Information Ofcr .... Dr. John MCGOWAN
18 Assoc VP Facilities/Grounds .... Col. Duane LAMB
18 Sr Assoc VP Campus Development .... Mr. Tim LEOPARD
19 Assoc VP Public Safety .... Dr. Ralph CLAYTON
21 Assoc Provost for Financial Affairs .... Mr. Jordan JOHNSON
20 Sr Assoc Provost Academic Affairs .... Dr. Luoheng HAN
20 Assoc Provost Academic Affairs .... Dr. Patty SOBECKY
15 Assoc VP Human Resources .... Ms. Nancy H. WHITTAKER
21 Assoc Vice President for Finance .... Ms. Julie SHELTON
21 Asst Vice Pres Finance & Operations .... Ms. Cheryl MOWDY
27 Assoc VP Communications .... Ms. Monica WATTS
88 Director Marketing .... Mr. Jimmy HART
29 Director of Alumni Affairs .... Mr. Calvin BROWN
85 Assoc Provost Internatl Educ .... Dr. Teresa WISE
06 University Registrar .... Dr. Kenneth H. FOSHEE
09 Director Inst Research/Assessment .... Dr. Lorne KUFFEL
36 Int Exec Director Career Center .... Dr. Schernavia HALL
84 Assoc VP Enrollment Mgmt .... Mr. Matthew MCLENDON
22 Exec Dir Institutional Compliance .... Dr. Marcy HUEY
37 Director of Student Financial Aid .... Ms. Helen ALLEN
39 Exec Director Housing/Res Cmty .... Mr. Matthew KERCH
40 Asst VP Enterprise Operations .... Ms. Teresa SHREVE
41 Athletic Director .... Mr. Greg BYRNE
43 Chief University Counsel .... Mr. Robin JONES
08 Dean of University Libraries .... Dr. Donald GILSTRAP
49 Dean of Arts & Sciences .... Dr. Joseph P. MESSINA
50 Dean Culverhouse Col of Business .... Dr. Kay M. PALAN
51 Dean Col of Cont Studies .... Dr. Jonathon HALBESLEBEN
53 Dean College of Education .... Dr. Peter HLEBOWITSH
54 Dean College of Engineering .... Dr. Clifford L. HENDERSON
58 Assoc Provost/Dean Graduate School .... Dr. Susan CARVALHO
59 Dean Human Environmental Sciences .... Dr. Stuart USDAN
60 Dean Col of Communication/Info Sci .... Dr. Brian S. BUTLER
61 Dean School of Law .... Dr. Mark E. BRANDON
62 Dir Sch of Library/Info Studies .... Dr. James ELMBORG
38 Manager Stdnt Support Svcs-Trio Pgm .... Ms. Wendy CHRISTIAN
96 Purchasing Manager .... Mr. Lane COX
76 Dean Cmty Health Sciences .... Dr. Ricky FRIEND
66 Dean Capstone College of Nursing .... Dr. Suzanne S. PREVOST
70 Dean School of Social Work .... Dr. Schnavia HATCHER
92 Interim Dean of Honors College .... Dr. Luoheng HAN
94 Dir Women & Gender Resource Ctr .... Ms. Elle SHAABAN-MAGANA
122 Exec Dir Fraternity/Sorority Life .... Ms. Patricia WILSON

*University of Alabama at Birmingham (A)

1720 2nd Avenue South, Birmingham AL 35294-0001
County: Jefferson FICE Identification: 001052
Unit ID: 100663
Telephone: (205) 934-4011 Carnegie Class: DU-Highest
FAX Number: N/A Calendar System: Semester
URL: www.uab.edu
Established: 1969 Annual Undergrad Tuition & Fees (In-State): $8,568
Enrollment: 22,563 Coed
Affiliation or Control: State IRS Status: 501(c)3
Highest Offering: Doctorate
Accreditation: SC, ANEST, ARCPA, ART, CACREP, CAEP, CAHIIM, CAMPEP, CEA, CLPSY, DENT, DIETC, DIETI, FEPAC, HSA, IPSY, MED, @MIDWF, MLS, MUS, NMT, NNPR, NURSE, OPT, OPTR, OT, PAST, PH, PTA, SPAA, SW, THEA

02 President .... Dr. Ray L. WATTS
05 Sr VP Academic Affairs & Provost .... Dr. Pam BENOIT
10 Sr VP Financial Affairs/Admin .... Dr. Brian BURNETT
17 CEO UAB Health System .... Dr. Will FERNIANY
111 Vice Pres Advancement .... Mr. Thomas I. BRANNAN
13 Vice Pres Info Technology/CIO .... Dr. Curtis A. CARVER, JR.
28 Vice Pres for Equity & Diversity .... Dr. Paulette P. DILWORTH
46 Vice Pres for Research .... Dr. Chris BROWN
63 Sr VP/Dean School of Medicine .... Dr. Selwyn M. VICKERS
20 Sr VProv Student/Faculty Success .... Vacant
32 Vice Pres Student Affairs .... Dr. John R. JONES, III
43 University Counsel .... Mr. W. John DANIEL
49 Dean College of Arts & Sciences .... Dr. Kecia M. THOMAS
50 Dean School of Business .... Dr. Eric JACK
52 Dean School of Dentistry .... Dr. Russell TAICHMAN
53 Interim Dean School of Education .... Dr. Michelle A. ROBINSON
54 Dean School of Engineering .... Dr. Jeffrey W. HOLMES
76 Dean Sch of Health Professions .... Dr. Andrew J. BUTLER
66 Dean School of Nursing .... Dr. Doreen C. HARPER
88 Dean School of Optometry .... Dr. Kelly NICHOLS
69 Dean School of Public Health .... Dr. Paul ERWIN
58 Dean Graduate School .... Dr. Lori L. MCMAHON
18 Sr Facilities Officer .... Mr. Greg PARSONS
29 Asst VP Alumni Affairs .... Dr. Jennifer R. BRELAND
110 Assoc Vice Pres Development .... Ms. Rebecca J. GORDON
26 Assoc VP Strategic Comm & CCO .... Mr. Jim BAKKEN
105 AVP Digital Strategy & Marketing .... Ms. Rosie O'BEIRNE
84 Vice Provost Enrollment Management .... Dr. Bradley BARNES
21 Chief Financial Officer .... Ms. Stephanie B. MULLINS
08 Dean of Libraries .... Ms. Kasia J. GONNERMAN
41 Director of Athletics .... Mr. Mark T. INGRAM
15 Chief Human Resources Officer .... Ms. Alesia M. JONES
09 Vice Provost Inst Effectiveness .... Ms. Eva LEWIS
19 Assoc VP Public Safety/Chief Police .... Mr. Anthony B. PURCELL
07 Exec Dir Admisson/Financial Assist .... Mr. Tyler M. PETERSON
37 Director of Financial Aid .... Ms. Helen M. MCINTYRE
06 University Registrar .... Ms. Cynthia TERRY
39 Exec Dir Student Housing & Dining .... Mr. Marc BOOKER
36 Director Career Services .... Mr. Brandon WRIGHT
38 Asst VP Student Dev/Health & Well .... Dr. Rebecca KENNEDY
04 Executive Asst to President .... Ms. Kay D. KIRK
106 Assoc Provost Academic Learning .... Dr. Pamela E. PAUSTIAN
96 Director of Purchasing .... Mr. Ron COLLINS
101 Board Liaison .... Ms. Kirsten N. BURDICK

*University of Alabama in Huntsville (B)

301 Sparkman Drive, Huntsville AL 35899-1911
County: Madison FICE Identification: 001055
Unit ID: 100706
Telephone: (256) 824-1000 Carnegie Class: DU-Highest
FAX Number: (256) 824-6073 Calendar System: Semester
URL: www.uah.edu
Established: 1950 Annual Undergrad Tuition & Fees (In-State): $11,338
Enrollment: 9,999 Coed
Affiliation or Control: State IRS Status: 501(c)3
Highest Offering: Doctorate
Accreditation: SC, ART, CAEP, MUS, NURSE

02 Interim President .... Dr. Charles L. KARR
05 Provost & Exec VP Academic Affairs .... Dr. David PULEO
10 VP Finance & Administration .... Mr. Todd BARRE
41 Director of Athletics .... Dr. Cade SMITH
43 Chief University Counsel .... Mr. Michael HUFF
32 VP of Student Affairs .... Dr. Kristi MOTTER
28 Int VP Diversity/Equity & Inclusion .... Ms. LaFreeda JORDAN
46 VP Research/Economic Development .... Dr. Robert LINDQUIST
86 Chief of External Affairs .... Ms. LaFreeda JORDAN
88 Assoc VP Research/Economic Dev .... Dr. Thomas M. KOSHUT
11 Assoc VP Finance & Business Svcs .... Mr. Robert LEONARD
13 CIO .... Mr. Malcolm RICE
20 Assistant Provost .... Dr. Suzanne SIMPSON
114 Associate VP Budgets & Fin Planning .... Mr. Chih LOO
26 Asst VP Marketing/Communications .... Ms. Elizabeth GIBISCH
15 Assoc VP Human Resources .... Ms. Laurel LONG
35 Dean of Students .... Dr. Ronnie HEBERT
116 Director Internal Audit .... Ms. Tharanee M. RAVINDRAN
85 Assoc Provost International Svcs .... Dr. Jon HAKKILA
25 AVP Contracts & Grants .... Ms. Gloria GREENE
88 Director Institute for Science Educ .... Dr. James A. MILLER
08 Director Library .... Dr. David P. MOORE
79 Dean Arts/Humanities/Soc Science .... Dr. Sean LANE
81 Dean College of Science .... Dr. Rainer STEINWANDT
50 Dean College Business Admin .... Dr. Jason GREENE
51 Interim Dean Prof & Cont Studies .... Dr. Jason GREENE
54 Dean College of Engineering .... Dr. Shankar MAHALINGAM
58 Dean Graduate Studies .... Dr. Jon HAKKILA
66 Dean College of Nursing .... Dr. Karen FRITH
53 Dean College of Education .... Dr. Beth QUICK
88 Dir of Cybersecurity Research & Edu .... Dr. Thomas MORRIS
37 Asst VP Student Affairs .... Mr. Patrick JAMES
23 Dir Faculty & Staff Clinic .... Dr. Louise O'KEEFE
19 Chief of Police .... Mr. Brian COZBY
06 Registrar .... Ms. Janet WALLER
07 Director Undergraduate Admissions .... Ms. Peggy MASTERS
29 VP Alumni Rels/Univ Advancement .... Ms. Mallie HALE
110 Sr Director Advancement Services .... Ms. Marcie T. EPPLING
23 Director Student Health Services .... Ms. Amber MCPHAIL
88 Regional Dir Small Bus Dev Ctr .... Ms. Hilary CLAYBOURNE
102 Asst Dir Corp & Foundation Gifts .... Ms. Katie S. THURSTON
112 Major Gifts Officer .... Dr. Helen LIEN
88 Director Library Computer Systems .... Mr. Jack DROST
90 Director Collaborative Learning Ctr .... Dr. Michelle GREENE
88 Director Research Institute .... Dr. Steven MESSERVY
88 Director Info Tech & Systems Center .... Dr. Sara GRAVES
88 Director Ctr for Applied Optics .... Dr. Patrick REARDON
88 Dir Ctr Mgmt & Econ Research .... Dr. Nicholas LOYD
88 Director Propulsion Research Center .... Dr. Robert FREDERICK
88 Dir Ctr Space Plasma/Aeronomic Res .... Dr. Gary ZANK
88 Director Earth Systems Science Ctr .... Dr. John R. CHRISTY
88 Director Event Services .... Mr. William HALL
104 Director Global Studies Program .... Dr. David JOHNSON
92 Dean of the Honors College .... Dr. William WILKERSON
18 Asst VP Facilities & Operations .... Mr. Greg SMITH
38 Director Counseling Services .... Ms. Emily EICHHORN
39 Director Student Life .... Ms. Nikki GOODE

University of Mobile (C)

5735 College Parkway, Mobile AL 36613-2842
County: Mobile FICE Identification: 001029
Unit ID: 101693
Telephone: (251) 675-5990 Carnegie Class: Masters/S
FAX Number: N/A Calendar System: Semester
URL: www.umobile.edu
Established: 1961 Annual Undergrad Tuition & Fees: $24,310
Enrollment: 2,016 Coed
Affiliation or Control: Southern Baptist IRS Status: 501(c)3
Highest Offering: Doctorate
Accreditation: SC, ACBSP, ANEST, MUS, NURSE

00 Chairman of the Board of Trustees .... Mr. Fred WILSON
01 President .... Dr. Lonnie BURNETT
05 VP for Academic Affairs .... Dr. Todd GREER
10 VP for Business & Financial Affairs .... Dr. Melvin SANSOM
111 VP for Advancement .... Dr. Bruce EARNEST
84 VP Enrollment & Student Life .... Mrs. Charity WITTNER
26 VP for Marketing/Public Relations .... Mrs. Lesa MOORE
21 Associate VP for Business Affairs .... Ms. Carol CAMP
37 Assoc VP for Financial Aid .... Ms. Marie BATSON
20 Asst VP for Academic Administration .... Dr. Pamela BUCHANAN MILLER
27 Asst VP for Campus Communications .... Mrs. Kathy L. DEAN
41 Int Director of Intercol Athletics .... Dr. Melvin SANSOM
07 Director for Admissions/Enrollment .... Mrs. Hali GIVENS
09 Senior Dir for Inst Research .... Mrs. Kim LEOUSIS
08 Director for Library Services .... Mr. Jeffrey D. CALAMETTI
15 Director for Human Resources .... Mrs. Diane BLACK
50 Dean School of Business .... Dr. Kathy DUNNING
53 Dean School of Education .... Dr. Debra CHANCEY
66 Dean School of Nursing .... Dr. Sarah BARNES-WITHERSPOON
57 Dean AL School of the Arts .... Dr. Al MILLER
85 Dean Office for Global Engagement .... Dr. Doug WILSON
88 Dean School of Health & Sports Sci .... Dr. Lori DELONG
49 Assoc Dean College of Arts/Sciences .... Dr. Matthew DOWNS
29 Dir of Alumni Programs .... Mrs. Allie RATCLIFF
121 Exec Dir for Student Success .... Mrs. Shirley SUTTERFIELD
06 Registrar .... Ms. Eileen GARDNER
13 Director of Information Technology .... Ms. Larkisha WINBUSH
89 Asst Dir for 1st Year Experience .... Mrs. Shanoa REED
19 Dir of Campus Opers & Risk Mgmt .... Ms. Vicki BURGIN
102 Exec Director of UM Foundation .... Mr. Brian BOYLE
32 Dean of Students .... Mr. Greg JOHNSON
04 Admin Assistant to the President .... Mrs. Barbara GREENE

University of Montevallo (D)

Station 6001, Montevallo AL 35115-6001
County: Shelby FICE Identification: 001004
Unit ID: 101709
Telephone: (205) 665-6000 Carnegie Class: Masters/M
FAX Number: N/A Calendar System: Semester
URL: www.montevallo.edu
Established: 1896 Annual Undergrad Tuition & Fees (In-State): $13,710
Enrollment: 2,600 Coed
Affiliation or Control: State IRS Status: 501(c)3
Highest Offering: Beyond Master's But Less Than Doctorate
Accreditation: SC, AAFCS, ART, CACREP, CAEPN, DIETC, MUS, SP, SW, THEA

01 President .... Dr. John W. STEWART, III
05 Provost and VP Academic Affairs .... Dr. Courtney BENTLEY
32 VP Student Affairs/Enrollment Mgmt .... Dr. Tammi DAHLE
11 VP Administration/CIO .... Dr. Kristalyn SCOTT LEE
18 Director Physical Plant .... Mr. Cody JONES
35 Dir Student Conduct/Dean Stdnt Affs .... Mr. Tony W. MILLER
06 Registrar .... Ms. Amanda FOX
08 Director Carmichael Library .... Dr. Charlotte FORD
07 Director Admissions .... Ms. Audrey CRAWFORD
37 Dir of Student Financial Services .... Ms. Nikki BRADBURY
38 Director Counseling Services/Center .... Mr. Joshua MILLER
19 Chief of Police .... Mr. Tim ALEXANDER
39 Dir Housing & Residence Life .... Mr. John DENSON
41 Director Athletics .... Mr. Mark RICHARD
15 Director of HR and Risk Management .... Ms. Barbara FORREST
51 Dir of Regional Inservice Center .... Ms. Brooke VEAZEY
09 Director of Institutional Research .... Mr. Jerome DEAN
49 Dean College Arts & Sciences .... Dr. Ruth TRUSS
50 Dean College of Business .... Dr. Aimee MELLON
53 Interim Dean College of Education .... Dr. Donna PLOESSL
57 Dean College of Fine Arts .... Dr. Steven PETERS
04 Spec Assistant Exec/Admin Affairs .... Ms. Carolyn JONES
10 Chief Financial/Business Officer .... Ms. Susan HAYES
13 Chief Information Technology Ofcr .... Dr. Joe WALSH

University of North Alabama (E)

One Harrison Plaza, Florence AL 35632-0001
County: Lauderdale FICE Identification: 001016
Unit ID: 101879
Telephone: (256) 765-4100 Carnegie Class: Masters/L
FAX Number: (256) 765-4644 Calendar System: Semester
URL: www.una.edu
Established: 1830 Annual Undergrad Tuition & Fees (In-State): $10,620
Enrollment: 8,086 Coed
Affiliation or Control: State IRS Status: 501(c)3
Highest Offering: Doctorate
Accreditation: SC, ART, CACREP, CAEP, CIDA, #JOUR, MUS, NURSE, SW

01 President .... Dr. Kenneth D. KITTS
05 Provost & EVP Academic Affairs .... Dr. Ross C. ALEXANDER
85 Senior Vice Provost Intl Affairs .... Dr. Chunsheng ZHANG
10 VP Business/Financial Affs .... Mr. Evan THORNTON
32 VP Student Affairs .... Dr. Kathleen C. WHITE
111 Vice President Advancement .... Mr. Kevin R. HASLAM
21 Assoc VP Business/Financial Affs .... Ms. Cindy H. CONLON
28 VP Diversity/Equity & Inclusion .... Dr. Ron K. PATTERSON
49 Dean College of Arts/Sci & Engr .... Dr. Sara Lynn BAIRD
50 Dean College of Business & Tech .... Dr. Gregory A. CARNES
53 Dean Col Education/Human Sciences .... Dr. Katie KINNEY
66 Dean Anderson College of Nursing .... Dr. Tera KIRKMAN

41 Director of Athletics ... Dr. Josh LOONEY
43 General Counsel ... Ms. Amber FITE-MORGAN
21 Controller ... Mr. Mike NELSON
37 Director Student Financial Aid ... Ms. Shauna JAMES
15 Asst VP for Human Resources ... Ms. Catherine D. WHITE
13 Exec Dir Info Technology Services ... Mr. Ethan HUMPHRES
26 Dir Univ Media & Public Relations ... Ms. Michelle EUBANKS
18 Int Dir Facilities Admin & Planning ... Ms. Cindy CONLON
19 Chief of University Police ... Mr. Les JACKSON
23 Exec Dir Health and Well-Being ... Ms. Sheena BURGREEN
07 Exec Dir Admissions & Enroll Innov ... Ms. Julie Y. TAYLOR
09 Director of Institutional Research ... Dr. Molly MATHIS
29 Director Alumni Relations ... Mr. Bishop ALEXANDER
06 Interim Registrar ... Mr. Mitch POWELL
38 Clinical Mgr Stdnt Counseling ... Ms. Carmen RICHTER
04 Senior Admin Asst to President ... Ms. Regina B. SHERRILL
89 Dir First Year Experience ... Ms. Tammy RHODES
25 Dir Grants/Sponsored Programs ... Dr. Kyrel BUCHANAN
08 University Librarian ... Mr. Derek MALONE
39 Director Housing & Resident Life ... Ms. Jennifer SUTTON
86 Director Government Relations ... Mr. Jason A. COCHRAN
103 Director Workforce Development ... Mr. Roger GARNER

University of South Alabama (A)

307 University Boulevard, N, Mobile AL 36688-0002
County: Mobile
FICE Identification: 001057
Unit ID: 102094
Telephone: (251) 460-6111
Carnegie Class: DU-Higher
FAX Number: (251) 461-1537
Calendar System: Semester
URL: www.southalabama.edu
Established: 1963
Annual Undergrad Tuition & Fees (In-State): $8,396
Enrollment: 14,224
Coed
Affiliation or Control: State
IRS Status: 501(c)3
Highest Offering: Doctorate
Accreditation: SC, ARCPA, AUD, CACREP, CAEP, EMT, MED, MUS, NURSE, OT, PSPSY, PTA, RAD, RTT, SP, SW

01 President ... Mr. Jo BONNER
05 Provost & Executive Vice President ... Dr. Andrea KENT
20 Exec Vice Provost Academic Affairs ... Dr. Charles GUEST
63 VP Med Affairs/Dean COM ... Dr. John MARYMONT
10 Int VP Financial Affairs & Admin ... Ms. Polly STOKLEY
30 VP Developmental/Alumni Relations ... Ms. Margaret SULLIVAN
46 VP for Research & Economic Dev ... Ms. Lynne CHRONISTER
43 General Counsel ... Ms. Kristen DUKES
58 AVP Academic Affs/Dean Grad Sch ... Dr. J. Harold PARDUE
121 Assoc VP Academic Success ... Dr. Nicole CARR
84 Int Assoc VP Enrollment Services ... Mr. Salvadore LIBERTO
108 Assoc VP IE/Dir Inst Assessment ... Dr. Angela COLEMAN
13 Asst VP & Dir Info Tech Svcs ... Mr. Chris CANNON
15 Asst VP Human Resources ... Mr. Gerald GATTIS
86 Exec Director Government Relations ... Mr. Nicholas LAWKIS
32 VP Student Affairs/Dean of Students ... Dr. Michael MITCHELL
88 Associate Director of Assessment ... Ms. Naima WELLS
26 VP of Marketing and Communications ... Vacant
41 Director Athletics ... Dr. Joel ERDMANN
07 Director Admissions ... Ms. Norma TANNER
88 Director Immigration ... Ms. Denise ROBB
09 Exec Dir IR/Planning & Analysis ... Dr. Gordon MILLS, JR.
06 Registrar ... Dr. Kelly OSTERBIND
29 Director Alumni Relations ... Ms. Karen EDWARDS
19 Chief of Police ... Mr. Zeke AULL, JR.
37 Director of Financial Aid ... Ms. Shannan WHITE
36 Director Career Services ... Ms. Bevley GREEN
18 Assoc VP/Director Facilities Mgmt ... Vacant
38 Director Student Counseling/Testing ... Dr. John FRIEND
28 Interim Chief Diversity Officer ... Dr. Joel BILLINGSLEY
96 Purchasing Manager ... Mr. Robert BROWN
54 Dean College of Engineering ... Dr. John USHER
51 Assoc VP Global USA ... Dr. Richard CARTER
49 Dean Arts & Sciences ... Dr. Andrzej WIERZBICKI
08 Exec Dir University Libraries ... Ms. Lorene FLANDERS
50 Interim Dean College of Business ... Dr. Alvin WILLIAMS
53 Interim Dean Educ & Prof Studies ... Dr. John KOVALESKI
66 Dean College of Nursing ... Dr. Heather HALL
76 Interim Dean Allied Health ... Dr. Susan GORDON-HICKEY
77 Interim Dean School of Computing ... Dr. J. Harold PARDUE
39 Assoc VP Auxiliary Services/Housing ... Dr. Chris CLEVELAND
04 Executive Asst to President ... Ms. Rita HARPER
101 Executive Asst Board Affairs ... Ms. Monica EZELL
104 Director Study Abroad ... Dr. Bri ARD
105 Asst Director Online Communication ... Mr. Ian HARBAUGH
22 HR Manager Benefits/EEO ... Ms. Yamayra BETLER
25 Mgr Grants & Contracts Acctg ... Mr. Lindsey SHEFFIELD
44 Assoc Dir Strategic Annual Campaign ... Ms. Tracy COLEMAN

The University of West Alabama (B)

100 US-11, Livingston, AL 35470, Livingston AL 35470
County: Sumter
FICE Identification: 001024
Unit ID: 101587
Telephone: (205) 652-3400
Carnegie Class: Masters/L
FAX Number: (205) 652-3718
Calendar System: Semester
URL: www.uwa.edu
Established: 1835
Annual Undergrad Tuition & Fees (In-State): $10,990
Enrollment: 5,734
Coed
Affiliation or Control: State
IRS Status: 501(c)3
Highest Offering: Doctorate
Accreditation: SC, ACBSP, ADNUR, CAATE, CAEP, NAEYC, NUR

01 President ... Dr. Ken TUCKER
05 Provost ... Dr. Tim EDWARDS
10 Interim VP Financial Affairs ... Mr. Clete BEARD
111 VP Institutional Advancement ... Dr. Chris THOMASON
32 VP Student Affairs ... Dr. Melissa HAAB
49 Interim Dean of Liberal Arts ... Dr. Richard SCHELLHAMMER
15 VP Human Resources ... Mr. Robert UPCHURCH
50 Dean of Business ... Dr. Willy HILL
53 Dean College of Education ... Dr. Jan MILLER
81 Dean of Natural Science/Math ... Dr. John MCCALL
58 Dean of Graduate Studies ... Dr. B.J KIMBROUGH
103 VP of Economic & WF Development ... Dr. Tina N. JONES
106 Dean Online Programs ... Dr. Jan MILLER
66 Chairperson of Nursing ... Dr. Mary HANKS
08 Director of Library ... Dr. Neil SNIDER
09 Institutional Effectiveness ... Dr. Angel JOWERS
41 Athletic Director ... Mr. Kent PARTRIDGE
35 Director of Student Life & Support ... Mr. Byron THETFORD
06 Interim Registrar ... Ms. Emily MCINNIS
37 Director Student Financial Aid ... Mr. Steve SMITH
25 Director of Sponsored Programs ... Mr. Rodney GRANEC
13 Director Information Systems ... Mr. Michael PRATT
18 Director of Physical Plant ... Mr. Bobby TRUELOVE
36 Career Service Coordinator ... Ms. Gena ROBBINS
29 Director Alumni Relations ... Ms. Katie BEARD
86 Director Government Relations ... Mr. Tom TARTT
07 Director of Admissions ... Ms. Libba BAKER
96 Director of Purchasing ... Ms. Janie WOOLDRIDGE
30 Director of Development ... Ms. Amanda MCRAE
26 Director Strategic Communications ... Ms. Betsy LUKER
19 Director of Security/Safety ... Chief Josette WHITE
88 Director Economic Development ... Ms. Allison BRANTLEY
101 Admin Assistant for Board Relations ... Ms. Toni TERRY
28 Chief Diversity Officer ... Dr. B. J KIMBROUGH
85 Dean of International Programs ... Dr. Mark DAVIS

ALASKA

Alaska Bible College (C)

248 East Elmwood Avenue, Palmer AK 99645
County: Matanuska-Susitna
FICE Identification: 008843
Unit ID: 102580
Telephone: (907) 745-3201
Carnegie Class: Spec-4-yr-Faith
FAX Number: (907) 745-3210
Calendar System: Semester
URL: www.akbible.edu
Established: 1966
Annual Undergrad Tuition & Fees: $9,700
Enrollment: 40
Coed
Affiliation or Control: Independent Non-Profit
IRS Status: 501(c)3
Highest Offering: Baccalaureate
Accreditation: BI

01 President ... Mr. David LEY
05 Vice Pres Academic Affairs ... Dr. Ben OLSON
32 Vice Pres Student Development ... Dr. Dan JARRELL
10 Vice Pres Business Admin ... Mr. Matthew COTE
42 Chaplain/Dir of Christian Ministry ... Mr. Justin ARCHULETTA
06 Registrar ... Vacant
08 Library Director ... Ms. Noel MAXWELL
07 Director of Admissions ... Mr. Josiah RICHARDSON
37 Director Financial Aid ... Ms. Christy COTE
26 Director of Communications ... Vacant
35 Dean of Students ... Vacant

Alaska Christian College (D)

35109 Royal Place, Soldotna AK 99669-9755
FICE Identification: 041386
Unit ID: 442523
Telephone: (907) 260-7422
Carnegie Class: Assoc/HT-High Trad
FAX Number: (907) 260-6722
Calendar System: Semester
URL: alaskacc.edu
Established: 2001
Annual Undergrad Tuition & Fees: $8,414
Enrollment: N/A
Coed
Affiliation or Control: Independent Non-Profit
IRS Status: 501(c)3
Highest Offering: Associate Degree
Accreditation: BI

01 President ... Dr. Keith J. HAMILTON
03 Executive Vice President ... Mr. Jeff SEIMERS
11 Vice President of Operations ... Mr. Sean OFFBECK
111 Vice President of Advancement ... Mr. Eric JOHNSON
05 Vice President Academic Affairs ... Ms. Lindsey HALLAM
06 Registrar ... Ms. Brittany WILLIAMS
32 Director of Student Life ... Mr. Jacob HOEKSTRA
07 Director of Admissions ... Mr. Jeffrey SMITH
13 Director of IT Services ... Mr. David WILEY
15 Finance & Human Resources Director ... Ms. April WEBER
37 Director of Financial Aid ... Ms. Krista PITSCH
18 Director of Facilities ... Mr. Harvey LUNDQUIST

Alaska Career College (E)

1415 E. Tudor Road, Anchorage AK 99507-1033
County: Anchorage
FICE Identification: 025410
Unit ID: 103501
Telephone: (907) 563-7575
Carnegie Class: Spec 2-yr-Other
FAX Number: (907) 563-8330
Calendar System: Other
URL: www.alaskacareercollege.edu
Established: 1985
Annual Undergrad Tuition & Fees: N/A
Enrollment: 412
Coed
Affiliation or Control: Proprietary
IRS Status: Proprietary
Highest Offering: Associate Degree
Accreditation: ACCSC

01 Director ... Ms. Linda STURE
36 Director of Career Services ... Mr. Chaz ALEXANDER
10 Chief Financial/Business Officer ... Ms. Jennifer DEITZ
18 Chief Facilities/Physical Plant Ofc ... Ms. Donna BLEVINS
37 Director Student Financial Aid ... Ms. Monica MATLOCK

Alaska Pacific University (F)

4101 University Drive, Anchorage AK 99508-4672
County: Anchorage
FICE Identification: 001061
Unit ID: 102669
Telephone: (907) 561-1266
Carnegie Class: Bac-Diverse
FAX Number: (907) 562-4276
Calendar System: Semester
URL: www.alaskapacific.edu
Established: 1959
Annual Undergrad Tuition & Fees: $20,760
Enrollment: 493
Coed
Affiliation or Control: Independent Non-Profit
IRS Status: 501(c)3
Highest Offering: Doctorate
Accreditation: NW, ADNUR, CAEPN, IACBE, NUR

01 President ... Dr. Janelle VANASSE
04 Executive Assistant to President ... Ms. Debbie ROLL
05 Provost ... Dr. Hilton HALLOCK
10 Chief Financial Officer ... Ms. Sheila KING
32 Dean of Students ... Mr. Ben HAHN
06 Registrar ... Vacant
84 Dean of Enrollment Services ... Ms. Toni RILEY
109 Director of Auxiliary Services ... Mr. Brian MCDERMOTT
37 Interim Director of Financial Aid ... Ms. Jo HOLLAND
18 Director Facilities Management ... Ms. Kathy MINCKS
13 Director Information Technology ... Mr. Kent ENGLISH
111 Chief Advancement Officer ... Ms. Laurie EVANS-DINNEEN
42 Chaplain ... Mr. Brian ANDERSON
15 Director Human Resources ... Ms. Kathleen WYRICK
29 Alumni/Donor Relations ... Mr. Christopher DEEN
117 Compliance/Risk Officer ... Mr. Robert MEYER
38 Dir of Career/Counseling/Disability ... Vacant
39 Dir Campus Life/Student Housing ... Mr. Chandler STROUP

Charter College (G)

2221 E. Northern Lights Blvd, Anchorage AK 99508
FICE Identification: 025769
Unit ID: 102845
Telephone: (907) 777-1300
Carnegie Class: Bac/Assoc-Mixed
FAX Number: N/A
Calendar System: Quarter
URL: www.chartercollege.edu
Established: 2010
Annual Undergrad Tuition & Fees: N/A
Enrollment: 2,120
Coed
Affiliation or Control: Proprietary
IRS Status: Proprietary
Highest Offering: Baccalaureate
Accreditation: ABHES, ADNUR

02 Campus Manager ... Gabriel GONZALES

Ilisagvik College (H)

PO Box 749, Barrow AK 99723
County: North Slope Borough
FICE Identification: 034613
Unit ID: 434584
Telephone: (907) 852-3333
Carnegie Class: Tribal
FAX Number: (907) 852-3003
Calendar System: Semester
URL: www.ilisagvik.edu
Established: 1996
Annual Undergrad Tuition & Fees: $4,780
Enrollment: 232
Coed
Affiliation or Control: Independent Non-Profit
IRS Status: 501(c)3
Highest Offering: Baccalaureate
Accreditation: NW, DTH

01 President ... Mrs. Justina WILHELM
11 Dean of Administration ... Mrs. Nicole EVANS
06 Registrar ... Ms. Fa'amamata TUFELE
05 Dean of Academic Affairs ... Vacant
15 Exec Director of Human Resources ... Ms. Robyn BURKE
18 Chief Facilities/Physical Plant ... Mr. Tom CARAWAY
111 Exec Dir Institutional Advancement ... Mrs. Caitlin WALLS
32 Dean of Students ... Mr. Hal HAYNES, JR.
37 Student Financial Aid Manager ... Mrs. Monica ROMERO-CURIEL
08 Chief Library Officer ... Ms. Teressa WILLIAMS
10 Chief Financial Officer ... Ms. Ann Marie CLARK
101 Executive Assistant/Board Secretary ... Mrs. Clarissa PELIA
13 IT Director ... Ms. Monica LUGO
04 Exec Assistant to the President ... Ms. Clarissa PELIA

*University of Alaska System (I)

2025 Yukon Drive, Suite 202, Fairbanks AK 99775-5000
County: Fairbanks
FICE Identification: 008005
Unit ID: 103529
Telephone: (907) 450-8000
Carnegie Class: N/A
FAX Number: (907) 450-8012
URL: www.alaska.edu

01 President ... Ms. Pat PITNEY
26 Vice President for Univ Relations ... Ms. Michelle RIZK
05 VP for Academics/Students/Research ... Dr. Paul LAYER
10 Chief Finance Officer/Controller ... Mr. Myron DOSCH
46 Chief Strategy/Planning/Budget Ofcr ... Ms. Michelle RIZK
09 AVP Data Strategy & Inst Research ... Ms. Gwendolyn GRUENIG
86 Assoc VP Public Affairs ... Ms. Robbie GRAHAM

43 General Counsel .... Mr. Matthew COOPER
15 Acting Chief HR Officer .... Mr. David BISHKO
13 Interim Chief Information Tech Ofcr .... Mr. John BOUCHER
101 Exec Officer Board of Regents .... Ms. Brandi BERG

*University of Alaska Anchorage (A)

3211 Providence Drive, Anchorage AK 99508-8000
County: Anchorage FICE Identification: 011462
Unit ID: 102553
Telephone: (907) 786-1800 Carnegie Class: Masters/L
FAX Number: (907) 786-4888 Calendar System: Semester
URL: www.uaa.alaska.edu
Established: 1954 Annual Undergrad Tuition & Fees (In-State): $8,622
Enrollment: 11,953 Coed
Affiliation or Control: State IRS Status: 501(c)3
Highest Offering: Doctorate
Accreditation: **NW**, ACFEI, ADNUR, ART, CAEP, CLPSY, CONST, CSHSE, DA, DH, DIET, DIETD, DIETI, EMT, MAC, MLS, MLTAD, MUS, NAEYC, NUR, NURSE, PH, PTAA, SURGT, SW

02 Chancellor .... Sean PARNELL
05 Provost .... Denise RUNGE
10 Interim Vice Chanc Admin Services .... Bill JACOB
84 Assoc Vice Chanc Enroll Svcs .... Lora VOLDEN
111 Vice Chanc University Advancement .... Megan OLSON
32 Vice Chancellor Student Affairs .... Bruce SCHULTZ
20 Vice Provost Undergrad Acad Affairs .... Susan KALINA
46 Assoc Vice Chancellor for Research .... Aaron DOTSON
13 Interim CIO/Assoc Vice Chanc ITS .... Benjamin SHIER
18 Assoc VC Facilities/Campus Svcs .... Kim MAHONEY
29 Asst Vice Chanc Alumni Relations .... Tanya PONT
121 Dir Acad/Multicultural Success .... Sara CALDWELL-KAN
35 Dean of Students .... Ben MORTON
37 Financial Aid Director .... Shauna GRANT
09 Director Institutional Research .... Daniel CAMPBELL
15 Chief Human Resources Officer .... Steven J. PATIN
85 Director Multicultural Center .... Vacant
26 Director of Philanthropy .... Brian IBSEN
35 Director Student Life & Leadership .... Zak CLARK
07 Interim Exec Director of Admissions .... Craig MEAD
41 Director Athletics .... Greg MYFORD
06 University Registrar .... Lindsey CHADWELL
08 Dean Consortium Library .... Stephen ROLLINS
63 Director WWAMI Biomedical Program .... Jane SHELBY
38 Director Student Health & Counsel .... Mary WOODRING
50 Dean Business & Public Policy .... John NOFSINGER
51 Dean Cmty & Tech College .... Raymond WEBER
76 Int Dean College of Health .... Andre ROSAY
54 Dean College of Engineering .... Kenrick MOCK
49 Dean College Arts & Sciences .... Jenny MCNULTY
92 Dean Honors College .... Claudia LAMPMAN
39 Exec Director Campus Services .... David WEAVER
28 Chief Diversity Officer .... Jennifer BOOZ

*University of Alaska Fairbanks (B)

505 South Chandlar Drive, Fairbanks AK 99775
County: Fairbanks North Star Borough FICE Identification: 001063
Unit ID: 102614
Telephone: (907) 474-7500 Carnegie Class: DU-Higher
FAX Number: (907) 474-5379 Calendar System: Semester
URL: www.uaf.edu
Established: 1917 Annual Undergrad Tuition & Fees (In-State): $7,176
Enrollment: 6,813 Coed
Affiliation or Control: State IRS Status: 501(c)3
Highest Offering: Doctorate
Accreditation: **NW**, CACREP, CAEP, EMT, MAC, NAEYC, SW

02 Chancellor .... Dr. Daniel M. WHITE
05 Provost .... Dr. Anupma PRAKASH
11 Vice Chancellor Administrative Svcs .... Ms. Julie QUEEN
18 Assoc Vice Chancellor Facilities .... Ms. Kellie FRITZE
32 Vice Chancellor Student Affairs .... Ms. Alexis KNABE
46 Vice Chancellor Research .... Dr. Nettie LA BELLE-HAMER
10 AVC for Financial Services .... Ms. Amanda WALL
30 Director of Development .... Ms. Morgan DULIAN
58 Director Graduate School .... Dr. Richard COLLINS
81 Dean Col of Natural Science/Math .... Dr. Kinchel DORNER
35 Assoc Vice Chanc for Student Life .... Mr. Alexis KNABE
31 VC Rural/Cmty & Native Educ .... Dr. Charlene STERN
12 Dean UAF Comm & Tech College .... Ms. Michele STALDER
88 Dean Col Fisheries & Ocean Sciences .... Dr. Bradley MORAN
50 Dean School of Management .... Dr. Mark HERRMANN
54 Dean Col of Engineering & Mines .... Dr. William SCHNABEL
88 Dir Intl Arctic Research Center .... Dr. Hajo EICKEN
88 Dir Institute of Arctic Biology .... Dr. Diane O'BRIEN
54 Int Dir Inst Northern Engineering .... Dr. David BARNES
15 Chief Human Resources Officer .... Mr. David BISHKO
19 Chief of Police .... Ms. Kathleen CATRON
37 Director Financial Aid .... Ms. Deanna L. DIERINGER
41 Director Athletics .... Dr. Brock ANUNDSON
35 Dean of Students .... Ms. Kaydee VAN FLEIN
56 Vice Provost for Extension/Outreach .... Dr. Pete PINNEY
109 Director of Aux/Recharge/Cntrct Ops .... Vacant
85 Director International Programs .... Ms. Joanna CRUZAN
88 Fire Chief .... Mr. Forrest KUIPER
88 Dir Institute of Marine Science .... Dr. Terry WHITLEDGE
49 Dean College of Liberal Arts .... Dr. Ellen LOPEZ
53 Director School of Education .... Dr. Amy VINLOVE
12 Director Bristol Bay Campus .... Ms. Sarah ANDREW
12 Dir Chukchi Campus .... Ms. Stacey GLASER
12 Dir Interior Alaska Campus .... Mr. Byron BLUEHORSE
12 Director Kuskokwim Campus .... Ms. Linda KURDA
12 Director Northwest Campus .... Ms. Barbara AMAROK
28 Director of Diversity & EO .... Ms. Margo GRIFFITH
23 Director Health and Counseling .... Dr. BJ ALDRICH
29 Exec Director Alumni Association .... Ms. Theresa BAKKER
06 Registrar .... Mr. Mike EARNEST
88 Director Geophysical Institute .... Dr. Robert MCCOY
21 Director Business Operations .... Ms. Briana WALTERS
121 Director Academic Advising Center .... Ms. Linda M. HAPSMITH
92 Director Honors Program .... Dr. Alex HIRSCH
09 Dir Planning/Analysis/Inst Research .... Vacant
111 Director University Advancement .... Ms. Samara TABER
08 Director of Libraries .... Ms. Karen JENSEN
88 Dir UA Museum of the North .... Dr. Patrick DRUCKENMILLER
13 Chief Info Technology Officer .... Ms. Martha MASON
22 Director for Disability Services .... Ms. Amber CAGWIN
96 Dir of Procurement & Contract Svcs .... Mr. John HEBARD
88 Director Wood Center Student Union .... Ms. Cody ROGERS
97 Vice Provost/Dean Gen Studies .... Dr. Alex FITTS
04 Assistant to the Chancellor .... Ms. Jeannie PHILLIPS
106 Executive Director for E-learning .... Dr. Owen GUTHRIE
07 Director Admissions .... Ms. Anna GAGNE-HAWES

*University of Alaska Southeast (C)

11066 Auke Lake Way, Juneau AK 99801
County: Juneau FICE Identification: 001065
Unit ID: 102632
Telephone: (907) 796-6100 Carnegie Class: Masters/M
FAX Number: N/A Calendar System: Semester
URL: www.uas.alaska.edu
Established: 1956 Annual Undergrad Tuition & Fees (In-State): $6,960
Enrollment: 2,070 Coed
Affiliation or Control: State IRS Status: 501(c)3
Highest Offering: Master's
Accreditation: **NW**, ACBSP, CAEP, CAHIIM, MAC

02 Chancellor .... Dr. Karen CAREY
05 Interim Provost .... Dr. Maren HAAVIG
84 VC Enrollment Mgmt & Stdnt Affs .... Ms. Lori KLEIN
75 Exec Dean of Career/Tech Educ .... Mr. Pete TRAXLER
46 Vice Provost for Research .... Dr. Maren HAAVIG
11 Vice Chanc Administration .... Mr. Michael CIRI
12 Sitka Campus Director .... Mr. Paul KRAFT
12 Ketchikan Campus Director .... Dr. Priscilla SCHULTE
49 Dean of Arts & Sciences .... Ms. Carin SILKAITIS
53 Int Director School of Education .... Ms. Mary Lou MADDEN
37 Financial Aid Director .... Ms. Janelle COOK
26 Exec Asst to Chanc/Public Rels Ofcr .... Ms. Keni CAMPBELL
06 Registrar .... Ms. Trisha LEE
09 Dir Institutional Effectiveness .... Ms. Kristen HANDLEY
10 Dir Business Operations .... Mr. Jon LASINSKI
15 Chief Human Resources Officer .... Mr. David BISHKO
18 Director Facilities Services .... Mr. Nathan LEIGH
08 Dean Library Services .... Ms. Elise TOMLINSON
13 Director Information/Technology .... Mr. Michael CIRI
30 Dir Development/Alumni Relations .... Ms. Lynne JOHNSON
21 Chief Budget Officer .... Ms. Julie VIGIL
22 Dep Dir Equity/Compliance/TIX .... Mr. Ryan WARK
32 Dean Students & Campus Life .... Ms. Jackie WILSON
88 Dir of PITAAS/AVC AK Native Pgms .... Ms. Ronalda CADIENTE-BROWN
88 Dir of AK Coastal Rainforest Center .... Mr. Jason FELDMAN
07 Dir of Admissions/Recruitment .... Ms. Lori KLEIN
105 Web Coordinator .... Mr. Colin OSTERHOUT
96 Procurement Services Manager .... Mr. Richard HITCHCOCK

*Prince William Sound Community College (D)

PO Box 97, 303 Lowe Street, Valdez AK 99686-0097
Telephone: (907) 834-1600 Identification: 666659
Accreditation: **&NW**

† Branch campus of University of Alaska Anchorage, Anchorage, AK

ARIZONA

Acacia University (E)

7665 South Research Drive, Tempe AZ 85284-1812
County: Maricopa Identification: 667017
Telephone: (480) 428-6034 Carnegie Class: Not Classified
FAX Number: (480) 428-6033 Calendar System: Other
URL: www.acacia.edu
Established: 2003 Annual Undergrad Tuition & Fees: N/A
Enrollment: N/A Coed
Affiliation or Control: Proprietary IRS Status: Proprietary
Highest Offering: Doctorate
Accreditation: **DEAC**

01 President .... Mr. Tim MOMAN
05 Provost/Executive Vice President .... Dr. Marilynn D. HENLEY
13 Vice President of Technology .... Mr. Michael TURICO

American InterContinental University (F)

2200 E. Germann Rd, Chandler AZ 85286
County: Maricopa FICE Identification: 021136
Unit ID: 445027
Telephone: (877) 701-3800 Carnegie Class: Masters/L
FAX Number: N/A Calendar System: Quarter
URL: www.aiuniv.edu
Established: 1970 Annual Undergrad Tuition & Fees: $11,646
Enrollment: 15,415 Coed
Affiliation or Control: Proprietary IRS Status: Proprietary
Highest Offering: Master's
Accreditation: **HLC**, AAQEP, ACBSP

01 President .... Mr. John KLINE
05 Provost & Chief Academic Officer .... Dr. Ruki JAYARAMAN
07 VP of Admissions .... Mrs. Trisha GANGER
32 VP of Strategic Student Operations .... Mr. Jeffrey SONNENBERG
88 VP Program Management .... Ms. April MIGEL
10 VP of Univ Policy/Administration .... Mr. Daniel SESSIONS
11 VP of Campus Operations .... Ms. Julia LEEMAN
09 VP Educational Alliances & IRC .... Mr. Walid KAAKOUSH
12 Campus Director-Atlanta .... Ms. Sharon SMITH
12 Campus Director-Houston .... Vacant

Arizona Christian University (G)

1 W. Firestorm Way, Glendale AZ 85306
County: Maricopa FICE Identification: 007113
Unit ID: 105899
Telephone: (602) 489-5300 Carnegie Class: Bac-Diverse
FAX Number: (602) 404-2159 Calendar System: Semester
URL: www.arizonachristian.edu
Established: 1960 Annual Undergrad Tuition & Fees: $29,250
Enrollment: 925 Coed
Affiliation or Control: Independent Non-Profit IRS Status: 501(c)3
Highest Offering: Baccalaureate
Accreditation: **HLC**

01 President .... Mr. Len MUNSIL
11 Chief Operating Officer .... Mr. James TITO
111 VP of University Engagement .... Mr. James GRIFFITHS
84 VP of Enrollment .... Mr. Jeff RUTTER
18 VP of Campus Operations .... Mr. Jon CLINE
05 Dean of Academic Affairs .... Dr. Edward CLAVELL
32 Interim Dean of Students .... Dr. Peter DRYER
26 VP of Marketing .... Dr. Zachariah GREEN
41 Asst Athletic Director .... Mr. Keith BAKER
10 Controller .... Mrs. Kelly BULLOCK
53 Asst Dean of School of Education .... Dr. Linnea LYDING
06 Registrar .... Mrs. Tracy MARTIN
09 AVP of Institutional Effectiveness .... Mr. Jeff PHILLIPS
49 Assistant Dean .... Dr. Carolyn PELA
30 Director of University Engagement .... Mrs. Allison PETEET
35 Director of Student Engagement .... Mr. Steven VALDEZ
41 Director of Athletics .... Dr. Peter DRYER
37 Director of Financial Aid .... Mrs. Lisa STONE
08 Head Librarian .... Mr. Robert OLIVERIO
19 Director of Campus Safety .... Mr. Corey QUINN
13 Director of Information Technology .... Mr. Jon CLINE
15 HR Administrator .... Ms. Kasey LYTTLE
113 Dir Student Accounts .... Ms. Kylie OTSTOT
39 Director of Resident Life .... Mr. Bryan STANLEY
04 Asst to President & Provost/COO .... Mrs. Julie ROSEN
84 Director of Enrollment Management .... Mr. David HOSKINSON
38 Director of Counseling Services .... Vacant
121 Director of Academic Services .... Mrs. Brenda SPEAR
120 LMS Administrator .... Ms. Courtney PHOENIX
29 Alumni Engagement Specialist .... Mr. Tim REED
07 Manager of Recruitment .... Mr. Joshua ESAU
42 Campus Pastor .... Mr. Travis TURNER

Arizona College-Mesa (H)

163 N. Dobson Road, Mesa AZ 85201
Telephone: (855) 706-8382 Identification: 770514
Accreditation: **ABHES**

Arizona College of Nursing (I)

1620 W. Fountainhead Pkwy, Ste 110, Tempe AZ 85282
County: Maricopa FICE Identification: 031150
Unit ID: 421708
Telephone: (855) 706-8382 Carnegie Class: Spec 2-yr-Health
FAX Number: N/A Calendar System: Other
URL: www.arizonacollege.edu
Established: 1991 Annual Undergrad Tuition & Fees: $15,841
Enrollment: 524 Coed
Affiliation or Control: Proprietary IRS Status: Proprietary
Highest Offering: Baccalaureate
Accreditation: **ABHES**, NURSE

01 President .... Mr. Nick MANSOUR
10 Vice President of Finance .... Mr. Ryan SVENDSEN

Arizona School of Acupuncture and Oriental Medicine (J)

2856 E Fort Lowell Rd., Tucson AZ 85716
County: Pima FICE Identification: 036955
Unit ID: 446039
Telephone: (520) 795-0787 Carnegie Class: Spec-4-yr-Other Health
FAX Number: (877) 222-4606 Calendar System: Quarter
URL: www.asaom.edu
Established: 1996 Annual Graduate Tuition & Fees: N/A
Enrollment: 13 Coed
Affiliation or Control: Proprietary IRS Status: Proprietary
Highest Offering: Master's; No Undergraduates

Accreditation: ACUP

00 Owner ... Mr. Jonathan HU
01 President ... Mr. Joshua HANNUM
05 Academic Dean ... Dr. Kara MICHALSEN
37 Director of Financial Programs ... Ms. Susan WAGNER
07 Admissions Officer ... Mr. Frank HARRIS
06 Registrar ... Ms. Haley HALL
63 Dean of Clinical Education ... Mr. Nathan ANDERSON

Arizona State University (A)

300 E. University Drive, Tempe AZ 85281
County: Maricopa FICE Identification: 001081
Unit ID: 104151
Telephone: (855) 278-5080 Carnegie Class: DU-Highest
FAX Number: N/A Calendar System: Semester
URL: www.asu.edu
Established: 1885 Annual Undergrad Tuition & Fees (In-State): $11,338
Enrollment: 74,795 Coed
Affiliation or Control: State IRS Status: 501(c)3
Highest Offering: Doctorate
Accreditation: HLC, AAB, ART, AUD, CAPRT, CIDA, CLPSY, CONST, COPSY, CR, DIETD, DIETI, IPSY, JOUR, LAW, LSAR, MLS, MUS, NURSE, PCSAS, PLNG, SP, SPAA, SW

01 President ... Dr. Michael M. CROW
05 Exec VP & University Provost ... Dr. Nancy GONZALES
46 Exec VP Knowledge Enterprise ... Dr. Sally C. MORTON
88 Exec Vice Pres Learning Enterprise ... Maria ANGUIANO
10 Exec VP Treasurer & CFO ... Dr. Morgan R. OLSEN
11 Exec VP & Chief Operating Officer ... Chris HOWARD
88 Vice Prov Academic Alliances ... Cheryl HYMAN
88 Vice Prov Academic Personnel ... Deborah CLARKE
28 Vice Prov Inclusion and Comm Eng ... Vacant
121 Vice Prov Student Success ... Arthur BLAKEMORE
20 Vice Prov Undergrad Education ... Anne JONES
92 Dean Barrett Honors College ... Tara WILLIAMS
50 Dean W.P. Carey School Business ... Ohad KADAN
57 Dean Herberger Inst for Design/Arts ... Dr. Steven J. TEPPER
54 Vice Prov/Dean Fulton Sch of Engr ... Dr. Kyle SQUIRES
88 Vice Pres/Vice Prov Global Futures ... Dr. Peter SCHLOSSER
58 Vice Prov/Dean Graduate College ... Dr. Elizabeth A. WENTZ
76 Dean Col Health Solutions ... Dr. Deborah L. HELITZER
49 Dean Col Integr Science & Arts ... Dr. Joanna GRABSKI
60 Dean Sch Journalism/Mass Comm ... Battinto BATTS, JR.
61 Interim Dean College of Law ... Zachary KRAMER
49 Dean Col Lib Arts & Sciences ... Dr. Patrick J. KENNEY
79 Dean Col Lib Arts & Sci/Humanities ... Dr. Jeffrey J. COHEN
81 Dean Col Lib Arts & Sci/Natl Sci ... Dr. Kenro KUSUMI
83 Int Dean Col Lib Arts & Sci/Soc Sci ... Dr. Patrick J. KENNEY
88 Dean New Col Interdisc Arts & Sci ... Dr. Todd R. SANDRIN
66 Dean Col Nursing/Health Innovation ... Dr. Judith F. KARSHMER
106 Dean Educ Initiatives/CEO EdPlus ... Dr. Philip R. REGIER
80 Dean Col Public Svc & Cmty Solution ... Dr. Cynthia LIETZ
53 Dean Mary Lou Fulton Teachers Col ... Dr. Carole G. BASILE
82 Dean/Dir Thunderbird Sch Global Mgt ... Dr. Sanjeev KHAGRAM
97 Vice Prov/Dean University College ... Dr. Sukhwant JHAJ
114 Vice Pres Budget Planning & Mgmt ... Matthew SMITH
93 Vice Pres Cultural Affairs ... Colleen JENNINGS-ROGGENSACK
32 Sr VP Educ Outreach & Stdnt Svcs ... Dr. James A. RUND
35 Vice Pres Student Services ... Dr. Joanne VOGEL
26 Vice Pres & Chief Brand Officer ... Jill ANDREWS
18 Vice Pres Facilities Dev & Mgmt ... Alexander KOHNEN
21 VP Finance & Deputy Treasurer ... Vacant
43 Sr Vice President & General Counsel ... Lisa LOO
86 Vice Pres Govt & Cmty Engagement ... Adam DEGUIRE
15 VP & Chief Human Resources Ofcr ... Vacant
88 VP Corp Engage/Strat Partnership ... Grace O'SULLIVAN
101 Sr Vice Pres/Sec of the University ... Dr. Christine K. WILKINSON
88 Vice Pres Social Advancement ... Bryan BRAYBOY
100 Sr VP Univ Affairs/Chief of Staff ... Jim O'BRIEN
41 Athletics Director & Vice President ... Raymond ANDERSON
88 Vice Pres Univ Business Services ... Nichol LUOMA
45 Sr Vice Pres & University Planner ... Richard H. STANLEY
84 Vice Pres Acad Enterprise Enroll ... Kent R. HOPKINS
13 Chief Information Officer ... Dr. Lev GONICK
08 University Librarian ... Dr. James O'DONNELL
06 University Registrar ... Lou Ann DENNY
07 Assoc Vice Pres Admission Svcs ... Matthew LOPEZ
19 Chief of Police ... Michael THOMPSON
37 AVP Financial Aid/Scholarship Svcs ... Melissa PIZZO
38 Assoc Vice Pres Counseling Svcs ... Aaron KRASNOW

Arizona Western College (B)

2020 South Avenue 8E, Yuma AZ 85365
County: Yuma FICE Identification: 001071
Unit ID: 104160
Telephone: (928) 317-6000 Carnegie Class: Assoc/HT-Mix Trad/Non
FAX Number: N/A Calendar System: Semester
URL: www.azwestern.edu
Established: 1963 Annual Undergrad Tuition & Fees (In-District): $2,840
Enrollment: 6,487 Coed
Affiliation or Control: State/Local IRS Status: Exempt
Highest Offering: Associate Degree
Accreditation: HLC, ADNUR, EMT, RAD

01 President ... Dr. Daniel P. CORR
05 Vice President Learning Services ... Vacant
10 VP Finance/Administration ... Mr. Ross POPPENBERGER
111 Vice President of Advancement ... Ms. Lori STOFFT
25 Director of Grants ... Ms. Rainier DISCHINGER
103 Interim Assoc Dean of Workforce ... Mr. Alfonso ZAVALA
32 Vice President for Student Services ... Mr. Bryan E. DOAK
75 VP Workforce Dev & Career Tech Educ ... Ms. Reetika DHAWAN
84 Associate Dean of Enrollment Svcs ... Ms. Ana ENGLISH
35 Dean of Students ... Dr. Nikki HAGE
21 Dir Financial Services/Controller ... Ms. Michelle LANDIS
15 Chief Human Resources Officer ... Ms. Karen M. JOHNSON
96 Dir Purchasing & Auxiliary Services ... Ms. Brenda SAWYER
18 Director of District Operations ... Mr. Steve ECKERT
13 Chief Information Officer ... Mr. Scott ESTES
08 Director of Library Services ... Ms. Angie CREEL
41 Director of Athletics ... Mr. Jerry SMITH
19 Chief of Police ... Mr. Stephen SUHO
28 Dir Diversity/Inclusion/Access ... Ms. Laura SANDIGO
12 Associate Dean La Paz County Svcs ... Ms. Kathy OCAMPO
12 Assoc Dean for South Yuma County ... Ms. Susanna ZAMBRANO
37 Director of Financial Aid ... Mr. Alan SANCHEZ
85 Coord of International Students ... Ms. Laura SANDIGO
106 Associate Dean for Distance Educ ... Vacant
88 Director of Testing Services ... Mrs. Holly M. BANES
105 Webmaster II ... Mr. Damien BATES
100 Chief of Staff ... Mrs. Ashley HERRINGTON
36 Director Career/Advisement Services ... Ms. Cristina C. GONZALEZ
101 Executive Assistant to the District ... Mrs. Ashley HERRINGTON
06 Registar ... Mrs. Debra VEGA
07 Director of Admissions ... Mrs. Debra VEGA
09 Director of Institutional Research ... Ms. Betty LOPEZ
20 Associate Academic Officer ... Dr. Joann CHANG
26 Assoc Dean Communications ... Ms. Mandy HEIL
102 Foundation Officer ... Ms. Laura KNARESBORO
30 Chief Development Officer ... Ms. Lori C. STOFFT
38 Director of Student Counseling ... Dr. Nikki HAGE

Aspen University (C)

4615 E Elwood Street, #100, Phoenix AZ 85040
FICE Identification: 040803
Unit ID: 454829
Telephone: (303) 333-4224 Carnegie Class: Spec-4-yr-Other Health
FAX Number: (303) 200-7428 Calendar System: Semester
URL: www.aspen.edu
Established: 1987 Annual Undergrad Tuition & Fees: $5,110
Enrollment: 9,563 Coed
Affiliation or Control: Proprietary IRS Status: Proprietary
Highest Offering: Doctorate
Accreditation: DEAC, NURSE

00 Chairman & CEO BOT ... Mr. Michael MATHEWS
01 President/Chief Academic Officer ... Dr. Cheri ST. ARNAULD
11 Chief Operating Officer ... Vacant
10 Chief Financial Officer ... Ms. Cheryl JULAKA
05 Provost ... Dr. Joanne WEISS
06 Registrar ... Ms. Katie BROWN

Benedictine University Mesa (D)

225 East Main Street, Mesa AZ 85201
Telephone: (602) 888-5000 Identification: 770068
Accreditation: &HLC

† Branch campus of Benedictine University, Lisle, IL

Brookline College (E)

2445 West Dunlap Avenue, Suite 100, Phoenix AZ 85021
County: Maricopa FICE Identification: 022188
Unit ID: 104090
Telephone: (602) 242-6265 Carnegie Class: Spec-4-yr-Other Health
FAX Number: (602) 973-2572 Calendar System: Other
URL: www.brooklinecollege.edu
Established: 1979 Annual Undergrad Tuition & Fees: N/A
Enrollment: 1,552 Coed
Affiliation or Control: Proprietary IRS Status: Proprietary
Highest Offering: Baccalaureate
Accreditation: ABHES, MLS, MLTAD, NURSE, PTAA

01 Campus Director ... Mr. Glen THARP
05 Director or Education ... Dr. Lenora SPICER

Brookline College (F)

1140 South Priest Drive, Tempe AZ 85281
Telephone: (480) 545-8755 Identification: 666403
Accreditation: ABHES, SURTEC

† Branch campus of Brookline College, Phoenix, AZ.

Brookline College (G)

5441 E 22nd Street, Suite 125, Tucson AZ 85711-5444
Telephone: (520) 748-9799 Identification: 666402
Accreditation: ABHES, SURTEC

† Branch campus of Brookline College, Phoeniz, AZ.

Bryan University (H)

350 West Washington Street, Ste 100, Tempe AZ 85281
County: Maricopa FICE Identification: 007164
Unit ID: 110219
Telephone: (602) 384-2555 Carnegie Class: Bac/Assoc-Mixed
FAX Number: (888) 458-0447 Calendar System: Quarter
URL: www.bryanuniversity.edu
Established: 1940 Annual Undergrad Tuition & Fees: $11,755
Enrollment: 1,350 Coed
Affiliation or Control: Proprietary IRS Status: Proprietary
Highest Offering: Master's
Accreditation: ACCSC, CAHIIM

01 President/COO ... Mr. Eric EVANS
03 Executive Vice President ... Mr. Dimitrios KRIARAS
05 Exec Dir Undergraduate Studies ... Mr. Nicholas KEELING
10 Chief Financial Officer ... Mr. David ROGERS
06 Registrar ... Ms. Hope BEJARANO
37 VP of Student Finance ... Ms. Roxane ROMERO
32 Dean of Students ... Dr. Dylan MATSUMORI

Carrington College - Mesa (I)

1001 W Southern Avenue, Suite 130, Mesa AZ 85210
Telephone: (480) 212-1600 FICE Identification: 023352
Accreditation: &WJ, ADNUR, DH, MAC, PTAA

† Regional accreditation is carried under the parent institution in Sacramento, CA.

Carrington College - Phoenix East (J)

2149 W Dunlap Avenue, Suite 103, Phoenix AZ 85021
Telephone: (602) 427-0660 Identification: 666248
Accreditation: &WJ, COARC, MAC

† Regional accreditation is carried under the parent institution in Sacramento, CA.

Carrington College - Phoenix North (K)

8503 N 27th Avenue, Phoenix AZ 85051
Telephone: (602) 393-5900 FICE Identification: 021006
Accreditation: &WJ, ADNUR

† Regional accreditation is carried under the parent institution in Sacramento, CA.

Carrington College - Tucson (L)

201 N. Bonita Avenue, Suite 101, Tucson AZ 85745
Telephone: (520) 888-5885 FICE Identification: 030898
Accreditation: &WJ, ADNUR, MAC

† Regional accreditation is carried under the parent institution in Sacramento, CA.

Central Arizona College (M)

8470 N Overfield Road, Coolidge AZ 85128-9779
County: Pinal FICE Identification: 007283
Unit ID: 104346
Telephone: (520) 494-5111 Carnegie Class: Assoc/HT-Mix Trad/Non
FAX Number: (520) 494-5008 Calendar System: Semester
URL: www.centralaz.edu
Established: 1961 Annual Undergrad Tuition & Fees (In-District): $2,580
Enrollment: 4,076 Coed
Affiliation or Control: Local IRS Status: 501(c)3
Highest Offering: Associate Degree
Accreditation: HLC, ADNUR, CAHIIM, DIETT, EMT, MAC, MLTAD, NAEYC, RAD

01 President ... Dr. Jacquelyn ELLIOTT
05 VP Academic Affairs ... Dr. Mary K. GILLILAND
32 VP Student Services ... Dr. Jenni CARDENAS
107 Academic Dean ... Dr. Tina BERRY
81 Academic Dean ... Vacant
10 VP/CFO Business Affairs ... Mr. Chris WODKA
15 Executive Dir Talent Development ... Vacant
08 Director Library Services ... Ms. Adriana SAAVEDRA
37 Director of Financial Aid ... Ms. Elisa JUAREZ
41 Athletic Director ... Ms. Shelby DAVIS
39 Director of Residence Life ... Ms. Rosemary RAMIREZ
18 Associate Director of Facilities ... Mr. Domingo BARRAGAN
96 Director of Purchasing ... Mr. Mark SALAZ
06 Registrar ... Ms. Veronica DURAN
84 Dir Enrollment Mgmt & Outreach ... Ms. Sandra LASCHER
21 Exec Dir Accounting Svc/Comptroller ... Ms. Luisa OTT
114 Exec Director Budget & Acctng ... Ms. Jody TRAVIS
30 Director Institutional Development ... Vacant
07 Dean of Enrollment Services ... Mr. Andrew LONG
04 Exec Asst to President & Gov Board ... Ms. Mary Lou HERNANDEZ
13 Chief Info Technology Officer (CIO) ... Mr. Cameron SANDERS
19 Chief of Police ... Mr. Gregory L. ROBERTS
26 Exec Dir PR & Marketing ... Ms. Angela ASKEY
09 Exec Dir Inst Effectiveness ... Mr. Dustin MARONEY
25 Director Resource Development ... Mr. Hugo STEINCAMP
121 Director of Advising ... Mr. Derek SHANK

Chamberlain University-Phoenix (N)

2149 West Dunlap Avenue, Phoenix AZ 85021
Telephone: (602) 331-2720 Identification: 770502
Accreditation: &HLC, NURSE

† Branch campus of Chamberlain University-Addison, Addison, IL

Cochise College (O)

901 N Colombo Avenue, Sierra Vista AZ 85635-2317
County: Cochise FICE Identification: 001072
Unit ID: 104425
Telephone: (800) 966-7943 Carnegie Class: Assoc/HVT-High Non
FAX Number: (520) 417-4006 Calendar System: Semester

URL: www.cochise.edu
Established: 1964 Annual Undergrad Tuition & Fees (In-District): $2,184
Enrollment: 3,327 Coed
Affiliation or Control: State/Local IRS Status: 170(c)1
Highest Offering: Associate Degree
Accreditation: HLC

01 Chief Executive Officer/President .... Dr. James D. ROTTWEILER
04 Executive Asst to President .... Ms. Crystal WHEELER
05 Executive VP for Academics .... Dr. James PEREY
11 VP Administration .... Dr. Wendy DAVIS
13 Chief Information Officer .... Mr. David LUNA
15 Executive Director Human Resources .... Mr. Wick LEWIS
102 Exec Dir Foundation & Ext Relations .... Ms. Denise HOYOS
49 Dean Liberal Arts .... Ms. Angela GARCIA
81 Dean Math and Sciences .... Dr. Thomas GUETZLOFF
76 Dean Nursing/Allied Health .... Ms. Beth HILL
50 Dean Business and Technology .... Dr. Kristy RITTER
56 Dean Outreach .... Ms. Barbara RICHARDSON
103 Dean of Workforce Development .... Mr. Karl GRIFFOR
84 Asst Dean Enroll Mgmt & Marketing .... Ms. Robyn MARTIN
88 Asst Dean Business & Technology .... Dr. Dale PORTER
88 Assistant Dean Military Programs . Mr. F. Cullen SCARBOROUGH
18 Dir Maintenance & Operations .... Mr. James BARROWS
06 Registrar .... Ms. Faye LUNA
08 Director Library Services .... Ms. Karly SCARBROUGH
96 Director Procurement Services .... Mr. Jeff MOUNTJOY
39 Director of Housing & Resident Life .... Ms. Manda BURKHART
117 Director Risk Management .... Mr. Ben WILSON
37 Director Student Financial Aid .... Ms. Karen EMMER
38 Director Counseling and Advising .... Dr. Miranda VIVIAN
88 Dir TRIO Student Support Services .... Ms. Gabriela AMAVIZCA
22 Director of Accessibility Services .... Ms. Nanette ROMO
66 Director Nursing .... Ms. Melesa ASHLINE
88 Director Aviation Programs .... Ms. Belinda BURNETT
55 Director Adult Education .... Mr. Peter HOOPER
88 Director Small Business Dev Center .... Mr. Mark SCHMITT
51 Ctr for Lifelong Learning Manager .... Ms. Ana SMITH
88 Director of Testing Services .... Ms. Rebecca WESTBY
113 Director of Business Office .... Ms. Sally APARICIO
25 Director Grants Management .... Ms. Celia JENKINS
90 Director User Support Services .... Mr. Jesus ARRIETA
88 Director of Compliance/Title IX .... Ms. Jessica MORGAN-TATE
21 Director Finance/Controller .... Ms. Carol HOLDEN
88 Director EMS Program .... Ms. Kelly JUVERA
88 Director of Cyber Security .... Ms. Michelle HIGGS
41 Director of Athletics .... Vacant
32 Vice President of Student Services .... Dr. Dana HORNE
119 Chief Info Security Officer .... Mr. Robert GIBBS
121 Dean of Academic Affairs .... Dr. Sheena BROWN
31 Exec Dean of Community Engagement .... Dr. Jennifer WANTZ
88 Exec Dir First Responders Academy .... Dr. Eric BROOKS

Cochise College (A)

4190 W. Highway 80, Douglas AZ 85607-6190
Telephone: (800) 966-7943 Identification: 770004
Accreditation: &HLC, ADNUR, EMT

Coconino Community College (B)

2800 S Lone Tree Road, Flagstaff AZ 86005
County: Coconino FICE Identification: 031004
Unit ID: 404426
Telephone: (928) 527-1222 Carnegie Class: Assoc/HT-Mix Trad/Non
FAX Number: (928) 226-4105 Calendar System: Semester
URL: www.coconino.edu
Established: 1991 Annual Undergrad Tuition & Fees (In-State): $3,119
Enrollment: 3,289 Coed
Affiliation or Control: State IRS Status: 501(c)3
Highest Offering: Associate Degree
Accreditation: HLC

01 President .... Dr. Colleen A. SMITH
30 Chief Development Officer .... Ms. Dianna SANCHEZ
05 Provost .... Dr. J. Nathaniel SOUTHERLAND
10 Executive Vice Pres/CFO .... Ms. Jami VAN ESS
32 Dean of Student Affairs .... Mr. Tony WILLIAMS
75 Dean of Career & Technical Educ .... Ms. Lisa BLANK
49 Dean of Arts & Sciences .... Dr. Kimberly BATTY-HERBERT
15 Exec Director for Human Resources .... Mr. Dietrich SAUER
09 Dir Institutional Research/Assess .... Mr. Michael MERICA
37 Director for Financial Aid/Vet Aff .... Mr. Robert VOYTEK
06 Registrar .... Ms. Robin JARECKI
04 Assistant to the President .... Ms. April SANDOVAL

Coconino County Community College Flagstaff Fourth Street Innovation Center (C)

3000 N Fourth Street, Flagstaff AZ 86004
Telephone: (928) 526-7600 Identification: 770005
Accreditation: &HLC

Cummings Gaduate Institute for Behavioral Health Studies (D)

2111 East Baseline Road, Suite E1, Tempe AZ 85283
County: Maricopa Identification: 667376
Telephone: (480) 285-1761 Carnegie Class: Not Classified
FAX Number: N/A Calendar System: Quarter
URL: https://cgi.edu/
Established: 2015 Annual Graduate Tuition & Fees: N/A
Enrollment: N/A Coed
Affiliation or Control: Independent Non-Profit IRS Status: 501(c)3
Highest Offering: Doctorate; No Undergraduates
Accreditation: DEAC

01 President/CEO .... Dr. Cara ENGLISH
05 Dir Instruction Electronic Campus .... Lori CHRISTIANSON
11 Chief Operating Officer .... Amanda HARRISON
26 Director of Marketing .... Melissa MCGURGAN
06 Registrar/Enrollment Coordinator .... Vicki HAYES
10 Controller/Office Manager .... Denice LANGE
51 Director of Continuing Education .... Dr. Alicia INIGUEZ

DeVry University - Phoenix Campus (E)

2149 W Dunlap Avenue, Phoenix AZ 85021
Telephone: (602) 749-7301 FICE Identification: 008322
Accreditation: &HLC, ACBSP

† Regional accreditation is carried under the parent institution in Downers Grove, IL.

Diné College (F)

One Circle Drive, Tsaile AZ 86556-9998
County: Apache FICE Identification: 008246
Unit ID: 105297
Telephone: (928) 724-6671 Carnegie Class: Tribal
FAX Number: (928) 724-3327 Calendar System: Semester
URL: www.dinecollege.edu
Established: 1968 Annual Undergrad Tuition & Fees (In-District): $1,410
Enrollment: 1,369 Coed
Affiliation or Control: Local IRS Status: 501(c)3
Highest Offering: Master's
Accreditation: HLC

01 President .... Dr. Charles ROESSEL
10 Vice Pres Finance/Administration .... Ms. Bo LEWIS
32 Vice Pres of Student Affairs .... Ms. Glennita HASKEY
05 Provost .... Dr. Geraldine GARRITY
86 Vice Pres External Affairs/PR .... Ms. Marie R. NEZ
06 Registrar .... Ms. Louise LITZIN
37 Financial Aid Officer .... Mr. Nolan S. BEGAYE
15 Dir Department of Human Resources .... Mr. Merle DAYZIE
18 Supt Maintenance Operations .... Mr. Leon JACKSON
21 Controller .... Ms. Raychelle LEONARD
46 Dir Inst Grants/Sponsored Projects .... Ms. Amanda MCNEILL

Dunlap-Stone University (G)

19820 North 7th Street, Suite 100, Phoenix AZ 85024
County: Maricopa Identification: 666315
Telephone: (602) 648-5750 Carnegie Class: Not Classified
FAX Number: (602) 648-5755 Calendar System: Other
URL: www.dunlap-stone.edu
Established: 1995 Annual Undergrad Tuition & Fees: N/A
Enrollment: N/A Coed
Affiliation or Control: Proprietary IRS Status: Proprietary
Highest Offering: Master's
Accreditation: DEAC

00 Chancellor .... Dr. Donald N. BURTON
01 President/Chief Academic Officer .... Mrs. Caulyne BARRON

Eastern Arizona College (H)

615 N Stadium Avenue, Thatcher AZ 85552-0769
County: Graham FICE Identification: 001073
Unit ID: 104577
Telephone: (928) 428-8233 Carnegie Class: Assoc/MT-VT-High Non
FAX Number: (928) 428-2578 Calendar System: Semester
URL: www.eac.edu
Established: 1888 Annual Undergrad Tuition & Fees (In-District): $2,700
Enrollment: 4,392 Coed
Affiliation or Control: State/Local IRS Status: 501(c)3
Highest Offering: Associate Degree
Accreditation: HLC, ADNUR, EMT

01 President .... Mr. Todd HAYNIE
05 Vice President of Academics .... Dr. Susan WOOD
11 Vice President of Administration .... Mr. Heston WELKER
13 Chief Information Officer .... Mr. Thomas THOMPSON
20 Dean of Instruction .... Dr. Phil MCBRIDE
20 Dean of Curriculum and Instruction .... Dr. Janice LAWHORN
32 Dean of Students .... Dr. Gary SORENSEN
06 Registrar .... Ms. Heather AUGENSTEIN
35 Dean of Student Services .... Mr. Kenny SMITH
12 Director of Discovery Park Campus .... Mr. Paul ANGER
21 Director Fiscal Control/Controller .... Mr. Troy AINSWORTH
37 Director of Financial Aid .... Mrs. Sharon MONTOYA
108 Director of Accreditation .... Mrs. Shannon SEBALLOS
08 Director of Library Services .... Mrs. Tammy POWERS
26 Dir of Marketing & Public Relations .... Mr. Kris MCBRIDE
18 Director of Physical Resources .... Mr. Jeremy HUGHES
102 Executive Director EAC Foundation .... Mr. David UDALL
35 Director of Student Life .... Mr. Danny BATTRAW
41 Athletic Director .... Mr. James BAGNALL
15 Director Admin Support/HR .... Mrs. Lydia NEWKIRK
04 Exec Asst to the President and DGB .... Mrs. Jodi KEIM
86 Special Asst Government Relations .... Mr. Keith ALEXANDER

Eastern Arizona College Gila Pueblo Campus (I)

8274 Six Shooter Canyon,PO Box 2656, Globe AZ 85502
Telephone: (928) 425-8481 Identification: 770008
Accreditation: &HLC

Eastern Arizona College Payson Campus (J)

201 North Mud Springs Rd,PO Box 359, Payson AZ 85547
Telephone: (928) 468-8039 Identification: 770009
Accreditation: &HLC

Embry-Riddle Aeronautical University-Prescott (K)

3700 Willow Creek Road, Prescott AZ 86301-3270
Telephone: (800) 888-3728 FICE Identification: 021047
Accreditation: &SC, AAB, ACBSP

† Regional accreditation is carried under the parent institution in Daytona Beach, FL.

Grand Canyon University (L)

3300 W Camelback Road, Phoenix AZ 85017-3030
County: Maricopa FICE Identification: 001074
Unit ID: 104717
Telephone: (602) 639-7500 Carnegie Class: DU-Mod
FAX Number: N/A Calendar System: Semester
URL: www.gcu.edu
Established: 1949 Annual Undergrad Tuition & Fees: $17,800
Enrollment: 103,427 Coed
Affiliation or Control: Independent Non-Profit IRS Status: 501(c)3
Highest Offering: Doctorate
Accreditation: HLC, AAQEP, ACBSP, CAATE, @DIET, NURSE, SW, THEOL

01 President/Chief Executive Officer .... Mr. Brian MUELLER
05 Provost .... Dr. Randy GIBB
10 Vice Pres Business/Finance .... Ms. Junette WEST
11 Chief Admin Ofcr/General Counsel .... Mr. Ray KASELONIS
13 Chief Information Officer .... Mr. Joseph MILDENHALL
20 Vice Provost .... Dr. Jennifer LECH
26 Exec Vice Pres of Marketing .... Ms. Christel MOSBY
41 Vice President of Athletics .... Ms. Jamie BOGGS
32 VP Student Svcs/Dean of Students .... Dr. Tim GRIFFIN
121 Vice Pres Student Success .... Dr. Joe VERES
110 Vice President Advancement .... Dr. T. Kale GOBER
37 Vice Pres Student Financial Aid .... Ms. Trish LEONARD
50 Dean Colangelo College Business .... Dr. Randy GIBB
53 Dean College of Education .... Dr. Meredith CRITCHFIELD
66 Dean College Nursing/Hlth Care Prof .... Dr. Lisa SMITH
49 Dean College Sci/Engineering/Tech .... Dr. K. Mark WOODEN
58 Dean College Doctoral Studies .... Dr. Michael BERGER
57 Dean College Arts and Media .... Dr. Craig DETWEILER
73 Dean College of Theology .... Dr. Jason HILES
79 Dean College Human/Social Science .... Dr. Sherman ELLIOTT

Harrison Middleton University (M)

3345 South Rural Road, Tempe AZ 85282-5404
County: Maricopa Identification: 666169
Telephone: (877) 248-6724 Carnegie Class: Not Classified
FAX Number: (800) 762-1622 Calendar System: Other
URL: www.hmu.edu
Established: 1998 Annual Graduate Tuition & Fees: N/A
Enrollment: N/A Coed
Affiliation or Control: Proprietary IRS Status: Proprietary
Highest Offering: Doctorate; No Undergraduates
Accreditation: DEAC

01 President .... Dr. Joseph COULSON
05 Exec Vice Pres of Education/CEO .... Mr. Michael CURD
51 VP/Dean Continuing Education .... Ms. Rebecca FISHER
06 Registrar/VP Accreditation .... Ms. Lauren GUTHRIE

Indian Bible College (N)

2237 E. Cedar Avenue, Flagstaff AZ 86004
County: Coconino Identification: 667317
Telephone: (928) 774-3890 Carnegie Class: Not Classified
FAX Number: (928) 774-2655 Calendar System: Semester
URL: www.indianbible.org
Established: 1958 Annual Undergrad Tuition & Fees: N/A
Enrollment: N/A Coed
Affiliation or Control: Independent Non-Profit IRS Status: 501(c)3
Highest Offering: Baccalaureate
Accreditation: BI

01 President .... Dr. Jason KOPPEN
32 EVP/Dean of Students .... Mr. Clint ROSS
05 Academic Dean .... Vacant
07 Director Admissions .... Mr. Daniel ESPLIN
08 Librarian .... Ms. Deedra DALLAS

International Baptist College and Seminary (O)

2211 W Germann Road, Chandler AZ 85286
County: Maricopa FICE Identification: 033473
Unit ID: 436614
Telephone: (480) 245-7903 Carnegie Class: Spec-4-yr-Faith
FAX Number: (480) 245-7909 Calendar System: Semester

URL: www.ibcs.edu
Established: 1980 Annual Undergrad Tuition & Fees: $12,900
Enrollment: 78 Coed
Affiliation or Control: Baptist IRS Status: 501(c)3
Highest Offering: Doctorate
Accreditation: TRACS

01 President ..... Pastor Nathan M. MESTLER
32 Dean of Students ..... Dr. Kristopher ENDEAN
05 Academic Dean ..... Dr. David SHUMATE
10 Chief Financial Officer ..... Vacant
20 Seminary Dean ..... Dr. David SHUMATE
30 Chief Development/Advancement ..... Vacant
07 Director of Admissions ..... Pastor Scott OLSON
09 Director of Inst Effectiveness ..... Mrs. Rebecca M. STERTZBACH
08 Media Center Director ..... Mr. Lee WILL
34 Dean of Women ..... Mrs. Marcia L. GAMMON
06 Registrar ..... Miss Brittany MOFFITT
37 Financial Aid Administrator ..... Mrs. Eliza MAYORAL
04 Exec Asst to President/Office Mgr ..... Mrs. Rebecca M. STERTZBACH

*Maricopa County Community College District Office (A)

2411 W 14th Street, Tempe AZ 85281-6941
County: Maricopa FICE Identification: 001075
Unit ID: 105136
Telephone: (480) 731-8000 Carnegie Class: N/A
FAX Number: (480) 731-8850
URL: www.maricopa.edu

01 Interim Chancellor ..... Dr. Steven R. GONZALES
05 Interim VC & Provost ..... Dr. Eric LESHINSKIE
102 President/CEO Foundation ..... Mr. Brian F. SPICKER
15 Chief Human Resources Officer ..... Ms. Georgetta KELLY
13 Vice Chancellor Information Tech ..... Dr. Mark KOAN
103 Chief Workforce/Econ Dev Officer ..... Ms. Darcy RENFRO
09 Assoc VC Inst Strategy/Rsrch/Effect ..... Mr. Matthew ASHCRAFT

*Chandler-Gilbert Community College (B)

2626 E Pecos Road, Chandler AZ 85225-2499
County: Maricopa FICE Identification: 030722
Unit ID: 364025
Telephone: (480) 732-7000 Carnegie Class: Assoc/HT-Mix Trad/Non
FAX Number: (480) 732-7090 Calendar System: Semester
URL: www.cgc.maricopa.edu
Established: 1992 Annual Undergrad Tuition & Fees (In-District): $2,070
Enrollment: 13,395 Coed
Affiliation or Control: State/Local IRS Status: 501(c)3
Highest Offering: Associate Degree
Accreditation: HLC, ADNUR

02 College President ..... Dr. Gregory PETERSON
04 Executive Assistant to President ..... Ms. Susan D. HAMS
05 Vice President Academic Affairs ..... Dr. William GUERRIERO
32 VP Student Affairs ..... Ms. Veronica HIPOLITO
11 VP Administrative Services ..... Mr. Bradley S. KENDREX
49 Dean of Arts and Sciences ..... Mr. Chris SCHNICK
20 Dean of Instruction ..... Ms. Gabriela ROSU
31 AVP of Institutional Advancement ..... Ms. Jenna KAHL
10 Assoc VP of Business Operations ..... Dr. Bernadette LA MAZZA
84 Dean of Enrollment Services ..... Dr. Felicia RAMIREZ-PEREZ
88 Dean of Student Development ..... Dr. Anne SUZUKI
07 Director Admissions ..... Mr. Paul TRAN
09 Director Planning & Research ..... Ms. Theresa WONG
36 Student Services Supervisor ..... Ms. Deb RUIZ
85 Dir International Education Program ..... Vacant
22 Dir Disability Resources & Svcs ..... Ms. Dawn GRUICHICH
18 Interim Facilities Director ..... Mr. Josh DODDROE
35 Director Student Life & Leadership ..... Mr. Michael GREENE
41 Athletic Director ..... Mr. Russ LUCE
19 College Police Commander ..... Mr. Charles MOUNT
37 Director Financial Aid ..... Dr. Timothy WOLSEY
88 Director Learning Center ..... Ms. Eva R. FALLETTA
88 Director Early Outreach Programs ..... Mr. Lambert YAZZIE
88 Director Instr Tech & Course Prod ..... Dr. Jeremy TUTTY
66 Division Chair Nursing ..... Dr. Jill ANDERSON
13 Int Dir Computer Labs/Instr Svcs ..... Ms. Sonya BRIESKE
113 Manager College Cashiers Office ..... Ms. Julie WRIGHT
15 Senior Human Resource Manager ..... Mr. Joe VARGAS

*Estrella Mountain Community College (C)

3000 N Dysart Road, Avondale AZ 85392
County: Maricopa FICE Identification: 031563
Unit ID: 384333
Telephone: (623) 935-8000 Carnegie Class: Assoc/HT-Mix Trad/Non
FAX Number: (623) 935-8008 Calendar System: Semester
URL: www.estrellamountain.edu
Established: 1990 Annual Undergrad Tuition & Fees (In-District): $2,070
Enrollment: 8,768 Coed
Affiliation or Control: State/Local IRS Status: 501(c)3
Highest Offering: Associate Degree
Accreditation: HLC, ADNUR

02 President ..... Dr. Rey RIVERA
11 Vice President Admin Services ..... Dr. Heather WEBER
32 Vice President Student Affairs ..... Dr. Patricia CARDENAS-ADAME
05 Vice Pres of Academic Affairs ..... Dr. Kimberley HARRELL
20 Dean of Academic Affairs ..... Dr. Sylvia ORR
35 Dean of Student Services ..... Ms. Laura DULGAR
09 Dean Planning/Rsrch/Effectiveness ..... Mr. John SNELLING
08 Division Chair Information Resource ..... Ms. Nikol PRICE
18 Director Facilities Planning/Devel ..... Vacant
13 Associate Vice President IT ..... Mr. Chad GALLIGAN
07 Dir Student Svcs Admissions/Records ..... Mr. Ralph CAMPBELL
10 Fiscal Director ..... Ms. Leda JOHNSON
102 Dir Corp Foundation Rels/Dev Ops ..... Mr. Jonathan P. ROBLES
37 Dir Student Svcs/Financial Aid ..... Ms. Rosanna SHORT
114 Fiscal Director Budget ..... Ms. Maggie CASTILLO
15 Director Human Resources ..... Mr. Teofilo FERRER

*GateWay Community College (D)

108 N 40th Street, Phoenix AZ 85034-1795
County: Maricopa FICE Identification: 008303
Unit ID: 105145
Telephone: (602) 286-8000 Carnegie Class: Assoc/HVT-Mix Trad/Non
FAX Number: (602) 286-8072 Calendar System: Semester
URL: www.gatewaycc.edu/
Established: 1968 Annual Undergrad Tuition & Fees (In-District): $2,070
Enrollment: 4,670 Coed
Affiliation or Control: State/Local IRS Status: 501(c)3
Highest Offering: Associate Degree
Accreditation: HLC, ADNUR, COARC, DMS, MAC, NDT, NMT, OTA, POLYT, PTAA, RAD, SURGT

02 Interim President ..... Dr. Amy DIAZ
05 Int Vice Pres Academic Affairs ..... Dr. Stephanie POLLIARD
32 Vice Pres Student Affairs ..... Dr. Delfina WILSON
11 Vice President Administrative Svcs ..... Mr. Tony ASTI
09 AVP Institutional Effectiveness ..... Dr. Cathy HERNANDEZ
114 Budget Fiscal Manager ..... Ms. Regina GUTIERREZ
10 AVP Administrative Services ..... Ms. Cecilia VILLA
13 AVP Information Tech/Facilities ..... Mr. Jose CANDANEDO
26 Director Marketing/Public Relations ..... Ms. Lindsey WILSON
111 AVP External Affairs ..... Ms. Kristin GUBSER
37 Director Student Financial Aid ..... Ms. Suzanne RINGLE
15 Human Resources Director ..... Ms. Mika DAVIS
06 Registrar/Dir Enrollment Svcs ..... Ms. Kristie FOK

*Glendale Community College (E)

6000 W Olive Avenue, Glendale AZ 85302-3006
County: Maricopa FICE Identification: 001076
Unit ID: 104708
Telephone: (623) 845-3000 Carnegie Class: Assoc/HT-Mix Trad/Non
FAX Number: (623) 845-3329 Calendar System: Semester
URL: www.gccaz.edu
Established: 1965 Annual Undergrad Tuition & Fees (In-District): $2,070
Enrollment: 14,374 Coed
Affiliation or Control: State/Local IRS Status: 170(c)1
Highest Offering: Associate Degree
Accreditation: HLC, ADNUR, EMT

02 President ..... Dr. Teresa LEYBA-RUIZ
05 VP Academic Affairs ..... Mr. Scott SCHULZ
32 VP Student Affairs ..... Ms. Monica CASTAÑEDA
11 VP Admin Services & CIO ..... Ms. Augustine ERPELDING
108 Assoc VP Inst Effectiveness ..... Dr. Alka ARORA SINGH
20 Dean of Academic Affairs ..... Dr. Fernando CAMOU
20 Dean of Acad Affs Career & Tech Ed ..... Dr. Susan CAMPBELL
20 Sr AVP of Academic Affairs ..... Dr. Lorelei CARVAJAL
84 Dean Enrollment Services ..... Vacant
35 Dean Student Life ..... Dr. Genesis TOOLE
12 Dean of Academic Affs/GCC North ..... Mr. Charles JEFFERY
37 Director Financial Aid ..... Ms. Annette LINDERS
18 Director Facilities ..... Mr. Al GONZALES
10 Director College Business Services ..... Ms. Kim GOLIS
26 Dir Sales Mktg & Public Rels ..... Mr. John HECKENLAIBLE
45 Dir Institutional Effectiveness ..... Mr. Kerry MITCHELL
15 Dir College Employee Svcs ..... Ms. June S. FESSENDEN
30 Director of Development ..... Ms. Frances MATEO
13 Director College Technology Svcs ..... Mr. Isaiah WASHINGTON
38 Dept Chair Counseling ..... Mr. Paul ROMO
08 Dept Chair Library ..... Mr. Frank TORRES
19 Police Commander ..... Ms. Debra PALOK
04 Admin Coordinator to College Pres ..... Ms. Esmeralda M. ACOSTA
41 Athletic Director ..... Mr. Peter OLISZCZAK
79 Dept Chair Art & Humanities ..... Mr. Brendan REGAN
81 Dept Chair Biology ..... Ms. Karen CONZELMAN
50 Dept Chair Business & Info Tech ..... Ms. Rachelle HALL
81 Dept Chair Chemistry ..... Ms. Debbie LEEDY
79 Dept Chair Comm & World Languages ..... Dr. Pam JORAANSTAD
60 Dept Chair Eng/Reading/Journalism ..... Mr. David MILLER
68 Dept Chair Fitness & Wellness ..... Ms. Lisa LEWIS
77 Dept Chair Math/Computer Science ..... Mr. Chris MILLER
66 Dept Chair Nursing ..... Dr. Susan MAYER
57 Dept Chair Performing Arts ..... Mr. Donald SMITH
73 Dept Chair Phil/Religious Stds ..... Mr. Peter LUPU
81 Dept Chair Physical Sciences ..... Mr. David RAFFAELLE
83 Dept Chair Psychology ..... Dr. Julie MORRISON
88 Dept Chair Public Safety Sciences ..... Mr. Chris COUGHLIN
83 Dept Chair Social Sciences ..... Mr. Dean WHEELER
72 Dept Chair Tech & Consumer Sciences ..... Ms. Angela JORDAN
88 Dept Chair Automotives ..... Mr. Jay COVEY

*Mesa Community College (F)

1833 W Southern Avenue, Mesa AZ 85202-4866
County: Maricopa FICE Identification: 001077
Unit ID: 105154
Telephone: (480) 461-7000 Carnegie Class: Assoc/HT-Mix Trad/Non
FAX Number: N/A Calendar System: Semester
URL: www.mesacc.edu/
Established: 1965 Annual Undergrad Tuition & Fees (In-District): $2,070
Enrollment: 16,948 Coed
Affiliation or Control: State/Local IRS Status: 501(c)3
Highest Offering: Associate Degree
Accreditation: HLC, ADNUR, DH, EMT

02 President ..... Dr. Tammy ROBINSON
05 Sr Assoc VP Academic Affairs ..... Dr. Nora REYES
32 Sr Assoc VP Student Affairs ..... Mrs. Carmen NEWLAND
11 Int Vice Pres Admin Services ..... Mr. Bradley KENDREX
13 VP Information Technology ..... Vacant
09 Assoc VP Inst Effectiveness ..... Dr. Dennis MITCHELL
111 AVP Institutional Advancement ..... Mrs. Marcy SNITZER
10 Assoc Vice Pres Admin Services ..... Ms. Mary DRIESSEN
20 Dean of Instruction ..... Mr. Michael VOSS
20 Dean of Instruction ..... Dr. Francis CANEDO
20 Dean of Instruction ..... Ms. Carol ACHS
76 Dean of Health Sciences ..... Ms. Mary BOYCE
84 Dean of Enrollment Development ..... Dr. Andrew STONE
35 Dean of Student Development ..... Dr. Julie VOLLER
30 Chief Development Officer ..... Mr. Christos CHRONIS
37 Dir Financial Aid/Scholarships ..... Ms. Patricia PEPPIN
19 Police Sergeant ..... Mr. Jack MCCLAREN
29 Director Alumni Relations ..... Ms. Marcy SNITZER
41 Athletic Director ..... Mr. John MULHERN
18 Director of Facilities ..... Mr. Steve AZEVEDO
06 Director of A&R & Registrar ..... Mr. Jeffrey RHOADS
15 Director of Human Resources ..... Mr. Garrett SMITH
08 Library Department Chair ..... Mr. Trevor SMITH
100 Chief of Staff ..... Mr. Juan DIARTE
106 eLearning Director ..... Ms. Laura BALLARD
108 Director of Assessment ..... Ms. Kimberly THOMPSON
26 Media Relations Manager ..... Ms. Stacy PICKAVANCE
28 College Diversity Officer ..... Ms. Nicole COLLINS
38 Counseling Department Chair ..... Dr. Angel BRANCH MOORE

*Paradise Valley Community College (G)

18401 N 32nd Street, Phoenix AZ 85032-1210
County: Maricopa FICE Identification: 026236
Unit ID: 364016
Telephone: (602) 787-6500 Carnegie Class: Assoc/HT-Mix Trad/Non
FAX Number: (602) 787-6625 Calendar System: Semester
URL: www.paradisevalley.edu
Established: 1985 Annual Undergrad Tuition & Fees (In-District): $2,070
Enrollment: 6,575 Coed
Affiliation or Control: State/Local IRS Status: 501(c)3
Highest Offering: Associate Degree
Accreditation: HLC, ADNUR, DIETT, EMT, NAEYC

02 President ..... Dr. Tiffany HUNTER
05 Vice President of Academic Affairs ..... Dr. Doug BERRY
11 VP Administrative Services ..... Mr. Herman GONZALEZ
32 Vice President of Student Affairs ..... Dr. Jana SCHWARTZ
20 Dean of Academic Affairs ..... Dr. Jamie MARTIN
84 Dean Admin Affs/Enrollment Services ..... Dr. Jen MILLER
15 Director Personnel Services ..... Dr. Kimberlin GLENN
10 Director Fiscal Services ..... Dr. Huu HOANG
18 Chief Facilities/Physical Plant ..... Mr. Bob GARCIA
37 Director Student Financial Aid ..... Ms. Kathaerine JOHNSON
38 Director Student Counseling ..... Dr. James RUBIN
06 Dean/Registrar ..... Mr. Frank AMPARO
36 Director Student Placement ..... Ms. Norma CHANDLER
26 Dir of Marketing/Public Relations ..... Ms. Tina MILLER
09 Dir Institutional Research/Effect ..... Dr. Sherri ONDRUS LEWIS
19 Director Security/Safety ..... Mr. Scott MEEK
41 Athletic Director ..... Ms. Christina HUNDLEY
30 Director of Development ..... Dr. Brianna DEGEUS

*Phoenix College (H)

1202 W Thomas Road, Phoenix AZ 85013-4234
County: Maricopa FICE Identification: 001078
Unit ID: 105428
Telephone: (602) 285-7777 Carnegie Class: Assoc/HT-Mix Trad/Non
FAX Number: (602) 285-7700 Calendar System: Semester
URL: www.pc.maricopa.edu
Established: 1920 Annual Undergrad Tuition & Fees (In-District): $2,070
Enrollment: 9,538 Coed
Affiliation or Control: State/Local IRS Status: 501(c)3
Highest Offering: Associate Degree
Accreditation: HLC, ADNUR, CAHIIM, DA, DH, EMT, HT, MLTAD

02 Interim President ..... Dr. Clyne NAMUO
05 VP of Academic Affairs ..... Dr. Kimberly BRITT
32 Vice Pres of Student Affairs ..... Dr. Heather KRUSE
11 VP Administrative Services ..... Mr. Paul DEROSE
15 Chief Human Resources Officer ..... Ms. Barbara CHERNER
13 Chief Information Ofcr/AVP IT ..... Mr. Paul ROSS
10 Assoc VP Business/Finance ..... Ms. Angela GENNA
20 Dean of Academic Affairs ..... Mr. Wilbert NELSON
35 Dean of Student Affairs ..... Ms. Julie VOLLER

07 Dir Admissions/Registration/Records ... Ms. Brenda STARCK
37 Director Financial Aid ... Ms. Cynthia RAMOS
30 Development Director ... Ms. Deborah SPOTTS
09 Dir Inst Plng/Rsrch/Effectiveness ... Mr. Eugene YE
18 Director of Facilities ... Mr. Douglas MCCARTHY
19 Director of College Safety ... Mr. Matt VERTHEIN
41 Athletic Director ... Ms. Kristine KINCAID
84 Director Advisement/Enrollment ... Ms. Felicia RAMIREZ-PEREZ
88 Int Director Student Leadership ... Ms. Diana MARTINEZ
88 Int Dean Industry/Public Service ... Ms. Maria REYES
26 PR Marketing Manager ... Ms. Erika KEENAN
88 Sr Program Analyst ... Ms. Kimberly ANDERSON
04 Senior Administrative Specialist ... Ms. Briana JORDAN
08 Department Chair Library ... Ms. Christine MOORE
121 Department Chair Counseling ... Mr. Robert VILLEGAS GOLD

*Rio Salado College (A)

2323 W 14th Street, Tempe AZ 85281-6950
County: Maricopa FICE Identification: 021775
Unit ID: 105668
Telephone: (480) 517-8000 Carnegie Class: Assoc/MT-VT-High Non
FAX Number: (480) 377-4719 Calendar System: Semester
URL: www.riosalado.edu
Established: 1978 Annual Undergrad Tuition & Fees (In-District): $2,070
Enrollment: 17,362 Coed
Affiliation or Control: State/Local IRS Status: 501(c)3
Highest Offering: Associate Degree
Accreditation: HLC, DH

02 President ... Dr. Kate SMITH
05 Vice President Academic Affairs ... Dr. Stella PEREZ
10 Vice Pres Administrative Svcs ... Ms. Michelle GATES
32 Vice Pres Student Affairs ... Dr. Greg PEREIRA
13 Vice Pres Technology/Infrastructure ... Mr. David O'SHEA
15 AVP Administrative & Employee Svcs ... Ms. Maria BELLINO
20 Dean of Instruction ... Mr. Rick KEMP
90 Assoc Dean Instruct Tech/Design ... Mr. Michael MEDLOCK
108 Dean of Institutional Effectiveness ... Ms. Karol SCHMIDT
84 Dean Stdnt Affs Enrollment Mgmt ... Dr. Ramona COX
35 Dean of Studnet Affairs ... Ms. Rachelle CLARKE
31 Dean Instruction & Cmty Development ... Dr. Tamara COCHRAN
88 Assoc Dean Community Standards ... Mr. Tafari OSAYANDE
21 Fiscal Director Business Svcs ... Mr. Anthony DISCALA
37 Director of Financial Aid ... Ms. Nanci REGEHR
09 Assoc Dean Institutional Research ... Mr. Zach LEWIS
07 Dir Admissions/Registration/Records ... Ms. Laurel REDMAN
18 Director of Facilities ... Mr. Richard OROS
19 Commander of Public Safety ... Ms. Cecilia STRABALA
16 Human Resources Director ... Ms. Anna FLORES
08 Library Faculty Co-Chair ... Ms. Karen DOCHERTY
08 Library Faculty Co-Chair ... Ms. Sarah STOHR
04 Admin Coordinator to President ... Ms. Kevyn MILLER

*Scottsdale Community College (B)

9000 E Chaparral, Scottsdale AZ 85256-2626
County: Maricopa FICE Identification: 008304
Unit ID: 105747
Telephone: (480) 423-6000 Carnegie Class: Assoc/HT-High Non
FAX Number: (480) 423-6200 Calendar System: Semester
URL: www.scottsdalecc.edu
Established: 1970 Annual Undergrad Tuition & Fees (In-District): $2,070
Enrollment: 7,634 Coed
Affiliation or Control: State/Local IRS Status: 501(c)3
Highest Offering: Associate Degree
Accreditation: HLC, ACFEI, ADNUR

02 President ... Dr. Eric LESHINSKIE
32 Vice Pres Student Affairs ... Dr. Donna YOUNG
05 Interim Vice Pres Academic Affairs ... Dr. Eddie LAMPEREZ
11 Vice Pres Administrative Services ... Ms. Colleen O'NEILL
13 AVP ITS/College CTO ... Mr. Vargha MOHEBBI
20 Interim Dean of Instruction ... Dr. Lucas MESSER
35 Dean of Student Affairs ... Ms. Larissa TRAIN
84 Dean of Enrollment Services ... Ms. Yolanda ESPINOZA
07 Director of Admissions ... Ms. Laura KRUEGER
09 Dir of Institutional Research/Plng ... Dr. Laurie COHEN
08 Director of Library Services ... Vacant
37 Director Financial Aid/Placement ... Ms. Stacie BECK
18 AVP Facilities Mgmt ... Mr. Tony MIELE
19 Director of College Safety ... Mr. Arlyn WALZ
41 Athletic Director ... Mr. Michael MCNALLY
121 Director Student Advisement ... Mr. Darryl GREELEY
04 Executive Assistant ... Ms. Donna COLE
10 Chief Business Officer ... Ms. Mirna ROSAS
15 Director Personnel Services ... Vacant

*South Mountain Community College (C)

7050 S 24th Street, Phoenix AZ 85042-5806
County: Maricopa FICE Identification: 021466
Unit ID: 105792
Telephone: (602) 243-8000 Carnegie Class: Assoc/HT-Mix Trad/Non
FAX Number: (602) 243-8329 Calendar System: Semester
URL: www.southmountaincc.edu
Established: 1979 Annual Undergrad Tuition & Fees (In-District): $2,070
Enrollment: 3,497 Coed
Affiliation or Control: State/Local IRS Status: 501(c)3
Highest Offering: Associate Degree
Accreditation: HLC

02 President ... Dr. Shari L. OLSON-NIKUNEN
05 Interim Vice Pres of Learning ... Ms. Bernice PORTERVINT
11 Vice Pres Administrative Svcs ... Dr. Janet L. ORTEGA
32 Vice Pres Student Affairs ... Dr. Osaro O. IGHODARO
09 Dean Research/Plng & Development ... Ms. Damita A. KALOOSTIAN
20 Interim Dean Academic Affairs ... Dr. Travis MAY
84 Dean Enrollment Services ... Ms. Dana FRASCA
37 Director Financial Aid ... Ms. Elizabeth CARLON
07 Director of Admission & Records ... Ms. Jean C. WATERMOLEN
10 Director College Business Services ... Mr. Mark W. MCCAIN
18 Director of Facilities ... Mr. David S. BANNENBERG
15 Human Resources Director ... Ms. Shanel CARTER
07 Recruitment and Outreach Supervisor ... Ms. Brittney MATTA
41 Associate Dean/Athletic Director ... Mr. Todd B. EASTIN
13 Chief Info Technology Officer ... Mr. Tim BUDWORTH

*Chandler-Gilbert Community College-Williams Campus (D)

7360 E Tahoe Avenue, Mesa AZ 85212-0908
Telephone: (480) 988-8000 Identification: 770178
Accreditation: &HLC, FUSER

*Glendale Community College North (E)

5727 W Happy Valley Road, Phoenix AZ 85310
Telephone: (623) 845-4000 Identification: 770179
Accreditation: &HLC

*Mesa Community College at Red Mountain (F)

7110 East McKellips Road, Mesa AZ 85207
Telephone: (480) 654-7200 Identification: 770180
Accreditation: &HLC

Midwestern University (G)

19555 N 59th Avenue, Glendale AZ 85308
Telephone: (623) 572-3400 Identification: 666001
Accreditation: &HLC, ANEST, ARCPA, CLPSY, DENT, OPT, OPTR, OSTEO, OT, PERF, PHAR, POD, PTA, SP, VET

† Regional accreditation is carried under the parent institution in Downers Grove, IL.

Mohave Community College (H)

1971 E. Jagerson Avenue, Kingman AZ 86409-1238
County: Mohave FICE Identification: 011864
Unit ID: 105206
Telephone: (866) 664-2832 Carnegie Class: Assoc/MT-VT-High Non
FAX Number: (928) 757-0836 Calendar System: Semester
URL: www.mohave.edu
Established: 1971 Annual Undergrad Tuition & Fees (In-District): $2,112
Enrollment: 3,654 Coed
Affiliation or Control: State/Local IRS Status: 501(c)3
Highest Offering: Associate Degree
Accreditation: HLC, ADNUR, DH, EMT, PTAA, RAD, SURGT

01 President ... Dr. Stacy S. KLIPPENSTEIN
03 Executive Vice President ... Dr. Tim CULVER
11 Vice Pres of Administrative Svcs ... Ms. Jennifer DIXON
32 Vice Pres Student & Cmty Engagement ... Dr. Tramaine RAUSAW
84 Dean of Enrollment and Student Svcs ... Ms. Ana MASTERSON
111 Chief Advancement Officer ... Mr. Shawn BRISTLE
13 Chief Information Officer ... Mr. Mark VANPELT
26 Chief Public Relations Officer ... Mr. James JARMAN
15 Chief Human Resources Officer ... Ms. Jennifer PICARD
12 Campus Dean Bullhead City ... Dr. Carolyn HAMBLIN
12 Campus Dean Lake Havasu ... Dr. Maria AYON
12 Campus Dean Neal Kingman ... Dr. Tramaine RAUSAW
12 Campus Dean North Mohave ... Mr. John CAWLEY
76 Dean of Health Professions ... Dr. Liliya TISHCHENKO
97 Dean General Education & Transfer ... Ms. Lucinda LEUGERS
103 Dean of Workforce & Partnerships ... Dr. Kirk LACY
18 Director of Facilities Managment ... Mr. Don MONTGOMERY
09 Director of Institutional Research ... Mr. Matt BUTCHER
04 Administrative Asst to President ... Ms. Amy CURLEY

National Paralegal College (I)

717 East Maryland Avenue, Phoenix AZ 85014-1561
County: Maricopa FICE Identification: 041574
Unit ID: 461023
Telephone: (800) 371-6105 Carnegie Class: Spec-4-yr-Law
FAX Number: (866) 347-2744 Calendar System: Other
URL: nationalparalegal.edu
Established: 2003 Annual Undergrad Tuition & Fees: $7,995
Enrollment: 693 Coed
Affiliation or Control: Proprietary IRS Status: Proprietary
Highest Offering: Master's
Accreditation: DEAC

01 President/CEO ... Avi KATZ
05 Dean/Director Education/CAO ... Stephen HAAS
13 Chief Technology Officer ... David COHEN
07 Director of Admissions ... Dana LUKSENBURG
37 Director Student Financial Aid ... Lisa PIMBER

Northern Arizona University (J)

South San Francisco Street, Flagstaff AZ 86011-0001
County: Coconino FICE Identification: 001082
Unit ID: 105330
Telephone: (928) 523-9011 Carnegie Class: DU-Higher
FAX Number: (928) 523-1848 Calendar System: Semester
URL: www.nau.edu
Established: 1899 Annual Undergrad Tuition & Fees (In-State): $11,896
Enrollment: 29,566 Coed
Affiliation or Control: State IRS Status: 501(c)3
Highest Offering: Doctorate
Accreditation: HLC, ACBSP, ACPHA, ARCPA, CAATE, CACREP, CAEP, CAPRT, CIDA, CLPSY, CONST, DH, @DIET, DIETD, EXSC, IPSY, MUS, NURSE, OT, PSPSY, PTA, SP, SPAA, SW, THEA

01 President ... Dr. Jose Luis CRUZ RIVERA
100 Chief of Staff ... Mr. Brian REGISTRAR
05 Int Provost & EVP Academic Affairs ... Dr. Karen PUGLIESI
10 SVP Univ Operations/Chief Fin Ofcr ... Mr. Bjorn FLUGSTAD
18 VP Capital Planning & Campus Ops ... Dr. Daniel T. OKOLI
46 Int Vice President for Research ... Dr. Jason WILDER
86 SVP Engagement/Public Affairs ... Ms. Christy FARLEY
41 VP Intercollegiate Athletics ... Ms. Mike MARLOW
93 VP of Native American Initiatives ... Dr. Chad S. HAMILL
88 Exec Dir Inst for Tribal Env Prof ... Dr. AnnMarie CHISCHILLY
88 Exec Dir Native Amer Cultural Ctr ... Dr. Ora MAREK-MARTINEZ
43 VP Legal Affairs/General Counsel ... Ms. Michelle G. PARKER
88 Vice Provost Academic Personnel ... Dr. Astrid KLOCKE
13 VP Tech/Chief Information Officer ... Dr. Steven C. BURRELL
32 VP of Student Affairs ... Dr. Margot SALTONSTALL
12 Assoc VP/Campus Exec Officer - Yuma ... Dr. Michael J. SABATH
15 VP/Chief Human Resources Officer ... Mr. Josh MACKEY
21 Associate VP Comptrollers Office ... Ms. Wendy A. SWARTZ
26 AVP of Communications ... Ms. Kim A. OTT
85 Assoc VP Center for Intl Education ... Mr. Daniel PALM
108 Chief Institutional Data Officer ... Ms. Laura A. JONES
111 Assoc VP for Advancement ... Ms. Bonnie BAKER
29 Director Alumni Engagement ... Ms. Stephanie SMITH
08 Dean/University Librarian ... Dr. Cynthia A. CHILDREY
53 Dean College of Education ... Dr. Ramona N. MELLOTT
54 Dean College Eng/Forestry/Nat Sci ... Vacant
50 Dean WA Franke College of Business ... Dr. Ashok SUBRAMANIAN
83 Dean Col Social/Behavioral Sciences ... Dr. John MASSERINI
76 Int Dean Col of Health/Human Svcs ... Dr. Roger BOUNDS
06 University Registrar ... Mr. Gordon WISCHMEIER
19 Chief of Police ... Ms. Missy FRESHOUR
22 Assoc VP Equity and Access Office ... Ms. Pamela HEINONEN
23 Asst VP Campus Health Services ... Ms. Julie A. RYAN
39 Interim Dir Housing/Residence Life ... Ms. Carolyn BURRELL
36 Dir Gateway Student Success Center ... Ms. Monica S. BAI
07 Director of Admissions ... Mr. Chad A. EICKHOFF
96 Assoc VP Contracts/Purch/Risk Mgmt ... Ms. Becky E. MCGAUGH
104 Director Center for Intl Education ... Ms. Angelina PALUMBO
37 Director Financial Aid ... Ms. Amanda CORNELIUS
16 Director Human Resource Programs ... Ms. Cynthia A. CHILCOAT
64 Director School of Music ... Mr. Todd SULLIVAN
94 Director Women and Gender Studies ... Ms. Sanjam AHLUWALIA
58 Dean Graduate College ... Dr. Maribeth WATWOOD
14 Director Information Tech Services ... Mr. Don CARTER
121 Exec Dir University Advising ... Ms. Terri L. HAYES
108 VP Strategy/Sr Assoc to Pres ... Dr. Laurie DICKSON
88 Int Associate VP Research ... Dr. Andrew KOPPISCH
106 Assoc VP NAU Online ... Ms. Gina K. VANCE
88 Assoc VP for Government Affairs ... Ms. Katy YANEZ
88 Assoc VP Educational Partnerships ... Ms. Kathrine H. YEAGER
25 Asst VP Sponsored Projects ... Ms. Stacia LEVY
88 Asst VP Research Compliance ... Dr. David M. FAGUY
122 Coord Fraternity/Sorority Life ... Ms. Marissa Irene GRIFFIN

Northern Arizona University Yuma Branch Campus (K)

2020 S Avenue 8E, Yuma AZ 85365
Telephone: (928) 317-6450 Identification: 770011
Accreditation: &HLC, SW

Northland Pioneer College (L)

PO Box 610, Holbrook AZ 86025-0610
County: Navajo FICE Identification: 011862
Unit ID: 105349
Telephone: (928) 524-7311 Carnegie Class: Assoc/HVT-High Non
FAX Number: (928) 524-7312 Calendar System: Semester
URL: www.npc.edu
Established: 1973 Annual Undergrad Tuition & Fees (In-State): $2,428
Enrollment: 2,700 Coed
Affiliation or Control: State IRS Status: 501(c)3
Highest Offering: Associate Degree
Accreditation: HLC, ADNUR, EMT

01 College President ... Dr. Chato HAZELBAKER
101 Secretary of the Institution/Board ... Mr. John Paul HEMPSEY
05 VP Learning & Student Services ... Dr. Mike SOLOMONSON
10 VP for Administrative Services ... Ms. Maderia ELLISON
13 Director Information Services (CIO) ... Vacant
49 Dean of Arts & Sciences ... Mr. Rickey JACKSON
103 Dean of Career/Technical Education ... Mr. Jeremy RAISOR
66 Nursing & Allied Health Director ... Ms. Ruth ZIMMERMAN
53 Dean of Education/College/Career Pr ... Ms. Gail CAMPBELL
106 Dean of Instructional Innovation ... Dr. Wei MA
15 Human Resources Director ... Vacant

84	Director of Enrollment Services	Vacant
06	Assistant Registrar	Ms. Deena GILLESPIE
32	Director of Student Services	Mr. Josh ROGERS
18	Director of Facilities and Vehicles	Mr. David HUISH
26	Dir of Marketing/Public Relations	Ms. Ann HESS
09	Director of Institutional Effective	Dr. Judy YIP-REYES
88	Director Small Business Development	Mr. Richard CHANICK
19	Director of Public Safety Education	Mr. Jon WISNER
102	Prgm Director NPC Friends & Family	Ms. Betsyann WILSON
37	Manager of Financial Aid Operations	Ms. Marletha BALOO
21	Controller	Ms. Amber HILL
08	Director of Library Services	Ms. Shannon MOTTER
96	Procurement Manager	Mr. Robert JOHNSON
88	Early College Coordinator	Ms. April HORNE
25	Grant Accountant	Ms. Donna SOSEMAN
04	Admin Assistant to the President	Mr. Paul HEMPSEY

Ottawa University Surprise, AZ　　　(A)
15950 N. Civic Center Plaza, Surprise AZ 85374
Telephone: (855) 546-1342　　Identification: 770982
Accreditation: &HLC

† Regional accreditation is carried under the parent institution in Ottawa, KS.

Penn Foster College　　　(B)
14300 N Northsight Blvd, Suite 125,
Scottsdale AZ 85260-3673

County: Maricopa　　FICE Identification: 004049
　　Unit ID: 211486
Telephone: (480) 947-6644　　Carnegie Class: Not Classified
FAX Number: N/A　　Calendar System: Other
URL: www.pennfoster.edu
Established: 1974　　Annual Undergrad Tuition & Fees: N/A
Enrollment: N/A　　Coed
Affiliation or Control: Proprietary　　IRS Status: Proprietary
Highest Offering: Baccalaureate
Accreditation: DEAC

01	Chief Executive Officer	Mr. Frank BRITT
05	Vice Pres Education/Academic Dean	Vacant
10	Chief Financial Officer	Mr. Thomas BLESSO
11	Chief Operating Officer	Ms. Dara WARN
26	Chief Marketing Officer	Ms. Cindy STARR
07	Vice Pres Admissions	Ms. Pat GAFFEY
13	SVP/Chief Technology Officer	Mr. Nial MCLOUGHLIN
21	VP Corp Controller	Mr. Thomas WISHARD
32	SVP Student Success	Mr. Mark SLAYTON
43	General Counsel	Ms. Heather MCALLISTER
15	SVP People/Human Resources	Mr. Joshua BUDWAY

Phoenix Institute of Herbal Medicine and Acupuncture　　　(C)
301 E Bethany Home Road, Ste A-100,
Phoenix AZ 85012-1275

County: Maricopa　　FICE Identification: 036175
　　Unit ID: 447698
Telephone: (602) 274-1885　　Carnegie Class: Spec-4yr-Other Health
FAX Number: (602) 274-1895　　Calendar System: Semester
URL: www.pihma.edu
Established: 1996　　Annual Graduate Tuition & Fees: N/A
Enrollment: 132　　Coed
Affiliation or Control: Proprietary　　IRS Status: Proprietary
Highest Offering: Master's; No Undergraduates
Accreditation: ACUP

01	President	Ms. Catherine NIEMIEC
05	Chief Academic Officer	Ms. Debbie MAJOR
07	Admissions	Ms. Lisa DUNN
06	Registrar	Ms. Judy DRAYER
30	Regulatory/Inst Development Ofcr	Mr. Jonathan LINDSEY

Phoenix Seminary　　　(D)
7901 E. Shea Boulevard, Scottsdale AZ 85260-5510
County: Maricopa　　FICE Identification: 034784
　　Unit ID: 381459
Telephone: (602) 850-8000　　Carnegie Class: Spec-4-yr-Faith
FAX Number: (602) 850-8080　　Calendar System: Semester
URL: www.ps.edu
Established: 1988　　Annual Graduate Tuition & Fees: N/A
Enrollment: 260　　Coed
Affiliation or Control: Interdenominational　　IRS Status: 501(c)3
Highest Offering: Doctorate; No Undergraduates
Accreditation: HLC, THEOL

01	President	Dr. Brian ARNOLD
00	Chancellor	Dr. Darryl L. DELHOUSAYE
05	Provost/EVP	Dr. J. Michael THIGPEN
32	Vice President Student Development	Vacant
20	Asst Dean Academic Services	Ms. Roma ROYER
06	Registrar	Mrs. Merry STENSON
84	Dir Enrollment & Student Services	Mr. Kody GIBSON
10	Comptroller	Mrs. Deborah ARNITZ
08	Director of Library Services	Dr. David S. HOGG
35	Dean of Students	Dr. Joshua ANDERSON
15	Human Resources Director	Ms. Nancy STOCKING

Pima Community College　　　(E)
4905 East Broadway Boulevard, Tucson AZ 85709-1005
County: Pima　　FICE Identification: 007266
　　Unit ID: 105525
Telephone: (520) 206-4500　　Carnegie Class: Assoc/HT-High Non
FAX Number: (520) 206-4535　　Calendar System: Semester
URL: www.pima.edu
Established: 1966　　Annual Undergrad Tuition & Fees (In-District): $2,250
Enrollment: 15,544　　Coed
Affiliation or Control: State/Local　　IRS Status: 501(c)3
Highest Offering: Associate Degree
Accreditation: HLC, ADNUR, COARC, DA, DH, DT, EMT, MLTAD, NAEYC, RAD

01	Chancellor	Mr. Lee D. LAMBERT
05	Provost/Chief Academic Ofcr	Dr. Dolores DURAN-CERDA
10	Exec Vice Chanc for Finance & Admin	Dr. David BEA
12	President of Campuses	Dr. David DORE
26	Vice Chancellor External Relations	Mr. Phillip BURDICK
43	General Counsel	Mr. Jeffrey SILVYN
100	Chief of Staff	Mr. Thomas DAVIS
15	Chief HR Officer	Ms. Carleen THOMPSON
88	Vice Chanc Academic Excellence	Dr. Morgan PHILLIPS
20	Vice Chanc Educational Services	Vacant
09	VC Strategy/Analytics & Research	Dr. Nicola RICHMOND
32	Vice Chanc Student Experience	Dr. Irene ROBLES-LOPEZ
18	Asst Vice Chancellor Facilities	Ms. Brandye D'LENA
21	Asst Vice Chanc Finance	Mr. Daniel SOZA
13	Asst VC Information Tech	Mr. Isaac ABBS
86	Exec Dir Media & Govt Rels	Ms. Elizabeth HOWELL
19	Acting Exec Dir College Police	Ms. Michelle NIEUWENHUIS
37	Acting Exec Dir of Financial Aid	Ms. Melissa STODDART
28	Ex Dir Diversity/Equity & Inclusion	Ms. Hilda LADNER
76	Dean of Allied Health Programs	Mr. James CRAIG
96	Director of Procurement	Mr. Terry ROBINSON
07	Director Admissions & Registrar	Mr. Michael TULINO
103	Vice Chanc Workforce Development	Dr. Ian ROARK
41	Athletic Director	Mr. Jim MONACO

Pima Community College Community Campus　　　(F)
401 North Bonita Avenue, Tucson AZ 85709
Telephone: (520) 206-3933　　Identification: 770016
Accreditation: &HLC

Pima Community College Desert Vista Campus　　　(G)
5901 South Calle Santa Cruz, Tucson AZ 85709
Telephone: (520) 206-5101　　Identification: 770017
Accreditation: &HLC, SURGT

Pima Community College Downtown Campus　　　(H)
1255 North Stone Avenue, Tucson AZ 85709-3000
Telephone: (520) 206-7171　　Identification: 770018
Accreditation: &HLC

Pima Community College East Campus　　　(I)
8181 East Irvington Road, Tucson AZ 85709
Telephone: (520) 206-7000　　Identification: 770019
Accreditation: &HLC

Pima Community College Northwest Campus　　　(J)
7600 North Shannon Road, Tucson AZ 85709-7200
Telephone: (520) 206-2200　　Identification: 770020
Accreditation: &HLC

Pima Community College West Campus　　　(K)
2202 West Anklam Road, Tucson AZ 85709-0001
Telephone: (520) 206-6600　　Identification: 770021
Accreditation: &HLC

Pima Medical Institute-East Valley　　　(L)
2160 S Power Road, Mesa AZ 85209
Telephone: (480) 898-9898　　Identification: 770515
Accreditation: ABHES

Pima Medical Institute-Mesa　　　(M)
957 S Dobson Road, Mesa AZ 85202-2903
Telephone: (480) 644-0267　　FICE Identification: 011570
Accreditation: ABHES, COARC, EMT, OTA, PTAA, RAD

Pima Medical Institute-Tucson　　　(N)
2121 N Craycroft Road, Bldg 1, Tucson AZ 85712
County: Pima　　FICE Identification: 022171
　　Unit ID: 105534
Telephone: (520) 326-1600　　Carnegie Class: Spec-4yr-Other Health
FAX Number: (520) 326-4125　　Calendar System: Other
URL: www.pmi.edu
Established: 1972　　Annual Undergrad Tuition & Fees: N/A
Enrollment: 1,970　　Coed
Affiliation or Control: Proprietary　　IRS Status: Proprietary

Highest Offering: Baccalaureate
Accreditation: ABHES, COARC, NURSE, OTA, PTAA, RAD

01	Campus Director	Mr. Dale BERG

Prescott College　　　(O)
220 Grove Avenue, Prescott AZ 86301-2912
County: Yavapai　　FICE Identification: 020653
　　Unit ID: 105589
Telephone: (928) 350-2100　　Carnegie Class: Masters/M
FAX Number: (928) 776-5137　　Calendar System: Semester
URL: www.prescott.edu
Established: 1966　　Annual Undergrad Tuition & Fees: $33,669
Enrollment: 970　　Coed
Affiliation or Control: Independent Non-Profit　　IRS Status: 501(c)3
Highest Offering: Doctorate
Accreditation: HLC, CACREP

01	President	Mr. John FLICKER
05	Executive Vice President & Provost	Dr. Paul BURKHARDT
10	Chief Financial Officer	Ms. Andrea JAECKEL
84	Dean Enrollment Management	Ms. Pamela DELANY
111	Chief Advancement Ofcr/Alumni Rels	Ms. Marie SMITH
32	Chief Student Affairs Officer	Ms. Kristine PREZIOSI
124	Director of Student Retention	Ms. Jerri BROWN
06	Registrar	Ms. Aimee WALKER
07	Director of Admissions	Ms. Chorissa BUTLER
09	Director of Institutional Research	Ms. Jerri BROWN
15	Director of Human Resources	Ms. Susan KRAUSE
39	Housing Director	Ms. Megan LETCHWORTH
18	Director of Facilities	Mr. Brad SINN
08	Dir of Library/Learning Commons	Ms. Zoe CARAS
13	Dir Information Technology Services	Vacant
29	Director of Alumni Relations	Ms. Marie SMITH
20	Associate Dean for Instruction	Ms. Erin LOTZ

The Refrigeration School　　　(P)
4210 E Washington Street, Phoenix AZ 85034-1816
County: Maricopa　　FICE Identification: 011689
　　Unit ID: 105659
Telephone: (602) 275-7133　　Carnegie Class: Spec 2-yr-Tech
FAX Number: (602) 267-4805　　Calendar System: Other
URL: www.refrigerationschool.com
Established: 1965　　Annual Undergrad Tuition & Fees: N/A
Enrollment: 897　　Coed
Affiliation or Control: Proprietary　　IRS Status: Proprietary
Highest Offering: Associate Degree
Accreditation: ACCSC

01	Campus President	Mr. David EAKER
32	Director of Student Services	Ms. Susan CONNELLY
07	Director of Admissions	Mr. John PALUMBO
06	Registrar	Ms. Clare WEISENBERGER
36	Director Student Placement	Ms. Jessica VASQUEZ

The School of Architecture　　　(Q)
6433 E. Doubletree Ranch Rd, Paradise Valley AZ 85253
County: Maricopa　　FICE Identification: 025332
　　Unit ID: 104665
Telephone: (480) 750-4470　　Carnegie Class: Spec-4-yr-Other
FAX Number: N/A　　Calendar System: Other
URL: www.tsoa.edu
Established: 1932　　Annual Undergrad Tuition & Fees: N/A
Enrollment: 10　　Coed
Affiliation or Control: Independent Non-Profit　　IRS Status: 501(c)3
Highest Offering: Master's
Accreditation: HLC

01	President	Dr. Chris LASCH
05	Dean	Ms. Stephanie LIN
08	Director of Libraries	Vacant
07	Dir Admissions/Student Services	Ms. Shelby HAMET
10	Chief Financial Officer	Ms. Nicole HOLLENBECK
39	Residence Academic Manager	Vacant
06	Registrar	Ms. Elaine MCEWEN

Sessions College for Professional Design　　　(R)
51 W. Third Street, Suite E-301, Tempe AZ 85281
County: Maricopa　　FICE Identification: 042176
　　Unit ID: 475839
Telephone: (480) 212-1704　　Carnegie Class: Spec 2-yr-A&S
FAX Number: (480) 212-1705　　Calendar System: Semester
URL: www.sessions.edu
Established: 1997　　Annual Undergrad Tuition & Fees: $10,740
Enrollment: 197　　Coed
Affiliation or Control: Proprietary　　IRS Status: Proprietary
Highest Offering: Baccalaureate
Accreditation: DEAC

00	CEO	Ms. Doris GRANATOWSKI
01	President	Mr. Gordon DRUMMOND
03	Executive Vice President	Mr. Louis J. SCHILT
05	Dean of Academic Affairs	Dr. Meryl EPSTEIN
11	Sr Director Tech/Operations	Mr. Jason WOLLARD
10	Chief Financial Officer	Ms. Carole Anne BAILO
32	Sr Dir Student Services/Acad Pgms	Mr. Tyler DRAKE

07 Sr Dir Admissions .... Ms. Kimberly O'HANION
37 Dir Financial Aid .... Ms. Debra RICHARDS

Sonoran Desert Institute (A)

1555 W University Drive, Suite 103, Tempe AZ 85281
County: Maricopa | Identification: 667057
Unit ID: 488077
Telephone: (480) 314-2102 | Carnegie Class: Spec 2-yr-Tech
FAX Number: (480) 314-2138 | Calendar System: Semester
URL: www.sdi.edu
Established: 2000 | Annual Undergrad Tuition & Fees: $10,630
Enrollment: 2,709 | Coed
Affiliation or Control: Proprietary | IRS Status: Proprietary
Highest Offering: Associate Degree
Accreditation: DEAC

01 President .... Traci LEE
05 Vice Pres Academic Affairs .... Mike OLSON
10 Vice Pres Finance .... Marc PROCHELLO
07 Director of Admissions .... Jason LARSON

Southwest College of Naturopathic Medicine & Health Sciences (B)

2140 E Broadway Road, Tempe AZ 85282-1751
County: Maricopa | FICE Identification: 031070
Unit ID: 420246
Telephone: (480) 858-9100 | Carnegie Class: Spec-4-yr-Other Health
FAX Number: (480) 858-9116 | Calendar System: Quarter
URL: www.scnm.edu
Established: 1993 | Annual Graduate Tuition & Fees: N/A
Enrollment: 509 | Coed
Affiliation or Control: Independent Non-Profit | IRS Status: 501(c)3
Highest Offering: First Professional Degree; No Undergraduates
Accreditation: HLC, NATUR

01 President/Chief Executive Officer .... Paul A. MITTMAN
05 Vice President of Academic Affairs .... Garrett THOMPSON
10 Vice Pres Finance & Administration .... Edward PODOL
32 Vice President Student Affairs .... Melissa WINQUIST
13 Chief Information Officer .... Vacant
04 Executive Asst to President .... Tracy LINDBERGH
06 Registrar .... Brian MCCARTHY
07 Director of Admissions .... Gina KAEGI
08 Head Librarian .... Sally HARVEY
103 Dir Workforce/Career Development .... Joanna HAGAN
108 Director Institutional Assessment .... Tammy ARAGON

Southwest Institute of Healing Arts (C)

1538 E. Southern Ave, Tempe AZ 85282
County: Maricopa | FICE Identification: 035933
Unit ID: 442879
Telephone: (480) 994-9244 | Carnegie Class: Spec 2-yr-Health
FAX Number: (480) 994-3228 | Calendar System: Other
URL: www.swiha.edu
Established: 1992 | Annual Undergrad Tuition & Fees: N/A
Enrollment: 846 | Coed
Affiliation or Control: Proprietary | IRS Status: Proprietary
Highest Offering: Associate Degree
Accreditation: CNCE

01 President/Founder .... Mrs. KC MILLER
11 Chief Exec Director SWIHA .... Ms. Pam BROWN
05 Dean of Education .... Ms. Shelley TOM
32 Dean of Student Services .... Dr. Bradley BOUTE
10 Dir Finance & Human Res/Controller .... Ms. Salisha TAMANDL
35 Associate Dean of Student Services .... Mrs. Angelica DIAZ
106 Associate Dean Online Student Svcs .... Ms. Bernadett BILACH
37 Director of Financial Aid .... Ms. Amber IMES

Tohono O'odham Community College (D)

PO Box 3129, Sells AZ 85634-3129
County: Pima | FICE Identification: 037844
Unit ID: 442781
Telephone: (520) 383-8401 | Carnegie Class: Tribal
FAX Number: (520) 383-0029 | Calendar System: Semester
URL: www.tocc.edu
Established: 1998 | Annual Undergrad Tuition & Fees: $932
Enrollment: 843 | Coed
Affiliation or Control: Tribal Control | IRS Status: 501(c)3
Highest Offering: Associate Degree
Accreditation: HLC

01 President .... Dr. Paul ROBERTSON
05 Academic Dean .... Dr. Curtis PETERSON
10 Int Vice Pres of Finance .... Ms. Joann MIGUEL
32 Dean of Student Services .... Vacant
75 Acad Chair Occupational Pgms .... Mr. George MIGUEL
97 Acad Chair for General Education .... Dr. Mario MONTES-HELU
06 Registrar .... Ms. Chandra CLAW
08 College Librarian .... Ms. Ofelia ZEPEDA
37 Financial Aid Officer .... Ms. Novia JAMES
30 Controller .... Mr. Michael MAINUS
15 Director Human Resources .... Ms. Stacy OWSLEY
09 Institutional Effectiveness Dir .... Mr. Blaine ANTONE

Triad Education (E)

3110 North Central Ave, Suite L-100, Phoenix AZ 85012
Telephone: (602) 954-3834 | Identification: 770550
Accreditation: ACCSC

† Branch campus of Triad Education, Los Angeles, CA

Universal Technical Institute (F)

10695 W Pierce Street, Avondale AZ 85323-7946
County: Maricopa | FICE Identification: 008221
Unit ID: 106041
Telephone: (623) 245-4600 | Carnegie Class: Spec 2-yr-Tech
FAX Number: (623) 245-4601 | Calendar System: Other
URL: www.uti.edu
Established: 1965 | Annual Undergrad Tuition & Fees: N/A
Enrollment: 1,845 | Coed
Affiliation or Control: Proprietary | IRS Status: Proprietary
Highest Offering: Associate Degree
Accreditation: ACCSC

01 Campus President .... Mr. Roger SPEER
11 Director of Operations .... Mr. Patrick BENNETT
32 Director Student Experience .... Ms. Lindsay KINGSLEY
07 Director Campus Admissions .... Ms. Theresa EMEHISER
36 Director of Graduate Employment .... Ms. Cheryl RADKE

University of Advancing Technology (G)

2625 W Baseline Road, Tempe AZ 85283-1056
County: Maricopa | FICE Identification: 025590
Unit ID: 363934
Telephone: (602) 383-8228 | Carnegie Class: Bac-Diverse
FAX Number: (602) 383-8250 | Calendar System: Other
URL: www.uat.edu
Established: 1983 | Annual Undergrad Tuition & Fees: $18,378
Enrollment: 836 | Coed
Affiliation or Control: Proprietary | IRS Status: Proprietary
Highest Offering: Master's
Accreditation: HLC

01 President .... Mr. Jason PISTILLO
05 Provost .... Mr. Dave BOLMAN
26 VP Marketing & Technology .... Ms. Valerie CIMAROSSA
11 Chief Operating Officer .... Mrs. Karla ARAGON-JOYCE
32 Dean of Students/Academic Operation .... Ms. Brandi BEALS
07 Dean of Recruitment and Development .... Ms. Megan BENSON
10 Senior Controller .... Ms. Jodi ROBINSON
113 Bursar .... Ms. Renee GRAUBERGER
06 Registrar .... Ms. Jenna BROCCHINI
37 Director of Financial Aid .... Ms. Elizabeth EASTIN
04 Executive Assistant .... Ms. Christine ROGERS
06 Registrar .... Ms. Katie KEISTNER

University of Arizona (H)

1200 E University Boulevard, Tucson AZ 85721-0001
County: Pima | FICE Identification: 001083
Unit ID: 104179
Telephone: (520) 621-2211 | Carnegie Class: DU-Highest
FAX Number: (520) 621-9323 | Calendar System: Semester
URL: www.arizona.edu
Established: 1885 | Annual Undergrad Tuition & Fees (In-State): $12,716
Enrollment: 45,601 | Coed
Affiliation or Control: State | IRS Status: Exempt
Highest Offering: Doctorate
Accreditation: HLC, ANEST, ART, AUD, CACREP, CAMPEP, CEA, CLPSY, DANCE, DIET, DIETD, IPSY, JOUR, LAW, LIB, LSAR, MED, MIDWF, MUS, NURSE, PCSAS, PERF, PH, PHAR, PLNG, SCPSY, SP, SPAA, THEA, #VET

01 President .... Dr. Robert C. ROBBINS
05 SVP/Provost/Chief Academic Ofcr .... Dr. Liesl FOLKS
10 Sr VP Business Affairs & CFO .... Ms. Lisa RULNEY
17 Sr VP Health Sciences .... Dr. Michael DAKE
45 VP Strategic Initiatives .... Dr. Jane HUNTER
43 SVP Legal Affairs/General Counsel .... Dr. Laura T. JOHNSON
32 VP Student Affairs .... Vacant
101 SVP/Sr Assoc to the Pres/Sec Univ .... Dr. Jon DUDAS
85 Associate VP Global Affairs .... Mr. Daniel PALM
88 VP Global Environmental Futures .... Dr. Joaquin RUIZ
84 VP Enroll Mgmt/Dean Admissions .... Dr. Kasandra K. URQUIDEZ
11 VP University Planning/Design/Ops .... Mr. Robert R. SMITH
15 VP/Chief Human Resources Officer .... Ms. Helena RODRIGUES
106 AVP Digital Learning Initiatives .... Ms. Melody BUCKNER
26 VP Communications .... Ms. Holly JENSEN
47 VP/Dn Agri/Life/Veterinary Science .... Dr. Shane C. BURGESS
20 Sr Vice Provost Academic Affairs .... Dr. Gail D. BURD
86 VP Government/Cmty Relations .... Mr. Steve VOELLER
45 Senior VP Research and Innovation .... Dr. Elizabeth R. CANTWELL
88 Director Bio5 Institute .... Dr. Jennifer K. BARTON
88 Sr Advisor Health Sci/Cmty Engage .... Dr. Sally J. REEL
09 Assoc VP Institutional Analysis .... Mr. James S. FLORIAN
88 Assoc VP Tech Parks Arizona .... Ms. Carol A. STEWART
108 Assoc Vice Prov Instruct/Assessment .... Dr. Lisa K. ELFRING
88 Assoc VP Research .... Mr. Neal R. ARMSTRONG
21 VP Financial Services .... Ms. Nicole SALAZAR
13 CIO/Director UITS .... Mr. Barry BRUMMUND
21 Assoc VP Finance Administration .... Ms. Marilyn TAYLOR
18 Asst VP Plng/Design & Construction .... Mr. Peter DOURLEIN
88 Asst VP Tribal Relations .... Ms. Karen F. BEGAY
114 VP/Chief Budget Officer .... Mr. Garth PERRY
18 Asst VP Facilities Management .... Mr. Christopher M. KOPACH
117 Chief Risk Ofcr/Risk Mgmt/Safety .... Mr. Miguel DELGADO
88 Asst VP Govt Affairs .... Mr. Ethan R. ORR
08 Dean of University Libraries .... Mr. Shan C. SUTTON
83 Dean Social/Behavioral Science .... Dr. John P. JONES
35 Vice Prov Campus Life/Dean Students .... Ms. Kendal H. WASHINGTON WHITE
92 Dean Honors College .... Dr. Terry L. HUNT
48 Dean Col Arch/Plng/Landscape Arch .... Dr. Nancy POLLOCK-ELLWAND
53 Dean Education .... Dr. Bruce JOHNSON
58 Vice Prov/Dean Graduate College .... Dr. Andrew H. CARNIE
61 Dean James E Rogers College of Law .... Dr. Marc L. MILLER
66 Dean College of Nursing .... Dr. Ida M. MOORE
12 Interim Dean UA South .... Dr. Linda DENNO
79 Dean College of Humanities .... Dr. Alain-Philippe DURAND
57 VP/Dean Fine Arts .... Dr. Andrew SCHULZ
54 Dean College of Engineering .... Dr. David HAHN
50 Dean Eller College of Management .... Mr. Jeffrey SCHATZBERG
69 Dean College of Public Health .... Dr. Iman A. HAKIM
74 Dean College of Veterinary Medicine .... Dr. Julie FUNK
63 Dean College of Med-Phoenix Campus .... Dr. Guy L. REED
63 Dean College of Medicine-Tucson .... Dr. Michael ABECASSIS
81 Dean College of Optical Sciences .... Dr. Thomas L. KOCH
67 Dean College of Pharmacy .... Dr. Rick SCHNELLMAN
28 AVP Institutional Equity .... Ms. Kristen KLOTZ
40 Int AVP Business Affs/Auxiliary Svc .... Ms. Debby L. SHIVELY
23 Int Co-Exec Director Campus Health .... Dr. David B. SALAFSKY
23 Int Co-Exec Director Campus Health .... Dr. Michael STILSON
88 Chief Data Officer/AVP UAIR .... Mr. Ravneet CHADHA
96 Dir Procurement & Contract Services .... Mr. Edward D. NASSER
25 Director Sponsored Proj/Services .... Mr. Paul SANDOVAL
37 Exec Dir Scholarships/Fin Aid .... Mr. Art YOUNG
41 VP/Director of Athletics .... Mr. Dave HEEKE
06 Office of the Registrar .... Mr. Alex UNDERWOOD
104 Exec Director Study Abroad .... Ms. Harmony R. DEFAZIO

University of Arizona Global Campus (I)

180 S. Arizona Ave., Suite 301, Chandler AZ 85225
County: Phoenix | FICE Identification: 001881
Unit ID: 154022
Telephone: (866) 711-1700 | Carnegie Class: DU-Mod
FAX Number: (866) 685-4091 | Calendar System: Semester
URL: https://www.uagc.edu/
Established: 1918 | Annual Undergrad Tuition & Fees: $14,278
Enrollment: 31,115 | Coed
Affiliation or Control: Proprietary | IRS Status: Proprietary
Highest Offering: Master's
Accreditation: WC, CAHIIM, IACBE, NURSE

01 University President/CEO .... Mr. Paul PASTOREK
05 Provost/SVP Academic Affairs .... Dr. Iris ORBILLE LAFFERTY
10 SVP Finance/Chief Finance Officer .... Ms. Lisa KEMP
11 SVP University Svcs & Strat Plng .... Ms. Sheri JONES
15 VP Human Resources .... Ms. Monique COOK
06 University Registrar/COO .... Ms. Katie SCHEIE
21 VP Accounting Controller .... Ms. Heather WEINMANN
32 AVP Student Affairs .... Ms. Poppy FITCH
88 AVP Center for Teaching/Learning .... Ms. Morgan JOHNSON
12 President Clinton Campus .... Dr. Charlie MINNICK
49 Dean College of Arts/Sciences .... Dr. Tony FARRELL
69 Dean College of Health/Human Svcs .... Dr. Laura SLIWINSKI
88 Dean Doctoral Studies .... Dr. Iris LAFFERTY
97 Dean Division of General Education .... Dr. Justin HARRISON
50 Dean Forbes School of Business .... Ms. Maja ZELIHIC
53 Dean College of Education .... Dr. Tony FARRELL
37 Dir Financial Aid & Policy .... Ms. Stephanie COWSERT
09 Director of Institutional Research .... Dr. Stephen NETTLES
101 Secretary of the Institution/Board .... Ms. Patricia OGDEN
29 Director Alumni Affairs .... Ms. Graciela WILLIAMSON
22 Title IX Coordinator .... Dr. Poppy FITCH
04 Executive Administrative Manager .... Ms. Thuy LIEN

The University of Arizona College of Applied Science & Technology (J)

1140 N Colombo Avenue, Sierra Vista AZ 85635
Telephone: (520) 626-2422 | Identification: 770024
Accreditation: &HLC, CSHSE

University of Arizona Phoenix Biomedical Campus (K)

550 E Van Buren Street, Phoenix AZ 85004
Telephone: (602) 827-2002 | Identification: 770023
Accreditation: &HLC, MED, PHAR

University of Phoenix (L)

4035 S Riverpoint Pkwy, Phoenix AZ 85040
County: Maricopa | FICE Identification: 020988
Unit ID: 484613
Telephone: (480) 557-2000 | Carnegie Class: DU-Mod
FAX Number: N/A | Calendar System: Other
URL: www.phoenix.edu
Established: 1976 | Annual Undergrad Tuition & Fees: $9,552
Enrollment: 89,763 | Coed
Affiliation or Control: Proprietary | IRS Status: Proprietary
Highest Offering: Doctorate

Accreditation: HLC, ACBSP, CACREP, HSA, NURSE, SW

01 Int President University of Phoenix ... Mr. Chris LYNNE
04 Assistant to the President ... Ms. Cindy WHIPPO
05 Chief Academic Officer/Provost ... Dr. John WOODS
10 Chief Financial Officer ... Mr. Chris LYNNE
45 Chief Strategy & Customer Officer ... Ms. Ruth VELORIA
11 Chief Operating Officer ... Mr. Raghu KRISHNAIAH
26 SVP/Chief Marketing Officer ... Mr. Steven GROSS
86 SVP Government Relations ... Mr. Eric RIZZO
13 Chief Information Officer ... Mr. Jamie SMITH
15 Chief Human Resources ... Ms. Cheryl NAUMANN
20 Vice Prov Sch of Advanced Studies ... Dr. Hinrich EYLERS
20 Vice Provost Colleges ... Ms. Doris SAVRON
84 SVP Enrollment Services ... Mr. Brett ROMNEY
21 VP Financial Services ... Mr. Bronson LEDBETTER
43 SVP & General Counsel ... Mr. Srini MEDI
06 Registrar ... Ms. Audra MCQUARIE
19 Director Security/Safety ... Mr. Steve LINDSEY
101 Secretary of the Institution/Board ... Ms. Kim KAUFFMAN
106 Director Online Education ... Mr. Hal D. MORGAN
28 Director of Diversity ... Ms. Saray LOPEZ
29 Director Alumni Affairs ... Mr. Chris G. CELAURO
37 Director Student Financial Aid ... Ms. Stacy TUCKER
96 Director of Purchasing ... Mrs. Marty DALLAS
108 Director Institutional Assessment ... Dr. Eve BILLINGS
50 Dean of Business ... Mr. Kevin WILHELMSEN
53 Dean of Education ... Dr. Pamela ROGGEMAN

Viridis Graduate Institute (A)

3345 South Rural Road, Tempe AZ 85282
County: Maricopa | Identification: 667375
Telephone: (805) 889-0169 | Carnegie Class: Not Classified
FAX Number: N/A | Calendar System: Trimester
URL: www.viridis.edu
Established: 2011 | Annual Undergrad Tuition & Fees: N/A
Enrollment: N/A | Coed
Affiliation or Control: Independent Non-Profit | IRS Status: 501(c)3
Highest Offering: Doctorate
Accreditation: DEAC

01 President/CAO ... Dr. Lori PYE
05 Academic Dean ... Dr. Leslie STOUPAS

Yavapai College (B)

1100 E Sheldon Street, Prescott AZ 86301-3297
County: Yavapai | FICE Identification: 001079
Unit ID: 106148
Telephone: (928) 445-7300 | Carnegie Class: Assoc/HT-Mix Trad/Non
FAX Number: (928) 777-3154 | Calendar System: Semester
URL: www.yc.edu
Established: 1966 | Annual Undergrad Tuition & Fees (In-District): $2,600
Enrollment: 6,009 | Coed
Affiliation or Control: Local | IRS Status: 501(c)3
Highest Offering: Associate Degree
Accreditation: HLC, ADNUR, EMT, IFSAC, RAD

01 President ... Dr. Lisa RHINE
05 Vice Pres of Academic Affairs ... Dr. Diane RYAN
10 Vice Pres Finance/Admin Svcs ... Dr. Clint EWELL
32 VP Community Rels/Student Dev ... Mr. Rodney JENKINS
20 Dean for Instructional Support ... Ms. Stacey HILTON
12 Dean Verde Valley Campus & Sedona ... Vacant
75 Dean Career Technical Education ... Mr. John MORGAN
76 Dean Health Sciences ... Vacant
88 Assoc Dean of Performing Arts ... Dr. Craig RALSTON
84 AVP Enrollment Management ... Ms. Tania SHELDAHL
27 Exec Dir of Marketing/Public Info ... Mr. Tyler RUMSEY
35 Assoc VP Student Development ... Ms. Diana DOWLING
09 Dir Inst Effectiveness & Research ... Dr. Tom HUGHES
15 Chief Human Resources Officer ... Vacant
19 Chief of Police ... Mr. Tyran PAYNE
21 Dir of Business Svcs & Controller ... Mr. Frank D'ANGELO
18 Director for Facilities ... Mr. David LAURENCE
13 Chief Information Officer ... Mr. Patrick BURNS
06 Registrar ... Ms. Sheila JARRELL
96 Director of Purchasing ... Mr. Ryan BOUWHUIS
04 Exec Asst to President ... Ms. Yvonne SANDOVAL
07 Director of Admissions ... Ms. Wendy PRESENT
29 Director of Dev/Alumni Affairs ... Ms. Kammie KOBYLESKI
102 Exec Dir YC Foundation ... Ms. Mary TALOSI
37 Director Student Financial Aid ... Mr. Raymond CEO

Yavapai College Verde Valley Campus (C)

601 Black Hills Drive, Clarkdale AZ 86324
Telephone: (928) 634-7501 | Identification: 770029
Accreditation: &HLC

ARKANSAS

Arkansas Baptist College (D)

1600 Dr. Martin Luther King Drive,
Little Rock AR 72202-6099
County: Pulaski | FICE Identification: 001087
Unit ID: 106306
Telephone: (501) 420-1200 | Carnegie Class: Bac/Assoc-Mixed
FAX Number: (501) 414-0861 | Calendar System: Semester
URL: www.arkansasbaptist.edu
Established: 1884 | Annual Undergrad Tuition & Fees: $8,760
Enrollment: 468 | Coed
Affiliation or Control: Baptist | IRS Status: 501(c)3
Highest Offering: Baccalaureate
Accreditation: HLC

01 President ... Dr. Carlos R. CLARK
05 VP for Academic & Student Affairs ... Dr. Tracey MOORE
10 VP for Business & Finance/CFO ... Ms. Camesha YOUNG
04 President's Executive Assistant ... Ms. Patsy BIGGS
21 Comptroller ... Vacant
111 VP for Institutional Advancement ... Mr. Jeff SELLERS
32 Dean of Student Affairs ... Dr. Vicki WILLIAMS
37 Director of Financial Aid ... Mr. Lloyd DIXON
100 Chief of Staff ... Ms. Shae BEARDEN
09 Dir of Institutional Research ... Ms. LaTrice SMALL
88 Ombudsman ... Dr. Vicki WILLIAMS
08 Director of Library/Media Services ... Ms. Jacqueline ELDRIDGE
26 Dir of Marketing ... Vacant
19 Director of Campus Safety ... Mr. Claiborn DURHAM
18 Director Facilities & Maintenance ... Mr. Larry THOMPSON
06 Registrar ... Ms. Delores VOLIBER
13 Director of Information Technology ... Vacant
15 Human Resources Director ... Mrs. Pamela BRIMLEY
41 Director of Athletics ... Mr. Bill INGRAM
39 Director Resident Life/Housing ... Vacant
07 Int Dir of Admissions & Recruitment ... Ms. Pamela CONARD
28 Dir Title III/Sponsored Programs ... Vacant

Arkansas Colleges of Health Education (E)

7000 Chad Colley Boulevard, Fort Smith AR 72916
County: Sebastian | FICE Identification: 042568
Unit ID: 488527
Telephone: (479) 308-2200 | Carnegie Class: Spec-4-yr-Med
FAX Number: (479) 308-2766 | Calendar System: Semester
URL: https://acheedu.org/
Established: 2017 | Annual Graduate Tuition & Fees: N/A
Enrollment: 678 | Coed
Affiliation or Control: Independent Non-Profit | IRS Status: 501(c)3
Highest Offering: Doctorate; No Undergraduates
Accreditation: HLC, OSTEO, @PTA

01 President & CEO ... Kyle D. PARKER
05 Vice Provost & VPAA ... Dr. Elizabeth MCCLAIN
100 Senior Executive Assistant ... Dr. Benny L. GOODEN
10 VP & CFO ... Dennis BAUER
45 VP & COO ... Les SMITH
13 VP & CTO ... Joel WEBB
63 Dean DO Program ... Dr. Rance MCCLAIN
63 Associate Dean Clinical Medicine ... Dr. John SEALEY
63 Assoc Dean Biomedicine ... Dr. Ross LONGLEY
20 Assoc Dean Academic Affairs ... Dr. Melissa EFURD
32 Assistant Dean Student Affairs ... Laurel MCINTOSH
58 Dean Physical Therapy ... Dr. Teressa BROWN
58 Dean Occupational Therapy ... Dr. Jennifer MOORE
58 Dean Physicians Assistant ... Dr. Henry LEMKE
58 Program Dir MSB ... Dr. Kenneth HENSLEY
29 Chair of External Alumni Relations ... Dr. Ray E. STOWERS
108 Director of Data Analytics ... Dr. Ashley GERHARDSON
08 Director of Library Services ... Zahra KAMAREI
38 Director of Mental Wellness ... Vacant
30 Director of Development ... Jackie KRUTSCH
19 Chief of Police ... Levi RISLEY
18 Director of Building & Grounds ... Eric BURNS
35 Director of Student Services ... Amanda EVENSON
06 Registrar ... Shawna MASON
37 Director of Financial Aid ... Glenna GILLIAM
07 Director of Admissions ... Kelly DEWITT
121 Academic Success Counselor ... Vacant
15 Assoc VP of Human Resources ... Barbara JETTON
16 Human Resources Manager ... Sheila BENTLEY
26 Exec Dir Marketing/Communications ... Susan DEVERO
96 Director of Procurement ... Dianna JORDAN

Arkansas Northeastern College (F)

2501 S Division Street, Blytheville AR 72315-5111
County: Mississippi | FICE Identification: 012860
Unit ID: 107327
Telephone: (870) 762-1020 | Carnegie Class: Assoc/MT-VT-Mix Trad/Non
FAX Number: (870) 763-3704 | Calendar System: Semester
URL: www.anc.edu
Established: 1974 | Annual Undergrad Tuition & Fees (In-District): $2,654
Enrollment: 1,358 | Coed
Affiliation or Control: State/Local | IRS Status: 501(c)3
Highest Offering: Associate Degree
Accreditation: HLC, DA, EMT

01 President ... Dr. James SHEMWELL
05 VP for Instruction/CAO ... Dr. Keith MCCLANAHAN
03 Executive Vice President ... Mrs. June WALTERS
10 Vice President for Administration ... Mr. Don RAY
13 VP Information Technology ... Mr. James W. MCCLAIN
103 VP Workforce/Economic Development ... Mr. Gene BENNETT
31 VP for Community Relations ... Dr. Blanchie HUNT
32 VP for Student Services ... Dr. Chris HEIGLE
26 Assoc VP for Dev/College Relations ... Ms. Rachel GIFFORD
66 Dean Nursing/Allied Hlth/PE/Rec ... Mrs. Brenda HOLIFIELD
49 Dean for Arts and Sciences ... Mr. Ryan PERKINS
36 Dean Advisement/Placement ... Dr. Bridget SHEMWELL
75 Dean for Allied Technologies ... Dr. Jamie FRAKES
106 Dean Academic Tech & Dist Educ ... Mr. Ken BARTON
10 Controller ... Ms. Jennifer JOHNSON
32 Director for Student Services ... Mrs. Courtney FISHER
31 Coordinator Community Education ... Ms. Kaci BELL
08 Director of College Library/AV ... Ms. Karen ELLIS
37 Director Financial Aid ... Mrs. Mindy WALKER
14 Associate Dean MITS ... Mr. James ODOM
15 Human Resources & ADA Coordinator ... Mrs. Tabatha HAMPTON
18 Director Physical Plant and Grounds ... Mr. Scott CREECY
88 Director Talent Search/Educ Opp Ctr ... Mrs. Lisa MCGHEE
04 Assistant to Board/President ... Ms. Marlene BANKS
06 Registrar ... Mrs. Rosemary LOWE
27 Media Director ... Mr. James HARTLEY

*Arkansas State University System (G)

501 Woodlane Drive, Suite 600, Little Rock AR 72201
County: Pulaski | Identification: 666187
Telephone: (501) 660-1000 | Carnegie Class: N/A
FAX Number: (501) 660-1010
URL: www.asusystem.edu

01 President ... Dr. Charles L. WELCH
04 Exec Assistant to the President ... Ms. Pam KAIL
10 Executive Vice President Finance ... Ms. Julie BATES
86 Vice Pres Governmental Relations ... Mr. Shane BROADWAY
26 Vice Pres Strategic Comm/Econ Dev ... Mr. Jeff HANKINS
43 Legal Counsel ... Mr. Brad PHELPS
09 VP for Strategic Research ... Mr. Eric ATCHISON
102 President ASU System Foundation ... Mr. Philip JACKSON
15 Assoc Vice President Benefits ... Dr. LeAnne PERKINS
116 Internal Auditor ... Ms. Jo LUNBECK
13 Chief Info Technology Officer ... Mr. Henry TORRES

*Arkansas State University-Beebe (H)

PO Box 1000, Beebe AR 72012-1000
County: White | FICE Identification: 001091
Unit ID: 106449
Telephone: (501) 882-3600 | Carnegie Class: Assoc/MT-VT-High Trad
FAX Number: (501) 882-8970 | Calendar System: Semester
URL: www.asub.edu
Established: 1927 | Annual Undergrad Tuition & Fees (In-State): $2,928
Enrollment: 2,982 | Coed
Affiliation or Control: State | IRS Status: 501(c)3
Highest Offering: Associate Degree
Accreditation: HLC, EMT, MLTAD, NAIT

02 Chancellor ... Dr. Jennifer METHVIN
100 Executive Assistant to Chancellor ... Ms. Kim GULLAHORN
05 Vice Chanc of Academics/CAO ... Dr. Jason GOODNER
12 Campus Ops Mgr ASU-Heber Springs ... Mr. Cody MCMICHAEL
12 Campus Operations Mgr ASU-Searcy ... Ms. LaShanda OWENS
10 Vice Chanc Finance/Admin/CFO ... Dr. Roger MOORE
13 VC Information Technology Services ... Mr. Wade FINCHER
32 Vice Chanc Student Services/CSSO ... Dr. David MAYES
111 Assoc VC Advancement ... Ms. Rose Mary JACKSON
15 Director Human Resources ... Ms. Teri ROPER
14 Director of End User Assessment ... Ms. Danya UTLEY
35 Dean Student Affairs ... Mr. Zack TUCKER
26 Director of Marketing/PR ... Ms. Hannah KELLER-FLANERY
06 University Registrar ... Dr. April MARTIN
08 Library Director ... Ms. Tracy D. SMITH
19 Police Commander ... Mr. James J. MARTIN
18 Director of Physical Plant ... Mr. Mark HASTINGS
37 Director Student Financial Aid ... Ms. Angela JONES
09 Assoc VC of Institutional Research ... Ms. Katie VAUGHN
21 Controller ... Ms. Kathy WARD
72 Director of Allied Health ... Mr. Joseph SCOTT
106 Director of Distance Learning ... Ms. Stephanie UNGERANK
96 Executive Director Procurement ... Ms. Robin LANCASTER
12 Campus Operations Mgr LRAFB ... Ms. LaShanda OWENS
07 Director of Admissions ... Mr. Tyler BITTLE
105 Webmaster ... Vacant
84 Coord Concurrent Enrollment ... Ms. Ashley HANKINS
121 Director of Advising & Learning ... Ms. Catherine BURTON

*Arkansas State University-Jonesboro (I)

PO Box 600, State University AR 72467
County: Craighead | FICE Identification: 001090
Unit ID: 106458
Telephone: (870) 972-2100 | Carnegie Class: DU-Higher
FAX Number: (870) 972-3465 | Calendar System: Semester
URL: www.astate.edu
Established: 1909 | Annual Undergrad Tuition & Fees (In-State): $7,315
Enrollment: 13,106 | Coed
Affiliation or Control: State | IRS Status: 501(c)3
Highest Offering: Doctorate
Accreditation: HLC, ADNUR, ANEST, ART, CAATE, CACREP, CAEP, CAEPN, CEA, COSMA, DIETC, DMS, EMT, JOUR, MLS, MLTAD, MUS, NASP, NUR, OT, OTA, PTA, PTAA, RAD, RADMAG, RTT, SP, SPAA, SW, THEA

02 Chancellor ... Dr. Todd SHIELDS
05 Provost & Exec VC Acad Affairs ... Dr. Alan UTTER
10 Exec VC Finance & Administration ... Dr. Len T. FREY
84 Vice Chancellor Enrollment Mgmt ... Dr. Thilla SIVAKUMARAN
111 Vice Chancellor Univ Advancement ... Dr. Erika CHUDY
28 VC for Diversity/Community Engage ... Dr. Lonnie WILLIAMS
41 VC of Intercollegiate Athletics ... Mr. Jeff PURINTON
32 VC of Student Affs/Dean of Stdnts ... Dr. Martha SPACK

20 Sr Assoc Vice Chancellor AAR Dr. Karen WHEELER
21 Sr Assoc Vice Chanc Finance/CFO Dr. Russ HANNAH
114 Asst Vice Chanc Budget Ms. Donna MCMILLIN
15 Asst VC Human Resources Ms. Lori WINN
46 Vice Provost for Research & Tech Dr. Thomas RISCH
13 Vice Pres Information Tech/CIO Mr. Henry TORRES
18 Asst Vice Chancellor Facilities Mr. David HANDWORK
88 Asst Vice Chanc Enrollment Services Mr. Terry FINNEY
108 Asst VC Institutional Effectiveness Dr. Fen YU
85 Exec Dir Global Engage/Outreach Dr. Thilla SIVAKUMARAN
06 Director of Records/Registration Ms. Tracy FINCH
07 Director of Admissions Ms. Pamela BOWIE
39 Director of Residence Life Ms. Natalie ESKEW
19 Chief University Police Mr. Randy MARTIN
22 Co-Director of Disability Services Ms. Dominique WHITE
22 Co-Director of Disability Services Mr. Blake WALKER
36 Director Career Services Ms. Tiffany JOHNSON
38 Director Counseling Center Dr. Phil HESTAND
29 Exec Dir Alumni Relations Ms. Lindsay BURNETT
26 Chief Communications Officer Dr. Bill SMITH
27 Director of Media Relations/Comm Mr. Tom MOORE
88 Dir of Digital Creative Services Mr. Todd CLARK
96 Dir Procurement & Travel Svcs Ms. Lisa GLASCO
04 Admin Assistant to the Chancellor Ms. Julie WYATT
08 Dir Library Mr. Jeff BAILEY
47 Dean College Agriculture/Technology Dr. Mickey LATOUR
81 Dean College Sciences & Math Dr. Lynn BOYD
50 Dean College of Business Dr. Melody LO
53 Dean Col of Educ & Behavioral Sci Dr. Mary Jane BRADLEY
60 Dean Liberal Arts & Communication Dr. Carl CATES
66 Dean College of Nursing Health Prof Dr. Susan N. HANRAHAN
97 Assoc VC Undergraduate Studies Dr. Jill SIMONS
58 Dean of Graduate School Dr. Cherisse JONES-BRANCH
54 Dean College of Engineering Dr. Abhijit BHATTACHARYYA
88 Asst for Administration for Provost Ms. Jeannie COSSEY

*Arkansas State University Mid-South (A)

2000 W Broadway Avenue,
West Memphis AR 72301-3829
County: Crittenden FICE Identification: 023482
Unit ID: 107318
Telephone: (870) 733-6722 Carnegie Class: Assoc/HT-High Non
FAX Number: (870) 733-6799 Calendar System: Semester
URL: www.asumidsouth.edu
Established: 1992 Annual Undergrad Tuition & Fees (In-District): $3,226
Enrollment: 1,203 Coed
Affiliation or Control: State/Local IRS Status: 501(c)3
Highest Offering: Associate Degree
Accreditation: HLC, COARC

02 Chancellor Dr. Debra WEST
05 Vice Chanc Learning/Instruction Mr. Jeff GRAY
10 Vice Chanc Finance & Administration Ms. JaNan ABERNATHY
111 Vice Chanc Inst Advancement Ms. Diane HAMPTON
32 Vice Chanc Student Affairs Mr. Jeremy REECE
103 Interim AVC Workforce Education Dr. Callie DUNAVIN
21 AVC Finance Ms. Emilee SIDES
37 Director of Financial Aid Ms. Crystal BURGER
08 Director of Library/Media Center Ms. Brandi KATTERJOHN
06 Registrar Ms. Leslie ANDERSON
15 Director of Human Resources Ms. Lisa HAGGARD
18 Director Facilities/Physical Plant Mr. Ben SASSER
13 AVC for Information Systems Tech Mr. Ernesto MUNIZ
09 AVC Institutional Research Dr. Michael LEJMAN
50 Dean of Business/Math/Comp Sci Ms. Karen MITCHUSSON
79 Dean of Liberal Arts and Education Ms. Tracy GIOVANETTI
76 Dean of Allied Health and Science Ms. Erin GORDON
121 Dir of Learning Success Center Ms. Stephanie KREHL
04 Administrative Asst to Chancellor Ms. Claudia OHNECK
19 Director Public Safety Mr. Ross PROCTOR
41 Athletic Director Mr. Chris PARKER
96 Business Manager Ms. Wendy CRAWFORD

*Arkansas State University-Mountain Home (B)

1600 S College Street, Mountain Home AR 72653-5326
County: Baxter Identification: 666311
Unit ID: 420538
Telephone: (870) 508-6100 Carnegie Class: Assoc/HVT-Mix Trad/Non
FAX Number: (870) 508-6287 Calendar System: Semester
URL: www.asumh.edu
Established: 1995 Annual Undergrad Tuition & Fees (In-District): $2,904
Enrollment: 1,271 Coed
Affiliation or Control: State/Local IRS Status: 501(c)3
Highest Offering: Associate Degree
Accreditation: HLC, EMT, FUSER, PTAA

02 Chancellor Dr. Robin MYERS
05 Provost/Vice Chanc Academic Affairs Dr. Tamara DANIEL
10 VC Operations/Dir Career Pthwys Ms. Laura YARBROUGH
18 Director of Maintenance Mr. Nickey L. ROBBINS
26 AVC Marketing/Community Relations Mrs. Christy C. KEIRN
32 Assoc Vice Chanc of Students Mr. William KIMBRIEL
37 Director Financial Aid Mr. Clay BERRY
08 Director of Library Ms. Tina BRADLEY
09 Dir of Inst Research/Effectiveness Mr. David CULLIPHER
07 Admissions Coordinator Ms. Stephanie BEAVER
04 Exec Assistant to the Chancellor Ms. Mary DOUGLAS

103 Director Workforce Development Mr. Victor BECK
13 Director of Computer Services Ms. Tamya STALLINGS
30 Development Officer Ms. Mollie MORGAN
15 Int Coordinator Human Resources Ms. Lindsey POWERS

*Arkansas State University-Newport (C)

7648 Victory Boulevard, Newport AR 72112-8912
County: Jackson Identification: 666153
Unit ID: 440402
Telephone: (870) 512-7800 Carnegie Class: Assoc/HVT-High Non
FAX Number: (870) 512-7807 Calendar System: Semester
URL: www.asun.edu
Established: 2001 Annual Undergrad Tuition & Fees (In-State): $2,856
Enrollment: 1,941 Coed
Affiliation or Control: State IRS Status: Exempt
Highest Offering: Associate Degree
Accreditation: HLC, SURGT

02 Chancellor Dr. Johnny M. MOORE
100 Chief of Staff Ms. Kristen SMITH
05 Vice Chancellor Academic Affairs Dr. Holly SMITH
10 Vice Chancellor Finance & Admin Mr. Adam ADAIR
32 Vice Chancellor Student Affairs Dr. Ashley BUCHMAN
103 Vice Chancellor Econ/Workforce Dev Mr. Jeff BOOKOUT
30 VC Leadership/Community Engagement Mr. Ike WHEELER
121 Dean of Student Success/Registrar Dr. Allen MOONEYHAN
72 Dean for Applied Science Mr. Robert BURGESS
97 Dean for General Education Mr. Joseph CAMPBELL
84 Dean of Enrollment Services Ms. Candace GROSS
88 Dean Leadership/Org Development Dr. Veronica MANNING
13 Director of IT Services Ms. Debbie KEYTON
15 Director Human Resources Ms. Sara MOSS
06 Assistant Registrar Ms. Phyllis WORTHINGTON
18 Director of Physical Plant Mr. Brian PETTIE
21 Controller Ms. Monika PHILLIPS
37 Director Financial Aid Ms. Stacey DUNLAP
09 Director of Institutional Research Ms. Christy MANN
19 Chief of Police Mr. Johnathan TUBBS
96 Director of Procurement Ms. Lee WEBB
66 Dean of Nursing/Allied Health Dr. Typhanie MYERS
36 Director of Career Pathways Ms. Cheryl CROSS
75 Director of Adult Education Mr. John KELLY
26 Director Marketing & Communications Mr. Jeremy SHIRLEY
111 Advancement Officer Ms. Teriann TURNER

*Arkansas State University-Three Rivers (D)

One College Circle, Malvern AR 72104-0816
County: Hot Spring FICE Identification: 009976
Unit ID: 107521
Telephone: (501) 337-5000 Carnegie Class: Assoc/HVT-High Non
FAX Number: N/A Calendar System: Semester
URL: www.asutr.edu
Established: 1969 Annual Undergrad Tuition & Fees (In-State): $3,458
Enrollment: 1,243 Coed
Affiliation or Control: State IRS Status: 501(c)3
Highest Offering: Associate Degree
Accreditation: HLC

01 Chancellor Dr. Steve ROOK
04 Executive Asst to Chancellor Ms. Mitzi OVERTURF
05 Vice Chancellor Academic Affairs Mr. Pat SIMMS
84 Vice Chancellor Enrollment Services Ms. Carla CRUTCHFIELD
10 Vice Chancellor Finance & Admin Mr. James WHITE
28 Vice Chancellor Student/Equity/Cmty Dr. Kim ARMSTRONG
111 AVC College Advancement Ms. Amber CHILDERS
13 AVC Information Technology Mr. Jacob BLAND
20 Dean of Combined Divisions Ms. Tricia BAAR
76 Dean of Health Sciences Ms. Melinda SANDERS
51 Director of Adult Education Dr. Casson BROCK
08 Director of Library Ms. Irene GIRGENTE
36 Director of Career Center Mr. John BRATTON
92 Director Honors College Ms. Tricia BAAR
88 Director Concurrent Enrollment Ms. Tara BRATTON
37 Director Financial Aid Ms. Angela SEXTON
36 Director Career Pathways Mr. Terral HARPER
88 Dir TRIO Student Support Services Ms. Vergina SMITH-JOACHIM
21 Controller Mr. Lee MATTHEWS
15 Director Human Resources Vacant
103 Director Workforce Development Mr. Mason ROBINSON
18 Director of Physical Plant Mr. Danny COTTRELL
07 Director of Admissions Ms. Keesha JOHNSON

Arkansas Tech University (E)

1509 North Boulder Avenue, Russellville AR 72801-2222
County: Pope FICE Identification: 001089
Unit ID: 106467
Telephone: (479) 968-0389 Carnegie Class: Masters/L
FAX Number: (479) 964-0522 Calendar System: Semester
URL: www.atu.edu
Established: 1909 Annual Undergrad Tuition & Fees (In-State): $7,668
Enrollment: 10,829 Coed
Affiliation or Control: State IRS Status: 501(c)3
Highest Offering: Doctorate
Accreditation: HLC, ACPHA, ART, CAEP, CAHIIM, CAPRT, CEA, MAC, MUS, NUR, PTAA

01 President Dr. Robin E. BOWEN
10 VP Administration/Finance Mrs. Laury FIORELLO
05 Int Exec VP Academic Affs/Provost Dr. Julie FURST-BOWE
32 Vice President Student Svcs Dr. Keegan NICHOLS
111 Vice President Advancement Mr. Jason GEIKEN
84 Interim AVP Enrollment Management Mr. Kevin SOLOMON
12 Chancellor Ozark Campus Mr. Bruce SIKES
43 University Counsel Mr. Edward ARMSTRONG
20 Assoc VP Academic Affairs Dr. Jeanine MYERS
110 Associate VP for Development Mr. Bryan FISHER
121 Asst VP Student Success Vacant
35 Assoc VP Student Affairs/Title IX Ms. Amy PENNINGTON
35 Chief Student Officer Ozark Campus Mr. Richard HARRIS
20 Chief Academic Officer Ozark Campus Ms. Sheila JACOBS
100 Chief of Staff Dr. Mary GUNTER
06 Registrar Ms. Tammy WEAVER
21 Controller Ms. Suzanne MCCALL
21 Assistant VP Admin & Finance Ms. Jami FISHER
08 Interim Director of Library Ms. Angela BLACK
86 Director Government Relations Vacant
114 Director of Budget Vacant
09 Director of Institutional Research Mr. Wyatt WATSON
13 Director Information Systems/CIO Mr. Ken WESTER
113 Director of Student Accounts Ms. Angela CROW
15 Director of Human Resources Ms. Melissa RIFFLE
37 Director Student Financial Aid Ms. Niki SCHWARTZ
29 Director Alumni Relations Mrs. Caroline KITCHENS
85 Assistant Dean of International Pgm Mrs. Sara CHRONISTER
18 Interim Director of Physical Plant Mr. Drew DICKEY
96 Director of Purchasing Ms. Jessica HOLLOWAY
92 Director of Honors Program Dr. Georgeanna WRIGHT
22 Director Affirmative Action Ms. Melissa RIFFLE
108 Dir Assessment/Inst Effectiveness Dr. Christine AUSTIN
105 Webmaster Vacant
19 Director Public Safety Mr. Josh MCMILLIAN
26 Director of University Relations Mr. Sam STRASNER
44 Director Annual Giving Programs Ms. Caroline VINING
07 Director of Admissions Ms. Jessica BROCK
41 Athletic Director Ms. Abby DAVIS
88 Director of Prospect Research Ms. Pam COOPER
112 Director of Gift Planning Ms. Peggy AYERS
53 Dean College of Education Dr. Linda BEAN
49 Dean Col Arts & Humanities Dr. Jeffrey CASS
50 Dean College of Business Dr. K. Russell JONES
54 Dn Col Engineering & Applied Sci Dr. Judy CEZEAUX
81 Dean College of Natural & Health Sc Dr. Jeff ROBERTSON
58 Interim Dean of Graduate College Dr. Sarah GORDON
28 Asst Dean Diversity & Inclusion Vacant
38 Assoc Dean Student Student Wellness Ms. Kristy DAVIS
39 Associate Dean Residence Life Mr. Delton GORDON
04 Exec Assistant to the President Ms. Jennifer FLEMING

Arkansas Tech University-Ozark Campus (F)

1700 Helberg Lane, Ozark AR 72949
Telephone: (479) 667-2117 Identification: 770003
Accreditation: &HLC, ADNUR, CAHIIM, CSHSE, CVT, EMT, OTA

Baptist Health College Little Rock (G)

11900 Colonel Glenn Rd, Ste 1000, Little Rock AR 72210
County: Pulaski FICE Identification: 031052
Unit ID: 106546
Telephone: (501) 202-6200 Carnegie Class: Spec 2-yr-Health
FAX Number: N/A Calendar System: Semester
URL: www.bhclr.edu
Established: 1921 Annual Undergrad Tuition & Fees: $11,750
Enrollment: 661 Coed
Affiliation or Control: Independent Non-Profit IRS Status: 501(c)3
Highest Offering: Associate Degree
Accreditation: ABHES, ADNUR, MLS, NMT, OTA, PNUR, POLYT, RAD, SURTEC

01 Chancellor Dr. Judy PILE
66 Dean of Nursing Laura HAMILTON
06 Registrar Kristin WADDELL
37 Financial Aid Administrator Natalie MARTIN
10 Coordinator Campus/Financial Svcs Dr. Jamie CLARK

Black River Technical College (H)

PO Box 468/1410 Hwy 304 East,
Pocahontas AR 72455-0468
County: Randolph FICE Identification: 020522
Unit ID: 106625
Telephone: (870) 248-4000 Carnegie Class: Assoc/HT-High Trad
FAX Number: (870) 248-4100 Calendar System: Semester
URL: www.blackrivertech.org
Established: 1991 Annual Undergrad Tuition & Fees (In-State): $4,118
Enrollment: 1,350 Coed
Affiliation or Control: State IRS Status: 501(c)3
Highest Offering: Associate Degree
Accreditation: HLC, COARC, EMT

01 President Dr. Martin EGGENSPERGER
05 VP for Academics Dr. Brad BAINE
32 VP for Student Affairs Mr. Jason SMITH
111 VP for Institutional Advancement Mrs. Karen LIEBHABER
10 VP for Finance and Administration Mrs. Rhonda STONE
37 Director of Financial Aid Mrs. Brandi CHESTER
06 Registrar Mrs. Kimberly BIGGER
04 Administrative Asst to President Mrs. Janna GUTHREY
106 Dir Online Education/E-learning Mrs. Regina MOORE

15 Director Personnel Services ..... Mrs. Julie EDINGTON
19 Director Security/Safety ..... Mr. Tony SAYLORS
96 Director of Purchasing ..... Mrs. Janice HARVEY
13 Chief Info Technology Officer (CIO) ..... Mr. Mike GREENE
18 Chief Facilities/Physical Plant ..... Mr. Trent INGRAM
09 Director of Institutional Research ..... Mrs. Shana SARTAIN
07 Director of Admissions ..... Mrs. Angie FRENCH
50 Dean or Director Business ..... Mr. Phillip DICKSON
53 Dean or Director Education ..... Mrs. Donna STATLER
08 Library Director ..... Mr. Mark WARNICK
35 Director of Student Development ..... Mr. Neal HARWELL

Bryan University (A)

3704 West Walnut Street, Rogers AR 72756-1825
Telephone: (479) 899-6644 Identification: 666252
Accreditation: ACICS

† Branch campus of Bryan University, Springfield, MO.

Central Baptist College (B)

1501 College Avenue, Conway AR 72034-6470
County: Faulkner FICE Identification: 001093
Unit ID: 106713
Telephone: (501) 329-6872 Carnegie Class: Bac-Diverse
FAX Number: (501) 329-2941 Calendar System: Semester
URL: www.cbc.edu
Established: 1952 Annual Undergrad Tuition & Fees: $17,100
Enrollment: 604 Coed
Affiliation or Control: Baptist IRS Status: 501(c)3
Highest Offering: Baccalaureate
Accreditation: HLC, CAEP

01 President ..... Mr. Terry KIMBROW
04 Admin Asst to President ..... Mrs. Peggy PILLOW
05 VP for Academic Affairs ..... Dr. Gary MCALLISTER
10 VP for Finance ..... Mr. Paul CHERRY
111 VP for Advancement ..... Vacant
84 VP for Enrollment Mgmt ..... Mr. Ryan JOHNSON
32 Assoc VP for Student Services ..... Mr. Chris MITCHELL
35 Director of Student Services ..... Mrs. Marieca ASHWORTH
06 Registrar ..... Mrs. Stacy JORDAN
07 Director of Admissions ..... Ms. Mary Catherine HARVISON
106 Director of Online Studies ..... Mr. Steve ELDER
08 Library Director ..... Mrs. Rachel WHITTINGHAM
26 Director of Public Relations ..... Mrs. Jessica FAULKNER
37 Director of Financial Aid ..... Mrs. Tonya HAMMONTREE
09 Institutional Research Analyst ..... Mrs. Gwenda WILLIAMS
41 Athletic Director ..... Mr. Lyle MIDDLETON
15 Director of Human Resources ..... Ms. Mechelle CARGILE
29 Director of Alumni Engagement ..... Mrs. Jessica FAULKNER
88 Military Relations Counselor ..... Mr. Patrick JACOB
18 Director of Physical Plant ..... Mr. Byron BAKER

Champion Christian College (C)

600 Garland Ave, Hot Springs AR 71913
County: Garland Identification: 667324
Unit ID: 492069
Telephone: (501) 623-2272 Carnegie Class: Bac/Assoc-Mixed
FAX Number: (501) 623-4262 Calendar System: Semester
URL: championchristiancollege.com
Established: 2005 Annual Undergrad Tuition & Fees: N/A
Enrollment: N/A Coed
Affiliation or Control: Independent Non-Profit IRS Status: 501(c)3
Highest Offering: Baccalaureate
Accreditation: TRACS

01 President ..... Dr. Eric CAPACI
03 Executive Vice President ..... Dr. Jeremy HORTON
05 Vice President of Academic Affairs ..... Mr. Elsen PORTUGAL
32 VP Student Affairs/Dir Admissions ..... Mr. Josiah CAPACI
06 Registrar ..... Mr. Kevin CONNOR
10 Vice President of Finance ..... Mrs. Marcia THOMAS

Crowley's Ridge College (D)

100 College Drive, Paragould AR 72450-9775
County: Greene FICE Identification: 001095
Unit ID: 106810
Telephone: (870) 236-6901 Carnegie Class: Bac-Diverse
FAX Number: (870) 236-7748 Calendar System: Semester
URL: www.crc.edu
Established: 1964 Annual Undergrad Tuition & Fees: $15,100
Enrollment: 192 Coed
Affiliation or Control: Churches Of Christ IRS Status: 501(c)3
Highest Offering: Baccalaureate
Accreditation: HLC, CAEP

01 President ..... Dr. Richard JOHNSON
05 Vice President for Academic Affairs ..... Dr. Brian DAVIS
32 Vice President for Student Affairs ..... Mr. Paul MCFADDEN
111 Chief Financial Officer ..... Mrs. Liz BROWN
06 Registrar ..... Mrs. Treka CLARK
37 Director Student Financial Services ..... Mrs. Shelly BEASLEY
26 Director Public Relations/Marketing ..... Mr. Matthew EMERY
07 Director Admissions ..... Mrs. Shelly BEASLEY
08 Director Learning Center ..... Mrs. Ashley HANKINS
10 Business Office Manager ..... Mrs. Sonia JOHNSON
13 Director of Inst Technology ..... Mr. Larry JOHNSON
15 Director of Human Services ..... Mrs. Andrea JOHNSON
11 Director of Campus Operations ..... Mr. Craig CUPP

East Arkansas Community College (E)

1700 Newcastle Road, Forrest City AR 72335-2204
County: Saint Francis FICE Identification: 012260
Unit ID: 106883
Telephone: (870) 633-4480 Carnegie Class: Assoc/MT-VT-Mix Trad/Non
FAX Number: (870) 633-7222 Calendar System: Semester
URL: www.eacc.edu
Established: 1974 Annual Undergrad Tuition & Fees (In-District): $3,225
Enrollment: 934 Coed
Affiliation or Control: State/Local IRS Status: Exempt
Highest Offering: Associate Degree
Accreditation: HLC, EMT

01 President ..... Dr. Cathie CLINE
05 Interim VP Academic Affairs ..... Mrs. Michelle WILSON
10 Vice President for Finance ..... Mr. Tanner MCKNIGHT
75 VP for Economic and Workforce Dev ..... Mr. Robert P. SUMMERS
37 Director Student Financial Aid ..... Ms. Janice WALLACE
08 Director Library Services ..... Mrs. Paige LAWS
26 Exec Dir of PR/Community Programs ..... Mrs. Lindsay MIDKIFF
15 Director of Human Resources ..... Mrs. Lindsi HUFFAKER
96 Purchasing Specialist ..... Mrs. Lisa SILER
31 Director of Community Education ..... Mrs. Logan BRASFIELD
121 Director of Advising & Counseling ..... Mr. Errin JAMES
97 Dean of General Education ..... Dr. Laura RIDDLE
32 Dean of Student Services ..... Mr. Adam O'NEAL
78 Dean of Vocational Education ..... Mr. Jack HILL
102 Director Foundation/Corporate Rels ..... Mrs. Niki JONES
103 Director Workforce Development ..... Mrs. Heather MCBRIDE
09 Director of Institutional Research ..... Mrs. Roni HORTON
13 Director of Computer Services ..... Mr. Ed ADAMS
06 Registrar ..... Ms. Jenna HAYES
19 Director Security/ Safety ..... Mr. Mark WILSON

Ecclesia College (F)

9653 Nations Drive, Springdale AR 72762-8159
County: Benton FICE Identification: 038553
Unit ID: 446233
Telephone: (479) 248-7236 Carnegie Class: Bac-Diverse
FAX Number: (479) 248-1455 Calendar System: Semester
URL: www.ecollege.edu
Established: 1975 Annual Undergrad Tuition & Fees: $15,950
Enrollment: 193 Coed
Affiliation or Control: Independent Non-Profit IRS Status: 501(c)3
Highest Offering: Master's
Accreditation: BI

01 President ..... Mr. Michael A. NOVAK
00 Chancellor ..... Ms. R. Inez PARIS
05 Academic Dean ..... Ms. Donna BROWN
10 Chief Financial Officer ..... Ms. Melissa K. RICKS
32 Dean of Students ..... Ms. Elizabeth NEWLUN
106 Academic Dean EC Online ..... Dr. Ben PASCUT
111 Director of Advancement ..... Mr. Michael A. NOVAK
37 Director Student Financial Aid ..... Mr. Don PRESTON
41 Athletic Director ..... Vacant
06 Registrar ..... Ms. Amanda VINCENT
08 Head Librarian ..... Mrs. Angela CRISS
103 Dean of Work ..... Ms. Elizabeth NEWLUN
84 Director of Enrollment ..... Mr. Chad E. HOWARD

Harding University Main Campus (G)

915 E. Market Avenue, Searcy AR 72149-5615
County: White FICE Identification: 001097
Unit ID: 107044
Telephone: (501) 279-4000 Carnegie Class: DU-Mod
FAX Number: (501) 279-4600 Calendar System: Semester
URL: www.harding.edu
Established: 1924 Annual Undergrad Tuition & Fees: $21,540
Enrollment: 4,617 Coed
Affiliation or Control: Churches Of Christ IRS Status: 501(c)3
Highest Offering: Doctorate
Accreditation: HLC, ACBSP, ARCPA, CACREP, CAEP, CIDA, @DIET, DIETD, MUS, NURSE, PHAR, PTA, SP, SW

01 President ..... Dr. Michael D. WILLIAMS
03 Executive Vice President ..... Dr. Jean-Noel THOMPSON
05 Provost ..... Dr. Marty SPEARS
10 Vice President Finance ..... Mrs. Tammy HALL
111 Vice President Advancement ..... Dr. Bryan BURKS
13 VP Information Systems & Technology ..... Mr. Keith CRONK
84 VP Enrollment Services ..... Mr. Steve LAKE
41 Athletic Director ..... Mr. Jeff MORGAN
29 Director of Alumni Relations ..... Mrs. Heather KEMPER
88 Dean College of Bible & Ministry ..... Dr. Monte COX
97 Dean of University College ..... Dr. Kevin KEHL
50 Dean College of Business ..... Dr. Al FRAZIER
53 Dean College of Education ..... Dr. Donny LEE
66 Dean College of Nursing ..... Dr. Susan KEHL
79 Dean College of Arts & Humanities ..... Dr. Warren CASEY
81 Dean College of Sciences ..... Dr. Zane GASTINEAU
76 Dean College of Allied Health ..... Dr. Mike MCGALLIARD
104 Exec Dir of International Programs ..... Dr. Audra PLEASANT
88 Asst VP Enrollment Management ..... Mr. David HALL
21 Senior Finance Officer ..... Mr. Tim JONES
32 VP Student Life/Dean Students ..... Mr. Zach NEAL
88 Asst VP of IS&T ..... Mr. Mike CHALENBURG
06 Registrar ..... Mr. Tod MARTIN
38 Director of Counseling ..... Dr. Lew MOORE
19 Director Security/Safety ..... Mr. Craig RUSSELL
26 VP of Communication/Enrollment ..... Mrs. Candice MOORE
37 Director Student Financial Aid ..... Dr. Jonathan ROBERTS
58 Director of Graduate Studies ..... Vacant
08 Librarian ..... Mrs. Jean WALDROP
18 Chief Facilities/Physical Plant ..... Mr. Danny DERAMUS
15 Asst Vice Pres Human Resources ..... Mr. David ROSS
09 Director of Institutional Research ..... Mr. Dustin HOWELL
96 Purchasing Coordinator ..... Mrs. Karen CARPER
35 Assistant Dean of Students ..... Mr. Marcus THOMAS
35 Assistant Dean of Students ..... Mrs. Kara ABSTON
35 Assistant Dean of Students ..... Mrs. Ranan HESTER
35 Assistant Dean of Students ..... Mr. Logan LIGHT
28 Diversity Services ..... Mrs. Tiffany BYERS
39 Director Student Housing ..... Mrs. Rhonda FOSTER
07 Senior Director of Admissions ..... Mr. Scott HANNIGAN

Henderson State University (H)

1100 Henderson Street, Arkadelphia AR 71999-0001
County: Clark FICE Identification: 001098
Unit ID: 107071
Telephone: (870) 230-5000 Carnegie Class: Masters/M
FAX Number: (870) 230-5144 Calendar System: Semester
URL: www.hsu.edu
Established: 1890 Annual Undergrad Tuition & Fees (In-State): $7,392
Enrollment: 3,163 Coed
Affiliation or Control: State IRS Status: 501(c)3
Highest Offering: Beyond Master's But Less Than Doctorate
Accreditation: HLC, ART, CACREP, CAEP, DIETD, MUS, NURSE

01 Chancellor ..... Dr. Charles AMBROSE
04 Admin Assistant to the Chancellor ..... Ms. Flora E. WEEKS
05 Int Provost/VC Academic Affairs ..... Mr. James HUNT
10 VC Finance & Administration ..... Ms. Rita FLEMING
32 VC Student Affs & Student Success ..... Dr. Brad PATTERSON
111 Interim VC Advancement ..... Ms. Tina HALL
43 General Counsel ..... Ms. Elaine KNEEBONE
35 Asst VC Student Engagement ..... Dr. Veronikha SALAZAR
39 Asst VC Housing/Community Standard ..... Dr. Nicole LAIRD
13 AVC Computer/Comm Svcs & CIO ..... Vacant
41 Director Athletics ..... Mr. Shawn JONES
26 Exec Director of Marketing/Comm ..... Ms. Tina HALL
49 Dean Ellis Col Arts/Sciences ..... Dr. Angela BOSWELL
50 Dean of School of Business ..... Dr. Marc MILLER
53 Dean Teachers College Henderson ..... Dr. Celya TAYLOR
58 Vice Provost/Dean of Grad School ..... Dr. Kenneth TAYLOR
06 Assoc Provost/Registrar ..... Dr. Elwyn MARTIN
08 Interim Director Huie Library ..... Ms. Lacy WOLFE
15 Director of Human Resources ..... Ms. Loretta BRANTLEY
19 Director of University Police ..... Mr. Jonathan CAMPBELL
38 Dir Student Health/Counseling Ctr ..... Ms. Renee WALLS
07 Assoc Provost Enrollment/Admissions ..... Ms. Ashlee DIXON
37 Director of Financial Aid ..... Ms. Lisa SMITH
92 Director of Honors College ..... Dr. C. Drew SMITH
96 Director of Purchasing ..... Vacant
72 Dir Academic Tech & Help Desk ..... Ms. Jennifer HOLBROOK
09 Director of Institutional Research ..... Ms. Ginger OTWELL
29 Director Alumni Engagement ..... Ms. Leah SEXTON
122 Asst Dir Stdnt Act-Greek Life ..... Ms. Emily BLANTON

Hendrix College (I)

1600 Washington Avenue, Conway AR 72032-3080
County: Faulkner FICE Identification: 001099
Unit ID: 107080
Telephone: (501) 329-6811 Carnegie Class: Bac-A&S
FAX Number: (501) 450-1200 Calendar System: Semester
URL: www.hendrix.edu
Established: 1876 Annual Undergrad Tuition & Fees: $49,490
Enrollment: 1,077 Coed
Affiliation or Control: United Methodist IRS Status: 501(c)3
Highest Offering: Master's
Accreditation: HLC

01 President ..... Mr. W. Ellis ARNOLD, III
04 Executive Assistant to President ..... Ms. Donna PLEMMONS
05 Provost ..... Dr. Terri BONEBRIGHT
26 Vice Pres Marketing Communications ..... Mr. Rob O'CONNOR
10 Executive Vice President & CFO ..... Mr. Tom SIEBENMORGEN
84 VP Enrollment/Dir Admissions ..... Mr. Ryan CASSELL
15 Vice Pres for Human Resources ..... Ms. Vicki LYNN
18 VP Operations/Facilities ..... Ms. Sharron RUSSELL
32 Exec VP Student Affs/Dean of Stdnts ..... Mr. Jim WILTGEN, JR.
27 Assoc VP Marketing Communications ..... Ms. Amy FORBUS
06 Registrar ..... Ms. Brenda ADAMS
08 Director of Libraries ..... Ms. Britt Anne MURPHY
13 VP Technology/Chief Info Officer ..... Mr. Sam NICHOLS
29 Director Alumni Relations ..... Ms. Pamela OWEN
41 Director of Athletics ..... Ms. Amy WEAVER
37 Director of Financial Aid ..... Ms. Kristina BURFORD
79 Area Head/Humanities ..... Dr. Rod MILLER
81 Area Head/Natural Sciences ..... Dr. Ann WRIGHT
83 Area Head/Social Sciences ..... Dr. Todd BERRYMAN
42 Chaplain ..... Rev. Ellen ALSTON
20 Associate Academic Officer ..... Dr. David SUTHERLAND
21 Associate Business Officer ..... Mr. Shawn MATHIS
36 Director Career Services ..... Ms. Leigh LASSITER-COUNTS
38 Director Student Counseling ..... Ms. Mary Anne SIEBERT
09 Director of Institutional Research ..... Vacant
28 Int VP for Diversity & Inclusion ..... Ms. Kesha BAOUA

Jackson Theological Seminary (A)

520 North Locust Street, North Little Rock AR 72114

County: Pulaski Identification: 667411
Telephone: (501) 429-8395 Carnegie Class: Not Classified
FAX Number: (501) 375-0306 Calendar System: Semester
URL: www.jtseminary.org
Established: 1886 Annual Undergrad Tuition & Fees: N/A
Enrollment: N/A Coed
Affiliation or Control: African Methodist Episcopal IRS Status: 501(c)3
Highest Offering: Master's
Accreditation: @TRACS

01 President & CEO ....Rev. Cecil L. WILLIAMS, JR.

Jefferson Regional Medical Center School of Nursing (B)

1600 W. 40th Avenue, Pine Bluff AR 71603

County: Jefferson FICE Identification: 023308
Unit ID: 107123
Telephone: (870) 541-7858 Carnegie Class: Spec 2-yr-Health
FAX Number: (870) 541-7807 Calendar System: Semester
URL: www.jrmc.org
Established: 1981 Annual Undergrad Tuition & Fees: N/A
Enrollment: 55 Coed
Affiliation or Control: Independent Non-Profit IRS Status: 501(c)3
Highest Offering: Associate Degree
Accreditation: ABHES

01 President & CEO .... Brian THOMAS
05 Vice Pres/Chief Academic Officer .... Bryan JACKSON
10 Vice Pres/Chief Financial Officer .... Jeremy JEFFREY
15 Chief Human Resources Officer .... Layton ANDERSON

John Brown University (C)

2000 W University Street, Siloam Springs AR 72761-2121

County: Benton FICE Identification: 001100
Unit ID: 107141
Telephone: (479) 524-9500 Carnegie Class: Masters/M
FAX Number: (479) 524-7278 Calendar System: Semester
URL: www.jbu.edu
Established: 1919 Annual Undergrad Tuition & Fees: $28,288
Enrollment: 2,343 Coed
Affiliation or Control: Independent Non-Profit IRS Status: 501(c)3
Highest Offering: Master's
Accreditation: HLC, ACBSP, CAEP, CONST, NURSE

01 President .... Dr. Charles POLLARD
10 Vice Pres Finance & Administration .... Dr. Kim HADLEY
84 Vice Pres Enrollment Management ....Mr. Donald W. CRANDALL
111 Vice Pres of University Advancement .... Dr. Jim KRALL
32 Vice Pres for Student Development .... Dr. Stephen T. BEERS
05 VP Academic Affairs/Dean of Faculty ....Dr. Ed ERICSON, III
42 Campus Pastor/Assoc Dean of Stdnts .... Vacant
06 Registrar .... Dr. Rebecca WEIMER
21 Controller .... Mr. Tom PERRY
13 Chief Information Systems Ofcr .... Mr. Paul NAST
18 Director of Facilities Services .... Mr. Steve BRANKLE
112 Director of Planned Giving .... Mr. Eric GREENHAW
08 Director of Library .... Ms. Taylor VANLANDINGHAM
85 Director International Programs .... Mr. Bill STEVENSON
29 Director of Alumni/Parent Relations .... Mr. Brad EDWARDS
37 Director of Financial Aid .... Mr. David BURNEY
07 JBU Online Recruiting .... Vacant
41 Athletic Director .... Ms. Robyn DAUGHERTY
04 Administrative Asst to President .... Ms. Kory J. DALE
09 Director of Institutional Research ....Mrs. Lynette DUNCAN
15 Chief Human Resources Officer ....Mrs. Amy FISHER
19 Director Security/Safety ....Mr. Scott WANZER
26 Director University Communications ....Ms. Julie GUMM
39 Director Residence Life .... Dr. Andre BROQUARD
108 Director Institutional Assessment .... Dr. Robert NORWOOD

Lyon College (D)

PO Box 2317, Batesville AR 72503-2317

County: Independence FICE Identification: 001088
Unit ID: 106342
Telephone: (870) 307-7000 Carnegie Class: Bac-A&S
FAX Number: (870) 307-7001 Calendar System: Semester
URL: https://www.lyon.edu/
Established: 1872 Annual Undergrad Tuition & Fees: $29,415
Enrollment: 665 Coed
Affiliation or Control: Presbyterian Church (U.S.A.) IRS Status: 501(c)3
Highest Offering: Baccalaureate
Accreditation: HLC, CAEP

01 President ....Dr. Melissa P. TAVERNER
05 Provost & Dean of Faculty ....Dr. Anthony GRAFTON
100 Chief of Staff/EVP Enrollment Svcs .... Vacant
32 VP Student Life & Dean of Students .... Ms. Danell HETRICK
111 Vice President of Advancement .... Dr. David HUTCHISON
89 Dean of First Year Studies .... Vacant
10 VP for Business & Finance .... Mr. Joseph D. BOTANA, II
08 Director Library .... Dr. Robert KRAPOHL
110 Executive Dir of Advancement .... Mrs. Gina GARRETT
07 Dean of Admission ....Mr. Thomas NEWTON
37 Executive Director of Financial Aid .... Mr. Tommy TUCKER
36 Director Career Development .... Mr. Patrick LYNCH
13 Director Information Services .... Mr. Jeremiah CHERWIEN
26 Director of Marketing/Comm .... Ms. Carol LANGSTON
41 Director of Athletics .... Mr. Kevin JENKINS
42 Chaplain .... Rev. Margaret ALSUP
53 Director of Teacher Education .... Dr. Kim CROSBY
38 Director Student Counseling .... Ms. Victoria HUTCHINSON
40 Director Bookstore ....Ms. Lisa WATTS
08 Head Librarian .... Vacant
23 Director of Health Services ....Mrs. Jennifer MORRISON
18 Chief Facilities/Physical Plant .... Mr. Brett RAY
20 Associate Provost ....Dr. Cassia OLIVEIRA
06 Registrar ....Mrs. Tami HALL
44 Director Annual Giving .... Vacant
09 Director of Institutional Research .... Mr. Randy PETERSON
15 Director of Human Resources ....Ms. Rebecca VARELA
29 Director of Alumni Affairs ....Mrs. Cindy BARBER
122 Residential Dir/Coord Greek Life ....Mr. Tyler TOBER
104 Director Study Abroad ....Mr. Joseph MACADE

National Park College (E)

101 College Drive,
Hot Springs National Park AR 71913-9174

County: Garland FICE Identification: 012105
Unit ID: 106980
Telephone: (501) 760-4222 Carnegie Class: Assoc/MT-VT-High Trad
FAX Number: (501) 760-4100 Calendar System: Semester
URL: www.np.edu
Established: 1973 Annual Undergrad Tuition & Fees (In-District): $5,000
Enrollment: 1,912 Coed
Affiliation or Control: State/Local IRS Status: 501(c)3
Highest Offering: Associate Degree
Accreditation: HLC, ACBSP, ACPHA, ADNUR, CAHIIM, COARC, EMT, MLTAD, RAD

01 President ....Dr. John HOGAN
05 Vice Pres Academic Affairs ....Dr. Wade DERDEN
10 Vice Pres Finance & Admin .... Ms. Kelli EMBRY
32 VP Student Affairs/Enrollment Mgmt ....Dr. Jerry THOMAS
26 VP External affairs/Chief of Staff .... Ms. Darla THURBER
13 Vice Pres Information Technology ....Mr. Blake BUTLER
103 Vice Pres Workforce ....Mr. Bill ALLISON
15 Vice Pres Human Resources .... Ms. Janet BREWER
35 Dean of Students .... Mr. John TUCKER
84 Dean of Enrollment Svcs/Stdnt Life .... Mr. Jason HUDNELL
09 Director Institutional Research .... Mr. Chris COBLE
08 Director of Library Services .... Ms. Lynn VALETUTTI
37 Director of Financial Aid ....Ms. Lisa HOPPER
102 Executive Director of Foundation ....Ms. Nicole HERNDON
06 Registrar .... Mr. Scott POST
04 Exec Assistant to the President .... Ms. Jill HOULIHAN
18 Director Physical Plant .... Mr. Brad HOPPER
41 Athletics Director .... Mr. Jason HUDNELL

North Arkansas College (F)

1515 Pioneer Drive, Harrison AR 72601-5599

County: Boone FICE Identification: 012261
Unit ID: 107460
Telephone: (870) 743-3000 Carnegie Class: Assoc/MT-VT-High Trad
FAX Number: (870) 391-3250 Calendar System: Semester
URL: www.northark.edu
Established: 1974 Annual Undergrad Tuition & Fees (In-District): $3,840
Enrollment: 1,604 Coed
Affiliation or Control: State/Local IRS Status: 501(c)3
Highest Offering: Associate Degree
Accreditation: HLC, ACBSP, ADNUR, EMT, MLTAD, RAD, SURGT

01 President .... Dr. Rick MASSENGALE
05 VP of Academic Affairs .... Dr. Matt CARDIN
10 Vice Pres Finance & Administration .... Mr. Richard STIPE
111 Vice Pres Institutional Advancement .... Dr. Rodney ARNOLD
04 Executive Assistant to President .... Mrs. Joetta ADAMS
49 Dean Arts & Science/Business & IT .... Mr. Chris LAFATA
66 Dean Nursing/Allied Hlth/Tech Pgms .....Dr. Josephine KERSHAW
103 Dean of Outreach & Workforce Dev ....Mrs. Nell BONDS
08 Student Resource Coordinator .... Mrs. Sharla HELLEN
108 Dir Institutional Effectiveness .... Mrs. Amanda KILBOURN
32 VP of Student Affairs ....Mrs. Tavonda BROWN
41 Athletic Director .... Mr. Bobby HOWARD
15 Director Human Resources .... Mrs. Kris GREENING
18 Chief Facilities/Physical Plant .... Mr. Kevin SOMERS
96 Director of Purchasing .... Mrs. Shari HOLT
37 Director Student Financial Aid .... Mrs. Jennifer HADDOCK
06 Registrar .... Mrs. Charla JENNINGS
07 Director of Admissions .... Mrs. Charla JENNINGS
26 Director of Public Relations .... Mrs. Micki SOMERS
31 Asst Dir of Community Education .... Ms. Sarah BING

NorthWest Arkansas Community College (G)

1 College Drive, Bentonville AR 72712-5091

County: Benton FICE Identification: 030633
Unit ID: 367459
Telephone: (479) 986-4000 Carnegie Class: Assoc/HT-Mix Trad/Non
FAX Number: (479) 619-4118 Calendar System: Semester
URL: www.nwacc.edu
Established: 1989 Annual Undergrad Tuition & Fees (In-District): $4,096
Enrollment: 7,411 Coed
Affiliation or Control: State/Local IRS Status: 501(c)3
Highest Offering: Associate Degree
Accreditation: HLC, ACBSP, ACFEI, ADNUR, CAHIIM, COARC, EMT, IFSAC, PTAA

01 President ....Dr. Dennis RITTLE
10 VP of Finance & Administration ....Mr. Al MASSRI
05 Vice Pres for Learning/CAO .... Dr. Ricky TOMPKINS
32 VP of Student Services .... Dr. Justin WHITE
36 VP of Career & Workforce Education .... Mr. Tim CORNELIUS
103 Dean of Workforce Education ....Dr. Megan BOLINDER
13 AVP IT/Chief Information Officer .... Mr. Jason DEGN
56 AVP of Washington Co Programs ....Ms. Brenda GREEN
88 Exec Dir Retail/Supplier Education ....Mr. Mark TUCKER
88 Executive Director of Operations .... Mr. Jack THOMPSON
51 Dean of Adult Education ....Mr. Ben ALDAMA
35 Dean of Students .... Vacant
30 Executive Director of Advancement .... Ms. Liz ANDERSON
20 Assoc VP Learning .... Dr. Diana JOHNSON
26 Exec Dir Cmty/Govt Rels/Marketing .... Mr. Grant HODGES
21 Controller ....Ms. Holly WESCOTT
06 Registrar .... Mr. Austin SCHADER
15 Exec Director Human Resources ....Ms. Beverly HILL
106 Assoc Dean of Distance Learning ....Dr. Kate BURKES
88 Director of Learning Resources .... Ms. Gwen DOBBS
84 Director of Enrollment Services .... Ms. Shannon CANTRELL
37 Director Student Financial Aid .... Ms. Michelle CORDELL
121 Exec Director of Student Success ....Mr. Eric VEST
109 Dir Food Services/Event Management .... Ms. Diane BOSS
88 Executive Director of Brightwater ....Mr. Marshall SHAFKOWITZ
09 Director of Institutional Research ....Ms. Kim PURDY
18 Director of Physical Plant ....Mr. Jim NELSON
77 Dean for Bus/Computer Information .... Dr. Christine DAVIS
76 Dean of Health Professions .... Mr. Mark WALLENMEYER
04 Exec Asst to President & BOT .... Ms. Lindsey WHITE
22 Exec Dir Policy/Risk & Comp .... Ms. Teresa TAYLOR
19 Interim Director of Public Safety .... Mr. Cecil WHITE
104 Director Global Intl Programs .... Mr. Jeremy YOUMANS
07 Director of Admissions ....Ms. Paula GULLEDGE
96 Director of Purchasing .... Ms. Jennifer LEWIS

Ouachita Baptist University (H)

410 Ouachita Street, Arkadelphia AR 71998-0001

County: Clark FICE Identification: 001102
Unit ID: 107512
Telephone: (870) 245-5000 Carnegie Class: Bac-A&S
FAX Number: (870) 245-5500 Calendar System: Semester
URL: www.obu.edu
Established: 1886 Annual Undergrad Tuition & Fees: $29,120
Enrollment: 1,704 Coed
Affiliation or Control: Southern Baptist IRS Status: 501(c)3
Highest Offering: Master's
Accreditation: HLC, CAEP, DIETD, @DIETI, MUS, NUR

01 President .... Dr. Ben R. SELLS
111 Vice Pres Institutional Advancement .... Dr. Keldon HENLEY
100 Chief of Staff .... Dr. Keldon HENLEY
05 Vice President Academic Affairs ....Dr. Justin K. HARDIN
10 Vice Pres for Finance .... Mr. Jason TOLBERT
32 Vice Pres for Student Development .... Dr. Rickey ROGERS
30 Vice President for Development ....Mrs. Terry G. PEEPLES
26 Asst to Pres for Comm/Mktg .... Mrs. Brooke ZIMNY
07 Director of Admissions Counseling .... Mrs. Lori MOTL
09 Director of Institutional Research .... Dr. Deborah ROOT
15 Director of Human Resources .... Mrs. Sherri PHELPS
18 Chief Facilities/Physical Plant ....Mr. Jonathan HUGHES
29 Director of Alumni Relations ....Mr. Jon MERRYMAN
35 Dean of Students ....Mr. Brandon TOLLETT
20 Assoc Vice Pres Academic Affairs .... Dr. Doug REED
36 Director of Career Services ....Mr. Adam WHEAT
38 University Counselor .... Mr. Dan JARBOE
08 Interim Director of Library Svcs .... Dr. Anping WU
06 Registrar/Director of Admissions .... Mrs. Susan ATKINSON
37 Director of Student Financial Svcs ....Mrs. Karen MATROS
92 Director Honors Program .... Dr. Barbara PEMBERTON
13 Chief Information Officer .... Mr. Bill PHELPS
39 Director of Residence Life ....Mr. Quantel WILLIAMS
41 Athletic Director .... Mr. David SHARP
43 University Counsel .... Mr. Bryan MCKINNEY
21 Director of Business Services .... Mrs. Kristi CLAY
40 Bookstore Manager ....Mrs. Jennifer FORTHMAN
57 Interim Dean of School of Fine Arts .... Dr. Ryan LEWIS
50 Dean of the School of Business .... Mr. Bryan MCKINNEY
53 Dean Sch of Interdisciplinary Stds ....Dr. Justin HARDIN
73 Dean School of Christian Studies .... Dr. Jeremy GREER
79 Dean School of Humanities & Educ ....Dr. Jeff ROOT
81 Dean School of Natural Sciences ....Dr. Tim KNIGHT
83 Dean School of Social Sciences ....Dr. Kevin (Casey) C. MOTL
101 Secretary of the Institution/Board ....Mrs. Tracey KNIGHT
108 Director Institutional Assessment .... Dr. Deborah ROOT
19 Director Security/Safety .... Mr. Jeff CROW
04 Executive Asst to the President ....Mrs. Tracey KNIGHT
104 VP Cmty/Intercultural Engagement .... Dr. Lewis SHEPHERD
106 Asst to Pres for Grad/Prof Studies .... Dr. Monica HARDIN

Ozarka College (I)

218 College Drive, Melbourne AR 72556

County: Izard FICE Identification: 020870
Unit ID: 107549
Telephone: (870) 368-2300 Carnegie Class: Assoc/HT-High Trad
FAX Number: (870) 368-2091 Calendar System: Semester
URL: www.ozarka.edu
Established: 1991 Annual Undergrad Tuition & Fees (In-State): $3,004
Enrollment: 1,033 Coed
Affiliation or Control: State IRS Status: 501(c)3

Highest Offering: Associate Degree
Accreditation: HLC, ACFEI, SURGT

01 President .... Dr. Richard L. DAWE
05 Vice President of Academic Affairs .... Dr. Chris LORCH
10 Exec Vice Pres of Finance/Admin .... Mrs. Tina WHEELIS
13 Chief Information Officer .... Mr. Scott PINKSTON
111 Vice President of Advancement .... Dr. Joshua WILSON
32 Vice Pres of Student Services .... Mrs. Zeda WILKERSON
04 Assistant to the President .... Ms. Valerie LONG
15 Director of Human Resources .... Ms. Deedra STEED
21 Business Manager .... Mrs. Amber RUSH
30 Vice Pres of Advancement .... Dr. Joshua WILSON
110 Assoc Director of Advancement .... Mrs. Suellen DAVIDSON
37 Director of Financial Aid .... Mrs. Tania WALLACE
110 Director of Planning/Spec Projects .... Ms. Kim WILSON
06 Registrar .... Mr. Dylan HEREKAMP
26 Dir Public Relations/Marketing .... Ms. Katie NORRIS
07 Director of Admissions .... Mr. McKenzie JACKSON

Philander Smith College (A)

900 W. Daisy L. Gatson Bates Drive,
Little Rock AR 72202-3799
County: Pulaski FICE Identification: 001103
Unit ID: 107600
Telephone: (501) 375-9845 Carnegie Class: Bac-Diverse
FAX Number: (501) 370-5277 Calendar System: Semester
URL: www.philander.edu
Established: 1877 Annual Undergrad Tuition & Fees: $13,014
Enrollment: 799 Coed
Affiliation or Control: United Methodist IRS Status: 501(c)3
Highest Offering: Baccalaureate
Accreditation: HLC, ACBSP, CAEP, SW

01 President .... Dr. Roderick L. SMOTHERS, SR.
04 Senior Exec Assistant to President .... Mrs. Anita L. HATLEY
03 Executive Vice President .... Vacant
100 Chief of Staff .... Dr. Kenyatta SHAMBURGER
05 Interim VP of Academic Affairs .... Dr. Shannon CLOWNEY-JOHNSON
32 VP of Student Affs/Enrollment Mgmt .... Dr. Gregory HUDSON
111 VP Institutional Advancement .... Mr. Charles KING
10 VP of Fiscal Affairs .... Vacant
108 Director Inst Effectiveness .... Dr. Laza RAZAFIMANJATO
06 Registrar .... Ms. Bertha OWENS
42 Chaplain/Dean of Religious Life .... Rev. Ronnie MILLER-YOW
35 Associate VP and Dean of Students .... Dr. Rhonda LOVELACE
15 Director of Human Resources .... Vacant
37 Director of Financial Aid .... Mr. Kevin BARNES
18 Director of Physical Plant .... Mr. Thaddeus SINGLETON
26 Director Marketing/Public Relations .... Vacant
88 Executive Director of WISE -P3 .... Mr. Glenn SERGEANT, SR.
07 Interim Director of Admissions .... Mr. Paul PERSON
08 Director of the Library .... Mrs. Kathy ANDERSON
29 Director of Alumni Relations .... Mrs. Shonta ARNOLD
41 Athletic Director .... Mr. Roderick SMOTHERS, JR.
13 Interim Chief Information Officer .... Dr. Mario BERRY
09 Director of Institutional Research .... Ms. Beverly RICHARDSON
19 Chief of Security .... Mr. Arthur WILLIAMS
51 Dir of Continuing Education (PSMI) .... Dr. Cedric STONE
88 Kendall Mission Center Director .... Vacant
40 Bookstore Manager .... Mr. Alvin HARRIS
17 Campus Nurse .... Ms. Deveta CROUTHER
88 Dean of Campus Culture .... Mr. Ronnie MILLER-YOW
81 Div Chair Natural/Physical Sciences .... Dr. Duane JACKSON
50 Div Chair of Business/Economics .... Dr. Cedric STONE
53 Div Chair of Education .... Dr. Charity SMITH
57 Div Chair Visual and Performing Art .... Dr. Carla CARTER
83 Div Chair Social Sciences .... Dr. Daniel EGBE
38 Director of Counseling Services .... Mrs. LaTisha JACKSON
39 Director of Housing and Res Life .... Mr. Jeremy CARTER
101 Secretary of the Institution/Board .... Mr. David L. LEWIS
105 Web Services .... Ms. Carmen BRADFORD
22 Director of Social Justice .... Vacant
36 Director Student Engagement .... Vacant
25 Chief Contract and Grants Administr .... Mrs. Latonya HAYES
30 Director of Development .... Mr. Kevin COOPER
96 Director of Purchasing .... Mr. Itya PONDWA

Shorter College (B)

604 Locust Street, North Little Rock AR 72114
County: Pulaski FICE Identification: 001105
Unit ID: 107840
Telephone: (501) 374-6305 Carnegie Class: Assoc/HT-High Trad
FAX Number: (501) 374-9333 Calendar System: Semester
URL: www.shortercollege.edu
Established: 1886 Annual Undergrad Tuition & Fees: $5,596
Enrollment: 223 Coed
Affiliation or Control: African Methodist Episcopal IRS Status: 501(c)3
Highest Offering: Associate Degree
Accreditation: TRACS

01 President .... Dr. O. Jerome GREEN
10 Chief Financial Officer .... Mr. George MACKEY
05 Dean Academic/Student Affairs .... Dr. Johnny JONES
07 Director of Admissions .... Mrs. Arnella HAYES-CARTER
15 Chief Human Resources Officer .... Mrs. Cordelia MITCHELL
18 Chief Facilities/Phys Plant Ofcr .... Mr. Nathan ALEXANDER
32 Assoc Dean Student/Academic Affairs .... Dr. Demetrius GILBERT
29 Director Alumni Affairs .... Vacant
37 Director Student Financial Aid .... Ms. Audra HINTON
35 Associate Student Affairs Officer .... Dr. Yvette WIMBERLY
06 Registrar .... Ms. Natalie VIERNA
04 Admin Assistant to the President .... Ms. Phyllis JOHNSON
08 Chief Library Officer .... Mr. Dessalines AGINNIES
09 Director of Institutional Research .... Ms. Tabatha SCOTT
103 Director Workforce Development .... Mr. Arnell WILLIS
41 Athletic Director .... Ms. Jenone BELL

South Arkansas Community College (C)

300 S West Avenue, PO Box 7010,
El Dorado AR 71731-7010
County: Union FICE Identification: 020746
Unit ID: 107974
Telephone: (870) 862-8131 Carnegie Class: Assoc/MT-VT-Mix Trad/Non
FAX Number: (870) 864-7190 Calendar System: Semester
URL: www.southark.edu
Established: 1992 Annual Undergrad Tuition & Fees (In-State): $3,012
Enrollment: 1,253 Coed
Affiliation or Control: State IRS Status: 501(c)3
Highest Offering: Associate Degree
Accreditation: HLC, EMT, PTAA, RAD, SURGT

01 President .... Dr. Bentley WALLACE
05 VP for Academic Affairs .... Dr. Stephanie TULLY-DARTEZ
32 Vice Pres for Student Services .... Dr. Derek MOORE
10 VP for Finance & Administration .... Mr. Carey TUCKER
13 Chief Info Ofcr/AVP Administration .... Dr. Tim KIRK
26 Dir Marketing & Public Relations .... Mr. Heath WALDROP
84 Director of Enrollment Services .... Vacant
08 Director Library Media Center .... Mr. Philip SHACKELFORD
37 Director of Financial Aid .... Ms. Veronda TATUM
04 Executive Asst to the President .... Ms. Kathy MODICA
15 Human Resources Director .... Mr. Bill FOWLER
18 Director of Physical Plant .... Vacant
30 Dir of Foundation/External Funding .... Ms. Cynthia REYNA
96 Director of Procurement/Budget .... Ms. Ann SOUTHALL
103 Dean Workforce & Continuing Educ .... Mr. Brooks WALTHALL
49 Dean Arts and Sciences .... Dr. James YATES
76 Dean Health Sciences .... Ms. Caroline HAMMOND
121 Dean Student Success .... Mr. Timothy R. JOHNSON

Southeast Arkansas College (D)

1900 Hazel Street, Pine Bluff AR 71603-3900
County: Jefferson FICE Identification: 005707
Unit ID: 107637
Telephone: (870) 543-5900 Carnegie Class: Assoc/HT-High Non
FAX Number: (870) 850-8636 Calendar System: Semester
URL: www.seark.edu
Established: 1991 Annual Undergrad Tuition & Fees (In-State): $3,855
Enrollment: 1,113 Coed
Affiliation or Control: State IRS Status: 501(c)3
Highest Offering: Associate Degree
Accreditation: HLC, ADNUR, COARC, EMT, RAD, SURGT

01 President .... Dr. Steven BLOOMBERG
05 Vice President Academic Affairs .... Dr. Stacy PFLUGER
32 Vice President Student Affairs .... Ms. Lozanne CALHOUN
10 Vice President Fiscal Affairs .... Ms. Debbie WALLACE
21 Controller .... Mr. Steve BALLARD
13 Director of Technology Services .... Ms. JoAnn DUPRA
06 Registrar/Director of Admissions .... Ms. Sherri ROBERTS
15 Human Resources .... Vacant
18 Chief Facilities/Physical Plant .... Mr. Jabe THROWER
37 Director Student Financial Aid .... Ms. Donna COX
04 Administrative Asst to President .... Ms. Wanda GRIMMETT
08 Director of Library .... Ms. Kim WILLIAMS
105 Webmaster .... Vacant
97 Interim Dean General Studies .... Dr. Melanie HAAS
66 Dean Nursing & Allied Health .... Ms. Joyce SCOTT
103 Dean Technical Studies/Wkforce Dev .... Ms. Lyric SEYMORE
09 Director of Institutional Research .... Ms. Phylesia DAVIS
30 Director of Development .... Ms. Barbara DUNN
36 Dir Workforce/Career Development .... Mr. Jeff PULLIAM
121 Director of Advising & Retention .... Mr. Gene WHITE
106 Coord Online Education/E-learning .... Ms. Meagan COATS
19 Director Security/Safety .... Mr. Scott GANN

Southern Arkansas University (E)

100 E University Street, Magnolia AR 71753-5000
County: Columbia FICE Identification: 001107
Unit ID: 107983
Telephone: (870) 235-4000 Carnegie Class: Masters/L
FAX Number: (870) 235-5005 Calendar System: Semester
URL: www.saumag.edu
Established: 1909 Annual Undergrad Tuition & Fees (In-State): $9,080
Enrollment: 4,432 Coed
Affiliation or Control: State IRS Status: 501(c)3
Highest Offering: Doctorate
Accreditation: HLC, CAEP, NUR, SW

01 President .... Dr. Trey BERRY
05 Provost/Vice Pres Academic Affairs .... Dr. David LANOUE
11 VP Administration/General Counsel .... Mr. Roger W. GILES
32 Vice President Student Affairs .... Dr. Donna Y. ALLEN
18 Director of Facilities .... Mr. Robert NASH
10 Vice President for Finance .... Ms. Shawana REED
30 Asst Vice President for Development .... Mr. Josh KEE
49 Dean Col Liberal & Performing Arts .... Dr. Deborah WILSON
50 Dean College of Business .... Dr. Robin SRONCE
53 Dean College of Education .... Dr. Kim K. BLOSS
81 Dean College of Science & Eng .... Dr. Abdel BACHRI
58 Dean School of Graduate Studies .... Dr. Connie WILSON
06 Registrar .... Ms. Marisa GRIPPO
84 Dean Enrollment Services .... Ms. Sarah E. JENNINGS
35 Associate Dean of Students .... Mr. Carey BAKER
08 Director of Library .... Dr. Del G. DUKE
13 Director Info Technology Services .... Mr. Mike A. ARGO
38 Director Counsel/Testing Center .... Ms. DeAnna TRACY
39 Dean of Housing .... Ms. Sandra E. MARTIN
29 Director of Alumni Affairs .... Vacant
110 Director of Development .... Ms. Macy BRASWELL
37 Director of Financial Aid .... Ms. Marcela C. MCRAE-BRUNSON
51 Director of Continuing Education .... Mr. Tyler HABA
41 Director of Athletics .... Mr. Steve BROWNING
121 Director Student Support Services .... Mrs. Stephanie MANNING
36 Director of Placement Services .... Vacant
28 Assoc Dean Multicultural Affairs .... Mr. Cledis D. STUART
27 Assoc Dir Communications Center .... Vacant
04 Asst to President .... Ms. LaTricia DAVIS
09 Director of Institutional Research .... Ms. Christine PACHECO
86 Director Government Relations .... Mrs. Sheryl EDWARDS
102 Director Foundation .... Ms. Macy BRASWELL
15 Human Resources Manager .... Ms. Tammy SIMS

Southern Arkansas University Tech (F)

6415 Spellman Road, Camden AR 71701
County: Calhoun FICE Identification: 007738
Unit ID: 107992
Telephone: (870) 574-4500 Carnegie Class: Assoc/HVT-Mix Trad/Non
FAX Number: N/A Calendar System: Semester
URL: www.sautech.edu
Established: 1968 Annual Undergrad Tuition & Fees (In-State): $4,571
Enrollment: 769 Coed
Affiliation or Control: State IRS Status: 501(c)3
Highest Offering: Associate Degree
Accreditation: HLC

01 Chancellor .... Dr. Jason MORRISON
10 VC for Finance & Administration .... Mrs. Gaye MANNING
05 VC for Academics & Planning .... Dr. Valerie WILSON
32 VC for Student Services .... Dr. Edward RICE
26 Dean of Communications/Development .... Mrs. Kim COKER
09 Dir Inst Effectiveness & Research .... Mrs. Rita GIVENS
84 Director of Enrollment Services .... Ms. Bailey CARL
103 Director of Career Pathways .... Ms. LaTonya REED
36 Director of Career Academy .... Mrs. Rachel GASTON
107 Director AETA & Workforce Education .... Mr. Randy HARPER
88 Director of AFTA .... Mr. Andy WOODY
13 Director of Technology Services .... Mr. Patrick GRAHAM
37 Director of Financial Aid .... Mrs. Connie RILEY
18 Director of Physical Plant .... Mr. Carl RAMSAY
35 Director of Student Life .... Mr. Courtney HAYGOOD
06 AVC Student Svcs/Registrar .... Mrs. Jenny SANDERS
121 Dir Student Success & Acad Engage .... Mr. Marcus COPELAND
04 Assistant to the Chancellor .... Vacant
15 Director Human Resources .... Mrs. Debbie BEASLEY
21 Controller .... Mr. Dale TOMMEY
96 Buyer .... Mrs. Angela FRY
51 Director of Adult Education .... Mrs. Barbara HAMILTON
19 Director Security/Safety .... Mr. Jud MITCHELL
41 Athletic Director .... Mrs. Amy DIEHL
07 Director of Admissions .... Vacant
108 Director Institutional Assessment .... Vacant

*University of Arkansas System Office (G)

2404 N University Avenue, Little Rock AR 72207-3608
County: Pulaski FICE Identification: 008008
Unit ID: 108056
Telephone: (501) 686-2500 Carnegie Class: N/A
FAX Number: (501) 686-2507
URL: www.uasys.edu

01 President .... Dr. Donald R. BOBBITT
04 Assistant to the President .... Ms. Angela HUDSON
05 Vice President Academic Affairs .... Dr. Michael K. MOORE
26 Vice President University Relations .... Ms. Melissa RUST
47 Vice President Agriculture .... Dr. Deacue FIELDS
10 Chief Financial Officer .... Mrs. Tara SMITH
43 General Counsel .... Mrs. JoAnn MAXEY
116 Chief Audit Executive .... Mrs. Laura CHEAK
30 Vice President Planning & Devel .... Mr. Christopher THOMASON
13 Chief Information Officer .... Mr. Steven FULKERSON
27 Director of Communications .... Mr. Nate HINKEL
15 AVP Benefits/Risk Management Svcs .... Mr. Steve WOOD
27 Sr Dir Policy & Public Affairs .... Mr. Ben BEAUMONT
114 Associate VP Finance .... Mrs. Chaundra HALL

*University of Arkansas Main Campus (H)

1125 W. Maple St., Fayetteville AR 72701-1201
County: Washington FICE Identification: 001108
Unit ID: 106397
Telephone: (479) 575-3836 Carnegie Class: DU-Highest
FAX Number: (479) 575-2361 Calendar System: Semester
URL: www.uark.edu

Established: 1871 Annual Undergrad Tuition & Fees (In-State): $9,384
Enrollment: 27,562 Coed
Affiliation or Control: State IRS Status: 501(c)3
Highest Offering: Doctorate
Accreditation: **HLC**, ART, CAATE, CACREP, CAEP, CIDA, CLPSY, DIETD, IPSY, JOUR, LAW, LSAR, MUS, NURSE, OT, PH, SP, SW, THEA

02 Interim Chancellor ....Mr. Charles F. ROBINSON
04 Executive Asst to the Chancellor ....Ms. Sally Ann ADAMS
05 Int Provost/VC Academic Affairs ....Dr. Terry MARTIN
10 Vice Chanc Finance & Admin ....Ms. Ann BORDELON
111 Vice Chanc for Advancement ....Mr. Mark POWER
86 Vice Chanc Governmental Relations ....Mr. Randy MASSANELLI
45 Vice Provost Planning ....Ms. Colleen BRINEY
46 Vice Chancellor for Econ Dev ....Mr. Mike MALONE
32 Interim Vice Chanc Student Affairs ....Ms. Melissa HARWOOD-ROM
84 Vice Prov Enrol Mgt/Dean Admissions ....Dr. Suzanne MCCRAY
100 Vice Chanc and Chief of Staff ....Dr. Laura JACOBS
25 AVC Research & Sponsored Pgms ....Vacant
15 Assoc Vice Chanc Human Resources ....Ms. Debbie MCLOUD
18 Assoc Vice Chanc Facilities Mgmt ....Mr. Scott TURLEY
21 Asst Vice Chancellor ....Ms. Jennifer JONES
26 Assoc Vice Chanc University Rels ....Mr. Mark RUSHING
08 Dean of Libraries ....Mr. Jason J. BATTLES
49 Dean of Arts & Sciences ....Dr. Todd G. SHIELDS
50 Dean Sam Walton College of Business ....Dr. Matthew WALLER
47 Interim Dean of Agriculture ....Dr. JF MEULLENET
53 Interim Dean Education/Health ....Dr. Kate MAMISEISHVILI
48 Dean of Architecture ....Mr. Peter MACKEITH
58 Dean of Graduate School ....Dr. Curt ROM
54 Dean of Engineering ....Dr. Kim NEEDY
92 Dean Honors College ....Dr. Lynda COON
61 Interim Dean of the Law School ....Ms. Cynthia NANCE
29 Assoc Vice Chanc for Alumni ....Ms. Brandy A. COX
22 Director of Equal Opportunity ....Ms. Danielle L. WOOD-WILLIAMS
07 Assoc Vice Prov Enroll/Dean Admiss ....Ms. Wendy D. STOUFFER
38 Dir of Counseling/Psych Services ....Dr. Josette CLINE
19 Director University Police ....Mr. Steve GAHAGANS
36 Exec Dir of Career Devel Center ....Ms. Angela S. WILLIAMS
13 Assoc Vice Chanc for Info Tech ....Mr. Steve KROGULL
06 Registrar ....Mr. Gary GUNDERMAN
96 Director of Purchasing ....Ms. Whitney SMITH
123 Director Graduate & Intl Admissions ....Ms. Patricia GAMBOA
37 Director of Financial Aid ....Mr. Phillip Andrew BLEVINS
09 Int Dir Inst Research & Assessment ....Mr. Doug MILES
102 Sr Dir Ofc Corporate & Found Rels ....Ms. Cherie RACHEL
104 Director Study Abroad ....Ms. Sarah L. MALLOY
41 Athletic Director ....Mr. Hunter YURACHEK
44 Director Annual Giving ....Ms. Robyn RIGGINS

*University of Arkansas at Fort Smith (A)

PO Box 3649, Fort Smith AR 72913-3649
County: Sebastian FICE Identification: 001110
Unit ID: 108092
Telephone: (479) 788-7000 Carnegie Class: Bac-Diverse
FAX Number: (479) 788-7003 Calendar System: Semester
URL: www.uafs.edu
Established: 1928 Annual Undergrad Tuition & Fees (In-District): $5,754
Enrollment: 5,887 Coed
Affiliation or Control: State/Local IRS Status: 501(c)3
Highest Offering: Master's
Accreditation: **HLC**, ART, CAEP, DH, DMS, MUS, NAIT, NURSE, RAD, SURGT, SW

02 Chancellor ....Dr. Terisa C. RILEY
05 Provost/Vice Chanc Academic Affairs ....Dr. Shadow ROBINSON
111 Vice Chancellor Univ Advancement ....Mr. Blake RICKMAN
10 Vice Chanc Finance & Administration ....Mr. Carey TUCKER
32 Vice Chancellor Student Affairs ....Dr. Lee KREHBIEL
58 Assoc Provost/Dir of Grad Studies ....Dr. Margaret TANNER
31 Assoc VC Campus/Cmty Events ....Mr. Stacey JONES
86 Director Govt & Univ Relations ....Dr. Ken WARDEN
20 Asst Prov Student Success/Retention ....Dr. Blake JOHNSON
100 Chief of Staff ....Ms. Jennifer BELT
76 Dean Col of Hlth Educ & Hum Sci ....Dr. Dean CANTU
50 Dean College of Business & Industry ....Dr. Latisha SETTLAGE
49 Dean Col of Arts & Sciences ....Dr. Paul HANKINS
15 Dir Human Resources/EEO Officer ....Mrs. Mandy KEYES
12 Dir Western AR Tech Ctr ....Ms. Amanda SEIDENZAHL
107 Dir of Student Professional Dev Ctr ....Ms. Susan KRAFFT
45 Asst Provost Inst Effectiveness ....Vacant
88 Director of Instructional Support ....Dr. Tara MISHRA
08 Director of Library Services ....Mr. Jason BYRD
39 Interim Director of Student Housing ....Ms. Stephanie LONDON
37 Director of Financial Aid ....Ms. Karen JEFFERS
07 Director of Admissions ....Vacant
121 Director of Advisement ....Ms. Julie MOSLEY
06 Registrar ....Mr. Wayne WOMACK
85 Dir of International Relations ....Mr. Nicolas PATTILLO
26 Dir Marketing/Communications ....Mr. Chris KELLY
41 Director of Athletics ....Mr. Curtis JANZ
96 Director of Procurement Services ....Ms. Rhonda CATON
27 Assoc Director of Strategic Comm ....Ms. Rachel PUTMAN
18 Director of Plant Operations ....Mr. Robert AIRO
103 Dir CBPD/Family Enterprise Ctr ....Mr. Kendall ROSS
13 Director Technology Services ....Mr. Terry MEADOWS
19 Dir Chief of University Police ....Mr. Ray OTTMAN
29 Director of Alumni Affairs ....Ms. Jasmine SMITH
112 Director of Planned Giving ....Ms. Anne THOMAS

36 Asst Director Career Services ....Mr. Jeff ADAMS
53 Executive Director Education ....Dr. Monica RILEY

*University of Arkansas - Grantham (B)

2404 North University Ave, Little Rock AR 72207
County: Pulaski FICE Identification: 004283
Unit ID: 442569
Telephone: (888) 947-2684 Carnegie Class: Masters/L
FAX Number: (913) 309-4949 Calendar System: Other
URL: www.grantham.edu
Established: 1951 Annual Undergrad Tuition & Fees: $8,280
Enrollment: 6,465 Coed
Affiliation or Control: Proprietary IRS Status: Proprietary
Highest Offering: Master's
Accreditation: **DEAC**, IACBE, NURSE

01 Chancellor/Interim President ....Dr. Lindsey BRIDGEMAN
05 Provost/Dean ....Dr. Bill ALLEN
15 Vice President Human Resources ....Tracy GALLERY
13 Chief Information Officer ....Baz ABOUELENEIN
37 Director Student Financial Service ....Lindsay BRIDGEMAN
26 AVP of Marketing Operations ....Stephen RENTSCHLER

*University of Arkansas at Little Rock (C)

2801 S University Avenue, Little Rock AR 72204-1099
County: Pulaski FICE Identification: 001101
Unit ID: 106245
Telephone: (501) 916-3000 Carnegie Class: DU-Higher
FAX Number: (501) 916-3915 Calendar System: Semester
URL: www.ualr.edu
Established: 1927 Annual Undergrad Tuition & Fees (In-State): $8,366
Enrollment: 8,899 Coed
Affiliation or Control: State IRS Status: 501(c)3
Highest Offering: Doctorate
Accreditation: **HLC**, ADNUR, ART, CAEP, CAMPEP, CONST, DENT, LAW, MUS, NUR, SPAA, SW

02 Chancellor ....Dr. Christina S. DRALE
05 Executive Vice Chancellor & Provost ....Dr. Ann BAIN
32 Vice Chancellor for Student Affairs ....Dr. William C. DECKER
10 Vice Chanc Finance & Administration ....Mr. Gerald J. GANZ
111 Vice Chancellor Advancement ....Mr. Christian O'NEAL
41 Director of Athletics ....Mr. George L. LEE
86 Vice Chancellor University Affairs ....Ms. Joni C. LEE
13 Associate Vice Chancellor & CIO ....Dr. Thomas BUNTON
06 Registrar ....Ms. Malissa MATHIS
15 Assoc VC of Human Resources ....Ms. LaTonda WILLIAMS
26 Dir Marketing & Brand Development ....Mr. Jeff HARMON
09 Assoc Provost & Chief Data Officer ....Dr. William C. DECKER
37 Director Financial Aid ....Mr. Jonathan B. COLEMAN
07 Director of Admissions ....Ms. Chelsea B. WARD
88 Assoc Prov for UALR Collect and Arc ....Dr. Deborah J. BALDWIN
19 Chief of Police ....Ms. Regina W. CARTER
25 Director Research & Sponsored Pgm ....Ms. Tammie L. CASH

*University of Arkansas for Medical Sciences (D)

4301 W Markham, Little Rock AR 72205-7199
County: Pulaski FICE Identification: 001109
Unit ID: 106263
Telephone: (501) 686-7000 Carnegie Class: Spec-4-yr-Eng
FAX Number: (501) 686-5905 Calendar System: Semester
URL: www.uams.edu
Established: 1879 Annual Undergrad Tuition & Fees (In-State): N/A
Enrollment: 2,907 Coed
Affiliation or Control: State IRS Status: 501(c)3
Highest Offering: Doctorate
Accreditation: **HLC**, ANEST, ARCPA, AUD, COARC, CYTO, DH, DIETI, DMS, HSA, IPSY, MED, MLS, NMT, NURSE, OT, PH, PHAR, PTA, RAD, SP

02 Chancellor ....Dr. Cam PATTERSON
05 Sr Vice Chanc Academic Affs/ Provost ....Dr. Stephanie F. GARDNER
63 EVC/Dean College of Medicine ....Dr. Susan SMYTH
10 Vice Chancellor Finance & CFO ....Ms. Amanda GEORGE
26 Vice Chanc Communications/Marketing ....Ms. Leslie W. TAYLOR
111 VC Institutional Advancement ....Mr. John ERCK
11 Vice Chanc Inst Support/COO ....Ms. Christina L. CLARK
28 VC Diversity/Equity & Inclusion ....Dr. Brian E. GITTENS
09 Vice Chancelor for Research ....Dr. Shuk-Mei HO
13 Assoc VC IT/CIO ....Vacant
08 Interim Library Director ....Ms. Libby INGRAM
15 Vice Chancellor for HR/Chief HR Off ....Dr. Danielle LOMBARD-SIMS
20 Asst Provost Teaching Lrng Support ....Dr. Steve E. BOONE
32 Assoc Provost Students & Admin ....Dr. Kristen STERBA
37 Director Financial Services ....Ms. Alisha MCREYNOLDS
76 Dean College of Health Professions ....Dr. Susan LONG
66 Dean College of Nursing ....Dr. Patricia COWAN
67 Dean College of Pharmacy ....Dr. Cindy STOWE
58 Dean of the Graduate School ....Dr. Robert E. MCGEHEE, JR.
69 Dean College of Public Health ....Dr. Mark WILLIAMS
06 Dir Enrollment Svcs/Chief Registrar ....Mr. Clinton D. EVERHART
39 Dir Campus Life/Stdnt Support Svcs ....Ms. Cheri D. GOFORTH
12 Vice Chanc Regional Campuses ....Dr. Richard TURNAGE

† Tuition figure is for Medical School. Other school's tuitions vary widely.

*University of Arkansas at Monticello (E)

346 University Drive, Monticello AR 71656-3596
County: Drew FICE Identification: 001085
Unit ID: 106485
Telephone: (870) 460-1020 Carnegie Class: Masters/M
FAX Number: (870) 460-1321 Calendar System: Semester
URL: www.uamont.edu
Established: 1909 Annual Undergrad Tuition & Fees (In-State): $7,909
Enrollment: 2,645 Coed
Affiliation or Control: State IRS Status: 501(c)3
Highest Offering: Master's
Accreditation: **HLC**, CNEA, EMT, MUS, SW

02 Chancellor ....Dr. Peggy DOSS
05 VC for Academic Affairs ....Ms. Crystal HALLEY
111 VC for Advancement ....Mr. Jeff WEAVER
32 VC for Student Engagement ....Dr. Moses GOLDMON
10 VC for Finance and Administration ....Mr. Alex BECKER
12 VC for UAM College of Tech-Crossett ....Ms. Linda RUSHING
12 VC for UAM College of Tech-McGehee ....Mr. Bob WARE
04 Assistant to the Chancellor ....Ms. Christy PACE
45 Exec Dir of Budget Mgmt ....Ms. Debbie GASAWAY
13 Chief Information Officer ....Ms. Anissa ROSS
86 Director of Government Relations ....Dr. John DAVIS
35 AVC/Dean of Students ....Vacant
07 Director of Admissions ....Ms. Mary WHITING
19 Director of University Police ....Mr. John KIDWELL
22 Dir Affirmative Action/EEO ....Ms. Sage LOYD
41 Director of Athletics ....Mr. Hud JACKSON
38 Director of Counseling/Testing ....Ms. Sydney HILL
37 Director of Financial Aid ....Mr. Brad FULLER
29 Director Alumni Affairs ....Mr. Jay HUGHES
08 Director of Library ....Mr. Daniel BOICE
26 Director of Marketing/Public Rels ....Ms. Kelsey ENGLERT
18 Director of Physical Plant ....Mr. Rusty RIPPEE
96 Director of Purchasing ....Ms. Gay PACE
06 Registrar ....Mr. Keith CHAMBLISS
39 Director of Housing ....Ms. Leanna PAYTON
15 Human Resources Manager ....Ms. Jennifer HARGIS

*University of Arkansas at Pine Bluff (F)

1200 N University Drive, Pine Bluff AR 71601-2799
County: Jefferson FICE Identification: 001086
Unit ID: 106412
Telephone: (870) 575-8000 Carnegie Class: Bac-Diverse
FAX Number: (870) 543-8009 Calendar System: Semester
URL: www.uapb.edu
Established: 1873 Annual Undergrad Tuition & Fees (In-State): $8,248
Enrollment: 2,668 Coed
Affiliation or Control: State IRS Status: 501(c)3
Highest Offering: Doctorate
Accreditation: **HLC**, AAFCS, ACBSP, ART, CAEP, MUS, NAIT, NURSE, SW

02 Chancellor ....Dr. Laurence B. ALEXANDER
05 Vice Chanc Academic Affairs ....Dr. Andrea STEWART
10 Vice Chanc Finance & Admin ....Dr. Carla M. MARTIN
32 Vice Chancellor Student Affairs ....Mr. Elbert BENNETT
45 Vice Chanc Research/Innovation ....Dr. Mansour MORTAZAVI
111 Vice Chanc Inst Advancement ....Mr. George COTTON
84 VC Enrollment Mgmt/Stdnt Success ....Vacant
100 Chief of Staff ....Mrs. Janet BROILES
41 Director of Athletics ....Mr. Chris ROBINSON
15 Director of Human Resources ....Mr. Christopher HICKMAN
13 Director of Technical Services ....Mrs. Willette TOTTEN
09 Director of Institutional Research ....Mrs. Margaret W. TAYLOR
06 Interim Registrar ....Ms. Aretha LACEFIELD
29 Director of Alumni Affairs ....Mr. John KUYKENDALL
08 Head Librarian ....Mr. Edward FONTENETTE
103 Dir Workforce/Career Development ....Mrs. Shirley CHERRY
108 Director Institutional Assessment ....Dr. Steve LOCHMANN
37 Director Student Financial Aid ....Mrs. Janice KEARNEY
22 Dir Affirmative Action/EEO ....Ms. Tonisha DAVIS
88 Interim Director of Recruitment ....Mrs. Constance CASTLE
07 Director of Admissions ....Vacant
18 Director Facilities/Physical Plant ....Mr. Terrell LANGLEY
19 Director Security/Safety ....Chief Maxcie THOMAS
30 Director of Development ....Vacant
50 Int Dean Sch of Business & Mgmt ....Mr. Lawrence AWOPETU
53 Dean School of Education ....Dr. Kimberly DAVIS
96 Director of Purchasing ....Mrs. Alisha LEWIS
104 Director Study Abroad ....Dr. Pamela MOORE
38 Director Student Counseling ....Mr. Leonardo GLOVER
39 Int Assoc Dean Residential Services ....Mr. Ralph OWENS
86 Director Government Relations ....Mr. John KUYKENDALL

*Cossatot Community College of the University of Arkansas (G)

183 College Drive, De Queen AR 71832
County: Sevier FICE Identification: 022209
Unit ID: 106795
Telephone: (870) 584-4471 Carnegie Class: Assoc/HT-Mix Trad/Non
FAX Number: N/A Calendar System: Semester
URL: www.cccua.edu
Established: 1991 Annual Undergrad Tuition & Fees (In-District): $3,960
Enrollment: 1,386 Coed
Affiliation or Control: State/Local IRS Status: 501(c)3
Highest Offering: Associate Degree

Accreditation: HLC, ACBSP, OTA, PTAA

02 Chancellor .... Dr. Steve COLE
05 Vice Chancellor of Academics .... Dr. Ashley AYLETT
45 VC of Planning and Facilities .... Mr. Mike KINKADE
10 Vice Chancellor Business/Finance .... Mrs. Charlotte JOHNSON
32 Director of Student Services .... Mrs. Suzanne WARD
37 Director Student Financial Aid .... Mrs. Denise HAMMOND
06 Registrar .... Ms. Jocelin GALVEZ
103 Dir of Public Svc/Workforce Dev .... Mrs. Tammy COLEMAN
12 Director of Ashdown Campus .... Mr. Barrett REED
15 Director of Human Resources .... Ms. Kelly PLUNK
13 Director of Technology .... Mr. Tony HARGROVE
30 Director of Development .... Mr. Dustin ROBERTS
04 Executive Assistant to Chancellor .... Ms. Wendy GARCIA
09 Director of Institutional Research .... Mrs. Tommi COBB

*Phillips Community College of the University of Arkansas (A)

PO Box 785, Helena AR 72342-0785
County: Phillips FICE Identification: 001104
Unit ID: 107619
Telephone: (870) 338-6474 Carnegie Class: Assoc/MT-VT-Mix Trad/Non
FAX Number: (870) 338-7542 Calendar System: Semester
URL: www.pccua.edu
Established: 1965 Annual Undergrad Tuition & Fees (In-District): $3,410
Enrollment: 1,093 Coed
Affiliation or Control: State/Local IRS Status: 501(c)3
Highest Offering: Associate Degree
Accreditation: HLC, ACBSP, ADNUR, MLTAD

02 Chancellor .... Dr. G. Keith PINCHBACK
05 Vice Chancellor for Instruction .... Dr. Deborah KING
10 Vice Chanc Finance & Administration .... Mr. Stan SULLIVANT
32 Vice Chanc Student Services .... Dr. Kimberley JOHNSON
30 Vice Chanc Col Advancement/Res Dev .... Mrs. Rhonda ST. COLUMBIA
12 Vice Chancellor Arkansas County .... Mrs. Kim KIRBY
84 Director Enrollment Management .... Vacant
13 Director IT .... Mr. Lee WILLIAMS
37 Director Financial Aid .... Ms. Barbra STEVENSON
15 Director Human Resources .... Ms. Ella JAMES

*University of Arkansas Community College at Batesville (B)

2005 White Drive, PO Box 3350,
Batesville AR 72503-3350
County: Independence FICE Identification: 020735
Unit ID: 106999
Telephone: (870) 612-2000 Carnegie Class: Assoc/HVT-High Trad
FAX Number: (870) 793-4988 Calendar System: Semester
URL: www.uaccb.edu
Established: 1975 Annual Undergrad Tuition & Fees (In-District): $2,862
Enrollment: 1,224 Coed
Affiliation or Control: State/Local IRS Status: 501(c)3
Highest Offering: Associate Degree
Accreditation: HLC, ADNUR, EMT

02 Chancellor .... Dr. Brian SHONK
04 Assistant to the Chancellor .... Ms. Jodie HIGHTOWER
05 Vice Chancellor for Academic Affs .... Dr. Holly SMITH
32 Vice Chanc Student Affairs .... Dr. Zach PERRINE
10 Chief Financial Officer .... Mr. Bruce HANKINS
88 Executive Dir of Special Projects .... Dr. Anne AUSTIN
49 Chair Div of Arts & Humanities .... Mr. Doug MUSE
50 Chair Div Business/Tech/Public Svc .... Ms. Jeanette YOUNGBLOOD
76 Chair Div Nursing/Allied Health .... Ms. Michelle BISHOP
81 Chair Div of Math and Science .... Mr. Douglas MUSE
75 Dir of Career and Tech Educ .... Dr. Zachery HARBER
09 Dir of Institutional Research .... Dr. Deltha SHARP
07 Director of Admissions .... Ms. Meagan AKINS
13 Director Information Services .... Ms. Crystal BLUE
06 Dir Student Information/Registrar .... Ms. Casey BROMLEY
37 Director of Financial Aid .... Ms. Debbie WYATT
111 Director of Advancement .... Ms. Shannon HANEY
18 Director of Maintenance .... Mr. Heath WOOLDRIDGE
36 Director Student Development .... Ms. Louise HUGHES
103 Dir of Workforce and Career Svcs .... Vacant
08 Director Library .... Mr. Jay STRICKLAND
21 Business Office Manager .... Ms. Jennifer SINELE
15 Human Resources Coordinator .... Ms. Julie JOHNSON
96 Purchasing Agent .... Ms. Peggy JACKSON
40 Bookstore Manager .... Ms. Luanne BARBER

*University of Arkansas Community College Hope-Texarkana (C)

PO Box 140, 2500 S Main Street, Hope AR 71802-0140
County: Hempstead FICE Identification: 005732
Unit ID: 107725
Telephone: (870) 777-5722 Carnegie Class: Assoc/MT-VT-Mix Trad/Non
FAX Number: (870) 777-5957 Calendar System: Semester
URL: https://www.uaht.edu/
Established: 1991 Annual Undergrad Tuition & Fees (In-State): $3,250
Enrollment: 1,211 Coed
Affiliation or Control: State IRS Status: 501(c)3
Highest Offering: Associate Degree
Accreditation: HLC, EMT, FUSER

02 Chancellor .... Dr. Christine HOLT
32 Vice Chanc Student Services .... Mr. Brian BERRY
05 Vice Chancellor for Academics .... Ms. Laura CLARK
10 Vice Chancellor for Finance .... Ms. Cindy LANCE
35 Dean of Students .... Mr. Christopher SMITH
108 Dean of Institutional Effectiveness .... Mr. John HOLLIS
111 Dir of Institutional Advancement .... Ms. Anna POWELL
88 Director of Hempstead Hall .... Ms. Amanda LANCE
13 Chief Info Technology Officer (CIO) .... Mr. Chuck JORDAN
06 Registrar .... Ms. Diana DAVIDSON
15 Human Resources Officer .... Ms. Kathryn HOPKINS

*University of Arkansas Community College at Morrilton (D)

1537 University Boulevard, Morrilton AR 72110-9601
County: Conway FICE Identification: 005245
Unit ID: 107585
Telephone: (501) 977-2000 Carnegie Class: Assoc/HT-High Trad
FAX Number: N/A Calendar System: Semester
URL: www.uaccm.edu
Established: 1961 Annual Undergrad Tuition & Fees (In-State): $3,456
Enrollment: 1,836 Coed
Affiliation or Control: State IRS Status: 501(c)3
Highest Offering: Associate Degree
Accreditation: HLC, NAEYC

02 Chancellor .... Ms. Lisa WILLENBERG
05 Vice Chancellor for Academics .... Dr. Richard COUNTS
10 Vice Chancellor for Finance .... Mr. Jeff MULLEN
32 Vice Chancellor Student Services .... Mr. Darren JONES
09 Director of Institutional Research .... Ms. Amanda BARTON
08 Librarian .... Mr. Justin LILLARD
06 Registrar .... Ms. Linda HOLLAND
37 Financial Aid Director .... Ms. Jennifer WILLIAMS
26 Dir Marketing & Public Relations .... Ms. Mary CLARK
13 Director of Information Tech/CIO .... Mr. Steve WALLACE
18 Director of the Physical Plant .... Mr. C. Allen HOLLOWAY
07 Director of Admissions .... Ms. Rachel MULLINS
103 Coord Workforce Devel/Cmty Educ .... Ms. Jessica ROHLMAN
15 Director Personnel Services .... Ms. Judy SANDERS
30 Chief Development .... Ms. Taylor HOLLAND
38 Director Student Counseling .... Mr. Cody DAVIS
96 Director of Purchasing .... Ms. Anna HALBROOK

*University of Arkansas - Pulaski Technical College (E)

3000 W Scenic Drive, North Little Rock AR 72118-3399
County: Pulaski FICE Identification: 020753
Unit ID: 107664
Telephone: (501) 812-2200 Carnegie Class: Assoc/HT-High Trad
FAX Number: (501) 771-2844 Calendar System: Semester
URL: www.uaptc.edu
Established: 1991 Annual Undergrad Tuition & Fees (In-State): $5,670
Enrollment: 4,810 Coed
Affiliation or Control: State IRS Status: 501(c)3
Highest Offering: Associate Degree
Accreditation: HLC, ACFEI, ACPHA, COARC, DA, EMT, NAEYC, OTA, SURGT

02 Chancellor .... Dr. Margaret ELLIBEE
05 Provost .... Vacant
10 Vice Chancellor for Finance .... Ms. Charlette MOORE
111 Vice Chancellor for Advancement .... Vacant
103 Director of Workforce/Comm Educ .... Ms. Sharon CANTRELL
32 Dean of Student Affairs .... Mr. Mason CAMPBELL
84 Dean of Admissions/Financial Aid .... Dr. John LEWIS
07 Director of Admissions .... Ms. Kyanna BEARD
08 Library Director .... Ms. Wendy DAVIS
18 Director of Physical Plant .... Mr. Bryan RUSHER
09 Inst Reporting & Research Coord .... Ms. Jennifer BLAYLOCK
96 Director of Purchasing .... Ms. Emily FISHER
13 Director of Information Services .... Mr. Robert DURHAM
15 Director of Human Resources .... Ms. Regina FOSSETTE
04 Assistant to the President .... Ms. Tena CARRIGAN
37 Director of Financial Aid .... Ms. Lori TAYLOR
26 Director Public Relations/Marketing .... Mr. Tim JONES
72 Dean Technical/Professional Studies .... Vacant
81 Dean Science/Math/Allied Health .... Dr. Marcio BRYANT HOWE
57 Dean Fine Arts/Humanities/Social Sc .... Dr. Christy OBERSTE
06 Registrar .... Dr. Ana HUNT
19 Director Security/Safety .... Mr. Mark STAFFORD
29 Director Alumni Affairs .... Ms. Adora CURRY

*University of Arkansas Rich Mountain (F)

1100 College Drive, Mena AR 71953-2500
County: Polk FICE Identification: 021111
Unit ID: 107743
Telephone: (479) 394-7622 Carnegie Class: Assoc/MT-VT-High Trad
FAX Number: (479) 394-7295 Calendar System: Semester
URL: www.uarichmountain.edu
Established: 1983 Annual Undergrad Tuition & Fees (In-District): $3,408
Enrollment: 798 Coed
Affiliation or Control: State/Local IRS Status: 501(c)3
Highest Offering: Associate Degree
Accreditation: HLC

02 Chancellor .... Dr. Phillip WILSON
05 Vice Chancellor Academic Affairs .... Dr. Krystal THRAILKILL
32 VC Student Affairs/Registrar .... Mr. Chad FIELDING
10 Vice Chancellor Administration/CFO .... Ms. Megan WHEELER
13 Chief Information Officer .... Mr. Brian CARNAHAN
08 Director Library Services .... Ms. Brenda MINER
37 Financial Aid Director .... Ms. Mary STANDERFER
30 Director Business Outreach .... Ms. LeAnn DILBECK
18 Associate Director Physical Plant .... Mr. Mike BECK
97 Director Adult Basic Education .... Ms. Julie GORDON
15 Director of Human Resources .... Ms. Julie SCHNELL
07 Director of Admissions .... Ms. Wendy MCDANIEL
21 Controller .... Ms. Patricia HALL
26 Dir Marketing/Community Relations .... Ms. LeAnn DILBECK
04 Executive Asst to Chancellor .... Ms. Yanel RIOS
88 Student Union Manager .... Mr. Jason WOOD
09 Coordinator Institutional Research .... Ms. Tammy ODOM
114 Budget Analysis Coordinator .... Ms. Amy LUDWIG
18 Constructions/Grounds Supervisor .... Mr. David DILBECK

*Phillips Community College of the University of Arkansas-DeWitt (G)

1210 Rice Belt Avenue, DeWitt AR 72042
Telephone: (870) 946-3506 Identification: 770174
Accreditation: &HLC

*Phillips Community College of the University of Arkansas-Stuttgart (H)

2807 Hwy 165 South, Stuttgart AR 72160-2408
Telephone: (870) 673-4201 Identification: 770175
Accreditation: &HLC

*University of Arkansas at Monticello College of Technology-Crossett (I)

1326 Highway 52 W, Crossett AR 71635
Telephone: (870) 364-6414 Identification: 770176
Accreditation: &HLC

*University of Arkansas at Monticello College of Technology-McGehee (J)

PO Box 747, McGehee AR 71654
Telephone: (870) 222-5360 Identification: 770177
Accreditation: &HLC

University of Central Arkansas (K)

201 Donaghey Avenue, Conway AR 72035-0001
County: Faulkner FICE Identification: 001092
Unit ID: 106704
Telephone: (501) 450-5000 Carnegie Class: DU-Mod
FAX Number: (501) 450-5003 Calendar System: Semester
URL: uca.edu
Established: 1907 Annual Undergrad Tuition & Fees (In-State): $9,338
Enrollment: 10,335 Coed
Affiliation or Control: State IRS Status: 501(c)3
Highest Offering: Doctorate
Accreditation: HLC, ART, CAATE, CAEP, CIDA, COPSY, DIET, DIETD, MUS, NURSE, OT, PTA, SCPSY, SP, THEA

01 President .... Dr. Houston D. DAVIS
05 Provost/Exec VP Academic Affairs .... Dr. Patricia S. POULTER
10 VP Finance/Administration .... Ms. Terri CANINO
32 VP Student Affairs .... Dr. Robin WILLIAMSON
43 General Counsel .... Mr. Warren READNOUR
22 Asc Gen Counsel/Compliance Officer .... Mr. Adam ROSE
26 Director of Media Relations .... Ms. Fredricka SHARKEY
111 VP for University Advancement .... Dr. Mary LACKIE
41 Athletic Director .... Dr. Brad TEAGUE
15 AVP Human Resources & Risk Mgmt .... Ms. Britni ELDER
100 Chief of Staff .... Ms. Amy WHITEHEAD
86 Director Gvt/External Relations .... Mr. Jeremy GILLAM
21 Controller .... Ms. Shakarie MURPHY
108 Assoc Provost Inst Effectiveness .... Dr. Jonathan A. GLENN
20 Associate Provost Academic Success .... Dr. Kurt A. BONIECKI
84 AVP Enrollment Management .... Dr. Kevin P. THOMAS
85 AVP Global Learning & Engagement .... Dr. Phillip BAILEY
58 Dean of Graduate School .... Dr. Angela BARLOW
50 Dean College of Business .... Dr. Michael HARGIS
53 Dean College of Education .... Dr. Victoria GROVES-SCOTT
76 Dean Col Health/Behavioral Science .... Dr. Nancy REESE
49 Dean Col Arts/Humanities/Soc Sci .... Dr. Thomas WILLIAMS
81 Dean Col Natural Sci/Math .... Dr. Steve ADDISON
35 Dean of Students .... Ms. Kelly OWENS
92 Dean of Honors College .... Dr. Patricia SMITH
07 Director of Admissions .... Dr. Courtney BRYANT
08 Library Director .... Mr. Rodney LIPPARD
06 Registrar .... Ms. Vicky SUMMERS
09 Director Institutional Research .... Ms. Amber L. HALL
13 Chief Information Officer .... Mr. Trevor SEIFERT
37 Director Student Financial Aid .... Ms. Cheryl C. LYONS
36 Exec Dir Career Services .... Dr. Kathy CLAYBORN
19 Chief University Police .... Mr. John MERGUIE
38 Director Counseling Center .... Dr. Susan SOBEL
39 AVP Housing & Residence Life .... Dr. Stephanie H. MCBRAYER
29 Director of Alumni Relations .... Ms. Alison TAYLOR
116 Director of Internal Audit .... Ms. Leslie CODDINGTON
18 AVP Campus Facilities .... Mr. Kevin CARTER
96 Director of Purchasing .... Ms. Cassandra MCCUIEN-SMITH
113 Director Student Accounts .... Ms. Sandra OTT

University of the Ozarks (A)

415 College Avenue, Clarksville AR 72830-2880
County: Johnson FICE Identification: 001094
Unit ID: 107558
Telephone: (479) 979-1000 Carnegie Class: Bac-Diverse
FAX Number: (479) 979-1355 Calendar System: Semester
URL: www.ozarks.edu
Established: 1834 Annual Undergrad Tuition & Fees: $25,950
Enrollment: 836 Coed
Affiliation or Control: Presbyterian Church (U.S.A.) IRS Status: 501(c)3
Highest Offering: Baccalaureate
Accreditation: HLC, CAEP

01 President .... Mr. Richard L. DUNSWORTH
05 Provost .... Vacant
10 VP for Finance & Administration .... Ms. Gloria ARCIA
26 Interim VP Marketing & Enrollment .... Ms. Amy LLOYD
07 Assistant Director of Admission .... Mr. Joseph HUGHES
42 Chaplain .... Rev. Jeremy WILHEMI
06 Registrar .... Ms. Monica FRIZZELL
08 Librarian .... Mr. Stuart P. STELZER
36 Director of Career Services .... Ms. Andrea COOPER
29 Director Alumni Affairs .... Mr. Justin MCCORMICK
41 Athletic Director .... Mr. Jimmy CLARK
27 Dir University/Public Relations .... Mr. Larry A. ISCH
111 VP of Advancement .... Ms. Lori A. MCBEE
88 Director Jones Learning Center .... Ms. Dody PELTS
09 Director of Institutional Research .... Ms. Cara FLINN
13 Director of Information Technology .... Ms. Vickie ALSTON
32 Dean of Students .... Ms. Teri THOMAS
81 Dean Div of Mathematics & Sciences .... Dr. Joel HAGAMAN
79 Dean Div Humanities & Fine Arts .... Dr. David DAILY
15 Human Resources Manager .... Ms. Karen SCHLUTERMAN
19 Director Security/Safety .... Mr. Larry GRAHAM
21 Controller .... Mr. Albert LEDING
18 Chief Facilities/Physical Plant .... Mr. Donny FROST
37 Dir of Student Financial Services .... Ms. Kim MADDOX
30 Director of Development .... Mr. Brian HENDERSON
04 Admin Assistant to the President .... Ms. Connie BOOTY
83 Dean Div of Social Sciences .... Dr. Christina SCOTT
38 Director Student Counseling .... Ms. Kaethe HOEHLING

Williams Baptist University (B)

60 W. Fulbright Avenue, Walnut Ridge AR 72476
County: Lawrence FICE Identification: 001106
Unit ID: 107877
Telephone: (870) 886-6741 Carnegie Class: Bac-Diverse
FAX Number: (870) 886-3924 Calendar System: Semester
URL: www.williamsbu.edu
Established: 1941 Annual Undergrad Tuition & Fees: $18,500
Enrollment: 618 Coed
Affiliation or Control: Southern Baptist IRS Status: 501(c)3
Highest Offering: Master's
Accreditation: HLC, CAEPN

01 President .... Dr. Stan NORMAN
05 Provost & EVP Campus Life .... Dr. Marvin SCHOENECKE
111 VP for University Advancement/COO .... Dr. Tim HUDDLESTON
13 VP Creative Services & Technology .... Dr. Brett COOPER
84 AVP for Enrollment Management .... Dr. Andrew WATSON
32 Dean of Students .... Ms. Amber N. GRADY
06 Registrar .... Ms. Tracy HENDERSON
04 Administrative Asst to President .... Ms. Shannon TOLSON
08 Director Library Services .... Mrs. Jennifer MATHIS
37 Director Student Financial Aid .... Dr. Andrew WATSON
124 Director Advising/Retention .... Mrs. Tonya BOLTON
42 AVP Acad Affs/Dir Campus Ministries .... Dr. Rhyne PUTMAN
18 Director Physical Plant .... Mr. Tony CONLEY
113 Bursar .... Mr. Aaron ANDREWS
14 Director Information Technologies .... Mr. Blake MCGINNIS
41 Athletic Director .... Mr. Jeff RIDER
15 Dir Human Resources/Payroll Ofc .... Ms. Morgan DURHAM

CALIFORNIA

Abraham Lincoln University (C)

100 W Broadway, Suite 600, Glendale CA 91210
County: Los Angeles Identification: 667049
Unit ID: 488031
Telephone: (213) 252-5100 Carnegie Class: Spec-4-yr-Law
FAX Number: N/A Calendar System: Semester
URL: www.alu.edu
Established: 1996 Annual Undergrad Tuition & Fees: $6,400
Enrollment: 265 Coed
Affiliation or Control: Proprietary IRS Status: Proprietary
Highest Offering: First Professional Degree
Accreditation: DEAC

01 President & CEO .... Dr. Leslie GARGIULO
05 Chief Academic Officer .... Dr. Robert ABEL, JR.
61 Vice President/Dean School of Law .... Ms. Jessica K. PARK
11 Chief Operations Officer .... Mr. Donald GARGIULO
20 Academic Program Coordinator .... Ms. Jokebed RENTERIA
06 Registrar .... Mr. Mark WILLS
07 Director of Admissions .... Vacant
37 Director of Financial Aid .... Ms. Kelli Jo MALAGON
13 Director of Technology .... Vacant
108 Assoc Dean Academic Operations .... Ms. Bernadette M. AGATON
121 Assoc Dean Academic Success .... Ms. Lydia G. LIBERIO
32 Student Services Coordinator .... Ms. Kylie O'BRIEN
88 Operations Coordinator .... Ms. Lidby LOPEZ
53 Dean of Faculty - University .... Dr. Joy KLOTZ

Academy for Jewish Religion, California (D)

1270 S Alfred Street, PO Box 351297,
Los Angeles CA 90035
County: Los Angeles FICE Identification: 041555
Unit ID: 457271
Telephone: (213) 884-4133 Carnegie Class: Spec-4-yr-Faith
FAX Number: N/A Calendar System: Semester
URL: www.ajrca.edu
Established: 2001 Annual Graduate Tuition & Fees: N/A
Enrollment: 61 Coed
Affiliation or Control: Jewish IRS Status: 501(c)3
Highest Offering: Master's; No Undergraduates
Accreditation: WC, PAST

01 President .... Rabbi Mel GOTTLIEB
05 VP/Dean of Chaplaincy School .... Rabbi Rochelle ROBINS
88 Dean of Cantorial School .... Rabbi Sam RADWINE
73 Dean of Rabbinical School .... Rabbi Tal SESSLER
58 Dean of MJS Program .... Cantor Jonathan FRIEDMANN
21 Controller .... Ms. Grace MAKOW
11 Director of Administration .... Ms. Lauren GOLDNER
10 Chief Financial Officer .... Dr. Alvin MARTIN
07 Director of Admissions/Recruitment .... Ms. Robin FEDERMAN
06 Coordinator Registration/Operations .... Ms. Elea FRIEDMAN
36 Director of Internships/Placement .... Rabbi Faith TESSLER
09 Director of Institutional Research .... Cantor Jonathan FRIEDMANN
37 Director Student Financial Aid .... Ms. Lauren GOLDNER

Academy of Art University (E)

79 New Montgomery Street,
San Francisco CA 94105-3410
County: San Francisco FICE Identification: 007531
Unit ID: 108232
Telephone: (415) 274-2200 Carnegie Class: Masters/L
FAX Number: (415) 274-8665 Calendar System: Semester
URL: www.academyart.edu
Established: 1929 Annual Undergrad Tuition & Fees: $24,664
Enrollment: 8,928 Coed
Affiliation or Control: Proprietary IRS Status: Proprietary
Highest Offering: Master's
Accreditation: WC, ART, CIDA

01 President .... Dr. Elisa STEPHENS
05 Chief Academic Officer .... Ms. Sue ROWLEY

Academy of Chinese Culture and Health Sciences (F)

1600 Broadway Street, Suite 200, Oakland CA 94612
County: Alameda FICE Identification: 032883
Unit ID: 108269
Telephone: (510) 763-7787 Carnegie Class: Spec-4-yr-Other Health
FAX Number: (510) 834-8646 Calendar System: Other
URL: www.acchs.edu
Established: 1982 Annual Undergrad Tuition & Fees: N/A
Enrollment: 97 Coed
Affiliation or Control: Independent Non-Profit IRS Status: 501(c)3
Highest Offering: Doctorate; No Lower Division
Accreditation: ACUP

01 Acting President .... Mr. Andres BELLA
03 Vice President .... Dr. Rong Yuan ZHAO
11 Vice President of Administration .... Ms. Julie WANG
05 Director of Education .... Zheng-jie KUO
06 Registrar .... Ms. Jessica DANG

Acupuncture and Integrative Medicine College-Berkeley (G)

2550 Shattuck Avenue, Berkeley CA 94704-2724
County: Alameda FICE Identification: 033274
Unit ID: 384306
Telephone: (510) 666-8248 Carnegie Class: Spec-4-yr-Other Health
FAX Number: (510) 666-0111 Calendar System: Trimester
URL: www.aimc.edu
Established: 1990 Annual Undergrad Tuition & Fees: N/A
Enrollment: 99 Coed
Affiliation or Control: Independent Non-Profit IRS Status: 501(c)3
Highest Offering: Doctorate; No Lower Division
Accreditation: ACUP

01 President .... Dr. David LEE
05 Academic Director .... Dr. Thomas SIEMANN
17 Acting Clinic Dean .... Ms. Nishanga BLISS
06 Registrar .... Ms. Shirlin DUDONIS
20 Chief Acad Admin Officer .... Ms. Robbyn KAWAGUCHI
08 Head Librarian .... Ms. Patricia WARD
32 Director of Student Services .... Ms. Robbyn KAWAGUCHI
10 Admin Director .... Ms. Shirlin DUDONIS

Advanced College (H)

13180 Paramount Boulevard, South Gate CA 90280-7956
County: Los Angeles FICE Identification: 037863
Unit ID: 444343
Telephone: (562) 408-6969 Carnegie Class: Spec 2-yr-Health
FAX Number: (562) 408-0471 Calendar System: Other
URL: www.advancedcollege.edu
Established: 1999 Annual Undergrad Tuition & Fees: N/A
Enrollment: 59 Coed
Affiliation or Control: Proprietary IRS Status: Proprietary
Highest Offering: Associate Degree
Accreditation: COE

01 Chief Executive Officer .... Mr. Amin VOHRA
37 Director Financial Aid .... Mr. Roberto QUINONES
05 Chief Academic Officer .... Mr. Ghazanfar MAHMOOD
11 Vice President .... Mr. Bharpur SINGH
108 Compliance Officer .... Ms. Rumaana R. KHAN
06 Registrar .... Ms. Kaoru ITO

Agape College of Business and Science (I)

1313 P Street, Fresno CA 93721
County: Fresno Identification: 667362
Telephone: (559) 486-1166 Carnegie Class: Not Classified
FAX Number: N/A Calendar System: Quarter
URL: www.acbscollege.org/
Established: 2006 Annual Undergrad Tuition & Fees: N/A
Enrollment: N/A Coed
Affiliation or Control: Independent Non-Profit IRS Status: 501(c)3
Highest Offering: Baccalaureate
Accreditation: ACICS

01 CEO/Chief Operating Officer .... Dr. Linda SCOTT
05 Chief Academic Officer .... Dr. Linda SCOTT
20 Dean of Schools .... Ms. Diana PADILLA

Alder Graduate School of Education (J)

2946 Broadway St., Ste B, Redwood City CA 94062
County: San Mateo Identification: 667356
Telephone: (650) 362-3997 Carnegie Class: Not Classified
FAX Number: N/A Calendar System: Semester
URL: aldergse.edu
Established: 2010 Annual Graduate Tuition & Fees: N/A
Enrollment: N/A Coed
Affiliation or Control: Independent Non-Profit IRS Status: 501(c)3
Highest Offering: Master's; No Undergraduates
Accreditation: WC

01 CEO/President .... Heather KIRKPATRICK
11 Chief Operating Officer .... Nimmi CHILAMKURTI
10 Chief Financial Officer .... Erik BROWN
05 Dean .... Shayna SULLIVAN
08 Instructional Research Librarian .... Leila ROD-WELCH
32 Director of Student Services .... Ivan A. IBARRA MORA

Alhambra Medical University (K)

2215 West Mission Road, Suite 280, Alhambra CA 91803
County: Los Angeles Identification: 667052
Unit ID: 487995
Telephone: (626) 289-7719 Carnegie Class: Spec-4-yr-Other Health
FAX Number: (626) 289-8641 Calendar System: Quarter
URL: www.amuedu.com
Established: 2005 Annual Graduate Tuition & Fees: N/A
Enrollment: 154 Coed
Affiliation or Control: Proprietary IRS Status: Proprietary
Highest Offering: Master's; No Undergraduates
Accreditation: ACUP

01 President .... Dr. Eric TUCKMAN
05 Academic Vice President .... Dr. David LEE
23 Director of University Clinic .... Elizabeth JIN
32 Dean of Students .... Megan HAH
07 Director of Admissions .... Qing MA
06 University Registrar .... Xiaoting DING
37 Financial Aid Director .... Luke CHEN

Allan Hancock College (L)

800 S College Drive, Santa Maria CA 93454-6399
County: Santa Barbara FICE Identification: 001111
Unit ID: 108807
Telephone: (805) 922-6966 Carnegie Class: Assoc/HT-Mix Trad/Non
FAX Number: (805) 347-9896 Calendar System: Semester
URL: www.hancockcollege.edu
Established: 1920 Annual Undergrad Tuition & Fees (In-District): $1,188
Enrollment: 10,248 Coed
Affiliation or Control: State/Local IRS Status: 501(c)3
Highest Offering: Associate Degree
Accreditation: WJ

01 Superintendent/President .... Dr. Kevin G. WALTHERS
04 Executive Asst to President .... Ms. Carmen S. CAMACHO
10 Assoc Supt/VP Finance/Admin .... Mr. Eric D. SMITH
05 Assoc Supt/VP Academic Affairs .... Dr. Robert CURRY

32	Assoc Supt/VP Student Services	Dr. Genevieve SIWABESSY
108	Vice Pres Inst Effectiveness	Dr. Paul MURPHY
15	Director Human Resources	Mr. Ruben RAMIREZ
35	Dean Student Services	Ms. Mary DOMINGUEZ
38	Dean Counseling & Matriculation	Ms. Yvonne TENIENTE
20	Dean Academic Affairs	Dr. Sean ABEL
20	Dean Academic Affairs	Dr. Sofia RAMIREZ-GELPI
20	Dean Academic Affairs	Ms. Margaret LAU
20	Dean Academic Affairs	Mr. Rick RANTZ
20	Dean Academic Affairs	Dr. Mary PATRICK
41	Assoc Dean Kines/Rec/Athletics	Ms. Kim ENSING
88	Assoc Dean Law Enforcement	Mr. Mitch MCCANN
111	Exec Director College Advancement	Dr. Jon HOOTEN
88	Artistic Director PCPA	Mr. Mark BOOHER
13	Dir Information Technology	Dr. Andy SPECHT
21	Director Business Services	Ms. Laura BECKER
07	Director Admissions & Records	Mr. David VASQUEZ
37	Director Student Financial Aid	Ms. Mary DOMINGUEZ
26	Dir Public Affairs/Publications	Ms. Lauren MILBOURNE
78	Dir Cooperative Work Experience	Mr. Thomas LAMICA
124	Director EOPS & Special Outreach	Vacant
18	Director Facilities	Vacant
19	District Police Chief	Ms. Catherine FARLEY
88	Director Cal-SOAP	Ms. Diana PEREZ
25	Director Institutional Grants	Dr. LeeAnne MCNULTY
88	Counselor/Coordinator MESA	Ms. Christine REED
88	Managing Director PCPA	Ms. Jennifer SCHWARTZ
88	Director Special Projects	Ms. Marina WASHBURN
88	Director Children's Center	Ms. Maria SUAREZ
88	Dir LAP/Stdt Hlth/Veteran's Success	Dr. Stephanie CROSBY
88	Director Public Safety	Mr. David WHITHAM
88	Dir Student Activities & Outreach	Ms. Stephanie ROBB
16	Asst Dir Human Resources	Ms. Janeal BLUE

*Alliant International University President's Office (A)

1475 66th Street, Emeryville CA 94608
County: San Francisco   Identification: 666132
Telephone: (415) 955-2100   Carnegie Class: N/A
FAX Number: (414) 955-2062
URL: www.alliant.edu

01	President	Mr. Andy VAUGHN
05	Provost/SVP Academic Affairs	Dr. Tracy HELLER
30	Sr Vice Pres Development/Inclusion	Dr. Mary OLING-SISAY
11	Sr Vice President of Operations	Ms. Amy KWIATKOWSKI
10	Interim Chief Financial Officer	Mr. Christoph WINTER
06	Registrar	Mr. Paul WELCH
15	Interim Human Resources Director	Ms. Melissa ROTHMEYER
13	Chief Information Officer	Mr. Joshua BLAZER
32	Vice President of Student Services	Ms. Amber ECKERT

*Alliant International University-San Diego (B)

10455 Pomerado Road, San Diego CA 92131-1799
County: San Diego   FICE Identification: 011117
   Unit ID: 110468
Telephone: (858) 635-4000   Carnegie Class: DU-Mod
FAX Number: (858) 693-8562   Calendar System: Semester
URL: www.alliant.edu
Established: 1952   Annual Undergrad Tuition & Fees: $13,680
Enrollment: 3,429   Coed
Affiliation or Control: Independent Non-Profit   IRS Status: 501(c)3
Highest Offering: Doctorate
Accreditation: **WC**, ACBSP, CLPSY, MFCD

12	Campus Director	Mr. Jose HERNANDEZ
05	Provost/Vice Pres Academic Affairs	Dr. Tracy HELLER
32	VP Student Services	Ms. Amber ECKERT

*Alliant International University-Fresno (C)

5130 E Clinton Way, Fresno CA 93727-2014
Telephone: (559) 456-2777   FICE Identification: 001158
Accreditation: **&WC**, CACREP, CLPSY, MFCD

*Alliant International University-Irvine (D)

2855 Michelle Drive, Suite 300, Irvine CA 92606
Telephone: (949) 812-7440   Identification: 666157
Accreditation: **&WC**, MFCD

*Alliant International University-Los Angeles (E)

1000 S Fremont Avenue, Unit 5,
Alhambra CA 91803-1360
Telephone: (626) 284-2777   FICE Identification: 010013
Accreditation: **&WC**, CLPSY, MFCD

*Alliant International University-San Francisco (F)

1475 66th Street, Emeryville CA 94608
Telephone: (415) 955-2100   FICE Identification: 011881
Accreditation: **&WC**, CLPSY, MFCD

AMDA College and Conservatory of the Performing Arts (G)

6305 Yucca Street, Los Angeles CA 90028
County: Los Angeles   Identification: 666721
Telephone: (323) 469-3300   Carnegie Class: Not Classified
FAX Number: (323) 469-1448   Calendar System: Semester
URL: www.amda.edu
Established: 1964   Annual Undergrad Tuition & Fees: N/A
Enrollment: N/A   Coed
Affiliation or Control: Independent Non-Profit   IRS Status: 501(c)3
Highest Offering: Master's
Accreditation: **WC**, THEA

01	President/Artistic Director	David MARTIN
05	Director of Education	Barry FINKEL
10	Chief Financial Officer	David SILVERMAN
07	Director Of Admissions	Joseph SIRIANO
37	Asst Director of Financial Aid	Sheena PONCE ALEGRE
20	Director of Education Services	Cynthia MOJ
32	Director of Student Services	Debra WALSH

*American Academy of Dramatic Arts, Los Angeles Campus (H)

1336 N La Brea Avenue, Hollywood CA 90028-7504
Telephone: (323) 464-2777   FICE Identification: 021069
Accreditation: **&M**, THEA

† Regional accreditation is carried under the parent institution in New York, NY.

American Career College-Los Angeles (I)

4021 Rosewood Avenue, Los Angeles CA 90004
County: Los Angeles   FICE Identification: 022418
   Unit ID: 109040
Telephone: (323) 668-7555   Carnegie Class: Spec 2-yr-Health
FAX Number: (322) 953-3654   Calendar System: Other
URL: www.americancareercollege.edu
Established: 1978   Annual Undergrad Tuition & Fees: N/A
Enrollment: 1,751   Coed
Affiliation or Control: Proprietary   IRS Status: Proprietary
Highest Offering: Associate Degree
Accreditation: ABHES, SURTEC

01	Executive Director	Ms. Lani TOWNSEND
05	Director of Education	Mr. Jamison WALLINGTON

American Career College-Ontario (J)

3130 East Sedona Court, Ontario CA 91764
County: San Bernardino   FICE Identification: 039713
   Unit ID: 447768
Telephone: (909) 218-3253   Carnegie Class: Spec 2-yr-Health
FAX Number: (909) 218-3340   Calendar System: Other
URL: www.americancareercollege.edu
Established: 2006   Annual Undergrad Tuition & Fees: N/A
Enrollment: 1,435   Coed
Affiliation or Control: Proprietary   IRS Status: Proprietary
Highest Offering: Associate Degree
Accreditation: ABHES, COARC

01	Executive Director	Tom BUSTAMANTE, JR.
05	Campus Director Education	Andrei LIVANU

American Career College-Orange County (K)

1200 North Magnolia Ave, Anaheim CA 92801
Telephone: (714) 763-9066   Identification: 667073
Accreditation: ABHES, COARC, OTA, PTAA, SURTEC

America Evangelical University (L)

1204 W. 163rd Street, Gardena CA 90247
County: Los Angeles   Identification: 667090
   Unit ID: 490081
Telephone: (323) 643-0301   Carnegie Class: Spec-4-yr-Faith
FAX Number: (323) 643-0302   Calendar System: Semester
URL: www.aeu.edu
Established: 2001   Annual Undergrad Tuition & Fees: $6,250
Enrollment: 165   Coed
Affiliation or Control: Independent Non-Profit   IRS Status: 501(c)3
Highest Offering: Doctorate
Accreditation: BI

01	President/CEO	Dr. Sanghoon LEE
05	Int Vice President for Academics	Rev. Sungho CHO
32	Dean of Stdnts/Spiritual Formation	Yoochang JUNG
45	Director of Planning	Brian KIM
11	Vice Pres for Administration	Rev. Sung Ho CHO
20	Academic Dean	Jongseock SHIN
30	Chief Development Officer	Brian KIM
08	Director of Library	Dr. Douho IM
06	Registrar	Jacob KIM
07	Director of Admissions	Miwon LEE
37	Director Financial Aid	Isaac JEON

American Film Institute Conservatory (M)

2021 N Western Avenue, Los Angeles CA 90027-1657
County: Los Angeles   FICE Identification: 022220
   Unit ID: 108870
Telephone: (323) 856-7600   Carnegie Class: Spec-4yr-Arts
FAX Number: (323) 467-4578   Calendar System: Semester
URL: www.afi.com
Established: 1969   Annual Graduate Tuition & Fees: N/A
Enrollment: 337   Coed
Affiliation or Control: Independent Non-Profit   IRS Status: 501(c)3
Highest Offering: Master's; No Undergraduates
Accreditation: **WC**

01	President/CEO	Mr. Bob GAZZALE
05	Dean AFI Conservatory/EVP	Ms. Susan RUSKIN
10	Chief Financial Officer	Mr. Lang FREDRICKSON
111	Chief Advancement Officer	Ms. Sandra CHEN-LAU
15	Chief Resources Officer	Ms. Roschoune FRANKLIN
26	Chief Communications Officer	Ms. Juli GOODWIN
11	Vice Dean of Administration	Ms. Yvette JUSSEAUME
20	Vice Dean of Academic Affairs	Mr. Tom ENGFER
88	Manager Thesis Production	Ms. Susan DRETZKA
57	Artistic Director	Vacant
06	Registrar	Vacant
37	Financial Aid Director	Ms. Robin BAILEY-CHEN
08	Librarian	Ms. Deborah COOPER
13	Director Information Technology	Vacant
113	Bursar	Ms. Jasmin CARROLL

American Jewish University (N)

15600 Mulholland Drive, Los Angeles CA 90077-1599
County: Los Angeles   FICE Identification: 002741
   Unit ID: 116846
Telephone: (310) 476-9777   Carnegie Class: Bac-A&S
FAX Number: (310) 471-1278   Calendar System: Semester
URL: www.aju.edu
Established: 1947   Annual Undergrad Tuition & Fees: $32,404
Enrollment: 93   Coed
Affiliation or Control: Independent Non-Profit   IRS Status: 501(c)3
Highest Offering: Master's
Accreditation: **WC**

01	President	Dr. Jeffrey HERBST
05	Chief Academic Officer	Dr. Robbie TOTTEN
10	VP Finance/Administration/CFO	Mr. Adrian BREITFELD
111	VP Advancement/Chief Dev Ofcr	Ms. Catherine SCHNEIDER
15	Director of Human Resources	Ms. Kathy SPIRA

American Medical Sciences Center (O)

225 West Broadway, Ste 410, Glendale CA 91204
County: Los Angeles   FICE Identification: 041597
   Unit ID: 461263
Telephone: (818) 240-6900   Carnegie Class: Spec 2-yr-Health
FAX Number: (818) 240-6902   Calendar System: Semester
URL: amsc.edu
Established: 1996   Annual Undergrad Tuition & Fees: N/A
Enrollment: 52   Coed
Affiliation or Control: Proprietary   IRS Status: Proprietary
Highest Offering: Baccalaureate
Accreditation: ABHES

01	Director	Mr. Vardan KARAGEZIAN

American University of Armenia (P)

1000 Broadway, Suite 280, Oakland CA 94607
County: Alameda   Identification: 666013
Telephone: (510) 925-4282   Carnegie Class: Not Classified
FAX Number: (510) 925-4283   Calendar System: Semester
URL: www.aua.edu
Established: 1991   Annual Undergrad Tuition & Fees: N/A
Enrollment: N/A   Coed
Affiliation or Control: Independent Non-Profit   IRS Status: 501(c)3
Highest Offering: Master's
Accreditation: **WC**

01	President	Dr. Karin MARKIDES
05	Provost	Dr. Brian ELLISON
11	Vice President Operations	Ashot GHAZARYAN
10	Vice President of Finance	Gevorg GOYUNYAN
30	VP Development	Gaiane KHACHATRIAN
06	Associate Registrar	Chaghig ARZROUNI-CHAHINIAN
26	Public Relations Coordinator	Vacant
07	Dir Admissions/Recruit/Intl Stdnts	Arina ZOHRABIAN
09	Institutional Research Manager	Vacant
08	Head Librarian	Satenik AVAKIAN
101	Secretary of the Institution/Board	Caren MEGHREBLIAN
15	Director Personnel Services	Arina BEKCHIAN
29	Director Alumni Relations	Narine PETROSYAN
13	Dir Information/Communications Tech	Berj GATRJYAN
50	Dean of Business and Economics	Eric VAN GENDEREN
69	Dean of Public Health	Varduhi PETROSYAN

American University of Health Sciences (A)

1600 E Hill Street, Building #1, Signal Hill CA 90755

County: Los Angeles — FICE Identification: 032253 — Unit ID: 433004

Telephone: (562) 988-2278 — Carnegie Class: Spec-4-yr-Other Health
FAX Number: (562) 988-1791 — Calendar System: Quarter
URL: www.auhs.edu
Established: 1994 — Annual Undergrad Tuition & Fees: $23,329
Enrollment: 408 — Coed
Affiliation or Control: Proprietary — IRS Status: Proprietary
Highest Offering: Doctorate
Accreditation: WC, NURSE, PHAR, TRACS

01 President ... Dr. Caroll RYAN
05 Provost ... Dr. Marilyn UVERO
10 Chief Financial/Business Officer ... Sandy SARGE
06 Registrar ... Alma PINEDA
07 Director of Admissions ... Lily NGUYEN
09 Director of Institutional Research ... Thomas VESSELLA
13 Chief Information Technology Office ... Don JAYATHILAKE
32 Chief Student Affairs/Student Life ... Genevieve (Ivy) JAVALUYAS
08 Librarian ... Rachel FRIEDMAN
04 Admin Assistant to the President ... Cynthia CHAMBERS
37 Director Student Financial Aid ... Venus CRUZ

Anaheim University (B)

1240 S State College Blvd, Ste 110,
Anaheim CA 92806-5152

County: Orange — Identification: 666651
Telephone: (714) 772-3330 — Carnegie Class: Not Classified
FAX Number: (714) 772-3331 — Calendar System: Other
URL: www.anaheim.edu
Established: 1996 — Annual Undergrad Tuition & Fees: N/A
Enrollment: N/A — Coed
Affiliation or Control: Proprietary — IRS Status: Proprietary
Highest Offering: Doctorate
Accreditation: DEAC

01 President ... Dr. Andrew E. HONEYCUTT
05 Vice President Academic Affairs ... Dr. Rod ELLIS
11 Vice Pres Administrative Affairs ... Ms. Kate STRAUSS
106 Dir Online Learning/Development ... Mr. David BRACEY
06 Registrar ... Ms. Elizabeth MAYS

Angeles College (C)

3440 Wilshire Boulevard, Suite 310,
Los Angeles CA 90010

County: Los Angeles — FICE Identification: 041604 — Unit ID: 457299

Telephone: (213) 487-2211 — Carnegie Class: Spec-4-yr-Other Health
FAX Number: (213) 487-2299 — Calendar System: Semester
URL: www.angelescollege.edu
Established: 2004 — Annual Undergrad Tuition & Fees: N/A
Enrollment: 303 — Coed
Affiliation or Control: Proprietary — IRS Status: Proprietary
Highest Offering: Baccalaureate
Accreditation: ABHES, NURSE

01 CEO/School Director ... Ms. Teresa KRAUSE

Angeles College-City of Industry (D)

17595 Almahurst Street, Suite 101-3,
City of Industry CA 91748

Telephone: (626) 965-5566 — Identification: 770518
Accreditation: ABHES

Antelope Valley College (E)

3041 W Avenue K, Lancaster CA 93536-5426

County: Los Angeles — FICE Identification: 001113 — Unit ID: 109350

Telephone: (661) 722-6300 — Carnegie Class: Bac/Assoc-Assoc Dom
FAX Number: (661) 722-6333 — Calendar System: Semester
URL: www.avc.edu
Established: 1929 — Annual Undergrad Tuition & Fees (In-District): $1,124
Enrollment: 12,057 — Coed
Affiliation or Control: State/Local — IRS Status: 501(c)3
Highest Offering: Baccalaureate
Accreditation: WJ, COARC, RAD

01 President/Superintendent ... Dr. Jennifer ZELLET
05 Interim VP Academic Affairs ... Dr. Howard DAVIS
32 Interim VP Student Services ... Dr. Jose RIVERA
15 Int Exec Director Human Resources ... Ms. Harmony MILLER
84 Dean Enrollment Services ... Ms. LaDonna TRIMBLE
35 Dean of Student Life ... Dr. Jill ZIMMERMAN
10 Exec Dir Fiscal/Financial Svcs ... Ms. Sarah MILLER
22 Dir Ofc Students with Disabilities ... Dr. Louis LUCERO
26 Exec Dir Marketing/Public Info ... Vacant
18 Exec Director Facilities Services ... Mrs. Dawn MCINTOSH
13 Exec Dir Information Technology ... Mr. Rick SHAW
111 Exec Dir Inst Advance & Foundation ... Ms. Dianne KNIPPEL
09 Director Inst Research & Planning ... Dr. Meeta GOEL
37 Director Financial Aid ... Ms. Nichelle WILLIAMS
76 Dean CTE ... Mr. Gregory BORMANN
79 Dean Arts & Humanities ... Mr. Nate DILLON
83 Dean Soc & Beh Sci/Bus/Comp Stds ... Mrs. Kathryn MITCHELL
38 Dean Counseling & Matriculation ... Ms. Rashitta BROWN-ELIZE
81 Dean of Math/Science & Engineering ... Dr. Christos VALIOTOS

Antiochian House of Studies (F)

1020 Baseline Road, La Verne CA 91750

County: Los Angeles — Identification: 667432
Telephone: (833) 468-2467 — Carnegie Class: Not Classified
FAX Number: N/A — Calendar System: Semester
URL: tahos.org
Established: 1980 — Annual Graduate Tuition & Fees: N/A
Enrollment: N/A — Coed
Affiliation or Control: Independent Non-Profit — IRS Status: 501(c)3
Highest Offering: Doctorate; No Undergraduates
Accreditation: THEOL

01 President ... V.Rev. Michel NAJIM

ArtCenter College of Design (G)

1700 Lida Street, Pasadena CA 91103-1999

County: Los Angeles — FICE Identification: 001116 — Unit ID: 109651

Telephone: (626) 396-2200 — Carnegie Class: Masters/S
FAX Number: N/A — Calendar System: Semester
URL: www.artcenter.edu
Established: 1930 — Annual Undergrad Tuition & Fees: $46,486
Enrollment: 2,182 — Coed
Affiliation or Control: Independent Non-Profit — IRS Status: 501(c)3
Highest Offering: Master's
Accreditation: WC, ART

01 President ... Ms. Karen HOFMANN
10 Chief Financial & Admin Officer ... Mr. Rich HALUSCHAK
05 Interim Provost ... Dr. Anne BURDICK
30 Sr Vice Pres Development ... Ms. Emily LASKIN
07 SVP Admissions/Enrollment Mgmt ... Mr. Tom STERN
88 VP Exhibitions/Director ARW Gallery ... Mr. Steve NOWLIN
13 VP Information Technology ... Ms. Theresa ZIX
26 VP Marketing & Communication ... Mr. Jered GOLD
15 Vice Pres Human Resources ... Ms. Lisa M. SANCHEZ
28 Vice President & Diversity Officer ... Dr. Aaron BRUCE
18 VP Facilities/Campus Planning ... Mr. Rollin HOMER
88 VP Professional Dev/Industry Engage ... Ms. Kristine BOWNE
32 Associate Provost Student Affairs ... Mr. Ray QUIROLGICO
08 College Librarian & Managing Dir ... Mr. Mario ASCENCIO
21 Controller ... Ms. Lina DEASE
37 Managing Director Financial Aid ... Ms. Cheryl GILLIES
06 Registrar/Director of Enrollment ... Mr. Greg YAMAMOTO
09 Director of Institutional Research ... Ms. Esmeralda NAVA
20 Director Academic Affairs ... Ms. Leslie JOHNSON
102 Sr Dir Foundation/Govt Relations ... Mr. Darryl MORI
36 Director of Career Development ... Ms. Amanda RAJOTTE
96 Director of Purchasing ... Ms. Monica MATSUO
19 Director Campus Security ... Mr. Jim FINCH
29 Director Alumni Affairs ... Ms. Keiko DOI

Asher College (H)

1215 Howe Street, Suite 101, Sacramento CA 95825

County: Sacramento — FICE Identification: 040573 — Unit ID: 447777

Telephone: (916) 900-2850 — Carnegie Class: Assoc/HVT-High Trad
FAX Number: (916) 649-9700 — Calendar System: Other
URL: www.asher.edu
Established: 1998 — Annual Undergrad Tuition & Fees: N/A
Enrollment: 748 — Coed
Affiliation or Control: Proprietary — IRS Status: Proprietary
Highest Offering: Associate Degree
Accreditation: CNCE

01 President ... David VICE
12 Campus Director Sacramento ... Linda FREEMAN
12 Campus Director Las Vegas ... Anne BUZAK
12 Campus Director Dallas ... Josh PAULSEN
88 Director of Compliance ... Kathryn JOHNSON
26 Director of Marketing ... Kim GASPER
37 Director Student Financial Aid ... Elona OWENS

ATA College (I)

1810 Gillespie Way, Suite 104, El Cajon CA 92020-1234

County: San Diego — FICE Identification: 035324 — Unit ID: 444361

Telephone: (619) 596-2766 — Carnegie Class: Assoc/HVT-High Trad
FAX Number: (619) 596-4526 — Calendar System: Other
URL: www.atacollege.edu
Established: 2000 — Annual Undergrad Tuition & Fees: N/A
Enrollment: 83 — Coed
Affiliation or Control: Proprietary — IRS Status: Proprietary
Highest Offering: Associate Degree
Accreditation: COE

01 President/CEO ... Henry MARENTES
11 Vice President of Operations ... Valerie PHILLIPS
88 Director of Compliance ... Nick FLEETWOOD
07 Director of Admissions ... Vacant
05 Director of Education ... James R. KYLE
06 Registrar ... Dionne SIMPSON
37 Financial Aid Officer ... Dionne SIMPSON
36 Career & College Advisor ... Ashley BARRETT

ATI College (J)

15141 Whittier Blvd, Ste 420, Whittier CA 90603

County: Los Angeles — FICE Identification: 037404 — Unit ID: 444325

Telephone: (562) 864-0506 — Carnegie Class: Not Classified
FAX Number: (562) 864-7806 — Calendar System: Semester
URL: www.ati.edu
Established: 1998 — Annual Undergrad Tuition & Fees: N/A
Enrollment: 83 — Coed
Affiliation or Control: Proprietary — IRS Status: Proprietary
Highest Offering: Baccalaureate
Accreditation: ACCSC

01 CEO/President ... Dr. Katherine CHO
05 Education Director ... Dr. Brian H. KIM

Azusa Pacific University (K)

901 E Alosta Avenue, Azusa CA 91702-7000

County: Los Angeles — FICE Identification: 001117 — Unit ID: 109785

Telephone: (626) 969-3434 — Carnegie Class: DU-Higher
FAX Number: (626) 969-7180 — Calendar System: Semester
URL: www.apu.edu
Established: 1899 — Annual Undergrad Tuition & Fees: $41,410
Enrollment: 9,006 — Coed
Affiliation or Control: Independent Non-Profit — IRS Status: 501(c)3
Highest Offering: Doctorate
Accreditation: WC, ART, CAATE, CAEPN, CLPSY, IACBE, MUS, NURSE, PTA, SW, THEOL

01 President ... Dr. Paul W. FERGUSON
05 Provost ... Dr. Rukshan FERNANDO
26 Exec Vice Pres External Affairs ... Mr. David E. BIXBY
32 Vice Pres for Student Affairs ... Dr. Shino SIMONS
10 Vice President Finance/Business/CFO ... Ms. Alanna CAJTHAML
43 General Counsel ... Mr. Chris JENNINGS
13 Vice President Admin/CIO ... Dr. Don DAVIS
84 VP Enrollment Management ... Dr. Heather PETRIDIS
20 Vice Provost Undergraduate Programs ... Dr. Vicky BOWDEN
35 AVP Student Life/Chief Judicial Ofc ... Mr. Willie HAMLETT
27 VP University Relations ... Dr. David PECK
49 Int Dean Col Liberal Arts/Sciences ... Dr. Denise EDWARDS-NEFF
83 Dean School Behav/Applied Sciences ... Dr. Robert WELSH
50 Int Dean School of Business Mgmt ... Dr. Roxanne HELM-STEVENS
53 Dean School of Education ... Dr. Anita HENCK
73 Dean Haggard School of Theology ... Dr. Robert DUKE
64 Dean College of of the Arts/Music ... Dr. Stephen JOHNSON
66 Dean School of Nursing ... Dr. Aja LESH
92 Dean Honors College ... Dr. David WEEKS
15 Vice President Human Resources ... Ms. Paola MARTINEZ
111 VP University Advancement ... Mr. Corbin HOORNBEEK
42 Campus Pastor ... Dr. Woody MOORWOOD
06 Associate Registrar-Undergraduate ... Ms. Mona MIKHAIL
41 Director Athletics ... Mr. Gary PINE
38 Director Counseling Center ... Dr. Bill FIALA
37 AVP for UG Academic Financial Svcs ... Mr. Jon KRIMMEL
36 Director Career Services ... Mr. AJ ZIMMERMAN
28 VP/Chief Diversity Officer ... Dr. Keith E. HALL

Barstow Community College District (L)

2700 Barstow Road, Barstow CA 92311-6699

County: San Bernardino — FICE Identification: 001119 — Unit ID: 109907

Telephone: (760) 252-2411 — Carnegie Class: Assoc/HVT-High Trad
FAX Number: (760) 252-1875 — Calendar System: Semester
URL: www.barstow.edu
Established: 1959 — Annual Undergrad Tuition & Fees (In-District): $1,104
Enrollment: 2,444 — Coed
Affiliation or Control: State/Local — IRS Status: 170(c)1
Highest Offering: Associate Degree
Accreditation: WJ

01 Superintendent/President ... Dr. Eva BAGG
04 Exec Assistant to the President ... Ms. Michelle HENDERSON
10 Vice President Admin Services ... Ms. DeeDee GARCIA
05 Int Vice Pres Academic Affairs ... Dr. Jennifer RODDEN
32 Vice Pres Student Services ... Mr. Henry L. COVARRUBIAS
15 Vice President of Human Resources ... Ms. Jennifer BURCHETT
20 Dean of Instruction OL & LSS ... Vacant
103 Dean Workforce & Econ Dev ... Ms. Sandi THOMAS
09 Dir Research Dev & Planning ... Ms. Lisa HOLMES
41 Athletic Director ... Mr. Mynor MENDOZA
26 Dir of Public Rels/Comm & Marketing ... Ms. Amanda SIMPSON
18 Director Maintenance & Operations ... Mr. Richard HERNANDEZ
21 Director Fiscal Services ... Ms. Pattie GRANADOS
13 Director of Information Technology ... Mr. Bryce PRUTSOS
84 Dean Enrollment Management & Svcs ... Ms. Heather MINEHART
35 Director Student Life & Dev ... Ms. Joann GARCIA
25 Director CTE Grants ... Mr. James LEE
88 Director Military Programs ... Mr. Robbie EVANS
88 Director Special Pgms & Svcs ... Ms. Christina CALDERON
16 Dir HR Org Dev & Process Imp ... Ms. Kim YOUNG
88 Civic Center & Event Manager ... Mr. Ed WILL

90 Dir Guided Path/Equity & Achvmt .... Ms. Melissa MEADOWS
14 Dir Inst Tech & OL Svcs .... Vacant
91 Dir Learning Support Svcs .... Mr. Bryan ASDEL
88 Dir Adult Educ Consortium .... Ms. Elean RIVERA
51 Dir Adult Educ & Basic Skills .... Mr. Elias VALENCIA
114 Budget Analyst .... Ms. Terri WALKER

Bergin University of Canine Studies (A)

10201 Old Redwood Highway, Penngrove CA 94951
County: Sonoma FICE Identification: 041763
Unit ID: 461643
Telephone: (707) 545-3647 Carnegie Class: Bac-Diverse
FAX Number: N/A Calendar System: Semester
URL: www.berginu.edu
Established: 1991 Annual Undergrad Tuition & Fees: N/A
Enrollment: 51 Coed
Affiliation or Control: Independent Non-Profit IRS Status: 501(c)3
Highest Offering: Master's
Accreditation: ACICS

01 President & Director of Education .... Dr. Bonita M. BERGIN
05 Chief Academic Officer .... Rebecca RICHARDSON
10 Chief Operating Officer .... Denise GREGERSEN
07 Director of Admissions Services .... Connie VAN GUILDER
06 Registrar .... Denise GREGERSEN
18 Facilities/Physical Plant Manager .... Eric JENSEN

Berkeley School of Theology (B)

2606 Dwight Way, Berkeley CA 94704-3097
County: Alameda FICE Identification: 001120
Unit ID: 108861
Telephone: (510) 841-1905 Carnegie Class: Spec-4-yr-Faith
FAX Number: (510) 841-2446 Calendar System: Semester
URL: https://www.bst.edu/
Established: 1871 Annual Graduate Tuition & Fees: N/A
Enrollment: 42 Coed
Affiliation or Control: American Baptist IRS Status: 501(c)3
Highest Offering: Doctorate; No Undergraduates
Accreditation: THEOL

01 President .... Dr. James E. BRENNEMAN
05 VP of Academics/Dean of Faculty .... Dr. LeAnn SNOW FLESHER
10 Vice Pres/Chief Financial Officer .... Ms. Yvonne WATSON
111 Vice Pres Institutional Advancement .... Dr. Charlotte TULLOS
32 Director of Student Services .... Ms. Kat A. CROSWELL
07 Director of Admissions .... Ms. Lia ROCHILL
06 Registrar .... Ms. Kat A. CROSWELL
04 Executive Asst to President .... Mr. Sam FIELDER

Bethesda University of California (C)

730 N Euclid Street, Anaheim CA 92801-4115
County: Orange FICE Identification: 032663
Unit ID: 110060
Telephone: (714) 517-1945 Carnegie Class: Bac-Diverse
FAX Number: (714) 683-1440 Calendar System: Semester
URL: www.buc.edu
Established: 1976 Annual Undergrad Tuition & Fees: $6,580
Enrollment: 399 Coed
Affiliation or Control: Independent Non-Profit IRS Status: 501(c)3
Highest Offering: Doctorate
Accreditation: BI, TRACS

01 President .... Dr. Seung Je Jeremiah CHO
10 Vice President/Chief Financial Ofcr .... Dr. Esther CHO
05 Chief Academic Officer .... Dr. Hyo In KIM
32 Chair of Student Affairs .... Prof. Hyun Bo SIM
06 Registrar/Academic Officer .... Ms. Seonhee OH
08 Librarian .... Ms. Rachel HWANG
07 Admissions Officer .... Ms. Jane CHIANG
37 Financial Aid Officer .... Ms. Yae Lee SHIN

Beverly Hills Design Institute (D)

8484 Wilshire Boulevard, Suite 730,
Beverly Hills CA 90211-3235
County: Los Angeles FICE Identification: 041855
Unit ID: 475635
Telephone: (310) 360-8888 Carnegie Class: Spec-4-yr-Other
FAX Number: (310) 857-6974 Calendar System: Quarter
URL: www.bhdi.edu
Established: 2005 Annual Undergrad Tuition & Fees: $23,220
Enrollment: 14 Coed
Affiliation or Control: Proprietary IRS Status: Proprietary
Highest Offering: Baccalaureate
Accreditation: ACICS

01 CEO .... Sonia ETE
05 Chief Academic Officer .... Douglas SPESERT
10 CFO/COO/Dir HR .... Thierry ETE
07 Director of Admissions/Career Svcs .... Brittany WISE
08 Director of Library .... Frida DICARLO

Biola University (E)

13800 Biola Avenue, La Mirada CA 90639-0001
County: Los Angeles FICE Identification: 001122
Unit ID: 110097
Telephone: (562) 903-6000 Carnegie Class: DU-Mod
FAX Number: (562) 903-4748 Calendar System: Semester
URL: www.biola.edu
Established: 1908 Annual Undergrad Tuition & Fees: $43,512
Enrollment: 5,815 Coed
Affiliation or Control: Independent Non-Profit IRS Status: 501(c)3
Highest Offering: Doctorate
Accreditation: WC, ACBSP, ART, CLPSY, IPSY, MUS, NURSE, SP, THEOL

01 President .... Dr. Barry H. COREY
05 Provost/Sr Vice President .... Dr. Matthew HALL
11 EVP Univ Operations & Finance .... Mr. Michael PIERCE
111 Interim VP Advancement .... Mrs. Heather CORDELL
26 VP Enrollment/Marketing & Comms .... Mr. Lee WILHITE
32 Interim VP Student Development .... Ms. Lisa IGRAM
10 VP Finance .... Mrs. Paula TKACH
88 VP Transformation .... Mr. David SHYNN
84 Assoc VP University Enrollment .... Ms. Fitsum MULAT
73 Interim Dean Talbot School Theology .... Dr. Tim PICKAVANCE
83 Dean Rosemead School Psychology .... Dr. Doug DAUGHERTY
88 Dean Cook Sch Intercultural Studies .... Vacant
53 Dean School of Education .... Dr. June HETZEL
50 Dean Crowell School of Business .... Dr. Gary LINDBLAD
81 Dean of Science/Tech & Health .... Dr. Matthew ROUSE
82 Dean Cinema & Media Arts .... Mr. Tom HALLEEN
57 Dean of Fine Arts & Comm .... Dr. Todd GUY
79 Dean of Humanities/Social Sciences .... Dr. Melissa B. SCHUBERT
97 Assoc Provost Curric & Instruction .... Dr. Cherry MCCABE
08 University Librarian .... Mr. Jeremy LABOSIER
42 Dean of Spiritual Development .... Dr. Todd PICKETT
06 University Registrar .... Ms. Cassandra HEATH
15 Chief Human Resources Officer .... Dr. Dave GRANT
21 Assoc VP of Finance .... Mr. Gordon HUMMEL
37 Sr Director Financial Aid .... Mr. Geoff MARSH
19 Assoc VP/Chief of Campus Safety .... Mr. John O. OJEISEKHOBA
13 Chief Information Officer .... Mr. Steven R. EARLE
36 Dir Career Development & Success .... Ms. Tiffany LEE
41 Sr Director of Athletics .... Dr. Bethany MILLER
40 Manager Bookstore .... Ms. Melissa C. CASTELLANO
18 Assoc VP of Facility and Aux Ops .... Mr. Brian PHILLIPS
27 Assoc VP of University Marketing .... Mr. Brian MILLER
38 Director Counseling Center .... Dr. Melanie TAYLOR
96 Sr Director Procurement .... Mrs. Breanna M. KLETT
120 Chief Education Technology Officer .... Mrs. Susan ISHII
43 University Legal Counsel .... Ms. Paula T. VICTOR
28 Chief Diversity Officer .... Ms. Tamra MALONE
100 Chief of Staff .... Mr. Brian J. SHOOK
108 Sr Associate Provost .... Dr. Tamara ANDERSON
04 Exec Assistant to the President .... Ms. Michele BYERLY

Butte College (F)

3536 Butte Campus Drive, Oroville CA 95965-8399
County: Butte FICE Identification: 008073
Unit ID: 110246
Telephone: (530) 895-2511 Carnegie Class: Assoc/HVT-High Trad
FAX Number: (530) 895-2345 Calendar System: Semester
URL: www.butte.edu
Established: 1966 Annual Undergrad Tuition & Fees (In-District): $1,368
Enrollment: 9,335 Coed
Affiliation or Control: State/Local IRS Status: 501(c)3
Highest Offering: Associate Degree
Accreditation: WJ, COARC, EMT

01 Superintendent/President .... Dr. Samia YAQUB
05 Vice Pres Instruction .... Ms. Virginia GULEFF
10 VP for Administration/CBO .... Mr. Andrew SULESKI
45 VP Institutional Effectiveness .... Mr. Gregory STOUP
32 Vice President Student Services .... Mr. Peter GITAU
20 Dean for Instruction .... Ms. Kam BULL
20 Dean for Instruction .... Dr. Carrie MONLUX
20 Dean for Instruction .... Ms. Denise ADAMS
20 Dean for Instruction .... Ms. Teresa DOYLE
37 Director Financial Aid/Vet Svcs .... Ms. Tammera SHINAR
35 Dean Student Services .... Mr. Clinton SLAUGHTER
35 Dean Student Services .... Mr. Brad ZUNIGA
15 Exec Director Human Resources .... Mr. Chris LITTLE
18 Dir Facilities Planning/Management .... Ms. Kim JONES
09 Director of Institutional Research .... Mr. Brian MURPHY
07 Director Admissions/Records .... Ms. Monica BOYES
103 Exec Dir Econ Workforce Development .... Ms. Linda ZORN
111 Director Institutional Advancement .... Ms. Lisa DELABY
41 Director Athletics/Kinesiology .... Mr. Craig RIGSBEE
13 Chief Technology Officer .... Vacant
21 Director Business Services .... Mr. Jim NICHOLAS
38 Coordinator of Counseling .... Ms. Debbie REYNOLDS
109 Director Auxiliary Services .... Mr. Steve DEMAGGIO
22 Director Student Equity .... Ms. Monica BROWN
100 Exec Asst to President & Board .... Ms. Shannon M. MCCOLLUM
108 Director Assessment .... Mr. Eric HOILAND
19 Chief of Police .... Mr. Casey CARLSON

Cabrillo College (G)

6500 Soquel Drive, Aptos CA 95003-3194
County: Santa Cruz FICE Identification: 001124
Unit ID: 110334
Telephone: (831) 479-6100 Carnegie Class: Assoc/HT-High Trad
FAX Number: (831) 479-6425 Calendar System: Semester
URL: www.cabrillo.edu
Established: 1959 Annual Undergrad Tuition & Fees (In-District): $1,270
Enrollment: 9,792 Coed
Affiliation or Control: State/Local IRS Status: 501(c)3
Highest Offering: Associate Degree
Accreditation: WJ, DH, RAD

01 Superintendent/President .... Dr. Matthew WETSTEIN
04 Executive Assistant .... Mrs. Ronnette SMITHCAMP
05 Vice Pres Instruction .... Dr. Robin MCFARLAND
10 VP Finance/Administrative Svcs .... Dr. Bradley OLIN
32 Vice Pres Student Svcs .... Ms. Amy LEHMAN-SEXTON
15 Vice Pres Human Resources .... Ms. Angela HOYT
13 Director Information Technology .... Ms. Spring ANDREWS
07 Director of Admissions/Records .... Mr. David CASTILLO
96 Dir Purchasing/Contracts/Risk Mgmt .... Mr. Michael ROBINS
26 Director Marketing & Communications .... Mrs. Kristin FABOS
21 Director Business Services .... Ms. Delana MILLER
31 Dir Community and Contract Ed .... Mr. Scott JOHNSON
18 Dir Planning & Facilities .... Mr. Jon SALISBURY
25 Dir Grants Development .... Ms. Carrie MULCAIRE
22 Dir Student Equity and Success .... Dr. Kofi AKINJIDE
121 Dir Student Resource and Support .... Ms. Karen REYES
08 Director Library .... Vacant
88 Dir Small Business Development Ctr .... Mr. Brandon NAPOLI
09 Dean Research/Planning/Inst Effect .... Mr. Terrence WILLETT
35 Dean Student Services .... Mrs. Michelle DONOHUE
38 Dean Counseling/Educ Support .... Mrs. Amy LEHMAN
102 Exec Dir Cabrillo Col Foundation .... Mrs. Eileen HILL
40 Bookstore Manager .... Ms. Linda CULLENS
37 Director Financial Aid .... Ms. Tootie TZIMBAL
103 Dean CTE & Workforce Development .... Ms. Gerlinde BRADY
106 Dean Online Education/E-learning .... Mrs. Rachel MAYO

Cal Northern School of Law (H)

1395 Ridgewood Drive, Ste 100, Chico CA 95973
County: Butte Identification: 667331
Telephone: (530) 891-6900 Carnegie Class: Not Classified
FAX Number: (530) 891-3429 Calendar System: Semester
URL: www.calnorthern.edu
Established: 1992 Annual Undergrad Tuition & Fees: N/A
Enrollment: N/A Coed
Affiliation or Control: Proprietary IRS Status: Proprietary
Highest Offering: First Professional Degree
Accreditation: WC

01 Dean and President .... Sandra BOOKS
09 Director of Institutional Research .... Martha WILSON
32 Dean of Students .... Douglas JACOBS

California Arts University (I)

4100 W. Commonwealth Ave #101, Fullerton CA 92833
County: Orange Identification: 667348
Unit ID: 494940
Telephone: (714) 222-1110 Carnegie Class: Spec-4-yr-Arts
FAX Number: (714) 907-1511 Calendar System: Semester
URL: https://www.cauniv.edu/
Established: Annual Undergrad Tuition & Fees: N/A
Enrollment: N/A Coed
Affiliation or Control: Independent Non-Profit IRS Status: 501(c)3
Highest Offering: Doctorate
Accreditation: TRACS

01 President .... Dr. Sae KWANG CHUNG
05 Academic Dean .... Dr. Don LEE
06 Registrar/Admissions Director .... Joy CHUNG
10 Business Manager .... Joel CHUNG
32 Student Dean/MA Program Director .... Dr. Yumi KIM

California Baptist University (J)

8432 Magnolia Avenue, Riverside CA 92504-3297
County: Riverside FICE Identification: 001125
Unit ID: 110361
Telephone: (951) 689-5771 Carnegie Class: Masters/L
FAX Number: N/A Calendar System: Semester
URL: www.calbaptist.edu
Established: 1950 Annual Undergrad Tuition & Fees: $36,340
Enrollment: 11,317 Coed
Affiliation or Control: Southern Baptist IRS Status: 501(c)3
Highest Offering: Doctorate
Accreditation: WC, ACBSP, ARCPA, CAATE, CLPSY, CONST, MUS, NURSE, PH, PTAA, RAD, SP, SW

01 President .... Dr. Ronald L. ELLIS
04 Admin Asst to the President .... Ms. Janie ARMENTROUT
05 VP for Academic Affairs/Provost .... Dr. Charles SANDS
10 VP for Finance & Administration .... Mr. Mark HOWE
84 VP Enrollment & Student Services .... Mr. Kent DACUS
26 VP for Marketing & Communication .... Vacant
43 VP and General Counsel .... Mr. Adam BURTON
88 VP for Global Initiatives .... Dr. Larry LINAMEN
111 VP for University Advancement .... Mr. Paul J. ELDRIDGE
48 Dean College of Architecture .... Mr. Mark A. ROBERSON
49 Dean College of Arts & Sciences .... Dr. Lisa HERNANDEZ
83 Dean Col Behavioral & Social Sci .... Dr. Jacqueline GUSTAFSON
54 Dean College of Engineering .... Dr. Phil VAN HAASTER
76 Dean College of Health Science .... Dr. David PEARSON
66 Dean College of Nursing .... Dr. Karen BRADLEY
50 Dean School of Business .... Dr. Tim GRAMLING
73 Dean School of Christian Ministries .... Dr. Chris MORGAN
53 Dean School of Education .... Dr. Robin DUNCAN
64 Dean School of Music .... Dr. Joseph BOLIN
88 Exec Dir Leadership Institute .... Dr. John SHOUP
106 Assoc VP of Academics .... Dr. Dirk DAVIS

20	Assoc Provost for Administration	Dr. Tracy WARD
108	Assoc Prov for Educ Effectiveness	Dr. Elizabeth MORRIS
06	University Registrar	Mr. Rich SIMPSON
08	Director of Library	Dr. Steve EMERSON
121	Director Student Success	Mr. Jeffrey TENNIS
124	Dean Academic Persistence & Support	Dr. Steve NEILSEN
20	Director Faculty Development	Dr. Ted MURCRAY
09	Director of Institutional Research	Dr. Brian NIEMEIER
124	Director of Academic Engagements	Mr. Brockton BRENNEMAN
21	Assoc VP for Financial Services	Mr. Calvin SPARKMAN
21	Assoc VP for Accounting	Ms. Jackie STILWELL
18	Assoc Dir Facilities Business Admin	Ms. Brenda FLORES
18	Assoc Dir Facilities Maint & Opers	Mr. Robert GURROLA
15	Director of Human Resources	Ms. Julie FRESQUEZ
13	Assoc VP of Technology	Dr. Tran HONG
119	Director of Info Security/Projects	Mr. Dale LEE
88	Director of Conferences & Events	Mr. Coreylon POLK
40	Director of Campus Store Operations	Mr. Greg REARDON
37	Director of Financial Aid	Mr. Joshua MOREY
32	Assoc VP for Student Services	Mr. Anthony LAMMONS
32	Assoc VP for Student Services	Mr. John MONTGOMERY
07	Asst VP for Admissions	Mr. Taylor NEECE
19	Director of Safety Services	Mr. John FREESE
41	Director of Athletics	Mr. Tyler MARIUCCI
39	Dir Residence Life & Housing Svcs	Mr. Daron HUBBERT
36	Director of Career Services	Ms. Lisa SINGER
27	Sr Dir Marketing & Communication	Mr. Jacob M. ROBERTSON
105	Director of Web Services	Mr. Daniel AKERS
85	Dean of International Programs	Mr. Bryan DAVIS
30	Sr Director of Development	Ms. Kim CUNNINGHAM
29	Sr Dir Alumni/Parent/Donor Engage	Mr. Joshua MOSS
44	Coordinator of Donor Stewardship	Ms. Joy LUNA

California Career College (A)

7003 Owensmouth Avenue, Canoga Park CA 91303

County: Los Angeles — FICE Identification: 039745
Unit ID: 447713
Telephone: (818) 710-1310 — Carnegie Class: Spec 2-yr-Health
FAX Number: (818) 710-1329 — Calendar System: Semester
URL: www.californiacareercollege.edu
Established: 2001 — Annual Undergrad Tuition & Fees: N/A
Enrollment: 159 — Coed
Affiliation or Control: Proprietary — IRS Status: Proprietary
Highest Offering: Associate Degree
Accreditation: **ABHES**

01	President/ADN Director	Susan NAIMI
10	General Counsel/CFO	Haleh NAIMI
07	Admissions Coord/Ofc of Registrar	Armenohy TELIME

California Christian College (B)

5364 E. Belmont Avenue, Fresno CA 93727

County: Fresno — FICE Identification: 008844
Unit ID: 110918
Telephone: (559) 251-4215 — Carnegie Class: Spec-4-yr-Faith
FAX Number: (559) 385-2329 — Calendar System: Semester
URL: www.calchristiancollege.edu
Established: 1955 — Annual Undergrad Tuition & Fees: $10,050
Enrollment: 13 — Coed
Affiliation or Control: Free Will Baptist — IRS Status: 501(c)3
Highest Offering: Baccalaureate
Accreditation: **TRACS**

01	President	Dr. Timothy M. POWELL
05	Vice Pres for Academic Affairs	Mrs. Joanna FELTS
06	Registrar	Vacant
10	Chief Financial Officer	Ms. Jennifer ARMSTRONG
09	Dir of Institutional Effectiveness	Ms. Jennifer WALLEY
08	Head Librarian	Mrs. Nanne SINGH
37	Student Finance Manager	Ms. Melinda SCROGGINS
07	Admissions/Recruitment Counselor	Mr. Manuel MARAVILLA
32	Dean of Students	Mr. Trent WALLEY
15	Human Resources Manager	Ms. Jennifer ARMSTRONG

California Coast University (C)

925 N. Spurgeon Street, Santa Ana CA 92701-3515

County: Orange — FICE Identification: 041276
Telephone: (714) 547-9625 — Carnegie Class: Not Classified
FAX Number: (714) 547-5777 — Calendar System: Other
URL: www.calcoast.edu
Established: 1973 — Annual Undergrad Tuition & Fees: N/A
Enrollment: N/A — Coed
Affiliation or Control: Proprietary — IRS Status: Proprietary
Highest Offering: Doctorate
Accreditation: **DEAC**

01	President	Dr. Thomas M. NEAL
03	Executive Vice President	Ms. Shelly MARQUARDT
32	Vice Pres of Student Affairs/CAO	Dr. Murl TUCKER
05	Director of Academic Affairs	Mr. Douglas PETRIKAT
06	Registrar	Ms. Angela CENINA
13	Dir Management Information Systems	Ms. Jojo SOBERANO

California College of the Arts (D)

1111 Eighth Street, San Francisco CA 94107-2247

County: San Francisco — FICE Identification: 001127
Unit ID: 110370
Telephone: (415) 703-9500 — Carnegie Class: Spec-4-yr-Arts
FAX Number: (510) 655-3541 — Calendar System: Semester
URL: www.cca.edu
Established: 1907 — Annual Undergrad Tuition & Fees: $51,137
Enrollment: 1,612 — Coed
Affiliation or Control: Independent Non-Profit — IRS Status: 501(c)3
Highest Offering: Master's
Accreditation: **WC**, ART

01	President	Mr. Stephen BEAL
05	Provost	Ms. Tammy Rae CARLAND
10	Chief Financial Officer	Mr. Nicholas ELSISHANS
111	Sr Vice President of Advancement	Ms. Susan AVILA
45	VP of Institutional Planning	Vacant
84	Vice Pres of Enrollment Svcs	Mr. Scott CLINE
26	Vice Pres Marketing/Comm Strategy	Ms. Ann WIENS
32	Vice President Student Affairs	Mr. George SEDANO
15	Assoc Vice Pres Human Resources	Ms. Maira LAZDINS
20	Associate Provost	Ms. Julianne KIRGIS
36	Director Career Development	Dr. Diana CHAVEZ
06	Registrar	Ms. Yun CHRISTENSON
37	Interim Director Financial Aid	Ms. Samantha DURANT DANCEL
29	Sr Mgr Alumni/Parent Engagement	Ms. Lisa JONAS
13	CIO/Sr VP Operations	Ms. Mara HANCOCK
07	Director Undergrad Admissions	Ms. Shiraz CHAVAN
38	Director Student Counseling	Vacant
88	Director Campus Planning	Mr. David MECKEL
18	VP for Operations/Capital Projects	Mr. Leigh SATA
123	Director Graduate Admissions	Mr. David MURRAY
09	Director of Institutional Research	Ms. Jennifer JURAS
96	Manager of Purchasing	Ms. Jackie CRADDOCK
04	Asst to the President & Board	Ms. Tayler HARRIMAN
08	Assoc VP of Libraries	Ms. Annemarie HAAR
104	Dir International Programs	Ms. Jessica MCMILLAN
19	Director Public Safety	Mr. Abe LEAL
28	Coordinator Diversity & Inclusion	Ms. Michelle CERAMI
35	Assoc Dir Student Life	Ms. Janeece HAYES
44	Assistant Annual Giving	Mr. Nathan BECKA
101	Special Asst & Board Liaison	Ms. Adriana LOBOVITS
102	Director Leadership Giving	Ms. Carleigh MCDONALD
105	Dir Content & Creative Strategy	Ms. Stephanie SMITH
108	Assoc Provost Accreditation & Curr	Ms. Dominick TRACY
86	Sr Dir of Inst Partnerships	Ms. Karen WEBER
90	Assoc Dir Academic Computing	Ms. Torreya CUMMINGS
91	Sr Dir Web & Infrastructure	Mr. Eli COCHRAN
41	Athletic Director	Vacant

California College of Music (E)

42 S. Catalina Avenue, Pasadena CA 91106

County: Los Angeles — Identification: 667402
Telephone: (626) 577-1751 — Carnegie Class: Not Classified
FAX Number: (626) 577-1765 — Calendar System: Quarter
URL: www.ccmla.edu
Established: 1999 — Annual Undergrad Tuition & Fees: N/A
Enrollment: N/A — Coed
Affiliation or Control: Proprietary — IRS Status: Proprietary
Highest Offering: Associate Degree
Accreditation: **MUS**

01	President/CEO	Michelle T. ISHII
05	Dean/Chief Academic Officer	Chris KAPICA

California Health Sciences University (F)

120 N. Clovis Ave, Clovis CA 93612

County: Fresno — Identification: 667218
Unit ID: 488572
Telephone: (559) 325-3600 — Carnegie Class: Spec-4-yr-Other Health
FAX Number: (559) 473-1487 — Calendar System: Semester
URL: https://chsu.edu/
Established: 2012 — Annual Graduate Tuition & Fees: N/A
Enrollment: 243 — Coed
Affiliation or Control: Proprietary — IRS Status: Proprietary
Highest Offering: Doctorate; No Undergraduates
Accreditation: **WC**, @OSTEO

01	President	Florence DUNN
04	Executive Asst to President	Kathleen HAEBERLE
05	COP Dean/Chief Academic Officer	Dr. Mark OKAMOTO
09	Dir Inst Assessmnt/Effectiveness/IR	Vacant
11	VP Operations/Facilities	Jimmy DUNN
10	Deputy Chief Financial Officer	Tanya BOHORQUEZ
13	Exec Dir of Info Technology	John BRIAR
32	Asst Dean of Student Affairs COP	Dr. Anitha SHENNOY
32	Asst Dean of Student Affairs COM	Susan ELY
06	Registrar	Janine DRAGNA
07	Director of Admissions	Leslie WILLIAMS
26	VP Marketing/Communications	Richele KLEISER
08	Librarian	Joanne MUELLENBACH
37	Director Student Financial Aid	Kevin HOOVER
15	VP of Human Resources	Carlita ROMERO-BEGLEY
19	Director Security/Safety	Timothy BOS
25	Director of Sponsored Programs	Karin CHAO-BUSHOVEN
30	Fund Development Manager	Chandler JAMESON
101	Secretary of the Institution/Board	Kathleen HAEBERLE
18	Chief Facilities/Physical Plnt Ofcr	James DUNN
28	Director of Diversity	Carlita ROMERO-BEGLEY

California Institute for Human Science (G)

701 Garden View Court, Encinitas CA 92024

County: San Diego — Identification: 667342
Telephone: (760) 634-1771 — Carnegie Class: Not Classified
FAX Number: N/A — Calendar System: Quarter
URL: www.cihs.edu
Established: 1992 — Annual Undergrad Tuition & Fees: N/A
Enrollment: N/A — Coed
Affiliation or Control: Independent Non-Profit — IRS Status: 501(c)3
Highest Offering: Doctorate
Accreditation: **WC**

01	President	Dr. Thomas BROPHY
05	Dean of Academic Affairs	Dr. William HOWE
07	Dean Admission/Enrollment Planning	Dr. Joel PILCO
32	Dean for Student Life	Vacant
10	CFO/Financial Controller/Bursar	Ms. Tamiko VOROS
31	Director Community Events	Dr. Ji Hyang PADMA

California Institute of Advanced Management (H)

1000 S. Fremont Avenue, #45, A10, Alhambra CA 91803

County: Los Angeles — FICE Identification: 042506
Unit ID: 487649
Telephone: (626) 350-1500 — Carnegie Class: Spec-4-yr-Bus
FAX Number: (626) 350-1515 — Calendar System: Other
URL: www.ciam.edu
Established: — Annual Graduate Tuition & Fees: N/A
Enrollment: 209 — Coed
Affiliation or Control: Independent Non-Profit — IRS Status: 501(c)3
Highest Offering: Master's; No Undergraduates
Accreditation: **WC**

01	President/CEO/COO	Ms. Jennie TA
05	Vice Pres Academic Affairs/Provost	Dr. Juan GARCIA
10	Chief Financial Officer	Mr. Salil SHARMA
43	General Counsel	Mr. Kien TIET
06	Registrar	Ms. Samantha SCOTT
07	Director of Admissions/Recruitment	Mr. Stephen JACOB
32	Dir Student Affairs	Dr. Jinny OH

California Institute of the Arts (I)

24700 McBean Parkway, Valencia CA 91355-2397

County: Los Angeles — FICE Identification: 001132
Unit ID: 111081
Telephone: (661) 255-1050 — Carnegie Class: Masters/M
FAX Number: (661) 254-8352 — Calendar System: Semester
URL: www.calarts.edu
Established: 1961 — Annual Undergrad Tuition & Fees: $53,466
Enrollment: 1,166 — Coed
Affiliation or Control: Independent Non-Profit — IRS Status: 501(c)3
Highest Offering: Doctorate
Accreditation: **WC**, DANCE

01	President	Ravi S. RAJAN
05	Provost/SVP Academic Affairs	Tracie COSTANTINO
10	Senior VP Finance/CFO	Vacant
111	Senior VP Advancement	Vacant
21	Assoc Vice President and Controller	Karla TALAVERA
15	VP/Chief Human Resources Ofcr	Bridgette WILDER
18	Assoc VP Facilities	Jesse SMITH
32	VP Student Experience	Brian HARLAN
84	VP Enrollment	Vacant
28	Institute Diversity Officer	Eva GRAHAM
08	Institute Librarian	Joan JOCSON-SINGH
57	Dean School of Art	Thomas LAWSON
64	Dean Herb Alpert School of Music	David ROSENBOOM
88	Dean School of Critical Studies	Amanda BEECH
88	Dean Sharon D Lund School of Dance	Dimitri CHAMBLAS
88	Dean School Film & Video	Abigail SEVERENCE
88	Dean School of Theater	Travis PRESTON
26	Executive Director Communications	Vacant
07	Exec Director Admissions/Enrollment	Steve CASTLES
37	Director of Financial Aid	Vacant
29	Director Alumni & Family Engagement	Harmony FREDERICK
22	Title IX/Dir Cmty Rights/Respons	Dionne SIMMONS
13	VP Institute Technology/CTO	Allan CHEN
101	Dir of Governance & Board Relations	Kiara BROWN
43	Director of Legal Affairs	Vacant
100	Chief of Staff	Chebon MARSHALL

California Institute of Arts & Technology (J)

2820 Camino Del Rio South, Ste 100,
San Diego CA 92108

County: San Diego — Identification: 667289
Unit ID: 490285
Telephone: (877) 559-3621 — Carnegie Class: Spec 2-yr-Tech
FAX Number: N/A — Calendar System: Other
URL: www.ciat.edu
Established: 2008 — Annual Undergrad Tuition & Fees: $15,390
Enrollment: 332 — Coed
Affiliation or Control: Proprietary — IRS Status: Proprietary
Highest Offering: Associate Degree
Accreditation: **CNCE**

01	President	Jamie DOYLE
05	Dean of Education	Melissa KINGSTON
11	Vice President for Compliance	Claire PARK
06	Registrar	Ed BRANCHEAU
26	Director of Marketing	Kirsten BARRERA
13	IT Director	Bashar QOPI

California Institute of Integral Studies (A)

1453 Mission Street, 4th Floor,
San Francisco CA 94103-2557

County: San Francisco
FICE Identification: 012154
Unit ID: 110316
Telephone: (415) 575-6100
Carnegie Class: DU-Mod
FAX Number: (415) 575-1264
Calendar System: Semester
URL: www.ciis.edu
Established: 1968
Annual Undergrad Tuition & Fees: N/A
Enrollment: 1,530
Coed
Affiliation or Control: Independent Non-Profit
IRS Status: 501(c)3
Highest Offering: Doctorate
Accreditation: WC, ACUP

01	President	Dr. Judie G. WEXLER
05	Provost	Dr. Kathy LITTLES
10	Controller	Ms. Tina O'GRADY
111	Vice President of Advancement	Ms. Jillian ELLIOT
32	Dean of Students	Ms. Yunny YIP
100	Chief of Staff	Dr. Richard BUGGS
20	Associate Provost	Ms. Michelle ENG
07	Director of Admissions	Ms. Ellen DURST
06	Registrar	Mr. Dan GURLER
26	Director of Communications	Ms. Lisa DENENMARK
37	Financial Aid Coordinator	Ms. Jennifer GRUCZELAK
18	Associate Director of Operations	Ms. Monica MUNJAL
04	Administrative Asst to President	Ms. Susan SORIANO
09	Director of Institutional Research	Ms. Lael FON
28	Director of Diversity	Ms. Rachel BRYANT
15	Human Resources Supervisor	Mr. Robert CROUCH

California Institute of Technology (B)

1200 E California Boulevard, Pasadena CA 91125-0001

County: Los Angeles
FICE Identification: 001131
Unit ID: 110404
Telephone: (626) 395-6811
Carnegie Class: DU-Highest
FAX Number: (626) 795-1547
Calendar System: Trimester
URL: www.caltech.edu
Established: 1891
Annual Undergrad Tuition & Fees: $56,862
Enrollment: 2,240
Coed
Affiliation or Control: Independent Non-Profit
IRS Status: 501(c)3
Highest Offering: Doctorate
Accreditation: WC

01	President	Dr. Thomas F. ROSENBAUM
101	Board Secretary	Ms. Cathy A. LIGHT
05	Provost	Dr. David A. TIRRELL
88	Vice President/Director JPL	Dr. Laurie LESHIN
10	VP of Admin/Chief Financial Officer	Ms. Karen SISSON
21	AVP for Finance & Treasurer	Ms. Sharon E. PATTERSON
111	VP for Advancement & Alumni Rels	Mr. Dexter F. BAILEY, JR.
45	VP for Strategy Implementation	Dr. Diana JERGOVIC
32	Vice President Student Affairs	Dr. Kevin M. GILMARTIN
43	General Counsel	Ms. Jennifer T. LUM
04	Asst Board Secretary/Sr Director	Ms. Debbie RODDAY
28	AVP of DEI & Assessment	Dr. Lindsey E. MALCOM-PIQUEUX
20	Vice Provost	Dr. Michelle EFFROS
20	Vice Provost	Dr. Kaushik BHATTACHARYA
15	Assoc Vice Pres Human Resources	Ms. Julia M. MCCALLIN
110	Assoc Vice President Development	Ms. Michelle R. CLARK
112	AVP for Campaigns	Ms. Diane M. BINNEY
86	External Relations Officer	Mr. Ken HARGREAVES
26	Chief Strat Communications Officer	Ms. Shayna CHABNER
81	Chair Biology & Biological Engr Div	Dr. Richard M. MURRAY
81	Chair Chemistry & Chemical Engr Div	Dr. Dennis A. DOUGHERTY
54	Chair Engr & Applied Science Div	Dr. Harry A. ATWATER
65	Chair Geology/Planet Science Div	Dr. John P. GROTZINGER
79	Chair Humanities/Social Science Div	Dr. Tracy DENNISON
81	Chair Physics/Math/Astro Division	Dr. Fiona HARRISON
06	Registrar	Ms. Christy SALINAS
84	AVP Stdnt Affs/Enroll/Career Svcs	Mr. Jarrid WHITNEY
08	University Librarian	Ms. Kara M. WHATLEY
13	Chief Information Officer	Mr. Jin CHANG
18	AVP for Facilities	Mr. David KANG
19	Chief of Campus Sec & Parking	Mr. Hampton CANTRELL
16	Exec Director of Human Resources	Ms. Tara KRUCKEBERG
23	Director Health Services	Dr. John Y. TSAI
25	Assoc VP of Research Admin	Dr. Richard P. SELIGMAN
117	Assoc VP Audit Svcs & Inst Comp	Ms. Pamela D. KOYZIS
29	AVP Alumni Rels/Exec Dir Alum Assn	Mr. Ralph AMOS
37	Director Financial Aid	Ms. Malina A. CHANG
109	AVP for Student Affairs Operations	Mr. Dimitris SAKELLARIOU
35	AVP Stdnt Affs & Residential Exper	Ms. Felicia HUNT
36	Director Career Development	Ms. Claire C. RALPH
40	Manager Bookstore	Ms. Karyn SEIXAS
41	Dir Athletics & Physical Education	Ms. Betsy MITCHELL
58	Dean of Graduate Studies	Mr. David C. CHAN
85	Assoc Dir International Student Pgm	Ms. Laura FLOWER KIM
96	Dir Purchasing & Payment Services	Ms. Tina LOWENTHAL
102	Director Foundation Relations	Ms. Nelly KHIDEKEL
104	Dir Fellowshp Advising/Study Abroad	Ms. Lauren B. STOLPER

38	AVP for Student Wellness	Vacant
39	Exec Dir Student Auxiliary Services	Ms. Maria A. KATSAS

California Intercontinental University (C)

2601 Main Street, Ste 250, Irvine CA 92614

County: Orange
Identification: 666670
Unit ID: 485546
Telephone: (866) 687-2258
Carnegie Class: DU-Mod
FAX Number: (949) 861-9431
Calendar System: Other
URL: www.caluniversity.edu
Established: 2003
Annual Undergrad Tuition & Fees: $10,805
Enrollment: 537
Coed
Affiliation or Control: Proprietary
IRS Status: Proprietary
Highest Offering: Doctorate
Accreditation: DEAC

01	Campus President	Mr. Richard MADRIGAL
06	Dir Academic Admin/Registrar	Ms. Gina BORELLI
05	Dean of Academics	Dr. Robert NEELY
07	Director of Admissions	Mr. Mike CRUZ
10	Chief Financial/Business Officer	Ms. Robyn FOURNIER
11	Director of Operations	Mr. David RODRIGUEZ

California Jazz Conservatory (D)

2087 Addison Street, Berkeley CA 94704

County: Alameda
Identification: 667217
Unit ID: 486488
Telephone: (510) 845-5373
Carnegie Class: Spec-4-yr-Arts
FAX Number: (510) 841-5373
Calendar System: Semester
URL: www.cjc.edu
Established: 2009
Annual Undergrad Tuition & Fees: $21,100
Enrollment: 35
Coed
Affiliation or Control: Independent Non-Profit
IRS Status: 501(c)3
Highest Offering: Master's
Accreditation: MUS

01	President	Susan MUSCARELLA
05	Dean of Instruction	Jeff DENSON
64	Director Jazz School at CJC	Rob EWING
11	Director of Operation	Max HODES
08	Head Librarian	Jayn PETTINGILL
06	Registrar	Tom WEEKS
37	Director of Financial Aid	Karen SHEPHERD
26	Director of Marketing/Public Rels	Paul FINGEROTE
10	Director of Finance	Tom LOW

California Lutheran University (E)

60 W Olsen Road, Thousand Oaks CA 91360-2787

County: Ventura
FICE Identification: 001133
Unit ID: 110413
Telephone: (805) 492-2411
Carnegie Class: Masters/L
FAX Number: (805) 493-3513
Calendar System: Semester
URL: www.callutheran.edu
Established: 1959
Annual Undergrad Tuition & Fees: $45,982
Enrollment: 4,027
Coed
Affiliation or Control: Evangelical Lutheran Church In America
IRS Status: 501(c)3
Highest Offering: Doctorate
Accreditation: WC, ACBSP, CLPSY, THEOL

01	President	Dr. Lori E. VARLOTTA
05	Provost/Vice Pres Academic Affairs	Dr. Leanne NEILSON
111	Vice Pres University Advancement	Dr. Regina BIDDINGS-MURO
10	Vice Pres Admin/Finance/Treasurer	Ms. Karen DAVIS
32	Vice Pres Stdnt Life/Dean of Stdnts	Ms. Melinda ROPER
84	VP Enrollment Mgmt/Student Success	Dr. Matthew WARD
13	Chief Information Officer	Mr. Zareh MARSELIAN
18	Assoc Vice Pres Facilities	Mr. Ryan VAN OMMEREN
100	Chief of Staff	Vacant
49	Dean College Arts & Sciences	Dr. Timothy HENGST
53	Dean of School of Education	Dr. Michael HILLIS
50	Dean of School of Management	Dr. Gerhard APFELTHALER
83	Dean Grad School of Psychology	Dr. Rick HOLIGROCKI
15	Asst VP for Human Resources	Ms. Patricia PARHAM
06	Assoc Prov Academic Svcs/Registrar	Ms. Maria KOHNKE
42	University Pastor	Rev. Scott ADAMS
42	Vice President Mission and Identity	Rev. Melissa MAXWELL-DOHERTY
41	Director of Athletics	Ms. Holly ROEPKE
107	Dean Sch for Profess/Cont Studies	Dr. Lisa BUONO
36	Director of Career Services	Ms. Cindy LEWIS
114	Exec Dir Budget/Financial Planning	Vacant
29	Dir Alumni and Family Relations	Ms. Rachel RONNING LINDGREN
38	Director Counseling Services	Vacant
19	Director Security/Safety	Mr. David HILKE
07	Dean of Undergrad Admissions	Mr. Falone SERNA
09	Assoc Provost Educ Effectiveness	Dr. Taiwo ANDE
37	Director of Financial Aid	Ms. Teresa POTTS
104	Asst Director Ofc of Educ Abroad	Dr. Matthew YATES
39	Asst Dean of Stdnts/Dir of Res Life	Dr. Christine PAUL
23	Director of Health Services	Mr. Saul MILLER
101	Mgr Pres Affairs/Board Relations	Ms. Ana GORMAN
44	Sr Director Annual Giving	Ms. Michelle SPURGEON
28	VP Talent/Culture & Diversity	Ms. Cristallea BUCHANAN
43	General Counsel	Mr. Thomas KNUDSEN

California Miramar University (F)

3550 Camino Del Rio N. Suite 208, San Diego CA 92108

County: San Diego
Identification: 666713
Unit ID: 480781
Telephone: (858) 653-3000
Carnegie Class: Spec-4-yr-Bus
FAX Number: (858) 653-6786
Calendar System: Other
URL: www.calmu.edu
Established: 2005
Annual Undergrad Tuition & Fees: $9,994
Enrollment: 174
Coed
Affiliation or Control: Proprietary
IRS Status: Proprietary
Highest Offering: Doctorate
Accreditation: DEAC

01	President/CEO	Bryan WALKER
05	Dean Academic Affairs	Bijan ZAYER
10	Chief Financial Officer	Jack THRIFT
07	International Admissions Director	Carol KULIS
06	Registrar	Marcelo DIFINI
37	Director Student Financial Aid	Dune TRINN
41	Athletic Director	Chris SHADE
13	Chief Information Officer	Farnaz GORJIAN

California Northstate University (G)

9700 West Taron Dr, Elk Grove CA 95757

County: Sacramento
Identification: 667020
Telephone: (916) 686-7400
Carnegie Class: Not Classified
FAX Number: (916) 686-8143
Calendar System: Semester
URL: www.cnsu.edu
Established: 2008
Annual Undergrad Tuition & Fees: N/A
Enrollment: N/A
Coed
Affiliation or Control: Independent Non-Profit
IRS Status: 501(c)3
Highest Offering: Doctorate
Accreditation: WC, CLPSY, DENT, #MED, PHAR

01	President	Dr. Alvin CHEUNG
05	VP Academic Affairs	Dr. Catherine YANG
63	VP Med Affs/Dean Col of Medicine	Dr. Joseph SILVA
10	VP of Finance/CFO	Ms. Shoua XIONG
11	VP of University Operations	Mr. Todd GALLAGHER
108	VP of Inst Rsrch/Quality/Assessment	Dr. Karen MCCLENDON
32	VP for Admissions & Student Service	Dr. Xiaodong FENG
43	Legal Counsel	Vacant
67	Dean of Pharmacy	Dr. Xiaodong FENG
08	Director of Library Resources	Mr. Scott MINOR
06	Registrar	Ms. Michelle WALKER
07	Asst Dean Admissions/Student Affs	Mr. Mark ETTENSOHN
76	Dean of Health Sciences	Dr. Heather BROWN

California Preparatory College (H)

1250 E. Cooley Drive, Colton CA 92324

County: San Bernardino
Identification: 667398
Telephone: (909) 370-4800
Carnegie Class: Not Classified
FAX Number: N/A
Calendar System: Semester
URL: www.calprepcollege.com
Established: 2007
Annual Undergrad Tuition & Fees: N/A
Enrollment: N/A
Coed
Affiliation or Control: Independent Non-Profit
IRS Status: 501(c)3
Highest Offering: Associate Degree
Accreditation: WJ

01	President/CEO	Gene EDELBACH
05	Academic Vice President	Dr. Jamie BIRD
32	Assoc Vice Pres for Student Life	Manual ALAMO, JR.

California Southern University (I)

3330 Harbor Boulevard, Costa Mesa CA 92626

Telephone: (800) 477-2254
Identification: 666770
Accreditation: &HLC, ACBSP, NURSE

*The California State University System Office (J)

401 Golden Shore, Long Beach CA 90802-4210

County: Los Angeles
FICE Identification: 001136
Unit ID: 110501
Telephone: (562) 951-4000
Carnegie Class: N/A
FAX Number: (562) 951-4986
URL: www.calstate.edu

01	Interim Chancellor	Dr. Jolene KOESTER
05	Exec VC Acad/Stdnt Affairs	Dr. Sylvia A. ALVA
10	Exec Vice Chancellor & CFO	Mr. Steve RELYEA
15	Vice Chancellor Human Resources	Ms. Evelyn NAZARIO
43	Exec Vice Chanc/General Counsel	Mr. Andrew JONES
116	Vice Chanc & Chief Audit Officer	Mr. Vlad MARINESCU
100	Chief of Staff	Ms. Michelle KISS

*California Polytechnic State University-San Luis Obispo (K)

1 Grand Avenue, San Luis Obispo CA 93407-9000

County: San Luis Obispo
FICE Identification: 001143
Unit ID: 110422
Telephone: (805) 756-1111
Carnegie Class: Masters/L
FAX Number: (805) 756-5400
Calendar System: Quarter
URL: www.calpoly.edu
Established: 1901
Annual Undergrad Tuition & Fees (In-State): $10,071
Enrollment: 22,440
Coed

Affiliation or Control: State IRS Status: 501(c)3
Highest Offering: Master's
Accreditation: WC, ART, CAPRT, CONST, DIETD, DIETI, JOUR, LSAR, MUS, PLNG

02 President .... Dr. Jeffrey D. ARMSTRONG
100 AVP & Chief of Staff .... Ms. Jessica DARIN
05 Provost .... Dr. Cynthia JACKSON-ELMOORE
32 Vice President Student Affairs .... Dr. Keith HUMPHREY
10 Senior Vice Pres Admin & Finance .... Ms. Cynthia VILLA
41 Athletic Director .... Mr. Don OBERHELMAN
13 Vice President ITS & CIO .... Mr. Bill BRITTON
88 CEO Cal Poly Corporation .... Mr. Cody VANDORN
21 Associate Vice Pres Financial Svcs .... Ms. Angela KRAETSCH
26 Chief Communications Officer .... Mr. Chris MURPHY
18 AVP Fac Mgmt & Development .... Mr. Mike MCCORMICK
39 AVP Stdnt Affs/Exec Dir of UH .... Dr. Jo CAMPBELL
15 Vice President University Personnel .... Dr. Al LIDDICOAT
30 Vice President for Univ Development .... Mr. Zachary K. SMITH
20 Assoc Vice Provost Acad Affairs .... Dr. Bruno GIBERTI
07 VP Strategic Enrollment Management .... Mr. Terrance HARRIS
84 Interim Dir Enrollment Plng & Mgmt .... Dr. Joseph BORZELLINO
88 Dir Ctr Teaching/Learning & Tech .... Mr. Patrick O'SULLIVAN
29 Exec Dir Alumni Engagement .... Ms. Amanda MCADAMS
19 Asst VP Pub Safety/Chf of Police .... Chief George HUGHES
06 University Registrar .... Mr. Cem SUNATA
28 Interim VP Diversity & Inclusion .... Dr. Denise ISOM
22 Asst VP Civil Rights and Compliance .... Ms. Maren HUFTON
23 AVP Health & Well Being .... Dr. Tina HADAWAY-MELLIS
38 Director of Counseling Services .... Dr. Andrea LAWSON
35 ASI Executive Director .... Ms. Michelle CRAWFORD
14 Deputy Chief Information Officer .... Mr. Ryan MATTESON
35 Dean of Students .... Dr. Joy M. PEDERSEN
103 AVP Corp Engagement & Industry .... Mr. Jim DUNNING
47 Dean Agriculture/Food & Env Sci .... Dr. Andrew THULIN
48 Dean Architect/Environmental Design .... Ms. Christine THEODOROPOULOS
50 Dean College of Business .... Dr. Damon FLEMMING
54 Dean College of Engineering .... Dr. Amy FLEISCHER
49 Dean College of Liberal Arts .... Dr. Philip J. WILLIAMS
81 Dean Science & Mathematics .... Dr. Dean WENDT
51 Interim Dean of Extended Education .... Dr. J. Kevin TAYLOR
08 Dean of Library Services .... Ms. Adriana POPESCU
58 Interim Dean of Graduate Educ .... Dr. Amanda LATHROP
53 Director School of Education .... Dr. J. Kevin TAYLOR
96 Asst VP Strat Business Sup Svcs .... Mr. Dru ZACHMEYER
37 Exec Director Fin Aid/Scholarship .... Ms. Gerrie HATTEN
36 Exec Director Career Services .... Vacant
09 Exec Director Inst Research .... Mr. Mauricio SAAVEDRA
121 Asst Vice Prov Univ Advising .... Ms. Beth MERRITT MILLER
104 Asst Vice Provost Intl Programs .... Ms. Caroline VANDERKAR
92 Director Honors Program .... Dr. Jasna JOVANOVIC
04 Executive Asst to President .... Ms. Barbara RISCHE
25 AVP for Research Admin .... Ms. Amy VELASCO
86 Director of Government Relations .... Mr. Justin WELLNER
108 Director Academic Assessment .... Dr. Michael NGUYEN
108 Dir Stdt Affs Assessment & Rsrch .... Dr. Kevin GRANT
44 Sr Director Planned Giving .... Ms. Allie BURNETT

*California State Polytechnic University-Humboldt (A)

1 Harpst Street, Arcata CA 95521-8222
County: Humboldt FICE Identification: 001149
Unit ID: 115755
Telephone: (707) 826-3011 Carnegie Class: Masters/L
FAX Number: (707) 826-5555 Calendar System: Semester
URL: www.humboldt.edu
Established: 1913 Annual Undergrad Tuition & Fees (In-State): $7,858
Enrollment: 6,612 Coed
Affiliation or Control: State IRS Status: 501(c)3
Highest Offering: Master's
Accreditation: WC, ART, IACBE, MUS, SW

02 President .... Dr. Tom JACKSON, JR.
100 Chief of Staff .... Mr. Timothy DOWNS
05 Provost/VP Academic Affairs .... Dr. Jenn CAPPS
20 AVP Academic Programs .... Dr. Carmen BUSTOS-WORKS
32 VP Student Success/Enrollment Mgmt .... Dr. Eboni FORD TURBOW
10 Vice Pres Admin & Finance .... Ms. Sherie GORDON
111 VP of University Advancement .... Mr. Frank WHITLATCH
15 AVP Human Resources .... Mr. Bruce CURL
88 AVP Development .... Ms. Deborah RICE
26 Sr Communication Officer .... Ms. Aileen YOO
18 Planning Director Facilities Mgmt .... Mr. Michael FISHER
84 Director of Enrollment Management .... Vacant
114 Director University Budget Office .... Ms. Amber BLAKESLEE
88 Director of Academic Resources .... Vacant
06 Registrar .... Ms. Jennifer ROBINSON
07 Director of Admissions .... Mr. Pedro MARTINEZ
08 Dean of Library .... Dr. Cyril OBERLANDER
44 Annual Giving Coordinator .... Ms. Marie FORREST-MURRAY
19 Chief of University Police .... Mr. Peter CRESS
41 Athletic Director .... Mr. Cooper JONES
121 AVP Student Success .... Dr. Stephen ST. ONGE
13 Chief Information Officer .... Ms. Bethany RIZZARDI
36 Director Career Devel Center .... Ms. Kathy THORNHILL
28 Diversity Officer .... Dr. Elavie NDURA
46 Executive Director Sponsored Pgms .... Ms. Kacie FLYNN
104 Study Abroad Coordinator .... Ms. Megan MEFFORD
35 Dean of Students .... Dr. Eboni TURNBOW
37 Director Student Financial Aid .... Ms. Peggy METZGER

96 Director of Contracts & Procurement .... Ms. Tawny FLEMING
90 Director ITS User Support .... Mr. Breck ROBINSON
09 Director Institutional Research .... Mr. Michael S. LE
23 Director Health/Counseling .... Vacant
38 Director Counseling & Psych Svcs .... Dr. Jennifer SANFORD
56 Dean of eLearning & Ext Education .... Dr. Cyril OBERLANDER
79 Dean Col Arts/Humanities/Soc Sci .... Dr. Jeff CRANE
107 Dean College Professional Studies .... Dr. Shawna YOUNG
65 Dean Col Natural Resources/Science .... Dr. Eric RIGGS
21 Controller .... Ms. Lynne SANDSTROM
06 Registrar eLearning & Ext Educ .... Ms. Deserie DONAE
105 Web Manager .... Mr. Matt HODGSON
29 Director Alumni Relations .... Ms. Stephanie LANE
04 Administrative Asst to President .... Ms. Paula PETERSEN
117 Dir of Risk Management & Safety .... Ms. Cris KOCZERA
16 AVP Faculty Affairs .... Dr. Simone ALOISIO
122 Student Life Coordinator-Greek Life .... Ms. Molly KRESL

*California State Polytechnic University-Pomona (B)

3801 W Temple Avenue, Pomona CA 91768-2557
County: Los Angeles FICE Identification: 001144
Unit ID: 110529
Telephone: (909) 869-7659 Carnegie Class: Masters/L
FAX Number: (909) 869-4535 Calendar System: Semester
URL: www.cpp.edu
Established: 1938 Annual Undergrad Tuition & Fees (In-State): $7,438
Enrollment: 30,014 Coed
Affiliation or Control: State IRS Status: 501(c)3
Highest Offering: Master's
Accreditation: WC, ACPHA, ART, CEA, CIDA, DIETD, DIETI, LSAR, MUS, NAEYC, PLNG, SPAA

02 President .... Dr. Soraya M. COLEY
05 Provost/VP Academic Affairs .... Dr. Jennifer L. BROWN
32 VP Student Affairs .... Ms. Christina GONZALES
111 VP University Advancement .... Mr. Daniel MONTPLAISIR
10 VP Administration and Finance/CFO .... Ms. Ysabel D. TRINIDAD
20 Assoc Provost Academic Planning .... Vacant
18 Sr AVP Facilities Planning & Mgmt .... Mr. Aaron KLEMM
35 AVP & Dean of Students .... Dr. Jonathan GRADY
84 Sr AVP Enrollment Services .... Ms. Jessica M. WAGONER
88 Exec Asst to the Provost .... Ms. Marissa M. MARTINEZ
46 AVP Research/Innovation/Econ Dev .... Dr. Craig LAMUNYON
26 Sr AVP for Strategic Communication .... Mr. Amon RAPPAPORT
21 Interim Assoc VP Finance/Admin .... Ms. Michelle D. CARDONA
35 AVP Student Affairs .... Dr. Megan M. STANG
31 Pres Assoc Cmty/Campus Partnership .... Dr. Reginald S. BLAYLOCK
13 Vice President IT & CIO .... Mr. John W. MCGUTHRY
09 Exec Dir Inst Rsrch/Plng/Analytics .... Ms. Jeanette G. BAEZ
15 AVP for Employee Org/Dev/Advance .... Ms. Kimberly ALLAIN
100 Chief of Staff .... Ms. Nicole A. HAWKES
04 Director of Administration .... Ms. Francine M. RAMIREZ
47 Interim Dean College of Agriculture .... Dr. Martin SANCHO-MADRIZ
49 Int Dean Col Letters/Arts/Soc Sci .... Dr. David HORNER
50 Dean Col of Business Admin .... Dr. Erik ROLLAND
54 Dean College of Engineering .... Dr. Alison A. BASKI
48 Dean Col Environmental Design .... Dr. Mary Anne AKERS
88 Int Dean Col of Hospitality Mgmt .... Dr. Margie JONES
81 Dean College of Science .... Dr. Alison BASKI
53 Int Dean Col Educ/Integrat Studies .... Dr. Hend GILLI-ELEWY
30 Assoc VP for Development .... Mr. Douglas NELSON
08 Dean University Library .... Ms. Pat HAWTHORNE
41 Director of Athletics .... Mr. Brian R. SWANSON
86 Assoc VP Govt & External Affairs .... Ms. Frances TEVES
19 Interim Chief of Police .... Mr. Erik MUNZENMAIER
88 Exec Dir Acad Rsrch & Acad Resource .... Ms. Lisa M. ROTUNNI
37 Dir Financial Aid/Scholarships .... Ms. Jeannette L. PHILLIPS
06 Registrar .... Mr. Daniel A. PARKS
88 Asst VP Outreach & Educ Partnernshp .... Mr. Ronald WHITENHILL
85 Int Dean College Prof & Global Educ .... Dr. Richard NAVARRO
28 Pres Assoc Inclus Excell/Diversity .... Vacant
29 Exec Dir Alumni/External Affairs .... Ms. Melissa RIORDAN
39 Int Exec Dir & Dir Residence Life .... Mr. Reyes LUNA
07 Director of Admissions .... Mr. Brandon TUCK
102 Director Corporate Relations .... Mr. David PORGES

*California State University-Bakersfield (C)

9001 Stockdale Highway, Bakersfield CA 93311-1022
County: Kern FICE Identification: 007993
Unit ID: 110486
Telephone: (661) 654-2782 Carnegie Class: Masters/L
FAX Number: (661) 654-3194 Calendar System: Semester
URL: www.csub.edu
Established: 1965 Annual Undergrad Tuition & Fees (In-State): $7,498
Enrollment: 11,745 Coed
Affiliation or Control: State IRS Status: 501(c)3
Highest Offering: Doctorate
Accreditation: WC, MUS, NURSE, SPAA, SW

02 President .... Dr. Lynnette ZELEZNY
100 Chief of Staff to the President .... Dr. Kristen WATSON
04 Admin Asst to the President .... Ms. Valerie STROM
05 Provost/VP Academic Affairs .... Dr. Vernon HARPER
10 Vice Pres Business/Admin Services .... Mr. Thom DAVIS
32 Vice President Student Affairs .... Dr. Thomas WALLACE
111 Interim VP University Advancement .... Mr. Heath NIEMEYER
20 Associate VP Faculty Affairs .... Dr. Debbie BOSCHINI
84 Assoc VP Enrollment Mgmt .... Dr. Dwayne CANTRELL
20 Assoc VP for Academic Affairs .... Dr. Debra JACKSON
85 Director of International Students .... Ms. Sonia SILVA
15 AVP Human Res/Administrative Svcs .... Ms. Lori BLODORN
13 AVP & Chief Information Officer .... Mr. Faust GORHAM
88 Spec Asst to Provost Academic Aff .... Ms. Leslie WILLIAMS
21 AVP & Chief Accounting Officer .... Ms. Queen KING
114 AVP & Chief Budget Officer .... Ms. Natasha HAYES
88 AVP Capital Planning & Design .... Mr. Joseph HEDGES
09 Asst VP Inst Rsrch/Plng/Assess .... Ms. Monica MALHOTRA
25 Interim AVP Grants/Resources .... Dr. Isabel SUMAYA
124 Assoc VP Student Affairs & Services .... Dr. Markel QUARLES
12 Dean CSUB Antelope Valley .... Dr. Elizabeth ADAMS
50 Interim Dean Business/Public Admin .... Dr. John STARK
83 Dean Social Sciences/Education .... Dr. James RODRIGUEZ
79 Dean Arts & Humanities .... Dr. Robert FRAKES
81 Int Dean Natural Sciences/Math/Eng .... Dr. Todd MCBRIDE
56 Dean Extended Educ/Global Outreach .... Dr. Mark NOVAK
104 Director International Success .... Ms. Yuri SAKAMAKI
88 Dir of Acad Opers & Support .... Ms. Lisa ZUZARTE
08 Dean University Library .... Ms. Sandra BOZARTH
06 University Registrar .... Ms. Jennifer MCCUNE
07 Director Admissions & Records .... Ms. Jennifer MCCUNE
29 Director Alumni Engagement .... Ms. Sarah HENDRICK
41 Interim Director of Athletics .... Ms. Cindy GOODMON
36 Dir for Career Educ/Cmty Engagement .... Ms. Katrina GILMORE
96 Asst VP for Business Services .... Mr. Michael CHAVEZ
38 Counseling Coordinator .... Ms. Janet MILLAR
37 Director Financial Aid .... Mr. Chad MORRIS
92 Director CSUB Honors Program .... Dr. Jacquelyn KEGLEY
39 Director Housing & Residential Life .... Ms. Crystal BECKS
117 Director Safety/Risk/Sustainability .... Mr. Tim RIDLEY
22 Dir Svcs Students w/Disabilities .... Ms. Janice CLAUSEN
23 Asst Director Health Services .... Ms. Erika DELAMAR
30 Director of Development .... Ms. Lauren FALK
88 Director Outreach Services .... Mr. Darius RIGGINS
19 Chief University Police .... Chief Marty WILLIAMSON
109 Director of Food Services .... Mr. Owen SMITH
18 Facilities Manager .... Mr. Scott WELLS
40 Bookstore Manager .... Mr. Richard SALCEDO
26 Director of Marketing & Comm .... Dr. Esra HASHEM
28 Chief Diversity Ofcr & Pres Asst .... Ms. Claudia CATOTA
44 Director Annual Giving/Stewardship .... Mr. Eric WEIS
27 Public Affairs Specialist .... Mr. Aaron WAN
22 Dir Equity/Inclusion/Compliance .... Mr. Marcus BROWN
102 Dir Corporate & Foundation Rels .... Ms. Heather PENNELLA
43 University Counsel .... Mr. Ronnie GOMEZ
122 VP Student Affairs & Centered Ent .... Mr. Emile (EJ) CALLAHAN

*California State University-Channel Islands (D)

1 University Drive, Camarillo CA 93012-8599
County: Ventura FICE Identification: 039803
Unit ID: 441937
Telephone: (805) 437-8400 Carnegie Class: Masters/S
FAX Number: (805) 437-8414 Calendar System: Semester
URL: www.csuci.edu
Established: 2002 Annual Undergrad Tuition & Fees (In-District): $6,802
Enrollment: 7,446 Coed
Affiliation or Control: State/Local IRS Status: 501(c)3
Highest Offering: Master's
Accreditation: WC, ACBSP, NURSE

02 President .... Dr. Richard YAO
05 Provost .... Dr. Mitch AVILA
32 Interim VP Student Affairs .... Ms. Toni DEBONI
111 VP University Advancement .... Ms. Nichole IPACH
100 Interim Chief of Staff .... Dr. Kaia TOLLEFSON
49 Dean of School of Arts & Sciences .... Dr. Vandana KOHLI
50 Int Dean MVS School of Bus & Econ .... Dr. Susan ANDRZEJEWSKI
84 Associate VP Enrollment Management .... Mr. Hung D. DANG
53 Dean of School of Education .... Dr. Brian SEVIER
25 Director Sponsored Programs .... Mr. Scott PEREZ
104 Assoc VP/Dean International Program .... Dr. Osman OZTURGUT
08 Dean of Library .... Ms. Alicia VIRTUE
88 Chief Academic Budget Officer .... Mr. Kirk R. ENGLAND
20 Assoc VP Academic Programs .... Dr. Jennifer E. PERRY
88 Assoc Vice Provost Innovation .... Ms. Jill LEAFSTEDT
121 Assoc Vice Provost Student Success .... Dr. Amanda M. QUINTERO
88 University Ombuds Officer .... Mr. Mark PATTERSON
38 Director Counseling & Psychological .... Ms. Kirsten G. OLSON
15 Interim Assistant VP Administrative .... Ms. Laurie NICHOLS
86 Sr Dir Community & Govt Relations .... Ms. Celina ZACARIAS
30 Director of University Development .... Mr. Richard S. LEROY
110 Dir Advancement Operations .... Mr. Christopher ABE
88 Dir University Events & Spec Pgms .... Ms. Alisaa BLOUGH
29 Dir Development/Alumni Engagement .... Dr. Amanda CARPENTER
112 Director Planned & Major Gifts .... Ms. Grace G. ROBINSON
44 Dir Annual Giving & Special Gifts .... Ms. Eva C. GOMEZ
19 Chief of Police .... Mr. Michael MORRIS
22 Int Title IX Administrative Sp .... Ms. Renee FUENTES
116 University Internal Auditor .... Ms. Penny MATTHEWS
35 Associate VP & Dean of Students .... Ms. Toni DEBONI
39 AVP Housing/Residential Educ & ASI .... Ms. Cindy DERRICO
88 Exec Dir Admin & Strategic Ops .... Ms. Dorothy R. AYER
06 Associate Registrar .... Ms. Colleen FOREST
07 AVP/Dir of Admissions & Records .... Ms. Ginger REYES
108 Assoc VP for SA/ROISS .... Dr. Charles E. OSIRIS
26 Exec Dir Communication & Marketing .... Ms. Nancy GILL
37 Dir Financial Aid & Scholarships .... Ms. Sunshine GARCIA

18 AVP Facilities Services ... Mr. Thomas M. HUNT
114 University Budget Officer ... Ms. Barbara A. REX
13 Chief Information Officer ... Mr. James AUGUST
88 Director Strategic Operations ... Mr. Nathan E. BOWDEN
04 Presidential Aide ... Ms. Alanna TREJO

*California State University-Chico (A)

400 W First Street, Chico CA 95929-0001
County: Butte | FICE Identification: 001146
Unit ID: 110538
Telephone: (530) 898-6116 | Carnegie Class: Masters/L
FAX Number: (530) 898-6824 | Calendar System: Semester
URL: www.csuchico.edu
Established: 1887 | Annual Undergrad Tuition & Fees (In-State): $7,864
Enrollment: 16,746 | Coed
Affiliation or Control: State | IRS Status: 501(c)3
Highest Offering: Master's
Accreditation: WC, ART, CAPRT, CONST, DIETD, DIETI, JOUR, NURSE, SP, SPAA, SW, THEA

02 President ... Dr. Gayle E. HUTCHINSON
100 Chief of Staff ... Dr. Seema SEHRAWAT
05 Provost/Vice Pres Academic Affairs ... Dr. Debra S. LARSON
10 Vice Pres Business & Finance ... Ms. Ann SHERMAN
32 VP Student Affairs/Dean Students ... Dr. Isaac BRUNDAGE
111 Vice Pres University Advancement ... Mr. Ahmad BOURA
13 Vice Pres Information Technology ... Dr. Monique SENDZE
46 Assoc Vice Pres Research ... Vacant
84 Assoc Vice Pres Enroll Management ... Mr. Jerry P. ROSS
119 Chief Info Security Officer ... Mr. Chris WITTHANS
21 Assoc VP Financial Svcs/Univ Budget ... Ms. Stacie CORONA
15 Assoc Vice Pres Human Resources ... Ms. Sheryl WOODWARD
16 Assoc Vice Pres OAPL ... Dr. Mahalley ALLEN
47 Dean College of Agriculture ... Dr. Patricia STOCK
51 Dean Continuing Education ... Ms. Clare VAN NESS
72 Dean Col Engr/Comp Sci/Const Mgmt ... Dr. Blake WENTZ
83 Dean Col Behavior & Social Sci ... Dr. Eddie VELA
50 Dean College of Business ... Dr. Terence LAU
79 Dean College Humanities ... Dr. Tracy BUTTS
81 Dean College Natural Sciences ... Dr. David M. HASSENZAHL
60 Dean Coll Communication & Educ ... Dr. Angela TRETHEWEY
20 Dean Undergraduate Education ... Ms. Kate MCCARTHY
58 Dean Graduate Studies ... Dr. Sharon A. BARRIOS
08 Dean Library ... Dr. John WANG
26 Director Univ Public Engagement ... Mr. Stephen B. CUMMINS
29 Director Alumni Relations ... Mr. Jay R. FRIEDMAN
09 Director Inst Research ... Mr. Thomas C. ROSENOW
06 University Registrar ... Mr. Michael C. DILLS-ALLEN
07 Director of Admissions ... Mr. Serge DESIR, JR.
36 Director Career Center ... Ms. Megan ODOM
37 Director Financial Aid/Scholarships ... Mr. Kentiner DAVID
18 Dir of Ops/Facilities Mgmt Svcs ... Mr. Randy SOUTHALL
96 Director of Procurement ... Ms. Sara RUMIANO
92 Director Univ Honors Program ... Mr. Jason NICE
35 Dir Stdnt Conduct/Rights/Respon ... Vacant
28 Chief Diversity Officer ... Vacant
04 Executive Asst to President ... Ms. Jennifer DA SILVA
104 AVP Intl Educ/Global Engagement ... Ms. Jennifer GRUBER
25 Chico State Enterprises CEO ... Ms. Mary SIDNEY
109 Exec Director Associated Students ... Ms. Jamie C. CLYDE
23 Int Director Student Health Center ... Ms. Carol HUSTON
38 Director Counseling ... Dr. Francisca DUENAS
39 Assoc Director University Housing ... Ms. Corinne KNAPP
41 Athletic Director ... Ms. Anita S. BARKER
53 Director School of Education ... Ms. Rebecca JUSTESON
19 Chief of Police ... Vacant
22 Director of Labor Relations ... Mr. Dylan SAAKE
30 Director of Development ... Ms. Daria BOOTH
43 University Counsel ... Mr. Stephen SILVER
122 Pgm Coord-Fraternity/Sorority Life ... Ms. Lesley CARON

*California State University-Dominguez Hills (B)

1000 E Victoria Street, Carson CA 90747-0005
County: Los Angeles | FICE Identification: 001141
Unit ID: 110547
Telephone: (310) 243-3696 | Carnegie Class: Masters/L
FAX Number: N/A | Calendar System: Semester
URL: www.csudh.edu
Established: 1960 | Annual Undergrad Tuition & Fees (In-State): $6,941
Enrollment: 18,687 | Coed
Affiliation or Control: State | IRS Status: 501(c)3
Highest Offering: Master's
Accreditation: WC, JOUR, MLS, MUS, NURSE, OPE, OT, SPAA, SW, THEA

02 President ... Dr. Thomas A. PARHAM
05 Provost/VP Academic Affairs ... Dr. Michael SPAGNA
10 VP Administration/Finance ... Ms. Deborah WALLACE
32 Vice President Student Affairs ... Dr. William FRANKLIN
111 VP Univ Advancement ... Mr. Scott BARRETT
13 VP/Chief Information Officer ... Mr. Chris MANRIQUEZ
35 AVP Stdnt Life/Dean of Stdnts ... Mr. Matthew SMITH
84 AVP Enrollment Management ... Dr. Deborah BRANDON
100 Chief of Staff ... Ms. Deborah ROBERSON
15 Int AVP Human Resources ... Ms. Monica PONCE
07 Interim Director of Admissions ... Ms. Christina RIOS
37 Associate Dir of Financial Aid ... Ms. Angela PROVENCIO
06 University Registrar ... Mr. John HILL
04 Senior Exec Asst & Operations Admin ... Ms. Susan SANDERS
41 Athletic Director ... Ms. Dena FREEMAN-PATTON
122 Student Engage Coord-Greek Life ... Ms. Christina IBARRA

*California State University-East Bay (C)

25800 Carlos Bee Boulevard, Hayward CA 94542-3001
County: Alameda | FICE Identification: 001138
Unit ID: 110574
Telephone: (510) 885-3000 | Carnegie Class: DU-Higher
FAX Number: N/A | Calendar System: Semester
URL: www.csueastbay.edu
Established: 1957 | Annual Undergrad Tuition & Fees (In-State): $6,890
Enrollment: 16,253 | Coed
Affiliation or Control: State | IRS Status: 501(c)3
Highest Offering: Doctorate
Accreditation: WC, MUS, NURSE, SP, SW

02 President ... Dr. Cathy SANDEEN
05 Provost/VP Academic Affairs ... Dr. Walt JACOBS
10 Vice Pres Admin & Finance/CFO ... Ms. Myeshia ARMSTRONG
111 Vice President Univ Advancement ... Ms. Evelyn BUCHANAN
32 Vice Pres Student Affairs ... Dr. Suzanne ESPINOZA
15 AVP Human Resources/Payroll Svcs ... Mr. Andre JOHNSON
84 Interim AVP Enrollment Management ... Ms. Angela SCHNEIDER
18 AVP Facilities Devel & Operations ... Ms. Winnie KWOFIE
41 AVP/Athletic Director ... Ms. Allison KERN
28 University Diversity Officer ... Ms. Kimberly BAKER-FLOWERS
100 Chief of Staff ... Mr. Derek AITKEN
49 Dean Col of Ltrs/Arts/Soc Sci ... Dr. Wendy NG
50 Interim Dean Col of Business/Econ ... Dr. Nancy MANGOLD
53 Dean Col of Educ/Allied Stds ... Dr. Robert WILLIAMS
81 Dean College of Science ... Dr. Jason SINGLEY
08 Dean of Libraries ... Dr. John WENZLER
13 CIO ... Dr. Jake HORNSBY
06 Interim Registrar ... Ms. Karen MUCCI
19 Chief University Police Department ... Mr. Mark FLORES
37 Director Student Financial Aid ... Ms. Sonia JETHANI
39 Dir Student Housing/Resident Life ... Mr. Mark ALMEIDA
43 Director Legal Services ... Ms. Shawna MCKEEVER
96 Director Procurement Services ... Mr. Jon MEWIN

*California State University-Fresno (D)

5200 N. Barton Avenue, Fresno CA 93740-8027
County: Fresno | FICE Identification: 001147
Unit ID: 110556
Telephone: (559) 278-4240 | Carnegie Class: DU-Higher
FAX Number: (559) 278-4715 | Calendar System: Semester
URL: www.csufresno.edu
Established: 1911 | Annual Undergrad Tuition & Fees (In-State): $6,643
Enrollment: 25,497 | Coed
Affiliation or Control: State | IRS Status: 501(c)3
Highest Offering: Doctorate
Accreditation: WC, AAQEP, ART, CAATE, CACREP, CAEPN, CAPRT, CIDA, CONST, DIETD, DIETI, MUS, NAIT, NURSE, PH, PTA, SP, SPAA, SW, THEA

02 President ... Dr. Saúl JIMÉNEZ-SANDOVAL
05 Provost/VP Academic Affairs ... Dr. Xuanning FU
10 VP Administration/CFO ... Dr. Deborah ADISHIAN-ASTONE
111 Vice Pres University Advancement ... Ms. Paula CASTADIO
32 VP Student Affs/Enroll Mgmt ... Dr. Carolyn COON
100 Chief of Staff ... Ms. Diana RALLS
43 General Counsel ... Mr. Darryl HAMM
26 AVP University Communications ... Ms. Lauren NICKERSON
09 Int Dir Institutional Effectiveness ... Dr. Yoshiko YAKAHASHI
15 AVP for Human Resources ... Ms. Marylou MENDOZA-MILLER
30 Assoc VP University Development ... Ms. Caty PEREZ
18 Associate Vice President Facilities ... Ms. Tinnah MEDINA
84 Assoc Vice Pres Enrollment Mgmt ... Ms. Malisa LEE
21 Assistant VP Financial Services ... Mr. John FUGATT
13 VP Info Tech/Chief Information Ofcr ... Ms. Bao JOHRI
20 Int Vice Provost ... Dr. Alam HASSON
51 Dean/AVP Continuing/Global Educ ... Dr. Scott MOORE
47 Dean Agricultural Science/Tech ... Dr. Dennis L. NEF
79 Int Dean of Arts & Humanities ... Dr. Honora CHAPMAN
50 Dean Craig School of Business ... Dr. Julie OLSON-BUCHANAN
53 Dean of Kremen School of Education ... Dr. Randy YERRICK
54 Dean of Engineering ... Dr. Ramakrishna NUNNA
76 Dean of Health/Human Services ... Dr. Denise SEABERT
83 Int Dean of Social Sciences ... Dr. Elizabeth LOWHAM
81 Dean of Science & Mathematics ... Dr. Christopher G. MEYER
97 Dean Undergraduate Studies ... Dr. Bernadette T. MUSCAT
08 Dean of Library Services ... Ms. Delritta HORNBUCKLE
58 Int Dean Research/Graduate Studies ... Dr. Joy GOTO
86 Exec Dir Government Relations ... Mr. Michael LUKENS
23 AVP of Student Health ... Dr. Janell MORILLO
19 Chief Police ... Mr. James WATSON
41 Director of Athletics ... Mr. Terrance TUMEY
37 Director of Financial Aid ... Ms. Kelly RUSSELL
29 Executive Director Alumni Relations ... Ms. Jacquelyn GLASENER
36 Int Dir Career Development Center ... Ms. Mary WILLIS
39 Director Univ Courtyard (Housing) ... Ms. Erin BOELE
96 Dir Procurement & Support Services ... Mr. Brian COTHAM
07 Director of Admissions/Recruitment ... Mr. Phong YANG
35 Int Assoc Dean Student Involvement ... Ms. Amy ALLEN
06 Registrar ... Ms. Laura YAGER
44 Director Annual Giving ... Ms. Patricia O'CONNOR
90 Director Academic Computing ... Dr. Brent AUERNHEIMER
38 Director Student Counseling ... Dr. Malia SHERMAN
112 Dir Donor Relations and Stewardship ... Ms. Breanne SCOGIN
12 Exec Dir CSUF Visalia Campus ... Dr. Luz GONZALEZ
14 Deputy Chief Information Officer ... Mr. Robert GUINN
16 Asst Exec Dir Aux Human Resources ... Ms. Nicole LANE
117 Manager Env Health/Safety/Risk Mgmt ... Ms. Lisa KAO

27 Dir Brand Strategy and Marketing ... Ms. Ashley ILIC
110 Exec Dir Advancement Services ... Ms. Leticia R. CANO
88 Dir Title IX and Clery Compliance .. Ms. Jamie PONTIUS-HOGAN
114 Manager Budget & Resource Planning ... Ms. Pam LEWIS
88 Dir of Advancement Operations ... Ms. Lori CLANTON

*California State University-Fullerton (E)

PO Box 34080, 800 N State Col Blvd, Fullerton CA 92831-3547
County: Orange | FICE Identification: 001137
Unit ID: 110565
Telephone: (657) 278-2011 | Carnegie Class: DU-Higher
FAX Number: (657) 278-2649 | Calendar System: Semester
URL: www.fullerton.edu
Established: 1957 | Annual Undergrad Tuition & Fees (In-State): $6,953
Enrollment: 42,051 | Coed
Affiliation or Control: State | IRS Status: 501(c)3
Highest Offering: Doctorate
Accreditation: WC, ANEST, ART, CAATE, CACREP, CAEPN, CSHSE, DANCE, IPSY, JOUR, MIDWF, MUS, NURSE, PH, SP, SPAA, SW, THEA

02 President ... Mr. Framroze (Fram) VIRJEE
100 Chief of Staff ... Ms. Danielle GARCIA
05 Provost & VP Academic Affairs ... Dr. Carolyn THOMAS
10 VP Admin & Finance/CFO ... Mr. Alexander PORTER
32 Vice President of Student Affairs ... Dr. Tonantzin OSEGUERA
111 VP University Advancement ... Mr. Greg SAKS
13 VP Info Tech/Chief Info Ofcr ... Mr. Amir DABIRIAN
15 VP of HR/Diversity & Inclusion ... Dr. David FORGUES
21 Director of Business Operations ... Mr. Robert SCIALDONE
16 COO HR/Diversity & Inclusion ... Ms. Tara GARCIA
43 University Counsel ... Ms. Catherine BARRAD
110 Assoc VP University Advancement ... Mr. Todd FRANDSEN
35 AVP Student Affairs ... Dr. Martha ENCISO
35 AVP Student Affairs ... Dr. Elizabeth ZAVALA-ACEVEZ
20 AVP Undergraduate Academic Programs ... Dr. Ed FINK
26 AVP Strategic Communications ... Ms. Ellen TREANOR
121 AVP Student Success ... Vacant
28 Int AVP Diversity/Inclusion/Equity ... Ms. Cecil CHIK
25 AVP Research and Sponsored Projects ... Dr. Binod TIWARI
12 AVP South County Ops/Initiatives ... Dr. Steve WALK
86 AVP Govt/ Community Relations ... Ms. Elva RUBALCAVA
16 AVP Human Resource Services ... Ms. Phenicia MCCULLOUGH
45 AVP for Resource Planning/ Budget ... Ms. Laleh GRAYLEE
88 Chief of Operations Stdnt Affs ... Ms. Chalea FORGUES
18 Int AVP Capital Planning/Fac Mgt ... Dr. Sarabdayal SINGH
29 AVP Alumni Relations ... Mr. Bill COLE
109 Exec Dir/CEO Auxiliary Svcs Corp ... Mr. Chuck KISSEL
08 Dean of the Library ... Dr. Emily BONNEY
07 Director of Admissions ... Vacant
36 Director Career Center ... Ms. Jennifer MOJARRO
40 Director Titan Shops ... Ms. Kimberly BALL
19 Chief University Police ... Mr. Carl JONES
37 Int Director Financial Aid ... Ms. Jessica BARCO
41 Director of Athletics ... Mr. James DONOVAN
96 Sr Director Contracts & Procurement ... Mr. Nelson NAGAI
35 Dean of Students ... Dr. Vincent VIGIL
94 Director Women's Center/Re-Entry ... Dr. Alyssa AVILA
88 Director Educational Partnerships ... Ms. Adriana BADILLO
39 Director Housing ... Mr. Larry MARTIN
89 Dir Univ Outreach/New Stdnt Pgm .Ms. Colleen A. MCDONOUGH
88 Dir Athletic Academic Services ... Ms. Meredith BASIL
88 Dir Center for Internship/Com Eng ... Ms. Dawn MACY
88 Dir Student Academic Services ... Dr. Rochelle WOODS
88 Dir Veteran Student Services ... Mr. Cameron COOK
38 Dir Counseling/Psych Svcs ... Mrs. Jaime SHEEHAN
14 AVP IT/Infrastructure Services ... Mr. Berhanu TADESSE
90 AVP IT/Academic Technology Svcs ... Mr. Willie PENG
51 AVP Extension/International Pgms ... Mr. Joe SHAPIRO
79 Dean Humanities/Social Sciences ... Dr. Sheryl FONTAINE
81 Dean Natural Sciences & Math ... Dr. Marie JOHNSON
50 Dean Mihaylo Col Business/Econ ... Mr. Sridhar SUNDARAM
83 Dean Health/Human Development ... Dr. Cindy GREENBERG
57 Interim Dean College of the Arts ... Mr. Arnold HOLLAND
53 Dean College of Education ... Dr. Lisa KIRTMAN
54 Dean Col Engineering & Comp Sci ... Dr. Susamma BARUA
60 Dean College of Communications ... Dr. Bey-Ling SHA
22 Title IX Coordinator ... Ms. Sarah BAUER
88 ASI Executive Director ... Dr. Dave EDWARDS
117 Executive Director Risk Mgmt ... Mr. John BEISNER
88 AVP Labor/Employee Relations ... Ms. Michelle TAPPER
88 University Controller ... Mr. Steven YIM
114 Dir of Acct Services & Fin Report ... Ms. Lynn GANAC
88 Director of Accounts Payable ... Ms. Mary Ann TORRES
113 Dir of Student Financial Services ... Ms. Pearl BOELTER
18 Director of Physical Plant ... Mr. Leonardo LOPEZ
88 Director of Construction ... Mr. Sarabdayal SINGH
88 Director of Planning and Design ... Mr. Emil ZORDILLA
88 Dir of Parking and Transportation ... Ms. Kristen JASKO
116 Dir of Audit Svcs & Coordination ... Ms. Cindy MERIDA
09 AVP Institutional Effectiveness ... Dr. Su SWARAT
20 COO Academic Affairs ... Mr. Mike STEELE
88 Exec Dir Academic Fin & Space Mgmt ... Ms. Alyssa ADAMSON
88 AVP Faculty Support Services ... Dr. Kristin STANG
04 Presidential Assistant ... Mrs. Sandra QUINTERO
06 Registrar ... Mr. Rob BODEEN
102 Director Foundation/Corporate Rels ... Ms. Lauren SIEVEN
104 Director Study Abroad ... Mr. Jack HOBSON
105 Director Web Services ... Mr. Mishu VU
106 Dir of Online Education/E-learning ... Ms. Shelli WYNANTS
112 Director Planned Giving ... Mr. Hart ROUSSEL
122 Coord Fraternity/Sorority Life ... Mr. Edwin ALARID

*California State University-Long Beach (A)

1250 Bellflower Boulevard, Long Beach CA 90840
County: Los Angeles FICE Identification: 001139
Unit ID: 110583
Telephone: (562) 985-4111 Carnegie Class: DU-Higher
FAX Number: (562) 985-5419 Calendar System: Semester
URL: www.csulb.edu
Established: 1949 Annual Undergrad Tuition & Fees (In-State): $6,834
Enrollment: 40,069 Coed
Affiliation or Control: State IRS Status: 501(c)3
Highest Offering: Doctorate
Accreditation: WC, AAFCS, ACPHA, ART, CAATE, CAPRT, CEA, CONST, DANCE, DIETD, DIETI, HSA, IPSY, JOUR, MUS, NURSE, PH, PTA, SP, SPAA, SW, THEA

02 President ..... Dr. Jane C. CONOLEY
05 Provost/Sr Vice Pres Academic Affs ... Dr. Karyn SCISSUM GUNN
11 Vice Pres Administration/Finance ..... Mr. Scott APEL
13 VP/Chief Information Officer ..... Dr. Min YAO
32 VP Student Affairs ..... Dr. Beth LESEN
30 Interim VP Univ Rels/Development ..... Mr. Jeff COOK
100 Chief of Staff ..... Mr. Chris FOWLER
10 Assoc VP Financial Management ..... Mr. Milton ORDONEZ
20 Assoc VP Undergraduate Studies ..... Dr. Kerry JOHNSON
23 Assoc Vice Pres Health & Wellness ..... Mr. Damian ZAVALA
104 AVP Intl Educ/Global Engagement ..... Dr. Jeet JOSHEE
18 AVP Facilities Services ..... Mr. Mark ZAKHOUR
58 Vice Provost/Dean Grad Studies ..... Dr. Jody CORMACK
20 Vice Provost Academic Planning ..... Dr. Dhushy SATHIANATHAN
46 AVP Univ Research/Economic Dev ..... Dr. Simon KIM
15 Interim AVP Human Resource Mgmt ..... Ms. Marita SWANSON
91 Assoc VP Academic Technology ..... Dr. Shariq AHMED
09 Director Institutional Research ..... Dr. Mahmoud ALBAWANEH
84 Asst VP Enrollment Services ..... Ms. Donna GREEN
14 Assoc VP Information Technology ..... Ms. Janet FOSTER
76 Dean College Health/Human Svcs ..... Dr. Monica LOUNSBERY
50 Dean College of Business ..... Dr. Michael SOLT
53 Interim Dean College of Education ..... Dr. Anna ORTIZ
54 Dean College of Engineering ..... Dr. Jinny RHEE
57 Acting Dean College of the Arts ..... Ms. Anne D'ZMURA
81 Dean College Natural Sciences/Math ..... Dr. Curtis BENNETT
49 Dean College of Liberal Arts ..... Dr. Deborah THIEN
51 Dean College Prof & Continuing Ed ..... Dr. Chris SWARAT
08 Interim Dean Library ..... Ms. Tracey MAYFIELD
06 University Registrar ..... Ms. Donna GREEN
39 Executive Dir Housing & Res Life ..... Mr. Corry COLONNA
16 Dir Staff Human Resources ..... Mr. Neil IACONO
41 Interim Director of Athletics ..... Mr. Ted KADOWAKI
07 Director of Admissions ..... Mr. Andrew WRIGHT
36 Dir Career Development Ctr ..... Ms. Erin BOOTH-CARO
23 Co-Director Health Services ..... Ms. Angela CONTE
23 Co-Director Health Services ..... Dr. Kimberly FODRAN
19 Chief University Police ..... Mr. John BROCKIE
38 Director Counseling/Psych Svcs ..... Ms. Amanda DE LOERA-MORALES
37 Interim Director Financial Aid ..... Ms. Donna GREEN
25 Senior Director Sponsored Programs ..... Ms. Maria REYES
102 Chief Op Ofcr/Rsrch Foundation ..... Dr. Brian NOWLIN
28 Director of Equity & Diversity ..... Ms. Larisa HAMADA
96 Director Procurement & Contracts ..... Mr. Michael PRUITT
109 49er Shops & ASI CFO ..... Mr. Gordon COPLEY
104 Director Education Abroad ..... Ms. Sharon OLSON
44 Director of Gift Planning ..... Ms. Sireth TORRES
26 AVP of University Relations ..... Mr. Christopher REESE
114 Assoc VP Budget & Univ Svcs ..... Ms. Kara PERKINS
88 Asst VP Administrative Services ..... Ms. Mishelle LAWS
20 Interim Assoc VP Faculty Affairs ..... Dr. Malcolm FINNEY
04 Deputy Chief of Staff ..... Ms. Coleen FOLLOWELL
108 Director Program Review/Assessment ..... Dr. Sharlene SAYEGH
22 Dir Affirmative Action/EEO ..... Ms. Larisa HAMADA
26 AVP Strategic Communications ..... Mr. Jeff COOK
116 Audit Liaison ..... Mr. Gene WOHLGEZOGEN
105 Director Web Services ..... Mr. Jesse SANTANA
86 Director Govt/Community Relations ..... Ms. Ricki BURGENER
29 Director Alumni Engagement ..... Ms. Noemi GUEVARA

*California State University-Los Angeles (B)

5151 State University Drive, Los Angeles CA 90032-8530
County: Los Angeles FICE Identification: 001140
Unit ID: 110592
Telephone: (323) 343-3000 Carnegie Class: Masters/L
FAX Number: (323) 343-2670 Calendar System: Semester
URL: www.calstatela.edu
Established: 1947 Annual Undergrad Tuition & Fees (In-State): $6,781
Enrollment: 26,745 Coed
Affiliation or Control: State IRS Status: 501(c)3
Highest Offering: Doctorate
Accreditation: WC, ABAI, ACAE, ART, CACREP, DIETD, MLS, MUS, NURSE, SP, SPAA, SW

02 President ..... Dr. William A. COVINO
11 Exec VP and Chief Operating Officer ..... Dr. Jose A. GOMEZ
05 Acting Provost/VP Academic Affairs ..... Dr. Jose A. GOMEZ
10 VP Administration & CFO ..... Dr. Joyce WILLIAMS
32 Vice President Student Life ..... Dr. Octavio VILLALPANDO
13 Chief Information Officer/AVP ITS ..... Ms. Chioma NDUBUISI
44 Vice Pres University Advancement ..... Mr. Robert AVALOS
84 Exec Director Enrollment Services ..... Dr. Margaret GARCIA
21 AVP Budget/Plng/Fiscal Compliance ..... Mr. John TCHENG
35 Int AVP Student Life/Dean Students ..... Ms. Danielle CHAMBERS
111 Assoc VP University Advancement ..... Vacant
46 AVP Research ..... Dr. Jeffrey UNDERWOOD
29 Exec Director Alumni Relations ..... Ms. Maria UBAGO
26 Assoc VP Comm/Public Affairs ..... Dr. Jocelyn STEWART
41 Exec Dir Intercollegiate Athletics ..... Dr. Daryl J. GROSS
83 Dean Natural & Social Sciences ..... Dr. Rene VELLANOWETH
88 Assoc Dean Natural/Social Sciences ..... Dr. Alison MCCURDY
08 Dean of the University Library ..... Mr. Carlos RODRIGUEZ
88 Assoc Dean of the Univ Library ..... Ms. Marla PEPPERS
06 University Registrar ..... Mr. Christopher COBB
58 Dean Graduate Studies ..... Dr. Karin A. ELLIOT BROWN
09 Asst VP Institutional Research ..... Dr. Sunny MOON
36 Dir Career Placement & Planning ..... Ms. Michelle LAVASZ
37 Director Student Financial Services ..... Ms. Tamie NGUYEN
23 Director Health Center ..... Ms. Grace CASTILLO-JOHNSON
39 Dir Housing Svcs/Residence Life ..... Mr. Leonard EDMOND
22 Director Equal Opportunity Pgm ..... Vacant
18 AVP Fac/Plng/Design & Construct ..... Ms. Barbara QUEEN
19 Chief of Police ..... Mr. Larry BOHANNON
15 AVP Human Resources Management ..... Ms. Susie VARELA
85 Director Intl Programs & Services ..... Vacant
43 University Counsel ..... Mr. Victor I. KING
07 Director Admissions & Recruitment ..... Mr. Vince LOPEZ
96 Director Procurement & Contracts ..... Vacant
28 Dir HR Equity/Div/Pol/Proc/Title IX ..... Ms. Mariel MULET
40 General Manager Bookstore ..... Ms. Elaine REED
20 Assoc Dean Undergrad Studies ..... Dr. Margaret GARCIA
49 Dean Arts & Letters ..... Dr. Stephen TRZASKOMA
88 Int Associate Dean Arts/Letters ..... Dr. Katherine WEISS
54 Int Dean Engr/Computer Science/Tech ..... Dr. Nancy WARTER-PEREZ
77 Assoc Dean Engr/Comp Sci/Tech ..... Dr. Mark TUFENKJAN
107 Dean Col of Profess/Global Studies ..... Dr. Harkmore LEE
88 Assoc Dean of Administration/PaGE ..... Vacant
76 Dean Health & Human Services ..... Dr. Ronald VOGEL
88 Assoc Dean Health & Human Svcs ..... Dr. Tony SINAY
88 Assoc Dean Health/Human Services ..... Dr. Veena PRABHU
53 Dean Charter Col of Education ..... Dr. Cheryl L. NEY
88 Assoc Dean Charter Col of Education ..... Dr. Mitch FRYLING
50 Dean Business & Economics ..... Dr. Tyrone JACKSON
88 Int Assoc Dean Business & Economics ..... Dr. Ramon CASTILLO
97 Dean Undergraduate Studies ..... Dr. Michelle HAWLEY
92 Director Honors College ..... Dr. Rennie SCHOEPFLIN
122 Coord Fraternity/Sorority Life ..... Mr. Chris BATTLE
88 Dean College of Ethnic Studies ..... Dr. Julianne MALVEAUX
88 Assoc Dean Col of Ethnic Studies ..... Dr. Dolores DELGADO BERNAL

† Grants Joint Doctoral degree in cooperation with the University of California-Los Angeles.

*CSU Maritime Academy (C)

200 Maritime Academy Drive, Vallejo CA 94590-0644
County: Solano FICE Identification: 001134
Unit ID: 111188
Telephone: (707) 654-1000 Carnegie Class: Bac-Diverse
FAX Number: (707) 654-1001 Calendar System: Semester
URL: www.csum.edu
Established: 1929 Annual Undergrad Tuition & Fees (In-State): $7,160
Enrollment: 952 Coed
Affiliation or Control: State IRS Status: 501(c)3
Highest Offering: Master's
Accreditation: WC, IACBE

02 President ..... RADM. Thomas A. CROPPER, USMS
05 Provost/VP Academic Affairs ..... Dr. Lori SCHROEDER
10 VP of Administration/Finance ..... Mr. Franz LOZANO
32 VP of Student Affairs ..... Ms. Kathleen MCMAHON
111 VP of University Advancement ..... Mr. Richard P. ORTEGA
15 AVP of Human Resources/Diversity ..... Mr. Michael MARTIN
13 Chief Information Officer ..... Ms. Tara M. HUGHES
100 Chief of Staff/AVP Univ Affairs ..... Ms. Karyn CORNELL
88 Master of Training Ship ..... Capt. Samuel R. PECOTA
20 Associate Vice Provost ..... Dr. Graham BENTON
112 Senior Development Officer ..... Ms. Linda SOLOW BOUWER
06 Registrar ..... Ms. Julia L. ODOM
08 Dean of Library ..... Ms. Michele VAN HOECK
07 Admissions Officer ..... Mr. Christopher P. ALDACO
37 Director of Financial Aid ..... Ms. Priscilla MUHA
109 AVP Enterprise Services ..... Mr. Mark GOODRICH
88 Director of SEAS ..... Ms. Vineeta DHILLON
35 Dean of Students ..... Mr. James DALSKE
18 AVP Facilities Management ..... Mr. Audun AABERG
19 Chief of Police Services ..... Chief Donny GORDON
21 University Controller ..... Mr. Rabi JOSEPH
41 Director of Athletics ..... Ms. Karen YODER
40 Bookstore Manager ..... Mr. Andre JIMENEZ
96 Director of Purchasing ..... Ms. Lorrie DINEEN-THACKERAY
09 Director of Institutional Research ..... Mr. Gary MOSER
29 Director of Alumni Relations ..... Ms. Theresa COSGROVE
101 Asst Director University Affairs ..... Ms. Jennifer HEMBREE
114 Budget Director ..... Mr. Andrew SOM
117 Director of Risk Management ..... Ms. Marianne SPOTORNO
36 Director Career Services ..... Ms. Wendy HIGGINS
23 Chief Medical Officer ..... Ms. Rebecca MILLER

*California State University-Monterey Bay (D)

100 Campus Center, Seaside CA 93955-8000
County: Monterey FICE Identification: 032603
Unit ID: 409698
Telephone: (831) 582-3000 Carnegie Class: Masters/L
FAX Number: (831) 582-3783 Calendar System: Semester
URL: www.csumb.edu
Established: 1994 Annual Undergrad Tuition & Fees (In-State): $7,147
Enrollment: 7,409 Coed
Affiliation or Control: State IRS Status: 501(c)3
Highest Offering: Master's
Accreditation: WC, #ARCPA, IPSY, NURSE, @SP, SW

02 President ..... Dr. Eduardo M. OCHOA
05 Provost ..... Dr. Katherine KANTARDJIEFF
10 Vice Pres Admin & Finance/CFO ..... Dr. Glen NELSON
30 Vice Pres University Development ..... Ms. Barbara ZAPPAS
32 VP Student Affairs & Enroll Service ..... Dr. John FRAIRE
45 VP for Strategic Initiatives ..... Dr. Lawrence SAMUELS
86 Director of Governmental Affairs ... Ms. Nicole HOLLINGSWORTH
35 Dean of Students/AVP Student Affs ..... Dr. Leslie WILLIAMS
21 Assoc Vice President for Finance ..... Mr. Stephen MACKEY
28 AVP for Inclusive Excellence ..... Dr. Brian CORPENING
108 AVP Institutional Effectiveness ..... Dr. Dan SHAPIRO
15 AVP for University Personnel ..... Ms. Natalie KING
06 Registrar ..... Ms. Sandra NAFFZIGER
13 Chief Information Officer ..... Dr. Chip LENNO
16 Director Employee & Labor Relations ..... Ms. Melanie CHAVEZ
37 Director Financial Aid ..... Ms. Angeles FUENTES
19 Chief of Police ..... Chief Earl LAWSON
18 AVP Facilities Services & Operation ..... Mr. Marcel FORTE
07 Director of Admissions ..... Ms. Kimberly GUANZON
29 Director Alumni Relations ..... Ms. Annie WARR
41 Athletic Director ..... Mr. Kirby GARRY
96 Director of Purchasing ..... Vacant

*California State University-Northridge (E)

18111 Nordhoff Street, Northridge CA 91330-0001
County: Los Angeles FICE Identification: 001153
Unit ID: 110608
Telephone: (818) 677-1200 Carnegie Class: Masters/L
FAX Number: N/A Calendar System: Semester
URL: www.csun.edu
Established: 1958 Annual Undergrad Tuition & Fees (In-State): $7,017
Enrollment: 40,381 Coed
Affiliation or Control: State IRS Status: 501(c)3
Highest Offering: Doctorate
Accreditation: WC, AAFCS, ART, CAATE, CAPRT, CIDA, CONST, DIETD, DIETI, HSA, IPSY, JOUR, MFCD, MUS, NURSE, PH, PTA, RAD, SP, SW, THEA

02 President ..... Dr. Erika D. BECK
05 Provost/Vice Pres Academic Affairs ..... Dr. Mary Beth WALKER
10 Vice President Admin Finance/CFO ..... Mr. Colin DONAHUE
32 VP Student Affairs/Dean of Students ..... Dr. William WATKINS
111 Int VP Univ Advancement/Found Pres ..... Dr. Thor STEINGRABER
13 Vice President IT/CIO ..... Ms. Hilary BAKER
88 Exec Director University Corp ..... Mr. Rick EVANS
20 Vice Provost Academic Affairs ..... Dr. Matthew CAHN
100 Chief of Staff ..... Ms. Genevieve EVANS TAYLOR
18 Assoc VP Facilities Dev/Operations ..... Mr. Ken ROSENTHAL
58 Assoc VP Graduate Studies ..... Dr. Amy LEVIN
21 Interim Assoc VP Financial Services ..... Mr. John VEATCH
15 Assoc VP of Human Resources ..... Ms. Kristina DE LA VEGA
29 Asst Vice Pres Alumni Relations ..... Ms. Shellie HADVINA
26 Assoc VP of Mktg/Comm ..... Mr. Jeffrey NOBLITT
121 Assoc VP for Student Success ..... Dr. Melanie BOCANEGRA
91 Assoc VP of Acad Resources/Planning .. Ms. Diane S. STEPHENS
07 Director of Admissions and Records ..... Mr. David R. DUFAULT-HUNTER
08 Dean University Library ..... Dr. Mark STOVER
51 Dean College of Extended Learning ..... Dr. Joyce A. FEUCHT-HAVIAR
79 Dean College of Humanities ..... Dr. Jeffrey REEDER
50 Dean College Business/Economics . Dr. Chandra SUBRAMANIAM
53 Dean College of Education ..... Dr. Shari A. TARVER-BEHRING
57 Dean College Arts/Media/Comm ..... Mr. Dan HOSKEN
83 Dean Col Social/Behavioral Sci ..... Dr. Yan Dominic SEARCY
76 Dean Col Health/Human Development ..... Dr. Farrell WEBB
81 Dean College Science & Math ..... Dr. Jerry STINNER
54 Dean College Engr/Computer Sci ..... Dr. Houssam TOUTANJI
09 Sr Dir Institutional Research ..... Dr. Janet S. OH
37 Director Financial Aid/Scholarships ..... Ms. Linda M. BRIGNONI
38 Director Univ Counseling Services ..... Dr. Julie L. PEARCE
36 Director Career Center ..... Ms. Ann N. MOREY
25 Dir Research/Graduate Studies ..... Ms. Hedy L. CARPENTER
18 Senior Dir Physical Plant Mgmt ..... Mr. Jason WANG
19 Director of Police Services ..... Chief Gregory MURPHY
22 Director of Equity/Diversity ..... Mr. Barrett MORRIS
86 AVP Government/Community Relations ... Mr. Rafael DE LA ROSA
23 Int Director Student Health Center ..... Dr. Lynne LANDETA
39 Dir of Stdnt Housing/Resident Life ..... Ms. Claire DAVIS
41 Dir of Intercollegiate Athletics ..... Mr. Michael IZZI
35 Dir Student Involvement/Development ..... Mr. Patrick BAILEY
92 Dir General Education Honors Pgm ..... Dr. Beth A. WIGHTMAN
96 Manager Purchasing ..... Ms. Deborah FLUGUM
06 Registrar ..... Mr. Todd WOLFE
28 Chief Div Ofcr/Title IX Coordinator ..... Ms. Natalie L. MASON-KINSEY

04 Exec Assistant to the President .... Ms. Elbi MAGANA
11 Dir of Administrative Operations .... Mr. Randy REYMALDO

*California State University-Sacramento (A)

6000 J Street, Sacramento CA 95819-2694
County: Sacramento FICE Identification: 001150
Unit ID: 110617
Telephone: (916) 278-6011 Carnegie Class: Masters/L
FAX Number: (916) 278-6664 Calendar System: Semester
URL: www.csus.edu
Established: 1947 Annual Undergrad Tuition & Fees (In-State): $7,418
Enrollment: 32,293 Coed
Affiliation or Control: State IRS Status: 501(c)3
Highest Offering: Doctorate
Accreditation: WC, ART, @AUD, CACREP, CAPRT, CONST, DIETD, DIETI, EMT, MUS, NURSE, PTA, SP, SW, THEA

02 President .... Dr. Robert S. NELSEN
05 Provost & VP Academic Affairs .... Dr. Carlos NEVAREZ
111 VP University Advancement .... Dr. Lisa CARDOZA
32 VP Student Affairs .... Dr. Edward MILLS
13 VP & Chief Information Officer .... Dr. Mark HENDRICKS
10 VP/CFO Admin & Business Affs .... Mr. Jonathan BOWMAN
15 Sr AVP Human Resources Management .... Ms. Machelle MARTIN
26 Assoc VP Public Affairs/Advocacy .... Mr. Nathan DIETRICH
46 AVP Research Innovation & Econ Dev .... Dr. Yvonne HARRIS
20 Vice Provost .... Dr. Tasha SOUZA
30 AVP University Development .... Ms. Tracy LATINO-NEWMAN
18 Assoc Vice Pres Facilities Mgmt .... Mr. Victor TAKAHASHI
84 AVP Enrollment & Student Svcs .... Dr. Steven M. SALCIDO
27 Senior Assoc VP Univ Communications .... Ms. Jeannie WONG
35 AVP Stdnt Affs/Engage/Dean Students .... Mr. Bill HEBERT
21 Assoc VP Financial Svcs .... Ms. Gina CURRY
07 Dir Outreach & Admissions .... Mr. Brian HENLEY
08 Library Dean .... Ms. Amy KAUTZMAN
29 Assoc VP Alumni Relations .... Ms. Jennifer BARBER
19 Chief of Police .... Mr. Chet MADISON, JR.
39 Dir of Strategic Initiatives .... Mr. Michael SPEROS
41 Director of Athletics .... Dr. Mark ORR
37 Director Financial Aid/Scholarships .... Ms. Anita KERMES
22 Director of Equal Opportunity .... Mr. William BISHOP
40 Bookstore Director .... Ms. Pam PARSONS
100 Chief of Staff .... Dr. Sarah BILLINGSLEY
06 University Registrar .... Ms. Michelle FAUL
85 Director of International Programs .... Ms. Stephanie INGVALDSON
23 AVP Student Health & Counseling Svc .... Dr. Joy STEWART-JAMES
96 Sr Dir/Chief Procurement Officer .... Ms. Nicole LACK
97 Dean Undergraduate Studies .... Dr. James GERMAN
49 Dean College of Arts & Letters .... Dr. Sheree MEYER
50 Dean College of Business Admin .... Dr. Jaydeep BALAKRISHNAN
53 Dean College of Education .... Dr. Alexander SIDORKIN
54 Dean Col of Engr/Computer Sci .... Dr. Kevan SHAFIZADEH
76 Dean College Health/Human Svcs .... Dr. Mary MAGUIRE
81 Dean Col of Natural Science/Math .... Dr. Lisa HAMMERSLEY
51 Dean College Continuing Educ .... Dr. Jenni MURPHY
83 Dean Col Soc Sci/Interdisc Stds .... Dr. Dianne HYSON
58 Dean Graduate Studies .... Dr. Chevelle NEWSOME
28 VP for Inclusive Excellence .... Dr. Mia SETTLES-TIDWELL
113 University Bursar .... Ms. Elena LARSON
112 Exec Dir Advance Stewardship .... Ms. Lisa WOODARD-MINK
44 Exec Dir Annual Giving .... Ms. Sharon TAKEDA
88 Exec Dir Ctr Innov/Entrepreneurship .... Mr. Cameron LAW
90 AVP Academic Technology .... Dr. Peggy KAY
88 Deputy Chief of Staff .... Dr. Kristen TUDOR

*California State University-San Bernardino (B)

5500 University Parkway, San Bernardino CA 92407-2393
County: San Bernardino FICE Identification: 001142
Unit ID: 110510
Telephone: (909) 537-5000 Carnegie Class: DU-Higher
FAX Number: N/A Calendar System: Quarter
URL: www.csusb.edu
Established: 1960 Annual Undergrad Tuition & Fees (In-State): $6,952
Enrollment: 19,689 Coed
Affiliation or Control: State IRS Status: 501(c)3
Highest Offering: Doctorate
Accreditation: WC, ART, CACREP, DIETD, MUS, NURSE, PH, SPAA, SW, THEA

02 President .... Dr. Tomas MORALES
05 Interim Provost/VP Academic Affairs .... Dr. Rafik MOHAMED
10 Vice Pres Administration/Finance .... Dr. Doug FREER
111 Vice Pres University Advancement .... Mr. Robert NAVA
13 Vice Pres ITS/CIO .... Dr. Samuel SUDHAKAR
28 Co-Chief Diversity Officer .... Dr. Daria GRAHAM
28 Co-Chief Diversity Officer .... Ms. Robin PHILLIPS
11 AVP of Operations/Administration .... Ms. Monica ALEJANDRE
29 AVP Alumni/Govt & Comm Relations .... Vacant
20 Interim Vice Provost .... Dr. Kelly CAMPBELL
46 Assoc Provost Research .... Dr. Dorota HUIZINGA
20 AVP Undergraduate Studies .... Dr. Leslie DAVIDSON-BOYD
21 Assoc VP Finance .... Mr. Michael AU-YEUNG
15 VP Human Resources .... Ms. Robin PHILLIPS
121 Director .... Mr. Jairo LEON
32 AVP Student Svcs/Dean of Students .... Dr. Daria GRAHAM
14 Assoc VP ITS .... Mr. Gerard AU
26 Assoc VP Strategic Communications .... Mr. Bob TENCZAR
88 Assoc Provost Faculty Affairs & Dev .... Dr. Kevin GRISHAM
22 Director Title IX & Gender Equity .... Ms. Cristina ALVAREZ
06 Int Director University Registrar .... Ms. Amy BRACEROS
07 Director of Outreach .... Ms. Tiffany BONNER
23 Interim Director Health Center .... Dr. Carolyn O'KEEFE
08 University Librarian .... Mr. Cesar CABALLERO
37 Director Financial Aid .... Ms. Diana MINOR
39 Assoc Dir Housing/Residential Life .... Ms. Holly ALLAR
18 Assoc VP Facilities Management .... Ms. Jennifer SORENSON
41 Director Athletics .... Mr. Shawn FARRELL
92 Director University Honors Program .... Dr. David MARSHALL
56 Dean Col of Extended Learning .... Dr. Tatiana KARMANOVA
83 Dean Col Social/Behavioral Sciences .... Dr. Rafik MOHAMED
53 Dean College of Education .... Dr. Chinaka DOMNWACHUKWU
50 Dean College of Business .... Dr. Lawrence D. ROSE
58 Dean Graduate Studies .... Dr. Dorota HUIZINGA
12 Dean CSUSB Palm Desert .... Dr. Jake ZHU
100 Chief of Staff .... Ms. Julie M. LAPPIN
102 Sr Dir Foundation/Corp Rels .... Ms. Annya DIXON
44 Operations Manager Annual Giving .... Ms. Carolina VAN ZEE
104 Study Abroad Coordinator .... Ms. Amy CHIEN
104 Study Abroad Coordinator .... Mr. Emilio RODRIGUEZ
09 Chief Data Officer .... Ms. Muriel LOPEZ-WAGNER
29 Director Alumni Affairs .... Ms. Crystal WYMER-LUCERO
104 Director of Education Abroad .... Dr. Sonja LIND
04 Admin Assistant to the President .... Ms. Katherine HARTLEY
106 Dean of E-learning .... Dr. Tatiana KARMANOVA
19 Chief of Police .... Ms. Nina JAMSEN
122 Dir Stdnt Engage-Frat/Sorority Life .... Ms. Jackie GARDNER

*California State University-San Marcos (C)

333 S Twin Oaks Valley Road, San Marcos CA 92096-0001
County: San Diego FICE Identification: 030113
Unit ID: 366711
Telephone: (760) 750-4000 Carnegie Class: Masters/L
FAX Number: (760) 750-4030 Calendar System: Semester
URL: www.csusm.edu
Established: 1989 Annual Undergrad Tuition & Fees (In-State): $7,712
Enrollment: 16,367 Coed
Affiliation or Control: State IRS Status: 501(c)3
Highest Offering: Doctorate
Accreditation: WC, IPSY, NURSE, PH, SP, SW

02 President .... Dr. Ellen J. NEUFELDT
04 Presidential Aide .... Ms. Viviana GARCIA
10 VP Finance/Admin Svcs & CFO .... Mr. Leon WYDEN
05 Provost/VP Academic Affairs .... Dr. Carl KEMNITZ
32 Vice President of Student Affairs .... Dr. Viridiana DIAZ
111 VP University Advancement .... Ms. Jessica BERGER
20 Dean Academic Programs .... Dr. Regina EISENBACH
45 Vice Prov Plng/Acad Resources .... Dr. Mary OLING-SISAY
84 Assoc Vice Pres Enrollment Mgmt .... Mr. Scott HAGG
15 Assoc VP Human Resource/Equal Oppty .... Ms. Erika GRAVETT
49 Dean Col Hum Arts/Behav & Soc Sci .... Dr. Liora GUBKIN
50 Dean Col Business Admin .... Dr. Ronald RAMIREZ
53 Dean Col Educ/Hlth/Human Svcs .... Dr. Jennifer OSTERGREN
08 Dean of Library Services .... Dr. Jennifer FABBI
81 Dean Col of Sci/Tech/Engr/Math .... Dr. Jackie TRISCHMAN
56 Dean of Extended Studies .... Mr. Godfrey GIBSON
13 Int Dean Instructional/Info Tech .... Mr. John HUMES
06 Registrar .... Ms. Lisa MEDINA
07 Dir Admissions & Univ Registrar .... Ms. Lisa MEDINA
100 Chief of Staff .... Ms. Sarah VILLARREAL
21 AVP Business and Fin Svcs .... Mr. Matias FARRE
29 Director Alumni/Parent Relations .... Ms. Lori BROCKETT
96 Exec Dir/AVP Business Development .... Mr. Will MARCHESE
121 Director Undergraduate Advising .... Mr. David MCMARTIN
09 Dir Inst Planning & Analysis .... Mr. Jeffrey MARKS
104 Executive Director Global Education .... Mr. Robert CAROLIN
18 AVP Facilities Dev & Mgmt .... Mr. Mark NORITA
19 Int Chief Univ Police Department .... Mr. Jesus FLORES
28 Chief Diversity Officer .... Dr. Aswad ALLEN
26 Chief Communications Officer .... Ms. Margaret CHANTUNG
39 Interim Director Student Housing .... Ms. Allie SERRANO
41 Athletic Director .... Ms. Jennifer MILO
88 AVP Faculty Affairs .... Ms. Michelle HUNT
44 Director Annual Programs .... Mr. Sean BRINER
86 Director Government Relations .... Mr. Ryan MAXSON
108 Int Dir Institutional Assessment .... Ms. Cameron STEVENSON
122 Coord Fraternity/Sorority Life .... Ms. Megan CEPPI

† Grants Joint Doctoral degree in cooperation with the University of California-San Diego.

*California State University-Stanislaus (D)

1 University Circle, Turlock CA 95382-0299
County: Stanislaus FICE Identification: 001157
Unit ID: 110495
Telephone: (209) 667-3122 Carnegie Class: Masters/L
FAX Number: N/A Calendar System: Semester
URL: www.csustan.edu
Established: 1957 Annual Undergrad Tuition & Fees (In-State): $7,584
Enrollment: 11,163 Coed
Affiliation or Control: State IRS Status: 170(c)1
Highest Offering: Doctorate
Accreditation: WC, ART, MUS, NURSE, SPAA, SW, THEA

02 President .... Dr. Ellen JUNN
05 Provost/VP Academic Affairs .... Dr. Rich OLGE
06 Registrar .... Ms. Lisa M. BERNARDO
10 VP Business/Finance/CFO .... Ms. Mary STEPHENS
32 VP Student Affairs .... Dr. Christine ERICKSON
111 VP University Advancement .... Dr. Michele LAHTI
84 VP Strategic Plng/Enroll Mgmt/Innov .... Dr. Gitanjali KAUL
15 Sr AVP HR/EO/Compliance .... Mr. Paul NORRIS
100 Dir Presidential Initiatives .... Ms. Neisha RHODES
79 Dean College Arts/Humanities & SS .... Dr. James A. TUEDIO
50 Dean College of Business Admin .... Dr. Thomas GOMEZ-ARIAS
53 Dean College of Education .... Dr. Oddmund R. MYHRE
81 Dean College of Science .... Dr. David EVANS
08 Dean Library Services .... Mr. Ron RODRIGUEZ
106 Dean Stockton Center .... Dr. Faimous HARRISON
51 Dean Extended Education .... Dr. Kari MILLER
07 Dir Admissions & Outreach .... Mr. Miguel PULIDO
41 Director Athletics .... Mr. Aaron ALLAIRE
35 AVP Student Affs/Dean of Students .... Dr. Heather DUNN CARLTON
21 Assoc VP Financial Services .... Ms. Regan LINDERMAN
13 Chief Information Officer .... Mr. Rafael ESPINOSA
18 Assoc VP Facilities Services .... Ms. Melody MAFFEI
26 Sr AVP Comm & Public Affairs .... Dr. Rosalee RUSH
19 Chief of Police .... Mr. Clint STRODE
09 Director of Institutional Research .... Dr. Dai LI
103 Director Career Development .... Ms. Julie SEDLEMEYER
28 Director of Diversity Center .... Ms. Carolina ALFARO
38 Director Student Counseling .... Ms. Cynthia BORGES-O'DELL
39 Dir Resident Life/Student Housing .... Ms. Renee GIANNINI
29 Director Alumni Affairs .... Vacant
30 Director of Development .... Mr. Jeff PORTO, JR.
44 Director Annual Giving .... Ms. Sandra SANTINI
04 Admin Assistant to the President .... Ms. Naraith LOPEZ
37 Director Student Financial Aid .... Ms. Belinda GARCIA
104 Director Study Abroad .... Ms. Brittany FENTRESS
122 Fraternity/Sorority Life Coord .... Ms. Julie ANAYA

*San Diego State University (E)

5500 Campanile Drive, San Diego CA 92182-8000
County: San Diego FICE Identification: 001151
Unit ID: 122409
Telephone: (619) 594-5200 Carnegie Class: DU-Higher
FAX Number: (619) 594-8894 Calendar System: Semester
URL: www.sdsu.edu
Established: 1897 Annual Undergrad Tuition & Fees (In-State): $7,720
Enrollment: 36,334 Coed
Affiliation or Control: State IRS Status: 501(c)3
Highest Offering: Doctorate
Accreditation: WC, ART, AUD, CAATE, CACREP, CAMPEP, CIDA, CLPSY, DIETD, HSA, JOUR, MFCD, NASP, NURSE, PH, PLNG, PTA, SP, SPAA, SW, THEA

02 President .... Dr. Adela DE LA TORRE
05 Provost .... Dr. Hector OCHOA
10 Int VP/CFO Business Affairs .... Ms. Agnes WONG NICKERSON
32 Vice Pres for Student Affairs .... Dr. J. Luke WOOD
30 VP Univ Relations & Development .... Ms. Adrienne VARGAS
46 Interim VP for Research .... Dr. Hala MADANAT
20 Assoc Vice Pres Academic Affairs .... Dr. Radmila PRISLIN
88 Assoc VP Real Estate Planning & Dev .... Mr. Robert SCHULZ
21 Int Assoc VP Financial Operations .... Ms. Crystal LITTLE
15 Associate VP Administration .... Ms. Jessica RENTTO
85 Int Associate VP for Global Affairs .... Dr. Christina ALFARO
26 AVP/Chief Comm Officer .... Dr. La Monica EVERETT-HAYNES
35 Int Assoc VP for Student Affairs .... Ms. Rashmi PRABA
35 Assoc VP for Student Affairs .... Dr. Andrea DOOLEY
35 Assoc VP for Student Affairs .... Dr. Antionette MARBRAY
35 Assoc VP for Student Affairs .... Dr. Randy TIMM
88 Asst VP Special Projects .... Mr. James S. HERRICK
100 Chief of Staff President's Office .... Ms. Brittany SANTOS-DERIEG
84 Int Assoc VP Enrollment Management .... Ms. Sandra TEMORES
38 Director Counseling/Psych Services .... Dr. Jennifer RIKARD
08 Int Dean Library/Information Access .... Mr. Patrick MCCARTHY
110 Int Associate VP for Development .... Ms. Mary DARLING
88 AVP & Exec Director Rsrch Found .... Ms. Michele GOETZ
51 Dean SDSU World Campus .... Dr. Radhika SESHAN
58 Assoc Dean Graduate & Rsrch Affairs .... Dr. Edmund BALSDON
49 Assoc VP AA/Student Achievement .... Dr. Norah SHULTZ
79 Dean of College Arts & Letters .... Dr. Monica CASPER
81 Dean of College of Sciences .... Dr. Jeffrey ROBERTS
54 Interim Dean College of Engineering .... Dr. Eugene OLEVSKY
50 Int Dean Fowler College of Business .... Dr. Bruce REINIG
76 Dean College Health/Human Svcs .... Dr. Steven P. HOOKER
53 Dean of College of Education .... Dr. Y. Barry CHUNG
12 Dean of Imperial Valley Campus .... Dr. Gregorio PONCE
57 Dean Prof Studies/Fine Arts .... Dr. Peggy SHANNON
117 Director of Emergency Services .... Ms. Kayli SINGER
28 CDO/AVP Faculty Diversity & Incl .... Dr. J. Luke WOOD
06 Registrar .... Vacant
07 Director of Admissions .... Ms. Sabrina CORTELL
36 Executive Director Career Services .... Dr. James TARBOX
39 Director Office of Housing Admin .... Ms. Cynthia CERVANTES
40 Assoc VP & CEO Aztec Shops .... Mr. Todd SUMMER
41 Director Intercollegiate Athletics .... Mr. John David WICKER
85 Dir International Student Center .... Mr. Noah HANSEN
88 Director Environ Health & Safety .... Mr. Terry GEE
13 Chief Tech Officer/Interim CIO .... Mr. Rick NORNHOLM
09 Dir Analytic Studies/Inst Research .... Ms. Jeanne STRONACH
86 Dir Govt & Comm Relations .... Ms. Rachel GREGG
96 Director Procurement Mgmt .... Ms. Tami FORD
21 University Controller .... Ms. Beth WARREM
18 Director of Facilities Services .... Mr. John FERRIS
22 Dir Educational Opportunity Program .... Ms. Miriam CASTANON

37	Dir Financial Aid & Scholarships	Ms. Rose PASENELLI
88	Ombudsman	Mr. Darrell HESS
39	Director of Residential Education	Dr. Kara BAUER
121	Dir Student Ability Success Ctr	Dr. Pamela STARR
88	Sr Director Enterprise Tech Svcs	Mr. Rick NORNHOLM
29	Asst VP Alumni Engagement	Mr. Jim HERRICK
04	Executive Asst to the President	Mr. Luis MURILLO
122	Student Life Advisor-Greek Life	Ms. Kayla SNOW

*San Francisco State University (A)

1600 Holloway Avenue, San Francisco CA 94132-1740

County: San Francisco — FICE Identification: 001154
Unit ID: 122597

Telephone: (415) 338-1111 — Carnegie Class: DU-Higher
FAX Number: (415) 338-2514 — Calendar System: Semester
URL: www.sfsu.edu
Established: 1899 — Annual Undergrad Tuition & Fees (In-State): $7,006
Enrollment: 27,349 — Coed
Affiliation or Control: State — IRS Status: 501(c)3
Highest Offering: Doctorate
Accreditation: WC, AAFCS, ART, CACREP, CAPRT, DIETD, DIETI, JOUR, MLS, MUS, NURSE, PH, PTA, SP, SPAA, SW, THEA

02	President	Dr. Lynn MAHONEY
05	Provost & VP Academic Affairs	Dr. Jennifer SUMMIT
111	Vice Pres University Advancement	Mr. Jeffrey JACKANICZ
32	VP Student Affairs/Enroll Mgmt	Dr. Jamillah MOORE
20	Vice Provost Academic Resources	Dr. Dwayne BANKS
46	Assoc VP Research Sponsored Pgms	Mr. Michael SCOTT
20	Assoc VP Academic Affairs Operation	Vacant
10	AVP Business Operations	Mr. Jay ORENDORFF
85	Interim AVP International Education	Dr. Marilyn JACKSON
13	AVP Information Technology Services	Mr. Nish MALIK
84	Senior AVP Enrollment Management	Ms. Katie LYNCH
15	Assoc VP Human Resources	Ms. Ingrid WILLIAMS
35	Assoc VP Student Affairs	Mr. Gene CHELBERG
100	Chief of Staff	Ms. Noriko LIM-TEPPER
53	Dean College Education	Dr. Cynthia GRUTZIK
88	Dean College Ethnic Studies	Dr. Amy SUEYOSHI
51	AVP/Dean of CELIA	Dr. Angie LIPSCHUETZ
69	Dean Col Health & Soc Science	Dr. Alvin ALVAREZ
79	Dean Col Lib Sci & Creative Arts	Dr. Andrew HARRIS
88	AVP Faculty Affairs & Prof Dev	Dr. Carleen MANDOLFO
58	Dean Graduate Studies	Dr. Sophie CLAVIER
97	Dean Undergraduate Education	Dr. Lori Beth WAY
102	Int President SF State	
	Foundation	Ms. Venesia THOMPSON-RAMSAY
08	University Librarian	Ms. Deborah C. MASTERS
90	Director Academic Technology	Vacant
117	Risk Manager	Mr. Michael BEATTY
39	Director Resident Life	Mr. David ROURKE
28	Int Dir Diversity/Student Equity	Mr. Christian LOZANO CUELLAR
07	Director Undergraduate Admissions	Mr. Fernando PENA
38	Director Counseling & Psych Svcs	Dr. Stephen CHEN
22	Dir Education Opportunity Program	Mr. Oscar M. GARDEA
19	Chief of Police/AVP Public Safety	Chief Reginald PARSON
88	Dir Environmental Health & Safety	Mr. Marc MAJEWSKI
18	AVP Facilities Services	Mr. Avinash RAHURKAR
04	Deputy Chief of Staff	Vacant
06	Registrar	Ms. Margo LANDY
37	Asst Dir Student Financial Aid	Mr. Charles B. GATES
41	Director of Athletics	Ms. Stephanie E. SHRIEVE-HAWKINS
86	Director Government/Cmty Relations	Vacant
50	Dean College of Business	Dr. Eugene SIVADAS

† Grants additional Doctoral degrees in cooperation with the UC-Berkeley and UC-San Francisco.

*San Jose State University (B)

One Washington Square, San Jose CA 95192-0001

County: Santa Clara — FICE Identification: 001155
Unit ID: 122755

Telephone: (408) 924-1000 — Carnegie Class: Masters/L
FAX Number: (408) 924-1018 — Calendar System: Semester
URL: www.sjsu.edu
Established: 1857 — Annual Undergrad Tuition & Fees (In-State): $7,852
Enrollment: 36,208 — Coed
Affiliation or Control: State — IRS Status: 501(c)3
Highest Offering: Doctorate
Accreditation: WC, ART, @AUD, CAPRT, CEA, DANCE, DIETD, DIETI, IPSY, JOUR, LIB, MLS, MUS, NAIT, NURSE, OT, PH, PLNG, SP, SPAA, SW, THEA

02	Interim President	Dr. Stephen PEREZ
05	Provost/Sr Vice Pres Acad Affs	Dr. Vincent DEL CASINO
10	VP Administration & Finance/CFO	Mr. Charles FAAS
32	Vice President Student Affairs	Mr. Patrick K. DAY
13	VP Information Technology/CIO	Mr. Bob LIM
100	VP Strategy/Chief of Staff	Ms. Lisa MILLORA
09	Assoc VP Research	Dr. Pamela STACKS
20	Sr Assoc VP Grad/Undergrad Programs	Dr. Thalia ANAGNOS
21	Assoc VP Finance	Ms. Marna GENES
18	Assoc VP for Facilities/Operations	Vacant
15	Senior AVP University Personnel	Ms. Joanne WRIGHT
26	AVP Strategic Comm/Public Affairs	Vacant
29	AVP Alumni Engagement and Giving	Mr. Brian BATES
35	Int AVP Student Services	Ms. Catherine VOSS PLAXTON
22	Chief Diversity Officer	Dr. Kathleen WONG (LAU)
51	Dean Col of Intl/Extended Studies	Dr. Ruth HUARD
84	Int Sr AVP Enrollment Mgmt	Ms. Coleetta MCELROY
08	Int Dean University Library	Ms. Ann AGEE
28	Sr Dir Equal Opport/Employee Rels	Ms. Julie PAISANT

06	University Registrar	Ms. Maria MARTINEZ
41	Director Intercollegiate Athletics	Ms. Marie TUITE
07	Dir Undergrad Admissions/Outreach	Ms. Deanna GONZALES
40	B&N Asst Dir Spartan Bookstore	Ms. Lisa TOWNS
38	Dir Counseling/Psychological Svcs	Mr. Kell FUJIMOTO
37	Assoc Dir Fin Aid/Scholarships	Ms. Carolyn GUEL
39	Dir University Housing Services	Mr. Kevin KINNEY
50	Dean Lucas Col/Grad Sch of Business	Dr. Dan MOSHAVI
53	Dean Connie L Lurie Col of Educ	Dr. Heather LATTIMER
54	Dean Charles W Davidson Col of Eng	Dr. Sheryl EHRMAN
79	Dean Col of Humanities and the Arts	Dr. Shannon MILLER
81	Dean College of Science	Dr. Michael KAUFMAN
83	Dean College Social Sciences	Dr. Walt JACOBS
04	Presidential Aide	Ms. Zaynna TELLO

*Sonoma State University (C)

1801 E Cotati Avenue, Rohnert Park CA 94928-3609

County: Sonoma — FICE Identification: 001156
Unit ID: 123572

Telephone: (707) 664-2880 — Carnegie Class: Masters/L
FAX Number: (707) 664-2505 — Calendar System: Semester
URL: www.sonoma.edu
Established: 1960 — Annual Undergrad Tuition & Fees (In-State): $7,952
Enrollment: 8,018 — Coed
Affiliation or Control: State — IRS Status: 501(c)3
Highest Offering: Master's
Accreditation: WC, ART, MUS, NURSE

02	Interim President	Dr. Ming-Tung (Mike) LEE
05	Provost/VP Academic Affairs	Ms. Karen MORANSKI
10	VP Administration/Finance/CFO	Mr. Monir AHMED
111	Vice President for Advancement	Mr. Mario PEREZ
32	VP Student Affairs	Mr. Gerald JONES
20	Assoc VP for Faculty Affairs	Dr. Deborah ROBERTS
18	Chief Planning Officer	Mr. Christopher DINNO
100	Chief of Staff/AVP Strat Initiative	Ms. Jerlena GRIFFIN-DESTA
21	Assoc VP for Admin & Finance	Mr. Neil MARKLEY
08	Dean of Library	Ms. Karen SCHNEIDER
79	Dean School of Arts & Humanities	Dr. Hollis ROBBINS
50	Dean School of Business/Economic	Vacant
81	Dean School Science & Technology	Ms. Elisabeth WADE
83	Dean of Social Sciences	Ms. Tori CARLETON
26	Public Rels/Govt Relations Officer	Vacant
06	Sr Dir Records/University Registrar	Mr. Sean JOHNSON
38	Dir of Counseling/Psych Services	Dr. Laura WILLIAMS
37	Director of Financial Aid	Ms. F. Shanon LITTLE
88	Dir of Dev for Intercol Athletics	Mr. Jose HILLA
19	Chief of Police	Mr. Nader OWEIS
109	Director Seawolf Services	Ms. Elizabeth O'BRIEN
07	Director of Admissions	Ms. Natalie KALOGIANNIS
84	Sr AVP Strategic Enrollment	Mr. Elias LOPEZ
29	Dir Advancement Svcs & Stewardship	Ms. Laurie OGG
15	AVP for Administration/Finance/HR	Vacant
96	Managing Dir for Purchasing	Ms. Jenifer BARNETT
28	AVP Strategic Initiatives/Diversity	Ms. Janelle ROSSI
30	Director of Development	Mr. Stephen ARNESON

California University of Management and Sciences (D)

1126 North Brookhurst St, Suite 200, Anaheim CA 92801

County: Orange — FICE Identification: 041331
Unit ID: 460075

Telephone: (714) 533-3946 — Carnegie Class: Not Classified
FAX Number: (714) 533-7778 — Calendar System: Quarter
URL: www.calums.edu
Established: 1998 — Annual Undergrad Tuition & Fees: N/A
Enrollment: N/A — Coed
Affiliation or Control: Independent Non-Profit — IRS Status: 501(c)3
Highest Offering: Master's
Accreditation: ACICS

01	President	Jessica M. MERTZ
10	Finance Officer	Hongjun AHN
05	Academic Dean	Sasha SAFARZADEH
11	Dean of Administration	Yukari NISHIOKA
07	Admissions Officer	CJ JOHNS
32	Student Services Advisor	Kholood JADALLA
08	Librarian	Lionnel YAMENTOU
06	Registrar	Hongjun AHN
85	International Student Advisor	Yukari NISHIOKA
15	Personnel Mgr	Jessica MERTZ

California University of Science and Medicine (E)

1501 Violet Street, Colton CA 92324

County: San Bernardino — Identification: 667343
Unit ID: 496043

Telephone: (909) 580-9661 — Carnegie Class: Spec-4-yr-Med
FAX Number: (909) 424-0345 — Calendar System: Semester
URL: https://www.cusm.org/
Established: 2015 — Annual Graduate Tuition & Fees: N/A
Enrollment: N/A — Coed
Affiliation or Control: Independent Non-Profit — IRS Status: 501(c)3
Highest Offering: Doctorate; No Undergraduates
Accreditation: @WC, #MED

01	President/Dean	Dr. Paul LYONS
10	Chief Financial/Operating Officer	Mr. Moe ABOUFARES

13	Chief Information Officer	Mr. Nasser SALOMON
63	Sr Assoc Dean Medical Education	Dr. Gordon GREEN
84	Exec Vice Dean Univ Rels & Admiss	Dr. Peter EVELAND

California University - Silicon Valley (F)

441 De Guigne Drive #201, Sunnyvale CA 94085

County: Santa Clara — Identification: 667207
Telephone: (408) 532-5567 — Carnegie Class: Not Classified
FAX Number: N/A — Calendar System: Trimester
URL: www.cusv.us
Established: 2013 — Annual Graduate Tuition & Fees: N/A
Enrollment: N/A — Coed
Affiliation or Control: Independent Non-Profit — IRS Status: 501(c)3
Highest Offering: Master's; No Undergraduates
Accreditation: ACUP

01	President	Philip YANG
05	Academic Dean	Cynthia MA

California Victor University (G)

708 W. Holt Avenue, Pomona CA 91768

County: Los Angeles — Identification: 667386
Telephone: (909) 671-4038 — Carnegie Class: Not Classified
FAX Number: (909) 671-4086 — Calendar System: Semester
URL: cavictorun.org
Established: 2010 — Annual Undergrad Tuition & Fees: N/A
Enrollment: N/A — Coed
Affiliation or Control: Non-denominational — IRS Status: 501(c)3
Highest Offering: Doctorate
Accreditation: TRACS

01	President	Dr. Benjamin HONG
05	Provost	Dr. Sung W. KIM
32	Dean of Student Affairs	Dr. Suk Young KIM

California Western School of Law (H)

225 Cedar Street, San Diego CA 92101-3046

County: San Diego — FICE Identification: 013103
Unit ID: 111391

Telephone: (619) 239-0391 — Carnegie Class: Spec-4-yr-Law
FAX Number: (619) 525-7092 — Calendar System: Trimester
URL: www.cwsl.edu
Established: 1924 — Annual Graduate Tuition & Fees: N/A
Enrollment: 796 — Coed
Affiliation or Control: Independent Non-Profit — IRS Status: 501(c)3
Highest Offering: First Professional Degree; No Undergraduates
Accreditation: @WC, LAW

01	President & Dean	Dean Sean M. SCOTT
05	Vice Dean	Dean Hannah BRENNER JOHNSON
46	Assoc Dean Research/Faculty Devel	Prof. Catherine HARDEE
88	Assoc Dean of Exper Learning	Prof. James COOPER
32	Asst Dean Students/Diversity	
	Svcs	Ms. Susan GARRETT FINSTER
36	Assistant Dean Career Services	Ms. Courtney MIKLUSAK
37	Director Financial Aid	Mr. William KAHLER
18	Exec Dir Facilities Management	Ms. Jolie L. CARTIER
08	Assoc Dean Law Library/Info Res	Prof. Philip T. GRAGG
10	Chief Financial Officer	Ms. Cindy BERTRAND
07	Asst Dean Admiss/Fin Aid/Diversity	Mr. Jorge GARCIA
06	Registrar	Mr. Jerome THOMPSON
26	Chief Marketing Officer	Mr. Chris VAN NOSTRAND
15	VP Administration	Mr. Dave BLAKE
111	VP Institutional Advancement	Ms. Dani DAWSON
100	Chief of Staff	Mr. Christopher E. BAIDOO
108	Assoc Dean Assessment/Teaching	Prof. Kenneth S. KLEIN

Calvary Chapel University (I)

8344 Clairemont Mesa Blvd, Ste 100, San Diego CA 92111

County: San Diego — Identification: 667372
Telephone: (954) 453-9228 — Carnegie Class: Not Classified
FAX Number: N/A — Calendar System: Other
URL: calvarychapeluniversity.com
Established: 2005 — Annual Undergrad Tuition & Fees: N/A
Enrollment: N/A — Coed
Affiliation or Control: Independent Non-Profit — IRS Status: 501(c)3
Highest Offering: Master's
Accreditation: TRACS

01	President	Dr. F. Chapin MARSH, III
05	Chief Academic Officer	Dr. Kathy MORALES
11	Chief Operating Officer	Ms. Laura NUNES
10	Chief Financial Officer	Ms. Nike OMOLE
07	Director of Admissions	Ms. Pamela PRINCE
15	Director of Human Resources	Ms. Evelyn NAJARRO

Career Care Institute (J)

43770 15th Street West, Ste 115, Lancaster CA 93534

County: Los Angeles — FICE Identification: 037974
Unit ID: 446118

Telephone: (661) 942-6204 — Carnegie Class: Spec 2-yr-Health
FAX Number: (661) 942-8130 — Calendar System: Other
URL: ccicolleges.edu
Established: 1998 — Annual Undergrad Tuition & Fees: N/A
Enrollment: N/A — Coed

Affiliation or Control: Proprietary IRS Status: Proprietary
Highest Offering: Associate Degree
Accreditation: COE

01 President ....Evelyn ORELLANA

Carnegie Mellon University Silicon Valley Campus (A)

PO Box 98, Moffett Field CA 94035
Telephone: (650) 335-2810 Identification: 770149
Accreditation: &M

† Branch campus of Carnegie Mellon University, Pittsburgh, PA

Caroline University (B)

3660 Wilshire Blvd, Ste 320, Los Angeles CA 90010
County: Los Angeles Identification: 667387
Telephone: (213) 246-4174 Carnegie Class: Not Classified
FAX Number: (213) 487-9199 Calendar System: Semester
URL: www.caroline.edu
Established: 2016 Annual Undergrad Tuition & Fees: N/A
Enrollment: N/A Coed
Affiliation or Control: Independent Non-Profit IRS Status: 501(c)3
Highest Offering: Doctorate
Accreditation: TRACS

01 President ....Dr. Jinsam LEE

*Carrington College - Administrative Office (C)

8909 Folsom Boulevard, Sacramento CA 95826
County: Sacramento Identification: 666086
Telephone: (916) 361-5100 Carnegie Class: N/A
FAX Number: (916) 381-1809
URL: www.carrington.edu

01 President Carrington Colleges ..... Mr. Mitch CHARLES
05 Provost/Vice Pres Academic Affairs ....Mr. Ravinder DAYAL
11 Regional VP of Operations ....Mr. Michael COMO
84 Sr Director Enrollment Services ....Mr. Dan SIMON
10 Sr Dir Finance & Infrastructure ....Vacant
15 AVP/Director of Human Resources ....Ms. Lea MARSHALL

*Carrington College - Sacramento (D)

8909 Folsom Boulevard, Sacramento CA 95826
County: Sacramento FICE Identification: 009748
Unit ID: 125532
Telephone: (916) 361-1660 Carnegie Class: Spec 2-yr-Health
FAX Number: (916) 361-6666 Calendar System: Other
URL: www.carrington.edu
Established: 1983 Annual Undergrad Tuition & Fees: N/A
Enrollment: 1,709 Coed
Affiliation or Control: Proprietary IRS Status: Proprietary
Highest Offering: Associate Degree
Accreditation: WJ, DH, MAC

02 Campus Director ....Cynthia BRYSON
121 Student Success Center Manager ....Becky CARDWELL

*Carrington College - Citrus Heights (E)

7301 Greenback Lane, Suite A, Citrus Heights CA 95621
Telephone: (916) 722-8200 Identification: 667042
Accreditation: &WJ, MAC

† Regional accreditation is carried under the parent institution in Sacramento, CA.

*Carrington College - Pleasant Hill (F)

380 Civic Drive, Suite 300, Pleasant Hill CA 94523
Telephone: (925) 609-6650 Identification: 666043
Accreditation: &WJ, COARC, MAC, PTAA

† Regional accreditation is carried under the parent institution in Sacramento, CA.

*Carrington College - Pomona (G)

901 Corporate Center Drive, #300, Pomona CA 91768
Telephone: (909) 868-5834 Identification: 770506
Accreditation: &WJ

† Regional accreditation is carried under the parent institution in Sacramento, CA.

*Carrington College - San Jose (H)

5883 Rue Ferrari, Suite 125, San Jose CA 95138
Telephone: (408) 960-0161 Identification: 666042
Accreditation: &WJ, DH, MAC, SURGT

† Regional accreditation is carried under the parent institution in Sacramento, CA.

*Carrington College - San Leandro (I)

15555 E 14th Street, Suite 500, San Leandro CA 94578
Telephone: (510) 276-3888 Identification: 666751

Accreditation: &WJ, MAC

† Regional accreditation is carried under the parent institution in Sacramento, CA.

*Carrington College - Stockton (J)

1313 W Robinhood Drive, Suite B, Stockton CA 95207
Telephone: (209) 956-1240 Identification: 666140
Accreditation: &WJ, MAC

† Regional accreditation is carried under the parent institution in Sacramento, CA.

Casa Loma College-Van Nuys (K)

6725 Kester Avenue, Van Nuys CA 91405
County: Los Angeles FICE Identification: 006731
Unit ID: 111638
Telephone: (818) 785-2726 Carnegie Class: Spec 2-yr-Health
FAX Number: (818) 785-2191 Calendar System: Other
URL: www.casalomacollege.edu
Established: 1966 Annual Undergrad Tuition & Fees: N/A
Enrollment: 164 Coed
Affiliation or Control: Independent Non-Profit IRS Status: 501(c)3
Highest Offering: Baccalaureate
Accreditation: ABHES, PTAA

01 President ....Dr. Scott SAND
05 Dean of Education ....Vacant
06 Registrar ....Ms. Kimberly DUNCAN
32 Director of Student Affairs ......Mr. Nicholas WALSH-DAVIS
37 Director Student Financial Aid ....Ms. Christy RUOFF
08 Head Librarian ....Ms. Jennifer MEYER
13 Chief Info Technology Officer ....Mr. Cyrill REISER
15 Chief Human Resources Officer ....Ms. Veronica PANTOJA

CBD College (L)

3699 Wilshire Boulevard, 4th Floor,
Los Angeles CA 90010
County: Los Angeles FICE Identification: 032503
Unit ID: 439367
Telephone: (213) 427-2200 Carnegie Class: Spec 2-yr-Health
FAX Number: (213) 427-9278 Calendar System: Other
URL: www.cbd.edu
Established: 1982 Annual Undergrad Tuition & Fees: N/A
Enrollment: 974 Coed
Affiliation or Control: Independent Non-Profit IRS Status: 501(c)3
Highest Offering: Baccalaureate
Accreditation: ABHES, DMS, OTA, PTAA, SURTEC

01 President ....Mr. Alan HESHEL
05 Chief Academic Officer ....Randall SANSOM
10 Chief Operating Officer ....Patricia KOUROPOVA
106 Online Dean of Education ....Chanel MARTINEZ
32 Dir Student Affairs/Career Services ....Ivan REYNOSO
07 Director of Admissions ....Jim HAYES
37 Director of Financial Aid ......Michael RENDON-THOFSON
13 Chief Technology Officer ....Randall SANSOM

Cedars-Sinai Graduate School of Biomedical Sciences (M)

8700 Beverly Boulevard, Los Angeles CA 90048
County: Los Angeles Identification: 667071
Telephone: (310) 423-8294 Carnegie Class: Not Classified
FAX Number: N/A Calendar System: Trimester
URL: www.cedars-sinai.org/education/graduate-school.html
Established: 1902 Annual Graduate Tuition & Fees: N/A
Enrollment: N/A Coed
Affiliation or Control: Independent Non-Profit IRS Status: 501(c)3
Highest Offering: Doctorate; No Undergraduates
Accreditation: WC

01 President/CEO ....Mr. Thomas PRISELAC
03 Executive Vice President ....Dr. John JENRETTE
05 Dean/Exec Vice Pres Academic Affs ....Dr. Shlomo MELMED
10 Exec Vice Pres Finance/CFO ......Mr. Edward PRUNCHUNAS
15 SVP/Chief Human Resources Ofcr ......Mr. Andrew ORTIZ

Central Coast College (N)

111 East Navajo Dr., Ste 100, Salinas CA 93906
County: Monterey FICE Identification: 026023
Unit ID: 378105
Telephone: (831) 424-6767 Carnegie Class: Spec 2-yr-Other
FAX Number: (831) 753-9954 Calendar System: Quarter
URL: www.centralcoastcollege.edu
Established: 1983 Annual Undergrad Tuition & Fees: N/A
Enrollment: N/A Coed
Affiliation or Control: Proprietary IRS Status: Proprietary
Highest Offering: Associate Degree
Accreditation: CNCE

01 President/CEO ....LeeAnn ROHMANN

Cerritos College (O)

11110 Alondra Boulevard, Norwalk CA 90650-6298
County: Los Angeles FICE Identification: 001161
Unit ID: 111887

Telephone: (562) 860-2451 Carnegie Class: Assoc/HT-High Trad
FAX Number: (562) 467-5005 Calendar System: Semester
URL: www.cerritos.edu
Established: 1955 Annual Undergrad Tuition & Fees (In-District): $1,404
Enrollment: 20,406 Coed
Affiliation or Control: State/Local IRS Status: 501(c)3
Highest Offering: Associate Degree
Accreditation: WJ, ADNUR, DA, DH, PTAA

01 President ....Dr. Jose L. FIERRO
04 Executive Assistant ....Ms. Andrea WITTIG
05 Vice President Academic Affairs ....Mr. Rick MIRANDA
10 Vice President Business Services ....Mr. Felipe LOPEZ
32 Acting VP Student Services ....Dr. Elizabeth MILLER
15 Vice President Human Resources ....Vacant
20 Dean Acad Affs/Strategic Init ......Dr. Linda CLOWERS
84 Dean Enrollment Services ....Ms. Yvette TAFOYA
38 Dean of Counseling Services ....Vacant
86 Dir College/Govt Rels & Pub Affs ....Ms. Miya WALKER
88 Dean Stdnt Access/Wellness Svcs ..Dr. Christopher ELQUIZABAL
121 Dean Student Equity & Success ....Mr. Lui AMADOR
50 Interim Dean Business/Humanities/SS ....Dr. Michael ALLEN
57 Dean Fine Arts/Communications ......Dr. Gary PRITCHARD
76 Dean Health Occupations ....Dr. Elizabeth RILEY
88 Dean Academic Success ....Ms. Shawna BASKETTE
49 Dean Liberal Arts ....Dr. Frank MIXSON
68 Dean Health/PE/Dance/Athl ....Dr. Rory NATIVIDAD
54 Dean Sci/Engineering/Math ....Mr. Andrew VINES
72 Dean Technology ....Dr. Yannick REAL
13 Director Information Technology ......Mr. Patrick O'DONNELL
21 Director of Fiscal Services ......Mr. Noorali DELAWALLA
35 Dean of Student Services ....Dr. Elizabeth MILLER
36 Dir of Career/Assessment Services ....Ms. Theresa LOPEZ
18 Director Physical Plant & Const Svc ....Mr. Anthony PARKER
102 Exec Dir Foundation/Inst Advance ......Ms. Carol KRUMBACH
103 Director Community Advancement ......Ms. Bellegran GOMEZ
96 Dir Purchasing/Contract Admin ....Mr. Mark LOGAN
16 Director Human Resources/Risk Mgmt ......Ms. Nancy BUVINGER
19 Chief of Campus Police ....Mr. Don MUELLER
51 Assoc Dn Adult Educ/Diversity Pgms ...Ms. Graciela VASQUEZ
31 Temp Director Community Education ......Ms. Graciela VASQUEZ
88 Director Child Development Center ....Ms. Debra WARD
88 Operations Manager ....Mr. Carlos SERNA
88 Payroll Manager ....Ms. Deanna HART
114 Budget Manager ....Mr. Conrad SELORIO
14 Manager Information Technology ......Mr. Javier BANUELOS
23 Assoc Dean Student Health Wellness ....Dr. Hillary MENNELLA
88 Director of Student Program Svcs ....Ms. Norma RODRIGUEZ
09 Dir Inst Effect/Research & Planning ....Dr. Amber HROCH
88 Sector Nvg Adv Trans Tech Projects ....Ms. Jannet MALIG
28 Dir Diver/Compliance/Title IX Coord ..Dr. Lauren ELAN HELSPER
88 EOPS Assistant Director ....Dr. Patricia ROBBINS SMITH
89 Dir Educational Partnerships & Pgm ....Ms. Colleen MCKINLEY
88 Dual Enrollment Manager ....Dr. Laura TCHULLUIAN
88 Accounting Manager ....Ms. Kathy BURGOS
88 Facilities Manager ....Vacant
29 Director Alumni Relations ....Mr. Jason BORQUERO
30 Senior Development Officer ....Ms. Martha PELAYO
37 Financial Aid Asst Director ....Ms. Jaime QUIROZ
06 Asst Dir Admissions/Records ....Ms. Sonia GONZALEZ
41 Athletic Director ....Ms. Maria V. CASTRO
88 Case Manager Basic Needs ....Ms. Pamela SEPULVEDA
88 Mgr Partnershp Adult Acad/Career Ed ....Ms. Sherryl CARTER
88 Captain Campus Police Services ....Mr. Wayne REHNELT

*Chabot-Las Positas Community College District (P)

7600 Dublin Blvd., 3rd Flr., Dublin CA 94568
County: Alameda Identification: 666925
Telephone: (925) 485-5208 Carnegie Class: N/A
FAX Number: (925) 485-5256
URL: www.clpccd.org

01 Chancellor ....Mr. Ronald GERHARD
10 Vice Chanc Business Svcs ....Mr. Jonah NICHOLAS
05 Vice Chanc Educational
    Svcs ....Ms. Theresa FLEISCHER ROWLAND
15 Vice Chanc Human Resource Svcs ....Mr. Wyman FONG
18 Vice Chanc Facilities/Bond Program ......Mr. Owen LETCHER
13 Chief Technology Officer ....Mr. Bruce GRIFFIN

*Chabot College (Q)

25555 Hesperian Boulevard, Hayward CA 94545-2400
County: Alameda FICE Identification: 001162
Unit ID: 111920
Telephone: (510) 723-6600 Carnegie Class: Assoc/HT-High Trad
FAX Number: (510) 782-9315 Calendar System: Semester
URL: www.chabotcollege.edu
Established: 1961 Annual Undergrad Tuition & Fees (In-District): $1,150
Enrollment: 11,922 Coed
Affiliation or Control: State/Local IRS Status: 501(c)3
Highest Offering: Associate Degree
Accreditation: WJ, ART, DH, MAC, MUS, NAEYC

02 President ....Dr. Susan S. SPERLING
05 VP Academic Services ....Dr. Jamal COOKS
32 Vice President Student Services ....Dr. Matthew KRITSCHER
11 Vice Pres Administrative Services ......Mr. Dale WAGONER
10 Actg Chief Financial Officer ....Mr. Dale WAGONER
04 Exec Asst to the College President ....Ms. Kirti REDDY

08 Librarian ... Vacant
38 Interim Dean Counseling ... Ms. Sadie ASHRAF
41 Interim Dean Health/PE/Athletics ... Dr. Jamal COOKS
07 Dir Admissions & Records/Registrar ... Mrs. Paulette LINO
37 Director of Financial Aid ... Mrs. Kathryn MEDINA
19 Director Safety & Security ... Vacant
09 Int Dir Institutional Effectiveness ... Mr. Brian GOO
15 Director Human Resources ... Dr. Wyman FONG
18 Chief Facilities/Physical Plant ... Mr. Walter BELVINS
111 Exec Director Inst Advancement ... Ms. Yvonne WU CRAIG
35 Dir Student Life/Student Services ... Mr. Arnold PAGUIO
96 Manager Purchasing/Warehouse Svcs ... Ms. Marie HAMPTON

*Las Positas College (A)

3000 Campus Hill Drive, Livermore CA 94551-7623
County: Alameda — FICE Identification: 030357
Unit ID: 366401
Telephone: (925) 424-1000 — Carnegie Class: Assoc/HT-High Trad
FAX Number: (925) 443-0742 — Calendar System: Semester
URL: www.laspositascollege.edu
Established: 1975 — Annual Undergrad Tuition & Fees (In-District): $1,168
Enrollment: 8,005 — Coed
Affiliation or Control: State/Local — IRS Status: 501(c)3
Highest Offering: Associate Degree
Accreditation: WJ, EMT

02 President ... Dr. Dyrell FOSTER
05 Vice President Academic Svcs ... Dr. Kristina WHALEN
32 Vice President Student Svcs ... Dr. Jeanne WILSON
11 Vice President Admin Services ... Ms. Anette RAICHBART
04 Exec Assistant to the President ... Ms. Sheri MOORE
35 Dean of Student Services ... Mr. Joel GAGNON
49 Dean Arts & Humanities ... Ms. Amy MATTERN
81 Dean Math/Science/Eng/Public Safety ... Dr. Nan HO
69 Dn Pub Saf/Adv Mfg/Trans/Hlth/Kin ... Mr. Kevin KRAMER
50 Dn Business/Soc Sci/Lrng Resources ... Mr. Stuart MCELDERRY
84 Dean of Enrollment Services ... Ms. Tamica WARD
45 Director of Research & Planning ... Mr. Rajinder SAMRA
37 Financial Aid/Veterans Assistance ... Ms. Andi SCHREIBMAN
19 Campus Safety Supervisor ... Mr. Sean PRATHER
08 Head Librarian ... Dr. Tina INZERILLA
102 Executive Director LPC Foundation ... Mr. Kenneth COOPER
41 Athletic Director ... Mr. James GIACOMAZZI
10 Associate Business Officer ... Ms. Sui SONG
18 Project Planner/Manager Facilities ... Ms. Ann KROLL
06 Registrar ... Vacant
88 Project Manager CTE ... Ms. Vicki SHIPMAN
88 Director Child Development Center ... Ms. Angela LOPEZ

Chaffey College (B)

5885 Haven Avenue, Rancho Cucamonga CA 91737-3002
County: San Bernardino — FICE Identification: 001163
Unit ID: 111939
Telephone: (909) 652-6000 — Carnegie Class: Assoc/HT-High Trad
FAX Number: (909) 652-6006 — Calendar System: Semester
URL: www.chaffey.edu
Established: 1883 — Annual Undergrad Tuition & Fees (In-State): $1,180
Enrollment: 20,025 — Coed
Affiliation or Control: State — IRS Status: 501(c)3
Highest Offering: Associate Degree
Accreditation: WJ, ADNUR, DA, RAD

01 Superintendent/President ... Dr. Henry D. SHANNON
11 Assoc Supt Administrative Services ... Mr. Troy AMENT
10 Assoc Supt Bus Svcs/Econ Dev ... Ms. Lisa BAILEY
05 Assoc Supt Instruction/Inst Effect ... Dr. Laura HOPE
32 Associate Supt Student Services ... Ms. Alisha ROSAS
09 Dean Inst Research/Research Dev ... Mr. Jim FILLPOT
29 Director Alumni Relations ... Ms. Janeth RODRIGUEZ
85 Director International Students ... Vacant
35 Dean Student Life ... Mr. Christopher BRUNELLE
84 Executive Director Enrollment Svcs ... Ms. Janeth RODRIGUEZ
21 Exec Director Business Services ... Ms. Kim ERICKSON
13 Director Technical Services ... Mr. Michael FINK
23 Director Student Health Services ... Vacant
37 Director Financial Aid ... Ms. Patricia BOPKO
109 Director Auxiliary Services ... Vacant
114 Exec Dir Fiscal & Audit Svcs ... Mr. Patrick CABILDO
88 Director Museum Gallery ... Ms. Rebecca TRAWICK
18 Manager Facilities Development ... Ms. Sarah RILEY
12 Dean Chino Campus ... Dr. Teresa HULL
88 Dean Visual Performing Arts ... Ms. Misty BURRUEL
50 Dean Business & Applied Tech ... Dr. Yolanda FRIDAY
81 Dean Mathematics & Science ... Mr. Michael WANGLER
83 Dean Social/Behavioral Sciences ... Dr. Corene SCHWARTZ
79 Dean Language Arts ... Dr. Jason CHEVALIER
38 Dean Counseling & Matriculation ... Mr. Michael MCCLELLAN
12 Dean Fontana Campus ... Ms. Amy NEVAREZ
76 Dean Health Sciences ... Mr. Eric SORENSON
04 Exec Assistant Supt/Pres Office ... Ms. Julie SANCHEZ
41 Director Athletics ... Dr. Timi BROWN
86 Manager Government Relations ... Ms. Janeth RODRIGUEZ
15 Director Human Resources ... Ms. Susan HARDIE
102 Director Foundation ... Ms. Heather PARSONS
103 Executive Director Economic Dev ... Ms. Sheneui WEBER
28 Director of Diversity ... Ms. Tomeika CARTER
96 Interim Director of Purchasing ... Ms. Ashira MURPHY

Chamberlain University-Sacramento (C)

10971 Sun Center Drive, Rancho Cordova CA 95670
Telephone: (916) 330-3410 — Identification: 770978
Accreditation: &HLC, NURSE

† Branch campus of Chamberlain University-Addison, Addison, IL

Chapman University (D)

One University Drive, Orange CA 92866-1099
County: Orange — FICE Identification: 001164
Unit ID: 111948
Telephone: (714) 997-6815 — Carnegie Class: DU-Higher
FAX Number: (714) 997-6713 — Calendar System: 4/1/4
URL: www.chapman.edu
Established: 1861 — Annual Undergrad Tuition & Fees: $57,214
Enrollment: 9,761 — Coed
Affiliation or Control: Christian Church (Disciples Of Christ)
IRS Status: 501(c)3
Highest Offering: Doctorate
Accreditation: WC, ARCPA, CAEP, DANCE, LAW, MFCD, MUS, NASP, PHAR, PTA, SP, THEA

01 President ... Dr. Daniele C. STRUPPA
05 Exec VP/Provost & CAO ... Dr. Norma BOUCHARD
03 Executive Vice President & COO ... Mr. Harold W. HEWITT, JR.
111 Exec VP University Advancement ... Dr. Matt PARLOW
32 VP & Dean of Students ... Dr. Jerry PRICE
84 VP/Dean Enrollment Management ... Mr. Michael PELLY
11 Vice Provost of Operations/Finance ... Dr. Raymond SFEIR
09 Vice Prov Inst Effect & Fac Affairs ... Mr. Joseph SLOWENSKY
49 Dean Wilkinson Col Hum/Soc Sci ... Dr. Jennifer KEENE
61 Interim Dean School of Law ... Dr. Marisa S. CIANCIARULO
50 Dean School Business/Economics ... Dr. Henrik CRONQVIST
67 Interim Dean School of Pharmacy ... Dr. Rennolds OSTROM
121 Director of Academic Advising ... Mr. Roberto CORONEL
53 Dean College of Educ Studies ... Dr. Roxanne GREITZ MILLER
57 Dean College of Film/Media Arts ... Mr. Stephen GALLOWAY
57 Dean College of Performing Arts ... Dr. Guilio ONGARO
83 Dean Col Health/Behavioral Sciences ... Dr. Janeen M. HILL
81 Dean College of Science/Tech ... Dr. Michael IBBA
54 Dean School of Engineering ... Dr. L. Andrew LYON
57 Executive Dir Center for Arts ... Mr. Richard T. BRYANT
104 Director Ctr for Global Education ... Ms. Kristin BEAVERS
97 Vice Provost Undergrad Education ... Dr. Nina LENOIR
45 VP Campus Planning & Design ... Ms. Collette CREPPELL
15 Vice President/CHRO ... Mr. Brian POWELL
43 Assoc Vice Pres of Legal Affairs ... Ms. Janine DUMONTELLE
10 Assoc Vice President & Controller ... Mr. Brian THOMASON
07 Asst VP of Undergrad Admissions ... Ms. Marcela MEJIA MARTINEZ
26 VP of Strategic Marketing ... Ms. Jamie CEMAN
18 VP Facilities ... Mr. Rick TURNER
27 Director Public Relations ... Ms. Cerise VALENZUELA METZGER
08 Dean of Library ... Dr. Kevin ROSS
29 Asst VP Strategic Engagement/Dev ... Ms. Kim GREENHALL
13 VP/Chief Information Officer ... Ms. Helen NORRIS
31 VP of Community Relations ... Ms. Alisa DRISCOLL
09 Director of Institutional Research ... Dr. Marisol ARREDONDO SAMSON
06 Registrar ... Ms. Jan MCCUEN
46 Actg VP Rsrch/Sponsored Pgms Admin ... Dr. Janeen HILL
28 VP of Diversity/Equity/Inclusion ... Dr. Reginald C. STEWART
37 Director Undergrad Financial Aid ... Mr. David CARNEVALE
85 Manager International Scholars ... Ms. Susan SAMS
19 Chief of Public Safety ... Mr. Rick GONZALEZ
39 Director Residence Life ... Mr. David SUNDBY
41 Athletic Director ... Mr. Terry BOESEL
42 Dean of the Chapel ... Dr. Gail STEARNS
04 Associate to the President ... Dr. Christina MARSHALL
88 Exec Assistant to the Provost ... Ms. Shehani REEDER
23 Director Student Health Services ... Ms. Jacqueline DEATS
35 Asst VP for Student Affairs ... Dr. Chris HUTCHISON
36 Asst VP Career & Professional Dev ... Ms. Jennifer KIM
38 Dir Psychological Counseling Svcs ... Dr. Andrew KAMI
96 Director Purchasing ... Mr. Adey OYENUGA
04 Executive Asst to the President ... Ms. Erika CURIEL
58 Vice Provost for Graduate Educ ... Dr. Jason KELLER
102 Dir Corporate/Foundation Relations ... Mr. Mike STRINGER
44 Asst VP Legacy Planning ... Mr. David MOORE
90 Asst VP Educational Technology ... Dr. Jana REMY
105 Webmaster ... Mr. Ramiro LANDEROS
25 Dir of Sponsored Projects Svcs ... Vacant
108 Assoc VP Assessment/Student Success ... Dr. Brad PETITFILS
22 Director of Equal Opportunity ... Mr. Albert ROBERSON

Charles R. Drew University of Medicine & Science (E)

1731 E 120th Street, Los Angeles CA 90059-3025
County: Los Angeles — FICE Identification: 010365
Unit ID: 111966
Telephone: (323) 563-4800 — Carnegie Class: Spec-4-yr-Other Health
FAX Number: (323) 563-5987 — Calendar System: Semester
URL: www.cdrewu.edu
Established: 1966 — Annual Undergrad Tuition & Fees: $14,002
Enrollment: 872 — Coed
Affiliation or Control: Independent Non-Profit — IRS Status: 501(c)3
Highest Offering: Doctorate
Accreditation: WC, ARCPA, NURSE, PH, RAD

01 President & CEO ... Dr. David M. CARLISLE
05 EVP Academic Affairs/Provost ... Dr. Sylvia O. MANNING
100 Chief of Staff ... Vacant
45 VP Research & Health Affairs ... Dr. Jadutt VADGAMA
111 SVP Advancement & Operations ... Ms. Angela L. MINNIEFIELD
10 VP Finance/Chief Business Officer ... Mr. Carl MCLANEY
15 Int Chief Human Resources Ofcr ... Ms. Angela MINNIEFIELD
63 Dean College of Medicine ... Dr. Deborah PROTHROW-STITH
66 Dean School of Nursing ... Dr. Gail WASHINGTON
76 Dean College of Science & Health ... Dr. Monica FERRINI
20 Asst Provost Faculty Affairs ... Dr. William SHAY
32 Dean Student Affairs ... Dr. Keosha PARTLOW
20 Sr Assoc Dean Academic Affairs ... Vacant
09 Dir Inst Research & Effectiveness ... Dr. Susana SANTOS
21 Chief Financial Officer ... Ms. Elizabeth BASKERVILLE
08 Director Health Sciences Library ... Dr. Darlene PARKER-KELLY
06 Registrar ... Ms. Raquel MUNOZ
84 Director of Enrollment Management ... Ms. Vanessa RIGGINS
13 Chief Information Officer ... Mr. Aaron WEATHERSBY

Charter College-Oxnard (F)

2000 Outlet Center Drive, Suite 150, Oxnard CA 93036
Telephone: (805) 973-1240 — Identification: 666675
Accreditation: ABHES

† Branch campus of Charter College, Vancouver, WA

Chicago School of Professional Psychology (G)

707 Wilshire Blvd. Suite 600, Los Angeles CA 90017
County: Los Angeles — FICE Identification: 021553
Unit ID: 455664
Telephone: (213) 615-2700 — Carnegie Class: Spec-4-yr-Other Health
FAX Number: (213) 615-7274 — Calendar System: Semester
URL: www.thechicagoschool.edu
Established: 2008 — Annual Undergrad Tuition & Fees: $12,524
Enrollment: 3,131 — Coed
Affiliation or Control: Independent Non-Profit — IRS Status: 501(c)3
Highest Offering: Doctorate
Accreditation: WC, CLPSY

01 President ... Dr. Michele NEALON
05 Vice Pres AA/Chief Academic Officer ... Dr. Ted SCHOLZ
10 Sr Director of Business Operations ... Mr. Chris JACKSON
32 Dean for Student Success ... Ms. Jennifer STRIPE PORTILLO
15 Vice Pres Human Resources ... Dr. David IWANE
11 Chief Operating Officer ... Dr. Michael FALOTICO
111 Director Inst Advancement ... Mr. Anthony MACK
26 Director of Communications ... Mr. Victor ABALOS
04 Administrative Asst to President ... Ms. Adriana KLEIMAN
06 National Registrar ... Ms. Jennifer STROBEL
08 University Librarian ... Mr. David SIBLEY
100 Chief of Staff ... Ms. Shari MIKOS
101 Secretary of the Institution/Board ... Ms. Patti TYRA
19 Director of Facilities ... Mr. Brian LA BELLE
37 Regional Assoc Director of Fin Aid ... Mr. Seph RODRIGUEZ
09 Director of Institutional Research ... Mr. Kevin MCPHERSON
108 Dir Institutional Effectiveness ... Ms. Virginia QUINONEZ
07 AVP of Admissions ... Ms. Christina SHADE

China Evangelical Seminary North America (H)

1520 W. Cameron Avenue Ste 275,
West Covina CA 91790
County: Los Angeles — Identification: 667256
Telephone: (626) 917-9482 — Carnegie Class: Not Classified
FAX Number: (626) 851-1371 — Calendar System: Quarter
URL: www.cesna.edu
Established: 2007 — Annual Graduate Tuition & Fees: N/A
Enrollment: N/A — Coed
Affiliation or Control: Non-denominational — IRS Status: 501(c)3
Highest Offering: Doctorate; No Undergraduates
Accreditation: THEOL

01 President ... Dr. Katheryn LEUNG
05 Academic Dean ... Dr. Raymond HSU
11 Chief of Administration ... Rev. Hokeung C. CHAN
30 Chief Development/Advancement ... Dr. Tina LIU
37 Director Student Financial Aid ... Dr. Chun M. FONG
08 Chief Library Officer ... Dr. Jean WU
13 Chief Info Technology Ofcr (CIO) ... Dr. Frank LIU

Christian Witness Theological Seminary (I)

1975 Concourse Drive, San Jose CA 95131
County: Santa Clara — Identification: 667255
Telephone: (408) 433-2280 — Carnegie Class: Not Classified
FAX Number: (408) 433-9855 — Calendar System: Semester
URL: www.cwts.edu
Established: 1978 — Annual Graduate Tuition & Fees: N/A
Enrollment: N/A — Coed
Affiliation or Control: Interdenominational — IRS Status: 501(c)3
Highest Offering: Doctorate; No Undergraduates
Accreditation: THEOL

01 President ... RevDr. Luke TSAI

11 Vice President Administration ..... Rev. James IP
05 Academic Dean ..... Dr. Peter TIE
07 Director of Admissions ..... Dr. Kevin CHEN
32 Dean of Student Affairs ..... Rev. Andrew LO
15 Director of Human Resources ..... Ms. Theresa WANG

Church Divinity School of the Pacific (A)

2451 Ridge Road, Berkeley CA 94709-1217
County: Alameda FICE Identification: 001165
Unit ID: 112127
Telephone: (510) 204-0700 Carnegie Class: Spec-4-yr-Faith
FAX Number: N/A Calendar System: Semester
URL: www.cdsp.edu
Established: 1893 Annual Graduate Tuition & Fees: N/A
Enrollment: 71 Coed
Affiliation or Control: Protestant Episcopal IRS Status: 501(c)3
Highest Offering: Doctorate; No Undergraduates
Accreditation: THEOL

01 Interim President & Dean ..... RtRev. Kirk SMITH
03 Vice President & COO ..... Rev. John DWYER
05 Dean Academic Affairs ..... Rev Dr. Ruth MEYERS
32 Director Student Services ..... Rev. Michael BARHAM
15 Director of Human Resources ..... Mr. Dennis HENDRICKS
20 Associate Dean Academic Affairs ..... Rev. Mark HEARN
10 Manager of Operations ..... Ms. Alissa FENCSIK
06 Registrar ..... Mr. Bob KRAMISH
04 Executive Assistant ..... Ms. Meghan RITCHIE

Citrus College (B)

1000 W Foothill Boulevard, Glendora CA 91741-1899
County: Los Angeles FICE Identification: 001166
Unit ID: 112172
Telephone: (626) 963-0323 Carnegie Class: Assoc/HT-High Trad
FAX Number: (626) 914-8618 Calendar System: Semester
URL: www.citruscollege.edu
Established: 1915 Annual Undergrad Tuition & Fees (In-District): $1,194
Enrollment: 11,863 Coed
Affiliation or Control: State/Local IRS Status: 501(c)3
Highest Offering: Associate Degree
Accreditation: WJ, DA

01 Superintendent/President ..... Dr. Greg SCHULZ
05 Vice President Academic Affairs ..... Dr. Joumana MCGOWAN
32 Vice President Student Services ..... Dr. Richard RAMS
10 Vice Pres Finance/Admin Services ..... Ms. Claudette E. DAIN
07 Dean Enrollment Services ..... Dr. Gerald SEQUEIRA
51 Dean Career/Tech & Cont Educ ..... Mr. Michael WANGLER
38 Dean of Counseling ..... Dr. Nicole SMITH
15 Director Human Resources ..... Dr. Robert L. SAMMIS
102 Director Foundation ..... Ms. Christina M. GARCIA
35 Dean of Students ..... Dr. Maryann TOLANO-LEVEQUE
18 Director Facilities & Construction ..... Mr. Fred DIAMOND
09 Director of Institutional Research ..... Dr. Lan HAO
06 Registrar ..... Ms. Cynthia ARRIETA
37 Director Financial Aid ..... Mr. Stephen FAHEY
21 Director of Fiscal Services ..... Mr. Wade ELLIS
28 Manager HR/Staff Diversity ..... Ms. Brenda FINK
13 Chief Information Services Officer ..... Mr. Robert HUGHES
19 Director of Campus Safety ..... Mr. Benjamin MACIAS
83 Dean Social/Behavioral Sciences/DE ..... Dr. Dana HESTER
41 Dean Kinesiology/Athletics/Health ..... Mr. Junior DOMINGO
79 Dean Language Arts & Library ..... Dr. Gina HOGAN
65 Dean Natural/Physical Sci & Health ..... Dr. Eric RABITOY
57 Dean Visual & Performing Arts ..... Mr. John VAUGHAN
81 Dean Math & Business ..... Ms. Victoria DOMINGUEZ
22 Director EOPS CARE CalWORKS ..... Ms. Sarah GONZALES-TAPIA
25 Dir Grants/Development Oversight ..... Dr. Marianne SMITH
101 Secretary of the Institution/Board ..... Ms. Christine A. LINK
109 Director of Business Services ..... Mr. Shawn JONES
26 Exec Dir of Cmty & External Rels ..... Ms. Melissa UTSUKI
88 Director Haugh Performing Arts Ctr ..... Ms. Tiina MITTLER
76 Director Health Sciences ..... Ms. Salima ALLAHBACHAYO
121 Director Student Support Svcs ..... Ms. Jessica LOPEZ-JIMINEZ
40 Enterprise Services Manager ..... Mr. Eric MAGALLON

City College of San Francisco (C)

50 Frida Kahlo Way, E200, San Francisco CA 94112
County: San Francisco FICE Identification: 001167
Unit ID: 112190
Telephone: (415) 239-3000 Carnegie Class: Assoc/MT-VT-High Trad
FAX Number: (415) 239-3919 Calendar System: Semester
URL: www.ccsf.edu
Established: 1935 Annual Undergrad Tuition & Fees (In-District): $1,165
Enrollment: 19,707 Coed
Affiliation or Control: State/Local IRS Status: 501(c)3
Highest Offering: Associate Degree
Accreditation: WJ, ACFEI, CAHIIM, DA, EMT, MAC, RAD

01 Chancellor ..... Dr. David MARTIN
11 Sr Vice Chanc Admin/Stdnt Affs ..... Vacant
05 Vice Chancellor Academic Affairs ..... Mr. Thomas BOEGEL
10 Vice Chancellor Finance/Admin & CFO ..... Mr. John AL-AMIN
108 Dean of Institutional Effectiveness ..... Dr. Pam MERY
12 Dean Civic Center Campus ..... Dr. Geisce LY
12 Dean Southeast Campus ..... Mr. Torrance BYNUM
12 Dean Mission Campus ..... Mr. Vinicio LOPEZ
12 Dean Downtown/Business School ..... Dr. Geisce LY
32 Vice Chanc of Student Affairs ..... Dr. Lisa COOPER WILKINS
37 Dean Financial Aid/Student Success ..... Mr. Guillermo VILLANUEVA
07 Dean Admissions & Records ..... Vacant
20 Assoc Vice Chanc of Instruction ..... Ms. Edith KAEUPER
103 Int Dean Workforce Development ..... Mr. John HALPIN
15 Assoc Vice Chanc Human Resources ..... Ms. Clara STARR
121 Dean Student Support Services ..... Ms. Lidia JENKINS
22 Assoc Dean Student Equity ..... Ms. Tessa HENDERSON-BROWN
12 Dean Chinatown/Contract & Cont Ed ..... Ms. Kit DAI
57 Dean Sch of Visual/Performing Arts ..... Vacant
83 Dean Behavioral/Social Sci ..... Ms. Jill YEE
81 Dean Science/Math/Technology/Engr ..... Mr. David YEE
68 Dean J Adams Campus/Sch Hlth Educ ..... Ms. Edie KAEUPER
30 Assoc Vice Chanc Institutional Dev ..... Ms. Kristin CHARLES
13 Technical Operations Manager ..... Mr. Tim RYAN
16 Int Director Employee Relations ..... Ms. Cassandra LAWSON
18 Director Buildings/Grounds ..... Mr. Jimmy KIRK
96 Dean of Purchasing ..... Mr. Garth KWIECIEN
19 Chief of Police/Public Safety ..... Mr. Mario VASQUEZ
22 ADA Compliance Officer ..... Vacant
25 Int Dean Grants/EAP ..... Ms. Wendy MILLER
06 Assoc Dean Admission & Records ..... Ms. Monika LIU
101 Liaison to the Board of Trustees ..... Ms. Linda SHAW
41 Athletic Director ..... Mr. Harold BROWN
43 Dir Legal Services/General Counsel ..... Vacant
26 Director of External Affairs ..... Vacant
04 Assistant to the Chancellor ..... Ms. Grace ESTEBAN
08 Dean Library ..... Ms. Cynthia DEWAR
100 Chief of Staff ..... Vacant
106 Dean Online Education/E-learning ..... Ms. Cynthia DEWAR

City of Hope (D)

1500 East Duarte Road, Duarte CA 91010-3000
County: Los Angeles FICE Identification: 035924
Unit ID: 441238
Telephone: (626) 256-4673 Carnegie Class: Spec-4-yr-Other Health
FAX Number: (626) 301-8105 Calendar System: Semester
URL: www.cityofhope.org
Established: 1994 Annual Graduate Tuition & Fees: N/A
Enrollment: 90 Coed
Affiliation or Control: Independent Non-Profit IRS Status: 501(c)3
Highest Offering: Doctorate; No Undergraduates
Accreditation: WC, RTT

01 President/CEO ..... Robert STONE
05 Provost/Chief Scientific Officer ..... Dr. Steven T. ROSEN
11 Interim Chief Operating Officer ..... Vince JENSEN
10 Chief Financial Officer ..... Jennifer PARKHURST
26 Sr VP & Chief Marketing/Comm Ofcr ..... Gulden MESARA
28 Sr VP/Chief Diversity Officer ..... Angela L. TALTON
43 General Counsel/Secretary ..... Cristin O'CALLAHAN
15 Chief Human Resource Officer ..... Kety DURON
58 Dean of Graduate School ..... Dr. John J. ROSSI
06 Registrar ..... Tracy KURZY
07 Director of Admissions ..... Vacant
08 Head Librarian ..... Andrea LYNCH

*The Claremont College Services (E)

101 South Mills Avenue, Claremont CA 91711-5053
County: Los Angeles Identification: 666003
Telephone: (909) 621-8026 Carnegie Class: N/A
FAX Number: (909) 621-8517
URL: https://services.claremont.edu

01 Chief Executive Officer ..... Mr. Stig LANESSKOG
10 Int VPfor Finance/Treasurer ..... Ms. Vanessa AGUIRRE
32 Vice President of Student Affairs ..... Ms. Janet SMITH DICKERSON
21 AVP Financial Services/Controller ..... Ms. Mia ALONZO
26 Director of Communications ..... Ms. Laura MUNA-LANDA
19 Asst Vice Pres Campus Safety ..... Mr. Stan SKIPWORTH
13 Chief Information Officer ..... Mr. Chuck THOMPSON
101 Sec to Board/AVP Cmty Relations ..... Mr. Colin TUDOR
08 Dean TCC Library ..... Ms. Janet BISHOP
15 Director Human Resources ..... Ms. Crystal ROSETTI

*Claremont Graduate University (F)

150 E 10th Street, Claremont CA 91711-5909
County: Los Angeles FICE Identification: 001169
Unit ID: 112251
Telephone: (909) 621-8000 Carnegie Class: DU-Higher
FAX Number: (909) 621-8390 Calendar System: Semester
URL: www.cgu.edu
Established: 1925 Annual Graduate Tuition & Fees: N/A
Enrollment: 1,949 Coed
Affiliation or Control: Independent Non-Profit IRS Status: 501(c)3
Highest Offering: Doctorate; No Undergraduates
Accreditation: WC, PH

02 President ..... Dr. Len JESSUP
04 Exec Asst to the President ..... Ms. Cindy BIERMAN
05 Exec Vice President and Provost ..... Dr. Patricia EASTON
45 VP Strategic Initiatives ..... Dr. Diane CHASE
10 VP Finance/Admin/CFO ..... Ms. Mary Ann RODRIGUEZ
111 VP for Advancement ..... Ms. Kristen ANDERSEN-DALEY
84 Asst VP Enroll/Dean of Admissions ..... Mr. Timothy COUNCIL
46 Assoc Provost for Research ..... Dr. Eusebio ALVARO
108 Assoc Prov for Inst Effectiveness ..... Dr. Jody WATERS
15 AVP for Human Resources ..... Ms. Alejandra GAYTAN
47 Botany Center ..... Dr. Lucinda MCDADE
50 Drucker-Ito Grad School of Mgt ..... Dr. David SPROTT
83 Behavioral & Organizational Sci ..... Dr. Michelle BLIGH
69 Community & Global Health ..... Dr. Jay ORR
53 Educational Studies ..... Dr. DeLacy GANLEY
77 Center for Information Science ..... Vacant
81 Mathematical Sciences Institute ..... Dr. Marina CHUGUNOVA
82 Politics & Economics ..... Dr. Michelle BLIGH
73 Arts and Humanities ..... Dr. Lori Anne FERRELL
09 Institutional Research Officer ..... Dr. Yumi HUANG
08 Library Dean ..... Dr. Janet BISHOP
19 Director of Campus Safety ..... Mr. Ernest DIDIER
21 Assoc VP Finance/Admin ..... Mr. Juan HERNANDEZ
29 Director of Alumni Engagement ..... Ms. Kala KARDEN
32 Asst VP Stdnt Affs/Dean of Students ..... Ms. Quamina CARTER
36 Director of Career Development ..... Ms. Michelle PONCE
37 Director Student Financial Aid ..... Ms. Kristal GAMA
85 Director of International Students ..... Ms. Heather CASE
06 Registrar ..... Ms. Sarah JAQUES-ROSS
18 AVP of Facilities and Aux Services ..... Ms. Lindsay GIRARDIN
90 AVP Tech & Info Systems ..... Mr. Manoj CHITRE
91 Dir of Enterprise Infrastructure ..... Mr. Ryan ZISKA
106 Asst Dir Digital Learning ..... Dr. Aimee GARTEN
101 Secretary to the Board ..... Ms. Chris ARMSTRONG

*Claremont McKenna College (G)

500 E 9th Street, Claremont CA 91711-6400
County: Los Angeles FICE Identification: 001170
Unit ID: 112260
Telephone: (909) 621-8111 Carnegie Class: Bac-A&S
FAX Number: (909) 621-8790 Calendar System: Semester
URL: www.claremontmckenna.edu
Established: 1946 Annual Undergrad Tuition & Fees: $56,475
Enrollment: 1,264 Coed
Affiliation or Control: Independent Non-Profit IRS Status: 501(c)3
Highest Offering: Master's
Accreditation: WC

02 President and CEO ..... Hiram E. CHODOSH
05 VP Academic Affs/Dean of Faculty ..... Heather ANTECOL
111 Vice President for Advancement ..... Michelle CHAMBERLAIN
10 VP Campus Plng/Cap Proj/Spec Couns ..... Matt BIBBENS
32 Vice President for Student Affairs ..... Sharon BASSO
115 Vice Pres/Chief Investment Officer ..... James J. FLOYD
29 Asst Vice Pres Alumni/Parent Rels ..... Evan RUTTER
07 Assoc Vice President for Admissions ..... Jennifer SANDOVAL DANCS
26 Assoc VP Public Affs/Communications ..... Vacant
92 Dean of Robert Day Scholars Program ..... Michelle CHAMBERLAIN
06 Registrar/AVP Academic Affairs ..... Elizabeth MORGAN
15 Asst Vice Pres for Human Resources ..... Dana NAGENGAST
104 Director of Off-Campus Study ..... Kristen MALLORY
41 Director of Athletics ..... Erica PERKINS JASPER
04 Special Assistant to the President ..... Dorothy BUCHANAN

*Claremont School of Theology (H)

1325 N College Avenue, Claremont CA 91711-3199
County: Los Angeles FICE Identification: 001288
Unit ID: 124283
Telephone: (909) 447-2500 Carnegie Class: Spec-4-yr-Faith
FAX Number: (909) 626-7062 Calendar System: Semester
URL: www.cst.edu
Established: 1885 Annual Graduate Tuition & Fees: N/A
Enrollment: 287 Coed
Affiliation or Control: United Methodist IRS Status: 501(c)3
Highest Offering: Doctorate; No Undergraduates
Accreditation: WC, THEOL

02 President ..... Dr. Jeffrey KUAN
04 Exec Assistant to the President ..... Ms. Maria Lise IANNUZZI
10 Chief Financial Officer ..... Mr. David ROBYDEK
05 Acting VP Academic Affairs & Dean ..... Dr. Andrew DREITCER
88 Vice President for Intl Relations ..... Dr. JongOh LEE
20 Associate Dean ..... Vacant
08 Dean of Library & Info Services ..... Vacant
32 Interim Dean Students & Disability ..... Dr. Clemette HASKINS
26 Interim VP Communications ..... Rev. Steve HORSWILL-JOHNSTON
27 Director of Communications ..... Ms. Kendra FREDRICKSON-LAOUINI
30 Director Donor Stewardship/Database ..... Mr. Dmitri POTEMKIN
07 Dir Admissions/Enrollment/Fin Svcs ..... Ms. Tomeka JACOBS
06 Registrar ..... Ms. Sansu WOODMANCY
78 Director of Field Education ..... Ms. Barbara NIXON
28 Campus Diversity Officer ..... Vacant

*Keck Graduate Institute (I)

535 Watson Drive, Claremont CA 91711-4817
County: Los Angeles FICE Identification: 038533
Unit ID: 440031
Telephone: (909) 607-7855 Carnegie Class: Masters/L
FAX Number: (909) 607-8086 Calendar System: Semester
URL: www.kgi.edu
Established: 1997 Annual Graduate Tuition & Fees: N/A
Enrollment: 631 Coed
Affiliation or Control: Independent Non-Profit IRS Status: 501(c)3
Highest Offering: Doctorate; No Undergraduates
Accreditation: WC, #ARCPA, PHAR

00 Board Chair ..... James WIDERGREN

02 President/CEO .... Dr. Sheldon M. SCHUSTER
04 Exec Asst to Pres & Secy BOT .... Patricia ROBIDOUX
05 Chief Academic Officer .... Vacant
10 CFO & COO .... Dr. Kelly ESPERIAS
06 Registrar & Dir Student Info Mgmt .... Melissa S. BROWN
32 Dean of Students .... Dr. Cynthia MARTINEZ
88 Dean School of Applied Life Science .... Dr. Martin ZDANOWICZ
67 Dean Sch of Pharmacy & Health Sci .... Dr. Martin ZDANOWICZ
46 Dean of Research .... Larry GRILL
123 Dean of Admissions/Financial Aid .... Sofia TORO
35 Director Student & Campus Life .... Andrea MOZQUEDA
21 Asst VP Finance & Business Svcs .... David CARTER
15 Asst VP Human Resources .... Cheryl MERRITT
16 Manager Human Resources .... Michelle VEGA
18 Asst VP Campus Operations .... Mark BENNETT
37 Director Financial Aid .... Maryville TUZON
09 Director of Institutional Research .... Vacant
111 VP Institutional Development .... Sharlene RISDON-JACKSON
88 Sr Director Inst Development .... Juliet NUSBAUM
25 Dir Sponsored Research Services .... Kirsten TORGUSON
26 Sr Dir Marketing & Communications .... Ivan ALBER
120 Dir Instructional Design & Dev .... George BRADFORD
13 Director IT .... Mark BENNETT
07 Dean of Admissions .... Sofia TORO
102 Sr Dir Corporate Partnerships .... Shannon BRAUN

Claremont Lincoln University (A)

150 West 1st Street, Claremont CA 91711

County: Los Angeles — Identification: 667215
Unit ID: 488387
Telephone: (909) 667-4411 — Carnegie Class: Spec-4-yr-Bus
FAX Number: (909) 399-3443 — Calendar System: Quarter
URL: claremontlincoln.edu
Established: 2011 — Annual Graduate Tuition & Fees: N/A
Enrollment: 300 — Coed
Affiliation or Control: Independent Non-Profit — IRS Status: 501(c)3
Highest Offering: Master's; No Undergraduates
Accreditation: WC

01 CEO/President .... Dr. Lynn PRIDDY
11 EVP/Chief Operating Officer .... Mr. Joseph SALLUSTIO
05 VP for Academic Affairs/CAO .... Dr. Joanna BAUER
32 Dean of Student Svcs/Registrar .... Ms. Karen KRAKER
20 Dean of Academic Affairs .... Dr. Nita EVANS
111 VP for University Advancement .... Vacant
10 Chief Financial Officer .... Ms. Linda RABITOY
35 Student Services Advisor .... Ms. Clair BACA
04 Executive Asst to President .... Ms. Judy MORAVITZ
30 Director of Development .... Ms. Sara GERTLER
15 Dir Admin Svcs/Chief HR Ofcr .... Ms. Nancy BARNES
37 Director Student Financial Aid .... Mr. Cesar PEREZ

CNI College (B)

1610 East St. Andrew Place, Santa Ana CA 92705

County: Orange — FICE Identification: 032423
Unit ID: 433013
Telephone: (714) 437-9697 — Carnegie Class: Spec-4-yr-Other Health
FAX Number: (714) 437-9356 — Calendar System: Other
URL: www.cnicollege.edu
Established: 1994 — Annual Undergrad Tuition & Fees: N/A
Enrollment: 522 — Coed
Affiliation or Control: Proprietary — IRS Status: Proprietary
Highest Offering: Baccalaureate
Accreditation: ABHES, NURSE, SURTEC

01 President .... Mr. James BUFFINGTON

*Coast Community College District Administration Offices (C)

1370 Adams Avenue, Costa Mesa CA 92626-5429

County: Orange — FICE Identification: 008711
Unit ID: 112376
Telephone: (714) 438-4600 — Carnegie Class: N/A
FAX Number: (714) 438-4882
URL: www.cccd.edu

01 Chancellor .... Dr. Whitney YAMAMURA
10 Vice Chancellor Finance & Adm Svcs .... Dr. Andrew DUNN
05 Vice Chanc Educ Svcs & Technology .... Dr. Andreea SERBAN
15 Vice Chanc Human Resources .... Dr. Marco BAEZA
26 Dir Public Affairs/Marketing .... Mr. Erik FALLIS
100 Director Chancellor Office Opers .... Ms. Julia L. CLEVENGER

*Coastline Community College (D)

11460 Warner Avenue, Fountain Valley CA 92708-2597

County: Orange — FICE Identification: 020635
Unit ID: 112385
Telephone: (714) 546-7600 — Carnegie Class: Assoc/HT-High Non
FAX Number: (714) 241-6277 — Calendar System: Semester
URL: www.coastline.edu
Established: 1976 — Annual Undergrad Tuition & Fees (In-District): $1,160
Enrollment: 8,826 — Coed
Affiliation or Control: State/Local — IRS Status: 501(c)3
Highest Offering: Associate Degree
Accreditation: WJ

02 President .... Dr. Vince RODRIGUEZ
05 Vice Pres of Instruction .... Dr. Isela OCEGUEDA
10 VP of Administrative Services .... Ms. Christine NGUYEN
32 Vice Pres Student Services .... Dr. Kate MUELLER
38 Dean Counseling/Matriculation .... Dr. Bruce KEELER
106 Assoc Dean of Distance Learning .... Mr. Bob NASH
12 Dean of Instruction Newport Beach .... Dr. Tom NEAL
12 Dean Instruct Tech Ed Garden Grove .... Dr. Nancy JONES
12 Dean Instruction Le Jao/Westminster .... Dr. Dana EMERSON
20 Dean Innovative Learning .... Dr. Shelly BLAIR
26 Director Public Relations/Marketing .... Ms. Dawn WILLSON
07 Director of Admissions/Records .... Ms. Jennifer MCDONALD
18 Director Maintenance & Operations .... Mr. Randy FLINT
21 Director Business Services .... Mr. Derek BUI
102 Exec Director College Foundation .... Ms. Mariam KHOSRAVANI
09 Dean Research/Plng/Effectiveness .... Dr. Aeron ZENTNER
24 Director of Electronic Media .... Ms. Judy GARVEY
15 Director of Personnel Services .... Ms. Renate DAVES
13 Director of Information Technology .... Mr. Dave THOMPSON
04 Admin Assistant to the President .... Vacant
19 Director Security/Safety .... Mr. Mike COLVER

*Golden West College (E)

15744 Golden West Street, Huntington Beach CA 92647-2748

County: Orange — FICE Identification: 001206
Unit ID: 115126
Telephone: (714) 892-7711 — Carnegie Class: Assoc/HT-Mix Trad/Non
FAX Number: (714) 895-8243 — Calendar System: Semester
URL: www.goldenwestcollege.edu
Established: 1966 — Annual Undergrad Tuition & Fees (In-District): $1,186
Enrollment: 11,396 — Coed
Affiliation or Control: State/Local — IRS Status: Exempt
Highest Offering: Associate Degree
Accreditation: WJ, ADNUR

02 President .... Mr. Tim MCGRATH
05 Vice Pres Instruction .... Ms. Meridith RANDALL
32 Vice Pres Student Services .... Dr. Claudia LEE
11 Vice Pres Admin Services .... Ms. Janet M. HOULIHAN
38 Dean Counseling .... Dr. Robyn BRAMMER
50 Executive Dean Business & Career Ed .... Mr. Christopher WHITESIDE
81 Interim Dean Math & Science .... Mr. Rick HICKS
49 Dean Arts & Letters .... Dr. David D. HUDSON
66 Dir School of Nursing .... Vacant
23 Director Student Health Center .... Dr. Judy CHENG
09 Dean Research/Plng/Inst Effect .... Dr. Kay NGUYEN
61 Dean Criminal Justice .... Mr. Ron LOWENBERG
35 Dean of Students & Library .... Ms. Carla MARTINEZ
84 Dean Enrollment Services .... Ms. Christina RYAN RODRIGUEZ
83 Dean Social Sci/Kines/Lrng Res .... Dr. Alex MIRANDA
15 Director Human Resources .... Ms. Leslile PICAZO
22 Dir DSPS .... Dr. Chad BOWMAN
10 Director Fiscal Services .... Mr. Paul WISNER
102 Director Foundation .... Mr. Bruce BERMAN
88 Coord Scholarships & Spec Events .... Ms. Valerie A. VENEGAS
07 Director of Admissions/Records .... Ms. Jennifer L. ORTBERG
37 Director of Financial Aid .... Ms. Adrienne BURTON
18 Director Maintenance & Operations .... Mr. Joseph B. DOWLING
41 Athletic Director .... Mr. Danny JOHNSON
04 Admin Asst to the President .... Ms. Diana RETES
19 Dir Public Safety/Emerg Prep .... Mr. Jon ARNOLD
35 Dir Student Life & Leadership Dev .... Mr. Frank CIRIONI
26 Dir Marketing & Public Relations .... Ms. Pam BRASHEAR
104 Dir of Global & Cultural Programs .... Ms. Melissa LYON
90 Dir Academic & User Support Svcs .... Mr. Kevin HARRISON
106 Dir Online Instruction .... Mr. Jorge ASCENCIO
31 Dir Community Educ & Swapmeet .... Vacant
88 Dir Guided Pathways/Dual Enroll .... Mr. Matt VALERIUS
88 Dir EOP&S .... Ms. Natalie TIMPSON

*Orange Coast College (F)

2701 Fairview Road, POB 5005, Costa Mesa CA 92626

County: Orange — FICE Identification: 001250
Unit ID: 120342
Telephone: (714) 432-5072 — Carnegie Class: Assoc/HT-High Trad
FAX Number: N/A — Calendar System: Semester
URL: www.orangecoastcollege.edu
Established: 1947 — Annual Undergrad Tuition & Fees (In-District): $1,188
Enrollment: 18,125 — Coed
Affiliation or Control: State/Local — IRS Status: 501(c)3
Highest Offering: Associate Degree
Accreditation: WJ, ACFEI, COARC, CVT, DA, DIETT, DMS, NDT, POLYT, RAD

02 President .... Dr. Angelica SUAREZ
05 Vice President of Instruction .... Ms. Michelle GRIMES-HILLMAN
32 Vice President Student Services .... Dr. Madjid NIROUMAND
10 Director of Fiscal Services .... Ms. Rachel KUBIK
11 Vice President Admin Services .... Dr. Richard PAGEL
84 Director Enrollment Services .... Ms. Rozanne CAPOCCIA-WHITE
38 Dean of Counseling .... Dr. Renee DE LONG
35 Dean of Students .... Dr. Derek VERGARA
28 Associate Dean Title IX .... Ms. Shannon QUIHUIZ
35 Director Student Life .... Mr. Michael MORVICE
26 Director Marketing & PR .... Mr. Juan GUTIERREZ
111 Exec Dir Inst Advancement/Found .... Mr. Douglas BENNETT
09 Admin Dir Research/Planning/IE .... Ms. Sheri STERNER
15 Director HR & Staff Development .... Ms. Rebecca MORGAN
07 Manager Enrollment Services .... Ms. Richelle PENALBA
18 Director Maintenance & Operations .... Mr. Enrique(Rick) GARCIA
37 Director Financial Aid .... Ms. Tanisha BRADFIELD
13 Director Information Technology .... Mr. Kevin HARRISON
23 Director Student Health Services .... Ms. Kelly DALY
88 Director Children's Center .... Ms. Patricia MENDOZA
68 Dean of Kinesiology & Athletics .... Dr. Michael SUTLIFF
72 Dean of Technology .... Vacant
50 Dean of Business & Computer Science .... Ms. Lisa KNUPPEL
83 Dean of Social & Behavioral Science .... Dr. Kevin HENSON
49 Dean of Literature & Languages .... Dr. Michael MANDELKERN
81 Dean of Math & Sciences .... Dr. Tara GIBLIN
88 Dean Consumer Health & Sciences .... Mr. Rodney FOSTER
57 Dean of Visual & Performing Arts .... Ms. Larissa NAZARENKO
25 Director CTE/Grants .... Ms. Lisa KNUPPEL
19 Director Campus Security .... Mr. James RUDY
40 Manager Bookstore .... Mr. Todd MURPHY
85 Assoc Dean Global Engagement Ctr .... Mr. Nathan JENSEN
121 Dean Student Success & Student Svcs .... Mr. Stephen TAMANAHA
04 Executive Asst to President .... Ms. Thuy NGUYEN
62 Dean Library Sci/Learning Support .... Mr. John TAYLOR
88 Director Maritime Center .... Ms. Sarah HIRSCH
22 Director Disabled Student Services .... Mr. Brian STOCKERT

The Colburn School (G)

200 S Grand Avenue, Los Angeles CA 90012-3007

County: Los Angeles — Identification: 666233
Telephone: (213) 621-2200 — Carnegie Class: Not Classified
FAX Number: (213) 621-2110 — Calendar System: Semester
URL: www.colburnschool.edu
Established: 2003 — Annual Undergrad Tuition & Fees: N/A
Enrollment: N/A — Coed
Affiliation or Control: Independent Non-Profit — IRS Status: 501(c)3
Highest Offering: Master's
Accreditation: MUS

01 President & CEO .... Mr. Sel KARDAN
05 Provost .... Dr. Adrian DALY
26 Vice President Communications .... Ms. Jennifer KALLEND
111 Vice President Advancement .... Ms. Annie WICKERT
15 Vice President Administration .... Ms. Linda CORMIER
10 Chief Financial Officer .... Ms. Maeesha MERCHANT

† Full room, board, and tuition are provided to accepted students through the school's endowment.

College of the Canyons (H)

26455 Rockwell Canyon Road, Santa Clarita CA 91355-1899

County: Los Angeles — FICE Identification: 008903
Unit ID: 111461
Telephone: (661) 259-7800 — Carnegie Class: Assoc/HT-Mix Trad/Non
FAX Number: (661) 259-8302 — Calendar System: Semester
URL: www.canyons.edu
Established: 1967 — Annual Undergrad Tuition & Fees (In-District): $1,156
Enrollment: 20,573 — Coed
Affiliation or Control: State/Local — IRS Status: 501(c)3
Highest Offering: Associate Degree
Accreditation: WJ, CNEA, MLTAD, NAEYC

01 Chancellor SCCCD & President COC .... Dr. Dianne G. VAN HOOK
03 Dep Chanc/Chief Diversity & Equity .... Dr. Diane FIERO
05 Asst Supt/VP Instruction .... Mr. Omar TORRES
10 Asst Supt/VP Business Services .... Ms. Sharlene COLEAL
15 Int Asst Supt/VP HR .... Dr. Rian MEDLIN
32 Asst Supt/VP Student Services .... Dr. Jasmine RUYS
18 Asst Supt/VP Facil Plng Op/Const .... Mr. Jim SCHRAGE
13 Asst Supt/VP Technology & Univ Ops .... Dr. James TEMPLE
103 VP Econ & Workforce Development .... Mr. Jeffrey FORREST
26 VP Public Info/Advoc/Ext Relations .... Mr. Eric HARNISH
12 VP Canyon County & Grants .... Dr. Ryan THEULE
21 Assoc VP Business Services .... Mr. Jason HINKLE
20 Assoc VP Instruction .... Mr. Luis GONZALEZ
45 Assoc VP Inst Research & Planning .... Dr. Daylene MEUSCHKE
35 Assoc VP Student Services .... Mr. Michael JOSLIN
51 Dean Acad Innovation & Cont Ed .... Ms. Diane AVERY
69 Dean Health Prof & Public Safety .... Ms. Kathy BAKHIT
85 Dean Intl Affairs/Global Engagement .... Dr. Jia-Yi CHENG-LEVINE
72 Dean School of Applied Tech .... Ms. Nadia COTTI
106 Dean Educ Tech/Lrng Res/Dist Educ .... Mr. James GLAPA-GROSSKLAG
81 Dean Math/Science & Engineering .... Ms. Ann HAMILTON
75 Dean Career and Technical Educ .... Ms. Harriet HAPPEL
79 Dean Schs of Human/Social/Beh Sci .... Mr. Andy MCCUTCHEON
109 Dean Campus Services & Ops (CCC) .... Mr. Anthony MICHAELIDES
68 Dean Ph Educ/Kinesiology/Athletics .... Mr. Steve RUYS
38 Dean Counseling .... Mr. Clinton SLAUGHTER
57 Dean Vis & Perf Arts/Dir of PAC .... Ms. Jennifer SMOLOS
37 Assoc Dean Student Financial Aid .... Mr. Tom BILBRUCK
07 Assoc Dean Admiss/Records/Veterans .... Mr. Steve ERWIN
88 Assoc Dean Lrng Resources/Dir TLC .... Ms. Mojdeh MAHN
96 Exec Dir Contracts Proc/Risk Mgmt .... Ms. April GRAHAM
88 Exec Dir Small Bus Devel Center .... Ms. Catherine GROOMS
14 Exec Dir Infrastructure & Info Sec .... Mr. Hsiawen HULL
88 Exec Director Employee Training .... Mr. John MILBURN
105 Exec Dir Enterprise Applications .... Ms. Lisa SAWYER
88 Director Employer Engagement .... Ms. Paula HODGE
88 Dir EOPS/CARE/CalWORKS/RISE .... Ms. Cyndi BENDEZU PALOMINO
113 Director Student Business Office .... Ms. Kathleen BENZ
88 Dir Prof Devel/Univ Ctr Operations .... Ms. Leslie CARR
88 Director Payroll .... Mr. Roy CASTILLO

88 Director Fiscal Services ... Ms. Balbir CHANDI
88 Director Grants Development ... Ms. Amber COLE
88 Dir Stdnt Resources & Basic Needs ... Ms. Sara COX
35 Dir Campus Life & Student Activity ... Ms. Kelly DAPP
88 Director Noncredit Enrollment Svcs ... Ms. Lisa FERRER PAVIK
88 MESA Program Director ... Ms. Amy FOOTE
31 Director of Community Relations ... Ms. Jasmine FOSTER
88 Director Academic Accommodations ... Mr. Wilbur FRANCIS
30 Director of Development ... Ms. Rane FRANKLIN
27 Managing Dir District Comm ... Mr. John GREEN
88 Dir EEO Leaves & Work Safety ... Dr. Lauren HELSPER
88 Director Intl Services and Programs ... Mr. Tim HONADEL
88 Dir Volunteer & Stdnt Employment ... Mr. Yasser ISSA
88 Director Art Galleries ... Ms. Pamela LEWIS
102 Dir Ops & Marketing (Foundation) ... Ms. Shawna LUBS
23 Director Student Health & Wellness ... Ms. Mary MANUEL
28 Director Diversity and Inclusion ... Mr. Flavio MEDINA-MARTIN
88 Assoc VP Facilities & Operations ... Mr. Jason MUNOZ
88 Director Public Relations & Sports ... Mr. Jesse MUNOZ
84 Director Enrollment Services ... Ms. Connie PALOZZOLO
88 Art Dir/Mgr Graphic Design ... Mr. Nicholas PAVIK
41 Athletic Director ... Mr. Chad PETERS
90 Dir Technology User Supp Svs ... Ms. Sally ROWLAND
19 Director Campus Safety ... Mr. Robert SADEH
25 Dir Grant/Categorical Accounting ... Ms. Carolyn SHAW
120 Interim Director Online Learning ... Ms. Joy SHOEMATE
124 Dir Outreach & School Relations ... Ms. Kari SOFFA
88 Director Veterans Resource Ctr ... Mr. Renard THOMAS
88 Dir Advertising/Social Media ... Ms. Wendy TRUJILLO
88 Dir Business Partnership/Work Engag ... Mr. Justin WALLACE
88 Director Custodial Svs ... Mr. Tony WARE
04 Special Assistant to the Chancellor ... Ms. Kristina HANCOCK
09 Director of Institutional Research ... Vacant

College of the Desert (A)

43-500 Monterey Avenue, Palm Desert CA 92260-9399
County: Riverside — FICE Identification: 001182
Unit ID: 113573
Telephone: (760) 346-8041 — Carnegie Class: Assoc/HT-High Trad
FAX Number: (760) 341-8678 — Calendar System: Semester
URL: www.collegeofthedesert.edu
Established: 1958 — Annual Undergrad Tuition & Fees (In-District): $1,383
Enrollment: 10,932 — Coed
Affiliation or Control: State/Local — IRS Status: 501(c)3
Highest Offering: Associate Degree
Accreditation: WJ

01 Superintendent/President ... Dr. Martha GARCIA
03 Interim Executive Vice President ... Dr. Christina TAFOYA
11 Interim Vice President Admin Svcs ... Mr. Dave VIGO
15 Vice President Human Resources ... Ms. Diana GALINDO
05 Interim Vice President Instruction ... Dr. Sara BUTLER
102 Executive Director Foundation ... Ms. Catherine ABBOTT
13 Exec Dir Educational Technology ... Mr. Stuart DAVIS
18 Director of Maintenance/Operations ... Mr. Brandon TOEPFER
37 Director Financial Aid ... Ms. Kristen MILLIGAN
21 Director Fiscal Services ... Mr. Tony CARRILLO
07 Director Admissions and Records ... Ms. Sonia GONZALEZ
12 Director Education Centers East ... Vacant
12 Director Education Centers West ... Mr. Scott ADKINS
19 Dir Pub Safety Dept/Emergency Prep ... Mr. Tim NAKAMURA
16 Director Human Resources ... Ms. Andrea STAEHLE
83 Dean of Social Science and Arts ... Ms. Sara BUTLER
04 Exec Assistant to the President ... Ms. Julia BREYER
04 Exec Assistant to the President ... Mr. Armando ROBLES
79 Dean of Communication & Humanities ... Mr. Dean PAPAS
88 Exec Director Bond & Facilities ... Mr. John WHITE
25 Director Institutional Grants ... Ms. Caroline MALONEY
35 Int Associate Dean Student Services ... Mr. Carlos MALDONADO
38 Dean Counseling Services ... Ms. Amanda PHILLIPS
20 Int Associate Dean of Instruction ... Mr. Gary PLUNKETT
50 Dean Applied Sciences and Business ... Dr. Douglas BENOIT
76 Int Dean Health Sci & Education ... Dr. Courtney DOUSSETT
84 Dean Enrollment Services ... Dr. Oscar ESPINOZA-PARRA
81 Dean of Math and Science ... Mr. Steven HOLMAN
26 Public Information Officer ... Ms. Marion CHAMPION

College of Marin (B)

835 College Avenue, Kentfield CA 94904-2590
County: Marin — FICE Identification: 001178
Unit ID: 118347
Telephone: (415) 457-8811 — Carnegie Class: Assoc/MT-VT-High Non
FAX Number: (415) 456-6017 — Calendar System: Semester
URL: www.marin.edu
Established: 1926 — Annual Undergrad Tuition & Fees (In-District): $1,494
Enrollment: 4,509 — Coed
Affiliation or Control: State/Local — IRS Status: 501(c)3
Highest Offering: Associate Degree
Accreditation: WJ, DA

01 Superintendent/President ... Dr. David Wain COON
32 Asst Supt/VP Stdnt Learning/Success ... Dr. Jonathan ELDRIDGE
10 Asst Supt/VP Ops & Admin Svcs ... Mr. Greg NELSON
05 Asst VP of Instruction ... Ms. Cari TORRES-BENAVIDES
15 Manager Employee & Labor Relations ... Ms. Connie LEHUA
84 Dean Enrollment Services ... Mr. Jon HORINEK
103 Dean Workforce Dev & Career Educ ... Dr. Alina R. VARONA
81 Dean Math/Sciences/Business ... Dr. Carol HERNANDEZ
49 Dean Arts & Humanities ... Ms. Lauren SERVAIS
21 Director Fiscal Services ... Ms. Peggy ISOZAKI
09 Dir of Institutional Effectiveness ... Ms. Holley SHAFER

37 Assoc Dir of Enrollment Services ... Ms. Emy BAGTAS-CARMONA
18 Dir Facil Planning & M&O ... Mr. Klaus CHRISTIANSEN
13 CIO & Director of IT ... Dr. Patrick EKOUE TOTOU
35 Dir Student Activities/Advocacy ... Ms. Sadika SULAIMAN HARA
19 Chief of Police ... Mr. Jeff MAROZICK
68 Dir Kinesiology & Athletics ... Mr. Ryan BYRNE
76 Health Sciences Program Admin ... Ms. Angela OLMANSON
51 Dir Cmty/Lifelong/Intl Education ... Vacant
22 Dir Student Accessibility Services ... Dr. Stormy C. MILLER
111 Director of Advancement ... Mr. Keith M. ROSENTHAL
26 Dir Marketing & Communications ... Ms. Nicole CRUZ
04 Exec Asst to Pres/Board ... Ms. Micol A. BENET
121 Dean Educational Success Programs ... Ms. Tonya HERSCH
43 General Counsel ... Ms. Mia ROBERTSHAW
88 Dir Child Development/Early Edu ... Dr. Corinna CALICA
08 Director of Library Services ... Vacant

College of the Sequoias (C)

915 S Mooney Boulevard, Visalia CA 93277-2234
County: Tulare — FICE Identification: 001186
Unit ID: 123217
Telephone: (559) 730-3700 — Carnegie Class: Assoc/HT-High Trad
FAX Number: (559) 730-3894 — Calendar System: Semester
URL: www.cos.edu
Established: 1925 — Annual Undergrad Tuition & Fees (In-District): $1,394
Enrollment: 12,571 — Coed
Affiliation or Control: State/Local — IRS Status: 501(c)3
Highest Offering: Associate Degree
Accreditation: WJ, PTAA

01 Superintendent/President ... Dr. Brent CALVIN
05 Vice President Academic Services ... Dr. Jennifer VEGA-LA SERNA
11 Vice President Administrative Svcs ... Mr. Ron BALLASTEROS-PEREZ
32 Vice President Student Services ... Ms. Jessica MORRISON
35 Dean Student Services ... Mr. Juan VAZQUEZ
35 Dean Student Services ... Ms. Michele BROCK
35 Dean Student Services ... Ms. Jenny SAE CHAO
12 Provost Tulare Center ... Dr. Louann WALDNER
12 Provost Hanford Center ... Dr. Kristin ROBINSON
81 Dean Science/Math/Eng ... Mr. Francisco BANUELOS
88 Dean Educ Support Services ... Ms. Angela SANCHEZ
49 Dean Arts & Letters ... Mr. Richard LUBBEN
50 Dean Business/Soc Sci/CFS ... Dr. Jesse WILCOXSON
09 Dean of Research ... Dr. Dali OZTURK
15 Dean Human Resources/Legal Affairs ... Mr. John BRATSCH
103 Dean CTE/Workforce Dev ... Dr. Jonna SCHENGEL
18 Dean Facilities ... Mr. Byron WOODS
13 Dean Info Technology ... Mr. Glen PROFETA
102 Exec Director Foundation ... Mr. Tim FOSTER
66 Dir Nursing/Allied Health ... Ms. Belen KERSTEN
08 Dir Library/Learning Resources ... Ms. Mai Soua LEE
88 Dir EOPS/CARE/NextUp ... Mr. Adrian BELTRAN
06 Registrar/Admissions Coordinator ... Ms. Velia RODRIGUEZ
41 Associate Dean/Athletic Director ... Mr. Brent DAVIS
19 Chief District Police ... Mr. Donnie CHARLES
37 Director Financial Aid ... Mr. David LOVERIN
40 Bookstore Manager ... Mr. Charles SLAGHT
88 Dir Access & Ability Center ... Ms. Lyndsi LITTEN
23 Director Health Center ... Ms. Joan DANIELS
88 Dir Foster Care/Independent Living ... Ms. Miriam SALLAM
35 Dir Student Activities/Affairs ... Mr. William HOBBS
121 Director Student Success ... Ms. Elise GARCIA
26 Dir Marketing & PR ... Ms. Lauren FISHBACK
04 Executive Asst to President ... Ms. Meghan TIERCE
114 Dir Budgets & Categorical Accts ... Ms. Leangela MILLER-HERNANDEZ
10 Chief Accounting Officer ... Ms. Linda MCCAULEY
106 Coord Distance Education ... Vacant
88 Coord Outcomes/Assessment ... Dr. Sarah HARRIS
109 Manager Food Services ... Mr. Zachary PATTERSON

College of the Siskiyous (D)

800 College Avenue, Weed CA 96094-2899
County: Siskiyou — FICE Identification: 001187
Unit ID: 123484
Telephone: (530) 938-5555 — Carnegie Class: Assoc/MT-VT-Mix Trad/Non
FAX Number: (530) 938-5506 — Calendar System: Semester
URL: www.siskiyous.edu
Established: 1957 — Annual Undergrad Tuition & Fees (In-District): $1,496
Enrollment: 1,276 — Coed
Affiliation or Control: State/Local — IRS Status: 501(c)3
Highest Offering: Associate Degree
Accreditation: WJ, EMT

01 Superintendent/President ... Dr. Char PERLAS
10 Vice President Administrative Svcs ... Vacant
05 Int Vice President Instruction ... Mr. Mark KLEVER
32 Acting Vice Pres Student Services ... Ms. Valerie ROBERTS
09 Int Dean Research/Development ... Dr. Nathan REXFORD
41 Assoc Dean Instruction/Dir Athletic ... Mr. Charles ROCHE
75 Dean Career & Technical Education ... Vacant
07 Director Admissions & Records ... Ms. Meghan WITHERELL
15 Int Director Human Resources ... Ms. Kelly GROPPI
18 Director Facilities ... Ms. Veronica RIVERA
111 Dir of Institutional Advancement ... Vacant
39 Director Student Housing ... Dr. Doug HAUGEN
26 Dir Comm Relations/Foundation ... Ms. Dawnie SLABAUGH
103 Director of Workforce Development ... Mr. Mark KLEVER
35 Director of Student Life ... Dr. Doug HAUGEN
36 Assoc Dean Student Success Programs ... Ms. Valerie ROBERTS

The Colleges of Law (E)

4475 Market Street, Ventura CA 93003
County: Ventura — Identification: 667229
Unit ID: 125037
Telephone: (805) 765-9300 — Carnegie Class: Spec-4-yr-Law
FAX Number: (805) 658-0529 — Calendar System: Semester
URL: www.collegesoflaw.edu
Established: 1969 — Annual Graduate Tuition & Fees: N/A
Enrollment: 230 — Coed
Affiliation or Control: Independent Non-Profit — IRS Status: 501(c)3
Highest Offering: Doctorate; No Undergraduates
Accreditation: WC

01 President/CEO ... Dr. Matthew NEHMER
05 Dean/Chief Academic Officer ... Ms. Jackie GARDINA
07 Associate Vice Pres of Admissions ... Mr. Shawn TAYLOR
06 Asst Dean & Registrar ... Ms. Barbara DOYLE
32 Student Services Manager ... Ms. Jennifer MACKIE
11 Director of Operations ... Ms. Alexis BURDICK
111 Sr Mgr Institutional Advancement ... Mr. Kryztofr KAINE
106 Assoc Dean Hybrid & Online Programs ... Ms. Andrea FUNK

Columbia College Hollywood (F)

18618 Oxnard Street, Tarzana CA 91356-1411
County: Los Angeles — FICE Identification: 021102
Unit ID: 112570
Telephone: (800) 785-0585 — Carnegie Class: Spec-4-yr-Arts
FAX Number: (818) 345-9053 — Calendar System: Quarter
URL: www.columbiacollege.edu
Established: 1952 — Annual Undergrad Tuition & Fees: $26,175
Enrollment: 760 — Coed
Affiliation or Control: Independent Non-Profit — IRS Status: 501(c)3
Highest Offering: Baccalaureate
Accreditation: WC

01 President/CEO ... Mr. Bill SMITH
10 Chief Financial Officer ... Mr. Greg BUBLITZ
26 Director of Marketing ... Ms. Casey SULLIVAN
84 Vice Pres Enrollment Services ... Ms. Wendi FRANCZYK
05 CAO/Dean of Academic Affairs ... Mr. David CARTER
11 VP Operations ... Mr. Patrick OLMSTEAD
32 VP Student Affairs ... Ms. Kelly PARKER
108 VP Institutional Effectiveness ... Ms. Lex SANDERSON
06 Registrar ... Ms. Ingrid ELIAS
36 Sr Dir Career Dev & Alumni Affairs ... Ms. Kelley LEWIS
37 Director Financial Aid ... Dr. Jason CUPP
121 Director of Student Success ... Ms. Jessica JOHNSON-MILLS
15 Director of Human Resources ... Ms. Rena WRIGHT
07 Assoc Director Admissions ... Mr. Lee HUGHES
13 Manager of IT and Production Svcs ... Mr. Stephen DELELLO
18 Facilities Manager ... Mr. Johnny MENDOZA

Community Christian College (G)

1174 Nevada Street, 2nd Floor, Redlands CA 92374
County: San Bernardino — FICE Identification: 038744
Unit ID: 446163
Telephone: (909) 794-1084 — Carnegie Class: Assoc/HT-High Non
FAX Number: (909) 794-1093 — Calendar System: Quarter
URL: www.cccollege.edu
Established: 1995 — Annual Undergrad Tuition & Fees: $9,750
Enrollment: 490 — Coed
Affiliation or Control: Independent Non-Profit — IRS Status: 501(c)3
Highest Offering: Associate Degree
Accreditation: TRACS

01 President ... Mr. Brian CARROLL
05 Vice Pres of Academic Affairs ... Dr. Robert GEE
10 Vice Pres Finance/Operations ... Mr. Richard DURANT
43 Corporate Counsel ... Mr. Robert ZIPRICK
32 Director of Student Services ... Vacant

Compton College (H)

1111 E Artesia Boulevard, Compton CA 90221-5393
County: Los Angeles — FICE Identification: 001188
Unit ID: 112686
Telephone: (310) 900-1600 — Carnegie Class: Assoc/MT-VT-High Non
FAX Number: N/A — Calendar System: Semester
URL: www.compton.edu
Established: 1927 — Annual Undergrad Tuition & Fees (In-State): $1,142
Enrollment: 4,612 — Coed
Affiliation or Control: State — IRS Status: 501(c)3
Highest Offering: Associate Degree
Accreditation: WJ

01 President/CEO ... Dr. Keith CURRY
05 Vice Pres Academic Affairs ... Ms. Sheri BERGER
32 Vice Pres Student Services ... Ms. Nicole JONES
10 Vice Pres Administrative Svcs ... Mr. Abdul NASSER
15 Acting VP Human Resources ... Mr. Ibrahim ALI
41 Dir Student Development/Athletics ... Mr. Andree PACHECO
08 Director Learning Resources ... Vacant
88 Director CalWORKs & DSPS ... Ms. Michelle GARCIA
22 Director EOP & S/CARE ... Ms. Christine ALDRICH
108 Director Institutional Effectivenes ... Ms. Lauren SOSENKO
37 Director Financial Aid ... Mr. Keith COBB
88 Dir Educational Partnerships ... Ms. Nelly ALVARADO
21 Director Fiscal Affairs ... Mr. Ruben JAMES

18 Chief Facilities Officer .... Ms. Linda OWENS
13 Chief Technology Officer .... Vacant
07 Director Admissions & Records .... Ms. Richette BELL
06 Interim Assoc Registrar .... Mr. Brian DEAN
28 Dir Diversity/Compliance/Title IX .... Ms. Tina KUPERMAN
38 Dean Stdnt Counseling/Guided Pthwys .... Mr. Cesar JIMENEZ
96 Dir Purchasing/Auxilliary Svcs .... Mr. Reuben JAMES

† Regional accreditation is carried under the parent institution in Torrance, CA.

Concorde Career College (A)

12951 S. Euclid Street, Suite 101,
Garden Grove CA 92840-1451

County: Orange — FICE Identification: 008071
Unit ID: 123679
Telephone: (714) 703-1900 — Carnegie Class: Spec 2-yr-Health
FAX Number: (714) 530-8421 — Calendar System: Semester
URL: concorde.edu/campus/garden-grove-california
Established: 1960 — Annual Undergrad Tuition & Fees: N/A
Enrollment: 603 — Coed
Affiliation or Control: Proprietary — IRS Status: Proprietary
Highest Offering: Associate Degree
Accreditation: ACCSC, COARC, DH, PTAA

01 Campus President .... Ms. Lisa RHODES
05 Academic Dean .... Dr. Omid PARTO

Concorde Career College (B)

12412 Victory Boulevard, North Hollywood CA 91606-3134

County: Los Angeles — FICE Identification: 007607
Unit ID: 124937
Telephone: (818) 766-8151 — Carnegie Class: Spec 2-yr-Health
FAX Number: (818) 766-1587 — Calendar System: Quarter
URL: https://www.concorde.edu/campus/north-hollywood-california
Established: 1955 — Annual Undergrad Tuition & Fees: N/A
Enrollment: 613 — Coed
Affiliation or Control: Proprietary — IRS Status: Proprietary
Highest Offering: Associate Degree
Accreditation: ACCSC, COARC, PTAA

01 Campus President .... Garo GHAZARIAN
05 Academic Dean .... Walter GUEVARA
07 Director of Admissions .... Allan GUECO
37 Director Student Financial Aid .... Cynthia STEIN

Concorde Career College (C)

201 E Airport Drive, San Bernadino CA 92408

County: San Bernardino — FICE Identification: 008537
Unit ID: 124706
Telephone: (909) 884-8891 — Carnegie Class: Spec 2-yr-Health
FAX Number: (909) 884-1831 — Calendar System: Semester
URL: https://www.concorde.edu/campus/san-bernardino-california
Established: 1970 — Annual Undergrad Tuition & Fees: N/A
Enrollment: 638 — Coed
Affiliation or Control: Proprietary — IRS Status: Proprietary
Highest Offering: Associate Degree
Accreditation: ACCSC, COARC, DH, NDT, POLYT, SURGT

01 Campus President .... Tracy L. WEST
07 Director of Admissions .... Juan M. TELLEZ

Concorde Career College (D)

4393 Imperial Avenue, Suite 100,
San Diego CA 92113-1962

County: San Diego — FICE Identification: 007930
Unit ID: 120661
Telephone: (619) 688-0800 — Carnegie Class: Spec 2-yr-Health
FAX Number: (619) 220-4177 — Calendar System: Other
URL: https://www.concorde.edu/campus/san-diego-california
Established: 1966 — Annual Undergrad Tuition & Fees: N/A
Enrollment: 733 — Coed
Affiliation or Control: Proprietary — IRS Status: Proprietary
Highest Offering: Associate Degree
Accreditation: ACCSC, DH, PTAA, SURGT

01 Campus President .... Ms. Rachel SAFFEL
32 Dir of Student Affs/Title IX Coord .... Mr. Bill KILBY
07 Director of Admissions .... Ms. Renee CODNER

Concordia University Irvine (E)

1530 Concordia West, Irvine CA 92612-3299

County: Orange — FICE Identification: 020705
Unit ID: 112075
Telephone: (949) 854-8002 — Carnegie Class: DU-Mod
FAX Number: (949) 214-3520 — Calendar System: Semester
URL: www.cui.edu
Established: 1972 — Annual Undergrad Tuition & Fees: $38,000
Enrollment: 4,071 — Coed
Affiliation or Control: Lutheran Church - Missouri Synod
IRS Status: 501(c)3
Highest Offering: Doctorate
Accreditation: WC, CACREP, HSA, IACBE, MUS, NURSE

01 President .... Dr. Michael A. THOMAS
88 Vice Pres/Spec Asst to President .... Dr. Peter SENKBEIL
05 SVP/Provost .... RevDr. Scott ASHMON
111 Exec VP Advancement/Mktg/Comm .... Mr. Timothy J. JAEGER
10 Exec VP/Chief Financial Officer .... Mr. Kevin TILDEN
20 Assoc Provost .... Vacant
49 Dean School of Arts & Sciences .... Dr. Brett TAYLOR
50 Dean of Business .... Mr. George WRIGHT
107 Dean School of Professional Studies .... Mr. Mike SHURANCE
53 Dean School of Education .... Dr. Kent SCHLICHTEMEIER
73 Dean Christ College .... RevDr. Steven P. MUELLER
06 Registrar .... Ms. Dessa SOPER
09 Director of Institutional Research .... Mrs. Deborah LEE
32 VP Student Affairs/Dean of Students .... Mrs. Megan BOUSLAUGH
07 Director of Undergrad Admissions .... Vacant
123 Sr Director of Graduate Admissions .... Mr. Justin MOSCHINA
37 Director of Financial Aid .... Ms. Lori MCDONALD
113 Bursar .... Mr. Edgar LOPEZ
43 VP of Legal Affairs/General Counsel .... Mr. Ronald VAN BLARCOM
15 AVP of Human Resources .... Mrs. Melinda MARTINEZ
08 Director of Library Services .... Ms. Laura GUZMAN
41 Athletic Director .... Ms. Crystal ROSENTHAL
35 Assoc Dean of Students .... Ms. Kristy FOWLER
19 Director Security/Safety .... Mr. Steven RODRIGUEZ
29 Exec Director of Alumni Relations .... Mr. Michael BERGLER
24 Senior Director of Faculty Training .... Prof. John RANDALL
36 Director of Career Services .... Mrs. Victoria JAFFEE
13 Director of IT Services .... Mr. Chris HARRIS
28 Director of Inclusion/Diversity .... Dr. Terilyn WALKER
106 Exec Dir Innov Instruction & eLrng .... Dr. Jason NEBEN

*Contra Costa Community College District Office (F)

500 Court Street, Martinez CA 94553-1278

County: Contra Costa — FICE Identification: 001189
Unit ID: 112817
Telephone: (925) 229-1000 — Carnegie Class: N/A
FAX Number: (925) 370-2019
URL: www.4cd.edu

01 Interim Chancellor .... Ms. Mojdeh MEHDIZADEH
05 Exec VC Education and Technology .... Vacant
10 Exec VC Administrative Services .... Dr. Micaela OCHOA
20 Int VC Education and Technology .... Ms. Kelly SCHELIN
18 VC Facilities Plng/Construction .... Ms. Ines ZILDZIC
21 AVC/Chief Financial Officer .... Ms. Phyllis CARTER
15 AVC/Chief HR Officer .... Vacant

*Contra Costa College (G)

2600 Mission Bell Drive, San Pablo CA 94806-3195

County: Contra Costa — FICE Identification: 001190
Unit ID: 112826
Telephone: (510) 235-7800 — Carnegie Class: Assoc/HT-Mix Trad/Non
FAX Number: N/A — Calendar System: Semester
URL: www.contracosta.edu
Established: 1948 — Annual Undergrad Tuition & Fees (In-District): $1,312
Enrollment: 6,249 — Coed
Affiliation or Control: State/Local — IRS Status: 501(c)3
Highest Offering: Associate Degree
Accreditation: WJ

02 President .... Dr. Tia ROBINSON-COOPER
06 Vice Pres of Student Services-Inter .... Jason CIFRA
05 Vice Pres of Instruction .... Dr. Kimberly R. ROGERS
10 Vice Pres of Business & Admin Svcs .... Dr. Tim HARRISON
108 Dean Inst Effectiveness & Equity .... Dr. Mayra PADILLA
26 Director of Marketing/Media Design .... Mr. Larry WOMACK
30 Dir Foundation/College Advancement .... Ms. Sara MARCELLINO
20 Senior Dean of Instruction .... Vacant
49 Dean Liberal Arts .... Mr. Jason BERNER
76 Interim Dean AACE .... Ms. Sandra MOORE
83 Dean of NSAS .... Ms. René SPORER
32 Dean of Student Services .... Mr. Dennis FRANCO
84 Dean of Enrollment Services .... Mr. Rod SANTOS
103 Dean of Economic & Workforce Dev .... Mr. Evan DECKER
07 Director Admissions & Records .... Mr. Cole MOYER
41 Athletics Director .... Mr. John WADE
09 Director of Institutional Research .... Vacant
18 Buildings & Grounds Manager .... Mr. Bruce KING
88 Custodial Manager .... Mr. William TANDONGFOR
21 Business Services Supervisor .... Mr. Nick DIMITRI
37 Financial Aid Supervisor .... Ms. Monica RODRIGUEZ
04 Senior Exec Asst to the President .... Ms. Joy BRUCELAS

*Diablo Valley College (H)

321 Golf Club Road, Pleasant Hill CA 94523-1544

County: Contra Costa — FICE Identification: 001191
Unit ID: 113634
Telephone: (925) 685-1230 — Carnegie Class: Assoc/HT-High Trad
FAX Number: (925) 685-1551 — Calendar System: Semester
URL: www.dvc.edu
Established: 1949 — Annual Undergrad Tuition & Fees (In-District): $1,312
Enrollment: 18,693 — Coed
Affiliation or Control: State/Local — IRS Status: 501(c)3
Highest Offering: Associate Degree
Accreditation: WJ, ACFEI, DA, DH

02 President .... Ms. Susan LAMB
05 Int Vice President Instruction .... Ms. Kim SCHENK
32 Vice President Student Services .... Dr. Vicki FERGUSON
10 Vice Pres Business & Admin Svcs .... Mr. Todd HAMPTON
20 Int Sr Dean Curriculum & Instr .... Ms. Nikki MOULTRIE
84 Dean Outreach/Enroll Mgt/Matric .... Vacant
12 Senior Dean San Ramon Campus .... Ms. Kenyetta TRIBBLE
41 Dean of Health/Athletic Director .... Ms. Christine WORSLEY
08 Dean Library/Ed Tech & Lrng Support .... Mr. Rick ROBISON
26 Dir Marketing and Media Design .... Ms. Brandy HOWARD
57 Dean Arts and Communication .... Ms. Janette FUNARO
81 Dean Sciences .... Mr. Joe GORGA
83 Dean Social Science .... Mr. Obed VAZQUEZ
50 Dean Math and Engineering .... Ms. Despina PRAPAVESSI
06 Registrar/Admissions .... Mr. Gabriel HARVEN
35 Dean Student Support Services .... Ms. Emily STONE
09 Int Dean IE/ALO .... Ms. Lindsay KONG
102 Director of College Advancement .... Mr. Jim BLAIR
103 Sr Dean Career & Community Partners .... Ms. Beth ARMAN
88 Dean English & Equity Pedagogy .... Mr. James NOEL
28 Dean of Student Engagement & Equity .... Ms. Rosa ARMENDARIZ
50 Dean Business .... Mr. Charlie SHI

*Los Medanos College (I)

2700 E Leland Road, Pittsburg CA 94565-5197

County: Contra Costa — FICE Identification: 010340
Unit ID: 117894
Telephone: (925) 439-2181 — Carnegie Class: Assoc/HT-High Trad
FAX Number: (925) 427-1599 — Calendar System: Semester
URL: www.losmedanos.edu
Established: 1973 — Annual Undergrad Tuition & Fees (In-District): $1,312
Enrollment: 8,521 — Coed
Affiliation or Control: State/Local — IRS Status: 501(c)3
Highest Offering: Associate Degree
Accreditation: WJ

02 President .... Dr. Bob KRATOCHVIL
04 Senior Executive Assistant .... Ms. Jennifer ADAMS
05 VP of Instruction .... Ms. Natalie HANNUM
32 VP of Student Services .... Dr. Tanisha MAXWELL
10 VP Business & Admin Services .... Dr. Carlos MONTOYA
45 Sr Dean Plng & Inst Effectiveness .... Vacant
28 Dean of Equity & Inclusion .... Dr. Sabrina T. KWIST
81 Dean of Instruction .... Mr. Ryan PEDERSEN
75 Dean of Instruction .... Ms. Aprill NOGARR
79 Interim Dean of Instruction .... Mr. Dennis FRANCO
66 Assoc Dean Nursing & Allied Health .... Ms. Maryanne HICKS
38 Dean Counseling & Student Support .... Mr. Jeffrey BENFORD
121 Dean of Student Success .... Mr. David BELMAN
06 Dir Admissions & Records .... Ms. Rikki HALL
36 Director Transfer & Career Services .... Ms. Rachel ANICETTI
88 Director Early Childhood Lab School .... Ms. Angela FANTUZZI
35 Dir Student Life & Intl Student Pgm .... Ms. Teresea ARCHAGA
88 Interim Asst Dir EOPS/CARE .... Ms. Carissa CRAIG
88 Outreach/Assessment Svcs Mgr .... Vacant
40 Bookstore Manager .... Mr. Robert ESTRADA
22 Manager Disability Support Services .... Ms. Virginia RICHARDS
103 Pgm Mgr Workforce & Econ Dev .... Mr. Bill BANKHEAD
88 Custodial Manager .... Mr. Frank ICHIGAYA
21 Business Services Supervisor .... Mr. Jinpa THARCHIN
18 Dir Maintenance & Operations .... Mr. Michael SCHENONE
37 Interim Dir Financial Aid .... Ms. Tammy ORANJE
88 Office of Instruction Supervisor .... Ms. Eileen VALENZUELA
111 Dir College Advancement .... Vacant
26 Dir Marketing & Media Design .... Vacant
41 Athletic Director .... Mr. Richard VILLEGAS
19 Police Services .... Lt. Ryan HUDDLESTON

Contra Costa Medical Career College (J)

4041 Lone Tree Way, Ste 101, Antioch CA 94531

County: Contra Costa — FICE Identification: 042749
Unit ID: 491950
Telephone: (925) 757-2900 — Carnegie Class: Not Classified
FAX Number: (925) 757-5873 — Calendar System: Quarter
URL: www.ccmcc.edu
Established: 2007 — Annual Undergrad Tuition & Fees: N/A
Enrollment: N/A — Coed
Affiliation or Control: Proprietary — IRS Status: Proprietary
Highest Offering: Associate Degree
Accreditation: CNCE, SURTEC

01 President .... Stacey OROZCO

Copper Mountain College (K)

6162 Rotary Way, Box 1398, Joshua Tree CA 92252-6102

County: San Bernardino — FICE Identification: 035424
Unit ID: 395362
Telephone: (760) 366-3791 — Carnegie Class: Assoc/HT-High Trad
FAX Number: (760) 366-5255 — Calendar System: Semester
URL: www.cmccd.edu
Established: 1999 — Annual Undergrad Tuition & Fees (In-District): $1,112
Enrollment: 1,539 — Coed
Affiliation or Control: State/Local — IRS Status: 170(c)1
Highest Offering: Associate Degree
Accreditation: WJ

01 Superintendent/President .... Dr. Daren OTTEN
05 VP of Academic Affairs/CIO .... Dr. Melynie SCHIEL
49 Dean of Arts & Sciences .... Vacant
32 VP of Student Services/CSSO .... Ms. Jane ABELL

15 Chief Human Resources Ofcr ..... Ms. Bonnie BILGER
18 Director of Facilities & Operations ..... Mr. Kevin COLE
102 Executive Director of Foundation ..... Ms. Sandy SMITH
10 Chief Business Officer ..... Ms. Meredith PLUMMER
35 Dean of Student Services ..... Ms. Jennifer SPARLING
108 Dean of Institutional Effectiveness ..... Ms. Alma CORREA
66 Coordinator for Nursing Programs ..... Ms. Dawn PAGE
13 Dir of Information Technology ..... Mr. Roengsak CARTWRIGHT
26 Public Relations & Event Specialist ..... Ms. Jolie ALPIN
04 Executive Asst to the President ..... Ms. Crisandra KAUFFMANN
07 Admissions & Records Specialist ..... Ms. Maria CRUZ
08 Library Coordinator ..... Mr. Derek MONYPENY
41 Athletic Director ..... Mr. Ken SIMONDS

Cuesta College (A)

PO Box 8106, San Luis Obispo CA 93403-8106
County: San Luis Obispo FICE Identification: 001192
Unit ID: 113193
Telephone: (805) 546-3100 Carnegie Class: Assoc/HT-Mix Trad/Non
FAX Number: N/A Calendar System: Semester
URL: www.cuesta.edu
Established: 1963 Annual Undergrad Tuition & Fees (In-District): $1,338
Enrollment: 10,093 Coed
Affiliation or Control: State/Local IRS Status: 501(c)3
Highest Offering: Associate Degree
Accreditation: WJ, EMT

01 Superintendent/President ..... Dr. Jill STEARNS
05 VP/Asst Supt Instruction ..... Dr. Jason CURTIS
10 VP/Asst Supt Administrative Svcs ..... Mr. Dan TROY
32 VP/Asst Supt Stdnt Success/Supp Pgm ..... Dr. Elizabeth CORIA
15 Vice Pres Human Resource/Labor Rels . Ms. Melissa RICHERSON
35 Dean Stdnt Success/Support Pgm ..... Dr. Maria ESCOBEDO
35 Dean Stdnt Success/Support Pgm ..... Dr. Genevieve SIWABESSY
79 Dean of Instruct Arts/Hum/Math/Sci ..... Ms. Madeline MEDEIROS
103 Dean of Instruct Hlth/Workforce/Kin ..... Dr. John CASCAMO
09 Dean of Instruction IR & Cmty Engag ..... Dr. Ryan CARTNAL
111 Exec Dir Found/Inst Advancement ..... Ms. Shannon HILL
13 Exec Dir Information Technology ..... Mr. Keith STEARNS
35 Coordinator Student Life/Leadership ..... Dr. Anthony GUTIERREZ
66 Director of Nursing ..... Ms. Marcia SCOTT
19 Chief of Police/College Safety ..... Mr. David MILLARD
41 Director of Athletics ..... Mr. Robert MARIUCCI
18 Director of Facilities Services ..... Mr. Brian MCALISTER
84 Director Outreach/Enrollment Svcs ..... Dr. Jeffery ALEXANDER
37 Assoc Dean Financial Aid & Records ..... Ms. Zhrinna MCDONALD
31 Dir Workforce/Econ Devel Cmty Pgm ..... Dr. Matthew GREEN
23 Director of Health Services ..... Ms. Nicole JOHNSON
21 Director Fiscal Services ..... Mr. Chris GREEN
102 Director of Philanthropy ..... Ms. Michelle HANAFIAH
88 Director Foundation Fiscal Services ..... Mr. Richard CAMARILLO
25 Director of Grant Development ..... Vacant
04 Executive Asst to President ..... Mr. Todd FREDERICK
04 Executive Asst to President ..... Ms. Cindy DILBECK

The Culinary Institute of America at Greystone (B)

2555 Main Street, Saint Helena CA 94574-9504
Telephone: (707) 967-1100 Identification: 666260
Accreditation: &M

† Regional accreditation is carried under the parent institution in Hyde Park, NY.

Daybreak University (C)

1818 S. Western Ave #207, Los Angeles CA 90006
County: Los Angeles Identification: 667392
Telephone: (310) 739-0132 Carnegie Class: Not Classified
FAX Number: (270) 714-0317 Calendar System: Quarter
URL: www.daybreak.edu
Established: Annual Graduate Tuition & Fees: N/A
Enrollment: N/A Coed
Affiliation or Control: Independent Non-Profit IRS Status: 501(c)3
Highest Offering: Doctorate; No Undergraduates
Accreditation: TRACS

01 CEO/President ..... Dr. Jea EUN OH
05 Academic Dean ..... Dr. Hye JIN KIM
10 Business Manager/CFO ..... Ms. Kathy Y. KANG
32 Director of Student Services ..... Ms. Kyunghee BAEK
07 Director of Admisions/Registrar ..... Ms. Grace J. LEE

Deep Springs College (D)

HC 72 Box 45001, Via Dyer, NV 89010-9803
County: Inyo FICE Identification: 001194
Telephone: (760) 872-2000 Carnegie Class: Not Classified
FAX Number: N/A Calendar System: Other
URL: www.deepsprings.edu
Established: 1917 Annual Undergrad Tuition & Fees: $0
Enrollment: N/A Coed
Affiliation or Control: Independent Non-Profit IRS Status: 501(c)3
Highest Offering: Associate Degree
Accreditation: WJ

01 President ..... Ms. Sue DARLINGTON
05 Academic Dean & CFO ..... Mr. Ryan DERBY-TALBOT
88 Ranch Manager ..... Mr. Tim GIPSON
10 Operations Manager ..... Mr. Ciaran WILLIS
30 Development Director ..... Mr. Koll JENSEN
88 Chef/BH Manager ..... Mr. Brian SHULSE
88 Farm Foreman ..... Vacant
04 Office Manager ..... Vacant

† A scholarship covers the costs of tuition, room, and board for every student.

Design Institute of San Diego (E)

8555 Commerce Avenue, San Diego CA 92121-2685
County: San Diego FICE Identification: 022980
Unit ID: 113582
Telephone: (858) 566-1200 Carnegie Class: Spec-4-yr-Arts
FAX Number: (858) 566-2711 Calendar System: Semester
URL: www.disd.edu
Established: 1977 Annual Undergrad Tuition & Fees: $25,649
Enrollment: 130 Coed
Affiliation or Control: Proprietary IRS Status: Proprietary
Highest Offering: Master's
Accreditation: WC, CIDA

01 CEO ..... Ms. Margot DOUCETTE
11 Director of Operations ..... Ms. Jessyca HOUCHINS
10 Chief Financial Officer ..... Mr. Dennis DOUCETTE
05 Director of Academics ..... Ms. Natalia WORDEN
07 Admissions ..... Ms. Savanna MCDEDE
37 Financial Aid Director ..... Ms. Jackie GLORIA
32 Director of Student Services ..... Ms. Molly DISHMAN
08 Library Director ..... Ms. Lisa SCHATTMAN
06 Registrar ..... Ms. Tracy GULINO
36 Career Advisor ..... Mr. Crandon GUSTAFSON

Dharma Realm Buddhist University (F)

4951 Bodhi Way, Ukiah CA 95482
County: Sacramento Identification: 667334
Telephone: (707) 621-7000 Carnegie Class: Not Classified
FAX Number: N/A Calendar System: Semester
URL: www.drbu.org
Established: 1976 Annual Undergrad Tuition & Fees: N/A
Enrollment: N/A Coed
Affiliation or Control: Independent Non-Profit IRS Status: 501(c)3
Highest Offering: Master's
Accreditation: WC

01 President ..... Susan ROUNDS
10 VP Finance & Admin/Provost ..... Douglas POWERS
05 Dean of Academics ..... Martin VERHOEVEN
32 Dean of Students ..... Heng LIANG

Dominican School of Philosophy and Theology (G)

2301 Vine Street, Berkeley CA 94708-1816
County: Alameda FICE Identification: 001296
Unit ID: 113704
Telephone: (510) 849-2030 Carnegie Class: Masters/S
FAX Number: (510) 849-1372 Calendar System: Semester
URL: www.dspt.edu
Established: 1932 Annual Undergrad Tuition & Fees: N/A
Enrollment: 72 Coed
Affiliation or Control: Roman Catholic IRS Status: 501(c)3
Highest Offering: Master's
Accreditation: WC, THEOL

01 President ..... Fr. Allen MORAN
05 Academic Dean ..... Fr. Bryan KROMHOLTZ
10 Vice Pres Finance/Administration ..... Mr. Ian BROOKS
06 Registrar ..... Ms. Laura FEGLEY
37 Dir Student Services/Financial Aid ..... Ms. Kimberly HEBERT
09 Director of Institutional Research ..... Rev. Christopher RENZ

Dominican University of California (H)

50 Acacia Avenue, San Rafael CA 94901-2298
County: Marin FICE Identification: 001196
Unit ID: 113698
Telephone: (415) 457-4440 Carnegie Class: Masters/M
FAX Number: N/A Calendar System: Semester
URL: www.dominican.edu
Established: 1890 Annual Undergrad Tuition & Fees: $47,910
Enrollment: 1,837 Coed
Affiliation or Control: Independent Non-Profit IRS Status: 501(c)3
Highest Offering: Doctorate
Accreditation: WC, ARCPA, ART, NURSE, OT

01 President ..... Dr. Nicola PITCHFORD
05 VP Academic Affairs/Dean of Faculty ..... Ms. Mojgan BEHMAND
10 Int VP Finance and Administration ..... Mr. Robert HITE
32 Dean of Student Affairs ..... Dr. Paul RACCANELLO
84 Int Vice Pres Enrollment/Marketing ..... Mr. Brandon BOULTER
111 VP for Advancement & Public Affairs ..... Ms. Marly NORRIS
20 AVP Academic Affairs/Dean Dom Exp ..... Vacant
06 AVP Academic Svcs/Univ Registrar ..... Ms. Colette GALIANI
29 AVP Alumni Engagement/Annual Fund ..... Ms. Jessica JORDAN
27 Executive Director Communications ..... Ms. Sarah GARDNER
04 Exec Assistant President's Office ..... Ms. Sandy PEARSON
101 Special Asst to Pres/Board Sec ..... Ms. Jennifer KRENGEL
49 Dean Sch Liberal Arts & Education ..... Dr. Gigi GOKCEK
50 Dean Barowsky School of Business ..... Dr. Yung-Jae LEE
81 Dean Sch Health/Natural Science ..... Dr. Ruth RAMSEY
18 Executive Director Facilities Svcs ..... Mr. John HASHIZUME
08 University Librarian ..... Mr. Gary GORKA
09 Director of Institutional Research ..... Dr. Yu-Ti HUANG
37 Director Financial Aid ..... Ms. Zelotes SMITH
07 Director Undergrad Admissions ..... Ms. Maria GENTILE
15 Director Human Resources ..... Mr. Jesse ANDREWS
121 Sr Director Integrative Coaching ..... Ms. Naomi ELVOVE
92 Director Honors Program ..... Ms. Lynn SONDAG
38 Director Univ Counseling Services ..... Dr. Diane SUFFRIDGE
85 Sr Intl Officer & GEO Director ..... Dr. Kati BELL
41 Director of Athletics & Rec Sports ..... Ms. Amy HENKELMAN
102 Dir Foundation/Corp/Govt Relations ..... Ms. Lenice SMITH
30 Director of Development ..... Ms. Tracy STEMPEL HOGEN

Dongguk University Los Angeles (I)

440 Shatto Place, 2nd floor, Los Angeles CA 90020
County: Los Angeles FICE Identification: 031095
Unit ID: 122117
Telephone: (213) 487-0110 Carnegie Class: Spec-4-yr-Other Health
FAX Number: (213) 487-0527 Calendar System: Quarter
URL: www.dula.edu
Established: 1979 Annual Undergrad Tuition & Fees: N/A
Enrollment: 158 Coed
Affiliation or Control: Independent Non-Profit IRS Status: 501(c)3
Highest Offering: Master's; No Lower Division
Accreditation: ACUP

01 President ..... Dr. SeokJoo AUM
05 Dean of Academic Affairs ..... Dr. Yae CHANG
10 Chief Operating Officer/Finance Mgr ..... John JEON
07 Director of Admissions ..... Chan Ho KIM
32 Director Student Affairs/Registrar ..... Seung Wook KIM
18 Facilities Manager ..... Jongho KIM

El Camino College (J)

16007 Crenshaw Boulevard, Torrance CA 90506-0002
County: Los Angeles FICE Identification: 001197
Unit ID: 113980
Telephone: (310) 660-3593 Carnegie Class: Assoc/HT-High Trad
FAX Number: (310) 660-7798 Calendar System: Semester
URL: www.elcamino.edu
Established: 1947 Annual Undergrad Tuition & Fees (In-District): $1,144
Enrollment: 20,418 Coed
Affiliation or Control: State/Local IRS Status: 501(c)3
Highest Offering: Associate Degree
Accreditation: WJ, COARC, RAD

01 President ..... Dr. Brenda A. THAMES
05 Interim VP Academic Affairs ..... Dr. Jaquelyn SIMS
10 Interim VP Administrative Services ..... Ms. Ann TOMLINSON
32 Vice Pres Student Services ..... Mr. Ross MIYASHIRO
15 Vice Pres of Human Resources ..... Ms. Jane MIYASHIRO
111 Dean Community Advancement ..... Mr. Jose ANAYA
72 Dean Industry & Technology ..... Mr. David GONZALES
81 Dean Mathematics ..... Dr. Marlow LEMONS
50 Dean of Business ..... Dr. Virginia RAPP
83 Dean Behavioral & Social Science ..... Dr. Chris GOLD
68 Int Dean Health Science & Athletics ..... Mr. Russel SERR
57 Dean Fine Arts ..... Dr. Berkeley PRICE
76 Dean Natural Sciences ..... Dr. Amy GRANT
79 Dean Humanities ..... Ms. Debra BRECKHEIMER
08 Dean Library & Learning Resources ..... Dr. Crystle MARTIN
121 Dean Counseling & Student Success ..... Dr. Dipte PALEL
121 Dean of Student Support Services ..... Ms. Idania REYES
84 Dean of Enrollment Services ..... Mr. Robin DREIZLER
88 Director Special Resource Center ..... Mr. Gary GRECO
13 Chief Technology Officer ..... Mr. Loic AUDUSSEAU
26 Exec Dir Marketing/Communications ..... Ms. Ann O'BRIEN
106 Coordinator Distance Education ..... Dr. Moses WOLFENSTEIN
88 Director Public Safety ..... Chief Jeffrey BAUMUNK
66 Director of Nursing ..... Vacant
86 Public Info & Government Relations ..... Ms. Kerri WEBB
102 Executive Director Foundation ..... Ms. Andrea SALA
96 Dir Procurement & Risk Management ..... Vacant
40 Director of Bookstore ..... Ms. Julie BOURLIER
19 Chief of Campus Police ..... Mr. Michael TREVIS
18 Exec Dir Facilities Planning/Svcs ..... Mr. Jorge GUTIERREZ
35 Director of Student Development ..... Dr. Gregory TOYA
37 Director Student Financial Aid ..... Vacant
06 Registrar ..... Ms. Lillian JUSTICE
09 Dir Institutional Research/Planning ..... Ms. Viviana UNDA
28 Dir Title IX/Diversity & Inclusion ..... Dr. Jayne ISHIKAWA
21 Business Manager ..... Mr. Jeffrey HINSHAW
103 Director Career Education ..... Ms. Adriana ESTRADA
25 Grants Development & Management ..... Ms. Roberta BECKA
41 Interim Athletic Director ..... Mr. Jeff MIERA
04 Executive Asst to President ..... Ms. Rose MAHOWALD

Emperor's College (K)

1807-B Wilshire Boulevard, Santa Monica CA 90403-5678
County: Los Angeles FICE Identification: 026090
Unit ID: 114114
Telephone: (310) 453-8300 Carnegie Class: Spec-4-yr-Other Health
FAX Number: (310) 829-3838 Calendar System: Quarter
URL: www.emperors.edu
Established: 1983 Annual Undergrad Tuition & Fees: N/A
Enrollment: 228 Coed
Affiliation or Control: Proprietary IRS Status: Proprietary
Highest Offering: Doctorate

Accreditation: ACUP

01 Chief Executive Officer/President .... Yun KIM
05 Academic Dean .... Jacques MORAMARCO
63 Dean of Clinical Education .... Elizabeth FINE
11 Chief Operations Officer .... George PARK

Empire College (A)

3035 Cleveland Avenue, Santa Rosa CA 95403-2100
County: Sonoma | FICE Identification: 009032
Unit ID: 114123
Telephone: (707) 546-4000 | Carnegie Class: Bac/Assoc-Mixed
FAX Number: (707) 284-2817 | Calendar System: Trimester
URL: www.empcol.edu
Established: 1961 | Annual Undergrad Tuition & Fees: N/A
Enrollment: 241 | Coed
Affiliation or Control: Proprietary | IRS Status: Proprietary
Highest Offering: Master's
Accreditation: ACICS

01 President .... Mr. Roy HURD
26 Vice Pres Marketing/Administration .... Mrs. Sherie HURD

Epic Bible College & Graduate School (B)

4330 Auburn Boulevard, Sacramento CA 95841
County: Sacramento | FICE Identification: 034033
Unit ID: 124487
Telephone: (916) 348-4689 | Carnegie Class: Not Classified
FAX Number: (916) 468-0866 | Calendar System: Trimester
URL: www.EPIC.edu
Established: 1974 | Annual Undergrad Tuition & Fees: $9,689
Enrollment: 170 | Coed
Affiliation or Control: Independent Non-Profit | IRS Status: 501(c)3
Highest Offering: Doctorate
Accreditation: TRACS

01 President/CEO .... Dr. Ronald W. HARDEN
05 Vice President of Academics .... Dr. Greg L. HARTLEY
58 Director Graduate Studies .... Dr. Gene MAYNARD
73 Chair of Worship Arts .... Rev. Lane OLSON
08 Director Learning Resource .... Rev. Deborah MCCONKEY
37 Director of Financial Services .... Ms. Kandi MCGODMAN
06 Director of Records/Office Manager .... Mrs. Monida SLUPIK
106 Director of Online Program .... Dr. Scott BOND
26 Director Enrollment/Marketing .... Rev. Daniel HARDEN

Eternity Bible College (C)

2136 Winifred Street, Simi Valley CA 93063
County: Ventura | Identification: 667045
Telephone: (805) 581-1233 | Carnegie Class: Not Classified
FAX Number: (805) 581-1245 | Calendar System: Semester
URL: www.eternitybiblecollege.com
Established: 2004 | Annual Undergrad Tuition & Fees: N/A
Enrollment: N/A | Coed
Affiliation or Control: Independent Non-Profit | IRS Status: 501(c)3
Highest Offering: Baccalaureate
Accreditation: BI

01 President .... Spencer MACCUISH
05 Academic Dean .... Joshua WALKER
32 Dean of Students .... Chris KOTTRE
07 Director of Admissions .... Mary Beth DRAGOUN
10 Registrar/Finance Manager .... Ryan MCGLADDERY
35 Dir Student Life/Exec Asst .... Vacant

Evangelia University (D)

2660 West Woodland Drive, Suite 200,
Anaheim CA 92801-2650
County: Orange | Identification: 666640
Telephone: (714) 527-0691 | Carnegie Class: Not Classified
FAX Number: (714) 527-0693 | Calendar System: Other
URL: www.evangelia.edu
Established: 1999 | Annual Undergrad Tuition & Fees: N/A
Enrollment: N/A | Coed
Affiliation or Control: Reformed Presbyterian Church | IRS Status: 501(c)3
Highest Offering: Doctorate
Accreditation: THEOL, TRACS

01 President/CEO .... Dr. Sung Soo KIM
03 Vice President .... Dr. David CHO
05 Dean of Academic Affairs .... Dr. Soonhae KANG
11 Dean Admin/Chief Operating Officer .... Vacant
32 Dean of Student Affairs .... Ki Won HAN
10 Chief Financial Officer .... Dr. Chang Ho SON
06 Registrar/Foreign Student Advisor .... Charley LEE
08 Librarian .... Sue CHUN
106 Director of Distance Education .... Soonhae KANG

Feather River College (E)

570 Golden Eagle Avenue, Quincy CA 95971-9124
County: Plumas | FICE Identification: 008597
Unit ID: 114433
Telephone: (530) 283-0202 | Carnegie Class: Bac/Assoc-Assoc Dom
FAX Number: (530) 283-3757 | Calendar System: Semester
URL: www.frc.edu
Established: 1968 | Annual Undergrad Tuition & Fees (In-District): $1,465
Enrollment: 1,821 | Coed
Affiliation or Control: State/Local | IRS Status: Exempt
Highest Offering: Baccalaureate
Accreditation: WJ

01 Superintendent/President .... Dr. Kevin TRUTNA
10 Vice President Business Services .... Ms. Morgan TURNER
05 Vice President Instruction/CIO .... Dr. Derek LERCH
32 Vice President Student Services .... Ms. Carlie MCCARTHY
20 Assistant Dean of Instruction .... Dr. Kim BEATON
15 Director Human Resources/EEO .... Vacant
18 Director of Facilities .... Mr. Nick BOYD
07 Registrar/Dir of Admissions .... Ms. Gretchen BAUMGARTNER
37 Director Student Financial Aid .... Mr. Billy OGLE
96 Purchasing Agent .... Ms. Tamara CLINE
04 Administrative Asst to President .... Ms. Cynthia HALL
09 Director of Institutional Research .... Mr. Sean WHALEY
13 Director of Information Services .... Dr. Natalie PRESTA

FIDM/Fashion Institute of Design and Merchandising-Los Angeles (F)

919 S Grand Avenue, Los Angeles CA 90015-1421
County: Los Angeles | FICE Identification: 011112
Unit ID: 114354
Telephone: (213) 624-1200 | Carnegie Class: Bac/Assoc-Mixed
FAX Number: (213) 624-9354 | Calendar System: Quarter
URL: www.fidm.edu
Established: 1969 | Annual Undergrad Tuition & Fees: $32,645
Enrollment: 1,886 | Coed
Affiliation or Control: Proprietary | IRS Status: Proprietary
Highest Offering: Master's
Accreditation: #WC, ART

01 President .... Ms. Tonian HOHBERG
10 Vice President/Treasurer .... Ms. Tess STOLZER
26 Vice President Marketing/Admission .... Ms. Belinda HARDING
05 Vice President Education .... Ms. Barbara BUNDY
108 Dean of Accreditation .... Ms. Lisa SCHOENING
08 Director of the Idea Center .... Ms. Debbie SCHUVER
06 Registrar .... Mr. Michael GILBERT
37 Director Financial Aid .... Mr. Chris JENNINGS
27 Director Public Rels/Publicity .... Ms. Shirley WILSON
38 Personal Counselor .... Ms. Jessica CATTANI
96 Director College Services .... Ms. Ella VAN NORT
13 Director IT Technical Services .... Ms. Saima LATIF
15 Exec Director Human Resources .... Ms. Kim WETZEL
04 Executive Asst to President .... Ms. Megan NOWAK
104 Director International Affairs .... Ms. Sarah REPETTO
105 Director Web Mktg Ops/Publications .... Mr. Michael KAMINSKI
18 Director of FIDM Facilities .... Mr. John (Buddy) BOLOGNONE
19 Director of Security .... Mr. Todd J. ANDERSON
22 Title IX Coordinator .... Ms. Kim WETZEL
29 Director Alumni Relations .... Mr. Kevin KEELE
32 Manager Student Activities .... Ms. Angela LEAVITT
53 Dean of Education .... Ms. Sheryl RABINOVICH
90 Director Academic Computing .... Ms. Cheryl BENSMILLER

Fielding Graduate University (G)

2020 De La Vina Street, Santa Barbara CA 93105-3538
County: Santa Barbara | FICE Identification: 020961
Unit ID: 114549
Telephone: (800) 340-1099 | Carnegie Class: DU-Mod
FAX Number: (805) 687-9793 | Calendar System: Trimester
URL: www.fielding.edu
Established: 1974 | Annual Graduate Tuition & Fees: N/A
Enrollment: 1,071 | Coed
Affiliation or Control: Independent Non-Profit | IRS Status: 501(c)3
Highest Offering: Doctorate; No Undergraduates
Accreditation: WC, CLPSY

01 President .... Dr. Katrina S. ROGERS
04 Exec Asst to President .... Mr. Bryan LOPES
03 Distinguished Sr Advisor to Pres .... Dr. Orlando L. TAYLOR
10 VP and Chief Financial Officer .... Ms. Prema WINDOKUN
05 Provost & Senior VP .... Dr. Raj PARIKH
15 Director of Human Resources .... Mr. Dino FERRARE
06 Registrar/Dir of Curriculum Svcs .... Ms. Bridget BRADY
29 Director of Alumni Relations .... Ms. Hilary MOLINA
28 Chief Diversity Officer .... Vacant
07 Director of Admissions .... Ms. Erica FICHTER
09 Director of Institutional Research .... Ms. Marine DUMAS

Five Branches University, Graduate School of Traditional Chinese Medicine (H)

1885 Lundy Avenue, Suite 108, San Jose CA 95131
County: Santa Clara | Identification: 667008
Telephone: (408) 260-0208 | Carnegie Class: Not Classified
FAX Number: (408) 261-3166 | Calendar System: Trimester
URL: www.fivebranches.edu
Established: 2005 | Annual Undergrad Tuition & Fees: N/A
Enrollment: N/A | Coed
Affiliation or Control: Proprietary | IRS Status: Proprietary
Highest Offering: Doctorate; No Lower Division
Accreditation: ACUP

01 President/CEO .... Ron ZAIDMAN
05 VP Academic Affairs .... Joanna ZHAO
10 VP Finance .... Liana CHEN
13 VP Operations .... Gina HUANG
06 Registrar .... Ling ZHANG
58 Director of Doctoral Program .... Robyn GRIEVE
26 Director of Marketing .... Sean ZAIDMAN
37 Director of Financial Aid .... Daryl CULLEN
58 Associate Director Doctoral Program .... Debbie CHENG
84 Director of Enrollment .... Alex HU
56 Extension Program Admin .... Lykos YANG
23 Clinic Manager .... Joyce HE
08 Library & Facility Manager .... Songsong GAO
20 Associate Academic Dean .... Nick HANCOCK

Five Branches University, Graduate School of Traditional Chinese Medicine (I)

200 7th Avenue, Santa Cruz CA 95062-4669
County: Santa Cruz | FICE Identification: 031313
Unit ID: 114585
Telephone: (831) 476-9424 | Carnegie Class: Spec-4-yr-Other Health
FAX Number: (831) 476-8928 | Calendar System: Trimester
URL: www.fivebranches.edu
Established: 1984 | Annual Undergrad Tuition & Fees: N/A
Enrollment: 349 | Coed
Affiliation or Control: Proprietary | IRS Status: Proprietary
Highest Offering: Doctorate; No Lower Division
Accreditation: ACUP

01 President & CEO .... Ron ZAIDMAN
05 Vice President & Dean .... Joanna ZHAO
11 Vice President Operations .... Gina HUANG
10 Vice President Finance & Accounting .... Liana CHEN
26 Dir of Marketing & Communications .... Sean ZAIDMAN
08 Librarian .... Jim EMDY
06 Registrar San Jose .... Ling ZHANG
32 Director Student Services .... Andrea CARVALHO
07 Admissions Director .... Eleonor MENDELSON
37 Director Student Financial Aid .... Daryl CULLEN
56 Director Extension Programs .... Fay DENNIS
07 Director Bridge Program Admissions .... Tom DICKLIN

*Foothill-De Anza Community College District System Office (J)

12345 El Monte Road, Los Altos Hills CA 94022-4597
County: Santa Clara | FICE Identification: 009020
Unit ID: 114831
Telephone: (650) 949-6100 | Carnegie Class: N/A
FAX Number: (650) 941-6289
URL: www.fhda.edu

01 Chancellor .... Dr. Judy C. MINER
10 Vice Chancellor Business Services .... Ms. Susan CHEU
15 Vice Chancellor Human Resources .... Ms. Dorene NOVOTNY
13 Vice Chancellor Technology .... Mr. Joseph MOREAU
09 Exec Dir of Inst Research/Planning .... Mr. David ULATE
19 Chief of Police .... Mr. Daniel ACOSTA
26 Coordinator District Communication .... Ms. Becky BARTINDALE
102 Exec Dir Foundation .... Mr. Dennis CIMA
96 Director of Purchasing .... Ms. Maria CONTRERAS-TANORI

*De Anza College (K)

21250 Stevens Creek Boulevard,
Cupertino CA 95014-5793
County: Santa Clara | FICE Identification: 004480
Unit ID: 113333
Telephone: (408) 864-5678 | Carnegie Class: Assoc/MT-VT-Mix Trad/Non
FAX Number: (408) 864-8238 | Calendar System: Quarter
URL: www.deanza.edu
Established: 1967 | Annual Undergrad Tuition & Fees (In-District): $1,561
Enrollment: 18,649 | Coed
Affiliation or Control: State/Local | IRS Status: 501(c)3
Highest Offering: Associate Degree
Accreditation: WJ, MLTAD, NAEYC

02 President .... Dr. Lloyd HOLMES
05 Vice Pres of Instruction .... Ms. Christina G. ESPINOSA-PIEB
32 VP of Student Services .... Dr. Rob MIESO
10 VP Administrative Services .... Ms. Pam GREY
20 Assoc Vice Pres Instruction .... Mr. Thomas RAY
26 AVP Communications & External Rel .... Ms. Marisa SPATAFORE
35 Dean Student Development/EOPS .... Dr. Michele LEBLEU BURNS
38 Dean Counseling & Matriculation .... Ms. Laureen BALDUCCI
84 Dean Enrollment Services .... Ms. Nazy GALOYAN
37 Director Student Financial Aid .... Ms. Lisa MANDY
21 Director Fiscal Services .... Mr. Martin VALERA
18 Director College Operations .... Ms. Jennifer MAHATO
102 Exec Director Foundation .... Mr. Dennis CIMA
28 Dean Equity & Engagement .... Ms. Alicia CORTEZ
88 Assessment Center Supervisor .... Ms. Casie WHEAT
09 Institutional Researcher .... Dr. Mallory NEWELL
06 Supervisor Admissions and Records .... Mr. Barry JOHNSON
04 Executive Assistant to President .... Ms. Nathaly AGUILAR
08 Head Librarian .... Mr. Tom DOLEN
13 Chief Info Technology Officer (CIO) .... Mr. Joe MOREAU
41 Dean Physical Education & Athletics .... Mr. Eric MENDOZA
50 Dean Business/Comp Sys/Applied Tech .... Mr. Moaty FAYEK
15 Human Resources Technician .... Ms. Kit PERALES

*Foothill College (A)
12345 El Monte Road, Los Altos Hills CA 94022-4599
County: Santa Clara | FICE Identification: 001199
Unit ID: 114716
Telephone: (650) 949-7777 | Carnegie Class: Bac/Assoc-Assoc Dom
FAX Number: (650) 949-7375 | Calendar System: Quarter
URL: www.foothill.edu
Established: 1957 | Annual Undergrad Tuition & Fees (In-District): $1,563
Enrollment: 14,605 | Coed
Affiliation or Control: State/Local | IRS Status: 501(c)3
Highest Offering: Baccalaureate
Accreditation: WJ, COARC, DA, DH, DMS, EMT, RAD

02 Interim President ... Ms. Bernadine CHUCK FONG
04 Assistant to the President ... Ms. Veronica CASAS HERNANDEZ
10 VP Finance & Admin Services ... Mr. Bret WATSON
05 Int VP Instruction & Inst Research ... Mr. Kurt HUEG
20 Int Associate VP Instruction ... Mr. Paul STARER
20 Assoc Vice Pres Instruction ... Mr. Kurt HUEG
32 Associate VP Student Services ... Dr. Laurie SCOLARI
21 Associate VP Finance & Admin Svcs ... Mr. Bret WATSON
35 Dean Student Affairs & Activities ... Ms. Leticia MALDONADO
38 Dean Counseling & Special Programs ... Mr. Roosevelt CHARLES
28 Dean EOPS ... Ms. April HENDERSON
12 Campus Director Sunnyvale Center ... Mr. Craig GAWLICK
88 Dean Disabled Stdnt Svcs/Vet Pgms ... Ms. Neelam AGARWAL
40 Director Bookstore ... Mr. Romeo PAULE
84 Dean Enrollment Services ... Mr. Anthony CERVANTES
37 Director Financial Aid ... Mr. Kevin HARRAL
22 Dean of Equity/Diversity/Inclusion ... Dr. Ajani BYRD
23 Director Health Services ... Vacant
76 Dean Biology & Health Sciences ... Mr. Ram SUBRAMANIAM
106 Dean Foothill Online Learning ... Ms. Lene WHITLEY-PUTZ
57 Actg Dean Fine Arts/Communications ... Ms. Debbie LEE
79 Dean Language Arts & LRC ... Ms. Valerie FONG
81 Dean Physical Sci/Math & Engr ... Mr. Ram SUBRAMANIAM
09 Supervisor Institutional Research ... Ms. Ajani BYRD
41 Athletic Director ... Mr. Mike TEIJEIRO
103 Associate VP Workforce ... Ms. Teresa ONG

Franciscan School of Theology (B)
5998 Alcala Park, San Diego CA 92110
County: San Diego | FICE Identification: 011792
Unit ID: 114734
Telephone: (619) 574-5800 | Carnegie Class: Spec-4-yr-Faith
FAX Number: (619) 849-8431 | Calendar System: Semester
URL: www.fst.edu
Established: 1968 | Annual Graduate Tuition & Fees: N/A
Enrollment: 57 | Coed
Affiliation or Control: Independent Non-Profit | IRS Status: 501(c)3
Highest Offering: Master's; No Undergraduates
Accreditation: WC, THEOL

01 President ... Fr. Garrett GALVIN
10 VP Finance/Business Operations ... Ms. Kimberly RENNA
05 Vice President for Academic Affairs ... Sr. Juliet MOUSSEAU
07 Assoc Dir Admissions/Recruitment ... Mr. John GONZALES
30 Director of Development ... Ms. Andrea DELUCIA
32 Director of Student Services ... Sr. Kathy FLOOD
26 Marketing/Recruitment Coord ... Ms. Gigi BETANCOURT
110 Development Coordinator ... Ms. Mitchelle GREENLEE
04 Executive Assistant to President ... Ms. Rose WALTON
20 Coordinator for AA & Student Svs ... Mr. Brady YOUNG
51 Continued Education/FJI Coordinator ... Ms. Sharmeen ENAYAT

Fremont College (C)
18000 Studebaker Road, Suite 900A, Cerritos CA 90703
County: Los Angeles | FICE Identification: 030399
Unit ID: 372073
Telephone: (562) 809-5100 | Carnegie Class: Bac/Assoc-Mixed
FAX Number: (562) 809-7100 | Calendar System: Other
URL: https://fremont.edu
Established: 1985 | Annual Undergrad Tuition & Fees: N/A
Enrollment: 180 | Coed
Affiliation or Control: Proprietary | IRS Status: Proprietary
Highest Offering: Master's
Accreditation: ACCSC

01 Campus Director ... Tony WONG
06 Registrar ... Joyce BOYLAN
07 Director of Admissions & Marketing ... Brian RAMAGE
08 Librarian ... Alison QUIRION
10 Business Office/Database Specialist ... Phillip WANG
32 Director of Student Affairs ... Amy VARGAS
36 Director of Career Development ... Amber CRUZ
37 Director of Financial Aid ... Israel RODRIGUEZ

Fresno Pacific University (D)
1717 S Chestnut Avenue, Fresno CA 93702-4798
County: Fresno | FICE Identification: 001253
Unit ID: 114813
Telephone: (559) 453-2000 | Carnegie Class: Masters/L
FAX Number: (559) 453-2007 | Calendar System: Semester
URL: www.fresno.edu
Established: 1944 | Annual Undergrad Tuition & Fees: $33,452
Enrollment: 3,995 | Coed
Affiliation or Control: Mennonite Brethren Church | IRS Status: 501(c)3
Highest Offering: Master's
Accreditation: WC, NURSE, SW, THEOL

01 President ... Dr. André STEPHENS
05 Provost/Senior VP Academic Affairs ... Dr. D. Gayle COPELAND
10 Vice President Finance & Business ... Mr. Robert LIPPERT
26 Exec Dir of Public Relations ... Mrs. Rebecca BRADLEY
11 Vice Pres of Operations ... Vacant
84 Vice Pres Enrollment Mgmt ... Mr. Jon ENDICOTT
111 VP for Advancement/Exec Dir Found ... Mr. Donald GRIFFITH
32 Vice President Campus Life ... Mr. Dale SCULLY
73 VP & Dean of the Seminary ... Dr. Sharon TAN
50 Dean School of Business ... Dr. Katie FLEENER
79 Dean Sch of Human/Rel/Soc Sci ... Dr. Ron HERMS
53 Dean School of Education ... Dr. Gary GRAMENZ
78 Dean School of Natural Sciences ... Dr. Tara SIRVENT
08 Director of Library ... Mr. Kevin ENNS-REMPEL
36 Director of Career Resource Center ... Ms. Rose WINN
15 Human Resources Director ... Mr. Jordan SHARP
29 Director Alumni Development ... Ms. Ali SENA
37 Dir Student Financial Services ... Mr. David RICHARDS
41 Athletic Director ... Mr. Morgan WALKER
19 Chief of Campus Safety ... Mr. Javier CAMPOS
26 Chief Public Rels Ofcr/Dir Pubs ... Mr. Wayne STEFFEN
104 Dir International Pgms/Svcs Ofc ... Ms. Angela MUNEZ
07 Director of Admissions ... Mrs. Krista BROOKS
18 Facilities Manager ... Mr. Gary METCALF
04 Executive Asst to President ... Ms. Gwenevera E. BURKS
102 Dir Foundation/Corporate Relations ... Mr. Mark DEFFENBACHER
112 Dir of Found Dev & Legacy Gifts ... Mr. Steven REDEKOP
09 Director of Institutional Research ... Ms. Lisa FOSTER
13 CIO ITS ... Mr. James LONG
105 Director Web Services ... Mr. Justin GABLE
39 Asst Dean Stdnt Dev/Title IX Coord ... Ms. Pam SCHOCK
106 Director Center for Online Learning ... Dr. Henrietta SIEMENS
86 Director Government Relations ... Mr. Donald NORMAN
06 Registrar ... Ms. Danielle JEFFRESS
108 Director Institutional Assessment ... Ms. Candi ALEXANDER
25 Chief Contract and Grants Administr ... Ms. Anna JAMES MILLER
28 Interim Director of Diversity ... Dr. Jesse SALINAS
101 Secretary of the Institution/Board ... Ms. Gwenevera E. BURKS

Fuller Theological Seminary (E)
135 N Oakland Avenue, Pasadena CA 91182-1780
County: Los Angeles | FICE Identification: 001200
Unit ID: 114840
Telephone: (626) 584-5200 | Carnegie Class: Spec-4-yr-Faith
FAX Number: (626) 795-8767 | Calendar System: Quarter
URL: www.fuller.edu
Established: 1947 | Annual Graduate Tuition & Fees: N/A
Enrollment: 2,277 | Coed
Affiliation or Control: Independent Non-Profit | IRS Status: 501(c)3
Highest Offering: Doctorate; No Undergraduates
Accreditation: WC, CLPSY, THEOL

01 President ... Dr. Mark A. LABBERTON
05 CAO ... Dr. Alexis ABERNETHY
102 Chief of Philanthropy ... Mr. Kenneth ERFFMEYER
10 Chief Financial Officer ... Mr. Ray ASAD
26 Chief of Communications & Branding ... Ms. Dana VANVALIN
88 Chief of Leadership Formation ... Dr. Kara POWELL
73 Dean School of Mission & Theology ... Dr. Amos YONG
83 Dean School of Psychology ... Dr. Ted COSSE
13 Chief of Technology ... Mr. Jeff HARWELL
88 Assoc Dean Doctor of Ministry Pgm ... Dr. Kurt FREDRICKSON
15 Chief of HR & Org Development ... Mrs. Bernadette (BJ) O'HALLORAN
32 Chief Student Engagement/Success ... Mr. Marcus SUN
106 Chief of Teaching and Learning ... Mr. Tommy LISTER
43 Chief Counsel ... Mr. Lance GRIFFIN
108 Accreditation Liaison Officer ... Dr. Dave L. SCOTT
09 Director of Institutional Research ... Dr. Dave SCOTT
06 Registrar ... Mrs. Andrea EDIN
11 Chief Operating Officer ... Dr. Ted COSSE
39 Manager of Housing Services ... Ms. Lavina SEAWRIGHT
04 Assistant to President ... Mrs. Amanda MACINTOSH
18 Facilities Director ... Mr. Nathan MERRITT
109 Director of Auxiliary Services ... Mrs. Jeanne HANDOJO
85 Dir Student Affs/International Svcs ... Mr. Matthew JIN
37 Dir Student Financial Svcs ... Ms. Theresa COWAN
08 Director of the DAH Library ... Ms. Daniell WHITTINGTON
29 Exec Director Alumni Engagement ... Ms. Lily TSAU

Galaxy Medical College (F)
6400 Laurel Canyon Blvd, St 270,
North Hollywood CA 91606
County: Los Angeles | FICE Identification: 041596
Unit ID: 461254
Telephone: (818) 509-9970 | Carnegie Class: Not Classified
FAX Number: (818) 509-9935 | Calendar System: Semester
URL: www.galaxymedicalcollege.edu
Established: 2003 | Annual Undergrad Tuition & Fees: N/A
Enrollment: 41 | Coed
Affiliation or Control: Proprietary | IRS Status: Proprietary
Highest Offering: Associate Degree
Accreditation: ABHES

01 School Director ... Ms. Agun Anna KHACHATRYAN

Gateway Seminary (G)
3210 E. Guasti Rd, Ontario CA 91761-8642
County: San Bernadino | FICE Identification: 001204
Telephone: (909) 687-1800 | Carnegie Class: Not Classified
FAX Number: N/A | Calendar System: Semester
URL: www.gs.edu
Established: 1944 | Annual Graduate Tuition & Fees: N/A
Enrollment: N/A | Coed
Affiliation or Control: Southern Baptist | IRS Status: 501(c)3
Highest Offering: Doctorate; No Undergraduates
Accreditation: WC, THEOL

01 President ... Dr. Jeff IORG
111 Vice Pres Advancement ... Dr. Jeff JONES
05 Vice President Academic Affairs ... Dr. Alex STEWART
32 VP Enroll/Student Svcs/Dean Stdnts ... Dr. Adam GROZA
10 VP Business Services ... Mr. Ray TONG
21 Controller ... Mr. Harry WEAVER
06 Registrar ... Ms. Deena CARTER
08 Director of Library Services ... Dr. Jonathan MCCORMICK
12 Director PNW Campus ... Dr. Mark BRADLEY
12 Director Arizona Campus ... Dr. Dallas BIVINS
12 Director Rocky Mountain Campus ... Dr. Steve VETETO
13 Director Information Technology ... Mr. Steve POLCYN
15 Director Personnel Services ... Ms. Jennifer PALMER
18 Chief Facilities/Physical Plant ... Mr. Manny GUERRERO
30 Director of Development ... Mr. Tyler SANDERS
84 Director Enrollment Management ... Mr. Cameron SCHWEITZER
32 Director of Student Life ... Mr. Jaclyn BRITO

Gavilan College (H)
5055 Santa Teresa Boulevard, Gilroy CA 95020-9599
County: Santa Clara | FICE Identification: 001202
Unit ID: 114938
Telephone: (408) 848-4800 | Carnegie Class: Assoc/HT-High Trad
FAX Number: (408) 848-4801 | Calendar System: Semester
URL: www.gavilan.edu
Established: 1919 | Annual Undergrad Tuition & Fees (In-District): $1,166
Enrollment: 4,494 | Coed
Affiliation or Control: State/Local | IRS Status: 501(c)3
Highest Offering: Associate Degree
Accreditation: WJ

01 Superintendent/President ... Dr. Pedro AVILA
05 EVP Educational Programs/Services ... Ms. Renee CRAIG-MARIUS
11 Vice Pres Administrative Services ... Mr. Graciano MENDOZA
10 Interim Business Svcs Supervisor ... Mr. Joshua JOHNSON
21 Director Fiscal Services ... Ms. Theresa M. ANAYA
29 Alumni Relations ... Ms. Rosie ZEPEDA
08 Head Librarian ... Vacant
84 Dean Enrollment Services ... Dr. Julian WEST
88 Interim Dean Foundational Skills ... Dr. Randy BROWN
15 Dir Human Resources/Labor Relations ... Ms. Lucy ALVAREZ
18 Director of Facilities/Maintenance ... Mr. Jeff GOPP
13 Director Information Technology ... Mr. Kyle BILLUPS
26 Public Information Officer ... Ms. Rosie ZEPEDA
23 Student Health Nurse ... Vacant
40 Manager Bookstore ... Ms. Laura JIMENEZ
49 Dean Arts/Humanities/Social Sci ... Mr. Noah LYSTRUP
121 Dean Special Programs ... Ms. Carina CISNEROS
81 Dean of STEM/MESA & Library ... Ms. Jen NARI
41 Interim Athletic Director ... Ms. Susan DODD
96 Purchasing Specialist ... Ms. Jeanne ALAMDARI
04 Exec Assistant to the President ... Ms. Lisa N. SCOTT
09 Dir Institutional Research/Planning ... Vacant
51 Dir Community/Educ Partnerships ... Vacant
37 Dir Student Financial Aid ... Ms. Marina MARTINEZ
38 Student Counseling ... Ms. Celia MARQUEZ
06 Interim Dir Admis/Records/Registrar ... Ms. Irene HANETA
36 Dean Career Education/Workforce ... Ms. Susan SWEENEY
66 Assoc Dean Nursing/Allied Health ... Dr. Enna TREVATHAN

Glendale Career College (I)
240 N. Brand Blvd, Lower Level, Glendale CA 91203
County: Los Angeles | FICE Identification: 023385
Unit ID: 115010
Telephone: (818) 243-1131 | Carnegie Class: Spec 2-yr-Health
FAX Number: (818) 243-6028 | Calendar System: Semester
URL: www.glendalecareer.com
Established: 1946 | Annual Undergrad Tuition & Fees: N/A
Enrollment: 632 | Coed
Affiliation or Control: Proprietary | IRS Status: Proprietary
Highest Offering: Baccalaureate
Accreditation: ABHES, NURSE, SURGT, SURTEC

01 Executive Director ... Irma PIRONE

Glendale Community College (J)
1500 N Verdugo Road, Glendale CA 91208-2894
County: Los Angeles | FICE Identification: 001203
Unit ID: 115001
Telephone: (818) 240-1000 | Carnegie Class: Assoc/HT-High Trad
FAX Number: (818) 549-9436 | Calendar System: Semester
URL: www.glendale.edu
Established: 1927 | Annual Undergrad Tuition & Fees (In-District): $1,175
Enrollment: 12,973 | Coed
Affiliation or Control: State/Local | IRS Status: 501(c)3
Highest Offering: Associate Degree

Accreditation: WJ

01 Superintendent/President .... Dr. David VIAR
10 Exec Vice Pres Administrative Svcs .... Dr. Anthony CULPEPPER
05 Vice Pres Instructional Services .... Dr. Michael RITTERBROWN
32 Vice President Student Services .... Dr. Paul SCHLOSSMAN
51 Admin Dean Continuing/Cmty Educ .... Dr. Alfred RAMIREZ
15 VP Human Resources .... Ms. Victoria SIMMONS
45 Dean Research/Planning/Grants .... Dr. Edward KARPP
07 Director Admissions & Records .... Ms. Michelle MORA
20 Dean Instructional Services .... Ms. Agnes EGUARAS
103 Int Dean Workforce Development .... Mr. Federico SAUCEDO
32 Dean Student Affairs .... Ms. Tzoler OUKAYAN
35 Dean of Student Services .... Mr. Drew YAMANISHI
37 Assoc Dean Stdnt Financial Aid Svcs .Dr. Christina TANGALAKIS
21 Director Business Services .... Ms. Susan COURTEY
102 Exec Director College Foundation .... Ms. Lisa BROOKS
41 Assoc Dean Athletics .... Mr. Chris CICUTO
36 Assoc Dn Career Educ/Wkfrc Dev .... Vacant
31 Assoc Dean Cont/Community Education .... Dr. Ramona BARRIO-SOTILLO

Gnomon (A)

1015 N. Cahuenga Blvd, Los Angeles CA 90038
County: Los Angeles | FICE Identification: 040764 | Unit ID: 449384
Telephone: (323) 466-6663 | Carnegie Class: Spec-4-yr-Arts
FAX Number: (323) 466-6710 | Calendar System: Quarter
URL: www.gnomon.edu
Established: 1997 | Annual Undergrad Tuition & Fees: $31,554
Enrollment: 575 | Coed
Affiliation or Control: Proprietary | IRS Status: Proprietary
Highest Offering: Baccalaureate
Accreditation: ACCSC

01 President .... Alex ALVAREZ
11 Vice President/Chief Admin Officer .... Darrin KRUMWEIDE
84 Executive Director Enrollment .... Brian BRADFORD
06 Registrar .... Tina OLVERA

Golden Gate University (B)

536 Mission Street, San Francisco CA 94105-2968
County: San Francisco | FICE Identification: 001205 | Unit ID: 115083
Telephone: (415) 442-7000 | Carnegie Class: Masters/L
FAX Number: N/A | Calendar System: Trimester
URL: www.ggu.edu
Established: 1901 | Annual Undergrad Tuition & Fees: N/A
Enrollment: 2,472 | Coed
Affiliation or Control: Independent Non-Profit | IRS Status: 501(c)3
Highest Offering: Doctorate
Accreditation: WC, LAW

01 President .... Dr. David J. FIKE
05 VP of Academic Affairs .... Ms. Barbara H. KARLIN
10 Interim Chief Financial Officer .... Mr. Brad MITCHELL
30 Int Dir Development/Alumni Rels .... Mr. Chris SORENSON
61 Dean School of Law .... Mr. Colin CRAWFORD
50 Dean School of Business .... Dr. Gordon SWARTZ
58 Dean Graduate Programs .... Ms. Amy MCLELLAN
106 Director E-Learning .... Mr. Doug GEIER
32 Dean of Students & Student Affairs .... Ms. Kayla KRUPNICK-WALSH
08 Director University Library .... Mr. James KRUSLING
08 Associate Dean Law Library .... Mr. Michael DAW
06 University Registrar .... Mr. Steven LIND
13 Director Information Technology .... Mr. Daniel FORTSON
27 Director of Marketing .... Mr. Ryan BADOWSKI
09 Dir Financial Planning/Analysis .... Mr. Sathyapal MENON
18 Director Business Svcs/Facilities .... Mr. Mike KOPERSKI
21 Controller .... Ms. Grace LEE
37 Director Student Financial Aid .... Ms. Gabriela DE LA VEGA
108 Director Institutional Assessment .... Ms. Lisa KRAMER
15 Head Human Resources .... Ms. S. Jamila BUCKNER
97 Int Dean School Undergrad Studies .... Mr. Nate HINERMAN

Grace Mission University (C)

1645 West Valencia Drive, Fullerton CA 92833-3860
County: Orange | Identification: 666642 | Unit ID: 481058
Telephone: (714) 525-0088 | Carnegie Class: Spec-4-yr-Faith
FAX Number: (714) 525-0089 | Calendar System: Semester
URL: www.gm.edu
Established: 1995 | Annual Undergrad Tuition & Fees: $3,120
Enrollment: 234 | Coed
Affiliation or Control: Presbyterian Church (U.S.A.) | IRS Status: 501(c)3
Highest Offering: Doctorate
Accreditation: BI, THEOL, TRACS

01 President & CEO .... Dr. Kyunam CHOI
05 Academic Dean .... Dr. Hyunwan KIM
10 Chief Financial Officer .... Mr. Seongyul BAEK
32 Dean of Student Affairs .... Dr. Byounggu LEE
11 Dir Administration/Financial Aid .... Mr. James KOO
06 Registrar .... Ms. Min LEE
08 Librarian .... Ms. EunJa SEO
07 Director of Admissions .... Ms. Meesun LEE
30 Director of Development .... Mrs. Suok RHIE
26 Director of Public Relations .... Dr. Changsoo LEE
37 Director of Financial Aid .... Mr. James KOO

Grace University (D)

1560 Brookhollow Dr., Suite 209, Santa Ana CA 92705
County: Orange | Identification: 667422
Telephone: (714) 486-2318 | Carnegie Class: Not Classified
FAX Number: N/A | Calendar System: Quarter
URL: www.graceuniv.org
Established: | Annual Undergrad Tuition & Fees: N/A
Enrollment: N/A | Coed
Affiliation or Control: Non-denominational | IRS Status: 501(c)3
Highest Offering: Master's
Accreditation: TRACS

01 President .... John CHARITY

Graduate Theological Union (E)

2400 Ridge Road, Berkeley CA 94709-1212
County: Alameda | FICE Identification: 001207 | Unit ID: 115214
Telephone: (510) 649-2400 | Carnegie Class: Spec-4-yr-Faith
FAX Number: (510) 649-1417 | Calendar System: Semester
URL: www.gtu.edu
Established: 1962 | Annual Graduate Tuition & Fees: N/A
Enrollment: 213 | Coed
Affiliation or Control: Independent Non-Profit | IRS Status: 501(c)3
Highest Offering: Doctorate; No Undergraduates
Accreditation: WC, THEOL

01 President .... Dr. Uriah Y. KIM
05 Dean/Vice Pres Academic Affairs .... Dr. Jennifer DAVIDSON
10 Chief Financial Officer .... Mr. Mike CAIRNS
11 Chief Operating Officer .... Ms. Marie LUCERO
26 Chief Strategy Ofcr/VP Inst Advance .... Ms. Sephora MARKSON
32 Director of Student Life .... Ms. Chaitanya MOTUPALLI
08 Interim Library Director .... Ms. Beth KUMOR
06 Consortia Registrar .... Mr. John SEAL
18 Director of Facilities .... Mr. Curtis OSBORNE
15 Manager of Human Resources .... Ms. Sylvie TIONADO
37 Sr Dir of Financial Aid/Enrollment .... Ms. Denise MORITA
04 Exec Assistant to President .... Ms. Melissa HADDICK
35 Assoc Dean of Students .... Ms. Wendy ARCE
07 Asst Dir of Recruitment/Admissions .... Mr. Ben WOEHLER

*Grossmont-Cuyamaca Community College District (F)

8800 Grossmont College Drive, El Cajon CA 92020-1799
County: San Diego | FICE Identification: 007006 | Unit ID: 115287
Telephone: (619) 644-7010 | Carnegie Class: N/A
FAX Number: (619) 644-7936
URL: www.gcccd.edu

01 Chancellor .... Dr. Lynn NEAULT
10 Vice Chanc Business Services .... Ms. Sahar ABUSHABAN
15 Int Vice Chanc Human Resources .... Ms. Aimee GALLAGHER

*Cuyamaca College (G)

900 Rancho San Diego Parkway, El Cajon CA 92019-4304
County: San Diego | FICE Identification: 021113 | Unit ID: 113218
Telephone: (619) 660-4000 | Carnegie Class: Assoc/HT-Mix Trad/Non
FAX Number: (619) 660-4399 | Calendar System: Semester
URL: www.cuyamaca.edu
Established: 1978 | Annual Undergrad Tuition & Fees (In-District): $1,340
Enrollment: 8,720 | Coed
Affiliation or Control: State/Local | IRS Status: 501(c)3
Highest Offering: Associate Degree
Accreditation: WJ

02 President .... Dr. Julianna BARNES
05 Int Vice President Instruction .... Ms. Alicia MUNOZ
32 Vice Pres Student Services .... Ms. Jessica ROBINSON
11 Int Vice Pres Admin Services .... Ms. Nicole SALGADO
81 Int Dean of Math/Sci/Engineering .... Ms. Kim DUDZIK
79 Int Dean of Arts/Human/Social Sci .... Dr. Lauren HALSTED
72 Dean of Career Technical Education .... Mr. Larry MCLEMORE
08 Int Dean Learning/Tech Resources .... Ms. Jodi REED
41 Dean Athletics/Kines/Health Educ .... Dr. Cuauhtemoc CARBONI
35 Dean Student Affairs .... Dr. Lauren VAKNIN
38 Dean Counseling Services .... Ms. Nicole JONES
37 Director of Financial Aid .... Mr. Ray REYES
07 Director Admissions & Records .... Mr. Gregory VEGA
18 Director Facilities .... Mr. Francisco GONZALEZ
04 Executive Asst to President .... Ms. Valeri WILSON
09 Sr Dean Inst Effectiv/Succ/Equity .... Ms. Brianna HAYS
26 Director College & Cmty Relations .... Ms. Christianne PENUNURI
10 Int Business Svcs Supervisor .... Mr. Michael ERICKSON

*Grossmont College (H)

8800 Grossmont College Drive, El Cajon CA 92020-1799
County: San Diego | FICE Identification: 001208 | Unit ID: 115296
Telephone: (619) 644-7000 | Carnegie Class: Assoc/HT-High Trad
FAX Number: (619) 644-7922 | Calendar System: Semester
URL: www.grossmont.edu
Established: 1961 | Annual Undergrad Tuition & Fees (In-District): $1,332
Enrollment: 15,426 | Coed
Affiliation or Control: State/Local | IRS Status: 501(c)3
Highest Offering: Associate Degree
Accreditation: WJ, ADNUR, CEA, COARC, CVT, OTA

02 President .... Ms. Denise WHISENHUNT
05 Vice Pres of Academic Affairs .... Dr. Marshall FULBRIGHT
32 Vice Pres Student Services .... Dr. Marsha GABLE
07 Dean Admissions/Records/Fin Aid .... Mr. Aaron STARCK
38 Dean Counseling Svcs .... Ms. Martha CLAVELLE
72 Dean Career & Technical Workforce .... Mr. Javier AYALA
81 Int Dean Math/Natural Sci/Phys Educ .... Mr. Shawn HICKS
60 Int Dean Arts/Languages/Comm .... Mr. Steve BAKER
79 Dean English/Social & Behav Sci .... Mr. Agustin ALBARRAN
08 Dean of Learning Resources .... Dr. Tate HURVITZ
35 Dean Student Affairs .... Ms. Sara VARGHESE
10 Chief Business Officer .... Mr. Bill MCGREEVY
18 Chief Facilities/Physical Plant .... Mr. Loren HOLMQUIST
26 Int Chief Public Relations Officer .... Mr. David OGUL
36 Director Student Placement .... Ms. Renee NASORI
37 Director Student Financial Aid .... Mr. Michael COPENHAVER
96 Director of Purchasing .... Mr. Nahid RAZI
04 Executive Assistant to President .... Ms. Bernadette BLACK

Gurnick Academy of Medical Arts (I)

2121 S. El Camino Real Bldg C200, San Mateo CA 94403
County: San Mateo | FICE Identification: 041698 | Unit ID: 459213
Telephone: (650) 685-6616 | Carnegie Class: Spec-4-yr-Other Health
FAX Number: (650) 685-6640 | Calendar System: Other
URL: www.gurnick.edu
Established: 2004 | Annual Undergrad Tuition & Fees: N/A
Enrollment: 2,462 | Coed
Affiliation or Control: Proprietary | IRS Status: Proprietary
Highest Offering: Associate Degree
Accreditation: ABHES, DMS, PTAA, RAD

00 CEO .... Konstantin GOURJI
01 Campus Director .... Fred FARIDIAN
11 Chief Operating Officer .... Burke MALIN
05 Chief Academic Officer .... Larisa REVZINA

Hartnell College (J)

411 Central Avenue, Salinas CA 93901-1697
County: Monterey | FICE Identification: 001209 | Unit ID: 115393
Telephone: (831) 755-6700 | Carnegie Class: Assoc/HT-High Trad
FAX Number: (831) 755-6751 | Calendar System: Semester
URL: www.hartnell.edu
Established: 1920 | Annual Undergrad Tuition & Fees (In-District): $1,400
Enrollment: 8,673 | Coed
Affiliation or Control: State/Local | IRS Status: 501(c)3
Highest Offering: Associate Degree
Accreditation: WJ, ADNUR, #COARC, PNUR

01 Superintendent/President .... Mr. Michael GUTIERREZ
32 VP Student Affairs .... Dr. Romero JALOMO
10 VP Administrative Services .... Mr. Graciano MENDOZA
13 VP Information Technology .... Dr. Chelsy PHAM
05 VP Academic Affairs .... Dr. Cathryn WILKINSON
111 VP Advancement/Development .... Ms. Jackie CRUZ
15 VP Human Resources/EEO .... Ms. Dianna ROSE
21 Controller .... Mr. David TECHAIRA
18 Exec Dir Constr/Facilities Mgmt .... Mr. Joseph REYES
20 Dean Academic Aff Programs/Support .... Dr. Marianne FONTES
81 Dean Academic Affs Math/Science .... Ms. Sharon ALBERT
35 Director of Student Life .... Mr. Augustine NEVAREZ
26 Director of Communications .... Ms. Terri PYER
22 Dir of Student Affairs/EOPS .... Mr. Paul CASEY
66 Dean Academic Affairs/Nursing .... Dr. Debra KACZMAR
83 Dean Acad Affs Soc/Fine Lang Arts .... Ms. Joy COWDEN
20 Dean South County Educ Programs .... Mr. Mostafa GHOUS
04 Senior Executive Assistant .... Ms. Lucille SERRANO
84 Dean of Student Affairs/Enrol Svcs .... Ms. Maria CEJA
09 Director of Institutional Research .... Dr. Milena ANGELOVA
101 Secretary of the Institution/Board .... Ms. Lucille SERRANO
121 Dean of Student Affs Stdnt Success .... Ms. Carla JOHNSON
68 Dean Athletics/PE/Kinesiology .... Mr. Daniel TERESA
103 Dir Workforce/Career Development .... Ms. Sharon ALBERT
19 Dir Public Safety/Emergency Mgmt .... Mr. Daniel SCOTT

Harvey Mudd College (K)

301 Platt Boulevard, Claremont CA 91711-5990
County: Los Angeles | FICE Identification: 001171 | Unit ID: 115409
Telephone: (909) 621-8000 | Carnegie Class: Bac-A&S
FAX Number: (909) 621-8360 | Calendar System: Semester
URL: www.hmc.edu
Established: 1955 | Annual Undergrad Tuition & Fees: $58,660
Enrollment: 854 | Coed
Affiliation or Control: Independent Non-Profit | IRS Status: 501(c)3
Highest Offering: Baccalaureate
Accreditation: WC

01 President .... Dr. Maria M. KLAWE
111 Vice President Advancement .... Mr. Hieu NGUYEN
10 Vice President Admin/Fin/Treasurer .... Dr. Andrew R. DORANTES
05 VP Acad Affairs/Dean of the Faculty .... Dr. Lisa M. SULLIVAN
07 Vice Pres Admissions/Financial Aid .... Ms. Thyra BRIGGS
32 VP Student Affs/Dean Students .... Dr. Marco VALENZUELA
13 VP/CIO .... Mr. Joseph VAUGHAN

15	Senior Director for Human Resources	Ms. Dana NAGENGAST
18	Senior Director of Plant Operations	Mr. Daniel MADRIGAL
28	Assoc Dean Institutional Diversity	Dr. Jennifer ALANIS
06	Registrar	Mr. Mark ASHLEY
26	Chief Communications Officer	Mr. Tim HUSSEY
29	Director of Alumni Relations	Ms. Jennifer GREEN
37	Director of Student Financial Aid	Ms. Gilma LOPEZ
101	Director of Pres Ofc/Secy to Board	Ms. Karen ANGEMI
100	Chief of Staff	Ms. Karen ANGEMI
09	AVP for Institutional Research	Dr. Laura PALUCKI BLAKE
104	Director Study Abroad	Ms. Rhonda CHILES
30	AVP for Development	Vacant
86	Senior Director Corporate Relations	Ms. Colleen COXE

Haven University　　　　　　　　　(A)

12761 South Euclid Street, Garden Grove CA 92840

County: Orange　　　　　　　　　Identification: 667307
Telephone: (714) 592-7878　　　Carnegie Class: Not Classified
FAX Number: (714) 636-1725　　Calendar System: Semester
URL: haven.edu
Established: 1969　　　Annual Undergrad Tuition & Fees: N/A
Enrollment: N/A　　　　　　　　　　　　　　　　　　Coed
Affiliation or Control: Interdenominational　IRS Status: 501(c)3
Highest Offering: Doctorate
Accreditation: TRACS

01	President	Dr. Kang Won LEE
10	Dean of Administration	Dr. Brian K. TROTT
05	Dean of Academic Affairs	Dr. Joshua SMITH
32	Actg Dean of Student Services	Dr. Brian TROTT
07	Director of Admissions/Records	Dr. Linda TROTT

† Previously California Graduate School of Theology 2019

Hayfield University　　　　　　　　(B)

2495 Orangethorpe Avenue, Fullerton CA 92831

County: Orange　　　　　　　　　Identification: 667415
Telephone: (714) 738-1461　　　Carnegie Class: Not Classified
FAX Number: (714) 738-1440　　Calendar System: Semester
URL: www.hayfieldun.org
Established: 1995　　　Annual Undergrad Tuition & Fees: N/A
Enrollment: N/A　　　　　　　　　　　　　　　　　　Coed
Affiliation or Control: Independent Non-Profit　IRS Status: 501(c)3
Highest Offering: Master's
Accreditation: @BI

Healthcare Career College　　　(C)

8527 Alondra Boulevard, Suite 174, Paramount CA 90723

County: Los Angeles　　　　　FICE Identification: 041327
　　　　　　　　　　　　　　　　　　　　Unit ID: 450960
Telephone: (562) 804-1239　　　Carnegie Class: Spec 2-yr-Health
FAX Number: N/A　　　　　　　　Calendar System: Other
URL: www.healthcarecareercollege.edu
Established: 1998　　　Annual Undergrad Tuition & Fees: N/A
Enrollment: N/A　　　　　　　　　　　　　　　　　　Coed
Affiliation or Control: Proprietary　　IRS Status: Proprietary
Highest Offering: Associate Degree
Accreditation: COE

01	Chief Executive Officer	Amita GARG
06	Chief Academic Officer	Ramon GELUZ
07	Director of Admissions	Kelley LEE
10	Chief Financial/Business Officer	Hugo H. AGUILAR
11	Chief of Operations/Administration	Elenita SEBASTIAN
13	Chief Information Technology Office	Joey REOMA
36	Director Student Placement	Kelley LEE
37	Director Student Financial Aid	Norma MEZA
06	Registrar	Mariana SAURI

Henry Appenzeller University　(D)

1325 N College Avenue, #106, Claremont CA 91711

County: Orange　　　　　　　　　Identification: 667133
Telephone: (213) 386-0080　　　Carnegie Class: Not Classified
FAX Number: (213) 386-5229　　Calendar System: Semester
URL: mtsamerica.edu/
Established: 1880　　　Annual Undergrad Tuition & Fees: N/A
Enrollment: N/A　　　　　　　　　　　　　　　　　　Coed
Affiliation or Control: Independent Non-Profit　IRS Status: 501(c)3
Highest Offering: Master's
Accreditation: BI

01	President	Rev. David LIM

High Desert Medical College　　(E)

701 West Avenue K, Ste 123, Lancaster CA 93534

County: Los Angeles　　　　　FICE Identification: 042281
　　　　　　　　　　　　　　　　　　　　Unit ID: 484002
Telephone: (661) 940-9300　　　Carnegie Class: Spec 2-yr-Health
FAX Number: (661) 940-7319　　Calendar System: Semester
URL: www.hdmc.edu
Established: 2002　　　Annual Undergrad Tuition & Fees: N/A
Enrollment: 1,016　　　　　　　　　　　　　　　　Coed
Affiliation or Control: Proprietary　　IRS Status: Proprietary
Highest Offering: Associate Degree
Accreditation: CNCE

01	President/CEO	LeeAnn ROHMANN

High Tech High Graduate School　(F)
of Education

2150 Cushing Road, San Diego CA 92106

County: San Diego　　　　　　　Identification: 667118
　　　　　　　　　　　　　　　　　　　　Unit ID: 485403
Telephone: (619) 398-4902　　　Carnegie Class: Spec-4-yr-Other
FAX Number: (619) 758-1960　　Calendar System: Other
URL: https://hthgse.edu
Established: 2007　　　Annual Graduate Tuition & Fees: N/A
Enrollment: 76　　　　　　　　　　　　　　　　　　Coed
Affiliation or Control: Independent Non-Profit　IRS Status: 501(c)3
Highest Offering: Master's; No Undergraduates
Accreditation: WC

01	President	Ben DALEY
05	Dean	Kelly WILSON
32	Director Student Affairs	Hayley MURUGESAN

HIS University　　　　　　　　　　(G)

1245 West 6th Street, Corona CA 92882

County: Riverside　　　　　　　Identification: 667388
Telephone: (951) 372-8080　　　Carnegie Class: Not Classified
FAX Number: (951) 372-8070　　Calendar System: Semester
URL: www.hisuniversity.edu
Established: 2004　　　Annual Undergrad Tuition & Fees: N/A
Enrollment: N/A　　　　　　　　　　　　　　　　　Coed
Affiliation or Control: Independent Non-Profit　IRS Status: 501(c)3
Highest Offering: Doctorate
Accreditation: TRACS

01	President/CEO	Dr. Eun Soon YANG
05	Chief Academic Officer	Dr. Donna BROWN
11	Chief Operations Officer	Dr. Boo Un OH
10	Chief Finance Officer	Dr. Jean YOO
06	Registrar/Admin Assistant	Ms. Kathleen BAXTER

Holy Names University　　　　　(H)

3500 Mountain Boulevard, Oakland CA 94619-1699

County: Alameda　　　　　　　FICE Identification: 001183
　　　　　　　　　　　　　　　　　　　　Unit ID: 115728
Telephone: (510) 436-1000　　　Carnegie Class: Masters/S
FAX Number: (510) 436-1199　　Calendar System: Semester
URL: www.hnu.edu
Established: 1868　　　Annual Undergrad Tuition & Fees: $40,904
Enrollment: 1,014　　　　　　　　　　　　　　　　Coed
Affiliation or Control: Independent Non-Profit　IRS Status: 501(c)3
Highest Offering: Master's
Accreditation: WC, NURSE

01	President	Mr. Michael GROENER
05	Provost/VP for Academic Affairs	Dr. Kimberly BOWERS
10	VP for Finance/Admin	Ms. Jeanine HAWK
32	VP for Student Affairs	Ms. Laura LYNDON
84	VP for Enrollment Mgmt	Ms. Elizabeth MIHOPOULOS
111	VP for University Advancement	Ms. Mary BOIVIN-MCGHEE
88	VP for Mission Integration	Sr. Carol SELLMAN
18	VP for Facilities & Events	Mr. Luis GUERRA
06	Registrar	Mr. Stephen STICKA
08	Director of Library Services	Ms. Sylvia CONTRERAS
37	Director Financial Aid	Ms. Rose STADLER
42	Co-Director of Campus Ministry	Ms. Jenny GIRARD-MALLEY
42	Co-Director of Campus Ministry	Fr. Sal RAGUSA
41	Director of Athletics	Mr. Phil BILLECI-GARD
26	Director Marketing & Communications	Ms. Stephanie SILVA
13	Director Information Technology	Mr. Jay CASTILLO
15	Director Human Resources	Ms. Patricia BARTON
04	Executive Asst to President	Ms. Vicki TOM
09	Exec Dir of Institutional Research	Mr. John HOFMANN
39	Interim Director Residence Life	Ms. Angeline BANEZ
29	Director Alumni/Donor Relations	Ms. Kelsey LINDQUIST
100	Chief of Staff	Mr. John HOFMANN
102	Dir Foundation/Corporate Relations	Mr. Stefan AMRINE
19	Campus Safety Director	Vacant

Homestead Schools　　　　　　(I)

23800 Hawthorne Blvd, Suite 200, Torrance CA 90505

County: Los Angeles　　　　　FICE Identification: 041497
　　　　　　　　　　　　　　　　　　　　Unit ID: 457086
Telephone: (310) 791-9975　　　Carnegie Class: Spec-4-yr-Other Health
FAX Number: N/A　　　　　　　　Calendar System: Other
URL: homesteadschools.com
Established: 2007　　　Annual Undergrad Tuition & Fees: N/A
Enrollment: 129　　　　　　　　　　　　　　　　　Coed
Affiliation or Control: Independent Non-Profit　IRS Status: 501(c)3
Highest Offering: Master's
Accreditation: ABHES, NURSE

01	President/CEO	Mr. Vijay FADIA

Hope International University　　(J)

2500 E Nutwood Avenue, Fullerton CA 92831-3104

County: Orange　　　　　　　　FICE Identification: 001252
　　　　　　　　　　　　　　　　　　　　Unit ID: 120537
Telephone: (714) 879-3901　　　Carnegie Class: Masters/M
FAX Number: (714) 681-7451　　Calendar System: 4/1/4
URL: www.hiu.edu
Established: 1928　　　Annual Undergrad Tuition & Fees: $34,450

Enrollment: 1,201　　　　　　　　　　　　　　　　Coed
Affiliation or Control: Independent Non-Profit　IRS Status: 501(c)3
Highest Offering: Doctorate
Accreditation: WC, BI, IACBE, MFCD

01	President	Dr. Paul H. ALEXANDER
04	Exec Asst to the President	Mrs. Sandy PRINTY
05	Vice President for Academic Affairs	Dr. Steve EDGINGTON
49	Dean College of Arts and Sciences	Dr. Steve EDGINGTON
50	Dean College of Business & Mgmt	Dr. Lydia KNOPF
53	Dean College of Education	Dr. Douglas S. DOMENE
73	Dean Col of Ministry & Bible Stds	Dr. Carl TONEY
83	Dean College of Psych & Counseling	Dr. Laura L. STEELE
09	Director of Institutional Research	Dr. Hector GALANO
08	Librarian	Mrs. Robin HARTMAN
06	Registrar	Mr. Ron ARCHER
10	Vice President for Business/Finance	Mr. Tom MCGLINCHEY
37	Director Student Financial Services	Mrs. Shannon O'SHIELDS
15	Director of Human Resources	Ms. Espie FREE
13	Director of Information Technology	Mr. Darrell C. JONES
18	Director of Campus Facilities	Mr. Steve MULLINS
111	Vice Pres Institutional Advancement	Mr. Michael MULRYAN
26	Chief Public Relations Officer	Mr. Michael MULRYAN
32	Vice President for Student Affairs	Dr. Joshua ARNOLD
41	Athletic Director	Mr. John G. TUREK
42	Director Campus Ministry	Mr. Joey ROSS
85	Director of International Students	Mrs. Judy E. KIM
38	Director Student Counseling	Dr. Laura L. STEELE
36	Director of Career Development	Mrs. Stacey GERHART
84	Vice Pres for Enrollment Management	Mrs. Teresa L. SMITH
07	Director Undergraduate Admissions	Mr. Michael CRUZ
106	Dir Learning Technology	Ms. Micah N. ALSTON
108	Director Institutional Assessment	Mr. Andrew PAINE

Horizon University　　　　　　　(K)

2040 S. Brea Canyon Rd, Ste 100,
Diamond Bar CA 91765

County: Los Angeles　　　　　Identification: 667360
Telephone: (909) 895-7138　　　Carnegie Class: Not Classified
FAX Number: (909) 895-7143　　Calendar System: Quarter
URL: www.huca.edu
Established: 2007　　　Annual Undergrad Tuition & Fees: N/A
Enrollment: N/A　　　　　　　　　　　　　　　　　Coed
Affiliation or Control: Independent Non-Profit　IRS Status: 501(c)3
Highest Offering: Master's
Accreditation: TRACS

01	President	Henry KHOR
05	Director of Academics	Abraham OH
06	Registrar	Jerry CUI
07	Director of Admissions	Aron KIM
10	Chief Financial/Business Officer	Michael YANG
11	Director of Operations	Benjamin STARKEY
32	Director of Student Services	Qi DENG

Humphreys University　　　　　(L)

6650 Inglewood Street, Stockton CA 95207-3896

County: San Joaquin　　　　　FICE Identification: 001212
　　　　　　　　　　　　　　　　　　　　Unit ID: 115773
Telephone: (209) 478-0800　　　Carnegie Class: Masters/S
FAX Number: (209) 478-8721　　Calendar System: Quarter
URL: www.humphreys.edu
Established: 1896　　　Annual Undergrad Tuition & Fees: $14,580
Enrollment: 401　　　　　　　　　　　　　　　　　Coed
Affiliation or Control: Independent Non-Profit　IRS Status: 501(c)3
Highest Offering: First Professional Degree
Accreditation: WC

01	President	Dr. Robert G. HUMPHREYS, JR.
05	Dn Instruction/Dir Arts & Sciences	Ms. Cynthia BECERRA
11	Director of Administrative Services	Ms. Carrie CASTILLON
58	Dean of Graduate Studies	Dr. Jess BONDS
61	Dean Law School	Mr. Matthew REYNOLDS
09	Dean of Institutional Research	Dr. Lisa KOOREN
06	Registrar	Ms. Maria GARCIA-MILLER
07	Director of Admissions	Ms. Santa E. LOPEZ
37	Director Student Financial Aid	Ms. Rita FRANCO

Hussian College (formerly known as Studio　(M)
School)

1201 West 5th St., Ste F10, Los Angeles CA 90017

Telephone: (800) 762-1993　　Identification: 770969
Accreditation: ACCSC

† Branch campus of Hussian College, Philadelphia, PA

Imperial Valley College　　　　　(N)

380 E Aten Road, Imperial CA 92251-0158

County: Imperial　　　　　　　FICE Identification: 001214
　　　　　　　　　　　　　　　　　　　　Unit ID: 115861
Telephone: (760) 352-8320　　　Carnegie Class: Assoc/HT-High Trad
FAX Number: (760) 355-2663　　Calendar System: Semester
URL: www.imperial.edu
Established: 1922　　　Annual Undergrad Tuition & Fees (In-District): $1,126
Enrollment: 7,123　　　　　　　　　　　　　　　　Coed
Affiliation or Control: Local　　IRS Status: 501(c)3
Highest Offering: Associate Degree
Accreditation: WJ, EMT

01	Superintendent/President	Dr. Lennor JOHNSON
05	Int VP for Academic Services	Mr. David DRURY
32	Int VP for Student Services/Equity	Mr. Victor TORRES
10	VP for Administrative Services	Mr. Cesar VEGA
15	Assoc VP Human Resources	Mr. Clint C. DOUGHERTY
103	Dean Economic & Workforce Develop	Mr. Efrain SILVA
76	Dean of Health & Public Safety	Ms. Gail WARNER
49	Dean Arts/Letters/Learning Svcs	Mrs. Betsy LANE
84	Dean Student Affs/Enroll Svcs	Mr. James DALSKE
35	Dean Student Svcs/Special Proj	Ms. Alexis VILLA
07	Director of Admissions and Records	Mrs. Vikki CARR
37	Director of Financial Aid	Ms. Lisa SEALS
09	Assoc Dean Institutional Effective	Mr. Jose CARRILLO
59	Dir Child/Family/Consumer Sciences	Ms. Rebecca GREEN
26	Comm & Govt Relations Officer	Ms. Elizabeth ESPINOZA
13	Assoc VP Information Technology	Mr. Jeff ENZ
81	Int Dean of Math/Sciences	Dr. Cuauhtemoc CARBONI
102	Exec Director Foundation	Mr. Rod SMART
18	Dir Facilities Planning/Construct	Mr. Javier LUNA

Institute for Business and Technology (A)

2400 Walsh Avenue, Santa Clara CA 95051

County: Santa Clara — FICE Identification: 021283
Unit ID: 115931
Telephone: (408) 727-1060 — Carnegie Class: Spec 2-yr-Health
FAX Number: N/A — Calendar System: Semester
URL: www.ibttech.com
Established: 1965 — Annual Undergrad Tuition & Fees: N/A
Enrollment: 579 — Coed
Affiliation or Control: Proprietary — IRS Status: Proprietary
Highest Offering: Associate Degree
Accreditation: ACCSC

01	President/CEO	Peter MIKHAIL
05	Director of Education	Fred WIEHE
11	Campus Director	Guy ADAMS
06	Registrar	Crystal LOMBERA
36	Director of Career Services	Deidre THOMPSON

Institute of Buddhist Studies (B)

2140 Durant Avenue, Berkeley CA 94704

County: Alameda — Identification: 667312
Unit ID: 489335
Telephone: (510) 809-1444 — Carnegie Class: Not Classified
FAX Number: N/A — Calendar System: Semester
URL: www.shin-ibs.edu
Established: 1949 — Annual Graduate Tuition & Fees: N/A
Enrollment: 27 — Coed
Affiliation or Control: Independent Non-Profit — IRS Status: 501(c)3
Highest Offering: Master's; No Undergraduates
Accreditation: WC

00	Chancellor	Rev. Kodo UMEZU
01	President & Vice Pres Academic Affs	RevDr. David MATSUMOTO
30	Vice Pres Development	Vacant
32	Dean of Students	Dr. Scott MITCHELL
10	Director of Finance	Ms. Linda SHIOZAKI
06	Registrar	Ms. Helen TAGAWA

Institute of Technology (C)

564 West Herndon Avenue, Clovis CA 93612

County: Fresno — FICE Identification: 030675
Unit ID: 431141
Telephone: (559) 297-4500 — Carnegie Class: Assoc/HVT-Mix Trad/Non
FAX Number: (559) 297-5822 — Calendar System: Semester
URL: www.iot.edu
Established: — Annual Undergrad Tuition & Fees: N/A
Enrollment: 1,279 — Coed
Affiliation or Control: Proprietary — IRS Status: Proprietary
Highest Offering: Associate Degree
Accreditation: ACCSC, ACFEI, PTAA

01	President	Ron GARDNER
05	Director of Education	Carol SMITH
66	Director of Nursing	Paula RICHARDS
32	Director of Student Services	Melinda WOOD
07	Director of Admissions	Marissa MARZAN
06	Registrar	Maria VALDEZ
37	Director of Financial Aid	Sandi PUGH
36	Director of Career Services	Tim KEARN
08	Librarian	Laura HABERSTICH
18	Facilities Coordinator	Tony LEON

Institute of Technology (D)

5601 Stoddard Road, Modesto CA 95356

Telephone: (209) 572-7800 — Identification: 770554
Accreditation: ACCSC, ACFEI, @PTAA

Integrity College of Health (E)

1460 N. Lake Avenue, Ste 102, Pasadena CA 91104

County: Los Angeles — FICE Identification: 041816
Unit ID: 483373
Telephone: (626) 808-0215 — Carnegie Class: Not Classified
FAX Number: (626) 345-9618 — Calendar System: Other
URL: www.ich.edu

Established: 2007 — Annual Undergrad Tuition & Fees: N/A
Enrollment: N/A — Coed
Affiliation or Control: Proprietary — IRS Status: Proprietary
Highest Offering: Baccalaureate
Accreditation: ABHES, @CNEA

Intercoast College (F)

2235 East Garvey Ave North, West Covina CA 91791

County: Los Angelos — FICE Identification: 025594
Unit ID: 366289
Telephone: (626) 337-6800 — Carnegie Class: Spec 2-yr-Other
FAX Number: N/A — Calendar System: Other
URL: www.intercoast.edu
Established: 1985 — Annual Undergrad Tuition & Fees: N/A
Enrollment: 20 — Coed
Affiliation or Control: Proprietary — IRS Status: Proprietary
Highest Offering: Associate Degree
Accreditation: CNCE

00	President	Geeta A. BROWN
01	Campus Director	Christopher RUSH
106	Director Online Education	James CHEEKS
07	Director of Admissions	Joel MEDRANO

Interior Designers Institute (G)

1061 Camelback Road, Newport Beach CA 92660-3228

County: Orange — FICE Identification: 025203
Unit ID: 116226
Telephone: (949) 675-4451 — Carnegie Class: Spec-4-yr-Arts
FAX Number: (949) 759-0667 — Calendar System: Quarter
URL: www.idi.edu
Established: 1984 — Annual Undergrad Tuition & Fees: $20,250
Enrollment: 144 — Coed
Affiliation or Control: Proprietary — IRS Status: Proprietary
Highest Offering: Master's
Accreditation: ACCSC, CIDA

01	Executive Director	Ms. Judy DEATON
10	Controller	Ms. Shanen FOYE
07	Director of Admissions	Ms. Judy DEATON

International American University (H)

3440 Wilshire Blvd #1000, Los Angeles CA 90010

County: Los Angeles — Identification: 667389
Telephone: (213) 262-3939 — Carnegie Class: Not Classified
FAX Number: (213) 262-5758 — Calendar System: Other
URL: www.iaula.edu
Established: — Annual Undergrad Tuition & Fees: N/A
Enrollment: N/A — Coed
Affiliation or Control: Independent Non-Profit — IRS Status: 501(c)3
Highest Offering: Doctorate
Accreditation: TRACS

01	CEO	Ryan DOAN
05	Chief Academic Officer	Dr. Richard H. GAYER
32	Assoc Director Student Services	Susan TAN
10	Chief Financial Officer	Jay CHUNG
15	Assoc Director Human Resources	Sue KIM
06	Registrar	Md OSMAN

International Reformed University and Seminary (I)

125 S. Vermont Avenue, Los Angeles CA 90004

County: Los Angeles — Identification: 667132
Telephone: (213) 381-0081 — Carnegie Class: Not Classified
FAX Number: (213) 381-0010 — Calendar System: Semester
URL: www.irus.edu
Established: 1977 — Annual Undergrad Tuition & Fees: N/A
Enrollment: N/A — Coed
Affiliation or Control: Independent Non-Profit — IRS Status: 501(c)3
Highest Offering: Doctorate
Accreditation: BI

01	President	Dr. Hun Sung PARK
05	Academic Dean	Dr. Paul Kitae PARK
32	Dean of Students	Dr. Bocheon SEO
11	Dean of Administrative Services	Dr. Joha OH
108	Director of Assessment & Planning	Dr. Yumee RAH
08	Librarian	Ms. Hannah LEE
20	Director of Teaching & Learning Tec	Ms. Hala SUN

International Technological University (J)

2010 El Camino Real, #852, Santa Clara CA 95050

County: Santa Clara — Identification: 667070
Unit ID: 443128
Telephone: (888) 488-4968 — Carnegie Class: Masters/L
FAX Number: (408) 331-1026 — Calendar System: Trimester
URL: www.itu.edu
Established: 1994 — Annual Graduate Tuition & Fees: N/A
Enrollment: 299 — Coed
Affiliation or Control: Independent Non-Profit — IRS Status: 501(c)3
Highest Offering: Doctorate; No Undergraduates
Accreditation: WC, ACBSP

01	President and CEO	Yau-Gene CHAN
10	Chief Financial Officer	Wilson CHEUNG
11	Chief Operating Officer	Suman BHARGAVA
05	Chief Academic Officer	Dr. Mamoun SAMAHA
13	Chief Technology Officer	Dr. Mamoun SAMAHA
15	Human Resources Manager	Fusako TSUIKI
26	Director of Marketing	Eric PALMA
06	University Registrar	Daniel SUNG
116	Director of Compliance	Philip NG
85	Dir International Student Office	Dr. Concepcion SAENZ-CAMBRA
121	Academic Advisor	Hussam MOUGHARBEL

International Theological Seminary (K)

540 E Vine Avenue, West Covina CA 91790

County: Los Angeles — Identification: 666360
Unit ID: 396985
Telephone: (626) 448-0023 — Carnegie Class: Not Classified
FAX Number: (626) 350-6343 — Calendar System: Quarter
URL: www.itsla.edu
Established: 1982 — Annual Undergrad Tuition & Fees: N/A
Enrollment: N/A — Coed
Affiliation or Control: Independent Non-Profit — IRS Status: 501(c)3
Highest Offering: Doctorate
Accreditation: THEOL

01	President	Dr. James S. LEE
05	Vice Pres for Academic Affairs	Dr. Priscilla ADOYO
10	Vice Pres of Operation/Finance	Rev. Paul Zhao Hui YANG
32	Dean of Students	Dr. Premkumar DHARMARAJ
06	Registrar	Ms. Letty CHEN
08	Librarian	Ms. Susan LIU
04	Asst to President/Communication Dir	Ms. Ei MEREN GUSTO

John Paul the Great Catholic University (L)

220 West Grand Avenue, Escondido CA 92025

County: San Diego — FICE Identification: 041937
Unit ID: 462354
Telephone: (858) 653-6740 — Carnegie Class: Bac-Diverse
FAX Number: (858) 653-3791 — Calendar System: Quarter
URL: www.jpcatholic.com
Established: 2003 — Annual Undergrad Tuition & Fees: $27,100
Enrollment: 274 — Coed
Affiliation or Control: Independent Non-Profit — IRS Status: 501(c)3
Highest Offering: Master's
Accreditation: WC

01	President/Chief Academic Officer	Dr. Derry CONNOLLY
10	Chief Finance Officer/COO	Kevin MEZIERE
30	Chief Development Officer	Vacant
11	VP for Administration	Lidy CONNOLLY
07	VP of Admissions	Martin HAROLD
15	VP for Human Resources	Anna VELASCO
32	Dean of Students	Jason PATERSON
37	Director of Financial Aid	Lisa WILLIAMS
05	Registrar/AVP Academic Affairs	Nick HEYE
42	Director Campus Ministry	Austin SCHNEIDER
08	Librarian	Melanie QUINN
26	AVP for Marketing & Admissions	Joe HOUDE

Kaiser Permanente Bernard J Tyson School of Medicine (M)

98 S. Los Robles Avenue, Pasadena CA 91101

County: Los Angeles — Identification: 667404
Telephone: (888) 576-3348 — Carnegie Class: Not Classified
FAX Number: N/A — Calendar System: Semester
URL: www.medschool.kp.org
Established: 2016 — Annual Graduate Tuition & Fees: N/A
Enrollment: N/A — Coed
Affiliation or Control: Independent Non-Profit — IRS Status: 501(c)3
Highest Offering: First Professional Degree; No Undergraduates
Accreditation: #MED

01	Founding Dean & CEO	Dr. Mark A. SCHUSTER
10	SVP Administration/Finance	Walter HARRIS
05	Sr Assoc Dean Academic/Cmty Affairs	Dr. Maureen T. CONNELLY
32	Sr Assoc Dean Student Affairs	Dr. Anne EACKER

Kaiser Permanente School of Allied Health Sciences (N)

938 Marina Way South, Richmond CA 94804

County: Contra Costa — Identification: 667152
Telephone: (510) 231-5000 — Carnegie Class: Not Classified
FAX Number: (510) 231-5001 — Calendar System: Quarter
URL: www.kpsahs.edu
Established: 1989 — Annual Undergrad Tuition & Fees: N/A
Enrollment: N/A — Coed
Affiliation or Control: Proprietary — IRS Status: Proprietary
Highest Offering: Master's
Accreditation: WC, DMS, NMT, RAD

01	Regional School Administrator/CEO	James FITZGIBBON
63	Medical Director	Dr. C. Darryl JONES
05	Dean of Academic Affairs/CAO	John ROTH
10	Assoc Director of Finance/CFO	Pamela PRESSLEY

09 Dir Assessment/Inst Research ... Bert CHRISTENSEN
04 Admin Assistant to the President ... Diana K. JACKSON

*Kern Community College District (A)

2100 Chester Avenue, Bakersfield CA 93301-4099
County: Kern FICE Identification: 006994
Unit ID: 436313
Telephone: (661) 336-5100 Carnegie Class: N/A
FAX Number: (661) 336-5134
URL: www.kccd.edu

01 Chancellor ... Ms. Sonya CHRISTIAN
05 Vice Chanc Educational Services ... Mr. John MEANS
15 Vice Chanc Human Resources ... Ms. Dena RHOADES
10 Chief Financial Officer ... Mr. Michael GIACOMINI
13 Chief Technology Officer ... Mr. Gary MOSER
43 General Counsel ... Mr. Christopher HINE
103 Exec Dir Econ/Workforce Development ... Mr. David TEASDALE
09 Director of Institutional Research ... Mr. Bob NGO

*Bakersfield College (B)

1801 Panorama Drive, Bakersfield CA 93305-1299
County: Kern FICE Identification: 001118
Unit ID: 109819
Telephone: (661) 395-4011 Carnegie Class: Bac/Assoc-Assoc Dom
FAX Number: (661) 395-4241 Calendar System: Semester
URL: www.bakersfieldcollege.edu
Established: 1913 Annual Undergrad Tuition & Fees (In-District): $1,418
Enrollment: 24,903 Coed
Affiliation or Control: State/Local IRS Status: 501(c)3
Highest Offering: Baccalaureate
Accreditation: WJ, CAHIIM, EMT, @PTAA, RAD

02 Interim President ... Dr. Zav DADABHOY
05 Vice President Instruction ... Ms. Billie Jo RICE
10 VP Finance & Administrative Svcs ... Mr. Mike GIACOMINI
20 Assoc VP Instruction ... Ms. Jessica WOJTYSIAK
32 Int Vice Pres Student Affairs ... Ms. Imelda SIMOS-VALDEZ
09 Dean Institutional Effectiveness ... Mr. Craig HAYWARD
83 Dean of Instruction ... Dr. Rich MCCROW
49 Dean of Instruction ... Ms. Rebecca FARLEY
81 Dean of Instruction ... Dr. Stephen WALLER
20 Dean of Instruction ... Mr. Anthony CORDOVA
102 Exec Director Foundation ... Ms. Cheryl SCOTT
66 Dean of Instruction ... Ms. Carla GARD
53 Dean of Instruction ... Ms. Melinda WILMOT
54 Dean of Instruction ... Ms. Lora LARKIN
18 Exec Dir Facilities/Maintenance/Ops ... Mr. Marcos RODRIGUEZ
12 Director Delano Center ... Vacant
37 Director Financial Aid ... Ms. Jennifer ACHAN
84 Director Enrollment Services ... Ms. Michelle PENA
26 Dir Communication/Cmty Relations ... Ms. Norma ROJAS-MORA
13 Int Exec Dir Tech Support Svcs ... Mr. Brett REDD
41 Assoc Director of Athletics ... Mr. Keith FORD
15 Interim Human Resources Manager ... Ms. Amalia CALDERON

*Cerro Coso Community College (C)

3000 College Heights Boulevard,
Ridgecrest CA 93555-7777
County: Kern FICE Identification: 010111
Unit ID: 111896
Telephone: (760) 384-6100 Carnegie Class: Assoc/HT-High Non
FAX Number: (760) 375-4776 Calendar System: Semester
URL: www.cerrocoso.edu
Established: 1973 Annual Undergrad Tuition & Fees (In-District): $1,382
Enrollment: 5,159 Coed
Affiliation or Control: State/Local IRS Status: 501(c)3
Highest Offering: Associate Degree
Accreditation: WJ

02 President ... Dr. Sean C. HANCOCK
05 Vice President Instruction ... Dr. Corey MARVIN
10 Vice Pres Finance/Admin Services ... Ms. Lisa COUCH
32 Vice President of Student Services ... Ms. Heather OSTASH
20 Dean of Instruction ... Mr. Chad HOUCK
12 Dir Eastern Sierra College Center ... Ms. Deanna CAMPBELL
12 Dir of East Kern/Kern River Valley ... Ms. Lisa STEPHENS
75 Dean Career Technical Education ... Vacant
38 Dir of Counseling Svcs/SSSP ... Ms. Christine SMALL
07 Acting Dir Admiss/Records/Fin Aid ... Ms. Jessica KAWELMACHER
15 Manager Human Resources ... Ms. Resa HESS
88 Program Mgr Child Development Ctr ... Ms. Jessica KRALL
26 Dir Public Relations/Inst Advance ... Ms. Natalie DORRELL
13 Director Information Technology ... Mr. Michael CAMPBELL
35 Director Outreach Services ... Ms. Katie BACHMAN
106 Director Distance Education ... Ms. Rebecca PANG
04 Administrative Asst to President ... Ms. Jennifer CURTIS
41 Athletic Director ... Mr. John MCHENRY
18 Dir Maintenance/Operations ... Mr. Cody PAUXTIS
19 Director Security/Safety ... Mr. Kevin KING

*Porterville College (D)

100 E College Avenue, Porterville CA 93257-6058
County: Tulare FICE Identification: 001268
Unit ID: 121363
Telephone: (559) 791-2200 Carnegie Class: Assoc/HVT-High Trad
FAX Number: (559) 784-4779 Calendar System: Semester
URL: www.portervillecollege.edu
Established: 1927 Annual Undergrad Tuition & Fees (In-District): $1,409
Enrollment: 3,964 Coed
Affiliation or Control: State/Local IRS Status: 501(c)3
Highest Offering: Associate Degree
Accreditation: WJ

02 President ... Dr. Claudia HABIB
04 Administrative Asst to President ... Mrs. Felisa HANNAH
05 Vice President Instruction ... Dr. Thad RUSSELL
10 Vice Pres Finance & Admin Services ... Dr. Arlitha WILLIAMS-HARMON
32 Vice President Student Services ... Ms. Primavera ARVIZU
20 Int Dean Instruction ... Dr. Michelle MILLER-GALAZ
20 Int Dean Instruction ... Vacant
121 Dean Student Success and Counseling ... Mrs. Erin WINGFIELD
37 Director Financial Aid ... Mrs. Tiffany HAYNES
76 Assoc Dean Health Careers ... Ms. Kim BEHRENS
18 Director Maintenance & Operations ... Mr. John WORD
102 Exec Director PC Foundation ... Ms. Ramona CHIAPA
84 Director Enrollment Services ... Vacant
09 Director Institutional Research ... Mr. Michael CARLEY
13 Director Information Technology ... Mr. Jay NAVARRETTE
35 Director Student Services ... Mr. Frank RAMIREZ
08 Librarian ... Mr. Chris EBERT
41 Athletic Director ... Mr. Joseph CASCIO
21 Accounting Manager ... Mr. Kevin KERWIN
26 Manager Communications & Marketing ... Mr. Roger PEREZ
105 Web Content Editor ... Mr. Kevin OTT
15 Int Human Resources Manager ... Ms. Johanna FISHER
19 Manager Campus Safety & Security ... Mr. Todd DEARMORE

Kernel University (E)

905 S. Euclid Street #213, Fullerton CA 92833
County: Orange Identification: 667308
Telephone: (714) 995-9988 Carnegie Class: Not Classified
FAX Number: (714) 995-9989 Calendar System: Semester
URL: www.kernel.edu
Established: 1995 Annual Undergrad Tuition & Fees: N/A
Enrollment: N/A Coed
Affiliation or Control: Independent Non-Profit IRS Status: 501(c)3
Highest Offering: Doctorate
Accreditation: TRACS

01 President ... Matthew D. WOO
05 Academic Dean ... Byung-Dal KUM
10 Chief Financial Officer ... Trang Thithuy LE
07 Director Admissions & Registrar ... Timothy KING
32 Director of Student Services ... Priscilla M. WOO

La Sierra University (F)

4500 Riverwalk Parkway, Riverside CA 92505
County: Riverside FICE Identification: 001215
Unit ID: 117627
Telephone: (951) 785-2000 Carnegie Class: Masters/M
FAX Number: (951) 785-2901 Calendar System: Quarter
URL: www.lasierra.edu
Established: 1922 Annual Undergrad Tuition & Fees: $35,208
Enrollment: 1,993 Coed
Affiliation or Control: Seventh-day Adventist IRS Status: 501(c)3
Highest Offering: Doctorate
Accreditation: WC, MUS, SW, THEOL

01 President ... Dr. Joy A. FEHR
05 Provost ... Dr. April SUMMITT
10 Vice President for Finance ... Mr. David GERIGUIS
32 Vice President for Student Life ... Ms. Yamilet BAZAN
111 Vice Pres Advancement/Univ Rels ... Mr. Norman YERGEN
84 Int Vice Pres Enrollment Services ... Mr. Wayne DUNBAR
26 VP Communication/Integrated Mktg ... Dr. Marilyn THOMSEN
21 Associate Vice President Finance ... Ms. Pamela CHRISPENS
20 Associate Provost ... Ms. Cindy PARKHURST
49 Dean College Arts/Sciences ... Vacant
50 Dean School of Business ... Dr. John THOMAS
53 Dean School of Education ... Dr. Chang-Ho JI
73 Dean School of Divinity ... Dr. Friedbert NINOW
35 Dean of Student Life ... Ms. Marjorie ROBINSON
102 Exec Director University Foundation ... Mr. Larry GERATY
55 Director Adult Evening Program ... Ms. Nancy DITTEMORE
29 Alumni Director ... Ms. Julie NARDUCCI
15 Director Human Resources ... Ms. Dell Jean VAN FOSSEN
08 Director Library ... Ms. Kitty SIMMONS
37 Director Student Financial Services ... Ms. Esther KINZER
42 Director Campus Ministries ... Mr. Samuel E. LEONOR, JR.
13 Director Information Technology ... Mr. Geoff INGRAM
09 Director of Institutional Research ... Ms. Jan LONG
18 Director Physical Plant ... Mr. Al VALDEZ
38 Director Counseling Center ... Ms. Debra WRIGHT
92 Director Honors Program ... Dr. Douglas R. CLARK
07 Director of Admissions/Registrar ... Vacant
36 Career Advisor ... Mr. William PENICK
41 Athletic Director ... Mr. Javier KRUMM

Laguna College of Art & Design (G)

2222 Laguna Canyon Road,
Laguna Beach CA 92651-1136
County: Orange FICE Identification: 023305
Unit ID: 117168
Telephone: (949) 376-6000 Carnegie Class: Spec-4-yr-Arts
FAX Number: (949) 376-6009 Calendar System: Semester
URL: www.lcad.edu
Established: 1961 Annual Undergrad Tuition & Fees: $32,600
Enrollment: 782 Coed
Affiliation or Control: Independent Non-Profit IRS Status: 501(c)3
Highest Offering: Master's
Accreditation: WC, ART

01 President & CEO ... Mr. Steven J. BRITTAN
05 Provost/ALO ... Dr. Nicole LESHER
84 Vice Pres Enrollment Management ... Mr. Christopher BROWN
10 Chief Financial Officer ... Mr. Jim GODEK
06 Registrar ... Ms. Laura PATRICK
08 Library Director ... Mr. Rand BOYD
04 Exec Assistant to the President ... Ms. Kerri REDEKER
37 Sr Financial Aid Counselor ... Mr. Reginald WEST, JR.
09 Director of Institutional Research ... Ms. Laura PATRICK
15 Director Human Resources ... Ms. Agnes SANCHEZ
13 Chief Information Officer ... Mr. Matt MORTON
18 Director Facilities/Physical Plant ... Mr. Mark DAY
26 Dir of Marketing/Communications ... Mr. Bassem GIRGIS
19 Director Security/Safety ... Mr. Jim WOOLEY

Lake Tahoe Community College (H)

1 College Drive, South Lake Tahoe CA 96150-4524
County: El Dorado FICE Identification: 012907
Unit ID: 117195
Telephone: (530) 541-4660 Carnegie Class: Assoc/MT-VT-High Non
FAX Number: (530) 541-7852 Calendar System: Quarter
URL: www.ltcc.edu
Established: 1975 Annual Undergrad Tuition & Fees (In-District): $1,131
Enrollment: 2,332 Coed
Affiliation or Control: State/Local IRS Status: 501(c)3
Highest Offering: Associate Degree
Accreditation: WJ

01 Superintendent/President ... Mr. Jeff DEFRANCO
04 Executive Assistant to President ... Ms. Lisa SHAFER
05 VP Academic Affairs ... Dr. Raymond GAMBA
10 Vice Pres Administrative Svcs ... Ms. Russi EGAN
103 Dean of Workforce Devel/Instruction ... Mr. Brad DEEDS
32 VP Student Services ... Ms. Michelle BATISTA
20 Dean of Instruction ... Ms. Ali BISSONNETTE
08 Director of Library ... Ms. Melanie CHU
13 Director Information Tech Svcs ... Mr. Josh SMITH
84 Director Enrollment Services ... Mr. Steve BERRY
21 Director of Fiscal Services ... Mr. Ryan PHILPOTT
15 Director of Human Resources ... Ms. Shelley YOHNKA
18 Int Dir of Facilities/Operations ... Mr. Felix CHAGOYA
88 Dir Child Development Programs ... Ms. Leslie AMATO
37 Director Financial Aid ... Ms. Naomi FOLLETT
09 Dir of Institutional Effectiveness ... Dr. Elizabeth BALINT
26 Dir Marketing/Communications ... Ms. Diane LEWIS
102 Foundation Director ... Ms. Nancy HARRISON
40 Bookstore Manager ... Vacant
96 Purchasing Agent ... Ms. Heather CADE
41 Athletic Director ... Mr. Steve BERRY
28 Director of Equity ... Ms. Laura SALINAS

Lassen Community College (I)

PO Box 3000, 478-200 Highway 139,
Susanville CA 96130-3000
County: Lassen FICE Identification: 001217
Unit ID: 117274
Telephone: (530) 257-6181 Carnegie Class: Assoc/HT-Mix Trad/Non
FAX Number: (530) 251-8872 Calendar System: Semester
URL: www.lassencollege.edu
Established: 1925 Annual Undergrad Tuition & Fees (In-District): $1,127
Enrollment: 1,821 Coed
Affiliation or Control: State/Local IRS Status: 501(c)3
Highest Offering: Associate Degree
Accreditation: WJ

01 Superintendent/President ... Dr. Trevor D. ALBERTSON
04 Assistant to President ... Ms. Julie L. JOHNSTON
05 Int VP Academic Svcs/CIO ... Ms. Carie CAMACHO
20 Interim Dean of Instruction ... Ms. Colleen BAKER
20 Interim Dean of Instruction-CTE ... Ms. Michell WILLIAMS
11 Interim VP Administrative Services ... Vacant
32 Interim VP Student Services ... Ms. Roxanna HAYNES
35 Interim Assoc Dean Student Services ... Mr. Davis MURPHY
21 Director Fiscal Services ... Ms. Marguerite LEWMAN
121 Assoc Dean Student Success/Equity ... Ms. Brady REED
08 Librarian ... Ms. Shar MURPHY
13 Director Technology ... Mr. David CORLEY
35 Director Student Life ... Mr. Francis BEAUJON
41 Athletic Director ... Mr. Glen YONAN
18 Director Facilities/Operations ... Mr. Gregory COLLINS
15 Director Human Resources ... Ms. Vickie RAMSEY
09 Director of Institutional Research ... Dr. Randall JOSLIN
30 Director of Development/Alumni Rels ... Ms. Nicole KELLEY

Latin American Bible Institute (J)

14209 E. Lomitas Avenue, La Puente CA 91746
County: Los Angeles Identification: 667319
Telephone: (626) 968-1328 Carnegie Class: Not Classified
FAX Number: (626) 961-7253 Calendar System: Semester
URL: www.labi.edu
Established: 1926 Annual Undergrad Tuition & Fees: N/A
Enrollment: N/A Coed
Affiliation or Control: Independent Non-Profit IRS Status: 501(c)3
Highest Offering: Baccalaureate
Accreditation: BI

01 President ..... Dr. Marty HARRIS
05 Provost/Dean of Academic Affairs ..... Mr. Nehemias ROMERO
10 Chief Financial Officer ..... Ms. Gabriela MORA-ALVAREZ
32 Dean of Students ..... Ms. Yvette ROBLES
06 Registrar ..... Ms. Berenice VALENCIA
08 Librarian ..... Mr. Steve VALDEZ
18 Office/Facilities Manager ..... Ms. Erika RAMIREZ
15 Dir Human Resources/Asst to CFO ..... Ms. Terry BONFIL

Laurus College (A)

81 Higuera Street, Ste 110, San Luis Obispo CA 93401
County: San Luis Obispo — FICE Identification: 041414
Unit ID: 454786
Telephone: (805) 267-1690 — Carnegie Class: Bac/Assoc-Assoc Dom
FAX Number: (805) 352-1307 — Calendar System: Quarter
URL: www.lauruscollege.edu
Established: 2006 — Annual Undergrad Tuition & Fees: N/A
Enrollment: 897 — Coed
Affiliation or Control: Proprietary — IRS Status: Proprietary
Highest Offering: Baccalaureate
Accreditation: DEAC

00 President/CEO ..... Mr. James REDMOND
01 School Chancellor ..... Mr. Jeff REDMOND
32 VP Student Programs/Admiss Mngr ..... Ms. Cecilia MORTELA
37 Director Financial Aid ..... Mr. Tim REDMOND
06 Registrar ..... Mr. Leo CRAVEN
05 Director of Education ..... Ms. Melanie BRYANT

Learnet Academy (B)

3251 W. 6th Street, 2nd Floor, Los Angeles CA 90020
County: Los Angeles — Identification: 667223
Unit ID: 483221
Telephone: (213) 387-4242 — Carnegie Class: Spec 2-yr-Other
FAX Number: (213) 387-5365 — Calendar System: Other
URL: www.learnet.edu
Established: 1993 — Annual Undergrad Tuition & Fees: N/A
Enrollment: 72 — Coed
Affiliation or Control: Proprietary — IRS Status: Proprietary
Highest Offering: Associate Degree
Accreditation: ACCSC, CEA

01 Executive Director ..... Ms. Tia SHIN
05 Education Director ..... Mr. Agasi ASLANYAN

The Lee Strasberg Theatre Institute (C)

7936 Santa Monica Blvd, Los Angeles CA 90046
County: Los Angeles — Identification: 667413
Telephone: (323) 650-7777 — Carnegie Class: Not Classified
FAX Number: (323) 650-7770 — Calendar System: Quarter
URL: strasberg.edu
Established: 1969 — Annual Undergrad Tuition & Fees: N/A
Enrollment: N/A — Coed
Affiliation or Control: Proprietary — IRS Status: Proprietary
Highest Offering: Associate Degree
Accreditation: THEA

01 CEO/Creative Director ..... David STRASBERG

Life Chiropractic College West (D)

25001 Industrial Boulevard, Hayward CA 94545-2801
County: Alameda — FICE Identification: 022285
Unit ID: 117520
Telephone: (510) 780-4500 — Carnegie Class: Spec-4-yr-Other Health
FAX Number: (510) 780-4525 — Calendar System: Quarter
URL: www.lifewest.edu
Established: 1976 — Annual Undergrad Tuition & Fees: N/A
Enrollment: 598 — Coed
Affiliation or Control: Independent Non-Profit — IRS Status: 501(c)3
Highest Offering: First Professional Degree; No Lower Division
Accreditation: WC, CHIRO

01 President ..... Dr. Ron OBERSTEIN
05 Provost ..... Dr. Scott DONALDSON
17 Dean Clinical Operations ..... Dr. Lauren CLUM
45 Chief Strategy Officer ..... Dr. Marilyn AL-HASSAN
111 Exec Dir Institutional Advancement ..... Mr. Toure CARTER
10 Chief Financial Ofcr/Controller ..... Angelito TOLENTINO
46 Director of Research ..... Dr. Monica SMITH
51 Director of Continuing Education ..... Dr. Laurie ISENBERG
08 Learning Commons Director ..... Barbara DELLI GATTI
29 Director Alumni Relations ..... Dr. Joseph IBE
37 Director Financial Aid ..... Brenda JOHNSON
06 Registrar ..... Maria LOPEZ
15 Director Human Resources ..... Antoinette MCGILL
32 Student Life Manager ..... Danielle LORTA
40 Bookstore Manager ..... Vacant
41 Athletic Director ..... Adriaan FERRIS
84 Director of Enrollment ..... Marc MARTIN
108 Dir of Assessment & Inst Research ..... Vacant
04 Executive Assistant to President ..... Sharon SETO
07 Executive Director of Admissions ..... Daniel CARDENAS
88 Dean of Clinical Competency ..... Dr. Bruce CHESTER
28 Diversity & Inclusion Officer ..... Silvia BIELSER
43 General Counsel ..... Antoinette MCGILL
20 Dean of Acad Faculty/Educ Effective ..... Adam THOMPSON

Life Pacific University (E)

1100 W. Covina Boulevard, San Dimas CA 91773-3298
County: Los Angeles — FICE Identification: 022706
Unit ID: 117104
Telephone: (909) 599-5433 — Carnegie Class: Bac-Diverse
FAX Number: (909) 599-6690 — Calendar System: Semester
URL: www.lifepacific.edu
Established: 1923 — Annual Undergrad Tuition & Fees: $17,434
Enrollment: 604 — Coed
Affiliation or Control: Other — IRS Status: 501(c)3
Highest Offering: Master's
Accreditation: WC, BI

01 President ..... Ms. Angie RICHEY
04 Exec Assistant to the President ..... Mrs. Shellie DRISCOLL
05 Vice President Academic Affairs ..... Dr. Daniel RUARTE
84 Director Enrollment Management ..... Mr. Matthew TAPP
32 Assoc VP of Student Development ..... Mr. George BOSTANIC
10 CFO ..... Mr. Bob JOHANSEN
08 Librarian ..... Mr. Gary MERRIMAN
06 Registrar ..... Mrs. Amber BURNETT
18 Director of Facilities ..... Mr. Rick MEYER
37 Director of Financial Aid ..... Mrs. Luci PEREZ
09 Dean Institutional Effectiveness ..... Mr. Brian TOMHAVE
15 Human Resources Director ..... Ms. Heidi BONADIE
39 Director Residence Life ..... Mrs. Maria MCCRACKEN
41 Athletic Director ..... Mr. Tim COOK
13 IT Administrator (CIO) ..... Mr. Marlon ESTELLA
111 Chief Development/Advancement ..... Mrs. Lynnette LOZOYA

Lincoln Law School of Sacramento (F)

3140 J Street, Sacramento CA 95816
County: Sacramento — Identification: 667379
Telephone: (916) 446-1275 — Carnegie Class: Not Classified
FAX Number: N/A — Calendar System: Semester
URL: www.lincolnlaw.edu
Established: 1969 — Annual Graduate Tuition & Fees: N/A
Enrollment: N/A — Coed
Affiliation or Control: Proprietary — IRS Status: Proprietary
Highest Offering: First Professional Degree; No Undergraduates
Accreditation: WC

01 Chief Executive Officer ..... James SMOLICH

Lincoln University (G)

401 15th Street, Oakland CA 94612-2801
County: Alameda — FICE Identification: 006975
Unit ID: 117557
Telephone: (510) 628-8010 — Carnegie Class: Spec-4-yr-Bus
FAX Number: (510) 628-8012 — Calendar System: Semester
URL: www.lincolnuca.edu
Established: 1919 — Annual Undergrad Tuition & Fees: $11,390
Enrollment: 371 — Coed
Affiliation or Control: Independent Non-Profit — IRS Status: 501(c)3
Highest Offering: Doctorate
Accreditation: WC, IACBE

01 President ..... Dr. Mikhail BRODSKY
05 Provost/Chief Academic Officer ..... Dr. Marc SLAVIN
11 Administrative Vice President ..... Dr. Michael GUERRA
10 Chief Financial Officer/CIO ..... Mr. Albert LOH
32 Dean of Students ..... Mr. William HESS
07 Director of Admissions & Records ..... Ms. Peggy AU
08 Head Librarian ..... Ms. Nicole Y. MARSH
35 Director of Student Services ..... Ms. Ana Maria GOWER
41 Director of Athletics Program ..... Mr. Desmond GUMBS
13 Director of Computer Laboratory ..... Mr. Shakil SHRESTHA
06 Registrar ..... Ms. Maggie HUA
108 Dir of Accreditation/Compliance ..... Dr. Harpal DHILLON
09 Institutional Research Coordinator ..... Dr. Igor HIMELFARB
37 Director Student Financial Aid ..... Ms. Wendy VASQUEZ
18 Campus Property Manager ..... Mr. Mikk TEEVEER

Lional University (H)

1015 Mark Avenue, Carpinteria CA 93013-2912
County: Santa Barbara — FICE Identification: 042434
Unit ID: 485519
Telephone: (800) 650-4772 — Carnegie Class: Spec 2-yr-Other
FAX Number: N/A — Calendar System: Quarter
URL: https://www.lionel.edu/
Established: 1988 — Annual Undergrad Tuition & Fees: $10,107
Enrollment: 431 — Coed
Affiliation or Control: Proprietary — IRS Status: Proprietary
Highest Offering: Master's
Accreditation: DEAC

01 President ..... Alex HOFFMANN
05 Academic Dean/CAO ..... Alex HOFFMANN
06 Registrar ..... Holly HIGGINS

Logos Evangelical Seminary (I)

9358 Telstar Avenue, El Monte CA 91731-2816
County: Los Angeles — FICE Identification: 039454
Unit ID: 397553
Telephone: (626) 571-5110 — Carnegie Class: Not Classified
FAX Number: N/A — Calendar System: Semester
URL: www.logos-seminary.edu
Established: 1989 — Annual Graduate Tuition & Fees: N/A
Enrollment: N/A — Coed
Affiliation or Control: Other — IRS Status: 501(c)3
Highest Offering: Doctorate; No Undergraduates
Accreditation: WC, THEOL

01 President ..... Dr. James HWANG
05 Academic Dean ..... Dr. Chloe SUN
111 Director of Advancement ..... Rev. Mark SHEN
10 Director Finance/Administration ..... Mr. James TSAI
32 Dean of Students ..... Rev. Samuel LIU
12 Director Logos Training Institute ..... Vacant
04 Director of President's Office ..... Ms. Kathleen LIN
08 Head Librarian ..... Ms. Shelley SII
09 Institutional Research Specialist ..... Ms. Tracy BAI

Loma Linda University (J)

11139 Anderson Street, Loma Linda CA 92350
County: San Bernardino — FICE Identification: 001218
Unit ID: 117636
Telephone: (909) 558-1000 — Carnegie Class: DU-Higher
FAX Number: (909) 558-0242 — Calendar System: Quarter
URL: www.llu.edu
Established: 1905 — Annual Undergrad Tuition & Fees: N/A
Enrollment: 4,468 — Coed
Affiliation or Control: Seventh-day Adventist — IRS Status: 501(c)3
Highest Offering: Doctorate
Accreditation: WC, ANEST, ARCPA, CAHIIM, CAMPEP, CLPSY, COARC, CVT, CYTO, DENT, DH, DIETC, DMS, IPSY, MAC, MED, MFCD, MLS, #NMT, NURSE, OPE, OT, PA, PAST, PH, PHAR, PTA, PTAA, RAD, RTT, SP, SW

01 President ..... Dr. Richard H. HART
05 Provost ..... Dr. Ronald L. CARTER
10 Sr Vice President Financial Affairs ..... Mr. Rodney NEAL
111 Sr Vice President Advancement ..... Mrs. Rachelle BUSSELL
13 Vice President Information Systems ..... Dr. David P. HARRIS
32 VP Student Experience ..... Dr. Karl HAFFNER
46 VP for Research Affairs ..... Dr. Michael SAMARDZIJA
15 VP Human Resource Management ..... Vacant
63 Dean of Medicine ..... Dr. Tamara THOMAS
52 Dean of Dentistry ..... Dr. Robert HANDYSIDES
69 Acting Dean of Public Health ..... Dr. Dwight BARRETT
66 Dean of Nursing ..... Dr. Elizabeth (Becky) BOSSERT
76 Dean of Allied Health Professions ..... Dr. Craig R. JACKSON
67 Dean School of Pharmacy ..... Dr. Michael D. HOGUE
83 Dean School of Behavioral Health ..... Dr. Beverly J. BUCKLES
73 Dean School of Religion ..... Dr. Leo RANZOLIN
58 Int Exec Dir Faculty Grad Studies ..... Dr. Ronald L. CARTER
06 Director of Records ..... Ms. Erin SEHEULT
08 Director University Libraries ..... Ms. Shanalee TAMARES
38 Director of Counseling ..... Dr. William G. MURDOCH
43 General Legal Counsel ..... Mr. Kent A. HANSEN
35 Dean of Students ..... Ms. Lynette BATES
37 Director Student Financial Aid ..... Ms. Verdell SCHAEFER
09 Dir Educational Effectiveness ..... Dr. W. Ken NELSON
18 Director Campus Engineering ..... Mr. Randy STEVENS
96 Asst VP Supply Chain Management ..... Mr. Josh LUND
40 Campus Bookstore Manager ..... Ms. Arlene ALVAREZ
42 Campus Chaplain ..... Pastor Terry SWENSON

Long Beach City College (K)

4901 E Carson Street, Long Beach CA 90808-1780
County: Los Angeles — FICE Identification: 001219
Unit ID: 117645
Telephone: (562) 938-4111 — Carnegie Class: Assoc/HT-High Trad
FAX Number: (562) 938-4118 — Calendar System: Other
URL: www.lbcc.edu
Established: 1927 — Annual Undergrad Tuition & Fees (In-District): $1,556
Enrollment: 23,147 — Coed
Affiliation or Control: State/Local — IRS Status: 501(c)3
Highest Offering: Associate Degree
Accreditation: WJ, ADNUR

01 Superintendent/President ..... Dr. Mike MUN~OZ
05 Vice Pres Academic Affairs ..... Dr. Lee DOUGLAS
10 Vice Pres Business Services ..... Chip WEST
32 Exec Vice Pres Student Support Svcs ..... Dr. Nohel CORRAL
15 Vice Pres Human Resources ..... Dr. Loy NASHUA
13 Exec Director Information Systems ..... Robert CARMAN
16 Assoc VP Human Resources ..... Kristin OLSON
84 Dean Enrollment Services ..... Yvonne GUTIERREZ-SANDOVAL
103 VP Econ & Workforce Dev/Govt Affair ..... Melissa INFUSINO
75 Dean Career & Technical Education ..... Gene CARBONARO
38 Int Dean Counseling/Stdnt Supp Svcs ..... Javier VILLASENOR
20 Dean Academic Affairs ..... Kenna HILLMAN
22 Dean of Student Equity ..... Sonia DE LA TORRE-INIGUEZ
60 Dean Language Arts & Comms ..... Nicole GLICK
35 Interim Dean Student Affairs ..... Deborah MILLER-CALVERT
81 Dean of Science & Math ..... Moises GUTIERREZ
76 Dean of Health Sci & Kinesiology ..... Dr. Paul CREASON
09 Dean Inst Effectiveness ..... Dr. Heather Van VOLKINBURG
83 Dean Social Sciences & Arts ..... Elisabeth ORR
102 Exec Director Foundation ..... Paul KAMINSKI
26 Exec Dir Public Affairs & Marketing ..... Joshua CASTELLANOS
20 Int Assoc Dean Academic Services ..... Brent GILMORE
88 Int Chief Innovation Officer ..... Tracy CARMICHAEL
96 Director Business Support Svcs ..... Bob RAPOZA
21 Director Fiscal Services & Payroll ..... John THOMPSON
37 Director Financial Aid ..... Jason AVILA
41 Dn Kinesiology/Public Hlth/Athletic ..... Randy TOTORP
04 Int Exec Asst to the President ..... Lauren ZALE

101 Sr Exec Assistant Governing Board .... M'Shelle REECE
105 Deputy Director Network Services .... Mark GUIDAS
106 Assoc Dean Online Lrng/Educ Tech .... Hussam KASHOU
90 Dep Dir Acad Comp/Multimedia Svcs .... Tim HEFFERN

Los Angeles Academy of Figurative Art (A)

16926 Saticoy Street, Van Nuys CA 91406
County: Los Angeles | Identification: 667231 | Unit ID: 490124
Telephone: (818) 708-9232 | Carnegie Class: Spec-4-yr-Arts
FAX Number: (818) 474-8679 | Calendar System: Quarter
URL: www.laafa.edu
Established: 2002 | Annual Undergrad Tuition & Fees: $32,093
Enrollment: 5 | Coed
Affiliation or Control: Proprietary | IRS Status: Proprietary
Highest Offering: Baccalaureate
Accreditation: ART

01 President .... Maryam STORM

Los Angeles College of Music (B)

300 South Fair Oaks Avenue, Pasadena CA 91105
County: Los Angeles | FICE Identification: 038684 | Unit ID: 446385
Telephone: (626) 568-8850 | Carnegie Class: Spec-4-yr-Arts
FAX Number: (626) 568-8854 | Calendar System: Quarter
URL: www.lacm.edu
Established: 1996 | Annual Undergrad Tuition & Fees: $25,650
Enrollment: 249 | Coed
Affiliation or Control: Proprietary | IRS Status: Proprietary
Highest Offering: Master's
Accreditation: MUS

01 President .... Charles T. AYLESBURY
03 Executive Vice President .... Erin WORKMAN
06 Registrar .... Jorge OJEDA
05 Dean of Academics .... Dr. Daniel WALKER
37 Director of Financial Aid .... Bertha CHAVEZ
07 Director of Admissions .... Emilio RODRIGUEZ
10 Controller .... Kristin BARRIOS

*Los Angeles Community College District Office (C)

770 Wilshire Boulevard, Los Angeles CA 90017
County: Los Angeles | FICE Identification: 001221 | Unit ID: 117681
Telephone: (213) 891-2000 | Carnegie Class: N/A
FAX Number: N/A
URL: www.laccd.edu

01 Chancellor .... Dr. Francisco C. RODRIGUEZ
05 Int VC Educ Pgms/Inst Effectiveness .... Dr. Nicole ALBO-LOPEZ
43 General Counsel .... Ms. Maribel MEDINA
10 VC/Chief Financial Officer .... Mr. Jeannette L. GORDON
13 VC/Chief Information Officer .... Ms. Carmen LIDZ
15 Interim VC Human Resources .... Dr. Shairon ZINGSHEIM
18 Chief Facilities Executive .... Dr. Rueben C. SMITH
20 Deputy Chancellor .... Dr. Melinda A. NISH
103 Int VC Workforce Dev & Adult Educ .... Dr. Katrina VANDERWOUDE

*East Los Angeles College (D)

1301 Avenida Cesar Chavez, Monterey Park CA 91754-6001
County: Los Angeles | FICE Identification: 022260 | Unit ID: 113856
Telephone: (323) 265-8650 | Carnegie Class: Assoc/HT-Mix Trad/Non
FAX Number: (323) 265-8763 | Calendar System: Semester
URL: www.elac.edu
Established: 1945 | Annual Undergrad Tuition & Fees (In-District): $1,238
Enrollment: 33,397 | Coed
Affiliation or Control: State/Local | IRS Status: Exempt
Highest Offering: Associate Degree
Accreditation: WJ, CAHIIM, COARC

02 President .... Dr. Alberto J. ROMAN
05 Interim VP Instructional Services .... Ms. Mercedes YANEZ
11 VP Administrative Services .... Dr. Michael PASCUAL
32 VP Student Services .... Dr. Miguel DUENAS
81 Dean STEM .... Dr. Djuradj BABIC
07 Dean Student Services .... Ms. Danelle FALLERT
88 Dean Student Services .... Dr. Sonia LOPEZ
121 Dean Student Services .... Ms. Paulina PALOMINO
120 Dean Academic Affairs .... Ms. Gina CHELSTROM
89 Dean Student Services .... Dr. Vanessa OCHOA
88 Dean Student Services .... Ms. Grace HERNANDEZ
88 Dean Language Arts .... Mr. James KENNY
57 Dean Visual Arts/Dance/Athletics .... Ms. Ming-huei LAM
83 Dean Social Sciences .... Ms. Kerrin MCMAHAN
88 Assoc Vice President Admin Svcs .... Mr. Nghi NGHIEM
88 Dean Perform Arts & Design .... Mr. Alfonso RIOS
76 Dean Health & Human Svcs .... Ms. Angelica TOLEDO
51 Dean Continuing Education .... Dr. Juan URDIALES
09 Dean Inst Effectiveness .... Dr. Laura CRUZ-ATRIAN
10 College Financial Administrator .... Mr. Hao XIE

26 Public Information Officer .... Mr. Kevin JIMENEZ
15 Chief Human Resources Officer .... Ms. Maria ESTRADA
40 Bookstore Supervisor .... Mr. Miguel PEREZ
41 Athletic Director .... Mr. Bobby GODINEZ
08 Library Dept Chair .... Ms. Chonhee RHIM
88 Director Child Development Center .... Ms. Marcia CAGIGAS
04 Exec Assistant to the President .... Ms. Kristen M. VAN HALA
06 Registrar .... Vacant
19 Director Security/Safety .... Mr. Don RUBIO
37 Director Student Financial Aid .... Ms. Lindy FONG
18 Director of College Facilities .... Mr. Jose VILLARREAL

*Los Angeles City College (E)

855 N Vermont Avenue, Los Angeles CA 90029-9990
County: Los Angeles | FICE Identification: 001223 | Unit ID: 117788
Telephone: (323) 953-4000 | Carnegie Class: Assoc/HT-High Non
FAX Number: (323) 953-4013 | Calendar System: Semester
URL: www.lacitycollege.edu
Established: 1929 | Annual Undergrad Tuition & Fees (In-District): $1,238
Enrollment: 14,800 | Coed
Affiliation or Control: Local | IRS Status: 501(c)3
Highest Offering: Associate Degree
Accreditation: WJ, DT, RAD

02 President .... Dr. Mary GALLAGHER
05 Vice President Academic Affairs .... Dr. James LANCASTER
10 Vice President Administrative Svcs .... Mr. Joe DOMINGUEZ
32 Actg VP of Student Services .... Mr. Alen ANDRIASSIAN
88 VP Economic Soc Mobil & Innovation .... Ms. Marcy DRUMMOND
15 AVP Administrative Svcs/Personnel .... Mr. Michael PASCUAL
20 Dean of Academic Affairs .... Dr. Vi LY
103 Dean of Workforce Development .... Dr. Armando RIVERA-FIGUEROA
09 Dean of Institutional Effectiveness .... Dr. Anna BADALYAN
124 Assoc Dean of EOPS .... Ms. Niki HARRISON
37 Dean Financial Aid .... Dr. Saadia PORCHE
35 Actg Dean Office of Student Life .... Mr. Dimitrios SYNODINOS
40 Bookstore Manager .... Ms. Christi O'CONNOR
85 Dean of International Students .... Dr. Darren GROSCH
66 Dean of Nursing & Allied Health .... Dr. Ann HAMILTON
38 Counseling Chairperson .... Mr. Edward SONG
18 Facilities Director .... Mr. Kahlil HARRINGTON
04 Executive Assistant to President .... Vacant

*Los Angeles Harbor College (F)

1111 Figueroa Place, Wilmington CA 90744-2397
County: Los Angeles | FICE Identification: 001224 | Unit ID: 117690
Telephone: (310) 233-4000 | Carnegie Class: Assoc/HT-Mix Trad/Non
FAX Number: (310) 233-4660 | Calendar System: Semester
URL: www.lahc.edu
Established: 1949 | Annual Undergrad Tuition & Fees (In-District): $1,238
Enrollment: 8,101 | Coed
Affiliation or Control: State/Local | IRS Status: 501(c)3
Highest Offering: Associate Degree
Accreditation: WJ, ADNUR

02 President .... Dr. Luis DORADO
04 Executive Assistant to President .... Ms. Sylvia FILES
05 Vice Pres Academic Affairs .... Dr. Bobbi VILLALOBOS
10 Vice Pres Administrative Services .... Dr. Reagan ROMALI
32 Vice Pres Student Services .... Dr. Nicole ALBO-LOPEZ
21 Assoc Vice Pres Administrative Svcs .... Vacant
09 Dean of Institutional Effectiveness .... Dr. Edward PAI
20 Dean of Academic Affairs .... Dr. Chelvi SUBRAMANIAM
35 Dean Student Services .... Mr. Tiffany SERGIO
22 Dean Student Svcs/Acting Dean EWD .... Ms. Mercy YANEZ
35 Dean of Student Services .... Mrs. Dawn REID
20 Dean Acad Affs/Non-credit & Cmty Ed .... Ms. Priscilla LOPEZ
83 Div Chair Behavioral/Social Sci .... Mr. Son NGUYEN
50 Division Chairperson Business .... Ms. Wendy HOFFMAN
60 Div Chairperson Communications .... Ms. Ann WARREN
57 Div Chair Humanities/Fine Arts .... Mr. Juan BAEZ
81 Div Chairperson Math/Phys Science .... Ms. Farah SADDIGH
76 Div Chairperson Health Sciences .... Mrs. Lynn YAMAKAWA
68 Div Chairperson Physical Education .... Mr. Nabeel M. BARAKAT
59 Div Chair Sci/Family Consumer Stds .... Dr. Basil IBE
08 Division Chairperson Library .... Mr. Jonathan LEE
38 Division Chairperson Counseling .... Ms. Sara RUBIO
41 Athletic Director .... Mr. Dean DOWTY
37 Director Student Financial Aid .... Vacant
18 Facilities Manager .... Mr. Alex NELSON
13 Manager Information Technology .... Vacant
31 Community Services Manager .... Ms. Darin COSTA
85 International Student Program .... Ms. Jessica CRUZ
15 Payroll & Personnel Supervisor .... Ms. Hsin (Gina) PENG
88 Assoc Dean of STEM Pathways .... Ms. Mercy YANEZ
102 Foundation Development Officer .... Mr. Peter BOSTIC
06 Registrar .... Ms. Ruby GUERRERO
26 Chief Public Relations Officer .... Mr. Peter BOSTIC

*Los Angeles Mission College (G)

13356 Eldridge Avenue, Sylmar CA 91342-3244
County: Los Angeles | FICE Identification: 012550 | Unit ID: 117867
Telephone: (818) 364-7600 | Carnegie Class: Assoc/HT-High Non
FAX Number: (818) 364-7826 | Calendar System: Semester
URL: www.lamission.edu
Established: 1975 | Annual Undergrad Tuition & Fees (In-District): $1,238
Enrollment: 9,451 | Coed
Affiliation or Control: State/Local | IRS Status: 501(c)3
Highest Offering: Associate Degree
Accreditation: WJ

02 President .... Dr. Armida ORNELAS
05 Vice President Academic Affairs .... Dr. Laura B. CANTU
11 Vice President Administrative Svcs .... Mr. Robert PARKER
32 Vice President of Student Services .... Dr. Larry L. RESENDEZ
55 Dean of Adult Education .... Ms. Fabiola MORA
35 Dean of Student Services .... Ms. Ludi VILLEGAS-VIDAL
84 Dean of Enrollment Management .... Ms. Lorena LOPEZ
121 Dean of Student Success .... Mr. Carlos R. GONZALEZ
88 Dean of CTE .... Ms. Marla ULIANA
81 Dean of STEM .... Ms. Farisa MORALES
09 Dean of Institutional Effectiveness .... Dr. Sarah L. MASTER
20 Dean of Academic Affairs .... Ms. Madelline HERNANDEZ
26 Chief Public Relations Officer .... Vacant
88 Director Child Development Center .... Ms. Diane STEIN
41 Interim Athletic Director .... Mr. Joel GUNTERMAN
08 Head Librarian .... Mr. Albert YBARRA
38 Counseling Chairperson .... Ms. Angela PAN
37 Financial Aid Manager .... Mr. Dennis J. SCHROEDER
18 Facilities/Physical Plant Manager .... Mr. Andrew GOOD
88 EOP & S/Care Director .... Ms. Ludi VILLEGAS-VIDAL
04 Executive Asst to President .... Ms. Oliva AYALA
10 Chief Business Officer .... Mr. Jerry HUANG
102 Dir Foundation/Corporate Relations .... Mr. Robert PARKER
15 Personnel Services Assistant .... Mr. Pio CASTILLO
07 Director of Admissions/Records .... Ms. Martha RIOS
36 Director Student Placement .... Ms. Wendy RIVERA
96 Director of Purchasing .... Ms. Tara WARD
13 Chief Info Technology Officer (CIO) .... Mr. Mark HENDERSON

*Los Angeles Pierce College (H)

6201 Winnetka Avenue, Woodland Hills CA 91371-0001
County: Los Angeles | FICE Identification: 001226 | Unit ID: 117706
Telephone: (818) 710-4100 | Carnegie Class: Assoc/HT-Mix Trad/Non
FAX Number: N/A | Calendar System: Semester
URL: www.piercecollege.edu
Established: 1947 | Annual Undergrad Tuition & Fees (In-District): $1,238
Enrollment: 17,521 | Coed
Affiliation or Control: State/Local | IRS Status: 501(c)3
Highest Offering: Associate Degree
Accreditation: WJ

02 Interim President .... Ms. Ara AGUIAR
05 Int Vice President Academic Affairs . Dr. Donna-Mae VILLANUEVA
11 Vice President Administrative Svcs .... Mr. Rolf SCHLEICHER
32 Acting Vice Pres Student Services .... Mr. Juan Carlos ASTORGA
10 Assoc Vice President Admin Services .... Mr. Bruce ROSKY
08 Chair Library .... Ms. Lauren SASLOW
38 Chair Counseling .... Ms. Alyce MILLER
20 Dean of Academic Affairs .... Vacant
20 Dean of Academic Affairs .... Ms. Mary Anne GAVARRA-OH
20 Dean of Academic Affairs .... Ms. Susan RHI-KLEINERT
20 Dean of Academic Affairs .... Ms. Sharon DALMAGE
37 Director of Financial Aid .... Ms. Anafe ROBINSON
108 Dean Institutional Effectiveness .... Mr. Amari WILLIAMS
26 Public Information Officer .... Ms. Doreen CLAY
18 Director of College Facilities .... Mr. Paul NIEMAN
106 Dir Online Education/E-learning .... Ms. Wendy BASS KEER
121 Dean of Student Success .... Dr. Kalynda WEBBER MCLEAN
35 Dean Student Services .... Mr. William MARMOLEJO
06 Registrar .... Ms. Lorena LOPEZ
35 Dean of Student Services & Equity .... Dr. Genice SARCEDO-MAGRUDER
124 Dean of Student Engagement .... Mr. Juan Carlos ASTORGA

*Los Angeles Southwest College (I)

1600 W Imperial Highway, Los Angeles CA 90047-4899
County: Los Angeles | FICE Identification: 007047 | Unit ID: 117715
Telephone: (323) 241-5225 | Carnegie Class: Assoc/HT-High Non
FAX Number: (323) 241-5220 | Calendar System: Semester
URL: www.lasc.edu
Established: 1967 | Annual Undergrad Tuition & Fees (In-District): $1,238
Enrollment: 5,216 | Coed
Affiliation or Control: State/Local | IRS Status: 501(c)3
Highest Offering: Associate Degree
Accreditation: WJ

02 Interim President .... Dr. Anthony CULPEPPER
05 Vice President Academic Affairs .... Dr. Lawrence BRADFORD
32 Acting VP Student Services .... Dr. Jamail CARTER
10 Vice President Admin Services .... Vacant
111 Dean Institutional Advancement .... Mr. Jose Alfred GALLEGOS
103 Dean Career/Technical Education .... Vacant
20 Dean Academic Affairs .... Dr. Tangelia ALFRED
20 Dean Academic Affairs .... Dr. Kristi BLACKBURN
35 Dean Student Services .... Dr. Ralph DAVIS
88 Dean Special Programs & Services .... Ms. Jeanette MAGEE
55 Dean Adult Non-credit/Cont Educ .... Ms. Laura PEREZ
38 Chairperson Counseling .... Dr. Katrin WILSON
08 Chairperson Library .... Ms. Parissa SAMAIE
06 Registrar .... Vacant
18 Director of Facilities .... Mr. Preston MORTLEY
13 Regional Mgr College Tech Svcs .... Mr. Kirk YAMAMOTO
37 Financial Aid Manager .... Ms. Muniece BRUTON
26 College Public Relations Manager .... Mr. Ben DEMERS
04 Executive Assistant/Confidential .... Ms. Chauncine R. STEWART

*Los Angeles Trade-Technical College (A)

400 W Washington Boulevard,
Los Angeles CA 90015-4108
County: Los Angeles FICE Identification: 001227
Unit ID: 117724
Telephone: (213) 763-7000 Carnegie Class: Assoc/HVT-High Non
FAX Number: (213) 763-5393 Calendar System: Semester
URL: www.lattc.edu
Established: 1925 Annual Undergrad Tuition & Fees (In-District): $1,238
Enrollment: 11,285 Coed
Affiliation or Control: State/Local IRS Status: 501(c)3
Highest Offering: Associate Degree
Accreditation: WJ, ACFEI

02 Interim President .... Dr. Kathleen BURKE
11 VP Administrative Services .... Mr. Harry ZIOGAS
05 Vice President Academic Affairs .... Dr. Michael REESE
32 Vice Pres Student Affairs .... Dr. Amir LAW
20 Dean Academic Affairs & Workforce .... Mr. Vincent JACKSON
20 Dean Academic Affairs & Workforce .... Ms. Cynthia MORLEY-MOWER
20 Dean Academic Affairs & Workforce .... Dr. Ann HAMILTON
20 Dean Academic Affairs & Workforce ... Dr. Arineh ARZOUMANIAN
35 Dean Student Services .... Dr. Henan JOOF
26 Public Relations Manager .... Mr. David YSAIS
13 Mgr Information Technology .... Vacant

*Los Angeles Valley College (B)

5800 Fulton Avenue, Valley Glen CA 91401-4096
County: Los Angeles FICE Identification: 001228
Unit ID: 117733
Telephone: (818) 947-2600 Carnegie Class: Assoc/HT-Mix Trad/Non
FAX Number: N/A Calendar System: Semester
URL: www.lavc.edu
Established: 1949 Annual Undergrad Tuition & Fees (In-District): $1,238
Enrollment: 15,957 Coed
Affiliation or Control: State/Local IRS Status: 501(c)3
Highest Offering: Associate Degree
Accreditation: WJ, ADNUR, COARC

02 President .... Dr. Barry C. GRIBBONS
05 Vice President Academic Affairs .... Dr. Matthew JORDAN
10 Vice President Admin Services .... Ms. Sarah SONG
32 Vice President Student Services .... Mr. Florentino MANZANO
11 Associate VP Administrative Svcs .... Vacant
20 Dean Academic Affairs .... Dr. Brandon HILDRETH
20 Dean Academic Affairs .... Dr. Laurie NALEPA
20 Dean Academic Affairs .... Dr. Deborah A. DICESARE
20 Dean Academic Affairs .... Vacant
20 Dean Academic Affairs .... Dr. Carmen DOMINGUEZ
09 Dean Institutional Effectiveness .... Ms. Michelle R. FOWLES
35 Dean Student Life .... Dr. Elizabeth NEGRETE
88 Dean of Special Programs .... Dr. Sherri RODRIGUEZ
121 Dean Student Success & Support Svcs .... Dr. Sorangel HERNANDEZ
88 Associate Dean SSP .... Mr. David M. GREEN
35 Associate Dean Student Services .... Ms. Cecilia CRUZ
35 Associate Dean Student Services .... Dr. Alex OJEDA
102 Executive Director LAVC Foundation .... Vacant
41 Athletic Director .... Mr. Dave MALLAS
18 Director College Facilities .... Mr. William KARRAT
40 College Store Manager .... Ms. Mary JOHN
26 Public Relations Manager .... Ms. Jennifer C. BORUCKI
31 Community Services Manager .... Vacant
13 Regional Manager College Tech Svcs .... Dr. Mark HENDERSON
37 Financial Aid Manager .... Mr. Vernon D. BRIDGES
21 College Fiscal Administrator .... Mr. Robert MEDINA
06 Registrar .... Ms. Ashley DUNN
04 Executive Assistant .... Ms. Tanya A. SIRKIN

*West Los Angeles College (C)

9000 Overland Avenue, Culver City CA 90230-5002
County: Los Angeles FICE Identification: 008596
Unit ID: 125471
Telephone: (310) 287-4200 Carnegie Class: Bac/Assoc-Assoc Dom
FAX Number: (310) 841-0396 Calendar System: Semester
URL: www.wlac.edu
Established: 1969 Annual Undergrad Tuition & Fees (In-District): $1,238
Enrollment: 11,417 Coed
Affiliation or Control: State/Local IRS Status: 501(c)3
Highest Offering: Baccalaureate
Accreditation: WJ, DH

02 President .... Dr. James M. LIMBAUGH
05 VP Academic Affairs .... Dr. Jeffrey D. ARCHIBALD
11 VP Administrative Svcs .... Vacant
32 VP Student Services .... Dr. Roberto O. GONZALEZ
97 Dean General Education & Transfer .... Dr. Walter JONES
20 Dean Academic Affairs .... Dr. Mary-Jo APIGO
88 Dean of Apprenticeship .... Ms. Tiffany MILLER
51 Dean Adult & Cont Education .... Dr. Allison TOM-MIURA
76 Dean of Health Sciences .... Ms. Carmen DONES
20 Dean Teaching & Learning .... Vacant
09 Dean Institutional Effectiveness .... Mr. Artour ASLANIAN
22 Dean Student Services/Equity .... Mr. Angel VIRAMONTES
84 Dean Student Svcs/Enrollment .... Mr. Michael GOLTERMANN
35 Dean Student Svcs .... Ms. Angeles ABRAHAM
35 Dean Student Svcs .... Ms. Edna CORDOVA-CHAVARRY
35 Dean Student Svcs TRIO .... Dr. Celena ALCALA-BURKHARDT
41 Athletic Director .... Mr. Anthony JONES
40 College Enterprise Manager .... Vacant
10 Chief Financial Administrator .... Ms. Rasel MENENDEZ
18 Director of College Facilities .... Mr. Dean FELTON
37 Director Financial Aid .... Mr. Glenn SCHENK
13 Manager Info System .... Vacant
88 Operations Manager .... Mr. Bruce HICKS
19 Sheriff/Deputy .... Mr. Roberto GONZALEZ
88 Academic Senate President .... Dr. Patricia ZUK
26 Dir Advertising/Mktg/Public Rels .... Ms. Michelle LONG-COFFEE
102 Executive Director WLAC Foundation .Ms. Etelvina DE LA TORRE
08 Library Chair .... Ms. Susan TRUJILLO

Los Angeles County College of Nursing and Allied Health (D)

1237 North Mission Road, Los Angeles CA 90033-1083
County: Los Angeles FICE Identification: 006165
Unit ID: 117803
Telephone: (323) 409-5911 Carnegie Class: Spec 2-yr-Health
FAX Number: (323) 226-6343 Calendar System: Semester
URL: dhs.lacounty.gov/wps/portal/dhs/conah/
Established: 1895 Annual Undergrad Tuition & Fees (In-District): N/A
Enrollment: 200 Coed
Affiliation or Control: Local IRS Status: 501(c)3
Highest Offering: Associate Degree
Accreditation: WJ

01 Provost/Administrator .... Ms. Vivian BRANCHICK
66 Dean School of Nursing .... Ms. Mildred GONZALES
32 Dean Col Operations/Student Svcs .... Ms. Trina TRONGONE
108 Dean Institutional Effectiveness .... Ms. Herminia HONDA
38 Director Advisement/Counseling .... Ms. Maria CABALLERO
13 College Information Officer .... Mr. Visna KIENG
76 Dir Allied Healtlh Cont Education .... Ms. Irene DE LA TORRE

Los Angeles Film School (E)

6363 Sunset Boulevard, Hollywood CA 90028
County: Los Angeles FICE Identification: 040373
Unit ID: 436429
Telephone: (323) 860-0789 Carnegie Class: Spec-4-yr-Arts
FAX Number: (323) 646-0770 Calendar System: Other
URL: www.lafilm.edu
Established: 1999 Annual Undergrad Tuition & Fees: N/A
Enrollment: 5,669 Coed
Affiliation or Control: Proprietary IRS Status: Proprietary
Highest Offering: Baccalaureate
Accreditation: ACCSC

01 President .... Ms. Tammy ELLIOTT
05 Chief Academic Officer .... Dr. Kyle WOODY
06 Registrar .... Mr. Andrew NORTON
07 Director of Admissions .... Ms. Ernesta MENSAH
08 Chief Library Officer .... Ms. Georgina GARCIA-CAMPOS
10 Chief Financial/Business Officer .... Ms. Pamela PAYAWAL
13 Chief Information Technology Office .... Mr. Iyob ARAIA
15 Chief Human Resources Officer .... Ms. Judy NIMOY
18 Chief Facilities/Physical Plant Ofc .... Ms. Elizabeth MCDONALD
29 Director Alumni Affairs .... Vacant
36 Director Student Placement .... Ms. Angelia BIBB-SANDERS
37 Director Student Financial Aid .... Mr. Dustin WEIR
26 Chief Public Relations/Marketing .... Mr. James WINSTEAD
38 Director Student Counseling .... Ms. Yacine NDAO
88 Compliance Officer .... Mr. Mark DEBACCO
19 Director Security/Safety .... Mr. Michael MCFATRIDGE

Los Angeles Pacific College (F)

3325 Wilshire Boulevard, Ste 550,
Los Angeles CA 90010-1758
County: Los Angeles Identification: 667143
Telephone: (213) 384-2318 Carnegie Class: Not Classified
FAX Number: (213) 384-0419 Calendar System: Semester
URL: www.lapacific.net
Established: 1989 Annual Undergrad Tuition & Fees: N/A
Enrollment: N/A Coed
Affiliation or Control: Proprietary IRS Status: Proprietary
Highest Offering: Associate Degree
Accreditation: COE, CEA

01 President/Student Services Coord .... Ms. Mary YOON
10 Controller/Academic Director .... Mr. Ho Sung YOON

Los Angeles Pacific University (G)

300 N. Lone Hill Ave #200, San Dimas CA 91773
County: Los Angeles FICE Identification: 042788
Unit ID: 474863
Telephone: (858) 527-2768 Carnegie Class: Masters/M
FAX Number: (626) 276-7034 Calendar System: Semester
URL: www.lapu.edu
Established: 2014 Annual Undergrad Tuition & Fees: $10,800
Enrollment: 2,036 Coed
Affiliation or Control: Independent Non-Profit IRS Status: 501(c)3
Highest Offering: Master's
Accreditation: WC

01 President .... Dr. John REYNOLDS
11 Executive Vice Pres/COO .... Dr. Frank ROJAS
05 Vice Pres/Chief Academic Officer .... Dr. Wayne HERMAN

† Affiliated with Azusa Pacific University.

The Los Angeles Performing Arts Conservatory (H)

1404 Third Street Promenade, Santa Monica CA 90401
County: Los Angeles Identification: 667412
Telephone: (310) 656-8070 Carnegie Class: Not Classified
FAX Number: (310) 656-8069 Calendar System: Quarter
URL: www.laconservatory.com
Established: Annual Undergrad Tuition & Fees: N/A
Enrollment: N/A Coed
Affiliation or Control: Proprietary IRS Status: Proprietary
Highest Offering: Associate Degree
Accreditation: THEA

01 Founder & CEO .... Natalia LAZARUS

*Los Rios Community College District Office (I)

1919 Spanos Court, Sacramento CA 95825-3981
County: Sacramento FICE Identification: 001231
Unit ID: 117900
Telephone: (916) 568-3021 Carnegie Class: N/A
FAX Number: (916) 561-0574
URL: www.losrios.edu

01 Chancellor .... Dr. Brian KING
04 Chancellor's Executive Officer .... Ms. Jennifer DELUCCHI
10 Vice Chancellor Finance/Admin .... Mr. Mario RODRIGUEZ
05 Vice Chancellor Education/Tech .... Dr. Jamey NYE
30 Assoc Vice Chanc Resource Dev .... Ms. Paula ALLISON
26 Assoc Vice Chanc Comm/Media Rels .... Mr. Gabe ROSS
18 Assoc Vice Chanc Facilities Mgmt .... Mr. Pablo MANZO
15 Assoc Vice Chanc Human Resources .... Mr. Jake KNAPP
13 Assoc Vice Chanc IT .... Ms. Tamara ARMSTRONG
20 Assoc Vice Chanc Instruction .... Vacant
32 Int Dir Educ Svcs/Student Success .... Ms. Hannah BLODGETT
37 Director Financial Aid .... Mr. Roy BECKHORN
96 Director General Services .... Ms. Anita SINGH
09 Director Institutional Research .... Ms. Betty GLYER-CULVER

*American River College (J)

4700 College Oak Drive, Sacramento CA 95841-4286
County: Sacramento FICE Identification: 001232
Unit ID: 109208
Telephone: (916) 484-8011 Carnegie Class: Assoc/MT-VT-Mix Trad/Non
FAX Number: (916) 484-8674 Calendar System: Semester
URL: www.arc.losrios.edu
Established: 1955 Annual Undergrad Tuition & Fees (In-District): $1,288
Enrollment: 25,422 Coed
Affiliation or Control: State/Local IRS Status: 501(c)3
Highest Offering: Associate Degree
Accreditation: WJ, COARC, EMT, #FUSER

02 President .... Ms. Melanie DIXON
10 Vice President Admin Services .... Ms. Koue VANG
05 Vice President Instruction .... Dr. Frank KOBAYASHI
32 Vice President Student Services .... Dr. Jeff STEPHENSON
20 Assoc VP Instruction .... Dr. Kate JAQUES
84 Assoc VP Instruction/Enrollment Mgt .... Dr. Kale BRADEN
35 Assoc VP Student Services .... Mr. Chad FUNK
103 Assoc VP Workforce Development .... Dr. Derrick BOOTH
57 Dean Fine & Applied Arts .... Ms. Angela MILANO
07 Dean Enrollment Services .... Mr. Parrish GEARY
83 Dean Behavioral/Social Science .... Dr. Kathy SORENSEN
88 Dean English .... Mr. Doug HERNDON
79 Dean Humanities .... Ms. Diana HICKS
68 Int Dean Kinesiology/Athletics .... Ms. Kat SULLIVAN-TORREZ
81 Dean Mathematics .... Mr. Adam WINDHAM
56 Int Dean McClellan Center .... Ms. Charissa GORRE
35 Dean Student Services .... Ms. Kolleen OSTGAARD
09 Dean Inst Effectiveness/Innovation .... Dr. Adam KARP
66 Dean Health & Education .... Ms. Jan DELAPP
54 Int Dean Science/Engineering .... Mr. Narinedat MADRAMOOTOO
56 Dean Natomas Center .... Mr. Roger DAVIDSON
22 Dean Library/Learning Resource Ctr .... Dr. Joshua MOON JOHNSON
50 Dean Business/Computer Science .... Ms. Kirsten CORBIN
72 Dean Technical Education .... Mr. Gary AGUILAR
04 Administrative Asst to President .... Ms. Sue MCCOY
11 Director Administrative Services .... Ms. Cheryl SEARS
26 Public Information Officer .... Mr. Scott CROW
37 Financial Aid Supervisor .... Ms. Robin GALLOWGLAS
88 Dean DE/Virtual Ed Center .... Vacant
75 Dean Career Ed & Workforce Dev .... Ms. Raquel ARATA
38 Dean Counseling .... Ms. Nisha BECKHORN
124 Int Dean Student Engage/Completion .... Mr. Eric HANDY

*Cosumnes River College (K)

8401 Center Parkway, Sacramento CA 95823-5799
County: Sacramento FICE Identification: 007536
Unit ID: 113096
Telephone: (916) 691-7344 Carnegie Class: Assoc/MT-VT-Mix Trad/Non
FAX Number: (916) 691-7375 Calendar System: Semester
URL: www.crc.losrios.edu

Established: 1970 Annual Undergrad Tuition & Fees (In-District): $1,288
Enrollment: 14,667 Coed
Affiliation or Control: State/Local IRS Status: 501(c)3
Highest Offering: Associate Degree
Accreditation: WJ, CAHIIM, DMS, MAC

02 President ... Dr. Edward C. BUSH
04 Admin Assistant to the President ... Ms. Rachel LARSEN
26 Public Information Officer ... Ms. Kristie WEST
05 VP Instruction & Student Learning ... Dr. Robert MONTANEZ
09 VP Inst Equity/Research/Planning ... Dr. Claire OLIVEROS
10 VP Admin Services & Student Support ... Ms. Theresa TENA
32 AVP Student Services ... Mr. Tadael EMIRU
20 AVP Instruction/Student Learning ... Dr. Michael LAWLOR
103 Int AVP Econ/Workforce Develop ... Ms. Dana WASSMER
81 Dean Science/Engineering ... Ms. Banafsheh (Bani) AMINI
79 Dean GP&Grants/Eng & Lang Studies ... Dr. Alexander CASARENO
88 Dean of Auto/Const Tech/EGC ... Ms. Ashu MISHRA
13 Int Dean Library and Tech Service ... Ms. Nancy REITZ
83 Dean Social/Behavioral Science ... Dr. Emilie MITCHELL
38 Dean Couns & Student Services ... Ms. Hong PHAM
50 Dean Business & Computer Science ... Mr. Joel POWELL
41 Dean of Athletics ... Mr. Collin PREGLIASCO
84 Int Dean Student Svcs/Enroll Mgmt ... Ms. Joann RAMIREZ
60 Dean Arts/Media & Entertainment ... Mr. Brian RICKEL
108 Dean Inst Effect/Research/Planning ... Ms. Sabrina SENCIL
47 Int Dn Ag/Food/Nat Res/Hlth Hm Svc ... Mr. Kris HUBBARD
81 Dean Math/Stats ... Ms. Camille MORENO
40 Int Director College Store ... Mr. Steve JAMES
88 Director AANAPISI Grant ... Mr. Raul PASAMONTE
18 Dir Administrative Services ... Mr. Christopher RAINES
88 Dir Academic/Stdnt Supp Projects ... Dr. Tyler ROLLINS
88 Director HSI CASA ... Ms. Gladis SANCHEZ
88 Int Director TRIO SSS ... Ms. Aselia MELO
124 Int Dir Stdnt Equity/ Engagement ... Mr. Oscar MENDOZA PLASCENCIA
88 Int Dir TRIO Upward Bound ... Ms. Trinity WILSON
88 Dir Employer Partnership ... Ms. Shinder GILL
06 Registrar/Admissions & Records ... Mr. Richard ANDREWS
89 Director First Year Experience ... Vacant

*Folsom Lake College (A)

10 College Parkway, Folsom CA 95630-6798
County: Sacramento FICE Identification: 038713
Unit ID: 444219
Telephone: (916) 608-6500 Carnegie Class: Assoc/HT-Mix Trad/Non
FAX Number: N/A Calendar System: Semester
URL: www.flc.losrios.edu
Established: 2004 Annual Undergrad Tuition & Fees (In-District): $1,288
Enrollment: 9,542 Coed
Affiliation or Control: State/Local IRS Status: 501(c)3
Highest Offering: Associate Degree
Accreditation: WJ, MLTAD

02 President ... Dr. Whitney YAMAMURA
11 Vice Pres Administration ... Augustine CHAVEZ
05 Vice President Instruction ... Dr. Monica PACTOL
32 Vice President Student Services ... Vacant
12 Int Dean of Instruction RCC ... Carlos LOPEZ
12 Int Dean of Instruction EDC ... Dr. Mari PESHON MCGARRY
81 Dean Instruction BLIT/MSE ... Greg MCCORMAC
57 Dean of Instruction VAPA/LALI ... Dr. Francis FLETCHER
68 Dean of Instruction KHAN ... Matthew WRIGHT
72 Dean of Instruction CTE ... Victoria MARYATT
09 Int Dean Planning & Research ... Brian ROBINSON
35 Int Dean of Student Success ... Dr. Molly SENECAL
18 Director of Administrative Services ... Melissa WILLIAMS
10 Business Services Supervisor ... Tatyana ZABEGALIN
26 Communications/Public Info Ofcr ... Kristy HART
30 Director Donor Relations ... Michele STEINER
37 Financial Aid Supervisor ... Ali PADASH
07 Admissions & Records Supervisor ... Christine WURZER
40 College Store Manager ... Rob MULLIGAN
04 Assistant to the President ... Lindsey CAMPBELL

*Sacramento City College (B)

3835 Freeport Boulevard, Sacramento CA 95822-1386
County: Sacramento FICE Identification: 001233
Unit ID: 122180
Telephone: (916) 558-2111 Carnegie Class: Assoc/MT-VT-High Trad
FAX Number: (916) 558-2449 Calendar System: Semester
URL: www.scc.losrios.edu
Established: 1916 Annual Undergrad Tuition & Fees (In-State): $1,288
Enrollment: 20,027 Coed
Affiliation or Control: State Related IRS Status: 501(c)3
Highest Offering: Associate Degree
Accreditation: WJ, ADNUR, DA, DH, OTA, PTAA

02 Interim President ... Dr. Albert GARCIA
05 Interim Vice Pres of Instruction ... Dr. Robin IKEGAMI
10 Interim Vice Pres Admin Services ... Ms. Stephanie SMITH
32 Vice Pres Student Services ... Dr. Davin BROWN
20 Associate Vice Pres Instruction ... Dr. Rick HODGE
20 Associate Vice Pres Instruction ... Dr. Deborah SAKS
13 Dean Information Technology ... Mr. Kirk SOSA
37 Dean Financial Aid/Student Svcs ... Dr. Miguel MOLINA
46 Dean Planning/Research/Development ... Dr. Gayle PITMAN
121 Dean Counseling/Student Success ... Dr. Andre COLEMAN
40 Director College Store ... Ms. Maria HYDE
66 Director Nursing ... Ms. Carel MOUNTAIN
18 Director College Operations ... Ms. Margaret LEDNICKY
30 Director of Donor Relations ... Vacant
26 Comm & Public Information Officer ... Ms. Kaitlyn COLLIGNON
76 Interim Dean Sci & Allied Health ... Dr. Rose GIORDANO
50 Interim Dean Business ... Dr. Sandra CAMARENA
79 Dean Humanities/Fine Arts ... Mrs. Patti LEONARD
79 Dean Languages/Literature ... Ms. Marci SELVA
72 Interim Dean Advanced Technology ... Mr. Gary HARTLEY
68 Dean PE/Health/Athletics ... Mr. Mitchell L. CAMPBELL
81 Dean Statistics/Math/Engineering ... Ms. Angelena LAMBERT
83 Dean Behavioral/Social Science ... Mr. Dennis LEE
56 Dean Davis Center ... Dr. Andrea GAYTAN
56 Dean West Sacramento Ctr ... Dr. Andrea GAYTAN
06 Records & Admissions Officer ... Ms. Kim GOFF
04 Administrative Asst to President ... Mrs. Hannia PARKER
88 Director HSI-SAGE ... Vacant

Loyola Marymount University (C)

1 LMU Drive, Los Angeles CA 90045-2659
County: Los Angeles FICE Identification: 011649
Unit ID: 117946
Telephone: (310) 338-2700 Carnegie Class: DU-Higher
FAX Number: N/A Calendar System: Semester
URL: www.lmu.edu
Established: 1911 Annual Undergrad Tuition & Fees: $52,977
Enrollment: 9,686 Coed
Affiliation or Control: Roman Catholic IRS Status: 501(c)3
Highest Offering: Doctorate
Accreditation: WC, ACATE, CAEP, CAEPN, DANCE, LAW, MUS, THEA, THEOL

01 President ... Dr. Timothy L. SNYDER
00 Chancellor ... Fr. Michael ENGH
05 Exec Vice President & Provost ... Dr. Thomas POON
42 VP for Mission & Ministry ... Dr. John SEBASTIAN
20 Vice Provost for Academic Affairs ... Dr. David A. SAPP
84 Vice Provost Enrollment Management ... Dr. Maureen WEATHERALL
85 Vice Prov Global-Local Initiatives ... Dr. Roberta ESPINOZA
10 Sr Vice Pres/Chief Financial Ofcr ... Ms. Aimee UEN
111 Sr VP University Advancement ... Mr. Peter WILCH
32 Int SVP for Student Affairs ... Dr. Terri L. MANGIONE
11 EVP & Chief Administrative Officer ... Ms. Lynne B. SCARBORO
13 VP for Information Technology Svcs ... Ms. Tamara ARMSTRONG
35 VP Student Affairs/Dean Students ... Dr. Terri L. MANGIONE
15 Vice President for Human Resources ... Ms. Rebecca CHANDLER
18 VP for Construction and Planning ... Vacant
11 Vice President of Campus Operations ... Mr. Michael WONG
26 SVP Marketing/Communications ... Mr. John KIRALLA
28 VP Intercultural Affairs ... Vacant
36 Assoc Provost Career & Professional ... Ms. Kat WEAVER
20 Assoc Provost Undergraduate Educ ... Fr. José BADENES
106 Asc Prov Rsrch/Prof Dev/Online Lrng ... Dr. Kathleen WEAVER
109 Sr Dir Auxiliary/Business Services ... Mr. Andrew O'REILLY
100 Special Asst to President/COS ... Dr. John M. PARRISH
08 Dean University Library ... Ms. Kristine BRANCOLINI
06 University Registrar ... Dr. Jennifer SILVERMAN
61 SVP/Dean Loyola Law School ... Mr. Michael WATERSTONE
49 Dean College Liberal Arts ... Dr. Robbin D. CRABTREE
53 Dean Sch of Education ... Dr. Michelle D. YOUNG
50 Dean College of Business Admin ... Dr. Dayle SMITH
57 Dean Communication & Fine Arts ... Dr. Bryant K. ALEXANDER
54 Dean College of Science & Engineer ... Dr. Tina CHOE
88 Dean School of Film/Television ... Ms. Joanne MOORE
30 Sr Dir Development/Gift Planning ... Vacant
07 Asst Vice Prov Undergrad Admissions ... Mr. Thomas A. GUTTO
37 Associate Director of Financial Aid ... Mr. William BROOKS
41 Athletics Director ... Mr. Craig PINTENS
27 Social Media Manager ... Ms. Shelbey GALLIHER
09 Sr Dir Inst Rsrch/Decision Support ... Ms. Christine CHAVEZ
108 Sr Dir Educ Effectiveness/Assessmnt ... Dr. Rebecca HONG
29 Executive Director of Alumni Rels ... Ms. Lisa FARLAND
23 Director of Student Health Services ... Ms. Katherine ARCE
104 Director Study Abroad ... Dr. Lisa LOBERG
25 Dir Research & Sponsored Projects ... Ms. Angela ROCHAT
90 Sr Dir of Educational Technology ... Ms. Crista COPP
04 Executive Asst to President ... Ms. Debbie CAVANAGH
04 Admin Specialist to Ofc of the Pres ... Ms. Rosa CALDERON
102 Exec Dir Corp/Foundation Relations ... Ms. Michelle PLASSE
19 Chief of Public Safety ... Mr. Robbie WILLIAMS
22 EEO Officer and Title IX Coord ... Ms. Sara TRIVEDI
39 Director Student Housing ... Mr. Steven NYGAARD
43 General Counsel ... Mr. Harold A. BRIDGES
04 Admin Specialist to Ofc of the Pres ... Mr. Leo BUENO
38 Dir Student Psychological Services ... Ms. Kristin LINDEN

Marshall B. Ketchum University (D)

2575 Yorba Linda Boulevard, Fullerton CA 92831-1615
County: Orange FICE Identification: 001230
Unit ID: 123943
Telephone: (714) 449-7451 Carnegie Class: Spec-4-yr-Other Health
FAX Number: N/A Calendar System: Quarter
URL: www.ketchum.edu
Established: 1904 Annual Graduate Tuition & Fees: N/A
Enrollment: 738 Coed
Affiliation or Control: Independent Non-Profit IRS Status: 501(c)3
Highest Offering: Doctorate; No Undergraduates
Accreditation: WC, ARCPA, OPT, OPTR, PHAR

01 President ... Dr. Kevin L. ALEXANDER
111 Vice Pres University Advancement ... Ms. Joan RUBIO
100 Sr Vice President & Chief of Staff ... Dr. Julie A. SCHORNACK
32 Vice President for Student Affairs ... Dr. Carmen N. BARNHARDT
15 Vice Pres Human Resources ... Ms. Gail S. DEUTSCH
10 Senior Vice Pres Admin & Finance ... Mr. Frank SCOTTI
05 VP Educ Effectiveness/Academic Affs ... Dr. Judy ORTIZ
18 Director of Campus Operations ... Mr. Gregory SMITH
51 Director of Continuing Education ... Ms. Bonnie DELLATORRE
13 Director of Information Technology ... Mr. Samuel YOUNG
08 Director of Library Services ... Mr. Scott JOHNSON
23 Director of Special Clinic Programs ... Ms. Michele WHITECAVAGE
26 Director Marketing/Communications ... Ms. Erin HALES
88 Dean of Optometry ... Dr. Jennifer COYLE
67 Dean of Pharmacy ... Dr. Edward FISHER
88 Director PA Program ... Ms. Allison MOLLET
108 Dir Institutional Effectiveness ... Dr. Ajoy KOOMER
04 Executive Asst to the President ... Ms. Carole JOLLY
23 Assoc Dean Clinics ... Dr. Mark E. NAKANO
24 Director of Multi-Media Services ... Mr. Matt BRENEMAN
00 Chairman of the Board of Trustees ... Mr. Rick S. PRICE, II
31 Director of Community Relations ... Mr. Wayne HEIDLE
109 Auxiliary Services Manager ... Ms. Debra WOODS
06 Associate Registrar ... Ms. Lisa CASSIDY
19 Director Campus Safety/Security ... Mr. Craig COOPER
38 Director Univ Student Counseling ... Ms. Alyse KIRSCHEN
30 Director of Development ... Ms. Ruby FOSTER
21 Controller ... Ms. Lori JACKLIN
114 Sr Dir Financial Reporting & Budget ... Ms. Kim ELLEN
85 Dir Registration/Intl Student Svcs ... Ms. Lauren KIM
37 Director of Financial Aid ... Mr. Nicholas NOVELLO
35 Director University Student Affairs ... Mr. Karlos SANTOS-COY
113 Director of Student Accounts ... Ms. Arlene VILLARUZ

The Master's University & Seminary (E)

21726 Placerita Canyon Road,
Santa Clarita CA 91321-1200
County: Los Angeles FICE Identification: 001220
Unit ID: 117751
Telephone: (661) 259-3540 Carnegie Class: DU-Mod
FAX Number: N/A Calendar System: Semester
URL: www.masters.edu
Established: 1927 Annual Undergrad Tuition & Fees: $28,740
Enrollment: 2,449 Coed
Affiliation or Control: Independent Non-Profit IRS Status: 501(c)3
Highest Offering: Doctorate
Accreditation: WC, MUS

01 President ... Dr. Abner CHOU
125 Chancellor Emeritus ... Dr. John MACARTHUR
03 Executive Vice President ... Dr. John STEAD
05 Provost/Dean Online Learning ... Dr. Mitch HOPEWELL
58 Executive Vice President Seminary ... Dr. Nathan BUSENITZ
10 CFO/VP of Administration ... Mr. Todd KOSTJUK
84 VP/Chief Enroll & Marketing Ofcr ... Mr. Dariu DUMITRU
13 VP/Chief Information Officer ... Mr. Paul SEDY
30 Vice President of Development ... Mr. Luke CHERRY
09 Director of Institutional Research ... Mr. John MILTON
26 Director of Communications ... Mr. Mason NESBITT
32 VP of Student Life/Campus Minister ... Rev. Harry WALLS
06 Registrar ... Ms. Patty TSAI
08 Director Library Services ... Mr. John STONE
41 Athletic Director ... Mr. Chris BECK
37 Director Financial Aid ... Mr. Kenneth PIESTER
29 Director Alumni Affairs ... Mr. AJ WORK
04 Executive Assistant ... Ms. Nicole CASTELHANO
15 Director of Human Resources ... Ms. Kim WILSON
19 Director Security/Safety ... Mr. Bryan KORTCAMP
50 Dean Business ... Mr. Dwight HAM
53 Dean Education ... Dr. Jordan MORTON
07 Director of Admissions ... Ms. Sarah DYER
18 Director of Plant Operations ... Mr. Ralph BAROSH
38 Director Academic Resource Center ... Ms. Kara ANTARIKSA

† The Master's Seminary is located at 13248 Roscoe Boulevard, Sun Valley, CA 91352.

Mendocino College (F)

1000 Hensley Creek Road, Ukiah CA 95482-7821
County: Mendocino FICE Identification: 011672
Unit ID: 118684
Telephone: (707) 468-3000 Carnegie Class: Assoc/HT-High Non
FAX Number: (707) 468-3120 Calendar System: Semester
URL: www.mendocino.edu
Established: 1973 Annual Undergrad Tuition & Fees (In-District): $1,426
Enrollment: 3,338 Coed
Affiliation or Control: State/Local IRS Status: 501(c)3
Highest Offering: Associate Degree
Accreditation: WJ, PTAA

01 Superintendent/President ... Mr. Timothy KARAS
11 Vice Pres Admin Services ... Ms. Eileen CICHOCKI
05 Vice Pres Academic Affairs ... Ms. Debra POLAK
32 Vice Pres Student Services ... Mr. Ulises VELASCO
08 Head Librarian ... Mr. Robert PARMENTER
20 Dean of Instruction ... Ms. Rebecca MONTES
75 Dean Applied Academics ... Vacant
38 Dean of Counseling/Student Programs ... Mr. Antonio LOPEZ
10 Director Fiscal Services ... Mr. Joe ATHERTON
15 Director Human Resources ... Ms. Nicole MARIN
18 Director of Facilities ... Mr. MacAdam LOJOWSKY
26 Director Communications & Cmty Rels ... Vacant
41 Director of Athletics ... Mr. Matthew GORDON

13 Director Information Technology ... Mr. David JOHNSTON
09 Director of Institutional Research ... Ms. Minerva FLORES
07 Director Admissions/Registrar ... Ms. Anastasia SIMPSON-LOGG
37 Director of Financial Aid ... Ms. Yuliana SANDOVAL
04 Administrative Asst to President ... Ms. Mary LAMB
12 Director of Lake Center ... Ms. Monica FLORES
102 Exec Dir Mendocino Col Foundation ... Ms. Julie MCGOVERN
88 MESA/Stem Success Director ... Mr. Eric HOEFLER
12 Dean of Centers ... Dr. Amanda XU

Menlo College (A)

1000 El Camino Real, Atherton CA 94027-4301
County: San Mateo | FICE Identification: 001236
Unit ID: 118693
Telephone: (800) 556-3656 | Carnegie Class: Spec-4-yr-Bus
FAX Number: (650) 543-4085 | Calendar System: Semester
URL: www.menlo.edu
Established: 1927 | Annual Undergrad Tuition & Fees: $45,860
Enrollment: 826 | Coed
Affiliation or Control: Independent Non-Profit | IRS Status: 501(c)3
Highest Offering: Baccalaureate
Accreditation: WC

00 Board Chair ... Mr. Micah KANE
01 President ... Mr. Steven A. WEINER
05 Provost ... Vacant
84 VP Enrollment & Athletics ... Mr. Keith SPATARO
121 VP Student Success ... Dr. Angela SCHMIEDE
50 Dean for Business ... Dr. Mouwafac SIDAOUI
49 Dean for Arts & Sciences ... Dr. Melissa MICHELSON
21 Dir Finance & Business Affairs ... Ms. Rita YON
13 Director Information Technology ... Mr. Minh HUYNH
84 Dean of Enrollment Mgmt ... Ms. Priscila DESOUZA
08 Dean Library Services ... Ms. Emily STAMBAUGH
32 Dean of Student Affairs ... Mr. Devin CARR
09 Director IR & Assessment ... Dr. Kristina POWERS
29 Sr Dir Alumni Engagement & Dev ... Dr. Laura KOO
15 Assoc Director of Human Resources ... Ms. Cindy MCGREW
18 Director Facilities & Operations ... Mr. Robert TALBOTT
88 Director Internship Program ... Vacant
06 Registrar ... Ms. Cristine RABAGO
19 Director Security/Safety ... Mr. Taylor HENKEL
38 Director Student Counseling ... Vacant
39 Dir Resident Life/Student Housing ... Mr. Taylor HENKEL
04 Admin Assistant to the President ... Ms. Kaiya ORQUE

Merced College (B)

3600 M Street, Merced CA 95348-2898
County: Merced | FICE Identification: 001237
Unit ID: 118718
Telephone: (209) 384-6000 | Carnegie Class: Assoc/HT-High Trad
FAX Number: (209) 384-6043 | Calendar System: Semester
URL: www.mccd.edu
Established: 1962 | Annual Undergrad Tuition & Fees (In-District): $1,180
Enrollment: 10,645 | Coed
Affiliation or Control: State/Local | IRS Status: 501(c)3
Highest Offering: Associate Degree
Accreditation: WJ, DMS, RAD

01 President ... Mr. Chris VITELLI
04 Executive Assistant to President ... Ms. Krystal POLLINGER
05 VP of Instruction ... Ms. Karissa MOREHOUSE
32 VP of Student Services ... Mr. Michael MCCANDLESS
10 VP Administrative Services ... Mr. Joseph ALLISON
13 AVP of ITS ... Mr. Arlis BORTNER
12 Dean Los Banos Campus ... Ms. Jessina MORAN
111 AVP of External Relations ... Ms. Jill CUNNINGHAM
45 Dean Institutional Effectiveness ... Ms. Dee SIGISMOND
15 AVP of Human Resources ... Ms. Kelly AVILA
81 Dean Science/Math/Engineering ... Dr. Douglas KAIN
79 Acting Dean English & Humanities ... Mr. Travis HICKS
75 Dean Career Technical Education ... Vacant
50 Acting Dean Business/Workforce Dev ... Dr. Caroline DAWSON
83 Dean Social Sci/Fine & Perf Arts ... Mr. John ALBANO
22 Acting Dean Student Equity/Success ... Mr. Joe SERENA
26 Chief Public Relations Officer ... Ms. Jill CUNNINGHAM
06 Registrar & Dir Financial Aid ... Mrs. Traci VEYL
07 Acting Dir Admissions & Records ... Ms. Jeanette MARTIN
41 Athletic Director ... Mr. Steve CASSADY
96 Director of Purchasing ... Mr. Charles HERGENRAEDER

Meridian University (C)

47 Sixth Street, Petaluma CA 94952
County: Sonoma | Identification: 667300
Unit ID: 491808
Telephone: (707) 765-1836 | Carnegie Class: Spec-4-yr-Other Health
FAX Number: (707) 765-2351 | Calendar System: Other
URL: www.meridianuniversity.edu
Established: 1993 | Annual Graduate Tuition & Fees: N/A
Enrollment: N/A | Coed
Affiliation or Control: Proprietary | IRS Status: Proprietary
Highest Offering: Doctorate; No Undergraduates
Accreditation: WC

00 Chancellor ... Dr. Jean HOUSTON
01 CEO ... Dr. Aftab OMER
05 Vice President Academic Affairs ... Dr. Melissa SCHWARTZ
10 Dir Administration/CFO ... Mr. Rob GALL

Merit University (D)

3699 Wilshire Blvd., Ste 970, Los Angeles CA 90010
County: Los Angeles | Identification: 667293
Telephone: (213) 325-2760 | Carnegie Class: Not Classified
FAX Number: N/A | Calendar System: Quarter
URL: www.meritu.edu
Established: 2014 | Annual Graduate Tuition & Fees: N/A
Enrollment: N/A | Coed
Affiliation or Control: Proprietary | IRS Status: Proprietary
Highest Offering: Master's; No Undergraduates
Accreditation: ACICS

01 President ... Dr. Jae KIM
05 Dean of Academic Affairs ... Dr. Min KIM

Middlebury Institute of International Studies at Monterey (E)

460 Pierce Street, Monterey CA 93940-2691
Telephone: (831) 647-4100 | FICE Identification: 001241
Accreditation: &EH, CEA

† Regional accrediation is carried under parent institution Middlebury College, VT.

Minerva University (F)

14 Mint Plaza, Ste 300, San Francisco CA 94103
County: San Francisco | Identification: 667427
Unit ID: 484844
Telephone: (415) 649-7658 | Carnegie Class: Not Classified
FAX Number: N/A | Calendar System: Semester
URL: www.minerva.edu
Established: 2013 | Annual Undergrad Tuition & Fees: N/A
Enrollment: N/A | Coed
Affiliation or Control: Independent Non-Profit | IRS Status: 501(c)3
Highest Offering: Master's
Accreditation: WC

00 Founder & Chancellor ... Mr. Ben NELSON
01 President ... Mr. Mike MAGEE
05 Provost ... Dr. Vicki CHANDLER

MiraCosta College (G)

One Barnard Drive, Oceanside CA 92056-3899
County: San Diego | FICE Identification: 001239
Unit ID: 118912
Telephone: (760) 757-2121 | Carnegie Class: Bac/Assoc-Assoc Dom
FAX Number: (760) 795-6609 | Calendar System: Semester
URL: www.miracosta.edu
Established: 1934 | Annual Undergrad Tuition & Fees (In-District): $1,152
Enrollment: 12,645 | Coed
Affiliation or Control: State/Local | IRS Status: 501(c)3
Highest Offering: Baccalaureate
Accreditation: WJ

01 Superintendent/President ... Dr. Sunita COOKE
101 Exec Asst to Pres/Sec to BOT ... Ms. Julie BOLLERUD
04 Exec Assistant to Supt/President ... Ms. Jeanne KOSCHWANEZ
05 Asst Super/VP Instructional Svcs ... Ms. Denee PESCARMONA
32 Vice President Student Svcs ... Dr. Alketa WOJCIK
11 Vice President Administrative Svcs ... Mr. Tim FLOOD
15 Vice President Human Resources ... Mr. Charles NG
79 Dean Letters/Humanities/Comm ... Mr. Antonio ALARCON
08 AVP Library/Academic Info Svcs ... Dr. Anthony MACIEL
38 Dean Counseling/Student Devel ... Dr. Wendy STEWART
07 Dean Admissions/Student Support ... Mr. Freddy RAMIREZ
51 Dean Continuing/Community Education ... Dr. John MAKEVICH
49 Dean Arts/Intl Languages ... Mr. Jonathan FOHRMAN
81 Dean Math/Sciences ... Mr. Mike FINO
75 Dean Career/Technical Education ... Dr. Al TACCONE
10 Director Fiscal Services ... Ms. Katie WHITE
88 Director Small Business Dev Ctr ... Mr. Sudershan SHAUNAK
103 Dir Community Educ/Workforce Dev ... Ms. Linda KUROKAWA
06 Registrar ... Ms. Kathy RODRIGUEZ
09 Dean Research/Plng/Inst Effective ... Dr. Chris TAMAN
26 Dir Public Rels/Marketing/Comm ... Dr. Kristen HUYCK
111 VP Institutional Advancement ... Ms. Shannon STUBBLEFIELD
18 Director Facilities ... Mr. Tom MACIAS
37 Director Financial Aid ... Mr. Michael DEAR
117 District Risk & Safety Manager ... Mr. Justin CRAST
113 Bursar ... Ms. Kristin HITCHCOCK
16 Director Human Resources ... Vacant
36 Director Career Center ... Ms. Donna DAVIS
88 Faculty Director/Counselor ... Ms. Lise FLOCKEN
96 Director Purchasing/Material Mgmt ... Ms. Mina HERNANDEZ
124 Director Retention Services ... Dr. Edward POEHLERT
19 Chief of Police ... Ms. Val WARNER-SAADAT
106 Director Online Education ... Dr. James JULIUS
22 Dir Affirmative Action/Equal Opp ... Ms. Hayley SCHWARTZKOPF

Monterey Peninsula College (H)

980 Fremont Street, Monterey CA 93940-4799
County: Monterey | FICE Identification: 001242
Unit ID: 119067
Telephone: (831) 646-4000 | Carnegie Class: Assoc/HT-Mix Trad/Non
FAX Number: (831) 655-2627 | Calendar System: Semester
URL: www.mpc.edu
Established: 1947 | Annual Undergrad Tuition & Fees (In-District): $1,178
Enrollment: 7,154 | Coed
Affiliation or Control: State/Local | IRS Status: 501(c)3
Highest Offering: Associate Degree
Accreditation: WJ, ADNUR, EMT

01 Int Superintendent/President ... Mr. Mark ZACOVIC
05 VP of Academic Affairs ... Dr. Jon KNOLLE
11 VP Administrative Services ... Mr. Steve HAIGLER
32 VP of Student Services ... Mr. Laurence WALKER
20 Dean of Instruction ... Dr. Vincent VAN JOOLEN
20 Dean of Instruction ... Ms. Diane BOYNTON
20 Dean of Instruction ... Ms. Judith CUTTING
35 Interim Dean of Student Services ... Dr. LaKisha BRADLEY
45 Dean of PRIE ... Vacant
10 Controller ... Vacant
15 Chief Human Resources Office ... Mr. David BETTS
09 Director of Institutional Research ... Dr. Rosaleen RYAN
07 Director of Admissions & Records ... Ms. Nicole DUNNE
08 Director of Library ... Mr. Jeffery SUNDQUIST
37 Student Financial Services Director ... Vacant
41 Athletic Director/Dean of SS ... Ms. Wendy BATES
18 Facilities Operations Supervisor ... Mr. Pete OLSEN
96 Purchasing Agent ... Mr. Kevin HASKIN
19 Director of Security ... Vacant
04 Admin Assistant to the President ... Ms. Shawn ANDERSON
101 Secretary of the Institution/Board ... Ms. JoRene FINNELL
102 VP Advancement/MPC Foundation ... Ms. Rebecca MICHAEL
13 Director Information Systems ... Mr. Michael MIDKIFF
26 Dir Marketing & Communications ... Ms. Kristin DARKEN
22 Director Affirm Action/Equal Opp ... Mrs. Kayla VALENTINE

Mount Madonna Institute (I)

445 Summit Road, Watsonville CA 95076
County: Santa Cruz | Identification: 667380
Telephone: (408) 847-4060 | Carnegie Class: Not Classified
FAX Number: N/A | Calendar System: Semester
URL: www.mountmadonnainstitute.org
Established: 2006 | Annual Undergrad Tuition & Fees: N/A
Enrollment: N/A | Coed
Affiliation or Control: Independent Non-Profit | IRS Status: 501(c)3
Highest Offering: Master's
Accreditation: WC

01 Interim President ... Dr. Swarup WOOD
05 Interim Chief Academic Officer ... Kamalesh G. HOOVEN
10 Chief Financial Officer ... Shanti CRUDDAS

Mount Saint Mary's University (J)

12001 Chalon Road, Los Angeles CA 90049-1599
County: Los Angeles | FICE Identification: 001243
Unit ID: 119173
Telephone: (310) 954-4000 | Carnegie Class: Masters/L
FAX Number: (310) 954-4379 | Calendar System: Semester
URL: www.msmu.edu
Established: 1925 | Annual Undergrad Tuition & Fees: $44,474
Enrollment: 2,745 | Female
Affiliation or Control: Roman Catholic | IRS Status: 501(c)3
Highest Offering: Doctorate
Accreditation: WC, ACBSP, NURSE, PTA

01 President ... Dr. Ann MCELANEY-JOHNSON
05 Provost ... Dr. Robert J. PERRINS
111 Vice Pres Institutional Advancement ... Dr. Stephanie CUBBA
10 Vice Pres Administration & Finance ... Ms. Debra MARTIN
13 VP Strategic Initiatives ... Vacant
32 Vice President Student Affairs ... Dr. Linda MCMURDOCK
84 VP Enrollment Management ... Ms. Susan DILENO
20 Associate Provost & ALO ... Vacant
09 Dir Inst Planning/Research ... Ms. Maria NARVAEZ
55 Dean of Weekend College ... Ms. Suzanne WILLIAMS
88 Asst VP Enrollment Management ... Mr. Dean KILGOUR
06 Registrar ... Ms. Rocio DELEON
26 Director Communications/Marketing ... Ms. Debbie REAM
15 Chief Human Resources Officer ... Mr. Adam KAPLAN
18 Director of Facilities Mgmt ... Mr. Edwin TORRES
37 Director of Student Financing ... Ms. La Royce HOUSLEY
08 Director of MSMU Libraries ... Ms. Danielle SALOMON
28 VP Equity/Diversity and Justice ... Dr. Krishauna HINES-GAITHER
29 Director Alumni Relations ... Vacant
38 Director Student Counseling ... Dr. Susan SALEM
07 Director of Admissions ... Ms. Erika YAMASAKI
36 Director Career Services ... Vacant
04 Administrative Asst to President ... Ms. Lucille VILLEGAS
19 Director Security/Safety ... Vacant
35 Dean of Student Life ... Vacant
44 Gift Planning Officer ... Ms. Maria SOLANO
104 Study Away Coordinator ... Vacant
105 Web Manager ... Vacant
106 Int Dir Online Education/E-learning ... Mr. Chris TSANG
39 Director of Residence Life ... Ms. Michelle SALDANA
102 Director of Institutional Giving ... Ms. Megan UEBELACKER
30 Director of Development ... Mr. Kevin A. BARRY
41 Athletic Director ... Vacant
50 Dept Chair Business Administration ... Dr. Michelle FRENCH-HOLLOWAY
53 Dept Chair Education ... Dr. Carol JOHNSTON

Mt. San Antonio College (K)

1100 N Grand, Walnut CA 91789-1399
County: Los Angeles | FICE Identification: 001245
Unit ID: 119164
Telephone: (909) 274-7500 | Carnegie Class: Assoc/MT-VT-High Trad

FAX Number: N/A　　　　　　　　Calendar System: Semester
URL: www.mtsac.edu
Established: 1946　　Annual Undergrad Tuition & Fees (In-District): $1,350
Enrollment: 28,393　　　　　　　　　　　　　　　　Coed
Affiliation or Control: State/Local　　　　　　IRS Status: 501(c)3
Highest Offering: Associate Degree
Accreditation: **WJ**, COARC, EMT, HT, RAD

01	President/CEO	Dr. William T. SCROGGINS
05	Vice President Instruction	Ms. Kelly FOWLER
10	Vice President Administrative Svcs	Mr. Morris J. RODRIGUE
32	Vice President Student Services	Dr. Audrey YAMAGATA-NOJI
15	Vice President Human Resources	Ms. Sokha SONG
20	AVP Instruction	Dr. Meghan CHEN
88	Dean Instruction	Ms. Sylvia RUANO
08	Dean Library/Learning Resources	Dr. Romelia SALINAS
35	Assoc VP Student Services	Mr. Tom MAUCH
51	Provost School of Continuing Educ	Dr. Madelyn ARBALLO
13	Chief Technology Officer/Info Tech	Mr. Anthony MOORE
84	Dean Enrollment Management	Dr. George BRADSHAW
21	AVP Administrative Services	Vacant
102	Executive Director of Foundation	Mr. Bill LAMBERT
37	Director Financial Aid	Ms. Jenny PHU
117	Director Risk Management	Ms. Duetta LANGEVIN
46	Director Grants	Ms. Adrienne PRICE
26	Director Marketing/Communications	Ms. Uyen MAI
09	Dir Research/Inst Effectiveness	Ms. Patricia QUINONES
18	Exec Dir Facilities/Planning/Mgt	Mr. Gary NELLESEN
35	Director Student Life	Ms. Andrea SIMS
96	Director Purchasing/Printing/Mail	Ms. Angelic DAVIS
50	Dean Business	Ms. Jennifer GALBRAITH
68	Dean Kinesiology/Athletics/Dance	Mr. Joe JENNUM
79	Dean Humanities/Social Sciences	Dr. Karelyn HOOVER
72	Dean Tech/Health Science	Mr. Sam AGDASI
65	Dean Natural Sciences	Dr. Denise BAILEY
57	Dean Arts	Vacant
51	Dean School of Cont Education	Ms. Tammi PEARSON
04	Exec Asst to President & BOT	Ms. Carol NELSON
38	Dean of Counseling	Mr. Francisco DORAME

Mt. San Jacinto College　　　　　　(A)

1499 N State Street, San Jacinto CA 92583-2399
County: Riverside　　　　　　　　FICE Identification: 001246
　　　　　　　　　　　　　　　　　　Unit ID: 119216
Telephone: (951) 487-6752　　Carnegie Class: Assoc/MT-VT-High Trad
FAX Number: (951) 654-9712　　　Calendar System: Semester
URL: www.msjc.edu
Established: 1962　　Annual Undergrad Tuition & Fees (In-District): $1,406
Enrollment: 13,988　　　　　　　　　　　　　　　　Coed
Affiliation or Control: State/Local　　　　　　IRS Status: 501(c)3
Highest Offering: Associate Degree
Accreditation: **WJ**, DMS

01	Superintendent/President	Dr. Roger W. SCHULTZ
04	Executive Assistant to President	Ms. Kristen GRIMES
05	VP of Instruction	Dr. Jeremy BROWN
32	Interim VP of Student Svcs	Ms. Rebecca TEAGUE
10	VP of Business Svcs	Ms. Beth GOMEZ
15	VP of Human Resources	Ms. Jeannine STOKES
84	VP of Inst Effect/Enrollmnt Mgmt	Mr. Brandon MOORE
20	Provost of Instruction	Ms. Joyce JOHNSON
79	Dean of Academic Programs MVC	Ms. Rickianne RYCRAFT
97	Dean of Academic Programs SJC	Dr. Alma RAMIREZ
72	Dean of Instruction Comp/Tech	Mr. Micah ORLOFF
103	Dean Career Education MVC	Dr. Marilyn HARVEY
103	Dean Career Education SJC	Mr. Von LAWSON
81	Dean of Academic Programs MVC	Mr. Marc DONNHAUSER
21	Int Dean of Admin Svcs/Controller	Ms. Gail JENSEN
13	Dean of Information Technology	Mr. Brian ORLAUSKI
18	Dean of Facilities Plng/Cap Constr	Mr. Todd FRANCO
35	Interim Dean of Student Svcs	Ms. Barbara FOUNTAIN
41	Dean of Phys Ed & Athletics	Mr. Patrick SPRINGER
45	Exec Dean Institutional Planning	Ms. Rebecca TEAGUE
108	Dean Institutional Effectiveness	Dr. Carlos TOVARES
26	Public Information Officer	Ms. Karin MARRIOTT
37	Dean of Student Svcs	Ms. Dolores SMITH
66	Assoc Dean of Nursing/Allied Hlth	Ms. Hope FARQUHARSON
121	Assoc Dean of Instructional Svcs	Ms. Cheri NAISH
18	Dir Maintenance & Operations MVC	Mr. Brian TWITTY
09	Assoc Dean of Inst Research	Mr. Nikilos (Nik) MESARIS
07	Int Director of Enrollment Svcs	Ms. Elizabeth MASCARO
19	Director of Campus Safety	Mr. David PASEMAN
96	Dir of Procurement & General Svcs	Ms. Tamara CUNNINGHAM

Mount Tamalpais College　　　　　(B)

PO Box 492, San Quentin CA 94964
County: Marin　　　　　　　　　　Identification: 667400
Telephone: (415) 455-8088　　　Carnegie Class: Not Classified
FAX Number: N/A　　　　　　　　Calendar System: Semester
URL: www.mttamcollege.org
Established: 1996　　　　Annual Undergrad Tuition & Fees: N/A
Enrollment: N/A　　　　　　　　　　　　　　　　　Male
Affiliation or Control: Independent Non-Profit　　IRS Status: 501(c)3
Highest Offering: Associate Degree
Accreditation: **WJ**

01	President	Jody LEWEN
05	Chief Academic Officer	Amy JAMGOCHIAN
32	Director of Student Affairs	Vacant

MTI College　　　　　　　　　　(C)

5221 Madison Avenue, Sacramento CA 95841-3037
County: Sacramento　　　　　　　FICE Identification: 012912
　　　　　　　　　　　　　　　　　　Unit ID: 118198
Telephone: (916) 339-1500　　Carnegie Class: Assoc/HVT-Mix Trad/Non
FAX Number: (916) 339-0305　　　Calendar System: Quarter
URL: mticollege.edu
Established: 1965　　　　Annual Undergrad Tuition & Fees: N/A
Enrollment: 495　　　　　　　　　　　　　　　　　Coed
Affiliation or Control: Proprietary　　　　　　IRS Status: Proprietary
Highest Offering: Associate Degree
Accreditation: **WJ**

01	President	Mr. Michael A. ZIMMERMAN
10	Vice Pres/Chief Financial Officer	Mr. David W. ALLEN
11	Campus Director	Mr. Lawrence RICHMAN

Musicians Institute　　　　　　　(D)

6752 Hollywood Boulevard, Hollywood CA 90028
County: Los Angeles　　　　　　　FICE Identification: 021618
　　　　　　　　　　　　　　　　　　Unit ID: 119270
Telephone: (323) 462-1384　　Carnegie Class: Spec-4-yr-Arts
FAX Number: (323) 462-1575　　　Calendar System: Quarter
URL: www.mi.edu
Established: 1977　　Annual Undergrad Tuition & Fees: $24,795
Enrollment: 714　　　　　　　　　　　　　　　　　Coed
Affiliation or Control: Proprietary　　　　　　IRS Status: Proprietary
Highest Offering: Master's
Accreditation: **MUS**

01	President/CEO	Mr. Todd BERHORST
05	Chief Academic Officer	Dr. Rachel YOON
10	Chief Financial/Business Officer	Mr. Kengo KIDO
108	Director of Compliance	Vacant
06	Registrar Supervisor	Mr. Shaun VIETEN
13	Director of Information Technology	Mr. Tim METZ
37	Director Student Financial Aid	Ms. Melissa CUESTA BOOKER
07	Sr Director of Admissions	Mr. Jose HERNANDEZ

Napa Valley College　　　　　　　(E)

2277 Napa-Vallejo Highway, Napa CA 94558-6236
County: Napa　　　　　　　　　　FICE Identification: 001247
　　　　　　　　　　　　　　　　　　Unit ID: 119331
Telephone: (707) 256-7000　　Carnegie Class: Assoc/HT-High Trad
FAX Number: (707) 253-3015　　　Calendar System: Semester
URL: www.napavalley.edu
Established: 1942　　Annual Undergrad Tuition & Fees (In-District): $1,150
Enrollment: 4,931　　　　　　　　　　　　　　　　Coed
Affiliation or Control: State/Local　　　　　　IRS Status: 501(c)3
Highest Offering: Associate Degree
Accreditation: **WJ**, COARC, EMT

01	Acting Superintendent/President	Mr. Oscar DE HARO
05	Vice President Academic Affairs	Dr. Sara PARKER
10	Vice Pres Business/Finance	Mr. Douglas ROBERTS
32	Vice Pres Student Affs/Asst Supt	Mr. Oscar DEHARO
38	Dean Counseling Svcs/Stdnt Success	Mr. Howard WILLIS
20	Dean of Instruction	Ms. Maria VILLAGOMEZ
37	Dean Fin Aid/EOPS/Pre-Col TRIO Pgms	Ms. Patricia MORGAN
103	Dean Career Tech Educ/Workforce Dev	Ms. Miraglia GREGORY
13	Vice Pres Institutional Technology	Vacant
09	Dean Research Plng/Instl Effect	Dr. Robyn WORNALL
36	Dean Counselor/WA III	Mr. Howard WILLLIS
04	Exec Asst to the President	Ms. Kathy WRIGHT
07	Admissions/Records Officer	Ms. Margarita CEJA
15	AVP Human Resources	Ms. Charo ALBARRAN
26	Dir Public Affs/Communications/ PIO	Ms. Holly KRASSNER DAWSON
18	Director Facilities	Mr. Matt CHRISTENSEN
19	Director College Police	Mr. Kenneth L. ARNOLD
84	Dean Enrollment/Outreach Svcs	Ms. Jessica ERICKSON
88	Coordinator Trans Center	Ms. Marci SANCHEZ
28	Dir Diversity/Equity/Inclusivity	Mr. Craig ALIMO
111	Director Inst Advancement	Ms. Carollee CATTOLICA
96	Business Services Asst/Purchasing	Ms. Solange KADA
23	Director Student Health Services	Ms. Nancy TAMARISK

National Career College　　　　　(F)

14355 Roscoe Boulevard, Panorama City CA 91402
County: Los Angeles　　　　　　　FICE Identification: 041460
　　　　　　　　　　　　　　　　　　Unit ID: 455868
Telephone: (818) 988-2300　　Carnegie Class: Assoc/HVT-Mix Trad/Non
FAX Number: (818) 988-9944　　　Calendar System: Semester
URL: www.nccusa.edu
Established: 2005　　　　Annual Undergrad Tuition & Fees: N/A
Enrollment: 293　　　　　　　　　　　　　　　　　Coed
Affiliation or Control: Proprietary　　　　　　IRS Status: Proprietary
Highest Offering: Associate Degree
Accreditation: **ABHES**

01	Campus President	Dr. Wazkein BARBERIAN
11	Chief Operating Officer	Sam KSACHIKIAN
10	Director Finance/Compliance	Anna TOVMASYAN

National Polytechnic College　　　(G)

4105 South Street, Lakewood CA 90712
County: Los Angeles　　　　　　　FICE Identification: 039104
　　　　　　　　　　　　　　　　　　Unit ID: 447759

Telephone: (888) 243-2493　　Carnegie Class: Spec 2-yr-Health
FAX Number: (888) 640-7732　　　Calendar System: Semester
URL: www.npcollege.edu
Established: 1996　　　　Annual Undergrad Tuition & Fees: N/A
Enrollment: 185　　　　　　　　　　　　　　　　　Coed
Affiliation or Control: Proprietary　　　　　　IRS Status: Proprietary
Highest Offering: Associate Degree
Accreditation: **ACCSC**

01	CEO and President	Dariush (David) MADDAHI

National Test Pilot School　　　　(H)

PO Box 658, Mojave CA 93502-0658
County: Kern　　　　　　　　　　Identification: 667009
Telephone: (661) 824-2977　　　Carnegie Class: Not Classified
FAX Number: (661) 824-2943　　　Calendar System: Semester
URL: www.ntps.edu
Established: 1981　　　Annual Graduate Tuition & Fees: N/A
Enrollment: N/A　　　　　　　　　　　　　　　　　Coed
Affiliation or Control: Independent Non-Profit　　IRS Status: 501(c)3
Highest Offering: Master's; No Undergraduates
Accreditation: **WC**

01	President	Mr. James E. BROWN, III
05	Chief Academic Officer	Mr. Ilan ARUSH
11	COO/Head of Training	Mr. Luca CAMPELLO
54	Director NFTI	Vacant
13	Chief of Systems Academics	Mr. Bruce WILDER
88	Chief of FW P&FQ Academics	Mr. Jason PAQUIN
88	Chief FW Test Pilot Instructor	Mr. Adam FRANCKI
88	Chief RW Test Pilot Instructor	Ms. Andrea PINGITORE
06	Registrar/Student Services Rep	Ms. Diane MELO
04	Admin Assistant to the President	Ms. Tammy FISHER

National University　　　　　　　(I)

9388 Lightwave Avenue, San Diego CA 92123
County: San Diego　　　　　　　FICE Identification: 011460
　　　　　　　　　　　　　　　　　　Unit ID: 119605
Telephone: (858) 642-8000　　Carnegie Class: Masters/L
FAX Number: (858) 642-8714　　　Calendar System: Other
URL: www.nu.edu
Established: 1971　　Annual Undergrad Tuition & Fees: $13,320
Enrollment: 18,070　　　　　　　　　　　　　　　Coed
Affiliation or Control: Independent Non-Profit　　IRS Status: 501(c)3
Highest Offering: Doctorate
Accreditation: **WC**, AAQEP, ANEST, CAEPN, IACBE, NURSE, PH, RTT

00	Chancellor	Dr. Michael R. CUNNINGHAM
01	University President	Dr. Mark D. MILLIRON
05	EVP/Provost	Vacant

New York Film Academy, Los Angeles　(J)

3300 Riverside Drive, Burbank CA 91505
County: Burbank　　　　　　　　FICE Identification: 041188
　　　　　　　　　　　　　　　　　　Unit ID: 461148
Telephone: (818) 333-3558　　Carnegie Class: Spec-4-yr-Arts
FAX Number: (818) 333-3557　　　Calendar System: Semester
URL: www.nyfa.edu
Established: 2006　　Annual Undergrad Tuition & Fees: $33,834
Enrollment: 1,271　　　　　　　　　　　　　　　　Coed
Affiliation or Control: Proprietary　　　　　　IRS Status: Proprietary
Highest Offering: Master's
Accreditation: **WC**

01	Dean of the College	Mr. Dan MACKLER
03	Executive Vice President	Mr. David KLEIN
05	Dean of Faculty	Mr. Nunzio DEFILIPPIS
32	Dean of Students	Dr. Susan ASHE
10	Chief Financial Officer	Mr. Kirk LENGA
06	Registrar	Mr. Vince VOSKANIAN
07	Director of Admissions	Vacant
08	Head Librarian	Mr. Josh MOORMON
39	Housing Coordinator	Ms. Sarah MARPLES

NewSchool of Architecture and Design　(K)

1249 F Street, San Diego CA 92101-6634
County: San Diego　　　　　　　FICE Identification: 030439
　　　　　　　　　　　　　　　　　　Unit ID: 119775
Telephone: (619) 684-8800　　Carnegie Class: Masters/S
FAX Number: (619) 684-8880　　　Calendar System: Quarter
URL: www.newschoolarch.edu
Established: 1980　　Annual Undergrad Tuition & Fees: $29,427
Enrollment: 455　　　　　　　　　　　　　　　　　Coed
Affiliation or Control: Proprietary　　　　　　IRS Status: Proprietary
Highest Offering: Master's
Accreditation: **WC**

01	President	Dr. Gisela LOEHLEIN
05	Chief Academic Officer	Dr. Gisela LOEHLEIN
32	Dean Division of Student Affairs	Vacant
48	Dean School of Design	Dr. Elena PACENTI
88	Head of Architecture	Ms. Daniela DEUTSCH
89	Head of Construction Management	Mr. Stephen MATLEY
90	Head of Integrative Studies	Mr. Bruce MATTHES
06	Registrar	Allen MUTCHLER

Nobel University (A)

505 Shatto Place #300, Los Angeles CA 90020

County: Los Angeles	Identification: 667274
Telephone: (213) 382-1136	Carnegie Class: Not Classified
FAX Number: (213) 382-1187	Calendar System: Semester
URL: nobeluniversity.edu	
Established: 2000	Annual Undergrad Tuition & Fees: N/A
Enrollment: N/A	Coed
Affiliation or Control: Proprietary	IRS Status: Proprietary
Highest Offering: Master's	
Accreditation: ACICS	

01	President	Chong S. KIM
05	Chief Academic Officer/Provost	Michael KAHLER

*North Orange County Community College District (B)

1830 W Romneya Drive, Anaheim CA 92801-1819

County: Orange	FICE Identification: 009742
	Unit ID: 120023
Telephone: (714) 808-4500	Carnegie Class: N/A
FAX Number: (714) 808-4791	
URL: www.nocccd.edu	

01	Chancellor	Dr. Byron D. CLIFT BRELAND
10	Vice Chanc Finance/Facilities	Mr. Fred WILLIAMS
15	Vice Chancellor Human Resources	Ms. Irma RAMOS
05	Vice Chanc Educational Svcs/Tech	Dr. Cherry LI-BUGG
26	Director Public/Government Affairs	Ms. Kai STEARNS MOORE
04	Exec Admin Aide to Chancellor	Ms. Alba RECINOS
22	Dist Director Diversity/Compliance	Vacant

*Cypress College (C)

9200 Valley View, Cypress CA 90630-5897

County: Orange	FICE Identification: 001193
	Unit ID: 113236
Telephone: (714) 484-7000	Carnegie Class: Bac/Assoc-Assoc Dom
FAX Number: (714) 527-8238	Calendar System: Semester
URL: www.cypresscollege.edu	
Established: 1966	Annual Undergrad Tuition & Fees (In-District): $1,146
Enrollment: 15,325	Coed
Affiliation or Control: State/Local	IRS Status: 501(c)3
Highest Offering: Baccalaureate	
Accreditation: WJ, ADNUR, CAHIIM, DA, DH, DMS, FUSER, RAD	

02	President	Dr. JoAnna SCHILLING
05	Int Vice Pres Instruction	Dr. Kathleen REILAND
32	Vice President Student Services	Dr. Paul DE DIOS
10	Int Vice Pres Administrative Svcs	Dr. Stephen SCHOONMAKER
08	Dean Library/Learning Resource Ctr	Dr. Treisa CASSENS
79	Dean Language Arts	Ms. Janet VERA
121	Dean Counseling/Student Dev	Dr. Troy DAVIS
06	Registrar	Mr. David BOOZE
26	Director Campus Communications	Mr. Marc POSNER
102	Exec Dir Foundation/Community Rels	Mr. Howard KUMMERMAN
90	Manager Systems Technology Svcs	Mr. Jose SANCHEZ
37	Director Financial Aid	Ms. Gabriela DE LA CRUZ
09	Dir Institutional Research/Plng	Mr. Bryan VENTURA
18	Director Physical Plant/Facilities	Mr. Philip FLEMING
19	Director Campus Safety	Mr. Craig LEE
04	Exec Assistant to President	Ms. Kristi VALDEZ
68	Dean Physical Education/Kinesiology	Mr. Colin PRESTON
57	Dean Fine Arts	Dr. Kellori DOWER
50	Dean Business/CIS	Mr. Henry HUA
83	Dean Social Sciences	Ms. Lisa GAETJE
53	Int Dean Science Engineering & Math	Dr. David VAKIL
76	Int Dean Health Sciences	Dr. Stephen SCHOONMAKER
75	Dean Career Technical Education	Dr. Kathleen REILAND
113	Campus Accounting Manager	Ms. Dao DO
22	Director EOPS	Ms. AnnMarie RUELAS

*Fullerton College (D)

321 E Chapman Avenue, Fullerton CA 92832-2095

County: Orange	FICE Identification: 001201
	Unit ID: 114859
Telephone: (714) 992-7000	Carnegie Class: Assoc/HT-High Trad
FAX Number: (714) 992-9930	Calendar System: Semester
URL: www.fullcoll.edu	
Established: 1913	Annual Undergrad Tuition & Fees (In-District): $1,154
Enrollment: 21,427	Coed
Affiliation or Control: State/Local	IRS Status: 501(c)3
Highest Offering: Associate Degree	
Accreditation: WJ	

02	Interim President	Dr. Monte PEREZ
05	Vice President Instruction	Dr. Jose Ramon NUNEZ
32	Vice Pres Student Services	Dr. Gilbert CONTRERAS
11	Vice Pres Administrative Svcs	Mr. Rodrigo GARCIA
50	Dean Business & CIS	Mr. Carlos AYON
57	Interim Dean Fine Arts	Ms. Nicola DEDMON
79	Interim Dean Humanities	Ms. Kim ORLIJAN
77	Interim Dean Math/Computer Science	Mr. Carlos AYON
65	Dean Natural Sciences	Ms. Bridget SALZAMEDA
68	Dean Physical Education	Dr. David GROSSMAN
83	Dean Social Sciences	Dr. Jorge GAMBOA
72	Dean Technology & Engr	Mr. Kenneth STARKMAN

37	Director of Financial Aid	Mr. Greg RYAN
23	Director Behavioral Health Services	Mr. Dana TIMMERMANS
18	Dir Facilities/Physical Plant	Mr. Larry LARA
40	Manager of Follett Bookstore	Mr. Andrew DIAZ
35	Director Student Life/Leadership	Ms. Naomi ABESAMIS
06	Registrar	Ms. Rena MARTINEZ STLUKA
19	Director Campus Safety	Mr. Steve SELBY
38	Dean Counseling/Student Development	Dr. Jennifer LABOUNTY
08	Dean Library (LLR & ISPS)	Dr. Dani WILSON
07	Dean Admissions & Records	Mr. Albert ABUTIN
90	Academic Computing Technologies	Mr. Co HO
09	Dir Institutional Effectiveness	Mr. Daniel BERUMEN
88	Director Cadena Transfer Center	Ms. Cecilia ARRIAZA
26	Director Campus Communications	Ms. Lisa MCPHERON
04	Exec Assistant to the President	Ms. Jean FOSTER
121	Dean Student Support Services	Dr. Elaine LIPIZ GONZALEZ
15	Personnel Services Specialist	Ms. Liz LEDEZMA RENTERIA

Northcentral University (E)

11355 North Torrey Pines Road, La Jolla CA 92037

County: San Diego	FICE Identification: 038133
	Unit ID: 444130
Telephone: (866) 776-0331	Carnegie Class: DU-Mod
FAX Number: (844) 851-5889	Calendar System: Other
URL: www.ncu.edu	
Established: 1996	Annual Undergrad Tuition & Fees: N/A
Enrollment: 12,471	Coed
Affiliation or Control: Independent Non-Profit	IRS Status: 501(c)3
Highest Offering: Doctorate	
Accreditation: WC, AAQEP, ACBSP, MFCD, NURSE, SW	

01	President	Dr. David HARPOOL
05	Sr VP Academic Affairs	Dr. Colin MARLAIRE
10	Chief Finance Officer	Mr. Jamie NICKEL
32	VP Student and Financial Services	Vacant
07	VP Enrollment	Mr. Ken BOUTELLE
15	VP Human Resources	Ms. Angie WALKER
13	Chief Technology Learning Officer	Dr. Colin MARLAIRE
26	VP Communications/Advancement	Ms. Molly GUTTERUD
43	General Counsel	Dr. David HARPOOL
50	Dean School of Business	Dr. Eugene WILKERSON
53	Dean School of Education	Dr. Andy RIGGLE
76	Int Dean School of Health Sciences	Dr. Wittney JONES
83	Dean Sch of Social/Behavioral Sci	Dr. James BILLINGS
72	Dean School of Technology	Dr. Robert SAPP
09	Director Institutional Research	Vacant
108	Asst VP Inst Effectiveness/Planning	Dr. Heather HUSSEY
06	VP Univ Governance Policy/Stdnt Rec	Ms. Jennifer RACER
08	Director of Library Services	Ms. Amanda ZIEGLER

Northern California Bible College (F)

1799 Winchester Blvd, Campbell CA 95008

County: Santa Clara	Identification: 667349
Telephone: (925) 846-6464	Carnegie Class: Not Classified
FAX Number: N/A	Calendar System: Quarter
URL: www.ncbc.net	
Established: 1971	Annual Undergrad Tuition & Fees: N/A
Enrollment: N/A	Coed
Affiliation or Control: Independent Non-Profit	IRS Status: 501(c)3
Highest Offering: Master's	
Accreditation: TRACS	

01	President	Pastor Greg HOLSCLAW
05	Chief Academic Officer/Dean	Dr. Tracy HOLSCLAW

Notre Dame de Namur University (G)

1500 Ralston Avenue, Belmont CA 94002-1908

County: San Mateo	FICE Identification: 001179
	Unit ID: 120184
Telephone: (650) 508-3500	Carnegie Class: Masters/M
FAX Number: (650) 508-3477	Calendar System: Semester
URL: www.ndnu.edu	
Established: 1851	Annual Undergrad Tuition & Fees: N/A
Enrollment: 585	Coed
Affiliation or Control: Independent Non-Profit	IRS Status: 501(c)3
Highest Offering: Doctorate	
Accreditation: WC, ACBSP	

01	President	Dr. Lizbeth MARTIN
05	Provost & Senior Vice President	Dr. Greg WHITE
10	Vice Pres Finance & Administration	Mr. George PETERSON
111	Vice President for Advancement	Mr. Aric AGRESTI
53	Dean Education/Psychology	Dr. Caryl HODGES
37	Director Financial Aid	Mr. I. CHEN
08	Director Library Services	Dr. Caryl HODGES
18	Director Facilities	Ms. Jessica ROTH
21	Controller	Ms. Emiko YAMADA
04	Exec Assistant to the President	Ms. Summer BRUNI
15	Director of Human Resources	Dr. Karen D. WHITE
88	Director of Conferences & Events	Ms. Deidre SARGENT
06	Registrar	Ms. Jane KUBEL
07	Director of Admissions	Mr. Stephen LAGOS-MURPHY
84	Interim VP Enrollment Management	Mrs. Arlene CASH

Oak Valley College (H)

2759 Ayala Dr, Rialto CA 92324

County: San Bernardino	Identification: 667381
Telephone: (909) 554-3814	Carnegie Class: Not Classified
FAX Number: N/A	Calendar System: Trimester

URL: www.oakvalleycollege.org	
Established: 2016	Annual Undergrad Tuition & Fees: N/A
Enrollment: N/A	Coed
Affiliation or Control: Independent Non-Profit	IRS Status: 501(c)3
Highest Offering: Baccalaureate	
Accreditation: WC	

01	President	Eric BLUM
84	Vice Pres Enrollment	Erika PAGE
05	Dean/Chief Academic Officer	Afarah BOARD
32	Mgr Student/Faculty Svcs/Registrar	Megan GRAHAM

Occidental College (I)

1600 Campus Road, Los Angeles CA 90041-3314

County: Los Angeles	FICE Identification: 001249
	Unit ID: 120254
Telephone: (323) 259-2500	Carnegie Class: Bac-A&S
FAX Number: (323) 259-2958	Calendar System: Semester
URL: www.oxy.edu	
Established: 1887	Annual Undergrad Tuition & Fees: $56,576
Enrollment: 1,839	Coed
Affiliation or Control: Independent Non-Profit	IRS Status: 501(c)3
Highest Offering: Master's	
Accreditation: WC	

01	President	Dr. Harry J. ELAM, JR.
05	VP Academic Affairs/Dean of College	Dr. Wendy F. STERNBERG
10	Vice Pres Chief Operating Officer	Mr. Amos HIMMELSTEIN
111	Vice Pres Inst Advancement	Mr. Charlie CARDILLO
32	VP Student Affairs/Dean of Students	Mr. Rob FLOT
26	VP Marketing/Communications	Vacant
43	General Counsel	Ms. Nora KAHN
100	Chief of Staff	Ms. Priya SRIDHARAN
41	Athletic Dir/VP Student Affairs	Ms. Shanda NESS
18	Director of Facilities	Mr. David CALDWELL
84	VP of Enrollment	Ms. Maricela LIMAS MARTINEZ
13	VP ITS/Chief Technology Officer	Mr. James UHRICH
36	Exec Director Career Services	Ms. Jamila J. CHAMBERS
04	Exec Assistant to President	Ms. Gretchen A. SAALBACH
08	Library Director	Dr. Kevin MULROY
29	Director Alumni/Parent Engagement	Ms. Helena C. LAZARO
37	Director of Financial Aid	Ms. Cheryl Lynn REINSCHMIDT
15	AVP of Human Resources	Mr. Randy GLAZER
27	Director of Communications	Mr. Jim TRANQUADA
09	Director of Institutional Research	Ms. Jaclyn A. CAMERON
19	Director of Campus Safety	Mr. Rick TANKSLEY
101	Secretary of the Institution/Board	Ms. Marsha SCHNIRRING
122	Asst Dir Stdnt Involvemt-Greek Life	Ms. Shaneice WARFIELD
28	Vice President for Equity & Justice	Mr. David CARREON BRADLEY

Ohlone College (J)

43600 Mission Boulevard, Fremont CA 94539-0390

County: Alameda	FICE Identification: 004481
	Unit ID: 120290
Telephone: (510) 659-6000	Carnegie Class: Assoc/HVT-Mix Trad/Non
FAX Number: N/A	Calendar System: Semester
URL: www.ohlone.edu	
Established: 1966	Annual Undergrad Tuition & Fees (In-District): $1,196
Enrollment: 9,060	Coed
Affiliation or Control: State/Local	IRS Status: 501(c)3
Highest Offering: Associate Degree	
Accreditation: WJ, ADNUR, COARC, PTAA	

01	Superintendent/President	Dr. Eric BISHOP
05	VP Academic Affairs/Deputy Supt	Mr. Anthony DISALVO
10	VP Administrative/Tech Services	Dr. Christopher DELA ROSA
32	VP Student Services	Vacant
15	VP Human Resources/Training	Ms. Vy LE
13	Assoc Vice Pres Information Tech	Dr. Chris DELA ROSA
101	Asst to Pres/Board of Trustees	Ms. Shelby FOSTER
72	Dean Business & Career Tech Educ	Ms. Lesley BUEHLER
38	Dean Counseling/Student Success	Vacant
09	Exec Dean Research/Planning/ALC	Mr. Michael BOWMAN
84	Dean Enrollment Services	Mr. Michael LEIB
28	Exec Dean Equity/Campus Diversity	Dr. Melissa CERVANTES
83	Dean Social Science	Dr. Ghada AL-MASRI
76	Dean Health Sciences	Mr. Robert GABRIEL
83	Dean Language/Comm/Academic Success	Dr. Sean STEWART
81	Dean Science/Technology/Engr/Math	Ms. Lori SILVERMAN
88	Interim Dean Deaf Studies	Mr. Robert GABRIEL
68	Dean Kinesiology/Athletics/Arts	Mr. Chris WARDEN
102	Exec Dir Foundation/PR/Mktg	Mr. Binh NGUYEN
88	Director EOPS	Ms. Nancy NAVARRO-LECA
21	Exec Dir Business Services	Mr. Farhad SABIT
26	Dir Communications/Mktg	Mr. Greg LAWSON
19	Interim Chief Campus Police	Mr. Ben PERALTA
18	Dir Campus Dev/Operations	Mr. Oscar GUILLEN
37	Dir Financial Aid	Vacant
96	Dir Purchasing/Auxiliary Services	Mr. Alex LEBEDEFF
104	Dir International Programs/Services	Ms. Kristi RADKE
88	Dir Curriculum & Scheduling	Ms. Kimberly ROBBIE
04	Asst to Superintendent/President	Mr. Edgar HERNANDEZ
50	Dean of Business	Dr. Andrew LAMANQUE

Oikos University (K)

7901 Oakport St, Ste 3000, Oakland CA 94621

County: Alameda	Identification: 667212
Telephone: (510) 639-7879	Carnegie Class: Not Classified
FAX Number: (510) 639-7810	Calendar System: Semester
URL: www.oikos.edu	

Established: 2004   Annual Undergrad Tuition & Fees: N/A
Enrollment: N/A   Coed
Affiliation or Control: Independent Non-Profit   IRS Status: 501(c)3
Highest Offering: Doctorate
Accreditation: **TRACS**

01	President	Dr. Jongin KIM
05	Dean of Academics	Dr. Ki Wook MIN
32	Director of Students	Dr. Dongjin LEE
10	Chief Financial Officer	Dr. Jooman LEE

Olivet University   (A)
36401 Tripp Flats Road, Anza CA 92539

County: San Francisco   Identification: 666176
Telephone: (951) 763-0500   Carnegie Class: Not Classified
FAX Number: (415) 371-0003   Calendar System: Quarter
URL: www.olivetuniversity.edu
Established: 1992   Annual Undergrad Tuition & Fees: N/A
Enrollment: N/A   Coed
Affiliation or Control: Independent Non-Profit   IRS Status: 501(c)3
Highest Offering: Doctorate
Accreditation: **BI**

01	University President	Dr. Matthias GEBHARDT
05	Dean of Academic Affairs	Dr. Tracy DAVIS
32	Dean of Students	Dr. Julia TZENG
10	Chief Financial Officer	Mr. Barnabas JUNG
11	Chief Operating Officer/Chaplain	Dr. Walker TZENG

Otis College of Art and Design   (B)
9045 Lincoln Boulevard, Los Angeles CA 90045-3550

County: Los Angeles   FICE Identification: 001251
    Unit ID: 120403
Telephone: (310) 665-6800   Carnegie Class: Spec-4-yr-Arts
FAX Number: (310) 665-6805   Calendar System: Semester
URL: www.otis.edu
Established: 1918   Annual Undergrad Tuition & Fees: $49,680
Enrollment: 1,073   Coed
Affiliation or Control: Independent Non-Profit   IRS Status: 501(c)3
Highest Offering: Master's
Accreditation: **WC, ART**

00	Chair Board of Trustees	Ms. Mei-Lee NEY
01	President	Mr. Charles HIRSCHHORN
05	Provost	Ms. Jiseon Lee ISBARA
13	VP of IT and Operations	Mr. Ankush MAHINDRA
10	VP of Financial Services/CFO	Mr. Ankush MAHINDRA
32	VP of Campus Life	Dr. Laura KIRALLA
15	VP of Human Resources/Risk Mgmt	Ms. Karen HILL
26	VP of Communications and Marketing	Mr. Lawrence ALDAVA
111	VP of Institutional Advancement	Mr. Patrick MAHANY
35	Dean of Student Affairs	Dr. Nick NEGRETE
56	Dean of Extension	Mr. Mark MANROSE
84	Dean of Enrollment Mgmt	Dr. Samuel KIM
06	Registrar	Ms. Anna MANZANO
18	Chief Facilities/Operation Officer	Mr. Claude NICA
37	Director Student Fin Services	Ms. Natasha KOBRINSKY
09	Dir Inst Research & Effectiveness	Dr. Angila ROMIOUS
14	Director Technology Infrastructure	Mr. Matthew BALLARD
108	Asst Provost Assessment & Accred	Ms. Joanne MITCHELL
28	Asst Dean of Stdnt Affs/Title IX	Dr. Carol BRANCH
19	Chief Safety and Security Officer	Mr. Rick GONZALEZ
101	Board Relations Mgr	Ms. Doniell PETERS
04	Sr Exec Asst to President	Ms. Renee JONES
23	Director Student Health & Wellness	Dr. Julie SPENCER
39	Director Housing & Res Life	Ms. Morgan BROWN
29	Director Alumni Relations	Ms. Hazel MANDUJANO

Pacific College   (C)
3160 Redhill Avenue, Costa Mesa CA 92626-3402

County: Orange   FICE Identification: 032993
    Unit ID: 422695
Telephone: (800) 867-2243   Carnegie Class: Spec-4-yr-Other Health
FAX Number: (714) 662-1702   Calendar System: Semester
URL: www.pacific-college.edu
Established: 1993   Annual Undergrad Tuition & Fees: N/A
Enrollment: 249   Coed
Affiliation or Control: Proprietary   IRS Status: Proprietary
Highest Offering: Master's
Accreditation: **WC, NURSE**

01	President	Mr. William L. NELSON
03	Vice President Instruction	Ms. Donna WOO
11	Chief Financial/Operating Ofcr	Ms. Sandy SARGE

Pacific College of Health and Science   (D)
7445 Mission Valley Road, #104,
San Diego CA 92108-4408

County: San Diego   FICE Identification: 030277
    Unit ID: 378576
Telephone: (619) 574-6909   Carnegie Class: Spec-4-yr-Other Health
FAX Number: (619) 574-6641   Calendar System: Trimester
URL: https://www.pacificcollege.edu
Established: 1986   Annual Undergrad Tuition & Fees: $9,791
Enrollment: 967   Coed
Affiliation or Control: Proprietary   IRS Status: Proprietary
Highest Offering: Doctorate

Accreditation: **WC, ACUP**

01	President	Mr. Malcolm YOUNGREN
05	Vice Pres of Academic Affairs	Ms. Stacy GOMES
11	Chief Operating Officer	Mr. Malcolm YOUNGREN
10	Chief Financial Officer	Mr. Claudio PICO
26	Vice President Marketing	Ms. Nathalie TUROTTE
12	Director NY Campus	Mr. Malcolm YOUNGREN
12	Director CH Campus	Mr. Dave FRECH
07	Vice President Admissions	Ms. Justina-Jupiter POWELL
12	Director SD Campus	Ms. April PANIAGUA
06	Registrar	Mr. Ethan WEBSTER
23	Director of Clinical Services	Ms. Leng TANG-RITCHIE
08	Head Librarian	Ms. Patricia BENEFIEL
13	Information Technology Director	Mr. Greg RUSSO
88	Pacific Symposium	Mr. Todd LUGER
29	Director Alumni Affairs	Ms. Stacy GOMES

Pacific Oaks College   (E)
45 West Eureka Street, Pasadena CA 91103

County: Los Angeles   FICE Identification: 001255
    Unit ID: 120768
Telephone: (626) 529-8500   Carnegie Class: Masters/M
FAX Number: N/A   Calendar System: Semester
URL: www.pacificoaks.edu
Established: 1945   Annual Undergrad Tuition & Fees: $11,692
Enrollment: 1,238   Coed
Affiliation or Control: Independent Non-Profit   IRS Status: 501(c)3
Highest Offering: Master's
Accreditation: **WC, @SW**

01	President	Dr. Jack PADUNTIN
05	Vice Pres Academic Affairs	Dr. Bree COOK
32	Dean of Students	Mr. Michael LOPEZ-PATTON
15	VP Human Resources/Title IX Coord	Ms. Jane SAWYER
10	AVP Financial/Admin Operations	Ms. Yug Fon CHIQUITO
35	Dir Ctr Stdnt Achievemt/Res/Enrich	Ms. Pat MEDA
07	Acting Assoc Vice Pres Admissions	Mr. Nubian LONDON
04	Dir President's Ofc/Sec to Cabinet	Ms. Carrie ZALKIND
12	Campus Dean San Jose	Dr. Marcia BANKIRER
53	Int Dean School of Education	Mr. Jerell HILL
88	Int Dean School of CFP	Dr. Andrew KAMI
83	Dean School of Human Development	Dr. Terry WEBSTER
88	Exec Director Children's School	Ms. Judy KRAUSE
111	AVP Advancement/External Affairs	Ms. Johanna ATIENZA
06	Registrar	Ms. Mary BERBERIAN

Pacific School of Religion   (F)
1798 Scenic Avenue, Berkeley CA 94709-1323

County: Alameda   FICE Identification: 001256
    Unit ID: 120795
Telephone: (510) 849-8200   Carnegie Class: Spec-4-yr-Faith
FAX Number: (510) 845-8948   Calendar System: Semester
URL: www.psr.edu
Established: 1866   Annual Graduate Tuition & Fees: N/A
Enrollment: 100   Coed
Affiliation or Control: Independent Non-Profit   IRS Status: 501(c)3
Highest Offering: Doctorate; No Undergraduates
Accreditation: **WC, THEOL**

01	President	Rev. David VASQUEZ-LEVY
05	Vice Pres Academic Affairs/Dean	Dr. Susan ABRAHAM
30	Vice Pres Development	Mr. Jeffrey FISCHER-SMITH
26	Vice Pres Marketing/Enrollment	Mr. Murry EVANS
10	Vice Pres Finance/Administration	Ms. Natasha LEE
06	Asst Dean Academic Pgms/Registrar	Ms. Lyndsey REED
07	Dir Admissions/Financial Aid Ofcr	Mr. Keaton ANDREAS
32	Dir Community Life/Spiritual Care	Rev. Ann JEFFERSON
15	Director Human Resources	Ms. Sarah CONROY

Pacific States University   (G)
3424 Wilshire Boulevard, 12th Floor,
Los Angeles CA 90010

County: Los Angeles   FICE Identification: 031633
    Unit ID: 120838
Telephone: (323) 731-2383   Carnegie Class: Spec-4-yr-Bus
FAX Number: (323) 731-7276   Calendar System: Quarter
URL: www.psuca.edu
Established: 1928   Annual Undergrad Tuition & Fees: $12,960
Enrollment: 26   Coed
Affiliation or Control: Independent Non-Profit   IRS Status: 501(c)3
Highest Offering: Master's
Accreditation: **ACCSC**

01	Interim President	Mr. Matthew SHIN
05	Dean Academic Affairs	Dr. Heidi CROCKER
10	Asst Dean Finance/General Affairs	Miss Rosy LIM
37	Financial Aid	Mr. Moonsik KIM
26	Assoc Dean Public Rels/Student Affs	Ms. Sarah MIN
13	Dir General & Technology Svcs/MIS	Mr. Kuang Kai LU
08	University Librarian	Ms. Aurora AREVALO
07	Dir of Admissions	Ms. Maawiya AYEVA
32	Dir Student Services/Int Registrar	Vacant

Pacific Union College   (H)
1 Angwin Avenue, Angwin CA 94508-9797

County: Napa   FICE Identification: 001258
    Unit ID: 120865
Telephone: (707) 965-6311   Carnegie Class: Bac-Diverse
FAX Number: (707) 965-6390   Calendar System: Quarter

URL: www.puc.edu
Established: 1882   Annual Undergrad Tuition & Fees: $32,016
Enrollment: 959   Coed
Affiliation or Control: Seventh-day Adventist   IRS Status: 501(c)3
Highest Offering: Master's
Accreditation: **WC, ADNUR, ART, IACBE, MUS, NUR, SW**

01	President	Dr. Ralph TRECARTIN, JR.
05	Academic Dean/VP for Academic Admin	Mr. Milbert MARIANO
10	VP for Financial Administration	Mrs. Joy HIRDLER
32	VP for Student Life	Dr. Ryan SMITH
84	VP for Enroll/Marketing/Comm	Mr. Gene EDELBACH
111	VP for Alumni & Advancement	Ms. Kellie LIND
08	Director of Library Services	Mr. Patrick BENNER
37	Director Student Financial Services	Mr. Frederick WHITESIDE
13	Director of Information Technology	Mr. David RAI
06	Registrar	Ms. Susan WALTERS
15	Assoc VP Human Resources	Mr. Stacy NELSON
41	Director of Athletics	Mr. J.R ROGERS
38	Director Counseling Center	Mr. Michael JEFFERSON
18	Chief of Facilities Management	Mr. Dale WITHERS
20	AVP for Academic Administration	Dr. Lindsay MORTON
07	Director Admissions	Mr. Craig PHILPOTT
09	Director of Institutional Research	Mr. Serhii KALYNOVSKYI

Pacifica Graduate Institute   (I)
249 Lambert Road, Carpinteria CA 93013-3019

County: Carpinteria   FICE Identification: 031268
    Unit ID: 115746
Telephone: (805) 969-3626   Carnegie Class: Spec-4-yr-Other Health
FAX Number: (805) 565-1932   Calendar System: Quarter
URL: www.pacifica.edu
Established: 1974   Annual Graduate Tuition & Fees: N/A
Enrollment: 856   Coed
Affiliation or Control: Proprietary   IRS Status: Proprietary
Highest Offering: Doctorate; No Undergraduates
Accreditation: **WC**

01	President/CEO	Dr. Joseph CAMBRAY
05	Provost/ALO/VP Academic Affairs	Dr. Peter ROJCEWICZ
10	Chief Financial Officer	Mr. Larry BYER
43	General Counsel	Mr. Marvin RICHARDS
84	Sr Director of Enrollment Mgmt	Ms. Rica TORIBIO
37	Director of Financial Aid	Ms. Tracie TEAGUE
20	CoDir of Academic Affs/Student Svcs	Ms. Lauren LASTRA
20	CoDir of Academic Affs/Student Svcs	Mr. Nicholas SABATINO
06	Registrar	Ms. Francine MATAS
15	Director of Human Resources	Ms. Norma MESA
39	Director of Guest Services	Ms. Heather SLADE
29	Director of Alumni Relations	Ms. Dianne TRAVIS-TEAGUE
13	Director of Information Technology	Mr. Tim FRITZ
14	Director of Information Systems	Mr. Griff JONES
19	Dir of Facilities/Safety/Security	Mr. Adam BROWN
105	Director of Marketing/Webmaster	Mr. John ZIEGLER
09	Director of Institutional Research	Dr. Bill BILLET

Palmer College of Chiropractic, West Campus   (J)
90 E Tasman Drive, San Jose CA 95134-1617

Telephone: (408) 944-6000   FICE Identification: 021849
Accreditation: **&HLC, &CHIRO**

† Regional accreditation is carried under the parent institution in Davenport, IA.

Palo Alto University   (K)
1791 Arastradero Road, Palo Alto CA 94304

County: San Mateo   FICE Identification: 021383
    Unit ID: 120698
Telephone: (800) 818-6136   Carnegie Class: Spec-4-yr-Other Health
FAX Number: (650) 433-3888   Calendar System: Quarter
URL: www.paloaltou.edu
Established: 1975   Annual Undergrad Tuition & Fees: N/A
Enrollment: 1,163   Coed
Affiliation or Control: Independent Non-Profit   IRS Status: 501(c)3
Highest Offering: Doctorate
Accreditation: **WC, CACREP, CLPSY**

01	President	Dr. Maureen O'CONNOR
108	VP of Inst Effectiveness	Dr. James BRECKENRIDGE
05	Provost/VP for Academic Affairs	Dr. Erika CAMERON
10	VP for Business Affairs & CFO	Dr. June KLEIN
26	VP for External Affairs	Ms. Camille WATSON
107	VP for Continuing & Prof Studies	Dr. Patricia ZAPF
32	Dean of Students	Mr. Thom SHEPARD
101	Dir of Board/President Operations	Ms. Melanie MORRISON
30	Director of Development	Ms. Anne FARRAH
21	Assistant Controller	Ms. Maya RAMAKRISHNAN
15	Sr Human Resource Manager	Ms. Holly LINDLEY
07	VP of Admissions	Ms. Alaina DUNN
27	Director of External Affairs	Ms. Rebecca LEVY
13	Chief Information Officer	Mr. Fei YING
37	Director of Financial Aid	Ms. Jessica AYRES
06	Director of Registration	Ms. Nora MARQUEZ
17	Director of Gronowski Center	Dr. Sandra MACIAS
09	Director of Institutional Research	Ms. Jennifer LEHNER
08	Librarian & Dir Academic Tech	Mr. Scott HINES
113	Billing Supervisor	Ms. Anna LITSITSA
88	Dept Chair Counseling	Dr. William SNOW
83	Dept Chair Psychology	Dr. Kimberly BALSAM

Palo Verde College (A)

One College Drive, Blythe CA 92225-9561
County: Riverside FICE Identification: 001259
Unit ID: 120953
Telephone: (760) 921-5500 Carnegie Class: Assoc/HT-Mix Trad/Non
FAX Number: (760) 921-5590 Calendar System: Semester
URL: www.paloverde.edu
Established: 1947 Annual Undergrad Tuition & Fees (In-District): $1,288
Enrollment: 3,854 Coed
Affiliation or Control: State/Local IRS Status: 501(c)3
Highest Offering: Associate Degree
Accreditation: WJ

01 Superintendent/President .... Dr. Donald WALLACE
05 Int VP Instructional/Student Svcs .... Mr. William SMITH
15 Assoc Vice Pres Human Resources/EEO .... Ms. Cecilia GARCIA
04 Executive Asst to Supt/President .... Ms. Denise HUNT
66 Int Assoc Dean Nursing/Allied Hlth .... Dr. Theresa BECKER
32 Dean Instruction/Student Services .... Mr. Biju RAMAN
08 Librarian .... Ms. June TURNER
07 Director of Admissions and Records .... Ms. Shelley HAMILTON
88 Site Supervisor of Child Dev Center .... Vacant
09 Director of Institutional Research .... Vacant
18 Director Facilities and Operations .... Mr. Mario HALE
13 Director of Information Technology .... Vacant
35 Mgr of Student Life/Development .... Ms. Staci LEE
10 VP Administrative Svcs/Advancement .... Ms. Stephanie SLAGAN
106 Assoc Dean Correspondence Educ .... Ms. Maria KEHL
37 Acting Director of Financial Aid .... Ms. German DE LA PENA
101 Exec Asst to Supt/President/Board .... Ms. Carrie MULLION
102 Executive Director Foundation .... Ms. Stephanie SLAGAN
41 Director of Athletics .... Mr. Ryan COPPLE
38 Associate Dean of Counseling .... Ms. Irma GONZALEZ

Palomar College (B)

1140 W Mission Road, San Marcos CA 92069-1487
County: San Diego FICE Identification: 001260
Unit ID: 120971
Telephone: (760) 744-1150 Carnegie Class: Assoc/MT-VT-High Trad
FAX Number: (760) 744-8123 Calendar System: Semester
URL: www.palomar.edu
Established: 1946 Annual Undergrad Tuition & Fees (In-District): $1,344
Enrollment: 21,141 Coed
Affiliation or Control: State/Local IRS Status: 501(c)3
Highest Offering: Associate Degree
Accreditation: WJ, ADNUR, DA, EMT

01 Superintendent/President .... Dr. Star RIVERA-LACY
05 Int Asst Supt/Vice Pres Instruction .... Dr. Diane STUDINKA
32 Asst Supt/VP Student Services .... Dr. Vikash LAKHANI
10 Actg Asst Supt/VP Finance/Admn Svcs .... Ms. Nancy LANE
15 Asst Supt/VP Human Resources .... Mr. David MONTOYA
04 Exec Assistant to the President .... Ms. Michelle LAVIGUEUR
79 Dean Languages & Literature .... Dr. Fabienne CHAUDERLOT
81 Dean Math/Science & Engineering .... Ms. Patricia MENCHACA
38 Dean Counseling Services .... Ms. Leslie SALAS
75 Dean Career/Tech/Extended Educ .... Dr. Susan WYCHE
50 Dean Arts/Media/Bus & Comp Sci .... Mr. Justin SMILEY
83 Dean Social/Behavioral Sciences .... Ms. Teresa LAUGHLIN
13 Director Info Systems & Services .... Mr. Michael DAY
84 Director Enrollment Svcs/Admissions .... Dr. Kendyl MAGNUSON
09 Sr Director Institutional Research .... Ms. Michelle BARTON
18 Director of Facilities .... Mr. Chris MILLER
35 Director Student Affairs .... Ms. Sherry TITUS
37 Director Student Financial Aid .... Ms. Adriana LEE
26 Int Dir Comm/Mktg/Public Affairs .... Ms. Julie LANTHIER-BANDY
102 Executive Director for Foundation .... Ms. Stacy RUNGAITIS
19 Chief of Police .... Mr. Chris MOORE
23 Director Health Services .... Dr. Patrick SAVAIANO
41 Director Athletics .... Mr. Daniel LYNDS

Pardee RAND Graduate School of Policy Studies (C)

1776 Main Street, Santa Monica CA 90407-2138
County: Los Angeles FICE Identification: 010441
Unit ID: 121628
Telephone: (310) 393-0411 Carnegie Class: Spec-4-yr-Other
FAX Number: (310) 451-6978 Calendar System: Quarter
URL: www.prgs.edu
Established: 1970 Annual Graduate Tuition & Fees: N/A
Enrollment: 123 Coed
Affiliation or Control: Independent Non-Profit IRS Status: 501(c)3
Highest Offering: Doctorate; No Undergraduates
Accreditation: WC

01 Dean .... Dr. Nancy STAUDT
05 Associate Dean .... Ms. Rachel SWANGER
06 Registrar .... Mr. Alex DUKE
07 Asst Dean Admissions .... Ms. Stefanie HOWARD
20 Asst Dean for Academic Affairs .... Ms. Angel O'MAHONEY

Pasadena City College (D)

1570 E Colorado Boulevard, Pasadena CA 91106-2041
County: Los Angeles FICE Identification: 001261
Unit ID: 121044
Telephone: (626) 585-7123 Carnegie Class: Assoc/HT-High Trad
FAX Number: (626) 585-7910 Calendar System: Semester
URL: www.pasadena.edu
Established: 1924 Annual Undergrad Tuition & Fees (In-District): $1,212
Enrollment: 25,034 Coed
Affiliation or Control: State/Local IRS Status: 501(c)3
Highest Offering: Associate Degree
Accreditation: WJ, DA, DH, DT, MAC, RAD

01 Superintendent-President .... Dr. Erika A. ENDRIJONAS
05 Vice President Instruction .... Dr. Laura RAMIREZ
10 VP Business & Administrative Svcs .... Ms. Candace JONES
32 Vice President Student Services .... Dr. Cynthia OLIVO
15 Vice President Human Resources .... Mr. Bob BLIZINSKI
09 Exec Dir Inst Research/Planning .... Ms. Crystal KOLLROSS
56 Director Extension .... Ms. Elaine CHAPMAN
121 Dean Counseling & Student Success .... Mr. Armando DURAN
88 Dean Special Services .... Dr. Ketmani KOUANCHAO
84 Dir Admissions/Records/Enrollment .... Ms. Arlene REED
37 Director Financial Aid .... Mr. David HULL
13 Int Exec Dir Info Tech Services .... Mr. Roberto JURADO
26 Special Asst to Pres-Strat Comm/Mkt .... Mr. Alex BOEKELHEIDE
04 Exec Asst to President .... Ms. Armine GALUKYAN
19 Chief Police & Safety Services .... Mr. Steven MATCHAN
35 Dean Student Life .... Ms. Rebecca COBB
96 Director of Purchasing & Contracts .... Mr. George CHIDIAC
101 Executive Assistant to Trustees .... Ms. Mary THOMPSON
102 Executive Director Foundation .... Ms. Bobbi ABRAM
103 Exec Director Workforce Development .... Ms. Salvatrice CUMMO
28 AVP/Chief Diversity/Equity/Incl .... Dr. Kari BOLEN
21 Exec Director Fiscal Services .... Ms. Chedva WEINGART
41 Athletic Director .... Mr. Tony BARBONE

Pathways College (E)

320 N. Halstead Street, Pasadena CA 91107
County: Los Angeles Identification: 667396
Telephone: (888) 532-7282 Carnegie Class: Not Classified
FAX Number: N/A Calendar System: Trimester
URL: www.pathwayscollege.org
Established: 2015 Annual Undergrad Tuition & Fees: N/A
Enrollment: N/A Coed
Affiliation or Control: Independent Non-Profit IRS Status: 501(c)3
Highest Offering: Baccalaureate
Accreditation: WC

01 Chancellor .... John HALL, SR.
05 Chief Academic Officer .... Melinda LESTER

Patten University (F)

2433 Coolidge Avenue, Oakland CA 94601
County: Alameda Identification: 666982
Telephone: (626) 966-4576 Carnegie Class: Not Classified
FAX Number: (626) 915-1709 Calendar System: Other
URL: www.patten.edu
Established: 1969 Annual Graduate Tuition & Fees: N/A
Enrollment: N/A Coed
Affiliation or Control: Proprietary IRS Status: Proprietary
Highest Offering: Master's; No Undergraduates
Accreditation: DEAC

01 President .... Mr. Eugene V. WADE
06 Registrar .... Ms. Cathy DIAZ
05 Chief Academic Officer .... Dr. Nathan BREITLING
07 Dir Admissions/Student Achievement .... Ms. Laurie MEJIA

PCI College (G)

17215 Studebaker Rd Ste 310, Cerritos CA 90703
County: Los Angeles FICE Identification: 034793
Unit ID: 439871
Telephone: (562) 916-5055 Carnegie Class: Spec-4-yr-Other Health
FAX Number: (562) 916-5057 Calendar System: Semester
URL: www.pci-ed.com
Established: 1996 Annual Undergrad Tuition & Fees: N/A
Enrollment: 140 Coed
Affiliation or Control: Proprietary IRS Status: Proprietary
Highest Offering: Baccalaureate
Accreditation: ACCSC

01 CFO .... Ray KHAN

Pepperdine University (H)

24255 Pacific Coast Highway, Malibu CA 90263-0001
County: Los Angeles FICE Identification: 010149
Unit ID: 121150
Telephone: (310) 506-4000 Carnegie Class: DU-Mod
FAX Number: (310) 506-4861 Calendar System: Semester
URL: www.pepperdine.edu
Established: 1937 Annual Undergrad Tuition & Fees: $58,002
Enrollment: 9,554 Coed
Affiliation or Control: Church Of Christ IRS Status: 501(c)3
Highest Offering: Doctorate
Accreditation: WC, CLPSY, DIETD, LAW, MUS

01 President .... Mr. James A. GASH
100 VP/Chief of Staff .... Mr. Daniel DEWALT
45 Sr VP for Strategic Implementation .... Mr. Tim PERRIN
03 Executive Vice President .... Mr. Gary A. HANSON
04 Exec Assistant to the President .... Mrs. Cynthia PAVELL
05 Provost .... Dr. Jay BREWSTER
10 Chief Financial Officer .... Mr. Greg RAMIREZ
111 VP Advancement .... Ms. Lauren COSENTINO
115 Chief Investment Officer .... Mr. Jeffrey ROHDE
43 General Counsel .... Mr. Marc P. GOODMAN
11 Sr VP of Administration & COO .... Mr. Phil E. PHILLIPS
21 Chief Business Officer .... Ms. Nicolle TAYLOR
13 Chief Information Officer .... Mr. Jonathan SEE
26 Sr VP & Chief Marketing Officer .... Mr. Sean BURNETT
06 Assoc VP & University Registrar .... Mr. Hung V. LE
104 Dean of International Programs .... Ms. Beth LAUX
84 Dean of Admission/Enrollment Mgmt .... Dr. Kristy COLLINS
32 VP of Student Affairs .... Dr. Connie HORTON
08 Dean of Libraries .... Mr. Mark S. ROOSA
61 Dean of the Caruso School of Law .... Mr. Paul CARON
50 Dean Graziadio Business School .... Dr. Deryck VAN RENSBURG
53 Dean of Graduate School Educ/Psych .... Dr. Helen E. WILLIAMS
49 Dean of Seaver College .... Dr. Michael E. FELTNER
80 Dean of School of Public Policy .... Mr. Pete PETERSON
42 University Chaplain .... Ms. Sara BARTON
46 Vice Provost for Research and Strat .... Dr. Lee KATS
108 Assoc Provost Inst Effectiveness .... Dr. Seta KHAJARIAN
29 Vice Chanc Engagement & Mass Appeal .... Mr. Dave JOHNSON
15 Assoc VP Human Resources Officer .... Mr. Sean Mike PHILLIPS
88 Director of Ministry Outreach .... Mr. Michael COPE
39 Director of Housing Operations .... Dr. Robin GORE
88 Managing Dir Center for the Arts .... Ms. Rebecca CARSON
85 Dir Intl Student Services .... Ms. Brooke CUTLER
27 VP Integrated Mktg Communications .... Mr. Michael THOMAS
23 Dir Student Health Services .... Ms. Rebecca ROLDAN
36 Assoc Dean of Students/Career Ctr .... Mr. Brad D. DUDLEY
41 Director of Athletics .... Dr. Steven POTTS
88 Assoc VP Planning/Opers/Construct .... Mr. Lance BRIDGESMITH
18 Exec Dir Planning/Opers/Constr .... Ms. Carly MISCHKE
86 Dir Government/Regulatory Affairs .... Mr. Ricky ELDRIDGE
37 Dir of Seaver Financial Assistance .... Mrs. Janet LOCKHART
09 Director of Institutional Research .... Ms. Jazmine ZANE
112 Exec Dir Estate and Gift Planning .... Vacant
22 Director Disability Services .... Ms. Sandra HARRISON
116 Senior Assurance Associate .... Ms. Carla ANDERSON
102 Dir Corporate/Foundation Relations .... Ms. Sheila D. KING
28 Assoc VP & Title IX Coordinator .... Ms. LaShonda COLEMAN
44 Director Pepperdine Fund .... Vacant
101 Secretary of the Institution/Board .... Mrs. Joan DEMPSTER
96 Purchasing Manager .... Ms. Vanessa HIGHSMITH
07 Director of Admissions .... Vacant
103 Director Career and Coaching .... Ms. Marla PONTRELLI
105 Director Digital Marketing .... Mr. Mauricio ACEVEDO
106 Associate Provost E-learning .... Dr. David SMITH
25 Assistant Provost for Research .... Mrs. Katy CARR
30 Dir of Parent/Family Development .... Ms. Kimberly BARKIS
38 Director Counseling Center .... Dr. Nivla FITZPATRICK
122 Stdnt Orgs Coord-Greek Life .... Ms. Sabrina WILLISON
19 Director of Public Safety .... Ms. Dawn EMRICH

*Peralta Community Colleges District Office (I)

333 E Eighth Street, Oakland CA 94606-2889
County: Alameda FICE Identification: 001265
Unit ID: 121178
Telephone: (510) 466-7200 Carnegie Class: N/A
FAX Number: (510) 835-4078
URL: www.peralta.edu

01 Interim Chancellor .... Dr. Jannett N. JACKSON
05 Vice Chancellor of Academic Affairs .... Dr. Siri BROWN
10 Int VC Finance/Administration .... Mr. Adil AHMED
15 Int Vice Chanc HR/Employee Rels .... Dr. Ronald MCKINLEY
26 Exec Dir Public Rels/Comm/Mktg .... Mr. Mark JOHNSON

*Berkeley City College (J)

2050 Center Street, Berkeley CA 94704-1183
County: Alameda FICE Identification: 022427
Unit ID: 125170
Telephone: (510) 981-2800 Carnegie Class: Assoc/HT-High Non
FAX Number: (510) 841-7333 Calendar System: Semester
URL: www.berkeleycitycollege.edu
Established: 1974 Annual Undergrad Tuition & Fees (In-District): $1,167
Enrollment: 6,097 Coed
Affiliation or Control: State/Local IRS Status: 501(c)3
Highest Offering: Associate Degree
Accreditation: WJ

02 President .... Dr. Angelica GARCIA
05 Vice President Instruction .... Ms. Kuniko HAY
32 Vice President Student Services .... Dr. Stacey SHEARS
81 Int Dean Math/Sci/Business/AppTech .... Dr. Joya CHAVARIN
49 Dean Liberal Arts/Social Sciences .... Ms. Lisa R. COOK
35 Dean Student Support Services .... Ms. Brenda JOHNSON
10 Director Business Services & Admin .... Ms. Shirley SLAUGHTER
121 Assoc Dean Educational Success .... Mr. Martin DE MUCHA FLORES
26 Public Information Officer .... Dr. Felicia L. BRIDGES
15 Acting Vice Chancellor HR .... Dr. Ronald MCKINLEY
18 Acting Vice Chancellor General Svcs .... Msr. Atheria SMITH
21 Supervisor Business Services .... Mr. John PANG
09 Sr Research Analyst .... Dr. Phoumy SAYAVONG
04 Executive Assistant to President .... Ms. Cynthia REESE
84 Coordinator Enrollment Services .... Ms. Gail PENDLETON
37 Financial Aid Officer .... Ms. Loan NGUYEN

*College of Alameda (A)

555 Ralph Appezzato Memorial Pkwy,
Alameda CA 94501-2109
County: Alameda FICE Identification: 006720
Unit ID: 108667
Telephone: (510) 522-7221 Carnegie Class: Assoc/HT-High Non
FAX Number: (510) 337-0619 Calendar System: Semester
URL: www.alameda.peralta.edu
Established: 1968 Annual Undergrad Tuition & Fees (In-District): $1,167
Enrollment: 5,107 Coed
Affiliation or Control: State/Local IRS Status: 501(c)3
Highest Offering: Associate Degree
Accreditation: WJ, DA

02 President .... Dr. Nathaniel JONES, III
05 Vice President of Instruction .... Dr. Diana BAJRAMI
32 Vice President of Student Svcs .... Ms. Tina VASCONCELLOS
26 Chief Public Relations Officer .... Vacant
20 Acting Dean of STEAM .... Mr. Silvester HENDERSON
88 Dean Special Programs .... Vacant
84 Dean Enrollment Services .... Dr. Amy LEE
49 Dean Liberal Studies/Language Arts .... Ms. Lilia CELHAY
103 Dean Career/Workforce Education .... Ms. Eva JENNINGS
121 Assoc Dean of Educational Success .... Vacant
10 Vice President of Admin Services .... Mr. Augustine GILL
07 Admissions & Records Specialist .... Ms. Marcean BRYANT
35 Director of Campus Life .... Vacant
09 Director College Research/Planning .. Ms. Dominique BENAVIDES

*Laney College (B)

900 Fallon Street, Oakland CA 94607-4893
County: Alameda FICE Identification: 001266
Unit ID: 117247
Telephone: (510) 834-5740 Carnegie Class: Assoc/MT-VT-High Non
FAX Number: N/A Calendar System: Semester
URL: laney.edu
Established: 1953 Annual Undergrad Tuition & Fees (In-District): $1,167
Enrollment: 9,225 Coed
Affiliation or Control: State/Local IRS Status: 501(c)3
Highest Offering: Associate Degree
Accreditation: WJ

02 President .... Dr. Rudy BESIKOF
05 Vice President of Instruction .... Dr. Rebecca OPSATA
32 Vice Pres Student Services .... Dr. Marlon HALL
10 Vice Pres Administrative Services .... Dr. Dettie DEL ROSARIO
75 Dean Career & Technical Educ .... Ms. Alejandria TOMAS
84 Dean Enrollment Services .... Dr. Mildred LEWIS
79 Dean Humanities/Social Science .... Dr. Mark FIELDS
49 Dean Liberal Arts .... Ms. Elizabeth (Beth) MAHER
81 Dean Mathematics and Science .... Mr. Angel FUENTES
35 Dean Student Services .... Ms. Diane T. CHANG
121 Assoc Dean Educational Success .... Mr. Gary ALBURY
04 Executive Assistant to President .... Ms. Arlene LONTOC
18 Director of Facilities & Operations .... Ms. Amy MARSHALL
35 Dir Student Activities/Campus Life .... Ms. Atiya RASHADA
13 Director IT .... Mr. Balamurali SAMPATHRAJ
88 Director Gateway to College Pgm .... Mr. William R. OCHOA
88 Director of AANAPISI .... Mr. David LEE
41 Director Athletics .... Mr. John BEAM
109 Food Services Manager .... Mr. Neil BURMENKO
08 Head Librarian .... Ms. Evelyn LORD
37 Director of Financial Aid .... Ms. Jennifer MA

*Merritt College (C)

12500 Campus Drive, Oakland CA 94619-3196
County: Alameda FICE Identification: 001267
Unit ID: 118772
Telephone: (510) 531-4911 Carnegie Class: Assoc/MT-VT-High Non
FAX Number: (510) 436-2405 Calendar System: Semester
URL: www.merritt.edu
Established: 1953 Annual Undergrad Tuition & Fees (In-District): $1,167
Enrollment: 6,261 Coed
Affiliation or Control: State/Local IRS Status: 501(c)3
Highest Offering: Associate Degree
Accreditation: WJ, DIETT, HT, RAD

02 President .... Dr. David JOHNSON
05 Vice President of Instruction .... Ms. Denise RICHARDSON
32 Vice President of Student Services .... Dr. Lilia CHAVEZ
10 VP of Administrative Services .... Mr. Garth KWIECIEN
96 Vice Chancellor of General Services .... Dr. Sadiq IKHARO
15 Vice Chancellor for Human Resources .... Ms. Trudy LARGENT
20 Vice Chanc Educational Services .... Dr. Michael ORKIN
13 Assoc VC of Information Technology .... Mr. Calvin MADLOCK
25 Dean Special Programs & Grants .... Dr. Lilia CHAVEZ
84 Dean of Enrollment Services .... Ms. Ree'shemah THORTON
26 Exec Dir Marketing/Public Rels/Comm .... Mr. Jeffrey HEYMAN
08 Library Director .... Ms. Adoria WILLIAMS
06 Registrar .... Ms. Susana DE LA TORRE
35 Dir Student Activities/Campus Life .... Ms. Doris HANKINS
09 Director Research & Planning .... Mr. Nathan PELLEGRIN
101 Board Clerk .... Ms. Brenda MARTINEZ
102 Interim Exec Dir Foundation .... Ms. Kaia BURKETT
18 Facilities Director/Physical Plant .... Ms. Tara MARRERO
37 Director Financial Aid Svcs .... Vacant
41 Athletic Director .... Mr. Brock DRAZEN

Pima Medical Institute-Chula Vista (D)

780 Bay Boulevard, Suite 101,
Chula Vista CA 91910-5261
Telephone: (619) 425-3200 Identification: 666272
Accreditation: ABHES, SURTEC

† Branch campus of Pima Medical Institute, Tucson, AZ.

Pitzer College (E)

1050 N Mills Avenue, Claremont CA 91711-6110
County: Los Angeles FICE Identification: 001172
Unit ID: 121257
Telephone: (909) 621-8198 Carnegie Class: Bac-A&S
FAX Number: N/A Calendar System: Semester
URL: www.pitzer.edu
Established: 1963 Annual Undergrad Tuition & Fees: $55,878
Enrollment: 922 Coed
Affiliation or Control: Independent Non-Profit IRS Status: 501(c)3
Highest Offering: Baccalaureate
Accreditation: WC

01 Interim President .... Jill KLEIN
05 Vice Pres Acad Affs/Dean of Faculty .... Dr. Allen OMOTO
100 Chief of Staff .... Vacant
10 Chief Operating Ofcr/Treasurer .... Ms. Laura TROENDLE
111 VP Col Advancement/Communications .... Ms. Kimberly SHINER
07 VP Admissions/Financial Aid .... Ms. Yvonne BERUMEN
32 Vice Pres Student Affairs .... Ms. Sandra VASQUEZ
26 VP Strategic Initiatives/Cmty Rels .... Mr. Jim MARCHANT
20 Associate Dean of Faculty .... Mr. Phil ZUCKERMAN
20 Associate Dean of Faculty .... Ms. Susan PHILLIPS
06 Registrar .... Ms. Jannie GILSON
09 Director of Institutional Research .... Ms. Leeshawn CRADOC MOORE
15 AVP Human Resources and Payroll .... Ms. Deanna CABALLERO
18 Asst VP Facilities .... Ms. Patrice LANGEVIN
21 AVP Finance .... Ms. Pamela MADER
36 Director Career Services .... Mr. Brad THARPE
29 Director Alumni/Family Relations .... Ms. Jenna GOUGH
101 Sr Exec Asst/Secretary to the Board .... Ms. Melanie LACY SORENSON

Platt College (F)

1000 S Fremont Avenue, Ste A9W,
Alhambra CA 91803-8845
County: Los Angeles FICE Identification: 030627
Unit ID: 260789
Telephone: (626) 300-5444 Carnegie Class: Bac/Assoc-Mixed
FAX Number: (626) 457-8295 Calendar System: Other
URL: www.plattcollege.edu
Established: 1987 Annual Undergrad Tuition & Fees: $14,354
Enrollment: 717 Coed
Affiliation or Control: Proprietary IRS Status: Proprietary
Highest Offering: Baccalaureate
Accreditation: ACCSC, COARC

01 President .... Mr. Christopher BECKER
06 Registrar .... Ms. Cathy WOLFE
07 Director of Admissions .... Mr. Steven BROYLES

Platt College (G)

3700 Inland Empire Blvd, Ste 400, Ontario CA 91764-4906
Telephone: (909) 941-9410 Identification: 666056
Accreditation: ACCSC, COARC

† Branch campus of Platt College, Ahambra, CA.

Platt College (H)

6465 Sycamore Canyon Blvd, Ste 100,
Riverside CA 92507
Telephone: (951) 572-4300 Identification: 770561
Accreditation: ACCSC

Platt College (I)

6250 El Cajon Boulevard, San Diego CA 92115-3919
County: San Diego FICE Identification: 023043
Unit ID: 121275
Telephone: (619) 265-0107 Carnegie Class: Spec-4-yr-Arts
FAX Number: (619) 265-8655 Calendar System: Other
URL: www.platt.edu
Established: 1980 Annual Undergrad Tuition & Fees: $17,235
Enrollment: 96 Coed
Affiliation or Control: Proprietary IRS Status: Proprietary
Highest Offering: Baccalaureate
Accreditation: ACCSC

00 Chairman .... Mr. Robert D. LEIKER
01 President .... Mrs. Meg LEIKER
03 Vice President .... Mr. Alfred MEDRO
10 Chief Business Officer .... Ms. Marianne TAXTER
05 Director of Education .... Mr. Julio FRIZZA-POMPA

Point Loma Nazarene University (J)

3900 Lomaland Drive, San Diego CA 92106-2899
County: San Diego FICE Identification: 001262
Unit ID: 121309
Telephone: (619) 849-2200 Carnegie Class: Masters/L
FAX Number: (619) 849-2579 Calendar System: Semester
URL: www.pointloma.edu
Established: 1902 Annual Undergrad Tuition & Fees: $38,300
Enrollment: 4,616 Coed
Affiliation or Control: Church Of The Nazarene IRS Status: 501(c)3
Highest Offering: Doctorate
Accreditation: WC, ACBSP, #ARCPA, CAATE, DIETD, EMT, MUS, NURSE, SW

01 President .... Dr. Bob BROWER
05 Provost/Chief Academic Officer .... Dr. Kerry FULCHER
10 VP Finance & CFO .... Mr. Joe LALUZERNE
32 VP Student Life & Formation .... Dr. Mary PAUL
111 Vice President Univ Advancement .... Ms. Kelly SMITH
13 Vice President University Services .... Dr. Jeff BOLSTER
15 Assoc VP for Human Resources .... Ms. Samara TIMMS
58 AVP Grad & Post-Trad Pgm Enrollment ... Ms. Jamie BROWNLEE
28 AVP Diversity and Belonging .... Vacant
114 Assoc VP Accounting/Finance .... Ms. Janet CAPRARIO
84 Assoc VP Enrollment & Retention .... Dr. Scott SHOEMAKER
20 Vice Prov Academic Administration .... Dr. Holly IRWIN
108 Vice Prov Assessment & IE .... Ms. April CORDERO
35 Dean of Students .... Dr. Jake GILBERTSON
13 Chief Information Officer .... Mr. Corey FLING
09 Dir Institutional Research .... Mr. Brent GOODMAN
12 Interim Director of Wesleyan Center .... Dr. Sam POWELL
103 Executive Dir Strengths & Vocation .... Vacant
88 Exec Dir of Enrollment Mgmt .... Ms. Jeanne COCHRAN
26 Director of Communications .... Ms. Lora FLEMING
42 Ld Con for Mission Res & Pst Rel .... Dr. Ron BENEFIEL
88 Director of Community Ministries .... Ms. Dana HOJSACK
88 Director of Worship Arts .... Mr. George WILLIAMSON
49 Dean & Vice Prov for Acad Studies .... Dr. Jim DAICHENDT
97 Assoc Dean of General Education .... Dr. Ben CATER
07 Director Undergraduate Admissions .... Ms. Shannon HUTCHISON-CARAVEO
08 Director of Ryan Library .... Dr. Denise NELSON
56 Dean Extended Learning .... Dr. Dave PHILLIPS
06 Registrar .... Mr. John GUNTHER
88 Director of Records .... Ms. Cheryl GAUGHAN
26 Assoc Vice Pres for Marketing .... Ms. Sharon AYALA
121 Assoc Dean Stdnt Care & Engagement .... Mrs. Melanie WOLF
19 Director of Public Safety .... Mr. Mark RYAN
29 Director of Alumni Relations .... Ms. Kendall LUCAS
40 Bookstore Manager .... Mrs. Anya SELNER TAN
85 Dir Multicultural/Intl Stdnt Svcs .... Ms. Maya HOOD
41 Athletic Director .... Mr. Ethan HAMILTON
88 Director of Nicholson Commons .... Mr. Milton KARAHADIAN
104 Dir Intl Min Study Abroad .... Mr. Brian BECKER
36 Dir of Career Services .... Mr. Nick WOLF
106 Dir Instructional Technology .... Ms. Katie JACOBSON
39 Asst Dir Student Housing .... Ms. Molly PETERSEN
110 Exec Dir Advancement Operations .... Ms. Christina GARDNER
50 Dean of Business .... Mr. Dan BOTHE
53 Dean of Education .... Ms. Deb ERICKSON
101 Secretary of the Board .... Dr. Joe WATKINS
44 Director Annual/Planned Giving .... Mr. William BURFITT
37 Director Student Financial Services .... Ms. Molly PORTER
04 Admin Assistant to the President .... Mrs. Jackye PEACOCK
18 Assoc VP Facilities Operations .... Mr. Dan TORO

Pomona College (K)

550 N College Avenue, #206, Claremont CA 91711-6301
County: Los Angeles FICE Identification: 001173
Unit ID: 121345
Telephone: (909) 621-8000 Carnegie Class: Bac-A&S
FAX Number: (909) 621-8403 Calendar System: Semester
URL: www.pomona.edu
Established: 1887 Annual Undergrad Tuition & Fees: $54,774
Enrollment: 1,475 Coed
Affiliation or Control: Independent Non-Profit IRS Status: 501(c)3
Highest Offering: Baccalaureate
Accreditation: WC

01 President .... Dr. G. Gabrielle STARR
05 Vice President/Dean of College .... Dr. Yuqing Melanie WU
13 Chief Information Officer .... Mr. Jose RODRIGUEZ
10 Vice President/Treasurer .... Vacant
111 VP Institutional Advancement .... Ms. Maria WATSON
32 Vice President/Dean of Students .... Ms. Avis HINKSON
07 VP of Admissions & Financial Aid .... Mr. Seth ALLEN
26 Chief Communications Officer .... Mr. Mark KENDALL
100 Chief of Staff .... Ms. Christine CIAMBRIELLO
06 Registrar .... Ms. Erin Michelle COLLINS
27 Sr Director of Communications .... Ms. Patricia Zurita VEST
29 Asst VP Alumni & Parent Engagement .... Ms. Alisa FISHBACH
37 Interim Director Financial Aid .... Mr. Matthew BIERGANS
36 Dir Career Development Ofc .... Ms. Hazel RAJA
15 Director Human Resources .... Ms. Brenda RUSHFORTH
41 Athletic Director .... Ms. Miriam MERRILL
44 Director Annual Giving .... Ms. Lucy TAKAHASHI
21 Assoc Treasurer/Controller .... Ms. Mary Lou WOODS
09 Int Dir of Institutional Research .... Dr. Elizabeth GRAHAM
18 Chief Facilities/Physical Plant .... Mr. Robert ROBINSON
115 Chief Investment Officer .... Mr. David WALLACE

Premiere Career College (L)

12901 Ramona Blvd, Irwindale CA 91706
FICE Identification: 031258
Unit ID: 416458
Telephone: (626) 814-2080 Carnegie Class: Not Classified
FAX Number: N/A Calendar System: Other

URL: www.premierecollege.edu
Established: 1991   Annual Undergrad Tuition & Fees: N/A
Enrollment: N/A   Coed
Affiliation or Control: Proprietary   IRS Status: Proprietary
Highest Offering: Associate Degree
Accreditation: **ABHES**, SURGT, SURTEC

Presbyterian Theological Seminary in America (A)

15605 Carmenita Road, Santa Fe Springs CA 90670
County: Los Angeles   FICE Identification: 041228
   Unit ID: 490045
Telephone: (562) 926-1023   Carnegie Class: Spec-4-yr-Faith
FAX Number: (562) 926-1025   Calendar System: Semester
URL: www.ptsa.edu
Established: 1977   Annual Undergrad Tuition & Fees: $7,935
Enrollment: 171   Coed
Affiliation or Control: Presbyterian Church In America   IRS Status: 501(c)3
Highest Offering: First Professional Degree
Accreditation: **BI**, THEOL

01	President	Dr. Sang Meyng LEE
05	Dean of Academic Affairs/CAO	Rev. Rubin KIM
10	Chief Financial Officer	Rev. Myung Chul LEE
32	Dean of Student Affairs	Vacant
37	Director of Financial Aid	Mrs. Sunny KIM
08	Librarian	Ms. Dou Ho IM
21	Managing Treasurer/Accountant	Mrs. Judy KIM
06	Registrar	Mrs. Kyu Hae LEE
106	Dir Online Education/E-learning	Mr. Jang Hoon WOO
13	IT Director	Mr. Chul Heon JUNG

Presidio Graduate School (B)

649 Mission Street, Suite 500, San Francisco CA 94105
County: San Francisco   Identification: 667150
   Unit ID: 486433
Telephone: (415) 561-6555   Carnegie Class: Spec-4-yr-Bus
FAX Number: (415) 561-6483   Calendar System: Semester
URL: www.presidio.edu
Established: 2003   Annual Graduate Tuition & Fees: N/A
Enrollment: 152   Coed
Affiliation or Control: Independent Non-Profit   IRS Status: 501(c)3
Highest Offering: Master's; No Undergraduates
Accreditation: **WC**

01	President	Elizabeth MAW
05	Academic Dean/CAO	Dr. Maggie WINSLOW
10	CFO/Vice Pres of Operations	Vacant
32	VP Student Affairs/Enrollment/COO	Dr. Diana ASAAD
07	AVP of Admissions	Dr. Amanda OPPERMAN

Professional Golfers Career College (C)

26109 Ynez Road, Temecula CA 92591-6013
County: Riverside   FICE Identification: 033673
   Unit ID: 437750
Telephone: (951) 719-2994   Carnegie Class: Spec 2-yr-Other
FAX Number: (951) 719-1643   Calendar System: Semester
URL: www.golfcollege.edu
Established: 1990   Annual Undergrad Tuition & Fees: $16,844
Enrollment: 86   Coed
Affiliation or Control: Proprietary   IRS Status: Proprietary
Highest Offering: Associate Degree
Accreditation: **CNCE**

01	President	Dr. Tim SOMERVILLE
10	Chief Financial Officer	Sandi SOMERVILLE

Providence Christian College (D)

464 East Walnut Street, Pasadena CA 91101
County: Los Angeles   FICE Identification: 041539
   Unit ID: 455770
Telephone: (866) 323-0233   Carnegie Class: Bac-A&S
FAX Number: (626) 696-4040   Calendar System: Semester
URL: www.providencecc.edu
Established: 2002   Annual Undergrad Tuition & Fees: $33,396
Enrollment: 121   Coed
Affiliation or Control: Non-denominational   IRS Status: 501(c)3
Highest Offering: Baccalaureate
Accreditation: **WC**

01	President	Vacant
05	Vice Pres Academic Affairs	Dr. David CORBIN
10	Vice Pres Finance & Operations	Dawn DIRKSEN
111	Vice Pres Advancement	Michael KILEDJIAN
84	Vice Pres Enrollment	Pete HAMSTRA
06	Registrar	Elijah VILLAFANA
29	Alumni Relations Manager	Sevanna RICHMOND
32	Dean of Student/Athletic Affairs	Brian DEHAAN

*Rancho Santiago Community College District (E)

2323 N. Broadway, Santa Ana CA 92706-1640
County: Orange   FICE Identification: 006991
   Unit ID: 438665
Telephone: (714) 480-7300   Carnegie Class: N/A

FAX Number: (714) 796-3915
URL: www.rsccd.edu

01	Chancellor	Mr. Marvin MARTINEZ
10	VC Business & Fiscal Svcs	Ms. Iris INGRAM
05	Vice Chanc Educational Svcs	Mr. Enrique PEREZ
15	Vice Chanc Human Resources	Mr. Cheng Yu HOU
13	Asst Vice Chanc Info Tech Svcs	Mr. Jesse GONZALEZ
19	Chief District Safety & Security	Mr. Ralph WEBB
04	Exec Asst to the Chancellor	Ms. Debra GERARD

*Santa Ana College (F)

1530 W 17th Street, Santa Ana CA 92706-3398
County: Orange   FICE Identification: 001284
   Unit ID: 121619
Telephone: (714) 564-6000   Carnegie Class: Bac/Assoc-Assoc Dom
FAX Number: (714) 564-6379   Calendar System: Semester
URL: www.sac.edu
Established: 1915   Annual Undergrad Tuition & Fees (In-District): $1,160
Enrollment: 20,118   Coed
Affiliation or Control: State/Local   IRS Status: 501(c)3
Highest Offering: Baccalaureate
Accreditation: **WJ**, ADNUR, OTA

02	Interim President	Dr. Marilyn FLORES
05	Vice President Academic Affairs	Dr. Jeffrey N. LAMB
10	Vice Chanc Business Svcs	Iris I. INGRAM
51	Vice President Continuing Educ	Dr. James KENNEDY
32	Vice Pres Student Services	Dr. Vaniethia HUBBARD
11	Vice Pres Administrative Services	Dr. Bart HOFFMAN
07	Dean of Enrollment Services	Mark LIANG
06	Interim Registrar	Hung NGUYEN
35	Interim Assoc Dean Student Dev	Dr. Brenda ESTRADA
38	Dean Counseling	Dr. Maria DELA CRUZ
37	Assoc Dean of Financial Aid	Robert MANSON
111	Exec Director College Advancement	Christina ROMERO
18	Interim Director Phys Plant/Facil	Robert WARD
50	Dean Business Division	Madeline GRANT
41	Dean Kinesiology & Athletics	Dr. R. Douglas MANNING
57	Dean Fine & Performing Arts	Dr. Kellori DOWER
79	Dean Humanities/Social Sciences	Vacant
81	Dean Science/Math/Health Sci	Dr. Saeid EIDGAHY
103	Dir Career Education/Workforce Dev	Kimberly MATHEWS
56	Associate Dean EOPS	Vacant
88	Associate Dean DSPS	Dr. Veronica OFORLEA
04	Assistant to the President	Leisa SCHUMACHER
26	Interim Public Information Officer	Dalilah DAVALOZ
09	Director of College Research	Vacant
35	Assistant Dean Student Services	Teresa MERCADO-COTA
35	Dean Student Affairs	Alicia KRUIZENGA
20	Dean Academic Affairs	Dr. Fernando ORTIZ
88	Associate Dean Counseling	Dr. Armando SOTO
41	Athletic Director	Mary HEGARTY
66	Int Assoc Dean Health Sci/Nursing	Mary STECKLER
109	Director Auxiliary Services	Jennie ADAMS
72	Dean Human Svcs & Technology	Dr. Larisa SERGEYEVA

*Santiago Canyon College (G)

8045 E Chapman Avenue, Orange CA 92869-4512
County: Orange   FICE Identification: 036957
   Unit ID: 399212
Telephone: (714) 628-4900   Carnegie Class: Assoc/HT-High Trad
FAX Number: (714) 628-4723   Calendar System: Semester
URL: www.sccollege.edu
Established: 1997   Annual Undergrad Tuition & Fees (In-District): $1,156
Enrollment: 9,003   Coed
Affiliation or Control: State/Local   IRS Status: 501(c)3
Highest Offering: Associate Degree
Accreditation: **WJ**

02	Acting President	Dr. Arleen SATELE
04	Assistant to the President	Ms. Esther ODEGARD
32	Vice President Student Services	Dr. Melba CASTRO
05	Int Vice President Academic Affairs	Mr. Jose VARGAS
51	Vice President Continuing Educ	Dr. James KENNEDY
10	Vice Pres Administrative Services	Dr. Arleen SATELE
38	Dean Counseling	Dr. Jennifer COTO
81	Dean Math & Sci/Athletic Dir	Mr. Martin STRINGER
79	Dean Arts/Humanities/Social Sci	Dr. Michelle SAMURA
50	Dean Business/Career Educ	Ms. Elizabeth ARTEAGA
108	Dean Institutional Effectiveness	Mr. Aaron VOELCKER
20	Int Dean Instruct/Student Services	Mr. Joseph ALONZO
35	Asst Vice President Student Svcs	Dr. Loretta JORDAN
20	Associate Dean DSPS	Ms. Starr AVEDESIAN
07	Assoc Dean of Admissions & Records	Mr. Tuyen NGUYEN
37	Assoc Dean Fin Aid/Scholarships	Ms. Sheena TRAN
18	Facilities Manager	Mr. Chuck WALES

Reach University (H)

1221 Preservation Park Way, Ste 100, Oakland CA 94612
County: Alameda   Identification: 667313
Telephone: (510) 501-5075   Carnegie Class: Not Classified
FAX Number: (510) 868-2215   Calendar System: Semester
URL: www.reach.edu
Established: 2007   Annual Undergrad Tuition & Fees: N/A
Enrollment: N/A   Coed
Affiliation or Control: Independent Non-Profit   IRS Status: 501(c)3
Highest Offering: Master's
Accreditation: **WC**

01	University President	Joseph EDELHEIT ROSS
00	Chancellor	Mallory DWINAL-PALISCH
05	Chief Academic Ofcr/Dean Grad Inst	Liz BAHAM

Redwoods Community College District (I)

7351 Tompkins Hill Road, Eureka CA 95501-9300
County: Humboldt   FICE Identification: 001185
   Unit ID: 121707
Telephone: (707) 476-4100   Carnegie Class: Assoc/HVT-High Trad
FAX Number: (707) 476-4400   Calendar System: Semester
URL: https://www.redwoods.edu/
Established: 1964   Annual Undergrad Tuition & Fees (In-District): $1,147
Enrollment: 3,891   Coed
Affiliation or Control: State/Local   IRS Status: 501(c)3
Highest Offering: Associate Degree
Accreditation: **WJ**, DA, EMT

01	President/Superintendent	Dr. Keith FLAMER
05	VP of Instruction	Ms. Kerry MAYER
04	Exec Assistant to the President	Ms. Cynthia PETRUSHA
10	VP Administrative Services	Ms. Julia MORRISON
32	Int VP Student Services	Mr. Clinton SLAUGHTER
103	Director Workforce & Community Educ	Ms. Pru RATLIFF
12	Director Del Norte Campus	Mr. Rory JOHNSON
84	Dean of Enrollment Services	Ms. Rianne CONNOR
88	Director of Special Programs	Dr. Kintay JOHNSON
22	Director Disabled Student Pgm Svcs	Vacant
18	Director Maintenance & Operations	Mr. Steve MCKENZIE
102	Exec Dir of Foundation/Col Advance	Mr. Marty COELHO
08	Director Library Svcs/Acad Support	Vacant
19	Director of Public Safety	Ms. Kristy SEHER
88	Director Administration of Justice	Mr. Mike PERKINS
41	Director of PE & Athletics	Mr. Bob BROWN
09	Director Institutional Research	Mr. Paul CHOWN
26	Career Outreach & Marketing Manager	Ms. Molly BLAKEMORE
15	Manager of Human Resources	Ms. Tina WAHLUND

Regan Career Institute (J)

11350 Valley Blvd, El Monte CA 91731
County: Los Angeles   FICE Identification: 042554
   Unit ID: 490197
Telephone: (626) 455-0312   Carnegie Class: Not Classified
FAX Number: (626) 455-0316   Calendar System: Other
URL: www.rci.edu
Established: 2004   Annual Undergrad Tuition & Fees: N/A
Enrollment: 41   Coed
Affiliation or Control: Proprietary   IRS Status: Proprietary
Highest Offering: Associate Degree
Accreditation: **ABHES**

01	CEO	Regan YU
11	Managing Director	Julian LEE

Reiss-Davis Graduate Center (K)

3200 Motor Avenue, Los Angeles CA 90034
County: Los Angeles   Identification: 667332
Telephone: (310) 204-1666   Carnegie Class: Not Classified
FAX Number: N/A   Calendar System: Other
URL: www.reissdavis.org
Established: 1976   Annual Graduate Tuition & Fees: N/A
Enrollment: N/A   Coed
Affiliation or Control: Independent Non-Profit   IRS Status: 501(c)3
Highest Offering: Doctorate; No Undergraduates
Accreditation: **WC**

01	Chancellor & Director	Vacant
11	Director of Operations	Lourdes BROWN
05	Provost	Dr. Halyna KORNUTA
09	Institutional Research Analyst	Dr. Karen JAMES
06	Registrar	Mila JOVICIC
20	Academic Dean	Dr. Jens SCHMIDT

Rhombus University (L)

8050 La Mesa Blvd, La Mesa CA 91942
County: San Diego   Identification: 667430
Telephone: (858) 848-1766   Carnegie Class: Not Classified
FAX Number: (619) 463-2522   Calendar System: Semester
URL: rhombusuniversity.com
Established: 2018   Annual Graduate Tuition & Fees: N/A
Enrollment: N/A   Coed
Affiliation or Control: Proprietary   IRS Status: Proprietary
Highest Offering: Master's; No Undergraduates
Accreditation: **DEAC**

01	CEO	Dr. Ray HAYDEN

Rio Hondo College (M)

3600 Workman Mill Road, Whittier CA 90601-1699
County: Los Angeles   FICE Identification: 001269
   Unit ID: 121886
Telephone: (562) 692-0921   Carnegie Class: Bac/Assoc-Assoc Dom
FAX Number: N/A   Calendar System: Semester
URL: www.riohondo.edu
Established: 1960   Annual Undergrad Tuition & Fees (In-District): $1,360
Enrollment: 15,692   Coed
Affiliation or Control: State/Local   IRS Status: 501(c)3

Highest Offering: Baccalaureate
Accreditation: WJ, NAIT

01 Superintendent/President ... Dr. Marilyn FLORES
05 Vice Pres Academic Affairs ... Dr. Don MILLER
10 Vice President Finance/Business ... Dr. Stephen KIBUI
32 Vice President Student Services ... Dr. Earic DIXON-PETERS
86 Dir Govt & Community Relations ... Dr. Russell CASTANEDA-CALLEROS
15 Vice President Human Resources ... Ms. Tina KUPERMAN
26 Dir Marketing & Communications ... Ms. Ruthie RETANA
35 Dir Student Life & Leadership ... Ms. Shaina PHILLIPS
06 Dir Admin & Records/Registrar ... Ms. Leigh UNGER
38 Dean Counseling ... Ms. Lisa CHAVEZ
102 Int Exec Dir RHC Foundation ... Mr. Henry GEE
37 Dir Financial Aid/Scholarships ... Mr. Donald GORDON
18 Director of Facilities ... Vacant
96 Director of Contract Management ... Mr. Felix G. SARAO
04 Exec Assistant to President/Board ... Ms. Renee D. GALLEGOS
09 Dean Inst Research & Plng ... Dr. Caroline DURDELLA
20 Dean Educational Centers ... Ms. Yolanda EMERSON
41 Dean KDA/Athletic Director ... Ms. Nedra BROWN
50 Dean Business ... Ms. Gita RUNKLE

*Riverside Community College District (A)

3801 Market Street, Riverside CA 92501
County: Riverside Identification: 667039
Telephone: (951) 222-8800 Carnegie Class: N/A
FAX Number: (951) 682-5339
URL: www.rccd.edu

01 Chancellor ... Dr. Wolde-Ab ISAAC
05 VC Educ Svcs/Strategic Planning ... Dr. Susan MILLS
10 VC Business & Financial Svcs ... Mr. Aaron BROWN
15 VC Human Resources/Employee Rels ... Ms. Tammy FEW
111 VC Institutional Advancement ... Ms. Rebeccah GOLDWARE
12 President Moreno Valley College ... Dr. Robin STEINBACK
12 President Norco College ... Dr. Monica GREEN
12 President Riverside City College ... Vacant
43 General Counsel ... Mr. Keith DOBYNS

*Moreno Valley College (B)

16130 Lasselle Street, Moreno Valley CA 92551
County: Riverside FICE Identification: 041735
Unit ID: 460394
Telephone: (951) 571-6100 Carnegie Class: Assoc/HT-Mix Trad/Non
FAX Number: N/A Calendar System: Semester
URL: www.mvc.edu
Established: 2010 Annual Undergrad Tuition & Fees (In-District): $1,420
Enrollment: 9,158 Coed
Affiliation or Control: State/Local IRS Status: 501(c)3
Highest Offering: Associate Degree
Accreditation: WJ, DA, DH, EMT

02 President ... Dr. Robin L. STEINBACK
05 Int Vice Pres Academic Affairs ... Mrs. Ree AMEZQUITA
10 Vice Pres Business Services ... Mr. Majd ASKAR
32 Vice Pres of Student Services ... Mr. Christopher SWEETEN
20 Dean of Instruction ... Vacant
121 Dean Stdnt Success & Acad Support ... Mr. Tom VITZELIO
84 Director Enrollment Services ... Ms. Jamie CLIFTON
37 Director Stdnt Financial Services ... Vacant
18 Director of Facilities ... Mr. Ron KIRKPATRICK
35 Dean Student Development & Wellness ... Mrs. Brandi AVILA
38 Dean Student Success & Counseling ... Dr. Michael Paul WONG
124 Dean Enrollment Svcs & Engagement ... Mrs. Sandra MARTINEZ
89 Director First Year Experience ... Vacant
13 Manager Tech Support Services ... Vacant
23 Director Health Services ... Ms. Tracy BENNETT
88 Dean of Instruction Public Safety ... Mr. Phillip RAWLINGS
75 Dean STEM/CTE ... Dr. Kevin STEWART
88 Associate Dean CTE ... Mr. Eric ANTHONY
81 Director STEM Innovation ... Mr. Donnell LAYNE
88 Director TRIO Programs ... Mrs. Micki GRAYSON
109 Assistant Manager Food Services ... Ms. Julie HLEBASKO
22 Director Disability Support Svcs ... Vacant
88 Asst Dir Student Financial Services ... Mr. Carlos PONCE
88 Makerspace Project Supervisor ... Mr. Jason KENNEDY
88 Asst Director Upward Bound ... Ms. Angel ORTA-PEREZ
04 Executive Admin Asst to the Pres ... Ms. Eden ANDOM
108 Dean Institutional Effectiveness ... Mr. Jacob KEVARI
88 Early Childhood Educ Manager ... Mrs. Sandra RIVAS
88 Apprenticeship Director ... Mrs. Rosalinda RIVAS
88 Director Middle College High School ... Mr. Julio GONZALEZ
88 Mental Health Supervisor ... Dr. Lynnette NAVARRO SULLIVAN
88 Basic Needs & Wellness Supervisor ... Ms. Angie GORDON

*Norco College (C)

2001 Third Street, Norco CA 92860
County: Riverside FICE Identification: 041761
Unit ID: 460464
Telephone: (951) 372-7000 Carnegie Class: Assoc/HT-Mix Trad/Non
FAX Number: N/A Calendar System: Semester
URL: www.norcocollege.edu
Established: 2010 Annual Undergrad Tuition & Fees (In-District): $1,420
Enrollment: 10,261 Coed
Affiliation or Control: State/Local IRS Status: 501(c)3
Highest Offering: Associate Degree
Accreditation: WJ

02 President ... Dr. Monica GREEN
05 Vice Pres Academic Affairs ... Dr. Samuel LEE
32 Vice Pres Student Services ... Dr. Kaneesha TARRANT
10 Vice Pres Business Services ... Dr. Michael COLLINS
45 Vice Pres Planning and Development ... Dr. Kevin FLEMING
04 Executive Asst to President ... Ms. Denise TERRAZAS
84 Dean Enrollment Services ... Mr. Mark DEASIS
09 Dean Institutional Effectiveness ... Dr. Greg AYCOCK
13 Dean Technology/Learning Resources ... Mr. Damon NANCE
18 Director Facilities ... Mr. Steven MARSHALL
25 Dean Grants/Stdnt Equity Initiative ... Dr. Gustavo OCEGUERA
37 Director Student Financial Services ... Dr. Maria GONZALEZ
20 Dean Instruction ... Dr. Jason PARKS
20 Interim Dean Instruction ... Dr. Melissa BADER

*Riverside City College (D)

4800 Magnolia Avenue, Riverside CA 92506
County: Riverside FICE Identification: 001270
Unit ID: 121901
Telephone: (951) 222-8000 Carnegie Class: Assoc/HT-High Trad
FAX Number: (951) 222-8036 Calendar System: Semester
URL: www.rcc.edu
Established: 1916 Annual Undergrad Tuition & Fees (In-District): $1,420
Enrollment: 20,080 Coed
Affiliation or Control: State/Local IRS Status: 501(c)3
Highest Offering: Associate Degree
Accreditation: WJ, ACBSP, ADNUR, PNUR

02 President ... Dr. Gregory ANDERSON
05 Vice Pres Academic Affairs ... Dr. Lynn WRIGHT
10 VP Business Services ... Dr. Raymond WEST
32 Vice President Student Services ... Dr. FeRita CARTER
66 Dean School of Nursing ... Dr. Tammy VANT HUL
83 Dean Instruction Hum/Soc Sci ... Dr. Kristi WOODS
04 Exec Asst to the President ... Ms. Heidi GONSIER
30 Interim VP Planning & Dev ... Ms. Kristine DIMEMMO
121 Director Academic Support ... Ms. Inez MOORE
84 Dean Enrollment Services ... Ms. Kyla TEUFEL
35 Dean Student Services ... Dr. Thomas CRUZ-SOTO
41 Director Athletics ... Mr. James WOOLDRIDGE
23 Director Health Services ... Ms. Renee MARTIN THORNTON
19 Sergeant Safety & Police ... Mr. Robert KLEVENO

Sacramento Ultrasound Institute (E)

2233 Watt Avenue #150, Sacramento CA 95825
County: Sacramento Identification: 667264
Unit ID: 490160
Telephone: (916) 877-7977 Carnegie Class: Not Classified
FAX Number: (916) 481-4032 Calendar System: Other
URL: www.sui.edu
Established: 2002 Annual Undergrad Tuition & Fees: N/A
Enrollment: 28 Coed
Affiliation or Control: Proprietary IRS Status: Proprietary
Highest Offering: Associate Degree
Accreditation: ABHES

01 President/CEO ... Mrs. Sima DERMISHYAN

SAE Expression College (F)

6601 Shellmound Street, Emeryville CA 94608-1021
County: Alameda FICE Identification: 039733
Unit ID: 447458
Telephone: (510) 654-2934 Carnegie Class: Not Classified
FAX Number: (510) 658-3414 Calendar System: Semester
URL: www.sae.edu
Established: 1999 Annual Undergrad Tuition & Fees: $23,399
Enrollment: 182 Coed
Affiliation or Control: Proprietary IRS Status: Proprietary
Highest Offering: Baccalaureate
Accreditation: ACCSC

05 Director of Education ... Mr. Chris COLATOS
07 Admissions Manager ... Ms. Miok KIM

Saint John's Seminary (G)

5012 Seminary Road, Camarillo CA 93012-2500
County: Ventura FICE Identification: 001299
Unit ID: 123855
Telephone: (805) 482-2755 Carnegie Class: Not Classified
FAX Number: (805) 482-3470 Calendar System: Semester
URL: www.stjohnsem.edu
Established: 1939 Annual Graduate Tuition & Fees: N/A
Enrollment: N/A Male
Affiliation or Control: Roman Catholic IRS Status: 501(c)3
Highest Offering: Master's; No Undergraduates
Accreditation: WC, THEOL

01 Rector/President ... Rev. Marco A. DURAZO
03 Executive Vice President ... Rev. Slawomir SZKREDKA
05 Academic Dean ... Rev. John O'BRIEN
07 Director of Admissions ... Rev. Thinh PHAM
06 Registrar ... Mr. Brian CAMPOS
04 Administrative Asst to President ... Ms. Maria GAETA
10 Director of Finance ... Mr. Nalin ATAPATTY
15 Director Personnel Services ... Ms. Mary BISSINGER
18 Chief Facilities/Physical Plant ... Mr. Greg JULIUS
30 Chief Development/Advancement ... Ms. Linda CHABOLLA
32 Chief Student Affairs/Student Life ... Rev. Raymond MARQUEZ
96 Director of Purchasing ... Ms. Delia GALICIA
08 Chief Library Officer ... Dr. Victoria BRENNAN

St. Luke University (H)

1460 E. Holt Ave., Suite 72, Pomona CA 91767
County: Los Angeles Identification: 667299
Telephone: (909) 623-0302 Carnegie Class: Not Classified
FAX Number: (909) 623-0480 Calendar System: Semester
URL: https://www.stlukeuniv.edu/
Established: 2004 Annual Undergrad Tuition & Fees: N/A
Enrollment: N/A Coed
Affiliation or Control: Independent Non-Profit IRS Status: 501(c)3
Highest Offering: Doctorate
Accreditation: TRACS

01 Founder/President ... Rev. Young D. KIM
05 Chief Academic Officer ... Dr. Kyung Hwan KIM
10 Chief Financial Officer ... Mr. David KIM
11 Director of Administration ... Ms. Jung KIM
32 Director Student Affairs ... Rev. Taehoon LEE
06 Registrar ... Kun KWAK
08 Librarian ... Ricky STROBEL

Saint Mary's College of California (I)

1928 Saint Mary's Road, Moraga CA 94556-2744
County: Contra Costa FICE Identification: 001302
Unit ID: 123554
Telephone: (925) 631-4000 Carnegie Class: Masters/L
FAX Number: (925) 376-8497 Calendar System: 4/1/4
URL: www.stmarys-ca.edu
Established: 1863 Annual Undergrad Tuition & Fees: $50,660
Enrollment: 3,439 Coed
Affiliation or Control: Roman Catholic IRS Status: 501(c)3
Highest Offering: Doctorate
Accreditation: WC

01 President ... Dr. Richard G. PLUMB
10 VP for Finance & Administration ... Ms. Susan H. COLLINS
05 Executive Vice President & Provost ... Dr. Corey COOK
20 AVP Academic Programs/Planning ... Dr. Jennifer KULBECK
20 Interim VP Student Academics ... Dr. Aeleah SOINE
88 Interim Dean of Core ... Dr. Steve MILLER
111 VP Strategic Partnershp/Advancement ... Mr. Patrick CAREW
32 Vice President for Student Life ... Dr. Anthony GARRISON
26 Asst VP College Communication ... Vacant
88 Vice President for Mission ... Dr. Frances SWEENEY
84 Vice Pres Enrollment Management ... Ms. Shobi SIVADASAN
20 Assoc Provost for Faculty Affairs ... Dr. Jennifer HEUNG
43 General Counsel ... Vacant
53 Dean School of Education ... Dr. Carol Ann GITTENS
81 Dean School of Science ... Dr. Roy WENSLEY
49 Dean School Liberal Arts ... Dr. Sheila HUGHES
35 Dean of Students ... Dr. Jim SCIUTO
08 Dean Library & Academic Resources ... Ms. Lauren MACDONALD
42 Director Mission & Ministry ... Ms. Karin MCCLELLAND
15 Associate VP Human Resources ... Ms. Denise PARISH
29 Sr Director of Alumni Engagement ... Ms. Courtney CARMIGNANI
50 Dean School of Bus Admin/Economics ... Dr. Elizabeth DAVIS
06 Registrar ... Ms. Tracey DONALDSON
35 Associate Dean of Students ... Vacant
37 Interim Director of Financial Aid ... Ms. Joyce SONENBERG
88 Director of Kinesiology ... Dr. Claire WILLIAMS
57 Director MFA in Creative Writing ... Dr. Matthew ZAPRUDER
102 Dir Corporate & Foundation Rels ... Mr. Bill OLDS
13 Chief Technology Officer ... Mr. Francisco CHAVEZ
19 Director of Public Safety ... Mr. Hampton CANTRELL
38 Director of Counseling Center ... Ms. Dai L. TO
41 VP for Intercollegiate Athletics ... Mr. Michael J. MATOSO
88 Museum Administrator ... Mr. John SCHNEIDER
88 Int Director January Term Program ... Dr. Claire WILLIAMS
18 VP for Facilities Services ... Ms. Sarah SPERON
88 Director of Project Management ... Ms. Chelsea BUFFINGTON
46 Director of Office of Research ... Ms. Elizabeth GALLAGHER
36 Dir of Career Devel Center ... Ms. Beverly MCLEAN
23 Medical Director Health & Wellness ... Ms. Rachel SNOWDEN
86 Director Community & Govt Relations ... Vacant
94 Director Women's Resource Ctr ... Ms. Sharon SOBOTTA
88 Director of CILSA ... Dr. Jennifer PIGZA
88 Assistant Director of CILSA ... Vacant
21 AVP of Finance & Controller ... Ms. Gina ARMSTRONG-SMITH
104 Director Ctr International Programs ... Ms. Vanessa MARQUEZ
121 Dir Student Engage & Academic Svcs ... Mr. Michael HOFFSHIRE
09 Director of Institutional Research ... Ms. Carlissa JACKSON
89 Dir New Student/Family Programs ... Ms. Jennifer HERZOG
96 Accounts Payable/Purchasing Super ... Ms. Shannon MURRAY
39 Director Student Housing ... Vacant
04 Executive Asst to President ... Dr. David FORD
07 Dean of Admissions ... Ms. Sherie GILMORE-CLEVELAND

Saint Patrick's Seminary & University (J)

320 Middlefield Road, Menlo Park CA 94025-3596
County: San Mateo FICE Identification: 010074
Telephone: (650) 325-5621 Carnegie Class: Not Classified
FAX Number: (650) 323-5447 Calendar System: Semester
URL: www.stpsu.edu
Established: 1898 Annual Undergrad Tuition & Fees: N/A
Enrollment: N/A Male
Affiliation or Control: Roman Catholic IRS Status: 501(c)3

Highest Offering: Master's
Accreditation: WC, THEOL

01 President-Rector .... V.Rev. Mark DOHERTY
03 Vice Rector .... Rev. Anthony STOEPPEL
05 Academic Dean .... Dr. Margaret TUREK
10 Director of Operations .... Rev. Richard DIZON
09 Director of Institutional Research .... Dr. Jill FEGLEY

Saint Photios Orthodox Theological Seminary (A)

PO Box 797, 510 Collier Way, Etna CA 96027
County: Siskiyou — Identification: 667366
Telephone: (530) 467-3544 — Carnegie Class: Not Classified
FAX Number: (530) 638-4456 — Calendar System: Semester
URL: www.spots.edu
Established: 2015 — Annual Undergrad Tuition & Fees: N/A
Enrollment: N/A — Coed
Affiliation or Control: Independent Non-Profit — IRS Status: 501(c)3
Highest Offering: Master's
Accreditation: BI

01 Rector .... M Rev. Bishop AUXENTIOS
05 Dean .... V Rev. Archimandrite PATAPIOS
06 Registrar .... Ms. Gabrielle ASGARIAN
26 Communications & Development Dir .... Mr. Alexei BUSHUNOW
08 Librarian .... Ms. Esther SCHENONE
10 Treasurer .... Schemamonk CHRYSOSTOMOS
32 Director of Student Services .... Schemanun KYPRIANE
13 Information Technology Director .... Schemamonk VLASIE
42 Director of Spiritual Life .... V Rev. Archimandrite GREGORY

The Salvation Army College for Officer Training at Crestmont (B)

30840 Hawthorne Boulevard,
Rancho Palos Verdes CA 90275-5301
County: Los Angeles — FICE Identification: 036954
Telephone: (310) 265-6132 — Carnegie Class: Not Classified
FAX Number: N/A — Calendar System: Quarter
URL: www.crestmont.edu
Established: 1878 — Annual Undergrad Tuition & Fees: N/A
Enrollment: N/A — Coed
Affiliation or Control: Other — IRS Status: 501(c)3
Highest Offering: Associate Degree
Accreditation: WJ

01 Training Principal .... Major Nigel CROSS
03 Assistant Training Principal .... Major Amy REARDON
05 Director of Education .... Major Stacy CROSS
10 Director of Business Administration ... Major Premek KRAMERIUS
04 Exec Secretary to Trng Principal .... Ms. Patricia EVANS
09 Director of Institutional Research .... Dr. Duncan SUTTON
15 Director of Personnel .... Major Charity KRAMERIUS

Samuel Merritt University (C)

3100 Telegraph Avenue, Oakland CA 94609
County: Alameda — FICE Identification: 007012
Unit ID: 122296
Telephone: (800) 607-6377 — Carnegie Class: Spec-4-yr-Other Health
FAX Number: (510) 869-6525 — Calendar System: Semester
URL: www.samuelmerritt.edu
Established: 1909 — Annual Undergrad Tuition & Fees: N/A
Enrollment: 2,050 — Coed
Affiliation or Control: Independent Non-Profit — IRS Status: 501(c)3
Highest Offering: Doctorate
Accreditation: WC, ANEST, ARCPA, NURSE, OT, POD, PTA

01 President .... Dr. Ching-Hua WANG
05 Academic Vice President/Provost .... Dr. Fred BALDINI
10 Exec Vice Pres/Treasurer/CFO/COO .... Mr. Dave LAWLOR
32 Acting Vice Pres of Student Affairs .... Mr. Timothy CRANFORD
111 Vice Pres Advancement/Communication .... Mr. Al FRISONE
20 Asst Academic Vice President .... Dr. Celeste VILLANUEVA
20 Asst Academic Vice President .... Dr. Michael NEGRETE
04 Assistant to the President .... Ms. Carrie ARNETT
66 Dean & Professor of Nursing .... Dr. Lorna KENDRICK
88 Chair Dept Physical Therapy .... Dr. Nicole CHRISTENSEN
88 Chair Dept Occupational Therapy .... Dr. Kate HAYNER
88 Chair ABSN Program .... Ms. Marianne BIANGONE
88 Chair Physician Assistant Program .... Dr. Michael DEROSA
15 Exec Director Human Resources .... Ms. Eva HILLIARD
26 Director of Communications .... Mr. Jim MUYO
09 Director Institutional Research .... Ms. Nandini DASGUPTA
06 Registrar .... Ms. Anne SCHER
08 Library Director .... Ms. Hai-Thom SOTA
37 Director Financial Aid .... Mr. Tyler PRUETT
88 Chair Family Nurse Practitioner Pgm .... Ms. Rhonda RAMIREZ
18 Facilities Manager .... Mr. Timothy PARKER
07 Dean of Admission .... Mr. Blas GUERRERO
12 Site Manager Sacramento .... Ms. Marianne BIANGONE
13 Dir of Information Technology Svcs .... Mr. Marcus WALTON
100 Chief of Staff .... Ms. Emily PRIETO-TSEREGOUNIS
102 Exec Dir Corporate/Foundation Rels .... Ms. Cyndi WEINGARD
108 Director Institutional Assessment .... Ms. Leslie WASSON
19 Univ Safety & Security Specialist .... Mr. Trevor FLANARY
44 Director Annual Giving .... Ms. Jenna INGALLS

*San Bernardino Community College District (D)

550 E Hospitality Lane, Suite 200,
San Bernardino CA 92408
County: San Bernardino — Identification: 667040
Telephone: (909) 388-6900 — Carnegie Class: N/A
FAX Number: (909) 387-1102
URL: www.sbccd.org

01 Interim Chancellor .... Jose TORRES
10 Int Vice Chanc Business/Fiscal Svcs .... James BUYSSE
15 Vice Chanc Human Resources .... Kristina HANNON
111 Assoc VC Economic Development .... Richard GALOPE
13 Chief Technology Officer .... Luke BIXLER
32 Dean Student Svcs/Development .... Joe CABRALES

*Crafton Hills College (E)

11711 Sand Canyon Road, Yucaipa CA 92399-1799
County: San Bernardino — FICE Identification: 009272
Unit ID: 113111
Telephone: (909) 794-2161 — Carnegie Class: Assoc/HT-High Trad
FAX Number: (909) 794-0423 — Calendar System: Semester
URL: www.craftonhills.edu
Established: 1972 — Annual Undergrad Tuition & Fees (In-District): $1,178
Enrollment: 6,012 — Coed
Affiliation or Control: State/Local — IRS Status: 501(c)3
Highest Offering: Associate Degree
Accreditation: WJ, COARC, EMT

02 President .... Dr. Kevin HORAN
05 Vice Pres of Instruction .... Dr. Keith WURTZ
11 Vice President Administrative Svcs .... Mr. Mike STRONG
32 Vice President Student Services .... Dr. Delmy MONTENEGRO-SPENCER
35 Dean Stdnt Svcs/Stdnt Development .... Mr. Joe CABRALES
83 Dean Social/Info/Natural Science .... Dr. Van MUSE
49 Dean Letters/Arts/Math .... Dr. Kay WEISS
36 Dean Career Educ & Human Devel .... Mr. Daniel WORD
38 Dean Student Services/Counseling .... Mr. Mauro PENA
09 Dean Inst Effect/Research/Planning .... Dr. Giovanni SOSA
111 Director Institutional Advancement .... Ms. Michelle RIGGS
124 Director EOPS/CARE .... Dr. Rejoice CHAVIRA
37 Director Financial Aid .... Mr. John W. MUSKAVITCH
35 Director Student Life .... Dr. Ericka PADDOCK
18 Director Facilities .... Mr. Larry COOK
13 Director Technology Services .... Ms. Melissa OSHMAN
07 Director Admissions & Records .... Mr. Larry AYCOCK
04 Executive Asst to President .... Mrs. Cyndie ST. JEAN

*San Bernardino Valley College (F)

701 S Mt. Vernon Avenue,
San Bernardino CA 92410-2798
County: San Bernardino — FICE Identification: 001272
Unit ID: 123527
Telephone: (909) 384-4400 — Carnegie Class: Assoc/MT-VT-High Trad
FAX Number: N/A — Calendar System: Semester
URL: www.valleycollege.edu
Established: 1926 — Annual Undergrad Tuition & Fees (In-District): $1,328
Enrollment: 12,206 — Coed
Affiliation or Control: State/Local — IRS Status: 501(c)3
Highest Offering: Associate Degree
Accreditation: WJ, ADNUR

02 Int President .... Dr. Scott W. THAYER
11 Int VP Administrative Services .... Ms. Tenille C. NORRIS
05 VP Instruction .... Dr. Dina HUMBLE
32 Int VP Student Services .... Dr. Olivia ROSAS
121 Dean Acad Success & Learning Svcs .... Ms. Patricia QUACH
72 Dn Applied Tech/Trans/Cul Arts .... Ms. Vanessa THOMAS
79 Dean Arts & Humanities .... Ms. Leticia HECTOR
38 Dean Counseling/Matriculation .... Mr. Marco COTA
50 Dean Math/Bus/Computer Tech .... Dr. Stephanie LEWIS
09 Dean Research/Plng/Inst Effect/GD .... Dr. Joanna OXENDINE
81 Dean of Science .... Dr. John STANSKAS
83 Dean SS/Human Development & PE .... Dr. Wallace JOHNSON
22 Dean Student Equity & Success .... Ms. Carmen RODRIGUEZ
66 Int Assoc Dean Hlth Sci/Div Nursing .... Ms. Yolanda SIMENTAL
07 Director Admissions/Records .... Ms. April DALE-CARTER
68 Director Athletics .... Mr. Dave RUBIO
13 Int Director Campus Technology Svcs .... Mr. Aldo SIFUENTES
88 Int Director Child Development .... Ms. Sandy KARGE
30 Director Development .... Mr. Michael LAYNE
28 Director DSP&S .... Mr. Larry BRUNSON, JR.
124 Director EOP&S/CARE .... Ms. Joanne HINOJOSA
18 Director Facilities M&O .... Mr. Robert JENKINS
37 Director Financial Aid .... Mr. Sam TREJO
89 Director First Year Experience .... Ms. Sharaf WILLIAMS
08 Dir Library/Learning Support Svcs .... Mr. Ron HASTINGS
26 Director Marketing Creative Svcs/PA .... Mr. Paul BRATULIN
88 Director Police Academies .... Mr. Paul DENNIS
88 Director STEM-MESA .... Dr. Daniel J. MAYO
35 Director Student Life .... Dr. Raymond CARLOS
103 Mgr CalWORKS/Workforce Dev .... Ms. Shalita TILLMAN
51 AEBG Administrator .... Dr. Emma DIAZ
88 Supervisor Custodial .... Mr. Albert CAMACHO
88 Supervisor Food Services .... Mr. Erik MORDEN
88 Supervisor Maintenance & Grounds .... Mr. Kevin GRISHOW

San Diego Christian College (G)

200 Riverview Parkway, Santee CA 92071
County: San Diego — FICE Identification: 012031
Unit ID: 112084
Telephone: (619) 201-8700 — Carnegie Class: Masters/S
FAX Number: (619) 201-8749 — Calendar System: Semester
URL: www.sdcc.edu
Established: 1970 — Annual Undergrad Tuition & Fees: $33,312
Enrollment: 512 — Coed
Affiliation or Control: Independent Non-Profit — IRS Status: 501(c)3
Highest Offering: Master's
Accreditation: WC

01 President .... Dr. Kevin CORSINI
04 Exec Assistant to the President .... Ms. Kelly BUCHANAN
10 Chief Financial Officer .... Mr. Allen GARRETT
05 Int VP for Academics .... Dr. Katina EVANS
30 VP of Development .... Mr. Jim BODOR
11 VP of Operations .... Mr. Matt ZEALAND
32 Dean of Students .... Vacant
37 Sr Director of Financial Services .... Ms. Rina CAMPBELL
35 Director of Student Life .... Mr. Isaac DEAL
06 Registrar .... Vacant
07 Sr Dir of Recruitment & Outreach .... Ms. Kelly BUCHANAN
42 Director of Spiritual Life .... Mr. Steve JENKINS
15 Human Resources Specialist .... Ms. Kendra CHAMBERLAIN
08 Director of Library Services .... Mr. Matt OWEN
29 Manager of Alumni/Donor Relations .... Mr. Jim BODOR
09 Dean of Assessment and Planning .... Mrs. Lundie CARSTENSEN
41 Asst Athletic Director .... Mr. Nick FORTINI
23 Director of Health Services .... Mrs. Malia JENKINS
28 Director of Diversity .... Mr. Fred BLACKBURN
13 Chief Information Technology Ofcr .... Mr. Matt OWEN
45 Chief Institutional Planning Ofcr .... Mr. Bill CRAWFORD

*San Diego Community College District Administrative Offices (H)

3375 Camino Del Rio South, San Diego CA 92108-3883
County: San Diego — FICE Identification: 008895
Unit ID: 122320
Telephone: (619) 388-6500 — Carnegie Class: N/A
FAX Number: (619) 388-6913
URL: www.sdccd.edu

01 Chancellor .... Dr. Carlos O. TURNER CORTEZ
10 Exec Vice Chanc Business Tech Svcs .... Dr. Bonnie Ann DOWD
05 Vice Chanc Educational Services .... Dr. Susan TOPHAM
15 Vice Chancellor Human Resources .... Mr. Gregory A. SMITH
18 Vice Chanc Facilities Management .... Mr. Christopher MANIS
26 Director Comm & Public Relations .... Mr. Jack BERESFORD
04 Exec Assistant to the Chancellor .... Ms. Margaret LAMB
13 Chief Info Technology Officer .... Dr. Peter S. MAHARAJ
19 Chief of Police .... Mr. Joseph RAMOS
101 Board Recording Secretary .... Ms. Amanda FICKEN-DAVIS
106 Dean Online & Distributed Education .... Mr. Brian WESTON
30 Development Coordinator .... Ms. Lisa COLE-JONES
45 Chief Institutional Planning Office .... Ms. Natalia CORDOBA-VELÁSQUEZ
43 Director Legal Services .... Mr. Ljubisa KOSTIC

*San Diego City College (I)

1313 Park Boulevard, San Diego CA 92101-4787
County: San Diego — FICE Identification: 001273
Unit ID: 122339
Telephone: (619) 388-3400 — Carnegie Class: Assoc/HT-High Non
FAX Number: (619) 388-3063 — Calendar System: Semester
URL: www.sdcity.edu
Established: 1914 — Annual Undergrad Tuition & Fees (In-District): $1,144
Enrollment: 14,865 — Coed
Affiliation or Control: State/Local — IRS Status: 501(c)3
Highest Offering: Associate Degree
Accreditation: WJ, ADNUR

02 President .... Dr. Ricky SHABAZZ
04 Acting Executive Asst to President .... Ms. Ira GARCIA
10 VP of Administrative Services .... Dr. John PARKER
05 VP of Instruction .... Ms. Matilda CHAVEZ
32 VP of Student Services .... Mr. Marciano PEREZ, JR.
07 Dean Outreach and Enrollment Svcs .... Ms. Genevieve ESGUERRA
108 Dean Institutional Effectiveness .... Dr. Susan MURRAY
35 Acting Dean Student Affairs .... Dr. Adan SANCHEZ
83 Dean Behav & Soc Sci/Cons & Fam St .... Dr. Masa OMAE
08 Dean Information/Learning Tech .... Mr. Robbi EWELL
79 Dean Arts/Hum/Comm/Telecomm .... Ms. Jeanie TYLER
50 Acting Dean Bus/IT/Cosm/Eng/Trades .... Ms. Shana CARR
124 Dean Student Dev and Matriculation .... Dr. Juan Carlos REYNA
41 Dean Health/Ex Sci/Athletics .... Mr. Aaron DETTY
81 Dean Math/Sciences/Nursing Ed .... Dr. Leticia LOPEZ
66 Associate Dean Nursing Education .... Dr. Dometrives ARMSTRONG
103 Associate Dean Strong Workforce .... Dr. Sasha KNOX
22 Equal Opp Site Compliance Officer .... Mr. Edwin HIEL
40 Acting Supervisor Campus Store .... Mr. Sol MADRID
26 Public Information Officer .... Mr. Cesar GUMAPAS
88 Acting Coordinator DSPS .... Ms. Jamila DECARLI
37 Director Financial Aid .... Ms. Wendy WANG
18 Regional Facilities Officer .... Mr. Jay PURNELL
06 Acting Director Admin & Records .... Ms. Carolina VARGAS
38 Acting Coord Student Health Clinic .... Ms. Deborah HELM
36 Acting Director Transf/Career Ctr .... Ms. Melody VALENCIA

*San Diego Mesa College　(A)

7250 Mesa College Drive, San Diego CA 92111-4998
County: San Diego　　　　　　　　FICE Identification: 001275
　　　　　　　　　　　　　　　　　Unit ID: 122375
Telephone: (619) 388-2721　　　Carnegie Class: Bac/Assoc-Assoc Dom
FAX Number: (619) 388-2929　　Calendar System: Semester
URL: www.sdmesa.edu
Established: 1962　　Annual Undergrad Tuition & Fees (In-District): $1,144
Enrollment: 20,693　　　　　　　　　　　　　　　　　Coed
Affiliation or Control: State/Local　　　IRS Status: 501(c)3
Highest Offering: Baccalaureate
Accreditation: **WJ**, CAHIIM, DA, PTAA, RAD

02	President	Dr. Pamela T. LUSTER
05	Vice President Instruction	Dr. Isabel O'CONNOR
32	Vice Pres Student Services	Dr. Ashanti HANDS
10	Vice Pres Administrative Services	Mr. Lorenze LEGASPI
121	Dean Student Development	Ms. Aileen CRAKES
79	Dean Arts & Languages	Ms. Leslie SHIMAZAKI
76	Dean Health Sciences/Public Svc	Dr. Tina RECALDE
81	Dean School Math/Natural Sciences	Dr. Paloma VARGAS
50	Dean Sch Business Technology	Vacant
08	Dean Lrng Res/Academic Support	Dr. Andrew MACNEILL
68	Dean PE/Health Educ/Athletics Dir	Dr. Ryan SHUMAKER
79	Dean of Humanities	Ms. Linda HENSLEY
83	Actg Dn Social/Behav Sci/Mult Stds	Dr. Pearl LY
35	Dean Student Affairs	Ms. Victoria MILLER
93	Dean of Student Success/Equity	Mr. Larry MAXEY
108	Dean Institutional Effectiveness	Vacant
09	Assoc Dean Research & Planning	Dr. Bridget HERRIN
72	Assoc Dean Career Technical Educ	Ms. Monica ROMERO
26	Public Information Officer	Ms. Jennifer KEARNS
37	Financial Aid Officer	Ms. Gilda MALDONADO
07	Student Svcs Supervisor Admission	Ms. Ivonne ALVAREZ
04	Exec Asst to the President	Ms. Sara Beth CAIN

*San Diego Miramar College　(B)

10440 Black Mountain Road, San Diego CA 92126-2999
County: San Diego　　　　　　　FICE Identification: 011820
　　　　　　　　　　　　　　　　　Unit ID: 122384
Telephone: (619) 388-7800　　Carnegie Class: Assoc/HT-High Non
FAX Number: (619) 388-7901　　Calendar System: Semester
URL: www.sdmiramar.edu
Established: 1969　　Annual Undergrad Tuition & Fees (In-District): $1,144
Enrollment: 13,408　　　　　　　　　　　　　　　　　Coed
Affiliation or Control: State/Local　　　IRS Status: 501(c)3
Highest Offering: Associate Degree
Accreditation: **WJ**, ACBSP, MLTAD

02	President	Dr. Wesley LUNDBURG
05	Vice President Instruction	Dr. Michael ODU
32	Vice President Student Services	Mr. Adrian GONZALES
10	Vice President Admin Services	Mr. Brett BELL
49	Dean Liberal Arts	Dr. Lou ASCIONE
50	Dean Business/Tech/Workforce Init	Mr. Jesse LOPEZ
81	Dean Math/Bio/Exer/Phys Sci	Dr. Linda WOODS
19	Acting Dean Public Safety	Dr. Linda WOODS
108	Dean PRIE/Library & Technology	Dr. Daniel MIRAMONTEZ
35	Dean Student Affairs	Dr. Cheryl BARNARD
124	Dean Matriculation & Student Dev	Dr. Tonia TERESH
103	Associate Dean Career Education	Ms. Claudia ESTRADA-HOWELL
35	Associate Dean Outreach/School Rel	Mr. Truongson (Sonny) NGUYEN
04	Executive Assistant to President	Ms. Malia KUNST
26	Public Information Officer	Mr. Steve QUIS
37	Financial Aid Officer	Mr. Vincent NGO
07	Admissions & Records Officer	Ms. Dana STACK

San Diego Global Knowledge University　(C)

1095 K Street Suite B, San Diego CA 92101
County: San Diego　　　　　　　Identification: 667294
　　　　　　　　　　　　　　　　　Unit ID: 493512
Telephone: (619) 934-0797　　Carnegie Class: Spec-4-yr-Bus
FAX Number: N/A　　　　　　　　Calendar System: Semester
URL: www.sdgku.edu
Established: 2007　　Annual Undergrad Tuition & Fees: $6,476
Enrollment: 93　　　　　　　　　　　　　　　　　Coed
Affiliation or Control: Proprietary　　　IRS Status: Proprietary
Highest Offering: Master's
Accreditation: ACICS

01	President/CEO	Dr. Miguel A. CARDENAS
05	Chief Academic Officer	Dr. Miguel A. CARDENAS, JR.
07	Dir of Admissions & Registrar	Devahn PARKER
32	Director of Student Services	Beatriz ESCOBEDO
11	Director of Administration	Ilian ROSALES
08	Librarian	Briana OCHOA
10	Financial/Business Officer	Farah PALOMAS
13	Chief Information Technology Ofcr	Dr. Andres MEJIA
15	Chief Compliance Officer	Tonya PARKER-JONES

San Francisco Bay University　(D)

161 Mission Falls Ln, Ste 200, Fremont CA 94539-7833
County: Alameda　　　　　　　　Identification: 666759
　　　　　　　　　　　　　　　　　Unit ID: 120166
Telephone: (510) 592-9688　　Carnegie Class: Spec-4-yr-Other Tech
FAX Number: (510) 657-8975　　Calendar System: Trimester

URL: www.npu.edu
Established: 1984　　Annual Undergrad Tuition & Fees: $8,720
Enrollment: 33　　　　　　　　　　　　　　　　　Coed
Affiliation or Control: Independent Non-Profit　IRS Status: 501(c)3
Highest Offering: Master's
Accreditation: **WC**, CEA

01	President	Mr. Peter HSIEH
11	EVP/Chief Operating Officer	Mr. Paul CHOI
05	Chief Academic Officer	Ms. Nelly MANGAROVA
10	Chief Financial Officer	Ms. Anne SUTARDJI
43	General Transactions & Corp Counsel	Mr. Mark SCHULTZ
07	Dir of Admissions/Special Projects	Ms. Monica SINHA
06	Registrar/Sr Academic Advisor	Vacant
54	Dean of School of Engineering	Dr. Thawi IWAGOSHI
50	Dean of School of Business	Mr. James CONNOR
18	Director of Facilities	Mr. Jose MARTINEZ

San Francisco Conservatory of Music　(E)

50 Oak Street, San Francisco CA 94102-6011
County: San Francisco　　　　　FICE Identification: 001278
　　　　　　　　　　　　　　　　　Unit ID: 122506
Telephone: (415) 864-7326　　Carnegie Class: Spec-4-yr-Arts
FAX Number: (415) 503-6299　　Calendar System: Semester
URL: www.sfcm.edu
Established: 1917　　Annual Undergrad Tuition & Fees: $49,050
Enrollment: 410　　　　　　　　　　　　　　　　　Coed
Affiliation or Control: Independent Non-Profit　IRS Status: 501(c)3
Highest Offering: Beyond Master's But Less Than Doctorate
Accreditation: **WC**

01	President	David STULL
05	Provost and Dean	Jonas WRIGHT
10	Vice Pres Finance & Administration	Kathryn WITTENMYER
45	Vice Pres Marketing/Admissions/PR	Beth GINDICESSI
111	Vice Pres Advancement	Kathleen NICELY
20	Assoc Dean of Academic Affairs	Michael ROEST
32	Associate Dean of Student Life	Timothy DUNN
64	Assoc Dean for New Media/Music Tech	Taurin BARRERA
15	Assoc VP Human Resources	Michael PATTERSON
07	Director of Admission	Lisa NICKELS
37	Director of Financial Aid	Kellie GAINES
51	Acting Dir PreCollege/Cont Educ	Justin SUN
06	Registrar & VA Certifying Official	Connor CALLAGHAN
18	Chief Facilities Engineer	David MITCHELL
35	Asst Director of Student Affairs	Susannah WHITE
20	Exec Assistant to the Dean	Ava HARMON
04	Executive Assistant to President	Marina KENNEDY
102	Institutional Gifts Manager	Rhiannon LEWIS
19	Director Security/Safety	Stephanie MENDOZA
30	Chief Development/Advancement	Kathleen NICELY
44	Director of Legacy Giving	Nic MEREDITH

San Francisco Film School　(F)

155 Sansome Street 2nd Floor, San Francisco CA 94104
County: San Francisco　　　　　FICE Identification: 042340
　　　　　　　　　　　　　　　　　Unit ID: 486372
Telephone: (415) 824-7000　　Carnegie Class: Spec 2-yr-A&S
FAX Number: (415) 824-7007　　Calendar System: Semester
URL: sanfranciscofilmschool.edu
Established: 2005　　Annual Undergrad Tuition & Fees: N/A
Enrollment: 40　　　　　　　　　　　　　　　　　Coed
Affiliation or Control: Proprietary　　　IRS Status: Proprietary
Highest Offering: Associate Degree
Accreditation: COE

01	President	Jeremiah BIRNBAUM

San Joaquin College of Law　(G)

901 Fifth Street, Clovis CA 93612-1312
County: Fresno　　　　　　　　　FICE Identification: 025000
　　　　　　　　　　　　　　　　　Unit ID: 122649
Telephone: (559) 323-2100　　Carnegie Class: Spec-4-yr-Law
FAX Number: (559) 323-5566　　Calendar System: Semester
URL: www.sjcl.edu
Established: 1969　　Annual Graduate Tuition & Fees: N/A
Enrollment: 183　　　　　　　　　　　　　　　　　Coed
Affiliation or Control: Independent Non-Profit　IRS Status: 501(c)3
Highest Offering: Doctorate; No Undergraduates
Accreditation: **WC**

01	Dean	Janice L. PEARSON
18	Facilities Manager	Richard RODRIGUEZ
10	Chief Financial Officer	Jill A. WALLER-RANDLES
32	Director of Student Services	Joyce K. MORODOMI
37	Financial Aid Administrator	Melisa NILMEIER
08	Library Director	Mark MASTERS
26	Public Information Officer	Missy M. CARTIER
15	Chief of Personnel	Beth PITCOCK
30	Chief Development	Janice L. PEARSON
84	Director Enrollment Management	Diane M. STEEL
61	Law Program Coordinator	Pat A. SMITH
35	Dean of Students	Logan TENNERELLI

San Joaquin Delta College　(H)

5151 Pacific Avenue, Stockton CA 95207-6370
County: San Joaquin　　　　　　FICE Identification: 001280
　　　　　　　　　　　　　　　　　Unit ID: 122658

Telephone: (209) 954-5151　　Carnegie Class: Assoc/MT-VT-High Trad
FAX Number: (209) 954-7001　　Calendar System: Semester
URL: www.deltacollege.edu
Established: 1935　　Annual Undergrad Tuition & Fees (In-District): $1,288
Enrollment: 18,224　　　　　　　　　　　　　　　　　Coed
Affiliation or Control: State/Local　　　IRS Status: 501(c)3
Highest Offering: Associate Degree
Accreditation: **WJ**, ADNUR

01	Acting Superintendent/President	Dr. Lisa AGUILERA LAWRENSON
05	Asst Supt/VP of Instruction	Mr. Joseph GONZALES
32	Asst Supt/VP of Student Svcs	Dr. Lonita CORDOVA
10	Vice Pres of Administrative Svcs	Dr. Amanda PRESTON-NELSON
38	Dean Counseling & Special Svcs	Vacant
09	Dean Institutional Effectiveness	Ms. Tina AKERS
103	Dean Workforce/Economic Development	Vacant
108	Dean Student Learning & Assessment	Dr. Ginger HOLDEN
08	Div Dean Library/Learning Res/Lang	Ms. Sheli AYERS
12	Dean of Tracy Center	Dr. Jessie GARZA-RODERICK
26	Dir Marketing/Stdnt Outreach	Mr. Alex BREITLER
18	Director Facilities Management	Ms. Stacy PINOLA
07	Director of Admissions & Records	Vacant
37	Director of Financial Aid/Vet Svcs	Ms. Tina LENT
04	Exec Assistant to the President	Ms. Robin SADBERRY
19	District Police Chief	Mr. Robert DI PIERO
13	Director IT & Data Center Services	Ms. Chelsy PHAM
41	Athletic Director	Mr. Tony ESPINOZA
15	Human Resources Manager	Ms. Jennifer BOLAND

San Joaquin Valley College, Inc. - Visalia　(I)

8344 West Mineral King Avenue, Visalia CA 93291-9283
County: Tulare　　　　　　　　　FICE Identification: 021207
　　　　　　　　　　　　　　　　　Unit ID: 122685
Telephone: (559) 651-2500　　Carnegie Class: Spec-4-yr-Other Health
FAX Number: (559) 651-0574　　Calendar System: Other
URL: www.sjvc.edu/campuses/central-california/visalia
Established: 1977　　Annual Undergrad Tuition & Fees: N/A
Enrollment: 1,927　　　　　　　　　　　　　　　　　Coed
Affiliation or Control: Proprietary　　　IRS Status: Proprietary
Highest Offering: Baccalaureate
Accreditation: **WC**, COARC, DH

01	Campus President	Mr. Kenneth GUERRERO
05	Academic Dean	Ms. Amanda OGATA
07	VP Admissions/Grad Services	Mr. Anthony ROMO
11	VP Operations North	Mr. Scott HAGER

*San Joaquin Valley College-Antelope Valley (Lancaster)　(J)

42135 10th Street West, Ste 147, Lancaster CA 93534
Telephone: (661) 974-8282　　Identification: 770968
Accreditation: **&WC**

*San Joaquin Valley College-Bakersfield　(K)

201 New Stine Road, Bakersfield CA 93309-2668
Telephone: (661) 834-0126　　FICE Identification: 023135
Accreditation: **&WC**, COARC, SURGT

† Regional accreditation is carried under the parent institution in Visalia, CA.

*San Joaquin Valley College-Fresno　(L)

295 East Sierra Avenue, Fresno CA 93710-3616
Telephone: (559) 448-8282　　Identification: 666008
Accreditation: **&WC**, SURGT

† Regional accreditation is carried under the parent institution in Visalia, CA.

*San Joaquin Valley College-Fresno Trades Education Center　(M)

4985 East Andersen Avenue, Fresno CA 93727
Telephone: (559) 453-0123　　Identification: 666009
Accreditation: **&WC**

† Regional accreditation is carried under the parent institution in Visalia, CA.

*San Joaquin Valley College-Modesto　(N)

5380 Pirrone Road, Salida CA 95368-9090
Telephone: (209) 543-8800　　Identification: 666128
Accreditation: **&WC**

† Regional accreditation is carried under the parent institution in Visalia, CA.

*San Joaquin Valley College-Ontario　(O)

4580 Ontario Mills Parkway, Ontario CA 91764
Telephone: (909) 948-7582　　Identification: 666096
Accreditation: **&WC**, COARC

† Regional accreditation is carried under the parent institution in Visalia, CA.

San Joaquin Valley College-Rancho Cordova (A)

11050 Olson Drive, Suite 210,
Rancho Cordova CA 95670-5600
Telephone: (916) 638-7582 Identification: 666133
Accreditation: &WC, COARC, SURGT

† Regional accreditation is carried under the parent institution in Visalia, CA.

San Joaquin Valley College-Santa Maria (B)

303 E Plaza Drive, Santa Maria CA 93454
Telephone: (805) 608-3104 FICE Identification: 025780
Accreditation: &WC

San Joaquin Valley College-Temecula (C)

27270 Madison Avenue, Suite 103, Temecula CA 92590
Telephone: (951) 296-6015 Identification: 770507
Accreditation: &WC, COARC, SURGT

San Joaquin Valley College-Victor Valley (Hesperia) (D)

9331 Mariposa Road, Hesperia CA 92344-8000
Telephone: (760) 948-1947 Identification: 667044
Accreditation: &WC

† Regional accreditation is carried under the parent institution in Visalia, CA.

*San Jose/Evergreen Community College District (E)

40 South Market Street, San Jose CA 95113-2367
County: Santa Clara FICE Identification: 029042
Unit ID: 122737
Telephone: (408) 274-6700 Carnegie Class: N/A
FAX Number: (408) 531-8722
URL: www.sjeccd.edu

01 Chancellor .... Dr. Byron D. BRELAND
11 Vice Chanc Administrative Services .... Mr. Jorge L. ESCOBAR
15 Assoc Vice Chanc Human Resources .... Ms. Beatriz S. CHAIDEZ
13 Vice Chanc Information Tech Svcs .... Dr. Ben SEABERRY
18 AVC Physical Plant Dev/Operations .... Mr. Terrance DEGRAY
103 Int Exec Dir Workforce Innovation .... Ms. Alexandra DURAN
09 Exec Dir Inst Effect/Stdnt Success .... Ms. Ann MACHAMER
86 Exec Dir Government/External Affs .... Ms. Rosalie LEDESMA
10 Interim Controller .... Ms. Manuela KOPLIN
26 Dir Communications/Community Rels .... Mr. Sam HO
27 Marketing & Public Info Officer .... Mr. Ryan BROWN

*Evergreen Valley College (F)

3095 Yerba Buena Road, San Jose CA 95135-1598
County: Santa Clara FICE Identification: 012452
Unit ID: 114266
Telephone: (408) 274-7900 Carnegie Class: Assoc/HT-Mix Trad/Non
FAX Number: N/A Calendar System: Semester
URL: www.evc.edu
Established: 1975 Annual Undergrad Tuition & Fees (In-District): $1,448
Enrollment: 8,699 Coed
Affiliation or Control: State/Local IRS Status: 501(c)3
Highest Offering: Associate Degree
Accreditation: WJ, ADNUR

02 President .... Dr. Tammeil Y. GILKERSON
05 VP Academic Affairs .... Dr. Matais POUNCIL
32 VP Student Affairs .... Mr. Howard WILLIS
10 VP Administrative Services .... Ms. Andrea ALEXANDER
50 Div Dean Business & Workforce .... Vacant
66 Div Dean Nursing & Allied Health .... Ms. Shara CRARY
81 Div Dean Math/Science/Engineering .... Dr. Antoinette HERRERA
83 Div Dean Soc Sci/PE/Arts/Humanities .... Ms. Colleen CALDERON
84 Dean Enrollment Services .... Mr. Sam MORGAN
49 Div Dean Language Arts .... Mr. Robert GUTIERREZ
08 Div Dean Library/Lrng Res/Adult Ed .... Dr. Roberta KUNKEL
121 Div Dean Student Success/Counseling .... Dr. Victor GARZA, JR.
93 Director Student Svcs & Wellness .... Mr. Michael OSORIO
37 Director Fin Aid & Scholarship Pgm .... Ms. Ebonnie HOPKINS
35 Director Student Dev & Activities .... Ms. Raniyah JOHNSON
88 Director Special Programs .... Ms. Teresa DE LA CRUZ
20 Supervisor Academic Services .... Ms. Tina NGUYEN
13 Supervisor Campus Tech Svcs .... Mr. Eugenio CANOY
88 Dir Student Outreach & Recruitment .... Mr. Song-Ho TRAN
26 Dir Marketing/Public Relations .... Mr. Josh RUSSELL
18 Facilities Supervisor .... Mr. Vince CABADA

*San Jose City College (G)

2100 Moorpark Avenue, San Jose CA 95128-2799
County: Santa Clara FICE Identification: 001282
Unit ID: 122746
Telephone: (408) 298-2181 Carnegie Class: Assoc/MT-VT-Mix Trad/Non
FAX Number: (408) 298-1935 Calendar System: Semester
URL: www.sjcc.edu
Established: 1921 Annual Undergrad Tuition & Fees (In-District): $1,362
Enrollment: 8,378 Coed
Affiliation or Control: State/Local IRS Status: 501(c)3
Highest Offering: Associate Degree
Accreditation: WJ, DA, NAEYC

02 President .... Dr. Rowena TOMANENG
05 Vice President Academic Affairs .... Dr. Elizabeth PRATT
11 Vice Pres Administrative Services .... Mr. Christopher HAWKEN
32 Vice President Student Affairs .... Mr. William GARCIA
45 Vice Pres Strategic Partnerships .... Vacant
121 Dean Acad Success & Student Equity .... Dr. René ALVAREZ
41 Dean of Athletics & Kinesiology .... Mr. Lamel HARRIS
50 Dean Business/Workforce Development .... Dr. J. Edward STEVENSON
38 Int Dean Couns/Guidance/Matriculatn .... Mr. Song-Ho TRAN
79 Dean Humanities/Social Science .... Mr. William REYES-CUBIDES
49 Dean Language Arts .... Dr. Celia CRUZ-JOHNSON
81 Dean Mathematics/Sciences Division .... Dr. Misty STROUD
09 Dean Rsrch/Planning/Inst Effective .... Dr. Joyce LUI
07 Director of Admissions .... Ms. Teresa PAIZ
10 Director College Fiscal Services .... Ms. Victoria MENZIES
37 Director Financial Aid .... Mr. Takeo KUBO
26 Dir Marketing & Public Relations .... Mr. Daniel GARZA
88 Director METAS .... Dr. Enrique VELASCO
35 Director Student Life .... Mr. Blake BALAJADIA
88 Director Support Programs .... Vacant
04 Assistant to the President .... Ms. Darlene SPECHT

*San Mateo County Community College District Office (H)

3401 CSM Drive, San Mateo CA 94402-3651
County: San Mateo FICE Identification: 004697
Unit ID: 122782
Telephone: (650) 574-6500 Carnegie Class: N/A
FAX Number: (650) 574-6566
URL: www.smccd.edu

01 Chancellor .... Mr. Michael CLAIRE
15 Director of Human Resources .... Mr. David FEUNE
05 Vice Chanc Educ Svcs/Plng .... Dr. Aaron MCVEAN
18 Vice Chanc Facil Plng/Maint/Oper .... Mr. Jose NUNEZ
109 Vice Chanc Auxiliary Services .... Mr. Tom BAUER
100 Chief of Staff .... Mr. Mitchell A. BAILEY
104 Provost International Education .... Dr. Jing LUAN
10 Chief Financial Officer .... Ms. Bernata SLATER
13 Chief Technology Officer .... Mr. Daman GREWAL

*Cañada College (I)

4200 Farm Hill Boulevard, Redwood City CA 94061-1099
County: San Mateo FICE Identification: 006973
Unit ID: 111434
Telephone: (650) 306-3100 Carnegie Class: Assoc/HT-High Non
FAX Number: (650) 306-3457 Calendar System: Semester
URL: www.canadacollege.edu
Established: 1968 Annual Undergrad Tuition & Fees (In-District): $1,362
Enrollment: 5,231 Coed
Affiliation or Control: State/Local IRS Status: 501(c)3
Highest Offering: Associate Degree
Accreditation: WJ, RAD

02 Interim President .... Ms. Kim LOPEZ
05 VP Instruction .... Dr. Tammy ROBINSON
32 VP Student Services .... Dr. Manuel Alejandro PEREZ
11 VP Administrative Services .... Mr. Graciano MENDOZA
10 College Business Officer .... Ms. Mary Chries CONCHA THIA
38 Dean Counseling .... Mr. C. Max HARTMAN
06 Interim Registrar .... Ms. Maria LARA
26 Dir Cmty Relations & Marketing .... Ms. Megan RODRIGUEZ ANTONE
45 Dean PRIE .... Dr. Karen ENGEL
37 Int Director Financial Aid Services .... Ms. Andrea GARCIA-RITTGERS
18 Facility Manager .... Ms. Karen PINKHAM
103 Dean Business/Design/Workforce .... Ms. Hyla LACEFIELD
79 Dean Humanities & Soc Sci .... Mr. James CARRANZA
81 Dean Science & Tech .... Mr. Ameer THOMPSON
121 Dean Acad Support & Learning Tech .... Mr. David REED
84 Int Dean Enrollment Services .... Mr. Wissem BENNANI

*College of San Mateo (J)

1700 W Hillsdale Boulevard, San Mateo CA 94402-3795
County: San Mateo FICE Identification: 001181
Unit ID: 122791
Telephone: (650) 574-6161 Carnegie Class: Assoc/HT-Mix Trad/Non
FAX Number: (650) 574-6680 Calendar System: Semester
URL: www.collegeofsanmateo.edu
Established: 1922 Annual Undergrad Tuition & Fees (In-District): $1,434
Enrollment: 7,494 Coed
Affiliation or Control: State/Local IRS Status: 501(c)3
Highest Offering: Associate Degree
Accreditation: WJ, DA

02 Interim President .... Ms. Kim LOPEZ
05 Int Vice President Instruction .... Ms. Carla GRANDY
10 Int Vice Pres Administrative Svcs .... Mr. Anthony DJEDI
32 Acting Vice Pres Student Services .... Ms. Kristi RIDGWAY
84 Dean Enrollment Svcs/Support Pgms .... Ms. Lizette BRICKER
38 Dean Counsel/Advis/Matriculation .... Ms. Krystal DUNCAN
09 Int Dean Plng/Research/Inst Effect .... Dr. Hilary GOODKIND
20 Dean Academic Support/Learning Tech .... Ms. Tarana CHAPPIE
35 Dean Student Services/Counseling .... Ms. Marsha RAMEZANE
79 Dean Language Arts Division .... Dr. Chris GIBSON
68 Dean Kinesiology/Athletics Division .... Mr. Andreas WOLF
81 Dean Math/Science Division .... Dr. Charlene FRONTIERA
83 Dean Creative Arts/Social Sci Div .... Dr. Laura DEMSETZ
50 Dean Business & Technology Division .... Mr. Francisco GOMEZ
06 Registrar .... Mr. Steven TRINH
37 Director Financial Aid Services .... Ms. Claudia I. MENJIVAR
26 Dir Marketing/Comm/Public Relations .... Ms. Cherie COLIN
18 Dir Maintenance/Operations .... Ms. Michele RUDOVSKY
15 Chief Human Resources Officer .... Ms. Marie BILLIE
96 Purchasing Services Supervisor .... Mr. Bob DOMENICI

*Skyline College (K)

3300 College Drive, San Bruno CA 94066-1698
County: San Mateo FICE Identification: 007713
Unit ID: 123509
Telephone: (650) 738-4100 Carnegie Class: Bac/Assoc-Assoc Dom
FAX Number: (650) 738-4338 Calendar System: Semester
URL: www.skylinecollege.edu
Established: 1969 Annual Undergrad Tuition & Fees (In-District): $1,464
Enrollment: 8,747 Coed
Affiliation or Control: State/Local IRS Status: 501(c)3
Highest Offering: Baccalaureate
Accreditation: WJ, ACBSP, COARC, SURGT

02 President .... Dr. Melissa MORENO
05 Vice President Instruction .... Dr. Vinicio LOPEZ
11 Vice Pres Administrative Services .... Mr. Joseph MORELLO
32 Vice President Student Services .... Dr. Newin ORANTE
84 Dean Enrollment Svcs/Financial Aid .... Mr. William MINNICH
09 Dean Plng/Research/Inst Effective .... Ms. Ingrid VARGAS
83 Dean Soc Sciences/Creative Arts .... Ms. Danni REDDING LAPUZ
50 Dean Business/Educ/Prof Pgm .... Mr. Michael KANE
60 Dean Language Arts/Learning Res .... Mr. Christopher GIBSON
68 Int Dean Kinesiology/Athl/Dance .... Mr. Dino NOMICOS
81 Acting Dean Science/Math/Technology .... Dr. Jing FOLSOM
38 Dean Counsel/Advis/Matric .... Dr. Luis ESCOBAR
103 Dean Strat Partnerships/WF Devel .... Mr. Russell WALDON
85 Int Dean Global Learning Programs .... Mr. Zaid GHORI
121 Dean Acad Support & Learning Tech .... Mr. Rolin MOE
88 Dean Student Equity/Support Svcs .... Dr. Cheryl JOHNSON
103 Director SparkPoint at Skyline Col .... Mr. Chad THOMPSON
26 Dir Community Rels/Marketing .... Ms. Cherie COLIN
08 Director Learning Commons .... Ms. Gabriela NOCITO
22 Exec Dir of the Equity Institute .... Dr. O'KenZoe SELASSIE-OKPE
06 Registrar .... Ms. Susan LORENZO
04 Executive Asst to President .... Mrs. Theresa TENTES
104 Director Study Abroad .... Vacant
18 Facilities Operation Manager .... Mr. John DOCTOR
19 Public Safety Captain .... Mr. Jim VANGELE
37 Director Student Financial Aid .... Ms. Ariackna SOLER
21 Finance and Operations Manager .... Mr. Paul CASSIDY

Sanford Burnham Prebys Medical Discovery Institute (L)

10901 North Torrey Pines Road, La Jolla CA 92037
County: San Diego Identification: 667069
Unit ID: 481535
Telephone: (858) 646-3100 Carnegie Class: Spec-4-yr-Other Health
FAX Number: (858) 646-3199 Calendar System: Quarter
URL: www.sbpdiscovery.org
Established: 2005 Annual Graduate Tuition & Fees: N/A
Enrollment: 26 Coed
Affiliation or Control: Independent Non-Profit IRS Status: 501(c)3
Highest Offering: Doctorate; No Undergraduates
Accreditation: WC

01 President .... Dr. Kristiina VUORI
10 Chief Financial Officer .... Mr. Amar DUVVUR
05 Dean Grad Sch Biomedical Sciences .... Dr. Guy SALVESEN
15 Chief Human Resources Officer .... Mr. Doug BATTISTA
88 Sr Vice Pres Drug Discovery/Devel .... Dr. Michael JACKSON
30 Chief Development Officer .... Ms. Christine DITTMER
100 Vice Pres/Chief of Staff .... Ms. Tara MARATHE
26 VP Communications/General Counsel .... Mr. Scott TOCHER

Santa Barbara City College (M)

721 Cliff Drive, Santa Barbara CA 93109-2394
County: Santa Barbara FICE Identification: 001285
Unit ID: 122889
Telephone: (805) 965-0581 Carnegie Class: Assoc/HT-High Trad
FAX Number: (805) 963-7222 Calendar System: Semester
URL: www.sbcc.edu
Established: 1909 Annual Undergrad Tuition & Fees (In-District): $1,374
Enrollment: 12,525 Coed
Affiliation or Control: State/Local IRS Status: 501(c)3
Highest Offering: Associate Degree
Accreditation: WJ, ADNUR, CAHIIM, RAD

01 Interim Superintendent/President .... Dr. Kindred MURILLO
05 VP Academic Affairs .... Dr. Maria L. VILLAGOMEZ
10 VP Business Services .... Ms. Lyndsay MAAS
15 VP Human Resources .... Mr. Michael SHANAHAN
13 Exec Dir Information Technology .... Dr. Dean NEVINS
56 VP Sch of Extended Learning .... Dr. Melissa MORENO
72 Dean Educational Programs .... Mr. Arturo RODRIGUEZ
76 Dean Educational Programs .... Dr. Alan PRICE
81 Dean Educational Programs .... Dr. Jens-Uwe KUHN

57 Dean Educational Programs .... Dr. Priscilla MORA
72 Dean Educational Programs .... Mr. Kenley NEUFELD
50 Dean Educational Programs .... Ms. Carola SMITH
32 VP Student Affairs .... Ms. Paloma ARNOLD
07 Assoc Dean Admissions/Stdnt Support .... Dr. Christopher JOHNSON
08 Librarian .... Ms. Elizabeth BOWMAN
102 Exec Dir Foundation for SBCC .... Mr. Geoff GREEN
09 Dir Institutional Research & Plng .... Dr. Z. REISZ
26 Exec Dir Public Affs/Communications .... Ms. Martha SWANSON
37 Director of Student Financial Aid .... Ms. Maureen GOLDBERG
18 Director of Facilities .... Mr. Robert MORALES
85 Director International Students .... Ms. Carola SMITH
06 Director of Records .... Mr. Michael MEDEL
96 Manager of Purchasing .... Mr. Robert MORALES
04 Executive Asst to President .... Ms. Jasmine TUAZON
19 Director Security/Safety .... Mr. Erik FRICKE
41 Athletic Director .... Mr. Rocco CONSTANTINO
84 Coordinator for Enrollment Services .... Ms. Vanessa PELTON
28 Director of Diversity .... Mr. Luis GIRALDO

Santa Clara University (A)

500 El Camino Real, Santa Clara CA 95053-0001
County: Santa Clara — FICE Identification: 001326
Unit ID: 122931
Telephone: (408) 554-4000 — Carnegie Class: DU-Mod
FAX Number: (408) 554-2700 — Calendar System: Quarter
URL: www.scu.edu
Established: 1851 — Annual Undergrad Tuition & Fees: $52,998
Enrollment: 8,616 — Coed
Affiliation or Control: Independent Non-Profit — IRS Status: 501(c)3
Highest Offering: Doctorate
Accreditation: WC, IPSY, LAW, THEOL

01 President .... Dr. Julie SULLIVAN
05 Acting Co-Provost .... Ms. Kate MORRIS
05 Acting Co-Provost .... Dr. Ed RYAN
10 Vice President Finance/Admin .... Mr. Michael CROWLEY
43 Senior Counsel .... Mr. John OTTOBONI
111 Vice President University Relations .... Mr. James LYONS
100 Chief of Staff to the President .... Ms. Molly MCDONALD
49 Dean of Arts & Sciences .... Dr. Daniel PRESS
50 Dean of Business .... Dr. Ed GRIER
53 Dean Educ & Counseling Psych .... Dr. Sabrina ZIRKEL
54 Dean of Engineering .... Dr. Elaine SCOTT
61 Dean of Law .... Mr. Michael KAUFMAN
73 Dean of JST .... Rev. Joseph MUELLER, SJ
20 Vice Provost Academic Affairs .... Dr. Kate MORRIS
32 Vice Provost and Dean Student Life .... Ms. Jeanne ROSENBERGER
84 Vice President for Enrollment Mgmt .... Ms. Eva BLANCO
13 CIO/Vice Provost Info Services .... Dr. Robert OWEN
20 Assoc Provost Undergraduate Studies .... Dr. Katharine HEINTZ
88 Assoc Vice Provost Faculty Devel .... Dr. Eileen R. ELROD
07 Dean Undergraduate Admission .... Ms. Becky KONOWICZ
37 Dean University Financial Aid Svcs .... Ms. Nan MERZ
21 Assoc Vice Pres Finance/Controller .... Ms. Ramona SAUTER
15 Director of Human Resources .... Mr. Agustin RUIZ
30 Assoc Vice President Development .... Mr. Mike J. WALLACE
109 Asst Vice Pres Auxiliary Services .... Mr. Sam FLORIO
35 Assoc Dean for Student Life .... Mr. Matthew DUNCAN
06 University Registrar .... Mr. Duane VOIGT
29 Asst Vice President Alumni Rels .... Ms. Kathy KALE
41 Athletics Director .... Dr. Renee BAUMGARTNER
90 Deputy CIO Academic Technology .... Ms. Nancy CUTLER
09 Director Institutional Research .... Ms. Barbara A. STEWART
25 Director Sponsored Projects .... Ms. Mary-Ellen FORTINI
38 Director Health & Counseling Svcs .... Dr. Jill ROVARIS
85 Assoc Provost International Pgm .... Ms. Susan POPKO
115 Chief Investment Officer .... Mr. John E. KERRIGAN
18 Director of Facilities .... Ms. Marissa PIMENTEL
96 Director University Support Service .... Mr. Ed MERRYMAN
19 Director Campus Safety Services .... Mr. Philip BELTRAN
42 Vice President Mission and Ministry .... Dr. Alison BENDERS
22 Int Director EO & Title IX .... Ms. Jenna ELLIOTT
88 Director de Saisset Museum .... Ms. Rebecca M. SCHAPP
88 Exec Dir Markkula Ctr Applied Ethic .... Mr. Don HEIDER
110 Assoc Vice President Development .... Ms. Nancy T. CALDERON
28 VP Diversity/Equity & Inclusion .... Dr. Shá DUNCAN SMITH
44 Asst Vice President Advance Svcs .... Mr. Jeff BEACHY
92 Director University Honors Program .... Dr. Naomi LEVY
94 Director Women & Gender Studies .... Dr. Linda GARBER
93 Director Ethnic Studies .... Dr. Anna C. SAMPAIO
04 Exec Assistant to the President .... Ms. Lisa MCMAHON
104 Assoc Provost International Pgms .... Ms. Susan POPKO
26 AVP Marketing & Communications .... Ms. Celine SCHMIDEK
39 Director of Residence Life .... Ms. Heather DUMAS-DYER

Santa Monica College (B)

1900 Pico Boulevard, Santa Monica CA 90405-1628
County: Los Angeles — FICE Identification: 001286
Unit ID: 122977
Telephone: (310) 434-4000 — Carnegie Class: Bac/Assoc-Assoc Dom
FAX Number: (310) 434-4386 — Calendar System: Semester
URL: www.smc.edu
Established: 1929 — Annual Undergrad Tuition & Fees (In-District): $1,148
Enrollment: 25,948 — Coed
Affiliation or Control: State/Local — IRS Status: 501(c)3
Highest Offering: Associate Degree
Accreditation: WJ, ADNUR, #COARC, NAEYC

01 Superintendent/President .... Dr. Kathryn E. JEFFERY
10 Vice President Business/Admin .... Mr. Christopher BONVENUTO
15 Vice President Human Resources .... Ms. Sherri LEE-LEWIS
05 Int VP Academic Affairs .... Mr. Jason BEARDSLEY
84 Vice Pres Enrollment Development .... Dr. Teresita RODRIGUEZ
32 Vice President Student Affairs .... Mr. Michael TUITASI
20 Dean Academic Affairs .... Dr. Dione CARTER
21 Controller .... Ms. Irma HARO
16 Dean Human Resources .... Dr. Tre'Shawn HALL-BAKER
08 Dir Library & Information Services .... Mr. Steve HUNT
28 Dean Equity/Pathways/Inclusion .... Dr. Maria MUNOZ
85 Dean International Education .... Mr. Pressian NICOLOV
56 Dean Noncredit/External Programs .... Mr. Scott SILVERMAN
38 Interim Dean Counseling .... Ms. Janet ROBINSON
13 Chief Director Info Technology .... Mr. Marc DRESCHER
88 Dean Education Enterprise .... Mr. Mitch HESKEL
43 Campus Counsel .... Mr. Robert MYERS
106 Int Assoc Dean Online Svcs/Support .... Ms. Tammara WHITAKER
35 Int Associate Dean of Students Life .... Mr. Thomas BUI
76 Associate Dean of Health Sciences .... Mr. Eric WILLIAMS
26 Public Information Officer .... Ms. Grace SMITH
31 Dean Community & Academic Relations .... Dr. Kiersten ELLIOTT
86 Sr Director Government Relations .... Mr. Don GIRARD
88 Dean Enrollment Services .... Dr. Esau TOVAR
37 Assoc Dean Financial Aid/Scholarshp .... Ms. Tracie HUNTER
18 Director Facilities Mgmt/Operations .... Vacant
109 Director Auxiliary Services .... Mr. David DEVER
114 Budget Manager .... Ms. Veronica DIAZ
09 Dean Institutional Research .... Ms. Hannah LAWLER
104 Assoc Dean International Education .... Ms. Catherine WEIR
41 Asst Director Athletics .... Mr. Reggie ELLIS
88 Director of Grants/SMC Foundation .... Ms. Tracy BEIDLEMAN
88 Director of Classified Personnel .... Ms. Carol LONG
91 Director Network Services .... Mr. Matthew KIAMAN
25 Director of Contracts .... Mr. Charlie YEN
96 Director Procurement/Contracts .... Ms. Nyla COTTON
19 Chief of Campus Police .... Mr. Johnnie ADAMS
04 Admin Asst to the President .... Ms. Letty KILIAN
40 Bookstore Manager .... Mr. David DEVER
103 Dean Academic Affairs .... Dr. Patricia RAMOS
101 Coordinator Board of Trustees .... Ms. Lisa ROSE
88 Director Radio Station (KCRW) .... Ms. Jennifer FERRO
88 Assoc Dean Facilities Programming .... Ms. Linda SULLIVAN
88 Dir Sustainability Coordination .... Mr. Ferris KAWAR
88 Dir Instr Services/External Pgms .... Ms. Maral HYELER
88 Dir Supplemental Instruct/Tutoring .... Ms. Wendi DEMORST
88 Int Assoc Dean Career/Technical Ed .... Ms. Sasha KING
105 Director Web/Social Media Strategy .... Mr. Paul TRAUTWEIN
102 Dean Foundation/Inst Advancement .... Dr. Lizzy MOORE
23 Associate Dean Health & Well-Being .... Vacant
124 Assoc Dean Outreach/Onboarding .... Mr. Jose HERNANDEZ
88 Chief Director Business Services .... Ms. Kim TRAN

Santa Rosa Junior College (C)

1501 Mendocino Avenue, Santa Rosa CA 95401-4395
County: Sonoma — FICE Identification: 001287
Unit ID: 123013
Telephone: (707) 527-4011 — Carnegie Class: Assoc/HT-Mix Trad/Non
FAX Number: (707) 527-4816 — Calendar System: Semester
URL: www.santarosa.edu
Established: 1918 — Annual Undergrad Tuition & Fees (In-District): $1,324
Enrollment: 16,757 — Coed
Affiliation or Control: State/Local — IRS Status: 501(c)3
Highest Offering: Associate Degree
Accreditation: WJ, DH, DIETT, EMT, RAD

01 Superintendent/President .... Dr. Frank CHONG
05 VP Academic Affairs .... Mr. Robert HOLCOMB
10 VP Finance and Admin Services .... Ms. Kate JOLLEY
32 VP Student Svcs/Asst Superintendent .... Mr. Pedro AVILA
15 VP Human Resources .... Mr. Gene DURAND
88 Sr Director Capital Projects .... Mr. Serafin FERNANDEZ
75 Dean Career/Tech Ed/Economic Dev .... Mr. Jerry MILLER
18 Director Facilities Operations .... Vacant
88 Dean Curriculum/Education Support .... Mr. Josh ADAMS
49 Dean Liberal Arts & Sciences .... Vacant
08 Sr Dean Learning Res/Educ Tech .... Ms. Phyllis USINA
19 Dean Public Safety .... Ms. April CHAPMAN
81 Dean Sci/Tech/Engr/Math .... Mr. Victor TAM
17 Dean Health Sciences .... Ms. Deborah CHIGAZOLA
50 Dean Business/Professional Studies .... Mr. Joshua ADAMS
79 Dean Arts & Humanities .... Mr. Kerry LOEWEN
79 Dean Language Arts/Acad Foundation .... Mr. Robert HOLCOMB
41 Dean Kinesiology/Dance/Athletic Dir .... Mr. Matthew MARKOVITCH
22 Dean Disabled Students Pgm & Svcs .... Ms. Kim STARKE
84 Dean Instr/Enrollment Svcs Petaluma .... Ms. Catherine WILLIAMS
35 Dean Student Services Petaluma .... Mr. Matthew LONG
88 Mgr Child Development Services .... Ms. Maleese WARNER
121 Sr Dean Counseling & Stdnt Success .... Ms. Li COLLIER
47 Dean Agriculture/Natural Resources .... Mr. Benjamin GOLDSTEIN
19 Chief of Police .... Mr. Robert BROWNLEE
13 Sr Dir Information Technology .... Mr. Kevin SNYDER
103 Dean Workforce Development .... Mr. Brad DAVIS
21 Director of Finance .... Ms. Whitney SCHULTZ
37 Int Director Student Financial Svcs .... Ms. Rachael CUTCHER
23 Director Student Health Services .... Ms. Susan QUINN
09 Director Institutional Research .... Dr. KC GREANEY
35 Sr Dean of Students .... Mr. Robert ETHINGTON
96 Dir Purchasing & Risk Mgmt .... Ms. Stephanie JARRETT
40 Director Bookstore .... Vacant
102 Executive Director Foundation .... Ms. J. MULLINEAUX
66 Associate Degree Nursing Program .... Ms. Anna VALDEZ
06 Dean Acad Records/Intl Admissions .... Ms. Freyja PEREIRA
07 Director Admissions/Enrollment Svcs .... Ms. Vayta SMITH
31 Director Community Education .... Mr. Jeffrey RHOADES
16 Director Human Resources .... Ms. Sarah HOPKINS
26 Dir District & Community Relations .... Ms. Erin BRICKER
90 Manager Instructional Computing .... Mr. Michael ROTH
24 Manager Media Services Petaluma .... Mr. Matt PEARSON
04 Exec Assistant to the President .... Ms. Zehra SONKAYNAR

Saybrook University (D)

55 Eureka Street, Pasadena CA 91103
County: Alameda — FICE Identification: 021206
Unit ID: 123095
Telephone: (626) 316-5300 — Carnegie Class: DU-Mod
FAX Number: (510) 455-7046 — Calendar System: Semester
URL: www.saybrook.edu
Established: 1971 — Annual Graduate Tuition & Fees: N/A
Enrollment: 785 — Coed
Affiliation or Control: Independent Non-Profit — IRS Status: 501(c)3
Highest Offering: Doctorate; No Undergraduates
Accreditation: WC, CACREP

01 President .... Dr. Nathan LONG
05 VP Academics Affairs .... Dr. Robyn PARKER
07 VP Admissions .... Ms. Karyn LEE
10 AVP Business Operations/CFO .... Ms. Jolene PRUITT
32 AVP of Student Affairs .... Ms. Shaniece MCGILL
09 AVP Institutional Advancement .... Ms. Carmen BOWEN
06 Registrar .... Ms. Crystal ISHIHARA
08 Library Director .... Ms. Laura RICE
04 Executive Assistant .... Ms. Val SMITH
26 Dir University Relations .... Ms. Carmen BOWAN
15 Human Resources Coordinator .... Ms. Krystiel HUDSON
20 Dir Academic Affairs/Admin/Projects .... Ms. Julia SONDEJ

Scripps College (E)

1030 Columbia Avenue, Claremont CA 91711
County: Los Angeles — FICE Identification: 001174
Unit ID: 123165
Telephone: (909) 621-8000 — Carnegie Class: Bac-A&S
FAX Number: (909) 621-8323 — Calendar System: Semester
URL: www.scrippscollege.edu
Established: 1926 — Annual Undergrad Tuition & Fees: $57,188
Enrollment: 958 — Female
Affiliation or Control: Independent Non-Profit — IRS Status: 501(c)3
Highest Offering: Baccalaureate
Accreditation: WC

01 President .... Ms. Suzanne KEEN
05 VP Acad Affs/Dean of Faculty .... Ms. Amy MARCUS-NEWHALL
111 VP for External Rels/Advancement .... Ms. Binti HARVEY
10 VP for Business Affairs/Treasurer .... Mr. Dean CALVO
32 VP Student Affs/Dean of Stdnts .... Ms. Sha BRADLEY
84 Vice President for Enrollment .... Ms. Victoria ROMERO
101 VP/Secretary of Board of Trustees .... Ms. Denise NELSON NASH
04 Executive Asst to the President .... Ms. Maria MANCERA
20 Associate Dean of Faculty .... Ms. Jennifer ARMSTRONG
15 AVP of Human Capital & Risk Mgmt .... Ms. Jennifer L. BERKLAS
09 Dir of Assessment/Inst Research .... Ms. Eulena JONSSON
08 Dir of Ella Strong Denison Library .... Ms. Jennifer MARTINEZ WORMSER
06 Registrar .... Ms. Kelly HOGENCAMP
37 Director of Financial Aid .... Mr. Patrick MOORE
36 Assistant Dir Center for Leadership .... Ms. Gretchen MALDONADO
13 Exec Dir of Information Technology .... Mr. Jeff SESSLER
18 Exec Director of Facilities .... Mr. Josh REEDER
104 Director of Off-Campus Study .... Ms. Neva BARKER

The Scripps Research Institute (F)

10550 N Torrey Pines Road, TPC19, La Jolla CA 92037-1000
County: San Diego — FICE Identification: 033213
Unit ID: 435338
Telephone: (858) 784-8469 — Carnegie Class: Not Classified
FAX Number: (858) 784-2802 — Calendar System: Quarter
URL: www.scripps.edu
Established: 1989 — Annual Graduate Tuition & Fees: N/A
Enrollment: N/A — Coed
Affiliation or Control: Independent Non-Profit — IRS Status: 501(c)3
Highest Offering: Doctorate; No Undergraduates
Accreditation: WC

01 President/CEO .... Dr. Peter G. SCHULTZ
46 EVP/Director Scripps Research .... Dr. Eric TOPOL
05 EVP Research & Academic Affairs .... Dr. James R. WILLIAMSON
26 VP Marketing/Communications .... Ms. Anna-Marie ROONEY
15 VP Human Resources .... Ms. Karen HAGGENMILLER
11 Chief Operating Officer .... Dr. Matthew TREMBLAY
10 Chief Financial Officer/Treasurer .... Ms. Alice FENG

Shasta Bible College and Graduate School (G)

2951 Goodwater Avenue, Redding CA 96002-1544
County: Shasta — FICE Identification: 023593
Unit ID: 123280
Telephone: (530) 221-4275 — Carnegie Class: Spec-4-yr-Faith
FAX Number: (530) 221-6929 — Calendar System: Semester
URL: www.shasta.edu
Established: 1972 — Annual Undergrad Tuition & Fees: $12,860

Enrollment: 41 Coed
Affiliation or Control: Independent Non-Profit IRS Status: 501(c)3
Highest Offering: Master's
Accreditation: TRACS

01 President/CEO Dr. David R. NICHOLAS
04 Exec Assistant to the President Ms. Jane DEANGELO
05 Vice President of Academics Dr. Stephen G. BROWN
32 Vice President of Student Services Mr. George A. GUNN
10 Chief Finance Officer Mr. Eric BROWN
49 Dean Undergraduate Studies Mrs. Faith MCCARTHY
34 Dean of Women Mrs. Donna R. NICHOLAS
18 Director Maintenance Mr. Ted RIVERS
06 Registrar Mrs. Faith MCCARTHY
37 Director of Financial Aid Ms. Linda ILES
08 Head Librarian Mrs. Virginia M. WILLIAMS

Shasta College (A)

PO Box 496006, 11555 Old Oregon Tr, Redding CA 96049-6006
County: Shasta FICE Identification: 001289
Unit ID: 123299
Telephone: (530) 242-7500 Carnegie Class: Bac/Assoc-Assoc Dom
FAX Number: (530) 225-4990 Calendar System: Semester
URL: www.shastacollege.edu
Established: 1950 Annual Undergrad Tuition & Fees (In-District): $1,187
Enrollment: 8,121 Coed
Affiliation or Control: State/Local IRS Status: Exempt
Highest Offering: Baccalaureate
Accreditation: WJ, CAHIIM, DH, @PTAA

01 Superintendent/President Dr. Joe WYSE
04 Asst to Superintendent/President Ms. Andree BLANCHIER
102 Executive Director SC Foundation Ms. Eva JIMENEZ
10 Asst Supt/VP of Admin Svcs Ms. Jill AULT
05 Asst Supt/VP of Instruction Dr. Frank NIGRO
32 Asst Supt/VP of Student Services Dr. Kevin O'RORKE
103 Asst Supt/VP of EWD Ms. Eva JIMENEZ
15 AVP of Human Resources Dr. Marrianne WILLIAMS
16 Director of Human Resources Ms. Amy WESTLUND
84 AVP of SS/Dean Enrollment Services Dr. Timothy JOHNSTON
35 Dean Student Services Ms. Sandra HAMILTON SLANE
35 Int Assoc Dean of Student Services Dr. Zhanjing (John) YU
57 Dean Arts/Communication/Soc Science Ms. Stacey BARTLETT
50 Dean Business/Ag/Ind/Tech/Safety Mr. Zachary ZWEIGLE
56 Dean Extended Education Dr. Andy FIELDS
76 Dean Health Sciences Ms. Ioanna IATRIDIS
88 Dir Hlth Sci Operations & Outreach Ms. Kim GILES
08 Exec Dean Educ Tech/Lrng Svcs/Rsrch Mr. William BREITBACH
68 Dean Phys Education and Athletics Mr. Mike MARI
81 Dean Science/Language Arts/Math Mr. Carlos REYES
09 Dn Innovation/Strategic Initiative Dr. Kate MAHAR
13 AVP of Info Services & Tech Ms. Becky MCCALL
21 Comptroller Ms. Jill AULT
19 Director of Campus Safety Mr. Lonnie SEAY
88 Director of Center of Excellence Ms. Sara PHILLIPS
109 Director of Food Services Ms. Denise AXTELL
25 Director of Grant Development Ms. Amy WEBB
14 Director of Information Technology Mr. James CRANDALL
35 Assoc Dean of Student Services Ms. Buffy TANNER
26 Director of Marketing & Outreach Mr. Peter GRIGGS
18 Director of Physical Plant Mr. George ESTRADA
39 Director Residence Life Mr. Nick WEBB
88 Int Dir Lrng Svcs & Special Pgms Ms. Tina DUENAS
81 Director of TRIO Ms. Sue HUIZINGA

Sierra College (B)

5100 Sierra College Blvd., Rocklin CA 95677
County: Placer FICE Identification: 001290
Unit ID: 123341
Telephone: (916) 624-3333 Carnegie Class: Assoc/MT-VT-High Trad
FAX Number: N/A Calendar System: Semester
URL: www.sierracollege.edu
Established: 1914 Annual Undergrad Tuition & Fees (In-District): $1,156
Enrollment: 17,503 Coed
Affiliation or Control: State/Local IRS Status: 501(c)3
Highest Offering: Associate Degree
Accreditation: WJ

01 Superintendent/President Mr. William H. DUNCAN
05 Supt/Vice President Instruction Dr. Rebecca BOCCHICCHIO
10 Vice Pres Administrative Services Mr. Erik SKINNER
32 Vice Pres Student Services Dr. James E. TODD
04 Exec Assistant Presidents Office Ms. Stacey CARROLL
08 Dean Library/Learn Rsc/Stdnt Engage Ms. Carolyn NORMAN
50 Dean Business & Technology Ms. Amy SCHULZ
81 Dean Science & Mathematics Dr. Randy LEHR
49 Dean Liberal Arts Dr. Anne FLEISCHMANN
41 Dean Phys Ed/Athletics Dir Ms. Rachel JOHNSON
09 Dean Planning/Research/Res Devel Mr. Erik COOPER
66 Dean Nursing & Allied Health Ms. Nancy JAMES
13 Chief Information Officer/ITS Mr. Tom BENTON
114 Dir of Budget & Financial Planning Ms. Judy AHLQUIST
15 Director Human Resources Mr. Cameron ABBOTT
18 Dir of Facilities & Construction Ms. Laura DOTY
37 Director Financial Aid Dr. Linda WILLIAMS
31 Community Education Pgm Manager Ms. Jill ALCORN
22 Director EEO/Diversity & Title IX Ms. LaToya JACKSON
26 Dir Marketing/Community Relations Mr. Joshua D. MORGAN
39 Residence Life Supervisor Ms. Cortney MAGORIAN
84 Dir Enrol Svcs/Registrar/Admissions Ms. Mariella CRANDALL

Simpson University (C)

2211 College View Drive, Redding CA 96003-8606
County: Shasta FICE Identification: 001291
Unit ID: 123457
Telephone: (530) 224-5600 Carnegie Class: Bac-A&S
FAX Number: (530) 226-4860 Calendar System: Semester
URL: www.simpsonu.edu
Established: 1921 Annual Undergrad Tuition & Fees: $33,630
Enrollment: 855 Coed
Affiliation or Control: The Christian And Missionary Alliance
IRS Status: 501(c)3
Highest Offering: Master's
Accreditation: WC, NURSE

00 Chair of the Board of Trustees Dr. James POSTMA
01 President Dr. Norman D. HALL
11 Chief Operating Officer Mr. Walter QUIRK
05 Provost Dr. Dale H. SIMMONS
10 Chief Financial Officer Mr. Timothy N. DIETZ
84 Chief Business Dev Ofcr/Dean Enroll Mr. Tony SMARRELLA
88 Faculty President Dr. Scott BARNETT
111 Dean of Advancement Mr. Ken WHITE
26 Director of Marketing Mr. Tony SMARRELLA
73 Executive Dean AW Tozer Seminary Dr. Patrick A. BLEWETT
53 Exec Dean of Education/Diversity Vacant
66 Dean School of Nursing Dr. Misty D. SMITH
88 Director Degree Completion Ms. Wendy J. SMITH
88 Director of Veterans Success Center Mr. Andrew TUGGLE
13 Director of Information Technology Mr. Ryan OPFER
41 Director of Athletics Vacant
32 Dean of Students/Title IX Coord Mr. Mark C. ENDRASKE
38 Director of Wellness Center Vacant
15 Director of Human Resources Mrs. Lindsey HARRIS
109 Director of Campus Operations Mr. Paul R. DAVIS
20 Dean/College of Arts & Sciences Dr. John AYABE
121 Associate Dean of Student Services Mr. Alex THIEMANN
35 Associate Dean of Campus Life Ms. Sarah A. JOBSON
08 Director of Library Service Ms. Heather MCCULLEY
21 Controller Ms. Juile CASE
06 Registrar Mrs. Adrienne CURRINGTON
04 Exec Assistant to the President Mrs. Elise WILSON
19 Campus Safety Operations Coord Mr. Dennis SMITH
40 Bookstore Manager Vacant
26 Communications Specialist Ms. Erin CLENDENEN
28 Executive Dean of Diversity Vacant
29 Director Alumni & Church Relations Mr. Raymond VAN GILST
37 Director Student Financial Services Ms. Shondra DICKSON
58 Director of M.A. Org Leadership Dr. Daniel SLOAN
50 Chair of Business Department Dr. Paul WOOD
60 Chair of Communications Dept Mrs. Molly RUPERT
81 Chair of Science and Math Dept Dr. Berkeley SHORTHILL
64 Chair of Music Department Dr. Steve KIM
82 Chair of History & Poli Science Dr. Tim ORR
09 Director of Institutional Research Mr. Michael MCNAIR

Sofia University (D)

1069 E Meadow Circle, Palo Alto CA 94303-4231
County: Santa Clara FICE Identification: 022676
Unit ID: 110778
Telephone: (888) 820-1484 Carnegie Class: Spec-4-yr-Other
FAX Number: (650) 459-5400 Calendar System: Quarter
URL: www.sofia.edu
Established: 1975 Annual Undergrad Tuition & Fees: N/A
Enrollment: 1,514 Coed
Affiliation or Control: Proprietary IRS Status: Proprietary
Highest Offering: Doctorate
Accreditation: WC

01 President Dr. Allan CAHOON
05 Provost & CAO Dr. Carol LEE HUMPHREYS
10 VP Admin & CFO Mr. Chris NGUYEN
32 Dean Student Services Ms. Rosalie COOK
15 Director of HR/Chief of Staff Ms. Renate KROGDAHL
88 Principal Designated Sch Official Ms. Raisa VELAZQUEZ
06 Registrar Ms. Karina SULAIMAN
07 Director of Admissions Ms. Penny LI

† Formerly Institute of Transpersonal Psychology.

Soka University of America (E)

1 University Drive, Aliso Viejo CA 92656-8081
County: Orange FICE Identification: 038144
Unit ID: 399911
Telephone: (949) 480-4000 Carnegie Class: Bac-A&S
FAX Number: (949) 480-4001 Calendar System: Semester
URL: www.soka.edu
Established: 2001 Annual Undergrad Tuition & Fees: $33,962
Enrollment: 403 Coed
Affiliation or Control: Independent Non-Profit IRS Status: 501(c)3
Highest Offering: Master's
Accreditation: WC

01 President/CAO/Prof of Economics Dr. Edward M. FEASEL
101 Exec Asst to President/Board Sec Mr. Hiro SAKAI
05 Exec Vice Pres for Academic Affairs Dr. Michael WEINER
10 Exec VP for Fin & Admin/CFO/CIO Mr. Archibald E. ASAWA
09 VP Inst Rsch/Dean of Graduate Sch Dr. Tomoko TAKAHASHI
15 Exec VP for Univ Comm/CHRO Ms. Katherine KING
46 VP Sponsored Research/Ext Acad Rels Dr. Bryan E. PENPRASE
88 Vice Pres Mission Integration Dr. Kevin MONCRIEF
84 Dean of Enrollment Services Mr. Andrew WOOLSEY
32 Dean of Students Dr. Hyon J. MOON
11 Chief of Operations Mr. Tom HARKENRIDER
43 Vice Pres/University Counsel Mr. David WELCH
39 Assoc Dean of Students Ms. Michelle HOBBY-MEARS
19 Director of Public Safety Mr. Don HODGSON
26 Exec Dir of Strategic Mktg & Comm Mr. Martin BECK
41 Director of Athletics & Recreation Mr. Mike MOORE
35 Director of Student Services Mr. Brian DURICK
30 Exec Director of Development Ms. Linda KENNEDY
13 Exec Director of InfoTechnology Mr. John MIN
44 Exec Director of Intl Development Ms. Toshiko SATO
104 Dir Study Abroad & Intl Internships Mr. Alex H. OKUDA
06 Registrar Ms. Nancy YOSHIMURA
08 Director of Library Mr. Hiroko TONONO
37 Director Student Financial Aid Mr. Scott BRANDOS
96 Director of Purchasing Ms. Kathy CRILLY

Solano Community College (F)

4000 Suisun Valley Road, Fairfield CA 94534-3197
County: Solano FICE Identification: 001292
Unit ID: 123563
Telephone: (707) 864-7000 Carnegie Class: Bac/Assoc-Assoc Dom
FAX Number: (707) 864-0361 Calendar System: Semester
URL: www.solano.edu
Established: 1945 Annual Undergrad Tuition & Fees (In-District): $1,168
Enrollment: 9,251 Coed
Affiliation or Control: State/Local IRS Status: 501(c)3
Highest Offering: Baccalaureate
Accreditation: WJ

01 Superintendent/President Dr. Celia ESPOSITO-NOY
05 VP Academic Affairs Dr. David WILLIAMS
10 Vice President Finance & Admin Vacant
13 Interim Chief Technology Officer Mr. James (Kimo) CALILAN
32 Vice President Student Services Ms. Lisa NEELEY
38 Dean Counseling/Special Services Dr. Kristin CONNER
37 Director Financial Aid Vacant
09 Dean Research and Planning Vacant
84 Dean of Enrollment Services Ms. Alysa BORELLI
15 Human Resources Director Mr. Salavatore ABBATE
18 Director Facilities Mr. Lucky LOFTON
88 Director Children's Programs Ms. Christie SPECK
103 Assoc Dean Workforce Development Vacant
26 Outreach/Public Relations Manager Vacant
96 Purchasing Tech/Buyer Ms. Laura SCOTT
36 Career & Job Placement Coordinator Ms. Patricia YOUNG
49 Dean School of Liberal Arts Mr. Neil GLINES
83 Dean Sch of Social/Behav Science Mr. Sandy LAMBA
81 Dean School Math/Science Mr. Joseph RYAN
72 Dean Sch Applied Tech Education Vacant
76 Dean of Health Sciences Dr. Sheila HUDSON
20 Dean Academic Support Services Dr. Shirley LEWIS
41 Director of Athletics Mr. Erik VISSER

South Baylo University (G)

1126 N. Brookhurst Street, Anaheim CA 92801-1702
County: Orange FICE Identification: 025973
Unit ID: 123633
Telephone: (714) 533-1495 Carnegie Class: Spec-4-yr-Other Health
FAX Number: (714) 533-6040 Calendar System: Quarter
URL: www.southbaylo.edu
Established: 1977 Annual Undergrad Tuition & Fees: N/A
Enrollment: 306 Coed
Affiliation or Control: Independent Non-Profit IRS Status: 501(c)3
Highest Offering: Doctorate
Accreditation: ACUP

01 President Dr. Bonifacio Bonny GARCIA
43 Vice President/General Counsel Dr. Janet LY
05 Academic Dean Dr. Pia MELEN
15 Personnel Director Ms. Sohila MOHIYEDDINI
17 Director of Clinics Dr. Sandjaya TRI
10 Director of Finance Ms. Michelle JANG
06 Registrar Dr. Woo Jin HAN
07 Director of Admissions Ms. Seon KIM
58 Master Program Director Dr. Hyo Jeong KANG
58 Doctoral Program Director Dr. Joseph SUH
32 Program Student Advisor Dr. Henry CHOI
88 Doctoral Clerkship Coordinator Dr. Anne AHN
35 Student/Alumni Coordinator Mr. Chanhwi JUNG
85 International Student Advisor Dr. Woo Jin HAN
13 Director IT Systems Mr. James KIM
37 Financial Aid Officer Ms. Mimi PARK
38 CCE Coordinator Dr. Henry CHOI
08 University Librarian Dr. Edwin FOLLICK
18 Chief of Facilities Mr. Yong Hee PARK

South Coast College (H)

2011 W Chapman Avenue, Orange CA 92868-2609
County: Orange FICE Identification: 022774
Unit ID: 123642
Telephone: (714) 867-5009 Carnegie Class: Spec 2-yr-Other
FAX Number: (714) 867-5026 Calendar System: Quarter
URL: www.southcoastcollege.com
Established: 1961 Annual Undergrad Tuition & Fees: $13,073
Enrollment: 254 Coed
Affiliation or Control: Proprietary IRS Status: Proprietary
Highest Offering: Associate Degree

Accreditation: ACCSC

01 President Ms. Jean GONZALEZ
10 Dean Finance & Admin Ms. Jila ANDELIBI
11 Director of Operations Mr. Kevin MAGNER
37 Director of Financial Aid Mr. Michael LY
06 Registrar Ms. Yoshiko IZUMI

*South Orange County Community College District (A)

28000 Marguerite Parkway, Mission Viejo CA 92692-3697
County: Orange FICE Identification: 033433
Unit ID: 432144
Telephone: (949) 582-4850 Carnegie Class: N/A
FAX Number: (949) 364-2726
URL: www.socccd.edu

01 Chancellor Dr. Julianna M. BARNES
05 Vice Chanc Educational & Tech Svcs Dr. Christopher MCDONALD
15 Vice Chancellor Human Resources Ms. Cindy VYSKOCIL
10 Vice Chancellor Business Svcs Ms. Ann-Marie GABEL
26 Chief Communications Officer Ms. Letitia CLARK
12 President Saddleback College Dr. Elliot STERN
12 President Irvine Valley College Dr. John HERNANDEZ

*Irvine Valley College (B)

5500 Irvine Center Drive, Irvine CA 92618-4399
County: Orange FICE Identification: 025395
Unit ID: 116439
Telephone: (949) 451-5100 Carnegie Class: Assoc/HT-Mix Trad/Non
FAX Number: (949) 451-5270 Calendar System: Semester
URL: www.ivc.edu
Established: 1979 Annual Undergrad Tuition & Fees (In-District): $1,146
Enrollment: 12,199 Coed
Affiliation or Control: State/Local IRS Status: 501(c)3
Highest Offering: Associate Degree
Accreditation: WJ

02 President Dr. John C. HERNANDEZ
100 Manager Office of the President Ms. Sandy JEFFRIES
05 Vice President Instruction Mr. Rick MIRANDA
32 Vice President Student Services Dr. Martha MCDONALD
11 Vice President Admin Services Mr. Davit KHACHATRYAN
26 Exec Dir Marketing/Creative Svcs Ms. Diane G. OAKS
102 Exec Director College Foundation Ms. Elissa ORANSKY
41 Dean Kinesiology/Health/Athletics Dr. Keith SHACKLEFORD
83 Dean Social & Behavioral Sciences Dr. Traci FAHIMI
38 Dean Counseling Services Dr. Angel HERNANDEZ
09 Dir Research/Planning/Accreditation Dr. Loris FAGIOLI
19 Chief of Police Mr. Scott KENNEDY
79 Dean Liberal Arts Dr. Brooke BUI
103 Dean Career & Continuing Educ Ms. Debbie VANSCHOELANDT
81 Dean Math/Sciences and Engr Dr. Lianna ZHAO
57 Dean The Arts Mr. Joseph POSHEK
84 Dean of Enrollment Services Mr. Corey RODGERS
23 Asst Dean Health/Wellness/Vet Svcs Ms. Nancy MONTGOMERY
37 Director of Financial Aid Mr. Korey LINDLEY
85 Dir International Student Programs Ms. Christina DELGADO
18 Director IVC Facilities Mr. Jeffrey HURLBUT
44 Director Annual Giving/Devel Svcs Ms. Karen ORLANDO
35 Assistant Dean of Students Mr. Amrik JOHAL
88 Manager of Outreach Services Mr. Frank RIVERA
22 Manager of Student Equity Ms. Erin POLLARD
124 Dir Student Recruitment Dr. Deejay SANTIAGO
13 Director Technology Services Mr. Nick WILKENING
06 Registrar/Admissions/Records Mr. Ruben GUZMAN

*Saddleback College (C)

28000 Marguerite Parkway, Mission Viejo CA 92692-3635
County: Orange FICE Identification: 008918
Unit ID: 122205
Telephone: (949) 582-4500 Carnegie Class: Assoc/HT-Mix Trad/Non
FAX Number: (949) 347-0438 Calendar System: Semester
URL: www.saddleback.edu
Established: 1968 Annual Undergrad Tuition & Fees (In-District): $1,330
Enrollment: 18,984 Coed
Affiliation or Control: State/Local IRS Status: 501(c)3
Highest Offering: Associate Degree
Accreditation: WJ, ADNUR, CAHIIM, EMT, NAEYC

02 President Dr. Elliot STERN
05 Vice President of Instruction Ms. Tram VO-KUMAMOTO
10 Vice Pres Administrative Svcs Mr. Cory WATHEN
32 Vice President of Student Services Dr. Juan AVALOS
20 Asst VP Cmty Ed/Emeritus & K-12 Dr. Karima FELDHUS
84 Dean of Enrollment Services Mr. Christian ALVARADO
100 Manager Office of the President Mr. Ryan BROOK
45 Director Planning/Research/Accred Ms. Shouka TORABI
06 Registrar Dr. James M. FEIGERT
19 Chief Of Police Mr. Pat HIGA
26 Dir Marketing/Communications Ms. Jennie MCCUE
102 Exec Dir College Foundation Ms. Elizabeth MCCANN
35 Director Student Life Mr. Christopher HARGRAVES
88 Assistant Dean Emeritus Institute Mr. Dan PREDOEHL
44 Director Annual/Planned Giving Ms. Erin MCHENRY
66 Director of Nursing Ms. Dee OLIVERI
18 Dir Facilities/Maint/Operation Mr. Timothy WOOTTON
23 Director Student Health Center Dr. Jeanne HARRIS-CALDWELL
13 Director Technology Services Dr. Anthony MACIEL
37 Director Financial Assistance Ms. Amber GALLAGHER
96 Director of Purchasing Mr. Nicholas NEWKIRK
85 Director of Intl Student Program Ms. Angela YANG
92 Honors Program Ms. Alannah ROSENBERG
38 Dean Counseling Svcs/Special Pgms Ms. Penny SKAFF
57 Dean Fine Arts Dr. Scott FARTHING
50 Dean Bus Science/Econ/Workforce Dev Dr. John JARAMILLO
76 Dean Health Sciences/Human Svcs Dr. Sherrie LOEWEN
81 Dean Math/Science & Engineering Dr. Akira NITTA
79 Dean Liberal Arts/Learning Res Dr. Kevin O'CONNOR
106 Dean Online Education/Learning Res Dr. Marina AMINY
72 Dean Advanced Tech Appl Science Dr. Anthony TENG
68 Dean Kinesiology/Athletic Director Mr. Daniel CLAUSS
83 Dean Social/Behavioral Sciences Dr. Christina HINKLE
121 Director Learning Assistance Dr. Kim D'ARCY
22 Dean Student Equity & Spec Programs Dr. Georgina GUY
103 Dir Economic/Workforce Development Mr. Israel DOMINGUEZ
25 Director Fiscal Contract Services Ms. Roxanne METZ
41 Athletic Director Mr. Randy TOTORP

Southern California Institute of Architecture (D)

960 E 3rd Street, Los Angeles CA 90013-1822
County: Los Angeles FICE Identification: 020758
Unit ID: 123952
Telephone: (213) 613-2200 Carnegie Class: Spec-4-yr-Other
FAX Number: (213) 613-2260 Calendar System: Semester
URL: www.sciarc.edu
Established: 1972 Annual Undergrad Tuition & Fees: $49,278
Enrollment: 481 Coed
Affiliation or Control: Independent Non-Profit IRS Status: 501(c)3
Highest Offering: Master's
Accreditation: WC

01 Director Mr. Herman DIAZ ALONSO
05 Vice Director/Chief Academic Ofcr Mr. John ENRIGHT
10 Chief Financial Officer Ms. Sue GOSNEY
11 Chief Administration Officer Mr. Paul HOLLIDAY
13 Chief Information Officer Mr. Vic JABRASSIAN
111 Chief Advancement Officer Ms. Kate O'NEAL
30 Assoc Director Development Vacant
58 Graduate Program Chair Ms. Elena MANFERDINI
48 Acting Undergrad Program Co-Chair Mr. William VIRGIL
48 Acting Undergrad Program Co-Chair Mr. Darin JOHNSTONE
04 Executive Assistant to Director Ms. Kian BROWN
07 Director Admissions Mr. Angel MONTES
26 Communications Director Ms. Stephanie ATLAN
15 Human Resources Director Ms. Liliana CLOUGH
06 Registrar/International Advisor Ms. Lisa RUSSO
37 Financial Aid Manager Ms. Marisela DE LA TORRE
08 Library Manager Mr. Kevin MCMAHON
88 Wood & Metal Shop Manager Mr. Rodney ROJAS
18 Facilities Director Mr. Emil TATEVOSIAN
20 Academic Affairs Coordinator Ms. Andrea YOUNG
19 Security Manager Mr. Reginald BENSON

Southern California Institute of Technology (E)

525 North Muller Street, Anaheim CA 92801-5454
County: Orange FICE Identification: 031136
Unit ID: 399869
Telephone: (714) 300-0300 Carnegie Class: Spec-4-yr-Other Tech
FAX Number: (714) 300-0311 Calendar System: Quarter
URL: www.scitech.edu
Established: 1987 Annual Undergrad Tuition & Fees: $18,390
Enrollment: 568 Coed
Affiliation or Control: Proprietary IRS Status: Proprietary
Highest Offering: Baccalaureate
Accreditation: ACCSC

01 President Dr. Parviz SHAMS
03 Vice President Mrs. Nazila SHAMS
11 Director of Operations Mr. Arian SHAMS

Southern California Seminary (F)

2075 E Madison Ave, El Cajon CA 92019-1108
County: San Diego FICE Identification: 033323
Unit ID: 117575
Telephone: (619) 201-8999 Carnegie Class: Bac-Diverse
FAX Number: (619) 201-8975 Calendar System: Trimester
URL: www.socalsem.edu
Established: 1946 Annual Undergrad Tuition & Fees: $16,884
Enrollment: 174 Coed
Affiliation or Control: Independent Non-Profit IRS Status: 501(c)3
Highest Offering: Doctorate
Accreditation: THEOL, TRACS

00 Chancellor Dr. David JEREMIAH
01 President Dr. Gary F. COOMBS
05 Provost & Chief Academic Officer Dr. Gino PASQUARIELLO
83 Dean Grad Sch Behavioral Science Dr. Elizabeth ELENWO
73 Dean of Biblical Studies/Theology Dr. James I. FAZIO
06 Registrar Mr. Brian BARGA
32 Director of Student Services Ms. Lisa PACHECO
37 Financial Aid Counselor Ms. Brianna ANDERSON
08 Library Director Miss Jennifer EWING
07 Admissions Officer Mr. Leroy HILL
113 Student Accounts Ms. Erin NEILL

Southern California State University (G)

3470 Wilshire Blvd, Ste 380, Los Angeles CA 90010
County: Los Angeles Identification: 667374
Telephone: (213) 382-5300 Carnegie Class: Not Classified
FAX Number: (213) 403-5636 Calendar System: Quarter
URL: https://scsuniversity.edu/
Established: 2012 Annual Undergrad Tuition & Fees: N/A
Enrollment: N/A Coed
Affiliation or Control: Independent Non-Profit IRS Status: 501(c)3
Highest Offering: Master's
Accreditation: TRACS

Southern California University of Health Sciences (H)

16200 E Amber Valley Drive, Whittier CA 90604-4051
County: Los Angeles FICE Identification: 001229
Unit ID: 117672
Telephone: (562) 947-8755 Carnegie Class: Spec-4-yr-Other Health
FAX Number: (562) 947-5724 Calendar System: Trimester
URL: www.scuhs.edu
Established: 1911 Annual Undergrad Tuition & Fees: N/A
Enrollment: 1,225 Coed
Affiliation or Control: Independent Non-Profit IRS Status: 501(c)3
Highest Offering: First Professional Degree
Accreditation: WC, ACUP, #ARCPA, CHIRO

01 President Dr. John SCARINGE
100 VP Operations/Chief of Staff Mr. Chuck SWEET
05 Provost/Chief Academic Officer Dr. Tamara ROZHON
10 VP Finance/CFO Mr. Thomas K. ARENDT
17 VP SCU Health Sys/Chief Clin Ofcr Dr. Melissa NAGARE
04 Exec Asst to President/BOR Ms. Michelle BERNHEIM
07 Asst VP Admissions Mr. Erick DE LA ROSA
32 Asst VP Student & Alumni Services Ms. Shelby GUGEL
106 AVP Online Educiation Ms. Meghan CHANDLER
88 AVP Clinical COS/Clinic Admin Mr. Robb RUSSELL
20 Asst Provost Academic Initiatives Dr. Michael RAMCHARAN
20 Asst Provost Academic Admin Dr. Jonathon EGAN
88 Dean LACC Dr. Ana CAMPOS FACCHINATO
63 Dean College of Eastern Medicine Dr. Jenny YU
37 Director of Financial Aid Ms. Eulanie MORALES
06 Assistant Registrar Ms. Raquel CHANG
81 Division Dean Accelerated Sciences Dr. Winmar WAY
21 Director of Accounting Mrs. Kelly GALLO
109 Asst VP Auxiliary Operations Mr. Joseph EGGLESTON
08 Integrative Support & Tech/LRC Mr. Joshua SHULMAN
88 Payroll Specialist Ms. Cindy SCHEIBEL
29 Director Alumni Services Dr. Elizabeth ROBLEDO
18 Director of Physical Plant Mr. Bob HARRISON
88 Assistant Controller Mrs. Christine HUYNH
121 Asst Dean Student Success Ms. Samaneh SADRI
26 Exec Dir Marketing & Admissions Mr. Jim BRENNER
45 Executive Director Finance Ms. Jennifer HAUSCH
88 Director Faculty/Dev/Excellence Mr. Vincent WIGGINS
09 AVP Institutional/Academic Insight Mr. Kris KRISHNAN
15 Director of People & Culture Ms. Siti WILLIAMS
13 Director Information Systems Mr. Bradley KUHN

Southern States University (I)

2855 Michelle Drive 380, Irvine CA 92606
Telephone: (949) 833-8868 Identification: 770629
Accreditation: ACICS

Southern States University (J)

1094 Cudahy Place, Suite 120, San Diego CA 92110
County: San Diego Identification: 667108
Unit ID: 490063
Telephone: (619) 298-1829 Carnegie Class: Spec-4-yr-Bus
FAX Number: (619) 704-0175 Calendar System: Quarter
URL: www.ssu.edu
Established: 1985 Annual Undergrad Tuition & Fees: $5,913
Enrollment: 358 Coed
Affiliation or Control: Proprietary IRS Status: Proprietary
Highest Offering: Master's
Accreditation: ACICS

01 Chancellor John D. TUCKER
05 Chief Academic Officer Charlotte HISLOP
06 Univ Registrar/Compliance Officer Wendy DU
08 University Librarian Christine WALCZYK
37 Financial Aid/Human Resources Mgr Denise MASTRO

Southwestern College (K)

900 Otay Lakes Road, Chula Vista CA 91910-7299
County: San Diego FICE Identification: 001294
Unit ID: 123800
Telephone: (619) 421-6700 Carnegie Class: Assoc/HT-High Trad
FAX Number: (619) 482-6413 Calendar System: Semester
URL: www.swccd.edu
Established: 1961 Annual Undergrad Tuition & Fees (In-District): $1,340
Enrollment: 17,621 Coed
Affiliation or Control: State/Local IRS Status: 501(c)3
Highest Offering: Associate Degree
Accreditation: WJ, ADNUR, DH, EMT, MLTAD, SURGT

01 Superintendent/President .... Dr. Mark SANCHEZ
05 Asst Supt/VP Academic Affairs .... Ms. Isabelle SABER
10 Asst Supt/VP Business & Fin Affs .... Dr. Kelly HALL
32 Int Asst Supt/VP Student Affairs .... Ms. Rachel FISCHER
12 Dn High Ed Ctr Otay Mesa .... Ms. Silvia CORNEJO
12 Dn High Ed Ctr Natl City/Crown Cove .... Ms. Christine PERRI
79 Dean Language & Literature .... Dr. Joel LEVINE
81 Dean Math/Science Engineering .... Dr. Silvia NADALET
68 Int Dean Wellness/Ex Sci/Athletics .... Ms. Jennifer HARPER
50 Dean Business & Technology .... Dr. Mink STAVENGA
57 Dean School of Arts/Comm and SS .... Dr. Cynthia MCGREGOR
09 Dean Inst Research & Planning .... Mr. Guillermo ABASOLO
108 Dean Inst Effect/Dir of Foundation .... Ms. Mia MCCLELLAN
26 Chief Public Info/Govt Relations .... Ms. Lillian LEOPOLD
15 Exec Asst Supt/VP Human Resources .... Ms. Janene MCINTYRE
88 Director Payroll Services .... Ms. Kimberly FROST
88 Dir Center Ops HEC San Ysidro .... Ms. Patricia BARTOW
88 Dir Rest Justice & Off Campus Pgm .... Ms. Patrice MILKOVICH
37 Director Financial Aid/Veterans .... Ms. Suzanne WOODS
07 Director Admissions/Records .... Mr. Nicholas MONTEZ
35 Interim Dean Student Services .... Ms. Rachel FISCHER
88 Int Dir Disability Support Svcs .... Mr. Stephen BROWN
22 Director EOPS .... Mr. Omar ORIHUELA
88 Director Child Development Ctr .... Ms. Isabel CARRASCO
22 Exec Officer of Equity & Engagement .... Ms. Janelle WILLIAMS
04 Special Assistant to Super/Pres .... Ms. Zaneta ENCARNACION
13 Chief Info Technology Officer (CIO) .... Vacant
28 Dir Equity Programs & Svcs .... Dr. Guadalupe CORONA
102 Executive Director Foundation .... Ms. Sofia ROBITAILLE
88 Director Student Development .... Mr. Ronnie HANDS
88 Director of Police Academy .... Mr. David ESPIRITU
103 Dean Cont Educ & Workforce Dev .... Ms. Jennifer LEWIS
88 Director EMT & Paramedic .... Mr. Jason HUMS
52 Director Dental Hygiene .... Ms. Gay TEEL
66 Sr Dir Nursing & Health Occupations .... Ms. Samantha GIRARD
88 Director MLT .... Ms. Deanna REINACHER
16 Director for Human Resources .... Ms. Angela RIGGS
88 Director of ER and Title IX .... Ms. Meng ZHANG
51 Dir Cont Education & Spec Projects .... Ms. Myesha JACKSON
109 Int Food Services Ops Supervisor .... Ms. Claudia ACOSTA
18 Int Dir Facilities Ops & Planning .... Ms. Aurora AYALA
21 Director of Finance .... Ms. Rizza DELA CUADRA

Southwestern Law School (A)

3050 Wilshire Boulevard, Los Angeles CA 90010-1106
County: Los Angeles — FICE Identification: 001295
Unit ID: 123970
Telephone: (213) 738-6700 — Carnegie Class: Spec-4-yr-Law
FAX Number: (213) 383-1688 — Calendar System: Semester
URL: www.swlaw.edu
Established: 1911 — Annual Graduate Tuition & Fees: N/A
Enrollment: 886 — Coed
Affiliation or Control: Independent Non-Profit — IRS Status: 501(c)3
Highest Offering: Doctorate; No Undergraduates
Accreditation: LAW

00 Chairman of the Board .... Ms. Lauren LEITCHMAN
01 President and Dean .... Ms. Darby DICKERSON
100 Chief of Staff/Asst Corporate Sec .... Ms. Marisela CERVANTES
43 General Counsel & Corporate Sec .... Ms. Julie XANDERS
10 Chief Financial Officer .... Vacant
13 Chief Information Officer .... Mr. Sean MURPHY
26 Chief Comm & Marketing Officer .... Ms. Hillary KANE
05 Vice Dean/Co-Dir of Externship .... Ms. Anahid GHARAKHANIAN
05 Vice Dean .... Ms. Julie WATERSTONE
20 Assoc Dean of Innovation & Admin .... Ms. Natalie RODRIGUEZ
11 Assoc Dean of Operations & Risk .... Ms. Marcie CANAL
32 Assoc Dean of Student Affairs .... Dr. Robert MENA
28 Dean of Students/Diversity Affairs .... Ms. Nydia DUEÑEZ
06 Registrar .... Mr. Wesley HOLLAND
111 VP for Institutional Advancement .... Mr. Jeff POLTORAK
09 Assoc Dean for Research .... Ms. Hila KEREN
88 Assoc Dean for Learning Outcomes .... Ms. Tracy TURNER
110 Assoc Dean for Institutional Advanc .... Ms. Debra L. LEATHERS
08 Assoc Dean and Law Library Director .... Ms. Margaret HALL
36 Assoc Dean of Career Services .... Vacant
88 Assoc Dean for SCALE .... Ms. Harriet M. ROLNICK
88 Assoc Dean Strategic Initiatives .... Mr. Byron G. STIER
07 Assoc Dean of Admissions .... Ms. Lisa L. GEAR
37 Director of Financial Aid .... Ms. Lina BORJORQUEZ
88 Director of Student Services .... Mr. Zachary BRUNING
09 Dir of Research and Data Management .... Ms. Margarita NUNEZ
88 Director of Legal Clinics .... Ms. Andrea RAMOS
19 Director of Campus Safety .... Vacant
44 Director of Annual Giving .... Ms. Emily CARDINAS
29 Director of Alumni Relations .... Ms. Cheryll AMORSOLO
88 Assoc Dean Biederman EML Institute .... Ms. Orly RAVID
21 Controller .... Ms. Phi RAMLI
22 Asst Gen Counsel/Title IX Coord .... Ms. Jessica JOHNSON
92 Co-Director of Moot Court Honors .... Ms. Catherine CARPENTER
88 Director of Writing Center .... Ms. Alexandra D'ITALIA
92 Co-Director of Trial Ad Honors .... Mr. Bill H. SEKI
92 Co-Director of Trial Ad Honors .... Mr. Joseph P. ESPOSITO
92 Co-Director of Negotiation Honors .... Ms. Cristina C. KNOLTON
55 Co-Director of Evening Program .... Ms. Bridgette DEGYARFAS
39 Property Manager of Residences .... Ms. Michelle TAFOYA
104 Dir of London Study Abroad Program .... Ms. Tamara MOORE
88 Director of Public Service Program .... Ms. Michelle TAKAGISHI-ALMEIDA
18 Building Engineer .... Mr. Juan CAMPOS
35 Sr Assoc Dir for Student Affairs .... Ms. Charlyne YUE
27 Asst Director Comm & Marketing .... Mr. Steven B. LOPEZ
88 Assoc Dir SA/Prin Des Schl Offic .... Ms. Sylvia VILLALPANDO
04 Dean's Office Assistant .... Ms. Jane C. FRANCIS

Spartan College of Aeronautics and Technology (B)

8911 Aviation Blvd, Inglewood CA 90301
County: Los Angeles — FICE Identification: 025964
Unit ID: 413680
Telephone: (310) 879-0554 — Carnegie Class: Spec 2-yr-Tech
FAX Number: N/A — Calendar System: Other
URL: www.spartan.edu
Established: 2014 — Annual Undergrad Tuition & Fees: N/A
Enrollment: 391 — Coed
Affiliation or Control: Proprietary — IRS Status: Proprietary
Highest Offering: Associate Degree
Accreditation: COE

01 President .... Mr. Chris TUREN

Stanbridge University (C)

2041 Business Center Dr., Suite 107, Irvine CA 92612
County: Orange — FICE Identification: 038893
Unit ID: 446561
Telephone: (949) 794-9090 — Carnegie Class: Spec-4-yr-Other Health
FAX Number: (949) 794-9098 — Calendar System: Other
URL: www.stanbridge.edu
Established: 1996 — Annual Undergrad Tuition & Fees: N/A
Enrollment: 1,698 — Coed
Affiliation or Control: Proprietary — IRS Status: Proprietary
Highest Offering: Master's
Accreditation: ACCSC, NURSE, OT, OTA, PTAA

01 Chief Executive Officer .... Mr. Yasith WEERASURIYA
10 Chief Financial Officer .... Ms. Nazi MASOUM
05 Vice Pres of Instruction .... Dr. Kelly HAMILTON
13 Exec VP Internet & Media Technology .... Mr. Monir BOKTOR
105 VP of Information/Web Technology .... Mr. Jesse DAVIS
66 Director of VN Program .... Ms. Renee HYPOLITE
88 Asst Program Director VN .... Ms. Kandace HUSTED
66 Director of RN/BSN Programs .... Dr. Minerva VALDENOR
88 Asst Program Director BSN .... Ms. Kelli PAUL
76 Director of OTA Program .... Mr. Satch PURCELL
76 Director of PTA Program .... Dr. Lauren EBERHARDT
32 Dir of Student Services .... Ms. Cynthia BARAHONA
37 Director of Financial Aid .... Mr. Brian SILVANO
07 Director of Admission Operations .... Mr. Greg LOW
74 Director of ASVT Program .... Dr. Brittany AGUILAR
88 Asst Program Director ASVT .... Ms. Maribel FORT
08 Librarian .... Mr. Fred POLING
36 Director of Career Services .... Dr. Yara WILLIAM
97 Director of GE Program .... Dr. Jason GOFF

Stanford University (D)

450 Jane Stanford Way, Stanford CA 94305-2004
County: Santa Clara — FICE Identification: 001305
Unit ID: 243744
Telephone: (650) 723-2300 — Carnegie Class: DU-Highest
FAX Number: (650) 725-6847 — Calendar System: Quarter
URL: www.stanford.edu
Established: 1885 — Annual Undergrad Tuition & Fees: $56,169
Enrollment: 15,953 — Coed
Affiliation or Control: Independent Non-Profit — IRS Status: 501(c)3
Highest Offering: Doctorate
Accreditation: WC, ARCPA, CAMPEP, IPSY, LAW, MED, PDPSY

01 President .... Dr. Marc TESSIER-LAVIGNE
43 Vice President & General Counsel .... Ms. Debra L. ZUMWALT
05 Provost .... Dr. Persis DRELL
26 VP/Chief External Relations Ofcr .... Mr. Martin SHELL
10 Vice President Business Affairs/CFO .... Mr. Randy LIVINGSTON
30 Vice Pres for Development .... Mr. Jon DENNEY
86 Sr Assoc VP for Public Affairs .... Mr. Ryan ADESNIK
15 Vice President for Human Resources .... Ms. Elizabeth ZACHARIAS
27 Vice President for Communications .... Ms. Farnaz KHADEM
29 President of Alumni Association .... Vacant
46 Vice Provost/Dean of Research .... Dr. Kathryn A. MOLER
20 Vice Provost Undergrad Education .... Dr. Sarah CHURCH
20 Vice Provost for Academic Affairs .... Dr. Stephanie KALFAYAN
88 Vice Provost Faculty Development .... Ms. Karen COOK
18 Vice President for Land & Buildings .... Mr. Robert C. REIDY
114 Vice Provost Budget & Auxiliaries .... Mr. Timothy R. WARNER
32 Vice Provost Student Affairs .... Ms. Susie BRUBAKER-COLE
100 Chief of Staff .... Ms. Megan PIERSON
106 Vice Prov Teaching & Learning .... Mr. Michael KELLER
63 Dean School of Medicine .... Dr. Lloyd MINOR
50 Dean Graduate School Business .... Dr. Jonathan LEVIN
65 Dean School of Earth Sciences .... Dr. Stephen GRAHAM
53 Dean School of Education .... Dr. Daniel SCHWARTZ
54 Dean School of Engineering .... Dr. Jennifer WIDOM
49 Dean School Humanities & Sciences .... Dr. Debra SATZ
61 Dean School of Law .... Ms. Jenny S. MARTINEZ
87 Dean Summer Session/Cont Stds .... Dr. Charles L. JUNKERMAN
42 Dean for Religious Life .... Dr. Tiffany STEINWERT
88 Director Hoover Institution .... Ms. Condoleezza RICE
88 Director SLAC .... Mr. Chi-Chang KAO
13 Chief Information Officer .... Mr. Steve GALLAGHER
08 Vice Provost/University Librarian .... Mr. Michael A. KELLER
41 Athletic Director .... Mr. Bernard MUIR
07 Dean of Admission and Financial Aid .... Mr. Richard H. SHAW, JR.
88 CEO Stanford Management Company .... Mr. Robert WALLACE
06 Registrar .... Ms. Johanna METZGAR
36 Director Career Development Center .... Mr. Farouk DEY
09 Dir Inst Research/Assessment .... Ms. Corrie POTTER
37 Director of Student Financial Aid .... Ms. Karen S. COOPER
27 AVP Stanford News Service .... Ms. Donna LOVELL
19 Director Public Safety .... Ms. Laura L. WILSON
96 AVP Procurement Services .... Ms. Cindy WILKINSON
35 Dir Prof Dev/Student Activities .... Ms. Ellen OH
38 Director Student Counseling .... Dr. Ronald ALBURCHER
102 Sr Dir Foundation/Corp Relations .... Ms. Kathy VEIT
88 Director Knight-Hennessy Scholars .... Dr. John L. HENNESSY
122 Asst Dean/Dir Frat/Sorority Life .... Ms. Amanda RODRIGUEZ

Stanton University (E)

9618 Garden Grove Blvd., Ste 201,
Garden Grove CA 92844
County: Orange — Identification: 667370
Telephone: (714) 539-6561 — Carnegie Class: Not Classified
FAX Number: (714) 539-6542 — Calendar System: Quarter
URL: https://stanton.edu/
Established: 1996 — Annual Undergrad Tuition & Fees: N/A
Enrollment: N/A — Coed
Affiliation or Control: Independent Non-Profit — IRS Status: 501(c)3
Highest Offering: Master's
Accreditation: WC

01 President .... Dr. David K. KIM
05 Chief Academic Officer .... Dr. Louna HALLAK
20 Director Academic Affairs .... Mr. Anhtu NGUYEN
10 Director of Business Affairs .... Ms. Han Na KIM
32 Director of Student Affairs .... Mr. Daniel KIM
07 Director of Admissions and Records .... Ms. Jean CHO
06 Registrar .... Ms. Raquel CRUZ
15 Director of Human Resources .... Ms. Jean CHO

Starr King School for the Ministry (F)

414 13th Street, Suite 700, Oakland CA 94612
County: Oakland — FICE Identification: 004080
Unit ID: 123916
Telephone: (510) 430-3335 — Carnegie Class: Spec-4-yr-Faith
FAX Number: N/A — Calendar System: Semester
URL: www.sksm.edu
Established: 1904 — Annual Graduate Tuition & Fees: N/A
Enrollment: 87 — Coed
Affiliation or Control: Unitarian Universalist — IRS Status: 501(c)3
Highest Offering: Doctorate; No Undergraduates
Accreditation: THEOL

01 President .... Rev. Rosemary BRAY MCNATT
111 Vice President Advancement .... Mr. Charles CLARK
10 Acting VP for Finance & Admin .... Mr. Michael BADALOV
05 Dean of the Faculty .... Dr. Gabriella LETTINI
35 Dean of Students .... Dr. Chris SCHELIN
06 Registrar .... Ms. Juliet CHAN
07 Director Admissions & Recruitment .... Mr. Matthew WATERMAN
20 Coordinator of Academic Programs .... Ms. Kim MOEBIUS
106 Director Online Education .... Dr. Hugo CORDOVA QUERO
26 Communications Officer .... Mr. Xander HUFFMAN
18 Facilities Director .... Mr. Fred WILLIAMSON
88 Director of Spiritual Care .... Ms. Jacqueline DUHART
04 Exec Asst to President & Dir of Ops .... Ms. Teresa JOYE
44 Director Annual Giving .... Ms. Erica TOYAMA

*State Center Community College District (G)

1171 Fulton Street, Fresno CA 93721
County: Fresno — FICE Identification: 001306
Unit ID: 123925
Telephone: (559) 243-7100 — Carnegie Class: N/A
FAX Number: N/A
URL: www.scccd.edu

01 Chancellor .... Dr. Carole GOLDSMITH
10 Vice Chancellor Finance & Admin .... Ms. Cheryl SULLIVAN
05 VC Educ Svcs/Inst Effectiveness .... Mr. Jerome COUNTEE
15 Vice Chanc Human Resources .... Ms. Julianna MOSIER
11 Vice Chancellor Operations & IS .... Ms. Christine MIKTARIAN
26 Exec Dir Pub/Legislative Rels .... Ms. Lucy RUIZ
102 Executive Director Foundation .... Mr. Rico GUERRERO
43 General Counsel .... Mr. Matthew BESMER
25 Dir Grants/External Funding .... Ms. Oxana AGHAEI
16 Director Human Resources .... Ms. Samerah CAMPBELL
96 Director of Purchasing .... Mr. Randy VOGT
21 Director of Finance .... Mr. William SCHOFIELD
13 Chief Technology Officer .... Dr. Ben SEABERRY
16 Director of Classified Personnel .... Vacant

*Clovis Community College (H)

10309 N. Willow Avenue, Fresno CA 93730
County: Fresno — Identification: 667125
Unit ID: 489201
Telephone: (559) 325-5200 — Carnegie Class: Assoc/HT-High Non
FAX Number: (559) 499-6065 — Calendar System: Semester
URL: www.cloviscollege.edu
Established: 2007 — Annual Undergrad Tuition & Fees (In-District): $1,304
Enrollment: 8,868 — Coed
Affiliation or Control: State/Local — IRS Status: 501(c)3

Highest Offering: Associate Degree
Accreditation: WJ, OTA

02 President .... Dr. Lori BENNETT
04 Assistant to the President ..... Ms. Bonnie BOONTHAVONGKHAM
05 VP Instruction .... Ms. Monica CHAHAL
10 VP Administrative Services .... Ms. Lorrie HOPPER
32 VP Student Services .... Mr. Marco J. DE LA GARZA
83 Dean of Instruction Social Sciences .... Dr. Ruben DIAZ
81 Dean Instruction Physical/CS/DE .... Dr. Derek DORMEDY
79 Dean Instruct Humanities/Athletics .... Dr. James ORTEZ
76 Dean Instruct Natural & Health Sci .... Dr. Laura A. HILL
35 Dean of Students Services .... Ms. Kira TIPPINS
35 Dean of Student Services .... Ms. Gurdeep HEBERT
13 Director of Technology .... Mr. Teng HER
26 Director of Marketing .... Ms. Stephanie BABB
27 Director of DSP&S .... Dr. Jacquelyn RUBALCABA
09 Director of Institutional Research .... Mr. Ryan FEYK-MINEY
37 Director of Financial Aid .... Ms. Rebecca KINLOW
38 Director of SBDC .... Mr. Rich MOSTERT
41 Director of Athletics .... Mr. James SEWELL
18 Custodian Manager .... Mr. Sergio SALINAS
07 Admissions & Records Manager .... Ms. Reynani CHAPPEL
21 Business Office Manager .... Ms. Kimberly DUONG
88 Child Development Lab Manager .... Ms. Monica MARQUEZ
124 Director of Relations and Outreach .... Ms. Emilee SLATER

*Fresno City College (A)

1101 E University Avenue, Fresno CA 93741-0002
County: Fresno — FICE Identification: 001307 — Unit ID: 114789
Telephone: (559) 442-4200 — Carnegie Class: Assoc/MT-VT-Mix Trad/Non
FAX Number: (559) 499-6045 — Calendar System: Semester
URL: www.fresnocitycollege.edu
Established: 1910 — Annual Undergrad Tuition & Fees (In-District): $1,304
Enrollment: 22,278 — Coed
Affiliation or Control: State/Local — IRS Status: 501(c)3
Highest Offering: Associate Degree
Accreditation: WJ, COARC, DH, RAD

02 Interim President .... Dr. Marlon HALL
05 Vice President of Instruction .... Mr. Don LOPEZ
32 VP of Student Services .... Dr. Lataria HALL
10 Vice Pres Administrative Services .... Mr. Omar GUTIERREZ
108 VP of Educ Svcs/Inst Effectiveness .... Dr. Robert PIMENTEL
07 District Dir Admissions & Records .... Ms. Robin TORRES
121 Dean Student Success/Learning .... Dr. Donna COOPER
50 Dean Business Division .... Dr. Tim WOODS
57 Dean Fine/Performing/Comm Arts .... Ms. Cyndie LUNA
79 Dean Humanities Division .... Ms. Tabitha VILLALBA
54 Dean Math/Science/Engineering Div .... Ms. Shirley MCMANUS
83 Dean Social Sciences Division ... Ms. Cherylyn CRILL-HORNSBY
76 Dean Health Sciences Division .... Ms. Lorraine SMITH
72 Dean Applied Technology Division .... Dr. Becky BARABE
38 Dean Counseling/Guidance .... Ms. Monica CUEVAS
35 Dean of Student Services .... Mr. Sean HENDERSON
75 Dean Educ Svcs/Pathway Effective .... Mr. Gurminder SANGHA
22 Director of Student Equity .... Dr. Raymond RAMIREZ
88 Dir Disabled Stdnt Pgms & Svcs .... Ms. Susan ARRIOLA
09 Dir Institutional Research .... Dr. Alex ADAMS
88 Director Police Academy .... Mr. Gary FIEF
35 Director of Student Activities .... Dr. Ernie MARTINEZ
26 Director Marketing/Communications .... Ms. Cris M. BREMER
37 Director Financial Aid .... Ms. Mikki JOHNSON
27 Public Information Officer .... Ms. Kathleen BONILLA
41 Assoc Dean Athletics .... Mr. Derrick JOHNSON
106 Dir Distance Education/Inst Tech .... Dr. Jodie STEELEY
72 Director of Technology .... Ms. Jennifer LAVAL
88 Dir College Relations & Outreach .... Mr. Nickolas LUCIO
66 Director of Nursing .... Ms. Keisha LEWIS
88 Director CalWORKs Program .... Ms. Mary Beth MOSSETTE
06 Director Admissions & Records .... Ms. Mirna DUARTE
88 Director TRIO Programs .... Mr. Bernardo REYNOSO
124 Director EOPS/CARE .... Mr. Thomas GAXIOLA-ROWLES
38 Dir Counseling/Special Programs .... Dr. George ALVARADO

*Madera Community College (B)

30277 Avenue 12, Madera CA 93638
County: Madera — Identification: 667399
Telephone: (559) 675-4800 — Carnegie Class: Not Classified
FAX Number: N/A — Calendar System: Semester
URL: www.maderacenter.com
Established: 1996 — Annual Undergrad Tuition & Fees (In-District): N/A
Enrollment: N/A — Coed
Affiliation or Control: State/Local — IRS Status: 501(c)3
Highest Offering: Associate Degree
Accreditation: WJ

02 Campus President .... Mr. Angel REYNA

*Reedley College (C)

995 N Reed Avenue, Reedley CA 93654-2099
County: Fresno — FICE Identification: 001308 — Unit ID: 117052
Telephone: (559) 494-3000 — Carnegie Class: Assoc/HT-High Non
FAX Number: N/A — Calendar System: Semester
URL: www.reedleycollege.edu
Established: 1926 — Annual Undergrad Tuition & Fees (In-District): $1,304
Enrollment: 6,796 — Coed
Affiliation or Control: State/Local — IRS Status: 501(c)3
Highest Offering: Associate Degree

Accreditation: WJ

02 College President .... Dr. Jerry L. BUCKLEY
05 Vice President of Instruction .... Mr. Dale VAN DAM
11 Vice Pres Administrative Svcs .... Ms. Melanie HIGHFILL
32 Vice Pres of Student Services ...... Ms. Natalie CULVER-DOCKINS
35 Dean of Student Services .... Ms. Shannon SOLIS
47 Dean of Instruction Agri/Nat Res .... Mr. David CLARK
79 Dean of Instruction Humanities .... Dr. G. Todd DAVIS
81 Dean Instruct Math/Sci/Tech/PE/Hlth .... Mr. Juan BEDOLLA
121 Dean Student Success & Achievement .... Dr. Sandra FUENTES
09 Int Dir IR/Effectiveness & Planning .... Ms. Janice OFFENBACH
26 Dir Marketing/Communications .... Mr. George TAKATA
28 Director DSP&S .... Dr. Samuel MORGAN
22 Director EOPS .... Mr. Mario GONZALES
13 Director of Technology .... Mr. Dan DEMMERS
37 Financial Aid Manager .... Ms. Christina CAZARES
07 Admissions & Records Mgr/Registrar .... Ms. Monique GARZA
08 Librarian .... Ms. Allie KENYON
41 Director of Athletics .... Dr. David SANTESTEBAN
04 Exec Assistant to the President .... Ms. Sarina NAVARRO

Stockton Christian Life College (D)

9023 West Lane, Stockton CA 95210
County: San Joaquin — Identification: 667333
Telephone: (209) 476-7840 — Carnegie Class: Not Classified
FAX Number: (209) 476-7868 — Calendar System: Semester
URL: www.clc.edu
Established: 1949 — Annual Undergrad Tuition & Fees: N/A
Enrollment: N/A — Coed
Affiliation or Control: Independent Non-Profit — IRS Status: 501(c)3
Highest Offering: Baccalaureate
Accreditation: WC

01 President & CEO .... Rev. Eli LOPEZ
11 Chief Operations Officer .... Rev. Laird G. SILLIMON
05 Chief Academic Officer .... Rev. Micah JOHNSON
32 Dean of Students .... Richard BISHOP
10 Chief Financial Officer .... Dr. William RIDDELL
113 Student Financial Services Asst .... Joshua ABREGO
04 Special Asst to the CEO .... Vacant
06 Registrar .... Jennifer C. LLAMAS
124 Recruitment & Retention .... Joanne GRESHAM
09 Director of Institutional Research .... Kenneth FITZPATRICK
105 Web/Media Services/Creative Design .... Josh RIVAS
108 Office of Assessment .... Israel RODRIGUEZ
121 Academic Advising .... Jasmin JOHNSON
13 Director of Information Technology ...... Timothy KHADVONGSINH
15 Director of Human Resources .... James LANGSTON
29 Alumni Affairs .... Sheila WILEY
53 General Education Chair .... Tina ROYER
73 Bible & Theology Chair .... William RIDDELL
96 Purchasing .... Connie SMITH
106 Dir of Online Svcs/Lrng Resources .... Regina LOPEZ
22 Title IX Coordinator .... Tamara FITZPATRICK
07 Director of Admissions .... Laird SILLIMON
44 Capital Development .... Sheila WILEY
50 Business Degree Program Chair .... Tamara FITZPATRICK

SUM Bible College and Theological Seminary (E)

1101 Investment Blvd, Suite 200, Eldorado Hills CA 95762
County: El Dorado — FICE Identification: 037524 — Unit ID: 447953
Telephone: (916) 306-1628 — Carnegie Class: Spec-4-yr-Faith
FAX Number: (510) 568-1024 — Calendar System: Trimester
URL: www.sum.edu
Established: 1999 — Annual Undergrad Tuition & Fees: $10,604
Enrollment: 584 — Coed
Affiliation or Control: Independent Non-Profit — IRS Status: 501(c)3
Highest Offering: Master's
Accreditation: WC, BI

01 President/Chancellor .... Rev. George NEAU
05 Chief Academic Officer .... Dr. Sanejo LEONARD
20 Vice President Cohort Development .... Rev. Melanie FRANCIS
10 Chief Financial Officer .... Ms. Lisa GODDARD
88 Assistant VP of Cohort Development .... Mr. Brendan BAGNELL
09 Director Institutional Research .... Dr. Benjamin KIM
08 Librarian .... Mr. Gary AVERILL
88 Faculty Chair .... Dr. Brandon KERTSON
20 Assoc Academic Dean .... Dr. Aaron YOM
06 Registrar .... Mr. Daniel ARROYO
28 Director of Diversity .... Dr. Aaron YOM

† Affiliated with School of Urban Missions-New Orleans, Gretna, LA.

Taft College (F)

29 Cougar Court, Taft CA 93268-2329
County: Kern — FICE Identification: 001309 — Unit ID: 124113
Telephone: (661) 763-7700 — Carnegie Class: Assoc/HT-High Non
FAX Number: (661) 763-7703 — Calendar System: Semester
URL: www.taftcollege.edu
Established: 1922 — Annual Undergrad Tuition & Fees (In-District): $1,104
Enrollment: 3,566 — Coed
Affiliation or Control: State/Local — IRS Status: 501(c)3
Highest Offering: Associate Degree
Accreditation: WJ, DH

01 Superintendent/President .... Dr. Debra DANIELS
10 Exec Vice Pres/Administrative Svcs .... Mr. Brock MCMURRAY
05 Vice President of Instruction .... Dr. Leslie MINOR
32 Vice Pres of Student Services .... Vacant
15 Vice President of Human Resources ... Ms. Heather DEL ROSARIO
04 Assistant to the President .... Ms. Sarah CRISS
30 Director Foundation & Development .... Ms. Sheri HORN BUNK
13 Director Information Services .... Ms. Xiaonong LI
08 Research and Instruction Librarian .... Ms. Terri SMITH
26 Exec Dir Marketing/Cmty Relations .... Ms. Susan GROVEMAN
09 Director Inst Research/Assessment .... Ms. Xiaohong LI
41 Director Athletics .... Ms. Kanoe BANDY
21 Director of Fiscal Services .... Ms. Amanda BAUER
07 Director of Admissions & Records .... Ms. Rebecca MUNILLO
18 Supervisor Facilities and Planning .... Mr. Richard TREECE
37 Director Student Financial Aid .... Ms. Barbara AMERIO
121 Dean of Student Success .... Vacant

Taft Law School (G)

3700 South Susan Street, Office 200, Santa Ana CA 92704-6954
County: Orange — Identification: 666398
Telephone: (714) 850-4800 — Carnegie Class: Not Classified
FAX Number: (714) 708-2082 — Calendar System: Other
URL: www.taftu.edu
Established: 1976 — Annual Undergrad Tuition & Fees: N/A
Enrollment: N/A — Coed
Affiliation or Control: Proprietary — IRS Status: Proprietary
Highest Offering: Doctorate
Accreditation: DEAC

02 Dean .... Ms. Melody JOLLY
07 Dean of Admissions .... Ms. Joan L. SLAVIN
11 Director of Administration .... Ms. Christine A. BALDWIN
37 Director of Financial Aid .... Ms. Lauren C. CROSWELL

Teachers College of San Joaquin (H)

2721 Transworld Dr, Stockton CA 95206
County: San Joaquin — Identification: 667087 — Unit ID: 488800
Telephone: (209) 468-4926 — Carnegie Class: Spec-4-yr-Other
FAX Number: (209) 468-9124 — Calendar System: Semester
URL: teacherscollegesj.edu
Established: 2009 — Annual Graduate Tuition & Fees: N/A
Enrollment: 868 — Coed
Affiliation or Control: State — IRS Status: 501(c)3
Highest Offering: Master's; No Undergraduates
Accreditation: WC

01 President .... Dr. Diane CARNAHAN
58 Director Graduate Studies .... Dr. Crescentia THOMAS
04 Senior Admin Asst to President .... Ms. Victoria L. DE PRATER
10 Chief Business Officer .... Mr. Scott ANDERSON
88 Director of Credential Programs .... Ms. Michele BADOVINAC
09 Director of Institutional Research .... Dr. Katherine BURNS

Theatre of Arts (I)

6472 Santa Monica Boulevard, Hollywood CA 90038
County: Los Angeles — Identification: 667098 — Unit ID: 486123
Telephone: (323) 463-2500 — Carnegie Class: Spec 2-yr-A&S
FAX Number: (323) 463-2500 — Calendar System: Trimester
URL: www.toa.edu
Established: 1927 — Annual Undergrad Tuition & Fees: $19,800
Enrollment: 22 — Coed
Affiliation or Control: Proprietary — IRS Status: Proprietary
Highest Offering: Associate Degree
Accreditation: THEA

01 Campus Director .... David LAW
37 Dir Student Financial Services .... Norma CELLS
06 Registrar .... Amanda ALVAREZ
07 Director of Admissions .... Reece CROSS

Thomas Aquinas College (J)

10,000 Ojai Road, Santa Paula CA 93060-9621
County: Ventura — FICE Identification: 023580 — Unit ID: 124292
Telephone: (805) 525-4417 — Carnegie Class: Bac-A&S
FAX Number: (805) 525-9342 — Calendar System: Semester
URL: www.thomasaquinas.edu
Established: 1971 — Annual Undergrad Tuition & Fees: $26,000
Enrollment: 462 — Coed
Affiliation or Control: Independent Non-Profit — IRS Status: 501(c)3
Highest Offering: Baccalaureate
Accreditation: WC

01 President .... Dr. Paul O'REILLY
04 Executive Assistant to President .... Miss Sarah JIMENEZ
88 Director of Special Projects .... Mrs. Anne S. FORSYTH
111 Vice President for Advancement .... Dr. Paul J. O'REILLY
30 Executive Director of Advancement .... Mr. James LINK
43 General Counsel .... Mr. John Q. MASTELLER
10 Vice Pres for Finance .... Mr. Dennis K. MCCARTHY
11 VP for Operations .... Mr. Mark KRETSCHMER
05 Academic Dean .... Dr. John GOYETTE
112 Director of Gift Planning .... Mr. Paul F. BLEWETT

29 Director of Alumni/Parent Relations ..... Mr. Robert A. BAGDAZIAN
07 Director of Admissions .... Mr. Jonathan P. DALY
44 Annual Fund Manager .... Ms. Heather TIFFANY
37 Director of Financial Aid .... Mr. Gregory J. BECHER
15 Director of Human Resources .... Vacant
08 Librarian .... Ms. Richena CURPHEY
32 Asst Dean for Student Affairs .... Dr. Jared KUEBLER
42 Chaplain .... Rev. John CHUNG
27 Dir of Communications/Marketing ...... Mr. Christopher WEINKOPF
88 Advancement Database Manager .... Mr. Francis DONNELLY
13 Chief Information Technology Office .... Mr. Pat NICHOLS
18 Chief Facilities/Physical Plant Ofc .... Mr. Clark TULBERG
102 Dir Foundation/Corporate Relations .... Mrs. Sharon REISER

Thomas Jefferson School of Law (A)

701 B Street, Ste. 110, San Diego CA 92101
County: San Diego FICE Identification: 010854
Unit ID: 126049
Telephone: (619) 297-9700 Carnegie Class: Spec-4-yr-Law
FAX Number: (619) 961-4370 Calendar System: Semester
URL: www.tjsl.edu
Established: 1969 Annual Graduate Tuition & Fees: N/A
Enrollment: 247 Coed
Affiliation or Control: Independent Non-Profit IRS Status: 501(c)3
Highest Offering: Doctorate; No Undergraduates
Accreditation: WC, LAW

01 President & General Counsel .... Karin K. SHERR
05 Assoc Dean Acad Affairs & Professor ...... Dean Steve SEMERARO
10 VP and Chief Financial Officer .... Nancy VU
32 Assistant Dean for Student Affairs .... Lisa FERREIRA
84 Asst Dean of Enrollment Mgmt .. Michelle SLAUGHTER ALLISON
88 Non-JD Enrol Mgr/Instruct Designer .... Nancy ANZALONE
08 Library Director .... Robert WICKMAN
36 Director of Career Services .... Judybeth TROPP
20 Director of Academic Administration .... Natasha DABNEY
37 Director of Financial Assistance .... Marc BERMAN
06 Registrar .... Carrie KAZYAKA
21 Financial Operations Specialist .... Vacant
88 Externship Director/Pro Bono .... Judybeth TROPP
15 Director of Human Resources .... Lisa CHIGOS
13 Director of IT .... Gil SUSANA

Touro University California (B)

1310 Club Drive, Vallejo CA 94592
County: Solano FICE Identification: 041426
Unit ID: 459736
Telephone: (707) 638-5200 Carnegie Class: Spec-4-yr-Med
FAX Number: (707) 638-5255 Calendar System: Trimester
URL: www.tu.edu
Established: 1997 Annual Undergrad Tuition & Fees: N/A
Enrollment: 1,321 Coed
Affiliation or Control: Independent Non-Profit IRS Status: 501(c)3
Highest Offering: Doctorate
Accreditation: WC, ARCPA, NURSE, &OSTEO, PH, PHAR

00 President & CEO Univ System .... Dr. Alan KADISH
02 CEO/Sr Provost Touro Western Div .... Hon. Shelley BERKLEY
05 Provost & Chief Academic Officer .... Dr. Sarah SWEITZER
32 Dean of Student Affairs .... Dr. Steven JACOBSON
35 Associate Dean of Students .... Dr. James BINKERD
07 Director of Admissions .... Mr. Steven DAVIS
09 AVP Institutional Effectiveness .... Dr. Meiling TANG
10 Dir of Fiscal Affairs & Accounting .... Ms. Amber SHOMO
15 Director Employee Relations .... Ms. Kathy LOWE
11 Associate VP of Administration .... Vacant
08 Director University Library .... Ms. Tamara TRUJILLO
63 Dean College of Osteopathic Med .... Dr. Michael CLEARFIELD
67 Dean College of Pharmacy .... Mr. James SCOTT
53 Dean Col of Education & Health Sci .... Dr. Lisa NORTON
13 Director of Information Technology .... Mr. Scott OLDS
111 AVP Univ Advancement .... Ms. Andrea GARCIA
37 Financial Aid Director .... Ms. Kim KANE
35 Director of Campus Life .... Rabbi Elchonon TENENBAUM
23 Asst Dir of Student Health Center .... Ms. Marcia GREENE
06 Registrar .... Mr. Ron TRAVENICK

Touro University Worldwide (C)

10601 Calle Lee Ste 179, Los Alamitos CA 90720
County: Orange FICE Identification: 041425
Unit ID: 459727
Telephone: (818) 575-6800 Carnegie Class: Masters/L
FAX Number: (818) 707-0316 Calendar System: Semester
URL: www.tuw.edu
Established: 2005 Annual Undergrad Tuition & Fees: N/A
Enrollment: 2,131 Coed
Affiliation or Control: Independent Non-Profit IRS Status: 501(c)3
Highest Offering: Doctorate
Accreditation: WC, MFCD, @SW

01 Interim CEO .... Mr. Roy FINALY
05 Provost & Chief Academic Officer .... Dr. Shelia LEWIS
10 Chief Financial Officer (CFO) .... Mr. Jayson CAPUNO
11 Chief Operating Officer (COO) .... Mr. Roy FINALY
15 Exec Dir Human Resources/Admin .... Mrs. Melody ERBES
06 Registrar/Exec Dir Enrollment Mgmt .... Ms. Wei REN

Touro College Los Angeles (D)

1317 N Crescent Heights Blvd, West Hollywood CA 90046
Telephone: (310) 822-9700 Identification: 770944
Accreditation: &WC

† Branch campus of Touro University Worldwide, Los Alamitos, CA.

Triad Education (E)

3580 Wilshire Boulevard, 4th Floor,
Los Angeles CA 90010
County: Los Angeles FICE Identification: 036393
Unit ID: 441229
Telephone: (310) 289-5123 Carnegie Class: Spec-4-yr-Other Health
FAX Number: (310) 289-5136 Calendar System: Quarter
URL: www.wcui.edu
Established: 1998 Annual Undergrad Tuition & Fees: $18,600
Enrollment: 809 Coed
Affiliation or Control: Proprietary IRS Status: Proprietary
Highest Offering: Baccalaureate
Accreditation: ACCSC

01 CEO/Campus Director .... Ms. Myra CHASON
06 Registrar .... Ms. Erika BRIZUELA
07 Director of Admissions .... Ms. Leslie SANTANA
10 Assisant Campus Director .... Ms. Mieke WIBOWO
11 Chief of Operations .... Mr. Andrew HIGH
36 Director Career Development .... Ms. Elai ZEINA
37 Director Student Financial Aid .... Ms. Dora RUIZ
29 Director Alumni/Continuing Educ .... Mr. Tommy SHIN
05 Director Education .... Mr. Michael STEWART

Triad Education (F)

3700 E. Inland Empire Blvd, Ste 235, Ontario CA 91764
Telephone: (909) 483-3808 Identification: 770942
Accreditation: ACCSC

† Main campus is Triad Education in Los Angeles, CA.

Trident University International (G)

5757 Plaza Drive, Suite 100, Cypress CA 90630
County: Orange FICE Identification: 041279
Unit ID: 450979
Telephone: (714) 816-0366 Carnegie Class: Not Classified
FAX Number: (714) 816-0367 Calendar System: Semester
URL: www.trident.edu
Established: 1998 Annual Undergrad Tuition & Fees: N/A
Enrollment: N/A Coed
Affiliation or Control: Proprietary IRS Status: Proprietary
Highest Offering: Doctorate
Accreditation: WC

01 President/CEO .... Mr. John KLINE
03 Senior Vice President .... Mr. Travis ALLEN
05 Provost/Chief Academic Officer .... Dr. Ruki JAYARAMAN
10 Chief Financial Officer .... Vacant
13 Chief Information Officer .... Mr. Vahid SHARIAT
07 Vice President of Admissions .... Ms. Christina HOANG
53 Dean College of Education .... Dr. Heidi SMITH
50 Dean GJ Col Business/Info Systems .... Dr. Lisa MOHANTY
76 Dean Educ/Health Sciences .... Dr. Mickey SHACHAR
04 Executive Assistant .... Ms. Patricia PARKS
06 Registrar .... Vacant
37 Student Finance Manager .... Ms. Brittney DRAKE
09 Director of Institutional Research .... Dr. Heidi SATO
08 Librarian .... Ms. Leslie ANDERSEN
21 Director of Financial Operation .... Vacant
18 Facilities Manager .... Mr. Fred WILSON
101 Board of Trustees Secretary .... Mr. Stanley MENGEL

Trinity Law School (H)

2200 N Grand Avenue, Santa Ana CA 92705
Telephone: (714) 836-7500 Identification: 770098
Accreditation: &HLC

† Branch campus of Trinity International University, Deerfield, IL

Union University of California (I)

14200 Goldenwest Street, Westminster CA 92683
County: Orange Identification: 667269
Telephone: (714) 903-2762 Carnegie Class: Not Classified
FAX Number: N/A Calendar System: Semester
URL: www.uuc.edu
Established: 1986 Annual Graduate Tuition & Fees: N/A
Enrollment: N/A Coed
Affiliation or Control: Independent Non-Profit IRS Status: 501(c)3
Highest Offering: Doctorate; No Undergraduates
Accreditation: DEAC

01 President/CEO .... Dr. Linh DOAN
04 Special Assistant to President .... Dr. Son Xuan NGUYEN
05 Vice President Academic Affairs .... Dr. Michael HUNG TRUONG
32 Vice Pres Student Affairs .... Vacant
10 Vice Pres Finance/CFO .... Mr. Tom DUONG
13 EVP/COO/CIO .... Mr. Philip NGUYEN
07 Director Admissions/Registrar .... Vacant

United States University (J)

7675 Mission Valley Road, San Diego CA 92108
County: San Diego FICE Identification: 040053
Unit ID: 447050
Telephone: (619) 876-4250 Carnegie Class: Spec-4-yr-Other Health
FAX Number: N/A Calendar System: Semester
URL: www.usuniversity.edu
Established: 1997 Annual Undergrad Tuition & Fees: $6,480
Enrollment: 1,981 Coed
Affiliation or Control: Proprietary IRS Status: Proprietary
Highest Offering: Doctorate
Accreditation: WC, NURSE

01 President and CEO .... Dr. Steven A. STARGARDTER
05 Provost/Chief Academic Officer .... Vacant
84 VP of Enroll Mgmt/Stdnt Svcs/Mktg .... Vacant
37 VP Student Financial Aid .... Jennifer ROBINSON
10 Chief Financial Officer .... Mr. Ming TAN
20 Assoc Provost Accred/Curriculum .... Dr. Elizabeth ARCHER
07 Director of Enrollment/Admissions .... Mr. Ken COOK
06 Registrar .... David NORIEGA
29 Director Alumni Relations .... Vacant
85 International Student Advisor .... Tina RICAFRENTE

Unitek College (K)

4670 Auto Mall Parkway, Fremont CA 94538
County: Alameda FICE Identification: 041697
Unit ID: 459204
Telephone: (888) 775-1514 Carnegie Class: Spec-4-yr-Other Health
FAX Number: (510) 249-9125 Calendar System: Other
URL: www.unitekcollege.edu
Established: 1992 Annual Undergrad Tuition & Fees: $35,284
Enrollment: 3,618 Coed
Affiliation or Control: Proprietary IRS Status: Proprietary
Highest Offering: Baccalaureate
Accreditation: ACCSC, NURSE

00 CEO .... Ms. Janis PAULSON
02 Fremont Campus Director .... Mr. Frederick HOLLAND

University of Antelope Valley (L)

44055 Sierra Hwy, Lancaster CA 93534
County: Los Angeles FICE Identification: 034275
Unit ID: 442930
Telephone: (661) 726-1911 Carnegie Class: Bac-Diverse
FAX Number: (661) 726-5158 Calendar System: Other
URL: www.uav.edu
Established: 1997 Annual Undergrad Tuition & Fees: N/A
Enrollment: 731 Coed
Affiliation or Control: Proprietary IRS Status: Proprietary
Highest Offering: Master's
Accreditation: WC, EMT

01 President .... Mr. Marco JOHNSON
10 Vice President Admin/CFO .... Dr. Barry RYAN
05 Dean of Academic Affairs .... Ms. Chonnea HARRIS
32 Dean of Student Affairs .... Mr. Ronald FELTS
37 Financial Aid Director .... Ms. Maricela GUZMAN
09 Dir Institutional Effectiveness .... Ms. Crystal STEPHENS
13 Director Information Technology .... Mr. Noel SANCHEZ
36 Director Career Services .... Ms. Karyn FRAHM
07 Director of Admissions .... Ms. Susan OROSCO

*University of California Office of the President (M)

1111 Franklin Street, 12th Floor, Oakland CA 94607-5200
County: Alameda FICE Identification: 001311
Unit ID: 124557
Telephone: (510) 987-0700 Carnegie Class: N/A
FAX Number: (510) 987-0328
URL: www.ucop.edu

01 President .... Michael V. DRAKE
05 Provost/EVP Academic Affairs .... Michael BROWN
10 EVP/Chief Financial Officer .... Nathan E. BROSTROM
11 EVP/Chief Operating Officer .... Rachael NAVA
17 Exec Vice Pres UC Health .... Carrie BYINGTON
26 SVP External Rels/Communications .... Claire HOLMES
27 AVP External Rels/Communications .... Diana HARVEY
108 SVP Compliance/Audit Services .... Alexander BUSTAMANTE
47 VP Agriculture/Natural Resources .... Glenda HUMISTON
115 Vice President of Investments .... Jagdeep S. BACHHER
09 Vice Pres Inst Rsrch/Acad Planning .... Pamela BROWN
88 VP Office of National Laboratories .... Craig LEASURE
15 Int Vice Pres Human Resources .... Cheryl LLOYD
43 General Counsel/VP Legal Affairs .... Charles F. ROBINSON
32 Vice President Student Affairs .... Yvette GULLATT
13 VP/CIO Information Technology Svcs .... Tom ANDRIOLA
28 Vice Prov Equity/Diversity/Inclus .... Yvette GULLATT
20 Vice Provost Academic Personnel .... Susan CARLSON
21 Assoc VP Budget Analysis/Planning .... David ALCOCER
04 Exec Assistant to the President .... Sutton BENNETT

*University of California-Berkeley (N)

Berkeley CA 94720-0001
County: Alameda FICE Identification: 001312
Unit ID: 110635
Telephone: (510) 642-6000 Carnegie Class: DU-Highest

FAX Number: (510) 643-5499 Calendar System: Semester
URL: www.berkeley.edu
Established: 1868 Annual Undergrad Tuition & Fees (In-State): $14,312
Enrollment: 42,327 Coed
Affiliation or Control: State IRS Status: 501(c)3
Highest Offering: Doctorate
Accreditation: WC, CLPSY, @DIET, DIETD, IPSY, LAW, LSAR, OPT, OPTR, PCSAS, PH, PLNG, SCPSY, SW

02 Chancellor Carol CHRIST
05 Exec Vice Chancellor/Provost Benjamin HERMALIN
11 Vice Chancellor Administration Marc FISHER
10 Vice Chance/Chief Financial Officer Rosemarie RAE
46 Vice Chancellor for Research Kathy YELICK
32 Vice Chancellor Student Affairs Steve SUTTON
30 Vice Chanc Univ Dev/Alumni Rels Julie HOOPER
88 Vice Chanc Undergrad Education Cathy KOSHLAND
22 Vice Chanc Equity & Inclusion Dania MATOS
43 Chief Campus Counsel David ROBINSON
100 Ast Vice Chanc/Chief of Staff Ann JEFFREY
25 Asst VC Research Admin & Compliance Patrick SCHLESINGER
13 AVC Info Technology/Chief Info Ofcr Jen STRINGER
07 Exec Dir of Admissions Eric ASKINS
87 AVC/Dean Summer Session/Stdy Abroad Richard RUSSO
26 AVC Communications/Public Affairs Diana HARVEY
21 Asst Vice Chanc Finance/Controller Vacant
35 Assc Vice Chanc/Dean of Students Sunny LEE
37 Asst VC/Dir Fin Aid & Scholarship Cruz GRIMALDO
08 University Librarian Jeffrey MACKIE-MASON
06 Registrar Walter WONG
38 Dir Counseling & Psychological Svcs Vacant
36 Director Career Center Thomas C. DEVLIN
41 Director of Athletics James KNOWLTON
58 Vice Prov/Dean of Graduate Division Lisa GARCIA BEDOLLA
61 Dean Boalt School of Law Erwin CHEMERINSKY
88 Dean School of Optometry John FLANAGAN
54 Dean College of Engineering Tsu-Jae KING LIU
88 Dean of Environmental Design Jennifer WOLCH
65 Dean College of Natural Resources David D. ACKERLY
50 Dean Haas School of Business Richard K. LYONS
70 Dean School of Social Welfare Jeffrey EDELSON
72 Dean School of Information AnnaLee SAXENIAN
69 Dean School of Public Health Michael C. LU
53 Int Dean Berkeley Sch of Education Christopher EDLEY, JR.
60 Dean Graduate School of Journalism Geeta ANAND
81 Dean College of Chemistry Douglas S. CLARK
80 Dean Goldman School Public Policy Henry E. BRADY
79 Dean of Arts and Humanities Anthony CASCARDI
81 Dean of Biological Sciences Michael R. BOTCHAN
81 Dean Mathematical/Physical Sciences Steven KAHN
49 Exec Dean Col of Letters & Sciences Jennifer JOHNSON-HANKS
97 Dean of the Undergrad Division Bob JACOBSON
56 Dean of University Extension Rick RUSSO

*University of California-Davis (A)

One Shields Avenue, Davis CA 95616-5270
County: Yolo FICE Identification: 001313
Unit ID: 110644
Telephone: (530) 752-1011 Carnegie Class: DU-Highest
FAX Number: N/A Calendar System: Quarter
URL: www.ucdavis.edu
Established: 1905 Annual Undergrad Tuition & Fees (In-State): $14,597
Enrollment: 39,074 Coed
Affiliation or Control: State IRS Status: 501(c)3
Highest Offering: Doctorate
Accreditation: WC, ARCPA, CAMPEP, DIETD, DIETI, IPSY, LAW, LSAR, MED, MLS, NURSE, PAST, PH, VET

02 Chancellor Dr. Gary S. MAY
05 Provost & Exec Vice Chancellor Dr. May CROUGHAN
100 Associate Chancellor/Chief of Staff Mr. Karl M. ENGELBACH
26 Chief Marketing & Comm Officer Ms. Dana TOPOUSIS
46 Vice Chancellor Research Dr. Prasant MOHAPATRA
30 Vice Chanc Dev/Alumni Relations Dr. Shaun B. KEISTER
32 Vice Chancellor Student Affairs Dr. Pablo G. REGUERIN
10 VC Finance/Operation & Admin Vacant
28 VC Diversity/Equity/Inclusion Ms. Renetta GARRISON
17 VC Human Hlth Sci/CEO UC Davis Hlth Dr. David A. LUBARSKY
66 Assoc VC/Dean Sch of Nursing Dr. Heather M. YOUNG
31 Assoc Exec VC Campus Cmty Relations Mr. Rahim REED
11 Asst VC Office of the COO Mr. Blair STEPHENSON
88 Exec Assoc VC Research Dr. Cindy M. KIEL
88 Assoc Vice Provost Global Affairs Dr. Ermias KEBREAB
88 Assoc Vice Provost Global Affairs Dr. Fadi FATHALLAH
88 Assoc VC Research Dr. Paul DODD
88 Assoc VC Research Dr. Dushyant PATHAK
15 Chief Human Resources Officer Ms. Christine LOVELY
110 Assoc VC Development Mr. Jason L. WOHLMAN
110 Assoc VC Development Mr. Paul PROKOP
88 Assoc VC Development Health Sci Ms. Chong U. PORTER
39 Int Assoc VC Student Affs/Aux Svcs Mr. Mike SHEEHAN
35 Assoc VC Student Affairs/Stdnt Life Dr. Sheri ATKINSON
84 Assoc VC Enrollment Management Mr. Donlad E. HUNT
88 Assoc VC Safety Services Mr. Eric KVIGNE
88 Assoc VC Design & Construct Mr. Jim CARROLL
18 Assoc VC Facilities Management Mr. Allen TOLLEFSON
45 AVC Campus Plng/Env Stewardship Mr. Robert B. SEGAR
88 Asst VC Student Affairs Div Svcs Mr. Cory N. VU
86 Int Lead Govt & Cmty Relations Ms. Mabel SALON
21 Asst VC & Campus Controller Mr. Matt OKAMOTO
88 Asst Exec Vice Chanc Provost Ofc Mr. Karl MOHR
114 Asst VC Budget Ms. Sarah MANGUM
88 Asst VC Capital Plng & Real Estate Mr. Grant ROCKWELL
88 Asst VC Development Outreach Ms. Angela JOENS
88 Asst VC Development Ms. Beth BRENNER
112 Asst VC Planned Giving Mr. Brian CASEY
102 Asst VC Foundation & Corp Giving Vacant
88 Asst VC Student Affs & Chf of Staff Ms. Emily PRIETO-TSEREGOUNIS
29 AVC/Exec Director Alumni Relations Mr. Richard R. ENGEL
13 CIO & VP Info/Educ Tech Ms. Viji MURALI
97 VP & Dean Undergraduate Educ Dr. Carolyn THOMAS
58 VP Grad Educ/Dean Grad Stds Dr. Jean-Pierre DELPLANQUE
20 Vice Provost Academic Affairs Dr. Phil KASS
104 VP & Assoc Chanc Global Affairs Dr. Joanna REGULSKA
47 Dean Agricultural/Environ Sci Dr. Helene DILLARD
81 Dean Biological Sciences Dr. Mark WINEY
54 Dean Engineering Dr. Jennifer SINCLAIR CURTIS
49 Int Dean College of Letters/Science Mr. Ari KELMAN
61 Dean School of Law Dr. Kevin R. JOHNSON
50 Dean Grad School of Management Dr. H. Rao UNNAVA
74 Dean Veterinary Medicine Dr. Michael D. LAIRMORE
53 Dean School of Education Dr. Lauren LINDSTROM
51 Dean Div of Cont/Prof Education Dr. Susan D. CATRON
63 Interim Dean School of Medicine Dr. Lars BERGLUND
88 Exec Director Mondavi Center Dr. Don F. ROTH
109 Exec Dir Campus Rec/Unions Mr. Jason LORGAN
36 Exec Dir Internship & Career Center Ms. Marcie KIRK-HOLLAND
23 Exec Student Health Services Dr. Margaret WALTER
37 Director Financial Aid Ms. Deborah G. AGEE
88 Medical Director Dr. Cindy M. SCHORZMAN
38 Director Student Health Counseling Dr. Sarah HAHN
41 Dir Intercollegiate Athletics Mr. Rocko DELUCA
116 Dir Audit & Mgmt Advisory Services Ms. Leslyn KRAUS
88 Int Director Student Health Admin Ms. Julienne DEGEYTER
19 Chief of Police Chief Joseph FARROW
43 Chief Campus Counsel Mr. Michael SWEENEY
06 Interim University Registrar Mr. David R. FLORES
08 University Librarian Ms. MacKenzie SMITH
122 Asst Dir Sorority/Fraternity Life Ms. Valerie LAMARRE-LAURENT

*University of California-Hastings College of the Law (B)

200 McAllister Street, San Francisco CA 94102-4978
County: San Francisco FICE Identification: 003947
Unit ID: 110398
Telephone: (415) 565-4600 Carnegie Class: Spec-4-yr-Law
FAX Number: (415) 565-4865 Calendar System: Semester
URL: www.uchastings.edu
Established: 1878 Annual Graduate Tuition & Fees: N/A
Enrollment: 1,026 Coed
Affiliation or Control: State IRS Status: 501(c)3
Highest Offering: First Professional Degree; No Undergraduates
Accreditation: WC, LAW

02 Chancellor and Dean Dean David L. FAIGMAN
05 Academic Dean and Provost Mr. Morris RATNER
43 General Counsel Mr. John DIPAOLO
10 Chief Financial Officer Mr. David SEWARD
11 Chief Operating Officer Ms. Rhiannon BAILARD
13 Chief Information Officer Mr. Adam HAMILTON
30 Chief Development Officer Mr. Eric DUMBLETON
08 Assoc Dean Library and Technology Ms. Camilla TUBBS
32 Dean of Students Ms. Grace HUM
84 Sr Asst Dean Enrollment Management Ms. June SAKAMOTO
15 Chief Human Resources Officer Mr. Andrew SCOTT
35 Director of Student Services Ms. Emily HAAN
06 Registrar Ms. Sarah REED
07 Director of Admissions Mr. Bryan ZERBE
36 Asst Dean Career & Professional Dev Ms. Amy KIMMEL
26 Chief Communications Officer Ms. Elizabeth MOORE
09 Dir of Accreditation & Assessment Ms. Andrea BING
93 Director LEOP Ms. Elizabeth MCGRIFF
28 Director of DEI Initiatives Mr. Mario LOPEZ
100 Chief of Staff and Assistant C&D Dr. Jenny KWON
21 Controller Ms. Sandra PLENSKI
37 Director Financial Aid Ms. Angie HARRIS
109 Property Manager Mr. Jarda BRYCH
18 Director of Facilities Mr. Danny DE LEON
96 Director of Business Services Mr. Adrian BROWN
30 Sr Director of Development Ms. Robin DRYSDALE
110 Director of Development Ms. Liz MAGGI
112 Director of Planned Giving Ms. Tracy WHITLOCK
29 Exec Director of Alumni Assoc. Ms. Meredith JAGGARD
04 Executive Assistant Ms. Sonia CHAHAL
19 Dir of Safety/Emerg Preparedness Mr. Noah SKINNER
25 Chief Contract/Grants Administrator Mr. Yael NADEL-CADAXA

*University of California-Irvine (C)

Campus Drive, Irvine CA 92697-0001
County: Orange FICE Identification: 001314
Unit ID: 110653
Telephone: (949) 824-5011 Carnegie Class: DU-Highest
FAX Number: N/A Calendar System: Quarter
URL: www.uci.edu
Established: 1965 Annual Undergrad Tuition & Fees (In-State): $13,753
Enrollment: 36,303 Coed
Affiliation or Control: State IRS Status: 501(c)3
Highest Offering: Doctorate
Accreditation: WC, CAMPEP, CEA, IPSY, LAW, MACTE, MED, MLS, NURSE, PH, PHAR, PLNG

02 Chancellor Howard A. GILLMAN
05 Provost & Exec Vice Chancellor Hal S. STERN
10 CFO & Vice Chanc Div of Fin & Admin Mary Lou D. ORTIZ
46 Vice Chancellor Research Pramod KHARGONEKAR
32 Vice Chancellor Student Affairs Willie L. BANKS
111 Vice Chanc Univ Advancemnt & Alumni Brian T. HERVEY
17 Vice Chancellor Health Affairs Steve GOLDSTEIN
15 Vice Chancellor & Chief HR Exec Ramona AGRELA
28 VC Equity/Diversity/Inclusion Douglas M. HAYNES
22 Vice Chanc Equal Opp & Compliance Kirsten K. QUANBECK
26 Vice Chanc Comms & Public Affairs Sherry MAIN
13 Vice Chanc Info Technology & Data Tom ANDRIOLA
20 Vice Prov for Acad Plng & Inst Res Roxane COHEN SILVER
88 Vice Provost for Academic Personnel Diane K. O'DOWD
97 VP & Dean Undergrad Education Michael DENNIN
58 VP & Dean Graduate Division Gillian R. HAYES
84 Vice Provost Enrollment Management Patricia MORALES
100 Associate Chancellor/Chief of Staff Lars T. WALTON
20 Assoc Prov and Chief of Staff Kate BRIGMAN
88 Assoc Chancellor Sustainability Wendell BRASE
35 Asst VC Stdnt Affs/Chief of Staff Edgar J. DORMITORIO
35 Assoc Vice Chanc/Dean of Students Rameen A. TALESH
23 Assoc VC COHS /Assoc Dean SOM Rebecca BRUSUELAS-JAMES
23 Assoc VC & Chief of Staff Hlth Affs Sheefteh KHALILI
14 Assoc VC/Chief Info Officer Kian COLESTOCK
21 Assoc Vice Chanc Admin/Business Svc Richard COULON
88 Chief Global Affairs & Assoc VC Victoria JONES
114 Asst Vice Chancellor Budget Katherine GALLARDO
06 University Registrar Elizabeth C. BENNETT
43 Chief Campus Counsel Andrea GUNN EATON
36 Assoc Vice Prov Div Career Pathway Suzanne C. HELBIG
09 Assoc VP Inst Research & Dec Supprt Ryan M. CHERLAND
37 Dir Financial Aid & Scholarship Rebecca SANCHEZ
41 Director Intercollegiate Athletics Paula Y. SMITH
88 Museum Director Kim KANATANI
88 Chief Innovation Officer Errol ARKILIC
88 Exec Dir Bus Transformation Ofcr Saroj SHARMA
51 Interim Dean Div of Cont Educ Ian GIBSON
08 University Librarian Lorelei A. TANJI
49 Dean Claire Trevor Sch of the Arts Tiffany Ana LOPEZ
81 Dean School of Biological Sciences Frank LAFERLA
50 Dean Paul Merage School of Business Ian O. WILLIAMSON
53 Dean School of Education Frances E. CONTRERAS
54 Stacey Nicholas Dean of Engineering Magnus B. EGERSTEDT
79 Dean School of Humanities Tyrus MILLER
77 Dean Bren Sch of Info & Comp Sci Marios PAPAEFTHYMIOU
61 Dean School of Law Austen PARRISH
81 Dean School of Physical Sciences James BULLOCK
83 Dean School of Social Ecology Jon B. GOULD
83 Dean School of Social Sciences William M. MAURER
63 Dean School of Medicine Michael STAMOS
66 Dean School of Nursing Mark LAZENBY
67 Dean Pharmacy & Pharmaceutical Sci Jan HIRSCH
69 Dir & Founding Dean Pgm in Pub Hlth Bernadette BODEN-ALBALA
88 Chair Academic Senate Georg STRIEDTER

*University of California-Los Angeles (D)

405 Hilgard Avenue, Los Angeles CA 90095-1405
County: Los Angeles FICE Identification: 001315
Unit ID: 110662
Telephone: (310) 825-4321 Carnegie Class: DU-Highest
FAX Number: N/A Calendar System: Quarter
URL: www.ucla.edu
Established: 1919 Annual Undergrad Tuition & Fees (In-State): $13,249
Enrollment: 44,589 Coed
Affiliation or Control: State IRS Status: 501(c)3
Highest Offering: Doctorate
Accreditation: WC, CAMPEP, CLPSY, CYTO, DENT, EMT, IPSY, LAW, LIB, MAC, MED, NURSE, PAST, PCSAS, PH, PLNG, RAD, SW, THEA

02 Chancellor Gene D. BLOCK
05 Int Exec Vice Chancellor & Provost Michael S. LEVINE
11 Administrative Vice Chancellor Michael J. BECK
10 Int Vice Chancellor/CFO Allison BAIRD-JAMES
15 Vice Chancellor Academic Personnel Michael LEVINE
28 VC Equity/Diversity & Inclusion Anna S. BRADLEY
26 Vice Chancellor External Affairs Rhea TURTELTAUB
23 Vice Chancellor Health Sciences John MAZZIOTTA
43 Vice Chancellor Legal Affairs Louise C. NELSON
46 Vice Chancellor Research Roger WAKIMOTO
32 Vice Chancellor Student Affairs Monroe GORDEN, JR.
58 Vice Provost & Dean Graduate Educ Susan ETTNER
20 Vice Provost & Dean Undergrad Educ Adriana GALVAN
13 Vice Provost Information Technology James DAVIS
88 Vice Prov Inst of American Cultures David K. YOO
88 VProv Interdiscip/Cross-Campus Affs Timothy BREWER
104 Vice Prov Intl Studies/Global Engmt C. Cindy FAN
14 Assoc VC/Chief Information Officer Lucy AVETISYAN
116 AVC & Chief Compliance/Audit Ofcr Mark C. KRAUSE
17 President UCLA Health Johnese Maria SPISSO
79 Dean of Humanities David SCHABERG
88 Dean of Life Sciences Tracy L. JOHNSON
81 Dean of Physical Sciences Miguel GARCIA-GARIBAY
83 Dean of Social Sciences Darnell HUNT
52 Dean School of Dentistry Paul KREBSBACH
48 Dean Sch of the Arts & Arch Brett STEELE
53 Dean Grad Sch Educ & Info Studies Christina CHRISTIE
54 Dean Sch of Eng & App Sci Jayathi Y. MURTHY
61 Dean School of Law Jennifer L. MNOOKIN

50 Dean Graduate School of Mgmt ....Antonio BERNARDO
63 Int Dean School of Medicine ....Steven DUBINETT
64 Dean School of Music ....Eileen STREMPEL
66 Dean School of Nursing ....Lin ZHAN
80 Dean School of Public Affairs ....Gary M. SEGURA
69 Dean Sch of Public Health ....Ronald S. BROOKMEYER
88 Dean School of Theater Film & TV ....Brian KITE
51 Dean Continuing Ed and Extension ....Eric BULLARD
88 Assoc VC Academic Planning & Budget ....Jeff ROTH
29 Assoc VC Alumni Affairs/Advancemnt ....Julie SINA
16 Assoc VC Campus Human Resources ....Lubbe LEVIN
21 Assoc Vice Chancellor/Controller ....Allison BAIRD-JAMES
30 Assoc VC Development ....Laura PARKER
84 Vice Provost Enrollment Management ....Youlonda COPELAND-MORGAN
35 Asst VC of Student Development ....Suzanne SEPLOW
35 Asst VC of Campus Life ....Mick DELUCA
27 Exec Dir Comm/Public Outreach ....Steve RITEA
20 Assistant Provost ....Emily ROSE
20 Assistant Provost ....Margaret LEAL-SOTELO
18 Asst VC Facilities Management ....Kelly J. SCHMADER
86 Assoc VC Govt/Community Relations ....Jennifer POULAKIDAS
39 Asst VC Housing & Hospitality Svcs ....Peter ANGELIS
25 Asst VC Research/Compliance ....Ann M. POLLACK
04 Executive Asst to the Chancellor ....Rena TORRES
88 Executive Director ASUCLA ....Pouria ABBASSI
09 Executive Director Inst Research ....Adam SUGANO
88 Director Volunteer Center ....Ashley LOVE-SMITH
96 Dir Campus Purchasing & Payables ....William S. PROPST
36 Int Director Career Center ....Christine WILSON
85 Int Dir Ctr for Internat'l Students ....Sam NAHIDI
37 Exec Director Financial Aid Office ....Marvin SMITH
41 Director Intercollegiate Athletics ....Martin JARMOND
90 Chief Technologist ....Scott FRIEDMAN
38 Exec Dir Couns & Psych Svcs ....Nicole GREEN
07 Director Undergraduate Admission ....Gary A. CLARK
06 Registrar ....Frank Y. WADA
08 University Librarian ....Virginia STEEL
19 Chief of Police ....Tony LEE
100 Chief of Staff ....Yolanda GORMAN
102 Exec Dir Foundation/Corporate Rels ....Stellar KIM
122 Dir Ofc Fraternity/Sorority Life ....Lindsey GOLDSTEIN

*University of California-Merced (A)

5200 North Lake Road, Merced CA 95343

County: Merced
FICE Identification: 041271
Unit ID: 445188
Telephone: (209) 228-4400
Carnegie Class: DU-Higher
FAX Number: (209) 228-4424
Calendar System: Semester
URL: www.ucmerced.edu
Established: 2005
Annual Undergrad Tuition & Fees (In-District): $14,100
Enrollment: 9,018
Coed
Affiliation or Control: State/Local
IRS Status: 501(c)3
Highest Offering: Doctorate
Accreditation: WC

02 Chancellor ....Dr. Juan SANCHEZ MUNOZ
05 Provost/Exec Vice Chancellor ....Dr. Gregg CAMFIELD
10 Interim Chief Financial Officer ....Dr. Kurt SCHNIER
30 VC Strat Partnerships/External Affs ....Ed KLOTZBIER
32 Vice Chancellor Student Affairs ....Dr. Charles NIES
114 Vice Chancellor Budget/Planning ....Mike RILEY
58 Int Vice Provost/Graduate Dean ....Dr. Chris KELLO
84 Assoc Vice Chanc Enrollment Mgmt ....Jill ORCUTT
26 Asst Vice Chanc Univ Communications ....Ed KLOTZBIER
46 Int Vice Chanc Research/Econ Dev ....Dr. Marjorie ZATZ
20 Vice Provost/Dean UG Education ....Sarah FREY
86 Exec Director of Govt Relations ....Cori LUCERO
04 Exec Assistant to the Chancellor ....Molly ELAZIER
13 Int AVC Information Technology ....Nick DUGAN
65 Dean Natural Sciences ....Dr. Betsy DUMONT
79 Interim Dean School of SSHA ....Jeffrey GILGER
54 Dean Engineering ....Dr. Mark MATSUMOTO
07 Director of Admissions ....Dustin NOJI
06 University Registrar ....Erin WEBB
37 Director of Financial Aid ....Ron RADNEY
41 Director of Campus Athletics & Rec ....David DUNHAM
23 Assoc Vice Chanc Health & Wellness ....Vacant
85 Director of International Affairs ....Garett GIETZEN
08 University Librarian ....Haipeng LI
39 AVC Housing/Residence/Stdnt Life ....Martin REED
43 Chief Campus Counsel ....Stella NGAI
100 Associate Chancellor/Chief of Staff ....Dr. Luanna PUTNEY
19 Chief of Police ....Chou HER
09 Director of Inclusive Research ....Andres HERNANDEZ
15 Chief Human Resources Officer ....Nicole POLLACK
18 Chief Facilities/Physical Plant Ofc ....Michael MCLEOD
21 Associate Business Officer ....Connie MCBRIDE
28 Vice Chanc/Chief Diversity Officer ....Delia SAENZ
29 Dir Alumni Affairs/Mktg/Public Rels ....Chris ABRESCY
36 Exec Director Student Placement ....Brian O'BRUBA
38 Int Director Student Counseling ....Tania GONZALEZ
96 Director of Purchasing ....Stephanie ZUNIGA
122 Coord Fraternity/Sorority Life ....Hayley MONTOYA

*University of California-Riverside (B)

900 University Avenue, Riverside CA 92521

County: Riverside
FICE Identification: 001316
Unit ID: 110671
Telephone: (951) 827-1012
Carnegie Class: DU-Highest
FAX Number: N/A
Calendar System: Quarter
URL: www.ucr.edu
Established: 1954
Annual Undergrad Tuition & Fees (In-State): $14,024
Enrollment: 26,434
Coed
Affiliation or Control: State
IRS Status: 501(c)3
Highest Offering: Doctorate
Accreditation: WC, IPSY, MED, SCPSY

02 Chancellor ....Dr. Kim A. WILCOX
100 Associate Chancellor ....Dr. Christine VICTORINO
05 Provost/Exec Vice Chanc ....Dr. Elizabeth WATKINS
10 CFO & Vice Chanc Planning & Budget ....Mr. Gerry BOMOTTI
32 Vice Chancellor Student Affairs ....Dr. Brian HAYNES
111 Vice Chanc University Advancement ....Ms. Monique DOZIER
46 Vice Chanc Research & Econ Dev ....Dr. Rodolfo H. TORRES
63 Dean School of Med/CEO Clin Affs ....Dr. Deborah DEAS
20 Vice Provost Academic Personnel ....Dr. Daniel R. JESKE
18 Assoc Vice Chanc Facilities Svcs ....Mr. Adam M. SCHNIREL
84 Assoc Vice Chanc Enrollment Svcs ....Ms. Emily D. ENGELSCHALL
30 Assoc Vice Chanc Development ....Ms. Marie SCHULTZ
09 Assoc Vice Chanc for Research ....Mr. Charles GREER
28 VC & Chief Diversity Officer ....Dr. Mariam LAM
58 Dean Graduate Division ....Dr. Shaun BOWLER
50 Dean School of Business Admin ....Dr. Yunzeng WANG
53 Interim Dean School of Education ....Dr. Louie F. RODRIGUEZ
54 Dean Bourns College of Engineering ....Dr. Christopher LYNCH
79 Dean Col of Humanities/Arts/Soc Sci ....Dr. Daryle WILLIAMS
81 Dean Col of Nat and Agr Sciences ....Dr. Kathryn UHRICH
06 Registrar ....Ms. Bracken J. DAILEY
80 Dean School of Public Policy ....Dr. Anil DEOLALIKAR
36 Director Career Center ....Mr. Sean GIL
37 Director Financial Aid ....Mr. Jose A. AGUILAR
38 Director Counseling Center ....Dr. Elizabeth MONDRAGON
07 Interim Director of Admissions ....Mr. Alex RUIZ
21 Assoc VC Business & Financial Svcs ....Ms. Bobbi MCCRACKEN
08 Head Librarian ....Mr. Steven MANDEVILLE-GAMBLE
04 Int Exec Asst to the Chancellor ....Mr. George RUELAS
41 Athletics Director ....Mr. Wesley MALLETTE
13 Assoc Vice Chanc ITS/CIO ....Mr. Matthew GUNKEL
15 Interim Assoc VC Human Resources ....Mr. John HENDERSON
26 Asst VC & Chief Communications Ofcr ....Mr. Johnny CRUZ
43 Chief Campus Counsel ....Vacant
86 AVC Govt/Community Relations ....Ms. Elizabeth ROMERO
102 Exec Dir Foundation Development ....Mr. Bryan CARLSON
104 Director of Education Abroad ....Dr. Karolyn ANDREWS
108 Asst VC Institutional Research ....Mr. Scott HEIL
109 Assoc Vice Chanc Auxiliary Svcs ....Ms. Heidi M. SCRIBNER
44 Director Gift Administration ....Ms. Lisa M. WILSON
88 AVC Health/Well-Being & Safety ....Dr. Denise WOODS

*University of California-San Diego (C)

9500 Gilman Drive, La Jolla CA 92093-0014

County: San Diego
FICE Identification: 001317
Unit ID: 110680
Telephone: (858) 534-2230
Carnegie Class: DU-Highest
FAX Number: (858) 534-6523
Calendar System: Quarter
URL: www.ucsd.edu
Established: 1960
Annual Undergrad Tuition & Fees (In-State): $14,648
Enrollment: 39,576
Coed
Affiliation or Control: State
IRS Status: 501(c)3
Highest Offering: Doctorate
Accreditation: WC, AUD, CAMPEP, CEA, CLPSY, DIETI, DMS, IPSY, LC, MED, MLS, PAST, PDPSY, PHAR

02 Chancellor ....Dr. Pradeep K. KHOSLA
05 EVC Academic Affairs ....Dr. Elizabeth H. SIMMONS
46 Vice Chancellor Research ....Dr. Corinne PEEK-ASA
63 VC Health Science/Dean Sch Med ....Dr. Steven GARFIN
65 Vice Chancellor Marine Sciences ....Dr. Margaret LEINEN
32 VC Student Affairs ....Dr. Alysson SATTERLUND
10 VC and Chief Financial Officer ....Mr. Pierre-Yves OUILLET
11 Vice Chanc Resource Mgmt/Planning ....Mr. Gary C. MATTHEWS
28 VC for Equity/Diversity & Inclusion ....Dr. Becky R. PETITT
111 Vice Chancellor Advancement ....Vacant
43 Chief Campus Counsel ....Mr. Daniel W. PARK
100 Associate Chancellor/Chief of Staff ....Mr. Jeff GATTAS
22 Chief Ethics and Compliance Officer ....Ms. Judith BRUNER
88 Associate Chancellor ....Dr. Kelly KISH
13 Chief Information Officer ....Mr. Vince KELLEN
88 Assoc VC Public Programs ....Dr. Mary L. WALSHOK
21 AVC Business Fin Svcs/Controller ....Ms. Cheryl ROSS
08 University Librarian ....Dr. Erik T. MITCHELL
88 Director Policy Admin ....Ms. Paula J. JOHNSON
23 Exec Dir Student Health/Wellness ....Vacant
26 Chief Comm/Marketing Ofcr ....Ms. Anne L. BUCKLEY
20 Sr Assoc VC Academic Affairs ....Dr. Robert E. CONTINETTI
20 AVC Education Innovation ....Dr. Carlos JENSEN
15 Chief Human Resources Officer ....Vacant
88 Sr Assoc Vice Chancellor Research ....Dr. Miroslav KRSTIC
88 AVC Innovation & Commercialization ....Mr. Paul W. ROBEN
84 Assoc Vice Chanc Enrollment Mgmt ....Mr. Jim RAWLINS
06 University Registrar ....Ms. Cindy G. LYONS
17 CEO UCSD Medical Center ....Ms. Patty MAYSENT
35 Asst VC Student Life ....Ms. Patricia MAHAFFEY
96 Assoc Controller/Chief Procurement ....Mr. Ted JOHNSON
35 AVC Student Retention Success ....Dr. Maruth FIGUEROA
54 Dean Jacobs Sch of Engineering ....Dr. Albert P. PISANO
49 Dean Arts & Humanities ....Dr. Cristina DELLA COLETTA
81 Dean Div of Biological Sciences ....Dr. Kit POGLIANO
83 Dean of Social Sciences ....Dr. Carol A. PADDEN
50 Dean Rady School of Management ....Dr. Lisa D. ORDONEZ
81 Dean Div of Physical Science ....Dr. Steven E. BOGGS
82 Dean Global Policy and Strategy ....Dr. Caroline FREUND
58 Dean Graduate Studies ....Dr. Kit POGLIANO
12 Provost John Muir College ....Dr. K. Wayne YANG
12 Prov Thurgood Marshall Coll ....Dr. Leslie CARVER
12 Provost Earl Warren College ....Dr. Marisa A. ABRAJANO
12 Provost Revelle College ....Dr. Paul K. YU
12 Provost Eleanor Roosevelt College ....Dr. Ivan EVANS
12 Provost Sixth College ....Dr. Lakshmi CHILUKURI
12 Provost Seventh College ....Dr. Kate ANTONOVICS
38 Director Stdt Psych/Counseling Svcs ....Dr. Reina JUAREZ
18 AVC EH&S and Facilities Management ....Mr. Stephen B. JACKSON
97 Dean of Undergraduate Education ....Dr. John C. MOORE
41 Intercollegiate Athletics Director ....Mr. Earl W. EDWARDS
19 Police Chief Community Safety ....Vacant

*University of California-San Francisco (D)

513 Parnassus Avenue, Box 0402,
San Francisco CA 94143

County: San Francisco
FICE Identification: 001319
Unit ID: 110699
Telephone: (415) 476-1000
Carnegie Class: Spec-4-yr-Eng
FAX Number: N/A
Calendar System: Quarter
URL: www.ucsf.edu
Established: 1864
Annual Graduate Tuition & Fees: N/A
Enrollment: 3,201
Coed
Affiliation or Control: State
IRS Status: 501(c)3
Highest Offering: Doctorate; No Undergraduates
Accreditation: WC, CAMPEP, DENT, DIETI, IPSY, MED, MIDWF, NURSE, PAST, PHAR, PTA

02 Chancellor ....Dr. Sam HAWGOOD
03 Executive Vice Chancellor & Provost ....Dr. Daniel H. LOWENSTEIN
15 SVP/Assoc VC Human Resources ....Mr. Corey JACKSON
100 Associate Chancellor ....Dr. Theresa O'BRIEN
10 Senior VC Finance & Administration ....Ms. Erin S. GORE
21 Sr Assoc VC & CFO ....Mr. Michael CLUNE
05 Vice Provost Academic Affairs ....Dr. Brian ALLDREDGE
32 Vice Prov Student Academic Affairs ....Dr. Nicquet BLAKE
30 VC Univ Development/Alumni Rels ....Ms. Erin HICKEY
26 Vice Chanc Communications ....Mr. Won HA
86 VC Community & Govt Relations ....Ms. Francesca VEGA
28 VC Diversity & Outreach ....Dr. Renee NAVARRO
13 Assoc VC & Chief Info Officer ....Mr. Joseph BENGFORT
109 Int Sr Assoc VC Campus Life Svcs ....Ms. Rebecca DARO
18 Assoc VC Camp Plng/Campus Architect ....Ms. Alicia MURASAKI
20 Int Vice Dean Academic Affairs ....Dr. Paul GARCIA
37 Director Student Financial Aid ....Mr. Jerry LOPEZ
43 Chief Campus Counsel ....Ms. Greta SCHNETZLER
08 University Librarian/Asst VC ....Mr. Chris SHAFFER
63 Dean School of Medicine/VC Med Affs ....Dr. Talmadge E. KING, JR.
19 Chief of Police ....Mr. Michael DENSON
66 Dean School of Nursing ....Dr. Catherine GILLISS
52 Dean School of Dentistry ....Dr. Michael REDDY
67 Dean School of Pharmacy ....Dr. Kathy GIACOMINI
58 Dean Graduate Division ....Dr. Nicquet BLAKE
96 Assoc VC/Chief Procurement Officer ....Mr. Justin SULLIVAN
06 Registrar/Asst VC Student Info ....Mr. Douglas CARLSON
88 Associate Registrar ....Mr. Jeff HARTER
36 Asst VC Career Advancement ....Mr. William LINDSTAEDT
23 Asst VC Student Health & Counseling ....Dr. Jill ROVARIS
09 Director Institutional Research ....Dr. Ning WANG

*University of California-Santa Barbara (E)

552 University Road, Santa Barbara CA 93106-0001

County: Santa Barbara
FICE Identification: 001320
Unit ID: 110705
Telephone: (805) 893-8000
Carnegie Class: DU-Highest
FAX Number: N/A
Calendar System: Quarter
URL: www.ucsb.edu
Established: 1909
Annual Undergrad Tuition & Fees (In-State): $14,406
Enrollment: 26,179
Coed
Affiliation or Control: State
IRS Status: 501(c)3
Highest Offering: Doctorate
Accreditation: WC, IPSY, PSPSY

02 Chancellor ....Dr. Henry T. YANG
04 Exec Assistant to the Chancellor ....Ms. Diane O'BRIEN
05 Executive Vice Chancellor Academics ....Dr. David B. MARSHALL
46 Vice Chancellor Research ....Dr. Joe INCANDELA
11 Vice Chancellor Admin Services ....Mr. Garry MAC PHERSON
32 Vice Chancellor Student Affairs ....Dr. Margaret KLAWUNN
10 AVC/Controller Bus & Fin Svc ....Mr. Jim R. CORKILL
15 Int Vice Pres Human Resources ....Ms. Cheryl LLOYD
28 VC Diversity/Equity/Acad Policy ....Ms. Belinda ROBNETT
20 AVC/Dean Undergraduate Education ....Dr. Jeffrey STOPPLE
30 Assoc Vice Chancellor Development ....Ms. Beverly COLGATE
26 AVC Public Affairs & Communications ....Mr. John LONGBRAKE
84 AVC Enrollment Services ....Mr. Mike MILLER
121 Acting AVC Student Acad Support Svc ....Ms. Lupe GARCIA
114 Asst Chanc Fin & Resource Mgmt ....Mr. Chuck HAINES
29 Assoc Director Alumni Affairs ....Ms. Samantha PUTNAM
13 AVC IT & Chief Information Officer ....Mr. Josh BRIGHT
88 Interim Dean Col Creative Studies ....Dr. Kathy FOLTZ
54 Dean College of Engineering ....Dr. Rod ALFERNESS
58 Dean Graduate Division ....Dr. Carol GENETTI
53 Dean Gevirtz Grad Sch Educ ....Dr. Jeffrey MILEM
65 Dean Bren School of Env Sci & Mgmt ....Dr. Steven D. GAINES
51 Dean Professional and Cont Educ ....Dr. Robert YORK

35 Dean of Student Life .... Ms. Katya ARMISTEAD
49 Exec Dean College Letters & Sci .... Dr. Pierre WILTZIUS
79 Dean Humanities & Fine Arts .... Dr. John MAJEWSKI
87 Director Summer Sessions .... Dr. James FORD
83 Dean Social Sciences .... Dr. Charles R. HALE
85 Dir International Students/Scholars .... Dr. Simran SINGH
06 Registrar .... Ms. Leesa BECK
16 Director Human Resources .... Vacant
37 Director Financial Aid .... Dr. Michael MILLER
116 Acting Dir Audit & Advisory Service .... Ms. Jessie MASEK
07 Director Admissions .... Ms. Lisa PRZEKOP
09 Director Institutional Research .... Dr. Steven C. VELASCO
23 Exec Director Student Health Svcs .... Dr. Mary FERRIS
39 AVC Housing/Dining & Aux Enterprise .... Mr. Wilfred E. BROWN
40 Director of UCSB Bookstore .... Mr. Mark BEISECKER
19 Chief of Police .... James BROCK
41 Director Intercollegiate Athletics .... Mr. John MCCUTCHEON
86 Dir Governmental Relations .... Ms. Kirsten DESHLER
21 Director Finance/Administration .... Vacant
08 University Librarian .... Ms. Kristin ANTELMAN
89 Director Orientation Programs .... Ms. Tricia RASCON
88 Acting Director Capital Development .... Mr. Mark NOCCIOLO
88 Director Campus Planning & Design .... Ms. Alissa HUMMER
88 Executive Director Arts & Lectures .... Ms. Celesta BILLECI
22 Director Disabled Students Pgm .... Mr. Gary R. WHITE
104 Dir Campus Education Abroad Program .... Dr. Juan E. CAMPO
88 Director Env Health & Safety .... Mr. John STERRITT
28 Director MultiCultural Center .... Ms. Zaveeni KHAN-MARCUS
38 Assoc Dir Counseling & Psych Svcs .... Dr. Brian OLOWUDE
94 Director Women's Center .... Ms. Kim EQUINOA
88 Campus Ombudsman .... Ms. Caroline ADAMS
88 Exec Dir Instructional Devel .... Mr. George H. MICHAELS
36 Director Career Services .... Mr. Ignacio GALLARDO
43 Chief Campus Counsel .... Ms. Nancy G. HAMILL
22 Dir EO & Discrimination Prevention .... Mr. Ricardo ALCAINO
88 Dir Design & Construction .... Mr. Julie HENDRICKS
88 Director Univ Center/Events Center .... Mr. Gary LAWRENCE
88 Director of Recreation .... Mr. Jeff HUSKEY
92 Honors Program Analyst .... Ms. Summer HOWATT-NAB
108 Institutional Assessment Coord .... Dr. Amanda BREY
44 Director Annual Giving .... Mr. Brandon FRIESEN

*University of California-Santa Cruz (A)

1156 High Street, Santa Cruz CA 95064-1077
County: Santa Cruz
FICE Identification: 001321
Unit ID: 110714
Telephone: (831) 459-0111
Carnegie Class: DU-Highest
FAX Number: (831) 459-0146
Calendar System: Quarter
URL: www.ucsc.edu
Established: 1965
Annual Undergrad Tuition & Fees (In-State): $14,025
Enrollment: 19,161
Coed
Affiliation or Control: State
IRS Status: 501(c)3
Highest Offering: Doctorate
Accreditation: WC, IPSY

02 Chancellor .... Dr. Cynthia LARIVE
05 Campus Provost/Exec Vice Chancellor .... Dr. Lori KLETZER
100 Assoc Chanc & Chief of Staff .... Dr. Anna FINN
10 Int VC Finance Ops & Administration .... Mr. Biju KAMALESWARAN
45 Assoc VC Budget Analysis & Planning ... Ms. Kimberly REGISTER
46 Int Vice Chancellor Research .... Dr. John MACMILLAN
30 Vice Chanc Univ Relations .... Mr. Mark DELOS REYES DAVIS
13 VC Information Technology .... Dr. Aisha JACKSON
20 Vice Prov/Dean Undergrad Educ .... Dr. Richard HUGHEY
20 Vice Provost Academic Affairs .... Dr. Herbert LEE
84 Assoc VC Enrollment Mgmt .... Ms. Michelle L. WHITTINGHAM
32 Vice Chanc Student Affairs/ Success .... Dr. Akirah BRADLEY-ARMSTRONG
16 Asst Vice Prov Academic Personnel .... Ms. Grace MCCLINTOCK
18 Campus Architect .... Mr. Felix ANG
15 Assoc VC/Chief HR Officer .... Mr. Steve STEIN
08 University Librarian .... Ms. Elizabeth COWELL
79 Dean of Humanities .... Dr. Jasmine ALINDER
81 Dean Physical & Biological Sci .... Dr. Paul KOCH
57 Dean of the Arts .... Dr. Celine PARREÑAS SHIMIZU
83 Dean of Social Sciences .... Dr. Katharyne MITCHELL
54 Dean of Engineering .... Dr. Alexander WOLF
58 Vice Prov/Dean of Grad Studies .... Dr. Peter BIEHL
65 Director Institute Marine Sciences .... Dr. Daniel COSTA
81 Director Institute Particle Physics .... Dr. Jason NIELSEN
88 Int Director UCO/Lick Observatory .... Dr. Connie ROCKOSI
12 Provost Stevenson College .... Dr. Matt O'HARA
12 Provost Cowell College .... Dr. Alan CHRISTY
12 Provost Crown College .... Dr. Manel CAMPS
12 Provost Merrill College .... Dr. Elizabeth ABRAMS
12 Provost Porter College .... Dr. Sean KEILEN
12 Provost Kresge College .... Dr. Mayanthi FERNANDO
12 Provost Rachel Carson College .... Dr. Sue CARTER
12 Provost College Nine & Ten .... Dr. Flora LU
12 Provost Oakes College .... Dr. Marcia OCHOA
06 Registrar .... Mr. Tchad SANGER
09 Director Institutional Research .... Dr. Julian L. FERNALD
37 Director Financial Aid/Operations .... Mr. Patrick REGISTER
28 Asst VC & Chief Diversity Officer .... Dr. Judith ESTRADA
29 Director of Alumni Relations .... Ms. Shayna KENT
26 Dir Marketing/Communications .... Ms. Lisa NIELSEN
86 Director Government Relations .... Ms. Melissa WHATLEY
38 Int Assc VC Student Health/Wellness .... Dr. Gary DUNN
07 Director of Admissions .... Ms. Blia YANG
41 Director Athletics/ Recreation .... Ms. Susan WITTMANN HARRIMAN

108 Asst Director for Assessment .... Dr. Anna SHER
102 Dir Foundation Relations .... Ms. Sarah CARLE
104 Director of Global Learning .... Ms. Alice MICHEL
106 Director of Online Education .... Mr. Michael TASSIO
43 Chief Campus Counsel .... Dr. Lorena PENALOZA
44 Director Annual Giving .... Ms. Marissa FULLUM-CAMPBELL

University of East-West Medicine (B)

595 Lawrence Expressway, Sunnyvale CA 94085
County: Santa Clara
FICE Identification: 039953
Unit ID: 447801
Telephone: (408) 733-1878
Carnegie Class: Spec-4-yr-Other Health
FAX Number: (408) 636-7705
Calendar System: Trimester
URL: www.uewm.edu
Established: 1997
Annual Undergrad Tuition & Fees: N/A
Enrollment: 119
Coed
Affiliation or Control: Proprietary
IRS Status: Proprietary
Highest Offering: Master's
Accreditation: ACUP

01 President .... Dr. Eric TAO
05 VP Academic Affairs .... Dr. Bei LIU
30 VP Development .... Dr. Yingqiu WANG
07 Director of Admissions/Admin .... Dr. Sharon ZHOU
37 Director of Financial Aid/Govt Rels .... Ms. Hui-Ping LO

University of La Verne (C)

1950 Third Street, La Verne CA 91750-4443
County: Los Angeles
FICE Identification: 001216
Unit ID: 117140
Telephone: (909) 593-3511
Carnegie Class: DU-Mod
FAX Number: (909) 593-0965
Calendar System: Semester
URL: www.laverne.edu
Established: 1891
Annual Undergrad Tuition & Fees: $45,850
Enrollment: 6,983
Coed
Affiliation or Control: Independent Non-Profit
IRS Status: 501(c)3
Highest Offering: Doctorate
Accreditation: WC, #ARCPA, CAATE, CLPSY, LAW, SPAA

01 President .... Dr. Devorah A. LIEBERMAN
05 Provost & Vice President .... Dr. Kerop JANOYAN
10 Chief Financial Officer .... Mr. Avedis (Avo) KECHICHIAN
111 Vice President Univ Advancement .... Mrs. Sherri MYLOTT
84 Vice Pres Strategic Enrollment Mgmt .... Mrs. Mary AGUAYO
50 Dean College Business/Public Mgmt .... Dr. Emmeline DE PILLIS
53 Int Dean College Educ/Org Ldrship .... Dr. MD HAQUE
61 Dean College of Law .... Mr. Kevin MARSHALL
32 Chief Student Affairs Officer .... Mr. Juan REGALADO
12 Associate Provost Grad Program/ROC .... Dr. Kristan VENEGAS
07 Director of Undergraduate Admission .... Dr. Adam WU
124 AVP Acad Support/Retent Svcs .... Mr. Carlos CERVANTES
21 Associate Vice President of Finance .... Ms. Lori K. GORDIEN
18 Sr Dir Physical Plant Ops & Svcs .... Mr. Garth JONES
29 Sr Dir Advancement Oper & Services .... Ms. Bianca ROMERO
38 Dir Counseling & Psych Services .... Dr. Elleni R. KOULOS
37 Director of Financial Aid .... Ms. Laura EVANS
113 Exec Director Student Accounts .... Ms. Xochitl E. MARTINEZ
96 Director Purchasing & Procurement .... Mrs. Deborah S. DEACY
28 Director Multicultural Affairs .... Dr. Daniel L. LOERA
23 Director of Health Services .... Ms. Jamie SOLIS
88 Dir Center for Adv/Teaching & Lrng .... Mr. Jeremy SCHNEIDER
121 Director Academic Success Center .... Ms. Savannah GARCIA
41 Athletic Director .... Mr. Scott WINTERBURN
06 Registrar .... Mr. Adam EVANS
08 University Librarian .... Dr. Vinaya L. TRIPURANENI
28 Chief Diversity Officer .... Dr. Alexandra BURREL
42 Chaplain/Dir of Campus Ministry .... Dr. Zandra L. WAGONER
90 Sr Dir Admission Oper/Tech Svcs .... Mrs. Loreto D'MONTE
88 Asst Director of Civic Engagement .... Ms. Julissa ESPINOZA
04 Dir President Office/Board Affairs .... Dr. Shannon CAPALDI
19 Director Security/Safety .... Mr. Ruben IBARRA
26 AVP of Strategic Communications .... Mr. Rod LEVEQUE
36 Director of Career Services .... Ms. Amanda MILLER
122 Dir Stdnt Life/Dev-Greek Life .... Mr. Adam WONG
09 Asst Dir Institutional Research .... Mr. James SCHIRMER

University Massachusetts Global (D)

16355 Laguna Canyon Road, 1st Floor, Irvine CA 92618
County: Orange
FICE Identification: 041618
Unit ID: 262086
Telephone: (949) 753-4774
Carnegie Class: DU-Mod
FAX Number: (714) 753-7875
Calendar System: Other
URL: www.umassglobal.edu
Established: 1958
Annual Undergrad Tuition & Fees: $12,480
Enrollment: 10,986
Coed
Affiliation or Control: Independent Non-Profit
IRS Status: 501(c)3
Highest Offering: Doctorate
Accreditation: WC, CAEPN, NURSE, SW

01 Chancellor .... Dr. Gary BRAHM
10 Exec Vice Chancellor/CFO .... Mr. Phillip DOOLITTLE
32 EVC Enrollment/Student Affairs .... Ms. Saskia KNIGHT
11 Campus Director .... Ms. Melissa REYES
05 Exec VC Acad Affs/CAO/Provost .... Mr. Charles BULLOCK
06 Registrar .... Vacant

† A member of the Chapman University System.

University of the Pacific (E)

3601 Pacific Avenue, Stockton CA 95211-0197
County: San Joaquin
FICE Identification: 001329
Unit ID: 120883
Telephone: (209) 946-2011
Carnegie Class: DU-Mod
FAX Number: (209) 946-2845
Calendar System: Semester
URL: www.pacific.edu
Established: 1851
Annual Undergrad Tuition & Fees: $51,094
Enrollment: 6,263
Coed
Affiliation or Control: Independent Non-Profit
IRS Status: 501(c)3
Highest Offering: Doctorate
Accreditation: WC, ACAE, ARCPA, AUD, CAATE, CEA, DENT, DH, @DIET, IPSY, LAW, MUS, NASP, PHAR, PTA, SP, @SW

01 President .... Christopher CALLAHAN
05 Provost/VP Academic Affairs .... Dr. Maria PALLAVICINI
11 Chief Operating Officer .... Ken MULLEN
10 VP Business & Finance/CFO .... James WALSH
32 VP Student Life .... Maria Q. BLANDIZZI
30 VP Development & Alumni Relations .... Scott BIEDERMANN
13 VP Technology/CIO .... Art SPRECHER
21 Assoc VP Business & Finance .... Ron ELLISON
84 VP Enrollment Management .... Dr. Chris FERGUSON
26 Assoc VP Marketing & Communication .... Marge GREY
119 Assoc VP Info Security/CISO .... Ken KERRICK
115 Asst VP Treasury/Chf Invest Ofcr .... Jol MANILAY
04 Exec Asst to the President .... Ashley WILLIAMS
49 Dean College of the Pacific .... Rena FRADEN
50 Dean Eberhardt School of Business .... Charles MOSES
52 Dean Dugoni School of Dentistry .... Nader NADERSHAHI
53 Dean Benerd School of Education .... Patricia CAMPBELL
54 Dean Sch Engineering/Computer Sci .... Elizabeth ORWIN
61 Dean McGeorge School of Law .... Michael H. SCHWARTZ
64 Dean Conservatory of Music .... Peter WITTE
67 Dean Long School Pharm/Hlth Sci .... Phillip R. OPPENHEIMER
36 Assoc VP/Exec Dir Career Dev .... Tom VECCHIONE
08 Int Dean University Library .... Edie SPARKS
58 Interim Dean Graduate School .... Cyd JENEFSKY
51 Dean University College .... Patricia CAMPBELL
25 Sponsored Pgms Administrator .... Vacant
29 AVP Alumni Relations .... Kelli PAGE
37 Exec Director Financial Aid .... Aquila GALGON
07 Interim Exec Director Admissions .... Jonathan LATTA
06 Assoc University Registrar .... Michael SNYDER
09 Assoc Prov Inst Research .... Mike ROGERS
35 Exec Director Campus Life .... Marc FALKENSTEIN
96 Director Purchasing .... Ronda MARR
92 Director Honors Program .... Balint SZATARAY
93 Dir Intercultural Student Success .... Vacant
94 Director Gender Studies .... Traci ROBERTS-CAMPS
38 Director Counseling Services .... Stacie TURKS
39 Exec Director Residential Life .... Joe BERTHIAUME
41 Director of Athletics .... Janet LUCAS
42 Director Religious & Spiritual Life .... Laura STEED
15 Asst VP Human Resources .... Linda JEFFERS
40 Director Bookstore .... Nicole CASTILLO
19 Exec Director Public Safety .... Grant BEDFORD
18 Director Physical Plant .... Steve GREENWOD
82 Director School Intl Studies .... Dr. William HERRIN
110 Sr Assoc VP Development .... Scott BIEDERMANN
88 Asst VP Development .... Judy NAGAI
100 Chief of Staff to the President .... Vacant
104 Dir International Programs Services .... Ryan GRIFFITH
43 General Counsel .... Kevin MILLS
12 Director Sacramento Campus .... Dr. Patrick FAVERTY
88 Asst Dean Admissions .... Tracy SIMMONS
117 Director Enterprise Risk Mgmt .... Roberta MARTOZA
116 Director Internal Audit .... Randy SCHWANTES
114 Director University Budget .... Jonallie PARRA
105 Director Web Services .... Vacant
108 Vice Prov Strategy/Educ Effective .... Cyd JENEFSKY
22 Director Affirmative Action/EEO .... Deborah FREEMAN
44 Exec Director Annual Giving .... Michael RICHMOND
90 Asst VP Tech Customer Experience .... Peggy KAY
91 Asst Dir Integrated Services .... Raoul VILLALPANDO
88 Asst VP Development .... Molly BYRNE
101 Exec Director Board of Regents .... Janine SWANSON
102 Asst Dir Corp/Foundation Relations .... Emily NOVICK

University of the People (F)

595 East Colorado Blvd Ste 623, Pasadena CA 91101
County: Los Angeles
Identification: 667160
Unit ID: 488846
Telephone: (626) 264-8880
Carnegie Class: Masters/L
FAX Number: N/A
Calendar System: Other
URL: www.uopeople.edu
Established: 2009
Annual Undergrad Tuition & Fees: $1,200
Enrollment: 43,722
Coed
Affiliation or Control: Independent Non-Profit
IRS Status: 501(c)3
Highest Offering: Master's
Accreditation: @WC, DEAC

01 President & Founder .... Mr. Shai RESHEF
05 Provost .... Dr. Marie CINI
11 Sr Vice Pres Operations .... Mr. Rami ISH-HURVITZ
45 VP for Strategy & Planning .... Mr. Yoav VENTURA
84 Sr Vice President Enrollment .... Mr. Asaf WOLFF
13 Vice Pres Information Svcs/Libraria .... Mr. James G. NEAL
15 Vice Pres Human Resources .... Ms. Galit TAMIR
10 Chief Financial Officer .... Vacant
37 Financial Aid Officer .... Vacant

University of Phoenix Central Valley Campus (A)

45 River Park Place West, Suite 201,
Fresno CA 93720-1552
Telephone: (559) 312-1133 Identification: 770190
Accreditation: &HLC, ACBSP

† Branch campus of University of Phoenix, Phoenix, AZ-No longer enrolling new students

University of Phoenix Sacramento Valley Campus (B)

2860 Gateway Oaks Drive, Sacramento CA 95833-4334
Telephone: (800) 266-2107 Identification: 770191
Accreditation: &HLC, ACBSP

† Branch campus of University of Phoenix, Phoenix, AZ-No longer enrolling new students

University of Phoenix San Diego Campus (C)

9645 Granite Ridge Dr, Suite 200,
San Diego CA 92123-2658
Telephone: (800) 473-4346 Identification: 770192
Accreditation: &HLC, ACBSP

† Branch campus of University of Phoenix, Phoenix, AZ-No longer enrolling new students

University of Phoenix Southern California Campus (D)

3110 E. Guasti Rd, Ontario CA 91761
Telephone: (800) 888-1968 Identification: 770189
Accreditation: &HLC, ACBSP

† Branch campus of University of Phoenix, Phoenix, AZ-No longer enrolling new students

University of Redlands (E)

PO Box 3080, Redlands CA 92373-0999
County: San Bernardino FICE Identification: 001322
Unit ID: 121691
Telephone: (909) 793-2121 Carnegie Class: Masters/L
FAX Number: (909) 793-2029 Calendar System: Semester
URL: www.redlands.edu
Established: 1907 Annual Undergrad Tuition & Fees: $52,500
Enrollment: 4,566 Coed
Affiliation or Control: Independent Non-Profit IRS Status: 501(c)3
Highest Offering: Doctorate
Accreditation: WC, ACBSP, MUS, PAST, SP, THEOL

01 President ... Ms. Krista L. NEWKIRK
05 Provost/Chief Academic Officer ... Dr. Kathy OGREN
10 Vice Pres Finance & CFO ... Mr. Kevin M. DYERLY
32 University Dean of Student Affairs ... Dr. Donna EDDLEMAN
84 Vice President for Enrollment ... Vacant
111 Vice Pres for Advancement ... Ms. Tamara M. JOSSERAND
11 Vice President Administration ... Dr. Michelle L. ROGERS
26 Chief Communications Officer ... Ms. Mika ONO
43 General Counsel ... Mr. Brent G. GERATY
100 Chief of Staff ... Ms. Jennifer L. THOMPSON
53 Dean School of Education ... Dr. Mario MARTINEZ
50 Dean School of Business ... Dr. Thomas HORAN
49 Interim Dean Col of Arts & Sciences ... Dr. Steven WUHS
64 Dean School of Music ... Dr. Joseph MODICA
21 Director Financial Ops & Controller ... Ms. Patricia M. CAUDLE
28 Sr Diversity & Inclusion Officer ... Mr. Christopher L. JONES
42 Chaplain ... Vacant
06 Registrar ... Ms. Maria JOHNSON
104 Director Study Abroad ... Mr. Leo ROWLAND
37 Director of Financial Aid ... Ms. Emily BAKER
08 Director of Library Services ... Vacant
15 Human Resources Supervisor ... Ms. Brittney BRAY
09 Asst Provost Institutional Research ... Dr. Yan XIE
19 Chief of Public Safety ... Mr. Jeffrey TALBOTT
18 Director of Facilities Management ... Mr. Roger CELLINI
29 Director of Alumni Relations ... Ms. Shelli STOCKTON
20 Asst Dean of Academic/Student Life ... Ms. Amy WILMS
38 Director Student Counseling Ctr ... Dr. Matt GRAGG
41 Director of PE & Athletics ... Mr. Jeffrey MARTINEZ
36 Director Student Employment ... Ms. Kathryn WOOD
07 Director of Admissions ... Ms. Belinda SANDOVAL
13 Chief Information Officer ... Mr. Steve GARCIA
04 Executive Assistant to President ... Vacant
39 Director of Student Housing ... Ms. Cassandra MORTON
88 Dir Military & Veteran Services ... Ms. Monique POPE
44 Director Annual Giving ... Ms. Molly WIDDICOMBE
88 Dir Community Service Learning ... Mr. Tony MUELLER
103 Exec Dir Career & Prof Dev ... Dr. Kelly DRIES

University of St. Augustine for Health Sciences (F)

700 Windy Point Drive, San Marcos CA 92069
County: San Diego FICE Identification: 031713
Unit ID: 367954
Telephone: (800) 241-1027 Carnegie Class: Spec-4-yr-Other Health
FAX Number: N/A Calendar System: Trimester
URL: www.usa.edu
Established: 1979 Annual Graduate Tuition & Fees: N/A
Enrollment: 4,711 Coed
Affiliation or Control: Proprietary IRS Status: Proprietary
Highest Offering: Doctorate; No Undergraduates
Accreditation: WC, NURSE, OT, PTA

01 CEO/Interim President ... Ms. Vivian SANCHEZ
05 Chief Academic Officer/Exec Dean ... Dr. Brian GOLDSTEIN
10 Interim CFO ... Mr. Patrick GRAMLING
15 Exec Director Human Resources ... Ms. Susan WAUGH
13 Exec Director IT ... Mr. Matt MOLINE
09 Director of Institutional Research ... Ms. Nga PHAN
37 Director Student Financial Aid ... Ms. Vanessa FLOWERS
84 Director Enrollment Management ... Ms. Julie GONICK
06 Registrar ... Ms. Diane RONDINELLI
08 Director Library Services ... Ms. Julie EVENER
106 Dean of Online Education ... Dr. Maria PUZZIFERRO
18 Exec Dir Campus Opers & Facilities ... Ms. Sylvia BERENGUER

University of Saint Katherine (G)

1637 Capalina Road, San Marcos CA 92069
County: San Diego Identification: 667263
Unit ID: 488785
Telephone: (760) 471-1316 Carnegie Class: Bac-Diverse
FAX Number: (760) 704-1314 Calendar System: Semester
URL: www.usk.edu
Established: Annual Undergrad Tuition & Fees: N/A
Enrollment: N/A Coed
Affiliation or Control: Independent Non-Profit IRS Status: 501(c)3
Highest Offering: Master's
Accreditation: WC

01 President & Founder ... Dr. Frank PAPATHEOFANIS
05 Chief Academic Officer ... Dr. Tina KEATING
10 Chief Financial Officer ... Charlotte FOWLER
09 Dir of Inst Research/Effectiveness ... Hilari TARAZI
07 Dean of Admissions/Registrar ... Marina TRIGONIS
32 Director of Student Affairs ... Dr. Tina KEATING

University of San Diego (H)

5998 Alcala Park, San Diego CA 92110-2492
County: San Diego FICE Identification: 010395
Unit ID: 122436
Telephone: (619) 260-4600 Carnegie Class: DU-Higher
FAX Number: (619) 260-6833 Calendar System: 4/1/4
URL: www.sandiego.edu
Established: 1949 Annual Undergrad Tuition & Fees: $52,864
Enrollment: 8,861 Coed
Affiliation or Control: Roman Catholic IRS Status: 501(c)3
Highest Offering: Doctorate
Accreditation: WC, CACREP, CEA, IPSY, LAW, MFCD, NURSE

01 President ... Dr. James T. HARRIS
04 Special Assistant to the President ... Ms. Elaine ATENCIO
05 Vice President & Provost ... Dr. Gail F. BAKER
10 VP Finance/Chief Financial Officer ... Ms. Katy ROIG
45 VP Inst Effectiveness/Strat Init ... Dr. Andrew ALLEN
42 Vice President Mission Integration ... Dr. Michael LOVETTE-COLYER
32 Vice President Student Affairs ... Ms. Charlotte JOHNSON
111 Vice President Univ Advancement ... Mr. Richard P. VIRGIN
11 Vice President Univ Operations ... Mr. Ky L. SNYDER
49 Dean College of Arts & Sciences ... Dr. Noelle NORTON
50 Dean School of Business ... Dr. Timothy KEANE
54 Dean Shiley-Marcos School of Engr ... Dr. Chell ROBERTS
61 Dean School of Law ... Mr. Robert SCHAPIRO
53 Dean Sch Leadership/Educ Sciences . Dr. Kimberly WHITE-SMITH
66 Dean Sch Nursing/Health Sci ... Dr. Jane GEORGES
88 Dean School of Peace Studies ... Dr. Patricia MARQUEZ
08 Dean University Library ... Dr. Theresa BYRD
43 General Counsel & Advisor to Pres ... Mr. Thomas SKINNER
20 Int Vice Provost Academic Affairs ... Dr. Roger PACE
13 Chief Information Officer ... Dr. Elazar HAREL
06 University Registrar ... Ms. Elizabeth SILVA
46 Associate Provost Research & Dev ... Dr. Truc NGO
28 Vice Prov Diversity/Equity/Inclus ... Dr. Regina DIXON-REEVES
88 Assoc Provost International Affairs ... Dr. James BOLENDER
21 Controller ... Ms. Maria SANCHEZ
114 Budget Director ... Ms. Marie DAVIS
41 Assoc VP & Exec Dir of Athletics ... Mr. Bill MCGILLIS
84 Asst VP Enrollment Management ... Mr. Stephen F. PULTZ
15 AVP & Chief Human Resources Officer ... Ms. Karen HAGGENMILLER
18 Asst VP Facilities Management ... Mr. Andre HUTCHINSON
30 Assoc Vice President Development ... Ms. Sandra CIALLELLA
26 AVP University Marketing & Comm ... Mr. Peter MARLOW
44 Asst VP Advancement Operations ... Mr. Philip GARLAND
86 Asst Vice Pres Cmty/Local/Govt Rels ... Vacant
19 Asst Vice Pres Public Safety ... Mr. James MIYASHIRO
35 Asst VP & Dean of Students ... Dr. Nicole WHITNER
35 Asst VP Student Life ... Dr. Cynthia AVERY
109 Asst VP Auxiliary Services ... Mr. Andre MALLIE
07 Director of Admissions & Enrollment ... Ms. Minh-Ha HOANG
123 Assoc Dir Graduate Admissions ... Ms. Erika GARWOOD
09 Dir Inst Research & Planning ... Dr. Margaret LEARY
108 Dir Inst Effectiveness/Strat Init ... Dr. Elizabeth GIDDENS
90 Sr Director Customer Support ... Ms. Shahra MESHKATY
91 Sr Dir Enterprise Applications ... Ms. Steffanie HOIE
102 Director Foundation Relations ... Mr. Bruce EDWARDS
112 Director Major & Planned Giving ... Ms. Erin JONES
29 Senior Director Alumni Relations ... Mr. Charles BASS
36 Interim Director Career Development ... Ms. Rhonda HARLEY
37 Director Financial Aid Services ... Ms. Kellie NEHRING
113 Dir Student Financial Services ... Ms. Rosemary STALLBAUMER
92 Director Honors Program ... Dr. Susannah STERN
39 Asst Dean of Students ... Mr. Luke LACROIX
85 Dir International Students/Scholars ... Ms. Chia-Yen LIN
104 Asst Provost International Affairs ... Dr. Kira A. ESPIRITU
93 Director Multicultural Commons ... Dr. Mayte PEREZ-FRANCO
27 Sr Director Media Relations ... Ms. Lissette MARTINEZ
96 Director Procurement Services ... Ms. Theresa L. ROBINSON HARRIS
25 Director Sponsored Programs ... Ms. Traci MERRILL
23 Director Student Health Center ... Dr. Kimberly WOODRUFF
40 Director Bookstore ... Mr. James THRAILKILL
106 Dir Online Education ... Ms. Roxanne MORRISON
22 Dir Title IX/EEO ... Dr. Nicole A. SCHUESSLER VELOZ
117 Director Risk Management ... Ms. Robin ESKOW
118 Director Benefits ... Vacant
88 AVP Student Wellness ... Dr. Chris BURDEN

University of San Francisco (I)

2130 Fulton Street, San Francisco CA 94117-1080
County: San Francisco FICE Identification: 001325
Unit ID: 122612
Telephone: (415) 422-5555 Carnegie Class: DU-Mod
FAX Number: (415) 422-2303 Calendar System: 4/1/4
URL: www.usfca.edu
Established: 1855 Annual Undergrad Tuition & Fees: $52,482
Enrollment: 10,068 Coed
Affiliation or Control: Roman Catholic IRS Status: 501(c)3
Highest Offering: Doctorate
Accreditation: WC, CLPSY, IPSY, LAW, NURSE, PH, SPAA

01 President ... Rev. Paul J. FITZGERALD, SJ
05 Provost & VP Acad Affairs ... Dr. Chinyere OPARAH
10 Vice President Business & Finance ... Mr. Charles E. CROSS
26 Vice Pres Marketing/Communications ... Ms. Ellen RYDER
30 Interim Vice President Development .. Ms. Lindsey MCCLENAHAN
43 General Counsel ... Ms. Donna J. DAVIS
13 Vice President IT & CIO ... Mr. Opinder BAWA
20 Senior Vice Provost Acad Affairs ... Dr. Shirley MCGUIRE
32 Vice Provost Student Life ... Ms. Julie J. ORIO
28 Vice Prov Equity/Inclusion ... Ms. Sheila S. MCKOY
114 Vice Prov Inst Budget/Plng/Analytic ... Vacant
84 Vice Provost Strategic Enroll Mgmt ... Ms. April CRABTREE
61 Dean School of Law ... Ms. Susan FREIWALD
49 Dean College Arts & Science ... Dr. Eileen FUNG
08 Dean of University Library ... Dr. Shawn CALHOUN
53 Dean School of Education ... Dr. Shabnam KOIRALA-AZAD
66 Dean School of Nursing/Health Prof ... Dr. Eileen FRY-BOWERS
50 Dean School of Management ... Mr. Otgontsetseg ERHEMJAMTS
18 Assoc Vice Pres Facilities Mgmt ... Mr. Michael E. LONDON
21 Assoc Vice Pres Finance & Treasury ... Ms. Stacy LEWIS
15 Assoc Vice Pres Human Resources ... Ms. Diane NELSON
114 AVP Accounting & Business Svcs ... Mr. Desmond DAIR
88 Rector of Jesuit Community ... Rev. Timothy S. GODFREY, SJ
42 Assoc Director University Ministry ... Ms. Angelica QUIONEZ
37 Asst Vice Prov Student Fin Svcs ... Ms. Angelika WILLIAMS
04 Exec Asst to President/Sec BOT ... Ms. Jaci E. NEESAM
27 Media Relations Specialist ... Ms. Kellie SAMSON
45 Assoc Vice Prov Planning and Budget ... Mr. Michael J. HARRINGTON
110 Sr Assoc VP Development ... Vacant
06 Assoc Dean University Registrar ... Mr. Robert L. BROMFIELD
96 Dir Purchasing & Ancillary Svc ... Ms. Janet L. TEYMOURTASH
38 Senior Dir Counseling & Psych Svcs ... Dr. Barbara J. THOMAS
36 Senior Director Career Svcs ... Mr. Alex HOCHMAN
19 Senior Director of Public Safety ... Dr. Daniel L. LAWSON
123 Asst Vice Prov Graduate Enrollment ... Vacant
88 Asst Vice Prov Integ Enrollment Mgt ... Mr. Patrick KAO
104 Director Ctr for Global Education ... Ms. Sharon F. LI
07 Asst Vice Prov Undergrad Admissions ... Ms. Ariana PISTORINO
85 Director Intl Student/Scholar Svcs ... Ms. Marcella PITCHER DEPROTO
41 Director of Athletics ... Ms. Joan MCDERMOTT
29 Assoc VP for Development ... Ms. Leslie WETZEL
44 Assoc VP Annual Giving ... Ms. Chantel SMITH
102 Sr Dir Corp/Foundation Relations ... Ms. Mary BUSSI
29 Director University Initiatives ... Mr. Bill CARTWRIGHT
16 Dir of Employee Relations ... Ms. Liliana ROJAS
09 AVP Institutional Research ... Vacant
39 Sr Dir Student Housing/Resident Ed ... Mr. Torry BROUILLARD-BRUCE
24 Dir Ctr Learning Instruct & Tech ... Dr. John BANSAVICH
105 Sr Dir Web & Digital Communication ... Ms. Marlene K. TOM
108 AVP Educ Effectiveness/Assessment ... Ms. Deborah PANTER
25 AVP Sponsored Programs ... Ms. Camille COLEY
22 Asst Dean/Director Disability Svcs ... Mr. Tom MERRELL
14 AVP & Dir Educ Technology Services ... Mr. David KIRMSE
88 Asst Vice Prov Enroll Communication ... Ms. Katherine EDWARDS
116 AVP Tax Compliance & Internal Audit ... Mr. Dominic DAHER
101 Secretary of the Board ... Ms. Jaci NEESAM

University of Silicon Andhra (J)

1521 California Circle, Milpitas CA 95035
County: Santa Clara Identification: 667397
Telephone: (844) 872-8680 Carnegie Class: Not Classified
FAX Number: N/A Calendar System: Semester
URL: www.universityofsiliconandhra.org
Established: Annual Graduate Tuition & Fees: N/A
Enrollment: N/A Coed
Affiliation or Control: Independent Non-Profit IRS Status: 501(c)3
Highest Offering: Master's; No Undergraduates

Accreditation: WC

01 President/CEO .... Anand KUCHIBHOTLA
05 Provost .... Raju CHAMARTHI
10 Vice Pres Finance/Administration .... Vacant
32 Manager Student Services .... Mamatha KUCHIBHOTLA
07 Manager Admissions .... Sridevi GANTI

University of Silicon Valley (A)

191 Baypointe Parkway, San Jose CA 95134-1697
County: Santa Clara FICE Identification: 001177
Unit ID: 112394
Telephone: (408) 498-5100 Carnegie Class: Bac-Diverse
FAX Number: (408) 877-7373 Calendar System: Trimester
URL: https://usv.edu/
Established: 1887 Annual Undergrad Tuition & Fees: $21,784
Enrollment: 524 Coed
Affiliation or Control: Proprietary IRS Status: Proprietary
Highest Offering: Master's
Accreditation: WC

01 CEO and President .... Mr. Charles RESTIVO
05 Provost/Chief Academic Officer .... Dr. Brian SHEPARD
10 Chief Financial Officer .... Ms. Ilona KREYNIS
84 VP of Enrollment .... Mr. Eric RAJASALU
13 VP Info Technology/Campus Svcs .... Dr. Andrey FEDIN
09 Vice Pres Inst Research & QA .... Ms. Milla ZLATANOV
07 Director of Admissions .... Ms. Jonelle TATE
88 Chief Compliance Officer .... Dr. Reba SMITH
20 Dean of Education .... Mr. Jerome SOLOMON
32 Dean of Students .... Ms. Carolus BROWN
06 Registrar .... Ms. Angela ACUNA
04 Executive Assistant to President .... Ms. Monique TAYLOR
36 Dir Career Services .... Mr. Jason ARANA
08 Librarian & Resource Center Manager . Ms. Louise PASTERNACK
37 Director of Financial Aid .... Ms. Stacey VALENTINE
15 Director of Human Resources .... Ms. Leslie ANDERSON

University of South Los Angeles (B)

1045 W Redondo Beach Blvd, Ste 200,
Gardena CA 90247
County: Los Angeles Identification: 667326
Telephone: (310) 756-0001 Carnegie Class: Not Classified
FAX Number: (310) 756-0004 Calendar System: Quarter
URL: www.uosla.org
Established: 1993 Annual Undergrad Tuition & Fees: N/A
Enrollment: N/A Coed
Affiliation or Control: Proprietary IRS Status: Proprietary
Highest Offering: Doctorate
Accreditation: TRACS

01 Chancellor .... Dr. Peter CHOI
11 Vice Chanc Admin & Student Affs .... Dr. Richard KANG
10 CFO & Director of Admin .... Jackie JUNG
05 Chief Academic Officer .... Dr. Guy LANGVARDT
32 Dean of Student Affairs .... Dr. Tania MAYNC
07 Dir of Admiss & Records/Registrar .... Vacant

University of Southern California (C)

University Park Campus, Los Angeles CA 90089-0012
County: Los Angeles FICE Identification: 001328
Unit ID: 123961
Telephone: (213) 740-2111 Carnegie Class: DU-Highest
FAX Number: N/A Calendar System: Semester
URL: www.usc.edu
Established: 1880 Annual Undergrad Tuition & Fees: $60,275
Enrollment: 46,287 Coed
Affiliation or Control: Independent Non-Profit IRS Status: 501(c)3
Highest Offering: Doctorate
Accreditation: WC, ANEST, ARCPA, CAEP, CLPSY, DENT, DIETC, HSA, IPSY, JOUR, LAW, LIB, LSAR, MED, NURSE, OT, PCSAS, PDPSY, PH, PHAR, PLNG, PTA, @SP, SPAA, SW

01 President .... Dr. Carol L. FOLT
05 Provost & SVP Academic Affairs .... Dr. Charles F. ZUKOSKI
26 SVP University Relations .... Mr. Samuel GARRISON
111 Int Sr VP University Advancement .... Ms. Tracey VRANICH
17 CEO for USC Health .... Mr. Rodney HANNERS
115 Chief Investment Officer .... Ms. Amy DIAMOND
27 SVP/Chief Communication Officer .... Mr. Kyle HENLEY
10 Sr VP Finance & CFO .... Mr. James STATEN
41 Athletic Director .... Mr. Mike BOHN
15 Sr VP Human Resources .... Ms. Felicia WASHINGTON
11 Sr VP Administration .... Mr. David W. WRIGHT
43 Senior VP and General Counsel .... Mr. Beong-Soo KIM
32 Interim VP for Student Affairs .... Dr. Monique ALLARD
84 VP for Enrollment Management .... Dr. Kedra ISHOP
46 VP for Research .... Dr. Ishwar PURI
88 VP for Athletic Compliance .... Mr. Michael BLANTON
18 Interim VP Capital Construction .... Mr. Christopher TOOMEY
88 VP Health Sciences Advancement .... Ms. Kathryn CARRICO
88 VP of Professionalism/Ethics .... Mr. Michael BLANTON
100 Chief of Staff .... Ms. Rene K. PAK
60 Dean Annenberg School Communication .... Dr. Willow C. BAY
48 Dean School of Architecture .... Vacant
50 Dean Marshall School of Business .... Mr. Geoff GARRETT
88 Dean School of Cinematic Arts .... Dr. Elizabeth M. DALEY
88 Dean Kaufman School of Dance .... Ms. Julia M. RITTER
52 Dean Ostrow School of Dentistry .... Dr. Avishai SADAN
53 Dean Rossier School of Education .... Dr. Pedro NOGUERA
54 Dean Viterbi School of Engineering .... Dr. Yannis C. YORTSOS
57 Dean Roski School of Fine Arts .... Ms. Haven LIN-KIRK
88 Dean Davis School of Gerontology .... Dr. Pinchas COHEN
61 Dean Gould School of Law .... Dr. Andrew GUZMAN
63 Dean Keck School of Medicine .... Dr. Carolyn MELTZER
64 Int Dean Thornton School of Music .... Mr. Josh KUN
67 Dean School of Pharmacy .... Dr. Vassilios PAPADOPOULOS
70 Dean School of Social Work .... Dr. Sarah GEHLERT
88 Dean School of Dramatic Arts .... Ms. Emily ROXWORTHY
80 Dean School of Public Policy .... Dr. Dana GOLDMAN
49 Dean Dornsife Col Ltrs/Arts & Sci .... Dr. Amber D. MILLER
42 Dean Religious Life .... Dr. Varun SONI
06 Registrar .... Dr. Frank CHANG
08 Dean University Libraries .... Vacant
07 Dean of Admission .... Mr. Timothy BRUNOLD
37 Dean of Financial Aid .... Mr. Thomas MCWHORTER
110 AVP Advancement Communications .... Mr. Sam LOPEZ
38 Associate Vice Provost .... Dr. Ilene ROSENSTEIN
88 Vice Provost and Senior Advisor .... Dr. Martin L. LEVINE
58 Vice Prov for Graduate Programs .... Dr. Sally PRATT
20 Vice Prov for Undergraduate Program .... Dr. Andrea HODGE
13 Chief Information Officer .... Dr. Douglas SHOOK
20 Vice Prov Academic Ops .... Dr. Mark TODD
88 Exec Dir USC Stevens Ctr for Innov .... Ms. Jennifer DYER
85 VP of Global Initiatives .... Dr. Anthony BAILEY
20 Vice Prov for Acad/Faculty Affairs .... Dr. Elizabeth GRADDY
122 Coord Fraternity/Sorority Life .... Ms. Diana TORRES

University of the West (D)

1409 Walnut Grove Avenue, Rosemead CA 91770-3709
County: Los Angeles FICE Identification: 036963
Unit ID: 449870
Telephone: (626) 571-8811 Carnegie Class: Bac-A&S
FAX Number: (626) 571-1413 Calendar System: Semester
URL: www.uwest.edu
Established: 1991 Annual Undergrad Tuition & Fees: $13,556
Enrollment: 238 Coed
Affiliation or Control: Independent Non-Profit IRS Status: 501(c)3
Highest Offering: Doctorate
Accreditation: WC

01 President .... Dr. Minh-hoa TA
05 Chief Academic Officer .... Dr. Jane IWAMURA
32 Chief Student Services Officer .... Ms. Vanessa KARAM
10 Chief Financial Officer .... Ms. Amy CHONG
13 Director Information Technology .... Mr. Rafael WU
08 Director of Library .... Ms. Ling Ling KUO
06 Registrar .... Ms. Jeanette ANDERSON
07 Enrollment/Admissions Coordinator .... Ms. Nadia SIMONE
35 Student Life Coordinator .... Mr. Eddie ESCALANTE
73 Chair of Religious Studies .... Dr. Miroj SHAKYA
50 Chair of Business Admin .... Dr. Bill CHEN
97 Chair of General Education .... Dr. Kanae OMURA
83 Chair of Psychology .... Dr. Elizabeth BURKE
88 Acting Chair of English .... Ms. Jennifer AVILA
04 Exec Assistant to the President .... Ms. Grace HSIAO
37 Director Financial Aid .... Ms. Lezli FANG
39 Coordinator Housing/Resident Life .. Mr. Eduardo (Eddie) BERNAL
15 Human Resources Assistant .... Ms. Joey CHOW

University of West Los Angeles (E)

9800 La Cienga Blvd., 12th Floor,
Inglewood CA 90301-4423
County: Los Angeles Identification: 667301
Unit ID: 484862
Telephone: (310) 342-5200 Carnegie Class: Spec-4-yr-Law
FAX Number: N/A Calendar System: Semester
URL: www.uwla.edu
Established: 1966 Annual Undergrad Tuition & Fees: N/A
Enrollment: 229 Coed
Affiliation or Control: Proprietary IRS Status: Proprietary
Highest Offering: First Professional Degree
Accreditation: WC

01 President/COO .... Robert BROWN
10 Chief Financial Officer .... Ryan FULLMER
07 SVP Admissions/Recruitment/Mktg .... Troy BROWN
43 VP/General Counsel .... Tiffany CLINTON
11 VP/Director Business Office .... Johnetta HEGWOOD
05 Provost/Dean School of Law .... Jay FRYKBERG
09 Director Institutional Research .... Jesse ALDAVA

Valley College of Medical Careers (F)

8399 Topanga Canyon Blvd Ste 200, West Hills CA 91304
County: Los Angeles FICE Identification: 041145
Unit ID: 449445
Telephone: (818) 883-9002 Carnegie Class: Spec 2-yr-Health
FAX Number: (818) 883-9003 Calendar System: Semester
URL: https://www.valleycollegeofmedicalcareers.info/vcmc.html
Established: Annual Undergrad Tuition & Fees: N/A
Enrollment: 129 Coed
Affiliation or Control: Proprietary IRS Status: Proprietary
Highest Offering: Associate Degree
Accreditation: ABHES

01 President .... Mr. Ronny SUSSMAN

Vanguard University of Southern California (G)

55 Fair Drive, Costa Mesa CA 92626-6597
County: Orange FICE Identification: 001293
Unit ID: 123651
Telephone: (714) 556-3610 Carnegie Class: Masters/M
FAX Number: (714) 957-9317 Calendar System: Semester
URL: www.vanguard.edu
Established: 1920 Annual Undergrad Tuition & Fees: $36,550
Enrollment: 2,289 Coed
Affiliation or Control: Assemblies Of God Church IRS Status: 501(c)3
Highest Offering: Master's
Accreditation: WC, MUS, NURSE, THEA

01 President .... Dr. Michael J. BEALS
100 Dir Org Strategy/Compliance .... Ms. Shree CARTER
04 Exec Assistant to the President .... Mrs. Alexis SCHNOOR
05 Provost/SVP Academic Affairs .... Dr. Pete MENJARES
49 Assoc Provost/Dean Col Arts & Sci .... Dr. Michael D. WILSON
107 Dean Professional Studies .... Vacant
73 Director of Graduate Religion .... Dr. Roger HEUSER
58 Director for Graduate Education .... Dr. Sylvia KANE
83 Director for Graduate Psychology .... Vacant
06 Dean Academic Records/Registrar .... Ms. Julie COWEN
104 Director Global Outreach/Educ .... Ms. Kayli HILLEBRAND
09 VP of Institutional Research .... Mr. John KIM
08 Head Librarian .... Ms. Pamela CRENSHAW
41 Athletic Director .... Mr. Jeff BUSSELL
10 Vice President Finance/CFO .... Mr. Jeremy MOSER
21 Controller .... Ms. Jill ROBINSON
96 Director of Fiscal Management .... Ms. Katy MCINTOSH
19 Dir of Campus Safety Services .... Mr. Kenton FERRIN
13 Director Informational Technology .... Mr. Sean MACLEAN
15 Senior Director of Human Resources .... Mr. Joe BAFFA
18 Director of Facility Operations .... Vacant
40 Bookstore Manager .... Ms. Stephanie BUNT
101 Board Professional .... Ms. Shree CARTER
42 Associate University Pastor .... Rev. Michael WHITFORD
32 VP of Student Affs/Dean of Students .... Dr. Tim YOUNG
39 Student Housing Coordinator .... Ms. Megan SISK
121 Dir Stdnt Success/Acad Res/Fam Rels .... Ms. Amanda LEBRECHT
38 Director of Counseling Services .... Dr. Doug HUTCHINSON
36 Career Planning Coordinator .... Vacant
28 Chief Diversity Officer .... Mr. Pete MENJARES
84 VP for Enrollment Management .... Ms. Kim JOHNSON
07 Director of Admissions Recruitment .... Vacant
123 Dir of Grad/Prof Studies Admissions .... Vacant
37 Assoc Dir of Student Financial Aid .... Ms. Denise PENA
111 VP University Advancement .... Mr. Justin MCINTEE
44 Director of Annual Fund .... Vacant
29 Director of Alumni Engagement .... Mrs. Laura CAPO
26 Chief Communications Officer .... Vacant
86 Director of Veteran/Government Rels .... Ms. Shree CARTER
102 Director of External Relations .... Vacant
108 Director Institutional Assessment .... Ms. Ludmilla PRASLOVA
106 Dean of Teaching and Learning .... Ms. Bonni STACHOWIAK

*Ventura County Community College District (H)

761 East Daily Drive, Suite 200, Camarillo CA 93010
County: Ventura FICE Identification: 006863
Unit ID: 125019
Telephone: (805) 652-5500 Carnegie Class: N/A
FAX Number: N/A
URL: www.vcccd.edu

01 Chancellor .... Dr. Greg GILLESPIE
10 Vice Chanc Business Svcs/Fin Mgmt .... Dr. David EL FATTAL
15 Vice Chanc of Human Resources .... Ms. Laura BARROSO
108 Vice Chancellor Inst Effectiveness .... Dr. Cynthia HERRERA
13 Assoc Vice Chanc of IT .... Mr. Dan WATKINS
12 Moorpark College President .... Dr. Julius SOKENU
12 Oxnard College President .... Mr. Luis SANCHEZ
12 Ventura College President .... Dr. Kimberly HOFFMANS
26 Director Public Relations/Marketing .... Ms. Patti BLAIR

*Moorpark College (I)

7075 Campus Road, Moorpark CA 93021-1695
County: Ventura FICE Identification: 007115
Unit ID: 119137
Telephone: (805) 378-1400 Carnegie Class: Assoc/HT-High Trad
FAX Number: (805) 378-1499 Calendar System: Semester
URL: www.moorparkcollege.edu
Established: 1967 Annual Undergrad Tuition & Fees (In-State): $1,394
Enrollment: 14,361 Coed
Affiliation or Control: State IRS Status: 501(c)3
Highest Offering: Associate Degree
Accreditation: WJ, ADNUR, RAD

02 President .... Dr. Julius SOKENU
05 Vice President Academic Affairs .... Dr. John FORBES
10 Vice President Business Services .... Dr. Jennifer CLARK
32 Vice President Student Support .... Dr. Amanuel GEBRU
04 Executive Assistant to President .... Ms. Linda RESENDIZ
20 Dean of Student Learning .... Dr. Josepha BACA
20 Dean of Student Learning .... Ms. Priscilla MORA
20 Dean of Student Learning .... Mr. Monica GARCIA
20 Dean of Student Learning .... Mr. Robert CABRAL

20 Dean of Student Learning .... Mr. Matthew CALFIN
20 Dean of Student Learning .... Ms. Khushnur DADABHOY
20 Dean of Student Learning .... Mr. Oleg BESPALOV
20 Dean of Student Learning .... Ms. Carol HIGASHIDA
18 Director Maintenance/Operations .... Mr. John SINUTKO
109 College Fiscal Services Supervisor .... Ms. Michele PERRY
13 Director Information Technology .... Mr. Dan MCMICHAEL
113 Bursar .... Ms. Lindy CHAU
23 Director Student Health Services .... Ms. Allison CASE BARTON
41 Athletic Director .... Mr. Matt CRATER
121 Supervisor Student Success Services .... Ms. Claudia SITLINGTON
37 Student Financial Aid Officer .... Ms. Kim KORINKE
06 Registrar .... Mr. David ANTER
111 Director of Inst Advancement .... Ms. Deborah KLEIN
35 Student Activities Specialist .... Ms. Kristen ROBINSON
85 Director International Students .... Ms. Claudia WILROY

*Oxnard College (A)

4000 S Rose Avenue, Oxnard CA 93033-6699

County: Ventura FICE Identification: 012842
Unit ID: 120421
Telephone: (805) 678-5800 Carnegie Class: Assoc/HT-High Trad
FAX Number: (805) 678-5806 Calendar System: Semester
URL: www.oxnardcollege.edu
Established: 1975 Annual Undergrad Tuition & Fees (In-District): $1,394
Enrollment: 6,994 Coed
Affiliation or Control: State/Local IRS Status: 501(c)3
Highest Offering: Associate Degree
Accreditation: WJ, DH, IFSAC

02 President .... Mr. Luis P. SANCHEZ
05 Vice Pres Academic Affairs .... Dr. Art SANDFORD
10 Vice Pres Business Services .... Mr. Christopher RENBARGER
32 Vice Pres Student Development .... Dr. Oscar COBIAN
79 Dean Library & Liberal Studies .... Dr. Luis GONZALEZ
75 Dean Career & Technical Education .... Dr. Armine DERDIARIAN
81 Dean Math/Science/Hlth/PE/Athletics .... Dr. Carolyn INOUYE
09 Dean Inst Effectiveness .... Dr. Keller MAGENAU
121 Dean Student Success .... Ms. Leah ALARCON
18 Director Maintenance/Operations .... Mr. Bob SUBE
41 Director of Athletics .... Mr. Jonas CRAWFORD
06 Registrar .... Mr. Joel DIAZ
88 Director STEM .... Dr. Marcella KLEIN-WILLIAMS
37 Financial Aid Officer .... Ms. Linda FAASUA
109 College Services Supervisor .... Mr. Gilbert DOWNS
04 Exec Assistant to the President .... Ms. Karla BANKS
13 Chief Information Technology Office .... Mr. Michael ALEXANDER
19 Dean of Public Safety .... Mr. Matthew JEWETT

*Ventura College (B)

4667 Telegraph Road, Ventura CA 93003-3899

County: Ventura FICE Identification: 001334
Unit ID: 125028
Telephone: (805) 289-6000 Carnegie Class: Assoc/HT-High Trad
FAX Number: (805) 289-6466 Calendar System: Semester
URL: www.venturacollege.edu
Established: 1925 Annual Undergrad Tuition & Fees (In-District): $1,394
Enrollment: 11,789 Coed
Affiliation or Control: State/Local IRS Status: 501(c)3
Highest Offering: Associate Degree
Accreditation: WJ, ADNUR, EMT

02 President .... Dr. Kim HOFFMANS
05 Vice President Academic Affairs .... Dr. Jennifer KALFSBEEK-GOETZ
32 Vice Pres Student Affairs .... Dr. Damien A. PEÑA
10 Vice Pres Business/Admin Services .... Ms. Cathy BOJORQUEZ
04 Exec Assistant to the President .... Ms. Andrea RAMBO
108 Dean Institutional Effectiveness .... Mr. Phillip BRIGGS
38 Dean Counseling/Student Engagement .... Ms. Leticia CANALES
68 Dean Health/Kines/Ath/Perf Ar .... Mr. Bernard GIBSON
83 Dean Behav & Social Sci/Lang .... Ms. Lisa PUTNAM
103 Dean Career Education .... Ms. Debbie NEWCOMB
103 Dean Career Education .... Ms. Felicia DUEÑAS
81 Dean Eng/Math/Lrng Resources .... Ms. Boglarka KISS
12 Dean East Campus & Stdnt Engage .... Dr. Jesus VEGA
102 Executive Director Foundation .... Ms. Anne KING
06 Registrar .... Ms. Gabriella ASAMSAMA-ACUNA
18 Director Maintenance/Operations .... Mr. Jesse SLUDER
35 Coordinator Student Activities .... Ms. Jessica PEREZ
37 Financial Aid Officer .... Ms. Alma RODRIGUEZ
09 Institutional Research .... Mr. Michael CALLAHAN
23 Director Student Health Center .... Ms. Mary JONES
19 Campus Police .... Lt. Mike PALLOTO
26 Director Marketing and Outreach .... Ms. Vanessa STOTLER
41 Athletic Director .... Mr. Jimmy WALKER

Veritas International University (C)

3000 W. MacArthur Blvd, Suite 207, Santa Ana CA 92704

County: Orange Identification: 667103
Telephone: (714) 966-8500 Carnegie Class: Not Classified
FAX Number: (714) 966-8510 Calendar System: Semester
URL: www.ves.edu
Established: 2008 Annual Undergrad Tuition & Fees: N/A
Enrollment: N/A Coed
Affiliation or Control: Independent Non-Profit IRS Status: 501(c)3
Highest Offering: Doctorate
Accreditation: TRACS

01 President .... Joseph M. HOLDEN
07 Director of Admissions .... Peter DIAZ
05 Academic Dean .... Frank CORREA
08 Library Director .... Joe MCELROY
10 Chief Business Officer .... Megan YORIMITSU
09 Dir Inst Effectiveness/Assessment .... Frank CORREA
32 Director Student Affairs/Careers .... Deborah DELARGY
15 Business Manager/Human Resources .... Megan YORIMITSU

Victor Valley College (D)

18422 Bear Valley Road, Victorville CA 92395-5850

County: San Bernardino FICE Identification: 001335
Unit ID: 125091
Telephone: (760) 245-4271 Carnegie Class: Assoc/MT-VT-Mix Trad/Non
FAX Number: (760) 245-9019 Calendar System: Semester
URL: www.vvc.edu
Established: 1961 Annual Undergrad Tuition & Fees (In-District): $1,424
Enrollment: 10,777 Coed
Affiliation or Control: State/Local IRS Status: 501(c)3
Highest Offering: Associate Degree
Accreditation: WJ, COARC, EMT

01 Superintendent/President .... Dr. Daniel W. WALDEN
05 Vice President Instruction .... Dr. Todd SCOTT
10 Deputy Supt/Exec VP Admin Svcs .... Mr. John NAHLEN
32 Vice President Student Development .... Dr. Karen ENGELSEN
15 Vice President Human Resources .... Ms. Monica MARTINEZ
72 Dean Public Safety/Industrial Tech .... Ms. McKenzie TARANGO
79 Dean Humanities/Arts & Social Sci .... Ms. Jacqueline AUGUSTINE
21 Director Fiscal Services .... Ms. Shawntee MILTON
07 Director of Admissions .... Mr. David VAZQUEZ
26 Director Public Info/Marketing .... Mr. Robert SEWELL
41 Director Athletics/Athletic Trainer .... Mr. Arthur LOPEZ
18 Exec Dir Facilities/Operations .... Mr. John NAHLEN
37 Director Financial Aid .... Mr. Jason JUDKINS
109 Director Auxiliary Services/ASB Adv .... Mrs. Deanna SANABRIA
35 Assoc VP Matriculation & Athletics .... Mr. Arthur LOPEZ
19 Chief Campus Police .... Mr. Leonard KNIGHT
13 Chief Information Officer .... Mr. Yogesh MARIMUTHU
88 Dir EOPS/CARE/CALWORKS .... Mr. Carl SMITH
09 Exec Dean Inst Effectiveness .... Ms. Virginia MORAN
04 Executive Asst to President .... Mrs. Michelle PAINTER
08 Head Librarian .... Ms. Leslie HUINER
102 Exec Dir Foundation .... Mrs. Kirsten ACOSTA
104 Facilitator Study Abroad .... Vacant
103 Director Workforce Development .... Ms. Frank CASTANOS

Virscend University (E)

16490 Bake Parkway Ste 100, Irvine CA 92618

County: Orange Identification: 667414
Telephone: (949) 502-6252 Carnegie Class: Not Classified
FAX Number: N/A Calendar System: Semester
URL: www.virscend.com
Established: Annual Undergrad Tuition & Fees: N/A
Enrollment: N/A Coed
Affiliation or Control: Proprietary IRS Status: Proprietary
Highest Offering: Master's
Accreditation: @WC

01 President .... Dr. Robert CHI
10 Chief Financial Officer .... Ms. Leslie CHEN

Weimar University (F)

20601 W. Paoli Lane, Weimar CA 95736

County: Placer Identification: 667302
Telephone: (530) 422-7927 Carnegie Class: Not Classified
FAX Number: N/A Calendar System: Semester
URL: www.weimar.edu
Established: 1978 Annual Undergrad Tuition & Fees: N/A
Enrollment: N/A Coed
Affiliation or Control: Independent Non-Profit IRS Status: 501(c)3
Highest Offering: Master's
Accreditation: WC, ADNUR, NUR

01 President .... Neil NEDLEY
05 Vice President Academic Affairs .... George ARAYA
10 Chief Financial Officer .... Dale NORTHROP
09 Director of Institutional Research .... Christina HARRIS
32 Director Student Services .... Rodolfo RAMIREZ
84 Director of Enrollment Management .... Wanda SWENSEN
06 Registrar .... Erica KINJO

West Coast Baptist College (G)

4010 E. Lancaster Boulevard, Lancaster CA 93535

County: Los Angeles Identification: 667268
Telephone: (661) 946-2274 Carnegie Class: Not Classified
FAX Number: (661) 946-4510 Calendar System: Semester
URL: www.wcbc.edu
Established: 1995 Annual Undergrad Tuition & Fees: N/A
Enrollment: N/A Coed
Affiliation or Control: Baptist IRS Status: 501(c)3
Highest Offering: Master's
Accreditation: TRACS

01 Founder & President .... Dr. Paul CHAPPELL
03 Exec Vice Pres/Chief Operating Ofcr .... Dr. John GOETSCH
05 Chief Academic Officer .... Mr. Tobias ENGLAND
11 Dean of Administrative Affairs .... Dr. Jerry GODDARD
32 Vice Pres Student Services .... Dr. Mark RASMUSSEN
06 Registrar .... Ms. Kristi LONGHOFER

West Coast University (H)

151 Innovation Dr., Irvine CA 92617

Telephone: (949) 783-4800 Identification: 770480
Accreditation: &WC, DH, @SP

West Coast University (I)

12215 Victory Boulevard, North Hollywood CA 91606-3206

County: Los Angeles FICE Identification: 036983
Unit ID: 443331
Telephone: (818) 299-5500 Carnegie Class: Spec-4-yr-Other Health
FAX Number: (818) 299-5545 Calendar System: Semester
URL: www.westcoastuniversity.edu
Established: 1909 Annual Undergrad Tuition & Fees: $35,110
Enrollment: 2,413 Coed
Affiliation or Control: Proprietary IRS Status: Proprietary
Highest Offering: Doctorate
Accreditation: WC, #ARCPA, NURSE, OT, PHAR, PTA

01 Co-President .... Dr. Jeb EGBERT
11 Executive Director .... Ms. Debra THIBODEAUX
10 Chief Financial Officer .... Mr. Scott MEHLBERGER
05 Chief Learning Officer .... Dr. Jeb EGBERT
66 Int Dean College of Nursing .... Dr. Chiarina PIAZZA
20 Academic Dean .... Dr. Miriam KAHAN
07 Director of Admissions .... Ms. Monica ENGLERT
37 Director of Financial Aid .... Ms. Tracy CABUCO
32 Director of Student Affairs .... Ms. Hilary CROCKER
08 Librarian .... Ms. Julie OSHIRO
06 Registrar .... Ms. Felicia LOCKHART

West Coast University (J)

2855 E Guasti Road, Suite 100, Ontario CA 91761

Telephone: (909) 467-6100 Identification: 770484
Accreditation: &WC

*West Hills Community College District (K)

275 Phelps Avenue, Coalinga CA 93210

County: Fresno Identification: 667041
Telephone: (559) 934-2180 Carnegie Class: N/A
FAX Number: (559) 934-2810
URL: www.westhillscollege.com

01 Chancellor .... Dr. Kristin CLARK
10 Vice Chanc Business & Fiscal Svcs .... Ms. Shanna AHRENS
05 Assoc VC Educ & Student Services .... Dr. Luca LEWIS
15 Assoc VC Human Resources .... Ms. Becky CAZARES
13 Assoc VC Information Technology .... Mr. Jeff SEED
102 Exec Director WHCC Foundation .... Mr. Alex PEREZ
09 Dir of Accred/Research/Inst Eff .... Mr. Kyle CRIDER
26 Dir of Marketing/Comm/Public Info .... Ms. Amber MYRICK
14 Dir of Info Technology Systems .... Mr. Shaun VETTER
21 Director of Fiscal Services .... Ms. Christine ALCARAZ
16 Director of Human Resources .... Ms. Kimberlee DAVIS
25 Director of Grants .... Mr. Brian BOOMER
103 Director of Special Grant Programs .... Mr. Cecilio MORA
103 Director of Special Grant Programs .... Mr. Francisco LOPEZ
103 Director of Contract Training .... Mr. David CASTILLO
88 Dir of Apprenticeship Programs .... Mr. Nickolas TRUJILLO
88 Dir of Child Development Centers .... Ms. Isabella GUTIERREZ
04 Executive Assistant to Chancellor .... Ms. Donna ISAAC

*West Hills College Coalinga (L)

300 Cherry Lane, Coalinga CA 93210-1399

County: Fresno FICE Identification: 001176
Unit ID: 125462
Telephone: (559) 934-2000 Carnegie Class: Assoc/MT-VT-High Non
FAX Number: N/A Calendar System: Semester
URL: www.westhillscollege.com/coalinga
Established: 1932 Annual Undergrad Tuition & Fees (In-District): $1,380
Enrollment: 4,229 Coed
Affiliation or Control: State/Local IRS Status: Exempt
Highest Offering: Associate Degree
Accreditation: WJ

02 President .... Dr. Carla TWEED
05 Vice Pres of Educational Services .... Mr. Samasoni AUNAI
32 Vice President of Student Services .... Ms. Angela TOS
20 Dean of Educational Services .... Dr. Justin GARCIA
12 Dean of Firebaugh Center .... Ms. Bethany MATOS
35 Dean of Student Services .... Mr. Javier CAZARES
41 Associate Dean of Athletics .... Mr. Joe HASH
28 Director of Title IV Projects .... Ms. April BETTERSON
07 Dir Admissions & Records/Registrar .... Ms. Rosalind TOLIVER
37 Director of Financial Aid .... Mr. Octavio CRUZ
25 Dir Special Grants/Dual Enrollment .... Mr. Richard AGUILAR
88 Director of MESA .... Mr. Zack SOTO
47 Director of Farm of the Future .... Mr. Terry BRASE
18 Dir of Maintenance & Operations .... Mr. Shaun BAILEY
04 Administrative Asst to President .... Ms. Amy MARTINEZ

*West Hills College Lemoore (A)

555 College Avenue, Lemoore CA 93245-9248
County: Kings FICE Identification: 041113
Unit ID: 448594
Telephone: (559) 925-3000 Carnegie Class: Assoc/HT-Mix Trad/Non
FAX Number: (559) 924-1243 Calendar System: Semester
URL: www.westhillscollege.com/lemoore
Established: 2002 Annual Undergrad Tuition & Fees (In-District): $1,380
Enrollment: 3,932 Coed
Affiliation or Control: State/Local IRS Status: Exempt
Highest Offering: Associate Degree
Accreditation: WJ, EMT

02 President .... Mr. James PRESTON
05 Vice President of Educational Svcs .. Mr. Christopher WHITESIDE
32 Vice President of Student Services .... Mr. Valentin GARCIA
20 Dean of Educational Services .... Dr. Kurt STERLING
35 Dean of Student Services .... Mr. Elmer AGUILAR
75 Dean of Career & Tech Education .... Ms. Kris COSTA
103 Assoc Dean of Categorical Programs .... Ms. Maria De La Luz GONZALEZ
41 Associate Dean of Athletics .... Ms. Andrea PICCHI
06 Director Admiss & Records/Registrar .... Mr. Nestor LOMELI
37 Director of Financial Aid .... Ms. Kathleen SCHOENECKER
88 Director of Upward Bound .... Mr. Oscar VILLARREAL
66 Director of Nursing .... Ms. Kathryn DEFEDE
84 Dir Outreach and Recruitment .... Ms. Callie BRANAN
18 Dir of Maintenance & Operations .... Mr. Joshua ALLEN
88 Director of HOPE Initiative .... Ms. Zara SIMS
04 Administrative Asst to President .... Ms. Dawne TROTH

*West Valley-Mission Community College District (B)

14000 Fruitvale Avenue, Saratoga CA 95070-5698
County: Santa Clara FICE Identification: 029139
Unit ID: 125222
Telephone: (408) 741-2011 Carnegie Class: N/A
FAX Number: (408) 867-8273
URL: www.wvm.edu

01 Chancellor .... Mr. Bradley J. DAVIS
04 Exec Assistant to Chancellor/BOT .... Ms. Rebecca ALVAREZ
15 Assoc Vice Chanc Human Resources .... Mr. Eric RAMONES
13 Assoc Vice Chanc Info/Educ Tech .... Mr. Dan BORGES
18 Assoc VC Facility Dev & Operations .... Mr. Javier CASTRUITA
19 Chief of Police .... Mr. Dalton Chris ROLEN
10 Assoc Vice Chanc Finance/Admin .... Ms. Ngoc CHIM
86 Assoc VC Govt Rels/Public Comm .... Mr. Manny CAPPELLO

*Mission College (C)

3000 Mission College Boulevard, Santa Clara CA 95054-1897
County: Santa Clara FICE Identification: 021191
Unit ID: 118930
Telephone: (408) 855-5000 Carnegie Class: Assoc/HT-Mix Trad/Non
FAX Number: N/A Calendar System: Semester
URL: www.missioncollege.edu
Established: 1976 Annual Undergrad Tuition & Fees (In-District): $1,200
Enrollment: 6,504 Coed
Affiliation or Control: State/Local IRS Status: 501(c)3
Highest Offering: Associate Degree
Accreditation: WJ

02 President .... Dr. Seher AWAN
05 Vice President of Instruction .... Ms. Lorrie RANCK
32 Vice President Student Services .... Dr. Omar MURILLO
11 Vice Pres Administrative Services .... Mr. Danny NGUYEN
13 Vice Chancellor Info Technology .... Mr. Dan BORGES
15 Vice Chance Human Resources .... Mr. Eric RAMONES
35 Dean of Student Support Services .... Mr. Richard ALFARO
20 Dean of Instruction .... Ms. Valerie JENSEN
26 Director of Marketing/Public Rels .... Mr. Niall ADLER
50 Dean Business/Tech & Kinesiology .... Mr. Jeff PALLIN
19 Chief of Police .... Lt. Chris ROLEN
18 Manager of Facilities .... Mr. Don HOUSTON
07 Director of Admissions .... Vacant
09 Director of Institutional Research .... Mr. Brian GOO
84 Dean Enroll & Financial Svcs .... Ms. Veronica MARTINEZ
04 Sr Exec Assistant to the President .... Ms. Milani ZEPEDA
76 Dean of Health Occupations .... Ms. Yuko KAWASAKI
81 Dean of Math/Science & Engineering .... Mr. Clement LAM
83 Dean Humanities/Social Sci & Art .... Mr. Brian MILLER
75 Dean of Career Education .... Ms. Jackie ESCAJEDA
101 Exec Asst of the Board of Trustees .... Ms. Rebecca ALVAREZ
102 Assistant to Advancement/Foundation .... Ms. Nicole AGUINALDO
103 Director Workforce Development .... Mr. Rob GAMBLE
104 Director of International Programs .... Ms. Chigusa KATOKU
22 Director Student Equity & Success .... Mr. Ken SONGCO
41 Athletic Director .... Mr. John VLAHOS
96 Director of Purchasing .... Mr. Michael ROBINS

*West Valley College (D)

14000 Fruitvale Avenue, Saratoga CA 95070-5698
County: Santa Clara FICE Identification: 001338
Unit ID: 125499
Telephone: (408) 867-2200 Carnegie Class: Assoc/HT-Mix Trad/Non
FAX Number: (408) 867-5033 Calendar System: Semester
URL: www.westvalley.edu
Established: 1963 Annual Undergrad Tuition & Fees (In-District): $1,486
Enrollment: 7,513 Coed
Affiliation or Control: State/Local IRS Status: 501(c)3
Highest Offering: Associate Degree
Accreditation: WJ, ART, MUS

02 President .... Ms. Stephanie KASHIMA
05 VP Instruction .... Ms. Stacy GLEIXNER
32 VP Student Services .... Ms. Debra GRIFFITH
10 VP Administrative Services .... Ms. Marilyn MORIKANG
20 Dean Instruction .... Mr. Chris DYER
111 Executive Director of Advancement .... Ms. Melissa JOHNS
36 Dean Career Pgm/Wrkforce Dev .... Mr. Bradley WEISBERG
26 Director Marketing/Communications .... Vacant
121 Dean Academic Counseling .... Mr. Murrell GREEN
100 Assoc Vice Chanc Human Resources .... Mr. Eric RAMONES
57 Dean School of Art & Design .... Ms. Shannon PRICE
22 Dir of Student Equity Experience .... Ms. Stacy NOJIMA
18 Chief Facilities/Physical Plant .... Mr. Bill TAYLOR
37 Dir Student Financial Aid/Admiss .... Vacant
41 Dean of Athletics .... Mr. John VLAHOS

Westcliff University (E)

17877 Von Karan Avenue, #400, Irvine CA 92614
County: Orange Identification: 667203
Unit ID: 490133
Telephone: (888) 491-8686 Carnegie Class: Spec-4-yr-Bus
FAX Number: (888) 409-7306 Calendar System: Trimester
URL: www.westcliff.edu
Established: 1993 Annual Undergrad Tuition & Fees: $13,560
Enrollment: 3,214 Coed
Affiliation or Control: Proprietary IRS Status: Proprietary
Highest Offering: Doctorate
Accreditation: WC, ACBSP, LAW

01 CEO/President .... Dr. Anthony LEE
05 CAO/VP Academic Affairs .... Dr. Julie CIANCIO
10 Chief Financial Officer .... Mr. Sean MURRAY
06 Director of Registrar Office .... Ms. Amanda OLMOS

Western Covenant University (F)

680 Wilshire Place, Ste 310, Los Angeles CA 90005
County: Los Angeles Identification: 667350
Telephone: (213) 293-1771 Carnegie Class: Not Classified
FAX Number: (213) 896-7265 Calendar System: Quarter
URL: www.wcuniversity.edu
Established: 2014 Annual Undergrad Tuition & Fees: N/A
Enrollment: N/A Coed
Affiliation or Control: Independent Non-Profit IRS Status: 501(c)3
Highest Offering: Master's
Accreditation: TRACS

01 President/CEO .... David K. OH
05 Chief Academic Officer .... Ilsoo LEE
10 Chief Financial Officer .... Vacant

Western University of Health Sciences (G)

309 E 2nd Street, Pomona CA 91766-1854
County: Los Angeles FICE Identification: 024827
Unit ID: 112525
Telephone: (909) 623-6116 Carnegie Class: Spec-4-yr-Med
FAX Number: N/A Calendar System: Semester
URL: www.westernu.edu
Established: 1977 Annual Graduate Tuition & Fees: N/A
Enrollment: 3,813 Coed
Affiliation or Control: Independent Non-Profit IRS Status: 501(c)3
Highest Offering: Doctorate; No Undergraduates
Accreditation: WC, ARCPA, DENT, NURSE, OPT, OSTEO, PHAR, POD, PTA, VET

01 President .... Dr. Robin FARIAS-EISNER
05 Interim Provost & CAO .... Dr. Paula CRONE
10 Interim CFO & Treasurer .... Mr. Joshua MCFARLEN
11 Sr VP & COO .... Dr. Clive HOUSTON-BROWN
46 Interim Sr VP Research .... Dr. Bradley HENSON
32 SVP Univ Student Affs/Enroll Mgmt . Dr. Beverly SANKS GUIDRY
111 Sr VP University Advancement .... Dr. Diane ABRAHAM
15 VP Human Resources Admin .... Ms. Linda EMILIO
13 Assoc VP of IT & Deputy COO .... Ms. Denise CORNISH
88 Assoc VP Ctr for Excel in Teach/Lrn .... Tim WOOD
25 Asst VP Spons Pgms/Contract Mgmt .... Mr. Matthew KATZ
20 Associate Provost for Academic Dev .... Dr. Elizabeth REGA
106 Associate Provost Online Education .... Mr. Jonathan DAITCH
88 Associate Provost Ventures .... Dr. Dean SMYLIE
18 Exec Dir Facilities/Physical Plant .... Mr. Todd CLARK
86 VP of Community & Gov Affairs .... Mr. Jeffery KEATING
07 Director Admissions .... Ms. Marie ANDERSON
17 Exec Dir for Patient Ctr Clinic .... Dr. Robert WARREN
08 Dir University Library .... Ms. Karoline ALMANZAR
37 Co-Director of Financial Aid .... Ms. Theresa POULLARD
37 Co-Director of Financial Aid .... Ms. Linda FRENZA
14 Senior Director IT/Business Process .... Ms. Denise WILCOX
96 Director of Procurement Services .... Mr. Michael BUTLER
26 VP & Chief Communications Officer .... Ms. Barbara O'MALLEY
88 Sr VP IEPE .... Dr. Stephanie BOWLIN
09 Director of Institutional Research .... Dr. Juan RAMIREZ
40 Campus Store Director .... Mr. Jesse CORRINGTON
63 Actg Dean Col of Osteopathic Med .... Dr. David CONNETT
52 Dean College of Dental Medicine .. Dr. Steven W. FRIEDRICHSEN
67 Dean College of Pharmacy .... Dr. Sunil PRABHU
88 Founding Dean College of Optometry .... Dr. Elizabeth HOPPE
88 Dean College of Podiatry .... Dr. Kathleen SATTERFIELD
76 Dean Col of Health Sciences .... Dr. Dee SCHILLING
66 Dean Col of Graduate Nursing .... Dr. Mary LOPEZ
74 Dean College of Veterinary Medicine .... Dr. Phil NELSON
63 Chr Dept Osteopath Manipulative Med .... Dr. Rebecca GIUSTI
88 Chair Dept of Physical Therapy .... Dr. Harsha DEOGHARE
88 Chair Dept of Health Sciences .... Ms. Jeanine BORLAND
88 Chair Physician Assistant Program .... Mr. Roy GUIZADO
63 Chair Department Family Medicine .... Dr. Kay KALOUSEK
06 Registrar .... Mr. Ivan NOE
19 Director Security/Safety .... Mr. David SEVESIND
29 Exec Director Alumni Relations .... Ms. Susan TERRAZAS
04 Executive Asst to President .... Ms. Liz PAWELL
102 Dir Foundation/Corporate Relations .... Ms. Leah SCHUELER
44 Exec Director of Annual Giving .... Ms. Kimberly CABRAL
16 Assoc VP Human Resources .... Ms. Cynthia FERRINI
43 Acting General Counsel .... Ms. Simone MILLER
88 Exec Director University Compliance .... Ms. Trena RICH
28 VP for HEAR .... Dr. Suresh APPAVOO

Westminster Theological Seminary in California (H)

1725 Bear Valley Parkway, Escondido CA 92027-4128
County: San Diego FICE Identification: 022768
Unit ID: 125718
Telephone: (760) 480-8474 Carnegie Class: Spec-4-yr-Faith
FAX Number: (760) 480-0252 Calendar System: Semester
URL: www.wscal.edu
Established: 1979 Annual Graduate Tuition & Fees: N/A
Enrollment: 134 Coed
Affiliation or Control: Independent Non-Profit IRS Status: 501(c)3
Highest Offering: Master's; No Undergraduates
Accreditation: WC, THEOL

01 President .... Rev. Joel KIM
05 Academic Dean .... Dr. Ryan GLOMSRUD
11 Vice President for Administration .... Dr. Marcus MCARTHUR
111 Vice President for Advancement .... Ms. Dawn DOORN
10 Chief Financial Officer .... Mr. Brett WATSON
84 VP for Enrollment Management .... Mr. Mark MACVEY
08 Library Director .... Mr. James LUND
32 Dean of Students .... Rev. Charles TEDRICK
06 Registrar .... Mr. Ryan THOMAS

Westmont College (I)

955 La Paz Road, Santa Barbara CA 93108-1089
County: Santa Barbara FICE Identification: 001341
Unit ID: 125727
Telephone: (805) 565-6000 Carnegie Class: Bac-A&S
FAX Number: (805) 565-7006 Calendar System: Semester
URL: www.westmont.edu
Established: 1937 Annual Undergrad Tuition & Fees: $48,180
Enrollment: 1,226 Coed
Affiliation or Control: Independent Non-Profit IRS Status: 501(c)3
Highest Offering: Baccalaureate
Accreditation: WC, MUS

01 President .... Dr. Gayle D. BEEBE
05 Provost .... Dr. Kim DENU
10 VP Finance .... Mr. Douglas W. JONES
32 VP Student Life/Dean of Students .... Dr. Edee SCHULZE
111 VP for Advancement & IT .... Dr. Reed L. SHEARD
84 VP Enrollment/Mktg/Communications .... Mrs. Irene NELLER
121 Dean of Student Success/Engagement .... Dr. Angela D'AMOUR
39 Dean of Students for Res Life .... Dr. Stu CLEEK
06 Registrar .... Mrs. Michelle M. HARDLEY
20 Vice Provost .... Dr. Patti HUNTER
12 Executive Dir of Westmont Downtown .... Dr. Rick OSTRANDER
15 Associate VP of Human Resources .... Mrs. Greta BRUNEEL
18 Director of Physical Plant .... Mr. Thomas BEVERIDGE
21 Controller .... Mr. Paul V. LARSON
23 Director of Student Health Services .... Dr. Rob HUGHES
09 Dir of Research/Planning & Implem .... Dr. Tim LOOMER
19 Chief of Public Safety .... Mr. William BOYD
26 Director of Public Events .... Mrs. Mary Pat WHITNEY
36 Director of Career/Development .... Mr. Paul BRADFORD
37 Director of Financial Aid .... Mr. Sean SMITH
38 Director Counseling Services .... Dr. Eric NELSON
39 Director of Housing/Parking .... Mr. Jon YOUNG
40 Asst Director Bookstore .... Mrs. Joanne GISH
41 Athletic Director .... Mr. Robert RUIZ
42 Campus Pastor .... Dr. Scott LISEA
96 Assc Dir Procurement/Auxiliary Svcs .... Mr. Bill GROENEVELD
28 Director of Intercultural Programs .... Mr. Blake THOMAS
88 Dean of Curriculum/Educ Effective .... Dr. Tatiana NAZARENKO
07 Senior Director of Admission .... Mr. Mike MCKINNISS
88 Dir of Institutional Resilience .... Mr. Jason TAVAREZ
88 Associate Dean of Faculty .... Dr. Eileen MCQUADE
88 Assistant VP for Advancement .... Mrs. Sarah CAMP
110 Assoc VP for Advancement .... Mr. Steve BAKER
112 Assistant VP for Major Gifts .... Mr. Alex NIZET
27 Dir of Marketing & Recruitment .... Mrs. Dominique LOFTUS
88 Dir of Conference Services .... Mrs. Melinda HARRIMAN
08 Dir of Library & Information Svcs .... Mrs. Jana MAYFIELD MULLEN
04 Admin Assistant to the President .... Mrs. Addie SMITH

Whittier College (A)

13406 E Philadelphia St, PO Box 634,
Whittier CA 90608-4413
County: Los Angeles FICE Identification: 001342
Unit ID: 125763
Telephone: (562) 907-4200 Carnegie Class: Bac-A&S
FAX Number: (562) 907-4242 Calendar System: 4/1/4
URL: www.whittier.edu
Established: 1887 Annual Undergrad Tuition & Fees: $49,514
Enrollment: 1,564 Coed
Affiliation or Control: Independent Non-Profit IRS Status: 501(c)3
Highest Offering: Doctorate
Accreditation: WC, SW

01 President .... Dr. Linda OUBRÉ
10 Vice Pres Finance & Administration .... Mr. James DUNKELMAN
05 VP Acad Affs/Dean of Faculty .... Dr. Sal JOHNSTON
88 VP of Innovation & New Ventures .... Mr. Timothy ANDERSON
84 VP Enrollment Management .... Mr. Falone SERNA
30 VP Development .... Ms. Eva SEVCIKOVA
32 Interim VP & Dean of Students ... Dr. Deanna MERINO CONTINO
37 Director of Student Financial Aid .... Ms. Julie ALDAMA
08 Interim Library Director and System .... Mr. Nick VELKAVRH
20 Dir Whtr Scholar Pgm/Assc Acad Dean .... Ms. Andrea REHN
26 VP Marketing & Communication .... Ms. Ana Lilia BARRAZA
13 Director of Computing Services .... Mr. Troy GREENUP
09 Dir of Institutional Research .... Mr. Gary WHISENAND
41 Director of Athletics .... Mr. Rock CARTER
62 Dir Lib Educ Pgm/Assoc Acad Dean .... Dr. Fritz SMITH
15 VP/Chief Administrative Officer .... Ms. Cynthia JOSEPH
19 Director of Campus Safety .... Mr. Jose PADILLA
06 Registrar .... Ms. Julie T. KHELLA

William Carey International University (B)

1605 East Elizabeth St, Pasadena CA 91104
County: Los Angeles Identification: 667383
Telephone: (626) 398-2222 Carnegie Class: Not Classified
FAX Number: N/A Calendar System: Trimester
URL: www.wciu.edu
Established: 1977 Annual Graduate Tuition & Fees: N/A
Enrollment: N/A Coed
Affiliation or Control: Independent Non-Profit IRS Status: 501(c)3
Highest Offering: Master's; No Undergraduates
Accreditation: DEAC

01 Acting President .... Dr. Peter MCLALLEN
05 Vice President of Academic Affairs .... Dr. Daniel LOW
03 Executive Vice President .... Vacant
10 Controller .... Mr. John HUSMAN
06 Registrar .... Mr. Tom RUTHERFORD

William Jessup University (C)

2121 University Avenue, Rocklin CA 95765-3707
County: Placer FICE Identification: 001281
Unit ID: 122728
Telephone: (916) 577-2200 Carnegie Class: Masters/M
FAX Number: (916) 577-2203 Calendar System: Semester
URL: www.jessup.edu
Established: 1939 Annual Undergrad Tuition & Fees: $37,000
Enrollment: 1,840 Coed
Affiliation or Control: Independent Non-Profit IRS Status: 501(c)3
Highest Offering: Master's
Accreditation: WC, #ACBSP

01 President .... Dr. John JACKSON
13 Chief Operating Officer .... Mrs. Judy RENTZ
05 Vice Pres Academic Affairs .... Dr. Phil ESCAMILLA
10 Chief Financial Officer .... Mrs. Diane AHN
30 Chief Development Officer .... Mr. Gordon FLINN
108 Accreditation Liaison Officer .... Dr. Kay LLOVIO
15 Human Resources Manager .... Ms. Linda GIUSTI
111 Assoc VP of Advancement .... Mr. David PINESCHI
84 Assoc VP of Enrollment Management .... Mr. Steve JIN
13 Assoc VP of Information Services .... Mr. Ben HUFFMAN
51 Assoc VP of Prof & Cont Education .... Dr. Linda SOMMERVILLE
20 AVP of Strategic Academic Projects .... Dr. Erin HILL
32 Assoc VP of Student Services .... Mr. Kevin PISCHKE
50 Dean of School of Business .... Dr. Stephen STROMBECK
53 Dean of School of Education .... Dr. Nathan HERZOG
81 Dean of School of Nat/Appl Science .. Dr. George STUBBLEFIELD
83 Dean of School of Psychology .... Dr. Jeff STONE
73 Dean of Sch of Theology/Leadership .... Dr. David TIMMS
06 Registrar .... Mrs. Tina PETERSEN
07 Director Admissions (Non Trad) .... Mrs. Angela SWITZER
07 Director Admissions (Trad UG) .... Mrs. Cathy MORGAN
29 Director Alumni Affairs .... Mrs. Marcie LEMOS
41 Director Athletics .... Mr. Lance VON VOGT
19 Director Campus Safety .... Mr. Paul YBARRA
36 Director Career & Life Planning .... Ms. Christy JEWELL
88 Director Church Relations .... Mr. Jim JESSUP
26 Director Communications & Marketing .... Mr. Aaron ROBBINS
09 Director Institutional Research .... Mrs. Karen LAMBRECHTSEN
08 Director Library Services .... Ms. Belinda SILVA
37 Director Student Financial Services .... Mr. John SWAN
35 Director Student Life .... Mr. Brandon FARMER
121 Director Student Success & Advising .... Dr. Denise WOLF
42 Campus Pastor .... Mr. PJ GARZA

Woodbury University (D)

7500 North Glenoaks Boulevard, Burbank CA 91504-7520
County: Los Angeles FICE Identification: 001343
Unit ID: 125897
Telephone: (818) 767-0888 Carnegie Class: Masters/S
FAX Number: (818) 767-3470 Calendar System: Semester
URL: www.woodbury.edu
Established: 1884 Annual Undergrad Tuition & Fees: $42,596
Enrollment: 1,132 Coed
Affiliation or Control: Independent Non-Profit IRS Status: 501(c)3
Highest Offering: Master's
Accreditation: WC, ACBSP, ART, CIDA

01 President .... David M. STEELE-FIGUEREDO
101 Secretary of the Institution/Board .... Seta JAVOR
05 Senior Vice Pres Academic Affairs .... Randy STAUFFER
10 VP Finance & Accounting .... David LEUNG
15 VP Administration & Human Resources .... Natalie AVALOS
84 Assoc VP Admissions .... Sabrina TAYLOR
30 VP Development & Marketing .... David MASCARINA
13 VP Information Technology .... Eric WANG
32 Dean of Students .... Tracci JOHNSON
50 Dean School of Business .... Joan MARQUES
48 Dean School of Architecture .... Ingalill WAHLROOS-RITTER
07 Director of Admissions .... Ani BONIADI
20 Dean of Faculty .... Christoph KORNER
49 Int Dean College of Liberal Arts .... Reuben ELLIS
09 Director of Institutional Research .... Christie RAINEY
82 Dean of International Affairs .... Mauro DIAZ
08 University Librarian .... Nedra PETERSON
06 Registrar .... Adam BROWN
19 Director Security/Safety .... Natalie AVALOS
04 Admin Assistant to the President .... Andrea BRUNO

World Mission University (E)

500 Shatto Place, Suite 600, Los Angeles CA 90020-1789
County: Los Angeles FICE Identification: 038683
Unit ID: 401223
Telephone: (213) 385-2322 Carnegie Class: Spec-4-yr-Faith
FAX Number: (213) 385-2332 Calendar System: Semester
URL: www.wmu.edu
Established: 1989 Annual Undergrad Tuition & Fees: $6,440
Enrollment: 370 Coed
Affiliation or Control: Independent Non-Profit IRS Status: 501(c)3
Highest Offering: First Professional Degree
Accreditation: BI, THEOL

01 President .... Dr. Paul S. LIM
05 Vice President/Chief Acad Officer .... Dr. Seon Mook SHIN
32 Dean of Student Affairs .... Dr. Im Sang YOON
10 Chief Financial Officer .... Rev. Paul J. LIM
06 Registrar .... Ms. Ju Young BAEK
37 Dir Financial Aid/Admissions Coord .... Ms. KyungHae KIM

The Wright Institute (F)

2728 Durant Avenue, Berkeley CA 94704-1796
County: Alameda FICE Identification: 008846
Unit ID: 126012
Telephone: (510) 841-9230 Carnegie Class: Spec-4-yr-Other Health
FAX Number: (510) 841-0167 Calendar System: Trimester
URL: www.wi.edu
Established: 1969 Annual Graduate Tuition & Fees: N/A
Enrollment: 514 Coed
Affiliation or Control: Independent Non-Profit IRS Status: 501(c)3
Highest Offering: Doctorate; No Undergraduates
Accreditation: WC, CLPSY, IPSY

01 President .... Mr. Peter DYBWAD
05 VP for Academic Affairs .... Dr. Gilbert NEWMAN
10 VP of Finance & Administrative Affs .... Ms. Tricia O'REILLY
32 Dean of Students/Registrar .... Ms. Ginny MORGAN
07 Dir of Admissions/Student Svcs .... Mr. John PITTS
08 Library Director .... Mr. Jason STRAUSS
37 Director of Financial Aid .... Ms. Mindy BERGERON

Yeshiva Ohr Elchonon Chabad/ West Coast Talmudical Seminary (G)

7215 Waring Avenue, Los Angeles CA 90046-7660
County: Los Angeles FICE Identification: 022624
Unit ID: 126076
Telephone: (323) 937-3763 Carnegie Class: Spec-4-yr-Faith
FAX Number: (323) 937-9456 Calendar System: Semester
URL: www.yoec.edu
Established: 1953 Annual Undergrad Tuition & Fees: $15,700
Enrollment: 135 Male
Affiliation or Control: Independent Non-Profit IRS Status: 501(c)3
Highest Offering: Baccalaureate
Accreditation: RABN

01 Chief Executive Officer .... Rabbi Ezra B. SCHOCHET
03 Executive Vice President .... Rabbi Mendel SPALTER
05 Curriculum Super/Education Counsel .... Rabbi Shimon RAICHIK
37 Director Student Financial Aid .... Mrs. Hendy TAUBER
06 Registrar .... Rabbi Chaim CITRON
38 Director Student Counseling .... Rabbi Mendel SCHAPIRO
08 Head Librarian .... Rabbi Ben Zion OSTER

Yo San University of Traditional Chinese Medicine (H)

13315 W Washington Boulevard, Los Angeles CA 90066
County: Los Angeles FICE Identification: 030982
Unit ID: 401250
Telephone: (310) 577-3000 Carnegie Class: Spec-4-yr-Other Health
FAX Number: (310) 577-3033 Calendar System: Trimester
URL: www.yosan.edu
Established: 1989 Annual Undergrad Tuition & Fees: N/A
Enrollment: 136 Coed
Affiliation or Control: Independent Non-Profit IRS Status: 501(c)3
Highest Offering: Doctorate; No Lower Division
Accreditation: ACUP

01 President/CEO .... Dr. Lawrence LAU
10 Chief Financial Officer .... Bruce KARIYA
06 Director Operations & Registrar .... Tora FLINT
63 Dean MATCM Program .... Dr. Brady CHIN
63 Dean DAOM Program .... Dr. Robert HOFFMAN
84 Director Enrollment Management .... Daouia AMRIR
37 Financial Aid Coordinator .... Vacant
32 Library Svcs & Student Affairs Ofcr .... Sean GATES

*Yosemite Community College District (I)

PO Box 4065, Modesto CA 95352-4065
County: Stanislaus FICE Identification: 009146
Unit ID: 126100
Telephone: (209) 575-6509 Carnegie Class: N/A
FAX Number: (209) 575-6565
URL: www.yosemite.edu

01 Chancellor .... Mr. Henry YONG
11 Vice Chancellor Administrative Svcs .... Mr. Trevor STEWART
05 Vice Chancellor Educ Support Svcs .... Mr. G. H JAVAHERIPOUR
13 Sr Dir Information Technology .... Mr. Joshua HASH
04 Executive Assistant to Chancellor .... Ms. Graciela MOLINA
26 District Director Public Affairs .... Vacant
15 Sr Director Human Resources .... Ms. Kathren PRITCHARD
19 Dir District Security/Comp & EP .... Vacant
117 Dir Risk Management/Purch & Rec .... Ms. Dorothy PIMENTEL

*Columbia College (J)

11600 Columbia College Drive, Sonora CA 95370-8580
County: Tuolumne FICE Identification: 007707
Unit ID: 112561
Telephone: (209) 588-5100 Carnegie Class: Assoc/HT-High Trad
FAX Number: (209) 588-5104 Calendar System: Semester
URL: www.gocolumbia.edu
Established: 1968 Annual Undergrad Tuition & Fees (In-District): $1,270
Enrollment: 2,132 Coed
Affiliation or Control: State/Local IRS Status: 501(c)3
Highest Offering: Associate Degree
Accreditation: WJ, ACFEI

02 President .... Dr. Lena TRAN
05 Vice Pres Instruction .... Dr. Raelene JUAREZ
11 VP College & Administrative Svcs .... Vacant
32 Vice Pres Student Services .... Dr. Melissa RABY
72 Dean Instruct Svcs/Career Tech Educ .... Mr. Steve AMADOR
49 Dean of Instruction/Arts & Sciences .... Ms. Raelene JUAREZ
41 Athletic Director .... Ms. LaDeane HANSTEN
37 Financial Aid Manager .... Ms. Marnie SHIVELY
10 Fiscal Services Supervisor .... Ms. Amy MCKINNEY
30 Director of Development .... Ms. Amy NILSON
06 Registrar .... Ms. Lesley MICHTAVY
09 Research Analyst .... Mr. Matthew CONNOT
124 Director of Outreach/Retention .... Mr. Michael IGOE
18 Campus Facilities Manager .... Mr. Steve ANDRADE

*Modesto Junior College (K)

435 College Avenue, Modesto CA 95350-9977
County: Stanislaus FICE Identification: 001240
Unit ID: 118976
Telephone: (209) 575-6550 Carnegie Class: Bac/Assoc-Assoc Dom
FAX Number: (209) 575-6630 Calendar System: Semester
URL: www.mjc.edu
Established: 1921 Annual Undergrad Tuition & Fees (In-District): $1,270
Enrollment: 16,365 Coed
Affiliation or Control: State/Local IRS Status: 501(c)3
Highest Offering: Baccalaureate
Accreditation: WJ, COARC, MAC

02 President .... Dr. Santanu BANDYOPADHYAY
05 Vice President for Instruction .... Dr. Brian SANDERS
32 Vice Pres for Student Services .... Dr. Andrea WILSON
10 VP College & Administrative Svcs .... Dr. Sarah SCHRADER
121 Vice Chanc of Educ Support Svcs .... Mr. G.H JAVAHERIPOUR
57 Div Dean Arts/Humanities/Comm .... Mr. Robert STEVENSON
83 Div Dean Business/Behav/Social Sci .... Dr. Nancy SILL
76 Div Dean Inst/All Hlth/Fam/Con Sci .... Ms. Martha ROBLES
79 Dean Literature/Language Arts .... Ms. Jillian DALY
54 Div Dean Science/Math/Engineering .... Dr. Laura MAKI
47 Dean Agri/Envir Science/Tech Ed .... Dr. Donald BORGES
88 Dean Public Safety/Tech Ed/Cmty Ed .... Mr. Pedro MENDEZ
09 Dean Institutional Effectiveness ... Mrs. Komal BANDYOPADHYAY
07 Director Admissions & Records .... Ms. Sonya OVIEDO

37 Director Student Financial Svcs ....Ms. Aurelia GONZALEZ
26 Director of Public Relations ....Mrs. Jeanette FONTANA
04 Exec Assistant to the President ....Mrs. Sabrina MIRANDA
08 Director Library & Learning Center ....Ms. Olga CASTANEDA
101 Exec Assistant to the Chancellor ....Ms. Graciela MOLINA
102 Executive Director of Foundation ....Mr. Keenon KRICK
103 Dean Workforce Dev & Lifelong Lrng ....Ms. Vickie MULVANEY-TRASK
106 Dean Instruction & Student Lrng ....Mr. Patrick BETTENCOURT
19 Manager of Campus Safety Operations ....Mr. Harry DAVIS
41 AD/Dean of Physical/Rec/Health Educ ....Mr. Nick STAVRIANOUDAKIS

The Young Americans College of Performing Arts (A)

1132 Olympic Dr, Corona CA 92881

County: Riverside | Identification: 667330 | Unit ID: 493619

Telephone: (951) 493-6753 | Carnegie Class: Spec 2-yr-A&S

FAX Number: (951) 493-6793 | Calendar System: Semester

URL: yacollege.edu

Established: 2002 | Annual Undergrad Tuition & Fees: $14,030

Enrollment: 27 | Coed

Affiliation or Control: Independent Non-Profit | IRS Status: 501(c)3

Highest Offering: Associate Degree

Accreditation: WJ

01 Chief Executive Officer ....Mr. Leif GREEN
05 Dean of Instruction ....Mr. Mohammad SHAHISAMAN
32 Dean of Students ....Ms. Kisha BASHKIHARATEE
10 Vice President of Finance ....Mrs. Tayla FRANKLIN

*Yuba Community College District (B)

3301 E. Onstott Road, Yuba City CA 95991

County: Yuba | Identification: 666478

Telephone: (530) 741-6700 | Carnegie Class: N/A

FAX Number: N/A

URL: www.yccd.edu

01 Interim Chancellor ....Dr. James L. HOUPIS
05 VC Educ Planning & Services ....Dr. Sonja LOLLAND
11 VC Administrative Services ....Ms. Kuldeep KAUR
32 Vice Pres Student Services ....Ms. Tonia TERESH
13 Chief Technology Officer ....Mr. Devin CROSBY
25 Grants/Research/Development Officer ....Vacant
15 Chief Human Resources Officer ....Ms. Maribel GAYTAN
37 Director of Financial Aid ....Ms. Kimberly REED
10 Director of Fiscal Services ....Mr. Divinder BAINS

*Woodland Community College (C)

2300 East Gibson Road, Woodland CA 95776-5156

County: Yolo | FICE Identification: 041438 | Unit ID: 455512

Telephone: (530) 661-5700 | Carnegie Class: Assoc/HVT-High Non

FAX Number: (530) 666-9028 | Calendar System: Semester

URL: https://wcc.yccd.edu/

Established: 2008 | Annual Undergrad Tuition & Fees (In-District): $1,124

Enrollment: 4,598 | Coed

Affiliation or Control: State/Local | IRS Status: 501(c)3

Highest Offering: Associate Degree

Accreditation: WJ

02 President ....Dr. Art PIMENTEL
05 Vice Pres Academic/Student Svcs ....Ms. Kasey GARDNER
32 VP Student Services ....Ms. Lisceth BRAZIL-CRUZ
04 Executive Asst to President ....Mr. Edwin ORTEGA BELTRAN
88 Int Exec Asst to Vice President ....Ms. Pamela PIMENTEL
75 Dean Career Tech Educ/Workforce Dev ....Ms. Sandra FOWLER
49 Dean Arts and Sciences ....Ms. Shannon REED
121 Dean Student Succes/Inst Effective ....Dr. Lisceth BRAZIL-CRUZ
37 Director Student Financial Aid ....Ms. Kimberly REED
06 District Registrar ....Ms. Sonya HORN
07 District Director of Matriculation ....Ms. Ariana VELASCO

*Yuba College (D)

2088 N Beale Road, Marysville CA 95901-7699

County: Yuba | FICE Identification: 001344 | Unit ID: 126119

Telephone: (530) 741-6700 | Carnegie Class: Assoc/HVT-Mix Trad/Non

FAX Number: (530) 741-3541 | Calendar System: Semester

URL: https://yc.yccd.edu/

Established: 1927 | Annual Undergrad Tuition & Fees (In-District): $1,128

Enrollment: 5,175 | Coed

Affiliation or Control: State/Local | IRS Status: 501(c)3

Highest Offering: Associate Degree

Accreditation: WJ, RAD

02 President ....Dr. Tawny M. DOTSON
05 Vice President of Instruction ....Mr. Jeremy BROWN
32 Vice President of Student Services ....Dr. Tonia TERESH
103 Dean of CTE & Workforce Development ....Mr. Dwayne NEWMAN
09 Dean Inst Research/Student Success ....Mr. Jeremy BROWN
38 Director Counseling ....Ms. Cristina SANCHEZ
88 Dir Child Dev Center/Foster Care ....Ms. Karen STANIS
66 Director Nursing/Allied Health .... Ms. Toni CHRISTOPHERSON
19 Director Public Safety ....Mr. Mark COVINGTON
57 Dean of Arts & Education ....Ms. Kristina VANNUCCI

37 Director Financial Aid ....Mr. Martin GUTIERREZ
68 Director Athletics/Health/PE ....Mr. Erick BURNS
81 Dean STEM & Outreach Centers ....Dr. Michael BAGLEY
121 Director Academic Excellence ....Vacant
04 Exec Assistant to the President ....Ms. Zulema ZERMENO
06 Registrar ....Ms. Sonya HORN
84 Director of Enrollment Services ....Vacant
10 Chief Financial/Business Officer ....Ms. Kuldeep KAUR
101 Secretary of the Institution/Board ....Ms. Kathryn WILKINS
102 Director Foundation/Corporate Rels ....Mr. Jay LOWDEN
15 Chief Human Resources Officer ....Mr. Jake HURLEY

Zaytuna College (E)

2401 Le Conte Avenue, Berkeley CA 94709

County: Alameda | Identification: 667230 | Unit ID: 458575

Telephone: (510) 356-4760 | Carnegie Class: Not Classified

FAX Number: (510) 327-2688 | Calendar System: Semester

URL: www.zaytuna.edu

Established: 2009 | Annual Undergrad Tuition & Fees: $19,250

Enrollment: N/A | Coed

Affiliation or Control: Independent Non-Profit | IRS Status: 501(c)3

Highest Offering: Master's

Accreditation: WC

01 President ....Hamza YUSUF
05 Provost ....Dr. Omar QURESHI
20 Dean of Faculty ....Dr. Mark Damien DELP
32 Director of Student Life ....Dawood YASIN
108 Dir of Inst Effectiveness/Plng ....Sumaira AKHTAR
07 Director of Admissions ....Faisal HAMID
15 Human Reources Manager ....Pepy PRAWIRA
10 Director of Administrative Svcs ....Naima JAMESON

COLORADO

Adams State University (F)

208 Edgemont Boulevard, Alamosa CO 81101-2320

County: Alamosa | FICE Identification: 001345 | Unit ID: 126182

Telephone: (719) 587-7011 | Carnegie Class: Masters/L

FAX Number: N/A | Calendar System: Semester

URL: www.adams.edu

Established: 1921 | Annual Undergrad Tuition & Fees (In-State): $9,560

Enrollment: 3,164 | Coed

Affiliation or Control: State | IRS Status: 501(c)3

Highest Offering: Doctorate

Accreditation: HLC, CACREP, MUS, NURSE

01 Interim President ....Dr. David D. TANDBERG
04 Executive Asst to the President ....Ms. Carol OSBORN
05 VP for Academic Affairs ....Dr. Kent BUCHANAN
26 VP CE&C ....Mr. Bruce ROSENGRANT
18 Director of Facilities Services ....Vacant
10 Chief Financial Officer ....Ms. Heather HEERSINK
20 Associate VP for Academic Affairs ....Ms. Margaret DOELL
32 Interim VP for Student Services ....Ms. Diane BRITTINGHAM
09 Senior Research Analyst ....Dr. Lee ALLARD
08 Director Library ....Mr. Jeffrey BULLINGTON
37 Director Student Financial Aid ....Ms. Heidi MARKEY
06 Registrar ....Ms. Belen MAESTAS
13 Chief Information Officer ....Mr. Kevin S. DANIEL
41 Athletic Director ....Ms. Katelyn SMITH
109 Director of Auxiliary Services ....Mr. Bruce DEL TONDO
28 Director of Diversity ....Vacant
38 Director Counseling/Career Svcs ....Ms. Aftin GILLESPIE
25 Chief Contract and Grants Administr ....Ms. Tawney BECKER
15 Director Human Resources ....Ms. Tracy ROGERS
102 Executive Director ASU Foundation ....Ms. Tammy L. LOPEZ
29 Director Alumni and Donor Relations ..... Ms. Ashley A. MAESTAS
39 Int Dir Res Life/Student Housing ....Mr. Mark PITTMAN
96 Director of Purchasing ....Ms. Renee VIGIL
19 Dir Adams State Univ Police Dept ....Ms. Erika DEROUIN
40 Director Bookstore ....Ms. Amy GOODWIN
50 School Director Business ....Dr. Liz HENSLEY
81 School Director STEM ....Dr. Matt NEHRING
53 School Director Education ....Dr. Curtis L. GARCIA
57 School Director V&PA ....Dr. John TAYLOR
88 School Director Kinesiology ....Dr. Terry DUPLER
88 School Director Counselor Educ ....Dr. Cheri MEDER
79 School Dir Humanities & Social Sci ....Dr. Colleen SCHAFFNER
66 School Director Nursing ....Dr. Melissa MILNER

Aims Community College (G)

Box 69, Greeley CO 80632-0069

County: Weld | FICE Identification: 007582 | Unit ID: 126207

Telephone: (970) 330-8008 | Carnegie Class: Assoc/HT-High Non

FAX Number: N/A | Calendar System: Semester

URL: www.aims.edu

Established: 1967 | Annual Undergrad Tuition & Fees (In-District): $2,762

Enrollment: 5,981 | Coed

Affiliation or Control: Local | IRS Status: 501(c)3

Highest Offering: Associate Degree

Accreditation: HLC, ADNUR, EMT, IFSAC, SURGT

01 President ....Dr. Leah L. BORNSTEIN
05 Executive Vice Pres & Academic Affs .... Dr. Russ ROTHAMER

10 VP Admin Services ....Mr. Chuck JENSEN
32 Vice President Student Affairs ....Vacant
26 Vice President Cmty & College Rels ....Vacant
20 Associate VP Academic Affairs ....Vacant
49 Dean Arts & Sciences ....Mr. Scott REICHEL
50 Dean Business & Technology ....Mr. Jim VERNON
80 Dean Public Svcs & Transportation .... Dr. Susan MORELAND
76 Dean Allied Health & Wellness ....Mr. Terry ANDERSON
35 Dean of Students ....Ms. Shannon MCCASLAND
102 Executive Director Foundation ....Ms. Kelly JACKSON
15 Exec Director/CHRO Employee Service ....Ms. Dee SHULTZ
09 Int Exec Dir Inst Research/Assess ....Mr. Jeffrey ADCOCK
114 Budget Director/Asst Controller ....Mr. Paul LIND
18 Exec Director Facilities/Operations ....Mr. Michael MILLSAPPS
37 Executive Director Financial Aid .... Mr. Chris PETERSON
06 Registrar ....Ms. Kelley CHRISTMAN
13 Exec Director IT Admin Services ....Ms. Andria BRABO
21 Assistant VP/Controller ....Ms. Kailey BLOCK
27 Exec Dir Comm/Public Info Ofcr ....Mr. Zachary MCFARLANE
12 Exec Campus Dir Loveland ....Ms. Heather LELCHOOK
12 Exec Campus Dir Windsor ....Ms. Mary GABRIEL
12 Exec Campus Dir Fort Lupton ....Ms. Julie LUEKENGA
04 Admin Assistant to the President ....Ms. Megan SELF

Arapahoe Community College (H)

5900 S Santa Fe Drive, Littleton CO 80120

County: Arapahoe | FICE Identification: 001346 | Unit ID: 126289

Telephone: (303) 797-4222 | Carnegie Class: Assoc/MT-VT-High Non

FAX Number: (303) 797-5935 | Calendar System: Semester

URL: www.arapahoe.edu

Established: 1965 | Annual Undergrad Tuition & Fees (In-State): $4,027

Enrollment: 12,001 | Coed

Affiliation or Control: State | IRS Status: Exempt

Highest Offering: Baccalaureate

Accreditation: HLC, ADNUR, CAHIIM, EMT, FUSER, MLTAD, NAEYC, NUR, PTAA

01 President ....Dr. Stephanie FUJII
05 Provost & Vice Pres of Instruction ....Dr. Cheryl CALHOUN
32 Vice President of Student Affairs ....Dr. Lisa MATYE EDWARDS
10 VP of Finance & Admin Svcs ....Dr. Belinda AARON
103 Vice Pres of Workforce/Economic Dev ....Dr. Eric DUNKER
35 Dean of Students ....Ms. Jennifer HUSUM
124 Exec Dir of Advising & Retention ....Mr. Mark NELSON
84 Assoc Dean of Enrollment Services ....Vacant
37 Director of Financial Aid ....Ms. Ariel MENDEZ
79 AVP/Dean Comm/Hum/Arts/Design ....Dr. Danielle STAPLES
81 Dean Mathematics & Sciences ....Vacant
69 Dean of Health and Public Services ....Dr. Darius NAVRAN
102 Executive Director Foundation ....Ms. Courtney LOEHFELM
13 Chief Information Technology Ofcr ....Mr. Jeff NESHEIM
21 AVP Fiscal & Admin Svcs ....Ms. Jill BECKER-LUTZ
19 Chief of Police ....Mr. Joseph MORRIS
09 Director Institutional Research ....Mr. Yared BELETE
08 Director Learning Resource Center ....Ms. Lisa CHESTNUT
26 Dir of Marketing/Public Relations .... Ms. Tina GRIESHEIMER
22 Assoc Dean Compliance & Equity ....Vacant
96 Purchasing Manager ....Mr. Daniel HOHN
15 Director Human Resources ....Ms. Angela JOHNSON
04 Executive Assistant ....Vacant
108 Exec Dir Institutional Assessment .... Dr. Terry BARMANN
06 Registrar ....Ms. Theresa GROFF
106 Director E-learning ....Ms. Lee C. CHRISTOPHER
28 Chief Inclusive Excellence Officer ....Ms. Quill PHILLIPS

Auguste Escoffier School of Culinary Arts (I)

637 South Broadway, Ste H, Boulder CO 80305

County: Boulder | FICE Identification: 037763 | Unit ID: 454810

Telephone: (303) 494-7988 | Carnegie Class: Spec 2-yr-A&S

FAX Number: N/A | Calendar System: Quarter

URL: www.escoffier.edu

Established: | Annual Undergrad Tuition & Fees: N/A

Enrollment: 7,600 | Coed

Affiliation or Control: Proprietary | IRS Status: Proprietary

Highest Offering: Associate Degree

Accreditation: CNCE, ACFEI

01 President ....Kirk BACHMANN
07 Director of Admissions ....Vacant
37 Director of Financial Aid ....*Jordan HAGEN
36 Director of Career Services ....Kate SWEASY
06 Registrar and Compliance Manager ....Vacant

Augustine Institute (J)

6160 S. Syracuse Way #310, Greenwood Village CO 80111

County: Arapahoe | Identification: 667219

Telephone: (303) 937-4420 | Carnegie Class: Not Classified

FAX Number: (303) 468-2933 | Calendar System: Semester

URL: augustineinstitute.org

Established: 2005 | Annual Graduate Tuition & Fees: N/A

Enrollment: N/A | Coed

Affiliation or Control: Roman Catholic | IRS Status: 501(c)3

Highest Offering: Master's; No Undergraduates

Accreditation: THEOL

01 President Mr. Tim GRAY
05 Academic Dean Dr. Sean INNERST
10 Chief Financial Officer Ms. Angie PARSONS

Bel-Rea Institute of Animal Technology (A)

1681 S Dayton Street, Denver CO 80247-3048
County: Arapahoe FICE Identification: 012670
Unit ID: 126359
Telephone: (303) 751-8700 Carnegie Class: Spec 2-yr-Health
FAX Number: (303) 751-9969 Calendar System: Quarter
URL: www.belrea.edu
Established: 1971 Annual Undergrad Tuition & Fees: $12,338
Enrollment: 306 Coed
Affiliation or Control: Proprietary IRS Status: Proprietary
Highest Offering: Associate Degree
Accreditation: ACCSC

01 President/Dean of Education Nolan RUCKER
11 Chief Operating & Compliance Ofcr Tracy PETERSON
04 Administrative Assistant Mimi PFAFF
32 Director Student Services John GANZAR
10 Director of Business and Financial Stacey SLOAN
18 Facilities Director Walter FRANKEWICZ
07 Admissions Manager Natalie ALAMAT
37 Financial Aid Manager Stasi BOTTINELLI
06 Registrar Jennifer HILLGROVE

College for Financial Planning (B)

9000 E. Nichols Avenue #200, Centennial CO 80112
County: Denver Identification: 666809
Telephone: (303) 220-1200 Carnegie Class: Not Classified
FAX Number: (303) 220-4940 Calendar System: Other
URL: www.cffp.edu
Established: 1972 Annual Graduate Tuition & Fees: N/A
Enrollment: N/A Coed
Affiliation or Control: Proprietary IRS Status: Proprietary
Highest Offering: Master's; No Undergraduates
Accreditation: HLC

01 President Mr. Dirk PANTONE
05 Vice Pres Academic Affairs/Provost Dr. Amy RELL

Colorado Academy of Veterinary Technology (C)

2766 Janitell Road, Colorado Springs CO 80906
County: El Paso FICE Identification: 041850
Unit ID: 461953
Telephone: (719) 219-9636 Carnegie Class: Spec 2-yr-Health
FAX Number: (719) 302-5577 Calendar System: Quarter
URL: www.cavt.edu
Established: 2007 Annual Undergrad Tuition & Fees: $17,354
Enrollment: 65 Coed
Affiliation or Control: Proprietary IRS Status: Proprietary
Highest Offering: Associate Degree
Accreditation: COE

01 CEO/Registrar Dr. Steve RUBIN
05 Program Director Ms. Stephanie WINTERS
38 Dir Student Counseling/Fin Aid Mrs. Traci THOMPSON
07 Admissions Officer Ms. Amanda TROSDAD

Colorado Christian University (D)

8787 W Alameda Avenue, Lakewood CO 80226-7499
County: Jefferson FICE Identification: 009401
Unit ID: 126669
Telephone: (303) 963-3000 Carnegie Class: Masters/L
FAX Number: (303) 963-3001 Calendar System: Semester
URL: www.ccu.edu
Established: 1914 Annual Undergrad Tuition & Fees: $34,750
Enrollment: 7,839 Coed
Affiliation or Control: Independent Non-Profit IRS Status: 501(c)3
Highest Offering: Doctorate
Accreditation: HLC, CACREP, MUS, NURSE

01 President Dr. Donald W. SWEETING
10 Executive Vice President/CFO Mr. Daniel L. COHRS
05 VP of Academic Affairs CUS Dr. Janet M. BLACK
05 VP of Academic Affairs CAGS Dr. Sarah SCHERLING
111 VP of University Advancement Mr. Eric HOGUE
18 VP of Campus Development Mr. Shannon DREYFUSS
32 VP of Enrollment & Student Life Mr. Jim S. MCCORMICK
35 Asst VP Stdnt Pgm/Dean of Students Ms. Sharon M. FELKER
84 VP of Enrollment CAGS Ms. Allison BURKHART
121 VP of Student Success Mr. Roger CHANDLER
50 Dean School of Business/Leadership Dr. Peter KERR
114 Chief Budget Officer Mr. Iain WIGHTMAN
72 Dean School of Business/Technology Dr. Mellani J. DAY
53 Dean School of Education Dr. Debora SCHEFFEL
83 Dean of Social Science & Humanities Dr. Ryan HARTWIG
53 Dean School of Education Prof Dr. Wendy WENDOVER
64 Dean School of Music Mr. Steven T. TAYLOR
73 Dean School of Theology Dr. David KOTTER
66 Dean of Nursing & Sciences Dr. Barbara WHITE
73 Dean of Biblical Studies & Theology Dr. Earl WAGGONER
07 Dir of Undergraduate Admissions Ms. Jo Leda MARTIN
43 University Counsel Mr. Thomas SCHEFFEL
21 Controller Mr. David SCHULL
06 University Registrar Mr. Jeremy WALLACE
41 Athletic Director Mr. Brian WALL
38 Director of Counseling Services Ms. Alisa SHANKS
88 Director of Centennial Institute Mr. Jeff HUNT
18 Director of Facilities Mr. Mathew J. GOTHARD
37 Asst VP of Financial Aid Mr. Steve M. WOODBURN
23 Director of Health Services Ms. Anita LIEBSCH
15 Asst VP Human Resources Mr. Rick GARRIS
13 Asst VP Information Systems/CIO Ms. Renee MARTIN
08 Library Director Ms. Gayle C. GUNDERSON
36 Director of Life Directions Center Ms. Leah SMITH
39 Director of Residence Life Mr. Neal ANDERSON
19 Director of Security Mr. John MAXFIELD
29 Director Alumni Relations Ms. Kara JOHNSTON
105 Asst VP of Creative Services Ms. Chris FRANZ
106 Asst VP of Technical Support Mr. Jordan HEERSINK
04 Executive Assistant to President Ms. Betsy SIMPSON

Colorado College (E)

14 E Cache La Poudre St.,
Colorado Springs CO 80903-3294
County: El Paso FICE Identification: 001347
Unit ID: 126678
Telephone: (719) 389-6000 Carnegie Class: Bac-A&S
FAX Number: (719) 634-4180 Calendar System: Other
URL: www.coloradocollege.edu
Established: 1874 Annual Undergrad Tuition & Fees: $60,864
Enrollment: 2,050 Coed
Affiliation or Control: Independent Non-Profit IRS Status: 501(c)3
Highest Offering: Master's
Accreditation: HLC

01 President Ms. L. Song RICHARDSON
03 SVP Mr. Mike EDMONDS
05 VP/Dean of Faculty Dr. Emily CHAN
05 VP/Dean of College Mr. Pedro DE ARAUJO
10 SVP Finance & Administration Mr. Robert G. MOORE
111 VP for Advancement Ms. Mary Ann GRAFFEO
100 EVP/Chief of Staff Ms. Manya WHITAKER
84 VP of Enrollment Mr. Mark HATCH
32 VP of Student Life/Dean of Students Ms. Rochelle DICKEY
13 Director Tech Solutions Services Mr. Tulio WOLFORD
119 Director IT Application & Security Ms. Katharina GROVES
45 AVP for Inst Planning/Effectiveness Ms. Lyrae WILLIAMS
110 Assoc VP Advancement Operations Ms. Molly BODNAR
37 Director of Financial Aid Ms. Shannon AMUNDSON
06 Registrar Mr. Phillip C. APODACA
26 VP of Communications/Marketing Mr. Todd WOODWARD
41 VP/Director of Athletics Mrs. Lesley IRVINE
104 Director of Global Education Mr. Allen BERTSCHE
15 Interim Assoc VP of Human Resources Ms. Laurie MOZINGO
07 Director of Admission Mr. Matthew BONSER
18 Assoc VP of Facilities Ms. Amber BRANNIGAN
19 Director of Campus Safety Ms. Cathy BUCKLEY
08 College Librarian Mr. Dustin FIFE
36 Director of the Career Center Ms. Megan NICKLAUS
29 Director of Family/Alumni Relations Ms. Brenda SOTO
09 Director Assessment/Program Review Dr. Amanda UDIS-KESSLER
21 Assoc VP of Finance Mrs. Lori SEAGER
105 Director of Web & Digital Media Ms. Karen TO
38 Director of Counseling Center Dr. Bill DOVE
22 Director of Accessibility Resources Ms. Jan EDWARDS
103 Dir Collaborative Cmty Engagement Ms. Jordan RADKE
04 Executive Asst to the President Ms. Lori HAMACHER

Colorado Mesa University (F)

1100 North Avenue, Grand Junction CO 81501-3122
County: Mesa FICE Identification: 001358
Unit ID: 127556
Telephone: (970) 248-1020 Carnegie Class: Bac-Diverse
FAX Number: (970) 248-1076 Calendar System: Semester
URL: www.coloradomesa.edu
Established: 1925 Annual Undergrad Tuition & Fees (In-State): $8,686
Enrollment: 9,110 Coed
Affiliation or Control: State IRS Status: 501(c)3
Highest Offering: Doctorate
Accreditation: HLC, ADNUR, #ARCPA, CAATE, MLTAD, MUS, NURSE, PNUR, RAD, SURGT, SW

01 President Mr. John MARSHALL
05 Vice Pres Academic Affairs Dr. Cher HENDRICKS
10 Vice President Financial/Admin Svcs Ms. Michelle QUINN
12 Actg Vice Pres Community College Ms. Brigitte SUNDERMANN
109 Asst Vice Pres Auxiliary Services Mr. Andy RODRIGUEZ
32 VP of Student Services Ms. Jody DIERS
13 VP of Information Technology/Comm Mr. Jeremy BROWN
08 Library Director Ms. Sylvia RAEL
30 Director of Development Vacant
37 Director Financial Aid Mr. Curt MARTIN
26 Director of Media Relations Vacant
06 Registrar Ms. Holly TEAL
09 Dir of Inst Research/Assessment Ms. Heather MCKIM
18 Actg Dir Facilities/Physical Plant Mr. David DETWILER
29 Director Alumni Relations Mr. Jared MEIER
07 Director of Admissions Vacant
15 Director of Human Resources Ms. Jill KNUCKLES
28 Director of Diversity Mr. Bob LANG
41 Co-Athletic Director Ms. Erin HILTNER
41 Co-Athletic Director Mr. Bryan ROOKS
96 Purchasing Manager Ms. Suzanne ELLINWOOD
108 Director Institutional Assessment Dr. Morgan BRIDGE
39 Director Residence Life Ms. Emily BOLLINGER
04 Admin Assistant to the President Ms. Nicole ALLEN
100 Chief of Staff Ms. Liz HOWELL
84 AVP Enrollment Management Ms. Kimberly MEDINA

Colorado Mesa University-Montrose Campus (G)

245 South Cascade Avenue, Montrose CO 81401
Telephone: (970) 249-7009 Identification: 770031
Accreditation: &HLC

Colorado Mountain College (H)

802 Grand Avenue, Glenwood Springs CO 81602-3961
County: Garfield FICE Identification: 004506
Unit ID: 126711
Telephone: (970) 945-8691 Carnegie Class: Bac/Assoc-Mixed
FAX Number: (970) 947-8385 Calendar System: Semester
URL: www.coloradomtn.edu
Established: 1965 Annual Undergrad Tuition & Fees (In-District): $4,740
Enrollment: 5,315 Coed
Affiliation or Control: Local IRS Status: 501(c)3
Highest Offering: Baccalaureate
Accreditation: HLC, ADNUR, EMT, NAEYC, NUR

01 President Dr. Carrie BESNETTE HAUSER
05 VP Academic Affairs Ms. Kathryn REGJO
10 Vice Pres Fiscal Affairs Ms. Mary BOYD
32 VP Student Affairs Mr. Shane LARSON
15 Director of Human Resources Ms. Angela WURTSMITH
26 Public Relations Officer Ms. Debbie CRAWFORD
13 Chief Information Officer Vacant
37 Director of Financial Aid Ms. Janelle COOK
18 Director of College Facilities Mr. Sean NESBITT
27 Director of Marketing/Publications Mr. Brian BARKER
96 Director of Purchasing Ms. Julie HANSON
04 Administrative Asst to President Ms. Debbie NOVAK
100 COO/Chief of Staff Dr. Matt GIANNESCHI
43 Dir Legal Services/General Counsel Mr. Richard GONZALES
06 Registrar Ms. Natalie TORRES
09 Director of Institutional Research Ms. Veneeya KINION
28 Senior Inclusivity Officer Mr. Richard GONZALES

Colorado Mountain College Alpine Campus (I)

1275 Crawford Avenue, Steamboat Springs CO 80487
Telephone: (970) 870-4444 Identification: 770038
Accreditation: &HLC

Colorado Mountain College Aspen (J)

0255 Sage Way, Aspen CO 81611
Telephone: (970) 925-7740 Identification: 770032
Accreditation: &HLC

Colorado Mountain College Leadville (K)

901 South Hwy 24, Leadville CO 80461
Telephone: (719) 486-2105 Identification: 770036
Accreditation: &HLC

Colorado Mountain College Rifle (L)

3695 Airport Road, Rifle CO 81650
Telephone: (970) 625-1871 Identification: 770037
Accreditation: &HLC

Colorado Mountain College Roaring Fork Campus-Spring Valley (M)

690 Colorado Avenue, Carbondale CO 81623
Telephone: (970) 963-2172 Identification: 770035
Accreditation: &HLC

Colorado Mountain College Summit Campus-Breckinridge Center (N)

PO Box 2208/107 Denison Placer Dr,
Breckinridge CO 80424
Telephone: (970) 453-6757 Identification: 770033
Accreditation: &HLC

Colorado Mountain College Vail Valley Campus at Edwards (O)

150 Miller Ranch Road, Edwards CO 81632
Telephone: (970) 569-2900 Identification: 770034
Accreditation: &HLC, MAC

Colorado Northwestern Community College (P)

500 Kennedy Drive, Rangely CO 81648-3598
County: Rio Blanco FICE Identification: 001359
Unit ID: 126748
Telephone: (970) 675-2261 Carnegie Class: Assoc/MT-VT-Mix Trad/Non

FAX Number: (970) 675-5046 Calendar System: Semester
URL: www.cncc.edu
Established: 1962 Annual Undergrad Tuition & Fees (In-District): $4,140
Enrollment: 993 Coed
Affiliation or Control: State/Local IRS Status: 170(c)1
Highest Offering: Associate Degree
Accreditation: HLC, ADNUR, DH

01 President ... Dr. Lisa JONES
32 Vice Pres Student Services ... Mr. David HARDMAN
05 Vice Pres Instruction ... Mr. Keith PETERSON
10 Vice Pres Business/Administration ... Mr. James CALDWELL
13 Director of Information Technology ... Mr. Fred BYERS
06 Registrar ... Ms. Grace STEWART
08 Library Director ... Ms. Leana COX
26 Director of Marketing ... Mr. Reuben TALBOT
15 Executive Director Human Resources ... Ms. Angie MILLER
111 Executive Director Advancement ... Ms. Sue SAMANIEGO
18 Facilities Director ... Mr. Nic LAFEVRE
09 Exec Dir of Institutional Research ... Ms. Kelly SCOTT
121 Director of Student Support ... Ms. Talitha HEJL
37 Financial Aid Director ... Ms. Merrie BYERS
49 Dean of Arts & Science ... Mr. Jesse LAROSE
75 Dean of CTE ... Ms. Meghan DAVIS
41 Athletics Director ... Ms. Candra ROBIE
113 Bursar ... Ms. Janet MACKAY
103 Dean Workforce Education ... Ms. Sasha NELSON
96 Purchasing Coordinator ... Ms. Kathy KOTTENSTETTE
04 Admin Assistant to the President ... Vacant
106 Assoc Dean Learning Technology ... Mr. Nicholas SWAILS
21 Controller ... Ms. Jennifer BARKER
25 Chief Contract and Grants Administr ... Mr. Rob SATTERLY
39 Associate Dean of Students ... Ms. Jen REA

Colorado School of Mines (A)

1500 Illinois Street, Golden CO 80401-1843
County: Jefferson FICE Identification: 001348
Unit ID: 126775
Telephone: (303) 273-3000 Carnegie Class: DU-Highest
FAX Number: (303) 273-3278 Calendar System: Semester
URL: www.mines.edu
Established: 1874 Annual Undergrad Tuition & Fees (In-State): $19,100
Enrollment: 6,744 Coed
Affiliation or Control: State IRS Status: 501(c)3
Highest Offering: Doctorate
Accreditation: HLC

01 President ... Dr. Paul C. JOHNSON
05 Provost ... Dr. Richard HOLZ
11 EVP Administration & Operations ... Kirsten VOLPI
100 Chief of Staff/VP External Rels ... Peter HAN
32 Vice Pres Student LIfe ... Dr. Dan FOX
88 VP Global Initiatives ... Dr. John BRADFORD
46 VP Research & Tech Transfer ... Dr. Walter COPAN
111 Pres for Institutional Advancement ... Brian WINKELBAUER
65 Dean Earth Resources & Environ Pgms ... Dr. Terri HOGUE
92 Exec Dir Univ Honors/Scholars Pgms ... Dr. Toni LEFTON
88 Dean Energy & Materials Pgm ... Dr. John BERGER
43 Vice Pres & General Counsel ... Anne WALKER
84 Assoc Prov Enrollment Management ... Lori KESTER
58 Dean Graduate Studies ... Dr. Tim BARBARI
20 Assoc Provost ... Dr. Andrew HERRING
35 AVP Student Service & Admin ... Rebecca FLINTOFT
15 Chief Human Resources Officer ... Christine HOMER
11 AVP Infrastructure & Operations ... Jason SLOWINSKI
13 Chief Information Officer ... Andrew MOORE
26 Chief Marketing Officer ... Jason HUGHES
35 Dean of Students ... Dr. Derek MORGAN
88 Assoc Dean of Students ... Colin TERRY
04 Sr Executive Asst to the President ... Tammy STRANGE
41 Athletic Director ... David HANSBURG
08 University Librarian ... Carol SMITH
88 Dir of Trefny Innov & Instruction ... Deborah JORDAN
37 Director of Financial Aid ... Jill ROBERTSON
88 Director of WISEM ... Annette PILKINGTON
09 Director of Institutional Research ... Tricia DOUTHIT
06 Registrar ... Paul MYSKIW
93 Dir Multicultural Engineering Pgm ... Dr. Stepheny BEAUCHAMP
29 Director Alumni Relations ... Damian FRIEND
91 Director Enterprise Systems ... John OBRECHT
104 Asst Provost for International Affs ... Dr. David WRIGHT
108 Sr Assessment Associate ... Megan SANDERS
44 Senior Director Annual Giving ... Sara POND
102 Dir Foundation/Corporate Relations ... Emily KELTON
38 Dir of Counseling Center ... Sandra SIMS
96 Director of Procurement/Contracting ... Ryan MCGUIRK
27 Director Communication Center ... Allyce HORAN
21 Controller ... Noelle SANCHEZ
115 Associate Treasurer ... Kevin GRAVINA
25 Director Research Admin ... Johanna EAGAN
109 Dir Student Life Business Admin ... Lisa GOBERIS
114 Director Budget ... Chris STOPPEL
113 Bursar ... Jenny PHOU
16 Dir Human Resources ... Melanie ULRICH
28 Director of Diversity ... Dr. Amy LANDIS
19 Director Public Safety ... Dustin OLSON
18 Director Facilities Mgmt ... Samuel CRISPIN
119 Chief Information Security Officer ... Phillip ROMIG
07 Exec Director of Admissions ... Dale GAUBATZ
123 Director of Graduate Admissions ... Megan STEELMAN
39 Director Housing/Residence Life ... Mary ELLIOTT
121 Dir of Acad Services and Advising ... Jennifer DRUMM
85 Asst Provost International Affairs ... David WRIGHT
117 Exec Dir of Bus Ops/Risk Mgmt ... Natalie VEGA
88 Manager Classroom Technology ... Sara SCHWARZ
89 Dir New Student/Trans Services ... Jessica KEEFER
88 Dir of Title IX Programs ... Katryn SCHMALZEL
88 Dir Office Design & Construction ... Mike BOWKER
88 Dir of Research Compliance ... Ralph BROWN
88 Dir Infrastructure Solutions ... Jorge RICARDINO CSAPO
88 Director Business Services ... Anna WELSCOTT
88 Dir Entrepreneurship/Innovator ... Werner KUHR
88 Dir Intramural & Club Sports ... John HOWARD
88 Dir Acad Affairs Operations ... Jennie KENNEY
88 Dir of Campus Events ... Brandy BURGESS
88 Dir of Fitness ... Heather HAMILTON
88 Dir Intramurals ... Adam HICKLE
88 Dir Administrative Processing Svcs ... Janice LANDER
88 Dir of Student Activities ... Kelsi STREICH
88 Dir of Wellness Programs ... Emma GRIFFIS
88 Dir Outdoor Recreation ... Nathanael BONDI
88 Dir Research & Technology Transfer ... William VAUGHAN
88 Dir Research Development ... Lisa KINZEL
88 Dir Facilities/Aquatics ... Bradford AVENIA
22 Dir Student Disability Services ... Marla DRAPER
88 Manager Application Systems ... Bryan SIEBUHR
88 Exec Dir Envir Health & Safety ... Barbara O'KANE
88 Museum Curator ... Renata LAFLER

Colorado School of Trades (B)

1575 Hoyt Street, Lakewood CO 80215-2996
County: Jefferson FICE Identification: 011572
Unit ID: 126784
Telephone: (303) 233-4697 Carnegie Class: Spec 2-yr-Tech
FAX Number: (303) 233-4723 Calendar System: Other
URL: www.schooloftrades.edu
Established: 1947 Annual Undergrad Tuition & Fees: N/A
Enrollment: 96 Coed
Affiliation or Control: Proprietary IRS Status: Proprietary
Highest Offering: Associate Degree
Accreditation: ACCSC

01 President ... Mr. Ryan LISHNER

Colorado School of Traditional Chinese Medicine (C)

1441 York Street, Suite 302, Denver CO 80206-2127
County: Denver FICE Identification: 036863
Unit ID: 381352
Telephone: (303) 329-6355 Carnegie Class: Spec-4-yr-Other Health
FAX Number: (303) 388-8165 Calendar System: Trimester
URL: www.cstcm.edu
Established: 1989 Annual Undergrad Tuition & Fees: N/A
Enrollment: 84 Coed
Affiliation or Control: Proprietary IRS Status: Proprietary
Highest Offering: Master's
Accreditation: ACUP

01 President ... Mark H. MANTON
11 Administrative Director ... Songtao ZHOU
05 Int Academic Dean/Dean of Faculty ... Parago JONES
20 Assistant Academic Dean ... Christopher SHIFLETT
17 Clinic Director ... Robin VAN MAARTH
88 Assistant Clinic Director ... Carol RIDSDALE
37 Financial Aid Administrator ... Joel SPENCER
10 Finance Administrator ... Yanyun WANG
06 Registrar ... Christine SCHULTZE
07 Recruiting Director ... Timothy FARAD
88 Administrator for the Dean ... Sam MACDONALD

*Colorado State University System Office (D)

555 17th Street, Suite 1000, Denver CO 80202
County: Denver FICE Identification: 033437
Telephone: (303) 534-6290 Carnegie Class: N/A
FAX Number: (303) 534-6298
URL: www.csusystem.edu

01 Chancellor ... Dr. Tony FRANK
10 SVP Admin & Govt Relations/CFO ... Mr. Henry SOBANET
43 General Counsel ... Mr. Jason JOHNSON
05 Chief Academic Officer ... Dr. Rick MIRANDA
88 Chief Educational Innovation Ofcr ... Dr. Becky TAKEDA-TINKER
13 Chief Information Officer ... Mr. Patrick BURNS
26 AVC for External Relations ... Ms. Tiana KENNEDY

*Colorado State University (E)

200 W. Lake Street, Fort Collins CO 80523-0015
County: Larimer FICE Identification: 001350
Unit ID: 126818
Telephone: (970) 491-1101 Carnegie Class: DU-Highest
FAX Number: (970) 491-0501 Calendar System: Semester
URL: www.colostate.edu
Established: 1870 Annual Undergrad Tuition & Fees (In-State): $11,814
Enrollment: 32,428 Coed
Affiliation or Control: State IRS Status: 501(c)3
Highest Offering: Doctorate
Accreditation: HLC, ART, CACREP, CAEPT, CEA, CIDA, CONST, COPSY, DIETC, DIETD, IPSY, JOUR, LSAR, MFCD, MUS, OT, PH, SW, VET

02 President ... Ms. Joyce E. MCCONNELL
05 Senior Exec Vice Pres/Provost ... Dr. Mary PEDERSEN
46 Vice President for Research ... Dr. Alan S. RUDOLPH
32 Vice Pres Student Affairs ... Dr. Blanche M. HUGHES
11 VP for University Operations ... Ms. Lynn JOHNSON
111 VP University Advancement ... Ms. Kim TOBIN
84 Vice Pres for Enrollment/Access ... Ms. Leslie TAYLOR
26 VP for University Communications ... Ms. Yolanda BEVILL
56 VP Outreach and Engagement ... Dr. Blake NAUGHTON
13 VP for IT ... Mr. Brandon BERNIER
20 Vice Prov for Undergraduate Affairs ... Dr. Kelly LONG
58 Vice Provost Graduate Affairs ... Dr. Mary STOMBERGER
85 Vice Provost for International Affs ... Ms. Kathleen FAIRFAX
36 Director Career Services ... Mr. Jon CLEVELAND
28 VP for Inclusive Excellence ... Dr. Kauline CIPRIANI
29 Exec Director Alumni Relations ... Ms. Kristi BOHLENDER
41 Athletic Director ... Mr. Joe PARKER
35 Dean of Students ... Dr. Jody DONOVAN
43 Deputy General Counsel ... Ms. Jannine R. MOHR
47 Dean Agriculture Sciences ... Dr. James PRITCHETT
76 Dean Applied Human Sciences ... Dr. Lise YOUNGBLADE
50 Dean of Business ... Dr. Beth WALKER
54 Dean of Engineering ... Dr. David MCLEAN
49 Dean of Liberal Arts ... Dr. Ben WITHERS
65 Dean of Natural Resources ... Dr. John HAYES
81 Dean of Natural Sciences ... Dr. Janice L. NERGER
74 Dean of Veterinary Med & Biomed Sci ... Dr. Mark STETTER
08 Dean of Libraries ... Dr. Karen ESTLUND
06 Registrar ... Ms. D. TOBIASSEN BAITINGER
18 Chief Facilities/Physical Plant ... Mr. Tom SATTERLY
22 VP for Equity/Equal Oppty/Title IX ... Ms. Diana PRIETO
37 Director of Student Financial Aid ... Mr. Joe DONLAY
39 Exec Dir Housing & Dining Services ... Dr. Mari STROMBOM
40 Director of Bookstore ... Mr. John PARRY
96 Director of Procurement Services ... Ms. Linda MESERVE
92 Director University Honors Program ... Dr. Donald MYKLES
94 Director Center for Women's Studies ... Dr. Caridad SOUZA
09 Vice Provost Institutional Research ... Dr. Laura JENSEN
100 Chief of Staff Office of the Pres ... Ms. Ann CLAYCOMB

*Colorado State University Global (F)

585 Salida Way, Aurora CO 80011
County: Arapahoe FICE Identification: 042087
Unit ID: 476975
Telephone: (800) 462-7845 Carnegie Class: Masters/L
FAX Number: N/A Calendar System: Trimester
URL: https://csuglobal.edu
Established: 2008 Annual Undergrad Tuition & Fees (In-State): $8,400
Enrollment: 12,578 Coed
Affiliation or Control: State IRS Status: 170(c)1
Highest Offering: Master's
Accreditation: HLC, ACBSP

02 President ... Pamela TONEY
05 EVP/Provost ... Dr. Paul SAVORY
26 VP Strategic Engagement ... Dr. Sandra JONES
10 VP Finance/Administration ... Patti ARROYO
32 VP Student & Faculty Ops ... Dr. Angela HERNQUIST

*Colorado State University-Pueblo (G)

2200 Bonforte Boulevard, Pueblo CO 81001-4901
County: Pueblo FICE Identification: 001365
Unit ID: 128106
Telephone: (719) 549-2100 Carnegie Class: Masters/M
FAX Number: (719) 549-2650 Calendar System: Semester
URL: www.csupueblo.edu
Established: 1933 Annual Undergrad Tuition & Fees (In-State): $8,591
Enrollment: 5,925 Coed
Affiliation or Control: State IRS Status: 501(c)3
Highest Offering: Doctorate
Accreditation: HLC, CAATE, MUS, NUR, SW

02 President ... Dr. Timothy MOTTET
05 Int Provost/EVP for Academic Affs ... Dr. Chad KINNEY
11 VP for Operations & Advancement ... Dr. Donna SOUDER HODGE
84 VP Enrollment Mgmt/Extended Studies ... Dr. Kristyn WHITE DAVIS
100 Chief of Staff ... Ms. Niki TOUSSAINT
10 Chief Financial Officer/Controller ... Ms. Juanita PENA
32 Sr Assoc VP Student Affairs & Dean ... Dr. Marie HUMPHREY
41 VP for Athletics & Strategic Ptnrs ... Dr. Paul PLINSKE
18 Asst VP Operations & Advancement ... Dr. Derek LOPEZ
108 Exec Dir Assessment/Inst Effect ... Dr. Helen CAPRIOGLIO
26 Exec Dir Marketing/Communications ... Mr. Greg HOYE
121 Exec Dir Persistence/Pack Initiativ ... Mr. John SANDOVAL
07 Int Exec Dir Enroll & Stdnt Exp ... Mr. Lee SAUNDERS
88 Int Exec Dir Enroll Strat & Comp ... Ms. Tiffany KINGREY
88 Int Exec Dir Trio & Upward Bound ... Mr. Jacobo VARELA
79 Dean Col of Humanities/Arts/Soc Sci ... Ms. Leticia STEFFEN
76 Dean Col Health/Education/Nursing ... Mr. Joe FRANTA
08 Dean Library Services ... Ms. Rhonda GONZALES
50 Dean Hasan School of Business ... Dr. Steve NORMAN
58 Dean of Graduate Studies ... Dr. Misty SAILORS
56 Dean of Extended Studies ... Dr. Kathryn STARKEY
81 Dean Col Science/Tech/Engr/Math ... Dr. David LEHMPUHL
97 Dean Undergraduate & Stdnt Success ... Dr. Stuart BENKERT
23 Assoc Dean Stdnt Health Services ... Ms. Carolyn DAUGHERTY
88 Assc Dean Humanities/Art/SocSci ... Mr. Juan MORALES
88 Assc Dean Health/Education/Nursing ... Mr. Jeff PIQUETTE
35 Asst Dean SEAL & Student Life ... Ms. Gena ALFONSO
35 Asst Dean Student Sprt & Advocacy ... Ms. Bonnie FRULAND
39 Asst Dean Student Life ... Ms. Gwendolyn YOUNG

88 Assoc Dean Health & Human Mvmnt .... Dr. Carol FOUST
22 Director & Title IX Coordinator .... Ms. Nicole FERGUSON
15 Director Human Resource Operations .... Ms. Jen QUINTANA
43 Deputy General Counsel .... Ms. Johnna DOYLE
96 Int Director of Purchasing .... Mr. Chris FENDRICH
09 Dir Institutional Research/Analysis .... Mr. Corey SHILLING
06 Registrar .... Ms. Carol LARSON
109 Int Director Auxiliary Services .... Ms. Chris SMITH
36 Director Career Center .... Ms. Michelle GJERDE
37 Director Student Financial Services .... Ms. Monica HARDWICK
114 Budget Director .... Ms. Margaret BREWER
88 Director English Language Institute .... Ms. Jeanne GIBSON
88 Director Disability Resource Center .... Mr. Justin HINIKER
88 Director Inst of Cannabis Research .... Dr. Chad KINNEY
88 Director Student Recreation .... Ms. Emily BACH MCELWAIN
90 Director of Academic Technology .... Mr. Adam POCIUS
88 Senior Associate Athletic Director .... Ms. Christie WARD
09 Senior Director of Reserach .... Dr. John WILLIAMSON
102 President/CEO Foundation .... Mr. Todd KELLY
13 Executive Director of IT .... Vacant
29 Director Alumni Relations .... Vacant

Colorado Technical University (A)

3151 South Vaughn Way, Suite 150, Aurora CO 80014
Telephone: (303) 632-2300 Identification: 666732
Accreditation: &HLC, ACBSP

† Regional accreditation is carried under the parent institution in Colorado Springs, CO.

Colorado Technical University (B)

4435 N Chestnut Street, Colorado Springs CO 80907-3896
County: El Paso FICE Identification: 010148
Unit ID: 126827
Telephone: (719) 598-0200 Carnegie Class: DU-Mod
FAX Number: (719) 598-3740 Calendar System: Quarter
URL: www.coloradotech.edu
Established: 1965 Annual Undergrad Tuition & Fees: $12,573
Enrollment: 28,244 Coed
Affiliation or Control: Proprietary IRS Status: Proprietary
Highest Offering: Doctorate
Accreditation: HLC, ACBSP, NURSE

01 President .... Mr. Andrew HURST
05 Chief Academic Officer/Provost .... Dr. Connie JOHNSON
10 Vice President Finance .... Ms. Erin KRAFT
07 Vice President of Admissions .... Mr. Keith ARMSTRONG
11 VP Univ Strategy/Operations .... Ms. Elise BASKEL
32 Vice President Student Affairs .... Ms. Terri HINES
20 Vice Provost .... Vacant

Community College of Aurora (C)

16000 E Centre Tech Parkway, Aurora CO 80011-9036
County: Arapahoe FICE Identification: 022769
Unit ID: 126863
Telephone: (303) 360-4700 Carnegie Class: Assoc/HT-High Non
FAX Number: (303) 360-4761 Calendar System: Semester
URL: www.ccaurora.edu
Established: 1983 Annual Undergrad Tuition & Fees (In-State): $3,940
Enrollment: 7,835 Coed
Affiliation or Control: State IRS Status: 501(c)3
Highest Offering: Associate Degree
Accreditation: HLC, EMT

01 President .... Dr. Mordecai I. BROWNLEE
05 Vice President Academic Success .... Dr. Bobby PACE
28 Vice President DEI .... Dr. Angela MARQUEZ
84 Interim VP Enrollment Management .... Mr. Chris TOMBARI
15 Vice Pres of Human Resources .... Ms. Cindy HESSE
11 VP of Administrative Services .... Ms. Lynne WINCHELL
10 Controller .... Mr. Eddie STORZ
32 Dean of Students & Chief SAO .... Dr. Reyna ANAYA
88 Dean Concurrent Enrollment .... Ms. Michelle PACHECO
72 Dean Technical Education .... Dr. Jim DELUNG
19 Director of Security .... Mr. Travis HOGAN
121 Interim Director Advising .... Ms. Tanika VAUGHN
13 Director Information Technology .... Ms. Eduardo PERALTA
18 Associate VP Administrative Svcs .... Mr. John BOTTELBERGHE
26 Executive Director Strategic Comms .... Mr. Blair LEE
37 Director Financial Aid .... Mr. John YOUNG
06 Registrar/Director Admissions .... Ms. Kristen CUSACK
08 Director Library Services .... Mr. Dan LAWRENCE
09 Director of Institutional Research .... Dr. HyeKyung LEE
102 Exec Dir CCA Foundation .... Mr. John WOLFKILL
22 College Equity Officer .... Dr. Angela MARQUEZ
88 Dean Academic Effectiveness .... Ms. Ana MARTIN-MEJIA
106 Dean Online & Blended Learning .... Dr. Jenn DALE
97 Dean General Education .... Dr. Brandon FERES
108 Dean Strategy/Assessment & Perf .... Dr. Kathryn SKULLEY
103 Dean Workforce Development .... Dr. Julie STEWART
81 Dean STEM .... Dr. Susan YOUNG
04 Admin Assistant to the President .... Mr. David MURPHY

Community College of Denver (D)

Campus Box 201, PO Box 173363,
Denver CO 80217-3363
County: Denver FICE Identification: 009542
Unit ID: 126942
Telephone: (303) 556-2400 Carnegie Class: Bac/Assoc-Assoc Dom
FAX Number: (303) 556-8555 Calendar System: Semester
URL: www.ccd.edu
Established: 1967 Annual Undergrad Tuition & Fees (In-State): $4,788
Enrollment: 7,273 Coed
Affiliation or Control: State IRS Status: 501(c)3
Highest Offering: Baccalaureate
Accreditation: HLC, CSHSE, DH, RAD, SURGT

01 President .... Dr. Marielena DESANCTIS
05 Provost/Chief Academic Officer .... Ms. Ruthanne ORIHUELA
10 Vice Pres Finance & Admin/CFO .... Ms. Kathryn KAOUDIS
32 Vice Pres Student Affairs .... Vacant
84 VP of Enrollment Administration . Ms. Gillian MCKNIGHT-TUTEIN
83 Dean Arts/Behavioral & Social Sci .... Dr. Robert STUDINGER
76 Dean Health & Natural Sciences .... Dr. Fida OBEIDI
89 Dean Math/English & FYE .... Mr. Peter LINDSTROM
50 Dean Business/Industry & Tech .... Mr. Thomas WILLIAMS
20 Dean of Instruction .... Dr. Kaylah ZELIG
124 Dean Student Success/Enroll Admin .... Mrs. Tina GARCIA
35 Director of Student Life .... Ms. Kathryn MAHONEY
37 Director Financial Aid .... Ms. Theresa LAVIN
15 Exec Director Human Resources .... Ms. Shana STOVALL
09 Director Institutional Research .... Ms. Katherine HILL
06 Registrar/Dir Registration & Recs .... Ms. Anastacia RODRIGUEZ
18 Dir Emergency Prep & Facilities .... Mr. Nick GODDARD
102 Foundation Director .... Ms. Leah GOSS
13 IT Service Manager .... Ms. Claudia FORBES

Concorde Career College (E)

111 N Havana Street, Aurora CO 80010-4314
County: Arapahoe FICE Identification: 008871
Unit ID: 126687
Telephone: (303) 861-1151 Carnegie Class: Spec 2-yr-Health
FAX Number: (303) 839-5478 Calendar System: Other
URL: https://www.concorde.edu/campus/aurora-colorado
Established: 1969 Annual Undergrad Tuition & Fees: N/A
Enrollment: 329 Coed
Affiliation or Control: Proprietary IRS Status: Proprietary
Highest Offering: Associate Degree
Accreditation: ACCSC, COARC, DH, PNUR, PTAA, RAD, SURGT

01 Campus President .... Mr. Thomas WICKE
05 Academic Dean .... Ms. Sue KUHL
37 Director of Financial Aid .... Ms. Kimberly MARTINEZ
07 Director of Admissions .... Ms. Mary GORDY

Denver College of Nursing (F)

1401 19th Street, Denver CO 80202
County: Denver FICE Identification: 041483
Unit ID: 454856
Telephone: (303) 292-0015 Carnegie Class: Spec-4-yr-Other Health
FAX Number: (720) 974-0290 Calendar System: Quarter
URL: https://www.denvercollegeofnursing.edu/
Established: 2003 Annual Undergrad Tuition & Fees: N/A
Enrollment: 1,042 Coed
Affiliation or Control: Proprietary IRS Status: Proprietary
Highest Offering: Master's
Accreditation: HLC, ADNUR, NUR, NURSE

01 President .... Dr. Cathy MAXWELL
10 Director of Business Operations .... Mr. Tim HEINTZ
32 Director of Student Services .... Mr. Michael RUSCHIVAL
05 Dean/Dir of Nursing Education Pgms .... Dr. Z. JoAnna HILL
37 Director of Financial Aid .... Ms. Geri REICHMUTH
07 Director of Admissions .... Mr. Jeff JOHNSON
06 Registrar .... Mr. Jacob DENNING

Denver Seminary (G)

6399 S Santa Fe Drive, Littleton CO 80120-2912
County: Arapahoe FICE Identification: 001352
Unit ID: 126979
Telephone: (303) 761-2482 Carnegie Class: Masters/M
FAX Number: (303) 761-8060 Calendar System: Semester
URL: www.denverseminary.edu
Established: 1950 Annual Graduate Tuition & Fees: N/A
Enrollment: 856 Coed
Affiliation or Control: Interdenominational IRS Status: 501(c)3
Highest Offering: Doctorate; No Undergraduates
Accreditation: HLC, CACREP, PAST, THEOL

01 President .... Dr. Mark S. YOUNG
05 VP Academic Affairs/Dean .... Dr. Don PAYNE
111 Vice President of Advancement .... Mr. Chris JOHNSON
10 Vice President of Finance .... Ms. Deborah KELLAR
32 VP Student Life & Enrollment Mgmt .... Mr. Dusty DI SANTO
100 Chief of Staff .... Mr. Josh BLEEKER
15 Director of Human Resources .... Mrs. Wendi GOWING
06 Registrar .... Ms. Georgia WRIGHT
08 Director of Library Services .... Mr. Matt WASIELEWSKI
26 Sr Director of Communications .... Mrs. Andrea WEYAND
109 Sr Dir of Physical Campus Opers .... Mr. Biagio BURRIESCI
21 Controller/Dir Financial Services .... Ms. Diana SMITH
35 Dean of Students .... Mrs. Kristy MCGARVEY
04 Executive Asst to the President .... Mrs. Christy GROSVENOR
37 Director of Financial Aid .... Mrs. Gina KELBERT
105 Director Web Services .... Mrs. Katie LARIC
73 Director of DMin Program .... Dr. Marshall SHELLEY
84 Director of Enrollment Management .... Vacant
09 Dir Office of Innov & Educ System .... Mr. David HIONIDES
13 Director of Information Systems .... Mr. Jason ADAMS

56 Assoc Dean Innovation/Ed Systems .... Mr. Tim KOLLER
28 Assoc Dean for Ethnic Communities .... Mr. Wilmer RAMIREZ
106 Associate Dean of Educational Tech .... Mr. Aaron JOHNSON
18 Associate Director of Facilities .... Vacant
88 Asst Director of DMinistry .... Ms. Angie WARD

Fort Lewis College (H)

1000 Rim Drive, Durango CO 81301-3999
County: La Plata FICE Identification: 001353
Unit ID: 127185
Telephone: (970) 247-7010 Carnegie Class: Bac-Diverse
FAX Number: (970) 247-7175 Calendar System: Semester
URL: www.fortlewis.edu
Established: 1911 Annual Undergrad Tuition & Fees (In-State): $8,896
Enrollment: 3,469 Coed
Affiliation or Control: State IRS Status: 170(c)1
Highest Offering: Master's
Accreditation: HLC, MUS

01 President .... Dr. Tom STRITIKUS
05 Provost/Vice Pres Academic Affairs .... Dr. Cheryl NIXON
10 Vice Pres Finance & Administration ..... Mr. Steven J. SCHWARTZ
111 Vice President for Advancement .... Ms. Melissa MOUNT
32 Dean Student Engagement .... Mr. Jeffrey DUPONT
06 Registrar .... Vacant
21 Chief Financial Officer .... Ms. Samantha GALLAGHER
21 Controller .... Ms. Holly ESTELLE
25 Dir of Sponsored Research .... Vacant
37 Director Financial Aid .... Mr. Jedidiah GILDEN
07 Director of Admission .... Ms. Jess SAVAGE
38 Dir Counseling Center .... Ms. Amie BRYANT
08 Director of the Library .... Ms. Astrid OLIVER
15 Dir Human Res/Equal Opportunity .... Ms. Erin BEEZLEY
41 Athletic Director .... Vacant
13 Director Computing & Telecomm .... Mr. Matt MCGLAMERY
29 Director Alumni Engagement .... Mr. Ryan LAZO
96 Director of Purchasing .... Ms. April ZION
26 Public Relations Officer .... Ms. Lauren SAVAGE
49 Dean Arts and Science .... Vacant
50 Dean Sch of Business Admin .... Dr. Steven M. ELIAS
53 Dean of Teacher Education .... Dr. Jennifer TRUJILLO
04 Admin Assistant to the President .... Ms. Vikki AGOVINO
09 Director of Institutional Research .... Ms. Orien S. MCGLAMERY
18 Chief Facilities/Physical Plant Ofc .... Mr. Jeff MILLER
19 Director Security/Safety .... Mr. Brett DEMING
28 Director of Diversity .... Vacant
39 Dir Resident Life/Student Housing .... Mr. Edgar ANAYA

Front Range Community College (I)

3645 W 112th Avenue, Westminster CO 80031-2105
County: Adams FICE Identification: 007933
Unit ID: 127200
Telephone: (303) 404-5000 Carnegie Class: Assoc/MT-VT-High Non
FAX Number: (303) 466-1623 Calendar System: Semester
URL: www.frontrange.edu
Established: 1968 Annual Undergrad Tuition & Fees (In-State): $4,032
Enrollment: 18,703 Coed
Affiliation or Control: State IRS Status: 501(c)3
Highest Offering: Baccalaureate
Accreditation: HLC, ADNUR, CAHIIM, DA, NAEYC, NURSE, SURGT

02 President .... Dr. Colleen SIMPSON
04 Asst to the President .... Ms. Denise BUCHER
10 VP Finance/Administration .... Mr. Duane RISSE
05 VP Acad Affairs & Online Learning .... Dr. Rebecca WOULFE
12 VP Westminster Campus/Brighton Ctr .... Dr. Tricia JOHNSON
12 Vice Pres Larimer Campus .... Dr. Jean RUNYON
12 Vice Pres Boulder County Campus .... Dr. Aparna PALMER
84 VP Enrollment Svs & Student Success .... Mr. Matt JAMISON
15 Exec Director of Human Resources .... Ms. JoAnne WILKINSON
102 Exec Director of Foundation .... Vacant
26 Lead Dir Marketing/Communications .... Ms. Marian MAHARAS
28 Exec Director of Equity & Inclusion .... Dr. Krishna PATTISAPU
18 Assoc VP Facilities Planning/Mgmt .... Mr. Derek BROWN
20 Dean of Instruction Larimer .... Ms. Anne Marie JACOBSON
20 Dean of Instruction Larimer .... Mr. Nicholas SPEZZA
20 Dean of Instruction Boulder County .... Mr. Matt JAMISON
20 Dean of Instruction Westminster .... Mr. Hector GARZA
20 Dean of Instruction Westminster .... Ms. Erin FARB
20 Dean of Instruction Westminster .... Ms. April MENZIES
20 Dean of Instruction Boulder County .... Ms. MaryLee GEARY
20 Dean of Instruction Boulder County .... Ms. Deborah CRAVEN
32 Dean of Student Svcs Boulder County .... Vacant
106 Dean of Std Affairs/Online Learning .... Mr. Chico GARCIA
32 Dean of Student Svcs Westminster .... Ms. Erica INGALLS
09 Director of Institutional Research .... Ms. Kim WALLACE
114 Director of Budget & Auxiliary Svcs .... Ms. Karen STEINER
06 Registrar .... Ms. Sonia GONZALES
07 Director of Admissions .... Vacant
37 Dir of Financial Aid Larimer .... Mr. David LUCCI
08 Librarian .... Vacant
18 Director of Facilities Westminster .... Mr. David CRAWFORD
18 Director of Facilities Larimer .... Mr. Mike BARANOVIC
35 Director Student Life Westminster .... Vacant
35 Director Student Life Larimer ...... Ms. Mary BRANTON-HOUSLEY
35 Dir Student Life Boulder County .... Ms. Amanda CLANCY
27 Public Information Officer .... Ms. Jessica PETERSON
13 Dir of Information Technology Svcs .... Vacant
19 Dir Campus Security/Preparedness .... Mr. Carl PEASTER

Front Range Community College-Boulder County Campus (A)

2190 Miller Drive, Longmont CO 80501
Telephone: (303) 678-3722 Identification: 770041
Accreditation: &HLC

Front Range Community College Larimer Campus (B)

4616 S Shields Street, Fort Collins CO 80526
Telephone: (970) 226-2500 Identification: 770040
Accreditation: &HLC, ADNUR, PNUR

Holmes Institute of Consciousness Studies (C)

573 Park Point Drive, Golden CO 80401
County: Jefferson Identification: 666255
Telephone: (720) 496-1370 Carnegie Class: Not Classified
FAX Number: (303) 526-0913 Calendar System: Quarter
URL: www.holmesinstitute.edu
Established: 1972 Annual Graduate Tuition & Fees: N/A
Enrollment: N/A Coed
Affiliation or Control: Other IRS Status: 501(c)3
Highest Offering: Master's; No Undergraduates
Accreditation: DEAC

01 President/Manager .... Rev. CC COLTRAIN
06 Registrar .... Mr. Dan HERFURT
05 Chief Academic Officer .... Dr. Greg SALYER

IBMC College (D)

3842 South Mason Street, Fort Collins CO 80526
County: Larimer FICE Identification: 030063
Unit ID: 372329
Telephone: (970) 223-2669 Carnegie Class: Spec 2-yr-Health
FAX Number: (970) 223-2796 Calendar System: Quarter
URL: www.ibmc.edu
Established: 1987 Annual Undergrad Tuition & Fees: $14,400
Enrollment: 408 Coed
Affiliation or Control: Proprietary IRS Status: Proprietary
Highest Offering: Associate Degree
Accreditation: ACCSC

01 CEO .... Mr. Steven STEELE
05 Director of Education .... Ms. Katie WILKINSON
06 Registrar .... Ms. Jami ZENNER

IBMC College (E)

2863 35th Avenue, Greeley CO 80634-9421
Telephone: (970) 356-4733 Identification: 770631
Accreditation: ACCSC

Iliff School of Theology (F)

2323 E. Iliff Ave, Denver CO 80210-4798
County: Denver FICE Identification: 001354
Unit ID: 127273
Telephone: (303) 744-1287 Carnegie Class: Spec-4-yr-Faith
FAX Number: (303) 765-1141 Calendar System: Quarter
URL: www.iliff.edu
Established: 1892 Annual Graduate Tuition & Fees: N/A
Enrollment: 215 Coed
Affiliation or Control: United Methodist IRS Status: 501(c)3
Highest Offering: Doctorate; No Undergraduates
Accreditation: HLC, THEOL

01 President and CEO .... Rev Dr. Thomas V. WOLFE
05 Vice Pres/Dean Academic Affairs .... Rev Dr. Boyung LEE
10 VP of Business Affairs/Controller .... Mr. Jason WARR
84 VP of Enrollment Management .... Dr. Stephanie KRUSEMARK
111 VP of Institutional Advancement .... Vacant
09 VP of Innovation/Learning and IR .... Dr. Theodore M. VIAL
42 Dean of the Chapel .... Rev Dr. Cathie KELSEY
26 Director of Communications .... Dr. Soon Beng YEAP
06 Registrar .... Ms. Kylie A. PARISH
13 Chief Information Officer .... Vacant
04 Executive Asst to President .... Mrs. Alisha ENO
18 Dir of Facilities Mgmt .... Mr. Anthony CHICCO
15 Director of Human Resources .... Ms. Caran WARE JOSEPH
11 Chief Operating Officer .... Ms. Caran WARE JOSEPH
37 Director Student Financial Aid .... Ms. Goldie ECTOR
101 Assistant Secretary of the Board .... Mrs. Alisha ENO

Institute of Business and Medical Careers (G)

2315 North Main Street, Longmont CO 80501
Telephone: (303) 651-6819 Identification: 770630
Accreditation: ACCSC

Institute of Taoist Education and Acupuncture (H)

317 West South Boulder Road, Ste 5, Louisville CO 80027
County: Boulder FICE Identification: 041212
Unit ID: 454838
Telephone: (720) 890-8922 Carnegie Class: Spec-4-yr-Other Health
FAX Number: (720) 890-7719 Calendar System: Other
URL: www.itea.edu
Established: 1996 Annual Graduate Tuition & Fees: N/A
Enrollment: 28 Coed
Affiliation or Control: Independent Non-Profit IRS Status: 501(c)3
Highest Offering: Master's; No Undergraduates
Accreditation: ACUP

01 President .... Hilary SKELLON
05 Vice President .... Brittany SANELLI
06 Registrar .... Kale DENNIS
10 Financial Administrator .... Kathy KNAUS

IntelliTec College (I)

2315 E Pikes Peak Avenue,
Colorado Springs CO 80909-6096
County: El Paso FICE Identification: 022537
Unit ID: 128179
Telephone: (719) 632-7626 Carnegie Class: Spec 2-yr-Tech
FAX Number: (719) 632-7451 Calendar System: Quarter
URL: www.intellitec.edu
Established: 1965 Annual Undergrad Tuition & Fees: N/A
Enrollment: 585 Coed
Affiliation or Control: Proprietary IRS Status: Proprietary
Highest Offering: Associate Degree
Accreditation: ACCSC

00 President .... Wayne ZELLNER
02 Campus Director .... David SCOTT
07 Director of Academics .... Catherine LECKMAN

Lamar Community College (J)

2401 S Main, Lamar CO 81052-3999
County: Prowers FICE Identification: 001355
Unit ID: 127389
Telephone: (719) 336-2248 Carnegie Class: Assoc/MT-VT-Mix Trad/Non
FAX Number: (719) 336-2448 Calendar System: Semester
URL: www.lamarcc.edu
Established: 1937 Annual Undergrad Tuition & Fees (In-State): $4,133
Enrollment: 723 Coed
Affiliation or Control: State IRS Status: 501(c)3
Highest Offering: Associate Degree
Accreditation: HLC, ADNUR

01 President .... Dr. Linda LUJAN
05 VP Academic Services/Student Svcs .... Mr. Larry MCLEMORE
11 VP Admin Svcs/Inst Effectiveness .... Mr. Chad DE BONO
20 Dean of Academic Services .... Mr. Kyle LASLEY
26 Director of Communication .... Vacant
06 Registrar .... Vacant
08 Library Tech .... Ms. Jennifer GOODLAND
18 Director of Facilities .... Mr. Sean LIRLEY
15 Director Personnel Services .... Ms. Shelly TOMBLESON
39 Director Student Housing .... Vacant
38 Director Student Counseling .... Mrs. Julie JONES
96 Director of Purchasing .... Ms. Ava BAIR
41 Athletic Director .... Mr. Scott CRAMPTON
37 Director Financial Aid .... Ms. Shealynn MCCRACKEN
07 Director of Admissions .... Vacant
21 Controller .... Mrs. Aubrie CLEAVINGER
111 Dir Inst Advancement/Foundation Dir .... Mrs. Anne-Marie CRAMPTON
09 Coordinator Institutional Research .... Ms. Kim WALLACE
84 Coord for Concurrent Enrollment .... Mr. Del CHASE
04 Admin Assistant to the President .... Ms. Misti FRONTERHOUSE
13 Chief Information Technology Ofcr .... Mr. Robert VAZQUEZ

Lincoln College of Technology (K)

11194 East 45th Avenue, Denver CO 80239
County: Denver FICE Identification: 007547
Unit ID: 126951
Telephone: (303) 722-5724 Carnegie Class: Spec 2-yr-Tech
FAX Number: (303) 778-8264 Calendar System: Semester
URL: www.lincolntech.edu
Established: 1963 Annual Undergrad Tuition & Fees: N/A
Enrollment: 1,529 Coed
Affiliation or Control: Proprietary IRS Status: Proprietary
Highest Offering: Associate Degree
Accreditation: ACCSC

01 Campus President .... Dr. Kelly THUMM MOORE
07 Sr Director of Admissions .... Ms. Jennifer HASH
05 Academic Dean .... Ms. Colleen LOTT
04 Administrative Asst to President .... Vacant
06 Registrar .... Ms. Stacy SWINBURN
36 Director of Career Services .... Ms. LeeDel COHENOUR
11 Director of Admin Services .... Ms. Christine GRAY
37 Director of Financial Aid .... Ms. Carrie HOCK
13 IT Administrator .... Vacant
18 Chf Facilities/Physical Plant Ofcr .... Mr. Brandon MORTON

Metropolitan State University of Denver (L)

PO Box 173362, Campus Box 48, Denver CO 80217-3362
County: Denver FICE Identification: 001360
Unit ID: 127565
Telephone: (303) 556-5740 Carnegie Class: Masters/L
FAX Number: (303) 556-3912 Calendar System: Semester
URL: https://www.msudenver.edu/
Established: 1963 Annual Undergrad Tuition & Fees (In-State): $8,693
Enrollment: 19,086 Coed
Affiliation or Control: State IRS Status: 501(c)3
Highest Offering: Master's
Accreditation: HLC, ART, CAATE, COSMA, CSHSE, DIETD, @DIETI, EXSC, MLS, MUS, NUR, NURSE, @SP, SW, THEA

01 President .... Dr. Janine A. DAVIDSON
05 Provost/EVP Academic Affairs .... Dr. Alfred W. TATUM
10 Vice Pres Admin/Finance & COO .... Mr. Larry SAMPLER
111 VP Advancement/Exec Dir Foundation .... Ms. Christine MARQUEZ-HUDSON
32 VP Student Affairs .... Dr. Will SIMPKINS
28 VP Ofc of Diversity/Inclusion .... Dr. Michael BENITEZ, JR.
45 Interim VP Strategy .... Mr. Eric MASON
43 General Counsel/Secretary to Board .... Mr. David FINE
13 AVP Info Technology Services/CIO .... Mr. Kevin TAYLOR
84 Assoc VP Enrollment Services .... Ms. Mary SAUCEDA
35 AVP Stdnt Engage & Well/Dean Stdnts .... Dr. Braelin PANTEL
29 Asst VP Strategic Engagement .... Ms. Jamie HURST
50 Dean School Business .... Dr. Ann B. MURPHY
107 Int Dean Sch Professional Studies .... Dr. Rebecca TRAMMELL
15 AVP Human Resources .... Ms. Stacy M. DVERGSDAL
06 Registrar .... Ms. Connie SANDERS
37 Interim Director Financial Aid .... Mr. Michael NGUYEN
41 Athletic Director .... Dr. G. Anthony GRANT
36 Assoc VP Classroom 2 Career Hub .... Dr. Adrienne MARTINEZ
07 Director of Admissions .... Mr. Vaughn TOLAND
09 Director of Data & Analytics .... Mr. Sean PETRANOVICH
04 Exec Assistant to the President .... Ms. Summer VALDEZ
106 Director Online Learning .... Dr. Matt GRISWOLD
25 Chief Contract/Grants Administrator .... Ms. Betsy JINKS
53 Dean School of Education .... Dr. Liz HINDE
100 Chief of Staff .... Mr. Edward BROWN

Morgan Community College (M)

920 Barlow Road, Fort Morgan CO 80701-4399
County: Morgan FICE Identification: 009981
Unit ID: 127617
Telephone: (970) 542-3100 Carnegie Class: Assoc/HVT-High Non
FAX Number: (970) 542-3115 Calendar System: Semester
URL: www.morgancc.edu
Established: 1967 Annual Undergrad Tuition & Fees (In-State): $3,850
Enrollment: 1,376 Coed
Affiliation or Control: State IRS Status: Exempt
Highest Offering: Baccalaureate
Accreditation: HLC, ADNUR, NURSE, PTAA

01 President .... Dr. Curt FREED
10 Vice Pres Finance/Admin Services .... Ms. Tracy SCHNEIDER
05 Vice President of Instruction .... Ms. Kathy FRISBIE
32 Vice President of Student Services .... Mr. Scott SCHOLES
04 Assistant to the President .... Ms. Jane FRIES
20 Dean of Gen Ed & Health Sciences .... Dr. Christiane OLIVO
103 Dean of Workforce Development .... Mr. John PROUTY
06 Registrar .... Vacant
26 Dir of Comm/Mktg & Recruitment .... Ms. Ariella GONZALES-VONDY
30 Director of Development .... Ms. Roberta BIGALK
37 Director of Financial Aid .... Ms. Sally SHAWCROFT
15 Director of Human Resources .... Ms. Julie BEYDLER
07 Director of Admissions & Advising .... Ms. Maria CARDENAS
08 Director of Learning Resources .... Ms. April AMACK
96 Director of Purchasing .... Ms. Chloe HIRSCHFELD
13 Director Information Technology .... Mr. Mark FRASCO
18 Director of Physical Facilities .... Mr. Gene KIND
40 College Store Manager .... Ms. Karissa SCHULTE

Naropa University (N)

2130 Arapahoe Avenue, Boulder CO 80302-6697
County: Boulder FICE Identification: 021175
Unit ID: 127653
Telephone: (303) 444-0202 Carnegie Class: Masters/M
FAX Number: (303) 444-0410 Calendar System: Semester
URL: www.naropa.edu
Established: 1974 Annual Undergrad Tuition & Fees: $34,600
Enrollment: 855 Coed
Affiliation or Control: Independent Non-Profit IRS Status: 501(c)3
Highest Offering: Master's
Accreditation: HLC, ACATE

01 President .... Mr. Charles G. LIEF
100 Special Advisor to the President .... Ms. Joy VALANIA
05 Chief Academic Officer .... Ms. Sue WEST
10 Vice President of Operations/CFO .... Mr. Tyler KELSCH
84 VP Enroll/Marketing/Student Success .... Ms. Ann Marie KLOTZ
30 Int Vice President of Development .... Mr. Jason EMBRY
21 AVP for Budget/Financial Affairs .... Ms. Yvonne GATES
108 Sr Advisor for Inst Effectiveness .... Ms. Cheryl BARBOUR
13 Director of IT .... Mr. David EDMINSTER
28 VP Mission/Culture/Inclusive Cmty .... Ms. Regina SMITH
38 Director Counseling Center .... Ms. Jo-Lynne PARKS
06 Registrar .... Vacant
08 Library Director .... Ms. Amanda RYBIN KOOB
18 Director of Safety/Facilities & Ops .... Mr. Aaron COOK
37 Dir Student Financial Services .... Ms. Jessica BREJC
15 Director of Human Resources .... Mr. Kert HUBIN
106 Director of Online Education .... Mr. Jirka HLADIS

Nazarene Bible College (A)

1465 Kelly Johnson Blvd, Colorado Springs CO 80920
County: El Paso FICE Identification: 013007
Unit ID: 127714
Telephone: (719) 884-5000 Carnegie Class: Spec-4-yr-Faith
FAX Number: (719) 884-5199 Calendar System: Trimester
URL: nbc.edu
Established: 1964 Annual Undergrad Tuition & Fees: $10,320
Enrollment: 608 Coed
Affiliation or Control: Church Of The Nazarene IRS Status: 501(c)3
Highest Offering: Baccalaureate
Accreditation: #HLC, BI

01 President .... Dr. Scott J. SHERWOOD
05 Provost .... Dr. Alan D. LYKE
10 Vice President for Finance .... Mrs. Shirley A. CADLE
37 Financial Aid Officer .... Mrs. Jan EDWARDS
06 Registrar .... Rev. Duane A. MATHIAS
13 Chief Information Officer .... Mr. Fred R. PHILLIPS
04 Executive Asst to President .... Rev. Susan P. MCKEITHEN
09 Institutional Research .... Dr. David M. CHURCH
15 Director Personnel Services .... Mrs. Carol A. CRIPPEN
29 Director Alumni Relations .... Rev. Susan P. MCKEITHEN
90 Director Academic Computing .... Vacant
07 Director of Admissions/Enrollment .... Rev. Will E. MACKEY
88 Exec Asst to VP Academic Affairs .... Ms. Karen COLSTON
88 Exec Assist to VP for Finance .... Ms. Michelle D. AVERY
08 Librarian .... Mr. Addison LUCCHI
88 Recruiting Representative .... Dr. Gary HAINES
88 Alliance Director .... Vacant
88 Admissions Counselor .... Ms. Winda LOVETT
88 Academic Advisor .... Mr. Stephen EDWARDS
121 Academic Advisor .... Mr. Aaron HOFFMAN
26 Communications Manager .... Ms. Michelle D. AVERY

Northeastern Junior College (B)

100 College Avenue, Sterling CO 80751-2399
County: Logan FICE Identification: 001361
Unit ID: 127732
Telephone: (970) 521-6600 Carnegie Class: Assoc/MT-VT-Mix Trad/Non
FAX Number: (970) 522-4945 Calendar System: Semester
URL: www.njc.edu
Established: 1941 Annual Undergrad Tuition & Fees (In-State): $5,288
Enrollment: 1,293 Coed
Affiliation or Control: State IRS Status: 501(c)3
Highest Offering: Associate Degree
Accreditation: HLC, ADNUR

01 President .... RADM. Michael WHITE, RET.
05 Vice President Instruction .... Dr. Sam SOLIMAN
10 Vice Pres Finance & Administration .... Ms. Lisa LEFEVRE
32 Vice President Student Services .... Mr. Steven SMITH
29 Alumni Director .... Ms. Heather BRUNGARDT
102 Executive Director NJC Foundation .... Ms. Vivian HADLEY
06 Director Records/Admission Process .... Ms. Lisa SCHAEFER
37 Director of Financial Aid .... Ms. Ashley UNREIN
39 Dir Resident Life/Student Activity .... Mr. Timothy STAHLEY
18 Physical Plant Director .... Mr. Tracey KNOX
15 Human Resources Director .... Ms. Jeri ESTRADA
41 Athletic Director .... Ms. Marci HENRY
96 Director of Purchasing .... Ms. Martha GAREIS
09 Dir of Inst Research/Plng/Devel .... Ms. Leslie WEINSHEIM
26 Director of Communications .... Ms. Jesse QUINLIN
21 Controller .... Ms. Judy MCFADDEN
13 Director Information Technology .... Ms. Cherie BRUNGARDT
40 Bookstore Director .... Ms. Heather BRUNGARDT
04 Executive Asst to President .... Ms. Shawn ROSE
07 Director of Admissions .... Ms. Camille ROSE
106 Dir Online Education/E-learning .... Vacant
108 Director Institutional Assessment .... Ms. Catheryne TRENKLE
25 Chief Contracts/Grants Admin .... Vacant

Otero College (C)

1802 Colorado Avenue, La Junta CO 81050-3346
County: Otero FICE Identification: 001362
Unit ID: 127778
Telephone: (719) 384-6800 Carnegie Class: Assoc/HVT-Mix Trad/Non
FAX Number: (719) 384-6933 Calendar System: Semester
URL: www.otero.edu
Established: 1941 Annual Undergrad Tuition & Fees (In-State): $4,100
Enrollment: 1,216 Coed
Affiliation or Control: State IRS Status: 501(c)3
Highest Offering: Associate Degree
Accreditation: HLC, ADNUR, MLTAD

01 President .... Dr. Timothy ALVAREZ
10 Vice Pres Business & Admin .... Mrs. Jennifer JOHNSTON
05 VP Academic & Student Affairs .... Mrs. Rana BROWN
84 Assoc VP Enrollment Management .... Mrs. Angela MOORE
20 Assoc VP Academic Affairs .... Mrs. Chelsea HERASINGH
32 Dean of Student Affairs .... Mr. Gary ADDINGTON
15 Director of Human Resources .... Mrs. Kelsey BARBEE
18 Director of Physical Plant .... Mr. David GIRARD
40 Bookstore Coordinator .... Mrs. Taylor DONNELL
37 Director of Financial Aid .... Mrs. Amber ASBURY
109 Director of Auxiliary Services .... Mr. Dillon MARTIN
26 Dir of Communications/Development .... Mrs. Angela MOORE
13 Director of Computer Services .... Mr. Shawn BORTON
09 Director of Institutional Research .... Vacant
04 Exec Admin Asst to the President .... Ms. Sarah PETRAMALA
41 Athletic Director .... Mr. Chris CARRILLO
06 Registrar .... Mrs. Kim JUUL

Pikes Peak State College (D)

5675 S Academy Boulevard,
Colorado Springs CO 80906-5498
County: El Paso FICE Identification: 008896
Unit ID: 127820
Telephone: (719) 502-2000 Carnegie Class: Bac/Assoc-Assoc Dom
FAX Number: (719) 502-2201 Calendar System: Semester
URL: www.pikespeak.edu
Established: 1968 Annual Undergrad Tuition & Fees (In-State): $3,967
Enrollment: 12,506 Coed
Affiliation or Control: State IRS Status: 501(c)3
Highest Offering: Baccalaureate
Accreditation: HLC, ACFEI, ADNUR, DA, EMT, NAEYC, NURSE, PTAA, SURGT

01 President .... Dr. Lance BOLTON
04 Exec Assistant to the President .... Vacant
05 Vice Pres of Instruction .... Ms. Jacquelyn GAITERS-JORDAN
32 Vice President Student Services .... Mr. Homer WESLEY
10 Vice Pres Administrative Services .... Mr. Duane RISSE
103 Vice Pres of Workforce Development .... Vacant
35 Assoc Vice Pres of Student Services .... Ms. Dawna HAYNES
88 Director of Instructional Support .... Ms. Rose ANGRY
37 Director of Financial Aid .... Mr. Ronald SWARTWOOD
08 Director of Libraries .... Ms. Carole OLDS
15 Exec Dir of Human Resource Services .... Mr. Carlton BROOKS
26 Exec Dir Marketing/Communications .... Mr. Warren EPSTEIN
28 Exec Director of Diversity/Equity .... Mr. Keith BARNES
21 Director of Business Svcs .... Mr. Alberto TEIXEIRA
06 Registrar/Coordinator of Records .... Ms. Twila HUMPHREY
07 Director of Admissions .... Mr. Kevin HUDGENS
102 Exec Director of Foundation .... Ms. Lisa JAMES
18 Director Facilities .... Mr. Roland SCOBEE
13 Chief Technology Officer .... Mr. Cyrille PARENT
19 Dir Public Safety/Emergency Mgmt .... Mr. Jim BARRENTINE
09 Exec Dir of Inst Effectiveness .... Dr. Patrica DIWARA
88 Director of Advising & Testing .... Mr. Lincoln WULF
96 Director of Purchasing .... Ms. Rockie HURRELL
38 Director Counseling Center .... Ms. Yolanda HARRIS
109 Director Auxiliary Services .... Ms. Lorelle DAVIES
09 Director of Institutional Research .... Vacant
88 Project Dir of Stdnt Support Svcs .... Mr. Michael COUILLARD
76 Dean Health and Science .... Ms. Kristen JOHNSON
81 Dean Mathematics & English .... Mr. Joe SOUTHCOTT
50 Dean Business/Public Service/SS .... Mr. Rob HUDSON
60 Dean Comm/Humanities/Tech Studies .... Ms. Fran HETRICK
88 Dean of High School Programs .... Ms. Chelsy HARRIS
20 Dean of Academic Resources .. Ms. Jacquelyn GAITERS-JORDAN

Pima Medical Institute (E)

13750 E. Mississippi Avenue, Aurora CO 80012
County: Arapahoe FICE Identification: 041771
Unit ID: 461689
Telephone: (303) 368-7462 Carnegie Class: Spec 2-yr-Health
FAX Number: N/A Calendar System: Other
URL: pmi.edu
Established: 2012 Annual Undergrad Tuition & Fees: N/A
Enrollment: 362 Coed
Affiliation or Control: Proprietary IRS Status: Proprietary
Highest Offering: Associate Degree
Accreditation: ABHES

01 Campus Director .... Ms. Terri SPENCER

Pima Medical Institute-Colorado Springs (F)

5725 Mark Dabling Blvd, Suite 150,
Colorado Springs CO 80919
Telephone: (719) 482-7462 Identification: 770516
Accreditation: ABHES

† Branch campus of Pima Medical Institute-Tucson, Tucson, AZ

Pima Medical Institute-Denver (G)

7475 Dakin Street, Suite 100, Denver CO 80221
Telephone: (303) 426-1800 Identification: 666171
Accreditation: ABHES, COARC, OTA, PTAA, RAD

† Branch campus of Pima Medical Institute, Tucson, AZ.

Platt College (H)

3100 S Parker Road, Suite 200, Aurora CO 80014-3141
County: Arapahoe FICE Identification: 030149
Unit ID: 260813
Telephone: (303) 369-5151 Carnegie Class: Spec-4-yr-Other Health
FAX Number: (303) 745-1433 Calendar System: Quarter
URL: www.plattcolorado.edu
Established: 1986 Annual Undergrad Tuition & Fees: $20,590
Enrollment: 227 Coed
Affiliation or Control: Proprietary IRS Status: Proprietary
Highest Offering: Baccalaureate
Accreditation: ACCSC, NUR

00 Owner .... Mr. Jerald B. SIRBU
01 President .... Dr. Julie BASLER
10 Chief Financial Officer .... Mr. Robert CRAVER
37 Director of Financial Aid .... Mr. Michael J. VIGIL
08 Head Librarian .... Ms. Laura CULLERTON
66 Dean College of Nursing .... Dr. Frances RICKER
06 Registrar .... Ms. Antonia DALPIAZ
07 Admissions Representative .... Ms. Samantha SINGLETON
13 Coordinator of IT Services .... Mr. Mark FINKEN

Pueblo Community College (I)

900 W Orman Avenue, Pueblo CO 81004-1499
County: Pueblo FICE Identification: 021163
Unit ID: 127884
Telephone: (719) 549-3200 Carnegie Class: Bac/Assoc-Assoc Dom
FAX Number: (719) 544-1179 Calendar System: Semester
URL: www.pueblocc.edu
Established: 1933 Annual Undergrad Tuition & Fees (In-State): $4,520
Enrollment: 5,551 Coed
Affiliation or Control: State IRS Status: 501(c)3
Highest Offering: Baccalaureate
Accreditation: HLC, ACFEI, ADNUR, CAHIIM, COARC, DH, EMT, OTA, PTAA, SURGT

01 President .... Dr. Patricia ERJAVEC
04 Executive Asst to President .... Ms. Julie JIMENEZ
10 VP of Administration and Finance .... Mr. Robert GONZALES
05 VP of Academic Support .... Dr. Quincy ROSE-SEWELL
32 VP of Student Success .... Dr. Heather SPEED
15 VP of Human Resources .... Vacant
12 Interim Executive Dean PCCSW Campus .... Dr. Kevin ATEN
12 Executive Dean Fremont Campus .... Vacant
76 Dean Health & Public Safety .... Dr. Andrew MILLER
49 Dean Arts & Sciences .... Dr. Young KIM
50 Dean Business & Advanced Technology ... Dr. Jennifer SHERMAN
88 Dean Medical & Behavioral Health .... Dr. Rajashree PANDIT
26 Director Marketing/Communications .... Ms. Erin HERGERT
09 Director Institutional Research .... Dr. Cory BUTTS
13 Dir Information Technology Services .... Mr. Bryan CRAWFORD
88 Exec Dir Pueblo Corporate College .... Ms. Amanda CORUM
102 Director of PCC Foundation .... Ms. Martha SIMMONS
07 Dir Admissions & Records/Registrar .... Ms. Barbara BENEDICT
21 Controller .... Ms. Robin ARWOOD
37 Director Financial Aid .... Ms. Pamela GRABLE
18 Director Facilities Services .... Vacant
08 Director Library Services .... Ms. Christina MCGRATH
35 Dean of Students .... Mr. Vernon JAMES
96 Director Purchasing .... Mr. Edmond INIGUEZ
121 Dir Student Support & Outreach Svcs .... Mr. Michael GAGE
120 Multimedia Tech Specialist .... Mr. Robin LEACH
06 Registrar .... Ms. Barbara BENEDICT
19 Director Public Safety .... Mr. William BROWN

Pueblo Community College Fremont Campus (J)

51320 W Highway 50, Canon City CO 81212
Telephone: (719) 296-6100 Identification: 770042
Accreditation: &HLC

Pueblo Community College Southwest Campus (K)

33057 Highway 160, Mancos CO 81328
Telephone: (970) 564-6200 Identification: 770044
Accreditation: &HLC

Red Rocks Community College (L)

13300 W Sixth Avenue, Lakewood CO 80228-1255
County: Jefferson FICE Identification: 009543
Unit ID: 127909
Telephone: (303) 914-6600 Carnegie Class: Bac/Assoc-Assoc Dom
FAX Number: (303) 914-6666 Calendar System: Semester
URL: www.rrcc.edu
Established: 1969 Annual Undergrad Tuition & Fees (In-State): $4,379
Enrollment: 6,029 Coed
Affiliation or Control: State IRS Status: 501(c)3
Highest Offering: Master's
Accreditation: HLC, ARCPA, MAC, NAEYC, RAD

01 President .... Dr. Michele HANEY
04 Exec Assistant to the President .... Ms. Kathy SCHISSLER
10 Vice Pres Administrative Services .... Mr. Bryan BRYANT
05 Vice President Academic Affairs .... Dr. Beverly CLARK, III
32 Director of Student Affairs .... Dr. Armando BURCIAGA
121 Vice Pres Student Success .... Dr. Lisa FOWLER
103 Vice Pres Workforce/Community Devel .... Ms. Angela KING
20 Dean Academic Services .... Vacant
20 Dean Instructional Services .... Ms. Barbra SOBHANI
20 Dn Instructional Svcs Arvada Campus .... Ms. Jennifer KROETCH
13 Dean Instructional Technology .... Mr. Jon JOHNSON
88 Dean of Instruct/Exec Dir RMEC-OSHA .... Vacant
85 Director International Education .... Vacant
07 Dir Student Recruit/Advising/Admiss .... Vacant
21 Controller .... Ms. Holly GENTRY
37 Director Financial Aid .... Ms. Shannon WEBBER
06 Dean Enrollment Services .... Vacant
18 Director Facilities .... Mr. Mark BANA
15 Exec Director Human Resources .... Ms. Patty DAVIES
102 Assoc VP of Inst Advancement .... Vacant
26 Director Marketing/Communications .... Vacant
35 Director Campus Life .... Dr. Steven ZEEH
88 Dir Childhood Ed & Support Svcs .... Ms. Janiece KNEPPE

09 Director Institutional Research ... Mr. Charles DUELL
96 Coordinator Purchasing ... Ms. Renee MURILLO
36 Director Student Outreach ... Vacant
46 Exec Dir Planning/Rsrch/Inst Effect ... Mr. Derek GRUBB
28 Dir of Diversity/Equity/Involvement ... Ms. Jen MACKEN
88 Assoc Dean of Enrollment Management .. Ms. Jen BROADWATER
124 Director Advising/Transfer/Tutoring ... Ms. Yvanna CORELLA

Red Rocks Community College Arvada Campus (A)

10280 W. 55th Avenue, Arvada CO 80002
Telephone: (303) 914-6010 Identification: 770045
Accreditation: &HLC

Regis University (B)

3333 Regis Boulevard, #B-4, Denver CO 80221-1099
County: Denver FICE Identification: 001363
Unit ID: 127918
Telephone: (303) 458-4100 Carnegie Class: DU-Mod
FAX Number: (303) 964-5449 Calendar System: Semester
URL: www.regis.edu
Established: 1877 Annual Undergrad Tuition & Fees: $38,558
Enrollment: 6,310 Coed
Affiliation or Control: Roman Catholic IRS Status: 501(c)3
Highest Offering: Doctorate
Accreditation: HLC, CACREP, CAHIIM, EXSC, MFCD, NURSE, PHAR, PTA

01 President ... Rev. John P. FITZGIBBONS, SJ
43 Chief Legal Officer ... Dr. Janelle RAMSEL
05 Provost ... Dr. Janet HOUSER
10 Sr Vice President/CFO ... Dr. Salvador D. ACEVES
111 Vice President Advancement ... Ms. Myrna HALL
100 Chief of Staff to President ... Ms. Terri CAMPBELL
88 Vice President Mission ... Fr. Kevin F. BURKE, SJ
32 Vice President Student Affairs ... Dr. Barbara WILCOTS
50 Dean of Regis College ... Dr. Thomas BOWIE
109 Assoc VP Auxiliary & Business Svcs ... Mr. Josef RILL
15 Assoc VP Human Resources ... Dr. Liz WHITMORE
18 Assoc VP Physical Plant ... Mr. Michael J. REDMOND
26 Assoc VP Marketing/Communication ... Mr. Todd COHEN
110 Asst VP University Advancement ... Ms. Abigail PALSIC
29 Asst VP Alumni Engagement Pgms ... Ms. Margaret LINN-ADDISON
13 Chief Information Officer ... Mr. Jaganmohan GUDUR
77 Dean Anderson College ... Dr. Shari PLANTZ-MASTERS
76 Dean Health Professions ... Dr. Linda OSTERLUND
88 Assoc Dean Health Professions ... Dr. Tristen AMADOR
66 Dean School of Nursing ... Dr. Catherine WITT
08 Dean of Libraries ... Dr. Erin MCCAFFREY
35 Dean of Students ... Mr. Patrick ROMERO-ALDAZ
07 Dean of Admissions ... Ms. Kim FRISCH
37 Director Financial Aid ... Ms. Cindy HEJL
06 Director Registration ... Ms. Cathy GORRELL
06 Director Academic Records ... Ms. Terry GAURMER
38 Dir Counseling/Personal Dev ... Ms. Melissa AURINGER
19 Director of Campus Safety ... Mr. Lance JONES
88 Director of Advancement Services ... Ms. Jean CAMBER
42 Director of University Ministry ... Mr. Kyle TURNER
41 Asst VP/Director Athletics ... Mr. David SPAFFORD
04 Executive Assistant to President ... Ms. Rita CONTRERAS
39 Assoc Dir Resident Life/Housing ... Mr. Eric BARNES
28 Associate Provost Diversity ... Dr. Nicki GONZALES
44 Assistant Director Annual Giving ... Mr. Alec THORNTON

Rocky Mountain College of Art & Design (C)

1600 Pierce Street, Lakewood CO 80214-1433
County: Denver FICE Identification: 007649
Unit ID: 127945
Telephone: (303) 753-6046 Carnegie Class: Bac-Diverse
FAX Number: (303) 759-4970 Calendar System: Semester
URL: www.rmcad.edu
Established: 1963 Annual Undergrad Tuition & Fees: $20,725
Enrollment: 1,643 Coed
Affiliation or Control: Proprietary IRS Status: Proprietary
Highest Offering: Master's
Accreditation: HLC, ART, CIDA

01 President ... Mr. Brent FITCH
05 Senior Vice President Academic Affairs ... Dr. Darcy OROZCO
26 Senior Vice Pres of Marketing ... Mr. Daron RODRIGUEZ
07 Vice President of Admissions ... Mr. Brian BELLIVEAU
32 Dean of Students ... Mr. Robert FLADRY
108 Director Accreditation/Compliance ... Dr. Terence BRENNAN

Rocky Vista University (D)

8401 South Chambers Road, Parker CO 80112
County: Douglas Identification: 667002
Unit ID: 480790
Telephone: (303) 373-2008 Carnegie Class: Spec-4-yr-Med
FAX Number: N/A Calendar System: Other
URL: www.rvu.edu
Established: 2006 Annual Graduate Tuition & Fees: N/A
Enrollment: 1,332 Coed
Affiliation or Control: Proprietary IRS Status: Proprietary
Highest Offering: Doctorate; No Undergraduates
Accreditation: HLC, #ARCPA, OSTEO

01 President ... Dr. David FORSTEIN
04 Executive Administrative Assistant ... Ms. Michele SOBCZYK
05 Provost ... Dr. David FORSTEIN
09 VP for Institutional Effectiveness ... Vacant
84 VP of Enrollment Mgmt/Ext Relations ... Ms. Julie ROSENTHAL
88 Compliance Coordinator ... Ms. Laura DEMENT
10 VP Finance & Controller ... Mr. David IRONS
37 Dir Student Financial Svc ... Ms. Fran LATA
32 Assoc Dean Student Affairs ... Dr. David ROOS
06 Registrar ... Mr. David PALTZA
08 Director of Library Services ... Dr. Brian SCHWARTZ
19 Manager Security/Safety ... Mr. Andrew STEVENS
15 VP of Human Resources ... Mr. Jerry ARMSTRONG
101 Secretary of the Institution/Board ... Ms. Michele SOBCZYK
38 Mental Health & Wellness Counselor ... Ms. Karen ROBINSON
39 Director Resident Life/Student Hous ... Ms. Vielane VAN NOY
63 Dean RVUCOM/VP of Faculty ... Dr. Heather FERRILL
13 Manager Information Services ... Mr. Brad ELLIS

St. John Vianney Theological Seminary (E)

1300 S Steele Street, Denver CO 80210-2526
County: Denver Identification: 666127
Telephone: (303) 282-3427 Carnegie Class: Not Classified
FAX Number: (303) 282-3453 Calendar System: Semester
URL: www.sjvdenver.edu
Established: 1999 Annual Graduate Tuition & Fees: N/A
Enrollment: N/A Male
Affiliation or Control: Roman Catholic IRS Status: 501(c)3
Highest Offering: Master's; No Undergraduates
Accreditation: THEOL

01 Rector ... VRev. Daniel S. LEONARD
03 Vice Rector ... Rev. John NEPIL
05 Academic Dean ... Dr. Alphonso PINTO
10 Director of Finance ... Ms. Vanesa GARCIA
08 Library Director ... Mr. Stephen SWEENEY
06 Registrar ... Ms. Denise SEERY
04 Administrative Asst to President ... Ms. Val CAREY

Southwest Acupuncture College (F)

6630 Gunpark Drive Suite 200, Boulder CO 80301-3339
Telephone: (303) 581-9955 Identification: 666618
Accreditation: ACUP

† Branch campus of Southwest Acupuncture College, Santa Fe, NM.

Spartan College of Aeronautics and Technology (G)

10851 W 120th Avenue, Broomfield CO 80021-3401
County: Broomfield FICE Identification: 007297
Unit ID: 126605
Telephone: (303) 466-1714 Carnegie Class: Spec 2-yr-Tech
FAX Number: (303) 496-0211 Calendar System: Other
URL: www.spartan.edu
Established: 1965 Annual Undergrad Tuition & Fees: $14,199
Enrollment: 292 Coed
Affiliation or Control: Proprietary IRS Status: Proprietary
Highest Offering: Associate Degree
Accreditation: ACCSC

01 Campus President ... Mr. Nicholas BROWN
05 Dean of Academic Affairs ... Mr. Dwayne ISBELL
07 Director of Admissions ... Mr. Jeremy COOPER
32 Dean of Student Affairs ... Mr. Corey O'BRIEN
06 Registrar ... Ms. Antonia MURPHY
37 Director of Student Finance ... Mr. Nicholas DIMANNA

The Taft University System (H)

3333 South Wadsworth Blvd, Ste D228, Lakewood CO 80227
County: Jefferson FICE Identification: 041004
Unit ID: 454689
Telephone: (303) 867-1155 Carnegie Class: DU-Mod
FAX Number: (303) 867-1156 Calendar System: Semester
URL: www.taft.edu
Established: 1976 Annual Undergrad Tuition & Fees: N/A
Enrollment: 614 Coed
Affiliation or Control: Proprietary IRS Status: Proprietary
Highest Offering: Doctorate
Accreditation: DEAC

01 President ... Dr. Neil A. JOHNSON
11 Director Administration/Registrar ... Ms. Christine A. BALDWIN
50 Dean School of Business ... Dr. Anita CASSARD
53 Dean School of Education ... Dr. Barry RESNICK
05 Chief Academic Officer ... Dr. Neil A. JOHNSON
07 Director of Admissions ... Ms. Ni PHAM
26 Director of Digital Marketing ... Ms. Megan MENENDEZ
32 Director of Student Affairs ... Ms. Stephanie ESTLOW
37 Director Student Financial Aid ... Ms. Deanna SANDOVAL
45 Chief Institutional Planning Ofcr ... Dr. Richard BOOROM

† Tuition varies by degree program.

Trinidad State College (I)

600 Prospect, Trinidad CO 81082-2396
County: Las Animas FICE Identification: 001368
Unit ID: 128258
Telephone: (719) 846-5011 Carnegie Class: Assoc/MT-VT-Mix Trad/Non
FAX Number: N/A Calendar System: Semester
URL: www.trinidadstate.edu
Established: 1925 Annual Undergrad Tuition & Fees (In-State): $5,299
Enrollment: 1,404 Coed
Affiliation or Control: State IRS Status: 501(c)3
Highest Offering: Baccalaureate
Accreditation: HLC, ADNUR, NURSE

01 President ... Dr. Rhonda EPPER
05 Vice President of Academic Affairs ... Dr. Lynette BATES
11 Vice Pres Administrative Services ... Ms. Shannon SHIVELEY
10 Controller ... Ms. Amanda VIGIL
20 Dean of Instruction ... Ms. LoriRae HAMILTON
124 Dean Student Retention/Completion ... Mr. Alfredo BURCIAGA
37 Asst Director Financial Aid ... Ms. Christina SISNEROS
06 Registrar ... Ms. Christy HOLDEN
18 Director of Physical Plant Opers ... Mr. Danny ROGERS
12 Vice President Valley Campus ... Mr. James KYNOR
106 Dir Online Educ/Dir of Technology ... Mr. Ira WILLIAMSON
04 Admin Asst to President ... Ms. Linda PERRY
41 Athletic Director ... Mr. Michael SALBATO
09 Director of Institutional Research ... Ms. Annette LUJAN
15 Human Resources Director ... Ms. Yvette ATENCIO
39 Housing Director ... Mr. Omar CANO
84 Director Enrollment Management ... Mr. Alfredo BURCIAGA

Trinidad State College San Luis Valley Campus (J)

1011 Main Street, Alamosa CO 81101
Telephone: (719) 589-7000 Identification: 770047
Accreditation: &HLC

UCH Memorial Hospital School Of Radiologic Technology (K)

2420 E. Pikes Peak Avenue, Colorado Springs CO 80910
County: El Paso Identification: 667097
Telephone: (719) 365-8291 Carnegie Class: Not Classified
FAX Number: (719) 365-5374 Calendar System: Semester
URL: www.uchealth.org/radschool
Established: 1969 Annual Undergrad Tuition & Fees: N/A
Enrollment: N/A Coed
Affiliation or Control: Independent Non-Profit IRS Status: 501(c)3
Highest Offering: Associate Degree
Accreditation: RAD

01 Director ... Elaine R. IVAN
05 Dean of Education ... Jarad MUASAU
11 Administrator ... Joseph DAILY
06 Registrar/Clinical Coordinator ... Danielle MASSAGEE
07 Director of Admissions ... Elaine R. IVAN
08 Librarian ... Megan MCCREIGHT

*University of Colorado System Office (L)

1800 Grant Street, Suite 800, Denver CO 80203
County: Denver FICE Identification: 007996
Unit ID: 128300
Telephone: (303) 860-5600 Carnegie Class: N/A
FAX Number: (303) 860-5610
URL: www.cu.edu

01 President ... Mr. Todd SALIMAN
05 Vice Pres Academic Affairs ... Dr. Michael LIGHTNER
100 Senior VP & Chief of Staff ... Mr. Leonard DINEGAR
10 Sr Assoc VP Business Ops & CFO ... Vacant
43 VP/University Counsel/Secy Board ... Mr. Jeremy HUETH
111 Interim Assoc VP for Advancement ... Ms. Annie BACCARY
15 Sr AVP/Chief Human Resource Ofcr ... Vacant
86 Sr Assoc VP State Relations ... Ms. Heather RETZKO
26 Assoc VP University Relations ... Mr. Mike SANDLER
21 Asst VP & University Controller ... Mr. Robert KUEHLER
13 Asst VP & Chief Information Ofcr ... Mr. Scott MUNSON
27 Sr Asst VP for University Relations ... Ms. Elizabeth COLLINS
88 Asst VP External Rels & Advocacy ... Mr. Tony SALAZAR
45 Asst VP Strategic Initiatives ... Ms. Angelique FOSTER
28 Chief Diversity Officer ... Vacant
86 Sr Associate VP Fed Rels Outreach ... Mr. Jack WALDORF
22 Chief Compliance Officer Title IX ... Ms. Valerie SIMONS
88 Treasurer ... Mr. Tony VU

*University of Colorado Boulder (M)

Regent Drive At Broadway, Boulder CO 80309-0001
County: Boulder FICE Identification: 001370
Unit ID: 126614
Telephone: (303) 492-1411 Carnegie Class: DU-Highest
FAX Number: N/A Calendar System: Semester
URL: www.colorado.edu
Established: 1876 Annual Undergrad Tuition & Fees (In-State): $12,466
Enrollment: 37,437 Coed
Affiliation or Control: State IRS Status: 501(c)3
Highest Offering: Doctorate

Accreditation: HLC, AUD, CEA, CLPSY, IPSY, JOUR, LAW, MUS, SP

02 Chancellor ... Dr. Phillip P. DISTEFANO
05 Provost & Exec VC for Acad Affairs ... Dr. Russell MOORE
11 Chief Operating Officer ... Mr. Patrick O'ROURKE
111 Vice Chanc for Advancement . Ms. Katy HERBERT KOTLARCZYK
28 Senior Vice Chanc for DEI ... Dr. Sonia DELUCA FERNÁNDEZ
32 Acting Vice Chanc Student Affairs ... Mr. Austin J. BANKS
88 Int VC Infrastruc/Sustainability ... Mr. Chris EWING
46 Vice Chancellor for Research ... Dr. Terri FIEZ
10 Chief Financial Officer ... Ms. Carla HO-A
15 Interim Chief HR Officer ... Dr. Merna JACOBSEN
13 Sr Assoc VC for IT/Chief Info Ofcr ... Dr. Marin STANEK
20 Exec Vice Prov Acad Resource Mgmt ... Dr. Ann SCHMIESING
22 AVC & Title IX Coordinator ... Ms. Llen POMERY
108 Sr Vice Prov Acad Plng/Assessment ... Dr. Katherine EGGERT
20 Dean & Vice Provost of Undergrad Ed ... Dr. Daryl J. MAEDA
58 Dean of the Graduate School ... Dr. E. Scott ADLER
26 Senior Assoc VC Strategic Comm ... Mr. Jon LESLIE
84 Assoc VC of Enrollment Mgt ... Mr. Kevin MACLENNAN
20 Assoc Vice Chanc Faculty Affairs ... Dr. Michele N. MOSES
88 AVC Integrity/Safety/Compliance ... Mr. Dan JONES
18 Acting Assoc VC for Facilities Mgmt ... Mr. Brian LINDOERFER
29 Asst Vice Chanc Alumni Relations ... Mr. Ryan CHREIST
08 Dean of Libraries ... Mr. Robert H. MCDONALD
49 Interim Dean of Arts & Sciences ... Dr. James WHITE
50 Dean of Business ... Dr. Sharon MATUSIK
51 Dean of Division of Continuing Educ ... Dr. Sara THOMPSON
53 Dean of Education ... Dr. Katherine SCHULTZ
54 Interim Dean of Engineering ... Dr. Keith MOLENAAR
61 Dean of Law ... Dr. Lolita BUCKNER INNISS
60 Dean of Media/Communications/Info ... Dr. Lori BERGEN
64 Dean of Music ... Dr. John DAVIS
37 Director of Financial Aid ... Ms. Ofelia A. MORALES
09 Dir of Institutional Research ... Mr. Robert STUBBS
41 Athletic Director ... Mr. Rick GEORGE
06 Registrar ... Dr. Kristi WOLD-MCCORMICK
07 Exec Director of Admissions ... Mr. Clark BRIGGER
35 Acting Dean of Students ... Mr. Devin CRAMER
43 Sr Managing Assoc Univ Counsel ... Ms. Elvira U. STREHLE-HENSON
100 Chief of Staff ... Ms. Catherine SHEA
36 Director of Career Services ... Ms. Lisa LOVETT
25 Dir of Contracts and Grants ... Mr. Gary HENRY
19 Chief of Police ... Ms. Doreen JOKERST
88 Director of Museum ... Dr. Patrick KOCIOLEK
104 Director of Education Abroad ... Ms. Sylvie BURNET-JONES
38 Dir Counseling & Psychiatric Svcs ... Ms. Jennifer KOCH

*University of Colorado Colorado Springs (A)

1420 Austin Bluffs Parkway, Colorado Springs CO 80918
County: El Paso — FICE Identification: 004509
Unit ID: 126580
Telephone: (719) 255-8227 — Carnegie Class: DU-Higher
FAX Number: (719) 255-3362 — Calendar System: Semester
URL: www.uccs.edu
Established: 1965 — Annual Undergrad Tuition & Fees (In-State): $8,580
Enrollment: 12,380 — Coed
Affiliation or Control: State — IRS Status: 501(c)3
Highest Offering: Doctorate
Accreditation: HLC, CAATE, CACREP, CLPSY, DIET, DIETD, NURSE, SPAA, @SW

02 Chancellor ... Dr. Venkat REDDY
05 Provost/VC Academic Affairs ... Dr. Nancy MARCHAND-MARTELLA
10 Interim VC Admin & Finance ... Karl SPIECKER
111 VC University Advancement ... Martin WOOD
32 VC Student Affairs ... Carlos GARCIA
20 Assoc VC Academic Affairs ... Dr. Susan TAYLOR
18 Chief Facilities/Physical Plant ... Vacant
43 Assistant Legal Counsel ... Tia LUBER
13 Asst VC Info Technology ... Harper JOHNSON
46 Assoc VC Research ... Dr. Jessi L. SMITH
25 Director of Sponsored Programs ... Gwen GENNARO
09 Director of Institutional Research ... Dr. Robyn MARSCHKE
119 Director Cybersecurity ... Gretchen BLISS
15 Asst Vice Chanc Human Resources ... Vacant
19 Director Police Operations ... Clayton GARNER
37 Director Financial Aid ... Jevita ROGERS
26 Asst VC Marketing Communications ... Chris VALENTINE
38 Director Student Counseling ... Dr. Benek ALTAYLI
41 Director of Athletics ... Nathan GIBSON
29 Director Alumni Relations ... Joanna BEAN
35 Dean of Students ... Amanda ALLEE
49 Dean of Letters/Arts/Science ... Dr. Lynn VIDLER
50 Dean of Business ... Dr. Karen MARKEL
53 Dean of Education ... Vacant
54 Dean of Engineering ... Dr. Don RABERN
80 Dean of Public Affairs ... Dr. George REED
66 Dean Nursing/Health Sciences ... Dr. Kevin LAUDNER
58 Dean of Graduate School ... Dr. Kelli KLEBE
08 Dean of Library ... Seth PORTER
39 Director Campus Housing ... Ralph GIESE
06 Registrar ... Tracy BARBER
07 Dir of Admissions/Recruitment ... Chris BEISWANGER
04 Executive Asst to the Chancellor ... Elizabeth WYATT
105 Director Web Services ... Craig DECKER
40 Director of Bookstore ... Paul DENISTON
104 Director Study Abroad ... Dr. Mandy HANSEN
106 Director of Extended Studies ... Candida BENNETT

30 Director of Development ... Melinda HAGEMANN
100 Chief of Staff ... Andrea CORDOVA
28 VC Diversity ... Rame HANNA
84 Dir of Enrollment Mgmt ... Mathew COX
86 Director of Partnerships & Govt ... Jenifer FURDA

*University of Colorado Denver | Anschutz Medical Campus (B)

13001 East 17th Place, Aurora CO 80045
County: Denver — FICE Identification: 004508
Unit ID: 126562
Telephone: (303) 556-2400 — Carnegie Class: DU-Highest
FAX Number: N/A — Calendar System: Semester
URL: https://www.cuanschutz.edu/
Established: 1912 — Annual Undergrad Tuition & Fees (In-State): $9,401
Enrollment: 24,723 — Coed
Affiliation or Control: State — IRS Status: 501(c)3
Highest Offering: Doctorate
Accreditation: HLC, AA, ARCPA, CACREP, CAMPEP, CLPSY, DENT, DMS, HSA, IPSY, LSAR, MED, MFCD, MIDWF, NURSE, PAST, PH, PHAR, PLNG, PTA, SCPSY, SPAA

02 Chancellor - CU Anschutz Med Campus ... Mr. Donald M. ELLIMAN, JR.
00 Chancellor - CU Denver ... Dr. Michelle MARKS
17 VC Health Affairs/Dean Medical Sch ... Dr. John J. REILLY, JR.
46 Vice Chancellor for Research ... Dr. Thomas FLAIG
10 EVC Admin/Finance & CFO ... Ms. Terri C. CARROTHERS
26 VC Marketing/Communications ... Ms. Kathy GREEN
05 Provost & EVC Academic/Student Affs ... Dr. Roderick NAIRN
111 Vice Chanc of Advancement Anschutz ... Mr. Scott ARTHUR
32 Int VProv/SVC Student Success ... Ms. Alana JONES
52 Dean School of Dental Medicine ... Dr. Denise KASSEBAUM
66 Dean College of Nursing ... Dr. Elias PROVENCIO-VASQUEZ
67 Dean School of Pharmacy ... Dr. Ralph ALTIERE
69 Dean CO School of Public Health ... Dr. David GOFF
58 Dean Graduate School ... Dr. David ENGELKE
64 Dean College of Arts/Media ... Dr. Laurence KAPTAIN
80 Dean School of Public Affairs ... Dr. Paul TESKE
49 Dean College Liberal Arts & Sci ... Dr. Pamela JANSMA
48 Dean College of Arch/Planning ... Mr. Mark GELERNTER
50 Dean Business School ... Ms. Sueann AMBRON
53 Dean School of Education ... Dr. Rebecca KANTOR
54 Dean College of Engineering ... Dr. Marc INGBER
88 Assoc Vice Chancellor for Research ... Dr. Robert DAMRAUER
20 Assoc VC Academic Affairs ... Dr. Laura GOODWIN
28 Assoc VC Diversity/Inclusion/Equity ... Ms. Regina RICHARDS
21 Assoc VC Finance/Controller ... Ms. E. Kim HUBER
18 Assoc VC Facilities Management ... Mr. David C. TURNQUIST
20 Assoc VC of Academic Planning ... Dr. Terry POTTER
15 Assoc VC Human Resources ... Ms. Carolyn BROWNAWELL
13 Asst VC Information Technology Svcs ... Vacant
106 Asst VC Acad Tech/Extended Learning ... Mr. Robert TOLSMA
84 Asst VC UG Admissions/K-12 Outreach ... Mr. Chris DOWEN
09 Asst VC Institutional Research ... Dr. Christine STROUP-BENHAM
121 Asst VC Student Success ... Ms. Peggy LORE
35 Interim Asst VC University Life ... Mr. Sam KIM
06 Asst VC Univ Registrar ... Ms. Lara MEDLEY
08 Director Auraria Library ... Dr. Mary SOMERVILLE
08 Interim Dir Health Sciences Library ... Ms. Melissa DESANTIS
27 Director PR/Media Relations ... Vacant
37 Director Financial Aid Svcs ... Mr. Justin JARAMILLO
19 Chief of Police ... Mr. Doug ABRAHAM
29 Director Alumni Relations ... Ms. Joy FRENCH
43 Assistant University Counsel ... Mr. Christopher PUCKETT
23 AVC of Health for Student Success ... Dr. Kristin KUSHMIDER
104 Director International Education ... Mr. John SUNNYGARD
45 Chief Institutional Planning ... Vacant

University of Denver (C)

2199 S. University Blvd., Denver CO 80208-0001
County: Denver — FICE Identification: 001371
Unit ID: 127060
Telephone: (303) 871-2000 — Carnegie Class: DU-Highest
FAX Number: (303) 871-3301 — Calendar System: Quarter
URL: www.du.edu
Established: 1864 — Annual Undergrad Tuition & Fees: $53,775
Enrollment: 13,856 — Coed
Affiliation or Control: Independent Non-Profit — IRS Status: 501(c)3
Highest Offering: Doctorate
Accreditation: HLC, ART, CACREP, CAEP, CLPSY, COPSY, IPSY, LAW, LIB, MPCAC, MUS, SCPSY, SW

01 Chancellor ... Dr. Jeremy HAEFNER
05 Provost & Exec Vice Chancellor ... Dr. Mary CLARK
43 Vice Chanc Legal Affs/Gen Counsel ... Mr. Paul H. CHAN
32 Vice Chancellor Student Affairs ... Mr. Todd ADAMS
10 SVC Business/Financial Affairs ... Ms. Leslie BRUNELLI
100 Chief of Staff/Sr Vice Chancellor ... Dr. Nancy NICELY
41 Vice Chanc Athletics and Recreation ... Mr. Joshua BERLO
111 Senior VC University Advancement ... Ms. Val OTTEN
26 Vice Chancellor Communications ... Ms. Renea MORRIS
13 Vice Chancellor/Chief Info Officer ... Mr. Russell KAURLOTO
84 Vice Chancellor for Enrollment ... Mr. Todd RINEHART
37 Assoc Vice Chanc Financial Aid ... Mr. John E. GUDVANGEN
88 Director of Chancellor Engagement ... Ms. Allison RIOLA
20 Vice Provost Academic Program ... Dr. Jennifer KARAS
07 AVC Enroll/Dir Undergrad Admissions ... Mr. Derek DUBOSE
35 AVC Student Affs/Inclusive Excel ... Dr. Niki LATINO
86 Assoc VC Government/Cmty Relations .. Ms. Stephanie O'MALLEY

28 VC Diversity/Equity/Inclusion ... Dr. Christpher M. WHITT
58 Senior Vice Prov Research/Grad Ed ... Dr. Corinne LENGSFELD
08 Dean/Dir University Libraries ... Mr. Michael LEVINE-CLARK
20 Senior Vice Provost Academic Admin ... Dr. Linda KOSTEN
30 Assoc Vice Chanc Univ Development ... Ms. Meriel HUGHES
06 Registrar ... Mr. Dennis M. BECKER
21 Controller ... Mr. Andrew CULLEN
29 Dir Alumni/Career/Prof Development ... Ms. Cindy HYMAN
22 Dir Diversity & Equal Opportunity ... Dr. Kristin DEAL
18 Assoc Vice Chancellor Facilities ... Mr. Allan WILSON
09 Asst Vice Provost Inst Research ... Dr. Mike FURNO
15 Vice Chancellor Human Resources ... Mr. Jeff BANKS
19 Director Campus Safety ... Mr. Michael BUNKER
113 Dir Student Financial Services ... Ms. Janet BURKHARDT
91 Assoc Vice Chanc EAS/Deputy CIO ... Ms. Rohini ANANTHAKRISHNAN
38 Exec Dir Health/Counseling Center ... Dr. Michael J. LAFARR
54 Dean Engr/Computer Science ... Dr. Michelle SABICK
79 Dean Arts/Humanities/Social Science ... Dr. Rhonda GONZALES
81 Dean Natural Science & Mathematics .. Dr. Andrei KUTATELADZE
50 Dean College of Business ... Mr. Vivek CHOUDHURY
61 Dean College of Law ... Dr. Bruce SMITH
82 Dean Graduate Sch of Intl Studies ... Mr. Fritz MAYER
70 Dean Graduate School of Social Work ... Dr. Amanda MCBRIDE
55 Dean University College ... Mr. Michael MCGUIRE
53 Dean College of Education ... Dr. Michelle KNIGHT-MANUEL
88 Exec Director Newman Center ... Ms. Aisha AHMAD-POST
88 Exec Dir Conference Event Services ... Ms. Amanda FUDALA
57 Director School of Art/Art History ... Dr. Annabeth HEADRICK
101 Secretary of the Institution/Board ... Ms. Nancy NICELY
105 Senior Digital Design and Architect ... Mr. Matt ESCHENBAUM
88 Director University Teaching ... Ms. Virgina PITTS
108 Director of Academic Assessment ... Mr. Stephen RILEY
122 Assc Dir Fraternity/Sorority Life ... Mr. Christopher MIOFSKY
104 Director Intl Students/Scholarship ... Ms. Theresa JOHNSON
39 Dir Resident Life/Student Housing ... Ms. Shana ALSTON

University of Northern Colorado (D)

501 20th Street, Greeley CO 80639-6900
County: Weld — FICE Identification: 001349
Unit ID: 127741
Telephone: (970) 351-1890 — Carnegie Class: DU-Mod
FAX Number: (970) 351-1880 — Calendar System: Semester
URL: www.unco.edu
Established: 1889 — Annual Undergrad Tuition & Fees (In-State): $10,062
Enrollment: 11,460 — Coed
Affiliation or Control: State — IRS Status: 501(c)3
Highest Offering: Doctorate
Accreditation: HLC, AUD, CAATE, CACREP, CEA, COPSY, DIETD, DIETI, IPSY, MUS, NASP, NURSE, PH, SCPSY, SP, THEA

01 President ... Mr. Andrew FEINSTEIN
05 Provost/Exec Vice President ... Dr. Kirsten FLEMING
10 Sr Vice Pres/Chief Finance Officer ... Mr. Dale PRATT
43 Vice President/General Counsel . Ms. Jacquie RICH FREDERICKS
111 VP for Advancement ... Ms. Allie STEG HASKETT
32 VP for Student Affairs ... Dr. Cedric HOWARD
58 Assoc VP Research/Dean Grad School ... Dr. Jeri Annette LYONS
29 AVP Alumni Relations ... Ms. Lyndsey CRUM
20 Ast VP Undergrad Stds/Dean Univ Col ... Vacant
114 Asst Vice Pres Budgets/Analysis ... Mr. Dale PRATT
13 Asst Vice President Info Technology ... Vacant
110 Asst VP for Development ... Ms. Jenny SHOOP
28 VP for Diversity/Equity/Inclusion ... Mr. Tobias GUZMAN
26 AVP Marketing ... Ms. Deborah FARRIS
79 Dean Humanities/Social Sciences ... Dr. Laura CONNOLLY
50 Dean Business ... Ms. SherRhonda GIBBS
53 Dean Education/Behavioral Sciences ... Mr. Jared STALLONES
76 Dean Natural & Health Sciences ... Dr. Kamel HADDAD
57 Dean Performing Visual Arts ... Ms. Cristina GOLETTI
08 Dean University Libraries ... Ms. Jennifer NUTEFALL
35 AVP Stdnt Engage/Dean of Students ... Dr. Gardiner TUCKER
102 President University Foundation ... Mr. Rod ESCH
06 Registrar ... Mr. Charlie COUCH
07 Director of Admissions ... Ms. Erika PEPMEYER
37 Dir Student Financial Resources ... Mr. Marty SOMERO
36 Director of Career Services ... Vacant
15 Director of Human Resources ... Vacant
18 Director Facilities Management ... Mr. Kirk LEICHLITER
41 Director of Athletics ... Mr. Darren DUNN
39 Director of Residential Education ... Vacant
38 Director Student Counseling ... Ms. Heather HELM
19 Chief of University Police ... Mr. Aaron CARMICHAEL
44 Director of Annual Giving ... Vacant
27 Dir News & Public Relations ... Ms. Deanna HERBERT
96 Director of Purchasing ... Mr. John CHAPLAIN
85 Director Ctr for International Educ ... Ms. Olga BARON
104 Director Study Abroad ... Ms. Jeanne MARION
108 Director Institutional Assessment ... Ms. Kim BLACK
04 Exec Assistant to President ... Ms. Lori RILEY
100 Chief of Staff ... Ms. Jennifer ALMQUIST
105 Director Web Services ... Vacant
106 Dir Online Education/E-learning ... Vacant
22 Dir Affirmative Action/EEO ... Mr. Larry LOFTEN
122 Asst Dir Fraternity/Sorority Life ... Ms. Patricia HARTLEY

U.S. Career Institute (E)

2001 Lowe Street, Fort Collins CO 80525
County: Larimer — Identification: 666776
Telephone: (970) 207-4500 — Carnegie Class: Not Classified
FAX Number: (970) 223-1678 — Calendar System: Other
URL: www.uscareerinstitute.edu
Established: 1981 — Annual Undergrad Tuition & Fees: N/A

Enrollment: N/A　Coed
Affiliation or Control: Proprietary　IRS Status: Proprietary
Highest Offering: Associate Degree
Accreditation: DEAC

01 President ..... Mr. Earl WESTON
05 Vice Pres of Academics/Compliance ..... Ms. Janet PERRY
32 Vice Pres Student Affairs/Marketing ..... Ms. Holly COOK
10 CFO ..... Mr. Dan THOMAS
07 Director Admissions/Student Rels ..... Ms. Jennifer MANNS
25 Sr Dir Workforce Development ..... Ms. Regina SERRANO
25 Sr Dir of Corp Partnerships/Bus Dev ..... Mr. Rob FERSHTMAN

Western Colorado Community College-Tilman M. Bishop Campus (A)

2508 Blichmann Avenue, Grand Junction CO 81505
Telephone: (970) 255-2600　Identification: 770030
Accreditation: &HLC

Western Colorado University (B)

1 Western Way, Gunnison CO 81231-0001
County: Gunnison　FICE Identification: 001372
Unit ID: 128391
Telephone: (970) 943-0120　Carnegie Class: Masters/M
FAX Number: (970) 943-7069　Calendar System: Semester
URL: www.western.edu
Established: 1901　Annual Undergrad Tuition & Fees (In-State): $10,646
Enrollment: 3,203　Coed
Affiliation or Control: State　IRS Status: 501(c)3
Highest Offering: Master's
Accreditation: HLC, MUS

01 President ..... Mr. Brad BACA
11 Exec Vice Pres and COO ..... Vacant
05 Interim Provost ..... Ms. Jessica YOUNG
111 Vice Pres Advancement ..... Mr. Mike LAPLANTE
10 VP Finance & Administration/CFO ..... Ms. Julie BACA
121 VP Student Success/Enrollment ..... Dr. Abel CHAVEZ
32 VP Student Affairs/Dean of Students ..... Mr. Gary PIERSON
20 Assoc Vice Pres Academic Affairs ..... Dr. Kevin ALEXANDER
35 AVP Student Affairs/Title IX Admin ..... Mr. Chris LUEKENGA
06 Registrar ..... Ms. Laurel BECKER
37 Director of Financial Aid ..... Ms. Carrie SHAW
104 Dir Intl Student Pgms/Study Abroad ..... Ms. Katie WHEATON
41 Athletic Director ..... Mr. Miles VAN HEE
15 Director of Human Resources ..... Ms. Kim GAILEY
40 Director Retail Operations ..... Ms. Teri HAUS
13 Chief Information Ofcr/IT Director ..... Mr. Chad ROBINSON
08 Director Library Services ..... Mr. Dustin FIFE
39 Director of Residence Life ..... Ms. Shelley JANSEN
36 Career Services Coordinator ..... Mr. Craig BEEBE
29 Director of Alumni Relations ..... Ms. Ann JOHNSTON
44 Director Annual & Special Gifts ..... Mr. Tom BURGRAFF
28 Director of Multicultural Center ..... Ms. Sally ROMERO
07 Dir Recruitment/Admissions ..... Vacant
96 Business Services Manager ..... Ms. Sherry FORD
04 Admin Assistant to the President ..... Ms. Joy KEAN
105 Director Web Services ..... Mr. RJ TONEY
106 Director Online Education ..... Mr. Dustin FIFE
18 Chief Facilities/Physical Plant Ofc ..... Mr. Bryce HANNA
19 Director Security/Safety ..... Mr. Nathan KUBES
25 Chief Contract Grants Admin ..... Ms. Janice WELBORN
50 Dean School of Business ..... Mr. Peter SHERMAN

CONNECTICUT

Albertus Magnus College (C)

700 Prospect Street, New Haven CT 06511-1189
County: New Haven　FICE Identification: 001374
Unit ID: 128498
Telephone: (203) 773-8550　Carnegie Class: Masters/M
FAX Number: (203) 773-9539　Calendar System: Semester
URL: www.albertus.edu
Established: 1925　Annual Undergrad Tuition & Fees: $35,410
Enrollment: 1,384　Coed
Affiliation or Control: Independent Non-Profit　IRS Status: 501(c)3
Highest Offering: Master's
Accreditation: EH, ACATE, IACBE

01 President ..... Dr. Marc M. CAMILLE
05 Vice Pres Academic Affairs ..... Dr. Sean P. O'CONNELL
10 Int Vice Pres Finance/Treasurer ..... Ms. JoAnne WILLIAMS
13 VP Information Technology Services ..... Dr. Steven GSTALDER
32 Vice President for Student Services ..... Mr. Andrew FOSTER
84 VP Enrollment Mgmt & Marketing ..... Ms. Andrea E. KOVACS
111 Vice President for Advancement ..... Ms. Mary YOUNG
88 Executive Director College Events ..... Ms. Carolyn A. BEHAN KRAUS
35 Asst Dean Campus Act/Orientation ..... Ms. Erin MORRELL
21 Controller ..... Mr. David LAVALLEY
06 Registrar ..... Mrs. Melissa DELUCIA
113 Bursar ..... Mr. Terence MCPARTLAND
08 Director Library/Information Svcs ..... Vacant
09 Dir Inst Research & Assessment ..... Mr. Jeffrey E. LUOMA
37 Director Financial Aid ..... Mrs. Michelle COCHRAN
41 Director of Athletics ..... Mr. James ABROMAITIS
58 Director MALS Program ..... Vacant
121 Director of Academic Advising ..... Ms. Heather WOTTON
92 Co-Director of Honors Program ..... Mr. Jonathan SOZEK
92 Co-Director of Honors Program ..... Vacant
11 Asst VP Operations ..... Mr. James A. SCHAFRICK
15 Director Human Resources ..... Ms. Renee SULLIVAN
36 Director Career Services ..... Mr. Patrick CLIFFORD
42 Coord of Dominican Ministries ..... Ms. Hallie DOUGLAS
18 Supervisor of Facilities Services ..... Mr. Dan SECORE
04 Administrative Asst to President ..... Ms. Lynne M. HENNESSY
07 Director of Admissions ..... Mr. Ben AMARONE
107 Dean Prof & Graduate Studies ..... Ms. Annette BOSLEY-BOYCE
29 Director Alumni & Parent Engagement ..... Ms. Anissa CONNOR
39 Director Resident Life & Community ..... Ms. Haley MCCONVILLE
44 Director Annual & Individual Giving ..... Ms. Siobhan LIDINGTON
105 Director Web Services ..... Mr. Daniel ALVES
108 Director Institutional Assessment ..... Mr. Jeffrey LUOMA
19 Director Security/Safety ..... Mr. Zachariah MIHALY
50 Dean of Business ..... Mr. William ANISKOVICH
96 Director of Purchasing ..... Mr. James SCHAFRICK

Charter Oak State College (D)

55 Paul Manafort Drive, New Britain CT 06053-2142
County: Hartford　FICE Identification: 029171
Unit ID: 128780
Telephone: (860) 515-3800　Carnegie Class: Bac-A&S
FAX Number: (860) 606-9615　Calendar System: Other
URL: www.charteroak.edu
Established: 1973　Annual Undergrad Tuition & Fees (In-State): $8,553
Enrollment: 1,634　Coed
Affiliation or Control: State　IRS Status: 501(c)3
Highest Offering: Master's
Accreditation: EH, CAHIIM, NURSE

01 President ..... Mr. Edward KLONOSKI
05 Provost ..... Dr. David FERREIRA
10 Chief Financial/Administrative Ofcr ..... Mr. Michael J. MORIARTY
13 Chief Information Officer ..... Vacant
09 Dir Institutional Effectiveness ..... Mr. Michael BRODERICK
06 Registrar ..... Ms. Jennifer WASHINGTON
37 Dir Financial Aid/Veterans Benefits ..... Mr. Ralph BRASURE, III
20 Director Academic Services ..... Ms. Wanda WARSHAUER
07 Director Admissions ..... Ms. Lori GAGNE PENDLETON
88 Dir Prior Learning Assessment Pgm ..... Ms. Linda WILDER
26 Director Marketing/Public Relations ..... Ms. Carolyn HEBERT
04 Administrative Asst to President ..... Ms. Carol HALL
30 Assoc Director Development ..... Ms. Carol HALL
105 Web Developer ..... Mr. Jon ELLIS
15 Director Personnel Services ..... Ms. Rowena MCGOLDRICK
29 Director Alumni Relations ..... Ms. Carol HALL

*Connecticut Board of Regents for Higher Education (E)

61 Woodland Street, Hartford CT 06105-2345
County: Hartford　Identification: 666656
Telephone: (860) 723-0000　Carnegie Class: N/A
FAX Number: (860) 723-0009
URL: www.ct.edu

01 President CTCU ..... Mr. Terrence CHENG
05 Provost/SVP Acad & Student Affairs ..... Dr. Jane GATES
88 VP for CT State Universities ..... Dr. Elsa NUNEZ
88 VP for Cmty Colleges at CT BOR ..... Vacant
15 VP for Human Resources ..... Mr. Andrew KRIPP
18 VP Facilities/RE/Infrastruct Plng ..... Mr. Keith EPSTEIN
10 Chief Financial Officer ..... Mr. Benjamin BARNES
13 Chief Information Officer ..... Mr. Joseph TOLISANO
101 Assoc Director Board Affairs ..... Ms. Erin FITZGERALD
04 Admin Assistant to the President ..... Ms. Victoria Lee THOMAS
100 Chief of Staff ..... Dr. Alice PRITCHARD
26 Asst Dir Public Relations/Marketing ..... Ms. Terri RAIMONDI
09 AVP Research/System Effectiveness ..... Dr. William GAMMELL
43 Dir Legal Services/General Counsel ..... Ms. Ernestine WEAVER
27 Director of Communications ..... Ms. Leigh APPLEBY

*Central Connecticut State University (F)

1615 Stanley Street, New Britain CT 06050-4010
County: Hartford　FICE Identification: 001378
Unit ID: 128771
Telephone: (860) 832-3000　Carnegie Class: Masters/L
FAX Number: (860) 832-3033　Calendar System: Semester
URL: www.ccsu.edu
Established: 1849　Annual Undergrad Tuition & Fees (In-State): $11,502
Enrollment: 10,652　Coed
Affiliation or Control: State　IRS Status: 501(c)3
Highest Offering: Doctorate
Accreditation: EH, ANEST, CAATE, CACREP, CAEPN, CONST, EXSC, MFCD, MUS, NAIT, NURSE, SW

02 President ..... Dr. Zulma R. TORO
04 Exec Assistant to the President ..... Ms. Susan MATTERAZZO
05 Interim Provost/VPAA ..... Dr. Kimberly KOSTELIS
32 VP Student Affairs ..... Dr. Kellie BYRD DANSO
35 Associate Dean Student Affairs ..... Mr. Ramon HERNANDEZ
43 University Counsel ..... Ms. Stacy VOTTO
11 Chief Operations Officer ..... Mr. Sal CINTORINO
114 Chief Budget & Compliance Officer ..... Ms. Lisa BUCHER
15 Chief Human Resources Officer ..... Ms. Anna SUSKI-LENCZEWSKI
28 VP for Equity & Inclusion ..... Dr. Craig WRIGHT
49 Dean Liberal Arts/Soc Sciences ..... Dr. Robert WOLFF
50 Interim Dean School of Business ..... Dr. Lisa FRANK
53 Int Dean School Educ/Prof Studies ..... Dr. James MULROONEY
54 Int Dean School Engr/Science/Tech ..... Dr. Jeremiah JARRETT
104 Dir Center International Education ..... Dr. Momar NDIAYE
51 Dir Continuing Educ/Cmty Engagement ..... Ms. Christa STERLING
07 Director Admissions & Recruitment ..... Mr. Lawrence HALL
41 Director Athletics ..... Mr. Thomas PINCINCE
39 Director Residence Life ..... Ms. Jean ALICANDRO
19 Interim Director Public Safety ..... Mr. Christopher CERVONI
37 Director Financial Aid ..... Ms. Keri LUPACHINO
26 Int AVP Marketing & Communications ..... Ms. Janice PALMER
08 Director Library Services ..... Mr. Carl ANTONUCCI
36 Dir Career Success Center ..... Mr. Paul ROSSITTO
23 Dir Student Wellness Svcs ..... Dr. Michael RUSSO
06 Registrar ..... Mr. Patrick TUCKER
38 Coordinator Office Wellness Educ ..... Mr. Jonathan POHL
21 University Controller ..... Ms. Julie DEFALCO
96 Contract Compliance/Procurement ..... Mr. Charles ZSEBIK
09 Dir Inst Research/Assessment ..... Ms. Yvonne KIRBY
13 Chief Info Technology Officer ..... Dr. George CLAFFEY
84 Assoc VP Enrollment Management ..... Dr. Christina ROBINSON

*Eastern Connecticut State University (G)

83 Windham Street, Willimantic CT 06226-2295
County: Windham　FICE Identification: 001425
Unit ID: 129215
Telephone: (860) 465-5000　Carnegie Class: Masters/S
FAX Number: (860) 465-4690　Calendar System: Semester
URL: www.easternct.edu
Established: 1889　Annual Undergrad Tuition & Fees (In-State): $12,304
Enrollment: 4,644　Coed
Affiliation or Control: State　IRS Status: 501(c)3
Highest Offering: Master's
Accreditation: EH, CAEP, SW

02 President ..... Dr. Elsa M. NUNEZ
05 Provost ..... Dr. William SALKA
10 VP Finance/Administration ..... Mr. James R. HOWARTH
32 Interim Vice Pres Student Affairs ..... Ms. Michelle DELANEY
111 Vice Pres Institutional Advance ..... Mr. Kenneth J. DELISA
28 VP Equity & Diversity ..... Dr. LaMar COLEMAN
35 Interim Dean of Students ..... Ms. Kemesha WILMOT
13 Chief Information Officer ..... Mr. Garry BOZYLINSKY
09 Dean of Academic Analytics ..... Dr. Jennifer BROWN
41 Director of Athletics ..... Ms. Lori RUNKSMEIER
08 Director of Library Services ..... Ms. Janice WILSON
84 Dir of Enrollment Mgmt/Fin Aid ..... Mr. Christopher DORSEY
36 Director of Career Services ..... Mr. Clifford MARRETT
29 Director of Alumni Affairs ..... Mr. Michael STENKO
06 Registrar ..... Ms. Jennifer HUOPPI
19 Police Chief & Dir of Public Safety ..... Mr. Stephen TAVARES
39 Director Housing/Residence Life ..... Ms. Angela BAZIN
40 Director of Bookstore ..... Ms. Allyson HALL
42 Director of Campus Ministry ..... Rev. Laurence LAPOINTE
18 Dir of Facilities Mgmt/Planning ..... Ms. Renee KEECH
26 Director University Relations ..... Mr. Edward H. OSBORN
49 Dean of Arts & Sciences ..... Dr. Emily TODD
58 Dean Educ/Prof Studies/Grad Pgm ..... Dr. Niti PANDEY
96 Assoc Dir Fiscal Affs/Acquisition ..... Ms. Terry O'BRIEN
38 Dir Counseling/Psych Svcs ..... Dr. Bryce CRAPSER
07 Director of Admissions ..... Mr. Christopher DORSEY
21 University Controller ..... Ms. Shirley AUDET
14 Director IT ..... Mr. Andrew JOHNSON
110 Director Institutional Advancement ..... Mr. Joesph MCGANN
88 Director Energy Institute ..... Dr. Patricia SZCZYS
15 Chief Human Resources Officer ..... Mr. Kenneth DELISA
04 Admin Assistant to the President ..... Ms. Maureen ZAVODJANCIK

*Southern Connecticut State University (H)

501 Crescent Street, New Haven CT 06515-0901
County: New Haven　FICE Identification: 001406
Unit ID: 130493
Telephone: (203) 392-7278　Carnegie Class: Masters/L
FAX Number: N/A　Calendar System: Semester
URL: www.southernct.edu
Established: 1893　Annual Undergrad Tuition & Fees (In-State): $11,802
Enrollment: 9,331　Coed
Affiliation or Control: State　IRS Status: 501(c)3
Highest Offering: Doctorate
Accreditation: EH, CAATE, CACREP, CAEP, CAPRT, #COARC, EXSC, LIB, MFCD, MUS, NURSE, PH, SP, SW

02 President ..... Dr. Joe BERTOLINO
04 Admin Assistant to the President ..... Ms. Charmaine R. LLOYD
05 Provost/Vice Pres Acad Affairs ..... Dr. Robert PREZANT
10 EVP for Finance & Administration ..... Mr. Mark ROZEWSKI
32 Vice Pres Student Affairs ..... Dr. Tracy TYREE
111 Vice President Inst Advancement ..... Dr. Michael KINGAN
28 VP of Diversity & Equity Pgm ..... Dr. Diane M. ARIZA
84 Assoc VP for Enrollment Management ..... Dr. Julie EDSTROM
15 Chief Human Resources Officer ..... Dr. Melitha PRZYGODA
18 Assoc VP Capital Budgeting/Fac Ops ..... Mr. Eric LESSNE
13 VP Tech/Chief Information Officer ..... Dr. Dennis REIMAN
49 Dean School Arts & Sciences ..... Dr. Bruce KALK
50 Dean School of Business ..... Dr. Jennifer ROBIN
53 Dean School Education ..... Dr. Stephen HEGEDUS
58 Dean School Graduate Studies ..... Dr. Manohar SINGH

70 Int Dean School Health/Human Svcs ... Dr. Sandra BULMER
41 Director of Athletics ... Mr. Christopher BARKER
26 Director of Public Affairs ... Mr. Patrick DILGER
29 Director Alumni Affairs ... Mr. Gregory BERNARD
07 Director Admissions ... Mr. Alick LETANG
06 Registrar ... Ms. Alicia CARROLL
08 Director of Library Services ... Dr. Clara OGBAA
19 Director of Public Safety ... Mr. Joseph M. DOOLEY
25 Director of Sponsored Research ... Ms. Amy TAYLOR
37 Director of Financial Aid ... Ms. Sage C. STACHOWIAK
23 Director of Health Services ... Dr. Diane S. MORGENTHALER
35 Dean of Student Affairs ... Dr. Jules TETREAULT
88 Assoc VP for Strategic Initiatives ... Dr. Colleen Q. BIELITZ
38 Director of Counseling Services ... Dr. Nick PINKERTON
21 University Controller ... Ms. Loren LOOMIS HUBBELL
92 Director of Honors Program ... Dr. Terese GEMME
94 Director of Women's Studies ... Dr. Yi-Chun Tricia LIN
121 Dir of Academic & Career Advising ... Mr. Harry TWYMAN
39 Director of Residence Life ... Mr. Robert C. DEMEZZO

*Western Connecticut State University (A)

181 White Street, Danbury CT 06810-6885
County: Fairfield FICE Identification: 001380
Unit ID: 130776
Telephone: (203) 837-8200 Carnegie Class: Masters/M
FAX Number: (203) 837-8276 Calendar System: Semester
URL: www.wcsu.edu
Established: 1903 Annual Undergrad Tuition & Fees (In-State): $11,781
Enrollment: 5,246 Coed
Affiliation or Control: State IRS Status: 501(c)3
Highest Offering: Doctorate
Accreditation: EH, ART, CACREP, CAEP, MUS, NURSE, PH, SW, THEA

02 Interim President ... Dr. Paul B. BERAN
05 Provost/Vice Pres Academic Affairs ... Dr. Missy ALEXANDER
10 Chief Financial Officer ... Ms. Beatrice FEVRY
32 VP Student Affairs ... Dr. Keith BETTS
111 Int VP of Inst Advancement ... Ms. Lynne LEBARRON
57 Dean of Visual/Performing Arts ... Mr. Brian VERNON
35 Dean of Student Affairs ... Dr. Walter CRAMER
49 Dean Macricostas Sch Arts & Sci ... Dr. Michelle L. BROWN
50 Int Dean of Ancell Sch of Business ... Dr. Joan PALLADINO
107 Int Dean Sch of Prof Studies ... Dr. Joan PALLADINO
15 Chief Human Resources Officer ... Mr. Frederic W. CRATTY
13 Chief Information Officer ... Mr. John DEROSA
21 Director Fiscal Affairs/Controller ... Mr. Peter ROSA
28 Chief Diversity Officer ... Ms. Jesenia MINIER
06 Registrar ... Dr. Debra ZAVATKAY
08 Director of Library Services ... Ms. Veronica KENAUSIS
09 Director Inst Research/Assessment ... Dr. Jerome WILCOX
25 Director of Grant/Programs ... Vacant
38 Director of Counseling Svcs ... Dr. Rée GUNTER
37 Director of Financial Aid ... Ms. Melissa STEPHENS
36 Director of Career Services ... Ms. Kathleen LINDENMAYER
88 Special Assistant to the President ... Mr. Paul STEINMETZ
39 Director Housing & Residence Life ... Mr. Ron MASON
35 Dir Center for Student Involvement ... Mr. Dennis LESZKO
41 Director of Athletics ... Ms. Lori MAZZA
29 Director of Alumni Relations ... Mr. Thomas CRUCITTI
07 Director of Admissions ... Mr. Luis SANTIAGO
88 Dir of Planning & Engineering ... Mr. Daniel CASSINELLI
11 Director of Administrative Services ... Ms. Amy LOPEZ
18 Int Assoc VP for Campus Planning ... Ms. Deanna CIBERY-SCHAAB
88 Dir Event & Conf Mgmt ... Mr. John MURPHY
114 Director of Fin Planning & Budgets ... Mr. Mufu WENG
27 Assoc Dir of Public Relations ... Ms. Sherri HILL
19 Chief of Police ... Mr. Richard GUERRERA
14 Digital Information Officer ... Ms. Rebecca WOODWARD
04 Exec Asst to President ... Ms. Mary O'CONNOR
84 Assoc VP Enrollment Services ... Mr. Jay MURRAY
30 Major Gifts Officer ... Ms. Julie PRYOR-BENNETT

*Asnuntuck Community College (B)

170 Elm Street, Enfield CT 06082-3800
County: Hartford FICE Identification: 011150
Unit ID: 128577
Telephone: (860) 253-3000 Carnegie Class: Assoc/HVT-Mix Trad/Non
FAX Number: (860) 253-3014 Calendar System: Semester
URL: www.asnuntuck.edu
Established: 1972 Annual Undergrad Tuition & Fees (In-State): $4,556
Enrollment: 1,304 Coed
Affiliation or Control: State IRS Status: 501(c)3
Highest Offering: Associate Degree
Accreditation: EH, NAEYC

01 Chief Executive Officer ... Dr. Michelle COACH
04 Exec Asst to Chief Exec Officer ... Ms. Maura KERNAN
05 Interim Dean of Academic Affairs ... Mr. Tim ST. JAMES
88 Int Dean of Prison Educ/Special Pgm ... Dr. Teresa FOLEY
32 Interim Dean of Student Services ... Mr. Tim ST. JAMES
88 Interim Dean of AMTC ... Ms. Mary BIDWELL
15 HR Generalist ... Ms. Erin RANSFORD
11 Associate Dean of Campus Operations ... Mr. Alfredo DIMAURO
10 Assoc Dir Finance/Admin ... Ms. Niki RITTENHOUSE
06 Interim Registrar ... Ms. Stacey MUSULIN
88 Interim Assistant Registrar ... Mr. Jeff SHUMAN
37 Financial Aid Lead ... Ms. Monica KEDZIOR
09 Dir Plng/Rsrch/Inst Effectiveness ... Ms. Caitlin BOGER-HAWKINS
102 Executive Dir of the Foundation ... Mr. Keith MADORE
103 Chief Regional Workforce Dev Ofcr ... Ms. Eileen PELTIER
18 Bldg Superintendent III/Bldg Svcs ... Mr. Joseph MULLER
75 Dir Business/Tech & Industry Trng ... Mr. Gary CARRA
13 Acting Asst Director of IT ... Mr. Charles KNUREK
121 Dir Ctr for Advising/Stdnt Achvmt ... Ms. Emily SANTANIELLO

*Capital Community College (C)

950 Main Street, Hartford CT 06103-1207
County: Hartford FICE Identification: 007635
Unit ID: 129367
Telephone: (860) 906-5000 Carnegie Class: Assoc/HVT-Mix Trad/Non
FAX Number: (860) 520-7906 Calendar System: Semester
URL: www.capitalcc.edu
Established: 1967 Annual Undergrad Tuition & Fees (In-State): $4,556
Enrollment: 2,715 Coed
Affiliation or Control: State IRS Status: 501(c)3
Highest Offering: Associate Degree
Accreditation: EH, ADNUR, EMT, MAC, NAEYC, RAD

02 Chief Executive Officer ... Dr. G. Duncan HARRIS
32 Dean of Students & Faculty ... Dr. Jason SCAPPATICCI
05 Interim Dean of Academics ... Mr. Michael PROULX
11 Associate Dean of Campus Operations ... Mr. Jose COLON
51 Interim Dir of Non-Credit Programs ... Ms. Odile DILONE
09 Director of Institutional Research ... Ms. Jenny WANG
10 Director Finance/Administration ... Mr. Ted HALE
06 Registrar ... Mr. Argelio MARRERO
08 Director of Library Services ... Mr. Daniel LEWIS
84 Director Student Development Svcs ... Ms. Marsha BALL-DAVIS
37 Director of Financial Aid ... Ms. Margaret MALASPINA
13 Interim Asst Director of IMT ... Mr. Alfredo BRITO
76 Dir Cont Educ Nurse/Allied Health ... Vacant
26 Dir of Marketing/Public Relations ... Ms. Vivian NABETA
15 Human Resources Generalist ... Ms. Frances LEON
111 Int Dir Institutional Advancement ... Dr. G. Duncan HARRIS
04 Executive Assistant ... Ms. Liza ITURRINO
18 Chief Facilities ... Mr. John BOUDREAU
19 Director Security/Safety ... Mr. Joel WHITE

*Gateway Community College (D)

20 Church St., New Haven CT 06510-5970
County: New Haven FICE Identification: 008037
Unit ID: 130396
Telephone: (203) 285-2000 Carnegie Class: Assoc/MT-VT-High Trad
FAX Number: (203) 285-2018 Calendar System: Semester
URL: www.gatewayct.edu
Established: 1968 Annual Undergrad Tuition & Fees (In-State): $4,496
Enrollment: 6,003 Coed
Affiliation or Control: State IRS Status: 501(c)3
Highest Offering: Associate Degree
Accreditation: EH, ADNUR, DIETT, DMS, NAEYC, NMT, RAD, RTT, SURGT

02 Chief Executive Officer ... Dr. William T. BROWN
30 Dean of Devel/Community Partnership ... Ms. Mary Ellen CODY
05 Dean of Academics ... Dr. Mark KOSINSKI
51 Dean of Cont Educ/Workforce Develop ... Vacant
15 Regional Human Resources Manager ... Vacant
04 Executive Assistant to President ... Ms. Tanya R. GIBBS
09 Director Institutional Research ... Dr. Vincent P. TONG
26 Assoc Dn Communications/Marketing ... Ms. Evelyn GARD
10 Int Director Finance/Admin Svcs ... Ms. Lutisha PERSHAD
08 Director Library ... Mr. Miguel A. GARCIA, III
36 Director Career Services ... Ms. Leigh ROBERTS
37 Director Financial Aid ... Mr. Raymond ZEEK
124 Int Dir Advising/Retention ... Ms. Kathleen AHERN
32 Director of Student Activities ... Mr. Alfred GUANTE
24 Director of Educational Technology ... Mr. Alfonzo LEWIS
25 Grants Development Specialist ... Ms. Andrea MACNOW
13 Director Information Technology ... Mr. Lawrence SALAY
88 Director Early Learning Center ... Ms. Sarah CHAMBERS
121 Director of Academic Support ... Ms. Clara MENA
50 Chair Business Department ... Vacant
79 Chair Humanities Department ... Ms. Susan CHENARD
83 Chair Social Sciences Department ... Mr. Jonah COHEN
88 Coord Early Childhood Education ... Ms. Carmelita E. VALENCIA-DAYE
88 Coord Drug/Alcohol Rehab Counseling ... Vacant
67 Coordinator Pharmacy Tech Program ... Ms. Louise A. PETROKA
81 Chair Math/Natural Sci Department ... Mr. Rocky TREMBLAY
88 Director Dietetic Technician Pgm ... Ms. Marcia DORAN
76 Director Allied Health ... Ms. Sheila SOLERNOU
54 Dir Engineering/Applied Technology ... Mr. Eric F. FLYNN
18 Chief Facilities/Physical Plant ... Mr. Lucian SIMONE
06 Registrar/Dir Enrollment Mgmt ... Ms. Maribel LOPEZ

*Housatonic Community College (E)

900 Lafayette Boulevard, Bridgeport CT 06604-4704
County: Fairfield FICE Identification: 004513
Unit ID: 129543
Telephone: (203) 332-5000 Carnegie Class: Assoc/MT-VT-High Trad
FAX Number: (203) 332-5123 Calendar System: Semester
URL: www.housatonic.edu
Established: 1967 Annual Undergrad Tuition & Fees (In-State): $4,496
Enrollment: 3,821 Coed
Affiliation or Control: State IRS Status: 501(c)3
Highest Offering: Associate Degree
Accreditation: EH, NAEYC, SURGT

02 Chief Executive Officer ... Dr. Dwayne SMITH
05 Int Dean of Faculty/Students ... Ms. Robin AVANT
11 Associate Dean of Campus Operations ... Mr. Mario PIERCE
32 Dean of Student Services ... Vacant
20 Dir Academic Advising/Success ... Ms. Jeanine GIBSON
06 Registrar & Director of Enrollment ... Mr. James CONNOLLY
07 Director of Admissions ... Mr. Earl GRAHAM
08 Interim Director Library Services ... Ms. Curleen ELLIOTT
37 Director of Financial Aid ... Mr. Omar LIVINGSTON
26 Assoc Dean Communications/Marketing ... Vacant
19 Director of Security ... Vacant
09 Director Institutional Research ... Dr. Vincent TONG
13 Assistant Director of IT ... Mr. Bruce BOMELEY
15 HR Generalist ... Ms. Ashley NICHOLSON
30 Director of Community Campus Rels ... Mr. Richard DUPONT
10 Director of Finance/Admin Svcs ... Ms. Teresa ORAVETZ
18 Coordinator of Facilities ... Vacant
04 Executive Asst to CEO ... Ms. Jessica CARL
38 Director Counseling/Wellness ... Ms. Lisa SLADE
102 Exec Director of HCC Foundation ... Ms. Kristy JELENIK
121 Int Director Academic Support Ctr ... Mr. Andrew PELLETIER

*Manchester Community College (F)

PO Box 1046, Great Path, Manchester CT 06045-1046
County: Hartford FICE Identification: 001392
Unit ID: 129695
Telephone: (860) 512-3000 Carnegie Class: Assoc/MT-VT-High Trad
FAX Number: (860) 512-3631 Calendar System: Semester
URL: www.manchestercc.edu
Established: 1963 Annual Undergrad Tuition & Fees (In-State): $4,516
Enrollment: 4,448 Coed
Affiliation or Control: State IRS Status: 501(c)3
Highest Offering: Associate Degree
Accreditation: EH, ACFEI, COARC, DA, MUS, NAEYC, OTA, RAD, RTT, SURGT

02 Chief Executive Officer ... Dr. Nicole ESPOSITO
05 Int Dean Academic/Student Affairs ... Dr. Fatma SALMAN
32 Interim Dean of Student Affairs ... Mr. Peter HARRIS
11 Dean of Administrative Affairs ... Vacant
102 Int Executive Dir MCC Foundation ... Ms. Susan ALSTON
20 Associate Dean of Academic Affairs ... Dr. Pamela MITCHELL
10 Dir Finance & Admin Services ... Ms. Regina FERRANTE
07 Int Assoc Director of Admissions ... Ms. Mariah THOMAS
06 Registrar ... Ms. Anita SPARROW
08 Dir Library Svcs/Educational Tech ... Ms. Deborah HERMAN
13 Int Dir of Information Technology ... Mr. Edgar CHAVARRIAGA
09 Director Plng/Research & Assessment ... Mr. David NIELSEN
15 Director of Human Resources ... Vacant
18 Dir Facilities Management/ Planning ... Ms. Darlene MANCINI-BROWN
26 Dir Marketing and Public Relations ... Ms. Charlene TAPPAN
37 Director of Financial Aid ... Ms. Anna TORRES
79 Director of Liberal & Creative Arts ... Ms. Samantha GONZALEZ
35 Int Director of Student Activities ... Mr. Trent J. BARBER
30 Dir of Development & Alumni Affairs ... Ms. Diana REID
36 Dir Career Svcs/Veteran Affairs ... Ms. Julie GREENE
84 Dir of Enrollment Management ... Ms. Sara VINCENT
04 Interim Executive Assistant ... Ms. Karyn CASE
103 Assoc Dean Cont Ed/Workforce Dev ... Mr. Miguel PIGOTT
90 Director of Academic Support Ctr ... Mr. Brian CLEARY
28 Chief Diversity Officer ... Ms. Debra FREUND
96 Assoc Director of Purchasing ... Mr. Paul MOUNDS

*Middlesex Community College (G)

100 Training Hill Road, Middletown CT 06457-4889
County: Middlesex FICE Identification: 008038
Unit ID: 129756
Telephone: (860) 343-5800 Carnegie Class: Assoc/MT-VT-Mix Trad/Non
FAX Number: (860) 344-7488 Calendar System: Semester
URL: www.mxcc.edu
Established: 1966 Annual Undergrad Tuition & Fees (In-State): $4,476
Enrollment: 2,106 Coed
Affiliation or Control: State IRS Status: 501(c)3
Highest Offering: Associate Degree
Accreditation: EH, CAHIIM, NAEYC, OPD, RAD

02 Interim Chief Executive Officer ... Ms. Kimberly HOGAN
05 Dean of Academic & Student Affairs ... Dr. Donna BONTATIBUS
11 Dean of Administration ... Ms. Kimberly HOGAN
32 Assoc Dean of Student Affairs ... Dr. Sara HANSON
04 Executive Assistant to the CEO ... Ms. Corey MARTELL
08 Director of the Learning Commons ... Ms. Melissa BEHNEY
09 Director of Institutional Research ... Dr. Paul CARMICHAEL
13 Director Information Technology ... Ms. Annie SCOTT
15 Reg Mgr Human Resources ... Ms. Shaylah CARBONE
37 Director Financial Aid ... Ms. Irene MARTIN
10 Assoc Dir of Finance/Administration ... Ms. Ashley LABBADIA
124 Retention Specialist ... Ms. Yhara ZELINKA
22 Disability Services Coordinator ... Ms. Hilary PHELPS
06 Registrar ... Ms. Joanne FAUST
18 Chief Facilities/Physical Plant ... Mr. Steven CHESTER
84 Reg Associate Dean of Enrollment ... Ms. Jean MAIN

*Naugatuck Valley Community College (H)

750 Chase Parkway, Waterbury CT 06708-3089
County: New Haven FICE Identification: 006982
Unit ID: 129729
Telephone: (203) 575-8044 Carnegie Class: Assoc/MT-VT-High Trad
FAX Number: (203) 575-8096 Calendar System: Semester
URL: www.nv.edu

Established: 1964 Annual Undergrad Tuition & Fees (In-State): $4,516
Enrollment: 5,083 Coed
Affiliation or Control: State IRS Status: 501(c)3
Highest Offering: Associate Degree
Accreditation: EH, ADNUR, COARC, NAEYC, PTAA, RAD

02 Chief Executive Officer .... Dr. Lisa DRESDNER
11 Interim Dean of Administration .... Ms. Dana ELM
05 Interim Dean of Academic Affairs .... Mr. Antonio SANTIAGO
30 Associate Dean of Development .... Ms. Angela CHAPMAN
32 Dean of Student Services .... Ms. Sarah GAGER
13 Assoc Dean Information Technology .... Vacant
06 Interim Registrar .... Ms. Lisa CALABRESE
37 Director of Financial Aid .... Ms. Catherine HARDY
84 Assoc Dean of Enrollment Management .... Vacant
08 Director Learning Resource Ctr .... Ms. Jaime HAMMOND
10 Director of Finance/Admin Services .... Ms. Lisa PALEN
35 Director of Student Activities .... Ms. Karen BLAKE
18 Chief Facilities/Physical Plant .... Vacant
09 Int Dir of Institutional Research .... Ms. Sohair OMAR
121 Dir of Student Development Services .... Ms. Bonnie GOULET
15 Director of Human Resources .... Vacant
26 Director of Marketing .... Vacant

*Northwestern Connecticut Community-Technical College (A)

Park Place E, Winsted CT 06098-1798
County: Litchfield FICE Identification: 001398
Unit ID: 130040
Telephone: (860) 738-6300 Carnegie Class: Assoc/MT-VT-High Trad
FAX Number: (860) 738-6488 Calendar System: Semester
URL: www.nwcc.commnet.edu/
Established: 1965 Annual Undergrad Tuition & Fees (In-State): $4,516
Enrollment: 1,228 Coed
Affiliation or Control: State IRS Status: 501(c)3
Highest Offering: Associate Degree
Accreditation: EH, ADNUR, NAEYC

02 President .... Dr. Michael ROOKE
05 Dean of Academic & Student Affairs .... Dr. David FERREIRA
07 Associate Dean of Enrollment .... Ms. Kalia KELLOGG
11 Associate Dean of Campus Operations .... Mr. Brian PLESSINGER
08 Director of Library Services .... Mr. James PATTERSON
06 Registrar .... Ms. Debra ZAVATKAY
15 Director of Human Resources .... Ms. Wendy BOVIA
32 Dir of Student Development .... Ms. Ruth GONZALEZ
09 Director of Institutional Research .... Ms. Caitlin BOGER-HAWKINS
26 Director Marketing/Public Relations .... Mr. Grantley ADAMS
10 Director Financial/Admin Services .... Ms. Kimberly DRAGAN
04 Admin Assistant to the President .... Ms. Susan A. STILLER
13 Chief Information Technology Ofcr .... Mr. Richard COUTANT

*Norwalk Community College (B)

188 Richards Avenue, Norwalk CT 06854-1655
County: Fairfield FICE Identification: 001399
Unit ID: 130004
Telephone: (203) 857-7000 Carnegie Class: Assoc/MT-VT-Mix Trad/Non
FAX Number: (203) 857-7287 Calendar System: Semester
URL: www.norwalk.edu
Established: 1961 Annual Undergrad Tuition & Fees (In-State): $4,546
Enrollment: 4,420 Coed
Affiliation or Control: State IRS Status: 501(c)3
Highest Offering: Associate Degree
Accreditation: EH, ADNUR, COARC, MAC, NAEYC, PTAA

02 Chief Executive Officer .... Ms. Cheryl DEVONISH
32 Dean of Students .... Vacant
05 Dean of Faculty/Students .... Dr. G. Anthony PEFFER
30 Executive Director of Development .... Ms. Carrie BERNIER
103 Dir Ext Stds/Workforce Development .... Mr. Jon DEBENEDICTIS
10 Director of Finance/Administration .... Ms. Carrie MCGEE-YUROFF
08 Director of Library Services .... Ms. Alison WANG
37 Director Financial Aid .... Ms. Fany STUBBS
66 Int Director of Nursing Education .... Dr. Ezechiel DOMINIQUE
06 Registrar .... Mr. Steve MENDES
15 Human Resources Generalist .... Ms. Erica RAMOS
26 Marketing/ Public Relations Assoc .... Mr. Mario HAIMINDRA
38 Director Student Counseling .... Ms. Catherine MILLER
07 Director of Admissions .... Mr. Curtis ANTRUM
18 Chief Facilities/Physical Plant .... Mr. Craig CARLSON
04 Executive Asst to CEO .... Mrs. Thomasina L. CALISE
09 Director of Institutional Research .... Ms. Rachael DIPIETRO

*Quinebaug Valley Community College (C)

742 Upper Maple Street, Danielson CT 06239-1440
County: Windham FICE Identification: 010530
Unit ID: 130217
Telephone: (860) 932-4000 Carnegie Class: Assoc/MT-VT-High Trad
FAX Number: (860) 932-4306 Calendar System: Semester
URL: www.qvcc.edu
Established: 1971 Annual Undergrad Tuition & Fees (In-State): $4,506
Enrollment: 1,161 Coed
Affiliation or Control: State IRS Status: 501(c)3
Highest Offering: Associate Degree
Accreditation: EH, MLTAB, NAEYC

02 Chief Executive Officer .... Dr. Karen HYNICK
05 Dean Academic Affs & Student Svcs .... Vacant
11 Dean of Administrative Services .... Vacant
08 Director of Library Services .... Mr. Matthew HALL
37 Assoc Dir of Student Financial Aid .... Vacant
09 Director of Institutional Research .... Mr. Patrick KELLER
10 Dir Finance/Administrative Svcs .... Ms. Alessandra LUNDBERG
18 Chief Facilities/Physical Plant .... Mr. Martin CHARETTE
26 Chief Public Relations Officer .... Vacant
111 Dir of Institutional Advancement .... Ms. Monique WOLANIN
32 Assoc Dean Student Development .... Vacant
27 Coordinator of Marketing .... Ms. Paige CARITO
07 Associate Director of Admissions .... Ms. Sarah HENDRICK
04 Administrative Asst to President .... Ms. Jennifer GREEN
13 Chief Info Technology Officer (CIO) .... Mr. Jeremy ESPESETH
15 Director Personnel Services .... Ms. Karla DESJARDINS
29 Director Alumni Relations .... Ms. Sarah WOLFBURG
06 Registrar .... Ms. Nicole MARCOUX-BOWEN

*Three Rivers Community College (D)

574 New London Turnpike, Norwich CT 06360
County: New London FICE Identification: 009765
Unit ID: 129808
Telephone: (860) 215-9000 Carnegie Class: Assoc/MT-VT-High Trad
FAX Number: (860) 215-9901 Calendar System: Semester
URL: www.threerivers.edu
Established: 1963 Annual Undergrad Tuition & Fees (In-State): $4,556
Enrollment: 3,160 Coed
Affiliation or Control: State IRS Status: 501(c)3
Highest Offering: Associate Degree
Accreditation: EH, ADNUR, NAEYC

02 President .... Dr. Mary Ellen JUKOSKI
05 Interim Dean Academics/Student Svcs .... Dr. Kem BARFIELD
11 Dean of Administration .... Mr. Stephen H. GOETCHIUS
13 Acting Director of IT .... Mr. Skye COHEN
111 Dir Institutional Advancement .... Ms. Betty BAILLARGEON
06 Registrar .... Mr. Kevin KELLY
08 Director Library Services .... Ms. Pamela WILLIAMS
37 Actg Dir Student Financial Aid .... Ms. Hong Yu KOVIC
18 Director of Facilities .... Mr. Arnie DELAROSSA
09 Office of Institutional Research .... Mr. Patrick KELLER
26 Int Dir of Marketing/Public Rels .... Ms. Alexa SHELTON
90 Dir of Educational Technology .... Ms. Amanda CAFFARY
04 Exec Assistant to President .... Ms. April HODSON
07 Acting Director of Admissions .... Ms. Michelle MASON
35 Acting Dir of Student Activities .... Ms. Alycia ZIEGLER
103 Acting Director of Non-Credit Pgms .... Ms. Erin SULLIVAN

*Tunxis Community College (E)

271 Scott Swamp Road, Farmington CT 06032-3187
County: Hartford FICE Identification: 009764
Unit ID: 130606
Telephone: (860) 773-1300 Carnegie Class: Assoc/MT-VT-High Trad
FAX Number: N/A Calendar System: Semester
URL: www.tunxis.edu/
Established: 1969 Annual Undergrad Tuition & Fees (In-State): $4,556
Enrollment: 3,365 Coed
Affiliation or Control: State IRS Status: 501(c)3
Highest Offering: Associate Degree
Accreditation: EH, ACBSP, DA, DH, NAEYC

02 Regional President .... Dr. James P. LOMBELLA
10 Chief Regional Fiscal Officer .... Mr. Gennaro DEANGELIS
11 Campus CEO .... Dr. Darryl REOME
05 Interim Dean of Academic Affairs .... Ms. Amy FEEST
09 Director of Institutional Research .... Dr. Qing Lin MACK
21 Dir Finance/Administrative Services .... Ms. Nancy ESCHENBRENNER
32 Dean of Student Affairs .... Mr. Charles CLEARY
13 Interim Director of Info Technology .... Mr. Peter HAFFNER
15 Regional HR Manager .... Ms. Wendy BOVIA
18 Director of Facilities .... Mr. John LODOVICO
26 Interim Director Marketing & PR .... Ms. Melissa LAMAR
06 Interim Registrar .... Ms. Magaly CORREA
12 Director Tunxis@Bristol .... Mr. Victor MITCHELL
35 Director of Student Activities .... Mr. Christopher LAPORTE
88 Director Early Childhood Center .... Ms. Debra COLLINS
102 Executive Director TXCC Foundation .... Mr. Keith MADORE
90 Director of Education Technology .... Ms. Adrianne DUNHAM
124 Dir College Transition and Outreach .... Mr. Peter MCCLUSKEY
103 Chief Reg Workforce Dev Officer .... Ms. Eileen PELTIER
84 Interim Assoc Dean of Enrollment .... Ms. Jean MAIN
07 Associate Director of Admissions .... Ms. Ashkhen STRACK
07 Associate Director of Admissions .... Ms. Alison MCCARTHY
37 Director Financial Aid Services .... Ms. Sandy VITALE
28 Interim VP Diversity and Equity .... Dr. Kimberly JAMES
72 Director STEAM & Adv Manufacturing .... Mr. Mathew SPINELLI

Connecticut College (F)

270 Mohegan Avenue, New London CT 06320-4125
County: New London FICE Identification: 001379
Unit ID: 128902
Telephone: (860) 447-1911 Carnegie Class: Bac-A&S
FAX Number: (860) 439-2700 Calendar System: Semester
URL: www.conncoll.edu
Established: 1911 Annual Undergrad Tuition & Fees: $59,025
Enrollment: 1,737 Coed
Affiliation or Control: Independent Non-Profit IRS Status: 501(c)3
Highest Offering: Master's
Accreditation: EH

01 President .... Dr. Katherine BERGERON
05 Dean of the Faculty .... Dr. Danielle EGAN
10 Vice Pres Finance and Admin .... Vacant
111 Vice President College Advancement .... Ms. Kimberly VERSTANDIG
08 Vice Pres of Info Svcs/Librarian .... Dr. W. Lee HISLE
26 Vice President Communications .... Mr. John CRAMER
07 VP of Admission & Financial Aid .... Mr. Andrew STRICKLER
15 VP Human Resources .... Mr. Reginald H. WHITE
20 Dean of the College .... Dr. Erika J. SMITH
32 Dean of Students .... Dr. Victor J. ARCELUS
28 Dean of Institution Equity and Incl .... Dr. Rodmon KING
20 Associate Dean of Faculty .... Dr. Deborah EASTMAN
06 Registrar .... Ms. Elisabeth S. LABRIOLA
09 Director of Institutional Research .... Dr. John D. NUGENT
21 Controller .... Ms. Amanda B. MAYFIELD
37 Director of Financial Aid .... Mr. Sean MARTIN
41 Director of Athletics .... Ms. Maureen WHITE
29 Director of Alumni Relations .... Ms. Tori MCKENNA
38 Director Student Counseling Service .... Dr. Janet D. SPOLTORE
96 Director of Purchasing .... Ms. Kristi KERR
04 Executive Asst to the President .... Ms. Lauren MIDDLETON
102 Dir Foundation/Corporate Relations .... Ms. Naima GHERBI
13 Asst VP Enterprise/Tech Systems .... Vacant
19 Director Security/Safety .... Ms. Mary SAVAGE
36 Director Student Placement .... Ms. Persephone HALL
39 Director Student Housing .... Dr. Sara ROTHENBERGER
44 Director Annual or Planned Giving .... Ms. Ellen BREMNER
104 Director Study Abroad .... Ms. Shirley PARSON
18 Chf Facilities/Physical Plant Ofcr .... Mr. Thomas HOBAICA
105 Director Web Services .... Ms. Christelle LACHAPELLE

Fairfield University (G)

1073 N Benson Road, Fairfield CT 06824-5195
County: Fairfield FICE Identification: 001385
Unit ID: 129242
Telephone: (203) 254-4000 Carnegie Class: DU-Mod
FAX Number: (203) 254-4101 Calendar System: Semester
URL: www.fairfield.edu
Established: 1942 Annual Undergrad Tuition & Fees: $51,325
Enrollment: 5,513 Coed
Affiliation or Control: Roman Catholic IRS Status: 501(c)3
Highest Offering: Doctorate
Accreditation: EH, ANEST, CACREP, CAEP, @DIET, MFCD, MIDWF, NURSE, SW

01 University President .... Dr. Mark R. NEMEC
42 University Chaplain .... Rev. Keith A. MACZKIEWICZ
42 Chaplain/Dir of Mission .... Rev. Gerry R. BLASZCZAK, SJ
05 Provost .... Dr. Christine SIEGEL
10 VP Finance/CFO and Treasurer .... Mr. Michael TRAFECANTE
111 Vice Pres Univ Advancement .... Mr. Wally HALAS
15 Vice President of Human Resources .... Mr. Scott ESPOSITO
88 Vice Pres for Mission and Ministry .... Rev. Paul ROURKE, SJ
26 VP Marketing and Communications .... Ms. Jennifer ANDERSON
84 VP Strategic Enrollment Management .... Mr. Corry D. UNIS
32 Vice President for Student Life .... Ms. Karen A. DONOGHUE
88 Vice Provost Undergrad Excellence .... Dr. Mark LIGAS
58 Vice Prov Grad/Cont & Prof Stds .... Dr. Walter RANKIN
18 Vice President Facilities Mgmt .... Mr. David W. FRASSINELLI
38 Assoc VP Health & Wellness .... Dr. Susan N. BIRGE
109 Asst Vice Pres Auxiliary Services .... Mr. James D. FITZPATRICK
88 Assoc VP SC & Cmty Engagement .... Dr. Jocelyn BORYCZKA
09 Dir Institutional Research .... Ms. Amy BOCZER
06 University Registrar .... Ms. Lynn M. KOHRN
13 Chief Information Officer .... Mr. Jonathan CARROLL
37 Director of Financial Aid .... Ms. Diana M. DRAPER
36 Dir Career & Professional Dev .... Ms. Cathleen M. BORGMAN
29 Asst Vice Pres of Alumni Relations .... Ms. Janet A. CANEPA
19 Director of Public Safety .... Mr. Todd A. PELAZZA
41 Director of Athletics .... Mr. Paul SCHLICKMANN
49 Dean College Arts & Science .... Dr. Richard GREENWALD
50 Dean Dolan Sch of Business .... Dr. Zhan LI
54 Dean School of Engineering .... Dr. Andres CARRANO
66 Dean School of Nursing/Health Stds .... Dr. Meredith W. KAZER
53 Dean Grad Sch of Educ & Human Dev .... Dr. Laurie GRUPP
88 Asst VP Ofc of Conference & Events .... Mr. Matthew A. DINNAN
35 Dean of Students .... Mr. William H. JOHNSON
39 Sr Assoc Dir Residence Life .... Mr. Charles SOUSA
104 Assoc Vice Provost Global Strategy .... Ms. Jennifer EWALD
92 Co-Director of Honors Program .... Dr. Laura NASH
08 Dean of Library/Univ Librarian .... Ms. Christina MCGOWAN
23 Director of the Health Center .... Ms. Julia A. DUFFY
16 Asst VP HR Operations .... Ms. Faith HUNT
96 Director of Purchasing .... Mr. Peter PEREZ

Goodwin University (H)

One Riverside Drive, East Hartford CT 06118-2777
County: Hartford FICE Identification: 022449
Unit ID: 129154
Telephone: (860) 528-4111 Carnegie Class: Bac/Assoc-Mixed
FAX Number: (860) 291-9550 Calendar System: Semester
URL: www.goodwin.edu
Established: 1999 Annual Undergrad Tuition & Fees: $20,998
Enrollment: 3,312 Coed
Affiliation or Control: Independent Non-Profit IRS Status: 501(c)3
Highest Offering: Master's
Accreditation: EH, ADNUR, COARC, DH, FUSER, HT, MAC, NURSE, OTA

01 President .... Mr. Mark E. SCHEINBERG

05 VP Academic Affs/Dean Faculty .... Vacant
10 Vice President for Finance/CFO .... Mr. Eddie MEYER
03 Sr Vice President .... Mr. Todd J. ANDREWS
18 Vice Pres Facilities/Technology .... Mr. Bryant L. HARRELL
84 Vice Pres Enrollment/Mktg/Comm .... Vacant
15 VP Human Resources .... Ms. Jean WHITE
32 Vice Pres Student Affairs .... Mr. Michael PARDALES
108 VP Inst Effectiveness .... Dr. Melissa QUINLAN
88 Asst VP Strategy/Business Devel .... Dr. Clifford THERMER
84 Asst VP Enrollment Services .... Mr. Nicholas LENTINO
08 Director of Library Services .... Mr. Scott HUGHES
36 Director of Career Services .... Vacant
26 Dir Marketing/Communications .... Mr. Phil MOORE
21 Sr Director of Finance/Controller .... Mr. Bryan SOLTIS
13 Director Information Technology .... Mr. John RUGGIRELLO
37 Sr Director of Financial Aid .... Ms. Bonnie SOLTZ-KNOWLTON
07 Director of Admissions .... Mr. Dan WILLIAMSON
09 Director of Institutional Research .... Ms. Grace LIBBY
106 Director of Online Learning .... Dr. Lisa MANLEY
06 Registrar .... Ms. Allison MISKY
29 Alumni Rels/Stdnt Engagement Coord .. Ms. Vanessa PERGOLIZZI
04 Executive Assistant to President .... Ms. Alyse MARION
66 Director of Nursing .... Ms. Vivienne FRIDAY
19 Dir of Campus Safety & Security .... Mr. Richard VIBBERTS

Hartford International University for Religion and Peace (A)

77 Sherman Street, Hartford CT 06105-2260
County: Hartford FICE Identification: 001387
Unit ID: 129491
Telephone: (860) 509-9500 Carnegie Class: Masters/S
FAX Number: (860) 509-9509 Calendar System: Semester
URL: www.hartfordinternational.edu
Established: 1834 Annual Graduate Tuition & Fees: N/A
Enrollment: 120 Coed
Affiliation or Control: Independent Non-Profit IRS Status: 501(c)3
Highest Offering: Doctorate; No Undergraduates
Accreditation: EH, THEOL

01 President .... Dr. Joel LOHR
05 Acting Academic Dean .... Dr. Deena GRANT
07 Director of Recruitment/Enrollment .... Ms. Kalia KELLOGG
08 Director Library Services .... Ms. Karla GRAFTON
10 Chief Business Officer .... Mr. Michael SANDNER
06 Registrar/Financial Aid Coord .... Vacant
04 Exec Assistant to the President .... Vacant
26 Director of Communications .... Ms. Susan SCHOENBERGER
15 Acting Director Human Resources .... Mr. Michael SANDNER
100 Chief of Staff/DEI Officer .... Ms. Lorraine BROWNE
107 Director Exec/Profess Education .... Ms. Katy O'LEARY
18 Director of Fac/Campus Operations .... Mr. Francis FITZGERALD

Holy Apostles College and Seminary (B)

33 Prospect Hill Road, Cromwell CT 06416-2027
County: Middlesex FICE Identification: 001389
Unit ID: 129534
Telephone: (860) 632-3010 Carnegie Class: Masters/M
FAX Number: (860) 632-3030 Calendar System: Semester
URL: www.holyapostles.edu
Established: 1956 Annual Undergrad Tuition & Fees: $8,720
Enrollment: 648 Coed
Affiliation or Control: Roman Catholic IRS Status: 501(c)3
Highest Offering: Beyond Master's But Less Than Doctorate
Accreditation: EH, THEOL

01 President & Rector .... VRev. Peter S. KUCER, MSA
11 Vice President of Administration .... Dr. Thomas SABBAGH
05 Chief Academic Officer .... Dr. Leslie DENARDIS
10 Chief Financial Officer .... Mr. William RUSSELL
08 Director of Library Services .... Ms. Clare ADAMO
07 Director of Admissions .... Ms. Jacqueline REISS
04 Admin Assistant to the President .... Mrs. Alicia FLECK
06 Registrar .... Mrs. Sudarat (Pon) OLMER
09 Director of Institutional Research .... Dr. Cynthia TOOLIN
105 Director Web Services .... Mrs. Jennifer MURPHY
106 Director Online Learning .... Mrs. Jennifer AREL
13 IT Coordinator .... Mr. Matthew GONZALEZ
18 Chf Facilities/Physical Plant Ofcr .... Mr. Kurt O'BRIEN
19 Security and Campus Affairs Officer .... Mr. Matthew GONZALEZ
37 Director Student Financial Aid .... Mr. Jason GILL

Mitchell College (C)

437 Pequot Avenue, New London CT 06320-4498
County: New London FICE Identification: 001393
Unit ID: 129774
Telephone: (860) 701-5000 Carnegie Class: Bac-Diverse
FAX Number: (860) 701-5090 Calendar System: Semester
URL: www.mitchell.edu
Established: 1938 Annual Undergrad Tuition & Fees: $35,072
Enrollment: 599 Coed
Affiliation or Control: Independent Non-Profit IRS Status: 501(c)3
Highest Offering: Baccalaureate
Accreditation: EH

01 President .... Dr. Tracy ESPY
05 VP Academic Affs/Dean of College .... Dr. Elizabeth BEAULIEU
84 VP for Enrollment Mgmt/Athletics .... Mr. Jamie ROMEO
07 Director of Admission/Financial Aid .... Mr. Kelby CHAPPELLE
41 Director of Athletics .... Mr. Matthew FINLAYSON
111 Chief Advancement/Alumni Affair .... Ms. Nancy COWSER
06 Registrar .... Ms. Amy VAN OOT
88 Director of Thames @ Mitchell .... Ms. Beverly SCULLY
10 Chief Financial/Business Officer .... Mr. Robert PERUZZOTTI
20 Assoc Dn Acad Affs/First Year Exp .... Ms. Jennifer R. WELSH
18 Director of Facilities .... Mr. Joseph PARDEE
113 Bursar .... Ms. Amanda CARTER
04 Executive Asst to the President .... Ms. Kristen PISANI
32 Dean Student Experience/Belonging .... Dr. Alicia MARTINEZ
121 Asst Dean of Advising/Stdnt Support .. Ms. Christina CHAPPELLE
38 Director Health & Wellness .... Ms. Kerry PHELON
19 Director Security/Safety .... Mr. Erik COSTA
26 Director of Marketing .... Ms. Lisa STINSON
36 Director Career Services .... Mr. Paul DUNN
15 Human Resource Manager .... Ms. Aruna IYER
39 Director of Residence Life .... Mr. Matthew BRANCACCIO

Paier College (D)

491 University Avenue, Bridgeport CT 06604
County: New Haven FICE Identification: 007459
Unit ID: 130110
Telephone: (203) 287-3031 Carnegie Class: Bac-Diverse
FAX Number: (203) 287-3021 Calendar System: Semester
URL: www.paier.edu
Established: 1946 Annual Undergrad Tuition & Fees: $19,670
Enrollment: 128 Coed
Affiliation or Control: Proprietary IRS Status: Proprietary
Highest Offering: Baccalaureate
Accreditation: ACCSC

01 President .... Mr. Joseph BIERBAUM
03 Provost .... Mr. James PAGE
05 Dean of the College .... Ms. Tammy VAZ
57 Director Design/Graphics .... Mr. Peter MISERENDINO
102 Director Foundation/Arts .... Mr. Robert E. ZAPPALORTI
08 Librarian .... Ms. Beth HARRIS
37 Director Student Financial Aid .... Mr. John DE ROSE
32 Director of Student Services .... Mr. Pedro RODRIGUEZ
88 Director Interior Design .... Mr. Pierre STRAUCH
88 Director Photography .... Mr. Peter BENSON
07 Director of Admissions .... Ms. Deena MARTINELLI

Post University (E)

800 Country Club Road, Waterbury CT 06723-2540
County: New Haven FICE Identification: 001401
Unit ID: 130183
Telephone: (203) 596-4500 Carnegie Class: Masters/L
FAX Number: (203) 841-1163 Calendar System: Semester
URL: www.post.edu
Established: 1890 Annual Undergrad Tuition & Fees: $16,610
Enrollment: 13,844 Coed
Affiliation or Control: Proprietary IRS Status: Proprietary
Highest Offering: Doctorate
Accreditation: EH, ACBSP, NAEYC, NUR, NURSE

01 Chief Executive Officer & President .... Mr. John L. HOPKINS
03 Sr Vice President .... Mr. Scott ALLEN
05 Provost/CAO .... Dr. Elizabeth JOHNSON
11 Chief Operations Officer .... Mr. Bobby REESE
10 Chief Financial Officer .... Mr. Dan STREEK
13 Chief Information Tech Officer .... Mr. Greg THEISEN
15 VP of Associate Experience .... Mr. Wesley DEBNAM
86 Chief Regulatory Officer .... Ms. Elaine NEELY
41 Director of Athletics .... Mr. Ronnie PALMER
50 Dean of School of Business .... Dr. Jeremy BAUER
80 Dean John P Burke Sch Pub Svcs & Ed .... Dr. James WHITLEY
49 Dean of School of Arts & Sciences .... Dr. Dylan CLYNE

Quinnipiac University (F)

275 Mount Carmel Avenue, Hamden CT 06518-1908
County: New Haven FICE Identification: 001402
Unit ID: 130226
Telephone: (203) 582-8200 Carnegie Class: DU-Mod
FAX Number: (203) 582-4703 Calendar System: Semester
URL: www.quinnipiac.edu
Established: 1929 Annual Undergrad Tuition & Fees: $50,760
Enrollment: 9,746 Coed
Affiliation or Control: Independent Non-Profit IRS Status: 501(c)3
Highest Offering: First Professional Degree
Accreditation: EH, ANEST, ARCPA, CAATE, CAEP, LAW, MED, NURSE, OT, PA, PERF, PTA, RAD, SW

01 President .... Dr. Judy D. OLIAN
05 Provost .... Dr. Debra J. LIEBOWITZ
100 Vice President/Chief of Staff .... Dr. Bethany C. ZEMBA
10 Chief Financial Officer .... Mr. Mark VARHOLAK
26 Vice Pres Marketing/Communications .... Mr. Daryl RICHARD
18 Vice Pres Facilities & Capital Plng .... Mr. Salvatore FILARDI
15 Gen Counsel/VP for Human Resources .... Ms. Elicia SPEARMAN
07 Dean of Admissions .... Ms. Karissa PECKHAM
114 Assoc VP Budget & Fin Planning .... Mr. Sandip PATEL
30 Vice Pres Devel & Alumni Affairs .... Mr. Todd SLOAN
32 Vice President & Dean of Students .... Dr. Monique DRUCKER
13 Chief Information Officer .... Mr. Matt ROMEO
20 VP for Acad Innovation & Effective .... Dr. Annalisa ZINN
27 AVP Integrated Mktg Communications .... Mr. James P. RYAN
27 Assoc VP for Public Relations .... Mr. John MORGAN
06 Registrar .... Vacant
28 VP for Equity & Inclusion .... Mr. Donald C. SAWYER
35 Assoc Dean Student Affairs .... Ms. Lynn Nicole HENDRICKS
39 Director of Resident Life .... Mr. Mark DEVILBISS
23 Dir of Student Health Services .... Ms. Christy CHASE
38 Exec Director of Health & Wellness .... Ms. Kerry PATTON
19 Chief of Public Safety .... Chief Otoniel REYES
08 Director of Arnold Bernhard Library .... Mr. Robert JOVEN
41 Director of Athletics & Recreation .... Mr. Greg AMODIO
40 Campus Store Manager .... Ms. Cheryl CARTIER
104 Director of International Svcs .... Ms. Erin SABATO
21 Assoc VP for Finance/Controller .... Mr. Stephen A. ALLEGRETTO
96 Manager of Strategic Sourcing .... Ms. Daniella VIZZIELLO
29 Sr Dir Parent/Family Development .... Vacant
37 Director of Financial Aid .... Ms. Victoria HAMPTON
108 Dir Institutional Assess/Research .... Ms. Sungah KIM
90 Director of Academic Technology .... Ms. Lauren ERARDI
66 Dean School of Nursing .... Dr. Lisa G. O'CONNOR
50 Dean School of Business .... Dr. Holly RAIDER
49 Dean College of Arts & Sciences .... Dr. Adam ROTH
76 Dean School of Health Sciences .... Dr. Janelle CHIASERA
61 Dean School of Law .... Dr. Jennifer G. BROWN
60 Dean School of Communications .... Mr. Chris G. ROUSH
53 Dean School of Education .... Dr. Anne M. DICHELE
63 Dean School of Medicine .... Dr. Philip BOISELLE
54 Dean School of Engineering .... Dr. Taskin KOCAK
94 Director of Women's Studies .... Dr. Jennifer SACCO
04 Sr Exec Assistant to President .... Ms. Gina FALCIGNO
44 Director Annual Giving .... Mr. Andy BERNSTEIN
122 Dir Campus Life-Frat/Sorority Life .... Ms. Avery MOSES

Rensselaer at Hartford (G)

275 Windsor Street, Hartford CT 06120-2991
Telephone: (860) 548-2400 FICE Identification: 002804
Accreditation: &M

† Regional accreditation is carried under the parent institution, Rensselaer Polytechnic Institute, NY.

Sacred Heart University (H)

5151 Park Avenue, Fairfield CT 06825-1000
County: Fairfield FICE Identification: 001403
Unit ID: 130253
Telephone: (203) 371-7999 Carnegie Class: DU-Mod
FAX Number: (203) 365-7652 Calendar System: Semester
URL: www.sacredheart.edu
Established: 1963 Annual Undergrad Tuition & Fees: $44,350
Enrollment: 9,313 Coed
Affiliation or Control: Independent Non-Profit IRS Status: 501(c)3
Highest Offering: Doctorate
Accreditation: EH, ADNUR, ARCPA, CAATE, CAEP, CEA, NURSE, OT, PTA, RAD, SP, SW

01 President & CEO .... Dr. John J. PETILLO
05 Provost/VP Academic Affairs .... Dr. Robin CAUTIN
32 Sr VP Student Affairs & Athletics .... Mr. James M. BARQUINERO
11 Sr VP Administration & Planning .... Dr. David COPPOLA
15 VP Human Resources .... Mr. Robert M. HARDY
26 Chief of Staff/VP Mktg/Comm .... Mr. Michael L. IANNAZZI
88 VP Mission/Catholic Identity .... Fr. Anthony CIORRA
10 Sr VP Finance .... Mr. Philip J. MCCABE
13 VP Information Technology .... Ms. Shirley CANAAN
111 Interim VP University Advancement .... Ms. Marie MUHVIC
43 University General Counsel .... Mr. Michael D. LAROBINA
49 Acting Dean of Arts & Sciences .... Dr. Mark BEEKEY
50 Dean College of Business .... Dr. Martha J. CRAWFORD
76 Dean Col Health Professions .... Dr. Maura IVERSEN
53 Dean College of Education .... Dr. Michael ALFANO
66 Dean College of Nursing .... Dr. Karen DALEY
58 Dean Graduate Studies .... Dr. Brian V. CAROLAN
12 Dean St. Vincent's College .... Ms. Maryanne DAVIDSON
108 President University Acad Assembly .... Mr. Dom PINTO
07 Exec Director Undergrad Admissions .... Ms. Pam PILLO
06 Registrar .... Ms. Angela PITCHER

Trinity College (I)

300 Summit Street, Hartford CT 06106-3100
County: Hartford FICE Identification: 001414
Unit ID: 130590
Telephone: (860) 297-2000 Carnegie Class: Bac-A&S
FAX Number: (860) 297-5359 Calendar System: Semester
URL: www.trincoll.edu
Established: 1823 Annual Undergrad Tuition & Fees: $59,050
Enrollment: 2,241 Coed
Affiliation or Control: Independent Non-Profit IRS Status: 501(c)3
Highest Offering: Master's
Accreditation: EH

01 President .... Dr. Joanne BERGER-SWEENEY
10 Vice Pres Finance/CFO .... Mr. Dan HITCHELL
05 Dean of Faculty/VP Academic Affairs .... Dr. Sonia CARDENAS
13 Vice Pres Information Svcs/CIO .... Ms. Kristen ESHLEMAN
111 Vice Pres College Advancement .... Mr. Michael CASEY
32 Vice Pres Student Affairs .... Mr. Joseph DICHRISTINA
84 Vice Pres Enrollment/Stdnt Success .... Mr. Joseph DICHRISTINA
26 VP of Marketing/Communications .... Ms. Hellen HOM-DIAMOND
28 VP Diversity/Equity and Inclusion .... Ms. Anita DAVIS
43 General Counsel & Secretary .... Mr. Dickens MATHIEU
100 Chief of Staff/AVP External Affairs .... Mr. Jason ROJAS
15 AVP Human Resources .... Ms. Michelle CABRAL

07 Director of Admissions — Mr. Anthony T. BERRY
37 Director of Financial Aid — Ms. Ashley DUTTON
27 Interim Director of Media Relations — Ms. Kathryn ANDREWS
06 Registrar — Mr. Gabriel G. OLSZEWSKI
21 Director of Business Operations — Mr. Michael ELLIOTT
114 Budget Director — Ms. Marcia PHELAN JOHNSON
19 Director of Campus Safety — Mr. Robert LUKASKIEWICZ
30 Director of Development — Mr. Christopher FRENCH
21 Comptroller — Mr. Guy DRAPEAU
41 Director of Athletics — Mr. Drew GALBRAITH
09 Dir Analytics/Strategic Initiatives — Mr. David ANDRES
39 Director of Residential Life — Ms. Susan SALISBURY
42 College Chaplain — Rev. Marcus HALLEY
38 Director Student Counseling — Dr. Randolph LEE
96 Director of Purchasing — Mr. Michael S. ELLIOTT
82 Dean of Urban and Global Studies — Dr. Xiangming CHEN
29 Int Director of Alumni Relations — Ms. Julie H. CLOUTIER
08 Head Librarian — Ms. Janine S. KINEL
101 Special Assistant to the President — Ms. Karolina KWIECINSKA
88 Deputy Chief of Staff — Mr. Tom YELICH
04 Executive Asst to President — Ms. Patrice A. LEMOINE
108 Director Institutional Assessment — Mr. Mark HUGHES
22 Director Affirm Action/Equal Opp — Ms. Kate DURANTE
86 Director Government Relations — Mr. Jason ROJAS

University of Bridgeport (A)

126 Park Avenue, Bridgeport CT 06604-5620
County: Fairfield — FICE Identification: 001416
Unit ID: 128744
Telephone: (203) 576-4000 — Carnegie Class: DU-Mod
FAX Number: (203) 576-4653 — Calendar System: Semester
URL: www.bridgeport.edu
Established: 1927 — Annual Undergrad Tuition & Fees: $35,760
Enrollment: 4,155 — Coed
Affiliation or Control: Independent Non-Profit — IRS Status: 501(c)3
Highest Offering: Doctorate
Accreditation: EH, ACBSP, ACUP, ARCPA, ART, CACREP, CAEP, CHIRO, DH, MLS, NURSE

01 President — Dr. Danielle E. WILKEN
04 Executive Assistant to President — Ms. Brenda PIOLI
05 Provost & VP for Academic Affairs — Dr. Manyul E. IM
11 VP & Chief Admin Officer — Mr. Daniel NOONAN
10 VP of Finance/Chief Financial Ofcr — Mr. William GUERRERO
111 VP Advancement & College Initiative — Mr. Rich M. MCCARTY
41 VP Athletics — Mr. James MORAN
88 Chief Operating Officer for Admin — Mr. Robert SCHMIDT
32 Dean of Students — Mr. Craig LENNON
08 Director of Library — Mr. Scott HUGHES
15 Director Human Resources — Ms. Cheryl M. NYARADY
21 Controller — Mr. Malhar SHARMA
37 Director Financial Aid & Compliance — Ms. Jamie GRIEFF
19 Exec Director of Campus Security — Mrs. April J. VOURNELIS
121 Dir of Student & Academic Success — Ms. Jill JEMMOTT
38 Director of Counseling Services — Vacant
06 University Registrar — Ms. Carmen ROSA
85 Director of Intl Student Affairs — Ms. Yumin WANG
76 Dean College of Health Sciences — Dr. Michael CIOLFI
39 Director of Residential Life — Mrs. Cindy SANDERS
35 Dir Student Involvement — Ms. Kelli A. MEYER
30 Dir of Devel & Alumni Relations — Ms. Jhanay ABRAMS
23 Director of Health Center — Vacant
88 Director of Acupuncture Institute — Dr. Jennifer BRETT
40 Manager of the Bookstore — Mr. Richard HEBERT
36 Director of Career Services — Vacant
54 Dean Engr/Business/Education — Dr. Khaled M. ELLEITHY
49 Dean Arts & Sciences — Dr. Kathleen ENGELMANN
53 Dir School of Education — Dr. Nancy DEJARNETTE
88 Dir School of Chiropractic — Dr. Michael A. CIOLFI
50 Dir School of Business — Mr. Timonthy RAYNOR
52 Dir School of Dental Hygiene — Dr. Marion MANSKI
106 Associate Provost — Dr. Jaria ALJOE
88 Dir Physician Assistant Institute — Ms. Lauren WEINDLLING
91 Dir Acad & Campus Tech Services — Vacant
07 Dean of Admissions — Mr. Jeff MON
105 Web Master — Ms. Brittany LADD

University of Connecticut (B)

352 Mansfield Road, Storrs CT 06269-1048
County: Tolland — FICE Identification: 001417
Unit ID: 129020
Telephone: (860) 486-2337 — Carnegie Class: DU-Highest
FAX Number: (860) 486-2627 — Calendar System: Semester
URL: www.uconn.edu
Established: 1881 — Annual Undergrad Tuition & Fees (In-State): $17,834
Enrollment: 27,215 — Coed
Affiliation or Control: State — IRS Status: 501(c)3
Highest Offering: Doctorate
Accreditation: EH, ART, AUD, CAATE, CACREP, CAEPN, CEA, CLPSY, DIETC, DIETD, DIETI, DMOLS, IPSY, JOUR, LAW, LSAR, MLS, MUS, NURSE, PHAR, PTA, SCPSY, SP, SPAA, SW

01 Interim President — Radenka MARIC
100 Chief of Staff/General Counsel — Nicole GELSTON
05 Int Provost/EVP Academic Affairs — Anne D'ALLEVA
111 President & CEO UConn Foundation — Jake LEMON
17 Interim Exec VP Health Affs & CEO — Bruce LIANG
10 Interim VP for Finance and CFO — Lloyd BLANCHARD
32 Vice President for Student Affairs — Michael GILBERT
46 Interim VP for Rsrch/Innov & Entr — Pamir ALPAY
101 Exec Sec to Board/Dep Dir Athletics — Rachel RUBIN
26 Vice Pres for Communications — P. Tysen KENDIG
41 Director of Athletics — David BENEDICT
13 Vice President & Chief Info Officer — Michael MUNDRANE
114 Assoc VP for Budget & Planning — Lloyd BLANCHARD
19 Assoc VP for Public Safety — Hans RHYNHART
28 Vice Pres/Chief Diversity Officer — Franklin A. TUITT
22 Assoc VP for Institutional Equity — Letissa REID
09 AVP Inst Research & Effectiveness — Lloyd BLANCHARD
20 Sr Vice Prov for Academic Affairs — Jeffrey SHOULSON
20 Vice Prov Faculty/Staff/Stdnt Dev — Michael BRADFORD
84 VP Enrollment Planning & Mgmt — Nathan FUERST
08 Dean of Univ Library — Anne LANGLEY
12 Director Stamford Campus — David SOUDER
12 Director Avery Point Campus — Annemarie SEIFERT
12 Interim Director Waterbury Campus — Fumiko HOEFT
12 Director Hartford Campus — Mark OVERMYER-VELAZQUEZ
92 AVProv Enrich Pgms/Dir Honors Pgms — Jennifer LEASE BUTTS
25 AVP Research/Sponsored Pgm Svcs — Michael GLASGOW
86 Sr Director Government Relations — Joann LOMBARDO
06 Registrar — Gregory BOUQUOT
07 Director Undergrad Admissions — Vern GRANGER
37 Director Student Financial Aid — Suzanne PETERS
29 Asst Vice Pres Alumni Relations — Montique COTTON KELLY
23 Exec Dir Student Health/Wellness — Suzanne ONORATO
15 Exec Director of Human Resources — Aliza WILDER
96 Interim AVP Univ Business Svcs — Gregory DANIELS
47 Dean Col of Agric/Natural Resources — Indrajeet CHAUBEY
50 Dean School of Business — John ELLIOTT
53 Dean Neag School of Education — Jason IRIZARRY
54 Dean of Engineering — Kazem KAZEROUNIAN
88 Assoc Vice Prov Excell Teach/Lrng — Peter DIPLOCK
57 Dean of Fine Arts — Anne D'ALLEVA
58 Vice Prov Grad Ed/Dean Grad Sch — Kent HOLSINGER
61 Dean School of Law — Eboni S. NELSON
49 Dean Col of Lib Arts/Sciences — Juli WADE
66 Dean School of Nursing — Deborah A. CHYUN
67 Dean School of Pharmacy — Philip HRITCKO
70 Dean School of Social Work — Nina ROVINELLI HELLER
52 Dean of Dental Medicine — Steven LEPOWSKY
63 Dean School of Medicine — Bruce LIANG
38 Director of Mental Health — Kristina STEVENS
39 Executive Director Residential Life — Pamela SCHIPANI
27 AVP Communications/Sr Adv to Pres — Michael KIRK
88 AVP Plng/Design/Const/Chf Architect — Laura CRUICKSHANK
85 Vice President for Global Affairs — Daniel WEINER
36 Asst VProv/Exec Dir Career Services — James R. LOWE
121 Assoc Vice Prov for Student Success — Tadarrayl STARKE
88 Ombuds — James WOHL
88 Dir Institute for Materials Science — Steven L. SUIB
04 Executive Asst to President — Jennifer BURCKARDT
104 Director Education Abroad — Vacant
18 Assoc VP Facilities Ops & Bldg Svcs — P. Michael JEDNAK
112 VP of Principal and Planned Gifts — Brian OTIS
106 Dir Online Education/E-learning — Peter DIPLOCK
88 Dir Vet Affs & Military Programs — Alyssa KELLEHER

University of Connecticut Health Center (C)

263 Farmington Avenue, Farmington CT 06030-1827
Telephone: (860) 679-2000 — FICE Identification: 009867
Accreditation: &EH, DENT, MED, PH

† Regional accreditation is carried under the parent institution in Storrs, CT.

University of Connecticut School of Law (D)

55 Elizabeth Street, Hartford CT 06105-2290
Telephone: (860) 570-5000 — Identification: 770108
Accreditation: &EH, LAW

University of Hartford (E)

200 Bloomfield Avenue, West Hartford CT 06117-1599
County: Hartford — FICE Identification: 001422
Unit ID: 129525
Telephone: (860) 768-4100 — Carnegie Class: DU-Mod
FAX Number: (860) 768-4070 — Calendar System: Semester
URL: www.hartford.edu
Established: 1877 — Annual Undergrad Tuition & Fees: $43,560
Enrollment: 6,493 — Coed
Affiliation or Control: Independent Non-Profit — IRS Status: 501(c)3
Highest Offering: Doctorate
Accreditation: EH, ART, CAEPN, CLPSY, COARC, DANCE, MUS, NURSE, OPE, PTA, RAD, THEA

01 President — Dr. Gregory S. WOODWARD
05 Interim Provost/VP Academic Affairs — Dr. Katherine A. BLACK
11 Exec Vice Pres/Chief Operating Ofcr — Dr. Mark BOXER
111 Vice Pres Institutional Advancement — Ms. Kate PENDERGAST
32 Vice Pres Student Affs/Dean Stdnts — Dr. Aaron ISAACS
26 Vice Pres Marketing/Enrollment — Ms. Molly POLK
41 Acting VP Athletics/Recreation — Dr. Sharon BEVERLY
35 Assoc Vice Pres for Student Life — Vacant
58 Assoc Prov/Dean of Grad Studies — Vacant
07 Dean of Admission — Mr. Richard A. ZEISER
04 Exec Assistant to the President — Ms. Ilena ROSENSTEIN
08 Director University Libraries — Ms. Elizabeth DILL
06 Registrar — Ms. Natalie DURANT
38 Dir Counsel & Psychology Services — Dr. Jeffrey BURDA
36 Exec Dir Career/Prof Services — Ms. Brooke PENDERS
13 Asst VP Ops/Info Tech Svcs — Mr. Sebby SORRENTINO
19 Chief Public Safety — Mr. Michael KASELOUSKAS
23 Director Health Services — Ms. Amy WISNIEWSKI
24 Director User Services — Vacant
25 Director Sponsored Programs — Mr. Christopher STANDISH
18 Asst VP Capital Plng/Mgmt — Mr. Chris DUPUIS
104 Director International Center — Ms. Nicole KURKER-STEWART
108 Exec Dir Inst Effectiveness — Ms. Kathleen NEAL
94 Director of Women's Center — Vacant
88 Director of Student Conduct & Admin — Mr. David STENDER
96 Director of Procurement Svcs — Ms. Lisa CONDON
92 Director of University Honors — Dr. Claudia OAKES
58 Asst VP Grad and Prof Studies — Dr. R. J. MCGIVNEY
57 Dean Hartford Art School — Dr. Nancy M. STUART
72 Dean College Engineer/Tech/Arch — Dr. Hisham ALNAJJAR
49 Interim Dean College Arts & Science — Dr. Mark BLACKWELL
50 Dean Barney School of Business — Mr. Stephen MULREADY
53 Dean Col of Educ/Nurs/Hlth Prof — Dr. Cesarina THOMPSON
64 Dean Hartt School — Dr. Dale MERRILL
12 Interim Dean Hillyer College — Dr. Fran ALTVATER
27 Dir of Marketing/Communications — Mr. Jonathan EASTERBROOK
102 Dir Foundation/Corporate Relations — Vacant
15 Director HRD — Ms. Jen CONLEY
28 Asst VP Diversity/Equity/Cmty Eng — Ms. Christine GRANT
29 Senior Director Alumni Engagement — Ms. Caitlin TRINH
37 Director Student Financial Aid — Ms. Katherine PRESUTTI
39 Exec Dir Resident Life — Ms. Jill ENGEL-HELLMAN
44 Director Annual Giving — Ms. Erin POLLARD

University of New Haven (F)

300 Boston Post Road, West Haven CT 06516-1916
County: New Haven — FICE Identification: 001397
Unit ID: 129941
Telephone: (203) 932-7000 — Carnegie Class: Masters/L
FAX Number: (203) 931-6060 — Calendar System: Semester
URL: www.newhaven.edu
Established: 1920 — Annual Undergrad Tuition & Fees: $41,654
Enrollment: 6,961 — Coed
Affiliation or Control: Independent Non-Profit — IRS Status: 501(c)3
Highest Offering: Doctorate
Accreditation: EH, ART, CIDA, DH, DIET, DIETD, DIETI, FEPAC, HSA, @SP

01 Interim President — Dr. Sheahon ZENGER
00 Chancellor/CEO — Dr. Steven H. KAPLAN
05 Interim Provost/SVP of Acad Affairs — Dr. Mario GABOURY
10 VP of Finance & Administration — Mr. George S. SYNODI
84 VP of Enrollment & Student Success — Mr. Gregory EICHHORN
111 VP of Advancement — Mr. Brian OTIS
15 Assoc VP of HR and Org Dev — Ms. Jennifer CINQUE
100 VP and Chief of Staff — Ms. Jean HUSTED
41 Director of Athletics & Recreation — Dr. Sheahon ZENGER
28 VP for Diversity & Inclusion — Dr. Lorenzo BOYD
54 Dean Tagliatela Col Engineering — Dr. Ronald HARICHANDRAN
50 Dean College Business — Dr. Brian KENCH
76 Dean School of Health Sciences — Dr. Summer J. MCGEE
49 Dean of Arts & Sciences — Dr. Shaily MENON
83 Actg Dean Crim Justice/Forensic Sci — Dr. David SCHROEDER
20 Deputy Provost — Dr. Glenn MCGEE
32 Dean Stdnts/Chief Student Affs Ofcr — Dr. Ophelie ROWE-ALLEN
21 Associate VP for Finance — Mr. Patrick TORRE
18 Associate VP for Facilities — Mr. Lou ANNINO
19 Assoc VP for Public Safety/Admin — Mr. Ron QUAGLIANI
13 Assoc VP for Information Tech/CIO — Mr. Vincent P. MANGIACAPRA
113 Assoc VP Financial/Registrar Svcs — Mr. Marc MANIATIS
26 AVP of Marketing & Public Relations — Mr. Doug WHITING
16 Exec Director of Human Resources — Ms. Iris CALOVINE
09 Director Institutional Research — Ms. Susan TURNER
08 University Librarian — Ms. Hanko H. DOBI
37 Director of Financial Aid — Mr. Erin CHIARO
110 Assoc VP for Advancement Operations — Ms. Lisa HONAN
30 Associate VP for Development — Ms. Roslyn REABACK
06 University Registrar — Ms. Elizabeth REZENDES
19 Chief of University Police — Chief James T. GILMAN
35 Senior Associate Dean of Students — Mr. Ric BAKER
35 Exec Dir of Student Activities — Mr. Gregory OVEREND
39 Associate Dean of Residential Life — Ms. Nicole MCGRATH
07 Director of Undergrad Admissions — Ms. Jessica GODDU
123 Sr Exec Dir Graduate Admissions — Ms. Selina O'TOOLE
04 President's Office Coordinator — Ms. Jennifer FAZEKAS
91 Dir Enterprise Applications — Mr. Todd MCINERNEY
96 Director of Purchasing — Mr. Robert STEVENS
103 Exec Director of Career Development — Mr. Matthew CAPORALE
85 Exec Dir of International Services — Ms. Kathy KAUTZ
29 Director of Alumni Relations — Ms. Jennifer PJATAK
122 Coord Stdnt Orgs-Greek Life — Ms. Erin O'KEEFE

University of Saint Joseph (G)

1678 Asylum Avenue, West Hartford CT 06117-2791
County: Hartford — FICE Identification: 001409
Unit ID: 130314
Telephone: (860) 232-4571 — Carnegie Class: Masters/L
FAX Number: (860) 232-6927 — Calendar System: Semester
URL: www.usj.edu
Established: 1932 — Annual Undergrad Tuition & Fees: $41,736
Enrollment: 2,305 — Coed
Affiliation or Control: Roman Catholic — IRS Status: 501(c)3
Highest Offering: Doctorate
Accreditation: EH, ARCPA, CACREP, CAEP, DIETD, DIETI, NURSE, PHAR, SW

01 President — Dr. Rhona C. FREE
05 Provost — Dr. Michelle KALIS

10 VP Finance and Administration .... Ms. Lucy LUCKER
111 VP Inst Advancement .... Ms. Maggie PINNEY
84 VP Enrollment Management .... Ms. Kimberly CRONE
32 Dean of Student Affairs .... Mr. Brandon DAWSON
26 Dir Marketing & Communications .... Ms. Stacy ROUTHIER
67 Dean Sch Pharmacy/PA Studies .... Dr. Ahmed ABDELMAGEED
49 Dean Sch Arts/Sci/Business/Ed .... Dr. Raouf BOULES
76 Dean Sch Interdisc Health & Science .... Vacant
08 Librarian .... Ms. Roseanne KRZANOWSKI
06 Registrar .... Ms. Angela ANDERSON
41 Director of Athletics .... Ms. Amanda DEVITT
15 Director of Human Resources .... Ms. Deborah SPENCER
13 Director of Info Tech (CIO) .... Mr. Jason LAWRENCE
18 Director of Facilities .... Mr. Andrew LEVESQUE
19 Director of Public Safety .... Mr. Derrick MCBRIDE
07 Director of Admissions .... Dr. Molly MINER
114 Director Budget & Planning .... Ms. Mary HUNT
37 Director of Student Financial Svcs .... Ms. Stacey DOWNING
36 Dir Career Dev/Women's Ldrship Ctr .... Ms. Melanie SINCHE
28 Director of Diversity/Title IX .... Ms. Rayna DYTON-WHITE
23 Director of Health Services .... Ms. Janet FLINK
38 Director of Counseling & Wellness .... Dr. Meredith YUHAS
29 Dir of Alumni Rels/Annual Giving .... Ms. Katie BURKE
09 Research Analyst .... Mr. Chris LOSO
04 Exec Asst to President .... Ms. Ruth FOXMAN

Wesleyan University (A)

45 Wyllys Avenue, Middletown CT 06459
County: Middlesex FICE Identification: 001424
Unit ID: 130697
Telephone: (860) 685-2000 Carnegie Class: Bac-A&S
FAX Number: (860) 685-2001 Calendar System: Semester
URL: www.wesleyan.edu
Established: 1831 Annual Undergrad Tuition & Fees: $59,686
Enrollment: 3,053 Coed
Affiliation or Control: Independent Non-Profit IRS Status: 501(c)3
Highest Offering: Doctorate
Accreditation: EH

01 President .... Dr. Michael S. ROTH
05 Provost/SVP for Academic Affairs .... Dr. Nicole L. STANTON
10 SVP/Chief Admin Ofcr/Treasurer .... Mr. Andrew Y. TANAKA
100 Chief of Staff .... Ms. Anne LASKOWSKI
111 Vice President for Advancement .... Mr. Frantz WILLIAMS, JR.
28 Int VP Equity/Inclusion/Title IX .... Dr. Alison WILLIAMS
32 Vice Pres of Student Affairs .... Mr. Michael J. WHALEY
13 VP Information Technology/CIO .... Dr. David BAIRD
20 Associate Provost .... Dr. Mark HOVEY
20 Associate Provost .... Ms. Sheryl CULOTTA
18 Assoc Vice President for Facilities .... Ms. Joyce TOPSHE
35 Assoc Vice Pres/Dean of Students .... Mr. Richard CULLITON
58 Dir Cont Stds/Graduate Liberal Stds .... Ms. Jennifer M. CURRAN
07 Vice Pres/Dean Admissions/Fin Aid .... Mr. Amin Abdul-Malik GONZALEZ
06 Registrar .... Vacant
08 University Librarian .... Mr. Andrew W. WHITE
09 Director of Institutional Research .... Mr. Michael E. WHITCOMB
37 Director Financial Aid .... Mr. Robert D. COUGHLIN
36 Executive Dir of the Career Center .... Ms. Sharon CASTONGUAY
15 Assoc VP for Human Resources .... Ms. Lisa BROMMER
19 Director Public Safety .... Mr. Scott ROHDE
41 Director of Athletics .... Mr. Michael WHALEN
04 Special Assistant to the President .... Ms. Heather BROOKE
104 Director Study Abroad .... Ms. Emily GORLEWSKI
108 Associate Director for Assessment .... Ms. Rachael BARLOW
38 Dir of Counseling and Psych Svcs .... Ms. Jennifer D'ANDREA
39 Dir Resident Life/Student Housing .... Ms. Frances KOERTING
90 Director of Academic Technology .... Ms. Rachel SCHNEPPER
91 Senior Dir of Enterprise Systems .... Mr. Steve B. MACHUGA
96 Director of Purchasing .... Ms. Olga BOOKAS

Yale University (B)

3 Prospect Street, New Haven CT 06520
County: New Haven FICE Identification: 001426
Unit ID: 130794
Telephone: (203) 432-2550 Carnegie Class: DU-Highest
FAX Number: (203) 432-7105 Calendar System: Semester
URL: www.yale.edu
Established: 1701 Annual Undergrad Tuition & Fees: $57,700
Enrollment: 12,060 Coed
Affiliation or Control: Independent Non-Profit IRS Status: 501(c)3
Highest Offering: Doctorate
Accreditation: EH, ARCPA, CAMPEP, CLPSY, IPSY, LAW, MED, MIDWF, NURSE, PAST, PCSAS, PH, THEOL

01 President .... Peter SALOVEY
05 Provost .... Scott A. STROBEL
11 Senior Vice President Operations .... Jack F. CALLAHAN, JR.
32 Secretary & VP Student Affairs .... Kimberly GOFF-CREWS
10 Vice Pres Finance & CFO .... Stephen MURPHY
30 VP Development/Alumni Affairs .... Joan E. O'NEILL
43 Sr Vice President & General Counsel .... Alexander DREIER
15 Vice Pres Human Resources .... John WHELAN
46 Vice Provost of Research .... Peter SCHIFFER
88 Vice President Global Strategy .... Pericles LEWIS
20 Vice Prov Health Affairs and Acad .... Stephanie SPANGLER
20 Vice Provost Academic Resources .... J. Lloyd SUTTLE
18 VP Facilities & Campus Development .... John H. BOLLIER
20 Vice Provost .... Emily P. BAKEMEIER
26 Vice President for Communications .... Nathaniel NICKERSON
102 Assoc VP/Dir Corp & Found Rels .... Patricia E. PEDERSEN
08 Univ Librarian & Deputy Provost .... Susan GIBBONS
09 AVP Academic Business Ops/Strategy .... Tim PAVLIS
13 VP IT & Chief Information Ofcr .... John BARDEN
96 Assoc VP Administration Operations .... John A. MAYES
19 Dir Public Safety/Chief Univ Police .... Ronnell A. HIGGINS
06 University Registrar .... Emily SHANDLEY
07 Dean Undergraduate Admissions .... Jeremiah QUINLAN
29 Exec Director Assoc of Yale Alumni .... Weili CHENG
35 Sr Assoc Dean & Dean Student Affs .... Mark SCHENKER
22 Sr Dir Ofc Equal Opportunities .... Valarie J. STANLEY
23 Director University Health Services .... Dr. Paul GENECIN
25 Exec Dir Sponsored Projects .... Lisa MOSLEY
36 Assoc Dean/Director Career Services .... Jeanine DAMES
37 University Director Financial Aid .... Caesar T. STORLAZZI
112 Univ Director Planned Giving .... Marybeth CONGDON
39 Dir Grad & Prof Student Housing .... George E. LONGYEAR, JR.
41 Director Athletics .... Victoria CHUN
42 University Chaplain .... Sharon KUGLER
48 Dean of the School of Architecture .... Deborah BERKE
49 Dean of Yale College .... Pericles LEWIS
50 Dean School of Management .... Kerwin CHARLES
85 Director Intl Students & Scholars .... Ann KUHLMAN
54 Dean School of Engineering .... Jeffrey BROCK
57 Dean of the School of Art .... Marta KUZMA
58 Dean of Grad Sch Arts & Science .... Lynn COOLEY
57 Dean of the School of Drama .... James A. BUNDY
61 Dean of the Law School .... Heather GERKEN
64 Dean of the School of Music .... Robert L. BLOCKER
65 Dean Sch of Forestry & Environ Stds .... Indy BURKE
73 Dean of the Divinity School .... Gregory E. STERLING
88 Director Inst of Sacred Music .... Martin D. JEAN
63 Dean of School of Medicine .... Dr. Robert J. ALPERN
66 Dean of the School of Nursing .... Ann KURTH
69 Dean of Public Health .... Sten VERMUND
28 AVP Emp Engage/Chief Diversity Ofcr .... Deborah STANLEY-MCAULAY
104 Sr Assoc Dean Intl/Prof Experience .... Jane EDWARDS
88 Assoc VP New Haven Aff & Univ Prop .... Lauren ZUCKER
100 Chief of Staff/YSM Dean's Office .... Cynthia DWYER

DELAWARE

Delaware College of Art and Design (C)

600 N Market Street, Wilmington DE 19801-3007
County: New Castle FICE Identification: 041398
Unit ID: 432524
Telephone: (302) 622-8000 Carnegie Class: Spec 2-yr-A&S
FAX Number: (302) 622-8870 Calendar System: Semester
URL: www.dcad.edu
Established: 1997 Annual Undergrad Tuition & Fees: $25,770
Enrollment: 107 Coed
Affiliation or Control: Independent Non-Profit IRS Status: 501(c)3
Highest Offering: Associate Degree
Accreditation: M, ART

01 President .... Ms. Jean DAHLGREN
05 Academic Dean .... Ms. Katy RO
20 Assistant Dean .... Vacant
10 Director of Finance .... Mr. Richard SAVONA
08 Library Director .... Ms. Megan JOHNSON
30 Director of Development .... Ms. Meg CLIFTON NORTH
37 Director of Financial Aid .... Ms. Kathleen ELLIS-FOULTZ
32 Director of Student Life .... Ms. Mussa TRYTEK
07 Director of Admissions .... Mr. Randle REED
06 Registrar .... Mr. David CZARNECKI
04 Admin Assistant to the President .... Ms. Kristen A. BLANCHARD

Delaware State University (D)

1200 N DuPont Highway, Dover DE 19901-2275
County: Kent FICE Identification: 001428
Unit ID: 130934
Telephone: (302) 857-6060 Carnegie Class: Masters/M
FAX Number: N/A Calendar System: Semester
URL: www.desu.edu
Established: 1891 Annual Undergrad Tuition & Fees (In-State): $8,358
Enrollment: 4,739 Coed
Affiliation or Control: State IRS Status: 501(c)3
Highest Offering: Doctorate
Accreditation: M, ACPHA, CAEP, DIETC, NUR, SW

01 President .... Dr. Tony ALLEN
05 Provost/Exec Vice President .... Dr. Saundra DELAUDER
10 Vice President Finance .... Mr. Robert SCHROF
111 Vice Pres Inst Advancement .... Dr. Vita C. PICKRUM
12 Chief Administrator DSU Downtown .... Dr. Stacy L. DOWNING
84 Vice Pres Strategic Enrollment .... Mr. Antonio BOYLE
46 Assoc Vice President for Research .... Dr. Melissa HARRINGTON
13 VP/CIO .... Mr. Darrell MCMILLON
09 Exec Dir Research/Planning/Analytic .... Mr. Vaughn K. HOPKINS
15 Vice Pres Human Resources .... Ms. Irene HAWKINS
20 Associate Provost .... Dr. Bradley SKELCHER
11 Chief Operating Officer .... Mr. Cleon CAULEY
18 AVP of Facilities/Planning & Constr .... Mr. Bernard PRATT
45 AVP for Strategic Initiatives .... Mr. Terrell HOLMES
07 Exec Director of Admissions .... Mr. Kareem MCLEMORE
08 Dean University Libraries .... Ms. Rebecca BATSON
37 Exec Director of Financial Aid .... Vacant
29 Executive Director Alumni Relations .... Dr. Marcia TAYLOR
32 AVP Student Affairs .... Ms. Jasmine BUXTON
19 Chief of Public Safety .... Mr. Bobby L. CUMMINGS
38 Director of Counseling Services .... Mr. Michael MONK
27 Director News Services .... Mr. Carlos HOLMES
41 Director of Athletics .... Ms. Alecia S. GADSON
44 Director Annual Giving .... Ms. Dawn HOPKINS
86 VP for Govt/Community Relations .... Mrs. Jackie GRIFFITH
100 Chief of Staff .... Ms. Tamara L. STONER
104 AVP for International Affairs .... Dr. Fengshan LIU
105 Director Web Services .... Mr. Stuart GROOBY
58 Dean Grad & Extended Studies .... Dr. Patrice GILLIAM JOHNSON
26 AVP Marketing & Communications .... Dr. Dawn MOSLEY
39 Director Housing/Residential Educ .... Mr. Phillip HOLMES
50 Dean College of Business .... Dr. Michael H. CASSON, JR.
47 Interim Dean Agri/Science & Tech .... Dr. Cherese WINSTEAD
04 Exec Assistant to the President .... Ms. Vanessa D. NESBIT
51 Exec Director Adult/Continuing Educ .... Dr. Darren BLACKSTON
108 Director of Assessment .... Dr. Bina DANIEL
88 Deputy Chief Administrative Ofcr .... Dr. Francine EDWARDS
28 VP of Global Institute .... Mr. Sonel SHROPSHIRE
25 Director OSP .... Ms. Renee S. JONES
88 Dir Labor Relations & Diversity .... Ms. Pamela M. GRESHAM
30 Director of Development .... Ms. Gina SACCHETTI
45 Director Planning/Special Projects .... Ms. Charmaine BABB
53 Interim Dean CHESS .... Dr. Akwasi OSEI
54 Dean CAST .... Dr. Cherese WINSTEAD
90 Director Academic Technology .... Mr. Christopher D. GARLAND
96 Director of Purchasing .... Ms. Shawnie R. NOEL

Delaware Technical Community College, Orlando J. George Campus (E)

300 N. Orange Street, Wilmington DE 19801
Telephone: (302) 571-5300 Identification: 770855
Accreditation: &M, CAHIIM, COARC, DH, DMS, MAC, OTA, PTAA, RAD

Delaware Technical Community College, Owens Campus (F)

21179 College Drive, Georgetown DE 19947-0610
Telephone: (302) 259-6000 FICE Identification: 007053
Accreditation: &M, ADNUR, COARC, CSHSE, DMS, MLTAD, OTA, PNUR, PTAA, RAD

Delaware Technical Community College, Stanton Campus (G)

400 Stanton-Christiana Road, Newark DE 19713-2197
Telephone: (302) 454-3900 FICE Identification: 021449
Accreditation: &M, ACFEI, ADNUR, CSHSE, HT, NMT

Delaware Technical Community College, Terry Campus (H)

100 Campus Drive, Dover DE 19904-1383
County: Kent FICE Identification: 011727
Unit ID: 130907
Telephone: (302) 857-1000 Carnegie Class: Bac/Assoc-Assoc Dom
FAX Number: (302) 857-1096 Calendar System: Semester
URL: www.dtcc.edu/terry
Established: 1972 Annual Undergrad Tuition & Fees (In-State): $4,945
Enrollment: 12,955 Coed
Affiliation or Control: State IRS Status: 501(c)3
Highest Offering: Baccalaureate
Accreditation: M, ACFEI, ADNUR, CSHSE, EMT, NUR, PNUR, SURGT

01 Vice President & Campus Director .... Ms. Cornelia JOHNSON
05 Dean Instruction .... Mr. John M. BUCKLEY
32 Dean Student Affairs .... Ms. Kerri HARMON
26 Director Communication and Planning .... Dr. Lisa STRUSOWSKI
103 Director Workforce Development .... Ms. Kristen YENCER
15 Director of Human Resources .... Ms. Marybeth ROACH
18 Director of Facilities .... Mr. Ray PARSONS
10 Director Business Services .... Ms. Noelle SUGALSKI
88 Asst Director of Facilities .... Mr. Allan NELSON
20 Assistant Dean of Instruction .... Mr. Bill J. MORROW

Goldey-Beacom College (I)

4701 Limestone Road, Wilmington DE 19808-0551
County: New Castle FICE Identification: 001429
Unit ID: 130989
Telephone: (302) 998-8814 Carnegie Class: Masters/L
FAX Number: (302) 998-8631 Calendar System: Semester
URL: www.gbc.edu
Established: 1886 Annual Undergrad Tuition & Fees: $25,500
Enrollment: 1,184 Coed
Affiliation or Control: Independent Non-Profit IRS Status: 501(c)3
Highest Offering: Doctorate
Accreditation: M, ACBSP

01 President .... Dr. Colleen PERRY KEITH
10 Exec Vice President Admin/Finance .... Ms. Kristine M. SANTOMAURO
05 Provost/VP Academic Affairs .... Ms. Alison Boord WHITE
06 Assoc Provost/AVP Academic Affairs .... Dr. Joel WORDEN
32 VP of Student Affairs & Athletics .... Dr. Charles A. HAMMOND
84 Dean Enrollment Mgmt .... Vacant
06 Registrar .... Mr. Ryan QUANN

111 Exec Dir Institutional Advancement ....Mr. Larry EBY
41 Director of Athletics ....Mr. Jeremy BENOIT
30 Director of External Affairs ....Ms. Janine SORBELLO
18 Director of Facilities/Operations ....Mr. Meezie FOSTER
08 Director of Library/Learning Center ....Mr. Russell MICHALAK
36 Career Services Coordinator ....Ms. Elizabeth KIRKER
15 Asst VP Finance/HR ....Ms. Susan M. MANNERING
13 Chief Informaton Officer ....Mr. Peter RYSAVY
35 Dean of Students ....Ms. Jocelyn MOSES

University of Delaware (A)

104 Hullihen Hall, Newark DE 19716
County: New Castle FICE Identification: 001431
Unit ID: 130943
Telephone: (302) 831-2000 Carnegie Class: DU-Highest
FAX Number: (302) 831-8000 Calendar System: 4/1/4
URL: www.udel.edu
Established: 1743 Annual Undergrad Tuition & Fees (In-State): $14,660
Enrollment: 23,613 Coed
Affiliation or Control: State Related IRS Status: 501(c)3
Highest Offering: Doctorate
Accreditation: M, CAATE, CAEP, CEA, CLPSY, DIETD, DIETI, IPSY, LSAR, MLS, MUS, NASP, NURSE, PCSAS, PTA, SP, SPAA

01 President ....Dr. Dennis ASSANIS
05 Provost ....Dr. Laura CARLSON
03 Exec VP & Chief Operating Officer ....Mr. John LONG
15 VP & Chief Human Resources Officer ....Ms. Melissa L. BARD
101 Vice Pres & University Secretary ....Ms. Beth G. BRAND
26 VP Comm & Marketing ....Mr. Glenn CARTER
28 VP Institutional Equity ....Ms. Fatimah R. CONLEY
08 Vice Prov Libraries & Museums ....Mr. Trevor A. DAWES
30 VP Development & Alumni Relations ....Mr. James DICKER
43 Vice Pres and General Counsel ....Ms. Laure ERGIN
20 Vice Provost for Faculty Affairs ....Dr. Matt KINSERVIK
18 VP Facilities/Real Est/Aux Svcs ....Mr. Peter KRAWCHYK
46 Int VP Rsrch/Scholarship/Innovation ....Dr. Kelvin H. LEE
84 Vice Pres Enrollment Management ....Mr. Rodney MORRISON
20 Deputy Provost Academic Affairs ....Dr. Lynn OKAGAKI
10 Vice Pres Finance/Dept Treasurer ....Vacant
13 VP Information Technologies ....Ms. Sharon PITT
41 Dir Intercol Athletics & Rec Svcs ....Ms. Christine RAWAK
45 VP Strategic Planning & Analysis ....Ms. Mary M. REMMLER
32 Vice President for Student Life ....Dr. José-Luis RIERA
88 Vice Provost for Equity ....Dr. Michael VAUGHAN
47 Interim Dean Ag & Natural Resources ....Dr. Calvin KEELER
49 Dean Arts & Sciences ....Dr. John A. PELESKO
50 Dean Lerner Col Business & Econ ....Dr. Bruce WEBER
65 Interim Dean Earth Ocean & Environ ....Dr. Fabrice VERON
53 Dean Educ & Human Development ....Dr. Gary HENRY
54 Dean Engineering ....Dr. Levi T. THOMPSON
58 Dean Graduate College ....Dr. Louis ROSSI
76 Dean Health Sciences ....Dr. Kathleen MATT
92 Dean Honors College ....Dr. Michael J. CHAJES
80 Dean Biden Sch Pub Policy & Admin ....Dr. Maria P. ARISTIGUETA
51 AVP Professional/Cont Studies ....Dr. George IRVINE
09 AVP Inst Research & Effectiveness ....Mr. Richard J. REEVES
09 Director Institutional Research ....Dr. Heather A. KELLY
108 Dir Ctr Teach/Assessment/Lrng ....Dr. Matthew TREVETT-SMITH
29 AVP Alumni Engagement/Annual Giving ....Ms. Lauren E. SIMIONE
85 Assoc Prov Global Pgms & Svcs ....Mr. Ravi AMMIGAN
104 Assoc Dir Study Abroad ....Mr. Matthew DREXLER
37 Exec Dir Student Financial Svcs ....Ms. Mary BOOKER
36 Director Career Center ....Mr. Nathan ELTON
19 Assoc VP & Chief of Police ....Chief Patrick OGDEN
07 Exec Director Undergrad Admissions ....Dr. William D. ZANDER
123 Director of Graduate Admissions ....Mr. Michael ALEXO
16 Asst VP Talent Management ....Mr. Keith FOURNIER
16 Asst VP HR Support & Svcs ....Mr. Jared AUPPERLE
96 Manager Purchasing Services ....Mr. George WALUEFF
06 University Registrar ....Ms. Amanda STEELE-MIDDLETON
114 Sr Assoc VP & Chief Budget Officer ....Ms. Mandy MINNER
22 Interim Title IX Coordinator ....Ms. Danica A. MYERS
35 AVP Dean of Students ....Mr. Adam D. CANTLEY
38 Int Dir Ctr Counslng/Student Dev ....Dr. Raeshawn CHRESFIELD
23 Interim Dir Student Health Svcs ....Dr. Kelly FRICK
04 Exec Assistant to the President ....Ms. Susan L. WILLIAMS

Widener University Delaware Law School (B)

4601 Concord Pike, Wilmington DE 19803-0406
Telephone: (302) 477-2100 FICE Identification: 012962
Accreditation: &M, LAW

† Branch campus of Widener University in Pennsylvania. This listing reflects the administrators for the school of law for the Harrisburg (PA) and Delaware campuses.

Wilmington University (C)

320 N Dupont Highway, New Castle DE 19720-6491
County: New Castle FICE Identification: 007948
Unit ID: 131113
Telephone: (302) 356-4636 Carnegie Class: DU-Mod
FAX Number: (302) 328-5902 Calendar System: Trimester
URL: www.wilmu.edu
Established: 1967 Annual Undergrad Tuition & Fees: $11,480
Enrollment: 14,769 Coed
Affiliation or Control: Independent Non-Profit IRS Status: 501(c)3
Highest Offering: Doctorate
Accreditation: M, CACREP, CAEP, IACBE, NURSE

00 Chairman of the Board ....Hon. Joseph J. FARNAN, JR.
01 President ....Dr. LaVerne T. HARMON
100 Executive Director ....Ms. Donna M. QUINN
11 SVP/COO Administrative Operations ....Dr. Erin DIMARCO
10 SVP/CFO Financial Affairs ....Ms. Heather A. O'CONNELL
05 VP Academic Affairs ....Dr. James D. WILSON, JR.
43 VP Admin & Legal Affairs ....Dr. Christian A. TROWBRIDGE
32 VP Student Affairs/Alumni Rel/Devel ....Dr. Tina M. BARKSDALE
111 VP Institutional Advancement ....Dr. Jacque R. VARSALONA
35 AVP Student Affairs ....Dr. Regina C. ALLEN-SHARPE
19 AVP Admin & Legal Affairs ....Dr. Joseph P. AVIOLA
88 AVP Student Support & Financial Svc ....Dr. Bonnie L. KIRKPATRICK
21 Asst Vice President/Controller ....Vacant
88 AVP Student Trans/Dean of Location ....Mr. Robert P. MILLER
88 AVP Student Access & Success ....Dr. Mary Ann K. WESTERFIELD
106 AVP Admin Affs/Dean Online ....Dr. Sallie A. REISSMAN
88 AVP Partnerships & Comm Affairs ....Dr. Robert W. RESCIGNO
15 Asst Vice President/CHRO ....Dr. Nicole ROMANO
20 AVP Academic Affairs ....Dr. Denise Z. WELLS
20 AVP Academic Affairs ....Dr. Matthew H. DAVIS
108 Assistant Vice President ....Dr. Angela C. SUCHANIC
26 AVP University Relations ....Mr. Bill F. SWAIN
13 Asst Vice President/CIO ....Mr. Peter E. LUTUS
101 Liaison to the Board of Trustees ....Ms. Ashley R. MUNDY
88 Exec Director Admin & Legal Affairs ....Ms. Linda M. ANDRZJEWSKI
41 AVP & Athletics Director ....Dr. Stefanie A. WHITBY
06 Registrar ....Ms. Misty B. WILLIAMS
105 Sr Dir of Web/System Communications ....Mr. Kevin G. BARRY
14 Senior Dir Information Technology ....Mr. Brian C. BEARD
88 Sr Dir Academic Support Services ....Dr. Elizabeth P. JORDAN
07 Sr Director of Admissions ....Dr. Laura M. MORRIS
09 AVP Inst Research & Strategic Plng ....Dr. Dana S. CHAPMAN
53 Dean College of Educ & Lib Studies ....Dr. John C. GRAY
83 Dean College of Soc & Beh ....Dr. Edward L. GUTHRIE
50 Dean College of Business ....Dr. Kathy S. KENNEDY-RATAJACK
76 Dean College Health Prof & Nat Sci ....Dr. Aaron M. SEBACH
72 Dean College of Technology ....Dr. Anthony J. CARCILLO
88 Dir Center for Teaching Excellence ....Dr. Adrienne M. BEY
85 Director International Affairs ....Ms. Angelina L. BURNS
78 Director Cooperative Learning ....Dr. David C. CAFFO
29 Asst Director Alumni Relations ....Ms. Brandi D. REDDING
08 Director Library ....Mr. James M. MCCLOSKEY
37 Director Financial Aid ....Ms. Nicole L. MCDANIEL-SMITH
30 Director of Development ....Ms. Felicia K. QUINN
16 Sr Dir Human Resources ....Ms. Karen A. SHEATS
40 Bookstore Manager ....Ms. Carmen L. CASANOVA
89 Chair First Year Experience ....Dr. Matthew J. WILSON
118 Benefits Coordinator ....Ms. Jennifer L. WORKMAN

DISTRICT OF COLUMBIA

American University (D)

4400 Massachusetts Avenue, NW, Washington DC 20016
FICE Identification: 001434
Unit ID: 131159
Telephone: (202) 885-1000 Carnegie Class: DU-Higher
FAX Number: N/A Calendar System: Semester
URL: www.american.edu
Established: 1893 Annual Undergrad Tuition & Fees: $51,361
Enrollment: 14,001 Coed
Affiliation or Control: United Methodist IRS Status: 501(c)3
Highest Offering: Doctorate
Accreditation: M, CAEPN, CLPSY, IPSY, JOUR, LAW, MUS, PH, SPAA

01 President ....Sylvia M. BURWELL
05 Provost/Chief Academic Ofcr ....Dr. Peter STARR
30 Vice President Development & Alumni ....Courtney SURLS
10 Vice President Finance & Treasurer ....Dr. Bronte BURLEIGH-JONES
32 VP Campus Life/Incl Excel/UG Enroll ....Dr. Fanta AW
43 Vice President & General Counsel ....Traevena BYRD
20 Vice Provost for Academic Admin ....Prita PATEL
106 Vice Provost/Chief Online Officer ....Joseph RIQUELME
18 Asst VP Facilities Management ....Vincent HARKINS
35 Asst VP Campus Life ....Dr. Traci CALLANDRILLO
35 Dean of Students ....Jeffery BROWN
108 Asst Provost Inst Rsrch/Assessment ....Karen L. FROSLID JONES
30 AVP Development & Alumni Relations ....Raina LENNEY
21 Assoc VP of Finance/Asst Treasurer ....Laura MCANDREW
28 Asst VP Diversity/Equity/Inclusion ....Dr. Amanda TAYLOR
84 Vice Provost Undergrad Enrollment ....Dr. Sharon ALSTON
13 Vice President & CIO ....Steve MUNSON
15 VP People & External Affairs ....Seth GROSSMAN
20 Deputy Provost/Dean of Faculty ....Dr. Monica JACKSON
58 Dean Graduate/Professional Studies ....Dr. Wendy BOLAND
20 Dean UG Ed & VP Acad Student Svcs ....Dr. Jessica WATERS
49 Dean College Arts & Sciences ....Dr. Linda ALDOORY
60 Dean School of Communication ....Mr. Sam FULWOOD, III
50 Dean Kogod Sch of Business ....Dr. John T. DELANEY
61 Dean Washington College of Law ....Roger A. FAIRFAX, JR.
82 Dean School of Intl Service ....Dr. Shannon HADER
80 Dean School of Public Affairs ....Dr. Vicky WILKINS
16 Asst VP of Human Resources ....Beth MUHA
36 Exec Director Career Center ....Gihan FERNANDO
26 Vice President of Communication ....Matthew BENNETT
27 Asst Vice Pres Marketing ....Julie ZITO
06 Assistant University Registrar ....Dr. Michael GIESE
08 University Librarian ....Jeehyun DAVIS
21 AVP & University Controller ....Nicole BRESNAHAN

113 Dir Student Account Operations ....Darrell COOK
114 Asst VP Finance/Chief Budget Ofcr ....Nana AN
42 University Chaplain ....Rev. Bryant OSKVIG
19 AVP Risk/Safety/Transportation ....Daniel NICHOLS
37 Asst Vice Provost Financial Aid ....Brian LEE SANG
38 Exec Director Counseling Center ....Dr. Jeff VOLKMANN
102 Sr Dir Corporate/Foundation Rels ....Amy BUTLER
96 Sr Dir Contract Management ....Brian BLAIR
07 Asst Vice Provost UG Admission ....Dr. Andrea FELDER
85 Director Intl Student/Scholar Svcs ....Senem BAKAR
92 Interim Dir Univ Honors Program ....Dr. Jeffrey MIDDENTS
41 Director Athletics & Recreation ....Dr. William (Billy) WALKER
104 Asst Vice Prov & Exec Dir AU Abroad ....Sara E. DUMONT
45 AVP Planning & Project Mgmt ....Jonathan MCCANN
88 AVP Lifetime Phil/Special Campaigns ....Lee HOLSOPPLE
88 Asst Vice Prov UG Enroll Operations ....Robert LINSON
04 Senior Assistant to the President ....Stephanie LEIGH
22 Sr Dir Employee Relations/Recruit ....Deadre JOHNSON
09 Asst Provost Inst Res & Assessment ....Karen L. FROSLID JONES
88 Sr Dir Talent Development ....Michelle FREDERICK
53 Dean School of Education ....Dr. Cheryl HOLCOMB-MCCOY
86 AVP Community/Government Relations ....Ed FISHER
101 Asst Secretary to the Board ....Leslie WONG
46 Vice Provost for Research ....Dr. Diana BURLEY
31 Dir Community Relations ....Maria BARRY
88 Exec Dir Strategic Implementation ....Geralynn FRANCESCHINI
39 Director of Residence Life ....Lisa FREEMAN
119 Chief Information Security Officer ....Cathy HUBBS
14 AVP IT Customer Services ....Terry FERNANDEZ
93 Dir Ctr for Diversity & Inclusion ....Robin ADAMS
100 Chief of Staff Office of the Pres ....Sarah BALDASSARO

Bay Atlantic University (E)

1510 H Street NW, Washington DC 20005
Identification: 667329
Telephone: (844) 922-8228 Carnegie Class: Not Classified
FAX Number: N/A Calendar System: Semester
URL: www.bau.edu
Established: 2014 Annual Undergrad Tuition & Fees: N/A
Enrollment: N/A Coed
Affiliation or Control: Independent Non-Profit IRS Status: 501(c)3
Highest Offering: Master's
Accreditation: ACICS

01 President/CEO ....Dr. Sinem VATANARTIRAN
05 Chief Acad Ofcr/Inst Effectiveness ....Dr. Michelle LANDA
10 CFO ....Ms. Melek EDIB
06 Registrar ....Ms. Izel UGUR
08 Librarian ....Ms. Taylor NICKELS
32 Director of Student Services ....Mr. Alex ROSET
15 Director of Human Resources ....Ms. Angela MYERS
07 Dir Marketing/Admissions ....Ms. Linh TRUONG

Career Technical Institute (F)

1101 Vermont Ave NW Ste L002, Washington DC 20005
FICE Identification: 031043
Unit ID: 420370
Telephone: (202) 932-8988 Carnegie Class: Assoc/HVT-High Trad
FAX Number: N/A Calendar System: Quarter
URL: careertechnical.edu
Established: 2003 Annual Undergrad Tuition & Fees: N/A
Enrollment: N/A Coed
Affiliation or Control: Proprietary IRS Status: Proprietary
Highest Offering: Associate Degree
Accreditation: COE

01 President ....Moses RABI

The Catholic University of America (G)

620 Michigan Avenue, NE, Washington DC 20064-0002
FICE Identification: 001437
Unit ID: 131283
Telephone: (202) 319-5100 Carnegie Class: DU-Higher
FAX Number: (202) 319-4441 Calendar System: Semester
URL: www.cua.edu
Established: 1887 Annual Undergrad Tuition & Fees: $49,416
Enrollment: 5,366 Coed
Affiliation or Control: Roman Catholic IRS Status: 501(c)3
Highest Offering: Doctorate
Accreditation: M, CAEP, CLPSY, IPSY, LAW, LIB, MUS, NAEYC, NURSE, SW, THEOL

01 President ....Dr. Patrick KILPATRICK
100 Chief of Staff/Counselor to Pres ....Mr. Lawrence J. MORRIS
05 Provost ....Dr. Aaron DOMINGUEZ
10 Vice Pres Finance & Treasurer ....Mr. Robert M. SPECTER
32 Vice President Student Affairs ....Dr. Judi BIGGS GARBUIO
84 Acting Vice Pres Enrollment Mgmt ....Dr. Hasanna TYUS
85 Vice Provost for Global Strategies ....Dr. Duilia DE MELLO
11 Vice Provost for Administration ....Vacant
35 Assoc VP Student Life/Dean Students ....Mr. Jonathan C. SAWYER
43 General Counsel ....Mr. Matthew DOLAN
15 Sr Assoc VP for Admin/CHRO ....Mr. Matthew MCNALLY
18 Assoc VP Facilities Operations ....Ms. Debra NAUTA-RODRIGUEZ
41 Assoc VP & Director Athletics ....Dr. Sean M. SULLIVAN
39 Executive Director for Housing ....Mr. Timothy CARNEY
111 Vice Pres for Univ Advancement ....Mr. Scott REMBOLD

26 VP for University Communications .... Ms. Karna LOZOYA
110 Senior AVP Univ Advancement .... Ms. Deborah BROWN
88 Assoc VP University Advancement .... Mr. Greg NALESKI
25 Vice Provost Sponsored Research .... Mr. Ralph ALBANO
58 Dean Graduate Studies .... Dr. J. Steven BROWN
48 Dean of Architecture .... Mr. Mark FERGUSON
49 Dean of Arts & Sciences .... Dr. Thomas SMITH
50 Dean School of Business .... Dr. Andrew V. ABELA
54 Dean of Engineering .... Dr. John JUDGE
61 Dean of Law .... Mr. Stephen C. PAYNE
64 Dean of Music/Drama and Art .. Dr. Jacqueline LEARY-WARSAW
70 Dean Natl Cath Sch Social Svcs .... Dr. Jo Ann R. COE REGAN
66 Dean of Nursing .... Dr. Maria NOLAN
73 Dean Theology/Religious Studies ...... VRev. Mark MOROZOWICH
107 Dean Metro Sch Professional Studies .... Dr. Vincent KIERNAN
79 Dean of Philosophy .... Dr. John C. MCCARTHY
88 Dean of Canon Law .... Msgr. Ronny JENKINS
13 Chief Information Officer .... Mr. Matthew MCNALLY
08 Director of Libraries .... Mr. Stephen CONNAGHAN
06 Registrar .... Ms. Danielle SPINATO
36 Director of Career Services .... Mr. Anthony CHIAPPETTA
19 Assoc VP Public Safety & Emergency .... Mr. Kirk MCLEAN
38 Director of Counseling Center .... Dr. T. Monroe RAYBURN
23 Medical Director of Health Center .... Dr. Loretta STAUDT
37 Dir Student Financial Assistance .... Ms. Mindy SCHAEFFER
35 Assoc Dean of Students .... Ms. Heidi E. ZEICH
44 Director of Regional Engagement .... Mr. Patrick DAVEY
42 Director University Campus Ministry .... Vacant
09 Assoc VP Fin Plng/Inst Res/Assess .... Dr. Brian A. JOHNSTON
20 Vice Provost & Dean Undergrad .... Dr. Lynn MAYER
96 Director of Procurement .... Ms. Yssa RESURRECCION
22 Director Compliance/Title IX Coord .... Mr. Lou MEJIA
40 Manager Bookstore .... Mr. Brett MCMICHAEL
04 Exec Assistant to the President .... Ms. Ruth BARWICK
101 Secretary of the Board .... Mr. Lawrence J. MORRIS
102 Director Institutional Partnership .... Ms. Jo Anna NORRIS
105 Director Digital Strategy .... Vacant
29 Director of Alumni Engagement .... Mr. Chris JOHNSON

Chicago School of Professional Psychology-Washington DC (A)

901 15th Street NW, Washington DC 20005
Telephone: (202) 706-5000 Identification: 770493
Accreditation: &WC, CACREP, CLPSY

† Branch campus of Chicago School of Professional Psychology Los Angeles Campus, Los Angeles, CA

Gallaudet University (B)

800 Florida Avenue, NE, Washington DC 20002-3695
FICE Identification: 001443
Unit ID: 131450
Telephone: (202) 651-5005 Carnegie Class: DU-Mod
FAX Number: (202) 651-5508 Calendar System: Semester
URL: www.gallaudet.edu
Established: 1864 Annual Undergrad Tuition & Fees: $17,038
Enrollment: 1,451 Coed
Affiliation or Control: Independent Non-Profit IRS Status: 501(c)3
Highest Offering: Doctorate
Accreditation: M, ACBSP, AUD, CACREP, CAEP, CEA, CLPSY, SP, SW

01 President .... Ms. Roberta (Bobbi) CORDANO
11 Chief Operating Officer .... Mr. Dominic LACY
05 Interim Provost .... Dr. Jeffrey LEWIS
88 Interim Chief Bilingual Officer .... Dr. Laurene SIMMS
10 Chief Finance Officer .... Mr. Brad HERMES
30 Exec Dir Advance & Alumni Relations .... Mr. Nicholas GOULD
43 General Counsel .... Vacant
28 Interim Chief Diversity Officer .... Dr. Elizabeth MOORE
12 Chief Admin Ofcr L. Clerc Natl Ctr .... Ms. Nicole SUTLIFFE
20 Chief Academic Officer .... Ms. Marianne BELSKY
101 Board Liaison/Presidential Support ...... Ms. Kim BIANCO MAJERI
100 Chief of Staff to President .... Ms. Heather HARKER
45 Exec Dir Strategic Planning .... Ms. Susan JACOBY
20 Dean of Faculty .... Dr. Khadijat RASHID
58 Assoc Dean Grad School .... Dr. Beth GIBBONS
32 Dean Student Affairs .... Mr. Travis IMEL
07 Exec Dir Admission .... Mr. John SERRANO
121 Int Dir Academic & Career Success .... Dr. Robert SANCHEZ
96 Exec Dir Business Support Services .... Ms. Davina KWONG
18 Interim Director Facilities .... Mr. Richard FICARELLI
26 Chief Marketing/Undergrad Admiss .... Ms. Brandi RARUS
09 Director Institutional Research .... Ms. Lindsay BUCHKO
29 Director Alumni Engagement .... Ms. Rebecca RYDSTROM
15 Exec Director Human Resources
Svcs .... Ms. Christina SHEN-AUSTIN
13 Exec Director Technology Services .... Mr. Earl PARKS
14 Dir Enterprise Info Systems .... Mr. Daryl FRELICH
88 University Ombuds .... Ms. Elizabeth STONE
08 Dir Library Deaf Collection/Archive .... Ms. Amy MALM
22 Director Equal Opportunity Programs .... Ms. Sharrell MCCASKILL
06 Registrar .... Ms. Elice PATTERSON
88 Assoc Director of Admissions .... Ms. Young Hae PARK
88 Director of Operations .... Ms. Laureen OBERMILLER
102 Director Corporate and Foundation .... Dr. Allison POLK
104 Senior International Officer .... Dr. Charles REILLY
108 Director Institutional
Effectivenes .... Dr. Caroline KOBEK PEZZAROSSI
88 Manager Field Services .... Mr. Patrick RADER
36 Director Career Educ & Development .... Ms. Julie TIBBITT
37 Director Student Financial Aid .... Ms. Doryann BARNHARDT

38 Director Counseling and Psychologic .... Dr. Lauri RUSH
39 Dir Resident Life .... Mr. Andrew SCHEWE
41 Athletic Director .... Mr. Warren KELLER

George Washington University (C)

1918 F Street, NW, Washington DC 20052-0002
FICE Identification: 001444
Unit ID: 131469
Telephone: (202) 994-1000 Carnegie Class: DU-Highest
FAX Number: (202) 994-0458 Calendar System: Semester
URL: www.gwu.edu
Established: 1821 Annual Undergrad Tuition & Fees: $58,640
Enrollment: 27,017 Coed
Affiliation or Control: Independent Non-Profit IRS Status: 501(c)3
Highest Offering: Doctorate
Accreditation: M, ACATE, ARCPA, ART, CACREP, CAEPN, CIDA, CLPSY, FEPAC, HSA, IPSY, LAW, MED, MLS, NURSE, PH, PLNG, PTA, SP, SPAA

01 President .... Mr. Mark S. WRIGHTON
100 Chief of Staff President's Office .... Mr. Aristide J. COLLINS
05 Provost & Exec VP Academic Affairs . Dr. Christopher A. BRACEY
84 Vice Provost of Enrollment Mgmt .... Mr. Jay GOFF
30 Vice Pres for Dev/Alumni Relations .... Ms. Donna ARBIDE
10 Exec Vice President & CFO .... Mr. Mark DIAZ
43 Interim Senior VP & General Counsel .... Mr. Charles BARBER
26 Vice President External Relations .... Vacant
45 VP Financial Planning & Ops .... Mr. Jared ABRAMSON
114 Vice Provost of Budget and Finance .... Vacant
28 Vice Provost Diversity &
Inclusion .... Ms. Caroline LAGUERRE-BROWN
15 VP & Chief People Officer .... Ms. Dana BRADLEY
13 Interim Chief Technology Officer .... Mr. Jared W. JOHNSON
20 Vice Provost Faculty Affairs .... Dr. Christopher A. BRACEY
18 Assoc VP Facil Plng/Const & Mgmt .... Mr. David D. DENT
32 Dean of Student Experience .... Dr. Marcia L. PETTY
88 Assoc Provost Diversity &
Inclusion .... Ms. Helen CANNADAY SAULNY
90 Deputy Chief Academic Tech Officer .... Vacant
108 Assoc VP of Acad Plng & Assessment .... Dr. Cheryl BEIL
46 Vice President for Research .... Dr. Pamela NORRIS
88 AVP Budget & Financial Analysis .... Ms. Cynthia VILLAVERDE
21 Assoc VP & University Controller .... Ms. Neena ALI
09 Director Inst Research & Planning .... Mr. Joachim W. KNOP
86 Asst VP Government Relations .... Ms. Renee MCPHATTER
104 Associate VP for International Pgms .... Vacant
08 University Librarian .... Ms. Geneva HENRY
27 Asst VP for
Communications ... Ms. Sarah GEGENHEIMER BALDASSARO
27 Exec Dir of Media Relations .... Ms. Maralee B. CSELLAR
111 Associate VP Advancement Services .... Mr. Gail FERRIS
06 Registrar .... Ms. Elizabeth A. AMUNDSON
07 Dean of Undergrad Admissions .... Mr. Benjamin A. TOLL
38 Director Counseling Center .... Vacant
37 Executive Director Financial Aid .... Ms. Michelle C. ARCIERI
36 Asst Provost Career Center .... Ms. Rachel A. BROWN
85 Director International Services .... Ms. Jennifer H. DONAGHUE
19 VP Safety & Facilities .... Mr. Scott G. BURNOTES
22 Dir EEO & Affirmative Action .... Ms. Vickie FAIR
23 Director Student Health Services .... Dr. Isabel GOLDENBERG
40 Director GW Bookstore .... Ms. Janet F. UZZELL
107 Dean Col Professional Studies .... Dr. Melissa FEUER
49 Dean Columbian Col Arts/Sci .... Dr. Paul J. WAHLBECK
63 Dean Medicine & Health Sciences .... Dr. Barbara BASS
69 Dean School of Public Health .... Dr. Lynn R. GOLDMAN
61 Dean Law School .... Dr. Dayna B. MATTHEW
54 Dean Engineering/Applied Science .... Dr. John LACH
53 Dean Education/Human Development .... Dr. Michael J. FEUER
50 Dean School of Business .... Dr. Anuj MEHROTRA
82 Int Dean Elliott Sch Intl Affairs .... Dr. Ilana FELDMAN
66 Interim Dean School of Nursing .... Dr. Pamela SLAVEN-LEE
41 Director Athletics/Recreation .... Ms. Tanya VOGEL
92 Director University Honors Program .... Dr. Bethany E. KUNG
93 Director Multicultural Student Svc .... Mr. Michael R. TAPSCOTT
39 Director Student Housing .... Mr. Seth D. WEINSHEL

Georgetown University (D)

37th & O Streets, NW, Washington DC 20057-1947
FICE Identification: 001445
Unit ID: 131496
Telephone: (202) 687-0100 Carnegie Class: DU-Highest
FAX Number: N/A Calendar System: Semester
URL: www.georgetown.edu
Established: 1789 Annual Undergrad Tuition & Fees: $57,928
Enrollment: 19,371 Coed
Affiliation or Control: Roman Catholic IRS Status: 501(c)3
Highest Offering: Doctorate
Accreditation: M, ANEST, CAMPEP, CEA, HSA, LAW, MED, MIDWF, NURSE, PAST

01 President .... Dr. John (Jack) J. DEGIOIA
46 SVP Research/Chief Technology Ofcr ...... Dr. Spiros DIMOLITSAS
05 Provost .... Dr. Robert M. GROVES
17 Exec Vice Pres Health Sciences .... Dr. Edward B. HEALTON
61 Exec Vice Pres/Dean of Law School ...... Dr. William M. TREANOR
111 Vice Pres for Advancement .... Mr. R. Bartley MOORE
42 Vice Pres for Mission and Ministry .... Rev. Mark BOSCO, SJ
13 Vice Pres/CIO .... Mr. Judd NICHOLSON
26 VP Public Affairs & Strategic Dev .... Mr. Erik SMULSON
32 VP Student Affairs .... Vacant
28 VP for Inst Diversity & Equity .... Ms. Rosemary KILKENNY
19 Chief of Police Dept Public Safety .... Mr. Jay GRUBER
43 VP & General Counsel .... Ms. Lisa M. BROWN
85 VP for Global Engagement .... Dr. Thomas BANCHOFF
11 VP & COO Main Campus .... Mr. Darryl E. CHRISTMON
10 Sr AVP Budget/Financial Planning .... Vacant
109 Assoc VP for Auxiliary Services .... Ms. Joelle D. WIESE
118 AVP Benefits/Chief Benefits Officer .... Mr. Charles E. DESANTIS
20 Vice Provost Education .... Dr. Randall BASS
88 Vice Provost Research .... Dr. Janet MANN
20 Vice Provost Faculty .... Dr. Reena AGGARWAL
21 Assoc Vice President for Operations .... Ms. Christina ROBERTS
114 Asst VP Finance Planning & Budget .... Mr. Matthew C. GREAVES
06 Assoc VP & University Registrar .... Ms. Annamarie BIANCO
35 AVP Student Affairs/Dean Students .... Dr. Jeanne F. LORD
23 Asst VP for Student Health .... Dr. Vince C. WINKLERPRINS
08 University Librarian .... Vacant
88 Ex Dir Ctr New Designs Lrng/Schlrs .... Dr. Edward J. MALONEY
25 Senior Research Compliance Officer ...... Ms. Mary E. SCHMIEDEL
49 Dean Georgetown College .... Dr. Christopher CELENZA
82 Dean School Foreign Service .... Dr. Joel HELLMAN
50 Dean School of Business .... Dr. Paul A. ALMEIDA
63 Exec Dean Medical School .... Dr. Edward B. HEALTON
66 Dean Sch of Nursing/Health Stds .... Dr. Patricia CLOONAN
51 Dean Continuing Studies .... Dr. Kelly OTTER
58 Dean of Graduate School .... Vacant
80 Dean McCourt School Public Policy .... Dr. Michael A. BAILEY
31 Dir Partnerships & Cmty
Engagement .... Ms. Brenda ATKINSON-WILLOUGHBY
96 Asst VP Procurement .... Mr. O.T WELLS
104 Director of Global Education .... Mr. Craig RINKER
22 Director Affirmative Action Pgm .... Mr. Michael W. SMITH
24 Exec Dir Classroom Educ/Tech Svcs .... Mr. Mark J. COHEN
38 Director Counseling Center .... Dr. Philip W. MEILMAN
39 Director of Residence Life .... Ms. Stephanie J. LYNCH
108 Asst Dir CNDLS/Assessment .... Ms. Mindy MCWILLIAMS
112 Exec Director Gift Planning .... Mr. Stephen LINK
15 Exec Director Human Resources .... Ms. Devon JINAR

Howard University (E)

2400 Sixth Street, NW, Washington DC 20059-0001
FICE Identification: 001448
Unit ID: 131520
Telephone: (202) 806-6100 Carnegie Class: DU-Higher
FAX Number: (202) 806-5934 Calendar System: Semester
URL: https://howard.edu
Established: 1867 Annual Undergrad Tuition & Fees: $28,440
Enrollment: 10,859 Coed
Affiliation or Control: Independent Non-Profit IRS Status: 501(c)3
Highest Offering: Doctorate
Accreditation: M, ART, CAEP, CLPSY, COPSY, DENT, DH, DIETC, IPSY, JOUR, LAW, MED, MLS, MUS, NURSE, OT, PAST, PHAR, #PTA, #RTT, SP, SW, THEA, THEOL

01 President .... Dr. Wayne FREDERICK
05 Provost/Chief Academic Officer .... Dr. Anthony K. WUTOH
11 EVP/Chief Operating Officer .... Dr. Tashni-Ann DUBROY
43 SVP/General Counsel .... Ms. Florence PRIOLEAU
10 Chief Financial Ofcr/Treasurer .... Mr. Stephen GRAHAM
26 VP/Chief Communications Ofcr .... Mr. Frank TRAMBLE
15 VP/Chief Human Resources Ofcr .... Mr. Warren PETTY
30 SVP Development & Alumni Relations ...... Mr. David P. BENNETT
17 CEO University Hospital .... Ms. Anita JENKINS
45 VP & Secretary to the Board .... Ms. Christie TAYLOR
46 Assoc Provost Research/Grad Studies .... Dr. Gary L. HARRIS
20 Assoc Provost Undergraduate Studies ..... Dr. Kenneth ANDERSON
32 Vice President Student Affairs .... Dr. Cynthia EVERS
88 AVP Regulatory/Research Compliance .. Dr. Thomas O. OBISESAN
88 AVP for Faculty Development ...... Ms. Okianer CHRISTIAN-DARK
13 Interim Chief Information Officer .... Ms. Olga OSAGHAE
88 CIO Howard Univ Hospital .... Mr. Kevin DAWSON
100 Chief of Staff .... Dr. Allison BRYANT
58 Dean of Graduate School .... Dr. Dana WILLIAMS
49 Dean College of Arts/Sciences .... Dr. Rubin PATTERSON
50 Dean School of Business .... Dr. Anthony WILBON
61 Dean School of Law .... Ms. Danielle R. HOLLEY
63 Dean Medicine/VP Clinical Affairs .... Dr. Hugh E. MIGHTY
52 Dean College of Dentistry .... Dr. Andrea D. JACKSON
54 Dean Col Engineering/Architecture .... Dr. John M. ANDERSON
53 Dean School of Education .... Dr. Dawn WILLIAMS
60 Dean School of
Communications .... Dr. Gracie LAWSON-BORDERS
66 Dean Nursing/Allied Hlth Sc .... Dr. Gina S. BROWN
70 Dean School of Social Work .... Dr. Sandra CREWE
73 Dean School of Divinity .... Dr. Yolanda PIERCE
67 Interim Dean College of Pharmacy .... Dr. Oluwaranti AKIYODE
48 Director School of Architecture .... Prof. Hazel EDWARDS
76 Assoc Dean/Div Allied Health Sci .... Dr. Shirley J. JACKSON
66 Assoc Dean/Div of Nursing .... Ms. Tammi L. DAMAS
57 Dean College of Fine Arts .... Ms. Phylicia RASHAD
81 Assoc Dean/Div Natural Sciences .... Dr. Robert CATCHINGS
83 Interim Assoc Dean/Social Sciences .... Dr. Terri ADAMS
79 Associate Dean Humanities .... Dr. James J. DAVIS
06 Registrar/Director of Admissions .... Ms. Latrice BYAM
37 Director Financial Aid .... Vacant
42 Dean Andrew Rankin Chapel .... Dr. Bernard L. RICHARDSON
35 Dean Student Life & Activities .... Vacant
39 Int Dir Residence Life/Univ Housing .... Mr. Joe UTER
36 Director Career Services Office .... Dr. Joan M. BROWNE
08 Executive Director Libraries .... Ms. Rhea BALLARD-THROWER
08 Interim Director Law Library .... Ms. Eileen SANTOS
24 Dir Teaching/Learning/Assessmnt Ctr .... Dr. Helen BOND
16 Senior Director Human Resources .... Mr. Michael MCFADDEN

22 Dir Equal Employment Opportunity .... Mr. Antwan LOFTON
29 Director Alumni Relations .... Ms. Sharon STRANGE LEWIS
44 Principal Gift Officer .... Mr. Ken ASHWORTH
27 AVP of External Affairs .... Dr. Joe LEONARD
18 AVP Facilities .... Vacant
19 Chief of Campus Police .... Mr. Marcus LYLES
31 Director HU Community Association .... Ms. Maybelle T. BENNETT
109 Director Auxiliary Enterprises .... Mr. Antwan D. CLINTON
41 Athletics Director .... Mr. Kery DAVIS
23 Director Student Health Center .... Dr. Ebony R. COPELAND
40 Gen Manager Barnes & Noble at HU .... Mr. Alex BAMFO
94 Director of Women's Studies .... Vacant
18 Director Physical Facilities .... Mr. Victor MCNAUGHTON
108 Director Institutional Assessment .... Dr. Glenn A. PHILLIPS
88 Director Events & Protocol .... Mr. Andrew RIVERS

The Institute of World Politics (A)

1521 16th Street, NW, Washington DC 20036-1464

FICE Identification: 041144
Unit ID: 455804

Telephone: (202) 462-2101 — Carnegie Class: Spec-4-yr-Other
FAX Number: (202) 464-0335 — Calendar System: Semester
URL: www.iwp.edu
Established: 1990 — Annual Graduate Tuition & Fees: N/A
Enrollment: 120 — Coed
Affiliation or Control: Independent Non-Profit — IRS Status: 501(c)3
Highest Offering: Doctorate; No Undergraduates
Accreditation: M

01 Interim President .... Amb. Aldona WOS
03 Executive Vice President .... CAPT. Chris GLASS
32 SVP/Dean of Students .... Jason JOHNSRUD
05 Interim Dean of Academics .... Dr. James ROBBINS
13 Chief Information Officer .... Dean LANE
88 SVP Professional Affiliations .... Christine BALLLING
111 SVP Institutional Advancement .... Ariane E. SWEENEY
06 Registrar .... Iman RIDDICK
123 VP Graduate Recruitment .... Tim STEBBINS
29 VP Alumni Affs/Communications .... Katie BRIDGES
36 Director of Career Services .... Derrick DORTCH
37 Director of Financial Aid .... Thelbert SNOWDEN
08 Director of Library Services .... Dmitry KULIK
15 Director Human Resources .... Michelle B. RAY

Inter-American Defense College (B)

210 B Street SW, Bldg 52, Ft McNair,
Washington DC 20319-5008

County: USA — Identification: 667275
Telephone: (202) 646-1337 — Carnegie Class: Not Classified
FAX Number: N/A — Calendar System: Semester
URL: iadc.edu
Established: 1962 — Annual Graduate Tuition & Fees: N/A
Enrollment: N/A — Coed
Affiliation or Control: Independent Non-Profit — IRS Status: 501(c)3
Highest Offering: Master's; No Undergraduates
Accreditation: M, ACICS

01 Director .... MGen. James E. TAYLOR
05 Chief of Studies .... BGen. Jorge RAMIREZ ZUNIGA
03 Vice Director .... BGen. Leonardo CHAVES RODRIGUES

Moreland University (C)

1701 K Street NW, Ste 250, Washington DC 20006

Identification: 667305

Telephone: (844) 283-2246 — Carnegie Class: Not Classified
FAX Number: N/A — Calendar System: Other
URL: https://www.moreland.edu/
Established: 2012 — Annual Graduate Tuition & Fees: N/A
Enrollment: N/A — Coed
Affiliation or Control: Proprietary — IRS Status: Proprietary
Highest Offering: Master's; No Undergraduates
Accreditation: DEAC, CAEP

00 Founder/CEO .... Dr. Emily FEISTRITZER
01 President .... Dr. Kevin J. RUTH
05 Chief Learning Officer .... Ms. Kunali SANGHVI
10 Chief Financial Officer .... Mr. Richard FEISTRITZER
26 Vice Pres Marketing .... Vacant
11 Director of Operations .... Vacant
07 Admissions Officer .... Mr. Andre BARNES
06 Registrar .... Ms. Bernadette GORMALLY
08 Chief Library Officer .... Ms. Courtney STOLL
13 Chief Information Technology Ofcr . Mr. Manish BHATTACHARYA

Pontifical Faculty of the Immaculate Conception at the Dominican House of Studies (D)

487 Michigan Avenue, NE, Washington DC 20017-1585

FICE Identification: 012803
Unit ID: 131405

Telephone: (202) 495-3820 — Carnegie Class: Spec-4-yr-Faith
FAX Number: (202) 495-3873 — Calendar System: Semester
URL: www.dhs.edu
Established: 1902 — Annual Graduate Tuition & Fees: N/A
Enrollment: 83 — Coed
Affiliation or Control: Roman Catholic — IRS Status: 501(c)3
Highest Offering: Master's; No Undergraduates
Accreditation: M, THEOL

00 Chancellor .... VRev. Gerard TIMONER, OP
01 President .... VRev. Thomas PETRI, OP
05 Vice President/Academic Dean ..... VRev. Dominic LANGEVIN, OP
20 Secretary of Studies .... Fr. Brian CHRZASTEK, OP
08 Librarian .... Fr. John Martin RUIZ, OP
18 Acting Director of Facilities .... Ms. Shauna ROYE
42 Chaplain to Commuter Students .... Fr. James BRENT, OP
06 Registrar/Accred Liaison .... Ms. Audrey QUADE
10 Treasurer/Director of Financial Aid .... Ms. Shauna ROYE
111 Executive Assistant for Advancement .... Ms. Theresa RYLAND
13 IT Director .... Mr. Carlos MOLINA
04 Chief of Staff .... Mrs. Patricia WORK
88 Administrative Secretary .... Ms. Katie PARKER

Pontifical John Paul II Institute for Studies on Marriage and Family (E)

620 Michigan Ave, NE, McGivney Hall,
Washington DC 20064

FICE Identification: 041427
Unit ID: 455813

Telephone: (202) 526-3799 — Carnegie Class: Spec-4-yr-Faith
FAX Number: (202) 269-6090 — Calendar System: Other
URL: www.johnpaulii.edu
Established: 1988 — Annual Graduate Tuition & Fees: N/A
Enrollment: 74 — Coed
Affiliation or Control: Roman Catholic — IRS Status: 501(c)3
Highest Offering: Doctorate; No Undergraduates
Accreditation: M

01 President .... RevMsg. Philippe BORDEYNE
03 Vice President .... Carl A. ANDERSON
05 Provost .... Fr. Antonio LOPEZ
20 Dean for Academic Affairs .... David S. CRAWFORD
11 Assoc Dean Programs/Administration .... Nick J. BAGILEO
07 Director of Admissions .... Sara L. TRUDEAU

† Affiliated with The Catholic University of America, DC.

Quantic School of Business and Technology (F)

712 H Street NE, Suite 1802, Washington DC 20002

Identification: 667384

Telephone: (571) 483-8002 — Carnegie Class: Not Classified
FAX Number: N/A — Calendar System: Other
URL: https://quantic.edu
Established: 2016 — Annual Graduate Tuition & Fees: N/A
Enrollment: N/A — Coed
Affiliation or Control: Proprietary — IRS Status: Proprietary
Highest Offering: Master's; No Undergraduates
Accreditation: DEAC

01 President/CEO .... Bill FISHER
05 Chief Academic Officer .... Alexie HARPER

Saint Michael College of Allied Health (G)

1106 Bladensburg Road, NE, Washington DC 20002

Identification: 667226
Unit ID: 486424

Telephone: (202) 388-5500 — Carnegie Class: Spec 2-yr-Health
FAX Number: (202) 388-9588 — Calendar System: Other
URL: https://smcah.edu/
Established: 2007 — Annual Undergrad Tuition & Fees: $16,325
Enrollment: 124 — Coed
Affiliation or Control: Proprietary — IRS Status: Proprietary
Highest Offering: Associate Degree
Accreditation: COE, PNUR

01 President/CEO .... Dr. Michael ADEDOKUN
03 EVP/Campus Director .... Catherine ADEDOKUN

Strayer University (H)

1133 15th Street, NW, Suite 200,
Washington DC 20005-2710

FICE Identification: 001459
Unit ID: 131803

Telephone: (202) 379-7808 — Carnegie Class: Masters/S
FAX Number: (202) 419-1423 — Calendar System: Quarter
URL: www.strayer.edu
Established: 1892 — Annual Undergrad Tuition & Fees: $13,515
Enrollment: 745 — Coed
Affiliation or Control: Proprietary — IRS Status: Proprietary
Highest Offering: Master's
Accreditation: M, ACBSP

01 President .... Dr. Andrea BACKMAN
05 Provost/Chief Academic Ofcr .... Mr. Cale HOLMAN
20 Vice Provost of Academics .... Ms. Jennifer NEWELL
32 Dean of Students .... Dr. Christy KARNES
08 University Librarian .... Ms. Mary SNYDER
06 University Registrar .... Ms. Alison MORRISON
07 Vice President Admissions .... Dr. Amy DUNN
106 Global Online Campus Dean .... Ms. Elizabeth CARDOSO
20 Chamblee GA Campus Dean .... Ms. Tonya MOORE
12 Chamblee GA Campus Director .... Ms. Miriam SANCHEZ
20 Douglasville GA Campus Dean .... Dr. A. Fitzgerald JONES
12 Douglasville GA Campus Director .... Ms. Monica POINTER
12 Charleston SC Campus Director .... Mr. Scott ANDERSON
20 Jackson MS Campus Dean .... Dr. Dana EVANS
12 Allentown PA Campus Director .... Mr. Michael GRANT
12 Jackson MS Campus Director .... Ms. Angela MILLER
20 Cherry Hill NJ Campus Dean .... Dr. R. Renee THOMPSON
12 Cherry Hill NJ Campus Director .... Ms. Allegra GLIEM
20 San Antonio TX Campus Dean .... Mr. Kendall JOHNSON
20 Henrico VA Campus Dean .... Mr. Marcus RALPH
20 Chesterfield VA Campus Dean .... Dr. Carol WILLIAMS
20 Piscataway NJ Campus Dean .... Mr. Jared ELLISON
12 Piscataway NJ Campus Director .... Mr. Khioverny DUARTE
12 Warrendale PA Campus Director .... Ms. Molly MAZZARINI
20 Teays Valley WV Campus Dean .... Dr. Joel GOLDSTEIN
20 Warrendale PA Campus Dean .... Mr. Timothy GRIFFIN
20 Willingboro NJ Campus Dean .... Dr. A. Renee THOMPSON
12 Willingboro NJ Campus Director .... Ms. Allegra GLIEM
20 Knoxville TN Campus Dean .... Dr. Chelsie SWEPSON
20 Huntersville NC Campus Dean .... Dr. Jonita HENRY POWELL
12 Huntersville NC Campus Director .... Ms. Krystal MOREHEAD
12 Research Triangle Pk NC Campus Dir .... Mr. Patrick DIXON
12 San Antonio TX Campus Director .... Mr. Coner GILL
12 Henrico VA Campus Director .... Ms. Sarah HOYT
12 Knoxville TN Campus Director .... Mr. Jason ADKINS
20 Cedar Hill TX Campus Dean .... Dr. LeAllen HAWKINS
12 Lower Bucks PA Campus Director .... Ms. Lauren PLINER
12 Cedar Hill TX Campus Director .... Ms. Marisol GREENWOOD
20 Charleston SC Campus Dean .... Mr. Elliot DILLIHAY
20 Newport News VA Campus Dean .... Dr. Mavis CARR
20 North Austin TX Campus Dean .... Mr. Kendall JOHNSON
12 North Austin TX Campus Director .... Mr. Coner GILL
20 Morrow GA Campus Dean .... Dr. Shadrack KOROS
20 North Dallas TX Campus Dean .... Dr. T.A ESSEX
20 Lower Bucks PA Campus Dean .... Dr. Byron WESS
12 North Dallas TX Campus Director .... Ms. Kedecia RITCHIE-MITCHELL
12 Teays Valley WV Campus Director .... Ms. Christine VITO
20 Cobb County GA Campus Dean .... Dr. Timothy SHERMAN
12 Cobb County GA Campus Director .... Mr. Richard WYLIE
12 Virginia Beach VA Campus Director .... Mr. Patrick DIXON
12 Prince Georges MD Campus Director .... Ms. Candy COLLINS
20 Columbia SC Campus Dean .... Ms. Piper LORICK
12 Columbia SC Campus Director .... Mr. Ryan BUCKSON
12 Takoma Park DC Campus Director .... Mr. Cristen JONES
12 Newport News VA Campus Director .... Ms. Colette REID
20 Delaware County PA Campus Dean .... Ms. Cornelia ZAVADSKY
12 Delaware Cty PA Assoc Campus Dir .... Mr. Charles MCCARTHY
20 Fredericksburg VA Campus Dean .... Mr. Terrell MASON
12 Fredericksburg VA Campus Director .... Mr. Duan BUTLER
20 North Charlotte NC Campus Dean .... Ms. Shawna MAGBIE-CARR
20 Greensboro NC Campus Dean .... Ms. Melissa REID ALSTON
12 Greensboro NC Campus Director .... Ms. Dorende CRAIGG
20 Research Triangle Park NC Campus Dn .... Dr. JoeAnn PARKER
12 Maitland FL Campus Director .... Mr. Jason MARTINE
12 Morrow GA Campus Director .... Ms. Allisha OUSLEY
20 Greenville SC Campus Dean .... Dr. William DUERR
12 Greenville SC Campus Director .... Ms. Jeanne POINDEXTER
20 Loudoun VA Campus Dean .... Dr. Richelle RESTO
12 Loudoun VA Campus Director .... Ms. Ashley COLLINS
20 Manassas VA Campus Dean .... Ms. Leila STEGLICH
12 White Marsh MD Campus Director .... Mr. Leator KNUCKLES
12 Manassas VA Campus Director .... Mr. Debra SANFORD
20 North Raleigh NC Campus Dean .... Ms. Ashley CASTLE
12 North Raleigh NC Campus Director .... Mr. Jason HARRIS
12 North Charlotte NC Campus Director ..... Ms. Stephanie JOHNSON
20 Nashville TN Campus Dean .... Dr. Kimberly MALONE-HADDOX
12 Nashville TN Campus Director .... Ms. Kelley BUCKLEY
20 Owings Mills MD Campus Dean .... Ms. LaToya HALE
12 Owings Mills MD Campus Director .... Ms. Shawne SCOTT
20 Arlington VA Campus Dean .... Dr. Mimi GETACHEW
12 Center City PA Campus Director .... Mr. Isaac WALTERS
20 Shelby TN Campus Dean .... Dr. Clinton MILLER
20 Rockville MD Campus Dean .... Dr. Angel CLAY
20 Takoma Park DC Campus Dean .... Mr. Vishnu DZIDZIENYO
12 Shelby TN Campus Director .... Mr. Sam THOMAS
20 Maitland FL Campus Dean .... Ms. Judith ZAYAS
20 Prince Georges MD Campus Dean .... Dr. Camilla CRAIG
20 Decatur AL Campus Dean .... Dr. Andrain YELDELL JONES
12 Decatur AL Campus Director .... Ms. Julie PRYOR
20 Mobile AL Campus Dean .... Dr. Mark PANTALEO
12 Mobile AL Campus Director .... Mr. Justin SULLIVAN
12 Miramar FL Campus Director .... Ms. Esmerelda AVILA
20 Montgomery AL Campus Dean .... Mr. Kenneth MACON
12 Montgomery AL Campus Director .... Mr. Eric WALKER
12 Arlington VA Campus Director .... Ms. Patrice JONES
20 Wilmington DE Campus Dean .... Ms. Sharmina ELLIS
12 Wilmington DE Campus Director .... Mr. Michael GRANT
20 Tallahassee FL Campus Dean .... Ms. Gabrielle NAVAS
12 Tallahassee FL Campus Director .... Ms. Kristy KEGLEY
20 Chattanooga TN Campus Dean .... Dr. Clinton MILLER
12 Chattanooga TN Campus Director .... Ms. Jeanne POINDEXTER
20 El Paso TX Campus Dean ... Ms. Nicole FRANCISCO-CAMPBELL
20 Anne Arundel MD Campus Dean .... Ms. Aerin GILBERT
12 El Paso TX Campus Director .... Mr. Donald WHITE
12 Rockville MD Assoc Campus Director .... Ms. Asija PRITCHETT
20 Fort Worth TX Campus Dean .... Dr. Dennis CARLSON
12 Fort Worth TX Campus Director .... Ms. Latrissa JACOBS
20 Killeen TX Campus Dean .... Dr. David WELLS
12 Killeen TX Campus Director .... Mr. Nicholas PEREZ
20 South Charlotte NC Campus Dean .... Dr. Jeffrey ROMANCZUK
20 Tampa FL East Campus Dean .... Ms. DeNeen ATTORD
12 South Charlotte NC Campus Director .... Ms. Christine VITO

20 Virginia Beach VA Campus Dean .... Dr. JoeAnn PACE
12 Anne Arundel MD Campus Director .... Ms. Cherone VALLEY
12 Orlando FL East Campus Director .... Mr. Jason MARTINE
12 Tampa FL East Campus Director .... Mr. Jeffrey KEITH
20 Alexandria VA Campus Dean .... Dr. Peter DEDOMINICI
20 Woodbridge VA Campus Dean .... Dr. Ras ACOLASTE
20 Lithonia GA Campus Dean .... Ms. Tariva SMITH
12 Woodbridge VA Campus Director .... Ms. Toni THORTON
12 Thousand Oaks TN Campus Director .... Ms. Mara JEFFERSON
20 Thousand Oaks TN Campus Dean .... Mr. Stanley WOOTEN
20 Miramar FL Campus Dean .... Dr. Joann RAPHAEL
20 Washington DC Campus Dean .... Ms. Timera WILLIAMS
12 Savannah GA Campus Director .... Ms. Dora JENKINS
12 Washington DC Campus Director .... Ms. Diane CLARK-FAGGS
20 Palm Beach Gardens FL Campus Dean .... Dr. Joann RAPHAEL
20 White Marsh MD Campus Dean .... Ms. Tafadzwa NHIRA
12 Alexandria VA Assoc Campus Director .... Ms. Natalie THOMAS
20 Macon GA Assoc Campus Dean .... Mr. Akinola DARE
12 Macon GA Campus Director .... Ms. Clairesse QUADIR
12 Lithonia GA Campus Director .... Mr. Etuwe OTUYA
20 Center City PA Campus Dean .... Ms. Saadia OULAMINE
20 South Raleigh NC Campus Dean .... Ms. Kimberly WILLIAMS
12 Birmingham AL Campus Director .... Ms. Irina ROGERS
20 Birmingham AL Campus Dean .... Mr. Keith JOHNSON
20 Chesapeake VA Campus Dean .... Ms. Amber EAKIN
12 Chesapeake VA Campus Director .... Mr. Tom LOTITO
20 Northwest Houston TX Campus Dean .... Dr. Johnny JONES
20 Savannah GA Campus Dean .... Dr. Denise OGDEN
20 Huntsville AL Campus Dean .... Mr. Dustin VICK
12 Huntsville AL Campus Director .... Ms. Julie PRYOR
20 Little Rock AR Campus Dean .... Dr. Stephanie COX
12 Little Rock AR Campus Director .... Mr. Charles BLOCKETT
12 Palm Beach Gardens FL Campus Dir .... Ms. Cathy HUCKABY
20 Orlando FL East Campus Dean .... Ms. Judith ZAYAS
20 Baymeadows FL Campus Dean .... Ms. Sarah FRADEN
12 South Raleigh NC Campus Director .... Mr. Matthew KOCH
12 Baymeadows FL Campus Director .... Mr. Joshua NOVATON
12 Northwest Houston TX Campus Dir .... Ms. Tracey MARTIN
20 Fort Lauderdale FL Campus Dean .... Dr. Joann RAPHAEL
12 Fort Lauderdale FL Campus Director .... Mr. Geoffrey RAMGOLAM
20 Augusta GA Campus Dean .... Dr. Isaac MOONZWE
12 Augusta GA Campus Director .... Mr. Louis DAVIS
12 Chesterfield VA Campus Director .... Mr. Thomas BERNHARDT
20 Allentown PA Campus Dean .... Ms. Holli QUINN
20 Columbus GA Campus Dean .... Dr. Kanidrus PRATHER
12 Columbus GA Campus Director .... Mr. Jonathan MURRAY

Trinity Washington University (A)

125 Michigan Avenue, NE, Washington DC 20017-1090

FICE Identification: 001460
Unit ID: 131876

Telephone: (202) 884-9000 Carnegie Class: Masters/M
FAX Number: (202) 884-9229 Calendar System: Semester
URL: www.trinitydc.edu
Established: 1897 Annual Undergrad Tuition & Fees: $25,110
Enrollment: 1,846 Female
Affiliation or Control: Roman Catholic IRS Status: 501(c)3
Highest Offering: Master's
Accreditation: M, CACREP, CAEP, NURSE, OT

01 President .... Ms. Patricia A. MCGUIRE
05 Provost .... Dr. Carlota OCAMPO
10 Vice President Fiscal Affairs/CFO .... Mr. Grant GONZALEZ
111 Vice Pres Institutional Advancement .... Ms. Ann PAULEY
84 Vice Pres Enrollment Services .... Ms. Cathy GEIER
26 Vice Pres Media Relations .... Ms. Ann PAULEY
32 Vice President for Student Affairs .... Dr. Karen GERLACH
13 Chief Info Technology Officer (CIO) .... Mr. Michael BURBACK
30 Chief Development Officer .... Mr. Patrick KELLOGG
49 Dean College of Arts & Science .... Dr. Sita RAMAMURTI
53 Dean School of Education .... Dr. Jennifer HAUVER
107 Dean School of Professional Studies ...... Mr. Thomas MOSTOWY
66 Dean Sch Nursing/Health Professions .... Dr. Brigid NOONAN
35 Dean of Student Services .... Ms. Michelle BOWIE
15 Exec Director of Human Resources ..... Ms. Tracey PRINCE ROSS
41 Athletic Director .... Ms. Monique MCLEAN
42 Director of Campus Ministry .... Sr. Ann HOWARD
18 Director Facilities Services .... Mr. William (Bill) SHAFFER
08 University Librarian .... Ms. Trisha SMITH
21 Assoc Controller/Business Officer .... Ms. Danielle MADDEN
51 Director Continuing Education .... Ms. Katie OMENITSCH

University of the District of Columbia (B)

4200 Connecticut Avenue, NW,
Washington DC 20008-1174

FICE Identification: 001441
Unit ID: 131399

Telephone: (202) 274-5000 Carnegie Class: Masters/M
FAX Number: (202) 274-5304 Calendar System: Semester
URL: www.udc.edu
Established: 1976 Annual Undergrad Tuition & Fees (In-District): $6,152
Enrollment: 3,725 Coed
Affiliation or Control: Local IRS Status: 501(c)3
Highest Offering: First Professional Degree
Accreditation: M, ACBSP, ADNUR, CACREP, CAEP, COARC, DIETD, FUSER, LAW, NUR, SP, SW

01 President .... Mr. Ronald MASON, JR.
05 Chief Academic Officer .... Dr. Lawrence POTTER
32 Chief Student Devel & Success Ofcr .... Dr. William LATHAM
11 Chief Operating Officer .... Mr. David FRANKLIN
43 General Counsel .... Ms. Avis RUSSELL
100 Chief of Staff/Senior Vice Pres .... Ms. Monique GUILLORY
15 Vice President Human Resources ..... Ms. Lorinnsa BRIDGES-KEE
18 VP Real Estate & Facility Mgmt .... Mr. Javier DUSSAN
111 Vice President for Advancement .... Mr. Rodney TRAPP
13 Vice President Information Tech .... Mr. Suresh MURUGAN
26 Vice President Marketing and Comm .... Ms. Leeann HALL
10 Chief Financial Officer .... Mr. Roy LANE
49 Dean Arts & Sciences .... Dr. April MASSEY
50 Dean Sch Business & Public Admin .... Dr. Mohamad SEPEHRI
61 Dean School of Law .... Ms. Renee MCDONALD HUTCHINS
54 Dean Engineering/Applied Scis .... Dr. Devdas SHETTY
56 Dean CAUSES .... Dr. Dwane JONES
46 VP Research & Sponsored Programs .... Dr. Victor MCCRARY
84 Interim AVP Enrollment Services .... Ms. Nailah WILLIAMS
06 University Registrar .... Ms. Tiffany COOPER
37 Director Student Financial Aid .... Mr. Wayne MONTGOMERY
08 Director of Learning Resources .... Ms. Melba BROOME
25 Capital Program Officer .... Ms. Cassandra PARKER
41 Athletic Director .... Ms. Patricia A. THOMAS
88 General Manager UDC Cable TV .... Mr. Edward JONES, JR.
09 Dir of Institutional Effectiveness .... Mrs. Maria BYRD
38 Director Student Counseling .... Ms. Serena BUTLER-JOHNSON
121 AVP Student Success UDC-CC .... Ms. Hermina P. PETERS
103 Dean Workforce Development .... Ms. Mashonda SMITH
19 Interim Dir Public Safety .... Mr. Orlando TREADWELL
36 Exec Director Career Services .... Mr. Jared E. MOFFETT
86 Exec Director State & Local Affairs .... Ms. Annie WHATLEY
21 Deputy Chief Operating Officer .... Ms. Raysa LEER
81 Director STEM .... Ms. Barbara J. HOLMES
29 Director Alumni Affairs .... Ms. Phomika PALMER
97 Assistant Director of General Educ .... Ms. Kimberly CREWS
102 Director Sponsored Programs .... Ms. Laura-Lee DAVIDSON
13 Dir Information Technology .... Mr. Michael ROGERS
07 Director Admissions/TRIO Programs .... Ms. Saundra CARTER
101 Exec Secretary Office the Board .... Ms. Frenika RIVERS
35 Asst Director of Student Success .... Ms. Latosha BALDWIN
39 Director of Residence Life .... Mr. Quintin VEASLEY
96 Chief Contracting Officer .... Ms. Mary Ann HARRIS

University of the Potomac (C)

1401 H Street NW, Suite 100, Washington DC 20005

FICE Identification: 032183
Unit ID: 384412

Telephone: (202) 274-2303 Carnegie Class: Spec-4-yr-Bus
FAX Number: N/A Calendar System: Semester
URL: www.potomac.edu
Established: 1991 Annual Undergrad Tuition & Fees: $6,660
Enrollment: 232 Coed
Affiliation or Control: Proprietary IRS Status: Proprietary
Highest Offering: Doctorate
Accreditation: M

01 Interim President .... Andrea KEMP-CURTIS
05 Dean of Academics .... Dr. Sergei ANDRONIKOV
10 Chief Financial Officer .... Vacant
11 Chief Operating Officer .... Andrea FORD
08 Director of Learning Resource Ctr .... Edward ROBINSON

Wesley Theological Seminary (D)

4500 Massachusetts Avenue, NW,
Washington DC 20016-5690

FICE Identification: 001464
Unit ID: 131973

Telephone: (202) 885-8600 Carnegie Class: Spec-4-yr-Faith
FAX Number: (202) 885-8605 Calendar System: Semester
URL: www.wesleyseminary.edu
Established: 1882 Annual Graduate Tuition & Fees: N/A
Enrollment: 530 Coed
Affiliation or Control: United Methodist IRS Status: 501(c)3
Highest Offering: Doctorate; No Undergraduates
Accreditation: M, THEOL

01 President .... Dr. David MCALLISTER-WILSON
04 Executive Assistant to President .... Mrs. Janice M. HUDSON
10 Vice Pres Finance/CFO .... Mr. Jeffrey STRAITS
05 Dean .... Dr. Philip WINGEIER-RAYO
20 Associate Dean Academic Affairs .... Dr. Michael KOPPEL
32 Assoc Dean for Campus Life .... Dr. Asa LEE
88 Vice President of Intl Relations .... Dr. Kyunglim SHIN LEE
84 VP Strategic Initiative Enrollment .... Rev. Beth LUDLUM
30 Vice Pres Development .... Rev. Brian MCCOLLUM
21 Controller .... Mr. William WALKER
06 Registrar .... Mr. Joseph E. ARNOLD
88 Dir Luce Ctr for Arts & Religion .... Dr. Aaron ROSEN
31 Director Community Engagement Inst .... Dr. Lorena PARRISH
88 Director Ctr for Public Theology .... Mr. Michael MCCURRY
88 Faculty Dir Ctr Public Theology .... Mr. Rick ELGENDY
26 Director Communications/Marketing .... Ms. Sheila GEORGE
88 Director Doctor of Ministry Program .... Dr. Douglas TZAN
24 Director of Educational Technology .... Ms. Berkeley COLLINS
88 Director of Enrollment .... Ms. JaNice PARKS
88 Director Heal the Sick Initiative .... Thomas PRUSKI
15 Director Human Resources .... Dr. Josie HOOVER
39 Director of Housing .... Ms. Monica PETTY
85 Dir International Student Services .... Ms. Karen SANTIAGO
88 Dir Lewis Ctr Church Leadership .... Dr. F. Douglas POWE
08 Director of Library .... Mr. Andy KLENKLEN
88 Dir Practice Ministry in Mission .... Dr. Joseph BUSH
37 Director Student Financial Aid .... Mr. Dane SMITH
88 Director Writing Center .... Ms. Raedorah STEWART
18 Chief Facilities/Physical Plant .... Mr. Oscar PALENCIA
28 Diversity Officer .... Mr. Matt LYONS

FLORIDA

Academy for Five Element Acupuncture (E)

305 SE Second Avenue, Gainesville FL 32601-6811

County: Alachua FICE Identification: 035243
Unit ID: 451079

Telephone: (352) 335-2332 Carnegie Class: Spec-4-yr-Other Health
FAX Number: (352) 337-2535 Calendar System: Trimester
URL: www.acupuncturist.edu
Established: 1998 Annual Graduate Tuition & Fees: N/A
Enrollment: 91 Coed
Affiliation or Control: Independent Non-Profit IRS Status: 501(c)3
Highest Offering: Master's; No Undergraduates
Accreditation: ACUP

01 President .... Ms. Misti OXFORD-PICKERAL
10 Vice President Administration .... Ms. Joanne EPSTEIN
05 Academic Dean .... Mr. Chuck GRAHAM
32 Student Dean .... Ms. Patty GETFORD
10 Finance Director .... Ms. Odalis CRUZ
06 Registrar .... Ms. Jessica BABAKER
07 Admissions .... Ms. Isabelle WINZELER

Academy for Nursing and Health Occupations (F)

5154 Okeechobee Blvd #201, West Palm Beach FL 33417

County: Palm Beach FICE Identification: 033463
Unit ID: 412173

Telephone: (561) 683-1400 Carnegie Class: Spec 2-yr-Health
FAX Number: (561) 683-6773 Calendar System: Other
URL: www.anho.edu
Established: 1978 Annual Undergrad Tuition & Fees: N/A
Enrollment: 703 Coed
Affiliation or Control: Independent Non-Profit IRS Status: 501(c)3
Highest Offering: Associate Degree
Accreditation: COE, ADNUR

01 Executive Director .... Dr. Lois M. RICHARDS
05 Academic Dean .... Neala ASSER
32 Dean of Student Svcs .... Kacey ATKINSON
15 Compliance Educator/Chief HR Ofcr .... Renee WERNER
06 Registrar .... Elizabeth RODRIGUEZ
37 Financial Aid Director .... Kacey ATKINSON
07 Admissions Specialist .... Angela STILES
11 Director of Operations .... Marlo ARIAS
26 Chief Public Relations Officer .... Sherri ADDUCI
38 Director Student Counseling .... Dr. Lois M. RICHARDS
84 Director Enrollment Management .... Angela STILES

Acupuncture & Massage College (G)

10506 N Kendall Drive, Miami FL 33176-1509

County: Miami-Dade FICE Identification: 034145
Unit ID: 439969

Telephone: (305) 595-9500 Carnegie Class: Spec-4-yr-Other Health
FAX Number: (305) 595-2622 Calendar System: Semester
URL: www.amcollege.edu
Established: 1983 Annual Undergrad Tuition & Fees: $10,943
Enrollment: 171 Coed
Affiliation or Control: Proprietary IRS Status: Proprietary
Highest Offering: Master's
Accreditation: ACCSC, ACUP

01 President .... Ms. Christy WOOD
05 Academic Dean .... Dr. Yaly FLORES-SOTO
17 Clinic Director .... Dr. Jean Pierre CHACON
37 Financial Aid Director .... Mr. Guy JACKMAN
07 Admissions Director .... Mr. Joe CALARESO
06 Registrar/Student Services .... Ms. Maria GARCIA

Advance Science International College (H)

5190 North West 167 Street, Ste 200,
Miami Lakes FL 33014

County: Miami-Dade FICE Identification: 037573
Unit ID: 444334

Telephone: (305) 626-6007 Carnegie Class: Spec 2-yr-Health
FAX Number: N/A Calendar System: Semester
URL: asicollege.edu
Established: 1998 Annual Undergrad Tuition & Fees: N/A
Enrollment: 53 Coed
Affiliation or Control: Proprietary IRS Status: Proprietary
Highest Offering: Associate Degree
Accreditation: ACCSC

01 President/Director of School .... Pablo PEREZ

AdventHealth University (A)

671 Winyah Drive, Orlando FL 32803-1204
County: Orange   FICE Identification: 031155
     Unit ID: 133872
Telephone: (407) 303-9798   Carnegie Class: Spec-4-yr-Other Health
FAX Number: (407) 303-5671   Calendar System: Trimester
URL: www.ahu.edu
Established: 1992   Annual Undergrad Tuition & Fees: $19,800
Enrollment: 1,802   Coed
Affiliation or Control: Seventh-day Adventist   IRS Status: 501(c)3
Highest Offering: Doctorate
Accreditation: **SC**, ANEST, ARCPA, DMS, HSA, NMT, NURSE, OT, OTA, PTA, RAD

01	President	Dr. Edwin I. HERNANDEZ
05	Provost	Dr. Sandra DUNBAR-SMALLEY
11	SVP Operational Strategy	Dr. Deena SLOCKETT
10	Sr VP for Finance/CFO	Mr. Ruben O. MARTINEZ
32	Sr VP for Student Services	Dr. Stephen H. ROCHE
26	VP Marketing & Public Relations	Mr. Lonnie MIXON
106	Director AHU Online	Ms. Leanna NEUBRANDER
09	Dir of Inst Effectiveness/Accred	Mr. Joe HAWKINS
37	Director of Financial Aid	Ms. Daisy TABACHOW
06	Registrar	Dr. Janet CALDERON
88	Dir Ctr for Academic Achievement	Dr. Nkala BOOKER
08	Library Director	Mr. Neal SMITH
07	Director of Enrollment Services	Ms. Lillian GARRIDO
21	Chief Accountant	Mr. Grayson GOODMAN
39	Director of Residence Hall	Ms. Cassandra PHILOGENE
30	Director of Philanthropy	Dr. Carol BRADFIELD
15	Director of Human Resources	Ms. Jennifer CARPENTER
13	Director of Information Technology	Mr. Travis WOOLEY
04	Executive Asst to the President	Ms. Viviana CALANDRA
88	Chief Compliance Officer	Ms. Starr S. BENDER
29	Director Alumni Relations	Ms. Dawn H. CREFT
19	Director Security/Safety	Mr. Eric GOEBELBECKER

American Medical Academy (B)

12215 SW 112th Street, Miami FL 33186
County: Miami-Dade   FICE Identification: 041921
     Unit ID: 475714
Telephone: (305) 271-6555   Carnegie Class: Spec 2-yr-Health
FAX Number: (305) 271-6556   Calendar System: Semester
URL: www.ama.edu
Established: 2006   Annual Undergrad Tuition & Fees: N/A
Enrollment: 527   Coed
Affiliation or Control: Proprietary   IRS Status: Proprietary
Highest Offering: Baccalaureate
Accreditation: **ABHES**

01	Chief Executive Officer	Dr. Eduardo GUTIERREZ

*Ana G. Mendez University (C)

5575 S. Semoran Blvd. Suite 502, Orlando FL 32822
County: Orlando   Identification: 667292
Telephone: (407) 563-6501   Carnegie Class: Not Classified
FAX Number: N/A   Calendar System: Semester
URL: www.agmu.edu
Established: 2011   Annual Undergrad Tuition & Fees: N/A
Enrollment: N/A   Coed
Affiliation or Control: Independent Non-Profit   IRS Status: 501(c)3
Highest Offering: Doctorate
Accreditation: **M**

02	Chancellor	Dr. Gino Q. NATALICCHIO
03	Executive VP	Mr. Nicholas NATALIZIO
05	Vice Chancellor of Academic Affairs	Dr. Donna VIENS
32	Vice Chancellor of Student Affairs	Dr. Claire L. BRADY

*Ana G. Mendez University Metro Orlando Campus (D)

5601 S Semoran Boulevard, #55, Orlando FL 32822
Telephone: (407) 207-3363   Identification: 770921
Accreditation: **&M**

*Ana G. Mendez University South Florida Campus (E)

15201 NW 79th Court, Miami Lakes FL 33016
Telephone: (954) 885-5595   Identification: 770922
Accreditation: **&M**

*Ana G. Mendez University Tampa Bay Campus (F)

3655 West Waters Avenue, Tampa FL 33614
Telephone: (813) 932-7500   Identification: 770923
Accreditation: **&M**

Antigua College International (G)

14505 Commerce Way, Suite 522,
Miami Lakes FL 33016-1573
County: Miami-Dade   Identification: 667344
Telephone: (786) 391-1167   Carnegie Class: Not Classified
FAX Number: (786) 452-9265   Calendar System: Semester
URL: www.antigua.edu
Established: 2012   Annual Undergrad Tuition & Fees: N/A

Enrollment: N/A   Coed
Affiliation or Control: Proprietary   IRS Status: Proprietary
Highest Offering: Baccalaureate
Accreditation: **ABHES**, @CNEA

00	CEO	Diony ANTIGUA
01	President	Jose ANTIGUA
10	Chief Financial Officer	Brian ANTIGUA
08	Chief Library Officer	Dorthy HAMILTON

The Art Institute of Tampa, a branch of Miami International University of Art & Design (H)

4401 North Himes Avenue, Suite 150, Tampa FL 33614
Telephone: (813) 393-5321   Identification: 770935
Accreditation: **&SC**

† Branch campus of Miami International University of Art & Design, Miami, FL.

ATA Career Education-Spring Hill (I)

7351 Spring Hill Drive, Suite 11, Spring Hill FL 34606
Telephone: (866) 438-2432   Identification: 770521
Accreditation: **ABHES**

† Branch campus of ATA College, Louisville, KY

Atlantic Institute of Oriental Medicine (J)

100 E Broward Boulevard, Suite 100,
Fort Lauderdale FL 33301-3510
County: Broward   FICE Identification: 034296
     Unit ID: 439446
Telephone: (954) 763-9840   Carnegie Class: Spec-4-yr-Other Health
FAX Number: (954) 763-9844   Calendar System: Trimester
URL: www.atom.edu
Established: 1994   Annual Graduate Tuition & Fees: N/A
Enrollment: 174   Coed
Affiliation or Control: Independent Non-Profit   IRS Status: 501(c)3
Highest Offering: Doctorate; No Undergraduates
Accreditation: **ACUP**

01	President	Dr. Johanna C. YEN
03	Exec Vice Pres/DAOM Director	Dr. Di FU
05	Academic Dean	Allyson WILSON
10	Financial Officer	Celia MUNOZ
06	Registrar	Milagros FERREIRA
08	Head Librarian	Royal MONTGOMERY
37	Financial Aid Manager	Michelle WELDY

Atlantis University (K)

1011 Sunnybrook Road, Miami FL 33136
County: Miami-Dade   FICE Identification: 042339
     Unit ID: 485768
Telephone: (305) 377-8817   Carnegie Class: Masters/M
FAX Number: (305) 377-9557   Calendar System: Semester
URL: www.atlantisuniversity.edu
Established: 1975   Annual Undergrad Tuition & Fees: $10,800
Enrollment: 550   Coed
Affiliation or Control: Proprietary   IRS Status: Proprietary
Highest Offering: Master's
Accreditation: **ACCSC**, CEA

01	Chancellor/President	Omar PALACIOS
11	Executive Director/Dir Compliance	Carol PALACIOS
07	Director of Admissions	Juan CRUZ TORRES
06	Registrar	Alina RODRIGUEZ
36	Director Student Placement	Alex LIMA
37	Director Student Financial Aid	Ingrid AYALA

Ave Maria School of Law (L)

1025 Commons Circle, Naples FL 34119
County: Collier   FICE Identification: 036914
     Unit ID: 442295
Telephone: (239) 687-5300   Carnegie Class: Spec-4-yr-Law
FAX Number: (239) 353-3173   Calendar System: Semester
URL: www.avemarialaw.edu
Established: 2000   Annual Graduate Tuition & Fees: N/A
Enrollment: 286   Coed
Affiliation or Control: Roman Catholic   IRS Status: 501(c)3
Highest Offering: First Professional Degree; No Undergraduates
Accreditation: **LAW**

01	CEO and Dean	Mr. John CZARNETZKY
04	Executive Assistant to the Dean	Ms. Pamela KRAMER
05	Assoc Dean Academic Affairs	Ms. Maureen MILLIRON
32	Assoc Dean Student Engagement	Ms. Claire O'KEEFE
10	Assoc Dean Finance/Student Admin	Ms. Kaye CASTRO
08	Director of the Law Library	Mr. Ulysses JAEN
42	Chaplain	Msgr. Frank MCGRATH
06	Registrar	Ms. Jennifer DIAZ
37	Director of Financial Aid	Mr. Kevin MCGOWAN
111	Chief Advancement Officer	Ms. Donna HEISER
36	Director of Career Services	Ms. Jennifer LUCAS-ROSS
13	Chief Information Officer	Ms. Monica RENGIFO
07	Assoc Dean of Admiss/Stdnt Engage	Ms. Claire O'KEEFE
15	Human Resources Officer	Ms. Kathleen SHELMERDINE

Ave Maria University (M)

5050 Ave Maria Boulevard, Ave Maria FL 34142-9505
County: Collier   FICE Identification: 039413
     Unit ID: 446048
Telephone: (239) 280-2500   Carnegie Class: Bac-A&S
FAX Number: (239) 352-2392   Calendar System: Semester
URL: www.avemaria.edu
Established: 2003   Annual Undergrad Tuition & Fees: $23,188
Enrollment: 1,108   Coed
Affiliation or Control: Independent Non-Profit   IRS Status: 501(c)3
Highest Offering: Doctorate
Accreditation: **SC**, NUR

00	Chancellor	Mr. Thomas S. MONAGHAN
01	Interim President	Dr. Roger P. NUTT
05	VP Academic Affairs & Provost	Dr. Roger NUTT
10	VP Finance/Administration	Mr. Eugene MUNIN
30	VP Institutional Advancement	Mr. Tim DOCKERY
32	VP Student Affairs	Ms. Kimberly KING
26	VP Marketing/Communications	Mr. Kevin MURPHY
13	Chief Information Officer	Mr. Eddie DEJTHAI
07	AVP of Admissions	Ms. Dee GIPSON
06	Registrar	Ms. Kathryn DIONNE
41	Athletic Director	Mr. Joseph PATTERSON
42	Director of Campus Ministry	Fr. Rick MARTIGNETTI
44	Sr Director of Principal Gifts	Mr. Patrick O'CONNELL
35	Director of Student Life	Ms. Rachel FLOWERS
88	Director of Mission/Outreach	Mr. Kerry ESTES
08	Director of Library Services	Ms. Jennifer NODES
15	Director of Human Resources	Ms. Kathy PHELPS
18	Director Physical Plant	Mr. Brent JOHNSON
38	Director Counseling Services	Ms. AnaMaria LI-ROSI
39	Director Resident Life	Mr. Ryan WELCH
19	Director Security/Safety	Mr. Michael MILLER
37	Director Financial Aid	Ms. Sandra SHIMP
04	Admin Assistant to the President	Ms. Cristine BUZZANCA
29	Program Manager Alumni Relations	Ms. Paula SHUTE

Aviator College of Aeronautical Science & Technology (N)

3800 St. Lucie Boulevard, Fort Pierce FL 34946
County: Saint Lucie   FICE Identification: 039863
     Unit ID: 447847
Telephone: (772) 466-4822   Carnegie Class: Spec 2-yr-Tech
FAX Number: (772) 462-4886   Calendar System: Semester
URL: www.aviator.edu
Established: 1984   Annual Undergrad Tuition & Fees: $31,211
Enrollment: 305   Coed
Affiliation or Control: Proprietary   IRS Status: Proprietary
Highest Offering: Associate Degree
Accreditation: **ACCSC**, CEA

01	President	Mr. Michael E. COHEN
10	Sr Vice Pres/Chief Financial Ofcr	Ms. T.J METE
05	Vice Pres Academic Affairs	Mr. Pierre LAVIAL
06	Registrar/Director Student Services	Mrs. Calandria YEE-BULLOCK
37	Financial Aid Officer	Ms. Jacqueline ORTIZ
43	Legal Counsel/Compliance	Mr. Kendall PHILLIPS

Azure College (O)

3201 W Commercial Blvd, Suite 127,
Fort Lauderdale FL 33309
County: Highlands   Identification: 667116
     Unit ID: 483762
Telephone: (954) 500-2987   Carnegie Class: Not Classified
FAX Number: N/A   Calendar System: Quarter
URL: www.azure.edu
Established: 2004   Annual Undergrad Tuition & Fees: N/A
Enrollment: N/A   Coed
Affiliation or Control: Proprietary   IRS Status: Proprietary
Highest Offering: Baccalaureate
Accreditation: **ABHES**

01	Campus Director	Mr. Jose NAPOLEON

The Baptist College of Florida (P)

5400 College Drive, Graceville FL 32440-3306
County: Jackson   FICE Identification: 021596
     Unit ID: 132408
Telephone: (850) 263-3261   Carnegie Class: Bac-Diverse
FAX Number: (850) 263-9026   Calendar System: Semester
URL: www.baptistcollege.edu
Established: 1943   Annual Undergrad Tuition & Fees: $12,150
Enrollment: 418   Coed
Affiliation or Control: Southern Baptist   IRS Status: 501(c)3
Highest Offering: Master's
Accreditation: **SC**, MUS

01	President	Dr. Thomas A. KINCHEN
30	Vice President for Development	Vacant
05	Academic Dean	Dr. G. Robin JUMPER
06	Registrar	Ms. Stephanie W. ORR
13	Chief Information Technology Ofcr	Vacant
32	Director of Student Life/Marketing	Mrs. Sandra K. RICHARDS
09	Director of Institutional Research	Dr. Ed SCOTT

37 Director of Financial Aid & VA ....Mrs. Stephanie E. POWELL
18 Maintenance Director ....Mr. Olan C. STRICKLAND
10 Associate Business Officer ....Ms. Polly K. FLOYD
04 Administrative Asst to President ....Mrs. Laura L. SOWELL
08 Head Librarian ....Mrs. Della M. JUSTICE
39 Housing Manager ....Mrs. Rose A. STRICKLAND
41 Athletic Coordinator ....Mr. R. Neal POTTER
19 Director of Campus Safety ....Mr. Olan C. STRICKLAND

Barry University (A)

11300 NE Second Avenue, Miami Shores FL 33161-6695
County: Dade FICE Identification: 001466
Unit ID: 132471
Telephone: (305) 899-3000 Carnegie Class: DU-Mod
FAX Number: (305) 899-3054 Calendar System: Semester
URL: www.barry.edu
Established: 1940 Annual Undergrad Tuition & Fees: $30,940
Enrollment: 7,515 Coed
Affiliation or Control: Roman Catholic IRS Status: 501(c)3
Highest Offering: Doctorate
Accreditation: SC, ANEST, ARCPA, CAATE, CACREP, EXSC, HT, LAW, MACTE, MLS, NURSE, OT, POD, SW, THEOL

01 President ....Dr. Mike ALLEN
04 Administrative Coordinator ....Mr. Miguel A. CALVO, JR.
125 President Emerita ....Sr. Linda BEVILACQUA
05 Provost ....Dr. John D. MURRAY
20 Associate Provost ....Dr. Victor ROMANO
20 Associate Provost Extended Learning ....Dr. David KOPP
08 Director Library Services ....Dr. Jan FIGA
49 Dean College of Arts/Sciences ....Dr. Karen A. CALLAGHAN
10 Vice Pres Business & Finance ....Mrs. Susan ROSENTHAL
11 Vice Pres University Administration ....Mrs. Jennifer N. BOYD-PUGH
111 VP for Institutional Advancement ....Ms. Bernadine DOUGLAS
110 Assoc VP for Development ....Mr. Pietro BONACOSSA
32 VP Mission & Student Engagement ....Dr. Scott F. SMITH
13 VP Strategic Initiatives & CIO ....Ms. Yvette KOOTTUNGAL
43 General Counsel ....Mr. David DUDGEON
50 Dean School of Business ....Dr. Joan M. PHILLIPS
53 Dean School of Education ....Dr. Jill FARRELL
76 Dean College of Health Sciences ....Dr. John MCFADDEN
61 Dean School of Law ....Dr. Leticia M. DIAZ
63 Dean School of Podiatric Medicine ....Dr. Bryan CALDWELL
20 Associate Vice Provost ....Dr. Victor ROMANO
70 Dean School of Social Work ....Dr. Phyllis SCOTT
35 Associate VP & Dean of Students ....Dr. Maria L. ALVAREZ
29 Assoc VP Alum Rels & Annual Giving ....Vacant
84 Assoc Vice Pres Recruit & Admission ....Ms. Roxanna CRUZ
26 Associate VP Marketing ....Mr. Michel SILY
19 Director Public Safety & Emerg Mgt ....Mr. John BUHRMASTER
42 Chaplain ....Fr. Cristobal TORRES
06 University Registrar ....Ms. Viviana CARABANNA
39 Director Housing and Residence Life ....Mr. Matthew R. CAMERON
36 Director Career Services ....Mr. John MORIARTY
37 Director Financial Aid ....Mrs. Aida CLARO
92 Director Honors Program ....Dr. Pawena SIRIMANGKALA
38 Director Student Counseling Center ....Dr. Hossiella LONGORIA
123 Director of Graduate Admission ....Ms. Betsy THOMAS
09 Director Institutional Research ....Ms. Shaunette GRANT
41 Director of Athletics ....Mr. Michael COVONE
102 Dir Foundation Rels & Major Gifts ....Mr. Frank SAAVEDRA
27 Dir Marketing Product Dev & Design ....Mr. Miguel RAMIREZ
109 Dir Student Union & Food Services ....Mr. Mickie VOUTSINAS
25 Director Grant & Sponsored Programs ....Ms. Michelle GOODING
40 Manager Bookstore ....Mr. Jean REYES
96 Dir Procurement & Accounts Payable ....Ms. Brooke PALLOT
18 Director Facilities Management ....Mr. Raul GONZALEZ
44 Director Annual Giving ....Mr. Anthony DICKEY

Beacon College (B)

105 E Main Street, Leesburg FL 34748-5162
County: Lake FICE Identification: 033733
Unit ID: 384254
Telephone: (352) 787-7660 Carnegie Class: Bac-Diverse
FAX Number: (352) 787-0721 Calendar System: Semester
URL: www.beaconcollege.edu
Established: 1989 Annual Undergrad Tuition & Fees: $42,900
Enrollment: 427 Coed
Affiliation or Control: Independent Non-Profit IRS Status: 501(c)3
Highest Offering: Baccalaureate
Accreditation: SC

01 President ....Dr. George J. HAGERTY
00 Chairman of the Board of Trustees ....Dr. Daniel H. AVERBECK
05 Provost ....Dr. Shelly CHANDLER
111 VP for Institutional Advancement ....Mr. Richard KILLION
10 Chief Financial Officer ....Ms. Sandi RYSELL
84 VP of Enrollment Management ....Ms. Dale HEROLD
06 Registrar ....Ms. Carrie SANTAW
18 Director of Facilities ....Mr. David O'BRIEN
37 Dir Enroll Svcs & Financial Aid ....Ms. Stephanie KNIGHT
08 Director of Library Resources ....Ms. Gretchen DREIMILLER
13 Director of Information Technology ....Mr. Mac HUDSON
04 Exec Assistant to the President ....Ms. Tamara SYNDER
15 Director of Human Resources ....Ms. Linda ALLISON
36 Career Integration Manager ....Mr. Dustin BOISE
88 Director Health Promotion Svcs ....Ms. Tekayiha COLEMAN
19 Director of Campus Safety ....Mr. Jeffrey BAIRD
39 Director Student Housing ....Ms. Tanisha MCINTOSH

38 Dean Wellness/Student Dev ....Ms. Dana MANZO
44 Director Annual Giving ....Ms. Keri Jo PANNELLA
121 Dean Center for Student Success ....Dr. Oksana HAGERTY
07 Assoc VP Transition ....Mr. Alex MORRIS-WOOD
104 Consultant International Programs ....Dr. Andrea BRODE
11 Chief Operating Officer ....Dr. Brian BETIT
26 Assoc VP Communications ....Mr. Darryl OWENS
41 Director of Fitness & Athletics ....Mr. Gabe WATSON

Bethesda College of Health Sciences (C)

3800 S Congress Avenue, Suite 9,
Boynton Beach FL 33426
County: Palm Beach Identification: 667258
Telephone: (561) 364-3064 Carnegie Class: Not Classified
FAX Number: (561) 364-3059 Calendar System: Semester
URL: www.bethesdacollege.net
Established: 2011 Annual Undergrad Tuition & Fees: N/A
Enrollment: N/A Coed
Affiliation or Control: Independent Non-Profit IRS Status: 501(c)3
Highest Offering: Associate Degree
Accreditation: ACICS, ADNUR, RAD

01 Dean ....Jacqueline MARSHALL

Bethune Cookman University (D)

640 Dr. Mary McLeod Bethune Blvd,
Daytona Beach FL 32114-3099
County: Volusia FICE Identification: 001467
Unit ID: 132602
Telephone: (386) 481-2000 Carnegie Class: Bac-A&S
FAX Number: (386) 481-2010 Calendar System: Semester
URL: www.cookman.edu
Established: 1904 Annual Undergrad Tuition & Fees: $14,794
Enrollment: 2,845 Coed
Affiliation or Control: United Methodist IRS Status: 501(c)3
Highest Offering: Master's
Accreditation: SC, ACBSP, ACPHA, CAATE, CAEP, MUS, NUR, PH

01 Interim President ....Dr. Lawrence DRAKE
00 Chair Board of Trustees ....Mr. Belvin PERRY
03 Executive VP/Chief Innovation Ofcr ....Dr. Karen BEARDEN
10 CFO/VP for Businessl Affairs ....Vacant
05 SVP for Academic Affairs/Provost ....Dr. William BERRY
32 VP for Student Affairs ....Vacant
84 VP for Enrollment Mgmt/Stdnt Exp ....Mr. Anthony JONES
111 VP for Institutional Advancement ....Mrs. Sherry PARAMORE
13 CIO/VP for Information Technology ....Dr. Franklin E. PATTERSON
41 Director Intercollegiate Athletics ....Mr. Reggie THEUS
43 General Counsel ....Ms. Valencia GALLON-STUBBS
25 Director of Sponsored Research ....Ms. Chelsea WASHINGTON
50 Dean College of Business ....Dr. Lawrence DRAKE
49 Dean College of Arts & Humanities ....Dr. Jan BOULWARE
66 Dean School of Nursing & Health Sci ....Dr. Sandra TUCKER
81 Dean Science/Engineering and Math ....Dr. Herbert THOMPSON
08 Dean of the Library/Chief Librarian ....Dr. Tasha LUCAS-YOUMANS
19 Exec Director Campus Safety ....Mr. Gary PRICE
07 Dir Admissions & Recruitment ....Mr. Billy (Malik) DAJUSTE
04 Executive Asst to the President ....Ms. Fanita KIRKLAND LEWIS
37 Associate Director of Financial Aid ....Mr. Kevin MCCRARY
91 Director of Administrative Systems ....Ms. Anna HEIN
06 Registrar Director ....Ms. Tanya CRUMP-DICKENS
15 Exec Director of Human Resources ....Dr. Arlesia WELCH
42 Chaplain ....Rev. Kenya LOVELL
36 Director of Career Development ....Ms. Davita BONNER
26 Dir of Marketing & Communications ....Ms. Karen PARKS
88 Director of Testing ....Mr. James LAI
105 Director Web & Digital Strategies ....Mr. Robert TURNER
29 Exec Director Alumni Affairs ....Ms. Kimberly WOODARD
33 Dir Male Development Initiatives ....Mr. Jermaine MCKINNEY
121 Exec Dir Student Success/Retention ....Dr. Joan BROWNE
113 Director Student Accounts ....Mr. John MOETZ
108 Director Institutional Assessment ....Mrs. Jennifer DASH
09 Director of Institutional Research ....Ms. Sajida BARMEDA
122 Coord Stdnt Act/Orgs-Greek Life ....Ms. Cynthia B. GRAY

Braxton College (E)

27975 Old 41 Road, Suite 201, Bonita Springs FL 34135
County: Lee Identification: 667266
Telephone: (239) 992-4624 Carnegie Class: Not Classified
FAX Number: (239) 405-8024 Calendar System: Semester
URL: www.braxton.edu
Established: 2008 Annual Undergrad Tuition & Fees: N/A
Enrollment: N/A Coed
Affiliation or Control: Proprietary IRS Status: Proprietary
Highest Offering: Baccalaureate
Accreditation: ABHES

01 Medical Director/Founder ....Dr. Antonio GANDIA
05 Vice President of Academics ....Mr. Bill MCGRATH
07 VP Admissions & Compliance ....Mr. Richard GONZALEZ
13 Director of Information Technology ....Mr. Freddie BATISTA

Broward College (F)

111 E Las Olas Boulevard,
Fort Lauderdale FL 33301-2298
County: Broward FICE Identification: 001500
Unit ID: 132709
Telephone: (954) 201-7350 Carnegie Class: Bac/Assoc-Assoc Dom
FAX Number: (954) 201-7576 Calendar System: Trimester
URL: www.broward.edu
Established: 1959 Annual Undergrad Tuition & Fees (In-State): $2,830
Enrollment: 33,243 Coed
Affiliation or Control: State IRS Status: 501(c)3
Highest Offering: Baccalaureate
Accreditation: SC, ADNUR, ART, CAHIIM, COARC, DA, DH, DMS, EMT, MUS, NMT, NURSE, OPD, PTAA, RAD, RTT, THEA

01 President ....Mr. Gregory Adam HAILE
05 Provost/SVP Academic Affs ....Dr. Jeffrey NASSE
11 Sr Vice Pres Finance/Operations ....Mr. John DUNNUCK
32 Vice Provost Student Services ....Ms. Janice STUBBS
26 VP Communications & Cmty Relations ....Ms. Isabel GONZALEZ
10 Vice President Finance ....Mr. Caleb CORNELIUS
111 VP Advancement/Exec Dir Foundation ....Ms. Nancy R. BOTERO
13 VP Information Technology ....Mr. Tony CASCIOTTA
86 VP Policy/Govt Affairs/Gen Counsel ....Ms. Lacey HOFMEYER
103 Sr VP Workforce Development ....Dr. Mildred COYNE
100 Chief of Staff ....Ms. Isabel GONZALEZ
12 Campus President North Campus ....Dr. Sunem BEATON-GARCIA
12 Campus President Central Campus ....Dr. Stephen DUNNIVANT
12 Interim Campus Pres South Campus ....Dr. Sunem BEATON-GARCIA
18 Interim AVP Facilities ....Mr. Marcus WILSON
09 Chief Data Officer ....Vacant
45 AVP Inst Planning/Effectiveness ....Ms. Renee LAW
08 Dean of Libraries/ASCs ....Dr. Monique BLAKE
37 Asst Director Financial Aid ....Ms. Celestine HUNTLEY
15 Vice President Talent/Culture ....Ms. Sophia GALVIN
06 Registrar/AVP Academic Affairs ....Ms. Karen LEE MURPHY
29 Alumni Engagement/Maj Gifts Officer ....Ms. Jill HOROWITZ
04 Sr Exec Asst to the President ....Ms. Marisol CORTEZ-DIAZ
19 AVP Security/Safety ....Mr. Grant GUNDLE
25 Chief Contracts/Grants Admin ....Ms. Kareen TORRES
96 Director of Purchasing ....Dr. Judy SCHMELZER

Cambridge College (G)

5150 Linton Boulevard, Suite 340, Delray Beach FL 33484
County: Palm Beach FICE Identification: 040834
Unit ID: 454865
Telephone: (561) 381-4990 Carnegie Class: Spec 2-yr-Health
FAX Number: (561) 381-4992 Calendar System: Other
URL: www.cambridgehealth.edu
Established: Annual Undergrad Tuition & Fees: $14,908
Enrollment: 654 Coed
Affiliation or Control: Proprietary IRS Status: Proprietary
Highest Offering: Associate Degree
Accreditation: ABHES, DMS

01 Chancellor and CEO ....Dr. Terrence LAPIER

Cambridge Institute of Allied Health & Technology-Altamonte Springs (H)

460 E. Altamonte Drive, Third Floor,
Altamonte Springs FL 32701
County: Seminole FICE Identification: 038425
Unit ID: 446109
Telephone: (407) 265-8383 Carnegie Class: Spec 2-yr-Health
FAX Number: (407) 265-8384 Calendar System: Other
URL: www.cambridgehealth.edu
Established: Annual Undergrad Tuition & Fees: $15,330
Enrollment: 377 Coed
Affiliation or Control: Proprietary IRS Status: Proprietary
Highest Offering: Associate Degree
Accreditation: ABHES, DMS

00 President ....Dr. Terrance LAPIER
01 Campus Dean ....Gabriel GARCES
06 Registrar ....Kristie MORALES
08 Librarian Online ....Stacey CRAIN
37 Financial Aid Manager ....Monica ROBLES
36 Careers Services Director ....Theresa MANTOVANI

CBT Technology Institute (I)

8230 W. Flagler Street, Miami FL 33144
County: Miami-Dade FICE Identification: 030716
Unit ID: 417318
Telephone: (305) 273-4499 Carnegie Class: Not Classified
FAX Number: (305) 270-0779 Calendar System: Semester
URL: www.cbt.edu
Established: 1988 Annual Undergrad Tuition & Fees: N/A
Enrollment: N/A Coed
Affiliation or Control: Proprietary IRS Status: Proprietary
Highest Offering: Associate Degree
Accreditation: ACICS

00 CEO/President ....Mr. Luis LLERENA
01 Campus Director Flagler ....Ms. Yazmin PALMA
10 Finance Director/COO ....Ms. Maricel SPEZZACATENA
37 Financial Aid Director ....Mrs. Yazmin PALMA
13 Information Systems Manager ....Mr. Jorge CUBILLO
12 Campus Director Hialeah ....Ms. Alexandra RAMIREZ
05 Director of Academic Operations ....Mr. Hector DUENAS
07 Director of Admissions ....Mr. Ramani NICOLA

Center of Cinematography, Art & Television (A)

1637 NW 27th Avenue, Miami FL 33125
Telephone: (305) 634-0550 Identification: 770562
Accreditation: ACCSC

† Branch campus of Colegio de Cinematografia, Artes y Television, Bayamon, PR

Chamberlain University-Jacksonville (B)

5200 Belfort Road, Suite 100, Jacksonville FL 32256
Telephone: (904) 251-8100 Identification: 770501
Accreditation: &HLC, NURSE

† Branch campus of Chamberlain University-Addison, Addison, IL

Chamberlain University-Miramar (C)

2300 SW 145th Avenue, Miramar FL 33027
Telephone: (954) 885-3510 Identification: 770498
Accreditation: &HLC, NURSE

† Branch campus of Chamberlain University-Addison, Addison, IL

Chi University (D)

9650 West Highway 318, Reddick FL 32686
County: Marion Identification: 667354
Telephone: (352) 591-5385 Carnegie Class: Not Classified
FAX Number: (844) 873-2868 Calendar System: Other
URL: www.chiu.edu
Established: 1998 Annual Graduate Tuition & Fees: N/A
Enrollment: N/A Coed
Affiliation or Control: Proprietary IRS Status: Proprietary
Highest Offering: Master's; No Undergraduates
Accreditation: DEAC

01 President ... Dr. Huisheng XIE
03 Executive VP/Campus Director ... Mr. Zhen ZHAO
10 VP Finance ... Ms. Yanru ZHAO
05 Provost ... Dr. Lisa TREVISANELLO

Chipola College (E)

3094 Indian Circle, Marianna FL 32446-3065
County: Jackson FICE Identification: 001472
Unit ID: 133021
Telephone: (850) 526-2761 Carnegie Class: Bac/Assoc-Mixed
FAX Number: (850) 718-2388 Calendar System: Semester
URL: www.chipola.edu
Established: 1947 Annual Undergrad Tuition & Fees (In-District): $3,120
Enrollment: 1,943 Coed
Affiliation or Control: State/Local IRS Status: 501(c)3
Highest Offering: Baccalaureate
Accreditation: SC, ADNUR, EMT, NUR

01 President ... Dr. Sarah CLEMMONS
05 VP of Instructional Affairs ... Dr. Pam RENTZ
10 Vice Pres of Admin & Business Svcs ... Mr. Steve YOUNG
15 Assoc VP of HR/Equity/Title IX ... Mrs. Wendy PIPPEN
13 Associate VP Information Systems ... Mr. Dennis F. EVERETT
32 Assoc VP of Student Affairs ... Ms. Bonnie SMITH
108 Dean Assessment/Compliance & Grant ... Dr. Matthew HUGHES
18 Dir Facilities & Campus Operations ... Mr. Dennis KOSCIW
26 Director Public Relations ... Dr. Bryan C. CRAVEN
07 Dir of Enrollment Services ... Mr. Shannon MERCER
37 Director of Financial Aid ... Ms. Beverly HAMBRIGHT
41 Director of Athletics ... Mr. Jeff JOHNSON
06 Registrar ... Ms. Ashley HARVEY
04 Executive Assistant ... Ms. Jan CUMMINGS
103 Dean Workforce/Economic Development ... Mr. Darwin GILMORE
08 Dir of Learning Resources ... Ms. Vikki MILTON
102 Dir Found/Corporate Relations ... Ms. Julie FUQUA
50 Dean School of Business/Tech ... Dr. David BOUVIN
53 Dean School of Education ... Dr. Gina MCALLISTER
101 Secretary of the Institution/Board ... Dr. Sarah CLEMMONS
91 AVP Administrative Computing ... Mr. Dennis EVERETT

City College (F)

177 Montgomery Road, Altamonte Springs FL 32714
County: Seminole FICE Identification: 030799
Unit ID: 417327
Telephone: (407) 831-9816 Carnegie Class: Spec 2-yr-Health
FAX Number: (407) 831-1147 Calendar System: Quarter
URL: https://www.citycollege.edu/locations/altamonte-springs-orla
Established: 1997 Annual Undergrad Tuition & Fees: $15,056
Enrollment: 242 Coed
Affiliation or Control: Independent Non-Profit IRS Status: 501(c)3
Highest Offering: Associate Degree
Accreditation: ABHES, ADNUR, EMT, SURTEC

00 President ... Mrs. Esther FIKE-CURRY
02 Campus Director ... Mr. LeShawn ROBERTS

City College (G)

6565 Taft Street, Hollywood FL 33024
County: Broward FICE Identification: 025154
Unit ID: 244233
Telephone: (954) 744-1777 Carnegie Class: Bac/Assoc-Mixed
FAX Number: (954) 983-0118 Calendar System: Quarter
URL: www.citycollege.edu
Established: 1983 Annual Undergrad Tuition & Fees: $14,876
Enrollment: 297 Coed
Affiliation or Control: Independent Non-Profit IRS Status: 501(c)3
Highest Offering: Baccalaureate
Accreditation: ABHES, EMT, SURTEC

01 President ... R. Esther CURRY
05 Director of Academic Affairs ... Dr. Joseph CAPEBIANCO
36 Director of Career Development ... Vacant
07 Director of Admissions ... Stacey KRAHE
13 Director Information Technology ... Alan BUSHKIN
08 Director of Library ... Cathy DIETERLY
06 Registrar ... Michelle SANCHEZ
15 Director Human Resources ... Natasga GROYSMAN
37 Asst Director Student Financial Aid ... Patty PATTERSON
106 Dir Online Education/E-learning ... Dr. Suzanne MORRISON-WILLAIMS
108 Dir Institutional Effectiveness ... Heather PAYNE
18 Director of Facilities ... Donna VARELA

City College (H)

7001 NW Fourth Boulevard, Gainesville FL 32607
Telephone: (352) 415-4497 Identification: 666413
Accreditation: ABHES, EMT

† Branch campus of City College, Hollywood, FL.

City College (I)

9250 W Flagler Street, Miami FL 33174
Telephone: (305) 666-9242 Identification: 666414
Accreditation: ABHES, AT, EMT, SURTEC

† Branch campus of City College, Hollywood, FL.

College of Business and Technology - Cutler Bay (J)

19151 South Dixie Highway, Ste 205, Cutler Bay FL 33157
Telephone: (786) 693-8801 Identification: 770677
Accreditation: ACICS

College of Business and Technology - Hialeah Campus (K)

935 West 49th Street, Suite 203, Hialeah FL 33012
Telephone: (305) 273-4499 Identification: 770675
Accreditation: ACICS

College of Central Florida (L)

3001 S.W. College Road, Ocala FL 34474
County: Marion FICE Identification: 001471
Unit ID: 132851
Telephone: (352) 237-2111 Carnegie Class: Bac/Assoc-Mixed
FAX Number: (352) 291-4450 Calendar System: Semester
URL: www.cf.edu
Established: 1957 Annual Undergrad Tuition & Fees (In-District): $2,710
Enrollment: 6,150 Coed
Affiliation or Control: Local IRS Status: 501(c)3
Highest Offering: Baccalaureate
Accreditation: SC, ADNUR, CAHIIM, DA, EMT, NUR, PTAA, RAD, SURGT

01 President ... Dr. James D. HENNINGSEN
10 Vice Pres Administration & Finance ... Mr. Charles PRINCE
05 Vice President Academic Affairs ... Dr. Mark PAUGH
32 Vice President Student Affairs ... Dr. Saul REYES
12 Vice President Regional Campuses ... Dr. Vernon LAWTER, JR.
86 Director Government Relations ... Ms. Sara FENNESSY
09 VP Inst Effectiveness/College Rels ... Dr. Jillian RAMSAMMY
26 Director Marketing/Public Relations .. Ms. Lois BRAUCKMULLER
102 VP Development/CEO Foundation ... Mr. Christopher KNIFE
21 Assistant VP for Finance ... Mr. Steven ASH
12 Provost Jack Wilkinson Levy Campus . Ms. Holland MCGLASHAN
80 Dean Public Service/Criminal Just ... Mr. Charles MCINTOSH
75 Dean Bus Tech Careers & Tech Educ ... Dr. Rob WOLF
35 Dean Student Services ... Dr. Henri BENLOLO
49 Associate Vice Pres Arts & Sciences ... Dr. Allan DANUFF
121 Director Advising & Stdnt Success ... Ms. Chenita HART
103 Assoc Vice Pres Career & Prof Pgms ... Dr. Jennifer FRYNS
76 Dean Health Sciences ... Dr. Stephanie CORTES
106 Dean E-learning & Learning Resource ... Dr. Tamara VIVIANO-BRODERICK
37 Director Financial Aid ... Ms. Jean IMES
09 Dir Inst Research & Effectiveness ... Ms. Judy MENADIER
07 Dir Admissions/Stdnt Recruitment ... Dr. Raphel ROBINSON
18 Manager of Plant Operations ... Ms. Katherine HUNT
15 Director Human Resources ... Ms. Jennifer KLEPFER
35 Director Student Life ... Ms. Marjorie MCGEE
88 Director Student Support Services ... Dr. Lisa SMITH
41 Manager Athletics ... Mr. Marty SMITH
22 Director Access and Counsel Service ... Ms. Cindy PFRIENDER
88 Dir Stdnt Success & Educ Outreach ... Dr. Leonard EVERETT
88 Director Appleton Museum of Art ... Mr. Jason STEUBER
25 Director of Resource Dev/Accred ... Mr. Matt MATTHEWS
96 Dir Purchasing & Risk Mgmt ... Mr. Stewart TRAUTMAN
08 Library Director ... Vacant
19 Manager Public Safety ... Mr. Mickey GUERIN
109 Manager Printing & Postal Service ... Ms. Alivia GIBSON
109 Manager Conference & Food Service ... Ms. Cheryl CROSBY
13 Associate VP Information Technology ... Mr. Ron KIELTY
06 Director Enroll Services/Registrar ... Dr. Alton AUSTIN
30 Director of Development ... Ms. Traci MASON
28 Director of Diversity & Inclusion ... Dr. Mary Ann BEGLEY
100 Manager Office of the President ... Ms. Erin CARTER

The College of the Florida Keys (M)

5901 College Road, Key West FL 33040-4397
County: Monroe FICE Identification: 001485
Unit ID: 133960
Telephone: (305) 296-9081 Carnegie Class: Bac/Assoc-Assoc Dom
FAX Number: (305) 292-5155 Calendar System: Trimester
URL: www.cfk.edu
Established: 1963 Annual Undergrad Tuition & Fees (In-District): $3,276
Enrollment: 856 Coed
Affiliation or Control: State/Local IRS Status: 501(c)3
Highest Offering: Baccalaureate
Accreditation: SC, ADNUR

01 President ... Dr. Jonathan GUEVERRA
05 Vice President Academic Affairs ... Mrs. Brittany SYNDER
10 Vice Pres Business & Admin Svcs ... Vacant
111 Vice President Advancement ... Dr. Frank WOOD
84 Assoc Dean Enrollment Mgmt ... Mrs. Kathleen CLARK
19 Dir Institute for Public Safety ... Mrs. Cathy TORRES
04 Director President's Office ... Ms. Rachel OROPEZA
26 Dir Marketing and Public Relations ... Mrs. Amber ERNST-LEONARD
06 Registrar ... Mrs. Kathleen CLARK
08 Director Learning Resources ... Ms. Kristina NEIHOUSE
37 Director Financial Aid ... Mr. Jeffrey SMITH
18 Dir Purchasing & Plant Operations ... Mr. Greg O'FLYNN
13 Director of IT ... Vacant
15 Director Human Resources ... Mrs. Beren LINDENBERG
21 Controller ... Ms. Heather GARCIA
09 Director Institutional Research ... Vacant
81 Dean of Science & Nursing ... Mr. Mark ROBY
50 Dean Business and Marine Science ... Mr. Jack SUEBERT
49 Dean Arts & Sciences ... Mr. Michael MCPHERSON

Concorde Career Institute (N)

7259 Salisbury Road, Jacksonville FL 32256
County: Duval FICE Identification: 020896
Unit ID: 133845
Telephone: (904) 725-0525 Carnegie Class: Spec 2-yr-Health
FAX Number: (904) 721-9944 Calendar System: Semester
URL: https://www.concorde.edu/campus/jacksonville-florida
Established: 1988 Annual Undergrad Tuition & Fees: N/A
Enrollment: 555 Coed
Affiliation or Control: Proprietary IRS Status: Proprietary
Highest Offering: Associate Degree
Accreditation: ACCSC, COARC, PTAA, SURGT

01 Campus President ... Ned SNYDER, JR.
07 Director of Admissions ... Lee KELLY

Concorde Career Institute (O)

10933 Marks Way, Miramar FL 33025
County: Broward FICE Identification: 022751
Unit ID: 133854
Telephone: (954) 731-8880 Carnegie Class: Spec 2-yr-Health
FAX Number: (954) 484-2961 Calendar System: Other
URL: https://www.concorde.edu/campus/miramar-florida
Established: 1989 Annual Undergrad Tuition & Fees: N/A
Enrollment: 434 Coed
Affiliation or Control: Proprietary IRS Status: Proprietary
Highest Offering: Associate Degree
Accreditation: ACCSC, COARC, OTA, PTAA, SURGT

01 Campus President ... Robert BURNFIELD
07 Director of Admissions ... Brandon PAUL

Concorde Career Institute (P)

3444 McCrory Place, Orlando FL 32803
Telephone: (407) 812-3060 Identification: 770563
Accreditation: ACCSC, DH, SURGT

Concorde Career Institute (Q)

4202 West Spruce Street, Tampa FL 33607-4127
County: Hillsborough FICE Identification: 021727
Unit ID: 133863
Telephone: (813) 874-0094 Carnegie Class: Spec 2-yr-Health
FAX Number: (813) 872-6884 Calendar System: Other
URL: https://www.concorde.edu/campus/tampa-florida
Established: 1978 Annual Undergrad Tuition & Fees: N/A
Enrollment: 405 Coed
Affiliation or Control: Proprietary IRS Status: Proprietary
Highest Offering: Associate Degree
Accreditation: ACCSC, COARC, DH, DMS, SURGT

01 Campus President ... Ms. Debra WENINGER

Daytona College (R)

425 South Nova Road, Ormond Beach FL 32174-8449
County: Volusia FICE Identification: 039396
Unit ID: 447014
Telephone: (386) 267-0565 Carnegie Class: Spec 2-yr-Health

FAX Number: (386) 267-0567 | Calendar System: Semester
URL: www.daytonacollege.edu
Established: 1996 | Annual Undergrad Tuition & Fees: N/A
Enrollment: 236 | Coed
Affiliation or Control: Proprietary | IRS Status: Proprietary
Highest Offering: Baccalaureate
Accreditation: ACCSC, ADNUR

01 President/CEO .... Mr. Roger BRADLEY
05 Director of Education .... Dr. Khaliff ALI

Daytona State College (A)

PO Box 2811, Daytona Beach FL 32120-2811
County: Volusia | FICE Identification: 001475
Unit ID: 133386
Telephone: (386) 506-3000 | Carnegie Class: Bac/Assoc-Mixed
FAX Number: N/A | Calendar System: Semester
URL: www.DaytonaState.edu
Established: 1957 | Annual Undergrad Tuition & Fees (In-District): $3,106
Enrollment: 12,728 | Coed
Affiliation or Control: State/Local | IRS Status: 501(c)3
Highest Offering: Baccalaureate
Accreditation: SC, ADNUR, COARC, DA, DH, EMT, MAC, NUR, OTA, PTAA, RAD, SURGT

01 President .... Dr. Thomas LOBASSO
03 Executive Vice President .... Mr. Brian T. BABB
05 Provost .... Dr. Amy LOCKLEAR
10 VP Finance/Chief Business Officer .... Mr. Martin CASS
13 SVP Information Technology .... Mr. Roberto LOMBARDO
84 VP Enrollment Services .... Dr. Erik D'AQUINO
32 VP Student Development .... Ms. Cerese RAMOS
111 VP Advancement/Exec Dir Foundation .... Mr. Timothy NORTON
15 AVP Human Resources .... Ms. Robin BARR
103 AVP Workforce & Cont Educ .... Dr. Sherryl WEEMS
08 Head Librarian .... Ms. Mercedes CLEMENT
49 AVP Arts & Science .... Dr. Alycia EHLERT
76 AVP College of Health .... Dr. Colin CHESLEY
18 AVP Facilities Planning .... Mr. Christopher WAINWRIGHT
21 AVP Finance/Controller .... Ms. Tina MYERS
50 AVP Business/Engr & Tech .... Mr. Dante LEON
106 Director Instructional Resources .... Mr. Hector VALLE
09 Dir Institutional Research .... Dr. Andrea GIBSON
37 Director Financial Aid .... Ms. Heidi PINNEY
69 Int Dean School Health & Wellness .... Mr. Will DUNN
19 Director Campus Safety .... Mr. Paul BARNETT
12 Dean DeLand & Deltona Campuses .... Mr. Neil CLEMONS
12 Dean New Smyrna Beach Campus .... Mr. Clarence MCCLOUD
43 General Counsel .... Mr. Brian BABB
51 Director Ctr for Business/Industry .... Mr. Frank MERCER
35 Director Student Life .... Mr. Elijah HOUSER
121 Director Academic Advising .... Ms. Michelle GOLDYS
07 Director Admissions/Recruitment .... Ms. Karen SANDERS
22 Director of Equity & Inclusion .... Ms. Tanika CLEMONS
06 Director of Records/Registrar .... Ms. Carri BLACK HUDGINS
113 Director Student Accounts .... Ms. Cerese RAMOS
26 Director of Marketing .... Mr. Chris THOMES
09 Dean Institutional Effectiveness .... Ms. Alicia ALEXANDER
29 Director Alumni Relations .... Ms. Kristen HANSON
96 Exec Director of Business Services .... Ms. Elaine THIEL

Dolphin Research Center Training Institute (B)

58901 Overseas Hwy, Grassy Key FL 33050
County: Monroe | Identification: 667338
Telephone: (305) 289-1121 | Carnegie Class: Not Classified
FAX Number: N/A | Calendar System: Quarter
URL: https://dolphins.org/drcti
Established: 2012 | Annual Undergrad Tuition & Fees: N/A
Enrollment: N/A | Coed
Affiliation or Control: Independent Non-Profit | IRS Status: 501(c)3
Highest Offering: Associate Degree
Accreditation: ACCSC

01 President & CEO .... Rita IRWIN
05 Director .... Linda ERB
06 Registration/Enrollment Coordinator .... Allie PROSKOVEC
88 Licensing & Accreditation .... Deborah HUCKABEE
04 Admin Assistant to the President .... Amy BAYER
10 VP Finance/Chief Financial Officer .... Peggy MCGILL

Doral College (C)

PO Box 227368, Miami FL 33222
County: Miami-Dade | Identification: 667335
Telephone: (305) 463-7210 | Carnegie Class: Not Classified
FAX Number: (305) 477-3525 | Calendar System: Semester
URL: www.doral.edu
Established: 2011 | Annual Undergrad Tuition & Fees: N/A
Enrollment: N/A | Coed
Affiliation or Control: Independent Non-Profit | IRS Status: 501(c)3
Highest Offering: Baccalaureate
Accreditation: DEAC

01 President .... Judith MARTY
05 VP for Academic Affairs .... Guillermo RIVERA
32 VP for Student Affairs/Registrar .... Cristina GUERRA ROMERO
10 VP for Financial Affairs .... Manny DIAZ
15 Director of Human Resources .... Lisset YANES

Dragon Rises College of Oriental Medicine (D)

1000 NE 16th Ave., Building F, Gainesville FL 32601-4557
County: Alachua | FICE Identification: 038883
Unit ID: 449481
Telephone: (352) 371-2833 | Carnegie Class: Spec-4-yr-Other Health
FAX Number: (352) 244-0003 | Calendar System: Semester
URL: www.dragonrises.edu
Established: 2001 | Annual Undergrad Tuition & Fees: N/A
Enrollment: 42 | Coed
Affiliation or Control: Independent Non-Profit | IRS Status: 501(c)3
Highest Offering: Master's
Accreditation: ACUP

01 Director/CEO .... Ms. Karen MARTIN-BROWN
05 Academic Dean .... Dr. Eduardo ALVAREZ
07 Director of Admissions .... Ms. Christina MCNIEL
08 Chief Library Officer .... Mr. Daniel HORAK
13 Chief Information Technology Office .... Mr. Brandon WEINTRAUB

East West College of Natural Medicine (E)

3808 N Tamiami Trail, Sarasota FL 34234-5362
County: Sarasota | FICE Identification: 034297
Unit ID: 439394
Telephone: (941) 355-9080 | Carnegie Class: Spec-4-yr-Other Health
FAX Number: (941) 355-3243 | Calendar System: Trimester
URL: www.ewcollege.edu
Established: 1994 | Annual Undergrad Tuition & Fees: N/A
Enrollment: 79 | Coed
Affiliation or Control: Proprietary | IRS Status: Proprietary
Highest Offering: Master's
Accreditation: ACCSC, ACUP

01 President .... Dr. Yoseph FELEKE
05 VP/Academic Dean .... Dr. Hailin WU
07 Director of Admissions/Career Svcs .... Ms. Sherry INGBRITSEN

Eastern Florida State College (F)

3865 N. Wickham Road, Melbourne FL 32935
County: Brevard | FICE Identification: 001470
Unit ID: 132693
Telephone: (321) 632-1111 | Carnegie Class: Bac/Assoc-Mixed
FAX Number: (321) 633-4565 | Calendar System: Semester
URL: www.easternflorida.edu
Established: 1960 | Annual Undergrad Tuition & Fees (In-District): $2,496
Enrollment: 13,937 | Coed
Affiliation or Control: Local | IRS Status: 501(c)3
Highest Offering: Baccalaureate
Accreditation: SC, ADNUR, #COARC, DA, DH, DMS, EMT, MLTAD, NURSE, PTAA, RAD, SURGT

01 President .... Dr. James H. RICHEY
10 VP Operations/Chief Financial Ofcr .... Mr. Mark CHERRY
05 VP Academic & Student Affairs/CLO .... Dr. Randy FLETCHER
41 Assoc Vice Pres of Athletics .... Mr. Jeffrey CARR
18 AVP Facilities & Special Projects .... Mr. Stockton WHITTEN
15 AVP Human Resources .... Ms. Darla FERGUSON
20 AVP Academic Affairs .... Dr. Sandy HANDFIELD
32 AVP Student Affairs .... Dr. Laura SIDORAN
86 VP External Affairs .... Mr. Jack PARKER
26 AVP Communications .... Mr. John GLISCH
12 Provost Palm Bay Campus .... Dr. Wayne STEIN
12 Provost Cocoa Campus .... Dr. Dedra SIBLEY
12 Provost Titusville Campus/eLearning .... Dr. Philip SIMPSON
103 Executive Director Workforce Pgms .... Mr. Stephen TAYLOR
37 Director Collegewide Financial Aid .... Ms. Eileen BRZOZOWSKI
84 Dean Enrollment Mgmt .... Ms. Michelle LOUFEK
04 Executive Asst to the President .... Ms. Gina TAYLOR
06 Registrar .... Vacant
09 Exe Dir Plng/Assessment/CIRO .... Dr. Mark QUATHAMER
102 Director EFSC Foundation .... Vacant
36 Exec Dir Career Plng/Development .... Dr. Cathy CADY
13 Chief Information Technology Officer .... Mr. Bill WHITE
19 Director Security/Safety .... Mr. Joe AMBROSE
29 Director Alumni Affairs .... Ms. Tonya CHERRY
39 Dir Resident Life/Student Housing .... Ms. Lena COPELAND

Eckerd College (G)

4200 54th Avenue S, Saint Petersburg FL 33711-4700
County: Pinellas | FICE Identification: 001487
Unit ID: 133492
Telephone: (727) 867-1166 | Carnegie Class: Bac-A&S
FAX Number: (727) 864-1877 | Calendar System: 4/1/4
URL: www.eckerd.edu
Established: 1958 | Annual Undergrad Tuition & Fees: $47,704
Enrollment: 1,822 | Coed
Affiliation or Control: Presbyterian Church (U.S.A.) | IRS Status: 501(c)3
Highest Offering: Baccalaureate
Accreditation: SC

01 President .... Dr. Damian J. FERNANDEZ
05 VP Academic Affs/Dean of Faculty .... Dr. Suzan HARRISON
10 VP Business and Finance .... Mr. Christopher P. BRENNAN
03 VP and Secretary of the College .... Dr. Lisa A. METS
111 Vice President Advancement .... Mr. Matthew S. BISSET
107 VP/Dean for Executive Education .... Mr. Kelly KIRSCHNER
32 VP Student Life/Dean of Students .... Dr. James J. ANNARELLI
84 VP Enrollment Management .... Mr. John SULLIVAN
20 Assoc Dean Faculty Development .... Dr. Kathryn J. WATSON
26 VP Marketing and Communications .... Ms. Valerie GLIEM
15 Asst VP Human Resources .... Ms. Liana HEMINGWAY
09 Exec Director Inst Effectiveness .... Ms. Jacqueline MACNEIL
21 AVP/Controller .... Ms. Robin REMLEY
20 Assoc Dean/Exec Dir Acad Excellence .... Dr. Marjorie SANFILIPPO
110 Assoc VP Advancement .... Mr. Tom SCHNEIDER
11 Assistant VP Operations .... Mr. Adam COLBY
105 Dir Web/Marketing/Communication .... Mr. Michel FOUGERES
88 Director of ASPEC .... Mr. Ken WOLFE
104 Director of International Education .... Vacant
85 Dir International Student Programs .... Mr. Olivier DEBURE
13 Director of Information Technology .... Mr. Ashley BURT
06 Registrar .... Vacant
08 Director of Library .... Ms. Lisa JOHNSTON
38 Exec Director Counseling & Outreach .... Ms. Linda ABBOTT
29 Director Alumni Engagement .... Ms. Kyla SMITH
19 Director Campus Safety .... Ms. Tonya WOMACK
37 Director Financial Aid .... Dr. Pat E. WATKINS
41 Athletics Director .... Mr. Tom RYAN
07 Director of Admission .... Mr. Jacob BROWNE
42 Chaplain .... Rev. Doug MCMAHON
25 Director of Grant Development .... Ms. Anna RUTH
124 Asst Dean Students for Engagement .... Mr. Fred SABOTA
51 Associate Dean Cont Education .... Ms. Amy APICERNO
04 Exec Asst to President .... Ms. Jolene QATATO

ECPI University College of Nursing (H)

660 Century Point, Ste 1050,
Orlando (Lake Mary) FL 32746
Telephone: (407) 562-9100 | Identification: 770566
Accreditation: &SC, NURSE, @PTAA

† Branch campus of ECPI University, Virginia Beach, VA

Edward Waters College (I)

1658 Kings Road, Jacksonville FL 32209-6199
County: Duval | FICE Identification: 001478
Unit ID: 133526
Telephone: (904) 470-8000 | Carnegie Class: Bac-Diverse
FAX Number: (904) 470-8039 | Calendar System: Semester
URL: www.ewc.edu
Established: 1866 | Annual Undergrad Tuition & Fees: $14,878
Enrollment: 2,273 | Coed
Affiliation or Control: African Methodist Episcopal | IRS Status: 501(c)3
Highest Offering: Master's
Accreditation: SC, IACBE

01 President .... Dr. A. Zachary FAISON, JR.
11 Executive Vice President/COO .... Dr. Sharron T. BURNETT
05 Provost/Sr VP Academic Affairs .... Dr. Donna H. OLIVER
10 VP Finance Admin/Bus Innovation .... Mr. Randolph MITCHELL, JR.
111 VP Inst Advance/Dev/Mktg/Comm .... Vacant
84 VP Enroll Mgt/Strat Matriculant Svc .... Dr. Jennifer PRICE
121 VP Student Success/Engagement .... Mr. Jame'l R. HODGES
15 Director Human Resources .... Ms. Carla GRAVES
09 Director Institutional Research .... Mr. Brian SEYMORE
25 Dir Title III & Sponsored Pgms .... Vacant
06 Registrar .... Ms. Detrenyona CHESTER
20 Assoc Provost Acad Stdnt Success/RI .... Dr. Stephanie CAMPBELL
37 Director Financial Aid .... Ms. Janice NOWAK
88 Director Upward Bound .... Dr. Delacy SANFORD
36 Dir Career Development/Placement .... Mr. Roderick MOZEE
07 Exec Dir Admissions/Enrollment Mgmt .... Mr. Kendrick DUNKLIN
88 Director of Support Services .... Ms. Andrea M. CUMMINGS
31 Dir Community Resource Center .... Ms. Marie HEATH
13 Director IT .... Mr. David SIMFUKWE
08 Library Director .... Ms. Brenda HARRELL
26 Marketing/Communication Manager .... Vacant
29 Director of Alumni Affairs .... Vacant
38 Director Counseling Center .... Ms. Ragan SUMMERS
32 AVP Student Success and Engagement .... Dr. Tymon GRAHAM
96 Purchasing Clerk .... Vacant
04 Admin Assistant to the President .... Mrs. Delicia GEORGE
39 Dir Resident Life/Student Housing .... Mr. Carl MATTHEWS
44 Director Annual Giving .... Ms. Nicole POWELL

Embry-Riddle Aeronautical University-Daytona Beach (J)

1 Aerospace Boulevard, Daytona Beach FL 32114-3900
County: Volusia | FICE Identification: 001479
Unit ID: 133553
Telephone: (386) 226-6000 | Carnegie Class: Masters/L
FAX Number: N/A | Calendar System: Semester
URL: www.erau.edu
Established: 1926 | Annual Undergrad Tuition & Fees: $37,964
Enrollment: 8,797 | Coed
Affiliation or Control: Independent Non-Profit | IRS Status: 501(c)3
Highest Offering: Doctorate
Accreditation: SC, AAB, ACBSP, CEA, IFSAC

01 President .... Dr. Barry BUTLER
05 SVP Academic Affairs & Provost .... Mr. Lon D. MOELLER
10 SVP for Finance and CFO .... Dr. Randy B. HOWARD
30 SVP Philanthropy/Alumni Engagement .... Vacant
15 VP/Chief Human Resources Officer .... Mr. Brandon L. YOUNG

43 Vice President & General Counsel ... Mr. Charlie W. SEVASTOS
26 Exec Dir Enrol Mktg/Digital Strat ... Mr. Tim WALSH
27 AVP News & Research ... Ms. Ginger PINHOLSTER
84 VP Enrollment Management ... Dr. Jason RUCKERT
13 Chief Information Officer ... Ms. Becky L. VASQUEZ
09 Exec Dir of Institutional Research ... Ms. Maria FRANCO
29 Exec Dir Engagement Initiatives ... Mr. William G. THOMPSON
39 Dir of Housing & Res Life ... Mr. Edward j. WALICKI
41 Director of Athletics ... Mr. John M. PHILLIPS
04 Senior Executive Asst to President ... Ms. Chantal C. CRISWELL
104 Dir Office of Global Engagement ... Mrs. Sue A. MACCHIARELLA
108 Exec Dir of Academic Assessment ... Ms. Tiffany D. PHAGAN
32 Assoc Provost and Dean of Students ... Ms. Lisa S. KOLLAR
36 Executive Director of Career Svcs ... Vacant
37 Director Student Financial Aid ... Vacant
49 Dean College of Arts & Sciences ... Dr. Peter M. HOFFMANN
88 Dean College of Aviation ... Dr. Alan J. STOLZER
50 Dean O'Maley College of Business ... Dr. Shanan GIBSON
54 Dean College of Engineering ... Dr. James W. GREGORY
08 Hunt Library Director ... Ms. Anne M. CASEY
25 Chief Contract/Grants Administrator ... Dr. Nanette GUZMAN

Embry-Riddle Aeronautical University-Worldwide (A)

1 Aerospace Boulevard, Daytona Beach FL 32114-3900
Telephone: (800) 522-6787 Identification: 666089
Accreditation: &SC, AAB, ACBSP

† Regional accreditation is carried under the parent institution in Daytona Beach, FL.

Emergency Educational Institute (B)

3111 N. University Dr., Ste 300, Coral Springs FL 33065
County: Broward Identification: 667310
Telephone: (954) 753-6869 Carnegie Class: Not Classified
FAX Number: (954) 755-9050 Calendar System: Other
URL: www.eei.edu
Established: 2002 Annual Undergrad Tuition & Fees: N/A
Enrollment: N/A Coed
Affiliation or Control: Proprietary IRS Status: Proprietary
Highest Offering: Associate Degree
Accreditation: ABHES

01 CEO/Owner ... Michelle UGALDE
05 EMS Medical Director ... Antonio GANDIA

Everglades University (C)

5002 T-Rex Avenue, Suite 100,
Boca Raton FL 33431-4493
County: Palm Beach FICE Identification: 031085
Unit ID: 385619
Telephone: (888) 772-6077 Carnegie Class: Masters/S
FAX Number: (561) 912-1191 Calendar System: Semester
URL: www.evergladesuniversity.edu
Established: 1990 Annual Undergrad Tuition & Fees: $18,320
Enrollment: 2,247 Coed
Affiliation or Control: Independent Non-Profit IRS Status: 501(c)3
Highest Offering: Master's
Accreditation: SC

01 President/CEO ... Ms. Kristi L. MOLLIS
20 Curriculum and Faculty Developer ... Dr. Kimberly PAVLIK
12 Vice President Boca Raton Campus ... Mr. Mikkel DIXON
12 Vice President Miami Campus ... Ms. Debra COHEN
12 Vice President Orlando Campus ... Mrs. Charlene PURTLEBAUGH
12 Vice President Sarasota Campus ... Ms. Caroline KING
12 Vice President Tampa Campus ... Ms. Dina SIGANOS
12 Vice President Online Division ... Mr. Jeffrey DAY
05 Vice President of Academic Affairs ... Mr. Jared BEZET
37 Regional Director of Financial Aid ... Mrs. Seeta SINGH MOONILALL
10 Chief Financial Officer ... Mr. Joseph BERARDINELLI
26 Director of Marketing ... Ms. Kristi L. MOLLIS
84 Regional Dir Enrollment Management ... Mr. Ryan HEINTZ
09 Director of Inst Effectiveness ... Mr. Paul CASTELLANO
08 Director of Library ... Mr. James EVANS
04 Executive Asst to the President ... Mrs. Dawn YAP
88 Director of Military Affairs ... Mr. Dale TOWERY

Flagler College (D)

74 King Street, Saint Augustine FL 32084-4342
County: Saint Johns FICE Identification: 007893
Unit ID: 133711
Telephone: (904) 819-6200 Carnegie Class: Bac-Diverse
FAX Number: (904) 824-6017 Calendar System: Semester
URL: www.flagler.edu
Established: 1968 Annual Undergrad Tuition & Fees: $20,040
Enrollment: 2,687 Coed
Affiliation or Control: Independent Non-Profit IRS Status: 501(c)3
Highest Offering: Master's
Accreditation: SC

01 President ... Mr. John A. DELANEY
10 Interim VP Business Services & CFO ... Ms. Stacey MATTHEWS
111 VP of Institutional Advancement ... Ms. Kristina MYERS
05 Vice President Academic Affairs ... Dr. Art VANDEN HOUTEN
26 Vice Pres Marketing/Communications ... Ms. Carol BRANSON
09 Dean Inst Research & Effectiveness ... Ms. Jessica STOWELL
27 Director of Publications ... Mr. Brian L. THOMPSON
84 Vice Pres for Enrollment Mgmt ... Ms. Deborah L. THOMPSON
32 Interim VP of Student Affairs ... Mr. Everett MALCOLM
20 Dean of Academic Life ... Dr. Craig WOELFEL
35 Dean of Student Affairs ... Dr. Dirk HIBLER
38 Sr Dir for Health & Wellness ... Ms. Mary C. TINLIN
06 Registrar ... Vacant
37 Director of Financial Aid ... Ms. Sheia I. PLEASANT-DOINE
124 Dean of Student Engagement/Careers ... Ms. Tara STEVENSON
08 Director of Library Services ... Mr. Brian NESSELRODE
41 Director Intercollegiate Athletics ... Mr. Jud DAMON
19 Director of Safety & Security ... Mr. Don MCGRAN
40 Bookstore Manager ... Mr. Pete PREVITE
24 Dir of Network & Desktop Support ... Mr. William JACKSON
13 Chief Information Officer ... Ms. Gwen PECHAN
39 Dir of Res/Integrated Student Exp ... Ms. Kristina LOMBARDO
12 Dean Flagler College - Tallahassee ... Dr. Wayne RIGGS
22 Dir of Disability Services ... Mr. Phillip POWNALL
18 Superintendent of Plant & Grounds ... Mr. Victor CHENEY
100 VP/Chief of Staff ... Ms. Laura STEVENSON DUMAS
21 Director of Business Services ... Ms. Sarah PRODROMOU
29 Director of Alumni Relations ... Ms. Whitney W. SHAFER
30 Sr Director of Development ... Mr. Jeffrey DAVITT
15 VP/CHRO & DEIO ... Ms. Kelly TOASTON
88 Athletics Business Manager ... Ms. Karen HUDGINS
07 Dean of Admissions ... Ms. Rachel U. BRANCH
104 Director of the International Ctr ... Ms. Ashley SIMMONS COFFEY
105 Sr Dir Mktg/Comm/Brand Strategy ... Ms. Holly L. HILL
106 Dir Online Education & Inst Design ... Vacant
50 Dean Sch Business/Educ/Math ... Dr. Kurt SEBASTIAN
86 Director Government Relations ... Ms. Beth SWEENY
18 Executive Director of Facilities ... Mr. Joe BRUCE
04 Exec Admin Asst to the President ... Ms. Michelle HARBIDGE LITTLE
28 Director of Diversity ... Dr. Jessica KOBRYN

Florida Academy of Nursing (E)

12002 Miramar Parkway, Miramar FL 33025
County: Broward Identification: 667382
Telephone: (954) 322-1612 Carnegie Class: Not Classified
FAX Number: (954) 241-6842 Calendar System: Quarter
URL: www.fanstudent.com
Established: 2013 Annual Undergrad Tuition & Fees: N/A
Enrollment: N/A Coed
Affiliation or Control: Proprietary IRS Status: Proprietary
Highest Offering: Baccalaureate
Accreditation: ACCSC

01 Chief Executive Officer ... Ms. Lisa TELFER
66 Director of Nursing ... Ms. Irene ROMAN
10 Director of Finance ... Ms. Annette AGLIETTI
07 Director of Admissions ... Ms. Lisa-Anne SHAW

Florida Career College (F)

1743 N Congress Avenue, Boynton Beach FL 33426
Telephone: (561) 810-1810 Identification: 770678
Accreditation: COE

Florida Career College (G)

3750 West 18th Avenue, Hialeah FL 33012-7028
Telephone: (786) 534-0940 Identification: 666624
Accreditation: COE

Florida Career College (H)

3383 North State Road 7,
Lauderdale Lakes FL 33319-5617
Telephone: (954) 908-4700 Identification: 666622
Accreditation: COE

Florida Career College - Margate Campus (I)

3271 North State Road 7, Margate FL 33063
Telephone: (954) 935-7921 Identification: 770681
Accreditation: COE

Florida Career College (J)

1321 SW 107th Avenue, Suite 201B,
Miami FL 33174-2521
County: Miami-Dade FICE Identification: 023058
Unit ID: 133997
Telephone: (786) 534-0500 Carnegie Class: Spec 2-yr-Tech
FAX Number: (786) 534-0558 Calendar System: Quarter
URL: www.floridacareercollege.edu
Established: 1982 Annual Undergrad Tuition & Fees: N/A
Enrollment: 504 Coed
Affiliation or Control: Proprietary IRS Status: Proprietary
Highest Offering: Associate Degree
Accreditation: COE

01 Int Campus President/Exec Director ... Mr. Edward RITO
06 Registrar ... Ms. Roxana CACERES
05 Director of Education ... Mr. Max AMER

Florida Career College (K)

6058 Okeechobee Boulevard, West Palm Beach FL 33417
Telephone: (561) 408-9910 Identification: 770683
Accreditation: COE

Florida Coastal School of Law (L)

8787 Baypine, Jacksonville FL 32256-8528
County: Duval FICE Identification: 033743
Unit ID: 434715
Telephone: (904) 680-7700 Carnegie Class: Not Classified
FAX Number: N/A Calendar System: Semester
URL: www.fcsl.edu
Established: 1995 Annual Graduate Tuition & Fees: N/A
Enrollment: 194 Coed
Affiliation or Control: Proprietary IRS Status: Proprietary
Highest Offering: First Professional Degree; No Undergraduates
Accreditation: LAW

01 Dean/President ... Mr. Peter GOPLERUD
07 Director of Admissions ... Ms. Megan SCHADE
09 Mgr of Institutional Effectiveness ... Vacant
10 Comptroller ... Mr. Ron BAMBACUS

† School is in Teach-Out

Florida College (M)

119 N Glen Arven Avenue,
Temple Terrace FL 33617-5578
County: Hillsborough FICE Identification: 001482
Unit ID: 133809
Telephone: (813) 988-5131 Carnegie Class: Bac/Assoc-Mixed
FAX Number: (813) 899-6772 Calendar System: Semester
URL: www.floridacollege.edu
Established: 1944 Annual Undergrad Tuition & Fees: $18,060
Enrollment: 488 Coed
Affiliation or Control: Independent Non-Profit IRS Status: 501(c)3
Highest Offering: Baccalaureate
Accreditation: SC, MUS

01 President ... Dr. John WEAVER
05 Academic Dean ... Dr. Thomas H. HAMILTON
32 Dean of Student Services ... Mr. Mike BENSON
10 Chief Business Officer ... Mr. Jamie LEWIS
37 Director Student Financial Aid ... Ms. Erin MCALLISTER
07 Dir of Admissions & Retention Svcs ... Miss Virginia MANESS
09 Director of Institutional Research ... Mr. Ryan BARCLAY
121 Director of Advising ... Mrs. Holly CABINA
06 Registrar ... Mr. Ryan BARCLAY
08 Director of Library ... Ms. Jennifer KEARNEY
13 Director of Information Technology ... Mrs. Alyssa JOHNSON
30 Director of Development ... Mr. Adam OLSON
29 Director of Alumni Relations ... Mrs. Deborah BREWER
40 Manager of Bookstore ... Mrs. Carrie BLACK
88 Events Coordinator ... Mrs. Sierra SCHMIDT
41 Athletic Director ... Mr. Chase TEICHMANN
18 Chief Facilities/Physical Plant ... Mr. Tom GARLAND

Florida College of Integrative Medicine (N)

7100 Lake Ellenor Drive, Orlando FL 32809-5721
County: Orange FICE Identification: 032383
Unit ID: 434441
Telephone: (407) 888-8689 Carnegie Class: Spec-4-yr-Other Health
FAX Number: (407) 888-8211 Calendar System: Semester
URL: www.fcim.edu
Established: 1990 Annual Undergrad Tuition & Fees: N/A
Enrollment: 71 Coed
Affiliation or Control: Proprietary IRS Status: Proprietary
Highest Offering: Master's; No Lower Division
Accreditation: ACUP

01 President ... Mr. Lincoln Z. ZHAO
26 Vice Pres Marketing Develpment ... Ms. Jenjen HAN
108 Vice Pres/Chief Quality Officer ... Ms. Yuan-Yuan HAN
05 Dean of Academic Affairs ... Dr. Lin CHAI
10 Director of Finance ... Ms. Susan HOEH
07 Admissions Representative ... Ms. Michelle COLON
37 Dir of Financial Aid/Registrar ... Ms. Mary SIMMONS

Florida Education Institute (O)

5818 SW 8th Street, Miami FL 33144
County: Miami-Dade FICE Identification: 036276
Unit ID: 441423
Telephone: (305) 444-1515 Carnegie Class: Not Classified
FAX Number: N/A Calendar System: Quarter
URL: www.fei.edu
Established: 1994 Annual Undergrad Tuition & Fees: N/A
Enrollment: N/A Coed
Affiliation or Control: Proprietary IRS Status: Proprietary
Highest Offering: Associate Degree
Accreditation: COE

01 Campus Director ... Ramon VALENTI, III

Florida Gateway College (P)

149 SE College Place, Lake City FL 32025-2007
County: Columbia FICE Identification: 001501
Unit ID: 135160
Telephone: (386) 752-1822 Carnegie Class: Bac/Assoc-Mixed
FAX Number: (386) 755-1521 Calendar System: Semester

URL: www.fgc.edu
Established: 1947 Annual Undergrad Tuition & Fees (In-State): $3,100
Enrollment: 3,018 Coed
Affiliation or Control: State IRS Status: 501(c)3
Highest Offering: Baccalaureate
Accreditation: SC, ADNUR, CAHIIM, EMT, NAEYC, NURSE, #PTAA

01 President ... Dr. Lawrence BARRETT
10 Vice President Business Services ... Ms. Michelle HOLLOWAY
04 Assistant to the President ... Ms. Katy MCCRARY
05 Vice President for Academic Affairs ... Dr. Brian DOPSON
84 VP Enroll Mgmt & Student Affairs ... Mr. Anthony CARDENAS
20 Dean of Academic Pgm & Bacc Liaison ... Dr. Paula GAVIN
20 Associate Dean Academic Programs ... Dr. Matthew PEACE
13 Exec Dir Info Technology/CIO ... Mr. Travis GREEN
15 Executive Director Human Resources ... Ms. Cassie BUCKLES
72 Exec Dir of Tech Pgm & Public Svcs ... Mr. John JEWETT
53 Exec Dir Teacher Prep Programs ... Ms. Pamela CARSWELL
121 Director of Student Success ... Ms. Elizabeth MCCARDLE
37 Director Financial Aid ... Mr. Travis GEORGE
07 Assoc Dean Enrollment Management ... Ms. Kacey SCHRADER
32 Associate Dean Student Affairs ... Ms. Sandra TOMLINSON
06 Registrar & Dir of Enrollment Svcs ... Ms. Gayle HUNTER
21 Director Business Services ... Mr. Joseph HOLMES
09 Director of Inst Effect & Assess ... Dr. Natalie WRIGHT
66 Exec Director Nursing ... Dr. Shane NEELY-SMITH
18 Director Facilities ... Mr. Lance JONES
96 Director Procurement & Contracts ... Ms. Misty TAYLOR
27 Director Marketing ... Mr. Rob CHAPMAN
88 Director Dual Enrollment ... Ms. Julie CANNON
41 Athletic Director ... Ms. Rebecca GOLDEN
08 Director Library ... Ms. Christine BOATRIGHT
35 Director of Student Life ... Ms. Amy DEKLE
26 Exec Dir Public Info & Govt Rels ... Mr. Mike MCKEE
30 Exec Director Resource Development ... Mr. Lee PINCHOUCK
88 Dir ASDN & Certificate Program ... Ms. Patricia ORENDER

Florida Institute of Technology (A)

150 W University Boulevard, Melbourne FL 32901-6975
County: Brevard FICE Identification: 001469
Unit ID: 133881
Telephone: (321) 674-8000 Carnegie Class: DU-Higher
FAX Number: (321) 984-8461 Calendar System: Semester
URL: www.fit.edu
Established: 1958 Annual Undergrad Tuition & Fees: $43,246
Enrollment: 6,775 Coed
Affiliation or Control: Independent Non-Profit IRS Status: 501(c)3
Highest Offering: Doctorate
Accreditation: SC, AAB, ABAI, CLPSY, CONST, IACBE

01 Acting President ... Dr. Marco CARVALHO
04 Exec Asst to Pres ... Ms. Rebecca CROOK
05 Exec VP & Provost ... Dr. Marco CARVALHO
10 Chief Financial Officer ... Mr. Michael JONES
26 Chief Marketing Officer ... Mr. Andy MCILWRAITH
100 Executive VP Communication ... Dr. Wesley D. SUMNER
88 Interim Dean College of Aeronautics ... Dr. John E. DEATON
50 Dean College of Business ... Dr. Theodore RICHARDSON
54 Dean Col of Engineering/Science ... Dr. John HARRIS
83 Dean Col of Psych/Lib Arts ... Dr. Robert TAYLOR
08 Acting Dean of Libraries ... Ms. Nancy GARMER
30 Sr VP of Development ... Mr. Gary GRANT
84 Vice Pres Enrollment Mgmt ... Mr. Brian EHRLICH
13 Chief Information Officer ... Mr. Mark LUMSDEN
18 Vice Pres Facilities Operations ... Mr. Brian LESLIE
15 Int VP Human Resources ... Ms. Jessica VINSON
25 Director of Sponsored Programs ... Ms. Carolyn LOCKYER
37 AVP Enrollment Mgmt/Financial Aid ... Mr. Jay LALLY
09 VP for Compliance and Accreditation ... Ms. Jessica ICKES
20 Associate Provost ... Dr. Munevver SUBASI
86 Federal Government Programs Manager ... Dr. Tristan FIEDLER
21 Assistant VP/Controller ... Mr. Ken WILSON
32 Dean of Students ... Mr. David MCMAHAN
39 AVP Housing and Campus Services ... Mr. Gregory CONNELL
06 Registrar ... Ms. Caroline JOHNSTON
121 Director Academic Support Services ... Mr. Rodd NEWCOMBE
41 Director Athletics ... Mr. Jamie JOSS
19 Director Campus Security ... Mr. Frank IANNONE
36 Director Career Services ... Ms. Dona E. GAYNOR
38 Dir Counseling/Psychological Svcs ... Dr. Robyn TAPLEY
88 Director Creative Services ... Ms. Christena CALLAHAN
88 Dir Environ/Regulatory Compliance ... Mr. Selvin MCLEAN
85 Director Intl Student Services ... Ms. Jackie LINGNER
104 Director Study Abroad ... Ms. Heather WAUTLET
07 Exec Dir of Admissions ... Mr. Michael PERRY
28 Exec Dir Comp & Risk/Title IX ... Ms. Fanak BAARMAND
96 Asst Director of Procurement Svcs ... Ms. Denise FLUTIE
89 Dir of First Year Experience ... Dr. Jessica HA BITTNER
122 Dir Student Life & Orientation ... Ms. Cat NANNEY

Florida Memorial University (B)

15800 NW 42nd Avenue, Miami Gardens FL 33054-6199
County: Miami-Dade FICE Identification: 001486
Unit ID: 133979
Telephone: (305) 626-3600 Carnegie Class: Bac-Diverse
FAX Number: N/A Calendar System: Semester
URL: www.fmuniv.edu
Established: 1879 Annual Undergrad Tuition & Fees: $16,176
Enrollment: 928 Coed
Affiliation or Control: Independent Non-Profit IRS Status: 501(c)3
Highest Offering: Beyond Master's But Less Than Doctorate
Accreditation: SC, AAB, ACBSP, SW

01 President ... Dr. Jaffus HARDRICK
05 Provost & Executive VP ... Dr. Adrienne T. COOPER
32 AVP Student Aff/Dean of Students ... Dr. Kelley C. KIMPLE
20 Associate Provost ... Dr. Tameka B. HOBBS
04 Executive Assistant to President ... Ms. Amanda EDUN
49 Interim Dean of Arts and Sciences ... Dr. William E. HOPPER
10 Controller/AVP Finance & Admin ... Mr. Rodney SOBELSON
07 Director of Admissions ... Vacant
111 Vice Pres University Advancement ... Mr. Cory WITHERSPOON
45 Assc VP Institutional Effectiveness ... Dr. William E. HOPPER, JR.
88 Chair Aviation and Safety ... Dr. Jorge GUERRA
50 Dean School of Business ... Dr. J. Preston JONES
53 Dean School of Education ... Dr. Jacqueline HILL
81 Chair Health and Natural Sciences ... Dr. Rose Mary STIFFIN
83 Interim Chair Social Sciences ... Vacant
64 Chair Visual/Perf Arts ... Vacant
77 Chair Comp Science/Math & Tech ... Dr. Ben WONGSAROJ
79 Chair Humanities ... Dr. William HOBBS, III
124 Dir Ctr Acad Resources & Support ... Dr. Rebecca DEVEREAUX
08 Interim Director Library Services ... Ms. Cheryl WILCHER
37 Dir Financial Aid & Scholarships ... Mrs. Kimberly W. JONES
06 Registrar ... Dr. Prudence LEWIS-BHOLA
09 Director of Institutional Research ... Dr. Carlos CANAS
15 Director Human Resources ... Ms. Youseline POTEAU
41 Director Intercollegiate Athletics ... Mr. Jason HORN
36 Director Career Development Ctr ... Ms. Megan D. ADERELE
39 Director Housing & Residence Life ... Ms. Myra M. MCPHEE
19 Dir Campus Safety & Emergency Mgt ... Dr. Gregory A. SALTERS
18 Dir Facility Mgmt/Plant Operations ... Mr. David JACCARINO
42 Dean of Campus Ministry ... Dr. Jeffrey D. SWAIN
29 Director Alumni Affairs ... Vacant
35 Director Student Engagement ... Ms. Sharhonda L. FORD
85 International Student Advisor ... Mr. Trevor LEWIS
13 CIO/Director of IMT ... Mr. Henry MATOS
07 Assistant Director of Admissions ... Vacant
105 IT Solutions Engineer ... Mr. Joslin "Joe" ATHIS
26 VP Public Relations/Marketing ... Vacant
38 Dir Univ Counseling/Support Serv ... Dr. Jason-Anthony K. PRENDERGAST
30 Exec Dir Advancement/Alumni Affairs ... Mrs. Shelia P. COHEN
43 Legal Counsel ... Sonya A. MILLER, ESQ
84 Asst VP Enrollment Management ... Dr. Heather MUNNS

Florida National University Hialeah Campus (C)

4425 W. Jose Regueiro (20th) Ave,
Hialeah FL 33012-4108
County: Dade FICE Identification: 025476
Unit ID: 408844
Telephone: (305) 821-3333 Carnegie Class: Masters/M
FAX Number: (305) 362-0595 Calendar System: Semester
URL: www.fnu.edu
Established: 1982 Annual Undergrad Tuition & Fees: $13,688
Enrollment: 4,173 Coed
Affiliation or Control: Proprietary IRS Status: Proprietary
Highest Offering: Master's
Accreditation: SC, COARC, NURSE, PTAA

01 President/CEO ... Dr. Maria C. REGUEIRO
09 VP of Assessment & Research/FA Dir ... Mr. Omar SANCHEZ
11 Vice President of Operations ... Mr. Frank ANDREU
05 Vice President of Academic Affairs ... Dr. Anthony BERRIOS
12 Campus Dean ... Mrs. Yedi CEPERO
10 Controller ... Dr. Lourdes ANDREU
88 Director of Accreditation ... Dr. Kelly KRENKEL
07 University Admissions Director ... Mr. Guy PIERCE
88 Distance Learning Admissions Dir ... Mr. Calos CARVAJALINO
06 University Registrar ... Mr. Bradley ARNETTE ERZ
106 Director of Distance Learning ... Dr. Emry SOMNARAIN
32 Student Services Officer ... Mr. Seilyn SANTOS
50 Business & Economics Division Head ... Dr. Ernesto GONZALEZ
76 Allied Health Division Head ... Dr. Loreto ALMONTE
79 Humanities & Liberal Arts Div Head ... Dr. Nat W. HARDY
88 ESL Division Head ... Mr. Reynaldo ALES
66 Nursing Division Head ... Vacant
83 Social & Behavioral Sci Div Head ... Dr. Jose PEREZ
15 Human Resources Generalist ... Mrs. Monica ARTEAGA
41 Athletic Director ... Mr. Ryan RAPOSO
88 Military Admissions Advisor ... Mrs. Yolanda NAVARRO
31 Director Community Relations ... Vacant
36 Career Services Officer ... Mrs. Ariadne LOPEZ
26 Marketing Director ... Mrs. Sandra MARINO
108 Director Assessment & Research ... Mr. Rodrigo LOAIZA
08 Library Director ... Mrs. Ida TOMSHINSKY
121 Academic Advisor ... Dr. Rosa HERNANDEZ
13 Director of Information Technology ... Mr. Michael AMBROISE
16 Human Resources Generalist ... Mrs. Isel CASALES
88 Assistant Campus Dean ... Mr. Angel CORONEL
88 Assistant Campus Dean ... Dr. Juan TAPIA
88 Assistant Campus Dean ... Mr. Israel KATZ
85 International Student Advisor ... Mrs. Julia SANCHEZ
88 Director of Military Affairs ... Mr. Giancarlo APONTE
36 Career Services Director ... Mr. Angel URQUIOLA
88 Social Media Manager ... Mrs. Angelina ANGULO

Florida National University South Campus (D)

11865 SW 26th Street Unit H-3, Miami FL 33175
Telephone: (305) 821-3333 Identification: 666691
Accreditation: &SC, NURSE

† Regional accreditation is carried under the parent institution Florida National College, Hialeah, FL.

Florida National University Training Center (E)

4206 West 12th Avenue, Hialeah FL 33012
Telephone: (305) 821-3333 Identification: 666690
Accreditation: &SC

† Regional accreditation is carried under the parent institution Florida National College, Hialeah, FL.

Florida Southern College (F)

111 Lake Hollingsworth Drive, Lakeland FL 33801-5698
County: Polk FICE Identification: 001488
Unit ID: 134079
Telephone: (863) 680-4111 Carnegie Class: Masters/M
FAX Number: (863) 680-4112 Calendar System: Semester
URL: www.flsouthern.edu
Established: 1883 Annual Undergrad Tuition & Fees: $38,980
Enrollment: 3,413 Coed
Affiliation or Control: United Methodist IRS Status: 501(c)3
Highest Offering: Doctorate
Accreditation: SC, MLS, MUS, NURSE, PTA

01 President ... Dr. Anne B. KERR
05 Provost ... Dr. Brad HOLLINGSHEAD
10 Vice President Finance & Admin ... Mr. Terry DENNIS
84 VP Enrollment Management ... Mr. John GRUNDIG
20 Assoc Provost Experiential Educ ... Dr. Tracey TEDDER
30 VP Development ... Ms. Heather PHARRIS
32 VP of Student Development ... Dr. Susan FREEMAN
102 Asst VP Foundation/Corp Giving ... Ms. Kathy ELLIS
15 AVP Operations/HR Director ... Ms. Katherine PAWLAK
42 Chaplain ... Rev. Timothy S. WRIGHT
13 Chief Information Officer ... Ms. Francine NEILING
21 Controller ... Ms. Shelley MARUCA
104 Coordinator Student Travel ... Ms. Bridgette MCARTHUR
49 Dean Art and Sciences ... Dr. Sara HARDING
50 Dean Business and Free Enterprise ... Dr. Michael WEBER
53 Dean Education ... Dr. Victoria GIORDANO
66 Dean Nursing and Health Science ... Dr. Linda S. COMER
121 Dean of Student Success ... Ms. Shari SZABO
35 Asst Dean Accountab/Educ/Compliance ... Ms. Amanda BLOUNT
07 Director of Admissions ... Ms. Arden MITCHELL
123 Director of Adult & Graduate Admiss ... Ms. Kristen PINNER
44 Director Annual Giving ... Mr. Chad M. MAGNUSON
41 Director of Athletics ... Mr. Drew HOWARD
36 Executive Director Career Services ... Dr. Lauren ALBAUM
39 Director of Community Living ... Mr. Romel BOISER
23 Director of Health Services ... Ms. Katherine PAWLAK
112 Director of Major Gifts ... Ms. Sara OLSON
92 Director of Honors Program ... Dr. Roxanne BACK
09 Dir Inst Research/Effectiveness ... Ms. Jazmine EVERHEART
119 Sr Database Administrator ... Ms. Charnee BALL
08 Director of the Library ... Mr. Randall M. MACDONALD
28 Director Multicultural Appreciation ... Ms. Vanessa BECKHAM
26 AVP of Marketing ... Ms. Kassie PAIZIS
18 Director of Facilities Maintenance ... Mr. Jon CAMP
06 Registrar ... Ms. Lindsay THIBODAUX
19 Director of Security/Safety ... Mr. Eric RAUCH
38 Director of Student Counseling ... Mr. David ARANDA
37 Director of Student Financial Aid ... Mr. William L. HEALY
105 Director of Web Development ... Mr. James JARRETT
106 Director Teaching/Learning Ctr ... Ms. Autumn GRUBB
27 Director Communication/Marketing ... Vacant
04 Executive Asst to President ... Ms. LeeAnna CATULLO
40 Manager Bookstore ... Mr. James BAUER
122 Asst Dir Stdnt Involve-Greek Life ... Mr. Kirby THOMAS
108 Director IR/IE/A ... Ms. Jazmine EVERHEART
90 Academic ITS Director ... Mr. Toby SINGER

Florida SouthWestern State College (G)

8099 College Parkway, Fort Myers FL 33919-5566
County: Lee FICE Identification: 001477
Unit ID: 133508
Telephone: (239) 489-9300 Carnegie Class: Bac/Assoc-Mixed
FAX Number: N/A Calendar System: Semester
URL: www.fsw.edu
Established: 1961 Annual Undergrad Tuition & Fees (In-State): $3,401
Enrollment: 15,141 Coed
Affiliation or Control: State IRS Status: 501(c)3
Highest Offering: Baccalaureate
Accreditation: SC, ADNUR, CAHIIM, COARC, CVT, DH, EMT, NUR, RAD

01 President ... Dr. Jeffery ALLBRITTEN
100 Chief of Staff ... Dr. Henry PEEL
05 Provost ... Dr. Eileen DELUCA
32 Vice Provost Student Affairs ... Dr. Michele YOVANOVICH
11 VP of Operations/CFO ... Dr. Gina DOEBLE
43 General Counsel & Govt Relations ... Mr. Joe COLEMAN
50 Dean Business & Technology ... Dr. Mary MYERS
76 Dean Health Professions ... Dr. Tami SUCH
53 Dean Education and Charter Schools ... Dr. April FLEMING
79 Dean Arts/Hum & Social Sciences ... Dr. Deborah TEED
81 Dean Pure & Applied Sciences ... Dr. Elizabeth SCHOTT
41 Director Intercollegiate Athletics ... Mr. George SANDERS
114 AVP Budget & Financial Planning ... Mr. Tobias DISCENZA
84 AVP Enrollment Services ... Dr. Christy GILFERT
35 AVP Student Success ... Dr. April PALMER
12 Campus Director Collier ... Ms. Gail MURPHY
06 Registrar ... Ms. Brenda KNIGHT

13 Chief Information Officer ..... Mr. Jason DUDLEY
08 Director Library Services ..... Dr. Richard HODGES
112 Sr Director Devel & Major Gifts ..... Ms. Susan DESANTIS
26 Exec Director Marketing & Media ..... Mr. Greg TURCHETTA
108 AVP IR Assessment & Effectiveness ..... Dr. Joseph VAN GAALEN
12 Director Hendry/Glades Center ..... Ms. Amanda LEHRIAN
113 Bursar ..... Mr. Brent NELSON
19 Chief of Police ..... Dr. Jerry CONNOLLY
109 Director Auxiliary Services ..... Ms. Angela MCNATT
37 Director Student Financial Aid ..... Ms. Jodi WALKER
15 Chief HR & Organizational Dev Ofc ..... Ms. Susan BRONSTEIN
07 Director Admissions ..... Vacant
18 Dir Facilities Plng & Space Mgmt ..... Mr. JR SHERMAN
121 Director Academic Support Programs ..... Ms. Monica MOORE
39 Dir Housing & Res Life ..... Mr. Justin LONG
88 Director Adaptive Services ..... Ms. Angela HARTSELL
96 Director of Procurement Services ..... Ms. Lisa TUDOR
88 Director Testing Services ..... Mr. Jose ESTRADA
22 Title IX Coord Equity Officer ..... Ms. Lauren FRASSER
10 Director Finance and Accounting ..... Ms. Kathleen PORTER
102 Int Exec Dir/CEO Foundation ..... Mr. Kevin ANDERSON
30 Chief Development Officer ..... Dr. Joseph KRAMP
88 Director Exhibitions & Collections ..... Mr. Jade DELLINGER
88 Director Strategic Initiatives ..... Ms. Whitney RHYNE
88 Director Corp Training & Services ..... Mr. Adrian KERR
88 Director Simulation Education ..... Mr. Tommy MANN
104 Director International Education ..... Mr. Michael MESSINA
117 Director Risk Management ..... Ms. Lori WELCH
110 Senior Director Development ..... Ms. Heather CHESTER
88 Director Corporate Sponsorship ..... Mr. Matthew KERASTAMATIS
12 Campus Director Charlotte ..... Dr. Thomas RATH
88 Director Student Affairs ..... Mr. Andrae JONES
88 Director Academic Advising ..... Dr. Ashley KUHN
20 Vice Provost Academic Affairs ..... Dr. Martin MCCLINTON
36 Director Career Services ..... Dr. Angelette ARIAS

Florida State College at Jacksonville (A)

501 W State Street, Jacksonville FL 32202-4097
County: Duval FICE Identification: 001484
Unit ID: 133702
Telephone: (904) 646-2300 Carnegie Class: Bac/Assoc-Mixed
FAX Number: N/A Calendar System: Semester
URL: www.fscj.edu
Established: 1965 Annual Undergrad Tuition & Fees (In-District): $2,878
Enrollment: 22,344 Coed
Affiliation or Control: Local IRS Status: Exempt
Highest Offering: Baccalaureate
Accreditation: SC, ACBSP, ACFEI, ACPHA, ADNUR, CAHIIM, COARC, CVT, DA, DH, EMT, FUSER, HT, MLTAD, NUR, OTA, #PTAA, SURGT

01 College President ..... Dr. John AVENDANO
05 Provost/Vice President Academics ..... Dr. John WALL
10 Vice Pres of Business Services ..... Vacant
43 Assistant General Counsel ..... Mr. Romualdo MARQUINEZ
32 Vice President Student Services ..... Dr. Linda HERLOCKER
108 VP Institutional Effectiveness ..... Dr. Jerrett DUMOUCHEL
18 Assoc Vice Pres Facilities ..... Mr. Morris A. BELLICK, II
88 AVP Academic Operations ..... Dr. Rich TURNER
88 AVP Strategic Priorities ..... Dr. Deborah FONTAINE
35 AVP Student Support Services ..... Ms. Pamela WALKER
49 Assoc Provost Liberal Arts/Sciences ..... Dr. Ian NEUHARD
56 Executive Dir Outreach & Extension ..... Dr. Heather KENNEY
20 Assoc Prov Curriculum/Instruction ..... Dr. Kathleen CIEZ-VOLZ
21 AVP Finance ..... Mr. Stephen STANFORD
121 AVP Student Success ..... Dr. Erin RICHMAN
103 AVP Workforce Dev/Entrepreneurship ..... Dr. Cedrick GIBSON
84 AVP Enrollment Management ..... Ms. Jacquelyn THOMPSON
15 Chief Human Resource Officer ..... Mr. Mark LACEY
13 Chief Information Tech Officer ..... Mr. Ronald SMITH
28 Chief Ofcr Diversity/Equity/Inclsn ..... Ms. Lisa J. MOORE
88 Exec Director Artist Series ..... Dr. Milton A. RUSSOS
16 Exec Director Talent Acquisition ..... Ms. Lisa MOORE
91 Executive Director Enterprise App ..... Mr. Chris MARTIN
08 Executive Dean of Library Services ..... Dr. Tom MESSNER
14 Exec Dir Computer Infrastructure ..... Mr. Ron SMITH
88 Exec Dir Military Affs/Veteran Svcs ..... Mr. James W. STEVENSON
12 Executive Director of Nassau Center ..... Ms. Donna MARTIN
102 Executive Director Foundation ..... Mr. Cleve WARREN
96 Executive Director Purchasing ..... Ms. Randi BROKVIST
19 Director of Security ..... Mr. Gordon BASS
37 Director Financial Aid ..... Ms. Christine HIBBARD
41 Director of Athletics ..... Ms. Ginny ALEXANDER
25 Director of Resource Development ..... Ms. Jennifer PETERSON
06 Registrar ..... Ms. Jacqueline SCHMIDT
09 Director Student Analytics/Research ..... Mr. Gregory MICHALSKI
26 Chief Communications Officer ..... Ms. Jill K. JOHNSON
04 Administration Support Mgr OCP ..... Mr. Calvin LEAVELL
07 Director of Admissions ..... Ms. Megan DROSS
101 Administration Support Mgr OCP ..... Ms. Kimberli SODEK
92 Director Honors Program ..... Ms. Maria DONAIRE-CIRSOVIUS
105 Web Communications Manager ..... Mr. Michael AHMED
29 Development Officer ..... Ms. Danielle THOMPSON
30 Development Officer ..... Mr. Socrates RIVERS
44 Director Annual Giving ..... Ms. Danielle THOMPSON
50 Dean of Career Education ..... Ms. Annette BARRINEAU
53 Dean of Education & Human Svcs ..... Dr. Tara HALEY
54 Dean Engr Technology & Industry ..... Dr. Douglas BRAUER

Florida Technical College (B)

1199 S Woodland Boulevard, Deland FL 32720-7415
Telephone: (386) 734-3303 Identification: 666419
Accreditation: &M

Florida Technical College (C)

3831 West Vine Street, Suite 50, Kissimmee FL 34741
Telephone: (844) 402-3337 Identification: 770684
Accreditation: &M, ACFEI

Florida Technical College (D)

4715 South Florida Avenue, Suite 4,
Lakeland FL 33813-2101
Telephone: (866) 967-8822 FICE Identification: 025981
Accreditation: &M

Florida Technical College (E)

12900 Challenger Parkway, Orlando FL 32826
Telephone: (407) 447-7300 FICE Identification: 022187
Accreditation: &M

Florida Technical College (F)

12520 Pines Boulevard, Pembroke Pines FL 33027
Telephone: (844) 332-3409 Identification: 770685
Accreditation: &M

Fortis College (G)

19600 South Dixie Highway, Ste B, Cutler Bay FL 33157
Telephone: (786) 345-5300 Identification: 770565
Accreditation: ACCSC, ADNUR

† Branch campus of Fortis College, Centerville, OH.

Fortis College (H)

700 Blanding Boulevard, Suite 16, Orange Park FL 32065
County: Clay FICE Identification: 034343
Unit ID: 439792
Telephone: (904) 269-7086 Carnegie Class: Spec 2-yr-Health
FAX Number: (904) 269-6664 Calendar System: Semester
URL: www.fortis.edu
Established: 1985 Annual Undergrad Tuition & Fees: $15,060
Enrollment: 489 Coed
Affiliation or Control: Proprietary IRS Status: Proprietary
Highest Offering: Associate Degree
Accreditation: ACCSC, ADNUR, SURGT

01 Campus President ..... Mr. Ben SEDRINE
05 Academic Dean ..... Dr. Andrea JONES

Fortis Institute-Port St. Lucie (I)

9022 South US Highway 1, Port St. Lucie FL 34952
Telephone: (772) 221-9799 Identification: 770527
Accreditation: ABHES, ADNUR

† Branch campus of Fortis Institute, Baton Rouge, LA.

Full Sail University (J)

3300 University Boulevard, Winter Park FL 32792
County: Orange FICE Identification: 023621
Unit ID: 134237
Telephone: (407) 679-0100 Carnegie Class: Masters/L
FAX Number: (407) 679-9685 Calendar System: Other
URL: www.fullsail.edu
Established: 1979 Annual Undergrad Tuition & Fees: $25,820
Enrollment: 24,627 Coed
Affiliation or Control: Proprietary IRS Status: Proprietary
Highest Offering: Master's
Accreditation: ACCSC, CEA

01 President ..... Mr. Garry JONES
07 Sr Vice President of Admissions ..... Mr. Matt PENGRA

Future-Tech Institute (K)

3446 8th St, Ste 213, Miami FL 33135
County: Miami-Dade FICE Identification: 041164
Unit ID: 459310
Telephone: (305) 774-0227 Carnegie Class: Spec 2-yr-Health
FAX Number: (305) 445-2217 Calendar System: Semester
URL: www.futuretechinstitute.com
Established: 2000 Annual Undergrad Tuition & Fees: $17,863
Enrollment: 105 Coed
Affiliation or Control: Proprietary IRS Status: Proprietary
Highest Offering: Associate Degree
Accreditation: ACCSC

01 School Director ..... Ana MONCADA
10 Financial Director ..... Miriam HODGES
07 Admissions Director ..... David NEWCOMB
15 Human Resources Director ..... Ivania MONCADA

FVI School of Nursing and Technology (L)

7757 West Flagler St., Ste 220, Miami FL 33144
County: Miami-Dade FICE Identification: 042063
Unit ID: 476939
Telephone: (305) 665-1911 Carnegie Class: Not Classified
FAX Number: (305) 665-1917 Calendar System: Other
URL: www.fvi.edu
Established: 2007 Annual Undergrad Tuition & Fees: N/A
Enrollment: N/A Coed
Affiliation or Control: Proprietary IRS Status: Proprietary
Highest Offering: Associate Degree
Accreditation: COE

Galen College of Nursing (M)

10200 Dr Martin Luther King Jr St N,
St. Petersburg FL 33716
Telephone: (727) 577-1497 Identification: 770539
Accreditation: &SC, ADNUR, NURSE

† Branch campus of Galen College of Nursing, Louisville, KY

Genesis University (N)

4000 Alton Road, Miami Beach FL 33140
County: Miami-Dade Identification: 667431
Telephone: (845) 533-6100 Carnegie Class: Not Classified
FAX Number: N/A Calendar System: Semester
URL: www.genesis.edu
Established: 2001 Annual Undergrad Tuition & Fees: N/A
Enrollment: N/A Coed
Affiliation or Control: Independent Non-Profit IRS Status: 501(c)3
Highest Offering: Baccalaureate
Accreditation: DEAC

01 President ..... Robert FRANKEL

Gulf Coast State College (O)

5230 W Highway 98, Panama City FL 32401-1058
County: Bay FICE Identification: 001490
Unit ID: 134343
Telephone: (850) 769-1551 Carnegie Class: Bac/Assoc-Assoc Dom
FAX Number: (850) 913-3319 Calendar System: Semester
URL: www.gulfcoast.edu
Established: 1957 Annual Undergrad Tuition & Fees (In-State): $2,370
Enrollment: 4,410 Coed
Affiliation or Control: State Related IRS Status: 501(c)3
Highest Offering: Baccalaureate
Accreditation: SC, ACFEI, ADNUR, COARC, DA, DH, EMT, NURSE, PTAA, RAD, SURGA, SURGT

01 Interim President ..... Dr. Cheryl L. FLAX-HYMAN
10 Vice Pres Administration & Finance ..... Mr. John D. MERCER
05 VP Academic Affairs ..... Dr. Holly KUEHNER
32 VP Inst Effect & Student Affairs ..... Vacant
45 VP Economic Dev & Strategic Init ..... Mr. Glen MCDONALD
13 Chief Information Officer ..... Mr. Greg ELLER
08 Exec Director E-Learning & Library ..... Ms. Lori DRISCOLL
15 Exec Director of Human Resources ..... Mr. Lee WOOD
26 Exec Director Community Engagement ..... Ms. Katie MCCURDY
04 Executive Asst to President ..... Ms. Dottie TERRYN
96 Exec Dir Procurement & Auxil Svcs ..... Ms. Tonia LAWSON
37 Exec Director Student Financial Svc ..... Mr. Christopher J. WESTLAKE
09 Institutional Research Analyst ..... Ms. Amber COKER
19 Director Security/Safety ..... Dr. David THOMASEE
41 Athletic Director ..... Mr. Mike KANDLER
06 Registrar ..... Ms. Merissa HUDSON
21 Dean Business Affairs ..... Ms. Leslie HAPNER
35 Dean Student Life ..... Dr. Kelli WALSINGHAM
121 Dean Student Engagement ..... Mr. J. Loyd HARRIS

HCI College (P)

1764 North Congress Avenue,
West Palm Beach FL 33409
County: Palm Beach Identification: 667104
Unit ID: 490054
Telephone: (561) 586-0121 Carnegie Class: Spec-4-yr-Other Health
FAX Number: (561) 471-4010 Calendar System: Semester
URL: www.hci.edu
Established: 1993 Annual Undergrad Tuition & Fees: $17,670
Enrollment: 709 Coed
Affiliation or Control: Proprietary IRS Status: Proprietary
Highest Offering: Associate Degree
Accreditation: ACCSC

01 President/CEO ..... Pedro DE GUZMAN
10 Vice President Finance ..... Ryan MILLER
05 VP Academic/Regulatory Affairs ..... Dr. Arlette PETERSSON
11 Vice President Administration ..... Caren STEWART
12 Campus President WPB ..... David SHELPMAN, JR.

Herzing University (Q)

1865 SR 436, Winter Park FL 32792
Telephone: (407) 641-5227 Identification: 666422
Accreditation: &HLC, ADNUR, NURSE, PTAA

† Regional accreditation is carried under the parent institution in Madison, WI.

Hillsborough Community College (A)

39 Columbia Drive, Tampa FL 33606
County: Hillsborough FICE Identification: 007870
Unit ID: 134495
Telephone: (813) 253-7000 Carnegie Class: Assoc/HT-Mix Trad/Non
FAX Number: N/A Calendar System: Semester
URL: www.hccfl.edu
Established: 1968 Annual Undergrad Tuition & Fees (In-State): $2,506
Enrollment: 19,532 Coed
Affiliation or Control: State IRS Status: 501(c)3
Highest Offering: Baccalaureate
Accreditation: SC, ACFEI, ADNUR, COARC, CSHSE, DA, DH, DMS, EMT, MLS, MUS, NMT, OPD, RAD, RTT, SURGT

01 President .... Dr. Ken ATWATER
10 VP Administration/CFO .... Mr. Greg ROSE
05 VP for Academic Affairs .... Mr. Richard SENKER
13 VP IT/Chief Information Officer .... Mr. Daya PENDHARKAR
32 VP Student Services/Enrollment Mgt .... Dr. Ken RAY
12 Campus President Dale Mabry .... Dr. Paige NIEHAUS
12 Campus President Ybor City Campus .... Dr. Larissa BAIA
12 Campus President Plant City Campus .... Dr. Martyn CLAY
12 Campus President Brandon .... Dr. Deb KISH-JOHANSEN
12 Campus President South Shore Campus .... Dr. Jennifer CHINA
28 CDO for Equity & Diversity .... Ms. Annazette HOUSTON
26 Exec Dir Marketing/Public Relations .... Ms. Ashley CARL
45 VP Strategic Planning & Analysis .... Dr. Paul NAGY
102 Exec Director HCC Foundation .... Mr. Stephen SHEAR
43 College Attorney .... Ms. Martha Kaye KOEHLER
15 Exec Dir Human Resources .... Ms. Kristin SMUDER
21 Controller .... Ms. Rhonesia DENNARD
75 Associate VP AS Programs .... Dr. Brian MANN
88 Dean Associate in Arts Degrees Pgm .... Mr. Dustin E. LEMKE
90 Dir of Instructional Technology .... Dr. Mark LEWIS
20 Dean of Acad Affairs - Ybor City .... Dr. Keith BERRY
20 Dean of Acad Affairs - Plant City .... Dr. Anthony BORRELL
20 Dean of Academic Affairs - Brandon .... Dr. Patricia RAND
49 Dean of AS Programs - Brandon .... Dr. Randall ROCKEFELLER
49 Dean of AS Programs Ybor City .... Ms. Sheila RIOS
49 Dean of AS Programs - Dale Mabry .... Dr. Simone JENKINS
81 Dean AA Math/Science Dale Mabry .... Dr. Hikmat BC
76 Dean of Health Sciences .... Dr. Leif PENROSE
84 Director Enrollment Mgmt Tech .... Dr. Kayla D. CHARLES
37 Financial Aid Director .... Ms. Tierra SMITH
06 Registrar .... Ms. Nevaler DAVIS
18 Director Facilities/Physical Plant .... Mr. Ben MARSHALL
96 Director of Purchasing .... Ms. Vonda MELCHIOR
19 Director Security/Safety .... Mr. Garrett ALLEN
04 Exec Asst to the President .... Ms. Suzy HOLLEY
29 Director Alumni Affairs .... Vacant
30 Director of Development .... Ms. Lee LOWRY
101 Secretary of the Institution/Board .... Ms. Trudy CRUZ
103 Associate VP PSAV Programs .... Mr. John MEEKS
104 Director International Education .... Dr. Michael BRENNAN
108 Dir of Information Mgmt/Reporting .... Dr. Nicole JAGUSZTYN
39 Director Student Svcs Dale Mabry .... Mr. Joseph BENTROVATO
41 Athletic Director .... Ms. Sarah SUMMERFIELD
09 Director of Institutional Research .... Dr. Aiisa ZUJOVICH
86 Director Government Relations .... Mr. Eric JOHNSON
35 Dean Student Services Brandon .... Dr. Julie RICHARDSON
35 Dean Student Services Plant City .... Ms. Yaima SERRANO
35 Dean Student Services Ybor City .... Dr. David J. ROSS
20 Dean Academic Affairs South Shore .... Ms. Nadia KOTULA
120 Dir Online Education/E-learning .... Ms. Laurie SAYLOR
51 Director Cont Educ/Corp Training .... Mr. Ryan R. BUCKTHORPE
27 Director Public Rels & Marketing .... Ms. Angela M. EVEILLARD
88 Dir Networking & Telecommuncations .... Mr. Adrian D. MCCRAY
88 Director Professional Development .... Ms. Brenda A. WATKINS

Hobe Sound Bible College (B)

PO Box 1065, Hobe Sound FL 33475
County: Martin FICE Identification: 021889
Unit ID: 134510
Telephone: (772) 546-5534 Carnegie Class: Bac-Diverse
FAX Number: (772) 545-1422 Calendar System: Semester
URL: www.hsbc.edu
Established: 1960 Annual Undergrad Tuition & Fees: $7,048
Enrollment: 159 Coed
Affiliation or Control: Independent Non-Profit IRS Status: 501(c)3
Highest Offering: Master's
Accreditation: BI

01 President .... Dr. Daniel STETLER
05 Academic Dean .... Dr. Clifford W. CHURCHILL
10 Director of Finance .... Mr. Aaron HAMILTON
11 Director of Administrative Services .... Mr. Wesley HOLDEN
32 Director of Student Life .... Mr. John S. JONES
08 Librarian .... Mr. Phil JONES
106 Dean of HOBE Online .... Dr. Brent JONES
06 Registrar .... Vacant
07 Director of Admissions .... Ms. Jennifer PLANK
111 Dir Institutional Advancement/PR .... Mr. Paul STETLER
37 Director of Financial Aid .... Vacant

Hodges University (C)

4501 Colonial Blvd, Fort Myers FL 33966
County: Collier FICE Identification: 030375
Unit ID: 367884
Telephone: (239) 938-7700 Carnegie Class: Masters/S
FAX Number: (239) 598-6251 Calendar System: Trimester
URL: www.hodges.edu
Established: 1990 Annual Undergrad Tuition & Fees: $14,660
Enrollment: 700 Coed
Affiliation or Control: Independent Non-Profit IRS Status: 501(c)3
Highest Offering: Master's
Accreditation: SC, CACREP, DH, NUR, PTAA

01 President .... Dr. John D. MEYER
10 Exec Vice Pres Admin Operations/CFO .... Ms. Erica VOGT
05 EVP Academic Affairs/Provost .... Dr. Rigoberto RINCONES GOMEZ
26 VP Marketing/Public Info Ofcr .... Ms. Teresa M. ARAQUE
32 Asst Vice Pres Student Experience .... Mr. Joshua CARCOPA
84 Chief Enrollment Officer .... Mr. Gary BRACKEN
37 Director of Financial Aid .... Ms. Sheri MORAN
28 Chief Diversity Officer .... Ms. Gail B. WILLIAMS
50 Dean Johnson School of Business .... Dr. Todd KATZ
107 Dean Nichols School of Prof Studies .... Dr. Mary NUOSCE
97 Dean School of Liberal Studies .... Dr. Elsa P. ROGERS
72 Assoc Dean Fisher School of Tech .... Ms. Tracey M. LANHAM
76 Dir School of Health Sciences .... Dr. Diana C. SCHULTZ
108 Dir Institutional Effectiveness .... Mr. Christopher PARFITT
08 Director of the Library .... Vacant
13 Director of Information Technology .... Vacant
15 Director of Human Resources .... Ms. Tracey DURHAM
18 Dir Facilities Mgmt/Campus Security .... Mr. Skip L. CAMP
07 Director or Admissions .... Ms. Deborah CLARK
04 Executive Asst to President .... Ms. Victoria WALKER
06 University Registrar .... Ms. Nicole HURLEY

Hope College of Arts & Sciences (D)

1200 SW 3rd Street, Pompano Beach FL 33069
County: Broward FICE Identification: 042517
Unit ID: 488332
Telephone: (954) 532-9614 Carnegie Class: Spec 2-yr-Health
FAX Number: N/A Calendar System: Other
URL: www.hcas.edu
Established: 2011 Annual Undergrad Tuition & Fees: N/A
Enrollment: 122 Coed
Affiliation or Control: Proprietary IRS Status: Proprietary
Highest Offering: Baccalaureate
Accreditation: ACICS

05 Dean of Nursing .... Ms. Andre DERBY
13 Distance Learning/IT Director .... Mr. Felipe LOPEZ
37 Director of Financial Aid .... Ms. Carmen TIRADO
07 Admissions .... Mr. James DORNEVIL
06 Registrar .... Mr. Joseph GARVER

Indian River State College (E)

3209 Virginia Avenue, Fort Pierce FL 34981-5596
County: Saint Lucie FICE Identification: 001493
Unit ID: 134608
Telephone: (772) 462-4772 Carnegie Class: Bac/Assoc-Mixed
FAX Number: (772) 462-4796 Calendar System: Semester
URL: www.irsc.edu
Established: 1960 Annual Undergrad Tuition & Fees (In-District): $2,764
Enrollment: 15,236 Coed
Affiliation or Control: Local IRS Status: 501(c)3
Highest Offering: Baccalaureate
Accreditation: SC, ADNUR, CAHIIM, COARC, DA, DH, EMT, MAC, MLTAD, NUR, PTAA, RAD, SURGT

01 President .... Dr. Timothy MOORE
84 Vice President Student Success .... Ms. Elizabeth GASKIN
03 Exec VP Strategic Initiatives .... Mr. Michael HAGELOH
45 VP Institutional Effectiveness .... Dr. Angela BROWNING
05 Vice President Academic Affairs .... Dr. Heather BELMONT
10 Vice President Financial Services .... Dr. Marvin PYLES
32 Vice President Student Affairs .... Mr. Frank WATKINS
13 Vice President Institutional Tech .... Dr. Timothy MARSHALL
17 Dean Health Science .... Dr. Ann HUBBARD
12 Dean Northwest Center .... Ms. Adriene JEFFERSON
08 Admin Dir Library Services .... Ms. Mia TIGNOR
103 Dean Workforce Education .... Mr. William SOLOMON
12 Campus President St Lucie County .... Mr. Andrew TREADWELL
12 Campus President Okeechobee County .... Mr. Russ BROWN
12 Campus President Martin County .... Dr. Alessandro ANZALONE
12 Campus President Indian River Co .... Dr. Terri GRAHAM
49 Dean Liberal Arts .... Dr. Scott STEIN
66 Dean Nursing .... Dr. Patricia GAGLIANO
80 Dean Public Service Education .... Dr. Raimundo SOCORRO
50 Dean Business .... Dr. Prashanth PILLY
88 Exec Dir Innovation/Bus Development .... Dr. Kevin COOPER
53 Dean School of Education .... Dr. Kelly AMATUCCI
15 Vice President Human Resources .... Ms. Melissa PROCHASKA
18 Assoc VP Facilities .... Mr. Sean DONAHUE
81 Dean Science .... Dr. Anthony DRIBBEN
21 Assoc VP Finance .... Ms. Edith PACACHA
14 Exec Dir Enterprise Systems .... Ms. Heather GUTMAN
41 Director Athletics .... Mr. Scott KIMMELMAN
88 Title IX Coordinator .... Mrs. Adriene JEFFERSON
26 Assoc VP Communications/PIO .... Ms. Suzanne SELDES
36 Admin Dir Advising & Career Svcs .... Dr. Calvin WILLIAMS
37 Director Financial Aid .... Ms. Mary LEWIS
35 Director Student Development .... Ms. Rochelle POPP-FINCH
22 Equity Officer .... Ms. Adriene JEFFERSON
96 Purchasing Director .... Mr. Daniel VEST
19 Director Safety/Security .... Mr. Alan MONTGOMERY
07 Admin Dir Recruitment & Admissions .... Ms. Emily MASS
45 Admin Dir Planning/Budget/Auxil .... Ms. Victoria ORTIZ-LUCAS

International College of Health Sciences (F)

2300 S. Congress Avenue #105, Boynton Beach FL 33426
County: Palm Beach Identification: 667238
Telephone: (561) 202-6333 Carnegie Class: Not Classified
FAX Number: (561) 296-9647 Calendar System: Semester
URL: https://www.ichs.edu/
Established: Annual Undergrad Tuition & Fees: N/A
Enrollment: N/A Coed
Affiliation or Control: Proprietary IRS Status: Proprietary
Highest Offering: Master's
Accreditation: ACCSC, ADNUR, CVT, NUR

01 Campus President .... Karyn J. VIDAL
05 Director of Education .... Vacant

Jacksonville University (G)

2800 University Boulevard N, Jacksonville FL 32211-3394
County: Duval FICE Identification: 001495
Unit ID: 134945
Telephone: (904) 256-8000 Carnegie Class: Masters/L
FAX Number: N/A Calendar System: Semester
URL: www.ju.edu
Established: 1934 Annual Undergrad Tuition & Fees: $39,900
Enrollment: 4,053 Coed
Affiliation or Control: Independent Non-Profit IRS Status: 501(c)3
Highest Offering: Doctorate
Accreditation: SC, AAB, CACREP, #COARC, DANCE, DENT, MUS, NURSE, OT, SP

00 Chairman Board of Trustees .... Mr. Matthew KANE
01 President .... Mr. Timothy P. COST
05 Provost/SVPAA .... Dr. Christine SAPIENZA
10 SVP/CFO .... Mr. Randal FREEBOURN
32 SVP/Dean of Students .... Dr. Kristie GOVER
43 SVP/Chief Compliance/Legal/HR .... Ms. Allana FORTE
111 SVP Strategic Operations .... Mr. Scott BACON
41 SVP Athletic Director .... Mr. Alexander RICKER-GILBERT
86 SVP EDEE .... Ms. Margaret DEES
09 Exec Dir Institutional AESP .... Dr. William MILLER
06 Asst Vice President/Registrar .... Mr. Robert BERWICK
124 Assoc VP Student Experience .... Mr. Thomas TAGGART
20 Vice Provost .... Dr. Sherri JACKSON
13 Director/CIO .... Mr. Dominic VENETO
76 Dean BRCHS .... Dr. Mark TILLMAN
50 Dean College of Business .... Dr. Barbara RITTER
15 Sr Human Resources Specialist .... Ms. E'Lisa GREEN
57 Dean of Fine Arts .... Dr. Timothy SNYDER
49 Int Dean College of Arts & Sciences .... Dr. Timothy SNYDER
19 Director of Campus Security .... Mr. Kevin BENNETT
38 Director Counseling Center .... Dr. Kristin ALBERTS
39 Director of Residential Life .... Ms. Jenny BOYER
22 Director of Equity & Inclusion .... Ms. Patrice ABNER
35 Associate Dean of Students .... Ms. DaVina HAMILTON
35 Assistant Dean of Students .... Ms. Jamie BURKET
46 Dir Research & Sponsored Pgms .... Ms. Renee ROSSI
08 Director of the Library .... Ms. Casanna JACKSON
113 Bursar .... Ms. Marcia GIBAJA
37 Director of Financial Aid .... Mr. Charles MOORE
109 Exec Director of Campus Services .... Mr. Michael BOBBIN
18 Sr Director of Facilities Services .... Mr. Brendan MCCARTHY
110 Assoc Vice President of Development .... Ms. Leslie REDD
29 Sr Dir of Engage/Annual Philanth .... Ms. Lauren GRIFFITH
102 Dir Corporate/Foundation Relations .... Ms. Annie TUTT
112 Director Major Gifts .... Mr. Chipper HOFFMAN
26 Chief Public Relations Officer .... Ms. Laura PHELPS
105 Director Web Svc & Mkt Data .... Ms. Amanda BILLY
04 Exec Assistant to the President .... Ms. Debra HODGINS
42 Campus Minister .... Mr. Lance BEAUCHAMP
07 Director of Admissions .... Dr. Teresa MACGREGOR
108 Director Institutional Assessment .... Ms. Katelyn ARMSTRONG

Johnson University Florida (H)

1011 Bill Beck Boulevard, Kissimmee FL 34744-5301
Telephone: (407) 847-8966 FICE Identification: 021567
Accreditation: &SC, &BI

† Branch campus of Johnson University, Knoxville, TN

Jose Maria Vargas University (I)

10131 Pines Boulevard, Pembroke Pines FL 33026
County: Broward FICE Identification: 041620
Unit ID: 461281
Telephone: (954) 322-4460 Carnegie Class: Spec-4-yr-Other
FAX Number: (954) 322-4131 Calendar System: Semester
URL: www.jmvu.edu
Established: 2003 Annual Undergrad Tuition & Fees: $10,480
Enrollment: 111 Coed
Affiliation or Control: Proprietary IRS Status: Proprietary
Highest Offering: Master's
Accreditation: ACICS

01 President .... Dr. Alicia F. PARRA
05 Vice President Academic Affairs .... Ms. Lelis ORTIZ PARRA

Keiser University　(A)
1800 Business Park Blvd, Daytona Beach FL 32114
Telephone: (386) 274-5060　　　Identification: 770900
Accreditation: **&SC**, ACBSP, DMS, MAC, OTA, RAD

Keiser University　(B)
1900 West Commercial Blvd, Fort Lauderdale FL 33309
County: Broward　　　FICE Identification: 021519
　　　　　　　　　　　Unit ID: 135081
Telephone: (954) 776-4476　　Carnegie Class: DU-Mod
FAX Number: N/A　　　Calendar System: Semester
URL: www.keiseruniversity.edu
Established: 1977　　Annual Undergrad Tuition & Fees: $21,008
Enrollment: 20,330　　　　　　　　Coed
Affiliation or Control: Independent Non-Profit　IRS Status: 501(c)3
Highest Offering: Doctorate
Accreditation: SC, ACBSP, ADNUR, CAHIIM, COARC, DIETI, DMS, MLTAD, NURSE, OT, OTA, PTAA, RAD

01	Chancellor/CEO	Dr. Arthur KEISER
11	Executive Vice Chancellor/COO	Mr. Peter CROCITTO
05	Vice Chancellor of Academic Affairs	Dr. John SITES
31	Vice Chancellor of Community Rels	Mrs. Belinda KEISER
84	Vice Chancellor of Enrollment Mgmt	Ms. Teri DEL VECCHIO
10	Sr Vice Chancellor of Finance	Mr. Joseph BERARDINELLI
85	Vice Chancellor International Affs	Mr. Xun LI
26	Coord Multimedia/Public Relations	Ms. Marianly HERNANDEZ PRIMMER
06	Registrar	Ms. Jazmine FERNANDEZ
09	Asst Vice Chanc Institutional Rsrch	Dr. Syeda QADRI
29	Director Alumni Relations	Ms. Kerri PERCY
32	AVP Student Affairs/Student Life	Ms. Jacqueline BONERI

Keiser University　(C)
9100 Forum Corporate Pkwy, Fort Myers FL 33905
Telephone: (239) 277-1336　　　Identification: 770901
Accreditation: **&SC**, ACBSP, DMS, OTA, PTAA, RAD

Keiser University-Jacksonville Campus　(D)
6430 Southpoint Pkwy, Jacksonville FL 33216
Telephone: (904) 296-3440　　　Identification: 770902
Accreditation: **&SC**, ACBSP, ADNUR, OTA, PTAA, RAD

Keiser University　(E)
2400 Interstate Drive, Lakeland FL 33805
Telephone: (863) 682-6020　　　Identification: 770903
Accreditation: **&SC**, ACBSP, ADNUR, DIETC, NMT, #PTAA, RAD

Keiser University　(F)
900 South Babcock Street, Melbourne FL 32901
Telephone: (321) 409-4800　　　Identification: 770904
Accreditation: **&SC**, ACBSP, ACFEI, ADNUR, DIETC, DMS, OTA, PTAA, RAD

Keiser University　(G)
2101 NW 117th Avenue, Miami FL 33172
Telephone: (305) 596-2226　　　Identification: 770905
Accreditation: **&SC**, ACBSP, ADNUR, OTA, PTAA, RAD

Keiser University　(H)
3909 Tamiami Trail East, Naples FL 34112
Telephone: (239) 513-1135　　FICE Identification: 039393
Accreditation: **&SC**, ANEST

Keiser University　(I)
6300 US Hwy 19 North, New Port Richey FL 34652
Telephone: (727) 484-3110　　　Identification: 770854
Accreditation: **&SC**, DMS

Keiser University　(J)
5600 Lake Underhill Road, Orlando FL 32807
Telephone: (407) 273-5800　　　Identification: 770906
Accreditation: **&SC**, ACBSP, ADNUR, HT, MLS, MLTAD, OTA

Keiser University　(K)
1640 SW 145th Avenue, Pembroke Pines FL 33027
Telephone: (954) 431-4300　　　Identification: 770907
Accreditation: **&SC**, ACBSP, OTA

Keiser University　(L)
9400 Discovery Way, Port Saint Lucie FL 34987
Telephone: (772) 398-9990　　　Identification: 666289
Accreditation: **&SC**, ACBSP, ADNUR

† Regional accreditation is carried under the parent institution Keiser University, Fort Lauderdale, FL.

Keiser University　(M)
6151 Lake Osprey Drive, Sarasota FL 34240
Telephone: (941) 907-3900　　　Identification: 770908
Accreditation: **&SC**, ACBSP, ACFEI, ADNUR, #PTAA, RAD

Keiser University　(N)
1700 Halstead Blvd, Bldg 2, Tallahassee FL 32309
Telephone: (850) 906-9494　　　Identification: 770909
Accreditation: **&SC**, ACBSP, ACFEI, ADNUR, OTA

Keiser University　(O)
5002 West Waters Avenue, Tampa FL 33634
Telephone: (813) 885-4900　　　Identification: 770910
Accreditation: **&SC**, ACBSP, ADNUR, OTA, RAD

Keiser University　(P)
2085 Vista Parkway, West Palm Beach FL 33411-2719
Telephone: (561) 471-6000　　　Identification: 667032
Accreditation: **&SC**, ACBSP, ADNUR, CHIRO, OTA, #PTAA, RAD

† Regional accreditation is carried under the parent institution Keiser University, Fort Lauderdale, FL.

Keiser University at Clearwater　(Q)
16120 US Hwy 19 N, Clearwater FL 33764
Telephone: (727) 576-6500　　　Identification: 666758
Accreditation: **&SC**, ADNUR, SURGT

Key College　(R)
2810 E Oakland Park Blvd, STE 305,
Fort Lauderdale FL 33306
County: Broward　　　FICE Identification: 023251
　　　　　　　　　　　Unit ID: 134422
Telephone: (754) 312-2898　　Carnegie Class: Spec-4-yr-Law
FAX Number: (954) 900-3446　　Calendar System: Quarter
URL: www.keycollege.edu
Established: 1982　　Annual Undergrad Tuition & Fees: $11,085
Enrollment: 29　　　　　　　　　Coed
Affiliation or Control: Proprietary　　IRS Status: Proprietary
Highest Offering: Associate Degree
Accreditation: ACCSC

01	President	Mr. Ronald H. DOOLEY
05	EVP/Director of Academic Affairs	Ms. Marella DOOLEY
07	Director of Admissions	Mr. Ron DOOLEY
37	Director of Financial Services	Ms. Linda GOLAN
06	Registrar	Mr. Guy ETIENNE
08	Librarian	Ms. Barbara HIJEK
20	Academic Coordinator	Vacant
106	Information Technology Technician	Mr. Mark ROSE

Knox Theological Seminary　(S)
5555 N Federal Highway, Fort Lauderdale FL 33308-3209
County: Broward　　　FICE Identification: 039923
　　　　　　　　　　　Unit ID: 484288
Telephone: (954) 771-0376　　Carnegie Class: Not Classified
FAX Number: (954) 351-3343　　Calendar System: Semester
URL: www.knoxseminary.edu
Established: 1989　　Annual Undergrad Tuition & Fees: N/A
Enrollment: N/A　　　　　　　　Coed
Affiliation or Control: Independent Non-Profit　IRS Status: 501(c)3
Highest Offering: Doctorate
Accreditation: THEOL

01	President & CEO	Dr. Scott MANOR
05	Provost	Dr. Timothy SANSBURY
32	Dean of Students	Dr. Josh BRUCE
106	Director of Distance Education	Dr. Tim FOX
30	Director of Development	Mr. Matt TILL
06	Registrar	Ms. Lori GOTTSHALL
10	Director of Finance	Ms. Janet CUNNINGHAM
04	Administrative Asst to President	Ms. Stephanie ZAMORA
07	Senior Admissions Advisor	Mr. Derek FREDERICKSON
13	Director Information Technology	Mr. Chris ZAMORA
15	Director of Human Resources	Ms. Markita DUNCOMBE

Lake Erie College of Osteopathic Medicine Bradenton　(T)
5000 Lakewood Ranch Boulevard, Bradenton FL 34211
Telephone: (941) 756-0690　　　Identification: 770160
Accreditation: **&M**, DENT, **&**OSTEO, PHAR

† Branch campus of Lake Erie College of Osteopathic Medicine, Erie, PA

Lake-Sumter State College　(U)
9501 US Highway 441, Leesburg FL 34788-8751
County: Lake　　　FICE Identification: 001502
　　　　　　　　　　　Unit ID: 135188
Telephone: (352) 787-3747　　Carnegie Class: Bac/Assoc-Assoc Dom
FAX Number: (352) 365-3548　　Calendar System: Semester
URL: www.lssc.edu
Established: 1962　　Annual Undergrad Tuition & Fees (In-District): $3,292
Enrollment: 4,760　　　　　　　　Coed

Affiliation or Control: State/Local　　IRS Status: 501(c)3
Highest Offering: Baccalaureate
Accreditation: **SC**, ADNUR, NUR

01	Interim President	Dr. Heather BIGARD
10	Prov & Exec VP Admin/Business Svcs	Dr. Heather BIGARD
05	Senior VP Academic Affairs	Dr. Michael VITALE
21	Assoc VP Fin Svcs & Controller	Ms. Melinda BARBER
12	Assoc VP South Lake Expansion	Mr. Thom KIEFT
15	Dir Human Resources Operations	Ms. Beisy HERNANDEZ
13	Chief Information Officer	Mr. Nicholas KEMP
111	Sr VP Inst Advancement/Foundation	Dr. Laura BYRD
18	Director Facilities	Vacant
08	Dean of Library & Learning Center	Ms. Katie SACCO
35	Dean of Students	Ms. Carolyn SCOTT
97	Dean of General Studies	Ms. Karen HOGANS
66	Dean of Nursing	Vacant
26	Exec Dir Strategic Communication	Mr. Kevin YURASEK
37	Director Financial Aid	Ms. Arminta JOHNSON
06	Registrar	Ms. Caitlin MOORE
41	Exec Director Athletics	Mr. Michael K. MATULIA
106	Exec Dir Strategic Inn/Dig Educ	Mr. Mike NATHANSON
84	Exec Director Enrollment Mgmt	Vacant
96	Purchasing and Accounts Payable Mgr	Ms. Tammy SPENCER
04	Executive Asst to the President	Ms. Claudia MORRIS
103	Dean Workforce Development	Dr. Amy ALBEE

Larkin University　(V)
18301 North Miami Avenue, Suite 1, Miami FL 33169
County: Miami-Dade　　　Identification: 667288
Telephone: (305) 760-7500　　Carnegie Class: Not Classified
FAX Number: N/A　　　Calendar System: Semester
URL: ularkin.org
Established:　　　Annual Graduate Tuition & Fees: N/A
Enrollment: N/A　　　　　　　　Coed
Affiliation or Control: Independent Non-Profit　IRS Status: 501(c)3
Highest Offering: Doctorate; No Undergraduates
Accreditation: @SC, PHAR

01	Chief Executive Officer/President	Dr. Rudi H. ETTRICH
05	Director of Clinical Programs	Dr. Alexis ARANGO
67	Vice President/Dean of Pharmacy	Dr. Ruth E. NEMIRE
81	Vice Pres/Dean Biomedical Sci	Dr. Marti ECHOLS
10	Vice Pres of Finance/CFO	Alan FESSENDEN
13	Director of Technology	Dr. Jorge E. MACHADO
08	Director of the Library	Dr. Sharon ARGOV
15	Director of Human Resources	Ms. Frida MUSILA

Lynn University　(W)
3601 N Military Trail, Boca Raton FL 33431-5598
County: Palm Beach　　　FICE Identification: 001505
　　　　　　　　　　　Unit ID: 132657
Telephone: (561) 237-7000　　Carnegie Class: Masters/L
FAX Number: (561) 237-7100　　Calendar System: Semester
URL: www.lynn.edu
Established: 1962　　Annual Undergrad Tuition & Fees: $39,350
Enrollment: 3,232　　　　　　　　Coed
Affiliation or Control: Independent Non-Profit　IRS Status: 501(c)3
Highest Offering: Doctorate
Accreditation: SC, CACREP, IACBE, MUS

01	President	Dr. Kevin M. ROSS
00	President Emeritus	Dr. Donald E. ROSS
11	Sr Vice President Administration	Mr. Gregory J. MALFITANO
05	Vice President Academic Affairs	Dr. Katrina CARTER-TELLISON
84	Vice Pres Enrollment Management	Dr. Gareth FOWLES
32	Vice President for Student Life	Dr. Anthony ALTIERI
30	Vice Pres Development/Alumni Affs	Mr. Gregory J. MALFITANO
13	Chief Strategy & Technology Officer	Mr. Chris G. BONIFORTI
10	Chief Financial Officer/Treasurer	Mr. Thomas ROONEY
26	Chief Marketing Officer	Mrs. Sherrie WELDON
35	Dean of Students	Mr. Gary MARTIN
43	General Counsel	Mr. Michael ANTONELLO
20	Academic Dean	Mr. Mike PETROSKI
113	Exec Dir Stdnt Administrative Svcs	Ms. Evelyn C. NELSON
39	Director Housing & Residence Life	Ms. Meagan ELSBERRY
36	Executive Director Career Develop	Ms. Barbara CAMBIA
41	Director of Athletics	Mr. Devin CROSBY
109	Director Auxiliary Services	Mr. Matthew P. CHALOUX
23	Director Health Center	Ms. Rita ALBERT
27	Director of Marketing and Comm	Ms. Stephanie BROWN
07	Dir Undergraduate Admissions	Mr. Stefano PAPALEO
37	Dir of Financial Aid	Mr. John CHAMBERS
38	Director of the Counseling Center	Ms. Nicole R. OVEDIA
96	Director of Purchasing	Ms. Maria BIMONTE
06	Registrar	Ms. Jenifer SCHOLL
21	Director of Accounting	Mr. Michael C. BOLDUC
123	Dir Graduate & Online Admission	Mr. Steven PRUITT
09	Director of Institutional Research	Mrs. Lara MARTIN
15	Director of Employee Services	Mr. Aaron GREENBERG
40	Campus Store Manager	Ms. Monaco CASTRO
50	Dean College Business & Management	Mr. RT GOOD
49	Dean College of Arts & Sciences	Dr. Gary VILLA
88	Dean College of Aeronautics	Dr. Jeffrey C. JOHNSON
53	Dean Ross College of Education	Dr. Kathleen WEIGEL
60	Dean College Comm and Design	Dr. David L. JAFFE
64	Dean Conservatory of Music	Dr. Jon H. ROBERTSON
88	Exe Dir Inst Achievement Learning	Mr. Shaun EXSTEEN
08	Director of the Library	Ms. Amy FILIATREAU
104	Director of International Programs	Mrs. Erin GARCIA
19	Campus Safety Chief	Mr. John MCAVOY
44	Director Annual Programs	Ms. Lisa MILLER

Marconi International University (A)

141 NE 3rd Ave., 7th Floor, Miami FL 33132

County: Miami-Dade Identification: 667377
Telephone: (305) 266-7678 Carnegie Class: Not Classified
FAX Number: (786) 866-2106 Calendar System: Semester
URL: www.miuniversity.edu
Established: 2018 Annual Undergrad Tuition & Fees: N/A
Enrollment: N/A Coed
Affiliation or Control: Proprietary IRS Status: Proprietary
Highest Offering: Master's
Accreditation: ACICS

01 President .... Pablo CARDONA
03 Executive Vice President .... Rafael GARCIA
07 Director of Admissions .... Vacant
37 Director Student Financial Aid .... Elba CASTANOS
06 Registrar .... Heydi DAVILA
38 Director Student Counseling .... Alfredo VILLALOBOS

Med Academy (B)

3418 West 84th St., Ste 100, Hialeah FL 33018

County: Miami-Dade FICE Identification: 042447
Unit ID: 488059
Telephone: (786) 792-3350 Carnegie Class: Spec 2-yr-Health
FAX Number: N/A Calendar System: Quarter
Established: 2006 Annual Undergrad Tuition & Fees: N/A
Enrollment: N/A Coed
Affiliation or Control: Proprietary IRS Status: Proprietary
Highest Offering: Associate Degree
Accreditation: COE

01 Founder & CEO .... Mr. Juan REVUELTA

Mercy Hospital College of Nursing (C)

3663 South Miami Ave Ste 1500, Miami FL 33133

County: Miami-Dade Identification: 667222
Unit ID: 419217
Telephone: (305) 285-2777 Carnegie Class: Not Classified
FAX Number: (305) 285-2671 Calendar System: Semester
URL: www.mercymiami.com/professionals/college-of-nursing
Established: 2008 Annual Undergrad Tuition & Fees: N/A
Enrollment: 91 Coed
Affiliation or Control: Proprietary IRS Status: Proprietary
Highest Offering: Associate Degree
Accreditation: ABHES, ADNUR, PNUR

66 Dean .... Ms. Elizabeth HERNANDEZ

Meridian College (D)

7020 Professional Pkwy E, Sarasota FL 34240

County: Sarasota FICE Identification: 023268
Unit ID: 244279
Telephone: (941) 377-4880 Carnegie Class: Spec 2-yr-Health
FAX Number: (941) 378-2842 Calendar System: Other
URL: www.meridian.edu
Established: 1982 Annual Undergrad Tuition & Fees: N/A
Enrollment: 194 Coed
Affiliation or Control: Proprietary IRS Status: Proprietary
Highest Offering: Associate Degree
Accreditation: ACCSC

01 Campus Director/Student Svcs .... Mr. Patrick MCDERMOTT
07 Director of Admissions .... Ms. Kim MILES
36 Director Career Services .... Ms. Tracy FORDHAM

Miami Dade College (E)

300 NE Second Avenue, Miami FL 33132-2204

County: Miami-Dade County FICE Identification: 001506
Unit ID: 135717
Telephone: (305) 237-8888 Carnegie Class: Bac/Assoc-Assoc Dom
FAX Number: (305) 237-7913 Calendar System: Semester
URL: www.mdc.edu
Established: 1960 Annual Undergrad Tuition & Fees (In-State): $2,838
Enrollment: 46,523 Coed
Affiliation or Control: State IRS Status: 501(c)3
Highest Offering: Baccalaureate
Accreditation: SC, ADNUR, ARCPA, ART, CAHIIM, COARC, DANCE, DH, DMS, EMT, FUSER, HT, MLTAD, MUS, NMT, NUR, NURSE, OPD, PTAA, RAD, THEA

01 President .... Ms. Madeline PUMARIEGA
05 Executive Vice President & Provost .... Dr. Malou HARRISON
10 Sr Vice Provost/CFO/IT .... Mr. Jayson IROFF
11 Vice Provost Business Affairs .... Mr. Christopher STARLING
13 Vice Provost Information Tech/CIO .... Mr. Robert PARRONDO
18 Vice Provost Facilities .... Mr. Leobardo BOBADILLA
15 Vice Provost Human Resources .... Ms. Iliana CASTILLO-FRICK
108 VP Strategy & Inst Effectiveness .... Ms. Wanda SMITH
12 Campus President Hialeah .... Dr. Anthony CRUZ
12 Campus President Wolfson .... Ms. Beatriz GONZALEZ
12 Campus President Kendall .... Dr. Anthony CRUZ
12 Campus President Medical .... Dr. Bryan STEWART
12 Campus President North .... Mr. Fermin VAZQUEZ
12 Campus President EPC .... Dr. Alanka BROWN
12 Campus President Homestead .... Dr. Oscar LOYNAZ
12 Campus President West .... Dr. Beverly MOORE-GARCIA
21 Assoc Vice Prov Business Affs .... Ms. Delilah ALMEDA
32 Vice Prov Stdnt Affs/Chief Enroll .... Dr. Jaime ANZALOTTA
102 Executive Dir MDC Foundation .... Mr. Nelson HINCAPIE
37 Assoc VP Student Financial Services .... Ms. Mercedes AMAYA
06 Collegewide Registrar .... Dr. Elisabet VIZOSO
26 Chief Public Rels Officer/Dir Comm .... Mr. Juan MENDIETA
29 Director Alumni Relations .... Mr. Adlar GARCIA
35 Director Student Life .... Ms. Annielys SOSA
88 Dir Testing Admin/Pgm Evaluation .... Mr. Silvio RODRIGUEZ
22 Dir Equal Opportunity Pgm/ADA Coord .... Dr. Joy C. RUFF
121 Director Student Advisement .... Ms. Veronica GONZALES
84 Exc Dir Enrollment Management .... Mr. Miguel MURPHY
96 Director of Purchasing .... Mr. Roman MARTINEZ
41 Director Intercollegiate Athletics .... Ms. Alysia DYER
09 Director Research & Data Analysis .... Dr. Ivana FREDOTOVIC
43 Legal Counsel .... Mr. Javier LEY-SOTO
86 Director Governmental Affairs .... Mr. Mauricio MONTIEL
100 Chief of Staff .... Ms. Maryam LAGUNA BORREGO
103 Vice Provost Workforce Pgm .... Dr. Loretta OVUERAYE
104 Director Global Student Pgm .... Ms. Gabriela ESTEVES
105 College Webmaster .... Mr. Andrew SEAGA
08 Head Librarian/Dir Lrng Resources .... Mr. Erick DOMINICIS
85 Dir International Student Services .... Ms. Adriana MENKE
04 Exec Assistant to the President .... Ms. Nadia BERBICK

Miami International University of Art & Design (F)

1501 Biscayne Boulevard, Suite 100,
Miami FL 33132-1418

County: Miami-Dade FICE Identification: 008878
Unit ID: 134811
Telephone: (305) 428-5700 Carnegie Class: Bac-Diverse
FAX Number: (305) 374-7946 Calendar System: Quarter
URL: www.artinstitutes.edu/miami
Established: 1965 Annual Undergrad Tuition & Fees: $19,354
Enrollment: 934 Coed
Affiliation or Control: Independent Non-Profit IRS Status: 501(c)3
Highest Offering: Master's
Accreditation: SC, CIDA

01 President .... Ms. Leslie BAUGHMAN
05 Dean of Academic Affairs .... Mr. Alfonso GUTIERREZ
10 Dir Admin & Financial Services .... Mr. John C. STILLWAGGON
32 Dean of Student Affairs .... Ms. April BURT
08 Librarian .... Ms. Lisa CASTO

Miami Regional University (G)

700 S. Royal Poinciana Blvd #100,
Miami Springs FL 33166

County: Miami-Dade FICE Identification: 041284
Unit ID: 451103
Telephone: (305) 442-9223 Carnegie Class: Spec-4-yr-Other Health
FAX Number: (305) 442-8723 Calendar System: Other
URL: www.mru.edu
Established: 1996 Annual Undergrad Tuition & Fees: N/A
Enrollment: 818 Coed
Affiliation or Control: Proprietary IRS Status: Proprietary
Highest Offering: Doctorate
Accreditation: @SC, ACCSC, ADNUR, NUR

01 President & CEO .... Ophelia SANCHEZ
43 Exec Vice President/General Counsel .... Richard GRILLO
05 Provost/SVP Academic Affairs .... Dr. Dario A. CORTES
32 Senior Director Student Services .... Vacant
07 Assist VP Admissions .... Vacant
08 Librarian .... Katia NUNEZ
10 VP Finance/Enrollment .... Henry BABANI
15 VP Employee Affs/Public Relation .... Mitsy SOUSA
36 Lead Career Services Rep .... Mirizza MENENDEZ
37 Assoc VP Student Financial Aid .... Vacant

Millennia Atlantic University (MAU) (H)

3801 NW 97th Avenue, Suite 100, Doral FL 33178

County: Miami-Dade FICE Identification: 041825
Unit ID: 461883
Telephone: (786) 331-1000 Carnegie Class: Spec-4-yr-Bus
FAX Number: (305) 503-9680 Calendar System: Semester
URL: www.maufl.edu
Established: 2007 Annual Undergrad Tuition & Fees: $9,876
Enrollment: 196 Coed
Affiliation or Control: Proprietary IRS Status: Proprietary
Highest Offering: Master's
Accreditation: ACCSC

01 President .... Dr. Aristides MAZA-DUERTO
05 Director of Academic Programs .... Dr. Octavio MAZA
00 Chancellor .... Mr. Luis E. MARTINEZ
10 CFO/VP Admin & Finance .... Mrs. Orianna M. MOSS
20 Vice Director of Academic Programs .Mrs. Teresa L. FITZGERALD
06 Registrar .... Ms. Natasha ALEONG
37 Financial Aid Manager .... Ms. Latia JONES
26 Dir of Marketing & Admissions .... Ms. Alma I. UBILLA
36 Student Services and Placement Mgr .... Ms. Angela D. PENAS
08 Librarian .... Ms. Natasa HOGUE
113 Bursar .... Mrs. Jenice C. MAZA-DUERTO

New York Film Academy, South Beach (I)

420 Lincoln Rd #200, Miami Beach FL 33139

Telephone: (305) 534-6009 Identification: 770984
Accreditation: &WC

† Regional accreditation is carried under the parent institution in Burbank, CA.

North Broward Technical Center (J)

1871 West Hillsboro Blvd, Deerfield Beach FL 33442

County: Broward Identification: 667357
Telephone: (954) 427-8830 Carnegie Class: Not Classified
FAX Number: (954) 427-8836 Calendar System: Other
URL: nbtechcenter.com/
Established: Annual Undergrad Tuition & Fees: N/A
Enrollment: N/A Coed
Affiliation or Control: Proprietary IRS Status: Proprietary
Highest Offering: Associate Degree
Accreditation: ABHES

01 President/Program Manager .... Dr. Herard LAFRANCE

North Florida College (K)

325 NW Turner Davis Drive, Madison FL 32340-1610

County: Madison FICE Identification: 001508
Unit ID: 136145
Telephone: (850) 973-2288 Carnegie Class: Bac/Assoc-Assoc Dom
FAX Number: (850) 973-1696 Calendar System: Semester
URL: www.nfc.edu
Established: 1958 Annual Undergrad Tuition & Fees (In-State): $3,054
Enrollment: 1,181 Coed
Affiliation or Control: State IRS Status: 501(c)3
Highest Offering: Baccalaureate
Accreditation: SC, ADNUR, EMT, NUR

01 President .... Mr. John GROSSKOPF
05 VP of Academic/Student Affairs/CAO .... Ms. Jennifer PAGE
10 Chief Business Officer .... Mr. Micah RODGERS
15 Exec Director of Employee Services .... Mr. Tyler COODY
08 Director of Learning Resources .... Ms. Lynn WYCHE
103 Assoc Dean Econ Dev/Workforce Educ .... Mr. David DUNKLE
06 Registrar .... Ms. Lori PLEASANT
18 Chief Facilities/Physical Plant .... Mr. Glenn STRICKLAND
111 Dir College Advancement .... Ms. Allison FINLEY
102 Dir Foundation/Alumni Relations .... Ms. Traci MCCLUNG
37 Director Student Financial Aid .... Ms. Brooke TURNER
28 Director of Diversity/Equity .... Ms. Denise BELL
04 Executive Asst to President .... Ms. Michelle WHEELER
19 Director Security/Safety .... Mr. Larry AKERS

Northwest Florida State College (L)

100 College Boulevard, Niceville FL 32578-1295

County: Okaloosa FICE Identification: 001510
Unit ID: 136233
Telephone: (850) 678-5111 Carnegie Class: Bac/Assoc-Mixed
FAX Number: (850) 729-5215 Calendar System: Semester
URL: www.nwfsc.edu
Established: 1963 Annual Undergrad Tuition & Fees (In-State): $3,133
Enrollment: 5,004 Coed
Affiliation or Control: State IRS Status: 501(c)3
Highest Offering: Baccalaureate
Accreditation: SC, ADNUR, DA, EMT, NURSE, @PTAA, RAD

01 President .... Dr. Devin STEPHENSON
03 Senior Vice President .... Ms. Cristie KEDROSKI
05 Vice Pres of Academic Affairs .... Dr. Deidre PRICE
10 Vice Pres of Business Operations .... Mr. Randy WHITE
13 Chief Information Officer .... Mr. Cole ALLEN
09 AVP of Research & Assessment .... Ms. Pauline ANDERSON
43 General Counsel .... Ms. Whitney RUTHERFORD
04 Executive Assistant to President .... Ms. Melissa WOLF-BATES
49 Dean of Art and Sciences .... Dr. Dana BIGHAM-STEPHENS
88 Dean/CHS Principal .... Dr. Sandy ARTEAGA
75 Dean Career & Technical Education .... Dr. Michael ERNY
66 Dean Health Science & Public Safety .... Dr. Charlotte KUSS
121 Exec Dir Student Success Navigation .... Ms. Heather DIETZOLD
06 Exec Dir Acad Records/Enrollment .... Ms. Stephanie LINARD
37 Exec Dir Fin Planning/Scholarships .... Dr. Aimee WATTS
103 Exec Dir Workforce & Cont Educ .... Mr. Dennis BRAUN
15 Exec Dir Human Resources/Diversity .... Ms. Roberta MACKEY
25 Exec Dir of Grant Development .... Mr. Sam RENFROE
21 Exec Dir of Accounting/Finance .... Mr. Edward ROSENTEL
26 Exec Dir Strategic Communications .... Mr. Bryan BROOKS
106 Exec Dir of Academic Strategies .... Dr. Melanie JACKSON
08 Learning Commons Director .... Ms. Lisa HADDORFF
18 Facilities Director .... Mr. Patrick SWEENEY
19 Director of College Safety/Security .... Mr. Aaron MURRAY
102 Executive Director Foundation .... Mr. Chris STOWERS
57 Director Mattie Kelly Arts Center .... Ms. Jeanette SHIRES
41 Athletic Director .... Mr. Ramsey ROSS
96 Director of Purchasing .... Ms. Katherine ST. ONGE
113 Student Accounts & Billing Mgr .... Ms. Cecilia BELL

Nova Southeastern University (M)

3301 College Avenue, Fort Lauderdale FL 33314-7796

County: Broward FICE Identification: 001509
Unit ID: 136215
Telephone: (800) 541-6682 Carnegie Class: DU-Higher
FAX Number: (954) 262-3800 Calendar System: Trimester

URL: www.nova.edu
Established: 1964 Annual Undergrad Tuition & Fees: $33,430
Enrollment: 20,888 Coed
Affiliation or Control: Independent Non-Profit IRS Status: 501(c)3
Highest Offering: Doctorate
Accreditation: SC, AA, ACAE, ARCPA, AUD, CACREP, CAEP, CAHIIM, CLPSY, COARC, CVT, DENT, DIET, @DIETD, #DMS, IACBE, IPSY, LAW, #MED, MFCD, NURSE, OPT, OPTR, OSTEO, OT, PH, PHAR, PTA, SCPSY, SP, SPAA

01 President & CEO ... Dr. George L. HANBURY, II
05 Provost & EVP Academic Affairs ... Dr. Ronald J. CHENAIL
10 VP Finance/CFO ... Ms. Alyson SILVA
00 Chancellor Nova Southeastern Univ ... Mr. Ray FERRERO, JR.
17 Chancellor Health Professions Div ... Dr. Fred LIPPMAN
11 EVP/Chief Operating Officer ... Dr. Harry K. MOON
88 Sr VP for Trans Rsrch & Econ Dev ... Dr. Ken DAWSON-SCULLY
100 Deputy Chief of Staff ... Ms. Jennifer RAMOS
08 Interim VP Info Svcs/Univ Librarian ... Mr. James HUTCHENS
43 VP Legal Affairs ... Mr. Joel BERMAN
46 VP Research Tech Transfer ... Dr. Gary S. MARGULES
32 VP Student Affairs/Dean UG Studies ... Dr. Brad WILLIAMS
111 VP Univ Advancement/Chief of Staff ... Mr. Terry J. MULARKEY
13 VP Info Tech/Chief Info Ofcr ... Mr. Tom WEST
15 VP Human Resources ... Mr. Robert J. PIETRYKOWSKI
84 VP Enrollment and Stdnt Svcs ... Dr. Stephanie BROWN
21 VP Business Services ... Mr. Marc CROCQUET
106 VP Reg Campus & Online Educ ... Dr. Ricardo BELMAR
18 VP Facilities Mgmt ... Mr. Daniel ALFONSO
23 Vice Pres Clinical Operations ... Mr. Leonard POUNDS
26 VP University Relations ... Ms. Kyle FISHER
19 Director Public Safety ... Mr. Paul TURNER
09 VP Institutional Effectiveness ... Dr. Donald J. RUDAWSKY
108 Dir Accreditation/Acad Pgm Rev ... Mr. Adam ROSENTHAL
24 Exec Dir Ed Tech/Digital Media Prod ... Ms. Diane LIPPE
25 Director Sponsored Programs ... Ms. Cathy HARLAN
86 Exec Dir Licensure/State Relations ... Dr. Greg F. STIBER
12 Headmaster University School ... Dr. William KOPAS
27 Exec Dir University Publications ... Ms. Bernadette BRUCE
36 Asst Dean Academic & Prof Succes .. Ms. Mignon BISSONNETTE
29 VP Alumni Relations/Advance ... Ms. Alissa HECHTER
06 Dir University Registrar's Office ... Ms. G. Elaine N. POFF
41 Asst VP UA/Director Athletics ... Mr. Michael MOMINEY
88 Director Campus Recreation ... Mr. Tom VITUCCI
116 Executive Dir Internal Auditing ... Mr. Ron MIDEI
88 VP Compliance/Chief Integrity Ofcr ... Ms. Robin SUPLER
88 Dir Museum of Art ... Ms. Bonnie CLEARWATER
63 Dean College Osteopathic Medicine ... Dr. Elaine WALLACE
67 Dean College Pharmacy ... Dr. Michelle CLARK
88 Dean College Optometry ... Dr. Linda ROUSE
76 Interim Dean College of HC Sciences ... Dr. Guy NEHRENZ
54 Dean College Engineering/Computing ... Dr. Meline KEVORKIAN
61 Dean Shepard Broad Law Center ... Mr. José (Beto) R. JUÁREZ, JR.
49 Halmos College of Arts and Sciences . Dr. Holly BAUMGARTNER
66 Dean College of Nursing ... Dr. Marcella M. RUTHERFORD
50 Dean Huizenga Col of Bus/Entrepren ... Dr. Andrew ROSMAN
92 Dean Farquhar Honors College ... Dr. Andrea SHAW-NEVINS
83 Dean College of Psychology ... Dr. Karen GROSBY
52 Dean of Dental Medicine ... Dr. Steven KALTMAN
53 Dean Fischler College of Education ... Dr. Kimberly DURHAM
88 Dean College Allopathic Med ... Dr. Johannes VIEWEG
117 Exec Director NSUBIC ... Dr. John WENSVEEN
118 VP Operations of HPD ... Dr. Irving ROSENBAUM

NRI Institute of Health Sciences (A)

503 Royal Palm Blvd, Royal Palm Beach FL 33411
County: Palm Beach FICE Identification: 042108
Unit ID: 481252
Telephone: (561) 688-5112 Carnegie Class: Spec 2-yr-Health
FAX Number: (561) 688-5113 Calendar System: Semester
URL: www.nriinstitute.edu
Established: 2006 Annual Undergrad Tuition & Fees: N/A
Enrollment: 126 Coed
Affiliation or Control: Proprietary IRS Status: Proprietary
Highest Offering: Associate Degree
Accreditation: COE

01 President & Director ... Elizabeth STOLKOWSKI

Palm Beach Atlantic University (B)

901 S. Flagler Drive, West Palm Beach FL 33401
County: Palm Beach FICE Identification: 008849
Unit ID: 136330
Telephone: (561) 803-2000 Carnegie Class: DU-Mod
FAX Number: (561) 803-2186 Calendar System: Semester
URL: www.pba.edu
Established: 1968 Annual Undergrad Tuition & Fees: $33,475
Enrollment: 3,704 Coed
Affiliation or Control: Interdenominational IRS Status: 501(c)3
Highest Offering: Doctorate
Accreditation: SC, IACBE, MUS, NURSE, PHAR, THEOL

01 President ... Dr. Debra A. SCHWINN
05 Provost/CAO ... Dr. Chelly TEMPLETON
10 VP for Finance/Admin & CFO ... Dr. Stacie BOWIE
30 EVP for Advancement ... Mrs. Laura BISHOP
84 Vice President Enrollment Mgmt ... Dr. Nancy BRAINARD
15 VP of Human Resources ... Mrs. Cara WALD
32 Vice President Student Development ... Dr. Bob LUTZ
88 VP for Spiritual Development ... Dr. Bernard CUETO
13 VP Information Tech Svcs/CIO ... Mr. Scott BARNES
09 Asst Provost Rsrch/Effectiveness ... Mrs. Carolanne BROWN
96 AVP Auxiliary Svcs/Procurement ... Ms. AnnMarie TAYLOR
51 Dean MacArthur School of Leadership ... Dr. Nathan LANE
49 Dean School of Arts & Sciences ... Dr. Robert LLOYD
50 Dean School of Business ... Dr. Brian STROW
53 Dean School of Education ... Ms. Chelneca TEMPLETON
57 Dean School of Music/Fine Arts ... Mr. Jason LESTER
66 Dean School of Nursing ... Ms. Phyllis KING
67 Dean Gregory School of Pharmacy ... Dr. Dana STRACHAN
57 Dean of College of the Arts ... Dr. Jason LESTER
73 Dean School of Ministry ... Dr. Jonathan GRENZ
06 Registrar ... Ms. Kathy MAJZNER
08 Director of the Warren Library ... Mr. John DONCEVIC
20 Associate Provost for Instruction ... Dr. Nathan LANE
18 Director of Physical Plant ... Mr. Martin SHUTTERLY
35 Assistant Dean of Students ... Ms. Kate MAGRO
41 Director of Athletics ... Ms. Courtney LOVELY
42 Director of Campus Ministries ... Mr. Mark KAPRIVE

Palm Beach State College (C)

4200 Congress Avenue, Lake Worth FL 33461-4796
County: Palm Beach FICE Identification: 001512
Unit ID: 136358
Telephone: (561) 967-7222 Carnegie Class: Bac/Assoc-Assoc Dom
FAX Number: (561) 868-3504 Calendar System: Semester
URL: www.palmbeachstate.edu
Established: 1933 Annual Undergrad Tuition & Fees (In-State): $2,444
Enrollment: 26,666 Coed
Affiliation or Control: State IRS Status: 501(c)3
Highest Offering: Baccalaureate
Accreditation: SC, ACBSP, ADNUR, CAHIIM, COARC, DA, DH, DMS, EMT, MAC, NUR, RAD, SURGT

01 President ... Ms. Ava L. PARKER
05 VP of Academic Affairs ... Dr. Tunjarnika COLEMAN-FERRELL
88 VP of Academic Innovation/Strategy ... Dr. Roger YOHE
10 VP Administration/Business Services ... Mr. James DUFFIE
32 Vice President Student Services ... Dr. Peter BARBATIS
13 Chief Information Officer ... Mr. Ken L. LIBUTTI
31 Exec Director Community Engagement ... Ms. Rachael E. BONLARRON
43 General Counsel ... Mr. Kevin A. FERNANDER
111 Vice President Advancement ... Mr. David RUTHERFORD
20 Int Assoc VP Academic Affairs ... Dr. Holly L. BENNETT
103 Dean Workforce Educ/Development ... Mr. Rick REEDER
20 Provost Boca Raton ... Mr. Van P. WILLAIMS
20 Dean Academic Affairs Loxahatchee .. Ms. Kimberley LANCASTER
20 Int Prov Academic Affs Lake Worth ... Dr. Peter BARBATIS
20 Dean Academic Affairs Boca Raton ... Dr. Roy M. VARGAS
97 Int Dean Bachelor Degree Programs ... Dr. Don GLADNEY
20 Dean Curriculum ... Dr. Velmarie ALBERTINI
20 Exec Dean Belle Grade Campus ... Ms. Latanya L. MCNEAL
84 Dean Enrollment Management ... Dr. Stephen JOYNER
37 Director Financial Aid ... Mr. Eddie VIERA
09 Exec Dir Inst Rsrch/Effectiveness ... Mr. David WEBER
18 Facilities Director ... Mr. Bob PRIOLO
15 Exec Director Human Resources ... Mr. Michael PUSTIZZI
06 College Registrar ... Mr. Peter BIEGEL
96 Procurement Director ... Mr. David CHOJNACKI
25 Dir Resource & Grant Development ... Ms. Maureen CAPP
106 E-Learning Director ... Mr. Sidney BEITLER
108 Assessment Director ... Ms. Iva BERGERON
19 Security & Risk Management Director ... Ms. Delsa BUSH
76 Dean Health Services ... Dr. Edward WILLEY

Palmer College of Chiropractic, Florida Campus (D)

4777 City Center Parkway, Port Orange FL 32129-4153
Telephone: (386) 763-2709 Identification: 666330
Accreditation: &HLC, &CHIRO

† Regional accreditation is carried under the parent institution in Davenport, IA.

Pasco-Hernando State College (E)

10230 Ridge Road, New Port Richey FL 34654-5112
County: Pasco FICE Identification: 010652
Unit ID: 136400
Telephone: (727) 847-2727 Carnegie Class: Bac/Assoc-Mixed
FAX Number: (727) 816-1815 Calendar System: Semester
URL: www.phsc.edu
Established: 1972 Annual Undergrad Tuition & Fees (In-District): $3,155
Enrollment: 9,886 Coed
Affiliation or Control: State/Local IRS Status: 501(c)3
Highest Offering: Baccalaureate
Accreditation: SC, ADNUR, DH, EMT, NURSE, SURGT

01 President ... Dr. Timothy L. BEARD
05 Exec VP & Chief Academic Officer ... Dr. Stanley M. GIANNET
32 Sr VP & Chief Student Affs/Enroll ... Dr. Robert E. BADE
10 Sr VP of Financal Opers & CFO ... Mr. Brian S. HORN
12 Provost of the East Campus ... Dr. Edwin G. GOOLSBY
12 Interim Provost North Campus ... Mr. Reggie L. WILSON
12 Provost Spring Hill Campus ... Dr. Amy E. ANDERSON
12 Provost Porter Campus at Wiregrass ... Dr. Kevin F. O'FARRELL
103 Dean of Workforce Dev/Career/Tech ... Dr. Marcia M. AUSTIN
120 SVP & Chief Tech/Distance Ed Ofcr ... Dr. Melissa L. HARTS
84 Dean Stdnt Affairs & Enroll Mgmt .. Ms. Chiquita A. HENDERSON
20 Asst VP Academic Affairs ... Ms. Sonia B. THORN
49 Dean Arts and Sciences ... Dr. Gerene M. THOMPSON
18 Asst VP Facilities Mgmt ... Mr. Tony A. RIVAS
09 Assoc Dean Inst Effectiveness ... Ms. Carla M. ROSSITER-SMITH
13 Assoc Dean of Enterprise Systems ... Ms. Jan L. SCOTT
111 Assoc VP Alum/Col Rels/Exec Dir Fdn ... Dr. Lisa A. RICHARDSON
66 Associate Dean of Nursing ... Ms. Tennille I. O'CONNOR
07 Dean of Admissions & Enroll Mgmt ... Mr. Chris J. BIBBO
37 Dean Financial Aid ... Ms. Rebecca SHANAFELT
43 Asst VP of Policy/General Counsel ... Vacant
08 Director of Libraries ... Ms. Ingrid L. PURRENHAGE
26 Assoc Dean Marketing/Comm & Media ... Ms. Melanie WAXLER
18 Director of Facilities ... Mr. Keith V. BRAUN
15 Exec Director of Human Resources ... Mr. Darrell L. CLARK
109 Director of Auxiliary Services ... Mr. John D. COLLINS
22 Dir of Global & Multi Aware & Spec ... Mr. Imani D. ASUKILE
96 Procurement & Contract Admin Mgr ... Ms. Christy L. AULICINO
04 Executive Asst to President & DBOT ... Ms. Rhonda M. DODGE
29 Director Alumni & Donor Relations ... Ms. Michelle L. BULLWINKEL
41 Athletics Director/Instructor ... Mr. Stephen A. WINTERLING

Pensacola Christian College (F)

250 Brent Lane, Pensacola FL 32503
County: Escambia Identification: 667101
Telephone: (850) 478-8496 Carnegie Class: Not Classified
FAX Number: (850) 479-6552 Calendar System: Semester
URL: www.pcci.edu
Established: 1974 Annual Undergrad Tuition & Fees: N/A
Enrollment: N/A Coed
Affiliation or Control: Independent Non-Profit IRS Status: 501(c)3
Highest Offering: Doctorate
Accreditation: TRACS, NURSE

01 President ... Dr. Troy SHOEMAKER
03 Executive Vice President ... Dr. Jon LANDS
05 Academic Vice President ... Dr. Raylene COCHRAN
32 Vice President for Student Affairs ... Mr. Tim MCLAUGHLIN
10 Chief Financial Officer ... Mr. Jim THOMPSON
13 Chief Information Officer ... Mr. Troy ARWINE
11 Vice President for Operations ... Mr. Mike HARRISON
06 Registrar ... Mr. Adam SCHRODER
09 Dir Institutional Effectiveness ... Dr. Mark SMITH
41 Athletic Director ... Mr. Addison CALLEY
08 Chief Librarian ... Mr. Kelly GRANDSTAFF
07 Director of Admissions ... Mrs. Amy ABBOTT
106 Director of Online Learning ... Mr. Steve MARTIN
19 Chief of Safety and Security ... Mr. Reggie BARTKOWSKI

Pensacola State College (G)

1000 College Boulevard, Pensacola FL 32504-8998
County: Escambia FICE Identification: 001513
Unit ID: 136473
Telephone: (850) 484-1000 Carnegie Class: Bac/Assoc-Mixed
FAX Number: (850) 484-1826 Calendar System: Semester
URL: www.pensacolastate.edu
Established: 1948 Annual Undergrad Tuition & Fees (In-District): $2,364
Enrollment: 9,226 Coed
Affiliation or Control: Local IRS Status: 501(c)3
Highest Offering: Baccalaureate
Accreditation: SC, ACFEI, ADNUR, CAHIIM, DH, EMT, MAC, NUR, NURSE, PNUR, PTAA, RAD, SURGT

01 President ... Dr. Ed MEADOWS
05 VP Academic and Student Affairs ... Dr. Erin SPICER
11 VP Administrative Services ... Mr. Tom GILLIAM
10 VP Business Affairs ... Mrs. Anita KOVACS
20 Dean Bacc Studies/Academic Sup ... Dr. Kirk BRADLEY
20 Senior Dean Academic Affairs ... Dr. Brenda KELLY
12 Dean Milton Campus ... Ms. Jennifer HILL-FARON
76 Dean Health Sciences ... Dr. Dusti SLUDER
102 Exec Director College Foundation ... Ms. Andrea KRIEGER
13 Assoc VP Information Systems ... Mr. Michael JOHNSTON
32 Assoc VP Student Affairs ... Dr. Jon STEPHENSON
14 Exec Director ITS ... Mr. Steve WHITING
86 Associate VP Govt Relations ... Ms. Sandy RAY
26 Exec Dir Marketing/College Info ... Ms. Sheila NICHOLS
105 Coordinator Internet Systems ... Mr. Jason KING
28 Ex Dir Inst Diversity/Stdnt Conduct ... Dr. Lynsey LISTAU
06 Registrar ... Ms. Stephanie DENMARK
25 Dean Grants and Federal Programs ... Dr. Debbie DOUMA
18 Director Facilities and Planning ... Ms. Diane BRACKEN
88 Director Technology Support ... Ms. Liz GOMEZ
15 Director Human Resources ... Ms. Tammy HENDERSON
37 Dir Fin Aid/Veterans/Scholarships ... Ms. Joanne ROZBORSKI
75 Director Career & Technical Educ ... Ms. Deborah HOOKS
38 Director Student Support Services ... Ms. Rachelle BURNS
19 Director Public Safety ... Mr. Robert GOLEY
43 General Counsel ... Mr. Thomas J. GILLIAM
08 District Dept Head Libraries ... Ms. LisaMarie BARTUSIK
96 Director Purchasing ... Ms. Ted YOUNG
91 Director MIS Support ... Mr. Beau MCHENRY
21 Comptroller ... Ms. Nan JACKSON
29 Exec Director Alumni Affairs ... Ms. Hailey LOTZ
07 Director Admissions ... Ms. Samantha HILL
84 Assoc Dean Enrollment Management ... Dr. Amanda TURNER
41 Director Athletics ... Mr. Bryan LEWALLYN
35 Dean Student Affairs ... Ms. Kathy DUTREMBLE
12 Director South Santa Rosa Center ... Ms. Karen MCCABE
12 Director Century Center ... Ms. Sparkie HARRISON

51 Coordinator Continuing Education Ms. Tricia SHERIDAN
04 Exec Assistant to the President Ms. Patricia S. CREWS

Polk State College (A)

999 Avenue H, NE, Winter Haven FL 33881-4299
County: Polk FICE Identification: 001514
Unit ID: 136516
Telephone: (863) 297-1000 Carnegie Class: Bac/Assoc-Mixed
FAX Number: (863) 297-1065 Calendar System: Semester
URL: www.polk.edu
Established: 1964 Annual Undergrad Tuition & Fees (In-District): $3,366
Enrollment: 9,961 Coed
Affiliation or Control: Local IRS Status: 501(c)3
Highest Offering: Baccalaureate
Accreditation: SC, ADNUR, COARC, CVT, DMS, EMT, NUR, OTA, #PTAA, RAD

01 President Dr. Angela FALCONETTI
05 Interim Provost Academic Affairs Dr. Martha SANTIAGO
10 VP Business Admin/Finance Vacant
32 Senior VP Student Svcs & Campus Ops Mr. Reginal WEBB
111 VP Resource Dev/Exec Dir PSCF Mr. Jeff BALDWIN
09 VP Inst Effectiveness/Accred/Rsrch Dr. Mary CLARK
103 Vice Pres Workforce Educ/Econom Dev Dr. Orathai NORTHERN
13 VP Institutional Tech & Risk Mgmt Mr. Robert STACK
28 Chief Diversity Officer/Title IX Mr. Lonnie THOMPSON
26 VP Communications & Public Affairs Ms. Tamara SAKAGAWA
20 Dean of Academic Affairs-WH Ms. April ROBINSON
15 Interim Asst Dir Human Resources Ms. Kristen SYKES
35 Assoc VP Student Services-WH Mr. Lawrence PAKOWSKI
35 Dean of Student Services-LK Mr. Keith BONNEY
20 Dean of Academic Affairs- LK Mr. David SUTTON
21 Exec Dir Business Affs/Controller Mrs. Erin MONTGOMERY
84 Director Stdnt Enrollment/Registrar Ms. Susan MORGAN
37 Director Student Financial Svcs Ms. Lenora BURNETT
66 Interim Director of Nursing Dr. Joan CONNORS
102 CFO Foundation & Alumni Mrs. Cindy BAKER
18 District Director of Facilities Mr. George URBANO
103 Director Corporate College Mr. Howard DRAKE
88 Principal Chain of Lakes Coll HS Ms. Patrice BRYANT-THIGPEN
88 Principal Lakeland Collegiate HS Mr. Rick JEFFRIES
88 Director JDA Center Dr. Andy OGUNTOLA
41 Athletic Director Mr. Stanley CROMARTIE
96 Director of Purchasing Vacant
04 Sr Executive Asst to the President Mrs. Christine LEE
106 District Dir Learning Tech/Ldr Dev Mr. Cody MOYER
25 Director Grants Administration Ms. Jennifer FIORENZA
38 Dir Disability/Counseling Services Ms. Kim PEARSALL
43 Dir Legal Services/General Counsel Mr. Don WILSON
50 Program Director Business Ms. Maria LEHOCZKY
53 Director of Education Ms. Sharon KOCHANOWSKI
54 Pgm Dir Engr Tech/Academics/Bus Dr. Mori TOOSI

Polytechnic University of Puerto Rico (B)

8180 NW 36th Street, Suite 401, Miami FL 33166-6674
Telephone: (305) 418-8000 Identification: 666238
Accreditation: &M

† Regional accreditation is carried under the parent institution, Universidad Politecnica de Puerto Rico, San Juan, PR.

Polytechnic University of Puerto Rico-Orlando Campus (C)

550 N Econlockhatchee Trail, Orlando FL 32825
Telephone: (407) 677-7000 Identification: 770172
Accreditation: &M

† Branch campus of Universidad Politecnica De Puerto Rico, San Juan, PR

The Praxis Institute (D)

1850 SW 8th Street, 4th Floor, Miami FL 33135
County: Miami-Dade FICE Identification: 031147
Unit ID: 430582
Telephone: (305) 642-4104 Carnegie Class: Not Classified
FAX Number: (305) 642-6063 Calendar System: Semester
URL: www.praxis.edu
Established: 1988 Annual Undergrad Tuition & Fees: N/A
Enrollment: 405 Coed
Affiliation or Control: Proprietary IRS Status: Proprietary
Highest Offering: Associate Degree
Accreditation: COE, #OTA, PTAA

01 Executive Director Rebeca ALFIE
05 VP Acad Affs & Campus Director Dario ALFIE
06 Campus Registrar Zoila ESPINOSA

Premiere International College (E)

2055 Central Avenue, Fort Myers FL 33901
County: Lee Identification: 667295
Telephone: (239) 454-5000 Carnegie Class: Not Classified
FAX Number: (239) 454-0456 Calendar System: Quarter
URL: www.picollege.edu
Established: 2009 Annual Undergrad Tuition & Fees: N/A
Enrollment: N/A Coed
Affiliation or Control: Proprietary IRS Status: Proprietary
Highest Offering: Associate Degree
Accreditation: ABHES, ADNUR

01 CEO/Owner Cynthia RUE
05 Director of Education Dr. Lori BARNES

Rasmussen University - Fort Myers (F)

9160 Forum Corporate Pkwy STE 100, Fort Myers FL 33905
Telephone: (239) 477-2100 Identification: 667062
Accreditation: &HLC, ADNUR, MAAB, RAD

† Regional accreditation is carried under the parent institution in Saint Cloud, MN. The tuition figure is an average, actual tuition may vary.

Rasmussen University - Ocala (G)

4755 SW 46th Court, Ocala FL 34474
Telephone: (352) 629-1941 FICE Identification: 008501
Accreditation: &HLC, ADNUR, MAAB, PTAA, RAD

† Regional accreditation carried under the parent institution in Saint Cloud, MN. The tuition figure is an average, actual tuition may vary.

Rasmussen University - Tampa/Brandon (H)

330 Brandon Town Center Dr, Brandon FL 33511
Telephone: (813) 246-7600 Identification: 667067
Accreditation: &HLC, ADNUR, MAAB

† Regional accreditation is carried under the parent institution in Saint Cloud, MN. The tuition figure is an average, actual tuition may vary.

Reformed Theological Seminary (I)

1231 Reformation Drive, Oviedo FL 32765-7197
Telephone: (407) 366-9493 Identification: 666628
Accreditation: &SC, THEOL

† Regional accreditation is carried under the parent institution in Jackson, MS.

Ringling College of Art and Design (J)

2700 N Tamiami Trail, Sarasota FL 34234-5895
County: Sarasota FICE Identification: 012574
Unit ID: 136774
Telephone: (941) 351-5100 Carnegie Class: Spec-4-yr-Arts
FAX Number: (941) 359-7517 Calendar System: Semester
URL: www.ringling.edu
Established: 1931 Annual Undergrad Tuition & Fees: $49,540
Enrollment: 1,624 Coed
Affiliation or Control: Independent Non-Profit IRS Status: 501(c)3
Highest Offering: Baccalaureate
Accreditation: SC, ART

01 President Dr. Larry R. THOMPSON
03 Executive Vice President Dr. Tracy A. WAGNER
04 Executive Assistant to the Pres Ms. Kerry SCHAFFER
05 VP for Academic Affairs Dr. Peter MCALLISTER
84 VP for Enrollment Mgmt/Mktg Dr. Jason GOOD
20 Assoc VP for AA/Dean of Faculty Mr. David H. JACKSON
20 Assoc VP for AA/Dean of UG Studies Mr. Jeff SCHWARTZ
51 Dir Cont Stds/Special Pgms Dr. Phyllis BROWN
06 Registrar Ms. Amanda SHURTLEFF
36 Director Career Services Mr. Charles KOVACS
08 Dir of Library Services Dr. Kristina KEOGH
26 Dir Marketing/Digital Strategies Ms. Laura NEFF-HENDERSON
27 Editorial & PR Manager Ms. Chelsea GARNER-FERRIS
108 Director of Assessment Ms. Kelly BEACHLER
111 VP for Advancement Ms. Stacey CORLEY
110 Sr Director Constituent Engagement Ms. Jeney SLUSSER
112 Asst VP for Strategic Philanthropy Ms. Lora WEY
29 Dir Alumni Relations/Annual Giving Ms. Susan BOROZAN
10 VP for Finance & Administration Ms. Jennifer PRICE
21 Asst VP for Fin & Admn/Controller Ms. Shan-Mei PHILLIPS
18 Asst VP/Dir Facilities Operations Mr. Viron LYNCH
19 Director of Public Safety Mr. Jim GILMAN
37 Dir of Financial Aid Mr. Lee HARRELL
09 Asst VP for Planning & IE Dr. Pat MIZAK
15 Dir of Human Resources Mr. Darren MATHEWS
32 VP for Student Life/Dean Stdnts Dr. Tammy S. WALSH
39 Assoc Dean of Students/Res Life Vacant
35 Assoc Dean of Students/Student Dev Mr. Jekeyma ROBINSON
23 Assoc Dean/Dir Student Health Svcs Dr. Erin ROBINSON
07 Director of Admissions Mr. Gregg PRIGERSON
13 Dir of Institutional Technology Mr. Mahmoud PEGAH
90 Dir of Academic Computing Ms. Karissa MILLER
91 Dir of Administrative Computing Ms. Kris PEGAH
28 Assoc Dean Diversity & Inclusion Yoleidy ROSARIO
30 Asst Dir of Fundraising Events Ms. Logan JULIEN

The Robert E. Webber Institute for Worship Studies (K)

4001 Hendricks Ave, Jacksonville FL 32207
County: Duval Identification: 666616
Telephone: (904) 264-2172 Carnegie Class: Not Classified
FAX Number: (904) 379-5534 Calendar System: Semester
URL: www.iws.edu
Established: 1998 Annual Graduate Tuition & Fees: N/A
Enrollment: N/A Coed
Affiliation or Control: Independent Non-Profit IRS Status: 501(c)3
Highest Offering: Doctorate; No Undergraduates
Accreditation: BI, THEOL

01 Chief Executive Officer/President Dr. James R. HART
05 Academic Dean Dr. Dinelle FRANKLAND
10 VP of Finance & Administration Ms. Christi G. MATTESON
42 Chaplain RevDr. Nancy NETHERCOTT
84 Director of Enrollment Dr. Juan LOPEZ
08 Interim Librarian Ms. Jennifer NICHOLSON
29 Director Alumni Relations Dr. Kent L. WALTERS
24 Dir of Technical Services Dr. Samuel L. HOROWITZ
04 Asst to the President Vacant
32 Dir Student Services/Office Admin Ms. Mira SMETANIUK
13 Information Technology Coordinator Dr. Ken RUSHING
26 Dir of Missional Relations Dr. Frank FORTUNATO
84 Director of Recruitment Mr. Joseph JAMERSON
88 Director of Sessions Dr. Oluwatayo OLOYEDE
06 Registrar Ms. Catherine NANCE
07 Director of Admissions Dr. Juan LOPEZ

Rollins College (L)

1000 Holt Avenue, Winter Park FL 32789-4499
County: Orange FICE Identification: 001515
Unit ID: 136950
Telephone: (407) 646-2000 Carnegie Class: Masters/L
FAX Number: (407) 646-2600 Calendar System: Semester
URL: www.rollins.edu
Established: 1885 Annual Undergrad Tuition & Fees: $53,716
Enrollment: 3,104 Coed
Affiliation or Control: Independent Non-Profit IRS Status: 501(c)3
Highest Offering: Doctorate
Accreditation: SC, ABAI, CACREP, MUS

01 President Dr. Grant H. CORNWELL
05 VP Acad Affairs/Provost Dr. Susan R. SINGER
32 Vice President Student Affairs Ms. Donna LEE
10 Vice President Business/Finance Mr. Ed KANIA
13 Chief Information Officer Mr. Troy THOMASON
20 Dean of the Faculty Dr. Jennifer CAVENAUGH
35 Asst VP Stdnt Affs/Int Dn of Stdnts Mr. Leon HAYNER
84 VP of Enrollment Mgmt and Marketing Dr. Faye F. TYDLASKA
50 Dean Crummer Grad Sch of Business Dr. Deborah F. CROWN
55 Dean Holt School Dr. Robert SANDERS
42 Dean of Religious Life Rev. Katrina JENKINS
21 Assoc VP Finance/Asst Treasurer Mr. William SHORT
26 VP Communications & External Rels Mr. Sam STARK
15 Assoc VP Human Res/Risk Management Mr. Matt HAWKS
108 Asst Provost Inst Effectiveness Dr. Toni STROLLO HOLBROOK
41 Athletic Director Ms. Pennie PARKER
37 Director of Financial Aid Mr. Steve BOOKER
104 Director of International Programs Ms. Giselda BEAUDIN
07 Dean of Admission Ms. Zaire MCCOY
36 Asst VP of Career & Life Planning Dr. Lisa JOHNSON
18 Asst VP of Facilities Management Mr. Jeremy WILLIAMSON
19 Assistant VP Public Safety Mr. Ken MILLER
29 Sr Director Alumni Engagement Ms. Andria SILVA
111 VP for Institutional Advancement Ms. Laurie HOUCK
102 Director of Foundation Relations Mr. Joseph MONTI
06 Registrar Ms. Stephanie HENNING
40 Manager of Bookstore Ms. Mary VITELLI
04 Exec Assistant to the President Ms. Jillian SCHUMM
23 Director of Wellness Ms. Connie BRISCOE
25 Director Contracts/Grants Admin Ms. Devon MASSOT
35 Asst VP Student Affairs/Community Ms. Michele MEYER
08 Director of Olin Library Dr. Deborah PROSSER
88 Director of Institutional Analytics Mr. Meghal PARIKH
113 Director of Student Accounts/Bursar Mr. Cory BADEN

Saber College (M)

3990 West Flagler Street, Ste 103, Miami FL 33134
County: Miami-Dade FICE Identification: 036964
Unit ID: 449506
Telephone: (305) 443-9170 Carnegie Class: Spec 2-yr-Health
FAX Number: (305) 443-8441 Calendar System: Other
URL: www.sabercollege.edu
Established: 1972 Annual Undergrad Tuition & Fees: N/A
Enrollment: 41 Coed
Affiliation or Control: Independent Non-Profit IRS Status: 501(c)3
Highest Offering: Associate Degree
Accreditation: COE, PTAA

01 Chief Administrator Ms. Josefina HABIF
05 Dean of Academic Affairs Ms. Amarilis SOMOZA
66 Director Nursing Program Ms. Ronda MIMS
76 Dir Physical Therapist Asst Program Ms. Karen AROCHA

St. John Vianney College Seminary (N)

2900 SW 87th Avenue, Miami FL 33165-3244
County: Miami-Dade FICE Identification: 008075
Unit ID: 137272
Telephone: (305) 223-4561 Carnegie Class: Spec-4-yr-Faith
FAX Number: (305) 223-0650 Calendar System: Semester
URL: www.sjvcs.edu
Established: 1959 Annual Undergrad Tuition & Fees: $23,100
Enrollment: 77 Male
Affiliation or Control: Roman Catholic IRS Status: 501(c)3
Highest Offering: Master's
Accreditation: SC

01 Rector & President ....Rev. Pablo A. NAVARRO
32 Vice Rector/Dean of Students ....Rev. Bryan GARCIA
42 Coordinator Spiritual Formation ....Rev. Daniel MARTIN
05 Academic Dean ....Dr. Paola BERNARDINI
06 Registrar ....Dr. Pablo MARTINEZ
07 Director of Admissions ....Rev. Pablo A. NAVARRO
09 Director of Institutional Research ....Dr. Jose ORTA
10 Chief Financial/Business Officer ....Rev. Luis RIVERO
15 Chief Human Resources Officer ....Rev. Luis RIVERO
18 Chief Facilities/Physical Plant ....Rev. Pablo A. NAVARRO
26 Chief Public Relations Officer ....Mr. Iancarlo ARISPE
35 Associate Student Affairs Officer ....Rev. Bryan GARCIA
37 Director Student Financial Aid ....Dr. Pablo MARTINEZ-DIENTE
96 Director of Purchasing ....Rev. Luis RIVERO

St. Johns River State College (A)

5001 St. Johns Avenue, Palatka FL 32177-3897

County: Putnam — FICE Identification: 001523

Unit ID: 137281

Telephone: (386) 312-4200 — Carnegie Class: Bac/Assoc-Mixed

FAX Number: (386) 312-4229 — Calendar System: Semester

URL: www.sjrstate.edu

Established: 1958 — Annual Undergrad Tuition & Fees (In-District): $2,830

Enrollment: 6,828 — Coed

Affiliation or Control: State/Local — IRS Status: 501(c)3

Highest Offering: Baccalaureate

Accreditation: SC, ADNUR, ART, CAHIIM, COARC, EMT, NUR, RAD

01 President ....Mr. Joe PICKENS
05 Chief Academic Officer/Sr VP ....Dr. Melanie A. BROWN
10 Chief Business Officer/Sr VP ....Dr. Lynn POWERS
43 VP Legal Affairs/General Counsel ....Dr. Gilbert L. EVANS, JR.
09 VP/Chief Inst Research Officer ....Dr. Rosalind M. HUMERICK
32 VP Academic & Student Affairs ....Dr. Edward K. JORDAN
103 VP Workforce/CTE ....Vacant
13 Chief Information Officer ....Mr. Richard C. ANDERSON
20 Associate VP Academic Affairs ....Mr. Mike KELLER
108 Asst VP Assess/Research & Grants ....Dr. Ellen BURNS
35 Assistant VP Student Affairs ....Mr. Jack C. HALL
21 Assistant VP for Finance ....Mr. Randall PETERSON
15 Director of Human Resources ....Mr. Charles ROMER
80 Dean of Crim Justice/Public Safety ....Mr. Timothy ADAMS
49 Dean of Arts and Sciences ....Dr. Myrna L. ALLEN
102 Executive Director of Foundation ....Mr. Brian BERGEN
76 Dean of Allied Health ....Dr. Holly COULLIETTE
57 Dean of Florida School of the Arts ....Mr. Alain R. HENTSCHEL
06 Dean of Admissions and Records .Mrs. Susanne B. LINEBERGER
121 Dean of Academic Advising ....Ms. Jean WONDELL
88 Exec Dir Thrasher-Horne Center ....Mr. Bob OLSON
66 Dean of Nursing ....Dr. Diane P. PAGANO
75 Dean of Technical Education ....Dr. John W. PATERSON
55 Dean of Adult Education ....Dr. Melissa PERRY
08 Dean of Library Services ....Dr. Christina WILL
88 Assistant Dean/Arts & Sciences ....Mr. Royce D. BASS
88 Assistant Dean/Arts & Sciences ....Mr. Dustin W. LATTA
50 Director of Business Education ....Mr. Joel C. ABO
51 Dir of Dual Enroll & College Access ....Mrs. Meghan DEPUTY
77 Director of Computer Education ....Dr. John ETIENNE
37 Director of Financial Aid ....Ms. Suzanne M. EVANS
26 Director of Public Relations ....Mrs. Susan B. KESSLER
88 Director of Testing/Student Support ....Ms. Sarah TAYLOR

Saint Leo University (B)

33701 State Road 52 W, Saint Leo FL 33574-6665

County: Pasco — FICE Identification: 001526

Unit ID: 137032

Telephone: (352) 588-8200 — Carnegie Class: DU-Mod

FAX Number: (352) 588-8654 — Calendar System: Semester

URL: www.saintleo.edu

Established: 1889 — Annual Undergrad Tuition & Fees: $24,640

Enrollment: 9,832 — Coed

Affiliation or Control: Roman Catholic — IRS Status: 501(c)3

Highest Offering: Doctorate

Accreditation: SC, ACBSP, CEA, SW

01 President ....Dr. Jeffrey SENESE
05 VP Academic Affairs ....Dr. Mary SPOTO
84 VP University Enrollment Management ....Dr. Senthil KUMAR
10 VP Business Affairs/CFO ....Mr. John NISBET
111 VP University Advancement ....Ms. Carla WILLIS
32 VP Student Affairs ....Dr. Jen SHAW
03 Senior Vice President ....Ms. Melanie STORMS
04 Assistant to the President ....Ms. Abigail APPLETON
13 Chief Technology Officer ....Mr. Daron MCNAB
88 Associate VP Regional Accreditation ....Dr. Diane BALL
43 Associate VP/General Counsel ....Ms. Staci SHELLEY
15 AVP Human Resources ....Ms. Susan MARTIN
42 Chaplain for University Ministries ....Fr. Randall MEISSEN
35 Associate VP Student Affairs ....Mr. Kenneth POSNER
85 AVP Worldwide Student Services ....Mr. Shadel HAMILTON
38 Director Counseling Services ....Mr. Lawson JOLLY
49 Dean School of Arts & Sciences ....Dr. Heather PARKER
53 Dean School of Educ/Social Svcs ....Dr. Susan KINSELLA
50 Dean School of Business ....Vacant
58 Dir Grad Studies Criminal Justice ....Dr. Phillip NEELEY
58 Dir Grad Studies in Education ....Dr. Fern AEFSKY
70 Dir Grad Studies in Social Work ....Ms. Courtney WIEST
73 Dir Graduate Studies in Theology ....Dr. Randall WOODARD
88 Director Graduate Creative Writing ....Dr. Steven KISTULENTZ
06 Registrar ....Mrs. Karen HATFIELD
08 Director Library Services ....Dr. Doris VAN KAMPEN-BREIT

88 Asst VP of Learning Design ....Dr. Karen HAHN
88 Director Student Learning ....Vacant
39 Dir Residence Life & Leadership ....Vacant
88 Exec Dir Academic Administration ....Mr. Joseph TADEO
41 Director Intercollegiate Athletics ....Mr. Francis REIDY
18 AVP Facilities Management ....Mr. Jose CABAN
19 Director Campus Security & Safety ....Mr. Vincent D'AMBROSIO
22 Director Accessibility Services ....Mr. Michael BAILEY
29 Director Alumni Engagement ....Vacant
110 Director Advancement Services ....Vacant
85 Exec Director PDSO Global Affairs ....Ms. Paige RAMSEY-HAMACHER
16 Director Human Resources ....Ms. Jennifer ALEXANDER
21 Senior Assoc VP Finance ....Mr. James DETUCCIO
96 Mgr Accts Payable/Sponsor Billing ....Ms. Laura SOLBERG
114 Director of Budgets ....Vacant
116 Director Internal Audit Services ....Ms. Monica KESSEL
12 Asst VP Military Center Operations ....Vacant
12 Asst VP Tampa Region ....Mr. Tyler UPSHAW
12 Asst VP Florida Region ....Ms. Katie DEGNER
103 Learning & Development Manager ....Mr. Joe ARNER
109 Director Dining Services ....Mr. Justin BUSH
88 Executive Officer ....Ms. Marcia MALIA
37 Associate VP of Financial Aid ....Ms. Melinda CLARK
26 AVP University Communications ....Ms. Marie THORNSBERRY
108 Dir of Institutional Effectiveness ....Vacant
89 Director First Year Experience ....Ms. Dawn MCELVEEN
119 Director Information Security ....Mr. Darius LEWIS
121 Chief Ofcr World Wide Stdnt Success ....Ms. Zaheda HERMAN
09 Chief Institutional Officer ....Dr. William HAMILTON
122 Asst Dir Greek Life/Community Svc ....Ms. Brandee GREAVES

St. Petersburg College (C)

PO Box 13489, Saint Petersburg FL 33733-3489

County: Pinellas — FICE Identification: 001528

Unit ID: 137078

Telephone: (727) 341-4772 — Carnegie Class: Bac/Assoc-Mixed

FAX Number: (727) 341-3318 — Calendar System: Semester

URL: www.spcollege.edu

Established: 1927 — Annual Undergrad Tuition & Fees (In-District): $2,682

Enrollment: 26,430 — Coed

Affiliation or Control: Local — IRS Status: 501(c)3

Highest Offering: Baccalaureate

Accreditation: SC, ADNUR, CAHIIM, CEA, COARC, DH, EMT, FUSER, NURSE, PTAA, RAD

01 President ....Dr. Tonjua L. WILLIAMS
05 VP Academic Affairs ....Dr. Matthew LIAO-TROTH
32 VP Student Affairs ....Dr. Jamelle CONNER
10 VP Finance and Business Operations ....Janette HUNT
18 Associate VP Facilities/Inst ....Vacant
15 Chief Human Resources/Talent Ofcr ....Darryl WRIGHT-GREENE
111 VP Inst Advance/Exec Dir Foundation ....Jesse TURTLE
114 Associate VP Budgeting ....Dr. Hector LORA
13 VP Information Technology ....Dr. Patrick RINARD
37 Assoc VP Financial Asst Svcs ....Michael J. BENNETT
20 Assoc VP Academic Affs/Partnership ....Catherine C. KENNEDY
21 AVP Business & Financial Svcs ....Mike MEIGS
108 AVP Institutional Effect/Acad Svcs ....Dr. Sabrina CRAWFORD
103 Career Connections Director ....Dr. Jason KRUPP
43 General Counsel ....Mia CONZA
12 Provost Downtown/Midtown and PAL ....Dr. Eric CARVER
12 Provost SP Gibbs and Allstate Ctr ....Dr. Leslie HAFER
12 Provost Seminole/Health Ed Ctr ....Dr. Mark STRICKLAND
12 Provost Tarpon Springs Campus ....Dr. Rodrigo DAVIS
12 Provost Clearwater Campus/EpiCenter ....Dr. Tashika GRIFFITH
96 Director of Procurement/Asset Mgmt ....Karen REYNOLDS
38 Student Support Manager ....Vacant
61 Dean Col of Policy/Ethics/Leg Stds ....Dr. Susan S. DEMERS
83 Dean Social & Behavioral Sciences ....Dr. Joseph SMILEY
88 Associate VP Collegiate High School ....Vacant
50 Dean College of Business .Dr. Emmanuel HERNANDEZ-AGOSTO
81 Dean Mathematics ....Jimmy CHANG
65 Dean Natural Science ....Dr. Natavia MIDDLETON
79 Dean Humanities/Fine Arts ....Dr. Barbara HUBBARD
53 Dean College of Education ....Dr. Kimberly HARTMAN
60 Dean Communications ....Dr. Joseph LEOPOLD
76 Dean College of Health Sciences ....Dr. Deanna STENTIFORD
72 Dean College of Comp & Info Tech ....Vacant
66 Dean College of Nursing ....Dr. Louisana LOUIS
90 Exec Director Academic Technology ....Christopher HARVEY
110 Exec Director Advancement Svcs ....Theresa MCFARLAND
08 Exec Director Learning Resources ....Matthew BODIE
07 Director of Admissions and Records ....Eva CHRISTENSEN
88 Director of Academic Services ....Djuan FOX
104 Director International Programs ....Frank JURKOVIC
108 Dir Institutional Effectiveness ....Magaly TYMMS
14 Exec Dir Enterprise Systems ....Zoran STANISIC
19 Director College Security Services ....Daniel BARTO
25 Exec Dir of Grants Development .Dr. Gretchen MULLIN-SAWICKI
86 Director Government Relations ....Amol DHALIWAL
41 Athletic Director ....Davie GILL
26 AVP Marketing & Strategic Comm ....Rita FARLOW
30 Executive Director of Development ....Deborah SWINK
28 Equity Diversity and Incl Director ....Dr. Devona PIERRE
84 Exec Dir Student Affairs/Enroll Mgt ....Dr. Kellie ZIEMAK
04 Exec Assistant to the President ....Rebecca TURNER

St. Thomas University (D)

16401 NW 37th Avenue, Miami Gardens FL 33054-6498

County: Miami-Dade — FICE Identification: 001468

Unit ID: 137476

Telephone: (305) 625-6000 — Carnegie Class: DU-Mod

FAX Number: (305) 628-6510 — Calendar System: Semester

URL: www.stu.edu

Established: 1961 — Annual Undergrad Tuition & Fees: $32,940

Enrollment: 5,601 — Coed

Affiliation or Control: Roman Catholic — IRS Status: 501(c)3

Highest Offering: Doctorate

Accreditation: SC, LAW, NURSE, @THEOL

01 President ....Mr. David A. ARMSTRONG
05 Acting Provost Academic Affairs ....Ms. Michelle JOHNSON GARCIA
10 VP Admin/Chief Financial Officer ....Ms. Linda WAGNER
111 Vice Pres Philanthropy ....Ms. Robyn S. HOFFMAN
26 VP of Marketing/Communications ....Mr. Carlos A. DE YARZA
42 VP for Mission & Ministry ....Rev. Rafael CAPÓ
06 Registrar ....Mrs. Maria ABDEL
37 Director Financial Aid ....Ms. Margherite POWELL
21 Assoc VP Finance & Controller ....Mrs. Maribel SMITH
18 Facilities Supervisor ....Mr. Christopher TARRANT
15 Director of Human Resources ....Mr. John C. PRATS
41 Director of Athletics ....Mr. William E. RYCHEL
32 AVP of Student Affairs/Compliance ....Mr. Matthew ROCHE
121 Director of Student Success Center ....Ms. Gretell GARCIA
88 SACSCOC Liaison ....Dr. Pamela CINGEL
07 Director of Admissions ....Ms. Whitney E. BATTOE
04 Exec Admin Assistant to the Pres ....Ms. Marina UGALDE
84 VP of Enrollment ....Ms. Jameka A. WINDHAM
61 Law School Dean ....Mr. John MAKDISI

St. Vincent De Paul Regional Seminary (E)

10701 S Military Trail, Boynton Beach FL 33436-4899

County: Palm Beach — FICE Identification: 008223

Unit ID: 136701

Telephone: (561) 732-4424 — Carnegie Class: Spec-4-yr-Faith

FAX Number: (561) 737-2205 — Calendar System: Semester

URL: www.svdp.edu

Established: 1963 — Annual Graduate Tuition & Fees: N/A

Enrollment: 142 — Coed

Affiliation or Control: Roman Catholic — IRS Status: 501(c)3

Highest Offering: Master's; No Undergraduates

Accreditation: THEOL

01 Rector/President ....Rev. Alfredo I. HERNANDEZ
03 Vice Rector/Dean Human Formation ....Rev. Gregg CAGGIANELLI
05 Academic Dean ....Rev. Timothy CUSICK
10 Treasurer ....Mr. Keith PARKER
08 Director of the Library ....Mr. Arthur QUINN
04 Administrative Asst to President ....Ms. Sindy DELEON
09 Dir Inst Research/Assessment ....Dr. S. Mary KRYSIAK BITTAR
111 Chief Development/Advancement ....Ms. Deb LINDSAY
06 Registrar ....Mrs. Alicia RUEFF

San Ignacio University (F)

3905 NW 107th Ave, Suite 301, Doral FL 33178

County: Miami-Dade — Identification: 667130

Unit ID: 486239

Telephone: (305) 629-2929 — Carnegie Class: Spec-4-yr-Bus

FAX Number: N/A — Calendar System: Semester

URL: www.sanignaciouniversity.edu

Established: 2007 — Annual Undergrad Tuition & Fees: $10,400

Enrollment: 232 — Coed

Affiliation or Control: Proprietary — IRS Status: Proprietary

Highest Offering: Master's

Accreditation: ACICS

01 President ....Dr. Federico MARTINEZ
11 VP Operations/Corporate Affairs ....Ezer TOSSAS
05 Dean of Academic Affairs ....Dr. Althia ELLIS
08 Head Librarian ....Yaima BALLESTER
15 Human Resources Senior Coordinator ....Sascha BAS QUINTERO
37 Financial Aid Coordinator ....Fabiola LAGARDERE
10 Director of Administration/Finance ....Carmen RODRIGUEZ
06 Registrar ....Jennifer GONZALEZ
07 Recruitment Director ....Sasha GIRO

Santa Fe College (G)

3000 NW 83rd Street, Gainesville FL 32606-6200

County: Alachua — FICE Identification: 001519

Unit ID: 137096

Telephone: (352) 395-5000 — Carnegie Class: Bac/Assoc-Assoc Dom

FAX Number: (352) 395-5581 — Calendar System: Semester

URL: www.sfcollege.edu

Established: 1965 — Annual Undergrad Tuition & Fees (In-District): $2,563

Enrollment: 12,607 — Coed

Affiliation or Control: Local — IRS Status: 501(c)3

Highest Offering: Baccalaureate

Accreditation: SC, ADNUR, CAHIIM, COARC, CONST, CVT, DA, DH, DMS, EMT, MLS, NMT, NURSE, POLYT, PTAA, RAD, SURGT

01 President ....Dr. Paul BROADIE, II
05 Interim Provost/VP Academic Affairs ....Dr. Lisa ARMOUR
10 Chief Financial Ofcr/VP Admin Affs ....Mr. Andy BARNES
32 Vice President Student Affairs ....Dr. Naima BROWN
111 VP Office for Advancement ....Mr. Chuck CLEMONS
04 Assistant to the President ....Vacant
20 Assoc Vice Pres Academic Affairs ....Dr. Jodi LONG
20 Assoc Vice Pres Academic Affairs ....Dr. Stefanie WASCHULL

104	Asst VP Academic Affairs	Dr. Vilma FUENTES
13	Assoc VP Information Tech Services	Mr. Bill PENNEY
18	Assoc VP Gov Affs & Facilities Svcs	Mr. Liam MCCLAY
35	Assoc VP Student Affairs	Dr. Dan RODKIN
22	Dean Access and Inclusion	Vacant
25	Director Sponsored Projects	Ms. Claudia GRANT
35	Asst Vice Pres Student Affairs	Dr. Beatrice AWONIYI
43	General Counsel and Chief of Staff	Ms. Patti LOCASCIO
06	College Registrar	Mr. Michael HUTLEY
88	Dir High Sch Dual Enrollment Pgm	Ms. Jennifer HOMARD
121	Dir Advising & Career Exploration	Ms. Andrea EVANGELIST
41	Athletic Director	Mr. Greg MCVEY
08	Interim Director Library Service	Ms. Nance LEMPINEN-LEEDY
19	Director Institute of Public Safety	Mr. Tom ACKERMAN
35	Director of Student Life	Dr. Tracey REEVES
96	Director of Purchasing	Mr. David SHLAFER
28	Coordinator Col Achievement Pgm	Ms. Adrienne PROVOST
37	Director Student Financial Aid	Ms. Kamia MWANGO
15	Director Human Resources	Ms. Lela FRYE
09	Director of Institutional Research	Mr. Gary HARTGE
07	Coordinator Admissions & Advising	Ms. Carolyn DAS
26	Asst VP Marketing and Communication	Ms. Teri MCCLELLAN
110	Assoc VP Advancement	Mr. John HOOKER
106	Asst VP Academic Technologies	Ms. Page JERZAK

Schiller International University (A)

400 N. Tampa St., Suite 1700, Tampa FL 33602

County: Pinellas

FICE Identification: 023141
Unit ID: 404338

Telephone: (727) 736-5082
FAX Number: (727) 738-8405
URL: www.schiller.edu

Carnegie Class: Spec-4-yr-Bus
Calendar System: Semester

Established: 1964
Enrollment: 30
Affiliation or Control: Proprietary
Highest Offering: Master's
Accreditation: **ACICS**

Annual Undergrad Tuition & Fees: $14,360
Coed
IRS Status: Proprietary

05	Provost	Dr. Victoria BAMOND
32	Dean of Students	Ms. Jeanette ESPINAL

Seminole State College of Florida (B)

100 Weldon Boulevard, Sanford FL 32773-6199

County: Seminole

FICE Identification: 001520
Unit ID: 137209

Telephone: (407) 708-4722
FAX Number: (407) 708-2139
URL: www.seminolestate.edu

Carnegie Class: Bac/Assoc-Mixed
Calendar System: Semester

Established: 1965
Enrollment: 16,298
Affiliation or Control: Local
Highest Offering: Baccalaureate
Accreditation: **SC**, ACBSP, ADNUR, CAHIIM, CIDA, COARC, CONST, EMT, NUR, PTAA

Annual Undergrad Tuition & Fees (In-District): $3,131
Coed
IRS Status: 501(c)3

01	President	Dr. Georgia LORENZ
10	Vice Pres Business Operations/CFO	Mr. Joe MAZUR
05	VP Academic Affairs/CAO	Dr. Laura ROSS
32	VP Student Affairs	Dr. Johnny CRAIG
13	VP Information Resources/CIO	Dr. Dick HAMANN
30	VP Resource Develop & Economic Dev	Dr. John GYLLIN
21	Interim AVP Finance & Budget	Ms. Sandra LOCHNER
35	AVP Student Development	Dr. Jan LLOYD-LESLEY
07	Interim AVP Admissions	Ms. Lorie COACHMAN
12	Dean of Students Altamonte Springs	Mr. Jeffery GIBBS
12	Dean of Students Oviedo Campus	Mr. Jeffery GIBBS
20	AVP Academic Services	Dr. Lisa VALENTINO
50	AVP Sch Business/Health/Safety	Dr. Molly KOSTENBAUDER
54	AVP Engineering/Design & IT	Mr. Basim KHARTABIL
26	Dir College & Community Relations	Ms. Deborah RICHARD
91	Director Networks	Mr. Julio VALENTIN
38	Director Counseling and Advising	Ms. Deborah LYNCH
88	Director Curriculum	Ms. Carlene MCNEIL
15	AVP Human Resources	Ms. Mae ASHBY
06	Director Enrollment Svcs/Registrar	Ms. Barbara RODRIGUEZ-LAMAS
37	Executive Director Financial Aid	Ms. Ju'Coby TODD-WASHINGTON
09	Director Inst Effectiveness	Dr. Thomas HOKE
41	Director Intercollegiate Athletics	Mr. Kurt ESSER
36	Asst Director Career Development	Ms. Candace LEHMANN
14	AVP Information Technology	Vacant
106	Dir Online Education/E-learning	Mr. Brian CROSE
28	AVP Equity & Diversity/Title IX	Ms. Barbara COLEMAN-FOSTER
102	Dir Foundation Finance & Operations	Mr. Sean BARTH
110	Assistant Director of Development	Ms. Laura SCHUMACHER
04	Special Assistant to the President	Ms. Meghann SELLERS
19	Director Security/Safety	Mr. Miguel SIERRA
43	Director Legal Svcs/General Counsel	Mr. J. Paul CARLAND
103	Dean Workforce Development	Mr. Joseph HUSTON
18	Director Facilities	Mr. Douglas BENTLEY
96	Director of Purchasing	Vacant

South Florida Bible College (C)

2200 SW 10th Street, Deerfield Beach FL 33442

County: Broward

FICE Identification: 032643
Unit ID: 366003

Telephone: (954) 637-2268
FAX Number: (954) 719-3780
URL: www.sfbc.edu

Carnegie Class: Bac-Diverse
Calendar System: Semester

Established: 1985

Annual Undergrad Tuition & Fees: $7,140

Enrollment: 313
Affiliation or Control: Interdenominational
Highest Offering: Doctorate
Accreditation: **BI**

Coed
IRS Status: 501(c)3

01	President	Dr. Mary A. DRABIK
03	Vice President	Josiah STEPHAN
05	Chief Academic Officer	Dr. Jodyann REID
10	Chief Financial Officer	David SAYERS
06	Registrar	Dr. Michael RACKLEY
08	Librarian	Paula STEVENSON
20	Dean of Faculty	Dr. Esa AUTERO
32	Dean of Students	Vacant
29	Director Alumni Relations	Casey PALACIOUS
84	Director Enrollment Management	Germil AGENOR
13	Chief Info Technology Officer (CIO)	Vacant
04	Administrative Asst to President	Neeta PRAKASH
09	Director of Institutional Research	Davi BAKTHAKUMAR
15	Chief Human Resources Officer	Crystal BERTLING
19	Director Security/Safety	Hector PEREZ
37	Director Student Financial Aid	Dr. Thomas DRABIK
07	Director of Admissions	Jeremy SCOTT

South Florida State College (D)

600 W College Drive, Avon Park FL 33825-9399

County: Highlands

FICE Identification: 001522
Unit ID: 137315

Telephone: (863) 453-6661
FAX Number: (863) 453-0165
URL: www.southflorida.edu

Carnegie Class: Bac/Assoc-Mixed
Calendar System: Trimester

Established: 1965
Enrollment: 2,710
Affiliation or Control: Local
Highest Offering: Baccalaureate
Accreditation: **SC**, ADNUR, DA, DH, EMT, NUR, RAD

Annual Undergrad Tuition & Fees (In-District): $3,165
Coed
IRS Status: 501(c)3

01	President	Dr. Thomas C. LEITZEL
05	Vice Pres Educational/Stdnt Svcs	Dr. Sidney VALENTINE
10	Controller	Mrs. Theresa VOROUS
11	Vice Pres Administrative Services	Mr. Peter ELLIOTT
75	Dean Applied Science & Tech	Mr. Erik CHRISTENSEN
49	Dean Arts & Sciences	Dr. James HAWKER
28	Director Cultural Programs	Ms. Cynthia GARREN
111	Exec Dir Institutional Advancement	Mrs. Jamie BATEMAN
32	Dean Student Services	Mr. Mark BUKOWSKI
12	Director DeSoto Campus	Mrs. Asena MOTT
12	Director Hardee Campus	Ms. Teresa CRAWFORD
12	Director Lake Placid Center	Mr. Randall K. PAEPLOW
26	Director Community Relations	Mrs. Melissa KUEHNLE
106	Director eLearning	Vacant
15	Director Human Res/EA-EO & ADA Ofcr	Mr. Donald KESTERSON
18	Dir Remodeling/Reno & Maint	Dr. Robert E. FLORES
06	Registrar	Mr. Jonathan STERN
41	Athletic Director	Mr. Richard J. HITT
36	Director Career Development Center	Mr. Robert HAMPTON
37	Director Financial Aid	Mrs. Tina STETSON
13	Chief Information Officer	Dr. Christopher VAN DER KAAY
38	Chair Counseling	Mrs. Charla ELLERKER
08	Library Services	Ms. Lena PHELPS
96	Coordinator Purchasing	Mrs. Deborah OLSON
07	Director of Admissions	Vacant
76	Dean Division of Health Services	Dr. Michele HESTON

South University (E)

9801 Belevedere Road, Royal Palm Beach FL 33411

Telephone: (561) 273-6500
Identification: 666117

Accreditation: **&SC**, AA, ACBSP, ARCPA, CACREP, NURSE, PTAA

† Regional accreditation is carried under the parent institution in Savannah, GA.

South University (F)

4401 North Himes Ave Ste 175, Tampa FL 33614-7095

Telephone: (813) 393-3800
Identification: 770913

Accreditation: **&SC**, ACBSP, ARCPA, NURSE, OTA, PTAA

† Branch campus of South University, Savannah, GA

Southeastern College (G)

5875 NW 163rd Street, Ste 101, Miami Lakes FL 33014

Telephone: (305) 820-5003
Identification: 666290

Accreditation: **ACCSC**, ADNUR, DMS, SURGT

† Branch campus of Southeastern College, West Palm Beach, FL.

Southeastern College (H)

1756 North Congress Avenue, West Palm Beach FL 33409

County: Palm Beach

FICE Identification: 031239
Unit ID: 428170

Telephone: (561) 433-2330
FAX Number: (561) 433-9025
URL: www.sec.edu

Carnegie Class: Spec 2-yr-Health
Calendar System: Other

Established: 1988
Enrollment: 690
Affiliation or Control: Proprietary
Highest Offering: Associate Degree

Annual Undergrad Tuition & Fees: $20,246
Coed
IRS Status: Proprietary

Accreditation: **ACCSC**, DMS, SURGT

01	President	Ms. Dana HUTTON
05	Dean Academic Affairs	Ms. Doris COMBS
37	Director of Financial Aid	Mr. Travis SMITH
06	Registrar	Ms. Cindy GALT
32	Director Student Services	Ms. Latoya JAMES

Southeastern University (I)

1000 Longfellow Boulevard, Lakeland FL 33801-6099

County: Polk

FICE Identification: 001521
Unit ID: 137564

Telephone: (863) 667-5000
FAX Number: (863) 667-5200
URL: www.seu.edu

Carnegie Class: DU-Mod
Calendar System: Semester

Established: 1935
Enrollment: 9,546
Affiliation or Control: Assemblies Of God Church
Highest Offering: Doctorate
Accreditation: **SC**, ACBSP, NURSE, SW, THEOL

Annual Undergrad Tuition & Fees: $27,520
Coed
IRS Status: 501(c)3

01	President	Dr. Kent INGLE
03	Executive Vice President	Dr. James (Chris) OWEN
05	Provost	Dr. Meghan GRIFFIN
32	VP for Student Development	Mrs. Bethany THOMAS
84	VP for Enrollment	Mr. Roy ROWLAND, IV
09	VP Inst Research/Effectiveness	Dr. Cody LLOYD
10	VP for Finance	Mr. Phil SCHMITT
45	VP for Innovation and Communication	Dr. Michael STEINER
88	VP of Strategic Partnerships	Mr. Justin LATHROP
08	Director of Library Services	Mrs. Amy BEATTY
06	Registrar	Mrs. Melissa MAISENBACHER
121	Exec Dir Academic Advising	Ms. Carla COLLINS
37	Exec Dir Student Financial Services	Mr. Michael YOHE
88	Director of Hispanic Learning Ctr	Ms. Betania TORRES
07	Exec Director of Admissions Trad	Mrs. Sarah E. CLARK
15	Director Human Resources	Mr. Geoffrey OTT
09	Dir Research & Strategic Projects	Dr. Ken REAVES
29	Director Alumni Relations	Mr. Joel JOHNSON
18	Exec Dir Facilities/Physical Plant	Mr. Norman (Mike) M. ALDERMAN
20	Director Academic Auxiliary Svcs	Mrs. Laura C. BROWN
36	Director of Career Services	Vacant
121	Dir Academic Center for Enrichment	Mr. Paul CARTER
28	Dir of Multicultural Affairs	Ms. Bridget LEE
21	Senior Director Finance & Treasury	Vacant
88	Director Enrollment Marketing	Ms. Sofia RAMOS
38	Dir Counseling/Health & Wellness	Ms. Megan WAGNER
13	Chief Info Technology Officer (CIO)	Dr. Cody LLOYD
19	Director Security/Safety	Mr. David BRIGHT
20	Associate Provost	Mrs. Amy BRATTEN
35	Exec Dir of Student Services	Vacant
108	Director Institutional Effectiveness	Mr. Levi LARSON
41	Athletic Director	Mr. Drew WATSON
27	Chief Communications Officer	Mrs. Dana DAVIS
39	Dir Resident Life/Student Housing	Ms. Danielle EVERSOLE
26	VP for Marketing	Mr. Jamie ANDERSON

Southern Technical College (J)

1685 Medical Lane, Fort Myers FL 33907-1158

County: Lee

FICE Identification: 022788
Unit ID: 366553

Telephone: (239) 939-4766
FAX Number: (239) 790-2118
URL: www.southerntech.edu

Carnegie Class: Spec-4-yr-Other Health
Calendar System: Quarter

Established: 1974
Enrollment: 1,125
Affiliation or Control: Proprietary
Highest Offering: Associate Degree
Accreditation: **ACICS**, ADNUR, SURTEC

Annual Undergrad Tuition & Fees: $13,895
Coed
IRS Status: Proprietary

01	Executive Director	Mr. Mark GUTMANN
05	Director Education	Mr. Esmail DARIAROW

Southern Technical College-Auburndale (K)

450 Havendale Boulevard, Auburndale FL 33823

Telephone: (863) 551-1112
Identification: 770705

Accreditation: **ACCSC**

Southern Technical College (L)

1485 Florida Mall Avenue, Orlando FL 32809

County: Orange

FICE Identification: 039035
Unit ID: 446552

Telephone: (407) 438-6000
FAX Number: (407) 438-6005
URL: www.southerntech.edu

Carnegie Class: Assoc/HVT-High Trad
Calendar System: Quarter

Established:
Enrollment: 1,712
Affiliation or Control: Proprietary
Highest Offering: Associate Degree
Accreditation: **ACCSC**

Annual Undergrad Tuition & Fees: N/A
Coed
IRS Status: Proprietary

01	Executive Director	Sandra MUSKOPF
05	Director of Education	Rachel KINSER

Southern Technical College-Port Charlotte (M)

950 Tamiami Trail, Unit 109, Port Charlotte FL 33953

Telephone: (941) 391-8888
Identification: 770709

Accreditation: ACICS, SURTEC

Southern Technical College-Sanford (A)

2910 South Orlando Drive, Sanford FL 32773
Telephone: (407) 917-7658 Identification: 770704
Accreditation: ACCSC

Southern Technical College-Tampa (B)

3910 Riga Boulevard, Tampa FL 33619-1269
Telephone: (813) 630-4401 Identification: 770708
Accreditation: ACICS, DMS, SURTEC

State College of Florida, Manatee-Sarasota (C)

PO Box 1849, Bradenton FL 34206-7046
County: Manatee FICE Identification: 001504
Unit ID: 135391
Telephone: (941) 752-5000 Carnegie Class: Bac/Assoc-Mixed
FAX Number: (941) 727-6230 Calendar System: Semester
URL: www.scf.edu
Established: 1957 Annual Undergrad Tuition & Fees (In-District): $3,074
Enrollment: 9,242 Coed
Affiliation or Control: Local IRS Status: 501(c)3
Highest Offering: Baccalaureate
Accreditation: SC, ADNUR, DH, NUR, OTA, PTAA, RAD

01 President ... Dr. Carol F. PROBSTFELD
04 Exec Assistant to President ... Ms. Susan MARROCCO
10 VP Finance/Admin Services ... Ms. Julie JAKWAY
05 Executive Vice President & Provost ... Dr. Todd FRITCH
32 Dean Student Services ... Ms. Jaquelyn MCNEIL
108 VP Inst Research/Effectiveness ... Mr. Ryan HALE
06 College Registrar ... Mr. Billy C. BENTON
20 Assoc Prov Academic/Faculty Affairs ... Mr. Mike KIEFER
102 Executive Director SCF Foundation ... Ms. Cassandra HOLMES
12 Dean Lakewood Ranch ... Vacant
84 AVP Student/Enrollment Services ... Ms. Stacey SHARPLES
26 AVP Communications & Marketing ... Ms. Jamie M. SMITH
18 AVP Facilities ... Mr. Chris WELLMAN
103 Director Workforce Services ... Ms. Lee KOTWICKI
08 Director Library Services ... Ms. Margaret E. HAWKINS
09 Director Institutional Research ... Mr. Bryce PRIDE
13 Director IT Operations ... Ms. Karla LAUER
43 General Counsel ... Mr. Steve PROUTY
88 Head of SCF Collegiate School ... Ms. Kelly MONOD
106 Director Online Learning ... Mr. Gary BAKER
19 Director Public Safety ... Mr. Shawn PATTEN
15 Director Human Resources ... Mr. Paul BERKLE

*State University System of Florida, Board of Governors (D)

325 W Gaines Street, Suite 1614,
Tallahassee FL 32399-0400
County: Leon FICE Identification: 008068
Unit ID: 137449
Telephone: (850) 245-0466 Carnegie Class: N/A
FAX Number: (850) 245-9685
URL: www.flbog.edu

01 Chancellor ... Mr. Marshall M. CRISER, III
05 Vice Chanc Academic/Student Affairs ... Dr. Christy ENGLAND
10 Vice Chanc Budget & Finance ... Mr. Tim JONES
43 General Counsel ... Mrs. Vikki SHIRLEY
22 Inspector General & Compliance ... Mrs. Julie LEFTHERIS
101 Corporate Secretary ... Mrs. Vikki SHIRLEY
86 Assoc Vice Chanc Govt Relations ... Mrs. Kristin WHITAKER
04 Assistant to the Chancellor ... Mrs. Shannon M. TRUE
26 Director of Communications ... Mrs. Renee FARGASON
13 Chief Info Technology Officer (CIO) ... Mr. Gene KOVACS
15 Director Personnel Services ... Mrs. Abigail MARTIN
18 Chief Facilities/Physical Plant ... Mr. Kevin PICHARD
09 Chief Data Officer ... Mr. Jason JONES
106 Assoc VC Innovation & Online Educ ... Dr. Nancy C. MCKEE
28 Chief Diversity/Equity & Inclusion ... Dr. Traki L. TAYLOR

*Florida Agricultural and Mechanical University (E)

1601 S. Martin Luther King Jr. Blvd, Tallahassee FL 32307
County: Leon FICE Identification: 001480
Unit ID: 133650
Telephone: (850) 599-3000 Carnegie Class: DU-Higher
FAX Number: (850) 599-3952 Calendar System: Semester
URL: www.famu.edu
Established: 1887 Annual Undergrad Tuition & Fees (In-State): $5,785
Enrollment: 9,184 Coed
Affiliation or Control: State IRS Status: 501(c)3
Highest Offering: Doctorate
Accreditation: SC, ACBSP, CAEP, CAHIIM, COARC, HSA, JOUR, LAW, NUR, OT, PH, PHAR, PTA, SW

00 Chair Board of Trustees ... Mr. Kelvin LAWSON
02 President ... Dr. Larry ROBINSON
05 Provost/VP Academic Affairs ... Dr. Maurice EDINGTON
10 VP Finance & Administration/CFO ... Dr. Alan D. ROBERTSON
32 Vice President Student Affairs ... Dr. William HUDSON, JR.
46 VP Research ... Dr. Charles WEATHERFORD
111 VP Univ Advancement/Exec Dir Fndn ... Dr. Shawnta FRIDAY-STROUD
116 VP Audit ... Mr. Joseph MALESZEWSKI
45 VP Strategic Planning/Analysis/IE ... Ms. Beverly BARRINGTON
43 VP Legal Affairs/Gen Counsel ... Ms. Denise WALLACE
100 Chief of Staff/BOT Liaison ... Ms. Linda BARGE-MILES
41 VP and Director Athletics ... Mr. Kortne GOSHA
26 Interim Director Communications ... Mr. Keith MILES
86 Director Governmental Relations ... Ms. Danielle MCBETH
04 Executive Asst to the President ... Ms. Cynthia HENRY
117 Chief Ethics and Compliance Officer ... Ms. Rica CALHOUN
53 Dean Education ... Dr. Allyson WATSON
67 Dean Pharmacy ... Dr. Johnnie EARLY
72 Dean Science & Technology ... Dr. Richard ALO
47 Dean Agriculture & Food Sciences ... Dr. Robert TAYLOR
83 Dean Social Sci/Arts & Humanities ... Dr. Valencia E. MATTHEWS
54 Dean FAMU-FSU Engineering ... Dr. J. Murray GIBSON
61 Dean College of Law ... Dr. Deidre KELLER
48 Dean Architecture & Engr Tech ... Mr. Rodner WRIGHT
76 Dean Allied Health Sciences ... Dr. Cynthia HUGHES HARRIS
50 Dean Business and Industry ... Dr. Shawnta FRIDAY-STROUD
60 Int Dean Journalism/Graphic Comm ... Dr. Bettye GRABLE
65 Dean School of the Environment ... Dr. Victor IBEANUSI
66 Dean Nursing ... Dr. Shelley JOHNSON
58 Assoc Provost & Dean Grad Studies ... Dr. David JACKSON, JR.
08 Dean University Libraries ... Ms. Faye WATKINS
20 Assoc Provost for Undergrad Educ ... Dr. Lewis JOHNSON
20 Assoc Provost Faculty Affairs & Dev ... Dr. Genyne BOSTON
06 University Registrar ... Dr. Agatha ONWUNLI
89 Asst VP Freshman Studies ... Dr. Jennifer COLLINS
84 Assoc VP Enrollment Management ... Ms. Terri LITTLE-BERRY
37 Director Financial Aid ... Ms. Lisa STEWART
07 Interim Director Admissions ... Mr. Chester HOOD
19 Chief of Police/Dir Public Safety ... Mr. Terence CALLOWAY
35 Assoc VP Student Affairs ... Mr. Bomani SPELL
88 University Ombuds & Student Life ... Mr. Bryan F. SMITH
84 Assoc VP Student Affairs ... Mr. Nigel EDWARDS
13 Associate VP/CIO Info Tech Svcs ... Mr. Ronald HENRY
18 Assoc VP Facilities/Construction ... Mr. Chris HESSEL
15 Associate VP Human Resources ... Ms. Joyce INGRAM
28 Assoc VP HR/Director of Diversity ... Ms. Joyce INGRAM
09 Asst VP/Dir Institutional Research ... Dr. Khoi TO
21 Asst VP/Univ Controller ... Ms. Tonya JACKSON
104 Asst VP International Educ & Dev ... Dr. William HYNDMAN, III
88 Exec Dir Title III Programs ... Dr. Erick AKINS
105 Director ITS Services & Telecomm ... Mr. Ronald HENRY
36 Director Career Center ... Ms. Shereada HARRELL
25 Director Contracts & Grants ... Ms. Pamela BLOUNT
39 Director Student Housing ... Dr. Jennifer WILDER
38 Director Counseling Services ... Ms. Anika FIELDS
96 Director Procurement Services ... Ms. Mattie HOOD
23 Director Student Health Services ... Ms. Tanya TATUM
108 Director University Assessment ... Dr. Melanie WICINSKI
112 Asst VP Major/Principal Gifts ... Ms. Kimberly HANKERSON
30 Asst VP Fin Mgmt/Donor Relations ... Ms. Juanita JOHNSON
29 Asst VP Alumni Affairs ... Ms. Carmen CUMMINGS
22 Director EEO ... Ms. Carrie GAVIN
51 Director Continuing Education ... Ms. Phyllis WATSON
120 Director Instr Tech & Distance Ed ... Ms. Franzetta FITZ
109 Asst VP Administrative Services ... Ms. Rebecca BROWN
119 Chief Information Security Officer ... Mr. Clifford STOKES
114 Director University Budgets ... Ms. Nichole MURRY
122 Director of Student Activities ... Mr. Andre GREEN

*Florida Atlantic University (F)

PO Box 3091, 777 Glades Road,
Boca Raton FL 33431-0991
County: Palm Beach FICE Identification: 001481
Unit ID: 133669
Telephone: (561) 297-3000 Carnegie Class: DU-Higher
FAX Number: (561) 297-3942 Calendar System: Semester
URL: www.fau.edu
Established: 1961 Annual Undergrad Tuition & Fees (In-State): $4,879
Enrollment: 30,805 Coed
Affiliation or Control: State IRS Status: 501(c)3
Highest Offering: Doctorate
Accreditation: SC, CACREP, CAEP, CAMPEP, IPSY, MED, MUS, NURSE, PLNG, SP, SPAA, SW

02 President ... Dr. John KELLY
05 Int Provost/VP Academic Affairs ... Dr. Michele HAWKINS
10 Vice Pres Financial Affairs & CFO ... Mr. Gregory E. DUBOIS
46 Vice President Research ... Dr. Daniel FLYNN
11 Vice Pres Administrative Affairs ... Ms. Stacy VOLNICK
41 VP of Intercollegiate Athletics ... Mr. Brian WHITE
111 VP Inst Advancement/CEO/FAU Found ... Mr. Christopher J. DELISIO
26 Vice President Public Affairs ... Mr. Peter HULL
43 General Counsel ... Mr. David KIAN
20 Assoc Vice Prov Academic Personnel ... Dr. Teresa WILCOX
20 Senior Associate Provost ... Dr. Russ IVY
13 Assoc Provost IT/CIO ... Mr. Jason BALL
88 Assoc VP Administrative Affairs ... Dr. Larry FAERMAN
12 AVP Jupiter Campus/Dn Grad Studies ... Dr. Robert STACKMAN
12 Assoc VP Broward Campus ... Ms. Linda JOHNSON
106 Asst Provost of Online & Cont Educ ... Dr. Julie GOLDEN-BOTTI
88 Asst VP Academic Finance & Admin ... Ms. Iselgis GARCIA
88 Asst Provost Acad Opers & Planning ... Dr. James CAPP
108 Asst Provost IEA ... Dr. Ying LIU
35 Interim Dean of Students ... Ms. Audrey PUSEY
22 Exec Dir Equity/Inclusion/Compl ... Mr. Donovan P. DIAZ
37 Asst VP Financial Aid/New Student ... Ms. Tracy BOULUKOS
70 Dean Social Work/Criminal Justice ... Dr. Naelys LUNA
49 Dean of Arts & Letters ... Dr. Michael HORSWELL
50 Dean of Business ... Dr. Daniel GROPPER
53 Dean of Education ... Dr. Stephen SILVERMAN
54 Dean of Engineering/Comp Sci ... Dr. Stella BATALAMA
92 Dean of Honors College ... Dr. Justin PERRY
63 Dean of Medicine ... Dr. Julie PILITSIS
66 Dean of Nursing ... Dr. Safiya A. GEORGE DALMIDA
81 Dean of Science ... Dr. Valery FORBES
97 Int Dean Undergraduate Studies ... Dr. Dan MEEROFF
62 University Libraries Dean ... Dr. Linda M. GOLIAN-LUI
88 Asst Dean/PK-12 Sch/Educational Pgm ... Mr. Joel HERBST
15 Asst Vice Pres Human Resources ... Vacant
85 Asst Provost of Global Engagement ... Dr. Mihaela METIANU

*Florida Gulf Coast University (G)

10501 FGCU Boulevard S, Fort Myers FL 33965-6565
County: Lee FICE Identification: 032553
Unit ID: 433660
Telephone: (239) 590-1000 Carnegie Class: DU-Mod
FAX Number: (239) 590-1166 Calendar System: Semester
URL: www.fgcu.edu
Established: 1991 Annual Undergrad Tuition & Fees (In-State): $6,118
Enrollment: 15,358 Coed
Affiliation or Control: State IRS Status: 501(c)3
Highest Offering: Doctorate
Accreditation: SC, ACPHA, ANEST, ARCPA, CACREP, CAEP, DMOLS, IPSY, MLS, MUS, NURSE, OT, PTA, SPAA, SW

02 President ... Dr. Michael V. MARTIN
05 Executive VP & Provost ... Dr. Mark RIEGER
10 Vice Pres Admin Services/Finance ... Mr. David VAZQUEZ
111 VP Univ Advance/Exec Dir Foundation ... Ms. Katherine GREEN
88 VP/VProv Strategy/Pgm Innovation ... Dr. Aysegul TIMUR
43 Vice President & General Counsel ... Ms. Vee LEONARD
32 Vice Pres Stdnt Success/Enrol Mgmt ... Dr. Mitch CORDOVA
20 AVP Academic Pgms/Curriculum Devel ... Dr. Dawn KIRBY
45 AVP Planning & Inst Performance ... Dr. Sang Ki MIN
46 AVP Research & Sponsored Pgms ... Dr. Rosemary HIGGINS
26 AVP Marketing & Communications ... Ms. Alice WHEELWRIGHT
18 Asst VP Physical Plant ... Mr. Jim HEHL
04 Asst to Pres/University Ombuds ... Vacant
21 Assoc VP Admin Svcs & Finance ... Vacant
13 AVP & Chief Info Officer ... Ms. Mary BANKS
15 Sr Assoc VP Admin Svcs ... Ms. Sara STENSRUD
20 Assoc Provost/VP Academic Affs ... Dr. Tony BARRINGER
21 University Controller ... Ms. Renee GARCIA
35 Asst VP/Dean of Students ... Dr. Christopher BLAKELY
49 Int Dean College Arts & Sciences ... Dr. Clay MOTLEY
50 Dean Lutgert Col of Business ... Dr. Chris WESTLEY
53 Interim Dean College of Education ... Dr. Tom ROBERTS
76 Int Dean Col of Health/Human Svcs ... Dr. Shawn FELTON
54 Dean U.A. Whitaker Col Engineering ... Dr. Huzefa KAGDI
62 Dean Library Services ... Dr. Tracy ELLIOTT
38 Sr Dir Counseling/Wellness Svcs ... Dr. Jon L. BRUNNER
84 Assoc VP Enrollment Management ... Dr. Lisa JOHNSON
96 Director of Procurement Services ... Ms. Maryan EGAN
19 Chief University Police Dept ... Vacant
18 Director Facilities Planning ... Mr. Greg LARSON
37 AVP Stdnt Fin/Enroll/Business Svcs ... Mr. Jorge LOPEZ
06 University Registrar ... Mr. Christopher SAXBY
23 Medical Director ... Dr. Brian BOZZA
41 Director of Athletics ... Mr. Kenneth KAVANAGH
28 Dir EEC & Title IX Coord ... Ms. Precious GUNTER
85 Asst VP Acad Affairs Intl Programs ... Dr. Michael MCDONALD
106 Director Digital Learning ... Mr. David JAEGER
13 Deputy CIO/Chief Info Security Ofcr ... Mr. Sven HAHUES
36 Director Career Development Svcs ... Ms. Rose FULLER
29 Director Alumni Relations ... Ms. Kimberly WALLACE
92 Interim Dean Honors College ... Dr. Minh NGUYEN
09 Director Inst Research/Analysis ... Dr. Robert VINES
114 Director University Budgets ... Ms. Megan CLIPSE
39 Assoc VP Student Engagement ... Vacant
86 Director Government Relations ... Ms. Jennifer GOEN
88 Dir Environmental Health/Safety ... Ms. Rhonda HOLTZCLAW
51 Asst VP Innovative Educ/Partnership ... Ms. Kristen VANSELOW
88 General Manager/WGCU ... Mr. Corey LEWIS
40 Manager Barnes & Noble at FGCU ... Mr. Larry DAVIS
121 Dir Ctr Academic Achievement ... Ms. Lindsay SINGH
04 Dir of Operations/President's Ofc ... Ms. Beverly D. BROWN
07 Asst VP University Admissions ... Mr. Derrell PUSTIZZI
101 Director Board Relations ... Ms. Tiffany REYNOLDS
104 Asst Director Study Abroad ... Vacant
105 Director Web Services/AVP Marketing ... Mr. Jeffrey GARNER
108 Director Assessment/Accreditation ... Vacant
25 Director Research/Sponsored Pgms ... Ms. Donna GILMORE
30 Sr Director of Development ... Ms. Dolly FARRELL
122 Coord Fraternity/Sorority Life ... Mr. Michael RAFO

*Florida International University (H)

University Park, 11200 SW 8 Street, Miami FL 33199-0001
County: Miami-Dade FICE Identification: 009635
Unit ID: 133951
Telephone: (305) 348-2000 Carnegie Class: DU-Highest
FAX Number: N/A Calendar System: Semester
URL: www.fiu.edu
Established: 1965 Annual Undergrad Tuition & Fees (In-State): $6,565
Enrollment: 58,836 Coed
Affiliation or Control: State IRS Status: 501(c)3
Highest Offering: Doctorate

Accreditation: SC, ACPHA, ANEST, #ARCPA, ART, CAATE, CACREP, CAEP, CAHIIM, CIDA, CLPSY, CONST, DIETD, DIETI, FEPAC, HSA, IPSY, JOUR, LAW, LSAR, MED, MUS, NURSE, OPE, OT, PH, PTA, SP, SPAA, SW, THEA

01 Interim President ... Dr. Kenneth JESSELL
100 Chief of Staff ... Vacant
05 Int Provost/EVP/COO ... Dr. Elizabeth BEJAR
32 Int VP Student Affairs ... Mr. Charlie ANDREWS
88 VP for Engagement ... Mr. Saif ISHOOF
10 Interim CFO/VP for Administration ... Ms. Aime MARTINEZ
111 Sr Vice President for Advancement ... Mr. Howard LIPMAN
09 AVP Analysis/Info Mgmt ... Dr. Hiselgis PEREZ
35 Dean of Students ... Dr. Bares PELAEZ
46 Vice President of Research ... Dr. Andres GIL
13 Vice President/CIO ... Mr. Robert GRILLO
12 Vice Provost BBC ... Mr. Michael HEARON
84 VP Enrollment Mgmt Services ... Dr. Kevin COUGHLIN, JR.
88 Ombudsperson ... Dr. Sofia TRELLES
15 Sr Vice President Human Resources ... Ms. El Pagnier HUDSON
18 Assoc VP Facilities Operations ... Mr. John CAL
07 Dir Undergraduate Admissions ... Ms. Jody GLASSMAN
49 Dean Col Arts/Sciences/Educ ... Dr. Michael HEITHAUS
50 Dean College Business Admin ... Dr. Joanne LI
54 Dean Col Engineering/Computing ... Dr. John VOLAKIS
53 Director College of Education ... Dr. Laura DINEHART
88 Dean Sch Hospitality Mgmt ... Dr. Michael CHENG
82 Dean School Intl/Pub Affairs ... Dr. John STACK
66 Dean Col Nursing/Health Science ... Dr. Ora STRICKLAND
69 Dean College of Public Health ... Dr. Tomas GUILARTE
61 Dean College of Law ... Dr. Antony PAGE
63 Dean Col Medicine/SVP Health Affs ... Dr. Robert SACKSTEIN
92 Dean Honors College ... Dr. Juan Carlos ESPINOSA
48 Dean Col Comm/Architecture/Arts ... Dr. Brian SCHRINER
77 Dir Sch Computing/Info Sciences ... Dr. Sundararaj IYENGAR
38 Dir Stdnt Hlth & Counseling ... Dr. Todd LENGNICK
22 Director Equal Opportunity Program ... Ms. Shirlyon J. MCWHORTER
62 Dean of Libraries ... Dr. Anne PRESTAMO
41 Athletics Director ... Mr. Pete GARCIA
86 VP for Government Relations ... Ms. Michelle PALACIO
06 University Registrar ... Ms. Dulce BELTRAN
26 Sr Vice President Ext Relations ... Ms. Sandra GONZALEZ-LEVY
37 Director Student Financial Aid ... Mr. Francisco VALINES
36 Director Career Services ... Ms. Ivette DUARTE
23 Medical Director Stdnt Hlth Svcs ... Dr. Saara SCHWARTZ
39 Dir of Housing/Residential Life ... Mr. Joe PAULICK
28 Director Disability Student Svcs ... Dr. Amanda NIGUIDULA
116 Chief Audit Executive ... Mr. Trevor WILLIAMS
24 Dir University IT/Media Support ... Mr. Matthew HAGOOD
21 Associate VP and Univ Controller ... Ms. Katharine BROPHY
88 Dir Environmental Health/Safety ... Ms. Tamece KNOWLES
19 Chief of Police ... Chief Alexander CASAS
27 Asst VP Media Relations ... Ms. Maydel SANTANA-BRAVO
43 General Counsel ... Mr. Carlos CASTILLO
85 Sr Dir International Stdnt Svcs ... Ms. Alejandra PARRA
25 Assistant VP for Research ... Mr. Roberto GUTIERREZ
04 Assistant Chief of Staff ... Ms. Claudia GONZALEZ
102 Sr Dir Corp/Foundation Relations ... Ms. Karla HERNANDEZ

*Florida Polytechnic University (A)

4700 Research Way, Lakeland FL 33805-8531

County: Polk | Identification: 667279 | Unit ID: 482936

Telephone: (863) 583-9050 | Carnegie Class: Bac-Diverse
FAX Number: N/A | Calendar System: Semester
URL: www.floridapoly.edu
Established: 2012 | Annual Undergrad Tuition & Fees (In-State): $4,940
Enrollment: 1,422 | Coed
Affiliation or Control: State | IRS Status: 501(c)3
Highest Offering: Master's
Accreditation: SC

02 President ... Dr. Randy K. AVENT
05 Provost ... Dr. Terry PARKER
43 Vice President & General Counsel ... Miss Gina DEIULIO
111 Vice President Advancement ... Ms. Kathy BOWMAN
10 Vice President/CFO ... Mr. Mark MROCZKOWSKI
07 Vice Provost Admissions/Fin Aid ... Mr. Ben MATTHEW CORPUS
32 Vice Provost Student Affairs ... Ms. Kathryn MILLER
37 Director Financial Aid ... Ms. Carola MANN
15 Assoc Director Human Resources ... Ms. DeAnn DOLL
04 Admin Assistant to the President ... Ms. Michele RUSH
06 Registrar ... Mr. Andrew KONAPELSKY
09 Director of Institutional Research ... Mr. Kevin CALKINS
13 Chief Information Technology Office ... Mr. Mike DIECKMANN
18 Chief Facilities/Physical Plant Ofc ... Mr. David CALHOUN
19 Director Security/Safety ... Chief Richard HOLLAND

*Florida State University (B)

222 S. Copeland Street, Tallahassee FL 32306

County: Leon | FICE Identification: 001489 | Unit ID: 134097

Telephone: (850) 644-2525 | Carnegie Class: DU-Highest
FAX Number: (850) 644-9936 | Calendar System: Semester
URL: www.fsu.edu
Established: 1851 | Annual Undergrad Tuition & Fees (In-State): $5,656
Enrollment: 43,569 | Coed
Affiliation or Control: State | IRS Status: 501(c)3
Highest Offering: Doctorate
Accreditation: SC, ACATE, ANEST, #ARCPA, ART, CACREP, CEA, CIDA, CLPSY, DANCE, DIETD, DIETI, IPSY, LAW, LIB, MED, MFCD, MUS, NASP, NURSE, PH, PLNG, PSPSY, SP, SPAA, SW, THEA

02 President ... Dr. Richard MCCULLOUGH
05 Prov/Exec VP Academic Affairs ... Dr. James J. CLARK
10 VP for Finance & Administration ... Mr. Kyle CLARK
32 VP for Student Affairs ... Dr. Amy HECHT
46 Interim VP for Research ... Dr. Mark RILEY
45 VP Planning and Programs ... Vacant
102 Interim Exec VP for FSU Foundation ... Dr. Michael HARTLINE
41 VP & Director of Athletics ... Mr. Michael ALFORD
20 VP Faculty Development/Advancement ... Dr. Janet KISTNER
100 President Office Chief of Staff ... Ms. Marissa LANGSTON
88 Associate VP for Research ... Ms. Kerry PELUSO
18 Associate VP for Facilities ... Mr. Dave IRVIN
21 Associate VP for Finance & Admin ... Mr. Michael WILLIAMS
13 AVP Strat & Analytics/Interim CIO ... Mr. Rick BURNETTE
20 Associate VP for Academic Affairs ... Mr. Paul HARLACHER, JR.
15 AVP HR/Fin & Admin Chief of Staff ... Ms. Renisha GIBBS
11 Asst VP for Administrative Services ... Mr. Steven CONNER
20 Associate VP for Academic Affairs ... Mr. John BARNHILL
26 Asst VP for Univ Communications ... Mr. Dennis SCHNITTKER
88 Dir Academic Pgm Professional Svcs ... Mr. Bill LINDNER
49 Dean College of Arts & Sciences ... Dr. Sam HUCKABA
50 Dean College of Business ... Dr. Michael HARTLINE
53 Dean College of Education ... Dr. Damon ANDREW
59 Interim Dean Health & Human Svcs ... Dr. Damon ANDREW
60 Dean Communication & Information ... Dr. Larry DENNIS
66 Dean College of Nursing ... Dr. Jing WANG
88 Dean College of Criminology ... Dr. Thomas G. BLOMBERG
61 Dean College of Law ... Dr. Erin O'HARA O'CONNOR
83 Dean Social Sci & Public Policy ... Dr. Timothy CHAPIN
70 Interim Dean College of Social Work ... Dr. Craig STANLEY
88 Dean College of Motion Picture Arts ... Mr. Reb BRADDOCK
64 Dean College of Music ... Dr. Todd QUEEN
57 Dean College of Fine Arts ... Mr. James FRAZIER
54 Dean College of Engineering ... Dr. Suvranu DE
63 Dean College of Medicine ... Dr. John P. FOGARTY
58 Dean Graduate School ... Dr. Mark RILEY
97 Dean Undergraduate Studies ... Dr. Karen L. LAUGHLIN
12 Dean FSU Panama City Campus ... Dr. Randy HANNA
06 University Registrar ... Dr. Kimberly BARBER
92 Director University Honors Program ... Ms. Annette SCHWABE
37 Director Student Financial Aid ... Ms. Suzanne VICKERS
08 Dean of University Libraries ... Ms. Gale ETSCHMAIER
90 Sr Director Enterprise Applications ... Vacant
43 VP Legal Affairs & General Counsel ... Ms. Carolyn EGAN
104 Director of International Programs ... Dr. James E. PITTS
114 Chief Budget Officer ... Ms. Katie PERKINS
09 Director of Institutional Research ... Dr. James HUNT
86 Chief Legislative Affairs Officer ... Mr. Clay INGRAM
38 Director of Counseling & Psych Svcs ... Dr. Carlos J. GOMEZ
19 Asst VP Public Safety/ Police Chief ... Ms. Rhonda HARRIS
23 Director University Health Services ... Dr. Amy MAGNUSON
36 Director Career Center ... Ms. Myrna HOOVER
116 Chief Audit Officer ... Mr. Undra BALDWIN
28 Dir Equity/Diversity & Inclusion ... Ms. Michelle DOUGLAS
39 Exec Director University Housing ... Ms. Shannon STATEN
109 Director Student Business Services ... Mr. John BEMBRY
25 Sr Director Sponsored Research ... Ms. Pamela RAY
14 Sr Director Community Tech Services ... Mr. Kenneth JOHNSON
96 Chief Procurement Officer ... Ms. Rosey MURTON

*New College of Florida (C)

5800 Bay Shore Road, Sarasota FL 34243-2109

County: Sarasota | FICE Identification: 001507 | Unit ID: 262129

Telephone: (941) 487-4100 | Carnegie Class: Bac-A&S
FAX Number: (941) 487-4101 | Calendar System: 4/1/4
URL: www.ncf.edu
Established: 1960 | Annual Undergrad Tuition & Fees (In-State): $6,916
Enrollment: 675 | Coed
Affiliation or Control: State | IRS Status: 501(c)3
Highest Offering: Master's
Accreditation: SC

02 President ... Dr. Patricia OKKER
05 Provost ... Dr. Suzanne SHERMAN
10 Vice Pres Finance & Administration ... Mr. Chris KINSLEY
79 Chair of Humanities ... Dr. Miriam WALLACE
81 Chair of Natural Sciences ... Dr. Sandra GILCHRIST
83 Chair of Social Sciences ... Dr. Barbara HICKS
08 Interim Dean Cook Library ... Ms. Tammera RACE
84 Int Vice President of Enrollment ... Mr. David BOIVERT
32 Vice President of Student Affairs ... Ms. S. Marjorie THOMAS
28 Dean Outreach/Engage/Inclusion ... Vacant
07 Associate Dean of Admissions ... Ms. Sonia WU
20 Associate Academic Officer ... Dr. Emily HEFFERNAN
21 Associate Business Officer ... Ms. Melissa SHIPPEE
13 Dir of Information Technology ... Mr. Ben FOSS
14 Director of Technology Support ... Mr. Jeff SMITH
29 Asst Director Alumnae/i Association ... Ms. Kathleen MCCOY
06 Registrar ... Vacant
26 Director Marketing/Communications ... Ms. Cathy HELEAN
38 Director Counseling ... Dr. Anne E. FISHER
09 Director of Institutional Research ... Ms. Hui-Men WEN
100 Chief of Staff President's Office ... Dr. Bradley THIESSEN
15 Assoc VP of Human Resources ... Ms. Erika WORTHY
18 Chief Facilities/Physical Plant ... Vacant
96 Director of Purchasing ... Ms. Jean HARRIS
37 Director Student Financial Aid ... Ms. Tara KARAS
43 General Counsel ... Mr. David FUGETT
25 Contract Administrator ... Mr. Justin MILLER
30 Chief Development ... Ms. MaryAnne YOUNG
19 Chief of Police ... Vacant
39 Director Student Housing ... Vacant
41 Athletic Director ... Mr. Tyler FORTUNE
04 Administrative Asst to President ... Ms. Shelley WILBUR
104 Director Study Abroad ... Ms. Florence ZAMSKY
36 Director Student Placement ... Vacant

*University of Central Florida (D)

PO Box 160000, Orlando FL 32816-0001

County: Orange | FICE Identification: 003954 | Unit ID: 132903

Telephone: (407) 823-2000 | Carnegie Class: DU-Highest
FAX Number: N/A | Calendar System: Semester
URL: www.ucf.edu
Established: 1963 | Annual Undergrad Tuition & Fees (In-State): $6,368
Enrollment: 71,881 | Coed
Affiliation or Control: State | IRS Status: 501(c)3
Highest Offering: Doctorate
Accreditation: SC, CAATE, CACREP, CAHIIM, CEA, CLPSY, FEPAC, HSA, IPSY, MED, MLS, MUS, NURSE, PLNG, PTA, SP, SPAA, SW, THEA

02 President ... Dr. Alexander N. CARTWRIGHT
05 Provost/Vice Pres for Acad Affs ... Dr. Michael D. JOHNSON
11 VP & Chief Operating Officer ... Ms. Misty SHEPHERD
10 Senior VP for Admin and Finance ... Mr. Gerald HECTOR
43 Vice President/General Counsel ... Ms. Youndy C. COOK
32 Int VP Student Dev/Enrollment Svcs ... Dr. Adrienne O. FRAME
102 Int CEO Foundation/Int VP Adv ... Ms. Karen COCHRAN
31 Vice President Community Relations ... Ms. Helen DONEGAN
63 VP Health Affairs/Dean Med College ... Dr. Deborah GERMAN
41 Vice Pres & Dir of Athletics ... Mr. Terry MOHAJIR
49 Dean College of Arts & Humanities ... Mr. Jeffrey MOORE
50 Dean College of Business Admin ... Dr. Paul JARLEY
53 Dean Col of Comm Innovation & Educ ... Dr. Grant HAYES
54 Dean College of Engr/Comp Sci .. Dr. Michael GEORGIOPOULOS
76 Dean Col Health Prof/Sciences ... Dr. Christopher INGERSOLL
88 Dean Rosen College Hospitality Mgt ... Dr. Youcheng WANG
66 Dean College of Nursing ... Dr. Mary L. SOLE
88 Dean Col of Optics/Photonics ... Dr. David HAGAN
81 Dean College of Sciences ... Dr. Maggy TOMOVA
92 Dean Burnett Honors Col ... Dr. Sheila PINERES
13 VP Info Tech & Chief Info Officer ... Mr. Matthew J. HALL
100 Chief of Staff ... Mr. Mike KILBRIDE
35 Asst VP UCF Downtown Student Svcs ... Dr. Chanda TORRES
46 Assoc VP Research Administration ... Ms. Dorothy YATES
58 Vice Pres Res/Dean Grad Studies ... Dr. Elizabeth KLONOFF
09 Chief Analytics Officer ... Dr. M. Paige BORDEN
18 Assoc VP Facilities & Safety ... Mr. Duane SIEMEN
97 VProv/Dean Col Undergrad Studies ... Dr. Theodorea BERRY
111 Assoc VP for Advancement ... Mr. Jeff COATES
84 Assoc VP Enrollment Services ... Dr. Gordon CHAVIS
20 Vice Prov Faculty Excellence ... Dr. Jana JASINSKI
26 AVP Communications & Marketing ... Mr. Patrick BURT
37 Dir Student Financial Aid ... Ms. Alicia KEATON
06 University Registrar ... Mr. Brian BOYD
08 Interim Director Libraries ... Mr. Frank ALLEN
15 Assoc VP HR/Chief HR Officer ... Ms. Maureen BINDER
19 Assoc VP Safety & Chief of Police ... Mr. Carl METZGER
93 Dir Multicultural Acad Support Svcs ... Mr. Wayne JACKSON
14 AVP/COO UCF IT ... Mr. Michael SINK
38 Director Counseling Center ... Dr. Karen HOFMANN
22 Dir Office of Institutional Equity ... Ms. Nancy F. MYERS
23 Assoc VP Student Health Services ... Dr. Michael G. DEICHEN
39 Int Exec Dir Housing and Res Life ... Dr. Andrea J. TRINKLEIN
28 VP Diversity/Equity & Inclusion ... Dr. Andrea GUZMAN
96 Associate Director Procurement ... Ms. Nellie NIDO
36 Exec Director Career Services ... Ms. Lynn HANSEN
44 Associate VP of Annual Giving ... Ms. Heather JUNOD
86 VP Govt & Community Relations ... Ms. Janet D. OWEN

*University of Florida (E)

235 Tigert Hall, Gainesville FL 32611-9500

County: Alachua | FICE Identification: 001535 | Unit ID: 134130

Telephone: (352) 392-3261 | Carnegie Class: DU-Highest
FAX Number: (352) 392-8735 | Calendar System: Semester
URL: www.ufl.edu
Established: 1853 | Annual Undergrad Tuition & Fees (In-State): $6,381
Enrollment: 53,372 | Coed
Affiliation or Control: State | IRS Status: 501(c)3
Highest Offering: Doctorate
Accreditation: SC, ARCPA, ART, AUD, CACREP, CAEP, CAMPEP, CEA, CIDA, CLPSY, CONST, COPSY, DANCE, DENT, DIETD, DIETI, HSA, IFSAC, IPSY, JOUR, LAW, LSAR, MED, MUS, NURSE, OT, PH, PHAR, PLNG, PTA, SCPSY, SP, THEA, VET

02 President ... Dr. W. Kent FUCHS
05 Provost & Senior Vice President ... Dr. Joseph GLOVER
47 Vice Pres Agric/Natural Res ... Dr. Jay Scott ANGLE
17 Sr Vice Pres Health Affairs ... Dr. David NELSON
10 VP/Chief Financial Ofcr ... Dr. Christopher COWEN
11 Sr Vice Pres/Chief Operating Ofcr ... Dr. Charles E. LANE
111 Vice President Advancement ... Mr. Thomas J. MITCHELL
21 Vice President Business Affairs ... Mr. Curtis REYNOLDS
32 Vice President Student Affairs ... Dr. D'Andra MULL
86 Vice President Govt & Cmty Relation ... Mr. Mark KAPLAN
26 Int VP Strategic Comm & Marketing ... Mr. Steve ORLANDO

15 Vice Pres Human Resources .... Vacant
46 Vice President Research .... Dr. David P. NORTON
43 Vice President and General Counsel .... Ms. Amy M. HASS
13 Vice President & CIO .... Mr. Elias G. ELDAYRIE
84 Vice Pres Enroll Mgmt/Assoc Provost .... Dr. Mary PARKER
100 Exec Chief of Staff .... Dr. Winfred PHILLIPS
28 Chief Diversity Officer .... Vacant
86 Assoc VP Government Relations .... Vacant
88 Assoc Provost Teaching/ Technology .... Dr. William A. MCCOLLOUGH
27 Int Asst VP Communications .... Ms. Brittany WISE
21 AVP Business Affs/Finance/Admin .... Ms. Brandi RENTON
18 Asst VP Fac/Plng/Construction .... Mr. Carlos DOUGNAC
20 Associate Provost Academic Affairs .... Dr. Chris J. HASS
20 Assoc Provost Undergrad Affairs .... Dr. Angela LINDNER
09 Asst Provost/Dir Inst Research/Plng .... Dr. Cathy LEBO
35 Assoc Vice Pres/Dean of Students .... Ms. Heather WHITE
08 Dean University Libraries .... Ms. Judith RUSSELL
50 Dean of Business Administration .... Dr. Sabyasachi MITRA
49 Dean of Liberal Arts & Science .... Mr. David E. RICHARDSON
68 Dean of Health/Human Performance .... Dr. Michael B. REID
61 Dean of Law .... Ms. Laura A. ROSENBURY
66 Dean of Nursing .... Dr. Anna M. MCDANIEL
67 Dean of Pharmacy .... Dr. Julie A. JOHNSON
54 Dean of Engineering .... Dr. Cammy ABERNATHY
47 Dean Agricultural/Life Sciences .... Dr. R. Elaine TURNER
60 Dean of Journalism/Comm .... Dr. Hubert BROWN
76 Dean Pub Health/Health Professions .... Dr. Beth VIRNIG
53 Dean of Education .... Dr. Glenn GOOD
47 Dean IFAS Extension .... Dr. Andra D. JOHNSON
74 Dean of Veterinary Medicine .... Dr. Dana ZIMMEL
57 Dean of the Arts .... Dr. Onye OZUZU
48 Dean Design Construction Planning .... Dr. Chimay ANUMBA
63 Dean of Medicine .... Dr. Colleen KOCH
46 Dean of IFAS Research .... Dr. Robert GILBERT
52 Dean of Dentistry .... Dr. Isabel GARCIA
58 Dean Graduate School/Assoc Provost .... Dr. Nicole STEDMAN
65 Dir School Natural Res/Envir .... Dr. Thomas K. FRAZER
06 Interim University Registrar .... Ms. Donna KOLB
23 Int Director of Student Health .... Dr. David FELLER
38 Assoc Dir of Counseling & Well Ctr .... Dr. Alvin LAWRENCE
37 Director Student Financial Aid .... Ms. Donna KOLB
36 Sr Dir of Career Connections Ctr .... Ms. Ja'Net GLOVER
14 Director of Computer Center .... Mr. Timothy J. FITZPATRICK
19 Director of University Police .... Ms. Linda J. STUMP-KURNICK
24 Director of Academic Technology .... Dr. Mark MCCALLISTER
65 Director of Forestry .... Dr. Timothy L. WHITE
39 Director of Housing .... Ms. Tina KUHLENGEL HORVATH
41 Athletic Director .... Mr. Scott STRICKLIN
29 Int Exec Dir FL Alumni Affairs .... Mr. Brian DANFORTH
96 Director of Purchasing .... Ms. Lisa DEAL
07 Director of Admissions .... Mr. Rick BRYANT
04 Executive Asst to President .... Ms. Beth BOONE
106 Dir Online Education/E-learning .... Ms. Evangeline CUMMINGS
108 Director Institutional Assessment .... Dr. Timothy S. BROPHY
101 Secretary of the Institution/Board .... Mr. Mark KAPLAN

*University of North Florida (A)

1 UNF Drive, Jacksonville FL 32224-7699

County: Duval FICE Identification: 009841
Unit ID: 136172

Telephone: (904) 620-1000 Carnegie Class: DU-Higher
FAX Number: (904) 620-2414 Calendar System: Semester
URL: www.unf.edu
Established: 1965 Annual Undergrad Tuition & Fees (In-State): $6,389
Enrollment: 16,926 Coed
Affiliation or Control: State IRS Status: 501(c)3
Highest Offering: Doctorate
Accreditation: SC, ANEST, ART, CAATE, CACREP, CAEP, CAEPN, CONST, COSMA, DIET, DIETD, DIETI, EXSC, HSA, IPSY, JOUR, MUS, NURSE, PH, PTA, SPAA, SW

02 President .... Dr. Moez LIMAYEM
05 Provost .... Dr. Karen PATTERSON
86 VP Government & Community Relations .... Ms. Heather DUNCAN
43 VP/General Counsel .... Ms. Karen J. STONE
30 VP Development/Alumni Affairs .... Ms. Teresa NICHOLS
88 VP Data Analytics .... Dr. Bob J. COLEMAN
26 VP Marketing Communications .... Ms. Isabel PEASE
28 VP/Chief Diversity Officer .... Dr. Richmond WYNN
84 Assoc VP Enrollment Services .... Dr. Terrence CURRAN
116 Assoc VP & Compliance Officer .... Dr. Joann N. CAMPBELL
10 VP Admin & Finance .... Mr. Scott BENNETT
45 Asst VP Research .... Dr. John KANTNER
32 Assoc VP Student Affairs .... Ms. Ruth LOPEZ
35 Assoc VP Student Affairs .... Ms. Christine S. MALEK RICHARD
58 Assoc Provost .... Dr. John KANTNER
08 Dean of the Library .... Dr. Brent MAI
97 AVP Undergraduate Studies .... Dr. Susan PEREZ
50 Dean Coggin College of Business .... Dr. Richard J. BUTTIMER
49 Dean Arts & Sciences .... Dr. Kaveri SUBRAHMANYAM
53 Interim Dean College of Education .... Dr. Jennifer KANE
76 Dean Brooks College of Health .... Dr. Curt LOX
77 Dean Computing/Engr/Constr .... Dr. William KLOSTERMEYER
07 Director of Admissions .... Ms. Terry R. EVANS
22 Dir Equal Opportunity Programs .... Ms. Marlynn JONES
103 Dir Professional Dev Training .... Mr. Kelly G. HARRISON
13 Chief Information Technology Office .... Mr. Brian VERKAMP
114 Chief Budget Officer .... Mrs. Devany GROVES
21 Controller .... Ms. Valerie O. STEVENSON
88 Senior Associate Athletic Director .... Ms. Donna R. KIRK
88 Dir Environment Health/Safety .... Mr. Daniel D. ENDICOTT
22 Dir ADA Compliance .... Ms. Rocelia T. GONZALEZ
14 Assoc VP & CSIO .... Mr. Jeffrey A. DURFEE
21 Treasurer .... Mr. Michael S. NEGLIA
18 Dir Campus Planning .... Mr. Paul STEWART
88 Dir University Center .... Mr. George ANDROUIN
19 Dir Safety Security .... Mr. Francis J. MACKESY
88 Dir Child Development Center .... Ms. Mahreen N. MIAN
23 Dir Student Health Services .... Dr. Valerie A. MORRISON
39 Dir Housing Residence Life .... Mr. Robert J. BOYLE
41 Athletic Director .... Mr. Nick MORROW
88 Int Assoc VP Faculty Enhancement .... Dr. Gordon RAKITA
108 Asst VP of Inst Effectiveness .... Dr. Amanda KULP
37 Asst VP Student Financial Aid .... Ms. Anissa AGNE
06 Registrar .... Mr. Charles N. LEARCH
09 Asst VP IR and Performance .... Dr. Abby WILLCOX
88 Exec Dir FL Inst of Education .... Dr. Cheryl A. FOUNTAIN
88 Dir Small Business Dev Ctr .... Mr. Huston PULLEN
96 Dir Purchasing .... Ms. Shawn ASMUTH
51 Dean Continuing Education .... Ms. Abdullah E. EDYTHE
106 Asst VP Digital Learning/Innovation .... Dr. Deb MILLER
04 Admin Assistant to the President .... Ms. Alison CRUESS
101 Secretary of the Institution/ Board .... Ms. Ann FISHMAN
104 Director Study Abroad .... Dr. Luisa MARTINEZ
105 Director Web Services .... Ms. Katherine THOMPSON
15 Chief Human Resources Officer .... Ms. Carrie GUTH
29 Director Alumni Affairs .... Vacant
44 Director Annual Giving .... Ms. Kristine HERRINGTON
122 Assoc Dir Fraternity/Sorority Life .... Ms. Jen MIRANDA

*University of South Florida (B)

4202 E Fowler Avenue, SVC 2172, Tampa FL 33620-6100

County: Hillsborough FICE Identification: 001537
Unit ID: 137351

Telephone: (813) 974-2011 Carnegie Class: DU-Highest
FAX Number: N/A Calendar System: Semester
URL: www.usf.edu
Established: 1956 Annual Undergrad Tuition & Fees (In-State): $6,410
Enrollment: 50,626 Coed
Affiliation or Control: State IRS Status: 501(c)3
Highest Offering: Doctorate
Accreditation: SC, ABAI, ANEST, ARCPA, ART, AUD, CAATE, CACREP, CAEP, CAHIIM, CAMPEP, CEA, CLPSY, DANCE, DIETI, HSA, IPSY, LIB, MED, MUS, NURSE, PCSAS, PH, PHAR, PLNG, PTA, SCPSY, SP, SPAA, SW, THEA

02 President .... Dr. Rhea LAW
45 Sr VP Business/Financial Strategy .... Mr. David LECHNER
100 Chief of Staff President's Office .... Dr. Cynthia S. VISOT
43 General Counsel .... Mr. Gerard SOLIS
05 Int Provost/Chief Academic Officer .... Dr. Eric EISENBERT
15 Vice Provost for HR and Space Plng .... Vacant
20 Vice Provost for Plng/Perf & Acct .... Dr. Theresa H. CHISOLM
20 Vice Provost and VP USF World .... Vacant
104 Director Education Abroad .... Dr. Amanda C. MAURER
46 Sr Vice Pres Research & Innovation .... Dr. Paul SANBERG
111 SVP Advance/Alumni Affs/CEO Found .... Mr. Jay STROMAN
17 Sr Vice Pres USF Health .... Dr. Charles LOCKWOOD
58 Sr Vice Provost/Dean Grad School .... Dr. Dwayne SMITH
10 Vice Pres Business & Finance .... Mr. Nick TRIVUNOVICH
88 Assistant Treasurer .... Ms. Dawn M. RODRIGUEZ
11 Vice Pres Administrative Services .... Mr. Calvin WILLIAMS
18 Asst VP Physical Plant .... Mr. Chris DUFFY
32 Asst VP and Dean of Students .... Ms. Danielle MCDONALD
13 Vice Pres Information Technology .... Mr. Sidney FERNANDES
14 AVP Information Technology .... Ms. Jenny PAULSEN
14 AVP Information Technology .... Mr. Swapna CHACKRAVARTHY
105 Director Information Technology .... Mr. Christopher L. AKIN
29 Assoc Vice Pres Alumni Affairs .... Mr. Bill MCCAUSLAND
22 Chief Diversity Officer .... Dr. Haywood BROWN
121 Vice Provost for Student Success .... Dr. Paul J. DOSAL
16 Vice Pres Human Resources .... Ms. Angela SKLENKA
86 Asst Vice Pres Government Rels .... Mr. Mark WALSH
09 Asst VP Office of Decision Support .... Dr. Valeria GARCIA
88 University Ombudsman .... Mr. Steven D. PREVAUX
39 Asst VP Housing/Residential Educ .... Ms. Ana HERNANDEZ
83 Dean Behavioral/Community Sci .... Dr. Julianne SEROVICH
50 Dean Business Administration .... Dr. Moez LIMAYEM
53 Dean College of Education .... Dr. Robert C. KNOEPPEL
54 Dean Engineering .... Dr. Robert H. BISHOP
57 Dean College of the Arts .... Dr. James S. MOY
67 Dean College of Pharmacy .... Dr. Kevin B. SNEED
49 Dean Arts & Sciences .... Dr. Eric EISENBERG
92 Dean Honors College .... Dr. Charles H. ADAMS
88 Dean Marine Science .... Dr. Jacqueline DIXON
69 Dean Public Health .... Dr. Donna PETERSEN
88 Int Dean Global Sustainability .... Dr. Govindan PARAYIL
89 Dean Undergraduate Studies .... Dr. Paul ATCHLEY
106 Asst Vice Provost Innovative Educ .... Dr. Cynthia A. DELUCA
48 Dir Sch of Architecture/Cmty Design .... Mr. Robert MACLEOD
12 Regional Chanc Sarasota-Manatee .... Dr. Karen HOLBROOK
12 Reg Chanc USF St Petersburg .... Dr. Martin TADLOCK
21 Controller .... Ms. Jennifer CONDON
26 Director of Media Relations .... Mr. Adam FREEMAN
06 Registrar .... Vacant
114 University Budget Officer .... Ms. Nell PETERSON
37 Assoc VP Financial Aid .... Ms. Billie Jo HAMILTON
38 Director Counseling Center .... Dr. Scott STRADER
36 Asst Vice President Career Services .... Ms. Ruth Ann ATCHLEY
19 Chief of Police .... Mr. Chris DANIEL
08 USF Libraries Dean .... Dr. Todd CHAVEZ
41 Director of Athletics .... Mr. Michael KELLY
28 Director of Diversity & Inclusion .... Ms. Patsy FELICIANO
96 Int Director Purchasing & Property .... Mr. George COTTER

*University of South Florida St. Petersburg (C)

140 7th Avenue S, Saint Petersburg FL 33701-5016

Telephone: (727) 873-4873 FICE Identification: 009016
Accreditation: &SC, JOUR

*University of South Florida Sarasota-Manatee (D)

8350 North Tamiami Trail, Sarasota FL 34243

Telephone: (941) 359-4200 Identification: 667058
Accreditation: &SC, ACPHA

*University of West Florida (E)

11000 University Parkway, Pensacola FL 32514-5750

County: Escambia FICE Identification: 003955
Unit ID: 138354

Telephone: (850) 474-2000 Carnegie Class: Masters/L
FAX Number: (850) 474-3131 Calendar System: Semester
URL: uwf.edu
Established: 1963 Annual Undergrad Tuition & Fees (In-State): $6,360
Enrollment: 13,061 Coed
Affiliation or Control: State IRS Status: 501(c)3
Highest Offering: Doctorate
Accreditation: SC, CAEP, EXSC, MLS, MPCAC, MUS, NURSE, PH, SW

02 President .... Dr. Martha D. SAUNDERS
05 Provost & Senior Vice President .... Dr. George B. ELLENBERG
20 Vice Provost .... Dr. Michelle WILLIAMS
111 Vice Pres for Univ Advancement .... Dr. Howard J. REDDY
10 VP Finance & Administration .... Ms. Betsy BOWERS
32 VP Acad Engagement/Student Affs .... Dr. Gregory TOMSO
15 AVP Human Resources .... Ms. Jamie SPRAGUE
18 Int AVP Facilities/Operations .... Mr. Mel MANOR
21 AVP Finance/Controller .... Mr. Jeffrey DJERLEK
30 AVP for Development .... Mr. Brett BERG
119 AVP Cybersecurity .... Dr. Eman EL-SHEIKH
46 AVP of Research Administration .... Dr. Matthew SCHWARTZ
35 AVP/Dean of Students .... Dr. Mary ANDERSON
110 AVP of Advancement .... Mr. Daniel LUCAS
88 Chief Compliance Officer .... Mr. Matthew W. PACKARD
43 General Counsel .... Ms. Susan A. WOOLF
116 Chief Audit Executive .... Mrs. Cynthia TALBERT
19 Chief of University Police .... Mr. Marc COSSICH
49 Int Dean Arts/Social Sci/Humanities .... Dr. Amy MITCHELL-COOK
50 Dean College of Business .... Dr. Richard FOUNTAIN
107 Dean Education & Prof Studies .... Dr. William CRAWLEY
81 Dean Science/Engineering/Health .... Dr. Jaromy KUHL
08 Dean University Libraries .... Ms. Stephanie CLARK
58 Dean Graduate Programs .... Dr. Kuiyuan LI
13 Exec Dir/Chief Tech Officer ITS .... Mr. Geissler GOLDING
76 Interim Dean College of Health .... Dr. Steve BROWN
07 Executive Director of Admissions .... Ms. Katherine CONDON
09 Dir Institutional Research .... Mr. Christophe LIZEN
108 Dir Institutional Effectiveness .... Dr. Angela BRYAN
96 Director Procurement & Contracts .... Ms. Christine MILLER
109 Director Business/Auxiliary Svcs .... Mr. James ADAMS
124 Dir Student Involvement .... Ms. Lindsey WOODS
38 Exec Dir Counseling Services .... Mr. Michael MYERS
37 Director of Financial Aid .... Ms. Rachel CONWAY
84 Exec Dir of Enrollment Mgmt & Svcs .... Vacant
06 Registrar .... Mr. Adam BURGESS
39 Interim Dir of Housing/Res Life .... Mrs. Leigh PROUTY
22 Dir Equity & Diversity .... Dr. Vannee C. NGUYEN
92 Dir of Kugelman Honors Pgm .... Dr. Jocelyn EVANS
104 Asst Dir of International Programs .... Mr. Randolph SCOTT
26 Exec Dir Institutional Comm .... Vacant
29 Assoc Dir Alumni Relations .... Mrs. Katrina SCHUTTS
41 Athletic Director .... Mr. David SCOTT
86 Director for Governmental Relations .... Ms. Rachel WITBRACHT
101 Executive Specialist to BOT .... Ms. Becky LUNTSFORD

Stetson University (F)

421 N Woodland Boulevard, DeLand FL 32723-0001

County: Volusia FICE Identification: 001531
Unit ID: 137546

Telephone: (386) 822-7000 Carnegie Class: Masters/L
FAX Number: (386) 822-8832 Calendar System: Semester
URL: www.stetson.edu
Established: 1883 Annual Undergrad Tuition & Fees: $49,500
Enrollment: 4,462 Coed
Affiliation or Control: Independent Non-Profit IRS Status: 501(c)3
Highest Offering: Doctorate
Accreditation: SC, CACREP, CAEP, LAW, MUS

01 President .... Dr. Christopher ROELLKE
05 Exec VP & Provost .... Dr. Noel PAINTER
10 Exec Vice Pres & CFO .... Mr. F. Robert HUTH
30 VP for Devel & Alumni Engagement .... Ms. Krista BOFILL
84 VP Enrollment Management .... Mr. Ray NAULT
26 VP for University Marketing .... Mr. Bruce CHONG
32 Co-Int VP Campus Life/Stdnt Success .... Ms. Lynn SCHOENBERG
32 Co-Int VP Campus Life/Stdnt Success .... Dr. Larry CORRELL-HUGHES
61 Interim Dean College of Law .... Ms. Theresa RADWAN
49 Dean Col Arts & Sciences .... Dr. Elizabeth SKOMP
50 Interim Dean School of Business .... Dr. Yiorgos BAKAMITSOS
64 Dean of School of Music .... Dr. Washington GARCIA
08 Dean of duPont-Ball Library .... Ms. Susan RYAN
20 Assoc Provost for Faculty Develop .... Dr. Rosalie RICHARDS

06	Registrar	Ms. Terri RICHARDS
41	Director of Athletics	Mr. Jeffrey P. ALTIER
13	Assoc VP & CIO	Dr. Jose BERNIER
15	Assoc VP for Human Resources	Ms. Graciela DUFOUR
18	Assoc Vice Pres Facilities Mgmt	Mr. Scott THACKER
21	Assoc Vice Pres for Finance	Mr. Jeffrey MARGHEIM
114	VP Budget & Human Resources	Mr. Jeremy DIGORIO
36	Assoc Dir Career Development	Ms. Liz CONNOR
09	Dir Institutional Research	Mr. Colin MACFARLANE
104	Director of International Learning	Ms. Paula HENTZ
112	Asst VP for Devel/Alumni Engagement	Ms. Rina ARROYO
110	Assoc VP Dev & Communications	Ms. Amy GIPSON
07	Director of Admissions	Mr. Brian FORTMAN
37	Dir Student Financial Aid	Vacant
39	Exec Dir Residential Living/Lrng	Dr. Larry CORRELL-HUGHES
16	Director Human Resources	Ms. Betty WHITEMAN
96	Director of Purchasing	Ms. Valinda WIMER
19	Chief Public Safety	Mr. Francisco ORTIZ
04	Executive Asst to President	Ms. Joan BEASLEY
102	Dir Ofc of Grants/Sponsored Rsrch	Ms. Carol BUCKELS
38	Director Counseling Ctr	Dr. Leigh BAKER
105	Director Web Services	Mr. Gary SIPE
44	Director Donor Relations	Mr. Don BURRHUS
28	Director of Diversity	Ms. Carmen JOHNSON
29	Exec Director Alumni Affairs	Ms. Margo THOMAS

Suncoast College of Health (A)

6513 14th Street West #103, Bradenton FL 34207
County: Manatee — Identification: 667296
Telephone: (941) 727-2273 — Carnegie Class: Not Classified
FAX Number: (941) 727-2274 — Calendar System: Quarter
URL: www.suncoastcollege.edu
Established: — Annual Undergrad Tuition & Fees: N/A
Enrollment: N/A — Coed
Affiliation or Control: Proprietary — IRS Status: Proprietary
Highest Offering: Baccalaureate
Accreditation: **ACICS**

01	President	Reynoso SEIDE
05	Chief Academic Officer	Joyce LAING

Tallahassee Community College (B)

444 Appleyard Drive, Tallahassee FL 32304-2895
County: Leon — FICE Identification: 001533
— Unit ID: 137759
Telephone: (850) 201-6200 — Carnegie Class: Bac/Assoc-Assoc Dom
FAX Number: (850) 201-8682 — Calendar System: Semester
URL: www.tcc.fl.edu
Established: 1966 — Annual Undergrad Tuition & Fees (In-District): $2,026
Enrollment: 11,245 — Coed
Affiliation or Control: Local — IRS Status: 501(c)3
Highest Offering: Baccalaureate
Accreditation: **SC**, ADNUR, COARC, DA, DH, EMT, NUR, SURGT

01	President	Dr. Jim MURDAUGH
05	Provost/VP Academic Affairs	Dr. Calandra STRINGER
10	Vice Pres Administrative Svcs/CFO	Dr. Barbara WILLS
13	VP Information Technology	Mr. Bret INGERMAN
32	Vice President for Student Affs	Dr. Sheri ROWLAND
103	Vice Pres Workforce Innovation	Ms. Kimberly MOORE
26	VP Communications and Marketing	Ms. Candice GRAUSE
108	VP Institutional Effectiveness	Dr. Lei WANG
12	Exec Dir Florida Public Safety Inst	Mr. Steve OUTLAW
12	Exec Dir Wakulla Environmental Inst	Mr. Bob BALLARD
100	Chief of Staff	Ms. Candice GRAUSE
88	Dir of Business Process Improvement	Ms. Renae TOLSON
21	Asst Vice President Admin Services	Mr. Bobby JONES
20	Associate VP of Academic Affairs	Dr. Anthony JONES
79	Dean Communications & Humanities	Dr. Donmetrie CLARK
83	Dean Behavioral/Social Science/Educ	Dr. Bryan HOOPER
50	Dean Business Industry & Technology	Dr. Joey WALTER
97	Dean Transitional Studies	Dr. Sharisse TURNER
08	Director of Library Services	Vacant
76	Dean Health Care Professions	Ms. Stephanie SOLOMON
37	Director of Student Financial Svcs	Mr. William SPIERS
84	Dean of Enrollment Services	Ms. Christen GIVENS
36	Dean of Career & Academic Planning	Ms. Pamela JOHNSTON
35	Associate VP of Student Affairs	Dr. Gerald JONES
15	Director of Human Resources	Ms. Nyla DAVIS
102	Director of TCC Foundation	Ms. Heather MITCHELL
41	Director of Athletics	Mr. Chuck MOORE
18	Dir Facilities/Construction/Plng	Mr. Don HERR
09	Director of Institutional Research	Ms. Margaret THOMPSON
106	Dir of TCC Online	Vacant
85	Coord International Student Svcs	Ms. Ivonne NARVAEZ
14	Director of User Services	Mr. Chip SINGLETARY
14	Director of Enterprise Systems	Mr. Mike ROBECK
14	Director of IT Infrastructure	Mr. Jason FOWLER
114	Dir of Financial Svcs/Spons Mgmt	Ms. Amy BRADBURY
25	Director Grants & Special Projects	Mr. Steven SOLOMON
96	Dir of Purchasing/Auxiliary Svcs	Mr. Dustin FROST
19	Chief of Police	Mr. Wes HARDIN
43	Dir Legal Services/General Counsel	Mr. Craig KNOX
27	Director of Integrated Marketing	Ms. Suzi BAUGH
04	Executive Coordinator	Ms. Bertie CULBREATH

Talmudic College of Florida (C)

4000 Alton Road, Miami Beach FL 33140
County: Dade — FICE Identification: 025089
— Unit ID: 137777
Telephone: (305) 534-7050 — Carnegie Class: Spec-4-yr-Faith

FAX Number: (305) 534-8444 — Calendar System: Semester
URL: www.talmudicu.edu
Established: 1974 — Annual Undergrad Tuition & Fees: $13,250
Enrollment: 30 — Male
Affiliation or Control: Independent Non-Profit — IRS Status: 501(c)3
Highest Offering: Master's
Accreditation: **RABN**

01	President	Rabbi Yitzchak ZWEIG
05	Dean/Vice President	Rabbi Yochanan ZWEIG
06	Registrar	Rabbi Yitzchak WINKLER
37	Director Student Financial Aid	Ms. Sharon BRECHER
20	Director Educational Programs	Rabbi Akiva ZWEIG
07	Director of Admissions	Rabbi Yaakov BURSTYN

Taylor College (D)

5190 SE 125th Street, Belleview FL 34420
County: Marion — FICE Identification: 041166
— Unit ID: 449524
Telephone: (352) 245-4119 — Carnegie Class: Spec 2-yr-Health
FAX Number: (352) 245-0276 — Calendar System: Other
URL: www.taylorcollege.edu
Established: 1999 — Annual Undergrad Tuition & Fees: $12,039
Enrollment: 228 — Coed
Affiliation or Control: Proprietary — IRS Status: Proprietary
Highest Offering: Associate Degree
Accreditation: **ABHES**, ADNUR, PNUR, PTAA

01	President	Jeff GEORGESON
10	Sr Director Finance/Operations	Amy DINELLA
66	Director Nursing	Arlene SALIBA EL HABRE
76	Director Physical Therapy	Stacy CAMPBELL
53	Director General Education	Elizabeth THOMPSON
37	Director Financial Aid	Brandy BAUDOUX
36	Director Career Svcs/Compliance	Ingrid ZEKAN
06	Registrar	Susie BRADLEY

Trinity Baptist College (E)

800 Hammond Boulevard, Jacksonville FL 32221-1398
County: Duval — FICE Identification: 031019
— Unit ID: 137953
Telephone: (904) 596-2451 — Carnegie Class: Bac-Diverse
FAX Number: (904) 596-2532 — Calendar System: Semester
URL: www.tbc.edu
Established: 1974 — Annual Undergrad Tuition & Fees: $13,130
Enrollment: 362 — Coed
Affiliation or Control: Baptist — IRS Status: 501(c)3
Highest Offering: Master's
Accreditation: **TRACS**

00	Chancellor	Dr. Thomas C. MESSER
01	President/CEO	Mr. Mac HEAVENER
05	Senior Vice President	Dr. Matthew BEEMER
32	Vice President of Student Affairs	Mr. Jeremiah STANLEY
84	VP Enrollment Mgmt & Development	Mr. Matthew HEAVENER
37	Director of Financial Aid	Mr. Mark ELKINS
06	Registrar	Mrs. Shelby DOWNING
08	Head Librarian	Dr. John LUCY
10	Chief Business Officer	Ms. Cathy BALLARD
41	Athletic Director	Mr. John JONES
18	Chief Facilities/Physical Plant	Mr. Dennis RIFFLE
19	Director Security/Safety	Mr. John CASH, JR.
29	Director Alumni Relations	Vacant
07	Dean of Admissions	Mr. Seth GRAY
106	Dean or Director Online Education/E	Mrs. Teresa DUSTMAN
30	Director of Development	Mr. Michael HEAVENER

Trinity College of Florida (F)

2430 Welbilt Boulevard, Trinity FL 34655-4401
County: Pasco — FICE Identification: 030282
— Unit ID: 137962
Telephone: (727) 376-6911 — Carnegie Class: Bac-Diverse
FAX Number: (727) 376-0781 — Calendar System: Semester
URL: www.trinitycollege.edu
Established: 1932 — Annual Undergrad Tuition & Fees: $16,300
Enrollment: 214 — Coed
Affiliation or Control: Independent Non-Profit — IRS Status: 501(c)3
Highest Offering: Baccalaureate
Accreditation: **BI**

01	President	Dr. Mark T. O'FARRELL
32	Vice President Student Development	Rev. Al DEPOUTOT
05	Vice President Academic Affairs	Dr. Eric BARGERHUFF
111	Vice President for Advancement	Dr. Charlie MARTIN
10	VP Business and Finance	Vacant
06	Registrar	Mrs. Sheila M. JOHNSON
26	Asst VP Marketing/Communications	Vacant
07	Director of Admissions	Mr. Kenyata HAYES
04	Administrative Asst to President	Mrs. Billie O'FARRELL
08	Head Librarian	Dr. Krista MALLO
13	Chief Info Technology Ofcr/CIO	Mr. Cory JOY
84	Director Enrollment Management	Mr. Anthony ABELL
37	Director Student Financial Aid	Mrs. Karly DOOLEY

Ultimate Medical Academy-Clearwater (G)

1255 Cleveland Street, Clearwater FL 33755
County: Pinellas — FICE Identification: 035493
— Unit ID: 441371

Telephone: (727) 298-8685 — Carnegie Class: Spec 2-yr-Health
FAX Number: (727) 446-2489 — Calendar System: Semester
URL: www.ultimatemedical.edu
Established: 1998 — Annual Undergrad Tuition & Fees: N/A
Enrollment: 7,124 — Coed
Affiliation or Control: Independent Non-Profit — IRS Status: 501(c)3
Highest Offering: Associate Degree
Accreditation: **ABHES**

01	AVP/Campus Director	Dr. Rebecca SARLO

Ultimate Medical Academy Online-Tampa (H)

3101 W Dr. Martin Luther King Blvd, Tampa FL 33607
Telephone: (888) 205-2456 — Identification: 770528
Accreditation: **ABHES**, CAHIIM

United International College (I)

3130 Commerce Pkwy, Miramar FL 33025
County: Broward — Identification: 667155
— Unit ID: 486354
Telephone: (954) 607-4344 — Carnegie Class: Spec-4-yr-Bus
FAX Number: (954) 357-1766 — Calendar System: Semester
URL: https://www.uinternational.edu/
Established: 2001 — Annual Undergrad Tuition & Fees: $8,907
Enrollment: 56 — Coed
Affiliation or Control: Proprietary — IRS Status: Proprietary
Highest Offering: Master's
Accreditation: **ACICS**

01	President	Lydia BAUTISTA MOLLER
05	Academic Director	Angelica B. MOYANO

University of Fort Lauderdale (J)

4131 NW 16th Street, Lauderhill FL 33313
County: Broward — FICE Identification: 041563
— Unit ID: 457402
Telephone: (954) 486-7728 — Carnegie Class: Spec-4-yr-Other
FAX Number: (954) 486-7667 — Calendar System: Other
URL: www.uftl.edu
Established: 1995 — Annual Undergrad Tuition & Fees: $7,410
Enrollment: 57 — Coed
Affiliation or Control: Non-denominational — IRS Status: 501(c)3
Highest Offering: Doctorate
Accreditation: **TRACS**

00	Chancellor/CEO	Dr. Henry B. FERNANDEZ
01	President	Vacant
10	Chief Financial Officer	Dr. Brian HANKERSON
05	Chief Academic Officer	Dr. Dawn PIPER
09	VP of Inst Compliance/Effectiveness	Ms. Chloris UNDERWOOD
88	Dean College of Religious Studies	Dr. Ranny LEWIS
06	Registrar	Ms. Lenice BARNETT
07	Director Admissions/Student Svcs	Ms. Jacquelyn STRACHAN
37	Director Financial Aid	Mr. Larry MOORE
100	Executive Assistant to President	Vacant
08	Chief Library Officer	Mr. Gregory SIDBERRY
13	Chief Information Technology Office	Mr. Michael DRUMMOND

University of Miami (K)

1252 Memorial Drive, Coral Gables FL 33124
County: Miami-Dade — FICE Identification: 001536
— Unit ID: 135726
Telephone: (305) 284-2211 — Carnegie Class: DU-Highest
FAX Number: N/A — Calendar System: Semester
URL: www.miami.edu
Established: 1925 — Annual Undergrad Tuition & Fees: $53,682
Enrollment: 17,809 — Coed
Affiliation or Control: Independent Non-Profit — IRS Status: 501(c)3
Highest Offering: Doctorate
Accreditation: **SC**, ANEST, CAATE, CAMPEP, CEA, CLPSY, COPSY, DENT, HSA, IPSY, LAW, MED, MUS, NURSE, PH, PTA

01	President	Dr. Julio FRENK
05	Executive Vice President & Provost	Dr. Jeffrey DUERK
10	Exec VP Business/Finance & COO	Dr. Jacqueline TRAVISANO
21	Vice President & CFO	Mr. Brandon GILLILAND
17	University of Miami & UHealth CEO	Mr. Joseph ECHEVARRIA
111	SVP Development & Alumni Relations	Mr. Joshua FRIEDMAN
84	VP Enrollment Management	Mr. John G. HALLER
115	Treasurer/Chief Investment Officer	Mr. Charmel MAYNARD
18	VP Facilities Operations & Planning	Ms. Jessica BRUMLEY
26	VP University Communications	Ms. Jacqueline R. MENENDEZ
15	Interim CHRO University	Ms. Karen STIMMELL
43	Sr VP/General Counsel	Ms. Aileen M. UGALDE
32	Sr VP Student Affairs	Dr. Patricia A. WHITELY
00	Chairman Board of Trustees	Ms. Laurie SILVERS
100	President's Chief of Staff	Mr. Rodolfo J. FERNANDEZ
20	Dean Undergraduate Affairs	Dr. Maria STAMPINO
46	Vice Provost Research	Dr. Erin KOBETZ
20	Vice Provost Faculty Affairs	Dr. Guillermo PRADO
41	Vice President & Director Athletics	Mr. Dan RADAKOVICH
27	Executive Director Comm & PR	Ms. Megan M. ONDRIZEK
19	Chief of Police	Chief David A. RIVERO
63	Dean School of Medicine	Dr. Henri FORD
49	Dean College of Arts & Sciences	Dr. Leonidas G. BACHAS
48	Dean School of Architecture	Dr. Rodolphe EL-KHOURY
50	Dean Miami Business School	Dr. John A. QUELCH

60 Dean School Communication ... Dr. Karin J. WILKINS
53 Dean Education/Human Development ... Dr. Laura KOHN-WOOD
54 Dean College of Engineering ... Dr. Pratim BISWAS
61 Dean School of Law ... Dr. David YELLEN
64 Dean School of Music ... Dr. Shelton G. BERG
65 Dean Marine & Atmospheric Science ... Dr. Roni AVISSAR
66 Dean Nursing & Health Studies ... Dr. Cindy L. MUNRO
58 Dean Graduate School ... Dr. Guillermo PRADO
35 AVP Stdnt Affs & Dean of Students ... Dr. Ryan C. HOLMES
07 Asst VP Undergrad Admissions & Mktg ... Mr. Nate CROZIER
38 Director Student Counseling ... Dr. Rene MONTEAGUDO
85 Executive Director Intl Services ... Ms. Teresa S. DE LA GUARDIA
39 AVP Student Affs/Housing/Strat Init ... Mr. Richard SOBARAM
96 Executive Director Purchasing ... Ms. Susan R. MONTES
91 AVP Enterprise Business Solutions ... Mr. Anurag SARIN
119 Assoc VP and CISO ... Mr. Thomas MURPHY
90 AVP Chief Academic Tech Officer ... Mr. Allan GYORKE
14 Assoc VP Chief Network Officer ... Mr. Stewart SERUYA
109 Asst VP Auxiliary Services ... Ms. Ana ALVAREZ
51 Dean Continuing & Intl Education ... Dr. Rebecca MACMILLAN FOX
40 Director Bookstore ... Ms. Wendy SMITH
06 Registrar ... Ms. Karen J. BECKETT
08 Dean Libraries ... Dr. Charles ECKMAN
101 University Secretary ... Ms. Frances M. DAVIS
102 Exec Director Foundation Relations ... Ms. Joanna DE VELASCO
36 Assoc Dean & Exec Dir Career Svcs ... Mr. Christian GARCIA
104 Asst Dean & Director Study Abroad ... Ms. Devika M. MILNER
22 AVP Workplace Equity ... Ms. Beverly PRUITT
88 Assoc VP Business Services ... Mr. Humberto M. SPEZIANI
37 Exec Director Financial Assistance ... Mr. John HALLER
13 VP Information Technology & CIO ... Mr. Brad ROHRER
44 Assoc VP Engagement ... Ms. Erica ARROYO
114 AVP Financial Planning & Analysis ... Ms. Aintzane CELAYA
04 Administrative Manager to President ... Ms. Alicia BLATCHFORD
86 EVP External Affairs/Strategic Init ... Mr. Rodolfo J. FERNANDEZ
116 VP/Chief Audit/Compliance Officer ... Ms. Blanca MALAGON
117 Executive Director Risk Management ... Mr. Craig MCALLISTER
09 Assc Provost Institutional Research ... Dr. Dave BECHER
106 Exec Director Online Education ... Dr. Rebecca MACMILLAN FOX
108 Assoc Prov University Accreditation ... Ms. Patty MURPHY
30 Assoc VP Development & Alum Rels ... Ms. Beth BROWN
28 Title IX Coord/AVP Equity & Inclus ... Ms. Beverly PRUITT
29 Asst VP Alumni Relations ... Ms. Heather KOPEC
122 Asst Dn Stdnts/Advisor Greek Life ... Ms. Dayle W. WILSON
105 Exec Director Univ Online Comm ... Mr. Robert YUNK
25 Assoc VP Research Administration ... Ms. Laura KOZMA
112 Assoc VP Development ... Ms. Claudia GRILLO
118 Assoc VP Total Rewards ... Ms. Cristina ELGARRESTA

University of St. Augustine for Health Sciences (A)

One University Boulevard, St. Augustine FL 32086
Telephone: (904) 826-0084 Identification: 770939
Accreditation: &WC, OT, PTA

† Branch campus of University of St. Augustine for Health Sciences, San Marcos, CA.

University of Tampa (B)

401 W Kennedy Boulevard, Tampa FL 33606-1490
County: Hillsborough FICE Identification: 001538
Unit ID: 137847
Telephone: (813) 253-3333 Carnegie Class: Masters/L
FAX Number: (813) 258-7207 Calendar System: Other
URL: www.ut.edu
Established: 1931 Annual Undergrad Tuition & Fees: $30,884
Enrollment: 9,605 Coed
Affiliation or Control: Independent Non-Profit IRS Status: 501(c)3
Highest Offering: Doctorate
Accreditation: SC, #ARCPA, ART, CAATE, CAEP, COSMA, FEPAC, MUS, NURSE

01 President ... Dr. Ronald L. VAUGHN
05 Provost/Vice Pres Academic Affairs ... Dr. David STERN
10 Vice Pres Administration/Finance ... Mr. Kevin LAFFERTY
07 Vice Pres for Strategic Enrollment ... Mr. W. Michael HENDRICKS
30 Vice Pres Development/Univ Rels ... Mr. L. Keith TODD
11 Vice Pres Operations ... Dr. Monnie WERTZ
13 VP Information Technology/Security ... Ms. Tammy L. LOPER
32 Vice Pres Student Affairs ... Ms. Stephanie R. KREBS
20 Assoc Provost & Dean of Acad Svcs ... Mr. C. Jay PENDLETON
06 Registrar ... Ms. Michelle PELAEZ
08 Director of the Library ... Vacant
29 Director of Alumni Relations ... Vacant
37 Director of Financial Aid ... Ms. Jacqueline GALZERANO
26 Director of Public Information ... Mr. Eric D. CARDENAS
18 Director of Facilities Management ... Mr. J. Scot PHILLIPS
15 Vice Pres Human Resources ... Ms. Donna B. POPOVICH
84 AVP/Int Mgr Enrollment Management ... Mr. Brent W. BENNER
41 Athletic Director ... Mr. Larry J. MARFISE
40 Manager University Bookstore ... Ms. Courtenay RHODES
39 Director of Residence Life ... Ms. Sarah HART
22 Affirmative Action Officer ... Ms. Donna B. POPOVICH
19 Director of Campus Safety ... Mr. Kevin A. HOWELL
23 Director of Medical Services ... Ms. Sharon CHARLES
96 Director of Business Services ... Ms. Cara SPOTO
09 Director of Institutional Research ... Mr. Drew KELLY
92 Director of Honors Program ... Dr. Gary S. LUTER
50 Dean College of Business ... Dr. F. Frank GHANNADIAN
83 Dean Social Science/Math/Education ... Dr. Jack M. GELLER
81 Dean College Natural/Health Sci ... Dr. Paul GREENWOOD
57 Dean College of Arts/Letters ... Dr. David GUDELUNAS
51 Assoc Dean Graduate/Continuing Stds ... Dr. Donald D. MORRILL
89 Director of First Year Experience ... Ms. Edesa SCARBOROUGH
36 AVP Career Development & Engagement ... Mr. Timothy HARDING
104 Assoc Dean International Programs ... Dr. Anne Liese BUSCH
04 Exec Asst to Pres/Board Liaison ... Ms. Teresa PEREZ
28 Chief Diversity Officer ... Dr. Thomas WITHERSPOON

Valencia College (C)

PO Box 3028, Orlando FL 32802-3028
County: Orange FICE Identification: 006750
Unit ID: 138187
Telephone: (407) 299-5000 Carnegie Class: Bac/Assoc-Assoc Dom
FAX Number: (407) 426-8970 Calendar System: Semester
URL: www.valenciacollege.edu
Established: 1967 Annual Undergrad Tuition & Fees (In-State): $2,474
Enrollment: 45,949 Coed
Affiliation or Control: State IRS Status: 501(c)3
Highest Offering: Baccalaureate
Accreditation: SC, ADNUR, CAHIIM, CEA, COARC, CVT, DH, DMS, EMT, NURSE, RAD

01 President ... Dr. Kathleen A. PLINSKE
05 Provost & VP Academic Affairs ... Dr. Isis ARTZE VEGA
100 VP Inst Planning/Devel & COS ... Dr. Amy N. BOSLEY
107 VP Global/Prof & Cont Education ... Mr. Joe N. BATTISTA
10 VP Business Operations & CFO ... Mr. Loren J. BENDER
26 VP Public Affairs & Advancement ... Mr. Jay R. GALBRAITH, II
88 VP Tech/Research & Analytics ... Dr. Brandon MCKELVEY
15 VP Org Dev & Human Resources ... Ms. Carla L. MCKNIGHT
43 VP Policy & General Counsel ... Dr. Bill J. MULLOWNEY
32 VP Student Affairs ... Dr. Lesley J. FREDERICK
13 Chief Information Officer ... Vacant
12 Provost WEC ... Dr. Danny M. HOEY, JR.
12 Provost OSC & PNC ... Dr. Lancelot A. GOODEN
12 Interim Campus President OSC ... Dr. Melissa D. PEDONE
12 Provost DTC & WPC ... Dr. Wendy L. GIVOGLU
12 Provost EAC & LNC ... Dr. Sobia KHAN
12 Interim Campus President LNC/PNC ... Mr. Stanton G. REED
20 Dean Academic Affairs ... Ms. Michelle R. FOSTER
20 Dean Academic Affairs ... Dr. Molly MCINTIRE
20 Asst VP Academic Affairs ... Dr. Wendi M. DEW
88 Asst VP Partnerships Educ Equity ... Ms. Eda DAVIS-LOWE
103 Asst VP Career & Workforce Educ ... Dr. Nasser HEDAYAT
21 Asst VP Financial Services ... Ms. Jackie D. LASCH
51 Asst VP Global & Continuing Educ ... Ms. Lisa G. ELI
27 Asst VP Marketing ... Ms. Traci A. BJELLA
11 Asst VP Operations ... Mr. Paul ROONEY
28 Asst VP Equity & Access ... Mr. Ryan D. KANE
51 Asst VP Prof & Continuing Edu ... Dr. Carolyn R. MCMORRAN
25 Asst VP Resource Development ... Ms. Kristeen R. GAMMON
124 Asst VP Recruit/Enroll/Retention ... Dr. Amy E. PARKER
18 Asst VP Facilities & Maint Opers ... Mr. Shaun D. ANDREWS
37 Asst VP Fin Aid & Vet Affairs ... Mr. Daniel T. BARKOWITZ
88 Asst VP Analytics & Reporting ... Mr. Daryl J. DAVIS
114 Asst VP Budgets & Analysis ... Mr. Oscar J. CRISTANCHO MERCADO
07 Asst VP Admiss/Records & Grad ... Mr. Edwin SANCHEZ VELEZ
84 Associate VP Enrollment Management ... Dr. Sonya F. JOSEPH
88 Faculty Dir TLA ... Dr. Claudine BENTHAM
88 Sr Dir Policy & Legal Svcs ... Ms. Michelle T. SEVER
116 Dir Compliance & Audit ... Ms. Cynthia SANTIAGO-GUZMAN
88 Dir Curriculum & Articulation ... Dr. Cheryl ROBINSON
88 Dir Strategic Learning Initiatives ... Dr. Robyn M. BRIGHTON
09 Dir Institutional Effectiveness ... Mr. Darren A. SMITH
108 Dir Institutional Evaluation ... Vacant
118 Dir Total Rewards ... Mr. Tom E. KELLER
19 Managing Dir Safety/Security ... Mr. Mike D. FAVORIT
96 Managing Dir Procurement ... Ms. Yaremis P. FULLANA
90 Managing Dir Campus Tech Svcs ... Dr. Jamie D. ROST
105 Managing Dir Enterprise App Svcs ... Ms. Maureen E. WILLIAMS
119 Managing Dir Network & Security ... Mr. John E. KNIGHTS
119 Dir Information Security Opers ... Mr. Patrick L. CRISS
120 Dir Ent App Development ... Mr. Bortie TEH
29 Dir Alumni Engagement/Annual Giving ... Ms. Erin C. OHLSEN
113 Dir Student Financial Operations ... Ms. Donna K. MACDONALD
22 Dir Equal Opportunity ... Dr. Trisha L. WHITMIRE
109 Dir Auxiliary Services ... Mr. Jeffrey D. FILKO
109 Dir Auxiliary Services ... Ms. Mona Liza COLON
88 Assoc General Counsel ... Dr. Leslie B. GOLDEN
38 Dean of Counsel/Adv/Hol Stdnt Supp ... Dr. Andel P. FILS AIME
124 Dean Stdnt Engagement/Partnership ... Dr. Edna D. JONES MILLER
35 Dean of Student Services ... Mr. Joe M. SARRUBBO, JR.
35 Dean of Stdnt Enrollment & Records ... Dr. Jill M. SZENTMIKLOSI
20 Executive Dean LNC ... Dr. Mike BOSLEY
12 Executive Dean SPS ... Dr. Jeff W. GOLTZ
20 Executive Dean WPC ... Dr. Terri A. GRAHAM
20 Executive Dean DTC ... Dr. Eugene G. JONES, II
20 Executive Dean PNC ... Dr. Jennifer ROBERTSON
97 Dean Learning Support EAC ... Dr. Leonard C. BASS
97 Dean Learning Support OSC ... Dr. Landon P. SHEPHARD
97 Int Dean Learning Support WEC ... Ms. Jennifer TOMLINSON
66 Int Dean Nursing WEC ... Dr. Ruby ALVAREZ
76 Dean School of Allied Health ... Ms. Marie E. VASQUEZ-BROOKS
81 Dean Math WEC ... Dr. Paul D. BLANKENSHIP
81 Dean Math OSC ... Dr. Nichole A. SEGARRA
81 Dean Math EAC ... Ms. Keri S. SILER
49 Dean Arts & Humanities WEC ... Ms. Ana J. CALDERO FIGUEROA
60 Dean Comm/Languages OSC ... Ms. Jenni L. CAMPBELL
60 Dean Communications WEC ... Dr. Wesley T. JOHNSON
60 Dean Communications EAC ... Ms. Linda R. NEAL
79 Int Dean Human/Foreign Lang EAC ... Mr. Eric WALLMAN
75 Int Dean Career & Technical Pgm ... Dr. Sonia P. CASABLANCA
50 Dean Business/Info Tech/Pub Svc EAC ... Ms. Shara K. TSCHEULIN
50 Int Dean Business WEC ... Dr. Cheri L. CUTTER
54 Dean Engr/Computer Pgm & Tech ... Dr. Paul J. WILDER
83 Dean Social Science EAC ... Dr. Mark G. COLLINS
83 Dean Behav/Soc Science WEC ... Dr. Susan C. DUNN
79 Dean Humanities/Soc Science OSC ... Dr. Scott F. CREAMER
81 Dean Science OSC ... Dr. Anitza M. SAN MIGUEL
49 Dean Science EAC ... Dr. Jennifer L. SNYDER
49 Dean Science WEC ... Dr. Bob F. GESSNER
88 Dean School of Hospitality/Culinary ... Mr. Alex ERDMANN
57 Int Dean Sch of Arts/Entertainment ... Mr. Rob MCCAFFREY
08 Campus Director Library WEC ... Ms. Ruth S. SMITH
44 Chief Philanthropy Officer ... Ms. Angela J. MENDOLARO
102 Foundation President and CEO ... Vacant
04 Senior Executive Assistant ... Ms. Barbara E. HALSTEAD
00 Chair Board of Trustees ... Ms. Daisy LOPEZ-CID

Warner University (D)

13895 Highway 27, Lake Wales FL 33859-2549
County: Polk FICE Identification: 008848
Unit ID: 138275
Telephone: (863) 638-1426 Carnegie Class: Masters/S
FAX Number: (863) 638-1472 Calendar System: Semester
URL: www.warner.edu
Established: 1968 Annual Undergrad Tuition & Fees: $24,200
Enrollment: 978 Coed
Affiliation or Control: Church Of God IRS Status: 501(c)3
Highest Offering: Master's
Accreditation: SC, SW

01 President ... Dr. David A. HOAG
05 VP for Academic Affairs ... Dr. Gentry SUTTON
10 SVP Opers/Administraton/CFO ... Mr. Mike PICHA
111 Vice President for Advancement ... Mrs. Andrea THIES
84 VP for Enrollment Mgmt ... Mrs. Andrea THIES
32 VP of Student Life ... Mrs. Anne TOHME
06 AVP Student Success/Registrar ... Mrs. Sara F. KANE
37 Director Student Financial Aid ... Mrs. Mandy RAMOS
29 Alumni & Annual Fund Coord ... Ms. Abby CRAWFORD
18 Chief Facilities/Physical Plant ... Mr. Mark THOMAS
97 Director of General Studies ... Dr. Daniel JULICH
13 VP for Information Tech/Facilities ... Mr. Mark THOMAS
19 Director Campus Security ... Mrs. Janet CRAIGMILES
88 Director Academic Skills Ctr ... Ms. Morrisia STEWART
106 Assoc Dean Online Education ... Mr. Shawn TAYLOR
04 Executive Asst to President ... Mrs. Jenna BUCHANAN
15 VP for Human Resources ... Mrs. Janet CRAIGMILES
21 Director of Accounting ... Mrs. Mandy RAMOS
07 Director of Admissions ... Mrs. Scarlett JACKSON
41 Athletic Director ... Mrs. Chrissy MOSKOVITS

Webber International University (E)

1201 Scenic Highway N/P.O. Box 96, Babson Park FL 33827-0096
County: Polk FICE Identification: 001540
Unit ID: 138293
Telephone: (863) 638-1431 Carnegie Class: Bac-Diverse
FAX Number: (863) 638-2823 Calendar System: Semester
URL: www.webber.edu
Established: 1927 Annual Undergrad Tuition & Fees: $28,268
Enrollment: 812 Coed
Affiliation or Control: Independent Non-Profit IRS Status: 501(c)3
Highest Offering: Master's
Accreditation: SC, @OTA

01 President/CEO ... Dr. H. Keith WADE
05 Academic Dean/CAO ... Dr. Charles SHIEH
10 Vice President Finance ... Ms. Christina JORDON
09 VP of Inst Effectiveness/Research ... Dr. Nelson MARQUEZ
32 Campus VP of Student Life ... Mr. Jay CULVER
06 Vice Pres of Student Record Svcs ... Vacant
36 Dir Career Service & Cmty Outreach ... Mrs. Devyn MONTALVO
08 Director Library Services ... Ms. Sue DUNNING
41 Athletic Director ... Mr. Darren RICHIE
13 Director Information Technology ... Mr. Davius ROSIUS
18 Director of Campus Svcs/Maintenance ... Mr. Matt YENTES
40 Director of Bookstore ... Mr. Matt SALIBA
07 Director of Admissions ... Ms. Bobbi ANDREWS
20 Director of Academic Planning ... Ms. Lacy EDWARDS
50 Chair of Business Education ... Dr. Jeanette EBERLE
53 Chair of General Education Division ... Dr. Charles WUNKER
04 Executive Asst to President ... Ms. Gerlinde DANCY
19 Director Security/Safety ... Mr. Michael RITTER
29 Dir Annual Fund/Alumni Relations ... Ms. Jeanne LAWRIE
22 Assoc Dean Title IX Compliance ... Dr. Eileen FARCHMIN

West Coast University - Miami (F)

9250 NW 36th Street, Doral FL 33178
Telephone: (786) 501-7070 Identification: 770936
Accreditation: &WC, @CNEA

† Branch campus of West Coast University, North Hollywood, CA.

Westfield Business School (G)

1200 Brickell Avenue, Ste #680, Miami FL 33131
County: Miami-Dade Identification: 667425
Telephone: (305) 456-0289 Carnegie Class: Not Classified
FAX Number: N/A Calendar System: Semester

URL: https://en.westfield.edu
Established: 2012 Annual Graduate Tuition & Fees: N/A
Enrollment: N/A Coed
Affiliation or Control: Proprietary IRS Status: Proprietary
Highest Offering: Master's; No Undergraduates
Accreditation: ACICS

01 President .... Carlos E. MAZO

WMU - Cooley Law School Tampa Bay Campus (A)

9445 Camden Field Parkway, Riverview FL 33578
Telephone: (813) 419-5100 Identification: 770290
Accreditation: &HLC

† Branch campus of Western Michigan University Cooley Law School, Lansing, MI

Woodmont College (B)

16375 NE 18th Avenue Ste 304,
North Miami Beach FL 33162
County: Miami-Dade Identification: 667347
Telephone: (305) 944-0035 Carnegie Class: Not Classified
FAX Number: (305) 944-0335 Calendar System: Semester
URL: www.woodmontcollege.edu
Established: 2011 Annual Undergrad Tuition & Fees: N/A
Enrollment: N/A Coed
Affiliation or Control: Independent Non-Profit IRS Status: 501(c)3
Highest Offering: Baccalaureate
Accreditation: DEAC

01 President .... Rabbi Harold REICHMAN
03 Dean .... Chana PRERO
05 Educational Director .... Rabbi Hillel RUDOLPH
20 Assistant Academic Director .... Rabbi Ari ACKERMAN
11 Director & VP of Operations .... Tzipora KLAVER
07 Director Admissions/Recruitment .... Joelle NADJARI
06 Registrar/Student Services Director .... Elisheva STEINHART

Yeshiva Gedolah Rabbinical College (C)

1140 Alton Road, Miami Beach FL 33139-4708
County: Dade FICE Identification: 032563
Unit ID: 363712
Telephone: (305) 653-8770 Carnegie Class: Spec-4-yr-Faith
FAX Number: (305) 653-6790 Calendar System: Semester
URL: www.YGMiami.com
Established: 1973 Annual Undergrad Tuition & Fees: $8,300
Enrollment: 48 Male
Affiliation or Control: Independent Non-Profit IRS Status: 501(c)3
Highest Offering: Master's
Accreditation: RABN

01 Executive Vice President .... Rabbi Benzion KORF
05 Dean .... Rabbi Abraham KORF
06 Registrar .... Ayelet BORTUNK
07 Director of Admissions .... Rabbi Chaim STERN

GEORGIA

Abraham Baldwin Agricultural College (D)

ABAC 1 - 2802 Moore Highway, Tifton GA 31793-2601
County: Tift FICE Identification: 001541
Unit ID: 138558
Telephone: (229) 391-5001 Carnegie Class: Bac/Assoc-Mixed
FAX Number: (229) 391-5002 Calendar System: Semester
URL: www.abac.edu
Established: 1908 Annual Undergrad Tuition & Fees (In-State): $3,565
Enrollment: 3,990 Coed
Affiliation or Control: State IRS Status: 501(c)3
Highest Offering: Baccalaureate
Accreditation: SC, ADNUR, NUR

01 President .... Dr. Tracy BRUNDAGE
05 Provost and VP for Academic Affairs .... Dr. Jerry BAKER
10 VP for Finance and Operations .... Ms. Deidra A. JACKSON
111 Int VP External Affairs/Advancement .... Mr. Paul WILLIAMS
13 AVP for Info Tech/CTO .... Mr. Allen C. SAYLOR, JR.
12 Exec Dir ABAC at Bainbridge .... Dr. Michael KIRKLAND
08 Director of Library Services .... Mr. David EDENS
32 AVP for Student Affairs .... Ms. Donna WEBB
41 Athletic Director .... Dr. Alan KRAMER
06 Registrar .... Dr. Amy WILLIS
37 Director of Financial Aid .... Ms. Brenda TAYLOR-HICKEY
15 Director of Human Resources .... Mr. Richard SPANCAKE
26 Dir of Marketing/Communications .... Ms. Lindsey CARNEY
108 Director of Assessment .... Vacant
84 Dir Enrollment Mgmt/Admissions .... Ms. Donna WEBB
96 Director of Procurement .... Ms. Teri MATHIS
19 Chief of Police .... Mr. Frank STRICKLAND
04 Admin Associate to President .... Ms. Jordan BEARD
39 Director of Student Housing .... Dr. Chris S. KINSEY
30 Chief Development Officer .... Dr. Deidre MARTIN

† Part of the University System of Georgia.

Agnes Scott College (E)

141 E. College Avenue, Decatur GA 30030-3770
County: DeKalb FICE Identification: 001542
Unit ID: 138600
Telephone: (404) 471-6000 Carnegie Class: Bac-A&S
FAX Number: (404) 471-6067 Calendar System: Semester
URL: www.agnesscott.edu
Established: 1889 Annual Undergrad Tuition & Fees: $44,250
Enrollment: 1,080 Female
Affiliation or Control: Presbyterian Church (U.S.A.) IRS Status: 501(c)3
Highest Offering: Master's
Accreditation: SC

01 President .... Ms. Leocadia (Lee) I. ZAK
05 VP Academic Affairs/Dean of College .... Dr. Christine COZZENS
32 Int VP Student Affs/Dean Students .... Ms. Marti FESSENDEN
10 Int VP Business & Finance .... Mr. Scott RANDAZZA
111 VP for College Advancement .... Dr. Robiaun R. CHARLES
84 VP for Enrollment/Dean of Admission .... Ms. Alexa GAETA
26 VP Communications/Marketing .... Ms. Danita KNIGHT
22 VP for Equity & Inclusion .... Dr. Yves-Rose PORCENA
101 Associate VP & Board Secretary .... Ms. Lea Ann HUDSON
13 Assoc VP Technology .... Ms. LaNeta COUNTS
15 Associate VP for Human Resources .... Ms. Karen GILBERT
06 Registrar .... Ms. Gail N. MEIS
08 Director of Library Services .... Ms. Elizabeth BAGLEY
29 Senior Director Alumnae Relations .... Ms. Mary Frances KERR
18 Director of Facilities .... Mr. Dave MARDER
42 Chaplain .... Rev. Whitney B. LOCKARD
37 Director of Financial Aid .... Mr. Patrick BONONES
09 Director of Institutional Research .... Dr. Corey DUNN
07 Sr Director of Admissions .... Ms. Aimee S. KAHN-FOSS
23 Wellness Center Director .... Dr. Michelle HAMM
19 Director of Public Safety .... Mr. Henry HOPE
36 Director of Career Development .... Ms. Dawn KILLENBERG

Albany State University (F)

504 College Drive, Albany GA 31705-2796
County: Dougherty FICE Identification: 001544
Unit ID: 138716
Telephone: (229) 500-2000 Carnegie Class: Masters/M
FAX Number: N/A Calendar System: Semester
URL: https://www.asurams.edu
Established: 1903 Annual Undergrad Tuition & Fees (In-State): $5,934
Enrollment: 6,509 Coed
Affiliation or Control: State IRS Status: 501(c)3
Highest Offering: Beyond Master's But Less Than Doctorate
Accreditation: SC, ACBSP, ADNUR, CACREP, CAHIIM, COARC, DH, DMS, EMT, FEPAC, HT, MLTAD, NUR, OTA, PTAA, RAD, SPAA, SW

01 President .... Mrs. Marion FEDRICK
100 VP Univ Relations/Chief of Staff .... Dr. Wendy WILSON
05 Provost/VP Academic Affairs .... Dr. Angela PETERS
10 Int VP Admin & Finance .... Mr. Bruce SPRATT
13 Chief Information Offilcer .... Mr. William MOORE
84 VP Enrollment Mgmt/Student Success .... Mrs. Kenyatta JOHNSON
111 VP Institutional Advancement .... Mr. A.L FLEMING
32 VP Student Affairs .... Dr. Terry LINDSAY
108 VP Institutional Effectiveness .... Vacant
43 Chief Legal Affairs Officer .... Mr. Joel WRIGHT
116 Exec Dir Internal Audits .... Ms. Katherine KIKIVARAKIS
41 Director of Athletics .... Mr. Anthony DUCKWORTH
49 Dean College of Arts and Sciences .... Dr. Melanie HATCH
107 Dean Professional Studies .... Dr. Alicia JACKSON
76 Dean Health Professions .... Dr. Sarah BRINSON
19 Chief of Police .... Mr. Gregory ELDER
06 Registrar .... Mr. Frank MALINOWSKI
21 Controller .... Mr. Jeffrey HALL
53 Chair Teacher Education .... Dr. Rhonda PORTER
88 Chair Counseling Ed Leadership .... Dr. Deborah BEMBRY
57 Chair Visual & Performing Arts .... Dr. Marcia HOOD
65 Chair Biological Sciences .... Dr. Olabisi OJO
66 Chair Nursing .... Dr. Cathy WILLIAMS
68 Chair Health & Human Performance .... Dr. Timothy HUGHLEY
82 Chair History/Political Sci .... Dr. Babafemi ELUFIEDE
83 Chair Sociology & Psychology .... Dr. Hema DAVIS
70 Chair Social Work .... Dr. Barbara NOWAK
80 Chair Public Administration .... Dr. Peter NGWAFU
79 Chair English Modern Lang Mass Comm .... Dr. Henry MACK
60 Chair English/Mod Lang/Mass Comm .... Dr. Jeffrey MACK
81 Chair Math & Computer Sciences .... Dr. Robert OWOR
114 Chief Budget Officer .... Mrs. Marion RYANT
113 Bursar .... Ms. Jan ROGERS
18 Dir Facilities Management .... Mr. Oren HOWELL
15 Chief Human Resources Officer .... Ms. Ola TERRELL-JORDAN
91 Director Application Services .... Mr. Sekar PONNAR
120 Director Online/Distance Learning .... Ms. Domonique HINES
92 Director Honors Program .... Dr. Florence LYONS
104 Director International Programs .... Dr. Nneka-Nora OSAKWE
36 Director Career Services .... Ms. Tracy WILLIAMS
38 Director Counseling/Disability Svcs .... Dr. Stephanie HARRIS-JOLLY
23 Director Student Health Services .... Dr. Vicki PHILLIPS
07 Interim Director of Admissions .... Ms. Michele APPLING
37 Interim Director of Financial Aid .... Mr. John BODIFORD
08 Director Library Services .... Dr. LaVerne MCLAUGHLIN
30 Director of Development .... Mr. Andrew FLOYD
40 Director Bookstore .... Ms. Tara JOHNSON
44 Director of Annual Giving .... Mrs. Ossie POLITE-WILLIAMS
119 Chief Information Security Officer .... Mr. Travis BARRON
96 Director of Purchasing .... Mrs. Joy CAUSEY

121 Dir Academic Advising/Retention .... Ms. Carolyn BROWN
39 Director Housing & Residence Life .... Ms. Keigan EVANS
123 Director Graduate Programs .... Dr. Charles OCHIE
109 Interim Dir Auxiliary Svcs .... Mrs. Martha SNOW
122 Greek Life & Diversity Coord .... Mr. Anthony MORMAN

† Part of the University System of Georgia.

Albany Technical College (G)

1704 S Slappey Boulevard, Albany GA 31701-3587
County: Dougherty FICE Identification: 005601
Unit ID: 138682
Telephone: (229) 430-3500 Carnegie Class: Assoc/HVT-Mix Trad/Non
FAX Number: (229) 430-3594 Calendar System: Semester
URL: www.albanytech.edu
Established: 1961 Annual Undergrad Tuition & Fees (In-State): $2,996
Enrollment: 3,022 Coed
Affiliation or Control: State IRS Status: 501(c)3
Highest Offering: Associate Degree
Accreditation: SC, ADNUR, DA, EMT, MAC, PNUR, RAD, SURGT

01 Interim President .... Dr. Emmett L. GRISWOLD
100 Special Assistant to the President .... Mrs. Lorraine ALEXANDER
05 Vice Pres Academic Affairs .... Dr. Emmett GRISWOLD
10 Vice Pres Administrative Services .... Mrs. Kathy SKATES
26 Dir Public Relations/Marketing .... Mr. Bobby ELLIS
32 VP Student Affairs/Enrollment Mgmt .... Mrs. Barbara BROWN
36 Assoc Vice Pres of Career Svcs .... Mrs. Judy JIMMERSON
46 Vice President Economic Development .... Mr. Matt TRICE
55 Vice Pres of Adult Education .... Mrs. Linda COSTON
15 Executive Director Human Resources .... Mrs. Lola EDWARDS
09 Vice Pres Inst Effectiveness .... Ms. Angela DAVIS
51 Dean of Cont Educ & Off-Campus Pgm .... Mrs. Tracy WALLACE
55 Dean of Evening Administration .... Mr. Don LAYE
37 Director of Financial Aid .... Mrs. Helen CATT
20 Dean of Academic Affairs .... Ms. Lisa STEPHENS
20 Dean of Academic Affairs .... Ms. Tomekia COOPER
20 Dean of Academic Affairs .... Mrs. Lisa HARRELL
88 Assoc Dean Early Childhood .... Mrs. Angela ROBINSON
56 Academic Dean Instructional Tech .... Mrs. Troycia WEBB
18 Director of Facilities .... Mr. Mike ALLIGOOD
84 Director of Enrollment .... Mr. Kenneth WILLIAMS
21 Director of Accounting Services .... Ms. Janet HAYES
06 Registrar .... Ms. Kennosha HAWKINS
35 Director Student Activities .... Dr. Mary RICHARDSON
13 Director of Computer/Info Systems .... Mr. Dennis SLEDGE
04 Executive Asst to the President .... Mrs. Natasha PRICE
08 Chief Library Officer .... Mr. Roy CALHOUN
19 Director Security/Safety .... Mr. Kenneth SINGLETON

American InterContinental University - Atlanta (H)

6600 Peachtree-Dunwoody Rd NE, 500, Atlanta GA 30328
Telephone: (404) 965-6500 Identification: 666723
Accreditation: &HLC, ACBSP

† Regional accreditation is carried under the parent institution in Schaumburg, IL.

Andrew College (I)

501 College Street, Cuthbert GA 39840-5550
County: Randolph FICE Identification: 001545
Unit ID: 138761
Telephone: (229) 732-2171 Carnegie Class: Bac/Assoc-Assoc Dom
FAX Number: (229) 732-2176 Calendar System: Semester
URL: www.andrewcollege.edu
Established: 1854 Annual Undergrad Tuition & Fees: $19,172
Enrollment: 301 Coed
Affiliation or Control: United Methodist IRS Status: 501(c)3
Highest Offering: Baccalaureate
Accreditation: SC, CNEA, #COARC

01 President .... Dr. Linda R. BUCHANAN
05 Dean of Academic Affairs .... Mrs. Karan B. PITTMAN
10 Vice President for Finance .... Mrs. Julie CADLE
111 Vice President for Advancement .... Mr. Spencer SEALY
84 Vice President for Enrollment .... Mr. Andy GEETER
21 Controller .... Ms. Beth STRICKLAND
32 Dean of Student Affairs .... Mr. James MCCOY
41 Athletic Director .... Mr. Blake WILLIAMS
42 Chaplain .... Ms. Ivelisse QUINONES
08 Director of Library Services .... Ms. Mckenzie RAGAN
40 Director of Bookstore .... Ms. McKenzie RAGAN
26 Dir of Communications & Marketing .... Ms. Heather BRADLEY
06 Registrar .... Ms. Carol DOLBERRY
18 Director of Maintenance .... Mr. Charles CORSON
19 Campus Security/Synergy .... Mr. Leon PARAMORE
39 Director of Residence Life .... Vacant
105 Web Services .... Mr. Brice HERRIN
22 ADA Director .... Mrs. Carol DOLBERRY
09 Director of Student Success Ctr/IR .... Ms. Julia WILLIAMS
37 Director of Financial Aid .... Ms. Daphne HARDEN
15 Director of Human Resources .... Mrs. Jennifer MITCHELL

The Art Institute of Atlanta (J)

6600 Peachtree Dunwoody Road, Atlanta GA 30328-1635
County: Fulton FICE Identification: 009270
Unit ID: 138813
Telephone: (770) 394-8300 Carnegie Class: Bac-Diverse
FAX Number: (770) 394-0008 Calendar System: Quarter

URL: www.artinstitutes.edu/atlanta/
Established: 1949 Annual Undergrad Tuition & Fees: $19,354
Enrollment: 814 Coed
Affiliation or Control: Independent Non-Profit IRS Status: 501(c)3
Highest Offering: Baccalaureate
Accreditation: SC, ACFEI, CIDA

01 Campus President .... Dr. David N. PUGH
05 Interim Dean of Academic Affairs .... Dr. Priya PANDEY
84 Director of Enrollment .... Ms. Quinisha STORY
37 Director of Student Financial Svcs ... Ms. Angela DAVIS-HAYNES
09 Dir of Inst Effectiveness/ Research .... Dr. Christopher S. BJORNSTAD
06 Registrar .... Mr. Willis PONDER
36 Director of Career Services .... Ms. Vicky BOLLING
15 Human Resources Manager .... Mr. Daniel KLAAS

Ashworth College (A)

5051 Peachtree Corner Circle, Ste 2, Norcross GA 30092
County: Gwinnett Identification: 666106
Telephone: (770) 729-8400 Carnegie Class: Not Classified
FAX Number: (770) 729-9296 Calendar System: Semester
URL: www.ashworthcollege.edu
Established: 2000 Annual Undergrad Tuition & Fees: N/A
Enrollment: N/A Coed
Affiliation or Control: Proprietary IRS Status: Proprietary
Highest Offering: Master's
Accreditation: DEAC

01 President .... Ms. Misty FROST
05 Chief Learning Officer .... Dr. Andy SHEAN
06 Registrar .... Mr. Eric RYALL

Athens College of Ministry (B)

PO Box 7593, Athens GA 30604
County: Clarke Identification: 667306
Telephone: (706) 769-1472 Carnegie Class: Not Classified
FAX Number: (706) 769-1479 Calendar System: Semester
URL: www.acmin.org
Established: 2012 Annual Undergrad Tuition & Fees: N/A
Enrollment: N/A Coed
Affiliation or Control: Interdenominational IRS Status: 501(c)3
Highest Offering: Master's
Accreditation: TRACS

01 President .... Dr. Marcia WILBUR
05 Chief Academic Officer .... Dr. Jesse COYNE
32 Director of Student Affairs .... Mr. Alex FIELDS
58 Graduate Program Chair .... Dr. Todd GADDIS
10 CFO/Undergrad Program Chair .... Mr. Kurt GENTEMAN

Athens Technical College (C)

800 US Highway 29 N, Athens GA 30601-1500
County: Clarke FICE Identification: 005600
Unit ID: 246813
Telephone: (706) 355-5000 Carnegie Class: Assoc/HVT-Mix Trad/Non
FAX Number: (706) 369-5753 Calendar System: Semester
URL: www.athenstech.edu
Established: 1958 Annual Undergrad Tuition & Fees (In-State): $3,062
Enrollment: 4,294 Coed
Affiliation or Control: State IRS Status: 501(c)3
Highest Offering: Associate Degree
Accreditation: SC, ACBSP, ADNUR, CAHIIM, DA, DH, EMT, PTAA, RAD, SURGT

01 President .... Dr. Andrea D. DANIEL
05 Vice President Academic Affairs/IE .... Dr. Kristen DOUGLAS
32 Vice President Student Affairs .... Mr. Lenzy REID, III
10 Vice Pres Administrative Services .... Ms. Kathryn S. THOMAS
45 Vice President Economic Development .... Mr. Al MCCALL
106 Dean General Educ & Online Learning .. Ms. Shawana STANFORD
72 Dean TEM/Business & Educ .... Ms. Christine WOLFE
76 Dean Life Sciences/Public Safety .... Mr. Stuart FREW
88 Exec Director Economic Development .... Mr. Andrew PALMER
55 Exec Dir Adult Educ & Walton Campus .... Ms. Fabersha FLYNT
108 Exec Dir Inst Effectiveness .... Dr. Laurie MCDOWELL
37 Exec Dir Fin Aid/Student Accounts .... Mr. Octavius DAVIS
18 Executive Director Facilities .... Mr. Jim WALTER
26 Executive Director PR/Foundation .... Mr. Josh PAINE
19 Chief of Police .... Mr. John GAISSERT
06 Director Registration & Records .... Mr. Gabriel LINDO-ARDILA
07 Director Admissions .... Ms. Lauren WILLIAMS
08 Director Library Services .... Ms. Carol STANLEY
35 Director Student Activities .... Vacant
121 Director Student Support .... Ms. Jessica FELTS
15 Director Human Resources .... Ms. Sherri HEATH
111 Director Institutional Advancement .... Ms. Jen WELBORN
13 Director Information Technology .... Mr. David FLOYD
21 Director of Accounting .... Mr. Ryan STANLEY

Atlanta Institute of Music and Media (D)

2875 Breckenridge Blvd, #700, Duluth GA 30096
County: Gwinnett FICE Identification: 031045
Unit ID: 419244
Telephone: (770) 242-7716 Carnegie Class: Assoc/HT-High Trad
FAX Number: N/A Calendar System: Quarter
URL: www.aimm.edu
Established: 1985 Annual Undergrad Tuition & Fees: N/A
Enrollment: N/A Coed
Affiliation or Control: Proprietary IRS Status: Proprietary
Highest Offering: Associate Degree
Accreditation: COE

01 President .... Nite DRISCOLL

Atlanta Metropolitan State College (E)

1630 Metropolitan Parkway, SW, Atlanta GA 30310-4498
County: Fulton FICE Identification: 012165
Unit ID: 138901
Telephone: (404) 756-4000 Carnegie Class: Bac/Assoc-Mixed
FAX Number: (404) 756-4460 Calendar System: Semester
URL: www.atlm.edu
Established: 1974 Annual Undergrad Tuition & Fees (In-State): $3,505
Enrollment: 1,704 Coed
Affiliation or Control: State IRS Status: 501(c)3
Highest Offering: Baccalaureate
Accreditation: SC, ACBSP

01 President .... Dr. Georj LEWIS
05 Provost/VP Student Success .... Dr. James MCGEE
10 Int Vice President Fiscal Affairs .... Mr. Nick HENRY
32 Exec Dir Student Svcs/Admissions .... Dr. J.L WYATT
111 VP Strategic Marketing/Advancement .... Ms. Lauretta HANNON
21 Director of Business Services .... Ms. Dakiesha PICKETT
50 Dean Div Business/Information Tech .... Dr. Vincent MANGUM
79 Int Dean Div Humanities/Fine Arts .... Ms. Lisa MALLORY
81 Dean Div of Sci/Math/Health Profess .... Dr. Bryan MITCHELL
83 Int Dean Div of Social Sciences .... Mr. Harry AKOH
06 Registrar/Dir Enrollment Svcs .... Mr. Edward ROSSER
15 Chief Human Resources Officer .... Mrs. Mitzi WILLIAMS
08 Director of the Library .... Mr. Robert QUARLES
35 Dir of Student Life and Leadership .... Ms. Iris SHANKLIN
37 Int Director of Financial Aid .... Ms. Carol JONES
38 Dir of Counseling/Disability Svcs .... Dr. Dorothy WILLIAMS
13 Chief Information/Tech Officer .... Mr. Antonio TRAVIS
108 VP Institutional Effectiveness .... Dr. Mark CUNNINGHAM
19 Chief of Police .... Chief Willey GAMMON, JR.
35 Dir of Student Outreach & Access .... Mr. Stephen WOODALL
18 Dir Plant Operations/Facilities .... Mr. Keith WILLIAMS
40 Bookstore Manager .... Ms. Natasha LAVINE
26 Director of Communications .... Ms. Sonja ROBERTS
41 Athletic Director .... Vacant

† Part of the University System of Georgia.

Atlanta Technical College (F)

1560 Metropolitan Parkway, SW, Atlanta GA 30310-4446
County: Fulton FICE Identification: 008543
Unit ID: 138840
Telephone: (404) 225-4400 Carnegie Class: Assoc/HVT-Mix Trad/Non
FAX Number: N/A Calendar System: Semester
URL: www.atlantatech.edu
Established: 1967 Annual Undergrad Tuition & Fees (In-State): $3,084
Enrollment: 3,030 Coed
Affiliation or Control: State IRS Status: 501(c)3
Highest Offering: Associate Degree
Accreditation: SC, ACFEI, ADNUR, CAHIIM, DA, DH, EMT, MAC, PTAA, RAD

01 President .... Dr. Victoria SEALS
05 Exec VP Academic & Student Affairs .... Ms. Caroline ANGELO
11 Vice Pres Administrative Services .... Ms. Melanie SEWELL
30 Vice President Economic Development .... Ms. Yulonda DARDEN-BEAUFORD
04 Assistant to the President .... Dr. Joni WILLIAMS
26 VP Communications & Marketing .... Ms. Dorna WERDELIN
37 Director of Financial Aid .... Ms. Amanda ABERNATHY
84 Dean Enrollment Services .... Ms. Niya EADY
88 Dean Industrial and Transportation .... Dr. Ian TOPPIN
51 Director of Continuing Education .... Mr. Curtis HALTON
36 Director Career Placement .... Mr. Mario WHITE
50 Dean Business and Public Services .... Mr. Robert LEACH
69 Dean Health and Public Safety .... Dr. Katrina WALKER
06 Registrar .... Mr. Kenya DANIEL
15 Director Human Resources .... Ms. Georgina DUMAY
18 VP Operations and IT .... Ms. Gail EDWARDS
09 Dean of Institutional Research .... Mr. Britt PITRE
49 Dean Arts and Sciences .... Vacant
08 Director of Library Services .... Ms. Tosha BUSSEY
32 Dean of Students .... Ms. Mattie GOSS
13 Director of Information Technology .... Mr. Jeffrey SMITH
25 Director of Sponsored Programs .... Mr. Lance WISE
96 Procurement Officer .... Ms. Sylvell MANSFIELD
102 VP Advancement/Dir Foundation .... Ms. Shannon GEORGECINK
19 Chief Security/Safety .... Mr. Charles SPANN
100 Chief of Staff .... Dr. Joni WILLIAMS
29 Director Alumni Affairs .... Ms. Staphea CAMPBELL
35 Director Student Affairs/Life .... Ms. Dessie HALL

Atlanta's John Marshall Law School (G)

245 Peachtree Center Ave Ste 1900, Atlanta GA 30303
County: Fulton FICE Identification: 031733
Unit ID: 138929
Telephone: (678) 916-2600 Carnegie Class: Spec-4-yr-Law
FAX Number: (404) 873-3802 Calendar System: Semester
URL: www.johnmarshall.edu
Established: 1933 Annual Graduate Tuition & Fees: N/A
Enrollment: 299 Coed
Affiliation or Control: Proprietary IRS Status: Proprietary
Highest Offering: First Professional Degree; No Undergraduates
Accreditation: LAW

01 Dean/CEO .... Mr. Jace C. GATEWOOD
32 Assoc Dean of Students .... Ms. Sheryl E. HARRISON-MERCER
10 CFO .... Mr. Duane WRIGHT
06 Registrar .... Ms. Cheryl FEREBEE
26 Asst Dir Marketing & Communications .... Ms. Hilary WALDO
07 Exec Director of Admissions .... Mrs. Rebecca MILTER
37 Director of Financial Aid .... Ms. Michelle COOPER
29 Alumni Director .... Mr. AJ DOCETT
36 Associate Dean of Career Svcs .... Dr. Bridgett ORTEGA
05 Assoc Dean for Academic Program .... Mr. Scott BOONE
20 Assoc Dean of Academic Admin .... Ms. Judith BARGER
35 Asst Dean of Student Svs .... Ms. Hope JAMISON
08 Director of Law Library .... Mr. Michael LYNCH
15 Director of Human Resources .... Ms. Cynthia DAVENPORTE
04 Executive Assistant to the Dean/CEO .... Mrs. Erika S. MURRAY
84 Director of Recruitment .... Mr. Marc REECE
09 Director of Institutional Research .... Ms. Phylicia THOMPSON
13 Chief Information Technology Office .... Mr. Harold BIEBER
30 Chief Development Officer .... Mrs. Wendy AINA
88 Director of Academic Achievement .... Mr. Scot GOINS

Augusta Technical College (H)

3200 Augusta Tech Drive, Augusta GA 30906-3399
County: Richmond FICE Identification: 005599
Unit ID: 138956
Telephone: (706) 771-4000 Carnegie Class: Assoc/HVT-High Trad
FAX Number: (706) 771-4016 Calendar System: Semester
URL: www.augustatech.edu
Established: 1961 Annual Undergrad Tuition & Fees (In-District): $3,232
Enrollment: 3,863 Coed
Affiliation or Control: State/Local IRS Status: 501(c)3
Highest Offering: Associate Degree
Accreditation: SC, ADNUR, CAHIIM, COARC, CVT, DA, DMS, MAC, NAEYC, OTA, PNUR, RAD, #SURGT

01 President .... Dr. Jermaine WHIRL
05 Provost .... Dr. Melissa FRANK-ALSTON
10 Vice Pres Administrative Services .... Ms. Sherrick JOHNSON
32 Vice Pres Student Affairs .... Dr. Nichole SPENCER
88 Vice President Economic Development .... Dr. Rebecca STOUT
108 Dir Institutional Advancement .... Mrs. Beverly PELTIER
13 Dir Information Technology .... Mr. Pete WILKINSON
37 Director Financial Aid .... Ms. Cicely HARPE
84 Director Enrollment Services .... Ms. Christine BALL
06 Registrar .... Ms. Melissa BURCH
21 Director Accounting .... Ms. Sherrick L. JOHNSON
26 Dir Cmty Engagements/Public Rels .... Ms. Kimberly HOLDEN
15 Director Human Resources .... Ms. Shannon PATTERSON
36 Director Career Services .... Ms. Donna WENDT
08 Head Librarian .... Ms. Katrina COOKS
18 Facilities Director .... Mr. Chris GAY
19 Director Security/Safety .... Mr. Mike ANCHOR
04 Administrative Asst to President .... Vacant
12 Coordinator Waynesboro Campus .... Mr. Greg COURSEY
12 Coordinator Thomson Campus .... Ms. Jeanette LOWE
88 High School Coordinator .... Mrs. Jan BLACKBURN
20 Dean Academic Affairs .... Mrs. Julie LANGHAM
76 Dean School of Health Sciences .... Dr. Kristie SEARCY
50 Dean School of Business .... Ms. Elizabeth A. JULIAN
49 Dean School of Arts & Sciences .... Mr. John RICHARDSON
54 Dn Aviation/Indust/Engineering Tech .... Mr. Quentin COOKS
106 Dean of Info Tech/Dist Educ/Lib .... Mrs. Tammy O'BRIEN
107 Dean Public/Professional Services .... Dr. Kellie MCELROY HOOPER
88 Dean Cyber Media & Design .... Mrs. Tammy O'BRIEN

Augusta University (I)

1120 Fifteenth Street, Augusta GA 30912-0004
County: Richmond FICE Identification: 001579
Unit ID: 482149
Telephone: (706) 721-0211 Carnegie Class: DU-Higher
FAX Number: N/A Calendar System: Semester
URL: www.augusta.edu
Established: 1828 Annual Undergrad Tuition & Fees (In-State): $9,022
Enrollment: 8,920 Coed
Affiliation or Control: State IRS Status: 501(c)3
Highest Offering: Doctorate
Accreditation: SC, ANEST, ARCPA, ART, CACREP, CAHIIM, CAMPEP, COARC, DENT, DH, DIETI, EMT, IPSY, MED, MIL, MLS, MPCAC, MUS, NMT, NURSE, OT, PH, PTA, RTT, SPAA, SW

01 President .... Dr. Brooks A. KEEL
05 Exec VP for Acad Affairs/Provost .... Dr. Neil J. MACKINNON
10 EVP Finance/CBO .... Ms. Yvonne TURNER
11 EVP Operations .... Ms. Karla LEEPER
31 EVP Ext Relations/Chief of Staff .... Mr. Russell KEEN
43 General Counsel/VP Legal Affairs .... Mr. Chris MELCHER
17 EVP Medical Affairs/Dean Medicine .... Dr. David HESS
86 EVP Strategic Partnerships/Econ Dev .... Mr. W. Michael SHAFFER
46 Senior Vice President for Research .... Dr. Michael DIAMOND
30 Interim VP of Development .... Ms. Eileen BRANDON
15 Enterprise VP Human Resources .... Ms. Rebecca CARROLL
20 Assoc Provost Faculty Affairs .... Dr. Kathy BROWDER
84 VP Enrollment/Student Affairs .... Dr. Susan B. DAVIES
09 VP Institutional Effectiveness .... Ms. Mickey WILLIFORD
109 AVP Campus Services/Chief Aux Ofcr .... Mr. Dale HARTENBURG
18 VP Facilities Service .... Mr. Ronald BOOTH
26 VP Communications & Marketing .... Mr. Mark LANE
20 Vice Prov Instruction/Innovation .... Dr. Zach KELEHEAR

21 Vice Pres for Finance .... Ms. Corrina WARNER
102 VP University Foundations .... Mr. Stephen R. LAMB
88 VP & CMO for Health System .... Dr. Phillip L. COULE
106 Dean of AU Online/Assoc Provost .... Dr. Marc AUSTIN
58 Dean of The Graduate School .... Dr. Jennifer SULLIVAN
76 Dean Col of Allied Health Sciences .... Dr. Lester PRETLOW
52 Dean Dental College of GA .... Dr. Carol LEFEBVRE
66 Dean College of Nursing .... Dr. Tanya SUDIA
77 Dean Sch of Computer/Cyber Science .... Dr. Alex SCHWARZMANN
50 Dean Hull College of Business .... Dr. Richard M. FRANZA
49 Dean College Arts/Hum/Soc Sci .... Dr. Kim DAVIES
53 Dean College of Education .... Dr. Judi WILSON
81 Dean College of Science & Math .... Dr. John SUTHERLAND
08 Dean of University Libraries .... Mr. Bradley WARREN
116 VP Audit/Compl/Ethics/Risk Mgmt .... Mr. Clay SPROUSE
28 Interim Chief Diversity Officer .... Dr. Garrett GREEN
13 VP Information Technology/CIO .... Dr. Michael CASDORPH
88 Director Georgia Cancer Center .... Dr. Jorge CORTES
06 Registrar .... Ms. Heather B. METRESS
113 Bursar .... Ms. Beth WELSH
41 Director of Athletics .... Vacant
19 Assistant VP Public Safety & Police .... Chief James LYON
96 Director Supply Management .... Mr. Greg WOODLIEF
88 Asst Chief Aux Services Officer .... Mr. Karl MUNSCHY
32 Asst VP and Dean of Students .... Dr. Scott WALLACE
37 Director of Financial Aid .... Ms. Debra TURNER
07 Director of Admissions .... Ms. Jacqueline DUCA
04 Exec Admin Asst to President .... Vacant
104 Director Study Abroad .... Ms. Katherine GREGO
22 Affirmative Action/EEO Officer .... Mr. Steven GOLDBERG
29 Director Alumni Engagement .... Ms. Kim KOSS
36 Director Career Services .... Ms. Julie GOLEY
38 Director Student Counseling .... Ms. Elena PETROVA
39 Director Student Housing .... Dr. Heather SCHNELLER
105 Director Web and Digital Services .... Mr. Davin MILLER

† Part of the University System of Georgia.

Berry College (A)

2277 Martha Berry Highway, NW, Mount Berry GA 30149
County: Floyd FICE Identification: 001554
Unit ID: 139144
Telephone: (706) 232-5374 Carnegie Class: Masters/S
FAX Number: (706) 236-2238 Calendar System: Semester
URL: www.berry.edu
Established: 1902 Annual Undergrad Tuition & Fees: $37,946
Enrollment: 2,125 Coed
Affiliation or Control: Independent Non-Profit IRS Status: 501(c)3
Highest Offering: Beyond Master's But Less Than Doctorate
Accreditation: SC, MUS, NURSE

01 President .... Dr. Stephen R. BRIGGS
05 Provost .... Dr. Mary K. BOYD
10 Vice President Finance .... Mr. Brian I. ERB
32 VP Student Affairs/Dean of Students .... Ms. Lindsey TAYLOR
111 Vice Pres Institutional Advancement .... Ms. Cynthia COURT
84 VP of Enrollment Management .... Dr. Andrew BRESSETTE
26 VP Marketing & Communications .... Ms. Nancy REWIS
100 Chief of Staff .... Ms. Debbie HEIDA
42 Chaplain .... Rev. Jonathan HUGGINS
19 Asst VP Campus Police/Emergency Mgt .... Mr. Gary WILL
50 Dean Campbell School of Business .... Dr. Joyce HEAMES
53 Interim Dean Charter School of Educ .... Dr. Alan HUGHES
79 Dean School Humanities/Arts/Soc Sci .. Dr. Gabriel BARRENECHE
66 Director of Nursing .... Dr. Carolyn REILLY
81 Dean School of Math/Nat Sci .... Dr. Alice SUROVIEC
88 Dean of Personal & Professional Dev .... Dr. Marc HUNSAKER
20 Associate Provost .... Dr. David SLADE
39 Assoc Dean Students/Residence Life .... Mrs. Lindsay NORMAN
07 Dir of Admission/Enroll Management .... Mr. Glenn GETCHELL
30 Asst VP Campaign/Leadership Giving ...... Mr. Scott BREITHAUPT
08 Director of the Library .... Ms. Sherre L. HARRINGTON
29 Director of Alumni Affairs .... Ms. Jennifer SCHAKNOWSKI
13 Chief Information Officer .... Ms. Penny EVANS-PLANTS
38 Director of Counseling Center .... Ms. Rebecca SMITH
37 Director Financial Aid .... Ms. Noemi SARRION-CORTES
09 Dir Institutional Research .... Dr. Bryce DURBIN
46 Dir Research & Sponsored Programs .... Ms. Laura TAYLOR
18 Director Physical Plant .... Mr. Todd BRADFORD
92 Director Honors Program .... Dr. Lauren HELLER
94 Director Women's Studies .... Dr. Susan CONRADSEN
96 Director Purchasing .... Mr. Brad BARRIS
85 Director International Experiences .... Dr. Elizabeth DAVIS
15 Director Human Resources .... Mr. Wayne PHIPPS
43 Director of Legal Services .... Mr. Danny PRICE
06 Registrar .... Dr. Bryce DURBIN
41 Director of Athletics .... Dr. Angel MASON
121 Associate Dean for Student Success .... Ms. Anna SHARPE
44 Director of Annual Giving .... Ms. Anne WILSON
35 Director Student Activities .... Ms. Cecily CROW
23 Director Health & Wellness Center .... Ms. Emma CORDLE
88 Associate Dir Academic Transitions .... Ms. Sarah KAUFMAN

Beulah Heights University (B)

892 Berne Street, SE, PO Box 18145,
Atlanta GA 30316-1873
County: Fulton FICE Identification: 030763
Unit ID: 139153
Telephone: (404) 627-2681 Carnegie Class: Bac-A&S
FAX Number: (404) 627-0702 Calendar System: Semester
URL: www.beulah.edu
Established: 1918 Annual Undergrad Tuition & Fees: $8,492
Enrollment: 565 Coed
Affiliation or Control: Other Protestant IRS Status: 501(c)3
Highest Offering: Doctorate
Accreditation: BI, TRACS

01 President .... Dr. Benson M. KARANJA
04 Administrative Asst to President .... Ms. Meirielly BECCA
11 Chief Operating Officer .... Mr. Peter KARANJA
05 Vice Pres/Dean Academic Affairs .... Dr. Rodney JACKSON
88 Vice Pres Asian Affairs .... Dr. Kyung Soo JHO
32 Vice Pres Student Success .... Dr. Wes WILSON
20 Associate Academic Dean .... Dr. Alicia PLANT
42 Dean of Chapel .... Vacant
06 University Registrar .... Ms. Georgia SKINNER
10 Director of Finance/Comptroller .... Vacant
37 Director of Financial Aid .... Dr. Gina D. GARLINGTON
07 Director of Admissions .... Ms. Divine ZUMBI
73 Chair Religious Studies .... Dr. Brian K. HODGES
08 Director of Library Services .... Mr. Michael JOHNSON
15 Director of Human Resources .... Vacant
39 Dir Resident Life/Student Housing .... Vacant
108 Director Institutional Assessment .... Dr. Chavonne STEWART

Brenau University (C)

500 Washington Street, SE, Gainesville GA 30501-3668
County: Hall FICE Identification: 001556
Unit ID: 139199
Telephone: (770) 534-6299 Carnegie Class: DU-Mod
FAX Number: (770) 534-6114 Calendar System: Semester
URL: www.brenau.edu
Established: 1878 Annual Undergrad Tuition & Fees: $31,720
Enrollment: 2,813 Coed
Affiliation or Control: Independent Non-Profit IRS Status: 501(c)3
Highest Offering: Doctorate
Accreditation: SC, ACBSP, #ARCPA, CIDA, MPCAC, NURSE, OT, PTA

01 President .... Dr. Anne A. SKLEDER
03 Executive VP/CFO .... Dr. David L. BARNETT
05 Provost & VP For Academic Affairs .... Dr. James C. ECK
100 Chief of Staff .... Ms. Jody Y. WALL
10 Vice President Financial Services .... Mr. Toby R. HINTON
84 Vice Pres Enrollment Management .... Vacant
111 Vice Pres External Relations .... Mr. J. Matthew THOMAS
13 Vice Pres Information Technology .... Mr. Chip L. ANDREWS
32 Int VP of Student Services .... Dr. Debra DOBKINS
09 Director of Research & Planning .... Ms. Claudia GEORGE
37 Assoc VP & Dir Financial Aid .... Ms. Pam J. BARRETT
21 Director of Accounting Operations .... Ms. Jennifer KELLEY
15 Asst VP Director of Human Resources ...... Ms. Kelley L. MADDOX
36 Director of Career Services .... Ms. Michelle MCGOWAN
121 Director of Learning Center .... Vacant
41 Vice President of Athletics .... Mr. Mike LOCHSTAMPFOR
53 Dean College of Education .... Dr. Eugene WILLIAMS
76 Dean College of Health Sciences .... Dr. Gale H. STARICH
50 Dean College Business & Comm .... Vacant
79 Dean Coll of Fine Arts & Humanities .... Dr. Andrea C. BIRCH
08 Dean of Library Services .... Ms. Linda KERN
07 Executive Director for Admissions .... Mr. Nathan R. GOSS
06 Registrar & Dir of Student Records .... Ms. Barbara WILSON
29 Exec Director Alumni .... Dr. Ashley CARTER
19 Director Campus Safety & Security .... Ms. Paula DAMPIER
104 Director Study Abroad .... Vacant
122 Assc Dir Stdnt Engage-Greek Life .... Vacant
39 Dir Resident Life/Student Housing .... Ms. Tammy STRINGER

Brewton-Parker College (D)

201 David-Eliza Fountain Circle,
Mount Vernon GA 30445-0197
County: Montgomery FICE Identification: 001557
Unit ID: 139205
Telephone: (912) 583-2241 Carnegie Class: Bac-Diverse
FAX Number: (912) 583-4498 Calendar System: Semester
URL: www.bpc.edu
Established: 1904 Annual Undergrad Tuition & Fees: $18,900
Enrollment: 835 Coed
Affiliation or Control: Baptist IRS Status: 501(c)3
Highest Offering: Baccalaureate
Accreditation: SC

01 President .... Dr. Steven F. ECHOLS
04 Executive Asst to President .... Ms. Laura HAY
43 General Counsel .... Mr. Thomas EVERETT
10 Chief Financial Officer .... Dr. Nicole SHEPARD
05 Provost & Senior Vice President .... Dr. Robert M. BRIAN
32 Director of Student Life .... Mr. Adam STANLEY
88 Assoc Prov External Programs .... Ms. Lynn ADDISON
84 VP of Enrollment Svcs & Athletics .... Mr. Chris DOOLEY
11 Director of Operations .... Mr. Ted TOWNS
15 Director Human Resources .... Ms. Keri NESTER
37 Director of Financial Aid .... Mr. Chris DOOLEY
07 Director of Admissions .... Ms. Michelle HARTER
38 Dir Counseling Services .... Mr. Thadeus HOLLOWAY
06 Registrar .... Dr. Deokhyo KIM
09 Dir of Inst Effectiveness/Research .... Ms. Toni BANKS
26 Dir Public Relations & Marketing .... Mrs. Miranda SIMMONS
111 Director of Advancement .... Mr. Chad RITCHIE
50 Chair Business .... Mr. Karl HAY
53 Chair Education/Behavioral Sci .... Dr. Justin RUSSELL
79 Chair Christian Studies/Humanities .... Dr. Grant LILFORD
81 Chair Math & Natural Sciences .... Dr. Helene PETERS
42 Campus Pastor .... Mr. Steve EDWARDS
13 Chief Information Technology Office .... Mr. Michael STEINMETZ
08 Director of Library Services .... Mr. John SHAFFETT
19 Director Security/Safety .... Mr. Robert BRIDGES
39 Dir Resident Life/Student Housing .... Ms. Cheyenne HINSON

Cambridge Institute of Allied Health & Technology (E)

5669 Peachtree Dunwoody Rd, Ste 100, Atlanta GA 30342
Telephone: (404) 255-4500 Identification: 770938
Accreditation: ABHES, DMS

† Branch campus of Cambridge Institute of Allied Health and Technology, Delray Beach, FL.

Central Georgia Technical College (F)

80 Cohen Walker Drive, Warner Robins GA 31088
County: Houston FICE Identification: 005763
Unit ID: 483045
Telephone: (478) 988-6800 Carnegie Class: Assoc/HVT-Mix Trad/Non
FAX Number: (478) 757-3454 Calendar System: Semester
URL: www.centralgatech.edu
Established: 1966 Annual Undergrad Tuition & Fees (In-State): $3,042
Enrollment: 8,140 Coed
Affiliation or Control: State IRS Status: 501(c)3
Highest Offering: Associate Degree
Accreditation: SC, ADNUR, CVT, DH, EMT, MLTAD, PNUR, POLYT, PTAA, RAD, SURGT

01 President .... Dr. Ivan ALLEN
03 Executive Vice President .... Mr. Jeff SCRUGGS
05 Vice President Academic Affairs .... Dr. Amy HOLLOWAY
10 Vice President Admin/Fin Svcs .... Dr. Michelle SINIARD
32 Vice President Student Affairs .... Dr. Craig JACKSON
31 Vice President Economic Development .... Ms. Andrea GRINER
13 Chief Information Officer .... Dr. Brian SNELGROVE
06 Registrar .... Ms. Sonja JENKINS
111 Asst VP for Advancement .... Ms. Tonya MCCLURE
08 Director Library & Media Services .... Ms. Allison REPZYNSKI
15 Executive Director Human Resources .... Ms. Carol DOMINY
18 Facilities Director .... Mr. Robert DOMINY
51 Director of Continuing Education .... Ms. Ann LEAR
04 Admin Assistant to the President .... Ms. Danielle STEELE
09 Director of Institutional Research .... Ms. Bonnie QUINN
104 Director Study Abroad .... Mr. Rick HUTTO
22 Dir Affirmative Action/Equal Opp .... Ms. Cathy JOHNSON
26 Dir Marketing & Public Relations .... Dr. Janet KELLY
38 Exec Dir for Counseling Svcs .... Ms. Tonja SIMMONS
84 Director Enrollment Management .... Ms. Brandi MITCHEM

Chamberlain University-Atlanta (G)

5775 Peachtree-Dunwoody Rd NE,A100,
Atlanta GA 30342
Telephone: (404) 250-8500 Identification: 770504
Accreditation: &HLC, NURSE

† Branch campus of Chamberlain University-Addison, Addison, IL

Chattahoochee Technical College (H)

980 South Cobb Drive, Marietta GA 30060
County: Cobb FICE Identification: 030290
Unit ID: 140331
Telephone: (770) 528-4545 Carnegie Class: Assoc/HVT-Mix Trad/Non
FAX Number: (770) 975-4126 Calendar System: Quarter
URL: www.chattahoocheetech.edu
Established: 1981 Annual Undergrad Tuition & Fees (In-State): $3,120
Enrollment: 9,432 Coed
Affiliation or Control: State IRS Status: 501(c)3
Highest Offering: Associate Degree
Accreditation: SC, ADNUR, EMT, MAC, MLTAD, OTA, PTAA, RAD, SURGT

01 President .... Dr. Ron NEWCOMB
04 Exec Asst to President .... Ms. Tammy COLLUM
05 Exec Vice President for Instruction .... Dr. Jason TANNER
11 EVP for Opers/Administrative Svcs .... Ms. Heather PENCE
32 Vice President Student Affairs .... Ms. Missy CUSSACK
18 Vice President for Facilities .... Mr. David SIMMONS
15 Vice President Human Resources .... Mr. Ron PRICE
26 Vice President Advancement .... Ms. Jennifer NELSON

Clark Atlanta University (I)

223 James P. Brawley Drive, SW, Atlanta GA 30314-4391
County: Fulton FICE Identification: 001559
Unit ID: 138947
Telephone: (404) 880-8000 Carnegie Class: DU-Higher
FAX Number: N/A Calendar System: Semester
URL: www.cau.edu
Established: 1988 Annual Undergrad Tuition & Fees: $21,695
Enrollment: 3,776 Coed
Affiliation or Control: United Methodist IRS Status: 501(c)3
Highest Offering: Doctorate
Accreditation: SC, CACREP, CAEP, SPAA, SW

01 President .... Dr. George T. FRENCH, JR.
05 Provost & SVP for Academic Affairs .... Dr. G. Dale WESSON
111 Vice President Institutional Advanc .... Dr. Richard LUCAS

10 Exec VP/CFO & Chief Strategy Ofcr .... Dr. Lanze THOMPSON
29 VP for Alumni Rels & Engagement ...Dr. Lorri L. SADDLER-RICE
46 Int Asst VP Rsrch & Sponsored Pgms .... Dr. Shafiq KHAN
20 Assoc Provost .... Dr. Calvin BROWN
13 Assoc VP/Chief Info Ofcr .... Mr. Charles COOPER
21 Assoc VP & Controller .... Vacant
84 VP Enrollment Mgmt & Retention .... Ms. Cherise Y. PETERS
09 VP Planning/Assess/Inst Rsrch .... Dr. Lauren LOPEZ
43 General Counsel ....Ms. Jennifer ERVIN
06 University Registrar .... Ms. Susan GIBSON
26 Dir of News & Media Relations ..... Ms. Jolene BUTTS-FREEMAN
58 Dean of Graduate Education .... Dr. Jamie PLEASANT
15 Sr VP Org Dev/Chief People Officer .... Ms. Debra HOYT
38 Director University Counseling Ctr .... Dr. Vicki JESTER
32 Int Dean Student Svcs Campus Life .... Dr. Cynthia CLEM
37 Director Student Financial Aid .... Mr. James STOTTS
96 Director of Purchasing ....Ms. Donna BYRD
41 Interim Athletics Director ....Mr. Willie SLATER
49 Dean Arts & Sciences ....Dr. Jaideep CHAUDHARY
50 Dean School of Business ....Dr. Silvanus UDOKA
53 Dean School of Education .... Dr. J. Fidel TURNER
70 Dean School of Social Work ....Dr. Jenny L. JONES
19 Chief of Public Safety & AVP ....Chief Debra A. WILLIAMS
23 Director Health Services ....Ms. Caroline B. RICHARDS
25 Director Grants & Contracts/Account .... Ms. Rotesha HARRIS
39 Director of Residence Life ....Mr. Larance CARTER
24 Director Instructional Media ....Mr. Frank EDWARDS
101 Coordinator for Board Relations .... Ms. Natalie BAKER
104 Coordinator Multicultural Affairs ....Ms. Gwen WADE
22 University Compliance Officer ....Ms. Karen SOLINSKI
18 Vice President of Facilities ....Ms. Bonita DUKES
108 Exec Dir Institutional Assessment ....Vacant
04 Sr Executive Asst to President ....Ms. Toni FANNIN
100 Interim Chief of Staff ....Ms. Verlanda TATE
102 Asst VP IAUR ....Ms. Quisa FOSTER
106 Assoc Provost Online Lrng/Cont Educ .... Dr. Mary A. HOOPER

Clayton State University (A)

2000 Clayton State Boulevard, Morrow GA 30260-0285
County: Clayton FICE Identification: 008976
Unit ID: 139311
Telephone: (678) 466-4000 Carnegie Class: Masters/M
FAX Number: (770) 961-3700 Calendar System: Semester
URL: www.clayton.edu
Established: 1969 Annual Undergrad Tuition & Fees (In-State): $5,568
Enrollment: 7,052 Coed
Affiliation or Control: State IRS Status: 501(c)3
Highest Offering: Master's
Accreditation: SC, DH, EXSC, MPCAC, MUS, NURSE

01 Interim President ....Ms. Kerry L. HEYWARD
05 Interim Provost/VP Academic Affairs .... Dr. Jill LANE
10 VP for Operations/Planning/Budget .... Ms. Corlis CUMMINGS
32 Interim VP for Student Affairs ....Mr. Jeff JACOBS
111 Interim VP University Advancement ....Ms. Asia HAUTER
13 Interim VP Info Tech & Svcs/CIO ....Mr. James PETE
20 Associate Provost ....Vacant
35 Assistant Vice Pres Student Affairs .... Dr. Allen WARD
84 Interim VP Enrollment Management .... Dr. Eric TACK
41 Director of Athletics .... Mr. Ryan ERLACHER
88 Executive Director of Spivey Hall .... Mr. Katherine LEHMAN
15 Director Human Resources & Services ....Mr. Rodney BYRD
49 Dean of Arts & Sciences .... Dr. Nasser MOMAYEZI
50 Dean of Business ....Dr. Jacob CHACKO
76 Dean of Health ....Vacant
81 Dean Information/Mathematical Sci .... Dr. Ebrahim KHOSRAVI
08 Dean of Library Services .... Dr. Sonya GAITHER
124 Director Advising & Retention .... Mr. Eric TACK
88 Exec Director Assessment/Online ....Mr. Justin MAYS
51 Exec Director Continuing Education ....Mr. Reginald TURNER
06 University Registrar ....Ms. Rebecca GMEINER
07 Interim Exec Director of Admissions . Ms. Ceimone STRICKLAND
109 Asst VP of Auxiliary Services ....Vacant
26 Asst VP Marketing/Communications ....Ms. Asia HAUTER
18 AVP of Facilities Management .... Mr. Harun BISWAS
19 Director of Public Safety ....Chief J. Michael KEENER
09 Dean of Institutional Research .... Dr. Narem REDDY
14 Assistant Vice President of ITS ....Mr. Charles READ
38 Director of Counseling Services .... Dr. Christine SMITH
37 Director Student Financial Aid .... Mr. Dolapo OGUNMAKIN
96 Procurement Manager ....Ms. Wanda POLITE
29 Director of Alumni Engagement .... Mr. Michael LITTLE
21 AVP Budget & Finance/Comptroller .... Ms. Akwai AGOONS
36 Director of Career Services ....Ms. Bridgette MCDONALD
121 Dir Center for Academic Success .... Ms. Jada MITCHELL
04 Exec Assistant to the President ....Ms. Brenda CARR
104 Director of International Programs .... Mr. Ryan PACKARD
39 Director of Housing/Residence Life ....Ms. Mya RICHARDSON-ECHOLS
44 Dir Annual Giving/Alumni Relations ....Mr. Michael LITTLE
86 Director Government Relations .... Mr. Jim FLOWERS

† Part of the University System of Georgia.

Coastal Pines Technical College (B)

1701 Carswell Avenue, Waycross GA 31503-4016
County: Ware FICE Identification: 005511
Unit ID: 485458
Telephone: (912) 287-6584 Carnegie Class: Assoc/HVT-High Non
FAX Number: N/A Calendar System: Semester
URL: www.coastalpines.edu
Established: 1965 Annual Undergrad Tuition & Fees (In-State): $2,759
Enrollment: 3,606 Coed
Affiliation or Control: State IRS Status: 501(c)3
Highest Offering: Associate Degree
Accreditation: SC, COARC, EMT, MAC, RAD, SURGT

01 President ....Mr. Lonnie ROBERTS
05 EVP & VP for Academic Affairs .... Ms. Amanda MORRIS
10 VP of Administrative Services .... Ms. Melissa LAMB
46 Vice Pres for Economic Development .... Dr. Pete SNELL
32 Vice President for Student Affairs ....Ms. Karla EUBANKS
06 Registrar .... Ms. Janet CARTER
111 Exec Dir of College Advancement .... Ms. Stephanie ROBERTS
18 Facilities Director .... Mr. Chad BOYETT
36 Career Placement & Develop Coord ....Vacant
37 Director Student Financial Aid ....Ms. Tina MANNING
108 VP for Institutional Effectiveness .... Mr. Vince E. JACKSON
07 Exec Dir of Admissions ....Mr. Austin JOHNSON
15 Human Resources Director .... Ms. Katrina HOWARD
04 Administrative Asst to President ....Ms. Natasha KING
08 Director of Library Services ....Vacant
13 Exec Dir of Information Technology ....Mr. Derrell HARRIS
38 Director of Counseling & Spec Svcs ....Ms. Katie RUTLAND
19 Campus Police Chief ....Mr. Ethan JOHNSON

College of Coastal Georgia (C)

One College Drive, Brunswick GA 31520-3632
County: Glynn FICE Identification: 001558
Unit ID: 139250
Telephone: (912) 279-5700 Carnegie Class: Bac-Diverse
FAX Number: (912) 262-3072 Calendar System: Semester
URL: www.ccga.edu
Established: 1961 Annual Undergrad Tuition & Fees (In-State): $3,933
Enrollment: 3,457 Coed
Affiliation or Control: State IRS Status: 501(c)3
Highest Offering: Baccalaureate
Accreditation: SC, ACFEI, ADNUR, NUR, RAD

01 President ....Dr. Michelle JOHNSTON
05 Provost/VPAA ....Dr. Johnny EVANS
111 VP Advancement .... Mr. James BESSETTE
10 Vice President Business Affairs .... Ms. Michelle HAM
32 VP Student Affairs & Enrollment ....Dr. Jason W. UMFRESS
20 Asst VP Academic Affairs ....Dr. German VARGAS
20 Asst VP Academic Affairs .... Dr. Laura LYNCH
21 Fiscal Dir Budgets and Foundation ....Ms. Lorraine MOYER
84 Asst VP Recruitment & Admissions .... Mr. Scott ARGO
13 Chief Information Officer .... Mr. Alan OURS
19 Chief of Police ....Mr. Bryan SIPE
08 Dean of Library Services .... Ms. Debra HOLMES
35 Dean of Students .... Dr. Michael BUTCHER
49 Dean Sch of Arts & Sciences ....Dr. Andrea WALLACE
50 Dean Sch of Business & Public Mgmt .... Dr. William MOUNTS
66 Dean Sch of Nursing & Health Sci ....Dr. Lydia WATKINS
41 Director of Athletics ....Dr. William CARLTON
12 Director of Camden Center ....Mr. Joseph LODMELL
106 Director of E-Learning .... Dr. Lisa MCNEAL
09 Dir Institutional Effectiveness .... Dr. James LYNCH
15 AVP Human Resources & Auxiliary Svc ....Ms. Phyllis BROADWELL
18 Director of Facilities and Plant Op .... Mr. Paul MELCHOR
37 AVP of Financial Aid ....Ms. Terral HARRIS
06 Registrar .... Ms. Lisa LESSEIG
07 Asst Dir of Admissions Operations ....Ms. Shannon RIGGINS
04 Executive Asst President's Office ....Ms. Judy JOHNSTON
96 Procurement Director .... Ms. Deborah MILES
36 Director Career & Academic Advising ....Mr. Brian WEESE
38 Dir of Student Well-Being & Support ....Ms. Tashania GARNER
29 Asst Dir Development/Alumni Engage .... Ms. Casey HANAK
28 Director of Diversity Initiatives ....Mr. J. Quinton STAPLES
39 Assoc Dir Res Life & Housing .... Dr. Kurtis WATKINS

† Part of the University System of Georgia.

Columbia Theological Seminary (D)

P.O. Box 520, 701 S Columbia Drive,
Decatur GA 30031-0520
County: DeKalb FICE Identification: 001560
Unit ID: 139348
Telephone: (404) 378-8821 Carnegie Class: Spec-4-yr-Faith
FAX Number: (404) 377-9696 Calendar System: 4/1/4
URL: www.ctsnet.edu
Established: 1828 Annual Graduate Tuition & Fees: N/A
Enrollment: 201 Coed
Affiliation or Control: Presbyterian Church (U.S.A.) IRS Status: 501(c)3
Highest Offering: Doctorate; No Undergraduates
Accreditation: SC, THEOL

01 President ....Dr. Leanne VAN DYK
05 VP Academic Affairs ....Dr. Love L. SECHREST
10 VP Business and Finance ....Mr. Martin SADLER
32 VP Student Affs/Dean of Students ......Rev. Brandon T. MAXWELL
111 VP Advancement ....Mr. David M. HUFFINE
20 Assoc Dean Academic Administration .... RevDr. Ann Clay ADAMS
13 Assoc Dean Info Svcs/Dir of Library ....Dr. Kelly D. CAMPBELL
107 Assoc Dean Advanced Prof Studies ... Dr. Jeffery L. TRIBBLE, SR.
06 Registrar ....Mr. Mike MEDFORD
84 Int VP Enrollment/Student Affairs ......Mr. David E. BUCKINGHAM
26 Director Marketing/Communications .... Ms. Jennifer F. CUTHBERTSON
04 Executive Assistant to President ....Ms. Lucy BAUM
29 Director Alumni/Church Relations ....Rev. Julie BAILEY

Columbus State University (E)

4225 University Avenue, Columbus GA 31907-5645
County: Muscogee FICE Identification: 001561
Unit ID: 139366
Telephone: (706) 507-8800 Carnegie Class: Masters/L
FAX Number: (706) 568-2123 Calendar System: Semester
URL: www.columbusstate.edu
Established: 1958 Annual Undergrad Tuition & Fees (In-State): $6,241
Enrollment: 8,372 Coed
Affiliation or Control: State IRS Status: 501(c)3
Highest Offering: Doctorate
Accreditation: SC, ART, CACREP, MUS, NURSE, THEA

01 Interim President ....Dr. John M. FUCHKO, III
05 Int Provost/EVP Academic Affairs ....Dr. Patrick MCHENRY
10 VP Business & Finance .... Mr. Richard SEARS
32 VP Student Affairs/Enrollment Mgmt ....Dr. Gina SHEEKS
111 VP University Advancement .... Dr. Rocky KETTERING
13 Chief Information Officer ....Vacant
43 General Counsel .... Mr. Craig BURGESS
84 AVP for Enrollment Mgmt ....Mrs. Sallie MCMULLIN
100 Chief of Staff .... Dr. Ron WILLIAMS
50 Dean Turner College of Business .... Dr. Linda HADLEY
08 Dean of Libraries .... Dr. Alan KARASS
15 Director Human Resources ....Ms. Tamara WADE
09 Director Institutional Research .... Dr. Sri SITHARAMAN
41 Director Intercollegiate Athletics .... Mr. Todd REESER
07 Director of Admissions ....Ms. Kristin WILLIAMS
122 Coord Fraternity/Sorority Life .... Mr. William KEEN

† Part of the University System of Georgia.

Columbus Technical College (F)

928 Manchester Expressway, Columbus GA 31904-6572
County: Muscogee FICE Identification: 005624
Unit ID: 139357
Telephone: (706) 649-1800 Carnegie Class: Assoc/HVT-Mix Trad/Non
FAX Number: (706) 649-1885 Calendar System: Semester
URL: www.columbustech.edu
Established: 1961 Annual Undergrad Tuition & Fees (In-State): $3,042
Enrollment: 2,999 Coed
Affiliation or Control: State IRS Status: Exempt
Highest Offering: Associate Degree
Accreditation: SC, ADNUR, COARC, DA, DH, DMS, FUSER, MAC, RAD, SURGT

01 President ....Ms. Martha Ann TODD
11 VP Administrative Services .... Ms. Karen THOMAS
05 Vice President Academic Affairs ....Dr. Kermelle HENSLEY
32 Vice President Student Affairs .... Dr. Tara ASKEW
18 Vice President Operations .... Mr. Tommy WILSON
88 Vice President Economic Development ....Mr. James LOYD
51 Vice President of Adult Education ....Ms. April HOPSON
15 Director of Human Resources .... Mr. Henry GROSS
13 Director Information Technology ....Mr. Jonathan NORRED
111 Director Institutional Advancement .... Ms. Susan SEALY
06 Registrar .... Ms. Sylvia DANSBY
07 Director of Admissions ....Mr. Joseph WILSON
50 Dean of Business ....Ms. Nicole JACKSON

Covenant College (G)

14049 Scenic Highway, Lookout Mountain TN 30750-4164
County: Dade FICE Identification: 003484
Unit ID: 139393
Telephone: (706) 820-1560 Carnegie Class: Bac-A&S
FAX Number: (706) 820-2165 Calendar System: Semester
URL: www.covenant.edu
Established: 1955 Annual Undergrad Tuition & Fees: $36,710
Enrollment: 911 Coed
Affiliation or Control: Presbyterian Church In America IRS Status: 501(c)3
Highest Offering: Master's
Accreditation: SC

01 President ....Dr. J. Derek HALVORSON
05 Vice Pres of Academic Affairs ....Dr. Jeffrey B. HALL
10 Vice Pres of Finance & Operations .... Mr. Fred VERWOERD
30 Vice President of Development ....Mr. Marc ERICKSON
32 Vice Pres of Student Development ....Mr. Brad VOYLES
84 Asst VP of Enrollment Management .... Mr. Brad TOMAS
09 AVP for Institutional Effectiveness .... Dr. Karen NELSON
08 Director of Library Services .... Mr. John HOLBERG
06 Dean of Records and Registrar ....Mr. Rodney E. MILLER
42 Chaplain ....Mr. Grant LOWE
58 Dean Master of Education Pgm .... Dr. Jim DREXLER
21 Controller ....Mrs. Jennifer BLACK-PATEL
88 Campus Architect ....Mr. David NORTHCUTT
37 Director of Financial Aid ....Mr. Matthew BAZZEL
15 Director of Human Resources ....Mr. Tom DEWEY
41 Director of Athletics ....Mr. Tim SCEGGEL
13 Director of Technology Services .... Ms. Marjorie CROCKER
29 Director of Alumni Relations ......Ms. Sara Kaitlin VAN PUFFELEN
23 Director of Health Services ....Ms. Tina HOLT
26 Dir of Marketing & Communications .... Mr. John HORTON
121 Coordinator of Student Success .... Ms. Becca MOORE
36 Dir of Center for Calling & Career .... Mr. John PLATING
04 Admin Asst to Office of President .... Mrs. Cassandra JONES
19 Director of Safety & Security ....Mr. Keith MCCLEARN
109 Director of Business Operations .... Mr. Caleb MASK
104 Coordinator of Global Education .... Ms. Lindsay SAUNDS

Dalton State College (A)

650 College Drive, Dalton GA 30720-3797
County: Whitfield FICE Identification: 003956
Unit ID: 139463
Telephone: (706) 272-4436 Carnegie Class: Bac-Diverse
FAX Number: (706) 272-4588 Calendar System: Semester
URL: www.daltonstate.edu
Established: 1963 Annual Undergrad Tuition & Fees (In-State): $3,683
Enrollment: 4,794 Coed
Affiliation or Control: State IRS Status: 501(c)3
Highest Offering: Baccalaureate
Accreditation: SC, ADNUR, COARC, MLTAD, NUR, RAD, SW

01 President ... Dr. Margaret VENABLE
05 VP for Academic Affairs ... Dr. Bruno HICKS
10 Vice President Fiscal Affairs ... Mr. Nick HENRY
84 VP Student Affairs & Enroll Mgmt ... Dr. Jodi JOHNSON
20 Assistant Provost ... Dr. Tammy BYRON
37 Director of Financial Aid/Vet Svcs ... Ms. Carol JONES
08 Director Library Services ... Ms. Melissa WHITESELL
18 Director Plant Opers ... Mr. George BREWER
26 Director of Marketing ... Mr. Philip SCHLESINGER
111 Director Institutional Advancement ... Mr. David ELROD
32 Dean of Students ... Dr. Jami HALL
15 Director Human Resources ... Ms. Lori MCCARTY
96 Procurement Director ... Mr. Matthew SHIVER
13 Chief Information Officer ... Mr. Jeff MARSHALL
19 Director Public Safety ... Mr. Michael MASTERS
30 Development Coordinator ... Mr. Josh WILSON
39 Director Student Housing ... Mr. Tim REILLY
50 Dean School of Business ... Dr. Marilyn HELMS
53 Dean School of Education ... Dr. Sharon HIXON
49 Dean School of Arts & Sciences ... Dr. Randall GRIFFUS
76 Dean School of Health Professions ... Dr. Gina KERTULIS-TARTAR
06 Registrar ... Vacant
04 Executive Asst to President ... Ms. Mary Ellen GURLEY
07 Director of Admissions ... Mrs. Katherine LOGAN
41 Exec Dir Athletics & External Rels ... Mr. Jon JAUDON
104 Director Study Abroad ... Dr. Fernando GARCIA
38 Assoc Director of Counseling ... Ms. Jenny GUY
86 Dir Government & Alumni Relations ... Ms. Vallarie PRATT
108 Director Institutional Assessment ... Dr. Henry CODJOE
121 Exec Dir Advising & Student Success ... Dr. Elizabeth HUTCHINS

† Part of the University System of Georgia.

East Georgia State College (B)

131 College Circle, Swainsboro GA 30401-3643
County: Emanuel FICE Identification: 010997
Unit ID: 139621
Telephone: (478) 289-2000 Carnegie Class: Bac/Assoc-Assoc Dom
FAX Number: (478) 289-2038 Calendar System: Semester
URL: www.ega.edu
Established: 1973 Annual Undergrad Tuition & Fees (In-State): $3,136
Enrollment: 2,415 Coed
Affiliation or Control: State IRS Status: 501(c)3
Highest Offering: Baccalaureate
Accreditation: SC

01 President ... Dr. David L. SCHECTER
04 Exec Assistant to the President ... Mrs. Dana WRIGHT
100 Chief of Staff/Legal Counsel ... Mrs. Mary C. SMITH
05 Interim VP Academic/Student Affairs ... Dr. John CADLE
10 VP for Business Affairs ... Mr. Cliff GAY
13 VP for Information Technology ... Mr. Mike ROUNTREE
111 VP for Institutional Advancement ... Vacant
12 AVP for External Campuses ... Mr. Nick KELCH
20 AVP for Academic Affairs ... Dr. David CHEVALIER
25 AVP Data Analytics & Grants ... Dr. Da'Mon ANDREWS
19 Dir Public Safety/Chief of Police ... Vacant
41 Director of Athletics ... Mr. Chuck WIMBERLY
09 Dir of Strategic Plng/Inst Research ... Mr. David GRIBBIN
12 Interim Director of EGSC Statesboro ... Mrs. Courtney JOINER
22 AVP Student Conduct/Title IX ... Mrs. Sherrie HELMS
39 Director of Housing ... Ms. Tiera WILLIAMS
06 Registrar ... Ms. Lynette M. SAULSBERRY
07 Director of Admissions ... Mr. Mike MORAN
109 Director of Dining Operations ... Ms. Ruth UNDERWOOD
18 Director of Plant Operations ... Mr. David STEPTOE
08 Interim Library Director ... Ms. Meghan CREWS
15 Director of Human Resources ... Mrs. Tracy WOODS
106 Director of eLearning ... Mrs. Terri BROWN
121 Director of Academic Advising ... Ms. Deborah KITTRELL-MIKELL
124 Director of Retention ... Ms. Georgia MATHEWS
38 Int Dir Counseling/Disability Svcs ... Ms. Stephanie ROYALS
88 Director Financial Accounting ... Ms. Sheila D. WENTZ
113 Director of Accounting Svcs ... Ms. Vera M. WILLIAMS
37 Director Student Financial Aid ... Mr. Michael WERNON
104 Director Study Abroad ... Mr. Carmine PALUMBO

† Part of the University System of Georgia.

Emmanuel College (C)

181 Spring Street, Franklin Springs GA 30639
County: Franklin FICE Identification: 001563
Unit ID: 139630
Telephone: (706) 245-7226 Carnegie Class: Bac-Diverse
FAX Number: (706) 245-4424 Calendar System: Semester
URL: www.ec.edu
Established: 1919 Annual Undergrad Tuition & Fees: $21,220
Enrollment: 883 Coed
Affiliation or Control: Pentecostal Holiness Church IRS Status: 501(c)3
Highest Offering: Master's
Accreditation: SC

01 President ... Dr. Ronald WHITE
32 Vice President for Student Life ... Dr. Mandrake MILLER
05 Vice President for Academic Affairs ... Dr. Janet COLEMAN
10 Vice President for Finance ... Mr. Greg K. HEARN
30 Vice President for Development ... Mr. W. Brian JAMES
84 Vice Pres Enrollment Mgmt/Marketing ... Ms. Donna QUICK
08 Director of Library Services ... Ms. Deborah MILLIER
06 Registrar ... Mrs. Debra F. GRIZZLE
37 Director of Financial Aid ... Mrs. Lisa WILLIAMSON
13 Director of Information Technology ... Mr. Glenn TONEY
11 Assoc VP of Campus Operations ... Mr. Matt MCREE
41 Athletics Director ... Mr. Nate MOORMAN
42 Dir Spiritual Life/Campus Pastor ... Mr. Chris MAXWELL
15 Director of Human Resources ... Mrs. Joann HARPER
26 Chief Public Relations Officer ... Mrs. Ashley WESTBROOK
96 Director of Accounting Services ... Mrs. Anita RAY
18 Physical Plant Director ... Mr. Wayne CRIDER
09 Director of Institutional Research ... Ms. Sharon SYNAN
29 Director Alumni Relations ... Mr. Brian JAMES
36 Director of Career Services ... Vacant
04 Administrative Asst to President ... Mrs. Stefanie KAUP
19 Campus Safety Coordinator ... Mr. Greg HEARN
39 Director Student Housing ... Mrs. Sherri CAREY
07 Director of Admissions ... Ms. Kelley CHAPPA
106 Dir Online Education/E-learning ... Ms. Sharon SYNAN
20 Dean of Academics ... Ms. Jennifer BENSON
53 Dean of Education ... Dr. Vicki HOLLINSHEAD
38 Director Student Counseling ... Vacant
108 Director Institutional Assessment ... Dr. Cyndee PHILLIPS

Emory University (D)

201 Dowman Drive, Atlanta GA 30322-0001
County: DeKalb FICE Identification: 001564
Unit ID: 139658
Telephone: (404) 727-6123 Carnegie Class: DU-Highest
FAX Number: (404) 727-5997 Calendar System: Semester
URL: www.emory.edu
Established: 1836 Annual Undergrad Tuition & Fees: $53,868
Enrollment: 13,997 Coed
Affiliation or Control: United Methodist IRS Status: 501(c)3
Highest Offering: Doctorate
Accreditation: SC, AA, ANEST, ARCPA, CAATE, CAMPEP, CLPSY, DENT, IPSY, LAW, MED, MIDWF, NURSE, PAST, PCSAS, PH, PTA, RAD, THEOL

01 President ... Dr. Gregory L. FENVES
05 Provost/EVP Academic Affairs ... Dr. Ravi V. BELLAMKONDA
10 EVP Business & Admin/CFO ... Mr. Christopher AUGOSTINI
17 Int Exec Vice Pres Health Affairs ... Dr. David S. STEPHENS
88 Univ Ombuds Ofcr/Sr Advisor to Pres ... Ms. Lynell CADRAY
101 VP/Secretary of the University ... Ms. Allison K. DYKES
84 VP Enrollment Mgmt ... Dr. Paul P. MARTHERS
100 Chief of Staff ... Ms. Emily FISHER
32 Sr VP/Dean Campus Life ... Ms. Enku GELAYE
26 VP Communications and Marketing ... Mr. Luke ANDERSON
46 Sr Vice Pres for Research ... Dr. Deborah W. BRUNER
111 SVP Advancement/Alumni Engagement ... Mr. Joshua NEWTON
88 Senior Advisor to the Pres ... Dr. Robert M. FRANKLIN, JR.
43 Interim Sr Vice Pres & Gen Counsel ... Ms. Amy ADELMAN
114 SVP Strategic and Resource Planning ... Ms. Susan BONIFIELD
20 Interim VP for Academic Affairs ... Dr. Lanny S. LIEBESKIND
13 Enterprise CIO/Sr VP Lib Svcs ... Mr. Richard A. MENDOLA
117 VP Enterprise Risk Mgmt/COS ... Ms. Diana CARTER
116 Chief Audit Officer ... Mr. Scott J. STEVENSON
88 VP Research Admin ... Dr. Robert NOBLES
88 AVP/Chief Business Officer Research ... Ms. Melanie LAWRENCE
110 Sr AVP Engage/Comm/Mktg/Advance ... Mr. Cutler ANDREWS
112 Sr Assoc VP Principal Gifts ... Mr. Alex BROWN
27 Int AVP Ent Communications ... Ms. Laura E. DOUGLAS-BROWN
27 VP Academic Communications ... Ms. Minnie GLYMPH
15 VP Human Resources ... Ms. Theresa MILAZZO
15 VP Human Resources ... Mr. Del KING
20 Vice Prov Academic Planning ... Dr. Nancy BLIWISE
28 Vice Provost Equity/Inclusion ... Dr. Carol E. HENDERSON
36 VP Career and Prof Dev ... Dr. Branden GRIMMETT
20 VP Faculty Affairs ... Dr. Pearl DOWE
20 Assoc VP Undergrad Affairs ... Ms. Heather MUGG
86 VP Government & Cmty Affairs ... Ms. Cameron P. TAYLOR
58 Vice Provost/Dean Graduate Sch ... Dr. Kimberly R. JACOB ARRIOLA
85 VP Global Strat & Initiatives ... Dr. Philip WAINWRIGHT
88 Advisor ... Dr. Qiang XU
11 VP Business Operations ... Ms. Debby MOREY
45 VP Campus Services/Chief Plng Ofcr ... Mr. Robin MOREY
115 VP & Chief Investment Officer ... Mr. Srinivas PULAVARTI
21 VP for Finance & Treasury ... Ms. Belva WHITE
21 Assoc VP Finance & Controller ... Mr. Adam GREENFIELD
25 Assoc Vice President Research ... Dr. Todd SHERER
07 AVP Undergrad Enroll/Dean of Admiss ... Dr. John LATTING
97 Sr Assoc Dean Undergrad Education ... Dr. Joanne BRZINSKI
88 Chief Compliance Officer ... Ms. Kenya M. FAULKNER
20 Vice Prov Academic Innovation ... Dr. Paul WELTY
06 Assoc VP/University Registrar ... Ms. JoAnn MCKENZIE
19 Associate VP/Chief of Police ... Ms. Cheryl ELLIOTT
88 Asst Vice Prov Faculty Affairs ... Dr. Carol A. FLOWERS
37 Asst Vice Prov/Dir Student Fin Aid ... Mr. John LEACH
38 Assistant VP Counseling/Psych Svcs ... Dr. Keilan RICKARD
108 Asst Vice Prov Academic Pgm/Plng ... Dr. David M. JORDAN
88 Chief Resilience Officer ... Mr. Amir ST. CLAIR
49 Int Dean of Emory College ... Dr. Carla FREEMAN
12 Int Dean & CEO Oxford College ... Dr. Kenneth CARTER
63 Dean of Medicine ... Dr. Vikas P. SUKHATME
66 Dean of Nursing ... Dr. Linda MCCAULEY
73 Dean of Theology ... Dr. Jan LOVE
61 Dean of Law ... Ms. Mary Anne BOBINSKI
50 Dean of Business School ... Dr. Gareth JAMES
69 Dean of Public Health ... Dr. Daniele FALLIN
42 Univ Chaplain/Dean Spiritual Life ... Rev. Gregory MCGONIGLE
80 Pres & CEO of the Carter Center ... Ms. Paige E. ALEXANDER
36 Exec Director Career Service ... Mr. Paul FOWLER
44 Sr Director of Gift Planning ... Ms. Stephanie D. FROSTBAUM
39 Sr Director Residence Life ... Dr. Scott K. RAUSCH
39 Sr Director Housing Operations ... Ms. Elaine TURNER
40 Director Bookstore ... Mr. Bruce COVEY
88 Director Communications ... Mr. Adam CRISP
96 Asst VP Rsrch Admin/Dir OSP ... Ms. Holly SOMMERS
12 Director Yerkes Research Ctrs ... Dr. Paul JOHNSON
85 Dir Intl Student Scholar Program ... Ms. Shinsaeng KO
09 Asst VP Inst Rsrch/Decision Support ... Dr. Justin SHEPHERD
88 Director MC Carlos Museum ... Mr. Henry S. KIM
88 Director Center for Ethics ... Mr. Paul R. WOLPE
41 Asst VP Athletics/Recreation ... Ms. Keiko PRICE
08 Int Dean & University Librarian ... Ms. Lisa MACKLIN
122 Sr Dir Sorority/Fraternity Life ... Mr. Scott RAUSCH

Fort Valley State University (E)

1005 State University Drive, Fort Valley GA 31030-4313
County: Peach FICE Identification: 001566
Unit ID: 139719
Telephone: (478) 825-6211 Carnegie Class: Masters/S
FAX Number: (478) 825-6394 Calendar System: Semester
URL: www.fvsu.edu
Established: 1895 Annual Undergrad Tuition & Fees (In-State): $5,832
Enrollment: 3,079 Coed
Affiliation or Control: State IRS Status: 501(c)3
Highest Offering: Beyond Master's But Less Than Doctorate
Accreditation: SC, AAFCS, CACREP, SW

01 President ... Dr. Paul JONES
05 Provost/VP for Academic Affairs ... Dr. Olufunke FONTENOT
10 CBO/VP for Business & Finance ... Ms. Michelle MARTIN
111 VP for Advancement ... Mr. Anthony HOLLOMAN
32 VP Student Affairs & Enrollment ... Dr. Timothy HATCHETT
20 AVP Academic Affairs/Dean ... Dr. Robert DIBIE, III
56 Extension Administrator ... Dr. Mark LATTIMORE
49 Interim Dean Arts & Sciences ... Dr. Berlethia PITTS
21 Assistant Vice President/Controller ... Vacant
06 Registrar ... Ms. Sharee LAWRENCE
43 Dir of Legal/Government Affairs ... Ms. Emma WILLIAMS
13 Chief Information Officer ... Mr. Ndidi AKUTA
08 Director Hunt Memorial Library ... Mr. Frank MAHITAB
07 Exec Dir Recruitment/Admissions ... Mr. Alex THOMAS
84 AVP for Enrollment Management ... Vacant
29 Director Alumni Affairs ... Vacant
15 Chief Human Resources Officer ... Ms. Gena WILSON
19 Director of Campus Police/Safety ... Mr. Antonio FLETCHER
47 Dean Agriculture ... Dr. Ralph NOBLE
23 Dir of Student Health/Counseling ... Ms. Jacqueline CASKEY-JAMES
18 Director of Facilities Management ... Mr. Edwidge DUFRESNE
26 Chief Communications Officer ... Vacant
41 Director of Athletics ... Mr. Anthony HOLLOMAN
97 Exec Director of University College ... Dr. Jocelyn POWELL
53 Dean College of Education ... Dr. Beth DAY-HAIRSTON
22 Contracts/Compliance Coordinator ... Ms. Karin VINSON
25 Director of Sponsored Programs ... Ms. Joyce Y. JOHNSON
39 Director Student Housing ... Mr. Shawn MODENA
96 Director of Procurement ... Ms. Rebecca HORTON
88 Title III Director ... Ms. Danyell BARRY
100 Chief of Staff ... Mr. RJ MATHIS
106 Director Online Learning Office ... Dr. Darryl HANCOCK
30 Director of Development ... Mr. Jaron LUCAS
88 VP Economic Dev/Land Grant Affairs ... Dr. Govind KANNAN

† Part of the University System of Georgia.

Georgia Central University (F)

6789 Peachtree Industrial Boulevard, Atlanta GA 30360
County: DeKalb FICE Identification: 041565
Unit ID: 461236
Telephone: (678) 535-7771 Carnegie Class: Not Classified
FAX Number: N/A Calendar System: Semester
URL: www.gcuniv.edu
Established: 1993 Annual Undergrad Tuition & Fees: N/A
Enrollment: N/A Coed
Affiliation or Control: Independent Non-Profit IRS Status: 501(c)3
Highest Offering: Doctorate
Accreditation: THEOL

01 President ... Dr. Paul C. KIM
05 Vice President/Chief Acad Officer ... Dr. Sung Shik JANG
26 Vice President External Affairs ... Dr. Ho Yeon LEE
10 Chief Financial Officer ... Mr. Daniel KIM
07 Director of Admissions/Registrar ... Dr. In Sook KIM
20 Associate Dir of Academic Affairs ... Dr. Mia KANG
45 Director of Planning ... Dr. Randy S. JU
12 Dir of New Jersey Extension Site ... Dr. Sun Hee CHOI
13 Senior Director of IT ... Mr. Dong Hyuk BANG
106 Director of Distance Education ... Dr. Kyueil KWAK
18 Director of Maintenance ... Rev. Min Soo KIM

19 Director Security/Safety .... Mr. Samuel KIM
21 Director of Business Affairs .... Mr. Daniel KIM
108 Dir of Institutional Effectiveness .... Dr. Edmund K. RHEE
29 President of Alumni Relations .... Dr. Sun Ki JEONG
37 Director Student Financial Aid .... Dr. Hee Sook SONG
50 Dean School of Business .... Dr. Byung Won LEE
73 Dean School of Christianity .... Dr. Kyung Hun LEE
73 Dean School of Divinity .... Dr. Sung Shik JANG
64 Dean School of Music .... Dr. Hee Churl KIM
88 International Student Advisor .... Mr. Daniel KIM
08 Director of the Library .... Mr. Jarian R. JONES
32 Director Student Affairs/Chaplain .... Dr. Heeduck YOO

Georgia College & State University (A)

231 West Hancock Street, Milledgeville GA 31061-0490
County: Baldwin FICE Identification: 001602
Unit ID: 139861
Telephone: (478) 445-5004 Carnegie Class: Masters/L
FAX Number: (478) 445-1191 Calendar System: Semester
URL: www.gcsu.edu
Established: 1889 Annual Undergrad Tuition & Fees (In-State): $9,524
Enrollment: 6,873 Coed
Affiliation or Control: State IRS Status: 501(c)3
Highest Offering: Doctorate
Accreditation: SC, CAATE, CAEP, @MIDWF, MUS, NURSE, SPAA

01 President .... Ms. Cathy COX
04 Special Assistant to the President .... Ms. Monica STARLEY
05 Provost/VP for Academic Affairs .... Dr. Costas SPIROU
10 VP Finance/Administration .... Mr. Lee FRUITTICHER
32 Vice President for Student Life .... Dr. Shawn BROOKS
111 VP for University Advancement .... Ms. Shelley STRICKLAND
20 Assoc Provost Academic Affairs .... Dr. Holley ROBERTS
45 Assoc VP for Strategic Initiatives .... Dr. Mark PELTON
26 Assoc VP Strategic Communications .... Mr. Omar ODEH
84 Assoc VP for Enrollment Management .... Mr. Joel ROBINSON
109 Asst VP for Auxiliary Services .... Mr. Kyle CULLARS
114 Sr Dir for Budget Planning & Admin .... Mr. Russ WILLIAMS
49 Dean College of Arts & Sciences .... Dr. Eric TENBUS
50 Dean College of Business .... Dr. Micheal T. STRATTON
53 Dean College of Education .... Dr. Joseph PETERS
76 Dean College of Health Sciences .... Dr. Sheri NOVIELLO
39 Exec Director of University Housing .... Mr. Larry CHRISTENSON
88 Project Manager .... Mr. Mark BOWEN
19 Dir Public Safety & Chief of Police .... Mr. Brett STANELLE
09 Assoc VP of Institutional Research .... Dr. Chris FERLAND
13 Chief Information Officer .... Ms. Susan KERR
08 Director of Libraries .... Dr. Shaundra WALKER
36 Director Career Center .... Ms. Lauren EASOM
15 Chief Human Resources Officer .... Ms. Carol WARD
07 Executive Director of Admissions .... Mr. Javier FRANCISCO
06 Registrar .... Ms. Kay ANDERSON
41 Director of Athletics .... Mr. Wendell STATON
29 Asst Dir of Alumni Engagement .... Vacant
43 General Counsel .... Mr. Brett MONTROY
38 Director of Counseling Services .... Dr. Stephen WILSON
37 Director of Financial Aid .... Ms. Shannon SIMMONS
88 Sr Dir Materials Mgmt/Central Svcs .... Mr. Mark MEEKS
116 Dir of Internal Audit .... Ms. Stacy MULVANEY
35 Dean of Students .... Dr. Tom MILES
104 Asst VP for International Educ .... Dr. James CALLAGHAN
56 Exec Director of Rural Studies .... Dr. Veronica WOMACK
28 Int Chief Diversity Officer .... Ms. Jennifer GRAHAM

Georgia Gwinnett College (B)

1000 University Center Lane, Lawrenceville GA 30043
County: Gwinnett FICE Identification: 041429
Unit ID: 447689
Telephone: (678) 407-5000 Carnegie Class: Bac-Diverse
FAX Number: N/A Calendar System: Semester
URL: www.ggc.edu
Established: 2005 Annual Undergrad Tuition & Fees (In-District): $4,948
Enrollment: 11,627 Coed
Affiliation or Control: State/Local IRS Status: 501(c)3
Highest Offering: Baccalaureate
Accreditation: SC, CAEPN, NURSE

01 President .... Dr. Jann L. JOSEPH
05 SVP Academic/Stdnt Affairs/Provost .... Dr. George S. LOW
84 Vice Pres Enrollment Management .... Mr. Michael POLL
13 Vice Pres Information Technology .... Dr. Christine MILLER DIVINE
10 Vice Pres Business & Finanance .... Mr. Frank HARDYMON
121 Vice Pres Student Engagement & Succ .... Dr. Michelle ROSEMOND
04 Executive Asst to President .... Mrs. Luann CAUSLAND
15 Assoc Vice Pres Human Resources .... Ms. Katherine KYLE
11 Assoc Vice Pres Operations .... Mr. Terrance SCHNEIDER
26 Assoc Vice Pres Communications .... Mrs. Sloan JONES
111 Assoc Vice Pres Advancement .... Ms. Jennifer HENDRICKSON
50 Dean School of Business .... Dr. Tyler YU
53 Dean School of Education .... Dr. Bernard OLIVER
49 Dean School of Liberal Arts .... Dr. Teresa WINTERHALTER
81 Dean School Science/Technology .... Dr. Chavonda J. MILLS
76 Dean School of Health Sciences .... Dr. Diane WHITE
121 Dean Library Services .... Ms. Barbara MANN

Georgia Highlands College (C)

3175 Cedartown Highway, Rome GA 30161-3897
County: Floyd FICE Identification: 009507
Unit ID: 139700
Telephone: (706) 802-5000 Carnegie Class: Bac/Assoc-Mixed
FAX Number: (706) 295-6341 Calendar System: Semester
URL: www.highlands.edu
Established: 1970 Annual Undergrad Tuition & Fees (In-State): $3,344
Enrollment: 5,680 Coed
Affiliation or Control: State IRS Status: 501(c)3
Highest Offering: Baccalaureate
Accreditation: SC, ADNUR, DH, NUR

01 President .... Dr. Mike HOBBS
05 Interim CAO & Provost .... Dr. Sarah COAKLEY
10 VP Finance & Administration .... Mr. Jamie PETTY
13 Chief Information Officer .... Mr. Rob LALTRELLO
15 Chief Human Resource Officer .... Ms. Dana ITKOW
09 Dean Plng/Assess/Accred/Research .... Dr. Jesse BISHOP
12 Campus Dean Cartersville .... Ms. Leslie JOHNSON
12 Campus Dean Marietta .... Mr. Ken REAVES
119 Chief Information Security Officer .... Mr. Ian FLEMING
21 AVP of Finance and Administration .... Ms. Stephanie LOVELESS
20 Asst VP Academic Retention/Resource .... Ms. Michelle LOCKETT
84 Executive Dir Enrollment Management .... Ms. Jennifer HICKS
04 Executive Asst to the President .... Ms. Lillian ROBERTSON
08 Dean Libraries & College Testing .... Mr. Julius FLESCHNER
19 Police Chief/Dir of Campus Safety .... Mr. David HORACE
41 Director of Athletics .... Mr. Brandan HARRELL
18 Director of Facilities .... Mr. David VAN HOOK
26 Sr Dir Marketing & Communications .... Ms. Sheila JONES
12 Manager Floyd Campus/HR Adm Progrms .... Mr. Bradley GILMORE
12 Manager Paulding Site .... Ms. Christina HENGGELER
102 Director Foundation .... Ms. Liz JONES
38 Dir Student Support Services .... Ms. Dorothy MORGAN
06 Registrar .... Ms. Gina FLOYD
37 Director Financial Aid .... Ms. Donna CHILDRES
89 Coord Cocurricular/Transition Pgm .... Mr. Clifton PUCKETT
28 Director of Diversity .... Dr. Sean CALLAHAN
25 Grants Admin/Faculty Affairs .... Ms. Kristina SHANAHAN
104 Director Study Abroad .... Dr. Lisa JELLUM

† Part of the University System of Georgia.

Georgia Institute of Technology (D)

225 North Avenue, NW, Atlanta GA 30332-0002
County: Fulton FICE Identification: 001569
Unit ID: 139755
Telephone: (404) 894-2000 Carnegie Class: DU-Highest
FAX Number: (404) 894-1277 Calendar System: Semester
URL: www.gatech.edu
Established: 1885 Annual Undergrad Tuition & Fees (In-State): $12,852
Enrollment: 39,771 Coed
Affiliation or Control: State IRS Status: 501(c)3
Highest Offering: Doctorate
Accreditation: SC, ART, CAMPEP, CEA, IPSY, PLNG

01 President .... Dr. Ángel CABRERA
05 Provost/Exec VP Academic Affairs .... Dr. Steven W. MCLAUGHLIN
11 Interim EVP Administration/Finance .... Dr. Michael SHANNON
46 Executive Vice President Research .... Dr. Chaouki ABDALLAH
100 Senior VP/Chief of Staff .... Mr. Frank NEVILLE
30 Vice President Development .... Ms. Jennifer HOWE
26 Vice Pres Institute Communications .... Ms. Renee KOPKOWSKI
32 VP Student Engagement & Well-Being .... Dr. Luoluo HONG
88 SVP Georgia Tech Rsrch Inst .... Dr. James HUDGENS
88 VP Research Dev/Operations .... Dr. Robert BUTERA
86 Vice President Institute Relations .... Mr. Bert REEVES
88 Int VP Enterprise Innovation Inst .... Mr. David BRIDGES
10 Vice President Finance & Planning .... Mr. James FORTNER
29 President GT Alumni Assoc .... Mr. Dene SHEHEANE
58 Vice Prov Graduate/PostDoc Educ .... Dr. Bonnie FERRI
84 Vice Prov Enrollment Mgmt .... Dr. Paul KOHN
20 Vice Prov Undergraduate Education .... Dr. Steven GIRARDOT
35 Dean of Students/AVP Student Life .... Mr. John STEIN
43 Chief Legal Counsel .... Ms. Danette JOSLYN-GAUL
28 VP Diversity/Equity & Inclusion .... Dr. Archie ERVIN
15 Vice Pres Human Resources .... Ms. Skye DUCKETT
18 VP Infrastructure/Sustainability .... Ms. Maria CIMILLUCA
88 Assoc Vice Pres Campus Services .... Ms. Kasey HELTON
13 VP Information Tech/CIO .... Mr. Daren HUBBARD
41 Director of Athletics .... Mr. Todd STANSBURY
22 Exec Dir Staff Diversity/Inclusion .... Ms. Pearl ALEXANDER
49 Dean College of Liberal Arts .... Dr. Kaye HUSBANDS FEALING
48 Dean College of Design .... Dr. Ellen BASSETT
77 Dean College of Computing .... Dr. Charles ISBELL
54 Dean College of Engineering .... Dr. Raheem BEYAH
08 Dean Libraries .... Dr. Leslie SHARP
50 Dean Scheller College of Business .... Dr. Maryam ALAVI
81 Dean College of Sciences .... Dr. Susan LOZIER
06 Registrar .... Ms. Reta PIKOWSKY
40 Director Georgia Tech Bookstore .... Ms. Reshma PATEL
19 Director of Security & Police .... Mr. Robert CONNOLLY
107 Dean Professional Education .... Dr. Nelson BAKER
37 Director Student Financial Aid .... Ms. Marie MONS
23 Sr Director Student Health Svcs .... Dr. Benjamin HOLTON
85 Vice Prov International Initiatives .... Dr. Bernard KIPPELEN
104 Exec Dir International Education .... Ms. Amy HENRY
38 Director Counseling Center .... Dr. Carla BRADLEY
109 Senior Director Auxiliary Services .... Ms. Carolina AMERO
07 AVP/Exec Dir Undergrad Admissions .... Mr. Richard CLARK
96 Sr Director Procurement Services .... Mr. Ajay PATEL
114 Exec Dir Inst Budget Plng & Admin .... Ms. Jamie FERNANDES
88 Exec Director Strategic Consulting .... Dr. Sonia ALVAREZ-ROBINSON
113 Bursar .... Ms. Gloria KOBUS
09 Sr Dir Institutional Research .... Ms. Sandra KINNEY
108 Assoc Prov Academic Effectiveness .... Dr. Loraine PHILLIPS

† Part of the University System of Georgia.

Georgia Military College (E)

201 E Greene Street, Milledgeville GA 31061-3398
County: Baldwin FICE Identification: 001571
Unit ID: 485111
Telephone: (478) 387-4900 Carnegie Class: Bac/Assoc-Assoc Dom
FAX Number: N/A Calendar System: Quarter
URL: www.gmc.edu
Established: 1879 Annual Undergrad Tuition & Fees: $6,615
Enrollment: 7,501 Coed
Affiliation or Control: Independent Non-Profit IRS Status: 501(c)3
Highest Offering: Baccalaureate
Accreditation: SC

01 President .... LtGen. William B. CALDWELL, IV
05 Chief Academic Ofcr/Dn of Faculty .... Dr. Phillip M. HOLMES
10 Chief Financial Officer .... COL. James WATKINS
13 VP Info Technology/Online College .... Mr. Jody YEARWOOD
84 Senior VP of Enrollment Management .... Mr. Jody YEARWOOD
15 VP Human Resources .... Ms. Jill ROBBINS
21 Assoc Vice Pres Resource Management .... Ms. Susan MEEKS
06 Associate VP Academic Records .... Mr. David FULMER
32 Commandant .... COL. Steve PITT
30 Chief Institutional Devel Officer .... Mr. Mark STROM
09 Director Institutional Research .... Dr. Susan ISAAC
41 Athletic Director .... Mr. Rob MANCHESTER
18 Director Facilities/Engineer .... Mr. Jeff GRAY
08 Director of Library Services .... Ms. Erin NEWTON
19 Chief Security/Safety/Campus Police .... Mr. James HODNETT
26 Dir Communication/Public Relations .... Ms. Jobie SHIELDS
20 Academic Dean .... Ms. Laura BOOTH
04 Executive Asst to President .... Ms. Joelle TRUMBO
37 Director Student Financial Aid .... Ms. Alisa STEPHENS
100 Director of Staff/Dean of Students .... Ms. Jeannie ZIPPERER
29 Director Alumni Affairs .... Mr. Craig PORTWOOD
96 Director of Purchasing .... Mr. Mark ALAN

Georgia Northwestern Technical College (F)

One Maurice Culberson Drive, Rome GA 30161
County: Floyd FICE Identification: 005257
Unit ID: 139384
Telephone: (706) 295-6963 Carnegie Class: Assoc/HVT-Mix Trad/Non
FAX Number: (706) 295-6944 Calendar System: Semester
URL: www.gntc.edu
Established: 1966 Annual Undergrad Tuition & Fees (In-State): $3,062
Enrollment: 6,608 Coed
Affiliation or Control: State IRS Status: 501(c)3
Highest Offering: Associate Degree
Accreditation: SC, ADNUR, CAHIIM, COARC, DA, DMS, EMT, LC, MAC, PNUR, RAD, SURGT

01 President .... Dr. Heidi POPHAM
05 Vice President Academic Affairs .... Dr. Elizabeth ANDERSON
11 Vice Pres Administrative Services .... Ms. Kelly BARNES
30 Vice Pres Econ Development .... Ms. Stephanie SCEARCE
09 Vice President IE & Student Success .... Ms. Selena MAGNUSSON
51 Vice President Adult Education .... Ms. Melissa SHAW
32 Vice Pres Student Affairs .... Mr. Stuart PHILLIPS
20 Assoc Vice Pres Academic Affairs .... Ms. Jennifer LOUDERMILK
06 Registrar .... Ms. Dana WALKER
08 Director of Library Services .... Mr. John LASSITER
19 Director Safety & Security .... Mr. Chad CARDIN
37 Exec Director of Financial Aid .... Ms. Amber SUMNER
18 Director Facilities Management .... Mr. Jeffrey AGAN
26 Dir Marketing/Public Relations .... Ms. Amber JORDAN
15 Director of Human Resources .... Ms. Elizabeth BARKSDALE
04 Admin Assistant to the President .... Ms. Lisa ODOM
13 Director of IT .... Mr. Dennis THOMAS
102 Dir Foundation/Corporate Relations .... Ms. Lauretta HANNON

Georgia Piedmont Technical College (G)

495 N Indian Creek Drive, Clarkston GA 30021-2397
County: DeKalb FICE Identification: 005622
Unit ID: 244446
Telephone: (404) 297-9522 Carnegie Class: Assoc/HVT-Mix Trad/Non
FAX Number: (404) 297-4234 Calendar System: Semester
URL: www.gptc.edu
Established: 1961 Annual Undergrad Tuition & Fees (In-State): $3,178
Enrollment: 2,615 Coed
Affiliation or Control: State IRS Status: 501(c)3
Highest Offering: Associate Degree
Accreditation: SC, CAHIIM, EMT, #MAC, MLTAD

01 President .... Dr. Tavarez HOLSTON
04 Exec Dir & Spec Asst to President .... Ms. Kaitlin DUDLEY
05 EVP/VP Academic Affairs .... Mr. Cheree WILLIAMS
10 Vice Pres Finance/Administration .... Ms. Teresa BROWN
103 VP Economic Development .... Mr. Irvin CLARK
32 Vice Pres Student Affairs .... Ms. Shawn ADAMS
108 VP Institutional Effectiveness .... Ms. Britnee SHANDOR
111 Dir Inst Advancement/Foundation .... Mr. Cory THOMPSON
37 Director of Financial Aid .... Ms. Felicia AILSTER
35 Dean of Student Affairs .... Dr. Candice BUCKLEY
08 Director of Library Services .... Ms. Wendy WILMOTH
15 Director of Human Resources .... Ms. Sadie WASHINGTON
26 Exec Dir Marketing/Public Relations .... Ms. Cheryl MYERS
06 Registrar .... Ms. Matilda PEEPLES

07 Director Admissions/Recruiting .... Vacant
18 Director Facilities Services .... Mr. Gary WILKINS
13 Director of Information Technology .... Mr. Samuel LOCKETT

Georgia Southern University (A)

PO Box 8033, Statesboro GA 30460-8033
County: Bulloch FICE Identification: 001572
Unit ID: 139931
Telephone: (912) 478-4636 Carnegie Class: DU-Higher
FAX Number: N/A Calendar System: Semester
URL: www.georgiasouthern.edu
Established: 1906 Annual Undergrad Tuition & Fees (In-State): $6,485
Enrollment: 26,949 Coed
Affiliation or Control: State IRS Status: 501(c)3
Highest Offering: Doctorate
Accreditation: SC, ART, CAATE, CACREP, CAEPN, CAPRT, CIDA, CLPSY, COARC, CONST, CVT, DIETD, DIETI, DMS, HSA, IPSY, MLS, MUS, NMT, NURSE, PH, PTA, RAD, RTT, SP, SPAA, THEA

01 President .... Dr. Kyle MARRERO
05 Provost/VPAA .... Dr. Carl REIBER
10 VP Business & Finance .... Mr. Ron STALNAKER
84 Interim VP Enrollment Management .... Dr. Amy BALLAGH
32 VP Student Affairs .... Dr. Shay LITTLE
111 VP Univ Advancement .... Mr. Trip ADDISON
13 Interim Chief Information Officer .... Ms. Ashlea ANDERSON
09 Director of Institutional Research .... Mr. Chris OLSON
20 Vice Provost .... Dr. Diana CONE
35 AVP & Dean of Students .... Dr. Aileen DOWELL
35 Assoc VP Student Engagement .... Dr. Ken GASSIOT
28 AVP Inclusive Exc/CDO .... Dr. Dominique QUARLES
43 Executive Counsel .... Ms. Maura COPELAND
04 Exec Associate to the President .... Ms. Leigh PRICE
07 Director of Admissions .... Dr. Amy CLINES
58 Dean College of Graduate Studies .... Dr. Ashley WALKER
50 Dean Parker College of Business .... Dr. Allen AMASON
53 Dean College of Education .... Dr. Sharon SUBREENDUTH
76 Dean Waters College of Health Prof .... Dr. Whitney NASH
49 Dean Col of Behavioral/Social Sci .... Dr. Ryan SCHROEDER
49 Int Dean College Arts/Humanities .... Dr. John KRAFT
81 Int Dean Col Science/Mathematics .... Dr. Will LYNCH
54 Dean AEP College of Engineering .... Dr. Mohammad DAVOUD
51 Director Continuing Education .... Dr. Diane BADAKHSH
69 Dean JPH College of Public Health .... Dr. Stuart TEDDERS
08 Dean University Libraries .... Dr. Lisandra CARMICHAEL
88 Dir NCAA Compliance .... Mr. Keith ROUGHTON
116 Chief Auditor .... Ms. Katrina MCNAIR
26 VP Univ Communications & Marketing .... Dr. John LESTER
121 Director Academic Success Center .... Ms. Jessica WILLIAMSON
37 Director Financial Aid .... Ms. Tracey MINGO
06 Registrar .... Ms. Cassie MORGAN
109 Int Assoc VP Auxiliary Services .... Mr. Jeff BLYTHE
21 Assoc VP Finance .... Mr. Justin JANNEY
15 Int Assoc VP Human Resources .... Ms. Vickie SHAW
41 Athletic Director .... Mr. Jared BENKO
18 Assoc VP Facilities .... Ms. Katie TWINING
19 Director Public Safety .... Ms. Laura MCCULLOUGH
36 Director Career Services .... Ms. Caitlyn COFER
38 Director Counseling Services .... Dr. Jodi K. CALDWELL
23 Director Health Services .... Ms. Emily ROGERS
39 Exec Director University Housing .... Mr. Peter BLUTREICH
93 Int Dir Multicultural Student Ctr .... Ms. Laurely CAYCHO
88 Dir Leadership/Outreach .... Ms. Jodi KENNEDY
88 Director Advancement IT .... Ms. Jill GERIG
29 Director Alumni Relations .... Ms. Ava EDWARDS
88 Director Botanic Garden .... Ms. Carolyn ALTMAN
14 Director Technical Services .... Mr. Joey REEVES
88 Director Museum .... Dr. Brent THARP
88 Director Wildlife Educ/Raptor Ctr .... Mr. Steven M. HEIN
96 Director Procurement & Logistical .... Ms. Daphne BURCH
22 Director Equal Opp/Title IX .... Ms. Amber CULPEPPER
89 Asst Director First-Year Experience .... Ms. Brenda RICHARDSON
92 Dean Honors College .... Dr. Steven ENGEL
119 Chief Information Tech Security Ofc .... Vacant
88 Int Dir Centers Teaching/Technology .... Dr. Debbie WALKER
88 Dir Stdnt Affs/Disability Res Ctr .... Ms. Kelly WOODRUFF
102 Director Foundation Acct .... Ms. Tina ADAMS
100 Chief of Staff & External Affairs .... Ms. Annalee ASHLEY
104 Int Dir Global Engage/Study Abroad .... Ms. Kristin KASTING KARAM
108 AVP Institutional Effectiveness .... Dr. Delana GATCH
25 Dir Research Svcs/Sponsored Program .... Vacant
44 Director Annual Giving .... Vacant
86 Director Government Relations .... Ms. Annalee ASHLEY

† Part of the University System of Georgia.

Georgia Southwestern State University (B)

800 GA Southwestern State Univ Dr, Americus GA 31709-4693
County: Sumter FICE Identification: 001573
Unit ID: 139764
Telephone: (877) 871-4594 Carnegie Class: Masters/M
FAX Number: N/A Calendar System: Semester
URL: www.gsw.edu
Established: 1906 Annual Undergrad Tuition & Fees (In-State): $5,464
Enrollment: 3,162 Coed
Affiliation or Control: State IRS Status: 501(c)3
Highest Offering: Beyond Master's But Less Than Doctorate
Accreditation: SC, NURSE

01 President .... Dr. Neal R. WEAVER
10 Vice Pres Business & Finance .... Mr. Jeff HALL
05 Provost/VP for Academic Affairs .... Dr. Suzanne R. SMITH
32 Exec VP Student Engagement/Success .... Dr. Laura D. BOREN
13 Dir Information Technology/CIO .... Mr. Royce HACKETT
41 Athletic Director .... Mr. Mike LEEDER
84 Asst VP for Enrollment Management .... Dr. Gaye HAYES
102 Asst VP Advance/Exec Dir GSW Found .... Mr. Stephen SNYDER
26 Director Marketing & Communications .... Ms. Chelsea COLLINS
20 Associate VP of Academic Affairs .... Dr. Bryan P. DAVIS
08 Dean of the Library .... Ms. Ru STORY-HUFFMAN
49 Dean Arts & Sciences .... Dr. Kelly MCCOY
50 Dean Business & Computing .... Dr. Gaynor CHEOKAS
53 Dean of Education .... Dr. Rachel ABBOTT
66 Dean Nursing & Health Sciences .... Dr. Sandra DANIEL
09 Director Institutional Research .... Dr. Lisa A. COOPER
06 Registrar .... Ms. Krista SMITH
89 Director of First Year Experience .... Dr. David JENKINS
07 Dir of Recruitment & Admissions .... Mr. Jonathan H. SCOTT
37 Director of Financial Aid .... Mr. Michael WRIGHT
39 Director Residential & Campus Life .... Ms. LaToya STACKHOUSE
21 Comptroller .... Vacant
15 Director of Human Resources .... Ms. Gena WILSON
96 Purchasing Director .... Ms. Michelle W. UNDERWOOD
18 Physical Plant Director .... Mr. Jim POSEY
19 Director of Public Safety .... Chf. Michael LEWIS
113 Director of Student Accounts .... Ms. Christy BARRY
24 Technology Services Director .... Mr. Robert SLENKER
91 Director Enterprise Services .... Ms. Beverly CARROLL
105 Network Administrator .... Mr. Dean CRUMBLEY
119 Information Security Officer .... Mr. Andrew JERNIGAN
38 Asst Director of Counseling .... Ms. Alma G. KEITA
29 Alumni Engagement Specialist .... Ms. Angela SMITH
44 Annual Giving Specialist .... Ms. Kim COMER
04 Exec Assistant to the President .... Ms. Terry THORPE

† Part of the University System of Georgia.

Georgia State University (C)

PO Box 3999, Atlanta GA 30302-3999
County: Fulton FICE Identification: 001574
Unit ID: 139940
Telephone: (404) 413-2000 Carnegie Class: DU-Highest
FAX Number: (404) 413-1380 Calendar System: Semester
URL: www.gsu.edu
Established: 1913 Annual Undergrad Tuition & Fees (In-State): $9,286
Enrollment: 36,360 Coed
Affiliation or Control: State IRS Status: 501(c)3
Highest Offering: Doctorate
Accreditation: SC, ACPHA, ADNUR, ART, CACREP, CEA, CLPSY, COARC, COPSY, DH, DIETC, EXSC, HSA, IPSY, LAW, MUS, NURSE, OT, PH, PTA, SCPSY, SP, SPAA, SW

01 President .... Dr. M. Brian BLAKE
05 Provost & VP Academic Affairs .... Dr. Lisa ARMISTEAD
10 Sr VP Finance & Administration .... Dr. Jerry J. RACKLIFFE
12 Dean Perimeter College .... Dr. Cynthia Y. LESTER
46 VP Research/Economic Dev .... Dr. Timothy DENNING
32 SVP Student Engagement Success .... Dr. Allison CALHOUN-BROWN
111 Vice President Univ Advancement .... Mr. Jay KAHN
26 VP PR & Mktg Communications .... Mr. Don HALE
43 University Attorney .... Vacant
49 Dean Arts & Sciences .... Dr. Sara ROSEN
50 Dean Business .... Dr. Richard D. PHILLIPS
53 Dean Education & Human Development .... Dr. Paul A. ALBERTO
66 Dean Nursing/Health Professions .... Dr. Huanbiao MO
69 Dean Public Health .... Dr. Rodney LYN
61 Dean Law .... Ms. LaVonda REED
80 Dean Policy Studies .... Dr. Sally WALLACE
92 Dean Honors College .... Dr. Larry S. BERMAN
08 Dean Libraries .... Mr. Jeff STEELY
58 Dean Graduate Programs .... Dr. Lisa ARMISTEAD
09 Assoc Provost Inst Effectiveness .... Dr. Michael GALCHINSKY
82 Assc Prov International Initiatives .... Dr. Wolfgang SCHLOER
20 Assoc Provost Faculty Affairs .... Dr. Kavita PANDIT
88 Assistant Provost Admin Operations .... Mr. Christopher D. HILL
45 Assoc VP Research Integrity .... Dr. Brenda J. CHAPMAN
13 Chief Innovation Officer for IT .... Mr. Phil VENTIMIGLIA
18 Assoc VP Facilities .... Mr. Ramesh VAKAMUDI
21 Assoc VP Finance & Comptroller .... Mr. Bruce R. SPRATT
88 Assoc VP Central Development .... Ms. Tabatha MICHEL
102 Assoc VP GSU Foundation .... Mr. Dale J. PALMER
35 Dean of Students .... Ms. Lanette BROWN
37 Assoc VP Student Financial Svcs .... Mr. James BLACKBURN
27 Assoc VP Public Relations/Marketing .... Ms. Andrea JONES
07 Asst VP Undergraduate Admissions .... Mr. Scott M. BURKE
124 Asst VP Student Retention .... Dr. Allison CALHOUN-BROWN
29 Asst VP Alumni Relations .... Ms. Christina C. MILLION
15 AVP/Chief Human Resources Ofcr .... Ms. Ann WILLIAMSON
22 Asst VP Opp Dev/Diversity Educ .... Vacant
19 Asst VP/Chief University Police .... Mr. Joseph SPILLANE
06 Registrar .... Ms. Tarrah N. MIRUS
121 Exec Director Student Success .... Dr. Timothy M. RENICK
85 Dir Intl Students/Scholars Svcs .... Ms. Heather L. HOUSLEY
39 Director University Housing .... Ms. Shannon COREY
38 Director Psychological & Health Svc .... Dr. Jill LEE-BARBER
28 Director Diversity Programs .... Mr. John R. DAY
88 Director Application Engineering .... Mr. John M. BANDY, JR.
36 Director University Career Svcs .... Ms. Catherine NEINER
96 Dir of Business Services/Purchasing .... Mr. Michael E. DAVIDSON
116 Dir Univ Auditing & Advisory Svcs .... Ms. Wanda L. RILEY
117 Director Emergency Management .... Mr. Keith P. SUMAS

31 Sr Director Govt/Community Affairs .... Ms. Julie M. KERLIN
41 Athletic Director .... Mr. Charles G. COBB
04 Assistant to the President .... Ms. Ethel B. WRIGHT

† Part of the University System of Georgia.

Gordon State College (D)

419 College Dr., Barnesville GA 30204-1746
County: Lamar FICE Identification: 001575
Unit ID: 139968
Telephone: (678) 359-5555 Carnegie Class: Bac/Assoc-Mixed
FAX Number: (678) 359-5080 Calendar System: Semester
URL: www.gordonstate.edu
Established: 1852 Annual Undergrad Tuition & Fees (In-State): $3,789
Enrollment: 3,231 Coed
Affiliation or Control: State IRS Status: 501(c)3
Highest Offering: Baccalaureate
Accreditation: SC, ADNUR, NUR

01 President .... Dr. Kirk NOOKS
05 Provost & VP Academic Affairs .... Dr. Jeffery KNIGHTON
10 VP Finance and Administration .... Vacant
32 VP Enrollment Mgmt/Student Affairs .... Vacant
111 VP Institutional Advancement .... Ms. Montrese ADGER FULLER
20 Asst VP Innovative Education and SI .... Dr. Ric CALHOUN
08 Library Director .... Ms. Angiah DAVIS
09 Director of Institutional Research .... Mr. Britt LIFSEY
49 Dean School of Arts & Sciences .... Dr. Barry KICKLIGHTER
53 Dean School of Education .... Dr. Joseph JONES
66 Dean School of Nursing .... Dr. Victor VILCHIZ
121 Assistant VP Academic Excellence .... Vacant
21 Controller .... Ms. Felicia JESTER
15 Director of Human Resources .... Ms. Madelyn BROWN
113 Bursar .... Ms. Candice BROWN
114 Dir of Budgets & Aux Operations .... Vacant
18 Director of Facilities .... Mr. Reggie HAMM
37 Senior Director of Financial Aid .... Mrs. Jody DEFORE
13 Director of Information Technology .... Vacant
19 Director of Public Safety .... Vacant
41 Athletic Director .... Dr. Tonya MOORE
38 Director of Counseling Services .... Ms. Alicia DORTON
39 Director of Residence Life .... Ms. Tonya R. COLEMAN
35 Director of Student Activities .... Ms. Brienne MCDANIEL
06 Registrar .... Mrs. Kristi HAYES
30 Development Officer .... Vacant
26 Chief Public Information Officer .... Vacant
40 Bookstore Manager .... Ms. Teresa THOMPSON
04 Special Assistant to the President .... Ms. LaSha SANDERS
07 Director of Admissions .... Vacant
103 Director of Career Services .... Dr. Tonya MOORE
29 Alumni & Annual Fund Administrator .... Vacant

† Part of the University System of Georgia.

Gupton Jones College of Funeral Service (E)

5141 Snapfinger Woods Drive, Decatur GA 30035-4022
County: DeKalb FICE Identification: 010771
Unit ID: 139995
Telephone: (770) 593-2257 Carnegie Class: Spec 2-yr-A&S
FAX Number: (770) 593-1891 Calendar System: Quarter
URL: www.gupton-jones.edu
Established: 1920 Annual Undergrad Tuition & Fees: $11,970
Enrollment: 266 Coed
Affiliation or Control: Independent Non-Profit IRS Status: 501(c)3
Highest Offering: Associate Degree
Accreditation: FUSER

01 President .... Ms. Hope IGLEHART
05 Campus Dean .... Mr. Mark PALUMBO

Gwinnett College (F)

4230 Highway 29, Suite 11, Lilburn GA 30047-3447
County: Gwinnett FICE Identification: 025830
Unit ID: 140003
Telephone: (770) 381-7200 Carnegie Class: Assoc/HVT-High Non
FAX Number: (770) 381-0454 Calendar System: Other
URL: www.gwinnettcollege.com
Established: 1976 Annual Undergrad Tuition & Fees: $9,925
Enrollment: 225 Coed
Affiliation or Control: Proprietary IRS Status: Proprietary
Highest Offering: Associate Degree
Accreditation: ACICS

01 President .... Mr. Michael DAVIS
11 Campus Director .... Ms. Lisa MCLARIO
05 Director of Education .... Mr. Travis EACONA

Gwinnett College-Sandy Springs (G)

6690 Roswell Rd, NE, Ste 2200, Sandy Springs GA 30328
County: Fulton FICE Identification: 034183
Unit ID: 425250
Telephone: (770) 457-2021 Carnegie Class: Not Classified
FAX Number: (404) 574-2234 Calendar System: Other
URL: www.risingspirit.edu
Established: 1994 Annual Undergrad Tuition & Fees: N/A
Enrollment: 114 Coed
Affiliation or Control: Proprietary IRS Status: Proprietary
Highest Offering: Associate Degree

Accreditation: ACCSC

01 Campus Director .... Mr. Ty DAVIS

Gwinnett College-Marietta (A)

1130 North Chase Parkway, Suite 100, Marietta GA 30067
County: Cobb FICE Identification: 038044
Unit ID: 444714
Telephone: (770) 859-9779 Carnegie Class: Spec 2-yr-Health
FAX Number: (770) 859-9778 Calendar System: Quarter
URL: https://www.gwinnettcollege.edu/
Established: Annual Undergrad Tuition & Fees: N/A
Enrollment: 274 Coed
Affiliation or Control: Proprietary IRS Status: Proprietary
Highest Offering: Associate Degree
Accreditation: COE

01 President .... Mr. Lenny DAVIS
11 Campus Director .... Mr. Keith CRAVENS

Gwinnett Technical College (B)

5150 Sugarloaf Parkway, Lawrenceville GA 30043-5702
County: Gwinnett FICE Identification: 022884
Unit ID: 140012
Telephone: (770) 962-7580 Carnegie Class: Assoc/HVT-Mix Trad/Non
FAX Number: (770) 962-7985 Calendar System: Semester
URL: www.gwinnetttech.edu
Established: 1984 Annual Undergrad Tuition & Fees (In-State): $3,236
Enrollment: 8,576 Coed
Affiliation or Control: State IRS Status: 501(c)3
Highest Offering: Associate Degree
Accreditation: SC, ACFEI, ADNUR, CAHIIM, COARC, CONST, CVT, DA, DMS, EMT, MAC, NAEYC, RAD, SURGT

01 President .... Dr. D. Glen CANNON
05 VP of Academic Affairs .... Ms. Rebecca ALEXANDER
111 VP of Inst Advancement .... Mr. Charles MCKINNON
32 VP of Student Affairs .... Dr. Kohle PAUL
103 VP Economic Development .... Mr. Melvin EVERSON
13 VP Technology & Operations .... Mr. Galen MARTIN
15 VP of Human Resources .... Ms. LaShanta' COX
53 VP of Adult Education .... Ms. Stephanie ROOKS
11 VP Administrative Services .... Ms. Sonya MCDANIEL
19 Chief of Campus Police & Security .... Ms. Sandra PRYOR
84 Exec Dir Enrollment Processing ... Ms. Betsy HARRIS-BRACKETT
07 Exec Dir Enrollment Support .... Ms. Janelle PIERCE
08 Director of Library Services .... Ms. Deborah GEORGE
09 Exec Dir Inst Research/Effective .... Mr. William CRISSMAN
36 Director of Career Services .... Ms. Ave MILLER
37 Executive Director of Financial Aid .... Ms. Felicia AILSTER
06 Registrar .... Mr. Brad THOMAS
04 Exec Assistant to the President .... Ms. Melissa FLANAGAN

Helms College (C)

5171 Eisenhower Pkwy, Macon GA 31206-5309
County: Bibb FICE Identification: 042064
Unit ID: 481155
Telephone: (478) 471-4394 Carnegie Class: Spec 2-yr-A&S
FAX Number: N/A Calendar System: Quarter
URL: helms.edu
Established: 2007 Annual Undergrad Tuition & Fees: $13,460
Enrollment: 280 Coed
Affiliation or Control: Independent Non-Profit IRS Status: 501(c)3
Highest Offering: Associate Degree
Accreditation: CNCE

01 President .... Mr. James STIFF
05 Director of Education .... Mr. Bill DINDY
84 Vice Pres Enrollment Management .... Mr. Andrew ROBINSON
06 Registrar .... Ms. Freda GAINES
07 Sr Admissions Manager .... Ms. Ariel SMITH
36 Vice Pres Career Services .... Ms. Leah PONTANI
88 VP Hospitality Education .... Mr. Bruce OZGA

Herzing University (D)

50 Hurt Plaza SE, Suite 400, Atlanta GA 30303
Telephone: (404) 816-4533 FICE Identification: 020897
Accreditation: &HLC, NURSE

† Regional accreditation is carried under the parent institution in Madison, WI.

Hudson Taylor University (E)

2855 Rolling Pin Lane, Suwanee GA 30024
County: Gwinnett Identification: 667416
Telephone: (770) 831-8882 Carnegie Class: Not Classified
FAX Number: N/A Calendar System: Semester
URL: hudsontayloruniversity.org
Established: 2013 Annual Undergrad Tuition & Fees: N/A
Enrollment: N/A Coed
Affiliation or Control: Independent Non-Profit IRS Status: 501(c)3
Highest Offering: Doctorate
Accreditation: @BI

01 President .... Dr. David J. BREWER

Interactive College of Technology (F)

5303 New Peachtree Road, Chamblee GA 30341-2818
County: DeKalb FICE Identification: 022843
Unit ID: 138655
Telephone: (770) 216-2960 Carnegie Class: Assoc/HVT-Mix Trad/Non
FAX Number: (678) 287-3474 Calendar System: Semester
URL: www.ict.edu
Established: 1986 Annual Undergrad Tuition & Fees: $10,250
Enrollment: 730 Coed
Affiliation or Control: Proprietary IRS Status: Proprietary
Highest Offering: Associate Degree
Accreditation: COE

00 Chief Executive Officer .... Mr. Elmer R. SMITH
01 President/COO .... Mr. Thomas A. BLAIR
10 Chief Financial Officer .... Ms. Samona ROBERTS
03 Vice President/Campus Dir Chamblee .... Ms. Jo Ann KOCH
12 Campus Director Pasadena Texas .... Mr. Greg WEAVER
12 Campus Dir SW Houston Texas .... Ms. Diane NGUYEN
12 Campus Dir North Houston Texas .... Mr. Lee JONES
12 Campus Director Newport KY .... Ms. Christina JONES
12 Campus Director Morrow GA .... Mr. Greg KOCH
12 Campus Administrator Gainesville GA .... Ms. Sofia LUKAS
88 Senior Administrative Assistant .... Ms. Liesa PEAVY
26 Director of Marketing .... Mr. David COHEN
88 Director of Compliance .... Ms. Christina JONES
04 Administrative Asst to President .... Ms. Karen A. MILLER
06 Registrar .... Ms. Rosalind HOLT
07 Director of Admissions .... Ms. Nicole CARUSO
37 Director Student Financial Aid .... Ms. Nataliya CHORNIY

Interactive College of Technology (G)

2323-C Browns Bridge Road, Gainesville GA 30504
Telephone: (678) 456-0550 Identification: 770533
Accreditation: COE

Interactive College of Technology (H)

1580 Southlake Parkway, Morrow GA 30260
Telephone: (770) 960-1298 Identification: 770534
Accreditation: COE

Interdenominational Theological Center (I)

700 Martin L. King, Jr. Drive, SW, Atlanta GA 30314-4143
County: Fulton FICE Identification: 001568
Unit ID: 140146
Telephone: (404) 527-7700 Carnegie Class: Spec-4-yr-Faith
FAX Number: (404) 527-0901 Calendar System: Semester
URL: www.itc.edu
Established: 1958 Annual Graduate Tuition & Fees: N/A
Enrollment: 285 Coed
Affiliation or Control: Interdenominational IRS Status: 501(c)3
Highest Offering: Doctorate; No Undergraduates
Accreditation: SC, THEOL

01 President .... Rev. Matthew W. WILLIAMS
05 VP Academic & Stdnt Affairs/Provost .... Dr. Reginaldo BRAGA
10 Chief Financial Officer .... Ms. Paula SCOTMAN
111 VP Institutional Advancement .... Ms. Christina ALEXIS
06 Registrar .... Ms. Arlene V. CLARKE
07 Senior Admissions Officer .... Dr. Antonio PROCTOR
42 Chaplain .... Dr. Willie F. GOODMAN
20 Director of Institutional Learning .... Dr. Shontell STANFORD
04 Executive Assistant .... Ms. Brittany SESSIONS
39 Resident Life & Student Experience .... Ms. Angelicia HEATH-MCKENZIE
84 Sr Director of Enrollment Mgmt .Ms. Natasha JORDAN SHIVERS
119 IT Manager .... Mr. Tramane MOULTON

Kennesaw State University (J)

1000 Chastain Road, NW, Kennesaw GA 30144
County: Cobb FICE Identification: 001577
Unit ID: 486840
Telephone: (470) 578-6000 Carnegie Class: DU-Higher
FAX Number: (470) 578-9117 Calendar System: Semester
URL: www.kennesaw.edu
Established: 1963 Annual Undergrad Tuition & Fees (In-State): $6,436
Enrollment: 41,181 Coed
Affiliation or Control: State IRS Status: 501(c)3
Highest Offering: Doctorate
Accreditation: SC, ART, CONST, CSHSE, EXSC, MUS, NURSE, OPE, SPAA, SW, THEA

01 President .... Dr. Kathy S. SCHWAIG
10 VP Finance/Chief Business Officer .... Mr. Aaron HOWELL
108 EVP Institutional Effectiveness .... Ms. Danielle BUEHRER
05 Int Provost/VP Academic Affairs .... Dr. Ivan PULINKALA
111 VP Advancement/CEO Univ Foundation .... Mr. Lance BURCHETT
32 Vice Pres Student Affairs .... Mr. Eric ARNESON
11 Chief Administrative Officer .... Dr. Tricia CHASTAIN
26 VP External Affairs/Chief of Staff .... Mr. Alex MCGEE
27 AVP Marketing/Communications .... Ms. Alice WHEELWRIGHT
103 VP Economic Dev/Cmty Engagement .... Vacant
20 Assoc Vice Provost Academic Affs .... Dr. Marla BELL
20 Assoc Vice Pres for Curriculum .... Dr. Pamela COLE
97 Dean University College .... Dr. Lynn DISBROW
15 AVP Human Resources/CHRO .... Ms. Karen MCDONNELL
13 VP IT/Chief Information Officer .... Mr. Jeff DELANEY
84 Vice Pres Enrollment Svcs .... Ms. Brenda STOPHER
106 AVP Technology Enhanced Learning .... Vacant
88 AVP Strategic Comm/Issues Mgmt .... Ms. Tammy DEMEL
08 Asst Vice Pres for Library Services .... Dr. J. David EVANS
18 Asst Vice Pres Facilities Services .... Mr. Andrew YAKIMOVICH
09 Asst VP Institutional Research .... Dr. Phaedra CORSO
79 Dean Humanities/Social Science .... Dr. Shawn LONG
81 Dean College Science & Mathematics .Dr. Kojo MENSA-WILMOT
53 Dean Bagwell College of Education .... Dr. Cynthia REED
50 Dean Coles College of Business .... Dr. Robin CHERAMIE
76 Int Dean College Health/Human Svcs .... Dr. Scott GORDON
57 Dean College of the Arts .... Dr. Ivan PULINKALA
48 Int Dean Architecture/Constr Mgmt .... Dr. Kathryn BEDETTE
77 Dean Col Computing/Software Eng .... Dr. Jon PRESTON
58 Dean Graduate College .... Dr. Mike DISHMAN
92 Dean Honors College .... Dr. Rita BAILEY
51 Assoc Dean Continuing/Prof Educ ..... Dr. Timothy BLUMENTRITT
54 Assoc Dean of Engineering/Eng Tech .... Dr. Renee BUTLER
80 Dir Sch Government/Intl Affairs .... Dr. Kerwin SWINT
35 Dean of Students/AVP Student Affs .... Mr. Ronald BRIGG
121 Assoc VP/Dir Student Success Svcs .... Vacant
28 Int VP DIE/Chief Diversity Ofcr .... Dr. Sonia TOSON
06 Registrar .... Ms. Ana EDWARDS
91 Exec Dir Enterprise Systems & Svcs .... Vacant
37 Director Student Financial Aid .... Vacant
07 Exec Dir Undergraduate Admissions ...... Ms. Jacqueline QUIROGA
25 Director Procurement & Contracting .... Vacant
88 Exec Dir Internships & Coops .... Ms. Ana BAIDA
41 Director of Athletics .... Mr. Milton OVERTON
29 Director Alumni Relations .... Ms. Jyll KAFER
19 AVP Public Safety/Chief of Police .... Mr. Edward STEPHENS
100 Exec Admin to Pres/Chf of Protocol .... Mr. James TAYLOR
104 Education Abroad Program Coord .... Ms. Nicole MEANOR
105 Dir Web Services/Mobile Development .... Mr. Chris WARD
39 Director University Housing .... Mr. Christopher BRUNO
86 VP of Government Relations .... Ms. Julia AYERS
116 Chief Internal Auditor .... Mr. Jay THOMAS
88 Director of Financial Compliance .... Mr. Robert BRIDGES

† Part of the University System of Georgia.

LaGrange College (K)

601 Broad Street, La Grange GA 30240-2999
County: Troup FICE Identification: 001578
Unit ID: 140234
Telephone: (706) 880-8000 Carnegie Class: Bac-Diverse
FAX Number: (706) 880-8358 Calendar System: Semester
URL: www.lagrange.edu
Established: 1831 Annual Undergrad Tuition & Fees: $32,370
Enrollment: 854 Coed
Affiliation or Control: United Methodist IRS Status: 501(c)3
Highest Offering: Master's
Accreditation: SC, ACBSP, CACREP, NUR

01 President .... Dr. Susanna BAXTER
04 Executive Assistant to President .... Mrs. Lisa CORNELL
05 VP Academic Affairs .... Dr. Brian PETERSON
84 VP of Enrollment Mgmt & Student Exp .... Dr. John HEAD
06 Registrar .... Mrs. Amber BALDRIDGE
41 Director of Athletics & Rec .... Ms. Terlynn OLDS
08 Director of Library Services .... Ms. Kelly ANSLEY
09 Director Inst Effectiveness .... Dr. Carol YIN
36 Director Career Development Center .... Dr. Karen PRUETT
38 Director Counseling Center .... Mrs. Pamela TREMBLAY
20 Associate Provost .... Dr. Maranah SAUTER
39 Director Housing & Student Life .... Dr. Kerry WALLAERT
111 VP of Advancement .... Mrs. Rebecca ROTH NICKS
26 Sr Director Communications/Mktg .... Mr. Dean A. HARTMAN
37 Director Student Financial Aid .... Mrs. Michelle REEVES
110 Director of Development .... Mr. Mark E. DAVIS
29 Director Alumni & Cmty Relations .... Mrs. Martha W. PIRKLE
112 Major Gift Officer .... Vacant
07 Director of Admission .... Ms. Nicole MADDOX
105 Asst Director Communications & Mktg .... Vacant
10 VP of Finance & Operations .... Mr. Jerry FORSTER
21 Director of Finance .... Mrs. Patti D. HOXSIE
15 Director of Human Resources .... Ms. Lucinda MUNCY
18 Manager Facilities/Physical Plant .... Mr. Andrew LOWERY
19 Director of Security .... Mr. Wayne MICHAUX
13 Sr Director Information Technology .... Mr. James BLACKWOOD
42 Director Spiritual Life & Chaplain .... Dr. Adam ROBERTS
106 Director Online Instruction .... Dr. Jon ERNSTBERGER
91 Database Administrator .... Vacant
88 Events Coordinator .... Ms. Tammy ROGERS
122 Coord Fraternity/Sorority Life .... Ms. Alexandria ANDRADE
104 Director Study Abroad .... Ms. Michele RAPHOON

Lanier Technical College (L)

2535 Lanier Tech Drive, Gainesville GA 30507
County: Hall FICE Identification: 005254
Unit ID: 140243
Telephone: (770) 533-7000 Carnegie Class: Assoc/HVT-Mix Trad/Non
FAX Number: (678) 989-3107 Calendar System: Semester
URL: www.laniertech.edu
Established: 1964 Annual Undergrad Tuition & Fees (In-State): $3,666
Enrollment: 5,045 Coed
Affiliation or Control: State IRS Status: 501(c)3
Highest Offering: Associate Degree
Accreditation: SC, ADNUR, CAHIIM, DA, DH, EMT, MAC, PTAA, RAD, SURGT

01 President ... Mr. Tim MCDONALD
103 Vice President Economic Development ... Vacant
05 Vice President Academic Affairs ... Mrs. Donna BRINSON
45 Vice President IE ... Dr. Joanne P. TOLLESON
32 Vice President Student Affairs ... Ms. Nancy BEAVER
10 Vice Pres Administrative Services ... Mr. Les SALTER
13 Vice Pres Information Technology ... Mr. Anthony HARDY
04 Executive Assistant to President ... Ms. Karen MINOR
75 Dean Business/Public Safety/Profess ... Ms. Beth HEFNER
54 Dean Advanced Tech/Engr ... Mr. John DUNBAR
72 Dean of Applied Technology ... Mr. Christian TETZLAFF
97 Dean of General Education ... Ms. Kathy ALDEN
76 Dean of Allied Health ... Dr. Deanne COLLINS
12 Dean of Barrow Campus ... Mr. Chip REYNOLDS
12 Dean of Dawson Campus ... Mr. Troy LINSEY
12 Dean of Jackson Campus ... Mr. Chip REYNOLDS
09 Dir of Institutional Effectiveness ... Mr. Brad GADBERRY
111 Vice Pres Institutional Advancement ... Ms. Lauren TALLEY
07 Director of Admissions ... Ms. Holly BATES
06 Registrar ... Ms. Mandy RICHARDS
37 Director Student Financial Aid ... Ms. Courtney RAY
21 Director Administrative Services ... Ms. Teri AURORA
15 Director of Human Resources ... Ms. Jill CANTRELL
18 Director of Facilities ... Mr. Mike SCHMIDT
36 Career Services Coordinator ... Ms. Sarah CROWE
22 Disability Services Coordinator ... Ms. Allison HAYNES
08 Library Services Director ... Ms. Kathryn S. THOMPSON
19 College Police Chief ... Mr. Jeff STRICKLAND
96 Purchasing Agent ... Ms. Kathy PHAGAN

Life University (A)

1269 Barclay Circle, Marietta GA 30060-2996
County: Cobb FICE Identification: 020748
Unit ID: 140252
Telephone: (770) 426-2600 Carnegie Class: Masters/L
FAX Number: (770) 429-4819 Calendar System: Quarter
URL: www.life.edu
Established: 1974 Annual Undergrad Tuition & Fees: $13,596
Enrollment: 2,761 Coed
Affiliation or Control: Independent Non-Profit IRS Status: 501(c)3
Highest Offering: Doctorate
Accreditation: SC, CHIRO, DIETD, DIETI

01 President ... Dr. Rob SCOTT
125 Chancellor Emeritus ... Dr. Guy F. RIEKEMAN
05 SVP Academic Affairs ... Vacant
10 Exec VP of Finance ... Mr. William JARR
18 Director of Facilities ... Mr. Ignacio MANZANERA
41 Director of Athletics ... Ms. Jayme PENDERGAST
13 Chief Information Officer ... Vacant
88 Dean College of Chiropractic ... Dr. Leslie KING
20 VP for Academic Affairs ... Dr. Jana W. HOLWICK
104 VP Global Initiatives ... Dr. John DOWNES
14 Director Information Technology ... Mr. Thorton MUIR
29 Director Alumni Relations ... Ms. Darcie WALLACE
58 Assoc Dean Grad & Undergrad Studies ... Dr. Michael D. SMITH
88 Assoc Dean College of Chiropractic ... Dr. Michael CLUSSERATH
35 Dean of Students ... Dr. Janna BREDESON
106 Dean Online Education ... Dr. Richard BELCASTRO
23 Associate Dean of Clinics ... Dr. Bernadette LAVENDER
88 Associate Dean ... Dr. Mary Catherine FAUST
81 Chair Basic Sciences ... Dr. Mamie WARE
21 Controller ... Ms. Jo Ann MILLER
101 Board Secretary ... Ms. Nita LOONEY
114 Budget Director ... Ms. Amy MCILVANE
88 Director Student Advocacy ... Ms. Sandra TERRY
15 Director Human Resources ... Ms. Lisa REED
27 Exec Director of Marketing ... Ms. Shelly BATCHER
88 Dir of Student Administrative Svcs ... Ms. Melissa WATERS
08 Director of Library ... Ms. Kathleen WILLIAMS
37 Director Student Financial Aid ... Ms. Jessica MAGAZU
44 Director of Advancement Services ... Ms. Lauren NIELSON
108 Director of Inst Effectiveness ... Dr. Vince ERARIO
09 Director of Institutional Research ... Dr. Howard WRIGHT
06 Registrar ... Ms. Heather HOFFMAN
17 Executive Director Clinic Ops ... Dr. Shayan SHEYBANI
88 Director of Peak ... Dr. John MARKMAN
88 Assistant Dean Liberal Studies ... Dr. Christopher WELLS
121 Director of University Advising ... Ms. Tameka GLASS
121 Director Student Success ... Dr. Lisa RUBIN
88 Director Chiropractic Research ... Dr. Stephanie SULLIVAN
30 Director of Development ... Ms. Erin DANCER
88 Director Academic Support ... Dr. Nicoly MYLES
88 Director Clinics ... Dr. Steven MIRTSCHINK
88 Director CETL ... Mr. William WATSON
88 Director of the Harris Center ... Dr. Krista BOLINE
89 Assistant Dean Student Engagement ... Ms. Jennifer STROBLE
88 Division Chair Clinical Sciences ... Dr. Mark FERDARKO
36 Director of Career Services ... Ms. Susan DUDT
32 VP for Student Services ... Dr. Marc SCHNEIDER
113 Director Student Accounts ... Ms. Phyllis SHROPSHIRE
16 Employee Relations Officer ... Ms. Monica WARD
96 Interim Director of Purchasing ... Mr. Mel BURTON
39 Asst Dean Community Living ... Mr. Andre CLANTON
88 Director Special Events ... Ms. Brenda BOONE
22 Director Disability Services ... Dr. Genelle HANEY
88 Director Sports Information ... Mr. William HUDSPETH
11 VP of Operations ... Mr. John MCGEE
88 Director Clinical Education ... Dr. Melissa LOSCHIAVO
84 VP of Enrollment & Mktg ... Dr. Cynthia BOYD
26 VP of Professional Relations ... Dr. Gilles LAMARCHE
88 Presidential Liaison for Ext Rels ... Dr. Gerald CLUM
88 Chair Chiropractic Sciences ... Dr. Lydia DEVER
88 Asst Dean Natural Sciences ... Dr. Saphronia JOHNSON
88 Director of Post Graduate Educ ... Ms. Kathleen BANNISTER
88 Director Athletics Health Care ... Mr. Christopher MARKIE
88 Asst Dean Sports Health Science ... Dr. Richard WILLIAMS
88 Director Clinical Assessment ... Dr. Stephen PATERNO
88 Director of Training-CCISE ... Ms. Jennifer VALTOS
88 Director of Clinics ... Dr. Joseph FORESE
88 Director GR & UG Enrollment ... Mr. Keith JORDAN
88 Director Clinic Advising ... Dr. Frank SCHWITZ
88 Director Sports Information ... Mr. William MANGUM
84 Director Enrollment Operations ... Ms. Khrystal STANLEY
88 Dir Student Athletic Performance ... Mr. Tommy STUCKY

Luther Rice College and Seminary (B)

3038 Evans Mill Road, Lithonia GA 30038-2454
County: DeKalb FICE Identification: 031009
Unit ID: 135364
Telephone: (770) 484-1204 Carnegie Class: Spec-4-yr-Faith
FAX Number: (770) 484-1155 Calendar System: Semester
URL: www.lutherrice.edu
Established: 1962 Annual Undergrad Tuition & Fees: $8,448
Enrollment: 693 Coed
Affiliation or Control: Independent Non-Profit IRS Status: 501(c)3
Highest Offering: Doctorate
Accreditation: SC, BI, TRACS

01 President ... Dr. Steven STEINHILBER
10 Vice President Financial Affairs ... Mr. Casey KUFFREY
05 Vice President for Academic Affairs ... Dr. Evan POSEY
58 Director Doctor of Ministry Program ... Dr. Ron K. COBB
13 Chief Info Technology Officer (CIO) ... Mr. Ken STOKES

Mercer University (C)

1501 Mercer University Drive, Macon GA 31207-0003
County: Bibb FICE Identification: 001580
Unit ID: 140447
Telephone: (478) 301-2700 Carnegie Class: DU-Higher
FAX Number: (478) 301-2108 Calendar System: Semester
URL: www.mercer.edu
Established: 1833 Annual Undergrad Tuition & Fees: $37,808
Enrollment: 9,006 Coed
Affiliation or Control: Independent Non-Profit IRS Status: 501(c)3
Highest Offering: Doctorate
Accreditation: SC, ARCPA, CAATE, CACREP, CEA, CLPSY, LAW, MED, MFCD, MUS, NURSE, PH, PHAR, PTA, THEOL

01 President and CEO ... Mr. William D. UNDERWOOD
125 Chancellor ... Dr. R. Kirby GODSEY
10 Executive VP for Admin & Finance ... Dr. James S. NETHERTON
26 Sr VP for Mktg Comm/Chief of Staff ... Mr. Larry D. BRUMLEY
05 Provost ... Dr. D. Scott DAVIS
45 Sr VP for Strategic Initiatives ... Ms. Kellie APPEL
111 Sr VP for University Advancement ... Mr. John A. PATTERSON
110 Senior Assoc VP for Advancement ... Mr. Allen S. LONDON
84 Sr VP for Enrollment Management ... Dr. Penny L. ELKINS
43 Interim Sr VP & General Counsel ... Mr. Matthew R. HALL
13 Assoc VP & Chief Technology Officer ... Vacant
41 Director of Athletics ... Mr. Jim COLE
46 Assoc Dean & Sr Vice Prov for Rsrch ... Dr. Wayne C. GLASGOW
108 Vice Provost for Inst Effectiveness ... Dr. Danielle S. BUEHRER
21 Assoc VP for Finance & Treasurer ... Ms. Julia T. DAVIS
18 Assoc Vice President for Facilities ... Mr. Russell VULLO
15 Assoc Vice Pres for Human Resources ... Ms. Candace WHALEY
27 Asst VP for Mktg Communications ... Mr. Matthew R. SMITH
37 Assoc VP for Student Financial Plng ... Ms. Maria A. HAMMETT
32 VP Stdnt Affairs & Dean of Students ... Dr. Doug R. PEARSON
35 Assoc Dean of Student Services ... Dr. Stephen R. BROWN
39 Director of Residence Life ... Mr. Jeff TAKAC
49 Dean College of Liberal Arts & Sci ... Dr. Anita O. GUSTAFSON
61 Interim Dean School of Law ... Ms. Karen J. SNEDDON
67 Dean School of Pharmacy ... Dr. Brian CRABTREE
63 Dean School of Medicine ... Dr. Jean R. SUMNER
54 Dean School of Engineering ... Dr. Laura W. LACKEY
50 Dean School of Business ... Dr. Julie PETHERBRIDGE
73 Dean School of Theology ... Dr. C. Gregory DELOACH
53 Dean College of Education ... Dr. Thomas R. KOBALLA, JR.
66 Interim Dean College of Nursing ... Dr. Tammy D. BARBE
107 Dean Col of Prof Advancement ... Dr. Priscilla R. DANHEISER
64 Dean School of Music ... Dr. Gary G. GERBER
76 Dean Col of Health Professions ... Dr. Lisa M. LUNDQUIST
08 Vice Prov for University Libraries ... Dr. Jeffrey A. WALDROP
42 Univ Minister & Dean of Chapel ... Dr. Craig T. MCMAHAN
06 University Registrar ... Ms. Alba RODRIGUEZ
19 Director of Mercer Police ... Mr. Gary COLLINS
09 Director of Institutional Research ... Ms. Sarah E. MAY
36 Exec Dir Ctr for Career & Prof Dev ... Ms. Kim MEREDITH
38 Dir Counseling & Psychological Svcs ... Dr. Emily PIASSICK
96 Director of Purchasing ... Ms. Lisa J. BUTLER
04 Admin Asst to the President ... Ms. Vonne SHEFFIELD
29 Assoc VP & Exec Dir Alumni Assn ... Ms. Jill H. KINSELLA
86 VP for Government Relations ... Mr. Hugh D. SOSEBEE, JR.
07 Asst VP for Enrollment Mgmt ... Dr. Kelly L. HOLLOWAY
25 Director of Grants & Contracts ... Ms. DeLaine SAMPLES
105 Dir of Digital Communications ... Ms. Jennifer L. FALK
28 Dir of Div/Inclusion Initiatives ... Dr. Ansley A. BOOKER

Middle Georgia State University (D)

100 University Parkway, Macon GA 31206-5145
County: Bibb FICE Identification: 007728
Unit ID: 482158
Telephone: (478) 471-2700 Carnegie Class: Masters/M
FAX Number: (478) 471-2846 Calendar System: Semester
URL: www.mga.edu
Established: 2013 Annual Undergrad Tuition & Fees (In-State): $4,060
Enrollment: 8,404 Coed
Affiliation or Control: State IRS Status: 501(c)3
Highest Offering: Doctorate
Accreditation: SC, AAB, ADNUR, COARC, NUR, OTA, @SW

01 President ... Dr. Christopher BLAKE
05 Provost/Vice Pres Academic Affairs ... Dr. David JENKS
10 Interim VP Finance & Business ... Ms. Amanda FUNCHES
32 VP Student Affairs ... Dr. Jennifer BRANNON
111 VP Univ Advancement/Exec Dir Fdn ... Ms. Mary MCDONALD
20 Assistant Provost ... Dr. Rod MCRAE
20 Associate Provost ... Dr. Deepa ARORA
88 Special Assistant to Provost ... Dr. David FULLER
88 Special Assistant to the President ... Dr. Kevin CANTWELL
100 Chief of Staff/Govt Relations Ofcr ... Ms. Ember BISHOP BENTLEY
84 VP Enrollment Management ... Dr. Stephen SCHULTHEIS
13 Chief Information Officer ... Mr. Geoffrey DYER
43 Dir Legal Services/General Counsel ... Ms. Renee RAINEY
28 Dir Diversity/Inclusion & Equity ... Ms. Jenia BACOTE
26 VP Recruit/Mktg & Chief Mktg Ofcr ... Ms. Cheryl CARTY
15 Exec Dir Human Resources ... Ms. Pamela BOOKER
30 Exec Dir Development & Alumni Affs ... Ms. Julie DAVIS
35 Asst VP Student Affairs ... Dr. Michael STEWART
18 Asst VP Facilities ... Mr. David SIMS
19 Asst VP Risk Mgmt and Police Svcs ... Mr. Shane ROLAND
108 Dir Institutional Effectiveness ... Mr. Chris TSAVATEWA
21 Controller ... Mr. Brian STANLEY
06 Interim Registrar ... Mr. Jed EDGE
113 Bursar ... Ms. Ana EVANS
07 Director of Admissions ... Ms. Margo WOODHAM
29 Director Alumni Relations ... Ms. Natalie RISCHBIETER
41 Interim Director Athletics/Rec ... Mr. Jason WILLIAMS
109 Director Auxiliary Services ... Ms. Millicent PARKE
40 Director Campus Stores ... Vacant
36 Director Student Placement ... Dr. Mary ROBERTS
38 Director Counseling ... Ms. Predita HOWARD
37 Director Financial Aid ... Ms. Lora FOSKEY
09 Director Institutional Research ... Ms. Samantha BOSWELL
08 Director Library Services ... Ms. Tamatha LAMBERT
96 Director Purchasing ... Ms. Amy INGRAM
39 Director of Residence Life ... Ms. Jennifer SHINPAUGH
12 Director of Commuter Campuses ... Dr. Stephen SVONAVEC
121 Director Advising ... Ms. Sandy LITTLE-HERRING
58 Interim Dean of Grad Studies ... Dr. Loretta CLAYTON
88 Dean Aviation ... Mr. Adon CLARK
50 Dean of Business ... Dr. Marc MILLER
53 Dean of Education & Behavioral Sci ... Dr. David BIEK
81 Dean Health & Natural Sciences ... Dr. Tara UNDERWOOD
77 Dean Computing ... Dr. Alex KOOHANG
49 Dean Arts and Letters ... Dr. Mary WEARN
04 Admin Assistant to the President ... Ms. Carey WIMBERLY

† Part of the University System of Georgia.

Miller-Motte College (E)

3128 Deans Bridge Rd, Ste A, Augusta GA 30906
Telephone: (706) 396-8000 Identification: 770710
Accreditation: ACCSC

† Branch campus of Miller-Motte College, Chattanooga, TN.

Miller-Motte College (F)

1800 Box Road, Columbus GA 31907
Telephone: (706) 225-5000 Identification: 770711
Accreditation: ACCSC

† Branch campus of Miller-Motte College, Chattanooga, TN.

Miller-Motte College (G)

175 Tom Hill Sr Boulevard, Macon GA 31210
Telephone: (478) 803-4800 Identification: 770844
Accreditation: ACCSC

† Branch campus of Miller-Motte College, Chattanooga, TN.

Morehouse College (H)

830 Westview Drive SW, Atlanta GA 30314-3773
County: Fulton FICE Identification: 001582
Unit ID: 140553
Telephone: (404) 639-0999 Carnegie Class: Bac-A&S
FAX Number: (404) 681-2650 Calendar System: Semester
URL: www.morehouse.edu
Established: 1867 Annual Undergrad Tuition & Fees: $29,468
Enrollment: 2,152 Male
Affiliation or Control: Independent Non-Profit IRS Status: 501(c)3
Highest Offering: Baccalaureate
Accreditation: SC, MUS

01 President ... Dr. David A. THOMAS
05 Sr VP of Academic Affairs/Provost ... Dr. Kendrick T. BROWN
04 Sr Exec Assistant to the President ... Vacant
04 Exec Assistant to the President ... Ms. Nakia WASHINGTON
116 Chief Audit Officer ... Ms. Undria STALLING
10 SVP Business/Finance & CFO ... Ms. Undria STALLING
11 Sr VP & Chief Administrative Ofcr ... Ms. Karen MILLER

111 VP for Institutional Advancement ... Ms. Monique DOZIER
13 VP of Information Technology & CIO ... Mrs. Kimberley MARSHALL
26 VP Strategic Comm/Chief Mktg Ofcr ... Mr. Jose MALLABO
29 VP Ext Relations/Alumni Engagement ... Mr. Henry GOODGAME
43 VP Legal Affs/GC/Chief Compl Ofcr ... Mrs. Joy WHITE
32 VP Student Svcs/Dean of College ... Mr. Kevin BOOKER
19 Chief of Campus Police ... Chief Valerie DALTON
15 AVP for HR/Chief Compliance Officer ... Mrs. Cassandra TARVER-ROSS
84 VP of Enrollment Management ... Mr. Terrance DIXON
21 AVP & Controller ... Mr. Haskell RUFF
42 Dean Martin Luther King Jr Chapel ... Dr. Lawrence E. CARTER
06 Dean/Registrar ... Ms. Marie BROWN
35 Assoc Dean for Student Services ... Mr. Kevin BOOKER
07 Director Admissions & Recruitment ... Mr. Darryl ISOM
37 Director of Financial Aid ... Mr. Tarik BOYD
09 Dir Inst Research/Effectiveness ... Ms. Sharmyne EVANS
41 Athletic Director ... Mr. Curtis CAMPBELL
85 AVP Advancement/Ldrshp Initiatives ... Dr. Jann ADAMS
38 Director for Student Counseling ... Mr. Steven ALLWOOD
105 Director Web Services ... Ms. Kara WALKER
22 Dir Title IX/Ethics/Compliance ... Ms. Cassandra TARVER-ROSS
39 Sr Assoc Dean Residential Educ ... Mr. DeMarcus CREWS

Morehouse School of Medicine (A)

720 Westview Drive, SW, Atlanta GA 30310-1495
County: Fulton FICE Identification: 024821
Unit ID: 140562
Telephone: (404) 752-1500 Carnegie Class: Spec-4-yr-Med
FAX Number: (404) 752-1027 Calendar System: Semester
URL: www.msm.edu
Established: 1975 Annual Graduate Tuition & Fees: N/A
Enrollment: 665 Coed
Affiliation or Control: Independent Non-Profit IRS Status: 501(c)3
Highest Offering: Doctorate; No Undergraduates
Accreditation: SC, #ARCPA, MED, PH

01 President/Dean ... Dr. Valerie MONTGOMERY RICE
10 Sr Vice Pres Finance/CFO ... Dr. John CASE
43 Sr Vice President/General Counsel ... Mr. Michael RAMBERT
111 Sr Vice Pres of Inst Advancement ... Dr. Bennie L. HARRIS
46 VP/Ex Vice Dean Research/Acad Admin ... Ms. Sandra HARRIS-HOOKER
88 VP Operation at Morehouse Hlthcare ... Dr. Stewart WITHERELL
21 VP Finance/Strategic Financial Plng ... Ms. Katherine NAPIER
100 Chief of Staff/Chief Admin Ofcr ... Dr. Monique GUILLORY
26 Chief Marketing Officer ... Ms. Goldie TAYLOR
15 Chief Human Resources Officer ... Ms. Denise BRITT
102 Assoc VP Development/Advance ... Mr. John WHITE
20 Sr Assoc Dean Educational Affairs ... Dr. Martha ELKS
20 Assoc Dean Faculty Affairs ... Dr. Erika BROWN
86 Exec Director of Government Affairs ... Mr. Daniel DAWES
37 Director Student Fiscal Affairs ... Ms. Cynthia H. HANDY
08 Library Manager ... Mr. Joe SWANSON, JR.
29 Dir Alumni Constituent Engagement ... Ms. Rochelle LINDSEY
07 Assoc Dn Admissions/Student Affairs ... Dr. Ngozi F. ANACHEBE
116 Internal Audit Director ... Mr. Curt MENCER
22 Interim Chief Compliance Officer ... Ms. Alecia BELL
13 Chief Information Officer ... Mr. Reginald BRINSON
06 Registrar ... Ms. Angela FREEMAN
19 Dir Public Safety/Chief of Police ... Mr. Joseph CHEVALIER, JR.
09 Director of Institutional Research ... Ms. Grace SUN
18 Director of Facilities ... Mr. Michael FLOOD

Morris Brown College (B)

643 Martin Luther King Jr Drive, Atlanta GA 30314
County: Fulton Identification: 667423
Telephone: (404) 458-6085 Carnegie Class: Not Classified
FAX Number: N/A Calendar System: Semester
URL: morrisbrown.edu
Established: 1881 Annual Undergrad Tuition & Fees: N/A
Enrollment: N/A Coed
Affiliation or Control: Independent Non-Profit IRS Status: 501(c)3
Highest Offering: Baccalaureate
Accreditation: TRACS

01 President ... Dr. Kevin E. JAMES
05 Provost/SVP Academic Affairs ... Dr. Anthony B. JOHNSON
10 Chief Financial Officer ... Ms. Shermanetta CARTER
06 Registrar ... Mr. Donovan MCKELVEY
15 Director Human Resources/Facilities ... Mr. Jerome ROWLAND

North Georgia Technical College (C)

PO Box 65, Clarkesville GA 30523-0065
County: Habersham FICE Identification: 005619
Unit ID: 140678
Telephone: (706) 754-7700 Carnegie Class: Assoc/HVT-Mix Trad/Non
FAX Number: (706) 754-7777 Calendar System: Semester
URL: www.northgatech.edu
Established: 1943 Annual Undergrad Tuition & Fees (In-State): $3,022
Enrollment: 2,548 Coed
Affiliation or Control: State IRS Status: 501(c)3
Highest Offering: Associate Degree
Accreditation: SC, ACFEI, ADNUR, EMT, MAC, MLTAD

01 President ... John WILKINSON
05 Vice President for Academic Affairs ... Mindy GLANDER
32 Vice President for Student Affairs ... Dr. Vinson BURDETTE
11 Exec VP Administrative Services ... Dr. Michele SHIRLEY
30 VP of Economic Development ... Leslie MCFARLIN
26 VP Inst Advancement & Marketing ... Amy HULSEY
15 Human Resources Director ... Beth HAMMOND
18 Chief Facilities/Physical Plant ... Bryan HARTZOG
19 Chief of Campus Police ... David SAVAGE
111 Institutional Advancement Coord ... Leigh FOWLER
35 Campus Life Director ... Sherry SEAL
07 Director of Admissions ... Mallory HICKS
37 Financial Aid Director ... Audra JIMENEZ
20 Dean for Academic Affairs ... Michelle LIKINS
108 Institutional Effectiveness Dir ... Janet LOVELL
20 Dean for Academic Affairs ... Michelle OGLESBY
20 Dean for Academic Affairs ... Christy BIVINS
106 Education Technology Specialist ... Samantha MARCHANT
06 Registrar ... Kelsey MCINTIRE
13 Information Technology Director ... Savonda TURNER
96 Purchasing Specialist ... Jerri BEASLEY
08 Chief Library Officer ... Jamie WILKES

Oconee Fall Line Technical College-North Campus (D)

1189 Deepstep Road, Sandersville GA 31082-9337
County: Washington FICE Identification: 031555
Unit ID: 420431
Telephone: (478) 553-2050 Carnegie Class: Assoc/HVT-Mix Trad/Non
FAX Number: (478) 553-2118 Calendar System: Semester
URL: www.oftc.edu
Established: 1996 Annual Undergrad Tuition & Fees (In-State): $3,072
Enrollment: 1,835 Coed
Affiliation or Control: State IRS Status: 501(c)3
Highest Offering: Associate Degree
Accreditation: SC

01 President ... Ms. Erica HARDEN
05 Vice Pres Academic Affairs ... Ms. Michelle STRICKLAND
10 Vice Pres Administrative Services ... Ms. Rosemary SELBY
30 Vice Pres Economic Development ... Ms. Kim DAVID
32 Vice Pres Student Affairs ... Dr. Saketha ADAMS
49 Dean Arts & Sciences/Business Svcs ... Ms. Michele STRICKLAND
06 Registrar ... Ms. Jennifer THIGPEN
07 Admissions Assistant ... Ms. Tracey DARRISAW
15 Director Human Resources ... Ms. Lynn MCDONALD
21 Director of Administrative Services ... Ms. Penny KITCHENS
18 Director Facilities/Physical Plant ... Mr. Jim HARRISON
37 Financial Aid Manager ... Ms. Lori PARNELL
28 Dir of Spec Populations/Stdnt Life ... Ms. Susan HAMMOCK

Oconee Fall Line Technical College-South Campus (E)

560 Pinehill Road, Dublin GA 31021-1599
County: Laurens FICE Identification: 022795
Telephone: (478) 275-6589 Carnegie Class: Not Classified
FAX Number: (478) 275-6642 Calendar System: Semester
URL: www.oftc.edu
Established: 1984 Annual Undergrad Tuition & Fees (In-State): N/A
Enrollment: N/A Coed
Affiliation or Control: State IRS Status: 501(c)3
Highest Offering: Associate Degree
Accreditation: SC, COARC, DMS, MAC, RAD

01 President ... Ms. Erica I. HARDEN
05 Vice President of Academic Affairs ... Ms. Michelle STRICKLAND
09 VP Inst Effectiveness/Plng/Research ... Dr. Katie DAVIS
32 Dean Student Affairs ... Mr. Jay MULLIS
06 Registrar ... Ms. Jennifer THIGPEN
18 Director Facilities ... Mr. Ragan GREEN
111 Exec Dir Institutional Advancement ... Ms. Kathy AARON
76 Dean Allied Health/Prof Svcs ... Ms. Tammy BAYTO
37 Asst Director Financial Aid ... Ms. Teresa CRAFTON
08 Director Library Services ... Mr. Ben MULLIS
07 Admissions Assistant South ... Ms. Kimberly YOUNG
36 Coord Career Services ... Ms. Saketta BROWN
19 Coord Safety/Security ... Mr. Mark ROGERS
15 Director Human Resources ... Ms. Lynn J. MCDONALD

Ogeechee Technical College (F)

One Joseph E. Kennedy Boulevard, Statesboro GA 30458-8049
County: Bulloch FICE Identification: 030300
Unit ID: 366465
Telephone: (912) 681-5500 Carnegie Class: Assoc/HVT-Mix Trad/Non
FAX Number: (912) 486-7704 Calendar System: Semester
URL: www.ogeecheetech.edu
Established: 1986 Annual Undergrad Tuition & Fees (In-State): $3,140
Enrollment: 2,153 Coed
Affiliation or Control: State IRS Status: 170(c)1
Highest Offering: Associate Degree
Accreditation: SC, CAHIIM, DA, DMS, FUSER, MAC, OPD, RAD

01 President ... Ms. Lori S. DURDEN
04 Exec Assistant to the President ... Ms. Karen MOBLEY
05 Exec VP Academic & Student Affairs ... Dr. Ryan FOLEY
103 Vice President Economic Development ... Ms. Jan MOORE
108 VP Institutional Effectiveness ... Dr. Brandy TAYLOR
10 Vice President for Administration ... Ms. Eyvonne HART
13 VP Technology & Institutional Supp ... Mr. Jeff DAVIS
111 VP for College Advancement ... Ms. Michelle DAVIS
09 Director for Inst Research & Plng ... Ms. Kathryn FINCH
08 Director for Library Services ... Ms. Lisa LANIER
07 Director for Admissions ... Ms. Molly BICKERTON
06 Registrar ... Ms. Erica GRIFFIN
37 Director for Financial Aid ... Ms. Kristie SANDERS
15 Director for Human Resources ... Ms. Desire ALEXANDER
109 Exec Director Auxiliary Services ... Mr. J.J ALTMAN
18 Director for Plant Operations ... Mr. Charlie COLLINS
19 Director for Campus Safety ... Mr. Ryan MCNEAL
20 Dean for Academic Affairs ... Ms. Leanne ROBINSON
97 Senior Academic Dean ... Ms. Jennifer WITHERINGTON
20 Dean for Academic Affairs ... Mr. Neal OWENS
21 Asst VP for Administration ... Ms. Tonya VICKERS
55 Dean of Adult Education ... Ms. Samantha SMITH
35 Assistant VP for Student Affairs ... Ms. Christy RIKARD
36 Director for Career Placement ... Ms. Cindy PHILLIPS
51 Director for Continuing Education ... Ms. Dawn OLIVER
26 Exec Director for Public Relations ... Mr. Sean PAYNE
25 Director for Grants/Contracts ... Ms. Angie MCGLAMERY

Oglethorpe University (G)

4484 Peachtree Road, NE, Atlanta GA 30319-2797
County: DeKalb FICE Identification: 001586
Unit ID: 140696
Telephone: (404) 261-1441 Carnegie Class: Bac-A&S
FAX Number: N/A Calendar System: Semester
URL: www.oglethorpe.edu
Established: 1835 Annual Undergrad Tuition & Fees: $41,160
Enrollment: 1,452 Coed
Affiliation or Control: Independent Non-Profit IRS Status: 501(c)3
Highest Offering: Baccalaureate
Accreditation: SC

01 President ... Dr. Nicholas LADANY
05 Provost/VP Academic Affairs ... Dr. Kathryn MCCLYMOND
10 VP for Business & Finance/CFO ... Mr. Pete STOBIE
111 Vice Pres for Advancement ... Dr. Juan MCGRUDER
84 VP Enroll/Dean Fin Aid/Admissions ... Ms. Whitney LEWIS
26 VP Marketing/Communications ... Vacant
32 VP for Student Affairs ... Dr. Meredith RAIMONDO
20 Assistant Provost ... Mr. Brian COLDREN
04 Exec Assistant to the President ... Ms. Colleen DONALDSON
08 Int Univ Librarian/Library Director ... Mr. Eli ARNOLD
06 Registrar ... Mr. Brian COLDREN
09 VP for Institutional Research/Plng ... Dr. Carolyn MATA
41 Athletic Director ... Mr. Todd BROOKS
37 Director of Financial Aid ... Mr. Chris SUMMERS
39 Asst Director of Residence Life ... Mr. Blake PETTY
21 Director of Finance/Controller ... Mr. Mark BERGER
13 Chief Information Officer ... Ms. Tanya THOMPSON
27 Dir University Communications ... Ms. Renee VARY KEELE
29 Director of Alumni/Donor Relations ... Ms. Mary RINALDI WINN
36 Director of Career Development ... Ms. Erin SHERRILL
44 Director of Donor Relations ... Ms. Barb HENRY
15 Director Human Resources ... Ms. Sandy BUTLER
31 Director A_LAB for Civic Engagement ... Ms. Beth CONCEPCION
18 Director Facilities/Physical Plant ... Mr. Lance KNIGHT
40 Bookstore Manager ... Ms. Kathleen GUY

Pacific College of Technology (H)

3510 DeKalb Technology Parkway, Atlanta GA 30340
County: DeKalb Identification: 667239
Telephone: (770) 559-0580 Carnegie Class: Not Classified
FAX Number: (770) 609-6850 Calendar System: Quarter
URL: www.pacifictech.edu
Established: 1999 Annual Undergrad Tuition & Fees: N/A
Enrollment: N/A Coed
Affiliation or Control: Proprietary IRS Status: Proprietary
Highest Offering: Associate Degree
Accreditation: TRACS

01 President ... Mr. Alain GALLIE
05 Chief Academic Officer ... Dr. Jilou KODJO

Paine College (I)

1235 Fifteenth Street, Augusta GA 30901-3182
County: Richmond FICE Identification: 001587
Unit ID: 140720
Telephone: (706) 821-8200 Carnegie Class: Bac-A&S
FAX Number: (706) 821-8373 Calendar System: Semester
URL: www.paine.edu
Established: 1882 Annual Undergrad Tuition & Fees: $14,595
Enrollment: 189 Coed
Affiliation or Control: Multiple Protestant Denominations
IRS Status: 501(c)3
Highest Offering: Baccalaureate
Accreditation: TRACS

01 President ... Dr. Cheryl EVANS JONES
04 Admin Asst President's Office ... Ms. Whitney WASHINGTON
05 Acting VP Academic Affairs ... Dr. Marci MIDDLETON
10 VP Administrative & Fiscal Affs/CFO ... Mr. LeRoy SUMMERS, JR.
111 VP Institutional Advancement ... Ms. Helene T. CARTER
32 Vice President of Student Affairs ... Vacant
42 Campus Pastor ... Dr. Luther FELDER
41 Director of Athletics ... Mrs. Selina KOHN
50 Chair Business Dept ... Dr. Okoroafor NZEH
79 Chair Humanities Dept ... Dr. Nancy BOOKHART
81 Chair Math/Science/Tech Dept ... Vacant

60 Chair Media Studies Dept .... Ms. Amesha ARNOLD
83 Interim Chair Social Sciences Dept .... Dr. Elias E. ETINGE
09 Dir Inst Research/Assessment & Eval ..... Mrs. Alice M. SIMPKINS
08 Director Library/LRC .... Mrs. Alana LEWIS
06 Registrar .... Mrs. Symphoni WIGGINS
36 Director Career Services .... Mrs. April EWING
38 Dir Counseling & Wellness Ctr .... Ms. Jenease HORSTEAD
39 Residence Life Coordinator .... Mrs. Shelia PAIGE
19 Chief of Police .... Chief Jessica BROWN
13 Interim Dir Information Technology .... Mr. Jeffrey OWENS
37 Director of Financial Aid .... Ms. Consuelo QUINN BUSSEY
15 Coordinator Human Resources .... Mrs. Troyline GRIFFIN
29 Director Alumni Relations .... Vacant
26 Dir Communications & Marketing .... Vacant
25 Dir Sponsored Prog/Title III .... Mrs. April EWING
108 Dir of Assessment/Evaluation .... Vacant
24 Info Tech Mgr Learning Resources .... Mrs. Rosa L. MARTIN
07 Admissions Coordinator .... Mrs. Felicia FENNER
88 Sr Women's Athletics Administrator .... Ms. Kisha LUCETTE

Philadelphia College of Osteopathic Medicine Georgia Campus (A)

625 Old Peachtree Road NW, Suwanee GA 30024
Telephone: (678) 225-7500 Identification: 770165
Accreditation: &M, &OSTEO, PHAR, PTA

† Branch campus of Philadelphia College of Osteopathic Medicine, Philadelphia, PA

Piedmont University (B)

PO Box 10, Demorest GA 30535-0010
County: Habersham FICE Identification: 001588
Unit ID: 140818
Telephone: (706) 778-3000 Carnegie Class: Masters/L
FAX Number: (706) 776-0701 Calendar System: Semester
URL: www.piedmont.edu
Established: 1897 Annual Undergrad Tuition & Fees: $27,520
Enrollment: 2,350 Coed
Affiliation or Control: United Church Of Christ IRS Status: 501(c)3
Highest Offering: Doctorate
Accreditation: SC, ACBSP, CAATE, CVT, NUR

01 President .... Dr. James F. MELLICHAMP
05 Vice Pres Academic Affairs/Provost .... Dr. Daniel SILBER
10 Vice Pres Administration & Finance .... Mr. Brant WRIGHT
84 Vice Pres Enrollment Management .... Vacant
111 Vice President for Advancement .... Mr. Craig ROGERS
13 AVP of Information Technology .... Dr. Shahryar HEYDARI
04 Exec Assistant to the President .... Ms. Erin FORESTER
32 Dir Transition/Student Success .... Ms. Ineke DYER
07 AVP of Admiss/Undergrad Enrol Mgmt .... Ms. Cynthia L. PETERSON
08 Dean of Libraries/College Librarian .... Mr. Robert GLASS, JR.
06 Registrar .... Ms. Courtney THOMAS
09 Director of Institutional Research .... Mr. Jody ANDERSON
123 AVP Graduate Enrollment .... Ms. Kathleen CARTER
07 Director Undergraduate Admissions .... Ms. Brenda BOONSTRA
37 Director of Financial Aid .... Ms. Cathy NIX
42 Campus Minister .... Rev. Timothy GARVIN-LEIGHTON
15 AVP Human Resources .... Ms. Rose Mariee ALLISON
26 Dir Marketing/Communications .... Ms. Rachel PLEASANT
41 Dir of Intercollegiate Athletics .... Mr. Jim PEEPLES
21 AVP Finance/Controller/Human Res .... Ms. Kristi WILLIAMS
19 AVP Facilities Mgmt/Safety .... Mr. Fred BUCHER
66 Dean School of Nursing/Health Sci .... Dr. Julie BEHR
50 Dean School of Business Admin .... Dr. J. Kerry WALLER
49 Dean School of Arts & Sciences .... Dr. Steven NIMMO
53 Dean School of Education .... Dr. Kelly LAND

Point University (C)

507 West 10th St, West Point GA 31833
County: Troup FICE Identification: 001547
Unit ID: 138868
Telephone: (706) 385-1000 Carnegie Class: Bac-Diverse
FAX Number: (706) 645-9473 Calendar System: Semester
URL: www.point.edu
Established: 1937 Annual Undergrad Tuition & Fees: $21,850
Enrollment: 1,946 Coed
Affiliation or Control: Christian Churches And Churches of Christ
IRS Status: 501(c)3
Highest Offering: Master's
Accreditation: SC, SW

01 President .... Mr. Dean C. COLLINS
05 Chief Academic Officer .... Dr. Stephen WAERS
111 Chief Advancement & Enrollment Ofcr .... Dr. Stacy BARTLETT
124 Chief Student Dev & Retention Ofcr .... Bernard HILL
10 Chief Financial Officer .... Nadeena POWER
19 Chief of Security .... Eric FLOURNOY
15 Director of Human Resources .... Margaret HODGE
20 Vice Pres for Academic Initiative .... Dr. Chris DAVIS
13 Vice Pres for Info Technology .... Bill DORMINY
84 Dean of Enrollment Management .... Rusty HASSELL
121 Dean of Point Academic Support Svcs .... Valarie WILLIAMS
06 Registrar .... Cassidy WITT
37 Director of Financial Aid .... Rachal WORTHAM
113 Director of Student Accounts .... Amanda SCHMIDT
120 Director of Online Learning and Ins .... Kyle MALMBERG
32 Dean of Students .... Laura SCHAAF
26 Director of Communications .... Vacant
29 Director of Alumni and Church Rels .... Tavaris TAYLOR
41 Athletic Director .... Alan WILSON
08 Director of Library Resources .... Adam SOLOMON
09 Institutional Research Manager .... Amanda YANCEY
28 Chief Diversity Officer .... Leonard PHILLIPS

† Formerly Atlanta Christian College

Reformed University (D)

1724 Atkinson Road, Lawrenceville GA 30043
County: Gwinnett Identification: 667247
Unit ID: 490230
Telephone: (770) 232-2717 Carnegie Class: Spec-4-yr-Faith
FAX Number: N/A Calendar System: Semester
URL: https://www.runiv.edu/
Established: 1992 Annual Undergrad Tuition & Fees: $5,360
Enrollment: 168 Coed
Affiliation or Control: Presbyterian Church In America IRS Status: Exempt
Highest Offering: Master's
Accreditation: TRACS

01 President/Founder .... Dr. Jae Sig PARK
03 Vice President .... Dr. Jin O JEONG
05 Dean of Academic Affairs .... Dr. Kaylarge ELOI
07 Director of Admissions .... Dr. Zamira AKOBIROVA
08 Chief Library Officer .... Ms. Na Ryung KIM
10 Chief Financial Officer .... Mr. Tuan N. NGUYEN
85 International Student Advisor .... Dr. Veronica GARCIA
108 Director Institutional Assessment .... Dr. Wilton HEYLIGER
37 Director of Financial Aid .... Mr. Eric WEEMS

Reinhardt University (E)

7300 Reinhardt Circle, Waleska GA 30183-2981
County: Cherokee FICE Identification: 001589
Unit ID: 140872
Telephone: (770) 720-5600 Carnegie Class: Bac-Diverse
FAX Number: (770) 720-5602 Calendar System: Semester
URL: www.reinhardt.edu
Established: 1883 Annual Undergrad Tuition & Fees: $25,228
Enrollment: 1,399 Coed
Affiliation or Control: United Methodist IRS Status: 501(c)3
Highest Offering: Master's
Accreditation: SC, MUS, NURSE

01 President .... Dr. Mark A. ROBERTS
04 Sr Executive Assistant to President .... Mrs. Angela D. PHARR
05 VPAA .... Dr. John D. MILES
10 Chief Financial Officer .... Mrs. Stephanie R. OWENS
32 Dean of Students .... Dr. Walter P. MAY
84 Assoc VP for Enrollment Mgmt .... Mrs. Jennifer PRINE
41 Director of Athletics .... Mr. Jeffrey M. POURCHIER
101 Asst Secretary Board of Trustees .... Mrs. Angela D. PHARR
18 Director of Facilities Management .... Mr. Jeffrey DALE
26 VP for Marketing/Strategic Init .... Dr. Tish SZYMURSKI
13 Director of IT .... Mr. Cabot HOWELL
88 Director of Funk Heritage Ctr .... Mr. Jeff BISHOP
07 Director of Admissions .... Vacant
06 Registrar .... Ms. Janet M. RODNING
09 Director Institutional Research .... Vacant
08 Director of Library Services .... Mr. Joel C. LANGFORD
19 Director of Public Safety .... Mr. Jay R. DUNCAN
42 Coordinator of Spiritual Life .... Mr. Josh GARNER
21 Controller .... Ms. Beverly SMITH
37 Director Student Financial Aid .... Mr. Joseph STEELMAN
15 Director Human Resources .... Ms. Kristy L. DEBORD
39 Director of Residence Life .... Vacant
23 University Nurse .... Vacant
35 Asst Dean of Students .... Mrs. Jamie M. JOHNSTON
38 Director of Counseling Svcs .... Vacant
121 Dean Center for Student Success .... Dr. Melissa S. HICKMAN
36 Dir Vocation & Career Services .... Vacant
40 Bookstore Manager .... Vacant
49 Int Dean School Arts & Humanities .... Dr. Peggy M. MORLIER
81 Int Dean School of Math & Sciences .... Dr. Irma M. SANTORO
50 Int Dn McCamish Sch Bus/Sport Stdy .... Dr. Joseph W. MULLINS
53 Int Dean Price School of Education .... Ms. Tamara J. SMITH
64 Dean School of Performing Arts .... Dr. Fredrick A. TARRANT
107 Dean Sch Professional Studies .... Vacant
66 Dean School Nursing/Health Sciences .... Dr. D. LeAnne WILHITE
108 Director Institutional Effectivenes .... Dr. Linda J. MORGAN
30 Exec Dir Development/Stewardship .... Mrs. Dale S. MORRISSEY

SAE Institute Atlanta (F)

215 Peachtree Street NE, Suite 300, Atlanta GA 30303-1739
Telephone: (404) 526-9366 FICE Identification: 042066
Accreditation: ACCSC

Savannah College of Art and Design (G)

342 Bull Street, PO Box 3146, Savannah GA 31402-6263
County: Chatham FICE Identification: 021415
Unit ID: 140951
Telephone: (912) 525-5000 Carnegie Class: Masters/L
FAX Number: (912) 525-6263 Calendar System: Quarter
URL: www.scad.edu
Established: 1978 Annual Undergrad Tuition & Fees: $38,075
Enrollment: 14,265 Coed
Affiliation or Control: Independent Non-Profit IRS Status: 501(c)3
Highest Offering: Master's
Accreditation: SC, CIDA

01 President .... Mrs. Paula WALLACE
11 Chief Operating Officer .... Mr. Glenn WALLACE
10 Chief Financial Officer .... Mr. J.J WALLER
113 VP for Student Financial Services .... Mr. Scott LINZEY
03 VP for SCAD Savannah .... Mr. Darrell NAYLOR-JOHNSON
05 Chief Academic Officer .... Dr. Gokhan OZAYSIN
43 VP International & Legal Services .... Ms. Hannah FLOWER
112 VP Giving .... Ms. Audra PRICE PITTMAN
84 Sr VP Admission/Student Success .... Dr. Philip ALLETTO
13 Sr VP for Technology/Development .... Mr. Brad GRANT
106 VP for Operations .... Mr. John BUCKOVICH
15 Chief Human Resources Officer .... Ms. Lesley HANAK
09 VP for Institutional Effectiveness .... Ms. Erin O'LEARY
07 VP for Admission .... Mr. Steve MINEO
20 Dean of Academic Svcs Atlanta .... Mr. Dale CLIFFORD
18 Exec Dir of Physical Resources .... Ms. Helen MORGAN
37 Director of Financial Aid .... Ms. Kim BEVERIDGE
07 AVP for Admissions .... Ms. Jenny JAQUILLARD
41 Athletics Director .... Mr. Doug WOLLENBURG
38 Dir Counseling/Student Support Svc .... Ms. Aimee BELLMORE
06 Sr Dir of Registrar Services .... Ms. Sarah MCCARN
88 Dean of School of Building Arts .... Dr. Geoffrey TAYLOR
88 Dean of School Communication Arts .... Mr. Anthony FISHER
106 Dean Sch of Design/Exec Dir eLrng .... Mr. Victor ERMOLI
88 Dean of School of Digital Media .... Ms. Marilynn ALMY
57 Dean of School of Fine Arts .... Ms. Maureen GARVIN
49 Dean Sch Liberal Arts/Library Svcs .... Ms. Kate NEWELL
97 Dean School of Foundation Studies .... Ms. Maureen GARVIN
88 Dean of Entertainment Arts .... Ms. Andra REEVE-RABB
36 AVP for Career & Alumni Success .... Ms. Eleanor TWIFORD
20 AVP of Academic Services .... Mr. Jesus ROJAS
121 Dean of Student Success .... Ms. Leslie MIRANDA
35 Dean of Students Savannah .... Mr. David BLAKE
104 Director SCAD Study Abroad .... Ms. Catherine DUNCAN
39 Assoc Dean/Dir of Residence Life .... Mr. Jason RIGSBEE

Savannah State University (H)

3219 College Street, Savannah GA 31404-5308
County: Chatham FICE Identification: 001590
Unit ID: 140960
Telephone: (912) 358-3004 Carnegie Class: Masters/S
FAX Number: N/A Calendar System: Semester
URL: www.savannahstate.edu
Established: 1890 Annual Undergrad Tuition & Fees (In-State): $5,902
Enrollment: 3,488 Coed
Affiliation or Control: State IRS Status: 501(c)3
Highest Offering: Master's
Accreditation: SC, JOUR, SPAA, SW

01 University President .... Dr. Kimberly BALLARD-WASHINGTON
05 Interim Provost/VP Academic Affairs .... Dr. Sametria R. MCFALL
10 VP Business & Financial Affairs .... Ms. Megan DAVIDSON
32 VP Enrollment Mgmt/Student Affairs .... Mr. Raymond CLARKE
111 Interim VP University Advancement .... Ms. Shalonda MULGRAV
13 Exec Dir Info Technology Svcs .... Ms. Patricia OGDEN
50 Dean College Business Admin .... Dr. Sudesh MUJUMDAR
81 Dean Col Science & Tech .... Dr. Mohamad MUSTAFA
49 Dean Col Liberal Arts/Social Sci .... Dr. David MARSHALL
53 Interim Dean College of Education .... Dr. Cora THOMPSON
07 Director of Admissions for Recruit .... Mr. Brian DAWSEY
15 Chief Human Resources Officer .... Ms. Jacqueline STEPHERSON
08 Librarian .... Mr. Felix UNAEZE
19 Chief of Police .... Mr. Rennie WALTERS
30 Director Advancement .... Ms. Sheri ROUSE-MAINOR
18 Director Facilities/Physical Plant .... Mr. Randall LOWERY
43 Dir Legal Services/General Counsel .... Ms. Flora DEVINE
09 Int AVP Inst Rsrch/Plng/Assessment .... Dr. Jonathan LAMBRIGHT
29 Director Alumni Relations .... Ms. Barbara S. MYERS
37 Interim Director Financial Aid .... Ms. Tracey MINGO
41 Director Athletics .... Mr. Opio MASHARIKI
35 Director of Student Development .... Ms. Jacqueline AWE
06 Registrar .... Ms. Kathleen PLATT
04 Exec Asst to President .... Ms. Lisa SCIPIO
39 Director of Housing .... Mr. Michael SHARPE
100 Chief of Staff .... Vacant
106 Dir Online Education/E-learning .... Vacant
104 Asst Dir International Education .... Ms. Joline KEEVY
84 VP Enrollment Management .... Mr. Raymond CLARKE
38 Director Student Counseling .... Dr. Shawntell PHOENIX-MARTIN
96 Director of Purchasing .... Ms. Alicia WILLIAMS
30 Director of Development .... Mr. Phil COLE
35 AVP Student Affs/Dean of Students .... Ms. Bonita BRADLEY

† Part of the University System of Georgia.

Savannah Technical College (I)

5717 White Bluff Road, Savannah GA 31405-5521
County: Chatham FICE Identification: 005618
Unit ID: 140942
Telephone: (912) 443-5700 Carnegie Class: Assoc/HVT-Mix Trad/Non
FAX Number: (912) 443-5705 Calendar System: Semester
URL: www.savannahtech.edu
Established: 1967 Annual Undergrad Tuition & Fees (In-State): $3,042
Enrollment: 3,649 Coed
Affiliation or Control: State IRS Status: 501(c)3
Highest Offering: Associate Degree
Accreditation: SC, DA, DH, EMT, MAC, SURGT

01	President	Dr. Kathy S. LOVE
11	Vice Pres Administrative Services	Ms. Connie CLARK
05	Vice President for Academic Affairs	Ms. Ashley MORRIS
103	Vice President of Economic Dev	Dr. Brent STUBBS
108	VP of Institutional Effectiveness	Mr. Paul SCOTT
111	Exec Dir Inst Advancement & Comm	Ms. Gail EUBANKS
13	Exec Director Information Tech	Mr. Jamie DAVIS
07	Director of Admissions	Vacant
37	Director of Financial Aid	Mr. Letherio ZEIGLER
06	Registrar	Ms. Regina THOMAS-WILLIAMS
18	Director of Facilities	Mr. Gary STRICKLAND
15	Director Human Resources	Vacant
08	Library Services Director	Ms. Kaitlin DOTSON
26	Director of Communications	Ms. Amy SHAFFER
12	Campus Dean Liberty Campus	Ms. Terrie SELLERS
12	Campus Dean Effingham Campus	Dr. Tristam ALDRIDGE
96	Purchasing Manager	Mr. Kevin CHIEVES
76	Dean of Health Sciences	Ms. Stephanie DERFUS
50	Dean Business and Professional Svcs	Ms. Debra GEIGER
97	Dean of General Studies	Dr. Lonnie GRIFFIN
88	Dean of Industrial Technology	Mr. Daniel KRAUTHEIMER
88	Dean of Aviation Technology	Mr. Tal LOOS
56	Dean of Adult Education	Dr. Jacqueline KORENGEL
88	Military Outreach Coordinator	Vacant
91	Dir of Enterprise Technology Svcs	Ms. Tammy BRANNEN
19	Chief of Police	Mr. Wayne WILLCOX
36	Coordinator of Career Services	Ms. Rachel OBER
88	Student Navigator	Ms. Kelley RIFFE
88	High School Initiatives Coordinator	Ms. Hannah WATSON
22	Special Population Disability Svcs	Ms. Melanie WILDER

Shorter University (A)

315 Shorter Avenue, Rome GA 30165-4298

County: Floyd FICE Identification: 001591
Unit ID: 140988
Telephone: (706) 291-2121 Carnegie Class: Masters/S
FAX Number: (706) 236-1515 Calendar System: Semester
URL: www.shorter.edu
Established: 1873 Annual Undergrad Tuition & Fees: $22,810
Enrollment: 1,410 Coed
Affiliation or Control: Baptist IRS Status: 501(c)3
Highest Offering: Master's
Accreditation: SC, COSMA, MUS, NURSE

01	President	Dr. Donald V. DOWLESS
05	Provost	Dr. John D. REAMS
10	VP of Finance & CFO	Ms. Michelle STRICKLIN
84	Vice Pres Enrollment Management	Mrs. Colleen LASSITER
30	Vice President for Advancement	Dr. Ben BRUCE
32	VP Student Affairs/Dean of Students	Mr. Ken WHITLOW
26	Assoc VP University Communications	Vacant
06	Registrar	Mrs. Bethany BRADY
35	Director of Student Life	Ms. Julia BOLTON
08	Director of Library Services	Ms. Dorothy SMITH
09	Director of Inst Effectiveness	Dr. Earl KELLETT
37	Assoc Director of Financial Aid	Ms. Hannah ROGERS
15	Human Resources Manager	Mrs. Brenda LONG
13	Director of Information Technology	Mr. Jeff BRAMLETTE
38	Director of Student Support Svcs	Ms. Moriah PENDER
23	Director of Student Health Services	Ms. Loretta WILLIAMS
41	Athletic Director	Mr. Richard HENDRICKS
07	Director of Admissions	Mr. Patrick MCELHANEY
39	Dir Residence Life/Student Conduct	Mr. Billy WATSON
40	Bookstore Manager	Ms. Jan PEARSON
57	Dean School of the Arts	Dr. Tara WARFIELD
50	Dean College of Business	Dr. Heath HOOPER
53	Dean School of Education	Dr. Dana KING
66	Dean School of Nursing	Dr. Roxanne JOHNSTON
81	Dean Col of Natural Sci/Mathematics	Dr. Clint HELMS
79	Dean Col of Humanities/Soc Sciences	Dr. Earl KELLETT
73	Chair Dept of Christian Studies	Dr. Brent BASKIN
77	Chair Dept of Mathematics	Dr. Diana SWANAGAN
60	Chair Dept of Communication Arts	Dr. Bill MULLEN
83	Chair Dept of Social Sciences	Dr. Luciana PHILYAW
42	Campus Minister	Rev. David E. ROLAND

South Georgia State College (B)

100 W College Park Drive, Douglas GA 31533-5098

County: Coffee FICE Identification: 001592
Unit ID: 482699
Telephone: (912) 260-4200 Carnegie Class: Bac/Assoc-Mixed
FAX Number: (912) 260-4441 Calendar System: Semester
URL: www.sgsc.edu
Established: 1906 Annual Undergrad Tuition & Fees (In-State): $3,310
Enrollment: 2,028 Coed
Affiliation or Control: State IRS Status: 501(c)3
Highest Offering: Baccalaureate
Accreditation: SC, ADNUR, NUR

01	President	Dr. Ingrid THOMPSON-SELLERS
05	Vice Pres Academic/Student Affs	Dr. Robert PAGE
84	Vice Pres Enrollment Mgmt/Info Tech	Mr. Jimmy HARPER
10	Vice Pres Fiscal Affs/Admin	Ms. Michelle HAM
111	VP Advancement/Govt Rels/Athletics	Dr. Greg TANNER
12	Dir of Waycross Campus/Devel	Mr. Taylor HEREFORD
37	Director of Financial Aid	Mr. Doug TANNER
08	Director of Libraries	Ms. Lynn KELLY
06	Registrar	Ms. Ame WILKERSON
15	Director of Human Resources	Vacant
07	Director of Admissions	Ms. Arlena STANLEY
39	Dean of Students & Housing	Ms. Sandra ADAMS
09	Dir of Inst Effectiveness	Mr. Jim LYNCH
19	Director of Public Safety	Ms. Sonja MCCULLOCH
121	Associate VP Academic Success	Ms. Brandi ELLIOTT
66	Dean School of Nursing	Dr. Jaime CARTER
107	Dean School Arts & Prof Studies	Vacant
81	Dean School of Sciences	Dr. Charles JOHNSON
26	Asst Dir Marketing/Comm/Grants	Ms. Amy HANCOCK
89	Asst Director of Entry Programs	Ms. Joanne JONES
18	Director of Facilities	Mr. Daniel WARREN
124	Director Recruitment/Special Proj	Ms. Jaleen WASHINGTON
40	Bookstore Manager	Ms. Daphne FRENCH

† Part of the University System of Georgia.

South Georgia Technical College (C)

900 South Georgia Tech Parkway,
Americus GA 31709-8167

County: Sumter FICE Identification: 005617
Unit ID: 141006
Telephone: (229) 931-2394 Carnegie Class: Assoc/HVT-Mix Trad/Non
FAX Number: (229) 931-2924 Calendar System: Semester
URL: www.southgatech.edu
Established: 1948 Annual Undergrad Tuition & Fees (In-State): $3,662
Enrollment: 1,814 Coed
Affiliation or Control: State IRS Status: 501(c)3
Highest Offering: Associate Degree
Accreditation: SC

01	President	Dr. John WATFORD
05	Vice President for Academic Affairs	David KUIPERS
10	Vice Pres Administrative Services	Lea COE
32	Vice President of Student Affairs	Eulish KINCHENS
111	Vice Pres Institutional Advancement	Su Ann BIRD
18	Vice President of Operations	Karen WERLING
13	Technology Director	Vacant
84	Dean Enrollment Management	Julie PARTAIN
37	Director of Financial Aid	Kelly EVERETT
20	Dean of Academic Affairs	Dr. David FINLEY
15	Director Personnel Services	Vacant
21	Director of Accounting	Robin BELL
11	Director of Administrative Services	Mark BROOKS
06	Registrar	Kari BODREY
07	Director of Admissions	Candie WALTERS
41	Athletic Director	James FREY
38	Director Student Counseling	Jennifer ROBINSON
32	Asst Vice Pres of Student Affairs	Joshua CURTIN
08	Librarian	Jerry STOVALL
96	Purchasing Agent	Gail CLARY
19	Director Security/Safety	Sammy STONE
04	Admin Assistant to the President	Teresa O'BRYANT
51	Continuing Education Director	Paul FARR
21	Director of Business & Industry Svc	Michelle MCGOWAN
09	Director of Institutional Research	David KUIPERS

South University (D)

709 Mall Boulevard, Savannah GA 31406-4881

County: Chatham FICE Identification: 013039
Unit ID: 139579
Telephone: (912) 201-8000 Carnegie Class: Masters/L
FAX Number: (912) 201-8070 Calendar System: Quarter
URL: www.southuniversity.edu
Established: 1899 Annual Undergrad Tuition & Fees: $17,014
Enrollment: 818 Coed
Affiliation or Control: Independent Non-Profit IRS Status: 501(c)3
Highest Offering: Doctorate
Accreditation: SC, AA, ACBSP, ARCPA, CACREP, MAC, NURSE, PHAR, PTAA

01	Chancellor	Dr. Steven YOHO
12	Campus Director Montgomery Campus	Dr. Kandis STEELE
12	President West Palm Beach Campus	Dr. Mark EVERETT
12	Int President Columbia Campus	Dr. April TAYLOR
12	Campus Director Richmond Campus	Dr. Jason CRITTENDEN
12	President Tampa Campus	Mr. James F. MCCOY, JR.
12	Campus Dir Virginia Beach Campus	Dr. Donald JOHNSON
12	President Austin Campus	Dr. Jeffery MUSGROVE
12	Campus Coord High Point Campus	Ms. Sandy BARKER
12	President Savannah Campus	Dr. Valarie TRIMARCHI
13	Assoc Vice Chancellor Technology	Mr. Dustin BARRETT
88	Vice Chancellor Compliance	Ms. Deanna ECHOLS
10	Vice Chancellor for Finance	Mr. John PAPP
05	Vice Chancellor Academic Affairs	Dr. Brian MCAULAY
20	Assoc Vice Chan Academic Ops	Dr. Frances W. OBLANDER
04	Executive Assistant to Chancellor	Ms. Jocelyn PICCOLO
08	Asst Vice Chanc Univ Library	Ms. Nancy SPEISSER
06	University Registrar	Ms. Toni Lynn DEBORD
86	Director of State Licensing	Ms. Misty BLACKSTON
49	Dean College of Arts & Sciences	Dr. April TAYLOR
50	Dean College of Business	Dr. Cheryl NOLL
76	Dean College of Health Professions	Ms. Gina SCARBORO
66	Dean College of Nursing & PH	Dr. Mable H. SMITH
67	Dean School of Pharmacy	Dr. Dean ARNESON
07	Asst Vice Chancellor of Admissions	Ms. Ashley WEEKS
15	Vice Chancellor of Human Resources	Ms. Lynne HAINES
16	Director of Human Resources	Ms. Cathy GIRARDEAU
32	Vice Chancellor for Student Success	Ms. Alisa KROUSE
18	Director of Facilities	Mr. John BIALOWAS
26	VP Marketing	Mr. Ken BAKER
27	Dir Campus Marketing/Communications	Ms. Jennifer FLATT

Southeastern Technical College (E)

3001 E First Street, Vidalia GA 30474-8817

County: Toombs FICE Identification: 030665
Unit ID: 368911
Telephone: (912) 538-3100 Carnegie Class: Assoc/HVT-High Non
FAX Number: (912) 538-3156 Calendar System: Semester
URL: www.southeasterntech.edu
Established: 1989 Annual Undergrad Tuition & Fees (In-State): $3,127
Enrollment: 1,792 Coed
Affiliation or Control: State IRS Status: 501(c)3
Highest Offering: Associate Degree
Accreditation: SC, ADNUR, DH, EMT, MAC, MLTAD, RAD

01	President	Mr. Larry CALHOUN
05	Vice Pres Academic Affairs	Ms. Teresa COLEMAN
11	Vice Pres Administrative Services	Ms. Denise POWELL
32	Vice President Student Affairs	Dr. Barry DOTSON
84	Director Enrollment Services	Mr. Brad HART
15	Director of Human Resources	Ms. Lanie JONAS
06	Registrar	Ms. Amanda LIVELY
37	Director Financial Aid	Ms. Rebecca ETHRIDGE
36	Director Job Placement	Mr. Lance HELMS
103	Special Populations Coordinator	Ms. Helen THOMAS
40	Bookstore Manager	Ms. Stacy FREEMAN
26	Dir Marketing & Public Relations	Ms. Natalie OSBORNE
08	Head Librarian	Mrs. Leah DASHER
19	Director Security/Safety	Mr. Travis AKRIDGE

Southern Crescent Technical College (F)

501 Varsity Road, Griffin GA 30223-2042

County: Spalding FICE Identification: 005621
Unit ID: 139986
Telephone: (770) 228-7348 Carnegie Class: Assoc/HVT-Mix Trad/Non
FAX Number: (770) 229-3227 Calendar System: Semester
URL: www.sctech.edu
Established: 1963 Annual Undergrad Tuition & Fees (In-State): $3,126
Enrollment: 5,232 Coed
Affiliation or Control: State IRS Status: 501(c)3
Highest Offering: Associate Degree
Accreditation: SC, ACFEI, ADNUR, COARC, CVT, DA, EMT, MAC, PNUR, SURGT

01	President	Dr. Irvin T. CLARK, III
03	Executive Vice President	Dr. Mark ANDREWS
05	Vice Pres for Academic Affairs	Dr. Steve PEARCE
04	Exec Admin Asst to President	Ms. Kim SANTERRE
32	Vice Pres for Student Affairs	Dr. Xenia JOHNS
111	Vice President Advancement	Ms. Barbara Jo COOK
09	Vice Pres Inst Effectiveness	Dr. Chris DANIEL
18	AVP Facilities & Operations	Dr. Alan STANFIELD
06	Registrar	Ms. Monica GREEN
26	Dir Marketing & Public Relations	Ms. Anna TAYLOR
37	Director of Financial Aid	Dr. Michelle BEDFORD
49	Dean Arts & Sciences	Dr. Sean BRUMFIELD
76	Dean Allied Health & ParaMedicine	Ms. Kimberly REGISTER
75	Dean Film/Public Safety/Ind Tech	Mr. Lemuel MERCADO
50	Dean Business/CIS/Prof Services	Dr. Roslyn MCCURRY
84	Assoc Vice Pres of Enrollment Mgt	Dr. Drew TODD
15	Director of Human Resources	Ms. Sharon HILL
35	Director of Student Support Svcs	Ms. Cherryl BURKS
21	Director of Administrative Services	Ms. Stacy ACEY
36	Director of Career Placement & Acad	Ms. Annita WHITE
19	Campus Police Chief	Vacant
13	Chief Information Officer	Mr. Michael SHIVER
08	Director of Library Services	Ms. Denise BARBOUR
106	Dir of Online Education/E-learning	Dr. Jennifer EDWARDS

Southern Regional Technical College (G)

15689 US Highway 19 N, Thomasville GA 31792-2622

County: Thomas FICE Identification: 005615
Unit ID: 487162
Telephone: (229) 225-4096 Carnegie Class: Assoc/HVT-Mix Trad/Non
FAX Number: (229) 225-4330 Calendar System: Semester
URL: www.southernregional.edu
Established: 2015 Annual Undergrad Tuition & Fees (In-State): $3,002
Enrollment: 4,154 Coed
Affiliation or Control: State IRS Status: 501(c)3
Highest Offering: Associate Degree
Accreditation: SC, ADNUR, #COARC, EMT, MAC, MLTAD, RAD, SURGT

01	President	Mr. Jim GLASS
11	Vice Pres Administrative Services	Mr. Ross COX
05	Vice Pres Academic Affairs	Dr. Ron O'MEARA
32	Exec Vice President Student Affairs	Ms. Leigh WALLACE
103	Vice President Economic Development	Mr. Dennis LEE
09	VP Institutional Effectiveness	Dr. Vic BURKE
76	Dean School of Health Sciences	Ms. Carla BARROW
50	Dean School of Bus/Industrial Tech	Ms. Abby CARTER
107	Dean School of Professional Svcs	Ms. Tara RAKESTRAW
49	Dean School of Art and Sciences	Ms. Kathryn KENT
37	Director Financial Aid	Ms. Amy SCOGGINS
26	VP Marketing/Inst Devel/Public Rels	Dr. Amy MAISON
55	Director Adult Education	Mr. Andy SEMONES
07	Director of Admissions	Ms. Wanda HANCOCK
35	Director Student Affairs/Admissions	Ms. Lisa GRIFFIN
06	Registrar	Ms. Lora Beth SHORT

08 Executive Director Library Services ... Ms. Polly SWILLEY
36 Dir Career Services & Counseling ... Dr. Jeanine LONG
15 Coordinator Human Resources ... Mrs. Jennifer SIMPSON
18 Executive Director Facilities ... Mr. George GRIFFIN

Spelman College (A)

350 Spelman Lane, SW, Atlanta GA 30314-4399
County: Fulton   FICE Identification: 001594
Unit ID: 141060
Telephone: (404) 681-3643   Carnegie Class: Bac-A&S
FAX Number: N/A   Calendar System: Semester
URL: www.spelman.edu
Established: 1881   Annual Undergrad Tuition & Fees: $29,972
Enrollment: 2,207   Female
Affiliation or Control: Independent Non-Profit   IRS Status: 501(c)3
Highest Offering: Baccalaureate
Accreditation: SC, CAEPN, MUS

01 President ... Dr. Helene GAYLE
100 Chief of Staff/AVP Govt Relations ... Vacant
05 Interim Provost ... Dr. Dolores BRADLEY BRENNAN
10 CFO & VP Business & Financial Affs ... Ms. Dawn ALSTON
32 VP of Student Affairs ... Dr. Darryl HOLLOMAN
84 Sr VP of Enrollment Management ... Ms. Ingrid HAYES
111 Sr VP of Institutional Advancement ... Mr. Jessie BROOKS
45 VP of IR/Planning & Effectiveness ... Dr. Myra BURNETT
101 Sr VP/Secretary of College ... Dr. Terri REED
13 VP & Chief Info Officer ... Mr. John WILSON
26 VP Public Relations/Communications ... Ms. Lydia SERMONS
88 Executive Dir of Endowment Mgmt ... Ms. Rhonda HONEGAN
114 Director of Budgets & Contracts ... Ms. Asella BRAXTON
21 Controller ... Ms. April AUSTIN
27 Director of Communications ... Ms. Jazmyn BURTON
04 Special Assistant to the President ... Ms. Jarvis RIDGES
88 Dir Office of Civic Engagement ... Ms. Jilo TISDALE
20 Dean of Undergraduate Studies ... Dr. Desiree PEDESCLEAUX
42 Dean of Sisters Chapel ... Dr. Neichelle GUIDRY
06 Registrar ... Mr. John BROWN
07 Director of Admissions ... Ms. Chelsea HOLLEY
29 Director of Alumnae Operations ... Ms. Linda PATTON
37 Director of Financial Aid ... Ms. Lenora JACKSON
36 Director Career Planning/Devel ... Mr. Harold BELL
78 Director of Cooperative Education ... Vacant
15 Director of Human Resources ... Ms. Bernadette COHEN
38 Director of Counseling Services ... Dr. Ave MARSHALL
09 Director of Institutional Research ... Mr. James SANDERS
88 Director of Women's Resource Center . Dr. Beverly GUY-SHEFTAL
18 Director Facilities Mgmt & Svcs ... Mr. Arthur E. FRAZIER, III
19 Director of Public Safety ... Mr. Steve BOWSER
24 Technology Services Coordinator ... Ms. Belinda GRIFFITH
88 Dir of Corporate Rels/Partnerships ... Ms. Cassandra JOSEPH
102 Director of Foundation Relations ... Ms. Eda GARCIA
88 Director of Event Operations ... Ms. Heather HAWES
39 Dir of Housing & Residence Life ... Ms. Alison CUMMINGS
28 Coord Diversity & Inclusion Pgms ... Ms. Letitia J. DENARD
08 Library Director/CEO ... Ms. Loretta PARHAM
23 Director of Health Services ... Ms. Dana LLOYD
46 Assoc Provost of Research ... Dr. Tasha INNISS
35 Dean of Students ... Dr. Bonnie TAYLOR
40 Bookstore Manager ... Mr. Andrew HALL
96 Dir Administrative Support Svcs ... Ms. Jacqueline JAMES
21 AVP Business & Financial Affairs ... Ms. Marissa PACE
105 Asst Dir of Web Communications ... Ms. Ingrid LASSITER
44 Director Annual Giving ... Vacant

Thomas University (B)

1501 Millpond Road, Thomasville GA 31792-7499
County: Thomas   FICE Identification: 001555
Unit ID: 141167
Telephone: (229) 226-1621   Carnegie Class: Masters/M
FAX Number: (229) 226-1653   Calendar System: Semester
URL: www.thomasu.edu
Established: 1950   Annual Undergrad Tuition & Fees: $16,970
Enrollment: 1,303   Coed
Affiliation or Control: Independent Non-Profit   IRS Status: 501(c)3
Highest Offering: Master's
Accreditation: SC, CACREP, MLS, NUR, SW

01 President ... Dr. Andy SHEPPARD
05 Vice President of Academic Affairs ... Dr. John MEIS
32 Vice President Student Life ... Dr. Robert BOHMAN
84 VP Enrollment Management ... Dr. Susan BACKOFEN
08 Director of Library Services ... Ms. Tara HAGAN
30 Director of Development ... Mr. Kurt STRINGFELLOW
06 Registrar ... Mrs. Michelle WENDEL
09 Director of Institutional Research ... Dr. Dañáe JOHNSON
15 Director of Human Resources ... Ms. Christine LYONS
37 Director of Financial Aid ... Mr. Clifton MITCHELL
41 Director of Athletics ... Mr. Rick PEARCE
10 Controller ... Ms. Sue STONE
44 Director of Annual Fund ... Vacant
26 Director of Communications ... Mrs. Cindy MONTGOMERY
04 Assistant to the President ... Mrs. Linda M. HERNDON

Toccoa Falls College (C)

107 Kincaid Drive, Toccoa Falls GA 30598-0068
County: Stephens   FICE Identification: 001596
Unit ID: 141185
Telephone: (706) 886-6831   Carnegie Class: Bac-Diverse
FAX Number: (706) 282-6005   Calendar System: Semester
URL: www.tfc.edu
Established: 1907   Annual Undergrad Tuition & Fees: $21,120
Enrollment: 1,698   Coed
Affiliation or Control: The Christian And Missionary Alliance
IRS Status: 501(c)3
Highest Offering: Master's
Accreditation: SC, MUS, NURSE

01 President ... Dr. Robert M. MYERS
00 Chairman of the Board ... Mr. John W. ALLEN
04 Sr Exec Administrative Assistant ... Mrs. Paula S. ELKINS
32 VP Student Affairs ... Dr. Abigail H. DAVIS
10 Vice President for Finance ... Dr. Dewanna MOONEY
05 VP for Academic Affairs ... Dr. Kieran CLEMENTS
84 VP for Enrollment Services ... Mrs. Emily C. KERR
42 Director Spiritual Formation ... Mr. Jordan BROWN
09 Director Institutional Research ... Ms. Allison FERRON
39 Director Residence/Community Life ... Mrs. Katie THORNE
29 Director Alumni Assoc/Col Relations ... Mrs. Deborah WILKES
106 Dean of Online & Dual Enrollment Ed ... Mr. Andrew THORNE
37 Director Student Financial Aid ... Mr. Donovan SMITH
06 Registrar ... Mr. Kelly G. VICKERS
41 Athletic Director ... Mr. Caleb BARNES
18 Chief Facilities/Physical Plant ... Mr. Merlin SCHENCK
19 Director of Security/Safety ... Mr. Stephen JOHANNES
15 Director Human Resources ... Ms. Mary Kaye RITCHEY
40 Director of Business Services ... Mrs. Allison HOTALEN
66 Dean of Nursing ... Dr. Kristi HENDRIX
11 Associate VP for Operations ... Mr. Merlin SCHENCK
88 Assistant VP Enrollment ... Mr. Ronnie STEWART
08 Head Librarian ... Mrs. Selina SLATE
13 Information Technology Director ... Mr. Mark FERRON
30 Development Officer ... Vacant
121 Director of Academic Success ... Mrs. Nancy HYNDMAN
38 Dir Counseling/Career Svcs ... Mrs. Amy MARSHALL

Truett McConnell University (D)

100 Alumni Drive, Cleveland GA 30528-1264
County: White   FICE Identification: 001597
Unit ID: 141237
Telephone: (706) 865-2134   Carnegie Class: Bac-Diverse
FAX Number: (706) 243-4968   Calendar System: Semester
URL: www.truett.edu
Established: 1946   Annual Undergrad Tuition & Fees: $21,938
Enrollment: 2,923   Coed
Affiliation or Control: Baptist   IRS Status: 501(c)3
Highest Offering: Master's
Accreditation: SC, MUS, NURSE

01 President ... Dr. Emir CANER
05 VP Academic Services ... Dr. Brad REYNOLDS
10 VP Finance/Operations/CFO ... Dr. Jason GRAFFAGNINO
32 VP Student Life & Athletics ... Mrs. Jenni SHEPARD
111 VP Advancement & CSO ... Mr. Martin CARNES
26 VP Marketing & CBO ... Mr. Kevin STERNER
37 Assoc VP Enrollment & Financial Aid ... Mrs. Karli GREENFIELD
21 Assoc VP of Finance ... Mr. Paul WILLARD
88 Assoc VP Enterprise Data Mgmt ... Mr. Truitt FRANKLIN
07 Assoc VP Admissions ... Mr. Stephen PATTON
88 Director of Special Projects ... Mr. David EPPLING
04 Executive Assistant to President ... Ms. Cindy ERBELE
06 Registrar ... Mrs. Kamille GAUNTT
08 Director of Library Resources ... Dr. Phillip NOTT
22 Director of Special Support Svcs ... Ms. Nell HOYLE
18 Director of Facilities ... Mr. Justin COALLEY
09 Director Institutional Research ... Mrs. Melissa FORTNER
15 Director of Human Resources ... Ms. Rachael MEGGITT
86 Director of Public Policy ... Dr. John YARBROUGH
121 Director of Student Success ... Mr. Andrew GAILEY
19 Director of Campus Safety ... Mr. Kerry SEABOLT
120 Director of Online Learning ... Mr. Matthew WAYMACK
84 Director of Dual Enrollment ... Mr. Jerry YANDELL
88 Director of TMU Press ... Mr. Peter LUMPKINS
13 Director of Information Technology ... Mr. Brandon HAAG
39 Director of Student Life ... Mr. Nicolas GREENFIELD
60 Directory Marketing & Communication ... Mrs. Jenny GREGORY
42 Director of Church Relations ... Dr. David DRAKE
88 Director of Events & Grant Writing ... Mrs. Andrea MCCALL
29 Director Alumni Services ... Mrs. Cassandra ABERNATHY
40 Director of Campus Store Operations ... Mrs. Tracy MITCHELL
88 Director of Athletics Mkgt & Comm ... Mrs. Sara HARDEMAN
53 Dean of Education ... Mrs. Julie LUTZ

Underwood University (E)

2855 Rolling Pin Lane, Suite 200, Suwanee GA 30024
County: Gwinnett   Identification: 667361
Telephone: (770) 831-9500   Carnegie Class: Not Classified
FAX Number: (770) 831-8858   Calendar System: Semester
URL: underwooduniversity.com
Established: 2011   Annual Undergrad Tuition & Fees: N/A
Enrollment: N/A   Coed
Affiliation or Control: Independent Non-Profit   IRS Status: 501(c)3
Highest Offering: Doctorate
Accreditation: TRACS

01 President ... Richard S. YOON
05 VP/Chief Academic Officer ... Rev. Howoo LEE
07 Director of Admissions ... Vacant

University of Georgia (F)

Athens GA 30602-0001
County: Clarke   FICE Identification: 001598
Unit ID: 139959
Telephone: (706) 542-3000   Carnegie Class: DU-Highest
FAX Number: N/A   Calendar System: Semester
URL: www.uga.edu
Established: 1785   Annual Undergrad Tuition & Fees (In-State): $12,080
Enrollment: 39,147   Coed
Affiliation or Control: State   IRS Status: 501(c)3
Highest Offering: Doctorate
Accreditation: SC, AAFCS, ART, CAATE, CACREP, CEA, CIDA, CLPSY, COPSY, DANCE, DIETD, DIETI, JOUR, LAW, LSAR, MFCD, MPCAC, MUS, PCSAS, PH, PHAR, PLNG, SCPSY, SP, SPAA, SW, THEA, VET

01 President ... Mr. Jere W. MOREHEAD
100 Chief of Staff ... Dr. Kathy R. PHARR
04 Assistant to the President ... Ms. Sheila J. DAVIS
04 Assistant to the President ... Mr. Alton M. STANDIFER
04 Assistant to the President ... Dr. Nathan MOORE
05 Sr VP Academic Affs/Provost ... Dr. Jack HU
20 Vice Provost Academic Affairs ... Dr. Usha R. RODRIGUES
11 Vice Pres for Finance & Admin ... Mr. Ryan A. NESBIT
30 Vice Pres for Devel & Alumni Rels ... Mr. Kelly K. KERNER
20 Vice President for Instruction ... Dr. Marisa A. PAGNATTARO
46 Vice President for Research ... Dr. Karen J. BURG
88 Vice Pres Public Svc/Outreach ... Dr. Jennifer L. FRUM
32 Vice President Student Affairs ... Dr. Victor K. WILSON
86 Vice President for Govt Relations ... Mr. Griffin DOYLE
26 Vice President for Marketing & Comm ... Dr. Kathy R. PHARR
13 VP for Information Technology ... Dr. Timothy M. CHESTER
10 Sr Assoc VP Finance & Admin ... Mr. James N. SHORE
104 Assoc Provost of International Educ ... Dr. Martin KAGEL
28 Sr Vice Prov Diversity & Inclusion ... Dr. Michelle G. COOK
20 Int Assoc Prov for Academic Program ... Dr. Sarah COVERT
08 Assoc Provost/University Librarian ... Dr. Toby GRAHAM
88 Assoc Provost Faculty Affairs ... Ms. Elizabeth WEEKS
84 Assoc VP Admissions/Enroll Mgmt ... Vacant
21 Assoc VP Univ Business & Acct Svcs ... Mr. Chad CLEVELAND
18 Assoc VP Facilities Management ... Mr. Jeffrey BENJAMIN
15 Int AVP Human Resources ... Ms. Tamara FREEMAN
43 Executive Director Legal Affairs ... Mr. Michael RAEBER
49 Dean of Arts & Sciences ... Dr. Alan T. DORSEY
47 Dean of Agricultural & Environ Sci ... Dr. Nick T. PLACE
61 Dean of Law ... Mr. Peter RUTLEDGE
67 Dean of Pharmacy ... Dr. Kelly M. SMITH
65 Dean Forestry & Natural Resources ... Dr. Dale GREENE
53 Dean of Education ... Dr. Denise SPANGLER
58 Dean of the Graduate School ... Dr. Ronald WALCOTT
50 Dean of Business ... Dr. Benjamin C. AYERS
60 Dean Journalism & Mass Comm ... Dr. Charles N. DAVIS
59 Dean of Family & Consumer Sci ... Dr. Anisa ZVONKOVIC
74 Dean of Veterinary Medicine ... Dr. Lisa K. NOLAN
70 Dean of Social Work ... Dr. Philip HONG
48 Dean of Environment & Design ... Dr. Sonia A. HIRT
80 Dean Public/International Affs ... Dr. Matthew R. AUER
69 Dean of Public Health ... Dr. Marsha DAVIS
88 Interim Dean School of Ecology ... Dr. Sonia ALTIZER
63 Dean GRU/UGA Medical ... Dr. Shelley NUSS
54 Dean of Engineering ... Dr. Donald LEO
92 Dean of Honors College ... Dr. Margaret A. AMSTUTZ
41 Athletic Director ... Mr. Joshua BROOKS
22 Director of Equal Opportunity ... Ms. Qiana N. WILSON
06 Registrar ... Ms. Fiona B. LIKEN
19 Chief of Police ... Chief Daniel SILK
07 Director of Undergraduate Admission ... Mr. Barkley BARTON, II
37 Director of Student Financial Aid ... Ms. Nancy FERGUSON
36 Director of Career Services Center ... Mr. Scott T. WILLIAMS
39 Executive Director of Housing ... Ms. Linda KASPER
23 Interim Exec Dir of Health Services ... Dr. Beau SEAGRAVES
35 Dean of Students ... Dr. William M. MCDONALD
38 Dir Counseling/Psychological Svcs ... Dr. Ash THOMPSON
88 Director Georgia Center ... Dr. Stacy JONES
29 Exec Dir of Alumni Relations ... Ms. Meredith G. JOHNSON
110 Sr Exec Dir Dev & Alumni Relations . Ms. Margaret MCALLISTER
09 Int Dir of Institutional Research ... Mr. Allan AYCOCK
121 Director of Academic Enhancement ... Dr. Cara SIMMONS
94 Director Inst of Women's Studies ... Dr. Patricia RICHARDS
96 Director of Purchasing ... Mr. Robert CURRY
106 Dir Online Education/E-learning ... Dr. Stephen P. BALFOUR
108 Sr Director for Accreditation ... Mr. Allan AYCOCK
44 Exec Dir Annual or Planned Giving ... Ms. Heather DUISER
103 Director of Economic Development ... Mr. Matthew COLVIN

† Part of the University System of Georgia.

University of North Georgia (G)

82 College Circle, Dahlonega GA 30597-1001
County: Lumpkin   FICE Identification: 001585
Unit ID: 482680
Telephone: (706) 864-1800   Carnegie Class: Masters/L
FAX Number: (706) 864-1478   Calendar System: Semester
URL: ung.edu
Established: 1873   Annual Undergrad Tuition & Fees (In-State): $4,976
Enrollment: 19,793   Coed
Affiliation or Control: State   IRS Status: 501(c)3
Highest Offering: Doctorate
Accreditation: SC, ART, CAATE, CACREP, CAEP, CSHSE, NUR, PTA

01 President ... Dr. Bonita JACOBS
05 Provost & Senior VP Acad Affairs ... Dr. Chaudron GILLE

10 Sr VP Business & Finance ... Dr. Frank J. MCCONNELL
88 Sr VP Leadership & Global Engage ... Dr. Billy WELLS
32 VP Student Affairs ... Dr. James CONNEELY
12 VP of Gainesville Campus ... Dr. Richard OATES
111 VP of University Advancement ... Mr. Jeff TARNOWSKI
20 Vice Provost ... Dr. Steve LLOYD
108 Assoc Prov IE & Chief Research Ofcr ... Dr. Holly VERHASSELT
20 Assoc VP & Dean Univ College ... Dr. Carol ADAMS
21 AVP Financial Svcs & Comptroller ... Dr. Donna CALDWELL
109 AProv AS&RE & Int Oconee Camp Dir ... Mr. Gerald SULLIVAN
13 Chief Information Officer ... Mr. Steve MCLEOD
84 Assoc VP Enrollment Management ... Dr. Brett E. MORRIS
35 Asst VP Stdnt Affs & Dean of Stdnts ... Dr. Michelle BROWN
35 Assoc VPSA & Dean of Students ... Dr. Alyson PAUL
29 Exec Dir Alumni Relations & Annual ... Ms. Wendy HUGULEY ROTHIER
106 Exec Dir DETI ... Dr. Irene KOKKALA
07 Director of Undergrad Admissions ... Ms. Molly POTTS
07 Director of Cadet Admissions ... Mr. Mike IVY
92 Director of Honors Program ... Dr. Royce DANSBY-SPARKS
41 Director of Athletics ... Ms. Mary Rob PLUNKETT
116 Director of Internal Audit ... Ms. Jill HOLMAN
06 University Registrar ... Mr. Brett MERRITT
25 Director of Grants & Contracts ... Dr. Yolanda CARR
37 Director of Financial Aid ... Ms. Jill RAYNER
09 Director Institutional Research ... Ms. Linda ROWLAND
08 Dean of Libraries ... Dr. Joy BOLT
49 Dean College of Arts & Letters ... Dr. Christopher JESPERSEN
50 Dean M C College of Business ... Dr. Mary A. GOWAN
53 Dean of College of Education ... Dr. Sheri HARDEE
81 Dean College of Science & Math ... Dr. John LEYBA
76 Dean College of Health Sciences ... Dr. Carolynn DESANDRE
104 Assoc VP International Programs ... Ms. Sheila SCHULTE
15 Assoc VP Human Resources ... Ms. Beth ARBUTHNOT
18 Asst VP of Facilities ... Mr. Ken CROWE
19 Director of Public Safety ... Mr. Greg WILLIAMS
100 VP Univ Relations & Chief of Staff ... Dr. Kate MAINE
35 Commandant Corp of Cadets ... Col. Joseph MATTHEWS
36 Director of Career Services ... Ms. Diane FARRELL
38 Director Counseling Services ... Dr. Simon CORDERY
39 Director of Residence Life ... Ms. Treva SMITH
23 Director of Student Health Services ... Ms. Karen TOMLINSON
12 Exec Dir Cumming Campus ... Mr. Jason PRUITT
12 Exec Director Oconee Campus ... Vacant
108 Dir Accreditation & Assessment ... Ms. Betsy CANTRELL
51 Director Continuing Education ... Dr. Wendy ESTES
86 Exec Dir Gov Relations & Econ Dev ... Mr. Ben JARRAD
43 General Counsel ... Mr. Reggie LAMPKIN
96 Director Procurement ... Mr. Milton HANSEN
85 Int Dir Multicultural Student Affs ... Mr. Kyle MURPHY
04 Admin Asst to the President ... Ms. Ellen CORMACK
28 Director of Diversity & Inclusion ... Dr. Pablo MENDOZA
105 Director Web Services ... Ms. Joanie CHEMBARS
91 Asst CIO ... Mr. Rick CRAIN
26 AVP Communications & Marketing ... Ms. Sylvia CARSON

† Part of the University System of Georgia.

University of West Georgia (A)

1601 Maple Street, Carrollton GA 30118-0001
County: Carroll FICE Identification: 001601
Unit ID: 141334
Telephone: (678) 839-5000 Carnegie Class: DU-Mod
FAX Number: N/A Calendar System: Semester
URL: www.westga.edu
Established: 1906 Annual Undergrad Tuition & Fees (In-State): $6,521
Enrollment: 13,419 Coed
Affiliation or Control: State IRS Status: 501(c)3
Highest Offering: Doctorate
Accreditation: SC, ART, CACREP, JOUR, MUS, NURSE, SP, SPAA, THEA

01 President ... Dr. Brendan KELLY
05 Provost/Sr VP for Academic Affairs ... Dr. Jon PRESTON
10 VP Business & Financial Services ... Mr. Scott MCELROY
32 VP Student Affairs & Enroll Mgmnt ... Dr. André FORTUNE
88 VP for Strategic Enrollment Mgmt ... Ms. Kimberly SCRANAGE
111 VP for University Advancement ... Dr. Meredith BRUNEN
11 VP of Administrative Services ... Ms. Annemarie EADES
30 Exec Dir of Development ... Ms. Nichole FANNIN
35 AVP for Student Affairs ... Dr. Jennifer JORDAN
35 AVP and Dean of Students ... Dr. Lakiesa RAWLINSON
20 Assoc VP for Academic Affairs ... Dr. Jill DRAKE
20 Vice Provost & AVP for Acad Affairs ... Dr. Ralitsa AKINS
20 VP for Innovation & Research ... Dr. Daryush ILA
13 Asst VP of IT/CIO ... Mr. Dale DRIVER
50 Dean Richards College of Business ... Dr. Christopher JOHNSON
53 Dean College of Education ... Dr. Mike DISHMAN
81 Dn Arts/Culture/Scientific Inquiry ... Dr. Pauline GAGNON
92 Dean Honors College ... Dr. Janet DONOHOE
06 Registrar ... Ms. Donna HALEY
07 Interim Director of Admissions ... Mr. Dillon MONTES DE OCA
08 Dean of Libraries ... Ms. Andrea STANFIELD
37 Director Financial Aid ... Ms. Leigh Ann HUSSEY
36 Director Career Services ... Ms. Ginny Rae TURNER
51 Director Continuing Education ... Mr. Marty DAVIS
15 Asst VP/Chief HR Officer ... Ms. Terri WALTHOUR
18 Asst VP Campus Planning/Facilities ... Mr. Mark REEVES
19 Police Chief ... Dr. George E. WATSON
39 Dir Housing & Residence Life ... Ms. Cassidy NELSON
41 Director of Athletics ... Mr. Jason CARMICHAEL
38 Director Counseling Center ... Dr. Lisa ADAMS SOMERLOT
109 Sr Assoc VP Auxiliary Services ... Mr. Mark REEVES
108 Exec Dir Inst Effctvness/Assessment ... Ms. Ashlesha PAWAR

29 Exec Dir of Alumni Relations ... Ms. Allyson BRETCH
26 Assoc VP Constituent Rels/Engage ... Ms. Jami BOWER
58 Dean of the Graduate School ... Dr. Toby ZIGLAR
106 Dean USG eCore/Exec Dir Ext Lrng ... Dr. Melanie N. CLAY
43 University General Counsel ... Ms. Kristi CARMAN
102 Dir of Advancement Services ... Mr. Bart GILLESPIE
66 Dean Tanner School of Nursing ... Dr. Jennifer SCHUESSLER
22 Title IX Coord & Equal Opportunity ... Mr. Blake WINGO
100 Assoc VP/Chief of Staff to the Pres ... Mr. Russell CRUTCHFIELD
85 Dir Intl Student Admiss & Pgms ... Mr. Brett REICHERT
04 Exec Assistant to the President ... Ms. Tina BENNETT
104 Dir of Office of Education Abroad ... Dr. Anne GAQUERE-PARKER

† Part of the University System of Georgia.

*University System of Georgia Office (B)

270 Washington Street, SW, Atlanta GA 30334-9007
County: Fulton FICE Identification: 008290
Telephone: (404) 962-3000 Carnegie Class: N/A
FAX Number: (404) 962-3013
URL: www.usg.edu

01 Chancellor ... Dr. Sonny PERDUE
04 Executive Assistant to Chancellor ... Ms. Hailey GHEE
11 Exec Vice Chanc Administration ... Ms. Teresa MACCARTNEY
05 Exec Vice Chanc/Chief Academic Ofcr ... Dr. Ashwani MONGA
45 Exec VC Strategy/Fiscal Affairs ... Ms. Tracey COOK
116 VC for Internal Audit & Compliance ... Ms. Jenna WIESE
20 Vice Chancellor Academic Affairs ... Vacant
18 Vice Chancellor Facilities ... Ms. Sandra NEUSE
43 Vice Chancellor Legal Affairs ... Mr. Christopher MCGRAW
26 Vice Chancellor for Communications ... Vacant
13 Vice Chanc/Chief Information Ofcr ... Mr. Jonathan PIERSOL
10 Vice Chancellor for Fiscal Affairs ... Mr. Jeff DAVIS
32 Vice Chancellor for Student Affairs ... Vacant
30 Vice Chancellor for Development ... Mr. Kirby THOMPSON
88 Vice Chancellor Org Effectiveness ... Mr. Wesley HORNE
15 Vice Chancellor for Human Resources ... Dr. Juanita HICKS
09 Vice Chanc of Research & Policy ... Dr. Angela BELL
100 Vice Chancellor for Leadership ... Dr. Stuart RAYFIELD
86 VC for External Affairs & COS ... Ms. Ashley JONES

Valdosta State University (C)

1500 N Patterson Street, Valdosta GA 31698-0010
County: Lowndes FICE Identification: 001599
Unit ID: 141264
Telephone: (229) 333-5800 Carnegie Class: DU-Mod
FAX Number: (229) 333-7400 Calendar System: Semester
URL: www.valdosta.edu
Established: 1906 Annual Undergrad Tuition & Fees (In-State): $6,583
Enrollment: 12,304 Coed
Affiliation or Control: State IRS Status: 501(c)3
Highest Offering: Doctorate
Accreditation: SC, ART, CAATE, CACREP, CAEP, EXSC, LIB, MFCD, MUS, NURSE, SP, SPAA, SW, THEA

01 President ... Dr. Richard CARVAJAL
05 Provost & VPAA ... Dr. Robert T. SMITH
10 Vice President for Finance & Admin ... Ms. Traycee F. MARTIN
111 VP Univ Advancement/CEO Foundation . Mr. John D. CRAWFORD
32 VP for Student Affairs ... Dr. Vince MILLER
58 Assoc Prov Grad Studies & Research ... Dr. Becky K. DA CRUZ
20 Assoc Provost Acad Programs & Svcs ... Dr. Sharon L. GRAVETT
21 Associate VP for Finance & Admin ... Ms. Shannon MCGEE
79 Dean Col of Humanities & Social Sci ... Dr. James T. LAPLANT
81 Dean College of Science & Math ... Dr. Pierre Richard CORNELY
50 Dean College of Business Admin ... Dr. Karin P. ROLAND
57 Dean College of the Arts ... Mr. Arthur B. PEARCE
53 Dean Col of Educ & Human Svcs ... Dr. David SLYKHUIS
66 Dean Col of Nursing/Health Sci ... Dr. James C. PACE
92 Dean of Honors College ... Dr. Michael P. SAVOIE
08 Univ Librarian & Dean of Libraries ... Dr. Alan M. BERNSTEIN
06 Registrar ... Mr. Stanley JONES
106 Assoc Dir Ofc of Extended Lrng ... Ms. Marsha B. DUKES
13 Chief Information Officer ... Mr. Kevin J. OVERLAUR
121 VP Div of Student Success ... Dr. Rodney B. CARR
39 Dir Housing & Residence Life ... Vacant
41 Director of Athletics ... Mr. Herb REINHARD
37 Director of Financial Aid ... Mr. Douglas R. TANNER
36 Dir of Career Opportunities ... Ms. Carla C. JORDAN
29 Chief Governmental Relations & Alum ... Ms. Merritt WALL
15 Director of Human Resources ... Ms. Jeanine Y. BODDIE-LA VAN
88 Director Division Aerospace Studies ... Vacant
43 University Attorney ... Mr. Justin ARRINGTON
18 Dir Phys Plant & Facilities Plng ... Mr. Ray A. SABLE
26 Director of Strategic Communication ... Ms. Robbyn W. DESPAIN
38 Director of Counseling Center ... Dr. Tricia A. HALE
23 Director of Student Health Services ... Dr. Richard RICKMAN
19 Dir Public Safety/Police Chief ... Mr. Alan ROWE
108 Director of Inst Effectiveness ... Dr. Michael M. BLACK
88 Dir of Info Tech Svcs for Adv Svcs ... Ms. Amelia REAMS
100 Chief Officer to the President ... Ms. Melinda B. HARBAUGH
96 Dir of Procurement & Accounting ... Ms. Antolina E. PILGRIM
09 Director Inst Research ... Mr. Barrie D. FITZGERALD
104 Director of Intl Programs ... Dr. Ivan NIKOLOV
105 Director of Creative Services ... Mr. Jeff GRANT
28 Dir of Stdnt Diversity & Inclusion ... Ms. Sandra JONES
25 Dir Spons Pgm & Research Admin ... Ms. Elizabeth W. OLPHIE
116 Director of Internal Audit ... Ms. Heidi COX

† Part of the University System of Georgia.

Wesleyan College (D)

4760 Forsyth Road, Macon GA 31210-4462
County: Bibb FICE Identification: 001600
Unit ID: 141325
Telephone: (478) 477-1110 Carnegie Class: Bac-Diverse
FAX Number: (478) 757-4030 Calendar System: Semester
URL: www.wesleyancollege.edu
Established: 1836 Annual Undergrad Tuition & Fees: $25,190
Enrollment: 779 Female
Affiliation or Control: United Methodist IRS Status: 501(c)3
Highest Offering: Master's
Accreditation: SC, NURSE

01 President ... Ms. Meaghan K. BLIGHT
05 Provost/VP for Academic Affairs ... Dr. Melody A. BLAKE
111 VP Institutional Advancement ... Ms. Andrea G. WILLIFORD
10 Vice Pres Business/Finance & CFO ... Mr. Larry S. WAKEFIELD
32 Dean of Students ... Ms. Christy S. HENRY
84 VP for Strategic Enrollment ... Mr. Clinton G. HOBBS
06 Assistant Dean/Registrar ... Ms. Angie WRIGHT
04 Assistant to the President ... Mrs. Denise W. HOLLOWAY
08 Library Director ... Ms. Kristi PEAVY
13 Director of Computer Info Resources ... Ms. Jan TEDDERS
29 Director of Alumnae Affairs ... Ms. Cathy C. SNOW
26 Director of Communications ... Ms. Mary Ann HOWARD
44 Director of Annual Fund ... Ms. Whitney DAVIS
37 Director of Financial Aid ... Ms. Jayme HITCHCOCK
39 Director of Residence Life ... Ms. Erica WHITE
18 Director of Physical Plant ... Mr. James FLEENOR
41 Athletic Director ... Mr. William SPEROW
42 Chaplain ... Vacant
19 Director Security/Safety ... Mr. Jay BARTLETT
15 Director Human Resources ... Ms. Julie DANIEL
07 Director of Admissions ... Vacant
09 Director of Institutional Research ... Ms. Glenda FERGUSON
35 Chief Student Life Officer ... Ms. Abbie PRICE
36 Director Career Development ... Ms. Ivy WORD
38 Director Student Counseling ... Ms. Myrana CRAIG
109 Director of Auxiliary Services ... Ms. Andrea WILLIFORD
21 Associate Business Officer ... Ms. Quintress HOLLIS
22 Director of Disability and Advocacy ... Ms. Jill AMOS
28 Dir of Diversity/Inclusion/Equity ... Ms. Tonya PARKER
30 Chief Development Officer ... Mrs. Susan B. ALLEN

West Georgia Technical College (E)

176 Murphy Campus Boulevard, Waco GA 30182-2407
County: Haralson FICE Identification: 010487
Unit ID: 139278
Telephone: (770) 537-6000 Carnegie Class: Assoc/HVT-Mix Trad/Non
FAX Number: (770) 537-7976 Calendar System: Semester
URL: www.westgatech.edu
Established: 1968 Annual Undergrad Tuition & Fees (In-State): $3,052
Enrollment: 6,437 Coed
Affiliation or Control: State IRS Status: 501(c)3
Highest Offering: Associate Degree
Accreditation: SC, ACBSP, ADNUR, CAHIIM, DH, MAC, MLTAD, RAD, SURGT

01 President ... Dr. Julie POST
11 Executive VP Admin Services ... Ms. Carol REID
05 Vice President Academic Affairs ... Ms. Kristen BUOY
32 Vice President Student Affairs ... Dr. Tonya F. WHITLOCK
09 VP Institutional Effectiveness ... Vacant
103 VP Economic Development ... Ms. Angela BERCH
51 VP of Adult Education ... Vacant
08 Exec Director Library Services ... Ms. Michelle BARSOM
06 Registrar ... Mrs. Laura THORNTON
13 Dir Information Technology ... Mr. Ryan DAHLBERG
07 Director of Admissions ... Mrs. Lori BASHAM
18 Director Facilities ... Mr. Michael JILES
04 Executive Asst to President ... Mrs. Julia WATSON
36 Manager Career Services ... Ms. Zelma JONES
37 Director Student Financial Aid ... Mrs. Kim KELLEY
15 Director of Human Resources ... Mr. Donnie LAFFERTY
19 Chief of Police ... Mr. James PERRY
50 Dean Sch of Business & Public Svcs ... Ms. Babs RUSSELL
49 Dean Sch of Arts & Sciences ... Mr. Brian BARKLEY
54 Dean Sch of Trade & Technology ... Mr. Gary WELBORN
106 Director Online Learning ... Ms. Myranda STEPHENS
108 Director Institutional Assessment ... Mr. AJ THOMAS
26 Dir of Public Relations & Info ... Ms. Ashley COPELAND
111 Exec Dir of Institutional Advance ... Ms. Brittney HENDERSON
38 Director Student Counseling ... Ms. Kim CROCKETT

Wiregrass Georgia Technical College (F)

4089 Val Tech Road, Valdosta GA 31602
County: Lowndes FICE Identification: 005256
Unit ID: 141255
Telephone: (229) 333-2100 Carnegie Class: Assoc/HVT-High Non
FAX Number: (229) 333-2129 Calendar System: Semester
URL: www.wiregrass.edu
Established: 1963 Annual Undergrad Tuition & Fees (In-State): $3,152
Enrollment: 3,709 Coed
Affiliation or Control: State IRS Status: 501(c)3
Highest Offering: Associate Degree
Accreditation: SC, ADNUR, CAHIIM, DA, DH, EMT, MAC, OPD, PNUR, RAD, SURGT

01 President ... Ms. DeAnnia CLEMENTS
05 Exec VP Academic Affairs ... Ms. April MCDUFFIE
18 Vice President Facilities ... Ms. Lidell GREENWAY
11 VP for Administrative Services ... Ms. Keren WYNN
84 VP for Enrollment Management ... Ms. Shannon MCCONICO
108 Assoc VP for Inst Effectiveness ... Mrs. April MCDUFFIE
28 VP Community Affs/Minority Recruit ... Vacant
103 Assoc VP Economic Development ... Ms. Brandy WILKES
13 Chief Info Technology Officer (CIO) ... Mr. Casey THOMPSON
88 Dir Administrative Services ... Ms. Chymeka GIBBS
32 Dean of Student Affairs ... Ms. Shannon MCCONICO
26 Dir for Cmty/College Relations ... Ms. Lydia HUBERT
07 Executive Dir High School Services ... Ms. Brooke JARAMILLO
04 Executive Asst to President ... Ms. Cheryl ACREE
06 Registrar ... Ms. Julie DREXLER
08 Head Librarian ... Ms. Kathryn TOMLINSON
105 Director Web Services ... Mr. Steve SAULS
106 Exec Director Online Education ... Ms. Sabrina COX
15 Assoc VP of Human Resources ... Ms. Shalonda SANDERS
19 Chief of Police ... Mr. Tim ALLMOND
37 Financial Aid Coordinator ... Ms. Paula HERRING
96 Director of Purchasing ... Ms. Ronshekua SIMS
20 Dean of Academic Affairs ... Ms. Holly GREENE
49 Dean of Arts and Science ... Mr. Michael WILLIAMS
76 Dean of Allied Health ... Mr. Stevan VAN HOOK

Young Harris College (A)

1 College Street, Young Harris GA 30582-0098
County: Towns FICE Identification: 001604
Unit ID: 141361
Telephone: (706) 379-3111 Carnegie Class: Bac-A&S
FAX Number: (706) 379-4319 Calendar System: Semester
URL: www.yhc.edu
Established: 1886 Annual Undergrad Tuition & Fees: $29,667
Enrollment: 1,417 Coed
Affiliation or Control: United Methodist IRS Status: 501(c)3
Highest Offering: Master's
Accreditation: SC, MUS

01 President ... Dr. Drew L. VAN HORN
05 Provost ... Dr. Jason PIERCE
10 CFO ... Mr. Wade M. BENSON
32 Vice Preside of Student Development .. Dr. Laura WHITAKER-LEA
111 Vice President of Advancement ... Mr. Mark DOTSON
09 Asst VP for Institutional Research ... Ms. Rosemary R. ROYSTON
13 Chief Technology Officer ... Mr. Ken FANEUFF
29 Director of Alumni Engagement ... Ms. Dana ENSLEY
15 Director of Human Resources ... Ms. Naveela ASLAM
20 Assoc VP for Academic Affairs ... Dr. Keith DEFOOR
08 Dean of Library Services ... Ms. Debra MARCH
38 Director of Student Counseling ... Ms. Susan MURPHY
06 Registrar ... Ms. Tammy GIBSON
37 Director of Financial Aid ... Ms. Michelle BERNARD
26 Dir of Communication & Marketing ... Vacant
18 Director of Facilities ... Mr. Charles WALDROUP
41 Director of Athletics ... Ms. Jennifer RUSHTON
42 Chaplain & Dean of the Chapel ... Vacant
04 Executive Asst to the President ... Ms. Teresa KELLEY
30 Director of Development ... Ms. Bobbie THOMPSON
11 VP Operations/Finance ... Mr. Bo WRIGHT
39 Director of Residence Life ... Mr. Mark JESTEL
84 Asst VP of Enrollment Management ... Dr. Joy HAMM
19 Campus Police Chief ... Mr. Robbie RICH

HAWAII

Brigham Young University Hawaii (B)

55-220 Kulanui Street, Laie, Oahu HI 96762-1294
County: Honolulu FICE Identification: 001606
Unit ID: 230047
Telephone: (808) 675-3211 Carnegie Class: Bac-Diverse
FAX Number: (808) 675-3329 Calendar System: Semester
URL: www.byuh.edu
Established: 1955 Annual Undergrad Tuition & Fees: $5,890
Enrollment: 3,180 Coed
Affiliation or Control: Latter-day Saints IRS Status: 501(c)3
Highest Offering: Baccalaureate
Accreditation: WC, AAQEP, SW

01 University President ... Dr. John S. KAUWE, III
05 Academic Vice President ... Dr. Isaiah H. WALKER
10 Administrative Vice President ... Mr. Steve W. TUELLER
32 Student Life Vice President ... Mr. Jonathan K. KAU
11 Operations Vice President ... Mr. Kevin SCHLAG
111 Advancement Vice President ... Mrs. Laura TEVAGA
100 Chief of Staff ... Mr. Keni REID
108 Assoc Acad VP Curriculum/Assessment ... Dr. Rosalind RAM
20 Assoc Academic VP Faculty ... Dr. Yifen BEUS
73 Director of Religious Education ... Mr. Aaron SHUMWAY
81 Dean Faculty of Sciences ... Dr. Jess KOHLERT
77 Dean Faculty of Math/Computing ... Dr. James D. LEE
79 Dean Fac of Culture/Lang/Perf Arts ... Dr. Tevita KAILI
49 Dean Faculty of Arts & Letters ... Dr. Patricia PATRICK
50 Dean Faculty of Business/Government ... Dr. Brian HOUGHTON
53 Dean Faculty of Educ & Social Work ... Dr. Mark WOLFERSBERGER
13 Chief Information Officer ... Mrs. Arlene SEWELL
35 Dean of Students ... Mr. James FAUSTINO
08 Director Library & Academic Success ... Mr. Michael ALDRICH
114 Budget Director ... Mr. Michael TEJADA
21 Director of Financial Services ... Mr. Eric MARLER
19 Director Campus Safety/Security ... Mr. Anthony PICKARD
15 Director of Human Resources ... Mr. Reid MILLERBERG
18 Director Facilities Management ... Mr. Randy SHARP
23 Director of Health Services ... Mrs. Laurie ABREGANO
116 Chief Compliance Officer ... Mr. David GALLOWAY
88 Title IX Deputy Coordinator ... Mr. Leland SIKAHEMA
38 Dir Counseling/Disability Services ... Mrs. Rachel KEKAULA
39 Director of Campus Life ... Ms. Alison WHITING
109 Director Food Services ... Mr. David KEALA
06 Registrar ... Mrs. Daryl WHITFORD
88 Event Services & Outreach Manager ... Ms. Diedra ULII
40 Camp Store/Aux Services Manager ... Mr. David FONOIMOANA
07 Admissions Manager ... Mr. Maurice MO'O

† Affiliated with Brigham Young University, Provo, UT.

Chaminade University of Honolulu (C)

3140 Waialae Avenue, Honolulu HI 96816-1578
County: Honolulu FICE Identification: 001605
Unit ID: 141486
Telephone: (808) 735-4711 Carnegie Class: Masters/M
FAX Number: N/A Calendar System: Semester
URL: www.chaminade.edu
Established: 1955 Annual Undergrad Tuition & Fees: $26,914
Enrollment: 2,208 Coed
Affiliation or Control: Independent Non-Profit IRS Status: 501(c)3
Highest Offering: Doctorate
Accreditation: WC, CAEPT, CIDA, CLPSY, IACBE, MACTE, NURSE

01 President ... Dr. Lynn BABINGTON
05 Provost ... Dr. Lance ASKILDSON
111 VP for Institutional Advancement ... Mr. Gary CORDOVA
10 Vice President Finance/Facilities ... Ms. Aulani KAANOI
84 Dean of Enrollment Management ... Ms. Lisa TRUMBULL
32 VP of Student Affairs ... Ms. Allison JEROME
15 VP of HR & Legal Affairs ... Ms. Christine DENTON
26 VP Communications & Marketing ... Ms. Lisa FURUTA
90 Sr Dir Network/Desktop Services ... Mr. Jules SUKHABUT
29 Director of Alumni Relations ... Ms. Jeannie LUM
41 Director of Athletics ... Mr. Tom BUNING
42 Director of Campus Ministry ... Mr. Jeremiah CARTER
36 Dir Advising & Career Development ... Ms. Danielle MASUDA
18 Asst Dir of Facilities Operations ... Ms. Lori AUKAI-PAIA
21 Director of Finance ... Mr. Choong LIM
08 Director of Library ... Ms. Sharon LEPAGE
19 Director of Security ... Mr. Damien BARR
38 Director of Counseling Services ... Dr. Sharolyn TANI
06 Asst VP Student Success & Registrar ... Ms. Jennifer CREECH
37 Dean of Financial Aid ... Mr. Jeff SCOFIELD
09 Dir of Institutional Research ... Mr. Hieu NGUYEN

Hawaii Medical Institute Inc. DBA Hawaii Medical College (D)

1221 Kapiolani Blvd Suite 644, Honolulu HI 96814
County: Honolulu FICE Identification: 041822
Unit ID: 460756
Telephone: (808) 237-5140 Carnegie Class: Spec 2-yr-Health
FAX Number: (808) 237-5805 Calendar System: Other
URL: www.hmi.edu
Established: 2007 Annual Undergrad Tuition & Fees: $26,037
Enrollment: 150 Coed
Affiliation or Control: Proprietary IRS Status: Proprietary
Highest Offering: Associate Degree
Accreditation: CNCE

01 President/CEO ... Ashton CUDJOE
06 Registrar ... Jetta TOBIN
07 Director of Admissions ... Marie THORNTON
10 Chief Financial Officer ... Renz BELTRAN
15 Human Resources Administrator ... Josephine BUSANO
36 Director Career Services ... Dante JOHNSON
37 Director Financial Aid ... Jennifer OLEVSON
38 Director Student Counseling ... Cheryl CHAR
53 Director of Education ... Dr. Zachary OLIVER

Hawaii Pacific University (E)

1164 Bishop Street, Suite 800, Honolulu HI 96813-2882
County: Honolulu FICE Identification: 007279
Unit ID: 141644
Telephone: (808) 544-0200 Carnegie Class: Masters/L
FAX Number: (808) 544-1136 Calendar System: Semester
URL: www.hpu.edu
Established: 1965 Annual Undergrad Tuition & Fees: $29,300
Enrollment: 4,243 Coed
Affiliation or Control: Independent Non-Profit IRS Status: 501(c)3
Highest Offering: Doctorate
Accreditation: WC, AAQEP, NURSE, @PTA, SW

01 President ... Mr. John GOTANDA
00 President Emeritus ... Mr. Chatt G. WRIGHT
05 Sr VP and Provost ... Dr. Jennifer WALSH
11 Sr Vice Pres Admin/Gen Counsel ... Ms. Janet BOIVIN
10 Sr VP/Chief Financial Officer ... Mr. David KOSTECKI
84 Vice Pres Enrollment Management ... Mr. Greg GRAUMAN
26 VP/Chief Communication/Mktg Ofcr ... Mr. Jeffrey RICH
111 INt VP of Advancement ... Mr. Dennis HUNT
15 Int AVP of Human Resources ... Vacant
13 Assoc VP/Chief Information Officer ... Mr. Cody DOWN
32 AVP/Dean of Students ... Ms. Marites MCKEE
21 Associate VP/Controller ... Mr. James BRESE
06 AVP of Enrollment Management ... Ms. Sara SATO
18 AVP of Facilities Safety/Security ... Mr. Kevin G. MATSUKADO
50 Interim Dean College Business ... Mr. Mani SEHGAL
76 Dean College Health Society ... Dr. Halaevalu VAKALAHI
81 Dean Col Natural/Computational Sci ... Dr. Brenda JENSEN
49 Dean College of Liberal Arts ... Dr. Allison GOUGH
56 Dean College of Prof Studies ... Mr. Mani SEHGAL
07 Assoc Dir International Admissions ... Vacant
97 Asst Dean College of Prof Studies .. Dr. Valentina ABORDONADO
07 Director of Admissions ... Ms. Marissa BRATTON
104 Director Intl Exchange/Study Abroad ... Ms. Melissa MATSUBARA
37 Assoc Director Financial Aid ... Ms. Alyson MACHADO
41 Exec Director of Athletics ... Dr. Debbie SNELL
08 Actg Dir Libraries/Learning Commons ... Dr. Valentina ABORDONADO
29 Sr Dir Development/Alumni Relations ... Ms. Tara K. WILSON

Hawaii Tokai International College (F)

91-971 Farrington Hwy, Kapolei HI 96707
County: Honolulu FICE Identification: 037603
Telephone: (808) 983-4000 Carnegie Class: Not Classified
FAX Number: (808) 983-4107 Calendar System: Quarter
URL: www.htic.edu
Established: 1992 Annual Undergrad Tuition & Fees: N/A
Enrollment: N/A Coed
Affiliation or Control: Independent Non-Profit IRS Status: 501(c)3
Highest Offering: Associate Degree
Accreditation: WJ

01 Int Chancellor ... Dr. Naoto YOSHIKAWA
05 Int Vice Chanc of Academic Affairs ... Dr. Sandra WU-BOTT
32 Vice Chancellor of Student Affairs .. Ms. Kumiko YABE-DOMINGO
10 Executive Director ... Mr. Takahiro FUJIMURA
49 Dean of Liberal Arts ... Dr. Sandra WU-BOTT

Institute of Clinical Acupuncture and Oriental Medicine (G)

100 N Beretania Street, Suite 203 B, Honolulu HI 96817-4709
County: Honolulu FICE Identification: 037353
Unit ID: 444699
Telephone: (808) 521-2288 Carnegie Class: Spec-4-yr-Other Health
FAX Number: (808) 521-2271 Calendar System: Semester
URL: www.orientalmedicine.edu
Established: 1996 Annual Graduate Tuition & Fees: N/A
Enrollment: 54 Coed
Affiliation or Control: Proprietary IRS Status: Proprietary
Highest Offering: Master's; No Undergraduates
Accreditation: ACUP

01 President ... Dr. Wai Hoa LOW
05 Chancellor Academic Affairs ... Dr. Edmund BERNAUER
32 Director of Student Affairs ... Dr. Craig TWENTYMAN
10 Director of Finance ... Dr. Catherine Yu-Ling LOW
06 Registrar ... Ms. Jeanne BERNAUER

Pacific Rim Christian University (H)

2223 Ho'one'e Place, Honolulu HI 96819
County: Honolulu Identification: 667010
Unit ID: 457484
Telephone: (808) 518-4791 Carnegie Class: Bac-Diverse
FAX Number: (808) 670-3957 Calendar System: Semester
URL: www.pacrim.edu
Established: 1998 Annual Undergrad Tuition & Fees: $11,900
Enrollment: 147 Coed
Affiliation or Control: Independent Non-Profit IRS Status: 501(c)3
Highest Offering: Master's
Accreditation: BI

01 Interim President ... Craig PANKOW
05 Vice Pres Academics/Student Life ... Dr. Jennifer KELLY
84 Vice Pres Enrollment ... Craig PANKOW
07 Director of Admissions ... Jade RANESES
20 Dean of Academics/Student Life ... Vicki LEPICK
08 Library Director ... Karen CLARKE
37 Director of Financial Aid ... Eli JENNINGS
13 Director IT & Facilities ... James MCELMURRY
06 Registrar/Career Svcs Director ... Melodie GARCIA
35 Director of Student Life ... Garret CHANG
10 Director of Business Operations ... Erica JANSEN

*University of Hawaii System (I)

2444 Dole Street, Honolulu HI 96822
County: Honolulu FICE Identification: 007885
Unit ID: 141963
Telephone: (808) 956-8207 Carnegie Class: N/A
FAX Number: (808) 956-5286
URL: www.hawaii.edu

01 President ... Dr. David K. LASSNER
05 VP for Academic Strategy ... Dr. Debora HALBERT
46 VP for Research and Innovation ... Dr. Vassilis L. SYRMOS
43 VP for Legal Affs/Univ Gen Counsel ... Ms. Carrie K. OKINAGA
10 VP for Budget and Finance/CFO ... Mr. Kalbert K. YOUNG
88 VP for Community Colleges ... Dr. Erika L. LACRO

11 VP for Administration ... Ms. Jan N. GOUVEIA
13 VP for Information Tech/CIO ... Mr. Garret T. YOSHIMI
111 VP for Advancement/CEO UH Found ... Mr. Timothy DOLAN
32 Assoc VP Student Affairs ... Vacant
21 Director of Budget ... Mr. Michael M. NG
15 Sys Dir Human Resources ... Mr. Jeffery R. LONG
14 Director Management Info Systems ... Ms. Susan K. INOUYE
45 Interim Dir Ofc of Research Svcs ... Dr. Vassilis L. SYRMOS
21 AVP Budget & Finance/Controller ... Ms. Amy S. KUNZ
09 Director Data Govt & Operations ... Ms. Sandra K. FURUTO
22 Director EEO/AA ... Dr. Dee E. UWONO
26 Director of Communications ... Mr. Dan T. MEISENZAHL
101 Exec Administrator/Sec to the Board ... Ms. Kendra T. OISHI
86 Director Government Relations ... Ms. Stephanie C. KIM
100 Executive Asst to President ... Ms. Lynne K. MONACO
100 Executive Asst to President ... Ms. Amy M. LUKE
04 Admin & Fiscal Support Specialist ... Ms. Courtney N. DOMINGO

*University of Hawaii at Hilo (A)

200 W Kawili Street, Hilo HI 96720-4091
County: Hawaii FICE Identification: 001611
Unit ID: 141565
Telephone: (808) 932-7348 Carnegie Class: DU-Mod
FAX Number: (808) 932-7338 Calendar System: Semester
URL: www.hilo.hawaii.edu
Established: 1947 Annual Undergrad Tuition & Fees (In-State): $7,838
Enrollment: 3,165 Coed
Affiliation or Control: State IRS Status: 501(c)3
Highest Offering: Doctorate
Accreditation: WC, AAQEP, MPCAC, NUR, NURSE, PHAR

02 Chancellor ... Dr. Bonnie D. IRWIN
05 Vice Chancellor Academic Affairs ... Dr. Kristen RONEY
10 Int Vice Chanc Admin Affairs ... Mr. Kalei RAPOZA
46 Vice Chancellor for Research ... Vacant
32 Vice Chancellor Student Affairs ... Ms. Farrah-Marie GOMES
35 Assoc VC for Student Affairs ... Mr. Christopher HOLLAND
114 Exec Budget Director & Business Mgt ... Ms. Lois M. FUJIYOSHI
22 Director University Disability Svcs ... Ms. Susan SHIRACHI
15 Director Human Resources ... Ms. Lorena KAUHI
18 Director Facilities Planning ... Mr. Jerry WATANABE
26 Int Director University Relations ... Ms. Alyson KAKUGAWA-LEONG
08 University Librarian ... Mr. Joseph SANCHEZ
24 Director Media Relations ... Ms. Alyson Y. KAKUGAWA-LEONG
07 Director Admissions ... Ms. Katherine MCGINNIS
38 Clinical Team Leader ... Mr. Andrew POLLOI
39 Director of Housing ... Ms. Sherri AKAU
35 Director of Campus Center ... Ms. Lai Sha BUGADO
37 Director Financial Aid ... Ms. Sherrie PADILLA
06 University Registrar ... Ms. Chelsea KAY-WONG
49 Int Dean College of Arts & Sciences ... Dr. Michael BITTER
50 Int Dean Col of Business/Economics ... Dr. Kristen RONEY
67 Int Dean College of Pharmacy ... Dr. Miriam MOBLEY SMITH
47 Dean Col Agri/For/Nat Res Mgmt ... Dr. Bruce MATHEWS
51 Actg Dir Ctr for Community Engage ... Dr. Julie MOWRER
41 Director of Athletics ... Mr. Patrick J. GUILLEN
40 Bookstore Manager ... Ms. Margaret STANLEY
85 Exec Dir Intl Student Services ... Mr. James P. MELLON
09 Institutional Research Analyst ... Dr. Bradley THIESSEN
23 Director Medical Services ... Ms. Heather HIRATA
88 Dir College of Hawaiian Language ... Ms. Keiki KAWAI`AE`A
19 Director Security/Safety ... Mr. Richard MURRAY

*University of Hawaii at Manoa (B)

2500 Campus Road, Honolulu HI 96822-2217
County: Honolulu FICE Identification: 001610
Unit ID: 141574
Telephone: (808) 956-8111 Carnegie Class: DU-Highest
FAX Number: N/A Calendar System: Semester
URL: www.manoa.hawaii.edu
Established: 1907 Annual Undergrad Tuition & Fees (In-State): $12,186
Enrollment: 18,025 Coed
Affiliation or Control: State IRS Status: 501(c)3
Highest Offering: Doctorate
Accreditation: WC, AAQEP, CAATE, CEA, CLPSY, DH, DIETD, IPSY, LAW, LIB, MED, MLS, MUS, NURSE, PH, PLNG, SP, SPAA, SW

00 Chair Board of Regents ... Mr. Randolph G. MOORE
02 President ... Dr. David LASSNER
05 Provost ... Dr. Michael BRUNO
22 Dir & Title IX Coord ... Dr. Dee UWONO
88 Native Hawaiian Affairs Pgm Officer ... Dr. Kaiwipuni LIPE
10 VC Admin/Fin/Chief Business Ofcr ... Ms. Alexandra S. FRENCH
113 Bursar ... Mr. Derek M. SEU
96 Int Dir Procurement/Real Prop Mgmt ... Ms. Karlee C. HISASHIMA
116 Director Internal Audit ... Mr. Glenn Y. SHIZUMURA
21 Dir Finance & Accounting ... Vacant
20 Int Vice Provost for Academic Excel ... Dr. Laura LYONS
46 Int Vice Prov for Rsrch/Scholarship ... Dr. Christopher L. SABINE
88 Asst Vice Provost for Faculty Excel ... Dr. Noelani N. GOODYEAR-KAOPUA
32 Vice Provost for Student Success ... Dr. Lori IDETA
13 VP Info Technology/CIO UH System ... Mr. Garret YOSHIMI
06 UHM University Registrar ... Mr. Pheng XIONG
08 University Librarian ... Mr. Clement P. GUTHRO
37 Director Financial Aid Services ... Ms. Jodie M. KUBA
38 Dir Counseling/Student Devel Ctr ... Dr. Allyson M. TANOUYE
23 Director University Health Center ... Dr. Andrew W. NICHOLS
39 Dir Student Affairs/Housing ... Mr. Dean H. SHIMOMURA
40 Director University Bookstore ... Ms. Tricia R. EJIMA
41 Athletics Director ... Mr. David MATLIN
86 Director of Cmty/Govt Affairs ... Mr. Elmer KAAI
28 Asst Vice Provost for Diver/Inclus ... Dr. Christine QUEMUEL
36 Director of the Manoa Career Center ... Ms. Wendy SORA
88 Interim Dir UH Cancer Center ... Dr. Joe W. RAMOS, JR.
88 Dir Institute for Astronomy ... Mr. Doug A. SIMONS
88 Director Waikiki Aquarium ... Dr. Andrew ROSSITER
88 Dir Pacific Bioscience Research Ctr ... Dr. Marla J. BERRY
51 Dean Outreach College ... Dr. William G. CHISMAR
50 Dean Shidler College of Business ... Dr. V. Vance ROLEY
58 Dean Graduate Division ... Dr. Krystyna AUNE
88 Dean Sch of Travel Industry Mgt ... Mr. V. Vance ROLEY
53 Dean College of Education ... Dr. Nathan MURATA
54 Dean College of Engineering ... Dr. Brennon MORIOKA
47 Dean Col Trop Agric & Human Res ... Dr. Nicholas COMERFORD
63 Dean John A Burns Sch of Med ... Dr. Jerris R. HEDGES
66 Int Dean Atmospera-Walch Sch Nurs ... Dr. Clementina D. CERIA-ULEP
70 Int Dn Thom Sch Soc Wk/Public Hlth ... Dr. Tetine L. SENTEL
61 Dean Wm S Richardson Sch of Law ... Ms. Camille NELSON
48 Interim Dean School of Architecture ... Dr. William CHAPMAN
49 Dean College Arts & Humanities ... Dr. Peter ARNADE
81 Dean College Natural Sciences ... Dr. Aloysius HELMINCK
83 Dean College Social Sciences ... Dr. Denise E. KONAN
88 Int Dean Sch Ocean/Earth Sci & Tech ... Dr. Charles H. FLETCHER
88 Dean Pacific and Asian Studies ... Dr. R. Anderson SUTTON
88 Dean Sch of Hawaiian Knowledge ... Dr. Jonhathan OSORIO
09 Director Institutional Research ... Dr. Yang ZHANG
04 Asst to the Sr Exec ... Ms. Debra ISHII
04 Executive Assistant to President ... Ms. Amy LUKE
07 Director of Admissions ... Mr. Ryan YAMAGUCHI
101 Exec Administrator & Secy to BOR ... Ms. Kendra OISHI
104 Director Study Abroad ... Dr. Jack A. TAYLOR
11 VP Administration UH System ... Ms. Jan GOUVEIA
19 Chief Public Safety ... Vacant
25 Int Dir Research Services UH Sys ... Dr. Vassilis L. SYRMOS
26 Director Communications UH System ... Mr. Dan MEISENZAHL
43 VP Legal Affairs UH System ... Ms. Carrie OKINAGA
84 Vice Provost Enrollment Management ... Ms. Nikki K. CHUN
90 Asc VP Stdnt Aff/Dir Acad Tech UHS ... Vacant
102 VP Advance & CEO UH Foundation ... Mr. Tim DOLAN
109 Director Campus Services ... Mr. Kevin H. ISHIDA

*University of Hawaii - West Oahu (C)

91-1001 Farrington Highway, Kapolei HI 96707
County: Honolulu FICE Identification: 021078
Unit ID: 141981
Telephone: (808) 689-2800 Carnegie Class: Bac-Diverse
FAX Number: (808) 689-2771 Calendar System: Semester
URL: westoahu.hawaii.edu
Established: 1976 Annual Undergrad Tuition & Fees (In-State): $7,584
Enrollment: 3,168 Coed
Affiliation or Control: State IRS Status: 501(c)3
Highest Offering: Baccalaureate
Accreditation: WC, ACBSP, CAEP

02 Chancellor ... Dr. Maenette BENHAM
05 Vice Chanc Academic Affairs ... Dr. Jeffrey MONIZ
32 Int Vice Chanc for Student Affairs ... Dr. Jan JAVINAR
20 Assoc Vice Chanc Academic Affairs ... Dr. Alan ROSENFELD
11 Vice Chanc for Administration ... Mr. Kevin ISHIDA
84 Director for Enrollment Services ... Ms. Ellen KENOLIO
09 Director of Institutional Research ... Mr. John STANLEY
26 Director of Communications ... Ms. Leila SHIMOKAWA
08 Library Director ... Ms. Michiko JOSEPH
06 Registrar ... Ms. Vicky DEL PRADO
37 Director of Financial Aid ... Mr. James OSHIRO
15 Director of Human Resources ... Ms. Nancy K. NAKASONE
10 Fiscal Manager ... Ms. Sheri CHING
07 Director of Admissions ... Ms. Michelle COHEN
13 Chief Info Technology Officer ... Ms. Therese NAKADOMARI
18 Dir Facilities/Physical Plant Ofc ... Ms. Bonnie ARAKAWA

*University of Hawaii Community Colleges (D)

2444 Dole Street, Honolulu HI 96822-2411
County: Honolulu FICE Identification: 006751
Unit ID: 420592
Telephone: (808) 956-7038 Carnegie Class: N/A
FAX Number: (808) 956-9219
URL: www.hawaii.edu

01 Vice Pres for Community Colleges ... Dr. Erika L. LACRO
05 Assoc Vice Pres Academic Affairs ... Ms. Tammi CHUN-OYADOMARI
11 Assoc Vice Pres Admin/Cmty Col Oper ... Mr. Michael T. UNEBASAMI
04 Executive Assistant to the VP & Dir ... Ms. Deborah NAKAGAWA
10 Director Budget & Planning ... Mr. Lance YAMAMOTO
15 Director Human Resources ... Ms. Sandra UYENO
18 Director Facilities/Physical Plant ... Ms. Denise YOSHIMORI-YAMAMOTO
22 Director of Compliance and Title IX ... Ms. Christine CHUN

*Kapiolani Community College (E)

4303 Diamond Head Road, Honolulu HI 96816-4221
County: Honolulu FICE Identification: 001613
Unit ID: 141796
Telephone: (808) 734-9000 Carnegie Class: Assoc/MT-VT-High Non
FAX Number: N/A Calendar System: Semester
URL: www.kapiolani.hawaii.edu
Established: 1957 Annual Undergrad Tuition & Fees (In-State): $3,284
Enrollment: 6,369 Coed
Affiliation or Control: State IRS Status: 501(c)3
Highest Offering: Associate Degree
Accreditation: WJ, ACBSP, ACFEI, ACPHA, ADNUR, COARC, DA, EMT, MAC, MLTAD, OTA, PTAA, RAD, SURGT

02 Chancellor ... Dr. Louise PAGOTTO
05 Interim VC Academic Affairs ... Dr. Maria BAUTISTA
10 Vice Chancellor for Admin Services ... Mr. Brian FURUTO
32 Vice Chancellor Student Affairs ... Mr. Thomas KEOPUHIWA
49 Dean Arts and Sciences ... Mr. Nawa'a NAPOLEON
50 Dean Hospitality/Business/Legal ... Mr. John RICHARDS
76 Dean Health Programs ... Ms. Lisa RADAK
51 Dir Continuing Educ & Training ... Vacant
04 Exec Asst to the Chancellor ... Ms. Joanne WHITAKER
09 Dir Institutional Effectiveness ... Dr. Robert FRANCO
08 Interim Head Librarian ... Ms. Annie THOMAS
06 Registrar ... Ms. Jerilyn ENOKAWA
37 Financial Aid Officer ... Ms. Jennifer BRADLEY
109 Auxiliary Services Officer ... Mr. Sean NATHAN
51 Dean Community & Continuing Educ ... Dr. Carol HOSHIKO
30 Development Officer ... Ms. Linh HOANG POE
15 Int Manager Human Resources ... Ms. Linda RENIO
21 Fiscal Officer ... Mr. Justin KASHIWAEDA

*University of Hawaii - Hawaii Community College (F)

1175 Manono Street, Hilo HI 96720-5096
County: Hawaii FICE Identification: 005258
Unit ID: 383190
Telephone: (808) 934-2800 Carnegie Class: Assoc/HVT-High Trad
FAX Number: (808) 934-2501 Calendar System: Semester
URL: www.hawaii.hawaii.edu
Established: 1941 Annual Undergrad Tuition & Fees (In-State): $3,204
Enrollment: 2,430 Coed
Affiliation or Control: State IRS Status: 501(c)3
Highest Offering: Associate Degree
Accreditation: WJ, ACFEI, ADNUR

02 Chancellor ... Dr. Rachel H. SOLEMSAAS
05 Vice Chanc Academic Affairs ... Ms. Joni Y. ONISHI
10 Interim Vice Chanc Admin Affairs ... Mr. Kenneth K. KALEIWAHEA
32 Vice Chanc Student Affairs ... Ms. Dorinna CORTEZ
51 Director Continuing Educ/Training ... Ms. Jessica YAMAMOTO
37 Financial Aid Manager ... Vacant
12 Interim Director Palamanui ... Ms. Raynette (Kalei) HALEAMAU-KAM
15 Human Resource Manager ... Ms. Mari CHANG
06 Registrar/A&R Mgr ... Ms. Sherise TIOGANGCO
114 Budget Analyst ... Ms. Jodi MINE
04 Private Secretary to the Chancellor ... Ms. Callie MARTIN
19 Campus Safety and Security Chief ... Vacant
49 Dean for Liberal Arts & Public Svcs ... Dr. Melanie WILSON
88 Director of KoEC ... Dr. Kei-Lin CERF

*University of Hawaii Honolulu Community College (G)

874 Dillingham Boulevard, Honolulu HI 96817-4598
County: Honolulu FICE Identification: 001612
Unit ID: 141680
Telephone: (808) 845-9211 Carnegie Class: Assoc/HVT-Mix Trad/Non
FAX Number: (808) 845-9173 Calendar System: Semester
URL: www.honolulu.hawaii.edu
Established: 1920 Annual Undergrad Tuition & Fees (In-State): $3,174
Enrollment: 3,378 Coed
Affiliation or Control: State IRS Status: 501(c)3
Highest Offering: Associate Degree
Accreditation: WJ

02 Interim Chancellor ... Ms. Karen LEE
11 Vice Chancellor of Admin Svcs ... Mr. Derek INAFUKU
05 Int Vice Chancellor of Acad Affairs ... Ms. Susan NISHIDA
88 Int Dean Transport & Trades ... Ms. Preshess WILLETS-VAQUILAR
26 Int Dean Communications & Services ... Mr. Wayne SUNAHARA
08 Librarian ... Ms. Sarah MYHRE
37 Financial Aid Officer ... Ms. Heather FLORENDO
15 Human Resources Mgr/EEO/AA Coord ... Ms. Monique TINGKANG
32 Director Student Life & Development ... Ms. Emily Ann KUKULIES
06 Registrar ... Ms. Jennifer NAGUWA
09 Director Management Info & Research ... Mr. Steven SHIGEMOTO
36 Director Student Placement ... Ms. Silvan CHUNG
20 Dean University College ... Ms. Jennifer HIGA-KING
10 Fiscal Manager ... Ms. Myrna PATTERSON
121 Interim Dean of Academic Support ... Ms. Silvan CHUNG
13 Chief Info Technology Officer (CIO) ... Mr. Michael MEYER
35 Dean of Student Services ... Ms. Lara SUGIMOTO

*University of Hawaii Kauai Community College (H)

3-1901 Kaumualii Highway, Lihue HI 96766-9500
County: Kauai FICE Identification: 001614
Unit ID: 141802
Telephone: (808) 245-8311 Carnegie Class: Assoc/HVT-Mix Trad/Non
FAX Number: (808) 245-8220 Calendar System: Semester
URL: kauai.hawaii.edu/

Established: 1964 Annual Undergrad Tuition & Fees (In-State): $3,252
Enrollment: 1,461 Coed
Affiliation or Control: State IRS Status: 501(c)3
Highest Offering: Associate Degree
Accreditation: WJ, ACFEI, ADNUR, MAC

02 Chancellor ..... Dr. Joseph DAISY
05 Vice Chanc Academic Affairs ..... Dr. Frankie HARRISS
32 Vice Chanc Student Affairs ..... Ms. Margaret SANCHEZ
11 Vice Chanc Administrative Services ..... Mr. Calvin SHIRAI
10 Chief Financial Officer ..... Ms. Deanne KOSHI
51 Director Continuing Educ/Training ..... Mr. Calvin SHIRAI
08 Head Librarian ..... Mr. Robert KAJIWARA
37 Financial Aid Officer ..... Mr. Jeff ANDERSON
15 Human Resource Manager ..... Ms. JoRae BAPTISTE
35 Counselor/Student Life Coordinator ..... Mr. John CONSTANTINO
09 Dir Institutional Effect/Univ Ctr ..... Dr. Valerie BARKO

*University of Hawaii - Leeward Community College (A)

96-045 Ala Ike, Pearl City HI 96782-3393
County: Honolulu FICE Identification: 004549
Unit ID: 141811
Telephone: (808) 455-0011 Carnegie Class: Assoc/HT-High Non
FAX Number: (808) 455-0471 Calendar System: Semester
URL: www.leeward.hawaii.edu
Established: 1968 Annual Undergrad Tuition & Fees (In-State): $3,209
Enrollment: 6,363 Coed
Affiliation or Control: State IRS Status: 501(c)3
Highest Offering: Associate Degree
Accreditation: WJ, AAQEP, ACFEI, CAHIIM

02 Chancellor ..... Dr. Carlos PENALOZA
05 Vice Chanc Academic Affairs ..... Mr. Keala CHOCK
11 Vice Chanc Admin Services ..... Ms. Kelli BRANDVOLD
10 Fiscal Manager ..... Vacant
49 Dean Arts & Sciences ..... Mr. James GOODMAN
72 Dean Career & Tech Education ..... Mr. Ron UMEHIRA
32 Interim Dean Student Services ..... Ms. Kami KATO
20 Interim Dean of Academic Services ..... Ms. Leanne RISELEY
08 Librarian ..... Mr. Wayde OSHIRO
06 Registrar ..... Mr. Grant HELGESON
37 Financial Aid Officer ..... Mr. Gregg YOSHIMURA
18 Aux & Facilities Services Mgr ..... Mr. Grant OKAMURA
09 Interim Policy/Plng/Assess Coord ..... Ms. Jayne BOPP
26 Marketing Officer ..... Mr. Tad SAIKI
15 Human Resources Mgr/EEO/AA Coord ..... Ms. Lori Lei HAYASHI
13 Information Technology Coord ..... Mr. Byron WATANABE
12 Waianae Education Center Coord ..... Mr. Danny WYATT
24 Interim Media Coordinator ..... Ms. Rachael INAKE
35 Student Activities Coordinator ..... Ms. Lexer CHOU

*University of Hawaii Maui College (B)

310 Kaahumanu Avenue, Kahului HI 96732-1644
County: Maui FICE Identification: 001615
Unit ID: 141839
Telephone: (808) 984-3500 Carnegie Class: Bac/Assoc-Assoc Dom
FAX Number: (808) 984-3546 Calendar System: Semester
URL: maui.hawaii.edu
Established: 1931 Annual Undergrad Tuition & Fees (In-State): $3,278
Enrollment: 2,936 Coed
Affiliation or Control: State IRS Status: 501(c)3
Highest Offering: Baccalaureate
Accreditation: WC, ACFEI, ACPHA, ADNUR, DH, NAEYC

02 Chancellor ..... Dr. Lui HOKOANA
05 Vice Chanc Academic Affairs ..... Vacant
32 Vice Chancellor of Student Affs ..... Ms. Debra NAKAMA
10 Vice Chanc of Administrative Affs ..... Mr. David TAMANAHA
51 Director Continuing Educ/Training ..... Ms. Karen HANADA
08 Librarian ..... Ms. Ellen PETERSON
88 Director University Center Maui ..... Ms. Tomone Karen HANADA
07 Director of Admissions ..... Ms. Flora MORA
09 Director of Institutional Research ..... Vacant
15 Director Human Resources ..... Ms. Susan TOKUNAGA
18 Chief Facilities/Physical Plant ..... Mr. Melvin HIPOLITO
21 Fiscal Administrator ..... Ms. Cindy YAMAMOTO
30 Director of Development ..... Ms. Jocelyn Romero DEMIRBAG
36 Director Student Placement ..... Ms. Debra NAKAMA
37 Financial Aid Director ..... Ms. Davileigh NAE`OLE
38 Director Student Counseling ..... Mr. Shane PAYBA
06 Registrar ..... Ms. Flora MORA
19 Director Security/Safety ..... Ms. Angela GANNON

*University of Hawaii Windward Community College (C)

45-720 Keaahala Road, Kaneohe HI 96744-3598
County: Honolulu FICE Identification: 011220
Unit ID: 141990
Telephone: (808) 235-7400 Carnegie Class: Assoc/HT-High Non
FAX Number: (808) 247-5362 Calendar System: Semester
URL: www.windward.hawaii.edu
Established: 1972 Annual Undergrad Tuition & Fees (In-State): $3,194
Enrollment: 2,299 Coed
Affiliation or Control: State IRS Status: 501(c)3
Highest Offering: Associate Degree
Accreditation: WJ

02 Chancellor ..... Dr. Ardis ESCHENBERG
05 Vice Chancellor Academic Affairs ..... Mr. Charles S. SASAKI
32 Int Vice Chancellor Student Affairs ..... Dr. Jennifer BROWN
11 Int Vice Chanc Administrative Svcs ..... Mr. Lance YAMAMOTO
20 Dean of Academic Affairs Div I ..... Vacant
20 Int Dean of Academic Affairs Div II ..... Dr. David KRUPP
78 Int Dir Vocational/Cmty Education ..... Dr. Maria-Elena DIAZ
08 Head Librarian ..... Ms. Sarah Gilman SUR
06 Registrar ..... Ms. Farah DOIGUCHI
09 Director of Institutional Research ..... Vacant
37 Director Student Financial Aid ..... Ms. Anna CHAMBERLAIN
15 Personnel Officer ..... Ms. Karen CHO
26 Marketing/Public Relations Dir ..... Ms. Bonnie BEATSON
19 Director Security/Safety ..... Vacant

University of Phoenix Hawaii Campus (D)

949 Kamokila Blvd. Suite 101, Kapolei HI 96707
Telephone: (808) 536-2686 Identification: 770202
Accreditation: &HLC, ACBSP

† Branch campus of University of Phoenix, Phoenix, AZ-No longer enrolling new students

IDAHO

Boise Bible College (E)

8695 W Marigold Street, Boise ID 83714-1220
County: Ada FICE Identification: 022345
Unit ID: 142090
Telephone: (208) 376-7731 Carnegie Class: Spec-4-yr-Faith
FAX Number: (208) 376-7743 Calendar System: Semester
URL: www.boisebible.edu
Established: 1945 Annual Undergrad Tuition & Fees: $13,100
Enrollment: 101 Coed
Affiliation or Control: Christian Churches And Churches of Christ
IRS Status: 501(c)3
Highest Offering: Baccalaureate
Accreditation: BI

01 President ..... Dr. Derek VOORHEES
05 VP of Academic Affairs ..... Mr. Charles FABER
32 VP of Institutional Operations ..... Dr. Cody CHRISTENSEN
10 Director of Finance/Administration ..... Mr. Steven MARSHALL
111 VP of Institutional Advancement ..... Mr. Scott LERWICK
06 Registrar ..... Mr. Ross KNUDSEN
84 VP of Enrollment Management ..... Mr. Cody CHRISTENSEN
08 Librarian ..... Mrs. Julie RUSSELL
37 Financial Aid Director ..... Mr. Ben BISHOP
18 Director of Physical Plant ..... Mr. Daniel MATA
04 Executive Assistant to President ..... Mrs. Rhonda HETHERINGTON

Boise State University (F)

1910 University Drive, Boise ID 83725-1000
County: Ada FICE Identification: 001616
Unit ID: 142115
Telephone: (208) 426-1000 Carnegie Class: DU-Higher
FAX Number: (208) 426-3765 Calendar System: Semester
URL: www.boisestate.edu
Established: 1932 Annual Undergrad Tuition & Fees (In-State): $8,068
Enrollment: 24,069 Coed
Affiliation or Control: State IRS Status: 501(c)3
Highest Offering: Doctorate
Accreditation: NW, ART, CAATE, CACREP, CAEP, COARC, CONST, DMS, MUS, NURSE, RAD, SW, THEA

01 President ..... Dr. Marlene TROMP
05 Provost & Vice President ..... Dr. John BUCKWALTER
111 VP University Advancement ..... Mr. Matthew EWING
45 Academic Planning & Inst Effective ..... Dr. Zeynep HANSEN
97 Vice Provost Undergrad Studies ..... Dr. Susan SHADLE
10 Assoc VP and Bursar ..... Ms. Jo Ellen DINUCCI
110 Assoc VP for Advancement Svcs ..... Mr. Joseph BOEKE
32 Int VP Student Affairs/Enrollment ..... Dr. Edward WHIPPLE
46 VP Research & Econ Development ..... Dr. Nancy GLENN
13 Assoc VP/Chief Info Officer ..... Mr. Max DAVIS-JOHNSON
08 Interim Dean of Library ..... Dr. Tod COLEGROVE
35 Dean of Students ..... Dr. Chris WUTHRICH
84 Assoc VP Enrollment Service ..... Ms. Kris COLLINS
15 Assoc VP Human Resources ..... Ms. Catherine WEITZ
29 Executive Director Alumni Relations ..... Ms. Lisa GARDNER
17 Exec Dir of Health Services ..... Dr. Julia BEARD
06 Registrar ..... Ms. Mandy NELSON
19 Interim Assoc VP Public Safety ..... Mr. Jon UDA
09 Sr Exec Dir Inst Effectiveness ..... Dr. Shari ELLERTSON
07 Director of Admissions ..... Dr. Kelly TALBERT
26 Assoc VP for Comm/Mktg ..... Ms. Lauren GRISWOLD
41 Exec Director Athletics ..... Mr. Jeramiah DICKEY
38 Director Counseling Services ..... Dr. Matthew NIECE
37 Director of Financial Aid ..... Ms. Kelley CHRISTIANSON
51 Dean Extended Studies ..... Mr. Mark WHEELER
49 Dean of Arts & Sciences ..... Dr. Leslie DURHAM
50 Dean Business & Economics ..... Dr. Mark BANNISTER
53 Dean College of Education ..... Dr. James SATTERFIELD
58 Interim Dean Graduate College ..... Dr. Scott LOWE
76 Dean of Health Sciences ..... Dr. Tim DUNNAGAN
54 Dean of Engineering ..... Dr. JoAnn LIGHTY
88 Interim Dean of Innovation & Design ..... Dr. Shawn BENNER
104 Asst Prov for Global Educ ..... Dr. Gonzalo BRUCE
80 Dean School of Public Service ..... Dr. Angela BOS
104 Dir Intl Learning/Student Success ..... Ms. Corrine HENKE
36 Director Career Center ..... Ms. Debbie KAYLOR
106 Exec Director e-Campus Center ..... Ms. Christine BAUER
30 Sr Exec Development Director ..... Ms. Jennifer NEIL
100 VP for Univ Affairs/Chief of Staff ..... Ms. Alicia ESTEY
04 Admin Assistant to the President ..... Ms. Elise ALFORD
18 Chief Facilities/Physical Plnt Ofcr ..... Ms. Randi MCDERMOTT
43 General Counsel Office ..... Mr. Matt WILDE
86 Director Government Relations ..... Mr. Andrew MITZEL
90 Customer Care/CISO ..... Mr. Mark FITZGERALD

Brigham Young University-Idaho (G)

525 South Center Street, Rexburg ID 83460
County: Madison FICE Identification: 001625
Unit ID: 142522
Telephone: (208) 496-1411 Carnegie Class: Bac-Diverse
FAX Number: (208) 496-1103 Calendar System: Semester
URL: www.byui.edu
Established: 1888 Annual Undergrad Tuition & Fees: $4,300
Enrollment: 44,481 Coed
Affiliation or Control: Latter-day Saints IRS Status: 501(c)3
Highest Offering: Baccalaureate
Accreditation: NW, MUS, NURSE, PTAA, SW

01 President ..... Dr. Henry J. EYRING
05 Academic Vice President ..... Dr. Jon F. LINFORD
11 University Resources Vice President ..... Mr. Brett A. COOK
32 Student Life Vice President ..... Mrs. Amy R. LABAUGH
88 Online Vice President ..... Mr. Kendall D. PECK
45 Exec Strategy & Planning VP ..... Mr. Robert J. GARRETT
20 Assoc Academic VP Instruction ..... Mr. Sidney L. PALMER
20 Assoc Acad VP Curriculum ..... Dr. Van D. CHRISTMAN
121 Assoc Acad VP Student Success ..... Ms. Danae ROMRELL
35 Dean of Students ..... Mr. Wynn N. HILL
13 Chief Information Officer ..... Mr. Joe MCWILLIAMS
09 Inst Research Managing Director ..... Dr. Ben FRYAR
45 Institutional Planning Managing Dir ..... Mr. Aaron SANNS
06 Registrar ..... Mrs. Lauri D. ARENSMEYER
37 Financial Aid Director ..... Mr. Ken L. JACKSON
08 University Librarian ..... Mr. Chris OLSEN
10 Univ Operations Managing Director ..... Mr. Kyle R. WILLIAMS
15 Human Resources Director ..... Mrs. Beth BALDWIN
23 Student Health Services Director ..... Mr. Shaun ORR
38 Student Counseling Center Director ..... Mr. Reed J. STODDARD
19 University Public Safety Director ..... Mr. Stephen P. BUNNELL
07 Admissions Director ..... Mr. Riley HALL
29 Alumni Engagement Director ..... Mr. Steve J. DAVIS
36 Student Placement Mng Director ..... Mr. Derek R. FAY
26 University Relations Mng Director ..... Mr. Brett SAMPSON
30 Philanthropies Director ..... Ms. Tanise CHUNG-HOON
39 Housing & Student Living Director ..... Dr. Troy J. DOUGHERTY
43 Associate University Counsel ..... Mr. Josh FIGUEIRA
21 Financial Services Mng Director ..... Mr. Shane WEBSTER
88 Student Services Mng Director ..... Mrs. Jill EVANS
96 Purchasing & Travel Director ..... Mr. Mike B. THUESON
88 Student Activities Mng Director ..... Mr. Allen JONES
40 University Store Director ..... Mr. Brent G. ASHCRAFT
104 International Services Director ..... Mr. Bryan H. JUSTESEN
121 Student Success Mng Director ..... Mr. Sam R. BRUBAKER
109 Auxiliary Services Mng Director ..... Mr. Ryan J. BUTTARS
04 Assistant to the President ..... Mrs. Kathy L. WEBB
50 Dean of Business/Communications ..... Mr. Kirk GIFFORD
53 Dean of Education & Hum Dev ..... Mr. David R. PECK
54 Dean of Physical Sciences & Engr ..... Mr. Greg ROACH
88 Dean of Faculty Development ..... Mrs. Susan WARD
81 Dean of Agriculture & Life Sciences ..... Mr. John ZENGER
79 Dean of Language & Letters ..... Mr. Jason R. WILLIAMS
57 Dean of Performing & Visual Arts ..... Mr. Brian MEMMOTT
88 Dean of Interdisciplinary Studies ..... Mr. Kevin BROWER
88 Dean of Teacher Preparation ..... Mr. Scott GARDNER
106 Dean of Online Programs ..... Mr. Jake ROMNEY

Carrington College - Boise (H)

1122 N Liberty Street, Boise ID 83704-8741
Telephone: (208) 377-8080 FICE Identification: 022180
Accreditation: &WJ, ADNUR, DH, MAC, PNUR, PTAA

† Regional accreditation is carried under the parent institution in Sacramento, CA.

College of Eastern Idaho (I)

1600 S 25th E, Idaho Falls ID 83404-5788
County: Bonneville FICE Identification: 011133
Unit ID: 142179
Telephone: (208) 524-3000 Carnegie Class: Assoc/HVT-Mix Trad/Non
FAX Number: (208) 524-3007 Calendar System: Semester
URL: www.cei.edu
Established: 1969 Annual Undergrad Tuition & Fees (In-State): $4,126
Enrollment: 1,803 Coed
Affiliation or Control: State IRS Status: 501(c)3
Highest Offering: Associate Degree
Accreditation: NW, ADNUR, MAC, SURGT

01 President ..... Dr. Rick AMAN
10 Vice President of Finance and Admin ..... Mr. Byron MILES
05 VP Instruction/Student Affairs ..... Ms. Lori BARBER
06 Registrar ..... Mrs. Raquel CUEVAS
21 Controller ..... Mr. Don E. BOURNE
103 Mgr Workforce Trng/Cmty Education ..... Vacant

37 Financial Aid Director Mrs. Tiffany CLEVERLY
04 President Administrative Assistant Mrs. Amanda LOGAN
26 Director of College Relations Mr. Todd WIGHTMAN
102 Foundation Director Mr. David FACER
76 Health Care Technology Div Manager Ms. Jodene TRIMBLE
88 Trades/Industry Division Manager Mr. Kent E. BERGGREN
51 Adult Basic Education Div Manager Mrs. Sandra TAKAHASHI
09 Dir of Institutional Effectiveness Dr. Amy BRUMFIELD
13 Chief Info Technology Officer Mr. Ray FOX
15 Chief Human Resources Officer Dr. Mary TAYLOR
96 Director of Purchasing Ms. Heidi MOORE
00 Chairman of the Board Mr. Park PRICE
97 Dean of General Education Mr. Jacob HAEBERLE
75 Dean of Career/Technical Education Mr. Chuck BOHLEKE
76 Dean of Healthcare Dr. Angela SACKETT
32 Dean of Student Affairs Mr. Michael WALKER
08 Chief Library Officer Mr. Nathan BROWN
106 Director Online Learning Svcs Dr. Ryan FAULKNER
18 Director of Facilities Mr. Greg HORTON
38 Director Student Counseling Mrs. Hailey HOLLAND

The College of Idaho (A)

2112 Cleveland Boulevard, Caldwell ID 83605-4432
County: Canyon FICE Identification: 001617
Unit ID: 142294
Telephone: (208) 459-5011 Carnegie Class: Bac-Diverse
FAX Number: (208) 454-2077 Calendar System: Other
URL: www.collegeofidaho.edu
Established: 1891 Annual Undergrad Tuition & Fees: $32,855
Enrollment: 1,114 Coed
Affiliation or Control: Independent Non-Profit IRS Status: 501(c)3
Highest Offering: Master's
Accreditation: NW

01 Co-President Mr. Doug BRIGHAM
01 Co-President Mr. Jim EVERETT
05 Provost/Dean of Faculty Dr. David DOUGLASS
10 Vice Pres Finance/Administration Mr. Richard ERNE
32 Vice President Student Affairs Dr. Paul BENNION
84 Vice President for Enrollment Mgmt Mr. Brian BAVA
111 VP for College Relations Mr. Jack CAFFERTY
20 Associate Dean of Faculty Dr. Andrew GADES
20 Associate Dean of Faculty Dr. Lynda DANIELSON
06 Registrar Ms. Cassandra HEATH
41 Vice President of Athletics Ms. Reagan ROSSI
26 Dir of Marketing & Communications Mr. Joe HUGHES
29 Dir of Alumni & Parent Relations Ms. Danielle DOUGHERTY DURHAM
44 Director of Boone Fund Vacant
08 Director of Library Ms. Christine SCHUTZ
21 Controller Ms. Kim NAPOLI
37 Director of Financial Services Ms. Terri SCOTT
15 Human Resources Director Ms. Nancy JOHNSON-CASSULO
36 Director Student Placement Ms. Nicole CAMMANN
92 Director of Honors Program Dr. Rochelle JOHNSON
39 Director of Residential Life Mr. Matt GIER
93 Asst Dean of Students/Dir of Inclus Mr. Arnold HERNANDEZ
42 Campus Minister/Asc Dean Students Dr. Phil ROGERS
19 Director of Campus Safety Mr. Ben MOSLEY
09 Assc VP Institutional Effectiveness Mr. Mark HEIDRICH
07 Director of Admissions Mr. Mike BURDINE
40 College Store Manager Ms. Liza SAFFORD
23 Director of Health/Wellness Center Ms. Natalie DAVISON
04 Exec Asst to Co-Pres External Rels Ms. Adrianne BARBER
18 Chief Facilities/Physical Plant Mr. Richard ERNE
27 Director External Affairs & Events Ms. Deidre FRIEDLI
103 VP of High Impact Practices Ms. Latonia HANEY KEITH

College of Southern Idaho (B)

PO Box 1238, 315 Falls Avenue,
Twin Falls ID 83303-1238
County: Twin Falls FICE Identification: 001619
Unit ID: 142559
Telephone: (208) 733-9554 Carnegie Class: Assoc/MT-VT-High Non
FAX Number: (208) 736-3015 Calendar System: Semester
URL: www.csi.edu
Established: 1965 Annual Undergrad Tuition & Fees (In-District): $4,560
Enrollment: 7,321 Coed
Affiliation or Control: Local IRS Status: 501(c)3
Highest Offering: Baccalaureate
Accreditation: NW, ADNUR, DH, EMT, MAC, PTAA, RAD, SURGT

01 President Dr. L. Dean FISHER
00 Chairman of the Board Mr. Laird STONE
05 Provost Dr. Todd SCHWARZ
10 VP Finance & Administration Mr. Jeff HARMON
13 Chief Information Officer Mr. Ryan JUND
32 VP Student Life & Enroll Services Dr. Jonathan LORD
09 Dean of IE/ALO & Communication Mr. Chris BRAGG
04 Exec Admin Asst to President Ms. Ginger NUKAYA
21 Controller Ms. Kristy CARPENTER
20 Instructional Dean Ms. Tiffany SEELEY-CASE
20 Instructional Dean Dr. Barry PATE
20 Instructional Dean Dr. Jayson LLOYD
35 Dean of Students Mr. Jason OSTROWSKI
15 Director Human Resources Mr. Eric NIELSON
06 Registrar Ms. Jackie SMITH
37 Director of Student Financial Aid Ms. Jennifer J. ZIMMERS
08 Director of Library Dr. Elizabeth JOHNSON
102 Executive Director Foundation Ms. Erika ALLEN
103 Sr Director Workforce Development Ms. Janet PRETTI
14 Dir Application/Data Architecture Mr. Ed DITLEFSEN
14 Dir Systems/Network Architecture Mr. Bruce NUKAYA
41 Athletic Director Mr. Joel C. BATE
18 Director Physical Plant Mr. Spencer CUTLER
19 Director Security & Safety Mr. Keith THOMPSON
26 Director Marketing & Communication Mr. Matt HARTGRAVE
40 Bookstore Manager Ms. Jayme KETTERLING
92 Coordinator Honors Program Mr. Brian DOBBS

College of Western Idaho (C)

6056 Birch Lane, Nampa ID 83687
County: Canyon FICE Identification: 042118
Unit ID: 455114
Telephone: (208) 562-3000 Carnegie Class: Assoc/HT-High Non
FAX Number: (888) 562-3216 Calendar System: Semester
URL: cwi.edu
Established: 2007 Annual Undergrad Tuition & Fees (In-District): $4,336
Enrollment: 10,200 Coed
Affiliation or Control: Local IRS Status: 501(c)3
Highest Offering: Associate Degree
Accreditation: NW, ACBSP, ADNUR, DA, MAC, PTAA, SURGT

01 President Mr. Gordon JONES
05 Provost Ms. Denise ABERLE-CANNATA
11 Executive VP Operations Mr. Craig BROWN
86 VP College Relations Vacant
15 VP Human Resources Mr. Ryan HERRING
10 Vice Pres Finance & Administration Vacant
04 Executive Asst President's Office Ms. Janice MCGEHEE
13 Chief Information Officer Mr. Michael CHACON
84 AVP Enrollment & Student Services Mr. Patrick TANNER
103 AVP Economic Development Ms. Christi GILCHRIST
09 Exec Dir Inst Effectiveness Ms. Alexis MALEPEAI-RHODES
102 Director CWI Foundation Mr. Michael JENSEN
18 Exec Dir Facilities/Plng & Mgmt Mr. Jeff FLYNN
32 Dean of Students Mr. Chad TRISLER
57 Dean Arts & Humanities Mr. Justin VANCE
60 Dean Comm & Technology Ms. Kelly STEELY
76 Dean Health Mr. Aaron VON LINDERN
54 Dean Industry/Engr & Trades Mr. Pat NEAL
81 Dean Math & Science Ms. Kae JENSEN
83 Dean Social Sciences & Public Affs Ms. Courtney SANTILLAN
07 Dean Admissions & One Stop Mr. Luis CALOCA
121 Director Advising Ms. Erica COMPTON
37 Director Financial Aid Ms. Jenee SNYDER
06 Registrar Ms. Connie BLACK
55 Director Adult Education Mr. Jac WEBB
88 Director Business & Manufacturing Mr. Marc SWINNEY
88 Dean Center for Teaching & Learning Ms. Courtney COLBY BOND
88 Exec Dir Dual Credit Mr. Stephen CRUMRINE
08 Director Learning Commons Ms. Kim REED
26 Exec Dir Comm & Marketing Ms. Audrey ELDRIDGE
21 Comptroller Ms. Mary Jo HAYES
43 In-House General Counsel Ms. Andrea FONTAINE
88 Associate General Counsel Mr. James FRANCEL

Idaho College of Osteopathic Medicine (D)

1401 E. Central Drive, Meridian ID 83642
County: Ada Identification: 667328
Telephone: (208) 795-4266 Carnegie Class: Not Classified
FAX Number: N/A Calendar System: Semester
URL: www.idahocom.org
Established: 2016 Annual Graduate Tuition & Fees: N/A
Enrollment: N/A Coed
Affiliation or Control: Proprietary IRS Status: Proprietary
Highest Offering: First Professional Degree; No Undergraduates
Accreditation: OSTEO

01 President Dr. Tracy FARNSWORTH
05 Dean & Chief Academic Ofcr Dr. Thomas MOHR
07 Director of Admissions Janette MARTIN
37 Director of Financial Aid Nicole MCMILLIN
10 VP Finance/Chief Financial Officer Larry TISDALE
43 Chief Legal/Compliance Officer John FULLERTON

Idaho State University (E)

921 S 8th Ave, Pocatello ID 83209-0009
County: Bannock FICE Identification: 001620
Unit ID: 142276
Telephone: (208) 282-0211 Carnegie Class: DU-Higher
FAX Number: (208) 282-4000 Calendar System: Semester
URL: www.isu.edu
Established: 1901 Annual Undergrad Tuition & Fees (In-State): $7,872
Enrollment: 11,766 Coed
Affiliation or Control: State IRS Status: 501(c)3
Highest Offering: Doctorate
Accreditation: NW, ADNUR, ARCPA, AUD, CAATE, CACREP, CAEPN, CAHIIM, CLPSY, COARC, DENT, DH, DIETD, DIETI, EMT, MAC, MLS, MUS, NAEYC, NAIT, NURSE, OT, OTA, PH, PHAR, PTA, PTAA, RAD, SP, SW, THEA

01 President Dr. Kevin SATTERLEE
04 Executive Assistant to President Ms. Jennifer FORSHEE
05 Interim Provost Dr. Karen APPLEBY
10 VP Finance & Business Affairs Mr. Glen NELSON
111 Vice Pres of University Advancement Mr. Kyle MCGOWAN
32 Vice Pres Student Affairs Ms. Lyn REDINGTON
46 Vice President for Research Ms. Donna LYBECKER
17 VP Kasiska Division Health Sciences Dr. Rex FORCE
43 General Counsel/Chief Comp Officer Mr. Blake CHRISTENSEN
41 Athletic Director Ms. Pauline THIROS
20 Vice Provost Academic Affairs Ms. Joanne TOKLE
84 AVP for Enrollment Management Vacant
18 AVP for Facilities Services Ms. Cheryl HANSON
58 Dean of Graduate School Dr. Adam BRADFORD
54 Dean College Science & Engineering Dr. Scott SNYDER
67 Dean College of Pharmacy Dr. Walter L. FITZGERALD, JR.
50 Dean College of Business Mr. Shane HUNT
49 Dean College of Arts & Letters Dr. Kandi TURLEY-AMES
53 Dean College of Education Dr. Jean MCGIVNEY-BURELLE
72 Interim Dean College of Technology Ms. Debra RONNEBURG
12 Dean of Academic Pgm ISU-Meridian Vacant
12 Vice Provost/Dean for IF AA Dr. Lyle CASTLE
08 Dean & University Librarian Dr. Sandra SHROPSHIRE
06 Registrar & Dir of Undergrad Admiss Ms. Laura MCKENZIE
13 Chief Information Officer Ms. Renae SCOTT
29 Director Alumni Relations Mr. Ryan SARGENT
09 Director Institutional Research Mr. Vince MILLER
37 Dir Student Fin Aid/Scholarships Mr. James R. MARTIN
15 Director Human Resources Mr. Brian SAGENDORF
23 Director Student Health Center Vacant
22 Dir EEO/Affirm Action & Diversity Ms. Stacey GIBSON
19 Director Public Safety Mr. Lewis EAKINS
26 Assoc VP Marketing & Communication Mr. Stuart SUMMERS
86 Director Government Relations Vacant
88 Director Events Management Mr. George CASPER
35 Dean of Students Mr. Craig CHATRIAND
38 Director of Counseling & Testing Dr. Richard PONGRATZ
85 Assoc Dir Admiss/Intl Svcs Mr. Shawn BASCOM
07 Director Admissions & Recruitment Ms. Nicole JOSEPH
39 Director University Housing Mr. Craig THOMPSON
96 Interim Dir Purchasing Services Ms. Lisa LEYSHON
44 Director Annual Giving Vacant
100 Chief of Staff Ms. Dani DUNSTAN
25 Director Contract/Grants Accounting Ms. Lisa WOOD

Lewis-Clark State College (F)

500 8th Avenue, Lewiston ID 83501-2698
County: Nez Perce FICE Identification: 001621
Unit ID: 142328
Telephone: (208) 792-5272 Carnegie Class: Bac-Diverse
FAX Number: (208) 792-2831 Calendar System: Semester
URL: www.lcsc.edu
Established: 1893 Annual Undergrad Tuition & Fees (In-State): $6,982
Enrollment: 3,856 Coed
Affiliation or Control: State IRS Status: 501(c)3
Highest Offering: Baccalaureate
Accreditation: NW, CAEP, EMT, IACBE, MAC, NURSE, PTAA, RAD, SW

01 President Dr. Cynthia L. PEMBERTON
05 Provost/VP Academic Affairs Dr. Fredrick CHILSON
10 VP Finance and Administration Dr. Julie CREA
32 Sr Vice President Student Affairs Dr. Andrew HANSON
75 Dean Career & Technical Education Mr. Jeffrey OBER
107 Int Dean Professional Studies Dr. Luther MADDY
49 Dean Liberal Arts & Sciences Mr. Martin GIBBS
08 Director of Library Services Ms. Johanna BJORK
103 Director of Workforce Training Vacant
07 Director of Admissions/Recruitment Ms. Soo Lee BRUCE-SMITH
06 Registrar Mr. Ted UNZICKER
09 Dir Inst Research & Effectiveness Dr. Grace ANDERSON
13 Chief Technology Officer Mr. Marty GANG
41 Athletic Director Ms. Brooke HENZE
15 Director of Human Resources Ms. Vikki SWIFT-RAYMOND
26 Director Communications & Marketing Mr. Logan FOWLER
37 Director of Student Financial Aid Ms. Laura HUGHES
111 Director of College Advancement Ms. Erika ALLEN
18 Director of Physical Plant Mr. Tom GARRISON
121 Director of Advising Center Ms. Debra LYBYER
96 Director of Purchasing Ms. Sheila KOM
19 Director Security/Safety Vacant
04 Exec Assistant to the President Ms. Lori RUDDELL
106 Dir E-learning/Testing Ctr/Acces Ms. Dawn LESPERANCE
25 Assoc Dir Grants & Contracts Dr. Chris BELCHER
38 Dir Student Counseling/Health Svcs Mr. Doug STEELE
39 Director Resident Life Ms. Debbie KOLSTAD

Mercy In Action College of Midwifery (G)

3018 West Overland Rd, Boise ID 83705
County: Ada Identification: 667393
Telephone: (208) 258-9334 Carnegie Class: Not Classified
FAX Number: N/A Calendar System: Semester
URL: mercycollegeofmidwifery.edu
Established: 1991 Annual Undergrad Tuition & Fees: N/A
Enrollment: N/A Coed
Affiliation or Control: Independent Non-Profit IRS Status: 501(c)3
Highest Offering: Baccalaureate
Accreditation: MEAC

01 Executive Director Vicki PENWELL
05 Academic Director Kristen BENOIT

New Saint Andrews College (H)

PO Box 9025, Moscow ID 83843-1525
County: Latah Identification: 666166
Unit ID: 440396

Telephone: (208) 882-1566 Carnegie Class: Bac-A&S
FAX Number: (208) 882-4293 Calendar System: Other
URL: www.nsa.edu
Established: 1994 Annual Undergrad Tuition & Fees: $13,550
Enrollment: 221 Coed
Affiliation or Control: Independent Non-Profit IRS Status: 501(c)3
Highest Offering: Master's
Accreditation: TRACS

01 President .... Dr. Ben MERKLE
05 Academic Dean .... Dr. Timothy EDWARDS
73 Director Theology MA Program .... Dr. Timothy EDWARDS
53 Dir Classical Christian Studies Pgm .... Mr. Christopher SCHLECT
58 Director MFA Program .... Mr. Nate WILSON
06 Registrar .... Ms. Grace BURNETT
07 Director of Admissions .... Mrs. Brenda SCHLECT
08 Head Librarian .... Mr. Caleb HARRIS
30 Director of Development .... Mr. Derek MONJURE
84 Director of Recruiting .... Ms. Grace HENDRIX

North Idaho College (A)

1000 W Garden Avenue, Coeur d'Alene ID 83814-2199
County: Kootenai FICE Identification: 001623
Unit ID: 142443
Telephone: (208) 769-3300 Carnegie Class: Assoc/HT-Mix Trad/Non
FAX Number: (208) 765-2761 Calendar System: Semester
URL: www.nic.edu
Established: 1933 Annual Undergrad Tuition & Fees (In-District): $4,960
Enrollment: 4,737 Coed
Affiliation or Control: Local IRS Status: 501(c)3
Highest Offering: Associate Degree
Accreditation: NW, ADNUR, DH, MAC, MLTAD, PTAA, RAD, SURGT

01 President .... Dr. Nick SWAYNE
05 Interim Provost .... Dr. Kassie SILVAS
10 Int VP for Finance/Business Affairs .... Ms. Sarah GARCIA
32 Int Dean of Students .... Mr. Alex HARRIS
86 Chief Communications/Govt Rels Ofcr .... Ms. Laura RUMPLER
103 Int Dean Workforce Education .... Mr. Doug ANDERSON
97 Dean of General Studies .... Vacant
76 Dean of Health Prof & Nursing .... Ms. Christy DOYLE
07 Director of Admissions/Registrar .... Vacant
108 Accred Liaison Ofcr/Dir Plng/Effect .... Dr. Steve KURTZ
08 Library Director .... Mr. George MCALISTER
13 Chief Information Officer .... Mr. Ken WARDINSKY
15 Chief Human Resources Officer .... Ms. Karen HUBBARD
37 Director of Financial Aid .... Ms. Stephanie HOUSE
121 Dir of Advising/Student Success .... Ms. Ellen CRABTREE
18 Director of Facilities .... Mr. Garry STARK
30 Director of Development .... Ms. Rayelle ANDERSON
35 Director Student Involvement .... Ms. Dodi STILKEY
21 Controller .... Ms. Sarah GARCIA
72 Technology Coordinator .... Mr. Andy FINNEY
29 Alumni Relations Coordinator .... Ms. Pam NOAH
04 Sr Executive Assistant .... Ms. Shannon GOODRICH
106 Director of E-learning .... Dr. Thomas SCOTT
25 Grants Development Manager .... Vacant
41 Athletic Director .... Mr. Bobby LEE
19 Supervisor Campus Security .... Mr. Stuart WAGNER

Northwest Nazarene University (B)

623 S. University Boulevard, Nampa ID 83686-5897
County: Canyon FICE Identification: 001624
Unit ID: 142461
Telephone: (208) 467-8011 Carnegie Class: Masters/L
FAX Number: (208) 467-8099 Calendar System: Semester
URL: www.nnu.edu
Established: 1913 Annual Undergrad Tuition & Fees: $32,780
Enrollment: 2,109 Coed
Affiliation or Control: Church Of The Nazarene IRS Status: 501(c)3
Highest Offering: Doctorate
Accreditation: NW, ACBSP, CACREP, CAEPN, NURSE, SW, THEOL

01 President .... Mr. Joel K. PEARSALL
05 Vice Pres Academic Affairs/Dean .... Dr. Brad KURTZ-SHAW
10 Vice Pres Finance & Operations .... Mr. Steve EMERSON
32 Vice President Student Life .... Mrs. Karen L. PEARSON
111 Vice Pres for External Relations .... Mr. Mark WHEELER
84 Chief Admissions Officer .... Mrs. Stacey BERGGREN
26 Assoc Vice Pres for Marketing .... Mr. Mark CORK
41 Athletic Director .... Ms. Kelli LINDLEY
06 Registrar .... Vacant
07 Director of Admissions .... Mr. Richard R. VASQUEZ
123 Director of Graduate Admissions .... Mr. Toby SCHMIDT
124 Chief Retention Officer .... Mrs. Michele CORKISH
121 Dir of Student Success/Advising .... Mrs. Heidi TRACHT
08 Director of the Library .... Ms. Amy RICE
29 Director of Alumni Relations .... Mr. Darl L. BRUNER
51 Dir Center for Professional Devel .... Mrs. Christa SANDIDGE
120 Dir of Instructional Design/Tech .... Mrs. Bethany SCHULTZ
42 University Chaplain .... Rev. Grant MILLER
40 Campus Store Manager .... Ms. Gail D. WALKER
35 Assoc Vice Pres Student Engagement .... Vacant
38 Director of Wellness Center .... Dr. Bryon HEMPHILL
21 Controller .... Mr. John GREENTREE
31 Director of Community Life .... Mr. Andrew CORNELIUS
36 Director of Career Center .... Ms. Amanda F. MARBLE
13 Exec Director of Info Technology .... Mr. Todd BAKER
119 IT Security Officer .... Mrs. Mattie BRANHAM
37 Director of Financial Aid .... Mr. Dwight BERRETH
15 Director of Human Resources .... Ms. Heidi POWERS
91 Dir of Administrative Computing .... Mr. Brian C. STILLMAN
18 Chief Facilities/Physical Plant .... Ms. Denise SENNER
04 Administrative Asst to President .... Mrs. Michelle KUYKENDALL
09 Director of Institutional Research .... Dr. Duane SLEMMER
19 Director Security/Safety .... Mr. Scott CHANDLER

University of Idaho (C)

875 Perimeter Drive, Moscow ID 83844
County: Latah FICE Identification: 001626
Unit ID: 142285
Telephone: (208) 885-6111 Carnegie Class: DU-Higher
FAX Number: N/A Calendar System: Semester
URL: www.uidaho.edu
Established: 1889 Annual Undergrad Tuition & Fees (In-State): $8,304
Enrollment: 10,791 Coed
Affiliation or Control: State IRS Status: 501(c)3
Highest Offering: Doctorate
Accreditation: NW, ART, CAATE, CAEP, CAPRT, CEA, CIDA, DIET, DIETC, IPSY, #JOUR, LAW, LSAR, MUS, NAIT

01 President .... Mr. C. Scott GREEN
05 Provost & Executive VP .... Dr. Torrey LAWRENCE
10 VP Finance and Administration .... Mr. Brian R. FOISY
111 VP University Advancement .... Ms. Mary Kay MCFADDEN
13 VP Information Technology/CIO .... Mr. Dan EWART
46 VP Research & Econ Dev .... Dr. Christopher NOMURA
32 VP Stdnt Affs/Dean of Students .... Dr. Blaine ECKLES
84 Vice Provost Strategic Enroll Mgmt .... Mr. Dean KAHLER
20 Vice Prov Academic Initiatives .... Dr. Gwendolen GORSELSKY
20 Vice Provost for Faculty .... Dr. Diane KELLY-RILEY
26 Alumni Relations & AVP Comm .... Ms. Kathy BARNARD
41 Athletic Director .... Ms. Terry GAWLIK
43 General Counsel .... Mr. Jim CRAIG
103 CEO Boise Ctr/Sr Assoc to Pres .... Ms. Chandra ZENNER FORD
88 Special Asst Strategy .... Vacant
86 Special Asst State Govt Relations .... Mr. Joe STEGNER
28 Chf Div Ofcr/Exec Dir Tribal Rels .... Dr. Yolanda BISBEE
08 Dean Library Services .... Mr. Ben HUNTER
49 Dean Col of Ltrs/Arts/Social Sci .... Dr. Sean QUINLAN
47 Dean College of Agric/Life Sci .... Dr. Michael PARRELLA
50 Dean College of Business & Econ .... Dr. Marc CHOPIN
53 Dean Col of Educ/Hlth/Human Sci .... Ms. Brooke BLEVINS
54 Int Dean College of Engineering .... Mr. John CREPEAU
58 Dean Graduate Studies .... Dr. Jerry MCMURTY
65 Dean College of Natural Resources .... Dr. Michael PARRELLA
61 Dean College of Law .... Ms. Johanna KALB
48 Dean College of Art & Arch .... Dr. Shauna CORRY
81 Dean College of Science .... Dr. Ginger CARNEY
109 Asst VP Auxiliary Services .... Ms. Cami MCCLURE
15 Director of Human Resources .... Ms. Brandi TERWILLIGER
114 AVP Budget/Planning .... Ms. Trina MAHONEY
12 Executive Officer Coeur d'Alene Ctr .... Dr. Charles BUCK
12 Int Exec Officer Idaho Falls Ctr .... Dr. Lee OSTROM
18 Director Facilities .... Mr. Rusty VINEYARD
19 Exec Dir Environment Health/Safety .... Mr. Samir Shahat ABD EL-FATAH
117 Dir Emergency Mgmt & Security Sys .... Mr. Todd PERRY
108 IR Dir Inst Effectiveness & Accred .... Mr. Wes MCCLINTICK
37 Director Student Financial Aid .... Ms. Randi CROYLE
07 Assistant Vice Provost SEM .... Ms. Bobbi J. GERRY
38 Director Counseling & Testing Ctr .... Dr. Gregory LAMBETH
39 Director University Residences .... Ms. Dee Dee KANIKKEBERG
44 Director Annual Giving .... Ms. Stacy RAUCH
92 Director Honors Program .... Ms. Sandra REINEKE
93 Dir Multicultural Affairs .... Mr. Jesse MARTINEZ
94 Director Women's Center .... Ms. Lysa SALSBURY
40 Mgr VandalStore/Trademark .... Ms. Tricia DURGIN
96 Director Purchasing Services .... Ms. Julia MCILROY
36 Director Career Services .... Mr. Christopher COOK
25 Director Research Admin .... Ms. Deborah SHAVER
121 Exec Dir Student Success Initiative .... Ms. Cynthia CASTRO
06 Registrar .... Ms. Lindsey BROWN
102 Exec Director UI Foundation .... Ms. Joy FISHER
88 Dir Admissions Operations .... Ms. Melissa GOODWIN
22 Dir Civil Rights & Investigation .... Ms. Erin AGIDIUS
104 Director International Services .... Ms. Dana BROLLEY
100 Chief of Staff President's Office .... Ms. Brenda HELBLING
09 Director of Institutional Research .... Mr. Wes MCCLINTICK
29 Director Alumni Programs & Opers .... Ms. Marie DUNCAN
30 Senior Director of Development .... Mr. Jeff PILCHER

ILLINOIS

Adler University (D)

17 North Dearborn Street, Chicago IL 60602
County: Cook FICE Identification: 020681
Unit ID: 142832
Telephone: (312) 662-4000 Carnegie Class: Spec-4-yr-Other Health
FAX Number: (312) 662-4099 Calendar System: Semester
URL: www.adler.edu
Established: 1952 Annual Graduate Tuition & Fees: N/A
Enrollment: 1,726 Coed
Affiliation or Control: Independent Non-Profit IRS Status: 501(c)3
Highest Offering: Doctorate; No Undergraduates
Accreditation: HLC, CACREP, CLPSY, IPSY, MFCD

01 President .... Dr. Raymond E. CROSSMAN
101 Board Secy/Dir Ofc of the Pres .... Ms. Mitzi NORTON
11 Vice President Administration .... Mrs. Jo Beth CUP
05 Vice President Academic Affairs .... Dr. Wendy PASZKIEWICZ
10 Vice President Finance & IT .... Vacant
07 Vice President Admissions .... Mr. Craig HINES
28 VP Diversity & Inclusion .... Ms. Tamara JOHNSON
26 Vice President Communications .... Mr. Mark BRANSON
111 AVP Institutional Advancement .... Ms. Heather SCHUSTER
06 Registrar .... Ms. Sheba JONES
32 Assoc Vice President Student Affs .... Dr. Quincy PADEN
19 Ex Dir Inst Pub Safety/Soc Justice .... Dr. Elena QUINTANA
37 Director Student Financial Aid .... Mr. David NELSON
13 AVP Technology .... Mr. Jomar MCDONALD
12 Exec Dean Vancouver Campus .... Mr. Bradley O'HARA
106 Executive Dean Online Campus .... Dr. Michelle DENNIS
15 Vice Pres People/Culture .... Ms. Dona MCCULLOUGH
29 Director Alumni Relations .... Vacant
04 Administrative Asst to President .... Ms. Elizabeth BLONDEL
18 Chief Facilities/Physical Plant .... Mr. Tom ROHNER
43 Dir Legal Services/General Counsel .... Ms. Julie PROSCIA
08 Director Library Services .... Ms. Ariel ORLOV
102 Dir Foundation/Corporate Relations .... Ms. Ingrid PARKER
108 Dir Institutional Effectivenes .... Ms. Katy SELINKO

Ambria College of Nursing (E)

5210 Trillium Boulevard, Hoffman Estates IL 60192
County: Cook FICE Identification: 041247
Unit ID: 457527
Telephone: (847) 397-0300 Carnegie Class: Spec-4-yr-Other Health
FAX Number: (847) 397-0313 Calendar System: Other
URL: www.ambria.edu
Established: 2006 Annual Undergrad Tuition & Fees: N/A
Enrollment: 229 Coed
Affiliation or Control: Proprietary IRS Status: Proprietary
Highest Offering: Associate Degree
Accreditation: ABHES, ADNUR

01 President .... Jon OLIVEROS
66 Director of Nursing Education .... Sharon ORTEGA

American Academy of Art College (F)

332 S Michigan Avenue, Chicago IL 60604-4302
County: Cook FICE Identification: 001628
Unit ID: 142887
Telephone: (312) 461-0600 Carnegie Class: Spec-4-yr-Arts
FAX Number: (312) 294-9570 Calendar System: Semester
URL: www.aaart.edu
Established: 1923 Annual Undergrad Tuition & Fees: $35,270
Enrollment: 169 Coed
Affiliation or Control: Independent Non-Profit IRS Status: 501(c)3
Highest Offering: Baccalaureate
Accreditation: HLC

01 President .... Mr. Richard H. OTTO
05 Academic Dean .... Mr. Duncan WEBB
06 Registrar .... Ms. Marcia R. THOMAS
36 Career Services Coordinator .... Ms. Lindsay SANDBOTHE
37 Financial Aid Director .... Ms. Ione FITZGERALD
07 Director of Admissions .... Mr. Stuart ROSENBLOOM

American Islamic College (G)

640 W. Irving Park Rd, Chicago IL 60613
County: Cook Identification: 667378
Unit ID: 142957
Telephone: (773) 281-4700 Carnegie Class: Not Classified
FAX Number: N/A Calendar System: Semester
URL: www.aicusa.edu
Established: 1981 Annual Undergrad Tuition & Fees: $7,600
Enrollment: 16 Coed
Affiliation or Control: Independent Non-Profit IRS Status: 501(c)3
Highest Offering: Master's
Accreditation: @HLC

01 President .... Timothy J. GIANOTTI
10 VP Finance & Administration .... Randal MUHAMMAD

Augustana College (H)

639 38th Street, Rock Island IL 61201-2296
County: Rock Island FICE Identification: 001633
Unit ID: 143084
Telephone: (309) 794-7000 Carnegie Class: Bac-A&S
FAX Number: (309) 794-7422 Calendar System: 4/1/4
URL: www.augustana.edu
Established: 1860 Annual Undergrad Tuition & Fees: $45,136
Enrollment: 2,389 Coed
Affiliation or Control: Evangelical Lutheran Church In America
IRS Status: 501(c)3
Highest Offering: Baccalaureate
Accreditation: HLC, MUS, @SP

01 President .... Mr. Steven C. BAHLS
05 Provost and Dean of the College .... Dr. Wendy HILTON-MORROW
10 Vice Pres of Finance and Admin .... Mr. Kirk D. ANDERSON
30 Executive VP External Relations .... Mr. W. Kent BARNDS
32 VP/Dean of Student Life .... Dr. Wesley BROOKS
28 VP Diversity/Equity and Inclusion .... Dr. Monica SMITH
20 Associate Dean of the College .... Dr. Michael EGAN
20 Associate Dean of the College .... Dr. Kristin DOUGLAS
20 Associate Dean of the College .... Dr. Jessica SCHULTZ

42 Chaplain .... Rev. Melinda PUPILLO
06 College Registrar .... Ms. Liesl A. FOWLER
09 Asst Dean/Director Inst Research .... Dr. Tsooane MOLAPO
08 Director of the Library .... Dr. Chris SCHAFER
36 Associate VP Careers & Prof Devel .... Ms. Laura KESTNER-RICKETTS
13 Director of ITS .... Mr. Chris VAUGHAN
37 Director of Student Financial Aid .... Mr. John CAGE
96 Dir Financial Plng & Procurement .... Mr. Malhar SAHEED
19 Chief of Public Safety .... Mr. Thomas M. PHILLIS
41 Director of Athletics .... Mr. Mike ZAPOLSKI
15 Director Human Resources .... Mr. Brandon TIDWELL
18 Director Facilities Services .... Mr. Robert LANZEROTTI
38 Director Student Counseling .... Mr. William IAVARONE
35 Assistant Dean of Student Life .... Ms. Laura L. SCHNACK
26 Assistant VP of Comm & Marketing .... Ms. Keri RURSCH
29 Director Alumni/Parent Relations .... Ms. Kelly NOACK
07 Executive Director of Admissions .... Ms. Emma ADEBAYO
04 Executive Assistant to President .... Ms. Mary KOSKI
104 Dir Intl Student & Scholar Svcs .... Ms. Xong Sony YANG
43 Dir Legal Services/General Counsel .... Ms. Sheri L. CURRAN
100 Chief of Staff .... Mr. Kai SWANSON
102 Dir Foundation/Corporate Relations .... Ms. Lori RODERICK
39 Director of Residential Life .... Mr. Christopher BEYER
105 Director Web Services & News Media .... Ms. Leslie M. DUPREE
50 Dean of Business .... Dr. Amanda BAUGOUS
53 Dean of Education .... Dr. Michael SCARLETT
54 Dean of Engineering .... Dr. Nathan FRANK
86 Director Government Relations .... Mr. Kai SWANSON
44 Director Annual Giving .... Ms. Erin WILLIAMS

Aurora University (A)

347 S Gladstone Avenue, Aurora IL 60506-4892
County: Kane FICE Identification: 001634
Unit ID: 143118
Telephone: (630) 892-6431 Carnegie Class: DU-Mod
FAX Number: (630) 844-5463 Calendar System: Semester
URL: www.aurora.edu
Established: 1893 Annual Undergrad Tuition & Fees: $25,600
Enrollment: 6,265 Coed
Affiliation or Control: Independent Non-Profit IRS Status: 501(c)3
Highest Offering: Doctorate
Accreditation: HLC, CAATE, NURSE, SW

01 President .... Dr. Rebecca L. SHERRICK
05 Vice President for Academic Affairs .... Dr. Andrew PRALL
10 Sr Vice President for Finance .... Ms. Sharon MAXWELL
18 Chief Operating Officer .... Mr. Jeff KING
121 Sr Vice President Student Success .... Dr. Jennifer BUCKLEY
111 Sr Vice President for Advancement .... Ms. Meg HOWES
26 Sr VP for Enrollment and Marketing .... Ms. Deb MAUE
29 SVP Alumni Relations/Career Service .... Ms. Teri TOMASZKIEWICZ
15 Vice President of Human Resources .... Ms. Ann CHAN
32 Vice President for Student Life .... Dr. Amy GRAY
41 Vice President for Athletics .... Mr. James HAMAD
37 AVP for Student Financial Services .... Ms. Heather L. GRANART
21 University Controller .... Mr. John BRYANT
06 University Registrar .... Mr. Daniel WEBER
08 Director University Library .... Ms. Sarah MCHONE-CHASE
19 Chief of Police .... Mr. John MCIVOR
07 Dean of Undergrad Admissions .... Mr. Matt CRISMAN
76 Dean of College of Health Sciences .... Dr. Sarah RADTKE
70 Dean Sch of Social Work & Education .... Dr. Brenda BARNWELL
88 Faculty Development Liaison .... Dr. Julie HIPP
123 Dean of Graduate Enrollment .... Ms. Emily MORALES
50 Dean Col Liberal Arts & Businesss .... Vacant
106 Dean of Online Enroll/Cont Educ .... Dr. Donna LILJEGREN
20 Dean Academic Administration .... Dr. Mary TARLING
04 Sr Executive Assistant to President .... Ms. Becca FLAMINIO
09 Director of University Analytics .... Dr. Katie THARP
39 Asst Dean of Student Life .... Mr. Chris SMITH
101 Secretary of the Institution/Board .... Ms. Becca FLAMINIO
13 Chief Information Technology Office .... Mr. Hurstel HOWARD

Benedictine University (B)

5700 College Road, Lisle IL 60532-0900
County: DuPage FICE Identification: 001767
Unit ID: 145619
Telephone: (630) 829-6000 Carnegie Class: Masters/L
FAX Number: N/A Calendar System: Semester
URL: www.ben.edu
Established: 1887 Annual Undergrad Tuition & Fees: $34,290
Enrollment: 3,779 Coed
Affiliation or Control: Roman Catholic IRS Status: 501(c)3
Highest Offering: Doctorate
Accreditation: HLC, DIETD, DIETI, NURSE, PH

01 President .... Mr. Charles GREGORY
05 Provost/Chief Academic Officer .... Dr. Kenneth F. NEWBOLD, JR.
10 Int Chief Financial Officer .... Mr. John SCHADE
100 Chief of Staff .... Ms. Patricia ARIANO
13 Chief Information Officer .... Mr. Darren ROBARDS
32 Chief Student Engagement Officer .... Mr. Mark MCHORNEY
124 Chief Enroll/Retention Officer .... Ms. Karen CAMPANA
28 Associate Prov for Diversity/Equity .... Dr. Julie DOCKERY
20 Assoc Provost .... Dr. Cheryl HEINZ
42 Director University Ministry .... Ms. Carrie ANKENY
06 Registrar .... Mr. Jason HEIDENFELDER
08 Assoc Director Library Services .... Ms. Lou Ann DEGREVE
37 Director Financial Aid .... Mr. Adrian GONZALEZ
09 Director of Institutional Research .... Dr. Amy SHIN
36 Director Career Development .... Vacant
32 Dean of Students .... Mr. Marco MASINI
23 Director Health Services .... Vacant
50 Dean College of Business .... Dr. Darrell RADSON
81 Dean College of Science/Health .... Vacant
49 Dean College of Lib Arts .... Ms. Olga LAMBERT
51 Pgm Dir Adult/Profess Bus Pgms .... Ms. Larissa ADAMIEC
88 Chief Mission Officer .... Dr. Peter HUFF
11 Chief Operations Officer .... Vacant
35 Dir Student Activities/Recreation .... Mr. Harold WATSON
07 Director of Admissions .... Mr. Matthew JONES
04 Executive Asst to the President .... Ms. Deborah A. SUTLIFF
15 Human Resources Manager .... Ms. Kelly ZAPP
29 Director Alumni Relations .... Vacant
41 Director of Athletics .... Mr. Paul NELSON
43 Chief Compliance Ofcr/Legal Counsel .... Vacant
18 Dir Facilities Mgmt/Planning .... Mr. Bryan GOODWIN
86 Assoc Compliance Officer .... Mr. Kevin RAPPEL
25 Dir Office of Institutional Grants .... Ms. Cate CROTEAU
30 Director of Development .... Mr. Eric SOLBERG

Bexley Seabury (C)

1407 E 60th St, Chicago IL 60637
County: Cook FICE Identification: 037473
Unit ID: 443702
Telephone: (773) 380-6780 Carnegie Class: Spec-4-yr-Faith
FAX Number: (773) 380-6788 Calendar System: Semester
URL: www.bexleyseabury.edu
Established: 1824 Annual Graduate Tuition & Fees: N/A
Enrollment: 68 Coed
Affiliation or Control: Protestant Episcopal IRS Status: 501(c)3
Highest Offering: Doctorate; No Undergraduates
Accreditation: THEOL

01 President .... RevDr. Micah JACKSON
05 Academic Dean .... Mr. Jason FOUT
10 Chief Financial Officer .... Mr. Curt SHORT
07 Director of Admissions .... Mr. Jaime BRICENO

Black Hawk College (D)

6600 34th Avenue, Moline IL 61265-5899
County: Rock Island FICE Identification: 001638
Unit ID: 143279
Telephone: (309) 796-5000 Carnegie Class: Assoc/MT-VT-High Non
FAX Number: (309) 792-5976 Calendar System: Semester
URL: www.bhc.edu
Established: 1946 Annual Undergrad Tuition & Fees (In-District): $7,500
Enrollment: 3,743 Coed
Affiliation or Control: Local IRS Status: 501(c)3
Highest Offering: Associate Degree
Accreditation: HLC, ADNUR, EMT, PTAA, SURGT

01 President .... Mr. Tim WYNES
05 VP of Instruction .... Dr. Amy MAXEINER
10 VP Finance/Admin & Board Treasurer .... Mr. Steve FROMMELT
12 Executive Dean of East Campus .... Dr. Jeffry HAWES
15 Director of Human Resources .... Ms. Stacey CARY
19 Chief of Police .... Mr. Shawn CISNA
09 Director Plng & Inst Effectiveness .... Ms. Kathy MALCOLM
26 Director Marketing/Public Relations .... Mr. John MEINEKE
13 Co-CIO/IT Systems Manager .... Mr. Ryan WHITE
13 Co-CIO/Manager of Admin Systems .... Ms. Sandy COX
102 Exec Dir BHC Foundation QC Campus .... Ms. Maureen DICKINSON
51 Acting Dean Adult/Continuing Educ .... Ms. Barb COURVILLE
81 Academic Dean .... Mr. Ken NICKELS
04 Executive Asst to the President .... Ms. Heather BENNETT
36 Director Career Services Center .... Dr. Bruce STOREY
37 Director of Financial Aid .... Vacant
08 Librarian .... Ms. Ashtin TRIMBLE
55 Director Adult Education .... Ms. Bianca PERKINS
84 Dean Enrollment Mgmt .... Ms. Heather BJORGAN
40 Bookstore Manager Quad Cities .... Ms. Aimee MUHLEMAN
96 Purchasing Manager .... Mr. Mike MELEG
50 Dept Chair Business & Technology .... Ms. Carrie DELCOURT
79 Dept Chair Human/Languages/Journal .... Mr. Bill DESMOND
77 Dept Chair Mathematics/Comp Science .... Ms. Connie MCLEAN
54 Dept Chair Natural Science/Engrng .... Mr. Brian GLASER
83 Dept Chair Social Sciences .... Mr. Mark ESPOSITO
47 Department Chair Agriculture .... Dr. Jeffrey HAWES
66 Dept Chair Nursing .... Ms. Trudy STARR
76 Dept Chair Allied Health/HPE .... Ms. Dianne ABELS
38 Dept Chair Counseling .... Ms. Wendy BOCK
62 Dept Chair Lrg Resource Center .... Vacant
53 Dept Chair Psych/Sociology/Educ .... Dr. Traci DAVIS
72 Dept Chair Career Technologies .... Ms. Jamie HILL
18 Chief Facilities/Physical Plant .... Mr. Bob MCCHURCH

Black Hawk College East Campus (E)

26230 Black Hawk Road, Galva IL 61434
Telephone: (309) 854-1700 Identification: 770069
Accreditation: &HLC

Blackburn College (F)

700 College Avenue, Carlinville IL 62626-1498
County: Macoupin FICE Identification: 001639
Unit ID: 143288
Telephone: (217) 854-3231 Carnegie Class: Bac-Diverse
FAX Number: (217) 854-5700 Calendar System: Semester
URL: www.blackburn.edu
Established: 1837 Annual Undergrad Tuition & Fees: $24,950
Enrollment: 516 Coed
Affiliation or Control: Presbyterian Church (U.S.A.) IRS Status: 501(c)3
Highest Offering: Baccalaureate
Accreditation: HLC

01 President .... Dr. Mark L. BIERMANN
05 Provost .... Dr. Karla MCCAIN
10 Vice Pres Administration & Finance .... Ms. Sarah MOUCH
111 VP for Institutional Advancement .... Ms. Lauren DODGE
32 VP/Dean of Student Affairs .... Vacant
101 Exec Asst to Pres/Sec Bd Trustees .... Mrs. Shawna POE
102 Sr Dir of Devel/Foundation Rels .... Ms. Sarah KOPLINSKI
29 Exec Dir Advance/Alumni Relations .... Ms. Alisha KAPP
37 Director of Financial Aid .... Ms. Alexis BROWN
38 Director Counseling Services .... Mr. Tim MORENZ
06 College Registrar .... Mrs. Dianna RUYLE
41 Athletic Director .... Vacant
26 Dir of Marketing/Public Relations .... Mr. Kyle LOWDEN
09 Director of Institutional Research .... Dr. Kristi NELMS
21 Controller .... Vacant
44 Exec Dir for Annual Giving .... Ms. Teresa KIRK
84 Enrollment Services Administrator .... Mrs. Kathy RUITER
13 Chief Info Technology Officer (CIO) .... Mr. Jason CLONINGER
88 Dean of Work .... Ms. Judy STURGEON
07 Director of Admissions .... Dr. Steven LAMBERT
15 Chief Human Resources Officer .... Mr. Marshall PETTY
28 Director of Diversity .... Dr. Margaret LAWLER

Blessing-Rieman College of Nursing & Health Sciences (G)

3609 North Marx Drive, Quincy IL 62305-7005
County: Adams FICE Identification: 006214
Unit ID: 143297
Telephone: (217) 228-5520 Carnegie Class: Spec-4-yr-Other Health
FAX Number: (217) 223-4661 Calendar System: Semester
URL: www.brcn.edu
Established: 1891 Annual Undergrad Tuition & Fees: N/A
Enrollment: 177 Coed
Affiliation or Control: Independent Non-Profit IRS Status: 501(c)3
Highest Offering: Master's
Accreditation: HLC, CAHIIM, COARC, MLTAD, NURSE, RAD

01 President/CEO .... Dr. Brenda BESHEARS
05 Academic Dean .... Dr. Jan AKRIGHT
84 Dean of Enroll Mgmt/Business Mgr .... Ms. Jenna CRABTREE
06 Registrar .... Ms. Rachel CRAMSEY

Bradley University (H)

1501 W Bradley Avenue, Peoria IL 61625-0001
County: Peoria FICE Identification: 001641
Unit ID: 143358
Telephone: (309) 676-7611 Carnegie Class: DU-Mod
FAX Number: N/A Calendar System: Semester
URL: www.bradley.edu
Established: 1897 Annual Undergrad Tuition & Fees: $35,480
Enrollment: 5,855 Coed
Affiliation or Control: Independent Non-Profit IRS Status: 501(c)3
Highest Offering: Doctorate
Accreditation: HLC, ACPHA, ART, CACREP, CONST, DIET, DIETD, DIETI, MUS, NURSE, PTA, SW, THEA

01 President .... Mr. Stephen STANDIFIRD
05 Provost/Vice Pres Academic Affs .... Dr. Walter R. ZAKAHI
32 Vice President Student Affairs .... Mr. Nathan THOMAS
84 VP Enrollment Management .... Mr. Justin BALL
111 Vice President Advancement .... Ms. Erin GENOVESE
43 Vice Pres Legal Affairs/Gen Counsel .... Ms. Erin KASTBERG
41 VP for Intercollegiate Athletics .... Dr. Chris REYNOLDS
10 Chief Financial Officer .... Ms. Sheryl COX
19 Chief of Campus Police .... Mr. Brian JOSCHKO
20 Associate Provost .... Dr. Jobie SKAGGS
20 Assistant to the Provost .... Mrs. Tracy ZUERCHER
114 Assistant VP Budgeting and Planning .... Mr. Demetrius L. CARMICHAEL
50 Dean Col Business and Engineering .... Dr. Molly GRIBB
57 Dean Slane Col Commun/Fine Arts .... Dr. Jeffrey H. HUBERMAN
53 Dean Educ & Health Sciences .... Dr. Jessica CLARK
49 Dean Liberal Arts/Sciences .... Dr. Daniel MOON
106 Assist VP for Online/Distance Educ .... Dr. Rui LI
08 Exec Director of Library .... Mr. Todd SPIRES
39 Dir Ctr Residential Living/Ldrshp .... Mr. Ryan BAIR
36 Exec Dir Smith Career Center .... Mr. Jon NEIDY
29 Director of Alumni Relations .... Ms. Tory JENNETTEN
51 Interim Exec Dir Continuing Educ .... Ms. Michelle RIGGIO RARICK
06 Registrar .... Mr. Andreas KINDLER
37 Director Financial Aid .... Ms. Abigail GASHAW
15 Director of Human Resources .... Ms. Crystal ELLIOTT
18 Director Facilities Management .... Mr. Larry MCGUIRE
23 Medical Director Health Services .... Dr. Jessica HIGGS
13 Chief Information Officer .... Mr. Zach GORMAN
78 Director Springer Center .... Mrs. Dawn KOELTZOW
87 Dir Summer/Interim Sessions .... Ms. Janet LANGE
28 VP of Diversity/Equity/Inclusion .... Mr. Warren ANDERSON
92 Director of Honors Program .... Dr. Kyle DZAPO
94 Dir of Women's Studies & Gender .... Dr. Amy SCOTT
108 Dir of Institutional Effectiveness .... Ms. Jennifer G. BURGE
40 Manager Bookstore .... Mr. Paul KROENKE
88 Dir of Health Prof Advising Ctr .... Dr. Valerie BENNETT
61 Dir Center for Legal Studies .... Ms. Jerelyn MAHER

07 Asst Dir Admissions .... Mr. Joshua JONES
104 Director Study Abroad .... Dr. Christine BLOUCH

Carl Sandburg College (A)

2400 Tom L. Wilson Boulevard, Galesburg IL 61401-9576
County: Knox FICE Identification: 007265
Unit ID: 143613
Telephone: (309) 344-2518 Carnegie Class: Assoc/HT-Mix Trad/Non
FAX Number: (309) 344-1395 Calendar System: Semester
URL: www.sandburg.edu
Established: 1966 Annual Undergrad Tuition & Fees: $7,190
Enrollment: 1,755 Coed
Affiliation or Control: Independent Non-Profit IRS Status: 501(c)3
Highest Offering: Associate Degree
Accreditation: HLC, ADNUR, DH, EMT, FUSER, MAC, PNUR

01 President .... Dr. Seamus REILLY
37 Director Financial Aid .... Ms. Lisa HANSON
07 Director of Recruitment .... Ms. Zoe KUDLA-POLAY
41 Athletic Director .... Mr. Jerry THOR
06 Director of Admissions & Records .... Mr. Rick EDDY
19 Director of Public Safety .... Mr. Kipton CANFIELD
15 Director of Human Resources .... Ms. Gina KRUPPS
45 Dean of Institutional Planning .... Ms. Michelle JOHNSON
103 Dean Career/Technical Education .... Ms. Ellen BURNS
88 Director of Corporate & Leisure .... Vacant
12 Director of Branch Campus .... Dr. Ellen HENDERSON-GASSER
81 Assoc Dean Math/Natural Sciences .... Ms. Marjorie SMOLENSKY
05 VP of Academic Services .... Ms. Carrie HAWKINSON
20 Assoc VP Academic/Student Svcs/Plng .... Vacant
79 Assoc Dean Humanities/Fine Arts .... Mr. James HUTCHINGS
50 Assoc Dean Social & Business Sci .... Ms. Lara ROEMER
75 Assoc Dean CTHE .... Vacant
76 Dean of Health Professions .... Ms. Kristina GRAY
04 Assistant to President & Board .... Ms. Lindsey HUBER
32 VP of Student Services .... Mr. Steve NORTON
10 Chief Financial Officer/Treasurer .... Mr. Cory GALL
108 Dean Inst Effectiveness/HR .... Dr. Connie THURMAN
26 Director Marketing/Public Relations .... Ms. Brittany GRIMES
111 Director of Advancement .... Ms. Emily WEBEL
13 Director of Technology Services .... Mr. Rob STEVENS
84 Dean of Student Success .... Ms. Autumn SCOTT
121 Director of TRIO SSS .... Ms. Amy BURFORD
121 Director TRIO Upward Bound .... Vacant
121 Director TRIO UB Math Science .... Ms. Stephanie WOODARD

Carl Sandburg College The Branch Campus (B)

305 Sandburg Drive, Carthage IL 62321
Telephone: (217) 357-3129 Identification: 770071
Accreditation: &HLC

Catholic Theological Union (C)

5416 S Cornell Avenue, Chicago IL 60615-5698
County: Cook FICE Identification: 009232
Unit ID: 143659
Telephone: (773) 371-5400 Carnegie Class: Spec-4-yr-Faith
FAX Number: (773) 324-8490 Calendar System: Semester
URL: www.ctu.edu
Established: 1968 Annual Graduate Tuition & Fees: N/A
Enrollment: 227 Coed
Affiliation or Control: Roman Catholic IRS Status: 501(c)3
Highest Offering: Doctorate; No Undergraduates
Accreditation: THEOL

01 President .... Sr. Barbara E. REID, OP
05 Int Vice President/Academic Dean ..Rev. Ferdinand OKORIE, CMP
10 Vice Pres Administration & Finance .... Ms. Cindy GONYA
111 Vice Pres Institutional Advancement .... Ms. Colleen KENNEDY
30 Director of Development .... Ms. Rachel KUHN
08 Director of the Library .... Ms. Kristine VELDHEER
06 Registrar .... Mrs. Maria De Jesus LEMUS
07 Asst Director Admissions .... Ms. Sarai MARTINEZ
13 Director of Information Technology .... Ms. Latisha AIKONS
04 Assistant to the President .... Sr. Pam PAULOSKI, SP
84 Director Enrollment Management ..... Mrs. Ellen ROMER-NIEMIEC
104 Director Study Abroad .... Rev. Ferdinand OKORIE
106 Director Online Educ/E-learning .... Mr. Richard MAUNEY
18 Director Facilities .... Mr. Marty FITZGERALD
26 Communications Manager .... Ms. Madison CHASTAIN
29 Director Alumni Affairs .... Vacant
32 Manager of Events/Student Services .... Ms. LaTasha WEBSTER
15 Chief Human Resources Officer .... Ms. Carmen SALAS
36 Director Student Placement .... Ms. Christine HENDERSON

*Chamberlain University-Administrative Office (D)

500 Monroe Street, Suite 28, Chicago IL 60661
County: DuPage Identification: 667149
Telephone: (703) 416-7300 Carnegie Class: N/A
FAX Number: (703) 416-7490
URL: www.chamberlain.edu

01 President .... Dr. Karen COX
11 VP Campus Operations .... Dr. Patrick ROMBALSKI
05 Provost .... Dr. Carla SANDERSON
84 VP Enrollment Management .... Scott MURPHY
32 VP Student Services .... June MARLOWE
06 University Registrar .... Abbey MCELLIGOTT
09 Assoc Prov Inst Effect/Accred/ Rsrch .... Dr. Linda HOLLINGER-SMITH

*Chamberlain University-Addison (E)

1221 N. Swift Road, Addison IL 60101
County: DuPage FICE Identification: 006385
Unit ID: 454227
Telephone: (630) 953-3660 Carnegie Class: Spec-4-yr-Other Health
FAX Number: (630) 628-1154 Calendar System: Semester
URL: www.chamberlain.edu/addison
Established: 1889 Annual Undergrad Tuition & Fees: $20,381
Enrollment: 29,481 Coed
Affiliation or Control: Proprietary IRS Status: Proprietary
Highest Offering: Doctorate
Accreditation: HLC, CNEA, NURSE, SW

02 Campus President .... Dr. Jan SNOW
05 Dean Academic Affairs .... Crystal PAUNAN
32 Director Student Services .... Lisa PETSCHENKO
07 Director Admissions .... Roz CASTRO

† Master's and Doctorate programs are only offered online.

*Chamberlain University-Chicago (F)

3300 North Campbell Avenue, Chicago IL 60618
Telephone: (773) 961-3000 Identification: 770495
Accreditation: &HLC, #ARCPA, NURSE

*Chamberlain University-Tinley Park (G)

18624 West Creek Drive, Tinley Park IL 60477
Telephone: (708) 560-2000 Identification: 770496
Accreditation: &HLC, NURSE

Chicago College of Oriental Medicine (H)

180 N. Michigan Ave, Ste 1919, Chicago IL 60601
County: Cook Identification: 667406
Telephone: (312) 368-0900 Carnegie Class: Not Classified
FAX Number: (312) 368-1080 Calendar System: Trimester
URL: www.ccoom.org
Established: Annual Graduate Tuition & Fees: N/A
Enrollment: N/A Coed
Affiliation or Control: Proprietary IRS Status: Proprietary
Highest Offering: Master's; No Undergraduates
Accreditation: @ACUP

00 Chancellor/Founder .... Dr. Yong Gao WONG
01 President/COO .... Yili GUO

Chicago School of Professional Psychology-Chicago (I)

325 N Wells Street, Chicago IL 60654-8158
Telephone: (312) 329-6600 Identification: 770349
Accreditation: &WC, ABAI, CACREP, CLPSY, MPCAC, SCPSY

† Branch campus of Chicago School of Professional Psychology Los Angeles Campus, Los Angeles, CA

Chicago State University (J)

9501 S King Drive, Chicago IL 60628-1598
County: Cook FICE Identification: 001694
Unit ID: 144005
Telephone: (773) 995-2000 Carnegie Class: Masters/L
FAX Number: (773) 995-2563 Calendar System: Semester
URL: www.csu.edu
Established: 1867 Annual Undergrad Tuition & Fees (In-State): $11,204
Enrollment: 2,644 Coed
Affiliation or Control: State IRS Status: 501(c)3
Highest Offering: Doctorate
Accreditation: HLC, ACBSP, ART, CACREP, CAHIIM, CAPRT, LIB, MUS, NUR, OT, #PHAR, SW

01 President .... Ms. Zaldwaynaka (Z) SCOTT
05 Int Provost/SVP Academic Affairs .... Dr. Leslie A. ROUNDTREE
10 Vice President/CFO .... Mr. Craig DUETSCH
114 Executive Director Budget/Resource .... Vacant
13 Chief Information Officer .... Mr. Adel HADDAD
84 Int VP of Enrollment Management .... Dr. William SLIWA
11 Int VP Administrative Services .... Mr. Michael HOLMES
09 Dir Inst Effectiveness & Research .... Dr. Jane STOUT
32 Dean of Student Affairs & FYE .... Vacant
49 Dean Col of Arts & Sciences .... Dr. Elizabeth DAVIES, II
53 Dean Col of Education .... Dr. Larnell FLANNAGAN
67 Dean College of Pharmacy .... Dr. Matthew FETE
76 Interim Dean Col of Health Sciences .... Dr. Gregory PAVEZA
50 Dean College of Business .... Mr. Derrick K. COLLINS
08 Dean of Library/Instruct Services .... Vacant
51 Int Dean Cont Educ Nontrad Pgms .... Dr. Patrice BOYLES
92 Dean Honors College .... Dr. Steven ROWE
06 Registrar .... Mr. Caleb WESTBERG
37 Director of Financial Aid .... Ms. Rhonda SMITH
07 Int Dir of Admissions/Recruitment .... Dr. Martha Faye IKNER
26 VP of External Affairs .... Ms. Erin STEVA
15 Asst Director Talent Relation .... Vacant
36 Director of Career Development .... Vacant
18 Director Facilities/Physical Plant .... Mr. Joseph SIMONETTI
20 Assoc Provost Academic Affairs .... Dr. Bernard ROWAN
38 Director Counseling Center .... Dr. Christine BROWN
20 Assoc Provost Academic Innov Strat .... Dr. Mary DANIELS
25 Assoc VP of Sponsored Programs .... Vacant
43 Assoc VP Gen Counsel/Ethics Officer .... Ms. Robin HAWKINS
19 Chief of Police .... Mr. Eddie WELCH
39 Director Student Housing .... Mr. Robert KING
41 Interim Athletic Director .... Ms. Jessica POOLE
43 Interim General Counsel .... Mr. Walter PRYOR
100 Chief of Staff .... Mr. Kim H. TRAN
88 Deputy Chief of Staff .... Ms. Aspen CLEMONS
04 Special Asst to the President .... Mrs. Jimell BYRD-RENO

Chicago Theological Seminary (K)

1407 East 60th Street, Chicago IL 60637-1284
County: Cook FICE Identification: 001661
Unit ID: 144014
Telephone: (773) 896-2400 Carnegie Class: Spec-4-yr-Faith
FAX Number: (773) 643-1284 Calendar System: Semester
URL: www.ctschicago.edu
Established: 1855 Annual Graduate Tuition & Fees: N/A
Enrollment: 294 Coed
Affiliation or Control: United Church Of Christ IRS Status: 501(c)3
Highest Offering: Doctorate; No Undergraduates
Accreditation: HLC, THEOL

01 President .... Rev. Stephen G. RAY, JR.
05 VP Academic Affairs/Academic Dean . Dr. Stephanie B. CROWDER
10 Vice President for Finance & Admin .... Ms. Karen WALKER
111 Int Vice Pres for Advancement .... Mr. Chad R. SCHWICKERATH
32 VP Student Svcs/Dean of Students .... Mr. Jason FREY
06 Registrar .... Ms. Tina SHELTON
08 Director of the Lapp Learning Ctr .. Ms. Jasmine ABOU-EL-KHEIR
07 Director Recruitment/Admission .... Mr. Jason FREY
04 Assistant to the President .... Ms. Kim M. JOHNSON
26 Director of Communications .... Mr. Steven MCFARLAND
18 Director of Facilities .... Ms. Shauna WARREN

*City Colleges of Chicago (L)

180 N. Wabash, Suite 200, Chicago IL 60601
County: Cook FICE Identification: 001647
Unit ID: 144500
Telephone: (312) 553-2500 Carnegie Class: N/A
FAX Number: (312) 553-2699
URL: www.ccc.edu

01 Chancellor .... Mr. Juan SALGADO
05 Provost .... Dr. Mark POTTER
10 Chief Financial Officer .... Ms. Maribel RODRIGUEZ
13 Chief Information Officer .... Mr. Jerrold MARTIN
43 General Counsel .... Mr. Karla GOWEN
15 Chief Talent Officer .... Ms. Carol DUNNING
100 Chief of Staff and Strategy .... Ms. Veronica HERRERO

*City Colleges of Chicago Harold Washington College (M)

30 E Lake Street, Chicago IL 60601-2449
County: Cook FICE Identification: 001652
Unit ID: 144209
Telephone: (312) 553-5600 Carnegie Class: Assoc/HT-Mix Trad/Non
FAX Number: (312) 553-5964 Calendar System: Semester
URL: www.ccc.edu/hwc
Established: 1962 Annual Undergrad Tuition & Fees (In-District): $11,520
Enrollment: 6,479 Coed
Affiliation or Control: State/Local IRS Status: 501(c)3
Highest Offering: Associate Degree
Accreditation: HLC, ACBSP, NAEYC

02 President .... Dr. Daniel LOPEZ
05 Vice Pres Academic/Student Affairs .... Ms. Theresa CARLTON
10 Vice Pres Finance/Operations .... Mr. Kent LUSK
37 Director of Financial Aid .... Ms. Tenika BURNS
18 Chief Engineer .... Mr. Jeremy GONZALEZ
36 Executive Director COEB .... Vacant
08 Librarian .... Vacant
15 HR Business Partner .... Mrs. Morgan ARAUJO
20 Dean of Instruction .... Ms. Aimee KRALL-LANOUE
13 Director Information Technology .... Mr. Brandon HOPKINS
32 Dean of Student Services .... Ms. Jackie WERNER
35 Assoc Dean of Student Services .... Ms. Ainka CLEPPER
46 Asst Director Research/Planning .... Vacant
06 Registrar .... Ms. Manisha THOMPSON
19 Director of Security .... Ms. Bernessa TATE
09 Director Strategy/Initiatives .... Vacant
84 Dean of Enrollment .... Vacant

*City Colleges of Chicago Harry S Truman College (N)

1145 W Wilson Avenue, Chicago IL 60640-5691
County: Cook FICE Identification: 001648
Unit ID: 144184
Telephone: (773) 907-4700 Carnegie Class: Assoc/HT-High Non
FAX Number: (773) 907-4464 Calendar System: Semester
URL: www.trumancollege.edu
Established: 1956 Annual Undergrad Tuition & Fees (In-District): $11,520
Enrollment: 5,186 Coed
Affiliation or Control: State/Local IRS Status: 501(c)3
Highest Offering: Associate Degree
Accreditation: HLC, NAEYC

02 President ... Dr. Shawn L. JACKSON
05 VP Academic & Student Affairs ... Dr. Kate CONNOR
20 Dean of Instruction ... Dr. Susan MARCUS
06 Registrar ... Ms. My Linh TRAN
32 Dean of Student Services ... Ms. Mary Ann SOLEY
35 Associate Dean of Student Services ... Ms. Chanel BISHOP
56 Dean of Adult Education ... Dr. Lee M. JACKSON
20 Associate Dean of Instruction ... Ms. Gail GORDON-ALLEN
20 Associate Dean of Instruction ... Ms. Laura CHEATHAM
10 VP of Finance & Operations ... Mr. Thomas DUNHAM
19 Director of Security ... Mr. Andres DURBAK
37 Director of Financial Aid ... Ms. Maria PINTO
15 Human Resource Business Partner ... Mr. Michael ROBERTS
13 Interim Director of Info Technology ... Mr. David YEH
21 Business Manager ... Ms. Nina CAO
53 Dean of Education & Teacher Pgms ... Ms. Hollie WAREJAYE
88 Dir of Student Development Projects ... Ms. Aubrey SCHEFFEY
103 Director of Workforce Development ... Ms. Danielle WALLINGTON-HARRIS
18 Manager of Operations & Purchasing ... Mr. Charles TALBERT
35 Associate Dean of Student Services ... Ms. Allison ZURES
88 Associate Dean of Adult Education ... Mr. Steven TEREF
36 Dir of Career Planning & Placement ... Ms. Meredith GALLO-MURPHY
41 Director Intercollegiate Athletics ... Ms. Jasmine GREEN
22 Director of Disability Access Ctr ... Ms. Lauren DALEY
88 Director Teaching & Learning Pgms ... Ms. Leslie LAYMAN
04 Assistant to the President ... Ms. Zsa POPIELARCZYK
121 Director Student Support Svcs TRIO ... Mr. Anthony KWIATKOWSKI
84 Director of Enrollment Management ... Mr. Kisalan GLOVER
51 Dean of Career & Cont Educ Programs .. Dr. Vincent D. WIGGINS
09 Director of Research & Planning ... Mr. Sean HUDSON

*City Colleges of Chicago Kennedy-King College (A)

6301 South Halsted Street, Chicago IL 60621-3798
County: Cook FICE Identification: 001654
Unit ID: 144157
Telephone: (773) 602-5000 Carnegie Class: Assoc/MT-VT-High Non
FAX Number: N/A Calendar System: Semester
URL: www.ccc.edu/colleges/kennedy
Established: 1934 Annual Undergrad Tuition & Fees (In-District): $11,520
Enrollment: 1,878 Coed
Affiliation or Control: State/Local IRS Status: 501(c)3
Highest Offering: Associate Degree
Accreditation: HLC, NAEYC

02 Int President ... Dr. Katonja WEBB WALKER
05 Vice Pres Academic/Student Affairs ... Dr. Patricia ARMSTRONG
32 Int Dean Student Services ... Ms. Allison ROSE
72 Dean Dawson Tech Inst/Col to Career ... Ms. Lucretzia JAMISON
84 Dean Enrollment Management ... Ms. Tonishea TERRY-JACKSON
51 Dean Adult/Continuing Education ... Mr. Henry HORACE
20 Int Dean of Instruction ... Ms. Shandria HOLMES
35 Assoc Dean Student Services ... Dr. Zalika LANDRUM
88 Exec Dean Washburne Culinary Inst ... Dr. Jason LAFFERTY
37 Director Financial Aid ... Ms. Ashley BALLARD
13 Exec Dir Information Technology ... Mr. Lonnie WASHINGTON
121 Director Academic Support Services ... Ms. Shandria HOLMES
10 Exec Dir Business/Operations ... Mr. Baha AWADALLAH
06 Registrar ... Ms. Lacey LAVONDRA
04 Executive Office Manager ... Ms. Cris SAYRE
109 Director of Auxiliary Services ... Mr. Robert GRAHAM
45 Director Strategic Initiatives ... Mr. Patrick GIPSON
19 Director Security/Safety ... Mr. Hershey NORISE
41 Athletic Director ... Mr. Maurice CULPEPPER

*City Colleges of Chicago Olive-Harvey College (B)

10001 S Woodlawn Avenue, Chicago IL 60628-1645
County: Cook FICE Identification: 009767
Unit ID: 144175
Telephone: (773) 291-6100 Carnegie Class: Assoc/HT-High Non
FAX Number: (773) 291-6304 Calendar System: Semester
URL: www.ccc.edu/colleges/olive-harvey/pages/default.aspx
Established: 1970 Annual Undergrad Tuition & Fees (In-District): $11,520
Enrollment: 1,955 Coed
Affiliation or Control: State/Local IRS Status: 501(c)3
Highest Offering: Associate Degree
Accreditation: HLC, NAEYC

02 President ... Ms. Kimberly HOLLINGSWORTH
04 Executive Office Manager ... Mr. LeoNard APPLETON
05 Dean of Instruction ... Dr. Vance GRAY
81 Dean STEM/Ctr Teaching & Lrng ... Ms. Adamma LOTSU
32 Dean Student Services ... Ms. Michelle ADAMS
51 Dean Adult & Continuing Education ... Ms. Lautauscha DAVIS
72 Dean of College to Career ... Ms. LaTonya ARMSTRONG
35 Assoc Dean of Student Services ... Ms. Inesha B. KELLY
10 Exec Dir Bus/Admin/Auxiliary Svcs ... Mr. Richard SLATER
13 Director Information Technology ... Mr. Jason CAMPBELL
36 Director Career Planning/ Placement ... Ms. Charlene HAYMOND-BUSSELL
37 Director Financial Aid ... Mr. Richard HAYES
06 Registrar ... Ms. Nailah WATSON
19 Director Security & Safety ... Mr. Regynold JOHNSON
88 Director Child Development Center ... Ms. Carol PURNELL
41 Director of Athletics ... Mr. Rob FLETCHER
15 Director Human Resources ... Ms. Latasha LARRY

38 Manager Wellness Center ... Ms. LaTia LANE
18 Chief Engineer ... Mr. Robert LUMPKIN

*City Colleges of Chicago Richard J. Daley College (C)

7500 S Pulaski Road, Chicago IL 60652-1299
County: Cook FICE Identification: 001649
Unit ID: 144193
Telephone: (773) 838-7500 Carnegie Class: Assoc/MT-VT-High Non
FAX Number: (773) 838-7524 Calendar System: Semester
URL: daley.ccc.edu
Established: 1960 Annual Undergrad Tuition & Fees (In-District): $11,520
Enrollment: 4,929 Coed
Affiliation or Control: State/Local IRS Status: 501(c)3
Highest Offering: Associate Degree
Accreditation: HLC

02 President ... Dr. Janine E. JANOSKY
05 Vice Pres Academic/Student Affs ... Mr. Eric HOFFMAN
20 Dean of Instruction ... Ms. Cynthia MORENO
55 Senior Dean Adult Education ... Ms. Teresa GUIA
32 Dean of Student Development ... Mr. Douglas GEIGER
31 Dir Community Education Programs ... Ms. Silvia VILLA
10 Vice President Operations & Finance . Ms. Crystal WASHINGTON
18 Chief Engineer/Physical Plant ... Mr. John MARTIN
19 Director Security ... Mr. Ronald MARTIN
06 Registrar ... Ms. Jacqueline LLOYD
84 Director Enrollment Management ... Mr. Rafael GODINA
15 Human Resources Specialist ... Ms. Sylvia ROBLES
13 Director of Information Technology ... Ms. Karen ALLEN
37 Director Student Financial Aid ... Mr. Tom PANAS

*City Colleges of Chicago Wilbur Wright College (D)

4300 N Narragansett Avenue, Chicago IL 60634-1591
County: Cook FICE Identification: 001655
Unit ID: 144218
Telephone: (773) 777-7900 Carnegie Class: Assoc/HT-High Non
FAX Number: (773) 481-8185 Calendar System: Semester
URL: www.ccc.edu/wright
Established: 1934 Annual Undergrad Tuition & Fees (In-District): $11,520
Enrollment: 7,946 Coed
Affiliation or Control: State/Local IRS Status: 501(c)3
Highest Offering: Associate Degree
Accreditation: HLC, OTA

02 President ... Dr. David POTASH
00 Chancellor ... Mr. Juan SALGADO
05 VP Academic/Student Affairs ... Dr. Pamela MONACO
10 VP Finance/Operations ... Ms. Phoebe WOOD
20 Assoc Dean of Instruction ... Dr. Gabe ESTILL
32 Dean of Student Services ... Mrs. Romell MURDEN
121 Assoc Dean Student Svcs Advising ... Ms. Maria LLOPIZ
84 Dean of Enrollment Management ... Ms. Melissa CHAMPS
37 Executive Director Financial Aid ... Mr. Noberto VALENTIN
09 Dir Institutional Research/Plng ... Mr. Brian TRZEBIATOWSKI
13 Director Information Technology ... Mr. Jeff JIROUT
109 Director of Auxiliary Services ... Ms. Anna Marie MORALES
15 Human Resources Director ... Ms. Alison GUENGERICH
38 Director of Wellness Center ... Ms. Hoyam TANON
19 Director of Security ... Mr. Victor GUERRIERI
06 Registrar ... Ms. Sherrea WASHINGTON
41 Athletic Director ... Vacant
55 Senior Dean of Adult Education ... Ms. Inesha KELLY
51 Director Continuing Education ... Mr. Adam KASHUBA
78 Dean of HPVEC ... Vacant
31 Community Affairs Liaison ... Ms. Sandra PAYAN-CATAÑO
36 Associate Dean Careers Programs ... Ms. Billie DIAZ
101 Chief Advisor to the Board ... Ms. Tracey FLEMING
88 College Director Special Projects ... Ms. Yeisha BETANCOURT-RUIZ

*Malcolm X College, One of the City Colleges of Chicago (E)

1900 W. Jackson Boulevard, Chicago IL 60612-3197
County: Cook FICE Identification: 001650
Unit ID: 144166
Telephone: (312) 850-7000 Carnegie Class: Assoc/MT-VT-Mix Trad/Non
FAX Number: (312) 850-7039 Calendar System: Semester
URL: www.ccc.edu/malcolmx
Established: 1911 Annual Undergrad Tuition & Fees (In-District): $11,520
Enrollment: 7,273 Coed
Affiliation or Control: State/Local IRS Status: 501(c)3
Highest Offering: Associate Degree
Accreditation: HLC, ADNUR, CAHIIM, COARC, DH, EMT, FUSER, MAC, NAEYC, PTAA, RAD

01 President ... Mr. David SANDERS
05 Vice President of Academic Affairs . Mrs. Katonja WEBB-WALKER
108 VP Institutional Effectiveness ... Mrs. Annie ZALEWSKI
10 VP of Finance & Operations ... Ms. Tiffany DIXON
32 Dean Student Services ... Ms. Lisa WILLIS
15 HR Business Partner ... Mr. Seth BAKER
20 Dean Instruction ... Dr. Shawna BUSHELL
20 Associate Dean Instruction ... Ms. Glasetta BARKSDALE
20 Associate Dean Instruction ... Mr. Byron JAVIER
13 Director Information Technology ... Mr. Ben ROOHANI

06 Registrar ... Ms. Patrice JARRETT
35 Associate Dean of Student Services ... Mr. Brian HALL
37 Director Financial Aid ... Ms. Tiffany MORRISON
88 Director Child Care Center ... Ms. Saundra PARKER
19 Director Security/Public Safety ... Ms. Gissella LIMON
18 Chief Engineer ... Mr. John MORLEY
21 Business Manager ... Ms. Jennifer WILLIAMS
76 Dean Health Sciences Programs ... Mr. Roy WALKER, III
56 Dean Adult Education Programs ... Ms. Inesha KELLY
56 Dean of West Side Learning Center ... Ms. Barbara MESCHINO
51 Dean Continuing Education ... Ms. Lizz GARDNER
66 Dean of Nursing ... Ms. Tammy SCOTT-BRAND
121 Assoc Dean Student Development ... Vacant
88 Assoc Dean Health Careers ... Vacant
36 Dir Career Planning/Placement ... Mrs. Toya JOHNSON
103 Director Workforce Partnerships ... Ms. Rhonda HARDEMON
26 Director of Media Relations ... Vacant
46 Director Strategic Initiatives ... Ms. Pamela PERRY
109 Director of Auxiliary Services ... Ms. Jessica HOLLOWAY
09 Director of Research and Planning ... Mr. Steve DAMARJIAN
84 Director of Enrollment Management ... Mr. Rolando MARTINEZ
11 Exec Dir of Projects & Initiatives ... Ms. Elizabeth GMITTER
04 Executive Office Mgr Pres Office ... Mrs. Alanna S. WITHERSPOON

College of DuPage (F)

425 Fawell Boulevard, Glen Ellyn IL 60137-6599
County: DuPage FICE Identification: 006656
Unit ID: 144865
Telephone: (630) 942-2800 Carnegie Class: Assoc/HVT-High Non
FAX Number: (630) 858-9399 Calendar System: Semester
URL: www.cod.edu
Established: 1965 Annual Undergrad Tuition & Fees (In-District): $9,732
Enrollment: 21,010 Coed
Affiliation or Control: State/Local IRS Status: 501(c)3
Highest Offering: Associate Degree
Accreditation: HLC, ACFEI, ADNUR, ART, #AT, CAHIIM, COARC, CSHSE, DH, DMS, MAC, NMT, PTAA, RAD, SURGA, SURGT

01 President ... Dr. Brian CAPUTO
05 Provost ... Dr. Mark CURTIS-CHAVEZ
10 Chief Financial Ofcr/Treasurer ... Mr. Scott BRADY
45 VP Planning & Inst Effectiveness ... Mr. James BENTE
11 Vice Pres Administrative Affairs ... Ms. Ellen ROBERTS
15 Vice Pres Human Resources ... Ms. Maritza RUANO
111 VP Institutional Advancement ... Mr. Walter JOHNSON
26 VP Public Rels/Comm/Marketing ... Ms. Wendy E. PARKS
49 Dean Liberal Arts ... Dr. Robyn SCHIFFMAN
83 Dean Social & Behavioral Sci/Lib ... Mr. Mark RUDISILL
51 Dean Cont Ed/Extended Learning ... Dr. Joseph CASSIDY
81 Dean Science/Tech/Engineering/Math .. Ms. Jennifer CUMPSTSON
32 Dean Student Affairs ... Dr. Nathania MONTES
21 Controller ... Mr. David VALADEZ
13 Dir Information Technology Services ... Vacant
18 Dir Facilities Planning and Dev ... Mr. Don INMAN
121 Dir Pathways for Student Success ... Mr. Roberto VALADEZ
09 Director Research & Analytics ... Mr. James KOSTECKI
116 Dir Compliance/Internal Auditor ... Mr. James E. MARTNER
57 Director McAninch Arts Center ... Mrs. Diana MARTINEZ
41 Dir Athletics/Recreation Programs ... Mr. Ryan KAISER
19 Chief of Police ... Mr. Joseph MULLIN
79 Associate Dean Humanities ... Dr. Sandra MARTINS
86 Director Legislative Relations ... Ms. Wendy MCCAMBRIDGE
07 Int Director Admissions & Outreach ... Mr. Hardee JUSTIN

College of Lake County (G)

19351 W Washington Street, Grayslake IL 60030-1198
County: Lake FICE Identification: 007694
Unit ID: 146472
Telephone: (847) 543-2000 Carnegie Class: Assoc/HT-High Non
FAX Number: N/A Calendar System: Semester
URL: www.clcillinois.edu
Established: 1969 Annual Undergrad Tuition & Fees (In-District): $9,632
Enrollment: 11,854 Coed
Affiliation or Control: Local IRS Status: 501(c)3
Highest Offering: Associate Degree
Accreditation: HLC, ADNUR, CAHIIM, DH, MAC, RAD, SURGT

01 President ... Dr. Lori SUDDICK
10 Vice Pres Business Svcs/Finance/CFO ... Mr. Kevin APPLETON
32 Vice President Student Development ... Ms. Karen HLAVIN
05 Vice Pres Education/Chief Acad Ofcr ... Dr. Sonya WILLIAMS
103 VP Cmty & Workforce Partnership ... Dr. Ali O'BRIEN
12 Dean Southlake Campus ... Dr. Viki CVITKOVIC
12 Dean Lakeshore Campus ... Mr. Jesus RUIZ
08 Dean Library/Testing & Acad Success ... Ms. Tanya WOLTMANN
21 Controller ... Ms. Connie KRAVITZ
50 Dean of Business/Social Science Div ... Dr. Jeffrey STOMPER
76 Dean Biological/Health Sciences ... Mr. Jeet SAINI
79 Dean Comm Arts/Humanities/Fine Arts ... Mr. Sheldon WALCHER
54 Dean Engr/Math/Physical Science ... Mr. Richard AMMON
51 Dean Adult Basic Education/GED/ ESL ... Dr. Arlene SANTOS-GEORGE
103 Exec Director Community Programming ... Ms. Roneida MARTIN
26 Director Public Relations & Mktg ... Ms. Anne O'CONNELL
35 Dean Student Life ... Mr. Gabriel LARA
102 Executive Director CLC Foundation ... Mr. Kurt PETERSON
15 Exec Director Human Resources ... Ms. Sue FAY
88 Exec Dir James Lumber Ctr Perf Arts ... Ms. Gwethalyn BRONNER
09 Dir Inst Effect/Plng/Research ... Ms. Sandra VILLANUEVA

41 Director of Athletics Mr. Bradley UNGER
86 Dir Resource Dev/Legislative Affs Mr. Nick C. KALLIERIS
13 Chief Information Officer Mr. Greg KOZAK
14 Director User Services/User Support Mr. David AYKROID
88 Dir Application Svcs/Development Mr. Jay MEYER
35 Director Student Services Lakeshore Mr. David WEATHERSPOON
18 Director of Facilities Mr. Mike WELCH
88 Dir Children's Learning Center Ms. Carlotta CONLEY
22 Dir Ofc Students with Disabilities Mr. Thomas CROWE
19 Chief of Police Mr. Brian HENRY
36 Exec Dir Career/Placement Services Ms. Sylvia M. JOHNSON JONES
66 Director Nursing Education Vacant
23 Director Health Services Ms. Michelle M. GRACE
37 Director Financial Aid Mr. Vatistas VATISTAS
88 Director Educational Technology Mr. Scott RIAL
107 Director Professional Development Vacant
88 Director Technical Services Mr. James SENFT
07 Dir Student Recruiting/Onboarding Ms. Sharon SANDERS-FUNNYE
04 Exec Assistant to President Ms. Laura LABA
106 Director Online Student Success Ms. Meredith TUMILTY
121 Dir Student Success Strategy Mr. Nick BRANSON
109 Director Business Operations Ms. Patricia ARGOUDELIS

College of Lake County Lakeshore Campus (A)

33 North Genesee Street, Waukegan IL 60085
Telephone: (847) 543-2191 Identification: 770073
Accreditation: &HLC

College of Lake County Southlake Campus (B)

1120 South Milwaukee Avenue, Vernon Hills IL 60061
Telephone: (847) 543-6501 Identification: 770072
Accreditation: &HLC

Columbia College Chicago (C)

600 S Michigan Avenue, Chicago IL 60605-1996
County: Cook FICE Identification: 001665
Unit ID: 144281
Telephone: (312) 369-1000 Carnegie Class: Masters/M
FAX Number: (312) 369-8069 Calendar System: Semester
URL: www.colum.edu
Established: 1890 Annual Undergrad Tuition & Fees: $27,786
Enrollment: 6,769 Coed
Affiliation or Control: Independent Non-Profit IRS Status: 501(c)3
Highest Offering: Master's
Accreditation: HLC, CIDA

01 President and CEO Kwang-Wu KIM
05 SVP/Provost Marcella DAVID
10 Sr VP Business Affairs/CFO Jerry TARRER
32 VP Student Affairs Sharon WILSON-TAYLOR
84 VP Enrollment Management Michael JOSEPH
43 VP Legal Affairs/General Counsel Patricia BERGESON
30 VP Development/Alumni Relations Shawn WAX
100 Chief of Staff Laurent PERNOT
88 Special Asst Strategic Init Charles KIMBALL
07 Asst VP Undergrad Admissions Derek BRINKLEY
37 Assistant VP SFS Virginia JOHNSON
18 AVP Fac & Construction Ann KALAYIL
20 Sr Assoc Provost Nathan BAKKAM
26 AVP Strategic Comm & External Rels Lambrini LUKIDIS
19 Assoc VP Security Ronald SODINI
88 Assoc Provost Transfer Init AP Holly HERRERA
108 Assoc Provost AASL Neil PAGANO
15 Assoc AVP of Human Resources Norma DE JESUS
88 Assoc Provost Fac Research Dev Ames HAWKINS
116 Assoc VP/Chief Aud/Comp Ofcr Kristi PERITO
13 Assoc VP/CIO Kathie KOCH
114 Assoc VP Budget Plng/Analysis Jeffrey REUTER
20 Assoc Provost Acad Personnel Pegeen QUINN
20 Asst Provost Acad Services Brian MARTH
104 Asst Provost Global Education David COMP
35 Dean of Students Douglas ECK
57 Dean School Fine/Performing Arts Rosita SANDS
60 Dean School of Media Arts Eric FREEDMAN
49 Dean School Liberal Arts/Sciences Steven COREY
58 Dean of Graduate Studies Suzanne MCBRIDE
36 Assoc Dean Career Dev Ind Rel Erik FRIEDMAN
35 Assoc Dean Student Life Kari SOMMERS
88 Assistant Dean of Student Life Sheila CARTER
06 Interim Registrar Jim GINGRAS
88 Sr Dir Enroll Mktg Comm Andrew WHATLEY
29 Sr Director Alumni Relations Dirk MATTHEWS
119 Sr Dir IT Operations & Security Edgar MEDINA
16 Sr Director HR Patricia OLALDE
21 Dir Finance & Budget Analysis Marvery GRIFFIN
88 Dir Enrollment Systems & Data Sarah OSAKO
88 Director of Development Andrea ROHLFING
88 Director of Development Trish BAILEY
88 Director of Acad DEI/Acad Personnel Raquel MONROE
121 Director of Academic Advising Keith LUSSON
88 Dir Donor/Alumni Services Erin DAVID
44 Director Annual Giving Jessica WELTON
38 Director of Counseling Services Emily BATTLE
85 Dir Intl Student & Scholar Svcs Clare LAKE
39 Director of Residential Operations Mary OAKES
08 Director of the Library Jo CATES
88 Dir Pres Events & Residence Julie BURNS
88 Director Columbia Central Miriam NICHOLES
88 Director Student Center Andy DUTIL
88 Director ORM Robert PAASCH
09 Asst Director Inst Research Jaclyn SMITH
25 Grant & Contract Manager David WEINER
96 Procurement Director Bryon GILSTRAP
88 Manager of Operations Connie STANLEY
04 Exec Assistant to the President Yvonne SODE
88 Sr Administrative Assistant Marcus HAMLIN

Concordia University Chicago (D)

7400 Augusta Street, River Forest IL 60305-1499
County: Cook FICE Identification: 001666
Unit ID: 144351
Telephone: (708) 771-8300 Carnegie Class: Masters/L
FAX Number: (708) 209-3176 Calendar System: Semester
URL: www.cuchicago.edu
Established: 1864 Annual Undergrad Tuition & Fees: $33,636
Enrollment: 6,491 Coed
Affiliation or Control: Lutheran Church - Missouri Synod
IRS Status: 501(c)3
Highest Offering: Doctorate
Accreditation: HLC, #ACBSP, CACREP, CAEP, MUS

01 President Dr. Russell DAWN
05 Provost Dr. Erik ANKERBERG
10 Sr Vice Pres of Finance/CFO Mr. Randall K. BARFIELD
111 CEO Foundation/VP for Advancement Mr. Jeff HYNES
88 Asst Vice President for Enrollment Ms. Gwen E. KANELOS
26 AVP Univ Communications & Marketing Mr. Eric MATANYI
49 Interim Dean Col Theo/Arts/Hum Dr. Maja MISKOVIC
50 Dean College of Business Dr. Lynn HUNNICUTT
09 Dir Inst Planning & Effectiveness Dr. Elizabeth OWOLABI
37 Exec Director of Financial Aid Ms. Aida ASENCIO-PINTO
08 Director of Library Services Ms. Liesl COTTRILL
36 Director Career Services Mr. Gerald PINOTTI
11 Assoc Vice Pres for Administration Mr. Glen D. STEINER
38 Director Counseling Ctr Mr. Christopher JOHNSTON
109 Dir Conference & Aux Svcs Ms. Mary CESAR
41 Director of Athletics Mr. Peter D. GNAN
21 Controller Mr. Andrew WINKELMAN
42 University Pastor Rev. Jeffrey LEININGER
24 Director of Video Production Svcs Mr. James A. KOSINSKY
19 Director of Public Safety Mr. David WITKEN
96 Director of Purchasing Ms. Denise JAMES
91 Dir of Admin Information System Ms. Linda C. BERRY
123 Asst VP Grad Admission/Student Svcs Ms. Deborah NESS
04 Sr Exec Assistant to the President Ms. Casey KIMBERLY
15 Sr Director Human Resources Ms. Lisa CLEMENTE

Danville Area Community College (E)

2000 E Main Street, Danville IL 61832-5199
County: Vermilion FICE Identification: 001669
Unit ID: 144564
Telephone: (217) 443-3222 Carnegie Class: Assoc/MT-VT-High Non
FAX Number: (217) 443-8560 Calendar System: Semester
URL: www.dacc.edu
Established: 1949 Annual Undergrad Tuition & Fees (In-District): $8,325
Enrollment: 2,171 Coed
Affiliation or Control: State/Local IRS Status: 501(c)3
Highest Offering: Associate Degree
Accreditation: HLC, ADNUR, CAHIIM, MAC, RAD

01 President Dr. Stephen D. NACCO
11 VP Operations/Board Secretary Ms. Kerri L. THURMAN
05 VP Academic Affairs Dr. Carl BRIDGES
15 VP Human Resource/AA Ofcr/Labor Rel Ms. Jill A. CRANMORE
10 VP Finance/Chief Financial Officer Ms. Tammy L. BETANCOURT
32 VP Student Services Ms. Stacy L. EHMEN
35 Asst VP Student Services Mr. Brian C. HENSGEN
102 Foundation Executive Director Ms. Tonya L. HILL
26 Exec Director College Relations Ms. Lara L. CONKLIN
18 Exec Dir Maintenance & Facilities Mr. Doug ADAMS
81 Dean Math/Sciences & Health Prof Ms. Kathy R. STURGEON
49 Dean Liberal Arts & Library Service Dr. Penny J. MCCONNELL
50 Dean Business & Technology Ms. Terri CUMMINGS
09 Director Institutional Research Mr. Tom CAREY
88 Director Student Support Svcs/TRIO Ms. Shanay M. WRIGHT
21 Asst VP Finance Mr. Carl LEWIS
37 Director Financial Aid Ms. Sadie EDWARDS
91 Programmer/Systems Administrator Ms. Jessica MILES
10 Controller Ms. Whitney YODER
13 Director Information Technology Mr. Mark BARNES
41 Director Athletics Mr. Tim M. BUNTON
88 Director Small Business Development Mr. Earle STEINER
07 Director Admissions & Registrar Mr. Timothy MORGAN
103 Director Workforce/Recruitment Svcs Mr. Nick CATLETT
31 Coord Campus & Community Resources Ms. Dawn S. NASSER
19 Director Campus Safety Mr. Nathan HOWIE
12 Director Hoopeston Extension Site Ms. Karla J. COON
31 Senior Dir Community Engagement Ms. Laura M. HENSGEN
88 Exec Director Corporate Education Ms. Brittany WOODWORTH
88 Coordinator Corporate Education Ms. Kirsten J. JURCZAK
88 Director Medical Imagery Programs Ms. Tammy L. HOWARD
88 Director Health Info Technology Ms. Kelly JOHNSON
66 Director Nursing Ms. Susan KOSS
121 Dir Acad Advis/Couns/Transf Articu Ms. Stephane POTTS
88 Coord Recruitment/Social Media Asst Ms. Alexis SIMMONS

DePaul University (F)

1 E Jackson Boulevard, Chicago IL 60604-2287
County: Cook FICE Identification: 001671
Unit ID: 144740
Telephone: (312) 362-8610 Carnegie Class: DU-Higher
FAX Number: (312) 362-5322 Calendar System: Quarter
URL: www.depaul.edu
Established: 1898 Annual Undergrad Tuition & Fees: $41,202
Enrollment: 21,922 Coed
Affiliation or Control: Roman Catholic IRS Status: 501(c)3
Highest Offering: Doctorate
Accreditation: HLC, ANEST, CACREP, CLPSY, LAW, MUS, NURSE, PH, @SP, SPAA, SW

01 President Dr. A. Gabriel ESTEBAN
00 Chancellor Rev. Dennis H. HOLTSCHNEIDER, CM
05 Provost Dr. Salma GHANEM
10 Executive Vice President Mrs. Sherri SIDLER
32 VP Student Affairs Dr. Gene ZDZIARSKI
84 Vice Pres Enroll Mgmt/Marketing Dr. Soumitra GHOSH
111 Int Vice Pres for Advancement Ms. Lori SMEDLEY
15 Vice President Human Resources Ms. Stephanie SMITH
18 Vice President Facilities Operation Mr. Robert J. JANIS
43 VP/General Counsel & Secretary Ms. Kathryn STIEBER
29 Assoc VP Communication & Engagement Ms. Tracy KRAHL
28 VP Inst Diversity & Equity Dr. Elizabeth F. ORTIZ
26 VP Public Relations & Communication Ms. Linda BLAKLEY
121 Assoc Prov Student Success/Accred Dr. Caryn CHADEN
106 Assoc Prov Global Eng and Online Dr. GianMario BESANA
100 Chief of Staff Mr. Steve STOUTE
13 VP Information Services Mr. Robert MCCORMICK
35 Assoc Vice Pres Student Affairs Dr. Ashley KNIGHT
35 Assoc Vice Pres Student Affairs Mr. Rico TYLER
09 AVP Inst Research/Market Analytics Dr. Liz SANDERS
36 AVP Div Planning & Mgmt/Career Ctr Ms. Jane MCGRATH
42 Assoc VP University Ministry Mr. Mark LABOE
108 AVP & COS Student Affairs Dr. Ellen MEENTS-DECAIGNY
27 Exec Dir News & Integrated Content Ms. Carol HUGHES
21 VP for Finance & Controller Ms. Sherri SIDLER
90 Dir Faculty Instructional Tech Svcs Dr. Sharon GUAN
37 Int Assoc Vice Pres Financial Aid Ms. Karen LEVEQUE
25 Assoc Provost for Research Dr. Daniela STAN RAICU
19 Director Public Safety Mr. Robert WACHOWSKI
38 Director Student Counseling Dr. Jeffery LANFEAR
39 Director of Housing & Student Ctrs Mr. Rick MORECI
41 Athletics Director Mr. DeWayne PEEVY
06 Director of Registration/Records Ms. Patricia HUERTA
104 Director Study Abroad Ms. Martha MCGIVERN
123 AVP Graduate & Adult Admission Ms. Suzanne DEPEDER
07 Dean of Undergraduate Admission Vacant
77 Dean Computing & Digital Media Dr. David MILLER
49 Dean Liberal Arts & Social Sciences Dr. Guillermo VASQUEZ DE VELASCO
50 Int Dean Bus Coll/Grad Sch Bus Mr. Thomas DONLEY
60 Int Dean Col of Communication Dr. Alexandra MURPHY
64 Dean School of Music Dr. Ronald CALTABIANO
61 Dean College of Law Ms. Jennifer R. PEREA
57 Dean Theatre School Mr. John CULBERT
53 Dean School of Education Dr. Paul ZIONTS
51 Int Dean School for New Learning Dr. Don OPITZ
76 Dean Col of Science & Health Dr. Dorothy KOZLOWSKI
08 Head Librarian Vacant
04 Sr Executive Asst to President Ms. Phyllis GREGG
100 Deputy Chief of Staff Ms. Annette WILSON
86 Assoc VP Community & Govt Relations Mr. Peter COFFEY

*DeVry University - Home Office (G)

3005 Highland Parkway, Suite 100,
Downers Grove IL 60515
County: DuPage FICE Identification: 001672
Unit ID: 144777
Telephone: (630) 515-3000 Carnegie Class: N/A
FAX Number: (630) 571-0317
URL: www.devry.edu

01 President/CEO Mr. Thomas L. MONAHAN, III
26 Chief Marketing Officer Mr. Remberto DEL REAL
84 VP Enrollment Management Ms. Elise AWWAD
05 Provost/VP Academic Affairs Mr. Shantanu BOSE
13 VP Information Technology Mr. Chris CAMPBELL
15 VP Human Resources & Univ Relations Mr. David BARNETT
10 Chief Financial Officer Mr. John LORENZ

*DeVry University - Chicago Campus (H)

3300 N Campbell Avenue, Chicago IL 60618
County: Cook FICE Identification: 010727
Unit ID: 482477
Telephone: (773) 929-8500 Carnegie Class: Masters/L
FAX Number: (773) 348-1780 Calendar System: Semester
URL: www.devry.edu
Established: 1931 Annual Undergrad Tuition & Fees: $17,680
Enrollment: 20,832 Coed
Affiliation or Control: Proprietary IRS Status: Proprietary
Highest Offering: Master's
Accreditation: HLC, ACBSP, CAHIIM

02 Center Dean ... Ms. Ruth PINEDA

† Regional accreditation is carried under the parent institution in Downers Grove, IL.

Dominican University (A)

7900 W Division Street, River Forest IL 60305-1099
County: Cook FICE Identification: 001750
Unit ID: 148496
Telephone: (708) 366-2490 Carnegie Class: Masters/L
FAX Number: (708) 524-5990 Calendar System: Semester
URL: www.dom.edu
Established: 1901 Annual Undergrad Tuition & Fees: $35,420
Enrollment: 3,189 Coed
Affiliation or Control: Roman Catholic IRS Status: 501(c)3
Highest Offering: Doctorate
Accreditation: HLC, ARCPA, DIETC, DIETD, LIB, NURSE, SW

01 President ... Dr. Glena G. TEMPLE
05 Provost ... Vacant
20 Assoc Provost Strategic Initiatives ... Dr. Roberto CURCI
10 VP Finance/Business Affairs ... Mr. Mark TITZER
42 Interim VP of Mission and Ministry ... Mr. John DECOSTANZA
111 VP University Advancement ... Ms. Sara ACOSTA
121 VP Student Success & Engagement ... Dr. Barrington PRICE
84 VP Enrollment Management/Marketing ... Mr. Genaro BALCAZAR
13 Interim CIO ... Mr. Todd KLEINE
15 Exec Director Human Resources ... Ms. Roberta MCMAHON
28 Chief Diversity Officer ... Dr. Precious PORRAS
07 AVP Enroll Mgt/Dir Undergrad Admiss ... Mr. Glenn HAMILTON
20 Assistant Provost ... Mr. Matthew J. HLINAK
27 Exec Dir of External Engagement ... Ms. Leslie RODRIGUEZ
32 Dean of Students ... Ms. Norah COLLINS PIENTA
76 Interim Dean Borra College ... Dr. Tamara BLAND
83 Dean Applied/Social Sciences ... Dr. Jacob BUCHER
50 Dean Brennan School of Business ... Dr. Roberto CURCI
62 Director School Information Stds ... Ms. Kate MAREK
53 Director Teacher Educ Programs ... Ms. Josephine SARVIS
88 Assoc Dean/Licensure Pgm Coord ... Dr. Ben FREVILLE
51 Asst Dean Student Svcs Cont Stds ... Ms. Monica HALLORAN
70 Int Director School of Social Work ... Ms. Julie BACH
49 Dean Rosary College ... Mr. Chad ROHMAN
08 University Librarian ... Mr. Estevan MONTAÑO
06 Registrar ... Ms. Kelly M. SIMMONS
36 Director Career Development ... Ms. Keli WOJCIECHOWSKI
29 Director Alumnae/i Relations ... Ms. Vimla HOMAN
09 Dir Institutional Rsrch/Assessment ... Ms. Elizabeth SILK
88 AVP Student Enrollment Services ... Ms. Victoria SPIVAK
23 Director Wellness Center ... Ms. Elizabeth RITZMAN
41 AVP Athletics ... Mr. Erick BAUMANN
104 Director International Studies ... Dr. Sue PONREMY
04 Exec Dir of Planning/Asst to Pres ... Ms. Anne DEETER
102 Director Foundation/Corporate Rels ... Ms. Sharon RYAN
44 Director Annual Giving ... Ms. Sarah SULLIVAN
18 Chf Facilities/Physical Plant Ofcr ... Mr. James DEFILY
19 Director Security/Safety ... Ms. Sasha M. SANTIAGO

East-West University (B)

816 S Michigan Avenue, Chicago IL 60605
County: Cook FICE Identification: 021686
Unit ID: 144883
Telephone: (312) 939-0111 Carnegie Class: Bac-A&S
FAX Number: (312) 939-0083 Calendar System: Quarter
URL: www.eastwest.edu
Established: 1980 Annual Undergrad Tuition & Fees: $22,650
Enrollment: 419 Coed
Affiliation or Control: Independent Non-Profit IRS Status: 501(c)3
Highest Offering: Baccalaureate
Accreditation: HLC

01 Chancellor ... Dr. M. Wasiullah KHAN
05 Provost ... Dr. Madhu JAIN
20 Academic Dean ... Vacant
30 Dean Development/Univ Relations ... Mr. Zafar A. MALIK
32 Director Counseling/Student Affairs ... Ms. Colby CHAPMAN
37 Director of Financial Aid ... Mr. Cesar CAMPOS
06 Registrar ... Ms. Jacqueline MORALES ELIZONDO
04 Assistant to the Chancellor ... Mr. Kaleem KAMBOJ
19 Director of Security ... Mr. Tasleem RAJA
10 Director of Business ... Dr. Madhu JAIN
44 Dir Devel/Univ Rels/Publications ... Ms. Barbara ABRAJANO
26 Manager Public Relations ... Vacant
18 Facilities Manager ... Mr. Tasleem RAJA
85 International Student Advisor ... Ms. Kate PETEK
21 Associate Business Officer ... Vacant
84 Director Enrollment Management ... Ms. Sonya SLAUGHTER

Eastern Illinois University (C)

600 Lincoln Avenue, Charleston IL 61920-3099
County: Coles FICE Identification: 001674
Unit ID: 144892
Telephone: (217) 581-5000 Carnegie Class: Masters/L
FAX Number: (217) 581-2722 Calendar System: Semester
URL: www.eiu.edu
Established: 1895 Annual Undergrad Tuition & Fees (In-State): $12,136
Enrollment: 8,626 Coed
Affiliation or Control: State IRS Status: 501(c)3
Highest Offering: Beyond Master's But Less Than Doctorate
Accreditation: HLC, AAFCS, ART, CACREP, CAEP, DIETD, DIETI, JOUR, MUS, NURSE, SP, THEA

01 President ... Dr. David M. GLASSMAN
05 Provost/Vice Pres Academic Affairs ... Dr. Jay D. GATRELL
10 Vice Pres Business Affairs ... Mr. Matthew J. BIERMAN
32 Vice Pres Student Affairs ... Dr. Anne G. FLAHERTY
111 Vice Pres University Advancement ... Dr. Ken A. WETSTEIN
35 Special Asst to VP Student Affairs ... Dr. Jennifer L. SIPES
26 Dir Marketing/Communications ... Ms. Christy E. KILGORE
08 Dean of Library Services ... Mr. Zach NEWELL
92 Dean Honors College ... Dr. Richard ENGLAND
15 Director Human Resources ... Ms. Linda C. HOLLOWAY
22 Director Civil Rights/Diversity ... Dr. Shawn PEOPLES
45 Int Dir Planning/Budget/IR ... Mr. Lakshmikara PADMARAJU
07 Director of Admissions ... Ms. Kelly MILLER
37 Director of Financial Aid ... Ms. Amanda STARWALT
06 Registrar ... Mr. Brad BENNINGTON
18 Dir Facilities/Planning Management ... Mr. Timothy P. ZIMMER
96 Dir Procure/Disburse/Contract Svcs ... Ms. Danielle M. GREEN
38 Int Asst Dir of Counseling Center ... Ms. Lindsay WILSON
25 Director of Research & Grants ... Dr. Robert W. CHESNUT
41 Director of Athletics ... Mr. Thomas R. MICHAEL
93 Exec Dir Inclusion/Acad Engagement ... Dr. Mona DAVENPORT
39 Exec Dir of Housing/Dining Svcs ... Mr. Mark A. HUDSON
21 Dir Business Services/Treasurer ... Mr. Paul A. MCCANN
36 Director of Career Services ... Ms. Bobbi KINGERY
58 Dean Graduate School ... Dr. Ryan C. HENDRICKSON
76 Int Dean College Health/Human Svcs ... Dr. John R. STORSVED
50 Dean Lumpkin Col Bus and Tech ... Dr. Austin C. CHENEY
49 Dean College Liberal Arts/Sciences ... Dr. Barbara E. BONNEKESSEN
53 Dean College of Education ... Dr. Laretta HENDERSON
43 General Counsel ... Ms. Laura L. MCLAUGHLIN
84 Assoc VP Enrollment Management ... Mr. Josh L. NORMAN
13 Exec Director for ITS ... Mr. Ryan W. GIBSON

Elgin Community College (D)

1700 Spartan Drive, Elgin IL 60123-7193
County: Kane FICE Identification: 001675
Unit ID: 144944
Telephone: (847) 697-1000 Carnegie Class: Assoc/HT-Mix Trad/Non
FAX Number: (847) 214-7995 Calendar System: Semester
URL: www.elgin.edu
Established: 1949 Annual Undergrad Tuition & Fees (In-District): $7,140
Enrollment: 7,882 Coed
Affiliation or Control: Local IRS Status: 501(c)3
Highest Offering: Associate Degree
Accreditation: HLC, ADNUR, COMTA, CSHSE, DA, HT, MLTAD, PTAA, RAD, RADMAG, SURGT

01 President ... Dr. David SAM
10 VP Business & Finance ... Dr. Kimberly WAGNER
05 VP Teaching/Learning/Student Dev ... Dr. Peggy HEINRICH
20 Dean Academic Resources/Instruction ... Mr. Timothy MOORE
35 Dean of Students ... Mr. John LONG
50 Dean Sustain/Business/Career Tech ... Ms. Cathy TAYLOR
83 Dean Comm/Behavioral Sciences ... Dr. Kristina GARCIA
57 Dean Liberal/Visual/Performing Arts ... Dr. Mary PERKINS
32 Interim Asst VP Student Svcs & Dev ... Dr. Lourdes BLACKSMITH
88 Dean of Col Transitions/Partnership ... Dr. Kyla WEGMAN
51 Dean Adult Basic Education ... Dr. Elizabeth HOBSON
76 Dean Health Prof/Math/Science/Eng ... Dr. Wendy MILLER
103 Dean Workforce Dev/CE ... Dr. Gina DE ROSIER COOK
07 Assoc Dean of Admissions/Registrar ... Ms. Ann KALAS
18 Managing Director Facilities ... Mr. Cal BYRD
13 Chief Information Officer ... Dr. Michael CHAHINO
26 Int Chief Mktg/Comm Ofcr & Govt ... Dr. Toya WEBB
15 Chief Human Resources Officer ... Mr. Anthony RAY
30 Exec Dir Inst Advance/ECC Found ... Vacant
20 Asst VP Teaching/Lrng/Student Dev ... Ms. Annamarie SCHOPEN
45 VP Planning/Inst Effect/Tech ... Dr. Philip GARBER
09 Managing Dir Institutional Research ... Mr. David RUDDEN
37 Dean Enroll/Student Financial Svcs ... Ms. Amy PERRIN
21 Asst VP Business and Finance ... Ms. Heather SCHOLL
22 Paralegal/EEO/AA Title IX/FOIA Ofcr ... Ms. Marilyn PRENTICE
41 Director Athletics & Wellness ... Mr. Kent PAYNE
96 Managing Director Business Services ... Ms. Pam SINGLETON
121 Assoc Dean of Student Success ... Ms. Peggy GUNDRUM
35 Director Orientation/Student Life ... Ms. Amybeth MAURER
04 Sr Exec Asst to Pres/Board Recorder ... Ms. Diane KERRUISH
08 Assoc Dean of Library ... Ms. Shannon POHRTE
51 Assoc Dean of Adult Educ ... Ms. Marcia LUPTAK
43 General Counsel ... Mr. Respicio VAZQUEZ
19 Chief of Police ... Mr. David KINTZ
28 Exec Dir Equity/Diversity/Inclusion ... Dr. Anthony RAMOS
88 Assoc Dean CETAL ... Dr. Tyler ROEGER
88 Sr Dir Academic Pgm/Public Safety ... Mr. Ron TWO BULLS
88 Asst Dean College/High School Pgm ... Mr. Sean JENSEN

Elmhurst University (E)

190 Prospect Avenue, Elmhurst IL 60126-3296
County: DuPage FICE Identification: 001676
Unit ID: 144962
Telephone: (630) 279-4100 Carnegie Class: Masters/L
FAX Number: (630) 617-3282 Calendar System: 4/1/4
URL: www.elmhurst.edu
Established: 1871 Annual Undergrad Tuition & Fees: $38,654
Enrollment: 3,421 Coed
Affiliation or Control: United Church Of Christ IRS Status: 501(c)3
Highest Offering: Doctorate
Accreditation: HLC, NURSE, OT, SP

01 President ... Dr. Troy VANAKEN
10 VP for Business & Finance ... Mrs. Julie SUDERMAN
05 VP Academic Affs/Dean of Faculty ... Dr. Dean PRIBBENOW
13 VP for Operations & Technology ... Mr. Kurt ASHLEY
111 VP of Advancement ... Mr. Andrew KNAP
32 VP for Student Affairs ... Dr. Phil RIORDAN
07 VP for Admission ... Dr. Timothy RICORDATI
20 Associate Dean of Faculty ... Dr. Brian WILHITE
88 Exec Dir Center for Pro Excellence ... Mr. Martin GAHBAUER
18 Exec Director Facilities Management ... Mrs. Nora O'MALLEY
26 Exec Dir of Mktg & Communication ... Mr. Jonathan SHEARER
42 Chaplain ... Rev. H. Scott MATHENEY
06 Registrar ... Ms. Linda DUFORT
27 Sr Dir Communications/Public Affs ... Ms. Desiree CHEN-MENICHINI
08 Director of the Library ... Ms. Carolyn CIESLA
36 Director of Career Education ... Ms. Julie NOSAL
38 Director of Counseling Services ... Dr. Amy SWARR
29 Director of Alumni Engagement ... Mr. Jon-Pierre BRADLEY
15 Exec Director of Human Resources ... Mr. David CRONAN
19 Exec Dir of Campus Security ... Mr. Marc MOLINA
37 Director of Financial Services ... Mr. Nathan HANCOCK
07 Assistant Director of Admissions ... Mr. Tim AHLBERG
123 Sr Dir Grad Admission & Enrollment ... Mr. Tim PANFIL
39 Dir of Housing & Res Life ... Vacant
41 Director of Athletics ... Mr. Glen BRITTICH
04 Executive Asst to President ... Ms. Molly NIESPO
101 Asst to President Office & Trustees ... Ms. Britney HEALD
89 Sr Dir 1st Year & Intl Admission ... Ms. Christine GRENIER
53 Dept Chair Education ... Dr. Jeanne WHITE
108 Asst Dean for Assessment & Accred ... Dr. A. Andrew DAS
88 Asst Dean For Faculty Development ... Dr. Kimberly LAWLER-SAGARIN
09 Inst Research/Assessment Specialist ... Ms. Catherine NEAD
22 VP of Equity & Inclusion ... Mr. Bruce KING
104 Director of Study Away ... Ms. Melissa NEWHOUSE
25 Grants Coordinator ... Vacant

Erikson Institute (F)

451 N. Lasalle Street, Chicago IL 60654
County: Cook FICE Identification: 035103
Unit ID: 409254
Telephone: (312) 755-2250 Carnegie Class: Masters/M
FAX Number: (312) 755-0928 Calendar System: Semester
URL: www.erikson.edu
Established: 1966 Annual Graduate Tuition & Fees: N/A
Enrollment: 457 Coed
Affiliation or Control: Independent Non-Profit IRS Status: 501(c)3
Highest Offering: Master's; No Undergraduates
Accreditation: HLC, SW

01 President ... Mariana SOUTO-MANNING
05 VP for Academic Affairs ... Pamela EPLEY
10 Vice President Finance/CFO ... Patricia LAWSON
111 Vice Pres Institutional Advancement ... Maura DALY
06 Sr Dir Enrollment/Student Records ... David SAENZ
32 Dean of Students ... Ashley CURRY
26 Dir of Communications and Marketing ... Sheila HAENNICKE
30 Dir Development/Alumni Relations ... Patricia OFFER

Eureka College (G)

300 E College Avenue, Eureka IL 61530-1500
County: Woodford FICE Identification: 001678
Unit ID: 144971
Telephone: (309) 467-3721 Carnegie Class: Bac-Diverse
FAX Number: (309) 467-6386 Calendar System: Semester
URL: www.eureka.edu
Established: 1855 Annual Undergrad Tuition & Fees: $28,360
Enrollment: 511 Coed
Affiliation or Control: Christian Church (Disciples Of Christ)
IRS Status: 501(c)3
Highest Offering: Baccalaureate
Accreditation: HLC

01 President ... Dr. Jamel WRIGHT
04 Administrative Asst to President ... Mrs. Jyl ZUBIATE
05 Provost & Dean of the College ... Dr. Ann FULOP
10 VP of Finance/Facilities/CFO ... Mr. Craig MAYNARD
32 Dean of Students ... Dr. Norris CHASE
06 Registrar ... Ms. Kendi ONNEN
18 Director of Physical Plant ... Mr. Jeromy FOX
42 Chaplain ... Rev. Bruce M. FOWLKES
36 Director of Career Development ... Ms. Kelly BAY
13 Director of Computer Services ... Dr. Kanaka VIJITHA-KUMARA
37 Director of Financial Aid ... Mrs. Tammy CROTHERS
41 Athletic Director ... Mr. Bryan MOORE
29 Director Alumni Relations ... Mr. Matthew DAUGHENBAUGH
39 Director Student Housing ... Mrs. Lisa ALLEN
28 Chief Diversity Officer ... Dr. Jamel WRIGHT
26 Director of Communications ... Ms. Melody CRICKMAN
84 Dean of Enrollment Management ... Mr. Richard FLOYD
108 Director Institutional Assessment ... Dr. Ann FULOP
104 Director Study Abroad ... Dr. Emily EATON
19 Director of Campus Security ... Mr. Loren MARION

Flashpoint Chicago, a Campus of Columbia College Hollywood (H)

28 North Clark Street, Suite 500, Chicago IL 60602
Telephone: (312) 506-0600 Identification: 667083
Accreditation: &WC

Fox College (A)

18020 Oak Park Avenue, Tinley Park IL 60477
County: Cook FICE Identification: 025228
Unit ID: 145239
Telephone: (708) 444-4500 Carnegie Class: Assoc/HVT-Mix Trad/Non
FAX Number: (708) 444-4520 Calendar System: Semester
URL: www.foxcollege.edu
Established: 1932 Annual Undergrad Tuition & Fees: $15,340
Enrollment: 404 Coed
Affiliation or Control: Proprietary IRS Status: Proprietary
Highest Offering: Associate Degree
Accreditation: HLC, MAAB, OTA, PTAA

01 President Ms. Jackie FLYNN
05 hief Academic Officer Ms. Rachel KREFT
08 Head Librarian Mr. Matthew JOHNSON
11 Chief Administrative Officer Ms. Kerry DEMARS

Garrett-Evangelical Theological Seminary (B)

2121 Sheridan Road, Evanston IL 60201-3298
County: Cook FICE Identification: 001682
Unit ID: 145275
Telephone: (847) 866-3900 Carnegie Class: Spec-4-yr-Faith
FAX Number: (847) 866-3884 Calendar System: Semester
URL: www.garrett.edu
Established: 1853 Annual Graduate Tuition & Fees: N/A
Enrollment: 283 Coed
Affiliation or Control: United Methodist IRS Status: 501(c)3
Highest Offering: Doctorate; No Undergraduates
Accreditation: HLC, THEOL

01 President Dr. Javier A. VIERA
05 Vice Pres Academic Affairs/Dean Dr. Mai-Anh L. TRAN
112 Senior VP for Planned Giving Dr. David L. HEETLAND
30 Vice President of Development Mr. Joe EMMICK
84 Vice Pres Enrollment Mgmt Mr. Scott OSTLUND
45 VP Strategic Init/Partnerships Rev. Becky J. EBERHART
10 Vice President Business Affairs/CFO Mr. Kevin MILLER
15 AVP for Human Resources Ms. Carine VELAZQUEZ
06 Registrar/Dir of Academic Studies Ms. Krista MCNEIL
08 Director of United Library Dr. Lucy CHUNG
18 Senior Director of B&G Mr. Josten BERCZY
37 Director of Financial Aid Mr. Jason GILL
26 Chief Marketing/Communications Ofcr Mr. Shane NICHOLS
32 Dean of Student Life/Chaplain Rev. Karen MOSBY
04 Exec Assistant to the President Ms. April LONDON
07 Director of Admissions Rev. Katie FAHEY

Governors State University (C)

1 University Parkway, University Park IL 60484-0975
County: Will FICE Identification: 009145
Unit ID: 145336
Telephone: (708) 534-5000 Carnegie Class: Masters/L
FAX Number: (708) 534-4107 Calendar System: Semester
URL: www.govst.edu
Established: 1969 Annual Undergrad Tuition & Fees (In-State): $10,108
Enrollment: 4,650 Coed
Affiliation or Control: State IRS Status: 501(c)3
Highest Offering: Doctorate
Accreditation: HLC, CACREP, CAEP, HSA, NUR, OT, PTA, SP, SPAA, SW

01 President Dr. Cheryl F. GREEN
05 Provost/VP Academic Affairs Dr. Beverly SCHNELLER
111 VP Advancement/CEO Foundation Mr. William DAVIS
13 Assoc VP/CIO Information Tech Svcs Mr. Chuck PUSTZ
43 VP/General Counsel Ms. Therese NOHOS
45 Exec Dir Budget & Fin Planning Ms. Sandra ZURAWSKI
09 Exec Dir Institutional Research Mr. Robert STANLEY
29 Director of Alumni Assoc Vacant
50 Dean College of Business Dr. Jun ZHAO
49 Interim Dean College Arts/Sciences Dr. Jason ZINGSHEIM
76 Dean Col Health Professions Dr. Catherine BALTHAZAR
53 Dean College Education Dr. Shannon DERMER
08 Interim Dean University Library Dr. Dennis SWANSON
06 Registrar Mr. Timothy CARROLL
37 Exec Director Financial Aid Mr. John PERRY
20 Associate Provost/AVP Academic Affs Dr. Timothy FORDE
15 VP Human Resources Mr. Joshua ALLEN
18 Associate VP Facilities Mr. John POTEMPA
19 Dir Public Safety & Chief of Police Mr. James MCGEE
38 Dir Counseling and Wellness Center Dr. Freddy TUNG
36 Director of Career Services Ms. Darcie R. CAMPOS
96 AVP Procurement/Business Services Ms. Tracy SULLIVAN
32 Dean of Students Mr. Mushtaq CHOUDHARY
41 Athletic Director Mr. Anthony BATES
86 Exec Dir Government Affairs Ms. Maureen KELLY
04 Exec Assistant to the President Ms. Patricia Y. O'NEAL
10 VP Administration and Finance Dr. Corey BRADFORD, SR.
100 Chief of Staff Ms. Janelle CROWLEY
84 VP Student Affairs/Enrollment Mr. Paul MCGUINNESS

Greenville University (D)

315 E College, Greenville IL 62246
County: Bond FICE Identification: 001684
Unit ID: 145372
Telephone: (618) 664-7100 Carnegie Class: Masters/S
FAX Number: (618) 664-6841 Calendar System: 4/1/4
URL: www.greenville.edu
Established: 1892 Annual Undergrad Tuition & Fees: $28,956
Enrollment: 994 Coed
Affiliation or Control: Free Methodist IRS Status: 501(c)3
Highest Offering: Master's
Accreditation: HLC, CAEP, IACBE, SW

01 President Mrs. Suzanne DAVIS
05 Chief Academic Officer Dr. Kathryn TAYLOR
15 Chief Culture & Diversity Officer Mrs. Katrina LOPEZ LISS
10 Chief Financial Officer Mr. Mark BIDDINGER
21 Controller Mrs. Chiyo PALEN
30 Chief Philanthropy Officer Mr. Scott GIFFEN
111 Executive Director of Advancement Mr. Evan ABLA
26 Chief Marketing & Comm Officer Mrs. Terri SUNDERLAND
41 Athletic Director & Bus Dev Officer Mr. Tom ACKERMAN
110 Chief Econ Dev & Innovation Officer Mr. Breck NELSON
13 Chief Information Officer Mr. Patrick FARMER
84 Chief Enrollment Officer Mrs. Victoria CLARK
20 Associate Chief Academic Officer Dr. Eric WATTERSON
20 Dean of Faculty Mr. Mark THOMAS
88 Faculty Moderator Dr. Paul SUNDERLAND
88 Associate Faculty Moderator Dr. Michael LAUGHLIN
32 Chief Student Development Officer Mr. Ross BAKER
19 Dir of Comm Standards & Safety Mr. Shawn FOLES
06 Registrar Mrs. Michelle SUSSENBACH
37 Director of Financial Aid : Mr. David KESSINGER
112 Director of Major & Planned Gifts Mr. Brett BRANNON
18 Director of Facilities Mr. Todd SIEBERT
04 Director of President's Office Mrs. Regina ROBART
29 Director Alumni Affairs Mr. Dewayne NEELEY

Harper College (E)

1200 W Algonquin Road, Palatine IL 60067-7398
County: Cook FICE Identification: 003961
Unit ID: 149842
Telephone: (847) 925-6000 Carnegie Class: Assoc/HT-High Non
FAX Number: (847) 925-6034 Calendar System: Semester
URL: www.harpercollege.edu
Established: 1965 Annual Undergrad Tuition & Fees (In-District): $9,942
Enrollment: 12,199 Coed
Affiliation or Control: State/Local IRS Status: 501(c)3
Highest Offering: Associate Degree
Accreditation: HLC, ACBSP, ADNUR, CAHIIM, COMTA, DH, @DIETI, DMS, MAC, MUS, NAEYC, PNUR, PTAA, RAD, SURGT

01 President Dr. Avis PROCTOR
100 Chief of Staff Mr. Jeff JULIAN
05 Provost Dr. MaryAnn JANOSIK
10 Exec VP Finance & Admin Services Mr. Rob GALICK
11 VP Strat All & Innov/Brd Liaison Dr. Maria COONS
111 VP & Chief Advancement Officer Ms. Laura BROWN
103 VP Workforce Solutions Dr. Michele' SMITH
45 VP Planning/Research/Inst Eff Ms. Darlene SCHLENBECKER
28 VP Diversity/Equity/Inclusion Dr. Tamara JOHNSON
121 Assoc Provost Student Success Dr. Travaris HARRIS
20 Assoc Provost Curriculum/Inst Dr. Michael BATES
15 Chief Human Resources Officer Ms. Amanda DUVAL
13 Chief Information Officer Mr. Riaz YUSUFF
21 Controller Mr. Robert GRAPENTHIEN
18 Exec Dir of Facilities Management Ms. Nancy MEDINA
84 Assoc Provost Enrollment Svcs Mr. Robert PARZY
32 Assoc Provost Student Affairs Dr. Claudia MERCADO
75 Dean Career & Technical Programs Dr. Joanne IVORY
76 Dean Health Careers Dr. Kimberly CHAVIS
08 Dean Resources for Learning Ms. Njambi KAMOCHE
35 Dean of Students Ms. Mary Kay HARTON
50 Int Dean Business/Social Sciences Ms. Darice TROUT
81 Dean Mathematics & Science Ms. Kimberley POLLY
106 Dean Teaching/Learning/Distance Edu Vacant
49 Dean Liberal Arts Ms. Jaime RIEWERTS
102 Assoc Exec Dir Fndn/Dir Major Gifts Ms. Heather ZOLDAK
19 Chief of Police Mr. John LAWSON
27 Director Marketing Services Mr. Mike BARZACCHINI
36 Sr Dir Job Placement/Workforce Sol Ms. Kathleen CANFIELD
91 Director Client Systems Ms. Sue CONTARINO
09 Director Institutional Research Dr. Katherine COY
51 Director Adult Educational Dev Ms. Andrea FIEBIG
37 Dir Student Financial Assistance Ms. Laura MCGEE
66 Director Nursing Ms. Jennifer SMITH
06 Int Registrar/Sr Dir Enrollment Svc Ms. Sue SKORA
07 Dir Student Recruitment & Outreach Ms. Nicolette CISARIK DE JESUS
41 Director of Athletics & Fitness Vacant
88 Campus Architect Mr. Steve PETERSEN

Heartland Community College (F)

1500 W Raab Road, Normal IL 61761-9446
County: McLean FICE Identification: 030838
Unit ID: 384342
Telephone: (309) 268-8000 Carnegie Class: Assoc/HT-High Non
FAX Number: (309) 268-7999 Calendar System: Semester
URL: www.heartland.edu
Established: 1990 Annual Undergrad Tuition & Fees (In-District): $9,540
Enrollment: 4,485 Coed
Affiliation or Control: State/Local IRS Status: 501(c)3
Highest Offering: Associate Degree
Accreditation: HLC, ADNUR, MAC, PTAA, RAD

01 President Dr. Keith CORNILLE
05 Provost/Vice Pres Academic Affairs Dr. Rick PEARCE
10 Vice Pres Finance/Administration Ms. Letisha TREPAC
86 Vice Pres External Relations Ms. Kelli HILL
84 Vice Pres Enrollment/Student Svcs Dr. Sarah DIEL-HUNT
32 Assoc VP Enrollment/Student Service Dr. Amy PAWLIK
15 Exec Director Human Resources Mrs. Barb LEATHERS
18 Executive Director of Facilities Mr. Andy LITWILLER
13 Chief Information Officer Mr. Scott BROSS
26 Exec Director of Marketing Ms. Megan ROLFS
30 Exec Dir Development/Foundation Mr. Chris DOWNING
106 Exec Dir Online Educ/E-learning Dr. Anna CATTERSON
21 Controller Mr. Justin KNORR
07 Dean Enrollment Services Ms. Lindsay EICKHORST
37 Director of Financial Aid Mr. Todd BURNS
41 Director of Athletics Mr. Ryan KNOX
121 Dean of Student Success Ms. Kimberly KELLEY
06 Registrar Ms. Hannah MATHES
35 Director of Student Engagement Mr. Skylar GUIMOND
04 Executive Assistant Ms. Dana TUTTLE
22 Assoc Dir Equity/Complianc/Title IX Mr. Terrance BOND
96 Associate Director Business Office Ms. Jd DAVIS
09 Director of Institutional Research Mr. Dan HAGBERG

Hebrew Theological College (G)

7135 N Carpenter Road, Skokie IL 60077-3263
County: Cook FICE Identification: 001685
Unit ID: 145497
Telephone: (847) 982-2500 Carnegie Class: Bac-A&S
FAX Number: (847) 674-6381 Calendar System: Semester
URL: www.htc.edu
Established: 1922 Annual Undergrad Tuition & Fees: $13,760
Enrollment: 181 Coordinate
Affiliation or Control: Independent Non-Profit IRS Status: 501(c)3
Highest Offering: Master's
Accreditation: HLC

01 Chief Executive Officer Rabbi Shmuel SCHUMAN
05 Chief Academic Officer Vacant
20 Rosh Hayeshiva Vacant
11 Chief Operating Officer Mr. Sid SINGER
33 Mashgiach Ruchani-Dean Rabbi Zvi ZIMMERMAN
20 Dean Blitstein Institute for Women Dr. Chani TESSLER
34 Menahel Ruchani-Dean Inst for Women Rabbi Binyamin OLSTEIN
06 Registrar Rabbi Gavriel BACHRACH
07 Director of Admissions Rabbi Joshua ZISOOK
111 Director of Inst Advancement Mrs. Alexis GOLDSTEIN
44 Development Coordinator Rabbi Yaakov FRIEDMAN
33 Assistant Dean of Men's Division Dr. Michael VERDERAME
125 Chancellor Emeritus Dr. Jerold ISENBERG

† Separate campuses for male and female students. Part of the Touro College and University System.

Highland Community College (H)

2998 W Pearl City Road, Freeport IL 61032-9341
County: Stephenson FICE Identification: 001681
Unit ID: 145521
Telephone: (815) 235-6121 Carnegie Class: Assoc/MT-VT-High Non
FAX Number: (815) 235-6130 Calendar System: Semester
URL: www.highland.edu
Established: 1962 Annual Undergrad Tuition & Fees (In-District): $6,846
Enrollment: 1,276 Coed
Affiliation or Control: State/Local IRS Status: 501(c)3
Highest Offering: Associate Degree
Accreditation: HLC, ADNUR, MAC

01 President Mrs. Christina KUBERSKI
05 Interim VP Academic Services/CAO Mr. Jim PHILLIPS
10 Vice Pres Administrative Services Ms. Jill M. JANSSEN
50 VP Business/Tech & Community Pgms Mr. Scott R. ANDERSON
32 VP Student Dev & Support Svc/CSSO Ms. Elizabeth L. GERBER
79 Dean Humanities/Social Sci & FA Mr. Jim PHILLIPS
81 Dean Natural Science & Math Dr. Brendan C. DUTMER
66 Dean Nursing & Allied Health Dr. Stephanie EYMANN
51 Director Adult Education Programs Ms. Rachel FELDHAUS
41 Director Athletics Mr. Peter E. NORMAN
84 Director Enrollment & Records Mr. Jeremy BRADT
18 Director Facilities & Safety Mr. Kurt SIMPSON
37 Director Financial Aid Ms. Kathy BANGASSER
15 Director Human Resources Ms. Karen BROWN
09 Director Institutional Research Dr. Michelle THRUMAN
13 Director Information Technology Mr. Pete FINK
124 Director Retention & Learning Svcs Ms. Carolyn PETSCHE
26 Director Marketing/Community Rels Ms. Jeniece SMITH
88 Dir Retired & Senior Volunteer Pgm Ms. Cindi MIELKE
22 Director TRiO Services Mr. Anthony SAGO
88 Coordinator Upward Bound Program Mr. Ryan SHIRLEY
21 Manager Accounting Ms. Mary J. LLOYD
40 Manager Bookstore Ms. Madonna KEENEY
101 Exec Asst to President/Board Sec Ms. Terri A. GRIMES
102 Foundation Executive Director Mr. Jeff REINKE
112 Foundation Major Gift Officer Mr. Dan DICK
88 Foundation Director of Operations Ms. Patricia A. DUNN

Illinois Central College (I)

1 College Drive, East Peoria IL 61635-0001
County: Tazewell FICE Identification: 006753
Unit ID: 145682
Telephone: (309) 694-5422 Carnegie Class: Assoc/HT-High Non
FAX Number: (309) 694-5450 Calendar System: Semester
URL: www.icc.edu
Established: 1966 Annual Undergrad Tuition & Fees (In-District): $9,900

Enrollment: 7,813 Coed
Affiliation or Control: State/Local IRS Status: 501(c)3
Highest Offering: Associate Degree
Accreditation: HLC, ACFEI, ADNUR, COARC, DH, EMT, MAC, MLTAD, MUS, OTA, PNUR, PTAA, RAD, SURGT

01 President ... Dr. Sheila QUIRK-BAILEY
10 Exec VP Administration/Finance ... Mr. Bruce BUDDE
26 VP of Marketing/Advancement ... Ms. Kim ARMSTRONG
05 Interim VP of Academic Affairs ... Dr. Charles SWAIM
28 VP of Workforce & Diversity ... Dr. Arnitria SHAW
32 VP of Student Success ... Vacant
15 AVP of Human Resources ... Vacant
108 AVP of Inst Effect & Innovation ... Dr. Kari SCHIMMEL
102 Exec Dir Education Foundation ... Ms. Stephanie HOLMES
09 Exec Dir Inst Research & Planning ... Mr. David COOK
103 Exec Dir Workforce Operations ... Ms. Paula NACHTRIEB
35 Dean of Students ... Ms. Amy DAXENBICHLER
84 Dean of Enrollment Management ... Ms. Emily POINTS
51 Dean of Corp/Cont Education ... Ms. Julie HOWAR
36 Dean of College/Career Readiness ... Ms. Kamilah WILLIAMS
79 Dean of Humanities ... Dr. Lonetta OLIVER
81 Dean of Math/Science/Engineering ... Mr. Joe BERGMAN
50 Dean of Business/Legal/Info Systems ... Ms. Michelle WEGHORST
57 Dean of Arts & Communications ... Vacant
47 Dean of Agriculture/Industrial Tech ... Dr. Dana KING
76 Dean of Health Careers ... Ms. Wendee GUTH
18 Sr Director Facilities Services ... Mr. Jeff LAGROW
16 Director Human Resources ... Vacant
08 Director Library Services ... Ms. Cathryne KAUFMAN
41 Director Athletics & PE ... Mr. Rob BUSS
13 Director Network & Desktop Svc ... Mr. William NEWPORT
14 Director Enterprise Systems ... Mr. Brad FINLEY
104 Director Intl Educ Program ... Vacant
19 Campus Police Chief ... Ms. Erika SCHWIDERSKI
21 Controller ... Mr. Ed BABCOCK
22 Coordinator Access Services ... Ms. Kendra MOULTRIE-BELK
06 Registrar ... Vacant
04 Administrative Asst to President ... Ms. Kristen MOTT
101 Admin Asst to EVP/Sec to the Board ... Ms. Sue BULITTA

Illinois College (A)

1101 W College Avenue, Jacksonville IL 62650-2299
County: Morgan FICE Identification: 001688
Unit ID: 145691
Telephone: (217) 245-3000 Carnegie Class: Bac-A&S
FAX Number: (217) 245-3034 Calendar System: Semester
URL: www.ic.edu
Established: 1829 Annual Undergrad Tuition & Fees: $34,620
Enrollment: 1,154 Coed
Affiliation or Control: Independent Non-Profit IRS Status: 501(c)3
Highest Offering: Master's
Accreditation: HLC, NURSE

01 President ... Dr. Barbara A. FARLEY
05 Provost and Dean of the College ... Dr. Catharine E. O'CONNELL
10 Vice President of Business Affairs ... Mr. Kent SILTMAN
111 Vice President External Relations ... Ms. Stephanie CHIPMAN
20 Dean of the Faculty ... Dr. Laura COREY
32 Assoc Dean Students/Title IX Coord ... Dr. Jennie HEMINGWAY
07 Dean of Admiss & Stdnt Fin Svcs ... Mr. Evan WILSON
39 Exec Dir of Residential Life ... Mr. Denny SCHUMACHER
09 Exec Dir for Inst Research ... Dr. Robert A. SWEATMAN
06 Registrar ... Ms. Helen KUHN
13 Chief Info Technology Officer (CIO) ... Mr. Patrick BROWN
37 Associate Director of Financial Aid ... Ms. Rebecca BIRDSELL
30 Exec Dir of Development & Alumni ... Ms. Kris HOUSER
26 Director Marketing/Communications ... Mr. Bryan LEONARD
08 Library Director ... Mr. Luke BEATTY
18 Director of Facilities Operations ... Mr. Al DILLOW
36 Exec Dir of Career Readiness & EXL ... Ms. Kelly POOL
21 Controller ... Ms. Melissa J. DYSON
35 Dir Center for Student Involvement ... Ms. Karen K. HOMOLKA
42 Chaplain ... Mr. Tim MCGEE
15 Director of Human Resources ... Ms. Lauren HAYS
38 Lead Mental Health Counselor ... Ms. Leah HAMILTON
28 Dir of Diversity/Equity/Inclusion ... Ms. Valeria CUETO
41 Athletic Director ... Mr. Mike SNYDER

Illinois College of Optometry (B)

3241 S Michigan Avenue, Chicago IL 60616-3878
County: Cook FICE Identification: 001689
Unit ID: 145628
Telephone: (312) 225-1700 Carnegie Class: Spec-4-yr-Other Health
FAX Number: (312) 225-1724 Calendar System: Quarter
URL: www.ico.edu
Established: 1872 Annual Undergrad Tuition & Fees: N/A
Enrollment: 531 Coed
Affiliation or Control: Independent Non-Profit IRS Status: 501(c)3
Highest Offering: First Professional Degree
Accreditation: HLC, OPT, OPTR

01 President ... Dr. Mark K. COLIP
05 Vice Pres for Academic Affairs/Dean ... Dr. Stephanie MESSNER
10 VP for Finance & Business/CFO ... Ms. Christa OJEDA
111 VP for Strategy/Inst Advancement ... Dr. Leonard V. MESSNER
32 Dean of Student Affairs ... Dr. Erik MOTHERSBAUGH
06 Assoc Dean for Academic/Registrar ... Dr. Geoffrey GOODFELLOW
07 Director of Admissions ... Ms. Teisha JOHNSON
35 Assistant Dean for Student Success ... Ms. Beth KARMIS
84 Sr Dir of Enrollment Mgmt Tech ... Ms. Milissa BARTOLD
29 Director Alumni Relations ... Ms. Elizabeth GRANTNER
18 Chief Facilities/Physical Plant ... Mr. Gary YOUNG
08 Chief Library Officer ... Ms. Christine WEBER
13 Chief Info Technology Officer ... Mr. Amit CHOKSI
04 Chief Exec Asst to the President ... Ms. Maggie LOPEZ
19 Director Security/Safety ... Mr. Tim CAPPARELLI
36 Director of Career Development ... Ms. Daphne ANDERSON
09 Director of Institutional Research ... Dr. Yi PANG
15 Chief Human Resources Officer ... Ms. Gloria AJAYI

*Illinois Eastern Community Colleges System Office (C)

233 E Chestnut Street, Olney IL 62450-2298
County: Richland FICE Identification: 009135
Unit ID: 443368
Telephone: (618) 393-2982 Carnegie Class: N/A
FAX Number: (618) 392-4816
URL: www.iecc.edu

01 Chancellor ... Dr. Ryan GOWER
05 Assistant Dean of Academic Services ... Mrs. Alyssa MAGLONE
10 Chief Finance Officer/Treasurer ... Mr. Ryan HAWKINS
103 Associate Dean Workforce Education ... Ms. Kim UNDERWOOD
25 Pgm Dir of Grants and Compliance ... Mrs. Libby MCVICKER
85 Pgm Dir of International Stdnt Pgm ... Ms. Cassandra GOLDMAN
15 Director of Human Resources ... Mrs. Andrea MCDOWELL
88 Director TRIO Upward Bound ... Ms. Tiffany COWGER
108 Pgm Dir Inst Assessment/Effective ... Mr. Brandon WEGER
121 Director TRIO Student Support Svcs ... Mr. Wain DAVIS
06 Registrar ... Mr. Steve PATBERG
07 Assoc Dean of Admissions & Records ... Mrs. Amber MALONE
37 Program Director of Financial Aid ... Mrs. Krystle RIGGLE
84 Director Enrollment Management ... Mrs. Andrea LOLL

*Illinois Eastern Community Colleges Frontier Community College (D)

Frontier Drive, Fairfield IL 62837-9801
County: Wayne FICE Identification: 020744
Unit ID: 403469
Telephone: (618) 842-3711 Carnegie Class: Assoc/HT-High Non
FAX Number: (618) 842-4425 Calendar System: Semester
URL: www.iecc.edu/fcc
Established: 1976 Annual Undergrad Tuition & Fees (In-District): $9,992
Enrollment: 1,262 Coed
Affiliation or Control: State/Local IRS Status: 501(c)3
Highest Offering: Associate Degree
Accreditation: &HLC, ADNUR

02 President ... Dr. Gerald EDGREN, JR.
05 Dean of Instruction ... Dr. Paul BRUINSMA
51 Program Director of Adult Education ... Mr. Rodney RANES
10 Director of Business ... Mrs. Mary JOHNSTON
08 Dir of Instructional Support Svcs ... Ms. Lori NOE
41 Director of Athletics ... Ms. Amanda KOTCH
37 Coordinator of Financial Aid ... Ms. Justn YOUNG
50 Dean of Business & Industry ... Ms. Sharmila KAKAC

† Regional accreditation is carried under the parent institution Illinois Eastern Community Colleges System Office in Olney, IL.

*Illinois Eastern Community Colleges Lincoln Trail College (E)

11220 State Highway 1, Robinson IL 62454-5707
County: Crawford FICE Identification: 009786
Unit ID: 403478
Telephone: (618) 544-8657 Carnegie Class: Assoc/HT-Mix Trad/Non
FAX Number: (618) 544-7423 Calendar System: Semester
URL: www.iecc.edu/ltc
Established: 1969 Annual Undergrad Tuition & Fees (In-District): $9,435
Enrollment: 723 Coed
Affiliation or Control: State/Local IRS Status: 501(c)3
Highest Offering: Associate Degree
Accreditation: &HLC, ADNUR

02 President ... Dr. Zahi ATALLAH
05 Interim Dean of the College ... Dr. Zahi ATALLAH
37 Coordinator of Financial Aid ... Ms. Krystle RIGGLE
08 Dir of Instructional Support Svcs ... Ms. Rena GOWER
10 Director of Business ... Ms. Jamie HENRY
41 Athletics Compliance Coordinator ... Mr. Tyler BROWNING
26 Coord Public Information/Marketing ... Mr. Christopher FORDE

† Regional accreditation is carried under the parent institution Illinois Eastern Community Colleges System Office in Olney, IL.

*Illinois Eastern Community Colleges Olney Central College (F)

305 North West Street, Olney IL 62450-1099
County: Richland FICE Identification: 001742
Unit ID: 145707
Telephone: (618) 395-7777 Carnegie Class: Assoc/HVT-Mix Trad/Non
FAX Number: (618) 392-3293 Calendar System: Semester
URL: www.iecc.edu/occ
Established: 1962 Annual Undergrad Tuition & Fees (In-District): $9,435
Enrollment: 906 Coed
Affiliation or Control: State/Local IRS Status: 501(c)3
Highest Offering: Associate Degree
Accreditation: &HLC, ADNUR, RAD

02 Interim President ... Mr. Roger EDDY
05 Dean of Instruction ... Dr. Michael CONN
76 Assoc Dean of Allied Health ... Ms. Alani FREDERICK
88 Director Cosmetology ... Ms. Courtney MEADOWS
10 Director Business ... Mr. Doug SHIPMAN
41 Athletic Director/Coach ... Mr. Dennis CONLEY
37 Financial Aid Coordinator ... Ms. Taryn BUNTING

† Regional accreditation is carried under the parent institution Illinois Eastern Community Colleges System Office in Olney, IL.

*Illinois Eastern Community Colleges Wabash Valley College (G)

2200 College Drive, Mount Carmel IL 62863-2657
County: Wabash FICE Identification: 001779
Unit ID: 403487
Telephone: (618) 262-8641 Carnegie Class: Assoc/HVT-High Non
FAX Number: (618) 262-5347 Calendar System: Semester
URL: www.iecc.edu/wvc
Established: 1960 Annual Undergrad Tuition & Fees (In-District): $9,435
Enrollment: 2,222 Coed
Affiliation or Control: State/Local IRS Status: 501(c)3
Highest Offering: Associate Degree
Accreditation: &HLC, ADNUR, @PTAA

02 President ... Mr. Matt FOWLER
05 Dean of Instruction ... Mr. Robert CONN
121 Director of Academic Advising ... Mr. Tim ZIMMER
08 Director of LRC ... Ms. Sandy CRAIG
60 Director of Broadcasting ... Mr. Kyle PEACH
41 Athletic Director ... Mr. Mike CARPENTER
10 Director of Business ... Mrs. Reilly BAUMGART
37 Financial Aid Coordinator ... Ms. Trina DUNKEL

† Regional accreditation is carried under the parent institution Illinois Eastern Community Colleges System Office in Olney, IL.

Illinois Institute of Technology (H)

10 West 35th Street, Chicago IL 60616-3793
County: Cook FICE Identification: 001691
Unit ID: 145725
Telephone: (312) 567-3000 Carnegie Class: DU-Higher
FAX Number: (312) 567-3004 Calendar System: Semester
URL: www.iit.edu
Established: 1890 Annual Undergrad Tuition & Fees: $50,490
Enrollment: 6,325 Coed
Affiliation or Control: Independent Non-Profit IRS Status: 501(c)3
Highest Offering: Doctorate
Accreditation: HLC, CACREP, CEA, CLPSY, LSAR

01 President ... Dr. Raj ECHAMBADI
05 Provost/SVP Academic Affairs ... Dr. Peter KILPATRICK
84 Vice Pres Enrollment/Vice Provost ... Dr. Mike GOSZ
10 Int Vice Pres Finance/CFO ... Mr. Jeffrey BETHKE
18 VP Admin/Facilities/Pub Safety ... Mr. Bruce WATTS
111 Vice Pres Institutional Advancement ... Mr. Ernie ISEMINGER
85 Vice Pres International Affairs ... Dr. Darsh T. WASAN
86 Vice President External Affairs ... Mr. Jess GOODE
43 Interim General Counsel/Secretary ... Mr. Walter HAZLITT
88 President & Dir IIT Research Inst ... Dr. David MCCORMICK
88 VP & Dir Inst Food Safety & Health ... Dr. Robert BRACKETT
13 CIO & Vice Provost ... Mr. Ophir TRIGALO
28 Vice Provost Student Diversity ... Vacant
58 Vice Provost Grad Academic Affairs ... Dr. Jamshid MOHAMMADI
46 Vice Provost for Research ... Dr. Fred HICKERNELL
32 Vice Provost Student Affairs ... Ms. Katherine STETZ
61 Dean Chicago-Kent College of Law ... Dr. Anita K. KRUG
49 Interim Dean Col of Sci & Letters ... Dr. Xiaofan LI
54 Dean Armour Col of Engineering ... Dr. Natacha DEPAOLA
50 Dean Stuart School of Business ... Vacant
48 Dean College of Architecture ... Mr. Reed KROLOFF
83 Dean Lewis Col of Human Sciences ... Dr. Christine HIMES
12 Dean Institute of Design ... Mr. Denis WEIL
72 Dean School of Applied Technology ... Dr. Bob CARLSON
08 Interim Dean of Libraries ... Mr. Devin SAVAGE
88 Associate General Counsel ... Ms. Candida MIRANDA
21 Assoc VP Finance & Controller ... Mr. Ken JOHNSTON
15 Associate VP Human Resources ... Ms. Hilary HUDSON HOSEK
88 Assoc Vice Prov Grad Acad Affs ... Ms. Holli PRYOR HARRIS
41 Asst VP/Director of Athletics ... Ms. Usha GILMORE
07 AVP Undergraduate Admissions ... Ms. Toni RILEY
123 Asst VP Grad/Prof Admissions ... Mr. Rishab MALHOTRA
39 AVP Residence & Greek Life ... Vacant
14 Assoc CIO Enterprise Systems ... Mr. Vince BATTISTA
14 Assoc CIO Technology Infrastructure ... Mr. Ibukun OYEWOLE
14 Assoc CIO User & Technical Svcs ... Mr. Eric BREESE
23 Assoc VP Student Health & Wellness ... Ms. Anita OPDYCKE
29 Assoc VP Alumni & Donor Rels ... Vacant
96 Director of Purchasing ... Ms. Snow RUTKOWSKE
06 Interim Registrar ... Vacant
37 Asst VP of Financial Aid ... Ms. Elizabeth WAHLSTROM HELGREN
22 Director Diversity/Inclusions/EE ... Ms. Lisa MONTGOMERY
25 Director Sponsored Research ... Mr. Robert LAPOINTE
88 Dir Environmental Health & Safety ... Ms. Cynthia CHAFFEE
108 Director of Assessment ... Dr. Carol-Ann EMMONS
105 Director Web Development/Services ... Mr. Brian BAILEY
106 Dir IIT Online Tech Svcs ... Ms. Lauren WOODS
04 Director President's Office ... Ms. Sandra LAPORTE
90 Manager Academic Computing ... Vacant

Illinois Institute of Technology Downtown Campus (A)

565 W Adams Street, Chicago IL 60661
Telephone: (312) 906-5000 Identification: 770075
Accreditation: &HLC, LAW

Illinois Institute of Technology Rice Campus (B)

201 East Loop Road, Wheaton IL 60189
Telephone: (630) 682-6000 Identification: 770077
Accreditation: &HLC

Illinois State University (C)

201 S. School St., Campus Box 3490,
Normal IL 61761-2521
County: McLean FICE Identification: 001692
Unit ID: 145813
Telephone: (309) 438-2111 Carnegie Class: DU-Higher
FAX Number: N/A Calendar System: Semester
URL: https://illinoisstate.edu/
Established: 1857 Annual Undergrad Tuition & Fees (In-State): $15,319
Enrollment: 20,720 Coed
Affiliation or Control: State IRS Status: 501(c)3
Highest Offering: Doctorate
Accreditation: HLC, AAFCS, ART, AUD, CAATE, CAEP, CAEPN, CAHIIM, CAPRT, CIDA, CONST, DIETD, DIETI, IPSY, MLS, MUS, NAIT, NURSE, PH, SCPSY, SP, SW, THEA

01 President .... Dr. Terri KINZY
100 Assistant to President .... Ms. Kathleen KILLIAN
04 Administrative Asst to President .... Mr. Dave BENTLIN
05 VP Academic Affairs & Provost .... Dr. Aondover TARHULE
10 VP Finance & Planning .... Mr. Daniel STEPHENS
32 VP Student Affairs .... Dr. Levester JOHNSON
35 Assistant VP Student Affairs .... Vacant
111 VP University Advancement .... Mr. Pat VICKERMAN
13 Assoc VP & Chief Info Officer .... Mr. Charles EDAMALA
41 Director Intercollegiate Athletics .... Mr. Kyle BRENNAN
86 Director Governmental Relations .... Dr. Jonathan LACKLAND
28 Int Asst to Pres for Diversity/Incl .... Dr. Doris HOUSTON
43 General Counsel .... Ms. Jeannie BARRETT
22 Dir EOA Title IX Coord .... Mr. Jeff LANGE
20 Associate Provost .... Dr. Ani YAZEDJIAN
58 Assoc VP Grad Studies/Research .... Dr. Craig MCLAUCHLAN
88 Assoc VP Undergrad Education .... Dr. Amy HURD
85 Int Assoc VP Global Education .... Dr. Perry SCHOON
88 Asst VP Academic Planning .... Dr. J. Cooper CUTTING
121 Interim Asst VP Student Success .... Dr. Amelia NOEL-ELKINS
88 Interim Assoc VP Academic Admin .... Dr. Roberta TRITES
88 Assoc VP Acad Fiscal Mgmt .... Dr. Dan ELKINS
84 Assoc VP Enrollment Management .... Dr. Jana ALBRECHT
15 Assoc VP Human Resources .... Ms. Janice BONNEVILLE
21 Assoc VP Fin Admin/Comptroller .... Mr. Doug SCHNITTKER
18 Assoc VP Fac Mgmt/Planning & Opers .... Mr. Mike GEBEKE
114 Assistant VP Budget & Planning .... Ms. Sandra CAVI
35 Assistant VP Student Affairs .... Dr. Danielle MILLER-SCHUSTER
08 Dean University Libraries .... Dr. Dallas LONG
06 University Registrar .... Ms. Stacey RAMSEY
07 Director Admissions .... Mr. Jeff MAVROS
97 Interim Director University College .... Ms. Wendi WHITMAN
30 Executive Dir of Dev Fundraising .... Ms. Joy HUTCHCRAFT
37 Director Financial Aid .... Ms. Bridget CURL
29 Exec Director Alumni Engagement .... Ms. Kristin HARDING
88 Director Emeritus Intl Studies .... Mr. William SEMLAK
92 Acting Dir Honors Program .... Dr. Linda CLEMMONS
94 Director Women's Studies .... Dr. Alison BAILEY
96 Director of Purchasing Office .... Mr. Ernest OLSON
49 Int Dean College Arts & Sciences .... Dr. Diane ZOSKY
106 Chief Online Learning Officer .... Dr. Anthony PINA
50 Dean College Business .... Dr. Ajay SAMANT
53 Dean College Education .... Dr. Jim WOLFINGER
72 Dean College Applied Sci/Tech .... Dr. Todd MCLODA
57 Dean Wonsook Kim College Fine Arts .... Ms. Jean MILLER
66 Dean Mennonite College .... Dr. Judy NEUBRANDER
35 Assistant VP & Dean of Students .... Dr. John DAVENPORT
38 Director Student Counseling .... Dr. Sandy COLBS
39 Director University Housing .... Ms. Stacey MWILAMBWE
23 Director Student Health Services .... Dr. Christina NULTY
19 Chief University Police .... Mr. Aaron WOODRUFF
44 Director Annual Giving .... Ms. Jillian NELSON
27 Exec Dir University Marketing/Comm .... Mr. Brian BEAM
45 Dir Planning/Rsch/Policy Analysis .... Ms. Angela ENGEL
108 Director University Assessment .... Dr. Ryan SMITH
105 Director Web & Interactive Comm .... Mr. Arturo RAMIREZ

Illinois Valley Community College (D)

815 N Orlando Smith Road, Oglesby IL 61348-9692
County: La Salle FICE Identification: 001705
Unit ID: 145831
Telephone: (815) 224-2720 Carnegie Class: Assoc/HVT-Mix Trad/Non
FAX Number: (815) 224-3033 Calendar System: Semester
URL: www.ivcc.edu
Established: 1966 Annual Undergrad Tuition & Fees (In-District): $13,232
Enrollment: 2,413 Coed
Affiliation or Control: Local IRS Status: 501(c)3
Highest Offering: Associate Degree
Accreditation: HLC, ADNUR, DA, EMT, NAEYC

01 President .... Dr. Jerry M. CORCORAN
05 Vice Pres for Academic Affairs .... Dr. Gary ROBERTS
10 Vice Pres Business Svcs/Finance .... Dr. Matthew SEATON
20 Assoc Vice Pres Academic Affairs .... Ms. Bonnie L. CAMPBELL
32 Vice President Student Services .... Mr. Mark J. GRZYBOWSKI
24 Director of Learning Resources .... Dr. Patrice HESS
31 Exec Dir Cmty Relations/Marketing .... Mr. Francis R. BROLLEY
13 Dir of Information Technology Svcs .... Mr. Justin DENTON
51 Dir Cont Educ/Business Svcs .... Ms. Jennifer C. SCHERI
15 Director Human Resources .... Ms. Leslie A. HOFER
37 Director of Financial Aid .... Mr. Eric JOHNSON
07 Director of Admissions/Records .... Mr. Tom QUIGLEY
08 Public Services Librarian .... Ms. Stephanie REEDER
30 Director of Development .... Mr. Francis R. BROLLEY
96 Director of Purchasing .... Ms. Michelle L. CARBONI
18 Director of Facilities .... Mr. Scott CURLEY
09 Director of Institutional Research .... Mr. Matthew P. SUERTH
81 Dean Natural Science/Business .... Mr. Ron W. GROLEAU
66 Interim Director of Nursing .... Ms. Anna BRUCH
79 Dean Humanities/Fine Arts/Soc Sci .... Dr. Lirim NEZIROSKI
103 Dean Workforce Development .... Mr. Shane LANGE

Illinois Wesleyan University (E)

PO Box 2900, 1312 Park Street,
Bloomington IL 61702-2900
County: McLean FICE Identification: 001696
Unit ID: 145646
Telephone: (309) 556-1000 Carnegie Class: Bac-Diverse
FAX Number: (309) 556-3411 Calendar System: Other
URL: www.iwu.edu
Established: 1850 Annual Undergrad Tuition & Fees: $51,336
Enrollment: 1,636 Coed
Affiliation or Control: Independent Non-Profit IRS Status: 501(c)3
Highest Offering: Baccalaureate
Accreditation: HLC, MUS, NURSE

01 President .... Dr. S. Georgia NUGENT
05 Provost & Dean of Faculty .... Dr. Mark BRODL
10 Vice President Business & Finance .... Mr. Matt BIERMAN
30 Vice President for Advancement .... Mr. Steve SEIBRING
27 Director for Communications .... Ms. Ann AUBRY
32 VP Student Affairs/Dean Students .... Dr. Karla CARNEY-HALL
84 VP of Enrollment & Marketing .... Ms. LeAnn HUGHES
07 Dean Admissions/AVP Enrollment Mgmt .... Mr. Greg KING
09 AVP for Institutional Effectiveness .... Dr. Michael THOMPSON
86 Dir Government/Community Relations .... Mr. Carl F. TEICHMAN
04 Exec Assistant to the President .... Ms. Julie ANDERSON
20 Assoc Provost .... Prof. Rebecca ROESNER
20 Assoc Dean Curricular/Faculty Dev .... Vacant
15 Dir Human Resources/Title IX Coord .... Ms. Cindy LOTZ
13 Chief Technology Officer .... Mr. Leon LEWIS
110 Asst Vice Pres for Advancement .... Mr. Bob GERATY
29 Asst VP of Alumni Engagement .... Vacant
38 Exec Director Counseling/Health .... Dr. Vickie FOLSE
35 Asst VP Stdnt Affs/Dir Campus Life .... Dr. Kevin CAREY
08 University Librarian/Copyright Ofcr .... Ms. Stephanie DAVIS-KAHL
06 Registrar .... Dr. Leslie BETZ
42 Univ Chaplain/Assoc Dean Students .... Vacant
21 Controller .... Mr. John BRYANT
37 Director of Financial Aid .... Mr. Scott SEIBRING
64 Director of School of Music .... Dr. Franklin LAREY
57 Director of School of Art .... Prof. Julie JOHNSON
57 Director of School of Theatre Arts .... Dr. Jean KERR
66 Director of School of Nursing .... Dr. Vickie FOLSE
41 Director of Athletics .... Prof. Mike WAGNER
29 Director of Alumni Engagement .... Vacant
102 Dir Grants/Foundation Relations .... Mr. Dick FOLSE
44 Director of Wesleyan Annual Fund .... Ms. Elizabeth CHAMBERS-KLATT
36 Director of Career Center .... Mr. Warren KISTNER
18 Director of Physical Plant .... Mr. James J. BLUMBERG
88 Dir of Athletic Communications .... Ms. Katie GONZALES
93 Dean for Inclusion & Advocacy .... Mr. Prince ROBERTSON
35 Director of Student Involvement .... Vacant
94 Dir of Women's & Gender Studies .... Dr. Carole MYSCOFSKI
104 Director of International Office .... Ms. Stacey SHIMIZU
40 Bookstore Manager .... Ms. Sarah HASTINGS
26 Director of Marketing .... Mr. Andrew KREISS

Institute for Clinical Social Work (F)

1345 W. Argyle St, Chicago IL 60640
County: Cook FICE Identification: 025737
Unit ID: 145886
Telephone: (312) 935-4232 Carnegie Class: Spec-4-yr-Other Health
FAX Number: (312) 935-4255 Calendar System: Semester
URL: www.icsw.edu
Established: 1981 Annual Graduate Tuition & Fees: N/A
Enrollment: 128 Coed
Affiliation or Control: Independent Non-Profit IRS Status: 501(c)3
Highest Offering: Doctorate; No Undergraduates
Accreditation: HLC

01 President .... Dr. Michelle C. STEWART
10 Vice Pres Finance/Operations .... Mr. Michael BAUMAN
05 Academic Dean .... Dr. Joan SERVATIUS
37 Director of Student Financial Svcs .... Vacant
07 Dir of Admissions/Enrollment Mgmt .... Mr. Kenneth FRIERSON
32 Chief Student Affairs Officer .... Ms. Andrea DUNBAR

John A. Logan College (G)

700 Logan College Road, Carterville IL 62918-2500
County: Williamson FICE Identification: 008076
Unit ID: 146205
Telephone: (618) 985-2828 Carnegie Class: Assoc/HVT-High Non
FAX Number: (618) 985-2248 Calendar System: Semester
URL: www.jalc.edu
Established: 1967 Annual Undergrad Tuition & Fees (In-District): $5,506
Enrollment: 3,328 Coed
Affiliation or Control: State/Local IRS Status: 501(c)3
Highest Offering: Associate Degree
Accreditation: HLC, ADNUR, DA, DMS, MLTAD, OTA, SURGT

01 President .... Dr. Kirk OVERSTREET
05 Provost .... Ms. Melanie PECORD
10 VP Business Services and CFO .... Ms. Stacy BUCKINGHAM
32 Asst Provost of Student Affairs .... Ms. Christy STEWART
21 Controller .... Ms. Kara BEVIS
20 Asst Provost of Academic Affairs .... Dr. Stephanie HARTFORD
75 Assoc Dean of Career/Technical Educ .... Mr. Scott WERNSMAN
20 Assoc Dean of Academic Affairs .... Mr. Nathan ARNETT
103 Dir of Academic & Workforce Pgms .... Ms. Michelle HAMILTON
37 Director of Student Financial Asst .... Ms. Cheri RUSHING
26 Asst VP of Marketing/Comm/PR .... Dr. Steve O'KEEFE
35 Assoc Dean of Student Activities .... Ms. Adrienne BARKLEY-GIFFIN
36 Dir of Career Services and Intl Ed .... Ms. Beth STEPHENS
102 Executive Director of Foundation .... Ms. Staci SHAFER
66 Director of Nursing .... Ms. Kristin YOSANOVICH
88 Director of Testing Services .... Ms. Christy MCBRIDE
15 Asst VP of Human Resources .... Ms. Johnna HERREN
18 Dir Buildings and Grounds .... Mr. Jeremy MUELLER
09 Asst VP Institutional E & R .... Mr. Jordan MAYS
25 Grant Writer .... Dr. Tammy GWALTNEY
04 Senior Exec Asst to President .... Ms. Carmen CUTSINGER
101 Dir of LA/Spec Asst to Pres/BOT .... Ms. Susan MAY
28 Director of Diversity & Inclusion .... Ms. Toyin FOX
41 Athletic Director .... Mr. Greg STARRICK
113 Bursar .... Mr. Jason SNIDER
38 Director of Student Success .... Ms. Nikki BROOKS
121 Director Academic Advisement .... Ms. Stacy HOLLOWAY
96 Dir of Purchasing/Auxiliary Svcs .... Ms. Shannon NEWMAN
88 Dir Child Care Resources/Referral .... Ms. Missy BROWN
88 Director of ASE .... Ms. Crystal HOSSELTON
56 Director of Adult Education .... Ms. Karla TABING
88 Manager of Workforce Educ .... Ms. Emily SPANN
88 Asst VP of Integrated Technology .... Mr. Scott ELLIOTT
18 Director of Facility Services .... Mr. Chris NAEGELE
105 WebMaster .... Mr. Phillip LANE
106 Assoc Dean of Education Technology .... Ms. Krystal REAGAN
08 Director of Library Services .... Mr. Adam RUBIN
19 Chief of Police and Campus Security .... Mr. Allan WILLMORE

John Wood Community College (H)

1301 S 48th Street, Quincy IL 62305-8736
County: Adams FICE Identification: 012813
Unit ID: 146278
Telephone: (217) 224-6500 Carnegie Class: Assoc/MT-VT-High Trad
FAX Number: (217) 224-4208 Calendar System: Semester
URL: www.jwcc.edu
Established: 1974 Annual Undergrad Tuition & Fees (In-District): $8,190
Enrollment: 1,881 Coed
Affiliation or Control: State/Local IRS Status: 501(c)3
Highest Offering: Associate Degree
Accreditation: HLC, @CNEA, SURGT

01 President .... Mr. Michael ELBE
05 Vice President for Instruction .... Dr. Laurel KLINKENBERG
10 Dean Business Svcs/Inst Effective .... Mr. Joshua WELKER
49 Dean Arts and Sciences .... Ms. Rachel HANSEN
75 Dean Careers/Tech/Health Education .... Mr. David HETZLER
06 Registrar/Dean Records/Fin Aid .... Ms. Melanie LECHTENBERG
07 Director Admissions .... Ms. Kristen RITTERBUSCH
32 Dean Students/Enrollment Management .... Ms. Tracy ORNE
21 Director Fiscal Services .... Mr. John REINHARDT
121 Director Support Services .... Mr. Robert HODGSON
13 Director Information Technology .... Mr. Joshua BRUECK
08 Director Learning Resource Center .... Ms. Barbara LIEBER
26 Director Public Relations/Marketing .... Ms. Tracy HAGMAN
111 Director Advancement .... Ms. Barbara HOLTHAUS
15 Director Human Resources .... Ms. Dana KEPPNER
18 Director Physical Plant .... Mr. Lou BARTA
37 Director Financial Aid .... Ms. Melanie LECHTENBERG
19 Dean of Ops/Chief of Campus Police .... Mr. Bill LATOUR
41 Director Athletics .... Mr. Brad HOYT
40 Manager Campus Services .... Ms. Darla SNYDER
47 Dept Chair Ag Sciences .... Mr. Mike TENHOUSE
50 Dept Chair Business/Computer Sci .... Mr. Devron STERNKE
81 Department Chair Mathematics .... Ms. Brenda GRAFF
65 Dept Chair Natural Sci/Engineering .... Dr. Christopher KAELKE
79 Dept Chair Communications/Lang/Lit .... Mr. Todd SAXTON
83 Dept Chair Social/Behavior Science .... Ms. Beth REINHARDT
57 Dept Chair Fine Arts/Hum/Educ .... Mr. Steven SOEBBING
04 Executive Asst to President .... Ms. Leah BENZ

Joliet Junior College (I)

1215 Houbolt Road, Joliet IL 60431-8938
County: Will FICE Identification: 001699
Unit ID: 146296
Telephone: (815) 729-9020 Carnegie Class: Assoc/MT-VT-Mix Trad/Non
FAX Number: N/A Calendar System: Semester
URL: www.jjc.edu

Established: 1901 Annual Undergrad Tuition & Fees (In-District): $4,440
Enrollment: 10,267 Coed
Affiliation or Control: State/Local IRS Status: 501(c)3
Highest Offering: Associate Degree
Accreditation: HLC, ACBSP, ACFEI, ADNUR, CAHIIM, DMS, MUS

01 President .... Dr. Judy MITCHELL
10 VP Finance & Admin Services .... Dr. Cecil LUCY
05 VP Academic Affairs .... Dr. Amy GRAY
13 Chief Information Officer .... Mr. Jim SERR
32 VP Student Development .... Dr. Yolanda FARMER
07 Director Admissions & Recruitment .... Ms. Jennifer KLOBERDANZ
37 Director Financial Aid .... Ms. Deanna FISK
15 Chief HR Officer .... Dr. Nicole WHITEHEAD
16 Director Human Resources .... Ms. Judy CONNELLY
18 Sr Director Facility Services .... Mr. Patrick VAN DUYNE
109 Sr Director Business/Auxiliary Svcs .... Ms. Janice REEDUS
26 Exec Dir Commun/External Rels .... Ms. Kelly ROHDER-TONELLI
36 Director Career Services .... Vacant
41 Director Athletics .... Mr. Gregory BRAUN
21 Director Financial Svcs/Controller .... Mr. Jeffrey HEAP
19 Dir Campus Safety & Police Chief .... Mr. Brandon CAMPBELL
111 Ex Dir Inst Adv Exec Dir JJC Found .... Ms. Kristin MULVEY
09 Director of Institutional Research .... Mr. Joseph OFFERMANN
29 Mgr Annual Giving & Alumni Rels .... Ms. Jennifer DAVIS
49 Dean Arts & Sciences .... Vacant
103 Dean Applied Arts/Wrkforce Ed/Trng .... Ms. Amy MURPHY
75 Dean CTE .... Ms. Patty ZUCCARELLO
108 Sr Director Inst Effectiveness .... Ms. Kristin CIESEMIER
121 Dean of Student Success .... Dr. Angie KAYSEN-LUZBETAK
04 Executive Asst to President .... Mrs. Kelly ROGERS
101 Secretary of the Institution/Board .... Ms. Joan TIERNEY
104 International Education Coord .... Vacant
106 Dir Online Education/E-learning .... Mr. Chris OSTWINKLE
84 Dean of Enrollment Mgmt & Registrar .... Mr. Robert MORRIS
110 Asst Dir Inst Advancement .... Ms. Amanda QUINN

Judson University (A)

1151 N State Street, Elgin IL 60123-1498
County: Kane FICE Identification: 001700
Unit ID: 146339
Telephone: (847) 628-2500 Carnegie Class: Masters/S
FAX Number: (847) 628-1027 Calendar System: Semester
URL: www.judsonu.edu
Established: 1913 Annual Undergrad Tuition & Fees: $29,870
Enrollment: 1,173 Coed
Affiliation or Control: American Baptist IRS Status: 501(c)3
Highest Offering: Doctorate
Accreditation: HLC

01 President .... Dr. Gene CRUME
03 Executive Vice President .... Dr. Nikki FENNERN
05 Provost/Chief Academic Officer .... Dr. A. Gillian STEWART-WELLS
10 VP for Business Affairs .... Ms. Sarah TAYLOR
06 VP for Student Success & Registrar .... Ms. Virginia GUTH
20 Assoc Provost/Academic Curriculum .... Dr. Lanette POTEETE-YOUNG
08 Library Director .... Mr. Larry WILD
37 Director of Financial Aid .... Ms. Diana WINTON
26 Director of Comm & Marketing .... Ms. Mary DULABAUM
36 Director of Career Services .... Ms. Colleen JONES
38 Dir of Counseling & Wellness .... Ms. Belinda ADAME
18 Asst VP for Campus Operations .... Mr. Nick SALZMANN
41 Athletic Director .... Mr. Joel POPENFOOSE
89 Dir of 1st Year Exp & Persistence .... Ms. Jaimee BARTHA
85 International Advisor .... Ms. Andrea SINNAEVE
92 Honors Director .... Dr. James HALVERSON
101 Asst Sec to Board of Trustees .... Ms. Tena ROBOTHAM
09 Director of Institutional Research .... Mr. Chad BRIGGS
39 Coordinator Student Housing .... Ms. McKenna HAAS
88 RISE Program Director .... Ms. Gineen VARGAS
111 VP for Advancement and Alumni .... Ms. Kristen EGAN
32 Dean of Student Life & Leadership .... Ms. Aubree FLICKEMA
121 Dean Student Academic Support Svcs .... Ms. Heather JOHNSON
42 Dean of University Ministries .... Mr. Chris LASH
15 Human Resources Generalist .... Ms. Jennifer CHICAS

Kankakee Community College (B)

100 College Drive, Kankakee IL 60901-6505
County: Kankakee FICE Identification: 007690
Unit ID: 146348
Telephone: (815) 802-8100 Carnegie Class: Assoc/MT-VT-High Non
FAX Number: (815) 802-8101 Calendar System: Semester
URL: www.kcc.edu
Established: 1966 Annual Undergrad Tuition & Fees (In-District): $13,200
Enrollment: 2,245 Coed
Affiliation or Control: State/Local IRS Status: 501(c)3
Highest Offering: Associate Degree
Accreditation: HLC, ADNUR, COARC, MLTAD, PNUR, PTAA

01 President .... Dr. Michael BOYD
04 Exec Asst to Pres & BOT .... Ms. Karen SLAGER
05 Vice President Academic Affairs .... Vacant
10 Vice President Business Affairs .... Ms. Beth NUNLEY
06 Dir Enrollment Services/Registrar .... Ms. Michelle HASIK
32 Vice President Student Affairs .... Ms. Meredith PURCELL
09 Dir Inst Effectiveness/Assessment .... Dr. Lesley COOPER
31 Director Adult & Community Educ .... Mr. Gregg BEGLAU
103 Director of Workforce Development .... Ms. Monica LOWE
37 Director Financial Aid .... Ms. Kendra SOULIGNE
41 Director Athletics .... Mr. Todd POST
15 Director Human Resources .... Mr. David CAGLE
50 Dean Business & Technology .... Mr. Paul CARLSON
51 Dean Cont Educ & Career Svcs .... Ms. Mary POSING
18 Director Facilities .... Mr. Rob KENNEY
76 Dean Health Careers Div .... Ms. Sheri CAGLE
121 Director Student Success .... Mr. Jeremy KINGERY
76 Director Respiratory Therapist Pgm .... Ms. Jaclyn MONTEMAYER
76 Director Medical Lab Technology .... Ms. Lamanda BAADE
66 Director Nursing .... Ms. Kellee HAYES
88 Dir Physical Therapy Asst Pgm .... Ms. Jennifer BLANCHETTE
49 Dean Liberal Arts & Sciences .... Ms. Jennifer HUGGINS
76 Director Radiology Technology Pgm .... Ms. Rebecca SHERRY
13 Director Information Tech Svcs .... Mr. Michael O'CONNOR
102 Exec Director of KCC Foundation .... Vacant
88 Director Institutional Tech/Fac Dev .... Mr. Craig KEIGHER
08 Director of Library .... Ms. Tracy CONNER
26 Dir Marketing/Public Relations .... Ms. Kari NUGENT
101 Exec Asst to Pres & BOT .... Ms. Karen SLAGER
88 Director Support Services .... Ms. Kimberlee JEFFREYS
19 Chief Police & Dir Public Safety .... Mr. Eric SPRINGER

Kaskaskia College (C)

27210 College Road, Centralia IL 62801-7878
County: Clinton FICE Identification: 001701
Unit ID: 146366
Telephone: (618) 545-3000 Carnegie Class: Assoc/MT-VT-High Non
FAX Number: (618) 532-1990 Calendar System: Semester
URL: www.kaskaskia.edu
Established: 1940 Annual Undergrad Tuition & Fees (In-District): $7,530
Enrollment: 2,785 Coed
Affiliation or Control: State/Local IRS Status: 501(c)3
Highest Offering: Associate Degree
Accreditation: HLC, ADNUR, COARC, DA, EMT, PTAA, RAD

01 President .... Mr. George EVANS
11 Vice Pres Administrative Services .... Mrs. Judy HEMKER
05 Vice Pres Instructional Services .... Mrs. Julie OBERMARK
32 Vice President of Student Services .... Dr. Susan BATCHELOR
75 Dean Career & Technical Education .... Ms. Traci MASAU
49 Dean of Arts & Sciences .... Mrs. Kellie HENEGAR
66 Dean Nursing & Health Sciences .... Vacant
09 Dir Institutional Effectiveness .... Mr. Bruce FISCHER
108 Associate Dean of Inst Assessment .... Mr. Alan BOERNGEN
15 Director of Human Resources .... Mrs. Jill HERCULES
18 Director Facilities/Physical Plant .... Mr. Jennings CARTER
96 Director Purchasing/Auxiliary Svcs .... Mr. Craig ROPER
37 Director of Financial Aid .... Mrs. Jill KLOSTERMANN
76 Director of Radiologic Technology .... Mrs. Mimi POLCZYNSKI
13 Chief Information Officer .... Mr. George KRISS
26 Director of Marketing .... Mr. Travis HENSON
07 Dean of Enrollment Services .... Ms. Amy TROUTT
88 Regional Director of Educ Centers .... Mrs. Cheryl BOEHNE
111 Dir Inst Advancement Programs .... Mrs. Suzanne CHRIST
19 Director of Public Safety .... Mr. Todd WAGNER
04 Admin Assistant to the President .... Mrs. Cathy QUICK
06 Registrar .... Mrs. Jenna LAMMERS
08 Chief Library Officer .... Ms. Laura VAHLKAMP

Kishwaukee College (D)

21193 Malta Road, Malta IL 60150-9600
County: De Kalb FICE Identification: 007684
Unit ID: 146418
Telephone: (815) 825-2086 Carnegie Class: Assoc/MT-VT-Mix Trad/Non
FAX Number: (815) 825-2072 Calendar System: Semester
URL: www.kish.edu
Established: 1968 Annual Undergrad Tuition & Fees (In-District): $9,390
Enrollment: 2,626 Coed
Affiliation or Control: State/Local IRS Status: 501(c)3
Highest Offering: Associate Degree
Accreditation: HLC, ADNUR, EMT, RAD

01 President .... Dr. Laurie BOROWICZ
05 Chief Academic Officer .... Dr. Joanne KANTNER
20 Interim Vice President Instruction .... Ms. Barbara LEACH
32 Vice President Student Services .... Ms. Michelle ROTHMEYER
11 Exec Director of Campus Operations .... Mr. Dave DAMMON
20 Director Curriculum & Program Dev .... Ms. Terry Lyn FUNSTON
06 Enrollment Services & Registrar .... Ms. Tina SWIGER
49 Dean Liberal Arts/Science/Business .... Mr. Chase BUDZIAK
10 CFO .... Ms. Jill HANSEN
102 Exec Director College Relations .... Ms. Kayte HAMEL
13 Director Information Technology .... Mr. Robert MCGARRY
30 Director Development & Compliance .... Mr. Nick PIAZZA
15 Exec Dir Human Resources .... Ms. Cindy MCCLUSKEY
35 Director Student Involvement .... Mr. Scott KAWALL
04 Executive Assistant to President .... Ms. Carolyn CHRUSCIEL
66 Director of Nursing .... Ms. Angie DELMONT
09 Director of Institutional Research .... Mr. Matthew CRULL
103 Director of Business Partnerships .... Ms. LaCretia KONAN
25 Chief Contract/Grants Administrator .... Dr. Kayte HAMEL
37 Manager of Financial Aid .... Mr. Adam GISSELER
96 Purchasing Accountant .... Mr. Christopher BAILEY

Knox College (E)

2 E South Street, Galesburg IL 61401-4999
County: Knox FICE Identification: 001704
Unit ID: 146427
Telephone: (309) 341-7000 Carnegie Class: Bac-A&S
FAX Number: (309) 341-7090 Calendar System: Trimester
URL: www.knox.edu
Established: 1837 Annual Undergrad Tuition & Fees: $49,974
Enrollment: 1,154 Coed
Affiliation or Control: Independent Non-Profit IRS Status: 501(c)3
Highest Offering: Baccalaureate
Accreditation: HLC

01 President .... Dr. Andrew MCGADNEY
101 Secretary of the College .... Ms. Peggy J. WARE
05 Provost/Dean of College .... Dr. Michael A. SCHNEIDER
10 Vice Pres for Finance & Admin Svcs .... Mr. Paul W. EISENMENGER
111 Vice President for Advancement .... Ms. Beverly HOLMES
07 Vice Pres Enrollment/Dean of Admiss .... Mr. Paul R. STEENIS
32 VP for Student Development .... Vacant
45 VP for Strategic Initiatives .... Ms. Heather BUMPS
26 Executive Director of Communication .... Ms. Lisa K. VAN RIPER
06 Acting Registrar .... Dr. Jerry MINER
35 Dean of Students .... Ms. Debbie SOUTHERN
20 Associate Dean of College .... Dr. Timothy J. FOSTER
37 Director Financial Aid .... Ms. Leigh T. BRINSON
08 Librarian .... Ms. Anne THOMASON
36 Exec Dir Career Development .... Mr. Scott CRAWFORD
13 VP/CIO Information Technology Svcs .... Mr. Steven HALL
15 AVP Director Human Resources .... Ms. Amy CHAMBERS
18 Director Facilities Services .... Mr. Scott MAUST
21 Controller .... Ms. Sara A. KING
86 Dir Government & Community Relation .... Vacant
29 Dir Alumni Engagement/Annual Giving .... Ms. Sarah E. BYRD
38 Director of Counseling Services .... Ms. Janell J. MCGRUDER
19 Director Campus Safety .... Mr. Nathan R. KEMP
09 Dir Institutional Research/Assess .... Ms. Anna J. CLARK
102 Dir Corporate/Foundation Relations .... Ms. Jan K. WOLBERS
39 Assistant Dean for Campus Life .... Mr. Jake MCLEAN
41 Director of Athletics .... Ms. Daniella J. IRLE
28 Executive Director of DIE .... Ms. Tianna N. CERVANTEZ

Lake Forest College (F)

555 N Sheridan Road, Lake Forest IL 60045-2338
County: Lake FICE Identification: 001706
Unit ID: 146481
Telephone: (847) 234-3100 Carnegie Class: Bac-A&S
FAX Number: N/A Calendar System: Semester
URL: www.lakeforest.edu
Established: 1857 Annual Undergrad Tuition & Fees: $49,822
Enrollment: 1,583 Coed
Affiliation or Control: Independent Non-Profit IRS Status: 501(c)3
Highest Offering: Master's
Accreditation: HLC, IPSY

01 President .... Mr. Stephen D. SCHUTT
05 VP Student Affairs/Dean of Students .... Ms. Andrea CONNOR
04 Admin Assistant to the President .... Ms. Dominique ALLION
06 Registrar .... Mr. BJ WHITE
84 Vice President of Enrollment .... Mr. Chris ELLERTSON
08 Interim Director of the Library .... Ms. Kimberly HAZLETT
09 Assistant Director of IR .... Mr. Kyle DIEP
10 VP for Finance & Planning .... Ms. Lori SUNDBERG
104 Coordinator of Global Engagement .... Ms. Alexandra OLSON
13 Chief Information Officer .... Mr. Ravi AGARWAL
15 Director of Human Resources .... Ms. Agnes STEPEK
18 Director of Facilities Management .... Mr. Dave SIEBERT
19 Director of Public Safety .... Mr. Richard COHEN
37 AVP for Financial Aid .... Mr. Jerry CEBRZYNSKI
39 Interim Director of Residence Life .... Mr. Jordan AHLERSMEYER
41 Athletic Director .... Ms. Nicole PIEART

Lake Forest Graduate School of Management (G)

1905 W Field Court, Lake Forest IL 60045-4824
County: Lake FICE Identification: 023192
Unit ID: 146490
Telephone: (847) 234-5005 Carnegie Class: Spec-4-yr-Bus
FAX Number: (847) 295-3656 Calendar System: Semester
URL: www.lfgsm.edu
Established: 1946 Annual Graduate Tuition & Fees: N/A
Enrollment: 395 Coed
Affiliation or Control: Independent Non-Profit IRS Status: 501(c)3
Highest Offering: Master's; No Undergraduates
Accreditation: HLC

01 President .... Mr. Jeffrey J. ANDERSON
05 Chief Academic Officer .... Dr. Neil HOLMAN
10 VP Finance & CFO .... Mr. Thomas PEROZZI
06 Registrar .... Ms. Diana BOOTH
07 Sr Director of Admissions/Marketing .... Ms. Carolyn BRUNE
32 Director of Student Experience .... Ms. Currie GASCHE
09 Sr Manager Institutional Research .... Ms. Catherine KISSLING
37 Director of Financial Aid .... Ms. Connie ELDRIDGE
88 VP Corporate Learning .... Ms. Carrie BUCHWALD
04 Executive Assistant to President .... Ms. Dana KAECHELE
08 Chief Library Officer .... Dr. Neil HOLMAN

Lake Land College (H)

5001 Lake Land Boulevard, Mattoon IL 61938-9366
County: Coles FICE Identification: 007644
Unit ID: 146506
Telephone: (217) 234-5253 Carnegie Class: Assoc/HVT-High Non
FAX Number: (217) 234-5400 Calendar System: Semester
URL: https://www.lakelandcollege.edu
Established: 1966 Annual Undergrad Tuition & Fees (In-District): $8,104
Enrollment: 3,862 Coed

Affiliation or Control: State/Local IRS Status: 501(c)3
Highest Offering: Associate Degree
Accreditation: HLC, ADNUR, DH, EMT, MAC, PNUR, PTAA

01 President .... Dr. Josh BULLOCK
100 Chief of Staff .... Ms. Jean Anne HIGHLAND
10 VP for Business Services .... Mr. Greg NUXOLL
05 VP for Academic Services .... Mr. Ikemefuna NWOSU
32 Vice President for Student Services .... Ms. Valerie LYNCH
88 Dean of Correctional Pgms South .... Mr. Brandon YOUNG
88 Dean of Correctional Pgms North .... Ms. Jennifer BILLINGSLEY
07 Dean of Admission Services .... Mr. Jon VAN DYKE
88 Assoc Dean Corrections Taylorville .... Mr. Robert EIFERT
88 Assoc Dean Corrections Graham .... Ms. Justy ROTHE
88 Assoc Dean Corrections Western .... Ms. Amber ALEXANDER
88 Assoc Dean Correction IL River .... Ms. Deborah COLLINS
88 Assoc Dean Corrections Southwestern .... Mr. Harvey GROENNERT
88 Assoc Dean Kewanee .... Mr. Aaron SHERBEYN
88 Assoc Dean Correction Lincoln .... Mr. Randall INGMIRE
88 Assoc Dean DOC Logan .... Mr. Dustin KNOLLENBERG
88 Assoc Dean DOC Ill River .... Mr. BJ MCCULLUM
88 Assoc Dean Corrections Vandalia .... Ms. Tabitha WELCH
88 Assoc Dean Corrections Hill .... Mr. Chris WILLIAMS
88 Site Dir Corrections Vienna/Shawnee .... Mr. Rich PATERA
21 Comptroller .... Ms. Madge SHOOT
50 Dir Center for Business & Industry .... Ms. Bonnie MOORE
08 Director of Library Services .... Ms. Sarah HILL
26 Dir of Marketing/Public Relations .... Mrs. Kelly ALLEE
13 Chief Information Officer .... Mr. David STEWART
37 Dir of Financial Aid/Veteran Svcs .... Ms. Jennifer HEDGES
15 Director of Human Resources .... Ms. Dustha WAHLS
25 Dir Grants & Academic Operations .... Ms. Emily RAMAGE
35 Director Student Life .... Ms. Lisa SCHUMARD-SHELTON
103 Director Workforce Investment .... Ms. Jamie CORDA HADJAOUI
19 Chief of Police .... Mr. Jeff BRANSON
40 Manager of Bookstore .... Ms. Amanda ARENA
111 Exec Dir for College Advancement .... Ms. Christi DONSBACH
36 Director of Career Services .... Ms. Tina MOORE
18 Dir of Physical Plant Operations .... Mr. Scott RAWLINGS
41 Director of Athletics .... Mr. William JACKSON
09 Director of Institutional Research .... Dr. Mary BREER
88 Dir of Data Analytics .... Ms. Lisa COLE
88 Assoc Dean Harrisburg IYC .... Ms. Toni PARKS-PARTON
88 Assoc Dean Corrections St Charles .... Mr. Scott HORSCH
88 Assoc Dean Corrections Murphysboro .... Ms. Tomi GRAVATT
88 Assoc Dean Corrections Pickneyville .... Mr. Doug LAUMBATTUS
88 Associate Dean Corrections Sherida .... Mr. Alan MORTENSEN
88 Associate Dean Big Muddy .... Ms. Penny MURPHY
88 Assoc Dean Corrections East Moline .... Ms. Ginger MURRAY
88 Assoc Dean Corrections Southwest .... Ms. Serenna ARNDT
88 Assoc Dean Corrections Robinson .... Mr. Mike PATILLA
88 Associate Dean Joliet .... Mr. Garry SCOTT
88 Assoc Dean Corrections Dixon .... Mr. Keith STEVENSON
88 Assoc Dean Corrections Decatur .... Ms. Lora TAIRA
88 Assoc Dean Corrections Vienna .... Mr. Brian WATSON

Lakeview College of Nursing (A)

903 N Logan Avenue, Danville IL 61832-3788
County: Vermilion FICE Identification: 010501
Unit ID: 146533
Telephone: (217) 709-0920 Carnegie Class: Spec-4-yr-Other Health
FAX Number: (217) 709-0954 Calendar System: Semester
URL: www.lakeviewcol.edu
Established: 1987 Annual Undergrad Tuition & Fees: N/A
Enrollment: 162 Coed
Affiliation or Control: Independent Non-Profit IRS Status: 501(c)3
Highest Offering: Baccalaureate
Accreditation: HLC, NURSE

01 President .... Ms. Sheila MINGEE
05 Dean .... Ms. Lanette STUCKEY
06 Registrar/Director of Enrollment .... Ms. Connie YOUNG
37 Director of Financial Aid .... Ms. Janet INGARGIOLA
08 Library Director/IT Coordinator .... Ms. Miranda SHAKE
04 Administrative Asst to President .... Ms. Karlee THOMEN

Lewis and Clark Community College (B)

5800 Godfrey Road, Godfrey IL 62035-2466
County: Madison FICE Identification: 010020
Unit ID: 146603
Telephone: (618) 468-7000 Carnegie Class: Assoc/MT-VT-High Non
FAX Number: (618) 466-2798 Calendar System: Semester
URL: www.lc.edu
Established: 1970 Annual Undergrad Tuition & Fees (In-District): $9,552
Enrollment: 4,683 Coed
Affiliation or Control: State/Local IRS Status: 501(c)3
Highest Offering: Associate Degree
Accreditation: HLC, ADNUR, DA, DH, EMT, MAAB, OTA

01 President .... Dr. Ken TRZASKA
05 Vice President Academic Affairs .... Dr. Sue CZERWINSKI
32 Interim VP Student Affairs .... Mr. Tim BELL
11 Vice President Administration .... Ms. Lori ARTIS
10 Vice President Finance .... Mrs. Mary SCHULTE
114 Chief Budget Officer .... Mrs. Cindy MCCOY
88 Director Corp & Comm Learning .... Mrs. Kathy WILLIS
13 Chief Information Officer .... Mr. Ron WALL
09 Dir Institutional Res/Library Svcs .... Mr. Dennis KRIEB
06 Registrar .... Ms. Jessica HALE
41 Athletic Director .... Dr. Cedric BROWN
07 Dean Student Experience .... Dr. Cherise JACKSON
124 Dean Student Support Svc .... Dr. Sean HILL
15 Director Human Resources .... Mr. Gabe SPRINGER
18 Facilities Manager .... Mr. Wolf VEVERKA
19 Director Campus Safety .... Mr. Brad RAISH
26 Manager Marketing/Public Relations .... Ms. Laura INLOW
28 Director Diversity & Inclusion .... Ms. Mya LAWRENCE
30 Director of Development .... Ms. Debbie EDELMAN
37 Director Financial Aid .... Ms. Angela WEAVER
108 Exec Dir College Effect & Grant .... Mr. Brett REINERT
04 Admin Assistant to the President .... Mrs. Sue KEENER

Lewis University (C)

One University Parkway, Romeoville IL 60446-2200
County: Will FICE Identification: 001707
Unit ID: 146612
Telephone: (815) 838-0500 Carnegie Class: Masters/L
FAX Number: (815) 838-9456 Calendar System: Semester
URL: www.lewisu.edu
Established: 1932 Annual Undergrad Tuition & Fees: $34,478
Enrollment: 6,437 Coed
Affiliation or Control: Roman Catholic IRS Status: 501(c)3
Highest Offering: Doctorate
Accreditation: HLC, ACBSP, CACREP, EXSC, NURSE, OT, @SP, SW

01 President .... Dr. David J. LIVINGSTON
05 Provost .... Dr. Christopher SINDT
84 VP Enrollment Mgmt .... Ms. Ashley SKIDMORE
111 VP University Advancement .... Ms. Colleen AHEARN
10 Vice Pres for Finance & CFO .... Ms. Teresa KREJCI
07 Dir Admissions Systems & Operations .... Ms. Patti PURRI
32 Assoc Prov/Dean Student Services .... Ms. Katheryn SLATTERY
124 Associate Provost/Dean of Retention .... Ms. Mary DEGRAW
121 VP Mission/Assoc Prov Stdnt Success .... Dr. Kurt SCHACKMUTH
72 Dean Aviation/Science/Technology .... Dr. Christopher WHITE
50 Dean College Business .... Mr. Ryan BUTT
53 Int Dean Education/Social Sciences .... Dr. Christopher KLINE
79 Dean Humanities/Fine Arts/Comm .... Dr. Laura FRANKLIN
66 Dean Nursing & Health Sciences .... Dr. Susan MULLER
15 Chief Human Resources Officer .... Mr. David CRONAN
09 Assoc VP Inst Research/Planning .... Dr. Kang BAI
08 Director of Library .... Mr. Andrew LENAGHAN
06 Registrar .... Mr. Gilbert MARTINEZ
37 Director of Financial Aid .... Ms. Janeen DECHARINTE
26 Director Marketing/Communications .... Dr. Ramona LAMONTAGNE
41 Director of Athletics .... Dr. John PLANEK
38 Director of Counseling Services .... Ms. Jill WHITAKER
19 Chief of Police .... Mr. Michael ZEGADLO
42 Director of University Ministry .... Vacant
88 Dir of Meetings/Events/Conferences .... Ms. Julie PENNER
85 Director International Student Svcs .... Mr. Tyler KING
91 Director of Administrative Systems .... Ms. Johanna REBMAN
13 Chief Information Officer .... Dr. LeRoy BUTLER
29 Executive Dir of Alumni Engagement .... Ms. Mary Colleen AHEARN
96 Director of Opers and Purchasing .... Ms. Jennifer SKVARLA
36 Director of Career Services .... Dr. Julie COSIMO
04 Executive Asst to President .... Ms. Julie MARTINEZ
102 Dir Foundation & Corp Relations .... Ms. Jennifer DOHERTY
104 Director of Intl Study Abroad .... Mr. Christopher SWANSON
105 Director of Web Development .... Mr. Sylvain GOYETTE
18 Assoc VP for Facilities .... Mr. Keith KAMERON
102 Director of Corporate & Foundation .... Vacant
23 Director Health Services .... Ms. Lori FORBEAR
39 Director of Residence Life .... Vacant
30 Exec Director of Development .... Mr. Brandon HOEFT
28 VP for Diversity/Assoc Provost .... Dr. Kristi KELLY
122 Asst Dir Stdnt Act/Greek Life .... Mr. Javier RODRIGUEZ

Lincoln Christian University (D)

100 Campus View Drive, Lincoln IL 62656-2167
County: Logan FICE Identification: 001708
Unit ID: 146667
Telephone: (217) 732-3168 Carnegie Class: Masters/S
FAX Number: (217) 732-5914 Calendar System: Semester
URL: www.lincolnchristian.edu
Established: 1944 Annual Undergrad Tuition & Fees: $13,980
Enrollment: 581 Coed
Affiliation or Control: Christian Churches And Churches of Christ
IRS Status: 501(c)3
Highest Offering: Doctorate
Accreditation: HLC, CACREP, THEOL

01 President .... Dr. Silas MCCORMICK
10 Vice President of Finance .... Ms. Danielle FIELDS
32 VP of Student Development .... Mrs. Jill DICKEN
05 Int Vice President Academic Officer .... Dr. Peter VERKRUYSE
84 Vice Pres of Enrollment Management .... Mr. Mac INGMIRE
111 VP of Advancement/Alumni .... Mr. Brady CREMEENS
29 Director of Alumni Services .... Mr. Tracy THOMAS
08 Director of Library Services .... Vacant
101 Admin Asst to Pres/Secy Bd of Gov .... Mrs. Cindy POPEJOY
13 Director of Campus Technology .... Mr. Jeremiah PROCTOR
06 Registrar .... Mr. Shawn SMITH
07 Director of Enrollment .... Ms. Lindsay CLARK
15 Director of Human Resources .... Ms. Taylor PAYNE
18 Director of Facilities .... Mr. Dave RIGGS
20 Director of Academic Services .... Ms. Susan FARWELL
37 Director of Student Financial Aid .... Ms. Nancy SIDDENS

Lincoln College of Technology (E)

8317 West North Avenue, Melrose Park IL 60160-1605
County: Cook FICE Identification: 010316
Unit ID: 146700
Telephone: (708) 344-4700 Carnegie Class: Assoc/HVT-High Trad
FAX Number: (708) 345-4065 Calendar System: Semester
URL: www.lincolntech.edu
Established: 1950 Annual Undergrad Tuition & Fees: N/A
Enrollment: 944 Coed
Affiliation or Control: Proprietary IRS Status: Proprietary
Highest Offering: Associate Degree
Accreditation: ACCSC

01 Campus President .... Karen M. CLARK
05 Academic Dean .... Leon KELLEY
11 Director Administrative Services .... Karen STEPINA
36 Director of Career Services .... Nancy JOURNET
37 Director of Financial Aid .... Heather MACDONALD
04 Executive Assistant .... Mindy GUARINO
07 Director of Admissions .... Lushanda BYRD
08 Head Librarian .... Karen MCELWAIN

Lincoln Land Community College (F)

5250 Shepherd Road, PO Box 19256,
Springfield IL 62794-9256
County: Sangamon FICE Identification: 007170
Unit ID: 146685
Telephone: (217) 786-2200 Carnegie Class: Assoc/MT-VT-High Non
FAX Number: (217) 786-2468 Calendar System: Semester
URL: www.llcc.edu
Established: 1967 Annual Undergrad Tuition & Fees (In-District): $6,648
Enrollment: 4,977 Coed
Affiliation or Control: Local IRS Status: 501(c)3
Highest Offering: Associate Degree
Accreditation: HLC, ADNUR, COARC, NDT, OTA, PNUR, RAD, SURGT

01 President .... Dr. Charlotte J. WARREN
05 Vice President Academic Services .... Dr. Vern L. LINDQUIST
11 Vice President Administrative Svcs .... Mr. Bryan GLECKLER
32 Vice President Student Services .... Ms. Kelli SINCLAIR
26 Chief Communications Officer .... Ms. Lynn WHALEN
13 Chief Information Officer .... Mr. Esteban CRUZ
111 VP Advancement/Exec Dir Foundation .... Ms. Karen A. SANDERS
15 AVP Human Resources .... Ms. Nicole RALPH
10 AVP Finance .... Ms. Karie L. LONGHTA
121 Exec Director Academic Success .... Ms. Julie CLEVENGER
09 AVP IR and Effectiveness .... Dr. Tricia A. KUJAWA
57 Dean Arts & Communication .... Mr. Adam WATKINS
76 Dean Health Professions .... Dr. Cynthia L. MASKEY
20 AVP Academic Services .... Dr. Jason DOCKTER
81 Dean Mathematics/Computer Sciences .... Dr. Scott SEARCY
83 Dean Social Science & Business .... Mr. Kalith SMITH
79 Dean English & Humanities .... Dr. Joel DYKSTRA
47 Dean Natural & Agriculture Science .... Mr. Brent TODD
103 Dean Workforce Institute .... Ms. Nancy SWEET
84 AVP Enrollment Services .... Ms. Shanda BYER
86 AVP Corp/Govt Trng & Econ Devel .... Ms. Laurel BRETZ
08 Dean Library .... Ms. Tamara KUHN-SCHNELL
106 Dean Academic Innov/eLearning .... Ms. Becky PARTON
41 Director Athletics .... Mr. Ron RIGGLE
14 Director IT Systems .... Mr. Ben ROTH
14 Director IT Service and Support .... Vacant
18 Director Facilities .... Mr. David BRETSCHER
91 Director IT Development .... Vacant
66 Assoc Dean Nursing .... Ms. Sonja K. HARVEY
120 Dir Instructional Technology .... Mr. Barry P. LAMB
37 Director Financial Aid .... Ms. Allison MILLS
124 Director Student Transitions .... Mr. Chris BARRY
93 Dir Student Support Services .... Dr. Anne ARMBRUSTER
114 Dir Budget & Fiscal Services .... Mr. Jeremy BLISS
117 Dir Construction and EHS .... Mr. Timothy R. ERVIN
109 Director Campus Services .... Mr. Andrew BLAYLOCK
35 AVP Student Success .... Ms. Leslie R. JOHNSON
121 Director Student Success .... Mr. Alex BERRY
118 Director Employment & Benefits .... Ms. Kirsten TAYLOR
07 Director Admissions & Records .... Vacant
12 Director LLCC Litchfield .... Ms. Jessamine BLACKBURN
12 Director LLCC Jacksonville .... Ms. Keri MASON
12 Director LLCC Taylorville .... Ms. Dee KRUEGER
06 Registrar .... Ms. Robin ACKMAN
04 Admin Assistant to the President .... Ms. Mary E. DELLERT

Loyola University Chicago (G)

1032 W. Sheridan Road, Chicago IL 60660
County: Cook FICE Identification: 001710
Unit ID: 146719
Telephone: (773) 274-3000 Carnegie Class: DU-Higher
FAX Number: (312) 915-7003 Calendar System: Semester
URL: www.luc.edu
Established: 1870 Annual Undergrad Tuition & Fees: $46,060
Enrollment: 16,893 Coed
Affiliation or Control: Roman Catholic IRS Status: 501(c)3
Highest Offering: Doctorate
Accreditation: HLC, CAEP, CAMPEP, CLPSY, COPSY, DENT, DIETI, EMT, #FEPAC, LAW, MED, MLS, NURSE, PH, SCPSY, SW, THEA, THEOL

01 President .... Dr. Mark C. REED
05 Provost/Chief Academic Officer .... Dr. Margaret F. CALLAHAN
11 Sr VP Admin Services .... Mr. Thomas M. KELLY

10 Sr Vice Pres/CFO Mr. Wayne MAGDZIARZ
84 VP Enrollment Management Mr. Paul G. ROBERTS
32 VP Student Development Dr. Keith M. CHAMPAGNE
13 VP Information Services/CIO Ms. Susan M. MALISCH
26 Vice Pres Marketing/Communications Mr. Jeremy W. LANGFORD
15 VP Human Resources Ms. Winifred WILLIAMS
43 VP & General Counsel Ms. Pamela G. COSTAS
21 Vice Provost Finance & Operations Ms. Joanna PAPPAS
20 Assoc Provost Programs/Planning Dr. Robyn MALLETT
46 Vice Provost Research Services Dr. Meharvan SINGH
08 Interim Dir HSD Library Ms. Jonna PETERSON
88 Asst Prov Provost Office Ms. Michelle PENCYLA
20 Vice Provost Faculty Affairs Dr. Badia S. AHAD
121 Asst VP Student Academic Svcs Dr. Lester J. MANZANO
88 Assoc VP Capital Planning Ms. Jennifer R. CLARK
18 Senior Assoc VP Capital Facilities Ms. Kana HENNING
88 Assoc VP Capital Planning Mr. David BEALL
91 Assoc VP Informatics Mr. Ronald N. PRICE
14 Assoc VP Information Services Mr. Jim SIBENALLER
16 Assoc VP Human Resources Ms. Joan C. STASIAK
14 Assoc VP Information Services Mr. Dan VONDER HEIDE
88 Asst VP Facilities Mr. Michael LOFTSGAARDEN
35 Asst VP & Dean of Students Dr. William RODRIGUEZ
39 Dir Residence Life Dr. Des'mon TAYLOR
41 Athletic Director Mr. Steve WATSON
65 Dean School Environmental Sustain Dr. Nancy TUCHMAN
08 Dean Libraries Dr. Marianne P. RYAN
58 Dean Grad Sch/Vice Prov Grad Educ Dr. Emily BARMAN
49 Dean Arts & Sciences Dr. Peter J. SCHRAEDER
63 Dean School of Medicine Dr. Sam J. MARZO
66 Dean School of Nursing Dr. Lorna FINNEGAN
104 Director Study Abroad Dr. Brian JOHNSON
118 Dir Compensation & Benefits Vacant
19 Dir Campus Safety Mr. Thomas MURRAY
88 Assistant VP Campus Support Ms. Dawn M. COLLINS
12 Dir Lurec Operations Mr. Kevin GINTY
28 Asst Provost Acad Diversity Vacant
23 Asst VP/Dir of Wellness Center Ms. Joan HOLDEN
37 Asst VP Financial Assistance Mr. Tobyn L. FRIAR
42 Dir Campus Ministry Dr. Lisa REITER
88 Dir Enrollment Sys & Research Mr. Timothy HEUER
85 Dir Global Initiatives Mr. Fraser S. TURNER
09 Inter Co-Dir Inst Effectiveness Dr. Eilene EDEJER
09 Inter Co-Dir Inst Effectiveness Dr. Brian J. ERDMAN
07 Interim Dean Undergrad Admissions Mr. Todd M. MALONE
36 Dir Career Development Center Ms. Megan K. TISDALE
106 Dir Online Learning Mr. John GURNAK
88 Dir Vietnam Center Mr. Richard C. ALBRIGHT
04 Exec Asst to the President Ms. Kate PETERSON
100 Chief of Staff Rev. James PREHN
88 VP Mission Integration Dr. Claire NOONAN
88 Co-Int Dir Fac Cntr for Ign Pedagog Ms. Bridget COLACCHIO
88 Co-Int Dir Fac Cntr for Ign Pedago Dr. Jessica MANSBACH
94 Director Ctr for Women & Leadership Ms. Gabrielle M. BUCKLEY
29 Assoc Alumni Relations Dir Mr. Jeremiah MARTIN
38 Director Student Counseling Mr. David S. DE BOER
50 Dean of Business Dr. Michael BEHNAM
53 Interim Dean of Education Dr. Markeda L. NEWELL
86 VP Government Relations Mr. Philip D. HALE
96 Director of Purchasing Vacant
122 Asst Dir Sorority/Fraternity Life Ms. Emily KONEVAL

Loyola University Health Sciences Campus (A)

2160 S First Avenue, Maywood IL 60153
Telephone: (708) 216-9000 Identification: 770080
Accreditation: &HLC, PAST

Loyola University Water Tower Campus (B)

820 N Michigan Avenue, Chicago IL 60611
Telephone: (312) 915-6000 Identification: 770079
Accreditation: &HLC

Lutheran School of Theology at Chicago (C)

1100 E 55th Street, Chicago IL 60615-5199
County: Cook FICE Identification: 001712
Unit ID: 146728
Telephone: (773) 256-0700 Carnegie Class: Spec-4-yr-Faith
FAX Number: (773) 256-0782 Calendar System: Semester
URL: www.lstc.edu
Established: 1860 Annual Graduate Tuition & Fees: N/A
Enrollment: 145 Coed
Affiliation or Control: Evangelical Lutheran Church In America IRS Status: 501(c)3
Highest Offering: Doctorate; No Undergraduates
Accreditation: HLC, THEOL

01 President Dr. James NIEMAN
04 Assistant to the President Ms. Patti DEBIAS
108 Director Inst Effectiveness Vacant
05 Dean and VP for Academic Affairs Dr. Esther MENN
58 Director of Advanced Studies Dr. Mark SWANSON
42 Pastor to the Community Rev. Erik CHRISTENSEN
111 Vice President for Advancement Ms. Sandra H. NELSON
10 Vice President for Finance & Opers Mr. Richard VIVIAN
32 Dean of Student Services Dr. Scott CHALMERS
06 Registrar Vacant
26 Exec Dir of Strategic Mktg & Comm Ms. Keisha COWEN
08 Interim Director of Library Mr. Barry HOPKINS
13 Director of Information Technology Ms. Debra CRONIN
15 Chief Human Resources Officer Mr. Aaron COPLEY-SPIVEY
28 Director of Diversity Ms. Vimary COUVERTIER-CRUZ
18 Chief Facilities/Physical Plant Ofc Mr. Bob BERRIDGE
19 Director Security/Safety Dr. James FOSTER

MacCormac College (D)

29 E Madison Street 2nd Floor, Chicago IL 60602-4405
County: Cook FICE Identification: 001716
Unit ID: 146816
Telephone: (312) 922-1884 Carnegie Class: Assoc/MT-VT-High Trad
FAX Number: (312) 922-4286 Calendar System: Semester
URL: www.maccormac.edu
Established: 1904 Annual Undergrad Tuition & Fees: $12,700
Enrollment: 276 Coed
Affiliation or Control: Independent Non-Profit IRS Status: 501(c)3
Highest Offering: Associate Degree
Accreditation: HLC

00 Chancellor Dr. Grace ALEXIS STEPHENS
01 President/Dean of Finance Mr. Matt GAWENDA
10 Dean of Finance/Operations Mr. Matt GAWENDA
05 Dean Acad/Dean Student Affairs Dr. Kenya GROOMS
06 Registrar Ms. Mariza SILVA
37 Director of Financial Aid Ms. Jamieta HOSKINS
07 Director of Admission Mr. Wentreal HOLLAND
26 Dir Communications/Public Relations Mr. Adam HITZEMAN

McCormick Theological Seminary (E)

5460 S University Avenue, Chicago IL 60615-5108
County: Cook FICE Identification: 001721
Unit ID: 146977
Telephone: (773) 947-6300 Carnegie Class: Spec-4-yr-Faith
FAX Number: (773) 288-2612 Calendar System: 4/1/4
URL: www.mccormick.edu
Established: 1829 Annual Graduate Tuition & Fees: N/A
Enrollment: 221 Coed
Affiliation or Control: Presbyterian Church (U.S.A.) IRS Status: 501(c)3
Highest Offering: Doctorate; No Undergraduates
Accreditation: HLC, THEOL

01 President Mr. David CRAWFORD
00 Chair of the Board Ms. Connie LINDSEY
05 Vice Pres Acad Affs/Dean Faculty Dr. Steed DAVIDSON
30 Vice Pres Seminary Rels/Development Ms. Lisa M. DAGHER
06 Registrar Ms. Chandra WADE
29 Vice Pres Alumni/ae & Church Rels Rev. Nannette BANKS
08 Interim Director of JKM Library Mr. Barry HOPKINS
15 Director Human Resources Ms. Ashley WOODFAULK
37 Dir Student Financial Aid/Planning Mr. Nate RAMSEY
07 Sr Director Admissions/Enrollment Ms. Veronica JOHNSON
88 Assistant to the Dean Ms. Jennifer OULD
04 Assistant to the President Ms. Joyce LEACHMAN

McHenry County College (F)

8900 US Highway 14, Crystal Lake IL 60012-2796
County: McHenry FICE Identification: 007691
Unit ID: 147004
Telephone: (815) 455-3700 Carnegie Class: Assoc/HT-High Non
FAX Number: (815) 455-3999 Calendar System: Semester
URL: www.mchenry.edu
Established: 1967 Annual Undergrad Tuition & Fees (In-District): $11,862
Enrollment: 7,814 Coed
Affiliation or Control: State/Local IRS Status: 501(c)3
Highest Offering: Associate Degree
Accreditation: HLC, ADNUR, CAHIIM, EMT, OTA, PTAA

01 President Dr. Clinton E. GABBARD
101 Board Liaison Ms. Denisa SHALLO
05 VP Academic Affairs & Workforce Dev Dr. Arlene SANTOS-GEORGE
32 VP Student Affairs Dr. Talia KORONKIEWICZ
103 Assoc VP of Workforce Development Ms. Catherine JONES
20 Assoc VP for Academic Affairs Dr. Gina MCCONOUGHEY
26 VP Marketing/Comm & Development Ms. Christina HAGGERTY
27 Exec Dir Mktg & Creative Services Mr. Ryan KLOS
102 Exec Director MCC Foundation Mr. Brian DIBONA
25 Director of Grants Ms. Wendy LAUEN
88 Manager Conference & Event Services Ms. Katherine BELLEN
10 CFO/Treasurer Mr. Bob TENUTA
21 Asst VP of Finance Ms. Lynn COWLIN
19 Chief of Police Chief Thomas KRETSCHMER
18 Asst VP of Facilities Vacant
88 Director of Sustainability Ms. Kim HANKINS
40 Director of the MCC Store Ms. Alma WILHELM
109 Director Food Services Ms. Sandra JOHNSTON
96 Director of Business Services Mr. James JULISON
13 Chief Information Officer Mr. Timothy HOPKINS
119 Director Infrastructure & Security Mr. Rob RASMUSSEN
14 Director of Enterprise Applications Vacant
09 Director of Institutional Research Vacant
15 VP of Human Resources Vacant
88 Director Employee Development Ms. Luanne MAYORGA
16 Exec Director of Human Resources Ms. Carolyn WALSH
16 Director of HR Operations Ms. Anita ROEWER
35 Asst VP Student Affairs Ms. Sonia REISING
06 Director of Registration & Records Dr. Sara PIRAINO
41 Director Athletics/Intramural & Rec Ms. Karen WILEY
124 Director Student Engagement Dr. Rachael BOLDMAN
88 Director of Upward Bound Program Mr. Rene GOVEA
124 Dir of Student Retention & Conduct Ms. Lisa BRNCICH
22 Dir Access & Disability Services Ms. Chelsey WINSTERSTEEN
37 Director of Financial Aid Mr. Chris HEFTKA
08 Director of Library Vacant
89 Dir College & Career Readiness Vacant
20 Director of Teaching & Learning Dr. Holly REY
121 Director Student Success Dr. Jim DISRUDE
84 Director of Enrollment Services Ms. Amy CARZOLI
88 Director Pathways to Success Ms. Christina SWANSON
81 Dean of Math & Sciences Mr. O'Neil WRIGHT
85 Dean of Humanities & Social Science Ms. Daniela BRODERICK
69 Dean Social Science/Public Service Dr. Dawn KATZ
55 Exec Director of Adult Education Ms. Delia RODRIGUEZ
88 Manager Nursing Labs Ms. Misty MEINERS
75 Mgr PTA Clinical Education Ms. Angela WALLACE
72 Mgr Applied Technology Labs Mr. Casey JUSZCZYK
31 Director of Community Education Ms. Dori SULLINS
76 Assoc Dean Allied Health & HIT Ms. Chris COCLANIS-LODING
66 Director of Nursing Program Ms. Betsy SCHNOWSKE
48 Director of Ctr Agrarian Learning Ms. Sheri DOYEL
76 Dir OT Assistant Program Ms. Marlene VOGT
88 Mgr IL Small Business Development Mr. Mark PIEKOS
75 Dean Career & Technical Educ Mr. Tom MCGEE

McKendree University (G)

701 College Road, Lebanon IL 62254-9990
County: Saint Clair FICE Identification: 001722
Unit ID: 147013
Telephone: (618) 537-4481 Carnegie Class: Masters/M
FAX Number: (618) 537-6259 Calendar System: Semester
URL: www.mckendree.edu
Established: 1828 Annual Undergrad Tuition & Fees: $32,200
Enrollment: 2,200 Coed
Affiliation or Control: United Methodist IRS Status: 501(c)3
Highest Offering: Doctorate
Accreditation: HLC, CAATE, IACBE, NURSE

01 President Mr. Daniel C. DOBBINS
03 Senior Vice President Vacant
04 Exec Assistant to the President Ms. Yvonne STRODER
05 Provost/Dean of the University Dr. Tami EGGLESTON
10 Vice Pres Finance/Administration Dr. Marilee K. MONTANARO
07 Vice Pres Admission & Financial Aid Mr. Chris HALL
32 Vice President Student Affairs Dr. Joni BASTIAN
108 Associate Provost Inst Effective Dr. Tami EGGLESTON
20 Associate Provost for Curriculum Dr. J. Alan ALEWINE
100 VP of Operations/Chief of Staff Mr. Daryl R. HANCOCK
13 CIO/Director Information Technology Ms. Christine TWEEDY
06 Registrar/Asst Dean Ms. Debra LARSON
08 Director of Holman Library Ms. Paula MARTIN
21 Comptroller Mrs. Hilary B. SMITH
26 Exec Dir Marketing/Communications Mrs. Krysti H. CONNELLY
29 Director Alumni Relations Ms. Brandi BROWN-HARRIS
37 Director Financial Aid Ms. Ashley BYERS
36 Director Career Services Ms. Jennifer K. PICKERELL
15 Director of Human Resources Mr. Ricardo ORTEGA
27 Director Media Relations Ms. Lisa K. SANDERS
39 Director of Residence Life Mrs. Samantha ENGLAR
35 Director of Campus Activities Mr. Craig L. ROBERTSON
41 Athletic Director Mr. Anthony FRANCIS
42 Chaplain/Director Church Relations Rev Dr. B. Timothy HARRISON
40 Bookstore Director Ms. Amy BLASDEL
111 Director of Advancement Services Mr. Scott L. BILLHARTZ
19 Director Safety & Security Mr. Ranodore M. FOGGS
112 Director of Major Gifts Mrs. Whitney STRONG
113 Director of Student Accounts Ms. Kiara HARMON
28 Director of Diversity Mr. Brent W. REEVES
106 Dean of Online Dr. Melissa MEEKER
104 Director of Study Abroad Ms. Sandee POWERS
09 Director of Institutional Research Mrs. Jessica HOPKINS
44 Director Annual Giving Mrs. Holly E. SALLEE
122 Dir Res Life-Frat/Sorority Life Mr. Calvin WERTMAN

Meadville Lombard Theological School (H)

610 South Michigan Avenue, Chicago IL 60605
County: Cook FICE Identification: 001723
Unit ID: 147031
Telephone: (773) 256-3000 Carnegie Class: Spec-4-yr-Faith
FAX Number: (312) 327-7002 Calendar System: Semester
URL: www.meadville.edu
Established: 1844 Annual Graduate Tuition & Fees: N/A
Enrollment: 83 Coed
Affiliation or Control: Unitarian Universalist IRS Status: 501(c)3
Highest Offering: Doctorate; No Undergraduates
Accreditation: THEOL

01 President Dr. Elias ORTEGA
05 VP Academic/Student Affairs RevDr. Pamela LIGHTSEY
10 Vice Pres Finance & Administration Ms. Cynthia REDMAN
06 Registrar Ms. Elena JIMENEZ
30 Director of Development Ms. Evy LIPECKA

Methodist College (I)

7600 N. Academic Drive, Peoria IL 61615
County: Peoria FICE Identification: 006228
Unit ID: 147129
Telephone: (309) 672-5513 Carnegie Class: Spec-4-yr-Other Health

FAX Number: (309) 671-8303 Calendar System: Semester
URL: www.methodistcol.edu
Established: 2000 Annual Undergrad Tuition & Fees: $17,988
Enrollment: 595 Coed
Affiliation or Control: Independent Non-Profit IRS Status: 501(c)3
Highest Offering: Master's
Accreditation: HLC, MAC, NURSE, SW

01 Chancellor/President ....Dr. Laurie SHANDERSON
05 Vice Chancellor of Academic Affairs ....Dr. Amer QATANANI
11 Vice Chancellor of Operations ....Dr. Pedro SANTANA
10 Vice Pres of Financial Operations ....Dr. David BURKITT
66 Dean of Nursing ....Dr. Blanca MILLER
49 Chair of Arts & Sciences ....Dr. Octavian GABOR
84 Vice President Enrollment Mgmt ....Mr. Jason GARBER
06 Registrar ....Mr. Nate MCCOY
37 Director Financial Aid ....Ms. Angela ROBINSON
121 Director Center for Student Success ....Ms. Tricia FOX
08 Library Services Director ....Mr. Joel SHOEMAKER
19 Director Security/Safety ....Mr. Ryan SCHUBERT
113 Bursar ....Ms. Amy IRWIN
32 Director of Student Affairs ....Mr. Andre ALLEN
96 Supply Chain Lead ....Ms. Nancy REBHOLZ
37 Assistant Director Financial Aid ....Mr. Jeff GOOD
15 Human Resources Business Partner ....Ms. Jennifer WHITE
04 Executive Assistant ....Ms. Michelle HOUSTON

Midwest College of Oriental Medicine (A)

8950 Gross Point Road, STE 400, Skokie IL 60077
Telephone: (773) 975-1295 Identification: 666090
Accreditation: ACUP

† Branch campus of Midwest College of Oriental Medicine, Racine, WI

Midwestern Career College (B)

100 South Wacker Dr, LL1-50, Chicago IL 60606
County: Cook FICE Identification: 041390
Unit ID: 457536
Telephone: (312) 236-9000 Carnegie Class: Spec 2-yr-Health
FAX Number: (312) 277-1007 Calendar System: Other
URL: mccollege.edu
Established: 2004 Annual Undergrad Tuition & Fees: N/A
Enrollment: 655 Coed
Affiliation or Control: Proprietary IRS Status: Proprietary
Highest Offering: Associate Degree
Accreditation: COE, CEA, SURGT

01 President & CEO ....Mr. Jeremy OBERFELD

Midwestern University (C)

555 31st Street, Downers Grove IL 60515-1200
County: DuPage FICE Identification: 001657
Unit ID: 143853
Telephone: (630) 971-6080 Carnegie Class: Spec-4-yr-Med
FAX Number: N/A Calendar System: Quarter
URL: www.midwestern.edu
Established: 1900 Annual Undergrad Tuition & Fees: N/A
Enrollment: 2,980 Coed
Affiliation or Control: Independent Non-Profit IRS Status: 501(c)3
Highest Offering: Doctorate
Accreditation: HLC, ARCPA, CLPSY, DENT, OPT, OSTEO, OT, PHAR, PTA, SP

01 President/CEO ....Dr. Kathleen H. GOEPPINGER
10 VP/Chief Financial Officer ....Mr. Matthew SWEENEY
88 VP/Special Assistant to President ....Dr. Mary W L. LEE
05 SVP/CAO Optmtry/Pharm/Vet Ed/Admiss ....Dr. Joshua C. BAKER
05 VP/CAO Dental/Health Sciences Educ ....Dr. Kyle H. RAMSEY
05 VP/CAO Med/Grad Stds/Podiatric Med ....Dr. Yir Gloria YUEH
11 SVP Administration/Communications ....Ms. Angela L. MARTY
43 VP & General Counsel ....Ms. Barbara L. MCCLOUD
23 VP Clinical Operations ....Dr. Kaila DOUGHERTY
63 Dean Chicago Col Osteopathic Med ....Dr. Laura M. ROSCH
67 Dean Col Pharmacy Glendale/DG ....Dr. Mitchell R. EMERSON
76 Dean Col Health Sci Downers Grove ....Dr. Fred D. ROMANO
88 Dean Chicago College of Optometry ....Dr. Melissa A. SUCKOW
52 Dean College of Dental Medicine IL ....Dr. Harold J. HAERING
32 Dean of Students DG and Glendale ....Dr. Ross J. KOSINSKI
32 Assoc Dean Student Services ....Dr. Pamela JURGENS-TOEPKE
07 Director of Admissions ....Mr. Michael J. LAKEN
111 Dir Inst Advancement DG/Glendale ....Ms. Stacy GLASS
15 VP Human Res/Organizational Dev ....Ms. Amy B. GIBSON
18 Director of Operations DG Campus ....Mr. Kevin M. MCCORMICK
18 Director Operations Glendale Campus ....Mr. James CIWAY
13 Director Information Technology Svc ....Mr. Erik P. CARROLL
08 Dir Library DG & Glendale Campuses ....Ms. Rebecca A. CATON
09 Director of Institutional Research ....Ms. Donna M. WEGLARZ
06 Registrar ....Ms. Debra GRIECO
24 Director of Media Resources ....Ms. Kathleen A M. DOOLEY
46 Asst VP Research ....Dr. James M. WOODS
19 Director of Security ....Mr. Paul R. CREEKMORE
26 Asst VP Communications/Marketing ....Ms. Dana FAY
37 Director Stdnt Fin Svcs & Registrar ....Mr. Nathan ERNST
14 Dir IT Applications/Clinic Svcs ....Mr. James RUBINSTEIN
28 Director Diversity/Equity/Inclusion ....Ms. Victoria FRANKS
88 VP Operations DG/Glendale ....Mr. Daniel TAPIA
88 Dean AZ College of Optometry ....Dr. Alicia E. FEIS
74 Dean College of Veterinary Medicine ....Dr. Carla GARTRELL
63 Dean AZ Col of Osteo Medicine ....Dr. Lori A. KEMPER
88 Dean AZ College of Podiatric Med ....Dr. Jeffrey L. JENSEN
52 Dean College of Dental Medicine AZ ....Dr. Sheri BROWNSTEIN
76 Dean College of Health Sci Glendale ....Dr. Jared CHAMBERLAIN
58 Dean College of Graduate Studies ....Dr. Michael FAY
100 Chief of Staff ....Ms. Monica KRAMER

† Tuition varies by degree program.

Millikin University (D)

1184 W Main Street, Decatur IL 62522-2084
County: Macon FICE Identification: 001724
Unit ID: 147244
Telephone: (217) 424-6211 Carnegie Class: Bac-Diverse
FAX Number: (217) 424-3993 Calendar System: Semester
URL: www.millikin.edu
Established: 1901 Annual Undergrad Tuition & Fees: $39,592
Enrollment: 1,982 Coed
Affiliation or Control: Presbyterian Church (U.S.A.) IRS Status: 501(c)3
Highest Offering: Doctorate
Accreditation: HLC, ACBSP, ANEST, MUS, NURSE

01 President ....Dr. James REYNOLDS
05 Provost ....Mrs. Mary BLACK
10 Vice Pres Finance/Business Affs ....Ms. Ruby F. JAMES
111 Vice Pres University Development ....Ms. Gina L. BIANCHI
84 Interim VP Enrollment/Marketing ....Mr. David RHODES
32 Vice Pres Student Affairs ....Mrs. Raphaella PRANGE
100 Chief of Staff/Board Secretary ....Ms. Marilyn S. DAVIS
49 Interim Dean of Arts & Sciences ....Dr. Nancy CURTIN
57 Dean of Fine Arts ....Ms. Laura LEDFORD
107 Interim Dean Col of Prof Studies ....Dr. Elizabeth GEPHART
50 Dean Tabor School Business ....Mr. RJ PODESCHI
06 Registrar ....Mr. Alex BERRY
29 Sr Dir Alumni Engage/Annual Giving ....Mrs. Alyse KNUST
112 Sr Director Major Gifts ....Mr. Dan BAKER
25 Director of Grants ....Mrs. Anne-Marie BERK
13 Director of Technology ....Mrs. Amy BRILLEY
08 Director of the Library ....Ms. Amanda PIPPITT
30 Sr Director of Operations ....Mrs. Amanda PODESCHI
41 Director of Athletics ....Dr. Craig WHITE
53 Int Director of School of Education ....Dr. Chris CUNNINGS
88 Director Kirkland Fine Arts Center ....Mr. Bryan DIVER
104 Dir Center for Intl Education ....Ms. Briana QUINTENZ
15 Director Human Resources ....Ms. Diane L. LANE
21 Director Financial Services ....Mrs. Vicki A. WRIGLEY
38 Dir Stdnt Mental/Behav Health Svcs ....Mr. Christopher MORRELL
92 Director of Honors Program ....Dr. Michael HARTSOCK
37 Dean Admission/Financial Aid ....Mrs. Stacey HUBBARD
58 Director of MBA Program ....Mrs. Jaclyn CANTWELL
64 Director School of Music ....Dr. Brian K. JUSTISON
87 Director of Summer School ....Vacant
19 Dir Dept Public Safety/Chief Police ....Mr. Chris BALLARD
66 Director School of Nursing ....Dr. Elizabeth GEPHART
07 Director of Admission ....Mr. Kyle TAYLOR
39 Dean of Campus Life ....Mr. Paul LIDY
18 Director of Facilities Services ....Mr. James FRALEY
26 Director of Marketing ....Mrs. Kylee RONEY
09 Coord of Institutional Research ....Mrs. Laura A. BIRCH
105 Web Developer ....Mr. Matt CLARK
88 Dir Ctr for Acad/Prof Perf (CAPP) ....Mrs. Carrie PIERSON
106 Director Online Education ....Dr. Rachel BICICCHI
108 Director Institutional Assessment ....Dr. Jennifer SCHROEDER

Monmouth College (E)

700 E Broadway, Monmouth IL 61462-1963
County: Warren FICE Identification: 001725
Unit ID: 147341
Telephone: (800) 747-2687 Carnegie Class: Bac-A&S
FAX Number: (309) 457-2141 Calendar System: Semester
URL: www.monmouthcollege.edu
Established: 1853 Annual Undergrad Tuition & Fees: $41,330
Enrollment: 860 Coed
Affiliation or Control: Presbyterian Church (U.S.A.) IRS Status: 501(c)3
Highest Offering: Baccalaureate
Accreditation: HLC

01 President ....Dr. Clarence R. WYATT
05 Dean/Vice Pres Academic Affairs ....Dr. Mark WILLHARDT
10 Vice President Finance & Business ....Ms. Holly THARP
32 Vice Pres Stdnt Life/Dean Students ....Ms. Karen OGORZALEK
121 VP Stdnt Life/Dean Student Success ....Ms. Michelle MERRITT
84 Vice Pres for Enrollment Management ....Vacant
30 Vice Pres Development/College Rels ....Ms. Hannah MAHER
26 Assoc VP Communications/Marketing ....Mr. Duane BONIFER
07 Director of Admission ....Vacant
13 Chief Information Officer ....Mr. Nicholas CARLSON
06 Registrar ....Ms. Kristi HIPPEN
08 Director Hewes Library ....Ms. Sarah HENDERSON
15 Director of Personnel Services ....Ms. Stephanie KINKAID
18 Director Facilities Management ....Ms. Sarah YOUNG
20 Associate Dean of the Faculty ....Dr. Joan WERTZ
21 Controller ....Ms. Katherine WALL
09 Director Institutional Research ....Ms. Christine D. JOHNSTON
04 Admin Assistant to the President ....Ms. Amy WARRINGTON
29 Director Alumni Affairs ....Vacant
36 Director Student Placement ....Ms. Marni DUGAN
37 Director Student Financial Aid ....Ms. Jayne SCHRECK
38 Director Student Counseling ....Ms. Cindy BEADLES
122 Coord Fraternity/Sorority Life ....Ms. Karen OGORZALEK

Moody Bible Institute (F)

820 N LaSalle Boulevard, Chicago IL 60610-3263
County: Cook FICE Identification: 001727
Unit ID: 147369
Telephone: (312) 329-4000 Carnegie Class: Spec-4-yr-Faith
FAX Number: (312) 329-4109 Calendar System: Semester
URL: www.moody.edu
Established: 1886 Annual Undergrad Tuition & Fees: $13,970
Enrollment: 2,870 Coed
Affiliation or Control: Independent Non-Profit IRS Status: 501(c)3
Highest Offering: Master's
Accreditation: HLC, BI, MUS, THEOL

01 President ....Dr. Mark JOBE
05 Provost & Dean of Education ....Dr. Dwight A. PERRY
11 Chief Operating Officer ....Mr. Mark WAGNER
10 Chief Financial Officer ....Mr. Gregory R. THORNTON
43 VP & General Counsel ....Mrs. Janet A. STIVEN
20 VP & Dean of UG School ....Dr. Bryan O'NEAL
13 VP & Chief Information Officer ....Mr. John SAUCEDA
15 VP of Human Resources ....Mrs. Debbie ZELINSKI
26 VP & Chief Marketing Officer ....Mr. Sam CHOY
32 VP & Dean of Student Life ....Mr. William O. WASHINGTON
84 VP/Dean of Student Enrollment Svcs ....Dr. Heather SHALLEY
44 VP Donor Dev/Chief Development Ofcr ....Mr. Bruce EVERHART
12 VP & Dean of MTS ....Dr. Winfred NEELY
30 VP of Stewardship ....Mr. James ELLIOTT
08 Department Manager Library ....Mr. James PRESTON
06 Registrar/Director of Acad Records ....Mr. George MOSHER
29 Exec Director Alumni Association ....Mrs. Nancy HASTINGS
39 Associate Dean Residence Life ....Mr. Bruce R. NORQUIST
35 Associate Dean of Students ....Mrs. Rachel PUENTE
36 Assoc Dean of Career Development ....Mr. Patrick FRIEDLINE
38 Associate Dean Counseling Services ....Mr. Steve BRASEL
35 Associate Dean for Student Programs ....Mr. Joseph M. GONZALES, JR.
88 Director of Moody Aviation ....Mr. James A. CONRAD
108 Dir Center Teach/Lrng/Assessment ....Dr. Andrew BEATY
88 Director Instruct Design and Dev ....Mr. Kevin MAHAFFY
88 Director of Student Experience MDL ....Mr. John ENGELKEMIER
96 Manager of Procurement Services ....Mr. Stephen RICHARDSON
102 Dir Foundation/Corporate Relations ....Mr. Nathan MEDINA
21 Controller ....Ms. Linda WAHR
37 Director of Financial Aid ....Ms. Tammy EASTER
14 Technology Services Director ....Mr. Michael JANCHENKO
18 Division Manager of Facilities ....Mr. Bill BIELAWSKI
19 Deputy Chief of Public Safety ....Mr. Brian M. STOFFER
41 Athletic Director ....Mr. Daniel DUNN
23 Admin of Health Service ....Ms. Ann MEYER
04 Executive Assistant to President ....Ms. Mary OLIVA
28 Asst Dean of Multicultural Stdnts ....Mr. Edward JONES
20 Dean of Faculty ....Dr. Timothy SISK
88 Dean of Ops and Strategic Educ Init ....Mr. Doug MURPHY

† Tuition is paid through donor contributions. Fees are $1,950.00 per year.

Moraine Valley Community College (G)

9000 W College Parkway, Palos Hills IL 60465-0937
County: Cook FICE Identification: 007692
Unit ID: 147378
Telephone: (708) 974-4300 Carnegie Class: Assoc/MT-VT-High Non
FAX Number: (708) 974-1184 Calendar System: Semester
URL: www.morainevalley.edu
Established: 1967 Annual Undergrad Tuition & Fees (In-District): $8,095
Enrollment: 11,026 Coed
Affiliation or Control: State/Local IRS Status: 501(c)3
Highest Offering: Associate Degree
Accreditation: HLC, ACFEI, ADNUR, CAHIIM, COARC, MAC, POLYT, RAD

01 President ....Dr. Sylvia JENKINS
05 Vice President Academic Affairs ....Dr. Pamela HANEY
32 Vice President Student Devel ....Dr. Normah SALLEH-BARONE
11 Vice Pres Administrative Services ....Mr. Richard J. HENDRICKS
10 Vice Pres Financial & Business Svcs ....Ms. Theresa O'CARROLL
13 Vice Pres Information Technology ....Mr. Kamlesh SANGHVI
50 Dean Science/Business/Comp Tech ....Dr. Ryen NAGLE
49 Dean Liberal Arts ....Dr. Kiana BATTLE
124 Dean Student Engagement ....Dr. Scott FRIEDMAN
84 Dean Enrollment Services ....Mr. Dave MARCIAL
51 Exec Dir Corporate/Cmty & Cont Educ ....Mr. Steven PAPPAGEORGE
36 Dean Career Programs ....Dr. LoShay WILLIS
35 Dean Student Services ....Mr. Chester SHAW
88 Dean Learn Enrich & Col Readiness ....Mr. Michael MORSCHES
35 Dean of Students/Compliance Officer ....Mr. Kent MARSHALL
37 Director Financial Aid ....Mr. Justin PICHEY
09 Dir Inst Research/Plng/Effectivenes ....Dr. Sadya KHAN
19 Chief of Police ....Mr. Patrick TREACY
15 Chief Human Resources Officer ....Ms. Lynn HARRINGTON
07 Director of Admissions/Recruitment ....Mr. Andrew SARATA
18 Director Campus Operations ....Mr. Timothy KOSIEK
109 Director Auxiliary Services ....Mr. Kashif SHAH
23 Director Health Education Well Ctr ....Mr. William FINN
26 Chief Marketing/Communications Ofcr ....Ms. Clare BRINER
25 Director Resource Development ....Dr. Theresa PALLANTI
21 Controller ....Mr. Michael CIPOLLA
22 Director of Disability Services ....Mr. Nathan PAYOVICH
96 Director of Purchasing ....Ms. Jane BENTLEY
102 Executive Director Foundation ....Ms. Kristy MCGREAL
20 Dean Academic Development/Outreach ....Dr. Cynthia ANDERSON

20 Dean Academic Services ... Dr. Cherie MEADOR
08 Dean Learning Resource Center ... Ms. Terra JACOBSON
121 Dean Student Success ... Dr. Jo Ann JENKINS
88 Asst Dean of Enrollment Services ... Ms. Kathryn WACHTOR
101 Secretary of the Institution/Board ... Mr. Richard CALDWELL
108 Director Curriculum/Assessment ... Ms. Carrie BLIXT-DIAZ
29 Director Alumni & Annual Programs ... Ms. Patricia MEHALLICK
28 Exec Dir Diversity/Equity/Inclusion ... Mr. Rory SMITH
43 Compliance Officer ... Ms. Kelly GRAB

Morrison Institute of Technology (A)

701 Portland Avenue, Morrison IL 61270-2959
County: Whiteside FICE Identification: 008880
Unit ID: 147396
Telephone: (815) 772-7218 Carnegie Class: Spec 2-yr-Tech
FAX Number: (815) 772-7584 Calendar System: Semester
URL: www.morrisontech.edu
Established: 1973 Annual Undergrad Tuition & Fees: $17,400
Enrollment: 79 Coed
Affiliation or Control: Independent Non-Profit IRS Status: 501(c)3
Highest Offering: Associate Degree
Accreditation: COE

01 President/Chief Executive Officer ... Mr. Christopher D. SCOTT
05 Vice President Academic Affairs ... Mr. Scott CONNELLY
10 Vice President for Finance ... Mr. Richard PARKINSON
07 Vice President Admissions ... Ms. Jodie EAKER
111 Dean Institutional Advancement ... Mr. Greg J. TULLY
37 Financial Aid Director ... Ms. Lisa KRAMER

Morton College (B)

3801 S Central Avenue, Cicero IL 60804-4398
County: Cook FICE Identification: 001728
Unit ID: 147411
Telephone: (708) 656-8000 Carnegie Class: Assoc/HVT-Mix Trad/Non
FAX Number: (708) 656-3297 Calendar System: Semester
URL: www.morton.edu
Established: 1924 Annual Undergrad Tuition & Fees (In-District): $8,852
Enrollment: 3,618 Coed
Affiliation or Control: State/Local IRS Status: 501(c)3
Highest Offering: Associate Degree
Accreditation: HLC, ADNUR, PTAA

01 President ... Dr. Stanley FIELDS
05 Provost ... Dr. Keith MCLAUGHLIN
11 VP of Administrative Services ... Mr. Frank MARZULLO
51 Dean Adult/Career Tech Education ... Ms. Claudia MOSQUEDA
32 Dean of Student Services ... Ms. Marisol VELAZQUEZ
08 Assoc Dn Library/Instructional Tech ... Mr. Micheal KOTT
111 Exec Dir of Inst Advancement ... Ms. Blanca JARA
15 Director of Human Resources ... Vacant
31 Dir of Community & Continuing Educ ... Ms. Irina CLINE
09 Director Institutional Research ... Ms. Erin STRAUTS
18 Director of Facilities & Operations ... Mr. Joseph FLORIO
37 Director of Financial Aid ... Ms. Carissa DAVIS
06 Assoc Dean of Stdnt Svcs/Registrar ... Mr. Michael BROWN
10 CFO/Treasurer ... Ms. Mireya PEREZ
04 Admin Assistant to the President ... Ms. Maria ANDERSON
13 Chief Information Officer ... Mr. Ruben RUIZ
41 Athletic Director ... Mr. Jason NICHOLS

National Louis University (C)

122 S Michigan Avenue, Chicago IL 60603
County: Cook FICE Identification: 001733
Unit ID: 147536
Telephone: (888) 658-8632 Carnegie Class: DU-Mod
FAX Number: N/A Calendar System: Quarter
URL: www.nl.edu
Established: 1886 Annual Undergrad Tuition & Fees: $11,505
Enrollment: 7,402 Coed
Affiliation or Control: Independent Non-Profit IRS Status: 501(c)3
Highest Offering: Doctorate
Accreditation: HLC, ACFEI, CACREP, CAEP, CLPSY, IACBE, @SW

01 President ... Dr. Nivine MEGAHED
05 Provost ... Dr. Eddie PHILLIPS
111 VP Inst Advance & Communications . Mr. Christopher CHANTSON
15 Vice President Human Resources ... Mr. Tom BERGMANN
10 Vice Pres Finance & Administration ... Mr. Marty MICKEY
84 Vice Pres Enrollment & Marketing ... Mr. Richard YACONIS
32 VP of Student Affairs & Dean ... Dr. Aurelio VALENTE
13 VP of Operations & Technology ... Dr. Michael GRAHAM
20 Vice Prov Acad Pgm & Fac Dev ... Vacant
06 Vice Prov Advising & Univ Registrar ... Mr. Stephen NEER
50 Dean School of Business & IT ... Dr. Ignacio LOPEZ
53 Dean NCE ... Dr. Carolyn THEARD-GRIGGS
08 Exec Dir University Library ... Ms. Alexis CARSCADDEN
97 Dean Undergraduate College ... Ms. Aarti DHUPELIA
16 Director of Employment ... Ms. Amy KING
37 Exec Dir Student Financial Services ... Ms. Brigid CALLAHAN
108 Exec Dir Institutional Assessment ... Dr. Joseph LEVY
07 Director of Admissions ... Ms. Lori MARKUSON
28 Director of DEI ... Mr. Donald GILLIAM
35 Director of Student Experience ... Dr. Danielle LABAN
04 Administrative Asst to President ... Ms. Diane M. TRAUSCH
108 Director Institutional Assessment ... Ms. Mital PATEL
18 Dir Facilities Management ... Mr. Richard STERRETT
29 Director Alumni Relations ... Mr. Michael ZAROBE
91 Technical Director ... Mr. John MAZARIEGOS

96 Purchasing Coordinator ... Ms. Caryn SMITH
102 Exec Dir of IA ... Vacant
12 Florida Exec Director ... Mr. Anthony SPANO
45 Exec Dir Strategic Initiatives ... Mr. Andi KORITARI
44 Director Annual Giving ... Mr. Joel RITTLE
30 Dir External Funding & Grant Devel ... Ms. Arlene STRONG
36 Exec Dir Career Svcs & Placement ... Ms. Kristen HODGES
09 Director of Institutional Research ... Ms. Stacy VLAHAKIS
106 Dean Online Education ... Dr. BettyJo BOUCHEY
39 Director Residence Life ... Ms. Victoria MULLALY
103 Director Workforce Development ... Mr. Thackston LUNDY

National University of Health Sciences (D)

200 E Roosevelt Road, Lombard IL 60148-4583
County: DuPage FICE Identification: 001732
Unit ID: 147590
Telephone: (630) 629-2000 Carnegie Class: Spec-4-yr-Other Health
FAX Number: (630) 889-6600 Calendar System: Trimester
URL: www.nuhs.edu
Established: 1906 Annual Undergrad Tuition & Fees: N/A
Enrollment: 529 Coed
Affiliation or Control: Independent Non-Profit IRS Status: 501(c)3
Highest Offering: First Professional Degree
Accreditation: HLC, ACUP, CHIRO, COMTA, NATUR

01 President ... Dr. Joseph P D. STIEFEL
05 Vice President Academic Services ... Dr. Randy L. SWENSON
10 Vice President Business Services ... Mr. Ron MENSCHING
11 Vice Pres Administrative Services ... Ms. Tracy MCHUGH
76 Dean College Allied Health Sciences ... Dr. Candace PASSI
51 Dean College Postprofessional Educ ... Dr. Jenna GLENN
23 Dean of Clinics ... Dr. Theodore JOHNSON
107 Dean Col Professional Studies FL ... Dr. Daniel STRAUSS
107 Dean Col Professional Studies IL ... Dr. Sandra ROGERS
46 Dean of Research ... Dr. Gregory D. CRAMER
32 Dean of Students ... Ms. Yesenia MALDONADO
09 Dean forInstitutional Effectiveness ... Dr. Jerrilyn CAMBRON
88 Dean Accreditation ... Vacant
08 Director Learning Resource Center ... Ms. Patricia GENARDO
06 University Registrar ... Ms. Izabela DUBAK
07 Dir Communication/Enrollment Svcs ... Ms. Victoria SWEENEY
21 Director of Financial Services ... Ms. Sue UNGER
37 Director of Financial Aid ... Mr. Marc YAMBO
18 Director Maintenance & Facilities ... Mr. Mark GALVANONI
15 Director of Human Resources ... Mr. Andrew WOZNIAK
26 Dir Communications/Enrollment Svcs ... Ms. Victoria SWEENEY
30 Dir Alumni Relations & Development ... Mrs. Tracy MCHUGH
13 Dir Management Information Services ... Mr. Ron MENSCHING
40 Bookstore Manager ... Ms. Sue ROBERTSON
39 Coordinator of Housing ... Ms. Marilyn FREAD
88 Dean of Institutional Compliance ... Mr. Daniel DRISCOLL

North Central College (E)

30 N Brainard Street, Naperville IL 60540-4607
County: DuPage FICE Identification: 001734
Unit ID: 147660
Telephone: (630) 637-5100 Carnegie Class: Masters/S
FAX Number: (630) 637-5121 Calendar System: Trimester
URL: www.northcentralcollege.edu
Established: 1861 Annual Undergrad Tuition & Fees: $41,180
Enrollment: 2,832 Coed
Affiliation or Control: United Methodist IRS Status: 501(c)3
Highest Offering: Doctorate
Accreditation: HLC, #ARCPA, CAATE, @DIETD, OT

01 President ... Dr. Troy D. HAMMOND
04 Exec Assistant to the President ... Ms. Kimberly SALZBRUNN
05 Provost/VP Academic Affairs ... Dr. Abiodun GOKE-PARIOLA
10 VP of Finance/CFO ... Ms. Maryellen SKERIK
111 VP Institutional Advancement ... Mr. Rick E. SPENCER
84 VP Enrollment Management/Athletics ... Mr. Marty R. SAUER
32 VP Student Affs/Dean of Strat Init ... Ms. Kimberly SLUIS
11 VP for Operations ... Mr. Michael J. HUDSON
13 VP Information and Technology/CIO ... Mr. Matthew BURDEN
15 Asst Vice Pres Human Resources ... Ms. Mary SPREITZER
26 Asst VP External Affs/Sp Asst Pres ... Mr. James GODO
28 Chief Diversity Officer ... Dr. Rebecca GORDON
07 Dean of Admissions ... Ms. Martha A. STOLZE
123 Assoc Dean Graduate Enrollment/Svcs .. Ms. Wendy E. POCHOCKI
06 Registrar ... Ms. Katherine NORRIS
08 Director of the Library ... Vacant
36 Director of Career Development Ctr ... Ms. Haydee NUNEZ
37 Director of Financial Aid ... Mr. Kevin TOWNS
23 Director of the Dyson Wellness Ctr ... Ms. Tatiana SIFRI
41 Athletic Director ... Mr. James MILLER
39 Director of Residence Life ... Mr. Andrew W. ZOBAC
42 Campus Chaplain ... Rev. Eric DOOLITTLE
09 Asst Provost/Dir Inst Effect/Plng ... Mr. Peter S. BARGER
29 Exec Dir of Development/Alumni Affs ... Mr. Adrian M. ALDRICH
28 Asst Dean of Students/Dir MC Affs ... Ms. Dorothy J. PLEAS

North Park University (F)

3225 W Foster Avenue, Chicago IL 60625-4895
County: Cook FICE Identification: 001735
Unit ID: 147679
Telephone: (773) 244-6200 Carnegie Class: Masters/L
FAX Number: N/A Calendar System: Semester
URL: www.northpark.edu
Established: 1891 Annual Undergrad Tuition & Fees: $32,100
Enrollment: 2,831 Coed
Affiliation or Control: Evangelical Covenant Church Of America
IRS Status: 501(c)3
Highest Offering: Doctorate
Accreditation: HLC, CAATE, IACBE, MUS, NURSE, THEOL

01 President ... Mrs. Mary K. SURRIDGE
05 Provost ... Dr. Michael CARR
84 Vice Pres for Enrollment/Marketing ... Mr. Anthony L. SCOLA
111 Vice President for Advancement ... Vacant
32 VP for Student Engagement ... Dr. Franco X. GAYTAN
10 Vice Pres Finance & Admin/CFO ... Mr. Scott STENMARK
73 Seminary Dean/VP Church Relations ... Dr. David W. KERSTEN
100 Chief of Staff ... Ms. Melissa VELEZ-LUCE
35 AVP and Dean of Students ... Ms. Elizabeth FREDEC
49 Dean of College of Arts & Sciences ... Vacant
107 Dean School of Professional Studies ... Dr. Lori SCREMENTI
50 Dean School of Business & NFP Mgmt ... Dr. Ann HICKS
53 Int Dean School of Education ... Dr. Daniel WALSH
64 Dean School of Music ... Dr. Rebecca RYAN
66 Dean School of Nursing ... Dr. Cindy HUDSON
28 Dir Diversity & Intercultural Life ... Ms. Sharee MYRICKS
08 Dean Library & Academic Technology ... Ms. Kathryn MAIER-O'SHEA
07 Sr Director Undergraduate Admission ... Mr. Brady MARTINSON
123 Dir of Graduate & Adult Admissions ... Ms. Judy DONOR
23 Director Health & Wellness ... Ms. Laura EBNER
37 Director Financial Aid Services ... Ms. Carolyn LACH
13 CIO/Asst VP Information Technology ... Mr. Jeffrey K. LUNDBLAD
15 Asst VP of Human Resources ... Ms. Ingrid K. TENGLIN
18 Director of Physical Plant ... Mr. Carl H. WISTROM
19 Director of Security ... Mr. Elman MCCLAIN
21 Director of Finance/Comptroller ... Ms. Debbie WILLBURN
26 Dir Univ Marketing & Communications ... Mr. Joseph MILLER
41 Asst VP for Athletics & Sports Mgmt ... Mr. John BORN
42 Director University Ministries ... Mr. Anthony ZAMBLE
36 Asst Dir Career Svcs/Internships ... Ms. Tyra OWENS
06 Registrar ... Mr. Aaron D. SCHOOF
29 Alumni Relations Assoc Dir ... Ms. Kristin ENGLUND
104 Director of International Office ... Dr. Sumie SONG
39 Director Student Housing ... Mr. Aidan HOWORTH
108 Assoc Prov Institutional Assessment ... Ms. Lisa NCUBE
106 Assoc Dean Center for Online Educ ... Vacant
44 Director Annual Giving ... Mr. Justin PREVOST-SHULTZ

Northeastern Illinois University (G)

5500 N Saint Louis Avenue, Chicago IL 60625-4699
County: Cook FICE Identification: 001693
Unit ID: 147776
Telephone: (773) 583-4050 Carnegie Class: Masters/L
FAX Number: (773) 442-4900 Calendar System: Semester
URL: www.neiu.edu
Established: 1867 Annual Undergrad Tuition & Fees (In-State): $11,827
Enrollment: 7,119 Coed
Affiliation or Control: State IRS Status: 501(c)3
Highest Offering: Master's
Accreditation: HLC, ART, CACREP, CAEP, MUS, SW

01 President ... Dr. Gloria J. GIBSON
05 Provost & VP Academic Affairs ... Dr. Dennis ROME
07 Exec Director of Admissions ... Mr. Lamont VAUGHN
100 Chief of Staff ... Vacant
32 VP for Student Affs/Dean Students ... Dr. Terry MENA
111 Vice President Inst Advancement ... Ms. Liesl V. DOWNEY
10 Vice Pres Finance & Admin ... Mr. Manish KUMAR
26 Chief of Staff/CMO ... Vacant
20 Associate Academic Officer ... Dr. Shayne COFER
84 Assoc VP Enrollment Services ... Vacant
13 Interim Chief Information Officer ... Ms. Marsha HENFER
114 Executive Director Univ Budgets ... Dr. Michael WENZ
08 Dean Libraries ... Mr. Steven HARRIS
09 Exec Dir Inst Rsrch & Assessment ... Mr. Blase E. MASINI
15 Int Exec Director Human Resources ... Ms. Abby MURRAY
25 Director Sponsored Programs ... Ms. Sharon K. TODD
37 Director Financial Aid ... Dr. Maureen T. AMOS
50 Dean College Bus/Management ... Dr. Michael D. BEDELL
58 Dean College Graduate Studies & Res ... Dr. Michael J. STERN
88 Special Assistant to Provost ... Dr. Sandra BEYDA-LORIE
49 Dean College of Arts & Sciences ... Dr. Katrina BELL-JORDAN
18 Assoc Vice Pres Facilities Mgmt ... Ms. Nancy MEDINA
19 Director University Police Dept ... Mr. John ESCALANTE
21 Director Controller's Office ... Ms. Beni ORTIZ
22 Dir Equal Opportunity/AA & Ethics ... Ms. Natalie POTTS
86 Sr Exec Dir Government Relations ... Dr. Suleyma PEREZ
06 University Registrar ... Mr. Daniel R. WEBER
29 Director of Alumni Relations ... Ms. Damaris TAPIA
110 Director Institutional Advancement ... Mr. John L. BUTLER
96 Director Purchasing ... Ms. Victoria SANTIAGO
23 Director of Student Health Services ... Ms. Sharon HEIMBAUGH
38 Director Student Counseling ... Dr. Nancy EASTON
122 Dir Stdnt Ldrshp-Greek Life ... Ms. Veronica RODRIGUEZ

Northern Illinois University (H)

1425 W. Lincoln Way, De Kalb IL 60115-2828
County: De Kalb FICE Identification: 001737
Unit ID: 147703
Telephone: (815) 753-1000 Carnegie Class: DU-Higher
FAX Number: (815) 753-0198 Calendar System: Semester
URL: www.niu.edu
Established: 1895 Annual Undergrad Tuition & Fees (In-State): $12,352
Enrollment: 16,769 Coed
Affiliation or Control: State IRS Status: 501(c)3

Highest Offering: Doctorate
Accreditation: HLC, ART, AUD, CACREP, CAEP, CLPSY, DIETD, DIETI, IPSY, LAW, MFCD, MLS, MUS, NAIT, NURSE, PH, PTA, SCPSY, SP, SPAA, THEA

01 President ... Lisa C. FREEMAN
05 Executive Vice Pres & Provost ... Beth INGRAM
10 VP Administration & Finance/CFO ... Vacant
51 SAVP University Outreach ... Rena COTSONES
46 VP Research/Innovative Partnership ... Jerry BLAZEY
26 VP Enroll Mgmt/Mktg/Communications ... Sol JENSEN
43 General Counsel ... Bryan PERRY
111 Vice Pres University Advancement ... Catherine SQUIRES
13 Chief Information Officer ... Matt PARKS
09 Exec Dir Inst Research/Analytics ... Greg BARKER
18 AVP Facilities Mgmt/Campus Services ... John HECKMANN
15 Sr AVP for Human Resources ... William HODSON
32 VP Student Affairs ... Clint-Michael RENEAU
28 VP Diversity/Equity/Inclusion ... Vernese EDGHILL-WALDEN
20 Vice Provost ... Omar GHRAYEB
50 Dean of Business ... Balaji RAJAGOPALAN
53 Dean of Education ... Laurie ELISH-PIPER
54 Dean of Engineering/Engr Tech ... Donald PETERSON
61 Dean of Law ... Cassandra HILL
49 Dean Liberal Arts & Sciences ... Robert BRINKMANN
76 Int Dean Health & Human Sciences ... Beverly HENRY
57 Dean Visual & Performing Arts ... Paul KASSEL
58 Int Dean Graduate School ... Purush DAMODARAN
85 Interim Sr International Affairs ... Bradley BOND
12 Director Lorado Taft Field Campus ... Melanie COSTELLO
12 Director NIU Naperville ... Gina KENYON
06 Director/Registrar ... Cody SCHMITZ
37 Director of Student Financial Aid ... Anne HARDY
38 Dir Counseling/Consultation ... Timothy PAQUETTE
19 Police Chief/Public Safety ... Darren MITCHELL
41 AVP/Athletic Director ... Sean FRAZIER
39 Exec Dir Housing/Residential Svcs ... Dan PEDERSEN
22 Actg Dir Disability Resources Ctr ... Amanda NEWMAN
29 Dir Alumni Relations/Univ Advance ... Reggie BUSTINZA
96 Dir Procurement/Strategic Sourcing ... Antoinette BRIDGES
07 Director of Admissions ... Mayra LAGUNAS

Northern Seminary (A)

410 Warrenville Road, Suite 300, Lisle IL 60532
County: DuPage FICE Identification: 001736
Unit ID: 147697
Telephone: (630) 620-2180 Carnegie Class: Spec-4-yr-Faith
FAX Number: (630) 620-2190 Calendar System: Quarter
URL: www.seminary.edu
Established: 1913 Annual Graduate Tuition & Fees: N/A
Enrollment: 285 Coed
Affiliation or Control: American Baptist IRS Status: 501(c)3
Highest Offering: Doctorate; No Undergraduates
Accreditation: THEOL

01 President ... Dr. William D. SHIELL
04 Executive Assistant to President ... Ms. Amy S. DISANTO
05 Provost/Dean of Academic Affairs ... Dr. Lynn COHICK
07 Director of Enrollment ... Rev. Greg ARMSTRONG
06 Registrar ... Rev. Linda OWENS
32 Assoc Dean Student Svcs/Registrar ... Rev. Linda OWENS
09 Dean of Program Dev and Innovation ... Dr. Jason GILE

Northwestern College (B)

9400 S. Cicero Avenue, Oak Lawn IL 60453
County: Cook FICE Identification: 012362
Unit ID: 147749
Telephone: (708) 237-5050 Carnegie Class: Not Classified
FAX Number: (708) 237-5005 Calendar System: Quarter
URL: www.nc.edu
Established: 1902 Annual Undergrad Tuition & Fees: N/A
Enrollment: N/A Coed
Affiliation or Control: Proprietary IRS Status: Proprietary
Highest Offering: Baccalaureate
Accreditation: #HLC, ACBSP, CAHIIM, RAD

01 President ... Mr. Lawrence SCHUMACHER
11 Executive VP of Operations ... Mrs. Gail SCHUMACHER
10 Chief Financial Officer ... Ms. Cynthia BERRYMAN
05 Chief Academic Officer ... Ms. Tonya TROKA
13 Exec Dir of Information Technology ... Mr. Omar BERNAL
86 Government and Public Relations Dir ... Ms. Laura POLLASTRINI
08 Director of Library Services ... Ms. Sarah DULAY
37 Exec Dir of Student Financial Svcs ... Mrs. Teresa VALDEZ
18 Exec Dir of Project Management ... Ms. Lauren SCHUMACHER
66 Dean of Nursing ... Ms. Lauren SPRAGGINS
06 Registrar ... Ms. Tina MARFOE

Northwestern University (C)

633 Clark Street, Evanston IL 60208-3854
County: Cook FICE Identification: 001739
Unit ID: 147767
Telephone: (847) 491-8400 Carnegie Class: DU-Highest
FAX Number: (847) 467-3104 Calendar System: Quarter
URL: www.northwestern.edu
Established: 1851 Annual Undergrad Tuition & Fees: $58,701
Enrollment: 22,603 Coed
Affiliation or Control: Independent Non-Profit IRS Status: 501(c)3
Highest Offering: Doctorate
Accreditation: HLC, ARCPA, AUD, CACREP, CLPSY, IPSY, LAW, MED, MFCD, OPE, PCSAS, PH, PTA, SP

01 President ... Dr. Michael H. SCHILL
05 Provost ... Dr. Kathleen M. HAGERTY
10 Sr Vice President Business/Finance ... Mr. Craig JOHNSON
32 Vice President Student Affairs ... Ms. Patricia M. LAMPKIN
26 VP Global Marketing & Comm ... Vacant
45 Vice Pres Administration & Planning ... Ms. Marilyn MCCOY
13 Vice Pres Information Technology ... Mr. Sean B. REYNOLDS
30 Vice Pres for Alumni Rel & Devel ... Mr. Robert MCQUINN
85 VP of Intl Relations ... Dr. Dévora GRYNSPAN
46 Vice President Research ... Dr. Milan T. MRKSICH
43 Vice President/General Counsel ... Ms. Stephanie M. GRAHAM
18 Vice Pres of Facilities Management ... Mr. Alex DARRAGH
41 Vice Pres Athletics and Recreation ... Dr. Derrick GRAGG
15 Vice Pres for Human Resources ... Ms. Lorraine GOFFE
84 Dean Enrollment/AVP Stdnt Outreach ... Mr. Christopher WATSON
20 Assoc VP & Assoc Provost Academic ... Mr. Jake JULIA
21 Assoc Prov Operations/Facilities ... Mr. Mark J. FRANCIS
86 Spec Asst to Pres for Govt Rels ... Mr. Bruce LAYTON
04 Assistant to the President ... Mr. Eugene Y. LOWE, JR.
100 Chief of Staff ... Vacant
54 Dean Sch Engr/Applied Science ... Dr. Julio M. OTTINO
50 Dean Graduate School of Management ... Dr. Francesca CORNELLI
60 Dean School of Journalism ... Dr. Charles WHITAKER
64 Dean School of Music ... Dr. Toni-Marie MONTGOMERY
63 Dean School of Medicine ... Dr. Eric G. NEILSON
107 Dean School of Professional Studies ... Dr. Thomas F. GIBBONS
58 Dean Graduate School ... Dr. Kelly MAYO
60 Dean School of Communication ... Dr. E. Patrick JOHNSON
49 Dean College Arts & Science ... Mr. Adrian RANDOLPH
61 Dean School of Law ... Dr. Hari OSOFSKY
08 University Librarian ... Ms. Sarah M. PRITCHARD
36 Exec Dir of University Career Svcs ... Dr. Mark PRESNELL
35 Assistant VP of Student Engagement ... Dr. Kelly SCHAEFER
29 AVP Alumni Relations/Development ... Mr. David LIVELY
88 Assoc Vice President for Research ... Dr. Jian CAO
88 AVP for Rsrch/Innov & New Ventures ... Ms. Alicia LOFFLER
88 Assoc Vice President for Research ... Ms. Ann ADAMS
88 Assoc Vice President for Research ... Dr. Rex CHISHOLM
88 Assoc Vice President for Research ... Dr. Richard D'AQUILA
23 Exec Director Health Services ... Dr. Robert PALINKAS
39 Asst Dean of Students ... Ms. Mary GOLDENBERG
38 Director of Counseling/Psych Svcs ... Dr. John H. DUNKLE
42 University Chaplain ... Rev. Kristen GLASS PEREZ
88 Asst VP for Information ... Mr. Amit PRACHAND
88 AVP Program Review/Spec Project ... Ms. Megan BLACKWELDER
06 University Registrar ... Ms. Jacqualyn CASAZZA
37 Director Financial Aid ... Mr. Phil ASBURY
16 Dir HR Consulting & Policy ... Ms. Stephanie GRIFFIN
19 AVP/Chief of Police & Safety ... Mr. Bruce LEWIS
116 Assoc VP of Audit & Compliance ... Mr. Luke FIGORA
22 Dir Equal Oppty & Access ... Ms. Karen TAMBURRO
96 Exec Director of Procurement ... Mr. Jim KONRAD
28 Assoc Provost Diversity & Inclusion ... Dr. Sekile NZINGA

Oak Point University (D)

1431 N. Claremont Street, 6th Floor, Chicago IL 60622
County: Cook FICE Identification: 006250
Unit ID: 149763
Telephone: (773) 252-6464 Carnegie Class: Spec-4-yr-Other Health
FAX Number: (773) 227-5134 Calendar System: Semester
URL: www.oakpoint.edu
Established: 1982 Annual Undergrad Tuition & Fees: N/A
Enrollment: 753 Coed
Affiliation or Control: Independent Non-Profit IRS Status: 501(c)3
Highest Offering: Doctorate
Accreditation: HLC, NURSE, RAD

01 President ... Dr. Therese A. SCANLAN
03 Executive Vice President & CFO ... Mr. Matthew HUGHES
05 Dir Student Academic Success ... Ms. Marlena AVALOS
32 VP Student & Employee Affairs ... Vacant
35 Director of Student Life ... Mr. Eric HERNANDEZ
90 Asst Director Student Systems ... Ms. Valarie LINDSEY
37 Director Financial Aid ... Ms. Dominique COLYER
06 University Registrar ... Ms. LaTrina GARNER
84 Director of Enrollment Management ... Dr. Rochelle KERRIGAN
08 Director of Library Services ... Ms. Liesl COTTRELL
66 Dean of Nursing ... Dr. Melissa MURPHEY
04 Administrative Asst to President ... Ms. Barbara BAILEY
13 Asst Vice Pres of Technology/CIO ... Mr. Matthew HERTZOG
29 Director Alumni Affairs ... Ms. Vickie THORNLEY
09 Director of Institutional Research ... Ms. Watasha HALL
10 Director of Finance ... Mr. Larry KEMNETZ
30 Director of Development/Alumni Rels ... Ms. Vickie THORNLEY
15 Director of Human Resources ... Mr. Anthony RIBAUDO

Oakton Community College (E)

1600 E Golf Road, Des Plaines IL 60016-1256
County: Cook FICE Identification: 009896
Unit ID: 147800
Telephone: (847) 635-1600 Carnegie Class: Assoc/HT-High Non
FAX Number: (847) 635-1992 Calendar System: Semester
URL: www.oakton.edu
Established: 1969 Annual Undergrad Tuition & Fees (In-District): $10,446
Enrollment: 7,313 Coed
Affiliation or Control: Local IRS Status: 501(c)3
Highest Offering: Associate Degree
Accreditation: HLC, ADNUR, CAHIIM, MLTAD, PTAA

01 President ... Dr. Joianne L. SMITH
05 Provost/VP Academic Affairs ... Dr. Ileo LOTT
32 VP Student Affairs ... Dr. Karl BROOKS
10 VP Admininstrative Affairs ... Mr. Edwin CHANDRASEKAR
20 Asst VP Academic Affairs ... Ms. Anne BRENNAN
103 AVP Workforce Education ... Mr. Marc BATTISTA
35 Asst VP Student Affairs ... Ms. Juletta PATRICK
13 Chief Information Officer ... Mr. Prashant SHINDE
76 Dean Health Careers ... Ms. Maribel ALIMBOYOGUEN
81 Dean STEM ... Dr. Robert SOMPOLSKI
49 Dean Liberal Arts ... Ms. Linda KORBEL
51 Dean Adult & Cont Education ... Dr. Jesse IVORY
09 AVP Institutional Effectiveness ... Dr. Kelly BECKER
26 AVP Mktg & Comm/CAO ... Ms. Katherine SAWYER
08 Dean Library ... Mr. Jacob JEREMIAH
07 Dir of Admissions & Enrollment ... Mr. Roberto VALADEZ
35 Director of Student Life/Inclusion ... Mr. Shedrick DANIELS
121 Dean of Student Success ... Mr. Sebastian CONTRERAS, JR.
124 Dir of Student Learning/Engagement ... Ms. Leana CUELLAR
41 Senior Manager of Athletics ... Ms. Christine PACIERO
88 Dir Workforce Development ... Dr. Ruben HOWARD, II
21 Controller ... Mr. Andy WILLIAMS
15 Chief Human Resources Officer ... Dr. Colette HANDS
18 Director of Facilities ... Mr. Joseph SCIFO
14 Director Systems & Network Svcs ... Mr. John WADE
14 Dir of Software & User Svcs ... Ms. Renee KOZIMOR
06 Dir Financial Aid/Registrar ... Dr. Cheryl WARMANN
25 Dir of Grant Strategy/Development ... Mr. Al GRIPPE
11 Dir of Operations & Admin ... Ms. Robyn BAILEY
38 Dean of Wellness Services ... Dr. Mark KIEL
19 Chief of Police ... Mr. Jeffrey HOFFMANN
20 Dean Curriculum & Instruction ... Ms. Ruth WILLIAMS
106 Director Online Curriculum ... Dr. David KENDRICK
27 Director of Marketing ... Dr. Andrea LEHMACHER
84 Dean of Enrollment Management ... Mr. Matthew HUBER
88 Asst Financial Controller ... Mr. David HITTENMILLER
88 Asst Dir Enrollment for Equity ... Ms. Ella WHITEHEAD
88 Director Campus Technologies ... Mr. LeVon MCALLISTER

Olivet Nazarene University (F)

One University Avenue, Bourbonnais IL 60914-2345
County: Kankakee FICE Identification: 001741
Unit ID: 147828
Telephone: (815) 939-5011 Carnegie Class: Masters/L
FAX Number: (815) 935-4998 Calendar System: Semester
URL: www.olivet.edu
Established: 1907 Annual Undergrad Tuition & Fees: $36,950
Enrollment: 3,764 Coed
Affiliation or Control: Church Of The Nazarene IRS Status: 501(c)3
Highest Offering: Doctorate
Accreditation: HLC, CAATE, @DIET, DIETD, MUS, NURSE, SW

01 President ... Dr. Gregg A. CHENOWETH
10 EVP/Chief Financial Officer ... Dr. David J. PICKERING
05 Vice President Academic Affairs ... Dr. Stephen R. LOWE
32 Vice President Student Development ... Dr. Walter W. WEBB
111 Vice Pres Institutional Advancement ... Dr. Brian D. ALLEN
88 Vice Pres for ONU Global ... Mr. Ryan D. SPITTAL
29 Dir Alumni & University Relations ... Mr. Erinn M. PROEHL
06 University Registrar ... Dr. Mark C. MOUNTAIN
08 Dean of Library Services ... Mrs. Pam S. GREENLEE
26 Exec Director of Univ Relations ... Mrs. Susan M. WOLFF
113 Director of Undergraduate Revenue ... Mr. Greg S. BRUNER
13 Chief Information Officer ... Mr. Dennis E. SEYMOUR
41 Athletic Director ... Mr. Mike C. CONWAY
42 Chaplain ... RevDr. Mark E. HOLCOMB
30 Exec Director of Development ... Mr. Brian ALLEN
35 Director Student Activities ... Mrs. Kathy STEINACKER
38 Director Student Counseling ... Mrs. Lisa VANDER VEER
18 Chief Facilities/Physical Plant ... Mr. Rob LALUMENDRE
40 Bookstore Manager ... Mrs. Rachel PIAZZA
36 Director of Career Services ... Vacant
85 International Student Advisor ... Mrs. Darlene SWANSON
26 Director of Marketing ... Mr. Adam ASHER
19 Director Security/Safety ... Mr. Darren BLAIR
49 Dean College of Arts & Sciences ... Dr. Kent OLNEY
73 Dn Sch Theology/Christian Ministry ... Dr. David WINE
53 Chair Education Dept ... Dr. Lance KILPATRICK
107 Dean College Professional Studies ... Dr. Amber RESIDORI
64 Assoc Dean School of Music ... Dr. Don REDDICK
50 Assoc Dean School of Business ... Dr. Glen REWERTS
54 Chair Engineering Dept ... Dr. Joe SCHROEDER
04 Admin Assistant to the President ... Mrs. Amy ZABEL
15 Director of Human Resources ... Mr. Tom ASCHER

Parkland College (G)

2400 W Bradley Avenue, Champaign IL 61821-1899
County: Champaign FICE Identification: 007118
Unit ID: 147916
Telephone: (217) 351-2200 Carnegie Class: Assoc/MT-VT-High Non
FAX Number: (217) 351-2581 Calendar System: Semester
URL: www.parkland.edu
Established: 1966 Annual Undergrad Tuition & Fees (In-District): $11,580
Enrollment: 5,758 Coed
Affiliation or Control: State/Local IRS Status: 501(c)3
Highest Offering: Associate Degree
Accreditation: HLC, ADNUR, COARC, DH, EMT, MAC, OTA, RAD, SURGT

01 President ... Dr. Thomas R. RAMAGE
04 Asst to President/Board of Trustees ... Ms. Krystal GARRETT
03 Exec Vice President ... Dr. Pam LAU

05 Vice Pres Academic Services ... Dr. Nancy SUTTON
32 Vice President Student Services ... Dr. Mike TRAME
10 Vice Pres Administrative Svcs/ CFO ... Mr. Christopher M. RANDLES
26 VP Communications/External Affairs ... Ms. Stephanie STUART
35 Dean of Students ... Ms. Marietta TURNER
35 Director Student Life ... Ms. Tracy KLEPARSKI
09 Dean Institutional Effectiveness ... Mr. Kevin KNOTT
49 Dean Arts & Sciences ... Dr. Joseph WALWIK
75 Dean Career & Technical Education ... Mr. Derrick BAKER
66 Dean Health Professions ... Ms. Caroyln RAGSDALE
103 Asst Dean Adult Educ/Workforce Dev ... Ms. Tawanna NICKENS
102 Exec Dir Foundation/Alumni Affairs ... Ms. Tracy WAHFELDT
08 Assoc Dean Learning Commons ... Ms. Morgann QUILTY
31 Director Community Education ... Ms. Triss HENDERSON
27 Director Marketing/Public Rels ... Ms. Erin SHANNON
84 Dean Enrollment Mgmt ... Ms. Kristin SMIGIELSKI
41 Director Athletics ... Mr. Brendan MCHALE
38 Dean Counseling Services ... Ms. Stephanie DAVINGMAN
121 Director Advising Services ... Ms. Julia HAWTHORNE
07 Director Enrollment Services ... Mr. Tim WENDT
19 Director Public Safety ... Mr. Troy DANIELS
18 Director Physical Plant ... Mr. James BUSTARD
15 Assoc VP/Chief Human Resources ... Ms. Kathleen MCANDREW
21 Controller ... Mr. Dave DONSBACH
40 Manager of Bookstore ... Ms. Hayden SEIDEL
108 Director Assessment Center ... Mr. Michael BEHRENS
13 Chief Information Tech Officer ... Mr. Amin KASSEM

Prairie State College (A)

202 S Halsted Street, Chicago Heights IL 60411-8226
County: Cook FICE Identification: 001640
Unit ID: 148007
Telephone: (708) 709-3500 Carnegie Class: Assoc/MT-VT-High Non
FAX Number: (708) 709-3774 Calendar System: Semester
URL: www.prairiestate.edu
Established: 1957 Annual Undergrad Tuition & Fees (In-District): $9,342
Enrollment: 2,716 Coed
Affiliation or Control: State/Local IRS Status: 501(c)3
Highest Offering: Associate Degree
Accreditation: HLC, ADNUR, DH, @PTAA, SURGT

01 Interim President ... Dr. Thomas D. SABAN
10 Vice Pres Finance & Administration ... Dr. Thomas D. SABAN
05 Vice Pres Academic Affairs ... Mr. Elighie WILSON
32 VP Student Affs/Inst Effectiveness ... Dr. Michael D. ANTHONY
49 Dean Liberal Arts & Soc Sciences ... Vacant
81 Dean Math/Nat Scienc/Acad Standards ... Ms. Annette DOLPH
76 Dean Allied Health/Emerg Services ... Dr. Megan HUGHES
75 Dean Career and Tech Education ... Dr. Janice KAUSHAL
15 Exec Dir Human Resources ... Dr. Charmaine SEVIER
13 Exec Dir Info Technology Resources ... Mr. Gregory KAIN
56 Dean Adult Education ... Ms. Kim M. KUNCE
21 Controller/Dir of Business Svcs ... Ms. Cheri TAYLOR-LAWTON
08 Dean Learning Resources/Assess ... Vacant
28 Dean Equity/Inclusion ... Dr. Tiffany BREWER
35 Dean Student Dev/Campus Life ... Mr. Felix SIMPKINS
103 Exec Dir Workforce Dev/Cmty Educ ... Ms. Alisha CLARK
18 Exec Dir Facilities and Operations ... Mr. Timothy J. KOSIEK
111 Exec Dir Inst Advance & Foundation ... Ms. Deborah S. HAVIGHORST
84 Dean Enrollment Management ... Ms. Jaime M. MILLER
19 Chief of Police ... Mr. Anthony MARTIN, SR.
37 Director Financial Aid ... Ms. Grace MCGINNIS
09 Director Inst Research/Planning ... Dr. Adane G. KASSA
41 Director of Athletics ... Mr. Christopher J. KUCHTA
100 Chief of Staff ... Ms. Patricia G. TROST
108 Dir Inst Effect/Plng/Accreditation ... Ms. Jan BONAVIA

Principia College (B)

1 Maybeck Place, Elsah IL 62028-9799
County: Jersey FICE Identification: 001744
Unit ID: 148016
Telephone: (618) 374-2131 Carnegie Class: Bac-A&S
FAX Number: (618) 374-5500 Calendar System: Semester
URL: www.principiacollege.edu
Established: 1898 Annual Undergrad Tuition & Fees: $30,720
Enrollment: 340 Coed
Affiliation or Control: Independent Non-Profit IRS Status: 501(c)3
Highest Offering: Baccalaureate
Accreditation: HLC

01 President ... Mr. John W. WILLIAMS
00 Chief Executive Officer ... Mrs. Barbara BLACKWELL
05 Dean of Academics ... Dr. Meggan MADDEN
115 Chief Investment Officer ... Mr. Howard E. BERNER, JR.
10 Chief Financial/Business Officer ... Mr. Tom NICKELL
43 Legal Counsel ... Mr. Lee BARRON
06 Registrar ... Ms. Helen WILLS
32 Dean of Students ... Mrs. Maya DIETZ
08 Library Director ... Dr. Edith LIST
104 Director of Principia Abroad ... Mrs. Stephanie LOVSETH
41 Director of Athletics ... Mrs. Ann PIERSON
18 Director of Facilities ... Mr. Lee EUBANK
21 Controller ... Mr. Don MILLER
37 Director of Financial Aid ... Ms. Rachael STOCK
96 Purchasing Agent ... Mrs. Susan CURRY
09 Institutional Research Officer ... Ms. Roz HIBBS
26 Dir Marketing & Communications ... Mrs. Laurel WALTERS
07 Director of Admissions ... Mr. Lee ELLIS
15 Director of Human Resources ... Mrs. Beth TREVINO
04 Exec Assistant to the President ... Ms. Christina WILSON

Quincy University (C)

1800 College Avenue, Quincy IL 62301-2699
County: Adams FICE Identification: 001745
Unit ID: 148131
Telephone: (217) 228-5432 Carnegie Class: Bac-Diverse
FAX Number: (217) 228-5487 Calendar System: Semester
URL: www.quincy.edu
Established: 1860 Annual Undergrad Tuition & Fees: $31,160
Enrollment: 1,273 Coed
Affiliation or Control: Roman Catholic IRS Status: 501(c)3
Highest Offering: Master's
Accreditation: HLC, CACREP

00 Chair Board of Trustees ... Mr. Delmer MITCHELL
01 President ... Dr. Brian R. MCGEE
125 President Emeritus ... Mr. Phillip CONOVER
05 VP for Academic Affairs ... Dr. Teresa REED
42 VP for Mission & Ministry ... Fr. John DOCTOR, OFM
10 VP for Business/Finance ... Mr. Mark STRIEKER
84 VP Student Enrollment Management ... Mr. Tom OLIVER
32 VP for Student Development ... Dr. Christine TRACY
41 Athletic Director ... Mr. Josh RABE
111 VP for University Advancement ... Dr. Robert WYATT
04 Exec Assistant to the President ... Mrs. Julie BUDINE
101 Corporate Secretary ... Fr. John DOCTOR, OFM
21 Controller ... Mrs. Nora KLINGELE
20 Associate VP for Academic Affairs ... Dr. Kimberly HALE
06 Registrar ... Mrs. Nancy GEISSLER
50 Dean School of Business ... Dr. Cynthia HALIEMUN
08 Dean Library/Info Resources ... Ms. Patricia TOMCZAK
79 Dean School of Humanities ... Dr. Robert MANNING
81 Dean School of Science & Technology ... Dr. Lee ENGER
57 Dean School Fine Arts/Communication ... Dr. Christine DAMM
53 Dean School of Education/Human Svcs ... Dr. Kenneth OLIVER
13 Director of IT Services ... Mr. Michael MCCABE
26 Director Community Relations ... Ms. Chris BRENNEMANN
108 Director of Academic Assessment ... Dr. Barbara ROWLAND
92 Director Honors Program ... Dr. Daniel STRUDWICK
42 Director Campus Ministry ... Ms. Jessica HOWELL
110 Sr Director for Univ Advancement ... Mr. Matthew BERGMAN
37 Director Financial Aid ... Mrs. Kristi SHELTON
18 Director Facilities Management ... Mr. Troy PETER
39 Director Residence Life ... Mr. Joshua JACOBS
124 Director Student Engagement ... Mr. Trenton HENDERSON
19 Director Safety & Security ... Mr. Sam LATHROP
15 Director Human Resources ... Vacant
07 Director of Admissions ... Vacant
36 Director of Experiential Learning ... Mrs. Kristen LIESEN
96 Purchasing ... Ms. Jennifer TRUITT
25 Grant Writer ... Vacant
40 Manager Bookstore ... Mr. Mark HUGHES
09 Director of Institutional Research ... Ms. Mary BERGSTROM

Rasmussen University - Rockford (D)

6000 E. State Street, 4th Floor, Rockford IL 61108
Telephone: (815) 316-4800 Identification: 667065
Accreditation: &HLC, MAAB, SURGT

† Regional accreditation carried under the parent institution in Saint Cloud, MN. The tuition figure is an average, actual tuition may vary.

Rasmussen University - Romeoville/Joliet (E)

1400 West Normantown Road, Romeoville IL 60446
Telephone: (815) 306-2600 Identification: 667066
Accreditation: &HLC, MAAB, SURGT

† Regional accreditation carried under the parent institution in Saint Cloud, MN. The tuition figure is an average, actual tuition may vary.

Rend Lake College (F)

468 N Ken Gray Parkway, Ina IL 62846-9801
County: Jefferson FICE Identification: 007119
Unit ID: 148256
Telephone: (618) 437-5321 Carnegie Class: Assoc/MT-VT-High Non
FAX Number: (618) 437-5677 Calendar System: Semester
URL: www.rlc.edu
Established: 1967 Annual Undergrad Tuition & Fees (In-District): $6,000
Enrollment: 1,802 Coed
Affiliation or Control: State/Local IRS Status: 501(c)3
Highest Offering: Associate Degree
Accreditation: HLC, ADNUR, EMT, MAC, RAD

01 President ... Mr. Terry WILKERSON
05 VP of Instruction & Student Affairs ... Mrs. Lori RAGLAND
10 VP of Finance & Administration ... Mr. John GULLEY
32 Assoc VP of Academic & Student Svcs ... Mr. Henry LEECK
26 Assoc VP of Institutional Outreach ... Mr. Chad COPPLE
121 Assoc VP of CTE & Student Support ... Mrs. Kim WILKERSON
37 Director of Financial Aid ... Vacant
41 Athletic Director ... Mr. Tim WILLS
18 Director Physical Plant ... Mr. Donnie MILLENBINE
102 CEO of RLC Foundation ... Vacant
06 Director of Student Records ... Mrs. Kelly DOWNES
84 Dean of Enrollment Services ... Mrs. Vickie SCHULTE
15 Director of Human Resources ... Ms. Kim ROGERS

Richland Community College (G)

One College Park, Decatur IL 62521-8513
County: Macon FICE Identification: 010879
Unit ID: 148292
Telephone: (217) 875-7200 Carnegie Class: Assoc/HVT-High Non
FAX Number: (217) 875-6961 Calendar System: Semester
URL: www.richland.edu
Established: 1971 Annual Undergrad Tuition & Fees (In-District): $6,180
Enrollment: 2,235 Coed
Affiliation or Control: State/Local IRS Status: 501(c)3
Highest Offering: Associate Degree
Accreditation: HLC, ACFEI, ADNUR, CAHIIM, RAD, SURGT

01 President ... Dr. Cristobal (Cris) VALDEZ
10 Vice President of Finance & Admin ... Mr. Greg E. FLORIAN
05 Vice Pres Academic Services ... Dr. Denise CREWS
106 Director Online Learning ... Mrs. Kona JONES
111 AVP Inst Advance/Exec Dir Found ... Ms. Julie MELTON
29 Dir Scholarships/Alumni Development ... Mrs. Tricia CORDULACK
15 Director Human Resources ... Ms. Robin BOLLHORST
37 Asst Dir Financial Aid/Veteran Affs ... Ms. Jody BURTNETT
81 Dean Math & Sciences/Business Div ... Dr. Andy HYNDS
76 Dean of Health Professions ... Ms. Ellen COLBECK

Rock Valley College (H)

3301 N Mulford Road, Rockford IL 61114-5699
County: Winnebago FICE Identification: 001747
Unit ID: 148380
Telephone: (815) 921-7821 Carnegie Class: Assoc/MT-VT-High Non
FAX Number: N/A Calendar System: Semester
URL: www.rockvalleycollege.edu
Established: 1964 Annual Undergrad Tuition & Fees (In-District): $9,314
Enrollment: 5,762 Coed
Affiliation or Control: Local IRS Status: 501(c)3
Highest Offering: Associate Degree
Accreditation: HLC, ADNUR, COARC, DH

01 President ... Dr. Howard J. SPEARMAN
11 VP Operations ... Mr. Rick JENKS
05 VP Academic Affairs & CAO ... Dr. Amanda SMITH
10 VP Finance ... Ms. Ellen OLSON
22 VP Equity & Inclusion ... Mr. Keith R. BARNES
15 VP Human Resources ... Mr. Jim HANDLEY
32 VP Student Affairs ... Dr. Patrick PEYER
103 VP Industrl Partnershp/Cmty Engage ... Dr. Hansen STEWART
20 Exec Dir Outcomes Assessment ... Dr. Lisa MEHLIG
16 Executive Director Human Resources ... Vacant
09 VP Inst Effectiveness/Communication ... Ms. Heather SNIDER
30 Chief Development Officer ... Ms. Brittany FREIBERG
18 Exec Dir Facilities Planning & POM ... Ms. Janet TAYLOR
26 Exec Dir Col Comm/Marketing ... Ms. Jennifer THOMPSON
88 Director Theatre & Arts Park ... Mr. Christopher D. BRADY
19 Chief of Police ... Mr. Thomas YEHL
06 Registrar/Director Financial Aid ... Ms. Stacey KOLDER
04 Assistant to the President ... Ms. Ann KERWITZ
04 Assistant to the President ... Ms. Kris FUCHS
41 Athletic Director ... Mr. Darin MONROE
106 Exec Dir Online Dev/Innovation ... Ms. Kym BLANCHARD
13 Exec Dir Information Technology ... Ms. Danielle BAUMGARTNER

Rockford Career College (I)

1130 S. Alpine Road, Suite 100, Rockford IL 61108
County: Winnebago FICE Identification: 008545
Unit ID: 148399
Telephone: (815) 965-8616 Carnegie Class: Not Classified
FAX Number: (815) 965-0360 Calendar System: Quarter
URL: www.rockfordcareercollege.edu
Established: 1862 Annual Undergrad Tuition & Fees: N/A
Enrollment: N/A Coed
Affiliation or Control: Proprietary IRS Status: Proprietary
Highest Offering: Associate Degree
Accreditation: ACCSC, DMS, MAAB, MLTAB, SURTEC

00 President/CEO ... Mr. Stephen TAVE
01 Campus President ... Mr. Mike O'HERRON
05 Academic Dean ... Mr. Marc SHERROD
32 Dean of Students/Student Services ... Ms. Danielle HARRIOTT
06 Registrar/Director of Compliance ... Ms. Erin EGGEBRECHT
07 Director of Admissions ... Vacant
36 Director Career Services ... Ms. Melissa RIDGEWAY-HAGERMAN
37 Director of Financial Aid ... Ms. Denise ACKLEY
08 Library/Bookstore Coordinator ... Ms. Lena VERKUILEN

Rockford University (J)

5050 E State Street, Rockford IL 61108-2393
County: Winnebago FICE Identification: 001748
Unit ID: 148405
Telephone: (815) 226-4000 Carnegie Class: Masters/S
FAX Number: (815) 226-4119 Calendar System: Semester
URL: www.rockford.edu
Established: 1847 Annual Undergrad Tuition & Fees: $33,050
Enrollment: 1,272 Coed
Affiliation or Control: Independent Non-Profit IRS Status: 501(c)3
Highest Offering: Master's
Accreditation: HLC, IACBE, NUR

01 President ... Dr. Eric W. FULCOMER
05 VP of Academic Affairs/Provost ... Dr. Michael PERRY
111 VP for Institutional Advancement ... Vacant
10 VP for Finance/CFO ... Ms. Lisa CUSTARDO
21 Business Office Accounting Manager ... Mr. John DIRAIMONDO
84 VP Enrollment Management ... Dr. Michael QUINN

32 VP for Student Affairs ... Dr. Randy WORDEN
37 Assistant VP for SAS ... Mr. Todd FISCHER-FREE
11 Director of Operations ... Mr. Ed TOMASZKIEWICZ
13 Director of Information Technology ... Mr. Ryan CUSHING
123 Director of Adult & Grad Admissions ... Ms. Elizabeth NARDI
06 Registrar ... Ms. Anna J. JATTKOWSKI-HUDSON
04 Exec Assistant to the President ... Ms. Jen CUNNINGHAM
41 Director of Athletics ... Mr. Jason MULLIGAN
15 Director of Human Resources ... Ms. Monique DIVENTI
36 Director Career Services ... Ms. Chelsea MINOR
26 Director of Communications ... Vacant
09 Coordinator of IR ... Dr. Stephen KIM
85 Director of Global Affairs ... Ms. Maria DIEMER
23 Director Health Services ... Ms. Kristen CLARKE
18 Facilities Director ... Vacant
08 Head Librarian ... Mr. Andy NEWGREN
19 Director Security/Safety ... Mr. Tim TREVIER
29 Director Alumni Affairs ... Ms. Nicole RILEY
39 Dir Resident Life/Student Housing ... Mr. Scott MITCHELL

Roosevelt University (A)

430 S Michigan Avenue, Chicago IL 60605-1394
County: Cook FICE Identification: 001749
Unit ID: 148487
Telephone: (312) 341-3500 Carnegie Class: DU-Mod
FAX Number: (312) 341-3655 Calendar System: Semester
URL: www.roosevelt.edu
Established: 1945 Annual Undergrad Tuition & Fees: $31,493
Enrollment: 4,680 Coed
Affiliation or Control: Independent Non-Profit IRS Status: 501(c)3
Highest Offering: Doctorate
Accreditation: HLC, ACBSP, CACREP, CLPSY, MUS, NURSE, PHAR

01 President ... Dr. Ali MALEKZADEH
05 Int Provost/EVP Academic Affairs ... Dr. Mablene KRUEGER
10 Int Vice Pres Finance/Admin & CFO ... Ms. Arlene REGNERUS
84 Vice Pres Enrollment Mgmt ... Mr. Michael CASSIDY
100 Vice Pres/Chief of Staff/Sec of BOT ... Dr. Michael FORD
111 VP University Advancement ... Ms. Nicole BARRON
32 Int VP Student Affs/Dean Students ... Ms. Mablene KRUEGER
13 Chief Info Ofcr/VP InfoTech ... Mr. Neeraj KUMAR
15 Vice Pres Human Resources ... Ms. Toyia K. STEWART
09 Assoc VP Inst Research ... Mr. Joseph P. REGAN
105 Assist Vice Pres Web Development ... Mr. Aaron RESTER
43 Interim Assistant Legal Counseling ... Ms. Latoya LAING
21 Assoc VP Finance/Controller ... Mr. Patrick ALFORQUE
19 Shift Director of Campus Safety ... Mr. Paul HUERTA
85 Asst Dir of International Programs ... Mr. Ken GRANLE
46 Assoc Provost Research ... Dr. Mike MALY
121 Assoc Provost Student Success ... Ms. Katrina COAKLEY
49 Int Dean College Arts & Sciences ... Dr. Cami MCBRIDE
50 Dean College of Business ... Dr. Ryan PETTY
57 Dean College of Performing Arts ... Dr. Rudy MARCOZZI
53 Dean College of Education ... Dr. Thomas PHILION
67 Dean College of Pharmacy ... Dr. Melissa HOGAN
88 Int CEO Auditorium Theatre ... Mr. Rich REGAN
37 Director Financial Aid ... Ms. Michelle STIPP
39 Asst Dean Student Life & Housing ... Ms. Hilda RAMOS
41 Director of Athletics ... Mr. John JARAMILLO
08 Director of Libraries ... Mr. Estavan MONTANO
36 Director Career & Prof Development ... Ms. Jennifer WONDERLY
04 Exec Asst to President ... Ms. Kathy BLISS
07 Executive Director of Admissions ... Vacant
96 Mgr Purchasing & Business Affairs ... Ms. Veleicia DIVINITY

Rosalind Franklin University of Medicine & Science (B)

3333 Green Bay Road, North Chicago IL 60064-3095
County: Lake FICE Identification: 001659
Unit ID: 145558
Telephone: (847) 578-3000 Carnegie Class: Spec-4-yr-Med
FAX Number: (847) 578-3401 Calendar System: Quarter
URL: www.rosalindfranklin.edu
Established: 1912 Annual Undergrad Tuition & Fees: N/A
Enrollment: 2,099 Coed
Affiliation or Control: Independent Non-Profit IRS Status: 501(c)3
Highest Offering: Doctorate; No Lower Division
Accreditation: HLC, ANEST, ARCPA, CLPSY, MED, PA, PHAR, POD, PTA

01 President/CEO ... Dr. Wendy RHEAULT
05 Provost ... Dr. Nancy PARSLEY
67 Dean College of Pharmacy ... Dr. Marc ABEL
107 Dean College Health Professions ... Dr. John VITALE
58 Dean Sch Grad PostDoc Stds ... Dr. Joseph X. DIMARIO
63 Dean Scholl Col Podiatric Med ... Dr. Stephanie WU
63 Dean Chicago Medical Sch/VP Med Aff ... Dr. Archana CHATTERJEE
46 Exec VP Research ... Dr. Ronald S. KAPLAN
26 Senior VP University Enhancement ... Ms. Lee CONCHA
32 VP Student Success and Inclusion ... Ms. Rebecca DURKIN
66 Found Dean Nursing/VP Partnerships ... Dr. Sandra LARSON
20 VP Academic and Faculty Affairs ... Dr. Moreen CARVAN
111 VP Institutional Advancement ... Mr. Chad RUBACK
10 Exec VP Finance & Admin ... Mr. Gavin FARRY
100 Chief of Staff/SVP Univ Enhancement ... Ms. Lee CONCHA
20 AVP Academic and Faculty Affairs ... Dr. Robert INTINE
13 AVP Technology & Learning Resources ... Mr. Richard LOESCH
114 AVP Financial Plng & Analysis ... Ms. Christie TIPTON
35 AVP Student Affairs ... Ms. Shelly BRZYCKI
07 AVP Admissions/Recruitment ... Dr. Bryan MOODY
06 AVP Student Records/Registrar ... Mr. Jason CELIZ
37 AVP Student Financial Services ... Ms. Maryann DECAIRE
15 AVP Human Resources ... Ms. Sally J. MADDEN
21 Controller ... Ms. Emily NYBLAD
30 Exec Dir of Development ... Mr. George RATTIN
30 Exec Dir of Development ... Ms. Pamela LOWE
29 Exec Dir Alumni Relations ... Ms. Martha KELLY BATES
102 Dir Foundation & Grant Relations ... Ms. Shella BLUE
44 Dir Annual Giving ... Vacant
09 Director of Institutional Research ... Mr. Omer MINHAS
28 Exec Dir Diversity & Inclusion ... Dr. Heather M. KIND-KEPPEL
96 Dir Materials Management ... Mr. Vince BUTERA
19 Dir Campus Security ... Mr. Gordon BLANCHARD
121 Dir Academic Support ... Ms. Nydia STEWART
18 Dir Facilities Management ... Mr. Robert D. JACKSON
25 Dir Sponsored Research ... Ms. Dora ESPINOSA
08 Library Director ... Ms. Charlotte BEYER
16 Dir of Human Resources ... Ms. Mary TELL
118 Benefits Administrator ... Ms. Melissa HALEY
39 Coordinator for Residence Life ... Ms. Amber WOYAK
04 Executive Administrative Assistant ... Ms. Jean MINA
86 Director Government Relations ... Mr. Joseph PIASECKI

Rush University (C)

600 S Paulina, Chicago IL 60612-3832
County: Cook FICE Identification: 009800
Unit ID: 148511
Telephone: (312) 942-7100 Carnegie Class: Spec-4-yr-Med
FAX Number: (312) 942-2219 Calendar System: Semester
URL: www.rushu.rush.edu
Established: 1971 Annual Undergrad Tuition & Fees: N/A
Enrollment: 2,816 Coed
Affiliation or Control: Independent Non-Profit IRS Status: 501(c)3
Highest Offering: Doctorate
Accreditation: HLC, ANEST, ARCPA, AUD, BBT, CAMPEP, COARC, DIETI, DMS, HSA, IPSY, MED, MLS, NURSE, OT, PAST, PERF, SP

01 President Rush University ... Dr. Sherine E. GABRIEL
05 Provost/SVP Univ System for Health ... Dr. Susan L. FREEMAN
26 VP Corp/External Affairs ... Vacant
10 Sr VP/CFO/Treasurer ... Ms. Patricia S. O'NEIL
30 Senior Vice President Philanthropy ... Ms. Diane M. MCKEEVER
43 SVP Legal Affairs/Gen Counsel ... Mr. Carl BERGETZ
15 Chief Human Resources Ofcr/Sr VP ... Mr. Marcos B. DELEON
25 VP/Chief Compliance Office ... Dr. Cynthia E. BOYD
21 Chief Finance Business Officer ... Mr. Vince GATTUSO
28 Sr Dir Stdnt Diversity/Cmty Engage ... Dr. Sharon GATES
20 Vice Provost Academic Affairs ... Dr. David KATZ
20 Vice Provost Faculty Affairs ... Dr. Susanna CHUBINSKAYA
32 Vice Provost Student Affairs ... Ms. Gayle B. WARD
76 Dean Col of Health Sciences ... Dr. Charlotte ROYEEN
58 Dean Graduate College ... Dr. Andrew J. BEAN
66 Dean College of Nursing ... Dr. Chrisitne KENNEDY
63 Dean Rush Medical College ... Dr. Badrinath R. KONETY
88 Sr Assoc Dean Medical College ... Dr. Elizabeth A. BAKER
27 Assoc VP Marketing & Comm ... Mr. Ryan NAGDEMAN
08 Director Library ... Mr. Scott THOMPSON
35 Director Student Affairs ... Ms. Kapula PATALINGHUG
37 Dir Student Financial Aid ... Ms. Jill GABLE
38 Interim VP of Wellness ... Ms. Evelyn POCZATEK
29 Director Alumni Relations ... Ms. Krista GIUFFI
18 Director University Facilities ... Mr. Chris KANAKIS
21 Manager of Financial Affairs ... Mr. Patrick MCNULTY
102 Dir Foundation/Corporate Relations ... Ms. Sophia WOROBEC
19 Director Security Services ... Mr. Peter C. ARDNT
46 Interim Vice Provost Research ... Dr. Andrew J. BEAN
04 Exec Asst to the President ... Ms. Sheila M. GREENE
06 Registrar/Sr Dir Enroll Mgmt ... Ms. Brenda L. WEDDINGTON

SAE Institute Chicago (D)

820 N. Orleans St., Ste 125, Chicago IL 60610
Telephone: (312) 300-5685 Identification: 770970
Accreditation: ACCSC

† Branch campus of SAE Institute Nashville, Nashville, TN

Saint Anthony College of Nursing (E)

3301 N. Mulford Rd, Rockford IL 61114
County: Winnebago FICE Identification: 009987
Unit ID: 149028
Telephone: (815) 282-7900 Carnegie Class: Spec-4-yr-Other Health
FAX Number: (815) 282-7901 Calendar System: Semester
URL: https://www.osfhealthcare.org/sacn/
Established: 1915 Annual Undergrad Tuition & Fees: $27,460
Enrollment: 291 Coed
Affiliation or Control: Roman Catholic IRS Status: 501(c)3
Highest Offering: Doctorate
Accreditation: HLC, NURSE

01 Interim President ... Dr. Shannon K. LIZER
66 Dean Undergraduate Affairs ... Dr. Elizabeth M. CARSON
58 Int Dean Graduate Affairs/Research ... Dr. Michelle BRADY
32 Associate Dean Support Services ... Ms. Nancy A. SANDERS
08 College Librarian ... Ms. Hilaree LOMBARDO
37 Financial Aid Coordinator ... Ms. Serrita WOODS
04 Executive Secretary to President ... Ms. Teresa M. DAUGHERTY
09 Inst Effectiveness/Assessment Spec ... Ms. Elizabeth R. HARP
90 Educational Technology Coordinator ... Ms. Susan K. STAAB

St. Augustine College (F)

1345 West Argyle Street, Chicago IL 60640-3501
County: Cook FICE Identification: 021854
Unit ID: 148876
Telephone: (773) 878-8756 Carnegie Class: Bac/Assoc-Mixed
FAX Number: (773) 878-3719 Calendar System: Semester
URL: www.staugustine.edu
Established: 1980 Annual Undergrad Tuition & Fees: $12,120
Enrollment: 901 Coed
Affiliation or Control: Independent Non-Profit IRS Status: 501(c)3
Highest Offering: Baccalaureate
Accreditation: HLC, COARC, SW

01 President ... Dr. Reyes GONZALEZ
05 Provost ... Vacant
20 Dean Academic Affairs ... Dr. Andrea KOEPKE
10 COO/CFO ... Dr. Luyan LI
26 Exec Dir Marketing/ Communication ... Mr. Marco AMARO
103 Int Dir Workforce Development ... Dr. Pedro CEVALLOS-CANDAU
32 Dean of Students ... Dr. Juan OJEDA
108 Director Academic Effectiveness ... Dr. Ana GIL GARCIA
13 Director of IT ... Ms. Elba GONZALEZ
37 Director of Financial Aid ... Ms. Maria ZAMBONINO
15 Director Human Resources ... Ms. Nancy BOURQUE
07 Director of Admission ... Ms. Andrea SCHMOYER
08 Librarian ... Ms. Claudia CHOCIAY NICKSON
06 Registrar ... Ms. Karla MARTINEZ
09 Director of Institutional Research ... Mr. Robert MYERS

Saint Francis Medical Center College of Nursing (G)

511 NE Greenleaf Street, Peoria IL 61603-3783
County: Peoria FICE Identification: 006240
Unit ID: 148575
Telephone: (309) 655-2201 Carnegie Class: Spec-4-yr-Other Health
FAX Number: (309) 624-8973 Calendar System: Semester
URL: https://www.osfhealthcare.org/sfmccon/
Established: 1985 Annual Undergrad Tuition & Fees: N/A
Enrollment: 466 Coed
Affiliation or Control: Roman Catholic IRS Status: 501(c)3
Highest Offering: Doctorate
Accreditation: HLC, NURSE

01 President of the College ... Dr. Sandie S. SOLDWISCH
05 Interim Provost ... Dr. Shannon LIZER
58 Dean Graduate Program ... Dr. Kimberly A. MITCHELL
20 Dean Undergraduate Program ... Dr. Sue C. BROWN
32 Asst Dean of Support Services ... Mr. Kevin N. STEPHENS
07 Director of Admissions/Registrar ... Mr. Austin BLAIR
08 Librarian ... Mr. William KOMANECKI
38 College Counselor ... Mrs. Victoria KAMHI
37 Coord Student Fin/Financial Assist ... Mrs. Nancy S. PERRYMAN
113 Coord Student Finance/Accts Rec ... Ms. Alice C. EVANS
04 Executive Assistant ... Ms. Luann MORELOCK
108 Inst Effectiveness/Assessment Spec ... Mr. Ryan A. WILLIAMS

St. John's College (H)

729 E. Carpenter Street, Springfield IL 62702-5317
County: Sangamon FICE Identification: 030980
Unit ID: 148593
Telephone: (217) 525-5628 Carnegie Class: Spec-4-yr-Other Health
FAX Number: (217) 757-6870 Calendar System: Semester
URL: www.sjcs.edu
Established: 1991 Annual Undergrad Tuition & Fees: N/A
Enrollment: 118 Coed
Affiliation or Control: Independent Non-Profit IRS Status: 501(c)3
Highest Offering: Doctorate
Accreditation: HLC, NUR

01 Chancellor ... Dr. Charlene S. AARON
05 Dean of Academic Affairs ... Dr. Judy SHACKELFORD
07 Admissions Officer/Registrar ... Vacant
37 Financial Aid/Compliance Officer ... Mr. Timothy MARTEN

Saint Xavier University (I)

3700 W 103rd Street, Chicago IL 60655-3105
County: Cook FICE Identification: 001768
Unit ID: 148627
Telephone: (773) 298-3000 Carnegie Class: Masters/L
FAX Number: (773) 779-9061 Calendar System: Semester
URL: www.sxu.edu
Established: 1846 Annual Undergrad Tuition & Fees: $34,730
Enrollment: 3,764 Coed
Affiliation or Control: Roman Catholic IRS Status: 501(c)3
Highest Offering: Master's
Accreditation: HLC, CAEPN, MUS, NURSE, SP

01 President ... Dr. Laurie M. JOYNER
05 Provost ... Dr. Saib OTHMAN
10 Vice Pres Finance/Admin & CFO ... Mr. Daniel P. KLOTZBACH
28 Chief Diversity Officer ... Dr. Natalie PAGE
09 Exec Dir Institutional Research ... Dr. Kathleen CARLSON
26 AVP Marketing/Communications ... Ms. Deb RAPACZ
111 AVP University Advancement ... Ms. Erin R. MUELLER
84 AVP Strategic Enroll/Stdnt Success ... Mr. Brian HOTZFIELD
32 Dean of Students ... Ms. Katy THOMPSON
41 Director of Athletics ... Mr. Matt CUNNINGHAM

13 Chief Information Officer ... Ms. Molly GAIK
18 Director of Facilities Management ... Mr. Peter SKACH
109 Director Auxiliary Services ... Ms. Linda MORENO
37 Exec Director Financial Aid ... Ms. Susan SWISHER
21 Controller ... Ms. Diane STALLMANN
114 Dir Fin Planning/Analysis ... Ms. Julie CUPP
24 Director CIDAT ... Ms. Yue MA
08 Int Director Library ... Mr. John MCDONALD
06 Exec Dir Records & Registration ... Ms. Peggy REHFELD
19 Dir Public Safety/Chief of Police ... Mr. Melvin CORNELIUS
85 Dir Center International Education ... Ms. Kelly REIDY-FOX
121 AVP SEM & Stu Success ... Ms. Alison CHANDLER
38 Director Counseling Center ... Dr. Keiana WINTERS
49 Int Dean Arts & Sciences ... Dr. Gina ROSSETTI
66 Dean Sch Nursing & Health Sci ... Dr. Gwen GEORGE
15 Director of Human Resources ... Mr. Gerry HORAN
29 Dir Alumni Relations/Advancement ... Ms. Jeanmarie GAINER
100 Chief of Staff ... Ms. Maggie EAHEART

Sauk Valley Community College (A)

173 Illinois Route 2, Dixon IL 61021-9188
County: Lee
FICE Identification: 001752
Unit ID: 148672
Telephone: (815) 288-5511
Carnegie Class: Assoc/MT-VT-High Non
FAX Number: (815) 288-1880
Calendar System: Semester
URL: www.svcc.edu
Established: 1965
Annual Undergrad Tuition & Fees (In-District): $11,588
Enrollment: 1,386
Coed
Affiliation or Control: State/Local
IRS Status: 501(c)3
Highest Offering: Associate Degree
Accreditation: HLC, ADNUR, PNUR, RAD

01 President ... Dr. David M. HELLMICH
05 Vice Pres Academics/Student Svcs ... Mr. Jon D. MANDRELL
76 Dean of Health Professions ... Ms. Christine L. VINCENT
10 VP of Business Services ... Mr. Kent A. SORENSON
18 Director Facilities ... Mr. Richard A. GROLEAU
15 Director of Human Resources ... Ms. Kathryn C. SNOW
84 Director Enrollment Mgmt/Registrar ... Ms. Pamela S. MEDEMA
111 Dean of Institutional Advancement ... Ms. Lori A. CORTEZ
41 Director of Athletics ... Mr. Michael P. STEVENSON
37 Director of Financial Assistance ... Ms. Jennifer A. SCHULTZ
13 Dean of Information Technology ... Ms. Kathleen M. DIRKS
04 Assistant to the President & Board ... Vacant

School of the Art Institute of Chicago (B)

37 S Wabash, Chicago IL 60603-3103
County: Cook
FICE Identification: 001753
Unit ID: 143048
Telephone: (312) 899-5100
Carnegie Class: Spec-4-yr-Arts
FAX Number: (312) 263-0141
Calendar System: Semester
URL: www.saic.edu
Established: 1866
Annual Undergrad Tuition & Fees: $53,160
Enrollment: 3,132
Coed
Affiliation or Control: Independent Non-Profit
IRS Status: 501(c)3
Highest Offering: Master's
Accreditation: HLC, ACATE

01 President ... Dr. Elissa TENNY
43 Exec Vice Pres/General Counsel ... Ms. Leslie DARLING
05 Provost & SVP of Academic Affairs ... Mr. Martin BERGER
84 Vice Pres Enrollment Management ... Ms. Rose MILKOWSKI
111 VP for Institutional Advancement ... Ms. Stephanie OBERHAUSEN
10 Vice President Finance ... Mr. Brian ESKER
15 Vice President for Human Resources ... Mr. Michael NICOLAI
32 Vice Pres/Dean of Student Affairs ... Dr. Felice DUBLON
20 Vice Provost/Dean Cmty Engagement ... Mr. Paul COFFEY
18 Vice Pres Campus Operations ... Mr. Thomas BUECHELE
20 Int Dean of Faculty/VP Acad Affs ... Ms. Shawn Michelle SMITH
35 Dean of Student Life ... Ms. Deborah MARTIN
21 Exec Dir Academic Accounting ... Vacant
26 Exec Dir Enroll Mktg & Operations ... Ms. Maryann SCHAEFER
29 Exec Director Alumni Relations ... Ms. Ashley SPELL
38 Exec Director Wellness Center ... Dr. Joseph BEHEN
88 Exec Director Enrollment Services ... Ms. Jane BRUMITT
06 Director Registration & Records ... Ms. Christy MICELI
08 Exec Director of School Library ... Ms. Claire EIKE
24 Exec Dir Media/Instruct Resources ... Mr. Craig DOWNS
36 Dean Career & Prof Experience ... Ms. Rosalie SHEMMER
07 Assoc Dir of Undergrad Admissions ... Vacant
123 Director of Graduate Admissions ... Ms. Nicole HALL
37 Director of Student Financial Svcs ... Mr. Patrick JAMES
28 Director of Multicultural Affairs ... Ms. Rashayla BROWN
88 Director of Learning Center ... Ms. Valerie ST. GERMAIN
49 Dean of Undergraduate Studies ... Ms. Tiffany HOLMES
58 Dean of Graduate Studies ... Mr. Arnold KEMP
28 Dir of Acad Affairs/Diversity/Incl ... Dr. Christina GOMEZ

Shawnee Community College (C)

8364 Shawnee College Road, Ullin IL 62992-2206
County: Pulaski
FICE Identification: 007693
Unit ID: 148821
Telephone: (618) 634-3200
Carnegie Class: Assoc/MT-VT-High Non
FAX Number: (618) 634-3300
Calendar System: Semester
URL: www.shawneecc.edu
Established: 1967
Annual Undergrad Tuition & Fees (In-District): $6,090
Enrollment: 1,176
Coed
Affiliation or Control: Local
IRS Status: 501(c)3
Highest Offering: Associate Degree
Accreditation: HLC, MLTAD, OTA, SURGT

01 President ... Dr. Tim TAYLOR
05 Vice President Academic Affairs ... Dr. Darci CATHER
32 VP Student Success & Services ... Dr. Lisa PRICE
11 VP of Administrative Services ... Mr. Chris CLARK
04 Administrative Asst to President ... Ms. Tina DUDLEY
88 Dean of Transfer ... Dr. Kristin SHELBY
103 Dean of Workforce ... Dr. Gregory MASON
38 Student Support Services Director ... Ms. Amber SUGGS
07 Director of Recruitment & Retention ... Dr. Cara DOERR
37 Fin Aid/Coord Vet & Mil Personl ... Dr. Tammy CAPPS
41 Athletic Director ... Mr. John SPARKS
13 Director of Information Technology ... Mr. Dwayne FEHRENBACHER
12 Metropolis Ext Center Coordinator ... Ms. Beth CROWE
76 Dean of Allied Health ... Ms. Amanda HANNAN
08 Librarian ... Ms. Cecilia KNIGHT
06 Registrar ... Ms. Danielle BOYD
10 Director of Business Services ... Ms. Brandy WOODS
18 Facilities Director ... Mr. Don KOCH
09 Director of Institutional Research ... Dr. April TESKE
40 Bookstore Manager ... Ms. Stacy SIMPSON
22 Director of Student Success ... Ms. Mindy ASHBY
88 Director Business & Economic Devel ... Ms. Lydia DOVER
26 Executive Dir of Public Info & Mktg ... Mr. Kevin HUNSPERGER
36 Career Services Coordinator ... Ms. Blake GOFORTH
50 Dept Chair Business/Occup/Tech Dp ... Ms. Ruth SMITH
81 Dept Chair Math/Science ... Ms. Lori ARMSTRONG
79 Detp Chair Humanities ... Ms. Joella BASLER
76 Dept Chair Allied Health ... Ms. Kayla SAUERBRUNN
15 Exec Director of Human Resources ... Ms. Emily FORTHMAN
24 Learning Resources Coordinator ... Mr. Russ STOUP
56 Dir Cmty Educ & Outreach Centers ... Ms. Lindsay JOHNSON
88 Education Talent Search Director ... Ms. Jipaum ASKEW

South Suburban College (D)

15800 S State Street, South Holland IL 60473-1270
County: Cook
FICE Identification: 001769
Unit ID: 149365
Telephone: (708) 596-2000
Carnegie Class: Assoc/HT-High Non
FAX Number: (708) 210-5710
Calendar System: Semester
URL: www.ssc.edu
Established: 1927
Annual Undergrad Tuition & Fees (In-District): $11,033
Enrollment: 3,366
Coed
Affiliation or Control: State/Local
IRS Status: 501(c)3
Highest Offering: Associate Degree
Accreditation: HLC, CVT, OTA

01 President ... Dr. Lynette D. STOKES
05 Vice President Academic Services ... Dr. Tasha WILLIAMS
11 Vice Pres Administration ... Mr. Pat RUSH
32 VP Student/Enrollment Services ... Dr. Deborah BANESS KING
35 Dean Student Services ... Ms. Devon POWELL
09 AVP Accreditation/Inst Effective ... Dr. Ronald KAWANNA, JR.
49 Dean Liberal Arts/Sciences ... Dr. Anna HELWIG
76 Dean Allied Health/Career Programs ... Dr. Omar SHERIFF
66 Dean Nursing ... Dr. Linda BROWN-ALDRIDGE
56 Dean Adult/Continuing Education ... Dr. Matthew BEASLAND
51 Director Continuing Education ... Ms. Shirley DREWENSKI
10 Treasurer/Controller ... Mr. Tim POLLERT
26 Exec Dir Public Rels/Resource Dev ... Mr. Patrick RUSH
13 Exec Dir Information Technology ... Mr. John MCCORMACK
89 Director Recruitment/Retention Svcs ... Ms. Tiffane JONES
37 Director of Financial Aid ... Ms. Kendra PERDUE-SMITH
18 Director Physical Plant Services ... Mr. Justin PAPP
27 Dir Communication Svcs/Media Design ... Mrs. Lisa MILLER
41 Athletic Director ... Mr. Steve RUZICH
09 Director of Institutional Research ... Dr. Kevin RIORDAN
15 Director Human Resources ... Ms. Kimberly PIGATTI
06 Director Registration/Records ... Ms. Tenial WHITTED
07 Director of Recruitment ... Ms. Tiffane JONES

Southeastern Illinois College (E)

3575 College Road, Harrisburg IL 62946-4925
County: Saline
FICE Identification: 001757
Unit ID: 148937
Telephone: (618) 252-5400
Carnegie Class: Assoc/HVT-High Non
FAX Number: (618) 252-3156
Calendar System: Semester
URL: www.sic.edu
Established: 1960
Annual Undergrad Tuition & Fees (In-District): $6,060
Enrollment: 1,263
Coed
Affiliation or Control: State/Local
IRS Status: 501(c)3
Highest Offering: Associate Degree
Accreditation: HLC, ADNUR

01 President ... Dr. Jonah RICE
05 Vice President Instruction ... Dr. Karen WEISS
10 Exec Dean Administration/Bus Affs ... Ms. Lisa HITE
20 Exec Dean of Academic Services ... Dr. Tyler BILLMAN
32 Exec Dean Student Services ... Mrs. Kyla BURFORD
103 Assoc Dean Workforce & Cmty Educ ... Mrs. Lori COX
08 Assoc Dean of Learning Commons ... Ms. Karla LEWIS
84 Assoc Dir Enrollment Svcs/Registrar ... Mrs. Tiffany BRANNOCK
26 Exec Dir Marketing/Public Relations ... Ms. Angela WILSON
37 Financial Aid Director ... Ms. Michelle METTEN
13 Chief Information Officer ... Mr. Greg MCCULLOCH
76 Director Allied Health & Nursing ... Ms. Amy MURPHY
04 Exec Asst to President ... Mrs. Amanda PAYNE
18 Director of Environmental Services ... Mr. Ed FITZGERALD
15 Director of Human Resources ... Mrs. Sky FOWLER
09 Exec Dean Inst Effectiveness ... Mr. Chris BARR
28 Dir Bus Svcs/Coord of Diversity ... Ms. Erica GRIFFIN
41 Athletic Director ... Mr. Jeremy IRLBECK

*Southern Illinois University System (F)

Stone Center - 1400 Douglas Drive, Carbondale IL 62901
County: Jackson
FICE Identification: 008237
Unit ID: 149240
Telephone: (618) 536-3331
Carnegie Class: N/A
FAX Number: (618) 536-3404
URL: www.siusystem.edu

01 President ... Dr. Daniel F. MAHONY
05 VP Academic Innov/Planning/Partshp ... Dr. Gireesh GUPCHUP
10 SVP Fin/Admin Affs/Bd Treasurer ... Dr. Duane STUCKY
86 Exec Dir Governmental/Public Affs ... Mr. John CHARLES
116 Exec Dir of Internal Audits ... Ms. Kim LABONTE
43 General Counsel ... Mr. Lucas CRATER
04 Assistant to the President ... Ms. Paula S. KEITH
28 VP ADEI/Chief Diversity Officer ... Dr. Sheila CALDWELL

*Southern Illinois University Carbondale (G)

1265 Lincoln Drive, Carbondale IL 62901-6899
County: Jackson
FICE Identification: 001758
Unit ID: 149222
Telephone: (618) 453-2121
Carnegie Class: DU-Higher
FAX Number: (618) 453-3250
Calendar System: Semester
URL: siu.edu
Established: 1869
Annual Undergrad Tuition & Fees (In-State): $15,104
Enrollment: 11,366
Coed
Affiliation or Control: State
IRS Status: 501(c)3
Highest Offering: Doctorate
Accreditation: HLC, AAB, ABAI, ACPHA, ARCPA, ART, CAEP, CEA, CIDA, CLPSY, COPSY, DH, DIETD, DIETI, DMS, FUSER, IFSAC, IPSY, LAW, MED, MUS, NAIT, NURSE, PH, PTAA, RAD, RADDOS, RADMAG, RTT, SP, SPAA, SW, THEA

02 Chancellor ... Dr. Austin A. LANE
05 Provost/Vice Chanc Acad Affs ... Dr. Meera KOMARRAJU
32 Dean of Students ... Ms. Jennifer L. JONES-HALL
30 Assoc VC Development/Alumni Rels ... Mr. Jeffrey GLEIM
46 VC for Research ... Dr. Costas TSATSOULIS
10 Int Vice Chanc Admin & Finance ... Ms. Julie MCREYNOLDS
28 VC for Anti-Racism/Div/Eqty/Inc ... Dr. Paul FRAZIER
102 CFO SIU Foundation ... Ms. Cynthia CIGANOVICH
13 Interim Chief Info Officer ... Mr. Wil CLARK
84 Assoc Chancellor for Enrollment Mgt ... Mr. Wendell WILLIAMS
20 Int Assoc Provost for Acad Pgms ... Dr. Andrew YOUPA
100 Chief of Staff ... Mr. Matthew BAUGHMAN
49 Dean Liberal Arts ... Dr. Joddy MURRAY
50 Dean College of Business ... Dr. Terry CLARK
53 Dean School of Education ... Dr. M. Cecil SMITH
54 Dean College of Engineering ... Dr. Xiaoqing LIU
58 Assoc Dean/Dir of Grad School ... Dr. Stephen C. SHIH
61 Dean School of Law ... Dr. Camille DAVIDSON
63 Dean School of Medicine/Provost ... Dr. Jerry E. KRUSE
47 Dean College of Agriculture ... Dr. Eric BREVIK
76 Dean Health & Human Sciences ... Dr. Robert MORGAN
60 Interim Dean Arts and Media ... Mr. Olusegun OJEWUYI
08 Dean Library Affairs ... Mr. John H. POLLITZ
37 Interim Director Financial Aid ... Ms. Elyse WELLER
09 Director Institutional Research ... Mr. Wil CLARK
26 Chief Marketing & Comm Officer ... Mr. James POTTER
15 Int Director Human Resources ... Ms. Renee COLOMBO
39 Director University Housing ... Mr. Jon L. SHAFFER
85 Int Director International Educ ... Mr. Samuel BANDY
18 Director Facilities and Energy Mgmt ... Mr. Mark OWENS
19 Director of Public Safety ... Mr. Benjamin NEWMAN
23 Director Student Health Services ... Dr. Jamie CLARK
41 Int Intercollegiate Athletic Dir ... Mr. Matthew KUPEC
106 Int Exec Director Extended Campus ... Dr. Julie DUNSTON
06 Int Director Registrar's Office ... Ms. Rachel FRAZIER
38 Dir Student Counseling Center ... Dr. Jaime CLARK
96 Director Procurement Services ... Ms. Susan ZAMORA

*Southern Illinois University Edwardsville (H)

State Route 157, Edwardsville IL 62026
County: Madison
FICE Identification: 001759
Unit ID: 149231
Telephone: (618) 650-2000
Carnegie Class: DU-Mod
FAX Number: (618) 650-2270
Calendar System: Semester
URL: www.siue.edu
Established: 1957
Annual Undergrad Tuition & Fees (In-State): $12,219
Enrollment: 12,860
Coed
Affiliation or Control: State
IRS Status: 501(c)3
Highest Offering: Doctorate
Accreditation: HLC, ACATE, ANEST, ART, CAEPN, CAHIIM, CONST, DENT, @DIETC, EXSC, JOUR, MUS, NURSE, PH, PHAR, SP, SPAA, SW, THEA

02 Chancellor ... Dr. James T. MINOR
05 Provost/VC for Academic Affairs ... Dr. P. Denise COBB
10 Vice Chancellor for Admin ... Dr. Morris TAYLOR
111 VC Univ Adv & CEO SIUE Foundation ... Ms. Cathy TAYLOR
32 Vice Chanc for Student Affairs ... Dr. Jeffrey N. WAPLE
22 Equal Opp/Access & Title IX ... Ms. Jamie BALL
58 Assoc Prov Rsch/Dean Grad Sch ... Dr. Jerry B. WEINBERG

35 Dean of Students ... Vacant
13 Assoc VC for IT & CIO ... Mr. Steven HUFFSTUTLER
28 VC Equity/Diversity & Inclusion ... Dr. Jessica HARRIS
41 Director of Athletics ... Mr. Tim HALL
84 Assoc VC for Enrollment Management ... Dr. Scott BELOBRAJDIC
49 Dean College of Arts & Sciences ... Dr. Kevin LEONARD
50 Dean School of Business ... Dr. Timothy SCHOENECKER
52 Dean School of Dental Medicine ... Dr. Duane DOUGLAS
53 Dean Sch of Educ/Hlth & Hum Behav ... Dr. Robin HUGHES
54 Dean School of Engineering ... Dr. Cem KARACAL
66 Dean School of Nursing ... Vacant
67 Dean School of Pharmacy ... Dr. Mark S. LUER
08 Dean Library & Info Services ... Dr. Eric RUCKH
114 Budget Director ... Mr. William F. WINTER, JR.
26 Exec Dir Univ Marketing & Comm ... Vacant
88 Dir Grant Funded Pgm East StL Ctr ... Dr. Tim STAPLES
124 Dir Retention & Student Success ... Vacant
07 Director Undergraduate Admissions ... Mr. Todd C. BURRELL
29 Dir Constituent Rel & Special Proj ... Ms. Cathy N. TAYLOR
36 Director Career Development Center ... Ms. Susan SEIBERT
38 Director Counseling Services ... Vacant
18 Director Facilities Management ... Mr. Craig HOLAN
23 Director Health Service ... Ms. Riane B. GREENWALT
15 Director Human Resources ... Vacant
09 Dir Institutional Research/Studies ... Mr. Phillip M. BROWN
85 Exec Director International Affairs ... Dr. Mary WEISHAAR
96 Director of Purchasing ... Mr. Matthew BROWN
37 Director Student Financial Aid ... Ms. Mesha GARNER
39 Director University Housing ... Ms. Mallory SIDAROUS
19 Director University Police ... Mr. Kevin SCHMOLL
06 Registrar ... Ms. Laura A. STROM

* *Southern Illinois University Carbondale School of Medicine* (A)

PO Box 19620, Springfield IL 62794-9620
Telephone: (217) 545-8000 Identification: 770181
Accreditation: &HLC

Southwestern Illinois College (B)

2500 Carlyle Avenue, Belleville IL 62221-5899
County: Saint Clair FICE Identification: 001636
Unit ID: 143215
Telephone: (618) 235-2700 Carnegie Class: Assoc/MT-VT-High Non
FAX Number: (618) 277-0631 Calendar System: Semester
URL: www.swic.edu
Established: 1946 Annual Undergrad Tuition & Fees (In-District): $6,390
Enrollment: 6,906 Coed
Affiliation or Control: State/Local IRS Status: 501(c)3
Highest Offering: Associate Degree
Accreditation: HLC, ADNUR, CAHIIM, COARC, EMT, MAC, MLTAD, PTAA, RAD

01 President - District ... Mr. Nick J. MANCE
11 Chief Administrative Svcs Officer ... Mr. Bernie J. YSURSA, JR.
05 Chief Academic Officer ... Dr. Gina L. SEGOBIANO
15 Chief HR & Operations Officer ... Vacant
10 CFO/Board Treasurer ... Ms. Missy ROCHE
32 Chief Student Services Officer ... Ms. Danielle CHAMBERS
84 Exec Dir Enrollment Dev/Planning ... Mr. Robert TEBBE
13 Executive Director of IT ... Ms. Linda ANDRES
96 Director of Purchasing ... Mr. Mike R. THOMAS
49 Acting Dean Liberal Arts ... Dr. Ashley BECKER
81 Dean Math & Sciences ... Dr. Kimberly CHERRY-VOGT
50 Dean Business/Health/Homeland Sec ... Dr. Ashley BECKER
72 Dean Technical Ed & Workplace Dev ... Mr. Brad SPARKS
51 Director of Adult Education ... Ms. Mereadith SHIVERS
35 Associate Director Student Services ... Ms. Annjanee JONES
08 Librarian ... Ms. Jennifer BONE
100 Chief of Staff/Board Secretary ... Ms. Beverly J. FISS
102 Executive Director Foundation ... Ms. Rena THOELE
26 Communications Specialist/Assoc Dir ... Mr. Jim HAVERSTICK
37 Int Director Student Financial Aid ... Mr. Christopher MELVIN
41 Athletic Director ... Mr. Mike JUENGER
09 Compliance Officer ... Mr. Jeffrey EBEL
113 Director of Student Finance ... Ms. Myki RHODES

Spertus Institute for Jewish Learning and Leadership (C)

610 S Michigan Avenue, Chicago IL 60605
County: Cook FICE Identification: 001663
Unit ID: 148982
Telephone: (312) 322-1700 Carnegie Class: Spec-4-yr-Faith
FAX Number: (312) 922-6406 Calendar System: Quarter
URL: www.spertus.edu
Established: 1924 Annual Graduate Tuition & Fees: N/A
Enrollment: 117 Coed
Affiliation or Control: Independent Non-Profit IRS Status: 501(c)3
Highest Offering: Doctorate; No Undergraduates
Accreditation: HLC

01 President and CEO ... Dr. Dean P. BELL
05 Dean and Chief Academic Officer ... Dr. Keren FRAIMAN
10 Controller ... Mr. Doug PETERSON
37 Financial Aid Manager ... Ms. Judith WOOD
26 Dir Marketing & Communications ... Ms. Betsy GOMBERG
06 Registrar ... Ms. Victoria BLUM
18 Director of Operations ... Mr. Phil THOMPSON
15 Manager of Human Resources ... Ms. Lucia KELLEY

Spoon River College (D)

23235 N County Road 22, Canton IL 61520-9801
County: Fulton FICE Identification: 001643
Unit ID: 148991
Telephone: (309) 647-4645 Carnegie Class: Assoc/MT-VT-Mix Trad/Non
FAX Number: (309) 649-6235 Calendar System: Semester
URL: www.src.edu
Established: 1959 Annual Undergrad Tuition & Fees (In-District): $10,590
Enrollment: 1,239 Coed
Affiliation or Control: Local IRS Status: 501(c)3
Highest Offering: Associate Degree
Accreditation: HLC, ADNUR

01 President ... Mr. Curt OLDFIELD
05 Dean Instruction ... Ms. Holly NORTON
11 Vice President ... Mr. Brett STOLLER
04 Executive Asst to the President ... Ms. Julie HAMPTON
75 Dean Career & Technical Education ... Mr. Brad O'BRIEN
32 Dean Student Services ... Ms. Missy WILKINSON
66 Director Nursing ... Ms. Tamatha SCHLEICH
06 Dir of Records & Admissions ... Ms. Melissa WILKINSON
18 Director Facilities ... Mr. Bob A. HAILE
55 Dir Adult and Outreach Education ... Mr. Chad MURPHY
08 Librarian ... Ms. Jeannette GLOVER
13 Chief Information Officer ... Mr. Raj SIDDARAJU
41 Director Athletics/Student Life ... Mr. John BASSETT
109 Director Business & Auxil Services ... Ms. Sarah GRAY
37 Director Financial Aid ... Ms. Salinda Jo BRANSON
15 Director Human Resources ... Ms. Andrea THOMSON
14 Director Technology Services ... Mr. Dean CLARY
84 Director Enrollment Services ... Ms. Janet MUNSON
09 Coord Institutional Reporting ... Mr. Lucas BUCHEN
26 Director Marketing ... Ms. Sherri RADER
27 Coordinator Public Information ... Ms. Sally SHIELDS
102 Director Foundation ... Mr. Colin DAVIS

Taylor Business Institute (E)

180 N. Wabash Avenue, Ste. 500, Chicago IL 60601
County: Cook FICE Identification: 011810
Unit ID: 149310
Telephone: (312) 658-5100 Carnegie Class: Assoc/HVT-Mix Trad/Non
FAX Number: (312) 658-0867 Calendar System: Quarter
URL: www.tbiil.edu
Established: 1962 Annual Undergrad Tuition & Fees: $10,650
Enrollment: 100 Coed
Affiliation or Control: Proprietary IRS Status: Proprietary
Highest Offering: Associate Degree
Accreditation: HLC

01 President/CEO ... Janice C. PARKER
05 Dean/Chief Academic Officer ... Rakesh KUMAR
03 Executive Vice President ... Franklin PARKER
04 Admin Assistant to the President ... Gabriela OCHOA
06 Registrar ... Lena YOUNG
08 Chief Library Officer ... Michelle KOPTEROS
10 Chief Financial/Business Officer ... Kathy LI
13 Chief Information Technology Ofcr ... Antonio VARGAS
37 Director Student Financial Aid ... Florence DAVIS

Telshe Yeshiva-Chicago (F)

3535 W Foster Avenue, Chicago IL 60625-5598
County: Cook FICE Identification: 020732
Unit ID: 149329
Telephone: (773) 463-7738 Carnegie Class: Not Classified
FAX Number: (773) 463-2849 Calendar System: Semester
URL: https://telsheyeshivachicago.com/
Established: 1960 Annual Undergrad Tuition & Fees: $14,500
Enrollment: 94 Male
Affiliation or Control: Independent Non-Profit IRS Status: 501(c)3
Highest Offering: Second Talmudic Degree
Accreditation: RABN

01 President ... Rabbi Ephraim M. LEVIN
03 Executive Vice President ... Rabbi Yitzchok LEVIN
05 Associate Dean ... Rabbi Moshe SCHMELCZER
11 Administrative Director/Secretary ... Rabbi Shaya HOUPHMAN

Toyota Technological Institute at Chicago (G)

6045 South Kenwood Avenue, Chicago IL 60637
County: Cook Identification: 666367
Unit ID: 445054
Telephone: (773) 834-2500 Carnegie Class: Spec-4-yr-Other Tech
FAX Number: (773) 834-9881 Calendar System: Quarter
URL: www.ttic.edu
Established: 2003 Annual Graduate Tuition & Fees: N/A
Enrollment: 43 Coed
Affiliation or Control: Independent Non-Profit IRS Status: 501(c)3
Highest Offering: Doctorate; No Undergraduates
Accreditation: HLC

01 President ... Dr. Matthew TURK
10 Chief Financial Officer ... Ms. Jessica JACOBSON
58 Admin Director of Graduate Studies ... Ms. Chrissy COLEMAN
15 Dir HR/International Affs ... Ms. Amy MINICK

Trinity Christian College (H)

6601 W College Drive, Palos Heights IL 60463-0929
County: Cook FICE Identification: 001771
Unit ID: 149505
Telephone: (708) 597-3000 Carnegie Class: Bac-Diverse
FAX Number: (708) 239-4826 Calendar System: Semester
URL: www.trnty.edu
Established: 1959 Annual Undergrad Tuition & Fees: $32,075
Enrollment: 1,086 Coed
Affiliation or Control: Independent Non-Profit IRS Status: 501(c)3
Highest Offering: Master's
Accreditation: HLC, ACBSP, NURSE, SW

01 President ... Mr. Kurt D. DYKSTRA
05 Provost ... Dr. Aaron KUECKER
10 Vice Pres for Finance ... Mr. Michael S. TROCHUCK
32 Vice Pres for Student Life ... Mrs. Rebekah L. STARKENBURG
26 Vice Pres for Comm & Strategic Init ... Mr. Paul BOICE
111 Vice Pres for Advancement ... Vacant
110 Assoc VP for Advancement ... Mr. Dennis HARMS
42 Chaplain ... Vacant
08 Director of Library Services ... Mr. Kyle MCCARRELL
15 Director of Human Resources ... Ms. Julia FOUST
06 Registrar ... Ms. Jaynn TOBIAS-JOHNSON
09 Asst Registrar for Inst Research ... Ms. Kimberly WILLIAMS
21 Controller ... Mrs. Ashleigh VELASQUEZ
36 Director of Career Development ... Mr. Jeff TIMMER
29 Director of Alumni Relations ... Mr. Jeremy KLYN
19 Director Security/Safety ... Mr. Tom KAZEN
13 Director of Technology Systems ... Mr. Kevin JACOBS
14 Director of Technology Support ... Mr. Doug VAN WYNGARDEN
41 AVP Student LIfe/Dir of Athletics ... Mr. Mark HANNA
28 Dir of Multicultural Engagement ... Mrs. Nicole SAINT-VICTOR
85 Director of Off-Campus Programs ... Ms. Maria HODAPP
37 Director Financial Aid ... Mr. Michael SHIELDS
18 Director of Building/Grounds ... Mr. Tim TIMMONS
112 Director of Planned Giving ... Mr. Jeff ENFIELD
92 Director of Honors Program ... Dr. Craig MATTSON
38 Director of Counseling Services ... Dr. Stephanie GRISWOLD
04 Executive Assistant to President ... Ms. Deborah S. VINCENT
88 Senior Graphic Designer ... Ms. Jyne KING
105 Web Developer ... Ms. Diane BRUNSTING
50 Department Chair of Business ... Dr. Deborah L. WINDES
07 Assoc Dir Admissions Adult & Grad ... Mrs. Alexis HENDERSON

Trinity College of Nursing & Health Sciences (I)

2122 25th Avenue, Rock Island IL 61201-5317
County: Rock Island FICE Identification: 006225
Unit ID: 146755
Telephone: (309) 779-7700 Carnegie Class: Spec-4-yr-Other Health
FAX Number: (309) 779-7748 Calendar System: Semester
URL: www.trinitycollegeqc.edu
Established: 1994 Annual Undergrad Tuition & Fees: $28,244
Enrollment: 206 Coed
Affiliation or Control: Independent Non-Profit IRS Status: 501(c)3
Highest Offering: Master's
Accreditation: HLC, NURSE, RAD

01 Chancellor ... Dr. Tracy L. POELVOORDE
05 Dean of Nursing & Health Sciences ... Dr. Teresa WISCHMANN
10 Director of Business Services ... Ms. Rosemary BROWER
32 Director of Student Services ... Ms. Hilary HENKE
06 Registrar ... Ms. Cara BANKS

Trinity International University (J)

2065 Half Day Road, Deerfield IL 60015-1284
County: Lake FICE Identification: 001772
Unit ID: 149514
Telephone: (847) 945-8800 Carnegie Class: DU-Mod
FAX Number: (847) 317-7009 Calendar System: Semester
URL: www.tiu.edu
Established: 1897 Annual Undergrad Tuition & Fees: $33,298
Enrollment: 1,454 Coed
Affiliation or Control: Evangelical Free Church Of America
IRS Status: 501(c)3
Highest Offering: Doctorate
Accreditation: HLC, CACREP, THEOL

01 President ... Dr. Nicholas PERRIN
13 Chief Operating Officer/CIO ... Mr. Mike PETERSON
73 VP Education/Dean TEDS ... Dr. David PAO
05 Dean Trinity Col/Trinity Grad Sch ... Dr. Karen WROBBEL
61 Interim Dean of Law School ... Mr. Eric HALVORSON
88 VP Strategic Partnerships ... Ms. Amanda ONAPITO
32 VP for Student Life ... Mr. Mark MUHA
10 Chief Financial Officer ... Mr. Paul EISENMENGER
07 VP for Admissions ... Ms. Shawn WYNNE
18 AVP Facility & Event Services ... Ms. Julie WONG
30 AVP Advancement/University Rels ... Mr. Garrett LUCK
111 Interim VP University Advancement ... Mr. Dwight GIBSON
26 Director of Marketing/Communication ... Mr. Chris DONATO
90 Director of Acad/Desktop Computing ... Mr. Chris MILLER
21 Director of Business Services ... Mr. Jerry RUSCITTI
91 Director Administrative Computing ... Ms. Katie KEMP
19 Director of Security Services ... Mr. Aron FORCH
15 Director of Human Resources ... Ms. Dawn GREENE
06 University Registrar ... Mr. James ULRICH

08 Int Director Library Svcs ....Mr. Nathan THEBARGE
92 Director of Honors Program ....Dr. Joshua HELD
38 Director Student Care & Engagement ....Ms. Mary GUTHRIE
04 Exec Assistant to the President ....Vacant
41 Athletic Director ....Mr. Luke WARD
09 Director of Institutional Research ....Vacant

Triton College   (A)

2000 Fifth Avenue, River Grove IL 60171-1995
County: Cook   FICE Identification: 001773
                                         Unit ID: 149532
Telephone: (708) 456-0300   Carnegie Class: Assoc/MT-VT-High Non
FAX Number: (708) 583-3112   Calendar System: Semester
URL: www.triton.edu
Established: 1964   Annual Undergrad Tuition & Fees (In-District): $10,890
Enrollment: 8,819   Coed
Affiliation or Control: Local   IRS Status: 501(c)3
Highest Offering: Associate Degree
Accreditation: HLC, ACBSP, ADNUR, DMS, MAC, RAD, SURGT

01 President ....Ms. Mary-Rita MOORE
05 Vice President Academic Affairs ....Dr. Susan CAMPOS
84 Vice Pres Enroll Mgmt/Student Affs ..Dr. Jodi KOSLOW MARTIN
10 Vice President Business Services ....Mr. Sean SULLIVAN
26 Assoc VP Comm & Inst Advancement ....Vacant
101 Secretary for Brd of Trustees ....Ms. Susan PAGE
13 Assoc VP Information Systems ....Mr. Michael GARRITY
41 AVP Athletics/Athletic Activities ....Mr. Garrick ABEZETIAN
18 Assoc VP of Facilities ....Mr. John LAMBRECHT
15 Assoc VP Human Resources ....Mr. Joe KLINGER
20 Assoc VP Academic Innov Workforce ....Mr. Paul JENSEN
32 Dean of Students ....Vacant
124 Dean of Retention/Stdnt Engagement ....Ms. Denise JONES
49 Dean of Arts & Sciences ....Vacant
72 Dean of Business & Technology ....Dr. Jennifer DAVIDSON
51 Dean of Continuing Education ....Dr. Bianca SOLA-PERKINS
121 Dean of Academic Success ....Ms. Hilary MEYER
55 Dean of Adult Education ....Ms. Jacqueline LYNCH
07 Assoc Dean of Enrollment Services ....Ms. Patricia ZINGA
21 Executive Director of Finance ....Mr. James REYNOLDS
27 Executive Director of Marketing ....Mr. Sam TOLIA
09 Executive Director of Research ....Dr. Kurian THARAKUNNEL
25 Exec Dir Grants Development ....Vacant
86 Director Public Affairs ....Vacant
88 Special Assistant to the President ....Ms. Brenda WATKINS
04 Admin Assistant to the President ....Vacant
19 Police Chief ....Mr. Austin WEINSTOCK
45 Exec Dir Strategic Plng & Accred ....Dr. Purva RUSHI

University of Chicago   (B)

5801 S Ellis Avenue, Chicago IL 60637-1496
County: Cook   FICE Identification: 001774
                                         Unit ID: 144050
Telephone: (773) 702-1234   Carnegie Class: DU-Highest
FAX Number: N/A   Calendar System: Quarter
URL: www.uchicago.edu
Established: 1890   Annual Undergrad Tuition & Fees: $60,552
Enrollment: 17,834   Coed
Affiliation or Control: Independent Non-Profit   IRS Status: 501(c)3
Highest Offering: Doctorate
Accreditation: HLC, CAMPEP, IPSY, LAW, MED, SW, THEOL

01 President ....Paul ALIVISATOS
100 Executive VP & Chief of Staff ....Katie CALLOW-WRIGHT
05 Provost ....Ka Yee C. LEE
17 EVP for Medical Affairs/Dean of BSD ....Kenneth S. POLONSKY
88 EVP Science/Innovation/Strategy ....Balaji SRINIVASAN
10 Int VP/Chief Financial Officer ....Brett PADGETT
43 Vice President & General Counsel ....Kim TAYLOR
88 VP for National Laboratories ....Juan DE PABLO
26 Vice Pres for Communications ....Paul M. RAND
84 VP Enrollment/Stdnt Advancement ....James G. NONDORF
45 VP for Strategic Initiatives ....Darren REISBERG
29 VP for Alumni Rels & Development ....Sharon MARINE
86 VP for Civic Engagement/Ext Affairs ....Derek DOUGLAS
115 Int Vice Pres/Chief Investment Ofcr ....Patrick O'HARA
20 Vice Provost for Acad Affairs ....Jason MERCHANT
20 Vice Provost ....Daniel ABEBE
20 Vice Provost ....Michael HOPKINS
20 Vice Provost ....Melina HALE
46 Vice Provost for Research ....Vacant
28 Vice Provost ....Melissa GILLIAM
13 AVP/Chief Information Officer ....Kevin BOYD
22 Assoc Prov Equal Opportunity Pgms ....Bridget COLLIER
54 Dean of Molecular Engineering ....Matthew TIRRELL
83 Dean Division of Social Sciences ....Amanda WOODWARD
73 Int Dean of Divinity School ....David NIRENBERG
80 Dean Harris Sch of Public Policy ....Katherine BAICKER
51 Dean of Graham School Cont Educ ....Emily Lynn OSBORN
63 Dean Medicine ....Kenneth POLONSKY
79 Dean of Humanities Division ....Anne ROBERTSON
70 Dean Sch of Social Svcs Admin ....Deborah GORMAN-SMITH
61 Dean of the Law School ....Thomas MILES
50 Dean of Booth School of Business ....Madhav V. RAJAN
49 Dean of the College ....John W. BOYER
65 Dean Physical Sciences Division ....Angela V. OLINTO
42 Dean Rockefeller Memorial Chapel ....Maurice CHARLES
32 Dean of Students in University ....Michele RASMUSSEN
37 Senior Exec Director University Aid ....Amanda FIJAL
06 AVP/Registrar ....Scott CAMPBELL
57 Executive Director of UChicago Arts ....Bill MICHEL
88 Director of Oriental Institute ....Christopher WOODS

*University of Illinois System   (C)

506 S Wright Street, 364 HAB, Urbana IL 61801
County: Champaign   FICE Identification: 008001
                                         Unit ID: 149587
Telephone: (217) 333-3070   Carnegie Class: N/A
FAX Number: N/A
URL: www.uillinois.edu

01 President ....Dr. Timothy L. KILLEEN
12 Chancellor/Vice President (Chicago) ....Dr. Michael AMIRIDIS
12 Chancellor/Vice President (Sprgfld) ....Dr. Karen WHITNEY
12 Chancellor/Vice President (Urbana) ....Dr. Robert J. JONES
10 VP & Chief Financial Officer ....Mr. Avijit GHOSH
05 Int Exec Vice Pres and VPAA ....Mr. Avijit GHOSH
45 VP Economic Development/Innovation ....Dr. Jay WALSH
43 University Counsel ....Mr. Thomas R. BEARROWS
26 Int Dir for Univ Relations ....Ms. Kirsten A. RUBY
13 CIO & Sr Assoc VP ....Mr. Kelly J. BLOCK
15 Assoc VP Human Resources ....Ms. Jami PAINTER
101 Secretary Board of Trustees/Univ ....Mr. Greg KNOTT
102 President/CEO Univ Foundation ....Mr. James H. MOORE, JR.
29 Pres UIAA/Assoc VC for Alumni Rel ......Ms. Jennifer NEUBAUER
04 Admin Assistant to the President ....Ms. Kathy J. FOGERSON

*University of Illinois at Chicago   (D)

601 S Morgan, M/C 102, Chicago IL 60607-7128
County: Cook   FICE Identification: 001776
                                         Unit ID: 145600
Telephone: (312) 996-7000   Carnegie Class: DU-Highest
FAX Number: (312) 413-3393   Calendar System: Semester
URL: www.uic.edu
Established: 1896   Annual Undergrad Tuition & Fees (In-State): $14,098
Enrollment: 33,518   Coed
Affiliation or Control: State   IRS Status: 501(c)3
Highest Offering: Doctorate
Accreditation: HLC, ATECH, CAHIIM, CEA, CLPSY, DENT, DIETC, DIETD,
FEPAC, HSA, IPSY, MED, MIDWF, MIL, NURSE, OT, PH, PHAR, PLNG, PTA,
SPAA, SW

02 Interim Chancellor ....Dr. Javier REYES
05 Acting Provost/VC Academic Affairs ....Dr. Karen COLLEY
32 Vice Chancellor Student Affairs ....Mr. J. Rex TOLLIVER
11 Vice Chanc for Admin Svcs ....Mr. John CORONADO
46 Vice Chancellor for Research ....Dr. Joanna GRODEN
26 VC Chanc Strategic Marketing/
     Comm ....Ms. Chandra HARRIS-MCCRAY
17 CEO Hospital Administration ....Dr. Michael ZENN
29 Exec Director Alumni Engagement ....Ms. Caryn KORMAN
111 Vice Chanc for Advancement ....Mr. Thomas WAMSLEY
84 Vice Prov Acad/Enrollment Svcs ....Mr. Kevin BROWNE
20 Vice Provost for Faculty Affairs ....Dr. Nancy FREITAG
20 Vice Prov Undergrad Affairs ....Dr. Nikos VARELAS
88 Vice Provost for Global Engagement ....Dr. Neal R. MCCRILLIS
114 Vice Chanc for Budget/HR/Fin Admin ....Ms. Janet PARKER
35 Assoc Vice Chanc/Dean Student Affs ....Dr. Linda DEANNA
27 Senior Exec Director Public
     Affairs ....Ms. Sherri MCGINNIS GONZALEZ
23 Vice Chancellor Health Affairs ....Dr. Robert BARISH
10 Asst VP Business Svcs ....Ms. Gloria KEELEY
48 Dean Col of Arch/Design/Arts ....Dr. Rebecca RUGG
50 Dean College of Business Admin ....Dr. Michael B. MIKHAIL
52 Dean College of Dentistry ....Dr. Clark STANFORD
53 Dean College of Education ....Vacant
54 Dean College of Engineering ....Dr. Peter C. NELSON
76 Dean Col Applied Health Sciences ....Dr. Bo FERNHALL
58 Dean Graduate College ....Dr. Karen COLLEY
92 Dean Honors College ....Dr. Ralph KEEN
49 Dean College Liberal Arts/Sciences ....Dr. Astrida O. TANTILLO
63 Exec Dean College of Medicine ....Dr. Mark ROSENBLATT
66 Dean College of Nursing ....Dr. Terri E. WEAVER
67 Dean College of Pharmacy ....Dr. Glen SCHUMOCK
70 Dean College of Social Work ....Dr. Creasie HAIRSTON
69 Dean School of Public Health ....Dr. Wayne GILES
80 Dean Urban Planning/Public Affairs ......Dr. Michael A. PAGANO
43 University Counsel ....Mr. Thomas R. BEARROWS
08 University Librarian ....Ms. Mary CASE
88 Asst Univ Librarian Health Sciences .Ms. Kathryn H. CARPENTER
07 Sr Assoc Director Admissions ....Ms. Lauren B. MORRIS
41 Director Athletics ....Mr. Michael LIPITZ
38 Director Counseling Services ....Dr. Joseph HERMES
39 Director of Campus Housing ....Ms. Susan TEGGATZ
37 Director Financial Aid ....Ms. Kiely FLETCHER
09 Director of Institutional Research ....Mr. William C. HAYWARD
16 Assoc Vice Provost Faculty Affairs ....Ms. Angela L. YUDT
22 Director Access/Equity ....Ms. Caryn A. BILLS-WINDT
36 Director Career Services ....Vacant
13 CIO/Exec Dir Acad
     Computing ....Ms. Cynthia E. HERRERA LINDSTROM
56 Asst Vice Chanc Extended Campus ....Ms. Dara CROWFOOT
06 Registrar ....Mr. Robert DIXON
96 Director of Purchasing ....Ms. Debra MATLOCK
18 Exec Dir Operations/Maintenance ....Mr. Clarence F. BRIDGES
28 Vice Chanc Diversity/Equity/Engage ....Dr. Amalia PALLARES
100 Associate Provost/Chief of Staff ....Dr. Aisha EL-AMIN
104 Executive Director of Study Abroad ....Vacant
88 Vice Chancellor for Innovation ....Dr. TJ AUGUSTINE

*University of Illinois Springfield   (E)

One University Plaza, Springfield IL 62703-5407
County: Sangamon   FICE Identification: 009333
                                         Unit ID: 148654
Telephone: (217) 206-6600   Carnegie Class: Masters/L
FAX Number: (217) 206-6511   Calendar System: Semester
URL: www.uis.edu
Established: 1969   Annual Undergrad Tuition & Fees (In-State): $11,911
Enrollment: 4,146   Coed
Affiliation or Control: State   IRS Status: 501(c)3
Highest Offering: Doctorate
Accreditation: HLC, CAATE, CACREP, MLS, SPAA, SW

02 Interim Chancellor ....Dr. Karen WHITNEY
05 Vice Chancellor Acad Affs/Provost ....Dr. Dennis PAPINI
32 Int Vice Chancellor Student Affairs ....Ms. Ann COMERFORD
10 Interim Vice Chanc Finance/Admin ....Mr. Arnold HENNING
20 Int Assoc Vice Chanc Undergrad Educ ....Dr. Kathy NOVAK
58 Assoc Vice Chanc for Graduate Educ ....Dr. Cecilia CORNELL
88 Exec Dir Ctr State Policy & Ldrship ....Ms. Molly LAMB
110 Assoc Vice Chanc for Development ....Ms. Lisa WHELPLEY
29 Assoc Vice Chanc for Alumni Rels ....Mr. Charles SCHRAGE
30 Vice Chanc Dev/Sr VP UL Found ....Dr. Jeffrey D. LORBER
18 Assoc Chanc Admin Affs/Facilities ....Mr. Charles CODERKO
26 Assoc Chancellor for Public Affairs ....Ms. Kelsea GURSKI
21 Sr Business & Financial Coordinator ....Mr. Jason BANE
49 Int Dean Col Liberal Arts/Science ....Dr. Lan DONG
50 Dean College Business/Mgmt ....Dr. Somnath BHATTACHARYA
80 Dean Col Public Affs/Admin ....Dr. Robert SMITH
53 Int Dean College Educ/Human Svcs ......Dr. James ERMATINGER
15 Sr Director HR ....Ms. Melissa MLYNSKI
43 Legal Counsel ....Ms. Rhonda PERRY
08 Dean of Library ....Dr. Pattie PIOTROWSKI
27 Director Public Information ....Mr. Derek SCHNAPP
27 Director Marketing ....Ms. Jessie BURRELL
19 Interim Chief Campus Police ....Mr. Ross OWENS
06 Registrar ....Mr. Brian CLEVENGER
35 Director of Student Life ....Ms. Cynthia THOMPSON
41 Interim Director of Athletics ....Mr. Roy BROWN
09 Director Institutional Research ....Ms. Laura DORMAN
96 Director of Purchasing ....Ms. Jill MENEZES
37 Interim Dir Financial Assistance ....Ms. Laurie BUCK
38 Exec Director Counseling Center ....Dr. Bethany BILYEU
85 Director Intl Student Services ....Mr. Rick LANE
13 Assoc Provost for IT/CIO ....Mr. Tulio LLOSA
39 Director Campus Housing ....Mr. Brian KELLEY
07 Director of Admissions ....Ms. Kathryn KLEEMAN
28 Director of Diversity & Inclusion ....Mr. Justin ROSE
36 Director Career Development
     Center ....Ms. Katherine BATTEE-FREEMAN
84 Director Enrollment Management ....Ms. Natalie HERRING
86 Director Government Relations ....Ms. Joan SESTAK
104 Director Study Abroad ....Dr. Jonathan GOLDBERGBELLE
105 Director Web Services ....Ms. Jessica BAUMBERGER
106 Exec Dir Online/Prof & Engaged Lrng ....Dr. Vickie S. COOK

*University of Illinois Urbana-Champaign   (F)

601 E John Street, Champaign IL 61820-5711
County: Champaign   FICE Identification: 001775
                                         Unit ID: 145637
Telephone: (217) 333-6677   Carnegie Class: DU-Highest
FAX Number: N/A   Calendar System: Semester
URL: www.illinois.edu
Established: 1867   Annual Undergrad Tuition & Fees (In-State): $15,150
Enrollment: 52,679   Coed
Affiliation or Control: State   IRS Status: 501(c)3
Highest Offering: Doctorate
Accreditation: HLC, ART, #AUD, CEA, CLPSY, COPSY, DANCE, DIETD, DIETI,
IPSY, JOUR, LAW, LIB, LSAR, #MED, MUS, PCSAS, PH, PLNG, SP, SW, VET

00 Chief Executive Officer (President) ....Dr. Timothy L. KILLEEN
02 Chancellor ....Dr. Robert J. JONES
05 Prov/Vice Chanc Academic Affs ......Dr. Andreas C. CANGELLARIS
46 Vice Chanc Research & Innovation ....Dr. Susan MARTINIS
32 Vice Chancellor Student Affairs ....Dr. Danita BROWN YOUNG
111 VC Inst Advancement/Found Admin ....Mr. Barry BENSON
88 Associate Chanc Corp/Intl Relations ....Dr. Pradeep KHANNA
20 Exec Vice Provost Academic Affairs ....Dr. William BERNHARD
26 Exec Assoc Chanc for Public Engage ....Dr. Wanda E. WARD
11 Vice Chanc for Admin and Operations ..Mr. Michael DELORENZO
28 VC for Diversity/Equity/Inclusion ....Dr. Sean C. GARRICK
88 Assoc Prov Faculty Development ....Dr. Rosa Milagros SANTOS
100 Chief of Staff/Assoc Chanc ....Dr. Christopher SPAN
27 Associate Chanc Public Affairs ....Ms. Robin KALER
15 Senior Assoc Chancellor for HR ......Ms. Shari MICKEY-BOGGS
84 Assoc Prov Enrollment Mgmt ....Mr. Daniel MANN
88 Assoc Prov Capital Planning ....Mr. Paul REDMAN
114 Actg Assoc Chanc/Vice Prov Budget ....Ms. Vicky GRESS
104 Vice Prov Intl Pgms/Global Studies ...Ms. Reitumetse MABOKELA
20 Int Vice Prov for Undergrad Educ ....Dr. Lisa MONDA-AMAYA
21 Exec Assoc Provost Budget Planning ....Ms. Vicky GRESS
88 Exec Assoc Prov Acad Pgms/Policy ....Ms. Kristi KUNTZ
09 Asst Provost Management Info ....Dr. Amy EDWARDS
49 Dean Liberal Arts & Sciences ....Dr. Venetria PATTON
61 Dean Law ....Dr. Vikram AMAR
74 Dean Veterinary Medicine ....Dr. Peter CONSTABLE
54 Dean Engineering ....Dr. Rashid BASHIR
47 Interim Dean Agric/Consumer/Env Sci ....Dr. German BOLLERO
50 Dean Business ....Dr. Jeffrey BROWN
57 Dean Fine & Applied Arts ....Dr. Kevin HAMILTON
63 Dean CI College of Medicine ....Dr. Mark COHEN
70 Dean School of Social Work ....Dr. Steven ANDERSON
68 Dean Col Applied Health
     Sciences ....Dr. Cheryl HANLEY-MAXWELL
60 Dean College of Media ....Dr. Tracy SULKIN
58 Dean Graduate College ....Dr. Wojciech CHODZKO-ZAJKO

62 Dean School of Info Sciences .... Dr. Eunice SANTOS
53 Dean Education .... Dr. James D. ANDERSON
63 Actg Reg Dean Col Med/Urbana-Champ .... Dr. Janet JOKELA
48 Dir School of Architecture ... Mr. Francisco RODRIGUEZ-SUAREZ
16 Dean Labor & Employment Rels .... Dr. Fritz DRASGOW
08 University Librarian & Dean .... Dr. John P. WILKIN
13 Interim Chief Information Officer .... Mr. Scott GENUNG
35 Dean of Students .... Dr. Stephen BRYAN
56 Assoc Dean Extension & Outreach .... Dr. Sharon NICKOLS
41 Director Athletics .... Mr. Josh WHITMAN
10 Exec Director Business/Fin Affairs .... Ms. Ginger VELAZQUEZ
43 Deputy Campus Legal Counsel .... Mr. Scott RICE
22 Dir Equal Opportunity & Access .... Ms. Heidi JOHNSON
19 Exec Director Public Safety .... Ms. Alice CARY
18 Interim Exec Director Facilities .... Dr. Ehab KAMARAH
23 Director McKinley Health Center .... Dr. Robert D. PARKER, JR.
36 Director Career Services Center .... Ms. Jennifer NEEF
37 Director Student Financial Aid .... Ms. Michelle TRAME
38 Director Counseling Center .... Dr. Carla MCCOWAN
39 Exec Director Housing Division .... Ms. Alma SEALINE
88 Dir Ctr Innovative Teaching/Lrng .... Dr. Michel BELLINI
06 Registrar .... Ms. Meghan HAZEN
07 Director of Admissions .... Mr. Andy BORST
101 Secretary of the Institution/Board .... Mr. Gregory KNOTT
108 Assoc Prov for Planning/Assessment .... Dr. Staci J. PROVEZIS
86 Dir Community/Govt Relations .... Mr. Robert FLIDER

*University of Illinois at Chicago College of Medicine at Peoria (A)

One Illini Drive, Peoria IL 61605

Telephone: (309) 671-8402 Identification: 770182

Accreditation: &HLC

*University of Illinois at Chicago College of Medicine at Urbana (B)

Carle Forum LL, 611 West Park St, Urbana IL 61801

Telephone: (217) 333-5465 Identification: 770184

Accreditation: &HLC

*University of Illinois Chicago School of Law (C)

300 S. State Street, Chicago IL 60604-3968

Telephone: (312) 427-2737 FICE Identification: 001698

Accreditation: &HLC, LAW

*University of Illinois College of Medicine Rockford (D)

1601 Parkview Avenue, Rockford IL 61107

Telephone: (815) 395-0600 Identification: 770183

Accreditation: &HLC, PHAR

University of St. Francis (E)

500 N Wilcox Street, Joliet IL 60435-6188

County: Will FICE Identification: 001664
Unit ID: 148584

Telephone: (815) 740-3400 Carnegie Class: DU-Mod
FAX Number: (815) 740-4285 Calendar System: Semester
URL: www.stfrancis.edu
Established: 1920 Annual Undergrad Tuition & Fees: $35,000
Enrollment: 3,529 Coed
Affiliation or Control: Roman Catholic IRS Status: 501(c)3
Highest Offering: Doctorate
Accreditation: HLC, ACBSP, CAPRT, NURSE, RTT, SW

01 President .... Dr. Arvid C. JOHNSON
05 Provost/VP Academic Affairs .... Dr. Beth ROTH
10 VP Administration & Finance .... Ms. Julee A. GARD
84 VP Admissions/Mktg/Enrollment Svcs .... Mr. Eric WIGNALL
88 VP Mission Int & Univ Ministry .... Sr. Mary Elizabeth IMLER
13 VP Operations/Planning & Technology .... Mr. Terrance L. COTTRELL
111 VP for University Advancement .... Ms. Lisa SAMPALIS
49 Dean Col Arts & Sciences .... Dr. Elizabeth DAVIES
50 Dean Col Business/Health .... Dr. Shannon BROWN
53 Dean Col Education .... Dr. John S. GAMBRO
66 Dean Leach Col Nursing .... Dr. Yeijin YEOM
32 Dean Student Life .... Ms. Mollie ROCKAFELLOW
37 Exec Dir Financial Aid .... Mr. Bruce FOOTE
29 Dir Alumni Relations .... Ms. Aubrey L. KNIGHT
41 Dir Athletics .... Mr. Dave LAKETA
36 Dir Career Success Center .... Ms. Maribeth HEARN
38 Dir Counseling & Wellness .... Vacant
28 Dir Institutional Diversity .... Ms. Allison HEARD
07 Dir Undergrad Admissions .... Mr. Eric RUIZ
123 Dir Grad/Degree Completion Admiss .... Ms. Sandra L. SLOKA
27 Dir Marketing Services .... Ms. Julie FUTTERER
14 Dir Network Support Services .... Mr. Mark T. SNODGRASS
19 Dir Safety/Security .... Mr. Jason WILLIAMS
42 Dir University Ministry .... Vacant
06 Registrar .... Ms. Jennifer ETHRIDGE
08 Head Librarian .... Ms. Brigitte BELL
23 Coordinator of Health Services .... Ms. Phyllis M. PETERSON
09 Dir Enterprise Data & Analytics .... Ms. Rebecca R. GARLAND
44 Director Annual Giving .... Ms. Kimberly KALAFUT

University of Saint Mary of the Lake-Mundelein Seminary (F)

1000 E Maple Avenue, Mundelein IL 60060-1174

County: Lake FICE Identification: 001765
Unit ID: 148885

Telephone: (847) 566-6401 Carnegie Class: Spec-4-yr-Faith
FAX Number: (847) 566-7330 Calendar System: Semester
URL: www.usml.edu
Established: 1844 Annual Graduate Tuition & Fees: N/A
Enrollment: 186 Male
Affiliation or Control: Roman Catholic IRS Status: 501(c)3
Highest Offering: Doctorate; No Undergraduates
Accreditation: THEOL

00 Chancellor .... Card. Blase CUPICH
01 Rector/President .... V.Rev. John KARTJE
11 Chief Operating Officer .... Mr. James HEINEN
03 Vice Rector .... Rev. Jake BELTRAN
05 Provost .... Vacant
73 Pres/Pontifical Faculty of Theology .... Rev. Brendan LUPTON
10 Vice President for Finance .... Mr. John F. LEHOCKY
30 Vice President of Development .... Ms. Holly GIBOUT
20 Academic Dean .... Ms. Marie PITT-PAYNE
88 Dean of Formation .... Rev. Maina WAITHAKA
73 Director Pre-Theology Program .... Rev. Dennis SPIES
08 Library Director .... Dr. Christopher ROGERS
06 Director of Registration & Records .... Ms. Devona SEWELL
42 Director of Spiritual Life .... Dcn. Pat QUAGLIANA
85 Director of International Students .... Rev. Maina WAITHAKA
07 Director of Admissions .... Rev. Jacque BELTRAN
04 Exec Assistant to the President .... Ms. Mary BERTRAM
13 Chief Information Technology Ofcr .... Mr. Brian BICKETT
15 Chief Human Resources Officer .... Mrs. Elizabeth SANTILLI
19 Director Security/Safety .... Mr. John HUINKER
38 Director Student Counseling .... Rev. Carlos RODRIGUEZ
26 Dir Marketing & Communications .... Mr. David RAGLIN

VanderCook College of Music (G)

3140 S Federal Street, Chicago IL 60616-3731

County: Cook FICE Identification: 001778
Unit ID: 149639

Telephone: (312) 225-6288 Carnegie Class: Spec-4-yr-Other
FAX Number: (312) 225-5211 Calendar System: Semester
URL: www.vandercook.edu
Established: 1909 Annual Undergrad Tuition & Fees: $29,800
Enrollment: 313 Coed
Affiliation or Control: Independent Non-Profit IRS Status: 501(c)3
Highest Offering: Master's
Accreditation: HLC, MUS

01 President .... Dr. Roseanne K. ROSENTHAL
08 Head Librarian .... Mr. Robert DELAND
05 CAO/Dean of Undergrad Studies .... Ms. Stacey L. DOLAN
58 Dean of Graduate Studies .... Dr. Robert L. SINCLAIR
07 Director of Admissions .... Ms. Kimberly FARRIS
10 Chief Financial Officer .... Mr. Steven (JR) REMKE
37 Director of Financial Aid .... Ms. Sirena COVINGTON
13 Director Information Technologies .... Mr. Mohammad DARWISH
06 Registrar/Educational Placement Dir .... Mr. Peter BERGHOFF
26 Director Communications .... Vacant
29 Director Alumni Relations .... Ms. Cindy TOVAR

Waubonsee Community College (H)

Route 47 at Waubonsee Drive,
Sugar Grove IL 60554-9799

County: Kane FICE Identification: 006931
Unit ID: 149727

Telephone: (630) 466-7900 Carnegie Class: Assoc/MT-VT-High Non
FAX Number: (630) 466-7550 Calendar System: Semester
URL: www.waubonsee.edu
Established: 1966 Annual Undergrad Tuition & Fees (In-District): $9,271
Enrollment: 7,564 Coed
Affiliation or Control: Local IRS Status: 501(c)3
Highest Offering: Associate Degree
Accreditation: HLC, ADNUR, ART, CAHIIM, EMT, MAC

01 President .... Dr. Christine J. SOBEK
05 VP Educational Affairs .... Dr. Diane NYHAMMER
10 VP Finance & Administration .... Mr. Douglas MINTER
45 VP Strategy/Community Development .... Dr. Jamal SCOTT
32 VP Student Dev & Exec Dir Found .... Dr. Melinda L. TEJADA
21 Asst Vice President of Finance .... Ms. Darla S. CARDINE
103 Asst VP Education/Workforce Devel .... Ms. Suzette MURRAY
13 Chief Information Officer .... Mr. Terence FELTON
35 Asst VP Student Svc/Alumni Rels .... Dr. Scott PESKA
15 Exec Director Human Resources .... Ms. Michele NEEDHAM
26 Exec Dir Marketing/Communications .... Ms. Amanda GEIST
76 Dean Health Professions/Public Svc .... Mr. Jeffrey GREGOR
88 Dean Faculty Devel/Engagement .... Dr. Laura ORTIZ
49 Exec Dean Liberal Arts/Sciences .... Ms. Sharon GARCIA
83 Dean Soc Sciences/Educ/World Lang .... Vacant
124 Exec Dean Student Success/Retention .... Ms. Kelli SINCLAIR
56 Dean Adult Education .... Mr. Adam SCHAUER
50 Exec Dean Bus/Technology/Wrkfrc Ed .... Ms. Ne'Keisha STEPNEY
07 Dean for Admissions .... Ms. Faith LASHURE
04 Dir Pres Communications/Operations .... Ms. Kimberly CAPONI
37 Dir Student Financial Aid Services .... Dr. Charles BOUDREAU
09 Dean Inst Effective/Title V Proj .... Dr. Stacey RANDALL

35 Chief Diversity Ofcr/Dean of Stdnts .... Mr. Bernard LITTLE
19 Exec Dir Campus Safety/Operations .... Mr. Daniel LARSEN
06 Dir Registration/Records/Registrar .... Mr. Marc DALE
88 Dean Lrng Outcomes/Curric/Pgm Dev .... Dr. Kathleen GORSKI
121 Exec Dean for Academic Support .... Ms. Anita MOORE-BOHANNON
109 Dir Financial/Auxiliary Services .... Mr. Lei XIE
16 Dir Employee Development .... Mr. Tim BIZOUKAS

Western Illinois University (I)

1 University Circle, Macomb IL 61455-1390

County: McDonough FICE Identification: 001780
Unit ID: 149772

Telephone: (309) 298-1414 Carnegie Class: Masters/L
FAX Number: (309) 298-2400 Calendar System: Semester
URL: www.wiu.edu
Established: 1899 Annual Undergrad Tuition & Fees (In-State): $13,314
Enrollment: 7,490 Coed
Affiliation or Control: State IRS Status: 501(c)3
Highest Offering: Doctorate
Accreditation: HLC, ART, CACREP, CAPRT, CEA, DIETD, MPCAC, MUS, NURSE, SP, SW, THEA

01 President .... Dr. Guiyou HUANG
05 Provost/Academic VP .... Dr. Manoochehr ZOGHI
20 Assoc Prov & Assoc VP Academic Affs .... Dr. Mark MOSSMAN
10 Interim VP for Finance & Admin .... Ms. Shannon SUTTON
121 Interim VP Student Success .... Mr. John SMITH
111 Int VP Advancement/Alumni Relations .... Mr. Michael MURTAGH
29 Asst VP of Alumni Programs .... Ms. Amy SPELMAN
43 General Counsel .... Mrs. Elizabeth DUVALL
39 AVP Student Services/Housing .... Mr. John BIERNBAUM
86 Director of Government Relations .... Ms. Jeanette MALAFA
49 Dean College Arts/Sciences .... Dr. Susan MARTINELLI-FERNANDEZ
50 Dean College Business/Tech .... Dr. Craig CONRAD
53 Int Dean College Educ & Human Svcs .... Dr. Katrina DAYTNER
57 Dean Fine Arts & Communication .... Mr. William CLOW
08 Dean University Libraries .... Dr. Hector MAYMI-SUGRANES
92 Dean Centennial Honors College .... Dr. Lorette ODEN
64 Director School of Music .... Dr. Jefrey BROWN
06 Registrar .... Ms. Sarah LAWSON
13 Exec Dir University Technology/CIO .... Mr. Greg KAIN
26 Asst VP Communication .... Ms. Darcie R. SHINBERGER
09 Director Inst Research & Planning .... Ms. Angela BONIFAS
22 Dir Equal Opportunity & Access .... Vacant
37 Director Financial Aid .... Ms. Roberta J. SMITH
121 Dir Student Development/Success Ctr ... Ms. Samantha KLINGLER
15 Int Chief Human Resources Officer .... Mr. Bruce WESTERN
18 Asst VP for Facilities Management .... Mr. Troy RHOADS
19 Director Public Safety .... Mr. Derek WATTS
23 Director Health Center .... Ms. John W. SMITH
85 Assoc VP for Global Affairs .... Dr. Randy GLEAN
40 Retail Manager University Bookstore .... Mr. Jeff MOORE
41 Director Athletics .... Mr. Paul BUBB
102 Exec Director WIU Foundation .... Mr. Bradley BAINTER
07 Director Undergraduate Admissions .... Mr. Doug FREED
38 Int Director Student Counseling .... Ms. Cara CERULLO
04 Sr Exec Assistant to the President .... Ms. Athena BROOKS
96 Director of Purchasing .... Ms. Lora LIDAYWA
84 VP of Enrollment Management .... Dr. Amber SCHULTZ

Western Illinois University Quad Cities (J)

3300 River Drive, Moline IL 61265

Telephone: (309) 762-9481 Identification: 770100

Accreditation: &HLC

Wheaton College (K)

501 College Avenue, Wheaton IL 60187-5593

County: DuPage FICE Identification: 001781
Unit ID: 149781

Telephone: (630) 752-5000 Carnegie Class: Bac-A&S
FAX Number: (630) 752-5555 Calendar System: Semester
URL: www.wheaton.edu
Established: 1860 Annual Undergrad Tuition & Fees: $39,100
Enrollment: 2,908 Coed
Affiliation or Control: Independent Non-Profit IRS Status: 501(c)3
Highest Offering: Doctorate
Accreditation: HLC, CACREP, CLPSY, MFCD, MUS

01 President .... Dr. Philip G. RYKEN
05 Provost .... Dr. Karen LEE
10 VP for Finance .... Mr. Chad RYNBRANDT
32 Vice President Student Development .... Mr. Paul O. CHELSEN
111 VP Advancement/Alumni Rels .... Mr. Kirk FARNEY
84 Chief Enrollment Management Officer .... Mr. Silvio E. VAZQUEZ
93 Chief Intercultural Engagement Ofcr .... Dr. Vanessa QUAINOO
13 Chief Information Officer .... Mr. Alan WOLFF
29 Sr Dir Vocation & Alum Engagement .... Ms. Cindra STACKHOUSE TAETZSCH
04 Special Asst to the President .... Miss Marilee A. MELVIN
58 Dean of the Graduate School .... Dr. Scott MOREAU
79 Dean Biblical/Theol Studies .... Dr. David LAUBER
64 Dean Conservatory/Arts & Comm .... Dr. Michael WILDER
81 Dean Natural Sciences .... Dr. Becky EGGIMANN
83 Dean of Social Sciences & Education .... Dr. Bryan MCGRAW
104 Dean Global Programs & Studies ... Dr. Laura M. MONTGOMERY
83 Dean Psych/Counsel & Fam Therapy .... Dr. Sarah HALL
79 Dean Humanities .... Dr. Jeffry DAVIS

35 Dean of Student Engagement ... Dr. Steve IVESTER
08 Dean Library & Archives ... Mr. Brent ETZEL
20 Assistant Provost ... Dr. Sarah MIGLIO
21 Controller ... Mr. Carlos GARCIA
88 Exec Dir Billy Graham Ctr/Dean MML ... Dr. Ed STETZER
09 Dir Inst Research & Acad Operations ... Dr. Gary LARSON
06 Registrar ... Dr. Diane KRUSEMARK
18 Director of Facilities ... Mr. Jay BIESZKE
36 Dir Ctr Vocation & Career ... Vacant
15 Director of Human Resources ... Mrs. Karen TUCKER
07 Dir Undergraduate Admissions ... Mr. Jason KIRCHER
123 Dir Graduate Admissions ... Mr. Terrance CAMPBELL
37 Director Student Financial Svcs ... Ms. Karen BELLING
41 Director of Athletics ... Vacant
39 Dean of Residence Life ... Dr. Justin HETH
35 Dean of Student Wellness ... Dr. Toussaint WHETSTONE
38 Director of Student Care ... Ms. Carrie WILLIAMS
42 Chaplain ... Dr. Angulus WILSON
23 Dir Student Health Services ... Ms. Beth WALSH
26 Director Marketing Communications ... Mr. Joseph MOORE
19 Chief of Public Safety ... Mr. Robert F. NORRIS
117 Director Risk Management ... Ms. Amanda FRANKLIN
105 Director Web Communications ... Mrs. Rebecca LARSON
25 Academic Grants Officer ... Mrs. Virginia SHAFFER

Worsham College of Mortuary Science (A)

495 Northgate Parkway, Wheeling IL 60090-2646
County: Cook   FICE Identification: 001783
Unit ID: 369455
Telephone: (847) 808-8444   Carnegie Class: Spec 2-yr-A&S
FAX Number: (847) 808-8493   Calendar System: Quarter
URL: www.worsham.edu
Established: 1911   Annual Undergrad Tuition & Fees: $23,800
Enrollment: 171   Coed
Affiliation or Control: Proprietary   IRS Status: Proprietary
Highest Offering: Associate Degree
Accreditation: FUSER

01 Director ... Ms. Leili MCMURROUGH

INDIANA

American College of Education (B)

101 West Ohio Street, Suite 1200, Indianapolis IN 46204
County: Marion   Identification: 666242
Unit ID: 449889
Telephone: (800) 280-0307   Carnegie Class: Spec-4-yr-Other
FAX Number: N/A   Calendar System: Other
URL: www.ace.edu
Established: 2005   Annual Undergrad Tuition & Fees: N/A
Enrollment: 8,112   Coed
Affiliation or Control: Proprietary   IRS Status: Proprietary
Highest Offering: Doctorate
Accreditation: HLC, CAEP, NURSE

01 President & CEO ... Mr. Geordie HYLAND
05 Chief Academic Officer & Provost ... Ms. Stephanie HINSHAW
09 Vice Pres Institutional Analytics ... Dr. George MAKIYA
88 Dir Regulatory Affairs & Compliance ... Mr. Tom BROUWER
07 Director of Admissions ... Ms. Jeannie TAYLOR
04 Executive Asst to President ... Ms. Jill ALGATE
08 Director Library ... Dr. Sandra QUIATKOWSKI
10 Chief Financial Officer ... Mr. Bryce PETERSON
26 Chief Marketing Officer ... Vacant
13 VP Information Technology ... Mr. Swapnal SHAH
15 VP Human Resources ... Ms. KK BYLAND
108 VP Continuous Improvement ... Ms. Alison WITHERSPOON
06 Registrar ... Mr. David GASTON
28 Diversity & Inclusion Advisor ... Ms. Fawzia REZA
29 Alumni Engagement Officer ... Ms. Courtney SHELTON

Anabaptist Mennonite Biblical Seminary (C)

3003 Benham Avenue, Elkhart IN 46517-1999
County: Elkhart   FICE Identification: 001823
Unit ID: 151865
Telephone: (574) 295-3726   Carnegie Class: Spec-4-yr-Faith
FAX Number: (574) 295-0092   Calendar System: Semester
URL: www.ambs.edu
Established: 1946   Annual Graduate Tuition & Fees: N/A
Enrollment: 107   Coed
Affiliation or Control: Mennonite Church   IRS Status: 501(c)3
Highest Offering: Doctorate; No Undergraduates
Accreditation: THEOL

01 President ... Dr. David BOSHART
05 VP & Academic Dean ... Dr. Beverly K. LAPP
10 Vice Pres Administration/CFO ... Ms. Deanna A. RISSER
30 Director of Development ... Dr. Bob YODER
06 Assistant Dean & Registrar ... Mr. Scott JANZEN
08 Director of Library Services ... Mr. Karl STUTZMAN
84 Director of Enrollment ... Ms. Mary Ann WEBER
73 Director Inst of Mennonite Studies ... Dr. Jamie PITTS
04 Exec Asst to Pres/Academic Dean ... Ms. Karen S. STOLTZFUS
13 Director of Information Technology ... Mr. Brent GRABER
26 Dir of Marketing/Communications ... Ms. Melissa TROYER

Anderson University (D)

1100 E Fifth Street, Anderson IN 46012-3495
County: Madison   FICE Identification: 001785
Unit ID: 150066
Telephone: (765) 649-9071   Carnegie Class: Masters/S
FAX Number: (765) 641-3851   Calendar System: Semester
URL: www.anderson.edu
Established: 1917   Annual Undergrad Tuition & Fees: $32,100
Enrollment: 1,406   Coed
Affiliation or Control: Church Of God   IRS Status: 501(c)3
Highest Offering: Doctorate
Accreditation: HLC, ACBSP, CAATE, CAEP, MUS, NURSE, SW, THEOL

01 President ... Mr. John PISTOLE
05 Provost ... Dr. Courtney TAYLOR
10 Interim Vice President Finance ... Mr. Daniel COURTNEY
111 Vice President for Advancement ... Ms. Jennifer HUNT
84 VP Enrollment & Marketing ... Ms. Heather KIM
73 Dean Sch of Theology/Christian Min ... Dr. Nathan WILLOWBY
50 Dean Falls School of Business ... Dr. Lonnie LEEPER
79 Assoc Prov/Dn Humanities/Behav Sci ... Dr. Elizabeth IMAFUJI
64 Dean School Music/Theatre & Dance ... Dr. Jeffrey WRIGHT
66 Dean Sch Nursing & Kinesiology ... Dr. Lynn SCHMIDT
54 School of Science & Engineering ... Dr. Chad WALLACE
42 Campus Pastor ... Rev. Joshua TANDY
32 Asst Provost/Dean of Students ... Mr. Scott CAGNET
06 University Registrar ... Mr. Arthur LEAK
08 Director of Libraries ... Mr. James BELL
21 Assistant Treasurer/Controller ... Mrs. Suahil HOUSHOLDER
36 Center for Career & Calling ... Vacant
13 Director of Info Technology Svcs ... Mr. Michael TUCKER
37 Student Financial Services ... Mrs. Christina MAGGART
15 Director of Work Life Engagement ... Mr. Tim STATES
19 Director Police & Security Services ... Mr. Rick GARRETT
40 Bookstore Manager ... Mr. Dustin MARTIN
41 Athletic Director ... Ms. Marcie TAYLOR
38 Director Counseling Services ... Ms. Christal HELVERING
29 Director of Alumni Relations ... Mr. Trent PALMER
109 Manager Business & Auxiliary Svcs ... Mrs. Whitney JIMENEZ
04 Executive Asst to the President ... Mrs. Ronda REEMER
104 Director Study Abroad ... Vacant
108 Director Institutional Assessment ... Dr. Jaye ROGERS
39 Student Housing Coordinator ... Ms. Stacey CARPENTER
09 Director of Institutional Research ... Ms. Kim WOLFE
100 Special Assistant to the President ... Mr. Dan COURTNEY
105 Web Editor & Content Writer ... Mr. Michael BAKER
106 Asst Dir ITS/Instr Resource Center ... Ms. Jodie REMINDER
26 Asst VP Admissions/Marketing/Comm ... Ms. Mischon HART
28 Director Cultural Resource Center ... Mr. Brian MARTIN
30 Executive Director of Development ... Mr. Brent BAKER
44 Associate Director Annual Giving ... Mrs. Elyse CROMER
53 Director Teacher Education ... Dr. Katy SAMPLE

Ball State University (E)

2000 W. University Avenue, Muncie IN 47306-1099
County: Delaware   FICE Identification: 001786
Unit ID: 150136
Telephone: (765) 285-5555   Carnegie Class: DU-Higher
FAX Number: (765) 285-1461   Calendar System: Semester
URL: www.bsu.edu
Established: 1918   Annual Undergrad Tuition & Fees (In-State): $10,144
Enrollment: 21,597   Coed
Affiliation or Control: State   IRS Status: 501(c)3
Highest Offering: Doctorate
Accreditation: HLC, ART, AUD, CAATE, CACREP, CAEP, CEA, CIDA, COARC, CONST, COPSY, DANCE, DIETD, DIETI, IPSY, JOUR, LSAR, MUS, NURSE, PH, PLNG, RAD, SCPSY, SP, SW, THEA

01 President ... Mr. Geoffrey S. MEARNS
05 Provost/EVP Academic Affairs ... Dr. Susana RIVERA-MILLS
10 VP Business Affairs & Treasurer ... Mr. Alan FINN
32 VP of Student Affairs ... Ms. Ro-Anne ROYER ENGLE
84 VP Enrollment Mgmt & Planning ... Ms. Paula LUFF
43 VP & General Counsel ... Ms. Sali K. FALLING
13 VP for IT & Chief Information Ofcr ... Mr. Loren MALM
26 VP for Marketing and Comm ... Ms. Deedie K. DOWDLE
86 VP Government Relations ... Ms. Becca RICE
102 President and CEO BSU Foundation ... Ms. Jean K. CROSBY
41 Director Intercollegiate Athletics ... Ms. Beth GOETZ
20 Vice Provost for Academic Affairs ... Dr. Kecia MCBRIDE
88 Assoc Prov Entrepreneurial Learning ... Ms. Jennifer BLACKMER
09 AVP Inst Research & Decision Sppt ... Mr. Michael J. LANE
39 AVP Student Affairs/Dir of Housing ... Dr. Amanda R. KNERR
18 Assoc VP Facilities Planning/Mgmt ... Mr. James LOWE
109 Assoc VP Business/Auxiliary Svcs ... Ms. Julie HOPWOOD
07 AVP Enrollment/Exec Dir of Admiss ... Mr. Christopher T. MUNCHEL
08 Dean University Libraries ... Mr. Matthew SHAW
48 Dean Architecture/Planning ... Mr. David FERGUSON
79 Dean Col of Science/Humanities ... Dr. Maureen MCCARTHY
50 Dean Miller College of Business ... Dr. Steve FERRIS
53 Dean of Teachers College ... Dr. Anand MARRI
57 Dean College of Fine Arts ... Dr. Seth BECKMAN
58 Dean of Graduate School ... Dr. Adam R. BEACH
60 Dean Col of Comm/Info/Media ... Dr. Paaige K. TURNER
76 Dean College of Health ... Dr. Scott RUTLEDGE
92 Dean of Honors College ... Dr. John EMERT
88 Chief Entrepreneurship Officer ... Dr. Michael GOLDSBY
06 Registrar ... Ms. Erin MASON
37 Director Scholarships/Financial Aid ... Dr. John MCPHERSON
15 Director of Human Resources Svcs ... Ms. Kate STOSS
19 Director Public Safety ... Mr. James DUCKHAM
25 Director of Sponsored Projects Admn ... Ms. Liz HANEY
44 Senior Director Annual Giving ... Ms. Amanda HOLMQUIST
30 VP of Development ... Mr. Ray ALLEN
106 Asst Provost for Online Learning ... Dr. Trudi WEYERMANN
38 Director Counseling/Health Services ... Dr. Bill BETTS
36 AVP & Exec Dir Career Center ... Mr. Jim MCATEE
96 Director of Purchasing Services ... Mr. Roger HASSENZAHL
24 Dir of University Media Services ... Mr. Alan GORDON
88 Dir of Economic Development Policy ... Mr. David R. TERRELL
31 AVP for Community Engagement ... Ms. Delaina BOYD
104 Exec Dir Global Affairs ... Ms. Laurie COX
04 Exec Dir of Presidential Operations ... Ms. Stephanie K. ARRINGTON
45 Chief Strategy Officer ... Dr. Charlene M. ALEXANDER

Bethany Theological Seminary (F)

615 National Road W, Richmond IN 47374-4019
County: Wayne   FICE Identification: 001637
Unit ID: 143233
Telephone: (800) 287-8822   Carnegie Class: Spec-4-yr-Faith
FAX Number: (765) 983-1840   Calendar System: Semester
URL: www.bethanyseminary.edu
Established: 1905   Annual Graduate Tuition & Fees: N/A
Enrollment: 71   Coed
Affiliation or Control: Church Of The Brethren   IRS Status: 501(c)3
Highest Offering: Master's; No Undergraduates
Accreditation: HLC, THEOL

01 President ... RevDr. Jeffrey W. CARTER
05 Academic Dean ... Dr. Steven J. SCHWEITZER
10 Exec Dir of Finance/Administration ... Mrs. Tammy S. GLENN
30 Exec Dir Institutional Advancement ... Mr. Sam LOCKE
26 Director Marketing/Communications ... Mr. Jonathan GRAHAM
32 Director Student Development ... Ms. Karen DUHAI
12 Director Brethren Academy ... Mrs. Janet L. OBER LAMBERT
88 Director of the MA Program ... Mrs. Denise KETTERING-LANE
07 Exec Dir of Admissions/Student Svcs ... Mrs. Lori M. CURRENT
04 Admin Assistant to the President ... Mrs. Karen SCHROEDER
06 Registrar ... Ms. April VANLONDEN

Bethel University (G)

1001 Bethel Circle, Mishawaka IN 46545-5509
County: Saint Joseph   FICE Identification: 001787
Unit ID: 150145
Telephone: (574) 807-7000   Carnegie Class: Masters/S
FAX Number: (574) 807-7484   Calendar System: Semester
URL: www.betheluniversity.edu
Established: 1947   Annual Undergrad Tuition & Fees: $29,790
Enrollment: 1,362   Coed
Affiliation or Control: Missionary Church   IRS Status: 501(c)3
Highest Offering: Master's
Accreditation: HLC, ADNUR, CAEPN, MUS, NUR

01 President ... Dr. Barbara K. BELLEFEUILLE
05 VP for Academic Services ... Dr. Bradley D. SMITH
111 VP for Advancement ... Mr. Brent LAVIGNE
10 VP for Finance & Administration ... Mr. Jerry WHITE
32 VP for Student Development ... Dr. Shawn M. HOLTGREN
84 VP for Enrollment Management ... Mrs. Amanda SLAUGHTER
13 Senior Director of IT ... Ms. Patti J. FISHER
66 Dean of Nursing ... Dr. Deborah GILLUM
49 Dean of Arts & Sciences ... Dr. Janna MCLEAN
83 Dean of Humanities/Social Sciences ... Dr. Robby PRENKERT
35 Dean of Students ... Mrs. Julie BEAM
06 Registrar ... Mrs. Jeanne E. FOX
121 Director of Student Success ... Mrs. Rachel A. KENNEDY
36 Dir Career Devel/Global Engagement ... Mr. Tyler GRANT
37 Director Financial Aid ... Ms. Sabrina CITTE
26 Director Marketing & Communication ... Mrs. Lissa DIAZ
41 Director Athletics ... Mr. Tony NATALI
08 Director Library Services ... Mr. Mark J. ROOT
88 Director Teacher Certification ... Mrs. Kimberly J. MEYER
09 Director Institutional Research ... Dr. Raymond E. WHITEMAN
19 Director Campus Safety ... Mr. Paul E. NEEL
85 Director International Students ... Mrs. Susan A. MATTESON
91 Director Administrative Computing ... Mrs. Donna FAUDREE
29 Director Alumni Services ... Mrs. Emily S. SHERWOOD
07 Director of Admission ... Mrs. Christine DICKINSON
15 Director Human Resources ... Mrs. Lisa CUTTING
04 Administrative Asst to President ... Mrs. Miriam WERTZ
104 Director Global & Comm Engagement ... Mr. Tyler C. GRANT
108 Director Institutional Assessment ... Dr. Raymond E. WHITEMAN
18 Chief Facilities/Phys Plant Ofcr ... Mr. Joe ZAPPIA

Butler University (H)

4600 Sunset Avenue, Indianapolis IN 46208-3443
County: Marion   FICE Identification: 001788
Unit ID: 150163
Telephone: (317) 940-8000   Carnegie Class: Masters/L
FAX Number: (317) 940-9930   Calendar System: Semester
URL: www.butler.edu
Established: 1855   Annual Undergrad Tuition & Fees: $43,400
Enrollment: 5,544   Coed
Affiliation or Control: Independent Non-Profit   IRS Status: 501(c)3
Highest Offering: Doctorate
Accreditation: HLC, ARCPA, CACREP, CAEP, DANCE, IPSY, MUS, PHAR, THEA

01 President ... Mr. James M. DANKO
05 Provost/VP Academic Affairs ... Dr. Brooke BARNETT
10 Vice Pres of Finance/Administration ... Mr. Bruce E. ARICK
111 VP University Advancement ... Mr. Jonathan PURVIS
32 Vice President of Student Affairs ... Dr. Frank E. ROSS, III
41 VP & Director of Athletics ... Mr. Barry S. COLLIER
84 VP of Enrollment Management ... Ms. Lori GREENE
45 VP of Strategy and Innovation ... Ms. Melissa BECKWITH
43 General Counsel ... Ms. Claire AIGOTTI
57 Dean Jordan College Fine Arts ... Dr. Michelle JARVIS
50 Interim Dean School of Business ... Ms. Hilary BUTTRICK
49 Dean Liberal Arts & Science ... Dr. Jay R. HOWARD
53 Dean College of Education ... Dr. Brooke KANDEL-CISCO
67 Dean Pharmacy & Health Sciences ... Dr. Robert P. SOLTIS
60 Dean College of Communication ... Dr. Jay R. HOWARD
08 Dean of Libraries ... Dr. Julie L. MILLER
35 Int Dean Student Services ... Ms. Martha DZIWLIK
38 Asst Dean & Director Counseling Ctr ... Dr. Keith B. MAGNUS
18 AVP of Facilities ... Mr. Doug MORRIS
112 Exec Dir Major Gifts/Planned Giving ... Mr. Michael EIKENBERRY
15 Int Dir of Human Resources ... Mr. Mark OSHIER
26 AVP Marketing & Communication ... Ms. Stephanie JUDGE CRIPE
88 Interim Director Butler Arts Center ... Mr. Aaron HURT
114 Executive Budget Director ... Mr. Robert J. MARCUS
37 Director Financial Aid ... Ms. Melissa J. SMURDON
88 Dir University Events ... Ms. Beth A. ALEXANDER
39 Director Residence Life ... Ms. Karla K. CUNNINGHAM
09 Director Institutional Research ... Ms. Amia FOSTON
85 Director Global Education ... Ms. Jill MCKINNEY
36 Sr Director Career Services ... Mr. Gary R. BEAULIEU
27 Director of Creative Services ... Ms. Nancy LYZUN
28 Exec Dir Equity/Diversity/Inclusion ... Mr. Danny KIBBLE
86 Director of External Relations ... Mr. Michael KALTENMARK
07 Director of Admission ... Mr. Jerome DUEWEKE
06 Registrar ... Ms. Michele NEARY
13 AVP IT/Chief Information Officer ... Mr. Peter WILLIAMS
21 Controller ... Ms. Susan M. WESTERMEYER
40 Manager Bookstore ... Ms. Janine L. FRAINIER
96 Manager of Purchasing ... Ms. Shelly S. RABIDEAU
122 Dir Fraternity/Sorority Life ... Ms. Sarah COHEN

Calumet College of Saint Joseph (A)

2400 New York Avenue, Whiting IN 46394-2195
County: Lake — FICE Identification: 001834
Unit ID: 150172
Telephone: (219) 473-7770 — Carnegie Class: Masters/S
FAX Number: (219) 473-4259 — Calendar System: Semester
URL: www.ccsj.edu
Established: 1951 — Annual Undergrad Tuition & Fees: $20,470
Enrollment: 694 — Coed
Affiliation or Control: Roman Catholic — IRS Status: 501(c)3
Highest Offering: Master's
Accreditation: HLC

01 President ... Dr. Amy MCCORMACK
84 Sr Vice President for Enrollment ... Mr. Johnny CRAIG
05 Vice President Academic Affairs ... Dr. Derek SHOUBA
111 Dir of Institutional Advancement ... Ms. Ester DIAZ
10 VP Business & Finance ... Ms. Lynn MISKUS
32 VP Student Engagement & Retention ... Dr. Dionne JONES-MALONE
06 Registrar ... Ms. Diana FRANCIS
08 Director Instructional Support Svcs ... Dr. Keith WEROSH
09 Institutional Researcher ... Mr. Darren HENDERSON
26 Dir of Communications & PR ... Ms. Linda GAJEWSKI
41 Athletic Director ... Mr. Andy MARKS
37 Dir Financial Aid/Business Ofc Ops ... Mr. Chris ARTIM
13 Director of Computer Services ... Mr. Kevin KRIEPS
121 Director of Academic Advising ... Dr. Elaine BLAIR
07 Director of Enrollment Management ... Ms. Keli BURNS
15 Director of Human Resources ... Ms. Paula SHREVE
101 Secretary of the Institution/Board ... Mrs. Linda GAJEWSKI
105 Director of Web Services ... Mr. Tony KWINTERA
18 Chief Facilities/Physical Plant Ofc ... Mr. James BOND
25 Chief Contract and Grants Administr ... Dr. Ginger RODRIGUEZ
30 Director of Development ... Mrs. Ester DIAZ

Caris College (B)

2780 Jefferson Centre Way, Ste 103, Jeffersonville IN 47130
County: Clark — Identification: 667314
Unit ID: 491941
Telephone: (812) 258-9510 — Carnegie Class: Spec 2-yr-Health
FAX Number: N/A — Calendar System: Quarter
URL: www.cariscollege.edu
Established: 2015 — Annual Undergrad Tuition & Fees: N/A
Enrollment: N/A — Coed
Affiliation or Control: Proprietary — IRS Status: Proprietary
Highest Offering: Associate Degree
Accreditation: ABHES, DMS

01 President & CEO ... Mr. Bruce KEPLEY
11 Campus Director ... Ms. Brittany COTTONER
05 Director of Education ... Ms. Mandy HICKS
06 Registrar/Office Manager ... Ms. Brittany COFFEY
37 Director Financial Aid ... Ms. Heather LISCO
07 Director of Admissions ... Vacant

Chamberlain University-Indianapolis Campus (C)

9100 Keystone Crossing, Suite 300, Indianapolis IN 46240
Telephone: (317) 816-7335 — Identification: 770503
Accreditation: &HLC, NURSE

Christian Theological Seminary (D)

1000 W. 42nd Street, Indianapolis IN 46208-3301
County: Marion — FICE Identification: 001789
Unit ID: 150215
Telephone: (317) 924-1331 — Carnegie Class: Spec-4-yr-Faith
FAX Number: (317) 923-1961 — Calendar System: Semester
URL: www.cts.edu
Established: 1925 — Annual Graduate Tuition & Fees: N/A
Enrollment: 156 — Coed
Affiliation or Control: Christian Church (Disciples Of Christ)
IRS Status: 501(c)3
Highest Offering: Doctorate; No Undergraduates
Accreditation: HLC, MFCD, THEOL

01 President ... Dr. David M. MELLOTT
05 VP Academic Affs/Dean of Faculty ... Dr. Leah GUNNING-FRANCIS
10 Vice President Finance and Business ... Mr. F. Ward LOGAN
111 Vice President Advancement ... Ms. Kristin CHAMPA
32 Dean of Students ... Vacant
04 Admin Asst to President ... Ms. Valerie RUESS
21 Director of Finance ... Mr. Scott SIMS
08 Director of Library ... Dr. Scott SEAY
06 Registrar ... Mr. Matt SCHLIMGEN
75 Director of Field Education ... Rev. Martin WRIGHT
37 Director of Student Financial Aid ... Ms. Sandra MITCHELL-HOLDER
26 Director of Communications ... Rev. Nathan WILSON
13 Chief Information Tech Officer ... Mr. Jesse JOHNSON

College of Court Reporting, Inc. (E)

455 West Lincolnway, Valparaiso IN 46385
County: Lake — FICE Identification: 026158
Unit ID: 150251
Telephone: (866) 294-3974 — Carnegie Class: Spec 2-yr-Other
FAX Number: (219) 942-1631 — Calendar System: Semester
URL: www.ccr.edu
Established: 1984 — Annual Undergrad Tuition & Fees: $9,950
Enrollment: 123 — Coed
Affiliation or Control: Proprietary — IRS Status: Proprietary
Highest Offering: Associate Degree
Accreditation: DEAC

01 President/Executive Director ... Mr. Jeff T. MOODY
05 Director of Education ... Ms. Kay MOODY
07 Director of Admissions ... Ms. Nicky M. RODRIQUEZ
37 Director of Financial Aid ... Ms. Alice LEONARD
32 Director of Student Services ... Ms. Mindi BILLINGS

Concordia Theological Seminary (F)

6600 N Clinton Street, Fort Wayne IN 46825-4996
County: Allen — FICE Identification: 020876
Unit ID: 150288
Telephone: (260) 452-2100 — Carnegie Class: Spec-4-yr-Faith
FAX Number: (260) 452-2121 — Calendar System: Quarter
URL: www.ctsfw.edu
Established: 1846 — Annual Graduate Tuition & Fees: N/A
Enrollment: 295 — Male
Affiliation or Control: Lutheran Church - Missouri Synod
IRS Status: 501(c)3
Highest Offering: Doctorate; No Undergraduates
Accreditation: HLC, THEOL

01 President ... Dr. Lawrence R. RAST
05 Provost ... Dr. Charles A. GIESCHEN
36 Dir of Certification & Placement ... Dr. Jeffrey PULSE, II
32 Dean of Students ... Dr. Ryan M. TIETZ
11 Vice President of Operations ... Mr. Lance HOFFMAN
06 Registrar ... Mrs. Barbara A. WEGMAN
07 Director of Admissions ... Rev. Matthew WIETFELDT
08 Director of Library ... Prof. Robert V. ROETHEMEYER
15 Director of Human Resources ... Ms. Kali ANDERSON

DePauw University (G)

313 S Locust Street, Greencastle IN 46135-1772
County: Putnam — FICE Identification: 001792
Unit ID: 150400
Telephone: (765) 658-4800 — Carnegie Class: Bac-A&S
FAX Number: (765) 658-4177 — Calendar System: Semester
URL: www.depauw.edu
Established: 1837 — Annual Undergrad Tuition & Fees: $52,710
Enrollment: 1,752 — Coed
Affiliation or Control: United Methodist — IRS Status: 501(c)3
Highest Offering: Baccalaureate
Accreditation: HLC, MUS

01 President ... Dr. Lori WHITE
04 Executive Assistant to President ... Ms. Elizabeth DEMMINGS
05 VP for Academic Affairs ... Dr. David BERQUE
32 VP Student Affs/Dean of Students ... Dr. John Mark DAY
10 VP for Finance/Administration ... Dr. Andrea YOUNG
84 VP for Enrollment Management ... Ms. Mary Beth PETRIE
30 VP Development/Alumni Engagement ... Ms. Anne S. CUNNINGHAM
22 VP for Institutional Equity ... Dr. Dionne JACKSON
28 Exec Dir Ctr Diversity/Inclusion ... Dr. Holbrook HANKINSON
20 Dean of the Faculty ... Dr. Bridget L. GOURLEY
64 Dean of the School of Music ... Dr. David CUTLER
13 Chief Information Officer ... Ms. Carol L. SMITH
35 Assistant VP for Student Life ... Mr. Dorian SHAGER
06 Registrar ... Dr. LaTonya BRANHAM
15 Dir of Human Resources ... Ms. Angela D. NALLY
37 Assistant VP for Financial Aid ... Ms. Leslie MIDDLETON
41 Director of Athletics ... Ms. Stevie BAKER-WATSON
21 Assoc VP for Finance ... Mr. Travis W. LINNEWEBER
08 Director of Libraries ... Mr. Rick E. PROVINE
44 Director of Annual Giving ... Ms. Rosalie BLANKENSHIP
19 Director of Public Safety ... Ms. Charlene P. SHREWSBURY
07 Assoc Director of Admission ... Mr. Orlando RAMIREZ
18 Assoc VP for Facilities ... Mr. Warren WHITESELL
27 Director of Media Relations ... Ms. Mary DIETER
09 Director of Institutional Research ... Dr. William M. TOBIN
38 Director of Student Counseling ... Dr. Trevor YUHAS
39 Assistant Director of Housing ... Ms. Nicci COLLISI
36 Dir Career Dev/Advising/Interns ... Ms. Erin A. MAHONEY
26 Int VP of Comm and Marketing ... Dr. Sarah STEINKAMP
105 Director Web Services ... Ms. Andrea ADAMCHAK
14 Associate CIO ... Vacant
100 Chief of Staff ... Ms. Sarah STEINKAMP
104 Director of off-Campus Programs ... Mr. David CROUT
29 Exec Director Alumni Engagement ... Ms. Leslie SMITH

Earlham College and Earlham School of Religion (H)

801 National Road W, Richmond IN 47374-4095
County: Wayne — FICE Identification: 001793
Unit ID: 150455
Telephone: (765) 983-1200 — Carnegie Class: Bac-A&S
FAX Number: (765) 983-1304 — Calendar System: Semester
URL: www.earlham.edu
Established: 1847 — Annual Undergrad Tuition & Fees: $48,091
Enrollment: 815 — Coed
Affiliation or Control: Friends — IRS Status: 501(c)3
Highest Offering: Master's
Accreditation: HLC, THEOL

01 President ... Anne HOUTMAN
05 Vice President Academic Affairs ... Tara NATARAJAN
10 Vice President Business Affairs ... Stacy LUTZ DAVIDSON
73 Dean School of Religion ... Gretchen CASTLE
84 VP of Enrollment Management ... Phil BETZ
32 VP/Dean of Student Life ... Bonita WASHINGTON-LACY
20 Sr Associate VP Academic Affairs ... Michael DEIBEL
20 Associate Academic Dean for Faculty ... James LOGAN
111 VP for Institutional Advancement ... Kimberly TANNER
15 AVP for Human Resources/Safety/Risk ... Christopher LITTLE
29 Director of Alumni Relations ... Alyssa TEGELER
21 Controller ... Carrie ERVIN
06 Registrar ... Corrine DEIBEL
121 Int Dir Academic Enrichment Svcs ... Jenelle JOB
88 Admissions School of Religion ... Julie DISHMAM
41 Athletic Director ... Adam HUTCHINSON
13 Interim Dir of Computing Services ... Denise CRUM
37 Director of Financial Aid ... Katherine GOTTSCHALK
85 Director of International Programs ... Roger ADKINS
26 VP Marketing & Communications ... Kristen LAINSBURY
27 Director of Media Relations ... Brian ZIMMERMAN
19 Director of Public Safety ... Christopher LITTLE
08 Director of Library ... Amy BRYANT
28 Sr AVP Strat/Diversity Initiatives ... Gariot LOUIMA
04 Executive Assistant ... Alisha TRIANA
39 Director Residence Life ... Shane PETERS
09 Director of Institutional Research ... Vacant
38 Director Student Counseling ... Jessica SANFORD
102 Dir Foundation/Corporate Relations ... Sara PAULE
104 Director Study Abroad ... Vacant
105 Director Web Services ... Adam FRAZIER
44 Director Annual Giving ... Dakota COLLINS
07 Director of Admissions ... Erin HUTCHINSON

Faith Bible Seminary (I)

2000 Elmwood Ave, Lafayette IN 47904
County: Tippecanoe — Identification: 667250
Telephone: (765) 448-1986 — Carnegie Class: Not Classified
FAX Number: (765) 448-2985 — Calendar System: Semester
URL: www.faithlafayette.org/seminary
Established: 2005 — Annual Graduate Tuition & Fees: N/A
Enrollment: N/A — Coed
Affiliation or Control: Independent Non-Profit — IRS Status: 501(c)3
Highest Offering: Master's; No Undergraduates
Accreditation: BI

01 President ... Dr. Brent AUCOIN
05 Academic Dean ... Dr. Rob GREEN
84 Dean of Enrollment Management ... Mr. Kirk FATOOL

Fortis College (J)

9001 N Wesleyan Road Suite 101, Indianapolis IN 46268
Telephone: (317) 808-4800 — Identification: 770574
Accreditation: ACCSC, MAAB

† Branch campus of Fortis College, Centreville, OH.

Franklin College of Indiana (A)

101 Branigin Boulevard, Franklin IN 46131-2623
County: Johnson FICE Identification: 001798
Unit ID: 150604
Telephone: (317) 738-8000 Carnegie Class: Bac-A&S
FAX Number: (317) 738-8013 Calendar System: 4/1/4
URL: www.franklincollege.edu
Established: 1834 Annual Undergrad Tuition & Fees: $33,954
Enrollment: 994 Coed
Affiliation or Control: American Baptist IRS Status: 501(c)3
Highest Offering: Master's
Accreditation: HLC, #ARCPA, CAATE

01 President .... Mr. Kerry N. PRATHER
04 Assistant to the President .... Ms. Janet D. SCHANTZ
10 Vice President and CFO .... Mr. Kevin HONIGFORD
05 VP Acad Affs/Dean of College .... Dr. Kristin C. FLORA
84 VP for Enrollment & Marketing .... Mr. Thandabantu B. MACEO
111 VP for Institutional Advancement .... Mrs. Dana CUMMINGS
20 Associate Dean for Academic Affairs .... Dr. Sarah SUMMERS
32 VP for Student Dev/Dean of Students .... Dr. Andrew B. JONES
29 Dir Alumni Engage/Campus Prtnrshps .... Ms. Emily S. WOOD
06 Registrar .... Ms. Lisa MAHAN
18 AVP of Physical Facilities .... Mr. Thomas PATZ
38 Director of Counseling Center .... Mrs. Sara KINDER
121 Dean Student Success/Retention .... Dr. Andrew B. JONES
46 Director of Academic Partnerships .... Ms. Betsy SCHMIDT
110 Sr Dir Development/Planned Giving .... Mrs. Nora BREMS
37 Director of Financial Aid .... Mr. James VINCENT-DUNN
42 Director of Religious Life/ Chaplain .... Rev. Hannah ADAMS INGRAM
41 Director of Athletics .... Mr. Andrew HENDRICKS
13 Director of Info Tech Svcs .... Mr. Jason MCHENRY
36 Director Career Development .... Mr. Kirk J. BIXLER
88 Dir Professional Dev/Employer Rels .... Dr. Jeremy VAN ANDEL
104 Dir Office of Global Education .... Ms. Jennifer CATALDI
109 General Manager Parkhurst Dining .... Ms. Deva DUNCAN
44 AVP for Alumni Engage/Annual Giving .... Ms. Lee Ann JOURDAN
07 Director of Admissions .... Mr. Ryan MCCLARNON
27 Director of Communications .... Ms. Deidra BAUMGARDNER
26 Interim Director of Marketing .... Ms. Sandy SHOAF
08 Director of Library Services .... Ms. Denise SHOREY
19 Dir of Security/Title IX Coord .... Mr. Steve LEONARD
105 Website Administrator .... Ms. Sandy SHOAF
15 Director of Human Resources .... Mr. Matthew DUSING
22 Asst Vice Pres Physical Facilities .... Mr. Thomas PATZ
40 Bookstore Manager .... Mr. Matthew NEAU
21 Business Office Manager .... Mr. Bradley JONES
23 Coordinator Student Health Center .... Ms. Katy ALEXANDER
28 Director of Diversity & Inclusion .... Dr. Maegan POLLONAIS
50 Head Business/Computing/Math Div .... Dr. Justin GASH
53 Head Education Division .... Dr. Amy SCHULZ
79 Head Humanities Division .... Dr. Susan CRISAFULLI
60 Head Journalism Division .... Mr. Joel CRAMER
65 Head Natural Sciences Division .... Dr. Benjamin O'NEAL
83 Head Social Sciences Division .... Dr. Jason JIMERSON
57 Head Fine Arts Division .... Dr. Svetlana RAKIC
122 Dir Stdnt Involvement/Greek Life .... Mr. Ernest C. EVANS
39 Associate Dean of Students .... Ms. Kathryn DENNEHY

Goshen College (B)

1700 S Main Street, Goshen IN 46526-4794
County: Elkhart FICE Identification: 001799
Unit ID: 150668
Telephone: (574) 535-7000 Carnegie Class: Bac-Diverse
FAX Number: (574) 535-7060 Calendar System: Semester
URL: www.goshen.edu
Established: 1894 Annual Undergrad Tuition & Fees: $35,230
Enrollment: 899 Coed
Affiliation or Control: Mennonite Church IRS Status: 501(c)3
Highest Offering: Doctorate
Accreditation: HLC, CAEP, NURSE, SW

01 President .... Dr. Rebecca J. STOLTZFUS
05 VP Academic Affairs/Academic Dean .... Dr. Ann VENDRELY
10 Vice President for Finance .... Mr. Jim ALVAREZ
111 VP for Advancement .... Mr. Todd A. YODER
84 VP for Enroll Management/ Marketing .... Ms. Dominique BURGUNDER-JOHNSON
26 VP Communications & People Strategy .... Ms. Jodi BEYELER
32 VP for Student Life .... Dr. Gilberto PEREZ, JR.
66 Director of Undergraduate Nursing .... Ms. Jewel YODER
66 Director of Graduate Nursing .... Dr. Ruth STOLTZFUS
70 Director of Social Work .... Dr. Jeanne M. LIECHTY
53 Director of Elementary Teacher Educ .... Dr. Kathryn MEYER REIMER
08 Library Director .... Mr. Fritz HARTMAN
82 Director of International Education .... Dr. Jan BENDER SHETLER
53 Director of Secondary Education .... Dr. Suzanne EHST
13 Director of Information Tech Svcs .... Ms. Patricia GOODMAN
09 Director of Institutional Research .... Mr. Justin HEINZEKEHR
06 Registrar .... Dr. Jan KAUFFMAN
37 Director Student Financial Aid .... Mr. Stephen WOLMA
29 Director of Alumni/Parent Relations .... Dr. Dan LIECHTY
28 Dir Diversity/Equity & Inclusion .... Rev. LaKendra HARDWARE
42 Campus Minister .... Rev. Cathy STONER
36 Director of Career Services .... Mr. David KENDALL
18 Director of Facilities .... Ms. Cynthia GOOD KAUFMANN
15 Director of Human Resources .... Ms. Marlene PENNER
58 Director Adult & Graduate Studies .... Dr. Duane STOLTZFUS
19 Director Campus Safety & Housing .... Mr. Chad COLEMAN
04 Exec Assistant to the President .... Ms. Kathleen YODER
108 Director Institutional Assessment .... Mr. Justin HEINZEKEHR
41 Athletic Director .... Dr. Erica ALBERTIN
38 Director Student Counseling .... Vacant
07 Director of Undergraduate Admission .... Mr. Steve WOLMA

Grace College and Seminary (C)

200 Seminary Drive, Winona Lake IN 46590-1294
County: Kosciusko FICE Identification: 001800
Unit ID: 150677
Telephone: (574) 372-5100 Carnegie Class: Masters/M
FAX Number: (574) 372-5139 Calendar System: Semester
URL: www.grace.edu
Established: 1937 Annual Undergrad Tuition & Fees: $27,432
Enrollment: 1,901 Coed
Affiliation or Control: IRS Status: 501(c)3
Highest Offering: Doctorate
Accreditation: HLC, CACREP, CAEPN, THEOL

01 President .... Dr. Drew FLAMM
04 Exec Assistant to the President .... Mrs. Sarah E. PRATER
73 VP/Dean Seminary & Sch of Ministry .... Dr. Frederick CARDOZA, II
111 VP Advancement and Marketing .... Dr. Andrew R. FLAMM
10 VP of Financial Affairs/CFO .... Mr. Doug BAUMGARDNER
11 VP Administration & Compliance .... Dr. Carrie A. YOCUM
05 Provost .... Dr. Kevin ROBERTS
84 Associate VP Enrollment Management .... Dr. Mark A. POHL
11 Chief Operations Officer .... Mr. Paul G. BLAIR
32 Associate VP Student Affairs .... Mr. Aaron T. CRABTREE
49 Dean of School of Arts & Sciences .... Dr. Mark M. NORRIS
83 Dean of Sch of Behavioral Science .... Dr. Thomas J. EDGINGTON
50 Dean of School of Business .... Dr. Jeffrey K. FAWCETT
53 Dean of School of Education .... Dr. Cheryl BREMER
106 Dean School of Prof/Online Ed .... Dr. Timothy J. ZIEBARTH
121 Dean of Academic Engagement/ Success .... Mrs. Jacqueline S. SCHRAM
42 Dean of Chapel .... Mr. Brent T. MENCARELLI
06 Registrar .... Mr. Timothy J. ZIEBARTH
08 Dir Library Services .... Mrs. Tonya L. FAWCETT
13 Dir Information Technology .... Mr. Donald W. FLUKE
23 Dir Student Health & Counseling .... Dr. Debra S. MUSSER
37 Dir Student Financial Aid .... Mrs. Charlette R. SAUDERS
15 Chief Human Resource Officer .... Mr. Norman BAKHIT
26 Dir of Marketing .... Mr. Matthew R. METZGER
18 Director Physical Plant .... Mr. Keith DENLINGER
19 Director Security/Safety .... Mr. Glenn A. GOLDSMITH
29 Director Alumni Engagement .... Mr. Robert JACKSON
41 Director of Athletics .... Mr. Chad C. BRISCOE
36 Director Career Connections .... Mrs. Denise A. TERRY
07 Director of Admissions .... Dr. Mark POHL
30 Director of Development .... Mrs. Carrie VINEYARD
39 Director Residence Life .... Ms. Rebecca STOWERS

Hanover College (D)

517 Ball Drive, Hanover IN 47243
County: Jefferson FICE Identification: 001801
Unit ID: 150756
Telephone: (812) 866-7000 Carnegie Class: Bac-A&S
FAX Number: (812) 866-2164 Calendar System: Other
URL: www.hanover.edu
Established: 1827 Annual Undergrad Tuition & Fees: $39,650
Enrollment: 1,028 Coed
Affiliation or Control: Presbyterian Church (U.S.A.) IRS Status: 501(c)3
Highest Offering: Doctorate
Accreditation: HLC, CAEP, @PTA

01 President .... Dr. Lake LAMBERT, III
100 Chief of Staff/Exec Asst to Pres .... Shelley PREOCANIN
05 Provost/VP Academic Affairs .... Dr. Carey ADAMS
10 Vice President Business Affairs .... Morris VINCE
41 Vice President of Athletics .... Lynn HALL
111 Vice President College Advancement .... Melba RODRIGUEZ
84 Vice Pres Marketing/Enrollment .... Peter ASHLEY
32 Vice President/Dean Student Life .... Dr. Dewain LEE
35 Associate Dean of Student Outcomes .... Katy LOWE-SCHNEIDER
39 Assoc Dean Students Residence Life .... Lindsay FAULSTICK
06 Registrar .... Dr. Ken PRINCE
07 Exec Director of Admissions .... Rachel SCHMIDTKE
36 Exec Director Levett Career Center .... Jenny MOSS
13 Chief Technology Officer .... Kevin STORMER
42 Chaplain .... Catherine KNOTT
29 Director of Alumni Engagement .... Christy HUGHES
19 Director of Campus Safety .... Jim HICKERSON
08 Director of Duggan Library .... Kelly JOYCE
37 Assoc Director of Financial Aid .... Jennifer SHELLEY
23 Director of Health Services .... Christy OWNBEY
15 Director of Human Resources .... Heather BUHR
18 Director of Physical Plant .... Kevin BROWN
104 Director of Study Abroad .... Uschi APPELT
38 Director of Student Counseling .... Catherine LE SAUX
21 Controller .... Heather CHISM
88 Special Asst to the President .... Kay STOKES
122 Assc Dean Stdnts-Frat/Sorority Life .... Casey HECKLER

Holy Cross College (E)

PO Box 308, Notre Dame IN 46556-0308
County: Saint Joseph FICE Identification: 007263
Unit ID: 150774
Telephone: (574) 239-8400 Carnegie Class: Bac-A&S
FAX Number: (574) 239-8323 Calendar System: Semester
URL: www.hcc-nd.edu
Established: 1966 Annual Undergrad Tuition & Fees: $33,250
Enrollment: 455 Coed
Affiliation or Control: Roman Catholic IRS Status: 501(c)3
Highest Offering: Baccalaureate
Accreditation: HLC

01 President .... Rev. David TYSON, CSC
05 Interim Provost .... Dr. Michael GRIFFIN
10 Vice President of Finance .... Ms. Monica MARKOVICH
32 Dean & VP for Student Life .... Mr. Andrew POLANIECKI
26 AVP Communications & Development .... Ms. JudeAnne HASTINGS
20 Dean of the College .... Dr. Anthony MONTA
06 Registrar .... Ms. Hiroko HARRISON
07 Director of Admissions .... Ms. Marisa SIMON
38 Director of Student Counseling Svcs .... Mr. Thomas DEHORN
13 Director of Information Technology .... Mr. Douglas BLAIR
08 Director of Library Services .... Ms. Sarah KOLDA
42 Director of Campus Ministry .... Mr. Andrew OUELLETTE
15 Director of Human Resources .... Ms. Gwen DEMAEGD
19 Chief Security Officer .... Mr. Greg RUNNELS
29 Director of Career Development .... Mr. Adam DEBECK
96 Director of Purchasing .... Mr. John PAJAKOWSKI
26 Assoc Dir for Special Events .... Ms. Jodie BADMAN
04 Admin Assistant to the President .... Mrs. Diane WELIHAN
37 Director Student Financial Aid .... Mr. Rick GONSIOREK
41 Athletic Director .... Mr. Tom ROBBINS

Horizon University (F)

7700 Indian Lake Road, Indianapolis IN 46236
County: Marion FICE Identification: 041405
Unit ID: 457226
Telephone: (800) 553-4674 Carnegie Class: Spec-4-yr-Faith
FAX Number: N/A Calendar System: Semester
URL: www.horizonuniversity.edu
Established: 1993 Annual Undergrad Tuition & Fees: $9,300
Enrollment: 42 Coed
Affiliation or Control: Independent Non-Profit IRS Status: 501(c)3
Highest Offering: Master's
Accreditation: BI

01 President .... Dr. Randall DODGE
05 Academic Dean .... Mr. Dave KOSOBUCKI
11 Dean of Administration .... Vacant
10 Chief Financial Officer .... Ms. Debbie MARSHALL
32 Dean of Students .... Mr. Tracy GRAY
26 Dir Marketing/Communications .... Mr. Andrew LOCKERBIE
06 Registrar/Dir Student Financial Aid .... Mrs. Judy SLACK
07 Director of Admissions .... Miss Jacki CURTIS
13 Chief Information Tech Officer .... Mr. Dave LOVELL
19 Director Security/Safety .... Mr. Paul LANGE

Huntington University (G)

2303 College Avenue, Huntington IN 46750-9986
County: Huntington FICE Identification: 001803
Unit ID: 150941
Telephone: (260) 356-6000 Carnegie Class: Masters/S
FAX Number: (260) 359-4086 Calendar System: Semester
URL: www.huntington.edu
Established: 1897 Annual Undergrad Tuition & Fees: $26,846
Enrollment: 1,391 Coed
Affiliation or Control: United Brethren Church IRS Status: 501(c)3
Highest Offering: Doctorate
Accreditation: HLC, CAEP, NURSE, OT, OTA, SW

01 President .... Dr. Sherilyn R. EMBERTON
05 VP Academic Affairs/Dean Faculty .... Dr. Luke S. FETTERS
11 VP/Chief Operating Officer .... Dr. Russ J. DEGITZ
10 Vice Pres Finance & Treasurer .... Mrs. Connie C. BONNER
84 VP Enrollment Mgmt & Marketing .... Ms. Cindy N. SISSON
111 VP for Advancement .... Dr. Stephen T. WEINGART
32 VP for Student Life .... Dr. Ron L. COFFEY
04 Executive Asst to President .... Ms. Peg DEBOLT
42 VP for Spiritual Formation .... Rev. Arthur L. WILSON
58 Dir of Grad & Professional Programs .... Ms. Wendy S. SPEAKMAN
36 Dean Student Life/Career Dev .... Ms. Martha J. SMITH
37 Director of Financial Aid .... Ms. Lisa M. MONTANY
06 Registrar .... Ms. Beth A. DUBOIS
08 Director of Library Services .... Ms. Noelle C. KELLER
13 Dir Information/Technology Services .... Mr. Adam L. SKILES
88 Dir Academic Center for Excellence .... Ms. Erica A. MARSHALL
41 Athletic Director .... Ms. Lori L. CULLER
18 Director of Facilities .... Ms. Marcie NOFZIGER
29 Dir Alumni & Foundation Relations .... Vacant
19 Chief of Campus Police/Safety .... Mr. Keirsh A. COCHRAN
15 Director of Human Resources .... Mr. Andy MCKEE
93 Dir of Intercultural Enrichment .... Vacant
121 Director of Student Success .... Mr. Isaac C. BARBER
21 Sr Staff Accountant/Budget Analyst .... Mr. Joseph A. PRETORIUS
26 Chief Public Relations Officer .... Ms. Lynette D. FAGER
07 Director of Admissions .... Ms. Susanne M. WATSON
106 Dean of Online Education/E-learning .... Ms. Wendy S. SPEAKMAN
108 Director Institutional Assessment .... Dr. Andrew J. HOFFMAN
44 Director Annual Giving .... Ms. Marcy T. HAWKINS

Indiana State University (H)

200 N 7th Street, Terre Haute IN 47809-1902
County: Vigo FICE Identification: 001807
Unit ID: 151324
Telephone: (812) 237-6311 Carnegie Class: DU-Mod
FAX Number: N/A Calendar System: Semester
URL: indstate.edu

Established: 1865 Annual Undergrad Tuition & Fees (In-State): $9,466
Enrollment: 10,829 Coed
Affiliation or Control: State IRS Status: 501(c)3
Highest Offering: Doctorate
Accreditation: HLC, ARCPA, ART, CAATE, CACREP, CAEP, CIDA, CLPSY, CONST, DIETC, MUS, NAIT, NUR, OT, PTA, SCPSY, SP, SW

01 President Dr. Deborah CURTIS
100 Chief of Staff Ms. Teresa D. EXLINE
86 Exec Dir of Govt Rel/Univ Comm Mr. Greg J. GOODE
05 Provost/Vice Pres Academic Affs Dr. Christopher OLSEN
10 Sr VP Finance & Admin/Univ Treas Ms. Diann E. MCKEE
32 VP Student Affairs Dr. Michele SOLIZ
88 Vice Pres Univ Engagement Dr. Nancy B. ROGERS
111 Vice Pres Univ Advancement/CEO Fndn Ms. Andrea L. ANGEL
43 General Counsel Legal Affairs Ms. Bridget K. BUTWIN
20 Assoc VP Academic Affairs Dr. Susan POWERS
13 Int Assoc VP/Chief Info Officer Mr. Robert BARLEY
26 Int AVP Marketing Ms. Carrie LUTZ
07 Int Exec Dir Admissions/HS Rels Ms. Regina ATKINS
29 Exec Director of Alumni Engagement Mr. Rex KENDALL
15 Exec Director Human Resources Ms. Tami WEINZAPFEL-SMITH
14 Exec Dir Information Technology Mr. Yancy PHILLIPS
21 Assoc VP/Univ Controller Mr. Jeff JACSO
06 Registrar Dr. April HAY
22 AVP for Inclusive Excellence Dr. Rana JOHNSON
28 Exec Dir Multicultural Svcs & Pgms Dr. Elonda ERVIN
41 Director of Athletics Mr. Sherard CLINKSCALES
36 Executive Director Career Svcs Mr. Alex ALLEN
25 Director Sponsored Programs Ms. Liz METZGER
09 Director of Institutional Research Ms. Patty MCCLINTOCK
19 Director of Public Safety Ms. Michele BARRETT
96 Dir Purchasing/Central Receiving Mr. Kevin BARR
39 Executive Dir of Residential Life Dr. Amanda KNERR
38 Director of Student Counseling Dr. Kenneth CHEW
37 Director Student Financial Aid Ms. Donna SIMMONDS
49 Int Dean of Arts & Sciences Dr. Bassam YOUSIF
50 Dean of Business Dr. Terry DAUGHERTY
53 Dean of Education Dr. Janet BUCKENMEYER
68 Dean Health & Human Svcs Dr. Caroline MALLORY
72 Dean of Technology Dr. Nesli ALP
58 Dean of Grad/Professional Studies Dr. Denise COLLINS
08 Dean of Library Services Dr. Robin CRUMRIN
56 Director of Extended Learning Ms. Samantha PENNEY
35 Assoc VP Student Affairs Mr. Brooks MOORE
04 Admin Assistant to the President Ms. Kay PONSOT
105 Web Director Mr. TJ (Garrett) ROOD
106 Exec Director of Online Education Dr. Tim LONDON
108 Director Institutional Assessment Dr. Kelley WOODS-JOHNSON
44 Director Annual Giving Ms. Hilary DUNCAN

Indiana Tech (A)

1600 E Washington Boulevard, Fort Wayne IN 46803-1297
County: Allen FICE Identification: 001805
Unit ID: 151290
Telephone: (260) 422-5561 Carnegie Class: Masters/L
FAX Number: (260) 420-1453 Calendar System: Semester
URL: www.IndianaTech.edu
Established: 1930 Annual Undergrad Tuition & Fees: $28,000
Enrollment: 2,370 Coed
Affiliation or Control: Independent Non-Profit IRS Status: 501(c)3
Highest Offering: Doctorate
Accreditation: HLC, CAHIIM, IACBE

01 President Dr. Karl W. EINOLF
10 Exec VP Finance & Administration Ms. Judy K. ROY
05 VP for Academic Affairs Dr. Kathleen WATLAND
26 VP for Marketing & Communications Mr. Brian W. ENGELHART
84 VP for Enrollment Management Mr. Steve A. HERENDEEN
32 VP for Student Affairs Dr. Daniel J. STOKER
111 VP for Institutional Advancement Mr. Dan G. GRIGG
28 VP of Diversity & Inclusion Ms. Lisa D. GIVAN
11 Associate VP for Operations Ms. Sharon LOKUTA
50 Dean of Business Dr. Angie L. FINCANNON
97 Dean of General Studies Dr. Anne M. GULL
54 Dean of Engineering/Computer Sci Dr. Ying SHANG
58 Director Global Leadership Program Vacant
15 Human Resources Director Ms. Julie A. HENDRYX
21 Controller Ms. Shelly R. MUSOLF
13 VP Information Technology Svc Mr. Jeff S. LEICHTY
06 Registrar Ms. Heidi L. KANTENWEIN
08 Director of McMillen Library Mr. Brian A. HICKMAN
41 Athletic Director Ms. Jessie N. BIGGS
18 Dir Security & Facilities Mgmt Mr. R. Michael TOWNSLEY
37 Student Financial Services Director Mr. Scott W. THUM
07 Director of Admissions Mr. Robert N. CONFER
36 Dir Career Ctr/Regional Services Ms. Cynthia P. VERDUCE
39 Assoc VP Student Services Mr. Chris M. DICKSON
07 Director of Admissions Indianapolis Mr. Robert A. STASH
19 Director of Security Mr. Devin K. BLACKFORD
100 Dir of Advancement & Exec Opers Ms. Jennifer A. ROSS
25 Asst Dir of Advancement & Grants Ms. Erin E. JOHNSON
96 Director of Procurement Mr. Mark A. HUNSBERGER
04 Admin Assistant to the President Ms. Shayla D. CARLISLE
105 Web Developer Mr. Joel A. KUHN
112 Sr Dir of Institutional Advance Ms. Mary LASITS
29 Director of Alumni Relations Mrs. Kristi JARMUS
27 Director of Marketing/Communications Mr. Matthew S. BAIR
119 Information Security Officer Mr. Michael C. MULLEN

*Indiana University (B)

107 S. Indiana Ave., Bryan Hall 200,
Bloomington IN 47405-7000
County: Monroe FICE Identification: 008002
Unit ID: 151351
Telephone: (812) 855-4613 Carnegie Class: N/A
FAX Number: (812) 855-9586
URL: www.indiana.edu

01 President Dr. Pamela S. WHITTEN
05 EVP/Provost IUB Dr. Rahul SHRIVASTAV
03 Exec VP IU Vacant
20 Interim EVP Univ Academic Affairs Dr. Sue SCIAME-GIESECKE
46 Vice Pres for Research Dr. Fred H. CATE
28 VP Diversity/Equity/Multicult Aff Dr. James C. WIMBUSH
18 Vice Pres Capital Planning & Facil Dr. Thomas A. MORRISON
10 Vice President/CFO Mr. John SEJDINAJ
100 Chief of Staff Dr. Karen H. ADAMS
13 Vice President Info Tech/CIO Mr. Rob LOWDEN
43 Vice Pres/General Counsel Ms. Jacqueline A. SIMMONS
104 Vice Pres for International Affairs Ms. Hannah BUXBAUM
86 VP Gov Relations/Econ Engagement Mr. William B. STEPHAN
41 VP/Dir Intercollegiate Athletics Mr. Scott M. DOLSON
63 EVP Univ Clinical Affs/Dean Sch Med Dr. Jay L. HESS
15 VP Human Resources Mr. John WHELAN
84 Vice Provost Enrollment Management Dr. David B. JOHNSON
21 University Treasurer Mr. Donald S. LUKES
22 Dir Univ Ofc Institutional Equity Ms. Jennifer KINCAID
29 CEO/Exec Dir IU Alumni Assoc Mr. J. Thomas FORBES
102 Interim President/CEO IU Foundation Mr. J. Thomas FORBES
21 AVP/University Controller Ms. Anna K. JENSEN
116 AVP/Chief Audit Officer Mr. Stewart T. COBINE
04 Executive Asst to President Ms. Brittany F. SANTA
25 Exec Dir Grant Services Mr. Jim BECKER
32 Dean Students/V Prov Student Affair Mr. M. Dave O'GUINN
37 Univ Director of Financial Aid Ms. Jenny STEPHENS
19 AVP Public Safety/Inst Assurance Mr. Ben HUNTER
06 Associate Vice Provost & Registrar Mr. Mark MCCONAHAY
07 AV Prov/Exec Director of Admissions Ms. Sacha THIEME ARTERBERRY
08 Interim Dean University Libraries Ms. Diane M. DALLIS-COMENTALE
09 AVP Univ Inst Research/Reporting Mr. Todd J. SCHMITZ
101 Secretary of the Board Ms. Deborah A. LEMON
106 AVP/Director Office of Online Educ Dr. Chris J. FOLEY
39 Exec Dir Residential Pgms & Svcs Mr. Lukas D. LEFTWICH
44 IUF Exec Dir Mktg/Annual Giving Ms. Lindsey K. PEARSEY
50 Dean of Business Dr. Idalene F. KESNER
53 Interim Dean of Education Dr. Anastasia (Stacy) MORRONE
54 Interim Dean Info/Comp/Engineering Dr. Dennis GROTH
103 Exec Dir for Career Development Mr. Pat DONAHUE
96 Assoc VP for Procurement Mr. Baris KIYAR
26 Interim VP Comm & Marketing Ms. Rebecca CARL
27 Director of Media Relations Mr. Chuck CARNEY
38 Dir Student Counseling/Psych Svcs Dr. Denise HAYES

*Indiana University Bloomington (C)

107 S. Indiana Avenue, Bloomington IN 47405-7000
County: Monroe FICE Identification: 001809
Unit ID: 151351
Telephone: (812) 855-4848 Carnegie Class: Not Classified
FAX Number: (812) 855-5678 Calendar System: Semester
URL: www.iub.edu
Established: 1820 Annual Undergrad Tuition & Fees (In-State): N/A
Enrollment: N/A Coed
Affiliation or Control: State IRS Status: 501(c)3
Highest Offering: Doctorate
Accreditation: HLC, ART, AUD, CAATE, CAEP, CARTE, CEA, CIDA, CLPSY, COPSY, DIETD, IPSY, #JOUR, LAW, LIB, MPCAC, MUS, OPT, OPTR, PCSAS, PH, SCPSY, SP, SPAA, THEA

02 President Dr. Pamela WHITTEN
05 Exec VP & Provost Dr. Rahul SHRIVASTAV
03 Exec VP & Chancellor IUPUI Mr. Andrew KLEIN
10 Interim VP & CFO Mr. Sam ADAMS
17 Exec VP University Clinical Affairs Dr. Jay L. HESS
18 VP Capital Planning & Facilities Mr. Thomas A. MORRISON
46 VP for Research Mr. Fred H. CATE
28 VP Diversity/Equity and Multicult Mr. James WIMBUSH
86 VP for Govt Rels/Econ Engagement Mr. Bill STEPHAN
12 VP Regional Campuses/Online Educ Ms. Susan SCIAME-GIESECKE
32 VProv Stdnt Affairs/Dean of Stdnts Mr. Dave O'GUINN
13 VP of IT/Comms/Mktg & CIO Mr. Rob LOWDEN
20 Vice Prov for Undergraduate Educ Mr. Kurt ZORN
20 Vice Prov Faculty & Academic Affs Ms. Eliza PAVALKO
84 Vice Prov Enrollment Mgmt Mr. David JOHNSON
58 Vice Prov Grad Educ & Health Sci Mr. David DALEKE
21 Vice Prov Finance and Strategy Mr. Munirpallam A. VENKATARAMANAN
22 Vice Prov for Diversity/Inclusion Mr. John NIETO-PHILLIPS
21 Assoc VP & Univ Controller Ms. Anna JENSEN
15 VP Human Resources Mr. Todd RICHARDSON
104 VP for International Affairs Ms. Hannah BUXBAUM
116 Chief Audit Officer Ms. Lisa BEYMER
49 Executive Dean Col Arts & Sciences Mr. Rick VAN KOOTEN
08 Ruth Lilly Dean Univ Libraries Ms. Diane DALLIS-COMENTALE
50 Int Dean Kelley School of Business Mr. Ash SONI
53 Dean School of Education Ms. Anastasia MORRONE
69 Dean School of Public Health Mr. David ALLISON
88 Dean School of Optometry Dr. Joseph A. BONANNO
61 Dean School of Law Mr. Austen L. PARRISH
64 Dean Jacobs School of Music Ms. Abra BUSH
60 Int Dean Media School Mr. Walter GANTZ
57 Dean School of Art/Arch & Design Ms. Peg FAIMON
77 Dean Sch Informatics/Comp/Eng Ms. Joanna MILLUNCHICK
82 Int Dean Sch of Global/Intl Affs Mr. Nick CULLATHER
80 Dean School of Public/Env Affairs Dr. SiGn MOONEY
66 Dean School of Nursing Ms. Robin NEWHOUSE
92 Dean Hutton Honors College Mr. Andrea CICCARELLI
70 Dean of Social Work Dr. Tamara DAVIS
29 CEO Alumni Association Ms. Patricia RIVEIRE STUMPF
39 Exec Dir Residential Pgm & Svcs Mr. Lukas LEFTWICH
06 Assoc Vice Provost/Registrar Mr. Mark MCCONAHAY
43 VP & General Counsel Mr. Anthony PRATHER
19 Chief of Police Ms. Jill LEES
41 Vice President & Dir of Athletics Mr. Scott DOLSON
88 Dir Eskenazi Museum of Art Mr. David BRENNEMAN
07 Vice Prov & Exec Dir Admissions Ms. Sacha THIEME
100 Chief of Staff Ms. Brenda STOPHER
106 Assoc VP & Dir Online Education Mr. Chris FOLEY
88 University Treasurer Mr. Don LUKES
37 Dir Student Financial Assistance Ms. Jackie KENNEDY-FLETCHER
04 Exec Assistant to the President Ms. Vicki PETERMICHAEL
88 Vice Provost for Research Ms. Brea PERRY
26 Int Vice Prov Comm & Mktg Ms. Rebecca CARL
27 Dir Strategic Comm & Marketing Ms. Jessica PARRY

*Indiana University East (D)

2325 Chester Boulevard, Richmond IN 47374-1289
County: Wayne FICE Identification: 001811
Unit ID: 151388
Telephone: (765) 973-8200 Carnegie Class: Masters/S
FAX Number: N/A Calendar System: Semester
URL: www.iue.edu
Established: 1946 Annual Undergrad Tuition & Fees (In-State): $7,715
Enrollment: 3,434 Coed
Affiliation or Control: State IRS Status: 501(c)3
Highest Offering: Master's
Accreditation: HLC, ACBSP, CAEP, NUR

02 Interim Chancellor Dr. Michelle MALOTT
05 Interim EVC Academic Affairs Mr. TJ RIVARD
26 Interim VC External Affairs Mr. Todd DUKE
10 Vice Chancellor Admin & Finance Ms. Leisa JULIAN
32 Dean of Students Ms. Amy JARECKI
13 Interim Dir Information Technology Ms. Joy MAUPIN
30 Director of Gift Development Ms. Paula Kay KING
06 Director Office of Student Records Ms. Katie CHANEY
08 Director Library/Media Services Dr. Frances YATES
15 Director Human Resources Ms. Evelyn GORDON
36 Director Career Services Ms. Kara BELLEW
07 Executive Director of Admissions Ms. Molly VANDERPOOL
37 Exec Dir Fin Aid & Scholarships Ms. Sarah SOPER
121 Director Student Success Vacant
35 Director of Campus Life Ms. Rebeckah HESTER
113 Assistant Bursar Ms. Shelley DODSON
70 Director Social Work/Human Services Vacant
27 Director Communications & Marketing Mr. John DALTON
29 Director Alumni Relations Ms. Terry WIESEHAN
50 Dean Business/Economics Dr. Denise S. SMITH
83 Dean Humanities/Social Sciences Dr. Daren SNIDER
81 Dean Natural Science & Math Dr. Markus POMPER
66 Dean Nursing/Ctr Health Promotion Dr. Karen CLARK
53 Dean of Education Dr. Jerry WILDE
09 Director of Institutional Research Vacant
18 Director of Physical Facilities Mr. Gail SMOKER
41 Director of Athletics Mr. Joe GRIFFIN
38 Director of Behavioral Health Ms. Jennifer CLAYPOOLE
19 Chief Campus Police Mr. Scott DUNNING
22 Dir Affirmative Action/EEOC/TitleIX Ms. Tracy AMYX
28 Chief Diversity Ofcr/Special Asst Ms. Yemi MAHONEY

*Indiana University Kokomo (E)

2300 S Washington, Box 9003, Kokomo IN 46904-9003
County: Howard FICE Identification: 001814
Unit ID: 151333
Telephone: (765) 453-2000 Carnegie Class: Masters/S
FAX Number: (765) 455-9444 Calendar System: Semester
URL: www.iuk.edu
Established: 1945 Annual Undergrad Tuition & Fees (In-State): $7,715
Enrollment: 3,227 Coed
Affiliation or Control: State IRS Status: 501(c)3
Highest Offering: Master's
Accreditation: HLC, CAEP, NUR, NURSE, RAD

02 Chancellor Dr. Susan SCIAME-GIESECKE
05 Int Deputy Chanc/Exec VC Acad Affs Dr. Mark CANADA
10 Vice Chancellor for Finance Mr. Jared HAYMAN
20 Assoc Vice Chanc Academic Affairs Dr. Christina DOWNEY
20 Assoc VC for Academic Affairs Dr. Julie SAAM
32 Vice Chanc Student Affs/Enroll Mgmt Ms. Tess BARKER
111 Vice Chancellor for Advancement Ms. Crystal JONES
26 Asst VC Media & Marketing Ms. Marie LINDSKOOG
07 Asst VC for Admissions Ms. Angie SIDERS
08 Dean of the Library Ms. Yan HE
37 Director Financial Aid Ms. Dara JOHNSON
27 Dir External Rels/Public Affairs Ms. Catherine VALCKE
06 Asst VC for Academic Affs/Registrar Ms. Stacey THOMAS
100 Chief of Staff Ms. Sarah SARBER
36 Manager Career/Accessibility Center Ms. Tracy SPRINGER

28 Coord Stdnt Life & Campus Diversity ... Vacant
35 Dean of Students ... Ms. Audra DOWLING
18 Director Facilities/Physical Plant ... Mr. John SARBER
50 Dean School of Business ... Dr. Chitti GOVINDARAJULU
79 Dean Sch Humanities/Social Sciences ... Dr. Eric BAIN-SELBO
66 Dean School of Nursing ... Dr. Susan HENDRICKS
53 Dean School of Education ... Dr. Leah NELLIS
81 Dean School of Sciences ... Dr. Christian CHAURET
13 Chief Info Technology Officer (CIO) ... Mr. Nick RAY
15 Director Human Resources ... Ms. April EVANS
41 Athletic Director ... Mr. Greg COOPER
29 Director Alumni Affairs ... Mr. Benjamin A. LIECHTY
30 Director of Development ... Ms. Catherine CLEARWATERS

*Indiana University Northwest (A)

3400 Broadway, Gary IN 46408-1197
County: Lake — FICE Identification: 001815
Unit ID: 151360
Telephone: (219) 980-6500 — Carnegie Class: Masters/S
FAX Number: (219) 980-6670 — Calendar System: Semester
URL: www.iun.edu
Established: 1921 — Annual Undergrad Tuition & Fees (In-State): $7,715
Enrollment: 3,801 — Coed
Affiliation or Control: State — IRS Status: 501(c)3
Highest Offering: Master's
Accreditation: HLC, CAEP, CAHIIM, DA, DH, DMS, NUR, RAD, RTT, SPAA

02 Chancellor ... Mr. Ken IWAMA
100 Chief of Staff ... Ms. Amy J. DIAZ
05 Exec VC Academic Affairs ... Dr. Victoria ROMAN-LAGUNAS
32 AVC Student Affs/Dean of Students ... Ms. Beth TYLER
10 Vice Chancellor for Finance ... Ms. Michelle DICKERSON
111 VC Advancement & External Affs ... Ms. Jeri Pat GABBERT
13 Chief Information Officer ... Mr. Nick RAY
20 Assoc EVC Academic Affairs ... Dr. Cynthia O'DELL
20 Assoc EVC Academic Affairs ... Dr. Bala ARSHANAPALLI
09 Asst VC Inst Effectiveness & Rsrch ... Mr. John NOVAK
49 Dean College of Arts & Sciences ... Dr. Mark HOYERT
69 Interim Dean Health & Human Svcs ... Dr. Crystal SHANNON
50 Dean School of Business & Economics ... Dr. Cynthia ROBERTS
53 Interim Dean School of Education ... Dr. Mark SPERLING
80 Director Public & Environ Affs ... Dr. Eric LAMBERT
70 Director Social Work ... Dr. Darlene LYNCH
06 Registrar ... Mr. Peter ZACHOCKI
88 Director Pre-Professional Pgm ... Dr. Michael LAPOINTE
07 Director of Admissions ... Ms. Dorothy FRINK
37 Director Financial Aid ... Ms. Gina PIRTLE
36 Director Career & Placement ... Ms. Sharese DUDLEY
35 Director Student Activities ... Mr. Scott FULK
18 Exec Dir Facilities/Operations ... Mr. Kevin ELMORE
19 Director Security ... Mr. Monte DAVIS
29 Director Alumni Relations ... Vacant
66 Director Division of Nursing ... Dr. Crystal SHANNON
24 Director Instr Media ... Mr. Aaron PIGORS
08 Interim Dean of the Library ... Dr. Crystal SHANNON
21 Director of Accounting Services ... Vacant
25 Grant Coord/Senior Grant Writer ... Ms. Sandra MCMULLEN
15 Director Human Resources ... Ms. Mianta' DIMING
28 Dir Diversity/Equity/Multicult Affs ... Mr. James WALLACE, JR.
38 Director of Counseling Services ... Ms. Barbara A. DAHL
22 Director Inst Equity/Title IX ... Ms. Lita PENER
88 Dir Schlrshp in Teaching & Learning ... Dr. Christopher YOUNG
88 Dir Urban & Regional Excellence ... Dr. Ellen SZARLETA
105 Web Tech Services Manager ... Ms. Nicolle KRAUSE
106 Dir Online Education/E-learning ... Mr. Christopher YOUNG
41 Athletic Director ... Mr. Ryan SHELTON

*Indiana University-Purdue University Indianapolis (B)

420 University Blvd., Indianapolis IN 46202
County: Marion — FICE Identification: 001813
Unit ID: 151111
Telephone: (317) 274-5555 — Carnegie Class: DU-Higher
FAX Number: N/A — Calendar System: Semester
URL: www.iupui.edu
Established: 1969 — Annual Undergrad Tuition & Fees (In-State): $9,944
Enrollment: 29,390 — Coed
Affiliation or Control: State — IRS Status: 501(c)3
Highest Offering: Doctorate
Accreditation: HLC, AA, ACATE, ARCPA, ART, CACREP, CAEP, CAHIIM, CAMPEP, CIDA, CLPSY, COARC, CONST, CYTO, DA, DENT, DH, @DIETC, DIETI, DT, EMT, FEPAC, HSA, HT, IPSY, LAW, LIB, MED, MLS, MUS, NMT, NURSE, OT, PAST, PH, PTA, RAD, RADDOS, RTT, SPAA, SW

02 Interim Chancellor IUPUI ... Mr. Andrew R. KLEIN
100 Chief of Staff ... Ms. Margie SMITH-SIMMONS
28 Vice Chanc Diversity/Equity/Inclus ... Dr. Karen L. DACE
05 Exec Vice Chanc/Chief Acad Ofcr ... Dr. Kathy E. JOHNSON
10 Vice Chanc Finance & Admin ... Ms. Camy BROEKER
30 VP for Development/Foundation ... Ms. Dee METAJ
86 Vice Chanc Community Engagement ... Ms. Amy C. WARNER
32 Vice Chancellor Student Affairs ... Dr. Eric A. WELDY
46 Vice Chancellor Research ... Dr. Janice BLUM
08 Dean University Library ... Ms. Kristi L. PALMER
84 Assoc Vice Chanc Enrollment Mgmt ... Mr. PJ WOOLSTON
06 Registrar ... Ms. Kimberly LEWIS
113 Bursar ... Mr. Dan YOUNGBLOOD
26 Director of Communications ... Dr. Becky WOOD
22 Director Equal Opportunity ... Ms. Anne L. MITCHELL
38 Director Counseling & Psych Svcs ... Ms. Petra BATEK
39 Director Housing/Residence Life ... Mr. Mike PERRY
36 Director Career Services ... Ms. Amelia HURT
41 Director of Athletics ... Dr. Roderick D. PERRY
29 Managing Dir of Alumni Relations ... Ms. Kim MERRITT
09 Asst Vice Chanc Inst Research ... Dr. Michele J. HANSEN
07 Dir of Undergraduate Admissions ... Mr. Errol L. WINT
37 Exec Dir of Student Financial Svcs ... Ms. Lauren GREIDER
15 Senior HR Dir/Dir Fin Services ... Ms. Juletta TOLIVER
23 Director Student Health Services ... Dr. Scott RENSHAW
18 Assoc Vice Chan Campus Facility Svc ... Mr. Jeffrey PLAWECKI
19 Chief of Police ... Mr. Scott DUNNING
92 Dean Honors College ... Dr. Kristina H. SHEELER
45 Sr Advisor to the Chancellor Plng ... Dr. Stephen P. HUNDLEY
12 Vice Chanc & Dean IUPU Columbus ... Dr. Reinhold R. HILL
57 Dean Herron School of Art & Design ... Mr. Greg HULL
52 Dean School of Dentistry ... Dr. Carol A. MURDOCH-KINCH
54 Dean School of Engr/Technology ... Dr. David J. RUSSOMANNO
77 Sr Exec Asc Dn of Informatics/Comp ... Dr. Mathew J. PALAKAL
61 Dean McKinney Sch of Law ... Dr. Karen E. BRAVO
49 Dean School of Liberal Arts ... Dr. Tami EITLE
63 Dean School of Medicine ... Dr. Jay L. HESS
66 Dean School of Nursing ... Dr. Robin P. NEWHOUSE
68 Dean Sch of Health & Human Science ... Dr. Rafael E. BAHAMONDE
81 Interim Dean School of Science ... Dr. John F. DITUSA
70 Dean School of Social Work ... Dr. Tamara S. DAVIS
69 Dean Fairbanks Sch of Public Health ... Dr. Paul K. HALVERSON
88 Dean Lilly Fam Sch of Philanthropy ... Dr. Amir PASIC
53 Interim Dean School of Education ... Ms. Tambra JACKSON
80 Exec Assoc Dean Public/Environ Affs ... Dr. Jeremy CARTER
85 Assoc VC International Affairs ... Dr. Hilary E. KAHN
50 Exec Assoc Dean School of Business ... Ms. Julie MAGID
58 Vice Chanc Graduate Education ... Dr. Janice S. BLUM
89 Dean University College ... Dr. James M. GLADDEN
122 Coord Fraternity/Sorority Life ... Mr. Justin COX

*Indiana University South Bend (C)

1700 Mishawaka Avenue, South Bend IN 46634-7111
County: Saint Joseph — FICE Identification: 001816
Unit ID: 151342
Telephone: (574) 520-4872 — Carnegie Class: Masters/M
FAX Number: (574) 520-4834 — Calendar System: Semester
URL: www.iusb.edu
Established: 1940 — Annual Undergrad Tuition & Fees (In-State): $7,715
Enrollment: 4,942 — Coed
Affiliation or Control: State — IRS Status: 501(c)3
Highest Offering: Master's
Accreditation: HLC, CACREP, CAEP, DH, MLS, MUS, NURSE, @OT, RAD, @SP, SPAA

02 Chancellor ... Dr. Susan ELROD
05 Exec Vice Chanc Acad Affairs ... Ms. Jill PEARON
10 Vice Chanc Admin & Finance ... Mr. Andy WILLLIAMS
26 Vice Chanc Univ Relations/Advancev ... Mr. Rob DECLEENE
32 VC Student Affairs/Diversity ... Ms. Monica PORTER
100 Chief of Staff ... Ms. Elizabeth PAICE
13 Regional Chief Information Officer ... Mr. Nick RAY
20 Assoc Vice Chanc Academic Affs ... Dr. Doug MCMILLEN
84 Assoc Vice Chanc Enrollment Mgt ... Vacant
06 Registrar ... Mr. Keith DAWSON
41 Executive Director of Athletics ... Mr. Steve BRUCE
18 Director Facilities Management ... Mr. Michael PRATER
19 Director of Safety & Security ... Mr. Kurt M. MATZ
15 Director of Human Resources ... Ms. Deborah SCHMITT
29 Dir Alumni Affs/Campus Ceremonies ... Ms. Moira DYCZKO
27 Dir Comm/Marketing/Chief of Staff ... Ms. Paige RISSER
52 Director of Dental Auxiliary Educ ... Ms. Mallory EDMONDSON
51 Director of Extended Learning ... Mr. Mike MANCINI
38 Director Student Counseling Ctr ... Mr. Kevin GRIFFITH
07 Director of Admissions ... Ms. Connie PETERSON-MILLER
28 Director of Institutional Equity ... Ms. Laura HARLOW
30 Director of Development ... Ms. Dina HARRIS
39 Director of Student Housing ... Mr. Scott STRITTMATTER
21 Director of Accounting ... Vacant
37 Director of Financial Aid ... Ms. Lorie WILLIAMS
122 Assoc Dir-Sorority/Fraternity Life ... Ms. Sarah COHEN
08 Dean of Library Services ... Ms. Vicki BLOOM
50 Int Dean of Business & Economics ... Dr. Tracey ANDERSON
53 Dean School of Education ... Dr. Hope DAVIS
57 Interim Dean of the Arts ... Dr. Jorge MUNIZ
76 Dean Col of Health Sciences ... Dr. Thomas FISHER
49 Dean of Liberal Arts & Sciences ... Dr. Brenda PHILLIPS

*Indiana University Southeast (D)

4201 Grant Line Road, New Albany IN 47150-2158
County: Floyd — FICE Identification: 001817
Unit ID: 151379
Telephone: (812) 941-2333 — Carnegie Class: Masters/M
FAX Number: (812) 941-2475 — Calendar System: Semester
URL: www.ius.edu
Established: 1941 — Annual Undergrad Tuition & Fees (In-State): $7,715
Enrollment: 4,678 — Coed
Affiliation or Control: State — IRS Status: 501(c)3
Highest Offering: Master's
Accreditation: HLC, CAEP, CAHIIM, NURSE

02 Interim Chancellor ... Dr. Kelly A. RYAN
05 Interim Exec VC Academic Affairs ... Dr. Uric B. DUFRENE
10 VC Administration/Finance ... Mr. Dana C. WAVLE
84 VC Enrollment/Mktg/Student Affairs ... Ms. Amanda G. STONECIPHER
111 Int VC Advance/Alumni/External Affs ... Mr. Joseph M. GLOVER
20 Assoc VC Academic Affairs ... Dr. Donna J. DAHLGREN
13 Chief Information Officer ... Mr. Nicholas T. RAY
07 Director Admissions ... Mr. Chris CREWS
04 Exec Secretary to the Chancellor ... Ms. Donna J. HARVEY
35 Dean for Student Life ... Dr. Seuth CHALEUNPHONH
06 Registrar ... Mr. James (Jay) MCTYIER
37 Director Student Financial Aid ... Ms. Jennifer A. SHELLEY
08 Director Library Services ... Ms. Kate B. MOORE
36 Director Career Development ... Ms. Donna A. REED
18 Exec Dir of Facility Operations ... Mr. Robert C. POFF
14 Dir IT Communications & Support ... Mr. Steve BENNISON
41 Interim Director Athletics ... Ms. Amanda M. DAILEY-WEAVER
15 Acting Human Resources Manager ... Ms. Tammy J. ROYSE
09 Dir Institutional Effectiveness ... Mr. Ronald E. SEVERTIS, JR.
19 Chief Safety & Security ... Mr. Stephen MILLER
38 Dir Personal Counseling ... Dr. Michael DAY
26 Dir Marketing & Communications ... Ms. Nancy J. TRAFTON
79 Dean School Arts & Letters ... Mr. James HESSELMAN
81 Dean School Natural Sciences ... Dr. Elaine HAUB
83 Dean School Social Sciences ... Dr. Meghan C. KAHN
50 Dean School Business ... Dr. David EPLION
53 Dean School Education ... Dr. Faye M. CAMAHALAN
66 Interim Dean School Nursing ... Dr. Karen R. CLARK
46 Dean for Research & Grad Studies ... Dr. Lisa H. HOFFMAN
28 Director Staff Equity & Diversity ... Mr. James J. WILKERSON
121 Director of Advising ... Ms. Rebecca TURNER
113 Exec Director Accounting Services ... Ms. Ashley M. MCKAY
88 Academic Information Officer ... Mr. Steven KROLAK
30 Director Development ... Mr. David C. DEWITT
39 Dir Residence Life & Housing ... Ms. Abbie DUPAY

*Indiana University-Purdue University Columbus (E)

4601 Central Avenue, Columbus IN 47203
Telephone: (812) 348-7390 — Identification: 770185
Accreditation: &HLC, CAEP, NURSE

Indiana Wesleyan University (F)

4201 S Washington Street, Marion IN 46953-4999
County: Grant — FICE Identification: 001822
Unit ID: 151801
Telephone: (765) 674-6901 — Carnegie Class: Masters/S
FAX Number: (765) 677-2499 — Calendar System: 4/1/4
URL: www.indwes.edu
Established: 1920 — Annual Undergrad Tuition & Fees: $28,184
Enrollment: 3,108 — Coed
Affiliation or Control: Wesleyan Church — IRS Status: 501(c)3
Highest Offering: Doctorate
Accreditation: HLC, ACBSP, CAATE, CACREP, CAEP, EXSC, MFCD, MUS, NURSE, OT, OTA, @PTA, SW, THEOL

01 President ... Dr. David WRIGHT
05 Chief Academic Officer/Provost ... Dr. Stacy HAMMONS
12 Chancellor IWU-Marion ... Dr. Rod REED
12 Chancellor IWU-National & Global ... Dr. Matt LUCAS
28 VP for Diversity & Inclusion ... Ms. Diane MCDANIEL
10 Executive VP & CFO ... Mrs. Nancy SCHOONMAKER
11 President Wesley Seminary ... Dr. Colleen DERR
20 VP for Academic Affairs/CAPS ... Dr. Mike MANNING
20 VP for Academic Affairs/SON ... Dr. Barbara IHRKE
111 VP for Advancement ... Dr. Scott TURCOTT
20 Associate Provost ... Dr. Don SPROWL
26 VP Univ Communications ... Mr. Jerry SHEPHERD
27 VP Mktg/IWU-N&G ... Ms. Erica ELLIOTT
107 VP Life Calling & Integrative Lrng ... Dr. Brandon HILL
11 VP of Operations/Residential Campus ... Mr. John JONES
58 Dean Graduate School ... Dr. Joanne BARNES
73 Dean of the Seminary ... Dr. Abson JOSEPH
76 Dean School of Health Sciences ... Dr. Martin RICE
50 Dean Devoe School of Business ... Dr. Christopher DAVIS
37 Executive Director Financial Svcs ... Ms. Emily MATTISON
88 Dean of Developmental Learning ... Mr. Andrew PARKER
08 Director Library Resources ... Mrs. Shelia CARLBLOM
08 Director Off-campus Library Svcs ... Mrs. Jule KIND
29 Director of Alumni ... Vacant
07 Dir Admissions/Residential Educ ... Mr. Ian SLATER
15 Exec Director Human Resources ... Mr. Mark PEDERSON
06 University Registrar ... Mrs. Kim NICHOLSON
43 University Counsel ... Mr. Shawn MATTER
21 Controller ... Mrs. Tiffany LEWIS
41 VP for Student Dev & Athletics ... Mr. Mark DEMICHAEL
42 Dean of the Chapel ... Dr. John BRAY
92 Dean Honors College ... Mr. David RIGGS
09 Director Institutional Research ... Mr. Tony PARANDI
18 AVP Facilities Services ... Mr. Don ROWLEY
19 Director Campus Police ... Mr. Kyle BEAL
25 Director of Research Support ... Vacant
13 VP for Digital Transformation & CIO ... Mr. Scott GILREATH
121 Dean Center for Student Success ... Mr. Nathan HERRING
102 Dir Foundation/Corporate Relations ... Dr. Michael MOFFITT
04 Exec Assistant to the President ... Ms. Lynn MUNDAY
30 Director of Development ... Mr. Kenneth GRIFFIN
44 Director Annual Giving ... Vacant

International Business College (G)

7205 Shadeland Station, Indianapolis IN 46256-3997
County: Marion — FICE Identification: 004579
Unit ID: 151457

Telephone: (317) 813-2300
FAX Number: (317) 841-6419
URL: www.intlbusinesscollege.com
Established: 1889
Enrollment: N/A
Affiliation or Control: Proprietary
Highest Offering: Associate Degree
Accreditation: ACCSC, DA, MAC

Carnegie Class: Not Classified
Calendar System: Semester

Annual Undergrad Tuition & Fees: N/A
Coed
IRS Status: Proprietary

01	Campus Director	Ms. Amee AUGENSTEIN
05	Director of Education	Ms. Judith THAMES
32	Director of Student Services	Ms. Sarah LAWSON
36	Director of Career Services	Ms. Diane DALTON

*Ivy Tech Community College of (A) Indiana-Systems Office

50 W Fall Creek Parkway N Drive,
Indianapolis IN 46208-5752
County: Marion

FICE Identification: 008546
Unit ID: 363563

Telephone: (317) 921-4882
FAX Number: N/A
URL: www.ivytech.edu

Carnegie Class: N/A

01	President	Dr. Sue J. ELLSPERMANN
43	College Counsel	J.D LUX
04	Sr Administrative Asst to President	Angelina GONZALEZ
116	Asst VP Internal Audit	Mike DAVIS
05	Provost/Sr Vice President	Dr. Dean MCCURDY
10	SVP/Chief Financial Officer	Dominick CHASE
20	Vice Pres Academic Affairs	Dr. Russell D. BAKER
124	Asst VP Acad Transitions/Support	Gwenn ELDRIDGE
106	Asst VP Ed Tech and Ivy OnLine	Matthew PITTMAN
20	Asst VP Curriculum	Dr. Nichole STITT
20	Asst VP Curriculum	Vearl TURNPAUGH
20	Asst VP Curriculum	Glenn ROBERSON
102	SVP/Pres Ivy Tech Foundation	John MURPHY
112	Asst VP Philanthropy	Becky MILLER
30	Asst VP Development Operations	Annette FLICKINGER
88	Chief Financial Officer Foundation	Kevin HONIGFORD
100	EVP/Chief of Staff	Matt HAWKINS
45	Asst VP Strategy & Innovation	Lakshmi HASANADKA
88	Asst VP Continuous Improvement	Jeff KRAFT
15	Sr Vice President Human Resources	Julie LORTON-ROWLAND
16	VP Human Resources	Michaels MCNICHOLS
118	Asst VP Employee Benefits	Jen FISHER
88	Asst VP Talent Development	Kirsten BIEL
103	Sr VP Workforce & Career	Vacant
88	VP Information Technology	Linda CALVIN
109	VP Business Logistics/Supply Chain	Aaron BAUTE
66	VP Healthcare	Mary Anne SLOAN
72	VP Technology	Sue SMITH
36	VP Career Coaching/Employer Connect	Caroline DOWD-HIGGINS
88	Asst VP Workforce Operations	Dr. Stacy TOWNSLEY
26	Vice Pres Marketing & Communication	Jeff FANTER
27	Asst VP Marketing & Communications	Kelsey BATTEN
18	Vice Pres Cap Plng & Facilities	Amanda WILSON
86	VP Government Relations	Mary Jane MICHALAK
88	VP K-14 Initiatives	Dr. Rebecca RAHSCHULTE
28	VP Diversity/Equity & Belonging	Doneisha POSEY
88	Sr VP & Chief Strategy Offiicer	Kristen MORELAND
88	VP Strategic Operations	Michelle SIMMONS
88	VP Strategic Operations	Chad BOLSER
32	Vice President Student Success	Dr. Corey CLASEMANN-RYAN
35	Asst VP Student Life	Kat STREMIECKI
121	Asst VP Academic Advising	Susan HAWKINS-WILDING
114	VP Financial Planning & Mgmt	William BOGARD
113	Asst VP Cash/Debt Mgmt	Tom SKIDMORE
14	Chief Technology Officer	Thomas RIEBE
88	Asst VP Student Advocacy	Dr. Carey TREAGER-HUBER
13	Sr VP & Chief Information Officer	Matt ETCHISON
06	College Registrar	Ann YATER
21	Asst VP Accounting & Fin Reporting	Christy GELBACK-DIAZ
37	Asst VP Financial Aid	Vacant
19	VP Public Safety/Emer Preparedness	Jon BAREFOOT
84	Asst VP Enrollment Management	Sarah CLEVELAND

*Ivy Tech Community College of (B) Indiana-Indianapolis

50 W Fall Creek Parkway North Drive,
Indianapolis IN 46208-5752
County: Marion

FICE Identification: 009917
Unit ID: 150987

Telephone: (317) 921-4882
FAX Number: (317) 921-4753
URL: www.ivytech.edu/indianapolis/
Established: 1966
Enrollment: 63,809
Affiliation or Control: State
Highest Offering: Associate Degree
Accreditation: HLC, ACBSP, ACFEI, ACPHA, ART, CAHIIM, CNEA, COARC, CSHSE, FUSER, MAC, NAEYC, NAIT, RAD, SURGT

Carnegie Class: Assoc/MT-VT-High Non
Calendar System: Semester

Annual Undergrad Tuition & Fees (In-State): $4,637
Coed
IRS Status: 501(c)3

02	Chancellor	Dr. Lorenzo ESTERS
05	VC of Academic Affairs	Dr. Rod BROWN
32	VC of Student Affairs/Success	Dr. LaWanda JOBE
84	VC of Enrollment Services	Vacant
10	Executive Director of Finance	Vacant

15	Exec Director of Human Resources	Ms. Sara HAUGER
11	Exec Dir of Administrative Services	Mr. Aaron ROBERTS
103	Exec Dir of CCEC	Mr. Ben CARTER
30	Exec Director of Development	Mrs. Danielle STILES-POLK
35	Asst Vice Chanc Student Success	Mrs. Amy GRIFFIN
37	Director of Financial Aid	Mr. Andrew PENALVA
06	Registrar	Mr. Andrew PENALVA
09	Institutional Research Analyst	Mr. Christopher G. SLEPPPY
36	Director of Career Services	Ms. Rebecca PATTEN-LEMONS
96	Director of Purchasing	Ms. Carissa CARTWRIGHT-COLLINS
20	Asst Vice Chanc Academic Support	Ms. Rhonda ANGSMAN
26	Exec Dir Marketing/Communications	Mrs. Tracey ALLEN

*Ivy Tech Community College of Indiana- (C) Anderson

104 West 53rd Street, Anderson IN 46013-1502
Telephone: (800) 644-4882   Identification: 770239
Accreditation: &HLC, CNEA, DA, DH, MAC, NAIT

*Ivy Tech Community College of Indiana- (D) Bloomington

200 N Daniels Way, Bloomington IN 47404-9772
Telephone: (812) 332-1559   FICE Identification: 035213
Accreditation: &HLC, ACBSP, ACFEI, CNEA, COARC, CSHSE, EMT, NAEYC, NAIT, RTT

*Ivy Tech Community College of Indiana- (E) Columbus

4475 Central Avenue, Columbus IN 47203-1868
Telephone: (812) 372-9925   FICE Identification: 010038
Accreditation: &HLC, ACBSP, CNEA, CSHSE, DA, MAC, NAEYC, NAIT, SURGT

*Ivy Tech Community College of Indiana- (F) Evansville

3501 N First Avenue, Evansville IN 47710-1881
Telephone: (812) 426-2865   FICE Identification: 009925
Accreditation: &HLC, ACBSP, CNEA, CSHSE, EMT, MAC, NAEYC, NAIT, SURGT

*Ivy Tech Community College of Indiana-Fort (G) Wayne

3800 N Anthony Boulevard, Fort Wayne IN 46805-1489
Telephone: (260) 482-9171   FICE Identification: 009926
Accreditation: &HLC, ACBSP, ACFEI, CAHIIM, CNEA, COARC, COMTA, CSHSE, EMT, MAC, NAEYC, NAIT

*Ivy Tech Community College of Indiana- (H) Kokomo

1815 E Morgan Street, Box 1373, Kokomo IN 46903-1373
Telephone: (765) 459-0561   FICE Identification: 010041
Accreditation: &HLC, ACBSP, CNEA, CSHSE, DA, EMT, MAC, NAEYC, NAIT, SURGT

*Ivy Tech Community College of Indiana- (I) Lafayette

3101 S Creasy Lane, Box 6299, Lafayette IN 47903-6299
Telephone: (765) 269-5000   FICE Identification: 010039
Accreditation: &HLC, ACBSP, CNEA, COARC, CSHSE, DA, MAC, NAEYC, NAIT, SURGT

*Ivy Tech Community College of Indiana-Lake (J) County

1440 E 35th Avenue, Gary IN 46409-1499
Telephone: (219) 981-1111   FICE Identification: 010040
Accreditation: &HLC, ACBSP, ACFEI, CNEA, COARC, CSHSE, NAEYC, NAIT, PTAA

*Ivy Tech Community College of Indiana- (K) Lawrenceburg-Riverfront

50 Walnut Street, Lawrenceburg IN 47025
Telephone: (812) 537-4010   Identification: 770242
Accreditation: &HLC, CNEA, MAC, NAIT

Ivy Tech Community College Madison (L)

590 Ivy Tech Drive, Madison IN 47250-1883
Telephone: (812) 265-2580   FICE Identification: 009923
Accreditation: &HLC, ACBSP, CNEA, CSHSE, EMT, MAC, NAIT

*Ivy Tech Community College of Indiana- (M) Marion

261 S Commerce Drive, Marion IN 46953
Telephone: (765) 651-3100   Identification: 770244
Accreditation: &HLC, CNEA, NAIT

*Ivy Tech Community College of Indiana- (N) Michigan City

3714 Franklin Drive, Michigan City IN 46360
Telephone: (219) 879-9137   Identification: 770245

Accreditation: &HLC, CNEA, MAC, NAIT

*Ivy Tech Community College of Indiana- (O) Muncie

345 South High Street, Muncie IN 47305
Telephone: (765) 289-2291   FICE Identification: 009924
Accreditation: &HLC, ACBSP, ACFEI, CNEA, CSHSE, MAC, NAEYC, NAIT, PTAA, RAD, SURGT

*Ivy Tech Community College of Indiana- (P) Richmond

2357 Chester Boulevard, Richmond IN 47374-1298
Telephone: (765) 966-2656   FICE Identification: 010037
Accreditation: &HLC, ACBSP, CNEA, CSHSE, MAC, NAIT

*Ivy Tech Community College of Indiana- (Q) Sellersburg

8204 Highway 311, Sellersburg IN 47172-1897
Telephone: (812) 246-3301   FICE Identification: 010109
Accreditation: &HLC, ACBSP, CNEA, COARC, CSHSE, DA, MAC, MLTAD, NAEYC, NAIT, PTAA

*Ivy Tech Community College of Indiana- (R) South Bend/Elkhart

220 Dean Johnson Boulevard, South Bend IN 46601-3415
Telephone: (574) 289-7001   FICE Identification: 008423
Accreditation: &HLC, ACBSP, ACFEI, CNEA, COARC, CSHSE, DA, DH, EMT, MAC, MLTAD, NAEYC, NAIT

*Ivy Tech Community College of Indiana- (S) Terre Haute

8000 S. Education Drive, Terre Haute IN 47802-4833
Telephone: (812) 299-1121   FICE Identification: 008547
Accreditation: &HLC, ACBSP, CNEA, COARC, CSHSE, DMS, EMT, MAC, MLTAD, NAEYC, NAIT, RAD, SURGT

*Ivy Tech Community College of Indiana- (T) Valparaiso Campus

3100 Ivy Tech Drive, Valparaiso IN 46383
Telephone: (219) 464-8514   Identification: 770246
Accreditation: &HLC, CNEA, EMT, NAIT, SURGT

John Patrick University of Health (U) and Applied Sciences

100 E. Wayne Street, Suite 140, South Bend IN 46601
County: St. Joseph

Identification: 667156
Unit ID: 488776

Telephone: (574) 232-2408
FAX Number: (574) 232-2200
URL: www.jpu.edu
Established: 2009
Enrollment: 133
Affiliation or Control: Proprietary
Highest Offering: Master's
Accreditation: ACCSC, RADDOS

Carnegie Class: Spec-4-yr-Other Health
Calendar System: Semester

Annual Undergrad Tuition & Fees: $16,100
Coed
IRS Status: Proprietary

01	President/Dean	Brent D. MURPHY
11	Dir of Administrative Services	Betsy DATEMA
26	Dir of Marketing/Recruiting	Linda MURPHY

Lincoln College of Technology (V)

7225 Winton Drive, Building 128,
Indianapolis IN 46268-4198
County: Marion

FICE Identification: 007938
Unit ID: 151661

Telephone: (317) 632-5553
FAX Number: (317) 851-3273
URL: www.lincolntech.edu
Established: 1962
Enrollment: 999
Affiliation or Control: Proprietary
Highest Offering: Associate Degree
Accreditation: ACCSC

Carnegie Class: Spec 2-yr-Tech
Calendar System: Semester

Annual Undergrad Tuition & Fees: N/A
Coed
IRS Status: Proprietary

01	Campus President	Brent JENKINS
05	Academic Dean	Rodney ALLEE
11	Director of Administrative Services	Andy RAHIMI
37	Director Student Financial Aid	Alison JONES
07	Director of Admissions	Shannon BIGELOW
88	Co-Dir of High School Admissions	Charles LIVORNO
88	Co-Dir of High School Admissions	David RITZ
36	Director of Career Services	Christine JOYCE
13	IT Administrator	Blake BROOKS
18	Facilities Manager	Roger PARK
10	Business Office Coordinator	Dawn KEMP

Manchester University (W)

604 E College Avenue, North Manchester IN 46962-1225
County: Wabash

FICE Identification: 001820
Unit ID: 151777

Telephone: (260) 982-5000   Carnegie Class: Masters/S

FAX Number: (260) 982-5043 Calendar System: 4/1/4
URL: www.manchester.edu
Established: 1889 Annual Undergrad Tuition & Fees: $34,436
Enrollment: 1,449 Coed
Affiliation or Control: Church Of The Brethren IRS Status: 501(c)3
Highest Offering: Doctorate
Accreditation: HLC, CAATE, CAEP, @DIET, PHAR, SW

01 President .... Dr. David F. MCFADDEN
05 VP Academic Affairs .... Dr. Celia B. COOK-HUFFMAN
32 VP for Student Life .... Dr. Abby L. VAN VLERAH
10 Chief Business Officer/VP Finance .... Mr. Clair W. KNAPP, IV
17 VP Health Sciences/Dean Health Prof .... Vacant
111 Vice President Advancement .... Mrs. Melanie B. HARMON
84 VP for Enrollment/Marketing .... Mr. Ryon KAOPUIKI
67 Dean Pharmacy & Grad Life Sciences .... Dr. Walter (Tommy) T. SMITH
49 Dean of Arts & Sciences .... Dr. Judd CASE
50 Dean of College of Business .... Dr. Heather C. TWOMEY
20 Associate Dean Academic Affairs .... Dr. Stacy L. ERICKSON-PESETSKI
20 Associate Dean of Academic Programs .... Ms. Jennifer CAMPBELL
18 Asst VP for Facilities .... Ms. Alexis D. YOUNG
41 Athletic Director .... Mr. Rick ESPESET
40 Campus Bookstore Manager .... Ms. Heather K. GOCHENAUR
21 Controller .... Mr. Greg A. JARRETT
90 Instructional Designer .... Mr. Justin P. LUNSFORD
06 Registrar .... Ms. Audrey N. HAMPSHIRE
42 University Pastor .... Mrs. Bekah HOUFF
07 Director of Admissions .... Ms. Brandi C. CHAUNCEY
121 Director of Advising .... Ms. Mara YOUNGBAUER
29 Director of Alumni Relations .... Mrs. Megan E. SARBER
108 Director of Assessment .... Ms. Michelle J. CORDOVA-KIBIGER
36 Dir Career/Professional Development .... Ms. Tish KALITA
26 Director of Communications & Media .... Ms. Anne GREGORY
38 Director of Counseling .... Ms. April D. WHITE
24 Director of Educational Media .... Ms. Melissa RASMUSSEN
107 Director of Executive Education .... Vacant
25 Director of Grants .... Ms. Elena M. BOHLANDER
23 Director of Health Services .... Ms. Kristina A. WILSON
15 Director of Human Resources .... Ms. Brandee ESTES
09 Director of Institutional Research .... Mr. Adam HOHMAN
13 Director of ITS .... Mr. Olan E. GRIFFITHS
96 Director of Purchasing .... Ms. Heather K. GOCHENAUR
39 Asst Dir of Residence Life .... Ms. Jane WEBB
19 Director of Security .... Ms. Tina L. EDWARDS
35 Director Student Activities .... Ms. Samantha A. ALLEY
28 Dir Student Diversity/Inclusion .... Mr. Rudolph ROLLE
37 Director of Student Financial Aid .... Ms. Sherri L. SHOCKEY
104 Director of Study Abroad .... Ms. Thelma ROHRER
08 Director of the Library .... Ms. Darla V. HAINES
44 Director of the Manchester Fund .... Ms. Janeen W. KOOI
100 Executive Assistant to President .... Ms. Julie J. KNUTH
04 Administrative Asst to President .... Ms. Jill R. MANNS

Marian University (A)

3200 Cold Spring Road, Indianapolis IN 46222-1997
County: Marion FICE Identification: 001821
Unit ID: 151786
Telephone: (317) 955-6000 Carnegie Class: DU-Mod
FAX Number: (317) 955-6448 Calendar System: Semester
URL: www.marian.edu
Established: 1851 Annual Undergrad Tuition & Fees: $36,000
Enrollment: 3,706 Coed
Affiliation or Control: Roman Catholic IRS Status: 501(c)3
Highest Offering: Doctorate
Accreditation: HLC, ANEST, CAEP, IACBE, NURSE, OSTEO, SW

01 President .... Mr. Daniel J. ELSENER
05 EVP & Provost .... Dr. Alan SILVA
10 SVP Finance & Operations .... Mr. Greg GINDER
45 SVP Strategic Growth & Innovation .... Dr. Kenith BRITT
17 SVP for Health Professions .... Ms. Marsha CASEY
26 VP Enrollment/Mktg/Communication .... Mr. Brad R. WUCHER
42 VP Mission & Ministry .... Mr. Adam SETMEYER
32 VP Student Success & Engagement .... Ms. Ruth RODGERS
13 VP and Chief Information Officer .... Mr. Ray STANLEY
43 SVP Strat Ptnrshps/General Counsel .... Ms. Deborah LAWRENCE
111 VP Institutional Advancement .... Mr. John FINKE
88 VP for Mission Effectiveness .... Sr. Mary Beth GIANOLI
20 Assistant Provost .... Dr. Elizabeth OSIKA
20 Assistant Provost .... Dr. Jonathan LOWERY
20 Assistant Provost .... Mr. William HARTING
49 Dean of College of Arts & Sciences .... Vacant
50 Dean of Business .... Dr. Greg RAWSKI
53 Dean of Klipsch Educators College .... Dr. LaTonya TURNER
54 Dean of Engineering .... Dr. Binh TRAN
63 Dean of Medicine .... Dr. Amanda WRIGHT
66 Dean of Nursing .... Dr. Dorothy GOMEZ
37 Director of Financial Aid .... Ms. Chaunta REDFIELD
18 Director Campus Operations .... Mr. Evan HAWKINS
41 Director of Athletics .... Mr. Steve DOWNING
29 Dir Alumni/Parent Engagement .... Ms. Jennifer WANING
06 Registrar .... Ms. Jennifer SCHWARTZ
08 Library Director .... Ms. Jessica TRINOSKEY
35 Dean of Students .... Ms. Karen CANDLISH
88 Director Student Activities .... Ms. Sarah BALANA MOLTER
19 Chief of Police Services .... Mr. Robert RICHARDSON
27 Exec Dir Marketing Communications .... Ms. Maggie KUCIK
121 Director Academic Support Services .... Mrs. Marjorie BATIC
55 Exec Director Adult Programs .... Ms. Amy BENNETT
38 Director of Counseling Services .... Dr. Marla SMITH

09 Director of Institutional Research .... Ms. Brooke KILE
15 Director of Human Resources .... Ms. Amy KOCH
21 Director of Business Services .... Ms. Alice SHELTON
40 Bookstore Manager .... Ms. Jordan WILSON
04 Executive Asst to President .... Ms. Cyndi KAMP
39 Dir Residential & Commuter Life .... Ms. Kate DOTY

Martin University (B)

2186 North Sherman Drive, Indianapolis IN 46218
County: Marion FICE Identification: 021408
Unit ID: 151810
Telephone: (317) 543-3235 Carnegie Class: Bac-A&S
FAX Number: (317) 543-3257 Calendar System: Semester
URL: www.martin.edu
Established: 1977 Annual Undergrad Tuition & Fees: $13,200
Enrollment: 220 Coed
Affiliation or Control: Independent Non-Profit IRS Status: 501(c)3
Highest Offering: Master's
Accreditation: HLC

01 President .... Dr. Sean L. HUDDLESTON
05 EVP Academic Affairs/Provost .... Dr. Mattie JONES
09 Director of Institutional Research .... Mr. Omar K. HABAYEB
10 EVP Finance/Administration .... Mr. Bill NEWELL
84 VP of Enrollment Management .... Mr. Ezell F. MARRS, III
37 Director Financial Aid .... Ms. Qiana HALL
32 Director Student Success/Retention .... Ms. Krystal BROWN
111 VP of Institutional Advancement .... Dr. Kristie JOHNSON
13 VP of Information Technology .... Ms. Carol BRANSON
15 Manager Human Resources/Controller .... Ms. Gina COWHERD
28 Director of Diversity .... Mr. Davyd HALL

Mid-America College of Funeral Service (C)

3111 Hamburg Pike, Jeffersonville IN 47130-9630
County: Clark FICE Identification: 010618
Unit ID: 151962
Telephone: (812) 288-8878 Carnegie Class: Spec-4-yr-Arts
FAX Number: (812) 288-5942 Calendar System: Quarter
URL: www.mid-america.edu
Established: 1980 Annual Undergrad Tuition & Fees: $12,700
Enrollment: 92 Coed
Affiliation or Control: Independent Non-Profit IRS Status: 501(c)3
Highest Offering: Baccalaureate
Accreditation: FUSER

01 President .... Dr. Mitch MITCHELL
37 Dir of Financial Aid/Office Mgr .... Mr. Jason KESSINGER
08 Librarian .... Ms. Sonja PIERCE
07 Director of Admissions .... Ms. Victoria THOMAS

Mid-America Reformed Seminary (D)

229 Seminary Drive, Dyer IN 46311-1069
County: Lake FICE Identification: 039893
Unit ID: 373030
Telephone: (219) 864-2400 Carnegie Class: Not Classified
FAX Number: (219) 864-2410 Calendar System: Semester
URL: www.midamerica.edu
Established: 1981 Annual Graduate Tuition & Fees: N/A
Enrollment: N/A Coed
Affiliation or Control: Independent Non-Profit IRS Status: 501(c)3
Highest Offering: Master's; No Undergraduates
Accreditation: THEOL

01 President .... Dr. Cornelis VENEMA
32 Dean of Students .... Rev. Mark D. VANDER HART
111 Vice President of Advancement .... Mr. Mike DECKINGA
11 Vice President of Operations .... Mr. Keith LEMAHIEU
36 Director of Apprenticeship Program .... Rev. Mark D. VANDER HART
06 Registrar .... Rev. Alan STRANGE
84 Director of Enrollment Management .... Mr. Brian BLUMMER
108 Director Institutional Assessment .... Rev. Marcus MININGER
08 Theological Librarian .... Rev. Alan STRANGE
26 Manager Marketing/Digital/Pubs .... Mr. Jared LUTTJEBOER

Oakland City University (E)

138 N Lucretia Street, Oakland City IN 47660-1099
County: Gibson FICE Identification: 001824
Unit ID: 152099
Telephone: (812) 749-4781 Carnegie Class: DU-Mod
FAX Number: (812) 749-1233 Calendar System: Semester
URL: www.oak.edu
Established: 1885 Annual Undergrad Tuition & Fees: $24,990
Enrollment: 1,241 Coed
Affiliation or Control: Baptist IRS Status: 501(c)3
Highest Offering: Doctorate
Accreditation: HLC, CAEPN, IACBE, THEOL

01 President .... Dr. Ron DEMPSEY
11 Vice President for Administration .... Mr. Clint WOOLSEY
05 Acting VP Academic Affairs/Provost .... Dr. Ron DEMPSEY
10 Chief Financial Officer .... Mr. Todd WAHL
111 VP for University Advancement .... Mr. Brian BAKER
32 Assoc VP for Student Life .... Mr. Brad KNOTTS
50 Dean School of Business .... Dr. Cathy ROBB
53 Dean School of Education .... Dr. Pamela BARNES
73 Dean Religious Studies .... Dr. Ron MERCER

49 Dean of Arts and Science .... Dr. Justin MURPHY
108 Asst Provost for Assessment .... Dr. Paul BOWDRE
37 Director of Financial Aid .... Mrs. Nicole SHARP
22 Compliance Officer .... Dr. JC CAMPBELL
06 Registrar .... Mrs. Linda TIPTON
08 Director of Library .... Dr. Denise PINNICK
42 Campus Minister .... Vacant
18 Director of Facilities .... Mr. Greg BURKE
15 Director of Human Resource .... Mrs. Stephanie KIRBY
19 Chief of Security .... Mr. Mike MCGREGOR
35 Director of Student Activities .... Vacant
88 Director of Directions Program .... Mrs. Charity JULIAN
36 Dir Center for Calling & Career .... Ms. Brooksie SMITH
88 Interim Upward Bound Director .... Mrs. Charity JULIAN
21 Director of Business Office .... Mrs. Elizabeth CARLISLE
113 Students Account Manager .... Mrs. Anita MISKELL
88 Facilities Service Coordinator .... Mrs. Amy HELDT
04 Exec Assistant to President .... Mrs. Mary NOSSETT
07 Director of Admissions .... Ms. Jennifer LANTRIP
105 Director Web Services .... Mrs. Andrea TURNER
28 Asst VP for Diversity & Inclusion .... Dr. JC CAMPBELL
39 Dir Resident Life/Student Housing .... Vacant
41 Athletic Director .... Mr. T-Ray FLETCHER
13 Director of Information Technology .... Mr. Eric MURPHY
96 Director of Purchasing .... Ms. Candy PANCAKE
09 Director of Institutional Research .... Dr. Paul BOWDRE
30 Director of Development .... Mr. Todd MOSBY
44 Director of Annual Giving .... Mr. Weston WHITEHOUSE

Purdue University Global (F)

2550 Northwestern Ave, STE 1100,
West Lafayette IN 47906
County: Marion FICE Identification: 004586
Unit ID: 260901
Telephone: (317) 208-5311 Carnegie Class: Not Classified
FAX Number: N/A Calendar System: Quarter
URL: www.purdueglobal.edu
Established: 1937 Annual Undergrad Tuition & Fees (In-State): N/A
Enrollment: N/A Coed
Affiliation or Control: State IRS Status: 501(c)3
Highest Offering: Doctorate
Accreditation: HLC, ACBSP, CAHIIM, @CNEA, IFSAC, MAC, NURSE

01 Chancellor .... Dr. Frank DOOLEY
00 President .... Mr. Mitchell DANIELS, JR.
05 Provost .... Dr. John HARBOR
10 Chief Financial Officer .... Mr. Chris RUHL
20 VP Faculty & Academic Resources .... Dr. Carolyn NORSTROM
06 VP Strat/Acad Ops & Registrar .... Mr. Michael LORENZ

Purdue University Main Campus (G)

610 Purdue Mall, West Lafayette IN 47907-2040
County: Tippecanoe FICE Identification: 001825
Unit ID: 243780
Telephone: (765) 494-4600 Carnegie Class: DU-Highest
FAX Number: N/A Calendar System: Semester
URL: www.purdue.edu
Established: 1869 Annual Undergrad Tuition & Fees (In-State): $9,992
Enrollment: 46,655 Coed
Affiliation or Control: State IRS Status: 501(c)3
Highest Offering: Doctorate
Accreditation: HLC, AAB, ART, AUD, CAATE, CAEP, CAEPN, CAMPEP, CIDA, CLPSY, CONST, COPSY, DIETC, DIETD, IPSY, LSAR, NAIT, NURSE, PCSAS, PHAR, SP, THEA, VET

01 President .... Mr. Mitchell E. DANIELS, JR.
10 Chief Financial Officer & Treasurer .... Mr. Christopher A. RUHL
05 Provost/Exec VP for Acad Affairs .... Dr. Jay AKRIDGE
21 Sr VP Business Svcs/Asst Treasurer .... Mr. James S. ALMOND
26 Exec Vice Pres Communications .... Vacant
106 SVP Purdue Online .... Dr. Gary R. BERTOLINE
15 Vice President Human Resources .... Mr. Bill BELL
20 Int Vice Prov Teaching/Learning .... Dr. Jenna RICKUS
28 Vice Chanc Diversity/Inclusion .... Dr. John GATES
20 Vice Pres Faculty Affairs .... Dr. Peter HOLLENBECK
32 Vice Provost Student Life .... Dr. Beth MCCUSKEY
08 Dean of Libraries .... Ms. Beth MCNEIL
29 President & CEO Alumni Association .... Vacant
07 Dean Admiss/VP Enrollment Mgmt .... Dr. Kris WONG-DAVIS
37 Exec Director Financial Aid .... Ms. Heidi A. CARL
122 Dir of Fraternity/Sorority Life .... Mr. Brandon CUTLER

Purdue University Fort Wayne (H)

2101 E Coliseum Boulevard, Fort Wayne IN 46805-1499
County: Allen FICE Identification: 001828
Unit ID: 151102
Telephone: (260) 481-6100 Carnegie Class: Masters/M
FAX Number: (260) 481-6880 Calendar System: Semester
URL: www.pfw.edu
Established: 1964 Annual Undergrad Tuition & Fees (In-State): $8,730
Enrollment: 8,093 Coed
Affiliation or Control: State IRS Status: 501(c)3
Highest Offering: Doctorate
Accreditation: HLC, ART, CACREP, CAEP, MUS, PH, RAD, @SP, THEA

02 Chancellor .... Dr. Ronald ELSENBAUMER
05 Vice Chanc Academic Affairs .... Dr. Carl DRUMMOND
10 Vice Chanc Financial/Admin Affairs .... Mr. Glen NAKATA

84 Vice Chanc Enroll/Stdnt Experience .... Dr. Krissy CREAGER
30 Vice Chancellor for Development .... Vacant
26 Vice Chanc Marketing/Comm .... Jerry LEWIS
06 Assoc Vice Chanc/Registrar .... Dr. Cheryl HINE
49 Dean College of Liberal Arts .... Janet BADIA
20 Assoc Vice Chanc Academic Programs .... Dr. Terri SWIM
100 Chief of Staff .... Kimberly WAGNER
13 Chief Information Ofcr/Dir IT Svcs .... Mitch DAVIDSON
18 Associate Vice Chance of Facilities .... Greg JUSTICE
29 Director of Alumni Relations .... Emily VENDERLEY
08 Dean of Library .... Vacant
15 Associate VC HR/OIE .... Cynthia SPRINGER
41 Director of Athletics & Recreation .... Kelley HARTLEY-HUTTON
96 Director of Purchasing .... Pam THOMPSON
19 Chief of Police .... Tim POTTS
16 Associate Director of HR .... Christine M. MARCUCCILLI
85 Director International Programs .... Brian MYLREA
37 Director Financial Aid .... Douglas HESS
09 Director of Institutional Research .... Irah MODRY-CARON
51 Exec Director Continuing Studies .... Karen VANGORDER
81 Dean College of Science .... Dr. Ronald FRIEDMAN
72 Dean Engr Tech/Computer Sci .... Dr. Manoochehr ZOGHI
53 Director School of Education .... Dr. Isabel NUNEZ
50 Dean Business .... Dr. Melissa GRUYS
57 Dean Visual/Performing Arts .... John O'CONNELL
04 Admin Assistant to the Chancellor .... Gayle BELLAM
39 Dir Housing/Residential Education .... Jordyn HOGAN

Purdue University Northwest (A)

2200 169th Street, Hammond IN 46323-2094

County: Lake FICE Identification: 001827
Unit ID: 490805
Telephone: (219) 989-2204 Carnegie Class: Masters/L
FAX Number: (219) 989-2581 Calendar System: Semester
URL: www.pnw.edu
Established: 1946 Annual Undergrad Tuition & Fees (In-State): $7,942
Enrollment: 9,363 Coed
Affiliation or Control: State IRS Status: 501(c)3
Highest Offering: Doctorate
Accreditation: HLC, CACREP, CAEP, CEA, MFCD, NAIT, NUR, SW

01 Chancellor .... Dr. Thomas L. KEON
05 Vice Chanc Acad Affs & Provost .... Dr. Kenneth HOLFORD
10 Vice Chanc Finance & Admin .... Mr. Stephen TURNER
111 Vice Chanc for Inst Advancement .... Dr. Lisa GOODNIGHT
13 Vice Chanc Info Services .... Mr. Tim WINDERS
84 VC Enroll Mgmt & Student Affairs .... Ms. Elizabeth BABCOCK-DEPEW
26 Assoc Vice Chanc Marketing and Comm .... Ms. Kris FALZONE
20 Assoc Vice Chanc Academic Affairs ... Dr. Rebecca STANKOWSKI
21 Asst VC Finance & Business Svcs .... Ms. Kimberly THOMAS
32 Assoc Vice Chanc Stdnt Affs/DoS .... Dr. Colin FEWER
15 Asst Vice Chanc Human Resources .... Ms. Susan MILLER
83 Dean College of Hum Educ & Soc Sci .... Dr. Elaine CAREY
54 Int Dean College of Engr & Science .... Dr. Dietmar REMPFER
72 Dean College of Technology .... Dr. Niaz LATIF
50 Dean College of Business .... Dr. Rachel CLAPP-SMITH
66 Dean College of Nursing .... Dr. Lisa HOPP
53 Dean College of Humanity/Educ & SS .... Dr. Anne GREGORY
58 Director of Graduate Studies .... Ms. Joy COLWELL
06 Registrar .... Ms. Jennifer WILLIAMS
37 Exec Dir of Financial Aid .... Mr. Michael J. BIEL
41 Director of Athletics .... Mr. Richard J. COSTELLO
38 Director Counseling Center .... Dr. Kenneth JACKSON
46 Dir Research & Sponsored Programs .... Ms. Maja MARJANOVIC
07 Interim Exec Dir Undergrad Admiss .... Ms. Julie WIEJAK
96 Dir of Procurement/Auxiliary Svcs .... Ms. Jennifer HUPKE
39 Director Housing Residential Educ .... Ms. Korey WEST
92 Dean Honors College/Undergrad Study .... Dr. Jonathan SWARTS
88 Dir Acad Oper of Strat Initiatives .... Ms. Catharine OLSEN
90 Asst Vice Chanc Stdnt Success Tech .... Ms. Heather ZAMOJSKI
25 Director CVIS .... Dr. Chenn ZHOU
28 Director of Equity & Diversity .... Ms. Linda B. KNOX
36 Executive Director for Employer Eng .... Ms. Natalie CONNORS
88 AVC Campus Plng/Proj & Space Mgmt .... Mr. Jacob G. LENSON
29 Exec Dir PNW Alumni Community .... Ms. Ashley GERODIMOS
18 Senior Dir of Facilities & Grounds .... Mr. Scott PARSONS
124 Asst Dir Student Success/Retention .... Ms. Yesenia Noreeka AVALOS
100 Chief of Staff .... Dr. Lisa GOODNIGHT
19 Director of Public Safety .... Mr. Brian E. MILLER
30 Director of Development .... Ms. Deanna HARDWICK

Purdue University Northwest, Westville Campus (B)

1401 S US 421, Westville IN 46391

Telephone: (219) 785-5200 FICE Identification: 001826
Accreditation: &HLC

† Branch Campus of Purdue University Northwest, Hammond, IN.

Rose-Hulman Institute of Technology (C)

5500 Wabash Avenue, Terre Haute IN 47803-3920

County: Vigo FICE Identification: 001830
Unit ID: 152318
Telephone: (812) 877-1511 Carnegie Class: Spec-4-yr-Other Tech
FAX Number: (812) 877-9925 Calendar System: Quarter
URL: www.rose-hulman.edu
Established: 1874 Annual Undergrad Tuition & Fees: $52,914
Enrollment: 1,990 Coed
Affiliation or Control: Independent Non-Profit IRS Status: 501(c)3
Highest Offering: Master's
Accreditation: HLC

01 President .... Mr. Robert A. COONS
10 Vice President for Finance .... Mr. Matthew D. DAVIS
05 Provost & Vice Pres Academic Affs .... Dr. Richard E. STAMPER
111 VP Inst Advancement .... Mr. Steven P. BRADY
32 VP Student Affs & Dean of Students .... Mr. Erik Z. HAYES
26 VP Communications/Marketing .... Mr. Santhana NAIDU
15 Vice Pres Human/Environmental Svcs .... Ms. Megan C. ELLIOTT
84 Vice President Enrollment Mgmt .... Dr. Thomas BEAR
88 Sr Director Venture .... Mr. Brian C. DOUGHERTY
20 Dean of Faculty .... Dr. Russell L. WARLEY
88 Dir for Micronano Devices & Sys .... Dr. Azad SIAHMAKOUN
88 Associate Dean of Learning & Tech .... Dr. Kay C. DEE
13 Vice Pres Info Tech and CIO .... Dr. Wayne DENNISON
18 Director Facilities Operations .... Mr. Chad T. WEBER
36 Dir Career Services/Employee Rels .... Mr. Scott K. TIEKEN
07 Dean of Admissions .... Ms. Lisa M. NORTON
29 Interim Director Alumni Relations .... Mr. Charlie RICKER
37 Director of Financial Aid .... Ms. Melinda L. MIDDLETON
41 Director of Athletics .... Ms. Ayanna TWEEDY
28 Dir for the Center of Diversity .... Mr. Nick DAVIS
30 Executive Director of Development .... Vacant
110 Exec Director Advancement Service .... Ms. Jennifer KENZOR
06 Registrar .... Ms. Angie SMITH
08 Sr Director Logan Library & Info .... Ms. Bernadette EWEN
19 Director of Public Safety .... Vacant
40 Bookstore Manager .... Ms. Sheryl E. FULK
85 Dir of Intl Student Services .... Vacant
04 Exec Asst to the President/BOT .... Ms. Amy TIMBERMAN
21 Director of Business Operations .... Ms. Linda L. PRICE
11 Director Administrative Services .... Mr. Bryan T. BROMSTRUP
09 Director of Institutional Research .... Dr. Timothy CHOW
35 Assoc Dean of Student Affairs .... Mr. Ryan BRIMBERRY
35 Director of Student Services .... Ms. Kristen J. LOYD
24 Instructional Technology Manager .... Ms. Cheryl DAVIDSON
24 Emerging Digital Technologies Mgr .... Mr. Alan WARD
108 Sr Dir of Institutional Research .... Dr. Matthew D. LOVELL
38 Director Student Counseling Center .... Mr. Michael LATTA
39 Director Residence Life .... Mr. Cory PARDIECK

St. Anthony School of Echocardiography (D)

1201 S. Main Street, Crown Point IN 46307

County: Lake Identification: 667119
Telephone: (219) 757-6132 Carnegie Class: Not Classified
FAX Number: (219) 681-6725 Calendar System: Semester
URL: https://www.franciscanhealth.org/EchoSchoolNWI
Established: 2004 Annual Undergrad Tuition & Fees: N/A
Enrollment: N/A Coed
Affiliation or Control: Independent Non-Profit IRS Status: 501(c)3
Highest Offering: Associate Degree
Accreditation: DMS

01 Co-Program Director .... Lori HULT
05 Co-Program Director .... Karin KOLISZ

Saint Mary-of-the-Woods College (E)

1 St Mary of Woods College,
St Mary of the Woods IN 47876-1099

County: Vigo FICE Identification: 001835
Unit ID: 152381
Telephone: (812) 535-5151 Carnegie Class: Masters/S
FAX Number: (812) 535-5231 Calendar System: Semester
URL: www.smwc.edu
Established: 1840 Annual Undergrad Tuition & Fees: $31,150
Enrollment: 1,099 Coed
Affiliation or Control: Roman Catholic IRS Status: 501(c)3
Highest Offering: Doctorate
Accreditation: HLC, ACATE, MUS, NURSE

01 President .... Dr. Dottie KING
05 Provost VP Acad & Student Affairs .... Dr. Janet CLARK
10 VP for Finance & Administration .... Ms. Jaclyn WALTERS
111 VP for Advancement & Strategic Init .... Ms. Karen DYER
84 VP for Enrollment Management .... Mr. Brennan RANDOLPH
06 Registrar .... Ms. Deanna SMITHEE
32 Associate VP for Student Affairs .... Dr. Aimee JANSSEN-ROBINSON
37 AVP for Financial Aid & Admissions .... Ms. Darla HOPPER
21 Associate VP/Controller .... Ms. Kari WOLFE
110 Associate VP for Advancement .... Ms. Catherine SAUNDERS
28 VP for Diversity/Equity/Inclusion .... Ms. Dee REED
15 Associate VP of Human Resources .... Mr. Terry BOWE
29 Director of Alumni Relations .... Ms. Sarah MAHADY
08 Director of the Library .... Dr. Rusty TRYON
07 Executive Director of Admissions .... Mr. Chris LOZIER
20 Executive Director Academic Affairs .... Ms. Sara BOYER
18 Director of Facilities .... Mr. Brian ARCHER
09 Director of Institutional Research .... Mr. Mike KING
19 Director of Campus Security .... Mr. Greg EWING
04 Exec Assistant for the President .... Ms. Peggy NASH
108 Director of Assessment .... Ms. Kimberli ZORNES
38 Campus Counselor .... Ms. Kalista LAWRENCE

Saint Mary's College (F)

Notre Dame IN 46556

County: Saint Joseph FICE Identification: 001836
Unit ID: 152390
Telephone: (574) 284-4000 Carnegie Class: Bac-A&S
FAX Number: (574) 284-4716 Calendar System: Semester
URL: www.saintmarys.edu
Established: 1844 Annual Undergrad Tuition & Fees: $45,720
Enrollment: 1,581 Female
Affiliation or Control: Roman Catholic IRS Status: 501(c)3
Highest Offering: Doctorate
Accreditation: HLC, CAEP, MUS, NURSE, SP, SW

01 President .... Dr. Katie CONBOY
04 Special Asst to the President .... Ms. Michelle EGAN
05 Provost/Sr VP Academic Affairs .... Dr. Barbara MAY
111 Int Vice Pres Advancement .... Ms. Holly JOHNSON
84 VP Student Enrollment & Engagement .... Ms. Lori JOHNSON
10 Vice President Strategy & Finance .... Dr. Dana STRAIT
88 Interim Vice President for Mission .... Ms. Molly GOWER
43 General Counsel .... Vacant
28 Vice Pres of Inclusion & Equity .... Dr. Redgina HILL
121 Dean of Student Academic Services .... Dr. Karen CHAMBERS
06 Dir of Academic Advising/Registrar .... Ms. Nadia EWING
07 Director of Admission .... Ms. Sarah DVORAK
08 Director of Library .... Mr. Joseph THOMAS
09 Director of Institutional Research .... Ms. Julie SISCO
29 Director of Alumnae Relations .... Ms. Kara O'LEARY
37 Director of Financial Aid .... Ms. Kathleen M. BROWN
27 Director of Public Relations .... Ms. Lisa KNOX
38 Director of Health & Counseling .... Ms. Sarah GRANGER
13 Chief Information Officer .... Mr. Todd NORRIS
15 Director of Human Resources .... Ms. Kris URSCHEL
19 Director of Safety & Security .... Mr. James BAMBENEK
41 Director of Athletics .... Ms. Julie SCHROEDER-BIEK
42 Director of Campus Ministry .... Ms. Nicole LABADIE
18 Director of Facilities .... Mr. Benjamin BOWMAN
96 Director of Purchasing .... Ms. Kathleen CARLSON
88 Dir of Student Involvement/Advocacy .... Ms. Liz COULSTON BAUMANN
85 Dir Multicultural/Intl Student Svcs .... Ms. Adriana PETTY
04 Senior Exec Asst to the President .... Ms. Vicki WICKIZER

Saint Meinrad School of Theology (G)

200 Hill Drive, St. Meinrad IN 47577-1030

County: Spencer FICE Identification: 007276
Unit ID: 152451
Telephone: (812) 357-6611 Carnegie Class: Spec-4-yr-Faith
FAX Number: (812) 357-6964 Calendar System: Semester
URL: www.saintmeinrad.edu
Established: 1861 Annual Graduate Tuition & Fees: N/A
Enrollment: 176 Coed
Affiliation or Control: Roman Catholic IRS Status: 501(c)3
Highest Offering: Master's; No Undergraduates
Accreditation: HLC, THEOL

01 President & Rector .... Rev. Denis ROBINSON, OSB
03 Vice Rector .... Rev. Tobias COLGAN, OSB
05 Academic Dean .... Dr. Robert ALVIS
42 Director of Spiritual Formation .... Rev. Guerric DEBONA, OSB
20 Dir of Graduate Theology Programs .... Sr. Jeana VISEL, OSB
30 Vice President of Development .... Mr. Duane SCHAEFER
10 Business Manager & Treasurer .... Mrs. Lisa CASTLEBURY
08 Library Director .... Dr. Daniel KOLB
06 Registrar .... Mrs. Donna BALBACH
88 Dir of Clergy Formation Pgm .... Dcn. Ron PIRAU
114 Director of Budget .... Mrs. Pam DOWLAND
37 Director of Student Financial Aid .... Mrs. Ruth KRESS
26 Director of Communications .... Mrs. Mary Jeanne SCHUMACHER
29 Director of Alumni Relations .... Mr. Tim FLORIAN
38 Director of Student Counseling Ctr .... Sr. Diane PHARO, SCN
23 Director of Health Services .... Ms. Melissa DEWOLFE
04 Executive Secretary .... Mrs. Karen SCHERZER
13 Chief Info Technology Officer (CIO) .... Mr. Dave GRAMELSPACHER
105 Director Web Services .... Mr. James PAQUETTE
106 Dir Online Education/E-learning .... Sr. Jeana VISEL, OSB
15 Director Human Resources .... Ms. Jackie SCHERLE
07 Director of Admissions .... Dr. John SCHLACHTER
44 Director of Annual Giving .... Mr. Joe Paul HADEN
108 Director Institutional Assessment .... Dr. John SCHLACHTER
18 Chief Facilities/Physical Plant Ofc .... Mr. Mark HOFFMAN
101 Secretary of the Institution/Board .... Br. Francis DeSales WAGNER, OSB
19 Director Security/Safety .... Mr. Darren SROUFE
112 Director of Planned Giving .... Mr. Michael SCHUMWAY

St. Vincent College of Health Professions (H)

2001 West 86th Street, Indianapolis IN 46260

County: Marion Identification: 667315
Telephone: (317) 338-3879 Carnegie Class: Not Classified
FAX Number: (317) 338-3720 Calendar System: Semester
URL: www.stvincent.org
Established: 2015 Annual Undergrad Tuition & Fees: N/A
Enrollment: N/A Coed
Affiliation or Control: Independent Non-Profit IRS Status: 501(c)3
Highest Offering: Associate Degree
Accreditation: ABHES, DMS, EMT, RAD

01 President/Exec Dir Medical Educ .... Dr. Jeffrey ROTHENBERG
05 Dean/Program Director .... Mr. Mark ADKINS

Taylor University (A)

West 236 Reade Avenue, Upland IN 46989-1001
County: Grant — FICE Identification: 001838
Unit ID: 152530
Telephone: (765) 998-2751 — Carnegie Class: Bac-Diverse
FAX Number: (765) 998-4925 — Calendar System: 4/1/4
URL: www.taylor.edu
Established: 1846 — Annual Undergrad Tuition & Fees: $36,800
Enrollment: 2,110 — Coed
Affiliation or Control: Independent Non-Profit — IRS Status: 501(c)3
Highest Offering: Master's
Accreditation: **HLC**, ACBSP, CAEP, CEA, MUS, SW

01 President ... Dr. D. Michael LINDSAY
04 Admin Assistant to the President ... Ms. Shelly GRAMLING
100 VP for Strategy and Chief of Staff ... Mr. Will HAGEN
45 Special Assistant to the President ... Mr. Ron SUTHERLAND
05 Provost ... Dr. Jewerl MAXWELL
88 Admin Assistant to the Provost ... Ms. Deb CARPENTER
111 VP for University Advancement ... Dr. Michael FALDER
10 VP Business/Finance/CFO ... Mr. Stephen OLSON
32 VP Student Development ... Dr. Skip TRUDEAU
28 VP Intercult Ldrship/Church Rels ... Mr. Greg DYSON
13 Chief Information Officer ... Mr. Chris JONES
84 VP for Enrollment & Marketing ... Ms. Holly WHITBY
112 Director of Stewardship Planning ... Ms. Rachel GAMARRA
81 Dean of Sciences ... Dr. Grace JU MILLER
49 Dean Arts/Humanities/Bus & HE ... Dr. Nancy DAYTON
104 Dean International Programs ... Dr. Charles BRAINER
20 Dean Faculty Development/Dir BCTLE ... Dr. Barb BIRD
37 Assoc VP of Financial Aid ... Mr. Timothy NACE
07 Exec Director Admissions ... Mr. Andy GAMMONS
39 Assc Dean Res Life & Discipleship ... Ms. Julia HURLOW
06 Registrar ... Ms. Janet ROGERS
08 Director of Library ... Ms. Shannon BROOKS
108 Dir Assessment/Quality Improvements ... Dr. Kim CASE
09 Director IR/Assoc Registrar ... Dr. Edwin WELCH
88 Exec Director for Campaigns ... Mr. David RITCHIE
112 Assoc VP Advancement/Major Gifts ... Vacant
30 Exec Director of Development ... Ms. Kristie JACOBSON
29 Exec Dir Alumni & Parent Relations ... Mr. Brad YORDY
124 Dean of Student Engagement ... Dr. Drew MOSER
41 Director of Athletics ... Mr. Kyle GOULD
36 Director Calling and Career Office ... Mr. Jeff AUPPERLE
42 Campus Pastor ... Mr. Jon CAVANAGH
15 Director of Human Resources ... Vacant
106 Dir Online Learning & Inst Tech ... Ms. Carrie MEYER
18 Director of Facility Services ... Mr. Gregg HOLLOWAY
38 Director of Counseling Ctr ... Vacant
19 Chief of Police/Taylor Police ... Mr. Jeff WALLACE
21 Dir of Acctng/Financial Reporting ... Mr. David LLOYD
21 Director Financial Operations ... Ms. Michele BRAGG
118 Dir of Payroll & Benefits ... Vacant
114 Bursar/Student Accounts ... Ms. Jill THURMAN
90 Director Academic Computing ... Vacant
88 Director Lead Generation ... Ms. Christa SIEGELIN
119 Director Enterprise Infrastructure ... Mr. Steve ELWOOD
91 Director Enterprise Data Systems ... Mr. Mark LORA
24 Director of Media Services ... Mr. Jon OCHS
53 Director Transition to Teaching ... Ms. April DICKEY
26 Director of Media Relations ... Mr. Jim GARRINGER

TCM International Institute (B)

6337 Hollister Drive, Indianapolis IN 46224
County: Marion — Identification: 666333
Telephone: (317) 299-0333 — Carnegie Class: Not Classified
FAX Number: (317) 290-8607 — Calendar System: Semester
URL: www.tcmi.edu
Established: 1991 — Annual Graduate Tuition & Fees: N/A
Enrollment: N/A — Coed
Affiliation or Control: Independent Non-Profit — IRS Status: 501(c)3
Highest Offering: Master's; No Undergraduates
Accreditation: **HLC**

01 President ... Dr. Tony TWIST
05 VP Educational Advancement ... Dr. Richard JUSTICE
11 U.S. Director of Operations ... Ms. Carol FIELDS
10 Director of Finance ... Ms. Julie RICE

Trine University (C)

1 University Avenue, Angola IN 46703-1764
County: Steuben — FICE Identification: 001839
Unit ID: 152567
Telephone: (260) 665-4100 — Carnegie Class: Bac-Diverse
FAX Number: (260) 665-4292 — Calendar System: Semester
URL: www.trine.edu
Established: 1884 — Annual Undergrad Tuition & Fees: $33,490
Enrollment: 3,573 — Coed
Affiliation or Control: Independent Non-Profit — IRS Status: 501(c)3
Highest Offering: Doctorate
Accreditation: **HLC**, ACBSP, #ARCPA, CAEP, NURSE, PTA, @SP, SURGT

01 President ... Dr. Earl D. BROOKS, II
05 Vice President for Academic Affairs ... Dr. John SHANNON
10 Vice President Finance ... Ms. Kayla WARREN
84 Vice Pres Enrollment Management ... Ms. Kim BENNETT
100 VP Administration/Chief of Staff ... Ms. Gretchen MILLER
32 Dean of Students ... Mr. Francisco ORTIZ
26 VP Univ Marketing/Communications ... Mr. Dave JARZYNA
29 VP Alumni/Development ... Mr. David FRABONI
41 Athletic Director/Asst VP Athletics ... Mr. Matt LAND
49 Dean Jannen School of Arts & Sci ... Ms. Sarah FRANZEN
107 Asst VP Prof Studies/Trine Online ... Ms. Keirsten EBERTS
15 Human Resources ... Ms. Jamie NORTON
06 Registrar ... Ms. Debra F. HELMSING
08 Director of the Library ... Ms. Michelle BLANK
36 Director of Placement/Coop Educ ... Ms. Linda COOPER
09 Director Inst Planning/Analysis ... Ms. Christina ZUMBRUN

Union Bible College (D)

PO Box 900, Westfield IN 46074
County: Hamilton — Identification: 667253
Telephone: (317) 896-9324 — Carnegie Class: Not Classified
FAX Number: N/A — Calendar System: Semester
URL: www.ubca.org
Established: 1911 — Annual Undergrad Tuition & Fees: N/A
Enrollment: N/A — Coed
Affiliation or Control: Interdenominational — IRS Status: 501(c)3
Highest Offering: Baccalaureate
Accreditation: **BI**

01 President ... C. Adam BUCKLER
05 Vice Pres Academic Affairs ... John WHITAKER
10 Director of Finance ... Lanae WHITAKER
11 Director of Operations ... Scott WILLIAMS
32 Dean of Student Life ... Joe CAREY
09 Director of Institutional Research ... Isabel RUNDELL
06 Registrar ... Elizabeth DAVIS
07 Director of Admissions/Public Rels ... Phil HOARD

University of Evansville (E)

1800 Lincoln Avenue, Evansville IN 47722-1586
County: Vanderburgh — FICE Identification: 001795
Unit ID: 150534
Telephone: (812) 488-2000 — Carnegie Class: Masters/M
FAX Number: (812) 488-2320 — Calendar System: Semester
URL: www.evansville.edu
Established: 1854 — Annual Undergrad Tuition & Fees: $38,686
Enrollment: 2,323 — Coed
Affiliation or Control: United Methodist — IRS Status: 501(c)3
Highest Offering: Doctorate
Accreditation: **HLC**, ANEST, ARCPA, CAATE, CAEP, MUS, NUR, PTA

01 President ... Mr. Christopher M. PIETRUSZKIEWICZ
05 Exec VP Academic Affairs ... Dr. Michael AUSTIN
111 VP Advancement ... Ms. Abigail WERLING
10 VP Fiscal Affairs & Admin ... Ms. Donna TEAGUE
32 VP Student Affairs/Dean ... Dr. Rachel CARPENTER
108 Assoc Provost for Academic Affairs ... Dr. Dave DWYER
84 VP Enrollment/Marketing ... Dr. Jill G. GRIFFIN
35 Asst VP Student Affs/Dir Res Life ... Mr. Michael A. TESSIER
13 Chief Information Officer/OTS ... Mr. Michael SMITH
49 Dean of Arts & Sciences ... Dr. Ray LUTGRING
50 Dean College Business/Engineering ... Dr. Beverly BROCKMAN
53 Dean of Educ/Health Science ... Ms. Mary KESSLER
51 Sr Dir Ctr Advancement of Learning ... Ms. Cynthia FELTS
85 Director International Programs ... Dr. Patricia Lorena ANDUEZA
41 Director of Athletics ... Dr. Kenneth SIEGFRIED
26 Sr Dir Marketing/Communication ... Ms. Holly SMITH
06 University Registrar ... Ms. Keely CUTTS
08 University Librarian ... Mr. Robb WALTNER
42 University Chaplain ... Rev. Andy PAYTON
96 Manager of Admin Service/Purchasing ... Ms. Kim WINSETT
29 Sr Director of Alumni/Engagement ... Ms. Jennifer CALDERONE
36 Sr Dir Ctr Career Development ... Mrs. Dianna CUNDIFF
38 Director of Counseling/Health Educ ... Ms. Elizabeth MCCORMICK
37 Director of Student Financial Svcs ... Ms. Hilary HILLENBRAND
15 Dir of HR/Institutional Equity ... Mr. Keith GEHLHAUSEN
18 Exec Dir Facilities Mgmt & Plng ... Mr. Mike AVERETT
19 Chief of Safety & Security ... Mr. Jason CULLUM
104 Exec Dir/Dean Harlaxton College ... Dr. Holly CARTER
40 Director of Bookstore ... Ms. Becky LAMONT
28 Chief Diversity Officer ... Dr. Robert SHELBY
112 Sr Dir of Major Gifts/Campaigns ... Ms. Jennifer WHITAKER
121 Director of Academic Advising ... Vacant
07 Director of Admissions ... Mr. Kenton HARGIS
04 Exec Assistant to the President ... Ms. Patricia A. LIPPERT

University of Indianapolis (F)

1400 E Hanna Avenue, Indianapolis IN 46227-3697
County: Marion — FICE Identification: 001804
Unit ID: 151263
Telephone: (317) 788-3368 — Carnegie Class: DU-Mod
FAX Number: (317) 788-3300 — Calendar System: Semester
URL: www.uindy.edu
Established: 1902 — Annual Undergrad Tuition & Fees: $32,268
Enrollment: 5,638 — Coed
Affiliation or Control: United Methodist — IRS Status: 501(c)3
Highest Offering: Doctorate
Accreditation: **HLC**, ACBSP, ART, CAATE, CAEP, CLPSY, COARC, COSMA, @DIETI, EXSC, MPCAC, MUS, NURSE, OT, PTA, PTAA, SW

01 Interim President ... Mr. Phil TERRY
45 Exec VP for Innovation & Planning ... Dr. Neil PERDUE
05 Executive VP and Provost ... Dr. Chris PLOUFF
20 Deputy Provost ... Dr. Mary Beth BAGG
84 VP for Enrollment Services ... Vacant
10 VP & Chief Financial Officer ... Mr. Jason DUDICH
111 Vice President for Univ Advancement ... Mr. Philip THORNTON
41 VP for Intercollegiate Athletics ... Mr. Scott YOUNG
42 VP for Mission ... Dr. Michael G. CARTWRIGHT
43 Vice President & General Counsel ... Ms. Andrea NEWSOM
32 VP Stdnt/Campus Affs/Dean of Stdnts ... Ms. Kory M. VITANGELI
13 Interim Chief Information Officer ... Ms. Michelle DUMAN
13 Interim Chief Technology Officer ... Mr. Matthew WILSON
28 VP/Chief Incl & Equity Officer ... Dr. Amber SMITH
29 VP of Alumni/Univ Events/Ext Rel ... Mr. Andrew KOCHER
26 Assoc VP for Communications ... Mr. Garrison CARR
06 Registrar ... Ms. Josh HAYES
49 Dean College of Arts & Sciences ... Dr. Patrick VAN FLEET
50 Dean School of Business ... Dr. Lawrence BELCHER
53 Dean School of Education ... Dr. John KUYKENDALL
66 Dean School of Nursing ... Ms. Norma HALL
76 Dean College of Health Sciences ... Dr. Stephanie KELLY
83 Int Dean Applied Behavioral Science ... Dr. Erin FEKETE
108 Assoc VP for Accreditation ... Dr. Mary C. MOORE
07 Director Admissions/Recruit & Opers ... Ms. Katie ASHCRAFT
08 Library Director ... Ms. Marisa ALBRECHT
15 Director Human Resources ... Mrs. Erin P. FARRELL
37 Director of Financial Aid ... Mr. Nathan LOHR
58 Director Graduate Business Pgms ... Mr. Stephen A. TOKAR
18 Executive Director Facilities Mgmt ... Mr. Dave STATLER
19 Director Safety & Police Services ... Mr. David K. SELBY
31 Director of Service Learning ... Dr. Marianna K. FOULKROD
42 Chaplain/Dir Lantz Center ... Rev. Jeremiah GIBBS
85 Director International Division ... Ms. Marilyn O. CHASE
38 Director Counseling Center ... Dr. Kelly M. MILLER
40 Bookstore Manager ... Ms. Kimberly MILLION

University of Notre Dame (G)

400 Main Building, Notre Dame IN 46556
County: Saint Joseph — FICE Identification: 001840
Unit ID: 152080
Telephone: (574) 631-5000 — Carnegie Class: DU-Highest
FAX Number: (574) 631-6700 — Calendar System: Semester
URL: www.nd.edu
Established: 1842 — Annual Undergrad Tuition & Fees: $57,699
Enrollment: 12,809 — Coed
Affiliation or Control: Roman Catholic — IRS Status: 501(c)3
Highest Offering: Doctorate
Accreditation: **HLC**, ART, CLPSY, IPSY, LAW, THEOL

01 President ... Rev. John I. JENKINS, CSC
05 Provost ... Dr. John T. MCGREEVY
03 Executive Vice President ... Mr. Shannon B. CULLINAN
20 Vice Pres/Sr Associate Provost ... Dr. Christine M. MAZIAR
20 Vice Pres/Associate Provost ... Dr. Maura A. RYAN
89 Vice Pres Inst Transformation ... Dr. Hugh R. PAGE, JR.
85 VP/Provost Internationalization ... Dr. Michael PIPPENGER
32 Vice President for Student Affairs ... Rev. Gerard J. OLINGER
10 Vice President for Finance ... Mr. Trent A. GROCOCK
46 Vice President for Research ... Dr. Robert J. BERNHARD
43 Vice President & General Counsel ... Ms. Marianne CORR
115 Vice Pres/Chief Investment Ofcr ... Mr. Mike DONOVAN
41 Vice Pres & Director of Athletics ... Mr. John B. SWARBRICK, JR.
15 Vice Pres Human Resources ... Ms. Heather CHRISTOPHERSEN
26 Vice President University Relations ... Mr. Louis M. NANNI
27 VP Public Affairs/Communications ... Mr. Joel G. CURRAN
13 VP & Chief Information Officer ... Ms. Jane LIVINGSTON
88 VP Mission Engagement/Church Affs ... Rev. Austin COLLLINS, CSC
58 VP/Assoc Prov/Dean Graduate Sch ... Dr. Thomas FUJA
45 VP Strategic Planning ... Mr. David C. BAILEY
100 Vice President/Chief of Staff ... Ms. Ann M. FIRTH
19 Vice Pres Campus Safety/Univ Ops ... Mr. Mike SEAMON
28 Chief Diversity Officer ... Mr. Eric LOVE
84 Assoc VP Undergraduate Enrollment ... Ms. Micki KIDDER
18 VP Facilities & Design ... Mr. Douglas K. MARSH
109 Vice Pres Univ Enterprises/Events ... Ms. Micki KIDDER
06 Registrar ... Mr. Charles T. HURLEY
96 Director Procurement ... Mr. Gilberto CARLES
50 Dean College of Business ... Dr. Martijn CREMERS
61 Dean of Law School ... Fr. Marcus G. COLE
54 Interim Dean College of Engineering ... Dr. Thomas E. FUJA
49 Dean of Arts & Letters ... Dr. Sarah A. MUSTILLO
81 Dean of Science ... Dr. Santiago SCHNELL
48 Dean of Architecture ... Dr. Stefanos POLYZOIDES
82 Dean School of Global Affairs ... Dr. Scott APPLEBY
29 Exec Director Alumni Assoc ... Ms. Dolly DUFFY
08 Dir of University Libraries ... Mr. K. Matthew DAMES
42 Director of Campus Ministry ... Rev. Peter M. MCCORMICK, CSC
37 Dir of Student Financial Aid ... Ms. Mary B. NUCCIARONE
36 Director of Undergrad Career Svcs ... Ms. LoriAnn EDINBOROUGH
38 Director of Counseling Center ... Dr. Christine G. CONWAY
19 Director of Security/Police ... Ms. Keri Kei SHIBATA
07 Director of Admissions ... Ms. Christy PRATT
101 Secretary of the Institution/Board ... Ms. Carol MULLANEY
09 Director of Institutional Research ... Vacant
102 Dir Foundation/Corporate Relations ... Ms. Amanda RETARTHA
104 Director Study Abroad ... Ms. Judy HUTCHINSON
39 Director Student Housing ... Mr. Jonathan RETARTHA
04 Administrative Asst to President ... Ms. Sarah A. GOTSCH
86 Director Government Relations ... Mr. Timothy D. SEXTON
25 Chief Contract/Grants Administrator ... Mr. Josh TULLIS
30 Director of Development ... Mr. Stu FORTENER
44 Director Annual Giving ... Mr. Brian DISS
105 Director Web Services ... Ms. Tracy WEBER

University of Saint Francis (A)

2701 Spring Street, Fort Wayne IN 46808-3994
County: Allen FICE Identification: 001832
Unit ID: 152336
Telephone: (260) 399-7700 Carnegie Class: Masters/M
FAX Number: N/A Calendar System: Semester
URL: www.sf.edu
Established: 1890 Annual Undergrad Tuition & Fees: $32,420
Enrollment: 2,271 Coed
Affiliation or Control: Roman Catholic IRS Status: 501(c)3
Highest Offering: Doctorate
Accreditation: HLC, ACBSP, ADNUR, ARCPA, ART, CAEP, DIETC, MLTAD, NURSE, PTAA, RAD, SURGT, SW

01 President ... RevDr. Eric A. ZIMMER
05 VP Academic Affairs ... Dr. Lance B. RICHEY
10 VP Finance ... Mr. Craig M. TEETSEL
111 VP Institutional Advancement ... Ms. Ellen PAXTON
11 VP of Operations ... Mr. Richard A. BIENZ
32 VP Student Affairs/COS ... Mr. Robert PASTOOR
84 VP Enrollment Management ... Ms. Beth M. TERRELL
20 Assoc VP Academic Affairs ... Mrs. Trish J. BUGAJSKI, OFS
88 Assistant VP Mission Integration ... Sr. M. Anita HOLZMER, OSF
50 Dean Keith Busse School of Business ... Vacant
57 Dean School of Creative Arts ... Vacant
17 Dean School of Health Sciences ... Dr. Angela HARRELL
49 Dean Business/Arts & Sciences ... Dr. Andrea GEYER
12 Dean Crown Point Site ... Dr. Marsha M. KING
36 Exec Dir Acad & Career Devel Ctr ... Vacant
106 Exec Dir Enrollment Management .. Mrs. Michelle L. KUHLHORST
13 Exec Dir Univ Technology Svcs ... Vacant
21 VP for Finance ... Mr. Craig M. TEETSEL
06 Registrar ... Vacant
42 Chaplain ... Mr. John SHEEHAN
121 Director Academic Advising ... Ms. Melissa J. REESMAN
29 Director Alumni Relations ... Mr. Tony S. DIDIER
41 Director Athletics ... Mr. Michael H. MCCAFFREY
42 Director Campus Ministry ... Vacant
28 Dir Diversity & Inclusion ... Dr. Paul PORTER
102 Dir Found Relations/Grant Writer ... Ms. Jessica H. EGGERS-BUTTES
15 Dir Human Resources & Org Develop ... Mrs. Carol L. COFFEE
92 Dir John Duns Scotus Honors Program ... Dr. Kenneth A. BUGAJSKI
105 Director Marketing ... Mrs. Carla S. PYLE
88 Director Sports Information ... Mr. William J. SCOTT
88 Dir Student Service Learning/Engage .. Mrs. Katrina P. BOEDEKER
08 Assoc Dir Information/Instruc Svcs .. Mrs. Maureen E. MCMAHAN
37 Assistant Director Financial Aid ... Mr. Michael L. CARPENTER
16 Assistant Dir Human Resources ... Mr. Andy MCKEE
53 Chair Department of Education ... Dr. Mary E. REIPENHOFF
19 Supervisor Campus Safety/Security ... Mr. Edward A. LAROCQUE
18 Supervisor Maintenance/Grounds ... Mr. Ramon S. DEMOND
44 Principal Gift Officer ... Mr. Gerry GRIM
09 Research/Assessment Analyst ... Mrs. Kim E. DIETRICH
04 Executive Assistant to President ... Mrs. Melissa STUDEBAKER
109 Mgr Creative Dining Food Service ... Ms. Scott KAMMERER
40 Mgr Barnes & Noble Campus Shoppe ... Mrs. Robin HUFFMAN

University of Southern Indiana (B)

8600 University Boulevard, Evansville IN 47712-3596
County: Vanderburgh FICE Identification: 001808
Unit ID: 151306
Telephone: (812) 464-8600 Carnegie Class: Masters/L
FAX Number: (812) 464-1960 Calendar System: Semester
URL: www.usi.edu
Established: 1965 Annual Undergrad Tuition & Fees (In-State): $9,285
Enrollment: 10,203 Coed
Affiliation or Control: State IRS Status: 501(c)3
Highest Offering: Doctorate
Accreditation: HLC, ART, CAEP, CEA, COARC, COSMA, DA, DH, DIETD, DMS, EXSC, NURSE, OT, OTA, RAD, SW

01 President ... Dr. Ronald S. ROCHON
100 Sr Exec Assistant to the President ... Mrs. Carey BEURY
04 Exec Assistant to the President ... Mrs. Nita R. MUSICH
05 Provost ... Dr. Mohammed KHAYUM
10 Vice President for Finance & Admin ... Mr. Steven J. BRIDGES
32 VP for Student Affairs ... Dr. Khalilah DOSS
26 VP Marketing & Communications ... Mrs. Kindra L. STRUPP
20 Assoc Provost for Academic Affairs ... Dr. Shelly B. BLUNT
38 Director of Counseling Center ... Dr. Robin SANABRIA
21 Assoc VP Finance & Administration ... Ms. Mary A. HUPFER
86 Chief Government/Legal Affairs Ofcr ... Mr. Aaron C. TRUMP
09 Interim Chief Data Officer ... Mr. Gregory J. JOHNSON
58 Director of Graduate Studies ... Dr. Michael D. DIXON
06 Registrar ... Mrs. Sandy K. FRANK
84 Executive Director of Enrollment ... Mr. Rashad E. SMITH
08 Director of Library ... Ms. Marna M. HOSTETLER
30 VP for Dev/Pres USI Foundation ... Mr. David A. BOWER
92 Director Honors Program ... Dr. Sarah E. STEVENS
29 Dir Alumni Relations/Volunteer USI ... Mrs. Janet L. JOHNSON
37 Dir Student Financial Assistance ... Vacant
15 Interim Exec Dir of Human Resources ... Mrs. Sarah K. WILL
35 Dean of Students ... Dr. Jennifer R. HAMMAT
85 Exec Dir Center for Intl Programs ... Ms. Emilija ZLATKOVSKA
28 Exec Dir Multicultural Center ... Mrs. Pamela F. HOPSON
13 Chief Information Officer ... Mr. Austin SIDERS
90 Academic Services Coordinator ... Mr. Juzar AHMED
18 Dir of Facility Operations & Plng ... Mr. James E. WOLFE
96 Director of Procurement ... Mr. Jeffrey M. SPONN
27 Director of Univ Communications ... Mr. John A. FARLESS
19 Director of Public Safety ... Mr. Stephen L. BEQUETTE
39 Director of Housing/Residence Life ... Ms. Amy S. PRICE
41 Athletic Director ... Mr. Jon Mark HALL
50 Dean Romain College of Business ... Dr. Sudesh MUJUMDAR
49 Dean College of Liberal Arts ... Dr. Del DOUGHTY
66 Int Dean Col Nursing/Health Prof ... Dr. Connie F. SWENTY
81 Dean College of Sci/Engr/Educ ... Dr. Zane W. MITCHELL, JR.
51 Exec Dir of Outreach & Engagement .. Ms. Dawn M. STONEKING
120 Exec Dir of Online Learning ... Vacant
105 Director of Web Services ... Mrs. Brandi S. HESS
89 Assoc Dir Ctr Campus Life ... Ms. Jennifer GARRISON

Valparaiso University (C)

Valparaiso IN 46383-6493
County: Porter FICE Identification: 001842
Unit ID: 152600
Telephone: (219) 464-5000 Carnegie Class: DU-Mod
FAX Number: (219) 464-5381 Calendar System: Semester
URL: valpo.edu
Established: 1859 Annual Undergrad Tuition & Fees: $43,286
Enrollment: 3,122 Coed
Affiliation or Control: Lutheran IRS Status: 501(c)3
Highest Offering: Doctorate
Accreditation: HLC, #ARCPA, CACREP, CAEP, MUS, NURSE, SW

01 President ... Mr. Jose D. PADILLA
05 Provost/Exec VP for Academic Affs ... Mr. Eric W. JOHNSON
32 VP for Student Life ... Mr. Steve JANOWIAK
84 VP for Enroll/Mktg/Communications ... Mr. Brian O'ROURKE
58 Assoc Provost Graduate/Online Educ ... Mr. Mike TYLER
111 VP Advancement/Strat Initiatives ... Ms. Lisa HOLLANDER
110 AVP for Advancement ... Mr. Jason PETROVICH
26 Dir University Communications ... Mr. Michael FENTON
43 VP/General Counsel ... Mr. Darron C. FARHA
10 VP for Finance/Chief Operating Ofcr ... Mr. Mark VOLPATTI
100 Chief of Staff/Board Liaison ... Mrs. Rebekah AREVALO
92 Int Dean of Christ College ... Dr. Jennifer PROUGH
49 Int Dean College Arts & Sciences ... Dr. Gregg JOHNSON
54 Dean College of Engineering ... Dr. Doug TOUGAW
50 Dean College of Business Admin ... Dr. Niclas ERHARDT
66 Dean College of Nursing ... Dr. Karen ALLEN
62 Dean of Library Sciences ... Ms. Trisha MILEHAM
35 Dean of Students ... Mr. Ryan BLEVINS
88 Exec Dean of Enrollment ... Ms. Jennifer EASTHOPE
42 AVP for Mission & Spiritual Life ... Dr. Brian BECKSTROM
06 University Registrar ... Ms. Allison URBANCZYK
19 Chief University Police ... Mr. Charles GARBER, JR.
39 Asst Dean Students/Residential Life ... Mr. Ryan BYE
104 Dir of Study Abroad Programs ... Dr. Allison KROFT
85 Dir International Students/Scholars ... Ms. Janice LIN
29 Exec Dir Alumni Rels/Univ Guild ... Ms. Linda ROETTGER
15 Exec Dir Human Resource Services ... Ms. Deondra DEVITT
18 Exec Dir of Facilities ... Mr. Jason KUTCH
36 Director Career Center ... Ms. Lori MILTENBERGER
38 Director of Counseling Services ... Ms. Kim BOONE
41 Director Athletics ... Dr. Charles SMALL
20 Assoc Provost for Faculty Affairs ... Dr. Lissa YOGAN
21 AVP for Finance/Controller ... Ms. Tamara GINGERICH
28 Asst VP Diversity/Equity/Inclusion ... Ms. Angela VIDAL-RODRIGUEZ
09 Exec Dir Inst Effectiveness ... Ms. Melizza ZYGMUNT
42 University Pastor ... Dcs. Katherine MUSEUS DABAY
42 University Pastor ... Rev. James WETZSTEIN
37 Director of Financial Aid ... Ms. Karen KLIMCZYK
04 Exec Asst to President/Office Mgr ... Ms. Tammy BASICH
07 Exec Dir Undergraduate Admission ... Mr. Bart HARVEY
13 Chief Info Technology Officer (CIO) ... Mr. Dave SIERKOWSKI
86 Dir Government/Cmty Relations ... Ms. Kelly ANTHONY

Veritas Baptist College (D)

181 U.S. 50 East, Suite 204, Greendale IN 47025
County: Dearborn FICE Identification: 038626
Unit ID: 482228
Telephone: (812) 221-1714 Carnegie Class: Spec-4-yr-Faith
FAX Number: (540) 785-5441 Calendar System: Semester
URL: www.vbc.edu
Established: 1984 Annual Undergrad Tuition & Fees: $6,716
Enrollment: 216 Coed
Affiliation or Control: Baptist IRS Status: 501(c)3
Highest Offering: Master's
Accreditation: TRACS

01 President ... John EDMONDS
00 Chancellor ... Dr. Don FORRESTER
05 Academic Dean ... Ann RILL
10 Chief Financial Officer ... Sherry DAVIS
32 Director of Student Services ... Dr. Mike LESTER
37 Director Student Financial Aid ... Delaney JOHNSTON
07 Director of Admissions ... Michele E. CATLIN

Vincennes University (E)

1002 N First Street, Vincennes IN 47591-1504
County: Knox FICE Identification: 001843
Unit ID: 152637
Telephone: (812) 888-8888 Carnegie Class: Bac/Assoc-Mixed
FAX Number: (812) 888-5868 Calendar System: Semester
URL: www.vinu.edu
Established: 1801 Annual Undergrad Tuition & Fees (In-State): $6,251
Enrollment: 16,048 Coed
Affiliation or Control: State IRS Status: 501(c)3
Highest Offering: Baccalaureate
Accreditation: HLC, ACBSP, ADNUR, ART, CAEP, CAHIIM, FUSER, NUR, PNUR, PTAA, SURGT

01 President ... Dr. Charles R. JOHNSON
05 Provost/VP Instructional Services ... Dr. Laura TREANOR
86 Vice Pres Government Relations ... Mr. Tony HAHN
10 Vice Pres Financial Services ... Mr. Tim EATON
103 VP Workforce Dev/Comm Services ... Mr. David A. TUCKER
12 Asst Vice Pres/Dean Jasper Campus ... Mr. Christian BLOME
21 Assoc VP of Fin Svcs & Controller ... Ms. Conya R. WAMPLER
32 Asst Provost Student Affairs ... Ms. Whitney N. DAUGHERTY
20 Asst Provost Curriculum & Inst ... Mr. Rick A. KRIBS
26 Sr Director External Relations ... Ms. Sarah E. FORTUNE
07 Director of Admissions ... Mr. Ryan J. BARBAULD
09 Sr Dir Inst Effectiveness/Research ... Mr. Dale R. PIETRZAK
13 Director of Mgmt Information Center ... Vacant
88 Director of University Events ... Mrs. Laura CARIE
36 Director Career Center ... Ms. Donna TAYLOR-BOUCHIE
37 Director of Student Financial Aid ... Mr. Stanley J. WERNE
22 Dir Diverse Abilities/Accommodation ... Ms. Sarah Jill STEELE
40 Manager of Bookstore ... Ms. Karen R. FAULKNER
102 Executive Director VU Foundation ... Ms. Kristi R. DEETZ
41 Athletic Director ... Mr. Harry L. MEEKS
88 Project Excel Interim Director ... Ms. D'Lee THOMAS
29 Director of Alumni Programs ... Vacant
28 Director Multicultural Affairs ... Vacant
18 Director of Physical Plant ... Mr. William KROEGER
19 Int Director of Campus Police ... Mr. Adam DAUGHERTY
113 Bursar ... Ms. Terri PERRY
06 Registrar ... Ms. Rebecca K. LITTLE
35 Dean of Students ... Vacant
39 Assoc Dean Housing/Residence Life ... Vacant
27 Director of Multimedia & Analytics ... Mr. Ryan EVANCOE
96 Director of Procurement ... Mr. Michael L. MORRISON
121 Director Student Success Center ... Ms. Gaye WALTHALL
88 Dir Architectural Svcs/Facilities ... Mr. Andrew YOUNG
15 Director Human Resources/AAO ... Ms. Regina L. MCCORD-FITHIAN
76 Dean College Health Sci/Human Perf ... Ms. Michelle CUMMINS
50 Dean College of Business/Public Svc .. Ms. Susan BROCKSMITH
72 Dean College of Technology ... Mr. Ty FREED
81 Dean College of Sc/Engr/Math ... Mr. Curt COFFMAN
83 Dean Soc Sci/Perf Arts/Comm ... Dr. Cynthia RAGLE
79 Dean College of Humanities ... Ms. Joan PUCKETT
88 Dir Avia Tech Ctr Indianapolis ... Mr. Michael D. GEHRICH
88 Dean of Academic Early College ... Ms. Nicole SHANKLE
88 Dir Out of State Military Educ Pgm ... Mr. Matthew J. SCHWARTZ
88 Director Military Education Pgms ... Mr. Alex SIEVERS
88 Dir Plainfield Logistics Center ... Mr. Scott A. BACON
04 Administrative Asst to President ... Ms. Nancy A. IRWIN
88 Director International Recruitment ... Mr. Ze (Wade) CHEN
23 Dir University Primary Care Clinic ... Ms. Deborah A. BEDWELL
85 Director International Affairs ... Vacant
51 Asst VP Lifelong Learning ... Ms. Shanni E. SIMMONS

Vincennes University-Jasper Center (F)

850 College Avenue, Jasper IN 47546
Telephone: (812) 482-3030 Identification: 770107
Accreditation: &HLC

Wabash College (G)

301 W Wabash Avenue, PO Box 352,
Crawfordsville IN 47933-0352
County: Montgomery FICE Identification: 001844
Unit ID: 152673
Telephone: (765) 361-6100 Carnegie Class: Bac-A&S
FAX Number: (765) 361-6461 Calendar System: Semester
URL: www.wabash.edu
Established: 1832 Annual Undergrad Tuition & Fees: $45,850
Enrollment: 868 Male
Affiliation or Control: Independent Non-Profit IRS Status: 501(c)3
Highest Offering: Baccalaureate
Accreditation: HLC

01 President ... Dr. Scott E. FELLER
05 Acting Dean of the College ... Dr. Todd F. MCDORMAN
10 Chief Financial Officer & Treasurer ... Ms. Kendra COOKS
32 Dean of Students ... Dr. Gregory REDDING
111 Dean for Advancement/Development ... Ms. Michelle L. JANSSEN
84 Dean for Enrollment Management ... Mr. Charles (Chip) TIMMONS
07 Assoc Director of Admissions ... Mr. Matt BOWERS
28 Dean Prof Dev & Malcolm X Institute ... Mr. Steven L. JONES
100 Chief of Staff ... Mr. James L. AMIDON
20 Sr Associate Dean of the College ... Dr. Ann TAYLOR
08 Head Librarian & Dir Lilly Library ... Mr. Jeffery BECK
06 Registrar & Assoc Dean ... Dr. Jonathon D. JUMP
13 Director of IT Services ... Mr. Bradley K. WEAVER
37 Director of Financial Aid ... Mr. Alex DELONIS
35 Associate Dean of Students ... Mr. Marc WELCH
36 Director of Career Development ... Mr. Roland MORIN
29 Dir of Alumni & Parent Relations ... Mr. Steve HOFFMAN
109 Director of Business Auxiliaries ... Mr. Thomas E. KEEDY
41 Dir of Athletics & Campus Wellness ... Mr. Matt TANNEY
110 Associate Dean for Advancement ... Mr. Joseph R. KLEN
15 Director of Human Resources ... Ms. Catherine A. METZ
18 Director of Campus Services ... Mr. David MORGAN
21 Controller ... Mr. Douglas SMITH
38 Director of Counseling Services ... Ms. Jamie DOUGLAS
88 Director of Inquiries CILA ... Dr. Charles F. BLAICH

88 Dir Wabash Ctr Teaching/Learning Ms. Nancy Lynne WESTFIELD
19 Director of Safety and Security Mr. Nicholas GRAY
09 Director of Institutional Research Mr. David DALENBERG
101 Secretary of the Institution/Board Mr. James L. AMIDON, JR.
102 Dir Foundation/Corporate Relations Ms. Deborah WOODS
104 Director International Programs Ms. Amy WEIR
26 Chief Public Relations/Marketing Ms. Kimberly JOHNSON
96 Director of Purchasing Mr. Thomas E. KEEDY
04 Admin Assistant to the President Ms. Beverly CUNNINGHAM
44 Director Annual Giving Mr. Aaron SHELBY
28 Diversity/Equity and Inclusion Dr. Jill LAMBERTON

IOWA

Allen College (A)

1825 Logan Avenue, Waterloo IA 50703-1999
County: Black Hawk FICE Identification: 030691
Unit ID: 152798
Telephone: (319) 226-2000 Carnegie Class: Spec-4-yr-Other Health
FAX Number: (319) 226-2010 Calendar System: Semester
URL: www.allencollege.edu
Established: 1989 Annual Undergrad Tuition & Fees: $19,512
Enrollment: 678 Coed
Affiliation or Control: Independent Non-Profit IRS Status: 501(c)3
Highest Offering: Doctorate
Accreditation: HLC, DMS, MLS, NURSE, OT, @PTA, RAD

01 President Dr. Jared SELIGER
05 Provost Dr. Bob LOCH
10 Exec Director Business/Admin Svcs Ms. Denise HANSON
66 Dean School of Nursing Dr. Kendra WILLIAMS-PEREZ
76 Dean School of Health Sciences Dr. Peggy FORTSCH
84 Dean Enrollment Management Dr. Joanna RAMSDEN-MEIER
37 Director of Financial Aid Ms. Renae CARRILLO
24 Media Specialist Ms. Robin NICHOLSON
06 Registrar Ms. Michelle KOEHN
08 Director of Library Services Dr. Ruth YAN
07 Director of Admissions Ms. Molly QUINN
09 Coord Inst Research/Effectiveness Dr. Lisa BRODERSEN
04 Administrative Asst to President Ms. Rhonda GILBERT
28 Director of Diversity Vacant

Antioch School of Church Planting and Leadership Development (B)

2400 Oakwood Road, Ames IA 50014
County: Story Identification: 667026
Telephone: (515) 292-9694 Carnegie Class: Not Classified
FAX Number: (515) 292-1933 Calendar System: Other
URL: www.antiochschool.edu
Established: 2006 Annual Undergrad Tuition & Fees: N/A
Enrollment: N/A Coed
Affiliation or Control: Independent Non-Profit IRS Status: 501(c)3
Highest Offering: Doctorate
Accreditation: DEAC

01 President Jeff REED
05 Academic Dean Stephen KEMP

The Art of Education University (C)

518 Main Street, Ste A, Osage IA 50461
County: Mitchell Identification: 667385
Telephone: (515) 650-3198 Carnegie Class: Not Classified
FAX Number: N/A Calendar System: Other
URL: theartofeducation.edu
Established: 2011 Annual Graduate Tuition & Fees: N/A
Enrollment: N/A Coed
Affiliation or Control: Proprietary IRS Status: Proprietary
Highest Offering: Master's; No Undergraduates
Accreditation: DEAC

01 CEO & President Brent BINGHAM
05 Chief Academic Officer Cheryl HAYEK
10 Controller Gwen JASS
15 Director of Team & Culture Maria THOMAS
111 Chief Growth Officer EJ CAFFARO
124 Dean of Retention & Student Support Shannon LAUFFER
58 Dean of Graduate Studies Heather CROCKETT
108 Dean of Accreditation & Compliance Julie STRECKER
13 Director of Technology Scott RUSSELL
26 Director of Marketing and CX Deb DUBOIS
88 Chief Product Officer Chris POULTON
07 Director of Admissions Ryan O'MEALEY

*Board of Regents, State of Iowa (D)

11260 Aurora Avenue, Urbandale IA 50322-7905
County: Polk FICE Identification: 033443
Telephone: (515) 281-3934 Carnegie Class: N/A
FAX Number: (515) 281-6420
URL: www.iowaregents.edu

01 President Dr. Michael J. RICHARDS
00 Executive Director & COO Dr. Mark J. BRAUN
05 Chief Academic Officer Dr. Rachel L. BOON
43 Board Counsel Mrs. Aimee K. CLAEYS
04 Executive Assistant Mrs. Laura M. DICKSON

*Iowa State University (E)

1750 Beardshear Hall, 515 Morrill R, Ames IA 50011
County: Story FICE Identification: 001869
Unit ID: 153603
Telephone: (515) 294-4111 Carnegie Class: DU-Highest
FAX Number: (515) 294-2592 Calendar System: Semester
URL: www.iastate.edu
Established: 1858 Annual Undergrad Tuition & Fees (In-State): $9,316
Enrollment: 31,822 Coed
Affiliation or Control: State IRS Status: 501(c)3
Highest Offering: Doctorate
Accreditation: HLC, ACPHA, ART, CAATE, CEA, CIDA, COPSY, DIET, DIETD, IPSY, JOUR, LSAR, MUS, NAIT, PLNG, VET

02 President Dr. Wendy WINTERSTEEN
04 Assistant to the President Ms. Shirley J. KNIPFEL
43 University Counsel Mr. Michael E. NORTON
05 Sr Vice President and Provost Dr. Jonathan A. WICKERT
10 Sr VP for Operations & Finance Ms. Karen Kay CLINE
32 Sr Vice Pres for Student Affairs Dr. Toyia YOUNGER
88 Int VP for Econ Dev/Business Engag Mr. David P. SPALDING
46 Vice Pres Research Dr. Sarah M. NUSSER
56 Vice Pres Extension/Outreach Dr. John D. LAWRENCE
13 Vice Pres/Chief Info Officer Dr. Kristin P. CONSTANT
28 Vice Pres for Diversity & Inclusion Vacant
20 Associate Provost Academic Programs Dr. Ann Marie VANDERZANDEN
20 Assoc Prov Faculty Dr. Dawn BRATSCH-PRINCE
18 Assoc Vice Pres Facilities Planning Mr. Paul FULIGNI
15 Vice President Human Resources Ms. Kristi DARR
35 Assoc Vice Pres & Dean of Students Dr. Vernon J. HURTE
84 Assoc VP Stdnt Affs for Enroll Mgmt Ms. Laura J. DOERING
88 Assoc VP Strategic Relations/Comm Ms. Jacy R. JOHNSON
22 Asst Vice Pres Equal Opportunity Ms. Margo FOREMAN
19 Asst VP and Chief of Police Mr. Michael R. NEWTON
39 Asst VP for St Aff/Dir of Residence Dr. Peter D. ENGLIN
38 Asst VP Stdnt Health/Wellness Ms. Erin BALDWIN
30 President of ISU Foundation Ms. Larissa HOLTMYER-JONES
29 President of Alumni Association Dr. Jeffrey W. JOHNSON
41 Director of Athletics Mr. Jamie B. POLLARD
06 Registrar Dr. Jennifer SUCHAN
37 Director of Financial Aid Ms. Roberta L. JOHNSON
07 Director of Admissions Ms. Katharine JOHNSON SUSKI
09 Exec Director of Inst Research Dr. Karen A. ZUNKEL
104 Director Study Abroad Dr. Frank PETERS
91 Associate CIO Mr. David M. POPELKA
25 Assoc Director/Sponsored Pgm Admin Ms. Tamara R. POLASKI
88 Director Ames Laboratory Dr. Adam SCHWARTZ
96 Director of Procurement Mr. Cory L. HARMS
40 Director University Bookstore Ms. Rita M. PHILLIPS
102 Sr Dir Dev/Corporate Relations Mr. Mark BOECK
102 Sr Dir Dev/Foundation Relations Ms. Donna VAN PELT
44 Exec Dir of Annual & Special Giving Ms. Mary EVANSON
26 Director of University Marketing Ms. Carole A. CUSTER
27 Director of Communications Mr. Rob SCHWEERS
122 Dir Sorority/Fraternity Engagement Mr. Billy BOULDEN
58 Dean Graduate College Dr. William R. GRAVES
08 Dean of Library Services Ms. Hillary SEO
47 Dean College of Agriculture Dr. Daniel J. ROBISON
50 Dean College of Business Mr. David P. SPALDING
48 Dean College of Design Mr. Luis C. RICO-GUTIERREZ
53 Dean College of Human Sciences Dr. Laura JOLLY
54 Dean College of Engineering Dr. W. Samuel EASTERLING
49 Dean Col of Lib Arts & Sciences Dr. Beate SCHMITTMANN
74 Dean College of Veterinary Medicine Dr. Daniel L. GROOMS

*University of Iowa (F)

5 W. Jefferson St, Iowa City IA 52242
County: Johnson FICE Identification: 001892
Unit ID: 153658
Telephone: (319) 335-3565 Carnegie Class: DU-Highest
FAX Number: (319) 335-3560 Calendar System: Semester
URL: www.uiowa.edu
Established: 1847 Annual Undergrad Tuition & Fees (In-State): $9,606
Enrollment: 30,318 Coed
Affiliation or Control: State IRS Status: 501(c)3
Highest Offering: Doctorate
Accreditation: HLC, ANEST, ARCPA, AUD, CAATE, CACREP, CAMPEP, CEA, CLPSY, COPSY, DANCE, DENT, @DIET, DMS, EMT, HSA, IPSY, JOUR, LAW, LIB, MED, MFCD, MIDWF, MUS, NMT, NURSE, PAST, PCSAS, PERF, PH, PHAR, PLNG, PTA, RAD, RTT, SP, SW, THEA

02 President Dr. Barbara J. WILSON
05 Exec Vice Pres & Provost Dr. Kevin KREGEL
46 VP for Research Dr. Martin SCHOLTZ
10 SVP Fin & Ops/Chief Financial Ofcr Mr. Rod LEHNERTZ
32 Vice Pres Student Life Ms. Sarah HANSEN
17 VP Med Affairs/Dean College of Med Dr. J. Brooks JACKSON
30 Vice Pres External Relations Mr. Peter R. MATTHES
26 Asst VP External Relations Ms. Laura MCLERAN
88 Chief Innovation Officer Mr. Jon DARSEE
27 Senior Director Marketing Comm Mr. Ben HILL
20 Associate Provost Faculty Dr. Kevin KREGEL
28 AVP Diversity/Equity/Inclusion Dr. Liz TOVAR
97 Assoc Provost/Dean Univ College Dr. Tanya UDEN-HOLMAN
45 Sr Assoc Vice President Research Dr. Richard D. HICHWA
11 Assoc VP/Dir of Admin and Planning Mr. Donald J. SZESZYCKI
15 Assoc VP Human Resources Ms. Cheryl REARDON
18 Assoc VP/Dir Facilities Management Mr. Donald J. GUCKERT
13 Assoc Vice President & CIO Mr. Steven R. FLEAGLE
17 Interim CEO Univ Hosp & Clinics Ms. Kim HUNTER
25 Exec Director Sponsored Programs Ms. Jennifer LASSNER
19 Asst VP & Director Public Safety Mr. Scott BECKNER
85 Provost/Dean International Programs Mr. Russell GANIM
43 VP Legal Affairs & General Counsel Ms. Carroll REASONER
08 University Librarian Mr. John P. CULSHAW
102 Pres/CEO Univ Ctr for Advancement Ms. Lynette L. MARSHALL
44 Asst VP Annual Giving Ms. Erin ALLEN
07 Director Admissions/Enrollment Mr. Kirk R. KLUVER
37 Director Student Financial Aid Vacant
06 Interim Registrar/Assistant Provost Ms. Julie FELL
36 Director Career Center Ms. Angi MCKIE
38 Director Univ Counseling Services Dr. Barry SCHREIER
39 Asst VP Stdnt Life/Sr Dir Hous/Din Mr. Von STANGE
41 Director Athletics Administration Mr. Gary BARTA
49 Dean Col of Lib Arts & Sci Ms. Sara SANDERS
50 Dean College of Business Ms. Amy KRISTOF-BROWN
52 Dean College of Dentistry Dr. Clark STANFORD
53 Dean College of Education Dr. Daniel CLAY
54 Dean College of Engineering Ms. Harriet NEMBHARD
58 Assoc Provost/Dean Graduate College Ms. Amanda THEIN
61 Dean College of Law Dr. Kevin WASHBURN
66 Dean College of Nursing Dr. Julie ZERWIC
67 Dean College of Pharmacy Dr. Donald E. LETENDRE
69 Dean College of Public Health Dr. Edith PARKER
22 Dir Equal Opportunity/Diversity Ms. Jennifer A. MODESTOU
86 Director State Relations Mr. Keith SAUNDERS
40 Director University Bookstore Mr. George E. HERBERT
96 Assoc VP & Director Purchasing Ms. Deborah J. ZUMBACH
92 Interim Director Honors Program Ms. Emily HILL
87 Director Summer Session Dr. Marlys BOOTE
35 AVP/Dean of Students Dr. Angie REAMS
84 Assoc VP/Enrollment Management Dr. Brent GAGE
100 Chief of Staff Mr. Peter MATTHES
104 Director Study Abroad Mr. Douglas LEE
122 Assoc Dir Fraternity/Sorority Life Ms. ShirDonna LAWRENCE

*University of Northern Iowa (G)

1227 W 27th Street, Cedar Falls IA 50614-0001
County: Black Hawk FICE Identification: 001890
Unit ID: 154095
Telephone: (319) 273-2311 Carnegie Class: Masters/L
FAX Number: (319) 273-2885 Calendar System: Semester
URL: https://uni.edu/
Established: 1876 Annual Undergrad Tuition & Fees (In-State): $8,938
Enrollment: 9,507 Coed
Affiliation or Control: State IRS Status: 501(c)3
Highest Offering: Doctorate
Accreditation: HLC, CAATE, CACREP, CAPRT, CEA, CIDA, MUS, SP, SW, THEA

02 President Dr. Mark A. NOOK
05 Exec VP & Provost Dr. José HERRERA
10 Sr VP Finance & Operations Dr. Michael A. HAGER
32 VP for Student Life Dr. Heather HARBACH
111 Vice President for Univ Advancement Mr. Jim JERMIER
84 Sr Assoc VP Enroll Mgmt/Stdt Suc Dr. Kristin L. WOODS
18 Asst VP & Director Facilities Mgmt Mr. Michael W. ZWANZIGER
39 Exec Dir of Housing/Dining Admin Dr. Nicholas RAFANELLO
20 Assoc Provost Acad Affairs Dr. Patrick P. PEASE
20 Assoc Provost for Faculty Dr. John F. VALLENTINE
13 Chief Information Officer Ms. Marty L. MARK
09 Dir Inst Effectiveness & Planning Dr. Kristin MOSER
06 University Registrar Vacant
29 Director Alumni Relations Dr. Leslie J. PRIDEAUX
37 Director of Financial Aid Mr. Timothy L. BAKULA
15 Dir Human Resource Services Ms. Michelle C. BYERS
83 Dean Col Soc/Behav Sciences Dr. Brenda L. BASS
53 Dean College of Education Dr. Colleen S. MULHOLLAND
49 Dean Col Hum/Arts & Science Dr. John E. FRITCH
58 Assoc VP Research/Dean Grad College Vacant
50 Dean College of Business Dr. Leslie K. WILSON
35 Dean of Students Dr. Allyson RAFANELLO
38 Exec Dir Health & Rec Svcs Ms. Shelley M. O'CONNELL
22 Asst to Pres Compliance/Equity Mgmt Ms. Leah K. GUTKNECHT
41 Athletic Director Mr. David W. HARRIS
21 Controller/Treasurer Ms. Tonya GERBRACHT
86 State Relations Officer Ms. Mary C. BRAUN
104 Exec Director Intl Programs Vacant
97 Director Undergraduate Studies Dr. Deirdre A. HEISTAD
19 Chief of Police/Dir Public Safety Ms. Helen M. HAIRE
25 Dir Research & Sponsored Programs Mr. Tolif R. HUNT
43 University Counsel Mr. Timothy J. MCKENNA
109 Dir Business Operations Ms. Christina GEWEKE
28 Asst to Pres/Chief Div Officer Ms. Gwennette C. BERRY
112 VP for Principal Gifts Ms. Noreen M. HERMANSEN
36 Director Career Services Mr. Robert J. FREDERICK
101 Chief of Staff & Govt Rels Dr. Andrew MORSE
26 Director of University Relations Vacant
08 Dean of the Library Ms. Theresa WESTBROCK
04 Admin Assistant to the President Ms. Jennifer YARROW
07 Director of Admissions Dr. Terri CRUMLEY
44 Director Annual Giving Mr. Nathan CLAPHAM

Briar Cliff University (H)

3303 Rebecca Street, Sioux City IA 51104-2324
County: Woodbury FICE Identification: 001846
Unit ID: 152992
Telephone: (712) 279-5321 Carnegie Class: DU-Mod
FAX Number: (712) 279-5410 Calendar System: Semester
URL: www.briarcliff.edu
Established: 1929 Annual Undergrad Tuition & Fees: $33,308
Enrollment: 1,076 Coed

Affiliation or Control: Roman Catholic IRS Status: 501(c)3
Highest Offering: Doctorate
Accreditation: HLC, NURSE, PTA, SW

01 Interim President .... Dr. Patrick JACOBSON-SCHULTE
05 VP Academic Affairs .... Dr. Todd KNEALING
10 Interim VP Finance & Treasurer .... Ms. Ann OATMAN
26 VP University Relations .... Ms. Suzie FISCHER
84 VP Enrollment Management .... Mr. Matt THOMSEN
06 Registrar .... Mrs. Deidre ENGEL
08 Librarian/Dir Information Services .... Ms. Breanne KIRSCH
13 Director Computer Center .... Mr. Travis ANDERSON
36 Director Career Development .... Ms. Nicole MCGLAUFLIN
37 Director Financial Aid .... Ms. Maria SHAULIS
40 Director Bookstore .... Ms. Calista FJELDOS
41 VP Athletics & Operations .... Mr. Nic SCANDRETT
42 Director Campus Ministry .... Mr. Jason SALISBURY
18 Director Physical Plant .... Mr. Greg PRANKE
111 VP University Advancement .... Ms. Michelle BOE
15 Director Human Resources .... Ms. Theresa VANDENBERG
39 Director of Campus Life & Security .... Mr. Dave ARENS
38 Director Student Counseling .... Ms. Therese COPPLE
09 Director of Institutional Research .... Ms. Deidre ENGEL
30 Director of Philanthropy .... Ms. Amy DERBY
19 Director Security/Safety .... Mr. David ARENS
04 Admin Assistant to the President .... Ms. Bernice METZ

Buena Vista University (A)

610 W Fourth Street, Storm Lake IA 50588-1798
County: Buena Vista FICE Identification: 001847
Unit ID: 153001
Telephone: (712) 749-2351 Carnegie Class: Masters/M
FAX Number: (712) 749-2037 Calendar System: 4/1/4
URL: www.bvu.edu
Established: 1891 Annual Undergrad Tuition & Fees: $36,426
Enrollment: 1,863 Coed
Affiliation or Control: Presbyterian Church (U.S.A.) IRS Status: 501(c)3
Highest Offering: Master's
Accreditation: HLC, CACREP, SW

01 President .... Dr. Brian A. LENZMEIER
04 Assistant to the President .... Ms. Angie DYE
05 Provost/VP Academic Affairs .... Dr. Heidi MANNING
10 Vice Pres Finance & Administration .... Ms. Suzette RADKE
84 Vice Pres for Enrollment Management .... Dr. Brandon JOHNSON
32 Vice Pres Student Success .... Dr. Heather BLACK
111 Vice Pres University Advancement .... Ms. Joan CANTY
30 Assistant VP of Development .... Vacant
81 Dean School of Science .... Dr. Thom BONAGURA
50 Dean HWS School of Business .... Ms. Lisa BEST
53 Dean School of Education .... Dr. Brittany GARLING
49 Dean School of Liberal Arts ...... Dr. Dixee BARTHOLOMEW-FEIS
56 VP for Extended University Programs .... Ms. Jean BRAL
06 Registrar .... Ms. Stephanie WILHELM
07 Exec Director of Admissions .... Mr. Conner ELLINGHUYSEN
15 Human Resources Manager .... Vacant
08 Actg Dir of Library/Ref Librarian .... Ms. Jodie MORIN
26 Chief Marketing Officer .... Vacant
29 Director of Alumni Engagement .... Ms. Kristie SPOTTS
44 Director of Annual Campaigns .... Ms. Barbara AIONA
13 Chief Information Officer .... Mr. Joe MCLAIN
18 Interim Director Facilities Mgmt .... Mr. Andy TAYLOR
36 Dir Career & Personal Development .... Ms. Mandi MOLLRING
37 Director of Financial Assistance .... Ms. Patti DEMERS
28 Sr Dir of Diversity & Inclusion .... Mr. Joel BERRIEN
41 Athletic Director .... Mr. Scott BROWN
42 Chaplain .... Dr. Melanie HAUSER
19 Director of Campus Security .... Ms. Jessica GARLING
09 Institutional Researcher .... Mr. James E. HEWETT
96 Purchasing Administrator .... Ms. Tanya LANDGRAF

Central College (B)

812 University, Pella IA 50219-1999
County: Marion FICE Identification: 001850
Unit ID: 153108
Telephone: (641) 628-9000 Carnegie Class: Bac-A&S
FAX Number: N/A Calendar System: Semester
URL: www.central.edu
Established: 1853 Annual Undergrad Tuition & Fees: $18,600
Enrollment: 1,120 Coed
Affiliation or Control: Reformed Church In America IRS Status: 501(c)3
Highest Offering: Baccalaureate
Accreditation: HLC, MUS

01 President .... Dr. Mark L. PUTNAM
05 VP Academic Affairs/Dean of Faculty .... Dr. Mary M. STREY
111 Vice President Advancement .... Mrs. Sunny EIGHMY
10 Vice Pres for Finance & Admin .... Mrs. Karen TUMLINSON
32 VP Student Development .... Mrs. Carol WILLIAMSON
84 VP Enrollment Mgmt/Dean Admission ... Mr. Chevy FREIBURGER
20 Assoc Dean Curriculum/Faculty Dev .... Mr. Brian PETERSON
36 Assoc Dean Career Dev/Civic Engage .... Mrs. Jessica KLYN DE NOVELO
21 Controller/Assistant Treasurer .... Mr. Jeff SANGER
110 Director of Advancement Services .... Mrs. Peggy VAN DEN BERG
26 Dir of Integrated Mktg/Comm/Media .... Mrs. Denise LAMPHIER
13 Int Dir Information Technology .... Mrs. Deb BRUXVOORT
44 Dir Annual Giving & Alumni Engage .... Mr. Corey FALTER
37 Director Financial Aid .... Mr. Wayne DILLE
42 Chaplain .... Rev. Joe BRUMMEL
15 Director of Human Resources .... Ms. Paula RYAN
41 Athletics Director .... Mr. Eric VAN KLEY
18 Dir of Facilities Management .... Mr. Craig ROOSE
06 Registrar .... Ms. Leslie DUININK
04 Administrative Asst to President .... Ms. Carma STURTZ
09 Institutional Research Director .... Vacant
96 Dir of Purchasing & Facility Svcs .... Mrs. Janine FONTANA
112 Major Gifts Officer .... Mrs. Michelle WILKIE
27 Director of External Engagement .... Ms. Jenae SIKKINK
109 Director of Dining Services .... Mr. Iwan WILLIAMS
88 Director of Conferences/Events .... Mrs. Susan CANFIELD
53 Director of the Education Program .... Mrs. Jennifer DIERS

Clarke University (C)

1550 Clarke Drive, Dubuque IA 52001-3198
County: Dubuque FICE Identification: 001852
Unit ID: 153126
Telephone: (563) 588-6300 Carnegie Class: DU-Mod
FAX Number: (563) 588-6789 Calendar System: Semester
URL: www.clarke.edu
Established: 1843 Annual Undergrad Tuition & Fees: $35,750
Enrollment: 855 Coed
Affiliation or Control: Roman Catholic IRS Status: 501(c)3
Highest Offering: Doctorate
Accreditation: HLC, CAATE, MUS, NURSE, PTA, SW

01 President .... Dr. Thom D. CHESNEY
04 Exec Admin Assistant to President .... Ms. Kathy TEIG
05 Vice Pres Academic Affairs .... Dr. Eden WALES FREEDMAN
111 Vice Pres Institutional Advancement .... Mr. Bill BIEBUYCK
32 Vice President Student Life .... Ms. Kate ZANGER
10 Vice President Business & Finance .... Ms. Elizabeth MCGRATH
84 Vice President Enrollment Mgmt .... Ms. Julie CIRKS
06 Registrar .... Ms. Kristi BAGSTAD
08 Director of Library .... Ms. Susanne LEIBOLD
58 Dean College of Prof & Grad Studies .... Vacant
49 Dean College of Arts & Sciences .... Dr. David DIMATTIO
37 Director of Financial Aid .... Mr. Robert HOOVER
26 Director of Marketing .... Ms. Amy ERRTHUM
13 Chief Technology Officer .... Mr. Andy BELLINGS
18 Exec Dir of Facilities Management .... Mr. Steven KIRSCHBAUM
36 Asst Dir of Counseling/Career Svcs .... Ms. Becky HERRIG
15 Director of Human Resources .... Ms. Jody PFOHL
41 Director of Athletics .... Mr. Curt LONG
42 Director of Campus Ministry .... Sr. Kathleen SINCLAIR
40 Director of the Bookstore .... Ms. Sarah HAAS
23 Director of Health Services .... Ms. Tammy MOORE
90 Asst Dean Acad Affairs/Inst Supp .... Mr. Pat MADDUX
88 Dir Institute for Prof Excellence .... Ms. Liz KRUSE
07 Director of Admissions .... Ms. Ali BOYD
30 Exec Director of Development .... Ms. Courtney LEONARD
29 Director of Alumni Relations .... Ms. Kaley RIGDON
85 International Students Advisor .... Ms. Evelyn NADEAU
09 Dir Institutional Rsrch/Assessment .... Mr. James UHLENKAMP

Coe College (D)

1220 1st Avenue, NE, Cedar Rapids IA 52402-5092
County: Linn FICE Identification: 001854
Unit ID: 153144
Telephone: (319) 399-8000 Carnegie Class: Bac-A&S
FAX Number: (319) 399-8830 Calendar System: Semester
URL: www.coe.edu
Established: 1851 Annual Undergrad Tuition & Fees: $47,220
Enrollment: 1,394 Coed
Affiliation or Control: Independent Non-Profit IRS Status: 501(c)3
Highest Offering: Baccalaureate
Accreditation: HLC, MUS, NURSE

01 President .... Mr. David HAYES
05 Interim Provost .... Dr. Angela ZISKOWSKI
111 Vice Pres for Advancement .... Ms. Chantel OLUFSEN
84 VP for Enroll/Marketing/Inst Effect .... Ms. Julie STAKER
10 Chief Financial/Business Officer .... Ms. Angela CALHOUN
15 Director of Human Resources .... Ms. Mary Kay NATH
06 Registrar .... Mr. Jesse UPAH
08 Director Library Services .... Ms. Laura RISKEDAHL
29 Director Alumni Programs .... Mr. Michael GENESER
09 Director of Institutional Research .... Vacant
37 Director of Financial Aid .... Ms. Julie STAKER
20 Associate Dean .... Dr. Marc FALK
35 Dean of Students .... Ms. Keniese EVANS
85 International Student Advisor .... Mr. John CHAIMOV
42 Chaplain .... Ms. Jayne THOMPSON
41 Director of Athletics .... Mr. Steve COOK
18 Director of Physical Plant .... Ms. Lisa CIHA
36 Dir of Career Services .... Ms. Nanci YOUNG
04 Administrative Asst to President .... Ms. Kim PRIBYL
13 Chief Info Technology Officer .... Ms. Natalie MILKE
19 Director Security/Safety .... Mr. Carlos VELEZ
44 Director Annual/Planned Giving .... Ms. Rachel COHEN
122 Dir Stdnt Life-Greek Life .... Mr. Chandler ROBLES

Cornell College (E)

600 First Street SW, Mount Vernon IA 52314-1098
County: Linn FICE Identification: 001856
Unit ID: 153162
Telephone: (319) 895-4000 Carnegie Class: Bac-A&S
FAX Number: (319) 895-4492 Calendar System: Other
URL: www.cornellcollege.edu
Established: 1853 Annual Undergrad Tuition & Fees: $45,914
Enrollment: 1,002 Coed
Affiliation or Control: United Methodist IRS Status: 501(c)3
Highest Offering: Master's
Accreditation: HLC

01 President .... Mr. Jonathan BRAND
05 Provost/VP Acad & Student Affairs .... Dr. Ilene CRAWFORD
10 Interim VP/COO and CFO .... Mr. Dan HALL
84 Vice Pres Enrollment Management .... Ms. Wendy BECKEMEYER
88 Special Assistant to the President .... Mr. John W. HARP
111 Assoc VP Alumni/College Advancement ..... Ms. Kristi COLUMBUS
32 Assoc VP/Dean of Students .... Ms. Jackie WILSON
20 Associate Dean .... Dr. Kate KAUPER
20 Associate Dean .... Dr. Craig TEAGUE
09 Dir Institutional Effectiveness .... Ms. Angie BAUMAN POWER
37 Director of Student Financial Asst .... Ms. Pamela PERRY
06 Registrar .... Ms. Megan HICKS
08 College Librarian .... Mr. Gregory COTTON
30 Director of Development .... Mr. AJ PLUMMER
26 Senior Dir Marketing/Communications .... Ms. Jen VISSER
42 Chaplain .... Rev. Melea WHITE
41 Athletics Director .... Mr. Seth WING
18 Facilities Operations Manager .... Mr. Luke FISCHER
36 Senior Dir Berry Career Institute .... Ms. Jodi SCHAFER
38 Director Student Counseling .... Dr. Brenda C. LOVSTUEN
15 Director of Human Resources .... Ms. Stefanie BRAY
07 Director of Admission Operations .... Ms. Sharon GRICE
13 Director of Information Technology .... Mr. Jeff GIBSON
40 Manager Bookstore .... Ms. Vicki MOORE
04 Executive Asst to President .... Ms. RuthAnn SCHEER
19 Campus Safety Director .... Mr. Mark WINDER
28 Senior Diversity Officer .... Mr. Hemie COLLIER

Des Moines Area Community College (F)

2006 S Ankeny Boulevard, Ankeny IA 50023-3993
County: Polk FICE Identification: 007120
Unit ID: 153214
Telephone: (515) 964-6200 Carnegie Class: Assoc/MT-VT-High Non
FAX Number: N/A Calendar System: Semester
URL: www.dmacc.edu
Established: 1966 Annual Undergrad Tuition & Fees (In-District): $5,100
Enrollment: 23,051 Coed
Affiliation or Control: State/Local IRS Status: 501(c)3
Highest Offering: Associate Degree
Accreditation: HLC, ACFEI, ADNUR, COARC, DA, DH, EMT, FUSER, IFSAC, MAC, MLTAD, SURGT

01 President/CEO .... Mr. Rob DENSON
00 Chair Board of Directors .... Mr. Joe PUGEL
05 Vice President Academic Affairs .... Mr. M.D ISLEY
84 VP Enrollment Svcs/Student Success .... Ms. Shelli ALLEN
15 Executive Director Human Resources .... Dr. Jenifer OWENSON
09 Exec Dir Plng/Assessment & Data .... Dr. Deborah J. KEPPLE-MAMROS
20 Asst to the VP for Academic Affs .... Mr. Kyle COLLINS
13 Exec Dir Information Solutions .... Mr. Mark CLARK
100 Chief Innovation Officer .... Ms. Karen STILES
81 Dean Sciences & Humanities .... Mr. Jim STICK
72 Dean Industrial & Technology .... Dr. Jennifer FOSTER
50 Dean Business/Mgmt/Information Tech .. Dr. Jeanie MCCARVILLE
76 Dean Health/Public Service .... Mr. Art BROWN
55 Dean SEMSS .... Mr. Scott SCHULTZ
12 Provost Urban Campus .... Dr. Anne HOWSARE
12 Provost Boone Campus .... Mr. Andrew NELSON
12 Provost Carroll Campus .... Mr. Joel LUNDSTROM
12 Provost Newton Campus .... Dr. Joe DEHART
12 Provost West Campus .... Dr. Tony PAUSTIAN
18 Executive Director Physical Plant .... Mr. Greg MARTIN
102 Executive Director Foundation .... Ms. Tara CONNOLLY
51 Exec Dir Continuing Education .... Mr. Michael HOFFMAN
36 Director Student Development .... Mr. Wade ROBINSON
37 Director Financial Aid .... Mr. Jerry MCKEEN
26 Director Marketing/Public Relations .... Mr. Todd JONES
25 Director Grants/Contracts .... Ms. Deb KOUA
19 Dir Energy Mgt/Safety/Security .... Mr. Jay TIEFENTHALER
06 Registrar .... Ms. Heidi HEILSKOV
08 Head Librarian .... Ms. Rebecca FUNKE
101 Secretary of the Board .... Ms. Carolyn FARLOW
04 Admin Assistant to the President .... Ms. Dona BURA
10 Chief Financial/Business Officer .... Mr. Ben VOAKLANDER
108 Director Institutional Assessment .... Dr. Andrew NEUENDORF
28 Director of Diversity .... Ms. Naomi Sea Young WITTSTRUCK

Des Moines Area Community College Boone Campus (G)

1125 Hancock Drive, Boone IA 50036
Telephone: (515) 432-7203 Identification: 770048
Accreditation: &HLC

Des Moines Area Community College Carroll Campus (H)

906 North Grant Road, Carroll IA 51401-2525
Telephone: (712) 792-1755 Identification: 770049
Accreditation: &HLC

Des Moines Area Community College Newton Campus (I)

600 N 2nd Avenue West, Newton IA 50208
Telephone: (641) 791-3622 Identification: 770051
Accreditation: &HLC

Des Moines Area Community College Urban Campus (A)

1100 7th Street, Des Moines IA 50314
Telephone: (515) 244-4226 Identification: 770050
Accreditation: &HLC

Des Moines Area Community College West Des Moines Campus (B)

5959 Grand Avenue, West Des Moines IA 50266
Telephone: (515) 633-2407 Identification: 770052
Accreditation: &HLC

Des Moines University (C)

3200 Grand Avenue, Des Moines IA 50312-4198
County: Polk FICE Identification: 001855
Unit ID: 154156
Telephone: (515) 271-1400 Carnegie Class: Spec-4-yr-Med
FAX Number: (515) 271-1532 Calendar System: Other
URL: www.dmu.edu
Established: 1898 Annual Graduate Tuition & Fees: N/A
Enrollment: 1,559 Coed
Affiliation or Control: Independent Non-Profit IRS Status: 501(c)3
Highest Offering: First Professional Degree; No Undergraduates
Accreditation: HLC, ARCPA, HSA, OSTEO, PH, POD, PTA

01 President/CEO .... Dr. Angela L. WALKER FRANKLIN
10 Senior Vice President & CFO .... Mr. Mark PEIFFER
05 VP Academic/Student Affairs .... Ms. Kimberly BROWN
111 VP University Advancement .... Ms. Stephanie GREINER
86 Chief External & Govt Affs Officer .... Ms. Susan HUPPERT
46 Vice President for Research .... Vacant
06 Registrar .... Ms. Melinda SHERZER
08 Director of Library .... Vacant
15 Chief Human Resources Officer .... Dr. Marc WACHTFOGEL
13 Chief Information Officer .... Ms. Carolyn WEAVER
37 Director of Financial Aid .... Ms. Mary PAYNE
18 Director of Facilities Management .... Mr. John HARRIS
19 Building Services Manager .... Mr. Philip BAUGHMAN
108 Chief Compliance Officer .... Ms. Erika LINDEN
69 Director Public Health Program .... Dr. Rachel REIMER
26 Chief Strategic Comm Officer .... Mr. Mark DANES
76 Dean College Health Sciences .... Dr. Wallace BOEVE
63 Dean Col Podiatric Medicine/Surg .... Dr. Kevin SMITH
63 Dean Col Osteopathic Medicine .... Dr. Steven HALM
04 Executive Asst to President .... Ms. Christina HENDERSON
07 Sr Dir of Admissions/Recruitment .... Ms. Molly MOELLER
32 Director of Student Services .... Ms. Alicia LYNCH
28 Dir Multicult Affs/Chief Div Ofcr .... Dr. Richard SALAS
29 Director Alumni Relations .... Ms. Krystal KRUSE
101 Secretary of the Institution/Board .... Ms. Linda KADING
38 Director Student Counseling .... Dr. Ciara LEWIS
44 Director Annual Giving .... Ms. Melanie WEIBEL
25 Grants and Contract Manager .... Ms. Mollie LYON

† Tuition varies by degree program.

Divine Word College (D)

102 Jacoby Drive, SW, PO Box 380,
Epworth IA 52045-0380
County: Dubuque FICE Identification: 001858
Unit ID: 153241
Telephone: (563) 876-3353 Carnegie Class: Bac-A&S
FAX Number: (563) 876-3407 Calendar System: Semester
URL: www.dwci.edu
Established: 1918 Annual Undergrad Tuition & Fees: $13,780
Enrollment: 69 Coed
Affiliation or Control: Roman Catholic IRS Status: 501(c)3
Highest Offering: Baccalaureate
Accreditation: HLC, CEA

01 President .... Rev. Thomas ASCHEMAN, SVD
05 Vice President Academic Affairs ..Rev. John A. SZUKALSKI, SVD
32 VP Formation/Dean of Students .... Rev. Long Phi NGUYEN, SVD
07 Vice President Admissions .... Mr. Len UHAL
11 Vice President Operations .... Mr. Steven WINGER
30 Director Development .... Rev. Linh PHAM, SVD
26 Director Public Relations .... Ms. Sandy WILGENBUSCH
29 Director Alumni .... Rev. Thang HOANG, SVD
04 Executive Sec to the President .... Ms. Christine JACKSON
108 Director Inst Effectiveness .... Dr. Yasmin RIOUX
08 Director Library .... Mr. Daniel C. WILLIAMS
06 Registrar .... Ms. Kimberly BURNETT-HACKBARTH
104 Coordinator Study Abroad .... Rev. John A. SZUKALSKI, SVD
38 Counselor .... Sr. Aprilia UNTARTO, SSPS
42 Chaplain .... Rev. Sonny DECLASS, SVD
23 Coordinator Health Services .... Bro. Mike DECKER, SVD
37 Coordinator Financial Aid .... Ms. Carolyn WAECHTER
10 Director Business Office .... Ms. Marlene DECKER
13 Director Information Systems .... Mr. Brad FLORENCE
18 Director Maintenance .... Bro. Vinh TRINH, SVD

Dordt University (E)

700 7th St. NE, Sioux Center IA 51250-1697
County: Sioux FICE Identification: 001859
Unit ID: 153250
Telephone: (712) 722-6000 Carnegie Class: Masters/S
FAX Number: (712) 722-6035 Calendar System: Semester
URL: www.dordt.edu
Established: 1955 Annual Undergrad Tuition & Fees: $32,820
Enrollment: 1,662 Coed
Affiliation or Control: Christian Reformed Church IRS Status: 501(c)3
Highest Offering: Master's
Accreditation: HLC, NURSE, SW

01 President .... Dr. Erik HOEKSTRA
111 Vice President Advancement .... Mr. John BAAS
84 VP for Enrollment & Marketing .... Mr. Brandon HUISMAN
05 VP for Academic Affairs .... Dr. Leah ZUIDEMA
11 Vice President for Univ Operations .... Mr. Howard WILSON
85 Director of Global Education .... Mr. Adam ADAMS
10 Vice President for Finance & Risk .... Mrs. Stephanie BACCAM
37 Director Financial Aid .... Mr. Harlan HARMELINK
06 Registrar .... Mr. James BOS
88 Asst Dir for Research & Scholarship .... Vacant
58 Director Graduate Studies .... Dr. Steve HOLTROP
36 Career Services Coordinator .... Ms. Amy WESTRA
26 Marketing and Public Relations .... Ms. Sarah MOSS
18 Director Physical Plant .... Mr. Nate VAN NIEJENHUIS
32 Vice Pres for Student Success .... Mr. Robert TAYLOR
42 Chief of Staff/Dean of Chapel .... Rev. Aaron BAART
41 Director of Athletics .... Mr. Ross DOUMA
112 Director of Planned Giving .... Mr. Dave VANDER WERF
15 Director Human Resources .... Mrs. Sue DROOG
91 Director of Computer Services .... Mr. Brian VAN DONSELAAR
08 Director of Library Services .... Ms. Jennifer BREEMS
23 Director of Health Services .... Ms. Beth BAAS
88 Director Academic Skills Center .... Mrs. Sharon ROSENBOOM
04 Exec Admin Asst to President .... Mrs. LeeAnn MOERMAN
07 Director of Admissions .... Mr. Greg VAN DYKE
29 Director Alumni Affairs .... Mrs. Alicia BOWAR
30 Director of Development .... Mr. Lyle HUISMAN
39 Dir Resident Life/Student Housing .... Mr. Derek BUTEYN

Drake University (F)

2507 University Avenue, Des Moines IA 50311-4505
County: Polk FICE Identification: 001860
Unit ID: 153269
Telephone: (515) 271-2011 Carnegie Class: DU-Mod
FAX Number: (515) 271-3016 Calendar System: Semester
URL: www.drake.edu
Established: 1881 Annual Undergrad Tuition & Fees: $44,376
Enrollment: 4,774 Coed
Affiliation or Control: Independent Non-Profit IRS Status: 501(c)3
Highest Offering: Doctorate
Accreditation: HLC, ART, CAATE, CACREP, JOUR, LAW, MUS, OT, PHAR

01 President .... Mr. Earl F. MARTIN
05 Provost .... Dr. Sue MATTISON
10 Chief Financial Officer .... Mr. Adam VOIGTS
11 Chief Administrative Officer .... Ms. Venessa MACRO
111 Vice Pres University Advancement .... Mr. John SMITH
20 Deputy Provost for Academic Affairs .... Dr. Renee CRAMER
28 Assoc Prov for Equity & Inclusion .... Dr. Jennifer HARVEY
07 Dean of Admission .... Ms. Anne KREMER
32 Chief Student Affairs Officer .... Dr. Jerry PARKER
35 Assoc Provost Student Affairs .... Ms. Melissa STURM-SMITH
15 Human Resources Director .... Ms. Maureen DE ARMOND
13 Chief Tech Information Officer .... Ms. Keren FIORENZA
09 Dir of Inst Research & Assessment .... Mr. Kevin SAUNDERS
88 Director of Student Records .... Mr. Kevin P. MOENKHAUS
08 Dean Cowles Library .... Ms. Gillian GREMMELS
85 Exec Dir Global Eng & Intl Pgm .... Dr. Annique KIEL
19 Director Public Safety .... Mr. Scott LAW
26 Director University Communications .... Ms. Leslie MAYNES
29 Alumni/Parent Programs .... Mr. Andrew VERLENGIA
49 Dean Arts & Sciences .... Dr. Gesine GERHARD
53 Dean School Education .... Dr. Ryan WISE
61 Dean Law School .... Mr. Jerry ANDERSON
50 Dean Business/Public Administration . Mr. Alejandro HERNANDEZ
67 Dean Pharmacy/Health Science .... Dr. Renae CHESNUT
60 Dean Journalism/Mass Communications .... Dr. Catherine STAUB
41 Director Intercollegiate Athletics .... Mr. Brian HARDIN
37 Director Financial Aid .... Mr. Ryan ZANTINGH
38 Director University Counseling Ctr .... Dr. Mark KLOBERDANZ
92 Assistant Director Honors Program .... Ms. Charlene SKIDMORE
94 Director Women's Studies .... Dr. Nancy REINCKE
39 Director Office of Residence Life .... Ms. Lorissa SOWDEN
04 Asst to President .... Ms. Cheryle ANANIA
100 Chief of Staff .... Mr. Nate REAGEN
30 Director of Development .... Mr. John AMATO
06 Registrar .... Ms. Jenny TRAN-JOHNSON

*Eastern Iowa Community College District (G)

101 West Third Street, Davenport IA 52801-1221
County: Scott FICE Identification: 004075
Unit ID: 153311
Telephone: (563) 336-3300 Carnegie Class: N/A
FAX Number: (563) 322-0129
URL: www.eicc.edu

01 Chancellor .... Dr. Sonya J. WILLIAMS
30 Exec Dir Resource Development .... Dr. Ellen BLUTH
26 Associate Director Communications .... Ms. Johnna KERRES
10 Chief Business Officer .... Mr. Suteesh TANDON
101 Secretary of the Institution/Board .... Ms. Honey BEDELL
15 Director Personnel Services .... Ms. Deb SULLIVAN
18 Chief Facilities/Physical Plant .... Mr. Matt SCHMIT
84 Director Enrollment Management .... Ms. Erin SNYDER

*Clinton Community College (H)

1000 Lincoln Boulevard, Clinton IA 52732-6299
County: Clinton FICE Identification: 001853
Telephone: (563) 244-7001 Carnegie Class: Not Classified
FAX Number: (563) 244-7107 Calendar System: Semester
URL: www.eicc.edu
Established: 1966 Annual Undergrad Tuition & Fees (In-District): N/A
Enrollment: N/A Coed
Affiliation or Control: State/Local IRS Status: 501(c)3
Highest Offering: Associate Degree
Accreditation: &HLC, EMT

02 President .... Dr. Brian KELLY
05 Dean of the College .... Ms. Amy MADSEN-SMITH
32 Dean of Student Development .... Dr. Michelle ALLMENDINGER
102 Asst to Pres/Exec Dir Sharar Found .... Ms. Ann EISENMAN

† Regional accreditation is carried under the parent institution Eastern Iowa Community College District in Davenport, IA.

*Muscatine Community College (I)

152 Colorado Street, Muscatine IA 52761-5396
County: Muscatine FICE Identification: 001882
Telephone: (563) 288-6001 Carnegie Class: Not Classified
FAX Number: (563) 288-6074 Calendar System: Semester
URL: www.eicc.edu
Established: 1929 Annual Undergrad Tuition & Fees (In-District): N/A
Enrollment: N/A Coed
Affiliation or Control: State/Local IRS Status: 501(c)3
Highest Offering: Associate Degree
Accreditation: &HLC, EMT

02 President .... Dr. Naomi DEWINTER
04 Assistant to the President .... Ms. Lisa WIEGEL
05 Dean of the College .... Dr. Jeremy PICKARD
32 Dean of Student Development .... Ms. Shelly CRAM-RAHLF
06 Registrar .... Ms. Robin MITCHELL
08 Library Specialist .... Ms. Nancy LUIKART

† Regional accreditation is carried under the parent institution Eastern Iowa Community College District in Davenport, IA.

*Scott Community College (J)

500 Belmont Road, Bettendorf IA 52722-6804
County: Scott FICE Identification: 001885
Telephone: (563) 441-4001 Carnegie Class: Not Classified
FAX Number: (563) 441-4154 Calendar System: Semester
URL: www.eicc.edu
Established: 1966 Annual Undergrad Tuition & Fees (In-District): N/A
Enrollment: N/A Coed
Affiliation or Control: State/Local IRS Status: 501(c)3
Highest Offering: Associate Degree
Accreditation: &HLC, CAHIIM, DA, EMT, RAD, SURGT

02 President .... Dr. Ann LAWLER
05 Dean of Instruction .... Mr. Gabe KNIGHT
32 Dean of Student Development/Affs .... Dr. Michael BEANE
103 Dean Career Assistance Center .... Dr. Scott SCHNEIDER
11 Dean of Operations .... Dr. Matt SCHMIT
37 Director Student Financial Aid .... Ms. Katy RUSH
36 Job Placement Specialist .... Mr. Wayne COLE

† Regional accreditation is carried under the parent institution Eastern Iowa Community College District in Davenport, IA.

Emmaus Bible College (K)

2570 Asbury Road, Dubuque IA 52001-3096
County: Dubuque FICE Identification: 023289
Unit ID: 153302
Telephone: (563) 588-8000 Carnegie Class: Bac-Diverse
FAX Number: (563) 588-1216 Calendar System: Semester
URL: www.emmaus.edu
Established: 1941 Annual Undergrad Tuition & Fees: $19,250
Enrollment: 194 Coed
Affiliation or Control: Independent Non-Profit IRS Status: 501(c)3
Highest Offering: Baccalaureate
Accreditation: HLC, BI

01 President .... Mr. Philip BOOM
10 VP for Administration and Finance .... Mr. Joseph ABDY
05 Vice President for Academic Affairs .... Mr. Raju KUNJUMMEN
111 Vice President for Advancement .... Mr. Chad CUNNINGHAM
32 VP for Student Development .... Mr. Israel CHAVEZ
84 Vice President Enrollment & Mktg .... Mr. Tom KOOK
73 Chair Bible & Theology .... Dr. Mark STEVENSON
08 Librarian .... Mr. John H. RUSH
37 Financial Aid Officer .... Mr. Steve C. SEEMAN
21 Controller .... Mr. Steve M. JENSEN
06 Registrar .... Mrs. Janice G. BENNETT
106 Dir Online Education/E-learning .... Mr. Ray GUERRA
108 Director Institutional Assessment .... Vacant
29 Director Alumni Relations .... Vacant
41 Athletic Director .... Mr. Chris MCHUGH
07 Director Enrollment Management .... Ms. Laurel R. RASMUSSEN
18 Chief Facilities/Physical Plant .... Mr. Jeremy MAU
04 Administrative Asst to President .... Ms. Becky PERKINS
50 Chair Business Department .... Mr. Kim PARCHER
39 Dir Resident Life/Student Housing .... Ms. Anna HENNING
13 Director of Technology .... Mr. Mark NEWLAND

Faith Baptist Bible College and Seminary (A)

1900 NW 4th Street, Ankeny IA 50023-2152

County: Polk   FICE Identification: 007121
Unit ID: 153320

Telephone: (515) 964-0601   Carnegie Class: Bac-Diverse
FAX Number: (515) 964-1638   Calendar System: Semester
URL: www.faith.edu
Established: 1921   Annual Undergrad Tuition & Fees: $17,650
Enrollment: 504   Coed
Affiliation or Control: Independent Non-Profit   IRS Status: 501(c)3
Highest Offering: Doctorate
Accreditation: HLC, BI

01	President	Dr. James R. TILLOTSON
03	Executive Vice President	Dr. Martin T. HERRON
05	VP for Academic Services	Dr. Kenneth D. RATHBUN
73	Dean of Seminary	Dr. Douglas E. BROWN
10	VP for Business/CFO	Mr. Paul BRAY
111	VP for Advancement/Church Rels	Mr. Daniel H. BJOKNE
34	Dean of Women	Mrs. Sandy CAPON
32	Dean of Students	Mr. Noah KEPHART
26	Director of Communications	Mr. Andrew GOGERTY
06	Registrar	Mr. Jeff BUNJER
37	Director Student Financial Aid	Ms. Alice BUNJER
08	Head Librarian	Dr. Paul A. HARTOG
04	Administrative Asst to President	Miss Briana K. HARRIER
84	VP for Enrollment and Student Life	Mr. Mark L. DAVIS
106	Dir Online Education/E-learning	Mr. Charlie CARTER
41	Athletic Director	Mr. Brian S. FINCHAM

Graceland University (B)

1 University Place, Lamoni IA 50140-1699

County: Decatur   FICE Identification: 001866
Unit ID: 153366

Telephone: (641) 784-5000   Carnegie Class: Masters/L
FAX Number: (641) 784-5480   Calendar System: Trimester
URL: www.graceland.edu
Established: 1895   Annual Undergrad Tuition & Fees: $31,320
Enrollment: 1,517   Coed
Affiliation or Control: Other   IRS Status: 501(c)3
Highest Offering: Doctorate
Accreditation: HLC

01	President	Dr. Patricia H. DRAVES
05	Vice Pres for Academic Affairs	Dr. Joel SHROCK
10	Vice Pres Business/Finance	Mr. David SIDDALL
32	VP Student Life/Dean of Students	Mr. Dave SCHAAL
111	Vice President for Institutional Ad	Ms. Kristi HETTRICK
108	Exec Dir Planning & Effectiveness	Ms. Beth HIGDON
51	Director Graduate/Continuing Educ	Mr. Paul BINNICKER
39	Director of Residence Life	Ms. Morgan BRADFORD DIAZ
84	VP Enrollment & Strategic Growth	Ms. Deborah SKINNER
06	Registrar	Mrs. Peggy MOTHERSHEAD
29	Dir Annual Giving/Alumni Program	Mr. Colby CONNELY
15	Director Human Resources	Mrs. Ondrea GREENE
04	Executive Asst to President	Mrs. Jodi SEYMOUR
110	Senior Dir Advancement Services	Ms. Paula ANDERSON
85	Dir Intercultural/Student Success	Ms. Diana JONES
66	Dean School of Nursing	Dr. Jolene LYNN
13	Chief Information Officer	Ms. Talia BROWN
26	Chief Marketing Officer	Mr. Shane ADAMS
37	Dir of Student Financial Services	Ms. Reta GEORGE

Grand View University (C)

1200 Grandview Avenue, Des Moines IA 50316-1599

County: Polk   FICE Identification: 001867
Unit ID: 153375

Telephone: (515) 263-2800   Carnegie Class: Masters/S
FAX Number: (515) 263-6095   Calendar System: Semester
URL: www.grandview.edu
Established: 1896   Annual Undergrad Tuition & Fees: $29,792
Enrollment: 1,874   Coed
Affiliation or Control: Evangelical Lutheran Church In America
IRS Status: 501(c)3
Highest Offering: Master's
Accreditation: HLC, CAATE, NURSE, SW

01	President	Mr. Kent L. HENNING
04	Exec Admin Asst to the President	Ms. Corinna KING
05	Provost/Vice Pres Academic Affairs	Dr. Carl MOSES
79	Dean College of Humanities & Educ	Vacant
83	Dean College of Social/Nat Science	Dr. Paul RIDER
10	Vice Pres Administration & Finance	Mr. Christopher LEE
111	Vice President Advancement	Mr. William H. BURMA
84	Vice Pres Enrollment Management	Ms. Debbie M. BARGER
26	Vice Pres Marketing/Communications	Ms. Kendall DILLON
32	Vice President Student Affairs	Dr. Jay B. PRESCOTT
13	Vice President Information Svcs/CIO	Mr. Tim T. WHEELDON
37	Director Financial Aid	Vacant
20	Special Assistant to the Provost	Ms. Pamela M. CHRISTOFFERS
51	Dean Graduate/Adult Programs	Dr. Patricia A. WILLIAMS
35	Associate VP for Student Affairs	Mr. Jason K. BAUER
06	Registrar	Ms. Debbie K. GANNON
42	Senior Campus Pastor	Rev. Russell L. LACKEY
09	Director Inst Planning/Research	Ms. Debbie M. BARGER
36	Director Career Center	Ms. Susan M. STEARNS
08	Director of the Library	Ms. Pamela D. REES

40	Director Bookstore & Campus Svcs	Mr. Tim REGER
07	Director of Admissions	Mr. Ryan THOMPSON
18	Director Buildings & Grounds	Ms. Kim I. BUTLER
38	Director Leadership & Counseling	Mr. Kent A. SCHORNACK
28	Dir Multicultural & Cmty Outreach	Mr. Alex H. PIEDRAS
41	Athletic Director	Mr. Troy A. PLUMMER
15	Human Resources Manager	Ms. Erica L. KLUVER

Grinnell College (D)

1121 Park Street, Grinnell IA 50112-1690

County: Poweshiek   FICE Identification: 001868
Unit ID: 153384

Telephone: (641) 269-4000   Carnegie Class: Bac-A&S
FAX Number: (641) 269-3408   Calendar System: Semester
URL: www.grinnell.edu
Established: 1846   Annual Undergrad Tuition & Fees: $56,680
Enrollment: 1,493   Coed
Affiliation or Control: Independent Non-Profit   IRS Status: 501(c)3
Highest Offering: Baccalaureate
Accreditation: HLC

01	President	Anne HARRIS
100	Chief of Staff/VP Planning	Myrna HERNÁNDEZ
05	VP Academic Affairs/Dean of College	Beronda MONTGOMERY
30	Vice Pres Development/Alumni Rels	Jaci A. THIEDE
115	Chief Investment Officer	Jainen THAYER
10	VP for Finance/Treasurer of College	Germaine GROSS
20	Associate Dean of College	Cynthia HANSEN
20	Associate Dean of College	Jin FENG
20	Associate Dean of College	Timothy ARNER
07	VP Enroll/Dean Admission & Fin Aid	Joseph P. BAGNOLI
30	Director of Development Operations	Adam LAUG
37	Dir Student Fin Aid & Asst VP Enrol	Brad LINDBERG
15	VP of Human Resources	Jana L. GRIMES
26	Vice President for Communications	Ellen DE GRAFFENREID
06	Registrar	Catherine ASHTON
08	Librarian	Mark CHRISTEL
29	Director of Alumni Relations	Jayn CHANEY
13	Chief Information Tech Officer	Dave ROBINSON
85	Director Intl Student Services	Karen K. EDWARDS
40	Manager Bookstore	Cassandra J. WHERRY
41	Athletic Director	Andrew HAMILTON
23	Director of Health Services	Kasey HERBERS
121	Dean Student Success/Acad Advising	Joyce STERN
38	Dean for Health & Counseling	Terry MASON
18	Asst Vice Pres Facilities Mgmt	Richard WHITNEY
19	Dir of Campus Safety	James SHROPSHIRE
42	Chaplain/Dean of Rel Life	Deanna SHORB
102	Director Corp/Found/Govt Rels	Susan FERRARI
32	VP Student Affairs	Sarah MOSCHENROSS
35	AVP Student Affs/Dean of Students	Ben NEWHOUSE
31	VP Community Engagement/Strat Plng	Monica CHAVEZ-SILVA
36	Dean & Dir Career Life & Service	Mark PELTZ
04	Executive Asst to President	Karen DILLON
101	Secretary of the College	Meg JONES BAIR
104	Director of Off-Campus Study	Alicia STANLEY
28	Interim VP DEI/Chief Diversity Ofcr	Reed MARC
39	Director Residence Life	Dennis PERKINS
44	Director Annual Giving	Mae PARKER
96	Procurement Manager	Amanda JONES

Hawkeye Community College (E)

Box 8015, Waterloo IA 50704-8015

County: Black Hawk   FICE Identification: 004595
Unit ID: 153445

Telephone: (319) 296-2320   Carnegie Class: Assoc/HVT-Mix Trad/Non
FAX Number: (319) 296-2874   Calendar System: Semester
URL: www.hawkeyecollege.edu
Established: 1966   Annual Undergrad Tuition & Fees (In-District): $5,790
Enrollment: 5,042   Coed
Affiliation or Control: State/Local   IRS Status: 501(c)3
Highest Offering: Associate Degree
Accreditation: HLC, COARC, DA, DH, EMT, MAC, MLTAD, OTA, PTAA

01	President	Dr. Todd HOLCOMB
05	Provost & VP Academic Affairs	Ms. Lynn LAGRONE
10	Vice Pres Administration & Finance	Mr. Dan GILLEN
32	Vice Pres Student Affairs	Ms. Nina GRANT
111	Exec Dir Institutional Advancement	Ms. Heather BREMER-MILLER
15	Exec Dir Human Resource Services	Ms. Susan C. HAUBER
51	VP Strat Partner & Workforce Educ	Mr. Aaron SAUERBREI
50	Dean Business and IT	Mr. Robin GALLOWAY
49	Dean Human Svcs/Lib & Applied Arts	Ms. Catharine FREEMAN
75	Dean Applied Technologies	Mr. David GRUNKLEE
81	Dean Science & Health Science	Dr. Troy MORAN
35	Dean of Students	Ms. Nancy HENDERSON
41	Director of Athletics	Mr. Ethan CRAWFORD
21	Director Business Services	Ms. Julie THOMAS
13	Chief Information Officer	Mr. Brian MCCORMICK
08	Director Library Services	Ms. Candace HAVELY
18	Director Plant & Facilities	Mr. Terence FLYNN
06	Registrar/Records & Registration	Ms. Amy FROST
19	Dir Public Safety/Emergency Mgr	Mr. John KRAMER
09	Director Institutional Research	Ms. Connie BUHR
26	Exec Dir Public Relations/Marketing	Ms. Mary Pat MOORE
28	Director of Inclusion & Diversity	Ms. Rhonda MCRINA
12	Director Adult Learning Center	Ms. Laura HIDLEBAUGH
103	Dir Workforce/Career Development	Mr. Christopher HANNAN
37	Director Student Financial Aid	Ms. Gisella BAKER
25	Director of Grants & Resource Dev	Ms. Constance GRIMM

84	Assoc Dir of Enrollment Tech	Ms. Stephanie CHERRY
04	Assistant to President	Ms. Annette STAPLES
07	Assoc Director of Admissions	Ms. Holly GRIMM

Indian Hills Community College (F)

525 Grandview Avenue, Ottumwa IA 52501-1398

County: Wapello   FICE Identification: 008403
Unit ID: 153472

Telephone: (641) 683-5111   Carnegie Class: Assoc/HVT-Mix Trad/Non
FAX Number: (641) 683-5184   Calendar System: Quarter
URL: www.indianhills.edu
Established: 1966   Annual Undergrad Tuition & Fees (In-District): $4,440
Enrollment: 3,279   Coed
Affiliation or Control: State/Local   IRS Status: 501(c)3
Highest Offering: Associate Degree
Accreditation: HLC, ACFEI, CAHIIM, DA, DH, EMT, MLTAD, OTA, PTAA, RAD

01	President	Dr. Matt THOMPSON
10	Chief Financial Officer	Mr. Michael LEE
05	VP Learning/Engagement	Dr. Jill BUDDE
32	VP Student Development/Operations	Dr. Brett MONAGHAN
103	Exec Dean Career/Workforce Educ	Dr. Jennifer WILSON
49	Assoc Dean Arts & Sciences	Dr. Don WALTENBERGER
06	Exec Dean Enrollment Srvs/Registrar	Ms. Joni KELLEY
12	Dean Centerville Campus/Lrng Svcs	Ms. Noel GORDEN
102	Exec Dir Foundation/Development	Ms. Blaire SIEMS
13	Chief Information Officer	Mr. Cory LAMB
15	Director Human Resources	Mr. Zeke FLICK
18	Director Physical Facilities	Mr. Rick FOSDYCK
41	Associate Athletic Director	Mr. Ricky WEBSTER
88	Asst Chief Flight/Aviation Programs	Mr. Brian HAMMACK
07	Director of Admissions	Ms. Ranae MOLKENTHIN
09	Director of Institutional Research	Dr. Stephanie HOLLIMAN-GINKENS
26	Dir Marketing & Comm Relations	Dr. Bianca MYERS
35	Success Center	Ms. Rhonda CONRAD

Iowa Central Community College (G)

One Triton Circle, Fort Dodge IA 50501

County: Webster   FICE Identification: 001865
Unit ID: 153524

Telephone: (515) 576-7201   Carnegie Class: Assoc/MT-VT-Mix Trad/Non
FAX Number: (515) 576-7207   Calendar System: Semester
URL: www.iowacentral.edu
Established: 1966   Annual Undergrad Tuition & Fees (In-District): $5,700
Enrollment: 4,704   Coed
Affiliation or Control: Local   IRS Status: 501(c)3
Highest Offering: Associate Degree
Accreditation: HLC, DH, EMT, MAC, MLTAD, RAD

01	President	Dr. Jesse ULRICH
04	Assistant to the President	Mrs. Ally P. WALTER
05	Vice President of Instruction	Dr. Stacy MENTZER
32	Vice Pres Enroll Mgmt/Student Devel	Mr. Thomas J. BENEKE
10	Vice President of Business Affairs	Mrs. Angela A. MARTIN
86	VP External Affairs/Govt Rels	Mr. James B. KERSTEN
50	Business & Ind Technology Dean	Mr. Neale J. ADAMS
76	Health Sciences Dean	Mr. John HANSEN
49	Liberal Arts & Sciences Dean	Mrs. Jennifer M. CONDON
106	Distance Learning Dean	Mr. Timothy J. MARTIN
09	Inst Effectiveness Coord	Mrs. Randi GRUVER
30	Development/Alumni Rels Exec Dir	Mrs. Mary LUDWIG
103	Econ Wrkfc Dev/Cont Educ Exec Dir	Mrs. Shelly R. BLUNK
06	Registrar	Ms. Courtney A. KOPP
37	Financial Aid Director	Mr. Krystal CRANDALL
21	Business Office Director	Mr. Luke J. GROVE
15	Human Resources Director	Ms. Stacy IHRIG
41	Athletic Director	Mr. Kevin TWAIT
39	Housing Coordinator	Mr. Joel DORNATH
38	Mental Health Counselor	Vacant
35	Student Life & Activities Director	Mr. David L. PEARSON
88	Student Resource Center Director	Ms. Amy MOFFITT
18	Physical Facilities Director	Mr. Shan L. BEECHER
12	Storm Lake Center Director	Mr. Chris CLEVELAND
12	Webster City Center Director	Ms. Colette BERTRAN
26	Public Information Director	Mr. Paul A. DECOURSEY
13	Institutional Technology Director	Mr. Jeff A. NELSEN
13	Institutional Technology Director	Mr. Troy D. CRAMPTON
14	Sr Computer System Analyst	Mr. Warren K. BAUER
40	Bookstore Manager	Mrs. Samantha E. MCCLAIN

Iowa Lakes Community College (H)

19 S Seventh Street, Estherville IA 51334-2234

County: Emmet   FICE Identification: 001864
Unit ID: 153533

Telephone: (712) 362-2604   Carnegie Class: Assoc/HVT-Mix Trad/Non
FAX Number: (712) 362-8363   Calendar System: Semester
URL: www.iowalakes.edu
Established: 1967   Annual Undergrad Tuition & Fees (In-District): $6,748
Enrollment: 2,288   Coed
Affiliation or Control: State/Local   IRS Status: 501(c)3
Highest Offering: Associate Degree
Accreditation: HLC, MAC, SURGT

01	President	Mr. Scott STOKES
11	Vice President of Administration	Mr. Robert A. LEIFELD
12	Exec Dean Emmetsburg Campus	Mr. Kyle NORRIS
26	Exec Director of Marketing	Ms. Beth ELMAN
18	Exec Dir of Facilities Management	Ms. Delaine S. HINEY

15 Exec Director Human Resources .... Ms. Kathy A. MULLER
31 Exec Dir Cmty & Business Relations ....Ms. Jolene R. ROGERS
10 Chief Financial Officer ....Mr. Jeff D. SOPER
12 Exec Dean Estherville Campus .... Mr. Scott STOKES
32 Executive Dean of Students .... Ms. Julie R. WILLIAMS
111 Exec Dir Foundation/Govt Affairs .... Mr. Daniel LUTAT

Iowa Lakes Community College Emmetsburg Campus (A)

3200 College Drive, Emmetsburg IA 50536
Telephone: (712) 852-3554 Identification: 770055
Accreditation: &HLC

Iowa Lakes Community College Spencer Campus (B)

Gateway N 1900 Grand Ave, Ste B-1, Spencer IA 51301
Telephone: (712) 262-7141 Identification: 770056
Accreditation: &HLC

*Iowa Valley Community College District (C)

3702 S Center Street, Marshalltown IA 50158-4760
County: Marshall FICE Identification: 033436
Telephone: (641) 752-4643 Carnegie Class: N/A
FAX Number: (641) 754-1336
URL: www.iavalley.edu

01 President .... Dr. Kristie FISHER
51 Vice Pres Business & Cmty Solutions ......Ms. Jacque GOODMAN
11 Vice President of Administration ....Ms. Gena GARBER
13 Chief Information Officer ....Mr. Mike MOSHER
12 Provost Ellsworth Community College ....Dr. Barbara KLEIN
12 Provost Marshalltown Community Col ....Dr. Robin SHAFFER LILIENTHAL
12 Dean of Iowa Valley Grinnell ....Ms. Mary Anne NICKLE
26 Director of Marketing ....Ms. Julie EASTRIDGE
09 Institutional Researcher .... Dr. Lisa BREJA
04 Asst to President/Board Secretary .... Ms. Barbara JENNINGS
86 Director of Government Affairs .... Ms. Cynthia SCHULTE

*Ellsworth Community College (D)

1100 College Avenue, Iowa Falls IA 50126-1199
County: Hardin FICE Identification: 001862
Unit ID: 153296
Telephone: (641) 648-4611 Carnegie Class: Assoc/MT-VT-High Trad
FAX Number: (641) 648-3128 Calendar System: Semester
URL: https://www.iavalley.edu/
Established: 1890 Annual Undergrad Tuition & Fees (In-District): $4,968
Enrollment: 731 Coed
Affiliation or Control: State/Local IRS Status: 501(c)3
Highest Offering: Associate Degree
Accreditation: &HLC, MAC

02 Provost ....Dr. Martin REIMER
05 Dean of Academic Affairs .... Dr. Amanda ESTEY
32 Dean of Student Affairs ....Dr. Barb KLEIN
08 Library Service Manager ....Ms. Sandra GREUFE
32 Director of Athletics/Student Life .... Mr. Nate FORSYTH
37 Director Financial Aid ....Ms. Tara MILLER
44 Dir Annual Plan Giving/Dir Alum Rel ....Ms. Gwen GROEN
07 Director of Admissions .... Ms. Adriane SIETSEMA

† Regional accreditation is carried under the parent institution Iowa Valley Community College District in Marshalltown, IA.

*Marshalltown Community College (E)

3700 S Center Street, Marshalltown IA 50158
County: Marshall FICE Identification: 001875
Unit ID: 153922
Telephone: (641) 752-4643 Carnegie Class: Assoc/MT-VT-High Non
FAX Number: (641) 752-8149 Calendar System: Semester
URL: www.mcc.iavalley.edu
Established: 1927 Annual Undergrad Tuition & Fees (In-District): $4,968
Enrollment: 1,836 Coed
Affiliation or Control: State/Local IRS Status: 501(c)3
Highest Offering: Associate Degree
Accreditation: &HLC, DA

02 Chancellor .... Dr. Kristie FISHER
05 Provost ....Dr. Robin SHAFFER LILIENTHAL
10 Chief Financial Officer/Director HR .... Ms. Gena GARBER
20 Dean of Academic Affairs ....Mr. Vincent BOYD
84 Dean Enrollment/Student Life ....Ms. Angie REDMOND
32 Dean of Students/Learning Svcs/TRIO ....Mr. Nate CHUA
06 Dir of Student Success/Registrar .... Ms. Ashtyn BEEK
76 Assoc Dean of Health Occupations ....Ms. Beth JOHANNS
102 Executive Director MCC Foundation ....Ms. Carol GEIL
37 Financial Aid Administrator ....Ms. Rachael KOEHLER
26 Director of Marketing ....Ms. Julie EASTRIDGE
41 Director of Athletics ....Mr. John KRIEBS
39 Dir Student Engagement/Res Life .... Mr. Chris BREES
121 Sr Academic Advising Specialist ....Mr. Dan KEY
08 Library Services Manager ....Ms. Emily HORNER
40 MCC Bookstore Manager ....Ms. Paulla HARTMAN
07 Admissions Office Associate ....Ms. Amy GOOD

† Regional accreditation is carried under the parent institution Iowa Valley Community College District in Marshalltown, IA.

Iowa Wesleyan University (F)

601 N Main, Mount Pleasant IA 52641-1398
County: Henry FICE Identification: 001871
Unit ID: 153621
Telephone: (319) 385-8021 Carnegie Class: Bac-Diverse
FAX Number: (319) 385-6296 Calendar System: Semester
URL: www.iw.edu
Established: 1842 Annual Undergrad Tuition & Fees: $25,280
Enrollment: 704 Coed
Affiliation or Control: United Methodist IRS Status: 501(c)3
Highest Offering: Master's
Accreditation: HLC, NUR

01 President .... Ms. Chris PLUNKETT
05 Provost .... Dr. DeWayne FRAZIER
84 VP for Enrollment & Marketing .... Ms. Meg RICHTMAN
111 VP for Advancement & Athletics ....Mr. Derek ZANDER
32 Dean of Students .... Mr. Matthew KLUNDT
13 Director of IT .... Mr. Jim COLLINS
06 Registrar ....Ms. Megan HILLS
37 Senior Financial Aid Counselor ....Ms. LaShawnda ROBERTS
10 Controller & Director of Finance ....Ms. Deb LILLIE
15 Director of Human Resources .... Ms. Kathy MOOTHART
44 Director of Advancement Operations .... Ms. Amy FRANTZ
41 Associate Athletics Director .... Ms. Courtney CARL
18 Director of Physical Plant ....Mr. Sean GRAY
36 Director of Career Development ....Ms. Nikki GERLING
40 Bookstore Director .... Ms. Amy MABEUS
04 Asst to the President .... Ms. Mary NOTESTEIN
105 Webmaster .... Ms. Cindee VANDIJK
30 Development Director ....Mr. Jim PEDRICK
30 Development Director ....Mr. Adam MCLAUGHLIN
58 Director of Graduate Studies .... Ms. Valerie HENESSEE
39 Dir Resident Life/Student Housing ....Vacant
28 Director of Title IX & Diversity .... Ms. Tina YOUNG
29 Director for Alumni Engagement .... Ms. Diane DAVIS

Iowa Western Community College (G)

2700 College Road, Council Bluffs IA 51503-0567
County: Pottawattamie FICE Identification: 004598
Unit ID: 153630
Telephone: (712) 325-3200 Carnegie Class: Assoc/MT-VT-High Non
FAX Number: (712) 325-3424 Calendar System: Semester
URL: www.iwcc.edu
Established: 1966 Annual Undergrad Tuition & Fees (In-District): $6,120
Enrollment: 5,791 Coed
Affiliation or Control: State/Local IRS Status: 501(c)3
Highest Offering: Associate Degree
Accreditation: HLC, DA, DH, EMT, MAC, SURGT

01 President ....Dr. Daniel KINNEY
04 Assistant to the President ....Mrs. Erin MCKEE
05 Vice President for Academic Affairs .... Dr. Jennifer KRUGER
10 Vice President of Finance ....Mr. Edwin HOLTZ
32 Vice President for Student Services .... Ms. Kim HENRY
26 Vice Pres of Marketing/Public Rels ....Mr. Donald KOHLER
111 Vice Pres Institutional Advancement .... Mrs. Molly NOON
103 VP Economic/Workforce Devel ....Vacant
09 Dean Institutional Research/Accred ....Mrs. Tina KNAUSS
84 Dean Enrollment Services ....Mr. Thomas GILMORE
121 Dean of Academic Support ....Mrs. Samantha LARSON
35 Dean Student Life/Student Success .... Ms. Reanna HEIM
106 Dean Distance Educ/Pathway Dev .... Mr. Matthew MANCUSO
81 Dean Science/Tech/Engineering/Math ....Mrs. Barb GODDEN
79 Dean of Comm/Education/Fine Arts ....Mrs. Jenny KRUGER
76 Dean of Health & Sports Sciences ....Mrs. Barb GODDEN
51 Director of Continuing Education ....Vacant
50 Dean Ag/Bus/Computer Info/Soc Sci ....Mrs. Ambe DOWDELL-WHITE
06 Registrar .... Mrs. Jill CLARK
07 Director of Admissions ....Mrs. Nyssa GREER
15 Director of Human Resources ....Mrs. Robyn PORTER
29 Director of Alumni Relations ....Mrs. Stacy SHOCKEY
37 Director of Student Financial Aid ....Ms. Lisa MORRISON
21 Director Accounting ....Ms. Randi BISSEN
13 Director Information Technology ....Mrs. Victoria HOSKOVEC
41 Athletic Director ....Mr. Shane LARSON
39 Director of Residence Life .... Mr. Griffen FARRAR
18 Director Physical Plant .... Mr. Brian SUTTER
96 Director of Purchasing ....Mrs. Diane OSBAHR
40 College Store Manager .... Mrs. Maggie SOBCZYK-BARRON
88 Food Service Manager ....Mr. Stephan BRYANT

Kirkwood Community College (H)

6301 Kirkwood Blvd. SW, Cedar Rapids IA 52404
County: Linn FICE Identification: 004076
Unit ID: 153737
Telephone: (319) 398-5411 Carnegie Class: Assoc/HVT-Mix Trad/Non
FAX Number: (319) 398-1037 Calendar System: Semester
URL: www.kirkwood.edu
Established: 1966 Annual Undergrad Tuition & Fees (In-District): $5,140
Enrollment: 12,277 Coed
Affiliation or Control: Local IRS Status: 501(c)3
Highest Offering: Associate Degree
Accreditation: HLC, ACFEI, CNEA, COARC, DA, DH, DT, EMT, MAC, MLTAD, MUS, NDT, OTA, PTAA, SURGT

01 President .... Dr. Lori SUNDBERG
51 VP Cont Education/Training Svcs ....Ms. Jasmine ALMOAYYED
10 Vice President/Chief Fin/Oper Ofcr .... Mr. Jim CHOATE
111 Vice President Advancement ....Ms. Jody PELLERIN
05 Vice President Academic Affairs ....Dr. Jennifer BRADLEY
32 Vice President Student Services ....Mr. Jon BUSE
20 Assoc Vice President Acad Affairs ....Ms. Colette ATKINS
12 Dean Iowa City Campus ....Vacant
35 Executive Dean of Students ....Ms. Melissa PAYNE
15 Vice President Human Resources ....Mr. Wes FOWLER
13 Vice President Technology Services .... Mr. Jon NEFF
106 Dean Distance Learning ....Mr. Dave HUNT
07 Director Admissions .... Mr. Nick KETTMANN
18 VP Facilities & Public Safety ....Mr. Troy MCQUILLEN
25 Director Grants & Fed Programs ....Ms. Doris NYAGA
41 Athletic Director ....Mr. Doug WAGEMESTER
06 Registrar ....Ms. Dena RAUCH
110 Director of Advancement .... Ms. Jody DONALDSON
37 Financial Aid Director ....Mr. Matt FALDUTO
47 Dean Agriculture Science ....Mr. Scott ERMER
72 Dean Industrial Technology ....Dr. Emily LOGAN
79 Assoc Vice Pres Liberal Arts ....Dr. Brooke STRAHN-KOLLER
76 Dean Allied Health ....Ms. Nicky CLINE
83 Interim Dean Social Sciences ....Ms. Amanda HUMPHREY
81 Dean Math/Science .... Ms. Wendy JAMISON
66 Dean Nursing ....Dr. Kathryn DOLTER
76 Dean Health Occupations .... Ms. Katie LYMAN
50 Dean Business & Information Tech ....Ms. Tamara ALT
08 Dean Learning Services/Dir Library ....Mr. Arron WINGS
04 Asst to President .... Ms. Peg SPRENGELER
104 Dean Global Learning ....Ms. Dawn WOOD
19 Assoc Vice President Public Safety ... Mr. Andrew MACPHERSON
26 Exec Dir Communications/Marketing ....Mr. Kevin HANSEN
112 Director Planned & Endowed Giving ....Vacant
14 Exec Dir IT Infrastructure ....Mr. Darren ZABLOUDIL
21 Exec Director Finance ....Vacant
88 Dean Secondary Programs ....Ms. Carla ANDORF
09 Director Institutional Research .... Mr. Cort IVERSON
86 Government Relations .... Mr. Justin HOEHN
108 VP of Institutional Effectiveness .... Dr. Connie THURMAN
44 Director Annual Giving ....Mr. Eric WEILER

Loras College (I)

1450 Alta Vista, Dubuque IA 52004-0178
County: Dubuque FICE Identification: 001873
Unit ID: 153825
Telephone: (563) 588-7100 Carnegie Class: Bac-Diverse
FAX Number: (563) 588-7964 Calendar System: Semester
URL: www.loras.edu
Established: 1839 Annual Undergrad Tuition & Fees: $35,218
Enrollment: 1,404 Coed
Affiliation or Control: Roman Catholic IRS Status: 501(c)3
Highest Offering: Master's
Accreditation: HLC, CAATE, SW

01 President .... Mr. James E. COLLINS
05 Provost .... Dr. Donna N. HEALD
10 VP/COO ....Ms. Margaret A. TUNGSETH
03 Senior Vice President ....Dr. Mary Ellen CARROLL
111 VP Institutional Advancement ....Mr. Scott W. MCCLURE
32 VP Student Development .... Dr. Arthur W. SUNLEAF
04 Executive Assistant to President ....Ms. Heather L. JUNGBLUT
42 Chaplain ....Rev. Dustin L. VU
91 Sr Dir Technology Services ....Mr. Thomas D. KRUSE
26 VP of Marketing ....Ms. Demeri C. MULLIKIN
15 Dir Human Resources ....Mr. Troy M. WRIGHT
09 Director of Institutional Research ....Mr. Christopher R. FEIT
38 Director Center for Counseling ....Ms. Tricia S. BORELLI
07 Director of Admissions-UG ....Ms. Maria GENTILE
08 Library Director ....Ms. Kristen L. SMITH
35 Assistant Dean of Students ....Ms. Molly A. BURROWS-SCHUMACHER
41 Dir Intercollegiate Athletics ....Ms. Denise A. UDELHOFEN
18 Asst VP Physical Resources ....Mr. John R. MCDERMOTT
40 Director of Bookstore ....Ms. Angel M. BELL
23 Director of Health Center ....Ms. Tammy S. MARTI
42 Campus Ministry/P&J Coordinator .... Ms. Anastacia M. MCDERMOTT
06 Registrar ....Mr. Christopher R. FEIT
19 Dir Res Life & Campus Safety ....Ms. Molly A. BURROWS-SCHUMACHER
35 Assoc Dean of Students .... Ms. Kimberly A. WALSH
37 Director of Financial Planning ....Ms. Lesley A. BUSE
96 Controller for Business Office ....Ms. Rennie A. ROOT
36 Academic Internship Coordinator ....Ms. Jennifer L. WEBER
122 Stdnt Life Pgm Coord-Greek Life ....Ms. Bella BARRIOS
28 Director of Diversity ....Mr. Sergio PEREZ

Luther College (J)

700 College Drive, Decorah IA 52101-1045
County: Winneshiek FICE Identification: 001874
Unit ID: 153834
Telephone: (563) 387-2000 Carnegie Class: Bac-A&S
FAX Number: (563) 387-2158 Calendar System: Other
URL: www.luther.edu
Established: 1861 Annual Undergrad Tuition & Fees: $45,610
Enrollment: 1,802 Coed
Affiliation or Control: Evangelical Lutheran Church In America
IRS Status: 501(c)3
Highest Offering: Baccalaureate
Accreditation: HLC, MUS, NURSE, SW

01 President Dr. Jenifer K. WARD
04 Exec Assistant to the President Ms. Tara QUASS
00 Chair of the Board Mr. J. Robert PAULSON
41 Director Intercollegiate Athletics Ms. Renae HARTL
05 Provost Dr. Lynda SZYMANSKI
20 Associate Dean/Dir Faculty Devel Dr. Sean BURKE
88 Assistant to the Provost Ms. Arleen ORVIS
08 Library Director Mr. Ryan GJERDE
30 Vice President for Development Ms. Mary DUVALL
110 Senior Director of Development Mr. Nathan ERSIG
29 Exec Director of Alumni Relations Ms. Sherry B. ALCOCK
36 Director of the Career Center Ms. Sarah CROSE
26 VP for Mission and Communication Dr. Brad CHAMBERLAIN
27 Exec Dir Strategic Marketing/Comm Ms. Laura BARLAMENT
10 Vice President for Finance & Admin Mr. Andrew BAILEY
21 Controller Ms. Peggy LENSING
40 Director Book Shop/Union Services Ms. Deanna CASTERTON
15 Director Human Resources Mr. Matthew BILLS
09 Director Institutional Research Vacant
28 Chief Equity and Inclusion Officer Dr. Robert CLAY
28 Director of Diversity Center Ms. Wintlett TAYLOR-BROWNE
19 Director Security/Safety Mr. Robert HARRI
18 Director of Facilities Services Mr. Jay L. UTHOFF
13 Exec Dir Info Technology Svcs Ms. Diane GOSSMAN
119 Info Security Analyst/Sys Admin Mr. Matthew HAMMEN
124 Dean of Student Engagement Dr. Ashley BENSON
35 Assistant Dean Student Life Mr. Jake DYER
84 VP for Enrollment Management Ms. Karen HUNT
07 Director of Admissions Vacant
06 Registrar Dr. Richard BERNATZ
37 Director Financial Aid Operations Mr. Aaron STEFFENS
39 Asst Dean/Dir Residence Life Ms. Kristine FRANZEN
38 Director Counseling Service Ms. Meg HAMMES
42 Dir of College Ministries/Pastor Rev. Melissa BILLS
85 Exec Dir Ctr Global Learning Dr. Victoria CHRISTMAN

Maharishi International University (A)

1000 N 4th Street, Fairfield IA 52557-0001
County: Jefferson | FICE Identification: 011113
Unit ID: 153861
Telephone: (641) 472-7000 | Carnegie Class: Masters/L
FAX Number: (641) 472-1179 | Calendar System: Semester
URL: www.miu.edu
Established: 1971 | Annual Undergrad Tuition & Fees: $16,530
Enrollment: 2,015 | Coed
Affiliation or Control: Independent Non-Profit | IRS Status: 501(c)3
Highest Offering: Doctorate
Accreditation: HLC, IACBE

01 President Dr. John HAGELIN
05 VP Academic Affairs Dr. Craig PEARSON
11 Vice President of Operations Mr. Thomas BROOKS
30 VP Development & Alumni Relations Mr. Brad MYLETT
84 VP Enrollment & Student Affairs Mr. Rod EASON
20 Dean of Faculty Dr. Vicki ALEXANDER-HERRIOTT
10 Treasurer Mr. Michael SPIVAK
88 International Vice President Dr. Michael DILLBECK
88 International Vice President Dr. Susan DILLBECK
11 Chief Administrative Officer Mr. David TODT
43 Legal Counsel/Dean Global Develop Mr. Bill GOLDSTEIN
07 Dean of Admissions Mr. Ron BARNETT
32 Associate Dean of Students Vacant
06 Registrar Mr. Selin OZBUDAK
26 Media Relations Mr. Jim KARPEN
106 Dir Distance Educ/Intl Programs Mr. Dennis HEATON
27 Director of Press Mr. Harry BRIGHT
39 Director of Housing Mr. Mahmood ALI
37 Director of Student Financial Aid Mr. Dan WASIELEWSKI
13 Manager of Information Services Mr. Gilberto RODRIGUEZ
20 Dean Academic Programs Dr. Chris JONES
15 Director Human Resources Ms. Carol PASSOS
29 Director Alumni Mr. Paul STOKSTAD
36 Career Development Services Ms. Ayesha SENGUPTA
18 Chief Facilities/Physical Plant Mr. Nathan GERDES
49 Dean College of Arts & Sciences Dr. Chris JONES
77 Dean College of Computer Sci & Math Mr. Gregory GUTHRIE
58 Dean of Graduate School Dr. Frederick TRAVIS
04 Administrative Asst to President Ms. Jane AIKENS
08 Director of Library Ms. Rouzanna VARDANYAN
41 Athletic Director Mr. Dustin MATTHEWS
101 Secretary of the Board of Trustees Ms. Susan TRACY
19 Director of Security and Safety Ms. Beata NACSA
106 Dir Online Education/E-learning Mr. Eric LIU
38 Assoc Dir Student Support Services Ms. Leslie DOYLE
104 Director Study Abroad Dr. Cathy GORINI
105 Director Web Services Mr. Michael MATZKIN
35 Director Student Activities Mr. Chris GRACE

Mercy College of Health Sciences (B)

928 Sixth Avenue, Des Moines IA 50309-1239
County: Polk | FICE Identification: 006273
Unit ID: 153977
Telephone: (515) 643-3180 | Carnegie Class: Spec-4-yr-Other Health
FAX Number: (515) 643-6698 | Calendar System: Semester
URL: www.mchs.edu
Established: 1995 | Annual Undergrad Tuition & Fees: $18,332
Enrollment: 869 | Coed
Affiliation or Control: Roman Catholic | IRS Status: 501(c)3
Highest Offering: Master's
Accreditation: HLC, ADNUR, DMS, EMT, MLS, NURSE, PTAA, RAD, SURGT

01 President Dr. Douglas J. FIORE
05 Provost & VP Academic Affairs Dr. Nancy K. KERTZ
10 VP of Business & Regulatory Affairs Dr. Thomas LEAHY
106 Exec VP & Chancellor Mercy Col Plus Mr. Matthew ROMKEY
15 VP of Employee Engagement & HR Ms. Anne DENNIS
20 Academic Dean Dr. Ryan "Bud" MARR
08 Dir of Library and Media Services Ms. Jennie E. VER STEEG
06 Registrar Ms. Carolyn BUCKLIN
37 Senior Director Financial Aid Mr. Joe BROOKOVER
32 Dean of Student Affairs Ms. Lyneene RICHARDSON
13 Director of Information Technology Mr. David VON ARB
84 Director Enrollment Management Mr. Andrew GRESS
101 Board Liaison/Communications Spec Ms. Mackenzie KELLOGG

Morningside University (C)

1501 Morningside Avenue, Sioux City IA 51106-1751
County: Woodbury | FICE Identification: 001879
Unit ID: 154004
Telephone: (712) 274-5000 | Carnegie Class: Masters/L
FAX Number: (712) 274-5101 | Calendar System: Semester
URL: www.morningside.edu
Established: 1894 | Annual Undergrad Tuition & Fees: $33,970
Enrollment: 2,411 | Coed
Affiliation or Control: United Methodist | IRS Status: 501(c)3
Highest Offering: Doctorate
Accreditation: HLC, MUS, NURSE

01 President Dr. Albert MOSLEY
05 Vice President for Academic Affairs Dr. Christopher L. SPICER
10 Vice President Business & Finance Mr. Ronald A. JORGENSEN
32 Vice Pres Student Life & Enrollment Mrs. Terri A. CURRY
111 Vice Pres Institutional Advancement Vacant
26 Vice Pres University Engagement Mrs. Erin M. EDLUND
35 AVP Student Life/Dean of Students Dr. Karmen TEN NAPEL
20 Associate VP for Acad Affairs Dr. Brian MCFARLAND
06 Registrar Mrs. Jen DOLPHIN
37 Dir Financial Plng/AVP Inst Rsrch Ms. Karen WIESE
13 Exec Dir of Information Services Mr. Mike HUSMANN
29 Alumni Engagement Director Mr. Alex WATTERS
07 Director of Admissions Mrs. Steph PETERS
18 Director of Physical Plant Mr. Jason REYNOLDSON
19 Director of Security Mr. Brett LYON
23 Director of Student Health Ms. Judi NESWICK
36 AVP Career/Employee Engagement Ms. Stacie HAYS
40 Director of Bookstore Ms. Jodi STROHBEEN
41 Athletic Director Mr. Jim SYKES
42 Campus Ministry Rev. Andy NELSON
112 Director of Gift Planning Mr. Jonathan BLUM
15 Director Human Resources Ms. Cindy WELP
21 Controller Mr. Paul TREFT
04 Administrative Asst to President Mrs. Lisa KROHN
105 Web Dev/Digital Strategy Director Mr. Timothy COHOON
39 Director Residence Life Ms. Sheri HINEMAN
08 Library Director Mr. Adam FULLERTON
38 Personal Counselor Ms. Bobbi MEISTER
101 Secretary of the Institution/Board Mrs. Lisa KROHN
91 Director Administrative Computing Ms. Carla GREGG
30 Director of Development Mr. Mike FREEMAN
44 Director Annual Giving Ms. J.J MARLOW
53 Dean of Education Dr. Kelly CHANEY
96 Director of Purchasing Mr. Ronald A. JORGENSEN
22 Dir Affirmative Action/Equal Opp Ms. Cindy WELP
28 Director of Diversity Mr. Andre MCWELL
50 Dean of Business Dr. Darrel SANDALL

Mount Mercy University (D)

1330 Elmhurst Drive NE, Cedar Rapids IA 52402-4797
County: Linn | FICE Identification: 001880
Unit ID: 154013
Telephone: (319) 363-8213 | Carnegie Class: Masters/M
FAX Number: (319) 363-5270 | Calendar System: 4/1/4
URL: www.mtmercy.edu
Established: 1928 | Annual Undergrad Tuition & Fees: $35,506
Enrollment: 1,705 | Coed
Affiliation or Control: Roman Catholic | IRS Status: 501(c)3
Highest Offering: Doctorate
Accreditation: HLC, MFCD, NURSE, SW

01 President Mr. Todd OLSON
05 Provost/VP Academic Affairs Dr. Timothy LAURENT
10 VP for Business & Finance Ms. Anne GILLESPIE
84 VP Enrollment & Marketing Mr. Todd COLEMAN
30 VP of Development/Alumni Relations Ms. Brenda HAEFNER
42 VP of Mission and Ministry Sr. Linda BECHEN
32 Vice Pres for Student Success Dr. Nate KLEIN
20 Assoc Prov/Exec Dir Acad Innovation Dr. Tom CASTLE
06 Registrar Mr. Chance MCWORTHY
08 Director of Library Services Ms. Kristy RAINE
36 Director of Career Services Ms. Kalindi GARVIN
29 Asst VP for Alumni Development Ms. Lonna DREWELOW
37 Director of Financial Aid Ms. Bethany DAVENPORT
26 Director of Marketing Ms. Jamie JONES
41 Director of Athletics Mr. Paul GAVIN
38 Director of Counseling Ms. Karol WHITE
19 Director of Public Safety Mr. Joe CERRUTO
24 Academic Technology Librarian Mr. Greg ENNIS
15 Asst VP of Human Res/Operations Mr. Thomas DOERMANN
18 Director of Facilities Mr. Dennis GEHRING
92 Director of Honors Program Dr. Richard BARRETT
04 Assistant to the President Ms. Kim BLANKENHEIM
09 Exec Dir of Institutional Research Ms. Lori HEYING

North Iowa Area Community College (E)

500 College Drive, Mason City IA 50401-7299
County: Cerro Gordo | FICE Identification: 001877
Unit ID: 154059
Telephone: (641) 423-1264 | Carnegie Class: Assoc/MT-VT-Mix Trad/Non
FAX Number: (641) 423-1711 | Calendar System: Semester
URL: www.niacc.edu
Established: 1917 | Annual Undergrad Tuition & Fees (In-District): $5,791
Enrollment: 2,681 | Coed
Affiliation or Control: State/Local | IRS Status: 501(c)3
Highest Offering: Associate Degree
Accreditation: HLC, ADNUR, MAC, PTAA

01 President Dr. Steven D. SCHULZ
05 Vice President Academic Affairs Dr. Charlene K. WIDENER
10 Vice Pres Administrative Services Ms. Noele M. BEAVER
32 Vice President of Student Services Dr. Rachel L. MCGUIRE
111 Director Institutional Advancement Mrs. Molly H. KNOLL
88 Director of JPEC Mrs. Candi KARSJENS
15 VP Organizational Development/HR Dr. Shelly M. SCHMIT
06 Registrar Mrs. Michelle L. PETZNICK
83 Chair Hum/Human & Public Svcs/Bus Mr. Joe D. DAVIS
76 Chair Health Sciences & STEM Ms. Heather M. RISSLER
50 Chair Agriculture/Skilled Trades Ms. Laura L. WOOD
51 Dean of Continuing Education Mrs. Patti L. HANSON
37 Director of Financial Aid Mrs. Abbie STEINBERG
20 Director Learning Services Ms. Dalila A. SAJADIAN
13 Chief Information Officer Vacant
103 WIOA Title I Director Region 2 Vacant
121 Director of TRIO Mrs. Bridget SHULTZ
41 Director of Athletics Mr. Camron M. OLSON
18 Director of Facilities Management Mr. Tony A. PAPPAS
21 Comptroller Ms. Mindy R. EASTMAN
39 Director Student Housing Mr. Jeremy G. WINTERS
08 Librarian/Media Specialist Ms. Rhonda K. NESHEIM-KAUFFMAN
26 Dir Marketing/Community Relations Mrs. Valerie F. ZAHORSKI-SCHMIDT
88 Director Innovation/Acceleration Mr. Tom MOORE
88 Director SBDC Mr. Brook S. BOEHMLER
88 Director of School Partnerships Mr. Brian M. WOGEN
51 Dir of Operations/Continuing Educ Mrs. Constance J. GLANDON
88 Director of Sales & Programming Ms. Amy MARKHAM
09 Director of Institutional Research Dr. Shelly M. SCHMIT
102 Grant Writer/Inst Fund Devel Spec Ms. Jana T. GRZENDA
90 Educational Software Administrator Ms. Erica S. MCBRIDE
29 Director Alumni Relations Ms. Andrea J. MUJICA
07 Director of Admissions Dr. Rachel L. MCGUIRE
28 Director of Diversity Dr. Shelly M. SCHMIT
04 Administrative Asst to President Ms. Taylor Ann HENDRICKS
22 Director Affirmative Action/EEO Dr. Shelly M. SCHMIT

Northeast Iowa Community College (F)

Box 400, Calmar IA 52132-0400
County: Winneshiek | FICE Identification: 004587
Unit ID: 154110
Telephone: (844) 642-2338 | Carnegie Class: Assoc/HVT-High Non
FAX Number: (563) 562-3983 | Calendar System: Semester
URL: www.nicc.edu
Established: 1966 | Annual Undergrad Tuition & Fees (In-District): $6,000
Enrollment: 4,162 | Coed
Affiliation or Control: Local | IRS Status: 501(c)3
Highest Offering: Associate Degree
Accreditation: HLC, CAHIIM, CNEA, COARC, DA

01 President Dr. Liang C. WEE
10 Vice Pres Finance & Administration Mr. David W. DAHMS
05 VP Learning/Student Success Dr. Kathy J. NACOS-BURDS
46 Vice Pres Bus & Community Solutions Dr. Wendy A. MIHM-HEROLD
11 Assoc Vice President for Operations Ms. Rhonda K. SEIBERT
108 VP Inst Effectiveness/Advancement Ms. Wendy S. KNIGHT
15 Exec Director of Human Resources Ms. Connie KUENNEN
106 Dean of Instructional Innovation Mr. Kyle T. COLLINS
13 Exec Dir Computer Information Sys Mr. Craig R. MEIRICK
09 Director of Institutional Research Ms. Lor M. MILLER
103 Director Economic Development Mr. Gregory A. WILLGING
37 Director of Financial Aid Mr. Randy D. MASHEK
06 Director of Registration/Retention Ms. Sheila R. BECKER
36 Career Services Manager Mr. Chris E. ENTRINGER
84 Exec Director of Enrollment Mgmt Ms. Kristi L. STRIEF
26 Dir Marketing/News/Publications Ms. Shea A. HERBST

Northeast Iowa Community College Peosta Campus (G)

8342 NICC Drive, Peosta IA 52068
Telephone: (844) 642-2338 | Identification: 770063
Accreditation: &HLC, EMT, MAC, RAD

Northwest Iowa Community College (H)

603 W Park Street, Sheldon IA 51201-1046
County: Sioux | FICE Identification: 004600
Unit ID: 154129
Telephone: (712) 324-5061 | Carnegie Class: Assoc/HVT-High Non
FAX Number: (712) 324-4136 | Calendar System: Semester

URL: www.nwicc.edu
Established: 1966 Annual Undergrad Tuition & Fees (In-District): $6,390
Enrollment: 1,666 Coed
Affiliation or Control: State/Local IRS Status: 501(c)3
Highest Offering: Associate Degree
Accreditation: HLC, CAHIIM, RAD

01 President .... Dr. John HARTOG, III
05 Exec Dir Student & Academic Svcs .... Ms. Erin LATONA
111 Director College Advancement .... Ms. Kristi LANDIS
10 Exec Dir Operations & Finance .... Mr. Brian NASH
72 Dean Applied Technology .... Mr. Steve WALDSTEIN
49 Dean Arts & Sci/Business/Health .... Ms. Leah MURPHY
21 Director of Business Services .... Ms. Jessica WILLIAMS
37 Director Financial Aid .... Ms. Karna HOFMEYER
84 Director Enrollment Management .... Ms. Lisa L. STORY
08 Coordinator of Library Services .... Ms. Renee FRANKLIN
13 Director of Technology & Info Svcs .... Mr. Mike OLDENKAMP
88 Coordinator of TRIO .... Ms. Tracy GORTER
06 Registrar/Assoc Dean of Students .... Ms. Beth SIBENALLER-WOODALL
15 Director of Human Resources .... Ms. Renee CARLSON
26 Director Community Relations .... Ms. Kristin E. KOLLBAUM
18 Director Physical Facilities .... Mr. Randy BAARTMAN

Northwestern College (A)

101 Seventh Street, SW, Orange City IA 51041-1996
County: Sioux FICE Identification: 001883
Unit ID: 154101
Telephone: (712) 707-7000 Carnegie Class: Masters/M
FAX Number: (712) 707-7247 Calendar System: Semester
URL: www.nwciowa.edu
Established: 1882 Annual Undergrad Tuition & Fees: $32,920
Enrollment: 1,496 Coed
Affiliation or Control: Reformed Church In America IRS Status: 501(c)3
Highest Offering: Master's
Accreditation: HLC, #ARCPA, IACBE, NURSE, SW

01 President .... Mr. Gregory E. CHRISTY
32 Dean of Student Life .... Dr. Julie VERMEER ELLIOTT
05 Vice President for Academic Affairs .... Dr. D. Nathan PHINNEY
10 Vice President for Finance & Opers .... Mr. Kent WIERSEMA
111 Vice President Advancement .... Mr. Jay WIELENGA
84 Vice President Enrollment & Mktg .... Ms. Tamara FYNAARDT
41 Vice President for Athletics .... Dr. Micah PARKER
08 Director of the Library .... Ms. Greta GROND
06 Registrar .... Mr. Austin NYHOF
37 Director of Financial Aid .... Mr. Eric ANDERSON
13 Director of Computing Services .... Mr. Harlan R. JORGENSEN
26 Director of Public Relations .... Mr. Duane L. BEESON
36 Director of Career and Calling .... Dr. Elizabeth PITTS
38 Dir Student Counseling Services .... Dr. Sally EDMAN
18 Director of Maintenance/Operations .... Mr. Ryan MCEWEN
29 Director Alumni Relations .... Mr. Ross FERNSTRUM
15 Director of Human Resources .... Mrs. Mindy STITCHKA
09 Director of Institutional Research .... Dr. Jennifer SCHON
04 Administrative Asst to President .... Ms. Jill HAARSMA
19 Director Security/Safety .... Mr. Andrew VAN OMMEREN
07 Dean of Admissions .... Ms. Lori ZOMERMAAND
106 Dean of Graduate & Adult Learning .... Mr. Gary RICHARDSON
39 Dean of Residence Life .... Mr. Marlon HAVERDINK

Orion Technical College (B)

3940 Elmore Ave, Davenport IA 52807
County: Scott FICE Identification: 012064
Unit ID: 153427
Telephone: (563) 674-6633 Carnegie Class: Spec-4-yr-Other Tech
FAX Number: (563) 519-6496 Calendar System: Semester
URL: https://orion.edu/
Established: 1969 Annual Undergrad Tuition & Fees: $14,275
Enrollment: 120 Coed
Affiliation or Control: Proprietary IRS Status: Proprietary
Highest Offering: Baccalaureate
Accreditation: ACCSC, MAC

01 President/CEO .... Troy HARRIS
05 Dean of Academic Affairs .... Dr. Cynthia KRUPA
07 Campus Center Director .... Leslie GONZALEZ
10 Director of Financial & Admin .... Patricia MCCRACKEN
32 Dir Students/Career Services .... Karin EDWARDS
37 Director of Student Financial Aid .... Jay COTTO, JR.

Palmer College of Chiropractic (C)

1000 Brady Street, Davenport IA 52803-5287
County: Scott FICE Identification: 012300
Unit ID: 154174
Telephone: (563) 884-5000 Carnegie Class: Spec-4-yr-Other Health
FAX Number: (563) 884-5409 Calendar System: Trimester
URL: www.palmer.edu
Established: 1897 Annual Undergrad Tuition & Fees: N/A
Enrollment: 2,178 Coed
Affiliation or Control: Independent Non-Profit IRS Status: 501(c)3
Highest Offering: First Professional Degree
Accreditation: HLC, CHIRO

01 Chancellor .... Dr. Dennis M. MARCHIORI
05 College Provost .... Dr. Daniel J. WEINERT
88 Vice Chanc Inst Effectiveness .... Dr. Robert E. PERCUOCO
32 Vice Chancellor Student Affairs .... Dr. Kevin A. CUNNINGHAM
07 Vice Chancellor for Admissions .... Mr. Michael C. NORRIS
10 Vice Chancellor for Finance .... Ms. Jennifer RANDAZZO
26 Vice Chancellor for Mktg & Comm .... Mr. James O'CONNOR
111 VC for Institutional Advancement .... Ms. Barbara MELBOURNE
17 Exec Dean of Clinic Affairs .... Dr. Ron BOESCH
46 Dean of Research .... Dr. Cynthia LONG
20 Dean of Academic Affairs .... Dr. Michael TUNNING
20 Assoc Dean of Academic Affairs .... Dr. Ward JONES
88 Assoc Dean of Clinic Research .... Dr. Robert VINING
43 Exec Dir Legal Affairs .... Ms. Amber WELLS
101 Exec Director Board Affairs .... Ms. Lynne LINDSTROM
110 Exec Dir Advancement .... Ms. Clare THOMPSON
06 Senior Director/Registrar .... Ms. Mindy S. LEAHY
09 Sr Dir Inst Research/Effectiveness .... Dr. Dustin C. DERBY
88 Sr Dir Accreditation & Licensure .... Ms. Beth BARCLAY
21 Senior Dir for Financial Affairs .... Ms. Kathleen GRAVES
13 Senior Dir Information Technology .... Mr. Mark WISELEY
15 Senior Dir of Human Resources .... Mr. Barry PENCE
18 Senior Director of Facilities .... Mr. Michael ERNSTER
51 Sr Dir Continuing Education .... Dr. Mary FROST
37 Senior Dir of Financial Planning .... Ms. Abbey NAGLE-KUCH
108 Senior Director for Assessment .... Dr. Troy STARK
08 Senior Director of Library .... Ms. Christine DEINES
88 Sr Dir Quality Assurance/System Org .... Ms. Earlye A. JULIEN
19 Sr Dir Campus Safety and Security .... Mr. Brian SHARKEY
88 Sr Dir Clinic Operations .... Ms. Tara SCHULZ
27 Sr Dir Marketing .... Ms. Kimberly KENT
27 Sr Dir of Communication .... Ms. Jillian MCCLEARY
07 Director of Campus Enrollment .... Mr. Erik SELLAS
121 Dir of Academic Support Services .... Ms. Holly FISCHER

St. Ambrose University (D)

518 W Locust Street, Davenport IA 52803-2898
County: Scott FICE Identification: 001889
Unit ID: 154235
Telephone: (563) 333-6000 Carnegie Class: DU-Mod
FAX Number: (563) 333-6243 Calendar System: Semester
URL: www.sau.edu
Established: 1882 Annual Undergrad Tuition & Fees: $32,758
Enrollment: 3,003 Coed
Affiliation or Control: Roman Catholic IRS Status: 501(c)3
Highest Offering: Doctorate
Accreditation: HLC, ACBSP, ARCPA, NURSE, OT, PTA, SP, SW

01 President .... Dr. Amy C. NOVAK
05 Provost & VP Academic/Student Affs .... Dr. Paul KOCH
10 Vice President Finance .... Mr. Michael C. POSTER
42 Chaplain .... Rev. Ross EPPING
111 Assoc Vice Pres Advancement .... Ms. Anne M. GANNAWAY
84 Vice Pres Enrollment Management .... Mr. LeShane SADDLER
46 Assoc Vice Pres Assess/Research .... Dr. Tracy SCHUSTER-MATLOCK
11 Director Administrative Services .... Ms. Carol A. GLINES
26 VP for Communications .... Dr. Toby ARQUETTE
32 Dean of Students .... Mr. Christopher A. WAUGH
15 Director Human Resources .... Ms. Audrey D. BLAIR
13 Dir of Information Resources .... Ms. Shelly L. LOWERY
29 Dir Alumni Rels & Cmty Engagement .... Ms. Wendy A. PONDELL
37 Director Financial Aid .... Ms. Julie A. HAACK
38 Director Counseling .... Dr. Sarah E. OLIVER
18 Director Physical Plant .... Mr. Jim M. HANNON
06 Registrar .... Mr. Dan L. ZEIMET
23 Director of Health Services .... Ms. Nancy A. HINES
19 Director of Security .... Mr. Robert CHRISTOPHER
39 Conduct Manager Res Life .... Ms. Anjie M. SORENSON
08 Director of Library .... Mr. Luke BEATTY
36 Director Career Development .... Ms. Lindsay ADOLPHS
41 Athletic Director .... Mr. Michael S. HOLMES
40 Manager of Bookstore .... Mr. Cory W. SAMBDMAN
104 Coordinator Education Abroad .... Ms. Morghan LEMMENES
73 Director Masters Pastoral Theology .... Rev. Robert GRANT
88 Director Masters Criminal Justice .... Dr. Chrisopher C. BARNUM
49 Dean College Arts & Sciences .... Dr. Patrick C. ARCHER
50 Dean College Business .... Dr. Maritza ESPINA
76 Dean Health & Human Services .... Dr. Lynn J. KILBURG
55 Dean Academic Adult & Graduate Pgm .... Dr. Regina M. MATHESON
54 Chair Engineering & Physical Sci .... Dr. Mohamad S. EL-ZEIN
57 Chair Fine Arts .... Mr. Joseph D. LAPPIE
75 Director Occupational Therapy .... Dr. Jill L. SCHMIDT
88 Director Masters of Accounting .... Dr. Janene R. FINLEY
58 Director MBA Pgm .... Dr. Monica L. FORRET
28 Director of Diversity .... Mr. Ryan C. SADDLER
04 Senior Asst to President .... Ms. Jana M. SEUTTER
44 Exec Dir Campaigns/Leadershp Giving .... Mr. James R. STANGLE
53 Dir School of Education .... Dr. Gene F. BECHEN
31 Dir Corporate & Community Relations .... Mr. Broderick AMBROSE
106 Director Online Learning .... Mr. Donnie L. INGRAM
108 Director Institutional Assessment .... Dr. Tracy SCHUSTER-MATLOCK
96 Director of Purchasing .... Ms. Carol A. GLINES
22 Dir Compliance & Title IX Coord .... Mr. Kevin R. CARLSON

St. Luke's College (E)

2720 Stone Park Boulevard, Sioux City IA 51104-0010
County: Woodbury FICE Identification: 007291
Unit ID: 154262
Telephone: (712) 279-3149 Carnegie Class: Spec-4-yr-Other Health
FAX Number: (712) 233-8017 Calendar System: Semester
URL: www.stlukescollege.edu
Established: 1995 Annual Undergrad Tuition & Fees: $20,940
Enrollment: 211 Coed
Affiliation or Control: Independent Non-Profit IRS Status: 501(c)3
Highest Offering: Baccalaureate
Accreditation: HLC, ADNUR, COARC, MLS, NURSE, PAST, RAD

01 President .... Dr. Kendra ERICSON
05 Chief Academic Office/Provost .... Dr. Robert LOCH
32 Dean Student Services .... Ms. Danelle D. JOHANNSEN
20 Dean of Academics .... Dr. Lorraine SACINO MURPHY
66 Associate Dean Nursing .... Dr. Shannon MERK
06 Registrar .... Ms. Michelle FITCH
113 Bursar .... Ms. Lori MEIER
84 Enrollment Mgmt/Marketing Coord .... Ms. Sherry MCCARTHY
08 Dept Chair/Library .... Ms. Nancy ZUBROD
29 Alumni/Events Coordinator .... Vacant

Shiloh University (F)

1370 Highway 1, PO Box 846, Kalona IA 52247-0846
County: Washington Identification: 667095
Unit ID: 480499
Telephone: (319) 656-2447 Carnegie Class: Spec-4-yr-Faith
FAX Number: (319) 656-2448 Calendar System: Trimester
URL: https://shiloh.edu/
Established: 2006 Annual Undergrad Tuition & Fees: $5,250
Enrollment: 49 Coed
Affiliation or Control: Independent Non-Profit IRS Status: 501(c)3
Highest Offering: Doctorate
Accreditation: DEAC

01 President/Chief Academic Ofcr .... Dr. Mark GLENN
11 VP of Operations/Administration .... Mr. Chris REEVES
13 Vice President of Technology .... Mr. James WIRTHLIN
73 Dean BA New Testament/Biblical Pgm .... Dr. Steven TODD
58 Dean Doctoral Studies .... Dr. Mark GLENN
58 Dean Graduate Programs .... Dr. Ana I. WOOD
06 Registrar .... Mr. Joshua WHEELER
07 Admissions Coordinator .... Mr. Vania GOMEZ
08 Library Director .... Mrs. Julie MCPHAIL

Simpson College (G)

701 North C Street, Indianola IA 50125-1297
County: Warren FICE Identification: 001887
Unit ID: 154350
Telephone: (515) 961-6251 Carnegie Class: Bac-Diverse
FAX Number: (515) 961-1623 Calendar System: Other
URL: www.simpson.edu
Established: 1860 Annual Undergrad Tuition & Fees: $42,246
Enrollment: 1,267 Coed
Affiliation or Control: United Methodist IRS Status: 501(c)3
Highest Offering: Master's
Accreditation: HLC, MUS

01 President .... Ms. Marsha KELLIHER
05 Sr Vice Pres/Dean Academic Affairs .... Mr. John WOELL
10 Vice President Business/Finance .... Mr. Philip PENA
111 Vice President College Advancement .... Mr. Robert J. LANE
32 Vice President Student Development .... Dr. Heidi LEVINE
84 Vice President Enrollment .... Mr. Leigh MLODZIK
13 VP Info Svcs/Chief Info Officer .... Vacant
37 Asst VP Enrollment/Financial Aid .... Ms. Tracie PAVON
06 Registrar .... Ms. Jody RAGAN
35 Dean of Students .... Mr. Luke BEHAUNEK
26 Vice President Marketing and PR .... Vacant
08 Director of Library .... Ms. Cynthia M. DYER
15 Director of Human Resources .... Ms. Mary E. BARTLEY
36 Director of Career Services .... Ms. Bobbi SULLIVAN
41 Athletic Director .... Mr. Marty BELL
96 Director of Procurement .... Vacant
35 Assistant Dean of Students .... Mr. Richard O. RAMOS
42 Chaplain .... Rev. Mara BAILEY
18 Director Campus Services .... Vacant
21 Controller/Assistant VP .... Vacant
19 Coordinator of Campus Security .... Mr. Chris FRERICHS
51 Dean Adult Learning/Online Programs .... Ms. Amy GIESEKE
104 Director of International Education .... Mr. Jay WILKINSON
04 Director Presidential Initiatives .... Ms. Megan SHULTZ
29 Director Alumni Relations .... Mr. Andy ENGLISH

Simpson College West Des Moines (H)

1415 28th Street, #250, West Des Moines IA 50266
Telephone: (515) 309-3099 Identification: 770064
Accreditation: &HLC

Southeastern Community College (I)

1500 W Agency Road, PO Box 180,
West Burlington IA 52655-0180
County: Des Moines FICE Identification: 001848
Unit ID: 154378
Telephone: (319) 752-2731 Carnegie Class: Assoc/HVT-High Trad
FAX Number: (319) 752-4957 Calendar System: Semester
URL: www.scciowa.edu
Established: 1966 Annual Undergrad Tuition & Fees (In-District): $5,910
Enrollment: 2,260 Coed
Affiliation or Control: State/Local IRS Status: 501(c)3
Highest Offering: Associate Degree
Accreditation: HLC, @CNEA, COARC, EMT, MAC

01 President .... Dr. Michael ASH
05 Vice Pres of Academic Affairs .... Dr. Janet SHEPHERD
32 Vice President of Student Services .... Ms. Joan WILLIAMS

11 Vice Pres Administrative Services .... Mr. Kevin CARR
13 Vice President for IT Services .... Mr. Chuck CHRISMAN
111 Exec Director for Inst Advancement .... Ms. Val GIANNETTINO
37 Financial Aid Officer .... Ms. Sheri KNIPE
84 Enrollment Coordinator .... Ms. Dana CHRISMAN
06 Registrar .... Mr. Dennis MARINO
15 Director Human Resources .... Ms. Laurie HEMPEN
49 Dean Arts and Sciences .... Dr. Chris SEDLACK
76 Dean oi Health .... Ms. Kristi SCHROEDER
75 Dean Career/Technical Education .... Dr. Ashlee SPANNAGEL
26 Dir Marketing/Communications .... Mr. Jeff EBBING
04 Admin Assistant to the President .... Ms. Darcy BURDETTE
09 Director of Institutional Research .... Dr. Debra HAGEN

Southeastern Community College Keokuk Campus (A)

335 Messenger Road, Keokuk IA 52632
Telephone: (319) 313-1928 Identification: 770065
Accreditation: &HLC

Southwestern Community College (B)

1501 W Townline Street, Creston IA 50801-1098
County: Union FICE Identification: 001857
Unit ID: 154396
Telephone: (641) 782-7081 Carnegie Class: Assoc/MT-VT-Mix Trad/Non
FAX Number: (641) 782-3312 Calendar System: Semester
URL: www.swcciowa.edu
Established: 1966 Annual Undergrad Tuition & Fees (In-State): $6,336
Enrollment: 1,503 Coed
Affiliation or Control: State IRS Status: 501(c)3
Highest Offering: Associate Degree
Accreditation: HLC

01 President/CEO .... Dr. Majorie MCGUIRE-WELCH
05 Vice President Instruction .... Ms. Lindsay STOAKS
09 Vice President Inst Effectiveness .... Ms. Barbara GODDEN
10 Chief Financial Officer .... Mrs. Tia SAMO
32 Dean of Student Services .... Ms. Kim BISHOP
103 Asst Vice President of Economic Dev .... Mr. Wayne PANTINI
20 Asst Vice Pres of Instruction .... Mr. John FRANKLIN
102 Ex Director Education Foundation .... Ms. Caitlyn MAITLEN
106 Director of Distance Education .... Mr. Doug GREENE
15 Director of Human Resources .... Ms. Lana BARTMESS
26 Director Marketing/Enrollment Mgmt .... Mrs. Terri HIGGINS
08 Director Learning Resource Center .... Mrs. Ann COULTER
13 Director of Information Technology .... Mr. Scott HELM
37 Director of Financial Aid .... Ms. Kylee KLOMMHAUS
06 Registrar .... Ms. Alyssa RILEY
04 Administrative Asst to President .... Ms. Carmalee WOODS
07 Director of Admissions .... Ms. Lauren ENGLAND
39 Dir Resident Life/Student Housing .... Ms. Lindsay STUMPFF
41 Asst Athletic Director .... Mr. Doug NORTH
18 Director of Plant Services .... Mr. Marv GODDEN

University of Dubuque (C)

2000 University Avenue, Dubuque IA 52001-5099
County: Dubuque FICE Identification: 001891
Unit ID: 153278
Telephone: (563) 589-3115 Carnegie Class: Masters/M
FAX Number: (563) 589-3110 Calendar System: 4/1/4
URL: www.dbq.edu
Established: 1852 Annual Undergrad Tuition & Fees: $36,610
Enrollment: 2,180 Coed
Affiliation or Control: Presbyterian Church (U.S.A.) IRS Status: 501(c)3
Highest Offering: Doctorate
Accreditation: HLC, AAB, ARCPA, NURSE, THEOL

01 President .... Rev Dr. Jeffrey F. BULLOCK
04 Exec Admin to President/BOT .... Mrs. Sandra M. LUDESCHER
05 VP Academic Affairs/Dean of Faculty .... Dr. Mark WARD
84 VP Enroll Mgmt/Dean Admissions .... Mr. Robert BROSHOUS
10 Vice Pres Finance/Auxiliary Svcs .... Mr. James D. STEINER
84 Vice Pres Enrollment/Univ Rels .... Vacant
32 Dean of Student Formation .... Mr. Mike J. DURNIN
20 Dean of the Seminary .... Dr. Annette BOURLAND HUIZENGA
07 Sr Director of Admission .... Mr. Shane BESLER
13 Dir of Technology/Communications .... Ms. Sherry CUSICK
06 Registrar .... Ms. Kim WULFEKUHLE-ISAAC
08 Director of the Library .... Mr. Christopher DOLL
15 Director of Human Resources .... Ms. Julie MACTAGGART
37 AVP/Dean Student Financial Planning .... Ms. Teresa BRAHM
58 Dean for Acad Affs Grad/Adult Pgms .... Dr. Richardo CUNNINGHAM
36 Director Vocation/Civic Engagement .... Ms. Marie MAGUINA HELLER
29 Director for Alumni Engagement .... Ms. Katie KRAUS
40 Director of Campus Stores .... Ms. Margo KETELS
41 Director of Athletics .... Mr. Dan RUNKLE
18 Director of Facilities .... Mr. Craig KLOFT
88 Executive Director Heritage Center .... Mr. Thomas J. ROBBINS

Upper Iowa University (D)

605 Washington, Box 1857, Fayette IA 52142-1857
County: Fayette FICE Identification: 001893
Unit ID: 154493
Telephone: (563) 425-5200 Carnegie Class: Masters/L
FAX Number: (563) 425-5271 Calendar System: Semester
URL: www.uiu.edu
Established: 1857 Annual Undergrad Tuition & Fees: $32,945
Enrollment: 3,610 Coed
Affiliation or Control: Independent Non-Profit IRS Status: 501(c)3
Highest Offering: Master's
Accreditation: HLC, NURSE

01 President .... Dr. William R. DUFFY, II
05 VP Academic Affairs .... Dr. Doug BINSFELD
10 VP Finance .... Ms. Kathy FRANKEN
84 VP Enrollment Management .... Ms. Kathy FRANKEN
30 VP of External Affairs .... Mr. Andrew WENTHE
41 VP Athletics .... Mr. Rick HARTZELL
32 Dean Students .... Ms. Danielle CUSHION
12 South Central Region Director .... Ms. Cynthia BENTLEY
12 Director North Central .... Ms. Jen WEBB
07 Exec Director of Admissions .... Mrs. Kathy WENTHOLD
06 Registrar .... Mrs. Holly STREETER
08 Director Library Services .... Mr. Kelly DONOVAN
04 Exec Assistant to the President .... Mrs. Holly D. WOLFF
105 Director Internet Development .... Mr. Tony PHAN
21 Controller .... Mrs. Stacie BURINGTON
36 Director of Career Development .... Ms. Anne PUFFETT
35 Director Student Activities .... Vacant
26 Exec Dir Communications & Marketing .... Vacant
29 Director of Alumni Relations .... Mr. Andrew WENTHE
13 Director Information Technology .... Mr. Terry SMID
15 VP Human Resources .... Mr. Beau SUDTELGTE
88 Director Sports Info Services .... Mr. Howard THOMPSON
18 Exec Director of Facilities .... Mr. Jesse PLEGGENKUHLE
40 Bookstore Manager .... Ms. Janelle SOPPE
37 Director Student Financial Aid .... Ms. Kelli BELL
38 Director Student Counseling .... Ms. Crystal COLE
109 Campus Store Manager .... Mrs. Holly WOLFF

Waldorf University (E)

106 S 6th Street, Forest City IA 50436-1713
County: Winnebago FICE Identification: 001895
Unit ID: 154518
Telephone: (641) 585-2450 Carnegie Class: Masters/M
FAX Number: (641) 585-8194 Calendar System: Semester
URL: www.waldorf.edu
Established: 1903 Annual Undergrad Tuition & Fees: $23,088
Enrollment: 3,025 Coed
Affiliation or Control: Proprietary IRS Status: Proprietary
Highest Offering: Master's
Accreditation: HLC

01 President .... Dr. Robert ALSOP
05 Dean of Col/VP Academic Affs .... Dr. Vincent BEACH
10 Vice President Business Affairs .... Ms. Bev RETLAND
84 Vice President Enrollment .... Mr. Mike HEITKAMP
11 Vice President Plant/Ancillary Svcs .... Mr. Brian KEELY
04 Assistant to the President .... Ms. Cindy CARTER
32 Vice President of Student Life .... Mr. Jason RAMAKER
92 Dean of Honors Program .... Dr. Suzanne FALCK-YI
08 Library Director .... Ms. Sarah BEITING
29 Director of Alumni Affairs .... Ms. Jaclyn SIFERT
06 Registrar .... Mr. Darrell BARBOUR
37 Director of Financial Aid .... Mr. Duane POLSDOFER
18 Director of Facilities Services .... Mr. Tim SEVERSON
26 Marketing Director .... Ms. Tara KINGLAND
38 Counselor .... Mr. Nic DETERMANN
41 Athletic Director .... Mr. Chad GASSMAN
36 Director Student Placement .... Ms. Kathy ROLLEFSON
40 Bookstore Manager .... Ms. Karla SCHAEFER
15 Director Human Resources .... Ms. Dawn RAMAKER

Wartburg College (F)

100 Wartburg Boulevard, Waverly IA 50677-0903
County: Bremer FICE Identification: 001896
Unit ID: 154527
Telephone: (319) 352-8200 Carnegie Class: Bac-A&S
FAX Number: (319) 352-8247 Calendar System: 4/1/4
URL: www.wartburg.edu
Established: 1852 Annual Undergrad Tuition & Fees: $45,680
Enrollment: 1,563 Coed
Affiliation or Control: Evangelical Lutheran Church In America
IRS Status: 501(c)3
Highest Offering: Master's
Accreditation: HLC, MUS, SW

01 President .... Dr. Rebecca NEIDUSKI
05 VP Acad Affairs/Dean Faculty .... Dr. Debora JOHNSON-ROSS
32 VP Student Life/Dean Students .... Mr. Greg KNESER
10 VP for Finance and Administration .... Mr. Richard SEGGERMAN
111 VP for Institutional Advancement .... Mr. Scott C. LEISINGER
88 VP for Student Recruitment .... Mr. Eric R. WILLIS
07 Executive Director of Admissions .... Ms. Tara WINTER
06 Registrar .... Ms. Sheree S. COVERT
26 CMO & Director of Marketing .... Mr. Christopher KNUDSON
13 AVP for ITS & CIO .... Ms. Melanie ABBAS
08 Director Vogel Library .... Ms. Susan MEYERAAN
29 Dir Alumni & Parent Engagement .... Ms. Ellen ENGH
37 Executive Director of Financial Aid .... Ms. Jen L. SASSMAN
41 Director of Athletics .... Mr. John T. COCHRANE
42 Interim Dean of Spiritual Life .... Rev. Halcyon D. BJORNSTAD
18 Dir of Facilities & Special Project .... Mr. Scott SHARAR
39 Dir Res Life/Chief Student Conduct .... Vacant
121 Associate Dean of Students .... Mr. Derek N. SOLHEIM
43 Chief Compliance Officer .... Ms. Karen THALACKER
38 Director Counseling Services .... Ms. Stephanie R. NEWSOM
40 Store Mgr & Textbook Services Dir .... Vacant
85 Dir of International Student Svcs .... Mr. Zafrul AMIN
35 Assistant Dean of Students .... Ms. Lindsey LEONARD
09 Dir of Inst Research/Effectiveness .... Dr. Jeffrey A. JOHNSON
15 Executive Director of HR & Payroll .... Ms. Jamie HOLLAWAY
112 Senior Advancement Associate .... Ms. Bethany J. BROOKS
92 Wartburg Scholars Director .... Dr. Rachel E. CLARK
04 Exec Admin President Office/Sec BOR .... Ms. Janeen K. STEWART
20 Associate Dean of Academic Affairs .... Mr. Douglas D. KOSCHMEDER
28 Dir Multicultural Student Services .... Ms. Krystal MADLOCK
19 Dir of Campus Security & Safety .... Mr. Ryan M. WEGNER
88 Director of Financial Reporting .... Mr. Justin CROUSE

Wartburg Theological Seminary (G)

333 Wartburg Place, Dubuque IA 52003
County: Dubuque FICE Identification: 001897
Unit ID: 154536
Telephone: (563) 589-0200 Carnegie Class: Spec-4-yr-Faith
FAX Number: (563) 589-0333 Calendar System: 4/1/4
URL: www.wartburgseminary.edu
Established: 1854 Annual Graduate Tuition & Fees: N/A
Enrollment: 203 Coed
Affiliation or Control: Evangelical Lutheran Church In America
IRS Status: 501(c)3
Highest Offering: Master's; No Undergraduates
Accreditation: HLC, THEOL

01 President .... RevDr. Kristin K. LARGEN
05 Academic Dean of the Seminary .... RevDr. Nathan FRAMBACH
10 Vice Pres for Finance & Operations .... Mr. Andy B. WILLENBORG
30 Vice President for Development .... Mr. Paul K. ERBES
88 Vice Pres for Leadership Formation .... Dr. Kris STACHE
08 Library Director .... Ms. Susan J S. EBERTZ
06 Registrar/Admin Assistant to Dean .... Dr. Kevin L. ANDERSON
04 Executive Assistant .... Ms. Lynne BAUMHOVER
37 Director Student Financial Aid .... Ms. Barbara ROLING
07 Director of Admissions .... Ms. Jeanette PERRAULT

Western Iowa Tech Community College (H)

PO Box 5199, 4647 Stone Avenue,
Sioux City IA 51102-5199
County: Woodbury FICE Identification: 007316
Unit ID: 154572
Telephone: (712) 274-6400 Carnegie Class: Assoc/HVT-High Non
FAX Number: (712) 274-6412 Calendar System: Semester
URL: www.witcc.edu
Established: 1966 Annual Undergrad Tuition & Fees (In-District): $4,488
Enrollment: 5,360 Coed
Affiliation or Control: State/Local IRS Status: 501(c)3
Highest Offering: Associate Degree
Accreditation: HLC, ADNUR, DA, EMT, MAC, PNUR, #PTAA, SURGT

01 President .... Dr. Terry MURRELL
05 VP Learning .... Ms. Juline ALBERT
10 VP Finance/Administrative Svcs .... Mr. Troy JASMAN
15 Dean Human Resources .... Ms. Jackie PLENDL
13 Dean of Information Technologies .... Mr. Mike LOGAN
32 Dean of Students .... Ms. Tawnya BEERMANN
20 Executive Dean of Instruction .... Mr. Darin MOELLER
35 Director Student Support Services .... Ms. Sara KLATT
30 Exec Director College Development .... Mr. Matthew PFISTER
08 Library Manager .... Ms. Kendra BERGENSKE
88 Director Small Business Devel Ctr .... Mr. Todd RAUSCH
18 Director Physical Plant .... Mr. Kyle HUESER
06 Registrar .... Mr. Jason PALSMA
26 Director Marketing/Publications .... Ms. Andrea ROHLENA
37 Director of Financial Aid .... Mr. Merlyn KATHOL
04 Admin Assistant to the President .... Ms. Theresa PETTY
102 Dean of Outreach .... Ms. Christina BRANDON

William Penn University (I)

201 Trueblood Avenue, Oskaloosa IA 52577-1799
County: Mahaska FICE Identification: 001900
Unit ID: 154590
Telephone: (641) 673-1001 Carnegie Class: Bac-Diverse
FAX Number: (641) 673-1396 Calendar System: Semester
URL: www.wmpenn.edu
Established: 1873 Annual Undergrad Tuition & Fees: $26,600
Enrollment: 1,350 Coed
Affiliation or Control: Friends IRS Status: 501(c)3
Highest Offering: Master's
Accreditation: HLC, NURSE

01 President .... Mr. John OTTOSSON
05 Vice Pres for Academic Affairs .... Dr. Noel STAHLE
111 Vice Pres for Advancement .... Ms. Marsha RIORDAN
10 VP for Financial Operations .... Ms. Bonnie JOHNSON
84 VP for Retention & Evening Enroll .... Ms. Kerra STRONG
32 Dean of Students .... Ms. Heidi SCHOLES
108 Director of Assessment .... Dr. Jared PEARCE
06 Registrar .... Ms. DeAnne DOLL
37 Director of Financial Aid .... Ms. Cyndi PEIFFER
36 Career Services Coordinator .... Ms. Debbie STEVENS
08 Head Librarian .... Ms. Jennifer STERLING
15 Human Resource Coordinator .... Ms. Angella DURIAN-GAMBELL
35 Director of Student Activities .... Mr. Jon HAUGEN
09 Director of Institutional Research .... Mr. Michael EDWARDS

40 Bookstore Manager ... Vacant
83 Chair Div of Social/Behavioral Sci ... Dr. Michael COLLINS
72 Co-Chair Div of Applied Technology ... Dr. Ted MCCOY
72 Co-Chair Div of Applied Technology ... Mr. Jim HOEKSEMA
53 Chair Division of Education ... Ms. Cathy WILLIAMSON
50 Chair Div of Business Admin ... Mr. David MEINERT
79 Chair Division of Humanities ... Dr. Anita MEINERT
76 Chair Div of Health & Life Sciences ... Dr. Gary CHRISTOPHER
66 Chair Div of Nursing ... Dr. Kimberley BROWN
04 Executive Asst to President ... Ms. Angella DURIAN-GAMBELL
13 Director of Information Services ... Mr. William HUGHES
19 Director of Campus Safety ... Mr. Troy BOSTON
38 Campus Counselor ... Ms. Tyne SMITH
39 Director of Residence Life ... Ms. Tanya MAMMEN
41 Athletic Director ... Mr. Nik RULE
07 Director of Admissions ... Ms. Madison STEINKE
101 Secretary of the Institution/ Board ... Ms. Angella M. DURIAN-GAMBELL
29 Director Alumni Affairs ... Mr. James KOBUS

KANSAS

Allen County Community College (A)

1801 N Cottonwood, Iola KS 66749-1698
County: Allen FICE Identification: 001901
Unit ID: 154642
Telephone: (620) 901-6400 Carnegie Class: Assoc/HT-High Non
FAX Number: (620) 365-7406 Calendar System: Semester
URL: www.allencc.edu
Established: 1923 Annual Undergrad Tuition & Fees (In-District): $3,080
Enrollment: 2,113 Coed
Affiliation or Control: State/Local IRS Status: 501(c)3
Highest Offering: Associate Degree
Accreditation: HLC

01 President ... Dr. Bruce MOSES
05 Vice President for Academic Affairs ... Vacant
10 Chief Financial Officer ... Mrs. Roberta NICKELL
32 Vice Pres Student Affairs ... Ms. Cynthia JACOBSON
20 Dean for Academic Affairs Onsite ... Mrs. Tosca HARRIS
106 Dean for Academic Affairs Online ... Mrs. Rebecca BILDERBACK
08 Director of Library ... Mrs. Virginia SHAFFER
13 Director of MIS ... Mr. Doug DUNLAP
37 Director of Financial Aid ... Mrs. Kim MURRY
18 Director of Physical Plant Opers ... Mr. Ryan SIGG
84 Director of Advising & Enrollment ... Mrs. Nikki PETERS
41 Director of Athletics ... Mr. Doug DESMARTEAU
40 Director of Bookstore ... Mrs. Reine LOFLIN
85 Foreign Student Advisor ... Mr. Nate RODRIGUEZ
09 Director Inst Research/Reporting ... Mrs. Deanna CARPENTER
35 Director Student Life ... Mr. Josiah D'ALBINI
06 Registrar ... Mrs. Bobbie HAVILAND
15 Human Resources Specialist ... Mrs. Shellie REGEHR
30 Director of Development ... Ms. Lauren MAISBERGER
121 Director of Advisement ... Mrs. Nikki PETERS

Allen County Community College Burlingame Campus (B)

100 Bloomquist Drive, Burlingame KS 66413
Telephone: (785) 654-2416 Identification: 770249
Accreditation: &HLC

Baker University (C)

618 Eighth Street/PO Box 65,
Baldwin City KS 66006-0065
County: Douglas FICE Identification: 001903
Unit ID: 154688
Telephone: (785) 594-6451 Carnegie Class: DU-Mod
FAX Number: (785) 594-2522 Calendar System: 4/1/4
URL: www.bakeru.edu
Established: 1858 Annual Undergrad Tuition & Fees: $30,770
Enrollment: 2,279 Coed
Affiliation or Control: United Methodist IRS Status: 501(c)3
Highest Offering: Doctorate
Accreditation: HLC, ACBSP, CAEP, EXSC, MUS, NURSE

01 President ... Dr. Lynne MURRAY
111 Assoc VP of Advancement ... Mr. Nate HOUSER
84 Int VP Student Affs/Enrollment Mgmt ... Ms. Cassy BAILEY
10 Interim CFO ... Ms. Darla PRATHER
53 Interim Dean School of Education ... Dr. Verneda EDWARDS
66 Dean of School of Nursing ... Dr. Libby ROSEN
49 Dean College of Arts & Sciences ... Dr. Darcy RUSSELL
107 Dean SPGS ... Dr. Matthew BICE
41 Director of Athletics ... Ms. Susan DECKER
07 Director of Admissions ... Ms. Kylie WILLIAMSON
26 Exec Dir Marketing & Communications ... Ms. Courtney HALLER
06 University Registrar ... Ms. Ramie NATION
21 Chief Accounting Officer/Controller ... Ms. Melissa VAN LEIDEN
18 Dir of Physical Plant/Facility Ops ... Mr. Tommy WOOD
42 Minister to the University ... Rev. Kevin HOPKINS
37 Senior Director of Financial Aid ... Ms. Jana PARKS
15 Chief Human Resources Officer ... Ms. Cathy MCDONALD
32 Dean of Students ... Dr. Cassy BAILEY
09 Director of Institutional Research ... Mr. Eric HAYS
29 Director of Alumni Relations ... Mr. Doug BARTH
36 Director of Career Services ... Mr. Gary HANDY
38 Dir of Health & Counseling Center ... Dr. Tim HODGES

Baker University School of Professional and Graduate Studies (D)

PO Box 65, 615 Dearborn Street, Baldwin City KS 66006
Telephone: (785) 594-6451 Identification: 770250
Accreditation: &HLC

Barclay College (E)

607 N Kingman, Haviland KS 67059-0288
County: Kiowa FICE Identification: 001917
Unit ID: 155070
Telephone: (620) 862-5252 Carnegie Class: Bac-Diverse
FAX Number: (620) 862-5242 Calendar System: Semester
URL: www.barclaycollege.edu
Established: 1917 Annual Undergrad Tuition & Fees: $21,780
Enrollment: 215 Coed
Affiliation or Control: Independent Non-Profit IRS Status: 501(c)3
Highest Offering: Master's
Accreditation: HLC, BI

01 President ... Dr. Royce FRAZIER
00 Chancellor ... Dr. Adrian HALVERSTADT
05 VP Academic Services ... Dr. Derek BROWN
10 VP Business Services ... Mr. Lee ANDERS
32 VP Student Services ... Mr. Ryan HAASE
111 VP Institutional Advancement ... Mr. Mark MILLER
06 Registrar ... Mr. Aaron STOKES
37 Director Student Financial Aid ... Ms. Ginger MAGGARD
84 Director Enrollment Services ... Mr. Justin KENDALL
08 Director of Library ... Mrs. Jeannie ROSS
106 Dir Online Education/E-learning ... Mr. Aaron STOKES
13 Chief Info Technology Officer (CIO) ... Mr. Trent MAGGARD
15 Director Personnel Services ... Mrs. Gayle MORTIMER
18 Chief Facilities/Physical Plant ... Mr. CD FITCH
41 Athletic Director ... Mr. Shane SHETLEY

Barton County Community College (F)

245 NE 30th Road, Great Bend KS 67530-9107
County: Barton FICE Identification: 004608
Unit ID: 154697
Telephone: (620) 792-2701 Carnegie Class: Assoc/HT-High Non
FAX Number: (620) 792-5624 Calendar System: Semester
URL: www.bartonccc.edu
Established: 1965 Annual Undergrad Tuition & Fees (In-District): $3,776
Enrollment: 4,094 Coed
Affiliation or Control: State/Local IRS Status: 501(c)3
Highest Offering: Associate Degree
Accreditation: HLC, ADNUR, EMT, MLTAD

01 President ... Dr. Carl R. HEILMAN
11 VP of Administration ... Mr. Mark DEAN
05 VP of Instruction ... Mrs. Elaine SIMMONS
32 VP of Student Services ... Mrs. Angela MADDY
13 Chief Information Officer ... Mrs. Michelle KAISER
20 Dean of Academics ... Mr. Brian HOWE
88 Dean Military Acad/Tech Ed/Outrch ... Mr. Kurtis TEAL
37 Chief Accreditation/Dir Fin Aid ... Mrs. Myrna PERKINS
20 Assoc Dean of Instruction ... Mrs. Claudia MATHER
111 Exec Dir Institutional Advancement ... Mrs. Coleen CAPE
75 Exec Dir Workforce Trng & Econ Dev ... Ms. Mary FOLEY
76 Exec Dir Healthcare/Public Service ... Vacant
41 Director of Athletics ... Mr. Trevor ROLFS
25 Director of Grants ... Ms. Cathie OSHIRO
26 Dir of Public Relations & Marketing ... Mr. Brandon STEINERT
09 Director of Institutional Research ... Mr. Todd MOBRAY
04 Assistant to the President ... Ms. Amye SCHNEIDER
08 Director of Library & Archives ... Mrs. ReGina REYNOLDS-CASPER
21 Comptroller & Budget Manager ... Mr. Terry BARROW
15 Director of Human Resources ... Mrs. Julie KNOBLICH
07 Director of Admissions ... Ms. Tana COOPER
06 Registrar ... Mrs. Lori CROWTHER
40 Bookstore Manager ... Mrs. Connie KERNS
39 Director of Student Life ... Mr. Jonathan DIETZ
23 Nurse ... Vacant
121 Dir Testing/Advisement/Career Svc ... Mrs. Judy JACOBS
19 Coordinator of Facility Management ... Mr. Jim IRELAND
103 Dean of Workforce Training/Cmty Ed ... Dr. Kathy KOTTAS

Benedictine College (G)

1020 N 2nd Street, Atchison KS 66002-1499
County: Atchison FICE Identification: 010256
Unit ID: 154712
Telephone: (913) 367-5340 Carnegie Class: Bac-Diverse
FAX Number: (913) 367-6566 Calendar System: Semester
URL: www.benedictine.edu
Established: 1858 Annual Undergrad Tuition & Fees: $31,630
Enrollment: 2,217 Coed
Affiliation or Control: Roman Catholic IRS Status: 501(c)3
Highest Offering: Master's
Accreditation: HLC, MUS, NURSE

01 President ... Mr. Stephen D. MINNIS
05 Dean of the College ... Dr. Kimberly C. SHANKMAN
10 Chief Financial Officer ... Mr. Ronald J. OLINGER
111 Vice President Advancement ... Ms. Kelly J. VOWELS
84 Dean of Enrollment Management ... Mr. Pete HELGESEN
32 Vice President of Student Life ... Dr. Linda HENRY
35 Dean of Students ... Dr. Joseph WURTZ
41 Athletic Director ... Mr. Charles GARTENMAYER
26 Vice President for College Rels ... Mr. Tom HOOPES
20 Assoc Dean & Registrar ... Sr. Linda HERNDON, OSB
09 Director of Institutional Research ... Vacant
58 Exec Dir of Grad Business Programs ... Mr. Michael KING
58 Director of MASL/Asst Prof Educ ... Vacant
37 Director of Student Financial Aid ... Mr. Tony TANKING
27 Dir of Marketing & Communications ... Mr. Steve JOHNSON
38 Director of Counseling Center ... Vacant
23 Director of Student Health Services ... Ms. Janet ADRIAN
18 Director of Operations ... Mr. Matt FASSERO
13 Dir of Tech & Information Sys ... Mr. Chuck WELTE
88 Director of International Program ... Mr. Daniele MUSSO
08 Library Director ... Mr. Steven GROMATZKY
39 Director of Residence Life ... Mr. Eli PRUNEDA
113 Bursar ... Ms. Becky MILLER
36 Director of Career Services ... Ms. Megan KLEBBA
29 Director of Planned Giving & Alumni ... Mr. Tim ANDREWS
04 Exec Assistant to the President ... Mrs. Abby BARTLETT
15 Int Director of Human Resources ... Ms. Charo KELLEY
19 Security Account Manager ... Mr. Danny FAIRLEY
53 Chair Education Department ... Dr. Matthew RAMSEY
54 Chair Engineering Department ... Dr. Darrin MUGGLI

Bethany College (H)

335 E Swensson Street, Lindsborg KS 67456-1895
County: McPherson FICE Identification: 001904
Unit ID: 154721
Telephone: (785) 227-3380 Carnegie Class: Bac-Diverse
FAX Number: (785) 227-2004 Calendar System: 4/1/4
URL: www.bethanylb.edu
Established: 1881 Annual Undergrad Tuition & Fees: $30,820
Enrollment: 790 Coed
Affiliation or Control: Evangelical Lutheran Church In America
IRS Status: 501(c)3
Highest Offering: Baccalaureate
Accreditation: HLC, MUS

01 President ... Dr. Elizabeth K. MAUCH
05 VP of Academic and Student Affairs ... Dr. Adam PRYOR
10 Chief Financial Officer ... Ms. Krista HARRIS
06 Registrar ... Mr. Mark BANDRE
84 VP of Enrollment Management ... Mrs. Haley WESLEY
11 VP of Administration/Gen Counsel ... Ms. Amie BAUER
32 VP of Student Affairs ... Mr. Matt PFANNENSTIEL
41 Dean of Athletics and AD ... Ms. Laura MORENO
15 VP of Human Capital Management ... Mrs. Jeanne LUCAS
111 Executive Director for Advancement ... Mrs. Brenda MEYER
09 Director of Institutional Research ... Vacant
21 Controller ... Ms. Jennifer BROZOVICH
07 Director of Admissions & Operations ... Ms. Vicki CORNETT
113 Exec Dir of Student Financial Svcs ... Mr. Christoffer LARSEN
37 Interim Director of Financial Aid ... Mr. Jeffrey ROUSH
08 Dir of Wallerstedt Learning Center ... Ms. Denise K. CARSON
35 Director of Student Affairs ... Ms. Tessa PETERS
13 Director of Technology Services ... Mr. Joshua BIEBER
16 Director Human Resources ... Vacant
29 Interim Dir of Alumni Engagement ... Mrs. Jill FISHBURN
88 Sports Information Director ... Mr. Ricky ALEXANDER
110 Director of Advancement Services ... Ms. Laurie DENK
35 Director Campus Activities ... Vacant
38 Director of Clinical Counseling ... Ms. Ginny REYES
39 Director of Residential Education ... Vacant
14 Dir of Information Services ... Ms. Vicki CORNETT
26 Director of Publications ... Mr. Frank BALLEW
36 Director Career Services ... Vacant
121 Dir of Student Success Center ... Ms. Christi WICKS
20 Asst Dean of Acad Affairs ... Vacant
108 Spec Asst to Dean Assessment ... Dr. Duke ROGERS
97 Director of Core Education ... Dr. Mary Beth HARRIS
89 Dir of Ministry & 1st Yr Experience ... Vacant
18 Director of Campus Facilities ... Mr. Dean ALLMAN
40 Bookstore Manager ... Ms. Angie SHOGREN
42 Campus Pastor ... Vacant
04 Exec Assistant to President ... Mrs. Angela BARBER
57 Interim Dir of Digital & Media Arts ... Ms. Sarah MATHIA
53 Program Director Teacher Education ... Dr. Gretchen NORLAND
57 Chair of Theatre Department ... Mr. Greg LEGAULT
61 Chair of Criminal Justice Dept ... Mr. Randy REPP
88 Dir of Oratorio & Choral Activities ... Dr. Mark LUCAS
64 Chair of the Music Department ... Dr. Dan MASTERSON
73 Chair of Religion & Philosophy Dept ... Dr. John MULLEN
81 Chair of Math & Physics Dept ... Dr. Pari FORD
81 Chair of Biology & Chemistry Dept ... Dr. Lucas MCCORMICK
83 Dir of Psychology Department ... Ms. Andrea RING
106 Director of Program Innovation ... Vacant
88 Director of Food Services ... Mr. Kevin MCCOY
92 Honors Program Coordinator ... Dr. Kristin VAN TASSEL
105 Dir Web Services & Social Media ... Ms. Molly CARVER
28 Director of Multicultural Programs ... Vacant
50 Director Business Department ... Mr. Robert CARLSON
19 Director of Campus Safety ... Mr. Austin HAMPTON
96 Purchasing Specialist ... Ms. Melanie SCHALLOCK
88 Director of Path to Your Purpose ... Mr. Chad MOORE

Bethel College (I)

300 E 27th Street, North Newton KS 67117-0531
County: Harvey FICE Identification: 001905
Unit ID: 154749
Telephone: (316) 283-2500 Carnegie Class: Bac-Diverse
FAX Number: (316) 284-5286 Calendar System: 4/1/4
URL: www.bethelks.edu

Established: 1887   Annual Undergrad Tuition & Fees: $30,264
Enrollment: 484   Coed
Affiliation or Control: Mennonite Church   IRS Status: 501(c)3
Highest Offering: Baccalaureate
Accreditation: **HLC**, CAEP, NURSE, SW

01	President	Dr. Jonathan C. GERING
04	Assistant to the President	Ms. Rosa M. BARRERA
05	Vice President Academic Affairs	Dr. Robert W. MILLIMAN
32	Vice President Student Life	Mr. Samuel C. HAYNES
41	Athletic Director	Mr. Tony HOOPS
111	Vice President Advancement	Mr. Bradley A. KOHLMAN
10	VP for Business and Finance	Vacant
84	VP for Enrollment Management	Ms. Heidi HOSKINSON
06	Registrar	Ms. Marcia K. MILLER
26	Dir Marketing and Communications	Ms. Tricia CLARK
29	Director of Alumni Engagement	Mr. Bradley SCHMIDT
37	Director of Financial Aid	Mr. Clark OSWALD
30	Director of Development	Mr. Garrett WHORTON
08	Co-Director of Libraries	Mrs. Barbara THIESEN
08	Co-Director of Libraries	Mr. John THIESEN
42	Coordinator of Church Relations	Mr. Benjamin LICHTI
18	Director of Facilities	Mr. Adam AKERS
13	Chief Info Technology Officer (CIO)	Mr. Adam HAAG
38	Director of Student Wellness	Mrs. Jill HOOPES
15	Director of HR	Mrs. Janet FULMER
28	Dir Diversity/Equity & Inclusion	Vacant

Butler Community College   (A)
712 Rose Hill Road, Rose Hill KS 67133
Telephone: (316) 776-9429   Identification: 770256
Accreditation: **&HLC**

Butler County Community College   (B)
901 S. Haverhill Road, El Dorado KS 67042-3225
County: Butler   FICE Identification: 001906
    Unit ID: 154800
Telephone: (316) 321-2222   Carnegie Class: Assoc/HT-High Trad
FAX Number: (316) 322-3109   Calendar System: Semester
URL: www.butlercc.edu
Established: 1927   Annual Undergrad Tuition & Fees (In-District): $3,706
Enrollment: 7,175   Coed
Affiliation or Control: Local   IRS Status: 501(c)3
Highest Offering: Associate Degree
Accreditation: **HLC**, ADNUR

01	President	Dr. Kimberly KRULL
05	Vice President of Academics	Dr. Tom NEVILL
10	Vice President of Finance	Mr. Kent WILLIAMS
32	Vice President of Student Services	Mr. Bill RINKENBAUGH
111	Vice President of Advancement	Mr. Tom BORREGO
08	Director of Library Services	Ms. Judy BASTIN
06	Registrar	Ms. Willow DEAN
09	AVP of Research/Inst Effectiveness	Dr. Esam MOHAMMAD
15	Assoc VP of Human Resources	Ms. Shelley STULTZ
21	Associate Business Officer	Ms. Kim SHERWOOD
29	Director Alumni Relations	Vacant
36	Director Student Placement	Vacant
37	Director Student Financial Aid	Ms. Heather WARD
35	Associate VP of Student Services	Ms. Jessica OHMAN
26	Director of Institutional Marketing	Ms. Kelly SNEDDEN
18	Director Facilities	Mr. Ireland TURNER
96	Director of Purchasing	Ms. Yolanda HACKLER
07	Director of Admissions	Ms. Kirsten ALLEN
38	Director Student Counseling	Vacant
13	VP of Digital Transformation/CIO	Mr. Bill YOUNG
19	Director Security/Safety	Mr. Glendell HENDERSON
39	Director Residence Life	Mr. David NEWELL
41	Athletic Director	Mr. Todd CARTER
04	Executive Asst to the President	Ms. Jennifer HARTMAN
106	Dean Online Learning	Dr. Heather RINKENBAUGH

Butler of Andover   (C)
715 East 13th Street, Andover KS 67002-8551
Telephone: (316) 733-0071   Identification: 770253
Accreditation: **&HLC**

Butler of Council Grove   (D)
131 West Main, Council Grove KS 66846
Telephone: (620) 382-2183   Identification: 770254
Accreditation: **&HLC**

Butler of Marion   (E)
701 E. Main, Hill Building, Marion KS 66861
Telephone: (620) 382-2183   Identification: 770255
Accreditation: **&HLC**

Butler of McConnell   (F)
Ed Ctr, Bldg 412, 53474 Lawrence Ct,
McConnell AFB KS 67221
Telephone: (316) 681-3522   Identification: 770257
Accreditation: **&HLC**

Central Baptist Theological Seminary   (G)
6601 Monticello Road, Shawnee KS 66226-3513
County: Johnson   FICE Identification: 001907
    Unit ID: 154837
Telephone: (913) 667-5700   Carnegie Class: Not Classified
FAX Number: (913) 371-8110   Calendar System: Semester
URL: cbts.edu
Established: 1901   Annual Graduate Tuition & Fees: N/A
Enrollment: N/A   Coed
Affiliation or Control: Baptist   IRS Status: 501(c)3
Highest Offering: Doctorate; No Undergraduates
Accreditation: **HLC**, THEOL

01	President	Dr. Pam R. DURSO
05	Provost/Dean of the Seminary	Dr. Robert E. JOHNSON
10	Chief Financial/Administrative Ofcr	Mr. Scott D. WEDEL
30	Director of Development	Dr. Angela B. JACKSON
26	Director of Marketing	Mr. Craig DOTY
29	Director of Alumni Engagement	Ms. Jessica C. WILLIAMS
06	Registrar	Ms. Hana YOU

Central Christian College of Kansas   (H)
1200 S Main, PO Box 1403, McPherson KS 67460
County: McPherson   FICE Identification: 001908
    Unit ID: 154855
Telephone: (620) 241-0723   Carnegie Class: Bac-Diverse
FAX Number: (620) 241-6032   Calendar System: Semester
URL: www.centralchristian.edu
Established: 1884   Annual Undergrad Tuition & Fees: $20,100
Enrollment: 629   Coed
Affiliation or Control: Free Methodist   IRS Status: 501(c)3
Highest Offering: Master's
Accreditation: **HLC**

01	President	Dr. Leonard FAVARA, JR.
05	Chief Academic Officer	Dr. Lara VANDERHOOF
32	Chief Student Engagement Officer	Mrs. Cathy BROWN
10	Chief Financial Officer	Mrs. LeAnn MOORE
41	Athletic Director	Mr. Kyle MOODY
07	Director of Admissions/Marketing	Ms. Elizabeth CARON
06	Registrar	Mrs. Michele AUGUST
08	Library Director	Mrs. Bev KELLEY
18	Director of Physical Plant	Mr. Kelly PAULS
100	Chief of Staff	Mrs. Hannah LITWILLER
11	Chief Operations Officer	Col. Doug VANDERHOOF
104	Dir International Student Programs	Vacant
09	Institution Effectiveness Analyst	Mr. Matt MALONE
102	Exec Director CCC Foundation	Dr. David FERRELL
37	Director Student Financial Aid	Mrs. Lyndsi ROMERO
29	Director Alumni Affairs	Mrs. Adriane CARR
15	Accounts Payable/HR Officer	Mrs. Katy POTTER

Cleveland University - Kansas City   (I)
10850 Lowell Avenue, Overland Park KS 66210
County: Johnson   FICE Identification: 020907
    Unit ID: 177038
Telephone: (913) 234-0600   Carnegie Class: Spec-4yr-Other Health
FAX Number: (913) 234-0904   Calendar System: Trimester
URL: www.cleveland.edu
Established: 1922   Annual Undergrad Tuition & Fees: $14,400
Enrollment: 608   Coed
Affiliation or Control: Independent Non-Profit   IRS Status: 501(c)3
Highest Offering: First Professional Degree
Accreditation: **HLC**, CHIRO, OTA

01	President	Dr. Carl S. CLEVELAND, III
05	VP Academic Affairs	Dr. Diane BARTHOLOMEW
10	VP of Finance	Mr. David CLUTE
84	VP Growth and Innovation	Dr. Alex BACH
111	VP of Advancement	Ms. Jessica RAMIREZ
26	VP of Campus and Alumni Relations	Dr. Clark BECKLEY
15	Vice Pres HR/Organizational Devel	Dr. Dale MARRANT
63	Dean of Chiropractic Education	Dr. Jon WILSON
32	Dean of Student Affairs	Mr. David FOOSE
06	Registrar	Ms. Sarah SHELNUTT
21	Controller	Ms. Marla COPE
37	Director of Financial Aid	Ms. Danielle HICKS
09	Director of Research	Dr. Mark T. PFEFER
29	Director of Campus/Alumni Relations	Ms. Jalonna BOWIE
07	Director of Admissions	Ms. Melissa DENTON
08	Library Director	Ms. Simone BRIAND
18	Director of Facilities Management	Mr. Frank HANEY
04	Executive Assistant to President	Ms. Marjorie BRADSHAW

Cloud County Community College   (J)
2221 Campus Drive, Concordia KS 66901-1002
County: Cloud   FICE Identification: 001909
    Unit ID: 154907
Telephone: (785) 243-1435   Carnegie Class: Assoc/MT-VT-High Non
FAX Number: (785) 243-1459   Calendar System: Semester
URL: www.cloud.edu
Established: 1965   Annual Undergrad Tuition & Fees (In-District): $3,390
Enrollment: 1,589   Coed
Affiliation or Control: State/Local   IRS Status: 501(c)3
Highest Offering: Associate Degree

Accreditation: **#HLC**, ADNUR

01	President	Ms. Amber KNOETTGEN
05	Vice Pres for Academic Affairs	Ms. Kimberly ZANT
11	Vice Pres for Administrative Svcs	Mr. Caesar WOOD
13	Director of Information Technology	Mr. Thomas ROBERTS
111	Director Institutional Advancement	Vacant
84	Director of Enrollment Management	Ms. Britni TREMBLAY
08	Director of Library Services	Ms. Jennifer SCHROEDER
41	Athletic Director	Mr. Matthew BECHARD
06	Registrar	Ms. Cassie WURTZ
18	Chief Facilities/Physical Plant	Mr. Rex E. SICARD
26	Coordinator of Marketing	Ms. Jessica LEDUC
102	Dir Cloud County CC Foundation	Ms. Heather GENNETTE
37	Director Student Financial Aid	Ms. Suzi KNOETTGEN
124	Director Advising & Retention	Ms. Kris FARMER
15	Director of Human Resources	Ms. Christine WILSON
09	Director Institutional Research	Vacant

Coffeyville Community College   (K)
400 W 11th Street, Coffeyville KS 67337-5064
County: Montgomery   FICE Identification: 001910
    Unit ID: 154925
Telephone: (620) 251-7700   Carnegie Class: Assoc/HT-High Trad
FAX Number: (620) 252-7098   Calendar System: Semester
URL: www.coffeyville.edu
Established: 1923   Annual Undergrad Tuition & Fees (In-District): $3,040
Enrollment: 1,368   Coed
Affiliation or Control: State/Local   IRS Status: 501(c)3
Highest Offering: Associate Degree
Accreditation: **HLC**, EMT, MAC, MLTAD

01	President	Dr. Marlon THORNBURG
05	Vice President Academic Services	Ms. Aron POTTER
10	Vice Pres for Operations & Finance	Mr. Jeff MORRIS
88	VP for Innovation/Bus Initiatives	Dr. Marlon THORNBURG
12	Columbus Campus Coordinator	Ms. Kari SOPER
102	Exec Director College Foundation	Mr. Dickie ROLLS
32	Student Life Manager	Mr. Garrett FRANCIS
09	Dir Institutional Research/Records	Mr. Chuck REED
26	Sr Director College Relations	Ms. Yvonne HULL
121	Sr Director Academic Advising	Ms. Pam FEERER
45	Dir Institutional Effectiveness	Mr. Marty EVENSVOLD
37	Director of Financial Aid	Ms. Robin ADAMSON
15	Director of Human Resources	Mrs. Kelli BAUER
41	Athletics Director	Mr. Jeff LEIKER
18	Director of Maintenance	Ms. Kris WECH
106	Director of Distance Learning	Mr. Brad WEBER
40	Bookstore Manager	Mrs. Karen STRIMPLE
06	Interim Registrar	Ms. Kristin HORNER

Colby Community College   (L)
1255 S Range, Colby KS 67701-4099
County: Thomas   FICE Identification: 001911
    Unit ID: 154934
Telephone: (785) 462-3984   Carnegie Class: Assoc/MT-VT-High Non
FAX Number: (785) 460-4699   Calendar System: Semester
URL: www.colbycc.edu
Established: 1964   Annual Undergrad Tuition & Fees (In-District): $3,934
Enrollment: 1,327   Coed
Affiliation or Control: State/Local   IRS Status: 501(c)3
Highest Offering: Associate Degree
Accreditation: **HLC**, ADNUR, PTAA

01	President	Mr. Seth M. CARTER
05	Vice Pres of Academic Affairs	Dr. Tiffany EVANS
32	Vice President of Student Affairs	Ms. Nikol NOLAN
10	Vice President of Business Affairs	Mr. Justin VILLMER
08	Librarian	Mrs. Tara SCHROER
26	Director of Public Information	Mr. Doug JOHNSON
37	Director of Financial Aid	Ms. Kathy RAMSEY
111	Dir of Inst Advancement/Foundation	Ms. Jennifer SCHOENFELD
41	Athletic Director	Mr. Mike SADDLER
13	Senior IT Director	Ms. Angel MORRISON
06	Registrar	Ms. Brette HANKIN
15	Director of Human Resources	Ms. Kayla KENNEDY

Cowley College   (M)
125 S Second, PO Box 1147,
Arkansas City KS 67005-1147
County: Cowley   FICE Identification: 001902
    Unit ID: 154952
Telephone: (620) 442-0430   Carnegie Class: Assoc/MT-VT-High Non
FAX Number: (620) 441-5350   Calendar System: Semester
URL: www.cowley.edu
Established: 1922   Annual Undergrad Tuition & Fees (In-District): $3,750
Enrollment: 2,475   Coed
Affiliation or Control: Local   IRS Status: 501(c)3
Highest Offering: Associate Degree
Accreditation: **HLC**, EMT

01	President	Dr. Randy L. SMITH
05	Vice President of Academic Affairs	Dr. Michelle SCHOON
32	Vice President of Student Affairs	Ms. Kristi SHAW
10	Vice Pres of Finance/Administration	Ms. Holly HARPER
13	Vice Pres Information Technology	Mr. Paul ERDMANN
20	AVP Secondary Partnerships/Acad	Ms. Janice STOVER
41	Athletic Director	Mr. Jason O'TOOLE
35	Director of Student Life	Ms. Peyton CRAVENS

106 AVP Distance Learning & Site Mgmt .. Mr. Shelby HUDDLESTON
26 Dir Inst Comm/Public Relations ... Mr. Rama PEROO
06 Registrar ... Mr. Devin GRAVES
15 Director of Human Resources ... Ms. Jenette HANNA
11 Campus Operations Officer ... Ms. Janet GRACE
04 Admin Assistant to the President ... Ms. Tiffany VOLLMER
09 Director of Institutional Research ... Ms. Deborah PHELPS
37 Director Student Financial Aid ... Ms. Lena SPENCER
39 Dir Resident Life/Student Housing ... Ms. Lynlea BARTLETT

Dodge City Community College (A)

2501 N 14th Avenue, Dodge City KS 67801-2399
County: Ford FICE Identification: 001913
Unit ID: 154998
Telephone: (620) 225-1321 Carnegie Class: Assoc/MT-VT-Mix Trad/Non
FAX Number: (620) 227-9366 Calendar System: Semester
URL: www.dc3.edu
Established: 1935 Annual Undergrad Tuition & Fees (In-District): $3,990
Enrollment: 1,459 Coed
Affiliation or Control: State/Local IRS Status: 501(c)3
Highest Offering: Associate Degree
Accreditation: HLC, ADNUR

01 President ... Dr. Harold E. NOLTE, JR.
00 Chairman of the Board of Trustees ... Mr. Gary HARSHBERGER
05 Provost Flight Program ... Dr. Adam JOHN
10 VP of Administration/Finance & CFO ... Mr. Jeff CERMIN
32 VP of Student Affairs ... Dr. Jay KINZER
20 Vice President of Academic Affairs ... Dr. Jane HOLWERDA
102 Dir DCCC Foundation/Cmty Relations ... Mrs. Christina HASELHORST
55 Director Adult Learning Center ... Ms. Maria ROJAS
15 AVP of Admin & Human Resources ... Ms. Kristi OHLSCHWAGER
08 Director Learning Resource Center ... Mrs. Holly MERCER
66 Dean Nursing/Allied Health ... Dr. Mechele HAILEY
41 Athletic Director ... Mr. Jacob RIPPLE
37 Director of Financial Aid ... Vacant
18 Director of Facilities & Operations ... Mr. Jared STEVENS
04 Exec Asst to Pres/Clerk of Board ... Ms. Renee A. ALLEN
103 Dir Workforce Development/Title V ... Dr. Clayton TATRO
09 Dir of Inst Research/Accreditation ... Vacant
21 Financial Accountant ... Mrs. Marinita ARAGON
19 Director Security/Safety ... Mr. Joshua THOMPSON
84 AVP of Enrollment Mgmt/Registrar ... Dr. Christy JOHANSON
13 Chief Information Technology Office ... Mr. Michael WEBSTER
88 Coordinator of Dual Credit ... Mrs. Tammi FISCHER
106 Dean of Online Education/E-learning ... Dr. Jodi RUST
28 Dir of Student Support & Diversity ... Dr. Gregory ROBERTS
09 Exec Dir Inst Rsrch/Effectiveness ... Mr. Joseph BAUMANN
07 Director of Admissions ... Mrs. Emily WITHERSPOON

Donnelly College (B)

608 N 18th Street, Kansas City KS 66102-4298
County: Wyandotte FICE Identification: 001914
Unit ID: 155007
Telephone: (913) 621-8700 Carnegie Class: Bac/Assoc-Mixed
FAX Number: (913) 621-8719 Calendar System: Semester
URL: www.donnelly.edu
Established: 1949 Annual Undergrad Tuition & Fees: $8,100
Enrollment: 336 Coed
Affiliation or Control: Roman Catholic IRS Status: 501(c)3
Highest Offering: Baccalaureate
Accreditation: HLC

01 President ... Msgr. Stuart SWETLAND
05 VP of Academic & Student Affairs ... Mrs. Lisa STOOTHOFF
111 Vice President of Advancement ... Ms. Emily BUCKLEY
10 CFO ... Mr. Bernard BARRY
09 Institutional Effectiveness Coord ... Ms. Jennifer BALES
32 Director of Student Success ... Dr. Mary PFLANZ
06 Registrar ... Ms. Crystal WILBURN
07 Director of Admissions ... Ms. Katy SIEBERT

Emporia State University (C)

1 Kellogg Circle, Emporia KS 66801-5415
County: Lyon FICE Identification: 001927
Unit ID: 155025
Telephone: (620) 341-1200 Carnegie Class: Masters/L
FAX Number: (620) 341-5553 Calendar System: Semester
URL: www.emporia.edu
Established: 1863 Annual Undergrad Tuition & Fees (In-State): $6,971
Enrollment: 5,828 Coed
Affiliation or Control: State IRS Status: 501(c)3
Highest Offering: Doctorate
Accreditation: HLC, ACATE, ART, CAATE, CACREP, CAEP, CEA, LIB, MUS, NUR

01 President ... Mr. Ken HUSH
05 Interim Provost/VP Acad Affs ... Dr. Gary WYATT
11 VP Admin/Fiscal Affairs ... Ms. Diana E. KUHLMANN
32 Vice President Student Affairs ... Dr. James E. WILLIAMS
13 Vice President for Infrastructure ... Mr. Cory FALLDINE
09 Asst Provost Inst Effectiveness ... Dr. JoLanna KORD
85 Dean of International Education ... Mr. Mark DALY
35 Dean of Students ... Ms. Lynn M. HOBSON
102 President ESU Foundation ... Mr. Shane SHIVLEY
84 VP for Enrollment Management ... Dr. Shelly GEHRKE
29 Director of Alumni Relations ... Ms. Tiffany WILSON
88 Director Natl Teachers Hall of Fame ... Dr. Ken WEAVER
22 Affirmative Action Officer ... Mr. Ray LAUBER
53 Dean of The Teachers College ... Dr. Joan BREWER
49 Dean College of Liberal Arts/Sci ... Dr. R. Brent THOMAS
50 Dean School of Business ... Dr. Ed BASHAW
62 Dean School of Library/Info Mgmt ... Dr. Wooseob JEONG
58 Dean Graduate Studies ... Dr. James SPOTSWOOD
06 Registrar ... Ms. Sheila MARKOWITZ
08 Dean University Libraries/Archives ... Dr. Wooseob JEONG
106 Director Distance Education ... Dr. James SPOTSWOOD
37 Director Student Financial Aid ... Ms. Jaime MORRIS
36 Director Career Services ... Mr. Ryan HORSCH
38 Director Stdnt Wellness/Counseling ... Ms. Lindsay BAYS
26 Chief Marketing Officer ... Ms. Kelly HEINE
41 Director Athletics ... Vacant
18 Dir Facilities/Phys Plant ... Mr. Bill MCKERNON
15 Director Human Resources ... Mr. Ray LAUBER
23 Director Health Services ... Ms. Mary MCDANIEL ANSCHUTZ
39 Dir Residential Life/Orientation ... Ms. Cass COUGHLIN
40 Manager Bookstore ... Mr. Michael MCRELL
19 Chief Police & Safety ... Capt. Jerry COOK
43 General Counsel ... Mr. Kevin JOHNSON
21 Controller ... Ms. Pamela NORTON
92 Associate Provost Honors College ... Dr. Gary WYATT
28 Director Diversity & Inclusion ... Mr. Nyk ROBERTSON
04 Administrative Asst to President ... Ms. Sarah MCKERNAN
91 Assoc CIO Academic & User Support ... Dr. Rob GIBSON
07 Director of Admissions ... Ms. Lydia BARNHART

Flint Hills Technical College (D)

3301 W 18th Avenue, Emporia KS 66801-5957
County: Lyon FICE Identification: 005264
Unit ID: 155052
Telephone: (620) 343-4600 Carnegie Class: Assoc/HVT-High Non
FAX Number: (620) 343-4610 Calendar System: Semester
URL: www.fhtc.edu
Established: 1965 Annual Undergrad Tuition & Fees (In-District): $6,200
Enrollment: 1,222 Coed
Affiliation or Control: State/Local IRS Status: 501(c)3
Highest Offering: Associate Degree
Accreditation: HLC, DA, DH

01 President ... Dr. Caron DAUGHERTY
05 Vice Pres Instructional Services ... Mr. Steve LOEWEN
32 Vice Pres Student Services ... Ms. Lisa KIRMER
10 Vice Pres Business Services ... Mrs. Nancy THOMPSON
15 Director Personnel Services ... Mrs. Sandy WEEKS
37 Director Student Financial Aid ... Ms. Erica CLARK
84 Director Enrollment Management ... Ms. Brenda CARMICHAEL
04 Administrative Asst to President ... Ms. Jacqui ANDERSON
30 Chief Development/Advancement ... Mr. Mike CROUCH

Fort Hays State University (E)

600 Park Street, Hays KS 67601-4099
County: Ellis FICE Identification: 001915
Unit ID: 155061
Telephone: (785) 628-4000 Carnegie Class: Masters/L
FAX Number: (785) 628-4096 Calendar System: Semester
URL: www.fhsu.edu
Established: 1902 Annual Undergrad Tuition & Fees (In-State): $5,430
Enrollment: 15,033 Coed
Affiliation or Control: State IRS Status: 501(c)3
Highest Offering: Doctorate
Accreditation: HLC, CACREP, CAEP, MUS, NAIT, NURSE, RAD, SP, SW

01 President ... Dr. Tisa MASON
05 Provost ... Dr. Jill ARENSDORF
10 Vice Pres Administration & Finance ... Mr. Wesley WINTCH
32 Vice Pres Student Affairs ... Dr. Joseph LINN
35 Asst VP Student Affairs/Compliance ... Dr. Teresa CLOUNCH
88 Asst Provost/Learning Tech ... Dr. Andrew FELDSTEIN
09 Asst VP Institutional Effectiveness ... Vacant
58 Asst Provost/Dean Graduate Studies ... Dr. Angela POOL-FUNAI
84 Assoc VP Student Affairs/Enrollment ... Dr. Dennis KING
06 Registrar ... Mr. Craig KARLIN
07 Director of Admissions ... Mr. Jon ARMSTRONG
114 Director Budget & Planning ... Mr. Robert MANRY
36 Director Career Services ... Ms. Karen MCCULLOUGH
37 Dir Student Financial Aid ... Ms. Vanessa FLIPSE
26 Chief Communications Officer ... Mr. Scott CASON
08 Dean of Library Services ... Ms. Ginger WILLIAMS
15 Director Personnel Services ... Ms. Shannon LINDSEY
106 Asst Director FHSU Online ... Ms. Kayla HICKEL
53 Dean College Education ... Dr. Paul ADAMS
49 Int Dean Col Arts/Hum/Soc Sci ... Dr. Daniel BLANKENSHIP
50 Dean Col Bus/Entrepreneurship ... Dr. Muhammad CHISHTY
76 Dean Col Health/Behavior Sciences ... Dr. Jeff BRIGGS
88 Dir Building & Maint Operations ... Mr. Terry PFEIFER
121 Dir Acad Advise/Career Exploration ... Dr. Patricia L. GRIFFIN
28 Asst VP/Student Engagement ... Ms. Taylor KRILEY
19 Int Dir University Police Chief ... Mr. Nathan LANG
22 Univ Compliance Officer ... Ms. Amy SCHAFFER
102 President/CEO Foundation ... Mr. Jason WILLIBY
25 Interim Chief Contract/Grants Admin ... Dr. Whitney WHITAKER
41 Athletic Director ... Mr. Curtis HAMMEKE
104 Director Intl Student Services ... Ms. Carol SOLKO-OLLIFF
43 General Counsel ... Dr. Joe BAIN
81 Dean College Science/Tech/Math ... Dr. P. Grady DIXON
13 Director Information Technology ... Mr. Mark GRIFFIN
96 Director of Purchasing ... Ms. Kathy HERRMAN
39 Interim Director Residential Life ... Mr. RJ SCHNACK
04 Exec Assistant to the President ... Ms. Tara GARCIA
18 Director Facilities Planning ... Mr. Dana CUNNINGHAM
86 Director Government Relations ... Ms. Jennie ROSE

Fort Scott Community College (F)

2108 S Horton, Fort Scott KS 66701-3140
County: Bourbon FICE Identification: 001916
Unit ID: 155098
Telephone: (620) 223-2700 Carnegie Class: Assoc/MT-Mix Trad/Non
FAX Number: (620) 223-4927 Calendar System: Semester
URL: www.fortscott.edu
Established: 1919 Annual Undergrad Tuition & Fees (In-District): $3,510
Enrollment: 1,617 Coed
Affiliation or Control: State/Local IRS Status: 501(c)3
Highest Offering: Associate Degree
Accreditation: HLC, ADNUR

01 President ... Alysia JOHNSTON
05 VP of Academic Affairs ... Adam BORTH
10 Vice Pres of Finance and Operations ... Julie EICHENBERGER
32 Vice President of Student Affairs ... Tom HAVRON
13 Director of Research & Technology ... Jacob REICHARD
07 Director Admissions ... Brian LANCASTER
08 Director of Library ... Susie ARVIDSON
06 Registrar ... Courtney METCALF
26 Director of Strategic Communication ... Kassie FUGATE-CATE
66 Director Nursing ... Jordan HOWARD
14 Information Technology Director ... Jason SIMON
12 Dean Crawford County ... Santos MANRIQUE
12 Dean of Miami County Campus ... Buddy Jo TANCK
121 VP of Student Support Services ... Janet FANCHER
15 Human Resource Director ... Juley MCDANIEL
30 Director of Development/Alumni ... Jeff TADTMAN
37 Director Student Financial Aid ... Lillie GRUBB
88 Director of Gordon Parks Museum ... Kirk SHARP
21 Director Business Operations ... Marianne CULBERTSON
04 Administrative Asst to President ... Darlene WOOD
39 Director Student Housing ... Marci MYERS
25 Director Grants & Special Projects ... Ralph BEACHAM

Friends University (G)

2100 W University Avenue, Wichita KS 67213-3397
County: Sedgwick FICE Identification: 001918
Unit ID: 155089
Telephone: (316) 295-5000 Carnegie Class: Masters/L
FAX Number: (316) 295-5060 Calendar System: Semester
URL: www.friends.edu
Established: 1898 Annual Undergrad Tuition & Fees: $30,120
Enrollment: 1,671 Coed
Affiliation or Control: Independent Non-Profit IRS Status: 501(c)3
Highest Offering: Master's
Accreditation: HLC, CAEP, MFCD, MUS

01 President ... Dr. Amy BRAGG CAREY
04 Executive Asst to the President ... Ms. Natasha PEREZ
05 VP Academic Affairs & Academic Dean . Dr. Kenneth STOLTZFUS
10 VP of Finance & Administration ... Mr. Vernon DOLEZAL
32 VP of Student Affairs ... Dr. Guy CHMIELESKI
111 VP of Univ Advancement & Marketing ... Ms. Brie BOULANGER
84 VP of Enrollment Management ... Mr. Andy JOHNSON
06 University Registrar ... Mr. Eric SANFORD
20 Assoc Academic Dean ... Dr. Preston TODD
15 Senior Director of Human Resources ... Ms. Danita MASON
50 Chair Business & IT ... Dr. James LONG
57 Chair Fine Arts ... Dr. Nathanael MAY
81 Chair STEM ... Dr. Nora STRASSER
73 Chair Theology & Humanities ... Dr. Jeremy GALLEGOS
53 Chair Teacher Education ... Dr. Moses RUMANO
08 Director Library ... Mr. David MCCLURE
18 Chief Facilities/Physical Plant ... Mr. Roger DANLEY
07 Director Recruiting/CBASE Admiss ... Ms. Jordan AUDETTE
37 Director Financial Aid ... Ms. Crystal ROACH
42 Director Campus Ministries ... Mr. Michael JADERSTON
39 Director of Residence Life ... Ms. Lacey LANDENBERGER
27 Director of Marketing ... Ms. Rachel MILLARD
29 Director of Alumni Relations ... Ms. Jessica BOONE
12 Site Manager - Kansas City ... Ms. Christy CARTER
09 Director of Institutional Research ... Mr. Victor ROGERS
19 Director Security/Safety ... Mr. Richard VINROE
120 Dir Online Education/E-learning ... Ms. Nancy ARTAZ
41 AVP Athletics ... Dr. Rob RAMSEYER
91 Director Administrative Computing ... Mr. Roger SCALES
13 Director Infrastructure Technology ... Mr. Gil OLIVA
30 Senior Director of Development ... Ms. Sanya WILES

Garden City Community College (H)

801 Campus Drive, Garden City KS 67846-6398
County: Finney FICE Identification: 001919
Unit ID: 155104
Telephone: (620) 276-7611 Carnegie Class: Assoc/HT-High Trad
FAX Number: (620) 276-9573 Calendar System: Semester
URL: www.gcccks.edu
Established: 1919 Annual Undergrad Tuition & Fees (In-District): $3,360
Enrollment: 1,868 Coed
Affiliation or Control: Local IRS Status: 501(c)3
Highest Offering: Associate Degree
Accreditation: HLC, ADNUR, EMT

01 President/CEO ... Dr. Ryan RUDA
05 VP for Instructional Services ... Mr. Marc MALONE

32 VP Student Services/Asst AD ... Mr. Colin LAMB
10 Vice President Admin Services/CFO ... Ms. Karla ARMSTRONG
35 Exec Director of Student Services ... Ms. Tammy TABOR
06 Registrar ... Ms. Nancy UNRUH
103 Dean Technical Educ/Workforce Dev ... Mr. Chuck PFEIFER
15 Director of Human Resources ... Ms. Kellee MUNOZ
18 Dean Physical Plng/Facilities Mgmt ... Mr. Derek RAMOS
26 Director of Media Relations ... Ms. Melody BROOKS
37 Director Student Financial Aid ... Ms. Melinda HARRINGTON
39 Director Residential Life ... Vacant
20 Dean of Academics ... Mr. Phil TERPSTRA
04 Executive Assistant to President ... Ms. Jodie TEWELL
09 Director of Institutional Research ... Ms. Brenda BARRETT
21 Comptroller ... Ms. Debra NICHOLSON
19 Campus Police Chief ... Mr. Rodney DOZIER
08 Director Library Services ... Mr. Trent SMITH
44 Executive Director Endowment ... Mr. Jeremy GIGOT
41 Athletic Director ... Mr. Jeff TATUM
121 Director of Advising ... Ms. Leslie WENZEL
22 Coord Disability Svcs & Compliance ... Ms. Kari ADAMS
106 Director Online Services ... Ms. Jamie DURLER
07 Director of Admissions ... Ms. Sydnee SASSAMAN
13 Chief Information Technology Office ... Mr. Lance MILLER

Haskell Indian Nations University (A)

155 Indian Avenue, #5030, Lawrence KS 66046-4800
County: Douglas — FICE Identification: 010438
Unit ID: 155140
Telephone: (785) 749-8404 — Carnegie Class: Tribal
FAX Number: N/A — Calendar System: Semester
URL: www.haskell.edu
Established: 1884 — Annual Undergrad Tuition & Fees: $480
Enrollment: 731 — Coed
Affiliation or Control: Federal — IRS Status: Exempt
Highest Offering: Baccalaureate
Accreditation: HLC, CAEP

01 Acting President ... Ms. Tamarah PFEIFFER
05 Acting Vice Pres Academic Affairs ... Ms. Cheryl CHUCKLUCK
11 Vice President University Services ... Ms. Tonia SALVINI
10 Chief Finance Officer ... Ms. Marie THORNE
13 Chief Information Officer ... Mr. David FIRE
111 Acting Dir Academic Support Ctr ... Ms. Carrie CORNELIUS
39 Acting Dir Resident Housing ... Ms. Barbara STUMBLINGBEAR
37 Financial Aid Officer ... Ms. Carlene MORRIS
06 Registrar ... Ms. Lou HARA
07 Director of Admissions ... Ms. Dorothy D. STITES
09 Dir Instl Research/Sponsored Pgms ... Ms. Cynthia GROUNDS
36 Career Development Specialist ... Vacant
38 Director Student Counseling ... Vacant
15 Human Resources Liaison ... Vacant
96 Acquisitions ... Ms. Janice BEGAY
26 Special Asst to the President ... Ms. Mona GONZALES
18 Acting Facilities Manager ... Ms. Karla VAN NOY

Hesston College (B)

301 S. Main Street, Hesston KS 67062-8901
County: Harvey — FICE Identification: 001920
Unit ID: 155177
Telephone: (620) 327-4221 — Carnegie Class: Bac/Assoc-Mixed
FAX Number: (620) 327-8300 — Calendar System: Semester
URL: www.hesston.edu
Established: 1909 — Annual Undergrad Tuition & Fees: $28,440
Enrollment: 359 — Coed
Affiliation or Control: Mennonite Church — IRS Status: 501(c)3
Highest Offering: Baccalaureate
Accreditation: HLC, NURSE

01 President ... Dr. Joseph MANICKAM
05 Vice Pres of Academics ... Dr. Carren MOHAM
07 Vice Pres of Admissions ... Mr. Del HERSHBERGER
10 Vice Pres Finance & Auxiliary Svcs ... Mrs. Lisa GEORGE
32 Vice Pres Student Life ... Mrs. Deb ROTH
111 Vice Pres Advancement ... Mrs. Rachel SWARTZENDRUBER MILLER
110 Coordinator of Advancement Services ... Ms. Sheri ESAU
06 Registrar/Dean of Assessment ... Mrs. Sandra HIEBERT
21 Business Manager ... Mr. Karl BRUBAKER
37 Director of Financial Aid ... Ms. Dori ROTH
15 Director of Human Resources ... Ms. Monica MILLER

Highland Community College (C)

606 W Main, Highland KS 66035
County: Doniphan — FICE Identification: 001921
Unit ID: 155186
Telephone: (785) 442-6000 — Carnegie Class: Assoc/MT-VT-High Non
FAX Number: (785) 442-6100 — Calendar System: Semester
URL: www.highlandcc.edu
Established: 1858 — Annual Undergrad Tuition & Fees (In-District): $3,600
Enrollment: 2,700 — Coed
Affiliation or Control: Local — IRS Status: 501(c)3
Highest Offering: Associate Degree
Accreditation: HLC, ADNUR

01 President ... Ms. Deborah FOX
32 Vice President for Student Services ... Dr. Eric INGMIRE
10 Vice Pres for Finance/Operations ... Mr. Randy WILLY
05 Dean of Instruction ... Ms. Sharon KIBBE
72 Director of Technical Education ... Mr. Lucas HUNZIGER
06 Registrar ... Ms. Alice HAMILTON
37 Financial Aid Director ... Ms. Sarah WINDMEYER
13 Director of IT ... Mr. Marc JEAN
75 Director of HCC Technical Center ... Ms. Amy DULAC
09 Director of Institutional Research ... Mr. Jeffrey HURN
38 Campus Counselor ... Ms. Vanessa CHAVEZ
41 Athletic Director ... Dr. Bryan DORREL
08 Library Director ... Ms. Cindy DAVIS
18 Supervisor of Buildings & Grounds ... Mr. Rick BLEVINS
29 Director Alumni Relations ... Ms. Kelly TWOMBLY
39 Coord of Student Life ... Mr. Jacob DAVIS
15 Director of Human Resources ... Ms. Eileen C. GRONNIGER
26 Director of Marketing ... Ms. Stephanie PETERSON
40 Bookstore Coordinator ... Ms. Shannon WIEDMER
07 Director of Admissions ... Ms. Taylor MARRIOTT
106 Assoc Dean Online Educ/E-learning ... Ms. Denise PETERS
35 Director of Campus Life ... Mr. Zachariah HARRIS
04 Admin Assistant to the President ... Ms. Heather MEJIA

Hutchinson Community College (D)

1300 N Plum Street, Hutchinson KS 67501-5894
County: Reno — FICE Identification: 001923
Unit ID: 155195
Telephone: (620) 665-3500 — Carnegie Class: Assoc/MT-VT-High Non
FAX Number: (620) 665-3310 — Calendar System: Semester
URL: www.hutchcc.edu
Established: 1928 — Annual Undergrad Tuition & Fees (In-District): $3,480
Enrollment: 4,907 — Coed
Affiliation or Control: State/Local — IRS Status: 501(c)3
Highest Offering: Associate Degree
Accreditation: HLC, ADNUR, CAHIIM, COARC, EMT, PNUR, PTAA, RAD, SURGT

01 President ... Dr. Carter FILE
05 Vice President of Academic Affairs ... Dr. Cindy HOSS
10 Vice President Finance/Operations ... Ms. Julie BLANTON
103 VP Workforce Development/Outreach ... Mr. Bryce MCFARLAND
32 Vice President of Students ... Mr. Brett BRIGHT
26 Director of Marketing & Info ... Mr. Denny STOECKLEIN
13 Chief Information Officer ... Mr. Loren L. MORRIS
06 Registrar ... Mrs. Christina LONG
41 Athletic Director ... Mr. Josh GOOCH
15 Director of Personnel ... Mr. Brooks E. MANTOOTH
37 Financial Aid Officer ... Mr. Nathan BUCHE
07 Director of Admissions ... Mr. Corbin STROBEL
18 Director of Plant Facilities ... Mr. Don ROSE
39 Director of Residence Life ... Ms. Dana HINSHAW
29 Director Alumni Relations ... Mrs. Cindy KEAST
08 Coordinator of Library Services ... Mr. Brad FENWICK
09 Coord of Institutional Research ... Mr. Rex CHEEVER
106 Director Online Education ... Dr. Rhonda CORWIN

Independence Community College (E)

1057 West College Avenue,
Independence KS 67301-0708
County: Montgomery — FICE Identification: 001924
Unit ID: 155201
Telephone: (620) 331-4100 — Carnegie Class: Assoc/HT-Mix Trad/Non
FAX Number: (620) 331-5344 — Calendar System: Semester
URL: www.indycc.edu
Established: 1925 — Annual Undergrad Tuition & Fees (In-District): $4,650
Enrollment: 798 — Coed
Affiliation or Control: State/Local — IRS Status: 501(c)3
Highest Offering: Associate Degree
Accreditation: HLC

01 President ... Dr. Vincent BOWHAY
05 VP for Academic Affairs ... Ms. Taylor CRAWSHAW
10 VP for Administration/Finance ... Mr. Jonathan SADHOO
32 VP for Student Affairs ... Mr. David ADAMS
13 Interim Chief Information Officer ... Mr. Brett BERTIE
26 Marketing Coordinator ... Mrs. Kris FERGUSON
15 VP for Human Resources ... Ms. Lori BOOTS
102 Foundation Director ... Mr. Bryce SAIA
06 Registrar ... Ms. Wendy NIEMEYER
08 Director Library Services ... Ms. Sarah OWEN
18 Director of Maintenance/Facilities ... Mr. Benny BEURSKENS
37 Financial Aid Director ... Ms. Laura ALLISON
09 Dir of Institutional Research ... Ms. Anita CHAPPUIE
04 Executive Asst to President ... Mrs. Cherie STOCKTON
40 Bookstore Manager ... Ms. Toni BRUINGTON
88 Upward Bound Program Director ... Ms. Lindsey DONOVAN
106 Director of Online Education ... Vacant
121 Assoc Dean Tutoring/Accessibility ... Vacant
39 Student Housing General Manager ... Ms. Crystal PENROD
84 Director Enrollment/Retention Mgmt ... Vacant
41 Athletic Director ... Ms. Melissa ANDERSON

Johnson County Community College (F)

12345 College Boulevard, Overland Park KS 66210-1299
County: Johnson — FICE Identification: 008244
Unit ID: 155210
Telephone: (913) 469-8500 — Carnegie Class: Assoc/HT-High Non
FAX Number: (913) 469-2559 — Calendar System: Semester
URL: www.jccc.edu
Established: 1969 — Annual Undergrad Tuition & Fees (In-District): $3,360
Enrollment: 13,891 — Coed
Affiliation or Control: State/Local — IRS Status: 501(c)3
Highest Offering: Associate Degree
Accreditation: HLC, ACBSP, ACFEI, ADNUR, COARC, DH, EMT, IFSAC, NDT

01 President ... Dr. Andrew BOWNE
05 Exec Vice Pres Academic Affs/CAO ... Dr. Mickey MCCLOUD
32 Vice Pres Student Success/CSSO ... Vacant
11 Exec VP Admin & Finance/COO ... Mr. Mike NEAL
35 Interim EVP/Dean Learner Engage ... Ms. Pam VASSAR
84 Interim EVP/Dean Enrollment Svcs ... Ms. MargE SHELLEY
04 Special Assistant to the President ... Ms. Terri SCHLICHT
15 Vice President Human Resources ... Dr. Leslie HARDIN
51 Vice President Continuing Educ ... Ms. Elisa WALDMAN
26 VP Strategic Comm & Mktg ... Mr. Chris GRAY
13 Interim CIO ... Ms. Del LOVITT
111 VP Inst Advancement/Govt Affairs ... Ms. Kate ALLEN
108 Exec Dir Inst Effectiveness/Plng ... Mr. John CLAYTON
43 VP General Counsel ... Ms. Kelsey NAZAR
10 AVP Financial Services/CFO ... Ms. Rachel LIERZ
116 Director Audit/Advisory Svcs ... Vacant
18 AVP Campus Services/Facility Plng ... Mr. Tom HALL
20 AVP Instruction ... Dr. Gurbhushan SINGH
96 AVP Business Services ... Ms. Janelle VOGLER
117 Exec Dir Mission Cont/Risk Mgmt ... Dr. Sandra WARNER
06 Dir Enrollment Svcs/Registrar ... Ms. Leslie QUINN
88 Director Testing and Assessment ... Ms. Mary Ann DICKERSON
37 Director Financial Aid ... Ms. Christal WILLIAMS
07 Dir of Admissions & Recruitment ... Mr. Peter BELK
41 Interim Director of Athletics ... Mr. Ben CONRAD
08 Director Library Services ... Mr. Mark DAGANAAR
09 Director of Institutional Research ... Ms. Natalie ALLEMAN-BEYERS
92 Director Honors Program ... Ms. Anne DOTTER
88 Exec Director Sustainability ... Dr. Jay ANTLE
25 Exec Director Grants Development ... Ms. Malinda BRYAN-SMITH

Kansas Christian College (G)

7401 Metcalf, Overland Park KS 66204-1995
County: Johnson — Identification: 667134
Unit ID: 155308
Telephone: (913) 722-0272 — Carnegie Class: Bac/Assoc-Mixed
FAX Number: (913) 601-3826 — Calendar System: Semester
URL: www.kansaschristian.edu
Established: 1938 — Annual Undergrad Tuition & Fees: $9,340
Enrollment: 152 — Coed
Affiliation or Control: Independent Non-Profit — IRS Status: 501(c)3
Highest Offering: Baccalaureate
Accreditation: BI

01 President ... Mr. Chad POLLARD
00 Chairman of the Board ... Rev. Rodney L. DAVIS
101 Secretary of the Board ... Mr. Dwight PURTLE
05 Vice Pres Academic Affairs ... Dr. Dennis CROCKER
03 Executive Vice President ... Rev. Matthew LEE
41 Vice Pres of Athletic Development ... Dr. Jim POTEET
10 Vice Pres of Operations/Finance ... Mr. David CARPENTER
18 Director of Facilities ... Mr. Ben ALLRED
08 Head Librarian ... Mrs. Dorie SCOFIELD
06 Registrar ... Mr. Lucien FORTIER
09 Director of Institutional Research ... Mrs. Dorothy PURTLE
37 Director Student Financial Aid ... Mrs. Marcia KELLEY
04 Admin Assistant to the President ... Ms. Kim LEONARD
106 Dir Professional/Online Education ... Dr. Kenneth L. MERSCHBROCK
39 Dir Resident Life/Student Housing ... Mrs. Leandra MARTIN

Kansas City Kansas Community College (H)

7250 State Avenue, Kansas City KS 66112-3003
County: Wyandotte — FICE Identification: 001925
Unit ID: 155292
Telephone: (913) 334-1100 — Carnegie Class: Assoc/HVT-Mix Trad/Non
FAX Number: (913) 288-7609 — Calendar System: Semester
URL: www.kckcc.edu
Established: 1923 — Annual Undergrad Tuition & Fees (In-District): $3,300
Enrollment: 5,148 — Coed
Affiliation or Control: State/Local — IRS Status: 501(c)3
Highest Offering: Associate Degree
Accreditation: #HLC, ACBSP, ADNUR, COARC, EMT, FUSER, MAC, PTAA

01 President ... Dr. Greg MOSIER
10 Chief Financial Officer ... Mr. Michael BEACH
05 Vice Pres Academic Affairs ... Mr. Jerry POPE
32 VP Student Affairs & Enrollment ... Dr. Chris MEIERS
26 VP Strategic Initiatives & Outreach ... Ms. Tami BARTUNEK
81 Dean Math/Science/Business ... Dr. Ed KREMER
51 Director Continuing Education ... Mr. David BEACH
103 Exec Dir Entrep & Workforce Dev ... Vacant
79 Dean Arts/Communications/Humanities ... Dr. Donna BOHN
13 Chief Information Officer ... Mr. Peter GABRIEL
09 Dir of Institutional Effectiveness ... Mr. Henry HINKLE
76 Dean of Health Professions ... Dr. Tiffany BOHM
36 Director of Pioneer Career Center ... Ms. Marcia IRVINE
08 Director of the Learning Commons ... Ms. Amanda WILLIAMS
41 Director of Athletics ... Mr. Anthony (Tony) TOMPKINS
40 Director of Bookstore ... Mr. James GOWING
18 Director of Facility Services ... Mr. Chris GARDNER
19 Chief of Campus Police ... Chief Robert PUTZKE
14 Director of Computing Services ... Mr. Jim BENNETT
84 Dean of Student Services/Enrollment ... Dr. Shawn DERRITT
38 Director Counseling & Advocacy ... Ms. Linda WARNER
37 Director of Financial Aid ... Ms. Mary I. DORR

21 Controller .... Ms. Lesley STROHSCHEIN
92 Director of Honors/Phi Theta Kappa .... Dr. Stacy TUCKER
28 Equity/Inclusion & Multicul Center .... Vacant
24 Director Media Services Technology .... Mr. Randy ROYER
106 Director of Online Education .... Ms. Susan STUART
35 Director of Student Activities .... Ms. Andrica WILCOXEN
07 Interim Director of Admissions .... Ms. Emily BRATTIN
06 Registrar .... Ms. Theresa HOLLIDAY
15 Chief Human Resources Officer .... Ms. Christina MCGEE
88 Director Wellness Center .... Mr. Rob M. CRANE
66 Director of Nursing Education .... Ms. Susan ANDERSEN
72 Director Technical Programs .... Mr. Richard PIPER
72 Director Technical Programs Perkins .... Ms. Donna S. SHAWN
88 Director Performing Arts Center .... Mr. Gary MOSBY
04 Executive Admin Partner .... Ms. Risala ALLEN
105 Web Services .... Mr. Omar BRENES
22 Dir Affirmative Action/EEO .... Vacant
39 Student Resident Life Director .... Ms. Nicole WILBURN
102 Executive Director of Foundation .... Ms. Mary SPANGLER
25 Grant Coordinator II .... Ms. Connie NORTHUP
96 Purchasing Coordinator .... Ms. Linda BURGESS
108 Dean Academic Support/Assessment .... Ms. Cecelia BREWER

Kansas State University (A)

919 Mid-Campus Drive North, Manhattan KS 66506
County: Riley FICE Identification: 001928
Unit ID: 155399
Telephone: (785) 532-6250 Carnegie Class: DU-Highest
FAX Number: (785) 532-2120 Calendar System: Semester
URL: www.k-state.edu
Established: 1863 Annual Undergrad Tuition & Fees (In-State): $10,466
Enrollment: 20,854 Coed
Affiliation or Control: State IRS Status: 501(c)3
Highest Offering: Doctorate
Accreditation: HLC, ACPHA, #ARCPA, ART, CACREP, CAEPN, CEA, CIDA, CONST, DIETC, DIETD, IPSY, JOUR, LSAR, MFCD, MUS, PH, PLNG, SP, SPAA, SW, THEA, VET

01 President .... Dr. Richard H. LINTON
04 Exec Asst to the President .... Ms. Kristin J. HOLT
05 Provost & Executive Vice President .... Dr. Charles S. TABER
10 CFO & Dir Budget Planning .... Mr. Ethan E. ERICKSON
11 Int Vice President & COO .... Mr. Ethan E. ERICKSON
46 VP for Research .... Dr. David V. ROSOWSKY
32 VP Student Life/Dean of Students .... Dr. Thomas A. LANE
26 Int VP for Communications/Marketing .... Ms. Ashley N. MARTIN
15 VP Human Capital .... Mr. Jay W. STEPHENS
13 Chief Information Officer .... Dr. Gary L. PRATT
28 Int Chief Diversity/Inclusion Ofcr .... Dr. BeEtta L. STONEY
102 President/CEO of Foundation .... Mr. Greg WILLEMS
29 Alumni Association President .... Ms. Amy Button RENZ
41 Athletics Director .... Mr. Gene TAYLOR
43 General Counsel .... Ms. Shari F. CRITTENDON
100 Chief of Staff/Dir Community Rels .... Mr. Kevin J. NALETTE
86 Chief Governmental Rels Officer .... Dr. Susan K. PETERSON
88 Exec Dir Military/Veterans Affairs .... Dr. Arthur S. DE GROAT, II
84 Vice Provost Enrollment Mgmt .... Dr. Karen D. GOOS
121 Vice Provost Student Success .... Dr. Jeannie BROWN LEONARD
108 Int Assoc Prov Inst Effectiveness .... Dr. Tanya GONZALEZ
09 Assoc Prov Institutional Research .... Dr. Bin NING
22 Director Institutional Equity .... Ms. Stephanie LOTT
08 Dean of Libraries .... Dr. Joe MOCNIK
47 Dean of Agriculture .... Dr. J. Ernest MINTON
48 Dean Architecture/Planning & Design .... Mr. Timothy E. DE NOBLE
49 Int Dean of Arts & Sciences .... Dr. Christopher T. CULBERTSON
50 Dean of Business Admin .... Dr. Kevin P. GWINNER
106 Dean Global Campus .... Dr. Karen L. PEDERSEN
53 Dean of Education .... Dr. Debbie K. MERCER
54 Dean of Engineering .... Dr. Matt J. O'KEEFE
58 Vice Prov Grad Ed/Dean Grad School .... Dr. Claudia A. PETRESCU
59 Int Dean of Health & Human Science .... Dr. Craig A. HARMS
72 CEO/Dean Technology/Aviation .... Dr. Alysia H. STARKEY
74 Dean of Veterinary Medicine .... Dr. Bonnie R. RUSH
12 Dean & CEO K-State Olathe .... Dr. Jacqueline D. SPEARS
117 Univ Risk & Compliance Officer .... Mr. Elliot C. YOUNG
18 Assoc VP for Facilities .... Mr. Casey S. LAUER
19 Asst VP Univ Police & Public Safety .... Mr. Ronnie D. GRICE
96 Purchasing Manager .... Ms. Cathy OEHM
07 Exec Dir Recruitment/Admissions .... Ms. Tammy BYLAND
06 Registrar .... Ms. Kelley L. BRUNDAGE
37 Dir Student Fin Assistance .... Mr. Robert GAMEZ
39 Assoc VP Housing & Dining Svcs .... Mr. Derek A. JACKSON
36 Exec Director Career Center .... Dr. Kerri D. KELLER

Kansas State University Salina Aerospace and Technology Campus (B)

2310 Centennial Road, Salina KS 67401-8196
Telephone: (785) 826-2601 FICE Identification: 004611
Accreditation: &HLC, AAB

† Regional accreditation is carried under the parent institution in Manhattan, KS.

Kansas Wesleyan University (C)

100 E Claflin Avenue, Salina KS 67401-6196
County: Saline FICE Identification: 001929
Unit ID: 155414
Telephone: (785) 827-5541 Carnegie Class: Bac-Diverse
FAX Number: (785) 827-0927 Calendar System: Semester
URL: www.kwu.edu
Established: 1886 Annual Undergrad Tuition & Fees: $30,570
Enrollment: 803 Coed
Affiliation or Control: United Methodist IRS Status: 501(c)3
Highest Offering: Master's
Accreditation: HLC, NURSE, @SW

01 President and CEO .... Dr. Matthew R. THOMPSON
04 Executive Assistant to President .... Ms. Jan M. SHIRK
05 Provost .... Dr. Damon KRAFT
32 Vice President Student Development .... Ms. Bridget R. WEISER
10 Chief Finance Officer .... Ms. Rhonda BETHE
06 Registrar .... Mrs. Jasmin DAUNER
111 VP Advancement & Mktg/Admiss .... Mr. Kenneth OLIVER
37 Assoc Dir Student Financial Plng .... Ms. Michelle JENSEN
07 Director of Admissions .... Ms. Claire HOUK
88 Admin Assistant to EVP/Provost .... Ms. Jill KOSTER
121 Director of Student Success Center .... Mr. Bryan L. MCCULLAR
26 Director Marketing & Communications .... Mr. Brad SALOIS
08 Director of Library Services .... Ms. Kelley WEBER
24 Production Manager .... Mr. Paul GREEN
13 Director of Information Systems .... Mr. Justin TAYLOR
19 Director of Emergency Management .... Dr. Lonnie BOOKER
18 Director of Plant Operations .... Mr. John SWAGERTY
40 Manager of Yotee's .... Ms. Jennifer RYAN
42 Campus Minister .... Mr. Scott JAGODZINSKE
41 Athletic Director .... Mr. Steve WILSON
53 Director of Teacher Education .... Dr. Eileen ST. JOHN
79 Div Chair Humanities/Teach Educ .... Dr. Phil MECKLEY
76 Div Chair Nursing Educ & Health Sci .... Ms. Janeane HOUCHIN
83 Division Chair Social Sciences .... Dr. Steve HOEKSTRA
57 Division Chair Fine Arts .... Prof. Barbara J. NICKELL
81 Div Chair Natural Sciences/Math .... Dr. Dorothy HANNA
15 Human Resources Asst Director .... Ms. Becky MATHEWS
106 Academic Dean .... Dr. William BACKLIN
39 Resident Hall Director .... Mr. Charles STENNETT
29 Director Alumni Relations .... Vacant
25 Chief Contract & Grants Admin .... Ms. Melissa ANDERSON
38 Director Student Counseling .... Ms. Patsy STOCKHAM
28 Dir of Diversity & Student Success .... Dr. Allen D. SMITH

Labette Community College (D)

200 S 14th, Parsons KS 67357-4299
County: Labette FICE Identification: 001930
Unit ID: 155450
Telephone: (620) 421-6700 Carnegie Class: Assoc/MT-VT-Mix Trad/Non
FAX Number: (620) 421-0921 Calendar System: Semester
URL: www.labette.edu
Established: 1923 Annual Undergrad Tuition & Fees (In-District): $3,488
Enrollment: 1,464 Coed
Affiliation or Control: Local IRS Status: 501(c)3
Highest Offering: Associate Degree
Accreditation: HLC, ADNUR, COARC, DA, DMS, RAD

01 President .... Dr. Mark WATKINS
04 Executive Assistant to President .... Mrs. Heidi S. FLORA
05 Vice President Academic Affairs .... Dr. Jason SHARP
10 Vice President Finance & Operations .... Ms. Leanna J. DOHERTY
32 Vice President Student Affairs .... Ms. Tammy FUENTEZ
84 Dean of Enrollment Management .... Mrs. Theresa HUNDLEY
20 Dean of Instruction .... Dr. Kara WHEELER
13 Director of Information Technology .... Mrs. Jody BURZINSKI
08 Director of Library Services .... Mr. Scott M. ZOLLARS
18 Director of Physical Plant .... Mr. Kevin DOHERTY
66 Director of Nursing .... Mrs. Delyna BOHNENBLUST
41 Athletic Director .... Mr. Aaron J. KEAL
26 Director of Public Relations .... Mrs. Bethany KENDRICK
06 Assistant Registrar .... Ms. Cindy DYSON
15 Director of Human Relations .... Ms. Janice S. EVERY
37 Director Student Financial Aid .... Ms. Megan FUGATE
35 Student Life Coordinator .... Ms. Lauren HOLMES
40 Bookstore Specialist .... Ms. Tonya EVANS
103 Dir Workforce Educ/Career Training .... Mr. Ross HARPER
29 Dir Alumni Affairs/Resource Dev .... Mrs. Lindi FORBES
07 Director of Admissions .... Ms. Kylie LUCAS

Manhattan Area Technical College (E)

3136 Dickens Avenue, Manhattan KS 66503-2499
County: Riley FICE Identification: 005500
Unit ID: 155487
Telephone: (785) 587-2800 Carnegie Class: Assoc/HVT-High Non
FAX Number: (785) 587-2804 Calendar System: Semester
URL: www.manhattantech.edu
Established: 1965 Annual Undergrad Tuition & Fees (In-District): $7,440
Enrollment: 842 Coed
Affiliation or Control: State/Local IRS Status: 501(c)3
Highest Offering: Associate Degree
Accreditation: HLC, ADNUR, MLTAD

01 President/CEO .... Dr. James GENANDT
05 Vice Pres Student Success/CAO/CSSO .... Ms. Sarah PHILLIPS
11 Vice Pres Operations/CFO/CHRO .... Ms. Carmela JACOBS
13 Chief Information Security Officer .... Mr. Josh GFELLER
32 Dean Student Services .... Mr. Neil ROSS
75 Dean Career & Technical Education .... Mr. Nathan ROBERTS
06 Registrar .... Ms. Morgen STOECKLEIN
09 Dir Inst Reporting/Instruct Tech .... Ms. Kim WITHRODER
16 Human Resources Coordinator .... Ms. Jasmyn GRIFFIN
37 Director Financial Aid .... Ms. Laura WEISS-COOK

Manhattan Christian College (F)

1415 Anderson Avenue, Manhattan KS 66502-4081
County: Riley FICE Identification: 001931
Unit ID: 155496
Telephone: (785) 539-3571 Carnegie Class: Spec-4-yr-Faith
FAX Number: (785) 539-0832 Calendar System: Semester
URL: www.mccks.edu
Established: 1927 Annual Undergrad Tuition & Fees: $17,250
Enrollment: 170 Coed
Affiliation or Control: Christian Churches And Churches of Christ
IRS Status: 501(c)3
Highest Offering: Baccalaureate
Accreditation: HLC, BI

01 President .... Mr. J. Kevin INGRAM
05 Vice President for Academics .... Dr. Greg DELORT
10 VP for Financial & Admin Services .... Mr. Rob BERARD
32 Vice President for Student Life .... Dr. Rick L. WRIGHT
06 Registrar .... Ms. Jennifer ANDERSON
111 Director Institutional Advancement .... Mrs. Jolene K. RUPE
08 Director of Library Services .... Mr. Caleb MAY
41 Athletic Director .... Mr. Jordan STROM
29 Alumni Relations Director .... Mrs. Genae DENVER
04 Admin Asst to President .... Mrs. April WENDT
37 Director Student Financial Services .... Mrs. Trish RUNION
07 Director of Admissions .... Mr. Ben FIELD
13 Director of Information Technology .... Mr. JT VANGILDER
39 Director of Student Development .... Mr. Ben GROGG

McPherson College (G)

1600 E Euclid, PO Box 1402, McPherson KS 67460-1402
County: McPherson FICE Identification: 001933
Unit ID: 155511
Telephone: (620) 242-0400 Carnegie Class: Bac-Diverse
FAX Number: (620) 241-8443 Calendar System: 4/1/4
URL: www.mcpherson.edu
Established: 1887 Annual Undergrad Tuition & Fees: $31,154
Enrollment: 868 Coed
Affiliation or Control: Church Of The Brethren IRS Status: 501(c)3
Highest Offering: Master's
Accreditation: HLC, CAEP

01 President .... Mr. Michael P. SCHNEIDER
05 Provost/VP Academic Affairs .... Dr. Bruce CLARY
111 Vice President Advancement .... Mr. Roger BRIMMERMAN
10 Vice President for Finance .... Mr. Rick TUXHORN
84 VP Enrollment Management .... Ms. Christi HOPKINS
100 Chief of Staff .... Ms. Abby ARCHER-RIERSON
32 Director of Student Life .... Ms. Gabrielle WILLIAMS
36 Exec Director Career Services .... Ms. Amy BECKMAN
41 Athletic Director .... Mr. Andrew EHLING
06 Registrar .... Ms. Tricia HARTSHORN
37 Dir Financial Aid/Admissions Opers .... Ms. Sara BRUBAKER
08 Library Director .... Ms. Jaime MAKATCHE
26 Director of Public Relations .... Ms. Tina GOODWIN
15 Director Human Resources .... Mr. Marty SIGWING
29 Director Alumni Relations .... Ms. Monica RICE
18 Director of Facilities .... Mr. Marty SIGWING
07 Director of Admissions .... Mr. Josh HUBIN
09 Assoc Dean Inst Research/Assessment .... Ms. Cari LOTT
35 Operations Specialist Student Affs .... Mr. Justin WILTFONG

MidAmerica Nazarene University (H)

2030 E College Way, Olathe KS 66062-1899
County: Johnson FICE Identification: 007032
Unit ID: 155520
Telephone: (913) 782-3750 Carnegie Class: Masters/M
FAX Number: (913) 971-3290 Calendar System: Semester
URL: www.mnu.edu
Established: 1966 Annual Undergrad Tuition & Fees: $32,872
Enrollment: 1,636 Coed
Affiliation or Control: Church Of The Nazarene IRS Status: 501(c)3
Highest Offering: Master's
Accreditation: HLC, ACBSP, CACREP, CAEP, MUS, NURSE

01 President .... Dr. David J. SPITTAL
05 Vice Pres/Chief Academic Officer .... Dr. Nancy DAMRON
10 Vice President Finance .... Mr. Darrel ANDERSON
111 Vice Pres University Advancement .... Mr. Jon D. NORTH
32 Vice President Student Development .... Mr. Daniel RINCONES
46 Vice President Strategic Expansion .... Dr. Mark C. FORD
110 Assoc VP University Advancement .... Mr. Tim KEETON
42 University Chaplain .... Mr. Brady J. BRAATZ
13 Associate VP for Instructional Tech .... Dr. Martin CROSSLAND
09 Dir Institutional Effectiveness .... Dr. Jordan MANTHA
66 Dean School of Nursing .... Dr. Sarah MILLER
49 Dean College of Arts & Sciences .... Mr. Jamie MYRTLE
06 Registrar .... Mrs. Rhonda RILEY
08 Director Mabee Learning Commons .... Mr. Mark HAYSE
29 Director of Alumni Relations .... Mr. Pete S. BRUMBAUGH
37 Director of Student Financial Svcs .... Mr. Cathy L. COLAPIETRO
41 Athletic Director .... Mr. Todd L. GARRETT
15 Director of Human Resources .... Mr. Rich CLIFFE
18 Director of Facility Services .... Mr. Jon N. SPENCE
40 Director MERC/Postmaster .... Mr. Nikos KELLEPOURIS
19 Director of Campus Safety .... Mr. Richard M. PACHECO
121 Director Academic Success Center .... Ms. Giselle TAYLOR
04 Administrative Asst to President .... Mrs. Kelly GIBSON
103 Dir Workforce/Career Development .... Mrs. Linda ALEXANDER

104 Director Study Abroad .... Mr. James GARRISON
28 Coord Diversity/Cultural Competency .... Dr. Victoria HAYNES

Neosho County Community College (A)

800 W 14th Street, Chanute KS 66720-2699
County: Neosho FICE Identification: 001936
Unit ID: 155566
Telephone: (620) 431-2820 Carnegie Class: Assoc/HVT-Mix Trad/Non
FAX Number: N/A Calendar System: Semester
URL: www.neosho.edu
Established: 1935 Annual Undergrad Tuition & Fees (In-District): $5,032
Enrollment: 1,727 Coed
Affiliation or Control: Local IRS Status: 501(c)3
Highest Offering: Associate Degree
Accreditation: HLC, ACBSP, ADNUR, CAHIIM, OTA, SURGT

01 President .... Dr. Brian L. INBODY
05 Vice President Student Learning .... Dr. Sarah ROBB
11 Vice President for Operations .... Mr. Kerry RANABARGAR
10 Chief Financial Officer .... Ms. Sondra K. SOLANDER
103 Dean Outreach/Workforce Development ..... Ms. Brenda L. KRUMM
32 Dean of Student Services .... Ms. Kerrie COOMES
15 Director of Human Resources .... Ms. Karin JACOBSON
106 Dean for Ottawa & Online Campuses .... Dr. Marie GARDNER
13 Dean for Operations/CIO .... Vacant
30 Director of Development/Alumni Rels .... Ms. Kelly COLTER
08 Coordinator of Library Services .... Mr. Todd KNISPEL
37 Director Student Financial Aid .... Ms. Jennifer DAISY
66 Director of Nursing .... Ms. Pamela COVAULT
105 Dir of Tech Services/Webmaster .... Vacant
41 Athletic Director .... Ms. Riann MULLIS
85 Dir International Student Services .... Ms. Sarah CADWALLADER
06 Registrar .... Mr. Ryan ROSE
09 Coordinator/Institutional Research .... Ms. LuAnn HAUSER
40 Chanute Bookstore Coordinator .... Ms. Pamela EHMKE
26 Advertising/Media Coordinator .... Vacant
39 Director of Residence/Student Life .... Mr. Nick NOTHERN
04 AA to the President/Board Clerk .... Ms. Naomi REESE
18 Director of Facilities .... Mr. Devin DONALDSON
07 Director of Admissions .... Ms. Amy MORRIS

Newman University (B)

3100 McCormick, Wichita KS 67213-2097
County: Sedgwick FICE Identification: 001939
Unit ID: 155335
Telephone: (316) 942-4291 Carnegie Class: Masters/M
FAX Number: (316) 942-4483 Calendar System: Semester
URL: www.newmanu.edu
Established: 1933 Annual Undergrad Tuition & Fees: $33,000
Enrollment: 2,053 Coed
Affiliation or Control: Roman Catholic IRS Status: 501(c)3
Highest Offering: Doctorate
Accreditation: HLC, ANEST, CAEP, COARC, NURSE, OTA, RAD, SW

01 President .... Dr. Kathleen S. JAGGER
05 Vice Pres Academic Affairs .... Dr. Alden STOUT
10 VP Finance & Administration .... Mr. Anthony BEATA
84 VP Enrollment Mgt & Student Success .... Ms. Christine SCHNEIKART-LUEBBE
32 Vice Pres Student Affairs .... Vacant
20 Assoc VP Academic Affairs .... Dr. Jill FORT
42 Director of Campus Ministry .... Fr. Adam GRELINGER
29 Director of Alumni Relations .... Ms. Dana BEITEY
41 Director of Athletics .... Ms. Joanna PRYOR
08 Library Director .... Mr. Steve HAMERSKY
06 Registrar .... Ms. Lori A. GIBBON
37 Director of Financial Aid .... Ms. Myra PFANNENSTIEL
40 Director of Bookstore .... Vacant
13 Chief Information Officer .... Mr. Icer VAUGHAN
19 Director of Security .... Mr. Morris FLOYD
15 Director of Human Resources .... Vacant
21 Controller .... Ms. Diana GRIBLIN
39 Director Residence Life .... Vacant
35 Dean of Students .... Dr. Sara MATA
49 Dean of Arts & Sciences .... Dr. Lori STEINER
58 Dean School of Catholic Studies .... Fr. Joseph GILE
50 Interim Dean School of Business .... Fr. Joseph GILE
53 Interim Dean of Educ & Social Work .... Ms. Jessica BIRD
104 Director Study Abroad .... Dr. Cheryl GOLDEN
26 Director University Relations .... Mr. Clark SCHAFER
18 Chief Facilities/Plant .... Mr. Paco GONZALEZ
09 Director of Institutional Research .... Mr. William GRAVES
44 Director of Annual Giving .... Ms. Laura HARTLEY
04 Executive Asst/Sec of the Corp .... Ms. Gabrielle DODOSH
28 Director of Diversity .... Vacant

North Central Kansas Technical College (C)

PO Box 507, Beloit KS 67420-0507
County: Mitchell FICE Identification: 005265
Unit ID: 155593
Telephone: (785) 738-2276 Carnegie Class: Assoc/HVT-Mix Trad/Non
FAX Number: (785) 738-2903 Calendar System: Semester
URL: www.ncktc.edu
Established: 1964 Annual Undergrad Tuition & Fees (In-District): $7,324
Enrollment: 843 Coed
Affiliation or Control: State/Local IRS Status: 501(c)3
Highest Offering: Associate Degree
Accreditation: HLC, ADNUR

01 President .... Mr. Eric BURKS
10 VP of Finance & Hays Operations .... Ms. Diana BAUMANN
05 VP Student & Instructional Services .... Mr. Corey ISBELL
20 Dean of Instruction .... Ms. Jennifer BROWN
06 Registrar .... Ms. Judy HEIDRICK
32 Dean of Student Experience .... Mr. Shane BRITT
37 Financial Aid Director .... Ms. Leah BERGMANN
04 Administrative Asst to President .... Ms. Lois HANEL
102 Director of Advancement .... Ms. Mendi ANSCHUTZ
13 Chief Info Technology Officer (CIO) .... Mr. Robert MCCREIGHT
121 Dean of Student Success .... Ms. Jayme OWEN
26 Marketing Director .... Ms. Chandra FELDMAN
84 Dean of Enrollment Mgmt .... Ms. Tricia CLINE

North Central Kansas Technical College (D)

2205 Wheatland Avenue, Hays KS 67601
Telephone: (785) 625-2437 Identification: 770259
Accreditation: &HLC

Northwest Kansas Technical College (E)

1209 Harrison Street, PO Box 668,
Goodland KS 67735-3441
County: Sherman FICE Identification: 005267
Unit ID: 155618
Telephone: (785) 890-3641 Carnegie Class: Assoc/HVT-Mix Trad/Non
FAX Number: (785) 899-5711 Calendar System: Semester
URL: www.nwktc.edu
Established: 1964 Annual Undergrad Tuition & Fees (In-District): N/A
Enrollment: 676 Coed
Affiliation or Control: State/Local IRS Status: 501(c)3
Highest Offering: Associate Degree
Accreditation: HLC, COARC, MAC

01 President .... Mr. Ben SCHEARS
05 Dean of Academic Advancement .... Ms. Lisa BLAIR
11 Vice President of Operations .... Mrs. Sherri KNITIG
13 Vice Pres for Information Tech .... Mr. Brad BERGSMA
07 Director of Admissions .... Mrs. Mandy GARRETT
41 Athletic Director .... Mr. Rory KLING
30 Director of Endowment/Career Svcs .... Mrs. Kelly JAMES

Ottawa University (F)

1001 S Cedar Street, Ottawa KS 66067-3399
County: Franklin FICE Identification: 001937
Unit ID: 155627
Telephone: (785) 242-5200 Carnegie Class: Bac-Diverse
FAX Number: (785) 229-1020 Calendar System: Semester
URL: www.ottawa.edu
Established: 1865 Annual Undergrad Tuition & Fees: $32,180
Enrollment: 797 Coed
Affiliation or Control: American Baptist IRS Status: 501(c)3
Highest Offering: Doctorate
Accreditation: HLC, ACBSP, CAEP, NURSE

00 University President & CEO .... Dr. Bill TSUTSUI
02 President .... Dr. Reggies WENYIKA
05 University Provost & CAO .... Dr. Terry HAINES
10 VP & Chief Financial Officer .... Mr. Craig KISPERT
111 Vice President Advancement .... Ms. Janet PETERS
06 University Registrar .... Mrs. Margaret HERRON
26 Director Marketing/Board Operations .... Mrs. Lara BOYD
21 Controller & Dir Fiscal Operations .... Mr. Thomas CORLEY
15 Director Human Resources .... Ms. Joanna WALTERS
29 Director Alumni Programs .... Ms. Courtney KLAUS
08 Director Library Services .... Ms. Gloria CREED-DIKEOGU
41 Director Athletics .... Ms. Arabie CONNER
18 Director of Facilities .... Mr. David BIRD
20 Acting Academic Dean .... Dr. Kevin MARET
53 Dean School of Education .... Dr. Amy HOGAN
84 Director of Admissions & Enrollment .... Mr. Andy OTTO
50 Dean School of Business .... Dr. Marylou DEWALD
49 Dean School of Arts & Sciences .... Dr. Karen OHNESORGE
88 Associate VP University Compliance .... Ms. Carrie STEVENS
13 Director Software Solutions .... Ms. Brandi SERVAES
35 Dean of Student Life & Services .... Mr. Donald ANDERSON
44 Director Annual Giving .... Ms. Nori HALE
104 Dean Study Abroad Program .... Dr. Marylou DEWALD
106 Director Instr Design/Academic Tech .... Dr. Carine ULLOM
19 Safety/Security Supervisor .... Mr. Kevin MOORE
36 Career Services Coordinator .... Dr. Christine CURRIER
38 Director Student Counseling .... Ms. Angela SPRUILL
90 Chief Technical Officer .... Mr. Adam CAYLOR
37 Director Student Financial Aid .... Ms. Mary REED

† The Online division is included in the institution's enrollment count.

Ottawa University Overland Park, KS (G)

4370 W. 109th Street, Suite 200,
Overland Park KS 66211-1302
Telephone: (913) 266-8600 Identification: 666083
Accreditation: &HLC

† Regional accreditation is carried under the parent institution in Ottawa, KS.

Pittsburg State University (H)

1701 S Broadway, Pittsburg KS 66762-7500
County: Crawford FICE Identification: 001926
Unit ID: 155681
Telephone: (620) 231-7000 Carnegie Class: Masters/L
FAX Number: (620) 235-4080 Calendar System: Semester
URL: www.pittstate.edu
Established: 1903 Annual Undergrad Tuition & Fees (In-State): $7,504
Enrollment: 6,398 Coed
Affiliation or Control: State IRS Status: 501(c)3
Highest Offering: Doctorate
Accreditation: HLC, CAEP, CAPRT, CEA, MUS, NURSE, SW

01 President .... Dr. Daniel SHIPP
05 Provost & VP for Academic Affairs .... Dr. Howard SMITH
11 CFO & VP Administration .... Mr. Doug BALL
111 VP University Advancement .... Ms. Kathleen FLANNERY
06 Registrar .... Ms. Melinda ROELFS
32 VP Student Life .... Dr. Steve ERWIN
26 Chief Marketing & Comm Officer .... Ms. Abigail FERN
49 Dean of Arts & Sciences .... Dr. Mary Carol POMATTO
50 Dean of Business .... Dr. Paul GRIMES
53 Dean of Education .... Dr. James TRUELOVE
72 Dean of Technology .... Dr. Robert FRISBEE
08 Dean of Library Services .... Mr. Randy ROBERTS
108 Director of Assessment .... Ms. Nora HATTON
27 Director of Media Relations .... Ms. Andra STEFANONI
29 Dir Alumni Rels/Constituent Svcs .... Dr. Jon A. BARTLOW
13 Chief Information Officer .... Ms. Angela NERIA
15 Director Human Resource Services .... Ms. Lori DREILING
85 Director of International Programs .... Mr. Aaron HURT
45 Chief Strategy Officer .... Dr. Shawn NACCARATO
88 Director of Building Trades .... Mr. Tom AMERSHEK
18 Director of Services & Grounds .... Mr. Tim SENECAUT
19 Director of University Police .... Mr. Stu HITE
22 Director of Institutional Equity .... Ms. Lori DREILING
37 Director of Financial Aid .... Mr. Scott DONALDSON
41 Director Intercollegiate Athletics .... Mr. Jim JOHNSON
07 Director of Admissions .... Mr. Scott DONALDSON
36 Director Career Services .... Ms. Jaime DALTON
09 Director of Institutional Research .... Mr. Bill HOYT
96 Director of Purchasing .... Mr. Jim HUGHES
28 Senior Diversity Officer .... Ms. Deatrea ROSE
10 Controller .... Ms. Barbara J. WINTER
39 Director of University Housing .... Mr. Tom WESTHOFF
100 Chief of Staff .... Ms. Katie GEORGE
43 General Counsel .... Dr. Jamie BROOKSHER
30 Exec Director of Univ Development .... Ms. Becky MCDANIEL
114 Director of Budget .... Ms. Barbara WINTER
25 Chief Grants Administrator .... Ms. Cindy JOHNSON
122 Pgm Coord Fraternity/Sorority Life .... Vacant
44 Director Annual Giving .... Ms. Kati KARLESKINT

Pratt Community College (I)

348 NE SR 61, Pratt KS 67124-8432
County: Pratt FICE Identification: 001938
Unit ID: 155715
Telephone: (620) 672-2700 Carnegie Class: Assoc/MT-VT-High Non
FAX Number: (620) 450-2283 Calendar System: Semester
URL: www.prattcc.edu
Established: 1938 Annual Undergrad Tuition & Fees (In-District): $3,780
Enrollment: 1,164 Coed
Affiliation or Control: State/Local IRS Status: 501(c)3
Highest Offering: Associate Degree
Accreditation: HLC, ACBSP

01 President .... Dr. Mike CALVERT
05 Vice President Instruction .... Ms. Monette DEPEW
10 Vice President Finance/Operations .... Mr. Kent ADAMS
84 Vice Pres Student Enroll Management .... Ms. Lisa MILLER
30 Exec Director of Inst Advancement .... Mr. Barry FISHER
41 Director of Athletics .... Mr. Tim SWARTZENDRUBER
07 Director of Admissions .... Ms. Elizabeth BRITTON
06 Registrar .... Ms. Caitlin MILLER
13 Chief Information Officer .... Mr. Jerry SANKO
37 Director of Financial Aid .... Ms. Rose FRAME
08 Dir Linda Hunt Memorial Library .... Mr. Frank STAHL
15 Director of Personnel .... Ms. Rita PINKALL
21 Controller .... Ms. Christy WRIGHT
18 Director of Buildings & Grounds .... Mr. Al WIESE
39 Director of Residence Life .... Mr. Brad LUTHE
04 Administrative Asst to President .... Ms. Donna MEIER PFEIFER
29 Director Alumni Relations .... Mr. Barry FISHER
108 Director of Planning & Assessment .... Vacant
09 Director of Institutional Research .... Ms. Lisa KOLM
26 Chief Public Relations/Marketing .... Ms. Audra ROGERS
36 Director Student Placement .... Ms. Amy JACKSON

Rasmussen University-Kansas City/Overland Park (J)

11600 College Boulevard, Suite 100,
Overland Park KS 66210
Telephone: (913) 491-7870 Identification: 770489
Accreditation: &HLC, ADNUR

† Regional accreditation carried under the parent institution in Saint Cloud, MN. The tuition figure is an average, actual tuition may vary.

Saint Paul School of Theology (A)

13720 Roe Avenue, Building C, Leawood KS 66224
County: Johnson FICE Identification: 002509
Unit ID: 179317
Telephone: (913) 253-5000 Carnegie Class: Spec-4-yr-Faith
FAX Number: (913) 253-5075 Calendar System: Semester
URL: www.spst.edu
Established: 1958 Annual Graduate Tuition & Fees: N/A
Enrollment: 101 Coed
Affiliation or Control: United Methodist IRS Status: 501(c)3
Highest Offering: Doctorate; No Undergraduates
Accreditation: HLC, THEOL

01 President .... Rev. Neil B. BLAIR
05 VP Academic Affairs/Dean .... Dr. Sharon BETSWORTH
111 Vice President for Inst Advancement .... Mr. Jay SIMMONS
32 Associate Dean of Students .... Rev. Margaretta S. NARCISSE
06 Registrar/Dir of Financial Aid .... Ms. Michelle HATCHER
07 Director of Admissions .... Ms. Shannon HANCOCK
26 Director of Communications .... Mrs. Heather SNODGRASS
08 Librarian .... Mr. Richard LIANTONIO
10 CFO/COO .... Mr. Matthew MILLS

Salina Area Technical College (B)

2562 Centennial Road, Salina KS 67401
County: Saline FICE Identification: 005499
Unit ID: 155830
Telephone: (785) 309-3100 Carnegie Class: Assoc/HVT-High Non
FAX Number: (785) 309-3101 Calendar System: Semester
URL: www.salinatech.edu
Established: 1965 Annual Undergrad Tuition & Fees (In-District): $8,127
Enrollment: 697 Coed
Affiliation or Control: State/Local IRS Status: 501(c)3
Highest Offering: Associate Degree
Accreditation: HLC, DA, DH

01 President .... Mr. Gregory A. NICHOLS
05 Vice Pres of Instruction .... Mr. Stanton GARTIN
11 Vice Pres of Administrative Service .... Mrs. Jamie PALENSKE
32 Vice Pres of Student Services .... Mrs. Jennifer CALLIS
09 Director of Inst Research/Registrar .... Mrs. Denise R. HOEFFNER
15 Human Resources Coordinator .... Mrs. Tamera WILCOX
18 Director of Maintenance .... Mr. Dale CASTILLO
102 Exec Dir of SATC Foundation .... Vacant
84 Director Enrollment Management .... Vacant
37 Student Financial Aid Specialist .... Mrs. Racheal GALVAN
06 Registrar .... Mrs. Paige AYLWARD

Seward County Community College (C)

1801 N Kansas Avenue, Liberal KS 67901-2054
County: Seward FICE Identification: 008228
Unit ID: 155858
Telephone: (620) 624-1951 Carnegie Class: Assoc/HVT-Mix Trad/Non
FAX Number: (620) 417-1169 Calendar System: Semester
URL: www.sccc.edu
Established: 1967 Annual Undergrad Tuition & Fees (In-District): $3,648
Enrollment: 1,580 Coed
Affiliation or Control: State/Local IRS Status: 501(c)3
Highest Offering: Associate Degree
Accreditation: HLC, ADNUR, COARC, MLTAD, SURGT

01 Interim President .... Mr. Dennis SANDER
10 VP of Finance & Operations .... Mr. Dennis M. SANDER
05 Vice President of Academic Affairs .... Mr. Luke DOWELL
32 Vice President of Student Services .... Ms. Celeste DONOVAN
13 Chief Information Officer .... Mr. Louie S. LEMERT
06 Registrar .... Ms. Alaina M. RICE
26 Exec Dir of Marketing & PR .... Ms. Rachel C. COLEMAN
25 Executive Director of Grant Development .... Ms. Charity HORINEK
30 Chief Development Officer .... Mr. Kyle WOODROW
41 Director of Athletics .... Mr. Dan ARTAMENKO
04 Executive Assistant .... Ms. Karla MORALES
76 Dean of Allied Health .... Dr. Suzanne CAMPBELL
51 Dean Industrial Tech/Cont Educ .... Vacant
35 Dean of Students .... Ms. Annette HACKBARTH-ONSON
15 Director of Human Resources .... Ms. Charlotte PETERSON
09 Institutional Research/Data Analyst .... Ms. Teresa WEHMEIER
19 Security Supervisor/Asst DOF .... Mr. Wendall WEHMEIER
18 Director of Facilities .... Mr. Roger SCHEIB
39 Director of Student Living Center .... Ms. Jennifer L. MALIN
78 Director of Outreach .... Mr. Mike BAILEY
35 Dir of Student Life & Leadership .... Mr. Wade LYON
37 Director of Financial Aid .... Ms. Amy BRIDENSTINE
66 Director of Nursing .... Ms. Susan INGLAND
84 Director of Admissions .... Mr. Eric D. VOLDEN
50 Director of Business & Industry .... Mrs. Norma Jean DODGE
08 Director of Library Services .... Ms. Casandra NORIN
14 Network Administrator .... Mr. Doug BROWNE
40 Director of Bookstore .... Ms. Laci FURR
91 Systems Administrator .... Mr. Cecil STOLL
105 Website Specialist .... Mr. Craig DUSEK
07 Director of Admissions .... Mr. Eric VOLDEN
44 Assoc Director Annual Giving .... Ms. Sara THOMPSON

Southwestern College (D)

100 College Street, Winfield KS 67156-2499
County: Cowley FICE Identification: 001940
Unit ID: 155900
Telephone: (620) 229-6000 Carnegie Class: Bac-Diverse
FAX Number: (620) 229-6224 Calendar System: Semester
URL: www.sckans.edu
Established: 1885 Annual Undergrad Tuition & Fees: $33,250
Enrollment: 1,413 Coed
Affiliation or Control: United Methodist IRS Status: 501(c)3
Highest Offering: Doctorate
Accreditation: HLC, CAEP, MUS

01 President .... Dr. Elizabeth FROMBGEN
84 EVP for Enrollment .... Mr. Dean CLARK
05 VP Acad Affairs/Dean of the College .... Dr. Ross PETERSON-VEATCH
10 Vice President Finance/CFO .... Mr. Tony CROUCH
124 VP Student Retention & Success .... Dr. Dawn E. PLEAS
45 Exec Dir Institute for Discipleship .... Dr. Stephen K. WILKE
111 Vice Pres Institutional Advancement .... Vacant
26 VP Marketing/Communications .... Ms. Kaydee RIGGS-JOHNSON
32 VP Student Life/Dean Students .... Mr. Dan FALK
29 Director Alumni Programs .... Ms. Ashleigh HOLLIS
08 Library Director .... Vacant
37 Director Financial Aid .... Ms. Brenda D. HICKS
06 Registrar .... Ms. Sarah HALLINAN
41 Director of Athletics .... Ms. Jamie ADAMS
15 Director Human Resources .... Ms. Lonnie BOYD
04 Exec Asst to President .... Ms. Doreen FAST
42 Campus Minister .... Rev. Molly JUST
07 Assoc VP of Admissions .... Ms. Stephannie DELONG
19 Director Security/Safety .... Ms. Teresa NICHOLS
39 Dir Resident Life/Student Housing .... Mr. Jonathan AFFALTER

Sterling College (E)

125 W Cooper Street, Sterling KS 67579-1533
County: Rice FICE Identification: 001945
Unit ID: 155937
Telephone: (620) 278-2173 Carnegie Class: Bac-Diverse
FAX Number: N/A Calendar System: 4/1/4
URL: www.sterling.edu
Established: 1887 Annual Undergrad Tuition & Fees: $27,300
Enrollment: 678 Coed
Affiliation or Control: Presbyterian IRS Status: 501(c)3
Highest Offering: Master's
Accreditation: HLC, CAATE

01 President .... Dr. Scott RICH
05 Vice President Academic Affairs .... Dr. Ken BROWN
111 Vice President for Inst Advancement .... Mr. David EARLE
32 Vice President Student Life .... Mr. Jason BRIAR
11 Vice Pres Admin/Inst Initiatives .... Mr. David LANDIS
07 Vice President Enrollment .... Ms. Mitzi SUHLER
41 Vice President of Athletics .... Mr. Scott DOWNING
10 CFO/Financial Services .... Ms. Michelle HALL
20 Assoc Vice Pres Academic Affairs .... Dr. Erin LAUDERMILK
04 Exec Assistant to the President .... Ms. Renee DODSON
41 Assoc VP Athletics/Facility Mgmt .... Mr. Justin MORRIS
26 Dir Marketing/Pres Communications .... Mr. Brad EVENSON
37 Asst Director of Financial Aid .... Ms. Sara HIATT
06 Registrar .... Ms. Kendra GRIZZLE
29 Director of Alumni .... Ms. Susie CARNEY
42 Chaplain/AVP Student Life .... Mr. Paul BRANDES
08 Library Director .... Ms. Laurel WATNEY
36 Director of Career Services .... Mr. Terry EHRESMAN
15 Director Human Resources/Title IX .... Ms. Angie PLETT
04 Administrative Asst to President .... Vacant
30 Director of Development .... Mr. Aaron WEBER

Tabor College (F)

400 S Jefferson Street, Hillsboro KS 67063-1753
County: Marion FICE Identification: 001946
Unit ID: 155973
Telephone: (620) 947-3121 Carnegie Class: Bac-Diverse
FAX Number: (620) 947-2607 Calendar System: 4/1/4
URL: www.tabor.edu
Established: 1908 Annual Undergrad Tuition & Fees: $32,100
Enrollment: 642 Coed
Affiliation or Control: Mennonite Brethren Church IRS Status: 501(c)3
Highest Offering: Master's
Accreditation: HLC, MUS, NURSE, SW

01 President .... Dr. David JANZEN
05 Exec VP of Academics & Compliance .... Dr. Frank JOHNSON
10 Vice President Business/CFO .... Dr. Michael JAMES
111 Vice President Advancement .... Mr. Ronald BRAUN
11 Exec VP of Operations .... Mr. Rusty ALLEN
32 Dean of Student Life .... Mr. Emir RUIZ-ESPARZA
06 Registrar .... Mr. Scott FRANZ
08 Director of Library Services .... Ms. Janet WILLIAMS
37 Assoc Director of Financial Aid .... Ms. Cathy CASTLE
29 Director Alumni Relations .... Mr. Rod HAMM
26 Director of Communications .... Vacant
18 Director Facilities/Physical Plant .... Mr. Terry ENS
121 Director Student Success .... Mrs. Erica KRUCKENBERG
09 Institutional Research .... Mr. David FABER
13 Director IT Infrastructure .... Mr. Chris GLANZER
14 Director of IT Operations .... Mr. Wayne KLIEWER
15 Personnel/Benefits Manager .... Ms. Misty SMITHSON
04 Admin Assistant to the President .... Mrs. Miriam KLIEWER
07 Dean of Enrollment Mgmt .... Mr. Grant MYERS
36 Director Student Placement .... Mrs. Sydney FOUNTAIN

University of Kansas Main Campus (G)

1450 Jayhawk Boulevard, Room 230,
Lawrence KS 66045-7518
County: Douglas FICE Identification: 001948
Unit ID: 155317
Telephone: (785) 864-3131 Carnegie Class: DU-Highest
FAX Number: (785) 864-4120 Calendar System: Semester
URL: www.ku.edu
Established: 1866 Annual Undergrad Tuition & Fees (In-State): $11,166
Enrollment: 26,744 Coed
Affiliation or Control: State IRS Status: 501(c)3
Highest Offering: Doctorate
Accreditation: HLC, ABAI, ART, CAEP, CEA, CLPSY, COPSY, HSA, IPSY, JOUR, LAW, MPCAC, MUS, PH, PHAR, PLNG, SCPSY, SP, SPAA, SW

01 Chancellor .... Dr. Douglas A. GIROD
05 Provost/Exec Vice Chancellor .... Dr. Barbara BICHELMEYER
12 Exec Vice Chancellor - KUMC .... Dr. Robert SIMARI
10 Exec Vice Chancellor & CFO .... Mr. Jeffrey DEWITT
46 Vice Chancellor Research .... Dr. Simon ATKINSON
26 Vice Chanc Strategic Initiatives .... Vacant
43 General Counsel & Vice Chancellor .... Mr. Brian WHITE
116 Vice Chanc & Chief Audit Executive .... Mr. John A. CURRAN
100 Chief of Staff to Chancellor .... Ms. Julie N. MURRAY
32 Vice Provost for Student Affairs .... Dr. Tammara DURHAM
22 Vice Chanc Office of Civil Rights .... Vacant
15 Vice Provost for Administration .... Mr. Michael ROUNDS
20 Vice Provost Faculty Development .... Dr. Christopher BROWN
28 Acting Vice Provost DEIB .... Dr. Nicole HODGES PERSLEY
86 Assoc Vice Chanc State Relations .... Ms. Kelly WHITTEN
84 Vice Provost Enrollment Management .... Dr. Matt MELVIN
88 University Architect .... Mr. Mark REISKE
13 Chief Information Officer .... Dr. Mary WALSH
21 Vice Provost for Finance .... Mr. Jason HORNBERGER
30 President Endowment Association .... Mr. Dale SEUFERLING
29 President Alumni Association .... Mr. Heath J. PETERSON
104 Assoc VP International Affairs .... Dr. Charles BANKART
07 Director Admissions .... Ms. Lisa P. KRESS
06 University Registrar/Asst VP .... Ms. Tiffany ROBINSON
09 Chief Data Ofcr Analytics/Research .... Mr. Nick STEVENS
85 Interim Dir Intl Student Services .... Dr. Roberta POKPHANH
38 Director Counseling/Psych Services .... Dr. Michael MAESTAS
37 Director Financial Aid/Scholarships .... Ms. Angela KARLIN
36 Exec Director Career Center .... Mr. David GASTON
21 Sr Dir Financial Analysis/Reporting .... Ms. Katrina M. YOAKUM
41 Director Intercollegiate Athletics .... Mr. Travis GOFF
18 Director Facilities Service .... Mr. Shawn HARDING
93 Interim Dir Multicultural Affairs .... Ms. Jordan BRANDT
23 Medical Director Watkins Health .... Dr. Graig NICKEL
14 Dir Info Tech Business Operations .... Mr. Chris CROOK
39 Director Student Housing .... Ms. Sarah WATERS
92 Director Honors Program .... Dr. Sarah CRAWFORD-PARKER
40 Director KU Bookstore .... Ms. Jen O'CONNOR
51 Exec Dir Continuing Education .... Ms. Sharon D. GRAHAM
25 Assoc Dir Contract Negotiations .... Ms. Lucille MARINO
63 Exec Dean School of Medicine .... Dr. Akinlolu OJO
12 Dean of Edwards Campus .... Dr. Stuart DAY
49 Interim Dean Liberal Arts/Science .... Dr. John COLOMBO
61 Dean of Law .... Mr. Stephen W. MAZZA
54 Dean of Engineering .... Dr. Arvin AGAH
48 Dean Architecture & Design .... Dr. Mahbub RASHID
50 Dean of Business .... Dr. L. Paige FIELDS
67 Dean of Pharmacy .... Dr. Ron E. RAGAN
60 Dean of Journalism .... Dr. Ann M. BRILL
53 Dean of Education .... Dr. Rick GINSBERG
64 Dean of Music .... Dr. Robert L. WALZEL, JR.
70 Dean of Social Welfare .... Dr. Michelle CARNEY
08 Dean Libraries .... Mr. Kevin L. SMITH
19 Police Chief .... Mr. Nelson MOSLEY
122 Pgm Dir Sorority/Fraternity Life .... Ms. Sony HEATH

† Medical Center and Main campus enrollments should be combined for the total institution enrollment.

University of Kansas Medical Center (H)

3901 Rainbow Boulevard, Kansas City KS 66160-0001
Telephone: (913) 588-5000 FICE Identification: 024579
Accreditation: &HLC, ANEST, AUD, CAHIIM, CAMPEP, COARC, DIETI, DMOLS, DMS, IPSY, MED, MIDWF, MLS, NMT, NURSE, OT, PDPSY, PTA

† Enrollment at the Medical Center is included within the published enrollment for the University of Kansas Main Campus. Regional accreditation is carried under the parent institution in Lawrence, KS.

University of Saint Mary (I)

4100 S 4th Street, Leavenworth KS 66048-5082
County: Leavenworth FICE Identification: 001943
Unit ID: 155812
Telephone: (913) 682-5151 Carnegie Class: Masters/M
FAX Number: (913) 758-6140 Calendar System: Semester
URL: www.stmary.edu
Established: 1923 Annual Undergrad Tuition & Fees: $30,800
Enrollment: 1,229 Coed
Affiliation or Control: Roman Catholic IRS Status: 501(c)3
Highest Offering: Doctorate
Accreditation: HLC, CAATE, CAEP, CAHIIM, IACBE, NURSE, PTA, @SW

01 President .... Sr. Diane STEELE

05 Provost & Academic Vice President ...... Dr. Michelle METZINGER
10 VP Finance & Administrative Svcs ...... Ms. Nancy BRAMLETT
07 VP Admissions & Marketing ...... Mr. John SHULTZ
111 VP for Advancement ...... Mr. Mark BLANCK
41 VP of Athletics ...... Mr. Rob MILLER
32 VP for Student Life ...... Mr. Bob SCHUCHARDT
20 Academic Dean ...... Dr. Gwen LANDEVER
06 Registrar ...... Ms. Maureen SCHUCHARDT
09 Institutional Research & Assessment ...... Ms. Christine HAMILTON
26 Director of Marketing Operations ...... Ms. Sara BELL-BRITTON
37 Director of Financial Aid ...... Ms. Heidi REID
42 Campus Minister ...... Mr. Jude HUNTZ
112 Development Officer Planned Giving ...... Ms. Jane LIEBERT
15 Director Human Resources ...... Ms. Michelle CARMITCHEL
121 Director Keleher Learning Commons ...... Ms. Ashley CREEK
21 Controller ...... Ms. Nicole BIBLER
38 Campus Counselor ...... Dr. Christina DUNN CARPENTER
18 Director of Plant Operations ...... Mr. Mauricio RODRIGUEZ
40 Bookstore Manager ...... Ms. Cynthia FORRESTER
13 Director of Information Services ...... Mr. Marvin SOMMERFELD
04 Executive Administrative Assistant ...... Ms. Sharron LUCAS
19 Public Safety Coordinator ...... Ms. Adriana HABR
106 Educational Technologist ...... Vacant
29 Alumni Relations Manager ...... Ms. Alicia OTTO
30 Development Manager/Special Events ...... Ms. Kylie ADAMS

Washburn University (A)

1700 SW College Avenue, Topeka KS 66621-0001
County: Shawnee FICE Identification: 001949
Unit ID: 156082
Telephone: (785) 670-1010 Carnegie Class: Masters/M
FAX Number: (785) 670-1089 Calendar System: Semester
URL: www.washburn.edu
Established: 1865 Annual Undergrad Tuition & Fees (In-District): $8,762
Enrollment: 5,880 Coed
Affiliation or Control: Local IRS Status: 501(c)3
Highest Offering: Doctorate
Accreditation: HLC, ART, CAEP, CAHIIM, CEA, COARC, DMS, LAW, MUS, NURSE, OTA, PTAA, RAD, RTT, SURGT, SW

01 President ...... Dr. Jerry B. FARLEY
05 Interim Vice Pres Academic Affairs ...... Dr. Laura STEPHENSON
10 Vice Pres Admin & Treasurer ...... Mr. Luther G. LEE, IV
32 Vice President for Student Life ...... Dr. Eric GROSPITCH
04 Special Assistant to the President ...... Ms. Cynthia HOLTHAUS
84 Exec Director Enrollment Management ...... Dr. Richard W. LIEDTKE
43 University Legal Counsel ...... Mr. Marc FRIED
35 Assoc Vice Pres of Student Life ...... Mr. Joel BLUML
20 Assoc Vice Pres Acad Affairs ...... Dr. Jennifer BALL
102 President WU Foundation ...... Mr. Marshall MEEK
06 Registrar ...... Ms. Stephanie LANNING
08 Dean of Libraries ...... Dr. Alan BEARMAN
37 Director Student Financial Aid ...... Mr. Andy FOGEL
07 Director of Admissions ...... Mr. Joseph TINSLEY
15 Director of Human Resources ...... Ms. Teresa LEE
13 CIO/Int Dir Info Systems & Services ...... Mr. John HAVERTY
09 Director Strategic Analysis & Rep ...... Ms. Christa SMITH
49 Interim Dean College Arts/Sciences ...... Dr. Matt ARTERBURN
88 Dean School Applied Studies ...... Dr. Zach FRANK
61 Interim Dean School of Law ...... Dr. Jeffrey JACKSON
50 Dean School of Business ...... Dr. David SOLLARS
66 Dean School of Nursing ...... Dr. Jane CARPENTER
41 Director of Athletics ...... Mr. Loren FERRE
22 Director Equal Opportunity ...... Dr. Michelle GODINET
18 Director of Facility Services ...... Mr. Eric JUST
23 Director Health Services ...... Ms. Tiffany MCMANUS
29 Alumni Association Director ...... Ms. Susie HOFFMANN
39 Director Student Housing ...... Ms. Molly PIERSON
40 Director Ichabod Shop ...... Ms. Brielle BARRETT
35 Dir Student Involvement/Development ...... Mr. Isaiah COLLIER
38 Director Student Counseling ...... Ms. Crystal LEMING
26 Director of University Relations ...... Mr. Patrick EARLY
36 Director Career Services ...... Mr. Kent MCANALLY
19 Director of Police ...... Mr. Chris ENOS
28 Dir of Diversity & Inclusion ...... Ms. Danielle DEMPSEY-SWOPES
96 Director of Purchasing ...... Ms. Kathy PFLAUM

Wichita State University (B)

1845 N Fairmount, Wichita KS 67260-0001
County: Sedgwick FICE Identification: 001950
Unit ID: 156125
Telephone: (316) 978-3456 Carnegie Class: DU-Higher
FAX Number: (316) 978-3770 Calendar System: Semester
URL: www.wichita.edu
Established: 1895 Annual Undergrad Tuition & Fees (In-State): $8,433
Enrollment: 14,999 Coed
Affiliation or Control: State IRS Status: 501(c)3
Highest Offering: Doctorate
Accreditation: HLC, ARCPA, ART, AUD, CAATE, CACREP, CAEP, CLPSY, COSMA, DANCE, DENT, DH, MLS, MUS, NURSE, PTA, SP, SPAA, SW

01 President ...... Dr. Richard D. MUMA
05 Exec VP & Provost ...... Dr. Shirley LEFEVER
10 VP Administration & Finance ...... Mr. Werner M. GOLLING
32 VP Student Affairs ...... Dr. Teri HALL
43 General Counsel ...... Ms. Stacia BODEN
26 VP Strategic Communications ... Ms. Shelly COLEMAN-MARTINS
09 Chief Data Officer ...... Dr. David WRIGHT
84 Assoc VP Enrollment Management ...... Dr. Carolyn SHAW
20 Assoc VP Academic Affairs ...... Dr. Linnea GLENMAYE
46 VP Research & Technology Transfer ...... Dr. John S. TOMBLIN
28 Vice President for Diversity ...... Dr. Marche FLEMING-RANDLE
49 Dean Liberal Arts & Sciences ...... Dr. Andrew HIPPISLEY
50 Dean Barton School of Business ...... Dr. Larisa GENIN
53 Interim Dean Education ...... Dr. Clay STOLDT
54 Dean Engineering ...... Dr. Anthony MUSCAT
57 Dean Fine Arts ...... Dr. Rodney E. MILLER
76 Dean Health Professions ...... Dr. Greg HAND
58 Dean Graduate School ...... Dr. Coleen PUGH
08 Dean Libraries ...... Ms. Kathy DOWNES
86 Exec Director Government Relations ...... Mr. Andrew SCHLAPP
24 Dir Media Resources Center ...... Mr. John JONES
102 CEO & President WSU Foundation ...... Ms. Elizabeth H. KING
41 Director of Athletics ...... Mr. Kevin SAAL
15 Exec Director Human Resources ...... Ms. Judy ESPINOZA
114 Director Budgets ...... Mr. David MILLER
06 Registrar ...... Ms. Gina D. CRABTREE
07 Director Admissions ...... Mr. Bobby GANDU
37 Exec Director Financial Aid ...... Ms. Sheelu M. SURENDER
38 Director Counseling & Testing ...... Dr. Jessica PROVINES
18 Director Physical Plant ...... Mr. Eason BRYER
45 Director of Facilities Planning ...... Ms. Emily A. PATTERSON
19 Chief of University Police ...... Mr. Guy SCHROEDER
23 Director Student Health Services ...... Ms. Heather STAFFORD
39 Director Stdnt Housing & Resid Life ...... Mr. Scott JENSEN
88 Director Diversity & Inclusion ...... Ms. Alicia SANCHEZ
40 Manager Bookstore ...... Mr. Kevin J. KONDA
21 Assoc VP Financial Operations ...... Mr. Troy BRUNN
96 Director of Purchasing ...... Mr. Steven WHITE
29 Executive Director Alumni Assoc ...... Ms. Courtney MARSHALL
106 Executive Dir Online Learning ...... Ms. Anna PORCARO
22 Title IX Coordinator ...... Ms. Lucretia TAYLOR
105 Director Web Services ...... Mr. Tim HART
30 VP for Development ...... Mr. Darin KATER
44 Director Annual/Planned Giving ...... Mr. Michael LAMB
108 Director Institutional Assessment ...... Vacant
122 Dir Greek Relations/Programming ...... Vacant
04 Admin Assistant to the President ...... Ms. Susan JOHNSON
100 Chief of Staff ...... Mr. Zach GEARHART

Wichita State University Campus of Applied Sciences and Technology (C)

4004 N Webb Road, Wichita KS 67226-8101
County: Sedgwick FICE Identification: 005498
Unit ID: 156107
Telephone: (316) 677-9400 Carnegie Class: Assoc/HVT-High Non
FAX Number: (316) 677-9510 Calendar System: Semester
URL: https://wsutech.edu/
Established: 1965 Annual Undergrad Tuition & Fees (In-District): $6,602
Enrollment: 4,606 Coed
Affiliation or Control: State/Local IRS Status: 501(c)3
Highest Offering: Associate Degree
Accreditation: HLC, DA, SURGT

01 President ...... Dr. Sheree UTASH
05 Chief of Academic Affairs ...... Mr. Scott LUCAS
10 Vice Pres Finance/Administration ...... Ms. Marlo DOLEZAL
20 VP General Educ/Applied Tech ...... Dr. Jennifer SEYMOUR
32 Vice President Student Services ...... Mr. Justin PFEIFER
26 Exec Dir Strategic Communications ...... Mr. Andy MCFAYDEN
13 Exec Dir Information Tech ...... Mr. Randy ROEBUCK
15 Exec Director Human Resources ...... Ms. Judy MOUNT
09 Exec Dir Institutional Research ...... Ms. Kristen JOHNSTON

KENTUCKY

Alice Lloyd College (D)

100 Purpose Road, Pippa Passes KY 41844-9703
County: Knott FICE Identification: 001951
Unit ID: 156189
Telephone: (606) 368-2101 Carnegie Class: Bac-Diverse
FAX Number: (606) 368-6212 Calendar System: Semester
URL: www.alc.edu
Established: 1923 Annual Undergrad Tuition & Fees: $14,230
Enrollment: 569 Coed
Affiliation or Control: Independent Non-Profit IRS Status: 501(c)3
Highest Offering: Baccalaureate
Accreditation: SC

01 President ...... Dr. James O. STEPP
00 Chancellor ...... Dr. Joe A. STEPP
05 Vice President Academic Affairs ...... Dr. Charles MARSHALL
10 Business Manager ...... Mr. Jessie WILKS
32 Vice President Student Affairs ...... Mr. Scott CORNETT
07 Director of Admissions ...... Mrs. Mary TURNER
06 Registrar ...... Ms. Kala THORNSBURY
08 Director of Library ...... Ms. Jeannie GALLOWAY
37 Director of Financial Aid ...... Mr. Joseph LITTLE
88 Director of Student Work Program ...... Mr. Kerry RATLIFF
53 Director of Teacher Education ...... Mrs. Katrina SLONE
18 Director of Physical Plant ...... Mr. Ryan GIBSON
39 Director of Student Housing ...... Mr. John MILLS
29 Director of Alumni Relations ...... Mrs. Teresa GRENDER
121 Student Success Coordinator ...... Mrs. Christine STUMBO
26 Dir of Marketing & Communications ...... Ms. Jennifer HALL
09 Director of Institutional Research ...... Mrs. Katrina SLONE
30 Director of Development ...... Mrs. Allison SOUTHARD
102 Dir Foundation/Corporate Relations ...... Ms. Crystal JONES

41 Athletic Director ...... Mr. David HATFIELD
15 Human Resources Manager ...... Mr. Larry ADAMS
84 Director Enrollment Management ...... Mrs. Tori NAIRN

† Cost of tuition is guaranteed for students from 108 county territories.

American National University (E)

50 National College Boulevard, Pikeville KY 41501
County: Pike FICE Identification: 010489
Unit ID: 157021
Telephone: (606) 478-7200 Carnegie Class: Spec-4-yr-Other Health
FAX Number: (606) 437-4952 Calendar System: Quarter
URL: www.an.edu
Established: 1941 Annual Undergrad Tuition & Fees: $11,136
Enrollment: 210 Coed
Affiliation or Control: Proprietary IRS Status: Proprietary
Highest Offering: Baccalaureate
Accreditation: ABHES

01 Campus Director ...... Mr. James C. HESS

American National University (F)

4205 Dixie Highway, Louisville KY 40216
Telephone: (502) 447-7634 Identification: 666443
Accreditation: ABHES

† Branch campus of American National University, Pikeville, KY.

Asbury Theological Seminary (G)

204 N Lexington Avenue, Wilmore KY 40390-1199
County: Jessamine FICE Identification: 001953
Unit ID: 156222
Telephone: (859) 858-3581 Carnegie Class: Spec-4-yr-Faith
FAX Number: N/A Calendar System: 4/1/4
URL: www.asburyseminary.edu
Established: 1923 Annual Graduate Tuition & Fees: N/A
Enrollment: 1,755 Coed
Affiliation or Control: Independent Non-Profit IRS Status: 501(c)3
Highest Offering: Doctorate; No Undergraduates
Accreditation: SC, CACREP, THEOL

01 President ...... Dr. Timothy C. TENNENT
05 Provost/SVP of Academic Affairs ...... Dr. Gregg OKESSON
10 Vice Pres Finance/Admin/CFO ...... Mr. Bryan P. BLANKENSHIP
111 Vice President of Advancement ...... Mr. Jay MANSUR
88 Vice President Formation ...... Ms. Donna COVINGTON
84 Vice Pres Enrollment Management ...... Mr. Kevin BISH
20 Associate Provost ...... Dr. Christine L. JOHNSON
12 Assoc VP of Florida Campus ...... Mr. Steve GOBER
06 Registrar ...... Vacant
07 Director of Admissions ...... Mr. Randy OZAN
37 Director of Student Financial Aid ...... Ms. Rachael TUBB
18 Director of Facilities & Security ...... Mr. Brian U'REN
09 Dir Inst Effectiveness/Assessment ...... Dr. Alexandra H. ANDERSON
15 Director of Human Resources ...... Mrs. Barbara ANTROBUS
29 Director Alumni/Church Relations ...... Ms. Tammy CESSNA
73 Dean School of Theology & Formation ...... Dr. James THOBABEN
88 Dean ESJ School World of Missions ...... Dr. Gregg OKESSON
88 Dean School Biblical Interpretation ...... Dr. David BAUER
73 Dean Beeson Sch Practical Theology ...... Dr. Tom TUMBLIN
46 Dean Advanced Research Programs ...... Dr. Lalsangkima PACHUAU
04 Executive Asst to President ...... Ms. Angela CLOYD
08 Dean Library Info & Tech Services ...... Dr. Paul A. TIPPEY

Asbury University (H)

1 Macklem Drive, Wilmore KY 40390-1198
County: Jessamine FICE Identification: 001952
Unit ID: 156213
Telephone: (859) 858-3511 Carnegie Class: Masters/S
FAX Number: (859) 858-3921 Calendar System: Semester
URL: www.asbury.edu
Established: 1890 Annual Undergrad Tuition & Fees: $32,028
Enrollment: 1,741 Coed
Affiliation or Control: Independent Non-Profit IRS Status: 501(c)3
Highest Offering: Beyond Master's But Less Than Doctorate
Accreditation: SC, CAEPN, MUS, SW

01 President ...... Dr. Kevin J. BROWN
05 Provost ...... Dr. Timothy T. WOOSTER
10 VP Business Affairs & Treasurer ...... Mr. Glenn R. HAMILTON
32 VP Student Life & Dean of Students ...... Dr. Sarah T. BALDWIN
111 VP Inst Advance/Strat Partnerships ...... Dr. Mark J. TROYER
41 VP Athletics & Strategic Comms ...... Mr. Mark H. WHITWORTH
20 Vice Provost ...... Dr. Timothy G. CAMPBELL
50 Dean Howard Dayton Sch Business ...... Dr. Michael J. KANE
60 Dean of School of Comm Arts ...... Dr. James R. OWENS
53 Dean School of Education ...... Dr. Sharon G. BIXLER
81 Dean School Science/Health & Math ...... Dr. Vins H. SUTLIVE
49 Dean College of Arts & Sciences ...... Dr. Stephen K. CLEMENTS
07 Director of Admissions ...... Mr. Brandon J. COMBS
08 Director of Library Services ...... Mr. Jared L. PORTER
09 AVP Inst Research & Effectiveness ...... Dr. Paul STEPHENS
21 AVP Business Affairs ...... Mr. Gary E. HOWARD
13 AVP Information Tech Svcs/CIO ...... Mr. Paul J. DUPREE
15 Director of HR/Risk Mgt ...... Mr. Gregory R. MCGEE
19 Director of Safety & Security ...... Mr. David P. HAY
18 Director of Physical Plant ...... Mr. Eric C. MCMILLION
37 Director of Financial Aid ...... Mr. Ron M. ANDERSON

42 Assoc Dean for Spiritual Life ....Rev. Greg K. HASELOFF
85 AVP Intercultural Affairs ....Rev. Esther D. JADHAV
39 Assoc Dean for Community Life ....Mr. Joe W. BRUNER
36 Assoc Dean of Career & Calling ....Ms. Michelle B. KRATZER
38 Assoc Dean of Wholeness & Wellness ......Mr. Kevin M. BELLEW
112 Senior Planned Giving Officer ....Rev. Stuart A. SMITH
29 Director of Alumni Relations ....Ms. Lisa D. HARPER
26 Director Strategic Communications ....Mrs. Jennifer J. MCCHORD
06 Registrar ....Mrs. Sheryl VOIGTS
40 Manager of Bookstore ....Mr. C. David TRAMMELL
23 Director Student Health Services ....Mrs. Heidi L. SUNNY
04 Exec Assistant to the President ....Ms. Michelle C. BUTCHER

ATA College (A)

10200 Linn Station Road, Suite 125, Louisville KY 40223
County: Jefferson FICE Identification: 040383
Unit ID: 447935
Telephone: (502) 371-8383 Carnegie Class: Spec 2-yr-Health
FAX Number: (502) 371-8598 Calendar System: Quarter
URL: www.ata.edu
Established: 1994 Annual Undergrad Tuition & Fees: $13,120
Enrollment: 298 Coed
Affiliation or Control: Proprietary IRS Status: Proprietary
Highest Offering: Associate Degree
Accreditation: ABHES

01 President/CEO ....Mr. Donald A. JONES

Baptist Seminary of Kentucky (B)

400 E. College Street, Box 358, Georgetown KY 40324
County: Scott Identification: 667211
Telephone: (502) 863-8300 Carnegie Class: Not Classified
FAX Number: (502) 863-8300 Calendar System: Semester
URL: www.bsk.edu
Established: 2002 Annual Graduate Tuition & Fees: N/A
Enrollment: N/A Coed
Affiliation or Control: Independent Non-Profit IRS Status: 501(c)3
Highest Offering: Master's; No Undergraduates
Accreditation: THEOL

01 President ....Dr. David CASSADY
05 Academic Dean ....Dr. Dalen C. JACKSON
07 Director of Admissions ....Ms. Abby SIZEMORE
06 Registrar/Academic Coordinator ....Ms. Jessalynn CORNETT

Beckfield College (C)

16 Spiral Drive, Florence KY 41042-4866
County: Boone FICE Identification: 024911
Unit ID: 247065
Telephone: (859) 371-9393 Carnegie Class: Spec-4-yr-Other Health
FAX Number: (859) 371-5096 Calendar System: Quarter
URL: www.beckfield.edu
Established: 1984 Annual Undergrad Tuition & Fees: $13,295
Enrollment: 748 Coed
Affiliation or Control: Proprietary IRS Status: Proprietary
Highest Offering: Baccalaureate
Accreditation: ABHES, CNEA, NURSE

01 President/CFO ....Ms. Diane G. WOLFER
05 Vice Pres Education & Accreditation ....Mr. Lee FOLEY
37 Director Student Financial Services ....Mr. Jeff HUBER
13 Vice Pres Information Technology ....Mr. Charles WILSON
07 Director Admissions ....Mr. Jeff BAKER
36 Director Career Services ....Ms. Karen SHELDON
22 Director of Compliance ....Mr. Lee FOLEY
06 Registrar ....Ms. Jocelyn ROY
08 Director of Library Services ....Ms. Gayle ECABERT
50 Dean of Business/Technology ....Dr. Erica OKERE
66 Dean of Nursing ....Dr. Deborah SMITH-CLAY
76 Dean of Allied Health ....Ms. Kate BEHAN
97 Dean of General Education ....Ms. Mindy HODGES
88 Dean of Criminal Justice ....Ms. Brandy EXELER

Bellarmine University (D)

2001 Newburg Road, Louisville KY 40205-0671
County: Jefferson FICE Identification: 001954
Unit ID: 156286
Telephone: (502) 272-8000 Carnegie Class: DU-Mod
FAX Number: (502) 272-8033 Calendar System: Semester
URL: www.bellarmine.edu
Established: 1950 Annual Undergrad Tuition & Fees: $43,470
Enrollment: 3,293 Coed
Affiliation or Control: Independent Non-Profit IRS Status: 501(c)3
Highest Offering: Doctorate
Accreditation: SC, CAATE, CAEP, COARC, MLS, NURSE, PTA, RTT

01 President ....Dr. Susan M. DONOVAN
03 Senior Vice President ....Dr. Sean J. RYAN
05 Provost/Vice Pres Academic Affairs ....Dr. Paul GORE
20 Vice Provost ....Dr. Mark WIEGAND
10 Vice President for Admin & Finance ....Mr. Daniel FROCKT
32 Vice President for Student Affairs ....Dr. Helen G. RYAN
30 VP for Dev & Alumni Relations ....Vacant
84 VP for Enrollment/Marketing & Comm ....Dr. Mike MARSHALL
04 Administrative Asst to President ....Ms. Calene BALDWIN
50 Dean School of Business ....Dr. Daniel PETREE
53 Dean Annsley Frazier Thornton Educ ....Dr. Elizabeth DINKINS
49 Dean Bellarmine College ....Dr. Mary HUFF
66 Dean Nursing & Clinical Sciences ....Dr. Christy KANE
75 Dean Movement & Rehabilitation Sci ....Dr. Tony BROSKY
15 Chief Human Resources Officer ....Ms. Dana HUMMEL
21 Asst VP Business Affairs ....Ms. Denise BROWN-CORNELIUS
110 Associate VP Development ....Vacant
35 Associate VP Student Affairs ....Mr. Patrick ENGLERT
85 Dir Study Abroad & Intl Programs ....Dr. Mary Aurora GRANDINETTI
35 Dean of Students ....Dr. Leslie MAXIE
92 Director Honors Program ....Dr. Jonathan W. BLANDFORD
41 Athletic Director ....Mr. Scott P. WIEGANDT
18 Asst VP Facilities Management ....Mr. Jeffrey DEAN
123 Dean of Graduate Admission ....Dr. Sara Y. PETTINGILL
08 Director of the Library ....Dr. John K. STEMMER
19 Director of Safety & Security ....Ms. Debbie FOX
06 Registrar ....Ms. Ann E. OLSEN
96 Purchasing Assistant ....Ms. Sherry PILE
42 Director Campus Ministry ....Vacant
39 Dir Housing and Residence Life ....Dr. Lindsey GILMORE
76 Vice Prov Col of Health Professions ....Dr. Mark WIEGAND
13 Chief Information Officer ....Mr. Eric SATTERLY
28 Chief Div/Equity/Inclusion Ofcr ....Dr. Tomarra ADAMS
37 Director Student Financial Aid ....Ms. April TRETTER
36 AVP for Career & Cmty Engagement ... Dr. Elizabeth M. CASSADY
29 Assistant VP for Alumni Relations ....Mr. Peter W. KREMER
26 Director of Media Relations ....Mr. Jason A. CISSELL
38 Director of Counseling Center ....Dr. Gary PETIPRIN
09 Director of Institutional Research ....Vacant
45 Vice Provost for Inst Effectiveness ....Dr. James BRESLIN
100 Chief of Staff ....Dr. Angela RONE

Berea College (E)

101 Chestnut Street, Berea KY 40404-0003
County: Madison FICE Identification: 001955
Unit ID: 156295
Telephone: (859) 985-3000 Carnegie Class: Bac-A&S
FAX Number: N/A Calendar System: Semester
URL: www.berea.edu
Established: 1855 Annual Undergrad Tuition & Fees: $45,092
Enrollment: 1,432 Coed
Affiliation or Control: Independent Non-Profit IRS Status: 501(c)3
Highest Offering: Baccalaureate
Accreditation: SC, CAEP, NURSE

01 President ....Dr. Lyle D. ROELOFS
10 Vice President Finance ....Mr. Jeff S. AMBURGEY
29 VP Alumni/Comm/Philanthropy ....Dr. Chad BERRY
32 VP Labor and Student Life ....Dr. Channell BARBOUR
11 VP Operations and Sustainability ....Mr. Derrick SINGLETON
05 Provost ....Dr. Scott STEELE
45 VP Strategic Initiatives ....Ms. Teri THOMPSON
28 VP Diversity/Equity/Inclusion ....Dr. Dwayne MACK
20 Dean of the Faculty ....Dr. Matthew SADERHOLM
20 Associate Provost ....Dr. Eileen MCKIERNAN GONZALEZ
26 Assoc VP for Marketing/Comm ....Ms. Kim BROWN
30 AVP Philanthropic Operations ....Ms. Candis ARTHUR
35 Asst Vice Pres for Student Life ....Mr. Gus GERASSIMIDES
37 Dir of Student Financial Aid Svcs ....Ms. Andrea SPRY
38 Dir Counseling/Psychological Svcs ....Ms. Sue REIMONDO
112 Senior AVP for Philanthropy ....Ms. Teresa KASH DAVIS
108 Director of Academic Assessment ....Dr. Robert SMITH
13 Chief Information Officer ....Mr. Phillip LOGSDON
07 AVP of Admissions Operations ....Mr. Luke HODSON
88 Associate VP for Alumni Relations ....Ms. Jackie COLLIER
15 Associate VP of Human Resources ....Mr. Steve LAWSON
18 Assoc Director of Facilities Mgmt ....Mr. Jeff REED
88 Director of Appalachian Center ....Dr. Chris GREEN
09 Interim Dir Inst Rsrch/Assessment ....Ms. Clara CHAPMAN
27 Dir Publications/Media Relations ....Ms. Abbie DARST
08 Director of Library Services ....Mr. Calvin GROSS
41 Director of Athletics ....Mr. Ryan HESS
42 Dean of the Chapel ....Rev. LeSette WRIGHT
43 General Counsel ....Mr. Judge WILSON
19 Director of Public Safety ....Mr. Brad COLE
88 Director Black Cultural Center ....Ms. Kristina GAMBLE
88 Dean of Labor ....Mr. Collis ROBINSON
85 Director International Center ....Dr. Richard CAHILL
40 Retail Manager College Store ....Ms. Sarah CAUDILL
96 Purchasing Manager ....Ms. Aurelia BRANDENBURG
88 Director Ctr Teaching/Learning ... Ms. Leslie ORTQUIST-AHRENS
88 Director Woodson Center ....Dr. Jessica KLANDERUD
88 Director of CELTS ....Ms. Ashley COCHRANE
23 Director of Health and Wellness ....Ms. Jill GURTATOWSKI
88 Director of Internships ....Ms. Esther LIVINGSTON
103 Director of Career Development ....Ms. Amanda TUDOR
104 Education Abroad Advisor ....Ms. Kathryn KING
06 Registrar ....Ms. Judy GINTER
100 Executive Assistant to President ....Ms. Judy MOTT
105 Director Web Design/Development .... Mr. Charlie CAMPBELL
04 Executive Assistant to President ....Ms. Sherry THIELE
102 Dir Foundation Rels/Corporations ....Ms. Jenny AKINS
112 Exec Dir Planned Philanthropy ....Ms. Amy HARMON
89 Dir Student Success/Transition ....Dr. Chris LAKES
88 Director Bell Hooks Center .... Dr. M Shadee MALAKLOU
39 Asst Dir Housing ....Ms. Hannah TOLLIVER
44 Director Annual Giving ....Ms. Johanna HALL-RAPPOLEE

Brescia University (F)

717 Frederica Street, Owensboro KY 42301-3023
County: Daviess FICE Identification: 001958
Unit ID: 156356
Telephone: (270) 685-3131 Carnegie Class: Bac-Diverse
FAX Number: (270) 686-6422 Calendar System: Semester
URL: www.brescia.edu
Established: 1950 Annual Undergrad Tuition & Fees: $25,100
Enrollment: 986 Coed
Affiliation or Control: Roman Catholic IRS Status: 501(c)3
Highest Offering: Master's
Accreditation: SC, @SP, SW

01 President ....Rev. Larry HOSTETTER
03 Executive VP/Chief of Staff ....Dr. Lauren MCCRARY
05 Vice President & Academic Dean ....Mr. Jeffrey BARNETTE
10 Sr Vice President Business/Finance ....Mr. Dale CECIL
84 Sr VP of Enrollment ....Mr. Christopher HOUK
111 VP Institutional Advancement ....Ms. Sydney WARREN
32 Int VP of Stdnt Affs/Dean Students ....Mrs. Patricia LOVETT
39 Director Residence Life ....Vacant
35 Director Stdnts Act/Leadership Dev ....Mr. Isaac DUNCAN
06 Registrar ....Sr. Helena FISCHER, OSU
106 Director of Operations BU Online ....Ms. Shanda LARUE
38 Director of Counseling Center ....Ms. Eva G. ATKINSON
08 Director of Library Services ....Sr. Judith N. RINEY, OSU
88 Director of UCTL ....Dr. Anna KUTHY
15 Director of Human Resources ....Ms. Tammy S. KELLER
13 Director of Information Technology ....Mr. Chris FORD
18 Director of Physical Plant ....Mr. Mike WARD
37 Director of Financial Aid ....Ms. Kristi EIDSON
41 Director of Athletics ....Ms. Sarah GAYLER
26 Director of Public Relations ....Ms. Rachel WHELAN
29 Director of Alumni & Donor Rels ....Mr. Jake DAVIS
44 Director of Annual Giving ....Ms. Lauren OSOWICZ
112 Director of Major Gifts ....Ms. Sydney WARREN
09 Director of Institutional Research ....Ms. Stephanie CLARY
58 Director of Graduate Program-MBA ....Dr. Sandra O. OBILADE
42 Director of Campus Ministry ....Sr. Pam MUELLER, OSU
07 Director of Admissions ....Ms. Christy ROHNER
21 Asst Director Business & Finance ....Ms. Nancy W. REYNOLDS
36 Director of Career Services ....Ms. Morgan RUSSELBURG
20 Associate Academic Dean ....Ms. Amanda MORRIS
40 Bookstore Manager ....Ms. Megan MCCARTHY
19 Director Security/Safety ....Mr. Nick SPINKS

Campbellsville University (G)

1 Universty Drive, Campbellsville KY 42718-2799
County: Taylor FICE Identification: 001959
Unit ID: 156365
Telephone: (270) 789-5000 Carnegie Class: Masters/L
FAX Number: (270) 789-5050 Calendar System: Semester
URL: www.campbellsville.edu
Established: 1906 Annual Undergrad Tuition & Fees: $25,400
Enrollment: 12,771 Coed
Affiliation or Control: Baptist IRS Status: 501(c)3
Highest Offering: Doctorate
Accreditation: SC, CAEP, IACBE, MFCD, MUS, NUR, SW

01 President ....Dr. Joseph HOPKINS
11 SVP for Operations/Administration ....Mr. Otto TENNANT
05 Provost and VP for Academic Affairs ....Dr. Donna HEDGEPATH
30 Vice President for Development ....Dr. Benji KELLY
84 VP for Enrollment ....Dr. Shane GARRISON
32 VP for Student Svcs/Athletics ....Mr. Rusty HOLLINGSWORTH
20 Associate Academic Officer ....Dr. Jeanette PARKER
10 Vice President for Finance ....Mr. Tim JUDD
09 Director of Institutional Research ....Mrs. Anna PAVY
38 Director of Student Counseling ....Ms. Erin JARRETT
92 Director of Honors Program ....Dr. Craig L. ROGERS
40 Director of Bookstore ....Vacant
42 Director of Campus Ministries ....Mr. Jamie LAWRENCE
13 Director of Computing/Communication ....Mr. Eric SMITH
37 Director of Financial Aid ....Mrs. Robyn SOLLBERGER
29 Director of Alumni Relations ....Mrs. Ashley FOX
08 Director of Library Services ....Mrs. Kay ALSTON
15 Director of Personnel Services ....Mr. Jason LAWSON
18 Director of Maintenance ....Mr. Steve MORRIS
26 Director of News Information ....Mrs. Joan C. MCKINNEY
06 Registrar ....Mrs. Rita A. CREASON
04 Director for Presidential Operation ....Mrs. Kellie VAUGHN
96 Director of Purchasing ....Mrs. Lisa FERGUSON
88 Director of Custodial Services ....Mr. Bob STOTTS
19 Director Security/Safety ....Mr. Kyle DAVIS
35 Dean of Students ....Mr. Rusty WATKINS
39 Director of Residence Life ....Mr. Elijah COFFEY
86 Director Government Relations ....Dr. John CHOWNING
28 Director of Diversity ....Dr. Carey RUIZ
41 Athletic Director ....Mr. Jim HARDY

Centre College (H)

600 W Walnut Street, Danville KY 40422-1394
County: Boyle FICE Identification: 001961
Unit ID: 156408
Telephone: (859) 238-5200 Carnegie Class: Bac-A&S
FAX Number: (859) 238-6977 Calendar System: Other
URL: www.centre.edu
Established: 1819 Annual Undergrad Tuition & Fees: $44,300
Enrollment: 1,333 Coed
Affiliation or Control: Independent Non-Profit IRS Status: 501(c)3
Highest Offering: Baccalaureate
Accreditation: SC

01 President ....Dr. Milton C. MORELAND
05 Vice Pres Acad Affs/Dean of College ....Dr. Ellen S. GOLDEY

10 Vice Pres/CFO & Treasurer ... Mr. Brian G. HUTZLEY
32 Vice Pres for Student Life ... Ms. Barbara LOMONACO
30 VP Devel/Alumni Engagement ... Ms. Kelly KNETSCHE
43 VP for Legal Affairs/Gift Planning ... Mr. James P. LEAHEY
15 VP for Human Resources/Admin Svcs ... Mrs. Kay L. DRAKE
26 VP for Strategic Marketing/Comm ... Ms. Sarah NOLAN
53 Assoc Professor/Chair Education ... Dr. Sarah A. MURRAY
28 VP Diversity/Equity/Inclusion ... Dr. Andrea C. ABRAMS
45 Exec Dir Strategic Int & Ext Rels ... Mrs. Lesley S. BILBY
20 Associate Dean of the College ... Dr. Alex M. MCALLISTER
38 Director of Counseling Services ... Ms. Ann E. GOODWIN
104 Director of Global Citizenship ... Dr. Lori L. HARTMANN
08 Director of Library Services ... Ms. Carolyn A. FREY
37 Assoc Dean/Dir of Financial Aid ... Mr. Kevin D. LAMB
06 Registrar ... Mr. Thomas E. MANUEL
36 Dir Ctr for Career/Professional Dev ... Ms. Joy ASHER
39 Director Student Life & Housing ... Ms. Ann S. YOUNG
41 Director of Athletics & Recreation ... Mr. W. Bradley FIELDS
19 Director of Public Safety ... Mr. Kevin S. MILBY
09 Director of Institutional Research ... Ms. Katherine M. ANDREWS
13 Chief Information Officer ... Mr. Andrew J. RYAN
24 Dir Ctr for Teaching/Learning ... Ms. Nisha GUPTA
18 Director of Facilities Management ... Mr. Scott MESSER
21 Controller ... Mr. R. Scott OWENS
42 College Chaplain ... Mr. Jason CROSBY
96 Dir Procurement/Capital Projects ... Ms. Ann T. SMITH
29 Dir of Alumni & Family Engagement ... Ms. Megan H. MILBY
57 Director Norton Center for Arts ... Mr. Steven A. HOFFMAN
102 Dir Foundation/Corporate Relations ... Ms. Elizabeth E. GRAVES
122 Director of Greek Life ... Ms. Amanda PEARCE

Clear Creek Baptist Bible College (A)

300 Clear Creek Road, Pineville KY 40977-9754

County: Bell FICE Identification: 025356
Unit ID: 156417
Telephone: (606) 337-3196 Carnegie Class: Spec-4-yr-Faith
FAX Number: (606) 337-2372 Calendar System: Semester
URL: www.ccbbc.edu
Established: 1926 Annual Undergrad Tuition & Fees: $9,870
Enrollment: 131 Coed
Affiliation or Control: Southern Baptist IRS Status: 501(c)3
Highest Offering: Master's
Accreditation: SC, BI

01 President ... Dr. Donnie S. FOX
05 Academic Dean ... Dr. Jay SULFRIDGE
10 Director of Business Affairs ... Ms. Monique BAILEY
11 Administrative Dean ... Mr. Eric J. GREENE
111 Dean of Institutional Advancement ... Mr. Matthew BLACK
08 Director of Library Svcs ... Ms. Andrea FOX
42 Director Christian Service ... Rev. Joshua SMITH
18 Director of Physical Plant ... Mr. Allen SANDERS
37 Director Financial Aid ... Mr. Eddie BARKER
06 Registrar ... Dr. Jared STYLES
07 Director of Admissions ... Mr. Taylor HALEY
26 Director of College Relations ... Mr. Michael DELAND
13 Dir of Information Technologies ... Mr. Eric GREENE
56 Coord of Distance Education ... Mr. David DOWELL

Eastern Kentucky University (B)

521 Lancaster Avenue, Richmond KY 40475-3102

County: Madison FICE Identification: 001963
Unit ID: 156620
Telephone: (859) 622-1000 Carnegie Class: DU-Mod
FAX Number: (859) 622-2196 Calendar System: Semester
URL: www.eku.edu
Established: 1906 Annual Undergrad Tuition & Fees (In-State): $9,876
Enrollment: 14,465 Coed
Affiliation or Control: State IRS Status: 501(c)3
Highest Offering: Doctorate
Accreditation: SC, ADNUR, CAATE, CACREP, CAEP, CAHIIM, CAPRT, CLPSY, CONST, DIETD, EMT, FEPAC, IFSAC, MLS, MUS, NAIT, NURSE, OT, PH, SP, SPAA, SW

01 President ... Dr. David MCFADDIN
05 Provost/Exec VP Acad Affairs ... Dr. Sara ZEIGLER
20 Associate Provost ... Dr. Jennifer WIES
10 Senior VP of Finance & Admin ... Mr. Barry POYNTER
121 SVP Student Success/Inst Effective ... Dr. Tanlee WASSON
30 VP Univ Devel & Alumni Engagement ... Ms. Betina GARDNER
31 Assoc VP Univ Outreach & Engagement ... Ms. Jill PRICE
32 VP Student Life/Chief Diversity ... Dr. Dannie MOORE
84 Exec Dir Stdnt Success & Enroll Mgt ... Mr. Dan HENDRICKSON
124 Asst VP Retention & Graduation ... Dr. Gill HUNTER
21 AVP for Finance & Controller ... Mr. Brad COMPTON
86 AVP Govt & Cmty Relations ... Mr. Ethan WITT
32 Dean of Students ... Dr. Lara VANCE
26 Asst VP Communications & Brand Mgmt ... Mr. Doug CORNETT
26 Chief External Affairs Officer ... Ms. Kristi MIDDLETON
114 Exec Dir Budget/Fin Plng & Effect ... Mr. Ryan GREEN
49 Dean Letters/Arts/Social Sciences ... Dr. John BOWES
76 Dean Health Sciences ... Dr. Colleen SCHNECK
81 Dean STEM ... Dr. Tom OTIENO
53 Dean Education ... Dr. Sherry POWERS
61 Dean Justice/Safety/Military Sci ... Dr. Derek PAULSEN
43 University Counsel ... Ms. Dana FOHL
19 Chief of Police ... Mr. Brian MULLINS
08 Dean of Libraries ... Ms. Julie GEORGE
06 Registrar ... Ms. Shannon TIPTON
88 Dir Corporate Educ Partnerships ... Mr. Benton SHIREY

25 Director Sponsored Programs ... Mr. Gus BENSON
92 Exec Director Honors Program ... Dr. David COLEMAN
108 Sr Dir Inst Effectiveness/Research ... Dr. Bethany MILLER
09 Director IR & Data Analytics ... Mr. Chad ADKINS
50 Dean College of Business ... Dr. Tom MARTIN
85 Director International Student Svcs ... Vacant
38 Director Counseling Center ... Dr. Melissa BARTSCH
88 Int Sr Director Student Conduct ... Ms. Emily DAVIS
39 Int Exec Dir Housing & Res Life ... Ms. Karen PEAVLER
37 Dir Student Financial Assistance ... Vacant
23 Dir Student Health Services ... Dr. Brenda CAUDILL
15 Exec Dir HR & Inst Equity ... Mr. John DIXON
13 Chief Information Officer ... Mr. Jeff WHITAKER
41 VP & Director of Athletics ... Mr. Matt ROAN
96 Director University Procurement ... Ms. Micah HUNSUCKER
04 Manager Office of President ... Ms. Shelia ADAMS
100 Exec Dir Office of the President ... Dr. Ryan WILSON
27 Chief of Staff & Chief Comm Ofcr ... Ms. Colleen CHANEY
58 Dean Graduate Studies ... Dr. Ryan BAGGETT
110 Assoc VP Devlpmnt & Campgn Mgr ... Ms. Melissa GRINSTEAD
29 Assoc VP Dev & Alum Engagement ... Mr. Dan MCBRIDE
18 AVP Facilities & Safety ... Mr. Bryan MAKINEN
116 Director of Internal Audit ... Ms. Kelly WALKER
103 Dir Workforce Dev & Cmty Engage ... Dr. Susan CORNELIUS
22 Dir Office of Inst Equity ... Ms. Lindsey CARTER
106 Exec Dir e-Campus Learning ... Mr. Tim MATTHEWS
28 Exec Dir Diversity & Dev ... Ms. Rachel LOFTIS
109 Chief Auxiliary Services Officer ... Mr. Stephen CAUDILL
88 Exec Dir Operations & Innovations ... Ms. Carrie ERNST
104 Education Abroad Dir ... Ms. Jennifer WHITE

Frontier Nursing University (C)

2050, Lexington Road KY 40383

County: Woodford FICE Identification: 030070
Unit ID: 156727
Telephone: (859) 251-4700 Carnegie Class: Spec-4-yr-Other Health
FAX Number: N/A Calendar System: Quarter
URL: www.frontier.edu
Established: 1939 Annual Graduate Tuition & Fees: N/A
Enrollment: 2,436 Coed
Affiliation or Control: Independent Non-Profit IRS Status: 501(c)3
Highest Offering: Doctorate; No Undergraduates
Accreditation: SC, MIDWF, NUR

01 President ... Dr. Susan STONE
10 EVP for Finance/Facilities ... Mr. Michael STEINMETZ
05 Associate Dean of Academic Affairs ... Dr. Rachel MACK
66 Dean of Nursing ... Dr. Joan SLAGER
37 Associate Director of Financial Aid ... Mr. Andrew DEZARN
07 Director of Admissions ... Ms. Rainie BOGGS

Galen College of Nursing (D)

3050 Terra Crossing Boulevard, Louisville KY 40245

County: Jefferson FICE Identification: 030837
Unit ID: 156471
Telephone: (502) 410-6200 Carnegie Class: Spec-4-yr-Other Health
FAX Number: N/A Calendar System: Quarter
URL: www.galencollege.edu
Established: 1989 Annual Undergrad Tuition & Fees: N/A
Enrollment: 2,986 Coed
Affiliation or Control: Proprietary IRS Status: Proprietary
Highest Offering: Master's
Accreditation: SC, ADNUR, NUR, NURSE

02 Director of Campus Operations ... Mr. Marshall MOORE
106 Dean of Online Programs ... Dr. Kathy BURLINGAME
66 Dean ... Dr. Lisa PEAK

Georgetown College (E)

400 E College Street, Georgetown KY 40324-1696

County: Scott FICE Identification: 001964
Unit ID: 156745
Telephone: (502) 863-8000 Carnegie Class: Bac-A&S
FAX Number: (502) 868-8891 Calendar System: Semester
URL: www.georgetowncollege.edu
Established: 1829 Annual Undergrad Tuition & Fees: $40,800
Enrollment: 1,565 Coed
Affiliation or Control: Non-denominational IRS Status: 501(c)3
Highest Offering: Master's
Accreditation: SC, CAEP

01 President ... Dr. Rosemary ALLEN
05 Provost/EVP/CAO ... Dr. Jonathan SANDS WISE
10 CFO/Treasurer ... Mr. Rush SHERMAN
04 Exec Asst to President/Bd Secretary ... Ms. Leah STUBBS
111 Sr Vice President for Advancement ... Mr. John DAVIS
32 VP Student Life/Dean of Students ... Dr. Curtis SANDBERG
84 Vice President Enrollment Mgmt ... Ms. Linda OLSEN
13 Assoc VP for Info Tech Services ... Vacant
11 Vice President Business Operations ... Ms. Sally WIATROWSKI
41 Vice President of Athletics ... Mr. Brian EVANS
110 Asst VP Advancement/Community Rel ... Ms. Christy MAI
21 Controller ... Mr. Brad KAUFMAN
121 Assoc Dean Student Success ... Ms. Alexandra LOPEZ
42 Assoc Dean Student Life/Campus Min ... Mr. Bryan LANGLANDS
35 Assistant Dean of Students ... Mr. Terry EVANS
06 Assoc Dean Academic Svcs/Registrar ... Mr. Jason SNIDER
15 Director of Human Resources ... Ms. Debbie CLARK
113 Bursar ... Ms. Christy DOLAN

53 Interim Dean of Education ... Ms. Kim WALTERS-PARKER
07 Exec Director of Admissions ... Mr. Ticha CHIKUNI
37 Dir of Student Financial Planning ... Mr. Bob FULTZ
30 Director of Development ... Ms. Hanna KROSKIE
09 Director of Institutional Research ... Ms. Amber AUSTIN
08 Director of Library Services ... Mr. Andrew ADLER
29 Director of Alumni Relations ... Ms. Olivia COLEMAN-DUNN
26 Exec Dir Marketing/Communications ... Ms. Abigail MALIK
36 Dir Graves Ctr for Calling & Career ... Ms. Faith CRACRAFT
19 Director Campus Safety/Title IX ... Mr. Joshua MASTERSON
38 Director of Counseling/Health Svcs ... Vacant
18 Dir Facilities and Grounds ... Mr. Tyler LAWS
28 Director of Diversity ... Ms. Robbi BARBER
112 Director of Donor Relations ... Ms. Tammy OWENS
88 Director Faithways Academy ... Ms. Hollis DUDGEON
88 Coord Academic Success Initiatives ... Ms. Devin HARRIS-DAVIS
88 Assoc Athletic Director Compliance ... Ms. Kimberly CHANDLER

Interactive College of Technology (F)

76 Caruthers Road, Newport KY 41071

Telephone: (859) 282-8989 Identification: 770535
Accreditation: COE

† Branch campus of Interactive College of Technology, Chamblee, GA

Kentucky Christian University (G)

100 Academic Parkway, Grayson KY 41143-2205

County: Carter FICE Identification: 001965
Unit ID: 157100
Telephone: (606) 474-3000 Carnegie Class: Bac-Diverse
FAX Number: (606) 474-3189 Calendar System: Semester
URL: www.kcu.edu
Established: 1919 Annual Undergrad Tuition & Fees: $21,200
Enrollment: 689 Coed
Affiliation or Control: Christian Churches And Churches of Christ
IRS Status: 501(c)3
Highest Offering: Master's
Accreditation: SC, NURSE, SW

01 President/CEO ... Dr. Terry L. ALLCORN
10 VP of Business Operations ... Mr. Daniel R. WHITE
05 VP of Academic Affairs ... Mr. Calvin O. LINDELL
32 VP of Student Services ... Mr. Donald M. DAMRON
84 VP of Enrollment Mgmt & Athletics ... Mr. Corey C. FIPPS
30 Director of Development ... Mrs. Megan B. RAWLINGS
06 Registrar ... Mrs. Emily A. MILLER
13 Director of Campus Technology ... Mr. Greg C. RICHARDSON
08 Library Director ... Mrs. Naulayne R. ENDERS
108 Director Institutional Assessment ... Vacant
42 Campus Minister ... Mr. Jacob F. SHOCKEY
37 Director Financial Aid ... Mrs. Jennie M. BENDER
15 Human Resource Officer ... Mr. Terry L. YANKEY
38 Student Counseling Coordinator ... Mrs. Lori A. SMITH-WARD
39 Director of Residence Services ... Vacant
18 Director of Facilities ... Mr. Paul C. PEPPARD
29 Alumni Relations Officer ... Ms. Vicky L. MADDEN
58 Dean of the Graduate School ... Mr. Robert G. O'LYNN
07 Director of Enrollment Services ... Mrs. Sheree GREER
40 Manager of Retail Operations ... Mrs. Kyleigh M. PERRY-MCCLURE
105 Website Manager ... Mr. David A. BENNETT

*Kentucky Community and Technical College System (H)

300 N Main Street, Versailles KY 40383-1245

County: Woodford FICE Identification: 006724
Unit ID: 157854
Telephone: (859) 256-3100 Carnegie Class: N/A
FAX Number: (859) 256-3119
URL: www.kctcs.edu

01 President ... Mr. Paul CZARAPATA
00 Chancellor ... Dr. Kristin WILLIAMS
10 Vice President Finance/Admin Svcs ... Mr. Wendell FOLLOWELL
13 Vice President Information Tech ... Dr. Paul CZARAPATA
111 VP Institutional Advancement ... Mr. Benjamin MOHLER
32 Vice President Student Affairs ... Dr. Gloria MCCALL
103 Exec Dir Workforce Solutions ... Ms. Jessie SCHOOK
09 VC Research and Analysis ... Dr. Alicia CROUCH
100 Chief of Staff ... Ms. Hannah RIVERA

*Ashland Community and Technical College (I)

1400 College Drive, Ashland KY 41101-3617

County: Boyd FICE Identification: 001990
Unit ID: 156231
Telephone: (606) 326-2000 Carnegie Class: Assoc/HVT-Mix Trad/Non
FAX Number: (606) 326-2185 Calendar System: Semester
URL: www.ashland.kctcs.edu
Established: 1938 Annual Undergrad Tuition & Fees (In-State): $4,488
Enrollment: 2,400 Coed
Affiliation or Control: State IRS Status: 501(c)3
Highest Offering: Associate Degree
Accreditation: SC, ADNUR, COARC, IFSAC, NAEYC, SURGT

02 President ... Dr. Larry FERGUSON
32 Dean Student Success/Enroll Svcs ... Mr. Steven WOODBURN

10 Dean of Business Affairs ..... Ms. Karen BLEVINS
09 Dean Inst Effectiveness & Grants ..... Mr. Steve FLOUHOUSE
05 Dean of Academic Affairs ..... Dr. Todd BRAND
26 Director Marketing/Communications ..... Ms. Taylor ALEXANDER
30 Director of Resource Development ..... Ms. Brooke SEASOR
08 Director of Library Services ..... Ms. Pamela KLINEPETER
07 Director of Admissions/Registrar ..... Ms. Robin LEWIS
28 Director of Cultural Diversity ..... Mr. Alvin BAKER
15 Director of Human Resources ..... Ms. Kellie ALLEN
37 Director of Financial Aid ..... Mr. Adam CHAPMAN
121 Director of Student Support Svcs ..... Ms. Megan HORNE

*Big Sandy Community and Technical College (A)

1 Bert T. Combs Drive, Prestonburg KY 41653-9502
County: Floyd FICE Identification: 001996
Unit ID: 157553
Telephone: (606) 886-3863 Carnegie Class: Assoc/MT-VT-High Trad
FAX Number: (606) 886-2677 Calendar System: Semester
URL: www.bigsandy.kctcs.edu
Established: 1964 Annual Undergrad Tuition & Fees (In-State): $4,488
Enrollment: 2,426 Coed
Affiliation or Control: State IRS Status: 501(c)3
Highest Offering: Associate Degree
Accreditation: SC, COARC, DA, DH

02 Interim President/CEO ..... Dr. Telly SELLARS
32 Chief Student Affs Ofcr/Registrar ..... Mr. Jimmy WRIGHT
05 Provost/Chief Academic Officer ..... Dr. Denise KING
10 Chief Business Affairs Officer ..... Ms. Michelle MEEK
18 Director of Facilities Management ..... Mr. Randy HANEY
08 Director of Library Services ..... Ms. Judy HOWELL
15 Chief Human Resources Officer ..... Mr. Jackie CECIL
06 Registrar ..... Ms. Carla BRANHAM
37 Director of Financial Aid ..... Ms. Cathy HURD-CRANK
09 Director of Inst Effectiveness ..... Ms. Denese ATKINSON
14 Director of Information Technology ..... Mr. Casey MUSIC
40 Bookstore Manager ..... Ms. Stephanie JENKINS
26 Dir of Strategic Communications ..... Ms. Greta SLONE
28 Director of Cultural Diversity ..... Vacant
103 Director of Workforce/Economic Dev ..... Ms. Rachelle BURCHETT
04 Exec Admin Asst to President ..... Ms. Velissa MURPHY

*Bluegrass Community and Technical College (B)

500 Newtown Pike, Lexington KY 40508
County: Fayette FICE Identification: 009707
Unit ID: 156392
Telephone: (859) 246-6200 Carnegie Class: Assoc/MT-VT-High Trad
FAX Number: (859) 246-4664 Calendar System: Semester
URL: www.bluegrass.kctcs.edu
Established: 1965 Annual Undergrad Tuition & Fees (In-State): $4,568
Enrollment: 10,180 Coed
Affiliation or Control: State IRS Status: 501(c)3
Highest Offering: Associate Degree
Accreditation: SC, ADNUR, COARC, DH, DMS, IFSAC, MAC, RAD, SURGT

02 President ..... Dr. Koffi C. AKAKPO
05 VP of Academics/WFD/Provost ..... Dr. Gregory FEENEY
32 AVP Dean of Students ..... Ms. Tania CRAWFORD GROSS
10 VP Finance & Administration ..... Ms. Lisa G. BELL
111 VP Advancement & Org Development ..... Mr. Mark MANUEL
28 Assoc VP Diversity/Equity/Inclusion ..... Dr. Carlous YATES
20 Assoc Vice President Academics ..... Dr. Karen MAYO
20 Dean Academics ..... Dr. Valdis ZEPS
103 Dean of Academics/Workforce Devel ..... Ms. Pam HATCHER
121 Dean of Academic Support ..... Dr. Rebecca SIMMS
06 Assoc Dean of Student Records ..... Ms. Becky HARP-STEPHENS
37 Financial Aid Director ..... Ms. Runan EVANS
07 Admissions Director ..... Ms. Shelbie HUGLE
110 Associate VP Institutional Develop ..... Ms. Deborrah L. CATLETT
26 Assoc VP Strategic Communications ..... Ms. Michelle SJOGREN
79 Assistant Dean Humanities ..... Ms. Angella KING
76 Asst Dean Allied Health/Nat Science ..... Dr. Yasemin CONGLETON
66 Assistant Dean Nursing ..... Dr. Melinda BAKER
81 Asst Dean Mathematics/Statistics ..... Ms. Kausha MILLER
77 Asst Dean Business/CIS ..... Ms. Lauren CAMPBELL
72 Asst Dean Advanced Mfg and Trade ..... Mr. Ralph POTTER
83 Asst Dean Comm/Hist/Lang/Social Sci ..... Dr. Jenny JONES
08 Director Library/Tutoring Services ..... Ms. Terry BUCKNER
51 Director Adult Education ..... Mr. David STURGILL
106 Assistant Dean Distance Learning ..... Dr. Kevin DUNN
18 Director of Maintenance/Operations ..... Mr. Michael BALL
09 Director of Institutional Research ..... Mr. Aaron GAY
96 Director of Purchasing ..... Ms. Kimberly CAMERON
04 President's Executive Assistant ..... Ms. Liza MERRYMAN
19 Director Security/Safety ..... Mr. Scott COLEMAN

*Elizabethtown Community and Technical College (C)

600 College Street Road, Elizabethtown KY 42701
County: Hardin FICE Identification: 001991
Unit ID: 156648
Telephone: (270) 769-2371 Carnegie Class: Assoc/MT-VT-High Non
FAX Number: (270) 769-0736 Calendar System: Semester
URL: www.elizabethtown.kctcs.edu
Established: 1963 Annual Undergrad Tuition & Fees (In-State): $4,488
Enrollment: 5,850 Coed
Affiliation or Control: State IRS Status: 501(c)3
Highest Offering: Associate Degree
Accreditation: SC, ADNUR, COARC, DMS, IFSAC, RAD

02 President/CEO ..... Dr. Juston PATE
05 Interim Provost/CAO ..... Mr. Darrin POWELL
32 Chief Student Affairs Officer ..... Dr. Dale BUCKLES
103 Dean of Workforce Solutions ..... Mr. Michael HAZZARD
10 Dean of Business Affairs ..... Mr. Brent HOLSCLAW
15 Director of Human Resources ..... Ms. Whitney TAYLOR
06 Registrar ..... Mr. Bryan SMITH
13 Director of IT ..... Mr. Michael MEANOR
37 Director of Financial Aid ..... Mr. Michael BARLOW
111 Dean of Institutional Advancement ..... Ms. Megan STITH
26 Director of Public Relations ..... Ms. Sarah BERKSHIRE
24 Learning Center Coordinator ..... Ms. Pam HARPER
40 Bookstore Manager ..... Ms. Melissa WILSON
108 Director Inst Effectiveness ..... Ms. Sarah EDWARDS
18 Maintenance/Operations Supervisor ..... Mr. Charles COBB
57 Chair Div of Arts/Humanities ..... Ms. Jacqueline HAWKINS
81 Chair Div of Biological Science ..... Ms. Anna HAMILTON
81 Chair Div of Physical Science ..... Dr. Shawn KELLIE
75 Chair Div Occupational Technology ..... Mr. Thomas CSONKA
83 Chair Div Social & Behavioral Sci ..... Mr. John WALDRON
28 Director of Diversity ..... Ms. Jerisia LAMONS
04 Exec Admin Assistant to President ..... Ms. Emily ALLEN
105 Director Web Services ..... Ms. Deanna YATES
08 Director of Library Services ..... Ms. Katie MEYER
25 Dir of Grants & Sponsored Projects ..... Ms. Susan COOPER

*Gateway Community and Technical College (D)

500 Technology Way, Florence KY 41042
County: Boone FICE Identification: 005273
Unit ID: 157438
Telephone: (859) 441-4500 Carnegie Class: Assoc/HVT-Mix Trad/Non
FAX Number: (859) 341-6859 Calendar System: Semester
URL: www.gateway.kctcs.edu
Established: 1961 Annual Undergrad Tuition & Fees (In-State): $4,568
Enrollment: 4,299 Coed
Affiliation or Control: State IRS Status: 501(c)3
Highest Offering: Associate Degree
Accreditation: SC, CAHIIM, EMT, IFSAC

02 President/CEO ..... Dr. Fernando FIGUEROA
05 Provost and VP Academic Affairs ..... Dr. Teri VONHANDORF
49 Dean of Arts and Sciences ..... Dr. Susan SANTOS
50 Dean of Business/IT/Prof Services ..... Dr. Amy CARRINO
76 Dean of Health Professions ..... Ms. Amber CARTER
72 Dean of Manufacturing & Trans Tech ..... Mr. Sam COLLIER
35 AVP for Student Development ..... Ms. Mallis GRAVES
20 Associate VP Academic Services ..... Mr. Doug PENIX
38 Director of Counseling Services ..... Dr. Tiffany MINARD
84 Associate VP Enrollment ..... Mr. Andre WASHINGTON
06 Registrar ..... Ms. Ann SCHULTZ
18 Director Maintenance & Operations ..... Mr. Mike BAKER
19 Director Security/Safety ..... Mr. Matt BUNNING
37 Director of Financial Aid ..... Ms. Ellen TEEGARDEN
13 Director of Information Technology ..... Ms. Melissa SEARS
08 Director of Library ..... Ms. Elizabeth HARTLAUB
66 Director of Nursing ..... Ms. Michele SIMMS
89 Director Early College Initiatives ..... Ms. Shelby KRENTZ
108 Dean Institutional Effectiveness ..... Dr. Denise FRITSCH
26 Asst Dir Mktg & Communications ..... Mr. Patrick LAMPING
27 Asst Dir Mktg & Communications ..... Ms. Erica MARYE
30 VP Devel & External Relations ..... Ms. Adrijana KOWATSCH
10 VP Admin & Business Affairs ..... Mr. James YOUNGER
32 VP Student Development ..... Ms. Ingrid WASHINGTON
103 Associate VP Workforce Solutions ..... Ms. Christi GODMAN
15 VP of Human Resources ..... Ms. Amy HATFIELD
110 Director of Development ..... Vacant
04 Exec Admin Asst to President ..... Ms. Jane FRANTZ
28 AVP Inclusion Intervention Services ..... Dr. Tiffany MINARD

*Hazard Community and Technical College (E)

One Community College Drive, Hazard KY 41701-2402
County: Perry FICE Identification: 006962
Unit ID: 156790
Telephone: (606) 436-5721 Carnegie Class: Assoc/HVT-High Non
FAX Number: (606) 487-3604 Calendar System: Semester
URL: www.hazard.kctcs.edu
Established: 1968 Annual Undergrad Tuition & Fees (In-State): $4,488
Enrollment: 2,630 Coed
Affiliation or Control: State IRS Status: 501(c)3
Highest Offering: Associate Degree
Accreditation: SC, DMS, IFSAC, PTAA, RAD, SURGT

02 President/CEO ..... Dr. Jennifer LINDON
05 Chief Academic Officer ..... Dr. Ella STRONG
32 Chief Student Affairs Officer ..... Dr. Deronda MOBELINI
10 Chief Financial Officer ..... Ms. Connie WATTS
103 Dean of Workforce Solutions ..... Mrs. Keila MILLER
13 Chief Information Officer ..... Ms. Donna ROARK
15 Senior Director of Human Resources ..... Ms. Vickie COMBS
18 Dean of Operations ..... Mr. Stu FUGATE
26 Dir of Marketing & Communications ..... Mrs. Delcie COMBS
21 Dean of Business Services ..... Ms. Jackie HALL
08 Director Library Services ..... Mrs. Cathy BRANSON
97 Academic Dean General Education ..... Ms. Leila SMITH
75 Acad Dean Occupational Technologies ..... Mr. Tony BACK
76 Acad Dean Allied Health Sci ..... Ms. Mavis CLEMONS
06 Registrar ..... Ms. Libby PETERS
07 Director of Admissions ..... Mr. Scott GROSS
09 Coord of Inst Effectiveness ..... Ms. Lois PUFFER

*Henderson Community College (F)

2660 S Green Street, Henderson KY 42420-4699
County: Henderson FICE Identification: 001993
Unit ID: 156851
Telephone: (270) 827-1867 Carnegie Class: Assoc/MT-VT-Mix Trad/Non
FAX Number: (270) 831-9600 Calendar System: Semester
URL: www.henderson.kctcs.edu
Established: 1960 Annual Undergrad Tuition & Fees (In-State): $4,488
Enrollment: 1,331 Coed
Affiliation or Control: State IRS Status: 501(c)3
Highest Offering: Associate Degree
Accreditation: SC, ADNUR, MAC, MLTAD, NAEYC

02 President ..... Dr. Jason D. WARREN
05 Interim Dean of Academic Affairs ..... Mr. Mike KNECHT
10 Chief Business Officer ..... Vacant
111 Director of Advancement ..... Ms. Jennifer PRESTON
09 Director of Knowledge Management ..... Mr. Brian MCMURTRY
15 Director of Human Resources ..... Ms. Kim JONES
84 Dean of Enrollment Mgmt/Registrar ..... Dr. Chad PHILLIPS
08 Interim Library Director ..... Ms. Allison HORNING
66 Interim Director of Nursing ..... Ms. Sarah CRICK
57 Coordinator of Preston Arts Center ..... Ms. Stacey HOWELL
13 Director of Technology Solutions ..... Mr. Joe HEERDINK
18 Maintenance/Oper Supervisor ..... Vacant
36 Career Services Coordinator ..... Ms. Angela WATSON
37 Director Financial Aid ..... Ms. Whitney LAIRD
49 Div Chair Liberal Arts/Prof Studies ..... Ms. Lilia JOY
76 Div Chair Allied Health ..... Dr. Carole MATTINGLY
81 Div Chair STEM ..... Mr. Barry PHELPS
04 Administrative Asst to President ..... Ms. Karen GUESS
103 Coordinator Workforce Solutions ..... Ms. Amanda BLOHM-THOMPSON

*Hopkinsville Community College (G)

720 North Drive, PO Box 2100,
Hopkinsville KY 42241-2100
County: Christian FICE Identification: 001994
Unit ID: 156860
Telephone: (270) 707-3700 Carnegie Class: Assoc/MT-VT-Mix Trad/Non
FAX Number: (270) 886-0237 Calendar System: Semester
URL: www.hopkinsville.kctcs.edu
Established: 1965 Annual Undergrad Tuition & Fees (In-State): $4,488
Enrollment: 2,076 Coed
Affiliation or Control: State IRS Status: 501(c)3
Highest Offering: Associate Degree
Accreditation: SC, ADNUR, SURGT

02 President ..... Dr. Alissa YOUNG
04 Exec Admin Asst to President ..... Ms. Janice JONES
05 Chief Academic Affairs Officer ..... Dr. Chris BOYETT
10 Chief Business Affairs Officer ..... Dr. Dale LEATHERMAN
32 Chief Student Affairs Officer ..... Ms. Angel PRESCOTT
103 Chief Cmty/Workforce/Economic Dev ..... Ms. Carol KIRVES
06 Registrar ..... Ms. Tiffanie WITT
08 Director Library Services ..... Ms. Elysa PARKS
09 Dir Institutional Effectiveness ..... Ms. Allisha LEE
12 Director Fort Campbell Campus ..... Ms. Tara RASCOE
13 Director Information Technology ..... Mr. Joe GRACE
15 Director Human Resources ..... Ms. Lisa HARBOLD
18 Director Maintenance/Operations ..... Mr. Joe GARY
26 Director Marketing & Communication ..... Ms. Rena YOUNG
28 Cultural Diversity Coordinator ..... Ms. Angel PRESCOTT
30 Chief Institutional Advancement Ofc ..... Ms. Yvette EASTHAM
37 Director Financial Aid ..... Ms. Janet GUNTHER
38 Advising Center Director ..... Ms. Deloria SCOTT
40 Bookstore Director ..... Ms. Sheena KOCH
36 Coordinator Career Services ..... Ms. Kanya ALLEN
19 Safety Specialist ..... Vacant
49 Chair Liberal Arts and Sciences Div ..... Ms. Julia LAFFOON-JACKSON
72 Chr Professional/Technical Studies ..... Mr. Robert SMITH
66 Chair Nursing Division ..... Ms. Joyce LAMBRUNO
81 Chair Mathematics & Sciences Div ..... Mr. Pat RILEY
76 Chair Allied Health Division ..... Dr. Beth BEVERLY

*Jefferson Community and Technical College (H)

109 E Broadway, Louisville KY 40202-2000
County: Jefferson FICE Identification: 006961
Unit ID: 156921
Telephone: (502) 213-5333 Carnegie Class: Assoc/MT-VT-High Non
FAX Number: (502) 213-2115 Calendar System: Semester
URL: www.jefferson.kctcs.edu
Established: 1967 Annual Undergrad Tuition & Fees (In-State): $4,568
Enrollment: 12,196 Coed
Affiliation or Control: State IRS Status: 501(c)3
Highest Offering: Associate Degree
Accreditation: SC, ADNUR, CAHIIM, COARC, EMT, IFSAC, MAC, MLTAD, OTA, PTAA, RAD, SURGT

02 President ..... Dr. Ty J. HANDY
05 VP of Academic Affairs ..... Dr. Reneau WAGGONER

10 VP of Administration and CFO ... Mr. Gary DRYDEN, JR.
21 Controller ... Vacant
20 Dean Academic Affs Tech Pgms ... Vacant
97 Dean of General Education/Transfer ... Dr. Randy DAVIS
12 Coordinator Shelby Campus ... Dr. Michael SHELL
32 Dean Student Affs/Enrollment Mgmt ... Dr. Laura SMITH
08 Library Services Director ... Ms. Sheree WILLIAMS
13 Chief Information Technology Office ... Mr. Thomas ROGERS
09 Dir Inst Research/Effectiveness ... Dr. Brittany INGE
07 Director of Admissions ... Mr. Jimmy KIDD
28 Dir Diversity/Inclusion/Cmty Engage ... Ms. Tamara RUSSELL
06 Registrar ... Ms. Amanda TINDALL
26 Public Relations/Marketing ... Ms. Nikolette LANGDON
15 Human Resources Director ... Ms. Toni WHALEN
18 Facilities Director ... Ms. Pamela TURNER
37 Director of Financial Aid ... Ms. Lindsay DRISKELL
30 Inst Advance/Development Coord ... Ms. Karla HALL
38 Student Counseling ... Ms. Selena SANCHEZ
96 Director of Purchasing ... Ms. Tineke SANTOS
12 Director of Carrollton Campus ... Ms. Heather YOCUM
04 Administrative Asst to President ... Ms. Teresa B. HARPER
106 Dir Online Education/E-learning ... Mr. Aaron NUSZ
25 Chief Contracts/Grants Admin ... Ms. Joanna LYNCH
19 Chief Campus Safety/Security ... Vacant
103 Director Workforce Development ... Ms. Nickie COBB

*Madisonville Community College (A)

2000 College Drive, Madisonville KY 42431-9199
County: Hopkins FICE Identification: 009010
Unit ID: 157304
Telephone: (270) 821-2250 Carnegie Class: Assoc/HVT-High Non
FAX Number: (270) 824-1866 Calendar System: Semester
URL: www.madisonville.kctcs.edu
Established: 1968 Annual Undergrad Tuition & Fees (In-State): $4,488
Enrollment: 3,104 Coed
Affiliation or Control: State IRS Status: 501(c)3
Highest Offering: Associate Degree
Accreditation: SC, ADNUR, COARC, EMT, IFSAC, MLTAD, OTA, PTAA, RAD, SURGA, SURGT

02 President ... Dr. Cynthia S. KELLEY
05 Provost ... Vacant
10 Chief Business Affairs Officer ... Mr. Ray GILLASPIE
11 Vice Pres Quality Assurance & Admin ... Dr. Jay PARRENT
103 Director Workforce Solutions ... Mr. Mike DAVENPORT
25 Dir Grants/Planning & Effectiveness ... Mr. David A. SCHUERMER
19 Director of Public Protection ... Mr. Joe BLUE
21 Dean of Business Affairs ... Mr. Michael L. JOHNSON
20 Dean of Academic Affairs ... Ms. Lisa A. HOWERTON
32 Dean of Student Affairs ... Dr. Cathy A. VAUGHAN
84 Dean of Enrollment Management ... Ms. Aimee J. WILKERSON
13 Director of Information Technology ... Mr. Joe HEERDINK
111 Director of Advancement ... Ms. Raegina SCOTT
15 Director of Human Resources ... Ms. Kim JONES
04 Sr Admin Assistant to the President . Mr. Grayson P. HAGERMAN
72 Division Chair Applied Technology ... Mr. Matt LUCKETT
66 Div Chr Nursing/Related Tech ... Dr. Marsha WOODALL
79 Div Chr Humanities/Related Tech ... Ms. Christy ADKINS
83 Div Chr Social Science/Related Tech ... Ms. Natalie F. COOPER
81 Div Chr Mathematics and Sciences ... Ms. Dawn TILLEN
76 Div Chr Allied Health/Related Tech ... Ms. Tonia R. GIBSON
56 Extended Campus Director ... Ms. Britney HERNANDEZ-STEVENSON
06 Registrar ... Ms. Casie RICHARDSON
37 Director of Financial Aid ... Ms. Karen MILLER
26 Public Relations Coordinator ... Ms. Emily RAY
36 Director of Counseling Services ... Dr. Cathy A. VAUGHAN
08 Director of Library Services ... Mr. Colin MAGEE
28 Director of Cultural Diversity ... Mr. James H. BOWLES
40 Bookstore Manager ... Ms. Sonya L. PARKER

*Maysville Community and Technical College (B)

1755 US Highway 68, Maysville KY 41056-8910
County: Mason FICE Identification: 006960
Unit ID: 157331
Telephone: (606) 759-7141 Carnegie Class: Assoc/HVT-Mix Trad/Non
FAX Number: (606) 759-7176 Calendar System: Semester
URL: www.maysville.kctcs.edu
Established: 1968 Annual Undergrad Tuition & Fees (In-State): $4,488
Enrollment: 3,446 Coed
Affiliation or Control: State IRS Status: 501(c)3
Highest Offering: Associate Degree
Accreditation: SC, COARC, EMT, IFSAC, MAC, MLTAD, @PTAA

02 President ... Dr. Laura MCCULLOUGH
05 Provost ... Dr. Thomas WARE
10 Chief Finance Officer ... Ms. Barbara CAMPBELL
84 Chief Ofcr Enrollment/Student Svc ... Ms. Jessica KERN
11 Chief Operations Officer ... Mr. Russ WARD
20 Assoc Dean Academic Support Svc ... Dr. Dana CALLAND
09 Assoc Dean Institutional Rsrch/Plng ... Ms. Pam STAFFORD
08 Director Library Services ... Ms. Sonja EADS
13 Director Information Technology ... Mr. Brett CABLE
111 Director Advancement/Foundation ... Ms. Cara CLARKE
37 Director Financial Aid ... Ms. Sandy POWER
06 Registrar ... Ms. Lori GAUNCE
28 Director of Diversity ... Ms. Millicent HARDING
15 Int Director of Human Resources ... Ms. Amanda K. CONLEY
106 Coordinator of Remote Learning ... Ms. Hannah THORNTON
50 Div Chr Business/Info Technologies ... Ms. Natasha MADDOX
49 Div Chair Liberal Arts/Education ... Ms. Melinda WALKER
81 Div Chair Math/Science/Agriculture ... Dr. Angela FULTZ
76 Associate Dean Health Sciences ... Ms. Ginger CLARKE
72 Dept Chair Industrial Maint/Tech ... Mr. Robbie GRAVES

*Owensboro Community and Technical College (C)

4800 New Hartford Road, Owensboro KY 42303-1899
County: Daviess FICE Identification: 030345
Unit ID: 247940
Telephone: (270) 686-4400 Carnegie Class: Assoc/MT-VT-High Non
FAX Number: (270) 686-4496 Calendar System: Semester
URL: https://owensboro.kctcs.edu/
Established: 1986 Annual Undergrad Tuition & Fees (In-State): $4,488
Enrollment: 3,901 Coed
Affiliation or Control: State IRS Status: 501(c)3
Highest Offering: Associate Degree
Accreditation: SC, CNEA, EMT, IFSAC, MAC, RAD, SURGT

02 President/CEO ... Dr. Scott WILLIAMS
04 Assistant to the President ... Ms. Kittridge MIDKIFF
05 VP of Academic Affairs ... Dr. Veena SALLAN
32 VP of Student Affairs ... Mr. Kevin BEARDMORE
10 VP of Business Affairs ... Ms. Sarah PRICE
13 VP Information Technology ... Mr. James HARTZ
103 VP Workforce Solutions ... Ms. Cynthia FIORELLA
08 Library Services Director ... Ms. Donna ABELL
06 Registrar ... Ms. Christy ELLIS
15 Director of Human Resources ... Ms. Shanna BALLARD
37 Dean of Student Affairs ... Dr. Andrea BORREGARD
111 Dir Institutional Advancement ... Mr. Michael RODGERS
26 Director of Public Relations ... Ms. Bernadette TOYE-HALE
28 Director of Diversity ... Dr. Ade OREDEIN
96 Director of Purchasing ... Ms. Sarah PRICE
40 Bookstore Manager ... Ms. Sonya SOUTHARD
88 TV Production Manager ... Mr. John BRYENTON
07 Senior Admissions Advisor ... Ms. Linda CALHOUN
36 Career Resource/Placemnt Ctr Coord ... Ms. Katie BALLARD
79 Assoc Dean Humanities/Fine Arts ... Dr. Julia LEDFORD
49 Academic Dean Arts & Sciences ... Dr. Marc MALTBY
75 Assoc Dean Prof/Tech Studies ... Mr. Dean AUTRY
66 Associate Dean Nursing ... Ms. Terri LANHAM
20 Dean Acad Affs Prof/Tech ... Dr. Stacy EDDS-ELLIS
09 Coord Institutional Effectiveness ... Vacant
19 Director Security/Safety ... Mr. Jeff HENDRICKS

*Somerset Community College (D)

808 Monticello Street, Somerset KY 42501-2973
County: Pulaski FICE Identification: 001997
Unit ID: 157711
Telephone: (877) 629-9722 Carnegie Class: Assoc/HVT-High Trad
FAX Number: N/A Calendar System: Semester
URL: somerset.kctcs.edu
Established: 1965 Annual Undergrad Tuition & Fees (In-State): $4,488
Enrollment: 4,837 Coed
Affiliation or Control: State IRS Status: 501(c)3
Highest Offering: Associate Degree
Accreditation: SC, ADNUR, COARC, EMT, IFSAC, MLTAD, PTAA, RAD, SURGT

02 President/CEO ... Dr. Carey CASTLE
05 Senior VP of Academic Affairs ... Dr. Clint HAYES
10 Vice President of Administration ... Ms. Jill MEECE
84 Vice President of Enrollment Mgmt ... Dr. Karleen HOWARD
11 Vice President of Operations ... Mr. Larry ABBOTT
76 Dean for Health Sciences ... Dr. Ronald L. MEADE
09 VP of Institutional Effectiveness ... Mr. Bruce GOVER
32 Vice President of Student Affairs ... Ms. Tracy L. CASADA
103 VP of Workforce Solutions ... Ms. Alesa JOHNSON
111 VP of Institutional Advancement ... Ms. Cindy D. CLOUSE
49 Dean Arts and Sciences ... Mr. Jon BURLEW
81 Dean Math/Natural Science ... Dr. Michael GOLEMAN
50 Dean Business/Applied Tech ... Mr. Kevin BRADFORD
37 Director of Financial Aid ... Mr. Patrick MAYER
06 Registrar ... Ms. Jami EVANS
15 Director of Human Resources ... Ms. Mary POYNTER
28 Director of Equity/Inclusion ... Ms. Elaine WILSON
12 Director McCreary & Clinton Centers ... Ms. Jill LAWSON
12 Director Casey & Russell Centers ... Ms. Regina HAUGEN

*Southcentral Kentucky Community and Technical College (E)

1845 Loop Drive, Bowling Green KY 42101-9202
County: Warren FICE Identification: 005271
Unit ID: 156338
Telephone: (270) 901-1000 Carnegie Class: Assoc/MT-VT-Mix Trad/Non
FAX Number: (270) 901-1145 Calendar System: Semester
URL: www.bowlinggreen.kctcs.edu
Established: 1939 Annual Undergrad Tuition & Fees (In-State): $4,488
Enrollment: 4,137 Coed
Affiliation or Control: State IRS Status: 501(c)3
Highest Offering: Associate Degree
Accreditation: SC, COARC, IFSAC, RAD, SURGT

02 President & CEO ... Dr. Phillip W. NEAL
05 Provost ... Dr. James MCCASLIN
32 VP Student Services ... Ms. Brooke JUSTICE
10 Vice President Business Services ... Mr. Chris CUMENS
06 Registrar ... Ms. Amy CANNON
15 VP Administrative Services ... Ms. Sherri L. FORESTER
26 Director of Public Relations ... Ms. Rebecca LEE
111 Director of Inst Advancement ... Ms. Heather ROGERS
21 Assoc Vice President of Business ... Ms. Jennifer NOBLE
09 Director Institution Effectiveness ... Mr. Mark GARRETT

*Southeast Kentucky Community and Technical College (F)

700 College Road, Cumberland KY 40823-1099
County: Harlan FICE Identification: 001998
Unit ID: 157739
Telephone: (606) 589-2145 Carnegie Class: Assoc/MT-VT-Mix Trad/Non
FAX Number: (606) 589-3175 Calendar System: Semester
URL: www.southeast.kctcs.edu
Established: 1960 Annual Undergrad Tuition & Fees (In-State): $4,488
Enrollment: 2,505 Coed
Affiliation or Control: State IRS Status: 501(c)3
Highest Offering: Associate Degree
Accreditation: SC, ADNUR, COARC, EMT, PTAA, RAD, SURGT

02 President ... Dr. Vic ADAMS
05 Chief Academic Officer ... Dr. Kevin LAMBERT
10 Chief Business Affairs Officer ... Ms. Angela SIMPSON
111 Chief Institutional Advancemnt Ofcr ... Ms. Carrie BILLETT
32 Chief Student Affairs Officer ... Dr. Rebecca JOHNSON
20 Dean of Academic Affairs ... Dr. Erin REASOR
20 Dean of Academic Affairs ... Ms. Peggy CONKLIN
11 Dean of Administrative Services ... Mr. Paul BRYANT
15 Director Human Resources ... Ms. Sharon JOHNSON
08 Head Librarian ... Ms. Lynn COX
13 Director of Information Technology ... Mr. Merrill GALLOWAY
07 Director of Admissions ... Ms. Felicia CARROLL
37 Director Financial Aid ... Ms. Barbara GENT
06 Registrar ... Ms. Anita BARNHILL
09 Dean of Institutional Effectiveness ... Dr. Rick MASON
103 Dir Workforce/Career Development ... Ms. Sherri CLARK
18 Dir Maintenance/Operations ... Mr. Stephen LEWIS
28 Director of Diversity ... Mr. Ryland POPE
26 Director of Public Relations ... Ms. Amy SIMPSON
121 Director of Academic Advising ... Ms. Sherry TINSLEY
19 Director Security/Safety ... Mr. Kenneth LAYNE
04 Executive Administrative Assistant ... Ms. Julie BROOKS

*West Kentucky Community and Technical College (G)

4810 Alben Barkley Drive, Paducah KY 42002-7380
County: McCracken FICE Identification: 001979
Unit ID: 157483
Telephone: (270) 554-9200 Carnegie Class: Assoc/HVT-Mix Trad/Non
FAX Number: (270) 554-6217 Calendar System: Semester
URL: www.westkentucky.kctcs.edu
Established: 1909 Annual Undergrad Tuition & Fees (In-State): $4,488
Enrollment: 4,893 Coed
Affiliation or Control: State IRS Status: 501(c)3
Highest Offering: Associate Degree
Accreditation: SC, ACBSP, ACFEI, ADNUR, DA, DMS, IFSAC, MLTAD, NAEYC, PNUR, PTAA, RAD, SURGT

02 President/CEO ... Dr. Anton REECE
103 VP of Workforce Solutions ... Mr. Kevin O'NEILL
05 VP of Academic Affairs ... Dr. Renea AKIN
32 VP of Student Services ... Ms. Octavia LAWRENCE
11 VP of Administrative Services ... Mr. Shay NOLAN
10 Int VP Business Affairs ... Ms. Bridget CANTER
111 VP Institutional Advancement ... Ms. Lee EMMONS
20 Associate VP Academic Affairs ... Dr. Kate SENN
08 Library Services Director ... Ms. Amy SULLIVAN
37 Financial Aid Director ... Mr. Mark SMITH
26 Public Relations Director ... Ms. Janett BLYTHE
13 Director Information Technology ... Mr. Clay RYCKERT
15 Director Human Resources ... Ms. Bridget CANTER
06 Registrar/Dir of Admissions ... Mr. Trent JOHNSON
35 Student Activities Coordinator ... Ms. Amy ELMORE
79 Dean Humanities/Fine Arts/Soc Sci ... Mr. Britton SHURLEY
66 Dean Nursing Division ... Ms. Shari GHOLSON
76 Dean Allied Health Division ... Ms. Shari GHOLSON
75 Dean Applied Tech Division ... Ms. Stephanie MILLIKEN
81 Dean Math/Science & Computer ... Mr. Corey WADLINGTON
09 Associate VP of IE ... Ms. Geelyn WARREN
04 Administrative Asst to President ... Ms. Melissa ALLCOCK
19 Interim Director Security/Safety ... Mr. David WALLACE
28 Director of Diversity ... Vacant
29 Director Alumni Affairs ... Mr. Kyle FISHER
07 Director of Admissions ... Mr. Trent JOHNSON
106 Director Online Learning ... Dr. Kate SENN

Kentucky Mountain Bible College (H)

855 Highway 541, Jackson KY 41339
County: Breathitt FICE Identification: 030021
Unit ID: 157030
Telephone: (606) 693-5000 Carnegie Class: Bac-A&S
FAX Number: (888) 742-1124 Calendar System: Semester
URL: www.kmbc.edu
Established: 1931 Annual Undergrad Tuition & Fees: $9,760
Enrollment: 87 Coed
Affiliation or Control: Interdenominational IRS Status: 501(c)3
Highest Offering: Baccalaureate

Accreditation: BI

01 President ... Dr. Philip E. SPEAS
03 Executive Vice President ... Rev. Thomas LORIMER
05 Academic Dean ... Mr. Zane DARLAND
10 Chief Business Manager/CIO ... Mr. Steve A. LORIMER
08 Head Librarian ... Ms. Patricia A. BOWEN
06 Registrar ... Dr. Richard E. ENGLEHARDT
07 Chief Admissions Counselor ... Mr. David W. LORIMER
37 Director Student Financial Aid ... Mr. Joe RITTER
32 Dean of Students ... Rev. James H. NELSON
18 Chief Facilities/Physical Plant ... Rev. Doug DUNN
20 Associate Academic Officer ... Mrs. Sara BAGBY
29 Director of Alumni Relations ... Mrs. Hannah AVERY
106 Dir Online Education/E-learning ... Rev. Jason GOBEN
88 Title 9 Coordinator ... Miss Elizabeth DIETZ
108 Director Institutional Assessment ... Mr. Zane E. DARLAND
13 Chief Info Technology Officer ... Mr. Steve E. LORIMER
38 Director Student Counseling ... Mrs. Ruth E. DARLAND

Kentucky State University (A)

400 E Main Street, Frankfort KY 40601-2355
County: Franklin — FICE Identification: 001968
Unit ID: 157058
Telephone: (502) 597-6000 — Carnegie Class: Bac-Diverse
FAX Number: (502) 597-6490 — Calendar System: Semester
URL: www.kysu.edu
Established: 1886 — Annual Undergrad Tuition & Fees (In-State): $8,800
Enrollment: 2,290 — Coed
Affiliation or Control: State — IRS Status: 501(c)3
Highest Offering: Doctorate
Accreditation: SC, ACBSP, ADNUR, CAEP, MUS, NUR, SW

01 Interim President ... Dr. Ronald A. JOHNSON
100 Interim Chief of Staff ... Dr. Daarel BURNETTE
10 VP for Finance Administration ... Dr. Gerald SHIELDS
05 Provost & VP for Academic Affairs ... Dr. Leroy HAMILTON, JR.
26 VP Brand Identity & University Rels ... Dr. Clara R. ROSS STAMPS
32 Int VP Student Engage & Campus Life ... Dr. Bridgett GOLMAN
43 General Counsel ... Ms. Lisa K. LANG
86 Director of Government Affairs ... Mr. Darryl D. THOMPSON
20 Vice Provost for Academic Affairs ... Dr. Berkley KING, JR.
35 Dean of Students ... Dr. Charles HOLLOWAY
121 Assistant VP for Student Success ... Mr. Christopher D. CRIBBS
111 Exec Director of Inst Advancement ... Mr. Michael DECOURCY
13 Chief Information Officer ... Dr. Wendy D. DIXIE
41 Interim Director Athletics ... Mr. Ramon JOHNSON
47 Dean Col of Agriculture/Comp & Sci ... Dr. Kirk W. POMPER
79 Dean Col Humanities/Business/SocSci ... Dr. David SHABAZZ
92 Dean of Whitney M Young Honors Col ... Dr. Takeia ANTHONY
88 Chair School of Agric/Cmty & Envir ... Dr. Marcus BERNARD
88 Chair Sch Aquaculture & Aquatic Sci ... Dr. James H. TIDWELL
81 Chair STEM ... Dr. Chi SHEN
53 Chair School of Education ... Dr. Phillip H. CLAY
66 Program Admin School of Nursing ... Dr. Mary E. BROADDUS
70 Chair Sch of Social Work ... Dr. Mindy BROOKS-EAVES
83 Chair Sch Behavioral & Social Sci ... Ms. Laquida R. SMITH
88 Chair Sch of Humanities/Perf Arts ... Mr. Alvin E. LEVEL
80 Chair Sch of Public Administration ... Dr. Elgie C. MCFAYDEN, JR.
50 Chair School of Business ... Dr. Gary R. STRATTON
21 Controller ... Vacant
82 Chair Sch of Criminal Jus/Pol Sci ... Dr. Frederick A. WILLIAMS
60 Chair Div of Literature/Lang/Phil ... Mr. Daniel D. COLLUM
18 Dir Capital Plng & Facilities Mgmt ... Mr. Paul CABLE
15 Director Human Resource Svcs ... Ms. Candace RAGLIN
07 Dir BREDS/Admissions ... Ms. Jennifer WILLIAMS
37 Exec Director Financial Aid ... Ms. Russelle KEESE
31 Director Of Public Engagement ... Ms. Sonia P. SANDERS
27 Director of Communication ... Ms. Tanya D. CARR RANKIN
85 Dir International Affairs & Global ... Dr. Eric YANG
29 Director Alumni Relations ... Vacant
06 Registrar ... Ms. Yolanda S. BENSON
08 Director Library ... Ms. Sheila A. STUCKEY
106 Director of Instructional Design ... Dr. Michael DAILEY
19 Interim Chief of Police ... Ms. Barbara HAYES
09 Director Instituional Research ... Ms. Yuliana SUSANTO-ONG
108 Dir of Institutional Effectiveness ... Dr. Tierra F. TAYLOR
96 Director of Purchasing ... Ms. Karen BROWN
113 Bursar ... Ms. Natalie T. TURNER
39 Dir Resident Life/ Student Housing ... Mr. James GARRETT
114 Budget Manager ... Ms. Christina JONES
117 Safety and Compliance Officer ... Ms. Corinne SCHWAB
04 Exec Assistant to President ... Ms. Amy OLDS

Kentucky Wesleyan College (B)

3000 Frederica Street, Owensboro KY 42301
County: Daviess — FICE Identification: 001969
Unit ID: 157076
Telephone: (270) 926-3111 — Carnegie Class: Bac-Diverse
FAX Number: (270) 926-3112 — Calendar System: Semester
URL: www.kwc.edu
Established: 1858 — Annual Undergrad Tuition & Fees: $28,540
Enrollment: 887 — Coed
Affiliation or Control: United Methodist — IRS Status: 501(c)3
Highest Offering: Baccalaureate
Accreditation: SC, IACBE

01 President ... Dr. Thomas M. MITZEL
05 VP Acad Affairs/Dean of the College ... Dr. James P. COUSINS
10 Vice President of Finance ... Mr. Dan FRAZIER
124 VP of Exec Initiatives & Retention ... Mr. Scott E. KRAMER
32 VP of Student Services ... Ms. Rebecca MCQUEEN
13 Dir of Information Services ... Mr. Jeff ARNOLD
111 Vice President for Advancement ... Mr. Eddie KENNY
07 VP of Admissions and Financial Aid ... Mr. Matthew RUARK
06 Registrar ... Ms. Lindsey CROWE
09 Dir of Inst Effectiveness/Research ... Ms. Jenna BRASHEAR
15 Director of Human Resources ... Mrs. Linda B. KELLER
37 Director of Financial Aid ... Ms. Crystal HAMILTON
08 Director of Library Learning Center ... Vacant
41 Interim Director of Athletics ... Mr. Mark SHOOK
30 Dir of Development/Campus Relations ... Ms. Kathy RUTHERMAN
42 Director of Campus Ministries ... Mr. Shawn TOMES
110 Dir Development/Donor Rels ... Mr. M. Blake HARRISON
04 Assistant to President ... Ms. Chanda F. PRATER
106 Assoc Dean/Dir Online Education ... Mrs. Rebecca FRANCIS
36 Dir of Career Services ... Ms. Deborah JONES
39 Director of Residence Life ... Ms. Lori ETHERIDGE
29 Director Alumni Affairs ... Ms. Summer CRICK
38 Director Student Counseling ... Ms. Terri PETZOLD

Lexington Theological Seminary (C)

230 Lexington Green Circle, Ste 300, Lexington KY 40503
County: Fayette — FICE Identification: 001971
Unit ID: 157207
Telephone: (859) 252-0361 — Carnegie Class: Spec-4-yr-Faith
FAX Number: (859) 281-6042 — Calendar System: Other
URL: www.lextheo.edu
Established: 1865 — Annual Graduate Tuition & Fees: N/A
Enrollment: 88 — Coed
Affiliation or Control: Christian Church (Disciples Of Christ)
IRS Status: 501(c)3
Highest Offering: Doctorate; No Undergraduates
Accreditation: THEOL

01 President ... Dr. Charisse L. GILLETT
05 VP Academic Affairs/Dean ... RevDr. Loida MARTELL
111 Vice President for Advancement ... Mr. Mark V. BLANKENSHIP
10 Chief Financial Officer ... Mrs. Karen C. WAGERS
06 Registrar ... Ms. Windy KIDD
08 Librarian ... Ms. Dolores YILIBUW
13 Director Information Services ... Mr. Ben WYATT
07 Interim Dean of Admission ... Ms. Carol DEVINE
15 Director Personnel Services ... Ms. Karen C. WAGERS
18 Chief Facilities/Physical Plant ... Ms. Karen C. WAGERS
29 Director Alumni Relations ... Mr. Mark V. BLANKENSHIP
37 Director Student Financial Aid ... Ms. Windy KIDD
96 Director of Purchasing ... Ms. Robin VARNER

Lindsey Wilson College (D)

210 Lindsey Wilson Street, Columbia KY 42728-1298
County: Adair — FICE Identification: 001972
Unit ID: 157216
Telephone: (270) 384-2126 — Carnegie Class: Masters/L
FAX Number: (270) 384-8200 — Calendar System: Semester
URL: www.lindsey.edu
Established: 1903 — Annual Undergrad Tuition & Fees: $25,718
Enrollment: 2,764 — Coed
Affiliation or Control: United Methodist — IRS Status: 501(c)3
Highest Offering: Doctorate
Accreditation: SC, CACREP, CAEP, IACBE, NURSE

01 President ... Dr. William T. LUCKEY, JR.
00 Chancellor ... Dr. John B. BEGLEY
05 Vice President Academic Affairs ... Dr. Patricia PARRISH
10 Vice President Administration ... Mr. Mark COLEMAN
111 Vice President Advancement ... Mr. Kevin A. THOMPSON
04 Executive Assistant ... Mrs. Amy THOMPSON-WELLS
32 Vice Pres Student Svcs/Enroll Mgmt ... Dr. Dean ADAMS
37 Vice Pres Student Financial Svcs ... Vacant
35 Dean of Students ... Mr. Christopher SCHMIDT
07 Dean of Admissions ... Mrs. Traci M. POOLER
07 Director of Admissions ... Mrs. Charity F. FERGUSON
41 Athletic Director ... Mr. Willis POOLER, III
06 Registrar ... Mrs. Claudia FROEDGE
15 Director of Human Resources ... Mrs. Karen F. WRIGHT
88 Dir Civic Engagement & Stdnt Ldrshp ... Ms. Kisha BURTON
36 Director Career Services ... Vacant
08 Librarian ... Ms. Erin WOLFORD
18 Director of Physical Plant ... Mr. Robert KARAM
109 Director of Auxiliary Services ... Mr. Jeff WILLIS
40 Bookstore Manager ... Mrs. Amy M. COOPER
35 Director of Student Activities ... Mrs. Anna BUCKMAN
85 Dir International Student Programs ... Ms. Sabine EASTHAM
13 Director of Information Systems ... Mrs. Harriet B. GOLD
26 Public Relations Officer ... Mrs. Venus POPPLEWELL
29 Director of Alumni Affairs ... Ms. Lafawn NETTLES
19 Director Safety/Security ... Mr. Michael STATEN
42 Chaplain ... Mr. Benjamin MARTIN
37 Director Student Financial Services ... Ms. Marilyn RADFORD
38 Director Student Counseling ... Dr. Jeff CRANE
66 Director of Nursing ... Mrs. Emiley BUTTON

Louisville Presbyterian Theological Seminary (E)

1044 Alta Vista Road, Louisville KY 40205-1798
County: Jefferson — FICE Identification: 001974
Unit ID: 157298
Telephone: (502) 895-3411 — Carnegie Class: Spec-4-yr-Faith
FAX Number: (502) 895-1096 — Calendar System: 4/1/4
URL: www.lpts.edu
Established: 1853 — Annual Graduate Tuition & Fees: N/A
Enrollment: 151 — Coed
Affiliation or Control: Presbyterian Church (U.S.A.) — IRS Status: 501(c)3
Highest Offering: Doctorate; No Undergraduates
Accreditation: SC, MFCD, THEOL

01 President ... Dr. Alton POLLARD, III
111 VP Philanthropy & Stewardship ... Ms. Anne MONELL
10 Vice President for Finance & Admin ... Ms. Angela TRAYLOR
05 Dean of Seminary ... Dr. Debra MUMFORD
32 Dean of Community Life ... Dr. Kilen GRAY
20 Assoc Dean BCS/DMin Studies ... Dr. Angela COWSER
06 Registrar ... Ms. Erin HAMILTON
29 Dir of Annual Giving/Alum Relations ... Ms. Andrea STEVENS
13 Director of Data Management ... Ms. Heather GRIFFIN
26 Director of Communications ... Ms. Kassandra TURPIN
08 Interim Dir of Library Services ... Ms. Jill SHERMAN
21 Controller ... Ms. Peggy MEREDITH
78 Director of Field Education ... Mr. Marcus HONG
07 Director of Admissions ... Rev. Sandra MOON
18 Director of Facilities ... Mr. Todd MCWHORTER
04 Executive Coordinator to President ... Ms. Susan DILUCA

MedQuest College (F)

10400 Linn Station Rd, Ste 120, Louisville KY 40223
County: Jefferson — FICE Identification: 042293
Unit ID: 484066
Telephone: (502) 245-6177 — Carnegie Class: Spec 2-yr-Health
FAX Number: (502) 245-4438 — Calendar System: Other
URL: www.medquestcollege.edu
Established: 2010 — Annual Undergrad Tuition & Fees: N/A
Enrollment: 337 — Coed
Affiliation or Control: Proprietary — IRS Status: Proprietary
Highest Offering: Associate Degree
Accreditation: ABHES, DH

01 Executive Director ... Ms. Robin BOUGHEY
11 Louisville Campus Director ... Mr. Todd JAKUB

Midway University (G)

512 E Stephens Street, Midway KY 40347-1112
County: Woodford — FICE Identification: 001975
Unit ID: 157377
Telephone: (859) 846-4421 — Carnegie Class: Masters/S
FAX Number: (859) 846-5349 — Calendar System: Semester
URL: www.midway.edu
Established: 1847 — Annual Undergrad Tuition & Fees: $24,850
Enrollment: 1,381 — Coed
Affiliation or Control: Christian Church (Disciples Of Christ)
IRS Status: 501(c)3
Highest Offering: Master's
Accreditation: SC, ADNUR, NUR

01 President ... Dr. John P. MARSDEN
05 Interim VP of Academic Affairs ... Dr. Carrie J. CHRISTENSEN
04 Exec Assistant to the President ... Ms. Elisabet BORDT
10 Vice Pres of Finance/Administration ... Mrs. Leah B. RICE
111 Vice President of Advancement ... Mr. Timothy CULVER
26 Vice Pres of Marketing & Comm ... Mrs. Ellen D. GREGORY
07 VP of Admissions & Athletics ... Mr. William "Rusty" KENNEDY, II
88 Director Undergraduate Admissions ... Ms. Ashley DUDGEON
13 Dean of Online Admissions & CIO ... Dr. Salah SHAKIR
06 Registrar ... Ms. Susie POWERS
08 Director of Library Services ... Mr. Michael GARNER
14 Technical Support Specialist ... Mr. Jimmy ROWE
15 Exec Director of Human Resources ... Ms. Trish JONES
37 Director of Financial Aid ... Ms. Erin TEVES
18 Director of Facilities ... Mr. Russell FISHER
50 Dean Business/Equine/Sport Stds ... Dr. Mark A. GILL
49 Dean School of Arts & Sciences ... Vacant
76 Dean School of Health Sciences ... Dr. Diane CHLEBOWY
19 Director Security/Safety ... Mr. Ric JACOB
36 Director Office of Student Success ... Ms. Mackenzie HANES
32 Dean of Students ... Mr. Joseph RYAN
09 Director of Institutional Research ... Mr. Jeffrey SUMMERS
39 Asst Director Residence Life ... Ms. Katie MORGAN
29 Dir Alumni Affairs/Annual Giving ... Mrs. Michelle PETERSON

Morehead State University (H)

150 University Boulevard, Morehead KY 40351-1689
County: Rowan — FICE Identification: 001976
Unit ID: 157386
Telephone: (800) 585-6781 — Carnegie Class: Masters/L
FAX Number: N/A — Calendar System: Semester
URL: www.moreheadstate.edu
Established: 1887 — Annual Undergrad Tuition & Fees (In-State): $9,290
Enrollment: 9,304 — Coed
Affiliation or Control: State — IRS Status: 501(c)3
Highest Offering: Doctorate
Accreditation: SC, ADNUR, ART, CAEP, COARC, DMS, MPCAC, MUS, NAIT, NURSE, RAD, RADMAG, SPAA, SW, THEA

01 President ... Dr. Joseph A. MORGAN
05 Provost/VP for Academic Affairs ... Dr. Antony NORMAN
10 VP Fiscal Svcs/Chief Financial Ofcr ... Mrs. Mary FISTER-TUCKER
32 Vice Pres for Student Affairs ... Mr. Russell F. MAST
111 Vice Pres for Univ Advancement ... Mr. Richard HESTERBERG
20 Assoc Provost UG Educ/Stdnt Success ... Dr. Laurie L. COUCH
88 Director of Testing Center ... Ms. Sharon S. REYNOLDS

06 Registrar ... Ms. Kerry MURPHY
51 Asst VP Regional Educ & Outreach ... Dr. Dan J. CONNELL
84 Asst Vice Pres Enrollment Services ... Mr. Tim RHODES
18 AVP Facilities Management ... Mr. Kim H. OATMAN
109 Exec Director Auxiliary Services ... Vacant
29 Asst VP Alumni Relations & Develop ... Ms. Melinda C. HIGHLEY
13 Interim Chief Information Officer ... Mr. Rick PHILLIPS
35 AVP Student Life/Dean of Students ... Mr. Maxwell J. AMMONS
08 Dean of Library Services ... Dr. David L. GREGORY
07 Dir of Undergraduate Admissions ... Ms. Holly L. POLLOCK
09 Dir Inst Research & Analysis ... Mrs. Courtney ANDREWS
15 Interim Director of Human Resources ... Dr. Caroline ATKINS
19 Chief of Police ... Mr. Merrell J. HARRISON
21 Director Accounting/Financial Svcs ... Ms. Kelli D. OWEN
37 Director Financial Aid ... Ms. Denise M. TRUSTY
36 Director Career Services ... Ms. Megan BOONE
39 Director of Housing/Residence Educ ... Dr. Alan M. RUCKER
41 Director of Athletics ... Dr. James D. GORDON
43 General Counsel ... Ms. Jane FITZPATRICK
96 Director Procurement Services ... Ms. Andrea STONE
38 Director of Counseling/Health Svcs ... Ms. Goldie C. WILLIAMS
50 Dean Smith Col Business/Tech ... Dr. Johnathan K. NELSON
53 Interim Dean College of Education ... Dr. April D. MILLER
81 Dean College of Science ... Dr. Wayne C. MILLER
79 Interim Dean Arts/Hum/Soc Sciences ... Dr. Sylvia HENNEBERG
106 Director Distance Educ/Instr Design ... Mr. Xavier M. SCOTT
108 Director University Assessment ... Dr. Kim NETTLETON
88 Director of Military Initiatives ... Dr. Silas SESSION
114 Director Budgets ... Ms. Jessica COOPER
101 Secretary of the Board of Regents ... Ms. Jane V. FITZPATRICK
58 Director of Graduate School ... Dr. Susan MAXEY
46 Director Research & Sponsored Pgms ... Dr. Shannon L. HARR
122 Coord Fraternity/Sorority Life ... Vacant

Murray State University (A)

102 Curris Center, Murray, KY 42071,
Murray KY 42071-3318

County: Calloway — FICE Identification: 001977
Unit ID: 157401
Telephone: (270) 809-3011 — Carnegie Class: Masters/L
FAX Number: (270) 809-3413 — Calendar System: Semester
URL: www.murraystate.edu
Established: 1922 — Annual Undergrad Tuition & Fees (In-State): $9,168
Enrollment: 9,449 — Coed
Affiliation or Control: State — IRS Status: 501(c)3
Highest Offering: Doctorate
Accreditation: SC, ANEST, ART, CACREP, CAEP, #COARC, DIETD, DIETI, EXSC, JOUR, MPCAC, MUS, NURSE, OT, SP, SW, THEA

01 President ... Dr. Robert JACKSON
05 Provost and VP Academic Affairs ... Dr. Tim TODD
10 VP Finance and Administratve Svcs ... Jacklyn DUDLEY
32 VP Student Affairs/Enrollment Mgmt ... Dr. Don ROBERTSON
58 Assoc Provost ... Dr. Robert PERVINE
13 Chief Information Officer ... Brian VERKAMP
19 Chief of Police ... Jeffrey GENTRY
43 General Counsel ... Robert MILLER
102 President MSU Foundation ... Dr. David W. DURR
30 Executive Director of Development ... Dr. C. Tina BERNOT
29 Director of Alumni Relations ... Carrie MCGINNIS
15 Interim Director of Human Resources ... Courtney HIXON
09 Exec Dir Strategic Enrollment Mgmt ... Dr. K. Renee FISTER
86 Exec Dir Government/Inst Relations ... Jordan SMITH
18 Director of Facilities Management ... Jason YOUNGBLOOD
41 Director of Athletics ... Kevin SAAL
26 Exec Dir of Marketing/Communication ... Shawn TOUNEY
28 Exec Dir IDEA & Title IX Coord ... Camisha DUFFY
06 Registrar ... Tracy ROBERTS
113 Bursar/Dir Student Fin Services ... Wendy CAIN
101 Sr Exec Coord for Pres/Board Rels ... T. Jill HUNT
07 Dir Undergrad Admiss/Transfer Ctr ... Maria ROSA
123 Coord Graduate Admissions/Records ... Kaitlyn BURZYNSKI
36 Director of Career Services ... Matt PURDY
38 Dir University Counseling Services ... Angie TRZEPACZ
96 Director of Procurement Services ... Beth WARD
122 Coord Greek Life/Stdnt Ldrshp Pgms ... Ms. Kim NEWBERN

Northern Kentucky University (B)

Nunn Drive, Highland Heights KY 41099-0000

County: Campbell — FICE Identification: 009275
Unit ID: 157447
Telephone: (859) 572-5100 — Carnegie Class: DU-Mod
FAX Number: (859) 572-5566 — Calendar System: Semester
URL: www.nku.edu
Established: 1968 — Annual Undergrad Tuition & Fees (In-State): $10,296
Enrollment: 16,211 — Coed
Affiliation or Control: State — IRS Status: 501(c)3
Highest Offering: Doctorate
Accreditation: SC, ANEST, CAATE, CACREP, CAEP, COARC, CONST, LAW, MUS, NURSE, RAD, RTT, SPAA, SW

01 President ... Dr. Ashish VAIDYA
05 Provost/Exec VP Academic Affairs ... Dr. Matt CECIL
32 Vice Pres Student Affairs ... Dr. Eddie J. HOWARD, JR.
111 Vice Pres University Advancement ... Mr. Eric C. GENTRY
43 VP Legal Affairs & General Counsel ... Mr. Grant GARBER
20 Vice Prov Undergrad Academic Affs ... Vacant
84 VP Enrollment/Degree Management ... Vacant
58 Vice Prov Grad Educ/Rsrch/Outreach ... Ms. Samantha LANGLEY-TURNBAUGH
46 Vice Pres/Chief Strategy Officer ... Dr. Bonita BROWN
20 Assoc Provost Academic Admin ... Mr. Chad OGLE
13 Chief Information Officer ... Mr. Timothy FERGUSON
10 Chief Financial Officer ... Mr. Jeremy ALLTOP
28 Chief Div/Equity/Incl Ofcr/T IX ... Mr. Darryl A. PEAL
08 Dean of the Library ... Ms. Andrea FALCONE
35 AVP Student Affairs ... Mr. Arnie SLAUGHTER
86 Director of Economic Engagement ... Ms. Jenny SAND
49 Dean College of Arts & Sciences ... Dr. Diana MCGILL
50 Dean College of Business ... Dr. Hassan HASSABELNABY
88 Dean College of Informatics ... Dr. Kevin KIRBY
53 Dean College of Education ... Dr. Ginni FAIR
61 Dean Chase College of Law ... Ms. Judith DAAR
66 Dean College of Health Professions ... Dr. Dale STEPHENSON
18 Asst VP Facilities Management ... Mr. Syed ZAIDI
18 Director Operations & Maintenance ... Mr. Bill MOULTON
26 Asst VP Marketing & Communications ... Vacant
21 Dir Fin & Operational Auditing ... Mr. Larry MEYER
109 Dir Business Ops/Auxiliary Services ... Mr. Andy MEEKS
88 Sr Director Planning/Design/Const ... Ms. Mary Paula SCHUH
15 Senior Director Human Resources ... Ms. Lori SOUTHWOOD
21 Comptroller ... Vacant
19 Chief of Police ... Mr. John GAFFIN
96 Int Director Procurement Services ... Mr. Blaine GILMORE
92 Dean of Honors College ... Mr. James BUSS
07 Sr Dir Undergraduate Admissions ... Mr. Derrick ROBERTSON
104 Exec Dir Intl Education Center ... Dr. Francois LEROY
06 Registrar ... Mr. W. Allen COLE, III
37 AVP Enrollment & Financial Aid ... Ms. Leah STEWART
78 Exec Dir Ctr for Civic Engagement ... Mr. Mark NEIKIRK
25 Director Research/Grants/Contracts ... Ms. Mary UCCI
89 Director First Year Experience ... Ms. Amanda ANDREWS
09 Exec Dir Planning/Inst Research ... Vacant
88 Director Campus Recreation ... Vacant
38 Director Health/Counseling/Prev ... Ms. Amy CLARK
124 Director of Student Engagement ... Ms. Tiffany MAYSE
36 Director Career Services ... Mr. Bill FROUDE
41 Dir of Intercollegiate Athletics ... Mr. Ken BOTHOF

Simmons College of Kentucky (C)

1018 South 7th Street, Louisville KY 40203-3322

County: Jefferson — FICE Identification: 041780
Unit ID: 461759
Telephone: (502) 776-1443 — Carnegie Class: Bac-A&S
FAX Number: (502) 882-1903 — Calendar System: Semester
URL: www.simmonscollegeky.edu
Established: 1879 — Annual Undergrad Tuition & Fees: $6,990
Enrollment: 140 — Coed
Affiliation or Control: Baptist — IRS Status: 501(c)3
Highest Offering: Baccalaureate
Accreditation: BI

01 President ... Dr. Kevin W. COSBY
05 VP of Academic Affairs ... Mr. Javan REED
108 Executive VP Inst Effectiveness ... Dr. Ken B. JOBST
32 Vice Pres Student Affairs ... Dr. Walter MALONE, JR.
22 Title III Director ... Ms. Kathy WASHINGTON
06 Registrar ... Ms. Deborah THOMAS
11 Sr VP & COO ... Dr. Frank M. SMITH, JR.
30 VP of Development ... Mr. Glenn DAVIS
15 Manager of Human Resources ... Ms. Deborah MCDONALD
31 VP Cmty Engagement & Advancement ... Ms. Von PURDY
25 VP Research & Planning ... Ms. Candice HOLT
04 Admin Assistant to the President ... Ms. Cheri MILLS
09 Director of Institutional Research ... Dr. Ken JOBST
29 Director Alumni Affairs ... Ms. Rebecca GARDNER
41 Athletic Director ... Mr. Jerry EAVES

The Southern Baptist Theological Seminary (D)

2825 Lexington Road, Louisville KY 40280-2899

County: Jefferson — FICE Identification: 001982
Unit ID: 157748
Telephone: (502) 897-4011 — Carnegie Class: Spec-4-yr-Faith
FAX Number: (502) 899-1770 — Calendar System: Other
URL: www.sbts.edu
Established: 1859 — Annual Undergrad Tuition & Fees: $11,896
Enrollment: 4,337 — Coed
Affiliation or Control: Southern Baptist — IRS Status: 501(c)3
Highest Offering: Doctorate
Accreditation: SC, CAEP, MUS, THEOL

01 President ... Dr. R. Albert MOHLER, JR.
100 Chief of Staff/SVP Administration ... Mr. Jonathan AUSTIN
04 Exec Admin Asst Office of President ... Ms. Anna ARRASTIA
05 Sr VP Academic Admin/Provost ... Dr. Matthew HALL
111 Sr VP Institutional Advancement ... Mr. Craig PARKER
11 Vice President of Operations ... Mr. Andrew VINCENT
110 VP of Advancement/Communications ... Mr. Edward HEINZE
13 VP Campus Technology ... Mr. Jason HEATH
58 Vice President for Doctoral Studies ... Dr. Timothy Paul JONES
108 Assoc VP Institutional Assessment ... Dr. Joseph HARROD
84 Assoc VP Enrollment Management ... Mr. Matt MINIER
15 Assoc VP of Human Resources ... Mr. Brent SMALL
18 Chief Facilities/Physical Plant ... Mr. Henry LACHER
41 Director of Health & Recreation ... Mr. Michael MCCARTY
07 Director of Admissions ... Mr. Jeremy PELTON
08 Librarian ... Dr. Berry DRIVER
37 Manager of Financial Aid ... Mrs. Ana WILLIAMS
73 Dean of School of Theology ... Dr. Hershael YORK
88 Dean Missions Evangel Chrch Growth ... Dr. Paul AKIN
12 Dean Boyce College ... Dr. Dustin BRUCE
06 Registrar ... Mr. Norm CHUNG
39 Director of Campus Housing & Legacy ... Mr. Caleb DYE
106 Assoc VP for the Global Campus ... Mr. Brian RENSHAW

Spalding University (E)

845 S Third Street, Louisville KY 40203-2213

County: Jefferson — FICE Identification: 001960
Unit ID: 157757
Telephone: (502) 585-9911 — Carnegie Class: Masters/L
FAX Number: (502) 585-7158 — Calendar System: Other
URL: www.spalding.edu
Established: 1814 — Annual Undergrad Tuition & Fees: $25,975
Enrollment: 1,596 — Coed
Affiliation or Control: Independent Non-Profit — IRS Status: 501(c)3
Highest Offering: Doctorate
Accreditation: SC, CAATE, CAEP, CLPSY, IACBE, NURSE, OT, SW

01 President ... Ms. Tori MURDEN MCCLURE
05 Provost ... Dr. John BURDEN
111 Chief Advancement Officer ... Ms. Caroline HEINE
11 Chief of Staff/Dean of Operations ... Mr. Chris HART
58 Dean of Graduate Studies ... Dr. Kurt JEFFERSON
20 Dean of Undergraduate Education ... Dr. Tomarra ADAMS
32 Dean of Students ... Ms. Janelle RAE
10 Chief Financial Officer ... Mr. Rush SHERMAN
43 General Counsel ... Ms. Emily NORRIS
84 Dean of Enrollment Management ... Dr. Melissa CHASTAIN
121 Director Academic Advising Center ... Ms. Nikki SHEDLETSKY
06 Registrar ... Ms. Jennifer GOHMANN
13 Chief Information Officer ... Mr. Ezra KRUMHANSL
37 Director Financial Aid ... Ms. Michelle STANDRIDGE
15 Exec Dir of Human Resources ... Ms. Jennifer BROCKHOFF
09 Director of Inst Effectiveness ... Ms. Elizabeth DYER
41 Director of Athletics ... Mr. Roger BURKMAN
21 Controller ... Ms. Katherine WEYHING
18 JLL Facilities Manager ... Mr. Kevin WEBER
07 Director of Admissions ... Ms. Jill GAINES

Sullivan University (F)

3101 Bardstown Road, Louisville KY 40205-3000

County: Jefferson — FICE Identification: 004619
Unit ID: 157793
Telephone: (502) 456-6504 — Carnegie Class: Masters/L
FAX Number: (502) 456-0040 — Calendar System: Quarter
URL: www.sullivan.edu
Established: 1962 — Annual Undergrad Tuition & Fees: $13,860
Enrollment: 3,165 — Coed
Affiliation or Control: Proprietary — IRS Status: Proprietary
Highest Offering: Doctorate
Accreditation: SC, ARCPA, CAHIIM, CIDA, MAC, PHAR, RAD, SURGT

00 Chancellor/CEO Sullivan Univ System ... Mr. Glenn D. SULLIVAN
02 President ... Dr. Jay D. MARR
05 Sr VP for Academic Affairs/Provost ... Dr. Diana LAWRENCE
11 Sr Vice Pres for Administration ... Mr. Chris ERNST
10 Chief Financial Officer ... Mr. Patrick MCMURRAY
84 VP of Enrollment Mgmt ... Ms. Nina MARTINEZ
86 Vice Pres of Community Partnerships ... Mr. David KEENE
12 Vice Pres Lexington Campus ... Dr. David TUDOR
15 Director of Human Resources ... Ms. Rachel MAGUIRE
58 Assoc Provost/Dean Graduate School ... Dr. Tim SWENSON
88 Dean College of Hosp Studies ... Mr. David HENDRICKSEN
06 Registrar ... Ms. Kim MITCHELL
08 Sr Dir of University Libraries ... Dr. Jackie YOUNG
13 Director of IT Services ... Mr. Drew ARNETTE
36 Sr Dir of Career Svcs & Alumni Affs ... Mr. Sam MANNINO
37 Sr Dir Student Financial Planning ... Ms. Angela MILLER
40 Bookstore Manager ... Mr. Bryan NEEDY
96 Director of Purchasing ... Ms. Ann VEST
56 Dir of Ft Knox Extension Campus ... Ms. Barbara DEAN
88 University Ombudsman ... Mr. Jim KLEIN
18 Manager Campus Facilities ... Mr. Mike FOWLER

Thomas More University (G)

333 Thomas More Parkway,
Crestview Hills KY 41017-3495

County: Kenton — FICE Identification: 002001
Unit ID: 157809
Telephone: (859) 341-5800 — Carnegie Class: Masters/S
FAX Number: (859) 344-3345 — Calendar System: Semester
URL: www.thomasmore.edu
Established: 1921 — Annual Undergrad Tuition & Fees: $33,420
Enrollment: 2,037 — Coed
Affiliation or Control: Roman Catholic — IRS Status: 501(c)3
Highest Offering: Master's
Accreditation: SC, ACBSP, CAEP, NUR

01 President ... Dr. Joseph L. CHILLO
04 Exec Assistant to the President ... Ms. Charlene BARLOW
10 Chief Financial/Business Officer ... Mr. Mark A. GOSHORN
05 Interim VPAA ... Dr. Jay LANGGUTH
100 Chief of Staff/VP Strategy ... Ms. Kelly FRENCH
32 Chief of Student Affairs/Life ... Ms. Annabelle BAUTISTA
111 Vice Pres Institutional Advancement ... Mr. Kevin REYNOLDS
84 Dean of Enrollment ... Mr. Justin VOGEL
21 Controller ... Ms. Beth MALEY
37 Director of Financial Aid ... Mr. Mark MESSINGSCHLAGER

13 Director of IT ..... Mr. Sean KAPSAL
26 Dir Communications/Media Relations ..... Ms. Lyna KELLEY
41 Athletic Director ..... Mr. Terry D. CONNOR
42 Chaplain ..... Rev. Gerald E. TWADDELL
43 Director of Legal Services ..... Mr. Noah WELTE
19 Director of Campus Safety ..... Mr. Dennis LEHMKUHL
15 Director of Human Resources ..... Ms. Laura CUSTER
18 Director of Facilities ..... Mr. Joey ETHERIDGE
29 Director of Alumni ..... Vacant
36 Dir of Career Planning/Coop Educ ..... Ms. Robin NORTON
73 Director of Campus Ministry ..... Mr. Andrew COLE
08 Director of Library ..... Dr. John ERNST
06 Registrar ..... Ms. Michelle VEZINA
92 Director of Honors Program ..... Dr. Catherine SHERRON
44 Director Annual Giving ..... Mr. Flynn ASHLEY
113 Bursar ..... Mr. Robert FISHER
50 Dean of Business ..... Dr. Bruce ROSENTHAL
39 Coordinator of Residence Life ..... Vacant
09 Dir of Inst Planning/Effectiveness ..... Vacant

Transylvania University (A)

300 N Broadway, Lexington KY 40508-1797
County: Fayette | FICE Identification: 001987
Unit ID: 157818
Telephone: (859) 233-8300 | Carnegie Class: Bac-A&S
FAX Number: (859) 233-8797 | Calendar System: Other
URL: www.transy.edu
Established: 1780 | Annual Undergrad Tuition & Fees: $41,610
Enrollment: 963 | Coed
Affiliation or Control: Christian Church (Disciples Of Christ)
IRS Status: 501(c)3
Highest Offering: Baccalaureate
Accreditation: SC

01 President ..... Mr. Brien LEWIS
05 VP Acad Affs/Dean of the University ..... Dr. Rebecca THOMAS
10 Vice President Finance & Business ..... Mr. Marc MATHEWS
84 Interim VP for Enrollment ..... Mr. Johnnie JOHNSON
111 VP for Advancement ..... Mr. Shawn LYONS
32 VP for Student Affairs ..... Dr. Michael COVERT
13 VP for Information Technology ..... Ms. Deepa DUBAL
26 VP for Marketing & Communications ..... Ms. Megan MOLONEY
09 VP for Institutional Effectiveness ..... Dr. Rhyan M. CONYERS
41 VP for Athletics ..... Dr. Holly SHEILLEY
28 VP for Diversity and Inclusion ..... Dr. Deidra DENNIE
06 Registrar ..... Ms. Michelle RAWLINGS
08 Director of Library ..... Ms. Susan M. BROWN
104 Dir Global & Intercult Engagement ..... Ms. Courtney SMITH
20 Assistant Dean for Academic Affairs ..... Ms. Tracy DUNN
15 Director Human Resources ..... Ms. Alison BEGOR
18 Director of Facilities ..... Mr. Danny KNOX
19 Director Security/Safety ..... Mr. Joe MCCLURE
96 Director of Purchasing ..... Ms. Shawn T. SINGLETON
39 Director Residence Life ..... Mr. Keith JONES
37 Director of Financial Aid ..... Ms. Jennifer PRIEST
29 Director Alumni Relations ..... Ms. Natasa PAJIC MONGIARDO
04 Executive Assistant to President ..... Ms. Amanda TURCOTTE
88 Assist Athletic Dir for Compliance ..... Mr. Jeff CHANEY

Union College (B)

310 College Street, Barbourville KY 40906-1499
County: Knox | FICE Identification: 001988
Unit ID: 157863
Telephone: (606) 546-4151 | Carnegie Class: Masters/S
FAX Number: (606) 546-1217 | Calendar System: Other
URL: www.unionky.edu
Established: 1879 | Annual Undergrad Tuition & Fees: $28,000
Enrollment: 1,179 | Coed
Affiliation or Control: United Methodist | IRS Status: 501(c)3
Highest Offering: Master's
Accreditation: SC, CAEP, CAEPN, NURSE

01 President ..... Dr. Marcia HAWKINS
04 Executive Assistant to President ..... Ms. Sherry JENKINS
31 Exec Dir Cmty Rels & Events ..... Ms. Meghann CHESNUT
42 College Minister ..... Rev. David MILLER
05 VP for Academic Affairs ..... Dr. Marisa GREER
79 Dean School of Humanities ..... Dr. Karl WALLHAUSSER
58 Dean Professional and Grad Studies ..... Dr. David WILLIAMS
111 VP of Advancement/Communications ..... Mr. Brian STRUNK
26 Senior Director of Communications ..... Mrs. Maisie NELSON
29 Director of Alumni Relations ..... Mrs. Courtney OLIVER
84 VP for Enrollment Management ..... Vacant
32 Dean of Students ..... Mr. James BECKNELL
39 Director of Housing ..... Mr. Jason ELS
35 Assistant Director of Campus Life ..... Vacant
10 Chief Business Officer ..... Mr. Steve MORRIS
114 Asst VP Business/Financial Svcs ..... Mr. Randle TEAGUE
15 Exec Director of Human Resources ..... Ms. Lynn SMITH
118 Coordinator of Payroll/Benefits ..... Ms. Samantha NANTZ
21 Controller ..... Ms. Jessica JUSTICE
06 Registrar ..... Ms. Kathy INKSTER
18 Director of Physical Plant (NMRC) ..... Mr. Shain SIZEMORE
41 Athletic Director ..... Mr. Tim CURRY
09 Director of Institutional Research ..... Ms. Anisa JAMES
121 Associate Dean for Student Success ..... Ms. Stephanie SMITH
08 Head Librarian ..... Ms. Tara L. COOPER
37 Director of Financial Aid ..... Ms. Andra BUTLER
19 Safety Team Leader ..... Mr. Mike GRAY
13 Director of IT ..... Mr. Eric EVANS

105 Director Web Services ..... Mr. Phillip HORN
44 Director Annual Giving ..... Mr. Derrick REYNOLDS

University of the Cumberlands (C)

6191 College Station Drive, Williamsburg KY 40769-1372
County: Whitley | FICE Identification: 001962
Unit ID: 156541
Telephone: (606) 549-2200 | Carnegie Class: DU-Mod
FAX Number: (606) 539-4280 | Calendar System: Semester
URL: www.ucumberlands.edu
Established: 1888 | Annual Undergrad Tuition & Fees: $9,875
Enrollment: 19,110 | Coed
Affiliation or Control: Baptist | IRS Status: 501(c)3
Highest Offering: Doctorate
Accreditation: SC, ADNUR, ARCPA, CACREP, CAEP, IACBE, NURSE

01 President ..... Dr. Larry L. COCKRUM
05 EVP Academic Affs/Provost/Title IX ..... Dr. Emily COLEMAN
10 EVP Finance/Chief Financial Officer ..... Dr. Quentin YOUNG
11 EVP of Operations/COO ..... Mr. Travis WILSON
37 Director of Financial Aid ..... Mrs. Kimberly NOE
41 Director of Athletics ..... Mr. Chris KRAFTICK
13 EVP for Information Technology/CIO ..... Dr. Donnie GRIMES
84 EVP for Enrollment & Communication ..... Dr. Jerry JACKSON
06 Registrar ..... Ms. Kathryn MCCUNE
38 Director of School Counseling ..... Vacant
111 EVP Inst Advance/Chief of Staff ..... Mrs. Leslie C. RYSER
35 Dean Student Life ..... Vacant
15 VP of Human Resources ..... Mr. Steve ALLEN
42 Director of Church Relations ..... Dr. Rick FLEENOR
32 VP Student Affairs ..... Dr. Jamirae HOLBROOK
08 Director of Library ..... Ms. Jan WREN
123 Director of Graduate Admissions ..... Mrs. Shonda POWERS
18 Director of Plant Services ..... Mr. David ROOT
113 Director of Student Accounts ..... Mr. Derek MCINTOSH
29 Exec Director for Alumni Relations ..... Mrs. Erica HARRIS
30 VP for Development ..... Mr. Bill STOHLMAN

University of Kentucky (D)

101 Main Building, Lexington KY 40506-0003
County: Fayette | FICE Identification: 001989
Unit ID: 157085
Telephone: (859) 257-2000 | Carnegie Class: DU-Highest
FAX Number: (859) 257-4000 | Calendar System: Semester
URL: www.uky.edu
Established: 1865 | Annual Undergrad Tuition & Fees (In-State): $12,484
Enrollment: 29,986 | Coed
Affiliation or Control: State | IRS Status: 501(c)3
Highest Offering: Doctorate
Accreditation: SC, ARCPA, CAATE, CACREP, CAMPEP, CIDA, CLPSY, COPSY, DENT, DIETC, DIETD, DIETI, HSA, IPSY, JOUR, LAW, LIB, LSAR, MED, MFCD, MLS, MUS, NURSE, PAST, PCSAS, PH, PHAR, PTA, SCPSY, SP, SPAA, SW, THEA

01 President ..... Dr. Eli I. CAPILOUTO
46 Vice President Research ..... Dr. Lisa A. CASSIS
05 Provost ..... Dr. Robert DIPAOLA
11 Exec VP Finance/Administration ..... Dr. Eric N. MONDAY
17 Executive VP for Health Affairs ..... Dr. Mark NEWMAN
32 VP for Student Success ..... Dr. Kirsten TURNER
13 Chief Information Officer ..... Mr. Brian NICHOLS
35 Stdnt Affs/Dean of Students ..... Dr. Trisha CLEMENT MONTGOMERY
22 Actg Assoc VP Institutional Equity ..... Ms. Thalethia ROUTT
30 Acting VP for Philanthropy ..... Mr. Tom HARRIS
10 VP Health Affs/Chief Financial Ofcr ..... Mr. Craig COLLINS
45 VP Financial Planning & CBO ..... Ms. Angela S. MARTIN
18 VP Facilities Mgmt & Chief Facil ..... Ms. Mary S. VOSEVICH
28 VP Institutional Diversity ..... Dr. Katrice ALBERT
26 VP University Relations ..... Mr. Thomas W. HARRIS
15 Actg VP Human Resources Adm & CHRO ..... Ms. Gina DUGAS
19 Asst Vice Pres Public Safety ..... Mr. Anthany BEATTY
109 Assistant VP Auxiliary Services ..... Mr. Andrew SMITH
21 Assoc VP Res Admin & Fiscal Affs ..... Mr. Jack SUPPLEE, JR.
25 Exec Director Sponsored Projects ..... Ms. Kim C. CARTER
88 Assoc VP UKHC/EVPHA ..... Mr. Joe CLAYPOOL
58 Acting Dean Graduate School ..... Dr. Martha PETERSON
88 Assoc Provost Faculty Advancement ..... Dr. Gene T. LINEBERRY
84 Chief Enrollment Officer ..... Ms. Christine HARPER
08 Dean of Libraries ..... Dr. Doug WAY
27 Chief Communications Officer ..... Mr. Jay D. BLANTON
43 General Counsel ..... Mr. William E. THRO
41 Director Athletics ..... Mr. Mitch S. BARNHART
37 Exec Director Student Financial Aid ..... Ms. Kathy BIALK
09 Director of Inst Research ..... Dr. Chris THURINGER
36 Asst Dean for Career & Academic Exp ..... Mr. Ray R. CLERE
38 Director Counseling & Testing ..... Dr. Mary C. BOLIN
29 Associate Vice President for Alumni ..... Ms. Jill SMITH
21 Controller ..... Ms. Shanhong WANG
47 Dean of Agriculture/Food & Envir ..... Dr. Nancy M. COX
19 Chief of Police ..... Mr. Joseph W. MONROE
88 Acting Dean of Design ..... Dr. Ned CRANK
88 Int Exec Director Gatton Stdnt Ctr ..... Mr. Scott HENRY
49 Dean of Arts & Sciences ..... Dr. Ana FRANCO WATKINS
50 Dean of Business & Economics ..... Dr. Simon J. SHEATHER
53 Dean of Education ..... Dr. Julian VASQUEZ HEILIG
54 Dean of Engineering ..... Dr. Rudolph BUCHHEIT
57 Dean of Fine Arts ..... Mr. Mark SHANDA
60 Dean of Communication & Information ..... Dr. Jennifer GREER
61 Dean of Law ..... Dr. Mary DAVIS

70 Dean of Social Work ..... Dr. Justin (Jay) MILLER
76 Dean of Health Sciences ..... Dr. Scott M. LEPHART
52 Dean of Dentistry ..... Dr. Jeff OKESON
63 Acting Dean of Medicine ..... Dr. Charles GRIFFITH, III
66 Dean of Nursing ..... Dr. Janie H. HEATH
67 Dean of Pharmacy ..... Dr. Kip GUY
69 Acting Dean Public Health ..... Dr. Heather BUSH
92 Dean Lewis Honors College ..... Dr. Christian BRADY
96 Exec Director Purchasing & CPO ..... Mr. Barry SWANSON
108 Director of Inst Effectiveness ..... Ms. Nora HATTON
44 Director Annual Giving ..... Mr. Andrew PALMER
116 Chief Accountability Officer Audit ..... Mr. Joe REED
04 Exec Administrator to President ..... Ms. Brenda HEETER
06 Registrar ..... Ms. Kimberly TAYLOR
39 Dir Resident Life/Student Housing ..... Dr. Justin BLEVINS

University of Louisville (E)

2301 S Third Street, Louisville KY 40292-0001
County: Jefferson | FICE Identification: 001999
Unit ID: 157289
Telephone: (502) 852-5555 | Carnegie Class: DU-Highest
FAX Number: (502) 852-7013 | Calendar System: Semester
URL: www.louisville.edu
Established: 1798 | Annual Undergrad Tuition & Fees (In-State): $12,162
Enrollment: 22,211 | Coed
Affiliation or Control: State | IRS Status: 501(c)3
Highest Offering: Doctorate
Accreditation: SC, ACATE, AUD, CAEP, CAMPEP, CIDA, CLPSY, COPSY, COSMA, DENT, DH, EXSC, HSA, IPSY, LAW, MED, MFCD, MUS, NURSE, PH, PLNG, SP, SPAA, SW, THEA

01 Interim President ..... Dr. Lori STEWART GONZALEZ
05 Interim Provost ..... Dr. Gerry BRADLEY
17 Vice Pres Academic Medical Affairs ..... Dr. Toni GANZEL
46 Executive VP for Research ..... Dr. Kevin GARDNER
10 Vice Pres & Chief Financial Officer ..... Mr. Daniel DURBIN
11 Sr Assoc VP for Operations ..... Mr. Mark WATKINS
111 Vice Pres Univ Advancement ..... Dr. Jasmine FARRIER
32 VP Student Affs/Dean of Students ..... Dr. Michael MARDIS
13 Vice President & CIO ..... Mr. M. Rehan KHAN
31 Vice President Community Engagement ..... Dr. Ralph FITZPATRICK
15 Vice President Human Resources ..... Ms. Mary Elizabeth MILES
41 Interim Athletic Director ..... Mr. Josh HEIRD
18 Assoc VP Facilities/Physical Plant ..... Mr. Mark WATKINS
29 Asst VP for Alumni Relations ..... Mr. Josh HAWKINS
100 Chief of Staff for the President ..... Mr. Michael W. SMITH
43 General Counsel/VP Legal Affs ..... Ms. Angela CURRY
58 Vice Prov/Dean Grad Affs ..... Dr. Beth BOEHM
28 Sr Assoc VP Diversity/Equity ..... Dr. V. Faye JONES
20 Interim Sr Vice Provost ..... Dr. Gail DEPUY
108 Vice Prov Assmnt/Plng/Accountabil ..... Mr. Robert S. GOLDSTEIN
84 Vice Provost Enrollment Management ..... Mr. James BEGANY
106 Int Vice Prov Online Learning ..... Ms. Kristen BROWN
88 Dir Accreditation & Acad Planning ..... Ms. Kay VETTER
21 Controller/Treasurer ..... Ms. Beverly SANTAMOURIS
07 Executive Director Admissions ..... Ms. Jenny L. SAWYER
06 University Registrar ..... Mr. Scott A. BURKS
37 Dir Financial Aid Svcs ..... Mr. Joseph DABLOW
26 Sr AVP Communications/Marketing ..... Mr. John DREES
16 Asst Dir Employee Relations ..... Ms. Donna ERNST
19 Dir Public Safety/Chief of Police ..... Mr. Gary D. LEWIS, JR.
09 Exec Dir Inst Research & Planning ..... Ms. Becky PATTERSON
45 Director Inst Effectiveness ..... Dr. Katie PARTIN
39 Director Residence Admin ..... Dr. Thomas HARDY
105 Director of Brand Design ..... Mr. Brian A. FAUST
27 Director Media Relations ..... Mr. John KARMAN
116 Director Audit Services ..... Ms. Cheri JONES
92 Exec Director of Honors Program ..... Dr. Joy HART
96 Chief Procurement Officer ..... Ms. Sally MOLSBERGER
36 Director Career Development ..... Mr. Bill FLETCHER
38 Director Counseling Center ..... Ms. Aesha UQDAH
08 Dean of University Libraries ..... Mr. Robert FOX
49 Int Dean College Arts & Sciences ..... Dr. David OWEN
50 Dean College of Business ..... Dr. Todd MOORADIAN
52 Dean School of Dentistry ..... Dr. Gerry BRADLEY
53 Int Dean Col of Educ/Human Devel ..... Dr. Amy LINGO
70 Dean Kent School Social Work ..... Dr. David A. JENKINS
64 Dean School of Music ..... Dr. Teresa REED
61 Int Dean Brandeis School of Law ..... Mr. Lars SMITH
66 Dean School of Nursing ..... Dr. Sonya HARDING
54 Dean Speed School Engineering ..... Dr. Emmanuel COLLINS
63 Dean School of Medicine ..... Dr. Toni GANZEL
69 Dean Public Health/Information Sci ..... Dr. Craig H. BLAKELY
104 Director Study Abroad ..... Dr. Virginia HOSONO

University of Pikeville (F)

147 Sycamore Street, Pikeville KY 41501-1194
County: Pike | FICE Identification: 001980
Unit ID: 157535
Telephone: (606) 218-5250 | Carnegie Class: DU-Mod
FAX Number: (606) 218-5269 | Calendar System: Semester
URL: www.upike.edu
Established: 1889 | Annual Undergrad Tuition & Fees: $22,050
Enrollment: 2,240 | Coed
Affiliation or Control: Presbyterian Church (U.S.A.) | IRS Status: 501(c)3
Highest Offering: Doctorate
Accreditation: SC, CAEP, NUR, OPT, OPTR, OSTEO, SW

01 President ..... Dr. Burton J. WEBB
00 Chancellor ..... Mr. Paul E. PATTON

20 Assistant Provost of Academics .... Dr. Amanda J. SLONE
05 Provost .... Dr. Lori WERTH
49 Dean College Arts/Sciences .... Dr. Jennifer DUGAN
88 Dean College of Optometry .... Dr. Michael BACIGALUPI
50 Dean College of Business .... Dr. Chris HARRIS
53 Dean College of Education .... Vacant
10 Vice Pres Finance/Business Affairs .... Mr. Barry BENTLEY
111 Vice President for Advancement .... Mr. David HUTCHENS
26 Dir of Public Affairs/Advancement .... Mrs. Kelly ROWE-JONES
63 Dean KYCOM .... Dr. Joe KINGERY
32 Dean of Students .... Vacant
07 Dean of Admissions .... Mr. Gary JUSTICE
08 Director of Library Services .... Ms. Edna FUGATE
06 University Registrar .... Mrs. Gia POTTER
09 Director of Institutional Research .... Dr. Meg SIDLE
13 Senior Info Services Administrator .... Mr. Jonathan WILLIAMSON
18 Director for Facilities .... Mr. Charles ATKINSON
37 Director of Student Financial Svcs .... Mr. Daniel DONNER
15 AVP Operations/Human Resources .... Mr. Michael PACHECO
04 Executive Asst to President .... Mrs. Sherrie MARRS
19 Director Security/Safety .... Mr. Oliver Lee UPCHURCH
41 Athletic Director .... Mr. Kelly WELLS
105 Coordinator of New Media .... Mr. Larry EPLING
25 Chief Contracts/Grants Admin .... Mrs. Tiffany THACKER
29 Director Alumni Relations .... Ms. Lisa BLACKBURN
124 Assistant Provost of Retention .... Dr. Mathys MEYER
35 Assistant Dean of Student Affairs .... Mr. Chris ROBINSON
44 Director Annual or Planned Giving .... Vacant
104 Director Study Abroad .... Vacant
28 Director of Diversity .... Dr. Katrina RUGLESS

Western Kentucky University (A)

1906 College Heights Blvd, Bowling Green KY 42101-3576
County: Warren FICE Identification: 002002
Unit ID: 157951
Telephone: (270) 745-0111 Carnegie Class: DU-Mod
FAX Number: (270) 745-5387 Calendar System: Semester
URL: www.wku.edu
Established: 1906 Annual Undergrad Tuition & Fees (In-State): $10,802
Enrollment: 17,517 Coed
Affiliation or Control: State IRS Status: 501(c)3
Highest Offering: Doctorate
Accreditation: **SC**, ADNUR, ART, CACREP, CAEP, CAHIIM, CAPRT, DANCE, DH, DIETD, DIETI, JOUR, MUS, NAEYC, NAIT, NURSE, PH, PTA, SP, SPAA, SW, THEA

01 President .... Dr. Timothy C. CABONI
04 Assistant to the President .... Ms. Kim LANCASTER
05 Provost/VP Academic Affairs .... Dr. Robert FISCHER
46 Assoc Provost for Research .... Dr. Ranjit KOODALI
26 Assoc VP Marketing & Brand Strategy ... Mr. John-Mark FRANCIS
30 Assoc VP Philanthropy & Alumni .... Mr. John Paul BLAIR
29 Exec Director Alumni Engagement .... Mr. Anthony MCADOO
84 VP Enrollment & Student Experience .... Dr. Ethan LOGAN
10 Exec VP Strategy Operations/Finance .... Ms. Susan HOWARTH
07 Assistant VP for Enrollment .... Mr. Scott MCDONALD
106 Assoc VP Ext Learning & Outreach .... Dr. Beth LAVES
79 Dean Arts & Letters .... Dr. Terrance BROWN
50 Dean Business .... Dr. Christopher SHOOK
53 Dean Education/Behavioral Sci .... Dr. Corinne MURPHY
76 Dean Health & Human Services .... Dr. Tania BASTA
54 Dean Science & Engineering .... Dr. David BROWN
62 Dean Libraries .... Ms. Susann DEVRIES
21 Interim Chief Financial Officer .... Ms. Kristi SMITH
06 University Registrar .... Ms. Jennifer HAMMONDS
13 Assistant VP Information Technology .... Mr. Jeppie SUMPTER
15 Assistant VP and CHRO .... Ms. Andrea SHERRILL
27 Director of Media Relations .... Mr. Jace LUX
86 Director Govt & Community Relations .... Ms. Jennifer B. SMITH
121 Assistant VP Advising & Career Dev .... Mr. Christopher JENSEN
39 Assistant VP Housing/Residence Life .... Dr. Mike REAGLE
19 Chief of Police .... Mr. Mitch WALKER
102 Pres College Heights Foundation .... Dr. Donald L. SMITH
37 Dir Student Financial Assistance .... Mr. Bryson DAVIS
51 Dir Continuing & Professional Dev .... Mr. Derek OLIVE
09 Director Institutional Research .... Dr. Tuesdi HELBIG
22 Director EEO/Title IX/ADA .... Mr. Joshua HAYES
24 Dir Educational Telecommunications .... Mr. David BRINKLEY
41 Director Intercollegiate Athletics .... Mr. Todd M. STEWART
85 Assoc Provost Global Learning .... Mr. John SUNNYGARD
92 Exec Dir Honors College .... Dr. Craig COBANE
18 Chief Facilities Officer .... Mr. Bryan RUSSELL
28 Dir Student Conduct/Chief Diversity .... Mr. Michael CROWE
28 Asst Provost/Chief Diversity Ofcr .... Dr. Molly KERBY
38 Director Counseling & Testing Ctr .... Dr. Peggy CROWE
43 General Counsel .... Ms. Andrea ANDERSON

LOUISIANA

Bridges Christian College (B)

PO Box 15138, New Orleans LA 70175
County: Orleans Identification: 667417
Telephone: (855) 702-7434 Carnegie Class: Not Classified
FAX Number: N/A Calendar System: Trimester
URL: bridgeschristiancollege.com
Established: 2011 Annual Undergrad Tuition & Fees: N/A
Enrollment: N/A Coed
Affiliation or Control: Assemblies Of God Church IRS Status: 501(c)3
Highest Offering: Baccalaureate
Accreditation: **@BI**

01 President .... Dr. Richard MILLER

Centenary College of Louisiana (C)

PO Box 41188, Shreveport LA 71134-1188
County: Caddo FICE Identification: 002003
Unit ID: 158477
Telephone: (318) 869-5011 Carnegie Class: Bac-A&S
FAX Number: N/A Calendar System: Semester
URL: www.centenary.edu
Established: 1825 Annual Undergrad Tuition & Fees: $38,060
Enrollment: 563 Coed
Affiliation or Control: United Methodist IRS Status: 501(c)3
Highest Offering: Master's
Accreditation: **SC**, MUS

01 President .... Dr. Christopher HOLOMAN
04 Exec Assistant to the President .... Mrs. Connie WHITTINGTON
05 Provost & Dean of the College .... Dr. Karen SOUL
10 Vice President for Finance/Admin .... Mr. Bob BLUE
50 Dean of the School of Business .... Vacant
64 Dean of the School of Music .... Dr. Cory WIKAN
30 Vice Pres for Development .... Mr. Fred LANDRY
84 Vice President Enrollment & Mktg .... Mr. Calhoun ALLEN
20 Vice Provost for Academic Affairs .... Dr. Jeanne HAMMING
09 Assoc Prov Inst Rsrch & Planning .... Dr. Katherine BEARDEN
13 Director of Information Technology .... Mr. Scott MERRITT
21 Business Manager .... Mrs. Monica POWELL
41 Director of Athletics & Recreation .... Mr. David ORR
32 Dean of Students .... Mr. Mark MILLER
38 Director of Counseling .... Ms. Tina FELDT
37 Director of Financial Aid .... Mrs. Lynette VISKOZKI
08 Librarian .... Ms. Christy WRENN
26 Dir of Strategic Communications .... Mrs. Kate PEDROTTY
29 Director Alumni/Family Relations .... Ms. Katie CHOPIN
18 Director of Facilities .... Mr. Chris SAMPITE
25 Director Sponsored Research .... Ms. Patty J. ROBERTS
07 Director Admissions/Recruitment .... Ms. Lauren HAWKINS
15 Human Resources Director .... Ms. Edie CUMMINGS
19 Director of Public Safety .... Mr. Eddie WALKER
104 Director Study Abroad .... Mrs. Anne-Marie BRUNER-TRACEY
39 Director Res Life & Student Conduct .... Ms. Katherine SHAMBURGER
06 Registrar .... Mrs. Deborah SCARLATO

Chamberlain University-New Orleans (D)

400 Lebarre Road, Jefferson LA 70121
Telephone: (504) 565-7995 Identification: 770983
Accreditation: **&HLC**, NURSE

† Branch campus of Chamberlain University-Addison, Addison, IL

Delta College of Arts & Technology (E)

7380 Exchange Place, Baton Rouge LA 70806-3851
County: East Baton Rouge FICE Identification: 025383
Unit ID: 366270
Telephone: (225) 928-7770 Carnegie Class: Spec 2-yr-A&S
FAX Number: N/A Calendar System: Other
URL: www.deltacollege.com
Established: 1983 Annual Undergrad Tuition & Fees: N/A
Enrollment: N/A Coed
Affiliation or Control: Proprietary IRS Status: Proprietary
Highest Offering: Associate Degree
Accreditation: **COE**

01 Campus Director .... Mr. Richard WILSON

Dillard University (F)

2601 Gentilly Boulevard, New Orleans LA 70122-3097
County: Orleans FICE Identification: 002004
Unit ID: 158802
Telephone: (504) 283-8822 Carnegie Class: Bac-A&S
FAX Number: N/A Calendar System: Semester
URL: www.dillard.edu
Established: 1869 Annual Undergrad Tuition & Fees: $19,281
Enrollment: 1,215 Coed
Affiliation or Control: United Methodist IRS Status: 501(c)3
Highest Offering: Baccalaureate
Accreditation: **SC**, ACBSP, NUR

01 President .... Dr. Rochelle L. FORD
111 Vice Pres Inst Advancement .... Vacant
05 Provost/Sr VP for Academic Affairs .... Dr. Yolanda PAGE
32 Vice President for Student Success .... Dr. Roland BULLARD
43 VP for Legal Affairs .... Mr. Brendan GREENE
10 VP for Finance/CFO .... Mr. R. JOHNSON
84 Vice Pres Enrollment Management .... Vacant
07 Dir of Recruitment & Admissions .... Ms. Monica WHITE
18 Dir of Facilities Mgmt .... Vacant
36 Director of Career/Prof Services .... Mr. Jonathan WRIGHT
06 Dir of Records & Registration .... Mr. Robert MITCHELL, JR.
37 Dir Financial Aid/Scholarships .... Ms. Denise SPELLMAN
46 Assoc VP Research & Spons Programs .... Mr. Theodore CALLIER
30 Director of Development .... Mrs. Adrian GUY-ANDERSON
04 Exec Assistant to the President .... Ms. Kathy TAYLOR
31 Director Community Development .... Mr. Nick L. HARRIS
19 Chief of Police .... Ms. Angela HONORA
15 Director of Human Resources .... Mrs. Brittany RICHARDSON
26 Dir of Marketing/Communications .... Mr. Eddie FRANCIS

08 Director of Library/Learning .... Ms. Jennifer COLLINS
49 Dean of College of Arts & Sciences .... Dr. Eartha JOHNSON
103 Dir Workforce/Career Development .... Vacant
13 Chief Info Technology Officer (CIO) .... Mr. Cederic KONYAOLE
22 Dir Affirmative Action/EEO .... Ms. Sheila JUDGE
39 Director Student Housing .... Mr. Jamar SIMMONS
41 Athletic Director .... Vacant
50 Interim Dean of Business .... Dr. Richard IGWIKE
29 Director Alumni Relations .. Mrs. Rebecca ARMSTONG-ENGLISH
44 Annual Fund Officer .... Mr. Braxton MCSHAN
09 Director of Institutional Research .... Mr. Jacques J. DETIEGE

Fortis College (G)

14111 Airline Highway, Suite 101, Baton Rouge LA 70817
County: East Baton Rouge FICE Identification: 034803
Unit ID: 439738
Telephone: (225) 248-1015 Carnegie Class: Spec 2-yr-Health
FAX Number: (225) 248-9517 Calendar System: Other
URL: www.fortis.edu
Established: 1991 Annual Undergrad Tuition & Fees: $15,030
Enrollment: 408 Coed
Affiliation or Control: Proprietary IRS Status: Proprietary
Highest Offering: Associate Degree
Accreditation: **ABHES**, MLTAD, SURTEC

01 Campus President .... Kendra WILLIAMS
05 Int Dean of Education .... Trevonda HENDERSON

Franciscan Missionaries of Our Lady University (H)

5414 Brittany Drive, Baton Rouge LA 70808
County: East Baton Rouge FICE Identification: 031062
Unit ID: 160074
Telephone: (225) 768-1700 Carnegie Class: Spec-4-yr-Other Health
FAX Number: (225) 768-0811 Calendar System: Semester
URL: www.franu.edu
Established: 1923 Annual Undergrad Tuition & Fees: $14,535
Enrollment: 1,366 Coed
Affiliation or Control: Roman Catholic IRS Status: 501(c)3
Highest Offering: Doctorate
Accreditation: **SC**, ANEST, ARCPA, COARC, DIETI, MLS, NUR, PTA, PTAA, RAD

01 President .... Dr. Tina HOLLAND
05 Provost/VP for Academic Affairs .... Br. Edward VIOLETT
111 VP for Institutional Advancement .... Ms. Judith ROBERSON
10 VP for Operations & Finance .... Ms. Angelia BERCEGEAY
84 VP Enrollment Mgmt/Student Affairs .... Ms. Rebecca CANNON
88 VP for Mission Identity .... Sr. Martha Ann ABSHIRE
66 Dean School of Nursing .... Dr. Amy HALL
76 Dean School of Health Professions .... Dr. Susan STEELE-MOSES
32 Dean of Students .... Dr. Alison WELLS
49 Dean School of Arts & Sciences .... Dr. Brian RASH
37 Director Financial Aid .... Vacant
06 Registrar .... Ms. Kimberly JONES-JAMES
76 Director Physician Asst Program .... Ms. Sarah DEYO
76 Director Nurse Anesthesia Program .... Dr. Mandy BROUSSARD
76 Director Radiologic Technology .... Ms. Nicole ST. GERMAIN
76 Director Medical Lab Science .... Dr. Debbie FOX
76 Director Physical Therapist Asst .... Dr. Marty AIME
88 Dir Master of Health Administration .... Dr. Elaine PURDY
76 Director Respiratory Therapy .... Ms. Sue DAVIS
88 Dir Doctor of Physical Therapy Pgm .... Dr. Kirk NELSON
88 Director FNP Program .... Dr. Alicia BATES
88 Director Nutritional Sciences Prog .... Dr. Rachel FOURNET
88 Dir Simulated Clinical Educ .... Ms. Tabitha JONES-THOMAS
24 Director Learning Resource Center .... Ms. Jalan WOODWARD
13 Director of Information Systems .... Vacant
07 Director of Admissions .... Ms. Christy SEVIER
09 Asst Provost Inst Effectiveness .... Dr. Candi MCELHENY
04 Executive Asst to President .... Ms. Kimberly MELANCON
44 Director Annual Giving/Alumni Rels .... Mr. Corey WILLIAMS
113 Bursar .... Ms. Erin ELLIS
42 Director Campus Ministry .... Ms. Tammy VIDRINE
90 Director Educational Technology .... Ms. Liza MAYEUX
112 Director Donor Relations .... Ms. Aimee GREENE
88 Director Service Learning .... Dr. Rhoda REDDIX
08 Co-Director Library .... Mr. Lucas HUNTINGTON
08 Co-Director Library .... Ms. Maggie MCCANN
18 Director of Operations .... Ms. Denice DORSEY
19 Director Health and Safety .... Ms. Denise GILLESPIE
38 Director Counseling .... Dr. Lynn BROWNING
30 Director of Development .... Ms. Laura ST. BLANC
88 Director Quality Enhancement Plan .... Dr. Valerie SCHLUTER
15 Human Resources Business Partner .... Ms. Jennifer STRICKLAND
25 Contract and Grants Manager .... Mr. Mark OURSO
36 Director Career & Leadership .... Ms. Tinicia TURNER

Herzing University (I)

3900 North Causeway Blvd, Suite 800, Metarie LA 70002
Telephone: (504) 613-4295 Identification: 666450
Accreditation: **&HLC**, SURTEC

† Regional accreditation is carried under the parent institution in Madison, WI.

Infinity College (J)

117 W. Pinhook Road, Lafayette LA 70501
County: Lafayette FICE Identification: 042454
Unit ID: 485564
Telephone: (337) 261-9009 Carnegie Class: Not Classified

FAX Number: N/A Calendar System: Semester
URL: infinitycollege.edu
Established: Annual Undergrad Tuition & Fees: N/A
Enrollment: N/A Coed
Affiliation or Control: Proprietary IRS Status: Proprietary
Highest Offering: Associate Degree
Accreditation: COE

ITI Technical College (A)

13944 Airline Highway, Baton Rouge LA 70817-5998
County: East Baton Rouge FICE Identification: 021662
Unit ID: 159197
Telephone: (225) 752-4230 Carnegie Class: Spec 2-yr-Tech
FAX Number: (225) 756-0903 Calendar System: Quarter
URL: www.iticollege.edu
Established: 1973 Annual Undergrad Tuition & Fees: $11,156
Enrollment: 603 Coed
Affiliation or Control: Proprietary IRS Status: Proprietary
Highest Offering: Associate Degree
Accreditation: ACCSC

01 President ... Mr. Earl Joe MARTIN, III
03 Vice President ... Mr. Mark WORTHY
05 Dean of Education ... Ms. Carol BOUDREAUX
11 Administrative Director ... Mr. Michael CHAMPAGNE
07 Director of Admissions ... Mr. Shawn NORRIS

Louisiana Christian University (B)

1140 College Drive, Pineville LA 71359-0001
County: Rapides FICE Identification: 002007
Unit ID: 159568
Telephone: (318) 487-7000 Carnegie Class: Masters/S
FAX Number: (318) 487-7800 Calendar System: Semester
URL: www.lacollege.edu
Established: 1906 Annual Undergrad Tuition & Fees: $17,500
Enrollment: 1,153 Coed
Affiliation or Control: Southern Baptist IRS Status: 501(c)3
Highest Offering: Master's
Accreditation: SC, ACBSP, MUS, NURSE, PTAA, SW

01 President ... Dr. Rick BREWER
03 Executive Vice President ... Dr. David JEFFREYS
05 Provost/Vice Pres Academic Affairs ... Dr. Cheryl CLARK
10 Exec Dir or Finance/CFO ... Mrs. Evelyn DEAN
111 VP Advancement ... Vacant
32 AVP Stdnt Engagement/Enrichment ... Dr. Joshua DARA
06 Registrar ... Ms. Eileen DEBOER
07 Exec Director of Admissions ... Mrs. Renee MELDER
37 Director of Financial Aid ... Ms. Brandie BASS
08 Director of the Library ... Dr. Lillian PURDY
26 Coordinator of College Relations ... Dr. Elizabeth CHRISTIAN
13 Exec Dir of Information Technology ... Mr. Bryce SANDERS
18 Maintenance Facility Supervisor ... Mr. Walt GOODMAN
21 Director of Business Office ... Ms. Beverly INGRAM
39 Director of Residence Life ... Mr. Michael SUCHANEK
41 Athletic Director ... Mr. Reni MASON
42 Baptist Student Union Director ... Mr. Brad GILL
85 Director International Student Affs ... Mr. Orlando WORGES
36 Exec Dir of Calling and Career ... Mrs. Meredith RENNIER
38 Director of Mental Health ... Ms. Taylor DAUZAT
15 Executive Director Human Resources ... Mrs. Christelle CARLEY
40 Bookstore Manager ... Ms. Linda BILLINGSLEY
29 Exec Dir of Development/Alumni Affs ... Vacant
19 Chief of Safety & Security ... Mr. John DAUZAT
23 Coordinator of Health Services ... Ms. Janet SANDERS
04 Executive Asst President's Office ... Mrs. Lori SCOTT
26 Director of Marketing ... Mrs. Karen CARTER

*Louisiana Community & Technical College System (C)

265 S Foster Drive, Baton Rouge LA 70806-4104
County: East Baton Rouge Identification: 666188
Telephone: (225) 922-2800 Carnegie Class: N/A
FAX Number: (225) 922-2786
URL: www.lctcs.edu

01 President ... Dr. Monty SULLIVAN
05 Chief Education/Training Officer ... Dr. Wendi PALERMO
32 Chief Student Affairs Officer ... Dr. Amy CABLE
10 Chief Administrative Officer ... Mr. Joseph F. MARIN
26 Chief Public Affairs Officer ... Mr. Quintin TAYLOR

*Baton Rouge Community College (D)

201 Community College Drive,
Baton Rouge LA 70806-4156
County: East Baton Rouge FICE Identification: 037303
Unit ID: 437103
Telephone: (866) 217-9823 Carnegie Class: Assoc/MT-VT-High Trad
FAX Number: (225) 216-8100 Calendar System: Semester
URL: www.mybrcc.edu
Established: 1998 Annual Undergrad Tuition & Fees (In-District): $4,221
Enrollment: 7,376 Coed
Affiliation or Control: State/Local IRS Status: 501(c)3
Highest Offering: Associate Degree
Accreditation: SC, ACBSP, ACFEI, ADNUR, CONST, DMS, NAIT, SURGT

02 Chancellor ... Dr. Willie E. SMITH
04 Asst to the Chancellor ... Ms. Tuesday A. GRAY
26 Chief PR & Marketing Officer ... Ms. Kizzy PAYTON
05 VC Academic & Student Affairs ... Dr. Sarah BARLOW
103 Vice Chanc for Workforce Solutions ... Dr. Girard MELANCON
111 Vice Chanc for Inst Advance/Found ... Mr. Philip L. SMITH, JR.
10 Vice Chanc for Finance & Admin ... Mr. Corlin LEBLANC
21 Asst VC for Finance ... Ms. Lyndra SMITH
114 Director of Budgets ... Vacant
13 Chief Information Officer ... Mr. Ronald SOLOMON
15 Chief HR Officer ... Ms. Annette ARBONEAUX
19 Chief of Police ... Ms. Genoria TILLEY
25 Dir Grants Resource Center ... Ms. Ann ZANDERS
46 Dir of Business Process Improv ... Ms. Dionne ANDRUS
18 Chief Facilities Officer ... Mr. Anthony BROWN
29 Alumni Relations Manager ... Ms. Georgia SCOBEE
35 Assoc Dean of Students ... Ms. Stacia HARDY
36 Director of Career Services ... Ms. Lisa HIBNER
37 Director of Financial Aid ... Ms. Miracle DAVIS
41 Interim Athletic Director ... Ms. Paula LEE
121 Dir of Academic Learning Center ... Ms. Jeanne STACY
88 Upward Bound Program Director ... Ms. Darica SIMON
96 Director of Purchasing ... Ms. Hilary STEPHENSON
06 Registrar ... Ms. Taylor DAVID

*Bossier Parish Community College (E)

6220 East Texas Street, Bossier City LA 71111-6922
County: Bossier FICE Identification: 020554
Unit ID: 158431
Telephone: (318) 678-6000 Carnegie Class: Assoc/MT-VT-High Trad
FAX Number: (318) 678-6389 Calendar System: Semester
URL: www.bpcc.edu
Established: 1966 Annual Undergrad Tuition & Fees (In-District): $4,284
Enrollment: 6,090 Coed
Affiliation or Control: State/Local IRS Status: 501(c)3
Highest Offering: Associate Degree
Accreditation: SC, ACFEI, ADNUR, COARC, EMT, NAIT, OTA, PTAA, SURGT

02 Chancellor ... Dr. Douglas R. BATEMAN
05 VC Academic Affairs ... Ms. Lesa TAYLOR DUPREE
32 VC of Student Services ... Ms. Karen RECCHIA
10 Assoc VC Finance ... Mr. Raymond ABRAHAM
45 Assoc VC Inst Planning & Assessment .. Dr. Holly FRENCH-HART
103 Assoc VC Workforce Solutions ... Ms. Sandra HARVEY
08 Dean of Learning Resources ... Mr. Adrian CRAWFORD
37 Director Student Financial Aid ... Ms. Vicki TEMPLE
06 Registrar ... Mr. Richard COCKERHAM
15 Director of Human Resources ... Ms. Teri BASHARA
35 Director of Student Life ... Ms. Marjoree HARPER
13 Chief Information Officer ... Mr. Wesley BANGE
22 Diversity/Multicultural Affairs ... Ms. Marjoree HARPER
72 Dean of Educational Technology ... Mr. Charley CAMERON
18 Dir Physical Plant & Maintenance ... Mr. Chad JOHNSTON
111 Dir Institutional Advance/Grants ... Dr. Jennifer LAWRENCE
96 Director of Purchasing ... Ms. Gayle DOUCET
04 Exec Assistant to Chancellor ... Ms. Christy MOORE
84 Dean of Enrollment Management ... Ms. Kathy VERCHER
108 Dir Institutional Effectiveness ... Ms. Allison MARTIN
19 Chief of Campus Police ... Mr. Jimmy STEWART
60 Dean of Comm & Performing Arts ... Dr. Ray Scott CRAWFORD
50 Dean of Business ... Ms. Peggy FULLER
54 Dean of TEM ... Ms. Megan BANGE
66 Dean of Sci/Nursing/Allied Health ... Ms. Carolyn BURROUGHS
49 Dean of Liberal Arts ... Ms. Vicki DENNIS
83 Dean of Behavioral Social Sciences ... Ms. Kay BOSTON
121 Dean of Student Success ... Ms. Peggy FULLER
41 Athletic Director ... Ms. Karen RECCHIA
100 Chief of Staff ... Dr. Jennifer LAWRENCE

*Central Louisiana Technical College Avoyelles Campus (F)

508 Choupique Street, Cottonport LA 71327-3743
County: Avoyelles FICE Identification: 008317
Unit ID: 158237
Telephone: (318) 876-2401 Carnegie Class: Not Classified
FAX Number: (318) 876-2634 Calendar System: Semester
URL: https://www.cltcc.edu/campuses/ward-h-nash-avoyelles-campus
Established: 1938 Annual Undergrad Tuition & Fees (In-District): N/A
Enrollment: N/A Coed
Affiliation or Control: State/Local IRS Status: 501(c)3
Highest Offering: Associate Degree
Accreditation: COE

02 Interim Campus Dean ... Ms. Kathryn BROWN

*Central Louisiana Technical Community College (G)

516 Murray St., Alexandria LA 71301
County: Rapides FICE Identification: 005489
Unit ID: 158088
Telephone: (318) 487-5443 Carnegie Class: Spec 2-yr-Other
FAX Number: (318) 487-5970 Calendar System: Semester
URL: www.cltcc.edu
Established: 1965 Annual Undergrad Tuition & Fees (In-State): $4,098
Enrollment: 2,192 Coed
Affiliation or Control: State IRS Status: 501(c)3
Highest Offering: Associate Degree
Accreditation: COE

02 Chancellor ... Dr. James (Jimmy) R. SAWTELLE, III
10 Vice Chanc of Finance/Admin ... Ms. Amanda CAIN
05 EVC Academic & Student Affairs ... Dr. Heather POOLE
103 Vice Chanc Workforce Solutions ... Ms. Misty SLAYTER
04 Executive Admin Assistant ... Mr. Lee WILEY
06 Asst VC of Records & Retention ... Ms. Lynda GARVIN
08 Director of Library Services ... Ms. Daenel VAUGHN-TUCKER
09 Asst VC of Institutional Research ... Dr. Stephen COX
13 Chief Information Technology Ofcr ... Dr. Sharon LAYCOCK
15 Chief Human Resources Officer ... Ms. Angel MCGEE
37 Director Student Financial Aid ... Ms. Danielle JAMES

*Central Louisiana Technical & Community College-Huey P. Long Campus (H)

5960 Highway 167 N, PO Box 871, Winnfield LA 71483
County: Winn FICE Identification: 005480
Unit ID: 159090
Telephone: (318) 628-4342 Carnegie Class: Not Classified
FAX Number: (318) 628-7768 Calendar System: Semester
URL: www.cltcc.edu
Established: 1939 Annual Undergrad Tuition & Fees (In-District): N/A
Enrollment: N/A Coed
Affiliation or Control: State/Local IRS Status: 501(c)3
Highest Offering: Associate Degree
Accreditation: COE

05 Campus Dean & Director ... Mr. Jeff JOHNSON

*Delgado Community College (I)

615 City Park Avenue, New Orleans LA 70119-4399
County: Orleans FICE Identification: 004625
Unit ID: 158662
Telephone: (504) 671-5000 Carnegie Class: Assoc/MT-VT-High Trad
FAX Number: (504) 361-6699 Calendar System: Semester
URL: www.dcc.edu
Established: 1921 Annual Undergrad Tuition & Fees (In-District): $4,079
Enrollment: 13,251 Coed
Affiliation or Control: State/Local IRS Status: 501(c)3
Highest Offering: Associate Degree
Accreditation: SC, ACBSP, ACFEI, ACPHA, ADNUR, CAHIIM, COARC, DMS, EMT, FUSER, MLTAD, NAIT, NMT, OTA, POLYT, PTAA, RAD, RTT, SURGT

02 Chancellor ... Dr. Larissa LITTLETON STEIB
10 VC Business/Admin Affairs ... Mr. Ronald RUSSO
05 VC Academic & Stdnt Affs/Provost ... Dr. Cheryl MYERS
103 VC Wkfrc Dev/Tech Educ/Inst Advance ... Ms. Arlanda WILLIAMS
32 AVC Stdnt Affairs/Exec Dean SC ... Dr. Tamika DUPLESSIS
66 Exec Dean Charity Sch of Nursing ... Dr. Joan ELLIS
76 AVC Acad Affs/Dean Allied Health ... Mr. Harold GASPARD
60 Dean Communication Division ... Ms. Emily COSPER
81 Dean Science & Math ... Dr. Raymond DUPLESSIS
79 Dean Arts and Humanities ... Ms. Patrice MOORE
106 Dir Distance Lrng/Instruct Tech ... Ms. Angela CAMAILLE
12 Exec Dean West Bank/Dean Bus & Tech ... Dr. Peter CHO
12 Exec Dean Sidney Collier ... Dr. Theresa DEGRUY
15 Asst Vice Chanc for Human Resources ... Ms. Carla MAJOR
13 Chief Information Officer ... Mr. James P. HOBBS, III
21 Exec Dir Fin Svcs/Assoc Controller ... Ms. Amy LASZCZ
18 Asst VC Facilities & Planning ... Mr. James ROYER
04 Executive Asst to the Chancellor ... Dr. Traci SMOTHERS
72 Asst Dean Business & Technology ... Ms. Karen MUHSIN
09 Director Planning & Research ... Dr. Shawn LOHT
88 Exec Dir Curriculum & Pgm Devel ... Mr. Timothy STAMM
08 Dean Library ... Mr. Timothy STAMM
41 Athletic Director ... Mr. Joe SCHEUERMANN
06 College Registrar ... Ms. Maria CISNEROS
07 Director Admissions/Enrollment Svcs ... Ms. Michelle GRECO
44 Director Restricted Funds ... Ms. Sarah CAMANIA VINNETT
84 Director Enrollment Management ... Mrs. Michelle GRECO
121 Int Director Advising & Testing ... Mr. Warren ATKINS
96 Director Purchasing ... Ms. Tracey SHEFFIELD
19 Director Campus Police ... Mr. Warren RILEY

*L.E. Fletcher Technical Community College (J)

1407 Highway 311, Schriever LA 70395
County: Terrebonne FICE Identification: 005761
Unit ID: 160481
Telephone: (985) 448-7900 Carnegie Class: Assoc/MT-VT-High Trad
FAX Number: (985) 446-3308 Calendar System: Semester
URL: www.fletcher.edu
Established: 1948 Annual Undergrad Tuition & Fees (In-State): $3,981
Enrollment: 2,105 Coed
Affiliation or Control: State IRS Status: Exempt
Highest Offering: Associate Degree
Accreditation: SC, ACBSP, ADNUR, COARC, MLTAD, NAIT, PNUR, SURGT

02 Chancellor ... Dr. Kristine STRICKLAND
05 Vice Chanc Academic Affairs ... Vacant
10 Vice Chanc Finance/Administration ... Dr. Mark MCLEAN
06 Registrar ... Ms. Alexis KNIGHT
09 Dir Inst Research & Effectiveness ... Dr. Carrie CORTEZ
66 Dean of Nursing and Allied Health ... Ms. Danielle VAUCLIN
84 Executive Director of Enrollment ... Ms. Ana NANNEY

15 Director of Human Resources .... Ms. Gina MARCEL
100 Special Assistant to the Chancellor .... Mrs. Crystal GIENGER
08 Director of Library Services .... Mrs. Jodi DUET
26 VC Inst Advance/Strat Initiatives .... Mr. W. Chandler LEBOEUF
49 Dean of Liberal Arts/CDYC/Business .... Ms. Susan GUERRERO
96 Manager of Purchasing & Travel .... Ms. Jill SEVIER

*Louisiana Delta Community College (A)

7500 Millhaven Road, Monroe LA 71203
County: Ouachita Parish FICE Identification: 041301
Unit ID: 483212
Telephone: (318) 345-9000 Carnegie Class: Assoc/HVT-High Trad
FAX Number: N/A Calendar System: Semester
URL: www.ladelta.edu
Established: 2001 Annual Undergrad Tuition & Fees (In-District): $4,076
Enrollment: 3,874 Coed
Affiliation or Control: State/Local IRS Status: 501(c)3
Highest Offering: Associate Degree
Accreditation: SC, ADNUR, EMT, NAIT

02 Chancellor .... Dr. Randy E. ESTERS
05 Vice Chanc of Academic Affairs .... Vacant
10 CFO .... Ms. Naomi MITCHELL
103 Exec Dir of Workforce Development .... Vacant
30 Dir Inst Advancement/Development .... Ms. Missy AMY
13 Chief Information Officer .... Mr. Bradley MASTERS
26 Director of Public Relations .... Ms. Darian ATKINS
04 Admin Assistant to the President .... Mrs. Connie L. CARR
09 Dir of IR & Effectiveness .... Ms. Stacy LYNCH
106 Director Online Education/E-learnin .... Mrs. Sharon BOWMAN
15 Exec Director of Human Resources .... Ms. Kendra HOUGH
18 Director of Facilities .... Mr. Bobby GRAHAM
38 Director Student Counseling .... Mrs. Traci CLARK
06 Registrar .... Mrs. Gwenn HALL
07 Director of Recruitment/Admissions .... Mr. Michael ANDERSON
19 Director Security/Safety .... Mr. Downey BLACK
37 Director Student Financial Aid .... Mrs. Kimberly BRUCE
08 Chief Library Officer .... Ms. Amelia BRISTER

*Northshore Technical Community College (B)

65556 Centerpoint Blvd, Lacombe LA 70437
County: St. Tammany FICE Identification: 006756
Unit ID: 160667
Telephone: (985) 545-1500 Carnegie Class: Assoc/HVT-Mix Trad/Non
FAX Number: N/A Calendar System: Semester
URL: www.northshorecollege.edu
Established: 1930 Annual Undergrad Tuition & Fees (In-District): $4,103
Enrollment: 3,552 Coed
Affiliation or Control: State/Local IRS Status: 501(c)3
Highest Offering: Associate Degree
Accreditation: SC

02 Chancellor .... Dr. William S. WAINWRIGHT
05 Provost/Vice Chancellor of Academic .... Dr. Daniel ROBERTS
10 Vice Chancellor Finance & Admin .... Mr. Marc CHAUVIN
45 Vice Chanc Strategic Initiatives .... Dr. Jim CARLSON
32 Vice Chancellor of Student Affairs .... Dr. Christy MONTGOMERY
20 Associate Provost of Academics .... Dr. Paul DONALDSON
66 Assoc Provost Health Sci/Nursing .... Ms. Christi MARCEAUX
75 Associate Provost Technical Studies .... Mr. Dewayne LAMBERT
12 Dean of Campus Administration (LB) .... Ms. Kim FINCH
12 Dean of Campus Administration (LC) .... Ms. Sandy YAEGER
12 Dean Campus Administration (LF) .... Ms. Owen SMITH
12 Dean Campus Administration (LE) .... Dr. Lizette LEADER
09 Director of Institutional Research .... Dr. Melandie MCGEE
18 Director of Facilities .... Mr. Rocky BORK
08 Director of Library Services .... Ms. Cynthia KNIGHT
37 Director of Financial Aid .... Ms. Nichole LABAT
13 Director of Information Technology .... Mr. Christopher BLOHM
15 Director of Human Resources .... Ms. Christi BROWN
111 Director Institutional Advancement .... Ms. Mary SLAZER
103 Director of Workforce Training .... Ms. Bridget LABORDE
21 Director of Accounting .... Ms. Kimberly SHOWERS
07 Director of Admissions .... Ms. Alverneece JOHNSON
120 Director of Online Learning .... Ms. Amanda JACOB
25 Director, Grants & Resources .... Mr. David LLOYD
06 Registrar .... Ms. Sarah PINION
113 Bursar .... Ms. Lisa KILLENS
96 Purchasing Manager .... Ms. Sharon JONES

*Northwest Louisiana Technical Community College (C)

9500 Industrial Drive, Minden LA 71055
County: Webster FICE Identification: 009975
Unit ID: 160010
Telephone: (318) 371-3035 Carnegie Class: Spec 2-yr-Tech
FAX Number: (318) 371-3325 Calendar System: Trimester
URL: www.nltcc.edu
Established: 1952 Annual Undergrad Tuition & Fees (In-District): $4,109
Enrollment: 935 Coed
Affiliation or Control: State/Local IRS Status: 501(c)3
Highest Offering: Associate Degree
Accreditation: COE, NAIT

02 Chancellor .... Dr. Earl MEADOR
05 Vice Chancellor of Academics .... Dr. Jayda SPILLERS
10 Vice Chancellor of Finance .... Ms. Melanie SOTAK
15 Director of Human Resources .... Ms. Amber SAUNDERS
06 Registrar .... Ms. Stacy SHEPHERD
37 Director of Financial Aid .... Ms. Mary Helen SIMMS

*Northwest Louisiana Technical Community College Shreveport Campus (D)

2010 N Market Street, Shreveport LA 71137-8527
Telephone: (318) 676-7811 FICE Identification: 005469
Accreditation: COE

† Branch campus of Northwest Louisiana Technical College Northwest Campus, Minden, LA.

*Nunez Community College (E)

3710 Paris Road, Chalmette LA 70043-1297
County: Saint Bernard FICE Identification: 021661
Unit ID: 158884
Telephone: (504) 278-6200 Carnegie Class: Assoc/HVT-Mix Trad/Non
FAX Number: (504) 278-6480 Calendar System: Semester
URL: www.nunez.edu
Established: 1992 Annual Undergrad Tuition & Fees (In-District): $4,255
Enrollment: 2,166 Coed
Affiliation or Control: State/Local IRS Status: 501(c)3
Highest Offering: Associate Degree
Accreditation: SC, EMT, NAIT

02 Chancellor .... Dr. Tina M. TINNEY
121 VC Educ Training/Student Success .... Dr. Cherie K. LAROCCA
10 Chief Financial Officer .... Mr. Tai NGUYEN
15 Director Human Resources .... Vacant
20 Dean of Instruction .... Mr. Reggie POCHE
32 Asst VC Educ Training/Stdnt Success .... Mr. Leonard UNBEHAGEN
103 Director Workforce Development .... Mr. Brian GIBSON
06 Registrar .... Ms. Meg GREENFIELD
84 Dean Strategic Enroll/Stdnt Success .... Dr. April LAVERGNE
37 Director Financial Aid .... Ms. Treasure BURTCHAELL
26 Director of Communications .... Mr. Jason BROWNE
18 Director of Facilities Management .... Mr. Randy HARTZOG
30 AVC of Institutional Advancement .... Ms. Katherine LEMOINE
13 IT Manager .... Mr. Jason HOSCH

*River Parishes Community College (F)

925 West Edenborne Parkway, Gonzales LA 70737
County: Ascension FICE Identification: 037894
Unit ID: 436304
Telephone: (225) 743-8500 Carnegie Class: Assoc/MT-VT-Mix Trad/Non
FAX Number: (225) 644-8210 Calendar System: Semester
URL: www.rpcc.edu
Established: 1999 Annual Undergrad Tuition & Fees (In-District): $4,079
Enrollment: 2,755 Coed
Affiliation or Control: State/Local IRS Status: 501(c)3
Highest Offering: Associate Degree
Accreditation: SC, NAIT

02 Interim Chancellor .... Dr. Jim CARLSON
10 VC Business/Finance/Administration .... Charles CAMBRE
05 VC of Acad Affairs/Enroll & Effect .... Dr. Emily CAMPBELL
103 VC Workforce Development .... Vacant
111 Dir Advancement/RPCC Foundation .... Lillie MURPHY
32 AVC Student Svcs/Chief DEI Ofcr .... Monica MORRISON
37 Director Financial Aid .... Lisa JACKSON
07 Director of Admissions/Orientation .... Natasha JOHNSON
08 Director of Library Services .... Wendy JOHNSON
15 Human Resource Manager .... Aarika DORSEY
09 Director of Institutional Research .... Melba KENNEDY

*South Louisiana Community College (G)

1101 Bertrand Drive, Lafayette LA 70506-4124
County: Lafayette FICE Identification: 039563
Unit ID: 434061
Telephone: (337) 521-9000 Carnegie Class: Assoc/HVT-High Trad
FAX Number: (337) 521-9061 Calendar System: Semester
URL: www.solacc.edu
Established: 1998 Annual Undergrad Tuition & Fees (In-District): $4,205
Enrollment: 5,855 Coed
Affiliation or Control: State/Local IRS Status: 501(c)3
Highest Offering: Associate Degree
Accreditation: SC, ACFEI, ADNUR, EMT, MLTAD, NAIT

02 Chancellor .... Dr. Vincent JUNE
04 Exec Assistant to the Chancellor .... Ms. Kelly GREENE
10 Vice Chanc Finance & Administration .... Mr. Bryan GLATTER
103 Int Vice Chanc Econ & Work Dev .... Mr. Anthony BAHAM
108 Assoc Vice Chanc Inst Effectiveness .... Dr. Charles MILLER
05 Vice Chanc Acad & Student Affs .... Dr. Crystal LEE
32 Assoc Vice Chanc Student Affairs .... Dr. Timothy WISE
37 Director of Financial Aid .... Mrs. Tiffany WILLIAMS
08 Director of Library Services .... Ms. Katherine ROLFES
113 Director of Student Accounts .... Ms. Wendi ROBICHEAUX
21 Director of Accounting .... Ms. Carla ORTEGO
18 Director of Facilities .... Mr. Justin HERNANDEZ
15 Exec Dir Strategic Engr/Employ Svcs .... Ms. Alicia HULIN
06 Registrar .... Ms. Samantha SYLVESTER
19 Director Security/Safety .... Mr. Stephen NORTH
26 Director of Strategic Communication .... Ms. Anne FALGOUT
84 Int Director Enrollment Management .... Mr. Collise DUPONT
111 Vice Chanc Inst Advancement .... Ms. Lana FONTENOT
106 Director Distance Education .... Vacant
13 Director of Information Technology .... Mr. Nicholas PITRE
28 Director Student Engagement .... Ms. Erica PRECHT
79 Dean Liberal Arts & Humanities .... Dr. Stasia HERBERT-MCZEAL
81 Dean STEM/Transportation & Energy .... Ms. Tanya ST. JULIEN
66 Dean Nursing & Allied Health .... Dr. Carry DEATLEY
50 Dean Business/Info Tech & Tech Stds .... Mr. Sam HARB
25 Director of Grants Administrator .... Vacant
38 Dir Counseling & Disability Svcs .... Dr. Cheryl FRUGE
96 Purchasing Manager .... Ms. Nicole MANUEL
102 Exec Director Foundation .... Ms. Lana FONTENOT

*SOWELA Technical Community College (H)

PO Box 16950, Lake Charles LA 70616-6950
County: Calcasieu FICE Identification: 005467
Unit ID: 160579
Telephone: (337) 421-6565 Carnegie Class: Assoc/HVT-High Trad
FAX Number: (337) 491-2135 Calendar System: Semester
URL: www.sowela.edu
Established: 1938 Annual Undergrad Tuition & Fees (In-District): $4,265
Enrollment: 2,914 Coed
Affiliation or Control: State/Local IRS Status: 501(c)3
Highest Offering: Associate Degree
Accreditation: SC, ACBSP, ACFEI, ADNUR, NAIT, SURGT

02 Chancellor .... Dr. Neil ASPINWALL
04 Assistant to the Chancellor .... Mrs. Julie CARROLL
05 Vice Chancellor Academic Affairs .... Dr. Paula HELLUMS
10 Vice Chancellor Finance .... Ms. Jeanine NEWMAN
103 Exec Dir of Workforce Solutions .... Mr. David LAFARGUE
13 Exec Dir Information Technology .... Mr. Roy BERTUCCI
84 Exec Dir Enroll Mgmt/Stdnt Affs .... Ms. Pam BOERSIG
21 Controller .... Ms. Lindsey REPPOND
37 Director of Financial Aid .... Ms. Allison DERING
08 Director of Library Services .... Ms. Mary Frances SHERWOOD
15 Director of Human Resources .... Ms. Candy PARKER
32 Director of Student Support Svcs .... Vacant
18 Exec Dir Facilities Planning & Mgmt .... Mr. Adam REED
09 Exec Director Planning & Analysis .... Dr. Fitzpatrick U. ANYANWU
111 Exec Dir Institutional Advancement .... Ms. Nicole RASCOE
06 Registrar .... Ms. Laura LAFLEUR
36 Director Student Placement .... Mr. Joseph LAVERGNE
53 Dean of Education .... Ms. Stephanie SMITH

Louisiana Culinary Institute (I)

10550 Airline Highway, Baton Rouge LA 70816-4109
County: East Baton Rouge FICE Identification: 041123
Unit ID: 449612
Telephone: (225) 769-8820 Carnegie Class: Spec 2-yr-A&S
FAX Number: (225) 769-8792 Calendar System: Semester
URL: www.lci.edu
Established: 2002 Annual Undergrad Tuition & Fees: $14,575
Enrollment: 114 Coed
Affiliation or Control: Proprietary IRS Status: Proprietary
Highest Offering: Associate Degree
Accreditation: COE

01 Chief Executive Officer .... Keith RUSH
05 Director .... David TINER

*Louisiana State University Administration (J)

3810 W Lakeshore Drive, Baton Rouge LA 70808-4600
County: East Baton Rouge FICE Identification: 002009
Telephone: (225) 578-2111 Carnegie Class: N/A
FAX Number: (225) 578-5524
URL: www.lsu.edu

01 President .... Mr. William F. TATE, IV
05 Int Exec VP/Provost .... Dr. Matt LEE
10 Int Exec VP Finance & Admin/CFO .... Ms. Donna K. TORRES
84 VP Enrollment Management .... Mr. Jose AVILES
18 AVP Facilities/Property Oversight .... Mr. Tony LOMBARDO
32 VP Student Affairs .... Mr. Jeremiah SHINN
43 Vice Pres Legal Affairs/Gen Counsel .... Mr. Winston G. DECUIR, JR.
28 Vice Provost Diversity .... Mr. Dereck ROVARIS, SR.
116 System Director Internal Audit .... Mr. Chad BRACKIN

*Louisiana State University and Agricultural and Mechanical College (K)

Baton Rouge LA 70803-0100
County: East Baton Rouge FICE Identification: 002010
Unit ID: 159391
Telephone: (225) 578-3202 Carnegie Class: DU-Highest
FAX Number: (225) 578-6400 Calendar System: Semester
URL: www.lsu.edu
Established: 1860 Annual Undergrad Tuition & Fees (In-State): $11,962
Enrollment: 34,285 Coed
Affiliation or Control: State IRS Status: 501(c)3
Highest Offering: Doctorate

Accreditation: SC, ART, CAATE, CACREP, CAEP, CAMPEP, CIDA, CLPSY, CONST, COSMA, DIETD, IPSY, JOUR, LAW, LIB, LSAR, MUS, SCPSY, SP, SPAA, SW, THEA, VET

02 President .... Dr. William F. TATE, IV
05 Exec Vice Pres/Provost .... Dr. Roy HAGGERTY
43 VP Legal Affairs/General Counsel .... Mr. Winston G. DECUIR, JR.
10 Exec Vice Pres Finance & Admin/CFO .... Mr. Kimberly LEWIS
100 Chief of Staff .... Ms. Ashley ARCENEAUX
46 Vice Pres Research & Econ Dev .... Mr. Sam BENTLEY
32 Vice Pres Student Affairs .... Dr. Jeremiah SHINN
26 VP Strategic Communications .... Mr. Ernie BALLARD
102 President/CEO LSU Foundation .... Mr. Robert M. STUART, JR.
28 VP Inclusion/Civil Rights/TitleIX .... Mr. Todd MANUEL
20 Sr Vice Prov Academic Affairs .... Dr. Jane CASSIDY
20 Vice Prov Academic Programs .... Dr. Jacqueline BACH
106 Vice Prov Digital & Continuing Educ .... Ms. Kappie MUMPHREY
15 Assoc VP/Chief Human Resources Ofcr .... Mr. Clayton JONES
84 VP for Enrollment Management .... Mr. Jose AVILES
88 Vice President of Public Policy .... Dr. Jason J. DRODDY
45 Vice President of Strategy .... Mr. Mark BIEGER
85 Assoc VP International Programs .... Mr. Samba DIENG
37 Director Student Aid .... Ms. Amy MARIX
08 Dean LSU Libraries .... Mr. Stanley WILDER
79 Dean of Col Hum & Soc Sciences .... Dr. Troy BLANCHARD
54 Dean College of Engineering .... Dr. Judy WORNAT
47 Dean College of Agriculture .... Dr. Matthew LEE
50 Dean Ourso College of Business .... Dr. Jared LLORENS
64 Int Dean Col Music & Dramatic Arts .... Ms. Kristin SOSNOWSKY
81 Dean College of Science .... Dr. Cynthia PETERSON
62 Dir Sch of Library & Info Science .... Dr. Carol BARRY
53 Dean Col Human Science/Education .... Dr. Roland MITCHELL
57 Dean College of Art & Design .... Mr. Alkis TSOLAKIS
74 Dean Veterinary Medicine .... Dr. Oliver GARDEN
60 Int Dean Manship Sch of Mass Comm .... Dr. Josh GRIMM
92 Dean Honors College .... Dr. Jonathan H. EARLE
65 Dean Sch of Coast & Environ .... Dr. Christopher D'ELIA
88 Exec Dir University College .... Ms. Andrea JONES
35 Assoc Dean of Student Affairs .... Mr. Brandon COMMON
88 Sr Ex Dir SN Ctr Security Rsch Trng .... Mr. James OLSON
88 Exec Director Center Energy Stds .... Mr. David DISMUKES
29 President LSU Alumni Association .... Mr. Gordon MONK
88 Int Exec Director LSU Museum of Art ... Ms. Kristin SOSNOWSKY
18 Assoc VP for Fac & Prop Oversight .... Mr. Tony LOMBARDO
13 Assoc VP & Chief Technology Officer .... Mr. Craig WOOLLEY
75 Int Dir Sch Human Res Ed & Wk Dev .... Ms. Tracey RIZZUTO
80 Director Public Admin Institute .... Mr. Roy HEIDELBERG
27 Director LSU Press .... Ms. Alisa PLANT
41 Athletic Director .... Mr. Scott WOODWARD
06 University Registrar .... Mr. Clayton BENTON
36 Director Olinde Career Center .... Mr. Jesse G. DOWNS
09 Director of Institutional Research .... Mr. Bernie BRAUN
93 Director Multicultural Affairs .... Ms. Michelle CARTER
65 Director Museum of Natural Science .... Dr. Christopher AUSTIN
88 Director Rural Life Museum .... Mr. Bill STARK
96 Asst VP Procurement & Property Mgt .... Ms. Michele M. MONTERO
07 Director of Admissions .... Mr. Danny BARROW
19 Chief of LSU Police Dept .... Mr. Bart THOMPSON
39 Exec Director of Residential Life .... Mr. Peter TRENTACOSTE
101 Executive Director for the Board .... Dr. Monique F. CAIN
104 Director Study Abroad .... Dr. Angela MILLER
105 Director of Digital Communications .... Ms. Lori MARTIN

*Louisiana State University at Alexandria (A)

8100 Highway 71 S, Alexandria LA 71302-9121
County: Rapides | FICE Identification: 002011 | Unit ID: 159382
Telephone: (318) 445-3672 | Carnegie Class: Bac-Diverse
FAX Number: (318) 473-6418 | Calendar System: Semester
URL: www.lsua.edu
Established: 1959 | Annual Undergrad Tuition & Fees (In-State): $6,669
Enrollment: 3,706 | Coed
Affiliation or Control: State | IRS Status: 501(c)3
Highest Offering: Baccalaureate
Accreditation: SC, ACBSP, ADNUR, CAEP, MLS, MLTAD, NUR, #RAD

02 Chancellor .... Dr. Paul COREIL
05 Provost/VC Academic Affairs .... Dr. John ROWAN
10 Vice Chanc Finance/Admin Svcs .... Mr. Deron THAXTON
84 VC Enrollment & Student Engagement .... Dr. Abbey BAIN
50 Dean College of Business .... Dr. Randall DUPONT
83 Dean College of Social Sciences .... Dr. Mary TREUTING
49 Dean College of Liberal Arts .... Dr. Elizabeth BEARD
69 Dean College of Health & Human Svcs .... Dr. Haywood JOINER
81 Dean College of Nat Science & Math .... Dr. Nathan PONDER
111 Asst Vice Chanc Univ Advancement .. Ms. Melinda F. ANDERSON
88 Dept Chair Criminal Justice .... Ms. Beth WHITTINGTON
18 Director of Facility Services .... Mr. Kevin VERCHER
08 Director Library Services .... Ms. Michelle WALLER
37 Director of Financial Aid .... Mr. Jeff MASSEY
13 Exec Dir Info Educational Tech Svcs .... Mr. Jason NORMAND
15 Director Human Resource Management .... Ms. Lynette BURLEW
51 Director Continuing Education .... Ms. Lakeshia WILLIAMS
09 Dir Inst Research/Effectiveness .... Mr. Scott COLLEY
96 Dir Procurement Svcs/Property Mgmt .... Ms. Mary LEMOINE
41 Director Athletics .... Mr. Bob AUSTIN
06 Registrar .... Ms. Jerri WESTON
19 Chief of Police .... Mr. Donald COLLINS
04 Senior Exec Asst to Chancellor .... Ms. Chancey SLIDER
07 Director of Admissions .... Ms. Shelly GILL
106 Director Distance Learning .... Ms. Teresa SEYMOUR
26 Dir of Marketing & Communications .... Ms. Elizabeth JONSON

*Louisiana State University at Eunice (B)

2048 Johnson Highway, Eunice LA 70535-6726
County: Acadia | FICE Identification: 002012 | Unit ID: 159407
Telephone: (337) 457-7311 | Carnegie Class: Assoc/HVT-High Trad
FAX Number: (337) 546-6620 | Calendar System: Semester
URL: www.lsue.edu
Established: 1964 | Annual Undergrad Tuition & Fees (In-State): $4,730
Enrollment: 3,142 | Coed
Affiliation or Control: State | IRS Status: 501(c)3
Highest Offering: Associate Degree
Accreditation: SC, ACBSP, ADNUR, COARC, DMS, RAD, SURGT

02 Chancellor .... Dr. Nancee SORENSON
05 Vice Chancellor Academic Affairs .... Dr. John HAMLIN
84 Dean of Enrollment Management .... Vacant
10 Interim VC Business Affairs .... Ms. Amy GREAGOFF
32 Int Dean Student Affs/Enrollment .... Dr. Kyle D. SMITH
26 Interim Dir of Public Relations .... Mr. Travis WEBB
06 Registrar/Director of Admissions .... Mr. Donnie THIBODEAUX
37 Director of Financial Aid .... Ms. Jacqueline LA CHAPELLE
30 Dir Foundation & Inst Development .... Ms. Carey LAWSON
09 Dir Inst Effectiveness/Devel Educ .... Dr. Paul FOWLER
51 Dir Cont Educ/Workforce Innovation .... Vacant
18 Director Physical Plant .... Mr. Michael BROUSSARD
15 Director Personnel Services .... Vacant
81 Interim Dean Div of Sciences/Math .... Dr. Brandon BORILL
50 Dean Div Bus/Nursing/Allied Health .... Ms. Dotty MCDONALD
49 Interim Dean Div of Liberal Arts .... Dr. Michael ALLEMAN
13 Director Information Technology .... Mr. Stephen HEYWARD
41 Athletic Director .... Mr. Jeff WILLIS
08 Director of the Library .... Ms. Cassie JOBE-GANUCHEAU
19 Director Security/Safety .... Mr. Joseph C. LALONDE
39 Dir Resident Life/Student Housing .... Ms. Victoria THROOP
04 Executiv Assistant to the President .... Ms. Courtney FRUGE
28 Dir Diversity/Equal Opp/Affirm Act .... Ms. Katie TUCKER

*Louisiana State University Health Sciences Center-New Orleans (C)

433 Bolivar Street, New Orleans LA 70112-2223
County: Orleans | FICE Identification: 002014 | Unit ID: 159373
Telephone: (504) 568-4808 | Carnegie Class: Spec-4-yr-Med
FAX Number: N/A | Calendar System: Semester
URL: www.lsuhsc.edu
Established: 1931 | Annual Undergrad Tuition & Fees (In-State): N/A
Enrollment: 2,827 | Coed
Affiliation or Control: State | IRS Status: 501(c)3
Highest Offering: Doctorate
Accreditation: SC, ANEST, ARCPA, AUD, CACREP, COARC, CVT, DENT, DH, DT, IPSY, MED, MIDWF, MLS, NURSE, OT, PH, PTA, SP

02 Chancellor .... Dr. Larry H. HOLLIER
10 Vice Chancellor Finance/Admin .... Mr. Keith SCHROTH
05 Vice Chanc Acad Aff/Dean Grad Stds .... Dr. Joseph M. MOERSCHBAECHER
31 Vice Chanc Community Affairs .... Mr. Edwin MURRAY
17 Vice Chanc Clinic Affairs .... Dr. J. Chris WINTERS
28 Vice Chanc Diversity & Inclusion .... Dr. Timothy FAIR
102 President & CEO Foundation .... Mr. Matthew ALTIER
100 Chief of Staff .... Mr. Louis COLLETTA
43 Interim General Counsel .... Ms. Tammy SIMIEN
63 Dean Medicine NO .... Dr. Steve NELSON
52 Dean School of Dentistry .... Dr. Robert LAUGHLIN
66 Dean of Nursing .... Dr. Demetrius PORCHE
76 Dean Allied Health Professions .... Dr. Jimmy R. CAIRO
69 Dean of Public Health .... Dr. Dean SMITH
21 Assoc Vice Chanc Admin & Finance .... Ms. Wendy SIMONEAUX
103 Asst VC Econ Dev & Strat Initiative .... Mrs. Nicole HONOREE
13 Director Information Services .... Ms. Leslie L. CAPO
18 Assoc VC Properties & Facilities .... Mr. John BALL
13 Asst VC Information Technology .... Mr. Ken BOE
88 Exec Dir for Accounting Services .... Mrs. Arlean WEHLE
109 Dir Supply Chain & Aux Enterprise .... Mr. Rob PARKER
06 Registrar .... Ms. Alicia EDWARDS
08 Director of Libraries .... Mr. J. Dale PRINCE
37 Dir Student Financial Aid .... Mr. Patrick GORMAN
85 Director of International Services .... Ms. Remy E. ALLEN
108 Director Institutional Effectivenes .... Ms. Christine MANALLA
04 Administrative Officer .... Ms. Jennifer CRISP
45 Financial Planning Officer .... Mrs. Vy APOSTOLAKIS
116 Compliance Officer .... Ms. Lori FERRO

*Louisiana State University Health Sciences Center at Shreveport (D)

1501 Kings Highway, Shreveport LA 71103
County: Caddo | FICE Identification: 008067 | Unit ID: 435000
Telephone: (318) 675-5240 | Carnegie Class: Spec-4-yr-Med
FAX Number: (318) 675-5244 | Calendar System: Semester
URL: www.lsuhs.edu
Established: 1969 | Annual Undergrad Tuition & Fees (In-State): N/A
Enrollment: 982 | Coed
Affiliation or Control: State | IRS Status: Exempt
Highest Offering: Doctorate
Accreditation: SC, ARCPA, COARC, DENT, MED, MLS, OT, PH, PTA, SP

02 Chancellor .... Dr. Ghali E. GHALI
11 Vice Chancellor Administration .... Ms. Cindy RIVES
46 Vice Chancellor Research Affairs .... Dr. Chris KEVIL
05 Vice Chancellor Academic Affairs .... Dr. Alan KAYE
10 Chief Financial Officer .... Ms. Sheila FAOUR
43 Senior Legal Counsel .... Mr. Carranza PRYOR
76 Dean Sch Allied Health Prof .... Dr. Sharon DUNN
58 Dean School of Graduate Studies .... Dr. Chris KEVIL
17 Vice Chancellor Clinical Affairs .... Dr. Charles FOX
86 Vice Chancellor Government Affairs .... Dr. Markey PIERRE
26 Exec Dir Comm/Public Relations .... Ms. Lisa BABIN
13 Chief Info Technology Officer (CIO) .... Mr. Kenneth BROWN
07 Assoc Dean for Admissions SOM .... Dr. Wanda S. THOMAS
32 Asst Dean for Student Affairs SOM .... Dr. Debbie CHANDLER
15 Exec Director of Human Resources .... Ms. Lisa EBARB
23 Executive Director Medical Services .... Ms. Leisa OGLESBY
18 Chief Facilities/Physical Plant .... Mr. Marc GIBSON
19 Director of Public Safety .... Mr. Philip BURRIS
09 Exec Dir Planning & Effectiveness .... Mr. Jeffrey D. HOWELLS
25 Asst Vice Chancellor for Research .... Ms. Annella NELSON
06 Registrar .... Ms. Kim CARMEN
08 Executive Director of Library .... Mr. William OLMSTADT
37 Director Student Financial Aid .... Ms. Katraya WILLIAMS
28 Asst Vice Chancellor for Diversity .... Dr. Toni THIBEAUX
29 Director Alumni Relations .... Ms. Mary COBB
96 Director of Purchasing .... Ms. Mary A. TEMPLETON
63 Dean School of Medicine .... Dr. David F. LEWIS

† Tuition varies by degree program.

*Louisiana State University Shreveport (E)

One University Place, Shreveport LA 71115-2399
County: Caddo | FICE Identification: 002013 | Unit ID: 159416
Telephone: (318) 797-5000 | Carnegie Class: Masters/L
FAX Number: (318) 797-5180 | Calendar System: Semester
URL: www.lsus.edu
Established: 1967 | Annual Undergrad Tuition & Fees (In-State): $7,160
Enrollment: 9,955 | Coed
Affiliation or Control: State | IRS Status: 501(c)3
Highest Offering: Doctorate
Accreditation: SC, CACREP, CAEP, PH

02 Chancellor .... Mr. Lawrence S. CLARK
05 Provost/VC Academic Affairs .... Dr. Helen TAYLOR
10 Vice Chancellor Business Affairs .... Ms. Barbie CANNON
32 Assoc VC Dean of Students .... Dr. Paula ATKINS
102 Executive Director LSUS Foundation .... Ms. Laura PERDUE
29 Director Alumni Affairs .... Ms. Jazmin JERNIGAN
88 Vice Chanc Strategic Initiatives .... Dr. Julie LESSITER
06 Registrar .... Ms. Sherri BOHANNON
15 Director of Human Resource Mgmt .... Mr. Bill WOLFE
08 Dean Noel Memorial Library .... Mr. Brian SHERMAN
37 Director of Student Financial Aid .... Ms. Chelsey CHANCE
07 Director of Admissions .... Ms. Jennie BYNOG
38 Director Counseling Services .... Ms. Angela PELLERIN
13 Assoc VC & CIO/IT .... Mr. Shelby C. KEITH
40 Director of Bookstore .... Ms. Renee MARTIN
96 Director of Purchasing .... Mr. Bill WOLFE
26 Int Dir of Media/External Relations .... Ms. Erin SMITH
100 Chief of Staff .... Ms. Kim RAMSEY
19 Dir of University Police .... Mr. Donald W. WRAY
41 Athletic Director .... Mr. Lucas MORGAN
49 Dean of Arts and Sciences .... Dr. Tibor SZARVAS
58 Dean of Graduate Studies .... Dr. Sanjay T. MENON
50 Interim Dean of Business .... Dr. Mary L. WHITE
106 Director Online Learning .... Ms. Rhonda FAILEY
18 Dir Physical Plant/Facility Svcs .... Mr. Art SHILLING
53 Dean of Education/Human Development ... Dr. Dennis R. WISSING
28 Director of Diversity .... Dr. Kenna FRANKLIN

*University of New Orleans (F)

2000 Lakeshore Drive, New Orleans LA 70148-2000
County: Orleans | FICE Identification: 002015 | Unit ID: 159939
Telephone: (504) 280-6000 | Carnegie Class: DU-Higher
FAX Number: (504) 280-5522 | Calendar System: Semester
URL: www.uno.edu
Established: 1958 | Annual Undergrad Tuition & Fees (In-State): $9,072
Enrollment: 8,375 | Coed
Affiliation or Control: State | IRS Status: 501(c)3
Highest Offering: Doctorate
Accreditation: SC, ART, CACREP, CAEPN, MUS, PLNG, SPAA, THEA

02 President .... Dr. John W. NICKLOW
05 Provost/VP Academic Affairs .... Dr. Mahyar AMOUZEGAR
10 Int VP Business Affairs/CFO .... Ms. Joanne TERRANOVA
32 Associate VP and Dean of Students .... Dr. Carolyn GOLZ
13 Chief Information Officer .... Dr. Ray WANG
85 Asst Prov International Education .... Ms. Alea COT
19 Chief of Police .... Mr. Joshua RONDENO
50 Dean of Business Administration .. Dr. Pamela KENNETT-HENSEL
54 Dean of Engineering .... Dr. Lizette CHEVALIER
49 Dean Liberal Arts & Education .... Dr. Samuel GLADDEN
08 Dean Library/Information Services .... Dr. Ray WANG
81 Dean of Sciences .... Dr. Steve JOHNSON
06 University Registrar .... Ms. Kara BISCEGLIE
29 Director Alumni Affairs .... Ms. Rachel MASSEY

26 Chief Communications Officer ... Mr. Adam NORRIS
96 Director of Purchasing ... Ms. Susan VARBLE
41 VP/Director Athletics ... Mr. Tim DUNCAN
39 Director Student Housing ... Ms. Amanda ROBBINS
121 Director Learning Resource Center ... Ms. Margaret WILLIAMSON
04 Exec Asst to the President ... Ms. Elizabeth LAND
09 Dir Inst Effectiveness & Research ... Dr. Colby STOEVER
15 Assoc VP Human Resource Management ... Ms. Karen PAISANT
18 Assoc VP for Facility Services ... Mr. Mark PYLE
30 Exec Director of Univ Advancement ... Mr. Anthony GREGORIO
36 Director Career Services ... Ms. Celyn BOYKIN
37 Dir Student Financial Aid & Scholar ... Ms. Ann LOCKRIDGE
38 Director Student Counseling ... Ms. Portia GORDON
84 Assoc VP Admissions & Enrollment ... Ms. Mary Beth MARKS

Loyola University New Orleans (A)

6363 Saint Charles Avenue, New Orleans LA 70118-6195
County: Orleans FICE Identification: 002016
Unit ID: 159656
Telephone: (504) 865-3240 Carnegie Class: DU-Mod
FAX Number: (504) 865-3851 Calendar System: Semester
URL: www.loyno.edu
Established: 1912 Annual Undergrad Tuition & Fees: $42,278
Enrollment: 4,497 Coed
Affiliation or Control: Roman Catholic IRS Status: 501(c)3
Highest Offering: Doctorate
Accreditation: SC, CACREP, JOUR, LAW, MUS, NURSE

01 Interim President ... Fr. Justin DAFFRON, S.J.
04 Senior Exec Asst to the President ... Ms. Desiree RODRIGUEZ
05 Prov/Sr Vice Pres Academic Affairs ... Dr. Tanuja SINGH
10 VP COO/Finance/Admin ... Ms. Carol MARKOWITZ
111 VP University Advancement ... Mr. Chris WISEMAN
42 Interim VP for Mission & Identity ... Dr. Thomas RYAN
28 VP Equity and Inclusion ... Dr. Kedrick PERRY
84 VP Enrollment Management ... Mr. Nathan AMENT
13 Chief Information Officer ... Mr. Alan SCHOMAKER
43 General Counsel ... Ms. Sharonda WILLIAMS
29 Asst Vice Pres Alumni Engagement ... Ms. Laura E. LEIVA
14 Senior Director of IT ... Mr. Joe LOCASCIO
26 VP Marketing and Communications ... Ms. Rachel HOORMAN
11 Asst Vice Pres Administration ... Vacant
20 Vice Provost ... Dr. Uriel QUESADA
108 Coord Internal Reporting/Assessment ... Ms. Donna BOURGEOIS
27 Assoc Dir Public Affs/External Rels ... Ms. Patricia MURRET
06 Registrar ... Ms. Kathy R. GROS
15 Director of Human Resources ... Ms. Rachel DIRMANN
40 Bookstore Manager ... Mr. Maris HAZNERS
41 Director Athletics & Wellness ... Mr. Brett SIMPSON
36 Director Career Development Center ... Ms. Jill BOATRIGHT
32 VP for Student Affairs ... Dr. Alicia BOURQUE
19 Director University Police ... Mr. Todd W. WARREN
37 Director Scholarships/Financial Aid ... Ms. Anna DAIGLE
08 Director of the Law Library ... Mr. Brian BARNES
104 Dir Center for International Educ ... Ms. Mariette THOMAS
38 Director Counseling & Health Svcs ... Dr. Asia WONG
96 Director of Purchasing ... Ms. Lynn DAVIS
06 Dir Admin Services/Student Records ... Mr. Michael RACHAL
49 Dean Arts and Sciences ... Dr. Maria CALZADA
61 Dean of Law ... Dr. Madeleine LANDRIEU
64 Dean of Music and Media ... Mr. Kern MAASS
50 Dean of Business ... Dr. Michael CAPELLA
66 Dean Nursing/Health ... Dr. Shelli COLLINS
08 Dean of Libraries ... Ms. Deborah PROSSER
88 Director of Service Learning ... Ms. Typhanie JASPER-BUTLER
88 Director of Women's Resource Ctr ... Ms. Patricia BOYETT
92 Dir of University Honors Program ... Dr. Jonathan PETERSON
121 Director of Student Success Center ... Ms. Liz RAINEY
18 Senior Director of Facilities ... Vacant
25 Grants and Research Officer ... Ms. Anne WEAVER
117 Director of Risk Management ... Mr. John CAIN
39 Director of Residence Life ... Mr. Chris RICE

McCann School of Business and Technology (B)

2319 Louisville Avenue, Monroe LA 71201-6126
Telephone: (318) 323-2889 FICE Identification: 026068
Accreditation: ACCSC

† Branch campus of Miller-Motte College, Chattanooga, TN.

NationsUniversity (C)

650 Poydras St., Ste 1400, PMB 133,
New Orleans LA 70130
County: Orleans Identification: 667257
Telephone: (866) 617-6446 Carnegie Class: Not Classified
FAX Number: N/A Calendar System: Other
URL: www.nationsu.edu
Established: 1996 Annual Undergrad Tuition & Fees: N/A
Enrollment: N/A Coed
Affiliation or Control: Independent Non-Profit IRS Status: 501(c)3
Highest Offering: Master's
Accreditation: DEAC

01 President/CEO ... Dr. John BAXTER
00 Chancellor ... Dr. Mac LYNN
03 Vice Chancellor ... Dr. Herman ALEXANDER
05 Chief Academic Officer ... Dr. David B. SRYGLEY
06 Registrar ... Mrs. Mary V. MABERY
10 Chief Financiall Officer ... Mr. Tom BUSSELL
11 Chief of Operations/Administration ... Vacant
20 Dean of Faculty ... Dr. Richard YOUNGBLOOD
32 Director of Student Services ... Mrs. Gail HEIDERICH
26 Director of Communications ... Mr. Jon R. SLOAN
88 Director of Prison Services ... Mr. Randl BAXTER
13 Director of Technology ... Mr. Mike BUSH
90 IT Administrator ... Mr. Glenn BEVILLE

New Orleans Baptist Theological Seminary (D)

3939 Gentilly Boulevard, New Orleans LA 70126
County: Orleans FICE Identification: 002019
Unit ID: 159948
Telephone: (504) 282-4455 Carnegie Class: Spec-4-yr-Faith
FAX Number: (504) 283-3631 Calendar System: Semester
URL: www.nobts.edu
Established: 1917 Annual Undergrad Tuition & Fees: $9,320
Enrollment: 2,293 Coed
Affiliation or Control: Southern Baptist IRS Status: 501(c)3
Highest Offering: Doctorate
Accreditation: SC, MUS, THEOL

01 President ... Dr. James Kenneth DEW, JR.
05 Provost ... Dr. Norris C. GRUBBS
111 Vice Pres Institutional Advancement ... Dr. Mike WETZEL
10 Vice President for Business Admin ... Dr. Larry LYON
84 Assoc Vice President Enrollment ... Mr. Matthew JAMES
12 Dean Leavell College ... Dr. L. Thomas STRONG, III
32 AVP Student Affs/Dean of Students ... Dr. Craig GARRETT
06 Registrar ... Dr. Paul E. GREGOIRE, JR.
08 Dean of Libraries ... Dr. Jeff D. GRIFFIN
13 Assoc VP Information Technology ... Dr. Laurie S. WATTS
73 Assoc Dean Prof Doctoral Pgms ... Dr. Reggie R. OGEA
58 Assoc Dean Research Doctoral Pgms ... Dr. Charles A. RAY, JR.
35 Director of Student Services ... Mr. Conner HINTON
30 Director of Development ... Ms. Betty Lynn CAMPBELL
15 Director of Human Resources ... Ms. Shelly COOPER
26 Dir Office of Communications ... Mr. Gary D. MYERS
29 Director of Alumni Relations ... Mr. Robert SMITH
36 Director of Student Enlistment ... Mr. Michael REED
37 Director of Financial Aid ... Mr. Michael WANG
38 Director of Testing & Counseling ... Dr. Jeffery W. NAVE
88 Director of Innovative Learning ... Dr. Donna B. PEAVEY
41 Athletic Director ... Mr. Tim DUNCAN

Notre Dame Seminary, Graduate School of Theology (E)

2901 S Carrollton Avenue, New Orleans LA 70118-4391
County: Orleans FICE Identification: 002022
Unit ID: 160029
Telephone: (504) 866-7426 Carnegie Class: Not Classified
FAX Number: (504) 866-3119 Calendar System: Semester
URL: www.nds.edu
Established: 1923 Annual Undergrad Tuition & Fees: N/A
Enrollment: N/A Coed
Affiliation or Control: Roman Catholic IRS Status: 501(c)3
Highest Offering: Master's
Accreditation: SC, THEOL

01 President - Rector ... V.Rev. Joshua J. RODRIGUE, STD
05 Academic Dean ... Dr. Rebecca S. MALONEY
08 Director of Library ... Mr. Thomas B. BENDER, IV
09 Dir IE/Planning/Faculty Development ... Dr. Rebecca S. MALONEY
10 Business Manager ... Ms. Michelle W. KLEIN
06 Registrar ... Ms. Debora PANEPINTO

Remington College-Baton Rouge Campus (F)

4520 S Sherwood Forest Blvd, Baton Rouge LA 70816
Telephone: (225) 236-3200 Identification: 666449
Accreditation: ACCSC

† Branch campus of Remington College-Dallas Campus, Garland, TX

Remington College-Lafayette Campus (G)

4021-A Ambassador Caffery Pkwy #100,
Lafayette LA 70503
Telephone: (337) 981-4010 FICE Identification: 005203
Accreditation: ACCSC

† Branch campus of Remington College-Dallas Campus, Garland, TX

Remington College-Shreveport (H)

2106 Bert Kouns Industrial Loop, Shreveport LA 71118
Telephone: (318) 671-4000 Identification: 666302
Accreditation: ACCSC

† Branch campus of Remington College-Dallas Campus, Garland, TX

Saint Joseph Seminary College (I)

75376 River Road, Saint Benedict LA 70457-9999
County: Saint Tammany FICE Identification: 002027
Unit ID: 160409
Telephone: (985) 867-2232 Carnegie Class: Spec-4-yr-Faith
FAX Number: (985) 867-2270 Calendar System: Semester
URL: www.sjasc.edu
Established: 1891 Annual Undergrad Tuition & Fees: $21,550
Enrollment: 107 Male
Affiliation or Control: Roman Catholic IRS Status: 501(c)3
Highest Offering: Baccalaureate
Accreditation: SC

01 President & Rector ... V.Rev. Gregory M. BOQUET, OSB
05 Academic Dean ... Dr. Daniel P. BURNS
03 Vice-Rector ... Rev. Matthew CLARK, OSB
08 Librarian ... Ms. JoAnn MONTALBANO
10 Business Officer ... Mrs. Jennifer WHITEHOUSE
37 Director Financial Aid/Registrar ... Ms. Katie REYNOLDS
29 Director of Alumni Affairs ... Rev. Matthew CLARK, OSB
30 Director of Development ... Vacant
26 Director of Communications ... Ms. Sandy CUNNINGHAM
32 Dean of Students ... Br. Jerome AUBERT, OSB
108 Director Institutional Assessment ... Ms. Wendy VANDALEN
13 Chief Info Technology Officer ... Mr. Todd RUSSELL
18 Chief Facilities/Physical Plant ... Mr. Jim ROBEAU
04 Admin Assistant to the President ... Mrs. Cindy MARKHAM
15 Chief Human Resources Officer ... Mrs. Carla GRAVES
41 Athletic Director ... Mr. Brenton ADDISON

*Southern University and Agricultural & Mechanical College System (J)

JS Clark Admin Building, 4th Floor,
Baton Rouge LA 70813-0001
County: East Baton Rouge Parish FICE Identification: 009637
Unit ID: 160533
Telephone: (225) 771-4680 Carnegie Class: N/A
FAX Number: (225) 771-5522
URL: www.sus.edu

01 President-Chancellor ... Dr. Ray L. BELTON
05 Executive VCAA/Provost ... Dr. Bijoy K. SAHOO
10 System VP Finance/Business Affairs ... Mr. Flandus MCCLINTON
84 VC Enroll Mgmt & Student Success ... Dr. Jacqueline PREASTLY
13 Assoc VP Information Technology ... Dr. Gabriel FAGBEYIRO
106 Director Office of E-Learning ... Ms. Tracy BARLEY
30 CEO SU System Foundation ... Mr. Alfred E. HARRELL, III
43 General Counsel to the System/Board ... Ms. Corinne BLACHE
26 VP of External Affairs ... Dr. Robyn M. MERRICK
27 System Director of Communications ... Ms. Janene TATE
45 VP Strategic Planning ... Dr. V. Alexander APPEANING
06 Registrar ... Ms. Dianna GILBERT-DEPRON
07 Executive Director of Admissions ... Ms. Heather FREEMAN
104 Dean of International Education ... Dr. Barbara CARPENTER
29 Exec Dir Alumni Federation ... Ms. LaQuitta THOMAS
36 Director of Career Services ... Ms. Tamara F. MONTGOMERY
37 Director Student Financial Aid ... Ms. Taishieka DAVIS
38 Director Student Counseling ... Dr. ValaRay IRVIN
39 Director Student Housing ... Ms. Tracie A. ABRAHAM
41 Athletic Director ... Mr. Roman BANKS, JR.
50 Dean College of Business ... Dr. Donald ANDREWS
53 Director of Education ... Dr. VerJanis PEOPLES
54 Dean College of Sci/Engineering ... Dr. Patrick CARRIERE
96 Director of Purchasing ... Ms. Linda ANTOINE

*Southern University and A&M College (K)

Harding Boulevard, Baton Rouge LA 70813-0001
County: East Baton Rouge FICE Identification: 002025
Unit ID: 160621
Telephone: (225) 771-4500 Carnegie Class: DU-Higher
FAX Number: (225) 771-2018 Calendar System: Semester
URL: www.subr.edu
Established: 1880 Annual Undergrad Tuition & Fees (In-State): $9,340
Enrollment: 6,917 Coed
Affiliation or Control: State IRS Status: 501(c)3
Highest Offering: Doctorate
Accreditation: SC, CACREP, CAEP, DIETI, JOUR, MUS, NURSE, SP, SPAA, SW

02 President/Chancellor ... Dr. Ray BELTON
05 EVC Academic Affairs ... Dr. Bijoy K. SAHOO
100 Chief of Staff ... Dr. Katara A. WILLIAMS
10 Sys VP Finance and Admin ... Mr. Flandus MCCLINTON
45 System VP SPPIE ... Dr. Vladimir A. APPEANING
26 System VP External Affairs ... Dr. Robyn M. MERRICK
43 General Counsel ... Ms. Corinne BLACHE
15 AVP Human Resources ... Ms. Tracie J. WOODS
13 AVP for IT/Chief Information Ofcr ... Dr. Gabriel FAGBEYIRO
115 AVP of Finance & Treasury ... Ms. Catherine MILES
106 AVP Online Learning Services ... Ms. Tracy BARLEY
108 AVP SPPIE ... Dr. Toni L. MANOGIN
116 Exec Director Internal Audit ... Mr. Brian ADAMS
102 CEO SU System Foundation ... Mr. Alfred E. HARRELL
18 Exec Director Facilities ... Mr. Eli G. GUILLORY, III
29 Exec Dir SU Alumni Federation ... Mr. Derrick WARREN
114 VC Finance & Administration ... Mr. Benjamin PUGH
84 VC Enroll Management/Stdnt Success ... Dr. Jacqueline G. PREASTLY
32 VC for Student Affairs ... Dr. Frederick C. WALTON
46 VC Research & Strategic Initiatives ... Dr. Michael A. STUBBLEFIELD
41 Athletic Director ... Mr. Roman BANKS
124 AVC for Student Affairs ... Mr. Anthony JACKSON
21 AVC Finance and Administration ... Mrs. Monica MEALIE
121 Exec Dir Center Student Success ... Ms. Latrina COLLINS
35 Dean of Students ... Ms. Montrice O'NEAL

50 Dean College of Business — Dr. Donald R. ANDREWS
54 Dean Col of Sciences/Engineering — Dr. Patrick CARRIERE
80 Dean College of Government/Soc Sci — Dr. Damien EJIGIRI
79 Dean College of Humanities and IDS — Dr. Cynthia D. BRYANT
51 Asst Dean Continuing Education — Dr. Nadia GADSON
92 Dean of Honors College — Dr. Karen CROSBY
47 Chancellor/Dean Agr Rsrch & Ext Ctr — Dr. Orlando F. MCMEANS
66 Dean Nursing/Allied Health — Dr. Sandra BROWN
58 Dean of the Graduate School — Dr. Ashagre A. YIGLETU
53 Director School of Education — Dr. Verjanis PEOPLES
16 Director Human Resources — Ms. Dawn HARRIS
27 Director of Communications — Ms. Janene TATE
120 Director Online Education/E-learnin — Ms. Tracy BARLEY
96 Director of Purchasing — Mrs. Linda B. ANTOINE
06 Registrar — Mrs. Dianna DEPRON
37 Director of Financial Aid — Mrs. Taisheika DAVIS
39 Director Residential Housing — Mrs. Tracie A. ABRAHAM
07 Exec Dir Admissions/Recruitment — Ms. Heather FREEMAN
19 Chief of Police — Ms. Joycelyn JOHNSON
36 Director Career Services — Mrs. Tamara F. MONTGOMERY
09 Dir of Inst Research & Assessment — Mr. Srinivas R. GAVINI
25 Assoc Controller for Sponsored Pgm — Ms. Famika SARGENT
88 Assoc Controller for Financial Op — Mrs. Cary HOLLINS
08 Dean of Libraries — Mrs. Dawn KIGHT
104 Dean Intl Affairs & Univ Outreach — Dr. Barbara W. CARPENTER
105 Director Web Services — Ms. Rachel CARRIERE
38 Director Student Counseling — Dr. ValaRay J. IRVIN
04 Admin Assistant to the President — Ms. Patricia HANDY
101 Secretary of the Institution/Board — Mrs. Tracey TAYLOR JARELL
90 Director Academic Computing — Mr. Maurice PITTS
91 Director Administrative Computing — Ms. Willie FRANCOIS
103 Director Workforce Development — Dr. Michael A. STUBBLEFIELD
44 Director Annual Giving — Mr. Alfred HARRELL
86 Director Government Relations — Dr. Robyn MERRICK

*Southern University at New Orleans (A)

6400 Press Drive, New Orleans LA 70126-1009
County: Orleans — FICE Identification: 002026
Unit ID: 160630
Telephone: (504) 286-5000 — Carnegie Class: Masters/M
FAX Number: (504) 286-5131 — Calendar System: Semester
URL: www.suno.edu
Established: 1956 — Annual Undergrad Tuition & Fees (In-State): $7,059
Enrollment: 2,264 — Coed
Affiliation or Control: State — IRS Status: 501(c)3
Highest Offering: Master's
Accreditation: SC, AAFCS, CAEPN, CAHIIM, SW

02 Chancellor — Dr. James H. AMMONS, JR.
04 Exec Assoc to the Chancellor — Mr. Harry DOUGHTY
05 EVC for Academic Affairs & SACS — Dr. Gregory FORD
10 VC for Admin & Finance — Dr. Teresa HARDEE
32 VC Student Affs/Enroll Mgmt — Dr. Adriel HILTON
46 VC for Research/Title III Programs — Dr. Brenda W. JACKSON
111 VC Advance/Community Outreach — Dr. Kim RUGON
09 Dir IR/IE & Strategic Planning — Mrs. Ada KWANBUNBUMPEN
108 Lrng Outcomes/Assessment Coord — Ms. Safia JENKINS
25 Dir Grants & Sponsored Programs — Dr. William R. BELISLE
06 Registrar — Ms. Gilda DAVIS
21 Comptroller — Ms. Shawn M. CHARLES
08 Director of Library — Mrs. Shatiqua A. MOSBY-WILSON
36 Dir Career Counseling & Vet Liaison — Vacant
13 Int Dir of Information Technology — Mr. Peter BONNEE
15 Director of Human Resources — Ms. Dana DOUGLAS
19 Police Chief Campus Police — Mr. Bruce ADAMS
41 Director of Athletics — Vacant
26 Dir of Comm and Public Relations — Ms. Regine WILLIAMS
96 Director of Purchasing — Ms. Marilyn G. MANUEL
106 Director of E-Learning — Ms. Shelia WOOD
70 Dean School of Social Work — Dr. Rebecca CHAISSON
50 Dean College of Business/Pub Admin — Dr. Igwe E. UDEH
88 Director of Museum Studies — Dr. Haitham EID
58 Director of Graduate Studies — Ms. Deidrea JONES-HAZURE
49 Dean College of Arts & Sciences — Dr. Evelyn HARRELL
53 Dean College of Education — Dr. Willie JONES
22 Dir Svcs for Stdnts w/Disabilities — Vacant
35 Dir of Student Activities/Orgs — Ms. Rebecca GILLIAM
38 Dir of Student Development Center — Dr. Josephine OKORONKWO
121 Dir Student Support Services Pgm — Ms. Linda D. FREDERICK
88 Dir Ctr for African & American Stds — Dr. Clyde ROBERTSON
18 Director of Facilities Management — Mr. Derrick JAMES
37 Director Student Financial Aid — Ms. LaCharlotte GARRETT
07 Director of Admissions — Vacant

*Southern University at Shreveport-Louisiana (B)

3050 Martin Luther King Jr. Drive,
Shreveport LA 71107-4795
County: Caddo — FICE Identification: 007686
Unit ID: 160649
Telephone: (318) 670-6000 — Carnegie Class: Assoc/HVT-High Non
FAX Number: (318) 670-6374 — Calendar System: Semester
URL: www.susla.edu
Established: 1964 — Annual Undergrad Tuition & Fees (In-State): $4,789
Enrollment: 3,013 — Coed
Affiliation or Control: State — IRS Status: 501(c)3
Highest Offering: Associate Degree
Accreditation: SC, ADNUR, CAHIIM, COARC, DH, MLTAD, RAD, SURGT

02 Chancellor — Dr. Rodney A. ELLIS
05 Int VC Acad Affs/Workforce Dev — Mr. Lonnie MCCRAY
32 Vice Chanc Student Affairs — Ms. Melva WILLIAMS
10 Vice Chanc Finance/Administration — Mr. Antonius PEGUES
103 Assoc VC Cmty Outreach/WFD — Mrs. Janice B. SNEED
11 Chief Admin/Operations Officer — Ms. Leslie R. MCCLELLON
35 Asst Vice Chanc Student Affairs — Dr. Fatina ELLIOTT
09 Vice Chanc for RSPIE — Dr. Regina ROBINSON
21 Chief Financial Officer — Mrs. Brandy JACOBSEN
111 Chief Advancement Officer — Ms. Stephanie ROGERS
113 Director of Student Accounts — Ms. Katrina HEARD
06 Registrar — Dr. Lalita ROGERS
08 Library Director — Mrs. Jane O'RILEY
35 Director of Student Activities — Mrs. Rebecca GILLIAM
41 Int Athletic Director — Mr. Patrick WESLEY
07 Director of Admission & Recruitment — Mr. Jorge SOUSA, III
37 Director of Financial Aid — Ms. Katraya WILLIAMS
102 Exec Director SUSLA Foundation — Mr. Frank WILLIAMS, JR.
26 Dir University Relations/Marketing — Ms. Rasheeda SIMMONS
19 Chief University Police — Mr. Edward REYNOLDS
13 Dir Information Tech Center/CIO — Ms. Carolyn MILLER
121 Director Student Support Services — Ms. Karen COCO
38 University Counselor — Ms. Kaye L. WASHINGTON
15 Director Human Resources — Mr. Wayne H. BRYANT
18 Director Facilities & Risk — Vacant
114 University Budget Officer — Ms. Regina WINN
72 Director Radiologic Technology — Ms. Sheila SWIFT
88 Exec Dir TRIO Community Outreach — Ms. Betty C. FAGBEYIRO
52 Int Director Dental Hygiene — Ms. Lynne EATMAN
66 Director of Nursing — Dr. Tiffany VARNER

*Southern University Law Center (C)

PO Box 9294, Baton Rouge LA 70813
County: East Baton Rouge — Identification: 667233
Unit ID: 440916
Telephone: (225) 771-2552 — Carnegie Class: Spec-4-yr-Law
FAX Number: N/A — Calendar System: Semester
URL: www.sulc.edu
Established: 1947 — Annual Graduate Tuition & Fees: N/A
Enrollment: 843 — Coed
Affiliation or Control: State — IRS Status: 501(c)3
Highest Offering: First Professional Degree; No Undergraduates
Accreditation: SC, LAW

02 Chancellor — Mr. John K. PIERRE
05 Vice Chanc Academic Affairs — Mr. Shawn VANCE
06 Int Director Records & Registration — Mrs. Latonya WRIGHT
07 AVC/Dir of Admissions/Recruitment — Ms. Andrea LOVE
09 VC Inst Accountability/Accred — Ms. Regina JAMES
10 Vice Chanc Finance & Administration — Mr. Terry HALL
20 AVC Academic Support/Bar Prep — Ms. Cynthia REED
18 Director of Facilities — Ms. Angela GAINES
26 Director of External Affairs — Ms. Jasmine HUNTER
29 Director of Alumni Affairs — Ms. Robbin THOMAS
30 Director of Development — Vacant
32 Vice Chanc Student Affairs — Mr. Donald NORTH
36 Director of Career Services — Ms. Koshaneke GILBERT
37 Director of Financial Aid — Ms. Calaundra CLARKE
21 Assoc Vice Chanc Finance/Admin — Ms. Demetria GEORGE
35 Assoc Vice Chanc Student Affairs — Ms. Shenequa GREY
28 AVC Diversity/Equity/Inclusion — Ms. Kerii LANDRY-THOMAS
96 Director of Purchasing — Ms. Terry STEWARD

Tulane University (D)

6823 St. Charles Avenue, New Orleans LA 70118-5698
County: Orleans — FICE Identification: 002029
Unit ID: 160755
Telephone: (504) 865-5000 — Carnegie Class: DU-Highest
FAX Number: (504) 865-5202 — Calendar System: Semester
URL: www.tulane.edu
Established: 1834 — Annual Undergrad Tuition & Fees: $58,852
Enrollment: 13,927 — Coed
Affiliation or Control: Independent Non-Profit — IRS Status: 501(c)3
Highest Offering: Doctorate
Accreditation: SC, CAEPT, DIETI, HSA, IPSY, LAW, MED, PA, PH, SCPSY, SW

01 President — Mr. Michael A. FITTS
05 Sr Vice Pres Acad Affairs/Provost — Dr. Robin FORMAN
111 Sr Vice Pres for Advancement — Ms. Ginny WISE
11 SVP/Chief Operations Officer — Mr. Patrick NORTON
63 Sr Vice Pres/Dn School of Medicine — Dr. Lee L. HAMM
43 General Counsel — Ms. Victoria D. JOHNSON
13 CIO & VP Information Technology — Mr. Noel WONG
10 Vice President Finance & Controller — Mr. James WANDLING
115 Chief Investment Officer — Mr. Richard CHAU
32 VP Student Affairs — Dr. J. Davidson PORTER
58 Assoc Provost Graduate Studies — Dr. Michael CUNNINGHAM
84 VP Enrollment Management — Dr. Shawn ABBOTT
18 VP Facil/Campus Dev & Real Estate — Mr. Randolph PHILIPSON
26 Vice Pres University Communications — Mr. Ian MORRISON
46 Vice President for Research — Dr. Giovanni PIEDIMONTE
110 Vice President Advancement — Ms. Luann D. DOZIER
15 AVP Human Resources/Inst Equity — Mr. Jonathan SMALL
117 VP Enterprise Risk Management — Ms. Angela SUTTON
86 Assoc VP Government Relations — Ms. Sharon P. COURTNEY
109 Assoc VP Campus Operations — Dr. Brian JOHNSON
37 Assoc Vice President Financial Aid — Mr. Michael GOODMAN
114 Chief of Staff to the COO — Ms. Judy VITRANO
29 VP for Alumni Affairs — Ms. Lori HURVITZ
08 Dean Library & Academic Information — Mr. David BANUSH
36 Asst Dean & Dir NTC Career Svcs — Mr. Edward CRUZ
12 Director/CAO Nat Primate Res Ctr — Dr. Jay RAPPAPORT
27 Asst VP Communications — Mr. Michael J. STRECKER
96 Director Central Procurement Svcs — Mr. William VAN CLEAVE
41 Director Athletics — Mr. Troy DANNEN
51 Dean School of Prof Advancement — Dr. Suri DUITCH
49 Dean School of Liberal Arts — Dr. Brian EDWARDS
49 Dean Newcomb-Tulane College — Dr. Lee SKINNER
61 Dean School of Law — Mr. David D. MEYER
69 Dean Sch Public Health/Trop Med — Dr. Thomas LAVEIST
54 Dean School Science & Engineering — Dr. Kimberly FOSTER
48 Dean School of Architecture — Dr. Inaki ALDAY
50 Dean AB Freeman School of Business — Dr. Paulo GOES
70 Dean School of Social Work — Dr. Patrick BORDNICK
09 Asst Provost Assess/Inst Research — Ms. Jessica SHEDD
88 Executive Director of CELT — Dr. Toni WEISS
85 Assoc Dean Ctr for Global Education — Dr. Casey LOVE
88 CPS Executive Director — Dr. Agnieszka NANCE
04 Senior Aide to the President — Ms. Sharia TYLER
06 Registrar — Ms. Colette RAPHEL
101 Secretary to the Board — Ms. Cyndy ENGLISH
100 VP/Sec of the Corp/Chief of Staff — Mrs. Elizabeth BROWN

University of Holy Cross (E)

4123 Woodland Drive, New Orleans LA 70131-7399
County: Orleans — FICE Identification: 002023
Unit ID: 160065
Telephone: (504) 394-7744 — Carnegie Class: Masters/S
FAX Number: (504) 391-2421 — Calendar System: Semester
URL: www.uhcno.edu
Established: 1916 — Annual Undergrad Tuition & Fees: $15,280
Enrollment: 1,137 — Coed
Affiliation or Control: Roman Catholic — IRS Status: 501(c)3
Highest Offering: Doctorate
Accreditation: SC, CACREP, CAEP, IACBE, NDT, NUR, RAD

01 President — Dr. Stanton F. MCNEELY
05 Int Provost/VP Academic Affairs — Dr. Lisa M. SULLIVAN
10 Vice Pres for Finance & CFO — Mr. Chris BUNDICK
30 Vice Pres for Philanthropy/Planning — Vacant
84 Vice Pres Enrollment Management — Dr. Rosaria GUASTELLA
32 Assoc Vice Pres of Student Affairs — Ms. Meredith REED
88 Vice Pres for Mission Integration — Ms. Angela RUIZ
08 Director of Library Services — Ms. Diana SCHAUBHUT
83 Dean Couns/Educ/Business — Dr. Carolyn WHITE
66 Dean Nursing/Allied Health — Dr. Patricia PRECHTER
49 Dean Liberal Arts and Science — Dr. Michael LABRANCHE
32 Director Student Life — Ms. Mallory OTTAWAY
06 Registrar — Ms. Leslie M. JONES
42 Campus Minister — Ms. Angela RUIZ
15 Director Human Resources — Ms. Christine WATTS
44 Director of Annual Fund — Vacant
13 Int Director of Info Tech Services — Ms. Audrey B. CLEMENTS
37 Director of Financial Aid — Mr. Jason CALLICO
04 Administrative Asst to President — Vacant
19 Asst Director Campus Public Safety — Mr. Garry FLOT
26 Director Marketing/Communications — Ms. Jessica A. PIERCE
29 Director Alumni/Parent Relations — Mr. Matthew PICARD

*University of Louisiana System Office (F)

1201 N Third Street, Suite 7-300,
Baton Rouge LA 70802-5243
County: East Baton Rouge — FICE Identification: 033444
Unit ID: 247083
Telephone: (225) 342-6950 — Carnegie Class: N/A
FAX Number: (225) 342-6473
URL: www.ulsystem.net

01 President & CEO — Dr. James B. HENDERSON
11 Exec VP/Chief Operating Officer — Dr. Marcus JONES
05 Provost and VP for Academic Affairs — Dr. Jeannine KAHN
10 VP of Business and Finance — Mr. Eddie MECHE
32 VP for Student Affairs & Governance — Ms. Erica CALAIS
26 VP for External Affairs — Ms. Cami GEISMAN
04 Exec Asst to President & CEO — Ms. Sandra GREEN

*Grambling State University (G)

403 Main Street, Grambling LA 71245
County: Lincoln — FICE Identification: 002006
Unit ID: 159009
Telephone: (318) 274-3811 — Carnegie Class: Masters/L
FAX Number: (318) 274-6172 — Calendar System: Semester
URL: www.gram.edu
Established: 1901 — Annual Undergrad Tuition & Fees (In-State): $7,635
Enrollment: 5,438 — Coed
Affiliation or Control: State — IRS Status: 501(c)3
Highest Offering: Doctorate
Accreditation: SC, CAEPN, CAPRT, MUS, NUR, NURSE, SPAA, SW, THEA

02 President — Mr. Richard GALLOT, JR.
05 Provost/VP Academic Affairs — Dr. Connie WALTON
11 Chief Operating Officer — Ms. Penya MOSES
10 Vice President for Finance — Dr. Edwin LITOLFF
32 Interim VP of Student Affairs — Dr. Rudolph K. ELLIS
111 VP of Institutional Advancement — Ms. Melanie JONES
13 Chief Information Officer — Mr. Jay J. ELLIS
15 Director of Human Resources — Mr. Wayne BRYANT
19 University Police Chief — Mr. Rodney DEMERY
50 Dean College of Business — Dr. Donald WHITE

53 Dean College of Education ... Dr. Debbie THOMAS
49 Dean College of Arts & Sci ... Dr. Stacey D. DUHON
92 Dean Honors College ... Dr. Ellen SMILEY
18 Interim Director Facilities Mgmt ... Mr. Damien CHATMAN
09 Director of Institutional Research ... Dr. Shalena JOHNSON
41 VP of Intercollegiate Athletics ... Dr. Trayvean SCOTT
07 Director of Admissions ... Ms. Georgio DOUGLAS
06 University Registrar ... Mrs. Patricia J. HUTCHERSON
37 Dir Student Financial Aid ... Dr. Alan JACKSON
29 Exec Director of Alumni Affairs ... Vacant
23 Director of Health Services ... Mrs. Patrice OUTLEY
38 Director Counseling Center ... Dr. Coleen SPEED
39 Director of Residential Life ... Ms. Carnelia BARFIELD
96 Director of Purchasing ... Vacant
40 Manager University Bookstore ... Mr. Alfredo MORELOS
106 Director of Distance Learning ... Dr. Eldrie HAMILTON
88 Special Assistant to Provost and VP ... Mrs. Melody FORD
36 Director of Career Services ... Mrs. Kellye BLACKBURN
100 Chief of Staff ... Ms. Jazmine CHERRY
84 Director Enrollment Management ... Dr. Gavin HAMMS
91 Director Administrative Computing ... Mrs. Peggy HANLEY

*Louisiana Tech University (A)

PO Box 3168, Ruston LA 71272-0001

County: Lincoln FICE Identification: 002008
Unit ID: 159647
Telephone: (318) 257-0211 Carnegie Class: DU-Higher
FAX Number: (318) 257-2928 Calendar System: Quarter
URL: www.latech.edu
Established: 1894 Annual Undergrad Tuition & Fees (In-State): $10,065
Enrollment: 11,126 Coed
Affiliation or Control: State IRS Status: 501(c)3
Highest Offering: Doctorate
Accreditation: SC, AAB, AAFCS, ADNUR, ART, AUD, CACREP, CAEP, CAHIIM, CIDA, COPSY, DIETD, DIETI, MLS, MUS, SP

02 President ... Dr. Leslie K. GUICE
05 Provost ... Dr. Terry M. MCCONATHY
111 Vice President for Univ Advancement ... Mr. Brooks HULL
46 Chief Research & Innovation Officer ... Dr. Davy NORRIS, JR.
10 Vice President of Finance ... Mrs. Lisa L. COLE
11 AVP of Administration & Facilities ... Mr. Sam G. WALLACE
09 AVP Inst Effect/Research & Planning . Dr. Sheryl S. SHOEMAKER
88 AVP Acad Advancement & Partnerships ... Dr. Donna JOHNSON
58 AVP Research & Dean Grad School ... Dr. Ramu RAMACHANDRAN
88 AVP Research & Partnerships ... Dr. Sumeet DUA
32 AVP Student Advance/Dean Stdnt Life ... Dr. Dickie CRAWFORD
115 CFO & Exec Dir University Services ... Ms. Pam GILLEY
04 EA to Pres Compliance/Title IX ... Mrs. Carrie FLOURNOY
50 Dean of Business ... Dr. Chris MARTIN
53 Dean of Education ... Dr. Don N. SCHILLINGER
54 Dean of Engineering & Science ... Dr. Hisham HEGAB
65 Dean of Applied & Natural Sciences ... Dr. Gary KENNEDY
49 Dean of Liberal Arts ... Dr. Don KACZVINSKY
121 Dean Student Svcs & Acad Support ... Mrs. Stacy GILBERT
84 Dean Stdnt Engage/Undergrad Recruit ... Mr. Sam SPEED
116 Internal Auditor ... Mr. Robert GRAFTON
43 Legal Counsel ... Mr. Justin KAVALIR
26 Exec Dir University Communications ... Ms. Tonya OAKS SMITH
15 Director Human Resources ... Ms. Sheila TRAMMEL
113 Comptroller ... Vacant
07 Director of Admissions ... Vacant
13 Chief Info Technology Officer ... Mr. Tom HOOVER
91 Director of Computer Center ... Mr. Mike COLYAR
90 Interim Dir Infrastructure & IT ... Mr. Danny SCHALES
37 Director Student Financial Aid ... Ms. Aimee F. BAXTER
06 Registrar ... Vacant
08 Executive Director Libraries Svcs ... Vacant
38 Dir Career Ctr/Student Counseling ... Mr. Ron CATHEY
89 Director of Freshmen Studies ... Ms. Jennifer CARTER
92 Director of Honors Program ... Dr. Ernest RUFLETH
93 Director of Multicultural Affairs ... Ms. Devonia LOVE-VAUGHN
96 Director of Procurement ... Ms. Melissa HUGHES
18 Director Physical Plant ... Mr. Joe PEEL
41 Athletics Director ... Vacant
117 Director Envir Health & Safety ... Mr. Don BRASWELL
39 Dir Resident Life & Summer Camps ... Ms. Casey INGRAM
85 Director Intl Students/Scholars ... Mr. Jay LIGON
19 Chief University Police ... Mr. Randal HERMES
40 Director Bookstore ... Mr. Elliot JONES
118 HR Coordinator Benefits ... Ms. Taryn SOIGNIER
25 Director Sponsored Programs ... Ms. Courtney JARRELL
100 Coordinator of Planning & Advance ... Mr. Ryan W. RICHARD

*McNeese State University (B)

4205 Ryan Street, Lake Charles LA 70605

County: Calcasieu FICE Identification: 002017
Unit ID: 159717
Telephone: (337) 475-5000 Carnegie Class: Masters/L
FAX Number: (337) 475-5012 Calendar System: Semester
URL: www.mcneese.edu
Established: 1939 Annual Undergrad Tuition & Fees (In-State): $8,382
Enrollment: 7,284 Coed
Affiliation or Control: State IRS Status: 501(c)3
Highest Offering: Beyond Master's But Less Than Doctorate
Accreditation: SC, ABAI, ART, CACREP, CAEP, CAEPN, DIETD, DIETI, MLS, MUS, NURSE, RAD

02 President ... Dr. Daryl V. BURCKEL
05 Provost/VP Acad Affairs/EM ... Dr. Frederick LEMIEUX
10 VP Business Affairs ... Ms. Mona WHITE
111 VP University Advancement ... Dr. Wade ROUSSE
32 VP Student Affairs ... Dr. Christopher THOMAS
84 Assoc VP Enrollment Management ... Dr. Toby OSBURN
20 Asst VP Academic Affairs ... Ms. Jessica HUTCHINGS
47 Dean College of Agriculture ... Dr. Frederick LEMIEUX
50 Dean College of Business ... Dr. Shuming BAI
53 Dean College of Education ... Dr. Angelique OGEA
49 Dean College of Liberal Arts ... Dr. Michael BUCKLES
54 Dean Col of Science/Engr/Math ... Dr. Tim HALL
66 Int Dean Col of Nursing/Health Prof ... Dr. Ann WARNER
35 Dean Student Affairs ... Dr. Kedrick NICHOLAS
13 Chief Information Technology ... Mr. Chad THIBODEAUX
19 University Police Chief ... Mr. William SCHEUFENS
28 Director of Diversity ... Ms. Krisshunn YOUNGBLOOD
41 Director of Athletics ... Mr. Heath SCHROYER
18 Director Facilities & Plant Opers ... Mr. Kevin MARTIN
15 Dir Human Res/Student Employment ... Ms. Charlene R. ABBOTT
37 Director Student Financial Aid ... Ms. Taina J. SAVOIT
88 Director of Scholarships ... Ms. Ralynn F. CASTETE
07 Dir of Recruiting ... Ms. Kourtney ISTRE
96 Dir Purchasing/Property Control ... Ms. Roxane FONTENOT
29 Director Alumni Affairs ... Vacant
92 Director of Honors College ... Dr. Scott E. GOINS
14 Director of Univ Computing Services ... Mr. Alfred FRUGE
08 Director of Library ... Vacant
85 Director of International Programs ... Ms. Preble GIRARD
26 Director Public Relations ... Ms. Candace V. TOWNSEND
38 Director Student Counseling/Health ... Dr. Troy HIDALGO
106 Director of Electronic Learning ... Ms. Wendi PRATER
110 Director University Advancement ... Ms. Melissa NORTHCUTT
40 Bookstore Manager ... Ms. Donna MARTIN
06 Registrar ... Ms. Catrina BOENIG
04 Administrative Asst to President ... Ms. Deb KINGREY
122 Dir Stdnt Orgs-Frat & Sorority Life ... Ms. Jacqueline CLARK

*Nicholls State University (C)

906 East First Street, Thibodaux LA 70310-0001

County: Lafourche FICE Identification: 002005
Unit ID: 159966
Telephone: (985) 448-4003 Carnegie Class: Masters/M
FAX Number: (985) 448-4920 Calendar System: Semester
URL: www.nicholls.edu
Established: 1948 Annual Undergrad Tuition & Fees (In-State): $7,946
Enrollment: 6,769 Coed
Affiliation or Control: State IRS Status: 501(c)3
Highest Offering: Beyond Master's But Less Than Doctorate
Accreditation: SC, ART, CACREP, CAEPN, DIETD, DIETI, JOUR, MUS, NAIT, NURSE

02 President ... Dr. Jay CLUNE
05 Provost/VP Academic & Student Affs . Dr. Velma S. WESTBROOK
20 Vice Provost ... Dr. Todd KELLER
32 VP Stdnt Affairs/Dean of Students ... Dr. Michele E. CARUSO
18 Director of Facility/Proj Manager ... Ms. Danielle BREAUX
10 VP for Finance & Administration ... Mr. Terry BRAUD
45 AVP Strat/Inst Effect/Accred/Succes ... Mrs. Renee G. HICKS
81 Dean of Sciences & Technology ... Dr. John DOUCET
66 Dean of Nursing ... Dr. Velma S. WESTBROOK
50 Dean Business Administration ... Dr. Marilyn MACIK-FREY
53 Dean Educ/Behavioral Sciences ... Dr. Scot RADEMAKER
121 Director of Academic Services ... Ms. Cambria BOUZIGARD
09 Dir Assess/Institutional Research ... Ms. Melanie COLLINS
08 Director of Library ... Vacant
19 Director of University Police ... Mr. Alexander BARNES
36 Director of Career Services ... Ms. Katherine MABILE
37 Director of Student Financial Aid ... Ms. Casie TRICHE
13 Director of Computing Center ... Mr. Sam CAGLE
15 AVP of Human Resources/CDIO ... Dr. Steven H. KENNEY
26 Director of Communications ... Mr. Jerad DAVID
51 Dir of Continuing Education ... Mrs. Elizabeth MCCURRY
41 Athletic Director ... Mr. Jonathan TERRELL
29 Exec Dir Alumni & External Affairs ... Ms. Monique CROCHET
88 Exec Dir Leadership & Master's Pgm ... Dr. Eugene A. DIAL
06 Director Records & Registration ... Mr. Kelly J. RODRIGUE
07 Director of Admissions ... Vacant
39 Director Residential Living ... Mr. Alex COAD
84 Director of Enrollment Services ... Mrs. Courtney CASSARD
96 Director of Purchasing ... Mr. Terry G. DUPRE
46 Director Research & Sponsored Pgms ... Mrs. Debra BENOIT
58 Director of Graduate Programs ... Vacant
88 Director of Printing & Design ... Mr. Bruno RUGGIERO
109 Director of Auxiliary Services ... Ms. Margo BADEAUX
88 Coordinator of Veterans Services ... Mr. Gilberto BURBANTE
106 Dir Online Education/E-learning ... Dr. Andrew SIMONCELLI
49 Dean of Liberal Arts ... Mrs. Jean DONEGAN
04 Admin Assistant to the President ... Mrs. Allison FORD
108 Director Institutional Assessment ... Ms. Melanie COLLINS
35 Dean of Students ... Dr. Janice LYN
38 Director of Student Counseling ... Ms. Adrienne BOLTON
90 Director Academic Computing ... Mr. Perry LAWLESS
16 Director of Human Resources ... Ms. Alison HADAWAY
25 Chief Contract and Grants Administr ... Ms. Lacey CROCHET

*Northwestern State University (D)

310 Sam Sibley Drive, Suite 223,
Natchitoches LA 71497-0002

County: Natchitoches FICE Identification: 002021
Unit ID: 160038
Telephone: (318) 357-6441 Carnegie Class: Masters/L
FAX Number: (318) 357-4223 Calendar System: Semester
URL: www.nsula.edu
Established: 1884 Annual Undergrad Tuition & Fees (In-State): $8,672
Enrollment: 11,447 Coed
Affiliation or Control: State IRS Status: 501(c)3
Highest Offering: Doctorate
Accreditation: SC, ADNUR, ANEST, ART, CACREP, CAEP, MUS, NURSE, RAD, SW, THEA

02 President ... Dr. Marcus JONES
05 Provost/VP Academic Affairs ... Dr. Greg HANDEL
26 Vice President for External Affairs ... Mr. Jerry D. PIERCE
46 VP for Tech/Innovation/Econ Dev ... Dr. Darlene WILLIAMS
10 Chief Financial Officer ... Mr. Pat JONES
32 VP Student Exp/Dean of Students ... Ms. Reatha COX
53 Dean Col of Education/Human Dev ... Dr. Kimberly MCALISTER
49 Dean Col of Arts & Sciences ... Dr. Francene LEMOINE
66 Dean Col of Nursing & Allied Health ... Dr. Joel HICKS
50 Dean Col of Business & Tech ... Vacant
13 Chief Information Officer ... Mr. Ron WRIGHT
92 Interim Director Scholars College ... Dr. Thomas REYNOLDS
12 Exec Director CENLA Campus ... Mr. Jason PARKS
09 Director Institutional Research ... Ms. Dawn MITCHELL
84 Director of Enrollment Management ... Mrs. Jana LUCKY
11 Director University Affairs ... Ms. Jennifer KELLY
06 Registrar ... Mrs. Barbara PRESCOTT
08 Director of Libraries ... Ms. Abbie LANDRY
111 Asst VP External Affs/Univ Advance ... Mr. Drake OWENS
37 Director Student Financial Aid ... Ms. Lauren JACKSON
88 Asst Dir Creative & Performing Arts ... Mr. Scott BURRELL
27 Director NSU Press ... Mrs. Leah JACKSON
36 Director Counseling & Career Svcs ... Mrs. Rebecca BOONE
41 Athletic Director ... Mr. Greg BURKE
23 Director of Health Services ... Ms. Carla WALKER
07 Director of University Recruiting ... Vacant
15 Director Human Resources ... Ms. Lisa HARRIS
18 Physical Plant Director ... Mr. Dale WOHLETZ
96 Director of Purchasing ... Mr. Dale MARTIN
122 Dir Fraternal Ldrshp/Civic Engagemt ... Ms. Mary-Katherine HORTON

*Southeastern Louisiana University (E)

500 West University Avenue, Hammond LA 70402

County: Tangipahoa FICE Identification: 002024
Unit ID: 160612
Telephone: (985) 549-2000 Carnegie Class: Masters/L
FAX Number: (985) 549-2061 Calendar System: Semester
URL: www.southeastern.edu
Established: 1925 Annual Undergrad Tuition & Fees (In-State): $8,289
Enrollment: 14,426 Coed
Affiliation or Control: State IRS Status: 501(c)3
Highest Offering: Doctorate
Accreditation: SC, AAFCS, ART, CAATE, CACREP, CAEPN, COSMA, MUS, NAIT, NURSE, SP, SW

02 President ... Dr. John L. CRAIN
05 Provost/VP Academic Affairs ... Dr. Tena GOLDING
10 VP Administration/Finance ... Mr. Sam DOMIANO
111 Vice Pres University Advancement ... Ms. Wendy LAUDERDALE
32 Vice President Student Affairs ... Dr. Eric SUMMERS
84 Chief Enrollment Management Officer ... Dr. Kay MAURIN
13 Chief Information Officer ... Dr. Mike M. ASOODEH
21 Controller ... Ms. Khalli s. HAGAN
06 Registrar ... Ms. Aime ANDERSON
08 Int Director of Library ... Ms. Janie BRANHAM
36 Director Career Development Svcs ... Mr. Ken W. RIDGEDELL
109 Director Auxiliary Services ... Ms. Connie DAVIS
29 Director of Alumni Services ... Ms. Michelle BIGGS
39 Dir Student Housing & Resident Svcs ... Mr. Chris ASPRION
15 Director Human Resources ... Ms. Tara DUPRE
19 Director University Police ... Mr. Michael BECKNER
46 Dir Sponsored Research/Programs ... Ms. Cheryl HALL
41 Athletic Director ... Mr. Jay ARTIGUES
18 Director Facility Planning ... Mr. Ken D. HOWE
92 Director Honors Program ... Dr. Claire PROCOPIO
23 Director Health Services ... Ms. Andrea PEEVY
38 Director of the Counseling Center ... Dr. Peter EMERSON
37 Director Financial Aid ... Ms. Mandy HOFFMAN
09 Director Inst Research/Assessment ... Dr. Michelle HALL
26 Sr Dir Public Information/Marketing ... Dr. Mike RIVAULT
96 Dir Purchasing/Property Control ... Mr. Richard HIMBER
35 Dean of Students ... Mr. Gabe WILLIS
22 Coordinator EEO/ADA ... Mr. Gene E. PREGEANT
49 Dean Col Arts/Human/Soc Sciences ... Dr. Karen FONTENOT
50 Dean of College of Business ... Dr. Tara LOPEZ
53 Dean College of Education ... Dr. Paula CALDERON
66 Dean Col of Nursing & Health Sci ... Dr. Ann CARRUTH
72 Dean Col of Science & Technology ... Dr. Daniel MCCARTHY

*University of Louisiana at Lafayette (F)

104 University Circle, Lafayette LA 70503-0001

County: Lafayette FICE Identification: 002031
Unit ID: 160658
Telephone: (337) 482-1000 Carnegie Class: DU-Highest
FAX Number: (337) 482-6195 Calendar System: Semester
URL: www.louisiana.edu
Established: 1898 Annual Undergrad Tuition & Fees (In-State): $10,358
Enrollment: 16,450 Coed
Affiliation or Control: State IRS Status: 501(c)3
Highest Offering: Doctorate

Accreditation: SC, ACPHA, ART, CACREP, CAEP, CAHIIM, CIDA, JOUR, MUS, NAIT, NURSE, SP, THEA

02 President .... Dr. E. Joseph SAVOIE
05 Provost/VP for Academic Affairs .... Dr. Jaimie HEBERT
10 VP Administration & Finance .... Mr. Jerry L. LEBLANC
32 Vice President for Student Affairs .... Ms. Patricia COTTONHAM
111 VP University Advancement .... Mr. John BLOHM
46 Vice President for Research .... Dr. Ramesh KOLLURU
84 VP for Enrollment Management .... Dr. DeWayne BOWIE
13 Chief Information Officer .... Mr. Gene FIELDS
26 AVP Communications/Marketing .... Dr. Jennifer STEPHENS
11 Director of Administrative Services .... Vacant
21 Asst Vice Pres Financial Services .... Ms. Debra CALAIS
45 Asst VP Inst Effectiveness .... Dr. Blanca BAUER
20 Asst VP Academic Affairs .... Dr. Robert MCKINNEY
35 Dean of Students .... Dr. Margarita PEREZ
35 Assoc Dean Students/Dir Stdnt Life .... Ms. Heidie LINDSEY
25 Director of Research/Sponsored Pgms .... Vacant
91 Director of Information Systems .... Ms. Paula BREAUX
14 Director Computing Support Services .... Mr. Patrick LANDRY
08 Dean University Libraries .... Dr. Brian DOHERTY
07 Interim Director of UG Admissions .... Ms. Tasha EVANS
09 Director of Institutional Research .... Ms. Lisa LORD
55 Director University Connection .... Ms. Amanda DOYLE
37 Director of Financial Aid .... Ms. Cindy SHOWS-PEREZ
96 AVP Finance and Director Purchasing .... Ms. Marie FRANK
27 Editorial Director .... Dr. James SAVAGE
36 Director Career Services .... Ms. Kim A. BILLEAUDEAU
19 Chief of Police .... Mr. Timothy HANKS
23 Chief Administrator Officer SHS .... Ms. Madeline HUSBAND-ARDOIN
49 Dean Liberal Arts .... Dr. Jordan KELLMAN
54 Dean of Engineering .... Dr. Ahmed KHATTAB
53 Dean of Education .... Dr. Nathan ROBERTS
66 Dean of Nursing .... Dr. Melinda OBERLEITNER
58 Dean of Graduate School .... Dr. Mary FARMER-KAISER
50 Dean of Business Admin .... Dr. Linda NICHOLS
81 Dean of Sciences .... Dr. Azmy ACKLEH
97 Dean of University College .... Dr. Bobbie DECUIR
57 Interim Dean College of the Arts .... Mr. Michael MCCLURE
77 Director Ctr Adv Computer Studies .... Dr. Magdy A. BAYOUMI
18 Director Physical Plant .... Mr. Scott HEBERT
43 Director of Operational Review .... Ms. Megan BREAUX
39 Director Housing .... Ms. Dawn MILLER
40 Manager Bookstore .... Mr. Robert RICHARD
24 Director Univ Media/Printing Svcs .... Vacant
41 Vice President for Athletics .... Dr. Bryan MAGGARD
85 Exec Dir Global Engagement .... Dr. Gabriel CARRANZA
51 Director of Continuing Education .... Dr. Martha BRYANT
31 Dean of Community Service .... Mr. David YARBROUGH
29 Exec Director Alumni Affairs .... Mr. John Claude ARCENEAUX
112 Planned Giving Officer .... Vacant
38 Director Counseling and Testing .... Mr. Brian FREDERICK
15 AVP Finance and Admin/CHRO .... Mr. Paul THOMAS
06 Registrar .... Ms. Amy DESORMEAUX
120 Director of Distance Learning .... Dr. Claire ARABIE
92 Director of Honors Program .... Dr. Julia FREDERICK
121 Exec Director of Student Success .... Dr. Elizabeth GIROIR
89 Director of First-Year Experience .... Vacant
28 Interim Chief Diversity Officer .... Ms. Kiwana MCCLUNG
108 Director Planning Acad Initiatives .... Dr. Melissa LEWIS
30 Exec Director of Development .... Ms. Lisa CAPONE
44 Director Annual Giving .... Ms. Claire ST. ROMAIN
113 Bursar .... Mr. Kyle CALAIS
119 Director of IT Security .... Mr. Charles BROOME
39 Director of Residence Life .... Ms. Maylen ALDANA
105 Director of Digital Communications .... Ms. Aimee ABSHIRE
16 Deputy Chief Human Resources Office .... Ms. Lelanya DOUET
122 Asst Dir Engage/Ldrshp-Greek Life .... Mr. Jackson TIDWELL

*University of Louisiana at Monroe (A)

700 University Avenue, Monroe LA 71209-0001
County: Ouachita — FICE Identification: 002020
Unit ID: 159993
Telephone: (318) 342-1000 — Carnegie Class: DU-Mod
FAX Number: (318) 342-5161 — Calendar System: Semester
URL: www.ulm.edu
Established: 1931 — Annual Undergrad Tuition & Fees (In-State): $9,070
Enrollment: 8,888 — Coed
Affiliation or Control: State — IRS Status: 501(c)3
Highest Offering: Doctorate
Accreditation: SC, CACREP, CAEP, CONST, DH, EXSC, MFCD, MLS, MUS, NURSE, OT, OTA, PHAR, RAD, SP, SW

02 President .... Dr. Ronald L. BERRY
10 Vice President for Business Affairs .... Dr. William T. GRAVES
32 Vice President for Student Affairs .... Dr. Valerie FIELDS
05 Vice President for Academic Affairs .... Dr. Mark ARANT
13 VP for Info Svcs/Student Success .... Dr. Michael CAMILLE
84 VP Enrollment Mgmt & Univ Rels .... Ms. Lisa MILLER
43 Legal/Compliance Counsel .... Ms. Sherrye CARRADINE
41 Interim Director of Athletics .... Mr. Seth HALL
46 Chief Innovation & Research Officer .... Dr. John SUTHERLIN
07 Director Admissions & Scholarship .... Dr. Robyn JORDAN
26 Exec Dir of Mktg & Communications .... Dr. Brice JONES
96 Director of Purchasing .... Ms. Cheri PERKINS
116 Internal Audit .... Mr. Ferando CORDOVA
49 Dean Arts/Education & Sciences .... Dr. John PRATTE
50 Dean Business & Social Sciences .... Dr. Michelle MCEACHARN
67 Dean Pharmacy .... Dr. Glenn ANDERSON
76 Dean College Health Science .... Dr. Donald SIMPSON
58 Dean Graduate School .... Dr. Sushma KRISHNAMURTHY
108 Director Assessment and Evaluation .... Mrs. Allison L. THOMPSON
09 Dir Univ Planning/Analysis .... Mr. Jason CONSTANT
08 Director Library & Coord of Tech .... Mr. Charles HUGHES
106 Director of Online Education .... Ms. Joanna HUNTER
06 Registrar .... Mr. Anthony MALTA
37 Director Financial Aid Services .... Ms. Marla HERRINGTON
85 Dir Intl Student Program and Svcs .... Ms. Gina WHITE
124 Director of University Retention .... Ms. Patricia PATE
102 Executive Director Foundation .... Mrs. Susan CHAPPELL
39 Director Residential Life .... Ms. Tresea L. BUCKHAULTS
114 Budget Officer .... Mrs. Nicole WALKER
21 Controller .... Mr. Mark LABUDE
15 Director Human Resources .... Ms. Melissa DUCOTE
14 Director Computer Center .... Mr. Chance W. EPPINETTE
109 Exec Dir Auxiliary Enterprises .... Mr. Tommy WALPOLE
40 Manager University Bookstore .... Ms. Stacey CORDELL
18 Director Physical Plant Admin .... Mr. Chris RINGO
88 Facilities Planning Officer .... Mr. Michael DAVIS
22 Spec Projects Ofcr/Title IX Coord .... Ms. Treina KIMBLE
38 Director Counseling Center .... Ms. Karen FOSTER
19 Director of University Police .... Mr. Tom TORREGROSSA
36 Director Career Center .... Ms. Kristin CHANDLER
88 Dir Recreational Svcs/Facilities .... Mr. Brandon BRUSCATO
88 Technology and Comm Liaison .... Mr. Lindsey S. WILKERSON
29 Director of Alumni Affairs .... Ms. Sarah SIEREVELD
04 Assistant to the President .... Ms. Kathy MASTERS
25 Dir Sponsored Programs & Research .... Ms. Lawanna GILBERT-BELL
53 Director School of Education .... Dr. Myra LOVETT
88 Exec Dir Recruitment/Admissions .... Ms. Sami OWENS
28 Dir of Diversity/Equity & Inclusion .... Dr. Pamela SAULSBERRY

WorldQuant University (B)

201 S. Charles Ave, Ste 2500, New Orleans LA 70170
County: Orleans — Identification: 667408
Telephone: (504) 662-1946 — Carnegie Class: Not Classified
FAX Number: N/A — Calendar System: Other
URL: https://www.wqu.edu/
Established: 2015 — Annual Graduate Tuition & Fees: N/A
Enrollment: N/A — Coed
Affiliation or Control: Independent Non-Profit — IRS Status: 501(c)3
Highest Offering: Master's; No Undergraduates
Accreditation: DEAC

01 CEO .... Daphne KIS

Xavier University of Louisiana (C)

One Drexel Drive, New Orleans LA 70125-1098
County: Orleans — FICE Identification: 002032
Unit ID: 160904
Telephone: (504) 486-7411 — Carnegie Class: Masters/M
FAX Number: (504) 520-7904 — Calendar System: Semester
URL: www.xula.edu
Established: 1925 — Annual Undergrad Tuition & Fees: $25,822
Enrollment: 3,383 — Coed
Affiliation or Control: Roman Catholic — IRS Status: 501(c)3
Highest Offering: Doctorate
Accreditation: SC, ACBSP, #ARCPA, CACREP, CAEP, MUS, PHAR, @SP

01 President .... Dr. C. Reynold VERRET
05 Provost and Sr VP Academic Affairs .... Dr. Anne MCCALL
100 VP Administration & Chief of Staff .... Ms. Patrice BELL
116 Dir Office of Internal Audits .... Mr. William BOSTICK
45 AVP Strat & Plng/Dep Chief of Staff .... Dr. Rae BORDEN
09 Sr Assoc Provost & Chief IR Officer .... Dr. Marguerite GIGUETTE
20 Assoc Provost for Faculty Affairs .... Ms. Floristina PAYTON STEWART
20 Asst Provost & COO Acad Affairs .... Ms. Shellond CHESTER
121 Asst Provost for Student Success .... Dr. Nathaniel HOLMES
84 VP Enrollment Management .... Vacant
111 Vice President Inst Advancement .... Mr. Phillip D. ADAMS
32 Vice President Student Affairs .... Mr. Curtis WRIGHT
10 CFO and VP Fiscal Services .... Mr. Edward J. PHILLIPS
13 VP Technology Administration .... Dr. Mable J. MOORE
18 VP Facility Planning & Mgmt .... Mr. Marion BRACY
15 Assoc VP Human Resources .... Ms. Adicia WADDELL
110 Assoc VP Inst Advancement .... Ms. Kimberly REESE
46 Assoc VP Research/Sponsored Pgms .... Ms. Kaneisha B. AKINPELUMI
88 Asst VP & Director Title III .... Dr. Rachel THOMAS
14 Asst VP Tech/Deputy CIO .... Ms. Melva D. WILLIAMS
07 Sr Assoc Dir of Admissions .... Ms. Kendra LAWRENCE
19 Asst VP/Chief of Police .... Ms. Changamire DURALL
22 Asst VP Stdnt Affs/Dep Chf Inc Ofcr .... Ms. Kerri ALEXANDER
07 Asst VP Enrollment Mgmt .... Mr. Tony JACKSON
88 Assoc Dean Health & Wellness .... Ms. Virginia PELLERIN
49 Dean Col of Arts & Sciences .... Dr. Anderson SUNDA-MEYA
35 Asst Dean Student Life .... Mr. Darryl KELLER
41 Exec Dir Athletics & Recreation .... Mr. Nathan COCHRAN
88 Exec Dir Advancement Services .... Mrs. Kendra TIRCUIT
39 Exec Director Residential Education .... Ms. Chermele CHRISTY
101 Dir Board Relations Pres Office .... Ms. Kris POTTHARST
35 Dir Opers/Sp Asst to VP Stdnt Affs .... Ms. Anitra CALVIN
06 University Registrar .... Mrs. Avis STUARD
67 Dean College of Pharmacy .... Dr. Kathleen KENNEDY
116 Controller/Dir Fin Rep/Exec Audit .... Ms. Ingenue S. SCHEXNIDER-FIELDS
88 Director Payroll .... Ms. Joyce SANDIFER
23 Med Dir Student Health Services .... Dr. Robert MERCADEL
21 Director Operations .... Ms. Lori GIE
36 Director Career Services .... Ms. Tracey JACKSON
37 Director Financial Aid .... Ms. Carrie GLASS
38 Dir Counseling & Wellness Center .... Dr. Steven BYRD
08 Interim Director University Library .... Ms. Nancy HAMPTON
108 Dir Inst Rsrch & Effectiveness .... Dr. Clair WILKINS-GREEN
88 Dir Inst Compliance/Extern Report .... Dr. Treva A. LEE
29 Dir Alum Rels & Annual Giving .... Ms. Lacretia JONES
88 Sr DBA/Sr Systems Analyst .... Ms. Kanetra TILLOTSON
104 Dir Div of Global Engagement .... Dr. Yu JIANG
88 Dir Violence Prevention Educ .... Ms. Jennifer BODNAR
113 Bursar .... Ms. Patrica VAULTZ
88 Dir Inst of Blk Catholic Studies .... Dr. Kathleen D. BELLOW
42 Dir Ctr for Faith and Spirituality .... Mrs. Lisa L. MCCLAIN
91 Manager Datacenter Operations .... Vacant
88 Dir Environmental Health & Safety .... Mr. Raymond BROWN
25 Director Grants and Contracts .... Ms. Shirley B. MASSENBURG
88 Dir Xavier Exponential .... Dr. Shearon ROBERTS
102 Dir Foundation/Corp Relations .... Dr. Jeff A. HALE
88 Dir Ctr Adv of Teaching & Fac Dev .... Dr. Elizabeth HAMMER
88 Dir Data Science & Analytics .... Ms. Rebecca OSAKWE
88 Sr Conduct Officer/Parent Programs .... Ms. Judy BRACY
119 IT Security Officer .... Mr. Gregory JONES
26 Asst VP/Dir Marketing/Comm .... Ms. Ashley IRVIN HAWKINS
105 Mgr Website Content/Dev & Design .... Mr. Kai RHEA
42 Univ Chap/Spec Asst to Pres Cath Id .... Fr. Victor LAROCHE, OP
40 Manager Bookstore .... Ms. Rose NAQUIN
88 Dir Ctr Eq Just/Human Spirit .... Dr. Ciricie OLATUNJI

MAINE

Bates College (D)

2 Andrews Road, Lewiston ME 04240-6047
County: Androscoggin — FICE Identification: 002036
Unit ID: 160977
Telephone: (207) 786-6255 — Carnegie Class: Bac-A&S
FAX Number: (207) 786-6123 — Calendar System: Other
URL: www.bates.edu
Established: 1855 — Annual Undergrad Tuition & Fees: $57,353
Enrollment: 1,876 — Coed
Affiliation or Control: Independent Non-Profit — IRS Status: 501(c)3
Highest Offering: Baccalaureate
Accreditation: EH

01 President .... Dr. A. Clayton SPENCER
05 VP Academic Affairs/Dean of Faculty .... Dr. Malcolm HILL
10 VP Finance & Admin/Treasurer .... Mr. Geoffrey SWIFT
08 VP for ILS & College Librarian .... Ms. Patricia SCHOKNECHT
100 VP for Institutional Affairs .... Mr. Michael HUSSEY
111 VP Advancement .... Ms. Sarah R. PEARSON
26 VP Communications & Public Affairs .... Mr. Sean T. FINDLEN
32 VP for Campus Life & DOS .... Mr. Joshua MCINTOSH
84 VP Enrollment/Dean of Admission .... Ms. Leigh WEISENBURGER
21 Asst Vice Pres Financial Planning .... Mr. Douglas W. GINEVAN
20 Assoc Dean of Faculty .... Ms. Aslaug ASGEIRSDOTTIR
20 Assoc Dean of Faculty .... Ms. Krista M. ARONSON
31 Director of Community Partnerships .... Ms. Darby K. RAY
06 Registrar .... Ms. Mary MESERVE
09 Dir Inst Rsch/Analysis and Planning .... Mr. Tom MCGUINNESS
15 Asst VP Human Resources .... Ms. Hope BURNELL
29 Assistant VP of Alumni Engagement .... Ms. Heather CORBETT
18 Dir of Facilities Svcs Operations .... Mr. Jay PHILLIPS
88 Dir Capital Planning/Construction .... Ms. Pamela J. WICHROSKI
19 Director Campus Safety .... Mr. Paul MENICE
23 Director Student Health Support .... Vacant
37 Dir Student Financial Services .... Ms. Wendy G. GLASS
40 Dir Bookstore/Contract Officer .... Ms. Gail S. ST. PIERRE
36 Sr Assoc Dean of PW & Career Dev .... Mr. Allen DELONG
91 Dir Sys Development & Integration .... Ms. Eileen P. ZIMMERMAN
88 Director of Client Services .... Mr. Scott TINER
41 Director of Athletics .... Mr. Jason FEIN
42 Multifaith Chaplain .... Ms. Brittany LONGSDORF
39 Senior Assoc Dean of Students .... Ms. Erin FOSTER ZSIGA
102 Dir Corporate/Foundation Relations .... Ms. Rachel WRAY
104 Assoc Dean/Dir for Global Education .... Mr. Darren GALLANT
28 AVP and Chief Diversity Officer .... Ms. Noelle CHADDOCK
07 Sr Assoc Dean Admiss/Dir Intl Enrol .... Mr. Scott ALEXANDER
04 Exec Assistant to the President .... Ms. Claire B. SCHMOLL
45 Chief Institutional Planning Office .... Mr. Tom MCGUINNESS

† Tuition figure is a comprehensive fees figure.

Beal University (E)

99 Farm Road, Bangor ME 04401-6831
County: Penobscot — FICE Identification: 005204
Unit ID: 160995
Telephone: (207) 307-3900 — Carnegie Class: Assoc/HVT-High Trad
FAX Number: (207) 947-0208 — Calendar System: Semester
URL: www.beal.edu
Established: 1891 — Annual Undergrad Tuition & Fees: N/A
Enrollment: 493 — Coed
Affiliation or Control: Proprietary — IRS Status: Proprietary
Highest Offering: Master's
Accreditation: ACCSC, CAHIIM, MAC

01 President .... Ms. Sheryl DEWALT
84 VP Enrollment .... Mr. Jeff BURBINE
11 Chief Operations Officer .... Mr. Steve VILLETT
10 VP of Finance .... Ms. Renee DUNTON
09 Compliance Officer .... Mrs. Carol PRICE
05 Dean of Education .... Dr. Colleen KOOB

37	Director Student Financial Aid	Ms. Bonnie SHUMATE
06	Registrar	Ms. Olivia GAUVIN
08	Chief Librarian	Ms. Donna BANCROFT
18	Superintendent Physical Plant	Mr. Kevin HARDY
36	Director Career Services	Ms. Robin TARDIFF
66	Dean of Nursing	Dr. Colleen KOOB

Bowdoin College   (A)

255 Maine Street, Brunswick ME 04011
County: Cumberland   FICE Identification: 002038
                                              Unit ID: 161004
Telephone: (207) 725-3000   Carnegie Class: Bac-A&S
FAX Number: (207) 725-3123   Calendar System: Semester
URL: www.bowdoin.edu
Established: 1794   Annual Undergrad Tuition & Fees: $56,350
Enrollment: 1,777   Coed
Affiliation or Control: Independent Non-Profit   IRS Status: 501(c)3
Highest Offering: Master's
Accreditation: EH

01	President	Dr. Clayton ROSE
10	Sr VP Finance/Admin/Treasurer	Mr. Matthew ORLANDO
30	VP Devel & Alumni Relations	Mr. Michael P. ARCHIBALD
26	Sr VP Communications/Public Affairs	Mr. Scott W. HOOD
13	SVP/Chief Information Officer	Mr. Michael CATO
28	SVP Inclusion & Diversity	Mr. Michael E. REED
15	Vice President of Human Resources	Ms. Tama SPOERRI
32	SVP & Dean of Student Affairs	Ms. Janet LOHMANN
05	SVP/Dean for Academic Affairs	Ms. Jennifer SCANLON
07	Dean of Admissions/Financial Aid	Vacant
09	SVP Inst Rsrch/Analytics Consulting	Dr. Christina M. FINNERAN
29	Director Alumni Relations	Ms. Rodie F. LLOYD
08	College Librarian	Ms. Marjorie HASSEN
37	Director of Student Financial Aid	Mr. Mike ALBANO
06	Registrar	Ms. Martina DUNCAN
19	Executive Director of Security	Mr. Randall NICHOLS
36	Exec Dir Career Exploration & Dev	Ms. Kristin BRENNAN
38	Director of Counseling Service	Dr. Bernie HERSHBERGER
41	Director of Athletics	Mr. Timothy M. RYAN
23	Director of Health Services	Dr. Jeffrey MAHER
18	Int Dir Facilities Ops/Maintenance	Mr. Jeff TUTTLE
24	Instructional Media Librarian	Ms. Carmen M. GREENLEE
39	Director of Residential Life	Ms. Whitney HOGAN
109	Dir Dining & Bookstore Services	Ms. Mary M. KENNEDY
35	Director of Student Activities	Mr. Nate HINTZE
35	Dean of Students	Ms. Kristina Bethea ODEJIMI
88	Co-Director of the Museum of Art	Ms. Anne GOODYEAR
88	Co-Director of the Museum of Art	Mr. Frank GOODYEAR
88	Director of Capital Projects	Mr. Donald V. BORKOWSKI

Colby College   (B)

4000 Mayflower Hill, Waterville ME 04901-8840
County: Kennebec   FICE Identification: 002039
                                              Unit ID: 161086
Telephone: (207) 859-4000   Carnegie Class: Bac-A&S
FAX Number: (207) 859-4603   Calendar System: 4/1/4
URL: www.colby.edu
Established: 1813   Annual Undergrad Tuition & Fees: $59,430
Enrollment: 2,155   Coed
Affiliation or Control: Independent Non-Profit   IRS Status: 501(c)3
Highest Offering: Baccalaureate
Accreditation: EH

01	President	Dr. David A. GREENE
05	Provost and Dean of Faculty	Dr. Margaret T. MCFADDEN
10	Vice President Admin & CFO	Mr. Douglas C. TERP
111	VP/Chief Advancement Ofcr	Mr. Matt PROTO
32	Dean of the College	Dr. Karlene A. BURRELL-MCRAE
100	Vice President & Chief of Staff	Ms. Ruth JACKSON
07	AVP/Dean Admission & Financial Aid	Mr. Randi ARSENAULT
121	VP and Dean of Student Advancement	Dr. C. Andrew MCGADNEY
45	Vice President of Planning	Mr. Brian J. CLARK
43	VP/Gen Counsel/Sec of the Col	Mr. Richard Y. UCHIDA
41	VP/Director of Athletics	Mr. Mike WISECUP
20	Assoc Provost & Dean of Faculty	Dr. Russell R. JOHNSON
18	Asst VP Facilities and Campus Plng	Ms. Minakshi M. AMUNDSEN
35	Dean of Students	Ms. Barbara E. MOORE
15	Assoc Vice Pres Human Resources	Mr. Mark CROSBY
37	Asst Dean/Director Financial Aid	Ms. Jill A. PIERCE
06	Registrar	Ms. Lindsey C. NELSON
08	Director of the Colby Libraries	Ms. Lareese M. HALL
88	Director of Special Programs	Mr. Brian BRAY
19	Director of Safety	Mr. Wade P. BEHNKE
13	Int Chief Information Officer	Mr. Jason PARKHILL
23	Medical Director	Dr. Paul D. BERKNER
38	Director of Counseling Services	Dr. Eric S. JOHNSON
09	Dir Inst Research & Assessment	Ms. Rebecca H. BRODIGAN
21	AVP Finance/Controller	Ms. Alicia J. GARDINER
40	Director of the Bookstore	Ms. Barbara C. SHUTT
104	Director of Off-Campus Study	Dr. Nancy DOWNEY
102	Director of Grants/Sponsored Pgms	Mr. William C. LAYTON, III

College of the Atlantic   (C)

105 Eden Street, Bar Harbor ME 04609-1198
County: Hancock   FICE Identification: 011385
                                              Unit ID: 160959
Telephone: (207) 288-5015   Carnegie Class: Bac-A&S
FAX Number: (207) 288-3780   Calendar System: Trimester
URL: www.coa.edu

Established: 1969   Annual Undergrad Tuition & Fees: $43,542
Enrollment: 370   Coed
Affiliation or Control: Independent Non-Profit   IRS Status: 501(c)3
Highest Offering: Master's
Accreditation: EH

01	President	Dr. Darron COLLINS
05	Academic Dean	Dr. Ken HILL
10	Director Administrative Svcs	Ms. Marie STIVERS
32	Dean of Student Life	Ms. Sarah LUKE
111	Dean Institutional Advancement	Ms. Shawn KEELEY
07	Dean of Admission	Ms. Heather ALBERT-KNOPP
06	Registrar	Ms. Krystal POULIN
08	Director of Thorndike Library	Ms. Jane HULTBERG
21	Comptroller	Mrs. Melissa COOK
37	Int Director of Financial Aid	Ms. Linda BLACK
36	Director of Internship/Career Svcs	Ms. Jill BARLOW-KELLEY
26	Public Relations Mgr/Dir Comm	Mr. Rob LEVIN

Husson University   (D)

1 College Circle, Bangor ME 04401-2929
County: Penobscot   FICE Identification: 002043
                                              Unit ID: 487524
Telephone: (207) 941-7000   Carnegie Class: DU-Mod
FAX Number: (207) 941-7139   Calendar System: Semester
URL: www.husson.edu
Established: 1898   Annual Undergrad Tuition & Fees: $19,772
Enrollment: 3,473   Coed
Affiliation or Control: Independent Non-Profit   IRS Status: 501(c)3
Highest Offering: Doctorate
Accreditation: EH, CACREP, IACBE, NURSE, OT, PHAR, PTA

01	President	Dr. Robert A. CLARK
05	Sr VP for Academic Affairs/Provost	Dr. Lynne COY-OGAN
10	VP Finance & Admin/Treasurer	Craig HADLEY
111	Vice President for Advancement	Sara C. ROBINSON
84	VP Enrollment Management	Michael J. FOX
13	AVP Information Technology	Garth CORMIER
50	Dean College of Business	Dr. Marie HANSEN
67	Dean College of Health and Pharmacy	Dr. Rhonda WASKIEWICZ
49	Dean College of Science/Humanities	Dr. Patricia BIXEL
26	Exec Director of Communications	Eric GORDON
32	Dean of Student Life	Pamela KROPP-ANDERSON
53	Director School of Education	Vacant
07	Director of Admissions	Melissa ROSENBURGI
37	Director of Financial Aid	Anne TABOR
06	Registrar	Nancy FENDERS
09	Director of Institutional Research	Dr. Cristi CARSON
108	Director Institutional Assessment	Travis E. ALLEN
106	Dir Online and Extended Learning	Dr. David HAUS
36	Director Career Services	James WESTHOFF
41	Director of Athletics	Francis PERGOLIZZI
35	Int Assoc Dean Student Life	Troy MOREHOUSE
15	Exec Director Human Resources	Janet KELLE
29	Director of Alumni Relations	Keith PIEHLER
18	Director of Maintenance	Gary GEROW
08	Head Librarian	Susanna PATHAK
30	Director of Advancement Services	Sarah ROBINSON
04	Executive Assistant to President	Kandi HALE
100	Chief of Staff	Kandi HALE
19	Director Safety and Security	Chris GROTTON
38	Director of Counseling Services	Vacant
105	Director Digital Communications	Matthew GREEN-HAMANN
109	Assoc Vice Pres Auxiliary Services	Thomas WARREN

Institute for Doctoral Studies in the Visual Arts   (E)

795 Congress Street, Portland ME 04102
County: Cumberland   FICE Identification: 041888
                                              Unit ID: 462044
Telephone: (207) 879-8757   Carnegie Class: Masters/S
FAX Number: N/A   Calendar System: Semester
URL: www.idsva.edu
Established: 2007   Annual Graduate Tuition & Fees: N/A
Enrollment: 88   Coed
Affiliation or Control: Independent Non-Profit   IRS Status: 501(c)3
Highest Offering: Doctorate; No Undergraduates
Accreditation: EH

01	President	George SMITH
10	Exec Vice President/CFO	Amy CURTIS
05	Vice Pres Acad Affs/Dir of School	Dr. Simonetta MORO

The Landing School   (F)

286 River Road, Arundel ME 04046
County: York   FICE Identification: 023613
                                              Unit ID: 161208
Telephone: (207) 985-7976   Carnegie Class: Spec 2-yr-Tech
FAX Number: (207) 985-7942   Calendar System: Semester
URL: www.landingschool.edu
Established: 1978   Annual Undergrad Tuition & Fees: $25,012
Enrollment: 48   Coed
Affiliation or Control: Independent Non-Profit   IRS Status: 501(c)3
Highest Offering: Associate Degree
Accreditation: ACCSC

01	President/Chief Executive Officer	Mr. Frederick J. FAWCETT, III
10	Vice President of Finance	Ms. Kate BALDWIN

05	Dean of Education	Mr. Ken RUSINEK
18	Operations & Industry Relations	Vacant
07	Director of Admissions/Recruitment	Mr. Michael BOLES
08	Librarian	Mr. James CUMISKEY
37	Financial Aid & VA Administrator	Mrs. Jeanne BOUCHER
96	Director of Purchasing	Mr. Michael CROSBY

Maine College of Art   (G)

522 Congress St, Portland ME 04101
County: Cumberland   FICE Identification: 011673
                                              Unit ID: 161509
Telephone: (207) 699-5521   Carnegie Class: Spec-4-yr-Arts
FAX Number: (207) 775-5087   Calendar System: Semester
URL: www.meca.edu
Established: 1882   Annual Undergrad Tuition & Fees: $38,310
Enrollment: 435   Coed
Affiliation or Control: Independent Non-Profit   IRS Status: 501(c)3
Highest Offering: Master's
Accreditation: EH, ART

01	President	Ms. Laura FREID
03	Executive Vice President	Ms. Beth ELICKER
05	VP Academic Affairs/Dean of College	Mr. Ian ANDERSON
111	Assoc VP Institutional Advancement	Vacant
06	Registrar	Ms. Anne DENNISON
32	Director of Student Life	Vacant
07	Director of Admissions	Ms. Jennifer CAMPANARO
13	Director Technology	Mr. Seth CLAYTER
26	Dir of Marketing & Communications	Mr. Steve BOWDEN
10	Director of Business Services	Ms. Holly HIGGINS
37	Director of Financial Aid	Ms. Carri FRECHETTE
51	Director Continuing Studies	Ms. Nik BSULLAK
18	Director of Facilities	Mr. Douglas DOERING
08	Library Director	Ms. Shiva DARBANDI
04	Executive Assistant	Ms. Melissa SULLIVAN
29	Director Alumni Relations	Vacant
36	Director of Artists at Work	Ms. Jessica TOMLINSON
101	Secretary of the Institution/Board	Ms. Heather YORK
15	Chief Human Resources Officer	Ms. Tanya GUAY

Maine College of Health Professions   (H)

70 Middle Street, Lewiston ME 04240-7027
County: Androscoggin   FICE Identification: 006305
                                              Unit ID: 161022
Telephone: (207) 795-2840   Carnegie Class: Spec-4-yr-Other Health
FAX Number: (207) 795-2849   Calendar System: Semester
URL: www.mchp.edu
Established: 1891   Annual Undergrad Tuition & Fees: $13,905
Enrollment: 216   Coed
Affiliation or Control: Independent Non-Profit   IRS Status: 501(c)3
Highest Offering: Baccalaureate
Accreditation: EH, ADNUR, NURSE, PNUR, RAD

01	President	Dr. Monika BISSELL
10	Vice President of Finance	Ms. Lesa ROSE
05	VP of Academic/Student Affairs	Dr. Alexander CLIFFORD
88	Dean of Medical Imaging	Mrs. Judith RIPLEY
07	Director of Admissions	Vacant
06	Registrar/Financial Aid Counselor	Mrs. Nicole DEBLOIS
66	Dean of Nursing	Dr. Lynne GOTJEN
22	Title IX Coordinator	Dr. Alexander CLIFFORD

*Maine Community College System   (I)

323 State Street, Augusta ME 04330-7131
County: Kennebec   Identification: 666092
                                              Unit ID: 409713
Telephone: (207) 629-4000   Carnegie Class: N/A
FAX Number: (207) 629-4048
URL: www.mccs.me.edu

01	President	Mr. David DAIGLER
05	VP & Chief Academic Officer	Ms. Janet SORTOR
10	Chief Financial Officer	Mrs. Pamela REMIERES-MORIN
15	Chief Counsel Labor & Employment	Vacant
13	Chief Information/Security Officer	Mr. Scott FORTIN

*Central Maine Community College   (J)

1250 Turner Street, Auburn ME 04210-6498
County: Androscoggin   FICE Identification: 005276
                                              Unit ID: 161077
Telephone: (207) 755-5100   Carnegie Class: Assoc/MT-VT-High Trad
FAX Number: (207) 755-5491   Calendar System: Semester
URL: www.cmcc.edu
Established: 1964   Annual Undergrad Tuition & Fees (In-State): $3,844
Enrollment: 3,115   Coed
Affiliation or Control: State   IRS Status: 501(c)3
Highest Offering: Associate Degree
Accreditation: EH, ADNUR

02	Interim President	Ms. Betsy LIBBY
32	Dean of Student Services	Mr. Nicholas HAMEL
05	Interim Dean Academic Affairs	Ms. Margaret BREWER
13	Dean Info Tech/Chief Info Security	Mr. Robert BOUCHER
10	Dean of Finance & General Services	Ms. Maureen AUBE
103	Dean Workforce & Professional Dev	Ms. Michelle HAWLEY
04	Executive Asst to the President	Ms. Alyson DANIELS

06 Registrar .... Ms. Sonya SAMPSON
84 Associate Dean of Enrollment Mgmt .... Mr. Andrew MORONG
37 Director of Financial Aid .... Mr. John BOWIE
35 Assoc Dean of Student Services .... Mr. Grimes WILLIAMS
18 Manager Facilities/Central Svcs .... Ms. Kellie MORRIS
07 Interim Director of Admissions .... Mr. Connor SHEEHY
39 Director of Housing/Athletic Dir .... Mr. David GONYEA
15 Director of Human Resources .... Ms. Suzanna GALLANT
27 Director of Communications .... Ms. Heather B. SEYMOUR
121 Director of Learning & Advising .... Mr. Eric MEADER
21 Assoc Dean of Finance & Gen Svcs .... Ms. Allie JOHNSON
09 Director of Institutional Research .... Ms. Brianna DOYLE
08 Director of Learning Commons .... Ms. Judith MORENO

*Eastern Maine Community College (A)

354 Hogan Road, Bangor ME 04401-4280
County: Penobscot FICE Identification: 005277
Unit ID: 161138
Telephone: (207) 974-4600 Carnegie Class: Assoc/HVT-Mix Trad/Non
FAX Number: (207) 974-4608 Calendar System: Semester
URL: www.emcc.edu
Established: 1966 Annual Undergrad Tuition & Fees (In-State): $3,877
Enrollment: 2,042 Coed
Affiliation or Control: State IRS Status: 501(c)3
Highest Offering: Associate Degree
Accreditation: EH, ADNUR, EMT, MAC, RAD, SURGT

02 President .... Dr. Lisa LARSON
05 VP of Academic & Student Affairs .... Dr. Brian DOORE
10 Dir Finance & Auxiliary Services .... Mrs. Cynthia KASPRZAK
09 Director of Institutional Research .... Ms. Kelsey GILBERT
88 Professional Services Coordinator .... Vacant
07 Director of Admissions .... Ms. Stacy GREEN
15 Director of Human Resources .... Ms. Jody MACDONALD
08 Librarian .... Mr. William COOK
37 Director of Financial Aid .... Ms. Candace WARD
13 Dean of Communication/Info Tech .... Mr. Bert AUDETTE
18 Dir Facilities Mgmt/Student Life .... Vacant
111 Dir of Inst Advancement/Development .... Ms. Erica HUTCHINSON
04 Admin Asst to the President .... Ms. Terri ADAM
19 Director of Safety & Security .... Mr. David WILSON
38 Director of Student Advising .... Ms. Sarah SAWYER
39 Director of Residential Life .... Ms. Kris KELLEY
103 Director Workforce Development .... Mr. Christopher WINSTEAD
26 Dir Marketing & Public Relations .... Ms. Mariah HUGHES

*Kennebec Valley Community College (B)

92 Western Avenue, Fairfield ME 04937-1367
County: Somerset FICE Identification: 009826
Unit ID: 161192
Telephone: (207) 453-5000 Carnegie Class: Assoc/HVT-Mix Trad/Non
FAX Number: (207) 453-5010 Calendar System: Semester
URL: www.kvcc.me.edu
Established: 1970 Annual Undergrad Tuition & Fees (In-State): $3,882
Enrollment: 2,297 Coed
Affiliation or Control: State IRS Status: 501(c)3
Highest Offering: Associate Degree
Accreditation: EH, ACBSP, ADNUR, CAHIIM, COARC, EMT, MAC, OTA, PTAA, RAD

02 President .... Ms. Karen NORMANDIN
05 Academic Dean .... Ms. Kathy ENGLEHART
13 Dean of Tech/Chief Security Officer .... Mr. Kevin CASEY
32 Interim Dean Student Affairs .... Mr. Crichton MCKENNA
10 Dean of Finance & Administration .... Mr. Russell BEGIN
84 Asst Dean of Enrollment Management .... Ms. Teresa SMITH
06 Registrar .... Mr. Christian HANSEN
30 Director of Development .... Ms. Michelle WEBB
37 Director of Financial Aid .... Ms. Kathryn BLAIR
09 Director of Institutional Research .... Ms. Karen GLEW
100 Chief of Staff to the President .... Ms. Monica BRENNAN
103 Dean of Workforce Training .... Ms. Elizabeth FORTIN
18 Director of Operations & Compliance .... Ms. Brianne PUSHOR
19 Campus Safety & Security Manager .... Mr. Timothy MCDONALD

*Northern Maine Community College (C)

33 Edgemont Drive, Presque Isle ME 04769-2099
County: Aroostook FICE Identification: 005760
Unit ID: 161484
Telephone: (207) 768-2810 Carnegie Class: Assoc/HVT-Mix Trad/Non
FAX Number: (207) 768-2831 Calendar System: Semester
URL: www.nmcc.edu
Established: 1961 Annual Undergrad Tuition & Fees (In-State): $3,830
Enrollment: 775 Coed
Affiliation or Control: State IRS Status: 501(c)3
Highest Offering: Associate Degree
Accreditation: EH, ACBSP, ADNUR, EMT, MAC

02 President .... Mr. Timothy D. CROWLEY
05 Academic Dean .... Ms. Angela BUCK
32 Dean of Students .... Mr. Matthew GRILLO
10 Dean of Finance .... Mr. Michael WILLIAMS
51 Asst Dean Continuing Education .... Ms. Leah BUCK
30 Dean of Development/College Rels .... Dr. Dorothy MARTIN
07 Director of Admissions .... Ms. Wendy BRADSTREET
06 Registrar .... Ms. Shannon COOK
37 Director for Financial Aid .... Mr. Brian HALL
39 Director of Housing & Resident Life .... Mr. Jon A. BLANCHARD
38 Director of Counseling .... Ms. Tammy NELSON
18 Dean of Tech and Facilities .... Mr. Barry INGRAHAM
21 Business Manager .... Ms. Wendy CAVERHILL
40 College Store Manager .... Mr. Kenneth J. KELMER, JR.
08 Head Librarian .... Dr. Ann SPINNEY
19 College Safety/Security Officer .... Mr. Peter GOHEEN
15 Human Resource Coordinator .... Ms. Lindsy LEBLANC

*Southern Maine Community College (D)

2 Fort Road, South Portland ME 04106-1698
County: Cumberland FICE Identification: 005525
Unit ID: 161545
Telephone: (207) 741-5500 Carnegie Class: Assoc/MT-VT-Mix Trad/Non
FAX Number: (207) 741-5751 Calendar System: Semester
URL: www.smccme.edu
Established: 1946 Annual Undergrad Tuition & Fees (In-State): $3,880
Enrollment: 5,789 Coed
Affiliation or Control: State IRS Status: 501(c)3
Highest Offering: Associate Degree
Accreditation: EH, ACFEI, ADNUR, COARC, CVT, EMT, MAC, RAD

02 President/CEO .... Joseph L. CASSIDY
05 Vice President & Academic Dean .... Dr. Paul CHARPENTIER
11 Dean of Administration .... Tiffanie L. BENTLEY
32 Dean of Student Success/Enrollment .... Barbara CONNER
103 Dean of Workforce Development .... James WHITTEN
10 Dean of Finance .... Robert COOMBS
13 Dean of Data/Tech & Info Security .... Timothy DUNNE
88 Dean of Academic Excellence .... Dr. Matthew GOODMAN
88 Int Dean Bus & Cmty Partnerships .... Julie CHASE
04 Exec Assistant to the President .... Lori HALL
06 Assoc Dean of Registration/Registrr .... Jeremy DILL
121 Associate Dean of Student Success .... Kathleen DOAN
20 Assoc Dean Academics/Learning .... Holly GURNEY
39 Acting Assoc Dean of Students .... Jason SAUCIER
41 Assoc Dean Stdnt Life/Dir Athletics .... Matthew RICHARDS
114 Director of Budget & Financial Rpt .... Shaun GRAY
37 Director of Financial Aid Systems .... Michel LUSSIER
84 Assistant Dean of Enrollment Mgmt .... Amy LEE
19 Director Campus Security .... Joseph MANHARDT
18 Plant Maintenance Engineer III .... Vacant
40 Manager Campus Store .... Katharine DUCHETTE
113 Business Mgr Student Billing/Bursar .... Coleen LAPRISE
15 Director of Human Resources .... Diane ABRAMSON
38 Dir Counseling & Disability Svcs .... Sandra LYNHAM
27 Director of Communications .... Clarke CANFIELD
105 Director Web Services .... Ken POOLEY
106 Dir Online Education/E-learning .... Michael HART
36 Director Career & Transfer .... Adrienne LAROCHE

*Washington County Community College (E)

One College Drive, Calais ME 04619-9704
County: Washington FICE Identification: 009231
Unit ID: 161581
Telephone: (207) 454-1000 Carnegie Class: Assoc/HVT-High Trad
FAX Number: (207) 454-1092 Calendar System: Semester
URL: www.wccc.me.edu
Established: 1969 Annual Undergrad Tuition & Fees (In-State): $3,850
Enrollment: 354 Coed
Affiliation or Control: State IRS Status: 501(c)3
Highest Offering: Associate Degree
Accreditation: EH, MAC

02 President .... Mrs. Susan MINGO
05 Dean of Academic Affairs .... Mr. Darin MCGAW
10 Dean of Finance .... Ms. Desiree THOMPSON
15 Dir of HR/Devel/Communications .... Mrs. Tina ERSKINE
84 Dean Enrollment Mgmt/Student Svcs .... Mr. Tyler STOLDT
103 Dean of Workforce & Prof Dev .... Ms. Nichole SAWYER
37 Financial Aid Director .... Mrs. Linda FITZSIMMONS
39 Director of Res Life .... Ms. Karen GOOKIN
04 Exec Asst to the Pres/HR Coord .... Mrs. Robyn LEIGHTON
21 Business Manager .... Mrs. Ashley MACDONALD
18 Manager Facilities .... Mr. Richard RAMSEY
13 Information Systems Manager .... Mr. Jorge REYES
06 Registrar/Asst to Academic Dean .... Mrs. Donna GEEL
113 Student Accounts .... Mrs. Heather SMALE
08 Dir of Library & Learning Resources .... Vacant
22 Instructional Technologist/AAO .... Ms. Tatiana OSMOND

*York County Community College (F)

112 College Drive, Wells ME 04090-0529
County: York FICE Identification: 031229
Unit ID: 420440
Telephone: (207) 646-9282 Carnegie Class: Assoc/HT-High Non
FAX Number: (207) 646-9675 Calendar System: Semester
URL: www.yccc.edu
Established: 1994 Annual Undergrad Tuition & Fees (In-State): $3,720
Enrollment: 1,575 Coed
Affiliation or Control: State IRS Status: 501(c)3
Highest Offering: Associate Degree
Accreditation: EH

02 President .... Mr. Michael FISCHER
05 Acting Dean of Academics .... Dr. Tracey CORNELL
10 Dean of Finance & Administration .... Mr. Samuel ELLIS
32 Dean of Student Svcs .... Ms. Jennifer LANEY
09 Assoc Dean of Inst Research .... Vacant
103 Dir of Economic/Workforce Dev .... Ms. Caitlin GRANT
20 Assoc Academic Dean .... Ms. Amber TATNALL
30 Special Asst to the Pres & Dev Dir .... Vacant
06 Director of Registration/Records .... Ms. Jessica MASI
26 Dir of Marketing & Communications .... Ms. Stacy CHILICKI
37 Director Financial Aid .... Ms. Barbara WINCHELL
13 Director of Technology .... Vacant
19 Safety & Security Manager .... Mr. Mark PARADIS
21 Manager of Financial Services .... Mrs. Tracy SLATER
07 Director of Admissions/HS Relations .... Ms. Allyson GROCHMAL
18 Manager of Facilities .... Vacant
100 Chief of Staff .... Ms. Barbara OWEN

Maine Maritime Academy (G)

1 Pleasant Street, Castine ME 04420-0001
County: Hancock FICE Identification: 002044
Unit ID: 161299
Telephone: (207) 326-4311 Carnegie Class: Bac-Diverse
FAX Number: (207) 326-2218 Calendar System: Semester
URL: www.mainemaritime.edu
Established: 1941 Annual Undergrad Tuition & Fees (In-State): $14,058
Enrollment: 941 Coed
Affiliation or Control: State IRS Status: 501(c)3
Highest Offering: Master's
Accreditation: EH

01 President .... Dr. William J. BRENNAN
05 VP Academic Affairs .... Mr. Keith WILLIAMSON
10 VP Financial & Institutional Svcs .... Mr. Richard ROSEN
84 VP Stdnt Svcs/Enrollment Mgmt .... Dr. Elizabeth TRUE
111 Vice President for Advancement .... Mr. Christopher HALEY
15 Human Resource Officer .... Ms. Heidi PUGLIESE
32 Dean of Student Svcs/Enroll Mgmt .... Ms. Deidra DAVIS
36 Director of Career Services .... Mr. Bryce POTTER
07 Director of Admissions .... Ms. Kelly GUALTIERI
06 Registrar .... Ms. Amy GUTOW
29 Director Alumni Relations .... Mr. Jeff WRIGHT
37 Director Student Financial Aid .... Ms. Kathy HEATH
38 Director Student Counseling .... Mr. Paul FERREIRA
08 Director of Library Services .... Ms. Lauren STARBIRD
21 Director of Fiscal Operations .... Ms. Alice HERRICK
18 Director of Facilities Mgmt/Safety .... Mr. Peter STEWART
20 Dean of Faculty .... Dr. Susan LOOMIS
26 Director of College Relations .... Vacant
39 Director of Residential Life .... Ms. Janice FOLK
09 Director of Institutional Research .... Mr. Ryan KING
04 Exec Asst to Pres/Chief of Staff .... Ms. Janet ACKER
13 AVP/Chief Technology Officer .... Ms. Lisa ROY
19 Director of Safety & Compliance .... Mr. Peter STEWART
41 Director of Athletics .... Mr. Stephen PEED

Maine Media College (H)

70 Camden St., PO Box 200, Rockport ME 04856
County: Knox Identification: 667339
Telephone: (207) 236-8581 Carnegie Class: Not Classified
FAX Number: (207) 236-2558 Calendar System: Other
URL: www.mainemedia.edu
Established: 1973 Annual Graduate Tuition & Fees: N/A
Enrollment: N/A Coed
Affiliation or Control: Independent Non-Profit IRS Status: 501(c)3
Highest Offering: Master's; No Undergraduates
Accreditation: @EH

01 President .... Michael P. MANSFIELD
05 Provost .... Elizabeth GREENBERG
10 Dir of Finance & Administration .... Cathi FINNEMORE
06 Registrar/Dir Student Services .... Kerry CURREN
15 Human Resources/Business Manager .... Jane RICHARDSON

Saint Joseph's College of Maine (I)

278 Whites Bridge Road, Standish ME 04084-5236
County: Cumberland FICE Identification: 002051
Unit ID: 161518
Telephone: (207) 892-6766 Carnegie Class: Masters/L
FAX Number: (207) 893-7861 Calendar System: Semester
URL: www.sjcme.edu
Established: 1912 Annual Undergrad Tuition & Fees: $38,820
Enrollment: 1,967 Coed
Affiliation or Control: Roman Catholic IRS Status: 501(c)3
Highest Offering: Master's
Accreditation: EH, CAHIIM, NURSE, SW

01 President .... Dr. James S. DLUGOS
06 Associate Registrar .... Mr. Jon TUTTLE
08 Director Library .... Vacant
23 Director of Student Health Center .... Ms. Sheri PIERS
05 Sr VP for Learning & Programs .... Dr. Monique LA ROCQUE
10 Int Chief Finance Ofcr/Controller .... Ms. Karen SHEA
111 Sr Director of Advancement .... Ms. Liz SCHRAN
88 VP for Sponsorship & Mission .... Dr. Christopher FULLER
84 Interim Chief Enrollment Officer .... Ms. Monica CALZOLARI
32 AVP/CSAO/Dean of Campus Life .... Dr. Liz WIESEN
15 Asst Director Human Resources .... Ms. Heidi JACQUES
13 AVP Chief Information Officer .... Mr. Chip STILES
26 AVP & Chief Brand/Marketing Ofcr .... Mr. Oliver GRISWOLD
35 Director of Student Engagement .... Mr. Matthew GAWEL

Thomas College (A)

180 W River Road, Waterville ME 04901-5097
County: Kennebec
FICE Identification: 002052
Unit ID: 161563
Telephone: (207) 859-1111
Carnegie Class: Masters/S
FAX Number: (207) 859-1114
Calendar System: Semester
URL: www.thomas.edu
Established: 1894
Annual Undergrad Tuition & Fees: $28,430
Enrollment: 1,705
Coed
Affiliation or Control: Independent Non-Profit
IRS Status: 501(c)3
Highest Offering: Master's
Accreditation: EH

01 President ... Ms. Laurie G. LACHANCE
11 Chief Operating Officer ... Mr. Todd SMITH
05 Provost ... Dr. Thomas EDWARDS
10 Vice Pres Financial Affairs ... Ms. Joan PARKER-LOW
32 Vice President Student Affairs .. Ms. Lisa DESAUTELS-POLIQUIN
13 Vice Pres Information Services/CIO ... Mr. Christopher RHODA
30 Vice Pres Advancement ... Ms. Chelsea HOELLER
07 Director of Admissions ... Ms. Abby DOOLEY
26 Asst VP Marketing/Communications ... Mr. Robert FIELD
35 AVP Student Engage/Residential Life ... Mr. Jim DELORIE
15 Chief Human Resources Officer ... Ms. Michelle JOLER-LABBE
37 Sr Director Student Financial Svcs ... Ms. Jeannine ROSS
36 Sr Director of Early College ... Mr. Corey PELLETIER
18 Director Physical Plant ... Mr. Matt BRESLIN
06 Registrar ... Ms. Michelle YATES
04 Executive Asst to President ... Ms. Leta BILODEAU
41 Director of Athletics ... Mr. Christopher PARSONS
19 Director of Security/Safety ... Mr. Christopher SANTIAGO

Unity College (B)

70 Farm View Drive, New Glouchester ME 04260
County: Waldo
FICE Identification: 006858
Unit ID: 161572
Telephone: (207) 509-7100
Carnegie Class: Masters/S
FAX Number: (207) 512-1192
Calendar System: Other
URL: www.unity.edu
Established: 1965
Annual Undergrad Tuition & Fees: $12,640
Enrollment: 1,429
Coed
Affiliation or Control: Independent Non-Profit
IRS Status: 501(c)3
Highest Offering: Master's
Accreditation: EH

01 President ... Dr. Melik Peter KHOURY
88 VP of Hybrid Learning ... Mr. Zachary FALCON
106 VP of Distance Education ... Vacant
05 President of the Enterprise/CAO ... Dr. Erika LATTY
111 Chief Advancement Officer ... Vacant
100 Chief of Staff ... Vacant
101 Secretary to Board ... Ms. Christine MELANSON
04 Special Assistant to the President ... Ms. Maren MCGILLICUDDY
10 Director of Business Office ... Vacant
13 Director of IT ... Vacant
06 Registrar ... Ms. Kerry HAFFORD
30 Director of Development & Grants ... Vacant
32 Exec Director of Student Life ... Mr. Dan SUMMERS, II
09 Dir of Institutional Effectiveness ... Vacant
26 Executive Director Brand Strategy ... Ms. Alecia SUDMEYER
41 Director of Athletics & Wellness ... Vacant
109 Director of Dining Services ... Vacant
36 Director of Career Placement ... Ms. Wendi RICHARDS
88 Director Unity College Sky Lodge ... Mr. Casey MOREY
18 Dir of Facilities Management ... Mr. Christopher BOND
37 Dir Student Finance/Enrollment Svcs ... Ms. Sherry WATSON
23 Director of Wellness ... Vacant
15 Director Human Resources ... Ms. Gabrielle NIEWADOMSKI
08 Director Library & Info Services ... Vacant
39 Asst Dean of Students ... Mr. Stephen S. NASON
22 ADA Coord/Learning Specialist ... Vacant
88 Dean of Curricular Innovation ... Dr. Jennifer CARTIER
27 Assoc Dir of Media Relations ... Mr. Joseph HEGARTY
19 Director of Public Safety ... Mr. Dennis PICARD
40 Manager Bookstore ... Ms. Leigh JUSKEVICE

*University of Maine System (C)

15 Estabrooke Drive, Orono ME 04469
County: Penobscot
FICE Identification: 008012
Unit ID: 161280
Telephone: N/A
Carnegie Class: N/A
FAX Number: N/A
URL: www.maine.edu

01 Chancellor ... Mr. Dannel P. MALLOY
05 Vice Chancellor Academic Affairs ... Dr. Robert PLACIDO
10 Vice Chanc for Finance & Treasurer ... Mr. Ryan LOW
43 Interim General Counsel ... Ms. Patricia PEARD
86 Dir of Comm/Governmental Rels ... Ms. Samantha C. WARREN
101 Clerk of the Board ... Ms. Ellen DOUGHTY
32 AVC Stdnt Success/Credential Attain ... Ms. Rosa REDONNETT
13 Chief Information Officer ... Dr. David DEMERS
18 Int Chief General Services Officer ... Mr. Rudy GABRIELSON
15 Chief Human Resources Officer ... Ms. Loretta SHIELDS

*University of Maine (D)

168 College Avenue, Orono ME 04469-0001
County: Penobscot
FICE Identification: 002053
Unit ID: 161253
Telephone: (207) 581-1865
Carnegie Class: DU-Highest
FAX Number: (207) 581-1604
Calendar System: Semester
URL: www.umaine.edu
Established: 1865
Annual Undergrad Tuition & Fees (In-State): $11,744
Enrollment: 11,741
Coed
Affiliation or Control: State
IRS Status: 501(c)3
Highest Offering: Doctorate
Accreditation: EH, ART, CAATE, CAEP, CLPSY, DIETD, DIETI, IPSY, MUS, NURSE, SP, SW

02 President ... Dr. Joan FERRINI-MUNDY
05 EVP Academic Affairs/Provost ... Dr. John VOLIN
10 Int VP/Chief Business Officer ... Ms. Joanne YESTRAMSKI
102 Pres Univ of Maine Foundation ... Vacant
32 VP Student Life & Dean of Students ... Dr. Robert Q. DANA
46 Vice President for Research ... Dr. Kody VARAHRAMYAN
84 VP Enrollment Management ... Mr. Chris RICHARDS
88 VP Innovation/Economic Development ... Mr. James WARD, IV
15 Vice President of Human Resources ... Mr. Chris LINDSTROM
21 Chief Business Officer ... Mrs. Claire I. STRICKLAND
20 Sr Assoc Prov/Dean Undergrad Educ ... Dr. Jeffrey E. ST. JOHN
100 Chief of Staff ... Ms. Kimberly WHITEHEAD
08 Dean of Libraries ... Ms. Joyce V. RUMERY
13 Dir Project Mgt Ofc/Campus IT Ofcr ... Ms. Robin SHERMAN
18 Exec Dir Facilities/Capital Mgt Svc ... Mr. Stewart A. HARVEY
26 Sr Exec Dir Marketing/Communication ... Mr. Dan DEMERITT
109 Exec Director of Auxiliary Services ... Mr. Daniel H. STURRUP
25 Director Research Administration ... Mr. Christopher E. BOYNTON
06 Registrar ... Mr. W. Sam CARRELL
07 Director of Transfer Admissions ... Ms. Sharon M. OLIVER
37 Director of Financial Aid ... Ms. Connie SMITH
36 Director of Career Center ... Ms. Crisanne BLACKIE
09 Director Institutional Studies ... Dr. Debra ALLEN
85 Sr Director International Programs ... Ms. Sarah JOUGHIN
41 Athletic Director ... Mr. Ken RALPH
28 Director Equal Employment Diversity ... Vacant
19 Chief Police Dept ... Chief Roland J. LACROIX
29 Vice President Alumni Association ... Mr. John N. DIAMOND
40 Assoc Director of Retail Operations ... Mr. Dean GRAHAM
96 Director of Procurement Services ... Mr. Kevin CARR
38 Director Student Counseling ... Mr. Douglas P. JOHNSON
49 Dean Liberal Arts & Sciences ... Dr. Emily A. HADDAD
50 Dean Undergrad School of Business ... Ms. Faye GILBERT
50 Dean Graduate School of Business ... Dr. Michael WEBER
53 Dean Educ/Human Development ... Dr. Penny BISHOP
54 Dean Engineering ... Dr. Dana N. HUMPHREY
65 Dean Natural Science/Forestry/Agric ... Dr. Diane ROWLAND
51 Dean Lifelong Learning ... Dr. Monique M. LAROCQUE
58 Dean Graduate School ... Dr. Kody VARAHRAMYAN
04 Exec Assistant to the President ... Ms. Josette A. MCWILLIAMS
86 Director Government Relations ... Ms. Samantha WARREN
122 Asst Dir Fraternity/Sorority Life ... Ms. Jennifer DESMOND

*University of Maine at Augusta (E)

46 University Drive, Augusta ME 04330-9410
County: Kennebec
FICE Identification: 006760
Unit ID: 161217
Telephone: (207) 621-3000
Carnegie Class: Bac-Diverse
FAX Number: (207) 621-3116
Calendar System: Semester
URL: www.uma.edu
Established: 1965
Annual Undergrad Tuition & Fees (In-State): $8,378
Enrollment: 4,202
Coed
Affiliation or Control: State
IRS Status: 501(c)3
Highest Offering: Master's
Accreditation: EH, CSHSE, DA, DH, NUR

02 Interim President ... Dr. Joseph S. SZAKAS
05 Vice President/Provost ... Dr. Joseph S. SZAKAS
10 Interim Chief Business Officer ... Mr. Buster NEEL
111 Exec Dir of Advance & Strat Proj ... Ms. Joyce BLANCHARD
84 VP Enrollment Mgmt & Marketing ... Mr. Jonathan HENRY
08 Director of UMA Library Svcs ... Vacant
32 Dean of Students ... Ms. Sheri FRASER
107 Dean College of Prof Studies ... Ms. Brenda MCALEER
07 AVP Admission/Stdnt Financial Svcs ... Ms. Brandy FINCK
06 Registrar ... Ms. Ann CORBETT
15 Director of Human Resources ... Ms. Amie PARKER
18 Director of Facilities Management ... Mr. James W. KAUPPILA
38 Director of Counseling ... Ms. Jennifer MASCARO
121 Director of Advising ... Ms. Tricia DYER
26 Exec Dir Planning & Communications ... Ms. Domna GIATAS
49 Dean College of Arts & Sciences ... Dr. Pamela MACRAE
04 Exec Assistant to the President ... Ms. Renee SHERMAN
35 Director of Student Life/Athletics ... Vacant
09 Director of Institutional Research ... Dr. Hirosuke HONDA
19 Director Campus Safety & Security ... Mr. Robert MARDEN

*University of Maine at Farmington (F)

224 Main Street, Farmington ME 04938-1911
County: Franklin
FICE Identification: 002040
Unit ID: 161226
Telephone: (207) 778-7000
Carnegie Class: Bac-Diverse
FAX Number: (207) 778-7247
Calendar System: Semester
URL: www.umf.maine.edu
Established: 1864
Annual Undergrad Tuition & Fees (In-State): $9,572
Enrollment: 1,862
Coed
Affiliation or Control: State
IRS Status: 501(c)3
Highest Offering: Master's
Accreditation: EH, CAEP

02 Interim President ... Mr. Joseph MCDONNELL
05 Provost/VP Academic Affairs ... Dr. Eric BROWN
10 Chief Business Officer ... Ms. Laurie A. GARDNER
32 VP Student Affs/Enrollment Mgmt ... Ms. Christine WILSON
04 Admin Assistant to the President ... Ms. Amy PERREAULT
20 Assoc Provost ... Dr. Steven QUACKENBUSH
92 Director of Honors Program ... Dr. John D. MESSIER
121 Dir Student Development Center ... Ms. Katie FOURNIER
37 Financial Aid Director ... Mr. Ronald P. MILLIKEN
21 Director of Finance ... Ms. Kathleen P. FALCO
27 Assoc Director of Media Relations ... Ms. April C. MULHERIN
13 IT Operations Manager ... Ms. Nicole WOODHOUSE
41 Dir Athletics/Fitness & Recreation ... Ms. Julie A. DAVIS
35 Director Student Life ... Mr. Brian K. UFFORD
18 Director of Facilities Management ... Mr. Keenan FARWELL
19 Director of Public Safety ... Mr. Brock E. CATON
26 Dir of Marketing and Communications ... Ms. Ryan MASTRANGELO
07 Director of Admissions ... Ms. Lisa ELLRICH
09 Director of Institutional Research ... Mr. Nathan GRANT
111 Director for Advancement ... Vacant
29 Dir Alumni Relations/Annual Fund ... Ms. Kathleen O'DONNELL
88 Sustainability Coordinator ... Mr. Mark PIRES

*University of Maine at Fort Kent (G)

23 University Drive, Fort Kent ME 04743-1292
County: Aroostook
FICE Identification: 002041
Unit ID: 161235
Telephone: (207) 834-7500
Carnegie Class: Bac-Diverse
FAX Number: (207) 834-7503
Calendar System: Semester
URL: www.umfk.edu
Established: 1878
Annual Undergrad Tuition & Fees (In-State): $8,475
Enrollment: 1,624
Coed
Affiliation or Control: State
IRS Status: 501(c)3
Highest Offering: Baccalaureate
Accreditation: EH, NURSE

02 President/Provost ... Ms. Deborah HEDEEN
10 Chief Business Officer ... Ms. Pamela ASHBY
32 Dean of Students ... Mr. Matthew MORRIN
26 Dir Marketing & Communications ... Vacant
15 HR Business Partner ... Ms. Debra PELLETIER
08 Dean of Information Svcs/Library ... Ms. Leslie E. KELLY
66 Dean of Nursing/Int Assoc Prov AA ... Ms. Erin SOUCY
49 Int Dean Arts & Sciences/Prof Stds ... Dr. King GODWIN
37 Associate Director of Financial Aid ... Ms. Lisa MICHAUD
18 Director of Facilities Management ... Mr. Jason GUERRETTE
07 Director of Admissions ... Vacant
09 Assoc Dir of Institutional Research ... Vacant
30 Development Officer ... Ms. Shannon LUGDON
06 Interim Registrar ... Mr. Jacob THERIAULT
04 Admin Assistant to the President ... Ms. Lisa M. ROY
39 Dir Resident Life/Student Housing ... Ms. Theresa BIGGS
41 Athletic Director ... Ms. Carly FLOWERS

*University of Maine at Machias (H)

116 O'Brien Avenue, Machias ME 04654-1397
Telephone: (207) 255-1200
FICE Identification: 002055
Accreditation: &EH

*University of Maine at Presque Isle (I)

181 Main Street, Presque Isle ME 04769-2888
County: Aroostook
FICE Identification: 002033
Unit ID: 161341
Telephone: (207) 768-9400
Carnegie Class: Bac-Diverse
FAX Number: (207) 768-9608
Calendar System: Semester
URL: www.umpi.edu
Established: 1903
Annual Undergrad Tuition & Fees (In-State): $8,585
Enrollment: 1,467
Coed
Affiliation or Control: State
IRS Status: 501(c)3
Highest Offering: Baccalaureate
Accreditation: EH, MLTAD, PTAA, SW

02 President & Provost ... Dr. Raymond J. RICE
05 Director of Education ... Dr. Alana MARGESON
10 Chief Business/Operating Officer ... Ms. Betsy SAWHILL ESPE
49 Dean of Arts and Sciences ... Dr. Jason JOHNSTON
107 Dean of Professional Programs ... Ms. Barbara BLACKSTONE
111 Exec Dir for University Advancement ... Dr. Debbie ROARK
106 Dean of Competency Based Education ... Ms. Susan CHANG
32 Dean of Students ... Ms. Sarah COYER
35 Associate Dean of Students ... Ms. Heather MAZOROW
07 Director of Admissions ... Ms. Susan WHITE
06 Registrar ... Ms. Lisa M. SMITH
15 Human Resources Partner ... Ms. Melissa DEMERCHANT
08 Director of Library Services ... Mr. Allen MORRILL
36 Director of Career Preparation ... Ms. Nicole FOURNIER
41 Director of Athletics ... Mr. Daniel C. KANE
26 Director Marketing & Communications ... Ms. Rachel RICE
37 Director Student Financial Services ... Ms. Connie SMITH
18 Director of Facilities Management ... Mr. Joe MOIR
19 Director Security/Safety ... Mr. Frederick A. THOMAS
04 Assistant to the President/Provost ... Ms. Denise TROMBLEY
29 Director Alumni Affairs ... Mr. Craig C. CORMIER

*University of Southern Maine (J)

96 Falmouth Street, PO Box 9300,
Portland ME 04101-9300
County: Cumberland
FICE Identification: 002054
Unit ID: 161554
Telephone: (207) 780-4141
Carnegie Class: Masters/L

FAX Number: (207) 780-4933 Calendar System: Semester
URL: www.usm.maine.edu
Established: 1878 Annual Undergrad Tuition & Fees (In-State): $9,528
Enrollment: 8,022 Coed
Affiliation or Control: State IRS Status: 501(c)3
Highest Offering: Doctorate
Accreditation: EH, ART, CAATE, CACREP, CAEP, EXSC, LAW, MUS, NAIT, NURSE, OT, PH, SW

02 President .... Dr. Glenn T. CUMMINGS
05 Provost/EVP for ASA .... Dr. Jeannine UZZI
102 President USM Foundation .... Ms. Ainsely WALLACE
110 VP USM Foundation .... Ms. Corey HASCALL
15 VP Human Resources .... Ms. Natalie JONES
84 VP Enrollment Mgmt & Marketing .... Mr. Jared CASH
109 VP Corp Engagement/Auxiliary Svcs .... Ms. Jeanne PAQUETTE
10 COO & CBO .... Mr. Alexander PORTEOUS
20 Asst Provost Academic Affairs .... Dr. Susan MCWILLIAMS
09 Sr Assoc Institutional Research .... Ms. Patricia DAVIS
18 Exec Director Facilities Management .... Mr. John SOUTHER
08 University Librarian .... Mr. David NUTTY
108 Director Academic Assessment Ctr .... Ms. Susan L. KING
23 Director of Health Services .... Ms. Lisa BELANGER
26 Director Public Affairs .... Mr. Marc GLASS
37 Director Financial Aid .... Ms. Jami JANDREAU
121 Director Academic Advising .... Ms. Elizabeth HIGGINS
58 Director Graduate Studies .... Mr. Andrew KING
07 Director of Admissions .... Ms. Rachel MORALES
06 Registrar/Director of Registration .... Ms. Karin PIRES
106 Director Online Teaching/Learning .... Mr. Paul COCHRANE
41 Director of Athletics .... Mr. Al BEAN
39 Director of Residential Life .... Ms. Christina LOWERY
40 General Manager of USM Bookstore .... Ms. Catherine JOHNSON
61 Dean School of Law .... Ms. Leigh INGALLS SAUFLEY
50 Dean College of Mgmt/Human Svcs .... Dr. Joanne WILLIAMS
72 Dean College of Sci/Tech & Health .... Dr. Jeremy QUALLS
49 Dean Arts/Humanities/Soc Sci .... Dr. Adam TUCHINSKY
12 Int Dean Lewiston-Auburn College .... Dr. Brian TOY
94 Director of Women & Gender Studies .... Dr. Rose CLEARY
27 Director of Marketing .... Ms. Traci ST. PIERRE
46 Director of Research .... Ms. Kris SAHONCHIK

University of New England (A)

11 Hills Beach Road, Biddeford ME 04005-9988
County: York FICE Identification: 002050
Unit ID: 161457
Telephone: (207) 283-0171 Carnegie Class: DU-Higher
FAX Number: (207) 282-6379 Calendar System: Semester
URL: www.une.edu
Established: 1831 Annual Undergrad Tuition & Fees: $38,750
Enrollment: 7,208 Coed
Affiliation or Control: Independent Non-Profit IRS Status: 501(c)3
Highest Offering: Doctorate
Accreditation: EH, ACBSP, ANEST, ARCPA, CAATE, DENT, DH, @DIET, EXSC, NUR, OSTEO, OT, PH, PHAR, PTA, SW

01 President .... Dr. James HERBERT
04 Executive Asst to the President .... Ms. Holly HAMMOND NASS
05 Provost/Sr VP Academic Affairs .... Dr. Karen PARDUE
06 Registrar .... Ms. Kathy DAVIS
07 VP of University Admissions .... Mr. Scott STEINBERG
26 VP for Strategy & Communications .... Dr. Ellen BEAULIEU
18 Vice President for Operations .... Mr. Alan THIBEAULT
10 Senior Vice Pres Finance and Admin .... Mr. Phil SHAPIRO
111 Vice Pres Institutional Advancement .... Ms. Alicia FEREDAY
32 Asst VP of Student Affairs .... Ms. Jennifer DEBURRO
15 Associate VP Human Resources .... Ms. Bobbie KALLNER
82 VP Global Affairs .... Dr. Anouar MAJID
121 Associate Provost Student Success .... Mr. John TUMIEL
20 Associate Provost Academic Affairs .... Dr. Michael SHELDON
106 Dean College of Grad/Prof Studies .... Dr. Beth TAYLOR NOLAN
49 Dean College Arts & Sciences .... Dr. Jonathan MILLEN
76 Dean Health Professions .... Dr. Jen MORTON
63 Dean College Osteopathic Medicine .... Dr. Jane CARREIRO
67 Dean College of Pharmacy .... Dr. Emily DORNBLASER
52 Dean of College Dental Medicine .... Dr. Nicole KIMMES
62 Dean Library Services .... Ms. Beth DYER
46 Associate Provost Research/Scholars .... Dr. Karen HOUSEKNECHT
110 Assistant VP Inst Advancement .... Ms. Amy HAILE
09 Director for Institutional Research .... Ms. Kelly DUARTE
19 Director Campus Safety & Security .... Mr. Jeffrey GREENE
45 Associate Director for Planning .... Mr. Gregory HOGAN
08 Director Reference Services .... Ms. Barbara SWARTZLANDER
28 Dir Multicultural Student Affairs .... Vacant
25 Director Sponsored Programs .... Mr. Nicholas GERE
38 Assistant Provost Student Support .... Mr. Hahna PATTERSON
113 Asst VP Student Financial Services .... Mr. Paul HENDERSON
100 Senior Advisor to President .... Mr. John TUMIEL
104 Director Study Abroad/Global Educ .... Ms. Emily DRAGON
13 Chief Info Technology Officer (CIO) .... Mr. Craig LOFTUS
36 Director Career Services .... Ms. Donna GASPER JARVIS
102 Sr Dir Foundation/Corp Relations .... Ms. Marci BERNARD
41 Athletic Director .... Ms. Heather DAVIS
22 Title IX Coordinator .... Ms. Angela SHAMBARGER
39 Assoc Dir for Housing/Resident Life .... Mr. Anthony MONTALBANO
44 Director Annual Giving .... Ms. Anne WASHBURNE
108 Assoc Director of Assessment .... Ms. Jennifer MANDEL
21 Assistant VP of Financial Planning .... Mr. Matthew KOGUT
88 Assistant VP Compl/Finance & Admin .... Mr. Jeffery CROCKER

MARYLAND

Allegany College of Maryland (B)

12401 Willowbrook Road, SE, Cumberland MD 21502-2596
County: Allegany FICE Identification: 002057
Unit ID: 161688
Telephone: (301) 784-5000 Carnegie Class: Assoc/HVT-High Trad
FAX Number: (301) 784-5050 Calendar System: Semester
URL: www.allegany.edu
Established: 1961 Annual Undergrad Tuition & Fees (In-District): $8,270
Enrollment: 2,523 Coed
Affiliation or Control: Local IRS Status: 501(c)3
Highest Offering: Associate Degree
Accreditation: M, ADNUR, COARC, CSHSE, DH, MAC, MLTAD, OTA, PTAA

01 President .... Dr. Cynthia S. BAMBARA
05 Sr Vice Pres Instructional Affairs .... Dr. Kurt HOFFMAN
10 Vice President Finance/Admin .... Ms. Christina KILDUFF
111 VP Advancement/Community Rels .... Mr. David R. JONES
15 Director of Human Resources .... Ms. Melinda DUCKWORTH

Anne Arundel Community College (C)

101 College Parkway, Arnold MD 21012-1895
County: Anne Arundel FICE Identification: 002058
Unit ID: 161767
Telephone: (410) 777-2222 Carnegie Class: Assoc/MT-VT-Mix Trad/Non
FAX Number: (410) 777-2489 Calendar System: Semester
URL: www.aacc.edu
Established: 1961 Annual Undergrad Tuition & Fees (In-District): $8,540
Enrollment: 11,948 Coed
Affiliation or Control: State/Local IRS Status: 501(c)3
Highest Offering: Associate Degree
Accreditation: M, ACFEI, ACPHA, ADNUR, CSHSE, EMT, MAC, MLTAD, PTAA, RAD, SURGT

01 President .... Dr. Dawn S. LINDSAY
05 VP for Learning .... Dr. Tanya C. MILLNER
10 VP Learning Resources Management .... Ms. Melissa A. BEARDMORE
84 VP for Learner Support Services .... Ms. Felicia L. PATTERSON
106 Dean of Instructional Design .... Dr. Colleen EISENBEISER
20 Associate VP for Learning .... Dr. Alycia MARSHALL
30 Director of Development .... Mr. Vollie D. MELSON
32 Dean of Student Development .... Ms. Deneen DANGERFIELD
76 Dean of Health Sciences .... Dr. Elizabeth H. APPEL
66 Director of Nursing .... Ms. Beth Anne BATTURS
49 Dean School of Liberal Arts .... Dr. Alicia MORSE
50 Dean School of Business & Law .... Ms. Karen COOK
81 Dean School of Science & Technology .... Dr. Lance BOWEN
51 Dean Sch Cont Educ & Workforce Dev .... Dr. Kip KUNSMAN
22 Controller .... Ms. Martha D. ROTHSCHILD
21 Assoc VP for Learning Resource Mgmt .... Mr. Andrew P. LITTLE
13 VP Information & Instructional Tech .... Mr. Richard C. KRALEVICH
08 Director of Library .... Ms. Cynthia K. STEINHOFF
06 Registrar .... Ms. Nancy A. BEIER
09 Assoc VP Innovation Analytics .... Dr. Shuang LIU
15 Exec Director of Human Resources .... Ms. Suzanne L. BOYER
26 Exec Dir Strategic Communications .... Mr. Dan B. BAUM
37 Director of Financial Aid .... Ms. Tara CAREW
07 Dir Admissions/Enroll Development .... Ms. Cassandra S. MOORE
11 Exec Dir of Administrative Services .... Vacant
84 Dean Enrollment Services .... Dr. John F. GRABOWSKI
124 Dean of Student Success .... Ms. Bonnie J. GARRETT
35 Director of Student Engagement .... Ms. Amberdawn CHEATHAM
22 Chief Compliance & Fair Practices .... Dr. Tiffany F. BOYKIN
40 College Bookstore Manager .... Mr. Christopher WALSH
19 Director Public Safety .... Mr. Sean KAPFHAMMER
96 Director Purchasing/Contracting .... Ms. Melanie L. HENRICKSON
30 Director of Development .... Ms. Wendy THOMAS
23 Coordinator Health Services .... Ms. Beth A. MAYS
41 Athletic Director .... Mr. Duane HERR
88 Assistant Director Admissions .... Mr. Brian O'NEIL
94 Coordinator of Women's Studies .... Dr. Suzanne J. SPOOR
88 Director of Environmental Center .... Dr. M. Stephen AILSTOCK
88 Director Center Study Local Issues .... Dr. Daniel D. NATAF
88 Dir Homeland Sec/Crim Justice Inst .... Dr. Tyrone POWERS
53 Director TEACH Institute .... Ms. Candice PLACE
88 Director Hosp/Cul Arts/Tourism Inst .... Mr. Matthew HERRON
38 Coord Institute for the Future .... Mr. Steven T. HENICK
88 Dir Sarbanes Center/Pub & Cmty Svc .... Ms. Cathleen H. DOYLE
28 Chief Diversity Officer .... Dr. Tiffany BOYKIN
04 Special Asst to President .... Ms. Monica RAUSA WILLIAMS
18 Dir Facilities Plng & Construction .... Mr. James TAYLOR
25 Director Sponsored Programs .... Ms. Susan GALLAGHER
103 Director Corporate Training Group .... Ms. Sonja GLADWIN
105 Team Leader Media & Web .... Ms. Amanda SACHS

Bais HaMedrash & Mesivta of Baltimore (D)

6823 Old Pimlico Road, Baltimore MD 21209
County: Baltimore FICE Identification: 041884
Unit ID: 476601
Telephone: (410) 486-0006 Carnegie Class: Spec-4-yr-Faith
FAX Number: (410) 602-9738 Calendar System: Semester
Established: 1997 Annual Undergrad Tuition & Fees: $13,100
Enrollment: 60 Male
Affiliation or Control: Independent Non-Profit IRS Status: 501(c)3
Highest Offering: First Talmudic Degree
Accreditation: RABN

01 Rosh Yeshiva .... Rabbi Chaim COHEN

Baltimore City Community College (E)

2901 Liberty Heights Avenue, Baltimore MD 21215-7893
County: Baltimore City FICE Identification: 002061
Unit ID: 161864
Telephone: (410) 462-8300 Carnegie Class: Assoc/MT-VT-High Trad
FAX Number: (410) 462-7791 Calendar System: Semester
URL: www.bccc.edu
Established: 1947 Annual Undergrad Tuition & Fees (In-State): $3,314
Enrollment: 4,181 Coed
Affiliation or Control: State IRS Status: 501(c)3
Highest Offering: Associate Degree
Accreditation: M, ACBSP, ADNUR, CAHIIM, COARC, DH, EMT, PTAA, SURGT

01 President .... Dr. Debra L. MCCURDY
32 VP for Student Affairs .... Dr. Jade BORNE
05 VP Academic Affairs .... Dr. Laura CRIPPS
103 VP Workforce Dev/Cont Education .... Mr. Michael THOMAS
45 VP Institutional Rsrch/Effect/Plng .... Ms. Becky BURRELL
111 VP Advance/Strategic Partnership .... Vacant
18 Asst Vice Pres Facilities .... Ms. Katherine ZURLAGE
10 VP for Finance and Administration .... Mr. Steven HARDY
13 Chief Information Officer .... Mr. Michael RADING
43 General Counsel/Chief of Staff .... Ms. Maria E. RODRIGUEZ
84 Dean of Enrollment Management .... Ms. Sylvia ROCHESTER
21 Controller .... Ms. Eileen WAITSMAN
37 Director Financial Aid .... Ms. Saleem CHAUDHRY
08 Director Library/Media Services .... Vacant
15 Asst VP of Human Resources .... Mr. Charles HALL
09 Director of Institutional Research .... Ms. Eileen HAWKINS
26 Director of Marketing .... Mr. Michael BERENDS
96 Director of Procurement .... Ms. Anna LANSAW
35 Dir of Student Life & Engagement .... Ms. Elizabeth PURSWANI
106 Director of E-Learning .... Mr. Brian TERRILL
19 Director of Public Safety .... Vacant
41 Director of Athletics .... Dr. Darryl POPE
06 Registrar .... Ms. Sharon STODDARD
86 Director Government Relations .... Vacant
105 Director Web Services .... Mr. Christopher JORDAN
108 Director Institutional Assessment .... Ms. Nicole DEUTSCH

Capitol Technology University (F)

11301 Springfield Road, Laurel MD 20708-9759
County: Prince Georges FICE Identification: 001436
Unit ID: 162061
Telephone: (800) 950-1992 Carnegie Class: DU-Mod
FAX Number: (301) 369-2310 Calendar System: Semester
URL: www.captechu.edu
Established: 1927 Annual Undergrad Tuition & Fees: $26,874
Enrollment: 754 Coed
Affiliation or Control: Independent Non-Profit IRS Status: 501(c)3
Highest Offering: Doctorate
Accreditation: M

01 President .... Dr. Bradford L. SIMS
05 Vice President for Academic Affairs .... Dr. Richard BAKER
10 VP Finance .... Ms. Kathleen WERNER
84 Sr VP for Enrollment Mgmt & Mktg .... Ms. Dianne M. O'NEILL
20 AVP Academic Assessment .... Dr. Natasha MILLER
32 VP Student Engagement & Univ Devel .... Ms. Melinda BUNNELL-RHYNE
54 Chair Electrical Engineering .... Dr. Richard BAKER
06 Director of Registration & Records .... Mr. Greg HUGHES
08 Dir Library/Information Literacy .... Mr. Allen EXNER
15 Director Human Resources .... Ms. Shirley WASHINGTON
26 Director Communications .... Ms. Olivia BATHERSFIELD
30 AVP Development/Fundraising .... Vacant
07 Director Admissions .... Mr. Cameron NEWSOME
37 Director of Financial Aid .... Vacant
51 Director of Continuing Education .... Vacant
18 VP Facilities Management .... Mr. Gary BURKE
04 Executive Admin Asst to President .... Ms. Brielle O'BRIEN
103 Director of Career Services .... Ms. Constance HARRINGTON
106 Dir Online Education/E-learning .... Mr. William DRAYTON
13 Director Information Services .... Mr. Terrell MOORE
35 Dean of Students .... Mr. Jason KILMER

Carroll Community College (G)

1601 Washington Road, Westminster MD 21157-6913
County: Carroll FICE Identification: 031007
Unit ID: 405872
Telephone: (410) 386-8000 Carnegie Class: Assoc/MT-VT-Mix Trad/Non
FAX Number: (410) 386-8181 Calendar System: Semester
URL: www.carrollcc.edu
Established: 1993 Annual Undergrad Tuition & Fees (In-District): $6,588
Enrollment: 3,060 Coed
Affiliation or Control: Local IRS Status: 501(c)3
Highest Offering: Associate Degree
Accreditation: M, CNEA, EMT, PTAA

01 President .... Dr. James D. BALL
11 Exec Vice Pres Administration .... Mr. Alan M. SCHUMAN
05 Provost .... Dr. Rosalie MINCE
51 Vice Pres of Cont Educ/Training .... Dr. Kelly KOERMER
111 Exec Dir Inst Advance/College Fndn .... Mr. Steven WANTZ
26 Chief Communications Officer .... Vacant

50	Div Chair Business & Technology	Mr. Robert BROWN
60	Div Chair Communication Arts	Ms. Siobhan WRIGHT
76	Div Chair Allied Health/Nursing	Dr. Nancy PERRY
83	Div Chair Social Sciences/Health	Ms. Sharon BRUNNER
54	Div Chair Mathematics/Engineer	Ms. Brianna MCGINNIS
81	Div Chair Sciences	Dr. Raza KHAN
53	Div Chair Educ & Trans Studies	Ms. Susan SIES
79	Div Chair Arts/Humanities	Ms. Jessi HARDESTY
32	Assoc Prov Student Affs/Marketing	Dr. Kristie CRUMLEY
06	Sr Dir of Records/Stdnt Data Analy	Ms. Laurie SHIELDS
121	Sr Dir Advising/Ret/Student Place	Dr. April HERRING
84	Sr Director Enrollment Development	Ms. Candace EDWARDS
28	Dir Student Care/Integrity	Dr. DaVida ANDERSON
37	Director of Financial Aid	Mr. John GAY
35	Sr Director of Student Engagement	Ms. Jennifer SNYDER
08	Director of the Library	Mr. Jeremy GREEN
106	Director Online Learning	Ms. Andrea GRAVELLE
27	Sr Director Marketing	Dr. Maya DEMISHKEVICH
09	Dir Institutional Effectiveness	Mr. Gregory BRICCA
103	Sr Dir Corporate Svcs/Workforce Dev	Ms. Janet LADD
45	Dir CET Research/Strategic Analysis	Ms. Jean MARRIOTT
88	Sr Dir Career & Continuing Educ	Mr. Steven BERRY
55	Director Lifelong Learning	Ms. Kathy MAYAN
105	Assoc VP Admin/CIO	Ms. Patti DAVIS
10	Director Fiscal Affairs	Mr. Timothy LEAGUE
15	Director Human Resources	Ms. Lisa KUHN
18	Director Facilities Plng Management	Ms. Lisa AUGHENBAUGH
19	Chief of Campus Police	Mr. Brian LINTZ
88	Assoc VP Program Dev/Partnerships	Dr. Melody MOORE
22	Director Disability Support Svcs	Mr. Joseph TATELA
108	Assoc Provost Assess/Inst Effective	Dr. Michelle KLOSS
04	Executive Associate to President	Ms. Marianne ANDERSON
41	Athletic Director	Mr. Bill KELVEY

Cecil College (A)

One Seahawk Drive, North East MD 21901-1999

County: Cecil FICE Identification: 008308
Unit ID: 162104
Telephone: (410) 287-6060 Carnegie Class: Assoc/MT-VT-High Trad
FAX Number: (410) 287-1026 Calendar System: Semester
URL: www.cecil.edu
Established: 1968 Annual Undergrad Tuition & Fees (In-District): $8,040
Enrollment: 2,090 Coed
Affiliation or Control: State/Local IRS Status: 501(c)3
Highest Offering: Associate Degree
Accreditation: M, ADNUR, EMT, MAC, PTAA

01	President	Dr. Mary WAY BOLT
05	Vice President Academic Programs	Dr. Christy DRYER
10	Vice President Finance	Mr. Christopher MILLS
32	VP Students/Enrollment Management	Dr. Kimberly JOYCE
13	Sr Director of IT Services	Mr. Ian COOPER
111	VP Cmty/Govt Rels & College Advance	Ms. Chris Ann SZEP
15	Executive Director Human Resources	Ms. Michelle WILLIAMS
66	Dean Nursing/Allied Hlth/Hlth Sci	Ms. Nancy NORMAN-MARZELLA
49	Acting Dean Arts & Sciences	Dr. Veronica DOUGHERTY
18	Director of Facilities	Mr. Keith BROWN
37	Director of Financial Aid Services	Ms. Amanda SOLECKI
26	Director of Marketing	Ms. Amy HENDERSON
93	Director Minority Student Services	Ms. Mayra CASTILLO
09	Director of Institutional Research	Ms. Karen EQYPT
06	Director of Records & Registration	Ms. S. Tomeka SWAN
08	Director of Library Services	Ms. Amanda DEMERS
41	Director Athletics	Mr. Ed DURHAM
29	Coordinator Alumni Relations	Ms. Mary MOORE
04	Exec Assistant to the President	Ms. Sherry HARTMAN
21	Controller	Mr. Craig WHITEFORD
19	Director Security/Safety	Mr. Walt BEAUPRE
103	Director Workforce Development	Mr. Miles DEAN
101	Secretary of the Institution/Board	Dr. Mary W. BOLT
86	Director Government Relations	Vacant

Chesapeake College (B)

PO Box 8, 1000 College Circle, Wye Mills MD 21679-0008

County: Queen Annes FICE Identification: 004650
Unit ID: 162168
Telephone: (410) 822-5400 Carnegie Class: Assoc/MT-VT-High Trad
FAX Number: (410) 827-5800 Calendar System: Semester
URL: www.chesapeake.edu
Established: 1965 Annual Undergrad Tuition & Fees (In-District): $5,552
Enrollment: 1,904 Coed
Affiliation or Control: State/Local IRS Status: 501(c)3
Highest Offering: Associate Degree
Accreditation: M, ADNUR, EMT, PTAA, RAD, SURGT

01	President	Dr. Clifford COPPERSMITH
05	Vice President for Academics	Dr. David HARPER
11	VP for Administrative Services	Ms. Karen SMITH
32	VP for Student Success & Enrollment	Mr. Kamari COLLINS
106	Dean for Teaching and Learning	Dr. Chandra M. GIGLIOTTI
20	Dean for Faculty	Dr. Juliet SMITH
103	Int Dean Workforce Programs	Mr. Jason MULLEN
18	Director of Facilities	Vacant
15	Director of Human Resources	Vacant
37	Director of Financial Aid	Ms. Princess WILLIAMS
09	Dir Inst Plng/Research/Assessment	Mr. Chris HALL
26	Dir College Relations & Marketing	Ms. Danielle DARLING
06	Registrar	Mr. James A. DAVIDSON
84	Dean for Enrollment & Advising	Ms. Joan M. SEITZER
101	Exec Assoc to President/Board	Ms. Kate MAXWELL

13	Int Chief Information Tech Ofcr	Ms. Loretta EARLY
30	Director of Constituent Engagement	Ms. Michelle HALL

College of Southern Maryland (C)

PO Box 910, La Plata MD 20646-0910

County: Charles FICE Identification: 002064
Unit ID: 162122
Telephone: (301) 934-2251 Carnegie Class: Assoc/HT-Mix Trad/Non
FAX Number: (301) 934-7698 Calendar System: Semester
URL: www.csmd.edu
Established: 1958 Annual Undergrad Tuition & Fees (In-District): $6,870
Enrollment: 6,164 Coed
Affiliation or Control: Local IRS Status: 501(c)3
Highest Offering: Associate Degree
Accreditation: M, ACBSP, ADNUR, CAHIIM, EMT, MLTAD, PNUR, PTAA

01	President	Dr. Maureen MURPHY
05	Provost and VP Academic Affairs	Dr. Rodney REDMOND
84	VP Student Equity and Success	Dr. Tracy HARRIS
103	AVP Continuing Educ & Workforce Dev	Ms. Ellen FLOWERS-FIELDS
10	VP Financial & Admin Services	Vacant
11	VP Operations and Planning	Dr. William COMEY
43	Vice President/General Counsel	Mr. Craig PATENAUDE
100	Chief of Staff	Ms. Larisa PFEIFFER
09	AVP Plng/Inst Effective/Rsrch	Dr. Erin EBERSOLE
15	AVP of Human Resources	Mr. Ivan SMITH
26	AVP Marketing/Communication	Ms. Avis MCMILLON
37	Director Financial Assistance	Mr. Christian ZIMMERMANN
06	Dean Enrollment Services	Ms. Carol HARRISON
18	Exec Director of Facilities	Mr. Ron TOWARD
76	Dean Health Sciences	Dr. Laura POLK
32	Dean Student Development	Ms. Michelle RUBLE
109	Exec Dir Auxiliary Services	Ms. Marcy GANNON
07	Director Admissions Department	Mr. David JONES
96	Exec Dir of Procurement/Contracts	Mr. Joe PICCOLO
28	Exec Dir Diversity and Inclusion	Vacant
19	Exec Director Security/Safety	Mr. Bill BESSETTE
25	Grants Development Coordinator	Ms. Lesley QUATTLEBAUM
30	Exec Director Development	Ms. Chelsea BROWN
108	Director Institutional Assessment	Mr. Roland KEECH
86	Director Government Relations	Ms. Karen SMITH-HUPP

The Community College of Baltimore County (D)

7201 Rossville Blvd., Baltimore MD 21237-3899

County: Baltimore FICE Identification: 002063
Unit ID: 434672
Telephone: (443) 840-2222 Carnegie Class: Assoc/MT-VT-High Trad
FAX Number: (443) 840-1100 Calendar System: Semester
URL: www.ccbcmd.edu
Established: 1957 Annual Undergrad Tuition & Fees (In-District): $7,474
Enrollment: 17,573 Coed
Affiliation or Control: Local IRS Status: 501(c)3
Highest Offering: Associate Degree
Accreditation: M, ACBSP, ADNUR, ART, AT, CAHIIM, COARC, DANCE, DH, EMT, FUSER, HT, MAC, MLTAD, MUS, OTA, POLYT, RAD, RTT, SURGT, THEA

01	President	Dr. Sandra L. KURTINITIS
111	Vice Pres Institutional Advancement	Mr. Kenneth WESTARY
10	Vice Pres Finance/Administration	Ms. Melissa HOPP
05	Chancellor/VP Instruction	Dr. Joaquin MARTINEZ
51	VP External Outreach Initiative	Mr. Michael NETZER
26	Sr Director for Public Relations	Ms. Amy FILARDO
15	Senior Director Human Resources	Ms. Yvette BUNN JONES

Frederick Community College (E)

7932 Opossumtown Pike, Frederick MD 21702-2097

County: Frederick FICE Identification: 002071
Unit ID: 162557
Telephone: (301) 846-2400 Carnegie Class: Assoc/HVT-Mix Trad/Non
FAX Number: (301) 846-2498 Calendar System: Semester
URL: www.frederick.edu
Established: 1957 Annual Undergrad Tuition & Fees (In-District): $7,396
Enrollment: 5,756 Coed
Affiliation or Control: State/Local IRS Status: 501(c)3
Highest Offering: Associate Degree
Accreditation: M, ACFEI, ADNUR, COARC, @PTAA, SURGT

01	President	Dr. Annesa CHEEK
100	Chief of Staff	Ms. Avis BOYD
11	Chief of Operations	Mr. Lewis GODWIN
05	Provost/EVP Academic Affairs & CEWD	Dr. Tony HAWKINS
32	VP for Student Affairs	Dr. Nora CLARK
121	AVP for Student Success	Dr. Candice BALDWIN
25	Director of Grants	Ms. Pamela DUBITSKY
111	Exec Dir Institutional Advancement	Ms. Deborah POWELL
13	Interim Chief Information Officer	Mr. Adam RENO
50	AVP for AA/Dean Health/Bus/Tech/Sci	Dr. Sandy MCCOMBE WALLER
27	Director of Communications	Ms. Caroline COLE
10	Interim VP for Finance	Ms. Amy STAKE
21	Director of Finance	Ms. Shawn CHESNUTWOOD
84	AVP for Strategic Enrollment	Dr. Vell LYLES
06	Exec Dir of Registration & Records	Ms. Deirdre WEILMINSTER
49	AVP for AA/Dean of Liberal Arts	Dr. Brian STIPELMAN
124	Exec Director of Student Leadership	Ms. Jeanni WINSTON-MUIR

88	Spec Asst to President Inst Effect	Mr. Gerald BOYD
88	Director of Capital Planning	Mr. John ANZINGER
08	Director of Library Services	Ms. Colleen MCKNIGHT
09	Exec Dir Plng/Inst Effectiveness	Dr. Gohar FARAHANI
26	Exec Director of Marketing and Web	Mr. Michael BAISEY
04	Exec Assoc to the President & BOT	Ms. Kari MELVIN
103	AVP for Cont Educ/Workforce Dev	Dr. Molly CARLSON
117	Exec Director MACEM & Public Safety	Ms. Kathy FRANCIS
41	Director of Athletics	Mr. Larry JOHNSTON
88	Director of Clinical Education	Ms. Ashley DICKS
37	Director of Financial Aid	Ms. Nichole POLLARD
36	Exec Dir Career & Academic Planning	Dr. Chad ADERO
88	AVP for Center for Teaching	Dr. Nicole BAIRD
15	Director of Human Resources	Ms. Diana OLIVER
22	Dir of Disability Access Services	Dr. Kate KRAMER-JEFFERSON
88	Dir Veteran & Military Services	Ms. Amy COLDREN
109	Executive Director of Auxiliaries	Mr. Frederick HOCKENBERRY
66	Director of Nursing Education	Ms. Kyla NEWBOULD
19	Director of Public Safety	Ms. Robin SHUSKO
28	Interim Director for DEI	Dr. Andrea DARDELLO
55	Director of Adult Education	Ms. Jennifer SZABO
88	Director of Physical Therapy	Ms. Amelia IAMS
76	Director of Health Science	Mr. Jeffrey HAWK
88	Interim Director Children's Center	Ms. Cathy FLORIMBIO
88	Exec Dir Open Campus & Dual Enroll	Ms. Elizabeth DUFFY
88	Director for Testing Center Service	Dr. Alesha ROSEN
18	Director of Plant Operations	Vacant
40	Director College Store Operations	Ms. Kimberly MADDEN
35	AVP for Student Affairs	Dr. Benita RASHAW
113	Exec Dir Student Finance/Bursar	Ms. Jane BEATTY
91	Exec Dir Network Infrastructure	Mr. Scott REECE
24	Director Audio-Visual Tech	Mr. Bryan VALKO
14	Director of IT Technical Support	Mr. Michael MARSHALL

Garrett College (F)

687 Mosser Road, McHenry MD 21541

County: Garrett FICE Identification: 010014
Unit ID: 162609
Telephone: (301) 387-3000 Carnegie Class: Assoc/HT-High Trad
FAX Number: N/A Calendar System: Semester
URL: www.garrettcollege.edu
Established: 1967 Annual Undergrad Tuition & Fees (In-District): $8,848
Enrollment: 624 Coed
Affiliation or Control: State/Local IRS Status: 501(c)3
Highest Offering: Associate Degree
Accreditation: M, EMT

01	President	Dr. Richard MIDCAP
04	Executive Assistant to President	Ms. Marcia KNEPP
10	Dean of Business & Finance	Ms. Dallas OUELLETTE
32	Chief Student Affairs Officer	Mr. Robert KERNS
05	Dean of Academic Affairs	Dr. Ryan HARROD
51	Dean of Cont Educ/Workforce Devel	Ms. Julie YODER
13	Director of IT	Mr. Andrew DURST
30	Dir Develop/Exec Dir Foundation	Ms. Cherie KRUG
06	Assoc Dean Student Affs/Registrar	Ms. Kim DEGIOVANNI
37	Director of Financial Aid	Mr. Andrew HARVEY
08	Dir of Library/Learning Commons	Ms. Jennifer MESLENER
15	Director of Human Resources	Ms. Janis BUSH
26	Int Dir of Marketing and CS	Dr. Kelli SISLER
35	Director of Student Development	Mr. Rich SCHOFIELD
65	Dir of Natural Res/Wildlife Tech	Mr. Kevin DODGE
41	Co-Director of Athletics	Ms. Elizabeth SHOW
41	Co-Director of Athletics	Mr. Eric HALLENBECK
18	Director of Facilities	Ms. Kathy MEAGHER
121	Coord of Student Advis & Acad Supp	Ms. Ashley RUBY
96	Purchasing/Accounts Payable	Ms. Carolina DODGE
40	Bookstore Manager	Ms. Lois ANDERSON
105	Web Developer	Mr. David LANTZ
106	Coord of DL & Inst Design	Ms. Carla ZEIGLER
19	Coord of Safety & Security	Mr. Steven BAKER
07	Director of Admissions	Ms. Melissa WASS
25	Chief Contract/Grants Administrator	Ms. Kearstin HINEBAUGH
22	Director of Equity/Compliance & RM	Ms. Shelley MENEAR
09	Dir of Analytics/IR & Assessment	Dr. Kelli SISLER

Goucher College (G)

1021 Dulaney Valley Road, Baltimore MD 21204-2780

County: Baltimore FICE Identification: 002073
Unit ID: 162654
Telephone: (410) 337-6000 Carnegie Class: Bac-A&S
FAX Number: N/A Calendar System: Semester
URL: www.goucher.edu
Established: 1885 Annual Undergrad Tuition & Fees: $47,200
Enrollment: 2,015 Coed
Affiliation or Control: Independent Non-Profit IRS Status: 501(c)3
Highest Offering: Master's
Accreditation: M

01	President	Mr. Kent DEVEREAUX
05	Provost/Sr VP Academic Affairs	Dr. Elaine MEYER-LEE
111	Vice Pres Advancement	Ms. Michele Y. EWING
26	VP Marketing & External Relations	Ms. Stephanie COLDREN
13	Vice Pres for Technology & Planning	Mr. Bill LEIMBACH
43	General Counsel	Vacant
41	Assoc Dean Students/Dir Athletics	Dr. Andrew WU
07	Director of Admissions	Ms. Lisa HILL
08	Librarian	Vacant
29	Exec Dir for Alumnae/i Engagement	Ms. Jennifer PAWLO - JOHNSTONE
36	Director of Career Development	Ms. Traci MARTIN

58 Director Grad Program in Education .... Dr. Annalisa CZEZULIN
06 Registrar .... Ms. Genevieve COLE
37 Director Student Financial Services .... Ms. Stephanie ALFORD
105 Webmaster .... Mr. John PERRELLI
39 Director Residential Life .... Ms. Lindy BOBBIT
38 Director Student Counseling Center .... Ms. Monica NEEL
04 Admin Assistant to the President .... Ms. Christine STEWART
09 Director Institutional Effectivenes .... Ms. Shama AKHTAR
102 Asst Dir Foundation/Corporate Rels .... Ms. Janeisa LASHLEY
104 Director Study Abroad .... Dr. Luchen LI
11 Chief of Operations/Administration .... Mr. David VALENTINE
15 AVP Human Resources .... Ms. Kristi YOWELL
18 VP Campus Operations .... Mr. Erik THOMPSON
28 Assoc Dean Diversity/Equity/Inclus .... Mr. Juan HERNANDEZ
32 VP Student Affairs .... Dr. Aarika CAMP
44 Director Annual Giving .... Ms. Ali SCHILLER-SMITH
84 VP Enrollment Management .... Mr. Jonathan LINDSAY
91 Director Administrative Computing .... Mr. Robert SMITH

Hagerstown Community College (A)

11400 Robinwood Drive, Hagerstown MD 21742-6590
County: Washington FICE Identification: 002074
Unit ID: 162690
Telephone: (240) 500-2000 Carnegie Class: Assoc/MT-VT-Mix Trad/Non
FAX Number: (301) 393-3682 Calendar System: Semester
URL: www.hagerstowncc.edu
Established: 1946 Annual Undergrad Tuition & Fees (In-District): $6,360
Enrollment: 3,433 Coed
Affiliation or Control: State/Local IRS Status: 501(c)3
Highest Offering: Associate Degree
Accreditation: M, ADNUR, CAHIIM, DA, DH, EMT, PNUR, RAD

01 President .... Dr. James S. KLAUBER, SR.
05 VP of Academic Affs & Student Svcs .... Dr. David WARNER
10 Vice Pres Administration/ Finance .... Dr. Heike I. SOEFFKER-CULICERTO
32 Dean of Students .... Dr. Christine A. OHL-GIGLIOTTI
09 Dean Plng/Inst Effectiveness .... Ms. Carlee K. RANALLI
103 Dean Workforce Solutions & Cont Ed .... Ms. Theresa M. SHANK
18 Dir Facilities Management & Plng .... Mr. Vincent T. IPPOLITO
07 Dir of Admissions & Enrollment Mgmt .... Mr. Kevin L. CRAWFORD
111 Senior Director College Advancement .... Dr. Ashley N. WHALEY
26 Sr Dir Public Relations & Marketing .... Ms. Elizabeth L. KIRKPATRICK
37 Director of Financial Aid .... Dr. Charles M. SCHEETZ
106 Dean of Distance Education .... Ms. Vidda P. BEACHE
21 Director of Finance .... Mr. David C. BITTORF
88 Manager of Business Services .... Ms. Alicia K. CULLOP
66 Director of Nursing .... Ms. Karen S. HAMMOND
15 Exec Director of Human Resources .... Ms. Jennifer A. CHILDS
41 Dir Athletics/Phys Ed/Leisure Stds .... Mr. Robert C. ROHAN
13 Sr Dir Information Technology .... Mr. Craig M. FENTRESS
04 Exec Assistant to the President .... Ms. Barbara W. ROULETTE
06 Registrar .... Mr. Christopher BAER
19 Director Security/Safety .... Mr. Eric C. BYERS

Harford Community College (B)

401 Thomas Run Road, Bel Air MD 21015-1698
County: Harford FICE Identification: 002075
Unit ID: 162706
Telephone: (443) 412-2000 Carnegie Class: Assoc/MT-VT-High Trad
FAX Number: (443) 412-2120 Calendar System: Semester
URL: www.harford.edu
Established: 1957 Annual Undergrad Tuition & Fees (In-District): $6,065
Enrollment: 5,256 Coed
Affiliation or Control: Local IRS Status: 501(c)3
Highest Offering: Associate Degree
Accreditation: M, ADNUR, EMT, HT, MAC

01 President .... Dr. Theresa FELDER
05 Vice President Academic Affairs .... Dr. Timothy SHERWOOD
10 VP Finance & Administration .... Mr. Trevor JACKSON
32 VP Student Affairs .... Dr. Jacqueline JACKSON
13 Chief Information Officer .... Mr. Tom ALCIDE
84 Assoc VP Enrollment Services .... Mr. Patrick ELLIOTT
35 Assoc VP Student Development .... Ms. Jennie TOWNER
21 Director for Finance & Accounting .... Ms. Karina JACKSON
106 Dean Teaching/Learning/Innovation .... Dr. Karen M. REGE
18 Director for Campus Operations .... Mr. Lou CLAYPOOLE
37 Director Financial Aid .... Ms. Amy R. SPINNATO
06 Registrar .... Ms. Courtney MITCHELL
26 Director for Communications .... Ms. Nancy J. DYSARD
15 AVP Human Resources/Employee Dev .... Ms. Donna SHOPULSKI
30 Director College/Alumni Development .... Ms. Denise M. DREGIER
08 Dean of Information & Innovation .... Ms. Karen REGE
09 Director for Inst Effectiveness .... Vacant
38 Dir Advising/Career/Transfer Svcs .... Ms. J. Bonnie SULZBACH
40 Coordinator College Store .... Mr. Joseph BUSKIRK
07 Dir for Admissions .... Ms. Katie REYNOLDS
110 Event Coordinator & Gift Officer .... Ms. Jordan WILLIAMS
81 Dean Science/Tech/Engr/Math .... Ms. Pamela PAPE-LINDSTROM
83 Dean Behavioral & Social Sciences .... Mr. Tony WOHLERS
79 Dean of Arts & Humanities .... Mr. Todd ABRAMOVITZ
50 Dean of CEBAT .... Ms. Kelly KOERMER
66 Interim Dean of NAHP .... Ms. Sonia GALVAN
19 Director Security/Safety .... Vacant
41 Athletic Director .... Vacant

Hood College (C)

401 Rosemont Avenue, Frederick MD 21701-8575
County: Frederick FICE Identification: 002076
Unit ID: 162760
Telephone: (301) 663-3131 Carnegie Class: Masters/L
FAX Number: (301) 694-7653 Calendar System: Semester
URL: www.hood.edu
Established: 1893 Annual Undergrad Tuition & Fees: $42,300
Enrollment: 2,042 Coed
Affiliation or Control: Independent Non-Profit IRS Status: 501(c)3
Highest Offering: Doctorate
Accreditation: M, ACBSP, CACREP, @DIET, NURSE, SW

01 President .... Dr. Andrea E. CHAPDELAINE
05 Provost/VP Academic Affairs .... Dr. Deborah RICKER
10 Vice Pres Finance .... Mr. Robert KLINEDINST
111 VP for Institutional Advancement .... Ms. Nancy E. GILLECE
32 Dean of Students .... Dr. Ron WIAFE
84 VP Undergrad/Grad Enrollment .... Mr. William BROWN
26 VP Marketing/Communications Officer .... Ms. Laurie WARD
07 Director of Admissions .... Ms. Nikki BAMONTI
58 Dean of Graduate School .... Dr. April BOULTON
08 Director of Library Service .... Mr. Toby PETERSON
15 Director of Human Resources .... Ms. Christine TRAINI
13 Chief Technology Officer .... Mr. Bill HOBBS
04 Executive Asst to President .... Ms. Diane K. WISE
104 Director Study Abroad .... Mr. Scott PINCIKOWSKI
19 Director Security/Safety .... Mr. Thurmond MAYNARD
39 Director Student Housing .... Vacant
102 Dir Foundation/Corporate Relations .... Ms. Jaime CACCIOLA
06 Registrar .... Ms. Katie GROCKI
09 Director of Institutional Research .... Dr. Shaowei WU
29 Director Alumni Affairs .... Ms. Kellye GREENWALD
37 Director Student Financial Aid .... Ms. Sarah MARINER
41 Athletic Director .... Dr. Susan KOLB
44 Director Annual Giving .... Ms. Niccole ROLLS
28 VP for Community & Inclusivity .... Ms. Tammi SIMPSON

Howard Community College (D)

10901 Little Patuxent Parkway, Columbia MD 21044-3197
County: Howard FICE Identification: 008175
Unit ID: 162779
Telephone: (443) 518-1000 Carnegie Class: Assoc/HT-Mix Trad/Non
FAX Number: N/A Calendar System: Semester
URL: www.howardcc.edu
Established: 1966 Annual Undergrad Tuition & Fees (In-District): $6,408
Enrollment: 9,566 Coed
Affiliation or Control: State/Local IRS Status: 501(c)3
Highest Offering: Associate Degree
Accreditation: M, ACFEI, ACPHA, ADNUR, ART, CVT, DH, DMS, EMT, MLTAD, MUS, PNUR, PTAA, RAD

01 President .... Dr. Daria WILLIS
32 Vice President of Student Success .... Dr. Maria CURTIS
05 Vice Pres of Teaching and Learning .... Dr. Carl S. MOORE
10 Vice Pres of Administration/Finance .... Ms. Lynn C. COLEMAN
13 Vice Pres Information Technology .... Ms. Linda WU
51 Associate VP Cont Ed/Workforce Dev .... Ms. Minah C. WOO
84 Associate VP Enrollment Services .... Dr. Jennifer MCCLURE
35 AVP for Student Development .... Ms. Debra GREENE
15 Associate Vice Pres Human Resources .... Vacant
21 Associate Vice Pres of Finance .... Mr. Chris W. HESTON
18 Exec Dir Capital Proj/Facilities .... Mr. Charles W. NIGHTINGALE
100 Chief of Staff .... Ms. Cheryl CUDZILO
114 Director of Budget and Finance .... Ms. Verna A. BERNOI
30 Dir of Dev/Exec Dir Educ Foundation .... Ms. Melissa L. MATTEY
109 Director Auxiliary Services .... Mr. L. Dewey GRIM
19 Director of Public Safety .... Mr. G. William DAVIS
35 Director Student Life .... Ms. Aisha RIVERS
04 Exec Assistant to the President .... Ms. Molly F. HONG
96 Director of Procurement .... Mr. Domonic A. CUSIMANO
06 Registrar .... Ms. Katelyn PIPER
07 Director of Admissions & Advising .... Mrs. Mary C. O'ROURKE
104 Director of International Education .... Ms. Mary L. ALLEN
105 Web Enterprise Services Manager .... Mr. Roger F. STOTT
37 Director of Financial Aid Services .... Ms. Tamika BYBEE
41 Director of Athletics .... Mr. Michael SMELKINSON
26 Exec Dir Public Relations/Mktg .... Ms. Elizabeth S. HOMAN
09 Exec Dir Plng/Research & Org Dev .... Ms. Zoe A. IRVIN
38 Director Counseling & Career Svcs .... Dr. Jay J. COUGHLIN, III
20 Assoc Vice Pres Academic Affairs .... Dr. Laura J. CRIPPS

Johns Hopkins University (E)

3400 N. Charles Street, Baltimore MD 21218-2680
County: Independent City FICE Identification: 002077
Unit ID: 162928
Telephone: (410) 516-8000 Carnegie Class: DU-Highest
FAX Number: N/A Calendar System: Semester
URL: www.jhu.edu
Established: 1876 Annual Undergrad Tuition & Fees: $54,160
Enrollment: 28,890 Coed
Affiliation or Control: Independent Non-Profit IRS Status: 501(c)3
Highest Offering: Doctorate
Accreditation: M, ANEST, CACREP, CAMPEP, DIET, DIETC, DMS, HSA, IPSY, MED, MIL, NMT, NURSE, PH

01 President .... Mr. Ronald J. DANIELS
100 Vice President/Chief of Staff .... Ms. Kerry A. ATES
05 Provost & Sr VP Acad Affs .... Dr. Sunil KUMAR
17 Int CEO Johns Hopkins Medicine .... Dr. Theodore DEWEESE
10 Sr VP Finance & Administration .... Mr. Laurent HELLER
30 VP for Development & Alum Relations .... Mr. Fritz SCHROEDER
26 Vice Pres for Communications .... Mr. Andrew GREEN
43 Vice Pres/General Counsel .... Mr. Paul PINEAU
86 Vice Pres State and Local Affairs .... Ms. Maria TILDON
18 Vice Pres Facilities/Real Estate .... Mr. Robert MCLEAN
15 Vice Pres Human Resources .... Mr. Pierre JOANIS
21 Vice Pres/CFO & Treasurer .... Ms. Helene GRADY
115 Vice Pres Chief Investment Officer .... Mr. Jason PERLIONI
117 Vice Provost and Chief Risk Officer .... Dr. Jonathan LINKS
32 Vice Prov Student Affairs .... Ms. Rachelle HERNANDEZ
36 Vice Provost Career Services .... Dr. Farouk DEY
20 Vice Provost Faculty Affairs .... Dr. Ralph ETIENNE-CUMMINGS
07 Vice Provost Admiss & Fin Aid .... Mr. David PHILLIPS
23 Vice Prov Student Health .... Mr. Kevin SHOLLENBERGER
28 Vice Prov/Chief Diversity Officer .... Dr. Katrina CALDWELL
58 Vice Prov Grad and Prof Education .... Dr. Nancy KASS
13 Int Vice Provost and CIO .... Mr. Dean ZARRIELLO
22 Vice Provost Institutional Equity .... Ms. Shanon SHUMPERT
46 Vice Provost Research .... Dr. Denis WIRTZ
09 Vice Provost Institutional Research .... Dr. Ratna SARKAR
88 Assoc Vice Prov International Svcs .... Mr. James BRAILER
06 University Registrar .... Ms. Amynah MITHANI
82 Dean School Adv Intl Studies .... Mr. James STEINBERG
49 Dean Krieger Sch Arts/Sciences .... Dr. Christopher CELENZA
50 Dean Carey Business School .... Dr. Alexander TRIANTIS
53 Dean School of Education .... Dr. Christopher MORPHEW
54 Dean Whiting Sch Engineering .... Dr. Ed SCHLESINGER
63 Int Dean School of Medicine .... Dr. Theodore DEWEESE
66 Dean School of Nursing .... Dr. Sarah SZANTON
69 Dean Bloomberg School Public Health .... Dr. Ellen MACKENZIE
08 Dean Sheridan Libraries and Museums .... Mr. Winston G. TABB
64 Dean Peabody Institute .... Dr. Fred BRONSTEIN
88 Director Applied Physics Lab .... Mr. Ralph SEMMEL
96 Chief Procurement Officer .... Mr. Brian SMITH
21 Controller .... Mr. Scott JONAS
19 Vice President for Public Safety .... Dr. Branville BARD, JR.
116 Exec Director Internal Audits .... Mr. James JARRELL
27 Director Strategic Communications .... Ms. Marianne VON NORDECK
104 Director Study Abroad .... Ms. Jessica MERVIS
41 Athletic Director .... Ms. Jennifer BAKER
101 Secretary of the Institution/Board .... Ms. Maureen MARSH
04 Admin Assistant to the President .... Ms. Jodi MILLER
37 Assoc Vice Provost Financial Aid .... Mr. Tom MCDERMOTT

Lincoln College of Technology (F)

9325 Snowden River Parkway, Columbia MD 21046
County: Howard FICE Identification: 007936
Unit ID: 163028
Telephone: (410) 290-7100 Carnegie Class: Assoc/HVT-High Trad
FAX Number: (410) 290-7880 Calendar System: Quarter
URL: www.lincolntech.com
Established: 1978 Annual Undergrad Tuition & Fees: N/A
Enrollment: 870 Coed
Affiliation or Control: Proprietary IRS Status: Proprietary
Highest Offering: Associate Degree
Accreditation: ACCSC

01 Campus President .... Mr. Cory HUGHES

Loyola University Maryland (G)

4501 N Charles Street, Baltimore MD 21210-2694
County: Independent City FICE Identification: 002078
Unit ID: 163046
Telephone: (410) 617-2000 Carnegie Class: Masters/L
FAX Number: N/A Calendar System: Semester
URL: www.loyola.edu
Established: 1852 Annual Undergrad Tuition & Fees: $51,100
Enrollment: 5,282 Coed
Affiliation or Control: Roman Catholic IRS Status: 501(c)3
Highest Offering: Doctorate
Accreditation: M, CACREP, CLPSY, SP

01 President .... Mr. Terrence SAWYER
05 Acting Provost/VP Academic Affairs .... Dr. Cheryl MOORE-THOMAS
10 VP for Finance/Admin & Treasurer .... Mr. John COPPOLA
111 Interim Vice Pres for Advancement .... Mr. Brian M. OAKES
32 VP Student Development .... Dr. Deborah MELZER
84 Vice Pres Enrollment Management .... Mr. Eric NICHOLS
09 Director of Institutional Research .... Ms. Nicole JACOBS
13 CIO/Assoc Vice Pres Technology .... Mr. Randall SABA
18 Assoc VP Facilities/Campus Services .... Ms. Helen SCHNEIDER
15 Assoc Vice Pres for Human Resources .... Ms. Kathleen PARNELL
110 Asst Vice Pres for External Affairs .... Ms. Joan FLYNN
114 AVP Budget/Business Planning .... Mr. Sean FRANCIS
35 Asst Vice Pres Student Development .... Ms. Michelle CHEATEM
26 Assoc VP Marketing/Communications .... Ms. Kristen MCGUIRE
41 Asst VP/Director of Athletics .... Ms. Donna WOODRUFF
07 Dean Undergraduate Admissions .... Ms. Jennifer LOUDEN
123 Exec Dir of Graduate Admissions .... Ms. Maureen BUSH
27 Dir Marketing and Communications .... Ms. Rita BUETTNER
06 Director of Records .... Ms. Deborah MILLER
85 Dean of International Programs .... Dr. Andre COLOMBAT
08 Director of Library .... Ms. Katy O'NEILL
42 Director of Campus Ministry .... Mr. Sean BRAY
88 Executive Dir York Road Initiative .... Ms. Gia G. MCGINNIS
88 PM Women's Ctr/Sex Assault Prev .... Ms. Melissa LEES
28 Director ALANA Services .... Ms. Raven WILLIAMS

21 Controller ... Ms. Jill HECKLINGER
109 Director Event Svcs/Auxiliary Mgmt ... Mr. Joseph BRADLEY
88 Director Environment Health/Safety ... Mr. Thomas HETTLEMAN
19 Dir of Public Safety/Campus Police ... Mr. Adrian BLACK
29 Director Alumni Engagement ... Ms. Colleen RIOPKO
49 Dean College of Arts & Sciences ... Dr. Steve FOWL
53 Dean School of Education ... Dr. Afra HERSI
50 Dean Sellinger Sch Business & Mgmt ... Ms. Mary Ann SCULLY
83 Assoc Dean Social Sciences/Graduate ... Dr. Jeffrey BARNETT
50 Asst Dean for Business Programs ... Ms. Susan HASLER
88 Sr Assoc Director Facilities ... Mr. Joseph GRIFFIN
105 Dir Web Development/Design ... Mr. David BLOHM
100 Chief of Staff ... Ms. Stephanie COLDREN

Maple Springs Baptist Bible College & Seminary (A)

4130 Belt Road, Capitol Heights MD 20743-5712
County: Prince Georges — FICE Identification: 038224
Unit ID: 446394
Telephone: (301) 736-3631 — Carnegie Class: Spec-4-yr-Faith
FAX Number: (301) 735-6507 — Calendar System: Semester
URL: www.msbbcs.edu
Established: 1986 — Annual Undergrad Tuition & Fees: $5,400
Enrollment: N/A — Coed
Affiliation or Control: Baptist — IRS Status: 501(c)3
Highest Offering: Doctorate
Accreditation: TRACS

01 Acting President ... Dr. Carl KEELS
05 Vice President Academic Affairs ... Dr. Luther S. BUCK
10 Vice Pres Finance & Administration ... Mr. Keith DUKES
73 Academic Dean Seminary Division ... Dr. Dana A. VAN BRAKLE
73 Academic Dean Bible College Div ... Dr. Carl E. KEELS
30 Chief Development/Advancement Ofcr ... Dr. George HOLMES
06 Director Admissions & Records ... Rev. Alonzo K. JACKSON, SR.
09 Dir Institutional Plng/Assessment ... Dr. Marquez BALL
32 Director Student Affairs ... Dr. Catherine BORGES-JOHNSON
08 Dir Library/Instruc Resource Center ... Mr. Darren JONES
37 Director Financial Aid ... Rev. Himie PICKETT
07 Asst Dir of Admissions/Records ... Mr. Timothy L. WASHINGTON
21 Associate Business Officer ... Mrs. Diane JENKINS

Maryland Institute College of Art (B)

1300 W. Mount Royal Avenue, Baltimore MD 21217-4191
County: Independent City — FICE Identification: 002080
Unit ID: 163295
Telephone: (410) 669-9200 — Carnegie Class: Spec-4-yr-Arts
FAX Number: (410) 669-9206 — Calendar System: Semester
URL: www.mica.edu
Established: 1826 — Annual Undergrad Tuition & Fees: $49,190
Enrollment: 1,892 — Coed
Affiliation or Control: Independent Non-Profit — IRS Status: 501(c)3
Highest Offering: Master's
Accreditation: M, ART

01 President ... Mr. Samuel HOI
05 Vice Pres Academic Affairs/Provost ... Ms. Tiffany HOLMES
10 Vice Pres Finance & Business Svcs ... Mr. Martin LEMELLE
32 Vice Pres Student Affairs ... Mr. Michael PATTERSON
07 VP Admissions/Financial Aid ... Dr. Audrey TANNER
13 Vice Pres Technology Systems & Svcs ... Ms. Alexa KIM
111 Vice Pres for Advancement ... Mr. Don JONES
26 VP for Strategic Communications ... Mr. Christian LALLO
11 VP for Operations & Technology ... Ms. Alexa KIM
97 Vice Provost Open Studies ... Mr. David GRACYALNY
46 Vice Provost Research/Grad Studies ... Ms. Stacey SALAZAR
04 Executive Assistant to President ... Vacant
37 Assoc VP Financial Aid ... Mr. DeRodrick JONKINS
15 VP People Belonging Culture ... Ms. Shanna HINES
123 Director of Graduate Admissions ... Mr. Christopher HARRING
06 Assoc Dean Enrol Svcs/Registrar ... Ms. Christine PETERSON
114 Director Budget ... Ms. Brigitte SULLIVAN
39 Director Residence Life ... Mr. Robert ALICEA
36 Director Career Development ... Ms. Jeremy GOLDSTEIN
23 AVP Health Services ... Ms. Judith KINNEY
35 Director Student Activities ... Ms. Karol MARTINEZ-DOANE
08 Director & Head Librarian ... Ms. Heather SLANIA
44 Director Annual Fund ... Mr. Mansoor ALI
88 Director Exhibitions ... Vacant
88 Dir Data Mgmt/Registration Cont Std ... Ms. Sarah MARAVETZ
84 Dir Enroll Svcs/Stdnt Records/Rsrch ... Mr. Hadley GARBART
19 Director of Campus Safety ... Mr. Marlon BYRD
88 Director Events ... Mr. Jon LIPITZ
88 Director Operation Services ... Mr. Chris BOHASKA
102 Director Corp/Found/Govt Relations ... Ms. Sara WARREN
24 Director Technical Support Services ... Mr. John RHODES
105 Director Network Services ... Mr. David APAW
40 Manager College Store ... Ms. Kerri LITZ
28 Dir of Diversity/Equity/Inclusion ... Ms. Shannon INGRAM

Maryland University of Integrative Health (C)

7750 Montpelier Road, Laurel MD 20723-6010
County: Howard — FICE Identification: 025784
Unit ID: 164085
Telephone: (410) 888-9048 — Carnegie Class: Spec-4-yr-Other Health
FAX Number: (410) 888-9004 — Calendar System: Trimester
URL: www.muih.edu
Established: 1981 — Annual Graduate Tuition & Fees: N/A
Enrollment: 815 — Coed
Affiliation or Control: Independent Non-Profit — IRS Status: 501(c)3
Highest Offering: Doctorate; No Undergraduates
Accreditation: M, ACUP

01 President/CFO/COO ... Mr. Marc LEVIN
05 Provost/VP Academic Affairs ... Dr. Christina SAX
10 VP Finance/Administration ... Mr. James COBB, JR.
26 VP Marketing/Enrollment Management ... Mr. Nigel LONG
15 VP Human Enrichment ... Ms. Melissa L. CAHILL
20 Assoc Provost Academic Operations ... Ms. Mary Ellen HRUTKA
108 Asst Provost Acad Assessment/Accred ... Ms. Deneb FALABELLA
20 Dean of Academic Affairs ... Mr. James SNOW
32 Dean of Student Affairs ... Ms. Michelle COLEMAN
76 Asst Dean of Academic Affairs ... Dr. Kathleen WARNER
07 Director of Admissions ... Mr. Kevin GORE
37 Director Student Financial Aid ... Ms. Kristina DEAN
06 Registrar ... Ms. Rhonda STOKES
13 VP Information Technology ... Mr. Lesly ELVARD
04 Exec Asst to the President ... Ms. Mia MATHIS
08 Head Librarian ... Ms. Carissa HERNANDEZ
09 Director of Institutional Research ... Mr. Lawrence MCGILL

McDaniel College (D)

2 College Hill, Westminster MD 21157-4390
County: Carroll — FICE Identification: 002109
Unit ID: 164270
Telephone: (410) 848-7000 — Carnegie Class: Masters/L
FAX Number: (410) 857-2279 — Calendar System: Semester
URL: www.mcdaniel.edu
Established: 1867 — Annual Undergrad Tuition & Fees: $45,876
Enrollment: 2,931 — Coed
Affiliation or Control: Independent Non-Profit — IRS Status: 501(c)3
Highest Offering: Master's
Accreditation: M, CAEPN, SW

01 President ... Dr. Julia JASKEN
05 Acting Provost & Dean of Faculty ... Dr. Wendy MORRIS
10 Vice Pres Administration & Finance ... Mr. Eric SIMON
84 VP of Enrollment Management ... Ms. Janelle HOLMBOE
111 VP for Institutional Advancement ... Mr. David SEARS
32 Dean of Students ... Ms. Elizabeth TOWLE
41 Director Athletics ... Mr. Adam HERTZ
15 Assoc VP for Administration ... Ms. Jennifer GLENNON
29 Assoc VP Alumni & Parent Engagement ... Ms. Heidi REIGEL
111 Sr AVP of Institutional Advancement ... Mr. Chip JUNKIN
58 Dean Graduate/Prof Studies ... Dr. Vickie MAZER
10 Controller ... Ms. Julie FISHER
07 Dean of Admissions ... Ms. Jill CENTOFANTI
28 Assoc Provost Equity & Belonging ... Mr. Richard SMITH
89 Assoc Dean for Student Development ... Ms. Erin BENEVENTO
39 Director of Residence Life ... Mr. Michael ROBBINS
38 Director of Wellness Center ... Ms. Heidi HUBER
19 Director of Campus Safety ... Mr. Eric IMMLER
08 Director of Hoover Library ... Mr. David BRENNAN
92 Director of Honors Program ... Dr. Corey WRONSKI-MAYERSAK
06 Registrar ... Ms. Susan FIELDHOUSE
09 Director Institutional Research ... Ms. Robin DEWEY
106 Director Online Educ/E-learning ... Mr. Steve KERBY
15 Director Human Resources ... Ms. Rose MERCIER
13 Chief Information Officer ... Mr. Bill LEIMBACH
18 Assoc VP for Facilities Mgmt ... Mr. Andrew VAN DER STUYF
96 Director of Purchasing/Receiving ... Ms. Ellen RUGEMER
109 Dir Conferences/Auxiliary Services ... Ms. Mary J. COLBERT
26 Director of Public Relations ... Ms. Cheryl KNAUER
105 Website Manager ... Ms. Tara DUNSMORE
36 Assoc Dir Career Development ... Mr. Daniel DEHOLLANDER
104 Assoc Dir International Programs ... Ms. Brooke HAIN
37 Director of Financial Aid ... Ms. Kemia HIMON
30 Assoc VP Development ... Ms. Carolyn SALAZAR

Montgomery College (E)

9221 Corporate Boulevard, Rockville MD 20850
County: Montgomery — FICE Identification: 006911
Unit ID: 163426
Telephone: (240) 567-5267 — Carnegie Class: Assoc/HT-Mix Trad/Non
FAX Number: (240) 567-9129 — Calendar System: Semester
URL: www.montgomerycollege.edu
Established: 1946 — Annual Undergrad Tuition & Fees (In-District): $10,254
Enrollment: 20,037 — Coed
Affiliation or Control: Local — IRS Status: 501(c)3
Highest Offering: Associate Degree
Accreditation: M, ADNUR, ART, CAHIIM, DMS, MUS, NAEYC, POLYT, PTAA, RAD, SURGT

01 President ... Dr. Jermaine WILLIAMS
05 Sr VP for Academic Affairs ... Dr. Sanjay RAI
32 Sr VP for Student Affairs ... Dr. Monica R. BROWN
11 SVP Fiscal/Administrative Svcs ... Mr. Sherwin COLLETTE
111 Int SVP Advancement/Cmty Engagement ... Ms. Joyce MATTHEWS
100 Chief of Staff/Chief Strategy Ofcr ... Dr. Stephen D. CAIN
88 Deputy COS Pres Pub/Ops ... Dr. Meghan GIBBONS
88 Deputy COS Planning & Policy ... Dr. Kevin LONG
35 Assoc SVP for Student Affairs ... Dr. Melissa GREGORY
88 Dpt Ch Analytics/Insights Officer ... Ms. Nadine PORTER
20 Assoc SVP for Academic Affairs ... Dr. Carolyn TERRY
20 Assoc SVP for Academic Affairs ... Dr. Elena SAENZ
86 Chief Government Relations Officer ... Ms. Susan MADDEN
43 General Counsel ... Mr. Timothy D. DIETZ
04 Assistant to the President ... Ms. Lisannie MONTILLA
101 BOT/Spec Asst to the President ... Dr. Michelle T. SCOTT
101 Mgr of Bd of Trustees Svcs & Ops ... Ms. Lily LEE
12 Int VP & Provost Rockville Campus ... Mr. Eric BENJAMIN
12 VP & Provost Germantown Campus ... Vacant
12 VP & Prov Takoma Pk/Silver Spring C ... Dr. Brad J. STEWART
103 VP/Prov App Tech/Tech Ed/WD&CE ... Mr. George M. PAYNE
119 Int Chief Info Security Officer ... Ms. Nell FELDMAN
13 Chief Technology Officer ... Mr. Anwar KARIM
15 VP Human Res & Strat Talent Mgmt ... Ms. Krista WALKER
18 VP Facilities & Security ... Mr. Marvin J. MILLS
26 Assoc SVP Advance & Cmty Engagement ... Mr. Ray GILMER
25 Assoc SVP Advance/Cmty Engagement ... Ms. Rose GARVIN AQUILINO
106 VP E-Learning/Innov/Teaching Exc ... Dr. Michael MILLS
50 Dean Acct/Bus Admin/Econ/Paralegal ... Dr. Kathryn DAVIS
88 Acting Dean Eng/Dev Eng/Reading ... Dr. Elizabeth BENTON
50 Actg Dean Acct/Bus Admin/Econ ... Dr. John COLITON
83 Int Dean Anth/Cr Just/Ed/Psych/Soc ... Dr. Eric M. BENJAMIN
81 Dean Biology/Biotech/Chemistry ... Dr. James SNIEZEK
54 Dean Eng/Comp Sci/Netwk/Cyber Sec ... Dr. Muhammad KEHNEMOUYI
88 Chief Analytics & Insight Officer ... Mr. John HAMMAN
76 Int Dean Health Sci/Health/PE/Nurs ... Dr. Monique DAVIS
88 Dean ELAP Linguistics/Comm Studies ... Dr. Fiona GLADE
79 Dean Hist/PolSci/World Lang/Am Sign ... Dr. Sharon FECHTER
75 Dean Applied Tech & Gudelsky Inst ... Mr. Ed ROBERTS
50 Dean Bus Info/Tech/Safety ... Mr. Steve GREENFIELD
51 Dean Cmty Educ & Extended Learning ... Ms. Dorothy UMANS
51 Dean Adult Eng Lang & GED Programs ... Dr. Donna KINERNEY
81 Dean Mathematics/Dev Math/Stats ... Dr. Milton NASH
57 Dean Visual/Perform & Media Arts ... Dr. Frank TREZZA
35 Dean Stdnt Affairs Gtown Campus ... Dr. Jamin BARTOLOMEO
35 Dean Stdnt Affairs Rockville Campus ... Dr. Tonya MASON
35 Dean Stdnt Affairs TP/SS Campus ... Ms. Janee MCFADDEN
53 Dir School of Education ... Ms. Debra POESE
41 Athletic Director ... Ms. Tarlough GASQUE
30 Exec MC Foundation/VP Dev ... Ms. Joyce MATTHEWS
112 Director of Planned Giving ... Ms. Francene WALKER
88 Exec Dir H. Pinkney Life Sci Park ... Ms. Martha SCHOONMAKER
09 Dir Inst Research & Effectiveness ... Dr. Arlene BLAYLOCK
96 Dir of Procurement ... Mr. Patrick JOHNSON
37 Collegewide Dir of Financial Aid ... Ms. Judith M. TAYLOR
84 Dir Enroll Svcs & College Registrar ... Mr. Ernest CARTLEDGE
19 Int Dir Pub Safety/Emergency Mgmt ... Mr. Adam REID
28 Chief Equity & Diversity Officer ... Ms. Sharon BLAND
108 Dir of Assessment ... Dr. Cassandra JONES
102 Dir Corp and Foundation Relations ... Mr. Stuart TART
29 Dir Alumni Relations ... Mr. Greg ENLOE
08 Dir College Libraries & Info Svcs ... Ms. Suzette SPENCER
16 Dir Employee & Labor Relations ... Mr. Santo A. SCRIMENTI
104 Coord of Travel & Study Abroad ... Dr. Gregory MALVEAUX

Morgan State University (F)

1700 East Cold Spring Lane, Baltimore MD 21251-0001
County: Independent City — FICE Identification: 002083
Unit ID: 163453
Telephone: (443) 885-3333 — Carnegie Class: DU-Higher
FAX Number: (443) 885-3698 — Calendar System: Semester
URL: www.morgan.edu
Established: 1867 — Annual Undergrad Tuition & Fees (In-State): $7,628
Enrollment: 7,634 — Coed
Affiliation or Control: State — IRS Status: 501(c)3
Highest Offering: Doctorate
Accreditation: M, AAFCS, CAEPN, DIETD, JOUR, LSAR, MLS, MUS, NURSE, PH, PLNG, SW

01 President ... Dr. David WILSON
05 Provost/Sr VP Academic Affairs ... Dr. Hongtao YU
10 Vice Pres Finance & Management ... Mr. Sidney EVANS
13 Vice Pres for Technology & CIO ... Dr. Adebisi OLADIPUPO
32 Vice Pres Student Affairs ... Dr. Kevin BANKS
30 Vice Pres Institutional Advancement ... Ms. Donna HOWARD
84 VP for Enroll Mgmt/Student Success ... Dr. Kara TURNER
21 Assoc Vice Pres Finance/Deputy CFO ... Mr. David LACHINA
20 Assoc Vice Pres for Academic Affs ... Ms. Patricia WILLIAMS-LESSANE
35 Associate VP Student Affairs ... Vacant
100 Chief of Staff ... Dr. Don-Terry VEAL
49 Dean College of Liberal Arts ... Dr. Mbare NGOM
50 Dean School Business & Management ... Dr. Fikru BOGHOSSIAN
53 Dean School of Education ... Dr. Glenda PRIME
54 Dean School of Engineering ... Dr. Oscar BARTON
58 Dean of the Graduate School ... Dr. Mark GARRISON
48 Dean School of Architecture ... Dr. Mary Anne AKERS
70 Dean School of Social Work ... Dr. Anna MCPHATTER
69 Dean School of Community Health ... Dr. Kim SYDNOR
37 Director of Financial Aid ... Ms. Tanya WILKERSON
38 Director of Counseling Services ... Ms. Sonya CLYBURN
08 Director of Library ... Dr. Richard BRADBERRY
06 Director of Records/Registration ... Ms. Keisha CAMPBELL
07 Interim Director of Admissions ... Ms. Keisha CAMPBELL
36 Director of Career Development ... Ms. Seana COULTER
15 Assoc Vice Pres Human Resources ... Ms. Chevonie OYEGOKE
29 AVP Alumni Relations ... Ms. Heidi BRUCE
14 Sr Director Enterprise Services ... Mr. Gilbert MORGAN
86 Director Government Relations ... Mrs. Joan CARTER-CONWAY
09 Director of Institutional Research ... Ms. Cheryl ROLLINS
18 Director Physical Plant ... Vacant
26 Asst Vice Pres Public Relations ... Mr. Larry JONES
96 Director of Procurement ... Ms. Erin JAMES
28 Asst VP for Diversity/EEO/Title IX ... Ms. Tara BERRIEN
45 Asst Vice Pres Planning/Inst Effect ... Dr. Linda MEHLINGER
104 Director Study Abroad ... Mrs. Marisa GRAY
106 Dir Online Education/E-learning ... Ms. Cynthia BROWN-LAVEIST

108 Asst VP Institutional Assessment ... Dr. Solomon ALAO
19 Chief of Police ... Mr. Lance HATCHER
39 Director Residence Life & Housing ... Dr. Douglas GWYNN
41 Athletic Director ... Ms. Dena FREEMAN-PATTON
43 General Counsel ... Ms. Julie GOODWIN

Mount St. Mary's University (A)

16300 Old Emmitsburg Road,
Emmitsburg MD 21727-7799
County: Frederick | FICE Identification: 002086
Unit ID: 163462
Telephone: (301) 447-6122 | Carnegie Class: Masters/M
FAX Number: (301) 447-5634 | Calendar System: Semester
URL: www.msmary.edu
Established: 1808 | Annual Undergrad Tuition & Fees: $43,650
Enrollment: 2,560 | Coed
Affiliation or Control: Roman Catholic | IRS Status: 501(c)3
Highest Offering: Master's
Accreditation: M, CAEPN, CEA, IACBE, THEOL

01 President ... Dr. Timothy E. TRAINOR
05 Provost ... Dr. Boyd CREASMAN
03 Vice President/Seminary Rector ... Msgr. Andrew R. BAKER, S.T.D.
11 Executive Vice President ... Dr. Kraig E. SHEETZ
10 Vice Pres for Business & Finance ... Mr. William E. DAVIES
84 VP Enrollment/Marketing and Comm ... Mr. Jack J. CHIELLI
32 Vice President for Student Life ... Dr. Levi K. ESSES
28 Vice President for Equity & Success ... Dr. Paula M. WHETSEL-RIBEAU
111 Vice President for Advancement ... Mr. Robert J. BRENNAN
20 Assoc Provost ... Dr. David M. MCCARTHY
58 Assoc Provost Grad/Continuing Ed ... Dr. Jennifer L. STAIGER
49 Dean College of Liberal Arts ... Dr. Bryan J. ZYGMONT
50 Dean Richard J Bolte Sr Sch of Bus ... Dr. John NAURIGHT
81 Dean School Natural Science & Math ... Dr. Christine MCCAUSLIN
53 Dean School of Education ... Dr. Barbara A. MARINAK
04 Sr Exec Assistant to the President ... Ms. June B. MILLER
41 Director of Athletics ... Ms. Lynne P. ROBINSON
35 Dean of Students ... Vacant
42 Chaplain ... Fr. Martin O. MORAN, III
36 Director Career Center ... Mr. Matthew POUSS
108 Exec Dir Strat Plng/Inst Effective ... Dr. Jeffrey A. SIMMONS
37 Director of Financial Aid ... Ms. Brenda K. DAYHOFF
06 Registrar ... Mr. Christopher WEBER
07 Director of Admissions ... Mr. Eric M. DANIELSON
08 Director of the Library ... Ms. Jessica W. BOYER
26 Director of PR & Communications ... Ms. Donna J. KLINGER
30 Director of Development ... Ms. Kimberly T. JOHNSON
29 Director of Alumni Engagement ... Ms. Emily A. MYERS
88 Director of University Operations ... Ms. Maureen PLANT
15 Director of Human Resources ... Ms. Kristin M. HURLEY
38 Director Student Counseling ... Mr. Gerald T. ROOTH
19 Director of Public Safety ... Mr. Ronald HIBBARD
24 Director of Media Systems ... Ms. Lisa REED
21 Controller ... Ms. Christine SNEERINGER
114 Director of Budget ... Ms. Tina RYDER
92 Director of the Honors Program ... Dr. Sarah SCOTT
18 Director of Physical Plant ... Ms. Kimberly S. KLABE
13 Chief Information Technology Ofcr ... Mr. David KING

Ner Israel Rabbinical College (B)

400 Mount Wilson Lane, Baltimore MD 21208-1198
County: Baltimore | FICE Identification: 002087
Unit ID: 163532
Telephone: (410) 484-7200 | Carnegie Class: Spec-4-yr-Faith
FAX Number: (410) 484-3060 | Calendar System: Semester
URL: www.nirc.edu
Established: 1933 | Annual Undergrad Tuition & Fees: $12,400
Enrollment: 471 | Male
Affiliation or Control: Independent Non-Profit | IRS Status: 501(c)3
Highest Offering: Doctorate
Accreditation: RABN

01 President ... Rabbi Boruch Y. NEUBERGER
05 Chief Academic Officer ... Rabbi Aharon FELDMAN
88 Executive Director ... Mr. Jerome H. KADDEN
07 Director of Admissions ... Rabbi Beryl WEISBORD
11 Director of Administrative Services ... Mr. Larry RIBAKOW
06 Registrar ... Rabbi Joseph IFRAH
85 Foreign Student Advisor ... Rabbi Eliyahu HAKKAKIAN
30 Director of Development ... Rabbi Louis HOFFMAN
45 Director of Planning ... Rabbi Leonard OBERSTEIN
37 Director Student Financial Aid ... Rabbi Shmuel SCHACHTER
18 Chief Physical Plant ... Mr. David FRIEDMAN
08 Head Librarian ... Rabbi Avrohom SHNIDMAN
39 Director of Student Housing ... Rabbi Emanuel GOLDFEIZ
29 Associate Director Alumni Relations ... Rabbi Eli GREENGART

Notre Dame of Maryland University (C)

4701 N Charles Street, Baltimore MD 21210-2404
County: Independent City | FICE Identification: 002065
Unit ID: 163578
Telephone: (410) 435-0100 | Carnegie Class: Masters/L
FAX Number: (410) 532-5791 | Calendar System: Semester
URL: www.ndm.edu
Established: 1873 | Annual Undergrad Tuition & Fees: $39,675
Enrollment: 2,233 | Female
Affiliation or Control: Roman Catholic | IRS Status: 501(c)3
Highest Offering: Doctorate
Accreditation: M, ACBSP, CAEPN, CEA, NURSE, PHAR

01 President ... Dr. Marylou YAM
05 Vice President Academic Affairs ... Dr. Martha WALKER
111 Vice Pres Institutional Advancement ... Ms. Kelley KILDUFF
84 Vice Pres Enrollment Management ... Mr. Scott BRIELL
10 Vice Pres for Finance & Admin ... Mr. Sean DELANEY
32 Assoc Vice President Student Life ... Meaghan DAVIDSON
20 Associate VP Academic Affairs ... Dr. Suzan HARKNESS
37 Director of Financial Aid ... Mr. Christopher HANLON
100 Chief of Staff ... Mr. Gregory FITZGERALD
06 Registrar ... Ms. Susanna PRICE
36 Director Career Center ... Mr. Alan JONES
13 Director Information Technology ... Mr. Warren SZELISTOWSKI
29 Director of Alumnae Relations ... Ms. Alexandra DEJOHN
08 Librarian ... Ms. Mary O'NEILL
49 Assoc Dean School Arts/Sciences/Bus ... Vacant
07 Interim Director of Admissions ... Ms. Marci LEADBETTER
09 Dir Inst Research/Effectiveness ... Ms. Luz CACEDA
15 Director of Human Resources ... Ms. Theresa SHRADER
18 Director of Facility Management ... Vacant
21 Controller ... Ms. Victoria WASHINGTON
38 Director Counseling Center ... Vacant
19 Director of Public Safety ... Mr. Gene TAYLOR
40 Bookstore Manager ... Vacant
41 Athletic Director ... Ms. Ashley HODGES
42 Director Mission & Campus Ministry ... Ms. Julia CAMPAGNA
67 Dean School of Pharmacy ... Dr. Matthew SHIMODA
07 Director Pharmacy Admissions ... Mr. Larry SHATTUCK
25 Chief Contracts/Grants Admin ... Mr. Carroll GALVIN
26 Sr Dir University Communications ... Ms. Damita MCDONALD

Prince George's Community College (D)

301 Largo Road, Largo MD 20774-2199
County: Prince Georges | FICE Identification: 002089
Unit ID: 163657
Telephone: (301) 546-7422 | Carnegie Class: Assoc/HT-Mix Trad/Non
FAX Number: N/A | Calendar System: Semester
URL: www.pgcc.edu
Established: 1958 | Annual Undergrad Tuition & Fees (In-District): $6,026
Enrollment: 11,357 | Coed
Affiliation or Control: Local | IRS Status: 501(c)3
Highest Offering: Associate Degree
Accreditation: M, ADNUR, CAHIIM, COARC, EMT, MAC, NMT, RAD, SURGT

01 President ... Dr. Falecia D. WILLIAMS
05 Exec Vice Pres and Provost for TLSS ... Dr. Clayton A. RAILEY
32 Vice Pres Student Affairs ... Dr. Tyson J. BEALE
10 Vice Pres Admin/Financial Svcs ... Terri K. BACOTE-CHARLES
13 Vice Pres Enterprise Technology ... Dr. Rhonda SPELLS-FENTY
26 AVP of Strategy/Planning/Effect ... Vacant
103 Interim AVP Partnerships & Econ Dev ... Michael W. SMITH
15 AVP Human Resources (HROD) ... Dr. Lynne I. ADAMS
20 Sr Dir Curr/Programs/Regulation ... Laura ELLSWORTH
88 AVP Administrative Support ... Dr. Rachel N. BONAPARTE
121 Dean Student Success/Engagement ... Dr. Scheherazade W. FORMAN
76 Dean Health Sci/Business/Public Svc ... Angela D. ANDERSON
79 Dean Humanities/English/Social Sci ... Nicole A. CURRIER
84 Dean of Student Enrollment Services ... Vacant
54 Dean Science/Tech/Engr/Math ... Calvin E. STANSBURY
81 Interim Associate Dean STEM ... Regina R. BENTLEY
78 Dean of Adult & Community Education ... Barbara DENMAN
88 Associate Dean of HES ... Mirian TORAIN
23 Int Assoc Dean Health/Well/Hospital ... Wynnona WARE-JACKSON
09 Exec Dir Research/Assessment/Effect ... Vacant
88 Executive Director Adjunct Fac Dev ... Dr. Beverly REED
86 Senior Director of Compliance ... Susan V. WATSON
88 Associate Dean Health/PSCE ... Laura R. ELLSWORTH
27 Senior Director Comm/Marketing ... Angie D. CREWS
19 Chief of College/DPS ... Lawrence B. AMES, JR.
21 Controller/Financial Svcs & Opers ... Dwight WASHINGTON
12 Program Director Laurel College Ctr ... Vacant
55 Director of Adult Education ... Sara MCDONOUGH
109 Director of Auxiliary Services ... Vacant
88 Sr Director Prof and Org Dev ... Dr. Audrey DAVIS
12 Program Director UTC ... Dr. Rosa SMITH
88 Director Entrepreneurial Dev ... June EVANS
88 Director HR Compensation/Benefits ... Dr. Keith E. MURVIN
18 Executive Director of Facilities ... Vacant
111 Executive Director Inst Advancement ... Brenda MITCHELL
14 Executive Director ERP Applications ... William ANDERSON
88 Director Admin/Financial Support ... Toni E. HILL
96 Director of Procurement ... Vacant
08 Director Library/Learning Resources ... Priscilla C. THOMPSON
117 Director Emergency Management ... Dr. Meloyde R. BATTEN-MICKENS
88 Program Director Const/Energy/Trans ... Marra ANTHONY
88 Director Facilities Operations ... Clarence V. BRYANT
88 Director College/Career Transition ... Cecilia KNOX
36 Dir of Student Acad/Career Adv ... Crystal M. SMITH
37 Director Student Financial Aid ... Thelma ROSS
88 Program Director Disability Support ... Thomas MAYS
41 Director Intercollegiate Athl/Intr ... JoAnn TODARO
88 Program Director Student Engagement ... Paulett MCINTOSH
93 Director Student Support and Trio ... Dr. Roosevelt CHARLES
07 Director Recruitment/Admissions ... Ronald D. WEIST
06 Registrar ... Rachel A. POLETO
88 Principal Director Nat Cyberwatch ... Michael W. SMITH
119 Director Network Infrastructure/Adm ... Manuel A. ARRINGTON
88 Senior Director Tech Client Support ... Paulette R. FOXX-DAWODU
88 Director of ERP Solution Services ... Doris M. HARRIS
88 Director of Testing Center ... William GARDNER
28 Director Governance and Diversity ... Andristine M. ROBINSON
25 Director Grants/Resource Dev ... Anne SHEPARD
04 Exec Associate to the President ... Greta R. MARTIN
30 Assistant Director of Development ... Vacant
44 Manager Annual Giving & Alum Rels ... Robin P. HAWKINS

St. John's College (E)

60 College Avenue, Annapolis MD 21401
County: Anne Arundel | FICE Identification: 002092
Unit ID: 163976
Telephone: (410) 263-2371 | Carnegie Class: Bac-A&S
FAX Number: (410) 626-2886 | Calendar System: Semester
URL: www.sjc.edu
Established: 1784 | Annual Undergrad Tuition & Fees: $35,935
Enrollment: 446 | Coed
Affiliation or Control: Independent Non-Profit | IRS Status: 501(c)3
Highest Offering: Master's
Accreditation: M

01 President ... Ms. Nora V. DEMLEITNER
05 Dean of College ... Mr. Joseph MACFARLAND
30 VP Development/Alumni Relations ... Ms. Kelly BROWN
84 Vice President of Enrollment ... Mr. Benjamin BAUM
58 Assoc Dean for Graduate Program ... Ms. Emily LANGSTON
10 Treasurer/Financial Officer ... Ms. Ally GONTANG-HIGHFIELD
06 Registrar ... Mr. Alexander MYHRE
102 Director Corporate/Foundation Rels ... Ms. Susan BORDEN
37 Director of Financial Aid ... Mr. Steven BELL
08 Library Director ... Ms. Catherine DIXON
15 Director of Human Resources ... Ms. Sue GELENTER
18 Director of Buildings and Grounds ... Mr. John DAVIS
19 Director of Public Safety ... Mr. Robert MUECK
23 Director of Student Health ... Ms. Nancy CALABRESE
26 Director of Communications ... Ms. Carol CARPENTER
32 Director of Student Services ... Ms. Taylor WATERS
36 Director of Career Services ... Ms. Jaime DUNN
21 Controller ... Ms. Sarah MACDONALD
29 Director of Alumni Relations ... Mr. Chris AAMOT
20 Assistant to the Dean ... Ms. Heather LATHAM
04 Executive Asst to President ... Ms. Amy WEBB
40 Bookstore Manager ... Ms. Melinda ROONEY
41 Athletic Coordinator ... Ms. Rachel FLEMING

† See Affiliate: St. John's College at Santa Fe, NM.

St. Mary's College of Maryland (F)

47645 College Drive, Saint Mary's City MD 20686-3001
County: Saint Mary's | FICE Identification: 002095
Unit ID: 163912
Telephone: (240) 895-2000 | Carnegie Class: Bac-A&S
FAX Number: (240) 895-4462 | Calendar System: Semester
URL: www.smcm.edu
Established: 1840 | Annual Undergrad Tuition & Fees (In-State): $15,124
Enrollment: 1,508 | Coed
Affiliation or Control: State | IRS Status: 501(c)3
Highest Offering: Master's
Accreditation: M

01 President ... Dr. Tuajuanda C. JORDAN
05 Interim Provost and Dean of Faculty ... Dr. Katherine L. GANTZ
10 VP Business & Finance ... Mr. Paul A. PUSECKER
111 VP for Institutional Advancement ... Ms. Carolyn S. CURRY
84 VP Enrollment Management ... Mr. David L. HAUTANEN, JR.
32 VP for Student Affairs ... Dr. Jerri D. HOWLAND
28 VP Equity & Strategic Initiatives ... Dr. Dereck J. ROVARIS, SR.
21 Asst Vice President for Finance ... Mr. Christopher J. TRUE
101 Exec Assistant to President ... Ms. Betsy BARRETO
22 Asst VP of Equity and Inclusion ... Mr. Michael K. DUNN
88 Director of Equity Programming ... Dr. Jose R. BALLESTEROS
26 Asst VP of Marketing/Communication ... Vacant
31 Community Relations Liaison ... Mr. Kelsey R. BUSH
35 Exec Dir Student Life/Dean Students ... Mr. Derek M. YOUNG
29 Director Alumni Relations ... Mr. David M. SUSHINSKY
06 Registrar ... Mr. Nickolas B. TULLEY
37 Director of Financial Aid ... Mr. Rob W. MADDOX
88 Director Enrollment Operations ... Dr. Bhargavi BANDI
07 Director of Admission ... Mr. Ryan M. MYZAK
38 Exec Dir of the Wellness Center ... Vacant
41 Director of Athletics/Recreation ... Ms. Crystal L. GIBSON
20 Interim Associate Provost ... Dr. Jeffrey J. BYRD
18 Director of Physical Plant ... Mr. Bradley D. NEWKIRK
19 Interim Director of Public Safety ... Mr. Christopher COONS
40 Director of the Campus Store ... Mr. Richard T. WAGNER
15 Asst VP of Human Resources ... Ms. Shannon K. JARBOE
23 Asst Director of Health Services ... Ms. Deborah A. BELLO
88 Asst Director Counseling Svcs ... Ms. Jessica L. JOLLY
121 Exec Dir Enroll for Student Success ... Ms. Kathleen L. PUSECKER
124 Assoc Dean Retention/Stdnt Success ... Ms. Joanne A. GOLDWATER
13 Asst VP of Information Technology ... Ms. Jenell SARGENT
44 Sr Devel Ofcr Annual Giving ... Mr. Richard J. EDGAR
08 Interim Dir of Library/Media Svcs ... Ms. Katherine H. RYNER
102 Dir Corporate/Foundation Relations ... Ms. Lauren K. SAMPSON
21 Comptroller/Director of Accounting ... Mr. Gabriel A. MBOMEH
43 Assistant Attorney General ... Ms. Allison J. BOYLE
16 Assoc Dir Human Resources ... Mr. Melvin A. MCCLINTOCK
25 Director of Sponsored Research ... Vacant
109 Procurement Ofcr/Dir of Auxiliary ... Mr. Patrick G. HUNT
92 Director DeSousa Brent Scholars Pgm ... Vacant

88 Director Events and Conferences ... Ms. Peggy R. AUD
30 Asst VP Development ... Ms. Karen C. RALEY
104 Director of International Education ... Ms. Aurora MARGARITA-GOLDKAMP
36 Exec Dir Ctr Career & Prof Dev ... Ms. Cynthia W. GREB
88 Dir of Career Development ... Mr. Geoffrey C. LEWIS
04 Executive Asst to President ... Ms. Jennifer L. SIVAK
09 Director of Institutional Research ... Dr. Anne Marie BRADY
105 Director Web Services ... Ms. Jeannette L. MODIC
108 Coordinator of Assessment ... Dr. Katy E. ARNETT
88 Director of Accessibility Services ... Ms. Dana M. KIERAN

Saint Mary's Seminary and University (A)

5400 Roland Avenue, Baltimore MD 21210-1994
County: Baltimore City FICE Identification: 002096
Unit ID: 163842
Telephone: (410) 864-4000 Carnegie Class: Not Classified
FAX Number: (410) 864-4278 Calendar System: Semester
URL: www.stmarys.edu
Established: 1791 Annual Undergrad Tuition & Fees: N/A
Enrollment: N/A Coed
Affiliation or Control: Roman Catholic IRS Status: 501(c)3
Highest Offering: First Professional Degree
Accreditation: M, THEOL

01 President/Rector ... Rev. Phillip J. BROWN
10 Vice President for Finance ... Ms. Victoria V. SEMANIE
111 Vice Pres Advancement/Admin ... Mrs. Elizabeth L. VISCONAGE
05 Dean School of Theology ... Rev. Gladstone STEVENS
73 Dean St Mary's Ecumenical Institute ... Dr. D. Brent LAYTHAM
73 Dean Ecclesiastical Fac/Sch Theol ... Rev. Thomas BURKE
06 University Registrar ... Ms. Paula M. THIGPEN
113 Ecumenical Inst Billing Officer ... Ms. Marcia HANCOCK
08 Director of Knott Library ... Mr. Thomas RASZEWSKI
13 Director Information Services ... Mr. Arryn MILNE
84 Director of Recruitment ... Ms. Kaye GUIDUGLI

The SANS Technology Institute (B)

11200 Rockville Pike, Suite 200,
North Bethesda MD 20852
County: Montgomery Identification: 667006
Telephone: (301) 654-7267 Carnegie Class: Not Classified
FAX Number: (301) 951-0140 Calendar System: Other
URL: https://www.sans.edu/
Established: 2006 Annual Graduate Tuition & Fees: N/A
Enrollment: N/A Coed
Affiliation or Control: Proprietary IRS Status: Proprietary
Highest Offering: Master's; No Undergraduates
Accreditation: M

01 President ... Mr. Ed SKOUDIS
03 Executive Director ... Mr. Eric PATTERSON

Stevenson University (C)

1525 Greenspring Valley Road,
Stevenson MD 21153-0641
County: Baltimore FICE Identification: 002107
Unit ID: 164173
Telephone: (410) 486-7000 Carnegie Class: Masters/L
FAX Number: (410) 486-3552 Calendar System: Semester
URL: www.stevenson.edu
Established: 1947 Annual Undergrad Tuition & Fees: $37,868
Enrollment: 3,492 Coed
Affiliation or Control: Independent Non-Profit IRS Status: 501(c)3
Highest Offering: Doctorate
Accreditation: M, CSHSE, IACBE, MLS, NURSE

01 President ... Dr. Elliot HIRSHMAN
04 Assistant to President ... Ms. Lauree WOODRING
05 Exec VP Academic Affairs/Provost ... Dr. Susan T. GORMAN
10 Vice Pres Administration & Finance ... Ms. Melanie EDMONDSON
111 Vice Pres University Advancement ... Mr. Chris VAUGHAN
84 Vice Pres Enrollment Management ... Mr. Mark J. HERGAN
32 Int Vice President Student Affairs ... Mr. Eric RIVERA
26 VP Marketing/Digital Communications ... Mr. John BUETTNER
15 Vice Pres for Human Resources ... Mr. Dave JORDAN
100 Vice President & Chief of Staff ... Ms. Sue B. KENNEY
36 Director Career Connection Center ... Mr. Matthew SEILER
81 Sr AVP Academic Affairs/Research ... Dr. Meredith DURMOWICZ
53 Associate Dean of Education ... Dr. Beth KOBETT
120 Dean/Vice Provost Online Learning ... Dr. Ali ESKANDARIAN
79 Dean Sch of Humanities/Social Sci ... Dr. Ricardo PHIPPS
88 Dean Sch Design/Int Dean SHS/VProv ... Ms. Amanda HOSTALKA
13 Chief Information Officer ... Mr. Karl BANTILLO
23 Asst Vice President Wellness Center ... Dr. Linda REYMANN
66 Dean Sch Nursing/Health Professions ... Dr. Marie BARRY
18 Asst VP Facilities & Campus Safety ... Mr. James MUSTARD
37 Director Financial Aid ... Ms. Melanie MASON
35 Assoc Vice Pres/Dean of Students ... Dr. Jeffrey M. KELLY
09 Dir Inst Research/Effectiveness ... Dr. May HSER
08 Director of Library Services ... Ms. Sara GODBEE
06 Registrar ... Ms. Rhonda STOKES
19 Director of Security ... Mr. Steve GOSSAGE
41 Director Athletics ... Mr. Brett C. ADAMS
109 Asst VP Property Mgmt/Campus Svcs ... Mr. Robert REED
29 Asst VP Annual Giving/Alumni Rels ... Ms. Allison CUNEO
22 Director of Disability Services ... Dr. Kimberly MCMANUS

*The University System of Maryland Office (D)

701 E. Pratt St., Baltimore MD 21202
FICE Identification: 007959
Unit ID: 164146
Telephone: (301) 445-2740 Carnegie Class: N/A
FAX Number: (301) 445-1931
URL: www.usmd.edu

01 Chancellor ... Dr. Jay A. PERMAN
05 Sr VC Academic Affairs ... Dr. Joann BOUGHMAN
10 Vice Chanc Admin & Finance ... Ms. Ellen HERBST
111 VC Advancement & CEO USM Foundation ... Mr. Leonard R. RALEY
86 VC Governmental Relations ... Mr. Patrick N. HOGAN
26 VC for Communications ... Mr. Timothy J. MCDONOUGH
20 Assoc Vice Chanc Academic Affairs ... Dr. Antoinette COLEMAN
13 Assistant VC for IT & Interim CIO ... Mr. Michael EISMEIER
100 Chief of Staff to Chancellor ... Ms. Denise WILKERSON
116 Director Internal Audit ... Mr. David MOSCA
114 Director Budget Analysis ... Ms. Colleen AUBURGER

*University of Maryland College Park (E)

1101 Miller Administration Building,
College Park MD 20742
County: Prince Georges FICE Identification: 002103
Unit ID: 163286
Telephone: (301) 405-1000 Carnegie Class: DU-Highest
FAX Number: (301) 314-9560 Calendar System: Semester
URL: www.umd.edu
Established: 1856 Annual Undergrad Tuition & Fees (In-State): $10,779
Enrollment: 40,709 Coed
Affiliation or Control: State IRS Status: 501(c)3
Highest Offering: Doctorate
Accreditation: M, AAQEP, AUD, CEA, CLPSY, COPSY, DANCE, DIETD, DIETI, IPSY, JOUR, LIB, LSAR, MFCD, MUS, PCSAS, PH, PLNG, SCPSY, SP, SPAA

02 President ... Dr. Darryll J. PINES
05 Senior Vice President & Provost ... Dr. Jennifer K. RICE
100 Asst to President & Chief of Staff ... Ms. Michele A. EASTMAN
11 Vice President & Chief Admin Ofcr ... Mr. Carlo COLELLA
32 Vice President for Student Affairs ... Dr. Patty PERILLO
111 Vice President University Relations ... Dr. Matthew HODGE
46 Vice President for Research ... Dr. Gregory F. BALL
13 Vice President and CIO ... Dr. Jeffrey K. HOLLINGSWORTH
10 VP & Chief Financial Officer ... Mr. Greg OLER
43 Vice President and General Counsel ... Mr. Michael R. POTERALA
28 Vice Pres for Diversity & Inclusion ... Dr. Georgina DODGE
26 VP Marketing & Communications ... Mr. Brian ULLMANN
47 Dean Col Agriculture/Natl Resources ... Dr. Craig BEYROUTY
48 Dean School of Architecture ... Dr. Dawn JOURDAN
79 Dean College Arts & Humanities ... Dr. Stephanie SHONEKAN
83 Dean Col Behavioral/Social Sciences ... Dr. Susan RIVERA
50 Dean Smith School of Business ... Dr. Prabhudev KONANA
81 Dean Col of Comp/Math/Natural Sci ... Dr. Amitabh VARSHNEY
53 Dean College of Education ... Dr. Kimberly GRIFFIN
54 Dean Clark Sch of Engineering ... Dr. Samuel GRAHAM
69 Dean School of Public Health ... Dr. Boris D. LUSHNIAK
60 Dean Merrill College of Journalism ... Ms. Lucy A. DALGLISH
62 Dean College of Information Studies ... Dr. Keith MARZULLO
80 Dean School of Public Policy ... Dr. Robert C. ORR
20 Dean Undergraduate Studies ... Dr. William A. COHEN
58 Dean Graduate School ... Dr. Steve FETTER
08 Dean of the Libraries ... Dr. Adriene LIM
85 Assoc VP International Affairs ... Dr. Ross D. LEWIN
20 AVP Acad Affairs/Finance Personnel ... Mr. Dylan BAKER
09 Int AVP Inst Research & Planning ... Ms. Michelle APPEL
84 Assoc VP Enrollment Management ... Ms. Barbara A. GILL
20 Assoc Provost Faculty Affairs ... Dr. John BERTOT
108 Assoc Provost Acad Planning & Pgms ... Dr. Elizabeth J. BEISE
88 Special Assistant to the Provost ... Dr. KerryAnn O'MEARA
20 Assoc Prov Enterprise Resource Plng ... Dr. Jack BLANCHARD
20 AVP Academic Innovation and Tech ... Dr. Marcio OLIVEIRA
07 Asst VP Enrollment Management ... Ms. Shannon GUNDY
06 Exec Dir and University Registrar ... Dr. Adrian R. CORNELIUS
92 Executive Director Honors College ... Dr. Peter MALLIOS
37 Director Student Financial Aid ... Mr. Dawit LEMMA
104 Dir Intl Student & Scholar Services ... Ms. Susan-Ellis DOUGHERTY
18 Assoc VP & Chief Facilities Officer ... Mr. Charles R. REUNING
96 Asst VP Procurement Str Sourcing ... Ms. Kimberly WATSON
15 Asst VP Human Resources ... Ms. Rythee LAMBERT-JONES
88 Asst VP for Real Estate ... Mr. Edward MAGINNIS, JR.
88 Asst VP Administration Finance ... Ms. Anne MARTENS
19 Dir Pub Safety/Chief Campus Police ... Mr. David B. MITCHELL
117 Exec Dir Env Safety/Sustain/Risk ... Ms. Maureen KOTLAS
21 Controller ... Ms. Lillian NASH
113 Bursar/Assoc Comptroller ... Ms. Alisa ABADINSKY
35 Sr Assoc VP for Student Affairs ... Dr. Warren KELLEY
35 Asst VP and Dean of Students ... Dr. Andrea GOODWIN
35 Asst VP for Student Affairs ... Dr. James MCSHAY
35 Int Asst VP for Student Affairs ... Ms. Colleen WRIGHT-RIVA
36 Director University Career Center ... Ms. Allynn POWELL
109 Director Stamp Student Union ... Dr. Marsha A. GUENZLER-STEVENS
23 Director University Health Center ... Dr. Spyridon MARINOPOULOS
38 Director Counseling Center ... Dr. Chetan JOSHI
122 Director Fraternity Sorority Life ... Dr. Matthew SUPPLE
39 Director Resident Life ... Mr. Dennis PASSARELLA-GEORGE

30 AVP University Development ... Mr. Jim HARRIS
29 AVP Alumni and Donor Relations ... Ms. Amy EICHHORST
110 AVP Univ Relations CFO UMCPF ... Ms. Cynthia ALLEN
112 Asst VP University Relations ... Ms. Beth JAVIER-WONG
88 Assoc VP for Research ... Ms. Denise CLARK
88 Assoc VP Research Development ... Mr. Eric CHAPMAN
103 AVP Innovation/Econ Development ... Dr. Dean CHANG
25 Asst VP Research Administration ... Ms. Wendy MONTGOMERY
88 Asst VP Sponsored Programs ... Mr. Marchon JACKSON
14 Asst VP Chief Technology Officer ... Ms. Tripti SINHA
91 Asst VP Enterprise Engineering ... Mr. Axel PERSAUD
119 Director Chief IT Security Officer ... Mr. Gerry SNEERINGER
90 Senior Director Enterprise Planning ... Mr. Joseph DRASIN
86 Exec Director Government Relations ... Mr. Ross STERN
41 Director Intercollegiate Athletics ... Mr. Damon EVANS

*University of Maryland, Baltimore (F)

220 Arch Street, 14th Floor, Baltimore MD 21201-1508
County: Independent City FICE Identification: 002104
Unit ID: 163259
Telephone: (410) 706-7002 Carnegie Class: Spec-4-yr-Eng
FAX Number: (410) 706-0500 Calendar System: Semester
URL: www.umaryland.edu
Established: 1807 Annual Undergrad Tuition & Fees (In-State): N/A
Enrollment: 7,137 Coed
Affiliation or Control: State IRS Status: 501(c)3
Highest Offering: Doctorate
Accreditation: M, ANEST, ARCPA, CAMPEP, DENT, DH, DIETI, IPSY, LAW, MED, MLS, NURSE, PA, PH, PHAR, PTA, RADDOS, SW

02 President ... Dr. Bruce E. JARRELL
05 Provost/Exec Vice President ... Dr. Roger J. WARD
10 Chief Admin & Finance Officer/VP ... Ms. Dawn M. RHODES
25 VP/Chf Enterprise/Econ Dev Ofcr ... Mr. James L. HUGHES
13 VP/Chief Information Officer ... Dr. Peter J. MURRAY
46 VP of Research ... Mr. Gregory F. BALL
32 Vice Prov & Vice Dean Graduate Sch ... Dr. Flavius LILLY
26 Sr VP External Relations ... Ms. Jennifer B. LITCHMAN
28 VP & Chief Diversity/Equity & Incl ... Dr. Diane FORBES BERTHOUND
30 Int Chief Philanthropy Officer/VP ... Mr. James L. HUGHES
86 Chief Govt Affairs Officer/AVP ... Mr. Kevin P. KELLY
43 Chief University Counsel ... Ms. Susan GILLETTE
19 Police Chief ... Dep. Thomas A. LEONE
108 VP & Chief Accountability Officer ... Dr. Susan BUSKIRK
18 Assoc VP Facilities & Operations ... Mr. Terry MORSE
15 Assoc VP Human Resources ... Ms. Malika MONGER
37 Assoc VP Student Financial Asst ... Ms. Patricia A. SCOTT
113 VP Budget & Finance ... Mr. Scott BITNER
27 Assoc VP Communications/Public Affs ... Ms. Laura A. KOZAK
14 Asst VP Information Technology ... Mr. Fred SMITH
09 Asst VP Inst Rsrch & Accountability ... Mr. Gregory C. SPENGLER
96 AVP Strategic Sourcing/Acquisition ... Mr. John JENSEN
88 AVP Sponsored Projects Accounting ... Ms. Laura SCARANTINO
88 AVP ORD Marketing & Operations ... Ms. Linda KENDERDINE
88 AVP ORD Sponsored Programs Admin ... Mr. Dennis PAFFRATH
88 AVP ORD Technology Transfer ... Mr. Philip ROBILOTTO
88 AVP ORD Center for Clinical Trials ... Mr. Michael ROLLOR
88 AVP ORD Economic Development ... Ms. Jane SHAAB
102 Treasurer & Dir of Operations UMBF ... Ms. Pamela HECKLER
08 Dean Health Sci/Human Svc Libr ... Ms. Mary J. TOOEY
90 Exec Dir Enterprise Applications ... Mr. Michael SMITH
31 Exec Dir Cmty Initiatives/Engage ... Vacant
06 Director Records & Registration ... Mr. Ryan HOLTZ
16 Director Benefits & Compensation ... Ms. Patricia HOFFMANN
22 Director EEO/Affirmative Action ... Ms. Sheila GREENWOOD-BLACKSHEAR
28 Director Diversity and Inclusion ... Ms. Mikhel A. KUSHNER
85 Director International Services ... Ms. Amy RAMIREZ
38 Director Counseling ... Ms. Emilia K. PETRILLO
41 Director Univ Recreation & Fitness ... Mr. William P. CROCKETT
23 Director Student Health Center ... Dr. James BARONAS
35 Director Student Services ... Ms. Cynthia E. RICE
39 Director of UM Housing ... Ms. Margaret SCHOTTO
21 Director of Financial Services ... Mr. Larry MILLER
105 Dir Web Dev Interactive Media ... Mr. Amir CHAMSAZ
58 Dean Graduate School ... Dr. Roger J. WARD
52 Dean School of Dentistry ... Dr. Mark A. REYNOLDS
61 Dean School of Law ... Ms. Renee MCDONALD HUTCHINS
63 Dean Sch of Medicine/Medical Affs ... Dr. Mark T. GLADWIN
66 Dean School of Nursing ... Dr. Jane M. KIRSCHLING
67 Dean School of Pharmacy ... Dr. Natalie D. EDDINGTON
70 Dean School of Social Work ... Dr. Judy L. POSTMUS
04 Admin Assistant to the President ... Ms. Clara WOODLY

*University of Maryland Baltimore County (G)

1000 Hilltop Circle, Baltimore MD 21250-0001
County: Baltimore FICE Identification: 002105
Unit ID: 163268
Telephone: (410) 455-1000 Carnegie Class: DU-Highest
FAX Number: (410) 455-1210 Calendar System: 4/1/4
URL: www.umbc.edu
Established: 1966 Annual Undergrad Tuition & Fees (In-State): $9,420
Enrollment: 13,497 Coed
Affiliation or Control: State IRS Status: 501(c)3
Highest Offering: Doctorate
Accreditation: M, ABAI, CAEP, CLPSY, DANCE, DMS, EMT, IPSY, MUS, SW

02 President ... Dr. Valerie SHEARES ASHBY

05 Provost/Sr Vice Pres Academic Affs Dr. Philip ROUS
10 Vice Pres Finance/Administration Mrs. Kathy L. DETTLOFF
32 Vice President Student Affairs Dr. Nancy YOUNG
111 Vice Pres Institutional Advancement Mr. Gregory SIMMONS
13 Vice Pres Information Technology Mr. Jack J. SUESS
46 Vice President of Research Dr. Karl V. STEINER
49 Dean Col of Arts/Humanities/Soc Sci Dr. Kimberly MOFFITT
81 Dean Col Natural/Math Sciences Dr. William LACOURSE
54 Dean College of Engr/Info Tech Dr. Keith BOWMAN
84 Asst Dean Graduate Enrollment Mgmt Ms. K. Jill BARR
20 Vice Provost/Dean Undergrad Educ Dr. Katharine COLE
107 Vice Provost Professional Studies Dr. Christopher STEELE
20 Vice Provost Academic Affairs Dr. Antonio R. MOREIRA
58 Dean/Vice Provost for Graduate Educ Dr. Janet RUTLEDGE
15 Vice Provost Faculty Affairs Dr. Patrice MCDERMOTT
84 Vice Provost Enrollment Management Dr. Yvette MOZIE-ROSS
21 Assoc VP Financial Services Mr. Bryan CASEY
26 Assistant to Pres/Assoc VP Mktg/PR Ms. Lisa G. AKCHIN
11 Assoc VP Administrative Services Ms. Terry COOK
16 Chief HR Officer/Assoc VP Mrs. Valerie THOMAS
29 Director Alumni Relations Ms. Stanyell ODOM
88 Asst VP New•Media/Instruction Tech Mr. John FRITZ
18 Asst VP Facilities Management Mr. Lenn CARON
04 Senior Advisor to the President Dr. Peter HENDERSON
96 Director of Procurement Dr. Elizabeth MOSS
92 Director Honors College Dr. Simon STACEY
41 Dir Athletics/Physical Educ/Rec Dr. Brian BARRIO
19 Chief of University Police Mr. Bruce PERRY
36 Asst VP Career & Corp Partnership Ms. Caroline BAKER
23 Director Health Services Dr. Bruce HERMAN
37 Director Financial Aid Ms. Andrea CIPOLLA
25 Asst Director Sponsored Programs Mr. Stanley JACKSON
40 Director of the Bookstore Ms. Erin MCGONIGLE
85 Assoc Vice Prov International Educ Dr. David DIMARIA
08 Director Library Mr. Patrick DAWSON
06 Registrar Ms. Pamela HAWLEY
43 General Counsel Mr. David GLEASON
07 Asst Vice Prov Admiss/Orientation Mr. Dale BITTINGER
39 Director Residential Life Mr. John FOX
09 Director of Institutional Research Dr. Connie PIERSON
38 Director Student Counseling Dr. Bruce HERMAN
100 Chief of Staff President's Office Ms. Candace DODSON-REED
108 Director Institutional Assessment Mr. Robert CARPENTER
22 Dir Affirm Action/Equal Opportunity Mr. Bobbie HOYE
28 Director of Diversity Vacant
30 Director of Development Mr. Mike BUCCINO
44 Director Annual Giving Mr. Carl FOWLKES
90 Director Academic Computing Mr. Damian DOYLE
91 Director Administrative Computing Mr. Joseph KIRBY
88 Dean Erickson Sch of Aging Studies Dr. Dana BRADLEY
102 Director Foundation Relations Mr. Bruce LYONS
104 Assoc Dir Education Abroad Ms. Caylie MIDDLETON
122 Coord Campus Life-Greek Life Ms. Courtney CAMPBELL

*University of Maryland Center for Environmental Science (A)

PO Box 775, Cambridge MD 21613

County: Dorchester — Identification: 667159
Telephone: (410) 228-9250 — Carnegie Class: Not Classified
FAX Number: (410) 228-3843 — Calendar System: Semester
URL: www.umces.edu
Established: 1925 — Annual Graduate Tuition & Fees: N/A
Enrollment: N/A — Coed
Affiliation or Control: State — IRS Status: 501(c)3
Highest Offering: Doctorate; No Undergraduates
Accreditation: M

02 President Dr. Peter GOODWIN
05 Vice Pres for Education Dr. Larry SANFORD
10 Vice Pres for Finance/Admin Ms. Lynn REHN
04 Admin Assistant to the President Ms. Melissa HOLLAND
100 Chief of Staff Mr. Dave NEMAZIE

*University of Maryland Eastern Shore (B)

11868 Academic Oval, Princess Anne MD 21853-1299

County: Somerset — FICE Identification: 002106
Unit ID: 163338
Telephone: (410) 651-2200 — Carnegie Class: DU-Higher
FAX Number: (410) 651-6105 — Calendar System: Semester
URL: www.umes.edu
Established: 1886 — Annual Undergrad Tuition & Fees (In-State): $8,558
Enrollment: 2,646 — Coed
Affiliation or Control: State — IRS Status: 501(c)3
Highest Offering: Doctorate
Accreditation: M, AAFCS, ACPHA, #ARCPA, CACREP, CONST, DIETD, DIETI, PHAR, PTA

02 President Dr. Heidi M. ANDERSON
100 Chief of Staff Dr. Robert C. MOCK
05 Provost/VP Academic Affairs Dr. Rondall E. ALLEN
10 VP Administration and Finance Ms. Anastasia RODRIGUEZ
84 VP Enrollment Mgmt/Stdnt Engagement Ms. Latoya JENKINS
111 VP University Relations Mr. David A. BALCOM
13 Interim Chief Information Officer Dr. Urban WIGGINS
20 Vice Provost Academic Affairs Vacant
114 Budget Director Ms. Beatrice V. WRIGHT
15 Director of Human Resources Ms. Gertrude J. HAIRSTON
32 Asst VP Student Affairs Vacant
29 Director of Alumni Relations Mr. Kadeem C. TURNBULL
08 Director of Library Services Ms. Sharon D. BROOKS
37 Interim Director of Financial Aid Ms. Danena R. LIVINGSTON
23 Director of Student Health Services Ms. Sharone V. GRANT
96 Director of Procurement Ms. Jacqueline M. COLLINS
07 Director of Admissions Mr. Darryl D. ISOM
06 Registrar Ms. Debbie G. BLAKE
12 Int Gen Mgr Richard A Henson Center Ms. Ciera E. NIMMONS
36 Director of Career Services Dr. Theresa QUEENAN
09 Vice Provost DSV/IR Dr. Urban T. WIGGINS
19 Interim Director of Public Safety Mr. Mark TYLER
18 Director of Physical Plant Ms. Jicola R. JOYNES-STURGIS
39 Director of Residence Life Ms. Larita L. HUGEE
41 Director of Athletics Ms. Tara A. OWENS
21 Comptroller Ms. Bonita E. BYRD
46 Director of Sponsored Research Dr. Joseph S. PITULA
124 Director of CAAS Dr. TerCraig D. EDWARDS
88 Director of Upward Bound Dr. Nicole L. GALE
35 Coord Student Activities Vacant
88 Director of Title III Program Dr. LaTashia H. SWAIN-GILLIARD
26 Director of Public Relations Mr. Earl D. HOLLAND, JR.
30 Director Development Vacant
110 Director of Advancement Services Ms. Chenita R. REDDICK
51 Coordinator of Continuing Education Ms. Gretchen M. BOGGS
38 Director of Counseling Services Dr. Malkia L. JOHNSON
58 Dean Graduate Studies & Research Dr. Lakeisha L. HARRIS
47 Dean School Agric/Natural Sciences Dr. Moses T. KAIRO
57 Dean Sch Educ/Soc Sci/The Arts Dr. Marshall STEVENSON
50 Dean School Business & Tech Dr. Derrek B. DUNN
67 Int Dean Sch Pharm/Health Prof Dr. T. Sean VASAITIS
28 Director of Diversity Mr. Jason A. CASARES
04 Exec Admin Asst to the President Vacant
104 Int Director Center for Intl Educ Mr. Phillip BROUSSARD
105 Webmaster Mr. Jeremy W. TOWNSEND
106 Dir Center Inst Tech/Online Lrng Dr. Brian BERGEN-AURAND
43 General Counsel Mr. Matthew A. TAYLOR
86 Director Government Relations Mr. Jim N. MATHIAS
14 Director of Information Technology Mr. Rob A. LOPEZ

*University of Maryland Global Campus (C)

3501 University Boulevard East, Adelphi MD 20783-7998

County: Prince Georges — FICE Identification: 011644
Unit ID: 163204
Telephone: (301) 985-7000 — Carnegie Class: Masters/L
FAX Number: N/A — Calendar System: Semester
URL: www.umgc.edu
Established: 1947 — Annual Undergrad Tuition & Fees (In-State): $7,560
Enrollment: 58,526 — Coed
Affiliation or Control: State — IRS Status: 501(c)3
Highest Offering: Doctorate
Accreditation: M, AAQEP, CAEPN, CAHIIM, IACBE, NURSE

02 President Dr. Gregory FOWLER
05 Sr Vice Pres/Chief Academic Officer Ms. Blakely POMIETTO
32 Sr VP Student Affairs Ms. Martina HANSEN
26 Sr Vice President Communications Mr. Michael FREEDMAN
88 Sr VP Global Military Operations Mr. Lloyd MILES
45 Sr VP Institutional Effectiveness Vacant
11 Chief of Operations/Administration Mr. Joseph SERGI
100 Chief of Staff/Sr VP Strategy Mr. Nicholas EREMITA
10 Vice Pres Financial Operations Mr. Eugene D. LOCKETT, JR.
43 Vice President & General Counsel Ms. Sherri SAMPSON
15 Vice President Human Resources Ms. JulieAnn GARCIA
121 VP Student Success Ms. Susan HAWKINS-WILDING
86 Vice Pres Govt Affs/Strat Prtnrshp Mr. Frank J. PRINCIPE, JR.
111 Vice Pres Inst Advancement Ms. Cathy SWEET
28 VP/Chief Diversity Ofcr/Ombudsman Dr. Blair HAYES
07 Vice Pres Admissions Ms. Jamie JAYNES
18 Associate Vice President Facilities Mr. George TRUJILLO
86 Director of State Govt Relations Ms. Erin FAVAZZA
37 AVP Student Financial Aid Ms. Cheryl STORIE
88 VP and Dean School of Cyber & IT Dr. Douglas HARRISON
08 Assoc Provost of Library Services Mr. Stephen MILLER
06 Associate VP and Registrar Ms. Insiya BREAM
49 VP/Dean School of Arts and Sciences Ms. Sharon FROSS
09 Sr Director Institutional Research Mr. Wei ZHOU
04 Dir Exec Support & Operations Ms. Lisa JACKSON
19 Director Security Mr. William BROGAN
29 Assoc VP Alumni Programs Ms. Nikki SANDOVAL
50 VP/Dean School of Business Dr. Pamela CARTER

*Bowie State University (D)

14000 Jericho Park Road, Bowie MD 20715-3318

County: Prince Georges — FICE Identification: 002062
Unit ID: 162007
Telephone: (301) 860-4000 — Carnegie Class: Masters/L
FAX Number: (301) 860-3510 — Calendar System: Semester
URL: www.bowiestate.edu
Established: 1865 — Annual Undergrad Tuition & Fees (In-State): $8,444
Enrollment: 6,250 — Coed
Affiliation or Control: State — IRS Status: 501(c)3
Highest Offering: Doctorate
Accreditation: M, ACBSP, CACREP, CAEP, NUR, SPAA, SW

02 President Dr. Aminta BREAUX
05 Provost/Vice Pres Academic Affs Dr. Carl GOODMAN
10 VP Finance & Administration Mr. Anthony SAVIA
109 Assoc VP Auxiliary Services Mr. Wade HENLEY
21 Asst VP Finance & Administration Mr. Michael ATKINS
111 Vice Pres Institutional Advancement Mr. Brent SWINTON
43 Vice Pres & General Counsel Ms. Karen JOHNSON SHAHEED
13 VP Office of Information Technology Mr. Maurice A. TYLER
84 VP Enrollment Mgmt & Student Affs Dr. Brian CLEMMONS
88 Asst to Prov Institutional Effect Ms. Gayle M. FINK
06 University Registrar Ms. Shari CHRISTIE
36 Acting Director Career Services Ms. Rosetta PRICE
15 Sr Director of Human Resources Ms. Sheila HOBSON
19 Chief of Campus Police Mr. James W. BOOKER
58 Int Dean Sch of Grad Stds/Research Dr. Cosmos NWOKEAFOR
49 Dean College of Arts & Sciences Dr. George ACQUAAH
50 Dean College of Business Dr. Lawrence R. MCNEIL, JR.
53 Dean College of Education Dr. Rhonda JETER-TWILLEY
107 Dean College Professional Studies Dr. Cheryl H. BLACKMAN
92 Director UCE Honors Program Dr. Monika GROSS
41 Director Athletics Mr. Clyde DOUGHTY, JR.
26 Dir University Relations/ Marketing Ms. Cassandra M. ROBINSON
37 Director Financial Aid Ms. Deborah STANLEY
18 Director Facilities Mr. Darryl WILLIFORD
29 Director of Alumni Relations Ms. Carla HOPKINS
96 Director of Purchasing Mr. Steve A. JOST
09 Director of Institutional Research Ms. Shaunette GRANT
04 Administrative Asst to President Ms. Tanya P. JONES
108 Director Institutional Assessment Dr. Becky VERZINSKI
39 Asst Dir of Student Housing Ms. Tammy TIMBERS
44 Director Annual Giving Ms. Rosalind MUCHIRI
90 Director Academic Computing Dr. Fabio CHACON
100 Chief of Staff Mrs. Karen JOHNSON-SHAHEED
104 Director Study Abroad Mr. Patrick FRAZIER
105 Sr Graphic Designer Mr. Michael FLEISHMAN
86 Director Government Relations Mr. Derrick COLEY

*Coppin State University (E)

2500 W North Avenue, Baltimore MD 21216-3698

County: Baltimore City — FICE Identification: 002068
Unit ID: 162283
Telephone: (410) 951-3000 — Carnegie Class: Masters/S
FAX Number: (410) 333-5369 — Calendar System: Semester
URL: www.coppin.edu
Established: 1900 — Annual Undergrad Tuition & Fees (In-State): $6,716
Enrollment: 2,348 — Coed
Affiliation or Control: State — IRS Status: 501(c)3
Highest Offering: Doctorate
Accreditation: M, ACBSP, CACREP, CAEPN, CAHIIM, NURSE, SW

02 President Dr. Anthony L. JENKINS
05 Provost/VP Academic Affairs Dr. Pamela WILKS
111 VP Institutional Advancement Mr. Joshua HUMBERT
10 VP Administration & Finance Mr. Steve DANIK
32 VP Student Affairs/Enrollment Mgmt Dr. Stephan MOORE
13 VP Information Systems/CIO Dr. Ahmed EL-HAGGAN
45 Asst VP Planning/Assessment Mr. Michael BOWDEN
20 Asst VP Academic Operations Vacant
18 Asst VP Facilities Management Mr. Roy THOMAS
15 Assoc VP of Human Resources Dr. Lisa EARLY
07 Director of Admissions Ms. Jinawa MCNEIL
06 Registrar Ms. Karen BARLAND
21 Controller Mrs. Crystal MOSLEY
08 Director of the Library Dr. Mary WANZA
37 Director of Financial Aid Mr. Marcus BYRD
36 Director of Career Services Center Vacant
19 Chief of Public Safety Mr. Dameon R. CARTER, SR.
39 Director of Housing/Residence Life Ms. Jacquelyn WONSEY
41 Director of Athletics Mr. Derek CARTER
112 Donor Relations & Stewardship Coord Ms. Deidre JOHNSON
96 Asst Vice President of Procurement Mr. Thomas E. DAWSON, JR.
26 Director of Communications Ms. Robyne MCCULLOUGH
88 Director Quality Assurance Mr. Emmanuel OWUSU-SEKYERE
105 Senior Web Developer Ms. Melissa C. RIGBY
49 Dean CASE Dr. Leontye LEWIS
92 Dean Honors College & McNair Pgms Ms. DeChelle FORBES
58 Dean Graduate School Dr. Mary E. OWENS-SOUTHHALL
66 Dean of Nursing Dr. Tracey L. MURRAY
83 Dean Col of Behavioral/Social Sci Dr. Beverly O'BRYANT
50 Dean Col of Business Dr. Sadie GREGORY
04 Executive Assistant to President Ms. Daphine M. THOMAS
09 Director of Institutional Research Mr. Beryl HARRIS
29 Director Alumni Engagement Ms. Kimberly NELSON
38 Director Student Counseling Ms. Michelle REYNOLDS
100 Chief of Staff Ms. Angela GALEANO
25 Chief Contract/Grants Administrator Dr. Dianna J. VASS
44 Annual Fund Manager Vacant

*Frostburg State University (F)

101 Braddock Road, Frostburg MD 21532-2303

County: Allegany — FICE Identification: 002072
Unit ID: 162584
Telephone: (301) 687-4000 — Carnegie Class: Masters/L
FAX Number: (301) 687-7070 — Calendar System: Semester
URL: www.frostburg.edu
Established: 1898 — Annual Undergrad Tuition & Fees (In-State): $9,410
Enrollment: 4,857 — Coed
Affiliation or Control: State — IRS Status: 501(c)3
Highest Offering: Doctorate
Accreditation: M, #ARCPA, CAATE, CAEPN, CAPRT, EXSC, MPCAC, NURSE, SW

02 President Dr. Ronald NOWACZYK
05 Provost Dr. Traki L. TAYLOR

32 VP Student Affairs ... Dr. Artie TRAVIS
10 VP Admin & Finance ... Mr. Troy DONOWAY
111 VP University Advancement ... Mr. John SHORT
15 Chief Human Resources Officer ... Ms. Lisa HERSCH
43 University Counsel ... Mr. Bradford NIXON
20 Interim Associate Provost ... Dr. Benjamin NORRIS
35 Sr Assoc VP Student Affairs ... Dr. Jeff GRAHAM
26 Interim Asst VP Marketing/Comm ... Ms. Nicole MCDONALD
114 Asst VP Budget & Planning ... Ms. Denise MURPHY
49 Int Dean Col Liberal Arts/Sciences ... Dr. Michael MATHIAS
50 Dean College of Business ... Dr. Sudhir SINGH
53 Dean College of Education ... Dr. Boyce WILLIAMS
08 Director of the Library ... Ms. Lea MESSMAN-MANDICOTT
37 Director of Financial Aid ... Ms. Natalia KENNEDY
108 Interim Assistant VP Analytics ... Dr. Sara Beth BITTINGER
58 Interim Dir of Graduate Services ... Dr. Sara Beth BITTINGER
18 Interim Director Physical Plant ... Mr. John BREWER
36 Director Career & Prof Dev Ctr ... Ms. Amy SHIMKO
38 Director Counseling & Psych Svcs ... Vacant
40 Director of Bookstore ... Dr. Rachel FARRIS
41 Athletic Director ... Mr. Troy DELL
19 Chief University Police ... Col. Cynthia SMITH
13 Chief Information Officer ... Mr. Timothy PELESKY
29 Director of Alumni ... Ms. Shannon L. GRIBBLE
07 Director of Admissions ... Ms. Natalie WAGONER
28 Director of Diversity ... Ms. Robin WYNDER
14 Dir Networking/Telecommunications ... Mr. Gary TRENUM
96 Coord Procurement/Material Handling ... Mr. Alan R. SNYDER
23 Director Health Services ... Ms. Christina BURKE
39 Director Residence Life ... Ms. Kimberly HINDS-BRUSH
06 Registrar ... Dr. Jay HEGEMAN
102 Dir Foundation/Corporate Relations ... Ms. Janelle MOFFETT
104 Director Study Abroad ... Ms. Victoria GEARHART
105 Director Web Services ... Mr. Wade BLUEBAUGH
30 Director of Development ... Ms. Lynn KETTERMAN
86 VP Regional Dev & Engagement ... Mr. Al DELIA
09 Interim Dir Institutional Research ... Ms. Selina SMITH
04 Exec Admin Asst III to Pres ... Mrs. Donnell VANSKIVER
122 Asst Dir Fraternity/Sorority Life ... Ms. Jamie WINTERS

*Salisbury University (A)

1101 Camden Avenue, Salisbury MD 21801-6860
County: Wicomico FICE Identification: 002091
Unit ID: 163851
Telephone: (410) 543-6000 Carnegie Class: Masters/L
FAX Number: (410) 548-2587 Calendar System: Semester
URL: www.salisbury.edu
Established: 1925 Annual Undergrad Tuition & Fees (In-State): $10,044
Enrollment: 8,124 Coed
Affiliation or Control: State IRS Status: 501(c)3
Highest Offering: Doctorate
Accreditation: M, AAQEP, COARC, EXSC, MLS, MUS, NURSE, PH, SW

02 President ... Dr. Carolyn R. LEPRE
05 Provost/SVP of Academic Affairs ... Dr. Karen L. OLMSTEAD
100 Chief of Staff ... Mr. Eli J. MODLIN
10 VP Admin and Finance ... Dr. Janet WORMACK
32 Vice Pres of Student Affairs ... Dr. Dane R. FOUST
111 Vice Pres Advancement/External Affs ... Mr. Jason E. CURTIN
84 Asst VP of Enrollment Management ... Mr. Allen M. KOEHLER
22 Assoc VP Institutional Equity ... Mr. Humberto X. ARISTIZABAL
35 Associate VP of Student Affairs ... Vacant
20 Asst Provost for Faculty Success ... Dr. Jessica CLARK
85 Asst Provost for International Ed ... Dr. Brian N. STIEGLER
20 Assoc Vice Pres Academic Affairs ... Dr. Melissa M. BOOG
18 Assoc VP Facilities & Cap Mgmt ... Mr. Eric J. BERKHEIMER
35 Asst VP Student Affs/Dean Students ... Ms. Valerie J. RANDALL-LEE
13 Chief Information Officer ... Mr. Ken F. KUNDELL
26 Director of Public Relations ... Mr. Jason F. RHODES
27 Director of Marketing Strategy ... Ms. Katie M. CURTIN
41 Director of Athletics ... Dr. Gerard R. DIBARTOLO
92 Dean of Honors Program ... Dr. Andrew P. MARTINO
06 Registrar ... Mr. Martin J. HUNTER
07 Director of Admissions ... Ms. Elizabeth A. SKOGLUND
09 Special Asst to Pres for UARA ... Dr. Kara M. OWENS
08 Dn of Libraries/Instruct Resources ... Dr. Beatriz B. HARDY
38 Director of Counseling Center ... Ms. Laurie K. SCHERER
36 Director of Career Services ... Dr. Kevin C. FALLON
37 Director of Financial Aid ... Mr. Mason M. WHITE
15 Assoc VP for HR ... Ms. Lisa M. LEPORE
29 Dir Alumni Relations & Gift Develop ... Mr. Jayme E. BLOCK
23 Director of Student Health Services ... Vacant
35 Director Ct For Student Inv & Lead ... Ms. Tricia G. SMITH
86 Dir of Govt & Community Relations ... Mr. Eli J. MODLIN
43 General Counsel ... Ms. Karen A. TREBER
39 Director Housing/Residence Life ... Mr. David P. GUTOSKEY
19 Director of Public Safety ... Mr. Edwin L. LASHLEY
40 Director of Bookstore ... Ms. Lisa G. GRAY
18 Director of Physical Plant ... Mr. Jonathan A. COOPER
96 Director of Purchasing ... Mr. Jeff H. CANADA
81 Dean Henson Sch Science/Tech ... Dr. Michael S. SCOTT
50 Dean Perdue School of Business ... Dr. Christy H. WEER
49 Dean Fulton School of Liberal Arts ... Dr. Maarten L. PEREBOOM
53 Dean Seidel School of Education ... Dr. Laurie A. HENRY
76 Dean College of Health & Human Svcs ... Dr. Kelly A. FIALA
58 Dean Graduate Studies/Research ... Dr. Clifton P. GRIFFIN
88 Dir Ctr for Student Achievement ... Dr. Heather W. HOLMES
04 Asst to the President ... Ms. Tracy F. HAJIR

*Towson University (B)

8000 York Road, Baltimore MD 21252-0001
County: Baltimore FICE Identification: 002099
Unit ID: 164076
Telephone: (410) 704-2000 Carnegie Class: Masters/L
FAX Number: N/A Calendar System: 4/1/4
URL: www.towson.edu
Established: 1866 Annual Undergrad Tuition & Fees (In-State): $10,198
Enrollment: 21,917 Coed
Affiliation or Control: State IRS Status: 501(c)3
Highest Offering: Doctorate
Accreditation: M, ARCPA, AUD, CAATE, CAEPN, DANCE, FEPAC, IPSY, MPCAC, MUS, NURSE, OT, SP, THEA

02 President ... Dr. Kim SCHATZEL
05 Provost/Exec VP Academic Affs ... Dr. Melanie PERREAULT
10 Vice Pres Administration & Finance ... Mr. Benjamin LOWENTHAL
111 Vice Pres University Advancement ... Mr. Brian J. DEFILIPPIS
46 VP Strategic Prtship/Applied Rsrch ... Dr. Daraius IRANI
26 Vice Pres Comm/Media Relations ... Mr. Sean WELSH
22 Vice Pres of Inclusion & Equity ... Ms. Patricia BRADLEY
32 VP for Student Affairs ... Dr. Vernon HURTE
84 VP for Enrollment Management ... Dr. Boyd BRADSHAW
30 Assoc Vice President Development ... Mr. Todd LANGENBERG
29 Assoc Vice Pres Alumni Relations ... Ms. Lori B. ARMSTRONG
13 Assoc Vice President/CIO ... Mr. Jeffrey SCHMIDT
18 Assoc VP Facilities Management ... Mr. Kevin PETERSEN
21 AVP Financial Affairs ... Mr. Eric JONES
15 Vice Pres Op/Chief Human Resources ... Mr. C. Stephen JONES
35 Assoc Vice Pres Student Affairs ... Dr. Anthony SKEVAKIS
35 Asst Vice President Campus Life ... Mr. Matthew LENNO
39 Asst VP Housing & Residence Life ... Ms. Kelly HOOVER
37 Director for Financial Aid ... Mr. David HORNE
25 Asst VP Sponsored Programs/Research ... Ms. Nancy DUFAU
07 Asst VP University Admissions ... Ms. Amy MOFFATT
19 Dir Public Safety/Chief of Police ... Chief Charles HERRING
53 Dean College of Education ... Dr. Laurie MULLEN
50 Dean College of Business/Economics ... Dr. Shohreh A. KAYNAMA
49 Dean College of Liberal Arts ... Dr. Chris CHULOS
81 Dean J&M Fisher Col of Science/Math ... Dr. David VANKO
57 Dean Col of Fine Arts/Comm ... Dr. Regina CARLOW
76 Dean College of Health Professions ... Dr. Lisa PLOWFIELD
58 Dean Graduate Studies ... Dr. Sidd KAZA
92 Rector Honors College ... Dr. Terry COONEY
43 VP of Legal Affairs/Gen Counsel ... Ms. Sara SLAFF
08 Dean of University Libraries ... Dr. Suzanna YAUKEY
104 Director Study Abroad ... Ms. Liz SHEARER
94 Chair Women's & Gender Studies . Dr. Cindy H. GISSENDANNER
09 Director Institutional Research ... Mr. Tim BIBO, JR.
41 Director of Athletics ... Dr. Steven C. EIGENBROT
23 Director of Health Services ... Mr. Yu-Ling SHAO
40 Director of University Store ... Ms. Stacy ELOFIR
96 Director of Procurement ... Ms. Joselyn JOHNSON
38 Asst Dir/Clin Dir Counseling Ctr ... Dr. Alessandra PIERACCINI
36 Asst VP Career Center ... Ms. Lorie LOGAN-BENNETT
06 Assoc Dir Rcrds/Reg/Reenroll/Resid ... Ms. Heather SULLIVAN

*University of Baltimore (C)

1420 N Charles Street, Baltimore MD 21201-5779
County: Independent City FICE Identification: 002102
Unit ID: 161873
Telephone: (410) 837-4200 Carnegie Class: Masters/L
FAX Number: N/A Calendar System: Semester
URL: www.ubalt.edu
Established: 1925 Annual Undergrad Tuition & Fees (In-State): $9,096
Enrollment: 4,169 Coed
Affiliation or Control: State IRS Status: 501(c)3
Highest Offering: Doctorate
Accreditation: M, LAW, MPCAC, SPAA

02 President ... Mr. Kurt L. SCHMOKE
05 Interim Provost ... Ms. Catherine ANDERSEN
20 Associate Provost ... Dr. Candace CARACO
10 CFO/VP Administration & Finance ... Ms. Beth AMYOT
84 VP Enrollment Management ... Ms. Roxie SHABAZZ
111 Vice Pres Institutional Advancement ... Ms. Theresa SILANSKIS
86 VP Government & Public Affairs ... Ms. Anita HAREWOOD
18 VP Facil Mgmt/Campus Safety ... Mr. Neb SERTSU
13 Vice Pres Technology/CIO ... Mr. David BOBART
32 AssocVP Student Success & Services ... Ms. Nicole MARANO
31 Dir Office of Community Life ... Dr. Llatetra ESTERS
15 Assoc Vice Pres Human Resources ... Ms. Sally REED
09 Asst Vice Pres Institutional Rsrch ... Mr. Paul MONIODIS
28 Dir Diversity & Culture Center ... Vacant
08 Dean of Bogomolny Library ... Mr. Jeffrey HUTSON
19 Acting Captain UB Police ... Mr. Jason KUNZ
07 AVP Enrollment Services ... Mr. Mark JACQUE
96 Director of Procurement & Supply ... Ms. Joselyn JOHNSON
44 AVP Alumni & Donor Services ... Ms. Kate CRIMMINS
36 Director Career & Internship Center ... Ms. Lakeisha MATHEWS
06 Assistant Registrar ... Ms. Brenda DER
26 Manager Public Information ... Mr. Chris HART
80 Dean College of Public Affairs ... Dr. Roger HARTLEY
49 Dean College of Arts & Sci ... Dr. Christine SPENCER
61 Dean of the School of Law ... Dr. Ronald WEICH
50 Dean School of Business ... Mr. Murray DALZIEL
88 Dir Center for Education Access ... Dr. Karyn SCHULZ
21 AVP Admin & Finance ... Ms. Barbara AUGHENBAUGH
29 Director Alumni Relations ... Ms. Kelley CHASE
37 Executive Director Financial Aid ... Mr. Terry RICHARDS
25 Asst Provost Sponsored Research ... Ms. Margarita CARDONA

Washington Adventist University (D)

7600 Flower Avenue, Takoma Park MD 20912-7794
County: Montgomery FICE Identification: 002067
Unit ID: 162210
Telephone: (301) 891-4000 Carnegie Class: Masters/S
FAX Number: (301) 270-1618 Calendar System: Semester
URL: www.wau.edu
Established: 1904 Annual Undergrad Tuition & Fees: $25,200
Enrollment: 968 Coed
Affiliation or Control: Seventh-day Adventist IRS Status: 501(c)3
Highest Offering: Master's
Accreditation: M, MUS, NURSE, RAD

01 President ... Dr. Weymouth SPENCE
05 Provost ... Ms. Cheryl KISUNZU
10 Exec Vice Pres Finance ... Mr. Patrick FARLEY
11 Chief Inst Effectiveness/Technology ... Mr. Ricardo FLORES
32 Vice Pres Student Life ... Dr. Ralph JOHNSON
84 VP Enrollment ... Mr. Dirk WHATLEY
13 Exec Dir Information Technology ... Vacant
15 Assoc VP of Human Resources ... Ms. Jeannie WRIGHT
58 Dean Sch Grad/Professional Studies ... Ms. Brenda CHASE
121 Dean of Student Success ... Dr. Betty JOHNSON
06 Registrar ... Dr. Reginald GARCON
33 Dean of Men ... Mr. Tim NELSON
34 Dean of Women ... Ms. Ashlee CHAMBERS
08 Library Director ... Dr. Sarah GARIFO
30 Exec Dir Development/Alumni Rels ... Ms. Jennifer ALBURY
19 Director Safety & Security ... Mr. John CAKE
41 Athletic Director ... Mr. Jered LYONS
07 Director of Admissions/Recruitment ... Vacant
26 VP for Communications ... Mr. Everett WILES
78 Dir Coop Educ/Acad Support & Test ... Mr. Fitzroy THOMAS
18 Chief Facilities/Physical Plant ... Mr. Steve LAPHAM
37 Exec Director Student Financial Aid ... Vacant
38 Campus Counseling ... Vacant
40 Manager the College Bookstore ... Mr. Lloyd YUTUC
85 Director of International Students ... Dr. Beulah MANUEL
04 Executive Asst to President ... Ms. Lydée BATTLE
09 Director Institutional Research ... Mr. John PETERS

Washington College (E)

300 Washington Avenue, Chestertown MD 21620-1197
County: Kent FICE Identification: 002108
Unit ID: 164216
Telephone: (410) 778-2800 Carnegie Class: Bac-A&S
FAX Number: (410) 778-7850 Calendar System: Semester
URL: www.washcoll.edu
Established: 1782 Annual Undergrad Tuition & Fees: $48,214
Enrollment: 1,089 Coed
Affiliation or Control: Independent Non-Profit IRS Status: 501(c)3
Highest Offering: Master's
Accreditation: M

01 President ... Dr. Michael SOSULSKI
05 Provost/Dean of College ... Dr. Michael HARVEY
45 VP Planning & Policy/Chief of Staff ... Dr. Victor SENSENIG
10 Vice Pres Finance ... Dr. Teresa SMITH
111 Vice Pres College Advancement ... Ms. Susie CHASE
84 Vice Pres Enrollment Mgmt/Marketing ... Dr. Lorna HUNTER
32 VP Student Affairs/Dean of Students ... Dr. Sarah FEYERHERM
20 Asst Dn First Yr Exp/Stdnt Success ... Vacant
31 Director of Campus Special Events ... Ms. Gina RALSTON
41 Director of Athletics ... Mr. Thad MOORE
06 Registrar ... Ms. Rachelle MARKS
08 Director of Miller Library ... Ms. Mary Alice BALL
21 Controller ... Vacant
18 Associate VP for Facilities ... Mr. Vic COSTA
15 Director of Human Resources ... Ms. Carolyn BURTON
19 Director of Public Safety ... Ms. Pamela HOFFMAN
07 Director of Recruitment ... Mrs. Kelsey MILLER
37 Director of Financial Aid ... Ms. Jennifer GALLAGHER
39 Dir Res Life/Assoc Dean of Students ... Mr. Greg KRIKORIAN
23 Clinical Director Health Services ... Mrs. Lisa M. MARX
38 Director of Counseling Center ... Ms. Miranda ALTMAN
36 Director of Career Development ... Mrs. Nanette COOLEY
28 Asst Dean Stdnts/Dir Intercult Affs ... Ms. Carese BATES
40 Bookstore Manager ... Ms. Shannon WYBLE
122 Dir Stdnt Engage-Frat/Sorority Life ... Mr. Antoine JORDAN

Women's Institute of Torah Seminary (F)

6602 Park Heights Avenue, Baltimore MD 21215
County: Baltimore Identification: 667271
Unit ID: 491631
Telephone: (410) 358-3144 Carnegie Class: Spec-4-yr-Faith
FAX Number: (866) 990-1983 Calendar System: Semester
URL: www.wits.edu
Established: 1998 Annual Undergrad Tuition & Fees: N/A
Enrollment: N/A Female
Affiliation or Control: Jewish IRS Status: 501(c)3
Highest Offering: Baccalaureate
Accreditation: AIJS

01 President ... Dr. Aviva WEISBORD
05 Academic Dean ... Dr. Leslie G. KLEIN

Wor-Wic Community College (A)

32000 Campus Drive, Salisbury MD 21804-1486
County: Wicomico   FICE Identification: 020739
Unit ID: 164313
Telephone: (410) 334-2800   Carnegie Class: Assoc/HVT-High Trad
FAX Number: (410) 334-2951   Calendar System: Semester
URL: www.worwic.edu
Established: 1975   Annual Undergrad Tuition & Fees (In-District): $6,480
Enrollment: 2,705   Coed
Affiliation or Control: Local   IRS Status: 501(c)3
Highest Offering: Associate Degree
Accreditation: M, ACFEI, CNEA, EMT, OTA, PTAA, RAD

01 President .... Dr. Murray K. HOY
05 Vice Pres Academic Affairs .... Dr. Kristin L. MALLORY
84 Vice Pres Enroll Mgmt & Student Svc .... Dr. Bryan NEWTON
10 Vice Pres Administrative Services .... Ms. Jennifer A. SANDT
26 Vice Pres Institutional Affairs .... Dr. Reenie MCCORMICK
51 Dean Continuing Education .... Ms. Ruth E. BAKER
97 Dean General Education .... Dr. Patricia L. RILEY
76 Dean Health Professions .... Dr. Karie SOLEMBRINO
88 Dean Occupational & Emerging Tech .... Mr. Paul SILBERQUIT
07 Director Admissions & Records .... Ms. Angie N. HAYDEN
13 Chief Information Officer .... Ms. Ruth F. GILL
36 Director Career & Testing Services .... Ms. Lori SMOOT
37 Director Financial Aid .... Ms. Katie ABREU
21 Director Finance .... Ms. Megan H. SMITH
15 Executive Director Human Resources .... Ms. Karen BERKHEIMER
121 Director of Student Success .... Mr. Aaron PREBENDA
27 Director Marketing .... Ms. Janet S. KENNINGTON
09 Director Inst Research .... Ms. Carol A. MENZEL
30 Director Development .... Ms. Jessica HALES
06 Registrar .... Ms. Amanda MESSATZZIA
32 Sr Director of Student Development .... Dr. Deirdra G. JOHNSON
07 Sr Director Enrollment Services .... Vacant
08 Director of Library Services .... Ms. Diana MILLS
18 Sr Director Facilities Management .... Mr. Gregory D. GREY
96 Director Purchasing & Auxiliary Svc .... Ms. Allison M. CANADA
105 Web Developer .... Mr. Joshua W. TOWNSEND
19 Director Public Safety .... Mr. Linnie VANN, JR.
108 Dir Inst Assessment & Effectiveness .... Dr. Julio BIRMAN
88 Director Early College Initiatives .... Mr. Richard C. WEBSTER
25 Director Grants .... Ms. Jo Ellen BYNUM

Yeshiva College of the Nation's Capital (B)

1216 Arcola Avenue, Silver Spring MD 20902-3408
County: Montgomery   FICE Identification: 039373
Unit ID: 434937
Telephone: (301) 649-7077   Carnegie Class: Spec-4-yr-Faith
FAX Number: (301) 649-7053   Calendar System: Semester
URL: https://www.yeshiva.college/
Established: 1995   Annual Undergrad Tuition & Fees: $10,600
Enrollment: 31   Male
Affiliation or Control: Independent Non-Profit   IRS Status: 501(c)3
Highest Offering: Second Talmudic Degree
Accreditation: RABN

01 President .... Mr. Abe ZWANY
05 Rosh Yeshiva .... Rabbi Aaron LOPIANSKY
06 Registrar .... Ms. Maryanna WALLS
11 Administrator .... Rabbi Yitzi LABELL

MASSACHUSETTS

American International College (C)

1000 State Street, Springfield MA 01109-3155
County: Hampden   FICE Identification: 002114
Unit ID: 164447
Telephone: (413) 737-7000   Carnegie Class: DU-Mod
FAX Number: (413) 205-3084   Calendar System: Semester
URL: www.aic.edu
Established: 1885   Annual Undergrad Tuition & Fees: $38,220
Enrollment: 2,612   Coed
Affiliation or Control: Independent Non-Profit   IRS Status: 501(c)3
Highest Offering: Doctorate
Accreditation: EH, IACBE, NURSE, OT, PTA

01 President .... Dr. Hubert M. BENITEZ
05 Exec Vice Pres Academic Affairs .... Dr. Velmer BURTON
11 COO/Chief of Staff .... Ms. Nicolle M. CESTERO
13 Chief Information Officer .... Ms. Mimi ROYSTON
35 VP Student Affairs/Dean of Students .... Mr. Matthew SCOTT
10 Vice President for Finance .... Mr. Christopher GARRITY
111 Exec Dir of Institutional Advance .... Ms. Jennifer MCDONOUGH
26 Int Dir Marketing & Communications .... Mr. Michael ERIQUEZZO
123 Director of Graduate Admissions .... Ms. Hannah HARTZSCH
07 Vice Pres of UG Admissions .... Mr. Kerry COLE
41 Athletic Director .... Ms. Jessica CHAPIN
76 Dean Health Sciences .... Dr. Karen ROUSSEAU
49 Dean Business/Arts/Sciences .... Dr. Susanne SWANKER
53 Dean of Education .... Vacant
109 Associate VP for Auxiliary Services .... Mr. Jeffrey BEDNARZ
06 Registrar .... Ms. Pamela ROBINSON
08 Director of Library .... Ms. Estelle H. SPENCER
38 Director Counseling Center .... Dr. Renee ROSADO
36 Dir of Career Services .... Mr. J. A. MARSHALL
66 Interim Dir of Division of Nursing .... Dr. Ellen FURMAN
50 Int Director of Business Programs .... Dr. Robyn POOLE
37 Director for Financial Aid .... Mr. Stephen PODESZWA
04 Exec Admin Asst to President .... Ms. Lani KRETSCHMAR
108 Dir of Institutional Effectiveness .... Dr. Kristy HUNTLEY
15 Director of Human Resources .... Ms. Debra RICO

Amherst College (D)

PO Box 5000, Amherst MA 01002-5000
County: Hampshire   FICE Identification: 002115
Unit ID: 164465
Telephone: (413) 542-2000   Carnegie Class: Bac-A&S
FAX Number: (413) 542-2621   Calendar System: Semester
URL: www.amherst.edu
Established: 1821   Annual Undergrad Tuition & Fees: $60,890
Enrollment: 1,745   Coed
Affiliation or Control: Independent Non-Profit   IRS Status: 501(c)3
Highest Offering: Baccalaureate
Accreditation: EH

01 President .... Dr. Michael A. ELLIOTT
05 Provost/Dean of the Faculty .... Dr. Catherine A. EPSTEIN
10 Interim Chief Financial Officer .... Mr. Thomas J. DWYER
32 Chief Student Affairs Officer .... Ms. Liz AGOSTO
18 Interim Chief of Campus Operations .... Mr. David BREEN
07 Dean Admission/Financial Aid .... Dr. Matthew MCGANN
111 Chief Advancement Officer .... Ms. Betsy CANNON SMITH
43 Chief Policy Ofcr/General Counsel .... Ms. Lisa H. RUTHERFORD
28 Interim Chief Equity & Incl Ofcr .... Ms. Angie TISSI-GASSOWAY
13 Chief Information Officer .... Mr. David L. HAMILTON
101 Secretary of the Board of Trustees .... Ms. Dianne M. PIERMATTEI
100 Interim Chief of Staff .... Ms. Kathleen PERTZBORN
26 Chief Communications Officer .... Ms. Sandy GENELIUS
15 Chief Human Resources Officer .... Ms. Kate HARRINGTON
20 Assoc Provost/Dean of the Faculty .... Dr. John CHENEY
20 Assoc Provost/Dean of the Faculty .... Dr. Pawan H. DHINGRA
37 Dean of Financial Aid .... Ms. Gail W. HOLT
09 Director of Institutional Research .... Mr. Jesse D. BARBA
21 Controller .... Mr. Stephen M. NIGRO
06 Registrar .... Vacant
08 Director of the Library .... Mr. Martin L. GARNAR
23 Director of Student Health Services .... Dr. Emily M. JONES
38 Director of Counseling Center .... Dr. Darien F. MCFADDEN
41 Director of Athletics .... Mr. Donald R. FAULSTICK
36 Director of the Career Center .... Ms. Emily GRIFFEN
109 Director of Dining Services .... Mr. Joseph T. FLUECKIGER
19 Chief of Campus Police .... Mr. John B. CARTER

Anna Maria College (E)

50 Sunset Lane, Paxton MA 01612-1198
County: Worcester   FICE Identification: 002117
Unit ID: 164492
Telephone: (508) 849-3333   Carnegie Class: Masters/M
FAX Number: (508) 849-3311   Calendar System: Semester
URL: www.annamaria.edu
Established: 1946   Annual Undergrad Tuition & Fees: $39,470
Enrollment: 1,492   Coed
Affiliation or Control: Roman Catholic   IRS Status: 501(c)3
Highest Offering: Beyond Master's But Less Than Doctorate
Accreditation: EH, EMT, MUS, NUR, SW

01 President .... Ms. Mary Lou RETELLE
05 VP for Academic Affairs .... Dr. Christine L. HOLMES
10 Vice President/Chief Financial Ofcr .... Vacant
13 Exec VP/Chief Information Officer .... Mr. Michael MIERS
32 VP for Student Affairs .... Ms. Jessica ECKSTROM
84 Vice Pres for Enrollment .... Mr. John HAMEL
31 VP for External Relations/CCO .... Mr. Hugh DRUMMOND
09 Asst VP Institutional Research .... Ms. Irene IRUDAYAM
35 Assoc VP for Student Affairs .... Vacant
111 VP for Institutional Advancement .... Ms. Bridget LEUNG-ROGALA
26 Manager of Marketing/Communications .... Ms. Sloane PERRON
06 Registrar .... Mr. John DELANEY
88 Director of the Learning Center .... Mr. Dennis VANASSE
23 Director of Health Services .... Vacant
08 Director of Library Services .... Ms. Becca PAC
29 Director of Alumni Engagement .... Vacant
36 Director Career Counsel/Placement .... Vacant
37 Director Financial Aid .... Ms. Nicole LENARES
04 Executive Asst to the President .... Vacant
18 Director Physical Plant .... Mr. Matthew SIMPSON
41 Athletic Director .... Mr. Joseph BRADY
42 Director Campus Ministry .... Vacant
15 Director of Human Resources .... Ms. Corina HENDEA
88 Dean of Mission Effectiveness .... Sr. Rollande QUINTAL
51 Director Grad/Continuing Educ .... Mr. Paul VACCARO
19 Public Safety .... Lt. Guy BIBEAU
102 Corporate & Foundation Rels Ofcr .... Mr. Richard RICARDI
28 Dir of Diversity/Equity/Inclusion .... Mr. Sherman COWAN
39 Director of Residence Life .... Mr. Drew MELENDEZ

Assumption University (F)

500 Salisbury Street, Worcester MA 01609-1296
County: Worcester   FICE Identification: 002118
Unit ID: 164562
Telephone: (508) 767-7000   Carnegie Class: Masters/M
FAX Number: (508) 767-7169   Calendar System: Semester
URL: www.assumption.edu
Established: 1904   Annual Undergrad Tuition & Fees: $43,978
Enrollment: 2,448   Coed
Affiliation or Control: Roman Catholic   IRS Status: 501(c)3
Highest Offering: Beyond Master's But Less Than Doctorate
Accreditation: EH, CACREP, MPCAC

01 Interim President .... Dr. Greg S. WEINER
10 VP for Finance and Administration .... Mr. Peter D. WELLS
05 Interim Provost/Academic Vice Pres .... Dr. Paul DOUILLARD
121 Vice President for Student Success .... Dr. Conway C. CAMPBELL
42 Vice President Mission .... Rev. Richard E. LAMOUREUX, AA
84 Vice Pres for Enrollment Management .... Mr. William BOFFI
43 General Counsel .... Dr. Michael H. RUBINO
58 Dean School of Graduate Studies .... Dr. Kimberly A. SCHANDEL
50 Dean School of Business .... Mr. Patrick CULLEN
66 Dean School of Nursing .... Ms. Caitlin M. STOVER
49 Interim Dean Col of Liberal Arts .... Dr. Michele A. GRAVELINE
107 Dir of Professional Studies .... Vacant
76 Dean School of Health Professions .... Dr. Robert J. AMRIEN
07 Dean of Enrollment .... Ms. Katie MOULTON
20 Assoc VP Academic Affairs/Grant Dev .... Dr. Eloise KNOWLTON
20 Asst VP of Academic Affairs .... Dr. Jennifer K. MORRISON
13 Chief Information Technology Office .... Mr. Wayne ROBIN
42 Director of Campus Ministry .... Mr. Paul F. COVINO
38 Director of Counseling Services .... Mr. Frank DIBERT
08 Director of Library Services .... Mr. Vincent BOISSELLE
10 Director of Finance .... Ms. Cathleen R. CULLEN
09 Director Inst Research and Ac Asst .... Mr. Stuart J. MUNRO
06 Registrar .... Ms. Heather PECORARO
15 Director of Human Resources .... Mr. Robert CARSON
26 Exec Director of Comm/Marketing .... Ms. Maureen HALLEY
88 Assistant VP for Student Success .... Ms. Mary BRESNAHAN
110 Interim VP for Institutional Adv .... Ms. Melanie DEMARAIS
44 Director of Assumption Fund .... Mr. Timothy R. MARTIN
121 Director of Academic Support Center .... Dr. Allen A. BRUEHL
35 Assoc Dean of Students .... Mr. Joseph ZITO
41 Director of Athletics .... Mr. Eric GOBIEL
19 Director of Public Safety .... Mr. Steven B. CARL
23 Director of Health Services .... Ms. Sarah K. SHERWOOD
24 Director of Media Services .... Mr. Ted HALEY
37 Director of Financial Aid .... Ms. Monica M. BLONDIN
21 Director of Business Services .... Mr. Todd DERDERIAN
86 Exec Asst for Govt/Cmty Relations .... Mr. Daniel F. DITULLIO
36 Director of Career Services .... Ms. Shannon CURTIS
04 Exec Admin Asst to President .... Ms. Tiffany WILLIAMS
39 Director of Residential Life .... Mr. Benjamin A. KADAMUS

Babson College (G)

231 Forest Street, Babson Park MA 02457-0310
County: Norfolk   FICE Identification: 002121
Unit ID: 164580
Telephone: (781) 235-1200   Carnegie Class: Spec-4-yr-Bus
FAX Number: (781) 239-5231   Calendar System: Semester
URL: www.babson.edu
Established: 1919   Annual Undergrad Tuition & Fees: $54,144
Enrollment: 3,340   Coed
Affiliation or Control: Independent Non-Profit   IRS Status: 501(c)3
Highest Offering: Master's
Accreditation: EH

01 President .... Dr. Stephen SPINELLI
05 VP AA/Dean of the College .... Dr. Kenichi MATSUNO
111 Senior VP for Advancement .... Mr. Edward CHIU
10 Chief Administrative Officer .... Ms. Katherine CRAVEN
11 Chief Operating Officer .... Ms. Kelly LYNCH
26 VP/Chief Marketing Officer .... Mr. Kerry SALERNO
15 VP Human Resources .... Ms. Donna BONAPARTE
84 VP Enrollment Management .... Ms. Courtney MINDEN
43 VP and General Counsel .... Mr. Michael D. LAYISH
32 VP Learner Success/Dean of Campus .... Dr. Lawrence P. WARD
12 CEO Babson Global .... Mr. David ABDOW
04 Exec Assistant to the President .... Ms. Leila LAMOUREUX
12 CEO Babson Executive Education .... Ms. Karen HEBERT-MACCARO
13 VP & Chief Information Officer .... Mr. Phillip KNUTEL
31 VP Programming/Community Outreach .... Ms. Jane EDMONDS
28 Chief Diversity & Inclusion Officer .... Dr. Sadie BURTON-GOSS
18 AVP Facilities Mgmt & Construction .... Ms. Tricia LYONS
36 Dir Center for Career Development .... Ms. Cheri PAULSON
06 Registrar .... Ms. Linda KEAN
37 Dir Student Financial Aid .... Ms. Meredith A. STOVER
94 Exec Dir Ctr for Wms Entrep Ldrshp .... Dr. Susan DUFFY
19 ExDir Campus Safety/Chief of Police .... Ms. Erin CARCIA
41 Director of Athletics .... Mr. Michael LYNCH

Bard College at Simon's Rock (H)

84 Alford Road, Great Barrington MA 01230-9702
Telephone: (413) 644-4400   FICE Identification: 009645
Accreditation: &M

Bay Path University (I)

588 Longmeadow Street, Longmeadow MA 01106-2292
County: Hampden   FICE Identification: 002122
Unit ID: 164632
Telephone: (413) 565-1000   Carnegie Class: Masters/L
FAX Number: (413) 565-1105   Calendar System: Semester
URL: www.baypath.edu
Established: 1897   Annual Undergrad Tuition & Fees: $35,781
Enrollment: 3,224   Female
Affiliation or Control: Independent Non-Profit   IRS Status: 501(c)3
Highest Offering: Doctorate
Accreditation: EH, ARCPA, NURSE, OT

01 President Ms. Sandra J. DORAN
05 Int VP Academic Affairs/Provost Dr. John V. CARON
10 SVP Finance/Administrative Services Mr. Michael GIAMPIETRO
111 VP Development/Planned Giving Ms. Allison GEARING-KALILL
26 VP Univ Relations & Board Liaison Ms. Kathleen BOURQUE
45 Chief Strategy Officer Springfield Ms. Caron T. HOBIN
84 Vice Pres for Enrollment Mgmt Dr. Frank ROJAS
04 Assistant to the President Vacant
88 Deputy Chief Ops Effectiveness/TAWC Ms. Amanda GOULD
21 Controller Mr. John O'ROURKE
25 Asst Dean Research/Acad Resource Mr. Peter TESTORI
12 Director of the Concord Campus Ms. Karen CARLSON
27 Director of Univ Communications Ms. Kathleen WROBLEWSKI
37 Exec Dir of Student Financial Svcs Ms. Stephanie KING
36 Exec Dir Career & Life Planning Ms. Laureen CIRILLO
08 Director of the Library Vacant
06 Registrar Mr. Marshall BRADWAY
44 Associate Director of Annual Giving Ms. Amanda GENO
23 Director of Health Services Ms. Deborah BAKER
15 Asst VP & Dir of Human Resources Ms. Kathleen HALPIN-ROBBINS
18 Dir Facilities/Campus Services Mr. Paul E. STANTON
13 Exec Dir Information Mgmt Ms. Robin SAUNDERS
14 Director of IT Infrastructure Mr. Christopher KNERR
41 Director of Athletics Mr. Steven J. SMITH
88 Executive Director Brand Strategy Ms. Karen WOODS
32 Dean of Students/Engagement Ms. Dinah MOORE
94 Deputy Chief Learning Officer Ms. Maura DEVLIN
88 Dir Business Programs TAWC Ms. Piccus MEGAN
88 Dir MBA Entrepr Thnkg/Innov Practic Mr. Mo SATTAR
88 Dir Grad Pgms Nonprofit Mgmt/ Philan Ms. Sylvia DE HAAS PHILLIPS
49 Vice Provost/Dean Liberal Studies Ms. Kristine BARNETT
96 Exec Dir of Purchasing/Office Svcs Mr. Ted LETH-STEENSEN
102 Dir Foundation/Corporate Relations Ms. Janine MCVAY
53 Dean School Educ/Human/Hlth Sci Dr. Elizabeth FLEMING
81 Dean School of Science & Management Dr. Thomas LOPER
76 Dir Occupational Therapy Program Dr. Beverly ST. PIERRE
123 Dean Graduate Admissions Ms. Sheryl KOSAKOWSKI
57 Director MFA Program Ms. Leanna JAMES BLACKWELL
88 Director ABA Program Dr. Susan AINSLEIGH
88 Director PA Program Ms. Theresa RIETHLE
77 Dir Computer Sci & Cyber Security Mr. Matthew SMITH
88 Dir Higher Education Administration Ms. Lauren WAY
88 Dir Finance & Accounting Program Ms. Kara STEVENS
88 Program Director Genetic Counseling Ms. Janice BELINER
88 Program Director Healthcare Mgmt Ms. Theresa DEVITO
88 Director MS Leadership/Negotiation Mr. Joshua WEISS
88 Dir Ctr Excellence Women in Science Ms. Gina SEMPREBON
83 Director Graduate Psychology Pgm Mr. Mark BENANDER
88 Director MS Applied Data Science Ms. Ning JIA
88 Director Neuroscience Program Vacant
09 Director of Institutional Research Ms. Ashley MURACZEWSKI
39 Dir Resident Life/Student Housing Ms. Lindsie LAVIN

Bay State College (A)

31 St. James Avenue, Boston MA 02116-2975
County: Suffolk FICE Identification: 003965
Unit ID: 164641
Telephone: (617) 217-9000 Carnegie Class: Bac-Diverse
FAX Number: (617) 249-0400 Calendar System: Semester
URL: www.baystate.edu
Established: 1946 Annual Undergrad Tuition & Fees: $29,200
Enrollment: 691 Coed
Affiliation or Control: Proprietary IRS Status: Proprietary
Highest Offering: Baccalaureate
Accreditation: #EH, ADNUR, NURSE, PTAA

01 President Dr. Steven COMBS
05 Dean of Col/Chief Academic Officer Dr. Jeff MASON
32 Dean of Students Jeremy SHEPARD
10 Chief Financial Officer Kevin DERRIVAN
07 Dean of Admissions Justin SCHWARZ
09 Director of Institutional Research Dr. Jerome DEAN
06 Registrar Shannon GOO
08 Librarian Sherry COWAN
113 Student Account Admin/Bursar Vacant
36 Director Career Services Linh NGUYEN
38 Director Student Counseling Vacant
15 Director Human Resources Ethel DANIEL
13 Chief Info Technology Officer Jeffrey MYERS

Benjamin Franklin Institute of Technology (B)

41 Berkeley Street, Boston MA 02116-6296
County: Suffolk FICE Identification: 002151
Unit ID: 165884
Telephone: (617) 588-1368 Carnegie Class: Bac/Assoc-Mixed
FAX Number: (617) 482-3706 Calendar System: Semester
URL: www.bfit.edu
Established: 1908 Annual Undergrad Tuition & Fees: $17,550
Enrollment: 463 Coed
Affiliation or Control: Independent Non-Profit IRS Status: 501(c)3
Highest Offering: Baccalaureate
Accreditation: EH, OPD

01 Chief Executive Officer Aisha FRANCIS
125 President Emeritus Anthony BENOIT
05 Dean of Academic Affairs Marvin LOISEAU
10 Dean of Finance/Operations & CFO Kevin HEPNER
32 Dean of Students/Title IX Coord Jackie CORNOG
06 Registrar James KLASEN
08 Librarian Sharon B. BONK
07 Assoc Dean Admissions/Recruitment Calvin CONYERS
111 Chief Advancement Officer Angela JOHNSON
121 Director of Student Success Shawn AYALA
09 Director of Institutional Research James KLASEN
15 Director Human Resources Diane DANIELS
19 Director of Facilities Myftar MYRTAJ
36 Director of Career Services Emily LEOPOLD
37 Director Financial Aid Shani WILKERSON
04 Administrative Asst to President Vacant
13 Dean of Information Technology Larson ROGERS

Bentley University (C)

175 Forest Street, Waltham MA 02452-4705
County: Middlesex FICE Identification: 002124
Unit ID: 164739
Telephone: (781) 891-2000 Carnegie Class: Masters/L
FAX Number: (781) 891-2569 Calendar System: Semester
URL: www.bentley.edu
Established: 1917 Annual Undergrad Tuition & Fees: $53,790
Enrollment: 5,177 Coed
Affiliation or Control: Independent Non-Profit IRS Status: 501(c)3
Highest Offering: Doctorate
Accreditation: EH

01 President Dr. E. LaBrent CHRITE
43 VP General Counsel/Sec to Corp Ms. Judith MALONE
05 Provost/VP Academic Affairs Mr. Paul TESLUK
10 VP and Chief Financial Officer Ms. Maureen FORRESTER
111 VP University Advancement Vacant
32 VP Student Affairs Dr. J. Andrew SHEPARDSON
84 VP Enrollment Management Ms. Carolina FIGUEROA
13 VP Chief Information Officer Ms. Elizabeth HESS
49 Dean of Arts and Sciences Dr. Eric OCHES
50 Dean of Business/Grad School Dr. Sanjay PUTREVU
20 Associate Provost Dr. Patrick SCHOLTEN
121 Assoc Provost for Student Success Ms. Jane DE LEON - GRIFFIN
26 VP Marketing & Communications Mr. Christopher J. JOYCE
20 Assoc Provost Undergrad Education Ms. Catherina CARLSON
88 Director Grad Acad Advising Ms. Whitney KUHNLENZ
15 VP of Human Resources & CHRO Mr. George CANGIANO
21 Associate VP Finance & Operations Ms. Nancy ANTUNES
06 Registrar Ms. Aimee LETURMY
88 Ombudsperson Ms. Eliane MARKOFF
38 Director of Counseling Center Dr. Peter FORKNER
09 Director of Business Intelligence Ms. Kelly GIARDULLO
39 Assoc Dean Student Affairs/Res Ctr Mr. John PIGA
08 Director of Library Ms. Hope HOUSTON
90 Director Academic Tech Center Mr. Gaurav SHAH
25 Director of Sponsored Programs Ms. Susan RICHMAN
124 Assoc VP Enrollment Management Ms. Donna KENDALL
28 Chief Diversity & Inclusion Officer Ms. Katherine LAMPLEY
123 AVP Enrollment/Dir Grad Admissions Ms. Jennifer FLAGEL
18 Exec Director Facilities Management Mr. Thomas KANE
35 Dir of Student Pgm & Engagement Ms. Nicole CHABOT-WIEFERICH
04 Exec Asst to President Ms. Susan HAYES
104 Director of International Education Ms. Natalie SCHLEGEL
122 Sr Assc Dir Stdnt Pgms-Greek Life Mr. Matt GALEWSKI

Berklee College of Music (D)

1140 Boylston Street, Boston MA 02215-3693
County: Suffolk FICE Identification: 002126
Unit ID: 164748
Telephone: (617) 266-1400 Carnegie Class: Masters/L
FAX Number: (617) 247-6878 Calendar System: Semester
URL: www.berklee.edu
Established: 1945 Annual Undergrad Tuition & Fees: $45,660
Enrollment: 6,631 Coed
Affiliation or Control: Independent Non-Profit IRS Status: 501(c)3
Highest Offering: Master's
Accreditation: EH

01 President Erica MUHL
100 Chief of Staff Melissa HOWE
12 Int Exec Dir Boston Conservatory Lucinda CARTER
05 Provost & Exec VP Academic Affairs David BOGEN
32 Sr VP Student Enrollment/Engagement Betsy NEWMAN
106 SVP Pre-College/Online & Prof Pgms Deborah CAVALIER
84 VP Enrollment Marketing/Management Keiko BROOMHEAD
111 Sr VP Institutional Advancement Erin TUNNICLIFFE
10 SVP Fin/Admin/Chief Financial Ofcr Richard M. HISEY
88 Sr VP Intl Lrng/Exec Dir Berk Val María MARTINEZ ITURRIAGA
13 VP/Chief Information Officer Phil KNUTEL
15 VP Human Resources Eileen ALVITI
103 VP Educ Outreach/Social Entrepren Krystal BANFIELD
28 VP Diversity and Inclusion Lacretia FLASH
21 VP Finance Vacant
20 VP Acad Affs Boston Conservatory Andy VORES
20 Dean Acad Affairs Berklee Valenci Simone PILON
86 VP Community/Govt & Auxiliary Rels Kaitlin PASSAFARO
88 VP for Real Estate Vacant
85 Asst Vice Pres Global Initiative Jason CAMELIO
20 VP Academic Affairs/Vice Provost Jay KENNEDY
26 VP for External Affairs Tom RILEY
18 VP for Facilities Erin MCCABE
88 Dean Pre-Col/Online & Prof Pgms Sean HAGON
88 Dean of Prof Performance Div Ron SAVAGE
107 Dean of Prof Education Division Darla S. HANLEY
64 Dean of Music Boston Conservatory Michael SHINN
88 Dean of Dance Boston Conservatory Tommy NEBLETT
88 Dean of Theater Boston Conservator Scott EDMISTON
88 Dean Prof Writing & Music Tech Matthew NICHOLL
88 Dean of Africana Studies Emmett G. PRICE, III
06 Registrar Jeffrey KINNAMON
22 Chief Equity Ofcr/Title IX Coord Kelly DOWNES
39 Director of Campus Life Rosemary SHADOW
37 Director of Student Aid Services Kevin FIGUEIREDO
07 Dean of Admissions Damien S. BRACKEN
36 Assoc VP Career & Digital Strategy Stefanie HENNING
20 AVP Academic Affairs Robert LAGUEUX
111 Asst VP Institutional Advancement Beverly TRYON
35 AVP/Dean of Student Affairs Christopher READE
113 AVP Student Financial Svcs Katherine ANDERSON
88 AVP Global Program Dev Betsie BECKER
88 Asst VP Enrollment Strategy/Opers Michael MOYES
90 Asst VP Academic Tech Jerry SMITH
88 Asst VP Concert Operations Cathy HORN
14 Asst VP Systems/Networks & Info Sec Bob XAVIER
18 Assistant VP for Facilities Kevin ANDERSON
91 Asst VP Tech Training & Support Tony SULPRIZIO
08 Interim Dean Learning Resources Pablo VARGAS
09 Dean Inst Rsrch/Assessment/Accred Sharon KRAMER
19 Sr Dir Public Safety/Chief Police David RANSOM
121 VP Student Success Christopher KANDUS-FISHER
29 Director of Alumni Affairs Joseph DREESZEN
104 Assoc Director Study Abroad Tracey MELLOR
27 Sr Dir Marketing/Communications Janelle BROWNING
04 Sr Advisor to the President Stefano FALCONI
88 Chief of Staff Boston Conservatory Kimberly HAACK
88 Exec Dir Berklee NYC Stephen WEBBER

Boston Architectural College (E)

320 Newbury Street, Boston MA 02115-2795
County: Suffolk FICE Identification: 003966
Unit ID: 164872
Telephone: (617) 262-5000 Carnegie Class: Spec-4-yr-Arts
FAX Number: (617) 585-0111 Calendar System: Semester
URL: www.the-bac.edu
Established: 1889 Annual Undergrad Tuition & Fees: $21,924
Enrollment: 742 Coed
Affiliation or Control: Independent Non-Profit IRS Status: 501(c)3
Highest Offering: Master's
Accreditation: EH, CIDA, LSAR

01 President Mr. Mahesh DAAS
05 Vice President Academic Affairs Ms. Victoria LIPTAK
10 Vice President for Finance/Admin Mr. Sydney LEO
111 VP Institutional Advancement Ms. Heather SULLIVAN
84 VP of Enrollment Management Mr. James RYAN
18 Director of Facilities Ms. Ellen YEE
32 Assoc Vice Pres/Dean of Students Mr. Richard M. GRISWOLD
48 Dean Interior Architecture Ms. Denise RUSH
88 Dean Sch Landscape Architecture Ms. Maria BELLALTA
88 Dean School of Design Studies Mr. Donald HUNSICKER
48 Dean School of Architecture Ms. Karen L. NELSON
88 Dean & Faculty of Practice Mr. Len CHARNEY
13 Director of Information Technology Mr. Jason O'BRIEN
88 Dir of Master's Thesis Arch Mr. Ian TABERNER
88 Director of Digital Media Mr. Peter ATWOOD
78 Dir of Applied Learning in Practice Ms. Beth GARVER
88 Director of Media Arts Mr. Luis MONTALVO
08 Director of the Library Mr. Robert ADAMS
07 Director of Admissions Ms. Meredith SPINNATO
37 Director of Financial Aid Mr. Janice WILKOS-GREENBERG
06 Registrar Ms. Katherine KWOLEK
11 Dir of Administrative Operations Ms. Patti VAUGHN
88 Director of Foundation Studios Mr. Lee PETERS
15 Director of Human Resources Vacant
29 Dir of Special Events & Alumni Vacant
21 Assoc VP for Finance & Admin Ms. Diane MERCIER
121 Director Foundation Student Support Mr. Michael DANIELS
04 Executive Asst to President Ms. Shannon THORIN
26 Dir of Marketing & Communications Ms. Nancy FINN
39 Coordinator of Student Life Mr. Zachary TRIPSAS
90 Manager of IT Operations & Projects Ms. Janet MCCLAIN

Boston Baptist College (F)

950 Metropolitan Avenue, Hyde Park MA 02136
County: Suffolk FICE Identification: 032483
Unit ID: 164614
Telephone: (617) 364-3510 Carnegie Class: Spec-4-yr-Faith
FAX Number: (775) 245-1498 Calendar System: Semester
URL: www.boston.edu
Established: 1976 Annual Undergrad Tuition & Fees: $12,600
Enrollment: 60 Coed
Affiliation or Control: Baptist IRS Status: 501(c)3
Highest Offering: Baccalaureate
Accreditation: TRACS

01 President Rev. David V. MELTON
05 Vice President/Chief Academic Ofcr Rev. Randall WARD
11 Vice President for Operations Rev. Randall WARD
10 Chief Financial Officer Vacant
08 Head Librarian Mr. Fred TATRO

Boston College (A)

140 Commonwealth Avenue, Chestnut Hill MA 02467-3934
County: Middlesex FICE Identification: 002128
Unit ID: 164924
Telephone: (617) 552-3000 Carnegie Class: DU-Highest
FAX Number: (617) 552-8828 Calendar System: Semester
URL: www.bc.edu
Established: 1863 Annual Undergrad Tuition & Fees: $60,202
Enrollment: 14,934 Coed
Affiliation or Control: Roman Catholic IRS Status: 501(c)3
Highest Offering: Doctorate
Accreditation: EH, ANEST, COPSY, LAW, MPCAC, NURSE, SW, THEOL

01 President Rev. William P. LEAHY, S.J.
05 Provost & Dean of Faculties Dr. David QUIGLEY
03 Executive Vice President Mr. Michael J. LOCHHEAD
111 Senior VP University Advancement Vacant
04 Vice Pres/Exec Asst to President Mr. Kevin J. SHEA
10 Financial Vice President/Treasurer Mr. John D. BURKE
32 Vice Pres Student Affairs Ms. Shawna COOPER WHITEHEAD
15 Vice President for Human Resources Mr. David P. TRAINOR
13 Vice Pres Information Technology Mr. Michael J. BOURQUE
88 Vice Pres Univ Mission & Ministry Rev. John T. BUTLER, S.J.
86 Vice Pres Govt/Community Affairs Mr. Thomas J. KEADY
18 Vice Pres Facilities Management Mr. Daniel F. BOURQUE
09 Vice Pres Inst Research & Planning Ms. Mara HERMANO
88 VP & Exec Director PMISS Ms. Joy MOORE
20 Vice Provost Undergrad Acad Affairs Dr. Akua SARR
84 Vice Prov for Enrollment Management Mr. John MAHONEY, JR.
20 Vice Provost for Faculties Dr. Billy SOO
111 Interim Sr VP Univ Advancement Ms. Amy YANCEY
18 Assoc VP Capital Projects Ms. Mary S. NARDONE
29 Associate VP Alumni Relations Ms. Leah DECOSTA
16 Assoc VP Human Resources Mr. William MURPHY
109 Assoc VP Auxiliary Services Ms. Patricia A. BANDO
49 Dean Morrissey Col Arts & Sciences Rev. Gregory KALSCHEUR, S.J.
88 Assoc Dean of Strategic Initiatives Mr. David M. GOODMAN
53 Dean Lynch Sch Education/Human Dev Dr. Stanton WORTHAM
61 Interim Dean Law School Ms. Diane RING
50 Dean Carroll School of Management Dr. Andrew C. BOYNTON
66 Dean Connell School of Nursing Dr. Katherine GREGORY
70 Dean School of Social Work Dr. Gautam N. YADAMA
73 Dean School of Theology & Ministry Rev. Michael MCCARTHY, SJ
20 Dean Woods Col of Advancing Studies Ms. Karen MUNCASTER
35 Assoc VP Student Affairs Dr. Melinda STOOPS
08 University Librarian Dr. Thomas WALL
28 Exec Dir Institutional Diversity Ms. Patricia LOWE
06 Int Exec Director Student Services Vacant
07 Director Undergraduate Admissions Mr. Grant M. GOSSELIN
27 AVP Office of Univ Communications Mr. John B. DUNN
102 Assoc VP Schools & Org Giving Ms. Renee DECESARE
41 Director Athletics Mr. Blake JAMES
36 Assoc VP Student Affairs Mr. Joseph DUPONT
42 Assoc VP Campus Ministry Rev. Anthony PENNA
31 Director of Community Affairs Mr. William R. MILLS
38 Director of Univ Counseling Svcs Mr. Craig D. BURNS
37 Director Financial Aid Ms. Ebony MARSALA
23 Director Health Services Dr. Douglas COMEAU
39 Assoc VP Residential Life Mr. George A. AREY
25 Director Sponsored Programs Ms. Jennifer LOPEZ
19 Dir Public Safety/Chief of Police Mr. William B. EVANS
40 Director Bookstore Mr. Robert STEWART
43 General Counsel Ms. Nora FIELD
24 Director Media Technology Services Mr. David CORKUM
85 Dir Office of International Pgms Dr. Nick GOZIK
88 Dir Jesuit Inst/VProv Global Engage Rev. James F. KEENAN, SJ
93 Director AHANA/Intercultural Center Rev. Michael DAVIDSON
86 Director Governmental Relations Ms. Jeanne LEVESQUE
96 Director Procurement Services Mr. Paul MCGOWAN
108 AV Provost Assessment/Accreditation Dr. Jessica A. GREENE

Boston Graduate School of Psychoanalysis (B)

1581 Beacon Street, Brookline MA 02446-4602
County: Norfolk FICE Identification: 031943
Unit ID: 164915
Telephone: (617) 277-3915 Carnegie Class: Spec-4-yr-Other Health
FAX Number: (617) 277-0312 Calendar System: Semester
URL: www.bgsp.edu
Established: 1973 Annual Graduate Tuition & Fees: N/A
Enrollment: 142 Coed
Affiliation or Control: Independent Non-Profit IRS Status: 501(c)3
Highest Offering: Doctorate; No Undergraduates
Accreditation: EH

01 President Dr. Jane SNYDER
10 Vice President Finance Dr. Carol PANETTA
58 Dean of Graduate Studies Dr. Lynn PERLMAN
07 Director of Admissions Dr. Paula BERMAN
06 Registrar Ms. Dianne KAELI
37 Director of Financial Aid Ms. Stephanie WOOLBERT
21 Controller Ms. Gayle DOLAN
08 Head Librarian Ms. Amy COHEN-ROSE
88 Director of the Center for Research Dr. Stephen SOLDZ

Boston University (C)

One Silber Way, Boston MA 02215-1700
County: Suffolk FICE Identification: 002130
Unit ID: 164988
Telephone: (617) 353-2000 Carnegie Class: DU-Highest
FAX Number: N/A Calendar System: Semester
URL: www.bu.edu
Established: 1839 Annual Undergrad Tuition & Fees: $58,072
Enrollment: 32,718 Coed
Affiliation or Control: Independent Non-Profit IRS Status: 501(c)3
Highest Offering: Doctorate
Accreditation: EH, ARCPA, ART, CAATE, CACREP, CAHIIM, CEA, CLPSY, COPSY, DENT, DIETD, DIETI, FEPAC, HSA, IPSY, LAW, MED, MUS, OT, PCSAS, PH, PTA, SP, SW, THEOL

01 President Robert A. BROWN
05 University Provost Jean MORRISON
17 Provost Med Campus/Dean Sch of Med Karen H. ANTMAN
100 VP & Chief of Staff to President Douglas A. SEARS
10 SVP/CFO/Treas/Fin Affs & HR Gary W. NICKSA
26 Senior VP External Relations Stephen P. BURGAY
30 Senior VP Devel/Alumni Relations Karen ENGELBOURG
04 Exec Asst to President's Office Megan S. COHEN
49 Dean Col & Grad Sch Arts/Sciences Stan SCLAROFF
60 Dean College of Communication Mariette DICHRISTINA-GEROSA
53 Dean Wheelock Col of Educ & HD David CHARD
54 Dean College of Engineering Kenneth R. LUTCHEN
57 Dean College of Fine Arts Harvey YOUNG
97 Dean College General Studies Natalie MCKNIGHT
88 Dean School of Hospitality Admin Arun UPNEJA
61 Dean of School of Law Angela ONWUACHI-WILLIG
50 Dean Questrom School of Business Susan FOURNIER
42 Dean of Marsh Chapel Robert A. HILL
51 Dean Metropolitan College/Ext Ed Tanya ZLATEVA
76 Dean SAR Health & Rehab Sciences Christopher A. MOORE
70 Dean School of Social Work Jorge DELVA
73 Dean School of Theology G. Sujin PAK
82 Dean Pardee Sch of Global Studies Adil NAJAM
52 Int Dean Goldman Sch Dental Med Cataldo LEONE
69 Dean School of Public Health Sandro GALEA
32 Interim Assoc Prov/Dean of Students Jason CAMPBELL-FOSTER
46 VP & Assoc Provost Research Gloria WATERS
31 Int Assoc Provost Cmty/Inclusion Karin FIROZA
58 Assoc Provost Graduate Affairs Daniel L. KLEINMAN
58 Assoc Provost Graduate Affairs Neena VERMA
114 Assoc Provost Budget & Planning Patricia O'BRIEN
88 Chief of Staff Provost's Office Judith SANDONATO
88 Assoc Prov for Faculty Acad Svcs Maureen O'ROURKE
20 Assoc Provost Undergraduate Affairs Amie GRILLS
106 Assoc Prov Digital Lrng/ Innovation Chrysanthos (Chris) DELLAROCAS
88 Sp Advisor to Pres Financial Affs Martin J. HOWARD
11 Senior VP Operations Derek HOWE
109 Vice President Auxiliary Services Peter SMOKOWSKI
43 SVP/Board Sec/Gen Counsel Trustees Erika GEETTER
86 Vice President Federal Relations Jennifer GRODSKY
18 VP Campus Planning & Operations Michael DONOVAN
85 VP/Assoc Provost Global Programs Willis G. WANG
88 Assoc Prov Comp & Data Sciences Azer BESTAVROS
88 Assoc Prov Spec Proj & Emerging Pro Suzanne KENNEDY
13 VP Info Svcs & Tech/Chief Data Ofcr Tracy SCHROEDER
84 VP/Assoc Prov Enroll & Stdnt Admin Christine W. MCGUIRE
86 VP Government/Community Rels Jake SULLIVAN
27 VP Marketing & Creative Services Amy HOOK
115 Chief Investment Officer Lila HUNNEWELL
19 Exec Dir Pub Safety/Chief of Police Kelly A. NEE
39 VP/Exec Director of Housing Nishmin KASHYAP
103 Exec Dir Career Development Addye BUCKLEY-BURNELL
15 VP for Human Resources Amanda BAILEY
16 Exec Dir Talent Mgmt/HR Officer Patricia SHEEHAN
07 Assoc VP Enrol & Dean of Admissions Kelly A. WALTER
35 Assoc VP Enroll & Student Affairs Denise MOONEY
88 Assoc VP Stdnt Info Sys/Comm & PM Marylou O'DONNELL-RUNDLETT
25 Assoc VP Sponsored Programs Diane BALDWIN
114 VP Budget/Plng & Business Affairs Ines GARRANT
21 VP of Fin Opers & Univ Comptroller Nicole TIRELLA
29 VP for Alumni Engagement Erika JORDAN
91 SVP Applications & Enterprise Svcs Janet O'BRIEN
09 Asst VP Analytical Svcs & Inst Rsch Linette A. DECARIE
88 Asst VP PostAward Financial Opers Gretchen HARTIGAN
87 Assistant Dean Summer Term Erin SALIUS
35 Asst Dean Stdnt/Exec Dir Stdnt Act John BATTAGLINO, JR.
108 Interim Asst Prov Acad Assessment Megan M. SULLIVAN
44 Exec Director Annual Giving Scott GRAHAM
41 Asst VP & Director of Athletics Drew MARROCHELLO
06 Acting University Registrar Debbie MACALINTAL
96 Asst VP/Chief Procurement Officer Randall MOORE
104 Exec Director Study Abroad Gareth MCFEELY
37 Exec Dir Financial Assistance Julie WICKSTROM
85 Mng Dir Intl Student/Scholars Ofc Jeanne KELLEY
88 Director Howard Thurman Center Katherine J. KENNEDY
88 Director Center for Anti-Racism Ibram X. KENDI
09 Director Institutional Research Elizabeth CAMPBELL
22 Exec Dir Equal Opportunity Jean ESTEVEZ
36 Senior Asst Dir Student Employment Jim RIVERA
08 Interim University Librarian Mark NEWTON
88 General Manager Agganis Arena Kristoffer W. BRASSIL
88 Exec Director Physical Ed Rec/Dance Timothy MOORE
23 Chief Health Officer/Exec Dir SHS Judy T. PLATT
28 Senior Diversity Officer Andrea TAYLOR
102 Assoc VP Industry Engagement Marc SCATAMACCHIA
105 Sr Functional Analyst/Res Adm/Web Ron YEANY
38 Exec Director Student Wellbeing Carrie LANDA
90 Director of Research Computing Wayne GILMORE
88 Dir Ugrad Rsrch Opportunities Pgm John CELENZA
88 Director Institute Comp Sci & Eng Ioannis PASCHALIDIS

Brandeis University (D)

415 South Street, Waltham MA 02453
County: Middlesex FICE Identification: 002133
Unit ID: 165015
Telephone: (781) 736-2000 Carnegie Class: DU-Highest
FAX Number: (781) 736-8699 Calendar System: Semester
URL: www.brandeis.edu
Established: 1948 Annual Undergrad Tuition & Fees: $57,615
Enrollment: 5,440 Coed
Affiliation or Control: Independent Non-Profit IRS Status: 501(c)3
Highest Offering: Doctorate
Accreditation: EH

01 President Dr. Ronald D. LIEBOWITZ
05 Provost Dr. Carol A. FIERKE
10 Exec VP for Finance/Administration Mr. Stewart URETSKY
111 Interim Sr VP Inst Advancement Ms. Hannah PETERS
43 Sr VP and General Counsel Mr. Steven S. LOCKE
26 Sr VP of Communications/Marketing Mr. Dan KIM
21 Chief Financial Officer & Treasurer Dr. Samuel SOLOMON
28 Chief Diversity Officer Dr. LeManuel BITSÓI
100 Chief of Staff/Sr Advisor to Pres Ms. Meredith L. AINBINDER
18 Vice Pres for Campus Operations Dr. Lois A. STANLEY
29 VP of Alumni Relations Ms. Patsy FISHER
13 Chief Information Officer Dr. James LA CRETA
15 Vice Pres Human Resources Mr. Robin SWITZER
32 Interim VP of Student Affairs Ms. Andrea B. DINE
45 VP Planning/Institutional Research Mr. Dan FELDMAN
09 Director of Institutional Research Ms. Haley ROSENFELD
37 Asst VP Student Financial Services Ms. Sherri M. AVERY
49 Dean of Arts & Sciences Dr. Dorothy L. HODGSON
70 Int Dn Heller Sch Social Pol & Mgt Dr. Maria MADISON
50 Dean International Business Sch Dr. Kathryn GRADDY
06 University Registrar Dr. Mark S. HEWITT
08 University Librarian Mr. Matthew SHEEHY
07 Dean of Admissions/Financial Aid Ms. Jennifer WALKER
41 Athletic Director Ms. Lauren HAYNIE

Cambridge College (E)

500 Rutherford Avenue, Boston MA 02129
County: Suffolk FICE Identification: 021829
Unit ID: 165167
Telephone: (800) 877-4723 Carnegie Class: Masters/L
FAX Number: N/A Calendar System: Trimester
URL: www.cambridgecollege.edu
Established: 1971 Annual Undergrad Tuition & Fees: $16,266
Enrollment: 2,764 Coed
Affiliation or Control: Independent Non-Profit IRS Status: 501(c)3
Highest Offering: Doctorate
Accreditation: EH

01 President Deborah C. JACKSON
05 Provost/VP Academic Affairs Dr. Stephen HEALEY
10 CFO/VP of Finance & Administration Dennis J. MADIGAN
15 VP of Human Resources Lauretta SIGGERS
86 VP of Strategic Partnerships Phillip PAGE
45 VP of Innovation/Strat Initiatives Mark ROTONDO
111 VP of Institutional Advancement Tom CAHILL
106 Executive Director CC Global Howard HORTON
43 General Counsel Judith SIZER
20 Assoc Provost Student Learning Dr. Tracy MCLAUGHLIN-VOLPE
13 Director of Information Technology Achal KHATRI
113 Dir of Student Financial Services Christina GRIECCI
37 Director of Financial Aid Frank LAUDER
21 Controller Joe CULLEN
06 Registrar Amy CAVELIER
09 Senior Director Research/Planning Stephanie FUNDERBURG
12 Director of Puerto Rico Dr. Santiago MENDEZ-HERNANDEZ
12 Director of Southern California Courtney GRIFFIN
12 Director of Lawrence MA Vacapt
12 Executive Director Springfield MA Vacant
112 Dir Strategic Partnerships Alex MORR
29 Dir Annual Fund/Alumni Engagement Erik RYAN
26 AVP Marketing/Digital Strategy Maria VASALLO
97 Dean Undergraduate Studies Dr. James LEE
83 Dean School of Psychology and Educ Dr. Niti SETH
32 Asst Dean of Student Affairs Vera DIMOPLON
50 Interim Dean School of Mgmt Dr. Joseph MIGLIO
07 Senior Director Admission Vacant
121 Dir Undergrad Academic Advising Michael DICKINSON
04 Sr Exec Assistant to President Robyn CARROLL
08 Chief Library Officer Anthony VIOLA

Clark University (F)

950 Main Street, Worcester MA 01610-1477
County: Worcester FICE Identification: 002139
Unit ID: 165334
Telephone: (508) 793-7711 Carnegie Class: DU-Higher
FAX Number: (508) 793-7780 Calendar System: Semester
URL: www.clarku.edu
Established: 1887 Annual Undergrad Tuition & Fees: $48,602
Enrollment: 3,405 Coed
Affiliation or Control: Independent Non-Profit IRS Status: 501(c)3
Highest Offering: Doctorate
Accreditation: EH, CLPSY

01 President Dr. David B. FITHIAN
10 Executive VP/CFO & Treasurer Ms. Danielle MANNING

05 Provost & Vice Pres Academic Affs ....Dr. Sebastian ROYO
111 Interim VP Univ Advancement ....Mr. Jonathan KAPPEL
26 Vice Pres Marketing & Communication ....Ms. Jill FRIEDMAN
07 VP Admissions & Financial Aid ....Ms. Meredith TWOMBLY
13 Vice Pres for Information Tech/CIO ....Mr. Joseph KALINOWSKI
86 VP Government & Cmty Affairs .... Mr. Joseph CORAZZINI
45 VP Planning & Strategic Initiatives .... Mr. David CHEARO
100 Chief of Staff .... Mr. David CHEARO
32 Dean of Students .... Ms. Kamala KIEM
46 Dean of Research/Dean Grad Studies .... Dr. Yuko AOYAMA
49 Dean of the College ....Dr. Betsy HUANG
20 Dean of the Faculty ....Dr. Esther JONES
58 Dean School of Management ....Dr. Alan EISNER
107 Dean of School of Prof Studies ....Mr. John LABRIE
37 Director of Financial Assistance ....Ms. Jennifer LAWTON
08 University Librarian ....Ms. Laura ROBINSON
21 Controller/Asst Treasurer ....Ms. Anne RANDALL
36 Director Career Development ....Ms. Michelle FLINT
06 Registrar .... Mr. John OHOTNICKY
15 Dir of HR/Affirm Action .... Mr. David EVERITT
18 Director of Facilities Management .... Mr. Daniel RODERICK
41 Dir of Athletics & Recreation ....Ms. Trish CRONIN
45 Assoc VP Planning & Finance ....Mr. Paul WYKES
19 Chief of Campus Police .... Ms. Lauren MISALE
23 Director of Health Services ....Ms. Robin MCNALLY
28 VP & Chief Officer Diversity/Incl ....Ms. Margo FOREMAN
109 Business & Auxiliary Services Mgr .... Mr. Anthony PENNY
09 Dir Strat Analytics/Inst Research .... Ms. Elissa LU
104 Director Study Abroad .... Ms. Alissa BRIGGS
39 Dir Res Life & Housing .... Mr. Jess MONTECALVO
22 Title IX Coord ....Ms. Cherie SCRICCA
102 Dir Foundation/Corporate Relations ....Ms. Jennifer HITT
105 Dir of Digital Content Strategy .... Ms. Meredith KING
04 Executive Asst to the President ....Vacant
88 Dean Becker School Design & Tech ....Mr. Paul COTNOIR
43 VP/General Counsel ....Mr. Kendall ISAAC

College of the Holy Cross (A)

1 College Street, Worcester MA 01610-2395

County: Worcester FICE Identification: 002141
Unit ID: 166124
Telephone: (508) 793-2011 Carnegie Class: Bac-A&S
FAX Number: (508) 793-3030 Calendar System: Semester
URL: www.holycross.edu
Established: 1843 Annual Undergrad Tuition & Fees: $54,770
Enrollment: 2,970 Coed
Affiliation or Control: Roman Catholic IRS Status: 501(c)3
Highest Offering: Baccalaureate
Accreditation: EH, THEA

01 President ....Mr. Vincent D. ROUGEAU
04 Sr Exec Assistant to the President ....Ms. Melanie MITCHELL
10 VP Admin & Finance/Treasurer ....Ms. Dottie HAUVER
42 Vice President for Mission ....Vacant
84 Vice Provost for Enrollment Mgmt ....Mr. Cornell B. LESANE, II
05 Provost/Dean of the College .... Dr. Margaret FREIJE
26 VP for Communications ....Ms. Marisa GREGG
111 VP for Advancement ....Ms. Tracy BARLOK
32 VP Student Affairs/Dean of Students .... Ms. Michelle MURRAY
115 Chief Investment Officer ....Vacant
28 Assoc Provost for Diversity/Equity ....Mr. Amit TANEJA
20 Dean of the Faculty ....Dr. Ann Marie LESHKOWICH
20 Dean of the Faculty .... Dr. Mary EBBOTT
21 Director of Finance/Asst Treasurer ....Mr. Charles ESTAPHAN
22 Director of Title IX and EO .... Mr. Derek DEBOBES
06 Registrar .... Ms. Patricia RING
07 Int Director of Admissions ....Ms. Lynn VERRECCHIA
08 Director of Library Services .... Mr. Mark SHELTON
37 Director of Financial Aid .... Ms. Nicole CUNNINGHAM
25 Director of Sponsored Research .... Ms. Stacy RISEMAN
42 Director Ofc of College
Chaplains ....Ms. Marybeth KEARNS-BARRETT
88 Director Ctr Interdisc Studies ....Dr. Lorelle SEMLEY
36 Director of Career Planning ....Ms. Amy MURPHY
13 Director Information Tech Services ....Dr. Ellen J. KEOHANE
29 Director of Alumni Relations ....Ms. Kristyn M. DYER
19 Director of Public Safety .... Ms. Shawn DE JONG
35 Director of Campus Center ....Mr. Jeremiah O'CONNOR
18 Director of Physical Plant .... Mr. Scott M. MERRILL
41 Int Co-Dir Intercol Athletics ....Mr. Nick SMITH
41 Int Co-Dir Intercol Athletics ....Ms. Rose SHEA
21 Controller .... Ms. Charlene BELLOWS
38 Director Counseling Center ....Dr. Paul GALVINHILL
23 Health Services Director .... Ms. Kelsey R. DEVOE
15 Chief Human Resources Ofcr ....Ms. Marymichele DELANEY
96 Assistant Director Purchasing ....Mr. Scott SLABODEN
09 Ofc of Assessment/Research ....Dr. Denise BELL
86 Dir of Govt/Community Rels ....Mr. Jamie D. HOAG
43 General Counsel ....Ms. Elizabeth SMALL
104 Director Study Abroad .... Dr. Brittain SMITH

College of Our Lady of the Elms (B)

291 Springfield Street, Chicopee MA 01013-2839

County: Hampden FICE Identification: 002140
Unit ID: 167394
Telephone: (413) 594-2761 Carnegie Class: Masters/M
FAX Number: (413) 592-4871 Calendar System: Semester
URL: www.elms.edu
Established: 1928 Annual Undergrad Tuition & Fees: $38,391
Enrollment: 1,355 Coed
Affiliation or Control: Roman Catholic IRS Status: 501(c)3
Highest Offering: Doctorate
Accreditation: EH, IACBE, NURSE, SW

01 President ....Dr. Harry E. DUMAY
05 Vice President of Academic Affairs ....Dr. Walter C. BREAU
10 Vice Pres Finance/Administration ....Katie LONGLEY
84 VP Enrollment Mgmt & Marketing ....Jonathan SCULLY
111 VP Institutional Advancement ....Bernadette NOWAKOWSKI
32 VP Stdnt Affs/Chf Diversity Officer ....Vacant
35 Dean of Students ....Teresa WINTERS
07 Director of Admissions ....Jenna STOLARIK
20 AVP Academic Affs/Strat Initiatives ....Dr. Joyce HAMPTON
121 Asst Acad Dean for Student Support ....Nancy DAVIS
15 Director Human Resources/Personnel .... Cheryl SMITH
06 Registrar .... Brooke BEDARD
113 Bursar .... Kathleen CURRY
21 Controller ....Vacant
08 Director of Library ....Anthony FONSECA
26 Director of Marketing ....Vacant
37 Director of Financial Aid ....Michele JARVIS-LETTMAN
36 Director of Career Services ....J. MARSHALL
04 Executive Assistant to President ....Bevin PETERS
09 Dir of Inst Assessment & Research ....Karalee YVON
44 Exec Dir Annual Giving/Alumni Rels ....Lynn KORZA
18 Dir of Campus Operations & Planning ....Ron RICKEY
39 Dir of Residence Life ....Maira PANTOJA
19 Director of Public Safety ....Pablo MADERA
41 Director of Athletics ....Michael THEULEN
66 Interim Dean School of Nursing ....Dr. Teresa KUTA RESKE
58 Dean School of Grad & Prof Studies ..... Dr. Elizabeth HUKOWICZ
28 Dir of Diversity & Inclusion ....Jennifer SHOAFF
38 Director of Counseling Center ....Dr. Nicole HADDAD
23 Director of Health Center ....Jessie CHENIER
42 Director of Campus Ministry .... Eileen KIRK
120 Director of Educ Tech & IT Support ....Sara FLINK
119 Dir of IT Apps/Infrastructure/Sec ....Alexander ZMACZYNSKI
105 Web Manager ....Nate JASPER
104 Director of International Programs ....Octavio SEIJAS
101 Secretary of the Institution/Board ....Kristin KIRWAN

Conway School of Landscape Design (C)

88 Village Hill Road, Northampton MA 01060

County: Hampshire FICE Identification: 022743
Unit ID: 165495
Telephone: (413) 369-4044 Carnegie Class: Spec-4-yr-Other
FAX Number: (413) 203-6914 Calendar System: Trimester
URL: www.csld.edu
Established: 1972 Annual Graduate Tuition & Fees: N/A
Enrollment: 13 Coed
Affiliation or Control: Independent Non-Profit IRS Status: 501(c)3
Highest Offering: Master's; No Undergraduates
Accreditation: EH

01 Executive Director .... Mr. Bruce STEDMAN
05 Academic Director .... Mr. Ken BYRNE
10 Finance Manager .... Ms. Kara SCHNELL
11 Administrative Director .... Ms. Priscilla NOVITT
06 Registrar/Dir Alumni/Librarian .... Ms. Elaine WILLIAMSON
07 Admissions Manager ....Ms. Kate CHOLAKIS
18 Chief Facilities/Physical Plnt Ofcr ....Mr. David WEBER

Curry College (D)

1071 Blue Hill Avenue, Milton MA 02186-2395

County: Norfolk FICE Identification: 002143
Unit ID: 165529
Telephone: (617) 333-0500 Carnegie Class: Masters/S
FAX Number: (617) 979-3540 Calendar System: Semester
URL: www.curry.edu
Established: 1879 Annual Undergrad Tuition & Fees: $42,425
Enrollment: 2,410 Coed
Affiliation or Control: Independent Non-Profit IRS Status: 501(c)3
Highest Offering: Master's
Accreditation: EH, IACBE, NURSE

01 President ....Mr. Kenneth K. QUIGLEY, JR.
05 EVP Academic Affairs/Provost ....Dr. David SZCZERBACKI
111 VP Institutional Advancement .... Ms. Sally MURRAY
84 VP Enrollment Management ....Mr. Edmond CABELLON
10 EVP/Chief Financial Officer .... Mr. David M. ROSATI
15 Interim VP of Human Resources .... Ms. Diane TUCKER
07 Assoc VP & Dean of Admission .... Mr. Keith ROBICHAUD
32 VP of Student Affairs ....Ms. Maryellen M. KILEY
45 Special Advisor to the President ....Dr. Susan W. PENNINI
04 Exec Assistant to the President .... Ms. Amy M. BIANCHI
08 Director Library .... Ms. Katharine G. EASTMAN
13 Chief Information Officer ....Vacant
06 Registrar ....Ms. June KOUKOL
18 Director of Buildings & Grounds .... Mr. Robert G. O'CONNELL
26 Interim VP of Mktg/Communications ....Ms. Liz MATSON
36 Director of Global & Career Service ... Ms. Mireille MCLAUGHLIN
37 Assoc VP of Finance for SFS ....Ms. Stephanny J. ELIAS
35 Director of Student Services .... Dr. Kathryn BRUNING
09 Director of Institutional Research ....Ms. Jennifer DUNNE
105 Director Web Services ....Mr. John EAGAN
41 Athletic Director .... Mr. Vincent ERUZIONE
39 Asst Director Res Life .... Ms. Marcie HARRINGTON

Dean College (E)

99 Main Street, Franklin MA 02038-1994

County: Norfolk FICE Identification: 002144
Unit ID: 165574
Telephone: (508) 541-1508 Carnegie Class: Bac-Diverse
FAX Number: (508) 541-8726 Calendar System: Semester
URL: www.dean.edu
Established: 1865 Annual Undergrad Tuition & Fees: $41,318
Enrollment: 1,180 Coed
Affiliation or Control: Independent Non-Profit IRS Status: 501(c)3
Highest Offering: Baccalaureate
Accreditation: EH, IACBE

01 President ....Mr. Kenneth ELMORE
00 Chancellor ....Mr. Edward AUGUSTUS
100 Chief of Staff ....Ms. Sandra CAIN
05 VP Academic Affairs .... Dr. Scott SIBLEY
10 Vice Pres Financial Svcs/Treasurer .... Ms. Kathleen MCGUIRE
84 VP Enrollment & Retention .... Ms. Cindy T. KOZIL
111 Vice Pres Institutional Advancement ....Ms. Coleen RESNICK
13 VP/Chief Information Officer .... Mr. Darrell KULESZA
21 Assoc VP/Controller/Asst Treasurer .... Ms. Deb ANDERSON
07 Assoc VP Enrollment/Dean Admission ....Ms. Iris GODES
121 Assc VP Student Success/Career Plng .... Ms. Wendy ADLER
20 Asst VP Academic Affairs ....Ms. Melissa READ
18 Assoc VP Capital Plng/Facilities ....Mr. Brian KELLY
26 VP Marketing & Business Development ....Mr. Gregg CHALK
32 Dean of Students ....Mr. David DRUCKER
51 Dean School of Continuing Studies .... Mr. Paul RESTEN
49 Dean School of Liberal Arts .... Dr. Brad HASTINGS
57 Dean Palladino School of Dance/Arts ....Mr. Marc ARENTSEN
06 Registrar ....Ms. Louise MONAST
19 Dir Law Enforcement Services .... Mr. Ken CORKRAN
08 Director of the Library .... Mr. Stan SKRABUT
41 Athletic Director ....Mr. George MARTIN
39 Assistant Dean of Students .... Ms. Shannon OVERCASH
40 Director of Bookstore .... Ms. Jackie CALDERONE
37 AVP Student & Financial Plng/Svcs .... Ms. Dianne PLUMMER
07 Director Enrollment Operations ....Ms. Kathleen RYAN
36 Dir Career Planning/Internships ....Ms. Thea CERIO
38 Director of Counseling Services .... Ms. Mary Ann SILVESTRI
29 Director Alumni Relations ....Ms. Jennifer POLIMER

Eastern Nazarene College (F)

23 E Elm Avenue, Quincy MA 02170-2999

County: Norfolk FICE Identification: 002145
Unit ID: 165644
Telephone: (617) 745-3000 Carnegie Class: Masters/S
FAX Number: (617) 745-3907 Calendar System: 4/1/4
URL: www.enc.edu
Established: 1918 Annual Undergrad Tuition & Fees: $26,952
Enrollment: 699 Coed
Affiliation or Control: Church Of The Nazarene IRS Status: 501(c)3
Highest Offering: Master's
Accreditation: EH, SW

01 President .... Dr. Jack CONNELL
05 VP Academic Affairs/Academic Dean ....Dr. William MCCOY
10 Vice President for Finance/CFO .... Mr. Robert CORNELL
32 Vice Pres Student Devel/Title IX ....Mr. Ian SLATER
111 Vice President Inst Advancement ....Vacant
84 Vice President of Enrollment .... Mr. Tim REES
93 VP of Multicultural Affairs .... Mr. Robert BENJAMIN
07 Dir of Undergraduate Admission ....Ms. Lesley BRITTON
123 Dir Grad/Online/Adult Admissions .... Mr. James SHEETS
35 Dean of Students ....Ms. Kristen PIERCE
06 Registrar .... Mr. Timothy MCDONALD
37 Director of Financial Aid ....Mr. Troy MARTIN
08 Director of Library Services .... Ms. Amy HWANG
19 Director Safety and Security .... Mr. Joshua EISENBERG
38 Dir Counseling & Career Services ....Vacant
88 Curriculum Director ....Ms. Melinda SMITH
41 AVP of Athletics ....Dr. Bradford ZARGES
18 Director of Facilities .... Mr. James GARDNER
21 Controller ....Ms. Patricia CONSTANTINO
15 Director Human Resources .... Ms. Nadine PFAUTZ
40 Director Bookstore ....Vacant
13 Chief Information Officer ....Mr. Charles BURT
04 Executive Asst to the President ....Vacant
09 Director of Institutional Research .... Mr. Ryan PIESCO
29 Director of Donor Relations .... Ms. Kristen WILSON
36 Director Student Placement ....Vacant
29 Director of Alumni Relations .... Mr. Matthew CARPENTER
26 Dir of Marketing & Communications ..Ms. Taisha HENDRICKSON
88 Instructional Resource Ctr Coord .... Ms. Patricia VAZQUEZ

Emerson College (G)

120 Boylston Street, Boston MA 02116-4624

County: Suffolk FICE Identification: 002146
Unit ID: 165662
Telephone: (617) 824-8500 Carnegie Class: Masters/L
FAX Number: (617) 824-8511 Calendar System: Semester
URL: www.emerson.edu
Established: 1880 Annual Undergrad Tuition & Fees: $51,148
Enrollment: 5,115 Coed
Affiliation or Control: Independent Non-Profit IRS Status: 501(c)3
Highest Offering: Master's
Accreditation: EH, SP

01 Interim President .... Dr. William GILLIGAN
43 Vice President & General Counsel ....Ms. Meredith AINBINDER
10 Vice President for Admin & Finance ....Mr. Paul DWORKIS
05 Provost & VP of Academic Affairs .... Dr. Michaele WHELAN
13 VP for Information Technology .... Mr. Brian BASGEN

26	AVP Communications/Marketing	Ms. Sofiya CABALQUINTO
28	VP Social Justice Center	Dr. Sylvia SPEARS
84	Vice Pres Enrollment Management	Dr. Ruthanne MADSEN
21	Assoc Vice Pres for Finance	Mr. Robert BUTLER
15	Sr AVP for Human Resources	Ms. Shari STIER
29	AVP Alumni Engagement	Ms. Leigh GASPAR
86	VP Government/Community Relations	Ms. Margaret Ann INGS
09	AVP Institutional Research	Mr. Michael DUGGAN
58	Dean Grad Studies/AVP Acad Affairs	Ms. Jan ROBERTS-BRESLIN
32	Vice Pres/Dean of Students	Mr. James HOPPE
107	Exec Director Professional Studies	Ms. Lesley NICHOLS
08	Exec Director of Library & Learning	Ms. Cheryl MCGRATH
123	Director of Graduate Admission	Ms. Leanda MIRANDA
36	Director of Career Services	Ms. Carol SPECTOR
38	Director Counseling/Health Center	Mr. Brandin DEAR
41	Director Athletics	Ms. Patricia NICOL
39	Assoc Dean Campus Life	Mr. Erik MUURISEPP
21	Controller	Mr. Jonathan PEARSALL
06	Registrar	Mr. JP PESTANA
42	Campus Chaplain	Ms. Julie AVIS ROGERS
101	VP President's Office & BOT	Ms. Anne SHAUGHNESSY
18	Director of Facilities	Mr. Joseph KNOLL
37	Director Financial Aid	Ms. Angela GRANT
04	Sr Executive Assistant to President	Ms. Mary Beth PESSIA
104	Director Study Abroad	Mr. David GRIFFIN
19	Chief of Police	Mr. Robert SMITH
25	Exec Director Research/Scholarship	Mr. Eric ASETTA
111	VP Institutional Advancement	Mr. John MALCOLM

Emmanuel College (A)

400 The Fenway, Boston MA 02115-5798

County: Suffolk — FICE Identification: 002147 — Unit ID: 165671

Telephone: (617) 277-9340 — Carnegie Class: Bac-A&S

FAX Number: (617) 735-9877 — Calendar System: Semester

URL: https://www.emmanuel.edu/

Established: 1919 — Annual Undergrad Tuition & Fees: $42,516

Enrollment: 1,946 — Coed

Affiliation or Control: Roman Catholic — IRS Status: 501(c)3

Highest Offering: Master's

Accreditation: EH, NURSE

01	President	Sr. Janet EISNER, SND
100	Exec Asst to the President	Ms. Michelle ERICKSON
04	Sr Asst to the Pres	Ms. Laurel CLANTON BOLDEN
10	VP of Finance/Treasurer (CFO)	Sr. Anne DONOVAN, SND
05	VP Academic Affairs & Dean	Dr. Josef KURTZ
15	Vice President of Human Resources	Ms. Erin FARMER NOONAN
30	VP of Development	Ms. Danielle KELLERMANN
37	Assoc VP for Student Financial Svcs	Ms. Jennifer PORTER
26	VP of College Relations	Ms. Molly DILORENZO
45	VP Alumni Rels/Strategic Engagement	Ms. Kristen CONROY
42	VP of Mission and Ministry	Fr. Terrence DEVINO
84	Dean of Enrollment	Ms. Sandra ROBBINS
35	Dean of Students	Ms. Jennifer FORRY
09	Dean Inst Effect/Chief Data Ofcr	Dr. Beth ROSS
20	Dean Academic Admin/Grad & Prof Pgm	Ms. Cindy O'CALLAGHAN
88	Asst Dean Cmty Stdrds & Family Pgms	Ms. Mary Beth THOMAS
121	Assoc Dean of Academic Advising	Sr. Susan THORNELL, SND
79	Assoc Dean Humanities/Soc Science	Dr. Lisa STEPANSKI
66	Assoc Dean Nursing/Clinical Science	Dr. Diane SHEA
81	Assoc Dean of Sciences/Health	Dr. Paul MARCH
53	Associate Dean of Education	Sr. Karen HOKANSON, SND
50	Associate Dean of Business and Mgmt	Ms. Anne Marie PASQUALE
08	Assoc Dn of Library/Lrng Resources	Ms. Karen STORIN LINITZ
36	Executive Director Career Ctr	Ms. Maureen ASHBURN
41	Director of Athletics & Recreation	Mr. Brendan MCWILLIAMS
90	Director of Academic Resource Ctr	Ms. Wendy LABRON
09	Director of Institutional Research	Dr. Alison VALLEREUX
13	VP Information Resources/Planning	Mr. Sean PHILPOTT
19	Director Security/Safety	Mr. John KELLY
06	Registrar	Ms. Kimberly CAMASSO
28	AVP Diversity & Incl/Chief Div Ofcr	Mr. Jeffrey SMITH, JR.
39	Dean of Campus Life	Ms. Susan BENZIE

Endicott College (B)

376 Hale Street, Beverly MA 01915-2098

County: Essex — FICE Identification: 002148 — Unit ID: 165699

Telephone: (978) 927-0585 — Carnegie Class: Masters/L

FAX Number: (978) 927-0084 — Calendar System: 4/1/4

URL: www.endicott.edu

Established: 1939 — Annual Undergrad Tuition & Fees: $35,320

Enrollment: 4,287 — Coed

Affiliation or Control: Independent Non-Profit — IRS Status: 501(c)3

Highest Offering: Doctorate

Accreditation: EH, ACPHA, ART, CAATE, CIDA, COSMA, NUR, NURSE

01	President	Dr. Steven DISALVO
100	Chief of Staff	Ms. Jillian DUBMAN
10	Vice President of Finance/CFO	Mr. Tony FERULLO
05	Provost	Dr. Sara QUAY
111	Vice Pres Institutional Advancement	Mr. Patrick HEWETT
26	VP Student & External Engagement	Mr. Bryan CAIN
41	Asst Vice President/Dir Athletics	Dr. Brian WYLIE
32	VP Student Affs/Chief Divers Ofcr	Ms. Brandi JOHNSON
04	Executive Administrative Assistant	Ms. Frances POISSON
04	Executive Admin Asst to the Provost	Ms. Amy ASTOLFI
15	Vice President Human Resources	Mr. Aaron MORRISON
35	AVP & Dean of Students	Mr. Marlin NABORS
21	Assoc Vice Pres Business Office	Mr. Andrew COOLE
88	Exec Director Misselwood Events	Ms. Eileen GEYER
90	Assoc Dean of Academic Technology	Mr. Kent BARCLAY
07	VP/Dean of Admission	Ms. Meghan MONACO
06	Registrar	Ms. Rosa CADENA
08	Director Library	Mr. Brian COURTEMANCHE
37	Director of Financial Aid	Ms. Maria MORELLI
13	Chief Information Officer	Ms. Amy DONOVAN
38	Director Counseling Center	Ms. Maureen GEBHARDT
36	Dean Internship and Career Center	Ms. Dale MCLENNAN
09	AVP Research & Planning	Mr. Donny FEMINO
96	Director of Purchasing	Ms. Susan AYERS
85	Dean International Education	Dr. Warren JAFERIAN
49	Dean School of Arts & Sciences	Dr. Gene WONG
53	Dean of School of Education	Dr. Aubry THRELKELD
57	Dean Visual & Performing Arts	Mr. Mark TOWNER
68	Dean School of Sports Science	Dr. Deborah SWANTON
66	Dean School of Nursing & HS	Dr. Nancy MEEDZAN
50	Dean School of Business	Dr. Michael PAIGE
60	Dean School of Social SCM	Dr. Mark HERLIHY
19	Director Public Safety & Police	Ms. Kerry RAMSDELL
104	Study Abroad Advisor	Ms. Rachel FLEMMING
44	Director of Annual Giving	Ms. Sarah EARNEST
39	Assoc Dir Res Life & Housing Opers	Ms. Corie QUILL
121	Dir Student Success & Retention	Ms. Adrienne BELL
107	Dean of Professional Studies	Ms. Laura DOUGLASS
58	Dir of Grad Education/Fellowships	Dr. Aubry THRELKELD
58	Associate Dean ABA	Dr. Mary Jane WEISS
18	Director of Facilities	Mr. Rick GAGNON

FINE Mortuary College (C)

150 Kerry Place, Norwood MA 02062

County: Norfolk — FICE Identification: 033164 — Unit ID: 436599

Telephone: (781) 762-1211 — Carnegie Class: Spec 2-yr-A&S

FAX Number: (781) 762-7177 — Calendar System: Quarter

URL: www.fmc.edu

Established: 1996 — Annual Undergrad Tuition & Fees: $20,520

Enrollment: 100 — Coed

Affiliation or Control: Proprietary — IRS Status: Proprietary

Highest Offering: Associate Degree

Accreditation: FUSER

01	President	Mr. Kevin KOCH
05	Program Director	Ms. Melissa CYFERS
11	Campus Manager	Ms. Laura HEWEY

Fisher College (D)

118 Beacon Street, Boston MA 02116-1500

County: Suffolk — FICE Identification: 002150 — Unit ID: 165802

Telephone: (617) 236-8800 — Carnegie Class: Bac-Diverse

FAX Number: (617) 236-8858 — Calendar System: Semester

URL: www.fisher.edu

Established: 1903 — Annual Undergrad Tuition & Fees: $32,700

Enrollment: 1,419 — Coed

Affiliation or Control: Independent Non-Profit — IRS Status: 501(c)3

Highest Offering: Master's

Accreditation: EH, CAHIIM, IACBE, NURSE

01	President	Mr. Steven RICH
03	Executive Vice President	Ms. Ana DA CUNHA
05	Vice President Academic Affairs	Dr. Janet KUSER
10	VP for Finance and Administration	Vacant
84	VP of Enrollment Management	Mr. Robert MELARAGNI
107	VP Online/Graduate/Prof Studies	Ms. Kathleen EHLERS
111	VP Advancement & Alumni Engagement	Ms. Brenda SANCHEZ
32	Dean of Students	Ms. Shiela LALLY
88	Dean Intl Acad Oper/Curriculum Dev	Ms. Nancy PITHIS
49	Asst Dean School of Liberal Arts	Mr. Willem WALLINGA
06	College Registrar	Mr. Jesse AVALOS
41	Director of Athletics	Mr. Scott DULIN
15	Director of HR/Title IX Coord	Mr. William OPAVA
26	Dir Marketing & Communications	Vacant
07	Director of Admissions	Mr. Zacchary SONGER
113	Director of Student Accounts	Mr. Kevin KELLY
13	Director Systems/Client Services	Mr. Michael CUTILLO
18	Director of Facilities	Mr. Paul MCBRINE
37	Director of Financial Aid	Ms. Jennifer WILHELM
20	Dir Academic Advising/Support Ctr	Mr. Arthur ASBURY
19	Dir Public Safety/Chief of Police	Mr. Brian PERRIN
36	Director of Career Services	Ms. Ally BALDWIN
22	Director of Accessibility Service	Ms. Ferna PHILLIPS
113	College Bursar	Ms. Kristen MARTINEZ
08	College Librarian	Mr. Joshua MCKAIN
09	Director of Institutional Research	Mr. Roland PEARSALL
58	Assistant Dean Grad/MBA Programs	Dr. Neil TROTTA
39	Interim Director Student Housing	Ms. Shiela LALLY
124	Dir Student Engagement & Retention	Mr. Jesse FORD
105	Webmaster & Digital Content Coord	Ms. Elissa SPINNER
104	Director Study Abroad	Mr. Jesse FORD

Franklin W. Olin College of Engineering (E)

Olin Way, Needham MA 02492-1200

County: Norfolk — FICE Identification: 039463 — Unit ID: 441982

Telephone: (781) 292-2300 — Carnegie Class: Spec-4-yr-Other Tech

FAX Number: (781) 292-2210 — Calendar System: Semester

URL: www.olin.edu

Established: 1997 — Annual Undergrad Tuition & Fees: $57,356

Enrollment: 310 — Coed

Affiliation or Control: Independent Non-Profit — IRS Status: 501(c)3

Highest Offering: Baccalaureate

Accreditation: EH

01	President	Dr. Gilda A. BARABINO
04	Exec Asst to President	Ms. Katherine MCDONOUGH
05	Provost/Dean of Faculty	Mr. Mark SOMERVILLE
32	Dean of the College	Dr. Alisha SARANG-SIEMINSKI
06	Assoc Dean for Acad Pgms/Registrar	Ms. Linda T. CANAVAN
07	Dean of Admission and Financial Aid	Ms. Emily ROPER-DOTEN
37	Director of Financial Aid	Ms. Jean RICKER
08	Library Director	Ms. Callan BIGNOLI
10	VP for Financial Affairs & CFO	Ms. Donna GOLEMME
13	Chief Information Officer	Mr. Rick OSTERBERG
26	Assoc VP for Marketing & Comm	Ms. Anne-Marie DORNING
09	Director of Inst Research	Ms. Rebecca MATHEWS
11	Head of Operations	Mr. Jeremy GOODMAN
15	Director of Human Resources	Ms. Sharon WOODWARD

† All admitted students who enroll at Olin College receive an Olin Scholarship covering half tuition during the eight semesters of the baccalaureate program.

Gordon College (F)

255 Grapevine Road, Wenham MA 01984-1899

County: Essex — FICE Identification: 002153 — Unit ID: 165936

Telephone: (978) 927-2300 — Carnegie Class: Bac-A&S

FAX Number: (978) 867-4659 — Calendar System: Semester

URL: www.gordon.edu

Established: 1889 — Annual Undergrad Tuition & Fees: $39,230

Enrollment: 1,816 — Coed

Affiliation or Control: Independent Non-Profit — IRS Status: 501(c)3

Highest Offering: Master's

Accreditation: EH, MUS

01	President	Dr. Michael HAMOND
05	EVP for Academic Affairs	Dr. Sandy DONESKI
84	VP for Enrollment	Dr. Larry HOEZEE
10	VP for Finance/Business Development	Mr. John J. TRUSCHEL
07	AVP Enrollment	Ms. June BODONI
32	Vice President for Student Life	Mr. Daniel TYMANN
26	VP of Marketing and Communications	Mr. Rick SWEENEY
111	Acting VP of Advancement	Mr. Mark DILLON
08	Director of Library Services	Mr. Myron SCHIRER-SUTER
06	Registrar	Mrs. Alice A. FALCONE
13	Chief Information Officer	Mr. Christopher HANSEN
37	Sr Dir of Student Financial Svcs	Mr. Daniel O'CONNELL
15	AVP for Human Resources	Mr. Christopher JONES
18	Director of Facilities	Mr. Dima BORISYUK
21	Dir of Finance and Controller	Mr. Stephen LACORAZZA
110	AVP for Advancement	Mrs. Britt CARLSON
36	Exec Director of Career Services	Mr. Alexander LOWRY
96	Dir of Purchasing and Distribution	Mr. Michael NAWOICHIK
09	AVP of Strategy & Decision Support	Vacant
19	Chief of Police	Mr. Glenn DECKERT
88	Dir of Advancement Service	Mr. Rick HOUSTON
41	Director of Athletics	Mr. Jon TYMANN
105	Creative Dir and Web Team Lead	Mr. Stephen DAGLEY
35	Dean of Student Life	Mr. Terry CHAREK
124	Dean of Student Engagement	Dr. Nicholas ROWE
121	Dean of Student Success	Mr. Christopher CARLSON
100	Deputy Chief of Staff	Mr. William HAGEN
104	Dean Acad Init & Global Education	Dr. Jewerl MAXWELL

Gordon-Conwell Theological Seminary (G)

130 Essex Street, South Hamilton MA 01982-2317

County: Essex — FICE Identification: 009747 — Unit ID: 165945

Telephone: (978) 468-7111 — Carnegie Class: Spec-4-yr-Faith

FAX Number: (978) 468-6691 — Calendar System: Semester

URL: www.gordonconwell.edu

Established: 1884 — Annual Graduate Tuition & Fees: N/A

Enrollment: 1,489 — Coed

Affiliation or Control: Independent Non-Profit — IRS Status: 501(c)3

Highest Offering: Doctorate; No Undergraduates

Accreditation: EH, CACREP, THEOL

01	President	Dr. Scott W. SUNQUIST
10	Vice Pres Finance & Operations/CFO	Mr. Gregg HANSEN
111	Vice President of Advancement	Mr. Brian GARDNER
112	Director Planned Giving	Vacant
12	Dean of Boston Campus	Dr. Virginia WARD
12	Dean of Charlotte Campus	Dr. Gerald WHEATON
12	Dean of Hamilton Campus	Dr. Mateus DE CAMPOS
12	Dean of Jacksonville Campus	Dr. Bradley HOWELL
32	Dean of Students	Ms. Jana HOLIDAY
15	Director of Human Resources	Dr. Steven GREISDORF
13	Chief Information Officer	Dr. Alex KOH
18	Director of Physical Plant	Mr. Timothy INGRAHAM
08	Director of Libraries	Mr. Brad HOWELL
58	Dean of Doctor of Ministry	Dr. David CURRIE
37	Director of Financial Aid	Mr. Stacey T. GLIDDEN
40	Director of Support Services	Mr. David SHOREY
07	Director of Admissions	Mr. Chris ANDERSON
21	Controller & Dir Financial Svcs	Mrs. Heidi O'CONNOR

29 Director Alumni Relations ... Ms. Laura CARMER
39 Director Student Housing ... Mr. Jason STRZEPEK
06 Institutional Registrar ... Ms. Natalie CROWSON
100 Chief of Staff ... Mrs. Mia ERTEL
101 Secretary of the Institution/Board ... Mrs. Mia ERTEL
84 Director Enrollment Management ... Mr. Chris ANDERSON

Hampshire College (A)

893 West Street, Amherst MA 01002-3372
County: Hampshire | FICE Identification: 004661
Unit ID: 166018
Telephone: (413) 549-4600 | Carnegie Class: Bac-A&S
FAX Number: (413) 559-5584 | Calendar System: 4/1/4
URL: www.hampshire.edu
Established: 1965 | Annual Undergrad Tuition & Fees: $51,768
Enrollment: 522 | Coed
Affiliation or Control: Independent Non-Profit | IRS Status: 501(c)3
Highest Offering: Baccalaureate
Accreditation: EH

01 President ... Mr. Edward WINGENBACH
125 President Emeritus ... Dr. Jonathan LASH
101 Secretary of the College ... Vacant
05 Vice Pres Acad Affs/Dean of Faculty ... Mr. Christoph COX
32 VP Student Affairs/Dean of Students ... Ms. Zauyah WAITE
10 VP Finance & Admin/Treasurer ... Mr. Carl RIES
15 Director HR/Title IX Coord ... Vacant
111 Chief Advancement Officer ... Ms. Jennifer CHRISLER
20 AVP of Academic Affairs ... Ms. Yaniris FERNANDEZ
37 Dean of Financial Aid ... Mr. Fumio SUGIHARA
08 Director of Library ... Ms. Rachel BECKWITH
06 Director of Central Records ... Ms. Rachael GRAHAM
29 Director Alumni & Family Relations ... Ms. Melissa MILLS-DICK
36 Dir Career Options Resource Ctr ... Ms. Carin RANK
38 Director Student Counseling ... Dr. Eliza MCARDLE
04 Admin Assistant to the President ... Ms. Cathy HEWS
11 Chief of Operations/Administration ... Ms. Elizabeth CRAUN
07 Dean of Admissions ... Mr. Fumio SUGIHARA
28 Co-Dean of Institutional Diversity ... Ms. Amy JORDAN
28 Co-Dean of Institutional Diversity ... Ms. Roosbelinda CARDENAS

Harvard University (B)

1350 Massachusetts Ave, Cambridge MA 02138-3800
County: Middlesex | FICE Identification: 002155
Unit ID: 166027
Telephone: (617) 495-1000 | Carnegie Class: DU-Highest
FAX Number: (617) 495-0500 | Calendar System: Semester
URL: www.harvard.edu
Established: 1636 | Annual Undergrad Tuition & Fees: $54,002
Enrollment: 30,391 | Coed
Affiliation or Control: Independent Non-Profit | IRS Status: 501(c)3
Highest Offering: Doctorate
Accreditation: EH, CAMPEP, CLPSY, DENT, IPSY, LAW, LSAR, MED, PCSAS, PH, PLNG, THEOL

01 President ... Lawrence S. BACOW
05 Provost ... Alan GARBER
49 Dean Arts and Sciences ... Claudine GAY
58 Dean Graduate School of A&S ... Emma DENCH
50 Dean Harvard Business School ... Srikant DATAR
49 Dean Harvard College ... Rakesh KHURANA
51 Dean Continuing Educ/Extension ... Nancy COLEMAN
52 Dean School of Dental Medicine ... William V. GIANNOBILE
48 Dean Graduate School of Design ... Sarah M. WHITING
73 Dean Harvard Divinity School ... David N. HEMPTON
53 Dean Graduate School of Education ... Bridget T. LONG
54 Dean Engineering/Applied Sciences ... Francis J. DOYLE
80 Dean Kennedy School of Government ... Douglas ELMENDORF
61 Dean Harvard Law School ... John F. MANNING
63 Dean Harvard Medical School ... George Q. DALEY
69 Dean School of Public Health ... Michelle A. WILLIAMS
88 Dean Inst for Advanced Studies ... Tomiko BROWN-NAGIN
21 Treasurer ... Paul J. FINNEGAN
03 Executive Vice President ... Katherine N. LAPP
43 VP and General Counsel ... Diane E. LOPEZ
29 VP Alumni Affairs/Development ... Brian K. LEE
10 VP for Finance & CFO ... Thomas HOLLISTER
101 VP and Secretary of the University ... Marc GOODHEART
100 Chief of Staff & Strategic Advisor ... Patricia BELLINGER
26 VP Public Affairs and Communication ... Paul ANDREW
15 VP for Human Resources ... Manuel CUEVAS-TRISAN
45 VP Planning & Project Management ... Vacant
08 VP for the Harvard Library ... Martha J. WHITEHEAD
13 VP Info Technology/CIO ... Klara JELINKOVA
18 VP for Campus Services ... Meredith WEENICK

Hebrew College (C)

160 Herrick Road, Newton Centre MA 02459-2237
County: Middlesex | FICE Identification: 002157
Unit ID: 166045
Telephone: (617) 559-8600 | Carnegie Class: Spec-4-yr-Faith
FAX Number: (617) 559-8601 | Calendar System: Semester
URL: www.hebrewcollege.edu
Established: 1921 | Annual Undergrad Tuition & Fees: N/A
Enrollment: 137 | Coed
Affiliation or Control: Independent Non-Profit | IRS Status: 501(c)3
Highest Offering: Beyond Master's But Less Than Doctorate
Accreditation: EH

01 President ... Rabbi Sharon C. ANISFELD
03 Vice President ... Dr. Susie TANCHEL
05 Dean and Chief Academic Officer ... Rabbi Dan JUDSON
10 Chief Financial and Admin Officer ... Mr. Keith DROPKIN
32 Senior Director of Student Services ... Mr. Bob GIELOW
35 Dean of Students ... Rabbi Daniel KLEIN
06 Registrar ... Ms. Marcia SPELLMAN
15 Director of Human Resources ... Ms. Steffi BOBBIN
04 Executive Asst to the President ... Ms. Deena KANOPKIN
13 Director of Information Technology ... Mr. Jim KENN
08 Library Director ... Mr. Harvey SUKENIC

Hellenic College-Holy Cross Greek Orthodox School of Theology (D)

50 Goddard Avenue, Brookline MA 02445-7496
County: Norfolk | FICE Identification: 002154
Unit ID: 166054
Telephone: (617) 731-3500 | Carnegie Class: Bac-A&S
FAX Number: (617) 850-1460 | Calendar System: Semester
URL: www.hchc.edu
Established: 1937 | Annual Undergrad Tuition & Fees: $22,490
Enrollment: 126 | Coed
Affiliation or Control: Greek Orthodox | IRS Status: 501(c)3
Highest Offering: Master's
Accreditation: EH, THEOL

01 President ... Mr. George M. CANTONIS
73 Dean School of Theology ... Fr. George PARSENIOS
05 VP for Academic Affairs ... Dr. Diana DEMETRULIAS
111 VP Institutional Advancement ... Fr. Jim KATINAS
32 Dean of Students ... Fr. Michael KOUREMETIS
10 VP Admin Affs/Operations/Finance ... RevDcn. Gary ALEXANDER
07 Director of Enrollment Mgmt ... Dr. Bruce BECK
08 Library Director ... Bishop Joachim COTSONIS
37 Financial Aid Director ... Mr. Michael KIRCHMAIER
06 Registrar ... Mr. Jay OSTROSKY
13 Technology/Digital Media Mgr ... Mr. Emanuel SABAU
29 Director of Alumni Office ... Ms. Frances LEVAS
113 Bursar ... Mrs. Bernadette DEGREGORIS
40 Bookstore Manager ... Mr. Nicholas BOTSOLIS
39 Director of Housing/Security ... Ms. Constandina BROWN
15 Director of Human Resources ... Dean Gary ALEXANDER
30 Director of Development ... Ms. Frances LEVAS
45 Director Strategic Initiatives ... Dean Gary ALEXANDER
22 Coordinator Equity and Compliance ... RevDr. Philip HALIKIAS
04 Admin Assistant to the President ... Ms. Maureen PARSENIOS
09 Director of Institutional Research ... Fr. Nicholas METRAKOS
19 Director Security/Safety ... Ms. Marcie MOLINE

Hult International Business School (E)

One Education Street, Cambridge MA 02141-1805
County: Middlesex | FICE Identification: 041432
Unit ID: 164368
Telephone: (617) 746-1990 | Carnegie Class: Spec-4-yr-Bus
FAX Number: (617) 746-1991 | Calendar System: Other
URL: www.hult.edu
Established: 1964 | Annual Undergrad Tuition & Fees: $49,950
Enrollment: 1,814 | Coed
Affiliation or Control: Proprietary | IRS Status: Proprietary
Highest Offering: Doctorate
Accreditation: EH

01 President ... Dr. Stephen J. HODGES
05 Chief Academic Officer ... Dr. Johan ROOS
11 Chief Operating Officer ... Mr. David ARTHUR
10 Chief Financial Officer ... Mr. Martin ASP
13 Chief Technology Officer ... Mr. John PROKOS
36 Vice President Career Development ... Ms. Katharine BOSHKOFF
03 Executive Vice President UG ... Dr. Jannicke ROOS
03 Executive Vice President PG ... Ms. Melissa FREDETTE
88 Chief Innovation Officer ... Dr. Mukul KUMAR
20 Director of Central Academics ... Ms. Caroline HAYES
20 Dean of Central Academics ... Dr. Ian DOUGAL
12 Senior Associate Dean Boston Campus ... Ms. Mary DUTKIEWICZ
12 Dean San Francisco Campus ... Dr. Mona DHILLON
84 Regional Director Enrollment ... Mr. Steve WYNN
36 Dir of Career Services Boston ... Ms. Maggie DALEY
32 Dir Student Services Boston ... Ms. Nayeli VIVANCO
06 Registrar Boston Campus ... Vacant
06 Registrar San Francisco Campus ... Vacant
37 Director Student Financial Aid ... Ms. Karen VAN DYNE

Laboure College (F)

303 Adams Street, Milton MA 02186-4253
County: Suffolk | FICE Identification: 006324
Unit ID: 165264
Telephone: (617) 322-3500 | Carnegie Class: Spec-4-yr-Other Health
FAX Number: (617) 296-7947 | Calendar System: Trimester
URL: www.laboure.edu
Established: 1892 | Annual Undergrad Tuition & Fees: $32,813
Enrollment: 1,188 | Coed
Affiliation or Control: Roman Catholic | IRS Status: 501(c)3
Highest Offering: Baccalaureate
Accreditation: EH, ADNUR, NDT, NURSE, RTT

01 President ... Lily HSU
10 VP of Administration and Finance ... William MCDONALD
05 Vice Pres Institutional Excellence ... Marilyn GARDNER
84 VP of Enrollment Management ... Justin ROY
32 VP of Academic and Student Affairs ... Maria R. ALTOBELLO
35 Asst VP Student Affairs ... Matthew GREGORY
04 Executive Asst to President ... Megan D. CURRIVAN
06 Registrar ... John SACCO
08 Director of Library ... Anicia KUCHESKY
29 Director Alumni Affairs ... Katelyn DWYER
37 Director Student Financial Aid ... Erin HANLON
15 Director of Human Resources ... Daniella SATTERFIELD

Lasell University (G)

1844 Commonwealth Avenue, Newton MA 02466-2716
County: Middlesex | FICE Identification: 002158
Unit ID: 166391
Telephone: (617) 243-2000 | Carnegie Class: Masters/L
FAX Number: (617) 243-2389 | Calendar System: Semester
URL: www.lasell.edu
Established: 1851 | Annual Undergrad Tuition & Fees: $39,000
Enrollment: 1,951 | Coed
Affiliation or Control: Independent Non-Profit | IRS Status: 501(c)3
Highest Offering: Master's
Accreditation: EH, ACBSP, CAATE, EXSC, FEPAC

01 President ... Michael B. ALEXANDER
05 Provost ... Eric M. TURNER
10 VP Finance & Administration ... Derek PINTO
84 VP Enrollment & Marketing ... Chrystal PORTER
88 President Lasell Village ... Anne DOYLE
111 VP University Advancement ... Chelsea GWYTHER
28 Asst VP/Chief Diversity Officer ... Jesse TAURIAC
32 Asst VP/Dean of Student Affairs ... David HENNESSEY
76 Dean Health Sciences ... Cris HAVERTY
57 Dean Comms & The Arts ... Vacant
88 Dean Fashion ... Vacant
79 Dean Human/Educ/Just & Soc Sc ... Lori ROSENTHAL
50 Dean Business ... Matthew REILLY
110 Asst VP University Advancement ... Caroline WEATHERBEE
07 Director of Admission ... Yavuz KIREMIT
37 Dir Student Financial Planning ... Jennifer MULDOWNEY
09 Dir Institutional Research ... Eric LANTHIER
06 Registrar ... Linda ARCE
26 Dir Communications ... Ian MEROPOL
29 Dir Alumni Relations/Annual Giving ... Thomas WILLIAMS
89 Dir Student Act & Orientation ... Thomas MORGAN
23 Dir Health Services ... Richard ARNOLD
08 Dir Library ... Anna SARNESO
41 Dir Athletics ... Kristy WALTER
15 Dir Human Resources ... Julie GROOM
38 Dir Counseling Center ... Sharon HARRINGTON-HOPE
45 Assoc VP of Strategic Initiatives ... Adrienne FRANCIOSI
13 Chief Information Officer ... Jonathan GORHAM
19 Director of Public Safety ... Robert SHEA
43 Chief of Staff & General Counsel ... Jennifer OKEEFFE
04 Executive Asst to the President ... Henry PUGH
85 Dir International Student Services ... Maria ADKINS
105 Dir Marketing ... Christopher LYNETT
36 Dir Career Readiness & Intern Pgm ... Donnell TURNER
39 Dir Resident Life/Student Housing ... Scott LAMPHERE

Lesley University (H)

29 Everett Street, Cambridge MA 02138-2790
County: Middlesex | FICE Identification: 002160
Unit ID: 166452
Telephone: (617) 868-9600 | Carnegie Class: DU-Mod
FAX Number: (617) 349-8717 | Calendar System: Semester
URL: www.lesley.edu
Established: 1909 | Annual Undergrad Tuition & Fees: $29,550
Enrollment: 4,200 | Coed
Affiliation or Control: Independent Non-Profit | IRS Status: 501(c)3
Highest Offering: Doctorate
Accreditation: EH, ACATE, ACBSP, ART, SW

01 President ... Dr. Janet L. STEINMAYER
05 Provost/CAO ... Dr. Jonathan JEFFERSON
11 Vice President for Administration ... Ms. Marylou BATT
10 Vice President of Finance/CFO ... Ms. Diane KIMBALL
111 VP of Advancement ... Ms. Veronica JORGE-CURTIS
84 VP of Enrollment Initiatives ... Mr. Thomas ENGLEHARDT
114 VP for Budgeting & Fin Planning ... Vacant
43 Vic Pres & General Counsel ... Ms. Shirin PHILIPP
45 VP Strategy & Implementation ... Dr. MaryPat LOHSE
20 Asst Provost Academic Success ... Mr. Randi KORN
58 Int Dean Grad Sch Arts & Social Sci ... Dr. Sandra WALKER
53 Interim Dean School of Education ... Dr. Amy RUTSTEIN-RILEY
32 Dean of Student Life & Academic Dev ... Dr. Nathaniel MAYS
49 Dean College of Liberal Arts & Sci ... Dr. Steven SHAPIRO
57 Dean of College of Art and Design ... Dr. Amy DEINES
13 Assoc VP Info Technology ... Mr. Charles COOPER
123 AVP of Graduate Admissions ... Ms. Barbara SELMO
15 Director of Human Resources ... Ms. Samantha CARPINELLA
37 Director of Financial Aid ... Ms. Michelle HEYDE
08 Head of Libraries ... Ms. Abigail MANCINI
07 Asst Dir Undergrad Admissions ... Mr. Shawn KITHCART
108 Assoc Dir Assessment/Accreditation ... Ms. Se-Ah SIEGEL
09 Dir of Institutional Research ... Mr. Alexander WAGNER
04 Assistant to the President ... Vacant
06 Registrar ... Ms. Adrienne ZONDERMAN
28 Cmty Standards/EO/Title IX Admin ... Ms. Sana AMINI

Longy School of Music of Bard College (A)

27 Garden Street, Cambridge MA 02138
Telephone: (617) 876-0956 Identification: 770137
Accreditation: &M

† Branch campus of Bard College, Annandale-On-Hudson, NY

*Massachusetts Board of Higher Education (B)

One Ashburton Place, Room 1401,
Boston MA 02108-1696
County: Suffolk FICE Identification: 029283
Telephone: (617) 994-6950 Carnegie Class: N/A
FAX Number: (617) 727-6397
URL: www.mass.edu

01	Commissioner	Dr. Carlos SANTIAGO
103	Assoc Comm Workforce Development	Mr. David CEDRONE
45	Senior Assoc Comm Strategic Plng	Dr. Winifred M. HAGAN
09	Sr Comm Research/Planning	Vacant
43	Chief Legal Counsel	Ms. Dena PAPANIKOLAOU
10	Deputy Commissioner Admin/Finance	Vacant
37	Sr Dep Comm Student Financial Aid	Dr. Clantha MCCURDY

*University of Massachusetts System Office (C)

One Beacon Street, 31st Floor, Boston MA 02108
County: Suffolk FICE Identification: 008017
Unit ID: 166665
Telephone: (617) 287-7050 Carnegie Class: N/A
FAX Number: (617) 287-7167
URL: www.umassp.edu

01	President	Mr. Martin T. MEEHAN
03	Executive Vice President	Mr. James JULIAN, JR.
05	SVP Acad/Student Affs & Econ Dev	Dr. Katherine NEWMAN
10	Sr VP Admin/Finance & Treasurer	Ms. Lisa CALISE
26	Executive Director Communications	Mr. John HOEY
11	Deputy Chief Operating Officer	Ms. Susan KELLY
86	Associate VP of Govt Affairs	Mr. David MCDERMOTT
43	General Counsel	Mr. Gerard LEONE
13	Chief Information Officer	Vacant
101	Secretary to Board of Trustees	Ms. Zunilka BARRETT
116	Director for University Auditing	Mr. Kyle DAVID
15	Chief Human Resources Officer	Mr. John DUNLAP
106	CEO UMassOnline	Mr. Donald KILBURN

*University of Massachusetts (D)

Amherst MA 01003
County: Hampshire FICE Identification: 002221
Unit ID: 166629
Telephone: (413) 545-0111 Carnegie Class: DU-Highest
FAX Number: N/A Calendar System: Semester
URL: www.umass.edu
Established: 1863 Annual Undergrad Tuition & Fees (In-State): $16,439
Enrollment: 31,642 Coed
Affiliation or Control: State IRS Status: 501(c)3
Highest Offering: Doctorate
Accreditation: EH, ACPHA, ART, AUD, CLPSY, DIETD, DIETI, IPSY, LSAR, MUS, NASP, NURSE, PH, PLNG, SCPSY, SP

02	Chancellor	Dr. Kumble R. SUBBASWAMY
05	Sr VC/Provost Academic Affairs	Dr. Tricia R. SERIO
88	Assoc Chancellor for Compliance	Ms. Christine M. WILDA
28	VC Diversity/Equity/Inclusion	Ms. Nefertiti A. WALKER
100	Chief of Staff	Dr. Rolanda C. BURNEY
10	Vice Chancellor Admin/Finance	Mr. Andrew P. MANGELS
111	VC Advancement	Ms. Arwen S. DUFFY
46	VC Research & Engagement	Dr. Michael F. MALONE
32	VC Student Affairs/Campus Life	Dr. Brandi HEPHNER LABANC
26	VC University Relations	Mr. John KENNEDY
13	VC Information Services & CIO	Mr. Christopher P. MISRA
15	VC & Chief Human Resources Officer	Mr. William D. BRADY
41	Director of Athletics	Mr. Ryan BAMFORD
43	Senior Counsel	Mr. Brian W. BURKE
22	Assoc VC Equal Opportunity/Access	Ms. Kerri T. TILLET
20	Assoc Chancellor	Dr. Tilman WOLF
20	SVP Acad Affrs/Dean Undergrad Educ	Dr. Farshid HAJIR
88	Assoc Prov Interdisciplinary Stds	Dr. Joseph BARTOLOMEO
58	Vice Provost/Dean of Grad School	Dr. Jacqueline URLA
106	Sr Vice Provost Lifelong Learning	Dr. John WELLS
84	Vice Provost Enrollment Management	Dr. James ROCHE
20	Vice Provost Faculty Development	Dr. Michelle BUDIG
09	Exec Dir Strategic Analytics	Dr. Barb CHALFONTE
88	Assoc Provost Academic Personnel	Mr. Michael J. EAGEN
11	Assoc Prov Admin & Finance	Ms. Deborah M. GOULD
108	Assoc Prov Assessment/Educ Effect	Vacant
88	Assoc Provost Equity & Inclusion	Dr. Amel AHMED
85	Assoc Provost International Pgms	Dr. Kalpen TRIVEDI
121	Assoc Provost Student Success	Dr. Carolyn S. BASSETT
07	Director of Admissions	Mr. Michael DRISH
87	Coord Pre-College Programs	Ms. Erin O'ROURKE
06	Sr Assoc Graduate Registrar	Ms. Kate C. WOODMANSEE
37	Dir Financial Aid Services	Ms. Lauren LAMICA
06	University Registrar	Dr. Patrick SULLIVAN
92	Dean Commonwealth Honors College	Dr. Mari CASTEÑEDA
79	Dean Col Humanities & Fine Arts	Dr. Barbara KRAUTHAMER
77	Dean Col Computer & Info Sci	Dr. Laura M. HAAS
81	Int Dean Col Natural Science	Dr. Nathaniel WHITAKER
83	Dean Col Social & Behavioral Sci	Dr. R. Karl RETHEMEYER
53	Dean School of Education	Dr. Cynthia GERSTL-PEPIN
54	Dean College of Engineering	Dr. Sanjay RAMAN
50	Dean School of Management	Dr. Anne MASSEY
66	Dean College of Nursing	Dr. Allison VORDERSTRASSE
69	Dean Sch Public Health/Hlth Sci	Dr. Anna Maria SIEGA-RIZ
08	Dean of Libraries	Dr. Nandita S. MANI
56	Director of Extension	Ms. Jody L. JELLISON
47	Dir Stockbridge School Agriculture	Dr. Wesley AUTIO
57	Director Fine Arts Center	Ms. Jamilla DERIA
114	Budget Director	Ms. Lynn C. MCKENNA
109	Executive Dir Auxiliary Enterprises	Mr. Kenneth K. TOONG
113	Bursar	Ms. Erin SCHADEL
18	Assoc VC Facilities & Campus Svcs	Mr. Shane R. CONKLIN
19	Asst Vice Chancellor/Chief Police	Mr. Tyrone PARHAM
40	Director Univ Store	Ms. Melissa PETERSON
35	Dean of Students	Dr. Evelyn ASHLEY
39	Dir Residential Life/Student Svcs	Ms. Dawn BOND
89	Dir Assessment/Student Affairs	Dr. Marcy R. CLARK
104	Dir Education Abroad	Mr. Mark ECKMAN
122	Coord Fraternity/Sorority Life	Mr. Thomas J. MARTIN
23	Exec Dir University Health Services	Dr. George A. COREY
38	Dir Ctr Counseling & Psych Hlth	Dr. Melissa S. ROTKIEWICZ
36	Director Career Services	Ms. Candice J. SERAFINO
29	Asst VC Alumni Relations	Ms. Deborah GOODHIND
44	Exec Dir Annual Giving	Mr. Nathan ADAMS
27	Assoc VC University Relations	Dr. Nancy BUFFONE
88	Exec Dir News & Media Relations	Mr. Edward F. BLAGUSZEWSKI
88	Sr Dir Executive Communications	Ms. Amy C. GLYNN
86	Exec Dir Government Relations	Mr. Christopher DUNN
102	Exec Dir Foundation Relations	Dr. Marco C. MONOC
112	Assoc Director Planned Gifts	Mr. Joe JAYNE
25	Dir Grants & Contracts (Post-Award)	Ms. Carol SPRAGUE
90	Int Dir Instructional Innovation	Mr. Matthew DALTON
119	Chief Information Security Officer	Mr. Matthew DALTON
30	Assoc VC Development	Ms. Kimberly DUMPSON

*University of Massachusetts Boston (E)

100 Morrissey Boulevard, Boston MA 02125-3393
County: Suffolk FICE Identification: 002222
Unit ID: 166638
Telephone: (617) 287-5000 Carnegie Class: DU-Higher
FAX Number: (617) 265-7173 Calendar System: Semester
URL: www.umb.edu
Established: 1964 Annual Undergrad Tuition & Fees (In-State): $14,677
Enrollment: 16,259 Coed
Affiliation or Control: State IRS Status: 501(c)3
Highest Offering: Doctorate
Accreditation: EH, CACREP, CLPSY, COPSY, MPCAC, NURSE, SCPSY, SPAA

02	Chancellor	Dr. Marcelo M. SUAREZ-OROZCO
05	Provost/VC Academic Affairs	Dr. Joseph BERGER
03	Deputy Chancellor	Dr. Hannah SEVIAN
20	Associate Provost	Mr. Brian WHITE
10	Vice Chanc for Admin & Finance	Ms. Kathleen KIRLEIS
111	VC for University Advancement	Mr. Adam WISE
32	Int Vice Chancellor Student Affs	Ms. Shawn DEVEAU
84	Vice Chanc for Enrollment Managemen	Dr. John DREW
26	VC for Marketing & Engagement	Ms. Megan DELAGE SULLIVAN
15	Vice Chanc for Human Resources	Ms. Marie BOWEN
13	Vice Chanc Information Svcs/CIO	Mr. Ray LEFEBVRE
20	Assoc VP for Academic Affairs	Ms. Anita MILLER
45	AVP/Exec Dir Strategic Initiatives	Ms. Mya M. MANAGAWANG
41	Director of Athletics	Ms. Jacqueline SCHUMAN
86	Asst Chanc Govt Rels & Public Affs	Mr. Matt FENLON
22	Asst Chancellor/Equity & Inclusion	Ms. Georgianna MELENDEZ
53	Int Dean Col of Educ & Human Dev	Dr. Laura HAYDEN
66	Interim Dean College of Nursing	Dr. Rosanna DEMARCO
79	Dean of Liberal Arts	Dr. Tyson D. KING-MEADOWS
81	Dean of Math & Science	Dr. Robin COTE
50	Interim Dean College of Management	Dr. Arindam BANDOPADHYAYA
08	Interim Dean of Univ Libraries	Ms. Joanne RILEY
09	Assoc Prov Institutional Research	Mr. James J. HUGHES
92	Dean of Honors College	Vacant
82	Dean Sch Global Incl & Social Dev	Vacant
80	Int Dn Grad Sch Policy/Global Stds	Dr. Rita Kiki EDOZIE
58	VP Research & Dean of Grad Studies	Mr. Bala SUNDARAM
121	Vice Prov for Academic Support Svcs	Ms. Liya ESCALERA
100	Chief of Staff	Ms. Anne RILEY
27	Director of Communications	Mr. DeWayne LEHMAN
88	Dean of Faculty	Dr. Rajini SRIKANTH

*University of Massachusetts Dartmouth (F)

285 Old Westport Road, North Dartmouth MA 02747-2300
County: Bristol FICE Identification: 002210
Unit ID: 167987
Telephone: (508) 999-8000 Carnegie Class: DU-Higher
FAX Number: (508) 999-8901 Calendar System: Semester
URL: www.umassd.edu
Established: 1895 Annual Undergrad Tuition & Fees (In-State): $14,408
Enrollment: 7,869 Coed
Affiliation or Control: State IRS Status: 501(c)3
Highest Offering: Doctorate
Accreditation: EH, ART, CIDA, LAW, MLS, NURSE

01	Chancellor	Dr. Mark FULLER
05	Provost/VC Academic Affairs	Dr. Hanchen HUANG
100	Chief of Staff/ Exec Dir Comm	Ms. Robyn PIGGOTT
15	VC for Human Resources	Ms. Deborah MAJEWSKI
10	VC Administration & Finance	Mr. David GINGERELLA
111	VC University Advancement	Mr. Dean HICKEY
28	Chief Diversity Officer/Title IX	Mr. David GOMES
110	Asst VC Advancement Services	Ms. Valerie AU
16	Asst VC HR Operations	Ms. Kimberly PENNOCK
26	Director Strategic Comms/Media	Vacant
20	Assoc Provost UGRD/Faculty Affairs	Dr. Robert JONES
58	Assoc Provost Grad Studies	Dr. Tesfay MERESSI
46	VC Research & Innovation	Dr. Ramprasad BALASUBRAMANIAN
84	VC Enrollment Management	Mr. James ANDERSON
21	Assoc VC Admin & Finance	Ms. Susan AMATRUDO
18	Associate VC Facilities Management	Mr. James JERUE, JR.
32	Vice Chancellor Student Affairs	Dr. Kimberly SCOTT
13	Assoc VC IT/CIO	Mr. Holger DIPPEL
35	Assistant VC Student Success	Ms. Carol SPENCER-MONTEIRO
49	Dean College Arts & Science	Dr. Pauline ENTIN
50	Dean Charlton College Business	Dr. John WILLIAMS
54	Dean College of Engineering	Dr. Jean VANDERGHEYNST
66	Dean College of Nurse & Health Sci	Dr. Kimberly CHRISTOPHER
57	Dean College Visual Perf Arts	Dr. A. Lawrence JENKENS
88	Interim Dean School Marine Sci/ Tech	Dr. Jean VANDERGHEYNST
61	Dean School of Law	Dr. Eric MITNICK
08	Interim Dean Library Services	Ms. Dawn GROSS
51	Asst VC Online & Continuing Educ	Mr. David PEDRO
58	Dir Graduate Studies/Admissions	Mr. Scott WEBSTER
96	Assoc VC for Admin Operations	Mr. Michael LAGRASSA
21	Controller	Ms. Suzanne AUDET
88	Director Faculty Development	Mr. Jay ZYSK
94	Dir Center Women/Gender/Sexuality	Dr. Juli PARKER
121	Dir Advising/Support & Planning	Vacant
06	University Registrar	Ms. Audra CALLAHAN
07	Director of Admissions	Ms. Hanan KHAMIS
37	Director Financial Aid	Vacant
09	Dir Inst Research/Assessment	Ms. Tammy A. SILVA
19	Dir Public Safety/Chief of Police	Vacant
36	Director Career Development Center	Mr. Un Yeong PARK
38	Dir Counseling/Student Devel Ctr	Dr. Catherine PERRY
90	Exec Dir IT Service Assurance	Ms. Margaret S. DIAS
29	Director of Alumni Relations	Mr. Joshua SYLVESTER
18	Director Facilities/Physical Plant	Mr. Jeffrey LOURO
41	Director of Athletics	Ms. Lori HENDRICKS
23	Director of Health Services	Ms. Marianne SULLIVAN
39	Dir Housing/Residential Education	Ms. Lucinda POUDRIER-AARONSON
44	Asst VC for Annual Giving	Ms. Ellen CACCIA
27	Asst VC for Univ Marketing	Ms. Hillary SYLVIA
113	Bursar	Vacant
35	Associate Dean of Students	Ms. Shelly METIVIER SCOTT
104	Asst Director Study Abroad Pgms	Ms. Gina REIS
85	Exec Dir International Education	Mr. Daniel PIRBUDAGOV
93	Assoc Dir Fred Douglas Unity House	Mr. Lasella HALL
88	Director Academic Resource Center	Mr. Sokratis KOUMAS
105	Webmaster	Vacant
103	Dir Experiential Learning & Intern	Ms. Amelia ALBURN
106	Dir Center for Access & Success	Ms. Wendi CHAKA
25	Dir Research Administration	Ms. Megan HENNESSEY-GREENE
28	Director Diversity & Inclusion	Vacant
45	Assoc VC Capital Planning & Ops Mgt	Mr. Jeffrey MARTIN
103	Exec Dir Economic Development	Vacant
88	Asst VC Civic Engagement	Mr. Matthew ROY
88	Director of Academic Budget	Mr. Christopher VALADAO
44	Director of Annual Giving	Vacant
88	Dir Frederick Unity House	Ms. Moise SAINT-LOUIS
108	Director Institutional Assessment	Ms. Tammy SILVA
86	Director Government Relations	Mr. John QUINN

*University of Massachusetts Lowell (G)

1 University Avenue, Lowell MA 01854-2881
County: Middlesex FICE Identification: 002161
Unit ID: 166513
Telephone: (978) 934-4000 Carnegie Class: DU-Higher
FAX Number: (978) 934-3000 Calendar System: Semester
URL: www.uml.edu
Established: 1894 Annual Undergrad Tuition & Fees (In-State): $15,698
Enrollment: 18,150 Coed
Affiliation or Control: State IRS Status: 501(c)3
Highest Offering: Doctorate
Accreditation: EH, ART, CAMPEP, DIETC, @DIETD, MLS, MUS, NURSE, PTA

02	Chancellor	Dr. Julie CHEN
05	Provost & VC Academic/Student Affs	Dr. Joseph HARTMAN
10	VC Finance and Operations	Mr. Steven O'RIORDAN
26	VC University Relations	Vacant
46	VC Research/Economic Development	Vacant
111	Vice Chancellor for Advancement	Mr. John FEUDO
15	Assoc VC Human Resources	Mr. Michael RUTHERFORD
58	Vice Provost Grad & Prof Studies	Dr. Steven TELLO
18	Assoc VC Facilities Management	Ms. Jean ROBINSON
27	Assoc VC Marketing	Mr. Bryce HOFFMAN
20	Vice Provost Academic Affairs	Dr. Julie NASH
84	Dean Enrollment Management	Ms. Kerri JOHNSTON
41	Director of Athletics	Mr. Peter CASEY
49	Dean Col Fine Arts/Hum/Soc Sci	Dr. Luis FALCON

81 Dean Kennedy College of Sciences .... Dr. Noureddine MELIKECHI
54 Dean College of Engineering .... Dr. Jim SHERWOOD
76 Dean College of Health Sciences .... Dr. Shortie MCKINNEY
50 Dean Manning School of Business .. Dr. Sandra RICHTERMEYER
20 Dean Academic Services .... Ms. Kerry DONOHOE
06 Registrar .... Ms. Mai NGUYEN
28 Dean Equity & Inclusion .... Ms. Leslie WONG
37 Assoc Dean Enrollment/Dir Fin Aid .... Ms. Joyce MCLAUGHLIN
38 Director of Counseling Svcs .... Dr. Deborah EDELMAN-BLANK
29 Exec Dir Alumni & Donor Relations . Dr. Heather MAKREZ ALLEN
19 Chief Univ Police Dir Public Safety .... Mr. Randolph BRASHEARS
123 Asst Dean Graduate Recruitment .... Dr. Shahram HAYDARI
96 Chief Procurement Officer .... Mr. Thomas HOOLE
07 Asst Dean Undergrad Admissions .... Ms. Christine BRYAN
119 Dir Security Tech & UCAPS .... Mr. Jon VICTORINE
22 Assoc VC Equal Opportunity/Outreach .... Ms. Clara REYNOLDS
36 Assoc Dean Student Affs/Career Dev .... Mr. Gregory DENON
35 Dean Student Affairs & Enrichment .... Mr. James KOHL
23 Dir Student Health Svcs .... Ms. Diana WALKER MOYER
35 Dean Student Affairs & Wellness .... Ms. Brenda EVANS
13 Assoc VC Info Tech & CIO .... Mr. Michael CIPRIANO
104 Director Intl Exper/Study Abroad .... Ms. Fern MACKINNON
92 Dean Honors College .... Dr. Jenifer WHITTEN-WOODRING
100 Chief of Staff .... Mr. Chris MULLIN
44 Director Annual Giving .... Mr. Michael DEGUGLIELMO
86 Exec Director Government Relations .... Mr. D.J CORCORAN

*UMass Chan Medical School (A)

55 Lake Avenue N, Worcester MA 01655-0001
County: Worcester FICE Identification: 009756
Unit ID: 166708
Telephone: (508) 856-8989 Carnegie Class: Spec-4-yr-Eng
FAX Number: (508) 856-8181 Calendar System: Semester
URL: www.umassmed.edu
Established: 1962 Annual Graduate Tuition & Fees: N/A
Enrollment: 1,292 Coed
Affiliation or Control: State IRS Status: 501(c)3
Highest Offering: Doctorate; No Undergraduates
Accreditation: EH, IPSY, MED, NURSE

02 Chancellor & SVP Health Sciences .... Dr. Michael F. COLLINS
05 Provost/Dean/Exec Deputy Chancellor .... Dr. Terence R. FLOTTE
10 Exec VC Administration & Finance .... Mr. John LINDSTEDT
88 Exec VC Innovation and Business Dev .. Mr. Parth CHAKRABARTI
111 VC for Advancement .... Mr. John J. HAYES
28 VC Diversity & Inclusion .... Dr. Marlina DUNCAN
88 Exec Vice Chancellor MassBiologics .... Ms. Mireli W. FINO
11 Exec VC Commonwealth Medicine .... Ms. Lisa COLOMBO
86 VC for Government Relations .... Mr. John ERWIN
26 Vice Chancellor of Communications ...... Ms. Jennifer BERRYMAN
20 Vice Provost Faculty Affairs .... Dr. Mary AHN
88 Vice Prov/Sr Assoc Dean Educ Affs .... Dr. Anne LARKIN
63 Sr Assc Dean Clin Aff/Assc Dean GME ... Dr. Deborah DEMARCO
66 Dean Graduate School of Nursing .... Dr. Joan VITELLO
32 Interim Assoc Dean Student Affs .... Dr. Anne GARRISON
58 Dean Grad School Biomedical Science .... Dr. Mary Ellen LANE
18 Assoc VC Facilities Mgmt .... Mr. John T. BAKER
06 Registrar .... Mr. Michael F. BAKER
13 Chief Information Officer .... Mr. Greg WOLF
07 Assoc Dean for Admissions .... Dr. Mariann M. MANNO
37 Director Financial Aid .... Mr. Shawn MORRISSEY
08 Director of Library .... Dr. Mary PIORUN
100 Assoc VC for Mgmt/Chief of Staff ...... Mr. Brendan H. CHISHOLM
04 Spec Assistant to the Chancellor .... Mr. Luke GLYNN
46 Vice Prov Rsrch/Strat Initiatives .... Dr. Michael GREEN
88 Vice Provost for Clin/Trans Science ..... Dr. Katherine LUZURIAGA
88 Chief of Staff to Dean/Provost .... Ms. Kristen MAKI
88 Exec Asst to Dean/Prov/Exec Deputy .... Ms. Kimberly LAPERLE
04 Exec Assistant to the Chancellor .... Ms. Lisa BARRY
11 Dep EVC of Management .... Mr. James HEALY
15 Dep EVC People Strategy .... Ms. Deborah HARNOIS

*Bridgewater State University (B)

131 Summer Street, Bridgewater MA 02325-0001
County: Plymouth FICE Identification: 002183
Unit ID: 165024
Telephone: (508) 531-1000 Carnegie Class: Masters/L
FAX Number: N/A Calendar System: Semester
URL: www.bridgew.edu
Established: 1840 Annual Undergrad Tuition & Fees (In-State): $10,732
Enrollment: 10,651 Coed
Affiliation or Control: State IRS Status: 501(c)3
Highest Offering: Master's
Accreditation: EH, AAB, ART, CAATE, CACREP, MPCAC, MUS, SP, SPAA, SW

02 President .... Mr. Frederick CLARK
05 Provost & VP Academic Affairs .... Dr. Karim ISMAILI
10 Vice President and CFO .... Mr. Doug SHROPSHIRE
32 VP Student Affs/Enrollment Mgmt .... Dr. Joseph ORAVECZ
36 Int Asst VP Outreach and Engagement .... Ms. Diane BELL
15 VP Human Resources & Talent Mgmt .... Ms. Keri POWERS
26 VP Marketing & Communication .... Mr. Paul JEAN
28 VP of Student Success & Diversity .... Dr. Sabrina GENTLEWARRIOR
11 Vice President Operations .... Ms. Karen W. JASON
124 Int VP Outreach & Engagement .... Dr. Deniz LEUENBERGER
100 Chief of Staff/VP Plng & Strategy .... Dr. Deniz ZEYNEP LEUENBERGER
22 Assoc Director EOO/Title IX .... Ms. Danielle DEMERS
35 Asst VP & Dean of Students .... Ms. Elizabeth CHING-BUSH
84 Assoc Dean for Enrollment Services .... Mr. Todd AUDYATIS

20 Int Assoc Provost Faculty Affairs .... Dr. Nicole GLEN
45 Sr Assoc Provost/Chief Data Officer .... Dr. Michael YOUNG
79 Dean Col Humanities/Social Sci .... Dr. Arnaa ALCON
53 Dean Col Education/Allied Studies ..... Dr. Tom TONG-CHING WU
51 Dean Col of Continuing Studies .... Dr. David CRANE
50 Dean Ricciardi Col of Business .... Dr. Jeanean DAVIS-STREET
07 Dean of University Admissions .... Mr. Gregg A. MEYER
13 VP & Chief Information Officer .... Mr. Steve ZUROMSKI
06 Registrar .... Mr. Joseph WOLK
121 Exec Director Academic Achievement .... Ms. Laura FOLLONI
29 Exec Director Alumni Relations .... Ms. Ellen CUTTLE-OLIVER
30 Director Development .... Ms. Betsy DUBUQUE
41 Assoc VP Athletics & Wellness .... Dr. Marybeth LAMB
21 Director University Services .... Dr. Margarida BAGANHA
19 Chief of Police .... Mr. David TILLINGHAST
36 Director Career Services .... Mr. John PAGANELLI
37 AVP of Financial Aid .... Ms. Laura BIECHLER
23 Executive Director Wellness Center .... Dr. Christopher FRAZER
08 Dean Library Administration .... Mr. Kevin KIDD
93 Int Director Multicultural Affairs .... Mr. Michael WALSH
27 Director Creative Svcs/Publications .... Ms. Jaime KNIGHT
25 Director Grants/Sponsored Projects .... Ms. Mia ZOINO
96 Director of Procurement Services .... Dr. Jennifer PACHECO
28 Director of Institutional Diversity .... Dr. Luis F. PAREDES
81 Dean Bartlett Col Science & Math .... Vacant
58 Dean College of Graduate Studies ..... Dr. Lisa KRISSOFF BOEHM
09 Director of Institutional Research .... Vacant
88 Director Teaching and Learning .... Dr. Roben TOROSYAN
46 Asst Prov High Impact Ed Practices .... Dr. Jenny SHANAHAN
85 Assoc Dir Intl Students/Scholars .... Ms. Jennifer CURRIE
104 Director Study Abroad .... Mr. Michael SANDY
14 AVP Information Technology .... Ms. Kelley BARAN
105 Director of Web Development .... Ms. Eileen O'SULLIVAN
27 Asst VP & Chief Marketing Officer .... Ms. Eva GAFFNEY
88 AVP University News and Video .... Mr. David ROBICHAUD
38 Clinical Dir Counseling Center .... Ms. Donna SHIAVO
39 Dir Residence Life and Housing .... Mr. Justin MCCAULEY
108 Director of Assessment .... Dr. Ruth SLOTNICK
88 Exec Dir Martin Richard Institute .... Ms. Jill BECKWITH
88 Asst Provost for Global Engagement .... Dr. Wing-Kai TO
04 Dir Presidential Initiatives & Oper ... Ms. Kelly HESS SALISBURY
88 Special Advisor to the President .... Mr. Vinny DE MACEDO
97 Dean of Undergraduate Studies .... Dr. Rita MILLER

*Fitchburg State University (C)

160 Pearl Street, Fitchburg MA 01420-2697
County: Worcester FICE Identification: 002184
Unit ID: 165820
Telephone: (978) 345-2151 Carnegie Class: Masters/L
FAX Number: (978) 665-3693 Calendar System: Semester
URL: www.fitchburgstate.edu
Established: 1894 Annual Undergrad Tuition & Fees (In-State): $10,830
Enrollment: 6,728 Coed
Affiliation or Control: State IRS Status: 501(c)3
Highest Offering: Master's
Accreditation: EH, CSHSE, IACBE, NURSE

02 President .... Dr. Richard S. LAPIDUS
05 Provost/VP Academic Affairs .... Dr. Patricia MARSHALL
10 Vice Pres Finance & Administration .... Mr. Jay BRY
20 Associate VP Academic Affairs .... Dr. Franca BARRICELLI
32 Vice President Student Affairs .... Dr. Laura BAYLESS
111 Vice President of Inst Advancement .... Mr. Jeffrey WOLFMAN
21 AVP Finance & Administration .... Ms. Mary Beth MCKENZIE
84 Assoc VP Enrollment Management .... Mr. Richard TOOMEY
09 Asst VP Institutional Research .... Ms. Pamela MCCAFFERTY
15 Asst VP of Human Resources/Payroll .... Ms. Jessica MURDOCH
18 Asst VP Capital Planning .... Vacant
35 Asst Dean for Student Development .... Dr. Henry C. PARKINSON, III
06 Registrar .... Ms. Barbara CORMIER
41 Director Athletics .... Mr. Matthew BURKE
07 Director of Admissions .... Mr. Anthony TRODELLA
36 Director Career Counseling .... Ms. Lindsay CARPENTER CONNORS
38 Director Counseling .... Dr. Robert HYNES
29 Director of Alumni Relations .... Ms. Tanya CROWLEY
19 Director of Campus Police .... Chief Michael CLOUTIER
44 Manager of Annual Fund/Donor Rels .... Mr. Brian BERUBE
18 Dir Capital Planning & Construction .... Vacant
25 Director Grants & Sponsored Pgm .... Ms. Jeanette ROBICHAUD
37 Director Financial Aid .... Ms. Denise BRINDLE
106 Dir of Digital Learning .... Mr. Ralph FASANO
13 Chief Info Technology Officer (CIO) .... Mr. Stephen E. SWARTZ
39 Dean of the Library .... Ms. Jacalyn KREMER
04 Special Asst to President .... Ms. Gail M. DOIRON
53 Dean of Education .... Dr. Nancy MURRAY
81 Dean of Health & Natural Sciences ...... Dr. Jennifer HANSELMAN
58 Dean of Graduate & Cont Educ .... Dr. Becky COPPER GLENZ
49 Dean of Arts & Sciences .... Dr. Sara LEVINE
122 Coordinator of Greek Life .... Vacant
26 Chief Public Relations Officer .... Mr. Matthew BRUUN

*Framingham State University (D)

100 State Street, PO Box 9101,
Framingham MA 01701-9101
County: Middlesex FICE Identification: 002185
Unit ID: 165866
Telephone: (508) 620-1220 Carnegie Class: Masters/L
FAX Number: (508) 626-4592 Calendar System: Semester
URL: www.framingham.edu
Established: 1839 Annual Undergrad Tuition & Fees (In-State): $11,380
Enrollment: 4,876 Coed
Affiliation or Control: State IRS Status: 501(c)3
Highest Offering: Master's
Accreditation: EH, ART, CAEP, DIETC, DIETD, IACBE, NURSE

02 President .... Dr. Nancy NIEMI
03 Executive Vice President .... Dr. Dale M. HAMEL
05 Vice President Academic Affairs .... Dr. Kristen PORTER-UTLEY
32 Vice Pres Enrollment & Student Dev .... Dr. Lorretta HOLLOWAY
43 Vice President/General Counsel .... Ms. Ann MCDONALD
13 Associate Vice President .... Mr. Patrick LAUGHRAN
18 Assistant Vice President .... Ms. Patricia WHITNEY
84 Dean of Enrollment Management .... Mr. Jeremy SPENCER
35 Dean of Students .... Dr. Meg NOWAK
39 Associate Dean Student Affairs .... Mr. Glenn COCHRAN
07 Associate Dean Undergrad Admissions .... Ms. Shayna EDDY
88 Assistant Dean Student Affairs .... Dr. Christopher GREGORY
06 Executive Director/Registrar .... Mr. Mark R. POWERS
15 Asst Vice Pres Human Resources .... Ms. Kimberly DEXTER
19 Chief Public Safety .... Mr. John SANTORO
121 Director Academic Support .... Ms. LaDonna BRIDGES
108 Director Assessment .... Dr. Mark NICHOLAS
41 Director Athletics .... Mr. Thomas KELLEY
36 Director Career Services .... Vacant
37 Director Financial Aid .... Ms. Carla MINCHELLO
10 Director Financial Services .... Ms. Jeanne DEREE
89 Director First Year Programs .... Mr. Benjamin J. TRAPANICK
23 Director Health Services .... Ms. Ilene HOFRENNING
104 Director International Education .... Ms. Jane DECATUR
08 Director Library Services .... Mrs. Millie GONZALEZ
38 Director Counseling Center .... Dr. Ben DAY
88 Director Student Involvement .... Ms. Rachel LUCKING
113 Director Student Accounts .... Mr. Jeffrey MCMASTER
30 Director Development .... Mr. Eric GUSTAFSON
25 Director Grants/Sponsored Programs ...... Ms. Patricia BOSSANGE
09 Director Institutional Research .... Ms. Ann CASO
04 Executive Assistant .... Ms. Katie HEBERT
58 Dean of Graduate Studies .... Dr. Sunny TAM
26 Chief Public Relations Officer .... Mr. Daniel MAGAZU
29 Director of Alumni Relations .... Ms. Jennifer DEFRONZO

*Massachusetts College of Art and Design (E)

621 Huntington Avenue, Boston MA 02115-5882
County: Suffolk FICE Identification: 002180
Unit ID: 166674
Telephone: (617) 879-7000 Carnegie Class: Spec-4-yr-Arts
FAX Number: (617) 566-4034 Calendar System: Semester
URL: www.massart.edu
Established: 1873 Annual Undergrad Tuition & Fees (In-State): $14,200
Enrollment: 1,894 Coed
Affiliation or Control: State IRS Status: 501(c)3
Highest Offering: Master's
Accreditation: EH

02 President .... Dr. Mary K. GRANT
10 VP of Administration & Finance .... Mr. Robert PERRY
05 Provost & VP of Academic Affairs .... Dr. Brenda MOLIFE
32 Vice President Student Development .... Dr. Maureen KEEFE
111 Vice Pres Institutional Advancement .... Ms. Marjorie O'MALLEY
09 Exec Dir IR/Effectiveness/Planning .... Ms. Karalynn GAU
21 Asst VP Fiscal Affairs .... Ms. Gina SPAZIANI
100 VP Strategic Engage/Chief of Staff .... Mr. Robert CHAMBERS
07 Dean of Admissions/Enrollment .... Ms. Lauren WILSHUSEN
35 Assoc VP/Dean of Students .... Dr. Jamie COSTELLO
06 Registrar .... Mr. Jonathan RAND
37 Director of Financial Aid .... Mr. Aurelio RAMIREZ
88 Director MassArt Art Museum .... Ms. Lisa TUNG
08 Librarian .... Mr. Greg WALLACE
15 Interim Exec Dir Human Resources .... Ms. Sandra KNIGHT
28 Dean of Diversity .... Ms. Lyssa PALU-AY
22 Exec Director of Compliance .... Ms. Alisa CHAPMAN
18 Asst VP Facilities & Planning .... Mr. Howie LAROSEE
11 Exec Dir of Administrative Services .... Mr. James MCDAID
26 Exec Dir Marketing/Communications .... Ms. Ellen CARR
13 Chief Information Officer .... Mr. Patrick O'CONNOR
19 Chief of Police .... Ms. Deborah CRAFTS
104 Dir International Education Center ..... Ms. Erica PUCCIO O'BRIEN
38 Director Counseling & Wellness .... Dr. Shauna SUMMERS
29 Director Alumni Relations .... Ms. Darlene GILLAN
39 Director Student Housing .... Vacant

*Massachusetts College of Liberal Arts (F)

375 Church Street, North Adams MA 01247-4100
County: Berkshire FICE Identification: 002187
Unit ID: 167288
Telephone: (413) 662-5000 Carnegie Class: Bac-A&S
FAX Number: (413) 662-5010 Calendar System: Semester
URL: www.mcla.edu
Established: 1894 Annual Undergrad Tuition & Fees (In-State): $11,306
Enrollment: 1,202 Coed
Affiliation or Control: State IRS Status: 501(c)3
Highest Offering: Master's
Accreditation: EH, ACBSP, RAD

02 President .... Dr. James BIRGE
05 VP Academic Affairs .... Dr. Richard GLEJZER
45 VP Strategic Initiatives .... Ms. Gina PUC
10 VP Administration & Finance .... Mr. Joseph DASILVA

32 VP Student Affairs ... Dr. Jeannette SMITH
111 VP Institutional Advancement ... Mr. Robert ZIOMEK
28 Chief Diversity Officer ... Dr. Christopher MACDONALD-DENNIS
15 Executive Director Human Resources ... Ms. Barbara CHAPUT
04 Executive Assistant to President ... Ms. Lisa LESCARBEAU
26 Director Marketing & Communications ... Ms. Bernadette ALDEN
13 Chief Information Officer ... Mr. Ian BERGERON
20 Interim Dean Academic Affairs ... Dr. Ely JANIS
21 Comptroller ... Mr. Curt CELLANA
35 Dean of Students ... Ms. Heather QUIRE
20 Dean DGCE ... Ms. Theresa O'BRYANT
41 Director Athletics ... Ms. Laura MOONEY
08 Associate Dean Library Services ... Ms. Emily ALLING
51 Associate Dean DGCE ... Mr. Paul PETRITIS
66 Associate Dean Nursing ... Dr. Elizabeth FISCELLA
110 Senior Dir Inst Advancement ... Ms. Kate GIGLIOTTI
124 Executive Dir Student Persistence ... Ms. Kayla HOLLINS
07 Director Admissions ... Vacant
37 Director Student Financial Services ... Ms. Bonnie HOWLAND
38 Director Counseling Services ... Ms. Heidi RIELLO
19 Director Public Safety ... Mr. Daniel COLONNO
23 Director Health Services ... Dr. Jacki KRZANIK
39 Director Residential Programs ... Ms. Dianne MANNING
06 Dir Student Records/Registrar ... Vacant
09 Assistant Dir Effectiveness ... Mr. Jason CANALES
22 Dir Equal Opportunity & Title IX ... Vacant
120 Director Academic Technology ... Dr. Gerol PETRUZELLA
18 Assistant Dir Facilities ... Mr. Robert FORTINI
25 Director of Development for Grants ... Ms. Lynette BOND
108 Director Assessment ... Ms. Erin MILNE
105 Web and Applications Manager ... Mr. Steven PESOLA
114 Budget Manager ... Ms. Jennifer DIX
96 Purchasing Manager ... Mr. William NORCROSS

*Massachusetts Maritime Academy (A)

101 Academy Drive, Buzzards Bay MA 02532-3400
County: Barnstable | FICE Identification: 002181
Unit ID: 166692
Telephone: (508) 830-5000 | Carnegie Class: Masters/S
FAX Number: (508) 830-5090 | Calendar System: Semester
URL: www.maritime.edu
Established: 1891 | Annual Undergrad Tuition & Fees (In-State): $11,687
Enrollment: 1,637 | Coed
Affiliation or Control: State | IRS Status: 501(c)3
Highest Offering: Master's
Accreditation: EH, IACBE

02 President ... RADM. Francis X. MCDONALD
05 Vice President Academic Affairs ... CAPT. Brigid PAVILONIS
10 Vice Pres Finance ... Ms. Rose-Marie CASS
32 Vice Pres Student Services ... CAPT. Brigid PAVILONIS
111 Vice Pres External Affairs ... CAPT. Elizabeth SIMMONS
13 Vice President/CIO ... Ms. Anne Marie FALLON
18 Vice President Operations ... CAPT. Allen METCALFE
36 Director Career/Professional Svcs ... CDR. Maryanne RICHARDS
07 Director of Admissions ... CDR. Albert SEITZ
06 Director Student Records/Registrar ... Ms. Wendy MAYNARD
08 Director Library ... Ms. Carolyn MICHAUD
110 Assistant Dean of Advancement ... Ms. Kelley LESSARD
09 Director of Institutional Research ... Dr. Megan CUNNIFF
15 Dean Human Resources ... Mrs. Elizabeth BENWAY
29 Director Alumni Relations ... Ms. Kelley LESSARD
37 Director Student Financial Aid ... Mrs. Cathy KEDSKI
96 Director of Purchasing ... Mr. Paul AIROZO
41 Athletic Director ... Mr. Michael KELLEY
20 Dean of Undergraduate Studies ... Dr. James MCKENNA
58 Dean of Graduate & Continuing Educ ... CAPT. James MCDONALD
28 Dean of Diversity/Equity/Inclusion ... Mr. Michael ORTIZ
35 Commandant of Cadets/Dean, Students ... CDR. Patrick DILLON
19 Director Security/Safety ... Chief Christopher SLATTERY

*Salem State University (B)

352 Lafayette Street, Salem MA 01970-5353
County: Essex | FICE Identification: 002188
Unit ID: 167729
Telephone: (978) 542-6000 | Carnegie Class: Masters/L
FAX Number: (978) 542-6970 | Calendar System: Semester
URL: www.salemstate.edu
Established: 1854 | Annual Undergrad Tuition & Fees (In-State): $11,675
Enrollment: 7,242 | Coed
Affiliation or Control: State | IRS Status: 501(c)3
Highest Offering: Master's
Accreditation: EH, ART, CAATE, MUS, NMT, NURSE, OT, SW, THEA

02 President ... Mr. John KEENAN
05 Provost & Academic VP ... Dr. David J. SILVA
03 Executive Vice President ... Vacant
111 VP Institutional Advancement ... Ms. Cheryl CROUNSE
10 VP Finance and Facilities ... Ms. Karen HOUSE
43 VP & General Counsel ... Ms. Rita COLUCCI
26 Asst VP Marketing/Creative Svcs ... Mr. Corey CRONIN
13 CIO-CISO ... Mr. Curt KING
121 Vice President of Student Success ... Dr. Nate BRYANT
21 Assoc VP Financial Svcs ... Vacant
15 Assistant VP for HR & EEO ... Mr. Mark R. QUIGLEY
20 Assoc Provost ... Vacant
86 Senior Director External Relations ... Ms. Adria DUIJVESTEIJN
08 Director Library ... Ms. Elizabeth MCKEIGUE
50 Dean School of Business ... Dr. Raminder LUTHER
53 Dean of Education ... Dr. Joseph CAMBONE
58 Assoc Dean Sch Grad & Prof Studies ... Dr. Barbara LAYNE
49 Dean School of Arts & Sciences ... Dr. Brian TRAVERS
32 Dean of Students ... Mr. Shawn NEWTON
110 AVP Institutional Advancement ... Ms. Mandy RAY
04 Asst to Pres/Asst Secy to BOT ... Ms. Mayra CLARKE
19 Director Public Safety ... Mr. Gene R. LABONTE
41 Director Athletics ... Ms. Nicolle WOOD
06 Registrar ... Ms. Megan M. MILLER
84 Int VP for Enroll Mgmt/Marketing ... Ms. Bonnie GALINSKI
18 AVP Capital Plng/Business Affairs ... Vacant
28 Director of Diversity ... Mr. Thomas ALEXANDER
37 Director of Financial Aid ... Mr. Scott JEWELL
38 Asst Dean of Students/Wellness ... Ms. Elisa CASTILLO
96 Sr Director Purchasing/Vendor Rels ... Mr. Reynaldo RAMOS
25 Asst Dir Sponsored Pgms & Research ... Ms. Elaine MILO
07 Director of Admissions ... Ms. Jackie HAAS
45 Exec Dir Strategic Planning ... Dr. Chunju CHEN
39 Director Residence Life ... Ms. Joy SCHMELZER
76 Int Dean Col of Health & Human Svcs ... Dr. Sami ANSARI
04 Special Asst to President ... Ms. Lynne MONTAGUE
44 Director of Annual Giving ... Ms. Lori BOUDO

*Westfield State University (C)

577 Western Avenue, Westfield MA 01086-1630
County: Hampden | FICE Identification: 002189
Unit ID: 168263
Telephone: (413) 572-5300 | Carnegie Class: Masters/L
FAX Number: (413) 572-8147 | Calendar System: Semester
URL: www.westfield.ma.edu
Established: 1839 | Annual Undergrad Tuition & Fees (In-State): $11,139
Enrollment: 5,395 | Coed
Affiliation or Control: State | IRS Status: 501(c)3
Highest Offering: Beyond Master's But Less Than Doctorate
Accreditation: EH, AAQEP, ARCPA, CAATE, EXSC, MUS, NURSE, SW

02 President ... Dr. Linda THOMPSON
100 Chief of Staff ... Dr. Michael FREEMAN
05 Int Provost/VP Academic Affairs ... Dr. Juline MILLS
32 Vice Pres Student Affairs ... Vacant
84 VP Enrollment Management ... Mr. Dan FORSTER
10 VP Administration & Finance ... Mr. Stephen TAKSAR
111 Int VP Institutional Advancement ... Ms. Lisa MCMAHON
21 Assoc VP Administration/Finance ... Ms. Lisa FREEMAN
15 Asst VP Human Resources ... Dr. Jalisa D. WILLIAMS
124 Interim Dean of Faculty ... Dr. Enrique MORALES-DIAZ
49 Dean of Undergrad Studies ... Vacant
58 Dean Graduate/Continuing Educ ... Vacant
81 Int Dean College of Math & Sciences ... Dr. Jennifer HANSELMAN
53 Dean College Educ/Health/Human Svcs ... Dr. Juline MILLS
79 Int Dean Coll Arts/Human/Soc Sc ... Dr. Emily TODD
35 Dean of Students ... Ms. Maggie BALCH
06 Registrar ... Dr. Monique LOPEZ
09 Assoc Dean Inst Research/Assess ... Dr. Lisa PLANTEFABER
08 Dean Acad Info Svcs/Dir Library ... Mr. Thomas RAFFENSPERGER
39 Assoc Director Residential Life ... Dr. Joshua HETTRICK
19 Director Public Safety ... Mr. Tony CASCIANO
36 Director Career Services ... Mr. Junior DELGADO
90 Exec Director Acad Tech Services ... Mr. Christopher HIRTLE
13 Chief Information Officer ... Mr. Alan BLAIR
91 Director Admin Systems ... Vacant
18 Exec Dir Facilities/Capital Plan ... Ms. Maureen SOCHA
41 Director Athletics ... Mr. Richard LENFEST
38 Assoc Director Counseling Center ... Ms. Suzanna ADAMS
23 Interim Director Health Services ... Ms. Lisa BROSNAN
37 Director of Financial Aid ... Mr. Michael MAZEIKA
07 Director of Admissions ... Vacant
88 Assoc Dir of Admissions ... Ms. Emily GIBBINGS
96 Director of Procurement ... Mr. Gary DUGGAN
25 Director Grants Sponsored Programs ... Ms. Louann D'ANGELO
102 Dir Budget & Financial Planning ... Ms. Maria FEUERSTEIN
04 Executive Assistant to President ... Ms. Michelle LEDOUX
101 Admin Asst to Board of Trustees ... Ms. Jean BEAL
104 Director of International Program ... Vacant
88 Veteran & Military Svcs Coord ... Ms. Lisa DUCHARME
106 Dir Center for Instructional Tech ... Ms. Lynn ZAYAC
22 Dir Non-Discrimination Compliance ... Dr. Jalisa D. WILLIAMS
26 Acting Dir of Campus Communications ... Ms. Lorraine MARTINELLE
29 Director Alumni Relations ... Vacant

*Worcester State University (D)

486 Chandler Street, Worcester MA 01602-2597
County: Worcester | FICE Identification: 002190
Unit ID: 168430
Telephone: (508) 929-8000 | Carnegie Class: Masters/L
FAX Number: (508) 929-8191 | Calendar System: Semester
URL: www.worcester.edu
Established: 1874 | Annual Undergrad Tuition & Fees (In-State): $10,586
Enrollment: 5,724 | Coed
Affiliation or Control: State | IRS Status: Exempt
Highest Offering: Master's
Accreditation: EH, NURSE, OT, SP

02 President ... Mr. Barry M. MALONEY
05 Provost/VP of Academic Affairs ... Dr. Lois A. WIMS
10 Vice Pres Administration & Finance ... Ms. Kathleen EICHELROTH
32 VP of Student Affs/Dean of Stdnts ... Ms. Julie KAZARIAN
111 Vice Pres University Advancement ... Mr. Thomas MCNAMARA
84 Vice Pres for Enrollment Management ... Dr. Ryan FORSYTHE
20 Assoc VP for Academic Affairs ... Dr. Henry THERIAULT
21 Assoc VP Administration & Finance ... Ms. Robin QUILL
13 Assoc VP Univ Technology Svcs/CIO ... Dr. Anthony ADADE
58 Assoc VP CE & Dean Grad Stds ... Dr. Roberta KYLE
108 Asst VP for Assessment & Planning ... Dr. Sarah STROUT
81 Dean Sch of Health/Natural Sci ... Dr. Linda LARRIVEE
79 Dean Sch of Human & Social Sciences ... Dr. Russ POTTLE
53 Dean of Education ... Dr. Raynold LEWIS
51 Assoc Dean of Grad/Cont Educ ... Ms. Sara GRADY
88 Dir Alternatives Ind Devel Pgm ... Ms. Laxmi BISSOONDIAL
19 Chief of Campus Police ... Mr. Jason KAPURCH
100 Chief of Staff ... Mr. Carl HERRIN
26 AVP Communications/Marketing ... Ms. Maureen O. STOKES
08 Executive Director of the Library ... Mr. Matthew BEJUNE
43 Gen Counsel/Asst to the Pres ... Ms. Stacey LUSTER
18 Staff Associate of Facilities ... Mr. Stephen M. BANDARRA
37 Interim Dir of Financial Aid ... Ms. Jennifer ENGLISH
84 Dean of Enrollment ... Mr. Joseph DICARLO
39 Asst Dean & Dir Res Life/Housing ... Mr. Adrian GAGE
15 Exec Dir of HR & Benefits ... Vacant
113 Dir of Student Accounts/One Card ... Ms. Julie CARMEL
96 Dir Procurement/Business Manager ... Ms. Brenda BUSSEY
09 Director of Institutional Research ... Mr. Kenneth SMITH
38 Assoc Dean for Heath & Wellness ... Ms. Laura MURPHY
85 Director of International Programs ... Ms. Katey PALUMBO
36 Director of Career Services ... Ms. Melisa ALVES
41 Director of Athletics ... Mr. Michael A. MUDD
109 Director of Admin Support Services ... Ms. Nancy M. RAMSDELL
29 Executive Director Alumni ... Ms. Tara A. HANCOCK
30 Exec Dir of University Advancement ... Ms. Jodi M. BRIGGS-PICKETT
114 Dir of Budget/Planning/Policy Dev ... Ms. Anisa HOXHA
06 Registrar ... Ms. Julie A. CHAFFEE
04 Admin Assistant to the President ... Ms. Ashlynn R. ALLAIN
28 Director of Diversity ... Ms. Maria GARIEPY

*Berkshire Community College (E)

1350 West Street, Pittsfield MA 01201-5786
County: Berkshire | FICE Identification: 002167
Unit ID: 164775
Telephone: (413) 499-4660 | Carnegie Class: Assoc/MT-VT-High Trad
FAX Number: N/A | Calendar System: Semester
URL: www.berkshirecc.edu
Established: 1960 | Annual Undergrad Tuition & Fees (In-State): $5,492
Enrollment: 1,465 | Coed
Affiliation or Control: State | IRS Status: 501(c)3
Highest Offering: Associate Degree
Accreditation: EH, ADNUR, COARC, PTAA

02 President ... Dr. Ellen KENNEDY
10 VP Admininstration & Finance/CFO ... Ms. Andrea WADSWORTH
05 VP Academic Affairs ... Dr. Kierstyn HUNTER
84 VP Student Affairs & Enrollment Mgm ... Mr. Adam KLEPETAR
15 Exec Dir HR/Affirm Action Officer ... Ms. Melissa LOIODICE
32 Dean of Students ... Ms. Celia NORCROSS
06 Registrar ... Mr. Adam EMERSON
102 Exec Dir BCC Foundation ... Mr. Nick DELMOLINO
13 Director Information Technology ... Mr. William JENNINGS
84 Dean of Enrollment Management ... Vacant
37 Director Student Financial Aid ... Ms. Kelly OSORIO
08 Dean of Library & Learning Commons ... Mr. Richard FELVER
09 Dir Institutional Effectiveness ... Dr. Margaret STEPHENSON
18 Dir Facilities/Physical Plant ... Mr. Chris DEGRAY
19 Director of Safety & Security ... Mr. Ellis RICHARDSON
38 Senior Academic Counselor ... Ms. Lisa MATTILA
04 Assistant to the President ... Ms. Heather SEELY
105 Director Web Services ... Vacant
26 Chief Public Rels/Mktg/Commun Ofcr ... Mr. Jonah SYKES
29 Director Alumni Affairs ... Ms. Toni BUCKLEY
30 Director of Development ... Vacant
96 Director of Purchasing ... Vacant
108 Director Institutional Assessment ... Ms. Margaret STEPHENSON
25 Grants Administrator ... Ms. Gina STEC
41 Athletic Director ... Mr. Daryl SHREVE

*Bristol Community College (F)

777 Elsbree Street, Fall River MA 02720-7395
County: Bristol | FICE Identification: 002176
Unit ID: 165033
Telephone: (508) 678-2811 | Carnegie Class: Assoc/HT-High Trad
FAX Number: (508) 730-3270 | Calendar System: Semester
URL: www.bristolcc.edu
Established: 1965 | Annual Undergrad Tuition & Fees (In-State): $5,136
Enrollment: 6,256 | Coed
Affiliation or Control: State | IRS Status: 501(c)3
Highest Offering: Associate Degree
Accreditation: EH, ADNUR, DH, MAC, MLTAD, OTA

02 President ... Dr. Laura L. DOUGLAS
05 Vice President of Academic Affairs ... Dr. Suzanne BUGLIONE
50 Dean of Business & Exp Education ... Mr. Vidyanidhi REGE
79 Interim Dean of Arts & Humanities ... Ms. Jennifer PUNIELLO
83 Dean of Behavioral & Soc Sciences ... Dr. Kathleen PEARLE
76 Dean of Health Sciences ... Vacant
81 Dean of Math/Science & Engineering ... Dr. Sarmad SAMAN
10 VP of Administration & Finance ... Mr. Steven KENYON
32 VP of Student Svcs/Enrollment Mgmt ... Ms. Kate O'HARA
13 Chief Information & Data Officer ... Ms. Jo-Ann M. PELLETIER
26 VP Marketing and Communications ... Ms. Joyce BRENNAN
103 Acting VP of Economic/Business Dev ... Ms. Jennifer MENARD
32 Director Student/Family Engagement ... Ms. Emma MONTAGUE
84 Dean of Enrollment Mgmt ... Vacant
12 Dean of New Bedford Campus ... Ms. Shanna HOWELL
12 Dean of Attleboro Campus ... Vacant

06 Registrar ... Ms. Jennifer VINCENT
12 Dean of Taunton Center ... Mr. Robert REZENDES
25 Dean of Grant Development ... Ms. Jennifer MENARD
37 Director Financial Aid ... Ms. Kate O'HARA
38 Dean of Counseling ... Mr. Michael BENSINK
15 Executive Director of HR ... Mr. Gary CONVERTINO
30 Executive Director of Development ... Vacant
18 Director of Facilities Management ... Ms. Karen PARKER
19 Director Public Safety Preparedness ... Mr. Mark NATALY
21 Comptroller ... Mr. Keith TONI
11 Assoc VP Administration/Facilities ... Ms. Jo Ann BENTLEY
22 Dir of Disability Services ... Ms. Julie JODOIN-KRAUZYK
78 Director Coop Education ... Ms. Nicole HEANEY
106 Dean of Online Learning ... Mr. Michael MURPHY
92 Commonwealth Honors Coordinator ... Ms. Denise DIMARZIO
96 Director of Purchasing ... Ms. Philicia PACHECO
41 Athletic Director ... Mr. Derek VIVEIROS
04 Sr Executive Assistant to President ... Ms. Kathleen A. WORDELL

*Bunker Hill Community College (A)

250 New Rutherford Avenue, Boston MA 02129-2925
County: Suffolk FICE Identification: 011210
Unit ID: 165112
Telephone: (617) 228-2400 Carnegie Class: Assoc/HT-High Trad
FAX Number: (617) 228-2050 Calendar System: Semester
URL: www.bhcc.edu
Established: 1973 Annual Undergrad Tuition & Fees (In-State): $5,160
Enrollment: 9,924 Coed
Affiliation or Control: State IRS Status: 501(c)3
Highest Offering: Associate Degree
Accreditation: EH, ADNUR, CEA, DMS, EMT, MLTAD, RAD, SURGT

02 President ... Dr. Pam Y. EDDINGER
10 VP of Administration and Finance ... Mr. John PITCHER
05 VP Academic Affairs/Student Service ... Dr. James F. CANNIFF
15 AVP Human Resources/Labor Relations ... Ms. Molly AMBROSE
32 Dean of Students ... Ms. Julie B. ELKINS
26 Exec Director of Communications ... Ms. Karen NORTON
18 Facilities Manager ... Mr. John CHIRICHIELLO
79 Dean of Humanities ... Ms. Lori A. CATALLOZZI
54 Dean of Science/Engineering/Math ... Ms. Laura C. RUBIN
83 Dean Behavioral/Social Sciences ... Ms. Carlnita P. GREENE
107 Dean of Professional Studies ... Ms. Austin A. GILLILAND
76 Director Health Sciences ... Ms. Maryanne ATKINSON
12 Associate Provost Chelsea Campus ... Dr. Alice MURILLO
21 Comptroller ... Ms. Champa NAGAGE
25 Exec Director of Grants Development ... Mr. Steven A. ROLLER
35 Director of Student Services ... Mr. Sercan FENERCI
06 Registrar ... Ms. Susan G. MARTIN
08 Dir of Library/Learning Commons ... Mr. Oscar R. LANZA-GALINDO
13 Chief Information Officer ... Mr. Tim OGAWA
27 Executive Director of Marketing ... Ms. Karen M. NORTON
19 Executive Dir and Chief of Police ... Mr. Robert BARROWS
37 Exec Dir Student Financial Svcs ... Ms. Melissa HOLSTER
96 Director of Purchasing ... Mr. Mukti RAUT
84 Interim Dean Enrollment Management ... Ms. Alicia A. D'OYLEY
30 Exec Dir Development/BHCC Found ... Ms. Marilyn KUHAR
100 Exec Asst to the President ... Mr. George HALLSMITH
09 Dean Research and Assessment ... Ms. Arlene VALLIE
04 Staff Assistant to President ... Ms. Frances H. JARVIS
103 Director Workforce Development ... Ms. Kristen P. MCKENNA
105 Director of Digital Communications ... Ms. Nicole MORO
41 Athletic Director ... Vacant
07 Director of Admissions ... Ms. Francine S. KUPFERMAN
106 Associate Dean of Online Learning ... Ms. Grace MAH
104 Director Study Abroad ... Ms. Heather SHAPAZIAN
108 Director Institutional Assessment ... Ms. Marilyn A. ROTH
22 Chief Equity/Compliance Officer ... Ms. Nahomi CARLISLE
36 Associate Dean Student Placement ... Ms. Jacqueline MACMILLION-WILLIAMS
90 Director Academic Computing ... Mr. Kenneth M. KOZIKOWSKI

*Cape Cod Community College (B)

2240 Iyannough Road, West Barnstable MA 02668-1599
County: Barnstable FICE Identification: 002168
Unit ID: 165194
Telephone: (508) 362-2131 Carnegie Class: Assoc/MT-VT-Mix Trad/Non
FAX Number: (508) 362-3988 Calendar System: Semester
URL: www.capecod.edu
Established: 1960 Annual Undergrad Tuition & Fees (In-State): $5,352
Enrollment: 2,710 Coed
Affiliation or Control: State IRS Status: 501(c)3
Highest Offering: Associate Degree
Accreditation: EH, ADNUR, DH, FUSER, MAC, NAEYC

02 President ... Dr. John L. COX
05 Vice Pres Academic/Student Affairs ... Dr. Arlene RODRIGUEZ
10 Vice President Finance & Operations ... Mr. Christopher CLARK
18 Director Facilities ... Mr. Joseph MACKINNON
49 Dean Arts & Humanities ... Dr. Cathy MCCARRON
81 Dean Science/Tech/Math/Business ... Dr. Donald CRAMPTON
121 Dean Learning Res & Student Success ... Mr. David ZIEMBA
84 Dean Enroll Mgmt/Advising Services ... Ms. Christine MCCAREY
83 Dean Health/Social Sci/Human Svcs ... Mr. Patrick PRESTON
15 Associate VP Human Resources ... Mr. Paul ALEXANDER
13 Chief Info/Technology Officer ... Mr. Richard WIXSOM
07 Director Admissions ... Ms. Sheila VAUGHN
37 Director of Financial Aid ... Vacant
26 Dir Strat Communications/Marketing ... Mr. Patrick STONE
06 Registrar ... Ms. Lucina HOLMES
19 Chief Public Safety ... Ms. Maria PADILLA
04 Exec Assistant to President ... Ms. Mia HAZLETT
09 Dir Inst Research & Effectiveness ... Ms. Maureen O'SHEA

*Greenfield Community College (C)

1 College Drive, Greenfield MA 01301-9739
County: Franklin FICE Identification: 002169
Unit ID: 165981
Telephone: (413) 775-1000 Carnegie Class: Assoc/MT-VT-Mix Trad/Non
FAX Number: (413) 774-4676 Calendar System: Semester
URL: www.gcc.mass.edu
Established: 1962 Annual Undergrad Tuition & Fees (In-State): $5,570
Enrollment: 1,620 Coed
Affiliation or Control: State IRS Status: 501(c)3
Highest Offering: Associate Degree
Accreditation: EH, ADNUR, EMT, MAC, NAEYC

02 President ... Dr. Michelle SCHUTT
05 Chief Academic/Stdnt Affs Ofcr ... Ms. Mary Ellen FYDENKEVEZ
10 VP Finance/Chief Financial Officer ... Ms. Karen PHILLIPS
84 Dean of Enrollment Services ... Vacant
32 Dean of Students ... Ms. Anna BERRY
79 Int Dean Humanities ... Mr. Matthew BARLOW
81 Dean Engr/Math/Nurs & Sciences ... Ms. Mary Ellen FYDENKEVEZ
30 Exec Director Resource Development ... Ms. Regina CURTIS
18 Director Physical Plant ... Mr. Jeffrey MARQUES
37 Director Financial Aid ... Ms. Linda DESJARDINS
19 Director Public Safety ... Mr. Alex WILTZ
96 Director of Purchasing ... Mr. Ryan AIKEN
08 Head of Library Services ... Ms. Laura GARCIA
21 Comptroller ... Mr. Mark BOUDREAU
06 Registrar ... Ms. Holly FITZPATRICK
38 Co-Coord Learning Asst Programs ... Ms. Cynthia SNOW
38 Co-Coord Learning Asst Programs ... Mr. Norman BEEBE
88 Coordinator of Student Assessment ... Ms. Catherine DEVLIN
35 Coordinator of Student Activities ... Ms. Mary MCENTEE
04 Staff Assistant to President ... Ms. Shannon LARANGE
108 Director Institutional Assessment ... Ms. Marie BREHENY

*Holyoke Community College (D)

303 Homestead Avenue, Holyoke MA 01040-1099
County: Hampden FICE Identification: 002170
Unit ID: 166133
Telephone: (413) 538-7000 Carnegie Class: Assoc/HT-High Trad
FAX Number: (413) 534-8927 Calendar System: Semester
URL: www.hcc.edu
Established: 1946 Annual Undergrad Tuition & Fees (In-State): $5,378
Enrollment: 4,209 Coed
Affiliation or Control: State IRS Status: 501(c)3
Highest Offering: Associate Degree
Accreditation: EH, ADNUR, MUS, PNUR, RAD

02 President ... Dr. Christina ROYAL
111 Vice Pres Administration & Finance ... Mr. Narayan SAMPATH
05 Int VP Academic/Student Affairs ... Dr. Sharale MATHIS
111 Vice Pres Institutional Advancement ... Ms. Amanda SBRISCIA
103 Vice Pres for Business & Community ... Mr. Jeffrey HAYDEN
20 Assistant VP of Academic Admin ... Ms. Idelia SMITH
08 Dean Library ... Ms. Mary DIXEY
84 Dean of Enrollment Management ... Ms. Renee TASTAD
15 Dean Human Resources ... Vacant
36 Dean Coop Education & Career Svcs ... Vacant
06 Registrar ... Ms. Allison WROBEL
37 Director of Financial Aid ... Ms. Patricia BILLINGS
91 Director Administrative Computing ... Vacant
18 Dir Facilities & Engineering Svcs ... Mr. Dan CAMPBELL
10 Comptroller ... Mr. Curt FOSTER
13 Interim Chief Information Officer ... Mr. Walter KERCE
96 Asst Comptroller/Purchasing ... Ms. Maria BRUNELLE
09 Director Institutional Research ... Ms. Veena DHANKHER
26 Dir of Marketing/Public Relations ... Ms. JoAnne ROME
111 Dir of Institutional Advancement ... Mr. Patrick CARPENTER
35 Dean of Student Services ... Vacant
19 Interim Director Security/Safety ... Mr. Dale BROWN
07 Director Admissions & Onboarding ... Mr. Mark HUDGIK
100 Chief of Staff ... Vacant
22 Dir Affirm Action/Equal Opportunity ... Ms. Olivia L. KYNARD
41 Athletic Director ... Mr. Thomas STEWART
04 Admin Assistant to the President ... Ms. Karen DESJEANS

*Massachusetts Bay Community College (E)

50 Oakland Street, Wellesley Hills MA 02481-5357
County: Norfolk FICE Identification: 002171
Unit ID: 166647
Telephone: (781) 239-3000 Carnegie Class: Assoc/MT-VT-High Non
FAX Number: (781) 237-1061 Calendar System: Semester
URL: www.massbay.edu
Established: 1961 Annual Undergrad Tuition & Fees (In-State): $5,376
Enrollment: 3,762 Coed
Affiliation or Control: State IRS Status: 501(c)3
Highest Offering: Associate Degree
Accreditation: EH, ADNUR, EMT, NAEYC, PNUR, RAD, SURGT

02 President ... Dr. David PODELL
04 Executive Director Ofc of the Pres ... Ms. Karen BRITTON
05 VP for Academic Affairs and Provost ... Dr. Lynn HUNTER
10 VP for Finance & Administration ... Mr. Neil BUCKLEY
15 Exec Director of Human Resources ... Ms. Samaria STALLINGS
84 Asst VP Enrollment Management ... Ms. Lisa SLAVIN
32 VP for Student Development ... Dr. Elizabeth BLUMBERG
45 VP Institutional Effectiveness ... Dr. Courtney JACKSON
13 Chief Information Officer ... Mr. Michael LYONS
50 Dean Business & Prof Studies ... Dr. Susan MAGGIONI
102 Director of Corp Partnerships ... Ms. Phara BOYER
76 Dean Health Sciences Division ... Dr. Lynne DAVIS
20 Assistant Provost ... Dr. Christopher LA BARBERA
81 Dean STEM Division ... Dr. Chitra JAVDEKAR
06 Registrar ... Ms. Jennifer MCANDREW
21 AVP Finance & Admin ... Mr. Marcus EDWARD
88 Dir Academic Achievement Center ... Ms. Barbara BERNARD
121 Director of Academic Advising ... Ms. Sarah SALERNO
91 Director Administrative Computing ... Mr. Terry KRAMER
07 Assoc Dean of Admissions ... Ms. Alison MCCARTY
36 Director of Career & Internship Svc ... Ms. Julie GINN
38 Director of Counseling ... Mr. Jon EDWARDS
37 Director of Financial Aid ... Ms. Robyn BUTTERFIELD
18 Director of Facilities ... Mr. Joseph DELISLE
08 Director of Learning Services ... Mr. Timothy RIVARD
25 Director of Grants Development ... Ms. Sunny STICH
26 Asst VP Inst Advance/Mktg/Comms ... Mr. Jeremy SOLOMON
19 Director of Public Safety ... Mr. Vincent O'CONNELL
124 Associate Dean for Student Success ... Mr. Richard WILLIAMS
35 Coordinator Student Engagement ... Ms. Julie SCHLEICHER
28 Chief Diversity Officer ... Dr. Lynn MOORE
79 Dean Humanities/Social Sciences ... Ms. Nina KEERY
88 Int Dean of Automotive Technology ... Mr. Howie FERRIS
22 Director of Equity Compliance ... Ms. Lisa MACDONALD
41 Director of Athletics ... Mr. Adam NELSON
106 Assistant Director Online Education ... Ms. Bernadette SIBUMA
96 Dir Procurement & Business Opers ... Ms. Lauren CURLEY

*Massasoit Community College (F)

1 Massasoit Boulevard, Brockton MA 02302-3996
County: Plymouth FICE Identification: 002177
Unit ID: 166823
Telephone: (508) 588-9100 Carnegie Class: Assoc/HVT-Mix Trad/Non
FAX Number: (508) 427-1202 Calendar System: Semester
URL: www.massasoit.mass.edu
Established: 1966 Annual Undergrad Tuition & Fees (In-State): $5,160
Enrollment: 5,665 Coed
Affiliation or Control: State IRS Status: 501(c)3
Highest Offering: Associate Degree
Accreditation: EH, ADNUR, COARC, DA, EMT, MAC, NAEYC, RAD

02 President ... Dr. Ray DIPASQUALE
05 Provost Academic/Student Services ... Dr. Deanna YAMEEN
10 VP Administration/CFO ... Mr. William MITCHELL
32 Vice Provost Student Affairs ... Dr. Ruben BARATO
20 Vice Provost Academic Affairs ... Ms. Pamela WITCHER
111 Chief Advancement Officer ... Mr. Paul GRAND PRÉ
28 Chief Diversity Officer ... Ms. Yolanda DENNIS
13 CIO/Dir Enterprise Systems ... Mr. William MORRISON
09 Assoc Dean Institutional Research ... Ms. Mary GOODHUE LYNCH
26 Director of Communications/PR ... Ms. Sarah YUNITS
27 Director of Marketing & Creative ... Mr. James LYNCH
84 Dean of Enrollment Management ... Ms. Shilo HENRIQUES
35 Dean of Students ... Ms. Slandie DIEUJUSTE
07 Director of Admissions ... Ms. Michelle HUGHES
37 Director Student Financial Aid ... Mr. Todd HUGHES
06 Registrar ... Ms. Jannie GILSON
121 Director of Advisement & Counseling ... Ms. Alessandra MONTEIRO
41 Director of Athletics ... Mr. Benjamin WARNICK
21 Comptroller ... Ms. Patricia MARCELLA
18 Director Facilities/Physical Plant ... Mr. Gregory HABEREK
96 Director of Purchasing ... Mr. John CAFFELLE
29 Director Alumni Relations ... Vacant
50 Dean Business & Technology ... Dr. Michael ROGGOW
79 Dean Humanities/Communication Arts ... Dr. Harriette SCOTT
76 Interim Dean Allied Health ... Ms. Susan CLOVER
83 Dean Public Svc/Social Science ... Ms. Karyn BOUTIN
81 Dean Science & Math ... Mr. Douglas BROWN
72 Exec Dean Canton/Emergent Tech ... Ms. Carine SAUVIGNON
15 VP of Human Resources ... Ms. Margaret GAZZARA HESS
103 of Corporate Education ... Ms. Maryellen BRETT
100 Chief of Staff/AVP Strategy ... Ms. Lydia CAMARA
19 Chief of Police ... Mr. Christopher CUMMINGS

*Middlesex Community College (G)

591 Springs Road, Bedford MA 01730-1197
County: Middlesex FICE Identification: 009936
Unit ID: 166887
Telephone: (781) 280-3200 Carnegie Class: Assoc/HT-Mix Trad/Non
FAX Number: (781) 275-0741 Calendar System: Semester
URL: www.middlesex.mass.edu
Established: 1969 Annual Undergrad Tuition & Fees (In-State): $6,048
Enrollment: 6,885 Coed
Affiliation or Control: State IRS Status: 501(c)3
Highest Offering: Associate Degree
Accreditation: EH, ADNUR, CEA, DA, DH, DMS, DT, MAC, MLTAD, NAEYC, RAD

02 President ... Mr. Philip J. SISSON
05 Int Provost & VP Acad/Student Affs ... Ms. Arlene RODRIGUEZ
15 VP Human Resources ... Ms. Mary EMERICK
10 VP of Finance/CFO ... Mr. Frank NOCELLA
04 Exec Assistant Ofc of the President ... Ms. Donna CORBIN
32 AVP Student Affs/Dean of Students ... Ms. Pamela B. FLAHERTY
46 Dean Research & Planning ... Ms. Jennifer LUDDY

79 Dean Humanities and Social Sciences .... Mr. Matthew OLSON
72 Dean Bus/Educ & Public Service .... Ms. Judith HOGAN
17 Dean of Health and STEM .... Ms. Kathleen J. SWEENEY
107 Dean Professional/Instructional Dev .... Ms. Susan ANDERSON
22 Asst Dir HR/Affirm Action Officer .... Mr. Reginald NICHOLS
11 Vice Pres Administration .... Mr. Patrick E. COOK
96 Director of Procurement .... Mrs. Christina KELLEY
84 Dean of Enrollment Services .... Ms. Audrey NAHABEDIAN
111 Exec Dir Inst Advancement .... Ms. Judith M. BURKE
07 Dean of Admissions .... Ms. Camille BROWN
09 Dean Institutional Research .... Ms. Linda HEINEMAN
27 Exec Director Public Affairs .... Mr. Patrick COOK
26 Dir Marketing/Communication .... Ms. Elizabeth J. NOEL
29 Director of Alumni Affairs .... Ms. Amy LEE
37 Assoc Director of Financial Aid .... Ms. Mary MULLENS
21 Comptroller .... Ms. Kathy RICH
08 Director Library Services .... Ms. Donna MATURI
06 Registrar .... Ms. Kayla BOYD

*Mount Wachusett Community College (A)

444 Green Street, Gardner MA 01440-1000
County: Worcester FICE Identification: 002172
Unit ID: 166957
Telephone: (978) 632-6600 Carnegie Class: Assoc/HVT-High Trad
FAX Number: (978) 630-9559 Calendar System: Semester
URL: www.mwcc.edu
Established: 1963 Annual Undergrad Tuition & Fees (In-State): $5,668
Enrollment: 3,187 Coed
Affiliation or Control: State IRS Status: 501(c)3
Highest Offering: Associate Degree
Accreditation: EH, ADNUR, DA, DH, MLTAD, PNUR, PTAA

02 President .... Dr. James L. VANDER HOOVEN
05 Interim VP Academic Affairs .... Dr. John EISLER
103 VP Lifelong Learning/Wkfc Dev .... Mr. Adam DUGGAN
10 VP Finance & Administration .... Ms. Sandra QUAYE
26 VP Marketing/Communications .... Ms. Lea Ann SCALES
111 Exec Dir Resource & Strat Init Dev .... Ms. Heather LAYTON
15 VP Human Resources/Payroll .... Mr. Peter SENNETT
32 Interim VP Student Affairs .... Mr. Jason ZELESKY
08 Asst Dean Library Services .... Mr. Elliott BRANDOW
09 Asst Dean of Records/Inst Research .... Vacant
13 Executive Director IT .... Mr. Daniel HORLANDER
18 Director Maintenance/Mechanical Sys .... Mr. Glen FOX
68 Director Mount Fitness .... Mr. Jason SNOONIAN
19 Deputy Chief of Police .... Ms. Melissa CROTEAU
27 Director of Media Services .... Mr. Arthur COLLINS
04 Exec Asst to President & Fndn .... Ms. Jo-Ann MEAGHER
07 Dean of Admissions/Enrollment Mgmt .... Ms. Marcia ROSBURY-HENNE
37 Director Student Financial Services .... Ms. Heather RULAND
41 Athletic Director .... Vacant
102 Exec Dir Dev & MWCC Found Inc .... Ms. Carla ZOTTOLI
28 Chief Diversity Executive .... Ms. Stephanie WILLIAMS
50 Dean of Business .... Ms. Veronica GUAY
53 Dean of Education .... Ms. Laurie OCCHIPINTI

*North Shore Community College (B)

1 Ferncroft Road, PO Box 3340, Danvers MA 01923-0840
County: Essex FICE Identification: 002173
Unit ID: 167312
Telephone: (978) 762-4000 Carnegie Class: Assoc/MT-VT-High Trad
FAX Number: (978) 762-4020 Calendar System: Semester
URL: www.northshore.edu
Established: 1965 Annual Undergrad Tuition & Fees (In-State): $5,352
Enrollment: 4,783 Coed
Affiliation or Control: State IRS Status: 501(c)3
Highest Offering: Associate Degree
Accreditation: EH, ADNUR, COARC, FUSER, MAC, NAEYC, OTA, PNUR, PTAA, RAD, SURGT

02 President .... Dr. William HEINEMAN
05 Provost .... Dr. Jennifer MEZQUITA
20 Interim Vice Pres Academic Affairs .... Ms. Andrea DEFUSCO-SULLIVAN
10 Vice Pres Administration/Finance ..... Ms. Janice M. FORSSTROM
32 Interim VP Student Affairs .... Mr. Stephen CREAMER
28 Director of Diversity .... Mr. Nikki PELONIA
15 Chief People and Culture Officer .... Ms. Justine CARON
103 Dean Workforce Dev/Corp Educ .... Ms. Dianne PALTER-GILL
07 Exec Dir Admissions & Enrollment .... Ms. Kim ODUSAMI
08 Director Library/Tutoring .... Mr. Rex KRAJEWSKI
13 Dir of Networking/Info Services .... Mr. Gary HAM
37 Director of Financial Aid .... Ms. Susan SULLIVAN
09 Asst Vice Pres Planning & Research ...... Ms. Laurie LACHAPELLE
30 Director of Development .... Ms. Nicole MARCOTTE
18 Asst Vice Pres Facilities Mgmt .... Mr. Jamie WICKS
19 Campus Police Chief .... Mr. David COOK
21 Comptroller .... Ms. Eileen GERENZ
26 Director Public Relations/New Media .... Ms. Linda BRANTLEY
36 Director Student Placement .... Ms. Lynn MARCUS
121 Director Student Support & Advising .... Mr. Daniel O'NEILL
27 Director Marketing Communications .... Ms. Samantha MCGILLOWAY
40 Bookstore Manager .... Mr. Shawn CRONIN
06 Registrar .... Ms. Mary DULATRE
04 Staff Assistant to the President .... Ms. Susan MULVEY

*Northern Essex Community College (C)

100 Elliott Street, Haverhill MA 01830-2399
County: Essex FICE Identification: 002174
Unit ID: 167376
Telephone: (978) 556-3700 Carnegie Class: Assoc/MT-VT-High Trad
FAX Number: (978) 556-3729 Calendar System: Semester
URL: www.necc.mass.edu
Established: 1960 Annual Undergrad Tuition & Fees (In-State): $5,544
Enrollment: 4,715 Coed
Affiliation or Control: State IRS Status: 501(c)3
Highest Offering: Associate Degree
Accreditation: EH, ADNUR, COARC, CSHSE, DA, EMT, MAC, NAEYC, PNUR, POLYT, RAD

02 President .... Dr. Lane A. GLENN
05 Vice President of Academic Affairs .... Vacant
111 Vice Pres Institutional Advancement .... Ms. Allison DOLAN-WILSON
10 VP of Administration & Finance/ CFO .... Mr. Michael R. MCCARTHY
32 Vice President Student Affairs .... Ms. Jennifer MEZQUITA
12 VP of Lawrence Campus .... Dr. Noemi CUSTODIA-LORA
09 Dean of Institutional Research .... Ms. Audrey ELLIS
30 Dean of Development .... Vacant
35 Dean of Students .... Mr. Jonathan L. MILLER
103 Dir of Workforce Devel/Cont Educ ...... Mr. Alexander RODRIGUEZ
13 Chief Information Officer .... Mr. David MCASKILL
06 Registrar .... Ms. Sue SHAIN
37 Director of Financial Aid .... Ms. Despina LAMBROPOULOUS
26 Director of Public Relations .... Ms. Ernestine GREENSLADE
29 Director Alumni Relations .... Ms. Lindsey GRAHAM
18 Chief Facilities/Physical Plant .... Mr. Paul MIEDZIONOSKI
96 Director of Purchasing .... Ms. Elizabeth DONOVAN
100 Chief of Staff to President .... Ms. Cheryl GOODWIN
08 Chief Library Officer .... Mr. Michael HEARN
19 Director Security/Safety .... Ms. Deborah CRAFTS
41 Athletic Director .... Mr. Daniel BLAIR
04 Admin Assistant to the President .... Ms. Linda J. BUCKLEY
15 Chief Human Resources Officer .... Ms. Patricia M. GAURON

*Quinsigamond Community College (D)

670 W Boylston Street, Worcester MA 01606-2092
County: Worcester FICE Identification: 002175
Unit ID: 167534
Telephone: (508) 853-2300 Carnegie Class: Assoc/MT-VT-High Trad
FAX Number: (508) 852-6943 Calendar System: Semester
URL: www.qcc.edu
Established: 1963 Annual Undergrad Tuition & Fees (In-State): $5,830
Enrollment: 6,942 Coed
Affiliation or Control: State IRS Status: 501(c)3
Highest Offering: Associate Degree
Accreditation: EH, ADNUR, COARC, CSHSE, DA, DH, EMT, MAC, NAEYC, OTA, PNUR, RAD, SURGT

02 President .... Dr. Luis PEDRAJA
05 VP of Academic Affairs .... Dr. James KEANE
10 VP of Administration .... Mr. Stephen T. MARINI
32 VP of Student Enrollment/Develop .... Dr. Lillian M. ORTIZ
20 Associate VP Academic Affairs .... Ms. Kathy RENTSCH
30 VP for External Relations .... Dr. Viviana ABREU-HERNANDEZ
04 Executive Assistant to President .... Ms. Selina M. BORIA
21 Asst VP for Finance/Comptroller .... Ms. Debra A. LAFLASH
79 Dean Humanities & Education .... Mr. Brady HAMMOND
76 Dean Health Care .... Mr. C. Pat SCHMOHL
50 Dean Business/Engineer/Technology .... Ms. Betty LAUER
81 Dean Science & Mathematics .... Mr. Benjamin BENTON
06 Registrar .... Ms. Barbara ZAWALICH
62 Dean of Library Services .... Ms. Cary MORSE
09 Dean of Inst Research/Planning .... Dr. Ingrid SKADBERG
121 Associate VP of Student Success ... Ms. Michelle TUFAU-AFRIYIE
106 Dean of Digital Learning .... Mr. Ken DWYER
35 Director Student Life & Leadership .... Ms. Ashlee GIVINS
18 Executive Director of Facilities .... Mr. James RACKI
37 Director Student Financial Aid .... Ms. Karen GRANT
96 Purchasing Manager .... Ms. Juliana ESPOSITO
19 Chief of Campus Police .... Mr. Kevin RITACCO
26 Dir Institutional Communications .... Mr. Joshua MARTIN
38 Social Worker/Mental Health Couns .... Ms. Tina WELLS
28 Director Disability Services .... Ms. Kristen PROCTOR
35 Dean of Students .... Ms. Terry VECCHIO
07 Director of Admissions .... Ms. Ai Co ABERCROMBIE

*Roxbury Community College (E)

1234 Columbus Avenue,
Roxbury Crossing MA 02120-3423
County: Suffolk FICE Identification: 011930
Unit ID: 167631
Telephone: (617) 427-0060 Carnegie Class: Assoc/HT-High Trad
FAX Number: N/A Calendar System: Semester
URL: rcc.mass.edu
Established: 1973 Annual Undergrad Tuition & Fees (In-State): $5,784
Enrollment: 1,200 Coed
Affiliation or Control: State IRS Status: 501(c)3
Highest Offering: Associate Degree
Accreditation: EH

02 President .... Dr. Valerie R. ROBERSON
04 Executive Asst to the President .... Ms. Judy M. PUGH
05 Int VP Academic/Student Affairs .... Ms. Cecile REGNER
108 Exec VP Institutional Effectiveness .... Ms. Cecile REGNER
10 Vice President of Admin & Finance .... Vacant
32 Dean of Students .... Ms. Robyn SHAHID-BELLOT
103 Assoc VP Workforce Development .... Dr. Hillel SIMS
13 Chief Information Tech Officer .... Mr. Patrick KANGETHE
15 Exec Director Human Resources .... Ms. Sandra KNIGHT
08 Director of Library .... Mr. William HOAG
23 Director of Health Services .... Ms. Ruth HINES
30 Exec Dir Dev/Alumni/Foundation ...... Ms. Mishawn DAVIS-EYENE
06 Registrar .... Mr. Bryan D. JONES
26 Director Marketing/Communications .... Ms. Jordan SMOCK
57 Dir of Visual/Performing/Media Arts .... Vacant
37 Assoc Director Financial Aid .... Mr. Christopher LEWIS
25 Grants Research Specialist .... Ms. Cecile REGNER
09 Director of Institutional Research .... Vacant
19 Director Public Safety .... Mr. David ALBENESE
81 Dean of STEM .... Dr. Hillel SIMS
90 Director Academic Computing .... Vacant
41 Manager of RLTAC .... Mr. Jelani TOWNSELL

*Springfield Technical Community College (F)

Armory Square, Springfield MA 01105-1296
County: Hampden FICE Identification: 008078
Unit ID: 167905
Telephone: (413) 781-7822 Carnegie Class: Assoc/HVT-High Trad
FAX Number: (413) 755-6309 Calendar System: Semester
URL: www.stcc.edu
Established: 1967 Annual Undergrad Tuition & Fees (In-State): $5,560
Enrollment: 4,327 Coed
Affiliation or Control: State IRS Status: 501(c)3
Highest Offering: Associate Degree
Accreditation: EH, ADNUR, CAHIIM, COARC, DA, DH, DMS, MAC, MLTAD, OTA, PTAA, RAD, SURGT

02 President .... Dr. John B. COOK
05 VP of Academic Affairs .... Dr. Geraldine DE BERLY
10 VP of Administration/CFO .... Ms. Andrea NATHANSON
111 Int VP Advancement/External Affairs .... Dr. Shai BUTLER
32 VP Student Affairs .... Ms. Darcy KEMP
103 Asst VP Workforce Development .... Ms. Gladys N. FRANCO
13 VP/CIO .... Ms. Mary KASELOUSKAS
20 Dean of Academic Initiatives .... Mr. Matthew GRAVEL
04 Executive Asst to the President .... Ms. Nanette FLORES
66 Director of Nursing .... Ms. Lisa FUGIEL
76 Dean Health and Patient Simulation ..... Mr. Christopher D. SCOTT
81 Dean STEM .... Ms. Lara SHARP
107 Dean Liberal/Professional Studies .... Mr. Richard GRECO
96 Director Purchasing/Business Svcs .... Ms. Kerri KANE
07 Dean Enroll/Retention/Completion .... Dr. Samantha PLOURD
06 Registrar .... Mr. Anthony (Tony) SBALBI
41 Director of Athletics .... Mr. Jenkin GOULD
121 Director of Advising .... Vacant
26 Dir Marketing/Communications .... Vacant
36 Director of Coop/Career Placement .... Ms. Pamela WHITE
37 Int Dir of Student Financial Svcs .... Ms. Amy BELINA
88 Fiscal/Financial Project Manager .... Vacant
35 Coord Student Activities/Devel .... Ms. Andrea TARPEY
27 Coordinator of Media Relations .... Mr. James DANKO
114 Senior Director Finance/Budgets .... Mr. Jason COHEN
119 Sr Dir Infrastructure and Security .... Mr. Sean PETTIS
08 Dean Library Services .... Ms. Erica EYNOUF
21 Controller .... Mr. Jonathan TUDRYN
09 Dean of Institutional Research .... Vacant
108 Director of Assessment .... Dr. Tracey TROTTIER
22 Director of Access/Student Success . Mr. Jose LOPES-FIGUEROA
88 Director of Gateway to College .... Ms. Katara ROBINSON
25 Dir Grants Development & Admin ...... Ms. Kimberley BRODERICK
88 Senior Director of Accounting .... Ms. Dorothy UNGERER
101 Liaison to the Board of Trustees .... Ms. Nanette FLORES
19 Sr Director Public Safety .... Mr. Jose RIVERA

Massachusetts Institute of Technology (G)

77 Massachusetts Avenue, Cambridge MA 02139-4307
County: Middlesex FICE Identification: 002178
Unit ID: 166683
Telephone: (617) 253-1000 Carnegie Class: DU-Highest
FAX Number: N/A Calendar System: 4/1/4
URL: web.mit.edu
Established: 1861 Annual Undergrad Tuition & Fees: $53,450
Enrollment: 11,254 Coed
Affiliation or Control: Independent Non-Profit IRS Status: 501(c)3
Highest Offering: Doctorate
Accreditation: EH, PLNG

01 President .... Dr. L. Rafael REIF
88 Chair of the Corporation .... Ms. Diane GREENE
05 Provost .... Dr. Cynthia BARNHART
00 Chancellor .... Prof. Melissa NOBLES
46 Vice President for Research .... Prof. Maria T. ZUBER
106 Interim VP for Open Learning .... Prof. W. Eric L. GRIMSON
10 Exec Vice President & Treasurer .... Mr. Glen SHOR
101 VP & Secretary of the Corporation ...... Ms. Suzanne GLASSBURN
20 Chancellor for Academic Advancement . Prof. W. Eric L. GRIMSON
26 VP for Communications .... Mr. Alfred IRONSIDE
30 VP for Resource Development .... Ms. Julie LUCAS

115 President MIT Investment Mgmt Co .... Mr. Seth ALEXANDER
15 VP for Human Resources .... Ms. Ramona ALLLEN
18 VP Campus Services & Stewardship .... Mr. Joe HIGGINS
13 VP for IS&T .... Mr. Mark SILIS
21 Vice President for Finance .... Ms. Katie HAMMER
48 Dean Sch of Architecture & Planning .... Prof. Hashim SARKIS
54 Dean School of Engineering .... Prof. Anantha CHANDRAKASAN
79 Dean Sch Hum/Arts/Soc Sciences .... Prof. Agustín RAYO
81 Dean School of Science .... Prof. Nergis MAVALVALA
50 Dean Sloan School of Management .... Prof. David C. SCHMITTLEIN
77 Dean Schwarzman Col of Computing .... Dr. Daniel HUTTENLOCHER
106 Dean for Digital Learning .... Dr. Cynthia BREAZEAL
20 Associate Provost .... Prof. Philip S. KHOURY
20 Associate Provost .... Prof. Richard K. LESTER
20 Associate Provost/Assoc VP Research .... Prof. Krystyn VAN VLIET
08 Director of Libraries .... Ms. Chris BOURG
28 Institute Community & Equity Ofcr .... Mr. John DOZIER
58 Vice Chancellor UG & Grad Education .... Prof. Ian A. WAITZ
32 Vice Chancellor/Dean Student Life .... Dr. Suzy NELSON
88 Director Lincoln Laboratory .... Dr. Eric D. EVANS
12 Director MIT Washington DC Office .... Mr. David GOLDSTON
07 Dean of Admissions/Student Fin Svcs .... Mr. Stuart SCHMILL
23 Medical Dir & Head MIT Medical .... Dr. Cecilia Warpinski STUOPIS
45 Director of Campus Planning .... Mr. Jon ALVAREZ
102 Exec Dir Foundation Relations .... Ms. Alicia SANCHEZ
25 Asst Provost for Research Admin .... Ms. Colleen M. LESLIE
96 Dir of Strategic Sourcing/Contracts .... Ms. Lillian M. DEWITT
41 Director of Athletics .... Dr. G. Anthony GRANT
09 Director of Institutional Research .... Dr. Jonathan D. SCHWARZ
88 Director Teaching & Learning Lab .... Dr. Janet RANKIN
85 Assoc Dean & Dir Intl Students Ofc .... Mr. David ELWELL
36 Exec Dir Career Advising & Prof Dev .... Ms. Deborah L. LIVERMAN
93 Associate Dean and Director OME .... Ms. DiOnetta CRAYTON
06 Registrar .... Mr. Brian CANAVAN
27 Director & Publisher MIT Press .... Ms. Amy BRAND
39 Sr Assoc Dean Housing & Res Svs .... Mr. David FRIEDRICH
42 Chaplain to the Institute/Assc Dean .... Rev. Thea KEITH-LUCAS
38 Sr Assoc Dean Support & Wellbeing .... Mr. David RANDALL
94 Director Women's and Gender Studies .... Prof. Lerna EKMEKTIOGLU
104 Executive Director MISTI .... Ms. April JULICH PEREZ
24 Director MIT Audio Visual Services .... Mr. Christopher WAY
90 Associate Vice President Technology .... Mr. Olu BROWN
04 Exec Assistant to the President .... Ms. Karla CASEY
43 Vice President & General Counsel .... Mr. Mark DIVINCENZO
29 CEO MIT Alumni Association .... Ms. Whitney T. ESPICH

Massachusetts School of Law at Andover (A)

500 Federal Street, Andover MA 01810-1094

County: Essex FICE Identification: 032353
Unit ID: 369002

Telephone: (978) 681-0800 Carnegie Class: Spec-4-yr-Law
FAX Number: (978) 681-6330 Calendar System: Semester
URL: www.mslaw.edu
Established: 1988 Annual Graduate Tuition & Fees: N/A
Enrollment: 295 Coed
Affiliation or Control: Independent Non-Profit IRS Status: 501(c)3
Highest Offering: Doctorate; No Undergraduates
Accreditation: EH

00 Dean Emeritus .... Mr. Lawrence R. VELVEL
01 Dean .... Prof. Michael COYNE
10 Chief Financial Officer .... Mr. Clifford ABELSON
37 Director of Financial Aid .... Ms. Lynn BOWAB
06 Registrar .... Ms. Rosa FIGUEIREDO
07 Director of Admissions .... Mr. Rohit BHASIN
26 Director of Media .... Ms. Kathryn VILLARE
05 Dir Academic Svcs/Career Devel .... Ms. Paula COLBY-CLEMENTS
13 Director of Technology .... Mr. Mick COYNE
08 Director of Library .... Mr. Daniel HARAYDA

MCPHS University (B)

179 Longwood Avenue, Boston MA 02115-5896

County: Suffolk FICE Identification: 002165
Unit ID: 166656

Telephone: (617) 732-2800 Carnegie Class: Spec-4-yr-Other Health
FAX Number: (617) 732-2801 Calendar System: Semester
URL: www.mcphs.edu
Established: 1823 Annual Undergrad Tuition & Fees: $34,650
Enrollment: 7,501 Coed
Affiliation or Control: Independent Non-Profit IRS Status: 501(c)3
Highest Offering: Doctorate
Accreditation: EH, ARCPA, CVT, DH, DMS, NMT, NURSE, OPT, PH, PHAR, PTA, RAD, RTT

01 President .... Richard LESSARD
05 VP for Acad Affairs/Provost .... Dr. Caroline ZEIND
10 Chief Financial Officer .... Keith BELLUCCI
111 VP for Advancement & Chief of Staff .... Sue GORMAN
20 Assoc Provost Acad & Prof Affairs .... Dr. Jeanine MOUNT
09 Assoc Prov Inst Research/Effective .... Dr. Henriette PRANGER
106 Assoc Provost Academic Innovation .... Dr. Barbara MACAULAY
43 Assoc General Counsel/Legal Affs .... Mary TANONA
32 Assoc Provost for Student Success .... Dr. Craig MACK
67 Interim Dean of Pharmacy Boston .... Dr. Stephen KERR
67 Interim CAO WM/Dean of Pharmacy WM .... Dr. Anna MORIN
08 Dean Library & Learning Resources .... Richard KAPLAN
49 Dean School of Arts and Sciences .... Dr. Delia C. ANDERSON
88 Dean School of Healthcare Bus .... Michael SPOONER
66 Interim Dean of Nursing .... Tammy GRAVEL
107 Dean Sch of Prof Studies .... Carol STUCKEY
52 Int Dean Forsyth Sch of Dental Hyg .... Dr. Dianne SMALLIDGE
88 Director of Physical Therapy .... Dr. Frances KISTNER
88 Director of PA Studies Boston .... Christopher COOPER
88 Director of PA Studies Wor/Man .... Kristy ALTONGY-MAGEE
69 Director Master of Public Health .... Carly LEVY
88 Dean of Optometry .... Dr. Maryke NEIBERG
88 Dean of Acupuncture & Oriental Med .... Dennis MOSEMAN
75 Director of Occupational Therapy .... Dr. Douglas SIMMONS
15 Chief Human Resources Officer .... Kevin DOLAN
06 Admin Dean/University Registrar .... Stacey TAYLOR
13 Director of Information Svcs/CIO .... Tom SCANLON
12 Exec Director Wor/Man Campuses .... Dr. Seth P. WALL
88 Title IX Coordinator .... Dawn BALLOU
84 Chief Enrollment Officer .... Kathleen RYAN
96 Director of Purchasing .... Peg CRAWFORD
38 Exec Dir Counseling Services .... Molly PAYNE
26 Director of Communications .... Michael RATTY
18 Director of Facilities Boston .... Jeff WARD
18 Director of Facilities Worcester .... Glen WARD
19 Chief of Public Safety .... Kevin NOLAN
105 Manager of Web Services .... Charlene ROBERTSON
108 Exec Dir Inst Research & Assessment .... Laura UERLING
04 Special Assistant to the President .... Sheryl CHEAL
25 Program Director Regulatory Affairs .... Frederick FRANKHAUSER
28 Asst Dean Diversity & Inclusion .... Julia GOLDEN-BATTLE
29 Exec Dir Prof Career Dev/Alum Svcs .... Karen SINGLE
36 Dir Center for Prof Career Develop .... Melissa HAWKINS
36 Dir Center for Prof Career Devel WM .... Jeanette DOYLE
37 Director Student Financial Services .... Elizabeth GORHAM
104 Director Study Abroad .... Sara SANFORD
22 Director Affirm Action/Equal Opp .... Vacant
91 Director Administrative Computing .... Kevin MCGOVERN
13 Chief Academic Technology Officer .... Dr. Daniel JAMOUS
07 Director of Admission .... Alex COLE
39 Director of Residence Life .... Irene STEFANAKOS

MCPHS-Worcester Campus (C)

19 Foster Street, Worcester MA 01608-1715
Telephone: (508) 890-8855 Identification: 770112
Accreditation: &EH, ACUP, CVT, DMS, PHAR

Merrimack College (D)

315 Turnpike Street, North Andover MA 01845-5800

County: Essex FICE Identification: 002120
Unit ID: 166850

Telephone: (978) 837-5000 Carnegie Class: Masters/L
FAX Number: (978) 837-5222 Calendar System: Semester
URL: www.merrimack.edu
Established: 1947 Annual Undergrad Tuition & Fees: $45,074
Enrollment: 5,418 Coed
Affiliation or Control: Roman Catholic IRS Status: 501(c)3
Highest Offering: Master's
Accreditation: EH, CAATE, @DIET

01 President .... Dr. Christopher E. HOPEY
10 Executive Vice President & CFO .... Dr. Jeffrey DOGGETT
04 Director Office of the President .... Ms. Lisa JEBALI
05 Provost .... Dr. John (Sean) CONDON
45 VP Inst Effectiveness/Dir Plng .... Dr. Jonathan LYON
84 VP Enrollment/Dean of Admissions .... Dr. Darren CONINE
42 Vice Pres Mission & Ministry .... Rev. Raymond DLUGOS, OSA
30 VP Development/Alumni Relations .... Ms. Leila RICE
43 Vice President & General Counsel .... Mr. Nicholas MCDONALD
86 AVP Campus Planning & Development .... Mr. Felipe SCHWARZ
26 Vice Pres Marketing & Communication .... Ms. Courtney JOHANSON
32 VP Student Affairs/Dean Students .... Ms. Allison GILL
50 Dean Girard School of Business .... Dr. Kenneth RHEE
54 Dean Sch of Science & Engineering .... Dr. Jose SANCHEZ
49 Interim Dean of Liberal Arts .... Dr. Steven SCHERWATZKY
53 Dean School of Education .... Dr. Deborah MARGOLIS
76 Dean School Health Sciences .... Dr. Janet BLUM
37 Director Financial Aid .... Ms. Annette MACMULLIN
41 Director of Athletics .... Mr. Jeremy GIBSON
08 Director of the Library .... Ms. Kathy NIELSON
23 Director Hamel Health .... Vacant
19 Director of Police Services .... Mr. Michael DELGRECO
24 Dir of Media Instructional Services .... Mr. Kevin SALEMME
96 Director of Purchasing .... Mr. Michael MAGNER
06 Registrar .... Mr. Kevin GATELY
100 Chief of Staff .... Fr. Bryan KERNS, OSA
39 Dir Resident Life/Student Housing .... Mr. Antonio WILLIS-BERRY

MGH Institute of Health Professions (E)

36 1st Avenue, Boston MA 02129-4557

County: Suffolk FICE Identification: 022316
Unit ID: 166869

Telephone: (617) 726-2947 Carnegie Class: Spec-4-yr-Other Health
FAX Number: (617) 726-3716 Calendar System: Semester
URL: www.mghihp.edu
Established: 1977 Annual Undergrad Tuition & Fees: N/A
Enrollment: 1,269 Coed
Affiliation or Control: Independent Non-Profit IRS Status: 501(c)3
Highest Offering: Doctorate
Accreditation: EH, ARCPA, NURSE, OT, PTA, SP

01 President .... Dr. Paula MILONE-NUZZO
05 Provost/VP Academic Affairs .... Dr. Alex JOHNSON
10 VP Finance/Administration .... Mr. Atlas EVANS
11 Chief Operating Officer .... Mr. Denis STRATFORD
100 Chief of Staff .... Ms. Elizabeth PIPES
26 Chief Communications Officer .... Mr. Paul MURPHY
30 Chief Development Officer .... Ms. Clare MCCULLY

† Tuition varies by degree program.

Montserrat College of Art (F)

23 Essex Street, Beverly MA 01915-4508

County: Essex FICE Identification: 020630
Unit ID: 166911

Telephone: (978) 921-4242 Carnegie Class: Bac-Diverse
FAX Number: (978) 922-4268 Calendar System: Semester
URL: www.montserrat.edu
Established: 1970 Annual Undergrad Tuition & Fees: $35,300
Enrollment: 362 Coed
Affiliation or Control: Independent Non-Profit IRS Status: 501(c)3
Highest Offering: Baccalaureate
Accreditation: EH, ART

01 President .... Dr. Kurt T. STEINBERG
05 Dean of Academic Affairs/Faculty .... Mr. Brian PELLINEN
32 Dean of Students .... Ms. Maureen WARK
30 Associate Director of Development .... Ms. Allison RIEKE
26 Dean College Rels/Chief of Staff .... Ms. Jo BRODERICK
10 Dean of Finance/Administration .... Ms. Lisa SHAWNEY
13 Director of Information Technology .... Ms. Ari GROSVENOR
08 Librarian .... Ms. Eileen FITZGERALD
06 Registrar .... Mrs. Theresa SKELLY
15 Director of Human Resources .... Mr. Steven GREISDORF
07 Interim Director of Admissions .... Ms. Michela DAVOLA
04 Executive Asst to the President .... Ms. Olivia LEJEUNE
37 Director of Financial Aid .... Vacant
18 Facilities Manager .... Mr. James MCCARTHY
88 Dir Academic Access Studio .... Ms. Meagan GRANT
39 Director of Campus Life .... Ms. Tanya VATTANASIL

Mount Holyoke College (G)

50 College Street, South Hadley MA 01075-1424

County: Hampshire FICE Identification: 002192
Unit ID: 166939

Telephone: (413) 538-2000 Carnegie Class: Bac-A&S
FAX Number: (413) 538-2391 Calendar System: Semester
URL: www.mtholyoke.edu
Established: 1837 Annual Undergrad Tuition & Fees: $54,618
Enrollment: 2,040 Female
Affiliation or Control: Independent Non-Profit IRS Status: 501(c)3
Highest Offering: Master's
Accreditation: EH

01 Interim President .... Dr. Beverly D. TATUM
05 Provost and Dean of Faculty .... Lisa SULLIVAN
10 Interim VP Finance & Administration .... Mary Jo MAYDEW
84 VP Enrollment Management .... Robin RANDALL
111 VP for College Relations .... Kassandra JOLLEY
32 VP Student Life/Dean of Students .... Marcella RUNELL HALL
28 VP for Equity and Inclusion/CDO .... Kijua SANDERS-MCMURTRY
15 Assoc VP Human Resources .... Penny DAVIS
101 Chief of Staff/Sec of the College .... Bett SCHUMACHER
06 Registrar .... Elizabeth PYLE
13 Chief Information Officer .... Alex WIRTH-CAUCHON
29 Exec Director Alumnae Association .... Nancy PEREZ

New England College of Optometry (H)

424 Beacon Street, Boston MA 02115-1129

County: Suffolk FICE Identification: 002164
Unit ID: 167093

Telephone: (617) 266-2030 Carnegie Class: Spec-4-yr-Other Health
FAX Number: (617) 424-9202 Calendar System: Semester
URL: www.neco.edu
Established: 1894 Annual Undergrad Tuition & Fees: N/A
Enrollment: 528 Coed
Affiliation or Control: Independent Non-Profit IRS Status: 501(c)3
Highest Offering: Doctorate
Accreditation: EH, OPT, OPTR

01 President .... Dr. Howard B. PURCELL
125 President Emeritus .... Dr. Clifford SCOTT
05 VP & Dean of Academic Affairs .... Dr. Erik WEISSBERG
10 EVP Finance/Admin/CFO .... Ms. Traci LOGAN
86 VP Professional Affairs .... Dr. Gary CHU
20 Dean Academic Resources & Admin .... Dr. Sandra MOHR
17 Assoc Dean of Clinical Affairs .... Dr. Kristen BROWN
15 Exec Dir of Human Resources .... Ms. Elizabeth DAVIES
07 Director of Admissions .... Ms. Kristen TOBIN
37 Director Student Financial Aid .... Ms. Esther BANDOO-GOMES
06 Registrar .... Ms. Kathryn KWOLEK
08 Director of Library Services .... Ms. Heather EDMONDS
04 Executive Asst to the President .... Ms. Donna Marie FERRI
09 Director of Institutional Research .... Dr. Fuensanta VERA-DIAZ
18 Chief Facilities/Physical Plant .... Ms. Shawne GILLIES
26 Chief Public Relations Officer .... Ms. Lauri CRAWFORD
28 Diversity & Inclusion Liaison .... Ms. Simone JADCZAK
30 Chief Development Officer .... Mr. Andrew KALL

New England Conservatory of Music (A)

290 Huntington Avenue, Boston MA 02115-5018
County: Suffolk FICE Identification: 002194
Unit ID: 167057
Telephone: (617) 585-1100 Carnegie Class: Spec-4-yr-Arts
FAX Number: (617) 262-0500 Calendar System: Semester
URL: www.necmusic.edu
Established: 1867 Annual Undergrad Tuition & Fees: $52,440
Enrollment: 701 Coed
Affiliation or Control: Independent Non-Profit IRS Status: 501(c)3
Highest Offering: Doctorate
Accreditation: EH

01 President .... Ms. Andrea KALYN
05 Provost and Dean of Faculty .... Mr. Benjamin SOSLAND
10 Chief Financial Officer .... Mr. John SPINARD
111 SVP Institutional Advancement .... Ms. Kathleen KELLY
26 Dir Marketing/Brand Strategy .... Ms. Valerie SZEPIWDYCZ
32 Dean of Students/Campus Life .... Ms. Christina DAVIS
07 Asst Director of Admissions .... Mr. Zach SCHWARTZ
21 AVP for Finance/Controller .... Ms. Kristina MARTIN
18 Dir Facilities/Campus Security .... Mr. Chris HAYDEN
06 Registrar/Dir of Inst Research .... Mr. Robert WINKLEY
15 Director of Human Resources .... Vacant
13 Chief Information Officer .... Ms. Heather WOODS
38 Director of Counseling Services .... Vacant
23 Director of Health Services .... Ms. Leah MCKINNON-HOWE
20 Dean of Academic Affairs/Admin .... Ms. Alison GARNER

New England Law | Boston (B)

154 Stuart Street, Boston MA 02116-5687
County: Suffolk FICE Identification: 008916
Unit ID: 167215
Telephone: (617) 451-0010 Carnegie Class: Spec-4-yr-Law
FAX Number: (617) 422-7333 Calendar System: Semester
URL: www.nesl.edu
Established: 1908 Annual Undergrad Tuition & Fees: N/A
Enrollment: 904 Coed
Affiliation or Control: Independent Non-Profit IRS Status: 501(c)3
Highest Offering: First Professional Degree
Accreditation: LAW

01 President/CEO/Dean .... Mr. Scott BROWN
05 Associate Dean .... Ms. Allison M. DUSSIAS
05 Associate Dean .... Ms. Lisa FREUDENHEIM
07 Assoc Director of Admission .... Ms. Angela SMITH ROWE
10 Chief Financial Officer .... Ms. Anne Marie MARTORANA
13 Director of Information Technology .... Mr. Gareth FLANAGAN
26 Chief Marketing/Communications Ofcr .... Ms. Jennifer KELLY
08 Director of the Law Library .... Ms. Kristin C. MCCARTHY
36 Asst Director of Career Services .... Ms. Larissa BREWSTER
07 Dean of Admissions .... Mr. John CHALMERS
37 Director of Financial Aid .... Mr. Eric A. KRUPSKI
06 Registrar .... Ms. Lexi OBERACKER
18 Director of Facilities/Security .... Mr. Miguel ALVARADO
32 Director of Student Services .... Ms. Jacqui PILGRIM
30 Dir of Development/Alumni Rels .... Ms. Jocelyn J. COLETTI
88 Director of the Clinical Law Office .... Mr. Russell ENGLER

Nichols College (C)

Center Road, PO Box 5000, Dudley MA 01571-5000
County: Worcester FICE Identification: 002197
Unit ID: 167260
Telephone: (800) 470-3379 Carnegie Class: Masters/M
FAX Number: N/A Calendar System: Semester
URL: www.nichols.edu
Established: 1815 Annual Undergrad Tuition & Fees: $36,540
Enrollment: 1,518 Coed
Affiliation or Control: Independent Non-Profit IRS Status: 501(c)3
Highest Offering: Master's
Accreditation: EH, COSMA, IACBE

01 President .... Glenn M. SULMASY
05 Provost/VPAA .... Daniel J. BORGIA
111 Vice President for Advancement .... William C. PIECZYNSKI
84 Vice President for Enrollment .... Michael CROWLEY
41 Vice President for Athletics and AD .... Jack HAYES
10 VP for Business & Finance/CFO .... Jamie SKOWYRA
18 Vice President for Operations .... Robert W. LAVIGNE
26 AVP Advancement/Col Communications .... Susan VESHI
13 Chief Technology Officer .... Jared HAMILTON
58 Associate Director GPS .... Robin FRKAL
04 Assistant to the President .... Cari CYR
07 Director of Admissions .... Micheal RICCI
06 Associate Dean for Registration .... Betin ROBICHAUD
08 Director of Library .... Carrie GRIMSHAW
15 Director of Human Resources .... Darcy VANGEL
35 Associate Dean for Student Eng .... Janet NEWMAN
36 Director of Career Services .... Elizabeth HORGAN
37 Director of Financial Aid .... Lindsay LOUIS
38 Director of Wellness Canter .... Kate LOGAN
09 Dir of Inst Research & Reporting .... Emily REARDON
19 Director Public Safety .... Eric STREICH
35 Dean of Students .... Hillary J. THEOFANE
39 Director of Residence Life .... Jessica RYAN
28 Director CDEI .... Alicia MCKENZIE

Northeastern University (D)

360 Huntington Avenue, Boston MA 02115-0195
County: Suffolk FICE Identification: 002199
Unit ID: 167358
Telephone: (617) 373-2000 Carnegie Class: DU-Highest
FAX Number: N/A Calendar System: Semester
URL: www.northeastern.edu
Established: 1898 Annual Undergrad Tuition & Fees: $55,452
Enrollment: 22,905 Coed
Affiliation or Control: Independent Non-Profit IRS Status: 501(c)3
Highest Offering: Doctorate
Accreditation: EH, ANEST, ARCPA, COPSY, COSMA, LAW, NASP, NURSE, PH, PHAR, PTA, SCPSY, SP, SPAA

01 President .... Dr. Joseph E. AOUN
03 Chancellor and SVP for Learning .... Mr. Ken HENDERSON
04 Exec Assistant to the President .... Ms. Susan CROMWELL
05 Sr VP Academic Affairs and Provost .... Dr. David MADIGAN
100 Chief of Staff .... Mr. Stephen CHAN
111 Sr VP University Advancement .... Ms. Diane N. MACGILLIVRAY
43 Sr VP and General Counsel .... Ms. Mary STROTHER
26 Sr VP External Affairs .... Mr. Michael A. ARMINI
12 Seattle Campus Dean & CEO .... Mr. David THURMAN
12 Regional Dean & CEO Silicon Valley .... Ms. Hillary MICKELL
12 Regional Dean & CEO Charlotte .... Ms. Angela HOSKING
08 Vice Provost for Info Collaboration .... Dr. Dan COHEN
46 Sr Vice Prov Research .... Dr. David LUZZI
88 Sr Vice Chancellor Educ Innovation .... Dr. Constance YOWELL
20 Executive Vice Provost .... Dr. Thomas C. SHEAHAN
13 VP & CIO .... Mr. Cole CAMPLESE
84 Chief Enrollment Officer .... Mr. Satyajit DATTAGUPTA
88 Sr VP for Global Network .... Dr. Mary LUDDEN
32 Sr Vice Chancellor Student Affairs .... Ms. Madeleine A. ESTABROOK
30 VP Development .... Ms. Luanne KIRWIN
15 VP & Chief Human Resources Officer .... Ms. Michele GRAZULIS
20 Deputy Provost .... Ms. Carolyn BARGOOT
86 VP Federal Relations .... Mr. Jack CLINE
31 VP City & Community Engagement .... Mr. John M. TOBIN
117 Director of Risk Services .... Vacant
45 VP/Chief Campus Planning & Facil .... Ms. Kathy SPIEGELMAN
20 Sr Vice Provost Academic Affairs .... Ms. Debra FRANKO
12 CEO of the London Campus .... Mr. Robert FARQUAHARSON
28 Sr Vice Prov Chief Inclusion Ofcr .... Dr. Karl REID
76 Dean Health Sciences .... Dr. Carmen SCEPPA
37 Dean Student Financial Svcs .... Mr. Robert REDDY
12 Regional Dean & CEO Arlington .... Ms. Jamie J. MILLER
88 V Provost & Deputy General Counsel .... Ms. Lisa SINCLAIR
88 Vice Provost Faculty Diversity .... Dr. Phil HE
21 VP of Admin & Financial Planning .... Dr. Anthony RINI
88 AVP Research Administration .... Ms. Dana CARROLL
35 Vice Chancellor Dean of Students .... Dr. Chong KIM-WONG
09 AVP Inst Rsrch & Data Admin .... Ms. Rana GLASGAL
06 Assoc VP & University Registrar .... Vacant
27 VP Communications .... Ms. Renata NYUL
27 VP Marketing .... Ms. Rebecca ANZUONI
92 Director University Honors Program .... Ms. Laurie KRAMER
42 Exec Dir Spirituality & Dialogue .... Mr. Alexander KERN
19 VP Safety/Security & Policing .... Mr. Michael DAVIS
41 Director of Athletics .... Mr. James MADIGAN
10 Sr VP Finance & Treasurer .... Mr. Thomas NEDELL
77 Dean Khoury Col Comp Science .... Dr. Elizabeth MYNATT
54 Dean College of Engineering .... Dr. Gregory ABOWD
81 Dean College of Science .... Dr. Hazel SIVE
50 Int Dean D'Amore-McKim Col Business .... Dr. Emery TRAHAN
57 Dean College of Arts/Media/Design .... Dr. Elizabeth HUDSON
61 Dean School of Law .... Dr. James HACKNEY
83 Dean Col of Soc Sci & Humanities .... Dr. Uta POIGER
107 Dean College of Prof Studies .... Dr. Radhika SESHAN
12 Dean Toronto Campus .... Ms. Aliza LAKHANI
106 Chief Admin Officer Roux Institute .... Mr. Chris MALLETT
29 VP Alumni Relations .... Mr. Rick DAVIS
39 Dean Cultural/Resident/Spirit Life .... Mr. Robert JOSE
101 Secretary of the Institution/Board .... Ms. Camille KLUTTZ-LEACH

Northpoint Bible College (E)

320 South Main Street, Haverhill MA 01835
County: Essex FICE Identification: 035705
Unit ID: 217606
Telephone: (978) 478-3400 Carnegie Class: Spec-4-yr-Faith
FAX Number: (978) 478-3406 Calendar System: Semester
URL: www.northpoint.edu
Established: 1924 Annual Undergrad Tuition & Fees: $13,493
Enrollment: 294 Coed
Affiliation or Control: Assemblies Of God Church IRS Status: 501(c)3
Highest Offering: Master's
Accreditation: BI

01 President .... Rev Dr. David J. ARNETT
05 Academic Dean .... Rev Dr. Daniel HOWELL
32 Dean of Student Development .... Rev. Michael SCOTT
10 Financial Services Manager .... Mrs. Pam PERRON
84 Dean of Enrollment .... Rev Dr. David MUNLEY
37 Director of Financial Aid .... Miss Patricia STAUFFER
06 Registrar .... Mrs. Amber PHILLIPS
13 Chief Info Technology Officer (CIO) .... Vacant

Pope St. John XXIII National Seminary (F)

558 South Avenue, Weston MA 02493-2699
County: Middlesex FICE Identification: 002202
Unit ID: 167464
Telephone: (781) 899-5500 Carnegie Class: Spec-4-yr-Faith
FAX Number: (781) 899-9057 Calendar System: Semester
URL: www.psjs.edu
Established: 1964 Annual Graduate Tuition & Fees: N/A
Enrollment: 54 Male
Affiliation or Control: Roman Catholic IRS Status: 501(c)3
Highest Offering: Master's; No Undergraduates
Accreditation: THEOL

01 Rector and President .... Rev. Brian R. KIELY
03 Vice Rector .... Rev. Paul E. MICELI
05 Academic Dean .... Dr. Anthony KEATY
08 Librarian .... Mrs. Barbara NEEM
10 Business Manager .... Mrs. Kyle RYAN
06 Registrar .... Dr. Paul MICELI
30 Chief Development Officer .... Mrs. Kate FOLAN
32 Chief Student Life Officer .... Rev. Stephen LINEHAN

Quincy College (G)

1250 Hancock Street, Quincy MA 02169-4324
County: Norfolk FICE Identification: 002205
Unit ID: 167525
Telephone: (617) 984-1700 Carnegie Class: Assoc/HT-High Non
FAX Number: (617) 984-1779 Calendar System: Semester
URL: www.quincycollege.edu
Established: 1958 Annual Undergrad Tuition & Fees (In-District): $6,960
Enrollment: 3,154 Coed
Affiliation or Control: Local IRS Status: 501(c)3
Highest Offering: Associate Degree
Accreditation: EH, MLTAD, PTAA, SURGT

01 President .... Dr. Richard DECRISTOFARO
100 Chief of Staff/VP of Operations .... Mr. Christopher BELL
05 Chief Academic Officer .... Dr. Servet YATIN
45 SVP Strategic Initiatives .... Ms. Jennifer LUDDY
13 VP Technology & Mission Support .... Mr. Tom C. PHAM
43 General Counsel .... Ms. Jessica CHERRY
10 VP of Finance .... Mr. Martin AHERN
04 Exec Asst to President .... Ms. Meaghan SHEEHAN
108 Director Institutional Assessment .... Ms. Amanda COLLIGAN
12 Dean of Operations Plymouth Campus .... Ms. Catherine MALONEY
66 Dean of Nursing .... Dr. Diane GILLIS
49 Dean of Liberal Arts & Prof Program .... Dr. William CARROLL
81 Dean of Natural & Health Sciences .... Ms. Andrea MCLAIN
37 Assoc VP for Financial Aid .... Ms. Rose M. DEVITO
18 Dir of Admin Services & Facilities .... Mr. William C. HALL
15 Human Resources Analyst .... Ms. Yveline EXANTUS
26 Exec Dir of Comm & Marketing .... Mr. Matthew MCGOWAN
84 AVP of Enrollment Management .... Mr. Joshua TEFFT
106 Assoc Dean & Dir Online Learning .... Ms. Lisa DESRUISSEAUX
35 Student Development Specialist .... Mr. Matthew MESSIER
08 Librarian .... Ms. Sarah DOLAN
103 AVP Workforce Dev & Cmty Engagement .... Ms. Kate LOPCI
41 Athletic Director .... Mr. John RAYMER

Regis College (H)

235 Wellesley Street, Weston MA 02493-1571
County: Middlesex FICE Identification: 002206
Unit ID: 167598
Telephone: (781) 768-7000 Carnegie Class: Masters/L
FAX Number: (781) 768-8339 Calendar System: Semester
URL: www.regiscollege.edu
Established: 1927 Annual Undergrad Tuition & Fees: $43,715
Enrollment: 3,460 Coed
Affiliation or Control: Independent Non-Profit IRS Status: 501(c)3
Highest Offering: Doctorate
Accreditation: EH, ACBSP, ADNUR, DH, DMS, NMT, NUR, OT, RAD, SP, SW

01 President .... Dr. Antoinette M. HAYS
11 SVP/Chief Operating Officer .... Ms. Kara KOLOMITZ
10 VP Finance/Business & CFO .... Mr. Richard KELLEY
05 Vice President Academic Affairs .... Dr. Mary Erina DRISCOLL
26 Vice President of Marketing & Comm .... Vacant
123 Vice President Grad Enrollment .... Mr. Jonathan SMALL
111 Vice Pres Inst Advancement .... Ms. Staci SHEA
109 AVP Auxiliary and Business Svcs .... Mr. Michael O'KEEFE
28 AVP Inclusive Excellence/CDO .... Ms. Audrey GRACE
07 Dean of Undergraduate Admission .... Dr. Laura BERTONAZZI
37 Director of Financial Aid .... Ms. Tanya JEAN-FRANCOIS
06 Registrar .... Ms. Esther A. GHAZARIAN
15 AVP of Human Resources .... Ms. Joan D. SULLIVAN
18 Director of Physical Plant .... Mr. Joseph SHAUGHNESSY
21 Director Finance & Business .... Mr. Jonathan AMARI
29 Director of Alumni Relations .... Ms. Molly ZUCCARINI
32 VP Student Affairs & UG Enrollment .... Dr. Kara KOLOMITZ
23 Director of Health Services .... Ms. Tammi MAGAZZU
08 Director of Library .... Ms. Jane PECK
13 Chief Information Officer .... Ms. Kate KORZENDORFER
41 Dean of Athletics .... Ms. Pamela ROECKER
42 Director Campus Ministry .... Mr. Daniel LEAHY
31 Director of Housing .... Ms. Bridget BUONICONTI
35 Director of Student Engagement .... Ms. Gerena WALKER
104 Director Study Abroad .... Dr. Megan GIBBONS
19 Director of Campus Safety .... Mr. Craig DAVIS

Saint John's Seminary (A)

127 Lake Street, Brighton MA 02135-3898
County: Suffolk FICE Identification: 002214
Unit ID: 167677
Telephone: (617) 254-2610 Carnegie Class: Spec-4-yr-Faith
FAX Number: (617) 787-2336 Calendar System: Semester
URL: www.sjs.edu
Established: 1884 Annual Undergrad Tuition & Fees: N/A
Enrollment: 105 Coed
Affiliation or Control: Roman Catholic IRS Status: 501(c)3
Highest Offering: Master's
Accreditation: EH, THEOL

01 Rector .... Rev. Stephen SALOCKS
03 Vice Rector .... Rev. Thomas MACDONALD
10 Vice Pres Finance/Administration .... Ms. Patricia FRASER
05 Academic Dean .... Dr. Paul METILLY
32 Dean of Students .... Rev. Edward RILEY
07 Director of Admissions & Records ... Mrs. Maureen DEBERNARDI
08 Librarian .... Rev. Raymond VAN DE MOORTELL
108 Executive Institutional Assessment .... Mr. Tomasz KIERUL
04 Admin Assistant to the President .... Ms. Susan EDWARDS
06 Registrar .... Ms. Maureen DEBERNARDI

Sattler College (B)

100 Cambridge Street, Ste 1701, Boston MA 02114
County: Suffolk Identification: 667410
Telephone: (617) 420-1820 Carnegie Class: Not Classified
FAX Number: N/A Calendar System: Semester
URL: www.sattlercollege.org
Established: 2018 Annual Undergrad Tuition & Fees: N/A
Enrollment: N/A Coed
Affiliation or Control: Non-denominational IRS Status: 501(c)3
Highest Offering: Baccalaureate
Accreditation: TRACS

01 President .... Mr. Dean TAYLOR
05 Dean Academic Affairs .... Mr. Michael MILLER

Simmons University (C)

300 The Fenway, Boston MA 02115-5898
County: Suffolk FICE Identification: 002208
Unit ID: 167783
Telephone: (617) 521-2000 Carnegie Class: DU-Mod
FAX Number: (617) 521-3065 Calendar System: Semester
URL: www.simmons.edu
Established: 1899 Annual Undergrad Tuition & Fees: $41,917
Enrollment: 6,263 Coordinate
Affiliation or Control: Independent Non-Profit IRS Status: 501(c)3
Highest Offering: Doctorate
Accreditation: EH, ABAI, DIETD, DIETI, LIB, NURSE, PH, PTA, SW

01 President .... Lynn PERRY WOOTEN
04 Assistant to the President .... Alva CEDENO
05 Provost .... Russell PINIZZOTTO
111 Int VP Advancement .... Cate MCLAUGHLIN
10 VP/Chief Financial Ofcr/Treasurer .... Meghan KASS
20 Vice Provost .... Stephanie COSNER BERZIN
76 Dean Sch Nursing & Health Sciences .... Lepaine SHARP-MCHENRY
50 Dean School of Management .... Patricia H. DEYTON
32 Dean of Student Experience .... Rae-Anne BUTERA
06 Registrar/Dir Academic Records .... Shirley ALEXANDER-HUNT
08 Library Director .... Vivienne B. PIROLI
25 Director Sponsored Programs .... Elena GLATMAN
09 Director Institutional Research .... Lan GAO
36 Director Career Education Center .... Barbara ZERILLO
13 VP Technology/Chief Info Ofcr .... David BRUCE
18 VP Real Estate/Facilities Mgmt .... Laura BRINK
38 Clinical Director Counseling Svcs .... Sherri ETTINGER
41 Director Athletics .... Ali KANTOR
35 Assoc Dir Campus Rec/Stdnt Wellnes .... Ryan BRADSHAW
43 SVP/General Counsel/Chief of Staff .... Kathleen R. ROGERS
15 Assistant VP Human Resources .... Elizabeth HURLEY
28 Asst VP for Inclusion/Diversity .... Rachel DELEVEAUX

Smith College (D)

10 Elm Street, Northampton MA 01063-0001
County: Hampshire FICE Identification: 002209
Unit ID: 167835
Telephone: (413) 584-2700 Carnegie Class: Bac-A&S
FAX Number: (413) 585-2123 Calendar System: Semester
URL: www.smith.edu
Established: 1871 Annual Undergrad Tuition & Fees: $54,224
Enrollment: 2,504 Female
Affiliation or Control: Independent Non-Profit IRS Status: 501(c)3
Highest Offering: Doctorate
Accreditation: EH, SW

01 President .... Kathleen MCCARTNEY
05 Provost/Dean of the Faculty .... Michael THURSTON
10 VP for Finance & Administration .... David DESWERT
28 Vice President for Inclusion/Equity .... Floyd CHEUNG
30 SVP Alumnae Relations/Development .... Beth RAFFELD
32 VP Campus Life/Dean of the College .... Baishakhi TAYLOR
84 VP for Enrollment .... Joanna MAY
13 VP Information Technology .... Samantha EARP
45 VP for Strategic Initiatives .... Laurie FENLASON
26 VP College Relations/Communications .... Julia YAGER
100 Chief of Staff .... Joanna OLIN
101 Secretary Board of Trustees/College .... Elena PALLADINO
20 Associate Provost .... Bill PETERSON
20 Assoc Dean of Faculty/Academic Dev .... Héline VISENTIN
70 Dean School for Social Work .... Marianne YOSHIOKA
08 Dean of Libraries .... Vacant
09 AVP Analytics & Inst Research .... Cate ROWEN
15 Assoc VP for Human Resources .... Anne-Marie SZMYT
88 ED Sustainability/Campus Planning .... Dano J. WEISBORD
114 Dir of Budgets/Financial Planning .... Kate GOLA
18 AVP for Facilities & Operations .... Jim GRAY
21 Controller .... Matthew D. MOTYKA
22 Dir Equal Opportunity/Title IX .... Amy HUNTER
88 Dean of Multicultural Affairs .... LÆTanya B. RICHMOND
42 Dir of Religious/Spiritual Life .... Matilda CANTWELL
29 VP for Alumnae Relations .... Denise W. MATERRE
111 AVP for Advancement .... Sandra L. DOUCETT
110 AVP for Development .... Betsy CARPENTER
35 Dean of Students/Assoc Dean College .... Julianne OHOTNICKY
35 Associate Dean of Students .... Becky SHAW
39 Director of Residence Life .... Hannah L. DURRANT
38 Interim Dir of Health and Wellness .... Kris EVANS
88 Dean of Senior Class .... Danielle D. CARR RAMDATH
41 Director of Athletics .... Kristin HUGHES
104 Dean for International Study .... Rebecca HOVEY
85 Assoc Dean International Students .... Caitlin B. SZYMKOWICZ
88 Assoc Dean Integrative Learning .... Borjana MIKIC
36 Director Career Development Office .... Stacie HAGENBAUGH
88 Disability Services Director .... Laura M. RAUSCHER
07 Dean of Admission .... Deanna DIXON
06 Registrar .... Gretchen B. HERRINGER
37 Dir Student Financial Services .... David J. BELANGER
04 Executive Asst to the President .... Beth BERG

Springfield College (E)

263 Alden Street, Springfield MA 01109-3797
County: Hampden FICE Identification: 002211
Unit ID: 167899
Telephone: (413) 748-3000 Carnegie Class: DU-Mod
FAX Number: N/A Calendar System: Semester
URL: www.springfieldcollege.edu
Established: 1885 Annual Undergrad Tuition & Fees: $40,480
Enrollment: 3,068 Coed
Affiliation or Control: Independent Non-Profit IRS Status: 501(c)3
Highest Offering: Doctorate
Accreditation: EH, ACATE, ARCPA, CAATE, CACREP, CAPRT, COPSY, EXSC, IACBE, OT, PTA, SW

01 President .... Dr. Mary-Beth A. COOPER
100 Chief of Staff .... Dr. Kathleen A. MARTIN
05 Provost & VP Academic Affairs .... Dr. Mary Ann COUGHLIN
111 VP Institutional Advancement .... Ms. Beth ZAPATKA
10 VP for Finance & Admin .... Mr. Lester PRIMUS
32 VP for Student Affairs .... Dr. Slandie DIEUJUSTE
43 VP & General Counsel .... Vacant
28 VP for Inclusion/Cmty Engagement .... Dr. Calvin R. HILL
26 Vice President of Communications .... Vacant
20 Assoc VP Academic Affairs .... Dr. Elizabeth MORGAN
25 Assoc Director Grants/Spons Rsrch .... Mr. Anthony MOTYL
15 Director of Human Resources .... Vacant
30 Director of Development .... Ms. Laura METALLO
84 VP of Enrollment Management .... Dr. Stuart JONES
06 Registrar .... Mr. Marshall BRADWAY
08 Director of Library .... Ms. Andrea S. TAUPIER
29 Director of Alumni Relations .... Ms. Tamie KIDESS LUCEY
37 Director of Financial Aid .... Mr. Troy DAVIS
36 Director of Career Center .... Mr. Scott DRANKA
13 Chief Information Officer .... Mr. Anthony MUTTI
90 Director of Network Systems .... Mr. Nadim EL-KHOURY
38 Director of Counseling Center .... Mr. Brian KRYLOWICZ
19 Chief of Police .... Mr. Joseph TIRABOSCHI
85 Director of International Center .... Dr. Deborah ALM
42 Director Campus Ministry .... Mr. David MCMAHON
18 Director of Facilities/Campus Svcs .... Mr. Kevin ROY
41 Executive Director of Athletics .... Dr. Craig POISSON
96 Director of Purchasing .... Ms. Lita ADAMS
09 Director of Institutional Research .... Dr. Raldy LAGUILLES
102 Exec Dir Corporate Partnerships .... Mr. John WHITE
39 Director Housing & Residence Life .... Mr. Robert YANEZ

Stonehill College (F)

320 Washington Street, Easton MA 02357-6110
County: Bristol FICE Identification: 002217
Unit ID: 167996
Telephone: (508) 565-1000 Carnegie Class: Bac-A&S
FAX Number: (508) 565-1500 Calendar System: Semester
URL: www.stonehill.edu
Established: 1948 Annual Undergrad Tuition & Fees: $46,642
Enrollment: 2,504 Coed
Affiliation or Control: Roman Catholic IRS Status: 501(c)3
Highest Offering: Master's
Accreditation: EH

01 President .... Rev. John F. DENNING, CSC
100 Chief of Staff .... Mrs. Heather L. HEERMAN
05 Provost/VP for Academic Affairs .. Dr. DeBrenna LaFa AGBENYIGA
10 Vice Pres for Finance & Treasurer .... Ms. Jeanne FINLAYSON
111 Vice President for Advancement .... Mr. Doug SMITH
32 Vice President of Student Affairs .... Ms. Pauline DOBROWSKI
21 AVP for Finance & Operations .... Mr. Craig BINNEY
35 Assoc VP for Student Affairs .... Mr. Kevin PISKADLO
37 Asst VP for Student Fin Assistance .... Mr. William C. SMITH
04 Executive Asst to the President .... Ms. Kathy JOHNSON
20 Assoc Provost .... Dr. Craig KELLEY
43 Vice President and General Counsel .... Mr. Thomas V. FLYNN
21 Controller .... Ms. Jennifer MATHEWS
84 Vice Pres for Enrollment Management .... Mr. Joseph DACEY
06 Registrar .... Rev. Jeffrey L. ALLISON, CSC
09 Dir of Inst Research/Assessment .... Mr. Brian M. OLES
08 Director of College Library .... Ms. Jennifer M. MACAULAY
26 Dir of Media Rels & Communications .... Ms. Jill P. GODDARD
29 Director of Alumni Affairs .... Ms. Anne M. SANT
15 Director of Human Resources .... Mrs. Lily A. KRENTZMAN
38 Dir of Counseling & Testing Center ... Ms. Maria A. KAVANAUGH
13 Chief Information Officer .... Ms. Tamara ANDERSON
19 Chief of Police .... Ms. Rochelle RYAN
42 Director Campus Ministry .... Rev. Anthony SZAKALY, CSC
90 Assoc Dir of Instructional Tech .... Ms. Janice HARRISON
88 Director of Academic Development .... Ms. Bonnie L. TROUPE
91 Dir of Enterprise Infrastructure .... Mr. Thomas MCGRATH
23 Director of Health Services .... Mrs. Maria SULLIVAN
36 Director of Career Services .... Mr. Andrew M. LEAHY
41 Dir of Intercollegiate Athletics .... Mr. Dean R. O'KEEFE
92 Director of Honors Program .... Prof. Sarah GRACOMBE
121 Dir Academic Services/Advising .... Ms. Shannon D. BALLIRO
96 Director of Purchasing .... Mr. Gregory WOLFE
45 Asst VP for Planning & Budgeting .... Mr. Stephen BEAUREGARD
39 Director of Residence Life .... Ms. Ariana GULBIS
24 Dir of Media/Videography Services .... Mr. Michael PIETROWSKI
40 Manager of College Bookstore .... Mrs. Mary DUNCKLEE
18 Director of Facilities Management .... Mr. Bruce BOYER
104 Director International Programs .... Vacant
28 Director of Intercultural Affairs .... Ms. Kristine DIN
49 Dean School of Arts and Sciences .... Fr. Kevin SPICER
50 Dean School of Business .... Dr. Sam BELDONA
58 Dean of Graduate Studies .... Dr. Kirill M. BUMIN
123 Dean of Graduate Admissions .... Vacant
102 Dir of Corp/Foundation & Donor Rels .... Mrs. Marie C. KELLY
07 Dean of Undergraduate Admissions .... Mr. Scott SESESKE
27 Director of Marketing .... Mr. Shane LAPRADE
108 Dir of Inst Research & Assessment .... Mr. Brian OLES
44 Director the Annual Fund .... Ms. Lisa RICHARDS

Suffolk University (G)

8 Ashburton Place, Boston MA 02108-2770
County: Suffolk FICE Identification: 002218
Unit ID: 168005
Telephone: (617) 573-8000 Carnegie Class: DU-Mod
FAX Number: (617) 573-8353 Calendar System: Semester
URL: www.suffolk.edu
Established: 1906 Annual Undergrad Tuition & Fees: $41,648
Enrollment: 6,830 Coed
Affiliation or Control: Independent Non-Profit IRS Status: 501(c)3
Highest Offering: Doctorate
Accreditation: EH, ART, CIDA, CLPSY, HSA, IPSY, LAW, RADDOS, RTT, SPAA

01 President .... Dr. Marisa KELLY
05 Provost .... Dr. Julie SANDELL
10 Sr VP Finance/Admin/Treasurer .... Ms. Laura SANDER
111 Sr VP of Advancement .... Mr. Colm RENEHAN
09 AVP Assessment/Chief Data Officer .... Dr. Gary FIREMAN
84 VP of Admissions & Financial Aid .... Ms. Donna GRAND PRE
26 VP of Communications .... Mr. Greg GATLIN
86 Sr VP of External Affairs .... Mr. John A. NUCCI
37 AVP/Dir of Financial Aid .... Ms. Jennifer H. RICCIARDI
32 Interim VP/Dean of Students .... Ms. Laura FERRARI
06 AVP/University Registrar .... Ms. Mary LALLY
15 Chief HR Officer .... Mr. Boris LAZIC
28 VP Diversity/Access & Inclusion .... Ms. Joyya SMITH
13 Chief Information Officer .... Dr. Mark NESTOR
43 General Counsel .... Mr. Thomas DORER
49 Dean College Arts & Science .... Dr. Edie SPARKS
61 Dean of the Law School .... Mr. Andrew PERLMAN
50 Dean Sawyer Business School .... Dr. Amy ZENG
19 Interim Chief of University Police .... Mr. Jim CONNOLLY
04 Exec Assistant to the President .... Ms. Valerie VENTURA
25 AVP Research & Sponsored Programs .... Mr. Michael MULLAHY
44 Director of Individual Giving .... Mr. John IRVIN
07 Director of Undergraduate Admission .... Ms. Lark KRAJESKI
123 Director of Graduate Admission .... Ms. Heather O'LEARY
29 AVP Advancement/Alumni Relations .... Ms. Caitlin HAUGHEY
08 Director of Law Library .... Mr. Richard BUCKINGHAM
08 Director of Sawyer Library .... Mr. Gregory HEALD
36 Exec Dir Career Development Center .... Mr. Dave MERRY
41 Director of Athletics .... Mr. Cary MCCONNELL
39 Director of Residence Life .... Mr. Shigeo IWAMIYA
38 Dir Counseling/Health & Wellness .... Dr. Stephanie KENDALL
35 Dir Student Ldrship & Involvement .... Dr. Dave DEANGELIS
96 Manager of Purchasing Services .... Mr. John KINEAVY
18 AVP Facilities .... Ms. Ashley LINDSEY
104 Director Intl Education/Study Away .... Dr. Amy EWEN
106 Assoc Dean of Online Programs .... Dr. Tracey RILEY
124 AVP Retention .... Mr. Peter FOWLER
88 AVP Acad Planning & Accreditation .... Dr. Rachael KIPP
88 Dir Title IX & Clery Act Compliance .... Ms. Sheila CALKINS
117 Chief Risk Officer .... Ms. Karen KRUPPA
88 Interim Dean Law JD Admissions .... Mr. Brian REID

Tufts University (A)

419 Boston Avenue, Medford MA 02155
County: Middlesex
FICE Identification: 002219
Unit ID: 168148
Telephone: (617) 628-5000
Carnegie Class: DU-Highest
FAX Number: N/A
Calendar System: Semester
URL: www.tufts.edu
Established: 1852
Annual Undergrad Tuition & Fees: $60,862
Enrollment: 12,219
Coed
Affiliation or Control: Independent Non-Profit
IRS Status: 501(c)3
Highest Offering: Doctorate
Accreditation: EH, ARCPA, DENT, MED, OT, PH, PLNG, @PTA, VET

01	President	Dr. Anthony P. MONACO
100	Chief of Staff	Mr. Marty RAY
03	Executive Vice President	Mr. Michael HOWARD
05	Interim Provost & Senior Vice Pres	Ms. Caroline GENCO
43	SVP Univ Relations & Gen Counsel	Ms. Mary R. JEKA
111	SVP University Advancement	Mr. Eric C. JOHNSON
11	Vice President for Operations	Ms. Barbara STEIN
10	VP Finance/Treasurer	Mr. James HURLEY
15	VP for Human Resources	Ms. Kim RYAN
26	VP Communications/Marketing	Mr. Michael RODMAN
13	VP & CIO	Mr. Chris SEDORE
20	Vice Provost	Mr. Kevin DUNN
46	Associate Provost & Sr Intl Officer	Ms. Diana CHIGAS
09	Associate Provost	Dr. Dawn G. TERKLA
21	Administrative Associate Provost	Ms. Celia CAMPBELL
110	Sr VP University Advancement	Mr. Eric JOHNSON
28	Assoc Prov/Chief Diversity Officer	Dr. Joyce A. SACKEY
28	Assoc Prov/Chief Diversity Officer	Mr. Rob MACK
23	Director Adm & Ops Health/Wellness	Ms. Jennifer D. BERRIOS
37	Director of Financial Aid	Ms. Patricia REILLY
27	Executive Director Public Relations	Mr. Patrick COLLINS
36	Exec Director Career Services	Ms. Donna ESPOSITO
08	Director Tisch Library	Ms. Dorothy MEANEY
22	Exec Director Equal Opportunity	Ms. Jill A. ZELLMER
38	Director Mental Health Services	Dr. Julie S. ROSS
19	Executive Director Public Safety	Ms. Yolanda SMITH
49	Dean Arts & Sciences	Mr. James GLASER
54	Interim Dean of Engineering	Dr. Kyongbum LEE
57	Interim Dean of SMFA at Tufts	Mr. Nate HARRISON
58	Dean Grad School of A&S	Ms. Barbara BRIZUELA
61	Dean Fletcher Sch of Law/Diplomacy	Ms. Rachel KYTE
52	Dean of Dental Medicine	Dr. Nadeem KARIMBUX
74	Dean Cummings School Vet Med	Dr. Alastair CRIBB
63	Interim Dean Medical School	Dr. Helen BOUCHER
81	Dean Grad Sch Biomedical Sciences	Dr. Daniel JAY
76	Dean Friedman School	Dr. Dariush MOZAFFARIAN
80	Dean Tisch College of Civic Life	Dr. Dayna CUNNINGHAM
121	Dean Academic Adv & Undergrad Study	Dr. Carmen LOWE
122	Director Fraternity/Sorority Life	Vacant
32	Dean of Student Affairs	Ms. Camille LIZARRIBAR
07	Dean of Admissions/Enroll Mgmt	Mr. Joseph T. DUCK
96	Chief Procurement Officer	Ms. Nisreen BAGASRA
41	Director Athletics	Mr. John MORRIS
42	University Chaplain	Rev. Elyse NELSON WINGER
102	Sr Dir Corp & Foundation Relations	Ms. Ippolita A. CANTUTI-CASTELVETRI
104	Assoc Dean/Sr Director Global Educ	Ms. Melanie Mala GHOSH
39	Director Res Life & Learning	Vacant
112	Senior Director Gift Planning	Ms. Brooke ANDERSON
86	Exec Director Govt & Comm Relations	Mr. Rocco DIRICO
18	Senior Facilities Director	Mr. Cory POULIOT

Urban College of Boston (B)

2 Boylston St, Boston MA 02116
County: Suffolk
FICE Identification: 031305
Unit ID: 429128
Telephone: (617) 449-7070
Carnegie Class: Spec 2-yr-Other
FAX Number: (617) 830-3137
Calendar System: Semester
URL: www.urbancollege.edu
Established: 1993
Annual Undergrad Tuition & Fees: $7,124
Enrollment: 554
Coed
Affiliation or Control: Independent Non-Profit
IRS Status: 501(c)3
Highest Offering: Associate Degree
Accreditation: EH

01	President	Mr. Michael TAYLOR
05	Chief Academic Officer	Ms. Clea ANDREADIS
06	Registrar	Mr. Alexander WOLNIAK
84	Chief Student Services Officer	Dr. Keiko BROOMHEAD
37	Director of Financial Aid	Mr. David VERA
11	Director Operations and Finance	Ms. Karen LUCAS
30	Chief Advancement Officer	Ms. Caitlin CALLAHAN
10	Chief Financial/Business Officer	Ms. Mimoza VREKA

Wellesley College (C)

106 Central Street, Wellesley MA 02481-8203
County: Norfolk
FICE Identification: 002224
Unit ID: 168218
Telephone: (781) 283-1000
Carnegie Class: Bac-A&S
FAX Number: (781) 283-3639
Calendar System: Semester
URL: www.wellesley.edu
Established: 1875
Annual Undergrad Tuition & Fees: $58,448
Enrollment: 2,280
Female
Affiliation or Control: Independent Non-Profit
IRS Status: 501(c)3
Highest Offering: Baccalaureate
Accreditation: EH

01	President	Paula A. JOHNSON
05	Provost & Dean of the College	Andrew SHENNAN
10	VP Finance Administration/Treasurer	Piper ORTON
32	Vice Pres/Dean of Students	Sheilah SHAW HORTON
07	Dean of Admission/Financial Aid	Joy ST. JOHN
30	VP Development	Mary CASEY
26	Chief Communications Officer	Tara MURPHY
43	General Counsel	Karen PETRULAKIS
115	Chief Investment Officer	Debby KUENSTNER
15	Asst VP/Director Human Resources/EO	Carolyn SLABODEN
20	Dean of Academic Affairs	Michael JEFFRIES
20	Dean of Faculty Affairs	Megan NÚÑEZ
09	Assc Provost Institutional Planning	Pamela L. TAYLOR
28	Assc Prov Acad/Dir Dvrsty/Inclusion	Vacant
29	Executive Director Alumnae Assn	Kathryn MACKINTOSH
18	Asst VP Facilities Management/Plng	David CHAKRABORTY
13	Chief Information Officer	Ravi RAVISHANKER
36	Assoc Prov/Dir Exec Ctr Work/Svc	Jennifer POLLARD
101	Clerk Board of Trustees	Marianne B. COOLEY
06	Registrar	Carol SHANMUGARATNAM
37	Director of Student Financial Svcs	Kari DIFONZO
38	Administrative Counseling Svcs	Robin COOK-NOBLES
96	Purchasing Manager	Tina M. DOLAN
42	Dean Religious/Spiritual Life	Jacqueline MARQUEZ
35	Dir Student Involvement/Leadership	Jessica GRADY
04	Admin Assistant to the President	Teresa GARCIA
08	Director Library Collections	Karen BOHRER
104	Director Study Abroad	Jennifer THOMAS-STARCK
39	Dir Resident Life/Student Housing	Helen Y. WANG
41	Athletic Director	Bethany ELLIS

Wentworth Institute of Technology (D)

550 Huntington Avenue, Boston MA 02115-5998
County: Suffolk
FICE Identification: 002225
Unit ID: 168227
Telephone: (617) 989-4590
Carnegie Class: Masters/S
FAX Number: (617) 989-4591
Calendar System: Semester
URL: www.wit.edu
Established: 1904
Annual Undergrad Tuition & Fees: $35,970
Enrollment: 4,389
Coed
Affiliation or Control: Independent Non-Profit
IRS Status: 501(c)3
Highest Offering: Master's
Accreditation: EH, ART, CIDA, CONST

01	President	Dr. Mark A. THOMPSON
100	Chief of Staff	Mr. Erik COTE
04	Executive Coordinator	Mr. Edward CULLINANE
101	VP & University Secretary	Ms. Amy INTILLE
88	AVP Organizational Development	Ms. Courtney MCKENNA
86	Director of Cmty & Govt Relations	Ms. Johanna SENA
15	VP Employee Relations/Engagement	Ms. Melanie DESANTIS
111	VP Inst Advancement & Ext Rels	Ms. Crate HERBERT
43	VP and General Counsel	Ms. Lynn MCCORMICK
13	Vice Pres Technology Svcs/CIO	Mr. Vish PARADKAR
84	VP Enrollment Management	Ms. Kristin TICHENOR
28	VP Diversity/Equity/Inclusion	Ms. Nicole PRICE
19	AVP Public Safety/Chief of Police	Mr. Edgar RODRIGUEZ
10	Vice President Finance	Mr. Robert TOTINO
32	Interim VP Student Affairs	Ms. Courtney MCKENNA
11	Vice President Business	Mr. David A. WAHLSTROM
50	Interim Dean for Management	Mr. Ilyas BHATTI
48	Dean for Architecture & Design	Dr. Sedef DONAGER
81	Interim Dean Sciences & Humanities	Dr. Lizzie FALVEY
54	Interim Dean for Engineering	Dr. Ali KHABARI
77	Dean for Computing and Data Science	Dr. Durga SURESH-MENON
20	Associate Provost	Mr. Joseph MARTEL-FOLEY
20	Assoc Prov Learning & Paterships	Dr. Susan DUFFY
14	Assoc VP Information Technology	Mr. Jim MCFARLAND
21	Assoc Vice President Finance	Mr. David GILMORE
26	AVP Marketing & Communications	Mr. Ted REED
35	Dean of Students	Dr. Jennifer KOSSES
08	Interim Director of Library	Mr. Dan NEAL
06	Registrar	Ms. Joan ROMANO
36	Asst Provost Coops/Careers	Ms. Robbin BEAUCHAMP
37	Director Financial Aid	Ms. Anne-Marie CARUSO
38	Director of Counseling	Ms. Maura MULLIGAN
39	Director Housing & Residential Life	Ms. Kara CUCIO
88	Associate Athletic Director	Mr. William P. GORMAN
41	Director of Athletics	Ms. Cheryl AARON
18	Director of Physical Plant	Mr. John MARUJO
09	Asst Prov Inst Effectiveness	Ms. Lisa KEATING
29	Sr Exec Dir Devel & Alumni Rels	Ms. Angela JOHNSON
96	Dir of Purchasing & Auxiliary Svcs	Mr. Thomas KANE

Western New England University (E)

1215 Wilbraham Road, Springfield MA 01119-2684
County: Hampden
FICE Identification: 002226
Unit ID: 168254
Telephone: (413) 782-3111
Carnegie Class: DU-Mod
FAX Number: (413) 782-1746
Calendar System: Semester
URL: www.wne.edu
Established: 1919
Annual Undergrad Tuition & Fees: $39,216
Enrollment: 3,673
Coed
Affiliation or Control: Independent Non-Profit
IRS Status: 501(c)3
Highest Offering: Doctorate
Accreditation: EH, LAW, OT, PHAR, SW

01	President	Dr. Robert E. JOHNSON
04	Executive Asst to President	Ms. Robin SAVITT-KING
05	Provost/Sr VP Academic Affairs	Dr. A. Maria TOYODA
26	AVP for Marketing/External Affairs	Ms. Mercedes MASKALIK
10	Vice Pres Finance & Administration	Mr. Basil Andrew STEWART
84	VP Enrollment Mgmt/Marketing	Mr. Bryan J. GROSS
32	VP Student Affairs	Ms. Kristine GOODWIN
111	Vice President Advancement	Ms. Beverly J. DWIGHT
13	Chief Information Officer	Mr. Scott J. COOPEE
15	Chief Human Resources Officer	Vacant
61	Dean of the School of Law	Prof. Sudha SETTY
67	Dean of the College of Pharmacy	Dr. John PEZZUTO
49	Dean College of A&S	Dr. Marcus DAVIS
50	Dean of the College of Business	Dr. Sharianne WALKER
54	Dean of the College of Engineering	Dr. S. Hossein CHERAGHI
08	Int Director Law Library	Ms. Nicole BELBIN
39	Director Residence Life	Ms. Christina WILLENBROCK
28	Asst Dean of Diversity Programs	Mrs. Yvonne BOGLE
06	AVP Enroll Mgmt/Univ Registrar	Ms. Julie RICHARDSON
37	Director of Financial Aid	Ms. Kathleen CHAMBERS
41	Director of Athletics	Vacant
36	Director Career Development Center	Ms. Andrea ST. JAMES
38	Director of Counseling Services	Dr. Wayne D. CARPENTER
08	Director of D'Amour Library	Mrs. Priscilla L. PERKINS
23	Director of Health Services	Ms. Kathleen NOONE
18	Director of Facilities Management	Mr. David ROSINSKI
90	Dir Educational Technology Center	Mr. Steven NARMONTAS
91	Dir of Administrative Info Systems	Vacant
29	Director of Alumni Engagement	Ms. Katie DEBEER
25	Corporate/Foundation Relations Ofc	Vacant
42	Spiritual Life Coordinator	Vacant
19	Director of Public Safety	Mr. Adam WOODROW
11	Director Administrative Services	Ms. Arlene M. ROCK
07	Exec Dir of Undergrad Admissions	Mr. Christopher WYSTEPEK
123	Exec Dir of Graduate Admissions	Mr. Matthew FOX
20	Academic Scheduling Controller	Dr. Linda M. CHOJNICKI
09	Director Inst Research & Planning	Ms. Mary GREY
100	Chief of Staff	Mr. Curt HAMAKAWA

Wheaton College (F)

26 E Main Street, Norton MA 02766-2322
County: Bristol
FICE Identification: 002227
Unit ID: 168281
Telephone: (508) 286-8200
Carnegie Class: Bac-A&S
FAX Number: N/A
Calendar System: Semester
URL: www.wheatoncollege.edu
Established: 1834
Annual Undergrad Tuition & Fees: $56,366
Enrollment: 1,670
Coed
Affiliation or Control: Independent Non-Profit
IRS Status: 501(c)3
Highest Offering: Baccalaureate
Accreditation: EH

01	President	Ms. Michaele WHELAN
05	Interim Provost	Dr. Touba GHADESSI
10	VP Finance & Administration	Mr. Roger STACKPOOLE
111	Vice President College Advancement	Ms. Merritt CROWLEY
84	VP of Enrollment	Mr. Walter CAFFEY
32	VP Stdnt Affairs/Dean Stdnts	Mr. Darnell PARKER
26	VP Marketing and Communications	Mr. Gene P. BEGIN
37	Dean of Stdnt Aid/Admissions	Mr. Walter CAFFEY
15	Assoc VP Human Resources	Ms. Omaira ROY
18	Asst VP Business Svcs/Phys Plant	Mr. John M. SULLIVAN
27	Director of Communications	Ms. Sandy COLEMAN
13	Assistant VP Info Tech Services	Mr. Joe LACASCIO
121	Executive Dean of Student Success	Vacant
06	Registrar/Dean Academic Systems	Ms. Sally BUCKLEY
104	Dean Center for Global Education	Ms. Gretchen YOUNG
29	Director Alumni Relations	Ms. Courtney SHURTLEFF
44	Director Annual Fund	Vacant
102	Dir Corporate & Foundation Rels	Ms. Patricia DEMARCO
38	Director Counseling Center	Ms. Valerie TOBIA
07	Acting Director of Admission	Mr. Jeff CUTTING
09	Director of Institutional Research	Dr. Kimberly PUHALA
39	Director Stdnt Life/Housing	Mr. Edward T. BURNETT
19	Director Public Safety	Chief Robert WINSOR
41	Director of Athletics & Recreation	Mr. Gavin VIANO
14	Dir Information Tech Services	Ms. Regina CARVELL
36	Director of Career Services	Ms. Lisa GAVIGAN
101	Asst to President/Sec Brd Trustees	Ms. Kelsey ANDRADE
04	Executive Asst to President	Ms. Pam VAZ

William James College (G)

1 Wells Avenue, Newton MA 02459-3211
County: Middlesex
FICE Identification: 021636
Unit ID: 166717
Telephone: (617) 327-6777
Carnegie Class: Spec-4-yr-Other Health
FAX Number: (617) 327-4447
Calendar System: Semester
URL: www.williamjames.edu
Established: 1974
Annual Graduate Tuition & Fees: N/A
Enrollment: 805
Coed
Affiliation or Control: Independent Non-Profit
IRS Status: 501(c)3
Highest Offering: Doctorate; No Undergraduates
Accreditation: EH, CLPSY, IPSY, NASP, SCPSY

01	President	Dr. Nicholas COVINO
04	Director Office of the President	Ms. Lilly MANOLIS
05	Vice Pres Academic Affairs	Dr. Stacey LAMBERT
10	VP Finance & Operations	Mr. Daniel BRENT
37	Director Financial Aid	Ms. Hilary BAXTER
06	Registrar	Ms. Sonji PAIGE
32	Dean of Students	Vacant
07	Director of Admissions	Mr. Mario MURGA
51	Coordinator Cont Prof Education	Ms. Emily PIERCE
26	Sr Dir of Marketing/Communication	Mrs. Katie O'HARE

13 Dir Information Technology .... Mr. Jeff CHOO
08 Head Librarian .... Ms. Julia CLEMENT
15 Sr Director Human Resources .... Mrs. Ellen COLLINS
18 Facilities Manager .... Mr. Kevin COSTELLO
29 Dir Alumni Relations/Annual Giving .... Ms. Lynn ALBERDING
09 Director Institutional Research .... Dr. Vera MAUK
28 Director of Diversity .... Ms. Gloria NORONHA
102 Director Foundation/Corporate Relat .... Ms. Dawn GOODMAN

† Formerly Massachusetts School of Professional Psychology

Williams College (A)

880 Main Street, Williamstown MA 01267
County: Berkshire
FICE Identification: 002229
Unit ID: 168342
Telephone: (413) 597-3131
Carnegie Class: Bac-A&S
FAX Number: N/A
Calendar System: 4/1/4
URL: www.williams.edu
Established: 1793
Annual Undergrad Tuition & Fees: $50,450
Enrollment: 1,987
Coed
Affiliation or Control: Independent Non-Profit
IRS Status: 501(c)3
Highest Offering: Master's
Accreditation: EH

01 President .... Maud S. MANDEL
05 Provost .... Eiko M. SINIAWER
20 Dean of the Faculty .... Safa ZAKI
10 VP for Finance/Admin & Treasurer .... Michael F. WAGNER
28 VP Inst Diversity/Equity/Inclusion .... Leticia HAYNES
111 VP for College Relations .... Megan MOREY
26 Chief Communications Officer .... Jim REISCHE
04 Asst to Pres/Secretary of the Col .... Keli A. GAIL
20 Dean of the College .... Gretchen LONG
18 Assoc VP Campus Planning/ Operations .... Rita COPPOLA-WALLACE
06 Registrar .... Kath DUNLOP
07 Director of Admission .... Sulgi LIM
37 Director of Financial Aid .... Ashley BIANCHI
08 Director of Libraries .... Jonathan MILLER
21 Controller .... Susan S. HOGAN
29 Exec Director Alumni Relations .... Brooks L. FOEHL
15 Chief Human Resources Officer .... Danielle GONZALEZ
36 Exec Director of Career Center .... Donald J. KJELLEREN
109 Director of Dining Services .... Temesgen ARAYA
13 Chief Information Officer .... Barron KORALESKY
09 Assoc Prov Analytics/Inst Research .... Courtney WADE
23 Director Integrative Wellbeing Svcs .... Wendy ADAM
35 Sr Assoc Dean of Campus Life .... Douglas J. SCHIAZZA
41 Director of Athletics/PE .... Lisa M. MELENDY
42 Chaplain .... Valerie BAILEY FISCHER

Woods Hole Oceanographic Institution (B)

266 Woods Hole Road, Woods Hole MA 02543-1535
County: Barnstable
FICE Identification: 002230
Telephone: (508) 548-1400
Carnegie Class: Not Classified
FAX Number: N/A
Calendar System: 4/1/4
URL: www.whoi.edu
Established: 1930
Annual Graduate Tuition & Fees: N/A
Enrollment: N/A
Coed
Affiliation or Control: Independent Non-Profit
IRS Status: 501(c)3
Highest Offering: Doctorate; No Undergraduates
Accreditation: EH

01 President and Director .... Dr. Peter DE MENOCAL
04 Exec Assist to President/Director .... Ms. Jean LEOTE
09 Deputy Dir/VP for Research .... Dr. Rick MURRAY
05 VP of Academic Programs/Dean .... Dr. Margaret K. TIVEY
43 VP Bus & Legal Affs/Gen Counsel .... Mr. Christopher LAND
10 VP of Operations/CFO .... Ms. Kathryn LINK
18 VP Marine Facilities/Operations .... Mr. Robert MUNIER
30 Chief Development Officer .... Mr. Court CLAYTON
20 Associate Dean of Academic Programs .... Dr. Ann TARRANT
06 Registrar/Grad Administrator .... Ms. Meredith BITTRICH
08 Library Director .... Ms. Lisa RAYMOND
100 Sr Advisor to the President .... Mr. Colin REED
13 Sr Dir Information Services .... Mr. Keith GLAVIN
15 Chief Human Resources Officer .... Ms. Kathi BENJAMIN
25 Dir Grants and Contracts .... Ms. Jennifer CROCKETT
26 Chief Communications Officer .... Ms. Danielle FINO
86 Director Government Relations .... Mr. Peter HILL

Worcester Polytechnic Institute (C)

100 Institute Road, Worcester MA 01609-2280
County: Worcester
FICE Identification: 002233
Unit ID: 168421
Telephone: (508) 831-5000
Carnegie Class: DU-Higher
FAX Number: (508) 831-5753
Calendar System: Semester
URL: www.wpi.edu
Established: 1865
Annual Undergrad Tuition & Fees: $54,416
Enrollment: 6,920
Coed
Affiliation or Control: Independent Non-Profit
IRS Status: 501(c)3
Highest Offering: Doctorate
Accreditation: EH

01 Interim President .... Dr. Winston OLUWOLE SOBOYEJO
05 Interim Provost/SVP .... Dr. Art HEINRICHER
10 Executive Vice President & CFO .... Mr. Jeffrey S. SOLOMON
84 Senior Vice President Enrollment .... Ms. Kristin R. TICHENOR
111 VP for University Advancement .... Ms. Donna K. STOCK
26 VP/Chief Marketing Officer .... Ms. Maureen DEIANA
13 VP Information Technology/CIO .... Ms. Patricia L. PATRIA
18 Asst Vice President for Facilities .... Mr. Eric L. BEATTIE
15 VP Talent/Chief Diversity Ofcr .... Ms. Alicia MILLS
20 AVP Academic Affairs .... Mr. Kristopher SULLIVAN
32 Sr VP of Student Affairs .... Mr. Philip N. CLAY
43 SVP/General Counsel .... Mr. David BUNIS
36 Exec Director Career Devel Center .... Mr. Stefan KOPPI
100 Assoc VP/Chief of Staff .... Mr. Kyle SIEGEL
35 Asst VP & Dean of Students .... Mr. Greg SNODDY
07 Exec Director of Admissions .... Ms. Jennifer A. CLUETT
06 University Registrar .... Ms. Sarah L. MILES
27 AVP Public Relations .... Ms. Eileen BRANGAN MELL
96 Director of Procurement Services .... Ms. Laurie COLELLA
21 University Controller .... Mr. Patrick HITCHCOCK
21 Assoc VP of Finance .... Ms. Mary CALARESE
38 Assoc Dean/Dir Counseling/SDCC .... Mr. Charles C. MORSE
88 Associate Director LSBC .... Mr. Andrew BUTLER
37 Dir Student Aid/Financial Literacy .... Ms. Jessica SABOURIN
19 Dir Public Safety/Chief WPI Police .... Chief Cheryl A. MARTUNAS
28 Dir Diversity/Inclusive Excellence .... Mr. Rame HANNA
29 Asst VP Lifetime Engagement .... Ms. Monica ELLIS
122 Asc Dir Stdnt Activities-Greek Life .... Ms. Christine ZIEV

MICHIGAN

Adrian College (D)

110 S Madison Street, Adrian MI 49221-2575
County: Lenawee
FICE Identification: 002234
Unit ID: 168528
Telephone: (517) 265-5161
Carnegie Class: Bac-Diverse
FAX Number: (517) 264-3331
Calendar System: Semester
URL: www.adrian.edu
Established: 1859
Annual Undergrad Tuition & Fees: $38,730
Enrollment: 1,865
Coed
Affiliation or Control: United Methodist
IRS Status: 501(c)3
Highest Offering: Master's
Accreditation: HLC, CAATE, CAEP, SW

01 President .... Dr. Jeffrey R. DOCKING
05 Vice Pres/Dean for Academic Affairs .... Dr. Andrea MILNER
111 Vice Pres Institutional Advancement .... Mr. James MAHONY
84 Vice President of Enrollment .... Mr. Frank J. HRIBAR
10 Vice Pres Business Affairs/CFO .... Mr. Jerry WRIGHT
32 Dean of Student Affairs .... Mrs. Melinda SCHWYN
20 Asst Dean of Academic Affairs .... Dr. Katie RASMUSSEN
30 Director of Development .... Vacant
42 Chaplain/Director Church Relations .... Vacant
06 Registrar .... Ms. Kristina SCHWEIKERT
86 Dir of Govt & Foundation Relations .... Vacant
15 Director of Human Resources .... Ms. Christina CORSON
40 Bookstore Manager .... Ms. Rachelle M. DUFFY
93 The Inst of Cross Cultural Studies .... Dr. David GOLDBERG
29 Director Alumni Relations .... Ms. Jennifer CARLSON
41 Director of Athletics .... Mr. Michael DUFFY
19 Director of Campus Safety .... Mr. Wade BIETELCHIES
36 Director of Career Planning .... Mrs. Janna D'AMICO
88 Director of Conferences .... Ms. DeAnne LEWIN
38 Director of Counseling .... Ms. Kellie BERGER
08 Head Librarian .... Mr. David CRUSE
23 Director of Health Center .... Dr. Emily KIST
96 Director of Purchasing .... Ms. Donna WARD
37 Director of Financial Aid .... Ms. Lori KOSARUE
18 Director of Facilities .... Mr. Chris STIVER
09 Director of Institutional Research .... Ms. Beth L. HEISS
88 Director of Academic Services .... Mr. Stephen MITCHELL
100 Chief of Staff President's Office .... Mrs. Andrea SAYLOR

Albion College (E)

611 E Porter Street, Albion MI 49224-1831
County: Calhoun
FICE Identification: 002235
Unit ID: 168546
Telephone: (517) 629-1000
Carnegie Class: Bac-A&S
FAX Number: (517) 629-0509
Calendar System: Semester
URL: www.albion.edu
Established: 1835
Annual Undergrad Tuition & Fees: $50,775
Enrollment: 1,506
Coed
Affiliation or Control: United Methodist
IRS Status: 501(c)3
Highest Offering: Baccalaureate
Accreditation: HLC, CAEPT, MUS

01 Interim President .... Mr. Joe CALVARUSO
05 Provost .... Dr. Ron MOURAD
32 Vice Pres & Dean Student Affairs .... Mr. Leroy WRIGHT
84 Vice Pres of Enrollment .... Ms. Jamie KRUEGER
13 Assoc Vice Pres Info Svcs/CIO .... Ms. Robin MOHLER
07 Director of Admissions .... Ms. Mandy DUBIEL
39 Director Residential Life .... Mr. Marcus DAWSON
08 Director of Libraries .... Dr. Michael VAN HOUTEN
38 Director of Counseling .... Dr. Frank KELEMEN
37 Director of Financial Aid .... Mr. Trevor L. MARKOVICH
06 Registrar .... Dr. Andrew M. DUNHAM
109 Director Dining & Hospitality Svcs .... Mrs. Pat MILLER
18 Director of Facilities Operations .... Mr. Doug LADITKA
19 Director of Campus Safety .... Mr. Kenneth SNYDER
41 Athletic Director .... Mr. Matthew AREND
42 College Chaplain .... Rev. Donald PHILLIPS
15 Director of Human Resources .... Mrs. Lisa LOCKE
09 Director of Institutional Research .... Dr. Andrew DUNHAM
96 Director of Purchasing .... Mrs. Susan CLARK
20 Associate Academic Officer .... Vacant
28 Assoc Director Multicultural Affs .... Ms. Keena WILLIAMS
40 Manager of Bookstore .... Mr. Todd SHAYLER

Alma College (F)

614 W Superior Street, Alma MI 48801-1599
County: Gratiot
FICE Identification: 002236
Unit ID: 168591
Telephone: (989) 463-7111
Carnegie Class: Bac-Diverse
FAX Number: (989) 463-7277
Calendar System: Other
URL: www.alma.edu
Established: 1886
Annual Undergrad Tuition & Fees: $42,622
Enrollment: 1,435
Coed
Affiliation or Control: Independent Non-Profit
IRS Status: 501(c)3
Highest Offering: Master's
Accreditation: HLC, CAEP, MUS, NURSE

01 President .... Dr. Jeff ABERNATHY
05 Interim Provost .... Dr. Janie DIELS
11 SVP Admin/Chief Operating Officer .... Dr. Raymond BARCLAY
111 Vice President for Advancement .... Mr. Scott WILLS
07 Vice President for Admissions .... Vacant
32 Vice President for Student Affairs .... Mr. Damon BROWN
10 VP/Chief Financial Officer .... Mr. James CARMAN
04 Executive Asst to the President .... Mrs. Kelly MASLEY
06 Registrar .... Ms. Mariah ORZOLEK
20 Assistant Provost .... Ms. Susan M. DEEL
42 Senior Chaplain .... Rev Dr. Andrew POMERVILLE
37 Director of Financial Assistance .... Ms. Michelle MCNIER
08 Director of Library .... Mr. Matthew COLLINS
26 Associate VP of Marketing .... Ms. Melinda BOOTH
13 Chief Information Officer .... Mr. Kyle WARNER
18 Director Facilities & Service Mgmt .... Mr. Ryan STOUDT
15 Associate VP for Human Resources .... Vacant
21 Controller/Director of Auxil Svcs .... Ms. Cassie TENNANT
36 Director of Career/Personal Dev .... Ms. Carla JENSEN
35 Director of Student Engagement .... Mr. David K. BLANDFORD
38 Assoc VP for Counseling & Wellness .... Ms. Anne K. LAMBRECHT
09 Director for Institutional Research .... Mr. John MACARTHUR
41 Athletic Director .... Ms. Sarah DEHRING
29 Dir Alumni & Family Engagement .... Ms. Katie CROMBE
39 Director Resident Life .... Ms. Alice KRAMER

Alpena Community College (G)

665 Johnson Street, Alpena MI 49707-1495
County: Alpena
FICE Identification: 002237
Unit ID: 168607
Telephone: (989) 356-9021
Carnegie Class: Bac/Assoc-Assoc Dom
FAX Number: (989) 358-7553
Calendar System: Semester
URL: www.alpenacc.edu
Established: 1952
Annual Undergrad Tuition & Fees (In-District): $7,110
Enrollment: 1,436
Coed
Affiliation or Control: Local
IRS Status: 501(c)3
Highest Offering: Baccalaureate
Accreditation: HLC, ADNUR, PNUR

01 President .... Dr. Donald MACMASTER
05 Vice Pres of Instruction .... Mr. Steven FOSGARD
10 Vice Pres Administration/Finance .... Mr. Richard SUTHERLAND
32 Dean of Students .... Ms. Nancy SEGUIN
21 Controller .... Ms. Lyn KOWALEWSKY
20 Dean Learning Resource Center .... Ms. Wendy BROOKS
25 Director of TAACCT Grants .... Ms. Dawn STONE
13 Co-Director Mgmt Info Systems .... Vacant
13 Co-Director Mgmt Info Systems .... Mr. Mark GRUNDER
26 Dir Public Information/Marketing .... Mr. Jay WALTERREIT
40 Director of ACC Bookstore .... Mr. William MATZKE
102 Exec Dir Devel/ACC Foundation .... Ms. Brenda HERMAN
18 Director of Facilities Management .... Mr. Nicholas BREGE
06 Registrar .... Ms. Sheila RUPP
15 Director Human Resources .... Ms. Carolyn DAOUST
07 Director of Admissions .... Mr. Mike KOLLIEN
37 Director Financial Aid .... Mr. Robert ROOSE
35 Director Student Life Activities .... Ms. Cynthia DEROCHER

Andrews University (H)

8975 U.S. 31, Berrien Springs MI 49104-0001
County: Berrien
FICE Identification: 002238
Unit ID: 168740
Telephone: (269) 471-7771
Carnegie Class: DU-Mod
FAX Number: (269) 471-6900
Calendar System: Semester
URL: www.andrews.edu
Established: 1874
Annual Undergrad Tuition & Fees: $31,008
Enrollment: 3,162
Coed
Affiliation or Control: Seventh-day Adventist
IRS Status: 501(c)3
Highest Offering: Doctorate
Accreditation: HLC, CACREP, CAEP, COPSY, DIETD, DIETI, IACBE, MLS, MUS, NUR, PH, PTA, SP, SW, THEOL

01 President .... Dr. Andrea T. LUXTON
04 Senior Executive Asst to President .... Ms. Dalry B. PAYNE
05 Provost .... Dr. Christon ARTHUR
108 Assistant Provost Inst Assessment .... Dr. Anneris CORIA-NAVIA
10 Vice Pres Financial Admin .... Mr. Glenn MEEKMA
21 Asst VP Financial Admin .... Ms. Valencia MAWUNTU
37 Asst Vice Pres Stdt Financial Svcs .... Ms. Elynda A. BEDNEY
32 Vice Pres Student & Campus Life .... Dr. Frances M. FAEHNER
27 Spec Asst to Pres Univ/Public Affs .... Mr. Stephen D. PAYNE

88 Asst to President Strategic Affairs ....Mr. Kevin BROWN
26 Vice Pres Strategy/Mktg & Enroll ....Mr. Tony YANG
111 Vice President for Advancement ....Dr. Donald A. BEDNEY
28 VP University Culture & Inclusion ....Mr. Michael T. NIXON
43 General Counsel ....Ms. Gwendolyn POWELL BRASWELL
06 Registrar ....Ms. Aimee VITANGCOL REGOSO
49 Dean Col of Arts/Sciences/UG Educ ....Dr. Amy ROSENTHAL
76 Dean College of Health & Human Svcs ....Dr. Emmanuel RUDATSIKIRA
107 Dean College of Professions ....Dr. Kimberly PICHOT
73 Dean of Theological Seminary ....Dr. Jiri MOSKALA
58 Dean Graduate Studies ....Dr. Alayne THORPE
106 Dean Col of Education/Intl Svcs ....Dr. Alayne THORPE
08 Dean of Libraries ....Ms. Paulette M. JOHNSON
46 Dean of Research ....Dr. Gary BURDICK
13 Chief Information Officer ....Ms. Debra HINTZ
15 Associate VP Human Resources ....Mr. Darcy L. DE LEON
39 Dir of University Apartment Life ....Mr. Alfredo RUIZ
39 Dir of Residence Life ....Ms. Jennifer R. BURRILL
42 University Chaplain ....Mr. Jose BOURGET
85 Exec Dir Intl Student Services ....Dr. Christian STUART
92 Director of Honors Program ....Dr. L. Monique PITTMAN
38 Dir of Counseling/Testing Center ....Dr. Judith FISHER
123 Director of Graduate Admissions ....Ms. Jillian PANIGOT
07 Exec Dir UG Recruitment/Admissions ....Ms. Wendy KEOUGH
88 Dir of Bridge to Success Program ....Mr. Randy K. GRAVES
29 Director of Alumni Services ....Ms. Laura MALCOLM
19 Director of Campus Safety ....Mr. Benjamin PANIGOT
23 Director of Medical Services ....Dr. Lowell HAMEL
44 Director of Planned Giving ....Ms. Tari POPP
09 Director Institutional Research ....Dr. Sally NORTON
18 Director of Facilities Management ....Mr. Steve NASH
105 Manager of Web Communications ....Mr. Jason STRACK
88 Chair Intl Lang & Global Studies ....Dr. Pedro NAVIA
41 Director of Athletics ....Mr. Rob GETTYS
40 Manager of Bookstore ....Ms. Cynthia SWANSON

Aquinas College (A)

1700 Fulton St. E, Grand Rapids MI 49506-1799
County: Kent FICE Identification: 002239
Unit ID: 168786
Telephone: (616) 632-8900 Carnegie Class: Bac-A&S
FAX Number: (616) 732-4469 Calendar System: Semester
URL: www.aquinas.edu
Established: 1886 Annual Undergrad Tuition & Fees: $35,086
Enrollment: 1,517 Coed
Affiliation or Control: Roman Catholic IRS Status: 501(c)3
Highest Offering: Master's
Accreditation: HLC, CAEP

01 President ....Dr. Kevin G. QUINN
05 Provost/Dean of Faculty ....Dr. Stephen GERMIC
102 Vice Pres Foundation ....Ms. Gina COVERT
10 Vice Pres/Chief Financial Officer ....Ms. Lisa VANDEWEERT
84 Vice President Enrollment ....Ms. Erin CRAIG
04 Chief Exec Assistant to President ....Ms. Mary VARGAS
26 Assoc VP Marketing & Communication ....Ms. Marissa SURA
32 Assoc VP for Student Success ....Mr. Brian MATZKE
21 Controller ....Ms. Melisssa SNYDER
09 Dean of Institutional Effectiveness ....Vacant
53 Dean of School of Education ....Dr. Susan ENGLISH
06 Registrar ....Ms. Elizabeth FLORES
15 Director of Human Resources ....Ms. Lynda GROUP
38 Dir of Career & Counseling Services ....Ms. Sharon E. SMITH
51 Director of Continuing Education ....Vacant
104 Assoc Dir International Educ Pgms ....Mr. Tim RAMSAY
94 Director of Women's Studies ....Ms. Amy DUNHAM STRAND
92 Director of Honors Program ....Dr. Michelle DEROSE
58 Int Director of Graduate Management ....Dr. Linda HAGAN
18 Director of Maintenance ....Mr. Dale HAISMA
39 Dir Housing/Residence Life Exp ....Mr. David DURKEE
07 Director of Admissions ....Vacant
37 Director of Financial Aid ....Ms. Darcy KAMPFSCHULTE
35 Assoc VP for Student Affairs ....Mr. Nick DAVIDSON
42 Director Campus Ministry ....Vacant
13 Dir Information Technology & Svcs ....Vacant
29 Director of Alumni Engagement ....Ms. Alexa CAREY
35 Dir Student Leadership & Engagement ....Vacant
112 Senior Director of Philanthropy ....Ms. Mary SLAFKOSKY
36 Director of Career Services ....Dr. Dana HEBREARD
28 Director of Diversity & Inclusion ....Ms. Alicia LLOYD
40 Director Bookstore ....Ms. Heather THOMPSON
08 Library Director ....Ms. Shellie JEFFRIE
42 Campus Chaplain ....Rev. Stanley DRONGOWSKI, OP

*Baker Professional Services, Inc. (B)

1020 S. Washington St, Owosso MI 48867
County: Shiawassee Identification: 666923
Unit ID: 419572
Telephone: (989) 729-3350 Carnegie Class: N/A
FAX Number: (810) 766-2102
URL: www.baker.edu

01 Chief Executive Officer ....Bart DAIG
05 Chief Academic Officer ....Jill LANGEN
11 Chief Operating Officer ....Jacqueline SPICER
15 Chief Human Resources Officer ....Dana CLARK

*Baker College of Auburn Hills (C)

1500 University Drive, Auburn Hills MI 48326-2642
Telephone: (248) 276-8240 Identification: 666940
Accreditation: &HLC, CSHSE, IACBE, PTAA

*Baker College of Cadillac (D)

9600 E 13th Street, Cadillac MI 49601-9169
Telephone: (231) 876-3107 Identification: 666941
Accreditation: &HLC, CSHSE, IACBE, MAC, SURGT

*Baker College of Jackson (E)

2800 Springport Road, Jackson MI 49202-1299
Telephone: (517) 841-4528 FICE Identification: 004680
Accreditation: &HLC, CSHSE, IACBE, RTT

*Baker College of Muskegon (F)

1903 Marquette Avenue, Muskegon MI 49442-3404
Telephone: (231) 777-5248 FICE Identification: 002296
Accreditation: &HLC, ACFEI, CSHSE, IACBE, OTA, PTAA, RAD, SURGT

*Baker College of Owosso (G)

1020 South Washington, Owosso MI 48867-4400
County: Shiawassee FICE Identification: 004673
Unit ID: 168838
Telephone: (989) 729-3431 Carnegie Class: Masters/M
FAX Number: (989) 729-3441 Calendar System: Semester
URL: www.baker.edu
Established: 1983 Annual Undergrad Tuition & Fees: N/A
Enrollment: N/A Coed
Affiliation or Control: Independent Non-Profit IRS Status: 501(c)3
Highest Offering: Baccalaureate
Accreditation: HLC, ACFEI, CAEP, CAHIIM, CSHSE, DMS, IACBE, NAEYC, NURSE, OTA, PTAA, RAD

12 Campus Director ....Stavroula ERFOURTH
11 Chief Operating Officer ....Jacqueline SPICER

Bay College West Campus (H)

2801 N US 2, Iron Mountain MI 49801
Telephone: (906) 302-3000 Identification: 770262
Accreditation: &HLC

Bay Mills Community College (I)

12214 W Lakeshore Drive, Brimley MI 49715-9750
County: Chippewa FICE Identification: 030666
Unit ID: 380359
Telephone: (906) 248-3354 Carnegie Class: Tribal
FAX Number: (906) 248-3351 Calendar System: Semester
URL: www.bmcc.edu
Established: 1984 Annual Undergrad Tuition & Fees: $3,320
Enrollment: 438 Coed
Affiliation or Control: Tribal Control IRS Status: 501(c)3
Highest Offering: Baccalaureate
Accreditation: HLC

01 President ....Duane BEDELL
05 Vice President of Academic Affairs ....Samantha CAMERON
10 Vice Pres Business & Finance ....Laura POSTMA
32 Vice President of Student Affairs ....Wendy HEYRMAN
13 Chief Information Officer ....Chet KASPER
06 Registrar/Inst Info Systems Mgr ....Sherri SCHOFIELD
37 Director Student Financial Aid ....Tina MILLER
07 Director of Admissions ....Elaine LEHRE
25 Land Grant Dir/Accred Liaison Ofcr ....Stephen YANNI
30 Director of Development ....Kathy ADAIR
08 Library Director ....Megan CLARKE
15 Human Resources Director ....Stacey WALDEN
04 Exec Assistant to the President ....Samantha SCHROEDER

Bay de Noc Community College (J)

2001 N Lincoln Road, Escanaba MI 49829-2510
County: Delta FICE Identification: 002240
Unit ID: 168883
Telephone: (906) 786-5802 Carnegie Class: Assoc/MT-VT-Mix Trad/Non
FAX Number: (906) 789-6952 Calendar System: Semester
URL: www.baycollege.edu
Established: 1962 Annual Undergrad Tuition & Fees (In-District): $8,520
Enrollment: 1,898 Coed
Affiliation or Control: Local IRS Status: 501(c)3
Highest Offering: Associate Degree
Accreditation: HLC, ADNUR, EMT, MAC, NAEYC

01 President ....Dr. Laura COLEMAN
11 VP of Operations ....Ms. Eileen SPARPANA
10 VP of Finance ....Ms. Eileen SPARPANA
111 VP of College Advancement ....Ms. Kim CARNE
32 VP of Student Services ....Mr. Travis BLUME
49 VP of Arts & Sciences and DEB ....Dr. Amy REDDINGER
103 VP Business/Tech/Allied Health/WD ....Ms. Cindy CARTER
50 Dean Business &Technology ....Mr. Mark HIGHUM
37 Director of Financial Aid ....Ms. Ruth CARLSON
07 Director of Admissions ....Ms. Jessica LAMARCH
15 Director of Human Resources ....Ms. Beth BERUBE
18 Facilities Manager ....Mr. Steve CARLSON
76 Dean of Allied Health ....Mr. Mitchell CAMPBELL
49 Dean of Arts & Sciences ....Dr. Jessica VAN SLOOTEN

32 Director of Student Life ....Mr. Dave LAUR
04 Exec Admin Asst to President ....Mrs. Laura JOHNSON
06 Registrar ....Ms. Rebecca LANDENBERGER
106 Exec Director of Online Learning ....Mr. Joseph MOLD
19 Campus Security Clery Officer ....Mr. Marc MAYCUNICH
41 Athletic Director ....Mr. Matt JOHNSON
09 Director of Institutional Research ....Ms. Penny PAVLAT
08 Chief Library Officer ....Ms. Mariel CARTER
101 Secretary of the Institution/Board ....Mrs. Laura JOHNSON
13 Chief Information Technology Ofcr ....Mr. Justin IZZARD
28 Director of Diversity ....Dr. Amy REDDINGER

Calvin Theological Seminary (K)

3233 Burton Street, SE, Grand Rapids MI 49546-4387
County: Kent FICE Identification: 002242
Unit ID: 169099
Telephone: (616) 957-6036 Carnegie Class: Spec-4-yr-Faith
FAX Number: (616) 957-8621 Calendar System: Semester
URL: www.calvinseminary.edu
Established: 1876 Annual Graduate Tuition & Fees: N/A
Enrollment: 245 Coed
Affiliation or Control: Christian Reformed Church IRS Status: 501(c)3
Highest Offering: Doctorate; No Undergraduates
Accreditation: THEOL

01 President ....Rev. Julius T. MEDENBLIK
05 Dean of Faculty ....Dr. David RYLAARSDAM
20 Assoc Dean of Academic Programs ....Ms. Joan BEELEN
11 Chief of Operations/Administration ....Dr. Margaret MWENDA
06 Registrar ....Ms. Joan BEELEN
32 Dean of Students ....Rev. Jeff SAJDAK
08 Theological Librarian ....Vacant
10 Director of Finance ....Mr. Chris DINH
30 Director of Development ....Mr. Robert KNOOR
36 Director of Vocational Ministry ....Rev. Geoff VANDERMOLEN
26 Communications Director ....Ms. Annie MAS-SMITH
37 Director of Financial Aid ....Mrs. Jennifer SETTERGREN
15 Director of Human Resources ....Ms. Karen DE YOUNG

Calvin University (L)

3201 Burton Street, SE, Grand Rapids MI 49546-4388
County: Kent FICE Identification: 002241
Unit ID: 169080
Telephone: (616) 526-6000 Carnegie Class: Masters/S
FAX Number: (616) 526-8551 Calendar System: Trimester
URL: www.calvin.edu
Established: 1876 Annual Undergrad Tuition & Fees: $37,806
Enrollment: 3,307 Coed
Affiliation or Control: Christian Reformed Church IRS Status: 501(c)3
Highest Offering: Master's
Accreditation: HLC, CAEP, NURSE, SP, SW

01 President ....Dr. Wiebe K. BOER
05 Provost ....Dr. Noah TOLY
10 Vice President for Admin/Finance ....Mr. Timothy G. FENNEMA
111 Vice President for Advancement ....Mr. Gregory J. ELZINGA
84 Vice Pres Enrollment Strategy ....Mrs. Lauren J. JENSEN
32 Vice President Student Life ....Dr. Sarah VISSER
13 Assoc Vice President for IT & CIO ....Mr. Brian PAIGE
20 Associate Provost ....Dr. Kevin DEN DULK
28 Exec Assoc for Diversity/Inclusion ....Dr. Michelle LOYD-PAIGE
42 College Chaplain ....Dr. Mary HULST
15 Director of Human Resources ....Mr. Andrew L. GEORGE
08 Dean of the Library ....Mr. David MALONE
29 Dir of Alumni Engagement ....Mr. Jeff HAVERDINK
06 Director Academic Svcs/Registrar ....Mr. Thomas L. STEENWYK
35 Dean of Students ....Mr. John WITTE
88 Assoc Dean Campus Involve/Ldrshp ....Mr. JB BRITTON
22 Dir of Safer Spaces/Title IX Coord .....Ms. Jane E. HENDRIKSMA
20 Dean of Faculty Development ....Dr. David WUNDER
20 Dean of Academic Administration ....Dr. Laura DEHAAN
83 Acad Dean Lang/Soc Sci/Context Disc ....Dr. Bernita WOLTERS-FREDLUND
81 Acad Dean Educ/Kinesio/Nat Sci/Math ....Dr. Arlene HOOGEWERF
36 Director of Career Development ....Ms. Courtney BANKS
108 Mgr Inst Effectiveness & Analytics ....Mrs. Lauren AMICK
89 Dir Retention/1st Year Initiatives ....Mr. Todd DORNBOS
26 Dir Communications & Brand Steward ......Mr. Timothy L. ELLENS
19 Director of Campus Safety ....Mr. William T. CORNER
18 Dir of Facilities Planning & Sus ....Mr. Nicholas THOMPSON
24 Dir Instructional Resources Ctr ....Vacant
38 Director Counseling and Well Center ....Dr. Irene KRAEGEL
23 Director Health Services ....Dr. Laura CHAMPION
92 Director Honors Program ....Dr. Amy WILSTERMANN
41 Athletic Director ....Dr. James TIMMER, JR.
30 Director of Development ....Ms. Jodi COLE
104 Director Study Abroad ....Dr. Cynthia SLAGTER
105 Web Developer & Mgr of Web R&D ....Mr. Luke ROBINSON
37 Director of Financial Aid ....Mr. James KOEMAN
44 Director Annual Fund ....Ms. Melanie N. LYONS
53 Dean for Education ....Dr. Brian BOLT
07 Director of Undergraduate Admission .....Ms. Melissa ROUSSEAU
101 Exec Asst to Pres/Sec to BOT ....Ms. Sharolyn J. CHRISTIANS
25 Dir of Grants & Sponsored Research ....Ms. Beth DYKSTRA
39 Dir of University Housing ....Mr. Jay WISE
50 Dean of School of Business ....Dr. James LUDEMA

Central Michigan University (M)

1200 S. Franklin Street, Mount Pleasant MI 48859
County: Isabella FICE Identification: 002243
Unit ID: 169248

Telephone: (989) 774-4000 Carnegie Class: DU-Higher
FAX Number: N/A Calendar System: Semester
URL: www.cmich.edu
Established: 1892 Annual Undergrad Tuition & Fees (In-State): $12,960
Enrollment: 17,311 Coed
Affiliation or Control: State IRS Status: 501(c)3
Highest Offering: Doctorate
Accreditation: HLC, ART, ARCPA, AUD, CAATE, CACREP, CAEP, CAPRT, CEA, CIDA, CLPSY, COSMA, DIETD, DIETI, EXSC, #JOUR, MED, MUS, NAEYC, NURSE, PTA, SCPSY, SP, SPAA, SW

01 President ...... Dr. Robert O. DAVIES
05 Interim Executive VP/Provost ...... Dr. Richard M. ROTHAUS
20 Int Sr Vice Provost Acad Affairs ...... Dr. Dave K. PATTON
10 Vice Pres Finance/Admin Svcs ...... Mr. Nicholas K. LONG
86 Assoc Vice Pres Govt/Ext Relations ...... Mr. Toby ROTH, JR.
84 VP Student Recruitment & Retention ...... Ms. Jennifer E. DEHAEMERS
30 Exec Director Development ...... Ms. Jennifer M. COTTER
13 Vice President Info Technology/CIO ...... Mr. Jim BUJAKI
21 AVP Fin Svcs & Reporting/Controller ...... Ms. Mary M. HILL
26 VP Univ Comm & Chief Mktg Officer ...... Mr. John M. VEILLEUX
18 Assoc VP Facilities Management ...... Mr. Jonathan D. WEBB
109 Exec Dir Auxiliary Services ...... Mr. Calvin H. SEELYE, II
39 Exec Dir Res Life/Ldrshp & Pub Svcs ...... Ms. Kathleen GARDNER
88 Asst VP Univ Recr/Student Engage ...... Mr. Stan L. SHINGLES
15 Assoc VP Human Resources ...... Ms. Lori L. HELLA
20 Sr Vice Provost Academic Admin ...... Dr. Ray L. CHRISTIE
46 VP Research & Innovation/Grad Stds ...... Dr. David C. WEINDORF
30 Dir Stewardship & Donor Rels/Advan ...... Ms. Kelly M. BERRYHILL
08 Dean University Libraries ...... Dr. Kathy M. IRWIN
32 Int Assoc VP Student Affairs ...... Mr. Shaun HOLTGREIVE
29 Exec Dir Alumni Rels & Adv Engage ...... Ms. Marcie M. OTTEMAN
09 Exec Dir Academic Planning/Analysis ...... Dr. Robert M. ROE
22 Int Ex Dir Civil Rights/Inst Equity ...... Ms. Mary A. MARTINEZ
07 Exec Director Admissions ...... Vacant
43 Sr Assoc Dean Legal Affairs/CMED ...... Dr. Manuel R. RUPE
06 Registrar ...... Mr. Keith J. MALKOWSKI
37 Director Scholarships/Financial Aid ...... Vacant
36 Director Career Development Center ...... Mr. Robert K. VANDORIN
38 Exec Dir of Counseling Services ...... Ms. Melissa M. HUTCHINSON
114 Exec Dir Financial Plng & Budgets ...... Mr. Joseph L. GARRISON
27 Exec Director Communications ...... Ms. Ari HARRIS
19 Chief of Police ...... Mr. Larry S. KLAUS
40 Director CMU Bookstore ...... Mr. Barry D. WATERS
81 Interim Dean College Sci & Engr ...... Dr. David M. FORD
76 Dean College of Health Professions ...... Dr. Thomas J. MASTERSON, JR.
63 VP Health Aff/Dean College Medicine ...... Dr. George E. KIKANO
49 Interim Dean Liberal Arts & Soc Sci ...... Dr. Marcia M. TAYLOR
57 Interim Dean College Arts & Media ...... Dr. Elizabeth A. KIRBY
50 Dean Business Admin ...... Dr. Christopher R. MOBERG
53 Dean Education & Human Svcs ...... Dr. Paula E. LANCASTER
100 Chief of Staff to President ...... Ms. Mary Jane FLANAGAN
96 Dir Contract & Purchasing Svcs ...... Ms. Anne R. THRUSH
92 Director Honors Program ...... Ms. Nicole S. BARCO
104 Director Study Abroad ...... Ms. Dianne S. DESALVO
116 Director Internal Audit ...... Ms. Beth J. TIMMERMAN
44 Director of Annual Giving ...... Mr. Bryan L. GRIFFIN
115 Asst Controller Financial Services ...... Ms. Kimberly A. WAGESTER
88 Asst Controller Financial Reporting ...... Ms. Julia H. MONTROSS
117 Dir/Risk Mgmt Env Health & Safety ...... Mr. Benjamin S. COFFMAN
121 Exec Dir Student Success & Acad Adv ...... Dr. Evan L. MONTAGUE
41 Assoc VP/Dir Athletics ...... Ms. Amy G. FOLAN
111 Dir Advancement Operations & Budget ...... Ms. Kasie L. NATZEL

Chamberlain University-Troy (A)

200 Kirts Boulevard, Suite C, Troy MI 48084
Telephone: (248) 817-4140 Identification: 770851
Accreditation: &HLC, NURSE

† Branch campus of Chamberlain University-Addison, Addison, IL

Cleary University (B)

3750 Cleary Drive, Howell MI 48843
County: Livingston FICE Identification: 002246
Unit ID: 169327
Telephone: (800) 686-1883 Carnegie Class: Spec-4-yr-Bus
FAX Number: N/A Calendar System: Semester
URL: www.cleary.edu
Established: 1883 Annual Undergrad Tuition & Fees: $22,230
Enrollment: 658 Coed
Affiliation or Control: Independent Non-Profit IRS Status: 501(c)3
Highest Offering: Master's
Accreditation: HLC

01 President ...... Dr. Alan DRIMMER
05 Provost & Chief Acad Officer ...... Ms. Emily BARNES
10 VP of Finance ...... Ms. Shelly HOLANDA
111 SVP Institutional Advancement ...... Dr. Matt BENNETT
109 VP Auxiliary Services ...... Mr. Jeffrey BANE
04 Exec Director Ofc of the President ...... Ms. Grace R. FARLAY
21 Controller ...... Ms. Megan TEMBY
09 Institutional Research Analyst ...... Mr. Omar HABAYEB
37 Sr Financial Aid Coord ...... Ms. Brandy AKERS
84 VP Enrollment Management ...... Vacant
88 Academic Support Assoc ...... Ms. Deb SOUTHERLAND
36 Director of Career Development ...... Ms. Amy DENTON
41 Athletic Director ...... Ms. Heather BATEMAN
15 Human Resources Manager ...... Ms. Sandra HAYES
08 Instructional Librarian ...... Ms. Jane SCALES
18 Facilities Manager ...... Mr. George HORN
32 VP/Dean of Student Affairs ...... Ms. Heather BATEMAN
06 Registrar ...... Vacant
13 Executive Director of Technology ...... Mr. Max GROMAKOV
35 Associate Dean of Students ...... Mr. Matthew OLIVER
106 Instructional Design Manager ...... Ms. Kirsten SHEPARD
20 Dean of Academic Operations ...... Dr. Sara BARNWELL
97 Dean of Undergraduate Studies ...... Mr. David HAYES
58 Dean of Graduate Studies ...... Dr. Regina BANKS-HALL

College for Creative Studies (C)

201 East Kirby Street, Detroit MI 48202-4034
County: Wayne FICE Identification: 006771
Unit ID: 169442
Telephone: (313) 664-7400 Carnegie Class: Spec-4-yr-Arts
FAX Number: (313) 872-8377 Calendar System: Semester
URL: www.collegeforcreativestudies.edu
Established: 1906 Annual Undergrad Tuition & Fees: $47,585
Enrollment: 1,512 Coed
Affiliation or Control: Independent Non-Profit IRS Status: 501(c)3
Highest Offering: Master's
Accreditation: HLC, ART, CIDA

01 President ...... Dr. Donald L. TUSKI
04 Exec Asst to Pres/Asst Sec to Board ...... Ms. Sandra WILSON
11 Chief of Operations/ Administration ...... Ms. Aletha D. JORDAN-WILLIAMS
10 Vice Pres Finance ...... Ms. Kerri MCKAY
84 Vice Pres Enrollment & Student Svcs ...... Ms. Julie HINGELBERG
111 Vice Pres Institutional Advancement ...... Ms. Tracy MUSCAT
26 Vice Pres Strategy & Communication ...... Ms. Olga STELLA
28 Chief Diversity Officer/Asst Dean ...... Dr. Deirdre YOUNG
58 Dean Graduate Studies ...... Mr. Ian LAMBERT
97 Dean Undergraduate Studies ...... Mr. Tim FLATTERY
05 Dean of Academic Affairs ...... Ms. Nadine ASHTON
106 Exec Dir of Educational Technology ...... Mr. Ryan ANSEL
32 Dean of Students ...... Mr. Daniel LONG
123 Director Graduate Admissions ...... Mr. Anthony MICELI
07 Director Undergraduate Admissions ...... Ms. Carla GONZALEZ
37 Director Financial Aid ...... Mr. Matthew CATANESE
104 Director Study Abroad ...... Ms. Katherine CAMPBELL
06 Registrar ...... Ms. Karen LADUCER
51 Dir Continuing/Pre-College Studies ...... Ms. Jane STEWART
31 Dir of Community Arts Partnerships ...... Mr. Mikel BRESEE
08 Director Library ...... Ms. Rebecca PAD
18 Dir of Facilities & Campus Safety ...... Mr. Michael BRUGGEMAN
13 Director Information Technology ...... Mr. Greg FRASER
21 Director Business Services ...... Ms. Heather GOOD
15 Director Human Resources ...... Ms. Raquel DIROFF
110 Director Advancement Operations ...... Ms. Katie RUSAK
36 Director Career Services ...... Vacant
29 Assoc Dir Annual Giv/Alumni Rels ...... Mr. Anthony SPANGLER
38 Director Wellness & Counseling ...... Ms. Valerie WEISS
40 Manager Bookstore ...... Ms. Glen MORREN
39 Director of Residence Life ...... Mr. Ryan HARRISON
88 Exec Dir Strategic Ptnrshps/Pgms ...... Ms. Shannon MCPARTLON
27 Director of Marketing ...... Ms. Megan MESACK
44 Director of Campaigns & Major Gifts ...... Ms. Denise THOMAS
102 Dir of Foundation Relations ...... Ms. Alecia HANEY
96 Purchasing & Fixed Assets ...... Ms. Mary ROMEO TARTE

Compass College of Film and Media (D)

41 Sheldon Avenue SE, Grand Rapids MI 49503
County: Kent FICE Identification: 041633
Unit ID: 459417
Telephone: (616) 988-1000 Carnegie Class: Spec-4-yr-Arts
FAX Number: (616) 458-4676 Calendar System: Other
URL: www.compass.edu
Established: 2003 Annual Undergrad Tuition & Fees: $16,800
Enrollment: 72 Coed
Affiliation or Control: Independent Non-Profit IRS Status: 501(c)3
Highest Offering: Baccalaureate
Accreditation: ACCSC

01 President ...... Jay GREER
05 Dean of Education ...... William KAVAN
11 Vice President of Operations ...... Todd STAAL
10 Director Finance & Administration ...... Fred KOOISTRA
26 Manager of Marketing & Enrollment ...... Chuck KUHN
32 Director of Student Affairs ...... Ken BOERSMA
07 Admissions Counselor ...... Emmett BROWN
37 Financial Aid Manager ...... Lynne HEEREMA

Concordia University Ann Arbor (E)

4090 Geddes Road, Ann Arbor MI 48105-2797
Telephone: (734) 995-7300 FICE Identification: 002247
Accreditation: &HLC, #ARCPA, CAATE, CAEP

Cornerstone University (F)

1001 E Beltline Avenue, NE, Grand Rapids MI 49525-5897
County: Kent FICE Identification: 002266
Unit ID: 170037
Telephone: (616) 949-5300 Carnegie Class: Masters/L
FAX Number: (616) 222-1540 Calendar System: Semester
URL: www.cornerstone.edu
Established: 1941 Annual Undergrad Tuition & Fees: $26,250
Enrollment: 1,917 Coed
Affiliation or Control: Independent Non-Profit IRS Status: 501(c)3
Highest Offering: Doctorate
Accreditation: HLC, ACBSP, CAEP, SW, THEOL

01 President ...... Dr. Gerson MORENO-RIAÑO
03 Executive Vice President ...... Dr. Peter OSBORN
05 VP Traditional Undergrad Academics ...... Dr. Shawn NEWHOUSE
10 Chief Financial Officer ...... Mr. Scott STEWART
88 Vice President of Broadcasting ...... Vacant
32 VP of Student Development ...... Mr. Gerald LONGJOHN
111 VP of Advancement ...... Mr. Bob SACK
108 Dean of Assessment/Curriculum ...... Dr. Ryan ROBERTS
73 EVP Academic/Dean Grad Theol Stdnts ...... Dr. John VER BERKMOES
121 Assoc Dean Accr/Stdnt Success ...... Mrs. Emily GRATSON
35 Director of Student Services ...... Mr. Keith DEBOER
08 Director of Miller Library ...... Mrs. Laura WALTON
37 Director Financial Services ...... Mrs. Carol CARPENTER
21 Director of Finance and Accounting ...... Mr. Stephen POPP
41 Athletic Director ...... Mr. Aaron SAGRAVES
15 Dir Human Resources/Title IX Coord ...... Mrs. Emilie AZKOUL
19 Director of Campus Safety ...... Mr. Brandan BISHOP
29 Director of Alumni ...... Mr. Dennis GRAHAM
06 Registrar ...... Mrs. Gail DUHON
13 Dir Opers/New Media Tech ...... Mr. Dodd MORRIS
38 Director of the Counseling Center ...... Mr. Scott COUREY
92 Director of Honors Program ...... Mr. Don PERINI
84 Executive Director of Enrollment ...... Mrs. Lisa LINK
04 Administrative Asst to President ...... Ms. Samantha KENDRICK
28 Dir Diversity/Multicultural Affairs ...... Mr. Kenneth RUSSELL
18 Chf Facilities/Physical Plant Ofcr ...... Mr. Chris BYNUM
39 Dir Resident Life/ Student Housing ...... Mr. Mark MUHA

Cranbrook Academy of Art (G)

39221 Woodward Avenue, Bloomfield Hills MI 48304
County: Oakland FICE Identification: 002248
Unit ID: 169424
Telephone: (248) 645-3300 Carnegie Class: Spec-4-yr-Arts
FAX Number: (248) 645-3591 Calendar System: Semester
URL: www.cranbrookart.edu
Established: 1932 Annual Graduate Tuition & Fees: N/A
Enrollment: 126 Coed
Affiliation or Control: Independent Non-Profit IRS Status: 501(c)3
Highest Offering: Master's; No Undergraduates
Accreditation: HLC, ART

01 Interim Director ...... Rod SPEARIN
05 Interim Dean ...... Gretchen WILKINS
20 Dir Academic Programs & Library ...... Judy DYKI
30 Senior Director of Development ...... Autumn PARROTT
26 Director of Communications ...... Julie FRACKER
84 Mgr Enrollment & Financial Aid ...... Julia DELAGARZA
29 Alumni Relations & Recruitment Mgr ...... Elizabeth DIZIK
32 Dean of Student Services ...... Vanessa LUCERO-MAZEI
44 Director of Annual Giving ...... Kelly LEWIS-GUMP
04 Executive Assistant to the Director ...... Meghan LUZOD

Davenport University (H)

6191 Kraft Avenue, S.E., Grand Rapids MI 49512
County: Kent FICE Identification: 002249
Unit ID: 169479
Telephone: (616) 698-7111 Carnegie Class: Masters/L
FAX Number: N/A Calendar System: Semester
URL: www.davenport.edu
Established: 1866 Annual Undergrad Tuition & Fees: $20,260
Enrollment: 6,127 Coed
Affiliation or Control: Independent Non-Profit IRS Status: 501(c)3
Highest Offering: Master's
Accreditation: HLC, CAHIIM, COSMA, IACBE, NURSE, OT, PNUR

01 President ...... Dr. Richard J. PAPPAS
111 Exec VP Advancement ...... Ms. Rachel RENDER
46 Exec VP of Quality & Effectiveness ...... Dr. Scott EPSTEIN
15 Exec VP Human/Organizational Devel ...... Mr. Dave VENEKLASE
32 Exec VP Enrollment & Student Svcs ...... Dr. Walter O'NEILL
10 Exec Vice President for Finance/CFO ...... Mr. Michael S. VOLK
05 Exec VP Academics/Provost ...... Dr. Gilda GELY
26 EVP for Marketing/Communications ...... Ms. Deb COOPER
07 VP Admissions/Strategic Partnership ...... Mr. David LAWRENCE
09 VP for Institutional Research ...... Dr. Kathy ABOUFADEL
13 VP Information Technology/CIO ...... Mr. Ben WILLIAMS
18 VP Facilities Management ...... Mr. Damon P. GONZALES
50 Dean College of Business & Tech ...... Dr. Amy MANSFIELD
76 Dean College of Health Professions ...... Dr. Karen DALEY
49 Int Dean College of Arts/Sciences ...... Dr. Gerald G. NYAMBANE
106 Dean Global Campus ...... Mr. Brian MILLER
107 Dean College of Urban Education ...... Dr. Susan GUNN
37 Exec Dir Student Financial Services ...... Ms. Leah AALDERINK
29 Dir of Alumni & Donor Engagement ...... Ms. Whitney ENGE
21 Controller ...... Mr. Michael SLEVA
06 University Registrar ...... Mr. Christopher MARX
41 Director of Athletics ...... Mr. Paul LOWDEN
04 Administrative Asst to President ...... Ms. Lisa AMEND-TOMAS
28 Exec Dir Diversity/Equity/Inclusion ...... Ms. Latoya BOOKER
39 Exec Dir Campus Life ...... Mr. Joseph BISHOP
27 Exec Dir Communications & PR ...... Ms. Amy MILLER
105 Dir Web & Media Services ...... Mr. Josh ISAAK
25 Exec Dir Sponsored Pgms/AOR/CGO ...... Ms. Michele DAVIS
30 Exec Director of Development ...... Ms. Ana DOONAN
36 Exec Dir Career Services ...... Ms. Shelley LOWE
44 Assistant Director Annual Giving ...... Ms. Megan SJOLANDER
96 Dir Procurement & Retail Sales ...... Ms. Paula GLEASON-ZEEFF

Davenport University Great Lakes Bay Campus - Midland (A)
3555 E Patrick Road, Midland MI 48642
Telephone: (989) 835-5588 Identification: 770270
Accreditation: &HLC

Davenport University Holland (B)
643 S Waverly Road, Holland MI 49423
Telephone: (616) 395-4600 Identification: 770266
Accreditation: &HLC

Davenport University Lansing (C)
200 S. Grand Avenue, Lansing MI 48933
Telephone: (517) 484-2600 Identification: 770268
Accreditation: &HLC

Davenport University Warren (D)
27650 Dequindre Road, Warren MI 48092
Telephone: (586) 558-8700 Identification: 770272
Accreditation: &HLC

Delta College (E)
1961 Delta Road, University Center MI 48710-0001
County: Bay FICE Identification: 002251
Unit ID: 169521
Telephone: (989) 686-9000 Carnegie Class: Assoc/HT-High Trad
FAX Number: (989) 667-0620 Calendar System: Semester
URL: www.delta.edu
Established: 1961 Annual Undergrad Tuition & Fees (In-District): $6,680
Enrollment: 6,954 Coed
Affiliation or Control: Local IRS Status: 501(c)3
Highest Offering: Associate Degree
Accreditation: HLC, ADNUR, COARC, DA, DH, DMS, NAEYC, PTAA, RAD, SURGA, SURGT

01 President ... Dr. Michael H. GAVIN
10 Vice President Business/Finance ... Ms. Sarah DUFRESNE
32 VP Student & Educational Services ... Vacant
05 VP Instruction/Learning Services ... Dr. Reva CURRY
111 Exec Dir Institutional Advancement ... Ms. Pam CLARK
20 Dean of Teaching & Learning ... Dr. Martha CRAWMER
36 Dean Career Educ/Lrng Partnerships ... Mr. Eduardo SUNIGA
84 Dean of Enrollment Management ... Vacant
26 Dir Marketing & Public Information ... Ms. Leanne GOVITZ
108 Exec Dir Admin Svcs/Inst Effective ... Ms. Andrea L. URSUY
101 Asst to President/Board Secretary ... Ms. Andrea URSUY
25 Director of Corporate Services ... Ms. Jennifer CARROLL
37 Director of Financial Aid ... Ms. Lisa DAVIS
15 Director of Human Resources ... Ms. Loyce BROWN
18 Director of Facilities Management ... Vacant
07 Assoc Dean of Enrollment Management ... Mr. Jason PREMO
19 Director of Public Safety ... Mr. Robert BATTINKOFF
12 Director of Downtown Centers ... Ms. Kristy NELSON
121 Dean Student Reten/Empower/Compl ... Ms. Shelly RAUBE
49 Associate Dean Arts & Letters Div ... Mr. Jonathan GARN
50 Associate Dean Business & Tech Div ... Ms. Susan ROCHE
88 Associate Dean Health/Wellness Div ... Dr. Pete FOX
81 Associate Dean Science & Math Div ... Dr. Melissa HASWELL
83 Associate Dean Social Sciences Div ... Dr. Daniel ALLEN
21 Business Services Director ... Mr. Jonathan FOCO
09 Director of Institutional Research ... Dr. Jason YOUNG
06 Registrar ... Vacant
13 Chief Information Officer ... Vacant
40 Assistant Bookstore Manager ... Mr. Daniel FRANCKE
08 Mgr of Library Programs & Services ... Ms. Michele PRATT

Eastern Michigan University (F)
900 Oakwood St, Ypsilanti MI 48197-2207
County: Washtenaw FICE Identification: 002259
Unit ID: 169798
Telephone: (734) 487-1849 Carnegie Class: DU-Higher
FAX Number: (734) 481-1095 Calendar System: Semester
URL: www.emich.edu
Established: 1849 Annual Undergrad Tuition & Fees (In-State): $13,810
Enrollment: 16,294 Coed
Affiliation or Control: State IRS Status: 501(c)3
Highest Offering: Doctorate
Accreditation: HLC, ARCPA, ART, CAATE, CACREP, CAEP, CEA, CIDA, CLPSY, CONST, DIETC, MLS, MUS, NURSE, OPE, OT, SP, SPAA, SW

01 President ... Dr. James M. SMITH
05 Provost and Executive VP ... Dr. Rhonda LONGWORTH
10 Chief Financial Officer ... Mr. Michael VALDES
26 Vice President Communications ... Mr. Walter KRAFT
111 VP Advance/Exec Dir Foundation ... Mr. William SHEPARD
101 VP & Sec to the Board of Regents ... Ms. Vicki REAUME
41 Vice President/Dir Athletics ... Mr. Scott WETHERBEE
84 Vice Pres/Chief Enrollment Officer ... Mr. Kevin KUCERA
86 Int VP Govt/Cmty Relations ... Ms. Vicki REAUME
18 Exec Dir Facilities/Construct Plng ... Mr. Scott STORRAR
15 Assoc VP & Chief HR Officer ... Mr. Brett LAST
43 General Counsel ... Ms. Lauren LONDON
88 Assoc General Counsel ... Mr. Jeffrey AMMONS
13 Chief Information Officer ... Mr. Ron WOODY
19 Exec Dir Public Safety ... Mr. Matthew LIGE
100 Chief of Staff ... Mr. Leigh GREDEN
11 Assoc Prov/Assoc VP Administration ... Dr. James J. CARROLL, III
20 Assoc Prov/Assoc VP Acad Pgm Svcs ... Dr. Michael TEW
49 Dean Col of Art & Sciences ... Dr. Dana HELLER
50 Dean Col of Business ... Dr. Kenneth LORD
53 Dean Col of Education ... Dr. Ryan GILDERSLEEVE
69 Dean Col Health & Human Svcs ... Dr. Murali NAIR
72 Dean Col Engineering & Technology ... Dr. Mohamad QATU
58 Int Assc Prov/AVP Grad Stds/Rsrch ... Dr. Wade TORNQUIST
08 University Librarian ... Ms. Rhonda FOWLER
32 Sr AVP Student Affs/Dean Students ... Ms. Ellen GOLD
09 Dir Inst Research/Info Mgmt ... Mr. Xunhang (Hank) ZHOU
20 Int Asst VP Academic Affairs/AHR ... Dr. Kathleen STACEY
88 Exec Dir Foundation Operations/CFO ... Ms. Laura WILBANKS
88 Assoc Director Ombuds ... Ms. Julia HECK
27 Director Media Relations ... Ms. Melissa THRASHER
88 Dir Charter Schools Program ... Ms. Jolia HILL
92 Dean Honors College ... Dr. Ann EISENBERG
39 Dir Housing & Residence Life ... Ms. Jeanette ZALBA
114 Exec Dir Financial Plng & Budget ... Mr. Todd OHMER
112 Dir Planned Giving/Foundation ... Mr. Sam JENSEN
102 Assoc VP Advancement/Foundation ... Ms. Jill HUNSBERGER
88 Exec Dir Integrated Content ... Ms. Darcy GIFFORD
88 Gen Mgr WEMU-FM Public Radio ... Ms. Mary MOTHERWELL
06 Registrar ... Ms. Christina SHELL
124 Director of Engagement @ EMU ... Ms. Jessica ALEXANDER
37 Director Financial Aid ... Ms. Donna HOLUBIK
96 Director Purchasing ... Mr. Travis TEMEYER
22 Title IX Coordinator ... Vacant
21 Controller ... Ms. Sandra MULLALLY
88 Asst Controller/Student Bus Svcs ... Ms. Beth HARDCASTLE
91 Asst Dir Enterprise & Applic Svcs ... Mr. Kenneth R. ADKINS
28 Interim Chief Diversity Officer ... Dr. Doris FIELDS
88 Dir Disability Resource Ctr ... Dr. LaMarcus HOWARD
85 Dir Office of Intl Stdnt & Scholars ... Ms. Esther GUNEL
04 Admin Associate to the President ... Ms. Casey WOOSTER
29 Interim Exec Dir Alumni Affairs ... Ms. Mia MILTON
38 Director Student Counseling ... Dr. Lisa LAUTERBACH
122 Coord Stdnt Orgs-Greek Life ... Ms. Karen THOMPSON
07 Director of Admissions ... Mr. Alexander LANDEN
88 Exec Dir Plant Grounds Custodial Op ... Mr. Dieter OTTO

Ecumenical Theological Seminary (G)
2930 Woodward Avenue, Detroit MI 48201-3035
County: Wayne FICE Identification: 040024
Unit ID: 247162
Telephone: (313) 831-5200 Carnegie Class: Spec-4-yr-Faith
FAX Number: (313) 831-1353 Calendar System: Quarter
URL: www.etseminary.edu
Established: 1980 Annual Undergrad Tuition & Fees: N/A
Enrollment: 76 Coed
Affiliation or Control: Independent Non-Profit IRS Status: 501(c)3
Highest Offering: Doctorate
Accreditation: THEOL

01 President ... Dr. Kenneth E. HARRIS
05 Academic Dean/CAO ... Dr. Brandon GRAFIUS
10 Finance Officer/Business Mgmt ... Ms. Jacquelyn HINES
06 Registrar ... Mrs. Barbara PYE
07 Manager of Enrollment/Recruitment ... Mr. James NEELY, JR.
73 Director Doctor of Ministry Program ... Dr. Constance SIMON
58 Director of Masters Program ... Dr. James WADDELL

Ferris State University (H)
1201 S. State Street, Big Rapids MI 49307-2295
County: Mecosta FICE Identification: 002260
Unit ID: 169910
Telephone: (231) 591-2000 Carnegie Class: DU-Mod
FAX Number: (231) 591-3592 Calendar System: Semester
URL: www.ferris.edu
Established: 1884 Annual Undergrad Tuition & Fees (In-State): $12,376
Enrollment: 11,165 Coed
Affiliation or Control: State IRS Status: 501(c)3
Highest Offering: First Professional Degree
Accreditation: HLC, ACBSP, CAEP, CAHIIM, #COARC, CONST, DH, DMS, HSA, MLS, MLTAD, NMT, NURSE, OPT, OPTR, PHAR, RAD, SW

01 President ... Dr. David L. EISLER
05 Provost & VPAA ... Dr. Robert FLEISCHMAN
43 Vice President & General Counsel ... Mr. Miles J. POSTEMA
10 VP Administration & Finance ... Mr. Jim BACHMEIER
111 VP of Advancement & Mktg ... Ms. Shelly PEARCY
32 Vice President Student Affairs ... Dr. Jeanine WARD-ROOF
12 President KCAD ... Ms. Tara MCCRACKIN
56 Dean Extended and Intl Operations ... Dr. Steve REIFERT
28 VP for Diversity and Inclusion ... Dr. David PILGRIM
108 Int Assoc Provost Accreditation ... Ms. Mandy SEIFERLEIN
109 Assoc VP of Auxiliary Enterprises ... Ms. Gheretta HARRIS
21 Assistant VP of Finance ... Ms. Gail TAYLOR
110 Assoc VP for Advancement ... Mr. Bob MURRAY
15 Assoc VP Human Resources ... Ms. Fredericka HAYES
18 Assoc VP Physical Plant ... Mr. Chad STIRRETT
84 Associate Dean Enrollment Services ... Ms. Kathy LAKE
07 Dean Enroll Svcs/Dir Admissions ... Dr. Kristen SALOMONSON
114 Director Budget Planning/Analysis ... Ms. Amy WINKER
13 Chief Technology Officer ... Mr. Charlie WEAVER
19 Director of Public Safety ... Mr. John ALLEN
88 Mgr Stdnt Empl & Financial Aid Adv ... Ms. Lori DEFOREST
88 Assoc Dean of Student Life ... Mr. Nicholas CAMPAU
38 Director Counseling & Health Center ... Vacant
35 Dean of Student Life ... Ms. Joy PULSIFER
93 Dir Multicultural Student Svcs ... Dr. Danyelle GREGORY
88 Director for CLACS ... Ms. Angela ROMAN
88 Director University Recreation ... Mr. Justin HARDEN
29 Assoc VP for External Relations ... Mr. Jeremy MISHLER
09 Dir of Inst Research & Testing ... Ms. Mitzi DAY
39 Interim Director Residential Life ... Ms. Lisa ORTIZ
40 Manager Bookstore ... Ms. Sheree SCHROT
41 Director of Athletics ... Mr. Steve BROCKELBANK
44 Dir Annual Giving & Advance Svcs ... Ms. Jennifer YONTZ
49 Dean of Arts/Sciences & Education ... Dr. Randy CAGLE
50 Dean of Business ... Dr. Logan JONES
67 Dean of Pharmacy ... Dr. Steve DURST
76 Dean of Health Professions ... Dr. Lincoln GIBBS
63 Interim Dean MI College Optometry ... Dr. Daniel TAYLOR
72 Dean of Engineering Technology ... Mr. Michael STALEY
08 Interim Dean of FLITE ... Dr. Jason BENTLEY
04 Executive Asst to the President ... Ms. Terri COOK
101 Secretary to the Board of Trustees ... Ms. Karen HUISMAN
37 Asst Director Financial Aid ... Ms. Rebecca VOKES
06 Registrar ... Mr. Eric HANER
104 Asst Director Office of Intl Educ ... Ms. Lisa VONREICHBAUER
105 Web Developer ... Mr. Paul HOBART
22 Director of Equal Opportunity ... Ms. Kylie PIETTE
106 Exec Director Online Education ... Vacant
96 Procurement Manager ... Ms. Cindee WILCOX

Finlandia University (I)
601 Quincy Street, Hancock MI 49930-1882
County: Houghton FICE Identification: 002322
Unit ID: 172440
Telephone: (906) 487-7201 Carnegie Class: Bac-Diverse
FAX Number: (906) 487-7366 Calendar System: Semester
URL: www.finlandia.edu
Established: 1896 Annual Undergrad Tuition & Fees: $23,990
Enrollment: 402 Coed
Affiliation or Control: Evangelical Lutheran Church In America
IRS Status: 501(c)3
Highest Offering: Baccalaureate
Accreditation: HLC, NURSE, PTAA

01 President ... Dr. Philip JOHNSON
10 Int Chief Financial Officer ... Ms. Laura SIEDERS
05 VP Academic Affairs ... Dr. Fredi DE YAMPERT
111 VP External Relations & Advancement ... Vacant
04 Executive Administrative Assistant ... Ms. Doreen KORPELA
26 Director Marketing/Communications ... Mr. Jordan SHAWHAN
08 Head Librarian ... Ms. Rebecca DALY
32 Dean of Students & Enrollment ... Ms. Erin BARNETT
42 Campus Pastor ... Ms. Sarah SEMMLERSMITH
06 Registrar ... Mr. Darren BAUSANO
13 Director Information Technology ... Mr. Scott BLAKE
41 Athletic Director ... Mr. Curtis WITTENBERG
18 Director of Plant and Facilities ... Mr. Curt HAHKA
37 Director Financial Services ... Ms. Sandra TURNQUIST
40 Bookstore Manager ... Ms. April STEVENS
96 Purchaser ... Ms. Janine NOTTKE
15 Human Resources Manager ... Mr. Joe KOEPEL
07 Director of Admissions/Enrollment ... Mr. Anthony SCHWASS
19 Director of Campus Safety/Security ... Mr. Scott HENDRICKSON
39 Asst Dean of Stdnts Residence Life ... Ms. Annette SAWADOGO
49 Dean College of Arts & Sciences ... Dr. Jason OYADOMARI
57 Dean Intl School of Art & Design ... Ms. Denise VANDEVILLE
76 Dean College of Health Science ... Dr. Fredi DEYAMPERT
50 Dean Intl School of Business ... Mr. Kevin MANNINEN
22 Title IX Coordinator ... Vacant
09 Director of Institutional Research ... Mr. David BERTHOLF
106 Dir of Innovative & Online Lrng ... Dr. Michelle RAUCH
108 Director Institutional Assessment ... Mr. Neil KROMER

Glen Oaks Community College (J)
62249 Shimmel Road, Centreville MI 49032-9719
County: Saint Joseph FICE Identification: 002263
Unit ID: 169974
Telephone: (269) 467-9945 Carnegie Class: Assoc/MT-VT-High Non
FAX Number: (269) 467-4114 Calendar System: Semester
URL: www.glenoaks.edu
Established: 1965 Annual Undergrad Tuition & Fees (In-District): $5,328
Enrollment: 950 Coed
Affiliation or Control: Local IRS Status: 501(c)3
Highest Offering: Associate Degree
Accreditation: HLC, MAC

01 President ... Dr. David DEVIER
05 Vice President of Academics ... Dr. Adam CLOUTIER
10 Vice President of Finance & Admin ... Mr. Bruce ZAKRZEWSKI
32 Vice President of Student Services ... Ms. Tonya HOWDEN
66 Dean of Nursing ... Ms. Sara BIRCH
08 Director Learning Resources Center ... Ms. Trista NELSON
21 Accountant ... Ms. Jennifer DODSON
18 Director of Buildings/Grounds ... Mr. Larry DIEKMAN
07 Director of Admissions ... Ms. Sara KOHLER
37 Dir of Financial Aid/Scholarships ... Ms. Jean ZIMMERMAN
41 Director of Athletics ... Vacant
15 Personnel Coordinator ... Mr. Candy BOHACZ
26 Public Relations/Marketing ... Ms. Valorie JUERGENS
04 Exec Assoc Asst to the President ... Ms. Diane ZINSMASTER
06 Registrar ... Ms. Amy YOUNG
103 Director Workforce Development ... Mr. Paul AIVARS
39 Dir Resident Life/Student Housing ... Ms. Ayla WILDER

13	Chief Information Technology Office	Mr. Evan DEMBSKEY
22	Dir Affirmative Action/Equal Opp	Ms. Jamie YESH
108	Dir Inst Plng/Assessment/Research	Dr. Tammy RUSSELL
19	Director Security/Safety	Mr. Larry DIEKMAN
20	Dean of Academics	Dr. Madonna JACKSON
38	Director of Advising	Mr. Ben FRIES

Gogebic Community College (A)

E4946 Jackson Road, Ironwood MI 49938-1366

County: Gogebic FICE Identification: 002264
Unit ID: 169992

Telephone: (906) 932-4231 Carnegie Class: Assoc/HVT-High Trad
FAX Number: (906) 932-5541 Calendar System: Semester
URL: www.gogebic.edu
Established: 1931 Annual Undergrad Tuition & Fees (In-District): $6,808
Enrollment: 896 Coed
Affiliation or Control: Local IRS Status: 501(c)3
Highest Offering: Associate Degree
Accreditation: HLC

01	President	Dr. George MCNULTY
05	Vice Pres of Academic Affairs	Mr. David DARROW
10	Vice Pres of Business Services	Mr. Chad LASHUA
32	Vice Pres of Student Services	Dr. Jennifer SABOURIN
37	Director Financial Aid	Vacant
76	Director of Allied Health Program	Ms. Nicole ROWE
88	Director of Ski Area Management	Mr. James VANDERSPOEL
13	Director of Computer Services	Mr. Steve SPETS
07	Dir of Admission/Public Information	Ms. Kim ZECKOVICH
30	Dir of Institutional Development	Ms. Kelly MARZCAK
15	Director of Human Resources	Vacant
09	Institutional Researcher	Ms. Miranda HEGLUND
04	Executive Admin Asst to President	Ms. Roberta ANDERS
103	Director Workforce Development	Mr. Glen ACKERMAN-BEHR
39	Resident Community Manager	Vacant
06	Registrar	Ms. Kristin KENNEY

Grace Christian University (B)

1011 Aldon Street, SW, Grand Rapids MI 49509-1998

County: Kent FICE Identification: 002265
Unit ID: 170000

Telephone: (616) 538-2330 Carnegie Class: Bac-Diverse
FAX Number: (616) 538-0599 Calendar System: Semester
URL: www.gracechristian.edu
Established: 1939 Annual Undergrad Tuition & Fees: $14,160
Enrollment: 1,052 Coed
Affiliation or Control: Independent Non-Profit IRS Status: 501(c)3
Highest Offering: Master's
Accreditation: HLC, BI

01	President	Dr. Kenneth B. KEMPER
03	Exec Vice President	Mr. Brian P. SHERSTAD
05	Provost	Dr. Kim PILIECI
20	Assistant Provost	Dr. Timothy RUMLEY
10	Vice Pres Finance/Business Opers	Mr. Douglas VRIESMAN
32	Assoc Vice Pres Student Affairs	Mr. Kyle BOHL
06	Registrar	Ms. Victoria CUMINGS
111	Vice Pres Institutional Advancement	Mr. Stephen GOWDY
08	Director Library Services	Mrs. Erinn HUEBNER
37	Director of Financial Aid	Mr. Kurt POSTMA
13	Director of Information Technology	Mr. Robert ELUSKIE
18	Director of Maintenance	Mr. Nathan JOHNSON
41	Athletic Director	Mr. Cory JAMIESON
35	Dean of Students	Mr. Jim GAMBLE
26	Assoc Vice President of Marketing	Vacant
15	Assoc Vice Pres of Human Resources	Mrs. Sherea LACY
07	Director of Admissions on Campus	Mr. Aaron COPE
88	Director of Online Enrollment	Mrs. Madison HETZLER
04	Assistant to the President	Mr. Robert KILGO

† Name changed from Grace Bible College on July 1, 2018.

Grand Rapids Community College (C)

143 Bostwick Avenue NE, Grand Rapids MI 49503-3295

County: Kent FICE Identification: 002267
Unit ID: 170055

Telephone: (616) 234-4000 Carnegie Class: Assoc/MT-VT-High Trad
FAX Number: (616) 234-4005 Calendar System: Semester
URL: www.grcc.edu
Established: 1914 Annual Undergrad Tuition & Fees (In-District): $7,869
Enrollment: 12,107 Coed
Affiliation or Control: Local IRS Status: 501(c)3
Highest Offering: Associate Degree
Accreditation: HLC, ACFEI, ADNUR, ART, DA, DH, MAC, MUS, NAEYC, OTA, PNUR, RAD

01	Interim President	Dr. Juan R. OLIVAREZ
05	Prov/Exec VP Academic Affairs	Dr. Brian KNETL
10	Exec VP Business/Financial Services	Ms. Lisa FREIBURGER
13	VP & CIO Lrng Res/Tech Solutions	Mr. David ANDERSON
111	AVP Advancement/Exec Dir Foundation	Dr. Kathryn MULLINS
28	Chief Equity & Inclusion Officer	Dr. Afeni MCNEELY COBHAM
124	Dean of Student Success & Retention	Mr. Eric MULLEN
32	Assoc Provost/Dean Student Affairs	Vacant
49	Int Dean School of Arts & Sciences	Dr. Bill FABER
103	Exec Dir Workforce Training	Ms. Julie PARKS
26	Director of Communications	Mr. David MURRAY
37	Director of Financial Aid	Ms. Ann ISACKSON
15	Executive Director Human Resources	Ms. Cathy KUBIAK

06	Registrar	Ms. Valerie BUTTERFIELD
35	Director Student Activities	Ms. Caroline BLAIR
88	Assoc Director Student Employment	Ms. Luann WEDGE
08	Director of Library Services	Mr. Brian BEECHER
18	Executive Director of Facilities	Mr. Thomas J. SMITH
19	Chief of Campus Police	Ms. Rebecca R. WHITMAN
43	General Counsel	Ms. Kathy KEATING
96	Director Purchasing	Mr. Mansfield MATTHEWSON
12	Dean of Lakeshore Campus & Outreach	Mr. Daniel CLARK

Grand Valley State University (D)

1 Campus Drive, Allendale MI 49401-9403

County: Ottawa FICE Identification: 002268
Unit ID: 170082

Telephone: (616) 331-5000 Carnegie Class: DU-Mod
FAX Number: (616) 331-3503 Calendar System: Semester
URL: www.gvsu.edu
Established: 1960 Annual Undergrad Tuition & Fees (In-State): $13,244
Enrollment: 23,350 Coed
Affiliation or Control: State IRS Status: 501(c)3
Highest Offering: Doctorate
Accreditation: HLC, ARCPA, ART, @AUD, CAATE, CAEP, CAHIIM, CARTE, CVT, DIETC, DIETD, DMS, HSA, IPSY, MLS, MUS, NURSE, OT, PH, PTA, RADDOS, RTT, SP, SPAA, SW

01	President	Dr. Philomena V. MANTELLA
05	Provost/EVP Acad Affairs	Dr. Fatma MILI
100	Chief of Staff/VP Inclus & Equity	Dr. Jesse M. BERNAL
26	VP/Chief Pub Affs/Comm Ofcr/Sec BOT	Ms. Stacie R. BEHLER
10	Vice President for Finance & Admin	Dr. Greg SANIAL
84	Vice President Enrollment Develop	Dr. Brencleveton D. TRUSS
30	VP for Development/Exec Dir Fndn	Ms. Laura M. AIKENS
43	General Counsel	Ms. Pat SMITH
13	Vice President for IT/CDO	Dr. Miloš TOPIC
32	Vice President for Student Affairs	Dr. Jennifer L. HALL-JONES
35	Assoc VP & Dean of Students	Dr. Aaron HAIGHT
88	Asst VP for Student Affairs	Dr. Andy BEACHNAU
51	Vice Prov Grad & Lifetime Learning	Dr. Kara VAN DAM
46	Vice Prov for Research Admin	Dr. Robert SMART
20	Vice Prov Instruct Dev & Innovation	Dr. Christine RENER
20	Assoc VP Academic Affairs	Dr. Edward ABOUFADEL
20	Assoc VP Academic Affairs	Dr. Suzeanne BENET
20	Assoc VP Academic Affairs	Ms. Bonnie BOWEN
21	Assoc VP Business/Finance	Mr. Craig WIESCHHORSTER
114	Director of University Budgets	Ms. Jennifer SCHICK
15	Chief Human Resources Officer	Mr. Mychal COLEMAN
88	Asst VP ERM & Insurance Programs	Ms. Heather TAYLOR
27	Assoc VP for Univ Communications	Ms. Mary Eilleen LYON
18	Asst VP Facilities Services	Mr. Rence MEREDITH
88	Assoc VP for Facilities Planning	Ms. Karen INGLE
12	Assoc VP Fac Svcs GR & Reg Ctrs	Ms. Lisa HAYNES
28	Assoc VP for Equity & Compliance	Ms. Kathleen VANDERVEEN
35	Assoc VP Inclusion & Student Affs	Dr. Marlene KOWALSKI-BRAUN
04	Assoc VP & Exec Assoc to President	Dr. Robert KIMBALL
49	Dean Col of Liberal Arts & Sciences	Dr. Jennifer DRAKE
50	Dean Seidman Col of Business	Dr. Diana LAWSON
53	Dean Col of Educ & Comm Innovation	Dr. Sherril SOMAN
54	Dean Padnos Col Engr & Computing	Dr. Paul PLOTKOWSKI
76	Dean Col Health Professions	Dr. Ning Jackie ZHANG
88	Dean College Interdisc Studies	Dr. Mark SCHAUB
66	Acting Dean College of Nursing	Dr. Lola COKE
58	Assoc Vice Provost Graduate School	Dr. Jeffrey POTTEIGER
08	Dean University Libraries	Dr. Annie BELANGER
07	AVP for Admission & Recruitment	Mr. Daniel VELEZ
29	Director of Alumni Relations	Ms. Susan PROCTOR
36	Director of Career Center	Mr. Troy FARLEY
37	Assoc VP for Financial Aid	Ms. Michelle RHODES
39	Director of Housing & Res Life	Dr. Kyle BOONE
14	Assoc VP Information Technology	Mr. Emil DELGADO
09	Assoc VP Institutional Analysis	Dr. Philip BATTY
96	Director of Procurement Services	Mr. Aaron CACCAMO
19	Director Public Safety/Police Chief	Mr. Brandon DEHAAN
38	Director Univ Counseling Center	Dr. Amber ROBERTS
41	Athletic Director	Ms. Keri BECKER
21	Controller	Ms. Karen MUSHONG
88	General Manager WGVU	Mr. Jim RADEMAKER, II
06	Assoc VP & Registrar	Ms. Pam WELLS
22	Dir Title IX Coord & Equity Ofcr	Mr. Kevin CARMODY

Great Lakes Christian College (E)

6211 Willow Highway, Lansing MI 48917-1299

County: Eaton FICE Identification: 002269
Unit ID: 170091

Telephone: (517) 321-0242 Carnegie Class: Bac-Diverse
FAX Number: (517) 321-5902 Calendar System: Semester
URL: www.glcc.edu
Established: 1949 Annual Undergrad Tuition & Fees: $17,220
Enrollment: 169 Coed
Affiliation or Control: Christian Churches And Churches of Christ
IRS Status: 501(c)3
Highest Offering: Baccalaureate
Accreditation: HLC

01	President	Dr. Frank WELLER
10	Vice President Finance/Operations	Vacant
05	Vice President of Academic Affairs	Dr. Samuel C. LONG
111	Vice Pres Institutional Advancement	Mr. Philip E. BEAVERS
84	Vice Pres Enrollment Mgmt	Mr. Gregory STAUFFER
06	Registrar	Dr. Esther A. HETRICK

08	Director of Library Services	Mrs. Heather BUNCE
37	Financial Aid Director	Prof. Ryan APPLE
32	Dean of Students	Dr. Michael GILES
41	Athletic Director	Mr. Richard WESTERLUND
88	Director of Outreach Ministries	Mrs. Judy BEAVERS
18	Maintenance Supervisor	Vacant
04	Administrative Secretary	Vacant

Henry Ford College (F)

5101 Evergreen Road, Dearborn MI 48128-1495

County: Wayne FICE Identification: 002270
Unit ID: 170240

Telephone: (313) 845-9615 Carnegie Class: Bac/Assoc-Assoc Dom
FAX Number: (313) 845-9658 Calendar System: Semester
URL: www.hfcc.edu
Established: 1938 Annual Undergrad Tuition & Fees (In-District): $5,020
Enrollment: 11,345 Coed
Affiliation or Control: Local IRS Status: 501(c)3
Highest Offering: Baccalaureate
Accreditation: HLC, ACFEI, ADNUR, COARC, EMT, LC, MAC, PTAA, RAD, SURGT

01	President	Dr. Russell A. KAVALHUNA
10	Vice President Financial Services	Dr. John SATKOWSKI
32	Interim VP of Student Affairs	Ms. Holly DIAMOND
05	VP of Academic Affairs	Dr. Michael NEALON
111	Vice Pres of Inst Advancement	Mr. A. Reginald BEST, JR.
15	VP Strategy and HR	Dr. Lori GONKO
06	Exec Director Registration/Enroll	Ms. Holly DIAMOND
38	Assoc Dean Counseling	Mr. Ibrahim ATALLAH
50	Dean Business/Entrepreneurship/PD	Ms. Patricia CHATMAN
08	Director Library	Ms. Kate HARGER
13	Dir Network and Infrastructure	Mr. Joseph ZITNIK
26	VP of Marketing/Communications	Ms. Rhonda DELONG
37	Exec Director Student Financial Aid	Mr. Kevin J. CULLER
92	Director Honors Program	Vacant
96	Director Purchasing	Mr. Fred STEINER
40	Manager of College Store	Ms. Pamela HALL
04	Administrative Asst to President	Ms. Kathy DIMITRIOU
09	Director of Institutional Research	Mr. Jacob KROGOL
15	Director Personnel Services	Vacant
19	Director Security/Safety	Ms. Karen SCHOEN
41	Athletic Director	Ms. Rochelle TAYLOR
43	VP Legal Services/General Counsel	Ms. Amy CLARK
07	Director of Admissions	Vacant
18	Chief Facilities/Physical Plant Ofc	Mr. Reuben BRUKLEY

Hillsdale College (G)

33 East College Street, Hillsdale MI 49242-1298

County: Hillsdale FICE Identification: 002272
Unit ID: 170286

Telephone: (517) 437-7341 Carnegie Class: Bac-A&S
FAX Number: (517) 437-3923 Calendar System: Semester
URL: www.hillsdale.edu
Established: 1844 Annual Undergrad Tuition & Fees: $29,482
Enrollment: 1,543 Coed
Affiliation or Control: Independent Non-Profit IRS Status: 501(c)3
Highest Offering: Doctorate
Accreditation: HLC

01	President	Dr. Larry ARNN
05	Provost	Dr. Chris VANORMAN
11	VP & Chief Administrative Officer	Mr. Rich PEWE
43	VP & General Counsel	Mr. Robert NORTON
07	VP Admissions/Business Development	Mr. Doug BANBURY
26	VP External Affairs	Mr. Douglas JEFFREY
10	VP Finance	Mr. Patrick FLANNERY
111	VP Institutional Advancement	Mr. John CERVINI
88	VP Marketing	Mr. William GRAY
32	VP Student Affairs	Ms. Diane PHILIPP
27	Associate VP External Affairs	Mr. Timothy CASPAR
100	Chief Staff Officer	Mr. Mike HARNER
36	Executive Director Career Services	Mr. Ken KOOPMANS
15	Associate VP of HR	Ms. Janet MARSH
13	Associate VP for ITS	Mr. Jason SHERRILL
29	Executive Director Alumni Affairs	Ms. Colleen MCGINNESS
41	Director Athletics	Mr. Don BRUBACHER
19	Director Campus Security	Mr. William WHORLEY
40	Director College Bookstore	Ms. Cindy WILLING
37	Director Financial Aid	Mr. Rich MOEGGENBERG
23	Director Health Services	Mr. Brock LUTZ
08	Director Library	Ms. Maurine MCCOURRY
09	Director Institutional Research	Mr. Joshua TROJNIAK
18	Director Facilities	Mr. Dave BILLINGTON
35	Director Student Activities	Ms. Madelyn CLARK
42	Chaplain	Rev. Adam RICK
21	Controller	Ms. LeAnn CREGER
33	Dean of Men	Mr. Aaron PETERSEN
34	Dean of Women	Ms. Rebekah DELL
06	Registrar	Mr. Douglas MCARTHUR
04	Exec Assistant to the President	Ms. Grace BALKAN
88	Senior Advisor to the Provost	Mr. Mark MAIER

Hope College (H)

141 E 12th Street, Holland MI 49423-3607

County: Ottawa FICE Identification: 002273
Unit ID: 170301

Telephone: (616) 395-7000 Carnegie Class: Bac-A&S
FAX Number: (616) 395-7922 Calendar System: Semester
URL: www.hope.edu
Established: 1866 Annual Undergrad Tuition & Fees: $36,650

Enrollment: 3,061 Coed
Affiliation or Control: Reformed Church In America IRS Status: 501(c)3
Highest Offering: Baccalaureate
Accreditation: HLC, ART, CAEP, DANCE, MUS, NURSE, SW, THEA

01 President ....Mr. Matthew A. SCOGIN
05 Provost ....Dr. Gerald GRIFFIN
10 Vice Pres & Chief Financial Officer ....Mr. Thomas W. BYLSMA
07 Vice President for Admissions ....Mr. William VANDERBILT
111 VP of Philanthropy & Engagement ....Mr. Jeffrey PUCKETT
32 VP Student Devel/Dean of Students ....Dr. Richard A. FROST
26 VP for Public Affairs & Marketing ....Mrs. Jennifer FELLINGER
08 Dean of Libraries ....Ms. Kelly G. JACOBSMA
39 Assoc Dean of Students/Housing ....Dr. John E. JOBSON
22 Assc Dn Stdnts/Dir Ctr Div & Incl ....Vacant
94 Director of Women's/Gender Studies ....Dr. Virginia BEARD
81 Dean for Natural & Applied Sciences ....Dr. David G. VAN WYLEN
79 Dean for the Arts & Humanities ....Dr. Sandra L. VISSER
83 Dean for Social Sciences ....Dr. Scott D. VANDER STOEP
88 Dean of the Chapel ....Rev Dr. Trygve D. JOHNSON
37 Director of Financial Aid ....Ms. Jill NUTT
36 Assoc Dean for the Career Dev Ctr ....Mr. Dale F. AUSTIN
21 Director of Finance & Business Svcs ....Mr. Douglas VAN DYKEN
11 Director of Operations ....Ms. Kara SLATER
88 Director of Process and Innovation ....Mr. Carl E. HEIDEMAN
15 Director of Human Resources ....Mrs. Lori MULDER
40 Manager of Hope-Geneva Bookstore ....Mr. Craig THELEN
29 Exec Director of Alumni Engagement ....Mr. Scott TRAVIS
41 Director of Athletics ....Mr. Tim SCHOONVELD
42 Senior Chaplain ....Rev. Paul H. BOERSMA
38 Asst Dean/Director Counseling Ctr ....Dr. Kristen GRAY
04 Executive Asst to the President ....Mrs. Mary HOUSEHOLDER
19 Director Security/Safety ....Mr. Jeffrey HERTEL
13 Dir Computing/Info Technology ....Mr. Jeff PESTUN
30 Assoc VP & Campaign Director ....Mrs. Mary REMENSCHNEIDER
06 Registrar ....Mrs. Carol DE JONG
105 Director Web Communications ....Mr. Jason CASH
28 Chief Officer for Culture & Inclus ....Dr. Sonja TRENT-BROWN
44 Dir of Leadership & Annual Giving ....Ms. Dana GILL

Jackson College (A)

2111 Emmons Road, Jackson MI 49201-8399
County: Jackson FICE Identification: 002274
Unit ID: 170444
Telephone: (517) 787-0800 Carnegie Class: Bac/Assoc-Assoc Dom
FAX Number: (517) 796-8630 Calendar System: Semester
URL: www.jccmi.edu
Established: 1928 Annual Undergrad Tuition & Fees (In-District): $9,318
Enrollment: 4,140 Coed
Affiliation or Control: Local IRS Status: 501(c)3
Highest Offering: Baccalaureate
Accreditation: HLC, CNEA, COARC, DH, DMS, EMT, RAD

01 President/CEO ....Dr. Daniel J. PHELAN
11 Chief Legal/Talent/Equity/Admin ....Ms. Cindy ALLEN
10 Vice President of Finance/CFO ....Vacant
05 Chief Academic & Student Svcs Ofcr ....Mr. Jeremy FREW
102 Foundation Pres/Chief Campus Ops ....Mr. Jason VALENTE
06 Registrar ....Mr. Zakary MCNITT
111 Chief Advancement Officer ....Ms. Julie HAND
08 Library Director ....Ms. Jennifer MIKESELL
100 Chief of Staff ....Vacant
103 Dir Workforce/Career Development ....Ms. Tina MATZ
18 Vice President Facilities & IT ....Vacant
19 Director Safety & Security ....Mr. Jeffrey WHIPPLE
28 Chief Diversity Officer/Dir DEB ....Ms. Kelly CRUM
29 Dir Annual Giving & Alumni Rels ....Ms. Brigette ROBINSON
37 Director of Financial Aid ....Ms. Andrew SPOHN
39 Director of Residence Life ....Ms. Momo SALDANA
41 Exec Dir Athletics/Stdnt Devel ....Ms. Courtney IVAN
15 Director of Human Resources ....Ms. Joyce DUNBAR

Kalamazoo College (B)

1200 Academy Street, Kalamazoo MI 49006-3295
County: Kalamazoo FICE Identification: 002275
Unit ID: 170532
Telephone: (269) 337-7000 Carnegie Class: Bac-A&S
FAX Number: (269) 337-7251 Calendar System: Quarter
URL: www.kzoo.edu
Established: 1833 Annual Undergrad Tuition & Fees: $52,530
Enrollment: 1,451 Coed
Affiliation or Control: Independent Non-Profit IRS Status: 501(c)3
Highest Offering: Baccalaureate
Accreditation: HLC

01 President ....Dr. Jorge G. GONZALEZ
05 Provost ....Dr. Danette IFERT JOHNSON
10 VP for Business and Finance ....Ms. Lisa VANDEWEERT
111 VP for College Advancement ....Ms. Karen ISBLE
32 VP Student Devel & Dean of Students ....Mr. J. Malcolm SMITH
84 VP for Admission & Financial Aid ....Ms. Mj HUEBNER
85 Executive Director for Intl Pgms ....Dr. Margaret WIEDENHOEFT
13 Chief Information Officer ....Mr. Todd WATSON
21 Director of Finance ....Ms. Jodi BREITHART
09 Director of Inst Support/Research ....Dr. Tara WEBB
35 Assoc Dean of Stdnts/1st Yr Exper ....Ms. Dana JANSMA
06 Registrar ....Ms. Nicole KRAGT
15 AVP Human Resources ....Ms. Renee E. BOELCKE
07 Dean of Admission ....Ms. Suzanne LEPLEY
37 Dean of Financial Aid ....Ms. Becca MURPHY
18 Director of Facilities Management ....Ms. Susan K. LINDEMANN
40 Director Bookstore ....Ms. Deborah L. THOMPSON
29 Director of Alumni Relations ....Ms. Kimberly J. ALDRICH
38 Director of Student Counseling ....Vacant
121 Director of Advising ....Ms. Lesley J. CLINARD
36 Dir Center Career/Prof Development ....Dr. Tricia ZELAYA-LEON
04 Administrative Asst to President ....Ms. Melanie K. WILLIAMS
08 Head Librarian ....Dr. Stacy A. NOWICKI
102 Dir Foundation/Corporate Relations ....Ms. Maria NEWHOUSE
19 Director Security/Safety ....Mr. Timothy YOUNG
41 Athletic Director ....Ms. Rebecca S. HALL
88 Enrollment Data Specialist ....Mr. Dan KIBBY
30 Director of Development ....Mr. Andrew M. MILLER
44 Director Annual Giving ....Ms. Laurel S. PALMER

Kalamazoo Valley Community College (C)

6767 West O Avenue, PO Box 4070,
Kalamazoo MI 49003-4070
County: Kalamazoo FICE Identification: 006949
Unit ID: 170541
Telephone: (269) 488-4400 Carnegie Class: Assoc/HT-Mix Trad/Non
FAX Number: (269) 488-4220 Calendar System: Semester
URL: www.kvcc.edu
Established: 1966 Annual Undergrad Tuition & Fees (In-District): $6,100
Enrollment: 6,656 Coed
Affiliation or Control: Local IRS Status: 501(c)3
Highest Offering: Associate Degree
Accreditation: HLC, ACFEI, ADNUR, COARC, DH, EMT, MAC

01 President ....Dr. L. Marshall WASHINGTON
05 Provost & VP Instr/Student Success ....Dr. Paige EAGAN
11 VP Campus Plng & Operations ....Mr. Dannie ALEXANDER
10 Vice President Finance & Business ....Mr. Brian LUETH
15 Vice President for Human Resources ....Mr. Aaron HILLIARD
13 Vice Pres for Admin Svc/Info Tech ....Mr. Tim WELSH
31 VP for Strategic Business/Cmty Dev ....Mr. Craig JBARA
121 Dean of Student Success ....Vacant
108 AVP for Collab/Compliance/Analytics ....Dr. Tracy LABADIE
19 Director of Public Safety ....Mr. Donald BENTHIN
08 Director of Libraries ....Mr. Mark WALTERS
07 Dir Admissions/Registration/Records ....Ms. Sarah HUBBELL
09 Dir Planning/Research/Accred/Compl ....Mr. Dan MONDOUX
102 Exec Dir Foundation & Development ....Ms. Linda DEPTA
37 Director Financial Aid ....Ms. Alisha CEDERBERG
26 Director of Marketing ....Ms. Linda DEPTA
18 Dir Facilities/Construction Mgmt ....Mr. Dannie ALEXANDER
21 Director of Business Services ....Ms. Muriel HICE
28 Director of Diversity & Inclusion ....Mr. Trice BATSON
41 Athletic Director ....Mr. Russ PANICO
84 Director Enrollment Management ....Ms. Megan PAUKEN
124 Dir of Student Retention Completion ....Mr. Evan PAUKEN
04 Admin Assistant to the President ....Ms. Sherry WEBER
38 Dir Advising & Counseling ....Ms. Angela MARSH-PEEK

Kellogg Community College (D)

450 North Avenue, Battle Creek MI 49017-3397
County: Calhoun FICE Identification: 002276
Unit ID: 170550
Telephone: (269) 965-3931 Carnegie Class: Assoc/HVT-High Non
FAX Number: (269) 962-4290 Calendar System: Semester
URL: www.kellogg.edu
Established: 1956 Annual Undergrad Tuition & Fees (In-District): $6,967
Enrollment: 3,469 Coed
Affiliation or Control: Local IRS Status: 501(c)3
Highest Offering: Associate Degree
Accreditation: HLC, ADNUR, DH, EMT, MAC, NAEYC, NDT, PTAA, RAD

01 President ....Dr. Paul WATSON
05 Vice President Instruction ....Ms. Tonya FORBES
32 Vice Pres Student & Community Svcs ....Dr. Kay KECK
10 Chief Financial Officer ....Mr. Richard SCOTT
57 Chair Arts & Communication Dept ....Ms. Barbara SUDEIKIS
81 Chair Math & Science Dept ....Dr. Michael GOLDIN
49 Dean Arts and Sciences ....Ms. Dawn LARSEN
102 Executive Director KCC Foundation ....Ms. Teresa DURHAM
96 Director Purchasing ....Ms. Angela CLEVELAND
06 Registrar ....Ms. Colleen WRIGHT
08 Chief Library Officer ....Dr. Michele REID
41 Director Athletics & PE ....Mr. Drew FLEMING
12 Director of Grahl Center ....Ms. Shari DEEVERS
84 Dean Enrollment Mgmt ....Ms. Nikki JEWELL
15 Chief Human Resources Officer ....Ms. Vicki RIVERA
18 Dir Inst Facilities ....Mr. Brad FULLER
51 Director Lifelong Learning ....Ms. Mary GREEN
09 Director Inst Compliance Reporting ....Mr. John JONES
21 Director of Finance ....Ms. Tracy BEATTY
12 Director Regional Mfg Tech Center ....Mr. Nathan VENSKE
35 Dean Student & Community Services ....Ms. Terah ZAREMBA
26 VP Strategy/Relations/Comm ....Mr. Eric GREENE
40 Bookstore Manager ....Ms. Catherine JAMES
04 Manager President's Office ....Ms. Marcia CAMPBELL
103 Dean Workforce Development ....Dr. Dennis BASKIN
36 Director Career & Emp Services ....Mr. Patrick CASEY
37 Director Financial Aid ....Ms. Nicole MASTERS
121 Manager Academic Advising ....Ms. Donna MALASKI
19 Chief of Public Safety ....Mr. Austin SIMONS

Kendall College of Art and Design of Ferris State University (E)

17 Fountain Street, NW, Grand Rapids MI 49503
Telephone: (800) 676-2787 Identification: 770273
Accreditation: &HLC, ART, CIDA

Kettering University (F)

1700 University Avenue, Flint MI 48504-6214
County: Genesee FICE Identification: 002262
Unit ID: 169983
Telephone: (810) 762-9500 Carnegie Class: Masters/M
FAX Number: (810) 762-9837 Calendar System: Semester
URL: www.kettering.edu
Established: 1919 Annual Undergrad Tuition & Fees: $44,380
Enrollment: 2,030 Coed
Affiliation or Control: Independent Non-Profit IRS Status: 501(c)3
Highest Offering: Master's
Accreditation: HLC, ACBSP

01 President ....Dr. Robert K. MCMAHAN
04 Executive Administrative Officer ....Ms. Cindy SOPKO
05 Sr VP for Academic Affairs/Provost ....Dr. James ZHANG
10 VP Administration & Finance ....Mr. Tom AYERS
84 Interim VP of Enrollment Services ....Ms. Tracie JONES
32 VP Student Life & Dean of Students ....Mr. LB MCCUNE
111 Int VP of University Advancement ....Mr. Joe RIZZA
13 Interim Vice President of IT ....Mr. Geoff MARSH
106 VP Kettering Global ....Ms. Christine WALLACE
20 Associate Provost ....Dr. Kathryn SVINARICH
15 Acting Director of Human Resources ....Mr. Rob BLOSSER
102 Dir of Philanthropy Corp/Found ....Mr. Dale PILGER
29 Dir of Alumni Engagement ....Ms. Starr CORNELL
44 Dir of Philanthropy Indiv Giving ....Mr. David TINDALL
19 Director of Campus Safety ....Mr. Paul CRANE
37 Assoc Director Financial Aid ....Ms. Barb HUFFMAN
21 Controller ....Ms. Nancy FIKE
09 Director of Institutional Research ....Dr. Mark WOODS
58 Dean Grad Studies & Research ....Dr. Scott REEVE
18 Director Physical Plant ....Mr. Joseph ASPERGER
08 Director Library Services ....Ms. Dina MEIN
41 Director Athletics/Rec Service ....Mr. Michael L. SCHAAL
93 Director Minority Student Affairs ....Mr. Ricky BROWN
104 Director International Office ....Ms. Laura ALLEN
109 Director Auxiliary Services ....Ms. Nadine L. THOR
06 Registrar ....Ms. Judi LANGOLF
23 Director Wellness Center ....Ms. Cristina REED
39 Dir Student Life Programs ....Ms. Myra LUMPKIN
88 MI SBDC Regional Director ....Ms. Janis MUELLER
96 Purchasing Manager ....Ms. Kathleen A. REMENDER
14 Interim Dir IT Operations ....Mr. Jonathon CONQUEST
25 Contract/Grant Specialist ....Ms. Jodi L. DORR
105 Webmaster ....Ms. Donna WICKS
88 Dir Enrollment Events/Visitor Rels ....Ms. Kristin LUKOWSKI
88 Director University Events ....Ms. Chelsea BRADBURN
121 Asst Dir Academic Success Center ....Ms. Sam KLASKOW
54 Dean Engineering ....Dr. Craig HOFF
49 Dean Sciences/Liberal Arts ....Dr. Kathryn SVINARICH
50 Int Dean School of Management ....Dr. Haseeb AHMED
43 University Counsel ....Mr. Don ROCKWELL

Keweenaw Bay Ojibwa Community College (G)

111 Beartown Rd, PO Box 519, Baraga MI 49908
County: Baraga FICE Identification: 041647
Unit ID: 461315
Telephone: (906) 353-8400 Carnegie Class: Tribal
FAX Number: (906) 353-8107 Calendar System: Semester
URL: www.kbocc.edu
Established: 1975 Annual Undergrad Tuition & Fees (In-District): $4,400
Enrollment: 79 Coed
Affiliation or Control: Local IRS Status: 501(c)3
Highest Offering: Associate Degree
Accreditation: HLC

01 President ....Ms. Lori Ann SHERMAN
05 Dean of Academic Affairs ....Ms. Megan HAATAJA
32 Dean of Students ....Ms. Amanda NORDSTROM
07 Admissions Officer ....Ms. Betti SZAROLETTA
06 Registrar ....Ms. Michelle BIANCO
10 Chief Financial/ Business Officer ....Mr. Ryan PERRIGO
15 Chief Human Resources Officer ....Ms. Theresa BIANCO
37 Director Student Financial Aid ....Ms. Dalene CHOSA

Kirtland Community College (H)

4800 W. 4 Mile Road, Grayling MI 49738
County: Crawford FICE Identification: 007171
Unit ID: 170587
Telephone: (989) 275-5000 Carnegie Class: Assoc/HVT-High Non
FAX Number: (989) 563-5915 Calendar System: Semester
URL: www.kirtland.edu
Established: 1966 Annual Undergrad Tuition & Fees (In-District): $6,090
Enrollment: 1,330 Coed
Affiliation or Control: Local IRS Status: 501(c)3
Highest Offering: Associate Degree
Accreditation: HLC, CNEA, CVT, SURGT

01 President ....Dr. Thomas QUINN

05 Vice Pres of Academic Services .... Dr. Amy FUGATE
32 Vice Pres of Student Svcs/Registrar .... Dr. Michelle VYSKOCIL
10 Vice Pres of Business Services .... Mr. Chris BOWMAN
119 Director of IT .... Mr. Matt BIERMANN
75 Dean Occupational Programs .... Ms. Barbara WALDEN
08 Director of Library & Tutoring Svcs .... Ms. Deb SHUMAKER
37 Director of Financial Aid .... Ms. Kemmoree DUNCOMBE
18 Director of Facilities .... Mr. Ron SHARPE
15 Director of Human Resources .... Ms. Vanessa NOFFSINGER
09 Director of Institutional Research .... Mr. Nick BAKER
102 Foundation Director .... Vacant
26 Director of Public Information .... Vacant
07 Admissions Coordinator .... Ms. Cesalee KUFFEL
19 Director Security/Safety .... Mr. Jeffrey GORNO
21 Director of Finance .... Ms. Kristin BARNHART
00 Chair Board of Trustees .... Ms. MaryAnn FERRIGAN
103 Director Workforce Development .... Vacant
105 Director Web Services .... Ms. Marj ESCH
106 Dir of Online Education/E-learning .... Mr. David CABLE
49 Dean of Liberal Arts .... Mr. John THIEL

Kuyper College (A)

3333 East Beltline Avenue, NE,
Grand Rapids MI 49525-9749

County: Kent — FICE Identification: 002311
Unit ID: 171881
Telephone: (616) 222-3000 — Carnegie Class: Bac-Diverse
FAX Number: (616) 988-3608 — Calendar System: Semester
URL: www.kuyper.edu
Established: 1939 — Annual Undergrad Tuition & Fees: $23,970
Enrollment: 152 — Coed
Affiliation or Control: Independent Non-Profit — IRS Status: 501(c)3
Highest Offering: Master's
Accreditation: HLC, BI, SW

01 President .... Dr. Patricia HARRIS
05 Academic Dean .... Dr. Tim DETWILER
06 Registrar .... Dr. Andrea FRYLING
10 Controller/CFO .... Ms. Christine MULKA
111 Vice Pres for College Advancement .... Mr. Ken CAPISCIOLTO
07 Director of Admissions .... Mr. Kevin GILLIAM
37 Financial Aid Director .... Ms. Agnes M. RUSSELL
44 Manager of the Annual Fund .... Ms. Lisa RUSTICUS
04 Assistant to the President .... Ms. Alyssa BLOM
08 Director of Library Services .... Ms. Michelle NORQUIST
32 Dean of Students and Work .... Mr. Curt ESSENBURG
18 Maintenance Supervisor .... Mr. Tim CHUPP
29 Manager of Alumni Relations .... Ms. Lisa RUSTICUS
15 Director of Human Resources .... Ms. Annie FIELDS
13 Director Computing/Info Management .... Mr. Keith TORNO
20 Dir Academic Support/Academics .... Mr. Andrew ZWART
70 Program Director Social Work .... Ms. Jennifer COLIN
85 International Student Services .... Ms. Jana POSTMA
50 Director of Business Leadership .... Mr. Marc ANDREAS
106 Director of Online Learning .... Mr. Darwin GLASSFORD
19 Director of Campus Operations .... Mr. Ray THOMAS

Lake Michigan College (B)

2755 E Napier, Benton Harbor MI 49022-1899

County: Berrien — FICE Identification: 002277
Unit ID: 170620
Telephone: (269) 927-1000 — Carnegie Class: Bac/Assoc-Assoc Dom
FAX Number: N/A — Calendar System: Semester
URL: www.lakemichigancollege.edu
Established: 1946 — Annual Undergrad Tuition & Fees (In-District): $6,743
Enrollment: 2,499 — Coed
Affiliation or Control: Local — IRS Status: 501(c)3
Highest Offering: Baccalaureate
Accreditation: HLC, ADNUR, DA, DMS, MAC, RAD

01 President .... Dr. Trevor A. KUBATZKE
10 Chief Financial Officer .... Ms. Kelli HAHN
04 Senior Exec Asst to President .... Ms. Stephanie STEELE
05 VP Academics .... Vacant
32 VP Student Affairs .... Mr. Nygil LIKELY
103 Dean Career Education Workforce .... Dr. Ken FLOWERS
49 Dean Arts & Sciences .... Mr. Kris ZOOK
76 Dean Health Sciences .... Ms. Marla CLARK
102 Executive Director Foundation .... Mr. Doug SCHAFFER
31 Dir Community Outreach & Relations .... Ms. Barbara CRAIG
88 Manager Mainstage Services .... Mr. Mike NADOLSKI
18 Director Facilities Management .... Ms. Sara VANDERVEEN
26 Director Marketing & Communications .... Ms. Jennifer SHOEMAKER
06 Registrar .... Ms. Sara SKINNER
96 Purchasing Manager .... Mr. Nathan MAIN
90 Director Teaching/Learning Center .... Mr. Daniel C. CAMPBELL
08 Head Librarian .... Ms. Diane BAKER
09 Director of Institutional Research .... Vacant
19 Director Security/Safety .... Mr. Steve SILCOX
39 Dir Residence Life & Stdnt Conduct .... Ms. Melissa GRAU
41 Athletic Director .... Ms. Melissa GRAU
37 Director Financial Aid .... Vacant
07 Director Admission & Recruitment .... Ms. Caroline TUBBS
108 Dean of Accreditation/Plng/Quality .... Ms. Melissa EMERY
15 Executive Director Human Resources .... Vacant
28 Dean Diversity/Equity/Inclusion .... Mr. Cam HERTH

Lake Superior State University (C)

650 W Easterday Avenue,
Sault Sainte Marie MI 49783-1699

County: Chippewa — FICE Identification: 002293
Unit ID: 170639
Telephone: (906) 632-6841 — Carnegie Class: Bac-Diverse
FAX Number: (906) 635-2111 — Calendar System: Semester
URL: www.lssu.edu
Established: 1946 — Annual Undergrad Tuition & Fees (In-State): $12,744
Enrollment: 1,909 — Coed
Affiliation or Control: State — IRS Status: 501(c)3
Highest Offering: Baccalaureate
Accreditation: HLC, ACBSP, CAEP, EMT, MLS, NURSE

01 President .... Dr. Rodney S. HANLEY
05 Provost/VP Academic Affairs .... Dr. Lynn GILLETTE
32 Vice Pres Student Affairs .... Dr. Michael BEAZLEY
10 Vice President Finance .... Dr. Nafez ALYAN
111 Vice Pres Advancment .... Mr. Scott SMITH
26 Dean of Admissions and Marketing .... Mr. Fred PIERCE
81 Dean Science & Environment .... Dr. Steven JOHNSON
49 Dean of Educ & Liberal Arts .... Vacant
83 Dean Health and Behavior .... Dr. Kathy BERCHEM
50 Dean Innovations & Solutions .... Dr. Kimberly MULLER
06 Registrar .... Ms. Nancy NEVE
15 Director of Human Resources .... Ms. Wendy BEACH
36 Director of Academic Services .... Ms. Geralyn NARKIEWICZ
37 Interim Director of Financial Aid .... Ms. Katelynn COON
38 Director of Counseling .... Ms. Kristin LARSON
28 Diversity Ofcr/Asst Dir Housing .... Mr. Derric KNIGHT
96 Purchasing Manager .... Ms. Stacy CHARLES
23 Director Health Services .... Ms. Karen STOREY
41 Director of Athletics .... Dr. David DILES
40 Bookstore Manager .... Ms. Amber MCLEAN

Lansing Community College (D)

610 N Capitol Avenue, Lansing MI 48933

County: Ingham — FICE Identification: 002278
Unit ID: 170657
Telephone: (517) 483-1200 — Carnegie Class: Assoc/MT-VT-High Trad
FAX Number: (517) 483-1845 — Calendar System: Semester
URL: www.lcc.edu
Established: 1957 — Annual Undergrad Tuition & Fees (In-District): $7,160
Enrollment: 10,306 — Coed
Affiliation or Control: Local — IRS Status: 501(c)3
Highest Offering: Associate Degree
Accreditation: HLC, ADNUR, COMTA, CONST, DH, DMS, EMT, NAEYC, NDT, RAD, SURGT

01 President .... Dr. Steve ROBINSON
05 Provost/SVP Academic Affairs .... Dr. Sally WELCH
10 SVP Business Operations .... Dr. Seleana SAMUEL
21 Chief Financial Officer .... Mr. Don WILSKE
13 Chief Information Officer .... Mr. Bill GARLICK
11 Exec Dir Administrative Svcs .... Mr. Chris MACKERSIE
20 Associate VP Academic Affairs .... Vacant
30 Assoc VP External Affs/Development .... Dr. Toni GLASSCOE
76 Dean Health & Human Services .... Dr. Betsy BURGER
103 Dean Community Educ/Workforce Dev .... Mr. Bo GARCIA
49 Dean Arts & Sciences .... Ms. Andrea HOAGLAND
32 Dean Student Affairs .... Ms. Ronda MILLER
72 Dean Technical Careers .... Ms. Cathy WILHM
15 Exec Director Human Resources .... Mr. James MITCHELL
28 Chief Diversity Officer .... Dr. Tonya BAILEY
26 Director Public Affairs .... Ms. Marilyn TWINE
09 Exec Dir Center for Data Science .... Dr. Matt FALL

Lawrence Technological University (E)

21000 W Ten Mile Road, Southfield MI 48075-1058

County: Oakland — FICE Identification: 002279
Unit ID: 170675
Telephone: (248) 204-4000 — Carnegie Class: Masters/L
FAX Number: (248) 204-3727 — Calendar System: Semester
URL: www.ltu.edu
Established: 1932 — Annual Undergrad Tuition & Fees: $36,630
Enrollment: 2,812 — Coed
Affiliation or Control: Independent Non-Profit — IRS Status: 501(c)3
Highest Offering: Doctorate
Accreditation: HLC, #ARCPA, ART, CIDA, NURSE

01 President and CEO .... Dr. Tarek M. SOBH
04 Exec Assistant to the President .... Ms. Kayleigh REID
05 Provost .... Vacant
88 Exec Dir Marburger STEM Center .... Dr. Sibrina Nichelle COLLINS
10 Vice Pres Finance/Admin .... Ms. Linda L. HEIGHT
88 Spec Asst to Pres for Development .... Dr. Greg CASCIONE
26 Vice Pres Mktg & Public Affairs .... Ms. Renee TAMBEAU
20 Assistant Provost .... Mr. Jim JOLLY
84 Asst Provost Enrollment Management .... Ms. Lisa R. KUJAWA
48 Dean of Architecture & Design .... Mr. Karl DAUBMANN
49 Dean of Arts & Sciences .... Mr. Srini KAMBHAMPATI
54 Dean of Engineering .... Dr. Nabil F. GRACE
50 Dean of Management .... Dr. Bahman MIRSHAB
32 Dean of Students .... Mr. Kevin FINN
13 Interim Director IT Services .... Dr. Lynn MILLER-WIETECHA
07 Director of Admissions .... Ms. Jane T. ROHRBACK
06 University Registrar .... Ms. Noreen FERGUSON
08 Director Library .... Mr. Gary R. COCOZZOLI
18 Director of Campus Facilities .... Mr. Carey G. VALENTINE
14 Director Help Desk/Services .... Vacant
37 Director of Financial Aid .... Ms. Susie POLI-SMITH
41 Dir of Rec/Athletics & Wellness .... Mr. Scott TRUDEAU
36 Asst Director of Career Services .... Ms. Kerri SEACH
35 Assistant Dean of Students .... Ms. Cyndi SPOTTS
39 Director of Residence Life .... Ms. Kimberly JERDINE
86 Exec Director Business Outreach .... Mr. Mark J. BRUCKI
102 Dir of Corp & Foundations Relations .... Vacant
30 Exec Dir Development Operations .... Ms. Shannon TRANSIT
15 Assoc VP/Chief HR Officer .... Ms. Deshawn JOHNSON
40 Manager Campus Bookstore .... Mr. Rob NOBLE
109 General Manager Dining Services .... Ms. Jillian WILLIAMS
27 Dir of Univ Comm & Academic Editor .... Ms. Renee TAMBEAU
88 Managing Editor Univ News Bureau .... Mr. Matt ROUSH
19 Director of Campus Safety .... Mr. Steven J. BOGDALEK
31 Exec Dir of Outreach & Spec Events .... Ms. Robin LECLERC
110 Coordinator of Advancement Services .... Ms. Brande' OLIVER
88 University Architect .... Mr. Joseph C. VERYSER
121 Dir of Academic Achievement Center .... Dr. Gladys M. AVILES
09 Dir of Inst Research/Academic Plng .... Ms. Noreen FERGUSON
96 Purchasing Supervisor .... Ms. Michelle BUTKOVICH
105 Director of Web Services .... Mr. Christian FORREST
106 eLearning Architect & Pgm Producer .... Dr. Lynn MILLER-WIETECHA
29 Alumni Relations .... Mr. Jay REDMAN
28 Director of Diversity .... Dr. Caryn REED-HENDON

Macomb Community College (F)

14500 Twelve Mile Road, Warren MI 48088-3896

County: Macomb — FICE Identification: 008906
Unit ID: 170790
Telephone: (586) 445-7241 — Carnegie Class: Assoc/MT-VT-High Trad
FAX Number: (586) 445-7886 — Calendar System: Semester
URL: www.macomb.edu
Established: 1954 — Annual Undergrad Tuition & Fees (In-District): $5,975
Enrollment: 16,736 — Coed
Affiliation or Control: Local — IRS Status: 501(c)3
Highest Offering: Associate Degree
Accreditation: HLC, ACFEI, ADNUR, CAHIIM, COARC, EMT, IFSAC, MAC, NAEYC, OTA, PTAA, SURGT

01 President .... Dr. James O. SAWYER
05 Provost/VP for Learning Unit .... Dr. Leslie KELLOGG
10 Vice President for Business .... Ms. Elizabeth ARGIRI
15 Vice President for Human Resources .... Ms. Joline DAVIS
111 VP College Adv/Community Relations .... Dr. Kevin CHANDLER
26 Dean University Relations .... Vacant
32 Vice President for Student Services .... Ms. Jill M. LITTLE
49 Dean Arts & Sciences .... Dr. Marie PRITCHETT
76 Dean Health/Public Services .... Dr. Nara MIRIJANIAN
54 Dean Engineering & Adv Tech .... Mr. Donald HUTCHISON
50 Dean Business & Info Technology .... Dr. Michael BALSAMO
35 Dean of Student Success .... Dr. Susan BOYD
115 Director Finance & Investments .... Ms. Kathi POINDEXTER
88 Director Public Service Institute .... Mr. Michael LOPEZ
27 Director Marketing & Recruitment .... Ms. Audrey TAKACS
09 Director Institutional Research .... Ms. Deirdre SYMS
88 Director Special Research Projects .... Dr. Randall HICKMAN
06 Registrar/Dir Enrollment Services .... Dr. Carrie JEFFERS
102 Director MCC Foundation .... Ms. Christina AYAR
38 Dir Counseling & Academic Advising .... Ms. Michelle KOSS
96 Purchasing Administrator .... Mr. Dennis COSTELLO
41 Director of Athletics .... Mr. Bryan RIZZO
18 Director Facilities Management .... Mr. William SIMONSON
37 Director of Financial Aid .... Mr. Michael WILLIAMS
36 Director Career Employment Services .... Mr. Robert PENKALA
51 Dir Workforce Continuing Education .... Mr. Patrick ROUSE
13 CIO .... Mr. Michael ZIMMERMAN
08 Dean Libraries/Learning Resources .... Vacant
43 General Counsel .... Mr. Jeffrey STEELE

Madonna University (G)

36600 Schoolcraft Road, Livonia MI 48150-1176

County: Wayne — FICE Identification: 002282
Unit ID: 170806
Telephone: (734) 432-5300 — Carnegie Class: Masters/M
FAX Number: N/A — Calendar System: Semester
URL: www.madonna.edu
Established: 1937 — Annual Undergrad Tuition & Fees: $24,000
Enrollment: 2,792 — Coed
Affiliation or Control: Roman Catholic — IRS Status: 501(c)3
Highest Offering: Doctorate
Accreditation: HLC, ACBSP, CAEP, DIETD, FEPAC, NURSE, SW

01 Acting President .... Mr. Ian DAY
100 Chief of Staff .... Mr. John MONTGOMERY
05 Provost and VP for Academic Admin .... Dr. Deborah DUNN
32 VP for Student Affs/Mission Integr .... Dr. Christine BENSON
111 Vice President for Advancement .... Dr. Matthew RHEINECKER
35 Asst VP/Dean of Students/504 Coord .... Dr. Clifford CAMP
06 Asst VP Enrollment Svc & Registrar .... Ms. Dina DUBUIS
15 Asst VP/Chief Human Resources Ofcr .... Ms. Tracey DURDEN
28 Chief Diversity Officer .... Mr. Jesse COX
13 Chief Information Officer .... Mr. Joshua STOTTS
10 Controller .... Mr. Matthew BEATTIE
49 Dean College of Arts and Sciences .... Dr. Kevin EYSTER
50 Dean School of Business .... Dr. Tara KANE
53 Dean College of Education .... Dr. Karen OBSNIUK

106 Associate Dean of Online Education .... Dr. Elena QURESHI
108 Assoc Dean of Assessment .... Dr. Stewart WOOD
07 Executive Director of Admissions .... Mrs. Patricia EVERETT
26 Exec Director Comm and Events .... Ms. Karen SANBORN
41 Director of Athletics .... Mr. Scott KENNELL
35 Director of Campus Life .... Ms. Annaliese CORACE-LANGBEEN
36 Director of Career Development .... Mrs. Cierra SUTHERLAND
18 Director of Facilities Management .... Mr. Michael MATICH
89 Director of First-Year Experience .... Ms. Toni HENNING
123 Director Grad & Online Admissions .... Mrs. Sarah HERMANN
85 Director International Students .... Ms. Grace PHILSON
08 Director of Library Services .... Ms. Cynthia SIMPSON
27 Director of Marketing .... Ms. Jennifer KENNEDY
88 Director Nursing Simulation Lab .... Ms. Laura VAN HORN
39 Director of Residence Life .... Mr. Evan OWEN
88 Director of Special Events .... Mrs. Katie ALEXANDER
113 Director Student Financial Services .... Mr. Mark SCHROEDER
07 Director Undergraduate Admissions .... Mrs. Lauren NOBLES
121 Director Student Advising/Success .... Ms. Katherine SARTORI
88 Int Dir Center Personal Instruction .... Mrs. Allison PROUGH
09 Institutional Research Specialist .... Mr. David PIASECKI

MIAT College of Technology (A)

2955 South Haggerty Road, Canton MI 48188
County: Wayne FICE Identification: 020603
Unit ID: 169655
Telephone: (734) 423-2139 Carnegie Class: Spec 2-yr-Tech
FAX Number: (734) 858-5000 Calendar System: Other
URL: www.miat.edu
Established: Annual Undergrad Tuition & Fees: $12,838
Enrollment: 1,537 Coed
Affiliation or Control: Proprietary IRS Status: Proprietary
Highest Offering: Associate Degree
Accreditation: ACCSC

01 Campus President .... Ms. Jennifer PAUGH

Michigan School of Psychology (B)

26811 Orchard Lake Road,
Farmington Hills MI 48334-4512
County: Oakland FICE Identification: 021989
Unit ID: 169220
Telephone: (248) 476-1122 Carnegie Class: Spec-4-yr-Other Health
FAX Number: (248) 476-1125 Calendar System: Semester
URL: www.msp.edu
Established: 1981 Annual Graduate Tuition & Fees: N/A
Enrollment: 209 Coed
Affiliation or Control: Independent Non-Profit IRS Status: 501(c)3
Highest Offering: Doctorate; No Undergraduates
Accreditation: HLC, CLPSY

01 President/CEO .... Dr. Fran BROWN
03 Vice President/COO .... Ms. Diane ZALAPI
05 Dean of Academic Programs/CAO .... Vacant
88 Director of Clinical Training .... Vacant
15 Dir of HR/Inst Effectiveness .... Ms. Amanda MING
32 Dir of Student Svcs/Registrar .... Ms. Carrie PYEATT
37 Dir Financial Aid .... Mr. Roger MAKI-SCHRAMM
13 Dir of Info Tech & Campus Security .... Mr. Jeffrey CROSS
07 Coord Admissions/Student Engagement .... Ms. Kinsey TEKIELE
18 Director Facilities Management .... Mr. Ed KLATT

Michigan State University (C)

426 Auditorium Road, Room 450,
East Lansing MI 48824-1046
County: Ingham FICE Identification: 002290
Unit ID: 171100
Telephone: (517) 355-1855 Carnegie Class: DU-Highest
FAX Number: N/A Calendar System: Semester
URL: www.msu.edu
Established: 1855 Annual Undergrad Tuition & Fees (In-State): $14,460
Enrollment: 49,695 Coed
Affiliation or Control: State IRS Status: 501(c)3
Highest Offering: Doctorate
Accreditation: HLC, ANEST, #ARCPA, CAATE, CACREP, CAEP, CEA, CIDA, CLPSY, CONST, DIETD, DIETI, FEPAC, IPSY, JOUR, LAW, LSAR, MED, MFCD, MLS, MUS, NURSE, OSTEO, PCSAS, PLNG, SCPSY, SP, SW, VET

01 President .... Dr. Samuel L. STANLEY
05 Provost/EVP Academic Affairs .... Dr. Teresa K. WOODRUFF
11 Exec Vice Pres for Administration .... Dr. Melissa WOO
46 Vice Pres Research/Graduate Studies .... Dr. Doug GAGE
86 Vice Pres Governmental Relations .... Dr. Kathleen WILBUR
10 VP Finance/Treasurer .... Ms. Lisa FRACE
111 Vice Pres Univ Advancement .... Ms. Kim TOBIN
43 VP Legal Affairs/General Counsel .... Mr. Brian T. QUINN
18 VP Infrastructure Plng & Facilities .... Mr. Dan J. BOLLMAN
32 Vice President Student Life .... Mr. Vennie GORE
26 VP Communication & Brand Strategy .... Ms. Heather C. SWAIN
27 Vice Pres & Univ Spokesperson . Ms. Emily GERKIN GUERRANT
88 Assistant VP Research & Innovation .... Dr. J.R HAYWOOD
58 Assoc Prov and Dean Grad School .... Dr. Thomas JEITSCHKO
20 Int Assoc Prov/VP Acad/Human Res .... Ms. Ann E. AUSTIN
20 Assoc Prov/Dean Undergrad Educ .... Dr. Mark A. LARGENT
31 Int Assoc Prov Univ Outreach/ Engage .... Dr. Laurie A. VAN EGEREN
84 Assoc Provost Acad Svcs/Enroll Mgt .... Dr. Dave D. WEATHERSPOON
15 VP Human Resources .... Ms. Christina BROGDON
13 SVP Info Tech/Chief Info Ofcr .... Dr. Melissa WOO
88 Asst VP Ofc of Sponsored Programs .... Dr. Twila REIGHLEY
21 Controller .... Mr. Greg J. DEPPONG
07 Director of Admissions .... Mr. John AMBROSE
22 Dir Ofc of Institutional Diversity .... Ms. Debra MARTINEZ
28 VP and Chief Diversity Officer .... Dr. Jabbar R. BENNETT
29 Assoc VP for Alumni Relations .... Mr. Bob THOMAS
25 Director Contract & Grant Admin .... Ms. Evonne PEDAWI
36 Exec Dir Career Services/Placement .... Mr. Jeff BEAVERS
38 Director Counseling Center .... Dr. Mark F. PATISHNOCK
88 Dir MI AgBioResearch .... Dr. Doug D. BUHLER
56 Assoc Dir MSU Extension .... Mr. Patrick CUDNEY
37 Director of Financial Aid .... Mr. Anthony T. WILLIAMS, JR.
06 Registrar .... Mr. Steve SHABLIN
85 Director Intl Students/Scholars ... Dr. Krista MCCALLUM BEATTY
23 Director MSU Student Health Ctr .... Dr. Michael BROWN
92 Dean Honors College .... Dr. Christopher P. LONG
41 VP & Dir Intercollegiate Athletics .... Mr. Alan HALLER
08 Director of Libraries .... Mr. Terri MILLER
88 Dir Natl Supercond Cyclotron Lab ...... Dr. Thomas GLASMACHER
19 VP Public Safety/Chief of Police .... Mr. Marlon C. LYNCH
47 Dean Col Agricul/Natural Resources .... Dr. Kelly F. MILLENBAH
79 Dean College Arts & Letters .... Dr. Christopher P. LONG
49 Dean Res Col Arts/Humanities .... Dr. Dylan AT MINER
50 Dean Eli Broad Col of Business .... Dr. Judith WHIPPLE
60 Dean Col Communications/Arts & Sci .... Dr. Prabu DAVID
53 Dean College of Education .... Dr. Ann E. AUSTIN
54 Dean College of Engineering .... Dr. Leo C. KEMPEL
63 Dean College Human Medicine .... Dr. Aron SOUSA
82 Dean James Madison College .... Dr. Cameron G. THIES
61 Dean College of Law .... Linda S. GREENE
81 Int Dean Lyman Briggs College .... Dr. Kendra S. CHERUVELIL
64 Dean College of Music .... Dr. James B. FORGER
65 Dean College Natural Science .... Dr. Phillip M. DUXBURY
66 Dean College of Nursing .... Dr. Randolph RASCH
63 Dean Col Osteopathic Medicine .... Dr. Andrea AMALFITANO
83 Dean College of Social Sciences .... Dr. Mary A. FINN
74 Dean College Veterinary Medicine .... Dr. Birgit PUSCHNER
82 Dean Intl Studies & Programs .... Dr. Steven D. HANSON
04 Executive Asst to President .... Ms. Jesselyn NELSON
100 Chief of Staff .... Dr. Michael ZEIG
09 Director of Institutional Research .... Ms. Bethan CANTWELL
102 Dir Foundation/Corporate Relations .... Ms. Deepa SRIKANTA
105 Director Web Services .... Mr. Randy BROWN
39 Dir Resident Life/Student Housing .... Dr. Ray F. GASSER
44 Director Annual Giving .... Ms. Kathleen DENEAU
96 Director University Services .... Ms. Kristin DEMIR
104 Director Study Abroad .... Dr. Opal LEEMAN BARTZIS
122 Asst Dir Student Life-Greek Life .. Mr. Brian HERCLIFF-PROFFER

Michigan Technological University (D)

1400 Townsend Drive, Houghton MI 49931-1295
County: Houghton FICE Identification: 002292
Unit ID: 171128
Telephone: (906) 487-1885 Carnegie Class: DU-Higher
FAX Number: (906) 487-2935 Calendar System: Semester
URL: www.mtu.edu
Established: 1885 Annual Undergrad Tuition & Fees (In-State): $16,436
Enrollment: 6,873 Coed
Affiliation or Control: State IRS Status; 501(c)3
Highest Offering: Doctorate
Accreditation: HLC, CONST, MLS

01 President .... Dr. Richard J. KOUBEK
05 Interim Provost .... Dr. Andrew STORER
86 Vice Pres Governmental Relations .... Mr. William R. KORDENBROCK
46 Vice President for Research .... Dr. David D. REED
84 Vice Pres Univ Relations/Enrollment .... Dr. John B. LEHMAN
111 VP Advancement & Alumni Engagement .... Dr. Bill ROBERTS
32 VP Student Affairs/Dean of Students .... Dr. Wallace SOUTHERLAND, III
10 Interim CFO .... Dr. David D. REED
92 Dean Pavlis Honors College .... Dr. Jean KAMPE
26 Asst VP Univ Mktg/Communications .... Mr. Ian REPP
08 Director of the Library .... Mr. Joshua OLSON
09 Institutional Analysis .... Mr. Richard ELENICH
29 Asst VP of Alumni Engagement .... Ms. Jennifer LUCAS
06 Registrar .... Ms. Theresa K. JACQUES
07 Asst VP Enrollment Management .... Mr. Kyle RUBIN
15 Director Human Resources .... Ms. Renee HILLER
37 Director of Student Financial Svcs .... Ms. Alyssa FREDIN
36 Interim Director Career Services .... Ms. Chris HOHNHOLT
18 Exec Director Facilities Management .... Vacant
114 Exec Director Budget and Planning .... Ms. Debbie L. SHELDON
38 Acting Director Counseling Services .... Ms. Crystal MCLEOD
19 Director and Chief Public Safety .... Mr. Brian J. CADWELL
22 Exec Director Affirmative Programs .... Ms. Beth LUNDE-STOCKERO
96 Director of Purchasing .... Ms. Danielle CYRUS
58 Assoc Provost/Dean Graduate School .... Dr. Will CANTRELL
50 Dean School of Business & Economics ..... Dr. Dean L. JOHNSON
54 Dean College of Engineering .... Dr. Janet CALLAHAN
65 Dean School of Forestry .... Dr. Andrew J. STORER
49 Dean College of Sciences/Arts .... Dr. David HEMMER
77 Dean College of Computing .... Dr. Dennis LIVESAY
13 Chief Information Officer .... Mr. Joshua OLSON
41 Athletic Director .... Dr. Suzanne SANREGRET
25 Chief Contracts/Grants Admin .... Ms. Julie SEPPALA
39 Chief Housing Officer/Director .... Mr. Travis L. PIERCE
04 Dir Presidential Communications .... Ms. Heather L. HERMAN
28 Dir IPS/Assoc Dean Stdnt Engagement .... Ms. Kellie RAFFAELLI
43 General Counsel .... Ms. Sarah H. SCHULTE

Mid Michigan College (E)

1375 S Clare Avenue, Harrison MI 48625-9447
County: Clare FICE Identification: 006768
Unit ID: 171155
Telephone: (989) 386-6622 Carnegie Class: Assoc/MT-VT-Mix Trad/Non
FAX Number: N/A Calendar System: Semester
URL: www.midmich.edu
Established: 1965 Annual Undergrad Tuition & Fees (In-District): $7,364
Enrollment: 3,291 Coed
Affiliation or Control: State/Local IRS Status: 501(c)3
Highest Offering: Associate Degree
Accreditation: HLC, CNEA, MAC, PTAA, RAD

01 President .... Mr. Tim HOOD
05 VP of Academic Affairs & Outreach .... Dr. Scott MERTES
10 VP of Finance & Administration .... Ms. Lillian FRICK
32 Vice President of Student Services .... Dr. Matt MILLER
102 Exec Director of the Mid Foundation .... Mr. Thomas OLVER
15 Associate VP Human Resources .... Ms. Lori FASSETT
09 Asst VP Institutional Research .... Dr. Peter VELGUTH
04 Exec Asst to President & Trustees .... Ms. Amy LINCE

Monroe County Community College (F)

1555 S Raisinville Road, Monroe MI 48161-9746
County: Monroe FICE Identification: 002294
Unit ID: 171225
Telephone: (734) 242-7300 Carnegie Class: Assoc/MT-VT-Mix Trad/Non
FAX Number: (734) 242-9711 Calendar System: Semester
URL: www.monroeccc.edu
Established: 1964 Annual Undergrad Tuition & Fees (In-District): $5,600
Enrollment: 2,302 Coed
Affiliation or Control: Local IRS Status: 170(c)1
Highest Offering: Associate Degree
Accreditation: HLC, ADNUR, COARC, NAEYC

01 President .... Dr. Kojo QUARTEY
05 Vice President of Instruction .... Dr. Grace B. YACKEE
10 Vice Pres of Admin .... Ms. Suzanne M. WETZEL
84 Vice Pres Enroll Mgmt/Stdnt Success .... Mr. Scott BEHRENS
72 Dean of Applied Sci & Eng Tech .... Mr. Parmeshwar COOMAR
50 Dean of Business .... Mr. Leon LETTER
76 Dean of Health Sciences .... Ms. Kimberly LINDQUIST
79 Dean of Humanities/Social Science .... Mr. James LEDUC
81 Dean of Science/Mathematics .... Mr. Kevin COOPER
06 Registrar .... Ms. Tracy VOGT
07 Director of Admissions/Guidance .... Ms. Tracy PERRY
88 Director of Upward Bound .... Mr. Anthony QUINN
88 Int Dir of Respiratory Therapy .... Ms. Helen STRIPLING
21 Director of Financial Services .... Ms. Elizabeth HARTIG
18 Director Physical Plant .... Mr. Jack BURNS
109 Dir Auxiliary Services/Purchasing .... Ms. Kelly HEINZERLING
14 Director Data Processing Services .... Mr. James A. ROSS
37 Director of Financial Aid .... Ms. Valerie CULLER
36 Dir Business Devel/Employment Svcs .... Mr. Barry C. KINSEY
51 Director of Lifelong Learning .... Ms. Tina PILLARELLI
13 Manager Information Services .... Mr. Brian K. LAY
26 Director of Marketing/Communication .... Mr. Joseph VERKENNES
15 Director of Human Resources .... Ms. Linda TORBET
04 Exec Asst to President/Sec Board .... Ms. Penny R. DORCEY
09 Dir Inst Research/Eval/Accred .... Ms. Quri WYGONIK
102 Exec Director Foundation .... Mr. Joshua MYERS
19 Chief of Safety Services .... Mr. Charles ABEL
121 Dir Student Success .... Dr. Gerald MCCARTY, III

Montcalm Community College (G)

2800 College Drive, Sidney MI 48885-9723
County: Montcalm FICE Identification: 002295
Unit ID: 171234
Telephone: (989) 328-2111 Carnegie Class: Assoc/MT-VT-High Trad
FAX Number: (989) 328-2950 Calendar System: Semester
URL: www.montcalm.edu
Established: 1965 Annual Undergrad Tuition & Fees (In-District): $7,710
Enrollment: 1,414 Coed
Affiliation or Control: Local IRS Status: 501(c)3
Highest Offering: Associate Degree
Accreditation: HLC, CNEA

01 President .... Dr. Stacy YOUNG
05 Vice Pres for Academic Affairs .... Mr. Robert SPOHR
10 VP Administrative Services .... Ms. Connie STEWART
102 Exec Dir Inst Advance/Foundation .... Ms. Lisa LUND
32 Dean Student & Enrollment Svcs .... Ms. Debra ALEXANDER
37 Director of Financial Aid .... Ms. Jessica HERRICK
13 Director Information Tech Svcs .... Mr. David KOHN
09 Research Analyst .... Mr. Vladimir EDELMAN
26 Communications Director .... Ms. Shelly SPRINGBORN
15 Director of Human Resources .... Ms. Riki JENSEN
21 Director of Accounting .... Ms. Kire WIERDA
18 Director of Facilities .... Mr. Taylor MALE
66 Dean of Nursing & Health Careers .... Ms. Danielle ANDERSON
07 Recruitment Director .... Ms. Emily DIMET
88 Dean Industrial Ed & Workforce Trng .... Ms. Susan HATTO
103 Director Workforce Development .... Ms. Susan HATTO
08 Librarian .... Ms. Katie ARWOOD

Moody Theological Seminary-Michigan (A)

41550 E Ann Arbor Trail, Plymouth MI 48170-4308
Telephone: (734) 207-9581 FICE Identification: 031353
Accreditation: &HLC, THEOL

† Regional accreditation is carried under the parent institution Moody Bible Institute, Chicago, IL.

Mott Community College (B)

1401 E Court Street, Flint MI 48503-2089
County: Genesee FICE Identification: 002261
Unit ID: 169275
Telephone: (810) 762-0200 Carnegie Class: Assoc/HT-High Trad
FAX Number: (810) 762-0257 Calendar System: Semester
URL: www.mcc.edu
Established: 1923 Annual Undergrad Tuition & Fees (In-District): $5,149
Enrollment: 5,920 Coed
Affiliation or Control: Local IRS Status: 501(c)3
Highest Offering: Associate Degree
Accreditation: HLC, ACBSP, ADNUR, COARC, DA, DH, NAEYC, OTA, PTAA

01 President Dr. Beverly WALKER-GRIFFEA
32 VP Student Academic Success Mr. Jason WILSON
10 Chief Financial/Admin Ofcr Mr. Larry GAWTHROP
111 Assoc VP Institutional Advancement Mr. Dale WEIGHILL
15 Associate Vice President of HR Vacant
103 Assoc VP Workforce & Economic Dev Mr. Robert MATTHEWS
37 Exec Dir Student Financial Svcs Mr. Richard BORUSZEWSKI
20 Exec Dir of Academic Operations Ms. Dolores SHARPE
84 Exec Dir of Enrollment Management Mr. Jon CALDERWOOD
124 Dean Enrollment Mgmt & Retention Mr. Chris ENGLE
81 Dean of Math & Science Dr. Charles WADE
76 Dean of Health Sciences Dr. Rebecca MYSZENSKI
83 Dean Social Sciences & Fine Arts Vacant
50 Dean of Business Mr. Stephen SHUBERT
72 Dean of Technology Dr. Mark BANNATYNE
13 Chief Technology Officer Ms. Cheryl SHELTON
06 Registrar Ms. Michele TRAVER
36 Supervisor Student Employment Svcs Mr. Aron GERICS
08 Director of Library Mrs. Jill SODT
18 Exec Director Physical Plant Mr. Rodney WHITNEY
07 Director of Admissions Ms. Regina BROOMFIELD
41 Director Athletics/Campus Rec Mr. Al PERRY
09 Exec Dir Institutional Research Vacant
35 Student Life Coordinator Ms. Alexandria DOWDALL
96 Purchasing Manager Ms. Jody MICHAEL
04 Executive Asst to President Vacant
101 Board Relations Coordinator Mr. Michael SIMON
100 Chief of Staff Mrs. DeAndra LARKIN
102 Deputy Chief of Staff Mr. Jordan CLIMIE
112 Chief Development Officer Mrs. Lennetta CONEY

Muskegon Community College (C)

221 S Quarterline Road, Muskegon MI 49442-1493
County: Muskegon FICE Identification: 002297
Unit ID: 171304
Telephone: (231) 773-9131 Carnegie Class: Assoc/MT-VT-Mix Trad/Non
FAX Number: (231) 777-0440 Calendar System: Semester
URL: www.muskegoncc.edu
Established: 1926 Annual Undergrad Tuition & Fees (In-District): $10,750
Enrollment: 3,456 Coed
Affiliation or Control: Local IRS Status: Exempt
Highest Offering: Associate Degree
Accreditation: HLC, ADNUR, COARC, MAC, NAEYC

01 President Dr. Dale K. NESBARY
03 Provost/Executive Vice President Dr. John SELMON
05 VP for Academic Affairs Ms. Kelley CONRAD
10 VP Finance/Chief Advancement Ofcr Mr. Kenneth LONG
32 Dean of Student Services Ms. Sally BIRKAM
20 Dean of Instruction & Assessment Dr. Edward BREITENBACH
31 Dean of Community Outreach Ms. Trynette Lottie HARPS
06 Registrar Mr. Aaron RICHMAN
13 Chief Information Officer Dr. Steven WILSON
37 Assoc Director Financial Aid Ms. Jody ZERLAUT
09 Dir Institutional Research & Grants Mr. Eduardo BEDOYA
45 Director of Strategic Initiatives Ms. Tina DEE
15 Executive Director of HR Ms. Kristine ANDERSON
41 Dean of College Svcs & AD Mr. Marty MCDERMOTT
18 Physical Plant Director Mr. David STURGEON
29 Alumni & Donor Relations Manager Ms. Rachel STEWART
04 Executive Assistant to President Ms. Cindy S. DEBOEF

North Central Michigan College (D)

1515 Howard Street, Petoskey MI 49770-8717
County: Emmet FICE Identification: 002299
Unit ID: 171395
Telephone: (231) 348-6600 Carnegie Class: Assoc/HT-High Non
FAX Number: (231) 348-6628 Calendar System: Semester
URL: www.ncmich.edu
Established: 1958 Annual Undergrad Tuition & Fees (In-District): $6,776
Enrollment: 1,748 Coed
Affiliation or Control: Local IRS Status: 501(c)3
Highest Offering: Associate Degree
Accreditation: HLC, EMT

01 President Dr. David R. FINLEY
05 VP Academic Affairs Dr. Stephen STROM
10 VP of Finance & Facilities Dr. Tom ZEIDEL
32 VP of Student Services Renee DEYOUNG
26 VP of Marketing Carol LAENEN
102 Executive Director Foundation Chelsea PLATTE
08 Librarian Kendra LAKE
37 Director of Financial Aid Katie MALONE
18 Director of Physical Plant Ernst RUSCHE
84 Dir Enrollment Services/Registrar Joseph BALINSKI
21 Director of Business Services Troy SLATER
39 Director of Campus Housing Leon NASH
15 Director of Human Resources Lynn ECKERLE
40 Bookstore Manager Debbie MORRISON
49 Dean Liberal Arts Dr. Sara GLASGOW
66 Dean Nurs/Allied Hlth/Sci Brent LAFAIVE
50 Dean Business & Adjunct Faculty Michele ANDREWS
07 Director of Student Outreach Corey LANSING
13 Director of Information Services Vacant
88 Director of Resource Center Dallas CULVAHOUSE
04 Executive Asst to President Lea DIETZEL
06 Registrar Joseph BALINSKI
41 Athletic Director Ashley ANTONISHEN

Northern Michigan University (E)

1401 Presque Isle Avenue, Marquette MI 49855-5301
County: Marquette FICE Identification: 002301
Unit ID: 171456
Telephone: (906) 227-1000 Carnegie Class: Masters/M
FAX Number: (906) 227-2204 Calendar System: Semester
URL: www.nmu.edu
Established: 1899 Annual Undergrad Tuition & Fees (In-State): $12,402
Enrollment: 7,368 Coed
Affiliation or Control: State IRS Status: 501(c)3
Highest Offering: Doctorate
Accreditation: HLC, CAATE, CGTECH, DMOLS, MLS, MLTAD, MUS, NURSE, RAD, SURGT, SW

01 Interim President Dr. Kerri SCHUILING
05 Interim Provost/VP Academic Affairs Dr. Dale KAPLA
10 VP for Finance & Administration Mr. R. Gavin LEACH
102 CEO NMU Foundation Mr. Brad CANALE
09 Asst Provost/Dir of Inst Research Mr. Jason NICHOLAS
106 VP Extended Lrng/Cmty Engagement Dr. Steve VANDENAVOND
20 Int Assoc Prov/VP Academic Affs Dr. Leslie WARREN
58 Dean Graduate Education Dr. Lisa ECKERT
08 Dean Library/Instructional Support Dr. Leslie A. WARREN
32 Assistant VP/Dean of Students Dr. Christine G. GREER
49 Dean of Arts & Sciences Dr. Rob WINN
50 Dean Walker L Cisler Col Bus Prof. Carol JOHNSON
72 Dean Col of Technology/Occ Science Dr. Steve VANDENAVOND
06 Registrar Mr. Josh SANTIAGO
45 Asst to Pres Strategic Initiatives Ms. Cindy L. PAAVOLA
36 Dir of Acad & Career Advisement Mr. James G. GADZINSKI
37 Director of Financial Aid Mr. Michael R. ROTUNDO
38 Director Counseling Center Vacant
88 Director Glenn T Seaborg Center Mr. Chris STANDERFORD
41 Athletic Director Mr. Forrest KARR
19 Dir Public Safety/Police Services Mr. Michael J. BATH
39 Director Housing/Residence Life Ms. Catherine HARDENBERGH
07 Director of Admissions Ms. Gerri L. DANIELS
23 Chief of Staff/Physician Dr. Christopher KIRKPATRICK
15 Director of Human Resources Ms. Rhea DEVER
26 Asst VP Marketing & Communications Dr. Derek HALL
92 Director of Honors Program Dr. David H. WOOD
24 Director Broadcast & AV Services Mr. Pat L. LAKENEN
29 Exec Dir Alumni Ops/Annual Giving Ms. Robyn L. STILLE
40 Bookstore Manager Mr. Paul WRIGHT
18 Associate VP Eng & Plan/Facilities Ms. Kathy A. RICHARDS
13 Chief Technology Officer Mr. David W. MAKI
96 Manager of Purchasing Mr. Joseph OMBRELLO
86 Exec Dir of BOT & Govt Relations Ms. Deanna HEMMILA
04 Executive Assistant to President Ms. Laura GLOVER
101 Secretary Board of Trustees Ms. Cathy ANDREW
22 Dir Affirmative Action/EEO Ms. Janet KOSKI
53 Dean Teacher Educ/Dir of Educ Dr. Joe LUBIG
28 Chief Diversity Officer Vacant
103 Director Workforce Development Ms. Stephanie ZADROGA-LANGLOIS
105 Web Systems Director Mr. Eric JOHNSON
25 Director Grants & Contracts Ms. Stacy SCHWENKE
104 Director International Programs Ms. Diana VREELAND
30 Director of Development Ms. Jane SURRELL
44 Assoc Director Annual Giving Mr. Andrew HILL
122 Coord Ctr Stdnt Enrich-Greek Life Ms. Nichole SANDOVAL

Northwestern Michigan College (F)

1701 E Front Street, Traverse City MI 49686-3061
County: Grand Traverse FICE Identification: 002302
Unit ID: 171483
Telephone: (231) 995-1000 Carnegie Class: Bac/Assoc-Assoc Dom
FAX Number: (231) 995-1339 Calendar System: Semester
URL: www.nmc.edu
Established: 1951 Annual Undergrad Tuition & Fees (In-District): $8,280
Enrollment: 3,278 Coed
Affiliation or Control: Local IRS Status: 501(c)3
Highest Offering: Baccalaureate
Accreditation: HLC, ACFEI, ADNUR, DA, PNUR, SURGT

01 President Dr. Nick NISSLEY
100 Exec Dir Pres Ofc & Board Ops Ms. Lynne M. MORITZ
05 VP for Educational Services Dr. Stephen N. SICILIANO
10 VP Finance & Administration Mr. Troy KIERCZYNSKI
15 Associate VP of Human Resources Mr. Mark LIEBLING
13 VP for Student Svcs & Technology Mr. Todd NEIBAUER
102 Assoc VP of Resource Dev & Found Ms. Jennifer HRICIK
88 Exec Dir of Dennos Museum Center Mr. Craig A. HADLEY
107 VP Strategic Initiatives Mr. Jason SLADE
75 Dir of Bus Dev/Marine Center Mr. Ed BAILEY
88 Director of Aviation Mr. Alex BLOYE
29 Director Alumni Engagement Mr. Carly MCCALL
32 Dean of Students Ms. Lisa THOMAS
37 Director of Financial Aid Ms. Linda BERLIN
90 Director of Systems and LAN Mgmt Mr. Dan WASSON
50 Director of the Hagerty Center Mr. Chad SCHENKELBERGER
20 Dir Academic Business/Affairs Div Mr. Brian HEFFNER
08 Director of Library Services Ms. Kerrey WOUGHTER
92 Director of Learning Services Ms. Kari L. KAHLER
24 Director Educational Media Tech Ms. Terri GUSTAFSON
26 Exec Dir of PR/Marketing/Comm Ms. Diana FAIRBANKS
56 Director Extended Educ Services Ms. Laura MATCHETT
18 Director of Campus Services Mr. Paul PERRY
28 Supt Great Lakes Maritime Academy RAdm. Gerard ACHENBACH, USMS
06 Registrar Ms. Cindy DEEMER
07 Director of Admissions Ms. Cathryn CLAERHOUT
09 Dir Research Planning Effectiveness Ms. Joy EVANS GOODCHILD
30 Director of Development Vacant
88 Director of Water Studies Institute Mr. Hans VANSUMEREN
64 Director of Music Programs Mr. Jeffrey COBB
104 Director of International Services Mr. Jim BENSLEY
66 Director of Nursing Programs Ms. Tamella LIVENGOOD
23 Director of Health Services Ms. Renee R. JACOBSON
88 Director of Police Academy Mr. Gail KUROWSKI
39 Associate Dean of Campus & Res Life Dr. Marcus BENNETT
12 Director Great Lakes Culinary Inst Ms. Les ECKERT
36 Director of Advising Ms. Lindsey DICKINSON
28 Special Assist to the President DEI Dr. Marcus BENNETT

Northwood University (G)

4000 Whiting Drive, Midland MI 48640-2398
County: Midland FICE Identification: 004072
Unit ID: 171492
Telephone: (989) 837-4200 Carnegie Class: Spec-4-yr-Bus
FAX Number: (989) 837-4111 Calendar System: Semester
URL: www.northwood.edu
Established: 1959 Annual Undergrad Tuition & Fees: $29,480
Enrollment: 2,541 Coed
Affiliation or Control: Independent Non-Profit IRS Status: 501(c)3
Highest Offering: Doctorate
Accreditation: HLC, ACBSP

01 President Dr. Kent MACDONALD
05 VP of Academics and Provost Dr. Kristin STEHOUWER
10 VP Finance & Administration Mr. Brian MCLEOD
88 Director of The McNair Center Dr. Timothy G. NASH
84 VP Undergrad Enrollment & Fin Aid Ms. Susan POLI-SMITH
111 VP Advancement Mr. Murray E. KYTE
26 Senior Communications Officer Ms. Rachel VALDISERRI
32 Dean of Student Affairs Mr. Andy CRIPE
06 Registrar Dr. Marisa HERNANDEZ
123 VP Grad Enrollment & Prof Studies Dr. Matthew L. BENNETT
37 Financial Aid Director Ms. Christie M. MCDONALD
15 Asst VP HR & Perf Meas/Title IX Ms. Pamela L. CHRISTIE
29 Executive Director Alumni Relations Ms. Julie L. ADAMCZYK
19 Director Security and Safety Ms. April OWENS
39 Director Student & Residence Life Mr. Justin THOMASON
18 Physical Plant Director Mr. Steven P. SMITH
30 Chief Development/Engagement Ofcr Mr. Justin W. MARSHALL
41 Athletic Director Mr. Jeff CURTIS

Oakland Community College (H)

2480 Opdyke Road, Bloomfield Hills MI 48304-2266
County: Oakland FICE Identification: 002303
Unit ID: 171535
Telephone: (248) 341-2000 Carnegie Class: Assoc/HT-Mix Trad/Non
FAX Number: (248) 341-2099 Calendar System: Semester
URL: www.oaklandcc.edu
Established: 1964 Annual Undergrad Tuition & Fees (In-District): $4,712
Enrollment: 14,511 Coed
Affiliation or Control: State/Local IRS Status: 501(c)3
Highest Offering: Associate Degree
Accreditation: HLC, ACFEI, ADNUR, COARC, DH, DMS, MAC, RAD, SURGT

01 Chancellor Mr. Peter PROVENZANO, JR.
05 Provost Dr. Jennifer I. BERNE
11 Vice Chanc Administrative Services Ms. Bobbie REMIAS
32 Vice Chanc for Student Services Vacant
15 Vice Chancellor for HR & DEI Mr. Andre' POPLAR
13 Vice Chanc Info Technologies/CIO Mr. Robert MONTGOMERY
26 Vice Chanc Marketing/Communications Ms. Elizabeth R. SCHNELL
43 Vice Chanc for Legal Affairs Ms. Eileen K. HUSBAND
111 Vice Chancellor for Advancement Mr. Daniel J. JENUWINE
20 Associate Provost Mr. Joseph L. PETROSKY
20 Associate Provost Ms. Jolene J. CHAPMAN
04 Exec Administrator to Chancellor Ms. Cherie A. FOSTER
27 Dir of Marketing & Comm Ms. Shelia ACKER
35 Dean of Student Services Mr. Jahquan C. HAWKINS
35 Dean of Student Services Mr. Robert T. SPANN
35 Dean of Student Services Ms. Stacey N. JACKSON
66 Academic Dean Nursing/Health Prof Vacant

14 Exec Dir IT Infrastructure ... Mr. Chuck S. FLAGG
06 Registrar ... Mr. Stephen M. LINDEN
18 Director Physical Facilities ... Mr. Daniel P. CHEREWICK
19 Chief of Public Safety ... Mr. Paul J. MATYNKA
21 Controller ... Ms. Sharon K. CONVERSE
114 Director Budget & Financial Plng ... Mrs. Renee OSZUST
102 Exec Director OCC Foundation ... Mr. Daniel J. JENUWINE
36 Director of Career Svcs & Coop Ed ... Ms. Donna L. DUHAME-SCHMIDT
41 Athletic Director ... Ms. Jamie L. CORONA
96 Dir Purchasing/Auxiliary Svcs ... Ms. Sarah L. ROWLEY
37 Director Financial Res/Scholarships ... Ms. Wilma B. PORTER
81 Academic Dean Math & Sciences ... Mr. Ken M. WILLIAMS
80 Academic Dean Public Services/CREST ... Mr. David F. CECI
62 Academic Dean Learning Resources ... Ms. Mary Ann SHEBLE
83 Academic Dean Soc Sci & Human Svcs ... Mr. Kevin BRATTON
79 Academic Dean Comm/Art/Humanities ... Ms. Cindy L. CARBONE
89 Academic Dean College Readiness ... Ms. Beverly J. STANBROUGH
50 Acad Dean Bus & Info Technologies ... Mr. Tom M. HENDRICKS
88 Academic Dean EMIT ... Vacant
106 Academic Dean of Distance Learning ... Ms. Kayla S. LEBLANC
88 Foundation Coordinator ... Ms. Candy GEETER
88 Director Law Enforcement Training ... Mr. David F. CECI
07 Director of Admissions ... Mr. Jeremy M. GUC
09 Chief Strategy Officer ... Dr. Steven M. SIMPSON
86 Director Government Relations ... Ms. Eunice M. JEFFRIES
104 Director Global Education ... Ms. Eleonora G. BAGATELIA
105 Director Web Services ... Ms. Anna M. HANSARD
28 Director of Diversity ... Ms. Kristina M. MARSHALL
30 Director of Development ... Mr. Eric W. LOFQUIST

Oakland Community College Auburn Hills (A)

2900 Featherstone Road, Auburn Hills MI 48326-2845
Telephone: (248) 232-4100 Identification: 770281
Accreditation: &HLC, EMT

Oakland Community College Highland Lakes (B)

7350 Cooley Lake Road, Waterford MI 48327-4187
Telephone: (248) 942-3100 Identification: 770285
Accreditation: &HLC

Oakland Community College Orchard Ridge (C)

27055 Orchard Lake Road,
Farmington Hills MI 48334-4579
Telephone: (248) 522-3400 Identification: 770282
Accreditation: &HLC

Oakland Community College Royal Oak (D)

739 South Washington Avenue, Royal Oak MI 48067-3898
Telephone: (248) 246-2400 Identification: 770283
Accreditation: &HLC

Oakland Community College Southfield (E)

22322 Rutland Drive, Southfield MI 48075-4793
Telephone: (248) 341-2000 Identification: 770284
Accreditation: &HLC

Oakland University (F)

371 Wilson Boulevard, Rochester MI 48309-4400
County: Oakland FICE Identification: 002307
Unit ID: 171571
Telephone: (248) 370-2100 Carnegie Class: DU-Higher
FAX Number: N/A Calendar System: Semester
URL: www.oakland.edu
Established: 1957 Annual Undergrad Tuition & Fees (In-State): $13,934
Enrollment: 18,552 Coed
Affiliation or Control: State IRS Status: 501(c)3
Highest Offering: Doctorate
Accreditation: HLC, ANEST, CACREP, CAEP, DANCE, @DIETD, MED, MUS, NURSE, PH, PTA, RAD, SPAA, SW, THEA

01 President ... Dr. Ora PESCOVITZ
05 Sr VP Academic Affairs/Provost ... Dr. Britt RIOS-ELLIS
32 SVP Stdnt Affs/Chief Diversity Ofcr ... Mr. Glenn MCINTOSH
111 VP University Advancement ... Mr. Michael WESTFALL
10 Interim VP Finance & Administration ... Mr. James HARGETT
86 VP Government & Comm Relations ... Ms. Rochelle A. BLACK
100 Chief of Staff ... Mr. Josh MERCHANT
12 Executive Director Outreach ... Ms. Julie DICHTEL
66 Dean School of Nursing ... Vacant
54 Dean Engineering & Computer Science ... Dr. Louay M. CHAMRA
76 Dean School Health Sciences ... Dr. Kevin A. BALL
53 Dean Educ & Human Services ... Dr. Jon MARGERUM-LEYS
49 Dean College Arts & Sciences ... Dr. Elaine CAREY
50 Dean School of Business Admin ... Dr. Charles PIERCE
63 Dean School of Medicine ... Dr. Duane MEZWA
08 Dean University Library ... Ms. Polly BORUFF-JONES
20 Interim Associate Provost ... Dr. Amy BANES-BERCELI
46 VP for Research ... Dr. David A. STONE
24 Mgr Classroom Support/Tech Service ... Mr. John J. REESER
20 Asst VP Academic Affairs ... Ms. Peggy S. COOKE
88 Director Center for Excellence ... Dr. Judith ABLESER
88 Dir Eye Research Institute ... Dr. Mohamed AL-SHABRAWEY
88 Director FAJRI ... Dr. Sayed NASSAR
21 Assoc VP Finance & Administration ... Vacant
18 Assoc VP Facilities Management ... Vacant
15 VP Human Resources ... Ms. Joi M. CUNNINGHAM
102 AVP Princ Gifts/Campaign Strategy ... Ms. Alison K. GAUDREAU
35 Dean of Students ... Mr. Michael WADSWORTH
19 Chief of Police ... Mr. Mark B. GORDON
06 Registrar ... Ms. Tricia WESTERGAARD
44 Dir Annual Giving Program ... Ms. Kelly N. BRAULT
37 Director of Financial Aid ... Ms. Nancy FETZER
29 Sr Dir of Engagement ... Ms. Sue HELDEROP
26 VP Communications & Marketing ... Mr. John O. YOUNG
41 Athletics Director ... Mr. Steven WATERFIELD
16 AVP Academic Human Resources ... Vacant
39 Director of University Housing ... Vacant
36 Senior Director Career Services ... Mr. Wayne J. THIBODEAU
38 Director Counseling Center ... Dr. David J. SCHWARTZ
85 Director International Students ... Mr. David J. ARCHBOLD
22 Director Disability Support Svcs ... Mr. Sarah GUADALUPE
96 Director of Purchasing ... Mr. Mike RANGOS
43 VP General Counsel ... Mr. Boyd A. FARNAM
13 Chief Information Officer ... Ms. Bhavani KONERU
84 VP Enrollment Management ... Ms. Dawn M. AUBRY
58 Dean Graduate Education ... Dr. Brandy RANDALL
09 Director of Institutional Research ... Ms. Song YAN
104 Exec Director Global Engagement ... Ms. Rosemary MAX
106 Director of e-learning ... Dr. Shaun A. MOORE
114 Director Internal Audit ... Mr. David P. VARTANIAN

Olivet College (G)

320 S Main Street, Olivet MI 49076-9406
County: Eaton FICE Identification: 002308
Unit ID: 171599
Telephone: (269) 749-7000 Carnegie Class: Bac-Diverse
FAX Number: (269) 749-7600 Calendar System: Semester
URL: www.olivetcollege.edu
Established: 1844 Annual Undergrad Tuition & Fees: $30,126
Enrollment: 1,023 Coed
Affiliation or Control: Independent Non-Profit IRS Status: 501(c)3
Highest Offering: Master's
Accreditation: HLC, NURSE

01 President ... Dr. Steven M. COREY
05 Provost and Dean of the College ... Dr. Paul BURKHARDT
10 Vice President and CFO ... Mr. Mark DERUITER
07 Vice Pres Admissions ... Vacant
32 Assoc Provost Student Development ... Ms. KayDee PERRY
111 Vice Pres Advancement ... Ms. Vicki STOUFFER
13 Asst Vice President Technology ... Mr. Suresh ACHARYA
06 Registrar ... Ms. Leslie SULLIVAN
41 Athletic Director ... Ms. Haley DIRINGER
42 Director of Campus Ministries ... Mr. Michael F. FALES
36 Dir Career Services Network ... Dr. Amy RADFORD-POPP
37 Director of Student Financial Aid ... Ms. Libby JEAN
18 Director of Facilities ... Mr. Billy HASTINGS
94 Director of Women's Resource Center ... Ms. Cynthia NOYES
39 Student Housing ... Ms. Shawn HAGADON
15 Director of Human Resources ... Mrs. Terri GLASGOW
29 Director of Alumni Engagement ... Ms. Erin HOMER
04 Admin Asst to President ... Ms. Lori OTTO
08 Head Librarian ... Vacant
19 Director Security/Safety ... Mr. Phil REED
100 Chief of Staff ... Mr. Ryan SHOCKEY
26 Chief Public Relations Officer ... Ms. Michele MCCAULEY
28 Director of Diversity ... Dr. Linda LOGAN

Puritan Reformed Theological Seminary (H)

2965 Leonard Street NE, Grand Rapids MI 49525
County: Kent Identification: 667099
Telephone: (616) 977-0599 Carnegie Class: Not Classified
FAX Number: (616) 285-3246 Calendar System: Semester
URL: www.prts.edu
Established: 1995 Annual Graduate Tuition & Fees: N/A
Enrollment: N/A Coed
Affiliation or Control: Independent Non-Profit IRS Status: 501(c)3
Highest Offering: Doctorate; No Undergraduates
Accreditation: THEOL

01 President ... Dr. Joel R. BEEKE
05 VP for Academics/Academic Dean ... Dr. Michael BARRETT
10 Vice President for Operations ... Mr. Henk KLEYN
32 Dean of Students/Spiritual Form ... Dr. Mark KELDERMAN
06 Registrar/Director of Admissions ... Dr. Jonathon BEEKE
04 Administrative Asst to President ... Ms. Ann C. DYKEMA
26 Dir Development/Marketing ... Mr. Chris HANNA
08 Head Librarian ... Mrs. Laura LADWIG
106 Dir Online Education/E-learning ... Mr. Chris ENGELSMA
13 IT Director ... Mr. Seth HUCKSTEAD
24 Video Producer & Editor ... Mr. Darryl BRADFORD

Rochester University (I)

800 W Avon Road, Rochester Hills MI 48307-2764
County: Oakland FICE Identification: 002288
Unit ID: 170967
Telephone: (248) 218-2000 Carnegie Class: Bac-Diverse
FAX Number: (248) 487-9485 Calendar System: Semester
URL: https://rochesteru.edu/
Established: 1959 Annual Undergrad Tuition & Fees: $24,720
Enrollment: 1,231 Coed
Affiliation or Control: Independent Non-Profit IRS Status: 501(c)3
Highest Offering: Master's
Accreditation: HLC, NURSE

01 President ... Dr. Brian L. STOGNER
05 Provost ... Dr. Remylin BRUDER
101 Sr VP/Special Asst to President ... Mr. Klint A. PLEASANT
10 Exec VP/Chief Financial Officer ... Mr. Thomas D. RELLINGER
07 Vice President Admissions ... Mr. Scott SAMUELS
30 Vice Pres Development/Alumni Rels ... Mr. Steve MOORE
21 Controller ... Ms. Susan IDE
18 Director of Operations ... Mr. Jacob LAWLESS
50 Dir School of Business/Prof Studies ... Vacant
79 Dir School of Humanities ... Dr. Catherine PARKER
15 Director of Human Resources ... Mrs. Charity DAVIDSON
26 Dir of Communication Services ... Mr. Elliot JONES
32 Dean of Students ... Dr. Sharia HAYS
37 Director of Student Financial Svcs ... Mrs. Kara MILLER
08 Director of Library Services ... Mrs. Allison JIMENEZ
06 Registrar ... Ms. Rebekah PINCHBACK
108 Director of Assessment ... Dr. J. Mark MANRY
29 Director of Alumni ... Mr. Larry STEWART
121 Director of Advising ... Mrs. Debi RUTLEDGE
41 Director of Athletics ... Mr. Klint PLEASANT
42 Director of Spiritual Life ... Mr. Evan GREEN
19 Director of Safety & Security ... Mr. Jacob LAWLESS
13 Chief Information Technology Office ... Mr. Eric CAMPBELL
110 Director of Development ... Mrs. Jennifer PORTER
09 Director of Institutional Research ... Dr. Mark MANRY
104 GEO Coordinator ... Dr. Keith HUEY
53 Dir School of Education ... Dr. Melvin BLOHM
43 General Counsel ... Mr. Dennis VEARA
04 Admin Assistant to the President ... Mrs. Ginny A. MAY

Sacred Heart Major Seminary (J)

2701 Chicago Boulevard, Detroit MI 48206-1799
County: Wayne FICE Identification: 002313
Unit ID: 172033
Telephone: (313) 883-8501 Carnegie Class: Bac-A&S
FAX Number: (313) 883-8685 Calendar System: Semester
URL: www.shms.edu
Established: 1919 Annual Undergrad Tuition & Fees: $21,107
Enrollment: 418 Coed
Affiliation or Control: Roman Catholic IRS Status: 501(c)3
Highest Offering: Master's
Accreditation: HLC, THEOL

01 Rector & President ... Rev. Stephen BURR
32 Vice Rector/Dean of Seminarians ... Rev. Charles FOX
05 Dean of Studies ... Rev. Timothy LABOE
73 Dean of the Inst for Lay Ministry ... Vacant
10 Director Finance/Treasurer ... Ms. Ann Marie CONNOLLY
06 Registrar ... Ms. Leslie JONES
35 Director Undergraduate Seminarians ... Rev. Clint MCDONELL
88 Graduate Spiritual Director ... Rev. Daniel TRAPP
08 Library Director ... Ms. Teresa LUBIENICKI
58 Dir Graduate Pastoral Formation ... Rev. Stephen PULLIS
111 Alumni Relations/Marketing ... Mrs. Emily BERSCHBACK
18 Facilities Director ... Mr. John DUNCAN
07 Director of Admissions ... Mr. Patrick CASSADY
106 Dir of Distance Ed/Online Learning ... Mr. Ryan CAHILL
58 Director of Graduate Seminarians ... Rev. Pieter VAN ROOYEN

Saginaw Chippewa Tribal College (K)

2274 Enterprise Drive, Mount Pleasant MI 48858-2335
County: Isabella FICE Identification: 037723
Unit ID: 441070
Telephone: (989) 317-4760 Carnegie Class: Tribal
FAX Number: (989) 317-4781 Calendar System: Semester
URL: www.sagchip.edu
Established: 1998 Annual Undergrad Tuition & Fees: $2,210
Enrollment: 96 Coed
Affiliation or Control: Tribal Control IRS Status: 501(c)3
Highest Offering: Associate Degree
Accreditation: HLC

01 President ... Ms. Carla SINEWAY
32 Dean of Student Services ... Ms. Amanda FLAUGHER
07 Admissions Officer/Registrar ... Ms. Jacqueline GRAVERATTE
09 Dean of Research ... Ms. Tracy REED
111 Dean of Institutional Advancement ... Ms. Gena QUALLS
05 Dean of Academics ... Ms. Mary PELCHER
04 Admin Assistant to the President ... Ms. Gladys GATES

Saginaw Valley State University (L)

7400 Bay Road, University Center MI 48710-0001
County: Saginaw FICE Identification: 002314
Unit ID: 172051
Telephone: (989) 964-4000 Carnegie Class: Masters/L
FAX Number: (989) 964-0180 Calendar System: Semester
URL: www.svsu.edu
Established: 1963 Annual Undergrad Tuition & Fees (In-State): $10,814
Enrollment: 8,028 Coed
Affiliation or Control: State IRS Status: 501(c)3
Highest Offering: Doctorate
Accreditation: HLC, CAEP, CEA, MLS, MUS, NURSE, OT, SW

01 President ... Dr. Donald J. BACHAND
05 Provost/VP Academic Affairs ... Dr. Deborah R. HUNTLEY
10 Exec VP Admin & Business Affairs ... Mr. James G. MULADORE
29 Executive Director Alumni Relations ... Mr. Nic J. TAYLOR

32 Assoc Provost Student Affairs ... Vacant
28 Spec Asst to Pres Diversity Pgms ... Dr. Mamie T. THORNS
83 Assoc Dean Arts/Behavioral Sciences ... Dr. Carlos RAMET
49 Dean of Arts/Behavioral Sciences ... Dr. Marc H. PERETZ
15 AVP Admin/Business & Dir of HR ... Ms. Corrie PIOTROWSKI
53 Dean of College of Education ... Dr. James E. TARR
21 AVP Admin & Business Affairs/CBO ... Mr. Ronald E. PORTWINE
41 Athletic Director/AVP Legal Affairs ... Mr. John DECKER
114 AVP/Chief Financial Officer ... Ms. Susan L. CRANE
43 AVP/General Counsel ... Ms. Ellen E. CRANE
13 Exec Dir Information Tech Svcs ... Mr. Jim M. MAHER
07 Director of Admissions ... Ms. Jennifer K. PAHL
06 Registrar ... Dr. Clifford DORNE
36 Director Career Services ... Ms. Teresa M. GEORGE
88 Director Business Services ... Ms. Connie J. SCHWEITZER
08 Dir of Melvin J Zahnow Library ... Ms. Anita DEY
25 HHS Grant Project Manager ... Ms. Janet M. RENTSCH
37 Director Scholarships/Financial Aid ... Mr. Robert L. LEMUEL
16 Asst Director of Human Resources ... Mr. Eddie V. JONES
50 Dean of Carmona College of Business ... Dr. Jayati GHOSH
88 Dir Environmental Health & Safety ... Mr. Robert J. TUTSOCK
88 Dir Accessibility Resources/Accom ... Dr. Shawn Y. WILSON
102 Executive Director SVSU Foundation ... Mr. Andrew J. BETHUNE
96 Purchasing Manager ... Mr. Joshua M. WEBB
76 Dean of Health & Human Services ... Dr. Marcia DITMYER
09 Dir of Institutional Effectiveness ... Dr. Nicholas J. WAGNER
04 Exec Asst to the Pres/Sec to Board ... Mrs. Mary A. KOWALESKI
20 Assoc Provost for Academic Affairs ... Dr. Joshua J. ODE
86 Director of Governmental Affairs ... Mr. John L. KACZYNSKI
39 Dir Residential Life ... Dr. Nathan C. TOMSON
54 Dean of Engineering ... Dr. Andrew M. CHUBB
19 Chief of University Police ... Mr. Clifford A. BLOCK
18 Dir Facilities Planning/Construc ... Mr. Michael A. PAZDRO
51 Dir Cont Educ & Ext Project Mgmt ... Ms. Susan M. BRASSEUR
121 Dir Academic Advisement Center ... Mr. Gary V. BRASSEUR

St. Clair County Community College (A)

323 Erie Street, PO Box 5015, Port Huron MI 48061-5015
County: St. Clair FICE Identification: 002310
Unit ID: 172291
Telephone: (810) 984-3881 Carnegie Class: Assoc/HT-Mix Trad/Non
FAX Number: (810) 984-4730 Calendar System: Semester
URL: www.sc4.edu
Established: 1923 Annual Undergrad Tuition & Fees (In-District): $8,845
Enrollment: 3,315 Coed
Affiliation or Control: Local IRS Status: 501(c)3
Highest Offering: Associate Degree
Accreditation: HLC, ADNUR, #COARC, RAD

01 President ... Dr. Deborah SNYDER
11 Exec VP/Chief Operating Officer ... Mr. Kirk KRAMER
05 Chief Academic Ofcr/VP Acad Svcs ... Mr. Ethan FLICK
32 SVP/VP of Student Services ... Mr. Pete LACEY
10 Chief Financial Officer ... Ms. Becky GENTNER
15 VP of Human Resources ... Ms. Bethany MAYEA
26 VP of Marketing & Special Projects ... Ms. Kristin COPENHAVER
09 VP of Institutional Effectiveness ... Vacant
37 Dir of Financial Assistance/Svcs ... Ms. Josephine CASSAR
06 Registrar/Dir Veterans Services ... Ms. Carrie BEARSS
41 Director of Athletics ... Mr. Dale VOS
08 Assoc Dean Library Services ... Ms. Kendra LAKE

Schoolcraft College (B)

18600 Haggerty Road, Livonia MI 48152-2696
County: Wayne FICE Identification: 002315
Unit ID: 172200
Telephone: (734) 462-4400 Carnegie Class: Bac/Assoc-Assoc Dom
FAX Number: (734) 462-4340 Calendar System: Semester
URL: www.schoolcraft.edu
Established: 1961 Annual Undergrad Tuition & Fees (In-District): $5,364
Enrollment: 8,116 Coed
Affiliation or Control: Local IRS Status: Exempt
Highest Offering: Baccalaureate
Accreditation: HLC, ACFEI, ADNUR, CAHIIM, EMT, MAC, PNUR

01 President ... Dr. Glenn CERNY
10 Chief Financial Officer ... Mr. Jon LAMB
11 Chief Operations Officer ... Mr. Steven KAUFMAN
05 Chief Academic Officer ... Ms. Stacy WHIDDON
32 Chief Student Enrollment Officer ... Ms. Melissa SCHULTZ
13 Chief Technology Officer ... Mr. Jeff BORTON
32 Chief Student Services Officer ... Dr. Laurie KATTUAH-SNYDER
26 Chief Mktg & Communications Ofcr ... Vacant
19 Chief of Police ... Mr. Mark ENGSTROM
15 Chief HR & Risk Mgt Officer ... Ms. Brenda LEAVENS
30 Exec Director of Development ... Ms. Dawn MAGRETTA
35 Dean of Students ... Dr. Martin HEATOR
89 Dean New Student Experience ... Dr. Stacey STOVER
49 Dean Liberal Arts & Sciences ... Dr. Michele KELLY
75 Dean Occupational Pgm/Econ Dev ... Dr. Robert LEADLEY
108 Assoc Dn Opers/Curriculum/Assessmt ... Ms. Cindy CICCHELLI
66 Assoc Dean Nursing ... Dr. Deborah VENDITTELLI
88 Assoc Dean Public Safety Programs ... Dr. Gerald CHAMPAGNE
72 Assoc Dean Occupation Pgm/Engr Tech ... Ms. Amy JONES
76 Assoc Dean Health Professions ... Dr. David KESLER
53 Assoc Dean Occupational/Educ Pgms ... Dr. Dennis GENIG
36 Assoc Dean of Career Services ... Dr. Michael OLIVER
88 Assoc Dean of Student Relations ... Ms. Nicole WILSON-FENNELL
37 Director of Financial Aid ... Mr. Michael WILLIAMS
07 Director of Admissions ... Ms. Lisa BUSHAW
06 Registrar ... Ms. Tracy MILLER
51 Dir Personal & Prof Learning ... Ms. Jodie BECKLEY
85 Dir International Student Ctr ... Ms. Laura LESHOK
09 Dir Data Strategy & Effectiveness ... Ms. Michelle STANDO
112 Dir Major & Planned Gifts ... Mr. Christopher KELLY
44 Dir of Annual Gvg & Scholar Admin ... Ms. Carole BOOMS
121 Dir of Advising & Transfer ... Ms. Carol DWYER
41 Director of Athletics ... Ms. Cali CRAWFORD
117 Dir Risk Mgmt & HR Compliance ... Ms. Ann WHITE
18 Director Facilities ... Mr. Stephen GREEN
101 Chief of Staff ... Ms. Beth LAFOREST
04 Ofc Mgr & SC Tech Coordinator ... Ms. Elizabeth NOVAK
40 Director of Bookstore ... Ms. Lyndsay TAGAREL
96 Chief Proc & Business Svcs Ofcr ... Mr. Matthew WILSON
90 Exec Dir Acad & Admin Info Sys ... Ms. Laura CULLEN
88 Director of Academic Innovation ... Mr. Adam AUTHIER

Siena Heights University (C)

1247 Siena Heights Drive, Adrian MI 49221-1796
County: Lenawee FICE Identification: 002316
Unit ID: 172264
Telephone: (517) 263-0731 Carnegie Class: Masters/M
FAX Number: (517) 264-7704 Calendar System: Semester
URL: www.sienaheights.edu
Established: 1919 Annual Undergrad Tuition & Fees: $27,642
Enrollment: 2,036 Coed
Affiliation or Control: Roman Catholic IRS Status: 501(c)3
Highest Offering: Beyond Master's But Less Than Doctorate
Accreditation: HLC, ART, CAEP, NURSE, SW

01 President ... Dr. Peg ALBERT
10 Sr Vice Pres for Business/Finance ... Dr. Lee JOHNSON
111 Vice President for Advancement ... Mr. Daniel PENA
05 Vice President for Academic Affairs ... Dr. Emily BARNES
84 Vice Pres of Enrollment Mgmt Svcs ... Mr. George WOLF
32 Vice President for Student Affairs ... Mr. Michael ORLANDO
107 Dean of Professional Studies/Grad ... Dr. Cheri BETZ
49 Dean College of Arts and Science ... Dr. Susan SHELANGOSKIE
06 Registrar ... Mr. Christopher COX
07 Director of Admissions ... Ms. Trudy MOHRE
08 Director of Library ... Mrs. Melissa SISSEN
41 Director of Athletics ... Ms. Susan SYLJEBECK
15 Human Resource Director ... Ms. Frances JOHNSON
42 Director of Campus Ministry ... Sr. Mary JONES, OP
38 Director of Counseling Services ... Mrs. Sandy MORLEY
121 Director of Academic Advising ... Mr. Michael BLUMENAUER
18 Supt of Buildings & Grounds ... Mr. Brian BERTRAM
09 Director of Institutional Research ... Mrs. Lan NGUYEN
39 Director of Residence Life ... Ms. Samantha THACKER
19 Director of Campus Security ... Mrs. Cindy A. BIRDWELL
23 Director of Health Services ... Ms. Dawn E. MARSH
29 Director of Alumni Relations ... Mrs. Kate HAMILTON
36 Director of Career Services ... Mrs. Melissa TSUJI
28 Director of Diversity and Inclusion ... Mr. Christopher CARTER
26 Dir of Integrated Univ Marketing ... Mrs. Liesel RIGGS
37 Director Student Financial Aid ... Mrs. Linda PANCONE
21 Controller ... Mrs. Pamela HOWARD
44 Coordinator of Annual Fund ... Mrs. Shawna WILSON
04 Executive Assistant to President ... Mrs. Krissie BARNES

Southwestern Michigan College (D)

58900 Cherry Grove Road, Dowagiac MI 49047-9793
County: Cass FICE Identification: 002317
Unit ID: 172307
Telephone: (269) 782-1000 Carnegie Class: Assoc/MT-VT-High Trad
FAX Number: (269) 782-8414 Calendar System: Semester
URL: www.swmich.edu
Established: 1964 Annual Undergrad Tuition & Fees (In-District): $6,708
Enrollment: 1,759 Coed
Affiliation or Control: State/Local IRS Status: 501(c)3
Highest Offering: Associate Degree
Accreditation: HLC, ADNUR, CAHIIM

01 President ... Dr. Joseph ODENWALD
84 VP Enrollment Mgmt/Campus Life ... Mr. Brent BREWER
10 Senior VP Business Affairs & CFO ... Ms. Susan COULSTON
05 Provost ... Dr. David FLEMING
111 VP Institutional Advancement ... Mr. Michael O'BRIEN
12 Executive Director of Niles Campus ... Mr. Jason SMITH
13 Director of IT and CIO ... Mr. Mick VALERIS
66 Dean School Nursing/Health Services ... Dr. Melissa KENNEDY
49 Dean of Arts and Sciences ... Dr. Keith HOWELL
50 Dean of School of Business/Adv Tech ... Dr. Karen REILLY
32 Dean of Student Development ... Dr. Katie HANNAH
35 Executive Director of Student Life ... Mr. Jeffery HOOKS
121 Director of Academic Advising ... Ms. Kathie GRIES
18 Director of Buildings & Grounds ... Mr. John EBERHART
19 Director of Campus Security ... Mr. Lyndon PARRISH
37 Director of Financial Aid ... Ms. Lauren MOW
07 Director Admission/Educ Partnership ... Ms. Heather ZILE
88 Dir Educational Talent Search Pgm ... Ms. Maria KULKA
09 Director of Institutional Research ... Dr. Angela EVANS
15 Director of Human Resources ... Ms. Kristin REYNOLDS
06 Director of Records/Registrar ... Mr. Steven CARLSON
08 Director of Library Services ... Ms. Colleen WELSCH
21 Controller ... Ms. Michelle KITE
103 Manager of Workforce Development ... Ms. Megan KUPRES
88 Manager of Accounting ... Ms. Christy MANGUS
88 Manager of Dual Enrolled Students ... Mr. Brian DEVLESCHOWARD
26 Manager of Marketing ... Ms. Michelle ORLASKE
89 Manager First Year Experience ... Ms. Courtney HEMENWAY
41 Asst Director Campus Life/Athletics ... Mr. Jordan PITRE
88 Asst Director Campus Life/Clubs ... Mr. Branden POMPEY

Southwestern Michigan College Niles Area Campus (E)

33890 U.S. Highway 12, Niles MI 49120
Telephone: (800) 456-8675 Identification: 770286
Accreditation: &HLC

Spring Arbor University (F)

106 E Main Street, Spring Arbor MI 49283-9799
County: Jackson FICE Identification: 002318
Unit ID: 172334
Telephone: (517) 750-1200 Carnegie Class: Masters/L
FAX Number: (517) 750-6620 Calendar System: Semester
URL: www.arbor.edu
Established: 1873 Annual Undergrad Tuition & Fees: $30,472
Enrollment: 3,118 Coed
Affiliation or Control: Free Methodist IRS Status: 501(c)3
Highest Offering: Doctorate
Accreditation: HLC, CACREP, CAEP, NURSE, SW

01 University President ... Dr. Brent D. ELLIS
03 Executive Vice President ... Dr. Douglas A. WILCOXSON
05 VP for Academic Affairs ... Dr. Carol C. GREEN
10 VP for Finance & Administration ... Ms. Dawn SCHNITKEY
32 VP Student Development/Success ... Mr. Corey ROSS
84 VP Enrollment & Marketing ... Mr. Jon BAHR
20 AVP Acad Affairs/Dean Engineering ... Dr. Ron A. DELAP
15 Assistant VP for Human Resources ... Mrs. Kerry J. KLEE-TIESMAN
88 Chief Strategy Officer ... Dr. Kimberly RUPERT
04 Exec Assistant to the President ... Ms. Julie MORSE
13 Chief Technology Officer ... Mr. Randy G. MELTON
66 Dean School of Nursing & Health Sci ... Dr. Alvin V. KAUFFMAN
79 Dean School of Humanities ... Mr. Kim T. BOWEN
83 Dean School of Social Sciences ... Dr. Terry DARLING
50 Dean School of Business ... Dr. Caleb K. CHAN
53 Interim Dean School of Education ... Mr. John M. WILLIAMS
60 Dean School of Communication ... Mrs. Dorie A. SHELBY
35 Asst VP Student Development ... Mr. Dan VANDERHILL
06 Registrar ... Mrs. Sherri HENDRIX
07 Director of Enrollment Operations ... Vacant
21 Assistant VP Financial Services ... Mrs. Dawn I. SCHNITKEY
30 Executive Director of Development ... Mrs. Linda SCHAUB
26 Exec Dir Mktg & Communication ... Ms. Bethany L. LANDIS
41 Athletic Director ... Mr. Ryan T. COTTINGHAM
42 Chaplain ... Dr. Brian S. KONO
37 Director of Financial Aid ... Mr. Herbert K. ROTICH
09 Director Institutional Research ... Mr. Thomas P. KORMAN
121 Dir of Student Success Initiative ... Mrs. Laura S. BRECKNER
108 Director of Assessment ... Vacant
08 Director Library ... Mr. Robert D. BOLTON
18 Director of Physical Plant ... Mr. Marty FORTRESS
124 Director Retention & Fresh Programs ... Mrs. Carrie L. WILLIAMS
104 Director Cross Cultural Studies ... Mrs. Diane L. KURTZ
23 Exec Dir Student Health/Wellness ... Mrs. Mary BRODA
39 Associate Dean of Students ... Mr. Robert C. PRATT
36 Career Development Advisor ... Mr. Chad W. MELTON
19 Director Campus Safety ... Mr. Scott L. KREBILL
106 Assoc Dean External/SAU Online ... Mr. Gary R. TUCKER
28 Chief Diversity Officer ... Mr. Kevin BROWN
29 Director Alumni Relations ... Mr. Brian R. KNAPP
105 Web Architect ... Mr. Ryan J. KELLY
44 Director Annual Giving ... Mrs. Tricia A. CRAMER

SS. Cyril and Methodius Seminary (G)

3535 Commerce Road, Orchard Lake MI 48324-1623
County: Oakland FICE Identification: 037384
Unit ID: 260211
Telephone: (248) 836-1271 Carnegie Class: Not Classified
FAX Number: (248) 738-6735 Calendar System: Semester
URL: www.sscms.edu
Established: 1885 Annual Graduate Tuition & Fees: N/A
Enrollment: N/A Coed
Affiliation or Control: Roman Catholic IRS Status: 501(c)3
Highest Offering: Master's; No Undergraduates
Accreditation: THEOL

01 Rector/President ... V.Rev. Miroslaw KROL
03 Vice Rector ... Rev. Przemyslaw NOWAK
32 Dean of Human Formation ... Vacant
42 Dean of Spiritual Formation ... Rev. Lukasz IWANCZUK
05 Academic Dean ... Rev. Gregory A. BANAZAK

University of Detroit Mercy (H)

4001 W McNichols Road, Detroit MI 48221-3038
County: Wayne FICE Identification: 002323
Unit ID: 169716
Telephone: (313) 993-1000 Carnegie Class: DU-Mod
FAX Number: (313) 993-1229 Calendar System: Semester
URL: www.udmercy.edu
Established: 1877 Annual Undergrad Tuition & Fees: $29,562
Enrollment: 4,987 Coed
Affiliation or Control: Roman Catholic IRS Status: 501(c)3
Highest Offering: Doctorate

Accreditation: HLC, ANEST, ARCPA, CACREP, CAHIIM, CLPSY, DENT, DH, LAW, NASP, NURSE, SW

01 President .... Dr. Donald B. TAYLOR
05 Provost and VP for Academic Affairs .... Ms. Pamela ZARKOWSKI
10 VP for Business & Finance/CFO .... Mr. Thomas MANCEOR
111 VP for University Advancement .... Mr. Arnold D'AMBROSIO
84 VP Enrollment & Student Affairs .... Ms. Deborah STIEFFEL
88 Vice Pres for Mission Integration .... Vacant
101 University Secretary & Senior Atty .... Ms. Monica BARBOUR
18 Assoc Vice Pres Facil Management ...... Ms. Tamara BATCHELLER
15 Associate Vice Pres Human Resources .... Ms. Netina ANDING-MOORE
26 Assoc VP Marketing & Communications .... Mr. Gary ERWIN
13 Associate Vice President ITS .... Mr. Edward TRACY, II
06 Associate VP/Registrar .... Ms. Diane M. PRAET
44 Exec Director of Annual Giving .... Ms. Judy WERNETTE
112 Exec Director of Major Gifts .... Mr. Dennis CARLESSO
32 Dean of Students .... Ms. Monica WILLIAMS
08 Interim Dean of Libraries .... Ms. Marilyn DOW
09 Director of Institutional Research .... Ms. Shelley WAGNON
37 Director Scholarships & Fin Aid .... Ms. Jessica ROUSER
35 Associate Director of Student Life .... Ms. Dorothy STEWART
41 Director of Athletics .... Mr. Robert VOWELS
49 Dean College of Liberal Arts/Ed .... Dr. Mark DENHAM
61 Dean School of Law .... Ms. Jelani JEFFERSON EXUM
54 Dean College Engr & Science .... Dr. Katherine SNYDER
48 Dean School of Architecture .... Mr. Daniel PITERA
50 Dean Col Business Admin .... Dr. Joseph EISENHAUER
52 Dean School of Dentistry .... Dr. Mert AKSU
76 Interim Dean CHP/Nursing .... Dr. Janet BAIARDI
36 Dir Center for Career & Prof Devel .... Vacant
39 Director Residence Life .... Ms. Lanae GILL
04 Exec Asst to the President .... Ms. Lisa MACDONNELL
85 Dir of International Services .... Ms. Lilymae SWAN
38 Director of Wellness Center .... Ms. Annamaria SILVERI
92 Co-Director of Honors Program .... Dr. Evan PETERSON
92 Co-Director of Honors Program .... Dr. Juan Carlos FLORES
88 Coordinator of Advancement Systems .... Ms. Stephanie JONES
07 Executive Director of Admissions .... Ms. Tyra ROUNDS
20 AVP for Academic Administration .... Dr. Karen LEE
19 Director Public Safety .... Mr. Joel GALLIHUGH
25 Dir of Sponsored Research .... Ms. Ann SERRA
106 Dir Online Education/E-learning .... Ms. Jennifer DEAN
102 Dir Foundation/Corporate Relations .... Ms. Yvonne LINDSTROM
22 Title IX & Equity/Compliance Coord .... Ms. Megan NOVELL
29 Director Alumni Relations .... Ms. Margaret PATTISON
96 Director of Purchasing .... Ms. Stacey KING
28 Director of Diversity .... Vacant

University of Michigan-Ann Arbor (A)

1109 Geddes Ave. Suite 3190, Ann Arbor MI 48109
County: Washtenaw FICE Identification: 002325
Unit ID: 170976
Telephone: (734) 764-6270 Carnegie Class: DU-Highest
FAX Number: N/A Calendar System: Trimester
URL: umich.edu
Established: 1817 Annual Undergrad Tuition & Fees (In-State): $15,948
Enrollment: 47,907 Coed
Affiliation or Control: State IRS Status: 501(c)3
Highest Offering: Doctorate
Accreditation: HLC, ART, CAATE, CAEPT, CAMPEP, CLPSY, DANCE, DENT, DH, DIETD, DIETI, HSA, IPSY, LAW, LIB, LSAR, MED, MIDWF, MUS, NURSE, PCSAS, PDPSY, PH, PHAR, PLNG, SW

01 President .... Dr. Santa J. ONO
05 Provost/EVP Academic Affairs .... Dr. Laurie MCCAULEY
10 Exec Vice Pres/CFO .... Mr. Geoff S. CHATAS
17 Exec VP Medical Affairs/Dean Med .... Dr. Marschall S. RUNGE
30 Vice President Development .... Mr. Thomas A. BAIRD
32 VP Student Life .... Dr. Martino HARMON
46 Vice President for Research .... Dr. Rebecca M. CUNNINGHAM
86 Vice Pres Governmental Relations .... Mr. Chris KOLB
26 Vice Pres Communications .... Ms. Kallie B. MICHELS
43 Vice Pres/General Counsel .... Mr. Timothy G. LYNCH
101 Vice Pres/Sec of the University .... Ms. Sally J. CHURCHILL
04 Exec Asst to the President .... Ms. Erika J. HRABEC
100 Special Counsel to the President .... Ms. Liz M. BARRY
88 Special Counsel to the Provost .... Ms. Christine M. GERDES
114 Vice Provost Acad/Budget Affairs .... Dr. Thomas A. FINHOLT
20 Vice Provost Acad & Faculty Affairs .... Dr. Lori J. PIERCE
20 Vice Provost Acad & Faculty Affairs .... Dr. Sara B. BLAIR
58 V Prov Acad Affs/Dean Grad Studies .... Dr. Michael J. SOLOMON
88 Vice Provost Engaged Learning .... Dr. Valeria BERTACCO
85 Assoc VProv/Dir Global Engagement .... Dr. Amy CAREY
28 Vice Prov Diversity/Eqty/Inclusion .... Dr. Tabbye M. CHAVOUS
88 Vice Prov Acad Innovation .... Dr. James L. HILTON
84 Vice Prov for Enrollment Mgmt .... Ms. Adele BRUMFIELD
09 Assoc Vice Provost & Exec Dir OBP .... Ms. Tammy C. BIMER
07 Director Undergrad Admissions .... Ms. Erica L. SANDERS
22 AVP for Institutional Equity .... Ms. Tamiko STRICKMAN
18 Assoc VP Facilities/Operations .... Mr. Henry D. BAIER
21 Assoc VP Finance .... Mr. Brian T. SMITH
115 Chief Investment Officer .... Mr. Erik LUNDBERG
88 AVP Research Nat Sciences/Engr .... Dr. Bradford ORR
88 Asst VP and Chief of Staff Research .... Dr. Nicholas WIGGINTON
88 Assoc VP for Research .... Dr. Michael J. IMPERIALE
88 Asst VP Reg and Comp Oversight .... Ms. Lois BRAKO
88 Asst VP Animal Resources .... Dr. William KING
88 Asst VP Animal Pgm Comp Oversight .... Mr. William GREER
88 Asst VP Fed Rel for Research .... Ms. Kristina KO
88 Assoc VP for Research .... Dr. Kelly B. SEXTON
35 Assoc VP Student Life/Dean Stdnts .... Ms. Laura B. JONES
35 Assoc VP Student Life .... Ms. Anjali N. ANTURKAR
35 Assoc VP Student Life .... Mr. Kambiz KHALILI
15 Assoc VP for Human Resources ... Mr. Richard S. HOLCOMB, JR.
13 Chief Information Officer .... Dr. Ravi PENDSE
06 University Registrar .... Mr. Paul A. ROBINSON
96 Director Procurement Services .... Mr. Tony BURGER
38 Director Counseling & Psych Service .... Dr. Todd D. SEVIG
39 Director University Housing .... Mr. Rick GIBSON
23 Chief Health Officer .... Dr. Robert D. ERNST
88 Chief Mental Health Officer .... Dr. Lindsey MORTENSON
19 Exec Dir Pub Safety/Security .... Mr. Eddie L. WASHINGTON
37 Exec Director Financial Aid .... Ms. Tammie DURHAM
41 Director of Athletics .... Mr. Warde MANUEL
48 Dean Col Architecture/Urban Plng .... Dr. Jonathan MASSEY
49 Dean Col Literature/Science/Arts .... Dr. Anne L. CURZAN
54 Dean College of Engineering .... Dr. Alec D. GALLIMORE
61 Dean Law School .... Mr. Mark D. WEST
67 Dean College of Pharmacy .... Dr. Vicki ELLINGROD
65 Dean Sch Natural Resources/Environ . Dr. Jonathan T. OVERPECK
64 Dean School Music/Theatre & Dance .... Dr. David GIER
57 Dean School of Art & Design .... Mr. Carlos F. JACKSON
60 Dean Ross School of Business .... Ms. Sharon MATUSIK
52 Int Dean School of Dentistry .... Dr. Jan CHIN CHUN HU
53 Dean School of Education .... Dr. Elizabeth B. MOJE
62 Interim Dean School of Information .... Ms. Elizabeth YAKEL
68 Dean School of Kinesiology .... Dr. Lori PLOUTZ-SNYDER
66 Dean School of Nursing .... Dr. Patricia D. HURN
80 Int Dean School of Public Policy .... Dr. Celeste M. WATKINS-HAYES
70 Dean School of Social Work .... Dr. Kathryn (Beth) ANGELL
69 Dean School of Public Health .... Dr. F. DuBois BOWMAN
29 President Alumni Association .... Mr. Steve C. GRAFTON
102 Director Foundation/Corporate Rels .... Ms. Maureen MARTIN
44 Director Annual Giving .... Ms. Megan F. DOUD
122 Assoc Dean Stdnts-Dir Frat/Sor Life .... Mr. Travis MARTIN

University of Michigan-Dearborn (B)

4901 Evergreen Road, Dearborn MI 48128-1491
County: Wayne FICE Identification: 002326
Unit ID: 171137
Telephone: (313) 593-5000 Carnegie Class: Masters/L
FAX Number: (313) 593-5452 Calendar System: Semester
URL: www.umdearborn.edu
Established: 1959 Annual Undergrad Tuition & Fees (In-State): $13,552
Enrollment: 8,783 Coed
Affiliation or Control: State IRS Status: 501(c)3
Highest Offering: Doctorate
Accreditation: HLC, CAEP, CEA

01 Chancellor .... Dr. Dominico GRASSO
05 Int Prov/Exec VC Academic Affairs .... Dr. Gabriella SCARLATTA
10 Vice Chancellor Business Affairs .... Mr. Bryan DADEY
84 Vice Prov Enrollment Management .... Ms. Melissa STONE
111 Vice Chanc Inst Advancement .... Dr. Casandra ULBRICH
26 Vice Chanc for External Relations .... Mr. Kenneth KETTENBEIL
21 Director of Financial Services .... Mr. Noel HORNBACHER
06 Registrar .... Mr. Timothy TAYLOR
27 Director Communications/Marketing .... Ms. Beth MARMARELLI
86 Government Relations Manager .... Vacant
15 Director of Human Resources .... Ms. Rima BERRY-HUNG
29 Alumni Engagement .... Ms. Cristina FRENDO
20 Associate Provost Undergraduate .... Dr. Mitchel SOLLENBERGER
58 Associate Provost Graduate .... Dr. Maureen LINKER
13 Dir IT Strategy/Operations .... Ms. Carrie SHUMAKER
08 Assoc Provost & Dir of Library .... Dr. Maureen LINKER
09 Exec Dir of Institutional Research .... Ms. Becky CHADWICK
07 Director of Admissions .... Ms. Deb PEFFER
32 Dean of Students .... Dr. Amy FINLAY
37 Director of Financial Aid .... Ms. Katherine ALLEN
38 Director of Counseling .... Dr. Sara BYCZEK
36 Director of Career Services .... Ms. Regina M. STORRS
85 Director of International Affairs .... Mr. Francisco LOPEZ
18 Exec Dir of Facilities Operations .... Ms. Carol GLICK
19 Chief of Police .... Mr. Gary GORSKI
22 Director Institutional Equity .... Ms. Pam HEATLIE
28 Sp Counsel to Chanc for Inclusion .... Dr. Ann LAMPKIN-WILLIAMS
49 Dean Col Arts/Science/Letters .... Dr. Martin HERSHOCK
54 Dean Col of Engr/Computer Science .... Dr. Ghassan KRIDLI
50 Dean College of Business .... Dr. Raju BALAKRISHNAN
53 Dean College of Educ/Health/HS .. Dr. Ann LAMPKIN-WILLIAMS
88 Director of Enrollment Research .... Mr. Dan MERIAN
41 Interim Athletic Director .... Mr. Bryan EARL
102 Dir Foundation/Corporate Relations .... Ms. Cheryl DONOHOE
44 Director Annual Giving .... Ms. Eva GOGOLA
90 Director Academic Computing .... Ms. Carrie SHUMAKER
04 Exec Assistant to the Chancellor .... Ms. Michelle BARNES
100 Chief of Staff .... Ms. Keisha BLEVINS

University of Michigan-Flint (C)

303 E Kearsley Street, Flint MI 48502-1950
County: Genesee FICE Identification: 002327
Unit ID: 171146
Telephone: (810) 762-3000 Carnegie Class: DU-Mod
FAX Number: (810) 762-5725 Calendar System: Semester
URL: www.umflint.edu
Established: 1956 Annual Undergrad Tuition & Fees (In-State): $12,744
Enrollment: 6,829 Coed
Affiliation or Control: State IRS Status: 501(c)3
Highest Offering: Doctorate
Accreditation: HLC, ANEST, #ARCPA, CAEPN, #COARC, MUS, NURSE, OT, PH, PTA, RTT, SW

01 Chancellor .... Dr. Debasish DUTTA
05 Provost/VC Academic Affairs .... Dr. Sonja FEIST-PRICE
32 VC Campus Inclusion & Student Life .... Dr. Christopher GIORDANO
111 VC University Advancement .... Ms. Shari SCHRADER
121 Asst VC for Student Success .... Vacant
35 Assoc VC & Dean of Students .... Dr. Julie SNYDER
20 Interim VP for Academic Affairs .... Dr. Syagnik BANERJEE
26 Director of Marketing and Comm .... Mr. Robert KING
28 Director of Educational Oppty .... Dr. Tiese ROXBURY
08 Director of Library .... Dr. Jennifer DEAN
06 Registrar .... Ms. Karen A. ARNOULD
07 Admissions Director .... Mr. Joseph VAINNER
37 Director Financial Aid .... Ms. Lori VEDDER
15 Director Human Res/Affirm Action .... Ms. Beth MANNING
49 Int Dean College of Arts & Sciences .... Dr. Douglas KNERR
50 Dean School of Management .... Dr. Aneil MISHRA
66 Dean School of Nursing .... Dr. Cynthia MCCURREN
76 Dean College of Health Studies .... Dr. Donna FRY
53 Dean Educ & Human Services .... Dr. Beth KUBITSKEY
72 Dean College of Innovation & Tech .... Dr. Christopher A. PEARSON
106 Director of Online & Digital Educ .... Mr. Nicholas GASPAR
19 Director of Public Safety .... Mr. Raymond D. HALL
18 Dir Facilities Mgmt/Auxiliary Svcs .... Mr. George HAKIM
13 Director Info Technology Services .... Mr. Scott ARNST
121 Director Student Success Center .... Dr. Dawn MARKELL
46 Director of Research .... Dr. Kenneth SYLVESTER
21 Director of Financial Svcs & Budget .... Mr. Gerald GLASCO
88 Director Economic Development .... Ms. Paula NAS
96 Procurement Agent Senior .... Ms. Cynthia STAHMER
09 Director of Institutional Analysis .... Ms. Fawn SKARSTEN
04 Project Manager to the Chancellor .... Ms. Chelsea DUNCAN
29 Exec Director Alumni Relations .... Dr. Mary Jo SEKELSKY
92 Director Honors Program .... Dr. Melissa SRECKOVIC
88 Asst Dir Stdnt Involvement/Ldrship .... Mr. Chris DEEULIS
88 Dir Center Gender & Sexuality .... Ms. Samara HOUGH
88 Dir Thompson Center for T&L .... Dr. Laura MCLEMAN

Van Andel Institute Graduate School (D)

333 Bostwick Avenue NE, Grand Rapids MI 49503
County: Kent Identification: 667085
Telephone: (616) 234-5708 Carnegie Class: Not Classified
FAX Number: (616) 234-5709 Calendar System: Semester
URL: vaigs.vai.org
Established: 2005 Annual Graduate Tuition & Fees: N/A
Enrollment: N/A Coed
Affiliation or Control: Independent Non-Profit IRS Status: 501(c)3
Highest Offering: Doctorate; No Undergraduates
Accreditation: HLC

01 President/Dean of VAIGS .... Dr. Steven J. TRIEZENBERG
05 Assistant Dean of Graduate School .... Dr. Brian HAAB
32 Director Student Support Services .... Ms. Allison ROMAN
07 Director of Enrollment and Records .... Ms. Christy MAYO
108 Director Assessment & Prof Devel .... Mr. Taylor BOYD
04 Executive Asst to President .... Mrs. Susanne MILLER-SCHACHINGER
15 Vice President for Human Resources .... Ms. Linda ZARZECKI

Walsh College of Accountancy and Business Administration (E)

3838 Livernois Road, Troy MI 48083
County: Oakland FICE Identification: 004071
Unit ID: 172608
Telephone: (248) 689-8282 Carnegie Class: Spec-4-yr-Bus
FAX Number: (248) 689-9066 Calendar System: Semester
URL: www.walshcollege.edu
Established: 1922 Annual Undergrad Tuition & Fees: N/A
Enrollment: 1,744 Coed
Affiliation or Control: Independent Non-Profit IRS Status: 501(c)3
Highest Offering: Doctorate
Accreditation: HLC, ACBSP

01 President & CEO .... Dr. Michael P. LEVENS
05 Executive VP/Provost .... Dr. Suzanne SIEGLE
10 Vice President/CFO/Treasurer .... Ms. Teresa ESSHAKI
15 VP/Chief Human Resources/Admin Ofcr .... Ms. Elizabeth A. BARNES
26 VP/Chief Marketing Ofcr .... Ms. Patti SWANSON
84 VP/Chief Enrollment Mgmt Ofcr .... Mr. Jesus HERNANDEZ
100 Chief of Staff .... Mrs. Stephanie M. WHEELER
20 Asst VP Academic Admin .... Ms. Victoria R. SCAVONE
106 Director Office of Online Learning .... Mr. Drew SMITH
37 Director Financial Aid .... Ms. Heidi WISBY
18 Director Facilities/Auxiliary Svcs .... Ms. Christine STOUT
21 Controller .... Ms. Karen ST. ROMAIN
06 Director of Records/Registrar .... Ms. Stacy JOHNSON
13 Director of Info Technology .... Vacant
36 Director Career Services .... Ms. Brenda PAINE
20 Assoc Provost/Chair Doctoral Pgms .... Dr. Jenny TATSAK
29 Manager of Alumni Relations .... Ms. Melanie ESLAND
88 Chair Accounting .... Mr. John BLACK
88 Chair Finance & Economics .... Mr. John MOORE
88 Chair Decision Sciences .... Mr. Dave SCHIPPERS
88 Chair Taxation .... Mr. Richard DAVIDSON

08 Chief Library Officer .... Ms. Caryn NOEL
111 Interim Director of Advancement .... Mr. Scott TRUDELL

Washtenaw Community College (A)

4800 E Huron River Dr, Ann Arbor MI 48105-4800
County: Washtenaw FICE Identification: 002328
Unit ID: 172617
Telephone: (734) 973-3300 Carnegie Class: Assoc/HT-High Non
FAX Number: (734) 677-5413 Calendar System: Semester
URL: www.wccnet.edu
Established: 1965 Annual Undergrad Tuition & Fees (In-District): $4,176
Enrollment: 11,140 Coed
Affiliation or Control: Local IRS Status: 501(c)3
Highest Offering: Associate Degree
Accreditation: HLC, ACFEI, ADNUR, DA, PTAA, RAD, SURGT

01 President .... Dr. Rose B. BELLANCA
10 Vice Pres & Chief Financial Officer .... Mr. Terry BARNES
05 Interim VP of Instruction .... Dr. Victor VEGA
32 Provost Student & Academic Svcs .... Ms. Linda BLAKEY
111 AVP of College Advancement .... Ms. Tina CASOLI
51 VP Economic & Col Development .... Ms. Michelle MUELLER
84 VP of Strategic Enrollment Mgmt .... Vacant
108 Exec Dir Inst Effect/Plng & Accred .... Dr. Julie MORRISON
121 Dean Supp Svcs & Student Advocacy .... Vacant
50 Dean Business/Comp Technologies .... Ms. Eva SAMULSKI
81 Interim Dean Math/Sci/Engineering .... Dr. Tracy SCHWAB
76 Dean Health Sciences .... Dr. Shari LAMBERT
79 Dean Humanities/Soc & Behav Sci .... Dr. Scott BRITTEN
72 Dean Adv Tech/Public Svc Car .... Dr. Jimmie BABER, III
88 Dean Skilled Trade Training .... Ms. Marilyn DONHAM
28 Dean Stdnt Acc/Succ/Equity/Inclus .... Dr. Eric REED
103 VP & Chief Wrk/Cmty Dev Ofcr .... Mr. Brandon TUCKER
21 Controller .... Ms. Lynn GRACE
114 Dir Budget/Purchasing/Accts Payable .... Vacant
15 VP Labor Relations & CHRO .... Mr. Ted CWIEK
37 Director Financial Aid .... Vacant
09 Director Institutional Research .... Dr. Roger MOURAD
19 Chief Public Safety .... Mr. John LEACHER
88 Dir Student Development/Activities .... Mr. Peter LESHKEVICH
86 Dir of Government Relations .... Vacant
43 General Counsel .... Mr. Larry BARKOFF
100 Chief of Staff .... Ms. Vanessa BROOKS
06 Stdnt System Architect/Registrar .... Ms. Kathy CURRIE
106 Executive Director Online Education .... Vacant
35 Dean of Student Services .... Ms. Tracci JOHNSON
45 Exec Dir FP&A/Treasurer .... Mr. Ben HUNHOLZ

Wayne County Community College District (B)

801 W Fort Street, Detroit MI 48226-3010
County: Wayne FICE Identification: 009230
Unit ID: 172635
Telephone: (313) 496-2600 Carnegie Class: Assoc/HT-High Non
FAX Number: (313) 961-9439 Calendar System: Semester
URL: www.wcccd.edu
Established: 1967 Annual Undergrad Tuition & Fees (In-District): $3,263
Enrollment: 10,748 Coed
Affiliation or Control: State/Local IRS Status: 501(c)3
Highest Offering: Associate Degree
Accreditation: HLC, ADNUR, AT, DA, DH, EMT, SURGT

01 Chancellor .... Dr. Curtis L. IVERY
05 Dist Lead Vice Chanc Educ Affairs .... Dr. David BEAUMONT
88 Dist VC Acad Accountability/Policy .... Ms. CharMaine HINES
10 Deputy Chancellor/Chief Fiscal Ofcr .... Ms. Kim DICARO
15 Senior Vice Chancellor .... Mr. Furquan AHMED
09 Dist VC IE & Research .... Ms. Johnesa HODGE
32 Vice Chancellor for Student Svcs .... Mr. Brian SINGLETON
12 Campus President Downriver .... Dr. Patrick MCNALLY
12 Campus President CLI Downtown .... Mr. Brian SINGLETON
12 Campus President Ted Scott Campus .... Mr. Allan COSMA
12 Campus President Northwest .... Mr. Furquan AHMED
12 Campus President Eastern .... Mr. Mark SANFORD
17 District Provost Health Sciences .... Dr. Abby FREEMAN
26 Asst to Chanc for Communication .... Ms. Unbreen AMIR
28 Provost Diversity & Inclusion .... Dr. Fidelis D'CUNHA
13 Chief Technology Officer .... Mr. Yoseph DEMISSIE
19 Chief District Police Authority .... Mr. Darrick D. MUHAMMAD
104 Dist Dean International Programs .... Mr. David C. BUTTY
88 Assoc Provost MESUC .... Mr. Denis KARIC

Wayne County Community College District Downriver Campus (C)

21000 Northline Road, Taylor MI 48180
Telephone: (734) 946-3500 Identification: 770297
Accreditation: &HLC

Wayne County Community College District Downtown Campus (D)

1001 West Fort Street, Detroit MI 48226
Telephone: (313) 496-2758 Identification: 770926
Accreditation: &HLC

Wayne County Community College District Eastern Campus (E)

5901 Conner, Detroit MI 48213
Telephone: (313) 922-3311 Identification: 770295
Accreditation: &HLC

Wayne County Community College District Northwest Campus (F)

8200 West Outer Drive, Detroit MI 48219
Telephone: (313) 943-4000 Identification: 770296
Accreditation: &HLC

Wayne County Community College District Ted Scott Campus (G)

9555 Haggerty Road, Belleville MI 48111
Telephone: (734) 699-7008 Identification: 770294
Accreditation: &HLC, SURGA

Wayne State University (H)

42 W. Warren Ave., Detroit MI 48202-4095
County: Wayne FICE Identification: 002329
Unit ID: 172644
Telephone: (313) 577-2424 Carnegie Class: DU-Highest
FAX Number: (313) 577-8154 Calendar System: Semester
URL: www.wayne.edu
Established: 1868 Annual Undergrad Tuition & Fees (In-State): $13,517
Enrollment: 26,241 Coed
Affiliation or Control: State IRS Status: 501(c)3
Highest Offering: Doctorate
Accreditation: HLC, ACATE, ANEST, ARCPA, AUD, CAATE, CACREP, CAEP, CAMPEP, CEA, CLPSY, DANCE, DIETC, EXSC, FUSER, LAW, LIB, MED, MIDWF, MLS, MUS, NURSE, OT, PA, PH, PHAR, PLNG, PTA, RAD, RTT, SP, SPAA, SW

01 President .... Dr. M. Roy WILSON
100 Chief of Staff/VP Marketing & Comm .... Mr. Michael G. WRIGHT
05 Provost .... Dr. Mark KORNBLUH
10 VP Finance & Business/Treasurer/CFO .... Ms. Rebecca COOKE
43 Vice President and General Counsel .... Mr. Louis A. LESSEM
46 Vice President for Research .... Dr. Stephen M. LANIER
30 VP Development and Alumni Affairs .... Ms. Susan E. BURNS
86 VP Government and Community Affairs ... Mr. Patrick O. LINDSEY
20 Assoc Provost for Academic Affairs .... Dr. R. Darin ELLIS
88 VP for Economic Development .... Mr. Ned STAEBLER
32 VP for Academic/Student Affairs .... Dr. Ahmad EZZEDDINE
101 VP & Secretary to the BOG .... Ms. Julie H. MILLER
04 Assistant to the President .... Ms. Allison GUILLIOM
29 Assoc VP Alumni Relations .... Mr. Peter CABORN
15 Asst VP of Human Resources .... Ms. Debra WILLIAMS
18 Assoc VP Facilities/Planning/Mgmt .... Mr. Robert DAVENPORT
114 Sr Director of University Budget .... Ms. Brelanda MANDIJA
44 Associate VP of Individual Gifts .... Dr. Stephen E. HENRIE
35 Dean of Students .... Dr. David J. STRAUSS
07 Director Undergraduate Admissions .... Ms. Ericka JACKSON
26 Director of Communications .... Mr. Matthew T. LOCKWOOD
25 Asst VP Sponsored Program Admin .... Ms. Gail L. RYAN
37 Director of Student Financial Aid .... Ms. Catherine KAY
62 Dean School of Information Sciences .... Dr. Thomas WALKER
06 University Registrar .... Mr. Kurt KRUSCHINSKA
49 Dean College of Liberal Arts/Sci .... Dr. Stephanie HARTWELL
61 Dean Law School .... Mr. Richard BIERSCHBACH
63 Dean Sch of Medicine/VP Health Affs .... Dr. Mark SCHWEITZER
66 Dean College of Nursing .... Dr. Laurie LAUZON CLABO
54 Dean College of Engineering .... Dr. Ali ABOLMAALI
50 Dean Mike Ilitch School of Business .... Dr. Virginia FRANKE KLEIST
70 Dean School of Social Work .... Dr. Sheryl KUBIAK
67 Dean Col of Pharmacy & Health Sci .... Dr. Brian CUMMINGS
53 Interim Dean College of Education .... Dr. Boris BALTES
57 Dean College Fine/Perf & Comm Arts .... Dr. Hasan ELAHI
92 Dean Honors College .... Dr. John CORVINO
58 Dean Graduate School .... Dr. Amanda BRYANT-FRIEDRICH
96 Assistant VP of Procurement .... Mr. Kenneth DOHERTY
109 Assoc VP Business & Auxiliary Ops .... Mr. Timothy MICHAEL
88 Assoc VP Tech Commercialization .... Dr. Joan DUNBAR
41 Director of Athletics .... Mr. Robert FOURNIER
105 Director of Web Communications .... Mr. Nick DENARDIS
19 Chief of Police .... Mr. Anthony HOLT
22 Director Equal Opportunity .... Ms. Nikki WRIGHT
28 Assoc Provost Diversity & Inclusion .... Dr. Marquita CHAMBLEE
36 Director of Career Services .... Ms. Shawn PEWITT
39 Director Housing & Residential Life .... Ms. Nikki DUNHAM
108 Director Institutional Assessment .... Dr. Catherine BARRETTE
38 Director Student Counseling .... Dr. Jeffrey KUENTZEL
09 Director of Institutional Research .... Ms. Carly CIRILLI
09 Director of Institutional Research .... Mr. James MORRISSEY
102 Assoc VP Principal Gifts .... Ms. Tracy UTECH
21 Controller .... Ms. Tamaka BUTLER
44 Director of Annual Giving .... Ms. Joye CLARK
106 Manager Online Education/E-Lrng .... Ms. Stacy N. JACKSON
90 Assoc VP Academic Computing .... Mr. Rob THOMPSON

West Shore Community College (I)

3000 N. Stiles Road, Scottville MI 49454-0277
County: Mason FICE Identification: 007950
Unit ID: 172671
Telephone: (231) 845-6211 Carnegie Class: Assoc/MT-VT-High Non
FAX Number: (231) 843-5803 Calendar System: Semester
URL: www.westshore.edu
Established: 1967 Annual Undergrad Tuition & Fees (In-District): $4,480
Enrollment: 1,058 Coed
Affiliation or Control: Local IRS Status: 501(c)3
Highest Offering: Associate Degree
Accreditation: HLC, CNEA, EMT, NAEYC

01 President .... Mr. Scott WARD
05 VP of Academic & Student Services .... Dr. Mark KINNEY
04 Executive Assistant to President .... Ms. Lisa STANKOWSKI
26 Exec Director of College Relations .... Ms. Crystal YOUNG
49 Dean of Arts and Sciences .... Ms. Darby JOHNSEN
13 Director of Information Technology .... Vacant
24 Media Svcs & Learning Tech Coord .... Mr. Craig PETERSON
119 Network Administrator .... Mr. Terrence JOHNSON
75 Dean of Occupational Programs .... Vacant
32 Dean of Student Services .... Vacant
06 Registrar .... Ms. Jill SWEET
09 Director of Institutional Research .... Ms. Kathi DOAN
40 Director of Bookstore & Food Svcs .... Ms. Cheryl HOGAN
37 Director Financial Aid .... Ms. Candace HENRY-SCHRODER
91 Manager of Adm Computing Systems .... Mr. Ryan GREGORSKI
18 Director of Facilities & Recreation .... Mr. Michael A. MOORE
15 Director of Human Resources .... Ms. Debra CAMPBELL
16 Human Resources Specialist .... Ms. Jessica KEITH
08 Director of Library Services .... Ms. Patti SKINNER
23 Director of Wellness Center .... Ms. Julie PAGE-SMITH
10 Director of Accounting .... Ms. Conny BAX
84 Director of Enrollment Services .... Ms. Annie JACOBSON
04 Administrative Assistant .... Ms. Tasha DAULT
120 Learning Management Systems Analyst .... Mr. Tom ALWAY
66 Director of Nursing .... Ms. Shelley BOES
105 Web & Digital Media Specialist .... Mr. Cameron FOGGO

Western Michigan University (J)

1903 West Michigan Avenue, Kalamazoo MI 49008-5202
County: Kalamazoo FICE Identification: 002330
Unit ID: 172699
Telephone: (269) 387-1000 Carnegie Class: DU-Higher
FAX Number: (269) 387-0958 Calendar System: Semester
URL: wmich.edu
Established: 1903 Annual Undergrad Tuition & Fees (In-State): $13,017
Enrollment: 19,887 Coed
Affiliation or Control: State IRS Status: 501(c)3
Highest Offering: Doctorate
Accreditation: HLC, AAB, ABAI, #ARCPA, ART, AUD, CACREP, CAEP, CEA, CIDA, CLPSY, COPSY, DANCE, DIETD, DIETI, MUS, NURSE, OT, PTA, SP, SPAA, SW, THEA

01 President .... Dr. Edward B. MONTGOMERY
05 Provost/Vice Pres Academic Affairs ... Dr. Christopher CHEATHAM
10 Vice Pres Business & Finance/CFO .... Ms. Jan VAN DER KLEY
32 VP Student Affairs .... Dr. Diane K. ANDERSON
46 Vice President for Research .... Dr. Remzi SEKER
30 VP Development/Alumni Relations .... Ms. Kristen DEVRIES
86 Vice Pres Government Relations .... Mr. Jeff BRENEMAN
43 General Counsel .... Mr. Keith HAHN
28 VP for Diversity and Inclusion .... Dr. Candy MCCORKLE
21 Assoc Vice Pres Business & Finance .... Ms. Colleen SCARFF
15 Assoc Vice Pres Human Resources .... Dr. Warren L. HILLS
18 Assoc Vice Pres Facilities Mgmt .... Mr. Steve PERLAKY
35 Assoc VP of SA & Dean of Students .... Dr. Reetha RAVEENDRAN
35 Assoc VP for Student Affairs .... Dr. Barry OLSON
84 Assoc VP Enrollment Management .... Dr. Charles COTTON
88 Assoc Prov for Global Education .... Dr. Paulo ZAGALO-MELO
114 Exec Dir University Budgets .... Ms. Carrie PUCKETT
101 Chief of Staff/Sec Board Trustees .... Mr. Kahler B. SCHUEMANN
58 Dean Graduate College .... Dr. Christine BYRD-JACOBS
49 Dean of Arts & Sciences .... Dr. Carla M. KORETSKY
88 Dean of Aviation .... Dr. Raymond THOMPSON
50 Dean of Business .... Dr. Satish DESHPANDE
53 Dean of Education & Human Dev .... Dr. Kristal EHRHARDT
54 Dean of Engineer & Applied Sciences .... Dr. Steven BUTT
57 Dean of Fine Arts .... Mr. Daniel GUYETTE
76 Dean Health & Human Services .... Dr. Ron CISLER
92 Dean of Lee Honors College .... Dr. Irma LOPEZ
08 Dean of Libraries .... Ms. Julie A. GARRISON
26 Vice Pres Marketing/Strategic Comm .... Mr. Tony PROUDFOOT
27 Director Strategic Communications .... Ms. Paula M. DAVIS
06 Registrar .... Ms. Carrie CUMMING
07 Director Admissions .... Ms. Alicia KORNOWA
37 Dir Student Financial Aid .... Ms. Shashanta JAMES
41 Director of Athletics .... Mr. Dan BARTHOLOMAE
88 Dir of International Enrollment .... Mr. M.K MOHANAN
13 Chief Information Officer .... Mr. Andrew HOLMES
22 Exec Dir Institutional Equity .... Dr. Evelyn B. WINFIELD-THOMAS
104 Director Study Abroad .... Dr. Lee M. PENYAK
19 Dir Public Safety/Chief of Police .... Mr. Scott R. MERLO
25 Dir Grants/Contracts .... Ms. Betty J. MCKAIN
39 Director Residence Life .... Mr. Steven C. PALMER
122 Int Asst Dir Frat/Sorority Life .... Ms. Autumn JAGER
09 Director of Institutional Research .... Mr. Jason JACH

Western Michigan University Cooley Law School (K)

300 S Capitol Avenue, Lansing MI 48933
County: Ingham FICE Identification: 012627
Unit ID: 172477
Telephone: (517) 371-5140 Carnegie Class: Spec-4-yr-Law
FAX Number: (517) 334-5718 Calendar System: Semester
URL: www.cooley.edu
Established: 1972 Annual Graduate Tuition & Fees: N/A
Enrollment: 972 Coed

Affiliation or Control: Independent Non-Profit IRS Status: 501(c)3
Highest Offering: First Professional Degree; No Undergraduates
Accreditation: HLC, LAW

01 President and Dean .... James MCGRATH
100 Chief of Staff .... Frank AIELLO
04 Exec Asst to President/Sec .... Cherie BECK
10 Chief Financial Officer/COO .... Kathleen CONKLIN
08 Assoc Dean Library/Instruct Support .... Duane STROJNY
28 Senior Director DEI .... Jacqueline FREEMAN
108 Sr Dir Planning/Accreditation .... Laura LEDUC
32 Assoc Dean Academics/Students .... Amy TIMMER
84 SVP/Assoc Dean for Enrol/Stdnt Svcs .... Paul ZELENSKI
12 Assoc Dean Experiential Education .... Tracey BRAME
88 Assistant Dean Lansing Campus .... Erika BREITFELD
88 Assistant Dean Tampa Bay Campus .... Katherine GUSTAFSON
07 Assoc Dir Admissions/Financial Aid .... Melissa CRIPS
36 Dir Career/Professional Devel .... Karen POOLE
06 Registrar/Dir of Student Records .... Danielle HALL
40 Bookstore Manager .... Joelle TOPP
21 Controller .... Ronda BECK
29 Dir Advancement/Alumni Relations .... William ARNOLD
26 Sr Dir Communications .... Terry CARELLA
15 Director Human Resources .... Debra HIRSCH

Western Michigan University Homer Stryker MD School of Medicine (A)

1000 Oakland Dr, Kalamazoo MI 49008-8010
County: Kalamazoo Identification: 667287
Telephone: (269) 337-4400 Carnegie Class: Not Classified
FAX Number: N/A Calendar System: Semester
URL: med.wmich.edu
Established: 2012 Annual Graduate Tuition & Fees: N/A
Enrollment: N/A Coed
Affiliation or Control: Independent Non-Profit IRS Status: 501(c)3
Highest Offering: Doctorate; No Undergraduates
Accreditation: HLC, MED

01 Dean .... Dr. Paula TERMUHLEN
05 Assoc Dean Educational Affairs .... Dr. Michael BUSHA
20 Assoc Dean for Faculty Affairs .... Dr. Lisa E. GRAVES
10 Assoc Dean Administration/Finance .... Ms. Lori STRAUBE
32 Assoc Dean Student Affairs .... Dr. Peter ZIEMKOWSKI
30 Assoc Dean Devel/Alumni Affairs .... Dr. Jack MOSSER
36 Asst Dean Career Development .... Dr. Kevin KAVANAUGH
28 Asst Dean Diversity/Inclusiveness .... Vacant

Western Theological Seminary (B)

101 E 13th Street, Holland MI 49423-3622
County: Ottawa FICE Identification: 002331
Unit ID: 172705
Telephone: (616) 392-8555 Carnegie Class: Spec-4-yr-Faith
FAX Number: (616) 392-7717 Calendar System: Semester
URL: www.westernsem.edu
Established: 1866 Annual Graduate Tuition & Fees: N/A
Enrollment: 357 Coed
Affiliation or Control: Reformed Church In America IRS Status: 501(c)3
Highest Offering: Doctorate; No Undergraduates
Accreditation: THEOL

01 President .... Dr. Felix THEONUGRAHA
05 Academic Dean/VP Academic Affairs .... Dr. Kristen JOHNSON
10 Vice President of Finance .... Mr. Norman DONKERSLOOT
08 Director of the Library .... Vacant
06 Registrar .... Mr. Kyle WIGBOLDY
07 Director of Admissions .... Ms. Jill ENGLISH
15 Dir of Administration & Human Res .... Ms. Rayetta PEREZ
04 Executive Asst to the President .Ms. Lannette ZYLMAN-TENHAVE
30 Director of Development .... Mr. Andy BAST

Yeshiva Beth Yehuda - Yeshiva Gedolah of Greater Detroit (C)

24600 Greenfield, Oak Park MI 48237-1544
County: Oakland FICE Identification: 023638
Unit ID: 247773
Telephone: (248) 968-3360 Carnegie Class: Spec-4-yr-Faith
FAX Number: (248) 968-8613 Calendar System: Semester
Established: 1985 Annual Undergrad Tuition & Fees: $7,800
Enrollment: 55 Male
Affiliation or Control: Independent Non-Profit IRS Status: 501(c)3
Highest Offering: Doctorate
Accreditation: RABN

01 Dean .... Rabbi Y. BAKST
05 Assistant Dean .... Rabbi M. S. BAKST
11 Executive Administrator .... Rabbi P. RUSHNAWITZ
37 Director of Financial Aid .... Rabbi Y. BLITZ

MINNESOTA

Academy College (D)

1600 W. 82nd Street, Suite 100, Bloomington MN 55431
County: Hennepin FICE Identification: 020503
Unit ID: 172866
Telephone: (952) 851-0066 Carnegie Class: Spec-4-yr-Other Tech
FAX Number: (952) 851-0094 Calendar System: Quarter
URL: www.academycollege.edu
Established: 1936 Annual Undergrad Tuition & Fees: $18,699
Enrollment: 95 Coed
Affiliation or Control: Proprietary IRS Status: Proprietary
Highest Offering: Baccalaureate
Accreditation: ACCSC

01 President .... Nancy GRAZZINI-OLSON
05 Director of Education .... Alicia OLSON-STRILZUK
37 Financial Aid Rep .... Joshua TSCHIDA

Adler Graduate School (E)

10225 Yellow Circle Dr, Minnetonka MN 55343
County: Hennepin FICE Identification: 030519
Unit ID: 374024
Telephone: (612) 861-7554 Carnegie Class: Spec-4-yr-Other Health
FAX Number: (612) 861-7559 Calendar System: Semester
URL: www.alfredadler.edu
Established: 1969 Annual Graduate Tuition & Fees: N/A
Enrollment: 267 Coed
Affiliation or Control: Independent Non-Profit IRS Status: 501(c)3
Highest Offering: Master's; No Undergraduates
Accreditation: HLC, ACATE, CACREP

01 Interim President/CAO .... Dr. Solange RIBEIRO
10 CFO .... Vacant
108 Director of Assessment .... Dr. Nicole RANDICK
07 Director of Admissions .... Ms. Marcie CONRAD SKOGLUND
06 Registrar .... Ms. Debbie VELASCO
37 Director of Student Financial Aid .... Ms. Jeanette MAYNARD NELSON
08 Head Librarian .... Ms. Nicole MARCHAND
29 Director of Alumni Relations .... Ms. Evelyn HAAS
13 Information Technology Director .... Mr. Laurencio LECHUGA

American Academy of Health and Wellness (F)

2233 Hamline Ave N, Suite 432, Roseville MN 55113
County: Ramsey FICE Identification: 038333
Unit ID: 446002
Telephone: (651) 493-3622 Carnegie Class: Spec-4-yr-Other Health
FAX Number: N/A Calendar System: Trimester
URL: https://acupunctureschoolusa.com/
Established: 2020 Annual Graduate Tuition & Fees: N/A
Enrollment: 43 Coed
Affiliation or Control: Proprietary IRS Status: Proprietary
Highest Offering: Doctorate; No Undergraduates
Accreditation: ACUP

01 President .... Dr. Xiping ZHOU
02 Campus Director .... Leila NIELSEN
11 Chief Operation Officer .... Bruce SUN

Augsburg University (G)

2211 Riverside Avenue, Minneapolis MN 55454-1398
County: Hennepin FICE Identification: 002334
Unit ID: 173045
Telephone: (612) 330-1000 Carnegie Class: Masters/L
FAX Number: (612) 330-1649 Calendar System: Semester
URL: www.augsburg.edu
Established: 1869 Annual Undergrad Tuition & Fees: $40,005
Enrollment: 3,346 Coed
Affiliation or Control: Evangelical Lutheran Church In America
IRS Status: 501(c)3
Highest Offering: Doctorate
Accreditation: HLC, #ACBSP, ARCPA, CLPSY, MUS, NURSE, SW

01 President .... Dr. Paul C. PRIBBENOW
05 Provost and Chief Academic Officer .... Dr. Karen KAIVOLA
10 CFO and Senior Director of Finances .... Mr. John COSKRAN
111 VP Institutional Advancement .... Ms. Amy ALKIRE
11 VP and Chief Operating Officer .... Ms. Rebecca JOHN
84 VP Strategic Enrollment Management .... Mr. Robert GOULD
45 VP & Chief Strategy Officer .... Mr. Leif B. ANDERSON
107 Dean of Professional Studies .... Dr. Monica C. DEVERS
49 Dean of Arts & Sciences .... Dr. Ryan HAALAND
20 Asst Provost Academic Analytics .... Dr. Jordan ORZOFF
88 Asst Provost of Global Education .... Mr. Patrick MULVIHILL
32 Dean of Students .... Dr. Mike GREWE
121 VP for Student Experience & Success .... Ms. Catherine BISHOP
12 Director Rochester Program .... Mr. Jeremy UPDIKE
41 Athletic Director .... Mr. Jeffrey F. SWENSON
42 Campus Pastor .... Rev. Justin LIND-AYRES
28 VP for Equity and Inclusion .... Ms. Joanne REECK
37 Director of Financial Aid .... Ms. Amanda BURGESS
06 Assist Prov Acad Admin/Mgr Registr .... Dr. Marah JACOBSON-SCHULTE
07 Director Undergraduate Admissions .... Vacant
18 Director of Facilities Mgmt .... Mr. James ORCHARD
13 AVP Information Technology .... Mr. Scott KRAJEWSKI
26 Assoc Vice Pres & Chief Mktg Ofcr ... Mr. Stephen JENDRASZAK
38 Director Ctr Wellness & Counseling .... Ms. Ellie OLSON
15 HR Director/CHRO .... Ms. Dawn MILLER
08 Director Library Services .... Ms. Mary HOLLERICH
19 Director Public Safety .... Mr. Anthony J. ERCHUL
31 Director Community Relations .... Mr. Steve PEACOCK
88 Director StepUp Program .... Vacant
85 Dir International Student Svcs .... Vacant

88 Director University Events .... Ms. Sarah CASH-DARVELL
27 Dir Public Rel & Internal Comm .... Ms. Rachel FARRIS
88 Asst Provost Experiential Learning ...Ms. Elaine ESCHENBACHER
39 Director Residence Life .... Ms. Emily LONG
104 Exec Dir Global Initiatives .... Ms. Leah SPINOSA DE VEGA
25 Dir Research & Sponsored Programs .... Mr. John ANDERSON
09 Dir Inst Research & Effectiveness .... Ms. Kathryn HAHN
04 Executive Assistant to President .... Ms. Cyndi BERG
88 Dir Enrollment Systems & Analytics .... Ms. Stephanie RUCKEL
40 Bookstore Manager .... Mr. Sam GUNTER
96 Manager of Purchasing/Central Svcs .... Vacant

Bethany Global University (H)

6820 Auto Club Road, Suite C, Bloomington MN 55438
County: Hennepin Identification: 667136
Unit ID: 486284
Telephone: (952) 222-0699 Carnegie Class: Spec-4-yr-Faith
FAX Number: (952) 829-2753 Calendar System: Semester
URL: https://bethanygu.edu/
Established: 1948 Annual Undergrad Tuition & Fees: $15,450
Enrollment: 359 Coed
Affiliation or Control: Interdenominational IRS Status: 501(c)3
Highest Offering: Master's
Accreditation: BI

01 President .... Dr. David HASZ
04 Executive Asst to President .... La'Tia COLEMAN
84 Director of Enrollment .... Kenneth FREIRE
05 Dean of Academic Operations .... Jason HACHÉ
103 Dean of Work Education .... Brian SCHWARZ
58 Dean of Graduate Studies .... Dr. Darin KINDLE
10 Chief Financial/Business Officer .... David ENTLER
101 Secretary of the Institution/Board .... Ron HAVE
30 Chief Development/Advancement .... Mike MINICH
26 Director of Marketing .... Kenneth FREIRE
18 Chief Facilities/Physical Plant .... Matthew ADAIR
88 Global Internship Director .... Doug GOODMUNDSON
106 Director Online Educ/Partnerships .... Kenneth ORTIZ
34 Dean of Women/Student Life .... Bethany FREIRE
33 Dean of Men/Student Life .... Derek BROKKE
13 Network/Computer Administrator .... Chris ERICKSON
15 Director Human Resources .... Noemi HEDRICK
19 Director Security/Safety .... Matthew ADAIR
44 Donor Communications Specialist .... Vacant
37 Director Financial Aid .... Anna BERGH
06 Registrar .... Hannah LEVIN
36 Director Career Development .... Dr. Elisabeth WILSON
08 Head Librarian .... Vacant

Bethany Lutheran College (I)

700 Luther Drive, Mankato MN 56001-6163
County: Blue Earth FICE Identification: 002337
Unit ID: 173142
Telephone: (507) 344-7000 Carnegie Class: Bac-A&S
FAX Number: (507) 344-7376 Calendar System: Semester
URL: www.blc.edu
Established: 1911 Annual Undergrad Tuition & Fees: $28,380
Enrollment: 769 Coed
Affiliation or Control: Evangelical Lutheran Synod IRS Status: 501(c)3
Highest Offering: Master's
Accreditation: HLC, NURSE

01 President .... Dr. Gene R. PFEIFER
42 Dir Campus Spiritual Life/Chaplain ....Rev. Donald L. MOLDSTAD
05 Vice President of Academic Affairs .... Dr. Jason H. LOWREY
32 Vice President of Student Affairs .... Dr. Theodore E. MANTHE
10 VP of Finance & Administration .... Mr. Daniel L. MUNDAHL
111 Vice President of Advancement .... Mr. Bruce A. GRATZ
37 Director of Financial Aid .... Mr. Jeffrey W. YOUNGE
06 Registrar .... Mr. Sergio SALGADO
07 VP of Admissions & Enrollment .... Dr. Jeffrey C. LEMKE
15 Manager of Human Resources .... Mr. Joshua PEDERSON
08 Director of Library Services .... Ms. Alyssa K. INNIGER
13 Director of Information Technology .... Mr. John M. SEHLOFF
26 Dir of Institutional Communication .... Mr. Lance W. SCHWARTZ
41 Director of Athletics .... Mr. Donald M. WESTPHAL
29 Manager of Alumni Relations .... Mr. Jacob C. KRIER
09 Mgr Acad & Institutional Research .... Ms. Lisa A. SHUBERT
40 Bookstore Manager .... Mr. Daniel GERDTS
21 Controller .... Mr. Gregory W. COSTELLO
28 Coord Ctr for Intercultural Develop .... Vacant
38 Coord of Student Counseling .... Vacant
18 Director of Facilities .... Mr. Patrick E. HULL
108 Director of Assessment .... Dr. Theodore E. MANTHE
04 Executive Asst to President .... Mrs. Barbara J. DRESSEN
106 Director Online Learning .... Mr. Kevin ZIMMERMAN

Bethel University (J)

3900 Bethel Drive, Saint Paul MN 55112-6999
County: Ramsey FICE Identification: 009058
Unit ID: 173160
Telephone: (651) 638-6400 Carnegie Class: DU-Mod
FAX Number: (651) 638-6001 Calendar System: Semester
URL: www.bethel.edu
Established: 1871 Annual Undergrad Tuition & Fees: $39,030
Enrollment: 3,814 Coed
Affiliation or Control: Baptist IRS Status: 501(c)3
Highest Offering: Doctorate
Accreditation: HLC, ACBSP, ARCPA, MFCD, MIDWF, NURSE, SW, THEOL

01 President .... Mr. Ross ALLEN
100 Chief of Staff .... Ms. Jeanne OSGOOD
05 University Provost .... Dr. Robin RYLAARSDAM
10 Vice Pres Finance .... Mr. Scott MOATS
20 Assoc Provost - CAS .... Dr. Julie FINNERN
84 Vice Pres Enroll & Marketing .... Mr. Paul MCGINNISH
111 Vice Pres Univ Advancement .... Mr. Jim BENDER
46 Chief Inst Data/Research Officer .... Mr. Daniel NELSON
18 Vice Pres Facilities & ITS .... Mr. Mark POSNER
29 Exec Minister for Church Relations .... Dr. Dale DURIE
32 Vice Pres Student Experience .... Ms. Miranda POWERS
73 Dean of Seminary .... Dr. Peter VOGT
49 Dean of Academic Programs .... Dr. Barrett FISHER
108 Assoc Dean Inst Assess/Accred .... Dr. Joel FREDERICKSON
66 Dean Nursing/CAPS-GS Health/Med .... Dr. Diane DAHL
107 Dean Faculty Dev/Professional Pgms .... Mr. Ray VAN ARRAGON
104 Assoc Dean Off-Campus Programs .... Ms. Virginija WILCOX
35 Assoc VP of Student Life .... Ms. Erica LYNCH
08 Director of Libraries .... Mr. David R. STEWART
15 Chief Human Resources Ofcr .... Ms. Jenny MARCHINIAK
41 Athletic Director .... Mr. Greg PETERSON
37 Financial Aid Officer .... Mr. Jeffery D. OLSON
07 Director of CAS Admissions .... Mr. Adam HIPPE
07 Dir Seminary/CAPS/GS Admissions .... Ms. Janna COLLINS
06 University Registrar .... Ms. Cheryl FISK
36 Dir Vocation/Path & Partner .... Mr. Stan THOMPSON
19 Director Risk Mgmt/Safety/Security .... Vacant
40 Director Campus Stores .... Ms. Jill SONSTEBY
23 Director of Health Services .... Mrs. Elizabeth K. MILLER
96 Director of Purchasing .... Vacant
38 Director Student Counseling .... Dr. Miriam HILL
109 Dir of Campus Svcs & Operations .... Vacant
18 Director Facilities Tech Ops .... Mr. Glenn HOFER
28 VP Diversity/Equity/Inclusion .... Mr. Rahn FRANKLIN
29 Director Alumni & Family Relations .... Ms. Jennifer SCOTT

† The marriage and family therapy master's program at Bethel Seminary San Diego is accredited by the Commission on Accreditation for Marriage and Family Therapy Education (COAMFTE) of the American Association for Marriage and Family Therapy (AAMFT)

Bethlehem College & Seminary (A)

720 13th Avenue South, Minneapolis MN 55415
County: Hennepin | Identification: 667249
Unit ID: 486053
Telephone: (612) 455-3420 | Carnegie Class: Spec-4-yr-Faith
FAX Number: N/A | Calendar System: Semester
URL: bcsmn.edu
Established: 2009 | Annual Undergrad Tuition & Fees: $6,560
Enrollment: 210 | Coed
Affiliation or Control: Independent Non-Profit | IRS Status: 501(c)3
Highest Offering: Master's
Accreditation: BI

01 President .... Dr. Joseph RIGNEY
05 Academic Dean .... Dr. Brian TABB
11 VP of Administration & CFO .... Jason ABELL
111 VP of Advancement .... Rick SEGAL
07 Dean of Admissions .... Jonathon WOODYARD
88 Accreditation Coordinator .... Lance KRAMER
06 Registrar/Bursar & Dir Inst Rsrch .... Connie KOPISCHKE

Capella University (B)

225 S 6th Street, 9th Floor, Minneapolis MN 55402-4319
County: Hennepin | FICE Identification: 032673
Unit ID: 413413
Telephone: (888) 227-3552 | Carnegie Class: DU-Mod
FAX Number: (612) 977-5066 | Calendar System: Other
URL: www.capella.edu
Established: 1993 | Annual Undergrad Tuition & Fees: $14,148
Enrollment: 38,930 | Coed
Affiliation or Control: Proprietary | IRS Status: Proprietary
Highest Offering: Doctorate
Accreditation: HLC, ACBSP, CACREP, CAEP, MFCD, NURSE, SW

01 President .... Dr. Richard SENESE
05 SVP Academic Affairs/Provost .... Dr. Constance ST. GERMAIN
10 VP Finance .... Vacant

Carleton College (C)

1 N College Street, Northfield MN 55057-4001
County: Rice | FICE Identification: 002340
Unit ID: 173258
Telephone: (507) 222-4000 | Carnegie Class: Bac-A&S
FAX Number: N/A | Calendar System: Trimester
URL: www.carleton.edu
Established: 1866 | Annual Undergrad Tuition & Fees: $59,352
Enrollment: 1,940 | Coed
Affiliation or Control: Independent Non-Profit | IRS Status: 501(c)3
Highest Offering: Baccalaureate
Accreditation: HLC

01 President .... Ms. Alison R. BYERLY
05 Provost .... Ms. Michelle MATTSON
10 VP Business & Finance/Treasurer .... Mr. Eric J. RUNESTAD
111 Vice President External Relations .... Mr. Tommy BONNER
32 VP for Student Dev/Dean of Students .. Ms. Carolyn LIVINGSTON
07 VP and Dean of Admissions/Fin Aid .... Mr. Art RODRIGUEZ
100 Vice President/Chief of Staff .... Ms. Elise ESLINGER
26 Assoc VP for Communications .... Ms. Helen CLARKE
20 Associate Provost .... Mr. David LIBEN-NOWELL
121 Associate Provost .... Ms. Yansi PEREZ
88 Director of Student Fellowships .... Ms. Marynel RYAN VAN ZEE
35 Associate Dean of Students .... Mr. Trey WILLIAMS
35 Associate Dean of Students .... Ms. Sindy FLEMING
35 Associate Dean of Students .... Ms. Cathy CARLSON
37 Sr Assoc Dean & Dir Stdnt Fin Aid .... Ms. Danielle HAYDEN
42 Chaplain .... Rev. Carolyn FURE-SLOCUM
06 Registrar .... Ms. Theresa RODRIGUEZ
08 College Librarian .... Mr. Bradley SCHAFFNER
09 Asst VP Inst Research & Assessment .... Mr. Todd JAMISON
110 Asst VP for External Relations .... Ms. Becky ZRIMSEK
29 Director of Alumni Relations .... Mr. Michael THOMPSON
44 Director of Alumni Annual Fund .... Ms. Anita FISHER-EGGE
30 Assoc VP for Development .... Mr. Dan RUSTAD
112 Director of Planned Giving .... Ms. Melissa SAUNDERS
13 Chief Technology Officer .... Ms. Janet SCANNELL
15 Director of Human Resources .... Ms. Kerstin CARDENAS
39 Director of Residential Life .... Ms. Andrea ROBINSON
85 Director of Intercultural Life .... Ms. Renee FAULKNER
85 Director of International Life .... Ms. Liz CODY
104 Director of Off-Campus Studies .... Ms. Helena KAUFMAN
36 Director of the Career Center .... Mr. R.J HOLMES-LEOPOLD
23 Dir Student Health and Counseling .... Ms. Marit LYSNE
18 Dir of Facilities/Capital Planning .... Mr. Steven SPEHN
21 Comptroller .... Ms. Linda THORNTON
25 Director of the Grants Office .... Mr. Christopher TASSAVA
88 Dir Center for Learning/Teaching .... Ms. Victoria MORSE
109 Director of Auxiliary Services .... Mr. Jesse CASHMAN
41 Chair of Physical Educ/Athl/Rec .... Mr. Gerald YOUNG
19 Director of Security/Emergency Mgmt .... Mr. John BERMEL
105 Director of Web Services .... Ms. Julie ANDERSON
91 Dir of Enterprise Information Svcs .... Ms. Julie CREAMER
88 Director of Technology Support .... Mr. Adit BURKULE
90 Director of Academic Technology .... Ms. Wiebke KUHN

Central Baptist Theological Seminary of Minneapolis (D)

900 Forestview Lane N, Plymouth MN 55441-5934
County: Hennepin | Identification: 666050
Telephone: (763) 417-8250 | Carnegie Class: Not Classified
FAX Number: (763) 417-8258 | Calendar System: Semester
URL: www.centralseminary.edu
Established: 1956 | Annual Undergrad Tuition & Fees: N/A
Enrollment: N/A | Coed
Affiliation or Control: Baptist | IRS Status: 501(c)3
Highest Offering: Doctorate
Accreditation: THEOL

01 President .... Dr. Matthew D. MORRELL
03 Provost/EVP .... Dr. Brett J. WILLIAMS
111 Vice Pres of Advancement .... Mr. Ron GOTZMAN
07 Director Recruitment/Retention .... Dr. Matt SHRADER
06 Registrar .... Dr. L. Mark BRUFFEY
08 Chief Library Officer .... Dr. L. Mark BRUFFEY

*College of Medicine, Mayo Clinic (E)

200 First Street, Rochester MN 55905-3712
County: Olmsted | Identification: 666719
Telephone: (507) 284-2511 | Carnegie Class: N/A
FAX Number: (507) 284-0999
URL: www.mayo.edu

01 Chief Executive Officer .... Dr. John H. NOSEWORTHY
05 Exec Dean Mayo Clinic Alix Sch Med .... Dr. Fredric B. MEYER
46 Exec Dean for Research Mayo Clinic .... Dr. Greg GORES
15 Chair of Human Resources .... Ms. Cathy FRASER
30 Exec Dean of Development .... Dr. Michael CAMILLERI

*Mayo Medical School (F)

200 1st Street, SW, Rochester MN 55905-0001
County: Olmsted | FICE Identification: 011732
Unit ID: 173957
Telephone: (507) 538-4897 | Carnegie Class: Spec-4-yr-Eng
FAX Number: (507) 284-2634 | Calendar System: Other
URL: www.mayo.edu/mms
Established: 1971 | Annual Undergrad Tuition & Fees: $7,290
Enrollment: 1,223 | Coed
Affiliation or Control: Independent Non-Profit | IRS Status: 501(c)3
Highest Offering: First Professional Degree
Accreditation: HLC, MED

02 Dean .... Dr. Fredric B. MEYER
37 Director of Financial Aid .... Ms. Anne DAHLEN
06 Registrar .... Ms. Anne DAHLEN

*Mayo Clinic College of Medicine-Mayo Graduate School (G)

200 First Street, SW, Rochester MN 55905-0001
Telephone: (507) 538-1160 | FICE Identification: 011516
Accreditation: &HLC, CAMPEP, DENT, PDPSY

† Regional accreditation is carried under College of Medicine, Mayo Clinic.

*Mayo Clinic School of Health Sciences (H)

200 First St. SW, Siebens Bldg 3,
Rochester MN 55905-0001
Telephone: (507) 284-3293 | FICE Identification: 008182
Accreditation: &HLC, ACS, ANEST, #ARCPA, COARC, CVT, CYTO, DIETI, DMS, EMT, HT, MLS, NDT, NMT, PAST, PTA, RAD, RADMAG, RTT, SURGA

† Regional accreditation is carried under College of Medicine, Mayo Clinic.

College of Saint Benedict (I)

37 S College Avenue, Saint Joseph MN 56374-2099
County: Stearns | FICE Identification: 002341
Unit ID: 174747
Telephone: (320) 363-5011 | Carnegie Class: Bac-A&S
FAX Number: (320) 363-6099 | Calendar System: Semester
URL: www.csbsju.edu
Established: 1913 | Annual Undergrad Tuition & Fees: $48,444
Enrollment: 1,668 | Coordinate
Affiliation or Control: Roman Catholic | IRS Status: 501(c)3
Highest Offering: Doctorate
Accreditation: HLC, DIETD, MUS, NURSE

01 Interim President .... Dr. Laurie HAMEN
05 Provost Academic Affairs .... Dr. Richard ICE
32 Vice President Student Development .... Ms. Mary A. GELLER
111 VP Institutional Advancement .... Ms. Kathy HANSEN
10 Vice Pres Finance/Administration .... Ms. Susan M. PALMER
84 VP Enrollment Management/Marketing .... Mr. Nate DEHNE
110 Assoc VP Institutional Advancement .... Ms. Heather PIEPER-OLSON
18 Exec Director Facilities .... Mr. Ryan GIDEON
26 Sr Director of Public Relations .... Mr. Michael HEMMESCH
20 Academic Dean .... Dr. Barbara MAY
34 Dean of Students .... Ms. Jody L. TERHAAR
06 Registrar .... Ms. Julie E. GRUSKA
08 Director Library .... Ms. Kathy PARKER
37 Exec Director Financial Aid .... Mr. Stuart PERRY
38 Director of Counseling .... Dr. Mike J. EWING
15 Chief Human Resources Officer .... Ms. Erin MUCKERHEIDE
42 Interim Director of Campus Ministry .... Mr. Aaron VOTH
41 Athletic Director .... Ms. Kelly ANDERSON DIERCKS
13 Director of Info Technology Svc .... Ms. Casey GORDON
19 Director of Security .... Mr. Darren SWANSON
21 Controller .... Ms. Anne OBERMAN
36 Executive Director XPD .... Vacant
09 Assoc Dir of Institutional Research .... Ms. Karen KNUTSON
40 Director of Bookstores .... Ms. Tina STREIT
20 Dean of the Faculty .... Dr. Pamela BACON
07 Dean of Admission .... Ms. Karen BACKES

The College of Saint Scholastica (J)

1200 Kenwood Avenue, Duluth MN 55811-4199
County: Saint Louis | FICE Identification: 002343
Unit ID: 174899
Telephone: (218) 723-6000 | Carnegie Class: DU-Mod
FAX Number: (218) 723-6290 | Calendar System: Semester
URL: www.css.edu
Established: 1912 | Annual Undergrad Tuition & Fees: $39,410
Enrollment: 3,712 | Coed
Affiliation or Control: Roman Catholic | IRS Status: 501(c)3
Highest Offering: Doctorate
Accreditation: HLC, AAQEP, ARCPA, CAATE, CAHIIM, NURSE, OT, PTA, SW

01 President .... Dr. Barbara MCDONALD
05 Vice President Academic Affairs .... Mr. Ryan SANDEFER
32 Vice President for Student Affairs .... Mr. Steve LYONS
10 Vice President of Finance & CFO .... Mr. Marty PARSONS
11 Chief Operating Officer .... Ms. Diane VERTIN
28 Chief Diversity Office .... Dr. Amy BERGSTROM
13 Chief Information Officer .... Vacant

Concordia College (K)

901 8th Street S, Moorhead MN 56562-0001
County: Clay | FICE Identification: 002346
Unit ID: 173300
Telephone: (218) 299-4000 | Carnegie Class: Bac-A&S
FAX Number: (218) 299-3947 | Calendar System: Semester
URL: www.cord.edu
Established: 1891 | Annual Undergrad Tuition & Fees: $43,266
Enrollment: 1,973 | Coed
Affiliation or Control: Evangelical Lutheran Church In America
IRS Status: 501(c)3
Highest Offering: Master's
Accreditation: HLC, CAEP, DIETD, DIETI, MUS, NURSE, SW

01 President .... Dr. William J. CRAFT
05 Provost and Dean of the College .... Dr. Susan J. LARSON
10 Vice Pres Finance/Treasurer .... Ms. Linda J. BROWN
84 Vice Pres Enrollment and Marketing .... Mr. Karl A. STUMO
111 Vice Pres Advancement .... Rev. Terry BRANDT
32 VP Student Dev and Campus Life .... Dr. Lisa SETHRE-HOFSTAD
28 Chief Diversity Officer .... Dr. Edward ANTONIO
20 Associate Provost .... Dr. Stephanie L. AHLFELDT
100 Deputy to the President .... Dr. Jill M. ABBOTT
13 Exec Dir of Information Technology .... Mr. Erik RAMSTAD
07 Dir of Admission Operations .... Ms. Samantha AXVIG
06 Registrar .... Ms. Lisa M. SJOBERG

37	Assoc VP Enrollment & Financial Aid	Mr. Eric J. ADDINGTON
08	Library Director	Mrs. Laura K. PROBST
15	Director Human Resources	Ms. Peggy L. TORRANCE
29	Director Alumni Relations	Mr. Eric P. JOHNSON
26	Assoc VP Comm/Chief Mktg Officer	Mr. Josh D. LYSNE
18	Director of Facilities Management	Mr. Dallas FOSSUM
41	Athletic Director	Ms. Rachel D. BERGESON
42	Minister of Word and Sacrament	Rev. Dave ADAMS
42	Minister Faith & Spirituality	Mr. Jon LEISETH
19	Director of Security/Public Safety	Mr. William MACDONALD
04	Exec Asst to the President	Ms. Carrie ROGERS
104	Assoc Dean Global Learning	Dr. Per M. ANDERSON
108	Dir Institutional Effectiveness	Dr. Jasi O'CONNOR
25	Dir Found Rels/Research Grants	Ms. Jillain VEIL-EHNERT
30	Director of Development	Ms. Trina PISK HALL
39	Director Residence Life	Ms. Mikal C. KENFIELD
117	Director Risk Management	Mr. Roger T. OLSON
44	Director Annual Fund	Ms. Rachel M. CLARKE
36	Director of Career Center	Ms. Kris OLSON
38	Director of Counseling Center	Mr. Matthew RUTTEN

Concordia University, St. Paul   (A)

1282 Concordia Ave, Saint Paul MN 55104-5494

County: Ramsey
FICE Identification: 002347
Unit ID: 173328
Telephone: (651) 641-8278
Carnegie Class: Masters/L
FAX Number: (651) 659-0207
Calendar System: Semester
URL: www.csp.edu
Established: 1893
Annual Undergrad Tuition & Fees: $23,400
Enrollment: 5,585
Coed
Affiliation or Control: Lutheran Church - Missouri Synod
IRS Status: 501(c)3
Highest Offering: Doctorate
Accreditation: **HLC**, AAQEP, DMS, NURSE, OPE, PTA

01	President	RevDr. Brian FRIEDRICH
11	Provost/SVP for Administration	Dr. Eric E. LAMOTT
05	Vice President Academic Affairs	Dr. Kevin HALL
10	Vice President for Finance	RevDr. Michael H. DORNER
111	Vice President for Advancement	Mr. Mark HILL
84	VP for Enrollment Management	Dr. Kimberly CRAIG
32	Assoc VP Student Life	Mr. Jason M. RAHN
20	Assoc VP Academic Affairs	Dr. Katie FISCHER
20	Assoc VP Academic Affairs	Dr. Mark KOSCHMANN
108	Assoc VP for Assessment/Accred	Dr. Miriam LUEBKE
108	Assoc VP for Assessment/Accred	Ms. Milissa ORCHARD
28	Chief Diversity Officer	Mr. Mychal THOM
53	Dean Col of Education & Humanities	Mr. Lonn MALY
83	Dean Col Human Svcs/Behavioral Sci	Dr. Michael WALCHESKI
50	Dean College of Business	Mr. Mychal THOM
76	Dean College of Health & Science	Dr. Mandy BROSNAHAN
66	Dean College of Nursing	Ms. Hollie CALDWELL
88	Dean College of Kinesiology	Dr. Lana HUBERTY
88	Director of Diversity Center	Ms. Aqueelah ROBERSON
06	Registrar	Ms. Lynn LUNDQUIST
08	Director of Library Services	Mr. Jonathan B. NEILSON
26	Dir Univ Communications/Marketing	Mr. Nick SCHROEPFER
15	Director of Human Resources	Ms. Dee Ann KERR
37	Director of Financial Aid	Ms. Amanda MCCAUGHAN
07	Director Undergrad Admissions	Ms. Leah MARTIN
42	University Pastor	Rev. Thomas GUNDERMANN
121	Director of Traditional Advising	Ms. Gretchen WALTHER
09	Director of Institutional Research	Ms. Beth C. PETER
29	Director of Alumni Relations	Mrs. Rhonda K. PALMERSHEIM
41	Director of Athletics	Mrs. Regan M. MCATHIE
40	Bookstore Manager	Mr. Chad L. MASTEL
90	Director of Computer Services	Mr. Jonathan S. BREITBARTH
91	Director Administrative Computing	Ms. Beth C. PETER
19	Risk Manager	Mr. David GALLOWAY
24	Help Desk Coordinator	Mr. Daniel CARTER
44	Director Annual Giving	Ms. Staci POOLE
04	Admin Assistant to the President	Mr. William SCHULTZ
39	Asst Director of Residence Life	Mr. Jake WAKEM

Crown College   (B)

8700 College View Drive, Saint Bonifacius MN 55375-9001

County: Carver
FICE Identification: 002383
Unit ID: 174862
Telephone: (952) 446-4100
Carnegie Class: Masters/M
FAX Number: (952) 446-4149
Calendar System: Semester
URL: www.crown.edu
Established: 1916
Annual Undergrad Tuition & Fees: $27,980
Enrollment: 1,485
Coed
Affiliation or Control: The Christian And Missionary Alliance
IRS Status: 501(c)3
Highest Offering: Master's
Accreditation: **HLC**, NURSE

01	President	Dr. Andrew DENTON
10	VP Enrollment & Administration	Mr. Michael PRICE
05	VP Academic Affairs	Dr. Christopher MATHEWS
32	VP Student Development	Dr. Bill KUHN
58	AVP Sch Online Studies/Grad School	Dr. Fawn MCCRACKEN
26	Chief Marketing & Comms Officer	Mrs. Jen NISKA
15	Director of Human Resources	Mrs. Amy LUESSE
21	Controller	Mr. Ronald STRAKA
41	Athletic Director	Mr. Mike VIGUE
66	Director of Nursing	Mrs. Teresa NEWBY
06	Registrar	Dr. Cheryl FISK
37	Director of Financial Aid	Mrs. Allyson GILLETTE

124	Director Student Engagement	Mrs. Martha SWIFT
123	Director of Graduate Admissions	Ms. Maggie UNGER
18	Director of Facilities Services	Mr. Matt SHEPPARD
40	Director of Campus Store	Mrs. Sharie THOELKE
42	Chaplain	Dr. Bill KUHN
36	Dir Counseling & Career Services	Dr. Bill JOHNSON
13	Director of Technology Services	Mr. Paul FLAGSTAD
35	Dean of Students	Mr. Ezra JOHNSON
07	Director of Admission	Mr. Mitch FISK

Dunwoody College of Technology   (C)

818 Dunwoody Boulevard, Minneapolis MN 55403-1192

County: Hennepin
FICE Identification: 004641
Unit ID: 175227
Telephone: (612) 374-5800
Carnegie Class: Bac/Assoc-Mixed
FAX Number: (612) 381-9620
Calendar System: Semester
URL: www.dunwoody.edu
Established: 1914
Annual Undergrad Tuition & Fees: $23,122
Enrollment: 1,281
Coed
Affiliation or Control: Independent Non-Profit
IRS Status: 501(c)3
Highest Offering: Baccalaureate
Accreditation: **HLC**, CIDA, CONST, RAD

01	President	Dr. Rich WAGNER
05	Provost	Dr. Scott STALLMAN
84	Vice President Enrollment Mgmt	Ms. Cynthia OLSON
111	VP of Institutional Advancement	Mr. Brian NELSON
15	Vice President of Human Resources	Ms. Patricia EDMAN
10	VP of Administrative Svcs & CFO	Ms. Tammy MCGEE
100	Chief of Staff	Ms. Katie MALONE

Free Lutheran Bible College and Seminary   (D)

3134 East Medicine Lake Blvd, Plymouth MN 55441

County: Hennepin
Identification: 667235
Telephone: (763) 544-9501
Carnegie Class: Not Classified
FAX Number: (763) 412-2047
Calendar System: Semester
URL: www.flbc.edu
Established: 1964
Annual Graduate Tuition & Fees: N/A
Enrollment: N/A
Coed
Affiliation or Control: Independent Non-Profit
IRS Status: 501(c)3
Highest Offering: Master's; No Undergraduates
Accreditation: TRACS

01	President	Dr. Wade MOBLEY
05	Chief Academic Officer/Dean	Dr. James MOLSTRE
11	Vice President of Operations	Larry MYHRER
03	Vice President/Dean	Adam OSIER
06	Registrar	Sarah BIERLE
07	Director of Admissions	Josh JOHNSON
32	Director Student Life & Athletics	Dr. Brad BIERLE

Gustavus Adolphus College   (E)

800 W College Avenue, Saint Peter MN 56082-1498

County: Nicollet
FICE Identification: 002353
Unit ID: 173647
Telephone: (507) 933-8000
Carnegie Class: Bac-A&S
FAX Number: (507) 933-7041
Calendar System: Semester
URL: www.gustavus.edu
Established: 1862
Annual Undergrad Tuition & Fees: $48,789
Enrollment: 2,230
Coed
Affiliation or Control: Evangelical Lutheran Church In America
IRS Status: 501(c)3
Highest Offering: Master's
Accreditation: **HLC**, CAATE, NURSE

01	President	Ms. Rebecca M. BERGMAN
05	Provost and Dean of the College	Dr. Brenda S. KELLY
10	VP for Finance/Treasurer/CFO	Mr. Curtis J. KOWALESKI
07	AVP and Dean of Admission	Mr. Richard S. AUNE
07	AVP for Enrollment	Mr. Kirk CARLSON
111	VP for Institutional Advancement	Mr. Thomas W. YOUNG
32	VP for Student Life	Dr. JoNes R. VANHECKE
26	VP Marketing & Communication	Mr. Timothy R. KENNEDY
88	VP Mission/Strategy/Innovation	Dr. Kathi TUNHEIM
28	VP for Equity and Inclusion	Mr. Doug THOMPSON
28	Director Diversity Center	Mr. Thomas G. FLUNKER
09	Director Institutional Research	Mr. David A. MENK
08	Head Librarian	Ms. Michelle TWAIT
88	Director Church Relations	Rev. Grady I. ST. DENNIS
29	Dir Alumni and Parent Engagement	Ms. Angela ERICKSON
36	Exec Director Career Development	Mr. Andrew COSTON
06	Registrar	Ms. Deann SCHLOESSER
13	Dir Gustavus Technology Services	Ms. Tami AUNE
18	AVP Facilities	Mr. Travis JORDAN
37	Dean of Financial Aid	Mr. Jesus O. HERNANDEZ MEJIA
39	Director Residential Life	Mr. Anthony BETTENDORF
42	Interim Chaplain	Rev. Grady I. ST. DENNIS
35	Assistant VP for Student Life	Ms. Megan RUBLE
35	Assistant VP for Student Life	Mr. Charlie POTTS
41	Athletics Director	Mr. Thomas W. BROWN
15	Director Human Resources	Ms. Jacque CHRISTENSEN
19	Director Campus Security	Mr. Frederick SMITH
40	Manager Book Mark	Ms. Molly L. YONKERS
27	Dir Media Relations/Internal Comm	Mr. Jacob J. AKIN
04	Asst to the Pres & Sec of the Board	Ms. Jolene D. CHRISTENSEN

© COPYRIGHT HIGHER EDUCATION PUBLICATIONS, INC. 2022

Hamline University   (F)

1536 Hewitt Avenue, Saint Paul MN 55104-1284

County: Ramsey
FICE Identification: 002354
Unit ID: 173665
Telephone: (651) 523-2800
Carnegie Class: Masters/L
FAX Number: (651) 523-2899
Calendar System: 4/1/4
URL: www.hamline.edu
Established: 1854
Annual Undergrad Tuition & Fees: $45,145
Enrollment: 3,113
Coed
Affiliation or Control: United Methodist
IRS Status: 501(c)3
Highest Offering: Doctorate
Accreditation: **HLC**, CAEP, MUS

01	President	Dr. Fayneese S. MILLER
05	Interim Provost	Dr. Andy RUNDQUIST
10	Sr VP Business/Finance/Technology	Mr. Brent GUSTAFSON
111	VP Institutional Advancement	Mr. Mike TOMPOS
32	VP/Dean of Students	Ms. Patti KLEIN
43	VP/General Counsel	Ms. Catherine WASSBERG
84	Vice Pres Enrollment Management	Ms. Mai Nhia XIONG-CHAN
13	Assoc VP/Dir IT	Mr. Terry METZ
26	Assoc VP Marketing/Communications	Vacant
18	Assoc VP Facilities/Physical Plant	Mr. Ken DEHKES
50	Dean School of Business	Ms. Beth GUNDERSON
49	Dean College Liberal Arts	Ms. Marcela KOSTIHOVA
85	Ast Dn/Dir Multicult/Intl Stdt Affs	Mr. Carlos SNEED
06	University Registrar	Ms. Gwen SHERBURNE
37	Sr Director Financial Aid	Ms. Lynette WAHL
07	Director Undergraduate Admission	Ms. Holly COLLINS
15	Director Human Resources	Vacant
36	Dir Career Dev Center	Mr. Terry MIDDENDORF
41	Athletic Director	Mr. Jason VERDUGO
19	Director of Safety & Security	Ms. Illiana CANTU DELGADO
23	Director Counseling & Health Center	Ms. Hussein RAJPUT
35	Dir Student Leadership & Activities	Mr. Patrick HAUGHT
42	Chaplain & Director	Ms. Kelly FIGUEROA-RAY
96	Director of Purchasing	Vacant
04	Exec Assistant to the President	Ms. Elizabeth RADTKE
09	Director of Institutional Research	Ms. Tracy WILLIAMS
08	Head Librarian	Mr. Terry METZ
39	Director Student Housing	Vacant

Hazelden Betty Ford Graduate School of Addiction Studies   (G)

PO Box 11 (CO9), Center City MN 55012-0011

County: Chisago
FICE Identification: 040443
Unit ID: 173683
Telephone: (651) 213-4175
Carnegie Class: Spec-4-yr-Other Health
FAX Number: (651) 213-4710
Calendar System: Semester
URL: www.hazeldenbettyford.org
Established: 1999
Annual Graduate Tuition & Fees: N/A
Enrollment: 174
Coed
Affiliation or Control: Independent Non-Profit
IRS Status: 501(c)3
Highest Offering: Master's; No Undergraduates
Accreditation: HLC

01	President and CEO	Dr. Joseph LEE
05	VP of Education & Research	Dr. Valerie SLAYMAKER
88	Exec Asst to VP Education/Research	Ms. Denell BELLE ISLE
20	Dean	Dr. Roy KAMMER
07	Dir Enrollment & Student Services	Ms. LeAnn BROWN
06	Registrar	Ms. Debra MATTISON
88	Registrar of Administrative Service	Ms. Twyla RAMSDELL

Herzing University   (H)

435 Ford Rd, St. Louis Park MN 55426

Telephone: (763) 535-3000
FICE Identification: 011017
Accreditation: &HLC, DA, DH, NURSE, OTA, PTAA

† Regional accreditation is carried under the parent institution in Madison, WI.

Institute of Production and Recording   (I)

300 N. 1st Avenue, Suite 500, Minneapolis MN 55401

County: Hennepin
FICE Identification: 041302
Unit ID: 454616
Telephone: (612) 351-0631
Carnegie Class: Spec-4-yr-Arts
FAX Number: (612) 244-2801
Calendar System: Other
URL: www.ipr.edu
Established: 2002
Annual Undergrad Tuition & Fees: $22,635
Enrollment: 133
Coed
Affiliation or Control: Proprietary
IRS Status: Proprietary
Highest Offering: Associate Degree
Accreditation: ACCSC

01	Executive Director	Charlie BUEHLER
05	Associate Campus Director	Trey WODELE
06	Associate Dean/Registrar	Nathan O'BRIEN
07	Assoc Director of Admissions	Lindsey MUNDY
36	Director of Career Services	Kyle SHELSTAD
37	Financial Aid Manager	Ben DOEHNE
08	Librarian	Kalina KASTNER

Leech Lake Tribal College   (J)

6945 Little Wolf Rd., NW, Cass Lake MN 56633

County: Cass
FICE Identification: 030964
Unit ID: 413626

Telephone: (218) 335-4200 Carnegie Class: Tribal
FAX Number: (218) 335-4282 Calendar System: Semester
URL: www.lltc.edu
Established: 1990 Annual Undergrad Tuition & Fees: $4,850
Enrollment: 133 Coed
Affiliation or Control: Tribal Control IRS Status: 501(c)3
Highest Offering: Associate Degree
Accreditation: HLC

01 Interim President .... Helen ZAIKINA-MONTGOMERY
05 Dean of Academics .... Vikki HOWARD
10 Director of Finance .... Burt HOWARD
32 Dean of Student Services .... Jorge MENDOZA
09 Dir Institutional Rsrch/ Assessment .... Helen ZAIKINA-MONTGOMERY
84 Dir Enrollment Services/Registrar .... Stacey LUNDBERG
37 Financial Aid Director .... Glen SAWA
15 Director of Human Resources .... Carol WHITE

Luther Seminary (A)

2481 Como Avenue, Saint Paul MN 55108-1496
County: Ramsey FICE Identification: 002357
Unit ID: 173896
Telephone: (651) 641-3456 Carnegie Class: Spec-4-yr-Faith
FAX Number: (651) 641-3425 Calendar System: Semester
URL: www.luthersem.edu
Established: 1869 Annual Graduate Tuition & Fees: N/A
Enrollment: 501 Coed
Affiliation or Control: Evangelical Lutheran Church In America
IRS Status: 501(c)3
Highest Offering: Doctorate; No Undergraduates
Accreditation: HLC, THEOL

01 President .... RevDr. Robin STEINKE
05 Dean of Academic Affairs .... Dr. Terri ELTON
20 Dean of Faculty .... Dr. Rolf JACOBSON
10 VP Administration & Finance .... Mr. Michael MORROW
26 VP Seminary Relations .... Ms. Heidi DROEGEMUELLER
32 Interim Dean Students .... Dr. Leon RODRIGUES
21 Assoc Business Officer .... Mr. Gerri STEPANEK
35 Assoc Student Affairs Officer .... Ms. Sarah LUEDTKE-JONES
28 VP Inclusion/Belonging .... Dr. Leon RODRIGUES
15 Director of Human Resources .... Mr. Randy KYLE
06 Registrar .... Ms. Mary SPERANZA-REEDER
84 Director of Enrollment Services .... Ms. Jessi LECLEAR VACHTA
04 Admin Assistant to the President .... Ms. Gina LOTZER
09 Director of Institutional Research .... Mr. Ken REYNHOUT
18 Chief Facilities/Physical Plnt Ofcr .... Mr. Tom MULLANEY
29 Director Alumni Affairs .... Mr. Jake HENNES
37 Director Student Financial Aid .... Mr. Bill SILVA-BREEN

Lutheran Brethren Seminary (B)

1036 Alcott Avenue W, Fergus Falls MN 56537
County: Otter Tail Identification: 666644
Telephone: (218) 739-3375 Carnegie Class: Not Classified
FAX Number: N/A Calendar System: Semester
URL: www.lbs.edu
Established: 1903 Annual Graduate Tuition & Fees: N/A
Enrollment: N/A Coed
Affiliation or Control: Other IRS Status: 501(c)3
Highest Offering: Master's; No Undergraduates
Accreditation: TRACS

01 President .... Dr. David VEUM
05 Dean of the Seminary/CAO .... Dr. Brad PRIBBENOW
06 Registrar/Director of Admissions .... Dr. Gaylan MATHIESEN

Macalester College (C)

1600 Grand Avenue, Saint Paul MN 55105-1801
County: Ramsey FICE Identification: 002358
Unit ID: 173902
Telephone: (651) 696-6000 Carnegie Class: Bac-A&S
FAX Number: N/A Calendar System: Semester
URL: www.macalester.edu
Established: 1874 Annual Undergrad Tuition & Fees: $58,478
Enrollment: 2,049 Coed
Affiliation or Control: Presbyterian Church (U.S.A.) IRS Status: 501(c)3
Highest Offering: Baccalaureate
Accreditation: HLC

01 President .... Dr. Suzanne M. RIVERA
05 Exec VP & Provost .... Dr. Lisa ANDERSON-LEVY
115 Chief Investment Officer .... Mr. Gary D. MARTIN
111 VP Advancement .... Mr. Andrew BROWN
32 Assoc VP & Dean of Students .... Dr. Kathryn KAY COQUEMONT
10 Vice President Admin/Finance .... Ms. Patricia LANGER
13 VP ITS/CIO .... Ms. Jennifer HAAS
07 Vice Pres Admissions/Financial Aid .... Mr. Jeffrey S. ALLEN
28 VP Diversity/Equity & Inclusion .... Dr. Alina WONG
108 Vice Provost .... Dr. Paul OVERVOORDE
20 Dean of Faculty .... Dr. Thomas HALVERSON
85 Dean Annan Inst Global Citizenship .... Vacant
20 Director of Academic Programs .... Ms. Ann M. MINNICK
37 Director Student Financial Aid .... Ms. Jenae A. SCHMIDT
06 Registrar .... Mr. Timothy S. TRAFFIE
35 Assoc Dean of Students .... Mr. Andrew M. WELLS
15 Director Employment Services .... Mr. Bob GRAF
18 AVP of Facilities .... Mr. Nathan P. LIEF
41 Athletic Director .... Mr. Donnie A. BROOKS
04 Assist to President/Sec to Board .... Vacant
26 AVP Communications/Marketing .... Ms. Julie T. HURBANIS
29 Director Alumni Engagement .... Ms. Catie K. GARDNER SMITH
38 Director Health and Wellness Center .... Ms. Jen JACOBSEN
96 Dir Purchasing/Accounts Payable .... Mr. Matthew D. RUMPZA
105 Dir Digital Engagement & Ext Rel .... Ms. Sara C. SUELFLOW
84 Manager of Enrollment Systems .... Vacant
08 Head Librarian .... Ms. Angi FAIKS
102 Dir Foundation/Corporate Relations .... Ms. Michelle EPP
36 Dean of Career Exploration .... Vacant
19 Director of Security .... Mr. James E. KURTZ
09 Director Institutional Research .... Dr. Bethany L. MILLER

Martin Luther College (D)

1995 Luther Court, New Ulm MN 56073-3300
County: Brown FICE Identification: 002361
Unit ID: 173452
Telephone: (507) 354-8221 Carnegie Class: Spec-4-yr-Other
FAX Number: (507) 354-8225 Calendar System: Semester
URL: www.mlc-wels.edu
Established: 1995 Annual Undergrad Tuition & Fees: $16,420
Enrollment: 968 Coed
Affiliation or Control: Wisconsin Evangelical Lutheran Synod
IRS Status: 501(c)3
Highest Offering: Master's
Accreditation: HLC

01 President .... Rev. Richard L. GURGEL
05 Vice President for Academics .... Dr. Jeffery P. WIECHMAN
11 Vice President for Administration .... Prof. Scott D. SCHMUDLACH
32 Vice President Student Life .... Prof. Jeffrey L. SCHONE
53 Academic Dean Educational Ministry .... Prof. Benjamin P. CLEMONS
73 Academic Dean Pastoral Ministry .... Prof. James N. DANELL
10 Director of Finance .... Mrs. Carla J. HULKE
08 Director of Library Services .... Mrs. Linda KRAMER
37 Director of Financial Aid .... Mr. Mark D. BAUER
84 Vice Pres for Enrollment Management .... Prof. Theodore A. KLUG
58 Director Graduate Studies/Cont Educ .... Dr. John E. MEYER
88 Director of Clinical Experiences .... Prof. Adam D. PAVELCHIK
41 Director of Athletics .... Prof. James M. UNKE
42 Campus Pastor .... Dr. John C. BOEDER
13 Director of Technology .... Mr. Robert L. MARTENS
26 Director of Public Relations .... Prof. William A. PEKRUL
40 Bookstore Manager .... Mrs. Linette M. SCHARLEMANN
90 Director of Academic Computing .... Prof. Rachel M. FELD
29 Director Alumni Relations .... Mr. Stephen J. BALZA
108 Director Student Assessment .... Prof. Rebecca L. COX
06 Registrar .... Mrs. Gwen L. KRAL
09 Director of Institutional Research .... Prof. Rachel R. FREDRICH
15 Chief Human Resources Officer .... Mrs. Andrea E. WENDLAND
104 Director Study Abroad .... Mrs. Megan R. KASSUELKE
111 Vice President Mission Advancement .... Mr. Mark E. MAURICE

Minneapolis College of Art and Design (E)

2501 Stevens Avenue, Minneapolis MN 55404-4343
County: Hennepin FICE Identification: 002365
Unit ID: 174127
Telephone: (612) 874-3700 Carnegie Class: Spec-4-yr-Arts
FAX Number: (612) 874-3704 Calendar System: Semester
URL: www.mcad.edu
Established: 1886 Annual Undergrad Tuition & Fees: $41,794
Enrollment: 760 Coed
Affiliation or Control: Independent Non-Profit IRS Status: 501(c)3
Highest Offering: Master's
Accreditation: HLC, ART

01 President .... Mr. Sanjit SETHI
04 Exec Asst to President/Sec Board .... Mr. Nick RAVERTY
05 Vice President Academic Affairs .... Mr. Robert RANSICK
10 VP Finance/Chief Financial Officer .... Ms. Mary Alma NOONAN
11 Vice President Administration .... Vacant
111 VP Institutional Advancement .... Ms. Emily KESSLER
84 Vice Pres Enrollment Management .... Ms. Melissa HUYBRECHT
32 Vice President of Student Affairs .... Ms. Jen ZUCCOLA
26 VP Communication/Marketing Strategy .... Ms. Annie G. CLEVELAND
18 VP Operations and Technology .... Mr. Brock RASMUSSEN
06 Registrar .... Mr. River GORDON
51 Director of Continuing Education .... Ms. Lara ROY
08 Director of Library .... Ms. Amy BECKER
39 Director Student Housing .... Mr. Nate K. LUTZ
37 Director Student Financial Aid .... Ms. Laura LINK
20 Assoc VP Academic Affairs .... Ms. Melissa RANDS
19 Director of Public Safety .... Mr. Todd JONES
15 Sr Director Human Resources .... Ms. Hope DENARDO
21 Assoc VP of Finance .... Ms. Mary YANG THAO

*Minnesota State Colleges and Universities System Office (F)

30 7th Street East, Suite 350, Saint Paul MN 55101-4901
County: Ramsey FICE Identification: 009346
Unit ID: 428453
Telephone: (651) 201-1800 Carnegie Class: N/A
FAX Number: (651) 297-5550
URL: https://www.minnstate.edu/

01 Chancellor .... Devinder MALHOTRA
15 Vice Chancellor Human Resources .... Eric DAVIS
05 Sr Vice Chanc Academic/Student Affs .... Ron ANDERSON
10 Vice Chanc Finance/Facilities & CFO .... William MAKI
13 Vice Chanc Information Tech/CIO .... Jacquelyn MALCOLM
26 Chief Marketing/Communications Ofcr .... Noelle HAWTON
18 Assoc Vice Chancellor Facilities .... Brian D. YOLITZ
46 Assoc Vice Chanc Research/Planning .... Vacant
32 AVC Student Affairs/Enrollment Mgmt .... Brent GLASS
100 Chief of Staff .... Jaime SIMONSEN
16 Asst Dir Human Resources .... Jessica WHITE
28 Chief Diversity Officer .... Clyde WILSON PICKETT
102 Exec Dir System/Foundation Rels .... Vacant
43 General Counsel .... Gary CUNNINGHAM
45 System Dir Academic Pgms/Plng .... Jon DALAGER

*Alexandria Technical & Community College (G)

1601 Jefferson Street, Alexandria MN 56308-2796
County: Douglas FICE Identification: 005544
Unit ID: 172918
Telephone: (320) 762-4600 Carnegie Class: Assoc/HVT-High Non
FAX Number: (320) 762-4501 Calendar System: Semester
URL: www.alextech.edu
Established: 1961 Annual Undergrad Tuition & Fees (In-State): $5,649
Enrollment: 2,549 Coed
Affiliation or Control: State IRS Status: 501(c)3
Highest Offering: Associate Degree
Accreditation: HLC, CNEA, MLTAD

02 President .... Mr. Michael SEYMOUR
10 Chief Financial Officer .... Mr. David BJELLAND
05 VP of Academic & Student Affairs .... Mr. Scott BERGER
72 Dean of Technology .... Mr. Steve RICHARDS
66 Dean of Nursing and Health .... Ms. Merilee RETZLOFF
75 Dean of Law Enforcemnt/Transp/Manuf .... Mr. Sean JOHNS
37 Financial Aid Director .... Mr. Jon ERICKSON
22 Human Rights Officer .... Ms. Tamzin BUKOWSKI
36 Director Student Placement .... Mr. Patrick RUNNING
102 Foundation Executive Director .... Mr. Jeffrey WILD
06 Registrar .... Mr. Patrick RUNNING
18 Director of Facilities .... Mr. Joel SEELA
15 Chief Human Resources Officer .... Ms. Shari MALONEY
09 Director of Institutional Research .... Ms. Heather RONDEAU
07 Director of Admissions .... Ms. Lynn ARNQUIST
35 Director of Student Activities .... Ms. Cynthia HAARSTAD
88 Director of K-12 Initiatives .... Ms. Mary LENZ
04 Asst to Pres/Dir of Office Services .... Ms. Annette PAVEK
21 Director of Financial Operations .... Ms. Julie FENLASON
40 Bookstore Manager .... Mr. David BJELLAND
30 Development Officer .... Ms. Christine HARRIS
121 Director of Support Services .... Ms. Kaye MADIGAN
28 Campus Diversity Officer .... Ms. Cindy HAGER
26 Director Mktg & Communications .... Mr. Adam HAMMER
41 Athletic Director .... Mr. Sean JOHNS

*Anoka-Ramsey Community College (H)

11200 Mississippi Boulevard NW,
Coon Rapids MN 55433-3470
County: Anoka FICE Identification: 002332
Unit ID: 172963
Telephone: (763) 433-1100 Carnegie Class: Assoc/HT-High Non
FAX Number: (763) 433-1121 Calendar System: Semester
URL: www.anokaramsey.edu
Established: 1965 Annual Undergrad Tuition & Fees (In-State): $5,286
Enrollment: 8,482 Coed
Affiliation or Control: State IRS Status: 501(c)3
Highest Offering: Associate Degree
Accreditation: HLC, ACBSP, ADNUR, MUS, PTAA

02 President .... Dr. Kent HANSON
10 VP Finance & Administration .... Mr. Don LEWIS
05 Int VP Academic/Student Affairs .... Mr. Steve CRITTENDEN
32 Dean of Student Affairs .... Ms. Lisa HARRIS
50 Dean Business/World Lang/Soc Sci .... Mr. Scott STANKEY
09 Dean of Research & Assessment .... Ms. Nora MORRIS
66 Dean of Nursing and Allied Health .... Ms. Sandra KOHLER
81 Dean of STEM .... Ms. Becky KRYSTYNIAK
57 Dean of Arts & Letters .... Ms. Hannah OLIHA-DONALDSON
88 Dean of Academic/Community Outreach .... Ms. Shannon KIRKEIDE
20 Int Associate Dean .... Mr. Thom NORDIN
15 Chief HR Director .... Mr. Jay NELSON
26 Chief Marketing & Comm Officer .... Ms. Mary JACOBSON
13 Int Chief Information Officer .... Mr. Richard MALOTT
35 Dir Student Development/Engagement .... Mr. Michael OPOKU
114 Director of Budget Plng & Forecasts .... Mr. Dave AUNE
84 Director of Enrollment Management .... Mr. Ricky GONZALEZ
28 Director of Multicultural Affairs .... Ms. Venoreen BROWNE-BOATSWAIN
102 Director of Foundations .... Mr. Jamie BARTHEL
18 Director of Facilities .... Mr. Ken KARR
19 Director of Safety & Security .... Mr. Cliff ANDERSON
21 Director of Business Affairs .... Vacant
109 Director of Auxiliary Services .... Mr. Robert PEREZ
37 Director Financial Aid .... Mr. Bill VIKANDER
04 Executive Asst to President .... Ms. Margie SCHLUETER
100 Special Assistant to the President .... Ms. Jessica MEDEARIS
06 Registrar .... Ms. Rhonda KERN
28 VP of Equity & Inclusion .... Mr. Brandyn WOODARD

*Anoka Technical College　(A)

1355 W Highway 10, Anoka MN 55303-1590

County: Anoka　　　　　　　FICE Identification: 007350
　　　　　　　　　　　　　　　Unit ID: 172954
Telephone: (763) 576-4700　Carnegie Class: Assoc/HVT-High Trad
FAX Number: (763) 576-4715　Calendar System: Semester
URL: www.anokatech.edu
Established: 1967　Annual Undergrad Tuition & Fees (In-District): $5,812
Enrollment: 1,683　　　　　　　　　　　　　　　　　Coed
Affiliation or Control: State/Local　　　　IRS Status: 501(c)3
Highest Offering: Associate Degree
Accreditation: **HLC**, CAHIIM, MAC, OTA, PNUR, SURGT

02	President	Dr. Kent HANSON
05	Int VP Academic/Student Affairs	Dimitria HARDING
10	Vice Pres Finance & Admin	Donald LEWIS
28	Vice Pres Equity & Inclusion	Brandyn WOODARD
20	Academic Dean	Dawn EASLEY
04	Executive Asst to the President	Margie SCHLUETER
15	Chief Human Resource Officer	Jay NELSON
13	Chief Information Officer	Richard MALOTT
26	Director of Marketing	Mary JACOBSON
06	Director of Records	Laura KITTELSON
32	Dean of Student Affairs	Vacant
37	Financial Aid Director	Bill VIKANDER
08	Head Librarian	Susan BRETTSCHNEIDER
18	Chief Facilities/Physical Plant	Kenneth KARR
19	Director Security/Safety	Clifford ANDERSON
84	Director of Enrollment Services	LeAnna WANGERIN
09	Director of Institutional Research	Nora MORRIS
22	Director of Diversity	Venoreen BROWNE-BOATSWAIN

*Bemidji State University　(B)

1500 Birchmont Drive NE, Bemidji MN 56601-2699

County: Beltrami　　　　　　FICE Identification: 002336
　　　　　　　　　　　　　　　Unit ID: 173124
Telephone: (218) 755-2001　Carnegie Class: Masters/S
FAX Number: N/A　　　　　Calendar System: Semester
URL: www.bemidjistate.edu
Established: 1919　Annual Undergrad Tuition & Fees (In-State): $9,076
Enrollment: 4,577　　　　　　　　　　　　　　　　　Coed
Affiliation or Control: State　　　　　IRS Status: 501(c)3
Highest Offering: Master's
Accreditation: **HLC**, AAQEP, IACBE, MUS, NAIT, NURSE, SW

02	President	Dr. John L. HOFFMAN
05	Provost/VP Academic Affairs	Dr. Allen BEDFORD
10	VP Finance & Administration	Ms. Karen SNOREK
84	Exec Dir of Enrollment Management	Vacant
22	Affirmative Action & Accreditation	Vacant
08	Library & Library Services	Mr. Pete MCDONNELL
09	Int Dir Inst Research/Effectiveness	Dr. Julian LICATA
103	Dir Center for Professional Devel	Dr. Keith GORA
92	Director Honors Program	Dr. Patrick LEEPORT
85	Director International Program Ctr	Vacant
88	Co-Director Leadership Studies	Dr. Anna CARLSON
88	Co-Director Leadership Studies	Dr. Virgil BAKKEN
23	Dean Individual/Community Health	Dr. Jeffrey BELL
50	Dean Business/Math & Sciences	Dr. Marilyn YODER
88	Exec Dir MN Adv Manuf Ctr of Excell	Mr. Jeremy LEFFELMAN
88	Director MARS Program	Vacant
79	Dean Arts/Education & Humanities	Dr. Mary Theresa SEIG
32	VP for Student Life & Success	Mr. Travis GREENE
20	Assoc VP/Provost Academic Affairs	Dr. Randy WESTHOFF
93	Director American Indian Center	Ms. Chrissy DOWNWIND
93	Student Ctr/Diversity/Equity/Incl	Vacant
88	Director Campus Recreation	Ms. Kierstin HOVEN
88	Director Hobson Memorial Union	Ms. Nina JOHNSON
39	Director Housing & Res Life	Dr. Randall LUDEMAN
38	Int Dir Center Health/Counseling	Mr. Randy LUDEMAN
106	Director Distance Learning	Ms. Lynn JOHNSON
21	Business Manager	Mr. Ron BECKSTROM
18	Physical Plant Manager	Mr. Travis BARNES
19	Director Public Safety	Mr. Casey J. MCCARTHY
28	Campus Diversity Officer	Mr. Steven PARKER
15	Campus Human Resources Officer	Ms. Megan ZOTHMAN
13	Chief Information Officer	Ms. Sherry LAWDERMILT
07	Interim Director Admissions	Ms. Carola THORSON
37	Director Financial Aid	Ms. Stephanie BARD
06	Registrar	Ms. Kim GOURNEAU
121	Director Advising Success Center	Mr. Zak JOHNSON
36	Interim Director Career Services	Ms. Nancy HAUGEN
88	TRIO/SSS/UB/McNair	Ms. Kelli STEGGALL
22	Assoc Dir Accessibility Services	Mr. Christian BRECZINSKI
26	Exec Dir Communications & Mktg	Mr. Andy BARTLETT
41	Athletic Director	Ms. Brittany LAURITSEN
111	Exec Dir for University Advancement	Mr. Joshua CHRISTIANSON
29	Director Alumni Relations	Mr. Brett BAHR
58	Director Graduate Studies	Mr. George MCCONNELL

*Central Lakes College　(C)

501 W College Drive, Brainerd MN 56401-3900

County: Crow Wing　　　　FICE Identification: 002339
　　　　　　　　　　　　　　　Unit ID: 173203
Telephone: (218) 855-8000　Carnegie Class: Assoc/MT-VT-High Non
FAX Number: (218) 855-8057　Calendar System: Semester
URL: www.clcmn.edu
Established: 1938　Annual Undergrad Tuition & Fees (In-State): $5,759
Enrollment: 4,491　　　　　　　　　　　　　　　　　Coed
Affiliation or Control: State　　　　　IRS Status: 501(c)3

Highest Offering: Associate Degree
Accreditation: **HLC**, CNEA, DA, MAC

02	President	Dr. Hara D. CHARLIER
05	VP Academic & Student Affairs	Vacant
11	VP Administrative Services	Ms. Kari CHRISTIANSEN
12	Dean Staples Campus/CTE/Grants	Mr. David ENDICOTT
12	Dean Brainerd CTE/Customized Trng	Ms. Rebekah KENT
47	Dean of Agricultural Studies	Mr. Keith OLANDER
84	Dean of Enrollment/Student Success	Mr. Paul PREIMESBERGER
49	Dean of Liberal Arts	Ms. Anne NELSON FISHER
30	Director of Res Develop/CLC Found	Ms. Kate ADORNETTO
15	Director of Human Resources	Ms. Kristi LANE
07	Director of Admissions/Recruitment	Ms. Tambera GARZA
06	Registrar	Ms. Susan RUMPCA
08	Librarian	Mr. David BISSONETTE
37	Director Financial Aid	Mr. Mike BARNABY
14	Director of Technology/Support	Mr. Scott STREED
26	Director Marketing	Mr. Kenn DOLS
109	Director of Business/Auxil Services	Mr. Jonathan KNUTSON
88	Director of Trio Programs	Mr. Charles BLACKLANCE
18	Director Physical Plant/Facilities	Mr. James MCARDELL
28	Dean of Students/Equity/Inclusion	Ms. Mary SAM
04	Executive Asst to President	Ms. Jody LONGBELLA
09	Director of Institutional Research	Ms. Wendy ADAMSON
88	Director Small Business Dev Center	Ms. Rebecca ROWE
19	Director Security/Safety	Mr. Matthew KRUEGER
32	Director of Student Life	Mr. Erich HEPPNER

*Century College　(D)

3300 Century Avenue North,
White Bear Lake MN 55110-1894

County: Ramsey　　　　　　FICE Identification: 010546
　　　　　　　　　　　　　　　Unit ID: 175315
Telephone: (651) 779-3200　Carnegie Class: Assoc/MT-VT-Mix Trad/Non
FAX Number: N/A　　　　　Calendar System: Semester
URL: www.century.edu
Established: 1967　Annual Undergrad Tuition & Fees (In-State): $5,578
Enrollment: 8,203　　　　　　　　　　　　　　　　　Coed
Affiliation or Control: State　　　　　IRS Status: 501(c)3
Highest Offering: Associate Degree
Accreditation: **HLC**, ADNUR, DA, DH, EMT, MAC, MUS, RAD

02	President	Ms. Angelia MILLENDER
05	Provost/VP Academic & Student Affs	Ms. Pakou YANG
10	VP Finance & Administration	Mr. Patrick OPATZ
13	Assoc VP Information Tech/Admn Svcs	Mr. John ROHLEDER
84	Assoc Dean Enrollment Management	Ms. Ali PICKENS-OPOKU
96	Buyer Supervisor	Vacant
21	Director of Finance	Ms. Marilyn SMITH
102	Executive Director Foundation	Ms. Nora SLAWIK
06	Registrar	Ms. Kirsten FABOZZI
15	Director of Human Resources	Ms. Jodean THRONSON
07	Associate Director of Admissions	Mr. Robert BEAVER
37	Director of Financial Aid	Ms. Pam ENGEBRETSON
18	Physical Building Supervisor	Mr. Michael HOUFER
19	Director of Public Safety	Mr. Jason PHILIPP
76	Dean of Human Svcs & Health Sci	Ms. Beth HEIN
103	Dean Industry/English/Devel Ed//Lib	Vacant
66	Dean Nursing/CETC/Online Lrng Excel	Mr. Eric RIEDEL
81	Dean Science/Tech/Engr/Math	Vacant
49	Dean of Liberal Arts	Ms. Julie ZALOUDEK
35	Dean of Student Affairs	Ms. Kristin HAGEMAN
09	Dean of Institutional Effectiveness	Vacant
04	Executive Assistant to President	Ms. Christine MCGING
26	Director of Marketing	Mr. James STUMNE
28	Chief Diversity Officer	Ms. Rosa RODRIGUEZ

*Dakota County Technical College　(E)

1300 145th Street East, Rosemount MN 55068-2999

County: Dakota　　　　　　FICE Identification: 010402
　　　　　　　　　　　　　　　Unit ID: 173416
Telephone: (651) 423-8000　Carnegie Class: Assoc/HVT-High Trad
FAX Number: (651) 423-8775　Calendar System: Semester
URL: www.dctc.edu
Established: 1970　Annual Undergrad Tuition & Fees (In-District): $5,941
Enrollment: 2,319　　　　　　　　　　　　　　　　　Coed
Affiliation or Control: State/Local　　　　IRS Status: 501(c)3
Highest Offering: Associate Degree
Accreditation: **HLC**, CNEA, DA, MAC

02	President	Mr. Michael D. BERNDT
05	VP Academic Affairs	Mr. Mike MENDEZ
10	VP/Chief Financial Officer	Vacant
09	Director Institutional Research	Ms. Wendy MARSON
32	VP Student Affairs	Ms. Anne JOHNSON
88	Dean Transportation/Construct/Manuf	Mr. Jason WETZEL
49	Interim Dean Arts & Sciences	Mr. Martin SPRINGBORG
50	Dean Business/Design/Hlth/Human Svc	Ms. Jodi OSBORN
13	College Information Officer	Mr. Todd JAGERSON
06	Registrar/Enrollment Director	Ms. Jodie SWEARINGEN
18	Director of Operations	Mr. Paul DEMUTH
35	Director Student Life/Activities	Ms. Nicole MEULEMANS
07	Dir Recruitment & Admissions	Mr. Heath BAUMGARD
37	Director Financial Aid	Mr. Scott ROELKE
15	Director of Human Resources	Ms. Laina CARLSON
26	Dir Strategic Mktg/Communication	Ms. Lise FREKING
103	Director of Workforce Training & CE	Mr. Robert TREWARTHA
19	Director Security/Safety	Mr. Anthony PANGAL
04	Exec Assistant to the President	Mr. Peter MOUA

*Fond du Lac Tribal and Community College　(F)

2101 14th Street, Cloquet MN 55720-2984

County: Carlton　　　　　　FICE Identification: 031291
　　　　　　　　　　　　　　　Unit ID: 380368
Telephone: (218) 879-0800　Carnegie Class: Tribal
FAX Number: (218) 879-0814　Calendar System: Semester
URL: www.fdltcc.edu
Established: 1987　Annual Undergrad Tuition & Fees (In-State): $5,535
Enrollment: 1,639　　　　　　　　　　　　　　　　　Coed
Affiliation or Control: State　　　　　IRS Status: 501(c)3
Highest Offering: Baccalaureate
Accreditation: **HLC**, ADNUR

02	President	Ms. Stephanie HAMMITT
05	Vice President of Academics	Mr. Kelly MCCALLA
10	Chief Financial Officer	Mr. Bret BUSAKOWSKI
32	Dean of Student Affairs	Ms. Anita HANSON
26	Dir Marketing/Communications	Ms. Taylor WARNES
06	Registrar	Ms. Erica GELO
88	Disability Services/Student Service	Ms. Nancy OLSEN
13	Chief Information Officer	Mr. Peter ANGELOS
37	Director of Financial Aid	Mr. David SUTHERLAND
07	Director of Admissions	Ms. Katie GUSTAFSON
09	Director of Institutional Research	Mr. James EISENHAUER
124	Dir of Student Support Services	Ms. Peggy POITRA
62	Library Services	Mr. Keith CICH
30	Director of Development	Ms. Stephanie HAMMITT
39	Director of Housing	Mr. Jesse STIREWALT
15	Director of Human Resources	Ms. Marisa HAGGY
18	Chief Facilities/Physical Plant	Mr. Mark BERNHARDSON
40	Bookstore Coordinator	Ms. Bonnie BERNHARDSON
04	Executive Assistant to President	Ms. Mary SOYRING

*Hennepin Technical College　(G)

9000 Brooklyn Boulevard, Brooklyn Park MN 55445-2399

County: Hennepin　　　　　FICE Identification: 010491
　　　　　　　　　　　　　　　Unit ID: 173708
Telephone: (952) 995-1300　Carnegie Class: Assoc/HVT-Mix Trad/Non
FAX Number: (763) 488-2956　Calendar System: Semester
URL: www.hennepintech.edu
Established: 1972　Annual Undergrad Tuition & Fees (In-District): $5,494
Enrollment: 4,094　　　　　　　　　　　　　　　　　Coed
Affiliation or Control: State/Local　　　　IRS Status: 501(c)3
Highest Offering: Associate Degree
Accreditation: **HLC**, ACBSP, ACFEI, DA, MAC, PNUR

02	Interim President	Joy BODIN
05	VP Academic Affairs	Dr. Leanne ROGSTAD
10	Vice Pres Finance and Operations	Joe WIGHTKIN
32	Vice President of Student Affairs	Dr. Jessica LAURITSEN
15	Vice Pres Human Resources	Daniel LE GUEN-SCHMIDT
84	Dean of Enrollment Services	Debra NEWGARD
13	AVP of Tech & Inst Research	Shannon THOMAS
28	Associate VP of Equity & Inclusion	Vacant
111	Assoc VP of Advancement	Lisa YAEGER
09	Institutional Effectivenss Proj Mgr	Elizabeth GIESEKE
37	Director of Financial Aid	Tim JACOBSON
04	Executive Assistant to President	Jessica SCHULTZ
19	Director Security/Safety	Randy ROEHRICK
35	Dir Student Life/Career Development	Stephen HARPER
18	Director of Facilities	Heidi RICCI

*Inver Hills Community College　(H)

2500 80th Street E, Inver Grove Heights MN 55076-3224

County: Dakota　　　　　　FICE Identification: 009740
　　　　　　　　　　　　　　　Unit ID: 173799
Telephone: (651) 450-3000　Carnegie Class: Assoc/HT-High Non
FAX Number: (651) 450-3679　Calendar System: Semester
URL: www.inverhills.edu
Established: 1970　Annual Undergrad Tuition & Fees (In-State): $5,558
Enrollment: 4,071　　　　　　　　　　　　　　　　　Coed
Affiliation or Control: State　　　　　IRS Status: 501(c)3
Highest Offering: Associate Degree
Accreditation: **HLC**, ACBSP, ADNUR, EMT

02	President	Mr. Michael BERNDT
05	VP Academic Affairs	Dr. Elaina BLEIFIELD
32	Interim Vice Pres Student Affairs	Ms. Kari RUSCH-CURL
10	Vice Pres of Finance & Operations	Vacant
06	Registrar	Mr. Scott KLAEHN
76	Dean of Allied Health & Career Pgm	Mr. Christopher METSGAR
79	Dean of Liberal Arts	Dr. Barb CURCHACK
81	Dean of STEM/Social Sciences	Mr. Yohannes AGEGNEHU
102	Exec Dir Found & Advancement	Ms. Kimberly SHAFF
15	Human Resources Director	Ms. Laina CARLSON
08	Librarian	Ms. Julie BENOLKEN
121	Director of Academic Advising	Ms. Amanda BARKLIND
20	Director of Academic Affairs Opers	Mr. JT BEALKA
18	Director Facilities Plng/Management	Mr. Paul DEMUTH
37	Dir of Scholarship & Financial Aid	Mr. Scott ROELKE
09	Director of Institutional Research	Ms. Wendy MARSON
26	Dir of Strategic Marketing & Comm	Ms. Lise FREKING
13	College Information Officer	Mr. Todd JAGERSON
106	Director of Teaching and Learning	Vacant
88	Assoc Dean/Dir of Acad Lrng Support	Ms. Hilary DAHLMAN
103	Director of Workforce Training & CE	Mr. Robert TREWARTHA
84	Director of Outreach & Recruitment	Mr. Aaron SALASEK

88 Dir of Student Support Services .... Mr. Matt KRUGER
36 Director of Career Development .... Mr. Jared SCHARPEN
88 Director of K12 Partnerships .... Ms. Mary Jo GARDNER
14 Director of Technology .... Mr. Abel ASFAW
19 Director of Safety & Security .... Mr. Anthony PANGAL
04 Exec Assistant to the President .... Mr. Peter MOUA

*Lake Superior College (A)

2101 Trinity Road, Duluth MN 55811-3399
County: Saint Louis FICE Identification: 005757
Unit ID: 173461
Telephone: (218) 733-7600 Carnegie Class: Assoc/HVT-High Non
FAX Number: (218) 733-5937 Calendar System: Semester
URL: www.lsc.edu
Established: 1995 Annual Undergrad Tuition & Fees (In-State): $5,334
Enrollment: 4,762 Coed
Affiliation or Control: State IRS Status: 501(c)3
Highest Offering: Associate Degree
Accreditation: HLC, ADNUR, COARC, DH, MAC, MLTAD, PNUR, PTAA, RAD, SURGT

02 President .... Dr. Patricia L. ROGERS
05 VP Academic/Student Affairs .... Dr. Linda KINGSTON
11 VP Administration .... Mr. Al FINLAYSON
111 VP Advancement & External Relations .... Mr. Daniel FANNING
20 Int Assoc VP of Acad/Student Affs .... Ms. LaNita ROBINSON
50 Dean of Business/Industry .... Mr. Miles LUNAK
49 Dean Liberal Arts/Sciences .... Ms. Hanna ERPESTAD
76 Dean Allied Health/Nursing .... Ms. Anna SACKETTE-URNESS
103 Dean of Workforce & Community Dev .... Mr. Erik SIMONSON
09 IR/Accred Assessment/Research .... Ms. Denise MILLS-LEMIRE
07 Director of Admissions/Recruitment .... Ms. Kayti STOLP
15 AVP Human Resources .... Ms. Jestina VICHOREK
06 Registrar .... Ms. Melissa LENO
18 Physical Plant Director .... Mr. Mark CARDINAL
32 Dean of Students .... Mr. Wade GORDON
36 Director Career Services .... Ms. Kaitlyn STEFFEN
37 Director Student Financial Aid .... Vacant
21 Director Business Services .... Ms. Nickoel ANDERSON
13 Director Information Technology .... Mr. Steve FUDALLY
121 Director of Advising .... Mr. Keith TURNER
96 Purchasing Agent .... Mr. Michael FRANCISCO
04 Executive Asst to President .... Ms. Debbie JOHNSON
28 Director of Diversity .... Ms. Sarah LYONS

*Metropolitan State University (B)

700 E 7th Street, Saint Paul MN 55106-5000
County: Ramsey FICE Identification: 010374
Unit ID: 174020
Telephone: (651) 793-1300 Carnegie Class: Masters/M
FAX Number: (651) 793-1235 Calendar System: Semester
URL: www.metrostate.edu
Established: 1971 Annual Undergrad Tuition & Fees (In-State): $8,249
Enrollment: 7,552 Coed
Affiliation or Control: State IRS Status: 501(c)3
Highest Offering: Doctorate
Accreditation: HLC, ACBSP, ANEST, NURSE, SW

02 President .... Ms. Virginia ARTHUR
05 Prov/Exec VP Acad & Student Affs .... Dr. Amy GORT
10 VP for Finance and Operations .... Mr. Stephen KENT
102 Exec Dir of the Foundation .... Ms. Rachel HUGHES
22 VP of Equity & Inclusion .... Dr. Josefina LANDRIEU
84 VP Strategic Enrollment & Marketing .. Ms. Audrey BERGENGREN
07 Exec Dir Strategic Enroll & Admiss .... Ms. Carrie CARROLL
32 Dean of Students .... Dr. Maya SULLIVAN
13 VP Info Tech & Inst Research .... Mr. Stephen REED
21 Business Manager .... Ms. Miliite GEBREMICHAEL
15 Int VP Human Resource & Emp Exp .... Mr. Steve BARRETT
06 Registrar .... Mr. Daryl JOHNSON
37 Director Financial Aid .... Ms. Brittany LARSON
29 Director Alumni Relations .... Ms. Kristine HANSEN
81 Dean College of Sciences .... Dr. Kyle SWANSON
58 Dean College of Management .... Dr. Rassule HADIDI
88 Int Dean Col Individualized Stds .... Dr. Charles TEDDER
88 Dean School of Urban Education .... Dr. Paul SPIES
49 Dean College of Liberal Arts .... Dr. Shirin EDWIN
66 Dean College of Nursing/Health Sci .... Dr. Doris HILL
08 Dean Library/Information Services .... Ms. Beth CLAUSEN
121 Assoc Provost for Student Success .... Ms. Roberta (Bobbie) ANDERSON

*Minneapolis Community and Technical College (C)

1501 Hennepin Avenue, Minneapolis MN 55403-9810
County: Hennepin FICE Identification: 002362
Unit ID: 174136
Telephone: (612) 659-6000 Carnegie Class: Assoc/MT-VT-Mix Trad/Non
FAX Number: N/A Calendar System: Semester
URL: www.minneapolis.edu
Established: 1996 Annual Undergrad Tuition & Fees (In-State): $5,660
Enrollment: 6,429 Coed
Affiliation or Control: State IRS Status: 501(c)3
Highest Offering: Associate Degree
Accreditation: HLC, ADNUR, DA, POLYT

02 President .... Dr. Sharon PIERCE
05 Vice Pres Academic Affairs .... Dr. Gail O'KANE
10 Vice Pres Finance/Operations .... Mr. Christopher RAU
32 Vice President Student Affairs .... Mr. Patrick TROUP
28 VP Equity & Inclusion .... Dr. Trumanue LINDSEY, JR.
07 Director of Admissions .... Vacant
49 Dean of Liberal Arts .... Dr. Derrick LINDSTROM
81 Dean of Science & Mathematics .... Dr. Ben WENG
103 Interim Dir Workforce Development .... Ms. Amie DWYER
66 Dean of Nursing & Allied Health .... Dr. Traci KRAUSE
35 Dean of Students .... Ms. Becky NORDIN
15 VP of Human Resources .... Ms. Dianna CUSICK
13 VP of Information Technology .... Ms. Tiffni DEEB
84 Dean of Enrollment Management .... Ms. Heidi ALDES
108 Assoc VP of Inst Effectiveness .... Mr. Thomas WILLIAMSON
06 Registrar .... Ms. Michele COPELAND
08 Librarian .... Mr. Tom ELAND
37 Financial Aid Director .... Ms. Angela CHRISTENSEN
09 Dir of Institutional Effectiveness .... Mr. Fernando FURQUIM
18 Director Facilities .... Mr. Roger BROZ
19 Director of Public Safety .... Mr. Curt SCHMIDT
26 Assoc VP Marketing/Communications .... Ms. Kathy RUMPZA
35 Director Student Life .... Ms. Tara MARTINEZ

*Minnesota North College (D)

1515 E 25th Street, Hibbing MN 55746-3300
County: Saint Louis FICE Identification: 002355
Unit ID: 173735
Telephone: (218) 293-6850 Carnegie Class: Assoc/HVT-Mix Trad/Non
FAX Number: N/A Calendar System: Semester
URL: www.minnesotanorth.edu
Established: 2022 Annual Undergrad Tuition & Fees (In-State): $5,525
Enrollment: 913 Coed
Affiliation or Control: State IRS Status: 501(c)3
Highest Offering: Associate Degree
Accreditation: HLC, ADNUR, DA, MLTAD

02 President .... Dr. Michael RAICH
05 VP of Academic & Student Affairs .... Dr. Bart JOHNSON
20 College Dean .... Mr. Brad SCOTT
10 VP Finance & Facilities .... Ms. Stephanie POPE
32 Associate VP of Student Affairs .... Mr. Rick KANGAS
72 Academic Dean Career/Tech Programs .... Dr. Jessalyn SABIN
65 Academic Dean Natural Res/Hum Svcs .... Mr. Chris KOIVISTO
49 Academic Dean Liberal Arts/Transfer .... Mr. Aaron REINI
09 Institutional Research .... Ms. Tracey ROY
37 Director Student Financial Aid .... Ms. Jodi PONTINEN
18 Director of Facilities .... Mr. Dave MARSHALL
84 Dean of Enrollment .... Ms. Molly FRANZ
06 Registrar .... Ms. Allison GEISLER
13 Chief Info Technology Officer (CIO) .... Mr. Jerritt JOHNSTON
109 Director of College Services .... Mr. Jeff NELSON
08 Head Librarian .... Mr. Steve BEAN
15 Chief Human Resource/Diversity Ofcr .... Ms. Carmen BRADACH
19 Safety & Emergency Management Coord .... Vacant
88 Exec Dir of Customized Training/PR .... Dr. Trent JANEZICH
04 Exec Assistant to the President .... Ms. Elise LIND

*Minnesota North College - Itasca (E)

1851 E Highway 169, Grand Rapids MN 55744-3397
Telephone: (800) 996-6422 FICE Identification: 002356
Accreditation: &HLC, CNEA

*Minnesota North College - Mesabi Range Eveleth (F)

1100 Industrial Park Drive, Eveleth MN 55734
Telephone: (218) 741-3095 Identification: 770300
Accreditation: &HLC, CNEA

*Minnesota North College - Mesabi Range Virginia (G)

1001 Chestnut Street West, Virginia MN 55792
Telephone: (218) 741-3095 FICE Identification: 004009
Accreditation: &HLC, EMT

*Minnesota North College - Rainy River (H)

1501 Highway 71, International Falls MN 56649-2187
Telephone: (218) 285-7722 FICE Identification: 006775
Accreditation: HLC

*Minnesota North College - Vermilion (I)

1900 E Camp Street, Ely MN 55731-1998
Telephone: (218) 365-7200 FICE Identification: 002350
Accreditation: HLC

*Minnesota State College Southeast (J)

1250 Homer Road, Winona MN 55987-4897
County: Winona FICE Identification: 002393
Unit ID: 175263
Telephone: (507) 453-2700 Carnegie Class: Assoc/HVT-High Non
FAX Number: (507) 453-2715 Calendar System: Semester
URL: www.southeastmn.edu
Established: 1949 Annual Undergrad Tuition & Fees (In-District): $5,835
Enrollment: 1,912 Coed
Affiliation or Control: State/Local IRS Status: 501(c)3
Highest Offering: Associate Degree
Accreditation: HLC, PNUR, RAD

02 President .... Dr. Marsha DANIELSON
10 Vice Pres Finance/Administration .... Ms. Amy SCHMIDT
05 Vice President of Academic Affairs .... Mr. Chad DULL
32 VP of Student Affs/Dean of Students .... Mr. Josiah LITANT
13 Chief Information Officer .... Mr. Rick NAHRGANG
49 Int Dean of Liberal Arts & Sciences .... Ms. Jean EGBERT
72 Int Dean of Bus/Trade & Technology .... Ms. Dawn LUBHAN
15 Chief Human Resource Officer .... Ms. Megan ZECHES
84 Director of Secondary Relations .... Ms. Jeannie MEIDLINGER
07 Director of Admissions/Enrollment .... Dr. Tammy VONDRASEK
18 Plant Operations Supervisor .... Mr. Thomas HOFFMAN
29 Director of Alumni Relations .... Ms. Casie JOHNSON
26 Director of Marketing & Design .... Ms. Joanne THOMPSON
103 Director of Customized Training .... Vacant
27 Director of Communications .... Ms. Katryn CONLIN
21 Director of Business/Financial Svcs .... Ms. Lisa POZANC
16 HR Business Partner .... Ms. Alecia SPAGNOLETTI
19 Director of Security .... Mr. Chris CICHOSZ
04 Assistant to President .... Ms. Amy DRAZKOWSKI

*Minnesota State Community and Technical College (K)

1414 College Way, Fergus Falls MN 56537-1000
County: Otter Tail FICE Identification: 005541
Unit ID: 173559
Telephone: (218) 736-1500 Carnegie Class: Assoc/HVT-Mix Trad/Non
FAX Number: (218) 736-1510 Calendar System: Semester
URL: www.minnesota.edu
Established: 1960 Annual Undergrad Tuition & Fees (In-State): $5,560
Enrollment: 5,757 Coed
Affiliation or Control: State IRS Status: 501(c)3
Highest Offering: Associate Degree
Accreditation: HLC, CAHIIM, CNEA, DA, MLTAD, RAD

02 President .... Dr. Carrie BRIMHALL
05 Int VP Academic Affairs .... Dr. Matthew BORCHERDING
15 Chief of Human Resources .... Mrs. Dacia JOHNSON
06 Registrar .... Ms. Sharlene ALLEN
13 Chief Information Officer .... Vacant
10 Chief Finance Officer .... Mr. Pat NORDICK
32 Dean of Students .... Mr. Shawn ANDERSON
81 Dean School Science & Mathematics .... Dr. Matthew BORCHERDING
76 Dean Health Sci/Human Svcs/Nursing .... Dr. Ken KOMPELIEN
79 Dean of Liberal Arts & Humanities .... Ms. Anne THURMER
103 Exec Dir Workforce Dev Solutions .... Mr. G.L TUCKER
09 Dean of Inst Effect/Tech Solutions .... Dr. Steve ERICKSON
84 Dean of Enrollment .... Ms. Karen REILLY
50 Dean School of Business/Info Tech .... Ms. Marsha WEBER
26 Assoc Dean of Marketing & Outreach .... Ms. Karen REILLY
72 Dean School of Applied Technology .... Mr. Matthew LOESLIE
30 Chief Development & Alum Officer .... Mr. Melvin WHITNEY
36 Career Services Director .... Ms. Sue ZURN
08 College Librarian .... Ms. Kari OANES
04 Exec Assistant to the President .... Ms. Alyssa CAMPION
19 Director Safety & ER Preparedness .... Ms. Paula PEDERSON
102 Exec Dir Fergus Area Col Foundation .... Ms. Lori LARSON
37 Director of Financial Aid .... Ms. Wendy OLDS
39 Dir Campus Life & Housing .... Ms. David ROBERTS
35 Dir of Student Engagement .... Ms. Teresa STOLFUS
28 Dean of Equity & Inclusion .... Ms. Jocelyn SANTANA
88 Accessibility Resource Director .... Dr. Jon KRAGNESS
88 Accessibility Resource Director .... Ms. Jamie JENSEN
88 Compliance Officer .... Ms. Laura ZEIHER
88 Accessibility Res Dir/Acad Advisor .... Mr. Mark NELSON

*Minnesota State University, Mankato (L)

309 Wigley Administration Center,
Mankato MN 56001-6062
County: Blue Earth FICE Identification: 002360
Unit ID: 173920
Telephone: (507) 389-1111 Carnegie Class: Masters/L
FAX Number: (507) 389-6200 Calendar System: Semester
URL: www.mnsu.edu
Established: 1868 Annual Undergrad Tuition & Fees (In-State): $8,566
Enrollment: 14,761 Coed
Affiliation or Control: State IRS Status: Exempt
Highest Offering: Doctorate
Accreditation: HLC, AAB, ART, CAATE, CACREP, CAEP, CAPRT, CONST, DH, DIETD, MUS, NURSE, SP, SPAA, SW

02 President .... Dr. Edward INCH
05 Int Provost/SVP Academic Affairs .... Dr. Brian MARTENSEN
10 Vice Pres Finance & Administration .... Mr. Richard STRAKA
111 VP University Advancement .... Mr. Kent STANLEY
13 VP IT Solutions/CIO .... Mr. Mark JOHNSON
88 VP Strategic/Bus/Educ/Reg Prtnrshps .... Vacant
32 VP Student Affairs/Enrollment Mgmt .... Dr. David JONES
121 VP Stdnt Succ/Analytics/Integ Plng .... Ms. Lynn AKEY
100 Chief of Staff .... Ms. Sheri SARGENT
04 Exec Assistant to the President .... Ms. Juanita MILBRETT
20 Interim AVP for Undergrad Education .... Ms. Jennifer VELTSOS
28 Vice President Inst Diversity .... Mr. Henry MORRIS
18 Facilities Service Director .... Mr. David COWAN
06 University Registrar .... Mr. Marcius BROCK
07 Director of Admissions .... Mr. Brian JONES
08 Interim Dean Library Services .... Mr. Chris CORLEY

15 Director of Human Resources ... Mr. Steve BARRETT
36 Director Career Development ... Ms. Pamela WELLER-DENGEL
26 Director Media Relations ... Mr. Daniel BENSON
41 Dir of Intercollegiate Athletics ... Mr. Kevin BUISMAN
29 Director of Alumni Relations ... Mr. Ramon PINERO
22 Director Affirmative Action/Title I ... Ms. Linda ALVAREZ
37 Director Student Financial Services ... Ms. Jan MARBLE
58 AVP Graduate Studies/Research ... Dr. Stephen STOYNOFF
79 Interim Dean of Arts & Humanities ... Dr. Chris BROWN
53 Dean of Education ... Dr. Jean HAAR
50 Dean of Business ... Dr. Brenda FLANNERY
76 Dean Allied Health/Nursing ... Dr. Kristine RETHERFORD
81 Interim Dean CSET ... Dr. Aaron BUDGE
83 Dean Social/Behavioral Science ... Dr. Matt LAOYZA
104 Interim Dean Global Education ... Ms. Anne DAHLMAN
56 Dean University Extended Education ... Dr. Tom NORMAN
38 Director Student Counseling ... Ms. Kari MUCH
18 AVP Facilities Management ... Mr. Paul CORCORAN
114 AVP for Budget & Business Services ... Mr. Steve SMITH
19 Director Security/Safety ... Ms. Sandi SCHNORENBERG
39 Dean of Students/Res Life Director ... Ms. Cindy JANNEY
122 Asst Dir Stdnt Act-Frat/Sor Life ... Mr. John BULCOCK

*Minnesota State University Moorhead (A)

1104 7th Avenue S, Moorhead MN 56563-2996
County: Clay FICE Identification: 002367
Unit ID: 174358
Telephone: (218) 477-4000 Carnegie Class: Masters/L
FAX Number: (218) 477-2168 Calendar System: Semester
URL: www.mnstate.edu
Established: 1887 Annual Undergrad Tuition & Fees (In-State): $8,980
Enrollment: 5,547 Coed
Affiliation or Control: State IRS Status: 501(c)3
Highest Offering: Doctorate
Accreditation: HLC, ART, CACREP, CAEPN, CONST, HSA, MUS, NAIT, NURSE, SP, SW

02 President ... Dr. Anne BLACKHURST
05 VP Academic Affairs ... Dr. Arrick L. JACKSON
10 VP Finance & Administration ... Ms. Jean HOLLAAR
84 VP Enrollment Mgmt/Student Affairs ... Dr. Brenda AMENSON-HILL
29 VP Alumni Foundation ... Mr. Gary HAUGO
04 Assistant to the President ... Ms. Kathy M. LEHN
20 AVP Academic Affs & Dean Grad Stds ... Dr. Robert NAVA
28 Assoc Provost for DEI ... Dr. Frank C. KING, JR.
09 Dir Institutional Effectiveness ... Vacant
13 Chief Information Officer ... Mr. Daniel A. HECKAMAN
21 Comptroller ... Ms. Karen K. LESTER
50 Dean Business/Analytics & Comm ... Dr. Peter SHERMAN
49 Interim Dean Arts & Humanities ... Dr. Kyja KRISTJANSSON-NELSON
53 Dean Educ/Human Svcs/Grad Stds ... Dr. Ok-Hee LEE
81 Dean Science/Health/Environment ... Dr. Lisa NAWROT
58 Director of Graduate Studies ... Vacant
32 Dean of Students ... Ms. Kara GRAVLEY-STACK
15 VP Human Resources ... Ms. Ann HIEDEMAN
06 Registrar ... Ms. Heather M. SOLEIM
26 Chief Marketing Officer ... Mrs. Kirsten JENSEN
19 Director of Public Safety ... Mr. Ryan NELSON
37 Dir Financial Aid & Scholarships ... Ms. Melissa DINGMANN
23 Dir Hendrix Counseling Ctr ... Ms. Angela BELLANGER
22 Director of Accessibility Resources ... Mr. Chuck EADE
36 Director of Career Development ... Ms. Samantha GUST
07 Director of Admissions ... Mr. Tom REBURN
35 Exec Dir Student Union ... Mr. Layne ANDERSON
39 Dir Housing & Residential Life ... Ms. Heather PHILLIPS
85 Global Engagement Director ... Ms. Fumi CHEEVER
18 Exec Dir of Facilities Management ... Ms. Brenda NORRIS
40 Bookstore Supervisor ... Ms. Kim M. SAMSON
122 Asst Dir Campus Life-Frat/Sor Life ... Ms. Becky BOYLE JONES
89 Director of First Year Programs ... Ms. Julia ROLAND
08 Exec Dir Library Svcs/Online Lrng ... Ms. Karen QUALEY
41 Athletic Director ... Mr. Chad MARKUSON

*Minnesota West Community and Technical College (B)

1593 11th Avenue, Granite Falls MN 56241
County: Yellow Medicine FICE Identification: 005263
Unit ID: 173638
Telephone: (800) 658-2330 Carnegie Class: Assoc/HVT-High Non
FAX Number: (507) 372-5803 Calendar System: Semester
URL: www.mnwest.edu
Established: 1985 Annual Undergrad Tuition & Fees (In-State): $5,936
Enrollment: 3,253 Coed
Affiliation or Control: State IRS Status: 501(c)3
Highest Offering: Associate Degree
Accreditation: HLC, ADNUR, DA, MAC, MLTAD, RAD, SURGT

02 President ... Dr. Terry GAALSWYK
05 College Provost ... Dr. Arthur BROWN
10 VP of Finance & Facilities ... Ms. Jodi LANDGAARD
49 Dean Liberal Arts/IT ... Ms. Kayla WESTRA
66 Dean Science & Nursing ... Ms. Dawn GORDON
07 Director Admiss/Reg & Financial Aid ... Ms. Katie HERONIMUS
32 Dean Student Services & Enrollment ... Ms. Rebecca WEBER
28 Dean Equity/Inclusion/Student Dev ... Mr. Abdulahi FARAH ABDIGANNI
18 Chief Facilities/Physical Plant ... Mr. Dillon CARLSON
15 Chief Human Resources Officer ... Ms. Karen MILLER
102 Foundation Director ... Ms. Treva GRAVES
08 Director of Library Services ... Mr. Kip THORSON
21 Director of Financial Operations ... Ms. Diana FLISS
04 Admin Assistant to the President ... Ms. Alicia PAULSON
19 Safety Director ... Mr. Royce OVERLAND
84 Director of Enrollment ... Ms. Linda PESCH

*Normandale Community College (C)

9700 France Avenue S, Bloomington MN 55431-4399
County: Hennepin FICE Identification: 007954
Unit ID: 174428
Telephone: (952) 358-8200 Carnegie Class: Assoc/HT-High Non
FAX Number: (952) 358-8101 Calendar System: Semester
URL: www.normandale.edu
Established: 1968 Annual Undergrad Tuition & Fees (In-State): $5,679
Enrollment: 9,420 Coed
Affiliation or Control: State IRS Status: 501(c)3
Highest Offering: Associate Degree
Accreditation: HLC, ACBSP, ADNUR, ART, DH, MUS, THEA

02 President ... Dr. Joyce C. ESTER
04 Executive Assistant to President ... Mrs. Kris CRAIG
11 Vice President Administration ... Mrs. Jill BOLDENOW
05 Provost/Vice Pres of Academic Affs ... Dr. Kristina KELLER
32 Vice President of Student Affairs ... Mrs. Dara HAGEN
15 Vice Pres Human Resources ... Mrs. Jodee MCCALLUM
111 Vice President Advancement ... Vacant
09 Director of IR ... Vacant
50 Dean of Business & Social Sci ... Mr. Michael KIRCH
79 Dean of Humanities ... Dr. Jeffrey JUDGE
81 Dean of STEM ... Dr. Cary KOMOTO
76 Dean of Health Sciences ... Dr. Colleen BRICKLE
08 Dean of Academic Svcs & Library ... Mrs. Erin DALY
10 Assoc VP Finance & Accounting ... Ms. Norma KONSCHAK
13 Chief Information Officer ... Mr. Stephen WINCKELMAN
18 Assoc Vice Pres of Operations ... Mr. Patrick BUHL
84 Dean of Recruitment and Outreach ... Mr. Charles FRAME
35 Dean of Students ... Mr. Jason CARDINAL
26 Chief Public Relations Officer ... Mr. Steve GELLER
06 Registrar ... Ms. Tonya HANSON
07 Director of Admissions ... Ms. Nancy PATES
37 Director of Financial Aid & Scholar ... Mrs. Susan ANT
38 Assoc Director of Advising & Couns ... Ms. Kari RUSCH-CURL
19 Director of Public Safety ... Mr. Erik BENTLEY
106 Director of Online Learning ... Vacant
27 Director of Marketing Communication ... Mrs. Jennifer LEFLER
88 Accounting Supervisor ... Mrs. Cindy LADD
40 Bookstore Manager ... Mr. Chris PETERSON
25 Grant Development Director ... Mrs. Angela ARNOLD
22 Equity & Inclusion Officer ... Mr. John PARKER-DER BOGHOSSIAN
109 Director of Auxiliary Services ... Mr. Chris MIKKELSEN
102 Director Foundation/Corporate Rels ... Ms. Jane FENTON

*North Hennepin Community College (D)

7411 85th Avenue N, Brooklyn Park MN 55445-2299
County: Hennepin FICE Identification: 002370
Unit ID: 174376
Telephone: (763) 424-0702 Carnegie Class: Assoc/HT-High Non
FAX Number: (763) 424-0929 Calendar System: Semester
URL: www.nhcc.edu
Established: 1966 Annual Undergrad Tuition & Fees (In-State): $4,596
Enrollment: 5,756 Coed
Affiliation or Control: State IRS Status: 501(c)3
Highest Offering: Associate Degree
Accreditation: HLC, ACBSP, ADNUR, MLTAD

02 President ... Dr. Rolando GARCIA
05 Provost ... Dr. Jesse MASON
10 Int VP Finance & Facilities ... Ms. Dawn BELKO
13 Chief Information Officer ... Mr. Joseph COLLINS
32 Dean Student Development ... Ms. Lindsay FORT
08 Librarian ... Mr. Craig LARSON
06 Director of Admissions & Records ... Ms. Melissa LEIMBEK
15 Chief Human Resources Officer ... Ms. Victoria DEFORD
18 Director of Facilities ... Mr. Joshua BLACKWELL
102 Foundation Executive Director ... Mr. Dale FAGRE
28 Assoc Vice Pres Equity/Inclusion ... Dr. Eda WATTS
26 Dir Marketing/Communications ... Ms. Liz HOGENSON
09 Director of Institutional Research ... Ms. Dena COLEMER
19 Director of Public Safety ... Mr. Ibuchwa KISONGO
21 Int Business Manager ... Ms. Kristen HARINEN
49 Dean of Liberal Arts ... Mr. Anthony MILLER
50 Dean Business & Career Programs ... Dr. Nerita HUGHES
81 Dean of Math/Science ... Mr. Jayant ANAND
76 Int Dean of Nursing & Allied Health ... Dr. Julia UGORJI
60 Dean of Comm/Language/Fine Arts ... Ms. Kathy HENDRICKSON
121 Director Student Advising ... Ms. Sarah DOMAN-FLYGARE
04 Executive Assistant to President ... Ms. Nicole CARLSON
36 Director Student Placement ... Ms. Deb ATKINS
37 Director Student Financial Aid ... Ms. Kristi L'ALLIER

*Northland Community and Technical College (E)

1101 Highway One East, Thief River Falls MN 56701
County: Pennington FICE Identification: 002385
Unit ID: 174473
Telephone: (218) 683-8800 Carnegie Class: Assoc/HVT-Mix Trad/Non
FAX Number: (218) 683-8980 Calendar System: Semester
URL: www.northlandcollege.edu
Established: 1965 Annual Undergrad Tuition & Fees (In-State): $5,793
Enrollment: 2,962 Coed
Affiliation or Control: State IRS Status: 501(c)3
Highest Offering: Associate Degree
Accreditation: HLC, ADNUR, CNEA, COARC, EMT, OTA, PTAA, RAD, SURGT

02 President ... Dr. Sandy KIDDOO
10 VP of Admin Services/CFO ... Ms. Shannon JESME
04 Asst to President ... Ms. Julie FENNING
05 Int VP of Academic/Student Affairs ... Ms. Jodi STAUSS
15 Director of Human Resources ... Mr. Mike CURFMAN
103 Dir of Workforce Development ... Ms. Kirsten MICHALKE
102 Executive Director NCTC Foundation ... Mr. Lars DYRUD
121 Director Academic Success Ctr ... Ms. Sara JOHNSON
38 Counselor ... Ms. Kelsy BLOWERS
84 Dir of Enrollment Mgmt & Admission ... Ms. Nicki CARLSON
37 Director Student Financial Aid ... Ms. Lisa BOTTEM
32 Dean Student Affairs/Dir Athletics ... Dr. Jeff POOLE
18 Chief Facilities/Physical Plant ... Mr. Clinton CASTLE
26 Director of Marketing/Communication ... Mr. Chad SPERLING
06 Registrar ... Mr. Ben HOFFMAN
13 Director of Technology ... Ms. Stacey HRON
19 Director Security/Safety ... Mr. Cory FELLER

*Northwest Technical College (F)

905 Grant Avenue, SE, Bemidji MN 56601-4907
County: Beltrami FICE Identification: 005759
Unit ID: 173115
Telephone: (218) 333-6600 Carnegie Class: Assoc/HVT-High Non
FAX Number: (218) 333-6694 Calendar System: Semester
URL: www.ntcmn.edu
Established: 1966 Annual Undergrad Tuition & Fees (In-State): $5,731
Enrollment: 825 Coed
Affiliation or Control: State IRS Status: 501(c)3
Highest Offering: Associate Degree
Accreditation: HLC, ADNUR, DA, PNUR

02 President ... Dr. John HOFFMAN
05 Chief Academic Officer ... Vacant
06 Registrar ... Ms. Kim GOURNEAU
84 Director Enrollment/Marketing ... Mr. Charles ABBOTT

*Pine Technical and Community College (G)

900 Fourth Street, SE, Pine City MN 55063-2198
County: Pine FICE Identification: 005535
Unit ID: 174570
Telephone: (320) 629-5100 Carnegie Class: Assoc/HVT-High Non
FAX Number: (320) 629-5101 Calendar System: Semester
URL: www.pine.edu
Established: 1965 Annual Undergrad Tuition & Fees (In-State): $4,302
Enrollment: 1,724 Coed
Affiliation or Control: State IRS Status: 501(c)3
Highest Offering: Associate Degree
Accreditation: HLC, CNEA

02 President ... Mr. Joe MULFORD
05 Vice Pres Academic/Student Affairs ... Ms. Denine ROOD
13 Chief Information Officer ... Ms. Janis WEGNER
10 Chief Financial Officer ... Ms. Janis WEGNER
51 Dean of Continuing Educ/Custom Trng ... Ms. Wendy WALBURG
66 Dean Nursing/Health Science ... Vacant
06 Registrar ... Ms. Sarah DORN
15 Chief Human Resources Officer ... Ms. Amy KRUSE
26 Director Marketing/Communications ... Ms. Katie KOPPY
32 Director Student Affairs ... Ms. Kierstan PECK
18 Physical Plant Supervisor ... Mr. Steven LANGE
04 Executive Asst to President ... Ms. Sandi CARLISLE

*Ridgewater College (H)

PO Box 1097, 2101 15th Ave NW, Willmar MN 56201-1097
County: Kandiyohi FICE Identification: 005252
Unit ID: 175236
Telephone: (320) 222-5200 Carnegie Class: Assoc/HVT-Mix Trad/Non
FAX Number: (320) 222-5212 Calendar System: Semester
URL: www.ridgewater.edu
Established: 1961 Annual Undergrad Tuition & Fees (In-State): $5,958
Enrollment: 3,176 Coed
Affiliation or Control: State IRS Status: 501(c)3
Highest Offering: Associate Degree
Accreditation: HLC, ADNUR, EMT, MAC, PNUR

02 President ... Dr. Craig JOHNSON
05 Vice Pres Student Success ... Mr. Mike KUTZKE
10 Vice President Finance & Operations ... Mr. Daniel F. HOLTZ
51 Dean of Cust Trng & Cont Education ... Mr. Sam BOWEN
20 Dean of Instruction/Technical Pgms ... Mr. Matthew FEUERBORN
20 Dean Instruction/Liberal Arts/Sci ... Mr. Jeff MILLER
32 Dean of Student Services ... Ms. Heidi L. OLSON
21 Director of Business Services ... Ms. Cheryl A. NORLIEN
15 Director of Human Resources ... Ms. Tara STREY
66 Director of Nursing/Allied Health ... Ms. Mary LEYK
37 Director of Financial Aid ... Mr. James W. RICE
121 Director of Student Success ... Ms. Jennifer HEWERDINE
07 Admissions/Academic Advisor ... Ms. Amy BIRKLAND
41 Athletic Coordinator ... Mr. Todd M. THORSTAD

06 Registrar ... Ms. Kelli S. KIENITZ
26 Dir Communications/Mktg/Admissions ... Ms. Laura KUVAAS
102 VP Advancement/Foundation Exec Dir ... Ms. Kelly J. MAGNUSON
09 Dir Inst Research/Effectiveness/CIO ... Mr. Prabesh SHRESTHA
28 Dir Diversity/Equity/Inclusion ... Ms. Jehana SCHWANDT
18 Physical Plant Director ... Mr. Kip R. OVESON

*Riverland Community College (A)

1900 8th Avenue, NW, Austin MN 55912-1473
County: Mower FICE Identification: 002335
Unit ID: 173063
Telephone: (507) 433-0600 Carnegie Class: Assoc/MT-VT-High Non
FAX Number: (507) 433-0665 Calendar System: Semester
URL: www.riverland.edu
Established: 1940 Annual Undergrad Tuition & Fees (In-State): $5,826
Enrollment: 3,494 Coed
Affiliation or Control: State IRS Status: 501(c)3
Highest Offering: Associate Degree
Accreditation: HLC, ADNUR, MAC, PNUR, RAD

02 President ... Dr. Adenuga ATEWOLOGUN
05 VP of Academic & Student Affairs ... Ms. Barbara EMBACHER
10 VP of Finance & Operations ... Mr. Brad DOSS
15 VP of Employee Relations & HR ... Vacant
66 Dean of Nursing/Health & Wellness ... Ms. Laura BEASLEY
49 Int Dean Liberal Arts & Sciences ... Ms. Jen OUELLETTE-SCHRAMM
75 Dean Ag/Trans/Trade & Tech ... Mr. Ryan LANGEMEIER
32 Dean of Student Affairs ... Vacant
111 Dean of Institutional Advancement ... Ms. Janelle KOEPKE
50 Dean of Business/SS/Safety & CT ... Ms. Christy TRYHUS
06 Registrar ... Ms. Jen PATTERSON
07 Dir of Admissions & New Student Rel ... Ms. Nel ZELLAR
26 Exec Dir Communications/Media/Mktg ... Mr. James DOUGLASS
37 Director of Financial Aid ... Ms. Patty HEMANN
36 Dir of College Partnerships & Trans ... Ms. Jean KYLE
13 VP Technology & Learning Resources ... Mr. Mark BAAS
18 Physical Plant Supervisor ... Mr. Shawn O'CONNOR
96 Purchasing Agent ... Ms. Page PETERSEN
28 Diversity Officer ... Ms. Dani HEINY
08 Librarian ... Ms. Jeannie (Carol) DIGGS
19 Safety Administrator ... Mr. Mike HOWE
29 Director Grants/Alumni Relations ... Ms. Kim NELSON
41 Athletic Director ... Mr. Derek HAHN
04 Exec Assistant to the President ... Ms. Holly SHERMAN
09 Director of Institutional Research ... Mr. Pawel BUDA
39 Director Residential Life & Housing ... Ms. Alexis PERSONS

*Rochester Community and Technical College (B)

851 30th Avenue, SE, Rochester MN 55904-4999
County: Olmsted FICE Identification: 002373
Unit ID: 174738
Telephone: (507) 285-7210 Carnegie Class: Assoc/MT-VT-Mix Trad/Non
FAX Number: (507) 285-7496 Calendar System: Semester
URL: www.rctc.edu
Established: 1915 Annual Undergrad Tuition & Fees (In-State): $5,252
Enrollment: 5,115 Coed
Affiliation or Control: State IRS Status: 501(c)3
Highest Offering: Associate Degree
Accreditation: HLC, ACBSP, ADNUR, CAHIIM, DA, DH, PNUR, SURGT

02 President ... Dr. Jeffery BOYD
05 VP of Academic Affairs ... Ms. Michelle PYFFEROEN
10 Vice Pres Finance ... Mr. Steve SCHMALL
81 Dean Sciences & Health Professions ... Mr. Jason JADIN
49 Dean of Liberal Arts ... Dr. Brenda FRAME
75 Dean Career/Technical Education ... Dr. Matt BISSONETTE
18 Vice Pres Facilities ... Mr. Steve SCHMALL
15 Chief Human Resource Officer ... Vacant
13 Chief Information Officer ... Mr. Mir QADER
32 Chief Student Affairs Officer ... Dr. Teresa BROWN
103 Dir of Business/Workforce Dev ... Vacant
35 Student Life Coordinator ... Ms. Megan ROSS
06 Registrar ... Ms. Melanie CALLISTER
07 Director Admissions and Enrollment ... Ms. Alicia ZEONE
37 Director Financial Aid ... Ms. Beth DIEKMANN
09 Chief Inst Effectiveness Officer ... Dr. Morris THOMPSON
04 Executive Assistant to President ... Mrs. Judy KINGSBURY
21 Business Office Supervisor ... Ms. Kelly PYFFEREOEN
26 Chief Public Relations Officer ... Mr. Nate STOLTMAN
19 Director of Campus Safety/Security ... Mr. Scott MCCULLOUGH
40 Bookstore Coordinator ... Ms. Michelle DANIELSON
96 Purchasing Manager ... Ms. June MEITZNER
102 Foundation Executive Director ... Dr. Matt BISSONETTE
08 Head Librarian ... Ms. Mary DENNISON
22 Dir Affirmative Action/EEO ... Vacant
41 Athletic Director ... Mr. Mike LESTER
105 Director Web Services ... Mr. Darin HOFFMAN
30 Advancement Coordinator ... Ms. Kristin MANNIX

*St. Cloud State University (C)

720 4th Avenue S, Saint Cloud MN 56301-4498
County: Stearns FICE Identification: 002377
Unit ID: 174783
Telephone: (320) 308-0121 Carnegie Class: Masters/L
FAX Number: N/A Calendar System: Semester
URL: www.stcloudstate.edu
Established: 1869 Annual Undergrad Tuition & Fees (In-State): $8,779
Enrollment: 11,841 Coed
Affiliation or Control: State IRS Status: 501(c)3
Highest Offering: Doctorate
Accreditation: HLC, ABAI, ART, CACREP, HT, JOUR, MLS, MUS, NURSE, SP, SW

02 President ... Dr. Robbyn R. WACKER
04 Executive Asst to President ... Ms. Meredith L. ATHMAN
05 Provost/VP for Academic Affairs ... Dr. Dan GREGORY
10 Vice Pres for Finance/Admin ... Mr. Larry LEE
84 VP Enrollment Management ... Dr. Jason L. WOODS
45 Asst Provost for Inst Effectiveness ... Dr. Michele MUMM
111 Vice Pres University Advancement ... Mr. Nic KATONA
32 VP for Student Affairs ... Dr. Katrina RODRIGUEZ
43 Special Advisor to the President ... Dr. Judith P. SIMINOE
86 Director Univ/Legislative Relations ... Mr. Bernie OMANN
22 Equity & Access Officer ... Ms. Chocoletta SIMPSON
41 Director of Athletics ... Ms. Holly SCHREINER
15 VP for HR and Workplace Experience ... Ms. Renee HILLER
13 Deputy Chief Information Officer ... Mr. Phil THORSON
21 Director of Business Services ... Mr. Jeff WAGNER
26 Exec Dir Marketing & Communications ... Dr. Kathryn KLOBY
50 Dean Herberger Business School ... Dr. Katherina PATTIT
53 Dean School of Education ... Dr. Jennifer MUELLER
76 Dean School of Health/Human Service ... Dr. Shonda M. CRAFT
49 Dean College of Liberal Arts ... Dr. Mark SPRINGER
80 Dean School of Public Affairs ... Dr. King BANAIAN
81 Dean Science & Engineering ... Dr. Adel ALI
08 Dean University Library ... Ms. Rhonda HUISMAN
46 AP for Research/Sponsored Pgms ... Dr. Claudia TOMANY
97 Dean University College ... Dr. Feng-Ling JOHNSON
20 Exec Dir of Academic Resources ... Dr. Michele MUMM
35 Dean of Students ... Ms. Jen SELL MATZKE
07 AVP Student Recruit & Enrollment ... Vacant
06 Registrar and Student Records ... Mr. Tim MEENDERING
36 Executive Director Career Center ... Ms. Michelle SCHMITZ
37 Director of Financial Aid ... Mr. Mike T. URAN
38 Director of Counseling ... Dr. Jennifer ROCHELEAU DORHOLT
117 AVP Safety/Risk Management ... Vacant
09 Dir Analytics/Business Intelligence ... Mr. Tony KUNKEL
18 AVP Facilities Management ... Mr. Phil MOESSNER
88 Director American Indian Center ... Ms. Barbara K. MILLER
88 Int Director LGBT Resource Center ... Ms. Jane OLSEN
88 Director Lindgren Child Care Center ... Vacant
22 Director Student Accessibility Svcs ... Ms. Andria BELISLE
23 Director Student Health Services ... Vacant
94 Director Womens Center ... Ms. Jane OLSEN
19 Director Public Safety ... Vacant
85 Int AVP Intl Studies/Dir MSS ... Mr. Shahzad AHMAD

*Saint Cloud Technical and Community College (D)

1540 Northway Drive, Saint Cloud MN 56303-1240
County: Stearns FICE Identification: 005534
Unit ID: 174756
Telephone: (320) 308-5000 Carnegie Class: Assoc/HVT-High Trad
FAX Number: (320) 308-5981 Calendar System: Semester
URL: www.sctcc.edu
Established: 1948 Annual Undergrad Tuition & Fees (In-State): $5,631
Enrollment: 3,931 Coed
Affiliation or Control: State IRS Status: 501(c)3
Highest Offering: Associate Degree
Accreditation: HLC, CAHIIM, CVT, DA, DH, DMS, EMT, PNUR, SURGT

02 Interim President ... Ms. Lori KLOOS
05 VP of Academic Affairs ... Dr. Emmanuel AWUAH
32 Vice President Student Affairs ... Mr. Andrew PFLIPSEN
04 Assistant to the President ... Ms. Karen A. HIEMENZ
10 Vice Pres Admin/Chief Financial Ofc ... Mr. Daniel HOLTZ
22 VP Cult Fluency/Equity/Inclusion ... Ms. Debra LEIGH
75 Interim Dean Trade/Industry ... Mr. Aaron BARKER
81 Dean of Liberal Arts & Trans Stds ... Mr. Jeff KIRCHOFF
50 Dean of Business/IT & Online Lrng ... Ms. Shanda DAVIS
66 Dean of Nursing/Health ... Ms. Laurie JENSEN
06 Registrar ... Ms. Bretta EDWARDS
15 Dir Personnel Svcs/Affirm Action ... Ms. Tina BOYD
84 Dir of Recruitment & Outreach ... Ms. Karen BACKES
08 Head Librarian ... Ms. Mary JORDAN
19 Security/Safety Officer ... Ms. Carol BREWER
37 Director Student Financial Aid ... Ms. Anita G. BAUGH
36 Director Student Placement ... Ms. Lisa MOHR
40 Director Bookstore ... Mr. Aquirre REESE
41 Director of Athletics ... Mr. Nathaniel HIESTAND
18 Chief Facilities/Physical Plant ... Mr. Jason THEISEN
13 Chief Information Officer ... Mr. Tim FURR
21 Business Officer ... Ms. Diane ILLIES
96 Director of Purchasing ... Ms. Susan MEYER
08 Director Library ... Ms. Jennifer ERICKSON
22 Director Affirm Action/Equal Oppty ... Ms. Tina BOYD
30 Chief Devel/Dir Annual/Planned Giv ... Mr. Daniel LARSON
09 Director of Institutional Research ... Dr. Kenneth MATTHEWS
88 Director of K-12 Initiatives ... Ms. Susan JORDAHL

*Saint Paul College-A Community & Technical College (E)

235 Marshall Avenue, Saint Paul MN 55102-1800
County: Ramsey FICE Identification: 005533
Unit ID: 175041
Telephone: (651) 846-1703 Carnegie Class: Assoc/MT-VT-Mix Trad/Non
FAX Number: (651) 846-1451 Calendar System: Semester
URL: www.saintpaul.edu
Established: 1910 Annual Undergrad Tuition & Fees (In-State): $5,811
Enrollment: 5,823 Coed
Affiliation or Control: State IRS Status: 501(c)3
Highest Offering: Associate Degree
Accreditation: HLC, ACBSP, ACFEI, CAHIIM, COARC, MLTAD, PNUR, SURGT

02 President ... Dr. Deidra PEASLEE
10 Vice President Finance & Operations ... Mr. Scott WILSON
111 VP of Advancement/Communications ... Dr. Austin CALHOUN
05 VP of Academic/Student Affairs ... Mr. Gregory RATHERT
32 Assoc Vice Pres of Student Affairs ... Ms. Kay FRANCIS GARLAND
20 Assoc Vice Pres of Academic Affairs ... Ms. Sarah CARRICO
28 VP Diversity/Equity/Inclusion ... Ms. Wendy ROBERSON
27 Director of TRIO ... Ms. Mary VANG
103 Dean Workforce Trng/Continuing Educ ... Ms. Jennifer HUSTON
07 Director of Admissions ... Ms. Gabriela MILLER
15 Senior Human Resources Officer ... Mr. Craig MORRIS
13 Chief Information Officer ... Ms. Ellen ROSTER
06 Director Records/Registration ... Ms. Tarah SACHDEV
29 Director of Alumni Relations ... Mr. Logan SPINDLER
36 Director Student Placement ... Ms. Sheryl SAUL
38 Director Student Counseling ... Dr. Lisa HANES-GOODLANDER
18 Director Facilities/Physical Plant ... Mr. Matthew WILLIAMS
21 Business Office Manager ... Ms. Angela SHEVCHUK
37 Director of Student Financial Aid ... Ms. Bao YANG-MOUA
102 Exec Director of Foundation ... Mr. David KLINE
26 Dir Marketing/Recruitment ... Mr. Ryan MAYOR
76 Dean of Health Sciences/Services ... Dr. Julia BARTLETT
81 Dean Science/Technology/Eng & Math ... Dr. Enyinda ONUNWOR
50 Dean Business/Career Tech Educ ... Dr. Virginia HAYMAN BARBER
57 Dean Liberal & Fine Arts ... Ms. Avani SHAH
19 Director Pubic Safety ... Mr. Thomas BERGS
108 Dean of Academic Effectiveness ... Ms. Dianne GREGORY

*South Central College (F)

1920 Lee Boulevard, PO Box 1920,
North Mankato MN 56003
County: Nicollet FICE Identification: 005537
Unit ID: 173911
Telephone: (507) 389-7200 Carnegie Class: Assoc/HVT-Mix Trad/Non
FAX Number: (507) 388-9951 Calendar System: Semester
URL: www.southcentral.edu
Established: 1946 Annual Undergrad Tuition & Fees (In-District): $5,491
Enrollment: 2,653 Coed
Affiliation or Control: State/Local IRS Status: 501(c)3
Highest Offering: Associate Degree
Accreditation: HLC, ADNUR, DA, EMT, MAC, MLTAD, PNUR

02 President ... Dr. Annette PARKER
04 Exec Assistant to the President ... Ms. Susan JAMESON
05 Vice Pres Academic/Student Affs ... Dr. Jennifer FAGER
10 VP Finance/Operations ... Ms. Roxy TRAXLER
15 Chief Human Resources Officer ... Ms. Roxy TRAXLER
09 VP Research & Inst Effectiveness ... Dr. Narren BROWN
32 AVP of Student Affairs ... Ms. Judy ENDRES
49 Dean of Arts & Sciences ... Dr. Rick KURTZ
103 Dean Health Sci/Career/Tech Educ ... Dr. Dimitria HARDING
47 Dean of Agriculture ... Mr. Brad SCHLOESSER
50 Dean of Business & Industry ... Mr. Jim HANSON
26 Public Relations/Marketing Director ... Ms. Shelly MEGAW
28 Dir of Diversity/Equity & Inclusion ... Mr. John HARPER
37 Director of Financial Aid ... Ms. Bonnie SCHEFFLER
08 Librarian ... Ms. Heather BIEDERMANN
06 Registrar ... Ms. Amber EISEN SANCHEZ
102 Exec Director N Mankato Foundation ... Ms. Erin AANENSON
19 Safety & Security Program Manager ... Mr. Aronn OAKLAND
07 Director of Admissions ... Mr. Edel FERNANDEZ

*Southwest Minnesota State University (G)

1501 State Street, Marshall MN 56258-1598
County: Lyon FICE Identification: 002375
Unit ID: 175078
Telephone: (507) 537-7678 Carnegie Class: Masters/L
FAX Number: (507) 537-7154 Calendar System: Semester
URL: www.smsu.edu
Established: 1963 Annual Undergrad Tuition & Fees (In-State): $9,058
Enrollment: 7,259 Coed
Affiliation or Control: State IRS Status: 501(c)3
Highest Offering: Master's
Accreditation: HLC, EXSC, MUS, NURSE, SW

02 President ... Dr. Kumara JAYASURIYA
05 Provost ... Dr. Ross WASTVVEDT
10 VP Finance and Admin ... Ms. Debra KERKAERT
32 AVP Stdnt Affairs/Dean of Students ... Mr. Scott CROWELL
111 Exec Dir Advancement/Foundation ... Mr. Nathan POLFLIET
29 Sr Dir of Alumni Rels & Outreach ... Ms. Stacy FROST
49 Interim Dean Arts/Letters/Sciences ... Dr. Lori BAKER
50 Dean Bus/Ed/Grad/Prof Studies ... Dr. Raphael ONYEAGHALA
41 Athletic Director ... Ms. Jennifer FLOWERS
13 Chief Information Officer ... Mr. Dan BAUN
07 Director of Admission ... Mr. Jeremy REED
14 Director of Computer Services ... Mr. Shawn HEDMAN
06 Registrar ... Mr. Eric WHITE
19 Director University Public Safety ... Mr. Michael MUNFORD
28 Director Diversity & Inclusion ... Mr. Alex WOOD
15 Chief Human Resources/Affirm Action ... Ms. Nancy OLSON
18 Facilities & Physical Plant Manager ... Mr. Tony NUBILE
36 Director of Career Services ... Ms. Melissa SCHOLTEN
37 Director of Financial Aid ... Ms. Natasha BOE

38 University Counselor ... Vacant
96 Buyer Supervisor ... Ms. Christy JOHNSON
21 Business Manager ... Vacant
26 VP Govt Rels/Comm & Mktg ... Mr. Bill MULSO
04 Exec Admin Asst to President ... Ms. Chris ANDERSON
09 Director of Institutional Research ... Mr. Alan MATZNER
30 Director Development ... Mr. Rustin BUYSSE
44 Director Annual Giving ... Ms. Meredith HYATT

*Winona State University (A)

PO Box 5838, Winona MN 55987-0838
County: Winona　FICE Identification: 002394
Unit ID: 175272
Telephone: (507) 457-5000　Carnegie Class: Masters/M
FAX Number: (507) 457-5586　Calendar System: Quarter
URL: www.winona.edu
Established: 1858　Annual Undergrad Tuition & Fees (In-State): $9,780
Enrollment: 7,106　Coed
Affiliation or Control: State　IRS Status: 501(c)3
Highest Offering: Doctorate
Accreditation: HLC, CAATE, CACREP, MUS, NURSE, SW, THEA

02 President ... Dr. Scott R. OLSON
05 Provost/VP Academic Affairs/CAO ... Dr. Darrell NEWTON
10 VP Finance & Administration ... Mr. Scott ELLINGHUYSEN
111 VP University Advancement ... Mr. Jon OLSON
32 VP Enrollment & Student Life & Dev ... Ms. Denise MCDOWELL
13 AVP Academic Affairs/CIO ... Mr. Kenneth JANZ
38 Director of Counseling Services ... Dr. Benedict EZEOKE
54 Dean College of Science/Engineering ... Dr. Charla MIERTSCHIN
49 Dean College of Liberal Arts ... Dr. Peter MIENE
50 Dean College of Business ... Mr. Randall SKALBERG
53 Interim Dean College of Education ... Mr. Edward REILLY
66 Dean Col of Nursing/Health Science ... Dr. Julie ANDERSON
35 Dean of Students ... Ms. Karen JOHNSON
06 Sr Associate Registrar ... Ms. Tania SCHMIDT
84 Director Warrior Success Center ... Mr. Ron STREGE
37 Assistant Director of Financial Aid ... Ms. Charlene KREUZER
36 Associate Director Career Services ... Ms. Deanna GODDARD
07 Interim Director of Admissions ... Ms. Kendra WEBER
39 Residential College Program Coord ... Ms. Sarah OLCOTT
51 Exec Dir Outreach/Continuing Educ ... Vacant
29 Director of Alumni Engagement ... Ms. Tracy HALE
40 Bookstore Manager ... Ms. Jacqueline MALAY
44 Director Development ... Vacant
88 Director of International Svcs ... Ms. Kemale PINAR
19 Director of Security ... Mr. Christopher CICHOSZ
41 Athletic Director ... Mr. Eric SCHOH
18 Asst VP for Facilities Management ... Mr. James GOBLIRSCH
26 Director Marketing & Communications ... Ms. Andrea NORTHAM
94 Director of Women's Studies ... Dr. Tamara BERG
96 Director of Purchasing ... Ms. Laura MANN
28 Director of Cultural Diversity ... Mr. Jonathan LOCUST
15 Director of Human Resources ... Ms. Lori REED
04 Exec Admin Assistant to President ... Ms. Ingrid SPIES
122 Asst Dir Student Act-Greek Life ... Ms. Alex THOMPSON

*Anoka-Ramsey Community College Cambridge Campus (B)

300 Spirit River Drive South, Cambridge MN 55008-5704
Telephone: (763) 433-1100　Identification: 770298
Accreditation: &HLC

*Minnesota State Community and Technical College Detroit Lakes (C)

900 Highway 34 E, Detroit Lakes MN 56501
Telephone: (218) 846-3700　Identification: 770303
Accreditation: &HLC, CNEA

*Minnesota State Community and Technical College Moorhead (D)

1900 28th Avenue S, Moorhead MN 56560
Telephone: (218) 299-6500　Identification: 770304
Accreditation: &HLC, CNEA, CVT, DH, SURGT

*Minnesota State Community and Technical College Wadena (E)

405 Colfax Avenue SW, Wadena MN 56482
Telephone: (213) 631-7800　Identification: 770305
Accreditation: &HLC, CNEA

*Minnesota West Community and Technical College Canby Campus (F)

1011 First Street West, Canby MN 56220
Telephone: (507) 223-7252　Identification: 770306
Accreditation: &HLC

*Minnesota West Community and Technical College Jackson Campus (G)

401 West Street, Jackson MN 56143
Telephone: (547) 847-7920　Identification: 770308
Accreditation: &HLC

*Minnesota West Community and Technical College Pipestone Campus (H)

1314 North Hiawatha Ave/PO Box 250, Pipestone MN 56164
Telephone: (507) 825-6800　Identification: 770309
Accreditation: &HLC, CAHIIM

*Minnesota West Community and Technical College Worthington Campus (I)

1450 Collegeway, Worthington MN 56187
Telephone: (507) 372-3464　Identification: 770310
Accreditation: &HLC, PNUR

*Northland Community and Technical College East Grand Forks Campus (J)

2022 Central Avenue NE, East Grand Forks MN 56721
Telephone: (218) 793-2800　Identification: 770311
Accreditation: &HLC, DIETT

*Riverland Community College Albert Lea Campus (K)

2200 Riverland Drive, Albert Lea MN 56007
Telephone: (507) 379-3300　Identification: 770313
Accreditation: &HLC

*South Central College Faribault Campus (L)

1225 Third Street SW, Faribault MN 55021
Telephone: (507) 332-5800　Identification: 770314
Accreditation: &HLC

*Winona State University-Rochester (M)

859 30th Avenue SE, Rochester MN 55904
Telephone: (800) 366-5418　Identification: 770317
Accreditation: &HLC

Mitchell Hamline School of Law (N)

875 Summit Avenue, Saint Paul MN 55105-3076
County: Ramsey　FICE Identification: 002391
Unit ID: 175281
Telephone: (651) 227-9171　Carnegie Class: Spec-4-yr-Law
FAX Number: (651) 290-6414　Calendar System: Semester
URL: www.mitchellhamline.edu
Established: 1900　Annual Graduate Tuition & Fees: N/A
Enrollment: 1,242　Coed
Affiliation or Control: Independent Non-Profit　IRS Status: 501(c)3
Highest Offering: First Professional Degree; No Undergraduates
Accreditation: LAW

01 President & Dean ... Mr. Anthony S. NIEDWIECKI
04 Exec Asst to President & Dean ... Ms. Lynette M. FRACTION
05 Vice Dean Academic & Faculty Affs ... Mr. Jim HILBERT
30 VP of Development & Alumni Affairs ... Ms. Leslie WRIGHT
15 Director Human Resources ... Mr. Michael FREER
13 Senior Academic Technology Officer ... Mr. Gregory DUHL
10 VP Finance & Administration ... Ms. Tressa C. RIES
31 VP Cmty Relations & Operations ... Ms. Christine SZAJ
84 Vice Pres of Enrollment ... Ms. Ann GEMMELL
08 Interim Director of Law Library ... Ms. Lisa HEIDENREICH
28 VP of DEI ... Mr. Michael BIRCHARD
36 Dean for Career Development ... Ms. Leanne FUITH
06 Interim Registrar ... Ms. Katie KUEHL
37 Director of Financial Aid ... Mr. Nick ANDERSON
96 Purchasing Manager ... Ms. Paula B. MERTH
19 Director Facilities & Security ... Mr. John BENTFIELD
32 Dean of Student Affairs ... Ms. Lynn LEMOINE
121 Dean of Academic Excellence ... Ms. Dena SONBOL
26 Asst Director of Marketing ... Mr. Doug BELDEN

North Central University (O)

910 Elliot Avenue, Minneapolis MN 55404-1391
County: Hennepin　FICE Identification: 002369
Unit ID: 174437
Telephone: (612) 343-4400　Carnegie Class: Bac-Diverse
FAX Number: (612) 343-4778　Calendar System: Semester
URL: www.northcentral.edu
Established: 1930　Annual Undergrad Tuition & Fees: $26,280
Enrollment: 1,062　Coed
Affiliation or Control: Assemblies Of God Church　IRS Status: 501(c)3
Highest Offering: Master's
Accreditation: HLC, SW

01 President ... Rev. Scott A. HAGAN
03 Executive Vice President ... Dr. Andrew C. DENTON
04 Executive Assistant to President ... Mrs. Kristie KERR
05 Provost ... Dr. Don L. TUCKER
10 Vice Pres Business & Operations ... Dr. Tim HAGER
20 VP for Academic Affairs ... Dr. Jason WENSCHLAG
84 VP Enrollment/Student Development ... Mrs. Beth HARSHBARGER
42 Assoc Vice Pres of Spiritual Life ... Mr. Joshua EDMON
57 Dean of the College of Fine Arts ... Mr. Larry C. BACH
50 Dean of College of Business & Tech ... Mr. Bill TIBBETTS
49 Dean of College of Arts & Sciences ... Dr. Desiree LIBENGOOD
88 Dean of Col of Church Leadership ... Dr. Allen TENNISON
32 Dean of Students ... Mr. Jeremy WILLIAMSON
41 Interim Director of Athletics ... Mr. Mike KNIPE
37 Director of Financial Aid ... Mr. Alex HINTZ
08 Library Director ... Mrs. Judy PRUITT
13 Director of Information Technology ... Mr. Colin MILLER
06 Registrar ... Ms. Mary MURPHY
09 Dir Inst Research/Effectiveness ... Ms. Erin WHITE
121 Exec Dir of Student Development ... Mr. Todd MONGER
18 Executive Director of Operations ... Mr. Jordan ROBERTSON
58 Dean College of Grad & Prof Educ ... Dr. Renea C. BRATHWAITE
15 Director of Human Resources ... Ms. Kate KETTERLING
19 Director Security/Safety ... Mr. Brent PETERS
111 Executive Director of Advancement ... Vacant
108 Dean of Assessment & Accreditation ... Ms. LaToya BURRELL
26 Director of Communications ... Ms. Nancy ZUGSCHWERT
29 Director Alumni Affairs ... Ms. Tabby FINTON

Northwestern Health Sciences University (P)

2501 W 84th Street, Bloomington MN 55431-1599
County: Hennepin　FICE Identification: 012328
Unit ID: 174507
Telephone: (952) 888-4777　Carnegie Class: Spec-4-yr-Other Health
FAX Number: (952) 888-6713　Calendar System: Trimester
URL: www.nwhealth.edu
Established: 1941　Annual Undergrad Tuition & Fees: $11,700
Enrollment: 1,132　Coed
Affiliation or Control: Independent Non-Profit　IRS Status: 501(c)3
Highest Offering: First Professional Degree
Accreditation: HLC, ACUP, CHIRO, COMTA, MAC, MLS, MLTAD, RTT

01 President and CEO ... Dr. Deborah BUSHWAY
05 VP of Academic Affairs ... Ms. Kim PEARCE
10 Chief Financial Officer ... Ms. Michelle HEGARTY
32 Dean of Students ... Mr. Anthony MOLINAR
15 VP of Human Resources ... Ms. Mary GALE
26 VP of Marketing & Events ... Vacant
30 VP of Development ... Ms. Linda KEILLOR BERG
07 Director of Admissions ... Ms. Erin KAHN
08 Director of Library Services ... Ms. Emily WAITZ
29 Manager Alumni Services ... Ms. Lilly MOKAMBA
51 Director of Continuing Education ... Ms. Deanna KOENIG
13 Chief Information Officer ... Mr. Cory MILLER
38 University Counselor ... Ms. Becky LAWYER
18 Director Facilities Management ... Mr. Kevin WOLPERN
96 Director Bookstore & Purchasing ... Ms. Jan HALLEEN
04 Administrative Asst to President ... Ms. Nancy JOHNSON
37 Director of Student Financial Svcs ... Ms. Karen SAMSTAD
76 Dean College of Health & Wellness ... Dr. Dale HEALEY
88 Dean College of Chiropractic ... Dr. Katie BURNS-RYAN
88 Dean College Acup & Chinese Med ... Dr. Jessica FRIER
06 Registrar ... Ms. Susan NEPPL

Oak Hills Christian College (Q)

1600 Oak Hills Road SW, Bemidji MN 56601-8826
County: Beltrami　FICE Identification: 009992
Unit ID: 174525
Telephone: (218) 751-8670　Carnegie Class: Bac-Diverse
FAX Number: (218) 751-8825　Calendar System: Semester
URL: www.oakhills.edu
Established: 1946　Annual Undergrad Tuition & Fees: $17,334
Enrollment: 103　Coed
Affiliation or Control: Interdenominational　IRS Status: 501(c)3
Highest Offering: Baccalaureate
Accreditation: BI

01 President ... Dr. Martin GIESE
05 Dean of the College ... Dr. Jeff WISDOM
11 Sr VP of Administration ... Dr. Rick WEINERT
111 VP of Inst Advancement & Marketing ... Ms. Leesa DRURY
32 Dean of Student Life ... Mr. Trevor ASHER
07 Director of Admissions ... Mr. Brad SPAULDING
19 Campus Mgr Safety/Security ... Mr. Brad DEJAGER
06 Registrar ... Ms. Jenny HODGSON
08 Library Director/IT Director ... Mr. Keith BUSH
37 Director of Financial Aid ... Ms. Mishele MCKAIN
10 Chief Business Officer ... Mr. Bruce KAEHNE
41 Athletic Director ... Mr. Jeremy ANDERSON
31 Dir of Church/Community Relations ... Mr. Jim HODGSON

*Rasmussen University Corporate Office (R)

8300 Norman Center Drive, Suite 300, Bloomington MN 55437
County: Hennepin　Identification: 667034
Unit ID: 17501405
Telephone: (952) 806-3910　Carnegie Class: N/A
FAX Number: (952) 831-0624
URL: www.rasmussen.edu

01 Acting President ... Javier MIYARES
05 Senior VP and Provost ... Dr. Savitri DIXON SAXON
10 Chief Financial Officer ... Mr. Kevin DELANO
84 Chief Enrollment Management Officer ... Mr. Don DEVITO
13 Chief Technology Officer ... Mr. Craig MCKIBBON
06 Registrar ... Ms. Juliana KLOCEK
07 VP Admissions/Student Experience ... Mr. Dwayne BERTOTTO
37 Director Student Financial Aid ... Ms. Catherine BREUER

*Rasmussen University - St. Cloud (A)

226 Park Avenue South, Saint Cloud MN 56301-3713
County: Stearns FICE Identification: 008694
Unit ID: 175014
Telephone: (320) 251-5600 Carnegie Class: Bac/Assoc-Mixed
FAX Number: (320) 251-3702 Calendar System: Quarter
URL: www.Rasmussen.edu
Established: 1902 Annual Undergrad Tuition & Fees: $12,233
Enrollment: 3,927 Coed
Affiliation or Control: Proprietary IRS Status: Proprietary
Highest Offering: Doctorate
Accreditation: HLC, ADNUR, CAHIIM, MAAB, NURSE, PNUR, SURGT

02 Campus Director .... Ms. Naomi MOGARD

† Regional accreditation carried under the parent institution in Lake Elmo, MN.

* *Rasmussen University - Bloomington* (B)

4400 W 78th St, 6th Floor, Bloomington MN 55435
Telephone: (952) 545-2000 FICE Identification: 011686
Accreditation: &HLC, ADNUR, CAHIIM, MAAB

† Regional accreditation carried under the parent institution in Saint Cloud, MN. The tuition figure is an average, actual tuition may vary.

* *Rasmussen University - Eagan* (C)

3500 Federal Drive, Eagan MN 55122-1346
Telephone: (651) 687-9000 FICE Identification: 004648
Accreditation: &HLC, CAHIIM, MAAB, PNUR

† Regional accreditation carried under the parent institution in Saint Cloud, MN. The tuition figure is an average, actual tuition may vary.

* *Rasmussen University - Mankato* (D)

1400 Madison Ave, Suite 510, Mankato MN 56001
Telephone: (507) 625-6556 FICE Identification: 025033
Accreditation: &HLC, ADNUR, CAHIIM, MAAB, PNUR

† Regional accreditation carried under the parent institution in Saint Cloud, MN.

Red Lake Nation College (E)

15480 Migizi Dr PO Box 576, Red Lake MN 56671
County: Beltrami Identification: 667311
Telephone: (218) 679-2860 Carnegie Class: Not Classified
FAX Number: (218) 679-3870 Calendar System: Semester
URL: www.rlnc.edu
Established: 2014 Annual Undergrad Tuition & Fees: N/A
Enrollment: N/A Coed
Affiliation or Control: Tribal Control IRS Status: 501(c)3
Highest Offering: Associate Degree
Accreditation: HLC

01 President .... Dan KING
05 Vice Pres Ops & Academic Affairs .... Mandy SCHRAM
32 Vice Pres Student Success .... Shieleen OMEN
10 CFO .... Tami NISWANDER
08 Director of Library Services .... Ignacio MENDEZ
06 Registrar .... Alexander KING
30 Director of Development .... Vacant

St. Catherine University (F)

2004 Randolph Avenue, Saint Paul MN 55105-1789
County: Ramsey FICE Identification: 002342
Unit ID: 175005
Telephone: (651) 690-6000 Carnegie Class: DU-Mod
FAX Number: N/A Calendar System: 4/1/4
URL: www.stkate.edu
Established: 1905 Annual Undergrad Tuition & Fees: $42,594
Enrollment: 4,277 Female
Affiliation or Control: Roman Catholic IRS Status: 501(c)3
Highest Offering: Doctorate
Accreditation: HLC, ACBSP, ARCPA, COARC, DIETD, DMS, EXSC, LIB, MACTE, NUR, OT, OTA, PH, PTA, PTAA, RAD, RTT, SW

01 President .... Ms. ReBecca K. ROLOFF
05 EVP and Provost .... Dr. Anita THOMAS
10 SVP and Chief Financial Officer .... Ms. Tracey GRAN
111 EVP and Chief Advancement Officer .... Ms. Elizabeth HALLORAN
04 Exec Assistant to the President .... Ms. Cynthia CONLEY
49 Dean Sch Humanities/Arts/Sci .... Vacant
76 Dean Health Sciences .... Dr. Lisa DUTTON
66 Dean Nursing .... Dr. Laura FERO
50 Dean of Business .... Mr. Benson K. WHITNEY
08 Library Director .... Ms. Emily ASCH
84 SVP Enrollment Management/Athletics .... Mr. John PYLE
30 Director of Development .... Ms. Elizabeth RIEDEL CARNEY
13 SVP and Chief Information Ofcr .... Ms. Jean GUEZMIR
15 SVP for HR/Equity & Inclusion .... Ms. Patricia PRATT-COOK
06 Registrar .... Ms. Cynthia EGENESS
29 Director of Alumnae Relations .... Ms. Mandy IVERSON
26 VP Marketing & Communications .... Dr. Toccara STARK
20 Assistant Provost .... Dr. Denise BAIRD
07 Associate VP of Admissions .... Ms. Cory PIPER-HAUSWIRTH
35 Associate Provost of Student Affair .... Mr. Matthew GOODWIN
37 AVP Enrollment/Financial Aid .... Ms. Elizabeth STEVENS
27 AVP Admission/Market Development .... Mr. Greg STEENSON
36 VP of Career Development .... Ms. May THAO-SCHUCK
16 Director of Human Resources .... Ms. Sarah SCHNELL
38 Director of Student Counseling .... Ms. Heide MALAT
92 Director of Honors Program .... Dr. Rafael CERVANTES
94 Director of Women's Studies .... Dr. Sharon DOHERTY
96 Director of Purchasing .... Mr. Michael HARA
28 Dir Multicultural/Intl Pgms & Svcs .... Vacant
41 Athletic Director .... Mr. Eric STACEY
19 Director of Public Safety .... Mr. Victor JURAN
22 Director of Equity and Inclusion .... Ms. Sandra MITCHELL

Saint John's University (G)

2850 Abbey Plaza, Box 2000, Collegeville MN 56321-2000
County: Stearns FICE Identification: 002379
Unit ID: 174792
Telephone: (320) 363-2011 Carnegie Class: Bac-A&S
FAX Number: (320) 363-2504 Calendar System: Semester
URL: www.csbsju.edu
Established: 1857 Annual Undergrad Tuition & Fees: $48,166
Enrollment: 1,668 Male
Affiliation or Control: Roman Catholic IRS Status: 501(c)3
Highest Offering: Master's
Accreditation: HLC, DIETD, MUS, NURSE, THEOL

01 Interim President .... Dr. James MULLIN
05 Provost Academic Affairs .... Dr. Richard ICE
20 Academic Dean .... Dr. Barbara MAY
20 Dean of the Faculty .... Dr. Pamela BACON
111 Vice President for Inst Advancement .... Mr. Rob CULLIGAN
32 Vice Pres Student Development .... Mr. Michael CONNOLLY
84 Vice Pres Enrollment Mgmt/Marketing .... Mr. Nathan DEHNE
10 Vice Pres Finance/Admin Services .... Mr. Richard ADAMSON
73 Dean School Theology .... Fr. Dale LAUNDERVILLE, OSB
35 Dean of Students .... Mr. Michael CONNOLLY
08 Director of Library .... Ms. Kathleen PARKER
06 Registrar .... Ms. Julie GRUSKA
26 Exec Director of Public Relations .... Mr. Michael HEMMESCH
37 Exec Director of Financial Aid .... Mr. Stuart PERRY
29 Exec Dir of University Relations .... Mr. Adam HERBST
15 Director Human Resources .... Ms. Carol ABELL
13 Director of Info Technology Svcs .... Ms. Casey GORDON

Saint Mary's University of Minnesota (H)

700 Terrace Heights, Winona MN 55987-1399
County: Winona FICE Identification: 002380
Unit ID: 174817
Telephone: (507) 452-4430 Carnegie Class: DU-Mod
FAX Number: (507) 457-1633 Calendar System: Semester
URL: www.smumn.edu
Established: 1912 Annual Undergrad Tuition & Fees: $38,280
Enrollment: 5,152 Coed
Affiliation or Control: Roman Catholic IRS Status: 501(c)3
Highest Offering: Doctorate
Accreditation: HLC, ANEST, COPSY, IACBE, MFCD, NMT, NURSE, SW

01 President .... Rev. James P. BURNS, IVD
10 Executive Vice President & CFO .... Mr. Benjamin MURRAY
05 Int Provost/Dean of Faculties .... Dr. Matthew GERLACH
18 Vice President of Facilities .... Mr. James BEDTKE
111 VP for Advancement .... Mr. Gary KLEIN
32 VP for Student Affairs .... Dr. Timothy GOSSEN
43 Senior VP and General Counsel .... Ms. Ann E. MERCHLEWITZ
26 VP for Marketing and Communication .... Ms. Kelly SHANNON
22 VP for Inclusion & Human Dignity .... Mr. Leon DIXON
42 VP for Mission and Ministry .... Dr. Marisa NARYKA
20 Vice Prov Faculties/Academic Affs .... Dr. Matt NOWAKOWSKI
84 Vice Provost for Enrollment Mgmt .... Mr. Timothy ALBERS
106 Vice Provost for Online Strategy .... Ms. Andrea CARROLL-GLOVER
111 AVP for Advancement .... Ms. Megan SADOWSKI
13 AVP for Information Technology .... Ms. Tianna JOHNSON
09 Asst VP Institutional Effectiveness .... Ms. Tracy LEHNERTZ
20 Director of Curriculum & Assessment .... Dr. Nicola IMBRACSIO
04 Exec Assistant to the President .... Vacant
06 Registrar .... Mr. Christopher VERCH
37 Director of Financial Aid .... Mr. Paul TERRIO
36 Dir Career Services & Internships .... Ms. Kerri CARLSON ANDERSON
08 Director of Library Services .... Ms. Laura OANES
19 Director of Campus Safety .... Mr. Timothy KAUPHUSMAN
88 Facilities Manager .... Mr. Timothy STENSGARD
29 Director Alumni Relations .... Mr. Robert FISHER
41 Director of Athletics .... Mr. Brian SISSON
15 Assistant VP for Human Resources .... Mr. David MILIOTIS
09 Director of Institutional Research .... Ms. Kara WENER
53 Dean School of Education .... Dr. Michael LOVORN
79 Dean of the College .... Dr. Darren ROW
108 Director Accreditation & Compliance .... Dr. Robin HEMENWAY
50 Dean School of Business .... Dr. Michelle WIESER
76 Dean Sciences & Health Professions .... Dr. Amy HEINZ
112 Director of Major & Planned Giving .... Mr. Matt MUSEL
100 Chief of Staff .... Mr. Andrew DIRKSEN
07 Director of Admissions .... Vacant
35 Dean of Students .... Ms. Nicole PETERSON
39 Director of Residence Life .... Ms. Andrea GETZIN
121 Dean of Student Success .... Ms. Alisa MACKSEY
120 Director of Instructional Tech .... Mr. Abram HEDTKE
88 Director of Access Services .... Mr. Billy BROOKS
44 Director Annual Giving .... Ms. Tracy HEASER

St. Olaf College (I)

1520 St. Olaf Avenue, Northfield MN 55057-1098
County: Rice FICE Identification: 002382
Unit ID: 174844
Telephone: (507) 786-2222 Carnegie Class: Bac-A&S
FAX Number: N/A Calendar System: 4/1/4
URL: wp.stolaf.edu
Established: 1874 Annual Undergrad Tuition & Fees: $51,450
Enrollment: 2,953 Coed
Affiliation or Control: Evangelical Lutheran Church In America
IRS Status: 501(c)3
Highest Offering: Baccalaureate
Accreditation: HLC, ART, DANCE, MUS, NURSE, SW, THEA

01 President .... Dr. David R. ANDERSON
05 Provost & Dean of the College .... Dr. Marci J. SORTOR
10 Vice Pres & Chief Financial Officer .... Ms. Janet K. HANSON
111 Vice Pres for Advancement .... Mr. Enoch BLAZIS
32 Vice Pres for Student Life .... Dr. Hassel Andre MORRISON
84 Vice Pres Enrollment/Col Relations .... Mr. Michael KYLE
88 Vice Pres for Mission .... Dr. Jo M. BELD
15 Vice Pres for Human Resources .... Ms. Leslie MOORE
43 General Counsel .... Mr. Carl CROSBY LEHMANN
28 Vice Pres for Equity & Inclusion .... Dr. Reginald H. MILES
20 Associate Provost .... Dr. Jason ENGBRECHT
06 Asst VP/Registrar .... Ms. Ericka K. PETERSON
89 Assoc Dean Interdisciplin/Gen Stds .... Dr. Karil KUCERA
81 Assoc Dean Natural Sciences & Math .... Dr. Kristina GARRETT
79 Assoc Dean Humanities .... Dr. Colin WELLS
57 Assoc Dean Fine Arts .... Dr. Alison J. FELDT
83 Assoc Dean Social Sciences .... Dr. Susan SMALLING
114 Asst VP/Budget & Auxiliary Ops .... Ms. Angela MATHEWS
07 Dean of Admissions & Financial Aid .... Mr. Chris GEORGE
35 Dean of Students .... Dr. Rosalyn EATON
35 Assoc Dean of Students .... Mr. Justin FLEMING
35 Assoc Dean of Students .... Mr. Timothy SCHROER
42 Campus Pastor .... Dr. Matthew MAROHL
13 Director of IT and Libraries .... Ms. Roberta LEMBKE
19 Director of Public Safety .... Mr. Derek KRUSE
41 Director of Athletics .... Mr. Ryan A. BOWLES
29 Dir of Engage/Alum/Parent Relations .... Ms. Ellen DRAEGER CATTADORIS
44 Director of Annual Giving .... Ms. Sara ELDRIDGE
38 Director of Counseling .... Dr. Stephen O'NEILL
26 Chief Marketing Officer .... Ms. Katie WARREN
75 Dir Piper Ctr for Vocation & Career .... Ms. Kirsten CAHOON
108 Assoc Dir of Eval & Assessment .... Ms. Kelsey THOMPSON
09 Director of Institutional Research .... Ms. Susan CANON
39 Asst Director of Residence Life .... Ms. Emily J. BUTTS
37 Director of Student Financial Aid .... Mr. Steve LINDLEY
102 Dir of Govt/Fndtn & Corp Relations .... Mr. Valeng CHA
104 Dir of Intl & Off-Campus Studies .... Dr. Jodi MALMGREN
04 Exec Assistant to the President .... Ms. Jennifer WHITSON

United Theological Seminary of the Twin Cities (J)

767 N. Eustis Street, Suite 140, St. Paul MN 55114
County: Ramsey FICE Identification: 002386
Unit ID: 175139
Telephone: (651) 633-4311 Carnegie Class: Spec-4-yr-Faith
FAX Number: (657) 309-8925 Calendar System: Trimester
URL: www.unitedseminary.edu
Established: 1962 Annual Graduate Tuition & Fees: N/A
Enrollment: 147 Coed
Affiliation or Control: United Church Of Christ IRS Status: 501(c)3
Highest Offering: Doctorate; No Undergraduates
Accreditation: HLC, THEOL

01 Interim President .... Dr. Molly T. MARSHALL
05 VP for Academic Affairs/Dean .... Dr. Kyle ROBERTS
10 VP for Finance/Admin & Strategy .... Mr. Jeff SWENSON
111 VP for Advancement .... Ms. Cindi Beth JOHNSON
26 Director of Marketing/Communication .... Ms. Laura LARSON
121 VP for Student Formation/Vocation .... Rev. Karen HUTT
84 Dir for Student Enrollment .... Ms. Ronny BRADTKE
08 Director of the Library .... Mr. Tim SENAPATIRATNE
88 Dir of Advanced Studies .... Mr. Demian WHEELER
73 Director of Theology and the Arts .... Ms. Jennifer AWES-FREEMAN
29 Dir of Alum Engagement/Giving .... Dr. Cindi Beth JOHNSON
88 Dir for Social Transformation .... Mr. Justin SABIA-TANIS
15 Dir Human Resources & Operations .... Ms. Vonda PEARSON
20 Dir Academic Ops & Distance Educ .... Mr. Matt STOLLENWERK
88 Dir of Formation .... Vacant
88 Dir Student Mentoring and Context .... Vacant
13 Director of Information Services .... Mr. Adam PFUHL
06 Registrar and Academic Advisor .... Ms. Hillary VAMSTAD
88 Operational Logistics/Special Event .... Vacant
04 Admin Assistant to the President .... Ms. Ashley HOVELL

University of Minnesota (K)

100 Church Street SE, 202 Morrill, Minneapolis MN 55455
County: Hennepin FICE Identification: 003969
Unit ID: 174066
Telephone: (612) 626-1616 Carnegie Class: DU-Highest
FAX Number: (612) 625-3875 Calendar System: Semester
URL: www.umn.edu
Established: 1851 Annual Undergrad Tuition & Fees (In-State): $15,027
Enrollment: 52,017 Coed
Affiliation or Control: State IRS Status: 501(c)3

Highest Offering: Doctorate
Accreditation: HLC, ANEST, AUD, CAHIIM, CAMPEP, CEA, CIDA, CLPSY, DENT, DH, DIETC, DIETD, DIETI, FUSER, HSA, IPSY, JOUR, LAW, LSAR, MED, MFCD, MIDWF, MLS, MUS, NURSE, OT, PCSAS, PH, PHAR, PLNG, PTA, RTT, SCPSY, SP, SPAA, SW, VET

01 President ... Dr. Joan T. GABEL
100 Senior Assistant to President ... Dr. Bill HALDEMAN
05 EVP Academic Affairs/Provost ... Dr. Rachel CROSON
10 Sr VP Finance & Operations ... Mr. Myron FRANS
46 Int Vice President for Research ... Dr. Michael` OAKES
58 Vice Prov/Dean Graduate Education ... Dr. Scott LANYON
20 Vice Prov/Dean Undergrad Education ... Dr. Robert MCMASTER
15 Int Vice President Human Resources ... Mr. Ken HORSTMAN
88 Vice Pres for University Services ... Mr. Michael BERTHELSEN
28 Vice Pres Equity and Diversity ... Dr. Michael GOH
13 VP/Chief Info Officer ... Mr. Jaime WASCALUS
43 General Counsel ... Mr. Doug PETERSON
102 President Univ Minnesota Foundation ... Vacant
25 Assoc VP Sponsored Projects Admin ... Ms. Pamela WEBB
26 Vice Pres for University Relations ... Mr. Matt KRAMER
18 Assoc VP/Chief of Facilities ... Mr. Bill PAULUS
32 VP Student Affairs/Dean of Students ... Mr. Calvin PHILLIPS
19 Chief of Police ... Vacant
08 University Librarian ... Dr. Wendy P. LOUGEE
06 Assoc Vice Provost/Registrar ... Ms. Sue N. VAN VOORHIS
07 Exec Director of Admissions ... Ms. Heidi MEYER
09 Director of Institutional Research ... Dr. John KELLOGG
22 Director Equal Oppty/Affirm Action ... Ms. Tina MARISAM
37 Director of Student Finance ... Ms. Tina FALKNER
40 Director of the U of M Bookstores ... Mr. Ross ROSATI
39 Dir of Housing & Residential Life ... Ms. Laurie L. MCLAUGHLIN
48 Dean College of Design ... Ms. Carol STROHECKER
86 Chief Government Relations Officer ... Mr. J.D BURTON
29 CEO Alumni Association ... Ms. Lisa LEWIS
38 Dir of Student Counseling Services ... Dr. Vesna HAMPEL-KOZAR
114 Associate VP for Budget/Finance ... Ms. Julie A. TONNESON
96 Director of Purchasing ... Ms. Beth TAPP
49 Dean of the College of Liberal Arts ... Mr. John COLEMAN
51 Dean Cont/Professional Studies ... Vacant
61 Dean of the Law School ... Mr. Garry JENKINS
74 Dean College of Veterinary Medicine ... Dr. Trevor R. AMES
63 Dean of the Medical School ... Dr. Jakub TOLAR
66 Dean of the School of Nursing ... Dr. Connie W. DELANEY
53 Dean College Education/Human Devel ... Dr. Jean K. QUAM
52 Dean of the School of Dentistry ... Dr. Gary C. ANDERSON
69 Dean of the School Public Health ... Dr. John FINNEGAN
54 Dean College of Science/Engineering ... Dr. Mostafa KAVEH
67 Dean of the College Pharmacy ... Dr. Lynda WELAGE
50 Dean Carlson School of Management ... Dr. Srilata A. ZAHEER
80 Dean Humphrey Sch of Pub Aff ... Dr. Laura BLOOMBERG
81 Dean College of Biological Science ... Dr. Valery E. FORBES
47 Dean Col Food/Agric/Natural Res Sci ... Mr. Brian BUHR
41 Director Intercollegiate Athletics ... Mr. Mark COYLE
27 Chief Public Relations Officer ... Mr. Chuck TOMBARGE
27 Chief Marketing Officer ... Ms. Ann ARONSON
21 Associate VP of Finance/Asst CFO ... Mr. Michael D. VOLNA
101 Secretary of the Institution/Board ... Mr. Brian STEEVES

University of Minnesota Duluth (A)

1049 University Drive, Duluth MN 55812-3011
County: Saint Louis — FICE Identification: 002388
Unit ID: 174233
Telephone: (218) 726-8000 — Carnegie Class: Masters/L
FAX Number: (218) 726-6254 — Calendar System: Semester
URL: www.d.umn.edu
Established: 1947 — Annual Undergrad Tuition & Fees (In-State): $13,576
Enrollment: 10,275 — Coed
Affiliation or Control: State — IRS Status: 501(c)3
Highest Offering: Doctorate
Accreditation: HLC, ART, CEA, MUS, PH, SP, SW

01 Chancellor ... Dr. Lendley C. BLACK
05 Int Exec Vice Chanc Acad Affairs ... Dr. Amy HIETAPELTO
32 Vice Chanc Stdnt Life/Dean Stdnts ... Dr. Lisa ERWIN
10 Int Vice Chanc Finance/Operations ... Ms. Sue BOSELL
06 Interim Registrar ... Mr. Tracey BOLEN
08 Director of Library ... Mr. Matt ROSENDAHL
37 Director Financial Aid ... Ms. Donna DAHLVANG
36 Director Career/Internship Svcs ... Ms. Jill KOLODZNE
13 Director Info Tech Sys/Services ... Dr. Jason DAVIS
84 AVC Enrollment Management ... Ms. Mary KEENAN
25 Senior Grant Administrator ... Ms. Claudia CARRANZA
41 Int Athletic Director ... Ms. Karen STROMME
15 AVC Human Resources ... Mr. Mark YURAN
07 Director Admissions ... Mr. Scott SCHULZ
18 Dir Facilities/Physical Plant ... Mr. John RASHID
29 Director Alumni Relations ... Mr. Matthew DUFFY
30 Chief Development Officer ... Ms. Tricia BUNTEN
114 Director of Budget and Analysis ... Mr. Greg SATHER
26 Chief Marketing & PR Officer-Duluth ... Ms. Lynne WILLIAMS
63 Int Dean School of Medicine ... Dr. Kevin DIEBEL
81 Dean College Science/Engineering ... Dr. Wendy REED
49 Dean Col Arts/Humanities & Soc Sci ... Dr. Jeremy YOUDE
53 Dean Col Education/Human Svc Prof ... Dr. Jill PINKNEY-PASTRANA
50 Int Dean School Business/Economics ... Dr. Praveen AGGARWAL
67 Dean School of Pharmacy ... Dr. Timothy STRATTON
58 AVC for Graduate Educ/Research ... Dr. Erik BROWN
19 Chief of Police ... Mr. Sean HULS
04 Executive Asst to the Chancellor ... Ms. Carlee WILLIAMS
104 Director Intl Programs & Services ... Mr. Karl MARKGRAF
39 Dir Resident Life/Student Housing ... Mr. Jeremy LEIFERMAN

University of Minnesota-Crookston (B)

2900 University Avenue, Crookston MN 56716-5001
County: Polk — FICE Identification: 004069
Unit ID: 174075
Telephone: (218) 281-6510 — Carnegie Class: Bac-Diverse
FAX Number: (218) 281-8040 — Calendar System: Semester
URL: www.crk.umn.edu
Established: 1965 — Annual Undergrad Tuition & Fees (In-State): $12,014
Enrollment: 2,530 — Coed
Affiliation or Control: State — IRS Status: 501(c)3
Highest Offering: Baccalaureate
Accreditation: HLC, ACBSP

01 Chancellor ... Dr. Mary HOLZ-CLAUSE
05 VC for Academic & Student Affairs ... Dr. John HOFFMAN
32 AVC Student Affairs/Enrollment ... Dr. Savala DEVOGE
18 Director Facilities/Operations ... Mr. Dave DANFORTH
10 Director of Finance/CFO ... Ms. Tricia SANDERS
15 Director Human Resources ... Mr. Griffin GILLESPIE
37 Director Financial Aid ... Ms. Kayla PAHLEN
26 Director of Communications ... Vacant
30 Dir Development/Alumni Relations ... Ms. Brandy CHAFFEE
08 Director Library ... Ms. Keri YOUNGSTRAND
36 Director Career/Counseling ... Mr. Tim MENARD
49 Head of Arts/Humanities/Soc Sci ... Dr. Kevin THOMPSON
47 Head Agriculture & Nat Resources ... Dr. Tony KERN
81 Head Math/Science/Technology ... Dr. Tony KERN
50 Head Business ... Dr. Mark HUGLEN
51 Director of Outreach ... Ms. Michelle CHRISTOPHERSON
06 Registrar ... Mr. Jason TANGQUIST
07 Director of Admissions/Enrollment ... Mr. Mike GRIFFIN
28 Dir Diversity/Equity/Belonging ... Mr. Christopher EHRHART
85 Dir of International Programs ... Ms. Sok Leng TAN

University of Minnesota-Morris (C)

600 E 4th Street, Morris MN 56267-2132
County: Stevens — FICE Identification: 002389
Unit ID: 174251
Telephone: (320) 589-6035 — Carnegie Class: Bac-A&S
FAX Number: (320) 589-6399 — Calendar System: Semester
URL: www.morris.umn.edu
Established: 1959 — Annual Undergrad Tuition & Fees (In-State): $13,578
Enrollment: 1,339 — Coed
Affiliation or Control: State — IRS Status: 501(c)3
Highest Offering: Baccalaureate
Accreditation: HLC

01 Acting Chancellor ... Dr. Janet S. ERICKSEN
05 Interim Vice Chanc Acad Affs/Dean ... Dr. Peh NG
32 Vice Chanc for Student Affairs ... Ms. Sandra OLSON-LOY
84 VC for Enroll Mgmt & Inst Effectiv ... Dr. Melissa BERT
10 Vice Chanc for Finance & Facilities ... Mr. Bryan HERRMANN
15 Vice Pres for Human Resources Admin ... Mr. Ken HORSTMAN
21 Finance Manager ... Ms. Melissa WROBLESKI
08 Head Librarian ... Ms. Angela VETSCH
06 Director of Registrar's Office ... Mr. Marcus MULLER
26 Director of Communications ... Vacant
29 Director of Alumni Relations ... Ms. Jennifer ZYCH HERRMANN
09 Director of Institutional Research ... Vacant
36 Assoc Director Career Services ... Ms. Cindy BOE
13 Information Technology Director ... Mr. Bill ZIMMERMAN
37 Director of Financial Aid ... Ms. Jill BEAUREGARD
93 Dir Multi Ethnic Student Program ... Ms. Tammy BERBERI
24 Director Educational Media ... Mr. Michael CIHAK
07 Director of Admissions ... Mr. Brian STUDEBAKER
108 Sr Dir Institutional Effectiveness ... Vacant
53 Chair of Education Division ... Dr. Michelle PAGE
81 Chair of Science/Math Division ... Dr. Rachel JOHNSON
79 Chair of Humanities Division ... Dr. Stacey ARONSON
83 Chair of Social Science Division ... Dr. Jennifer DEANE

University of Minnesota Rochester (D)

111 South Broadway, Suite 300, Rochester MN 55904
Telephone: (800) 947-0117 — Identification: 770316
Accreditation: &HLC, OT

University of Northwestern - St. Paul (E)

3003 Snelling Avenue N, Saint Paul MN 55113-1598
County: Ramsey — FICE Identification: 002371
Unit ID: 174491
Telephone: (651) 631-5100 — Carnegie Class: Masters/S
FAX Number: (651) 628-3339 — Calendar System: Semester
URL: www.unwsp.edu
Established: 1902 — Annual Undergrad Tuition & Fees: $33,200
Enrollment: 3,506 — Coed
Affiliation or Control: Independent Non-Profit — IRS Status: 501(c)3
Highest Offering: Master's
Accreditation: HLC, MUS, NURSE

01 President ... Dr. Corbin HOORNBEEK
05 Provost/Sr VP Academic Affairs ... Dr. Janet B. SOMMERS
88 Senior Vice President Media ... Mr. Jason R. SHARP
32 Vice Pres Student Life & HR ... Ms. Nina M. BARNES
111 Vice President for Advancement ... Dr. April L. MORETON
10 Vice President Finance/CFO ... Mr. John M. SOMMERVILLE
84 Vice President Enrollment Mgmt ... Mr. Erick P. KLEIN
18 Assoc VP Facility Ops & Planning ... Mr. Brian L. HUMPHRIES
15 Director of Human Resources ... Mrs. Pearl L. FERRIN
79 Dean College of Arts & Humanities ... Dr. Kirk D. MOSS
83 Dean College Behavioral/Natural Sci ... Vacant
107 Dean College Professional Studies ... Dr. Susan E. JOHNSON
58 Dean Graduate/Online & Adult Lrng ... Mr. Todd R. HARMENING
13 CIO ... Mr. Chad N. MILLER
21 Controller ... Ms. Kate M. MILLER
38 Director of Counseling Services ... Mr. Joseph M. BIANCARDI
121 Director of Academic Achievement ... Mrs. Ruth A. FRIES
37 Director of Financial Aid ... Ms. Hannah K. BLAHNIK
23 Director of Health Services ... Mrs. Alison L. PUTZ
08 Director of Library Services ... Mrs. Ruth A. MCGUIRE
19 Director of Public Safety ... Mr. Peter L. SOLA
28 Dir Intercultural Engage/Belonging ... Mr. Terrance J. ROLLERSON
96 Manager of Purchasing ... Ms. Cheryl A. GLASS
40 Manager Campus Store ... Mrs. Julienne N. ENTINGER
04 Executive Asst to President & Board ... Mrs. Ashley L. KINLEY
103 Dir of Career & Leadership Devel ... Ms. Kendra Q. DODD
06 Registrar ... Mr. Andy L. SIMPSON
112 Sr Dir Major Gifts/Planned Giving ... Mr. Dale R. ENGSKOV
29 Director Alumni & Parent Engagement ... Ms. Angel L. MOIN
07 Assoc VP Enrollment Management ... Mr. Bret M. HYDER
104 Director of Global Programs ... Ms. Kendra L. SUNDEEN
27 Associate VP of Marketing and Comm ... Dr. Greg L. JOHNSON
35 Dean of Students ... Mr. Jerod L. CORNELIUS
41 Athletic Director ... Dr. Mathew B. HILL
102 Dir NW Fund & Foundation Relations ... Mrs. April C. STENSGARD
117 Assoc VP of Business Services ... Mrs. Marla K. DENNISON
90 Sr Dir Project Mgmt/Academic Tech ... Mr. Joel T. JOHNSON
108 Dir Assessment/Acad Administration ... Mrs. Cheryl R. NORMAN
110 Director of Advancement Services ... Mr. Matt J. ANDERSON

† Formerly Northwestern College

University of Saint Thomas (F)

2115 Summit Avenue, Saint Paul MN 55105-1096
County: Ramsey — FICE Identification: 002345
Unit ID: 174914
Telephone: (651) 962-5000 — Carnegie Class: DU-Mod
FAX Number: (651) 962-6360 — Calendar System: 4/1/4
URL: www.stthomas.edu
Established: 1885 — Annual Undergrad Tuition & Fees: $47,383
Enrollment: 9,792 — Coed
Affiliation or Control: Roman Catholic — IRS Status: 501(c)3
Highest Offering: Doctorate
Accreditation: HLC, COPSY, IPSY, LAW, MUS, SW, THEOL

01 Interim President ... Mr. Rob VISCHER
05 EVP & Provost ... Dr. Eddy M. ROJAS
20 Rector/VP School of Divinity ... Fr. Joseph C. TAPHORN
32 VP For Student Affairs ... Dr. Karen M. LANGE
10 VP For Business Affairs/CFO ... Mr. Mark D. VANGSGARD
100 Chief of Staff ... Ms. Amy G. MCDONOUGH
13 VP Innovation & Technology/CIO ... Dr. Edmund U. CLARK
20 Vice Provost for Academic Affairs ... Dr. Wendy N. WYATT
84 VP Strategic Enrollment Mgmt ... Mr. Omar CORREA
21 AVP & Controller ... Ms. Katelyn L. SHEHU
18 VP for Facilities ... Mr. James M. BRUMMER
88 Executive Director Dining Services ... Dr. Pamela L. PETERSON
49 Int Dean College Arts & Sciences ... Dr. Mark D. STANSBURY-O'DONNELL
50 Dean Opus College of Business ... Dr. Laura DUNHAM
53 Int Dean School of Education ... Dr. Amy SMITH
76 VP/Dean Morrison Fam Col of Health ... Dr. MayKao Y. HANG
73 Academic Dean School of Divinity ... Dr. Christopher J. THOMPSON
61 Int Dean School of Law ... Mr. Joel A. NICHOLS
35 Dean of Students ... Ms. Linda M. BAUGHMAN
54 Dean School of Engineering ... Dr. Donald H. WEINKAUF
111 VP University Advancement ... Mr. Erik J. THURMAN
06 AVP of Student Data & Registrar ... Ms. Karen M. JULIAN
37 Director of Financial Aid ... Ms. Kristin A. ROACH
35 Director Campus Life ... Ms. Margaret D. CAHILL
29 AVP Careers/Alumni/Corporate ... Ms. Karen A. MCCOY
26 VP of Marketing/Insight/Comm/CMCO ... Ms. Kymm MARTINEZ
41 VP/Director of Athletics ... Dr. Phil J. ESTEN
40 Director Bookstore ... Mr. Stephen L. GRIFFIN
42 Director Campus Ministry ... Fr. Lawrence BLAKE
19 Director Public Safety ... Mr. Daniel J. MEUWISSEN
38 Exec Dir Center For Well Being ... Ms. Madonna K. MCDERMOTT
96 AVP Procurement Services ... Ms. Karen M. HARTHORN
88 Int Dean Dougherty Family College ... Dr. Buffy SMITH
88 VP For Mission ... Fr. Christopher J. COLLINS
15 VP & Chief Human Resources Officer ... Ms. Kathy R. ARNOLD
43 General Counsel ... Ms. Abigail CROUSE
125 President Emeritus ... Fr. Dennis J. DEASE
39 Director Residence Life ... Dr. Aaron M. MACKE
28 AVP For Inclusive Excellence ... Ms. Kha A. YANG
109 AVP For Auxiliary Services ... Mr. Mitchell KARSTENS

Walden University (G)

100 Washington Ave S, Suite 900, Minneapolis MN 55401
County: Hennepin — FICE Identification: 025042
Unit ID: 125231
Telephone: (866) 492-5336 — Carnegie Class: DU-Mod
FAX Number: (612) 338-5092 — Calendar System: Other
URL: www.waldenu.edu
Established: 1970 — Annual Undergrad Tuition & Fees: $12,180
Enrollment: 49,695 — Coed
Affiliation or Control: Proprietary — IRS Status: Proprietary
Highest Offering: Doctorate

Accreditation: HLC, ACBSP, CACREP, CAEP, NURSE, SW

01 President ... Mr. Michael BETZ
11 Sr VP Commercial Operations ... Mr. Jeff TOGNOLA
88 Chief Transform Ofcr & Sr VP SE ... Mr. Steven TOM
05 Provost and Chief Academic Officer ... Dr. Sue SUBOCZ
13 CIO ... Mr. Karthik VENKATESH
10 CFO ... Mr. Roger MCKINNEY
20 Vice Provost ... Dr. Savitri DIXON-SAXON
20 Vice Provost ... Dr. Andrea LINDELL
20 Vice Provost ... Dr. Marilyn POWELL
28 VP of Diversity/Equity & Inclusion ... Dr. Denise BOSTON
43 VP Asst General Counsel ... Ms. Staci SHELLEY
86 VP Government Relations ... Vacant
06 Registrar & Vice Provost ... Ms. Devon EDMUND
88 Assoc Vice Provost & Director ... Dr. Maleka INGRAM
72 Dean College of Management and Tech ... Dr. Karlyn BARILOVITS
83 Dean Sch of Counseling/Human Svcs ... Dr. Bill BARKLEY
53 Dean Sch Higher Ed/Ldrshp & Policy ... Dr. Kelly COSTNER
121 Dean Ctr for Academic Excellence ... Ms. Susanna DAVIDSEN
82 Dean Sch Public Pol Admin/Psych/CJ ... Dr. Shana GARRETT
88 Dean of Research/Exec Dir ... Dr. Laura LYNN
32 Dean Student Affairs/Alumni Engage ... Dr. Walter MCCOLLUM
70 Dean School of Social Work ... Dr. Lisa MOON
88 Dean Prod Strategy/Innov & Design ... Ms. Kathy STRANG
51 Dean Learning Pathways & SLL ... Dr. Barry SUGARMAN
76 Dean School of Health Sciences ... Dr. Jorg WESTERMANN
66 Dean Sch of Nursing ... Dr. George ZANGARO
53 Assoc Dean Sch Educ/Prof License ... Dr. Steve CANIPE
97 Assoc Dean Ctr for Gen Ed ... Dr. Sara MAKRIS
88 Assoc Dean Ctr for Faculty Excel ... Dr. Annie MORGAN
50 Assoc Dean Educ/Mgmt & Tech ... Ms. Joanna PATTERSON
58 Assoc Dean Sch High Educ/Leadership ... Dr. Pat THURMOND
76 Assoc Dean Health/SBS/Nursing ... Ms. Kristi TRAPP
15 Exec Dir of Human Resources ... Ms. Ivanie BRONSON
106 Exec Dir Ctr Competency-Based Educ ... Dr. Steven DANVER
46 Exec Dir Inst Research/Assessment ... Dr. Jim LENIO
107 Exec Dir Student Experiential Learn ... Dr. Mary RAEKER-REBEK
07 Director of Admissions ... Vacant
113 Bursar ... Ms. Linda ANTHONY
121 Sr Director Academic Advising ... Ms. Mandy OLSEN
08 Director of Library Services ... Ms. Michelle HAJDER
37 Director of Financial Aid ... Ms. Melvina JOHNSON
108 Dir of University Assessment ... Dr. Shari JORISSEN
26 Director of External Relations ... Ms. Sabrina RAM
88 Director Ctr for Social Change ... Dr. William SCHULZ

White Earth Tribal and Community College (A)

PO Box 478, Mahnomen MN 56557-0478
County: Mahnomen FICE Identification: 039214
Unit ID: 434751
Telephone: (218) 935-0417 Carnegie Class: Tribal
FAX Number: (218) 936-5814 Calendar System: Semester
URL: www.wetcc.edu
Established: 1997 Annual Undergrad Tuition & Fees: $4,568
Enrollment: 141 Coed
Affiliation or Control: Tribal Control IRS Status: 501(c)3
Highest Offering: Associate Degree
Accreditation: HLC

01 President ... Anna SHEPPARD
05 Provost ... Laura DRISCOLL
10 Finance Director ... Muriel STEWART
20 Academic Dean ... Frank OAKGROVE
32 Dean of Student Services ... Joan LAVOY
56 Community Extension Director ... Lisa BRUNNER
07 Admissions Coordinator ... Amber FOX
06 Registrar ... Lorraine LUFKINS
37 Financial Aid Coordinator ... Michelle WARREN
15 Human Resources Technician ... Jon KRULICH
18 Facilities Manager ... Paul PEMBERTON
13 IT Coordinator ... Jacob MCARTHUR
19 Security Guard ... Kurt HALVORSON
04 Admin Assistant to the President ... Indosa MONTOYA
103 Customized Educ Coordinator ... Bridget GUIZA
25 Grant Writer ... Virginia ANDERSON

MISSISSIPPI

Alcorn State University (B)

1000 ASU Drive, #359, Lorman MS 39096-7500
County: Claiborne FICE Identification: 002396
Unit ID: 175342
Telephone: (601) 877-6100 Carnegie Class: Masters/S
FAX Number: (601) 877-2975 Calendar System: Semester
URL: www.alcorn.edu
Established: 1871 Annual Undergrad Tuition & Fees (In-State): $7,290
Enrollment: 3,230 Coed
Affiliation or Control: State IRS Status: 501(c)3
Highest Offering: Doctorate
Accreditation: SC, ACBSP, ADNUR, CAEP, MUS, NAIT, NUR, SW

01 President ... Dr. Felecia M. NAVE
05 Provost/Sr VP for Academic Affairs ... Dr. Ontario S. WOODEN
04 Exec Asst to the President ... Ms. Karen R. SHEDRICK
116 Director of Internal Audit ... Ms. Tomeka L. MOORE
46 Chief Research Officer ... Dr. Keith MCGEE
10 SVP Finance/Admin Svcs/Opers/CFO ... Dr. Cornelius WOOTEN
32 VP for Student Affs & Enroll Mgmt ... Dr. Tracy M. COOK
111 VP Institutional Advancement ... Mr. Marcus D. WARD
26 VP Marketing/Communications ... Mr. Larry ORMAN
20 Assoc Prov Undergrad Educ & SS ... Dr. Joyce BUCKNER-BROWN
09 Assoc Prov Rsrch/Innov & Grad Educ ... Dr. Keith MCGEE
35 AVP Stdnt Dev/Dean of Students ... Dr. Natasha L. HUTSON
18 Assoc VP for Facilities Management ... Mr. Robert WATTS
21 Assoc VP for Finance ... Ms. Dana A. BROWN
27 Assoc VP Mktg/Comm & Senior Writer ... Ms. Maxine R. GREENLEAF
84 Asst VP for Enrollment Management ... Ms. Roslyn M. WHITE
39 Interim Director of Residence Life ... Ms. Yadonna WATTS
28 Dir of Educational Equity/Inclusion ... Mrs. Lljuna WEIR
88 Exec Dir of Strategic Acad Init ... Dr. Doris J. WARD
96 Purchasing Agent ... Ms. Mertha V. GEORGE
07 Director of Admissions/Recruiting ... Mr. Courtney SMITH
37 Director of Financial Aid ... Mrs. Juanita RUSSELL-EDWARDS
06 Registrar ... Dr. Tracee SMITH
08 Dean University Libraries ... Dr. Blanche SANDERS
47 Dean School of Agriculture ... Dr. Edmund BUCKNER
49 Dean School of Arts & Science ... Dr. Babu P. PATLOLLA
50 Interim Dean School of Business ... Dr. Babu GEORGE
53 Interim Dean School of Education ... Dr. Malinda BUTLER
66 Interim Dean School of Nursing ... Dr. Shirley EVERS-MANLY
89 Dean University College ... Dr. Valerie THOMPSON
13 Interim CIO Ctr for Info Tech Svcs ... Ms. Donna HAYDEN
15 AVP for Human Resources & Payroll ... Dr. Wanda FLEMING
88 Exec Dir SW MS Ctr Culture & Lrng ... Ms. Teresa BUSBY
36 Director Career Services ... Dr. Carolyn DAVIS
23 Director of Health & Disab Services ... Ms. Dorothy G. JACKSON-DAVIS
41 Director of Athletics ... Mr. Raynoid DEDEAUX
40 Follett Book Store ... Ms. Roshae LACEY
38 Director of Counseling & Testing ... Dr. Barbara MARTIN
108 Dir Institutional Rsrch/Assessment ... Dr. LaDonna EANOCHS
19 Chief of Campus Police ... Mr. Douglas STEWART
88 General Manager Sodexo ... Vacant
102 Exec Dir ASU Foundation ... Mr. Marcus D. WARD
88 Exec Dir Ofc of Univ Compliance ... Mr. Alfred GALTNEY
92 Director of Honors Program ... Dr. C. Edwards RHODES, II
25 Grants/Contract Administrator ... Mrs. Sallie MCMILLIAN
104 Director of International Affairs ... Dr. Dovi ALIPOE
88 Asst Athletic Dir for Compliance ... Mr. Jason POMPEY
29 Director Alumni Affairs ... Mrs. Kimberly M. MYLES
44 Director Annual Giving ... Mr. Marcus D. WARD

Belhaven University (C)

1500 Peachtree Street, Jackson MS 39202-1798
County: Hinds FICE Identification: 002397
Unit ID: 175421
Telephone: (601) 968-5940 Carnegie Class: DU-Mod
FAX Number: (601) 968-9998 Calendar System: Semester
URL: www.belhaven.edu
Established: 1883 Annual Undergrad Tuition & Fees: $27,025
Enrollment: 4,999 Coed
Affiliation or Control: Presbyterian Church (U.S.A.) IRS Status: 501(c)3
Highest Offering: Doctorate
Accreditation: SC, ART, DANCE, IACBE, MUS, NURSE, SW, THEA

01 President ... Dr. Roger PARROTT
05 Provost/Vice Pres Academic Affairs ... Dr. Bradford SMITH
58 VP for Adult/Graduate & Online Educ ... Dr. Audrey KELLEHER
84 VP of Enrollment and Marketing ... Mr. Kevin RUSSELL
10 CFO & VP Business Affairs ... Vacant
111 VP for University Advancement ... Mr. Jeff RICKLES
41 VP of Athletics ... Mr. Scott LITTLE
32 VP of Student Development ... Dr. Shelley SMITH
11 Asst VP Campus Operations ... Mr. David POTVIN
84 Assoc VP for Enrollment ... Mrs. Suzanne SULLIVAN
51 AVP for Adult/Graduate/Online ... Dr. Rick UPCHURCH
13 AVP of IT and Systems Admin ... Mrs. Stephanie STEELMAN
106 Dean of Adult/Grad/Online Studies ... Dr. Kim PREISMEYER
50 Dean of the School of Business ... Dr. Chip MASON
53 Dean of the School of Education ... Dr. David HAND
66 Dean of the School of Nursing ... Dr. Amy REX SMITH
79 Dean of Worldview Studies ... Dr. Tracy FORD
20 Dean of Curriculum ... Dr. Ken ELLIOTT
07 Assoc Director of Admission ... Mr. Michael HAWKINS
06 Registrar ... Ms. Lea Ann BETHANY
26 Director of University Relations ... Mr. Bryant BUTLER
13 Director Information Technology ... Mr. Bo MILLER
19 Director of Security ... Mr. David POTVIN
09 Dir Institutional Research ... Mr. Aaron PRITCHETT
08 Director of Libraries ... Mr. Chris CULLNANE, II
15 Director of Human Resources ... Mrs. Virginia HENDERSON
37 Director of Financial Services ... Mrs. Debbi BRASWELL
121 Director of Student Care ... Ms. Rebecca ROMINE
110 Director of Advancement/Alumni ... Mr. Frank LAWS
04 Admin Assistant to the President ... Mrs. Lea PARTRIDGE
18 Chf Facilities/Physical Plant Ofcr ... Mr. Wayne GREEN
121 Assoc VP of Academic Support ... Dr. Vicki WOLFE

Blue Mountain College (D)

201 W Main Street, PO Box 160,
Blue Mountain MS 38610-0160
County: Tippah FICE Identification: 002398
Unit ID: 175430
Telephone: (662) 685-4771 Carnegie Class: Bac-Diverse
FAX Number: (662) 685-4776 Calendar System: Semester
URL: www.bmc.edu
Established: 1873 Annual Undergrad Tuition & Fees: $15,800
Enrollment: 952 Coed
Affiliation or Control: Southern Baptist IRS Status: 501(c)3
Highest Offering: Master's
Accreditation: SC

01 President ... Dr. Barbara C. MCMILLIN
04 Admin Assistant to the President ... Mrs. Pam BOWMAN
05 Provost and Vice President ... Dr. Sharon B. ENZOR
53 Dean of Education ... Dr. Jenetta WADDELL
50 Dean of Business ... Dr. Anthony BULLARD
09 Director of Institutional Research ... Mr. Robert E. RUCKER
08 Director of Library Services ... Ms. Hannah JOHNSON
06 Registrar ... Mrs. Sheila D. FREEMAN
121 Director Teaching & Learning Center ... Dr. Delise TEAGUE
32 Dean of Students ... Mr. Philip RITCHEY
07 Vice Pres for Enrollment Services ... Mr. Lynn GIBSON
30 VP Community Rels/Dir BMC Found ... Vacant
37 Director of Financial Aid ... Mrs. Beverly HICKEY
10 Chief Financial Officer ... Mr. Steve ROBBINS
11 Chief Operating Officer ... Mrs. Joyce PETERS
40 Campus Store Manager ... Mrs. Dot M. LOCKE
41 Athletic Director ... Mr. Will LOWREY
42 Director Baptist Student Union ... Mrs. Tracy S. MOSER
13 Director of Information Services ... Mr. Kevin BAREFIELD
26 Dir of PR/Publications ... Ms. Emma L. AINSWORTH
29 Director of Alumni Relations ... Mrs. Kayce BRAGG
88 Director of Church Relations ... Dr. Ronald MEEKS

Coahoma Community College (E)

3240 Friars Point Road, Clarksdale MS 38614-9700
County: Coahoma FICE Identification: 002401
Unit ID: 175519
Telephone: (662) 627-2571 Carnegie Class: Assoc/HVT-High Trad
FAX Number: (662) 627-9451 Calendar System: Semester
URL: www.coahomacc.edu
Established: 1949 Annual Undergrad Tuition & Fees (In-District): $3,003
Enrollment: 1,612 Coed
Affiliation or Control: State/Local IRS Status: 501(c)3
Highest Offering: Associate Degree
Accreditation: SC, ADNUR, COARC, EMT, POLYT

01 President ... Dr. Valmadge T. TOWNER
05 Dean of Academics ... Dr. Rolanda BROWN
10 Chief Financial Officer ... Ms. Deborah VALENTINE
32 Director of Student Services ... Mrs. Karen DONE
09 Dir Inst Effectiveness/SACS Liaison ... Mrs. Margaret DIXON
30 Coordinator for Federal Programs ... Mrs. Marilyn STARKS
75 Dean of Career/Technical Education ... Dr. Larry WEBSTER
06 Registrar ... Dr. Nakisha WATTS
08 Dir Library/Instructional Resources ... Mrs. Rose LOCKETT
13 Director Computer Services ... Mr. Rob STALDER
19 Director of Safety ... Mr. Charles JONES
26 Chief Communication Officer ... Mr. Marriel HARDY
37 Director of Financial Aid ... Mr. Joseph MCKEE
15 Director of Employee Services ... Mr. Michael HOUSTON
51 Director of Educational Outreach ... Mr. William WADE
29 Director Alumni Relations ... Vacant
36 Director Student Placement ... Mrs. Trina COX
38 Coordinator of Student Counseling ... Dr. Renee HALL
04 Administrative Asst to President ... Ms. Yolanda D. MILLER
100 Chief of Staff ... Mr. Jerone SHAW
103 Dir Workforce/Career Development ... Mr. Steven JOSSELL
105 Director Web Services ... Mr. Ezra HOWARD
106 Online Education/E-learning Coord ... Ms. Monica MOORE JOHNSON
41 Interim Athletic Director ... Mr. Reggie HANKERSON

Concorde Career College (F)

7900 Airways Boulevard, Suite 103, Southaven MS 38671
Telephone: (662) 429-9909 Identification: 770540
Accreditation: COE

† Branch campus of Concorde Career College, Memphis, TN

Copiah-Lincoln Community College (G)

PO Box 649, Wesson MS 39191-0649
County: Copiah FICE Identification: 002402
Unit ID: 175573
Telephone: (601) 643-5101 Carnegie Class: Assoc/MT-VT-High Trad
FAX Number: (601) 643-8212 Calendar System: Semester
URL: www.colin.edu
Established: 1928 Annual Undergrad Tuition & Fees (In-State): $3,180
Enrollment: 2,907 Coed
Affiliation or Control: State IRS Status: 501(c)3
Highest Offering: Associate Degree
Accreditation: SC, ADNUR, COARC, MLTAD, RAD

01 President ... Dr. Jane HULON SIMS
04 Assistant to the President ... Mrs. Amber N. BRITT
10 Vice President Business Affairs ... Mr. Richard BAKER
03 Executive Vice Presdident ... Dr. Dewayne MIDDLETON
12 Vice Pres of the Natchez Campus ... Dr. Sandra BARNES
12 Vice President of the Wesson Campus ... Mrs. Jackie MARTIN
05 Dean of Academic Instructions ... Dr. Stephanie DUGUID
32 Dir of Enrollment/Student Services ... Mrs. Jordan STEPHENS
75 Dean Career & Technical Educ ... Mr. Brent DUGUID
31 Director of Community Programs ... Dr. Brenda ORR
41 Athletic Dir/Asst Dean of Students ... Mr. Bryan NOBILE
37 Director Student Financial Aid ... Mrs. Leslie SMITH

40 Director Bookstore Mr. Charles HART
08 Director of Library Resources Vacant
26 Director of Public Relations Mrs. Natalie DAVIS
13 Information Systems Specialist Ms. Deemie LETCHWORTH
19 Director of Security Mr. Thomas ROBERTS
09 Dir Inst Effectiv/Facilities Plng Mrs. Tiffany PERRYMAN
35 Dean of Students Mrs. Samantha SPEEG
102 Director of Foundation & Alumni Svc Mrs. Angela FURR
18 Director of Physical Plant Mr. Daniel CASE
66 Director of Assoc Degree Nursing Ms. Mary Ann FLINT
06 Student Records Manager Mrs. Gay LANGHAM
57 Chair Fine Arts Division Ms. Juanita PROFFITT
50 Chair Business Division Ms. Dana HALE
68 Chair Physical Education Division Ms. Dana HALE
77 Chair Math/Computer Science Div Mr. Eddie BRITT
79 Chair Humanities Division Mrs. Mary WARREN
82 Chair Social Science Division Mr. Keith STOVALL
81 Chair Science Division Dr. Kevin MCKONE
96 Director of Purchasing Mrs. Erin LIKENS
106 Director of E-learning Dr. Amanda HOOD
108 QEP Director Vacant
15 Human Resources Director Ms. Julia PARKER
39 Director Student Housing Mr. Allen KENT
91 Director of Technology/Info Systems Mr. James P. MCINNIS

Delta State University (A)

1003 W. Sunflower Rd., Cleveland MS 38733
County: Bolivar FICE Identification: 002403
Unit ID: 175616
Telephone: (662) 846-3000 Carnegie Class: Masters/L
FAX Number: (662) 846-4014 Calendar System: Semester
URL: www.deltastate.edu
Established: 1924 Annual Undergrad Tuition & Fees (In-State): $8,121
Enrollment: 2,999 Coed
Affiliation or Control: State IRS Status: 501(c)3
Highest Offering: Doctorate
Accreditation: SC, AAB, AAFCS, ACBSP, ART, CACREP, CAEP, DIETC, MUS, NURSE, SW

01 Interim President Dr. Everett E. CASTON
05 Provost/VP Academic Affairs Dr. Andy NOVOBILSKI
10 Vice President for Finance Mr. James RUTLEDGE
32 Vice President for Student Affairs Dr. Eddie LOVIN
111 Vice Pres Univ Advance & Ext Rels Mr. Rick MUNROE
100 Chief of Staff/VP Univ Relations Dr. Michelle A. ROBERTS
20 Associate Provost Dr. Beverly MOON
15 Director of Human Resources Ms. Lisa GIGER
41 Director of Athletics Mr. Mike KINNISON
49 Dean College of Arts & Sciences Dr. Ellen GREEN
50 Dean College of Business Dr. Billy MOORE
53 Dean College of Education Dr. Leslie GRIFFIN
66 Dean School of Nursing Dr. Vicki L. BINGHAM
08 Dean Library Services Mr. Jeff SLAGELL
58 Dean Graduate/Continuing Studies Dr. James GERALD
06 Registrar Ms. Emily C. DABNEY
13 Chief Information Officer Mr. Edwin CRAFT
21 Director of Financial Reporting Mr. Kelvin DAVIS
116 Internal Auditor Vacant
88 Executive Director BPAC Ms. Laura HOWELL
121 Executive Director Student Success Dr. Christy RIDDLE
37 Dir Student Financial Assistance Dr. Megan SMITH
38 Director Counsel/Stdnt Health Svcs Ms. Kashanta JACKSON
36 Director Career Services Ms. Nakikke JOHNSON
19 Director of Police Dept Mr. Jeffrey JOHNS
39 Director of Housing Ms. Julie JACKSON
26 Director of Media Relations Ms. Brittany DAVIS
25 Director Institutional Grants Ms. Heather MILLER
113 Director Student Business Svcs Mr. Mikhail COLLINS
106 Dir of Clinical Exp/Licensing/Acct Mrs. Anjanette POWERS
31 Director Delta Center Culture Learn Dr. Rolando HERTS
18 Director of Facilities Mgmt Mr. Gerald FINLEY
40 Manager of Bookstore Mr. James SOREY
109 Director of Food Services Vacant
07 Director of Admissions Vacant
09 Director of Institutional Research Ms. Chrisa MANSELL
30 Director of Development Dr. Lori SPENCER

East Central Community College (B)

PO Box 129, Decatur MS 39327-0129
County: Newton FICE Identification: 002404
Unit ID: 175643
Telephone: (601) 635-2111 Carnegie Class: Assoc/MT-VT-High Trad
FAX Number: (601) 635-4011 Calendar System: Semester
URL: www.eccc.edu
Established: 1928 Annual Undergrad Tuition & Fees (In-District): $3,150
Enrollment: 2,388 Coed
Affiliation or Control: Local IRS Status: 501(c)3
Highest Offering: Associate Degree
Accreditation: SC, ADNUR, SURGT

01 President Dr. Brent GREGORY
10 Vice Pres for Business Operations Mr. Mickey VANCE
03 Executive Vice President Mr. David CASE
26 VP for Public Information Mr. Bill WAGNON
106 Director of eLearning Education Ms. Alicia BEASLEY
51 Director of Adult Education/HSE Mrs. Alfreda THOMPSON
103 Director of Career & Tech Education Mr. Cody SPENCE
07 Director Admissions and Records Ms. Bridgett HITT
15 Director of Human Resources Mrs. Julie ROWZEE
18 Dir Facilities Planning & Project Mr. Artie FOREMAN
13 Dean of Information Technology Mr. Derek PACE
14 Assoc Dir Information Technology Mrs. Regena BOYKIN
37 Director of Financial Aid Mrs. Brenda B. CARSON
19 Chief of Police Mr. John HARRIS
57 Chairperson Fine Arts Division Mr. Chas EVANS
81 Chair Mathematics/Computer Science Ms. Cathryn MAY
83 Chairperson Social Sciences Mrs. Wanda HURLEY
76 Dean of Healthcare Education Dr. Donna EVERETT
81 Chairperson Science Division Mr. Curt SKIPPER
60 Chairperson Communications/ Language Mrs. Carol SHACKELFORD
04 Administrative Asst to President Mrs. Carol H. GERMANY
41 Director of Athletics Mr. Paul NIXON
32 Dean of Student Services Mr. James MILLER
84 Exec Dir for Enrollment Management Dr. Marie ROBERTS
102 Executive Director of Foundation Dr. Stacey HOLLINGSWORTH

East Mississippi Community College (C)

PO Box 158, Scooba MS 39358-0158
County: Kemper FICE Identification: 002405
Unit ID: 175652
Telephone: (662) 476-5000 Carnegie Class: Assoc/HVT-High Trad
FAX Number: (662) 476-5058 Calendar System: Semester
URL: www.eastms.edu
Established: 1927 Annual Undergrad Tuition & Fees (In-District): $3,740
Enrollment: 3,392 Coed
Affiliation or Control: State/Local IRS Status: Exempt
Highest Offering: Associate Degree
Accreditation: SC, ADNUR, FUSER, SURGT

01 President Dr. Scott ALSOBROOKS
05 VP of Instruction Dr. James RUSH
11 VP of Operations Dr. Paul MILLER
10 Chief Financial Officer Ms. Tammie HOLMES
103 Exec Dir of Cmty & Workforce Dev Dr. David CAMPBELL
84 VP for Enrollment Management Dr. Melanie SANDERS
04 Administrative Asst to President Ms. Nakishia WOODS
09 Dean of IR/Eff Grants/Special Pgms Mrs. Susan BAIRD
13 Director of Info Technology Mr. Michael TVARKUNAS
18 Director of Physical Plant Mr. Kyle YOUNGER
37 Director of Financial Aid Mr. Garry JONES
06 Registrar Mrs. Tammy PRATHER
88 Dir of Recruiting/GT Recruiter Mrs. Tawana BAUER
07 Director of Admissions Ms. Danielle HOPSON
40 Bookstore Manager Mrs. Jaimie CRAIG
26 Director of External Affairs Vacant
76 Dir Nurs Pgms/Assoc Dean Hlth Svcs Mrs. Jamonicia JOHNSON
32 Dean of Scooba Campus/Col Advance Mr. Tony MONTGOMERY
32 Dean of Students GT Campus Dr. Melanie SANDERS
41 Dean of Students/Athletic Director Ms. Sharon THOMPSON
19 Chief of Police Mr. Archer SALLIS
15 Director Human Resources Ms. Theresa HARPOLE
111 Exec Dir of CLG Advance/Athletics Vacant
20 Dean of Instruction GT Dr. Michael BUSBY
20 Dean of Instruction SC Dr. Jairus JOHNSON
106 Associate Dean of E-learning Mrs. Chris SQUARE
124 Dist Dir Advise/Retent/Stdnt Succ Dr. Nikita ASHFORTH-ASHWORTH
29 Exec Director Alumni Affairs Mrs. Gina COTTON
91 Director Administrative Computing Mr. Elanthus WICKS
39 Dir Resident Life/Student Housing Ms. Lapari MORANT

Hinds Community College (D)

PO Box 1100, Raymond MS 39154-1100
County: Hinds FICE Identification: 002407
Unit ID: 175786
Telephone: (601) 857-5261 Carnegie Class: Assoc/HVT-Mix Trad/Non
FAX Number: (601) 857-3518 Calendar System: Semester
URL: www.hindscc.edu
Established: 1917 Annual Undergrad Tuition & Fees (In-District): $3,450
Enrollment: 11,181 Coed
Affiliation or Control: State/Local IRS Status: 501(c)3
Highest Offering: Associate Degree
Accreditation: SC, ADNUR, CAHIIM, COARC, DA, DMS, EMT, MLTAD, PTAA, RAD, SURGT

01 President Dr. Stephen VACIK
10 VP Finance & Administration Mr. Vic PARKER
13 VP Planning/Effectiveness/Tech Dr. Keri COLE
05 VP of Instruction/Career & Tech Edu Ms. Sherry FRANKLIN
20 Academic Dean Mr. Gary FOX
20 Academic Dean Ms. Melissa K. BUIE
32 VP Student Services Dr. Jenny MILES
103 AVP Workforce/Community Development Mr. David G. CREEL
18 VP Facilities & Auxiliary Services Mr. Marvin MOAK
15 VP for Human Resources Ms. Andrea JANOUSH
100 Chief of Staff Mrs. Renee COTTON
84 Director Enrollment Services Ms. Kathryn B. COLE
08 Dean of Learning Resources Ms. Mary Beth APPLIN
76 Dean of Health Science NAHC Ms. Katharine ELLIOTT
37 Dir of Financial Aid & Veterans Svc Mrs. Deena MCINNIS
38 Dean Advisement/CT Counseling Ms. Jennifer SCOTT-GILMORE
41 Athletic Director Mr. Nathan WERREMEYER
09 Dir of Inst Research/Effectiveness Dr. Roddrick JONES
96 Director of Procurement Mr. Samuel LEMONIS
04 Administrative Assistant Ms. Jackie JACKSON
106 Dean of ELearning Mrs. Katherine PUCKETT
29 Alumni Coordinator Ms. Sydney LOVE
35 AVP Student Svcs/Dean of Students Mr. Deandre HOUSE
07 AVP Student Svcs/Admissions/Record Dr. Stephanie HUDSON
102 Executive Director Foundation Mr. Matthew W. JONES
19 Director Campus Safety Mr. Britt THOMAS
86 Exec Dir Legislative Affairs Dr. Ginger ROBBINS
88 VP Academic/Transfer Pgm Dr. Thomas WARE

Holmes Community College (E)

Hill Street, PO Box 369, Goodman MS 39079-0369
County: Holmes FICE Identification: 002408
Unit ID: 175810
Telephone: (662) 472-2312 Carnegie Class: Assoc/HVT-Mix Trad/Non
FAX Number: (662) 472-9152 Calendar System: Semester
URL: www.holmescc.edu
Established: 1925 Annual Undergrad Tuition & Fees (In-District): $3,410
Enrollment: 5,409 Coed
Affiliation or Control: Local IRS Status: 501(c)3
Highest Offering: Associate Degree
Accreditation: SC, ADNUR, EMT, OTA, PTAA, SURGT

01 President Dr. Jim HAFFEY
03 Executive Vice President Mr. Sonny SPARKS
09 VP Inst Research & Student Affairs Dr. Lindy MCCAIN
05 Vice Pres for Academic Programs Dr. Jenny B. JONES
12 Vice President Ridgeland Campus Dr. Don BURNHAM
12 Vice President Grenada Center Dr. Michelle BURNEY
72 Vice President CareerTech Education Dr. Amy WHITTINGTON
10 Vice Pres of Financial Services Mr. Sonny SPARKS
08 Librarian Mr. James THOMPSON
26 Director of Communications & Assoc Mr. Steve DIFFEY
103 Vice President of Workforce Develop Dr. Mike BLANKENSHIP
37 Director Student Financial Aid Mr. Clate HOLLEMAN
15 Director Personnel Services Ms. Julia BROWN
09 Director of Institutional Research Dr. Stephanie DIFFEY
18 Chief Facilities/Physical Plant Vacant
96 Director of Purchasing Mrs. Rosemary SELF
29 Director Alumni Relations Mrs. Katherine ELLARD
21 Business Manager Mr. Matt SURRELL
04 Exec Assistant to the President Mrs. Angie S. BURRELL
105 Director Marketing/Recruiting Mrs. Bronwyn MARTIN
106 Vice President Online Ed/E-learning Mrs. Tish STEWART
108 Director Institutional Research Dr. Stephanie DIFFEY
13 Director of Information Technology Mr. Kevin BAKER
19 Director of Public Safety Mr. Chris DILL
38 Student Academic Counselor Mrs. Simone MILLER
39 Dir Resident Life/Student Housing Mr. Terry FANCHER
41 Vice Pres/Director of Athletics Mr. Andy WOOD
50 VP/Academic Dean-Goodman Dr. Jenny BAILEY-JONES
53 Academic Dean-Ridgeland Dr. Tonya LAWRENCE

Itawamba Community College (F)

602 W Hill Street, Fulton MS 38843-1022
County: Itawamba FICE Identification: 002409
Unit ID: 175829
Telephone: (662) 862-8000 Carnegie Class: Assoc/MT-VT-High Trad
FAX Number: (662) 862-8036 Calendar System: Semester
URL: www.iccms.edu
Established: 1948 Annual Undergrad Tuition & Fees (In-District): $3,160
Enrollment: 4,696 Coed
Affiliation or Control: Local IRS Status: 501(c)3
Highest Offering: Associate Degree
Accreditation: SC, ADNUR, CAHIIM, COARC, EMT, OTA, PTAA, RAD, SURGT

01 President Mr. Jay S. ALLEN
100 Chief of Staff Mr. Tyler CAMP
05 Vice President of Instruction Dr. Michelle SUMEREL
10 VP Business Services Ms. Sandi SOUTH
32 VP Student Services Dr. Brad BOGGS
26 Dir Marketing/Comm Engagement Ms. Nina STROTHER
37 Director of Financial Aid Mr. Terry BLAND
24 Director of Library Ms. Holly GRAY
51 Director of Adult & Continuing Educ Mr. Josh GAMMILL
41 Athletic Director Mr. Chad CASE
111 Director of Advancement Mr. Michael UPTON
18 Director of Physical Plant Mr. John Wayne HARRIS
09 Director of Institutional Research Mrs. Elizabeth EDWARDS
15 VP of Human Resources/Admin Mr. Timothy C. SENTER
106 Dean of eLearning Ms. Denise GILLESPIE
76 Dean of Health Sciences Ms. Tonya VAUGHN
75 Dean of Career & Technical Educ Mr. Barry EMISON
39 Coordinator of Student Housing Ms. Kaitlyn STANFIELD
06 Registrar/Dir of Admissions Ms. Rachel STEELE
04 Admin Assistant to the President Ms. Brandy WHITE
19 Chief of Police Mr. Jason DICKINSON

Jackson State University (G)

1400 J. R. Lynch Street, Jackson MS 39217
County: Hinds FICE Identification: 002410
Unit ID: 175856
Telephone: (601) 979-2121 Carnegie Class: DU-Higher
FAX Number: (601) 979-2358 Calendar System: Semester
URL: www.jsums.edu
Established: 1877 Annual Undergrad Tuition & Fees (In-State): $8,445
Enrollment: 6,921 Coed
Affiliation or Control: State IRS Status: 501(c)3
Highest Offering: Doctorate
Accreditation: SC, ART, CACREP, CAEPN, CLPSY, MUS, NAIT, PH, PLNG, SP, SPAA, SW

01 President Mr. Thomas HUDSON

05	Provost/Senior VP Academic Affairs	Dr. Alisa MOSLEY
100	Vice President & Chief of Staff	Dr. Debra MAYS-JACKSON
10	SVP Finance/Administration	Dr. Arlitha WILLIAMS-HARMON
111	VP Institutional Advancement	Ms. Veronica M. COHEN
41	VP & Director of Athletics	Mr. Ashley ROBINSON
46	VP Research & Economic Dev	Dr. Joseph A. WHITTAKER
84	Assoc VP Enrollment Management	Vacant
32	VP for Student Life	Dr. Susan E. POWELL
114	Exec Dir Budget & Fin Analysis	Mrs. Tammiko HARRISON
21	Exec Dir Actg/Fin Rpts/Fiscal Comm	Mrs. Tracy STAPLETON
13	Chief Information Officer	Dr. Deborah DENT
15	Executive Director Human Resources	Mrs. Robin SPANN-PACK
43	General Counsel	Mr. Edward WATSON
50	Dean College of Business	Dr. Fidelis M. IKEM
53	Int Dean College Educ/Human Devel	Dr. Tracy HARRIS
49	Dean College of Liberal Arts	Dr. K. B TURNER
72	Dean College of Sci/Engr/Tech	Dr. Wilbur WALTERS
69	Dean College of Health Sciences	Dr. Girmay BERHIE
58	Dean Division of Graduate Studies	Dr. Preselfannie MCDANIELS
106	Executive Director JSU Online	Ms. Andrea JONES
08	Int Dean Div of Library & Info Res	Dr. Locord WILSON
97	Interim Dean University College	Dr. Shirley BURNETT
92	Assoc Dean Div of Honors College	Dr. Loria BROWN GORDAN
88	Assoc VP/Director of Title III	Dr. Mitchell SHEARS
14	Assoc VP Information Tech	Dr. Michael ROBINSON
35	AVP/Dean of Student Life	Dr. Laquala C. DIXON
51	Director of Lifelong Learning	Dr. Carlos WILSON
110	Asst VP Institutional Advancement	Mrs. Gwen CAPLES
116	Internal Auditor	Mr. Christopher THOMAS
85	Director JSU Global	Dr. Huie J. CUNNINGHAM
29	Dir Alumni/Constituency Relations	Mr. David HOWARD
18	Exec Dir for Business	Mr. Michael BOLDEN
88	Associate University Physician	Dr. Robert SMITH
37	Director of Financial Aid	Mr. Ozie RATCLIFF
39	Exec Director Housing & Residence	Vacant
06	Registrar	Dr. Harrison P. JOHNSON
23	Director of Health Center Services	Dr. Samuel JONES
88	Director MS Urban Research Ctr	Dr. Sam MOZEE, JR.
19	Director Public Safety	Mr. Thomas ALBRIGHT
26	Chief Communications Officer	Ms. Alonda THOMAS
22	Assistant Dir of Disability Service	Dr. Aaron RICHARDSON
40	Manager Bookstore	Ms. Dyonne CONNER
09	AVP Inst Research/Planning/Effect	Dr. La Toya HART
36	Executive Director Career Services	Ms. Lashanda JORDAN
38	Director Student Counseling	Ms. Shanice WHITE
21	Executive Director Business Office	Ms. Jewell HARRIS
22	Dir of Legal Oper/EEO-AA Officer	Ms. Tiffany DOCKINS
07	Dir Undergraduate Admissions	Mrs. Janieth ADAMS
90	Director Academic IT	Mr. Gregory ANDERSON
109	Director Auxiliary Services	Ms. Kameshia HILL
88	Ombudsman	Dr. Floressa HANNAH-JEFFERSON
88	Director Veteran & Military Center	Ms. Latoya REED
04	Admin Assistant to the President	Ms. Joyce JORDAN-GOODEN
122	Asst Dir Student Engage-Greek Life	Mr. Kenneth WILLIAMS

Jones County Junior College (A)

900 S Court Street, Ellisville MS 39437-3999

County: Jones

FICE Identification: 002411
Unit ID: 175883

Telephone: (601) 477-4000 Carnegie Class: Assoc/MT-VT-High Trad
FAX Number: (601) 477-4875 Calendar System: Semester
URL: www.jcjc.edu
Established: 1927 Annual Undergrad Tuition & Fees (In-District): $3,870
Enrollment: 4,535 Coed
Affiliation or Control: State/Local IRS Status: Exempt
Highest Offering: Associate Degree
Accreditation: SC, ACBSP, ADNUR, EMT, RAD

01	President	Dr. Jesse R. SMITH
05	Interim Chief Academic Officer	Mr. Rick YOUNGBLOOD
10	EVP/Chief Financial Officer	Mr. Rick YOUNGBLOOD
32	VP Student Affairs	Dr. Tessa FLOWERS
111	VP of Institutional Advancement	Mr. Joel CAIN
84	VP of Enrollment Management	Mr. Paul SPELL
13	VP of Information Technology	Mr. John Howard ROBERTSON
26	EVP/CMO/CIO/CEMO	Dr. Finee RUFFIN
18	Asst to the Pres Facilities Mgmt	Mr. Michael BRADSHAW
86	Asst to the Pres Govt Relations	Mr. Jim WALLEY
88	Asst to the Pres Leadership Trng	Dr. Sam JONES
04	Asst to the Pres Office Operations	Ms. Teresa WELCH
35	VP of Advancement and Athletics and	Mr. Joel CAIN
20	Dean of Academic Affairs	Dr. Jason DEDWYLDER
103	Dir of the Advanced Tech Center	Ms. Jennifer GRIFFITH
37	Director of Student Financial Aid	Ms. Kari DEDWYLDER
39	Director of Housing	Mr. Chuck ROBERTSON
40	Bookstore Manager	Ms. Lisa SIMS
41	Director of Athletics	Mr. Joel CAIN
15	Director of Human Resources	Mr. Luke HAMMONDS
96	Director of Purchasing	Ms. Daphne YEAGER
106	Dean of eLearning	Ms. Kandi JOHNSON
08	Head Librarian	Mr. Andrew SHARP
19	Chief Campus Police	Mr. Stan LIVINGSTON

Meridian Community College (B)

910 Highway 19 North, Meridian MS 39307-5890

County: Lauderdale

FICE Identification: 002413
Unit ID: 175935

Telephone: (601) 483-8241 Carnegie Class: Assoc/HVT-Mix Trad/Non
FAX Number: (601) 481-1305 Calendar System: Semester
URL: www.meridiancc.edu
Established: 1937 Annual Undergrad Tuition & Fees (In-District): $3,478
Enrollment: 3,003 Coed
Affiliation or Control: Local IRS Status: 501(c)3

Highest Offering: Associate Degree
Accreditation: SC, ADNUR, CAHIIM, COARC, DA, DH, EMT, MAC, MLTAD, PNUR, PTAA, RAD, SURGT

01	President	Dr. Thomas HUEBNER, JR.
04	Executive Assistant to President	Mrs. Lauren CLAY
05	VP for Academic Affairs	Mr. Michael THOMPSON
10	Chief Financial Officer	Mrs. Pam HARRISON
21	Assistant Chief Financial Officer	Mr. Drew EDWARDS
15	Director Human Resources	Ms. Angie PICKARD
18	Director Physical Plant	Mr. Adam FOREMAN
40	Bookstore Manager	Mrs. Cher WARREN
32	Interim VP Student Success	Mrs. Annette COOK
35	Dean of Student Services	Mrs. Deanna SMITH
121	Director Advising & Retention	Mrs. Kimberly RUSH
41	Athletic Director	Mr. Sander ATKINSON
07	Director of Admissions	Ms. Ashley TANKSLEY
124	Director Student Engagement	Mr. Brandon DEWEASE
37	Director Financial Aid	Ms. Nedra BRADLEY
06	Registrar	Ms. Deborah OLDHAM
19	Chief of Police	Mr. Nick KIRKLAND
39	Director Housing & Residence Life	Mr. Reginald DAVIS
20	Associate Dean Academic Affairs	Dr. Chad GRAHAM
13	Associate VP for Technology	Dr. Kelley GONZALES
09	Dean Institutional Effectiveness	Mrs. Valerie BISHOP
08	Director Library Services	Mr. Doug JERNIGAN
103	VP for Workforce Solutions	Mr. Joseph KNIGHT
103	Dean of Workforce Education	Dr. Lori SMITH
66	Assoc VP Nursing/Health Education	Dr. Lara COLLUM
25	Dir Workforce Grants & Development	Mrs. Lucy LAMBERTH
36	Career Center Director	Ms. Katrina GARRETT
111	VP Advancement/Exec Dir Foundation	Mrs. Leia HILL
26	Director of Public Information	Mrs. Kay THOMAS
105	Web Designer/Media Specialist	Ms. Desi ROSS

Millsaps College (C)

1701 N State Street, Jackson MS 39210-0001

County: Hinds

FICE Identification: 002414
Unit ID: 175980

Telephone: (601) 974-1000 Carnegie Class: Bac-A&S
FAX Number: (601) 974-1059 Calendar System: Semester
URL: www.millsaps.edu
Established: 1890 Annual Undergrad Tuition & Fees: $41,314
Enrollment: 712 Coed
Affiliation or Control: United Methodist IRS Status: 501(c)3
Highest Offering: Master's
Accreditation: SC

01	President	Dr. Rob PEARIGEN
05	Provost & Dean of the College	Dr. Keith DUNN
10	Vice President of Finance	Ms. Whitney EMRICH
111	VP for Institutional Advancement	Ms. Hope CARTER
32	Dean of Students	Ms. Megan JAMES
50	Dean of Else School of Management	Mr. Harvey FISER
84	Vice Pres for Enrollment	Ms. Beth CLARKE
79	Assoc Dean Arts & Humanities	Dr. Holly SYPNIEWSKI
28	Assoc Dean Intercul Affs/Cmty Life	Mr. Demetrius BROWN
81	Associate Dean Sciences Division	Dr. Stan GALICKI
82	AVP for International Initiatives	Ms. Molly WEST
37	Director of Financial Aid	Mrs. Isabelle HIGBEE
20	Director Academic Support Services	Dr. Jennifer LEWTON-YATES
51	Director of Continuing Education	Dr. Nola R. GIBSON
08	College Librarian	Ms. Jamie B. WILSON
36	Director of Career Center	Mr. Ryan COLVIN
41	Director of Athletics	Mr. Aaron PELCH
15	Dir of Human Resource Services	Ms. Julie DANIELS
42	Chaplain/Director Church Relations	Dr. Joey SHELTON
21	Controller	Mrs. Whitney EMRICH
06	Registrar	Dr. Ken THOMPSON
09	Director of Institutional Research	Mr. Ken THOMPSON
18	Director of Physical Plant	Mr. Michael SWITZER
29	Director Alumni Relations	Ms. Maribeth KITCHINGS
19	Director Security/Safety	Mr. John CONWAY
26	Director of Communications & Market	Mr. John SEWELL
04	Executive Asst to President	Mrs. Penta MOORE
100	Chief of Staff	Mr. Kenneth TOWNSEND
102	Dir Foundation/Corporate Relations	Mr. Lloyd GRAY
44	Director Annual Giving	Mr. Jim BURKE

Mississippi College (D)

200 W College Street, Clinton MS 39058-0001

County: Hinds

FICE Identification: 002415
Unit ID: 176053

Telephone: (601) 925-3000 Carnegie Class: DU-Mod
FAX Number: (601) 925-3276 Calendar System: Semester
URL: www.mc.edu
Established: 1826 Annual Undergrad Tuition & Fees: $19,308
Enrollment: 4,667 Coed
Affiliation or Control: Southern Baptist IRS Status: 501(c)3
Highest Offering: Doctorate
Accreditation: SC, ARCPA, CACREP, CAEP, CIDA, LAW, MUS, NAEYC, NURSE, SW

01	President	Dr. Blake THOMPSON
04	Chief Admin Support Officer	Ms. Shelia CARPENTER
10	COO/Chief Financial Officer	Ms. Laura JACKSON
05	Provost/Exec Vice President	Dr. Keith ELDER
29	VP & Exec Dir Alumni Assn	Dr. Jim TURCOTTE
58	Assoc Provost & Graduate Dean	Dr. Debbie NORRIS
32	Assoc VP for the Student Experience	Dr. Jonathan AMBROSE

06	Registrar	Ms. Megan PRITCHETT
09	Director of Institutional Research	Ms. Cassandra SESSOMS
08	Director of Library	Ms. Claudia CONKLIN
21	Controller	Ms. Ebby DEDEAUX
13	Chief Information Officer/CISO	Mr. Bill CRANFORD
38	Int Director of Student Counseling	Dr. James STRICKLAND
15	Director Human Resources	Ms. Donna SMITH
26	Assoc VP Marketing/Communications	Ms. Tracey HARRISON
18	Executive Director Physical Plant	Mr. Roe GRUBBS
39	Director of Residence Life	Mr. Seth BRILL
37	Director Student Financial Aid	Ms. Amanda BECK
84	Dean of Enrollment Services	Mr. Michael WRIGHT
88	Asst Dean Christian Leadership	Ms. Becca BENSON
19	Director of Public Safety	Mr. Mike WARREN
41	Director of Athletics	Mr. Kenny BIZOT
96	Director of Purchasing	Ms. Dana ELMORE
40	Manager Bookstore	Mr. Daniel HOWARD
36	Director of Career Services	Ms. Taylor ORMON
81	Dean School of Science/Mathematics	Dr. Stan BALDWIN
50	Dean School of Business Admin	Dr. Marcelo EDUARDO
79	Dean School of Humanities	Dr. Jonathan RANDLE
53	Dean School of Education	Dr. Cindy MELTON
73	Dean Sch Christian Studies/Fine Art	Dr. Wayne VAN HORN
61	Interim Dean School of Law	Dr. John ANDERSON
66	Dean School of Nursing	Dr. Kimberly SHARP
30	Executive Director of Development	Ms. Katrina PACE
43	VP Gen Counsel/Spec Asst to Pres	Dr. Bill TOWNSEND

Mississippi Delta Community College (E)

PO Box 668, Moorhead MS 38761-0668

County: Sunflower

FICE Identification: 002416
Unit ID: 176008

Telephone: (662) 246-6322 Carnegie Class: Assoc/MT-VT-Mix Trad/Non
FAX Number: (662) 246-6321 Calendar System: Semester
URL: www.msdelta.edu
Established: 1926 Annual Undergrad Tuition & Fees (In-District): $3,140
Enrollment: 2,096 Coed
Affiliation or Control: Local IRS Status: 501(c)3
Highest Offering: Associate Degree
Accreditation: SC, ADNUR, DH, MLTAD, PTAA, RAD

01	President	Dr. Tyrone JACKSON
05	Vice President of Instruction	Mrs. Teresa WEBSTER
10	Dean of Business Services	Mrs. Staci MILLER
88	Dean of GHEC Operations	Ms. Linda CLARK
103	VP of Workforce	Mr. Todd DONALD
15	Director of Human Resources	Mrs. Waunita R. JONES
37	Director of Financial Aid	Ms. Angela FANT
84	Dean of Enrollment Management	Mr. Jay GARY
13	Director Information Technologies	Mr. Torrey MOORE
08	Director of Library Services	Mrs. Kristi BARIOLA
124	Dean of Planning/Assessment	Mrs. Kate FAILING
18	Director of Maintenance	Vacant
108	VP of Enrollment & Effectiveness	Dr. Benjamin CLOYD
11	VP of Admin & Student Services	Dr. Steven JONES
04	Executive Asst to the President	Mrs. Debra BAKER
41	Athletic Director	Vacant
19	Director Security/Safety	Mr. Markricus HIBBLER
76	Dean of Allied Health	Mrs. Patricia KELLY
75	Dean of Career/Technical Education	Mrs. Suzanne THOMPSON
106	Coordinator of E-learning	Ms. Carmen BROWN
111	Exec Dir College Advancement/Alumni	Mr. Jim AYCOCK

Mississippi Gulf Coast Community College (F)

PO Box 609, Perkinston MS 39573-0012

County: Stone

FICE Identification: 002417
Unit ID: 176071

Telephone: (601) 928-5211 Carnegie Class: Assoc/HVT-High Trad
FAX Number: (601) 928-6386 Calendar System: Semester
URL: www.mgccc.edu
Established: 1911 Annual Undergrad Tuition & Fees (In-District): $3,750
Enrollment: 8,677 Coed
Affiliation or Control: Local IRS Status: Exempt
Highest Offering: Associate Degree
Accreditation: SC, ACFEI, ADNUR, #COARC, EMT, MAC, MLTAD, OTA, PNUR, PTAA, RAD, SURGT

01	President	Dr. Mary S. GRAHAM
05	Exec VP Teaching/Lrng/Cmty Campus	Dr. Jonathan WOODWARD
10	Exec VP Administration/Finance	Dr. Jason PUGH
12	VP Perkinston Campus (PC)	Dr. Ladd TAYLOR
12	VP Harrison County Campus (HCC)	Dr. Cedric BRADLEY
12	VP Jackson County Campus (JCC)	Dr. Tammy FRANKS
32	Exec VP Student Svcs/Enroll Mgmt	Dr. Phil BONFANTI
111	Exec VP Institutional Advancement	Dr. Suzi BROWN
103	AVP Teaching and Learning	Dr. Jordan SANDERSON
103	AVP Career & CTE for CC	Mr. John POELMA
15	Assoc VP Human Resources	Dr. Jared BURNS
09	EVP Technology & Research DO	Mr. Adam SWANSON
26	AVP Institutional Relations	Ms. Christen DUHE
84	Dean of Enrollment/Registrar DO	Dr. Kady PIETZ
106	Director of eLearning	Ms. Buffy MATTHEWS
96	Dir of Purchasing/Property Control	Mr. Jay NEWTON
50	Dean of Business Services	Mr. Wayne KUNTZ
50	Dean of Business Services PC	Mr. Jason FERGUSON
50	Dean of Business Services JC	Ms. Melissa DAVIS
50	Dean of Business Services HCC	Ms. Blythe KING

66 AVP School of Nursing & Health Prof .... Dr. Joan HENDRIX
75 Dean of Teaching & Learning PCC .... Dr. Bobby GHOSAL
75 Dean of Teaching & Learning HCC .... Dr. Emma MILLER
75 Dean of Teaching & Learning JCC .... Dr. Brad BAILEY
32 Dean Stdnt Svcs/Enroll Mgmt PC .... Dr. Jason BEVERLY
32 Dean Stdnt Svcs/Enroll Mgmt JCC .... Ms. Michelle SEKUL
20 AVP Teaching and Learning .... Dr. Erin RIGGINS
88 Admin Dean George County Center .... Dr. Lisa RHODES
39 Director Residential/Student Life .... Mr. Trey ROBERTSON
07 Director of Admissions/Rec JCC .... Ms. Miranda HEDMAN
07 Director of Admissions/Rec HCC .... Mr. Christopher BAGWELL
07 Director of Admissions/Rec PCC .... Ms. Mollie BARGER
37 Financial Aid Director JCC .... Ms. Angela BRADLEY
37 Financial Aid Director PCC .... Ms. Heather DEARMAN
37 Financial Aid Director HCC .... Ms. LaShanda CHAMBERLAIN
84 Director of Enrollment Services JCC .... Ms. Beth LOVORN
84 Director of Enrollment Services HCC .... Ms. Dawn BUCKLEY
84 Director of Enrollment Services PCC .... Ms. Paula RAINEY
04 Sr Exec Assistant to the President .... Ms. Natasha BAUCUM
21 Assoc VP Finance/Comptroller .... Ms. Shelly BENTZ
13 Chief Information Technology Ofcr .... Mr. Larry PICKERING
30 Dir Advancement/Foundation & Alumni ...... Ms. Veronica STUBBS
41 Athletic Director .... Mr. Steven CAMPBELL

Mississippi State University (A)

Lee Boulevard, Mississippi State MS 39762-5708
County: Oktibbeha   FICE Identification: 002423
Unit ID: 176080
Telephone: (662) 325-2323   Carnegie Class: DU-Highest
FAX Number: (662) 325-7455   Calendar System: Semester
URL: www.msstate.edu
Established: 1878   Annual Undergrad Tuition & Fees (In-State): $8,910
Enrollment: 22,986   Coed
Affiliation or Control: State   IRS Status: 501(c)3
Highest Offering: Doctorate
Accreditation: SC, AAFCS, #ARCPA, ART, CACREP, CAEPN, CIDA, CLPSY, CONST, DIETD, DIETI, IPSY, LSAR, MUS, SCPSY, SPAA, SW, VET

01 President .... Dr. Mark E. KEENUM
05 Provost/Executive VP .... Dr. David SHAW
46 VP Research & Econ Development .... Dr. Julie JORDAN
47 VP Agric/Forestry/Vet Med .... Dr. Keith COBLE
10 VP for Finance & Administration .... Mr. Don ZANT
32 VP for Student Affairs .... Dr. Regina HYATT
30 VP for Development and Alumni .... Mr. John P. RUSH
07 Assistant VP Enrollment .... Dr. John DICKERSON
41 Athletic Director .... Mr. John COHEN
43 General Counsel .... Ms. Joan LUCAS
28 VP for Access/Diversity & Inclusion .... Ms. Rasheda BODDIE-FORBES
15 Chief Human Resources Officer .... Ms. Leslie COREY
88 Special Assistant to the President .... Mr. Kyle STEWARD
26 Chief Communications Officer .... Mr. Sid SALTER
86 Special Assistant to the President .... Mr. Lee WEISKOPF
20 Executive Vice Provost .... Dr. Peter RYAN
13 Chief Information Officer .... Mr. Steve PARROTT
85 AVP International Institute .... Dr. Dan REYNOLDS
48 Dean Architecture/Art & Design .... Dr. Angi BOURGEOIS
49 Dean Arts & Sciences .... Dr. Rick TRAVIS
50 Dean Business .... Dr. Sharon OSWALD
53 Dean Education .... Dr. Teresa JAYROE
58 Dean Graduate School .... Dr. Peter RYAN
54 Dean Engineering .... Dr. Jason KEITH
65 Dean Forest Resources .... Dr. Wes BURGER
47 Dean Agric & Life Science .... Dr. Scott WILLARD
74 Dean Veterinary Medicine .... Dr. Kent H. HOBLET
12 Associate VP & Head of MSU-Meridian .... Dr. Terry CRUSE
92 Int Dean Honors College .... Dr. Tommy ANDERSON
08 Dean MSU Libraries .... Dr. Lis PANKL
56 Dir University Extension Service .... Dr. Gary JACKSON
88 Director Ag Experiment Station .... Dr. Scott WILLARD
06 Registrar .... Dr. John R. DICKERSON
106 Exec Director Distance Education .... Dr. Susan SEAL
36 Exec Director Career Center .... Ms. Bethany MILLS
35 Dean of Students .... Dr. Thomas BOURGEOIS
38 Director Counseling Services .... Ms. Luellyn SWITZER
37 Director Student Financial Aid .... Mr. Paul MCKINNEY
39 Exec Director Housing/Res Life .... Ms. Dei ALLARD
09 Director Institutional Research .... Dr. Tracey BAHAM
23 Medical Director .... Dr. Katrina POE
29 Director of Alumni Association .... Mr. Jeffrey DAVIS
112 Director of Planned Giving .... Mr. Wes GORDON
25 Director Sponsored Projects .... Mr. Kevin ENROTH
116 Director Internal Audit .... Ms. Leisa ERVIN
96 Exec Director Procurement/Contracts .... Mr. Don BUFFUM
19 Police Chief .... Mr. Vance RICE
122 Dir Fraternity/Sorority Life .... Dr. Jacqueline MULLEN

Mississippi University for Women (B)

1100 College Street, Columbus MS 39701-5800
County: Lowndes   FICE Identification: 002422
Unit ID: 176035
Telephone: (877) 462-8439   Carnegie Class: Masters/S
FAX Number: (662) 329-7297   Calendar System: Semester
URL: www.muw.edu
Established: 1884   Annual Undergrad Tuition & Fees (In-State): $7,525
Enrollment: 2,704   Coed
Affiliation or Control: State   IRS Status: 501(c)3
Highest Offering: Doctorate
Accreditation: SC, ACBSP, ADNUR, ART, CAEP, MUS, NURSE, SP

01 President .... Ms. Nora R. MILLER
05 Provost/Exec VP Academic Affairs .... Dr. Scott TOLLISON
10 Sr Vice Pres Administration & CFO .... Mr. Mark D. ELLARD
26 Exec Dir of University Relations .... Ms. Anika M. PERKINS
32 VP Student Affs/Dean of Students .... Ms. Jessica HARPOLE
20 Assoc Vice Pres Academic Affairs .... Dr. Martin HATTON
43 University Counsel .... Ms. Karen CLAY
49 Dean College Arts/Sciences .... Dr. Brian ANDERSON
50 Dean Business/Professional*Studies .... Dr. Marty A. BROCK
66 Dean College Nursing/SLP .... Dr. Brandy LARMON
08 Dean of Library Services .... Ms. Amanda C. POWERS
35 Dean of Students .... Ms. Jessica HARPOLE
58 Director Graduate Studies .... Dr. Martin HATTON
88 Director Outreach & Innovation .... Ms. Melinda LOWE
27 Chief Information Officer .... Ms. Carla LOWERY
06 Registrar .... Ms. Shannon LUCIUS
09 Director Inst Research & Assessment .... Ms. Jennifer MOORE
92 Director Honors College .... Dr. Kim WHITEHEAD
29 Dir Alumni Rels/Donor Engagement .... Dr. Anna H. OGBURN
30 Exec Dir Development & Alumni .... Ms. Andrea N. STEVENS
105 Web Communications Director .... Mr. Rich SOBOLEWSKI
21 Director University Accounting .... Ms. Susan SOBLEY
116 Internal Auditor .... Mr. Kenneth WIDNER
13 Director of Information Systems .... Mr. Aaron BROOKS
07 Director of Admissions .... Ms. Iika MCCARTER
37 Director Financial Aid .... Ms. Nicole PATRICK
15 Director Human Resources .... Ms. Laura QUINN
19 Chief of Police .... Mr. Randy G. VIBROCK
18 Interim Dir of Facilities Mgmt .... Mr. Jody KENNEDY
96 Director Resources Management .... Ms. Angie S. ATKINS
35 Director Student Life .... Ms. Mea ASHLEY
41 Dir Athletics & Recreation .... Ms. Jennifer CLAYBROOK
40 Director Bookstore .... Mr. Leonard COTTON
121 Director Student Success Center .... Dr. David BROOKING
109 Interim Mgr MUW Dining Svcs .... Mr. Matthew MOLINA
84 Enrollment Certification Officer .... Ms. Skyler HARGROVE
14 Director of Systems & Networks .... Mr. Rodney GODFREY
104 Coordinator Study Abroad .... Ms. Erinn HOLLOWAY
39 Director Housing & Residence Life ... Mr. Andrew MONEYMAKER

Mississippi Valley State University (C)

14000 Highway 82 W, Itta Bena MS 38941-1400
County: Leflore   FICE Identification: 002424
Unit ID: 176044
Telephone: (662) 254-9041   Carnegie Class: Masters/S
FAX Number: (662) 254-6709   Calendar System: Semester
URL: www.mvsu.edu
Established: 1950   Annual Undergrad Tuition & Fees (In-State): $6,746
Enrollment: 2,032   Coed
Affiliation or Control: State   IRS Status: 501(c)3
Highest Offering: Master's
Accreditation: SC, ACBSP, ART, CAEP, MUS, SW

01 President .... Dr. Jerryl BRIGGS, SR.
05 Provost/Sr VP Academic Affairs .... Dr. Kathie S. GOLDEN
32 VP Enrollment Mgmt/Student Affairs .. Dr. Thomas CALHOUN, JR.
20 Assoc VP Academic Affairs .... Dr. Abigail Sophia NEWSOME
09 Asst VP for IRE/Strat Planning .... Dr. Sharon FREEMAN
10 VP Business & Finance/CFO .... Ms. Joyce A. DIXON
100 Chief of Staff/Legislative Liaison .... Dr. LaShon F. BROOKS
111 Int Vice Pres for Univ Advancement .... Mr. Dameon SHAW
106 Asst VP for Distance & Online .... Dr. Kenneth DONE
39 Director Residence Life .... Mr. Raynaldo GILLUS
41 Director of Athletics .... Mrs. Dianthia FORD-KEE
16 Director of Student Records .... Mr. Jeffery LOGGINS
07 Director Admission/Recruitment .... Dr. Danisha WILLIAMS
08 Head Librarian .... Ms. Mantra HENDERSON
15 Director of Human Resources .... Mrs. Elizabeth HURSSEY
13 Director of Information Technology .... Vacant
37 Director of Financial Aid .... Mr. Letherio ZEIGLER
29 Manager of Alumni Relations .... Ms. Alyssa WEBB
26 Director of Comm/Mktg .... Mr. Donell MAXIE
19 Chief/Director University Police .... Mr. Xavier REDMOND
18 Director Facilities/Capital Project .... Mr. Terrence HURSSEY
36 Director Career Development .... Ms. Essie L. BRYANT
38 Dean of Student Development .... Dr. Yolanda JONES
50 Chair of Business Department .... Dr. Curressia BROWN
53 Acting Chair of Education Dept .... Dr. Theresa DUMAS
79 Chair English/Foreign Language .... Dr. John ZHENG
57 Acting Chair Fine Arts Department ... Dr. Kimberly BROADWATER
68 Chair Health/Phys Ed/Rec Dept .... Dr. Gloria ROSS
81 Chair of Math/Computer Science Dept .... Dr. Latonya GARNER
54 Acting Chair of Engineering Tech .... Mr. Antonio BROWNLOW
60 Chair Mass Communication Dept .... Vacant
88 Chair Criminal Justice .... Dr. Emmanual AMADI
70 Chair Social Work Department .... Dr. Catherine SINGLETON-WALKER
96 Director of Purchasing .... Ms. Carla M. WILLIAMS
04 Executive Asst to President .... Mrs. Auguster WALLACE
25 Director Sponsored Pgm/Title III .... Mr. Samuel MELTON, JR.
30 Director of Development .... Vacant

Northeast Mississippi Community College (D)

101 Cunningham Boulevard, Booneville MS 38829-1731
County: Prentiss   FICE Identification: 002426
Unit ID: 176169
Telephone: (662) 728-7751   Carnegie Class: Assoc/MT-VT-High Trad
FAX Number: (662) 728-1165   Calendar System: Semester
URL: www.nemcc.edu
Established: 1948   Annual Undergrad Tuition & Fees (In-District): $4,036
Enrollment: 3,243   Coed
Affiliation or Control: State/Local   IRS Status: 501(c)3
Highest Offering: Associate Degree
Accreditation: SC, ADNUR, COARC, DH, MAC, MLTAD, RAD

01 President .... Dr. Ricky G. FORD
03 Executive Vice President .... Dr. Craig-Ellis SASSER
103 VP Workforce Training/Economic Dev .... Nadara L. COLE
10 Vice President of Finance .... Chris MURPHY
26 Vice Pres of Public Information .... Tony FINCH
05 Vice President of Instruction .... Dr. Michelle BARAGONA
32 Vice President of Student Services .... Ray SCOTT
12 Vice Pres Satellite Campuses .... Ben SHAPPLEY
35 Assoc Vice Pres of Student Service .... Rod COGGIN
08 Library Director .... Ellice YAGER
96 Director of Purchasing .... Amber GARNER
37 Director of Financial Aid .... Greg WINDHAM
13 Director Computer Center .... Gregory SMITH
18 Director Facilities/Maintenance .... Brandon ELLIOTT
84 Dir of Enrollment Svcs/Registrar .... Chassie KELLY
15 Human Resources Officer .... Wesley FLOYD
04 Administrative Asst to President .... Misty DEVAUGHN
102 Dir Foundation/Corporate Relations .... Patrick D. EATON
106 Dir Online Education/E-learning .... Kim HARRIS
19 Chief of Security/Safety .... Anthony ANDERSON
09 Director of Institutional Research .... Dr. Kelli HEFNER
121 AVP of Student Success Center .... Britney WHITLEY
51 Director of Adult Education .... Laurie KESLER
41 Athletic Director .... Kent FARRIS
88 Director of Sports Information .... Blake LONG
88 New Albany Center Director/WIOA .... David GOODE

Northwest Mississippi Community College (E)

4975 Highway 51 N, Senatobia MS 38668-1703
County: Tate   FICE Identification: 002427
Unit ID: 176178
Telephone: (662) 562-3200   Carnegie Class: Assoc/MT-VT-High Trad
FAX Number: (662) 562-3911   Calendar System: Semester
URL: www.northwestms.edu
Established: 1927   Annual Undergrad Tuition & Fees (In-State): $3,390
Enrollment: 7,092   Coed
Affiliation or Control: State   IRS Status: 501(c)3
Highest Offering: Associate Degree
Accreditation: SC, ADNUR, COARC, EMT, FUSER, @PTAA

01 President .... Dr. Michael J. HEINDL
10 VP of Finance/Administration .... Mr. Jeff HORTON
31 VP for Community Relations .... Dr. Andrew DALE
05 Vice Pres of Instruction .... Dr. Matthew DOMAS
103 AVP Wrkfce Sol/Career Tech Educ .... Mr. Dwayne CASEY
84 AVP Stdnt Svcs/Enrolllment Mgmt .... Dr. Tonyalle V. RUSH
22 Disability Student Svcs Coordinator .... Ms. Missy KELSAY
26 Director of Communications .... Ms. Kayleigh MCCOOL
37 Director of Financial Aid .... Ms. LeKeisha MURRY-HIBBLER
36 Dir Student Development .... Ms. Candis WALKER
08 Director of Learning Resources .... Dr. Melissa WRIGHT
13 Director of Information Tech .... Mrs. Amy LATHAM
07 Director of Recruiting .... Mrs. Jere HERRINGTON
09 AVP Inst Research/Effectiveness .... Dr. Carolyn WILEY
18 Director of Physical Plant Building .... Mrs. Mary AYERS
19 Chief of Campus Police .... Mr. Zabe DAVIS
111 Exec Dir Inst Advancement .... Ms. Patti GORDON
32 District Dean of Student Services .... Dr. Tommy (TJ) WALKER
40 Director Bookstore .... Mr. Joel BOYLES
41 Director of Athletics .... Mr. Brian OAKES
96 Director of Purchasing .... Mrs. Ruth DUNLAP
15 Director of Human Resources .... Mrs. Erica STANFORD
21 Director of Accounting .... Mr. Matt SELLERS
06 Registrar .... Mrs. Angela DORTCH
29 Director Alumni Affairs .... Vacant

Pearl River Community College (F)

101 Highway 11 N, Poplarville MS 39470-2298
County: Pearl River   FICE Identification: 002430
Unit ID: 176239
Telephone: (601) 403-1000   Carnegie Class: Assoc/MT-VT-High Trad
FAX Number: (601) 403-1339   Calendar System: Semester
URL: www.prcc.edu
Established: 1909   Annual Undergrad Tuition & Fees (In-District): $3,500
Enrollment: 5,065   Coed
Affiliation or Control: State/Local   IRS Status: 501(c)3
Highest Offering: Associate Degree
Accreditation: SC, ADNUR, COARC, DA, DH, MLTAD, OTA, PTAA, RAD, SURGT

01 President .... Dr. Adam J. BREERWOOD
04 Exec Assistant to the President .... Ms. Maghan SMITH
05 Sr VP Poplarville Campus/Provost .... Dr. Martha L. SMITH
07 Director of Admissions and Records .... Ms. Tonia SEAL
09 VP for Planning & Inst Research .... Dr. Jennifer SEAL
103 Dean of Workforce/Cmty Dev .... Ms. Rebecca BROWN
106 Director of eLearning .... Ms. Michele MITCHELL
105 Webmaster .... Mr. Richard GLEBER
13 Chief Info Technology Officer (CIO) .... Mr. Matt LOGAN
15 Director of Human Resources .... Ms. Kelly REID
19 Director of Public Safety .... Mr. Don Butch RABY
29 Director Development/Alumni Rels .... Vacant
32 VP Poplarville Campus/Student Svcs .... Mr. Jeff LONG
75 Dean of Career & Technical Educ .... Dr. Amy TOWNSEND
86 Dir Government/Cmty Relations .... Ms. Angie KOTHMANN

Reformed Theological Seminary (A)

5422 Clinton Boulevard, Jackson MS 39209-3099
County: Hinds FICE Identification: 009193
Unit ID: 176284
Telephone: (601) 923-1600 Carnegie Class: Not Classified
FAX Number: (601) 923-1654 Calendar System: 4/1/4
URL: www.rts.edu
Established: 1965 Annual Graduate Tuition & Fees: N/A
Enrollment: N/A Coed
Affiliation or Control: Independent Non-Profit IRS Status: 501(c)3
Highest Offering: Doctorate; No Undergraduates
Accreditation: SC, CACREP, THEOL

00 Chancellor Emeritus Dr. Robert C. CANNADA, JR.
01 Chancellor/CEO Dr. J. Ligon DUNCAN
10 Chief Operations Financial Officer Mr. Bradley TISDALE
05 Provost and Chief Academic Officer Dr. Robert CARA
30 Sr Vice President for Development Mr. Matthew S. BRYSON
12 President Charlotte Campus Dr. Michael J. KRUGER
12 President Orlando Campus Dr. Scott R. SWAIN
12 President Jackson Campus Dr. Guy L. RICHARDSON
12 Executive Director Atlanta Campus Dr. Guy RICHARD
106 Exec Dir RTS Global/Distance Educ Mr. David R. JOHN, III
12 President Washington DC Dr. Scott REDD
12 Executive Director Dallas Campus Dr. Mark MCDOWELL
12 Executive Director Houston Campus Dr. Mark MCDOWELL
12 Executive Director NYC Campus Dr. Jay HARVEY
26 VP for Institutional Communications Mr. Phillip HOLMES
84 VP for Enrollment Management Mr. David VELDKAMP
21 VP for Finance Vacant

Rust College (B)

150 Rust Avenue, Holly Springs MS 38635-2328
County: Marshall FICE Identification: 002433
Unit ID: 176318
Telephone: (662) 252-8000 Carnegie Class: Bac-A&S
FAX Number: N/A Calendar System: Semester
URL: www.rustcollege.edu
Established: 1866 Annual Undergrad Tuition & Fees: $9,900
Enrollment: 623 Coed
Affiliation or Control: United Methodist IRS Status: 501(c)3
Highest Offering: Baccalaureate
Accreditation: SC, SW

01 President Dr. Ivy R. TAYLOR
100 Chief of Staff Mrs. Tiffani PERRY
10 Vice President for Finance Dr. Adell BROWN
05 Vice President for Academic Affairs Dr. Rolondus R. RICE
32 Vice Pres Student Engagement Vacant
84 Vice Pres Enrollment Management Dr. Jason K. JOHNSON
111 AVP of Advancement Mrs. Tiffiney GRAY
06 Interim Dir of Registration Service Mrs. Marilyn CURRY
08 Interim Library Director Mrs. Wanda PEGUES
13 CIO Ms. LaRita BREWSTER
35 Director Student Activities Ms. Kristen WALLACE
37 Director of Financial Aid Ms. Arlisha WALTON
25 Director Contracts & Grants Vacant
30 Director Alumni/Development Ms. Rosemary HICKS
89 Director FYE & Student Enrichment Ms. Talisa BOSWELL
21 Comptroller Mrs. Sandra C. DAWKINS
23 Director Student Health Services Vacant
39 Director Student Housing Mr. Austin RAYFORD
36 Director of Career Pathways Ms. Sandra BURKE
18 Director Physical Plant Vacant
83 Dean Division of Social Science Dr. Alfred J. STOVALL
15 Human Resources Manager Mrs. Angela WILLIAMS
19 Chief of Security Mr. Eric SCOTT
30 Director of Development Ms. Tiffaney GRAY
40 Bookstore Manager Mrs. Patricia HARRIS
42 College Chaplain Rev. Sapada THOMAS
96 Procurement Specialist Ms. Nashitka ROGERS
50 Dean Division of Business Mr. Richard FREDERICK
53 Dean Division of Education Dr. Marrix SEYMORE
79 Dean Division of Humanities Dr. Margaret DELASHMIT
81 Chair Division Science & Math Vacant
70 Chair Department of Social Work Ms. Debra BUTLER
105 Director Web Services Mr. Gino PETERSON
41 Athletic Director Mr. Jarvis STEPHEN
106 Dir Online Education/E-learning Vacant
09 Director of Institutional Research Vacant
04 Executive Administrative Assistant Ms. Evie FLETCHER
22 Dir Affirm Action/Equal Opportunity Mrs. Angela WILLIAMS
26 Director of Public Relations Ms. Mary LESUEUR
44 Director Annual Giving Ms. Kimberly WOODS
102 Dir Corp & Foundation Giving Mrs. Rita GIPSON-RAYFORD
104 Director Study Abroad Dr. James MOCK

Southeastern Baptist College (C)

4229 Highway 15 N, Laurel MS 39440-1096
County: Jones FICE Identification: 002435
Unit ID: 176336
Telephone: (601) 426-6346 Carnegie Class: Bac/Assoc-Mixed
FAX Number: (601) 426-6347 Calendar System: Semester
URL: www.southeasternbaptist.edu
Established: 1948 Annual Undergrad Tuition & Fees: $6,275
Enrollment: 62 Coed
Affiliation or Control: Baptist IRS Status: 501(c)3
Highest Offering: Baccalaureate
Accreditation: BI

01 President Dr. Scott CARSON
05 Academic Dean Mrs. Janice WALKER
06 Registrar Mrs. Caroline ADAMS
07 Director of Admissions Mrs. Anderle FOSTER
37 Director of Financial Aid Mrs. Ginny SINGLETON
08 Director of Library Mrs. Kathy ROBINSON
41 Director of Athletics Mr. Richard LOPEZ
13 Director Information Technology Mr. Hubert DYESS
09 Director of Institutional Research Mrs. Christina LUCAS

Southwest Mississippi Community College (D)

1156 College Drive, Summit MS 39666-9029
County: Pike FICE Identification: 002436
Unit ID: 176354
Telephone: (601) 276-2000 Carnegie Class: Assoc/MT-VT-High Trad
FAX Number: (601) 276-3888 Calendar System: Semester
URL: www.smcc.edu
Established: 1918 Annual Undergrad Tuition & Fees (In-District): $3,380
Enrollment: 1,888 Coed
Affiliation or Control: Local IRS Status: 501(c)3
Highest Offering: Associate Degree
Accreditation: SC, ADNUR, CAHIIM

01 President Dr. Steve BISHOP
05 Vice President for Instruction Ms. Alicia SHOWS
10 Vice President of Financial Affairs Mr. Andrew ALFORD
32 Vice President for Student Affairs Mr. Brent GREGORY
18 Vice Pres Physical Resources Mr. Bill TUCKER
06 Vice President Admissions/Registrar Mr. Matthew CALHOUN
75 Assoc Vice President for CTE Dr. Addie BOONE
37 Director Financial Aid Ms. Amber KELLY
09 Director of Institutional Research Mr. Matthew CALHOUN
08 Librarian Ms. Laura RIDDLE
39 Dir Student Activities/Housing Mrs. Lauren WOODWORTH

Tougaloo College (E)

500 West County Line Road, Tougaloo MS 39174-9999
County: Madison FICE Identification: 002439
Unit ID: 176406
Telephone: (601) 977-7730 Carnegie Class: Bac-A&S
FAX Number: (601) 977-7739 Calendar System: Semester
URL: www.tougaloo.edu
Established: 1869 Annual Undergrad Tuition & Fees: $10,861
Enrollment: 775 Coed
Affiliation or Control: United Church Of Christ IRS Status: 501(c)3
Highest Offering: Master's
Accreditation: SC

01 President Dr. Carmen J. WALTERS
05 Provost/VP for Academic Affairs Dr. Leon C. WILSON
10 CFO/VP for Finance and Admin Ms. Pacey BOWENS
84 VP of Enroll Mgmt/Student Services Dr. Whitney MCDOWELL-ROBINSON
111 VP for Institutional Advancement Mrs. Sandra HODGE
45 VP for Strategic Initiatives Soc Dr. Daphne CHAMBERLAIN
100 Chief of Staff Dr. Linda DANIELS
18 Asst VP for Facilities/Real Prop Mr. Claude E. BROWN
23 Executive Director for OWHC Mr. Gary ANDERSON
08 Director of Library Services Ms. Stefanie TAYLOR
13 Chief Information Officer Ms. LaMica JUSTICE
26 Dir of Communications/External Rels Dr. Ashley MCLAUGHLIN
37 Director of Student Financial Aid Mrs. Trena ROBINSON-YOUNG
06 Registrar Vacant
15 Director Human Resources Ms. Karen COLE
29 Director of Alumni Affairs Mrs. Doris BRIDGEMAN
36 Int Director of Career Services Dr. Melissa MCCOY
25 Dir of Sponsored Pgms/Research Vacant
88 Director of TRiO Dr. Valvia WILSON
38 Director of Counseling Services Dr. Shakebra YOUNG
96 Business Operations Manager Ms. Tracey MINOR
19 Director Security/Safety Ms. Edna DRAKE
39 Director Residential Life Ms. Latoya HAYMER
104 Director Study Abroad Education Vacant
105 Director Web Services Mr. D'Cory OWENS
41 Athletic Director Mr. Keith BARNES
04 Executive Asst to the President Mrs. Latona BANKS
07 Director of Admissions Mrs. D'Awana BLEDSOE
09 Director of Institutional Research Ms. Demetria HOWARD WHITE

University of Mississippi (F)

P.O. Box 1848, University MS 38677
County: Lafayette FICE Identification: 002440
Unit ID: 176017
Telephone: (662) 915-7211 Carnegie Class: DU-Highest
FAX Number: (662) 915-7010 Calendar System: Semester
URL: www.olemiss.edu
Established: 1844 Annual Undergrad Tuition & Fees (In-State): $8,828
Enrollment: 21,014 Coed
Affiliation or Control: State IRS Status: 501(c)3
Highest Offering: Doctorate
Accreditation: SC, ACPHA, ART, CACREP, CAEPN, CAPRT, CEA, CLPSY, DIETC, DIETD, FEPAC, JOUR, LAW, MUS, PHAR, SP, SW, THEA

01 Chancellor Dr. Glenn BOYCE
05 Provost/Exec Vice Chancellor Dr. Noel E. WILKIN
10 Vice Chanc Administration & Finance Mr. Steven HOLLEY
32 Vice Chancellor of Student Affairs Dr. Charlotte FANT PEGUES
46 VC Research/Sponsored Programs Dr. Josh GLADDEN
28 VC of Diversity/Cmty Engagement Ms. Shawnboda MEAD
30 Vice Chanc Development Mrs. Charlotte PARKS
26 Chief Marketing/Communications Ofcr Mr. Jim ZOOK
35 Asst VC Student Affs/Dean Students Dr. Brent MARSH
51 Assoc Prov/Dir Outreach/Cont Stds Dr. Tony AMMETER
08 Dean of Libraries Ms. Cecilia BOTERO
13 Chief Information Officer Mr. Nishanth RODRIGUES
110 Exec Director Development Mr. Denson HOLLIS
29 Exec Director of Alumni Affairs Mr. Kirk PURDOM
37 Director of Financial Aid Mrs. Laura DIVEN-BROWN
36 Director of Career Center Ms. Toni D. AVANT
41 VC of Intercollegiate Athletics Mr. Keith CARTER
15 Chief Human Resources Officer Ms. Andrea JEKABSONS
18 Director of Facilities Management Mr. Dean HANSEN
19 Dir/Chief Univ Police/Campus Safety Mr. Ray HAWKINS
38 Dir of University Counseling Center Dr. Quinton T. EDWARDS, JR.
23 Director University Health Services Mr. Alex LANGHART
39 AVC Student Affairs/Housing Mr. Lionel MATEN
09 Director Institutional Research Dr. Katie BUSBY
22 Dir Equal Oppty/Reg Compliance Ms. Rebecca B. BRESSLER
100 Special Assistant to the Chancellor Mrs. Sue T. KEISER
43 General Counsel & Chief Legal Ofcr Mr. David WHITCOMB
96 Director of Procurement Services Ms. Rachel R. BOST
06 Interim Registrar Mrs. Denise KNIGHTON
21 Controller Mrs. Nina JONES
07 Director of Admissions Mrs. Jody LOWE
50 Dean School of Business Admin Dr. Kendall B. CYREE
49 Dean College of Liberal Arts Dr. Lee COHEN
81 Dean School of Applied Sciences Dr. Peter W. GRANDJEAN
53 Dean School of Education Dr. David ROCK
54 Dean School of Engineering Dr. David PULEO
61 Dean School of Law Dr. Susan DUNCAN
67 Dean of the School of Pharmacy Dr. David D. ALLEN
88 Dean School of Accountancy Dr. W. Mark WILDER
60 Int Dean Sch Journalism/New Media Ms. Debora WENGER
58 Dean of the Graduate School Dr. Annette KLUCK
92 Dean of SM Barksdale Honors College Dr. Douglass SULLIVAN-GONZALEZ
86 Special Asst to Chanc for Govt Affs Mr. Perry SANSING
88 University Ombudsman Mr. Paul CAFFERA
116 Director of Audit Ms. Tanya SATTERFIELD
104 Sr Intl Ofcr/Director Study Abroad Ms. Blair MCELROY
44 Director Annual Giving Mrs. Maura LANGHART
39 Director of Student Housing Mr. John YAUN
84 Vice Chancellor Enrollment Mgmt Mr. Eduardo PRIETO
122 Asst Dir Fraternity/Sorority Life Mr. Jordan FREEMAN

University of Mississippi Medical Center (G)

2500 N State Street, Jackson MS 39216-4505
County: Hinds FICE Identification: 004688
Unit ID: 17601701
Telephone: (601) 984-1000 Carnegie Class: Not Classified
FAX Number: (601) 984-1013 Calendar System: Semester
URL: www.umc.edu
Established: 1955 Annual Undergrad Tuition & Fees (In-State): N/A
Enrollment: N/A Coed
Affiliation or Control: State IRS Status: 501(c)3
Highest Offering: Doctorate
Accreditation: SC, CAHIIM, DENT, DH, HT, IPSY, MED, MLS, NMT, NURSE, OT, PHAR, PTA, RAD, RADMAG

01 Vice Chancellor Health Affairs Dr. LouAnn WOODWARD
05 Assoc VC for Academic Affairs Dr. Scott M. RODGERS
23 Assoc VC for Clinical Affairs Dr. Alan E. JONES
46 Associate Vice Chanc Research Dr. Richard SUMMERS
10 Chief Financial Officer Mr. Nelson WEICHOLD
17 CEO Adult Hospitals Mr. Britt H. CREWSE
88 Chief Nursing Executive Dr. Kristina CHERRY
17 CEO Children's of Mississippi Dr. Guy B. GIESECKE
17 CEO Community Hospitals Ms. Dodie T. MCELMURRAY
26 Exec Dir Communications & Mktg Mr. Marc ROLPH
15 Chief Human Resources Officer Ms. Molly A. BRASFIELD
63 Vice Dean for Medical Educ SOM Dr. Loretta JACKSON-WILLIAMS
28 Chief Diversity & Inclusion Officer Dr. Juanyce TAYLOR
100 Chief of Staff to Vice Chancellor Dr. Brian RUTLEDGE
43 Chief Legal Officer Mr. William C. SMITH, III
11 Chief Administrative Officer Dr. Jonathan WILSON
76 Dean Sch Health Related Professions Dr. Angela BURRELL
69 Interim Dean School Pop Health Dr. Natalie W. GAUGHF
58 Dean Sch Grad Stds Health Sciences Dr. Joey GRANGER
66 Dean School of Nursing Dr. Julie SANFORD
52 Dean of School of Dentistry Dr. Sreenivas KOKA
67 Assoc Dean for Clinical Affs/SOPH Dr. Leigh A. ROSS

University of Southern Mississippi (H)

118 College Drive, #5001, Hattiesburg MS 39406-0001
County: Forrest FICE Identification: 002441
Unit ID: 176372
Telephone: (601) 266-1000 Carnegie Class: DU-Highest
FAX Number: (601) 266-5756 Calendar System: Semester
URL: www.usm.edu
Established: 1910 Annual Undergrad Tuition & Fees (In-State): $8,896
Enrollment: 14,606 Coed
Affiliation or Control: State IRS Status: 501(c)3
Highest Offering: Doctorate

Accreditation: SC, AAFCS, ANEST, ART, AUD, CAATE, CAEP, CIDA, CLPSY, CONST, COPSY, DANCE, DIETD, DIETI, JOUR, KIN, LIB, MFCD, MLS, MPCAC, MUS, NURSE, PH, SCPSY, SP, SW, THEA

01 President ... Dr. Rodney D. BENNETT
04 Executive Asst to the President ... Dr. Steven MILLER
05 Provost & SVP for Academic Affairs ... Dr. Steven MOSER
10 VP Finance & Administration ... Ms. Allyson EASTERWOOD
32 VP Student Affairs ... Dr. Deanna ANDERSON
12 Sr Assoc VP for Coastal Operations ... Dr. Shannon CAMPBELL
20 Exec Vice Provost ... Dr. Amy CHASTEEN
108 Sr Assoc Prov Inst Effectiveness ... Dr. Doug MASTERSON
46 VP for Research ... Dr. Gordon CANNON
50 Dean College Business ... Dr. Bret BECTON
66 Dean College Nursing ... Dr. Lachel STORY
49 Dean College Arts & Sciences ... Dr. Chris WINSTEAD
92 Interim Dean of Honors College ... Dr. Sabine HEINHORST
53 Dean College Educ & Human Sciences ... Dr. Trent GOULD
58 Dean Graduate School ... Dr. Karen COATS
08 Dean/University Librarian ... Dr. John EYE
18 Assoc VP Planning & Facilities Mgmt ... Dr. Chris CRENSHAW
13 Chief Information Officer ... Mr. David SLIMAN
06 Registrar ... Mr. Greg PIERCE
25 Asst VP for Research Administration ... Ms. Marcia LANDEN
45 Dir of Institutional Effectiveness ... Mrs. Kathryn LOWERY
29 Alumni Activities/Exec Director ... Mr. Jerry DEFATTA
36 Director Career Services ... Mr. Russell ANDERSON
22 Interim Title IX Coordinator ... Ms. Cristin REYNOLDS
38 Interim Dir Counseling Center ... Ms. April ESTILL
23 Director of Health Services ... Dr. Melissa ROBERTS
35 Dean of Students ... Ms. Sirena CANTRELL
15 Associate VP of Human Resources ... Mrs. Krystyna VARNADO
96 Director Procurement & Contracts ... Mr. Steve BALLEW
07 Asst Dir of Recruitment ... Ms. Susan W. SCOTT
88 Dir of Vet & Military Student Svcs ... Gen. Jeff HAMMOND
102 Exec Dir USM Foundation ... Ms. Stace L. MERCIER
104 Assoc VP for Intl Programs ... Dr. Daniel NORTON
106 Dir Office of Online Learning ... Dr. Tom HUTCHINSON
43 Dir Legal Services/General Counsel ... Mr. Robert D. GHOLSON
86 Vice President for External Affairs ... Mr. Chad DRISKELL
37 Director Student Financial Aid ... Mr. David WILLIAMSON
09 Director of Institutional Research ... Dr. Megan MCCAY
19 Chief of Police ... Chief Rusty KEYES
26 Chief Communications Officer ... Mr. James P. COLL
41 Director of Athletics ... Mr. Jeremy MCCLAIN
28 Chief Diversity Officer ... Ms. Kimbaya BROWN
122 Director Fraternity/Sorority Life ... Ms. Laura LAUGHLIN

Wesley Biblical Seminary (A)

1880 E County Line Rd, Ridgeland MS 39157
County: Madison | FICE Identification: 025162 | Unit ID: 176451
Telephone: (601) 366-8880 | Carnegie Class: Spec-4-yr-Faith
FAX Number: (601) 510-9114 | Calendar System: Semester
URL: www.wbs.edu
Established: 1974 | Annual Graduate Tuition & Fees: N/A
Enrollment: 158 | Coed
Affiliation or Control: Interdenominational | IRS Status: 501(c)3
Highest Offering: Master's; No Undergraduates
Accreditation: THEOL

01 President ... Dr. Matthew I. AYARS
05 VP Academic Affairs/Academic Dean ... Dr. Andy MILLER, III
10 VP of Business Affairs ... Mr. Ethan KELLY
84 VP of Enrollment ... Mr. Elijah FRIEDEMAN
30 Director of Development ... Mrs. Maribeth GIBSON
21 Director Business Affairs ... Ms. Peggy PRICE
08 Director of Library Services ... Ms. Grace ANDREWS
06 Registrar/Director Financial Aid ... Mr. Karl LUMAN

William Carey University (B)

710 William Carey Parkway, Hattiesburg MS 39401
County: Forrest | FICE Identification: 002447 | Unit ID: 176479
Telephone: (601) 318-6051 | Carnegie Class: DU-Mod
FAX Number: N/A | Calendar System: Trimester
URL: www.wmcarey.edu
Established: 1892 | Annual Undergrad Tuition & Fees: $13,650
Enrollment: 5,472 | Coed
Affiliation or Control: Southern Baptist | IRS Status: 501(c)3
Highest Offering: Doctorate
Accreditation: SC, CAEPN, CAHIIM, IACBE, MUS, NURSE, OSTEO, PHAR, PTA

01 President/Chief Executive Officer ... Dr. Ben BURNETT
03 Executive Vice President ... Vacant
05 Provost & VP for Academic Affairs ... Dr. Daniel CALDWELL
10 Vice Pres Business Affs/CFO ... Mr. Grant GUTHRIE
32 Vice Pres for Student Support ... Mrs. Valerie BRIDGEFORTH
46 Vice President Inst Effectiveness ... Dr. Bennie R. CROCKETT
88 VP for Spiritual Development ... Dr. Brett GOLSON
17 Associate VP for Health Programs ... Dr. Janet WILLIAMS
63 Dean College Osteopathic Medicine ... Dr. Italo SUBBARAO
12 Admin/Acad Dean Tradition Campus ... Dr. Cassandra CONNER
50 Dean School of Business ... Dr. Cheryl DALE
53 Dean School of Education ... Dr. Teresa POOLE
83 Dean Sch Natural/Behavioral Science ... Dr. Frank BAUGH
66 Dean School of Nursing ... Dr. Alicia NEWELL
49 Dean School of Arts & Letters ... Dr. Myron NOONKESTER
64 Dean School of Music ... Dr. Wes DYKES
58 Dean of Graduate Studies ... Dr. Frank BAUGH
73 Dean School of Ministry Studies ... Dr. Brett GOLSON
06 Registrar ... Ms. Leana WILSON
08 Dean Libraries & Learning Resource ... Mr. Reese POWELL
29 Alumni Director ... Mrs. Pam SHEARER
26 Coordinator of Media Relations ... Ms. Suzanne MONK
13 Chief Information Officer ... Mr. Jeff ANDREWS
92 Director of Honors Program ... Dr. David LOWERY
41 Athletic Director ... Mr. D. J PULLEY
18 Dir Facilities/Grounds/Maintenance ... Mr. Bob BLEVINS
15 Associate VP of Human Resources ... Dr. Deidre SHOWS
07 Director of Admissions ... Ms. Meagan E. SMITH
04 Administrative Asst to President ... Mrs. Charlotte GREEN
106 E-Learning Coordinator ... Ms. Shanna MURRAY-LUKE
102 Assoc VP for University Enhancement ... Dr. Angela HOUSTON
37 Director Student Financial Aid ... Mr. Dean PACE
39 Director of Housing ... Mr. Jared ACKLEY
43 General Legal Counsel ... Mrs. Julie HAWKINS
44 Annual Fund Director ... Mrs. Karen GOLSON

MISSOURI

A. T. Still University of Health Sciences (C)

800 W Jefferson Street, Kirksville MO 63501-1497
County: Adair | FICE Identification: 002477 | Unit ID: 177834
Telephone: (660) 626-2391 | Carnegie Class: Spec-4-yr-Med
FAX Number: (660) 626-2672 | Calendar System: Semester
URL: www.atsu.edu
Established: 1892 | Annual Graduate Tuition & Fees: N/A
Enrollment: 3,995 | Coed
Affiliation or Control: Independent Non-Profit | IRS Status: 501(c)3
Highest Offering: First Professional Degree; No Undergraduates
Accreditation: HLC, DENT, OSTEO, PH

01 President ... Dr. Craig PHELPS
05 Sr VP Academic Affairs ... Dr. Norman GEVITZ
63 Dean KCOM ... Dr. Margaret WILSON
32 VP Student Affairs ... Mrs. Lori HAXTON
111 VP University Advancement ... Dr. Shaun SOMMERER
43 VP & General Counsel ... Mr. Matthew HEEREN
10 VP Finance & Administration/CFO ... Ms. Dana FUNDERBURK
13 VP Info Technologies/Services ... Mr. Bryan KRUSNIAK
52 Dean MO Sch of Dentistry/Oral Hlth ... Dr. Dwight MCLEOD
58 Dean Col of Graduate Hlth Studies ... Dr. Don ALTMAN
52 Dean AZ Sch of Dentistry/Oral Hlth ... Dr. Robert TROMBLY
76 Dean AZ Sch of Health Sciences ... Dr. Ann Lee BURCH
63 Dean Sch of Osteo Med in AZ ... Dr. Jeffrey MORGAN
35 Assoc VP AZ Student Affairs ... Dr. Beth POPPRE
07 Asst VP Admissions ... Dr. David KOENECKE
88 VP Univ Strat Partnershps/Diversity ... Dr. Gary CLOUD
45 Sr VP Strat Planning & Univ Init ... Dr. O.T WENDEL
46 VP Research & Grants ... Mrs. Gaylah SUBLETTE
04 Asst to Pres & Secretary to BoT ... Mrs. Norine EITEL
06 Registrar ... Dr. Deanna HUNSAKER
08 University Librarian ... Mr. Harold BRIGHT
15 Asst VP Human Resources/AA Ofcr ... Mrs. Donna BROWN WYATT
18 Director Facilities/Plant Operation ... Mr. Robert EHRLICH
96 Director Purchasing ... Mr. Corey LOUDER
19 Director Security ... Mr. Jim HUGHES
28 VP of Diversity/Inclusion ... Mr. Clinton NORMORE
20 SVP Academic Affairs ... Dr. Ann BOYLE
110 Associate VP University Advancement ... Mr. Bob BEHNEN
51 Assistant VP Continuing Education ... Dr. Lloyd CLEAVER
21 Assistant VP for Finance ... Mrs. Tonya GRIMM
09 Director AT Still Research Inst ... Dr. Brian DEGENHARDT
29 Assoc Director Alumni Relations ... Mrs. Melody CHAMBERS

† Arizona campus accreditation includes ARPCA, AUD, CAATE, DENT, OSTEO, OT, PTA.SP

American Business & Technology University (D)

1018 West Saint Maartens Drive, Saint Joseph MO 64506
County: Buchanan | FICE Identification: 041187 | Unit ID: 457688
Telephone: (816) 279-7000 | Carnegie Class: Bac-Diverse
FAX Number: (888) 890-8190 | Calendar System: Other
URL: www.abtu.edu
Established: 2001 | Annual Undergrad Tuition & Fees: N/A
Enrollment: 353 | Coed
Affiliation or Control: Proprietary | IRS Status: Proprietary
Highest Offering: Master's
Accreditation: DEAC

01 University President ... Mr. Ramsey ATIEH
11 CEO ... Mr. Lute ATIEH
88 VP of Strategic Initiatives ... Mr. Eddie COLON
37 VP of Financial Aid/Compliance ... Dr. Michael CAMPBELL
05 Chief Academic Officer ... Dr. Michelle CHEASTY
13 Chief Information Officer ... Mr. Ramsey ATIEH
10 Chief Financial Officer ... Mr. Dan MARLOW
20 Program Development Officer ... Dr. Donald LADER
108 Accreditation/Compliance Officer ... Mr. Chad BREAZILE
06 Registrar ... Mrs. Kourtney DRAKE
07 Director of Admissions ... Mr. Richard LINGLE
29 Director Alumni/Career Services ... Ms. Debra HAYES

American Trade School (E)

3925 Industrial Drive, Saint Ann MO 63074
County: Saint Louis | FICE Identification: 041748 | Unit ID: 461573
Telephone: (314) 423-1900 | Carnegie Class: Spec 2-yr-Tech
FAX Number: (314) 423-1911 | Calendar System: Quarter
URL: www.americantradeschool.edu
Established: 2003 | Annual Undergrad Tuition & Fees: N/A
Enrollment: 128 | Coed
Affiliation or Control: Proprietary | IRS Status: Proprietary
Highest Offering: Associate Degree
Accreditation: ACCSC

01 Ceo/President/Director ... Mr. John VATTEROTT, JR.

Aquinas Institute of Theology (F)

23 South Spring Avenue, Saint Louis MO 63108-3323
County: City of Saint Louis | FICE Identification: 001632 | Unit ID: 176600
Telephone: (314) 256-8800 | Carnegie Class: Spec-4-yr-Faith
FAX Number: N/A | Calendar System: Semester
URL: www.ai.edu
Established: 1951 | Annual Graduate Tuition & Fees: N/A
Enrollment: 124 | Coed
Affiliation or Control: Roman Catholic | IRS Status: 501(c)3
Highest Offering: Doctorate; No Undergraduates
Accreditation: THEOL

01 President ... Rev. Mark WEDIG, OP
05 Academic Dean/VP ... Rev. Michael MASCARI, OP
11 Exec Director of Operations ... Br. John STEILBERG, OP
15 Director of Human Resources ... Mrs. Joan HART
20 Coordinator of Admin Affairs ... Ms. Mary URBANEK-MUELLER
84 Coordinator of Enrollment Mgmt ... Vacant
06 Registrar ... Ms. Mary URBANEK-MUELLER
13 Coordinator of Inst Technology ... Mr. Tim ROESSLEIN
26 Coordinator of Marketing & Comm ... Mr. Michael WINTERS
10 Chief Financial/Business Officer ... Mrs. Donna THRO
30 Coordinator of Development ... Ms. Erin HAMMOND

Assemblies of God Theological Seminary (G)

1111 N Glenstone Avenue, Springfield MO 65802-2131
County: Greene | FICE Identification: 012120 | Unit ID: 176619
Telephone: (417) 268-1000 | Carnegie Class: Not Classified
FAX Number: (417) 268-1001 | Calendar System: Semester
URL: www.agts.edu
Established: 1972 | Annual Graduate Tuition & Fees: N/A
Enrollment: N/A | Coed
Affiliation or Control: Assemblies Of God Church | IRS Status: 501(c)3
Highest Offering: Doctorate; No Undergraduates
Accreditation: THEOL

01 President of Evangel University ... Dr. Mike RAKES
05 EVP/Chief Academic Officer ... Dr. Jon SPENCE
84 Vice President of Enrollment ... Mr. Chris BELCHER
111 Vice President of Advancement ... Dr. Michael KOLSTAD
20 Associate Dean ... Dr. Paul W. LEWIS
20 Associate Dean ... Dr. Randy WALLS
88 Dir Intercultural Doctoral Studies ... Dr. Mike MCATEER
58 Dir PhD Biblical Interpr/Theology ... Dr. Paul W. LEWIS
58 Director DMin Program ... Dr. John A. BATTAGLIA
32 Student Life Coordinator ... Mr. Alex L. BRYANT
88 Veteran Center Coordinator ... Mr. Dane MOORE
08 Seminary & Instruction Librarian ... Ms. Katelyn DEWITT
06 Assistant Registrar Seminary ... Mrs. Kathy L. HARRISON
37 Financial Aid Counselor ... Ms. Amelia OBERBECK
29 Director Alumni Engagement ... Mr. Hector CRUZ
04 Admin Assistant to the President ... Ms. Angela DENSE
88 Executive Assistant to the Deans ... Mrs. Cara R. CROSS
26 Director of Public Relations & Adv ... Mrs. Erin HEDLUN

† The Seminary continues to offer its educational programs as a distinct unit within the consolidated Evangel University, Springfield, MO.

Avila University (H)

11901 Wornall Road, Kansas City MO 64145-9990
County: Jackson | FICE Identification: 002449 | Unit ID: 176628
Telephone: (816) 942-8400 | Carnegie Class: Masters/M
FAX Number: (816) 942-3362 | Calendar System: Semester
URL: www.avila.edu
Established: 1916 | Annual Undergrad Tuition & Fees: $21,115
Enrollment: 1,414 | Coed
Affiliation or Control: Roman Catholic | IRS Status: 501(c)3
Highest Offering: Master's
Accreditation: HLC, CAEP, IACBE, MPCAC, NURSE, RAD, SW

01 President ... Dr. Ron SLEPITZA
05 Provost/VP of Academic Affairs ... Dr. Ted WHAPHAM
10 Vice Pres for Finance/Admin Svcs ... Mr. Tim KLOCKO
84 VP for Enrollment & Athletics ... Dr. Alexandra ADAMS
32 AVP Student Development/Success ... Ms. Darby GOUGH
13 VP for Information Services ... Mr. Jon GAMBILL
26 Sr Dir Marketing/Communications ... Mr. Darren ROUBINEK
111 Interim VP of Advancement ... Ms. Maggie MOHRFELD

06	Registrar/Director Student Records	Ms. Michelle DRISCOLL
08	Director of Library	Ms. Becky NICHOLS
37	Director of Financial Aid	Mr. Michael PEPPLE
42	Dir Mission Effect/Campus Ministry	Mr. David M. ARMSTRONG
21	Controller	Mr. Joseph H. SJUTS
30	Sr Director of Development	Ms. Bailey CARR
41	Director of Athletics	Mr. Sean SUMME
15	Director of Human Resources	Ms. Nancy BURFORD
18	Director Campus Services	Vacant
40	Bookstore Manager	Mr. John A. TARANTO
38	Coord Counseling & Career Services	Ms. Taryn HODISON
04	University Executive Assistant	Ms. Malissa TOLLIVER
07	Dir of Undergraduate Admissions	Mr. Josh PARISSE
09	Director Institutional Research	Mr. Rusty MCLOUTH

Baptist Bible College   (A)

628 E Kearney St, Springfield MO 65803-3498
County: Greene   FICE Identification: 013208
Unit ID: 176664
Telephone: (417) 268-6000   Carnegie Class: Spec-4-yr-Faith
FAX Number: (800) 819-8330   Calendar System: Semester
URL: www.gobbc.edu
Established: 1950   Annual Undergrad Tuition & Fees: $14,890
Enrollment: 222   Coed
Affiliation or Control: Baptist   IRS Status: 501(c)3
Highest Offering: Master's
Accreditation: **HLC**, BI

01	President	Mr. Mark L. MILIONI
05	Academic Dean	Mr. Shannon L. MULFORD
10	Vice President of Financial Affairs	Mr. Jason L. TODD
18	Chief Facilities/Physical Plant	Mr. Chris C. WILLIAMS
06	Registrar	Mr. Terry A. ALLCORN
32	Director of Student Life	Ms. Chaneika POLK
84	Director of Enrollment Services	Mr. Brad COOKSEY
37	Director of Financial Aid	Mr. Brian RAINS
33	Dean of Men	Mr. Bill J. LEVERGOOD
34	Dean of Women	Mrs. Tina L. EBERT
30	Director of Development	Mr. Kelly ANDERSON
15	Director of Human Resources	Miss Emily MILIONI
19	Director of Security/Safety	Mr. Chad FUQUA
08	Director of Library Services	Mr. Jon JONES
04	Administrative Asst to President	Mrs. Barbara MILIONI
108	Dir of Institutional Effectiveness	Mr. Roland Q. DUDLEY
41	Athletic Director	Mr. Darin MEINDERS

Bolivar Technical College   (B)

1135 North Oakland Avenue, Bolivar MO 65613
County: Polk   FICE Identification: 042557
Unit ID: 490203
Telephone: (417) 777-5062   Carnegie Class: Spec 2-yr-Health
FAX Number: (417) 777-8908   Calendar System: Semester
URL: https://www.bolivarcollege.edu/
Established: 1996   Annual Undergrad Tuition & Fees: N/A
Enrollment: N/A   Coed
Affiliation or Control: Independent Non-Profit   IRS Status: 501(c)3
Highest Offering: Baccalaureate
Accreditation: **ABHES**

02	President/Campus Director	Ms. Charlotte GRAY
05	Vice President	Dr. William GRAY
07	Director Admissions	Ms. Nancy BRANNON
26	Marketing Director	Ms. Rachael HENEISE

Brookes Bible College   (C)

10257 St. Charles Rock Road, St Louis MO 63074
County: St. Louis   Identification: 667137
Telephone: (314) 773-0083   Carnegie Class: Not Classified
FAX Number: (314) 736-6293   Calendar System: Semester
URL: www.brookes.edu
Established: 1909   Annual Undergrad Tuition & Fees: N/A
Enrollment: N/A   Coed
Affiliation or Control: Independent Non-Profit   IRS Status: 501(c)3
Highest Offering: Baccalaureate
Accreditation: **BI**

01	President	Rev. Robert D. THURMAN, JR.
00	Chairman of the Board	Mr. Brian SANDERS
05	Chief Academic Officer	Dr. Jon DENNEY
106	Dean of Online Learning and Cohorts	Dr. R. Brian RICKETT
10	Chief Financial Officer	Mr. Brian TOENNIES
08	Librarian	Mrs. Amy PEARCE
111	Chief Advancement Officer	Vacant
32	Student Ministry Director	Mr. Verle CLINES
07	Director of Admissions	Mr. Obadiah MCADOO
108	Director Institutional Assessment	Dr. David AGRON
06	Registrar	Mr. Owen CORNELIUS

Bryan University   (D)

4255 Nature Center Way, Springfield MO 65804
County: Greene   FICE Identification: 030663
Unit ID: 369516
Telephone: (417) 862-5700   Carnegie Class: Bac/Assoc-Mixed
FAX Number: (417) 865-7144   Calendar System: Other
URL: www.bryanu.edu
Established: 1982   Annual Undergrad Tuition & Fees: $15,782
Enrollment: 275   Coed
Affiliation or Control: Proprietary   IRS Status: Proprietary
Highest Offering: Master's

Accreditation: **ACICS**

01	Executive Director	Mr. Scott HAAR

Calvary University   (E)

15800 Calvary Road, Kansas City MO 64147-1341
County: Cass   FICE Identification: 002450
Unit ID: 176789
Telephone: (816) 322-0110   Carnegie Class: Bac-Diverse
FAX Number: (816) 331-4474   Calendar System: Semester
URL: www.calvary.edu
Established: 1932   Annual Undergrad Tuition & Fees: $11,164
Enrollment: 469   Coed
Affiliation or Control: Independent Non-Profit   IRS Status: 501(c)3
Highest Offering: Doctorate
Accreditation: **HLC**, BI

01	President/CEO	Dr. Alexander GRANADOS
11	Chief Operating Officer/VP	Mr. Jeff CAMPA
10	Chief Financial Officer/VP	Dr. Tom STOLBERG
05	Chief Academic Officer/VP	Dr. Teddy BITNER
111	Chief Development Officer/VP	Mr. John MCGEE
41	Athletic Director	Miss Jeanette REGIER
97	Dean of the College	Dr. Luther SMITH
58	Dean of the Graduate School	Dr. Germaine WASHINGTON
73	Dean of the Seminary	Dr. Thomas BAURAIN
06	Registrar	Mr. Gary ROGERS
13	Director Information Technology	Mr. Aaron HEATH
19	Director of Security	Mr. Allen PRODOEHL
37	Director of Financial Aid	Vacant
08	Head Librarian	Miss Tiffany SMITH
108	Dir of Institutional Effectiveness	Dr. Allan HENDERSON
15	Human Resources Director	Mrs. Leslie LAMBKIN
29	Alumni Relations Coordinator	Mrs. Sara KLAASSEN
88	Practical Christian Ministries Dir	Mrs. Dawnita PHILLIPS
109	Director of Food Service	Mr. Joe DAPRA
105	Director Web Services	Vacant
32	Dean of Students	Mr. Joshua JOHNSON
35	Associate Dean of Students	Mrs. Jamie FRANZ
26	Dir of Marketing & Communications	Mr. Adam WEEKS
18	Director of Maintenance	Vacant
39	Residence Life Coordinator	Miss Alyssa PAYNE
04	Admin Assistant to the President	Miss Krista OWEN

Carver Baptist Bible College, Institute & Theological Seminary   (F)

8524 Blue Ridge Blvd, Kansas City MO 64138
County: Jackson   Identification: 667418
Telephone: (816) 333-1577   Carnegie Class: Not Classified
FAX Number: N/A   Calendar System: Semester
URL: carverbiblecollegekc.org
Established: 1942   Annual Undergrad Tuition & Fees: N/A
Enrollment: N/A   Coed
Affiliation or Control: Independent Non-Profit   IRS Status: 501(c)3
Highest Offering: Master's
Accreditation: **@BI**

01	President	Dr. Antoine D. RICHARDSON

Central Christian College of the Bible   (G)

911 E Urbandale Drive, Moberly MO 65270-1997
County: Randolph   FICE Identification: 022664
Unit ID: 176910
Telephone: (660) 263-3900   Carnegie Class: Spec-4-yr-Faith
FAX Number: (660) 263-3936   Calendar System: Semester
URL: www.cccb.edu
Established: 1957   Annual Undergrad Tuition & Fees: $9,250
Enrollment: 186   Coed
Affiliation or Control: Christian Churches And Churches of Christ
    IRS Status: 501(c)3
Highest Offering: Master's
Accreditation: **BI**

01	President	Dr. David B. FINCHER
05	Vice President of Academics	Mr. Shawn LINDSAY
10	Vice Pres of Business & Finance	Mrs. Lara LAWRENCE
84	Vice Pres Enrollment Mgt/Marketing	Mr. Brian TAYLOR
32	VP Student Development/Dean of Men	Mr. Darryl C. AMMON
111	Vice Pres Advancement/Operations	Mr. Janeil OWEN
07	Director of Admissions	Mr. Jeremiah RATLIFF
04	Exec Assistant to the President	Mrs. Sherry L. WALLIS
121	Dean of Student Success	Dr. Eric A. STEVENS
06	Registrar	Mr. Bill THOMAS
41	Athletic Director	Ms. Kori ZARZUTZKI
08	Head Librarian	Ms. Crystal APPLEGARTH
35	Dean of Students	Mr. Lucas REYNOLDS
37	Director of Financial Aid	Mrs. Elizabeth WALTER
13	Director of Information Technology	Mr. James WILLIAMSON
18	Physical Plant Manager	Mr. Mark E. DUNHAM
40	Bookstore Manager	Mrs. Tracey WILLIAMSON
39	Residence Director - Women	Ms. Cindy BINGAMON
39	Residence Director - Men	Mr. James WILLIAMSON
106	Director Online Education	Mr. James FRANKE
30	Director of Development	Mr. Kevin BROWN

107	Dean of Professional Studies	Mr. Brandon BRADLEY

† Onsite students accepted into a degree or certificate program will receive Full-Tuition Scholarship which equals cost of tuition up to 18 hrs/semester. Scholarship may be reduced from deficiencies in grades, Christian service, or chapel attendance.

Central Methodist University   (H)

411 Central Methodist Square, Fayette MO 65248-1198
County: Howard   FICE Identification: 002453
Unit ID: 445267
Telephone: (660) 248-3391   Carnegie Class: Masters/S
FAX Number: (660) 248-2287   Calendar System: Semester
URL: www.centralmethodist.edu
Established: 1854   Annual Undergrad Tuition & Fees: $6,430
Enrollment: 3,429   Coed
Affiliation or Control: United Methodist   IRS Status: 501(c)3
Highest Offering: Master's
Accreditation: **HLC**, CAATE, CACREP, MUS, NURSE, OTA, #PTAA

01	President	Dr. Roger D. DRAKE
05	Provost	Dr. Rita GULSTAD
13	VP Technology & Planning	Mr. Chad GAINES
111	VP Advancement/Alumni Rels	Mr. William SHEEHAN
32	VP for Student Life	Mr. Brad DIXON
84	VP Enrollment Management	Dr. Joseph PARISI
10	VP Finance & Administration	Ms. Julee SHERMAN
08	Director of Information Resources	Ms. Holly RAY
37	Director of Financial Aid	Ms. Kristine STODGEL
07	Director of Admissions	Ms. Maile RHORER
106	Asst Dean Online Programs	Ms. Stephanie BRINK
09	Coordinator Institutional Research	Ms. Amber MONNIG
26	Exec Dir Marketing Communications	Mr. Scott QUEEN
04	Administrative Asst to President	Ms. Whitney PARKS
15	Director of Human Resources	Ms. Kimberly THOMSON
06	Registrar	Ms. Brianne HILGEDICK
18	Chief Facilities/Physical Plant	Mr. Derry WISWALL
19	Campus Safety Officer	Mr. Don CLEAR
36	Dir Student Placement/Career Dev	Vacant
40	Bookstore Manager	Ms. Jill BARRINGHAUS
39	Coordinator of Residential Life	Mr. Jordan SCHWELLENBACH
29	Director Alumni Affairs	Ms. Stasia SHERMAN
41	Athletic Director	Mr. Jeffrey SHERMAN
44	Director Annual Giving	Ms. Alissa WATKINS

Chamberlain University-St. Louis   (I)

11830 Westline Industrial, Ste 106, St. Louis MO 63146
Telephone: (314) 991-6200   Identification: 770494
Accreditation: **&HLC**, NURSE

† Branch campus of Chamberlain University-Addison, Addison, IL

City Vision University   (J)

1100 E 11th Street, Kansas City MO 64106-3028
County: United States   FICE Identification: 041191
Unit ID: 457697
Telephone: (816) 960-2008   Carnegie Class: Bac-Diverse
FAX Number: (816) 256-8471   Calendar System: Other
URL: www.cityvision.edu
Established: 1998   Annual Undergrad Tuition & Fees: $6,000
Enrollment: 127   Coed
Affiliation or Control: Other   IRS Status: 501(c)3
Highest Offering: Master's
Accreditation: **DEAC**

01	Executive Director/President	Dr. Andrew SEARS
05	VP Academic Administration	Dr. Evan DONOVAN
83	Addiction Studies Department Chair	Mrs. Lynda MITTON
10	Financial Aid/Accounting Manager	Mrs. Traci HEDLUND
07	Director of Admissions	Ms. Nancy YOUNG

† Mail address is 31 Torrey St, Dorchester, MA 02124-3543.

College of the Ozarks   (K)

PO Box 17, Point Lookout MO 65726-0017
County: Taney   FICE Identification: 002500
Unit ID: 178697
Telephone: (417) 334-6411   Carnegie Class: Bac-Diverse
FAX Number: N/A   Calendar System: Semester
URL: www.cofo.edu
Established: 1906   Annual Undergrad Tuition & Fees: $19,960
Enrollment: 1,489   Coed
Affiliation or Control: Independent Non-Profit   IRS Status: 501(c)3
Highest Offering: Baccalaureate
Accreditation: **HLC**, ACFEI, DIETD, NURSE, TRACS

01	President	Dr. Brad S. JOHNSON
125	Chancellor	Dr. Jerry C. DAVIS
11	COO/VP Vocational Pgms	Dr. Weston T. WIEBE
05	VP Academic Affairs/Dean of College	Dr. Eric BOLGER
42	VP Christian Ministries/Dean Chapel	Dr. Justin CARSWELL
93	VP Cultural Affs/Dean Character Ed	Dr. Sue HEAD
07	VP Patriotic Activities/Dean Admiss	Dr. Marci LINSON
30	Dean of Development	Dr. Natalie RASNICK
103	Dean of Work Education	Dr. Nick SHARP
32	Dean of Students	Dr. Nick SHARP
88	Dean of the Lab School	Dr. Brad DOLLOFF
10	Business Manager	Mr. Greg STARK
13	Chief Info Technology Officer	Mr. Jeffrey K. SCHNEIDER

18 Chief Facilities/Physical Plant .... Mr. Jody BRASWELL
06 Registrar .... Mrs. Lacey MATTHEIS
26 Director of Public Relations .... Mrs. Valorie COLEMAN
29 Director of Alumni Affairs .... Mrs. Angela WILLIAMSON
36 Director of Career Center .... Mr. Jim FREEMAN
37 Director of Financial Aid .... Mr. Jeff FORD
19 Director of Security .... Mr. David KEMPF
96 Director of Purchasing .... Mr. Andy MCNEILL
41 Athletic Director .... Mr. Steve SHEPHERD
38 Student Counseling .... Mrs. Pat MCLEAN
08 Librarian/Library Science .... Ms. Gwen SIMMONS
88 Assistant to the Chancellor .... Mrs. Beth BLEVINS
04 Assistant to the President .... Mrs. Tamara J. SCHNEIDER

Columbia College (A)

1001 Rogers Street, Columbia MO 65216-0001
County: Boone FICE Identification: 002456
Unit ID: 177065
Telephone: (573) 875-8700 Carnegie Class: Masters/L
FAX Number: (573) 875-7209 Calendar System: Semester
URL: www.ccis.edu
Established: 1851 Annual Undergrad Tuition & Fees: $24,320
Enrollment: 8,347 Coed
Affiliation or Control: Christian Church (Disciples Of Christ)
IRS Status: 501(c)3
Highest Offering: Master's
Accreditation: HLC, ADNUR, MAC, NURSE

01 Interim President .... Dr. David R. RUSSELL
05 Provost/Vice Pres Academic Affairs .... Dr. Piyusha SINGH
51 VP Adult Higher Education .... Dr. Jeff MUSGROVE
11 SVP/Chief Operations Officer .... Mr. Kevin PALMER
111 Vice President of Advancement .... Ms. Suzanne ROTHWELL
10 Chief Financial Officer .... Mr. Bruce E. BOYER
32 Dean of Student Affairs .... Mr. Dave ROBERTS
18 Exec Director of Plant/Facilities .... Mr. Cliff JARVIS
26 AVP of Marketing .... Mr. Brad WUCHER
07 AVP of Admissions .... Ms. Stephanie JOHNSON
06 Registrar .... Ms. Jennifer THORPE
29 Sr Director of Alumni Relations .... Ms. Ann MERRIFIELD
27 Sr Director of Public Relations .... Mr. Sam FLEURY
37 Int Director of Financial Aid .... Ms. Coleen BROWN
08 Director of Stafford Library .... Ms. Janet CARUTHERS
106 Dir Online Academic Programs .... Ms. Kate BOULERSOX
35 Director of Student Activities .... Ms. Kim COKE
36 Director Career Services Center .... Mr. Dan GOMEZ-PALACIO
15 Executive Director Human Resources .... Ms. Michelle MCCAULLEY
13 Chief Information Officer .... Mr. Gary STANOWSKI
55 Sr Dir Adult Higher Educ Acad Spprt .... Mr. Eric CUNNINGHAM
41 Director of Athletics .... Mr. Robert BURCHARD
09 Director Institutional Research .... Ms. Shonda IRELAND
19 Director of Campus Safety .... Mr. Robert KLAUSMEYER
113 Bursar .... Ms. Denise GELINA

Conception Seminary College (B)

37174 State Highway VV, PO Box 502,
Conception MO 64433-0502
County: Nodaway FICE Identification: 002467
Unit ID: 177083
Telephone: (660) 944-3105 Carnegie Class: Spec-4-yr-Faith
FAX Number: (660) 944-2829 Calendar System: Semester
URL: www.conception.edu
Established: 1883 Annual Undergrad Tuition & Fees: $22,873
Enrollment: 42 Male
Affiliation or Control: Roman Catholic IRS Status: 501(c)3
Highest Offering: Baccalaureate
Accreditation: HLC

01 Rector & President .... VRev. Victor SCHINSTOCK, OSB
11 Director of Administration .... Mrs. Amy K. SCHIEBER
32 Vice Rector/Dean of Stdnts/ Chaplain .... Rev. Pachomius MEADE, OSB
05 Dean of Academic Affairs .... Dr. Lawrence J. WELCH
10 Business Manager/Dir Auxiliary Svcs .... Bro. Jacob KUBAJAK
30 Development Director .... Mrs. Jenny HUARD
07 Director of Admissions/Registrar .... Mrs. Jeanette SCHIEBER
37 Director of Student Financial Aid .... Bro. Justin J. HERNANDEZ
29 Director of Alumni .... Bro. Thomas SULLIVAN, OSB
08 Librarian .... Mr. Chris BRITE
26 Director of Communications .... Mrs. Kaity HOLTMAN
13 Director of Information Technology .... Mr. Tony MEISTER
38 Director of Counseling Services .... Rev. Duane REINERT
18 Chief Facilities/Physical Plant .... Mr. Mark WIEDERHOLT

Concorde Career College (C)

3239 Broadway Street, Kansas City MO 64111-2407
County: Jackson FICE Identification: 023616
Unit ID: 155283
Telephone: (816) 531-5223 Carnegie Class: Spec-4-yr-Other Health
FAX Number: (816) 756-3231 Calendar System: Other
URL: https://www.concorde.edu/campus/kansas-city-missouri
Established: 1986 Annual Undergrad Tuition & Fees: N/A
Enrollment: 323 Coed
Affiliation or Control: Proprietary IRS Status: Proprietary
Highest Offering: Baccalaureate
Accreditation: ACCSC, COARC, DH, PTAA

01 Campus President .... Kathrin PACKARD
05 Academic Dean .... Lisa BALZARETTI
07 Int Director of Admissions .... Alex VACA
32 Director of Student Affairs .... Dan GURULE
37 Director of Financial Aid .... Derrick PLAIN

Concordia Seminary (D)

801 Seminary Place, Saint Louis MO 63105-3168
County: Saint Louis FICE Identification: 002457
Unit ID: 177092
Telephone: (314) 505-7000 Carnegie Class: Spec-4-yr-Faith
FAX Number: (314) 505-7001 Calendar System: Semester
URL: www.csl.edu
Established: 1839 Annual Graduate Tuition & Fees: N/A
Enrollment: 596 Coed
Affiliation or Control: Lutheran Church - Missouri Synod
IRS Status: 501(c)3
Highest Offering: Doctorate; No Undergraduates
Accreditation: HLC, THEOL

01 President .... Rev Dr. Thomas J. EGGER
03 Executive Vice President/COO .... Mr. Michael LOUIS
05 Provost .... Rev Dr. Douglas L. RUTT
10 Sr VP for Finance/Administration .... Mr. Chad A. CATTOOR
111 Senior VP for Advancement .... Mrs. Vicki BIGGS
58 Dean of Advanced Studies .... Rev Dr. Joel ELOWSKY
06 Registrar .... Mrs. Beth R. MENNEKE
110 Executive Director Seminary Support .... Mrs. Kathleen LUTHER
20 Associate Provost .... Rev Dr. Benjamin HAUPT
88 Director Center for Hispanic Study .... Rev Dr. Leopoldo A. SANCHEZ
15 Director of Human Resources .... Mr. Thomas MYERS
18 Director Campus Facilities .... Mr. Martin HAGUE
36 Director of Placement .... Rev Dr. Glenn NIELSEN
37 Director of Student Financial Aid .... Mrs. Laura HEMMER
13 Chief Information Officer .... Mr. John KLINGER
29 Sr Coord Alumni Relations .... Ms. Melodie BOSTIC
04 Executive Asst to President .... Ms. Pamela K. DAVITZ
09 Director of Institutional Research .... Rev Dr. Alan BORCHERDING
44 Director Gift Operations .... Ms. Megan DUNCAN
51 Director Continuing Education .... Ms. Erika BENNETT
88 Managing Editor Sem Publication .... Ms. Melanie APPLEBAUM
84 Director Recruitment .... Rev. Micah A. GLENN
08 Director Library Services .... Rev Dr. Paul ROBINSON

Cottey College (E)

1000 W Austin Boulevard, Nevada MO 64772-2763
County: Vernon FICE Identification: 002458
Unit ID: 177117
Telephone: (417) 667-8181 Carnegie Class: Bac/Assoc-Mixed
FAX Number: (417) 667-8103 Calendar System: Semester
URL: www.cottey.edu
Established: 1884 Annual Undergrad Tuition & Fees: $22,770
Enrollment: 283 Female
Affiliation or Control: Independent Non-Profit IRS Status: 501(c)3
Highest Offering: Baccalaureate
Accreditation: HLC, MUS

01 President .... Dr. Stefanie NILES
05 VP Academic Affs/Dean of Faculty .... Dr. Joann BANGS
10 VP for Finance & Administration .... Ms. Kimberly MARSHALL
32 VP for Student Life .... Mr. Landon ADAMS
84 VP for Enrollment Mgmt & Marketing .... Mr. David HERINGER
30 Director of Development .... Ms. Staci KEYS
88 Dir of Enrollment/Comm & Research .... Ms. Angela MOORE
06 Registrar .... Mr. William STANFILL
08 Director of the Library .... Ms. Courtney TRAUTWEILER
18 Director Physical Plant .... Mr. Todd HEFNER
19 Manager of Campus Safety/Security .... Mr. Brett DAWN
15 Director of Human Resources .... Ms. McGee STOLLER
91 Director Administrative Computing .... Mr. Keith SPENCER
37 Director of Financial Aid .... Ms. Hannah MASTERS
90 Director Academic Computing .... Mr. Adam DEAN
39 Director of Housing .... Ms. Cindy SPENCER
41 Director of Athletics .... Ms. Maryann MITTS
40 Bookstore Manager .... Ms. Sherry PENNINGTON
09 Director of Institutional Research .... Ms. Annette ROBERTS
111 Associate VP Inst Advancement .... Ms. Christi ELLIS
38 Director of Health & Counseling Svc .... Ms. Jeanna SIMPSON
88 Director of Engagement Activities .... Ms. Amy HOLLENBURG
04 Director of the President's Office .... Ms. Catherine MORRIS
21 Controller .... Ms. Jeannine NIKODIM
108 Dir of Assessment & Inst Research .... Ms. Nancy KERBS
26 Director of Marketing .... Mr. Randon COFFEY
35 Director of Campus Activities & Cal .... Ms. Kristi KORB
109 Executive Chef & Director of Dining .... Ms. April MOSHER
88 Asst Dir Administrative Computing .... Mr. Justin MAYS
88 Accountant .... Ms. Alli SHINKLE

Covenant Theological Seminary (F)

12330 Conway Road, Saint Louis MO 63141-8697
County: Saint Louis FICE Identification: 004707
Unit ID: 177126
Telephone: (314) 434-4044 Carnegie Class: Spec-4-yr-Faith
FAX Number: (314) 434-4819 Calendar System: 4/1/4
URL: www.covenantseminary.edu
Established: 1956 Annual Graduate Tuition & Fees: N/A
Enrollment: 593 Coed
Affiliation or Control: Presbyterian Church In America IRS Status: 501(c)3
Highest Offering: Doctorate; No Undergraduates
Accreditation: HLC, THEOL

01 President .... RevDr. Thomas C. GIBBS
05 VP of Academics .... Dr. Jay SKLAR
10 VP of Business and Finance .... Mr. Jason ROBEY
111 Interim VP of Advancement .... Mr. Ken MCDONALD
08 Library Director .... Mr. Steve JAMIESON
20 Dean of Academic Administration .... Ms. Jessica SWIGART
32 Dean of Students .... Mr. Mark MCELMURRY
07 Director of Admissions .... Mr. Stuart MCCLURE
30 Sr Director of Business Development .... Mr. Ken MCDONALD
37 Director of Financial Aid .... Ms. Lori BODE
13 Director of Information Technology .... Mr. Ryan JOHNS
06 Registrar .... Ms. Betsy GASOSKE
29 Alumni/Placement Services Director .... Dr. Joel HATHAWAY
21 Controller .... Mr. Collin OHMS
26 Sr Director of Communications .... Mr. Kent NEEDLER
38 Associate Dean of Counseling .... Mrs. Sabrina HICKEL
35 Associate Dean of Student Life .... Ms. Lindsey DEJONG
88 Director of Accreditation Services .... Mrs. Shannon HATHAWAY
15 Assoc Director of Human Resources .... Mrs. Meagan BUCHHOLZ
106 Assoc Director of Online Learning .... Mr. Aaron GOLDSTEIN
18 Senior Director of Campus Operation .... Mr. Brian SKAMRA
84 Senior Director of Enrollment .... Mr. John CHUNG

Cox College (G)

1423 N Jefferson Avenue, Springfield MO 65802-1917
County: Greene FICE Identification: 020682
Unit ID: 176770
Telephone: (417) 269-3401 Carnegie Class: Spec-4-yr-Other Health
FAX Number: (417) 269-3581 Calendar System: Semester
URL: www.coxcollege.edu
Established: 1907 Annual Undergrad Tuition & Fees: $12,600
Enrollment: 975 Coed
Affiliation or Control: Independent Non-Profit IRS Status: 501(c)3
Highest Offering: Master's
Accreditation: HLC, ADNUR, DIETI, DMS, NURSE, OT, RAD

01 President .... Dr. Amy DEMELO
05 Vice Pres Acad Affairs/Inst Effect .... Vacant
10 Vice Pres Business/Finance .... Jayne BULLARD
32 VP Student Affs/Marketing/Comm/Dev .... Dr. Sonya HAYTER
37 Director of Financial Aid .... Steve NICHOLS
06 Registrar .... Ms. Monica LEWIN
113 Bursar .... Lianna MARSHALL
106 Chair E-Learning/General Education .... Heather SADE

Crowder College (H)

601 Laclede Avenue, Neosho MO 64850-9165
County: Newton FICE Identification: 002459
Unit ID: 177135
Telephone: (417) 451-3223 Carnegie Class: Assoc/MT-VT-High Trad
FAX Number: (417) 455-5702 Calendar System: Semester
URL: www.crowder.edu
Established: 1963 Annual Undergrad Tuition & Fees (In-District): $5,328
Enrollment: 4,194 Coed
Affiliation or Control: Local IRS Status: 501(c)3
Highest Offering: Associate Degree
Accreditation: HLC, ADNUR, EMT, OTA

01 President .... Dr. Katricia PIERSON
10 Vice President of Finance .... Mrs. Mickie MAHAN
05 Interim VP of Academic Affairs .... Dr. Chett DANIEL
32 Vice President of Student Affairs .... Mrs. Tiffany SLINKARD
26 Assoc VP of Information Services .... Vacant
75 Assoc VP of Careers & Tech Educ .... Dr. Phillip WITT
20 Assoc VP of Academic Affairs .... Mr. Keith ZOROMSKI
07 Director of Admissions .... Mr. JP DICKEY
09 Director of Institutional Research .... Vacant
08 Director of Lee Library .... Mr. Eric DEATHERAGE
27 Director of Public Information .... Mrs. Cindy BROWN
41 Athletic Director .... Vacant
37 Director of Financial Aid .... Mr. Jared BROWN
15 Director of Human Resources .... Mrs. Cassandra HALE
111 Dir of Institutional Advancement .... Mr. Jim CULLUMBER
40 Bookstore Manager .... Ms. Colleen HOLLAND
35 Assoc VP of Student Affairs .... Ms. Jamie WARD
13 Vice President of Info Services .... Mr. Al STADLER
04 Exec Assistant to the President .... Ms. Elizabeth ARMSTRONG
18 Chief Facilities/Physical Plnt Ofcr .... Mr. TJ ANGEL
25 Grants Director .... Ms. Kathy PARKER-COLLIER

Culver-Stockton College (I)

One College Hill, Canton MO 63435-1257
County: Lewis FICE Identification: 002460
Unit ID: 177144
Telephone: (573) 288-6000 Carnegie Class: Bac-Diverse
FAX Number: (573) 288-6611 Calendar System: Semester
URL: www.culver.edu
Established: 1853 Annual Undergrad Tuition & Fees: $27,740
Enrollment: 1,006 Coed
Affiliation or Control: Christian Church (Disciples Of Christ)
IRS Status: 501(c)3
Highest Offering: Master's
Accreditation: HLC, CAATE, IACBE, MUS

01 President .... Dr. Douglas PALMER
05 Provost/VPAA .... Dr. Lauren SCHELLENBERGER
32 Dean of Student Life .... Dr. Angela ROYAL
84 VP for Enrollment Management .... Dr. Kim GAITHER
111 VP for Advancement and Marketing .... Ms. Leslie PAYNE

06 Registrar/Director Inst Research .... Mrs. Chris HUEBOTTER
08 Librarian .... Dr. Katherine MARNEY
26 Dir of Communications & Marketing .... Ms. Alyssa HUMMEL
37 Director Financial Aid .... Mrs. Tina WISEMAN
29 Director of Alumni Programs .... Ms. Melissa DUBUQUE
91 Exec Dir Admin Systems/Services .... Dr. Joseph LIESEN
10 Chief Financial Officer .... Mrs. Diane BOZARTH
15 Exec Dir of Human Resources .... Mrs. Amy BAKER
35 Director of Student Engagement .... Mr. Bill BOXDORFER
42 Chaplain .... Rev. Wesley KNIGHT
41 Athletic Director .... Mr. Patrick ATWELL
40 Wildcat Warehouse Manager .... Mrs. Sharon FARR
04 Sr Assistant to the President .... Ms. Cindy FREELS
19 Director Campus Security & Facil .... Mr. Michael BRINGER
49 Chair Applied Liberal Arts/Sciences .... Dr. Scott GILTNER
50 Chair Business Education & Law .... Mrs. Julie STRAUS
57 Chair Fine Applied & Literary Arts .... Dr. Dylan MARNEY
58 Dean of Grad & Professional Studies .... Dr. Dell Ann JANNEY
92 Director of Honors Program .... Dr. Haidee HEATON
24 Circulation Coordinator .... Ms. Robyn LAMBERT
112 Dir Major Gifts & Estate Giving .... Ms. Courtney POURCIAUX
36 Dir of Career Services/Internship .... Ms. Robin JARVIS
124 Director of Retention .... Dr. Alissa BURGER
38 Dir Counseling/Student Wellness .... Ms. Susan MOON
09 Director of Institutional Research .... Mrs. Karla MCREYNOLDS
110 Director of Advancement Operations .... Mrs. Marjorie ELLISON
104 Director Study Abroad .... Dr. Melissa HOLT
122 Coord Fraternity/Sorority Life .... Mr. Bill BOXDORFER

Drury University (A)

900 N Benton Avenue, Springfield MO 65802-3791

County: Greene — FICE Identification: 002461 — Unit ID: 177214

Telephone: (417) 873-7879 — Carnegie Class: Masters/S
FAX Number: (417) 873-7529 — Calendar System: Semester
URL: www.drury.edu
Established: 1873 — Annual Undergrad Tuition & Fees: $31,215
Enrollment: 1,691 — Coed
Affiliation or Control: Independent Non-Profit — IRS Status: 501(c)3
Highest Offering: Master's
Accreditation: HLC, CAEP, MUS

01 President .... Dr. Timothy CLOYD
05 Executive Vice President/Provost .... Dr. Beth HARVILLE
10 EVP of Administrative Services/CFO .... Mr. Rob FRIDGE
32 EVP Student Affs/Dean of Students .... Dr. Tijuana S. JULIAN
43 Exec VP Univ Rels/General Counsel .... Mr. Aaron JONES
84 EVP Enrollment Management .... Mr. Kevin KROPF
111 Exec Vice Pres Advancement .... Ms. Marie MUHVIC
112 Senior VP of Major Gifts .... Mr. Wayne CHIPMAN
15 Director Human Resources .... Mrs. Jennifer BALTES
20 Assoc Provost Adult/Online/Grad .... Dr. Shannon CUFF
18 VP of Facilities Operations .... Mr. Brandon GAMMILL
41 VP & Director of Athletics .... Mrs. Nyla MILLESON
06 University Registrar .... Ms. Salia MANIS
13 VP of Technology Services .... Mr. Val SERAFIMOV
26 Exec Director of Marketing & Comm ... Mrs. Chelsea BALTIMORE
09 Director of Institutional Research .... Ms. Deborah DERDEN
21 University Controller .... Ms. Debbie O'NEAL
121 Assoc VP Ac Affrs/Dir Compass Cntr .... Dr. Jennifer JOSLIN
37 Director of Financial Aid .... Ms. Rebecca AHRENS
08 Director of FW Olin Library .... Mr. William GARVIN
36 Dir Career Planning & Development .... Mr. Brandon GASH
88 Dir Disability Support Services .... Ms. Lori SLATER
19 Director of Safety and Security .... Mr. Chris JOHNS
89 Dir Orientation/New Student Program .... Ms. Jennifer STEWART
39 Dir of Student Housing/Res Pgms .... Mr. Ethan SYKES
88 Director of Administrative Services .... Ms. Christie GARRISON
42 Chaplain .... Dr. Peter BROWNING
04 Executive Asst to President .... Mrs. Bonnie WILCOX
104 Associate Dean Intl Programs .... Dr. Thomas RUSSO
106 Director of Online Education .... Ms. Alexis SLYTER
07 Director of Admission .... Mrs. Kelli ROBERTS
88 Director of Advancement Services .... Mr. Michael SHRIMPTON
113 Director of Business Services .... Mrs. Jill HOLMES
50 Dean School of Business .... Dr. Jeffrey ZIMMERMAN
81 Dean Sch Natural & Math Sciences .... Mr. Albert KORIR
57 Dean School Comm/Fine & Perf Arts .... Dr. Allin SORENSON
83 Dean Sch Human & Social Sciences .... Dr. Jennifer SILVA-BROWN
48 Dean Hammons School of Architecture .... Dr. Robert WEDDLE
53 Dean School Education & Child Dev .... Ms. Natalie PRECISE
35 Assoc Dean of Students .... Mr. Chip PARKER
28 Assoc Dean of Diversity & Inclusion .... Mrs. Rosalyn THOMAS
110 Assoc VP of Advancement .... Ms. Melanie EARL-REPLOGLE
40 Director Univ Bookstore .... Ms. Valerie RAINS
122 Director of Greek Life .... Ms. Anna STARK
102 Director Foundation/Corporate Rels .... Mrs. Melissa ADLER

Drury University Ft. Leonard Wood Campus (B)

4904 Constitution Drive, Ft. Leonard Wood MO 65473

Telephone: (573) 329-4400 — Identification: 770319
Accreditation: &HLC

Drury University Rolla Campus (C)

1034 S. Bishop Avenue, Rolla MO 65401

Telephone: (573) 368-4959 — Identification: 770321
Accreditation: &HLC

East Central College (D)

1964 Prairie Dell Road, Union MO 63084-0529

County: Franklin — FICE Identification: 008862 — Unit ID: 177250

Telephone: (636) 584-6500 — Carnegie Class: Assoc/MT-VT-Mix Trad/Non
FAX Number: (636) 583-1897 — Calendar System: Semester
URL: www.eastcentral.edu
Established: 1968 — Annual Undergrad Tuition & Fees (In-District): $4,272
Enrollment: 2,593 — Coed
Affiliation or Control: Local — IRS Status: 501(c)3
Highest Offering: Associate Degree
Accreditation: HLC, ACFEI, ART, CAHIIM, EMT, MAC, MLTAD, MUS, NAIT, OTA

01 President .... Dr. C. Jon BAUER
10 Vice Pres Finance/Administration .... Ms. DeAnna CASSAT
05 Vice President Academic Affairs .... Ms. Robyn WALTER
32 Vice President Student Development .... Ms. Sarah LEASSNER
26 VP External Relations .... Mr. Joel DOEPKER
12 Director ECC Rolla .... Ms. Christina M. AYRES
102 Exec Director Foundation .... Ms. Bridgette KELCH
18 Director Facilities & Grounds .... Mr. Tot PRATT
08 Director of Library Services .... Ms. Lisa M. FARRELL
96 Purchasing Manager .... Ms. Melissa D. POPP
79 Dean of Instruction .... Ms. Ann BOEHMER
75 Dean of Career & Technical Educ .... Mr. Richard HUDANICK
81 Department Chair Math & Education .... Dr. Reginald BRIGHAM
79 Dept Chair English & Humanities .... Mr. Joshua STROUP
54 Dept Chair Science & Engineering .... Dr. Parvadha GOVINDASWAMY
83 Department Chair Social Sciences ...... Dr. William CUNNINGHAM
64 Dept Chair Fine & Performing Arts ....Vacant
15 Director Human Resources .... Ms. Carrie MYERS
76 Dean of Health Sciences .... Ms. Nancy MITCHELL
37 Director Financial Aid .... Mr. Jon GRUETT
06 Registrar .... Ms. Sarah SCROGGINS
21 Director Financial Svcs/Comptroller .... Ms. Annette MOORE
09 Director of Institutional Research .... Ms. Bethany L. LOHDEN
27 Director Communications/Marketing .... Mr. Gregg JONES
13 Director Information Technology .... Mr. Doug HOUSTON
40 Bookstore/Mail/Imaging Coordinator .... Mr. Doug A. AGEE
121 Director Advising & Counseling .... Mr. Paul LAMPE
103 Executive Director Workforce Devel .... Mr. Edward SHELTON
51 Coordinator Adult Educ & Literacy .... Ms. Alice WHALEN
24 Coordinator Instructional Design .... Mr. R. Chad BALDWIN
35 Coordinator Student Activities .... Ms. Carson MOWERY
04 Executive Asst to President .... Ms. Bonnie S. GARDNER
41 Athletic Director .... Mr. Jay MEHRHOFF
101 Secretary of the Institution/Board .... Ms. Bonnie GARDNER
07 Dir Early College & Admissions .... Ms. Megen STRUBBERG
30 Director of Development .... Ms. Bridgette KELCH
108 Director Institutional Assessment .... Dr. Michelle SMITH

Eden Theological Seminary (E)

475 E Lockwood Avenue,
Webster Groves MO 63119-3192

County: Saint Louis — FICE Identification: 002462 — Unit ID: 177278

Telephone: (314) 961-3627 — Carnegie Class: Spec-4-yr-Faith
FAX Number: (314) 962-9918 — Calendar System: 4/1/4
URL: www.eden.edu
Established: 1850 — Annual Graduate Tuition & Fees: N/A
Enrollment: 117 — Coed
Affiliation or Control: United Church Of Christ — IRS Status: 501(c)3
Highest Offering: Doctorate; No Undergraduates
Accreditation: HLC, THEOL

01 President .... Ms. Deborah KRAUSE
111 Vice President for Advancement .... Ms. Mary BLAUFUSS
05 Academic Dean .... Dr. Christopher GRUNDY
06 Registrar .... Ms. Michelle WOBBE
04 Exec Asst to the President .... Ms. Danita CARTER
32 Dean of the Seminary .... Dr. Sonja WILLIAMS
15 Director of Human Resources .... Ms. Denise STAUFFER
10 Director of Accounting .... Ms. Kelly JOHNSON
30 Director of Development .... Ms. Sandi BOEHLEIN
18 Chief Facilities/Physical Plant .... Mr. Todd THEISSEN
07 Director of Admissions .... Ms. Dana MCNAMARA
08 Chief Library Officer .... Mr. Scott HOLL
11 Dir Administration/Implementation .... Ms. Denise STAUFFER
13 Chief Information Technology Ofcr ...... Ms. Katie HOTZE-WILTON

Evangel University (F)

1111 N Glenstone, Springfield MO 65802-2191

County: Greene — FICE Identification: 002463 — Unit ID: 177339

Telephone: (417) 865-2815 — Carnegie Class: Masters/M
FAX Number: (417) 865-9599 — Calendar System: Semester
URL: www.evangel.edu
Established: 1955 — Annual Undergrad Tuition & Fees: $25,037
Enrollment: 1,999 — Coed
Affiliation or Control: Assemblies Of God Church — IRS Status: 501(c)3
Highest Offering: Doctorate
Accreditation: HLC, ACBSP, CACREP, MUS, SW

01 President .... Dr. Mike RAKES
10 Exec Vice Pres/VP Business/Finance .... Ms. Linda ALLEN
32 VP for Student Development .... Mr. Mark ENTZMINGER
111 Exec Vice Pres/Chief of Staff .... Dr. Michael KOLSTAD
05 VP for Academic Affairs/CAO .... Dr. Jon SPENCE
84 Vice Pres Enrollment Management .... Mr. Chris BELCHER
26 Direct Marketing/Communication Ofcr .... Mrs. Erin HEDLUN
18 Director of Physical Plant .... Mr. Brian HAUFF
41 Director of Athletics .... Dr. Dennis MCDONALD
06 Registrar .... Mrs. Connie CROSS
08 Librarian .... Mr. Richard OLIVER
19 Director of Public Safety .... Mr. Brian KEYES
38 Director of Counseling Services .... Vacant
30 Senior Development Officer .... Mr. Hector CRUZ
37 Dir of Student Financial Services .... Mrs. Valerie SHARP
36 Career Development/Placement .... Mrs. Shannon MCCLURE
23 Director of Health Services .... Ms. Susan BRYAN
21 Controller .... Mr. Dan EDWARDS
35 Director Student Life .... Miss Gina RENTSCHLER
15 Director of Human Resources .... Dr. Rob BARTELS
39 Housing Coordinator .... Mrs. Danielle POULSON-JONES
09 Director of Institutional Research .... Dr. Linda WELLBORN
04 Executive Asst to President .... Mrs. Angela DENSE
101 Secretary of the Institution/Board .... Mrs. Angela DENSE

Fontbonne University (G)

6800 Wydown Boulevard, Saint Louis MO 63105-3098

County: Saint Louis — FICE Identification: 002464 — Unit ID: 177418

Telephone: (314) 862-3456 — Carnegie Class: Masters/M
FAX Number: (314) 889-1451 — Calendar System: Semester
URL: www.fontbonne.edu
Established: 1923 — Annual Undergrad Tuition & Fees: $27,790
Enrollment: 1,112 — Coed
Affiliation or Control: Roman Catholic — IRS Status: 501(c)3
Highest Offering: Doctorate
Accreditation: HLC, ACBSP, DIETC, DIETD, SP, SW

01 President .... Dr. Nancy BLATTNER
05 Vice President Academic Affairs .... Dr. Adam WEYHAUPT
30 Vice President Advancement .... Ms. Kathleen BARNES
32 Vice President Student Affairs .... Ms. Heather FRENCH
10 Vice President Finance & Admin/CFO .... Mrs. Ann SPALL
84 Vice President Enrollment Mgmt .... Mr. Quinton CLAY
41 Vice President for Athletics .... Mrs. Maria BUCKEL
13 Director of Information Technology .... Ms. Julianne HAYES
35 Associate Vice Pres Student Affairs .... Dr. Janelle JULIAN
20 Associate VP Acad Affairs .... Vacant
35 Assistant VP for Student Affairs .... Vacant
49 Dean Arts & Sciences .... Dr. Gale RICE
50 Dean Global Business/Prof Studies .... Dr. Gale RICE
76 Dean Educ/Allied Health Prof .... Dr. Gale RICE
06 Registrar .... Ms. Katie PIACENTINI
15 Director Human Resources .... Mr. Steven LOHER
08 University Librarian .... Dr. Sharon MCCASLIN
22 Acad/Disabilities Resources Coord .... Mrs. Regina WADE JOHNSON
09 Director Institutional Research .... Mrs. Meaghan ONG
26 Director of Integrated Marketing .... Ms. Stephanie DANE
106 Director Online Programs .... Ms. Joanne MATTSON
121 Director Academic Advising .... Ms. Lee DELAET
85 Director International Affairs .... Ms. Caroline CLASBY
29 Director Alumni Relations .... Ms. Kate FLATLEY
28 Director Multicultural Affairs .... Ms. Deanna WILLIAMS
124 Dir Orientation & Stdnt Engagement .... Mr. Joel HERMANN
19 Director Public Safety .... Mr. Larry VERTREES
18 Director Physical Plant .... Vacant
04 Exec Asst Office of Pres/Board .... Mrs. Yvonne FARMER
121 Dir Student Success/Engagement .... Mr. Corey HAWKINS
36 Director Career Development .... Vacant
38 Director Counseling and Wellness .... Ms. Therese JACQUES
07 Associate VP Admission .... Ms. Jenny CHISM
37 Director Student Financial Aid .... Mr. Shawn MCCAW
39 Director Residential Life .... Mr. AJ FRIEDHOFF

Global University (H)

1211 South Glenstone Avenue,
Springfield MO 65804-1894

County: Greene — Identification: 666687 — Unit ID: 247296

Telephone: (800) 443-1083 — Carnegie Class: Not Classified
FAX Number: (417) 865-7167 — Calendar System: Other
URL: www.globaluniversity.edu
Established: 2000 — Annual Undergrad Tuition & Fees: N/A
Enrollment: N/A — Coed
Affiliation or Control: Assemblies Of God Church — IRS Status: 501(c)3
Highest Offering: Doctorate
Accreditation: HLC

01 President .... Dr. Gary SEEVERS, JR.
03 Executive Vice President .... Rev. Keith HEERMANN
05 Provost .... Dr. David L. DEGARMO
20 Vice Provost Academic Effectiveness ...... Dr. D. Bradley AUSBURY
58 Dean Graduate School/Theology .... Dr. Randy J. HEDLUN
73 Dean UG School Bible & Theology .... Dr. Kevin FOLK
13 VP Info Tech/Media Dept .... Mr. Wade W. PETTENGER
10 Vice President Finance .... Mr. Aron VAD
111 Vice President Advancement .... Vacant
07 Director of Enrollment Services .... Rev. Todd WAGGONER
06 Registrar .... Mrs. Lynne KROH
15 Director of Human Resources .... Ms. Jami NEMETI
04 Administrative Asst to President .... Mr. Gabriel RICHNER
08 Head Librarian .... Rev. Russ LANGFORD
09 Director of Institutional Research .... Dr. Brad AUSBURY
18 Chief Facilities/Physical Plant .... Mr. Bruce HAVENS

Goldfarb School of Nursing at Barnes-Jewish College (A)

4483 Duncan Avenue, Stop: 90-36-697,
Saint Louis MO 63110-1111
County: Saint Louis FICE Identification: 006389
Unit ID: 177719
Telephone: (314) 454-7055 Carnegie Class: Spec-4-yr-Other Health
FAX Number: (314) 362-9250 Calendar System: Trimester
URL: www.barnesjewishcollege.edu
Established: 1902 Annual Undergrad Tuition & Fees: N/A
Enrollment: 627 Coed
Affiliation or Control: Independent Non-Profit IRS Status: 501(c)3
Highest Offering: Doctorate
Accreditation: HLC, ANEST, NURSE

01 President ... Dr. Nancy RIDENOUR
10 Vice Dean for Finance/Admin ... Mr. Djuan COLEMAN
32 Vice Dean Student Affairs/Diversity ... Dr. Michael WARD
15 Vice Dean Human Res/Strat Effect ... Ms. Rosalynn BRYANT
05 Dean Academic Affairs ... Dr. Mayola ROWSER
46 Associate Dean for Research ... Vacant
08 Library & Info Services Director ... Ms. Renee GORRELL
21 Finance Director ... Ms. Linda STILLE
13 Director Information System ... Mr. Carlos PARDO
06 Registrar ... Dr. Samantha DEAN
84 Director Enrollment Management ... Ms. Stacy BOGIER
04 Administrative Asst to Dean ... Ms. Wanda CUMMINGS
29 Director Alumni Relations ... Dr. June COWELL-OATES
09 Dir Institutional Effectiveness ... Dr. George VINEYARD
26 Marketing Research Manager ... Ms. Angela WADE
100 Special Assistant to the President ... Deborah METTLACH

Graceland University (B)

1401 West Truman Road, Independence MO 64050-3434
Telephone: (816) 833-0524 Identification: 666262
Accreditation: &HLC, NURSE

† Regional accreditation is carried under the parent institution in Lamoni, IA.

Graduate School of the Stowers Institute for Medical Research (C)

1000 East 50th Street, Kansas City MO 64110
County: Jackson Identification: 667369
Telephone: (816) 926-4400 Carnegie Class: Not Classified
FAX Number: N/A Calendar System: Other
URL: www.stowers.org/gradschool
Established: 2012 Annual Graduate Tuition & Fees: N/A
Enrollment: N/A Coed
Affiliation or Control: Independent Non-Profit IRS Status: 501(c)3
Highest Offering: Doctorate; No Undergraduates
Accreditation: HLC

01 President ... Dr. Betty M. DREES
05 Dean ... Dr. Matthew GIBSON
10 Chief Financial Officer ... Penny SPENCE
11 Assoc Dean Administration/Registrar ... Susan WEIGEL
15 Human Resources Officer ... Vacant

Hannibal-LaGrange University (D)

2800 Palmyra Road, Hannibal MO 63401-1999
County: Marion FICE Identification: 009089
Unit ID: 177542
Telephone: (573) 221-3675 Carnegie Class: Bac-Diverse
FAX Number: (573) 221-6594 Calendar System: Semester
URL: www.hlg.edu
Established: 1858 Annual Undergrad Tuition & Fees: $24,000
Enrollment: 739 Coed
Affiliation or Control: Southern Baptist IRS Status: 501(c)3
Highest Offering: Master's
Accreditation: HLC, ADNUR, NURSE

01 Transitional President ... Dr. Rodney A. HARRISON
05 VP for Acad Admin/Dean of Faculty ... Dr. Robert J. MATZ
111 VP for Institutional Advancement ... Dr. Raymond W. CARTY
10 VP for Business & Finance ... Vacant
84 VP for Enrollment Management ... Mr. Tad WINGO
32 Dean of Students ... Vacant
06 Registrar/Director of Records ... Mr. Joseph GARNER, III
37 Director of Financial Aid ... Mr. Brice D. BAUMGARDNER
26 Marketing Coordinator ... Vacant
29 Dir Alumni Rels/Development ... Ms. Lauren YOUSE
36 Director Academic/Career Services ... Ms. Kathryn MARTIN
08 Library Director ... Mrs. Julie A. ANDRESEN
19 Chief Public Safety/Compliance Ofcr ... Mr. Abert HIGDON
39 Director of Residential Life ... Mrs. Ashley NEWTON
41 Athletic Director ... Mr. Clay BIGGS
40 Campus Store Manager ... Mrs. Susan A. BOOTH
07 Director of Admissions ... Vacant
30 Director of Development ... Mr. David DEXHEIMER
04 Admin Assistant to the President ... Mrs. Stephanie REECE
15 Chief Human Resources Officer ... Mrs. Jordahn LEONARD

Harris-Stowe State University (E)

3026 Laclede Avenue, Saint Louis MO 63103-2199
County: Independent City FICE Identification: 002466
Unit ID: 177551
Telephone: (314) 340-3366 Carnegie Class: Bac-Diverse
FAX Number: (314) 340-3399 Calendar System: Semester
URL: www.hssu.edu
Established: 1857 Annual Undergrad Tuition & Fees (In-State): $5,484
Enrollment: 1,400 Coed
Affiliation or Control: State IRS Status: 501(c)3
Highest Offering: Baccalaureate
Accreditation: HLC, ACBSP, CAEP

01 President ... Dr. LaTonia COLLINS SMITH
05 Interim Provost/VP Academic Affairs ... Dr. Edward HILL
10 Chief Financial Officer ... Dr. Terence FINLEY
13 Interim CIO ... Mr. Tahir YOUNAS
88 Spec Asst to Pres Spec Events/Proj ... Mr. Bennie GILLIAM-WILLIAMS
111 VP of Institutional Advancement ... Mr. Jeffrey L. SHAW
06 Registrar ... Dr. Chauvette MCELMURRY-GREEN
07 Dir Admissions/Advise/Retention ... Ms. Iris TABB
08 Coordinator of Special Services ... Ms. Linda ORZEL
37 Director Financial Assistance ... Mr. James GREEN
15 Director of Human Resources ... Ms. Romney EDWARDS
38 Director Counseling Services ... Dr. Cammie CONNOR
25 Exec Dir Title III/Sponsored Pgms ... Vacant
20 Director of Academic Success ... Mr. Sean SPINKS
41 Director of Athletics ... Ms. Dorianne JOHNSON
21 Director of Business Services ... Ms. Barbara A. MORROW
36 Dir Career/Engage/Experiential Lrng ... Ms. Victoria HARRIS
53 Dean College of Education ... Dr. Edward HILL
50 Dean Anhauser Busch Sch of Business ... Dr. Stacy HOLLINS
49 Dean College of Arts & Sciences ... Dr. Terry Daily DAVIS
19 Director Security/Safety ... Chief Eric SULLIVAN
32 VP/Dean of Student Success ... Dr. Shawn BAKER
04 Executive Asst to the President ... Ms. Karen MAY
26 Int VP Marketing & Communications ... Dr. Alandrea STEWART
39 Dir Residential Life/Stdnt Conduct ... Mr. Virgil PEARSON
84 Dean of Enrollment Management ... Dr. Manicia FINCH

Heartland Christian College (F)

321 Mercy Street, Bethel MO 63434
County: Shelby Identification: 667091
Telephone: (660) 284-4800 Carnegie Class: Not Classified
FAX Number: (680) 284-4098 Calendar System: Semester
URL: www.heartlandcollege.edu
Established: 1992 Annual Undergrad Tuition & Fees: N/A
Enrollment: N/A Coed
Affiliation or Control: Non-denominational IRS Status: 501(c)3
Highest Offering: Associate Degree
Accreditation: BI

01 President ... Kris R. PALMER
05 Chief Academic Officer ... Martha PALMER
10 CFO ... Nathan MAYES
06 Registrar ... Christie RIHANEK
08 Head Librarian ... Molly NICKERSON

Jefferson College (G)

1000 Viking Drive, Hillsboro MO 63050-2441
County: Jefferson FICE Identification: 002468
Unit ID: 177676
Telephone: (636) 481-3000 Carnegie Class: Assoc/MT-VT-High Trad
FAX Number: (636) 789-4012 Calendar System: Semester
URL: www.jeffco.edu
Established: 1963 Annual Undergrad Tuition & Fees (In-District): $5,940
Enrollment: 3,740 Coed
Affiliation or Control: State/Local IRS Status: 501(c)3
Highest Offering: Associate Degree
Accreditation: HLC, CAHIIM, EMT, OTA, PTAA, RAD

01 President ... Dr. Dena MCCAFFREY
04 Exec Asst to the President & Board ... Ms. Lisa VINYARD
05 Vice President of Instruction/CAO ... Dr. Chris DEGEARE
10 VP Finance & Administration ... Mr. Daryl GEHBAUER
32 VP Student Services ... Dr. Kimberly HARVEY-MANUS
20 Dean Integrated Plng/Academic Svcs ... Mr. Allan WAMSLEY
21 Controller ... Ms. Kathy KUHLMAN
15 Director of Human Resources ... Ms. Tasha WELSH
30 Exec Director of Development ... Mr. Blake TILLEY
26 Director of PR & Marketing ... Mr. Roger BARRENTINE
13 Director Information Technology ... Mr. Tracy JAMES
45 Dir Financial Reporting/Analysis ... Vacant
06 Registrar ... Ms. Stacey WILSON
50 Assoc Dean Business/Social Science ... Dr. Terry KITE
79 Assoc Dean Humanities ... Dr. Michael BOOKER
76 Assoc Dean Science & Health ... Mr. Kenny WILSON
81 Assoc Dean Math/Physics/Technology ... Ms. Maryanne ANGLIONGTO
37 Director Student Financial Services ... Ms. Sarah BRIGHT
84 Director Enrollment Services ... Ms. Holly LINCOLN
96 Director of Purchasing ... Ms. Sheree BELL
08 Director Library Services ... Ms. Lisa PRITCHARD
41 Director Athletics ... Mr. Robert DEUTSCHMAN
31 Director Business/Community Develop ... Vacant
18 Director Buildings & Grounds ... Mr. Dale RICHARDSON
19 Director Public Safety Programs ... Mr. Paul FERBER
66 Director of Nursing ... Ms. Amy MCDANIEL
121 Director Advising & Retention ... Ms. Kathy JOHNSTON
124 Director of Student Support Svcs ... Ms. Teresa SCHWARTZ
74 Director Veterinary Technology ... Ms. Dana NEVOIS
88 Director Child Care Center ... Ms. Stephanie CAGE
39 Director Residential & Student Life ... Vacant
55 Director Adult Educ/Literacy ... Ms. Julie JOHNS
07 Director of Admissions ... Ms. Carrie GREER
09 Director of Institutional Research ... Dr. Jude KYOORE

Kansas City Art Institute (H)

4415 Warwick Boulevard, Kansas City MO 64111-1874
County: Jackson FICE Identification: 002473
Unit ID: 177746
Telephone: (816) 472-4852 Carnegie Class: Spec-4-yr-Arts
FAX Number: (816) 472-3493 Calendar System: Semester
URL: www.kcai.edu
Established: 1885 Annual Undergrad Tuition & Fees: $40,100
Enrollment: 698 Coed
Affiliation or Control: Independent Non-Profit IRS Status: 501(c)3
Highest Offering: Baccalaureate
Accreditation: HLC, ART

01 The Nerman Family President ... Mr. Tony JONES
10 EVP for Administration/CFO ... Mr. Brian HENKE
05 EVP for Academic Affairs ... Dr. Bambi BURGARD
111 Exec VP for Advancement ... Ms. Nicolle RATLIFF
20 VP for Academic Affairs ... Dr. Milton KATZ
15 VP of Human Resources ... Vacant
13 Vice Pres/Chief Information Officer ... Vacant
32 VP/Dean of Student Affairs ... Ms. Gina GOLBA
110 VP for Advancement/General Counsel ... Ms. Emily HESS
20 Senior Academic Affairs Specialist ... Ms. Julia WELLES
26 Director of Communications and PR ... Mr. Whit BONES
06 Registrar ... Ms. Nancy EASTMAN
35 Assistant Dean of Student Affairs ... Mr. Joe TIMSON
38 Psychologist and Counseling Coord ... Ms. Elisabeth SUNDERMEIER
18 Facilities Director/Plant Services ... Ms. Roxie CURTIS
29 Manager of Alumni Relations ... Ms. Angelica DESIMIO
37 Director of Financial Aid ... Ms. Lori BAER
36 Dir of Acad Advising & Career Svcs ... Ms. Amanda HADJU
08 Director of Library ... Ms. M.J POEHLER
24 Director of Creative Media ... Mr. Aldo BACCHETTA
19 Director of Safety & Security ... Mr. Mike RAUNIG
109 Manager of Auxiliary Services ... Ms. Jennifer BOE
88 Director of H&R Block Artspace ... Ms. Raechell SMITH
21 Director of Finance & Accounting ... Ms. Breely BENNETT
04 Exec Admin Asst to President ... Ms. Sarah MCDONALD
39 Asst Dir of Housing & Student Activ ... Ms. Roxie KENNEDY
102 Dir Foundation/Corporate Relations ... Mr. Randy WILLIAMS
90 Director Academic Computing ... Ms. Evonne BRIONES
07 Director of Admissions ... Ms. Darcy DEAL
28 Director of Diversity ... Ms. Shawntae JONES

Kansas City University of Medicine & Biosciences (I)

1750 East Independence Avenue, Kansas City MO 64106
County: Jackson FICE Identification: 002474
Unit ID: 179812
Telephone: (816) 654-7000 Carnegie Class: Spec-4-yr-Med
FAX Number: (816) 654-7101 Calendar System: Semester
URL: www.kcumb.edu
Established: 1916 Annual Graduate Tuition & Fees: N/A
Enrollment: 1,275 Coed
Affiliation or Control: Independent Non-Profit IRS Status: 501(c)3
Highest Offering: First Professional Degree; No Undergraduates
Accreditation: HLC, CLPSY, DENT, OSTEO

01 President & CEO ... Dr. Marc B. HAHN
05 EVP Academic & Rsrch Affs/Provost ... Dr. Edward R. O'CONNOR
10 Exec VP Finance/Operations ... Mr. Joseph MASSMAN
31 Vice Pres Community Engagement ... Vacant
111 VP for Philanthropy/Alumni Rels ... Dr. Jennifer INGRAHAM
84 Vice Prov Student/Enrollment Svcs ... Dr. Kristine A. STEVENS
32 Assoc Provost Student Services ... Ms. Sara E. SELKIRK
17 Vice Pres Health Affairs ... Vacant
12 Dean Joplin Campus ... Dr. Laura ROSCH
76 Dean College of Biosciences ... Dr. Robert WHITE
20 Vice Dean/COM KCU ... Dr. G. Michael JOHNSON
35 Director Student Activities ... Dr. Catherine MCCOMB
100 Chief of Staff/Dir Govt Relations ... Dr. Brooke YODER
26 Exec Dir University Relations ... Ms. Lisa CAMBRIDGE
08 University Library Director ... Ms. Lori FITTERLING
15 Director Human Resources ... Ms. Jamie HIRSHEY
13 Director of Information Technology ... Vacant
37 Director of Financial Aid ... Ms. Kristi NICHOL
63 Campus Dean COM Kansas City ... Dr. Josh COX
19 Director Campus Operations ... Mr. James HERRINGTON
38 Director Counseling and Support Svc ... Ms. Beth EPLEY
29 Director Alumni Development ... Dr. Alex HOPKINS
07 Assoc Director of Admissions ... Ms. Brooke SONGBIRD

Kenrick-Glennon Seminary, Kenrick School of Theology (J)

5200 Glennon Drive, Saint Louis MO 63119-4399
County: Saint Louis FICE Identification: 002476
Unit ID: 177816
Telephone: (314) 792-6100 Carnegie Class: Spec-4-yr-Faith
FAX Number: (314) 792-6500 Calendar System: Semester
URL: www.kenrick.edu
Established: 1893 Annual Undergrad Tuition & Fees: N/A
Enrollment: 68 Male
Affiliation or Control: Roman Catholic IRS Status: 501(c)3
Highest Offering: Master's

Accreditation: HLC, THEOL

01 President/Rector ... Rev. Paul HOESING
03 Vice Rector for Formation ... Rev. Shane DEMAN
73 Dir Pre-Theol & Asst Vice Rector ... Rev. Fadi AURO
05 Academic Dean ... Dr. Edward HOGAN
88 Director of Spiritual Formation ... Rev. Kristian TEATER
08 Director of Library ... Dr. David MORRIS
42 Director of Worship ... Rev. Don ANSTOETTER
30 Director of Development ... Mrs. Kate SAUERBURGER
06 Registrar ... Mr. Andy BOSSALLER
10 Director of Operations & Finance ... Mr. Greg NOVAK

Lincoln University (A)

820 Chestnut Street, Jefferson City MO 65101-3537
County: Cole FICE Identification: 002479
Unit ID: 177940
Telephone: (573) 681-5000 Carnegie Class: Bac-Diverse
FAX Number: (573) 681-5566 Calendar System: Semester
URL: www.lincolnu.edu
Established: 1866 Annual Undergrad Tuition & Fees (In-State): $8,370
Enrollment: 2,012 Coed
Affiliation or Control: State IRS Status: 501(c)3
Highest Offering: Beyond Master's But Less Than Doctorate
Accreditation: HLC, ACBSP, ADNUR, NUR, SW

01 President ... Dr. John MOSELEY
100 Director Strategic Initiatives ... Dr. Darius WATSON
05 VP Academic Affairs/Provost ... Dr. Michael SELF
10 VP Administration/Finance ... Mr. Jeffrey BARLOW
111 VP Advancement/Athletics/Recreation ... Mr. Kevin WILSON
19 VP Campus Culture & Chief of Police ... Mr. Gary HILL
21 Asst VP Admin/Finance & Controller ... Mrs. Stacey SCHULTE
32 VP Student Affairs/Enrollment Mgmt ... Dr. Zakiya BROWN
26 Director of University Relations ... Vacant
49 Dean Arts/Sciences ... Dr. Sunder BALASUBRAMANIAN
47 Dean of Ag/Natural Sciences ... Vacant
107 Dean Professional Studies ... Dr. Ann MCSWAIN
13 Chief Information Officer ... Mr. John FANDREY
08 University Librarian ... Ms. Waheedah BILAL
15 Director Human Resources ... Vacant
06 Registrar ... Mr. Blaine BREDEMAN
113 Bursar ... Vacant
114 Director of Accounting ... Ms. Kathy MUENKS
96 Director of Purchasing ... Mr. Damon NUNN
86 Governmental Liaison ... Mr. Carlos GRAHAM
36 Director of Career Services ... Mrs. Elizabeth JORDAN
25 Mgr Sponsored Programs/Title III ... Ms. Regina ANDERSON
09 Director of Institutional Research ... Mrs. Beth NOLTE
37 Director Student Financial Services ... Ms. Cynthia WANSING
18 Director of Facilities and Planning ... Mr. Jeffrey TURNER
23 Director Student Health Services ... Mrs. Leasa WEGHORST
121 Director Academic Success Center ... Ms. Qubieinique GREER
85 Director for Global Education ... Ms. Jeannie CULBERSON
22 Dir Affirmative Action/EEO ... Vacant
100 Chief of Staff ... Mr. Jeremy FAULK

Lindenwood University (B)

209 S Kingshighway, Saint Charles MO 63301-1695
County: Saint Charles FICE Identification: 002480
Unit ID: 177968
Telephone: (636) 949-2000 Carnegie Class: Masters/L
FAX Number: (636) 949-4910 Calendar System: Semester
URL: www.lindenwood.edu
Established: 1827 Annual Undergrad Tuition & Fees: $18,100
Enrollment: 7,382 Coed
Affiliation or Control: Independent Non-Profit IRS Status: 501(c)3
Highest Offering: Doctorate
Accreditation: HLC, ACBSP, CAATE, CAEPT, SW

01 President ... Dr. John R. PORTER
05 Int Provost/SVP Academic Affairs ... Dr. Bethany ALDEN-RIVERS
111 VP Advancement & Communications ... Mr. Orrie COVERT
15 Vice Pres Human Resources ... Dr. Deb AYRES
84 SVP Enroll Mgmt/Student Engagement ... Mr. Terry WHITTUM
10 Chief Financial Officer ... Mr. Rick BANIAK
11 VP Operations ... Dr. Diane MOORE
41 VP Athletics ... Mr. Brad WACHLER
13 VP Information Technology ... Mr. TJ RAINS
45 VP Strategy & Innovation ... Mr. Rob WESTERVELT
43 General Counsel ... Mr. Mark FALKOWSKI
32 Associate VP Student Affairs ... Ms. Kelly MOYICH
88 Assoc VP Operations ... Mr. Tim CRUTCHLEY
88 Assoc VP Enrollment Management ... Ms. Sara WIEDMAN
04 Executive Asst to the President ... Mrs. Nicole SULLIVAN
20 Assistant Provost ... Ms. Kate HERRELL
53 Dean School of Education ... Dr. Anthony SCHEFFLER
79 Dean School of Arts & Humanities ... Dr. Kathi VOSEVICH
50 Dean Business/Entrepreneurship ... Dr. Molly HUDGINS
81 Dean School of Sciences ... Dr. Cynthia SCHROEDER
08 Dean of Library Services ... Ms. Elizabeth MACDONALD
06 Registrar ... Ms. Christine HANNAR
108 Assoc VP/Chief Assessment Officer ... Dr. Bethany ALDEN-RIVERS
07 Asst VP Enrollment Management ... Ms. Kara SCHILLI
110 Assistant VP Advancement ... Mr. Brian BRUNNER
16 Assistant VP HR ... Ms. Amanda PRICE
42 Chaplain ... Dr. Nichole TORBITZKY
21 Asst VP Fiscal Affairs ... Mr. John PLUNKETT
89 Director of First Year Programs ... Mrs. Sarah LEASSNER
106 Dir Online Education/E-learning ... Dr. Hannah KOHLER
19 Director Security/Safety ... Mr. Ryan ANDERSON
26 Director of Communications ... Ms. Julee MITSLER
38 Director Student Counseling ... Mr. Jonathan HUNN
09 Director of Institutional Research ... Dr. Peter WEITZEL
29 Director Alumni Relations ... Ms. Rachael HEUERMANN
104 Asst Director Study Abroad ... Ms. Elizabeth SNELL
105 Webmaster ... Mr. Jason WAACK
27 Director Marketing ... Ms. Jessica SCHROER
09 Director Research and Compliance ... Mr. Michael LEARY

Logan University (C)

1851 Schoettler Road, Chesterfield MO 63017
County: Saint Louis FICE Identification: 004703
Unit ID: 177986
Telephone: (636) 227-2100 Carnegie Class: Spec-4-yr-Other Health
FAX Number: N/A Calendar System: Trimester
URL: www.logan.edu
Established: 1935 Annual Undergrad Tuition & Fees: $6,700
Enrollment: 1,806 Coed
Affiliation or Control: Independent Non-Profit IRS Status: 501(c)3
Highest Offering: First Professional Degree
Accreditation: HLC, CHIRO, @DIET

01 President ... Dr. Clay MCDONALD
05 VP Academic Affairs ... Dr. Brian MCAULAY
46 VP Innovation and Research ... Dr. Vincent DEBONO
84 VP Enrollment Management ... Dr. Natacha DOUGLAS
111 VP Institutional Advancement ... Ms. Theresa FLECK
13 VP Information Tech/CIO ... Dr. Brad HOUGH
10 VP Admin Services/CFO ... Mr. Adil KHAN
15 VP Human Resources ... Ms. Nichole NICHOLS
09 VP Strategic Perf/Cont Improv ... Dr. Lee VAN DUSEN

Maryville University of Saint Louis (D)

650 Maryville University Drive,
Saint Louis MO 63141-7299
County: Saint Louis FICE Identification: 002482
Unit ID: 178059
Telephone: (314) 529-9300 Carnegie Class: DU-Mod
FAX Number: (314) 529-9900 Calendar System: Semester
URL: www.maryville.edu
Established: 1872 Annual Undergrad Tuition & Fees: $27,166
Enrollment: 10,979 Coed
Affiliation or Control: Independent Non-Profit IRS Status: 501(c)3
Highest Offering: Doctorate
Accreditation: HLC, ACBSP, ART, CACREP, CIDA, MUS, NURSE, OT, PTA, SP, @SW

01 President ... Dr. Mark LOMBARDI
05 Vice Pres Academic Affairs ... Ms. Jennifer YUKNA
10 Vice Pres Finance & Facilities ... Dr. Steve MANDEVILLE
84 Vice President Enrollment ... Ms. Shani LENORE
86 VP Community/Gov Relations ... Ms. Laraine DAVIS
32 VP for Student Life ... Dr. Nina CALDWELL
121 VP for Student Success ... Dr. Jennifer MCCLUSKEY
26 Exec Dir Mktg & Communications ... Ms. Gabrielle YOUNG
20 Associate VP Academic Affairs ... Ms. Laura ROSS
46 VP Strategic Trends ... Mr. Jeff MILLER
100 Chief of Staff ... Ms. Jessica NORRIS
50 Dean School of Business ... Dr. Tammy GOCIAL
53 Dean School of Education ... Dr. Mascheal SCHAPPE
76 Dean School Health Professions ... Dr. Michelle JENKINS
49 Int Dean College Arts & Sciences ... Dr. Jason TELFORD
106 Dean Adult & Online Education ... Ms. Katherine LOUTHAN
88 VP for Operational Excellence ... Dr. Stephanie ELFRINK
07 Asst Vice Pres Enrollment ... Ms. Melissa MACE
29 Director of Alumni Affairs ... Mr. Andrew FOX
42 Dir Campus Ministry & Comm Service ... Mr. Stephen DISALVO
35 Dean of Students ... Mr. Joseph FITZGERALD
36 Director Career & Prof Development ... Ms. Erin BOSWELL
21 Controller/Dir Finance ... Ms. Nikki PAYNE
37 Senior Director of Financial Aid ... Ms. Liesl FLANAGAN
23 Director of Health & Wellness ... Ms. Suzanne JAUDES
28 Sr Advisor to Pres for Access/Oppty ... Dr. Turan MULLINS
13 Chief Technology Officer ... Mr. Doug GLAZE
09 Dir Info Resources/Data Analytics ... Mr. Jonathan SCHLERETH
90 Dir Learning Design & Technology ... Ms. Pamela BRYAN WILLIAMS
18 Senior Project Manager ... Ms. Angela WARNER
112 Director of Planned Gifts ... Mr. Michael SCHROEDER
102 Dir Foundation/Corp Relations ... Mr. Michael WHITLEY
19 Director of Public Safety ... Vacant
39 Director of Residential Life ... Vacant
104 Assoc VP/Dir Ctr for Global Educ ... Dr. James HARF
88 Asst Athletic Dir Communications ... Mr. Charles YAHNG
88 AVP Ops Systems/Quality Assurance ... Ms. Elizabeth STACEY
88 Director Fresh Ideas Food Services ... Ms. Linda THACKER
38 Director Personal Counseling ... Ms. Jennifer HENRY
30 Exec Director Devel & Alumni Rels ... Ms. Fay FETICK
88 Assoc VP Ctr for Institution Values ... Dr. Alden CRADDOCK
04 Executive Asst to President ... Ms. Maria-Louisa KNIERIM
109 Director of Auxiliary Operations ... Mr. Damon MITCHELL
105 Assoc Director Web Strategy ... Ms. Kate BOELHAUF
41 Director of Athletics & Recreation ... Mr. Lonnie FOLKS
101 Secretary of the Board ... Ms. Jessica NORRIS
103 Chief of Corp Partnership Acquis ... Mr. Scott CHADWICK
15 Director of Human Resources ... Ms. Natasha TASSON

*Metropolitan Community College - Kansas City Administrative Center (E)

3200 Broadway, Kansas City MO 64111-2429
County: Jackson FICE Identification: 009137
Unit ID: 177995
Telephone: (816) 604-1000 Carnegie Class: N/A
FAX Number: (816) 759-1158
URL: www.mcckc.edu

01 Chancellor ... Dr. Kimberly BEATTY
101 Chancellor's Asst/Board Secretary ... Ms. Cindy K. JOHNSON
12 President Penn Valley ... Dr. Tyjaun LEE
12 President Blue River/Bus & Tech ... Dr. Thomas MEYER
12 President Longview ... Dr. Dan HOCOY
12 President MW ... Dr. Larry RIDEAUX
05 VC of Instruction & CAO ... Dr. Suzanne GOCHIS
32 VC Student Success/Engagement ... Dr. Kathrine SWANSON
10 Vice Chanc Admin Svcs/CFO ... Dr. Donald CHRUSCIEL
09 VC Inst Effectiveness/Research/Tech ... Dr. John CHAWANA
100 Chief Legal Officer ... Ms. Sandra GARCIA
20 AVC Academic Affairs ... Dr. Dreand JOHNSON
35 AVC Student Svcs/Enrollment ... Dr. Karen MOORE
18 Chief Facilities Officer ... Mr. Jeffrey ULLMANN
15 AVC/Chief Human Resources Officer ... Dr. Rosemary MARTIN
103 AVC Workforce & Economic Dev ... Dr. Alicia DICKENS
37 AVC Student Financial Services ... Ms. Dena NORRIS
21 AVC Financial Svcs & Admin Sys ... Ms. Patricia A. AMICK
111 AVC of Advancement ... Ms. Jessica RAMIREZ
13 AVC of Information Technology ... Dr. Barcus JACKSON
106 VP Online Instruction/Student Svcs ... Dr. Deanna SYNDER
108 Exec Dir Curriculum & Assessment ... Ms. Tammie MAY
19 Chief of Campus Police ... Mr. Londell JAMERSON, JR.
28 VP Diversity/Equity/Inclusion ... Mr. Warren HAYNES
09 Executive Director Inst Research ... Mrs. Melissa GIESE
114 Exec Director Budget and Planning ... Ms. Britney DOMANN
96 Executive Director of Procurement ... Mr. Mitch BORCHERS
26 Exec Dir Communications/Marketing ... Mr. Blake FRY
88 Dir of Support Services PS ... Mr. Domenick R. BROUILLETTE
22 Director Student Disability Svcs ... Ms. Kim FERNANDES
19 Director of Public Safety ... Mr. Rusty SULLIVAN
88 Dir of CTE Accountability & Comp ... Ms. Teresa A. LONEY
06 Registrar ... Mr. Ryan MEADOR
41 Athletic Director ... Mr. Brian BECHTEL
43 Associate General Counsel ... Ms. Andrea SCHATZ
88 Director of Enterprise/PM/P&IE ... Mr. Ed FOLEY

*Metropolitan Community College - Blue River (F)

20301 E 78 Highway, Independence MO 64057-2053
County: Jackson FICE Identification: 032613
Telephone: (816) 604-1000 Carnegie Class: Not Classified
FAX Number: N/A Calendar System: Semester
URL: www.mcckc.edu
Established: 1997 Annual Undergrad Tuition & Fees (In-District): N/A
Enrollment: N/A Coed
Affiliation or Control: State/Local IRS Status: 501(c)3
Highest Offering: Associate Degree
Accreditation: &HLC

02 President ... Dr. Thomas W. MEYER
03 Vice President ... Dr. Ryan CRIDER
04 Sr Exec Admin Asst to the President ... Mrs. Karla DEATHERAGE
05 Int Dean of Instruction ... Mrs. Cheryl WINTER
32 Dean of Student Development/Enroll ... Dr. Jonathan L. BURKE
11 Director of Campus Operations ... Mrs. Kimberly POINDEXTER
19 Campus Police Sergeant ... SGT. Larry MCCREA
18 Facilities Superintendent ... Mr. Clint JOHNSON

† Regional accreditation is carried under the parent institution Metropolitan Community College-Kansas City Administrative Center in Kansas City, MO.

*Metropolitan Community College - Business and Technology (G)

20301 East 78 Highway, Independence MO 64057-2052
County: Jackson Identification: 666295
Telephone: (816) 604-1000 Carnegie Class: Not Classified
FAX Number: (816) 482-5256 Calendar System: Semester
URL: www.mcckc.edu/btc
Established: 1995 Annual Undergrad Tuition & Fees (In-District): N/A
Enrollment: N/A Coed
Affiliation or Control: Local IRS Status: 501(c)3
Highest Offering: Associate Degree
Accreditation: &HLC

02 President ... Dr. Thomas MEYER
05 VP Instruction/Student Services ... Dr. Ryan CRIDER
20 Dean of Instruction ... Mrs. Cheryl WINTER
32 Dean Student Development/Enrollment ... Dr. Jon BURKE
10 Director of Campus Operations ... Mrs. Kim POINDEXTER
04 Sr Exec Admin Asst to the President ... Mrs. Karla DEATHERAGE

† Regional accreditation is carried under the parent institution Metropolitan Community College-Kansas City Administrative Center in Kansas City, MO.

*Metropolitan Community College - Longview (H)

500 SW Longview Road, Lee's Summit MO 64081-2105
County: Jackson FICE Identification: 009140
Telephone: (816) 604-2144 Carnegie Class: Not Classified

FAX Number: (816) 672-2025 Calendar System: Semester
URL: www.mcckc.edu
Established: 1969 Annual Undergrad Tuition & Fees (In-District): N/A
Enrollment: N/A Coed
Affiliation or Control: Local IRS Status: 501(c)3
Highest Offering: Associate Degree
Accreditation: &HLC

02 President ... Dr. Kathrine SWANSON
05 Vice Pres Instruction/Student Svcs ... Dr. David OEHLER
20 Interim Dean of Instruction ... Ms. Gretchen BLYTHE
32 Dean Student Devel/Enrollment Mgmt ... Dr. Diana BOYD MCELROY
11 Interim Director Campus Operations ... Ms. Tahmeka THOMPSON
37 Financial Aid Manager ... Ms. Lisa L. FANNAN
124 Student Retention Manager ... Dr. Joe BARNHILL

† Regional accreditation is carried under the parent institution Metropolitan Community College-Kansas City Administrative Center in Kansas City, MO.

*Metropolitan Community College - Maple Woods (A)

2601 NE Barry Road, Kansas City MO 64156-1299
County: Clay FICE Identification: 009139
Telephone: (816) 604-1000 Carnegie Class: Not Classified
FAX Number: (816) 437-3049 Calendar System: Semester
URL: www.mcckc.edu
Established: 1968 Annual Undergrad Tuition & Fees (In-District): N/A
Enrollment: N/A Coed
Affiliation or Control: Local IRS Status: 501(c)3
Highest Offering: Associate Degree
Accreditation: &HLC

02 President ... Dr. Laarry RIDEAUX, JR.
03 Executive Vice President ... Dr. Ellen CROWE
05 Dean Instruction ... Mr. James R. MOES
32 Dean Student Devel/Enrollment ... Mr. Terrell TIGNER
11 Director of Campus Operations ... Ms. Kim GREENE
08 Librarian ... Mrs. Linda CARTER
41 Athletic Director ... Vacant
37 Financial Aid Manager ... Mrs. Robin STIMAC
18 Physical Facilities Superintendent ... Vacant

† Regional accreditation is carried under the parent institution Metropolitan Community College-Kansas City Administrative Center in Kansas City, MO.

*Metropolitan Community College - Penn Valley (B)

3201 Southwest Trafficway, Kansas City MO 64111-2764
County: Jackson FICE Identification: 002484
Telephone: (816) 604-1000 Carnegie Class: Not Classified
FAX Number: (816) 759-4161 Calendar System: Semester
URL: www.mcckc.edu
Established: 1915 Annual Undergrad Tuition & Fees (In-District): N/A
Enrollment: N/A Coed
Affiliation or Control: Local IRS Status: 501(c)3
Highest Offering: Associate Degree
Accreditation: &HLC, ADNUR, CAHIIM, DA, EMT, OTA, PTAA, RAD, SURGT

02 President ... Dr. Tyjaun LEE
05 VP of Instruction & Student Svcs ... Mr. Jon MARSHALL
20 Dean of Instruction ... Vacant
32 Dean of Student Development ... Ms. Samaiyah JONES SCOTT
08 Librarian ... Mr. Michael KORKLAN
13 NUS Department Director ... Vacant
18 Sr Facilities Svcs Superintendent ... Mr. James MANTHEY
19 Campus Police Captain ... Cpt. Ronald REILLY
84 Enrollment Manager ... Mr. Carlton FOWLER
41 Athletic Programs Manager ... Mr. Marcus HARVEY
37 Financial Aid Manager ... Ms. Becka STOW
10 Business Office Supervisor ... Vacant
36 Career Services Coordinator ... Mr. Evan PENNINGTON
11 Director of Campus Operations ... Vacant

† Regional accreditation is carried under the parent institution Metropolitan Community College-Kansas City Administrative Center in Kansas City, MO.

Midwest Institute (C)

2 Soccer Park Road, Fenton MO 63026
County: St. Louis FICE Identification: 021211
Unit ID: 178183
Telephone: (314) 965-8363 Carnegie Class: Spec 2-yr-Health
FAX Number: N/A Calendar System: Other
URL: www.midwestinstitute.com
Established: 1965 Annual Undergrad Tuition & Fees: N/A
Enrollment: 297 Coed
Affiliation or Control: Proprietary IRS Status: Proprietary
Highest Offering: Associate Degree
Accreditation: ABHES

05 Director of Education ... Vacant

Midwest Institute-Earth City (D)

4260 Shoreline Drive, Earth City MO 63045
County: Saint Louis Identification: 667074
Telephone: (314) 344-4440 Carnegie Class: Not Classified
FAX Number: (314) 344-0495 Calendar System: Other
URL: www.midwestinstitute.com
Established: 1970 Annual Undergrad Tuition & Fees: N/A
Enrollment: N/A Coed
Affiliation or Control: Proprietary IRS Status: Proprietary
Highest Offering: Associate Degree
Accreditation: ABHES

01 President ... Vacant

Midwest University (E)

851 Parr Road, Wentzville MO 63385-0365
County: Saint Charles FICE Identification: 035283
Telephone: (636) 327-4645 Carnegie Class: Not Classified
FAX Number: (636) 327-4715 Calendar System: Semester
URL: www.midwest.edu
Established: 1986 Annual Undergrad Tuition & Fees: N/A
Enrollment: N/A Coed
Affiliation or Control: Independent Non-Profit IRS Status: 501(c)3
Highest Offering: Doctorate
Accreditation: BI

01 President ... Dr. James SONG
04 Executive Assistant to President ... Ms. Taylor BUMILLER
05 Academic Dean ... Dr. Hee Cheol LEE
06 Registrar/Admission ... Mr. Jeoung H. HAM
08 Director of Library Services ... Mrs. Mi Kyoung HWANG
10 Director of Finance ... Mr. In Cheol JANG
21 Business Office Manager ... Mrs. Bokhee SONG
45 Director of Planning & Marketing ... Mr. Jae Pil SONG
12 Korea Office Regional Director ... Dr. Jae M. SONG
12 Washington DC Regional Director ... Dr. Yoo K. KO
12 Director of Torrance Site ... Dr. Jong Yong LEE
12 Director of Irvine Site ... Dr. Sung T. JUNG
12 Director of Dallas Site ... Dr. Heung Shik KOH
07 Admission Counselor ... Mr. Sang Bae SEO
73 Dir Col & Grad School of Theology ... Dr. Myeong Hwan OH
64 Director of School of Music ... Dr. Emily HONG
12 Dir of MIRI ... Mr. Landon SONG
50 Dir Col & Grad School of Business ... Dr. Joseph PARK
53 Dir Col & Grad School of Education ... Mr. Landon SONG

Midwestern Baptist Theological Seminary (F)

5001 N Oak Trafficway, Kansas City MO 64118-4697
County: Clay FICE Identification: 002485
Unit ID: 178208
Telephone: (816) 414-3700 Carnegie Class: Spec-4-yr-Faith
FAX Number: (816) 414-3724 Calendar System: Semester
URL: www.mbts.edu
Established: 1957 Annual Undergrad Tuition & Fees: $8,410
Enrollment: 3,432 Coed
Affiliation or Control: Southern Baptist IRS Status: 501(c)3
Highest Offering: Doctorate
Accreditation: HLC, BI, THEOL

01 President ... Dr. Jason K. ALLEN
05 Provost/SVP Academic Admin ... Dr. Jason G. DUESING
10 VP for Inst Administration/Fin Svcs ... Mr. James J. KRAGENBRING
30 VP of Institutional Relations ... Mr. Charles W. SMITH, JR.
20 VP UG Stds/Dean Spurgeon College ... Dr. Samuel BIERIG
58 Dean of Graduate Studies ... Dr. Thor MADSEN
09 Dean of Institutional Effectiveness ... Dr. Rodney A. HARRISON
73 Dean of Postgraduate Studies ... Dr. Rodney A. HARRISON
32 VP Student Svcs/Dean of Students ... Dr. John Mark YEATS
20 Associate Dean ... Dr. Rustin UMSTATTD
13 Director of Info Technology ... Mr. David MEYER
06 Registrar ... Mr. Jared KATHCART
08 Librarian ... Ms. Kenette HARDER
84 VP Enrollment Mgmt ... Mr. Camden PULLIAM

Mineral Area College (G)

5270 Flat River Road, Park Hills MO 63601-2224
County: Saint Francois FICE Identification: 002486
Unit ID: 178217
Telephone: (573) 431-4593 Carnegie Class: Assoc/HT-High Trad
FAX Number: (573) 518-2164 Calendar System: Semester
URL: www.mineralarea.edu
Established: 1922 Annual Undergrad Tuition & Fees (In-District): $5,200
Enrollment: 2,410 Coed
Affiliation or Control: Local IRS Status: 501(c)3
Highest Offering: Associate Degree
Accreditation: HLC, EMT, MLTAD, PTAA

01 President ... Dr. Joe GILGOUR
05 Provost ... Mr. Roger MCMILLIAN
32 Dean of Student Services ... Ms. Julie SHEETS
10 VP of Finance & Administration ... Vacant
13 VP IT & Cybersecurity ... Mr. Andy WHITE
76 Dean of Health Professions ... Mrs. Angela ERICKSON
06 Registrar ... Ms. Connie HOLDER
09 Director of Institutional Research ... Ms. Lisa EDBURG
26 Exec Dir of College Communications ... Ms. Danielle BASLER
30 Executive Director of Development ... Mr. Kevin THURMAN
15 Executive Director Human Resources ... Ms. Kathryn NEFF
37 Director Student Financial Aid ... Ms. Julie CRABDREE
38 Director Student Counseling ... Vacant
18 General Services Director ... Mr. Rodney RESINGER
04 Administrative Asst to President ... Ms. Amy MCKENNA-JONES
08 Director of the Library ... Mr. Ryan HARRINGTON
19 Director Security/Safety ... Mr. Rich FLOTRON
39 Co-Director Student Housing ... Mr. Blake JONES
39 Co-Director Student Housing ... Mr. Jamie PICKEL
41 Athletic Director ... Mr. Jim GERWITZ

Missouri Baptist University (H)

One College Park Drive, Saint Louis MO 63141-8698
County: Saint Louis FICE Identification: 007540
Unit ID: 178244
Telephone: (314) 434-1115 Carnegie Class: Masters/L
FAX Number: (314) 434-7596 Calendar System: Semester
URL: www.mobap.edu
Established: 1964 Annual Undergrad Tuition & Fees: $29,360
Enrollment: 4,860 Coed
Affiliation or Control: Baptist IRS Status: 501(c)3
Highest Offering: Doctorate
Accreditation: HLC, CACREP, CAEP, @CNEA, EXSC, MUS, NURSE, @SW

01 President ... Dr. Keith L. ROSS
04 Assistant to the President ... Mrs. Janet MAYFIELD
05 Senior VP of Academic Affs/Provost ... Dr. Andy CHAMBERS
26 VP of Enroll/Mktg/Communications ... Mr. Bryce CHAPMAN
32 VP of Student Development ... Dr. Benjamin LION
10 VP for Business Affairs ... Mr. Oran WOODWORTH
20 Assoc VP for Academic Affs & Accred ... Dr. Lydia THEBEAU
58 Assoc VP for Grad Affairs ... Dr. Melanie BISHOP
29 Assoc Director for Alumni Relations ... Mrs. Abby KASSEBAUM
85 Director of International Services ... Ms. Marie TUDOR
09 Director Institutional Research ... Mr. Tim DELICATH
08 Director of Library Services ... Mrs. Zana SUEME
37 Director Financial Services ... Mr. Zach GREENLEE
111 Assoc VP for Univ Advancement ... Mrs. Ashlee JOHNSON
35 Assoc Dean Students ... Mrs. Amy GOODBERLET
41 Assoc VP & Director of Athletics ... Dr. Thomas SMITH
18 Director Campus Operations ... Mr. Andy HOUGH
06 Director of Records ... Mrs. Thea ABRAHAM
15 Director Personnel Services ... Mrs. Laurie WALLACE
13 Director of Information Systems ... Mr. Jerry MCKITTRICK
19 Director Public Safety ... Mr. Stephen HEIDKE
21 Controller ... Mrs. Pam SAVAGE
30 Development Officer ... Mrs. Ashlee JOHNSON
07 Exec Director of Admissions ... Mrs. Cynthia SUTTON
28 Diversity/Inclusion Initiative ... Vacant
66 Dean of School of Nursing ... Dr. Amber PYATT
106 Assoc VP for Extended Learning ... Dr. Amber HENRY
39 Dir of Student Life ... Mrs. Taira SCHERTZ
50 Dean of Business ... Dr. Karen KANNENBERG
53 Dean of Education ... Dr. Tammy COX

Missouri Southern State University (I)

3950 E Newman Road, Joplin MO 64801-1595
County: Jasper FICE Identification: 002488
Unit ID: 178341
Telephone: (417) 625-9300 Carnegie Class: Masters/S
FAX Number: (417) 625-3121 Calendar System: Semester
URL: www.mssu.edu
Established: 1965 Annual Undergrad Tuition & Fees (In-State): $6,964
Enrollment: 5,045 Coed
Affiliation or Control: State IRS Status: 501(c)3
Highest Offering: Master's
Accreditation: HLC, ACBSP, CAEP, COARC, DH, EMT, MUS, NUR, RAD, SW

01 President ... Dr. Dean A. VAN GALEN
05 Int Provost/VP Academic Affairs ... Ms. Lorinda HACKETT
32 Int VP Student Affairs/Enrollment ... Dr. Julie WENGERT
10 Vice President Business Affairs ... Mr. Rob YUST
30 Exec Vice Pres for Development ... Dr. Brad HODSON
20 Prov/Vice Pres Academic Affairs ... Dr. Wendy MCGRANE
06 Registrar ... Ms. Faustina ABRAHAM
08 Library Director ... Mr. James CAPECI
37 Director Student Financial Aid ... Ms. Becca L. DISKIN
21 Treasurer ... Mrs. Linda EIS
15 Director Human Resources ... Mr. Evan JEWSBURY
18 Director Facilities/Physical Plant ... Mr. Bryan GOODWIN
76 Int Dean College of Health Sciences ... Ms. Erica WIGHT
49 Dean College of Arts & Sciences ... Dr. Marsi ARCHER
53 Interim Dean College of Education ... Dr. Holly HACKETT
50 Dean Plaster College of Business ... Dr. Jeff ZIMMERMAN
04 Administrative Asst to President ... Ms. Laura BOYD
07 Director of Admissions ... Dr. Shellie HEWITT
104 Director Study Abroad ... Dr. Chad STEBBINS
106 Director Distance Learning ... Mr. Scott SNELL
108 Dir Institutional Effectiveness ... Vacant
19 Chief of Campus Police ... Mr. Kenneth KENNEDY
41 Director of Athletics ... Mr. Robert MALLORY
44 Director of Annual Giving ... Ms. Elisa BRYANT
114 Dir Budget & Operations ... Mr. Jeff GIBSON
26 Dir University Relations/Marketing ... Ms. Heather LESMEISTER
29 Director Alumni Relations ... Ms. Lee ELLIFF POUND
28 Director of Diversity ... Ms. Stacey CLAY
13 Chief Info Technology Officer (CIO) ... Mr. Don MIHULKA
39 Director Student Housing ... Mr. Joshua M. DOAK

Missouri State University (J)

901 S National Avenue, Springfield MO 65897-0027
County: Greene FICE Identification: 002503
Unit ID: 179566
Telephone: (417) 836-8500 Carnegie Class: DU-Mod
FAX Number: (417) 836-7669 Calendar System: Semester
URL: www.missouristate.edu
Established: 1905 Annual Undergrad Tuition & Fees (In-State): $7,938

Enrollment: 23,505 Coed
Affiliation or Control: State IRS Status: 501(c)3
Highest Offering: Doctorate
Accreditation: HLC, ACPHA, ADNUR, ANEST, ARCPA, AUD, CAATE, CACREP, CAPRT, CEA, CONST, DIETD, DIETI, MUS, NURSE, OT, PH, PTA, SP, SW, THEA

01 President ... Mr. Clifton M. SMART, III
05 Interim Provost ... Dr. John JASINSKI
12 Chancellor West Plains Campus ... Dr. Dennis LANCASTER
46 VP for Research/Economic Devel ... Dr. Bradley BODENHAUSEN
11 Vice Pres Administrative Services ... Mr. Matthew MORRIS
111 Vice Pres University Advancement ... Mr. W. Brent DUNN
32 VP Student Affairs & Dean of Stdts ... Dr. Dee SISCOE
26 VP Marketing and Communications ... Ms. Suzanne SHAW
20 Deputy Provost ... Dr. Christopher J. CRAIG
20 Associate Provost ... Dr. Kelly WOOD
20 Associate Provost ... Dr. Joye NORRIS
58 Dean of Grad College ... Dr. Julie J. MASTERSON
10 Chief Financial Officer ... Mr. Steve FOUCART
84 Associate VP Enrollment Mgmt & Svcs ... Mr. Rob HORNBERGER
08 Dean Library Services ... Mr. Thomas A. PETERS
28 Chief Diversity Officer ... Mr. H. Wes PRATT
09 Director of Institutional Research ... Dr. Michelle D. OLSEN
29 Exec Dir of Alumni Relations ... Vacant
15 Director of Human Resources ... Mr. Scot SCOBEE
37 Director of Student Financial Aid ... Mr. Rob MOORE
19 Director of University Safety ... Mr. David A. HALL
36 Director of the Career Center ... Dr. Kelly E. RAPP
13 Chief Information Officer ... Mr. Jeff P. COINER
100 Chief of Staff ... Mr. Ryan DEBOEF
23 Director of Health & Wellness Svcs ... Dr. Dave MUEGGE
92 Director Honors College ... Dr. John F. CHUCHIAK
18 Director Facilities Management ... Mr. Brad B. KIELHOFNER
96 Director of Procurement ... Mr. Mike WILLS
07 Director of Admissions ... Ms. Teresa HANEY
06 Asst VP Enrollment Mgmt/Registrar ... Ms. Angela YOUNG
49 Dean College Arts & Letters ... Dr. Shawn T. WAHL
79 Dean Col Humanities/Public Affairs ... Dr. Victor MATTHEWS
76 Dean Col Health/Human Services ... Dr. Mark SMITH
81 Dean Col Natural/Applied Science ... Dr. Tamera S. JAHNKE
53 Dean College of Education ... Vacant
50 Dean College of Business ... Dr. David B. MEINERT
85 Director of International Services ... Mr. Patrick M. PARNELL
105 Dir of Web Strategy and Devel ... Ms. Jessica J. SUMMERS
41 Athletic Director ... Mr. Kyle MOATS
43 General Counsel ... Ms. Rachael M. DOCKERY
04 Exec Assistant to the President ... Ms. Sherri L. CLOYD
101 Secretary of the Board ... Ms. Rowena STONE
102 Director Foundation/Corporate Rels ... Ms. Debbie BRANSON
104 Director Study Abroad ... Ms. Elizabeth C. STRONG
108 Assoc Prov Public Affs & Assessment ... Ms. Keri FRANKLIN
39 Dir Resident Life/Student Housing ... Ms. Teresa FREDERICK

Missouri State University - West Plains (A)

128 Garfield Avenue, West Plains MO 65775-2715
County: Howell FICE Identification: 031060
Unit ID: 179344
Telephone: (417) 255-7255 Carnegie Class: Assoc/HT-Mix Trad/Non
FAX Number: (417) 255-7962 Calendar System: Semester
URL: www.wp.missouristate.edu
Established: 1963 Annual Undergrad Tuition & Fees (In-State): $4,620
Enrollment: 1,920 Coed
Affiliation or Control: State IRS Status: 501(c)3
Highest Offering: Associate Degree
Accreditation: HLC

01 Chancellor ... Dr. Dennis LANCASTER
05 Dean of Academics ... Dr. Michael ORF
32 Dean of Student Services ... Dr. Angela TOTTY
20 Int Asst Dean of Academic Affairs ... Vacant
10 Director of Business/Support Svcs ... Mr. Crockett OAKS
30 Director of Development ... Mrs. Rachel PETERSON
26 Dir of Communications/Public Rels ... Mr. Dakota BATES
31 Director of Univ/Community Pgms ... Ms. Brenda POLYARD
06 Registrar ... Mrs. Laurie WALL
13 Dir Information Technology Services ... Mr. David YOUNG
18 Chief Facilities/Physical Plant ... Mr. Ron HENSLEY
04 Executive Asst to Chancellor ... Ms. Trish SMITH
08 Director Library Services ... Ms. Rebekah MCKINNEY
07 Coord of Admissions ... Mrs. Melissa JETT
09 Coord of Institutional Research ... Ms. Carrie STEEN
35 Coord Student Life and Development ... Mr. Jared CATES

Missouri Valley College (B)

500 E College, Marshall MO 65340-3197
County: Saline FICE Identification: 002489
Unit ID: 178369
Telephone: (660) 831-4000 Carnegie Class: Bac-Diverse
FAX Number: (660) 831-4039 Calendar System: Semester
URL: www.moval.edu
Established: 1889 Annual Undergrad Tuition & Fees: $21,500
Enrollment: 1,682 Coed
Affiliation or Control: Presbyterian Church (U.S.A.) IRS Status: 501(c)3
Highest Offering: Master's
Accreditation: HLC, NURSE

01 President ... Dr. Bonnie HUMPHREY
111 Vice Pres of External Relations ... Mr. Eric SAPPINGTON
32 Vice Pres Student Affairs ... Dr. Heath MORGAN
05 VP of Academic Affairs ... Dr. Diane BARTHOLOMEW
18 Vice Pres of Operations ... Mr. Tim SCHULTE
41 Exec Vice Pres/Athletic Director ... Mr. Tom FIFER
10 VP Business Svcs/Enrollment Mgmt ... Mr. Greg SILVEY
07 Director of Admissions ... Ms. Jessica GREEN
06 Registrar ... Ms. Marsha LASHLEY
21 Director Business Office ... Ms. Paula BURKE
08 Head Librarian ... Dr. Bryan CARSON
42 Director Campus Ministry ... Rev. Pam SEBASTIAN
09 Director of Institutional Research ... Dr. Tonia COMPTON
37 Director of Financial Aid ... Mr. Derek BOHNSACK
38 Director Counseling Center ... Ms. Teresa CESELSKI
13 Chief Information Officer ... Mr. Omar ALREFAE
26 Dir of Marketing & Public Relations ... Ms. Danielle DURHAM
19 Director of Public Safety ... Mr. Nick BOEHMER
29 Alumni Relations Director ... Ms. Jennifer SWIFT
04 Administrative Asst to President ... Ms. Brandy SCHULTE
15 Human Resources Manager ... Ms. Christi HICKS

Missouri Western State University (C)

4525 Downs Drive, Saint Joseph MO 64507-2294
County: Buchanan FICE Identification: 002490
Unit ID: 178387
Telephone: (816) 271-4200 Carnegie Class: Masters/S
FAX Number: N/A Calendar System: Semester
URL: www.missouriwestern.edu
Established: 1915 Annual Undergrad Tuition & Fees (In-State): $8,875
Enrollment: 4,911 Coed
Affiliation or Control: State IRS Status: 501(c)3
Highest Offering: Master's
Accreditation: HLC, CAEPN, CAHIIM, #COARC, MUS, NURSE, PTAA, SW

01 President ... Dr. Elizabeth KENNEDY
100 Chief of Staff ... Ms. Chris DUNN
05 Int Provost ... Mr. Marc MANGANARO
111 Vice Pres Univ Advancement ... Vacant
10 VP Finance & Administration ... Mr. Darrell MORRISON
32 Vice Pres for Student Affairs ... Ms. Melissa MACE
20 Int Vice Provost Academic Affairs ... Ms. Elise HEPWORTH
21 Assoc VP Financial Plng/Admin ... Vacant
84 Vice Pres Enrollment Mgmt ... Ms. Melissa MACE
81 Interim Dean Science & Health ... Dr. Crystal HARRIS
57 Dean of Fine Arts ... Vacant
49 Dean Liberal Arts ... Dr. Joel HYER
51 Dean of Western Institute ... Vacant
50 * Dean of Business & Prof Studies ... Dr. Logan JONES
35 AVP Student Affs & Dean of Students ... Mr. Brett BRUNER
06 Registrar ... Ms. Susan BRACCIANO
08 Director of Library ... Ms. Sally GIBSON
37 Director Student Financial Aid ... Ms. Cindy SPOTTS-CONRAD
13 Director of Information Technology ... Vacant
38 Director Student Counsel & Testing ... Mr. H. David BROWN
18 Director Physical Plant ... Mr. Bryan ADKINS
41 Vice President Intercol Athletics ... Vacant
15 Director of Human Resources ... Ms. Sara FREEMYER
86 Director of External Relations ... Vacant
26 Chief Communications Officer ... Ms. Becky DUNN
29 Exec Dir of Alumni Relations/Giving ... Ms. Kimberly WEDDLE
96 Purchasing Manager ... Ms. Kelly SLOAN
04 Executive Associate to President ... Ms. Betsy WRIGHT
36 Career Development Director ... Ms. Megan RANEY
39 Director Student Housing ... Mr. Nathan ROBERTS
19 Chief of University Police ... Ms. Jill VOLTMER

Moberly Area Community College (D)

101 College Avenue, Moberly MO 65270-1304
County: Randolph FICE Identification: 002491
Unit ID: 178448
Telephone: (660) 263-4100 Carnegie Class: Assoc/HT-High Non
FAX Number: (660) 263-6252 Calendar System: Semester
URL: www.macc.edu
Established: 1927 Annual Undergrad Tuition & Fees (In-District): $5,520
Enrollment: 4,878 Coed
Affiliation or Control: State/Local IRS Status: 501(c)3
Highest Offering: Associate Degree
Accreditation: HLC, MLTAD, OTA, SURGT

01 President ... Dr. Jeffery LASHLEY
10 Vice President for Finance ... Ms. Susan SPENCER
05 Vice President for Instruction ... Dr. Todd MARTIN
75 Dean Workforce Dev/Technical Educ ... Ms. Jo FEY
32 Dean Student Affairs & Enrollment ... Ms. Michele MCCALL
20 Dean of Academic Affairs ... Mr. Matthew CRIST
09 Dir Inst Reporting & Compliance ... Ms. Meghan HOLLERAN
21 Director Business Services ... Ms. Heather WITT
26 Dir Marketing and Public Relations ... Vacant
18 Director of Plant Operations ... Mr. Eric ROSS
13 Chief Information Officer ... Mr. Robert WIDEMAN
08 Dir Library & Academic Resources ... Ms. Donna MONNIG
15 Director of Human Resources ... Ms. Ann PARKS
14 Dir of Instructional Technology ... Ms. Susan BURDEN
37 Director of Financial Aid ... Ms. Amy HAGER
06 Registrar ... Ms. Julie PERKINS
29 Dir Inst Development & Alumni Svcs ... Ms. Elizabeth GREGORY
36 Dir Career and Technical Programs ... Ms. Suzi MCGARVEY
88 Director of Academic Services ... Ms. Katelyn WILSON
04 Executive Asst to President ... Ms. Tammi RICHARDSON
103 Exec Dir of Workforce Development ... Ms. Brandi GLOVER
19 Director Security & Residence Life ... Ms. Lori PERRY
76 Dean of Health Sciences ... Ms. Michelle FREY

Nazarene Theological Seminary (E)

1700 E Meyer Boulevard, Kansas City MO 64131-1263
County: Jackson FICE Identification: 002494
Unit ID: 178518
Telephone: (816) 268-5400 Carnegie Class: Spec-4-yr-Faith
FAX Number: (816) 268-5500 Calendar System: Semester
URL: www.nts.edu
Established: 1945 Annual Graduate Tuition & Fees: N/A
Enrollment: 160 Coed
Affiliation or Control: Church Of The Nazarene IRS Status: 501(c)3
Highest Offering: Doctorate; No Undergraduates
Accreditation: THEOL

01 President ... Dr. Jeren ROWELL
05 Dean of the Faculty ... Dr. Josh SWEEDEN
11 Dean for Administration ... Dr. Glenn MILLER
08 Director Library Service ... Mrs. Debra BRADSHAW
37 Financial Aid Coordinator ... Mrs. Cindy HOWARD
26 Director of Communications ... Dr. Jason VEACH
111 Dean for Advancement ... Rev. Timothy MCPHERSON
04 Admin Assistant to the President ... Mrs. Nancy MCPHERSON
13 Chief Information Technology Ofcr ... Dr. Stephen PORTER
123 Director of Graduate Admissions ... Dr. Levi JONES
07 Director of Admissions ... Mr. Derek DAVIS
101 Secretary of the Institution/Board ... Mr. Allen BROWN
15 Dir HR/Controller ... Ms. Carol NOLTING
29 Director Alumni Affairs ... Rev. Dana PREUSCH
38 Director Student Counseling ... Dr. William KIRKEMO
18 Chief Facilities/Physical Plant Ofc ... Mr. Steve GARROW

North Central Missouri College (F)

1301 Main Street, Trenton MO 64683-1824
County: Grundy FICE Identification: 002514
Unit ID: 179715
Telephone: (660) 359-3948 Carnegie Class: Assoc/HVT-High Trad
FAX Number: (660) 359-2211 Calendar System: Semester
URL: www.ncmissouri.edu
Established: 1925 Annual Undergrad Tuition & Fees (In-District): $5,670
Enrollment: 1,591 Coed
Affiliation or Control: Local IRS Status: 501(c)3
Highest Offering: Associate Degree
Accreditation: HLC, CNEA, MLTAD, OTA

01 President ... Dr. Lenny KLAVER
05 Vice President of Academics ... Dr. Tristan LONDRE
10 Vice President of Finance ... Mr. Tyson OTTO
32 Vice President of Student Affairs ... Dr. Kristen ALLEY
20 Dean of Instruction ... Dr. Mitchell HOLDER
06 Registrar ... Ms. Joni OAKS
13 Chief Information Officer ... Ms. Jennifer TRIPLETT
08 Librarian ... Ms. Beth CALDARELLO
37 Director of Financial Aid ... Ms. Kimberly MEEKER
30 Director Development ... Ms. Alicia ENDICOTT
40 Director Bookstore ... Ms. Cecilia MARSH
39 Director Student Housing ... Mr. Donnie HILLERMAN
41 Athletic Director ... Mr. Nate GAMET
18 Director of Facilities ... Mr. Randy YOUNG
105 Director Web Services ... Ms. Tami CAMPBELL
09 Director of Institutional Research ... Ms. Tara NOAH
07 Director of Admissions ... Ms. Megan PESTER
26 Chief Public Relations Officer ... Ms. Kristi HARRIS

Northwest Missouri State University (G)

800 University Drive, Maryville MO 64468-6015
County: Nodaway FICE Identification: 002496
Unit ID: 178624
Telephone: (660) 562-1212 Carnegie Class: Masters/L
FAX Number: (660) 562-1900 Calendar System: Trimester
URL: www.nwmissouri.edu
Established: 1905 Annual Undergrad Tuition & Fees (In-State): $8,500
Enrollment: 7,267 Coed
Affiliation or Control: State IRS Status: 501(c)3
Highest Offering: Beyond Master's But Less Than Doctorate
Accreditation: HLC, AAQEP, ACBSP, CAPRT, CNEA, DIETD, @DIETI, MUS

01 President ... Dr. Clarence GREEN
05 Provost ... Dr. Jamie HOOYMAN
10 VP of Finance & Administration ... Ms. Stacy CARRICK
32 VP of Student Affairs ... Dr. Matt BAKER
111 VP Univ Advance/Dir NW Foundation ... Ms. Mitzi G. MARCHANT
88 Interim VP of Culture ... Dr. Egon HEIDENDAL
58 Assoc Prov for Grad & Prof Studies ... Dr. Gregory HADDOCK
49 Assoc Prov Dean Col of Arts & Sci ... Dr. Michael STEINER
20 Assoc Prov Academic Ops & Dev ... Dr. Jay JOHNSON
53 Dean School of Education ... Dr. Timothy WALL
26 Exec Dir Marketing/Communications ... Mr. Brandon STANLEY
41 Director Athletics ... Mr. Andy PETERSON
15 AVP of Human Resources ... Ms. Krista BARCUS
13 AVP of IT ... Mr. Brennan LEHMAN
96 Director of Purchasing ... Ms. Alyssa PULLEY
21 AVP of Finance ... Ms. Mary COLLINS
18 AVP of Facility Services ... Mr. Dan HASLAG
84 AVP Admissions & Student Success ... Dr. Allison S. HOFFMANN
60 Director School of Comm/Mass Media ... Dr. Matt WALKER
47 Director School of Agriculture ... Mr. Rodney BARR
50 Director School of Business ... Dr. Ben BLACKFORD
77 Director School of Computer Science ... Ms. Joni ADKINS

76 Dir School of Health Sci & Wellness Dr. Terry LONG
04 Exec Asst to President Mr. Jacob WOOD
06 Registrar Ms. Terri VOGEL
07 Director of Admissions-Operations Ms. Tamera J. GROW
22 AVP Student Affairs/Title IX/Equity Mr. William R. SABIO
28 AVP Diversity/Inclusion Dr. Justin MALLETT
102 Director Corp Relations/Major Gifts Ms. Jill BROWN
37 Director Financial Assistance Mr. Charles MAYFIELD
23 AVP Stdnt Affs/Hlth/Well-Being Mr. Chris DAWE
36 Director Career Services Ms. Hannah CHRISTIAN
104 Director Intl Involvement Center Dr. Thomas MERLOT
105 Manager of Web Services Ms. Crystal D. WARD
106 Director NW Online & LTC Dr. Darla J. RUNYON
108 Assoc Dir Accreditation/Assessment Dr. Mike MCBRIDE
25 Grants Coordinator Mr. Ty T. PARSONS
38 Assistant Director Counseling Ms. Kristen S. PELTZ
14 Director Technology Services Mr. Merlin R. MILLER

Ozark Christian College (A)

1111 N Main Street, Joplin MO 64801-4804
County: Jasper FICE Identification: 022027
Unit ID: 178679
Telephone: (417) 626-1234 Carnegie Class: Spec-4-yr-Faith
FAX Number: (417) 624-0090 Calendar System: Semester
URL: occ.edu
Established: 1942 Annual Undergrad Tuition & Fees: $13,600
Enrollment: 629 Coed
Affiliation or Control: Independent Non-Profit IRS Status: 501(c)3
Highest Offering: Master's
Accreditation: HLC, BI

01 President Matt PROCTOR
03 Executive Vice President Damien SPIKEREIT
111 Exec VP of College Advancement Jim DALRYMPLE
05 Executive VP of Academics Chad RAGSDALE
20 Assoc Academic Dean Shane WOOD
88 Director Academic Operations Lisa WITTE
09 VP Inst Research & Effectiveness Teresa ROBERTS
32 VP of Student Affairs Andy STORMS
11 VP of Campus Operations David MCMILLIN
84 VP of Enrollment Robert WITTE
26 Director Marketing & Communications Amy STORMS
43 General Counsel Doug MILLER
15 Director of Human Resources Travis HALL
04 Admin Assistant to the President Kathy BOWERS
06 Registrar Jennifer MCMILLIN
07 Director of Admissions Marycruz HURLEY
08 Chief Library Officer Justin GILL
18 Chf Facilities/Physical Plant Ofcr Tim RUNYON
19 Director Security/Safety Monte SHOEMAKE
37 Student Financial Services Director Kim BALENTINE
41 Athletic Director Chris LAHM

Ozarks Technical Community College (B)

1001 E Chestnut Expressway, Springfield MO 65802-3625
County: Greene FICE Identification: 030830
Unit ID: 177472
Telephone: (417) 447-7500 Carnegie Class: Assoc/HVT-High Trad
FAX Number: N/A Calendar System: Semester
URL: www.otc.edu
Established: 1990 Annual Undergrad Tuition & Fees (In-District): $4,924
Enrollment: 11,237 Coed
Affiliation or Control: State/Local IRS Status: 501(c)3
Highest Offering: Associate Degree
Accreditation: HLC, ACFEI, ADNUR, CAHIIM, COARC, DA, DH, EMT, IFSAC, MLTAD, NAEYC, NAIT, OTA, PTAA, SURGT

01 Chancellor Dr. Hal L. HIGDON
100 Chief of Staff Ms. Amy BACON
101 Secretary to the Chancellor Ms. Jennifer HOGAN
05 Vice Chancellor Academic Affairs Dr. Tracy MCGRADY
11 Vice Chancellor Admin Services Mr. Rob RECTOR
32 Vice Chancellor Student Affairs Ms. Joan BARRETT
10 Vice Chancellor Finance Vacant
12 President Table Rock Campus Dr. Robert GRIFFITH
12 President Richwood Valley Campus Dr. Cliff DAVIS
13 Interim Chief Technology Officer Mr. Eric KYLE
15 Assoc VC Human Resources/Workforce Ms. Ocki HAAS
20 Dean of Academic Services Dr. Megan WEAVER
76 Dean of Allied Health Programs Dr. Aaron LIGHT
97 Dean of General Education Vacant
72 Dean of Technical Education Dr. Matthew HUDSON
103 Exec Dir Workforce Development Ms. Sherry COKER
06 Asst Registrar Records/Registration Ms. Amy BERGANT
38 Director of Counseling Services Vacant
26 Director Communications & Marketing Ms. Sarah BARGO
18 College Director Facilities/Grounds Mr. Raymond WADE
28 Title IX Coord/Col Dir Civil Rights Mr. Kevin LUEBBERING
37 College Director of Financial Aid Ms. Kim CARY
08 Director College Library Ms. Sarah FANCHER
88 Director College Library RVC/TRC Ms. Angela SWIFT
36 Director of Career Employment Svcs Vacant
102 Exec Director of OTC Foundation Ms. Amy BACON
09 Chief Research/Govt Affairs Officer Mr. Matthew SIMPSON
19 College Director Safety & Security Mr. Scott LEVEN
35 Dean of Students Ms. Joyce BATEMAN
88 Director Dual Credit/HS Admissions Ms. Piper WILSON
105 Director Web Services Mr. George LAMELZA
106 Dean Online Education/Faculty Dev Dr. Julie COLTHARP
25 Chief Strategy Officer Dr. Abigail BENZ
96 Director of Procurement Ms. Katie HIGHFILL
07 Director of Admissions/Registrar Mr. Scott FIEDLER
88 Exec Dir Ctr for Advanced Mfg Mr. Robert RANDOLPH
121 College Dir of Student Success Mr. Steve FOUSE
28 Director Diversity/Equity/Inclusion Mr. Daniel OGUNYEMI

Ozarks Technical Community College Richwood Valley (C)

3369 W Jackson Street, Nixa MO 65714
Telephone: (417) 447-7700 Identification: 770324
Accreditation: &HLC

Ozarks Technical Community College Table Rock Campus (D)

10698 Historic Highway, MO 165, Hollister MO 65672
Telephone: (417) 336-6239 Identification: 770325
Accreditation: &HLC

Park University (E)

8700 River Park Drive, Parkville MO 64152-3795
County: Platte FICE Identification: 002498
Unit ID: 178721
Telephone: (816) 741-2000 Carnegie Class: Masters/L
FAX Number: (816) 746-6423 Calendar System: Semester
URL: www.park.edu
Established: 1875 Annual Undergrad Tuition & Fees: $11,929
Enrollment: 10,165 Coed
Affiliation or Control: Independent Non-Profit IRS Status: 501(c)3
Highest Offering: Master's
Accreditation: HLC, ACBSP, NURSE, SW

01 President Mr. Shane SMEED
05 Provost Dr. Michelle MYERS
84 Chief Enrollment Management Officer Ms. Kena WOLF
10 Chief Financial Officer Mr. Gregg GIVENS
111 Chief Advancement Officer Mr. Nathan MARTICKE
20 Associate Provost Dr. Emily SALLEE
29 Assoc VP for External Relations Mr. Erik BERGRUD
32 Associate VP/Dean of Student Life Dr. Jayme UDEN
06 Registrar Dr. Cynthia OTTS
37 Director Student Financial Service Ms. Brynn BOLOGNA
15 Director Human Resources Ms. Cutrina CATLIN
41 Director of Athletics Ms. Kristin GILLETTE
85 Sr Director International Students Mr. Kevin VICKER
13 Assoc VP Information Technology Mr. James NELSON
19 Director of Campus Safety Mr. Jeffrey HURLEY
04 Executive Asst to the President Ms. Bobbi SHAW
50 Dean College of Management Mr. Kirby BROWN
49 Dean Liberal Arts & Sciences Dr. James PASLEY
53 Dean School for Education Dr. Timothy HANRAHAN
101 Asst Secretary to Board of Trustees Ms. Ami WISDOM
100 Chief of Staff Ms. Laure CHRISTENSEN
26 Assoc VP of Marketing Dr. Long HUYNH
27 Dir Communications/Public Relations Mr. Brad BILES
39 Director Student Housing Ms. Tonya WESSEL
21 Chief Business Officer Mr. Scott FERGERSON
09 Dir Institutional Effectiveness Ms. Jennifer HELLER
07 Assoc VP Enrollment Management Mr. Andrew DAVIS

Pinnacle Career Institute (F)

10301 Hickman Mills Drive, Kansas City MO 64137
County: Jackson FICE Identification: 010405
Unit ID: 177302
Telephone: (816) 331-5700 Carnegie Class: Not Classified
FAX Number: (816) 331-2026 Calendar System: Quarter
URL: www.pcitraining.edu
Established: 1953 Annual Undergrad Tuition & Fees: N/A
Enrollment: 508 Coed
Affiliation or Control: Proprietary IRS Status: Proprietary
Highest Offering: Associate Degree
Accreditation: ACCSC

01 Campus President Valerie BUJAK
05 Director of Education Kelly LAMB

Pinnacle Career Institute (G)

11500 Ambassador Dr Ste 221, Kansas City MO 64153
Telephone: (816) 331-5700 Identification: 770737
Accreditation: ACCSC

Ranken Technical College (H)

4431 Finney Avenue, Saint Louis MO 63113-2898
County: Saint Louis FICE Identification: 012500
Unit ID: 178891
Telephone: (314) 371-0236 Carnegie Class: Bac/Assoc-Assoc Dom
FAX Number: (314) 371-0241 Calendar System: Semester
URL: ranken.edu/
Established: 1907 Annual Undergrad Tuition & Fees: $15,947
Enrollment: 1,823 Coed
Affiliation or Control: Independent Non-Profit IRS Status: 501(c)3
Highest Offering: Baccalaureate
Accreditation: HLC, ACBSP

01 President Mr. Don J. POHL
10 Vice President for Finance & Admin Mr. Peter T. MURTAUGH
00 Chief Executive Officer Mr. Stan SHOUN
22 VP Diversity/Student Success Ms. Crystal HERRON
51 Dean of Continuing Education Mr. Keyvan GERAMI
05 VP Educ/Dean Academic Affairs Mr. Dan KANIA
84 Dean of Enrollment Management/Mktg Ms. Frank MILLER

Research College of Nursing (I)

2525 E Meyer Boulevard, Kansas City MO 64132-1133
County: Jackson FICE Identification: 006392
Unit ID: 178989
Telephone: (816) 995-2800 Carnegie Class: Spec-4-yr-Other Health
FAX Number: (816) 995-2817 Calendar System: Semester
URL: www.researchcollege.edu
Established: 1980 Annual Undergrad Tuition & Fees: N/A
Enrollment: 420 Coed
Affiliation or Control: Proprietary IRS Status: Proprietary
Highest Offering: Master's
Accreditation: HLC, NURSE

01 President Dr. Frederick P. ROBINSON
05 Dean Dr. Rebecca SAXTON
07 Director Admissions Ms. Leslie BURRY
37 Director Financial Aid Ms. Stacie WITHERS
24 Director LRC Vacant
13 Senior Technology Analyst Vacant
04 Exec Admin Asst to President/Dean Ms. Roseanne ZIMNY
06 Registrar Ms. Camelia WILLIAMS
08 Head Librarian Ms. Kitty SERLING
106 Dir Online Education/E-learning Ms. Sheryl MAX
111 Advancement & Development Officer Ms. Tiffany HAMLETT
113 Coordinator of Student Accounts Ms. Marcy SACKMAN
09 Director of Institutional Research Ms. Christine HAMMOND
88 Director of Instructional Design Mr. Matthew LIVENGOOD

Rockbridge Seminary (J)

3111 East Battlefield Street, Springfield MO 65804
County: Greene Identification: 667151
Telephone: (866) 931-4300 Carnegie Class: Not Classified
FAX Number: (866) 931-4300 Calendar System: Semester
URL: www.rockbridge.edu
Established: 2002 Annual Graduate Tuition & Fees: N/A
Enrollment: N/A Coed
Affiliation or Control: Independent Non-Profit IRS Status: 501(c)3
Highest Offering: Doctorate; No Undergraduates
Accreditation: DEAC

01 President Tommy HILLIKER
05 Chief Academic Officer Dr. Mark SIMPSON
08 Head Librarian Seth ALLEN
04 Administrative Asst to President Brenda CIRTIN
121 Director of Academic Coaching Linda GRABER

Rockhurst University (K)

1100 Rockhurst Road, Kansas City MO 64110-2561
County: Jackson FICE Identification: 002499
Unit ID: 179043
Telephone: (816) 501-4000 Carnegie Class: Masters/L
FAX Number: (816) 501-4588 Calendar System: Semester
URL: www.rockhurst.edu
Established: 1910 Annual Undergrad Tuition & Fees: $39,780
Enrollment: 3,688 Coed
Affiliation or Control: Roman Catholic IRS Status: 501(c)3
Highest Offering: Doctorate
Accreditation: HLC, CAEP, NURSE, OT, PTA, SP

01 President Dr. Sandra CASSADY
28 Chief Inclusion Officer Vacant
111 Vice President for Advancement Ms. Mary MOONEY BURNS
10 Interim Chief Financial Officer Mrs. Kris PACE
05 Provost & Senior VP Acad Affairs Dr. Douglas N. DUNHAM
45 VP Strategy and Innovation Vacant
88 Vice Pres Mission & Ministry Rev. Stephen HESS, S.J.
32 VP Stdnt Dev/Dean Stdnts/Athletics Dr. Matthew D. QUICK
13 Assoc VP of Technology Mr. Bart KLEIN
18 Assoc VP Facilities Operations Vacant
84 Vice President of Enrollment Svcs Dr. Carmen PANLILIO
26 Assoc VP of Marketing Mr. Dave HUNT
108 Dir of Institutional Effectiveness Ms. Annalisa GRAMLICH
121 Assoc Provost of Student Success Ms. Melinda PETTEGREW
35 Director of Student Life Ms. Emma RAPP
39 Assoc VP of Students/Dir Res Life Mr. Mark HETZLER
04 Sr Exec Assistant to the President Ms. Terry THOMAS
50 Dean College of Business Dr. Myles GARTLAND
49 Dean Arts & Sciences Dr. Jennifer FRIEND
66 Dean Nursing & Health Sciences Dr. Kris VACEK
08 Director Library Ms. Laura HORNE-POPP
06 Registrar Ms. Brenda LANEY
37 Director Student Financial Aid Ms. Jennifer WRIGHT
41 Director of Athletics Ms. Kristy BAYER
15 Director of Human Resources Ms. Jackie MICHAELS
91 Director of Infrastructure Services Mr. Michael CRAIG
36 Director of Career Center Mr. Michael J. THEOBALD
30 Exec Director of Development Ms. Paula MOSS
27 Director of University Relations Ms. Katherine FROHOFF
110 Director Advancement/Alumni Mr. Brent BLAZEK
42 Director of Campus Ministry Mr. Bill KRIEGE
19 Director Security/Safety Mr. Randy HOPKINS

38 Director of Student Counseling ..... Dr. Elbert DARDEN
31 Dir Community Relations & Outreach ..... Ms. Alicia R. DOUGLAS
07 Director of Operations/Admission ..... Ms. Annie LEHWALD
40 Director Bookstore ..... Vacant
09 Director of Inst Research ..... Mr. Kirk SKOGLUND
21 Controller ..... Ms. Kris PACE
104 Study Abroad Advisor ..... Ms. Paivi BYBEE
106 Director Center for E-learning ..... Ms. Becca HEDGE
88 Director of the Learning Center ..... Ms. Sara KEENAN
88 Director Center for Svc Learning ..... Dr. Julia VARGAS
29 Director Alumni Relations ..... Ms. Caroline CAMPBELL
54 Director Engineering Program ..... Dr. Deborah O'BANNON

St. Charles Community College (A)

4601 Mid Rivers Mall Drive, Cottleville MO 63376-2865
County: Saint Charles FICE Identification: 025306
Unit ID: 262031
Telephone: (636) 922-8000 Carnegie Class: Assoc/HT-High Trad
FAX Number: (636) 922-8352 Calendar System: Semester
URL: www.stchas.edu
Established: 1986 Annual Undergrad Tuition & Fees (In-District): $4,152
Enrollment: 6,014 Coed
Affiliation or Control: State/Local IRS Status: 501(c)3
Highest Offering: Associate Degree
Accreditation: HLC, ADNUR, CAHIIM, CEA, CSHSE, EMT, OTA

01 President ..... Dr. Barbara KAVALIER
05 VP Academic Affairs ..... Dr. Holly MARTIN
11 VP Administrative Services/COO ..... Mr. Todd GALBIERZ
32 VP Student Services ..... Mr. Dave LEENHOUTS
15 VP Human Resources ..... Ms. Terri EDRICH
26 VP Marketing/Student Life ..... Ms. Heather MCDORMAN
20 AVP Academic Affairs ..... Vacant
10 Asst VP Financial Services ..... Ms. Susan RUBEMEYER
124 AVP Col Transitions/Support Svcs ..Ms. Kathy BROCKGREITENS
103 AVP Corporate & Community Dev ..... Ms. Amanda SIZEMORE
35 Student Life Manager ..... Mr. James BRATCHER
102 Exec Director of the Foundation ..... Ms. Betsy SCHNEIDER
19 Exec Dir Public Safety/Facilities ..... Mr. Bob RONKOSKI
37 Director Financial Aid ..... Mr. David SEWARD
09 Director Institutional Research ..... Dr. Chris HUBBARD JACKSON
13 Exec Dir Information Technology ..... Mr. Don POPHAM
21 Director Financial Services ..... Ms. Barbara FUERST
121 Director Advising Svcs ..... Ms. Diane AMZEN
41 Director Athletics ..... Mr. Timothy BRIX
88 Director Technology Support ..... Ms. Lisa MOUSER
50 Dean Bus/Sci/Ed/Math/CompSci ..... Dr. Darren OSBURN
57 Dean Arts/Humanities/Soc Sci ..... Dr. Mara VORACHEK-WARREN
103 Assoc Dean Workforce Pgm & Svcs ..... Ms. Lauren DICKENS
36 Career Services Manager ..... Ms. Jenny HAHN SCHNIPPER
96 Purchasing Manager ..... Ms. Diana SCHOO
109 Asst Director Food Services ..... Ms. Laura GRANT
40 Asst Director Bookstore ..... Mr. Daniel GRANZOW
04 Sr Administrator Ofc of President ..... Ms. Amy SNYDER

Saint Louis College of Health Careers (B)

1297 N Highway Drive, Saint Louis MO 63026-1909
County: Saint Louis FICE Identification: 023405
Unit ID: 179511
Telephone: (636) 529-0000 Carnegie Class: Spec 2-yr-Health
FAX Number: (636) 489-2791 Calendar System: Semester
URL: www.slchc.edu
Established: 1981 Annual Undergrad Tuition & Fees: N/A
Enrollment: 100 Coed
Affiliation or Control: Proprietary IRS Status: Proprietary
Highest Offering: Master's
Accreditation: ABHES, COARC, OTA, PTAA

13 Chief Info Technology Officer ..... Mr. Alan PORTMAN
37 Director Student Financial Aid ..... Mr. Jim BELL
106 Dir Online Education/E-learning ..... Mrs. Tina LAKIN
01 Chief Executive Officer ..... Mr. Steven N. BARSAM
36 Director of Career Services ..... Ms. Danielle ALLEN
07 Director of Admissions ..... Mrs. Amy HYDE
06 Registrar ..... Ms. Tabatha HUTSON
05 Dean of Education ..... Ms. Cynthia MARTEN

*Saint Louis Community College - Cosand Center (C)

3221 McKelvey Road, Bridgeton MO 63044
County: Saint Louis FICE Identification: 002471
Unit ID: 179308
Telephone: (314) 539-5000 Carnegie Class: N/A
FAX Number: (314) 539-5170
URL: www.stlcc.edu

01 Chancellor ..... Dr. Jeff PITTMAN
05 Vice Chanc Academic Affairs ..... Dr. Andrew LANGREHR
10 Vice Chanc Finance/Administration ..... Mr. Paul ZINCK
32 Vice Chanc Student Affairs ..... Dr. Christine DAVIS
103 Assoc VC Workforce Solutions ..... Mr. Hart NELSON
13 Chief Information Officer ..... Mr. Keith HACKE
15 Assoc Vice Chanc Human Resources ..... Ms. Robin PHILLIPS
102 Executive Director STLCC Foundation ..... Ms. Jo-Ann DIGMAN
26 Exec Dir Marketing/Communication ..... Ms. Kedra TOLSON
09 Exec Dir of Inst Research/Planning ..... Ms. Kelli BURNS
112 Director of Grants ..... Vacant
06 Registrar ..... Vacant
04 Administrative Assoc to Chancellor ..... Ms. Yvonne BLOOM
101 Secretary of the Board ..... Ms. Jessica GROVE
106 Mgr Online Student Services ..... Ms. Stacey FOSTER
96 Assistant Controller ..... Ms. Cindy GREEN
19 Dir Public Safety/Emergency Mgmt ..... LtCol. Alfred ADKINS
43 Dir Legal Services/General Counsel ..... Vacant

*Saint Louis Community College at Florissant Valley (D)

3400 Pershall Road, Saint Louis MO 63135-1499
Telephone: (314) 513-4200 FICE Identification: 002470
Accreditation: &HLC, ADNUR, ART

*Saint Louis Community College at Forest Park (E)

5600 Oakland Avenue, Saint Louis MO 63110-1393
Telephone: (314) 644-9100 Identification: 667353
Accreditation: HLC, ACFEI, ADNUR, CAHIIM, COARC, DA, DH, DMS, EMT, FUSER, MLTAD, RAD, SURGT

*Saint Louis Community College at Meramec (F)

11333 Big Bend Road, Kirkwood MO 63122-5720
Telephone: (314) 984-7500 FICE Identification: 002472
Accreditation: &HLC, ADNUR, ART, OTA, PTAA

*Saint Louis Community College at Wildwood (G)

2645 Generations Drive, Wildwood MO 63040-1168
Telephone: (636) 422-2000 Identification: 667084
Accreditation: &HLC

Saint Louis University (H)

One Grand Boulevard, Saint Louis MO 63103-2097
FICE Identification: 002506
Unit ID: 179159
Telephone: (314) 977-2500 Carnegie Class: DU-Higher
FAX Number: (314) 977-3874 Calendar System: Semester
URL: www.slu.edu
Established: 1818 Annual Undergrad Tuition & Fees: $47,124
Enrollment: 12,229 Coed
Affiliation or Control: Roman Catholic IRS Status: 501(c)3
Highest Offering: Doctorate
Accreditation: HLC, AAB, ARCPA, ART, CAATE, CAHIIM, CEA, CLPSY, DENT, DIETD, DIETI, HSA, LAW, MED, MFCD, MLS, NMT, NURSE, OT, PH, PTA, RADMAG, RTT, SP, SW

01 President ..... Dr. Fred P. PESTELLO
05 Provost ..... Dr. Michael LEWIS
10 Vice Pres/Chief Financial Officer ..... Mr. David F. HEIMBURGER
18 Assoc VP Facilities Management ..... Mr. Michael LUCIDO
84 VP Enrollment/Retention Management ..... Ms. Kathleen DAVIS
12 Director Madrid Campus ..... Dr. Paul VITA
15 VP Human Resources ..... Mr. Mickey LUNA
26 VP Marketing and Communications ..... Ms. Anita BORGMEYER
43 Vice President/General Counsel ..... Ms. Danielle UY
32 VP Student Development ..... Dr. Sarah CUNNINGHAM
30 VP Development ..... Ms. Sheila M. MANION
42 Vice President for Mission/Identity ..... Fr. David SUWALSKY, SJ
13 VP Information Tech Svcs/CIO ..... Mr. Kyle COLLINS
23 Vice President for Medical Affairs ..... Dr. Christine JACOBS
27 Asst VP Marketing & Communications ..... Ms. Laura GEISER
29 Exec Development Director ..... Ms. Mary CONNOLLY
21 Assistant Controller ..... Mr. Fred R. WINKLER
35 Dean of Students ..... Dr. Donna BESS MYERS
54 Int Dean Science and Engineering ..... Dr. Scott DUELLMAN
49 Interim Dean Arts & Sciences ..... Dr. Donna LAVOIE
50 Dean Chaifetz School of Business ..... Dr. Barnali GUPTA
61 Dean of Law ..... Mr. William P. JOHNSON
63 Dean of Medical School ..... Dr. Christine JACOBS
79 Dean Philosophy & Letters ..... Dr. Randall ROSENBERG
53 Dean School of Education ..... Dr. Gary RITTER
08 University Librarian ..... Ms. Jennifer NUTEFALL
88 Director Ctr for Health Care Ethics ..... Dr. Jason EBERL
52 Exec Dir Ctr Advanced Dental Educ ..... Dr. John HATTON
46 Vice President for Research ..... Dr. Kenneth OLLIFF
19 Asst VP Public Safety/Emerg Prep ..... Ms. Melinda HEIKKINEN
06 University Registrar ..... Mr. Jay HAUGEN
07 AVP and Dean of Admission ..... Ms. Jean COX
37 AVP and Director Financial Aid ..... Ms. Cari S. WICKLIFFE
41 Athletics Director ..... Mr. Christopher V. MAY
85 Director International Services ..... Ms. Rebecca BAHAN
92 Director Honors Program ..... Mr. Robert PAMPEL
100 Chief of Staff ..... Mr. Bob GAGNE
88 Director Univ Museums/Galleries ..... Dr. Petruta LIPAN
110 Exec Development Director ..... Mr. Kent G. LEVAN
20 Assoc Provost Undergraduate Educ ..... Dr. Lisa DORSEY
58 Interim Assoc Provost Graduate Educ ..... Dr. April TREES
108 Associate Provost & Inst Assessment ..... Dr. Steven SANCHEZ
09 Assoc Prov & Dir of Inst Research ..... Ms. Stacey HARRINGTON
96 Director of Business Services ..... Mr. Jeff HOVEY
22 Dir Ofc of Inst Equity & Diversity ..... Mr. Justin LACY
86 Director Government Relations ..... Mr. Marc SCHEESSELE
28 Diversity/Community Engagement ..... Ms. Rochelle SMITH
103 Executive Dir Workforce Development ..... Ms. Katherine CAIN
105 Director Web Services ..... Mr. Mark RIMAR
38 Director Student Counseling ..... Dr. Knieba JONES-JOHNSON
101 Board & Council Administrator ..... Ms. Amelia ARNOLD
39 Dir Resident Life/Student Housing ..... Ms. Manisha FORD-THOMAS

Southeast Missouri Hospital College of Nursing and Health Sciences (I)

2001 William Street, Cape Girardeau MO 63703-5815
County: Cape Girardeau FICE Identification: 030709
Unit ID: 417734
Telephone: (573) 334-6825 Carnegie Class: Spec-4-yr-Other Health
FAX Number: (573) 339-7805 Calendar System: Semester
URL: www.sehcollege.edu
Established: 1990 Annual Undergrad Tuition & Fees: $13,301
Enrollment: 203 Coed
Affiliation or Control: Independent Non-Profit IRS Status: 501(c)3
Highest Offering: Baccalaureate
Accreditation: HLC, ADNUR, MLS, NURSE, RAD, SURGT

01 President ..... Dr. Steven D. LANGDON
05 Dean General Education/Student Svcs ..... Dr. Dedria A. BLAKELY
66 Dean of Nursing ..... Dr. Tonya BUTTRY
06 Registrar ..... Ms. Erica URY
37 Financial Aid Director ..... Ms. Cassandra HICKS
09 Inst Research Officer/Admissions ..... Ms. Rhonda VANDERGRIFF
10 Business Officer ..... Ms. Deanna SELLS

Southeast Missouri State University (J)

One University Plaza, Cape Girardeau MO 63701-4799
County: Cape Girardeau FICE Identification: 002501
Unit ID: 179557
Telephone: (573) 651-2000 Carnegie Class: Masters/L
FAX Number: (573) 651-2200 Calendar System: Semester
URL: www.semo.edu
Established: 1873 Annual Undergrad Tuition & Fees (In-State): $8,033
Enrollment: 10,001 Coed
Affiliation or Control: State IRS Status: 501(c)3
Highest Offering: Beyond Master's But Less Than Doctorate
Accreditation: HLC, ART, CAATE, CACREP, CAEP, CAPRT, CEA, CIDA, COSMA, DANCE, DIET, DIETD, JOUR, MUS, NAIT, NURSE, SP, SW, THEA

01 President ..... Dr. Carlos VARGAS
05 Provost ..... Dr. Michael GODARD
10 VP Finance & Administration ..... Mr. Brad SHERIFF
84 VP Enrollment Mgmt/Student Success ..... Dr. Debbie BELOW
111 VP University Advancement ..... Mrs. Trudy LEE
09 Director of Institutional Research ..... Mr. Eric CHAMBERS
100 Chief of Staff & Asst to the Pres ..... Mr. Chris MARTIN
58 Vice Provost & Dean Grad Studies ..... Dr. Doug KOCH
13 Asst Vice Pres Information Tech ..... Mr. Floyd DAVENPORT
32 AVP for Student Life ..... Dr. Bruce SKINNER
50 Dean Harrison Col of Bus & Comp ..... Dr. Alberto DAVILA
53 Dean Col of Educ/Hlth/Hum Stds ..... Dr. Joe PUJOL
79 Dean Col of Humanities/Soc Sci ..... Dr. Eric BAIN-SELBO
57 Dean Holland Col of Arts & Media ..... Ms. Rhonda WELLER STILSON
81 Dean Col of Sci/Tech/Engr/Math ..... Dr. Tamela RANDOLPH
35 Dean of Students ..... Mr. Trae MITTEN
08 Dean of Kent Library ..... Ms. Barbara GLACKIN
07 Director of Admissions ..... Ms. Lenell HAHN
35 Director of Campus Life & Event Svc ..... Ms. Michele IRBY
26 AVP Marketing & Comm ..... Ms. Tonya WELLS
41 Director of Athletics ..... Mr. Brady L. BARKE
29 Director Alumni Services ..... Mr. George GASSER
85 Exec Dir Intl Education & Svcs ..... Mr. Kevin TIMLIN
18 Director of Facilities Management ..... Ms. Angela MEYER
37 Director of Student Financial Svcs ..... Mr. Matt KEARNEY
15 Director of Human Resources ..... Ms. Alissa VANDEVEN
19 Dir of Public Safety/Trans ..... Ms. Beth GLAUS
06 Registrar ..... Ms. Sandy L. HINKLE
88 Director of Show Me Center ..... Mr. Wil GORMAN
92 Dir Jane Stephens Honors Pgm ..... Dr. Scott BRANDHORST
38 Int Dir Ctr Behav Health & Access ..... Ms. Dinia JENKINS
21 Asst VP Financial Svcs ..... Ms. Sue WILDE
39 Director of Residence Life ..... Dr. Kendra SKINNER

Southwest Baptist University (K)

1600 University Avenue, Bolivar MO 65613-2597
County: Polk FICE Identification: 002502
Unit ID: 179326
Telephone: (417) 328-5281 Carnegie Class: Masters/L
FAX Number: (417) 328-1514 Calendar System: Semester
URL: www.sbuniv.edu
Established: 1878 Annual Undergrad Tuition & Fees: $25,508
Enrollment: 3,039 Coed
Affiliation or Control: Southern Baptist IRS Status: 501(c)3
Highest Offering: Doctorate
Accreditation: #HLC, ACBSP, ADNUR, MUS, NUR, PTA, RAD, SW

00 Chairman of the Board ..... Dr. Eddie BUMPERS
01 President ..... Dr. Richard J. MELSON
05 Provost ..... Dr. Lee SKINKLE
45 VP Strategic Planning/Chf of Staff ..... Dr. Ryan GRIFFITH
111 VP for Institutional Advancement ..... Vacant
11 Vice President Administration ..... Vacant
84 Vice Pres Enrollment Management ..... Mr. Darren CROWDER

41 Athletic Director ... Mr. Clark SHEEHY
26 VP of Marketing & Graduate Studies ... Dr. Todd EARL
32 Vice Pres for Student Development ... Vacant
20 Assistant Provost ... Vacant
107 Dean College Professional Programs ... Dr. Troy BETHARDS
49 Dean College of Liberal Arts ... Dr. Holly HILL-STANFORD
76 Dean College of Health Professional . Dr. Brittney HENDRICKSON
08 Dean of University Libraries ... Vacant
13 Chief Technology Officer ... Mr. David BOLTON
37 Dir Student Financial Assistance ... Mrs. Karla GOUGHNOUR
91 Network Administrator ... Mr. Kevin KELLEY
19 Director Campus Security ... Mr. Mark GRABOWSKI
106 Sr Director of Teaching & Learning ... Ms. Angela CARR
42 Director University Ministries ... Vacant
18 Director Physical Plant ... Mr. Robbie BRYANT
06 Registrar ... Mrs. Roberta RASOR
39 Director Residence Life ... Mrs. Christina RUIZ
07 Director Undergraduate Admissions ... Ms. Natalie O'KEEFE
36 Director of Career Services ... Mrs. Shonna FORE
29 Director of Alumni Engagement ... Vacant
35 Director Student Activities ... Vacant
04 Executive Coordinator to President ... Mrs. Brittany EARL
108 Dir of Institutional Effectiveness ... Mr. Levi FOX
73 Division Head Dept Theology ... Dr. Dave QUACKENBOS
38 Director Counseling Services ... Vacant
10 Controller ... Ms. Terri ROGERS
15 Director of Human Resources ... Mrs. Sunny FULLER
40 Book Store Manager ... Mrs. Debbie LEWIS
12 Director of Springfield Campus ... Mr. Brian MCCARLEY
12 Director of Mtn View & Salem Campus ... Mrs. Shae MILLER
105 Director Web Services ... Ms. Rebekah WRIGHT

Southwest Baptist University Mountain View Campus (A)

PO Box 489, Mountain View MO 65548
Telephone: (417) 934-2999 Identification: 770326
Accreditation: &HLC

Southwest Baptist University Salem (B)

501 S Grand, Salem MO 65560
Telephone: (573) 729-7071 Identification: 770327
Accreditation: &HLC

Southwest Baptist University Springfield (C)

4431 S Fremont, Springfield MO 65804
Telephone: (417) 820-2069 Identification: 770328
Accreditation: &HLC

State Fair Community College (D)

3201 W 16th Street, Sedalia MO 65301-2199
County: Pettis FICE Identification: 008080
Unit ID: 179539
Telephone: (660) 596-7222 Carnegie Class: Assoc/MT-VT-High Trad
FAX Number: (660) 596-7335 Calendar System: Semester
URL: www.sfccmo.edu
Established: 1968 Annual Undergrad Tuition & Fees (In-District): $4,680
Enrollment: 3,928 Coed
Affiliation or Control: Local IRS Status: 501(c)3
Highest Offering: Associate Degree
Accreditation: HLC, CAHIIM, CONST, DH, DMS, MLTAD, OTA, RAD

01 President ... Dr. Brent BATES
05 VP for Educ/Student Support Svcs ... Vacant
10 VP for Finance/Administration & HR ... Mr. Keith ACUFF
20 Dean of Academic Affairs ... Mr. Jim CUNNINGHAM
75 Dean Vocational/Technical Studies ... Mr. Michael ROGG
121 Dean Student/Academic Support ... Mr. Daniel AVEGALIO
13 Chief Information Officer ... Mr. Mark HAVERLY
102 Exec Director SFCC Foundation ... Ms. Mary TREUNER
06 Registrar ... Mrs. Jennifer WILBANKS
37 Director of Financial Aid ... Mrs. Angel MEFFORD
18 Chief Facilities/Physical Plant ... Mr. Justin O'NEAL
21 Controller Business Officer ... Mrs. Diane BROCKMAN
26 Exec Dir Marketing/Communication ... Mr. Brad HENDERSON
04 Executive Asst to President ... Mrs. Lisa OESTERLE
41 Athletic Director ... Mr. Darren PANNIER
15 Exec Director Human Resources ... Ms. Rachel DAWSON
09 Exec Director Institutional Effect ... Mrs. Darci MCFAIL
19 Director Security/ Safety ... Mr. Curtis HAMMONDS
86 Legislative and Community Pgm Mgr ... Mrs. Jo Lynn TURLEY

State Technical College of Missouri (E)

One Technology Drive, Linn MO 65051-0479
County: Osage FICE Identification: 004711
Unit ID: 177977
Telephone: (573) 897-5000 Carnegie Class: Assoc/HVT-High Trad
FAX Number: N/A Calendar System: Semester
URL: www.statetechmo.edu
Established: 1961 Annual Undergrad Tuition & Fees (In-State): $6,510
Enrollment: 1,756 Coed
Affiliation or Control: State IRS Status: 501(c)3
Highest Offering: Associate Degree
Accreditation: HLC, DA, NAIT, PTAA, RAD

01 President ... Dr. Shawn STRONG
05 Vice President of Academic Affairs ... Ms. Angie GAINES
32 Vice President of Student Affairs ... Dr. Chris BOWSER
10 Vice President of Finance ... Ms. Jenny JACOBS
111 Vice President of Advancement ... Ms. Shannon GRUS
100 Chief of Staff ... Ms. Amy AMES
04 Executive Asst to the President ... Ms. Katy MINNIX
18 Director of Facilities ... Mr. Brad CREDE
13 Director of IT ... Vacant
26 Director of Marketing ... Mr. Brandon MCELWAIN
09 Director of Institutional Research ... Mr. Aaron KLIETHERMES
20 Dean of Curriculum and Instruction ... Ms. Janet CLANTON
72 Dean of Technology ... Mr. Chris MEUNKS
97 Dean of Professional Studies ... Mr. Ken THOMPSON

Stephens College (F)

1200 E Broadway, Columbia MO 65215-0001
County: Boone FICE Identification: 002512
Unit ID: 179548
Telephone: (573) 442-2211 Carnegie Class: Masters/S
FAX Number: (573) 876-7248 Calendar System: Semester
URL: www.stephens.edu
Established: 1833 Annual Undergrad Tuition & Fees: $23,385
Enrollment: 622 Female
Affiliation or Control: Independent Non-Profit IRS Status: 501(c)3
Highest Offering: Master's
Accreditation: HLC, ARCPA, CAHIIM

01 President ... Dr. Dianne LYNCH
10 Vice Pres Finance/Business/CFO ... Mr. Dane FUHRMAN
05 Vice Pres Academic Affairs ... Dr. Leslie WILLEY
111 Vice Pres Institutional Advancement ... Ms. Gina SHOLTIS
32 Vice Pres Student Development ... Dr. Laura NUNNELLY
26 VP of Marketing/Public Relations ... Mr. Derrell CARTER
84 Vice President Enrollment Mgmt ... Vacant
06 Registrar ... Ms. Linda SHARP
13 IT Director ... Vacant
41 Athletic Director ... Mr. Miguel PAREDES
37 Director of Financial Aid ... Ms. Keri GILBERT
04 Executive Asst to President ... Ms. Lita PISTONO
07 Director of Admissions ... Ms. Severin ROBERTS
08 Head Librarian ... Mr. Dan KAMMER
18 Director of Facilities Mgmt ... Vacant
19 Director Security/Safety ... Ms. Candy CORNMAN
39 Director of Residence Life ... Vacant
104 Study Abroad Coordinator ... Dr. James TERRY
108 Director Institutional Assessment ... Dr. Sharon SCHATTGEN
15 Director of Human Resources ... Mr. Michael BATES

Stevens Institute of Business & Arts (G)

1521 Washington Avenue, Saint Louis MO 63103
County: Saint Louis FICE Identification: 008552
Unit ID: 178767
Telephone: (314) 421-0949 Carnegie Class: Bac-Diverse
FAX Number: (314) 421-0304 Calendar System: Quarter
URL: www.siba.edu
Established: 1947 Annual Undergrad Tuition & Fees: $12,285
Enrollment: 109 Coed
Affiliation or Control: Proprietary IRS Status: Proprietary
Highest Offering: Baccalaureate
Accreditation: ACCSC

01 President ... Ms. Cynthia A. MUSTERMAN
05 Academic Dean & Registrar ... Ms. Emilee SCHNEFKE
37 Financial Aid Director ... Ms. Christa SIAMPOS
07 Director of Admissions ... Ms. Sara DORN
36 Career Services Director ... Mr. Steve ASHER

Texas County Technical College (H)

6915 S Highway 63 PO Box 314, Houston MO 65483
County: Texas FICE Identification: 035793
Unit ID: 441487
Telephone: (417) 967-5466 Carnegie Class: Spec 2-yr-Health
FAX Number: (417) 967-4604 Calendar System: Semester
URL: www.texascountytech.edu
Established: 1986 Annual Undergrad Tuition & Fees: $18,240
Enrollment: 52 Coed
Affiliation or Control: Independent Non-Profit IRS Status: 501(c)3
Highest Offering: Associate Degree
Accreditation: ABHES

01 President ... Ms. Charlotte GRAY
06 Campus Director/Registrar ... Ms. Clarice CASEBEER
37 Admissions/Financial Aid ... Ms. Chelsye SCANTLIN

Three Rivers College (I)

2080 Three Rivers Boulevard,
Poplar Bluff MO 63901-2350
County: Butler FICE Identification: 004713
Unit ID: 179645
Telephone: (573) 840-9600 Carnegie Class: Assoc/HT-High Trad
FAX Number: (573) 840-9604 Calendar System: Semester
URL: www.trcc.edu
Established: 1966 Annual Undergrad Tuition & Fees (In-State): $5,490
Enrollment: 2,759 Coed
Affiliation or Control: State IRS Status: 501(c)3
Highest Offering: Associate Degree
Accreditation: HLC, ADNUR, EMT, MLTAD, OTA

01 President ... Dr. Wesley A. PAYNE
10 Chief Financial Officer ... Ms. Charlotte EUBANK
05 Chief Academic Officer ... Dr. Sherry A. PHELAN
08 Director Library Services ... Dr. John LADUE
37 Director Financial Aid ... Ms. Regina MORRIS
06 Registrar ... Ms. Melanie HAMANN
32 Dean of Student Services ... Ms. Ann MATTHEWS
09 Chief Inst Effectiveness Officer ... Dr. Maribeth PAYNE
18 Chief Facilities/Physical Plant ... Mr. Rob TOMLINSON
15 Director Human Resources ... Ms. Kristina D. MCDANIEL
26 Chief Public Relations Officer ... Ms. Carrie FRANKLIN
30 Chief Development/Dir Alumni Rels ... Ms. Michelle REYNOLDS
84 Director Enrollment Management ... Ms. Brandi BROOKS
96 Dir Procurement/Risk Management ... Ms. Cambrea HALCUMB
04 Executive Asst to President ... Ms. Edie DILBECK
103 Dir Workforce Development ... Ms. Leann CLARK
13 Chief Info Technology Officer ... Mr. Steve ATWOOD
22 Dir Affirmative Action/EEO ... Ms. Kristina D. MCDANIEL
39 Director Student Housing ... Ms. Adrian JAMESON
19 Director Security/Safety ... Mr. Chuck STRATTON

Truman State University (J)

100 E Normal, Kirksville MO 63501-4221
County: Adair FICE Identification: 002495
Unit ID: 178615
Telephone: (660) 785-4000 Carnegie Class: Masters/M
FAX Number: (660) 785-4030 Calendar System: Semester
URL: www.truman.edu
Established: 1867 Annual Undergrad Tuition & Fees (In-State): $8,299
Enrollment: 4,655 Coed
Affiliation or Control: State IRS Status: 501(c)3
Highest Offering: Master's
Accreditation: HLC, AAQEP, CAATE, CAEP, MUS, NURSE, SP

01 President ... Dr. Susan L. THOMAS
05 Interim Provost ... Dr. Charles MCADAMS
111 Vice Pres for Univ Advancement ... Dr. Ernie T. HUGHES
10 VP for Admin Finance & Planning ... Mr. David RECTOR
84 VP Student Engage/Enrollment/Mktg ... Dr. Tyana LANGE
43 General Counsel ... Ms. Amy CLENDENNEN
21 Comptroller ... Mr. Mike GARZANELLI
41 Director of Athletics ... Mr. Jerry WOLLMERING
15 Director of Human Resources ... Ms. Melissa GARZANELLI
37 Financial Aid Director ... Ms. Marla FERNANDEZ
06 Registrar ... Ms. Nancy ASHER
13 Chief Information Officer ... Ms. Donna LISS
26 Director of Public Relations ... Mr. Travis MILES
20 Associate Provost ... Dr. Kevin M. MINCH
83 Dean Sch Social & Cultural Studies ... Dr. Elizabeth M. CLARK
50 Dean School of Business ... Dr. Rashmi PRASAD
81 Dean Sch of Science & Math ... Dr. Tim WALSTON
53 Dean Sch of Health Sci & Educ ... Dr. Lance RATCLIFF
49 Dean School of Arts & Letters ... Dr. Steve PARSONS

University of Central Missouri (K)

Administration Building, Room 101,
Warrensburg MO 64093-5299
County: Johnson FICE Identification: 002454
Unit ID: 176965
Telephone: (660) 543-4255 Carnegie Class: Masters/L
FAX Number: (660) 543-4200 Calendar System: Semester
URL: www.ucmo.edu
Established: 1871 Annual Undergrad Tuition & Fees (In-State): $8,306
Enrollment: 9,959 Coed
Affiliation or Control: State IRS Status: 501(c)3
Highest Offering: Beyond Master's But Less Than Doctorate
Accreditation: HLC, AAB, AAFCS, ART, CACREP, CAEPN, CEA, CIDA, @DIET, DIETD, MUS, NAIT, NURSE, SP, SW, THEA

01 President ... Dr. Roger BEST
101 Exec Asst to Pres/Asst Sec to Board ... Ms. Monica R. HUFFMAN
43 General Counsel ... Ms. Lindsay CHAPMAN
05 Provost & VP of Academic Affairs ... Dr. Phillip BRIDGMON
32 VP Student Experience/Engagement ... Dr. Sharlene GARBER BAX
10 Vice President Finance & Operations ... Mr. Bill HAWLEY
41 Vice Pres Intercollegiate Athletics ... Mr. Jerry M. HUGHES
20 Vice Prov Acad Pgms/Dean Grad Stds ... Dr. Tim CROWLEY
26 Vice Pres Integrated Mktg & Comm ... Ms. Susan SMEDLEY
35 Assoc VP Student Services/Title IX ... Dr. Corey L. BOWMAN
84 Exec Vice Provost Enroll Mgmt ... Dr. Randall LANGSTON
111 VP Advancement/External Engagement ... Ms. Courtney GODDARD
08 University Librarian ... Dr. Janette KLEIN
49 Dean Arts/Humanities/Soc Sci ... Dr. Mike SAWYER
72 Dean Health/Science/Tech ... Dr. Jeff ROBERTSON
50 Dean Business & Prof Studies ... Dr. Mark SUAZO
53 Dean of College of Education ... Dr. Ann MCCOY
13 Vice Provost for Technology & CIO ... Dr. James F. GRAHAM
06 Interim Registrar ... Ms. Heather MCGRATH
121 Director Academic Success Advisor ... Mr. Kenneth SCHUELLER
37 Dir Student Financial Assistance ... Mr. Tony LUBBERS
19 Interim Director of Public Safety ... Mr. Bill BRINKLEY
39 Sr Director of University Housing ... Dr. Brenda MOEDER
18 Assoc VP Capital Plng/Fac Mgmt ... Mr. Timothy CASTILAW
96 Director Purchasing ... Mr. Bob WALLA
15 Assoc VP Human Resources ... Ms. Ranea TAYLOR
40 Director of Univ Store & Textbooks ... Mr. Charles D. RUTT
106 Vice Prov Online & Learning Engage ... Dr. Laurel HOGUE
07 Asst VP for Admissions & Analytics ... Mr. Christopher LANG
38 Asst Director Counseling Center ... Dr. Jeanne WOON

36 Director Career Services ... Ms. Amber GOREHAM
09 Director of Institutional Research ... Dr. Meng CHEN
86 Director Governmental Relations ... Mr. David PEARCE
122 Dir of Residence/Greek Llife ... Mr. Alan NORDYKE

University of Health Sciences and Pharmacy in St. Louis (A)

1 Pharmacy Place, Saint Louis MO 63110-1088
County: Independent City — FICE Identification: 002504
Unit ID: 179265
Telephone: (314) 367-8700 — Carnegie Class: Spec-4-yr-Other Health
FAX Number: (314) 446-8304 — Calendar System: Semester
URL: www.uhsp.edu
Established: 1864 — Annual Undergrad Tuition & Fees: $30,147
Enrollment: 998 — Coed
Affiliation or Control: Independent Non-Profit — IRS Status: 501(c)3
Highest Offering: First Professional Degree
Accreditation: HLC, PHAR

01 President ... Dr. David D. ALLEN
100 Chief of Staff ... Dr. Michael SASS
05 VP Pgm Dev/Strategic Initiatives ... Dr. Brenda GLEASON
49 Interim Dean College of A&S ... Dr. Ehren BUCHOLTZ
58 Dean College of Graduate Studies ... Dr. Giovanni PAULETTI
69 Dean College of Global Pop Health ... Dr. David STEEB
67 Dean College of Pharmacy ... Dr. Terri WARHOLAK
28 VP Campus Life/Chief Diversity Ofcr ... Dr. Isaac BUTLER
43 General Counsel ... Mr. Kenneth FLEISCHMANN
84 VP Enrollment Mgmt/Mktg/Athletics ... Ms. Michele HOEFT
18 Vice President Operations ... Dr. Eric KNOLL
10 VP Finance and CFO ... Ms. Lisa VANSICKLE
46 VP Research/Scholarly Activities ... Dr. Pamela XAVERIUS
04 Exec Assistant to the President ... Ms. Trina WARREN
15 AVP HR & Title IX Coordinator ... Mr. Daniel BAUER
25 AVP Research Admin & Tech Transfer ... Ms. Brandi CLEMENTS
84 AVP Admissions/Chief Enrollment Ofc ... Ms. Jill GEBKE
41 Director Athletics/Fitness & Rec ... Ms. Jill HARTER
28 Director Diversity/Equity & Incl ... Mr. Harlan HODGE
32 AVP Student Success and Wellness ... Ms. Rebecca JONES
111 AVP Advancement ... Mr. Port KAIGLER
06 Registrar ... Ms. Laura KLOS
37 AVP Enrollment Mgmt & Financial Aid ... Ms. Kim LAMBORN
13 AVP Information Technology ... Mr. Zachary LEWIS
29 Director Alumni Relations ... Ms. Stephanie MAUZY
26 AVP Marketing/Chief Marketing Ofcr ... Ms. Kelsey MEYER
08 Library Director ... Ms. Jill NISSEN
21 Director of Finance ... Mr. David POOLE
88 Manager Institutional Events ... Ms. Randi POSCOVER
21 AVP Finance & Controller/Dir of IR ... Ms. Kayla REYNOLDS
36 Director Career Svcs/Employer Rels ... Dr. Jordan WATSON
109 AVP Facilities & Auxiliary Services ... Mr. Matthew WEVER
108 Assistant Director of IR ... Dr. Francis ANDERSON
39 Coordinator Residential Life ... Ms. Maryam OUECHANI
38 Director Counseling and Wellness ... Ms. Susan MOORE
44 Annual Giving Officer ... Vacant
19 Director Security/Safety ... Vacant

*University of Missouri System Administration (B)

105 Jesse Hall, Columbia MO 65211-3020
County: Boone — FICE Identification: 002515
Unit ID: 178439
Telephone: (573) 882-2011 — Carnegie Class: N/A
FAX Number: (573) 882-2721
URL: www.umsystem.edu

01 President ... Dr. Mun Y. CHOI
05 Provost/Exec VC Academic Affairs ... Dr. Latha RAMCHAND
10 Vice President Finance/CFO ... Mr. Ryan RAPP
28 Vice Chancellor of Incl/Div/Equity ... Dr. Maurice GIPSON
13 Vice President Info Technology ... Ms. Beth CHANCELLOR
15 Vice Pres Human Resource Svcs ... Ms. Marsha FISCHER
20 Sr Assoc Vice Pres Academic Affairs ... Vacant
88 Assistant Vice Chancellor ... Dr. John MIDDLETON
43 General Counsel ... Mr. Stephen J. OWENS
26 Chief Communications Officer ... Ms. Kamrhan FARWELL
17 CEO/COO UM Health Care ... Mr. Jonathan CARTRIGHT
21 Treasurer ... Mr. Tom F. RICHARDS
21 Controller ... Mr. Eric VOGELWEID
04 Executive Asst to President ... Ms. Janet WAIBEL
101 Secretary of the Board of Curators ... Ms. Cindy S. HARMON

*University of Missouri - Columbia (C)

Columbia MO 65211-0001
County: Boone — FICE Identification: 002516
Unit ID: 178396
Telephone: (573) 882-2121 — Carnegie Class: DU-Highest
FAX Number: (573) 882-9907 — Calendar System: Semester
URL: www.missouri.edu
Established: 1839 — Annual Undergrad Tuition & Fees (In-State): $10,723
Enrollment: 31,089 — Coed
Affiliation or Control: State — IRS Status: 501(c)3
Highest Offering: Doctorate
Accreditation: HLC, CAEP, CAHIIM, CAPRT, CEA, CIDA, CLPSY, COARC, COPSY, DIETC, DMS, HSA, IPSY, JOUR, LAW, LIB, MED, MUS, NMT, NURSE, OT, PCSAS, PH, PHAR, PTA, RAD, SCPSY, SP, SPAA, SW, VET

02 President and Chancellor ... Dr. Mun Y. CHOI
100 Chief of Staff ... Dr. John R. MIDDLETON
05 Prov/Exec Vice Chanc Acad Affs ... Dr. Latha RAMCHAND
20 Senior Vice Provost ... Dr. Matthew P. MARTENS
111 Vice Chanc Advancement ... Ms. Jackie A. LEWIS
56 Vice Chanc Extension & Engagement ... Dr. Marshall M. STEWART
10 Vice Chanc Finance & CBO ... Dr. Rhonda K. GIBLER
28 VC Inclusion/Diversty & Equity ... Dr. Maurice D. GIPSON
26 Vice Chanc/Chief Marketing & Comm ... Dr. Kamrhan M. FARWELL
11 Exec Vice Pres Finance/Operations ... Mr. Ryan D. RAPP
46 Vice Chanc Research/Econ Dev ... Dr. Thomas E. SPENCER
32 Vice Chanc Student Affairs ... Dr. William B. STACKMAN
110 Asst Vice Chanc Advancement ... Ms. Meichele A. FOSTER
22 Asst V Chanc Civil Rights/Title IX ... Dr. Andrea (Andy) S. HAYES
29 Assoc Vice Chanc Alumni Relations ... Mr. Todd A. MCCUBBIN
17 Exec Vice Chanc Health Affairs ... Dr. Richard J. BAROHN
84 Vice Prov Enrollment Mgmt ... Ms. Kim A. HUMPHREY
09 Exec Dir Institutional Research ... Dr. Mardy T. EIMERS
15 Vice Pres Human Resources ... Ms. Marsha B. FISCHER
85 Vice Prov International Programs ... Dr. Mary A. STEGMAIER
08 Vice Prov Libraries ... Ms. Deb H. WARD
20 Vice Prov Undergraduate Studies ... Dr. James N. SPAIN
17 Chief Exec Officer MU Health Care ... Dr. Jonathan W. CURTRIGHT
13 Chief Information Officer ... Ms. Beth C. CHANCELLOR
19 Police Chief University Police ... Mr. Brian WEIMER
35 Dean of Students ... Dr. William B. STACKMAN
23 Exec Dir Stdnt Health & Well-Being ... Dr. Jamie L. SHUTTER
06 University Registrar ... Ms. Brenda V. SELMAN
47 Dean Agri/Food & Natural Resources ... Dr. Christopher R. DAUBERT
49 Dean Arts & Science ... Dr. Cooper C. DRURY
50 Interim Dean Business ... Dr. Chris A. ROBERT
53 Interim Dean Education & Human Dev ... Dr. Timothy (Chris) C. RILEY-TILLMAN
54 Dean Engineering ... Dr. Noah D. MANRING
58 Dean Graduate School ... Dr. Jeni L. HART
76 Dean Health Professions ... Dr. Kristofer J. HAGGLUND
60 Dean Journalism ... Dr. David D. KURPIUS
61 Interim Dean Law ... Dr. Paul J. LITTON
63 Dean Medicine ... Dr. Richard J. BAROHN
66 Interim Dean Nursing ... Dr. Lori L. POPEJOY
74 Dean Veterinary Medicine ... Dr. Carolyn J. HENRY
07 Director Admissions ... Mr. Charles A. MAY
41 Director Athletics ... Ms. Desiree D. REED-FRANCOIS
40 Director Campus Retail ... Mr. Dale B. SANDERS
36 Director Career Center ... Dr. Rob M. MCDANIELS
105 Director Digital Service ... Mr. Kevin S. BAILEY
88 Director Disability Center ... Ms. Ashley M. BRICKLEY
92 Interim Director Honors College ... Ms. Catherine E. RYMPH
25 Director Sponsored Program Admin ... Mr. Craig A. DAVID
37 Exec Director Student Financial Aid ... Ms. Emily L. HAYNAM

*University of Missouri - Kansas City (D)

5100 Rockhill Road, Kansas City MO 64110-2499
County: Jackson — FICE Identification: 002518
Unit ID: 178402
Telephone: (816) 235-1000 — Carnegie Class: DU-Higher
FAX Number: (816) 235-1717 — Calendar System: Semester
URL: www.umkc.edu
Established: 1929 — Annual Undergrad Tuition & Fees (In-State): $10,145
Enrollment: 16,147 — Coed
Affiliation or Control: State — IRS Status: 501(c)3
Highest Offering: Doctorate
Accreditation: HLC, AA, ANEST, ARCPA, CAEP, CEA, CLPSY, COPSY, DANCE, DENT, DH, EMT, IPSY, LAW, MED, MPCAC, MUS, NURSE, OTA, PHAR, PLNG, SPAA, SW, THEA

02 Chancellor ... Dr. C. Mauli AGRAWAL
100 Chief of Staff ... Ms. Sheri GORMLEY
05 Provost ... Dr. Jennifer LUNDGREN
28 Int Vice Chanc Diversity/Inclusion ... Dr. Makini KING
10 Vice Chanc Finance/Administration ... Mr. Sean REEDER
21 Director Budgeting and Planning ... Ms. Karen WILKERSON
113 Director Cashiering ... Mr. Paul SCHWARTZ
104 Director International Affairs ... Dr. Joy STEVENSON
102 Interim Pres UMKC Foundation ... Ms. Shelly DOUCET
44 Director Annual Giving ... Ms. Dana CHAMBLIN
111 Vice Chanc External Relations ... Mr. Curt CRESPINO
41 Athletic Director ... Dr. Brandon MARTIN
13 Chief Information Officer ... Mr. Andrew GOODENOW
119 Information Security Officer ... Mr. Justin MALYN
15 Vice Chanc Human Resources ... Ms. Carol HINTZ
118 Employee Services ... Mr. Ted STAHL
20 Vice Provost Faculty Affairs ... Dr. Diane FILION
108 Vice Prov Curriculum & Assessment ... Dr. Kim MCNELEY
106 Asst Vice Provost Acad Innovation ... Dr. Molly MEAD
79 Dean Sch of Humanities & Social Sci ... Dr. Tamara FALICOV
50 Dean Bloch School of Management ... Dr. Brian KLAAS
81 Dean Sch Bio and Chemical Sciences ... Dr. Theodore WHITE
92 Director Honors Program ... Dr. Gayle LEVY
64 Dean of UMKC Conservatory ... Dr. Courtney CRAPPELL
52 Dean School of Dentistry ... Dr. Steven HAAS
53 Interim Dean School of Education ... Dr. Carolyn BARBER
54 Dean Sch of Science and Engineering ... Dr. Kevin Z. TRUMAN
61 Dean School of Law ... Ms. Barbara GLESNER FINES
63 Dean School of Medicine ... Dr. Mary Anne JACKSON
66 Int Dean Nursing & Health Studies ... Dr. Joy ROBERTS
67 Dean School of Pharmacy ... Dr. Russell B. MELCHERT
08 Dean University Libraries ... Dr. Cindy THOMPSON
58 Dean of Graduate Studies ... Dr. Chris LIU
20 Vice Provost Inst Effectiveness ... Dr. Kelli COX
84 Asst Vice Prov Enroll Management ... Mr. Doug SWINK
124 Sr Vice Prov Student Success ... Dr. Kristi HOLSINGER
32 Vice Prov/Dean Student Affairs ... Dr. Michele D. SMITH
88 Director Student Conduct ... Ms. Keishea BOYD
35 Director Student Involvement ... Mr. Todd WELLS
26 Vice Chanc Strategic Market & Comm ... Ms. Anne SPENNER
27 Director Media Relations ... Mr. John MARTELLARO
29 Director Alumni & Constituent Rels ... Ms. Kathryn HOUSTON
86 Asst Vice Chanc External Relations ... Mr. Troy LILLEBO
22 Title IX Coordinator ... Dr. KC ATCHINSON
121 Dir Academic Support & Mentoring ... Ms. Jessica BROOKS
07 Director Admissions ... Ms. Elora THOMAS
37 Director Student Financial Aid ... Mr. Scott YOUNG
06 Registrar ... Ms. Amy COLE
19 Chief Campus Police ... Mr. Michael BONGARTZ
40 Director Bookstore ... Mr. Pete EISENTRAGER
38 Director Counseling Services ... Dr. Arnold ABELS
94 Int Director Women's Center ... Ms. Arzie UMALI
36 Director Career Services ... Mr. Davlon MILLER
39 Director Residential Life ... Ms. Kristen TEMPLE
93 Dir Multicultural Student Affairs ... Ms. Keichanda DEES-BURNETT
109 Director Student Union ... Mr. Jody JEFFRIES
25 Business Manager for Admin Services ... Mr. Jeffery ROSS

*University of Missouri - Saint Louis (E)

1 University Boulevard, Saint Louis MO 63121-4400
County: Saint Louis — FICE Identification: 002519
Unit ID: 178420
Telephone: (314) 516-5000 — Carnegie Class: DU-Higher
FAX Number: (314) 516-5378 — Calendar System: Semester
URL: www.umsl.edu
Established: 1963 — Annual Undergrad Tuition & Fees (In-State): $10,573
Enrollment: 13,874 — Coed
Affiliation or Control: State — IRS Status: 501(c)3
Highest Offering: Doctorate
Accreditation: HLC, AAQEP, CACREP, CLPSY, IPSY, MUS, NURSE, OPT, OPTR, SPAA, SW

02 Chancellor ... Dr. Kristin SOBOLIK
05 Provost/Exec Vice Chanc Acad Affs ... Dr. Steven BERBERICH
10 VC Finance/Admn & CFO ... Ms. Tanika BUSCH
111 VC Univ Advancement ... Ms. Lisa CAPONE
26 Asst Vice Chanc Marketing/Comm ... Mr. Justin L. ROBERTS
28 VC Diversity/Equity/Inclusion ... Dr. Tanisha STEVENS
46 Vice Chancellor Research Admin ... Dr. Christopher SPILLING
58 Sr Director Graduate School ... Dr. Teresa THIEL
13 Chief Information Officer ... Mr. Kenneth L. VOSS
88 AVP Center for Teaching & Learning ... Dr. Keeta HOLMES
85 Exec Dir International Studies ... Ms. Liane CONSTANTINE
49 Int Dean College Arts & Sciences ... Dr. Francis GRADY
50 Dean College Business Admin ... Dr. Joan PHILLIPS
53 Dean College of Education ... Dr. Ann TAYLOR
66 Dean College of Nursing ... Dr. Roxanne K. VANDERMAUSE
92 Dean Honors College ... Dr. Edward MUNN SANCHEZ
88 Dean College of Optometry ... Dr. Keshia ELDER
08 Dean of Libraries ... Mr. Christopher DAMES
54 Dean Engineering Program ... Dr. Joseph O'SULLIVAN
35 AVP of Student Success ... Ms. Collette DIXON
103 VP for Student Affs/Workforce Dev ... Dr. Natissia SMALL
41 Director of Athletics ... Ms. Lori FLANAGAN
84 VC of Strategic Enrollment ... Dr. Reggie D. HILL
40 Asst Director Bookstore ... Ms. Stephanie EATON
36 Director Career Services ... Ms. Teresa A. BALESTRERI
06 Registrar ... Ms. Theresa KEUSS
39 Director Residential Life ... Ms. Jacquelyn WARREN
37 Director Student Financial Services ... Mr. Mitchell R. HESS
88 Dir MO Inst of Mental Health ... Dr. Robert H. PAUL
18 Int Exec Dir Facilities Mgmt ... Mr. Matthew G. PRSHA
21 Director of Finance & Accounting ... Mr. Randall VOGAN
15 Executive Director Human Resources ... Ms. Jill H. WOOD
19 Director Institutional Safety ... Mr. Dan FREET
09 Dir of Institutional Research ... Ms. Cynthia M. CONRAD
88 Interim GM St Louis Public Radio ... Mr. Tom LIVINGSTON
44 Assoc VC Engagement/Annual Giving ... Ms. Jennifer JEZEK-TAUSSIG
70 Dean Social Work ... Dr. Sharon JOHNSON
88 Dir of Ops-Touhill PAC ... Mr. Jason A. STAHR
88 Dir Comm Outreach/Leg Liason ... Ms. Patricia ZAHN
88 Dir Student Support/SUCCEED ... Mr. Jonathan LIDGUS
88 Dir Recreation/Wellness ... Ms. Yvette KELL
100 Chief of Staff ... Ms. Adella D. JONES
102 Director Foundation/Corporate Rels ... Ms. Elizabeth LANIER-SHIPP
29 Director Alumni Activities ... Mr. Phillip DONATO
30 AVC Univ Development ... Ms. Sharon FENOGLIO
86 AVC Comm/Econ Dev ... Mr. Karl GUENTHER

*Missouri University of Science & Technology (F)

300 W 13th Street, Rolla MO 65409-0001
County: Phelps — FICE Identification: 002517
Unit ID: 178411
Telephone: (573) 341-4111 — Carnegie Class: DU-Higher
FAX Number: (573) 341-4307 — Calendar System: Semester
URL: www.mst.edu
Established: 1870 — Annual Undergrad Tuition & Fees (In-State): $10,165
Enrollment: 7,642 — Coed
Affiliation or Control: State — IRS Status: 501(c)3
Highest Offering: Doctorate
Accreditation: HLC, CEA

02 Chancellor Dr. Mohammad DEHGHANI
05 Provost/Exec Vice Chanc Acad Affs Dr. Colin POTTS
10 Vice Chanc Finance/Operations Ms. Alysha M. O'NEIL
111 Vice Chanc University Advancement Ms. Joan M. NESBITT
32 Vice Chancellor Student Affairs Dr. Debra A G. ROBINSON
35 Assoc Vice Chanc Student Affairs Dr. James H. MURPHY
20 Int Deputy Provost Acad Excellence Dr. Richard K. BROW
121 Int Vice Provost Academic Support Dr. Kathryn NORTHCUT
84 Vice Provost Enrollment Mgmt Ms. Shobi SIVADASAN
54 VP/Dean Col Engr & Computing Dr. Richard WLEZIEN
49 Int VP/Dean Arts/Sciences/Business Dr. Kate DROWNE
08 Director of Library Dr. Oliver CHEN
13 Chief Information Officer Mr. Danny TANG
06 Registrar Ms. Deanne JACKSON
38 AVC Student Affairs/Support Svcs Dr. Edna GROVER-BISKER
41 Director of Athletics Mr. Mark E. MULLIN
23 Senior Dir Student Health Services Dr. Dennis S. GOODMAN
36 Dir Career Opportunities Center Mr. William ZWIKELMAIER
85 AP International/Cultural Affairs Dr. Jeanie HOFER
35 Director Student Life Mr. John GALLAGHER
39 Director Residential Life Dr. Dorie PAINE
07 Interim Director of Admissions Ms. Cathy TIPTON
29 Asst Vice Chanc Advancement Svcs Ms. Darlene RAMSAY
37 Director Student Financial Aid Ms. Bridgette K. BETZ
26 Chief Marketing/Communications Ofcr Mr. Andrew P. CAREAGA
18 Asst Vice Chanc Facilities Svcs Mr. Ted RUTH
40 Manager of University Bookstore Mr. Mark GALLARDO
19 Director University Police Mr. Douglas P. ROBERTS
27 Assoc Dir Strategic Communications Ms. Cheryl A. MCKAY
112 Director Planned Giving Mr. John HELD, II
28 Acting Chief Diversity Officer Ms. Anitra RIVERA
15 Director Human Resources Ms. Rhonda BYERS
09 Director Inst Research Data Mgmt Dr. Wayne R. JONES

Urshan College and Urshan Graduate School of Theology (A)

1151 Century Tel Dr., Wentzville MO 63385
County: St. Charles FICE Identification: 041461
Unit ID: 455099
Telephone: (314) 838-8858 Carnegie Class: Spec-4-yr-Faith
FAX Number: (636) 538-5317 Calendar System: Semester
URL: www.ugst.edu
Established: 2001 Annual Undergrad Tuition & Fees: N/A
Enrollment: 103 Coed
Affiliation or Control: Pentecostal/Charismatic Non-Denominational
IRS Status: 501(c)3
Highest Offering: Master's
Accreditation: HLC, THEOL

01 President Dr. Brent COLTHARP
03 Executive Vice President Rev. Jennie RUSSELL
05 Academic Dean Rev. David JOHNSON
32 Dean of Student Services Rev. Jonathan MCCLINTOCK
10 CFO Mrs. Ashley CHANCELLOR
06 Registrar Ms. Brook CROW
08 Head Librarian Dr. Gary ERICKSON
106 Director of Distance Learning Ms. Vinessa D'SA
26 Director of Marketing and Events Mr. David MOLINA
07 Director of Admissions Ms. Dinecia GATES
15 Chief Human Resources Officer Mrs. Marsha JOHNSTON
30 Development Ofcr/Dir Annual Giving Mrs. Phyllis JONES
36 Director Student Placement Ms. Amber WILLEFORD
37 Director Student Financial Aid Mr. Grant POLLARD
39 Director Student Housing Mrs. Alisha DUGAS
101 Secretary of the Institution/Board Rev. Terry BAUGHMAN
108 Dir Institutional Effectiveness Mrs. Wanda BAKER
09 Director of Institutional Research Dr. Cindy MILLER
18 Chief Facilities/Physical Plant Rev. Billy BABB
35 Assistant Dean of Student Services Mrs. Angela MCCLINTOCK
13 Chief Info Technology Officer Rev. Dewayne PRESSON

Washington University in St. Louis (B)

One Brookings Drive, Saint Louis MO 63130-4899
County: Saint Louis FICE Identification: 002520
Unit ID: 179867
Telephone: (314) 935-5100 Carnegie Class: DU-Highest
FAX Number: N/A Calendar System: Semester
URL: www.wustl.edu
Established: 1853 Annual Undergrad Tuition & Fees: $57,386
Enrollment: 15,449 Coed
Affiliation or Control: Independent Non-Profit IRS Status: 501(c)3
Highest Offering: Doctorate
Accreditation: HLC, ART, AUD, CLPSY, LAW, LSAR, OT, PCSAS, PH, PTA, SW

01 Chancellor Dr. Andrew D. MARTIN
05 Exec Vice Chancellor/Provost Dr. Beverly R. WENDLAND
11 Exec VC Administration Dr. Shantay N. BOLTON
63 Exec Vice Chanc/Dean of Medicine Dr. David H. PERLMUTTER
10 Exec VC for Finance/CFO Ms. Amy B. KWESKIN
111 Exec VC University Advancement Ms. Pamella A. HENSON
43 Vice Chanc/General Counsel Ms. Monica J. ALLEN
46 Interim VC for Research Dr. Mark E. LOWE
88 VC Innovation & Chief Commer Ofcr Dr. Dedric A. CARTER
15 VC Human Resources & Inst Equity Mr. Scot R. BEMIS
110 VC Medical Advancement Ms. Lynda HEANEY
13 VC Technology & Chief Info Officer Ms. Jessie MINTON
17 VC Clinical Affairs Dr. Paul J. SCHEEL
32 VC for Student Affairs Dr. Anna K. GONZALEZ
26 VC for Marketing & Communications Ms. Julie FLORY
21 VC Med Finance & Administration Mr. Richard J. STANTON
115 Chief Investment Officer Mr. Scott L. WILSON
17 VC Medical Education Dr. Eva M. AAGAARD
86 VC Government & Community Relations Ms. Pamela S. LOKKEN
61 Dean School of Law Dr. Russell K. OSGOOD
21 Assoc VC for Finance and Treasurer Ms. Amye KIM
49 Dean Faculty of Arts & Sciences Dr. Feng Sheng HU
54 Dean McKelvey School Dr. Aaron F. BOBICK
50 Interim Dean Olin Sch of Business Prof. Anjan THAKOR
97 Dean University College Dr. A. (Sean) S. ARMSTRONG
57 Dean Sam Fox Sch Design/Visual Arts Prof. Carmon COLANGELO
70 Co-Interim Dean Brown School Prof. Rodrigo REIS
70 Co-Interim Dean Brown School Prof. Tonya EDMOND
58 Interim Vice Dean Grad Educ Prof. Sophia HAYES
57 Dir College & Grad Sch of Art Prof. Amy G. HAUFT
48 Dir College of Architecture & Grad Prof. Heather WOOFTER
100 VC/Board Secretary/Chief of Staff Ms. Rebecca L. BROWN
07 Vice Prov Admissions/Financial Aid Ms. Ronne P. TURNER
110 Sr VC University Advancement Mr. William S. STOLL
27 Assoc VC Medical Public Affairs Ms. Joni L. WESTERHOUSE
28 Dean Center for Diversity/ Inclusion Dr. Mark KAMIMURA-JIMENEZ
85 Dir Bauer Leadership Center Prof. Kurt T. DIRKS
08 Vice Provost & Univ Librarian Ms. Mimi CALTER
35 Assoc Vice Chanc for Students/Dean Dr. Robert M. WILD
92 Assoc Dean Scholar Pgm Dr. Julia MACIAS
85 Interim Exec Dir Intl Students Ms. Ariel CARPENTER
36 Assoc VC for Student Affairs Dr. Mark KAMIMURA-JIMENEZ
18 Assoc VC Facilities Planning/Mgmt Mr. JD LONG, II
88 Asst VC Environ Health & Safety Mr. Lance FRANKLIN
88 Assoc VC Real Estate Ms. Mary B. CAMPBELL
72 Asst VC and Managing Director OTM Ms. Nichole R. MERCIER
23 Exec Dir Habif Health/Wellness Ctr Dr. Cheri LEBLANC
37 Asst VProvost/Dir Student Fin Svcs Mr. Michael J. RUNIEWICZ
41 Assoc VC/Dir of Athletics Mr. Anthony J. AZAMA
19 Interim Chief of Police Mr. David GOODWIN
06 University Registrar Ms. Keri A. DISCH
38 Director of Mental Health Services Dr. Thomas M. BROUNK
122 Asst Dir Campus Life-Frat/Sor Life Mr. James MCLENDON

Washington University School of Medicine in St. Louis (C)

660 Euclid Avenue, Saint Louis MO 63110
Telephone: (314) 360-5000 Identification: 770329
Accreditation: &HLC, CAMPEP, MED

Webster University (D)

470 E Lockwood, Webster Groves MO 63119-3141
County: Saint Louis FICE Identification: 002521
Unit ID: 179894
Telephone: (800) 981-9801 Carnegie Class: Masters/L
FAX Number: N/A Calendar System: Semester
URL: www.webster.edu
Established: 1915 Annual Undergrad Tuition & Fees: $28,700
Enrollment: 8,197 Coed
Affiliation or Control: Independent Non-Profit IRS Status: 501(c)3
Highest Offering: Doctorate
Accreditation: HLC, ACBSP, ANEST, CACREP, CAEP, MUS, NUR

00 Chancellor Dr. Elizabeth J. STROBLE
01 President Dr. Julian Z. SCHUSTER
10 Vice President & CFO Mr. Richard MEYER
13 Chief Information Officer Mr. Greg MALONE
101 Asst Chancellor/Univ Secretary Ms. Jeanelle WILEY
05 Vice President Academic Affairs Ms. Nancy HELLERUD
84 VP of Enrollment Mgmt Ms. Lisa BLAZER
20 AVP for Academic Affairs Dr. Thao DANG-WILLIAMS
32 AVP Stdnt Affs/Dean of Students Dr. John BUCK
04 Executive Asst to the Chancellor Ms. Dana SPREHE
50 Dean School Business/Technology Dr. Simone CUMMINGS
53 Interim Dean School of Education Dr. Stephanie MAHFOOD
57 Dean Leigh Gerdine Col of Fine Arts Mr. Paul STEGER
76 Dean College of Science and Health Dr. Michael HULSIZER
79 Dean Col of Humanities & Soc. Sci Dr. Danielle MACCARTNEY
60 Dean School of Communications Dr. Eric ROTHENBUHLER
08 Dean of University Libraries Ms. Eileen CONDON
15 Chief Human Resources Officer Ms. Cheryl FRITZ
27 AVP & Chief Comm Officer Ms. Lisa BROWN
30 VP Business Dev & Corp Partnerships Ms. Dawn JENSEN
37 AVP UG Admiss/Dir Financial Aid Mr. James MYERS
28 Chief Diversity Officer Mr. Vincent FLEWELLEN
06 Registrar Ms. Laura WAINZ
121 Senior Dir of Academic Advising Ms. Kyle MCCOOL
19 Senior Director Public Safety Mr. Rick GERGER
26 Dir Public Relations Mr. Patrick GIBLIN
90 Dir of Media Center Mr. Marty (Dewey) MARTIN
36 Dir Career Planning & Dev Center Mr. John LINK
29 Dir of Alumni Rel & Annual Fund Ms. Kelly DOPMAN
41 Director Athletics Mr. Scott KILGALLON
35 Director Student Engagement Ms. Jennifer STEWART
38 Director Counsel & Life Development Dr. Patrick STACK
96 Director of Procurement Ms. Jeanene GEORGE
09 Director of Inst Effectiveness Mr. Erik PALMORE
18 Manager of Facilities Operations Mr. Gilbert MORALES
104 Director of Study Abroad Ms. Kelly HEATH
07 AVP of New Student Enrollment Ms. Joanna FINCH
39 Dir Resident Life/Student Housing Ms. Anna DICKHERBER
44 AVP Advancement Services Mr. Ryan ELLIOT
86 AVP for Research Mr. Eric GOEDEREIS
106 AVP for Online Education Dr. Michelle LOYET
88 Sr Dir Military Campus Operations Mr. Ben BRINK

WellSpring School of Allied Health-Kansas City (E)

9140 Ward Pkwy Ste 100, Kansas City MO 64114
County: Jackson FICE Identification: 039704
Unit ID: 447999
Telephone: (816) 523-9140 Carnegie Class: Spec 2-yr-Health
FAX Number: (816) 437-7503 Calendar System: Other
URL: www.wellspring.edu
Established: 1988 Annual Undergrad Tuition & Fees: N/A
Enrollment: 173 Coed
Affiliation or Control: Proprietary IRS Status: Proprietary
Highest Offering: Associate Degree
Accreditation: ABHES

01 President Donald FARQUHARSON
11 VP of Campus Operations Robin O'CONNELL
05 Education Director Dan GERBER
10 Chief Financial/Business Officer Sandy DELAPP

Westminster College (F)

501 Westminster Avenue, Fulton MO 65251-1230
County: Callaway FICE Identification: 002523
Unit ID: 179946
Telephone: (573) 642-3361 Carnegie Class: Bac-A&S
FAX Number: (573) 592-5227 Calendar System: Semester
URL: www.wcmo.edu
Established: 1851 Annual Undergrad Tuition & Fees: $30,880
Enrollment: 609 Coed
Affiliation or Control: Independent Non-Profit IRS Status: 501(c)3
Highest Offering: Baccalaureate
Accreditation: HLC, ACBSP

01 President/Chief Transform Ofcr Mr. Donald P. LOFE, JR.
11 CFO/COO Dr. Steven TYRELL
05 VP of Academic Affairs Dr. Ingrid ILINCA
111 VP for Advancement Mr. JR ANDREWS
10 AVP Business/Controller Ms. Jennifer YELTON
26 Exec Dir Marketing/Communicationss Ms. Kristina BRIGHT
32 Dean of Student Life Dr. Kasi LACEY
84 VP of Enrollment Services Mr. Paul ORSCHELN
18 Exec Dir Plant Ops/Security Mr. Jack BENKE
20 Associate Dean of Faculty Dr. Linda WEBSTER
121 Associate Dean of Student Success Dr. Ingrid ILINCA
06 Registrar Mrs. Phyllis MASEK
07 Director of Admissions Vacant
13 AVP of IT Mr. Nick WATSON
37 AVP Enroll Mgmt/Dir Financial Aid Ms. Aimee BRISTOW
30 Director of Advancement Services Ms. Jeni WHITTINGTON
15 Director of Human Resources Ms. Mandy MARCH
19 Director of Campus Safety/Security Mr. Jack BENKE
41 Interim Athletic Director Mr. Todd CREAL
23 Exec Director Wellness Center Dr. Kasi LACEY
29 Dir Alumni Engagement Ms. Melanie BARGER
08 Director of Library Services Ms. Victoria KNIGHT
09 Dir of Inst Research/Assessment Mr. Matt KNUDTSON
42 Chaplain Rev. Kiva NICE-WEBB
04 Executive Asst to the President Mrs. Jessie JONES

William Jewell College (G)

500 College Hill, Liberty MO 64068-1896
County: Clay FICE Identification: 002524
Unit ID: 179955
Telephone: (816) 781-7700 Carnegie Class: Bac-Diverse
FAX Number: (816) 415-5027 Calendar System: Semester
URL: www.jewell.edu
Established: 1849 Annual Undergrad Tuition & Fees: $34,450
Enrollment: 751 Coed
Affiliation or Control: Independent Non-Profit IRS Status: 501(c)3
Highest Offering: Master's
Accreditation: HLC, MUS, NURSE

01 President Dr. Elizabeth MACLEOD WALLS
05 Provost Dr. Anne C. DEMA
10 Vice Pres for Finance & Operations Mr. Joseph GARCIA
111 Vice Pres Institutional Advancement Mr. Clark MORRIS
84 Vice Pres Enrollment & Marketing Mr. Eric BLAIR
28 Vice President Access & Engagement Dr. Rodney SMITH
45 Assoc VP Institutional Strategy Mr. Daniel HOLT
32 Dean of Student Life Ms. Shelly KING
07 Director of Student Recruitment Mr. William PALMER
06 Registrar Dr. Edwin H. LANE
08 Director of Library Services Ms. Rebecca HAMLETT
21 Director of Budget and Finance Ms. Deborah GREEN
13 Director of Information Technology Ms. Lan GUO
97 Assoc Dean Core Curriculum Dr. Gary ARMSTRONG
37 Asst VP & Director Financial Aid Mr. Thomas STUART
15 Director of Human Resources Ms. Julie DUBINSKY
18 Director of Facilities Management Ms. Stephany GUEST
57 Executive Director Harriman-Jewell Mr. Clark W. MORRIS
41 Director of Athletics Mr. Thomas EISENHAUER
36 Director of Career Development Ms. Marissa BLAND
38 Director of Counseling Services Ms. Tricia HAGER
29 Director of Alumni Relations Ms. Andrea MELOAN
104 Director of Global Studies Ms. Sara ROUND
04 Executive Asst to President Ms. Angela BASS
19 Director of Campus Safety Mr. Mike CRUTCHFIELD
26 Director of Marketing Ms. Cara DAHLOR
39 Director of Residence Life Mr. Ernie STUFFLEBEAN

90 Director of Teaching/Learning Tech .... Mr. Heath HASE
50 Chair Comm in Business & Leadership .... Dr. Kelli SCHUTTE
53 Chair Education .... Dr. Donna GARDNER
110 Assoc VP of Advancement .... Ms. Susan TIDEMAN
54 Chair of Engineering .... Dr. Will LINDQUIST

William Woods University (A)

One University Avenue, Fulton MO 65251-1098
County: Callaway FICE Identification: 002525
Unit ID: 179964
Telephone: (800) 995-3159 Carnegie Class: DU-Mod
FAX Number: (573) 592-1146 Calendar System: Semester
URL: www.williamwoods.edu
Established: 1870 Annual Undergrad Tuition & Fees: $25,930
Enrollment: 2,114 Coed
Affiliation or Control: Christian Church (Disciples Of Christ)
IRS Status: 501(c)3
Highest Offering: Doctorate
Accreditation: HLC, ACBSP, SW

01 President .... Dr. Jeremy L. MORELAND
05 Provost .... Dr. Aimee SAPP
10 Chief Financial Officer .... Stephen MANSDOERFER
13 Chief Information Officer .... Travis BOND
32 Chief Student Experience Officer .... Dr. Ted BLASHAK
84 Vice President of Enrollment Svcs .... Dr. Andy OTTO
35 Vice President of Student Life .... Tiffany NOLAN
111 Vice President of Advancement .... Kathy GROVES
26 Vice President of Media Relations .... John FOUGERE
27 Vice President of Communications .... Stephanie WELLS
41 Dir of Intercollegiate Athletics .... Jason VITTONE

MONTANA

Aaniiih Nakoda College (B)

PO Box 159, Harlem MT 59526-0159
County: Blaine FICE Identification: 025175
Unit ID: 180203
Telephone: (406) 353-2607 Carnegie Class: Tribal
FAX Number: (406) 353-2898 Calendar System: Semester
URL: www.ancollege.edu
Established: 1984 Annual Undergrad Tuition & Fees: $2,410
Enrollment: 143 Coed
Affiliation or Control: Tribal Control IRS Status: 501(c)3
Highest Offering: Associate Degree
Accreditation: NW

01 President .... Dr. Sean CHANDLER
05 Co-Dean of Academic Affairs .... Mr. Daniel KINSEY
05 Co-Dean of Academic Affairs .... Ms. Krisi SYVERTSON
32 Dean of Student Affairs .... Ms. Clarena BROCKIE
10 Comptroller .... Ms. Debra EVE
06 Registrar/Admissions Officer .... Mr. Kimberly BARROWS
37 Financial Aid Director .... Ms. Toma CAMPBELL
08 Library Director .... Ms. Eva ENGLISH
25 Sponsored Programs Director .... Mr. Scott FRISKICS
13 Manager Information Systems .... Mr. Harold H. HEPPNER
40 Bookstore Manager .... Ms. Kim BROCKIE
04 Assistant to the President .... Ms. Michele BROCKIE
09 Institutional Research Assistant .... Ms. Danielle JACKSON

Apollos University (C)

600 Central Avenue, Ste 215, Great Falls MT 59401
County: Cascade Identification: 667096
Telephone: (406) 604-4300 Carnegie Class: Not Classified
FAX Number: (866) 287-1938 Calendar System: Quarter
URL: apollos.edu
Established: 2005 Annual Undergrad Tuition & Fees: N/A
Enrollment: N/A Coed
Affiliation or Control: Proprietary IRS Status: Proprietary
Highest Offering: Doctorate
Accreditation: DEAC

00 CEO .... Dr. Paul EIDSON
01 President .... Dr. Scott EIDSON
05 EVP/Provost and CAO .... Dr. Robin WESTERIK
32 Exec Vice Pres Student Services .... Dr. Michelle FOX
10 Sr Exec Vice President Admin/CFO .... Dr. Kelly LANCASTER
15 Vice President Human Resources .. Dr. Amanda CERAR-DERBISH
07 Dir Admissions/Student Engagement . Ms. Regina BURCKHALTER
06 Registrar/Dir of Office Admin .... Ms. Shirley CASTRO

Blackfeet Community College (D)

Box 819, Browning MT 59417-0819
County: Glacier FICE Identification: 025106
Unit ID: 180054
Telephone: (406) 338-5441 Carnegie Class: Tribal
FAX Number: (406) 338-3272 Calendar System: Semester
URL: www.bfcc.edu
Established: 1974 Annual Undergrad Tuition & Fees: $3,370
Enrollment: 417 Coed
Affiliation or Control: Independent Non-Profit IRS Status: 501(c)3
Highest Offering: Associate Degree
Accreditation: NW

01 President .... Dr. Karla BIRD
05 Provost/Vice Pres Academic Affairs .... Mrs. Carol MURRAY
10 Vice Pres of Finance .... Ms. Lola WIPPERT
37 Director of Financial Aid .... Mrs. Gaylene DUCHARME
06 Registrar/Dir of Admissions .... Ms. Helen HORN
18 Chief Facilities/Physical Plant .... Mr. Smokey HENRIKSEN
15 Human Resources Director .... Ms. Daisy GILHAM-LOUIS

Carroll College (E)

1601 N Benton Avenue, Helena MT 59625-0002
County: Lewis And Clark FICE Identification: 002526
Unit ID: 180106
Telephone: (406) 447-4300 Carnegie Class: Bac-Diverse
FAX Number: (406) 447-4533 Calendar System: Semester
URL: www.carroll.edu
Established: 1909 Annual Undergrad Tuition & Fees: $37,262
Enrollment: 1,108 Coed
Affiliation or Control: Roman Catholic IRS Status: 501(c)3
Highest Offering: Master's
Accreditation: NW, IACBE, NURSE, @SW

01 President .... Dr. John E. CECH
04 Sr Executive Asst to the President .... Ms. Kara PAUL
05 Senior VP for Academic Affairs .... Dr. Jennifer GLOWIENKA
10 VP for Finance & Administration .... Ms. Lori PETERSON
32 VP for Mission & Student Engagement .... Dr. Michael MCMAHON
111 VP for Institutional Advancement .... Mr. Chris AIMONE
42 Director Campus Ministry-Chaplain .... Rev. Marc LENNEMAN
41 Athletic Director .... Mr. Charles GROSS
121 Dean of Students & Retention .... Ms. Annette WALSTAD
09 Int Dir of Institutional Research .... Mr. John RAMIREZ
06 Registrar .... Vacant
26 Director of Public Relations .... Ms. Sarah LAWLOR
37 Financial Aid Director .... Ms. Janet RIIS
36 Career Services & Internships .... Ms. Laurie RODRIGUEZ
15 Director Human Resources .... Ms. Karla SMITH
18 Director of Facilities .... Mr. Walter H. BISKUPIAK
35 Director Student Activities .... Mr. Patrick HARRIS
21 Controller .... Ms. Kari BRUSTKERN
13 Campus Computing/Info Tech Director .... Mr. Robert WHITED
29 Director Alumni Relations .... Ms. Renee WALL
07 Director of Admissions .... Mr. Richard HINTON
08 Chief Library Officer .... Ms. Jennifer OATES
19 Director Security/Safety .... Mr. Jason GRIMMIS
39 Dir Resident Life/Student Housing .... Mr. Zack ECKERDT

Chief Dull Knife College (F)

One College Drive, PO Box 98, Lame Deer MT 59043
County: Rosebud FICE Identification: 025452
Unit ID: 180160
Telephone: (406) 477-6215 Carnegie Class: Tribal
FAX Number: (406) 477-6219 Calendar System: Semester
URL: www.cdkc.edu
Established: 1975 Annual Undergrad Tuition & Fees: $2,260
Enrollment: N/A Coed
Affiliation or Control: Independent Non-Profit IRS Status: 501(c)3
Highest Offering: Associate Degree
Accreditation: NW

01 President/Int Dean Cultural Affairs .... Dr. Richard LITTLEBEAR
05 Vice President Academic Affairs .... Mr. William BRIGGS
32 Vice President Student Affairs .... Mr. Zane SPANG
37 Director Financial Aid .... Ms. Sabrina NEIMAN
08 Library Directory .... Ms. Adrienne VIOLETT
06 Registrar .... Mr. Joey DITONNO

Dawson Community College (G)

P.O. Box 421, Glendive MT 59330-0421
County: Dawson FICE Identification: 002529
Unit ID: 180151
Telephone: (406) 377-3396 Carnegie Class: Assoc/HT-High Non
FAX Number: (406) 377-8132 Calendar System: Semester
URL: www.dawson.edu
Established: 1940 Annual Undergrad Tuition & Fees (In-District): $5,580
Enrollment: 377 Coed
Affiliation or Control: State/Local IRS Status: 501(c)3
Highest Offering: Associate Degree
Accreditation: NW

01 President .... Mr. Justin VILLMER
06 Registrar .... Ms. Virginia BOYSUN
08 Library Director .... Ms. Jerusha SHIPSTEAD
37 Director of Financial Aid .... Ms. Jennifer ALMLI
13 Director of Information Technology .... Vacant
15 VP of Advancement & Human Resources .... Ms. Daisy NYBERG
103 Dir Workforce/Career Development .... Ms. Sara ENGLE
04 Executive Asst to the President .... Ms. Becca KLANG
10 Chief Financial/Business Officer .... Vacant
41 Athletic Director .... Mr. Joe PETERSON
102 Exec Director of the Foundation .... Mr. Dennis HARP
18 Chief Facilities/Phys Plant Ofcr .... Mr. Todd THOMPSON
26 Dir Marketing & Public Relations .... Vacant
96 Director of Purchasing .... Ms. Tammy REED
32 Assoc Dean of Students .... Mr. Justin BEACH
84 Director of Enrollment .... Ms. Erica MILNE
39 Dir Resident Life/Student Housing .... Mr. Peyton KOIVU

Flathead Valley Community College (H)

777 Grandview Drive, Kalispell MT 59901
County: Flathead FICE Identification: 006777
Unit ID: 180197
Telephone: (406) 756-3822 Carnegie Class: Assoc/MT-VT-High Non
FAX Number: (406) 756-3815 Calendar System: Semester
URL: www.fvcc.edu
Established: 1967 Annual Undergrad Tuition & Fees (In-District): $6,377
Enrollment: 2,049 Coed
Affiliation or Control: Local IRS Status: 501(c)3
Highest Offering: Associate Degree
Accreditation: NW, CNEA, EMT, MAC, MLTAD, PTAA, SURGT

01 President .... Dr. Jane A. KARAS
05 Vice President Academic Affairs .... Dr. Chris CLOUSE
10 VP Administration & Finance/CFO .... Ms. Beckie CHRISTIAENS
12 Pgm Director Lincoln County Campus .... Dr. Megan RAYOME
32 Dean of Students .... Ms. Kelly MURPHY
51 Dir Continuing Education .... Mr. Luke LAVIN
111 Chief Development Officer .... Mr. Tagen VINE
13 Exec Dir Information Technology .... Mr. Kent ROGERS
15 Exec Director of Human Resources .... Ms. Karen GLASSER
06 Registrar .... Ms. Amy KANEWISCHER
37 Dir of Financial Aid .... Ms. Crystal MORRIS
26 Exec Dir Marketing & Communication .... Ms. Allison LINVILLE
04 Senior Exec Assistant to President .... Ms. Suzanne DECAMP

Fort Peck Community College (I)

PO Box 398, Poplar MT 59255-0398
County: Roosevelt FICE Identification: 023430
Unit ID: 180212
Telephone: (406) 768-6300 Carnegie Class: Tribal
FAX Number: (406) 768-6301 Calendar System: Semester
URL: www.fpcc.edu
Established: 1978 Annual Undergrad Tuition & Fees: $2,250
Enrollment: 328 Coed
Affiliation or Control: Tribal Control IRS Status: 501(c)3
Highest Offering: Associate Degree
Accreditation: NW

01 President .... Ms. Haven GOURNEAU
05 Int Vice Pres Academic Affairs .... Ms. Carrie SHUMACHER
32 Vice President Student Services .... Mr. Elijah HOPKINS
30 Vice Pres Institutional Development .... Mr. Craig SMITH
10 Business Manager .... Ms. Rose ATKINSON
06 Registrar .... Ms. Michelle DAY
37 Financial Aid Officer .... Ms. Lanette CLARK
08 Head Librarian .... Mrs. Anita A. SCHEETZ

Little Big Horn College (J)

PO Box 370, Crow Agency MT 59022-0370
County: Big Horn FICE Identification: 022866
Unit ID: 180328
Telephone: (406) 638-3104 Carnegie Class: Tribal
FAX Number: (406) 638-3169 Calendar System: Semester
URL: www.lbhc.edu
Established: 1980 Annual Undergrad Tuition & Fees: $3,200
Enrollment: 211 Coed
Affiliation or Control: Tribal Control IRS Status: 501(c)3
Highest Offering: Associate Degree
Accreditation: NW

01 President .... Dr. David YARLOTT, JR.
05 Dean of Academics .... Dr. Emerson BULL CHIEF
32 Dean of Student Affairs .... Miss Patricia WHITEMAN
11 Dean of Administration .... Ms. Shaleen OLD COYOTE
06 Registrar .... Mr. William OLD CROW
08 Director of Library .... Mr. Tim BERNARDIS
13 Chief Information Officer .... Mr. Franklin COOPER
10 Chief Finance Officer .... Ms. Aldean GOOD LUCK
15 Director Human Resources .... Ms. Laura OROSCO
97 Dept Head/General Stds/Crow Stds .... Dr. Tim MCCLEARY
81 Dept Head/Math/Science/Technology .... Vacant
25 Director Sponsored Grants .... Ms. Frances EAGLEMAN
37 Financial Aid Director .... Ms. Beverly SNELL
41 Athletic Director .... Dr. Cheryl POLACEK

Miles Community College (K)

2715 Dickinson, Miles City MT 59301-4799
County: Custer FICE Identification: 002528
Unit ID: 180373
Telephone: (406) 874-6100 Carnegie Class: Assoc/MT-VT-High Non
FAX Number: (406) 874-6282 Calendar System: Semester
URL: www.milescc.edu
Established: 1939 Annual Undergrad Tuition & Fees (In-District): $5,910
Enrollment: 567 Coed
Affiliation or Control: State/Local IRS Status: 501(c)3
Highest Offering: Associate Degree
Accreditation: NW, ADNUR

01 President .... Mr. Ron SLINGER
05 Vice Pres of Academic Affairs .... Dr. Rita KRATKY
84 Dean of Enrollment Services .... Ms. Erin NIEDGE
32 Dean of Student Engagement .... Mr. Richard DESHIELDS
08 Director of Library .... Ms. Jerusha SHIPSTEAD
13 Information Technology Manager .... Mr. Dirk SCHMIDT

37 Director Student Financial Aid ... Ms. Danielle DINGES
18 Chief Facilities/Physical Plant ... Mr. Ross LAWRENCE
21 Business Services Director ... Ms. Nancy AABERGE
06 Registrar ... Ms. Carla CUMMINS
15 Dean of Admn Svcs & Human Resources ... Ms. Kylene PHIPPS
66 Nursing Program Director ... Ms. Diedre FITZGERALD
20 Associate Academic Officer ... Mr. Garth SLEIGHT
40 Manager Bookstore ... Ms. Michele TRIMBLE
04 Administrative Asst to President ... Ms. Candy LANEY
111 Dir of Institutional Advancement ... Ms. Elizabeth PATTEN
09 Dir of Institutional Research ... Mr. Loren LANCASTER

Montana Bible College (A)

20 Cornerstone Way, Bozeman MT 59718
County: Gallatin FICE Identification: 041403
Unit ID: 262165
Telephone: (406) 586-3585 Carnegie Class: Not Classified
FAX Number: N/A Calendar System: Semester
URL: www.montanabiblecollege.edu
Established: 1987 Annual Undergrad Tuition & Fees: $9,040
Enrollment: N/A Coed
Affiliation or Control: Independent Non-Profit IRS Status: 501(c)3
Highest Offering: Baccalaureate
Accreditation: BI

01 President ... Mr. Ryan WARD
05 Vice President of Academic Affairs ... Dr. Andre GAZAL
06 Registrar ... Mrs. Louise TURNER
08 Librarian ... Mrs. Jessica CARLSON
10 Vice President of Finance ... Mr. Les WALTON
84 Director of Enrollment Management ... Mr. Dan HOVESTOL
09 Dir Inst Effective/Dean of Students ... Ms. Jenni O'BRIAN
88 Discipleship Director ... Mr. Micah FORSYTHE

Montana Christian College (B)

1605 Danielson Rd, Kalispell MT 59901
County: Flathead Identification: 667254
Telephone: (406) 656-9950 Carnegie Class: Not Classified
FAX Number: N/A Calendar System: Semester
URL: www.yellowstonechristian.edu
Established: 1974 Annual Undergrad Tuition & Fees: N/A
Enrollment: N/A Coed
Affiliation or Control: Independent Non-Profit IRS Status: 501(c)3
Highest Offering: Baccalaureate
Accreditation: #BI

01 President ... Dr. Martin JONES
05 Int VP Academic Affairs ... Ms. Vanessa LUND
84 Dean of Enrollment ... Mr. Max SOFT
10 Chief Financial/Operations Officer ... Dr. Robert ESHLEMAN
32 Associate Dean of Students ... Miss Miranda CARTER
06 Registrar ... Vacant
41 Athletic Director ... Mr. Kyle SPENCER

*Montana University System Office (C)

560 North Park Avenue, 4th Floor, Helena MT 59620
County: Lewis And Clark FICE Identification: 029072
Unit ID: 180470
Telephone: (406) 449-9124 Carnegie Class: N/A
FAX Number: (406) 449-9171
URL: www.mus.edu

01 Commissioner Higher Education ... Mr. Clayton T. CHRISTIAN
05 Deputy Cmsr Academic/Student Affs ... Dr. Brock TESSMAN
45 Deputy Cmsr Budget/Plng/Chief Staff ... Mr. Tyler TREVOR
15 Deputy Cmsr Human Resources ... Mr. Kevin MCRAE
43 MUS Chief Legal Counsel ... Ms. Ali BOVINGDON
100 Chief of Staff ... Mr. Tyler TREVOR
118 Director of Benefits ... Mrs. Mary LACHENBRUCH
117 Director of Work Comp Risk Mgmt ... Ms. Leah Jo TIETZ
93 Dir Minority/Amer Ind Achievement ... Ms. Angela MCLEAN
13 OCHE IT Manager ... Ms. Edwina MORRISON
86 Deputy Cmsr Govt Rels/Public Affs ... Ms. Helen THIGPEN

*University of Montana - Missoula (D)

32 Campus Drive, Missoula MT 59812-0001
County: Missoula FICE Identification: 002536
Unit ID: 180489
Telephone: (406) 243-2311 Carnegie Class: DU-Highest
FAX Number: (406) 243-2797 Calendar System: Semester
URL: www.umt.edu
Established: 1893 Annual Undergrad Tuition & Fees (In-State): $7,430
Enrollment: 9,808 Coed
Affiliation or Control: State IRS Status: 501(c)3
Highest Offering: Doctorate
Accreditation: NW, ART, CAATE, CACREP, CAEPN, CLPSY, COARC, JOUR, LAW, MUS, PH, PHAR, PTA, SCPSY, SP, SPAA, SW, THEA

02 President ... Mr. Seth BODNAR
05 Exec Vice President/Provost ... Dr. Pardis MAHDAVI
100 Chief of Staff ... Ms. Kelly WEBSTER
10 Vice Pres for Admin & Finance ... Mr. Paul LASITER
84 AVP Enrollment Mgmt/Strategic Init ... Ms. Mary KRETA
26 VP Marketing & Communications ... Ms. Jenny PETTY
46 VP Research & Creative Scholarship ... Dr. Scott WHITTENBURG
45 AVP Strategic Planning & Assessment ... Ms. Dawn RESSEL
15 AVP Human Resource Services ... Ms. Terri PHILLIPS
20 Vice Provost for Academic Affairs ... Dr. Kimber MCKAY
32 Vice Provost for Student Success ... Ms. Sarah SWAGER
121 Exec Dir Student Success ... Mr. Brian FRENCH
43 Legal Counsel ... Ms. Lucy FRANCE
12 Director Mansfield Center ... Ms. Deena MANSOUR
88 Dir Broadcast Media Center ... Mr. Ray EKNESS
22 Dir Equal Oppty & Title IX Coord ... Ms. Alicia ARANT
06 Registrar ... Ms. Maria MANGOLD
18 Director Facilities Svcs ... Vacant
13 CIO ... Mr. Zach ROSSMILLER
38 Director Counseling ... Dr. Erinn GUZIK
36 Dir Exper Lrng/Career Success ... Dr. Andrea VERNON
37 Director of Financial Aid ... Ms. Emily WILLIAMSON
29 Director of Alumni ... Ms. LeAnn MEYER
102 President & CEO/UM Foundation ... Ms. Cindy WILLIAMS
19 Director of Public Safety ... Vacant
23 Director Curry Health Center ... Dr. Jeffrey ADAMS
39 Director Residence Life ... Ms. Sandra CURTIS
41 Athletic Director ... Mr. Kent HASLAM
85 Exec Director of Global Engagement ... Dr. Donna ANDERSON
08 Interim Dean Mansfield Library ... Dr. Barry BROWN
79 Int Dean Col Humanities/Sciences ... Dr. Julie BALDWIN
79 Int Dean Col Humanities/Sciences ... Dr. Matthew SEMANOFF
61 Interim Dean School of Law ... Ms. Elaine GAGLIARDI
65 Dean Col Forestry/Conservation ... Dr. Alan TOWNSEND
50 Dean College of Business ... Dr. Suzanne TILLEMAN
76 Dean Col of Health Professions ... Dr. Reed HUMPHREY
53 Dean College of Education ... Dr. Adrea LAWERANCE
57 Dean Col of Arts/Media ... Dr. Laurie BAEFSKY
67 Dean School of Pharmacy ... Dr. Marketa MARVANOVA
75 Dean Missoula College ... Dr. Thomas GALLAGHER
92 Dean Honors College ... Dr. Timothy NICHOLS
04 Admin Assistant to the President ... Ms. Jessica SHONTZ
07 Director of Admissions ... Ms. Emily FERGUSON STEGER
106 Director Online Education ... Dr. Julie WOLTER
122 Dir Fraternity/Sorority Involvement ... Ms. Lacey ZINKE
09 Interim Dir of Inst Research ... Ms. Pope ASHWORTH
103 Director Workforce Development ... Ms. Jasmine ZINK LAINE
104 Director Study Abroad ... Ms. Donna ANDERSON
108 Director Institutional Assessment ... Dr. Kimber MCKAY
28 Director of Inclusive Excellence ... Ms. Salena HILL
86 Director Government Relations ... Mr. Dave KUNTZ
96 Director of Purchasing ... Mr. Bob HLYNOSKY

*The University of Montana Western (E)

710 S Atlantic St, Dillon MT 59725-3598
County: Beaverhead FICE Identification: 002537
Unit ID: 180692
Telephone: (406) 683-7011 Carnegie Class: Bac-Diverse
FAX Number: (406) 683-7493 Calendar System: Other
URL: www.umwestern.edu
Established: 1893 Annual Undergrad Tuition & Fees (In-State): $5,747
Enrollment: 1,334 Coed
Affiliation or Control: State IRS Status: 501(c)3
Highest Offering: Baccalaureate
Accreditation: NW, CAEP, IACBE

02 Chancellor ... Mr. Michael L. REID
05 Interim Provost ... Dr. Ashley CARLSON
10 Int Vice Chancellor Admin/Finance ... Mrs. Susan BRIGGS
26 Director of Communications ... Mr. Matt RAFFETY
25 Dean of Outreach/Grants ... Ms. Anneliese RIPLEY
06 Registrar ... Ms. Charity WALTERS
07 Director of Admissions ... Mr. Matt ALLEN
08 Librarian ... Ms. Anne KISH
36 Director of Field Learning ... Vacant
41 Director of Athletics ... Mr. Bill WILSON
13 Director of Information Technology ... Mr. Mel EWING
32 Dean of Students ... Ms. Nicole HAZELBAKER
102 Director of Foundation/Alumni ... Ms. Roxanne ENGELLANT
37 Director of Student Financial Aid ... Ms. Louise DRIVER
38 Dir of Student Counseling/Wellness ... Mrs. Heidi PETERSON
15 Human Resources ... Ms. Patti LAKE
04 Administrative Asst to Chancellor ... Mrs. Hillary LOWELL
21 Dir Business Services/Controller ... Ms. Debra RICHARDSON
18 Director of Facilities Services ... Mr. Michael (Embee) BROWN
109 Senior Director Auxiliary Services ... Mr. Mike PIAZZOLA
39 Assistant Director Residence Life ... Ms. Bonita BONTRAGER
88 Dir Conference & Event Services ... Ms. Kathy SIMKINS
106 Director E-learning/Moodle ... Mr. Justin MASON

*Helena College University of Montana (F)

1115 N Roberts, Helena MT 59601-3098
County: Lewis and Clark FICE Identification: 007570
Unit ID: 180276
Telephone: (406) 447-6900 Carnegie Class: Assoc/HVT-High Non
FAX Number: (406) 447-6395 Calendar System: Semester
URL: www.HelenaCollege.edu
Established: 1939 Annual Undergrad Tuition & Fees (In-State): $3,507
Enrollment: 1,324 Coed
Affiliation or Control: State IRS Status: 501(c)3
Highest Offering: Associate Degree
Accreditation: NW, ADNUR

02 Dean/CEO ... Dr. Sandra BAUMAN
04 Exec Assistant to Dean/CEO ... Ms. Paige PAYNE
97 Exec Dir of Gen Educ/Transfer ... Ms. Robyn KIESLING
75 Exec Dir of Career Tech Educ & DE ... Ms. Stephanie HUNTHAUSEN
84 Exec Dir of Enrollment ... Ms. Sarah DELLWO
11 Asst Dean of Admin Affairs ... Ms. Tricia FISCUS
26 Director of Marketing/Communication ... Vacant
37 Exec Dir of Compliance/Fin Aid ... Ms. Valerie CURTIN
18 Dir of Maintenance & Facilities ... Mr. John RUTHERFORD
13 Director of IT Services ... Mr. Melvin EWING
08 Director of Library Learning Hub ... Ms. Della DUBBE
106 Dir eLearning & Faculty Development ... Ms. Amy KONG
66 Director of Nursing ... Ms. Debra RAPAPORT
124 Director of Retention Initiatives ... Ms. Ann WILLCOCKSON
16 Human Resources Specialist ... Ms. Mary TWARDOS
21 Director of Business & Retail Svcs ... Ms. Cari SCHWEN
40 Bookstore Director ... Vacant
51 Director of CEC/SBDC ... Mr. Ryan LOOMIS
09 Director of Institutional Research ... Ms. Jessie PATE

*Montana State University (G)

PO Box 172190, Bozeman MT 59717-2190
County: Gallatin FICE Identification: 002532
Unit ID: 180461
Telephone: (406) 994-2452 Carnegie Class: DU-Highest
FAX Number: (406) 994-1923 Calendar System: Semester
URL: www.montana.edu
Established: 1893 Annual Undergrad Tuition & Fees (In-State): $7,371
Enrollment: 16,218 Coed
Affiliation or Control: State IRS Status: 501(c)3
Highest Offering: Doctorate
Accreditation: NW, ART, CACREP, CAEP, DIETD, DIETI, IPSY, MLS, MUS, NURSE

02 President ... Dr. Waded CRUZADO
05 Exec VP Academic Affairs/Provost ... Dr. Robert MOKWA
20 Senior Vice Provost ... Dr. Durwood SOBEK
88 Vice Provost ... Dr. Steven SWINFORD
10 Vice Pres Admin/Finance ... Mr. Terry LEIST
32 Vice Pres Student Success ... Dr. Chris KEARNS
56 Executive Director Extension ... Dr. Cody STONE
46 VP Research & Econ Development ... Dr. Alison HARMON
13 Vice Pres for Information Tech/CIO ... Mr. Ryan KNUTSON
18 Assoc Vice Pres University Services ... Mr. John HOW
15 Assoc VP HR/Chief HR Officer ... Ms. Jeannette GREY GILBERT
102 President/CEO MSU Foundation ... Mr. Christopher D. MURRAY
104 Dean International Programs ... Dr. Kristof ZABA
26 Vice Pres Univ Communications ... Mr. Tracy ELLIG
88 Exec Director Museum of the Rockies ... Mr. Chris DOBBS
50 Interim Dean and Professor JJCB ... Dr. Daniel MILLER
53 Dean Education/Health/Human Dev ... Dr. Tricia SEIFERT
54 Dean Engineering ... Dr. Brett GUNNINK
49 Dean Letters & Science ... Dr. Yves IDZERDA
66 Dean Nursing ... Dr. Sarah SHANNON
08 Dean Libraries ... Doralyn ROSSMANN
35 Dean Students ... Dr. Matthew CAIRES
58 Dean Graduate School ... Dr. Craig OGILVIE
92 Dean Honors College ... Dr. Jeffrey HEYS
47 VP and Dean Agriculture ... Dr. Sreekala BAJWA
48 Dean Arts/Architecture ... Dr. Royce SMITH
63 Dir WWAMI Medical Educ Program ... Dr. Martin TEINTZE
07 Director Admissions ... Mr. Mike OUERT
22 Director Institutional Equity ... Ms. Kyleen BRESLIN
41 Director Athletics ... Mr. Leon COSTELLO
109 Assoc VP Auxiliary Services ... Mr. Duane MORRIS
36 Dir Allen Yarnell Center ... Dr. Carina BECK
38 Dir Counseling/Psych Services ... Dr. Elizabeth ASSERSON
56 Exec Director Extended University ... Dr. Kim OBBINK
37 Director Financial Aid ... Mr. James BROSCHEIT
43 Legal Counsel ... Ms. Kellie PETERSON
45 Director Planning & Analysis ... Dr. Chris FASTNOW
96 Director Procurement ... Mr. Brian O'CONNOR
06 Registrar ... Mr. Tony CAMPEAU
27 Director Marketing/Creative Service ... Ms. Julie KIPFER
19 Chief of University Police ... Mr. Michael STANLEY
100 Exec Assistant to the President ... Ms. Amber VESTAL
105 Director Web Communications ... Mr. Justin ARNDT
25 Asst Vice Pres for Research ... Ms. Sandy SWARD
39 Director Housing/Residence Life ... Mr. Jeff BONDY
14 Assoc Chief IT/CSO ... Mr. Adam EDELMAN
16 Dir Employee & Labor Relations ... Ms. Susan ALT
114 Dir University Budget Office ... Ms. Megan LASSO
88 Director Women's Center ... Ms. Elizabeth DANFORTH

*Montana State University Billings (H)

1500 University Drive, Billings MT 59101-0245
County: Yellowstone FICE Identification: 002530
Unit ID: 180179
Telephone: (406) 657-2011 Carnegie Class: Masters/M
FAX Number: (406) 657-2302 Calendar System: Semester
URL: www.msubillings.edu
Established: 1927 Annual Undergrad Tuition & Fees (In-State): $5,980
Enrollment: 4,000 Coed
Affiliation or Control: State IRS Status: 501(c)3
Highest Offering: Master's
Accreditation: NW, ABAI, ART, CAATE, CACREP, CAEP, EMT, IFSAC, MUS, NURSE, RAD

02 Chancellor ... Dr. Stefani HICSWA
10 Vice Chanc Administration/Finance ... Ms. Susan SIMMERS
05 Provost/Vice Chanc Academic Affairs ... Dr. Sepehr ESKANDARI
32 Vice Chanc Student Access & Success ... Dr. Kimberly HAYWORTH
102 President/CEO Foundation ... Ms. Krista MONTAGUE
29 Director Alumni Relations ... Ms. Abby MOERKERKE

08 Director Library Services ..... Ms. Darlene HERT
06 Registrar ..... Dr. Cheri JOHANNES
07 Director Admissions ..... Mr. Ed BROWN
15 Director Human Resources ..... Ms. Paula HIGHLANDER
36 Director Career Services ..... Dr. Becky LYONS
121 Director of Advising ..... Vacant
13 Chief Information Officer ..... Mr. Brett WEISZ
25 Dir Grants & Sponsored Pgms ..... Ms. Cindy BELL
26 Dir University Comm & Marketing ..... Ms. Maureen BRAKKE
09 Director Institutional Research ..... Ms. Joann STRYKER
18 Director Facility Services ..... Mr. Michael SWAVELY
58 Director Graduate Studies ..... Dr. Jana MARCETTE
41 Athletic Director ..... Mr. Michael BAZEMORE
19 Chief of Campus Police ..... Mr. Brandon GATLIN
37 Director Financial Aid ..... Mr. Thomas VALLES
40 Interim Director Campus Store ..... Ms. Lorie HAACKE
35 Dean of Student Engagement ..... Ms. Kathy KOTECKI
114 Assistant Vice Chancellor Finance ..... Ms. Heather HANNA
96 Director of Business Services ..... Ms. Barb SHAFER
121 Director Academic Support Center ..... Dr. Stephen FOGGATT
28 Dir Montana Ctr for Inclusive Educ ..... Dr. Tom MANTHEY
89 Exec Dir Undergrad Student Services ..... Ms. Julie PETTITT
88 Dir Native American Achievement Ctr .Ms. Sunny Day REAL BIRD
85 Exec Dir Intl Studies/Outreach ..... Dr. Paul FOSTER
106 Director e-Learning ..... Vacant
92 Dir of University Honors Program ..... Dr. Jana MARCETTE
49 Dean Liberal Arts & Social Sciences ..... Ms. Tami HAALAND
53 Int Dean of Education ..... Dr. Kurt TOENJES
50 Interim Dean of Business ..... Mr. Ed GARDING
12 Dean City College ..... Dr. Vicki TRIER
76 Dean Health Professions & Science ..... Dr. Kurt TOENJES
04 Exec Assistant to the Chancellor ..... Ms. Natalie PRESTON
39 Director Center for Engagement ..... Ms. Brandee SOENS
108 Director Assessment & Accreditation ..... Ms. Kathleen THATCHER

*Montana State University - Northern (A)

PO Box 7751, Havre MT 59501-7751

County: Hill | FICE Identification: 002533 | Unit ID: 180522
Telephone: (406) 265-3700 | Carnegie Class: Bac-Diverse
FAX Number: N/A | Calendar System: Semester
URL: www.msun.edu
Established: 1929 | Annual Undergrad Tuition & Fees (In-State): $5,955
Enrollment: 1,024 | Coed
Affiliation or Control: State | IRS Status: 501(c)3
Highest Offering: Master's
Accreditation: NW, ADNUR, NUR

02 Chancellor ..... Mr. Gregory D. KEGEL
05 Provost/VC Academic Affairs ..... Dr. Neil MOISEY
10 VC Finance & Administration ..... Vacant
102 Executive Director of Foundation ..... Ms. Shantel CRONK
72 Dean College Technical Sciences ..... Dr. Dave KRUEGER
32 Dean of Students ..... Mr. Corey KOPP
53 Int Dean Col Educ/Arts & Sciences ..... Dr. Darlene SELLERS
06 Director Admissions/Student Records .... Ms. Alisha SCHROEDER
66 Int Dean of Col of Health Sciences ..... Ms. Jaime DUKE
21 Controller ..... Mr. Chris WENDLAND
41 Athletic Director ..... Mr. Christian OBERQUELL
36 Director Career Center ..... Vacant
13 Interim Chief Info Tech Officer ..... Ms. Marianne HOPPE
37 Director of Financial Aid ..... Ms. Cindy SMALL
26 Director of University Relations ..... Mr. James POTTER
08 Director of Library ..... Ms. Vicki GIST
121 Director Student Support Services ..... Vacant
84 Exec Director Enrollment Mgmt ..... Ms. Maura GATCH
15 Director of Human Resources ..... Ms. Suzanne HUNGER
18 Facilities Manager ..... Mr. Dan ULMEN
29 Outreach Specialist ..... Ms. Lee LOUNDER
100 Chief of Staff ..... Ms. Rachel DEAN

*Great Falls College Montana State University (B)

2100 16th Avenue South, Great Falls MT 59405-4909

County: Cascade | FICE Identification: 009314 | Unit ID: 180249
Telephone: (406) 771-4300 | Carnegie Class: Assoc/MT-VT-High Non
FAX Number: (406) 771-4317 | Calendar System: Semester
URL: gfcmsu.edu
Established: 1969 | Annual Undergrad Tuition & Fees (In-State): $3,450
Enrollment: 1,071 | Coed
Affiliation or Control: State | IRS Status: 501(c)3
Highest Offering: Associate Degree
Accreditation: NW, CAHIIM, @CNEA, COARC, DA, DH, EMT, PTAA, SURGT

02 CEO/Dean ..... Dr. Stephanie ERDMANN
05 Exec Director of Instruction ..... Dr. Leanne FROST
32 Exec Dir Student Affairs & HR ..... Ms. Mary Kay BONILLA
26 Exec Dir Marketing & Comm Relations ..... Mr. Scott THOMPSON
13 Director of Technology ..... Mr. David BONILLA
18 Director of Facilities Services ..... Mr. Gary SMART
36 Director Advising & Career Services ..... Mr. Troy STODDARD
37 Director Student Financial Aid ..... Ms. Leah HABEL
40 Bookstore Manager ..... Mr. Steve HALSTED
11 Exec Director of Operations ..... Ms. Carmen ROBERTS
09 Dir Inst Research & Effectiveness ..... Dr. Eleazar ORTEGA
88 Dir Specialty Trades Trainings ..... Mr. Joel SIMS
97 Director of General Studies ..... Dr. Leanne FROST
76 Director of CTE/Health Sciences ..... Ms. Quincie JONES
06 Registrar ..... Ms. Dena WAGNER-FOSSEN
84 Director Recruitment & Enrollment ..... Ms. Shannon MARR
108 Dir Teaching & Learning Innovation ..... Ms. Mandy WRIGHT

*Montana Technological University (C)

1300 W Park Street, Butte MT 59701-8997

County: Silver Bow | FICE Identification: 002531 | Unit ID: 180416
Telephone: (800) 445-8324 | Carnegie Class: Masters/S
FAX Number: (406) 496-4710 | Calendar System: Semester
URL: www.mtech.edu
Established: 1900 | Annual Undergrad Tuition & Fees (In-State): $7,390
Enrollment: 1,650 | Coed
Affiliation or Control: State | IRS Status: 501(c)3
Highest Offering: Doctorate
Accreditation: NW, IACBE, NURSE

02 Chancellor ..... Dr. Les COOK
05 Provost/Vice Chanc Academic Affairs ..... Dr. Steve GAMMON
10 Business Officer/Controller ..... Ms. Carleen CASSIDY
11 VC for Administration & Finance ..... Mr. Ron MUFFICK
102 Int CEO Foundation ..... Mr. Gary KOLSTAD
84 Exec Dir Admissions/Enrollment ..... Ms. Leslie DICKERSON
46 VC Research & Dean Grad Sch ..... Ms. Angela LUEKING
65 Director Bureau of Mines & Geology ..... Dr. John J. METESH
88 Dir Inst of Educational Opportunity ..... Ms. Amy VERLANIC
36 Director Career Services ..... Ms. Sarah RAYMOND
08 Director Library ..... Mr. Scott JUSKIEWICZ
37 Director of Financial Aid ..... Ms. Shauna SAVAGE
18 Director of Physical Facilities ..... Mr. Layne SESSIONS
29 Director Alumni Affairs ..... Vacant
41 Athletic Director ..... Mr. Matt STEPAN
72 Dean College of Technology ..... Ms. Karen VANDAVEER
49 Dean Col Letters/Sci/Prof Studies ..... Dr. Michele HARDY
54 Dean School of Mines & Engineering ..... Dr. Ken LEE
39 Director Residence Life ..... Vacant
26 Director Public Relations ..... Ms. Amanda BADOVINAC
40 Bookstore Director ..... Ms. Laurie VANDEL
09 Director Institutional Research ..... Ms. Melissa KUMP
06 Registrar ..... Vacant
105 Webmaster ..... Mr. Eduardo PANTOJA
106 Director of Distance Learning ..... Vacant
13 Director of Information Technology ..... Ms. Jennifer SIMON
96 Dir Purchasing & Budgets ..... Ms. Kelsey KERBS
15 Dir Human Resources ..... Ms. Vanessa VAN DYK
25 Dir of Sponsored Programs ..... Ms. Joanne LEE
38 Director Student Counseling ..... Ms. Amy LORANG
100 Chief of Staff ..... Ms. Jodie DELAY

*City College at Montana State University Billings (D)

3803 Central Avenue, Billings MT 59102-4398

Telephone: (406) 247-3000 | FICE Identification: 010166
Accreditation: &NW, CNEA

† Regional accreditation is carried under the parent institution Montana State University-Billings, Billings, MT.

*Highlands College of Montana Tech (E)

25 Basin Creek Road, Butte MT 59701-9704

Telephone: (406) 496-3701 | FICE Identification: 009282
Accreditation: &NW

† Regional accreditation is carried under the parent institution Montana Tech of The University of Montanna, Butte, MT.

*Missoula College-University of Montana (F)

1205 East Broadway Street, Missoula MT 59802

Telephone: (406) 243-7811 | FICE Identification: 007561
Accreditation: &NW, ACFEI, ADNUR, SURGT

† Regional accreditation is carried under the parent institution The University of Montana-Missoula, Missoula, MT.

Rocky Mountain College (G)

1511 Poly Drive, Billings MT 59102-1796

County: Yellowstone | FICE Identification: 002534 | Unit ID: 180595
Telephone: (406) 657-1000 | Carnegie Class: Masters/S
FAX Number: (406) 259-9751 | Calendar System: Semester
URL: www.rocky.edu
Established: 1878 | Annual Undergrad Tuition & Fees: $30,586
Enrollment: 1,014 | Coed
Affiliation or Control: Interdenominational | IRS Status: 501(c)3
Highest Offering: Doctorate
Accreditation: NW, AAB, ARCPA, OT

01 President ..... Dr. Robert WILMOUTH
05 Provost ..... Mr. Anthony PILTZ
32 Vice President for Student Life ..... Mr. Bradley A. NASON
84 Vice President of Enrollment ..... Mr. Austin MAPSTON
20 Academic Vice President ..... Dr. Erin RESER
10 Chief Financial Officer ..... Ms. Melodie MILROY
88 Director of Educational Leadership ..... Dr. Stevie SCHMITZ
08 Director of the Library ..... Ms. Bobbi OTTE
13 Director of Information Technology ..... Mr. Daniel WOLTERS
18 Director of Campus Facilities ..... Mr. Keith NORTH
41 Director of Athletics ..... Mr. Jim KLEMANN
09 Director of Student Records ..... Ms. Erica JOHNSON
37 Director of Financial Assistance ..... Ms. Jessica FRANCISCHETTI
39 Director of Residence Life ..... Ms. Shaydean SAYE
04 Executive Assistant to the Pres ..... Ms. Tracy DAVIDSON
19 Director Security/Safety ..... Mr. Donald LAUX
91 Director Administrative Computing ..... Ms. Kellee PIERCE
15 Chief Human Resources Officer ..... Ms. Marcella BUSTER
07 Director of Admissions ..... Mr. Sean COLEMAN

Salish Kootenai College (H)

PO Box 70, Pablo MT 59855-0070

County: Lake | FICE Identification: 021434 | Unit ID: 180647
Telephone: (406) 275-4800 | Carnegie Class: Tribal
FAX Number: (406) 275-4801 | Calendar System: Quarter
URL: www.skc.edu
Established: 1977 | Annual Undergrad Tuition & Fees: $6,399
Enrollment: 716 | Coed
Affiliation or Control: Independent Non-Profit | IRS Status: 501(c)3
Highest Offering: Baccalaureate
Accreditation: NW, DA, NUR, SW

01 President ..... Dr. Sandra BOHAM
05 Vice President of Academic Affairs ..... Mr. Dan DURGLO
10 Vice Pres Business Affairs ..... Ms. Audrey PLOUFFE
32 Vice President of Student Affairs ..... Mr. Antony BERTHELOTE
06 Registrar ..... Ms. Cleo KENMILLE
07 Director of Admissions ..... Mr. Juan PEREZ
08 Library Director ..... Mr. Fred NOEL
37 Financial Aid Director ..... Ms. Jackie SWAIN
09 Dir Institutional Effectiveness ..... Vacant
15 HR Generalist/Title IX Coord ..... Ms. Tommie LINSEBIGLER
102 College Foundation Director ..... Mr. William N. ROBERTS
13 Chief Information Officer ..... Mr. Al ANDERSON
18 Physical Plant Operations Manager ..... Vacant
04 Admin Assistant to President ..... Ms. Anita BIG SPRING
100 Chief of Staff ..... Ms. Brandy COUTURE
25 Chief Contract/Grants Administrator ..... Mr. Greg GOULD
38 Director Student Counseling ..... Ms. Kellie CALDBECK
39 Dir Resident Life/Student Housing ..... Ms. Nihtawneemiw BOHAM
41 Athletic Director ..... Ms. Melissa TIENSVOLD
50 Dean of Business ..... Ms. Rachel ANDREWS-GOULD
53 Dean of Education ..... Mr. Douglas RUHMAN

Stone Child College (I)

8294 Upper Box Elder Road, Box Elder MT 59521-9796

County: Hill | FICE Identification: 026109 | Unit ID: 366340
Telephone: (406) 395-4875 | Carnegie Class: Tribal
FAX Number: (406) 395-4836 | Calendar System: Semester
URL: www.stonechild.edu/
Established: 1984 | Annual Undergrad Tuition & Fees: $2,645
Enrollment: 311 | Coed
Affiliation or Control: Tribal Control | IRS Status: 501(c)3
Highest Offering: Baccalaureate
Accreditation: NW

01 President ..... Ms. Cory SANGREY-BILLY
05 Dean of Academics ..... Ms. Wilma Jean TYNER
32 Dean of Student Services ..... Ms. Marquieta JILOT
10 Chief Financial Officer ..... Ms. Tiffany GALBAVY
15 Personnel Officer ..... Ms. Jessie DEMONTINEY
06 Registrar ..... Ms. Gaile TORRES
13 Network Systems Administrator ..... Mr. Paul GARCIA
40 Bookstore Manager ..... Mr. Colton GALBAVY
37 Financial Aid Officer ..... Ms. Jolin SUNCHILD
18 Facilities/Maintenance Supervisor ..... Mr. Gus BACON
08 Head Librarian ..... Ms. Joy BRIDWELL
41 Athletic Director ..... Mr. Cameron BILLY

University of Providence (J)

1301 20th Street S, Great Falls MT 59405-4996

County: Cascade | FICE Identification: 002527 | Unit ID: 180258
Telephone: (800) 856-9544 | Carnegie Class: Masters/S
FAX Number: (406) 791-5209 | Calendar System: Semester
URL: www.uprovidence.edu
Established: 1932 | Annual Undergrad Tuition & Fees: $26,662
Enrollment: 1,005 | Coed
Affiliation or Control: Roman Catholic | IRS Status: 501(c)3
Highest Offering: Master's
Accreditation: NW, CACREP, NURSE

01 President ..... Rev. Oliver J. DOYLE
05 Provost ..... Dr. Matthew REDINGER
10 CFO ..... Vacant
100 Chief of Staff to the President ..... Ms. Kylie CARRANZA
84 VP for Enrollment Management ..... Ms. Mackenzie STICK
03 Interim Mission Officer ..... Mr. Nicolas ESTRADA
111 VP for Advancement ..... Vacant
41 Athletics Director ..... Mr. Douglas HASHLEY
121 Dir of Academic Success Center ..... Mr. Greg STIVERS
21 Financial Controller ..... Ms. Jillian EHNOT
15 Director of Human Resources ..... Mrs. Melanie HOUGE
06 Registrar ..... Ms. Ashley KOEPKE
09 Director of Institutional Research ..... Dr. Gregory MADSON
106 Director of Distance Learning ..... Mr. Jim GRETCH
108 Director of Inst Effectiveness ..... Mr. Greg MADSON
88 Director of Campus Ministry ..... Mr. Nicolas ESTRADA

18 Director Physical Plant .... Mr. Chet PIETRYKOWSKI
08 Senior Librarian .... Ms. Susan LEE
04 Executive Asst to the President .... Mr. Jose I. GARRIGO
88 Executive Assistant to the Provost .... Ms. Lindsay BERG
26 Dir of Marketing & Communications .... Ms. Christina DAWIDOWICZ
07 Director of Admissions .... Ms. Katelyn MARSIK
101 Secretary of the Institution/Board .... Mr. Jose I. GARRIGO
103 Director Workforce Development .... Mr. Rodney JOHANSON
11 Chief of Operations/Administration .... Ms. Brittany BUDESKI
19 Director Security/Safety .... Mr. Matthew GRUNENWALD
37 Director Student Financial Aid .... Ms. Kelli ENGELHARDT

NEBRASKA

Bellevue University (A)

1000 Galvin Road S, Bellevue NE 68005-3098
County: Sarpy
FICE Identification: 009743
Unit ID: 180814
Telephone: (402) 293-2000
Carnegie Class: Masters/L
FAX Number: (402) 293-2020
Calendar System: Other
URL: www.bellevue.edu
Established: 1966
Annual Undergrad Tuition & Fees: $7,851
Enrollment: 13,059
Coed
Affiliation or Control: Independent Non-Profit
IRS Status: 501(c)3
Highest Offering: Doctorate
Accreditation: HLC, CACREP, IACBE, NURSE

01 President .... Dr. Mary B. HAWKINS
03 Executive Vice President .... Ms. Sherrye HUTCHERSON
11 Exec VP Administrative Services .... Mr. Matthew DAVIS
18 Asst VP Grounds/Security/Safety .... Mr. Scott ALTIC
72 Dean of College of Science & Tech .... Dr. Mary DOBRANSKY
50 Dean College of Business .... Dr. Rebecca MURDOCK
49 Dean College of Arts & Sciences .... Dr. Michelle EPPLER
04 Exec Assistant to the President .... Ms. Juanite HALL
37 Director Student Financial Aid .... Ms. Christopher SIMPSON
08 Sr Dir Library Services .... Ms. Robin BERNSTEIN
102 Foundation CEO .... Mr. John ERICKSON
41 Director of Athletics .... Mr. Ed LEHOTAK
40 Director Bookstore .... Vacant
10 Controller .... Ms. McKayla GOLLOGLY
108 Quality Assurance Programs Director .... Mr. Pete HEINEMAN
26 Sr Director Growth Marketing .... Ms. Julia DORIA
06 Registrar .... Ms. Colette LEWIS

Bryan College of Health Sciences (B)

1535 S 52nd St., Lincoln NE 68506
County: Lancaster
FICE Identification: 006399
Unit ID: 180878
Telephone: (402) 481-3801
Carnegie Class: Spec-4-yr-Other Health
FAX Number: (402) 481-8421
Calendar System: Semester
URL: www.bryanhealthcollege.edu
Established: 2001
Annual Undergrad Tuition & Fees: $18,216
Enrollment: 778
Coed
Affiliation or Control: Independent Non-Profit
IRS Status: 501(c)3
Highest Offering: Doctorate
Accreditation: HLC, ANEST, CVT, DMS, NUR

01 President .... Dr. Richard LLOYD
05 Provost .... Dr. Kelsi ANDERSON
97 Dean of Educational Development .... Dr. Kristy PLANDER
11 Dean of Operations .... Mr. Bill EVANS
66 Dean of Undergraduate Nursing .... Dr. Theresa DELAHOYDE
58 Dean of Graduate Studies .... Dr. Marcia KUBE
76 Dean of Healthcare Studies .... Dr. Amy KNOBBE
88 Dean of Nurse Anesthesia .... Dr. Sharon HADENFELDT
32 Dean of Students .... Dr. Alethea STOVALL
08 Director of Library Services .... Ms. Heather ST. CLAIR
06 Registrar .... Ms. Deann BAYNE
29 Student/Alumni Services Director .... Ms. Brenda NEEMANN
37 Financial Aid Director .... Ms. Maggie HACKWITH
113 Student Accounts Coordinator .... Ms. Alicia ARNOLD
106 Director of Digital Education .... Ms. Deb MAEDER
84 Dean of Enrollment and Marketing .... Ms. Ashley SCHROEDER
04 Executive Assistant .... Ms. Brandi BASURTO
09 It Systems Director/Inst Research .... Mr. Ryan MOORE

Central Community College (C)

PO Box 4903, Grand Island NE 68802-4903
County: Hall
FICE Identification: 020995
Unit ID: 180902
Telephone: (308) 398-4222
Carnegie Class: Assoc/HVT-High Non
FAX Number: (308) 398-7398
Calendar System: Semester
URL: www.cccneb.edu
Established: 1966
Annual Undergrad Tuition & Fees (In-District): $3,210
Enrollment: 5,974
Coed
Affiliation or Control: Local
IRS Status: 501(c)3
Highest Offering: Associate Degree
Accreditation: HLC, ADNUR, CAHIIM, DA, DH, EMT, MAC, MLTAD, OTA

01 College President .... Dr. Matthew GOTSCHALL
05 VP of Innovation & Instruction .... Dr. Candace WALTON
10 Vice President of Admin Services .... Mr. Joel KING
15 Vice President of Human Resources .... Vacant
12 Grand Island Campus President .... Dr. Marcie KEMNITZ
12 Columbus Campus President .... Dr. Kathy FUCHSER
12 Hastings Campus President .... Dr. Chris WADDLE
102 Foundation Executive Director .... Ms. Traci SKALBERG
97 Dean of Academic Educ .... Dr. Amy MANCINI
76 Dean of Health Sciences .... Ms. Sarah KORT
88 Dean of Skilled & Technical Science .... Dr. Nate ALLEN
84 Dean of Enrollment Management .... Ms. Janel WALTON
32 Dean of Student Success .... Dr. Beth PRZYMUS
51 Dean of Workforce Training/ Cont Ed .... Dr. Kelly CHRISTENSEN
06 Registrar .... Ms. Barb LARSON
09 Director of Institutional Research .... Mr. Brian MCDERMOTT
37 Area Director Student Financial Aid .... Vacant
41 Athletic Director .... Ms. Mary YOUNG
22 Equity and Compliance Manager .... Ms. Lauren SLAUGHTER
13 IT Services Manager .... Mr. Tom PETERS
29 Alumni Director .... Ms. Cheri BEDA
07 Admissions Director Columbus .... Vacant
07 Admissions Director Grand Island .... Ms. Erin LESIAK
07 Admissions Director Hastings .... Ms. Regina SOMER
96 Purchasing Manager .... Ms. Carmen TAYLOR
26 Sr Dir College Communications .... Mr. Scott MILLER
100 Chief of Staff .... Ms. Joni RANSOM

Central Community College Columbus Campus (D)

PO Box 1027, 4500 63rd Street,
Columbus NE 68602-1027
Telephone: (402) 564-7132
Identification: 770331
Accreditation: &HLC

Central Community College Hastings Campus (E)

550 S Technical Blvd, PO Box 1024,
Hastings NE 68902-1024
Telephone: (402) 463-9811
Identification: 770332
Accreditation: &HLC

CHI Health School of Radiologic Technology (F)

6901 North 72nd Street, Omaha NE 68122
County: Douglas
FICE Identification: 008492
Unit ID: 181145
Telephone: (402) 572-3650
Carnegie Class: Spec 2-yr-Health
FAX Number: (402) 398-6650
Calendar System: Semester
URL: www.chihealth.com/school-of-radiologic-technology
Established: 1953
Annual Undergrad Tuition & Fees: N/A
Enrollment: 15
Coed
Affiliation or Control: Independent Non-Profit
IRS Status: 501(c)3
Highest Offering: Associate Degree
Accreditation: RAD

01 Int CEO CHI Health .... Jeanett WOJTALEWICZ
10 Int Chief Financial Officer .... Nick O'TOOL
05 Chief Medical Officer .... Dr. Cary WARD

Clarkson College (G)

101 S 42nd Street, Omaha NE 68131-2739
County: Douglas
FICE Identification: 009862
Unit ID: 180832
Telephone: (402) 552-3100
Carnegie Class: Spec-4-yr-Other Health
FAX Number: (402) 552-3369
Calendar System: Semester
URL: www.clarksoncollege.edu
Established: 1888
Annual Undergrad Tuition & Fees: $14,496
Enrollment: 1,169
Coed
Affiliation or Control: Independent Non-Profit
IRS Status: 501(c)3
Highest Offering: Doctorate
Accreditation: HLC, ANEST, CAHIIM, NUR, PTAA, RAD

01 President .... Dr. Gary PACK
05 VP of Academic Affairs .... Dr. Andriea NEBEL
11 Vice Pres Operations .... Jina PAUL
10 Controller .... Robyn HANSEN
06 Registrar .... Natalie VRBKA
13 Director Technology Services .... Ryan SCHURMAN
08 Director Library Services .... Anne HEIMANN
97 Director General Education .... Lori BACHLE
50 Dir Health Care Business .... Carla DIRKSCHNEIDER
76 Dir Medical Imaging/Radiologic Tech .... Shelli WEDDUM
76 Dir Physical Therapist Asst Pgm .... Jessica NIEMANN

College of Saint Mary (H)

7000 Mercy Road, Omaha NE 68106-2606
County: Douglas
FICE Identification: 002540
Unit ID: 181604
Telephone: (402) 399-2400
Carnegie Class: Masters/M
FAX Number: (402) 399-2647
Calendar System: Semester
URL: www.csm.edu
Established: 1923
Annual Undergrad Tuition & Fees: $21,370
Enrollment: 1,024
Female
Affiliation or Control: Roman Catholic
IRS Status: 501(c)3
Highest Offering: Doctorate
Accreditation: HLC, ARCPA, NUR, OT, @PTA

01 President .... Dr. Maryanne STEVENS, RSM
03 Executive Vice President .... Dr. Sarah KOTTICH
10 VP of Financial Services .... Ms. Bridgette RENBARGER
05 VP of Academic & Student Affairs .... Dr. Kimbery ALLEN
84 VP of Enrollment Services .... Mr. John FROST
11 VP of Operations/COO .... Mr. Nate NEUFIND
111 VP of Alumnae & Donor Relations .... Ms. Terri CAMPBELL
121 Assistant Dean of Student Success .... Ms. Daniela ROJAS
38 Asst Dean Student Support Services .... Ms. Barbara TREADWAY
32 Assistant Dean of Student Life .... Mr. Kristofer CZERWIEC
08 Library Director .... Ms. Margaret EMONS
88 VP of Mission Integration .... Dr. Andrea STAPLETON
19 Director Security/Safety .... Mr. David FERBER
06 Registrar .... Mr. Anthony COLE
37 Chief Student Financial Aid Officer .... Ms. Beth SISK
28 Director of Multicultural Affairs .... Vacant
26 AVP for Marketing/Public Relations .... Ms. Brittney LONG
21 Controller .... Mr. Michael BEVERLY
15 Chief HR Officer .... Ms. Jessica HOCHSTEIN
40 Director Bookstore .... Mr. Steve WESTENBROEK
29 Senior Director Alumnae Relations .... Ms. Katty PETAK
39 Director Residence Life .... Ms. Larissa BUSTER
112 Director of Major Gifts .... Ms. Susan MEDINA
44 Annual Giving Officer .... Ms. Johnna THOMPSON
41 Athletic Director .... Mr. Jeff JOHNSON
18 Director Physical Plant .... Mr. Dan SPARGEN
42 Director Campus Ministry .... Vacant
13 Chief IT Officer .... Mr. Kevin SHOLL
04 Executive Asst to the President .... Ms. Robyn KNIFFEN

Concordia University (I)

800 N Columbia Avenue, Seward NE 68434-1599
County: Seward
FICE Identification: 002541
Unit ID: 180984
Telephone: (402) 643-3651
Carnegie Class: Masters/L
FAX Number: (402) 643-4073
Calendar System: Other
URL: www.cune.edu
Established: 1894
Annual Undergrad Tuition & Fees: $34,900
Enrollment: 3,224
Coed
Affiliation or Control: Lutheran Church - Missouri Synod
IRS Status: 501(c)3
Highest Offering: Master's
Accreditation: HLC, CAEP, CAEPN, IACBE, MUS

01 President .... Dr. Bernard BULL
05 Provost .... Dr. Timothy PREUSS
111 Vice President Inst Advancement .... Vacant
84 VP Enrollment & Marketing .... Mr. Gary MCDANIEL
32 Vice Pres for Student Affairs .... Mr. Gene BROOKS
10 Chief Financial Officer .... Mr. David KUMM
13 Chief Information Officer .... Mr. Curt SHERMAN
53 Dean of Educ/Health & Human Science .... Dr. Lorinda SANKEY
49 Interim Dean of Arts & Sciences .... Dr. Lisa ASHBY
50 Dean College of Business .... Mr. Jonathon MOBERLY
14 Dir Special IT Projects .... Dr. Kent EINSPAHR
08 Director of Library Services .... Mr. Philip HENDRICKSON
88 Dir of Education/Synodical Careers .... Mr. William SCHRANZ
29 Director Alumni/University Rels .... Mrs. Jennifer FURR
41 Athletic Director .... Mr. Devin SMITH
06 University Registrar .... Mr. Ed SIFFRING
42 Campus Pastor .... Rev. Ryan MATTHIAS
37 Director of Financial Aid .... Mr. Scott JENKINS
18 Facilities Director/Maintenance .... Mr. Dale NOVAK
15 Director of Human Resources .... Mr. Shawn ZOOK
07 Director Admission Operations .... Mr. Aaron ROBERTS
27 Director of Marketing/Communication .... Mr. Seth MERANDA
115 Sr Dir Strategic Initiatives/Invest .... Mr. Curt SHERMAN
110 Sr Dir of Advancement Operations .... Mrs. Leigh LEWIS
106 Dir Classroom Innov & Online Educ .... Ms. Angie WASSENMILLER
121 Director of Student Success .... Mrs. Daisha THOMAS
19 Director Security/Safety .... Mr. Ron DOWN
35 Director Student Development .... Ms. Rebekah FREED
43 Assoc VP Legal Affairs/Gen Counsel .... Mr. Kirby KLAPPENBACK
28 Multicult Spec/Asst Dir Stdnt Life .... Mr. Von THOMAS
30 Sr Dir Development & Engagement .... Mr. Scott SEEVERS

Creighton University (J)

2500 California Plaza, Omaha NE 68178-0001
County: Douglas
FICE Identification: 002542
Unit ID: 181002
Telephone: (402) 280-2700
Carnegie Class: DU-Higher
FAX Number: N/A
Calendar System: Semester
URL: www.creighton.edu
Established: 1878
Annual Undergrad Tuition & Fees: $43,018
Enrollment: 8,770
Coed
Affiliation or Control: Roman Catholic
IRS Status: 501(c)3
Highest Offering: Doctorate
Accreditation: HLC, #ARCPA, CAEP, CAMPEP, DENT, EMT, HSA, LAW, MED, NURSE, OT, PHAR, PTA, SW

01 President .... Rev. Daniel S. HENDRICKSON, SJ
00 Chairman Creighton University Board .... Mr. Nizar GHOUSSAINI
05 Provost .... Dr. Mardell A. WILSON
100 Spec Asst to Pres & Board Liaison .... Mr. Jeffrey J. FELDHAUS
04 Sr Exec Assistant President Office .... Ms. Natalie OLSEN
04 Exec Assistant President Office .... Mr. David L. BARNUM
101 Corporate Secretary .... Mr. James S. JANSEN
03 Executive Vice President .... Ms. Jan E. MADSEN
88 Vice President Mission & Ministry .... Vacant
88 Sr Dir Ignation Formation/Ministry .... Ms. Susan NAATZ
42 Interim Director Campus Ministry .... Ms. Kelly TADEO ORBIK
88 Director Ctr for Service & Justice .... Mr. Kenneth REED-BOULEY
88 Director Retreat Center .... Ms. Amy K. HOOVER

111 Vice President University Relations .... Mr. Matthew C. GERARD
112 Assistant VP Principal Gifts .... Mr. Mike T. FINDLEY
110 Asst VP University Relations .... Fr. Tom MERKEL, SJ
30 AVP Development AZ HSC Campus .... Vacant
30 Assistant VP of Development .... Ms. Cortney A. BAUER
88 AVP Athletic Development .... Mr. Adrian E. DOWELL
30 AVP Advancement Svcs & Dev Prog ... Ms. Amy M. MCELHANEY
29 Assistant VP Alumni Relations .... Vacant
88 Sr Philanthropic Advisor .... Mr. Steven A. SCHOLER
08 Asst Vice Provost Library Services ..... Ms. Elizabeth J. KISCADEN
106 Assoc VP Teaching & Learning Center .... Dr. Debra FORD
09 Director Institutional Research .... Dr. Kristin BUSCHER
06 Registrar .... Ms. Melinda J. STONER
22 Director Disability Accommodations .... Ms. Jacque KNEDLER
36 Director Career Center .... Mr. Jeremy M. FISHER
43 General Counsel .... Mr. James S. JANSEN
32 Vice Provost Student Life .... Dr. Tanya C. WINEGARD
121 Vice Provost for Student Success .... Dr. Wayne YOUNG
35 Assoc VP Student Engagement .... Dr. Michele K. BOGARD
41 Athletic Director .... Mr. Marcus BLOSSOM
39 Sr Dir Housing & Auxiliary Service .... Mr. Lucas NOVOTNY
39 Director of Residential Life .... Ms. Kristen SCHULING
88 Sr Dir Community Stdrds & Wellbeing .... Ms. Desiree NOWNES
93 Dir Creighton Intercultural Center .... Ms. Becky NICKERSON
88 Director of Recreation and Wellness .... Mr. Greg DURHAM
89 Dir Student Ldrshp/Involvement Ctr .... Ms. Katie M. KELSEY
84 VP Enrollment Mgmt & Univ Planning .... Dr. Mary E. CHASE
07 Director Admissions/Scholarships .... Ms. Sarah D. RICHARDSON
123 Dir Graduate and Adult Recruitment .... Ms. Elizabeth CHURCHICH
37 Director Student Financial Aid .... Ms. Janet SOLBERG
121 Sr Dir Acad Success & Educ Oppty .... Dr. Joe ECKLUND
49 Dean College of Arts & Sciences .... Dr. Bridget M. KEEGAN
50 Dean Heider College of Business .... Dr. Anthony R. HENDRICKSON
58 Interim Dean Graduate School .... Fr. Kevin FITZGERALD, SJ
52 Dean School of Dentistry .... Dr. Jillian WALLEN
61 Dean School of Law .... Mr. Joshua P. FERSHEE
63 Dean School of Medicine .... Dr. Robert W. DUNLAY
66 Dean College of Nursing .... Dr. Catherine M. TODERO
67 Int Dean Sch of Pharm/Health Prof .... Dr. Amy F. WILSON
26 Vice Pres Univ Comm & Marketing ... Ms. Heidi GRUNKEMEYER
27 Director Communication .... Mr. Rick C. DAVIS
105 Interim Director Web Strategy .... Ms. Beth CAVANAUGH
18 Assoc VP Facility Mgmt & Planning .... Mr. Derek SCOTT
19 Director Public Safety .... Mr. Michael D. REINER
21 Assoc VP Finance .... Mr. John J. JESSE, III
113 Assoc Director Business Office .... Ms. Ann M. O'DOWD
21 Assoc VP Finance .... Ms. Tara S. MCGUIRE
116 Director Internal Audit .... Mr. T. Paul TOMOSER
117 Risk Manager .... Ms. Katie BOOTON
88 Manager of Tax and GAAP .... Mr. Jason T. MCGILL
96 Sr Director Procurement .... Mr. Eric J. GILMORE
15 Assoc VP Human Resources .... Ms. Judi SZATKO
118 Sr Director Benefits & Compensation .... Ms. Molly BILLINGS
13 Vice Pres Information Technology .... Mr. Russ B. PEARLMAN
14 AVP Solution Delivery .... Dr. David RAMCHARAN
90 AVP Planning .... Mr. Scott TAYLOR
91 Senior Director IT Operations .... Mr. Mark MONGAR
119 Information Security Officer .... Mr. Bryan S. MCLAUGHLIN
24 IT Solutions Architect Learning Env .... Vacant
22 Exec Director Equity & Inclusion .... Ms. Allison S. TAYLOR
23 Medical Dir Student Health Services .... Vacant
25 Director Sponsored Programs Admin .... Ms. Beth J. HERR
28 Interim VP Inst Diversity/Inclusion .... Dr. Sarah WALKER
38 Director Counseling Services .... Dr. Jennifer PETER
40 Bookstore Manager .... Mr. Cory DAVIS
85 Vice Provost Global Engagement .... Dr. Rene L. PADILLA
86 Director Comm & Govt Relationships .... Mr. Chris T. RODGERS
92 Director Honors Program .... Dr. Jeffrey P. HAUSE
104 Global Programs Coordinator .... Ms. Lizzy E. CURRAN
104 Global Programs Coordinator .... Ms. Krista CUPICH
20 Vice President Compliance .... Ms. Tricia SHARRAR
20 VP Learning & Assessment .... Dr. Gail M. JENSEN

Doane University (A)

1014 Boswell Avenue, Crete NE 68333

County: Saline | FICE Identification: 002544
Unit ID: 181020
Telephone: (800) 333-6263 | Carnegie Class: Masters/L
FAX Number: (402) 826-8600 | Calendar System: 4/1/4
URL: www.doane.edu
Established: 1872 | Annual Undergrad Tuition & Fees: $36,800
Enrollment: 2,281 | Coed
Affiliation or Control: United Church Of Christ | IRS Status: 501(c)3
Highest Offering: Doctorate
Accreditation: HLC, CAEP, CAEPN, MUS

01 President .... Dr. Roger HUGHES
10 Chief Financial Officer .... Ms. Linda SCHOLTING
13 Chief Information Officer .... Mr. Derek BIERMAN
05 Chief Academic Officer .... Dr. Lorie COOK-BENJAMIN
28 VP for Diversity/Equity & Inclusion .... Mr. Luis SOTELO
108 Dir. of Institutional Effectiveness .... Dr. Kristopher WILLIAMS
41 Director of Athletics .... Mr. Mark WATESKA
84 Interim Vice Pres Enrollment .... Mr. Marty FYE
111 Vice President for Advancement .... Mr. Marty FYE
32 Vice President of Student Affairs .... Dr. Judy KAWAMOTO
15 Director of Human Resources .... Ms. Anne ZIOLA
04 Sr Exec Assistant to President .... Ms. Jenei SKILLETT
49 Dean College of Arts/Sciences .... Dr. Pedro MALIGO
50 Dean of the College of Business .... Dr. Jennifer BOSSARD
53 Dean College of Education .... Dr. Tim FREY

35 Dean of Students .... Ms. Megan FAILOR
21 Controller .... Vacant
06 Registrar .... Ms. Denise ELLIS
37 Director of Financial Aid .... Mr. Federico PENA, JR.
07 Director of Admissions .... Ms. Amber LINNERTZ
84 Director of Enrollment .... Ms. Kelli BACKMAN
12 Director of Omaha Campus .... Mr. Chris BRADY
12 Director of Lincoln Campus .... Ms. Angie KLASEK
113 Bursar .... Ms. Kelli SCHWEITZER
114 Dir of Financial Planning Analysis .... Mr. Joe MCCRACKEN
120 Director of Open Learning Academy .... Ms. Erin MAY
104 Director of International Programs .... Mr. Timothy BURGE
08 Director of Perkins Library .... Mr. Roger GETZ
121 Director of Student Support Service .... Ms. Anita HARKINS
121 Director of Academic Advising .... Ms. Ann KOOPMANN
26 Interim Exec Dir of Marketing .... Ms. MacKenzie JOBES
18 Dir of Facilities & Constr Proj .... Mr. Brian FLESNER
42 Dir of Religious & Spiritual Life .... Dr. Leah CECH
38 Director Counseling & Health .... Mr. Myron PARSLEY
23 Director of Student Health .... Ms. Kelly JIROVEC
39 Director of Res Life and Educ .... Mr. Brian STUTZ
88 Director of Campus Engagement .... Ms. Jayma AUSDEMORE
88 Dir of Veteran/Military Services .... Ms. Sarah MCNEEL
36 Dir Career/Leadership & Service .... Mr. Quint GEIS
09 Director of Institutional Research .... Dr. Raja TAYEH
19 Dir of Campus Safety/Assoc Dean .... Mr. Russ HEWITT
30 Senior Director of Development .... Ms. Jacqueline HINRICHSEN
44 Executive Director Annual Giving .... Ms. Julie RASGORSHEK
29 Director of Alumni Relation .... Mr. Michael STEHLIK
112 Dir Grants and Foundation Relations .... Ms. Sara ZULKOSKI
14 Director of Technology Operations .... Mr. Ryan DORSHORST
105 Director of Web App Services .... Mr. Amos JOSEPH
91 Service Center Director .... Ms. Quinn STRYKER
105 Director of Enterprise Services .... Mr. Steve GUGEL

Doane University (B)

303 North 52nd Street, Lincoln NE 68504

Telephone: (402) 466-4774 | Identification: 770334
Accreditation: &HLC, CACREP

Hastings College (C)

710 N Turner Avenue, Hastings NE 68902-0269

County: Adams | FICE Identification: 002548
Unit ID: 181127
Telephone: (402) 463-2402 | Carnegie Class: Bac-Diverse
FAX Number: (402) 461-7490 | Calendar System: 4/1/4
URL: www.hastings.edu
Established: 1882 | Annual Undergrad Tuition & Fees: $32,770
Enrollment: 982 | Coed
Affiliation or Control: Presbyterian Church (U.S.A.) | IRS Status: 501(c)3
Highest Offering: Master's
Accreditation: HLC, CAEP, MUS

01 Executive President .... Dr. Rich LLOYD
00 Chair of the Board .... Ms. Ann MARTIN
102 Executive Director of Foundation .... Mr. Gary FREEMAN
10 VP for Finance/CFO .... Ms. Stephanie OURADA
84 VP Access/Enrollment & Performance .... Dr. Annette VARGAS
05 VP of Academic & Student Affairs .... Dr. Jonas PRIDA
41 Athletic Director .... Mr. B.J PUMROY
32 Assoc Dean Academic/Student Affairs .... Dr. Kittie GRACE
112 Assoc VP for Planned & Major Gifts .... Mr. Michael KARLOFF
110 Assoc VP for Development .... Ms. Judee L. KONEN
06 Registrar .... Mr. Jim BOEVE
37 Director of Financial Aid .... Ms. Traci BOEVE
15 Director of Human Resources .... Ms. Jamie BATENHORST
26 Director of Marketing .... Mr. Michael HOWIE
29 AVP of External Relations .... Vacant
13 Director of IT .... Ms. Patty KINGSLEY
14 Network Administrator .... Mr. Josh KELLEY
18 Director Physical Plant Services .... Mr. Ron GRIGGS
93 Minority Students .... Dr. Moses DOGBEVIA
28 Pushkin Institute Director .... Dr. Rob BABCOCK
36 Director of Career Services .... Ms. Kimberly K. GRAVIETTE
23 Director Campus Health Services .... Vacant
42 Chaplain .... Vacant
35 Dean of Student Engagement .... Dr. Lisa SMITH
19 Director of Security/Safety .... Mr. Brian HESSLER
38 Director of Counseling Services .... Ms. Michelle MORGANFLASH
40 Bookstore Manager .... Ms. Brianna WEICHEL
88 Graphic Designer/Publisher .... Mrs. Camille KASTL
85 International Program Director .... Mr. Grant HUNTER
04 Executive Asst to President & VPAA .... Ms. Marin SUHR
07 Director of Admissions .... Ms. Chris SCHUKEI
09 Director of Institutional Research .... Dr. Kristin CHARLES
44 Director Annual Giving .... Ms. Alicia O'DONNELL

Little Priest Tribal College (D)

601 East College Drive, PO Box 270,
Winnebago NE 68071-0270

County: Thurston | FICE Identification: 033233
Unit ID: 434016
Telephone: (402) 878-2380 | Carnegie Class: Tribal
FAX Number: (402) 878-2380 | Calendar System: Semester
URL: www.littlepriest.edu
Established: 1996 | Annual Undergrad Tuition & Fees: $5,140
Enrollment: 113 | Coed
Affiliation or Control: Independent Non-Profit | IRS Status: 501(c)3
Highest Offering: Associate Degree
Accreditation: HLC

01 President .... Mr. Manoj PATIL
05 VP of Teaching and Learning .... Ms. Loretta BROBERG
10 VP of Finance and Operations .... Mr. Mark VASINA
07 Director of Admissions .... Mr. Darby YOUNG
37 Director of Financial Aid .... Ms. Yatty MOHAMMAD
15 Human Resource Coordinator .... Mrs. Angela KENT
32 Director of Student Support Service .... Ms. Trisha WEGNER
13 IT Director .... Mr. Morri CONWAY
25 Director of Grants .... Ms. Brenda CONWAY
09 Dir of Institutional Effectiveness .... Ms. Kavya MARIBOYINA
04 Exec Assistant to the President .... Ms. Carla KAI
19 Director Security/Safety .... Mr. Justin MCCAULEY

Mary Lanning Healthcare School of Radiology (E)

715 North St. Joseph Avenue, Hastings NE 68901

County: Adams | FICE Identification: 004431
Unit ID: 181251
Telephone: (402) 461-5177 | Carnegie Class: Not Classified
FAX Number: (402) 460-5059 | Calendar System: Other
URL: www.marylanning.org
Established: 1952 | Annual Undergrad Tuition & Fees: N/A
Enrollment: N/A | Coed
Affiliation or Control: Independent Non-Profit | IRS Status: 501(c)3
Highest Offering: Associate Degree
Accreditation: RAD

01 President and CEO .... Eric BARBER
05 Chief Medical Officer .... Dr. Adam HORN
10 Chief Financial Officer .... Shawn NORDBY
11 Chief Operating Officer .... Mark CALLAHAN
15 Vice Pres Human Resources .... Bruce CUTRIGHT

McCook Community College (F)

1205 East Third Street, McCook NE 69001

Telephone: (308) 345-8100 | Identification: 770337
Accreditation: &HLC, EMT

Metropolitan Community College (G)

PO Box 3777, Omaha NE 68103-0777

County: Douglas | FICE Identification: 012586
Unit ID: 181303
Telephone: (531) 622-2400 | Carnegie Class: Assoc/MT-VT-High Non
FAX Number: (402) 457-2395 | Calendar System: Quarter
URL: www.mccneb.edu
Established: 1974 | Annual Undergrad Tuition & Fees (In-District): $3,195
Enrollment: 13,244 | Coed
Affiliation or Control: State/Local | IRS Status: Exempt
Highest Offering: Associate Degree
Accreditation: HLC, ACBSP, ACFEI, ADNUR, CAHIIM, COARC, CSHSE, EMT, MAC

01 President .... Mr. Randy SCHMAILZL
100 Chief of Staff .... Ms. Patricia CRISLER
05 Vice President Academic Affairs .... Dr. Tom MCDONNELL
28 Assoc Vice Pres Equity/Diversity . Dr. Cynthia GOOCH-GRAYSON
15 Vice Pres for Human Resources .... Ms. Melissa BEBER
45 VP for Institutional Effectiveness .... Dr. Hank ROBINSON
32 Vice Pres for Student Affairs .... Dr. Maria VAZQUEZ
10 College Business Officer .... Ms. Brenda SCHUMACHER
26 College Marketing Officer .... Ms. Nannette RODRIGUEZ
11 Vice Pres of Planning & Operations .... Ms. Kay FRIESEN
18 Director Facilities Management .... Mr. Scott KARDELL
37 Director of Financial Aid .... Ms. Wilma HJELLUM
96 Director Administrative Management .... Ms. KT NELSON
19 Chief of Police/Dir Emergency Mgmt .... Mr. Dave FRIEND
13 Chief Information Officer .... Mr. Chad LYNCH
06 Registrar .... Ms. Albertha SCHMID
43 AVP Compliance/General Counsel .... Mr. Jim THIBODEAU
111 AVP for Advancement .... Ms. Amy RECKER
119 Director IT Risk and Compliance .... Ms. Jodie SNIDER
04 Executive Assistant to President .... Ms. Julie LANXON
103 AVP for Community & Workforce Dev .... Mr. Gary GIRARD

Metropolitan Community College Elkhorn Valley Campus (H)

829 North 204th Street, Elkhorn NE 68022

Telephone: (531) 622-5231 | Identification: 770335
Accreditation: &HLC

Metropolitan Community College South Omaha Campus (I)

2909 Edward Babe Gomez Avenue, Omaha NE 68107

Telephone: (531) 622-5231 | Identification: 770336
Accreditation: &HLC

Mid-Plains Community College (J)

601 W State Farm Road, North Platte NE 69101-9491

County: Lincoln | FICE Identification: 002557
Unit ID: 181312
Telephone: (800) 658-4308 | Carnegie Class: Assoc/MT-VT-High Non
FAX Number: (308) 535-3794 | Calendar System: Semester
URL: www.mpcc.edu
Established: 1926 | Annual Undergrad Tuition & Fees (In-District): $3,360
Enrollment: 2,075 | Coed
Affiliation or Control: State/Local | IRS Status: 501(c)3

Highest Offering: Associate Degree
Accreditation: HLC, ADNUR, DA, MLTAD

01 President ... Mr. Ryan PURDY
11 VP for Administrative Services ... Mr. Michael STEELE
05 VP for Academic Affairs ... Dr. Jody TOMANEK
09 Dir Institutional Effectiveness ... Mr. Tad PFEIFER
32 Dean of Student Life ... Dr. Brian OBERT
56 Associate Dean of Outreach ... Ms. Gail KNOTT
36 Director of Career Services ... Ms. Becky BARNER
84 Dir of Recruiting & Admissions ... Ms. Mindy HOPE
06 Registrar ... Ms. Lana STEWART
26 Dir Marketing & Public Relations ... Mr. Daniel STINMAN
15 Director of Human Resources ... Ms. Rebecca WRAGE
13 Dir Information Tech Svcs ... Mr. Trent WIESE
37 Dir of Student Financial Aid ... Ms. Erinn BROWN
04 Exec Assistant to the President ... Ms. Karen HALLER
108 Director Institutional Assessment ... Ms. Holly ANDREWS
18 Chief Fac/Physical Plant Ofcr ... Mr. Shawn ATEN
111 Director Institutional Advancement ... Mr. Jacob RISSLER
39 Dir Resident Life/Student Housing ... Mr. Jason OSMOTHERLY
41 Athletic Director ... Mr. Kevin O'CONNOR
07 Director of Admissions ... Ms. Donna MENKE
08 Chief Library Officer ... Ms. Kathleen WHEELER
103 Director Workforce Development ... Ms. Gail KNOTT

Mid-Plains Community College North Platte (A)

1101 Halligan Drive, North Platte NE 69101
Telephone: (308) 535-3600 Identification: 770338
Accreditation: &HLC

Midland University (B)

900 N Clarkson, Fremont NE 68025-4395
County: Dodge FICE Identification: 002553
Unit ID: 181330
Telephone: (402) 721-5480 Carnegie Class: Masters/S
FAX Number: (402) 721-0250 Calendar System: 4/1/4
URL: www.midlandu.edu
Established: 1883 Annual Undergrad Tuition & Fees: $35,528
Enrollment: 1,765 Coed
Affiliation or Control: Evangelical Lutheran Church In America
IRS Status: 501(c)3
Highest Offering: Master's
Accreditation: HLC, CAATE, NUR

01 President ... Ms. Jody HORNER
05 Chief Academic Officer ... Dr. Jamie SIMPSON
32 VP Stdnt Affs/Chief Diversity Ofcr ... Ms. Kristina CAMMARANO
11 Chief Operating Officer ... Ms. Jodi BENJAMIN
111 Vice Pres for Inst Advancement ... Ms. Laura ROBINETT
15 VP Human Resources ... Ms. Caryl JOHANNSEN
06 University Registrar ... Vacant
84 VP Undergrad Enrollment/Marketing ... Ms. Lori ETHIER
37 Director of Financial Aid ... Mr. Douglas WATSON
10 Chief Financial Officer ... Mr. Joe HARNISCH
41 Athletic Director ... Ms. Courtney THOMSEN
76 Dean College of Health Professions ... Dr. Linda QUINN
13 Chief Information Officer ... Mr. Shane PERRIEN
18 Director Facilities Management ... Vacant
44 Annual Giving Officer ... Ms. Katie CHATTERS

Myotherapy Institute (C)

245 S. 84th Street #100, Lincoln NE 68510
County: Lancaster FICE Identification: 032793
Unit ID: 434432
Telephone: (402) 421-7410 Carnegie Class: Spec 2-yr-Health
FAX Number: (402) 421-6736 Calendar System: Other
URL: www.myotherapy.edu
Established: 1992 Annual Undergrad Tuition & Fees: $16,750
Enrollment: 13 Coed
Affiliation or Control: Proprietary IRS Status: Proprietary
Highest Offering: Associate Degree
Accreditation: ACCSC

01 Director ... Ms. Sue KOZISEK

Nebraska Indian Community College (D)

1111 Hwy 75 - PO Box 428, Macy NE 68039-0428
County: Thurston FICE Identification: 025508
Unit ID: 181419
Telephone: (402) 494-2311 Carnegie Class: Tribal
FAX Number: (402) 837-4183 Calendar System: Semester
URL: www.thenicc.edu
Established: 1973 Annual Undergrad Tuition & Fees: $4,080
Enrollment: 210 Coed
Affiliation or Control: Tribal Control IRS Status: Exempt
Highest Offering: Associate Degree
Accreditation: HLC

01 President ... Dr. Michael OLTROGGE
05 Academic Dean ... Dr. Kristine SUDBECK
32 Dean Student Services ... Dawne PRICE
13 Chief Information Officer ... Justin KOCIAN
06 Registrar ... Troy MUNHOFEN
15 Human Resources Director ... Anthony WARRIOR
08 Library Director ... Susan TYNDALL

Nebraska Methodist College (E)

720 N 87th Street, Omaha NE 68114-2852
County: Douglas FICE Identification: 006404
Unit ID: 181297
Telephone: (402) 354-7000 Carnegie Class: Spec-4-yr-Other Health
FAX Number: (402) 354-7090 Calendar System: Semester
URL: www.methodistcollege.edu
Established: 1891 Annual Undergrad Tuition & Fees: $16,708
Enrollment: 1,212 Coed
Affiliation or Control: Independent Non-Profit IRS Status: 501(c)3
Highest Offering: Doctorate
Accreditation: HLC, COARC, DMS, NURSE, OT, PTAA, RAD, SURGT

01 President ... Dr. Deb CARLSON
05 Vice President Academic Affairs ... Dr. Amy CLARK
108 VP Institutional Effectiveness ... Ms. Lindsay SNIPES
84 Chief Enrollment/Bus Mgmt Officer ... Mrs. Jillian KRUMBACH
32 Chief Student Officer ... Ms. Sarah MURPHY
66 Dean of Nursing ... Ms. Sheila GARLAND
66 Pgm Director Undergrad Nursing ... Ms. Colleen WOODWARD
76 Dean Health Professions ... Ms. Kendra CRAVEN
58 Program Director Master's Nursing ... Dr. Marla KNIEWEL
49 Dean of Arts & Sciences ... Dr. Dean MANTERNACH
76 Director Physical Therapist Asst ... Ms. Shannon STRUBY
76 Director Respiratory Care ... Ms. Lisa FUCHS
88 Director Radiologic Technology ... Ms. Kate ROLLINS
88 Program Director Sonography ... Ms. Rebecca BOUCKAERT
88 Director Surgical Technology ... Ms. Janet MCADAMS
08 Director John Moritz Library ... Vacant
42 Coordinator Spiritual Development ... Ms. Kim HAIZLIP
29 Alumni Engagement Director ... Ms. Julie RAETHER
07 Director Enrollment Services ... Ms. Megan KOKENGE
06 Dir Student Records/Registration ... Ms. Alina BORKOWSKI
37 Director Financial Aid ... Ms. Penny JAMES
09 Director of Institutional Research ... Ms. Megan DREESZEN
04 Administrative Coordinator ... Ms. Lily KEOGH
26 Dir Marketing/Communications ... Ms. Emily PEKLO

*Nebraska State College System (F)

1327 H Street, Suite 200, Lincoln NE 68508
County: Lancaster FICE Identification: 033441
Telephone: (402) 471-2505 Carnegie Class: N/A
FAX Number: (402) 471-2669
URL: www.nscs.edu

01 Chancellor ... Dr. Paul D. TURMAN
43 General Counsel/VC for Empl Rels ... Ms. Kristin DIVEL
10 Vice Chancellor Finance/Admin ... Dr. Monte KRAMER
32 VC Student Affairs & Risk Mgmt ... Ms. Angela MELTON
18 Vice Chanc Facilities & Info Tech ... Mr. Steve HOTOVY
05 VC Acad Planning/Partnerships ... Dr. Judi KUPPER
21 Director of Financial Operations ... Mr. Robert HALADA
21 Director of Systemwide Accounting . Ms. Christina WUNDERLICH
13 System Data Analyst/Reports Devel ... Mr. Mike DUNKLE
26 Sys Dir Ext Rels/Communications ... Ms. Judi YORGES
22 System Director for Title IX ... Ms. Taylor SINCLAIR
15 Human Resource Specialist ... Ms. Kara VOGT

*Chadron State College (G)

1000 Main Street, Chadron NE 69337-2690
County: Dawes FICE Identification: 002539
Unit ID: 180948
Telephone: (308) 432-6000 Carnegie Class: Masters/M
FAX Number: (308) 432-6464 Calendar System: Semester
URL: www.csc.edu
Established: 1911 Annual Undergrad Tuition & Fees (In-State): $7,634
Enrollment: 2,330 Coed
Affiliation or Control: State IRS Status: 501(c)3
Highest Offering: Master's
Accreditation: HLC, ACBSP, CAEP, @DIETD, MUS, SW

02 President ... Dr. Randy RHINE
05 Vice President Academic Affairs ... Dr. James POWELL
10 Vice Pres Administration & Finance ... Ms. Kari GASWICK
84 VP Student Svcs/Enroll Mgmt ... Dr. Tami SELBY
13 Chief Information Officer ... Ms. Ann M. BURK
32 Dean Student Affairs ... Dr. Tara HART
58 Dean Graduate Studies/BEAMS ... Dr. Wendy WAUGH
49 Dean Essential Studies/Liberal Art ... Dr. James MARGETTS
107 Dean Prof Studies/Applied Sciences ... Vacant
21 Comptroller ... Ms. Melany HUGHES
09 Director Institutional Research ... Ms. Malinda LINEGAR
102 Chief Exec Officer CS Foundation ... Mr. Ben WATSON
06 Registrar ... Ms. Melissa MITCHELL
35 Assoc VP Student Services ... Vacant
07 Director of Admissions ... Ms. Sabrina FOX
37 Director Financial Aid ... Mr. Anthony MOREJON
15 Assoc VP Human Resources ... Ms. Anne DEMERSSEMAN
39 Director of Housing ... Mr. Austen STEPHENS
41 Athletics Director ... Mr. Joel SMITH
36 Director of Internships/Career Svcs ... Ms. Deena KENNELL
114 Budget Director ... Ms. Jordan HAEFLE
26 Director College Relations ... Mr. Alex HELMBRECHT
18 Director Facilities ... Mr. Todd BAUMANN
04 Admin Assistant to the President ... Ms. Julie HASZ

*Peru State College (H)

PO Box 10, Peru NE 68421-0010
County: Nemaha FICE Identification: 002559
Unit ID: 181534
Telephone: (402) 872-3815 Carnegie Class: Masters/M
FAX Number: (402) 872-2407 Calendar System: Semester
URL: www.peru.edu
Established: 1867 Annual Undergrad Tuition & Fees (In-State): $7,920
Enrollment: 1,902 Coed
Affiliation or Control: State IRS Status: 501(c)3
Highest Offering: Master's
Accreditation: HLC, CAEPN

02 President ... Dr. Michael EVANS
05 Vice Pres Academic Affairs ... Dr. Tim BORCHERS
10 Vice Pres Administration & Finance ... Ms. Jennifer RIEKEN
84 Vice Pres Enroll Mgmt & Stdnt Affs ... Dr. Jesse DORMAN
102 Exec Director PSC Foundation ... Mr. Ted HARSHBARGER
41 Director of Athletics ... Mr. Wayne ALBURY
26 Dir of Marketing & Communications ... Vacant
06 Dir Student Records/Col Registrar ... Ms. Heather RINNE
37 Director of Financial Aid ... Ms. Denise LICKTEIG
08 Director of Library ... Ms. Veronica MEIER
15 Director of Human Resources ... Ms. Eulanda CADE
18 Director Facility Services ... Mr. Keith BAILEY
21 Director of Business Services ... Ms. Julie COATNEY
07 Director of Admissions ... Ms. Cindy CAMMACK
38 Licensed Student Counselor ... Ms. Jamie EBERLY
108 Director Institutional Assessment ... Mr. Paul TRANA
13 Chief Info Technology Officer (CIO) ... Mr. Gene BEARDSLEE
19 Director Security/Safety ... Mr. Tim ROBERTSON
04 Admin Assistant to the President ... Ms. Amy MINCER

*Wayne State College (I)

1111 Main Street, Wayne NE 68787-1172
County: Wayne FICE Identification: 002566
Unit ID: 181783
Telephone: (402) 375-7000 Carnegie Class: Masters/L
FAX Number: (402) 375-7204 Calendar System: Semester
URL: www.wsc.edu
Established: 1909 Annual Undergrad Tuition & Fees (In-State): $7,428
Enrollment: 4,202 Coed
Affiliation or Control: State IRS Status: 501(c)3
Highest Offering: Beyond Master's But Less Than Doctorate
Accreditation: HLC, ART, CACREP, CAEP, DIETD, IACBE, MUS

02 President ... Dr. Marysz RAMES
05 Vice President Academic Affairs ... Mr. Steven ELLIOTT
20 Assoc VP for Academic Affairs ... Dr. Anne MCCARTHY
10 Vice Pres Admin/Finance ... Ms. Angela FREDRICKSON
21 Assoc VP Administration & Finance ... Ms. Barbara MEYER
102 CEO Foundation Office ... Mr. Kevin ARMSTRONG
32 Vice President of Student Affairs ... Mr. C.D DOUGLAS
13 Chief Information Officer ... Mr. Nick MUIR
37 Director Financial Aid ... Ms. Tiffany REED
07 Director of Admissions ... Mr. Kevin HALLE
38 Director of Counseling ... Ms. Alicia DORCEY MCINTOSH
39 Director of Residence Life ... Vacant
36 Director of Career Services ... Ms. Jason BARELMAN
26 Director College Relations ... Mr. Jay COLLIER
41 Director of Athletics ... Mr. Mike POWICKI
18 Director of Facility Services ... Mr. Kyle NELSEN
08 Director of Library Services ... Mr. David GRABER
06 Registrar ... Ms. Rebeka WILSON
112 Director of Major Gifts ... Ms. Melissa NELSEN
29 Director of Alumni Relations ... Ms. Amber SPERRY
15 Director of Human Resources ... Ms. Candace TIMMERMAN
79 Dean School of Arts & Humanities ... Dr. David BOHNERT
50 Dean Sch of Business & Technology ... Dr. Anne POWER
53 Dean Sch of Educ/Behavioral Science ... Dr. Nicholas SHUDAK
83 Dean Sch of Sci/Health/Crim Justice ... Dr. Ron LOGGINS
93 International/Multicultural Coord ... Mr. Edi HERNANDEZ
09 Director Institutional Research ... Ms. Jeannette BARRY
04 Admin Assistant to the President ... Ms. Joni BACKER
19 Campus Security Manager ... Mr. Jason MRSNY
78 Exec Dir Coop Educ & Indust Liaison ... Mr. Michael KEIBLER

Nebraska Wesleyan University (J)

5000 St. Paul Avenue, Lincoln NE 68504-2794
County: Lancaster FICE Identification: 002555
Unit ID: 181446
Telephone: (402) 466-2371 Carnegie Class: Masters/S
FAX Number: (402) 465-2179 Calendar System: Semester
URL: www.nebrwesleyan.edu
Established: 1887 Annual Undergrad Tuition & Fees: $36,854
Enrollment: 1,924 Coed
Affiliation or Control: United Methodist IRS Status: 501(c)3
Highest Offering: Master's
Accreditation: HLC, CAATE, MUS, NURSE, SW

01 President ... Dr. Darrin S. GOOD
00 Chair of the Board ... Ms. Cori VOKOUN
100 Chief of Staff ... Ms. Sara OLSON
05 Provost ... Dr. Graciela CANEIRO-LIVINGSTON
10 Vice Pres Finance/Administration ... Ms. Tish GADE-JONES
84 Vice President Enrollment Mgmt ... Mr. Bill MOTZER
111 Vice President Advancement ... Mr. John GREVING
32 Vice President Student Life ... Dr. Erin HOFFMAN
42 Univ Minister/Church Relations ... Rev. Eduardo BOUSSON
58 Dean of Graduate Programs ... Dr. Jennifer ZIEGLER
20 Dean of Undergraduate Programs ... Dr. Jodi RYTER
88 Assoc Prov Integral/Exper Learning ... Dr. Meghan WINCHELL
06 Asst Provost & Univ Registrar ... Ms. Brooke GLENN
21 Asst VP & Controller ... Mr. Greg D. MASCHMAN

121 Asst Dean Stdnt Success/Engagement ...... Ms. Karri SANDERSON
124 Asst Dean Stdnt Success/Persistence .... Ms. Candice HOWELL
39 Asst Dean Stdnt Success/Res Educ .... Ms. Brandi SESTAK
88 Asst Dean Stdnt Success/Campus Comm .. Ms. Janelle ANDREINI
41 Athletic Director .... Vacant
08 University Librarian .... Ms. Julie PINNELL
09 Data Analyst/IR Specialist .... Mr. Ricky HULL
38 Director Counseling Services .... Dr. Kimberly CORNER
07 Director of Admissions .... Mr. Gordie COFFIN
104 Director of Global Engagement .... Ms. Sarah BARR
102 Director of Foundation Relations .... Ms. Tara GREGG
23 Director Student Health Services .... Ms. Karri AHLSCHWEDE
13 Director of Computer Services .... Mr. Steven R. DOW
24 Director Instructional Technology .... Mr. Jay L. KAHLER
91 Director Administrative Systems .... Mr. Mark MURPHY
92 Director Wesleyan Honors Academy .... Dr. Marian BORGMANN-INGWERSEN
30 Director of Development .... Ms. Mary HAWK
36 Director Career Development .... Ms. Kim AFRANK
37 Director of Financial Aid .... Mr. Tom J. OCHSNER
15 Director of Human Resources .... Ms. Maria HARDER
18 Director of Physical Plant .... Mr. Jim RUZICKA
26 Director of Marketing .... Ms. Peggy S. HAIN
27 Director of Public Relations .... Mr. Hunter REEVES
105 Director Web Services .... Mr. Eric ASPEGREN
29 Director of Alumni Relations .... Ms. Shelley MCHUGH
04 Exec Asst to President .... Mr. Matt TEWES
28 Asst Director Diversity & Inclusion .... Ms. Wendy HUNT
44 Manager Annual Giving .... Ms. Ashley MURRAY-HANSEN
112 Planned Giving Officer .... Vacant
122 Asst Dn Stdnt Involve-Greek Life .... Ms. Karri SANDERSON-TOBLER

Northeast Community College (A)

801 E Benjamin, PO Box 469, Norfolk NE 68702-0469
County: Madison FICE Identification: 011667
Unit ID: 181491
Telephone: (402) 371-2020 Carnegie Class: Assoc/HVT-Mix Trad/Non
FAX Number: (402) 844-7400 Calendar System: Semester
URL: www.northeast.edu
Established: 1973 Annual Undergrad Tuition & Fees (In-District): $3,750
Enrollment: 5,105 Coed
Affiliation or Control: Local IRS Status: 501(c)3
Highest Offering: Associate Degree
Accreditation: HLC, ADNUR, CAHIIM, EMT, PTAA

01 President .... Dr. Leah BARRETT
10 VP Administrative Services .... Mr. Scott GRAY
13 Vice President Technology Services .... Mr. Paul FEILMEIER
32 Vice President Student Services .... Mrs. Amanda NIPP
30 VP Development/External Affairs .... Dr. Tracy L. KRUSE
05 VP Educational Services .... Vacant
15 Vice President Human Resources .... Ms. Jessica DVORAK
75 Dean of Applied Technology .... Ms. Shanelle GRUDZINSKI
50 Dean of Business .... Dr. Wade HERLEY
76 Dean of Health/Public Services .... Dr. Jeff HOFFMAN
81 Dean Science/Tech/Agric/Math .... Mrs. Tara SMYDRA
45 Dean of Institutional Effectiveness .... Mrs. Michela KEELER-STROM
18 Exec Director of Physical Plant .... Mr. Brandon MCLEAN
121 Dean of Student Success .... Ms. Shelley LAMMERS
61 Dean of Workforce Development .... Dr. Cyndi HANSON
06 Registrar .... Mrs. Makala MAPLE
37 Financial Aid Director .... Ms. Stacy DIECKMAN
96 Director of Purchasing .... Mr. Chris RUTTEN
66 Director of Nursing Programs .... Mrs. Karen K. WEIDNER
26 Director of Public Relations .... Mr. James CURRY
40 Retail Services Manager .... Mrs. Julie CARLSON
07 Director of Recruitment .... Mr. Anthony FAUST
35 Director of Student Activities .... Ms. Carissa KOLLATH
39 Director Res Life & Stdnt Conduct .... Dr. Emily NORMAN
114 Director of Budgeting .... Mrs. Chris MCKIBBON
09 VP Inst Research & Analytics .... Mrs. Danielle GIBSON
16 Dir Compensation & HR Compliance .... Mrs. Carly SALAK
104 Dir Global & Multicultural Engage .... Ms. Pam SAALFELD
19 Dir of Safety/Emer Preparedness .... Vacant
25 Chief Contract/Grants Administrator .... Mr. Kent WARNEKE
11 Exec Director Administrative Svcs .... Mrs. Coleen BRESSLER
08 Director of Library Services .... Vacant
38 Dir Student Care & Outreach .... Ms. Gina KRYSL
27 Exec Dir of Marketing/Recruitment .... Mrs. Jennifer GREVE
36 Director of Career Services .... Mrs. Terri HEGGEMEYER
04 Executive Assistant to President .... Mrs. Diane REIKOFSKI

Saint Gregory the Great Seminary (B)

800 Fletcher Road, Seward NE 68434-8145
County: Seward Identification: 667027
Unit ID: 486114
Telephone: (402) 643-4052 Carnegie Class: Not Classified
FAX Number: (402) 643-6964 Calendar System: Semester
URL: www.sggs.edu
Established: 1998 Annual Undergrad Tuition & Fees: N/A
Enrollment: N/A Male
Affiliation or Control: Roman Catholic IRS Status: 501(c)3
Highest Offering: Baccalaureate
Accreditation: HLC

01 Rector/President .... Rev. Brian KANE
05 Academic Dean .... RevFr. Matthew ROLLING
13 Vice Rector/Director of Technology .... Rev. John ROONEY

Southeast Community College (C)

4771 West Scott Road, Beatrice NE 68310-7042
Telephone: (402) 228-3468 Identification: 770341
Accreditation: &HLC

Southeast Community College (D)

301 S 68 Street Place, Lincoln NE 68510-2449
County: Lancaster FICE Identification: 025083
Unit ID: 181640
Telephone: (402) 323-3400 Carnegie Class: Assoc/HVT-Mix Trad/Non
FAX Number: (402) 323-3420 Calendar System: Semester
URL: www.southeast.edu
Established: 1973 Annual Undergrad Tuition & Fees (In-District): $2,664
Enrollment: 9,328 Coed
Affiliation or Control: State/Local IRS Status: 501(c)3
Highest Offering: Associate Degree
Accreditation: HLC, ACBSP, ACFEI, ADNUR, COARC, CSHSE, DA, EMT, MAC, MLTAD, NAEYC, PNUR, POLYT, PTAA, RAD, SURGA, SURGT

01 President .... Dr. Paul ILLICH
05 VP for Instruction .... Dr. Joel MICHAELIS
22 VP Access/Equity/Diversity .... Mr. Jose SOTO
11 VP Admin Svcs/Resource Devel .... Ms. Amy G. JORGENS
32 Vice Pres Student Services .... Ms. Bev CUMMINS
46 VP Research/Planning/Technology .... Mr. Ed KOSTER
15 Vice Pres Human Resources/Safety .... Mr. Bruce TANGEMAN
88 VP for Program Development .... Dr. Brett BRIGHT
106 Dean of Virtual Learning .... Mr. Bruce EXSTROM
35 Dean of Students .... Ms. Stacy RILEY
35 Dean of Students .... Ms. Toni LANDENBERGER
35 Dean of Students .... Ms. Theresa WEBSTER
84 Dean Student Enrollment .... Mr. Mike PEGRAM
37 Director of Financial Aid .... Ms. Melissa TROYER
06 Admin Director Registration .... Ms. Nancy MCCONKEY
07 Admin Director Admissions .... Ms. Kat KREIKEMEIER
26 Dir of Public Information/Marketing .... Mr. Stu OSTERTHUN
09 Admin Dir Institutional Research .... Ms. Robin MOORE
102 Foundation Director .... Ms. Michelle BIRKEL
90 Information Services Manager .... Mr. Alan BRUNKOW
04 Assistant to the President .... Ms. Katy NOVAK
88 Operations Assistant .... Ms. Amy BASSEN
51 Dean Continuing Education .... Ms. Amy CHESLEY
18 Director of Facilities .... Mr. Aaron EPPS
45 Admin Director Planning & Accred .... Ms. Shawna HERWICK

Southeast Community College (E)

600 State Street, Milford NE 68405-8498
Telephone: (402) 761-2131 Identification: 770342
Accreditation: &HLC

Summit Christian College (F)

2025 21st Street, Gering NE 69341
County: Scotts Bluff Identification: 667209
Unit ID: 181543
Telephone: (308) 632-6933 Carnegie Class: Spec-4-yr-Faith
FAX Number: N/A Calendar System: Semester
URL: www.summitcc.edu
Established: 1951 Annual Undergrad Tuition & Fees: $7,570
Enrollment: 34 Coed
Affiliation or Control: Independent Non-Profit IRS Status: 501(c)3
Highest Offering: Baccalaureate
Accreditation: BI

01 President .... David K. PARRISH
05 Academic Dean .... Scott GRIBBLE
88 Director of Operations .... Melissa PROHS
06 Registrar .... Kayleen COLLOPY
07 Director of Admissions .... Emilie YATES
88 Administrative Assistant .... Anne MULHOLLAND

Union College (G)

3800 S 48th Street, Lincoln NE 68506-4300
County: Lancaster FICE Identification: 002563
Unit ID: 181738
Telephone: (402) 486-2600 Carnegie Class: Bac-Diverse
FAX Number: (402) 486-2895 Calendar System: Semester
URL: www.ucollege.edu
Established: 1891 Annual Undergrad Tuition & Fees: $25,340
Enrollment: 757 Coed
Affiliation or Control: Seventh-day Adventist IRS Status: 501(c)3
Highest Offering: Master's
Accreditation: HLC, ARCPA, CAEP, NURSE, OTA, SW

01 President .... Dr. Vinita SAUDER
05 Vice President for Academic Admin .... Vacant
10 Vice President for Financial Admin .... Mr. Steve TRANA
32 Vice President Student Life .... Ms. Kim CANINE
111 Vice President for Advancement .... Ms. LuAnn DAVIS
42 Vice President for Spiritual Life .... Mr. David KABANJE
08 Library Director .... Ms. Bliss KUNTZ
13 Director of Information Systems .... Mr. Richard HENRIQUES
33 Dean of Men .... Mr. Daniel FORCE
06 Director Records/Registrar .... Ms. Rachael BOYD
07 Director Enrollment & Admissions .... Mr. Kevin ERICKSON
26 Director of Public Relations .... Mr. Ryan TELLER
29 Director Alumni Relations .... Ms. Peggy CARLSON
37 Director Student Financial Aid .... Ms. Laurie WHEELER
15 Human Resources Director .... Ms. Lisa R. FORBES
36 Career Center Coordinator .... Ms. Trina CRESS
09 Director of Institutional Research .... Mr. Tim SIMON
19 Director Security/Safety .... Mr. Dustin SAUDER
39 Dir Resident Life/Student Housing .... Mr. Chris CANINE

Universal College of Healing Arts (H)

8702 N 30th Street, Omaha NE 68112-1810
County: Douglas FICE Identification: 038214
Unit ID: 446598
Telephone: (402) 556-4456 Carnegie Class: Spec 2-yr-Health
FAX Number: N/A Calendar System: Semester
URL: www.ucha.edu
Established: 1995 Annual Undergrad Tuition & Fees: $11,327
Enrollment: 29 Coed
Affiliation or Control: Proprietary IRS Status: Proprietary
Highest Offering: Associate Degree
Accreditation: ABHES

01 President .... Ms. Paulette GENTHON
37 Director Student Financial Aid .... Ms. Patty EDEN

*University of Nebraska Central Administration (I)

3835 Holdrege, Lincoln NE 68583-0745
County: Lancaster FICE Identification: 008025
Unit ID: 181747
Telephone: (402) 472-8636 Carnegie Class: N/A
FAX Number: (402) 472-1237
URL: www.nebraska.edu

01 President .... Mr. Ted E. CARTER
05 Exec Vice President & Provost .... Dr. Jeffrey GOLD
10 Sr Vice Pres Business & Finance .... Mr. Chris KABOUREK
43 VP/General Counsel .... Mrs. Stacia PALSER
47 VP Agriculture/Natural Res .... Dr. Michael J. BOEHM
100 Chief of Staff .... Mr. Phillip BAKKEN
13 VP Information Technology .... Mr. Bret R. BLACKMAN
86 VP External Relations .... Mr. Heath M. MELLO
18 Assoc VP/Dir Facility Plng/Mgmt .... Mr. Ryan SWANSON
09 Asst VP/Dir Inst Research/Planning .... Vacant
88 Asst VP P-16 Initiatives .... Dr. Steven T. DUKE
85 Asst VP Global Strategy/Intl .... Vacant
26 Asst VP Ext Rels/Dir Mktg Brand .... Ms. Jacqueline M. OSTROWICKI
28 Chief Diversity/Inclusion Officer .... Ms. Stancia J. JENKINS
04 Exec Assistant to the President .... Ms. Jayne SUTTON
41 Athletic Director .... Mr. Trev ALBERTS
50 Dean of Business .... Dr. Kathleen A. FARRELL
53 Dean of Education .... Dr. Sherri JONES
54 Dean of Engineering .... Dr. Lance PEREZ

*University of Nebraska at Kearney (J)

2504 9th Avenue, Kearney NE 68849
County: Buffalo FICE Identification: 002551
Unit ID: 181215
Telephone: (308) 865-8208 Carnegie Class: Masters/L
FAX Number: (308) 865-8665 Calendar System: Semester
URL: www.unk.edu
Established: 1903 Annual Undergrad Tuition & Fees (In-State): $7,962
Enrollment: 6,225 Coed
Affiliation or Control: State IRS Status: 501(c)3
Highest Offering: Beyond Master's But Less Than Doctorate
Accreditation: HLC, CAATE, CACREP, CAEP, CIDA, MACTE, MUS, NAIT, SP, SW

02 Chancellor .... Mr. Douglas A. KRISTENSEN
05 Sr Vice Chanc Academic Affairs .... Ms. Kristen MAJOCHA
10 Vice Chanc Business & Finance .... Mr. Jon C. WATTS
84 VC for Enrollment Mgmt & Marketing ..... Ms. Kelly H. BARTLING
30 Vice President Development .... Mr. Lucas DART
13 AVP/Chief Information Officer .... Ms. Andrea CHILDRESS
21 Assoc Vice Chanc Business & Finance .... Ms. Jane SHELDON
49 Dean Arts & Sciences .... Dr. Ryan L. TETEN
50 Dean Business/Technology .... Dr. Tim E. JARES
53 Dean of Education .... Dr. Mark REID
100 Exec Assistant to the Chancellor .... Dr. John FALCONER
58 Dean Graduate Studies .... Dr. Mark ELLIS
32 Interim Dean of Student Affairs .... Mr. George HOLMAN
06 Dir Student Records/Registration .... Ms. Lisa NEAL
08 Dean of the Library .... Mr. Evan BOYD
36 Dir Academic Advising/Career Svcs .... Ms. Amy L. RUNDSTROM
07 Dir UG Recruitment/Admissions .... Ms. Jodi HOLT
18 Dir Facilities Mgmt & Planning .... Mr. Michael CREMERS
19 Director Police .... Mr. James F. DAVIS
22 Dir Affirm Action/Equal Opportunity .... Ms. Mary J. CHINNOCK PETROSKI
09 Director Academic Resources .... Ms. Megan M. FRYDA
26 Sr Dir Communications & Marketing .... Mr. Todd GOTTULA
29 Director Alumni Services .... Mr. Lucas DART
35 Director Student Life .... Ms. Renae ZIMMER
23 Director Counseling & Health Care .... Ms. Wendy L. SCHARDT
39 Director Residence Life .... Ms. Trelana DANIEL
40 Director Bookstore .... Mr. Len J. FANGMEYER
41 Director Intercollegiate Athletics .... Dr. Marc BAUER
88 Director Finance .... Ms. Jill PURDY
108 Director Assessment .... Dr. Beth D. HINGA
25 Director Sponsored Programs .... Mr. Travis REYNOLDS

85 Asst VC for International Educ .... Dr. Tim J. BURKINK
114 Budget Officer .... Ms. Chris MORAN
37 Director Financial Aid .... Ms. Mary SOMMERS
28 Director Diversity Outreach .... Mr. Juan GUZMAN
92 Director Honors Program .... Ms. Angela HOLLMAN
15 Director Human Resources .... Mr. Scott A. BENSON
109 Director Business Services .... Mr. Michael T. CHRISTEN

*University of Nebraska - Lincoln (A)

14th and R Streets, Lincoln NE 68588-0002
County: Lancaster FICE Identification: 002565
Unit ID: 181464
Telephone: (402) 472-7211 Carnegie Class: DU-Highest
FAX Number: (402) 472-2410 Calendar System: Semester
URL: www.unl.edu
Established: 1869 Annual Undergrad Tuition & Fees (In-State): $9,690
Enrollment: 25,108 Coed
Affiliation or Control: State IRS Status: 501(c)3
Highest Offering: Doctorate
Accreditation: HLC, ART, AUD, CAATE, CAEP, CIDA, CLPSY, COPSY, DANCE, DIET, DIETD, JOUR, LAW, LSAR, MFCD, MUS, PLNG, SCPSY, SP, THEA

02 Chancellor .... Dr. Ronnie D. GREEN
05 EVC for Academic Affairs .... Ms. Katherine ANKERSON
10 Int VC Business & Finance .... Ms. Mary LAGRANGE
32 VC Student Affairs .... Dr. Laurie BELLOWS
65 Vice Chanc Agric/Nat Resources .... Dr. Michael BOEHM
46 VC Rsrch/Economic Development .... Mr. Robert WILHELM
13 AVP Information Technology & CIO .... Mr. Heath TUTTLE
28 Vice Chanc Diversity/Inclusion .... Dr. Marco BARKER
124 Asst VC Academic Services .... Mr. James VOLKMER
86 Asst to Chanc Govt & Mil Relations .... Ms. Michelle WAITE
15 Asst Vice Chanc for Human Resources .... Mr. Bruce A. CURRIN
20 Sr Assoc Vice Chanc & Dean .... Dr. Amy GOODBURN
84 Int Asst VC for Enrollment Mgmt .... Mr. James S. VOLKMER
08 Dean University Libraries .... Ms. Claire STEWART
58 Assoc VC & Dean Grad Studies .... Dr. Debra HOPE
49 Dean Arts & Sciences .... Dr. Mark BUTTON
54 Dean Engineering .... Dr. Lance PEREZ
61 Dean of Law .... Dr. Richard MOBERLY
47 Dean Agric Science/Nat Resources .... Dr. Tiffany HENG-MOSS
50 Dean Business .... Dr. Kathy FARRELL
60 Dean Journalism/Mass Communications .... Dr. Shari VEIL
53 Dean Education & Human Sciences .... Dr. Sherri JONES
48 Int Dean College Architecture .... Ms. Sharon KUSKA
47 Dean Agricultural Research Division .... Dr. Archie CLUTTER
56 Dean/Dir Cooperative Extension .... Dr. Charles STOLTENOW
93 Director Educ Access & TRIO Pgms .... Ms. Catherine YAMAMOTO
57 Dean Fine & Performing Arts .... Dr. Andrew BELSER
37 Dir Scholarships/Financial Aid .... Mr. Justin C. BROWN
09 Dir Research/Analytics .... Mr. Jason CASEY
92 Director Honors Program .... Dr. Patrice MCMAHON
94 Director Women's Studies .... Dr. Marie-Chantal KALISA
06 University Registrar .... Mr. Steven BOOTON
36 Director Career Services Center .... Mr. Bill WATTS
19 Chief University Police Services .... Mr. Hassan RAMZAH
22 Equity/Compliance Investigator .... Ms. Meagan COUNLEY
23 Director University Health Center .... Ms. Jill LYNCH-SOSA
39 Director Housing & Dining .... Mr. Charlie FRANCIS
41 Director of Athletics .... Mr. Trev ALBERTS
106 Dir Distance Education Services .... Dr. Nancy ADEN-FOX
29 Exec Director Alumni Association .... Ms. Shelley ZABOROWSKI
26 Chief Communication/Mktg Ofcr .... Ms. Deb FIDDELKE
30 Chief Development .... Mr. Brian HASTINGS
38 Director Student Counseling .... Dr. Robert N. PORTNOY
96 Director of Procurement Services .... Ms. Maggie L. WITT
07 Director of Admissions .... Ms. Abby FREEMAN
100 Chief of Staff .... Dr. Michael ZELENY
104 Director Education Abroad .... Ms. Rebecca BASKERVILLE

*University of Nebraska Medical Center (B)

987020 Nebraska Medical Center, Omaha NE 68198-7020
County: Douglas FICE Identification: 006895
Unit ID: 181428
Telephone: (402) 559-4000 Carnegie Class: Spec-4-yr-Eng
FAX Number: (402) 559-4396 Calendar System: Semester
URL: www.unmc.edu
Established: 1869 Annual Undergrad Tuition & Fees (In-State): N/A
Enrollment: 3,699 Coed
Affiliation or Control: State IRS Status: 501(c)3
Highest Offering: Doctorate
Accreditation: HLC, ABAI, ARCPA, CAMPEP, CYTO, DENT, DH, DIET, DMS, MED, MLS, NURSE, PERF, PH, PHAR, PTA, RAD, RADMAG, RTT

02 Chancellor .... Dr. Jeffery P. GOLD
05 Sr Vice Chancellor Acad Affairs .... Dr. H. Dele O. DAVIES
10 Vice Chanc Business/Fin & Bus Dev .... Ms. Anne C. BARNES
46 Vice Chancellor Research .... Dr. Jennifer LARSEN
86 Vice Chancellor External Affairs .... Mr. Robert BARTEE
45 Vice Chanc Strategic Initiatives .... Vacant
20 Assoc Vice Chanc Academic Affairs .... Dr. Gary YEE
20 Assoc Vice Chancellor iEXCEL .... Dr. Pamela BOYERS
20 Assoc Vice Chanc Global/Stdnt Supp .... Dr. Jane MEZA
88 Assoc Vice Chanc Basic Sci Rsch .... Dr. Kenneth BAYLES
88 Assoc Vice Chancellor Research .... Dr. Christopher KRATOCHVIL
88 Assoc Vice Chanc Bus Development .... Dr. Rodney MARKIN
18 Assoc Vice Chanc Facilities .... Mr. Kenneth HANSEN
13 Assoc Vice Chancellor ITS .... Dr. Michael ASH
20 Asst Vice Chanc Acad Affs/Reg Comp .... Dr. Bruce GORDON
88 Asst VC Health Security Train/Educ .... Dr. John-Martin LOWE
23 Asst Vice Chanc Campus Wellness .... Dr. Steven WENGEL
20 Asst Vice Chanc Acad Affs .... Dr. Philip COVINGTON
21 Asst Vice Chanc Business & Finance .... Mr. Jeffrey D. MILLER
15 Asst Vice Chanc for Human Resources .... Ms. Sarah GLODEN CARLSON
08 Asst Vice Chanc & Director Library .... Ms. Emily J. MCELROY
58 Dean Graduate Studies .... Dr. H. Dele O. DAVIES
52 Dean College of Dentistry .... Dr. Janet GUTHMILLER
63 Dean College of Medicine .... Dr. Bradley E. BRITIGAN
66 Dean College of Nursing .... Dr. Juliann SEBASTIAN
67 Dean College of Pharmacy .... Dr. Keith OLSEN
69 Dean College of Public Health .... Dr. Ali KHAN
76 Dean College of Allied Health Prof .... Dr. Kyle P. MEYER
88 Dir Eppley Cancer Research Inst .... Dr. Kenneth H. COWAN
88 Director Munroe-Meyer Institute .... Dr. Karoly MIRNICS
43 Assoc Gen Counsel Hlth Sci .... Ms. Tara SCROGIN
37 Director Financial Aid Office .... Ms. Paula KOHLES
26 Director of Public Relations .... Mr. William O'NEILL
29 Director Alumni Relations .... Ms. Catherine MELLO
38 Exec Dir Counseling & Student Dev .... Dr. David S. CARVER
28 Director of Diversity .... Ms. Linda CUNNINGHAM
96 Director Procurement & Mtrls Mgt .... Mr. Robert JENNINGS
09 Director Institutional Research .... Ms. Jeanne FERBRACHE
19 Asst Vice Chanc/Chief of Police .... Ms. Charlotte EVANS

*University of Nebraska at Omaha (C)

6001 Dodge Street, Omaha NE 68182-0001
County: Douglas FICE Identification: 002554
Unit ID: 181394
Telephone: (402) 554-2262 Carnegie Class: DU-Higher
FAX Number: (402) 554-3555 Calendar System: Semester
URL: www.unomaha.edu
Established: 1908 Annual Undergrad Tuition & Fees (In-State): $8,136
Enrollment: 15,892 Coed
Affiliation or Control: State IRS Status: 501(c)3
Highest Offering: Doctorate
Accreditation: HLC, AAB, ART, CAATE, CACREP, CAEPN, MUS, SP, SPAA, SW

02 Chancellor .... Dr. Joanne LI
05 Sr Vice Chanc Acad/Student Affs .... Dr. Deborah SMITH-HOWELL
10 Vice Chanc Business & Finance .... Ms. Carol KIRCHNER
13 Chief Information Officer .... Mr. Bret BLACKMAN
84 Assoc Vice Chanc Enroll Mgmt Svcs .... Vacant
58 Dean Graduate Studies .... Dr. Juan CASAS
57 Dean Fine Arts/Communication/Media .... Dr. Michael HILT
53 Dean of Education .... Dr. Nancy EDICK
50 Dean of Business Administration .... Dr. Michelle TRAWICK
49 Dean of Arts & Sciences .... Dr. Melanie BLOOM
104 Associate Vice Chancellor Global .... Dr. Jane L. MEZA
72 Dean Info Science/Technology .... Dr. Martha GARCIA-MURILLO
80 Dean Public Affairs/Community .... Dr. John R. BARTLE
62 Dean of Library Services .... Mr. David E. RICHARDS
09 Dir Institutional Effectiveness .... Mr. Andrew ROBINSON
32 Int AVC Student Affs/Dean of Stdnts .... Ms. Cathy PETTID
15 Assoc VC Human Resources .... Ms. Aileen WARREN
18 Director Facilities Mgmt/Planning .... Mr. Larry MORGAN
06 Registrar .... Mr. Matt SCHILL
07 Director of Admissions .... Ms. Rashonda AUSTIN
37 Director Financial Aid .... Mr. Marty HABROCK
88 Director Student Testing Center .... Mr. John GOLKA
41 Vice Chanc/Director of Athletics .... Mr. Adrain DOWELL, JR.
29 President/CEO Alumni Association .... Vacant
26 Exec Dir University Communications .... Ms. Makayla MCMORRIS
96 Procurement Systems Coordinator .... Ms. Lynn MCALPINE
40 Manager Book Store .... Vacant
19 Director of Public Safety .... Ms. Charlotte EVANS
106 Director Online Educ/E-learning .... Dr. Jaci LINDBURG
28 Chief Diversity Officer .... Dr. A.T MILLER, JR.
122 Dir Stdnt Involve-Greek Life Adv .... Mr. Dustin WOLFE

*University of Nebraska - Nebraska College of Technical Agriculture (D)

404 E 7th Street, Curtis NE 69025-9502
County: Frontier FICE Identification: 007358
Unit ID: 181765
Telephone: (308) 367-4124 Carnegie Class: Spec 2-yr-Other
FAX Number: (308) 367-5203 Calendar System: Semester
URL: www.ncta.unl.edu
Established: 1913 Annual Undergrad Tuition & Fees (In-State): $5,483
Enrollment: 282 Coed
Affiliation or Control: State IRS Status: 501(c)3
Highest Offering: Associate Degree
Accreditation: HLC

02 Dean .... Dr. Larry GOSSEN
10 Assoc Dean Finance/Ops/Student Svcs .... Mrs. Jennifer A. MCCONVILLE
21 Business Manager .... Ms. Jan GILBERT
04 Administrative Associate to Dean .... Ms. Josi ARNOLD
06 Registrar .... Mrs. Victoria LUKE
08 Head Librarian .... Mr. Mo KHAMOUNA
09 Director of Institutional Research .... Ms. Mary RITTENHOUSE
39 Residence Life Manager .... Vacant

Western Nebraska Community College (E)

1601 E 27th Street, Scottsbluff NE 69361-1815
County: Scotts Bluff FICE Identification: 002560
Unit ID: 181817
Telephone: (308) 635-3606 Carnegie Class: Assoc/MT-VT-Mix Trad/Non
FAX Number: (308) 635-6100 Calendar System: Semester
URL: www.wncc.edu
Established: 1926 Annual Undergrad Tuition & Fees (In-District): $2,976
Enrollment: 1,625 Coed
Affiliation or Control: State/Local IRS Status: 501(c)3
Highest Offering: Associate Degree
Accreditation: HLC, CAHIIM, MLTAD, PNUR, SURGT

01 Interim President .... Mr. John MARRIN
05 Vice President of Educational Svcs .... Dr. Grant WILSON
10 Vice Pres Administrative Services .... Ms. Lynne KOSKI
84 Vice President of Enrollment .... Mr. William KNAPPER
15 Executive Director of HR .... Ms. Kathy AULT
88 Executive Director of Partnerships .... Ms. Paula ABBOTT
102 Foundation Executive Director .... Ms. Jennifer REISIG
108 Executive Director Assessment & IR .... Dr. Patrick FORTNEY
103 Dean of Instruction & Workforce Dev .... Dr. Charlie GREGORY
32 Executive Dean of Students .... Dr. Norman COLEY, JR.
121 Assoc Dean Instruct Support Svcs .... Ms. Ellen DILLON
35 Assistant Dean of Students .... Ms. Brynn ELLIOTT
06 Registrar .... Mr. Brian ELKINS
37 Financial Aid Director .... Ms. Sheila JOHNS
26 Public Relations & Marketing Dir .... Ms. Allison JUDY
38 Counseling Director .... Mr. Norman STEPHENSON
21 Accounting Services Director .... Mr. David KOEHLER
41 Athletic Director .... Mr. Ryan BURGNER
51 Lifelong Learning Director .... Ms. Lori STROMBERG
07 Admissions Director .... Ms. Gretchen FOSTER
29 Director Alumni Relations/Steward .... Ms. Mary SHEFFIELD
124 Student Engagement Director .... Ms. Megan WESCOAT
39 Residence Life Director .... Ms. Molly BONUCHI
13 Information Technology Director .... Mr. Loren MOENCH
40 Bookstore Operations Director .... Mr. Rich RIDDICK
19 Safety/Environmental Mgmt Director .... Mr. Josh VESPER
09 Institutional Research Officer .... Mr. Dustin EICKE
106 Instructional Tech Coordinator .... Ms. Heidi JACKSON
88 Academic Testing & Tutoring Coord .... Ms. Tammie KLEICH
08 Chief Library Officer .... Ms. Allison REISIG
28 Inclusion Coordinator .... Ms. Maricia GUZMAN
83 Div Chair Soc Sciences & Human Perf .... Ms. Jacklyn CAWIEZEL
76 Division Chair Health Sciences .... Vacant
81 Division Chair Math & Science .... Ms. Amy WINTERS
72 Division Chair Applied Tech .... Mr. Daniel JOPPA
79 Div Chair Acad Enrich/Lang/Fine Art .... Vacant
66 Nursing Program Director .... Ms. Rebecca KAUTZ
88 Surg Tech Program Director .... Ms. Marcene ELWELL
88 Health Info Technology Program Dir .... Ms. Nicole DANIELZUK
66 BNA Program Director .... Ms. Sherri YORGES
88 Med Lab Tech Program Director .... Vacant
88 EMS Program Director .... Mr. Ken BOSTON
04 Admin Assistant to the President .... Ms. Susan VERBECK

York College (F)

1125 E 8th Street, York NE 68467-2699
County: York FICE Identification: 002567
Unit ID: 181853
Telephone: (402) 363-5600 Carnegie Class: Bac-Diverse
FAX Number: (402) 363-5623 Calendar System: Semester
URL: www.york.edu
Established: 1890 Annual Undergrad Tuition & Fees: $19,810
Enrollment: 652 Coed
Affiliation or Control: Churches Of Christ IRS Status: 501(c)3
Highest Offering: Master's
Accreditation: HLC, CAEP

01 President .... Dr. Sam SMITH
05 Provost .... Dr. Shane MOUNTJOY
10 Vice President Finance & Operations .... Mr. Todd SHELDON
111 Vice Pres Advancement .... Mr. Jared STARK
42 VP for Spiritual Development .... Dr. Sam GARNER
32 VP for Student Development .... Mrs. Catherine SEUFFERLEIN
21 Business Manager .... Mr. Dan COLE
06 Registrar .... Mr. Jared LEINEN
35 Dean of Students .... Ms. Meghan SHRUCK
08 Director of Information Commons .... Vacant
26 Director of Publications .... Mr. Steddon L. SIKES
37 Financial Aid Director .... Mr. Brien ALLEY
40 Campus Store Manager .... Mrs. Janet RUSH
18 Supervisor Buildings & Grounds .... Mr. Bob GAVER
73 Chair Bible .... Dr. Frank E. WHEELER
88 Chair History .... Mr. Tim D. MCNEESE
50 Chair English .... Dr. Aleshia O'NEAL
81 Chair Math/Sciences .... Dr. Bryan KRETZ
57 Chair Performing Arts/Communication .... Dr. Clark A. ROUSH
29 Alumni Relations Officer .... Mr. Brent MAGNER
04 Executive Asst to President .... Mrs. Gayle A. GOOD
13 Chief Info Technology Officer (CIO) .... Mr. Joel COEHOORN
39 Director Student Housing .... Ms. Jennifer OTTE
106 Dir Online Education/E-learning .... Dr. Cheryl COUCH
07 Director of Admissions .... Mr. David ODOM
15 Human Resources Manager .... Mr. Dan COLE

NEVADA

Career College of Northern Nevada (G)

1421 Pullman Drive, Sparks NV 89434
County: Washoe FICE Identification: 026215
Unit ID: 181941
Telephone: (775) 241-4445 Carnegie Class: Assoc/HVT-Mix Trad/Non

FAX Number: (775) 856-0935 Calendar System: Quarter
URL: www.ccnn.edu
Established: 1984 Annual Undergrad Tuition & Fees: N/A
Enrollment: 385 Coed
Affiliation or Control: Proprietary IRS Status: Proprietary
Highest Offering: Associate Degree
Accreditation: ACCSC

01 President .... Mr. L. Nathan N. CLARK
05 Academic Dean .... Mr. Robert MCLAUGHLIN

Carrington College - Las Vegas (A)

5740 S Eastern Avenue, Suite 140, Las Vegas NV 89119
Telephone: (702) 688-4300 Identification: 770742
Accreditation: &WJ, COARC, MAC, PTAA

† Regional accreditation is carried under the parent institution in Sacramento, CA.

Carrington College - Reno (B)

5580 Kietzke Lane, Reno NV 89511
Telephone: (775) 335-2900 Identification: 770743
Accreditation: &WJ, ADNUR, MAC

† Regional accreditation is carried under the parent institution in Sacramento, CA.

Chamberlain University-Las Vegas (C)

9901 Covington Cross Drive, Las Vegas NV 89144
Telephone: (702) 786-1660 Identification: 770852
Accreditation: &HLC, NURSE

† Branch campus of Chamberlain University-Addison, Addison, IL

Las Vegas College (D)

8410 N Rafael Rivera Way, Las Vegas NV 89113
County: Clark FICE Identification: 022375
Unit ID: 182148
Telephone: (702) 567-1920 Carnegie Class: Spec 2-yr-Health
FAX Number: (702) 566-9725 Calendar System: Semester
URL: https://www.lvcollege.edu/
Established: 2004 Annual Undergrad Tuition & Fees: $14,903
Enrollment: 399 Coed
Affiliation or Control: Independent Non-Profit IRS Status: 501(c)3
Highest Offering: Associate Degree
Accreditation: ACCSC, ADNUR

01 CEO/CFO .... Peter MIKHAIL
03 Executive Vice President .... Bob ALLEN
05 Campus Director/Academic Dean .... David DOLBOW
06 Registrar .... Marjorie ZELAYA
07 Director of Admissions .... George VEGERANO

*Nevada System of Higher Education (E)

2601 Enterprise Road, Reno NV 89512-1666
County: Washoe FICE Identification: 008026
Unit ID: 182519
Telephone: (775) 784-4901 Carnegie Class: N/A
FAX Number: (775) 784-1127
URL: www.nevada.edu

01 Officer in Charge .... Ms. Crystal ABBA
05 VC Acad & Stdnt Affs/Cmty Colleges .... Ms. Crystal ABBA
10 Chief Financial Officer .... Mr. Andrew CLINGER
101 Chief of Staff of Board of Regents .... Mr. Michael FLORES
43 Chief General Counsel .... Mr. Joseph REYNOLDS
86 VC Public Affairs/Advancement .... Ms. Constance BROOKS

*College of Southern Nevada (F)

6375 W Charleston Boulevard, Las Vegas NV 89146-1139
County: Clark FICE Identification: 010362
Unit ID: 182005
Telephone: (702) 651-5000 Carnegie Class: Bac/Assoc-Assoc Dom
FAX Number: N/A Calendar System: Semester
URL: www.csn.edu
Established: 1971 Annual Undergrad Tuition & Fees (In-State): $3,878
Enrollment: 29,965 Coed
Affiliation or Control: State IRS Status: 501(c)3
Highest Offering: Baccalaureate
Accreditation: NW, ACBSP, ACFEI, ACPHA, ADNUR, CAHIIM, CEA, COARC, DA, DH, DMS, EMT, MAC, MLS, MLTAD, NUR, OPD, PNUR, PTAA, SURGT

02 President .... Dr. Federico ZARAGOZA
04 Executive Assistant .... Ms. Annette LORD
100 Chief of Staff .... Mr. Lawrence WEEKLY
10 VP for Finance & Administration .... Ms. Mary Kaye BAILEY
32 VP for Student Affairs .... Ms. Juanita CHRYSANTHOU
05 VP Academic Affairs .... Mr. James MCCOY
12 VP/Provost Henderson Campus .... Ms. Patricia A. CHARLTON
12 VP/Provost Charleston Campus .... Dr. Sonya PEARSON
12 VP/Provost North Las Vegas Campus .... Dr. Clarissa COTA
102 Exec Director CSN Foundation .... Vacant
18 AVP Facilities/Opers/Maint .... Ms. Sylvia KIM
43 Legal Counsel .... Mr. James MARTINES
06 Dir Student Affairs/Registrar .... Ms. Bernadette LOPEZ-GARRETT
103 Exec Dir Workforce Education .... Vacant
72 Dean Adv & Applied Technologies .... Dr. Michael SPANGLER
81 Dean Science & Math .... Dr. Douglas SIMS
83 Dean Social Sciences & Education .... Dr. Charles OKEKE
79 Interim Dean Arts & Letters .... Dr. Vartouhi ASHERIAN
76 Dean Health Sciences .... Ms. Janice GLASPER
50 Dean of Business .... Dr. Marcus JOHNSON
96 Associate VP of Purchasing .... Mr. Rolando MOSQUEDA
41 Director of Athletics .... Mr. L. Dexter IRVIN
114 Assoc Vice Pres Budget Services .... Ms. Lisa BAKKE
09 Exec Dir of Institutional Research .... Vacant
08 Interim Dir Library Services .... Ms. Emily KING
37 Associate VP for Financial Aid .... Mr. Tyler HEU
19 Chief of Police .... Mr. Adam GARCIA
13 Technology CIO .... Mr. Mugunth VAITHYLINGAM
15 Chief HR Officer .... Dr. Bill DIAL
28 Executive Director of Diversity .... Mr. Lawrence WEEKLY
106 Dir Online Education/E-learning .... Mr. Terry NORRIS
22 Director of Institutional Equity .... Dr. Armen ASHERIAN
86 Director Government Relations .... Ms. Mariana KIHUEN

*Great Basin College (G)

1500 College Parkway, Elko NV 89801-5032
County: Elko FICE Identification: 006977
Unit ID: 182306
Telephone: (775) 327-5002 Carnegie Class: Bac/Assoc-Mixed
FAX Number: (775) 327-5131 Calendar System: Semester
URL: www.gbcnv.edu
Established: 1967 Annual Undergrad Tuition & Fees (In-State): $3,248
Enrollment: 3,772 Coed
Affiliation or Control: State IRS Status: 501(c)3
Highest Offering: Baccalaureate
Accreditation: NW, ADNUR, CSHSE, DMS, EMT, NUR, RAD

02 President .... Ms. Joyce HELENS
05 VP for Student & Academic Affairs .... Dr. Jake HINTON-RIVERA
10 Vice President for Business Affairs .... Ms. Sonja SIBERT
111 Exec Dir Advancement/Communications .... Ms. Karrie BARRET
04 Assistant to the President .... Ms. Mardell DORSA
66 Dean of Health Sciences/Human Svcs .... Dr. Amber DONNELLI
49 Dean of Arts and Sciences .... Ms. Mary DOUCETTE
75 Dean of Applied Science .... Vacant
106 Dean of Distance Education .... Mr. Karl STEVENS
09 Dir Institutional Rsrch/Effective .... Vacant
37 Dir Student Financial Svcs & VA .... Mr. Scott NIELSEN
07 Director Enrollment Services .... Vacant
12 Director Ely Center .... Ms. Veronica NELSON
12 Director Winnemucca Center .... Ms. Becky COLEMAN
12 Director Pahrump Valley Center .... Ms. Diane WRIGHTMAN
51 Director Continuing Education .... Vacant
25 Director Grants .... Ms. Nicole MAHER
43 General Counsel .... Ms. Mary DUGAN

*Nevada State College (H)

1300 Nevada State Drive, Henderson NV 89002-9455
County: Clark FICE Identification: 041143
Unit ID: 441900
Telephone: (702) 992-2000 Carnegie Class: Bac-Diverse
FAX Number: (702) 992-2226 Calendar System: Semester
URL: www.nsc.edu
Established: 2002 Annual Undergrad Tuition & Fees (In-District): $6,075
Enrollment: 7,289 Coed
Affiliation or Control: State/Local IRS Status: 501(c)3
Highest Offering: Master's
Accreditation: NW, NURSE, SP

02 President .... Dr. DeRionne POLLARD
05 Provost/Exec Vice President .... Dr. Vickie SHIELDS
28 VP of College/Cmty Engagement .... Dr. Edith FERNANDEZ
10 SVP Finance & Business Operations .... Kevin BUTLER
53 Dean of Education .... Dr. Dennis POTTHOFF
49 Dean of Liberal Arts & Sciences .... Dr. Elizabeth GUNN
66 Dean of Nursing .... Dr. June EASTRIDGE
20 Executive Vice Provost .... Dr. Tony SCINTA
121 Vice Provost Student Success .... Dr. Gregory ROBINSON
15 Assoc VP of Human Resources .... Eric GILLILLAND
06 Registrar .... Adelfa SULLIVAN
08 Director of Library Services .... Nathaniel KING
09 Director of Institutional Research .... Dr. Sandip THANKI
37 Director Student Financial Aid .... Anthony MORRONE

*Truckee Meadows Community College (I)

7000 Dandini Boulevard, Reno NV 89512-3999
County: Washoe FICE Identification: 021077
Unit ID: 182500
Telephone: (775) 673-7000 Carnegie Class: Bac/Assoc-Assoc Dom
FAX Number: (775) 673-7108 Calendar System: Semester
URL: www.tmcc.edu
Established: 1971 Annual Undergrad Tuition & Fees (In-State): $2,862
Enrollment: 10,249 Coed
Affiliation or Control: State IRS Status: 501(c)3
Highest Offering: Associate Degree
Accreditation: NW, ACFEI, ADNUR, DA, DH, DIETT, EMT, NAEYC, RAD

02 President .... Dr. Karin HILGERSOM
04 Executive Assistant to President .... Ms. Melissa OLSEN
05 VP Academic Affairs .... Dr. Jeffrey ALEXANDER
26 Assoc VP Research/Mktg & Web Svcs .... Ms. Elena BUBNOVA
09 Director Institutional Research .... Ms. Cheryl SCOTT
32 VP Student Services & Diversity .... Ms. Estela LEVARIO GUTIERREZ
102 Exec Dir Foundation/Development .... Mrs. Gretchen SAWYER
07 Director Admissions & Records .... Mr. Andrew HUGHES
21 Controller Accounting Services .... Mr. Rich WILLIAMS
37 Director Financial Aid .... Ms. Leslie JIA
124 Exec Dir Retention and Support Svcs .... Ms. Joan STEINMAN
114 Exec Director Budget & Planning .... Ms. Elise BUNKOWSKI
15 Interim Director Human Resources .... Ms. Kim STUDEBAKER
103 Dir Workforce Devel/Cmty Education .... Vacant
08 Learning Commons Director .... Ms. Brandy SCARNATI
13 Chief Information Technology Office .... Mr. Thomas DOBBERT
19 Asst Vice Pres/Chief of Police .... Mr. Eric JAMES
28 Director of Diversity .... Ms. YeVonne ALLEN
41 Athletic Director .... Ms. Tina RUFF
18 Executive Director Facilities .... Dr. Ayodele AKINOLA

*University of Nevada, Las Vegas (J)

4505 S Maryland Parkway, Las Vegas NV 89154-1001
County: Clark FICE Identification: 002569
Unit ID: 182281
Telephone: (702) 895-3201 Carnegie Class: DU-Highest
FAX Number: (702) 895-1088 Calendar System: Semester
URL: www.unlv.edu
Established: 1957 Annual Undergrad Tuition & Fees (In-State): $8,685
Enrollment: 31,142 Coed
Affiliation or Control: State IRS Status: 501(c)3
Highest Offering: Doctorate
Accreditation: NW, ART, CAATE, CACREP, CAMPEP, CIDA, CLPSY, CONST, DENT, DIETD, DIETI, HSA, IPSY, LAW, LSAR, MED, MFCD, MUS, NURSE, PH, PTA, RAD, SPAA, SW

02 President .... Dr. Keith E. WHITFIELD
100 Chief of Staff .... Dr. Fred TREDUP
05 Executive Vice President & Provost .... Dr. Chris HEAVEY
10 SVP Finance & Business/CFO .... Mrs. Jean VOCK
41 Director of Athletics .... Mr. Erick HARPER
32 Int VP for Student Affairs .... Dr. B. Keith ROGERS
19 Vice Pres Public Safety .... Mr. Adam GARCIA
46 VP Research & Economic Development .... Dr. Bo BERNHARD
88 VP University Compliance .... Mr. Robert CORREALES
30 VP Philanthropy & Alumni Engagement .... Mr. Rickey MCCURRY
86 VP Govt & Community Affairs .... Mrs. Sabra NEWBY
26 VP Brand & Chief Marketing Officer .... Mr. Vince ALBERTA
28 VP Div Init/Chief Diversity Officer .... Mr. Seval YILDIRIM
43 General Counsel .... Mrs. Elda SIDHU
45 Exec Dir Strategic Initiatives .... Dr. Kyle KAALBERG
88 Senior Advisor to the President .... Dr. Tod FITZPATRICK
84 AVP Enrollment & Student Services .... Vacant
88 Asst VP Student Affairs/Finance .... Ms. Summer MUDD
35 Assoc VP for Student Affairs .... Dr. Renee WATSON
29 Sr Dir for Alumni Programs & Events .... Mr. Blake DOUGLAS
31 Int Exec Dir of Community Relations .... Mrs. Sue DIBELLA
15 VP Human Resources Officer .... Dr. Ericka SMITH
87 Vice Provost Educational Outreach .... Mr. Joseph MIERA
20 Vice Provost Academic Programs .... Dr. Javier RODRIGUEZ
20 Vice Provost for Undergraduate Educ .... Dr. Laurel PRITCHARD
09 Vice Provost Decision Support .... Dr. Brent DRAKE
13 Vice Provost Information Technology .... Dr. Lori TEMPLE
58 Dean of Graduate College .... Dr. Kate H. KORGAN
50 Interim Dean Business .... Dr. Paulette TANDY
49 Dean Liberal Arts .... Dr. Jennifer KEENE
53 Interim Dean of Education .... Dr. Danica HAYS
54 Dean of Engineering .... Dr. Rama VENKAT
66 Dean of Nursing .... Dr. Angela AMAR
63 Dean School of Medicine .... Dr. Marc J. KAHN
52 Dean School of Dental Medicine .... Dr. Lily T. GARCIA
61 Dean School of Law .... Mr. Daniel W. HAMILTON
81 Dean of Sciences .... Dr. Eric CHRONISTER
88 Dean College of Hotel Admin .... Dr. Stowe SHOEMAKER
57 Dean Fine Arts .... Dr. Nancy USCHER
08 Dean of Libraries .... Ms. Maggie FARRELL
88 Dean Urban Affairs .... Dr. Robert R. ULMER
92 Dean Honors College .... Dr. Andrew HANSON
121 Dean Academic Success Center .... Dr. Ann MCDONOUGH
88 Dean Community Health Sciences .... Dr. Shawn GERSTENBERGER
76 Dean Sch Allied Health Sciences .... Dr. Ronald T. BROWN
06 Registrar .... Dr. Sam FUGAZZOTTO
37 Dir Financial Aid & Scholarships .... Mr. Norm BEDFORD
39 Executive Director Residential Life .... Mr. Richard CLARK
38 AVP Student Wellness .... Dr. Jamie DAVIDSON
23 Director Student Health .... Ms. Kathy A. UNDERWOOD
96 Director Purchasing .... Ms. Sharrie MAYDEN
85 Dir International Students/Scholars .... Ms. Marianna PANOSSI
25 Director Sponsored Programs .... Ms. Lori CICCONE

*University of Nevada, Reno (K)

1664 N. Virginia Street, Reno NV 89557
County: Washoe FICE Identification: 002568
Unit ID: 182290
Telephone: (775) 784-1110 Carnegie Class: DU-Highest
FAX Number: (775) 784-1300 Calendar System: Semester
URL: www.unr.edu
Established: 1874 Annual Undergrad Tuition & Fees (In-State): $8,366
Enrollment: 20,722 Coed
Affiliation or Control: State IRS Status: 501(c)3
Highest Offering: Doctorate
Accreditation: NW, ABAI, #ARCPA, CACREP, CLPSY, DIETD, DIETI, IPSY, JOUR, MED, MUS, NURSE, PH, SP, SW

02 President .... Mr. Brian SANDOVAL
05 Exec Vice President & Provost .... Dr. Jeff THOMPSON
11 Vice Pres Administration & Finance .... Mr. Victor REDDING
63 Actg VP Health Sci/Dean Sch of Med .... Dr. Melissa PIASECKI
111 VP for Advancement .... Mr. Bill JOHNSON
32 Vice President for Student Services .... Dr. Shannon ELLIS
46 Vice President for Research .... Dr. Mridul GAUTAM
08 Dean of Libraries .... Dr. Catherine CARDWELL
20 Vice Prov Instr/Undergrad Programs .... Dr. David SHINTANI
20 Vice Provost Faculty Affairs .... Dr. Jill HEATON
58 Vice Provost/Dean Grad School .... Dr. Markus KEMMELMEIER
10 Assoc VP Business & Finance .... Ms. Sheri MENDEZ
84 Assoc VP Enrollment Services .... Dr. Melisa N. CHOROSZY
32 Dean of Students .... Dr. Leilani KUPO
45 Assoc VP Plng/Budget/Analysis .... Mr. Rashawn NORMAN
18 Asst Vice Pres Facilities Svcs .... Mr. Sean MCGOLDRICK
21 Controller .... Ms. Kara GRIFFIN
41 Director Athletics .... Mr. Doug KNUTH
96 Director Purchasing .... Mr. Raymond MORAN
19 Director University Police Svcs .... Mr. Eric JAMES
22 Dir Equal Opportunity & Title IX .... Ms. Maria DOUCETTPERRY
37 Director Financial Aid .... Ms. Lourdes GONZALES
39 Director Resident Life & Housing . Mr. Rodney L. AESCHLIMANN
23 Director Student Health Svcs .... Dr. Cheryl HUG-ENGLISH
09 Manager of Decision Support .... Mr. Cody CRIGG
86 Dir Govt Affairs & Ext Relations .... Mr. Michael FLORES
65 Dir Mackay Sch Mines/Earth Science .... Dr. Anna HUHTA
66 Interim Dean of Nursing .... Dr. Cameron DUNCAN
57 Director School of the Arts .... Dr. Tamara SCRONCE
25 Director Sponsored Projects .... Ms. Charlene HART
40 Director Wolf Shop .... Ms. Amy LEWIS
49 Interim Dean Liberal Arts .... Dr. Casilde ISABELLI
47 Dean Agriculture/Biotech/Nat Res .... Dr. William PAYNE
50 Dean Business Administration .... Dr. Gregory MOSIER
53 Dean of Education & Human Dev .. Dr. Donald EASTON-BROOKS
54 Dean Engineering .... Dr. Emmanuel MARAGAKIS
60 Dean School of Journalism .... Mr. Alan STAVITSKY
81 Dean College of Science .... Dr. Katherine MCCALL
70 Acting Dean School of Social Work .... Dr. Lillian WICHINSKY
07 Director of Admissions .... Dr. Stephen MAPLES
29 Director Alumni Relations .... Ms. Amy CAROTHERS
06 Associate Registrar .... Ms. Heather TURK FIECOAT
26 Exec Dir Marketing & Comm .... Ms. Kerri GARCIA
04 Executive Asst to President .... Ms. Aubrey FLORES
100 Chief of Staff .... Ms. Patricia RICHARD
104 Dir/CEO Univ Study Abroad Consort .... Dr. Alyssa NOTA
13 Chief Info Technology Officer (CIO) .... Mr. Steven SMITH
28 Dir Ctr for Student Cultural Dev .... Mr. Jose M. PULIDO LEON
43 General Counsel .... Ms. Mary DUGAN
112 Director of Planned Giving .... Ms. Lisa RILEY
69 Dean School of Public Health .... Dr. Mugi AKPINAR-ELCI

*Western Nevada College (A)

2201 W College Parkway, Carson City NV 89703-7316
County: Carson FICE Identification: 010363
Unit ID: 182564
Telephone: (775) 445-3000 Carnegie Class: Bac/Assoc-Assoc Dom
FAX Number: (775) 445-3051 Calendar System: Semester
URL: www.wnc.edu
Established: 1971 Annual Undergrad Tuition & Fees (In-State): $3,548
Enrollment: 3,495 Coed
Affiliation or Control: State IRS Status: 501(c)3
Highest Offering: Baccalaureate
Accreditation: NW, ADNUR

02 Interim President .... Dr. J. Kyle DALPE
04 Assistant to the President .... Ms. Deb CONRAD
05 VP of Academic & Student Affairs .... Dr. Dana RYAN
43 Deputy General Counsel .... Mr. Kiah BEVERLY
10 Chief Financial Officer .... Ms. Coral LOPEZ
88 Director Child Development Center .... Ms. Anna Lisa ACOSTA
38 Director of Counseling/Advising .... Ms. Piper MCCARTHY
18 Director Facilities Mgmt/Planning .... Mr. Jeff ERICKSON
37 Director Financial Aid .... Mr. John (JW) LAZZARI
08 Director of Learning & Innovation .... Mr. Ron BELBIN
07 Interim Director of Admissions .... Ms. Chelsie HAMTAK
102 Exec Director of WNC Foundation .... Ms. Niki GLADYS
09 Director of Institutional Research .... Ms. Cathy FULKERSON
13 Director of Computing Services .... Ms. Phyllis MASON
15 Director Human Resources .... Ms. Melody DULEY
35 Student Life Coordinator .... Ms. Heather RIKALO
49 Academic Director Liberal Arts .... Mr. Scott MORRISON
72 Academic Director Career & Tech Div .... Dr. Dana RYAN
66 Int Director Nursing/Allied Health .... Ms. Deborah INGRAFFIA STRONG
19 Police Services Commander .... Mr. Tod MILLER

Northwest Career College (B)

7398 Smoke Ranch Road, Las Vegas NV 89128
County: Clark FICE Identification: 038385
Unit ID: 445948
Telephone: (702) 254-7577 Carnegie Class: Assoc/HVT-Mix Trad/Non
FAX Number: (702) 256-9181 Calendar System: Other
URL: www.northwestcareercollege.edu
Established: 1997 Annual Undergrad Tuition & Fees: N/A
Enrollment: 1,723 Coed
Affiliation or Control: Proprietary IRS Status: Proprietary
Highest Offering: Associate Degree
Accreditation: ABHES

01 President/Founder .... Dr. John KENNY
05 Chief Academic Officer .... Dr. Stephanie KENNY
11 Chief Operating Officer .... Patrick KENNY
10 Chief Financial Officer .... Michael KENNY
37 Director of Financial Aid .... Dana MCILWAIN
36 Director of Career Services .... Tina SPENCER
09 Director of Compliance .... Thomas KENNY
07 Director of Admissions .... Sophia PALOMINO
13 Director of Technology .... Pablo CHACON
06 Registrar .... Century LEIGH

Pima Medical Institute-Las Vegas (C)

3333 E Flamingo Road, Las Vegas NV 89121-4329
Telephone: (702) 458-9650 Identification: 666273
Accreditation: ABHES, COARC, OTA, PTAA

† Branch campus of Pima Medical Institute, Tucson, AZ.

Roseman University of Health Sciences (D)

11 Sunset Way, Henderson NV 89014-2333
County: Clark FICE Identification: 040653
Unit ID: 445735
Telephone: (702) 990-4433 Carnegie Class: Spec-4-yr-Other Health
FAX Number: (702) 990-4435 Calendar System: Other
URL: www.roseman.edu
Established: 1999 Annual Undergrad Tuition & Fees: N/A
Enrollment: 1,554 Coed
Affiliation or Control: Independent Non-Profit IRS Status: 501(c)3
Highest Offering: Doctorate
Accreditation: NW, DENT, IACBE, NURSE, PHAR

01 President .... Dr. Renee COFFMAN
12 Chancellor Henderson Campus .... Dr. Eucharia E. NNADI
10 VP Business & Finance .... Mr. Doug DAWES
11 VP of Operations .... Mr. Terrell SPARKS
03 Vice President Executive Affairs .... Dr. Charles F. LACY
26 VP Communications & Partnerships .... Mr. Jason ROTH
09 VP Qual Assurance/Intercampus Cons .... Dr. Thomas METZGER
32 VP for Student Services .... Dr. Michael DEYOUNG
45 VP Strategic Implementation/Engage .... Ms. Vanessa MANIAGO
67 Dean College of Pharmacy .... Dr. Larry FANNIN
66 Dean College of Nursing .... Dr. Brian OXHORN
52 Dean College of Dental Medicine .... Dr. Frank LICARI
37 Director of Financial Aid .... Ms. Sally MICKELSON
15 Director of Human Resources .... Ms. Saralyn BARNES
08 Director of Library Services .... Ms. Tiffani GARRETT

Touro University Nevada (E)

874 American Pacific Drive, Henderson NV 89014
Telephone: (702) 777-8687 Identification: 770966
Accreditation: &WC, ARCPA, NURSE, &OSTEO, OT, PTA

† Branch campus of Touro University California, Vallejo, CA

University of Phoenix Las Vegas Campus (F)

3755 Breakthrough Way, Ste. 100,
Las Vegas NV 89135-3047
Telephone: (702) 352-2944 Identification: 770220
Accreditation: &HLC, ACBSP

† Branch campus of University of Phoenix, Phoenix, AZ-No longer enrolling new students

Wongu University of Oriental Medicine (G)

8620 S Eastern Avenue, Las Vegas NV 89123
County: Clark Identification: 667262
Unit ID: 488907
Telephone: (702) 463-2122 Carnegie Class: Spec-4-yr-Other Health
FAX Number: (702) 946-5050 Calendar System: Quarter
URL: www.wongu.edu
Established: 2012 Annual Graduate Tuition & Fees: N/A
Enrollment: 45 Coed
Affiliation or Control: Independent Non-Profit IRS Status: 501(c)3
Highest Offering: Master's; No Undergraduates
Accreditation: ACUP

01 Interim President .... Michael GIAMPAOLI
05 Academic Dean .... Dr. Sang HYUN LEE
10 Chief Financial Officer/HR .... Carolyn YANAI
06 Registrar/Financial Aid Officer .... Chau NGUYEN
07 Director Admissions/Marketing .... Michael GIAMPAOLI

NEW HAMPSHIRE

Colby-Sawyer College (H)

541 Main Street, New London NH 03257-7835
County: Merrimack FICE Identification: 002572
Unit ID: 182634
Telephone: (603) 526-3000 Carnegie Class: Bac-Diverse
FAX Number: N/A Calendar System: Semester
URL: www.colby-sawyer.edu
Established: 1837 Annual Undergrad Tuition & Fees: $44,930
Enrollment: 910 Coed
Affiliation or Control: Independent Non-Profit IRS Status: 501(c)3
Highest Offering: Master's
Accreditation: EH, ACBSP, CAATE, NURSE

01 President .... Dr. Susan D. STUEBNER
05 Academic Vice Pres/Dean of Faculty .... Dr. Laura A. SYKES
10 Vice Pres for Finance and Admin .... Ms. Karen I. BONEWALD
32 Vice Pres Stdnt Dev/Dean of Stdnts .... Ms. Robin BURROUGHS DAVIS
111 Vice President Advancement .... Mr. Daniel B. PARISH
07 Vice Pres Admissions/Financial Aid .... Ms. Anna D. MINER
26 Vice Pres Marketing/Communications .... Mr. Gregg MAZZOLA
15 Vice Pres Human Resources .... Dr. Ronnie J. PRICE, SR.
21 Controller/Assistant Treasurer .... Ms. Megan M. MILLER
09 Director Institutional Research .... Vacant
39 Director Residential Education .... Mr. Dave ZAMANSKY
37 Director of Financial Aid .... Ms. Beth W. RENZULLI
08 Director Library .... Ms. Malia M. EBEL
06 Registrar .... Ms. Siobhan SWANSON
13 Director Information Technology .... Mr. William ST. CYR
41 Director of Athletics .... Mr. Mitchell CAPELLE
88 Dir Student Lrng Collaborative ... Ms. Caren L. BALDWIN-DIMEO
44 Dir Annual Giving/Operations .... Mr. Luke GORMAN
29 Dir Alumni/Community Relations .... Ms. Tracey M. AUSTIN
19 Director of Campus Safety .... Mr. John YOUNG
18 Director of Facilities .... Mr. Domenic GIOIOSO, JR.
40 Bookstore Manager .... Ms. Malaika SIDMORE
23 Dir of Baird Health & Counsel Ctr .... Ms. Julie NICKNAIR-KEON
92 Wesson Honors Program Coord .... Mr. Russell MEDBERY
04 Admin Assistant to the President .... Ms. Megan E. OMAN
15 Director of Human Resources .... Ms. Heather ZAHN
28 Chief Diversity Officer .... Dr. Ronnie J. PRICE, SR.

*Community College System of New Hampshire (I)

26 College Drive, Concord NH 03301
County: Merrimack Identification: 666462
Telephone: (603) 230-3500 Carnegie Class: N/A
FAX Number: (603) 271-2725
URL: www.ccsnh.edu

01 Chancellor .... Dr. Mark RUBINSTEIN
11 Chief Operating Officer .... Scott FIELDS
26 Director of Communications .... Shannon REID
111 Chief Advancement Officer .... Tim ALLISON
13 Chief Information Technology Ofcr .... Barbara SPADA

*Great Bay Community College (J)

320 Corporate Drive, Portsmouth NH 03801-2879
County: Rockingham FICE Identification: 002583
Unit ID: 183150
Telephone: (603) 427-7600 Carnegie Class: Assoc/MT-VT-High Non
FAX Number: (603) 334-6308 Calendar System: Semester
URL: www.greatbay.edu
Established: 1945 Annual Undergrad Tuition & Fees (In-State): $7,200
Enrollment: 1,565 Coed
Affiliation or Control: State IRS Status: 501(c)3
Highest Offering: Associate Degree
Accreditation: EH, ACBSP, ADNUR, SURGT

02 President .... Dr. Cheryl LESSER
05 Vice President Academic Affairs .... Ms. Lisa MCCURLEY
32 VP Student Success/Enroll Mgmt .... Ms. Tina FAVARA
15 Senior Human Resources Officer .... Ms. Diane CARROLL
10 Chief Accounting Officer .... Mr. Tom ANDRUSKEVICH
37 Director Financial Aid .... Ms. Susan PROULX
06 Registrar .... Ms. Sandra HO
07 Director Admissions .... Mr. Steven GORMAN
08 Library Director .... Ms. Rebecca CLERKIN
04 Executive Asst to the President .... Mr. Christopher BLACKINGTON

*Lakes Region Community College (K)

379 Belmont Road, Laconia NH 03246-1364
County: Belknap FICE Identification: 007555
Unit ID: 183123
Telephone: (603) 524-3207 Carnegie Class: Assoc/HVT-High Non
FAX Number: (603) 527-2042 Calendar System: Semester
URL: www.lrcc.edu
Established: 1967 Annual Undergrad Tuition & Fees (In-District): $6,738
Enrollment: 697 Coed
Affiliation or Control: State/Local IRS Status: 501(c)3
Highest Offering: Associate Degree
Accreditation: EH, ADNUR, EMT

02 President .... Dr. Larissa BAIA
05 VP of Academic & Student Affairs .... Mr. Patrick CATE
10 Chief Financial Officer .... Ms. Marsha BOURDON
04 Executive Asst to President .... Ms. Elizabeth LAWTON
06 Registrar .... Vacant
102 Exec Director Foundation .... Mr. Tim ALLISON
07 Director of Admissions .... Mrs. Shawna YOUNG
37 Director Student Financial Aid .... Ms. Kristen PURRINGTON
26 Public Information Officer .... Ms. Carlene ROSE
103 Director Workforce Development .... Mr. Andrew DUNCAN
18 Chief Facilities/Physical Plnt Ofcr .... Mr. Roger LAJOIE
19 Director Security/Safety .... Mr. David STEVENS
21 Associate Business Officer .... Ms. Linda JENNINGS
35 Associate Student Affairs Officer .... Ms. Laura LEMIEN
39 Residence Director .... Mr. Eric WALSH

*Manchester Community College (A)

1066 Front Street, Manchester NH 03102-8518

County: Hillsborough FICE Identification: 002582
Unit ID: 183132
Telephone: (603) 206-8000 Carnegie Class: Assoc/MT-VT-High Non
FAX Number: (603) 668-5354 Calendar System: Semester
URL: www.mccnh.edu
Established: 1945 Annual Undergrad Tuition & Fees (In-State): $7,090
Enrollment: 2,263 Coed
Affiliation or Control: State IRS Status: 501(c)3
Highest Offering: Associate Degree
Accreditation: EH, ACBSP, ADNUR, MAC, NAEYC

02	President	Dr. Brian BICKNELL
05	Vice President Academic Affairs	Dr. Adriane LECHE
32	VP Students/Community Development	Megan CONN
07	Director of Admissions	Miho BEAN
26	Director of Marketing	Victoria JAFFE
37	Financial Aid Officer	Stephanie J. WELDON
06	Registrar	Evelyn R. PERRON
08	Library Director	Katie HAMILTON
09	Director Institutional Research	Dr. Jere TURNER
10	Business Affairs Officer	Kelly MARR
15	Human Resources Officer	Jeannie DIBELLA
40	Bookstore Manager	Cindy CORLISS
66	Nursing Director	Kimberly PERROTTA
21	Accountant I	Carol DESPATHY
13	Director Information Technology	Jean POTILLO
35	Director Student Life	Aileen CLAY
113	Bursar	Nathalie FERNS
04	Executive Asst to President	Michelle VECCHIARELLO
103	Dir Workforce/Career Development	Kristine DUDLEY
106	Dir Online Education/E-learning	Brian CHICK
18	Chief Facilities/Physical Plant	Joshua MURPHY
29	Director Alumni Relations	Vacant
19	Director of Campus Safety	Ronald PEDDLE

*Nashua Community College (B)

505 Amherst Street, Nashua NH 03063-1092

County: Hillsborough FICE Identification: 009236
Unit ID: 183141
Telephone: (603) 578-8900 Carnegie Class: Assoc/MT-VT-High Non
FAX Number: (603) 882-8690 Calendar System: Semester
URL: www.nashuacc.edu
Established: 1967 Annual Undergrad Tuition & Fees (In-State): $7,140
Enrollment: 1,352 Coed
Affiliation or Control: State IRS Status: 501(c)3
Highest Offering: Associate Degree
Accreditation: EH, ACBSP, ADNUR

02	President	Ms. Lucille A. JORDAN
05	Vice Pres Academic Affairs	Ms. Robyn GRISWOLD
32	Vice Pres Student & Community Affs	Ms. Lizbeth GONZALEZ
09	Assoc VP Inst Research/Acad Affs	Mr. Phil FRANKLAND
10	Chief Accounting Officer	Ms. Laurie BERNA
06	Registrar	Ms. Jennifer OLISZCZAK
37	Financial Aid Officer	Ms. Anne EULE
08	Director Library Services	Ms. Fran KEENAN
15	Human Resources Director	Ms. Catherine BARRY
18	Plant Maintenance Engineer	Mr. Scott BIENVENUE
19	Director of Security	Mr. Kyle METCALF
26	Director Marketing/Public Relations	Mr. Barry MEEHAN
04	Administrative Asst to President	Ms. Lucy JENKINS

*NHTI-Concord's Community College (C)

31 College Drive, Concord NH 03301-7412

County: Merrimack FICE Identification: 002581
Unit ID: 183099
Telephone: (603) 271-6484 Carnegie Class: Assoc/MT-VT-High Non
FAX Number: (603) 230-9311 Calendar System: Semester
URL: www.nhti.edu
Established: 1965 Annual Undergrad Tuition & Fees (In-State): $7,200
Enrollment: 2,945 Coed
Affiliation or Control: State IRS Status: 501(c)3
Highest Offering: Associate Degree
Accreditation: EH, #ACBSP, ADNUR, DA, DH, DMS, EMT, NAEYC, RAD, RTT

02	Interim President	Dr. Mark RUBINSTEIN
32	Interim VP Student Affairs	Dr. Rebecca DEAN
05	Vice President Academic Affairs	Dr. Andrew FISHER
10	Business Operations Officer	Ms. Marsha BOURDON
08	Coordinator of Library	Ms. Christine CHO
84	VP Student Success/Enrollment Mgmt	Dr. Rebecca DEAN
06	Registrar	Ms. Michele KARWOCKI
13	Enterprise Technology Manager	Mr. Todd BEDELL
26	Director of Communications	Dr. Anni JONES
36	Dir Residence Life/Career Counsel	Ms. Trish LORING
38	Counseling	Ms. Samantha ROBERTSON
37	Financial Aid Director	Ms. Sheri GONTHIER
19	Interim Director of Campus Safety	Mr. Jason WOVKANECH
41	Athletic Director	Mr. Paul HOGAN
15	Sr Human Resources Officer	Ms. Crystal MCINTYRE
28	Dir Cross-Cultural Education/ESOL	Ms. Dawn HIGGINS
96	Director of Purchasing	Mr. Robert BOWEN
106	Dir Online Learning	Ms. Trisha DIONNE
09	Director of Institutional Research	Mr. Gary GONTHIER
29	Director Alumni & Development	Ms. Laura A. SCOTT
39	Director Residence Life/Aux Srvs	Ms. Trish LORING

*River Valley Community College (D)

1 College Place, Claremont NH 03743-9707

County: Sullivan FICE Identification: 007560
Unit ID: 183114
Telephone: (603) 542-7744 Carnegie Class: Assoc/HVT-High Non
FAX Number: (603) 543-1844 Calendar System: Semester
URL: www.rivervalley.edu
Established: 1968 Annual Undergrad Tuition & Fees (In-State): $7,160
Enrollment: 694 Coed
Affiliation or Control: State IRS Status: 501(c)3
Highest Offering: Associate Degree
Accreditation: EH, ACBSP, ADNUR, COARC, MLTAD, OTA, PTAA, RAD

02	President	Alfred WILLIAMS
05	VP of Academic & Student Affairs	Jennifer COURNOYER
20	AVP of Academic & Student Affairs	Morgan SAILER
04	Exec Assistant to the President	Kate CROCKER
10	Chief Accounting Officer	Michelle LOCKWOOD
06	Registrar	Jillian DAVIS
84	Director of Enrollment	Suzanne GROENEWOLD
37	Director of Financial Aid	Julia DOWER
08	Director of Library Services	Sarah HEBERT
13	IT Manager	Shubhashish MATHEMA
15	Human Resource Coordinator	Connie SAMPSON

*White Mountains Community College (E)

2020 Riverside Drive, Berlin NH 03570-3799

County: Coos FICE Identification: 005291
Unit ID: 183105
Telephone: (603) 752-1113 Carnegie Class: Assoc/HVT-High Non
FAX Number: (603) 752-6335 Calendar System: Semester
URL: www.wmcc.edu
Established: 1966 Annual Undergrad Tuition & Fees (In-State): $7,050
Enrollment: 649 Coed
Affiliation or Control: State IRS Status: 501(c)3
Highest Offering: Associate Degree
Accreditation: EH, ADNUR, MAC

02	President	Dr. Charles LLOYD
05	Vice President Academic Affairs	Dr. Kristen MILLER
32	Vice President Student Affairs	Dr. Mark DESMARAIS
10	Chief Financial Officer	Vacant
15	Human Resources Officer	Gretchen TAILLON
12	Director of Academic Centers	Melanie ROBBINS
08	Director of Library Services	Melissa LAPLANTE
13	Director Computer Center	Vacant
06	Registrar	Laura PROVOST
18	Chief Facilities/Physical Plant	Scott LOCKE
40	Director Bookstore	Melissa COTE
22	Dir Affirmative Action/Equal Oppty	Vacant
91	Director Administrative Computing	Tammy VASHAW
84	Coordinator Enrollment Management	Christine GRANT
37	Asst Director Student Financial Aid	Angela LABONTE
09	Director of Institutional Research	Dr. Suzanne WASILESKI
38	Director Student Counseling	Jeff SWAYZE
04	Admin Assistant to the President	Gretchen TAILLON
19	Director Security/Safety	James ASTUTO
103	Director Workforce Development	Cynthia PIKE
50	Chair of Business Dept	Nikolaus NUTTING
53	Chair of Education Dept	Robin SCOTT
96	Coordinator of Purchasing	Cynthia MACKAY
121	Dir Student Success/Academic Advis	Nicole BOURQUE

Dartmouth College (F)

Hanover NH 03755-4030

County: Grafton FICE Identification: 002573
Unit ID: 182670
Telephone: (603) 646-1110 Carnegie Class: DU-Highest
FAX Number: N/A Calendar System: Quarter
URL: www.dartmouth.edu
Established: 1769 Annual Undergrad Tuition & Fees: $60,117
Enrollment: 6,292 Coed
Affiliation or Control: Independent Non-Profit IRS Status: 501(c)3
Highest Offering: Doctorate
Accreditation: EH, CAMPEP, IPSY, MED, PAST, PH

01	President	Dr. Philip J. HANLON
03	Executive Vice President	Mr. Richard G. MILLS
101	Secretary to Board of Trustees	Ms. Laura H. HERCOD
05	Provost	Dr. David F. KOTZ
111	Sr Vice President for Advancement	Mr. Robert W. LASHER
46	Vice Provost for Research	Dr. Dean R. MADDEN
10	CFO	Mr. R. Scott FREW
26	VP Communications	Mr. Justin ANDERSON
28	SVP/Senior Diversity Officer	Dr. Shontay DELALUE
15	Chief Human Resources Officer	Vacant
29	Vice President Alumni Relations	Ms. Cheryl A. BASCOMB
63	Dean Geisel Sch of Medicine	Dr. Duane A. COMPTON
18	VP of Campus Services	Mr. Josh KENISTON
43	General Counsel	Ms. Sandhya L. IYER
20	Dean of the College	Dr. Scott C. BROWN
06	Registrar	Mr. Eric PARSONS
07	VProv Enroll/Dean Admiss & Fin Aid	Mr. Lee A. COFFIN
37	Director of Financial Aid	Mr. Gordon D. KOFF
13	VP and Chief Information Officer	Mr. Mitchel W. DAVIS
08	Dean of Libraries	Ms. Susanne MEHRER
49	Dean of Faculty of Arts & Sciences	Dr. Elizabeth F. SMITH
50	Dean of Amos Tuck School	Dr. Matthew J. SLAUGHTER
54	Dean of the Thayer School	Dr. Alexis R. ABRAMSON
58	Dean of Graduate Studies	Dr. F. Jon KULL
42	Dean of Tucker Ctr/Col Chaplain	Rabbi Daveen H. LITWIN
41	Director of Athletics	Mr. Mike HARRITY
117	Director Risk Managment & Ins	Ms. Tina LEVENGOOD
23	Director of the Health Services	Dr. Mark H. REED
36	Dir Center for Prof Development	Ms. Monica WILSON
25	Dir Office of Sponsored Projects	Ms. Jill M. MORTALI
19	Director Safety & Security	Mr. Keiselim A. MONTAS
09	Assoc Prov Institutional Research	Dr. Elizabeth A. BARLOW
38	Dir Counseling/Human Development	Dr. Heather A. EARLE
22	Dir Equal Opportunity/Affirm Action	Vacant
96	Director of Procurement	Ms. Tammy L. MOFFATT
115	Chief Investment Officer	Ms. Alice A. RUTH
35	Assoc Dean for Student Affairs	Ms. Marianne H. THOMSON
21	Controller	Ms. Dianne J. INGALLS
04	Senior Executive Asst to President	Ms. Jennifer A. SHEPHERD
100	Chief of Staff	Ms. Laura H. HERCOD
104	Director Study Abroad	Ms. John G. TANSEY
105	Director Web Services	Mr. Jonathan CHIAPPA
106	Dir Digital Learning Initiatives	Mr. Joshua M. KIM
39	Director Residential Life	Mr. Michael W. WOOTEN

Franklin Pierce University (G)

40 University Drive, Rindge NH 03461-5046

County: Cheshire FICE Identification: 002575
Unit ID: 182795
Telephone: (603) 899-4000 Carnegie Class: Masters/M
FAX Number: (603) 899-6448 Calendar System: Semester
URL: www.franklinpierce.edu
Established: 1962 Annual Undergrad Tuition & Fees: $40,680
Enrollment: 1,928 Coed
Affiliation or Control: Independent Non-Profit IRS Status: 501(c)3
Highest Offering: Doctorate
Accreditation: EH, ARCPA, IACBE, NUR, PTA

01	President	Dr. Kim MOONEY
05	VP Academic Affairs/Provost	Dr. Catherine PADEN
10	Int Vice President Finance & CFO	Ms. Janet WALDRON
111	VP for University Advancement	Ms. Julie ZAHN
84	VP Enrollment & Univ Communications	Ms. Linda QUIMBY
32	Dean of Student Affairs	Dr. Andrew POLLOM
37	Assoc VP for Student Financial Svcs	Mr. Kenneth FERREIRA
41	Athletic Director	Ms. Rachel BURLESON
15	Director of Human Resources	Ms. Dawn BROUSSARD
06	University Registrar	Ms. Charlee EATON
08	University Librarian	Dr. Paul JENKINS
20	Exec Dean Assessment and Acad Aff	Dr. Sarah DANGELANTONIO
09	Executive Director of IR	Dr. Karen J. BROWN
79	Dean Coll Liberal Arts & Social Sci	Dr. Matthew KONIECZKA
76	Dean Coll of Health & Natural Sci	Dr. Priscilla MARSICOVETERE
50	Dean College of Business	Dr. Norman FAIOLA
36	Exec Director of Career Services	Mr. Pierre MORTON
110	Assc VP for University Advancement	Ms. Crystal NEUHAUSER
26	Director University Communication	Mr. Kenneth PHILLIPS
88	Asst Dean of Student Involvement	Mr. Scott ANSEVIN-ALLEN
39	Asst Dean Res Life & Comm Standard	Ms. Kathleen DOUGHERTY
21	Director of Finance & Accounting	Ms. Suzanne CARPENTER
18	Director of Plant Operations	Mr. Doug LEAR
28	Chief Diversity Officer	Dr. Pierre MORTON
96	Director of Purchasing	Ms. Chere HALLETT-ADAMS
104	Director Study Abroad	Ms. Patti VORFELD
13	Director of IT	Mr. Thomas TOLBERT
04	Executive Asst to the President	Ms. Heather RINGWALD

MCPHS-Manchester Campus (H)

1260 Elm Street, Manchester NH 03101
Telephone: (603) 314-0210 Identification: 770113
Accreditation: &EH, ARCPA, OT, PHAR

† Branch campus of MCPHS University, Boston, MA

New England College (I)

98 Bridge Street, Henniker NH 03242-3244

County: Merrimack FICE Identification: 002579
Unit ID: 182980
Telephone: (603) 428-2000 Carnegie Class: Masters/L
FAX Number: (603) 428-7230 Calendar System: Semester
URL: www.nec.edu
Established: 1946 Annual Undergrad Tuition & Fees: $39,648
Enrollment: 4,483 Coed
Affiliation or Control: Independent Non-Profit IRS Status: 501(c)3
Highest Offering: Doctorate
Accreditation: EH

01	Interim President	Dr. Wayne LESPERANCE
00	Chancellor	Dr. Michele D. PERKINS
05	Provost	Dr. Wayne LESPERANCE
88	Sr VP Academic Alliances	Dr. James MURTHA
10	Sr Vice President/CFO	Dr. Paula A. AMATO
08	Library Director	Ms. Chelsea HANRAHAN
108	Assoc Dean for Inst Effectiveness	Ms. Cynthia MARTIN
04	Admin Assistant to President	Ms. Holly HUDON
13	VP Technology	Mr. David RUBIN
06	Registrar	Ms. Beth DOWLING
32	Dean of Students	Mr. Jason BUCK

37 AVP of Student Financial Svcs .... Ms. Kristen BLASE
21 AVP of Finance and Administration .... Mr. Brian BOYER
36 Director Career/Life Planning .... Ms. Lindsay COATS
111 VP for Advancement .... Mr. Bill DEPTULA
15 Director of Human Resources .... Vacant
102 Director Legacy/Campaign Giving .... Mr. Gregory PALMER
18 AVP of Capital and Facilities Mgmt .... Mr. Dan GEARAN
19 Director Campus Safety .... Mr. Gregory PEPPER
35 Assoc Dean of Students .... Ms. Doreen LONG
41 Athletic Director .... Mr. Dave DECEW
09 Institutional Researcher .... Vacant
26 Exec Director Marketing/Comm .... Ms. Jen ROBERTSON
38 Director Mentoring .... Ms. Erin BROOKS
97 Dean of Undergraduate Programs .... Ms. Patricia CORBETT
14 Director Technology Services .... Vacant
28 Director of Diversity and Inclusion .... Ms. Erica SIGAUKE
29 Dir Annual Giving and Alumni Rels .... Ms. Anna TWOMBLY
50 Assoc Dean of Management ......Dr. Erin WILKINSON HARTUNG

Magdalen College of the Liberal Arts (A)

511 Kearsarge Mountain Road, Warner NH 03278-4012
County: Merrimack FICE Identification: 022233
Unit ID: 182917
Telephone: (603) 456-2656 Carnegie Class: Bac-A&S
FAX Number: (603) 456-2660 Calendar System: Semester
URL: https://magdalen.edu/
Established: 1973 Annual Undergrad Tuition & Fees: $24,000
Enrollment: 71 Coed
Affiliation or Control: Roman Catholic IRS Status: 501(c)3
Highest Offering: Baccalaureate
Accreditation: #EH

01 President .... Dr. Ryan MESSMORE
05 Academic Dean .... Dr. Brian FITZGERALD
32 Dean of Students .... Mr. Kenneth CRAMER
07 Director of Admissions .... Mrs. Michele MCKENNA
37 Director of Financial Aid .... Dr. Eric BUCK
08 Librarian .... Mrs. Marie LASHER
06 Registrar .... Ms. Catherine ORLOWSKI
10 Business Manager .... Mr. Victor PRIETO
15 Human Resources Officer .... Mrs. Michele MCKENNA
18 Facilities Manager .... Mr. John KLUCINEC
04 Admin Assistant to the President .... Mrs. Laura CRAMER

Rivier University (B)

420 S Main Street, Nashua NH 03060-5086
County: Hillsborough FICE Identification: 002586
Unit ID: 183211
Telephone: (603) 888-1311 Carnegie Class: Masters/M
FAX Number: (603) 897-8811 Calendar System: Semester
URL: www.rivier.edu
Established: 1933 Annual Undergrad Tuition & Fees: $34,510
Enrollment: 2,178 Coed
Affiliation or Control: Roman Catholic IRS Status: 501(c)3
Highest Offering: Doctorate
Accreditation: EH, ACBSP, ADNUR, NUR, PSPSY

01 President .... Sr. Paula Marie BULEY
05 Vice President for Academic Affairs .... Dr. Brian ERNSTING
10 Vice Pres Finance & Administration .... Mr. Steven PERROTTA
32 Vice President Student Affairs .... Mr. Kurt STIMELING
84 Vice Pres Enrollment Management .... Mr. Paul BROWER
111 Vice Pres University Advancement .... Ms. Karen COOPER
35 Asst Vice Pres Student Affairs .... Ms. Paula RANDAZZA
13 Chief Information Officer .... Ms. Heidi CROWELL
21 Controller .... Mr. John RIOUX
06 Registrar .... Ms. Dina BROWN
08 Library Director .... Mr. Daniel SPEIDEL
36 Director Academic & Career Advising .... Ms. Kerrie DAHL
37 Director of Financial Aid .... Ms. Kaydee RAFFERTY
15 Human Resources Manager .... Ms. Colleen MILLS
18 Director Facilities Management .... Mr. Richard PERRINE
14 Director Instructional Computing .... Sr. Martha VILLENEUVE
41 Director of Athletics .... Mr. Jonathan HARPER
42 Chaplain Campus Ministry .... Vacant
28 Multicult/Student Engagement Coord .... Mr. Ian WADE
29 Dir Alumni Relations/Special Events .... Ms. Joanne YOUNG
26 Director Marketing/Communication .... Vacant

Saint Anselm College (C)

100 Saint Anselm Drive, Manchester NH 03102-1310
County: Hillsborough FICE Identification: 002587
Unit ID: 183239
Telephone: (603) 641-7000 Carnegie Class: Bac-A&S
FAX Number: (603) 641-7116 Calendar System: Semester
URL: www.anselm.edu
Established: 1889 Annual Undergrad Tuition & Fees: $42,840
Enrollment: 2,019 Coed
Affiliation or Control: Roman Catholic IRS Status: 501(c)3
Highest Offering: Master's
Accreditation: EH, NURSE

01 President .... Dr. Joseph A. FAVAZZA
03 Executive Vice President .... Bro. Isaac MURPHY, OSB
05 Interim Vice Pres Academic Affairs .... Dr. Mark W. CRONIN
111 Sr VP College Advancement .... Mr. James P. FLANAGAN
125 President Emeritus .... Fr. Jonathan P. DEFELICE
20 Dean of the College .... Dr. Mark W. CRONIN
26 Exec Dir Col Comm & Mktg .... Mr. Paul PRONOVOST
10 Chief Financial Ofcr/Sr VP Finance .... Mr. William FURLONG
28 Chief Diversity Officer .... Dr. Ande DIAZ
29 Assistant VP Alumni & Programs .... Ms. Patrice RUSSELL
06 Registrar .... Ms. Tracy MORGAN
07 Dean of Admissions/VP Enrollment .... Mr. Steven GOETSCH
08 Interim Librarian .... Mr. John DILLON
37 Director of Financial Aid .... Ms. Elizabeth KEUFFEL
35 Dean of Students .... Dr. Alicia A. FINN
89 Dean of Freshmen .... Dr. Benjamin HORTON
121 Dean of Academic Excellence .... Dr. Christine A. GUSTAFSON
66 Exec Director of Nursing .... Dr. Maureen A. O'REILLY
04 Assistant to the President .... Ms. Valerie S. DIAZ
18 Director of Physical Plant .... Mr. Jonathan WOODCOCK
23 Director of Health Services .... Ms. Maura MARSHALL
41 Director of Athletics .... Mr. Daron MONTGOMERY
42 Director of Campus Ministry .... Dr. Susan S. GABERT
09 Director of Institutional Research .... Vacant
13 Chief Information Officer .... Mr. Steven MCDEVITT
15 Director Human Resources .... Ms. Molly MCKEAN
19 Director Security/Safety .... Mr. Robert BROWNE
53 Director Education Planning .... Dr. Laura WASIELEWSKI
28 Director Multicultural Center .... Dr. Wayne CURRIE
39 Director Student Housing .... Ms. Susan WEINTRAUB
104 Assoc Dir Study Abroad .... Ms. Jane BJERKLIE-BARRY
25 Dir Sponsored Programs & Research .... Ms. Mary MADER
44 Asst VP Individual Giving .... Mr. John DAVIS
86 Director Government Relations .... Mr. Neil LEVESQUE
102 Dir Foundation/Corporate Rels .... Ms. Sharon SWEET

St. Joseph School of Nursing (D)

5 Woodward Avenue, Nashua NH 03060
County: Hillsborough FICE Identification: 021404
Unit ID: 183248
Telephone: (603) 594-2567 Carnegie Class: Spec 2-yr-Health
FAX Number: (603) 578-5028 Calendar System: Semester
URL: www.sjson.edu
Established: 1908 Annual Undergrad Tuition & Fees: $22,764
Enrollment: 92 Coed
Affiliation or Control: Roman Catholic IRS Status: 501(c)3
Highest Offering: Associate Degree
Accreditation: ACCSC, ADNUR

01 Dean .... Vickie K. FIELER

Southern New Hampshire University (E)

2500 North River Road, Manchester NH 03106-1045
County: Hillsborough FICE Identification: 002580
Unit ID: 183026
Telephone: (603) 626-9100 Carnegie Class: Masters/L
FAX Number: (603) 645-9665 Calendar System: Semester
URL: www.snhu.edu
Established: 1932 Annual Undergrad Tuition & Fees: $9,650
Enrollment: 134,345 Coed
Affiliation or Control: Independent Non-Profit IRS Status: 501(c)3
Highest Offering: Doctorate
Accreditation: EH, ACBSP, CACREP, CAEPT, CAHIIM, NURSE

01 President .... Dr. Paul LEBLANC
04 Executive Assistant to President .... Ms. Alycia AVERY
03 Executive Vice President .... Dr. Adrian HAUGABROOK
05 Sr VP/Chief Academic Officer .. Dr. Kimberly BOGLE JUBINVILLE
88 Chief Operating Officer .... Ms. Amelia MANNING
15 Exec VP Human Resources .... Ms. Danielle STANTON
13 Exec VP Digital Transformation .... Mr. John JIBILIAN
54 EVP Col Engr/Tech/Aeronautics .... Dr. Kirk KOLENBRANDER
10 EVP F&A/Chief Financial Ofcr .... Mr. Kenneth LEE
100 Chief of Staff .... Ms. Beth PRIETO
11 EVP Campus Administration .... Mr. Donald BREZINSKI
26 SVP External Affairs/Communications .... Ms. Libby MAY
27 Chief Marketing Officer .... Ms. Alana BURNS
88 Chief Product Officer .... Mr. Travis WILLARD
43 Sr VP/General Counsel .... Ms. Yvette CLARK
28 SVP/Chief Diversity/Inclusion Ofcr .... Ms. Jada HEBRA
85 VP Assessment/Academic Ops GEM .... Ms. Rachael SEARS
20 Sr VP Global Campus .... Dr. Jennifer BATCHELOR
06 VP University Registrar .... Ms. Deanna BECHARD
32 VP Student Affairs Univ College .... Dr. Heather LORENZ
35 Chief Experience Officer .... Ms. Susan NATHAN

The Thomas More College of Liberal Arts (F)

6 Manchester Street, Merrimack NH 03054-4805
County: Hillsborough FICE Identification: 030431
Unit ID: 183275
Telephone: (603) 880-8308 Carnegie Class: Bac-A&S
FAX Number: (603) 880-9280 Calendar System: Semester
URL: www.thomasmorecollege.edu
Established: 1978 Annual Undergrad Tuition & Fees: $24,600
Enrollment: 80 Coed
Affiliation or Control: Independent Non-Profit IRS Status: 501(c)3
Highest Offering: Baccalaureate
Accreditation: EH

01 President .... Dr. William E. FAHEY
30 Exec VP/Director Inst Advancement .... Mr. Paul JACKSON
05 Academic Dean .... Dr. Walter THOMPSON
32 Dean of Students .... Mr. Denis KITZINGER
10 Director of Business .... Ms. Pamela BERNSTEIN
35 Director of Collegiate Life .... Dr. Sara KITZINGER
04 Executive Asst President's Office .... Ms. Valerie BURGESS
06 Registrar .... Ms. Pamela BERNSTEIN
07 Director of Admissions .... Mr. Zachary NACCASH
08 Librarian .... Ms. Alexis ROHLFING
18 Director of Buildings & Grounds .... Mr. Clark INGRAM

*University System of New Hampshire (G)

5 Chenell Drive, Suite 301, Concord NH 03301
County: Merrimack FICE Identification: 008027
Unit ID: 183327
Telephone: (603) 862-1800 Carnegie Class: N/A
FAX Number: (603) 862-0908
URL: usnh.edu

01 Chief Administrative Officer .... Ms. Catherine A. PROVENCHER
43 General Counsel .... Mr. Chad PIMENTEL
09 Dir of Institutional Research .... Ms. Heidi HEDEGARD
15 Chief Human Resource Officer .... Mr. James MCGRAIL
04 Admin Assistant to the President .... Ms. Tia MILLER
13 Chief Info Technology Officer (CIO) .... Mr. Bill POIRIER
26 Chief Public Relations Officer .... Ms. Lisa THORNE

*University of New Hampshire (H)

105 Main Street, Durham NH 03824
County: Strafford FICE Identification: 002589
Unit ID: 183044
Telephone: (603) 862-1234 Carnegie Class: DU-Highest
FAX Number: N/A Calendar System: Semester
URL: www.unh.edu
Established: 1866 Annual Undergrad Tuition & Fees (In-State): $18,938
Enrollment: 14,348 Coed
Affiliation or Control: State IRS Status: 501(c)3
Highest Offering: Doctorate
Accreditation: EH, CAATE, CAPRT, CARTE, DIETD, DIETI, IPSY, LAW, MFCD, MLS, MUS, NURSE, OT, PH, SP, SW

02 President .... Dr. James W. DEAN, JR.
05 Provost & VP for Academic Affairs .... Dr. Wayne E. JONES, JR.
10 Chief Financial Officer .... Mr. Marcel VERNON
13 Chief Information Officer .... Mr. Bill POIRIER
11 VP Administration/COO .... Mr. Christopher D. CLEMENT
111 VP Advancement .... Ms. Deborah DUTTON COX
41 Dir Intercollegiate Athletics .... Mr. Martin SCARANO
28 AVP Equity/Diversity/Chief Div Ofcr .... Ms. Nadine PETTY
100 Chief of Staff .... Ms. Megan W. DAVIS
20 Sr Vice Prov Academic Affairs .... Dr. Katherine ZIEMER
46 Sr Vice Provost for Research .... Dr. Marian MCCORD
32 Sr Vice Provost for Student Life .... Mr. Kenneth HOLMES
25 Asst Prov Contract Administration .... Mr. John WALLIN
47 Dean Life Sciences/Agriculture .... Dr. Jon M. WRAITH
49 Dean Liberal Arts .... Dr. Michele M. DILLON
54 Dean Engineering/Physical Sci .... Dr. Charles K. ZERCHER
50 Dean Paul College of Business .... Dr. Deborah M. MERRILL-SANDS
76 Dean Health & Human Services .... Dr. Michael FERRARA
61 Dean UNH School of Law .... Ms. Megan M. CARPENTER
12 Dean UNH at Manchester .... Dr. Michael P. DECELLE
88 Director Institute for EOS .... Dr. Harlan SPENCE
58 Dean Graduate School .... Dr. Cari A. MOORHEAD
08 Dean University Library .... Dr. Tara Lynn FULTON
56 Vice Provost University Outreach .... Dr. Kenneth J. LAVALLEY
84 Vice Provost Enrollment Management .... Dr. Pelema ELLIS
21 Assoc VP Business Affairs .... Mr. David J. MAY
18 Assoc VP Facilities .... Mr. William P. JANELLE
15 Assoc VP/Chief HR Officer .... Ms. Kathleen A. NEILS
21 Assoc VP for Finance .... Ms. Kerry L. SCALA
19 Assoc VP Public Safety & Risk Mgt .... Chief Paul M. DEAN
26 AVP Communications/Chief Mktg Ofcr .... Ms. Danielle O'NEIL
91 Sr Director for Center of Data .... Ms. Jackie SNOW
30 Assoc VP for Development .... Mr. Troy FINN
29 Assoc VP Alumni Affairs .... Ms. Susan ENTZ
88 Exec Dir Media Relations .... Ms. Erika MANTZ
39 Director Residential Life .... Ms. Ruth E. ABELMANN
23 Exec Director Health & Wellness .... Dr. Kevin E. CHARLES
25 Dir Sponsored Programs .... Ms. Louise GRIFFIN
22 Dir Affirmative Action & Equity ... Ms. Donna Marie SORRENTINO
06 Registrar .... Mr. Andrew G. COLBY
37 Dir Financial Aid .... Mr. Joel B. CARSTENS
38 Dir Psychological Services .... Dr. Shari A. ROBINSON
102 Sr Exec Dir Advance Fin/Foundation .... Mr. Erik E. GROSS
88 Dir Housing/Conf Services .... Ms. Katherine M. IRLA-CHESNEY
85 Dir Intl Students & Scholars .... Ms. Leila L. PAJE-MANALO
92 Dir Honors Program .... Dr. Lisa MACFARLANE
09 Dir Inst Research & Assessment .... Dr. Anne SHATTUCK
88 Dir Writing Program .... Dr. Edward A. MUELLER
07 Director of Admissions .... Vacant
16 Asst VP Human Resources .... Ms. Sari M. BENNETT
88 Asst VP Enterprise Comp .... Mr. William J. HALL
88 Sr VProv Engagement & Faculty Dev .... Dr. Leslie COUSE
90 Asst Vice Prov Digital Lrng & Comm .... Ms. Terri S. WINTERS

*Granite State College (I)

25 Hall Street, Concord NH 03301-7317
County: Merrimack FICE Identification: 031013
Unit ID: 183257
Telephone: (603) 228-3000 Carnegie Class: Masters/S

FAX Number: (603) 513-1389 Calendar System: Quarter
URL: www.granite.edu
Established: 1972 Annual Undergrad Tuition & Fees (In-State): $7,791
Enrollment: 1,879 Coed
Affiliation or Control: State IRS Status: 501(c)3
Highest Offering: Master's
Accreditation: EH, CAEPT, NURSE

02 President ... Mr. James DEAN
05 Provost/VP Academic Affairs ... Dr. Wayne JONES
10 Chief Financial Officer ... Mr. Marcel VERNON
84 VP Enrollment Management ... Ms. Tara PAYNE
53 Dean of School of Education ... Mr. Nick MARKS
24 Director of Educational Technology ... Ms. Reta CHAFFEE
08 Librarian ... Ms. Lia HORTON
88 Administrative Asst to Provost ... Ms. Susan L. ORR
15 Asst VP of Human Resources ... Ms. Maggie HYNDMAN
21 Asst VP of Finance ... Mr. Steve PERROTTA
18 Dir of Facilities/Safety/Sustain ... Mr. Peter CONKLIN
07 Asst VP Enrollment Ops/Admissions ... Ms. Christine WILLIAMS
121 Sr Dir of Advising/Stdnt Engagement ... Ms. Nicole HORNE
37 Director Student Financial Aid ... Mr. Mac BRODERICK
36 Director of Career Services ... Ms. Jan COVILLE
06 Registrar ... Ms. Cortney FRENCH
108 Dir Inst Effectiveness/Compliance ... Mr. Todd SLOVER
124 Director of Student Affairs ... Ms. Tiffany DOHERTY

*Keene State College (A)

229 Main Street, Keene NH 03435-0001
County: Cheshire FICE Identification: 002590
Unit ID: 183062
Telephone: (603) 352-1909 Carnegie Class: Bac-Diverse
FAX Number: (603) 358-2257 Calendar System: Semester
URL: www.keene.edu
Established: 1909 Annual Undergrad Tuition & Fees (In-State): $14,638
Enrollment: 3,210 Coed
Affiliation or Control: State IRS Status: 501(c)3
Highest Offering: Master's
Accreditation: EH, CAEPN, DIETD, DIETI, MUS, NURSE

02 President ... Dr. Melinda TREADWELL
05 Provost/VP Academic Affairs ... Dr. James BEEBY
84 VP Enrollment/Student Engagement ... Dr. MB LUFKIN
10 VP Finance & Administration ... Ms. Nathalie HOUDER
32 VP Student Affairs/Dean of Students ... Vacant
28 AVP Diversity & Inclusion ... Dr. Dottie MORRIS
111 VP Advancement/Constituent Rels ... Ms. Veronica ROSA
15 Director Human Resources ... Ms. Karen CRAWFORD
88 Dean of College Faculty ... Dr. Karrie KALICH
57 Dean Arts/Education & Humanities ... Vacant
08 Dean of Library ... Dr. Celia E. RABINOWITZ
13 Chief Information Officer ... Vacant
26 Director Strategic Communications ... Mr. Paul MILLER
20 Associate Provost ... Dr. Sue CASTRIOTTA
39 Assoc Dean Students/Dir Res Life ... Vacant
07 Director of Admissions ... Ms. Peggy RICHMOND
06 Registrar ... Vacant
37 Dir of Financial Aid/Scholarships ... Ms. Cathy MULLINS
38 Exec Dir Wellness Center ... Vacant
41 Athletic Director ... Mr. Philip RACICOT
09 Dir Inst Effectiveness & IR ... Vacant
18 Director Physical Plant ... Vacant
96 Campus Purchasing Director ... Ms. Renee HARLOW

*Plymouth State University (B)

17 High Street, MSC01, Plymouth NH 03264-1595
County: Grafton FICE Identification: 002591
Unit ID: 183080
Telephone: (603) 535-5000 Carnegie Class: Masters/L
FAX Number: (603) 535-2654 Calendar System: Semester
URL: www.plymouth.edu
Established: 1871 Annual Undergrad Tuition & Fees (In-State): $14,492
Enrollment: 4,491 Coed
Affiliation or Control: State IRS Status: 501(c)3
Highest Offering: Doctorate
Accreditation: EH, AAQEP, ACBSP, CAATE, CACREP, CAEP, NURSE, PTA, SW

02 President ... Dr. Donald L. BIRX
05 Provost/VP for Academic Affairs ... Dr. Nathaniel BOWDITCH
10 VP for Finance & Administration ... Ms. Tracy L. CLAYBAUGH
111 Director of Development ... Mr. John E. SCHEINMAN
26 Int VP of Comm/Enroll/Student Life ... Mr. Marlin COLLINGWOOD
13 USNH/UNH Chief Information Officer ... Mr. Bill POIRIER
21 Assoc VP Finance & Administration ... Ms. Mary BATCH
28 Chief Diversity Officer ... Mr. Alberto RAMOS
07 Interim Director of Admissions ... Mr. Matthew L. WALLACE
39 Dir Residence Life/Dining Svcs ... Ms. Amanda GRAZIOSO
108 Dir Institutional Effectiveness ... Ms. Melissa K. CHRISTENSEN
06 Registrar ... Ms. Tonya B. LABROSSE
30 Director of Development/Major Gifts ... Mr. John E. SCHEINMAN
29 Director of Alumni Relations ... Mr. Rodney EKSTROM
113 Director Student Financial Services ... Mr. Mac J. BRODERICK
15 Director of Human Resources ... Vacant
19 Dir Public Safety and Emer Planning . Mr. Steven H. TEMPERINO
41 Director of Athletics ... Ms. Kim M. BOWNES
18 Director of Physical Plant ... Mr. Stephen P. FOSTER
38 Dir of Counseling/Human Rel Center ... Dr. Robert W. ORF
22 Coordinator Title IX/504 ... Ms. Janette T. WIGGETT
08 Outreach Librarian ... Ms. Anne M. JUNG-MATHEWS
40 Bookstore Manager ... Mr. Steve RHEAUME
09 Director Inst Research/Innovation ... Vacant

Upper Valley Educators Institute (C)

194 Dartmouth College Hwy, Lebanon NH 03766
County: Grafton FICE Identification: 034373
Unit ID: 440004
Telephone: (603) 678-4888 Carnegie Class: Not Classified
FAX Number: (603) 678-4899 Calendar System: Other
URL: www.uvei.edu
Established: 1969 Annual Graduate Tuition & Fees: N/A
Enrollment: N/A Coed
Affiliation or Control: Independent Non-Profit IRS Status: 501(c)3
Highest Offering: Master's; No Undergraduates
Accreditation: @EH

01 Executive Director ... Dr. Page TOMPKINS

NEW JERSEY

Assumption College for Sisters (D)

200A Morris Avenue, Denville NJ 07834
County: Morris FICE Identification: 002595
Unit ID: 183600
Telephone: (973) 957-0188 Carnegie Class: Assoc/HT-High Trad
FAX Number: (973) 957-0190 Calendar System: Semester
URL: www.acs350.org
Established: 1953 Annual Undergrad Tuition & Fees: $5,773
Enrollment: 45 Female
Affiliation or Control: Roman Catholic IRS Status: 501(c)3
Highest Offering: Associate Degree
Accreditation: M

01 President/Chief of Development ... Sr. Joseph SPRING, SCC
05 Academic Dean ... Sr. Teresa BRUNO, SC
10 Treasurer/Institutional Advancement ... Mrs. Patricia MCGRADY
32 Chief Student Life Officer ... Sr. Marie LUU, SCC
06 Registrar ... Mrs. Barbara KELLY-VERGONA
13 Chf Information Technology Officer ... Mrs. Jean WEDEMEIER

Atlantic Cape Community College (E)

5100 Black Horse Pike, Mays Landing NJ 08330-2699
County: Atlantic FICE Identification: 002596
Unit ID: 183655
Telephone: (609) 343-4900 Carnegie Class: Assoc/HT-High Trad
FAX Number: (609) 343-4917 Calendar System: Semester
URL: www.atlantic.edu
Established: 1964 Annual Undergrad Tuition & Fees (In-District): $6,840
Enrollment: 4,464 Coed
Affiliation or Control: State/Local IRS Status: 501(c)3
Highest Offering: Associate Degree
Accreditation: M, ACFEI, ACPHA, ADNUR

01 President ... Dr. Barbara GABA
05 Senior VP of Academic Affairs ... Dr. Josette KATZ
32 Senior VP Student Affairs/Enroll ... Dr. Natalie DEVONISH
46 VP Inst Research/Chief Strategy ... Dr. Vanessa O'BRIEN-MCMASTERS
10 Chief Financial Officer ... Ms. Leslie JAMISON
11 Chief Business Officer ... Mr. George BOOSKOS
100 Chief of Staff/Chief Advance Ofcr ... Ms. Jean MCALISTER
13 Chief Information Officer ... Mr. John PIAZZA
26 Executive Director Marketing ... Ms. Laura BATCHELOR
12 Dean Cape May County Campus ... Ms. Maria KELLETT
49 Dean Professional & Liberal Studies ... Dr. Denise COULTER
06 Registrar ... Ms. Heather PETERSON
84 Senior Dir Enrollment & Recruitment ... Dr. Sattik DEB
37 Director Financial Aid ... Ms. Victoria DELAURENTIS
28 DEI Advocate & Judicial Officer ... Ms. Nancy PORFIDO
09 Director Institutional Research ... Mr. Luis MONTEFUSCO
96 Director Business Services ... Ms. Carol MELKONIAN
15 Director Human Resources ... Ms. Cindy DEFALCO
19 Director Security/Safety ... Mr. Clifton SUDLER
41 Director Athletics ... Mr. Jamal EDWARDS

Bais Medrash Mayan Hatorah (F)

101 Milton Avenue, Lakewood NJ 08701
County: Ocean Identification: 667280
Unit ID: 490513
Telephone: (732) 367-9900 Carnegie Class: Spec-4-yr-Faith
FAX Number: N/A Calendar System: Other
Established: Annual Undergrad Tuition & Fees: $10,650
Enrollment: 41 Male
Affiliation or Control: Independent Non-Profit IRS Status: 501(c)3
Highest Offering: Baccalaureate
Accreditation: AIJS

05 Dean ... Rabbi Abraham NEWMAN

Bais Medrash Toras Chesed (G)

910 Monmouth Avenue, Lakewood NJ 08701-1921
County: Ocean FICE Identification: 040813
Unit ID: 449658
Telephone: (732) 364-1220 Carnegie Class: Spec-4-yr-Faith
FAX Number: (732) 886-2323 Calendar System: Semester
Established: 1999 Annual Undergrad Tuition & Fees: $7,200
Enrollment: 150 Male
Affiliation or Control: Independent Non-Profit IRS Status: 501(c)3
Highest Offering: Baccalaureate
Accreditation: RABN

01 Dean ... Rabbi N. STEIN
37 Director of Financial Aid ... Mrs. H. WEISS

Bais Medrash Zichron Meir (H)

1500 Vermont Ave, Lakewood NJ 08701
County: Ocean Identification: 667259
Telephone: (732) 370-1560 Carnegie Class: Not Classified
FAX Number: (732) 363-7864 Calendar System: Semester
Established: 2013 Annual Undergrad Tuition & Fees: N/A
Enrollment: N/A Male
Affiliation or Control: Independent Non-Profit IRS Status: 501(c)3
Highest Offering: First Talmudic Degree
Accreditation: @RABN

01 CEO ... Zev MINTZ
10 CFO ... Nissim BASALA
37 Dir Student Financial Aid/Registrar ... Lipa EIDELMAN

Bergen Community College (I)

400 Paramus Road, Paramus NJ 07652-1595
County: Bergen FICE Identification: 004736
Unit ID: 183743
Telephone: (201) 447-7100 Carnegie Class: Assoc/HT-High Trad
FAX Number: (201) 447-9042 Calendar System: Semester
URL: www.bergen.edu
Established: 1965 Annual Undergrad Tuition & Fees (In-District): $8,281
Enrollment: 11,409 Coed
Affiliation or Control: State/Local IRS Status: 501(c)3
Highest Offering: Associate Degree
Accreditation: M, ADNUR, COARC, DH, DMS, EMT, MAC, RAD, RTT, SURGT

01 President ... Dr. Eric M. FRIEDMAN
05 Vice President of Academic Affairs ... Dr. Brock FISHER
32 Vice Pres Student Affairs ... Dr. Anthony J. TRUMP
19 Vice Pres of Facilities ... Mr. Nathaniel SAVIET
50 Int Dean Business/Arts/Social Sci ... Mr. Adam GOODELL
79 Dean of Humanities ... Mr. Adam GOODELL
76 Dean Health Professions ... Dr. Susan BARNARD
81 Dean Science/Math & Technology ... Ms. Emily VANDALOVSKY
51 Interim Exec Dir of Cont Educ ... Ms. Cinzia D'IORIO
08 Dean Library Services ... Mr. David MARKS
12 Dean of Off-Campus Sites ... Ms. Linda EMR
121 Dean of Student Support Services ... Ms. Jennifer REYES
15 Vice President of Human Resources ... Ms. Meredith GATZKE
18 Managing Director Physical Plant ... Mr. Michael HYJECK
13 Exec Dir of Info Technology/CIO ... Mr. Ronald SPAIDE
06 Managing Dir Registration/Records ... Ms. Jacqueline OTTEY
31 Director of Community/Cultural Affs ... Mr. Peter LEDONNE
101 Exec Asst Board of Trustees/Pres ... Ms. Maria FERRARA
29 Managing Director of Alumni Affairs ... Vacant
37 Managing Dir Stdnt Financial Ops ... Ms. Caroline OFODILE
102 Exec Dir Foundation/Development ... Mr. Ronald MILLER
25 Dir Grants Admin/Inst Effectiveness ... Dr. William YAKOWICZ
96 Director of Purchasing & Services ... Ms. Stephanie WEISE
26 Exec Dir Pub Rels & Community Cult ... Dr. Lawrence HLAVENKA
07 Managing Dir of Admissions ... Ms. Kathryn BRUNETTO

Berkeley College (J)

44 Rifle Camp Road, Woodland Park NJ 07424-3367
County: Passaic FICE Identification: 007502
Unit ID: 183789
Telephone: (973) 278-5400 Carnegie Class: Masters/S
FAX Number: N/A Calendar System: Semester
URL: www.berkeleycollege.edu
Established: 1931 Annual Undergrad Tuition & Fees: $27,000
Enrollment: 2,625 Coed
Affiliation or Control: Proprietary IRS Status: Proprietary
Highest Offering: Master's
Accreditation: M, CIDA, IACBE, MAC, #SURGT

00 Chairman of the Board ... Mr. Kevin L. LUING
01 President ... Dr. Diane RECINOS
03 Executive Vice President ... Mr. Tim LUING
05 Interim Provost ... Dr. Marianne VAKALIS
10 Vice President and Controller ... Mr. Stephen RUTKOWSKI
121 VP Academic Advisement ... Mr. Brian MAHER
32 VP Student Development/Campus Life ... Dr. Sherrille SHABAZZ
36 Vice President Career Services ... Ms. Amy SORICELLI
113 VP Student Finance &áInst Effect ... Mr. Will MOYA
13 Senior VP/Chief Information Officer ... Mr. Leonard DE BOTTON
88 VP Financial Aid Compliance ... Mr. Howard LESLIE
20 Asst Provost Teaching and Learning ... Ms. Dana HEIMLICH
50 Dean School of Business ... Dr. Joseph SCURALLI
76 Dean School Health Studies ... Vacant
107 Dean School of Professional Studies ... Dr. Marianne VAKALIS
106 Dean Online ... Dr. Joseph SCURALLI
58 Director MBA Program ... Dr. David GLAZER
58 Director MSN Program ... Ms. Eleni PELLAZGU
49 Director General Education ... Dr. Gregory HOTCHKISS
11 Campus Operating Officer ... Ms. LaTysha GAINES
37 Assoc VP Financial Aid ... Mr. Alejandro GUIRAL
15 VP Human Resources ... Ms. Karen J. CARPENTIERI
84 VP Graduate & Undergrad Enrollment ... Mr. David J. BERTONE
26 Dir Communications & Ext Relations ... Ms. Kelly DEPSEE
86 Senior VP Government Relations NJ ... Ms. Teri DUDA
06 Registrar ... Ms. Deborah PALICIA
29 AVP Alumni Relations & Career Svcs ... Mr. Michael IRIS

22 Director Accessibility Services ... Ms. Katherine WU
88 Asst VP Military & Veterans Affairs ... Mr. Edward J. DENNIS
38 Sr Director Personal Counseling ... Dr. Sandra COPPOLA
85 VP International Operations ... Dr. Nori JAFFER
123 Director Graduate Admissions ... Mr. Michael LINCOLN
18 Senior Vice President Operations ... Mr. Thomas ALESSANDRELLO
19 Asst VP Pub Safety/Emergency Mgmt ... Mr. Robert MAGUIRE
109 Senior Director Auxiliary Services ... Mr. Luis COLLAZO
119 Info Systems Security Manager ... Mr. Dana KILCREASE
09 Director of Institutional Research ... Ms. Rebecca J. DRENNEN

Best Care College (A)

68 South Harrison St, East Orange NJ 07018

County: Essex — FICE Identification: 041814 — Unit ID: 461865
Telephone: (973) 673-3900 — Carnegie Class: Not Classified
FAX Number: (973) 673-0597 — Calendar System: Trimester
URL: bestcarecollege.edu
Established: 1997 — Annual Undergrad Tuition & Fees: N/A
Enrollment: 31 — Coed
Affiliation or Control: Proprietary — IRS Status: Proprietary
Highest Offering: Associate Degree
Accreditation: ACICS

01 President ... Theodore FAYETTE

Beth Medrash Govoha (B)

617 Sixth Street, Lakewood NJ 08701-2797

County: Ocean — FICE Identification: 007947 — Unit ID: 183804
Telephone: (732) 367-1060 — Carnegie Class: Spec-4-yr-Faith
FAX Number: (732) 367-7487 — Calendar System: Semester
URL: www.yeshivanotices.org
Established: 1943 — Annual Undergrad Tuition & Fees: N/A
Enrollment: 7,159 — Male
Affiliation or Control: Independent Non-Profit — IRS Status: 501(c)3
Highest Offering: Master's
Accreditation: RABN

01 President/Chief Executive Officer ... Rabbi Yosef HEINEMANN
05 Chairman Academic Council ... Rabbi A. Malkiel KOTLER
10 Chief Financial Officer ... Mr. Isaac LEVINE
43 VP Finance/Corporate/Legal Affairs ... Rabbi Eli KUPERMAN
11 Vice President Admin/Campus Life ... Rabbi Yitzchok S. KOTLER
33 Dean of Students ... Rabbi Mattisyahu SALOMON
58 Dean of Graduate Studies ... Rabbi Yisroel NEUMAN
30 Vice President of Fundraising ... Rabbi Mordechai HERSKOWITZ
86 Director Government Affairs ... Mrs. Chanie JACOBOWITZ
06 Registrar ... Rabbi Moshe ROCKOVE
84 Director Enrollment Management ... Rabbi Gedalya A. GREEN
07 Director of Admissions ... Rabbi Avraham FEUER
08 Director Library/Research Programs ... Rabbi Benjamin SPIEGEL
36 Director of Placement ... Rabbi Yaakov SHULMAN
39 Director of Residence Halls ... Rabbi Yosef HOUSMAN
15 Director of Human Resources ... Mrs. Dina YELLIN
18 Director of Facilities ... Mr. Mottie MOSESON

Bloomfield College (C)

467 Franklin Street, Bloomfield NJ 07003-3425

County: Essex — FICE Identification: 002597 — Unit ID: 183822
Telephone: (973) 748-9000 — Carnegie Class: Bac-A&S
FAX Number: (973) 743-3998 — Calendar System: Semester
URL: www.bloomfield.edu
Established: 1868 — Annual Undergrad Tuition & Fees: $30,680
Enrollment: 1,533 — Coed
Affiliation or Control: Presbyterian Church (U.S.A.) — IRS Status: 501(c)3
Highest Offering: Master's
Accreditation: #M, CAEP, NURSE

01 President ... Dr. Marcheta P. EVANS
10 Vice President Finance/Admin ... Ms. Cynthia MCDANIEL
04 Administrative Asst to President ... Vacant
05 Vice President Academic Affairs ... Dr. Michael PALLADINO
84 VP Enrollment Mgmt ... Mr. Kevin CAVANAGH
32 VP Student Affairs ... Vacant
111 VP for Advancement ... Ms. Sarah LACZ
107 VP Global Affairs/Prof Studies ... Vacant
06 Registrar and Director of Advising ... Ms. Annette RAYMOND
09 Director Inst Research/Assessment ... Mr. Craigon CAMPBELL
79 Chair Div of Humanities ... Dr. Brandon FRALIX
83 Chair Div Social/Behavioral Science ... Dr. Daniel SKINNER
66 Chair Div of Nursing ... Dr. Frances MAL
81 Chair Div of Natural Science/Math ... Dr. Jim MURPHY
57 Chair Div Creative Arts Technology ... Prof. Yuichiro NISHIZAWA
50 Chair Div of Business ... Dr. Steven KREUTZER
53 Chair Div of Education ... Dr. Karen FASANELLA
08 Library Director ... Mr. Gregory REID
13 Director Enterprise Tech Services ... Mr. Andrew GERSTMAYR
36 Director of Ctr for Career Develop ... Vacant
37 Interim Director of Financial Aid ... Ms. Quincina LITTLEJOHN
35 Asst VP for Student Affairs ... Vacant
15 Assoc Director Human Resources ... Ms. Susan DACEY
07 Assoc Director Of Admissions ... Ms. Julia DELBAGNO
18 Supervisor of Buildings & Grounds ... Mr. Peter DOYLE
85 Coord Intl Admissions/Student Svcs ... Mr. Jorge FERNANDEZ
38 Director Personal Counseling ... Ms. Nicole PALAGANO
42 Dir Spiritual Life/College Chaplain ... Vacant

41 Director of Athletics ... Ms. Sheila WOOTEN
121 Dir Center Academic Development ... Ms. Leah BROWN-JOHNSON
19 Director of Security ... Mr. David REILLY
39 Director Res Educ & Housing ... Mr. Derrick HICKS
105 Webmaster ... Mr. Matt SHILLITANI
14 Director Institutional Technology ... Mr. Yifeng BAI

Brookdale Community College (D)

Newman Springs Road, Lincroft NJ 07738-1597

County: Monmouth — FICE Identification: 008404 — Unit ID: 183859
Telephone: (732) 842-1900 — Carnegie Class: Assoc/MT-VT-High Trad
FAX Number: (732) 224-2242 — Calendar System: Other
URL: www.brookdalecc.edu
Established: 1967 — Annual Undergrad Tuition & Fees (In-District): $8,804
Enrollment: 10,438 — Coed
Affiliation or Control: State/Local — IRS Status: 501(c)3
Highest Offering: Associate Degree
Accreditation: M, ACFEI, ADNUR, COARC, CSHSE, RAD

01 President ... Dr. David M. STOUT
05 Vice President for Academic Affairs ... Dr. Matthew REED
10 VP of Finance & Operations ... Ms. Teresa MANFREDA
86 Exec Dir Govt & Comm Rels ... Mr. Edward JOHNSON
32 Assoc VP of Student Affairs ... Dr. Yesenia MADAS
15 Assoc VP HR & Organizational Safety ... Ms. Patricia SENSI
08 Director of Library ... Mr. Steven CHUDNICK
45 Assoc VP Plng & Inst Effectiveness ... Dr. Nancy KEGELMAN
26 Int Exec Director College Relations ... Ms. Kathy KAMATANI
111 VP of Advancement ... Ms. Nancy KAARI
88 Dir of Student Life & Activities ... Ms. Lauren BRUTSMAN
37 Director of Financial Aid ... Ms. Stephanie FITZSIMMONS
25 Director Grants & Institutional Dev ... Ms. Laura V. QAISSAUNEE
35 Exec Dir Student Services ... Mr. Christopher JEUNE
06 Registrar ... Ms. Eleanor GLAZEWSKI
09 Dir of Inst Research/Evaluation ... Dr. Laura LONGO
104 Director of International Center ... Ms. Janice THOMAS
13 Chief Information Officer (CIO) ... Mr. George SOTIRION
19 Police Chief ... Mr. Robert KIMLER
41 Dir Athletics & Recreation ... Ms. Katelyn AMUNDSON
76 Dean of Health Sciences ... Dr. Jayne EDMAN
50 Dean Business/Social Science ... Dr. Norah KERR-MCCURRY
81 Int Dean of STEM ... Dr. Jim CROWDER
106 Assoc VP Educ Access/Innovation ... Dr. William BURNS
79 Dean Humanities Inst ... Dr. Christine WEBSTER-HANSEN
04 Senior Asst to President & BOT ... Ms. Cynthia GRUSKOS
18 Mgr Facilities/Construction ... Mr. Michael NAPARLO
84 Exec Dir Enrollment Services ... Ms. Mary Beth REILLY
51 Dean of Cont & Prof Studies ... Dr. Joan SCOCCO
43 Exec Assoc of Legal Services ... Ms. Bonnie PASSARELLA
36 Exec Dir Career & Transfer Pathways ... Dr. Sarah MCELROY
28 Dir Diversity/Inclusion & CCOG ... Ms. Angela KARIOTIS
07 Director of Admissions ... Ms. Kristin WORTHLEY

Caldwell University (E)

120 Bloomfield Avenue, Caldwell NJ 07006-5310

County: Essex — FICE Identification: 002598 — Unit ID: 183910
Telephone: (973) 618-3000 — Carnegie Class: Masters/M
FAX Number: (973) 618-3300 — Calendar System: Semester
URL: www.caldwell.edu
Established: 1939 — Annual Undergrad Tuition & Fees: $36,700
Enrollment: 2,274 — Coed
Affiliation or Control: Roman Catholic — IRS Status: 501(c)3
Highest Offering: Doctorate
Accreditation: M, ABAI, ACATE, ACBSP, CACREP, CAEP, NURSE

01 President ... Dr. Matt WHELAN
05 Vice President for Academic Affairs ... Dr. Peter UBERTACCIO
15 Vice President Operations ... Mrs. Sheila N. O'ROURKE
32 Vice President for Student Affairs ... Dr. Jose RODRIGUEZ
84 VP for Enrollment Management ... Mr. Jorge RODRIGUEZ
30 Vice Pres Development/Alumni Affs ... Mr. Kevin BOYLE
10 Vice President Finance ... Mr. Ketan GHANDI
50 Associate Dean School of Business ... Ms. Virginia RICH
53 Associate Dean School of Education ... Dr. Kevin BARNES
85 Director International Student Svcs ... Mr. Jan Marco JIRAS
112 Philanthropy Officer ... Ms. Christina HALL
06 University Registrar ... Ms. Rachel ROTH
08 Director of Library ... Ms. Victoria SWANSON
58 Associate VP for Academic Affairs ... Dr. Ellina CHERNOBILSKY
38 Executive Director of Counseling ... Ms. Robin DAVENPORT
39 Assistant Dean Residence Life ... Ms. Crystal LOPEZ
13 Assistant Vice President and CIO ... Mr. Anthony YANG
36 Dir Career Plng & Development ... Ms. Geraldine PERRET
37 Director Financial Aid ... Ms. Eileen FELSKE
41 Asst Vice Pres & Dir of Athletics ... Mr. Mark A. CORINO
26 Director News and Media Relations ... Ms. Colette LIDDY
19 Director Campus Safety ... Mr. Jeffrey CAMP
91 Exec Director Application Support ... Mr. David BOHNY
16 Asst VP of Human Resources ... Mrs. Michelle STAUSS
35 Asst Dean Student Engagement ... Mr. Timothy KESSLER-CLEARY
106 Dir Online Education ... Ms. Soheila KOBLER
04 Administrative Asst to President ... Vacant
09 Exec Dir of Inst Research/Planning ... Dr. Susan HAYES
124 Asst Dean Advisement and Retention ... Ms. Henrieta GENFI
102 Dir Foundation/Corporate Relations ... Ms. Pat LEVINS
105 Director Web Services ... Mr. Matt NETTER
29 Director Alumni Affairs ... Ms. Kate SOLOMON
07 Director of Admissions ... Ms. Martha ECHEVARRIA
18 Chief Facilities/Physical Plnt Ofcr ... Mr. Raymond WILLIAMS
44 Director Annual Giving ... Ms. Sharon DWYER

Camden County College (F)

PO Box 200, Blackwood NJ 08012-0200

County: Camden — FICE Identification: 006865 — Unit ID: 183938
Telephone: (856) 227-7200 — Carnegie Class: Assoc/HT-High Non
FAX Number: (856) 374-4894 — Calendar System: Semester
URL: www.camdencc.edu
Established: 1967 — Annual Undergrad Tuition & Fees (In-District): $4,680
Enrollment: 8,122 — Coed
Affiliation or Control: State/Local — IRS Status: 501(c)3
Highest Offering: Associate Degree
Accreditation: M, CAHIIM, DA, DH, DIETT, DNUR, OPD

01 President ... Dr. Lovell PUGH-BASSETT
45 VP Institutional Effectiveness ... Ms. Jocelyn LEWIS
05 Vice Pres Academic Affairs ... Dr. David EDWARDS
32 Exec Dean Student Affairs ... Ms. Anne DALY-EIMER
10 Exec Dir Finance & Planning ... Ms. Helen ANTONAKAKIS
11 Exec Dir Financial Admin Svcs ... Mr. Jack LIPSETT
15 Executive Director Human Resources ... Ms. Kathleen KANE
51 Exec Dean School/Cmty Academic Pgm ... Ms. Margo VENABLE
13 Chief Info Technology Officer (CIO) ... Mr. Jack POST
43 Dir Legal Services/General Counsel ... Mr. Karl MCCONNELL
108 Dean Academic Affairs ... Dr. Teresa A. SMITH
09 Dean Inst Research/Plng/Grants ... Dr. Rebecca FIDLER-SHEPPARD
81 Dean Math/Science/Health Careers ... Mr. John STEINER
79 Dean Liberal Arts/Profess Studies ... Dr. Michael NESTER
12 Exec Dean Camden City Campus ... Vacant
07 Dir Admissions/Registration Svcs ... Mr. Steve D'AMBROSIO
37 Executive Director of Financial Aid ... Ms. Felicia BRYANT
19 Director Public Safety ... Mr. John SCHUCK
29 External Resources Devel Associate ... Ms. Melissa DALY
88 Director of Testing ... Mr. Daniel MCMASTERS
26 Director of Communications ... Mr. Ronald TOMASELLO
08 Director Library Services ... Ms. Isabel GRAY
41 Athletic Director ... Vacant

Camden County College Camden City Campus (G)

200 N Broadway, Camden NJ 08102-1185

Telephone: (856) 338-1817 — Identification: 770126
Accreditation: &M

Centenary University (H)

400 Jefferson Street, Hackettstown NJ 07840-2100

County: Warren — FICE Identification: 002599 — Unit ID: 183974
Telephone: (908) 852-1400 — Carnegie Class: Masters/M
FAX Number: (908) 850-9508 — Calendar System: Semester
URL: www.centenaryuniversity.edu
Established: 1867 — Annual Undergrad Tuition & Fees: $34,498
Enrollment: 1,629 — Coed
Affiliation or Control: Independent Non-Profit — IRS Status: 501(c)3
Highest Offering: Doctorate
Accreditation: M, CAEP, CAEPT, IACBE, MLS, SW

01 President ... Dr. Bruce MURPHY
05 VP for Academic Affairs ... Dr. Amy D'OLIVO
10 VP for Business & Finance ... Mr. Denton STARGEL
84 VP for Enrollment Mgmt & Marketing ... Dr. Robert L. MILLER, JR.
32 VP for Student Life/Dean of Stdnts ... Ms. Kerry MULLINS
15 Director for Human Resources ... Ms. Christine ROSADO
18 Director of Facilities ... Mr. Jonathan MIRABAL
09 Coordinator Institutional Research ... Ms. Ying WANG
35 Sr Director Student Engagement ... Ms. Tiffany KUSHNER
06 Registrar ... Ms. Christine VANDENBERG
08 Int Dir Taylor Memorial Library ... Ms. Maryanne FEGAN
36 Asst Director Career Development ... Mr. Aaron RATZAN
41 Director of Athletics ... Mr. Travis SPENCER
19 Chief of Campus Safety ... Mr. Leonard KUNZ
38 Director of Counseling Center ... Vacant
13 Chief Information Officer ... Ms. Sharon AINSLEY
04 Exec Assistant to the President ... Ms. Claudia IZZI

Chamberlain University-North Brunswick (I)

630 US Highway One, North Brunswick NJ 08902

Telephone: (732) 875-1300 — Identification: 770850
Accreditation: &HLC, NURSE

† Branch campus of Chamberlain University-Addison, Addison, IL

The College of New Jersey (J)

2000 Pennington Road, Ewing NJ 08628-1104

County: Mercer — FICE Identification: 002642 — Unit ID: 187134
Telephone: (609) 771-1855 — Carnegie Class: Masters/L
FAX Number: (609) 637-5191 — Calendar System: Semester
URL: www.tcnj.edu
Established: 1855 — Annual Undergrad Tuition & Fees (In-State): $16,029
Enrollment: 7,783 — Coed
Affiliation or Control: State — IRS Status: 501(c)3
Highest Offering: Master's
Accreditation: M, ART, CACREP, CAEPN, MUS, NURSE

01 President ... Dr. Kathryn A. FOSTER

05 Provost/VP Academic Affairs ... Mr. Jeffrey OSBORN
10 Vice President & Treasurer ... Mr. Lloyd RICKETTS
43 Vice President & General Counsel ... Mr. Thomas MAHONEY
111 Vice Pres for College Advancement ... Mr. John DONOHUE
32 Vice President Student Affairs ... Mr. Sean STALLINGS
28 Vice Pres Inclusive Excellence ... Mr. James FELTON, III
84 Vice Pres Enrollment Management ... Ms. Lisa ANGELONI
15 Int Vice Pres of Human Resources ... Mr. Lee WEBSTER
11 VP for Operations ... Dr. Sharon BLANTON
100 Chief of Staff/Secy to Board ... Ms. Heather FEHN
30 Assoc Vice President of Development ... Mr. Charles WRIGHT
35 Asst Vice Pres Student Services ... Dr. Kelly HENNESSY
20 Vice Provost ... Dr. Timothy CLYDESDALE
57 Dean School of The Arts & Comm ... Dr. Maurice HALL
50 Dean School of Business ... Dr. Kathryn JERVIS
79 Dean Sch Humanities/Soc Sci ... Dr. Jane WONG
53 Dean School of Education ... Dr. Suzanne MCCOTTER
54 Interim Dean School of Engineering ... Dr. Steve O'BRIEN
66 Dean Nursing/Health/Exercise Sci ... Dr. Carole KENNER
81 Interim Dean School of Science ... Dr. Amanda NORVELL
58 Director for Grad Studies ... Mr. Michael ELLARD
37 Exec Dir of Student Fin Assistance ... Mr. Wil CASAINE
09 Assoc Provost Ctr Inst Effective ... Vacant
41 Exec Director of Athletics ... Ms. Amanda DEMARTINO
29 Director of Alumni Engagement ... Ms. Amy WALTON
26 Assoc VP Comm/Mktg/Brand Mgmt ... Mr. David MUHA
18 Director of Campus Construction ... Mr. William RUDEAU
23 Director for Health Services ... Ms. Janice VERMEYCHUK
06 Exec Director Records/Registration ... Mr. Frank COOPER
19 Director of Campus Police ... Chief Timothy GRANT
96 Exec Dir Procurement Services ... Mr. Anup KAPUR
07 Exec Dir Admissions/Enrollment Mgmt ... Ms. Grecia MONTERO
36 Director Career Center ... Ms. Shannon CONKLIN
38 AVP/Director Counseling/Psych Svcs ... Dr. Mark FOREST

County College of Morris (A)

214 Center Grove Road, Randolph NJ 07869-2086
County: Morris — FICE Identification: 007729
Unit ID: 184180
Telephone: (973) 328-5000 — Carnegie Class: Assoc/HT-Mix Trad/Non
FAX Number: (973) 328-1282 — Calendar System: Semester
URL: www.ccm.edu
Established: 1965 — Annual Undergrad Tuition & Fees (In-District): $9,720
Enrollment: 6,697 — Coed
Affiliation or Control: State/Local — IRS Status: 501(c)3
Highest Offering: Associate Degree
Accreditation: M, ACBSP, ADNUR, COARC, RAD

01 President ... Dr. Anthony J. IACONO
05 Vice President of Academic Affairs ... Dr. John MARLIN
10 Vice President of Business/Finance ... Ms. Karen VANDERHOOF
32 VP of Student Development ... Dr. Bette M. SIMMONS
102 Exec Dir Foundation ... Ms. Katie OLSEN
15 VP Human Resources & Labor Rels ... Ms. Vivyen RAY
09 Dean Inst Research ... Ms. Phebe SOLIMAN
114 Director Budget & Business Services ... Vacant
25 Director Resource Development ... Dr. Katrina BELL
07 Admissions Officer ... Ms. Donna TATARKA
37 Director Financial Aid ... Mr. Harvey WILLIS
06 Registrar ... Ms. Laura Lee BOWENS
26 Chief Public Relations Officer ... Ms. Kathleen BRUNET
29 Director Alumni Office ... Ms. Barbara CAPSOURAS
13 VP Institutional Effectiveness/CIO ... Mr. Robert STIRTON
08 Dean Learning Resource Ctr ... Ms. Heather CRAVEN
36 Director Career Svcs/Coop Education ... Ms. Denise SCHMIDT
38 Counseling Services Coordinator ... Ms. Janique CAFFIE
49 Interim Dean Liberal Arts ... Ms. Nieves GRUNEIRO
50 Dean Business/Math/Eng/Tech ... Dr. Kathleen NAASZ
76 Dean Health Prof/Natural Sciences ... Dr. Maria ISAZA
103 VP Workforce Dev/Prof Studies ... Mr. Patrick ENRIGHT
19 Director Security & Safety ... Mr. Steven ACKERMAN
41 Director Athletics ... Mr. Jack SULLIVAN
23 Health Services Coordinator ... Ms. Elizabeth HOBAN
18 Director of Plant & Maintenance ... Vacant
96 Manager of Purchasing ... Ms. Joanne KEARNS
40 Bookstore Manager ... Mr. Jeff LUBNOW

Drew University (B)

36 Madison Avenue, Madison NJ 07940-1493
County: Morris — FICE Identification: 002603
Unit ID: 184348
Telephone: (973) 408-3000 — Carnegie Class: Bac-A&S
FAX Number: N/A — Calendar System: 4/1/4
URL: www.drew.edu
Established: 1866 — Annual Undergrad Tuition & Fees: $40,960
Enrollment: 2,229 — Coed
Affiliation or Control: Independent Non-Profit — IRS Status: 501(c)3
Highest Offering: Doctorate
Accreditation: M, CAEP, THEOL

01 President ... Mr. Thomas SCHWARZ
05 Chief Academic Officer ... Dr. Jessica LAKIN
111 Vice Pres Advancement ... Mr. Bret SILVER
10 Interim Vice Pres Finance ... Mr. Michael WARD
73 Interim Dean Theological School ... Dr. Melanie JOHNSON-DEBAUFRE
08 University Librarian ... Mr. Andrew BONAMICI
32 Vice President Student Life ... Dr. Frank MERCKX
26 Director Communications & Marketing ... Ms. Kristen WILLIAMS
15 Director of Human Resources ... Ms. Maria FORCE
22 Title IX Coordinator ... Dr. Frank MERCKX
18 Director Facilities Operations ... Mr. Greg SMITH
07 Dean of Admissions ... Ms. Colby MCCARTHY
19 Director Public Safety ... Vacant
23 Director Health Services ... Ms. Joan GALBRAITH
35 Dean of Student Activities ... Ms. Michelle BRISSON
88 Director Theological Admissions ... Mr. Kevin D. MILLER
123 Director Graduate Admissions ... Mr. Kevin D. MILLER
09 Director Institutional Research ... Ms. Nadine HYLTON
41 Director Athletics ... Ms. Christa RACINE
06 Registrar ... Ms. Stephanie CALDWELL
40 Manager Bookstore ... Ms. Marie JOYNER
04 Administrative Asst to President ... Ms. Kathleen SUTHERLAND
100 Chief of Staff ... Ms. Barb BRESNAHAN
104 Director Study Abroad ... Ms. Stacy FISCHER
105 Webmaster ... Mr. Justin JACKSON
13 Interim Chief Technology Officer ... Mr. Christopher DARRELL
29 Director Alumni Relations ... Ms. Carol BASSIE
43 Director Legal Services ... Ms. Meredith PALMER
39 Dir Resident Life/Student Housing ... Ms. Stephanie PELHAM
20 Assoc Prov Exp Educ & Career ... Dr. Daniel PASCOE AGUILAR

Eastern International College (C)

684 Newark Avenue, Jersey City NJ 07306
County: Hudson — FICE Identification: 031226
Unit ID: 421878
Telephone: (201) 216-9901 — Carnegie Class: Spec-4-yr-Other Health
FAX Number: (201) 533-1027 — Calendar System: Semester
URL: www.eicollege.edu
Established: 1990 — Annual Undergrad Tuition & Fees: $16,442
Enrollment: 292 — Coed
Affiliation or Control: Proprietary — IRS Status: Proprietary
Highest Offering: Baccalaureate
Accreditation: M, ADNUR, CVT, DH

01 CEO/President ... Dr. Bashir MOHSEN
03 Acting Vice President ... Dr. Julius WANGIWANG
11 Dir of Opers/Student Svcs/HR ... Dr. Jennifer GONZALEZ
05 Dean of Academic Affairs & IT ... Dr. Melda YILDIZ
32 Student & Career Services Coord ... Ms. Mary KURZYNA
06 Registrar ... Mrs. Karen LOPEZ
113 Bursar ... Ms. Sheila SANCHEZ
37 Director Student Financial Aid ... Ms. Andrea OJEDA
07 Assoc Director of Admissions ... Ms. Kamlla RAMANAND
08 Library Director ... Ms. Emma TREVENA
38 Student Counseling Officer ... Ms. Maria BILLINGS

Eastwick College (D)

250 Moore Street, Hackensack NJ 07601
County: Bergen — Identification: 667131
Unit ID: 183488
Telephone: (201) 488-9400 — Carnegie Class: Assoc/HVT-Mix Trad/Non
FAX Number: (201) 488-1007 — Calendar System: Quarter
URL: www.eastwick.edu
Established: 1985 — Annual Undergrad Tuition & Fees: $16,797
Enrollment: 533 — Coed
Affiliation or Control: Proprietary — IRS Status: Proprietary
Highest Offering: Baccalaureate
Accreditation: ACCSC, FUSER

01 President ... Thomas M. EASTWICK
11 Campus Director Hackensack ... Mr. Abylash J. GEORGE
05 Dean of Academics ... Dawood GUIRGUIS

Eastwick College (E)

103 Park Avenue, Nutley NJ 07110
County: Essex — FICE Identification: 020923
Unit ID: 185721
Telephone: (973) 661-0600 — Carnegie Class: Spec 2-yr-Health
FAX Number: (973) 661-2954 — Calendar System: Quarter
URL: www.eastwick.edu
Established: 2014 — Annual Undergrad Tuition & Fees: $15,806
Enrollment: 455 — Coed
Affiliation or Control: Proprietary — IRS Status: Proprietary
Highest Offering: Associate Degree
Accreditation: ACCSC

01 President ... Thomas EASTWICK
11 Vice Pres of Operations ... Bhavna TAILOR
05 Dean of Academics ... Sameh FARAGALLA
06 Registrar ... Rocio SANCHEZ
13 Chief Information Technology Office ... Joseph NEYMAN
37 Director Student Financial Aid ... Marlyn RABELO

Eastwick College (F)

10 South Franklin Turnpike, Ramsey NJ 07446
County: Bergen — FICE Identification: 020537
Unit ID: 184959
Telephone: (201) 327-8877 — Carnegie Class: Spec-4-yr-Other Health
FAX Number: (201) 327-9054 — Calendar System: Other
URL: www.eastwick.edu
Established: 1968 — Annual Undergrad Tuition & Fees: $16,882
Enrollment: 781 — Coed
Affiliation or Control: Proprietary — IRS Status: Proprietary
Highest Offering: Baccalaureate
Accreditation: ACCSC, CVT, OTA, SURGT

01 President ... Thomas EASTWICK
05 Executive Vice President/Provost ... Rafael CASTILLA
11 Exec Vice Pres Operations ... Bhavna TAILOR
07 Director of Admissions ... Derek RUE
36 Director Career Development ... Jennifer BATE
37 Vice Pres of Financial Aid ... Christy DELAGUERRA

Essex County College (G)

303 University Avenue, Newark NJ 07102-1798
County: Essex — FICE Identification: 007107
Unit ID: 184481
Telephone: (973) 877-3000 — Carnegie Class: Assoc/MT-VT-High Trad
FAX Number: (973) 877-4465 — Calendar System: Other
URL: www.essex.edu
Established: 1966 — Annual Undergrad Tuition & Fees (In-District): $8,790
Enrollment: 6,360 — Coed
Affiliation or Control: State/Local — IRS Status: 501(c)3
Highest Offering: Associate Degree
Accreditation: M, ACBSP, ADNUR, OPD, PTAA, RAD

01 President ... Dr. Augustine A. BOAKYE
100 Special Assistant to the President ... Mr. Pavi JALLOH
04 Administrative Assistant ... Ms. Taniel MOORE
101 Liaison to the President/BOT ... Ms. Jonell CONGLETON
10 Senior Comptoller ... Ms. Kiswendsida KAPROU
21 Comptoller ... Mr. Evens WAGNAC
05 Exec Dean of Faculty & Academics ... Dr. Alvin WILLIAMS
108 Exec Dir Inst Planning/Assessment ... Mr. John RUNFELDT
111 Exec Dir Inst Advancement ... Mr. Alfred BUNDY
15 Exec Director Human Resources ... Ms. Yvette HENRY
13 Exec Dean/CIO Admin & Learning Tech ... Mr. Mohamed SEDDIKI
32 Dean Student Affairs ... Dr. Keith KIRKLAND
106 Assoc Dean Online Learning Resource ... Dr. Leigh BELLO-DECASTRO
20 Assoc Dean Academic Affairs-SP ... Dr. June PERSAUD
09 Director Institutional Research ... Dr. Jinsoo PARK
51 Dean Cmty/Continuing Educ/Wkfce Dev ... Dr. Elvira VIEIRA
35 Director Student Life/Development ... Mr. Jamil GRAHAM
18 Director Facilities Mgmt ... Mr. Jeff SHAPIRO
96 Director Purchasing ... Ms. Denise WILLIAMS
19 Director Public Safety ... Mr. Anthony CROMARTIE
37 Director Financial Aid ... Mr. David SMEDLEY
113 Director Bursar's Office ... Ms. Darlene MILLER
36 Director Student Devel & Counsel ... Dr. S. Aisha STEPLIGHT JOHNSON
88 Director Child Development Center ... Ms. Virginia FLANIGAN
41 Director Athletics ... Mr. Michael DOUGHTIE
24 Chief of Operations Media Prod Tech ... Mr. Eugene JACKSON
00 President Emeritus ... Dr. A. Zachary YAMBA
06 Registrar ... Dr. Renee OJO-OHIKUARE
84 Exec Director Enrollment Mgmt/Svcs ... Dr. Aylin BRANDON
43 General Counsel ... Ms. Christine SOTO
88 Director Men & Women of Excellence ... Mr. Ledawn HALL
102 Director Foundation/Corporate Rels ... Ms. Yvette JEFFERIES
103 Director Training Inc ... Mrs. Sanghamitra CHOUDHURY
104 Director Study Abroad ... Dr. Akil KHALFANI
08 Director MLK Library ... Vacant

Essex County College-West Essex Branch Campus (H)

730 West Bloomfield Avenue, West Caldwell NJ 07006
Telephone: (973) 877-6590 — Identification: 770127
Accreditation: &M

Fairleigh Dickinson University (I)

1000 River Road, Teaneck NJ 07666-1996
County: Bergen — FICE Identification: 002607
Unit ID: 184603
Telephone: (201) 692-2000 — Carnegie Class: Masters/L
FAX Number: N/A — Calendar System: Semester
URL: www.fdu.edu
Established: 1942 — Annual Undergrad Tuition & Fees: $42,240
Enrollment: 7,479 — Coed
Affiliation or Control: Independent Non-Profit — IRS Status: 501(c)3
Highest Offering: Doctorate
Accreditation: M, #ARCPA, CACREP, CAEP, CLPSY, NURSE, PHAR, @SW

01 President ... Dr. Christopher CAPUANO
43 General Counsel & CCO ... Mr. Edward SILVER
05 Univ Provost/SVP Academic Affairs ... Dr. Michael AVALTRONI
03 Sr VP for University Operations ... Dr. Robert PIGNATELLO
111 Sr Vice Pres University Advancement ... Mr. Jason AMORE
10 Senior VP for Finance & COO ... Ms. Hania FERRARA
18 VP for Facilities ... Mr. Richard A. FRICK
84 VP Enrollment/Planning & Effect ... Dr. Luke D. SCHULTHEIS
13 VP/Chief Information Officer ... Mr. Neal M. STURM
32 VP for Student Affairs/DOS ... Dr. Uchenna BAKER
07 AVP Admissions/Fin Aid/Enrollment ... Ms. Traci BANKS
26 Associate VP Communications ... Mr. Angelo CARFAGNA
15 Associate VP Human Resources ... Ms. Rose D'AMBROSIO
06 AVP Enrollment Services/Registrar ... Ms. Carol CREEKMORE
21 Assoc VP for Finance ... Mr. Frank BARRA
104 Vice Provost for International Affs ... Dr. Jason SCORZA
44 Manager of Donor Relations ... Mr. Richard DATZKO-BANTA
49 Dean Becton Col Arts & Sciences ... Dr. Benjamin RIFKIN
50 Dean College Business Admin ... Dr. Pierre BALTHAZARD
08 Assoc University Librarian-Florham ... Ms. Brigid BURKE
08 University Librarian ... Ms. Ana M. FONTOURA
88 Dir Public Administration Institute ... Dr. William ROBERTS
116 Director Internal Audit ... Ms. Agnes SCAGLIONE

53 Dir School of Education ... Dr. Vicki COHEN
66 Dir Sch of Nursing/Allied Health ... Dr. Minerva GUTTMAN
41 Director of Athletics-Metro ... Mr. Bradford D. HURLBUT
41 Director of Athletics-Florham ... Ms. Jennifer NOON
07 Asst VP & Dean of UG Admissions ... Mr. Kenneth SCHNEIDER
09 Director of Institutional Research ... Dr. Sam MICHALOWSKI
37 University Director Financial Aid ... Ms. Renee VOLAK
19 Dir Public Safety-Florham Campus ... Mr. Joseph VITIELLO
19 Director Public Safety-Metro Campus ... Mr. David A. MILES
12 Assoc VP Univ Operations Metro ... Dr. Steven NELSON
96 Director of Purchasing ... Ms. Juliette BROOKS
04 Assistant to the President ... Ms. Jeanne MAZZOLLA
25 Univ Dir Grants/Sponsored Projects ... Ms. Jane TSAMBIS
36 University Dir Career Development ... Ms. Donna ROBERTSON
117 Risk Manager ... Ms. Gail LEMAIRE
88 Florham Assoc Dean of Students ... Ms. Pamela MESSINA
88 Metro Assoc Dean of Students ... Ms. Juhi BHATT
29 Exec Dir of Alumni Engagement ... Ms. Laura REYNOLDS
44 Exec Dir of Annual Giving ... Mr. Kenneth LAM

Felician University (A)

262 S Main Street, Lodi NJ 07644-2198

County: Bergen | FICE Identification: 002610 | Unit ID: 184612
Telephone: (201) 559-6000 | Carnegie Class: Masters/M
FAX Number: (201) 559-6188 | Calendar System: Semester
URL: www.felician.edu
Established: 1942 | Annual Undergrad Tuition & Fees: $35,000
Enrollment: 2,556 | Coed
Affiliation or Control: Roman Catholic | IRS Status: 501(c)3
Highest Offering: Doctorate
Accreditation: M, COPSY, IACBE, MPCAC, NURSE, OT

01 President ... Mr. James W. CRAWFORD, III
05 Acting Vice Pres Academic Affairs ... Dr. Christine CLOUTIER MIHAL
20 Asst VP Academic Support Services ... Dr. Ann V. GUILLORY
10 VP for Business/Finance/CFO ... Mr. Thomas TRUCHAN
111 Vice Pres University Advancement ... Ms. Maura DENICOLA
84 VP Enroll Mgmt/Mktg & Registrar ... Ms. Priscilla KLYMENKO
11 Vice Pres Administration ... Vacant
32 VP Student Affairs/Dean of Students ... Dr. Ronald A. GRAY
123 Assoc Vice Pres Grad & Intl Enroll ... Mr. Michael SZAREK
13 Asst VP of Information Technology ... Mr. Christopher FINCH
07 AVP of Admissions ... Ms. Camile BRAKER-BALKUM
04 Exec Asst to Pres/Sec to Board ... Ms. Stephanie CACHEZ
15 Director of Human Resources ... Ms. Virginia TOPOLSKI
37 Exec Director Student Financial Aid ... Ms. Cynthia MONTALVO
39 Director of Residence Life ... Ms. Laura PIEROTTI
36 Director of Career Development Ctr ... Ms. Tiffany AUSTIN
24 Director Audio Visual Services ... Mr. Anthony KLYMENKO
88 Assoc Director Center for Learning ... Mr. Hamdi SHAHIN
53 Dean School of Education ... Dr. Stephanie MCGOWAN
49 Dean School of Arts/Science ... Dr. Mildred MIHLON
66 Dean School of Nursing ... Dr. Christine CLOUTIER MIHAL
50 Dean School of Business ... Dr. Heather PFLEGER
121 Dean Academic Success Programs ... Dr. Dolores HENCHY
23 Director Health Services ... Ms. Carolyn LEWIS
41 Director of Athletics ... Mr. Benjamin DINALLO, JR.
92 Director Honors Program ... Dr. Jeffrey BLANCHARD

Georgian Court University (B)

900 Lakewood Avenue, Lakewood NJ 08701-2697

County: Ocean | FICE Identification: 002608 | Unit ID: 184773
Telephone: (732) 987-2200 | Carnegie Class: Masters/L
FAX Number: N/A | Calendar System: Semester
URL: www.georgian.edu
Established: 1908 | Annual Undergrad Tuition & Fees: $33,640
Enrollment: 2,231 | Coed
Affiliation or Control: Roman Catholic | IRS Status: 501(c)3
Highest Offering: Master's
Accreditation: M, ACBSP, CACREP, CAEP, NURSE, SW

01 President ... Dr. Joseph R. MARBACH
05 Provost ... Dr. Janice WARNER
10 VP Finance/Chief Financial Officer ... Ms. Heather MEIER
111 Vice Pres Institutional Advancement ... Mr. Matthew MANFRA
84 VP of Enrollment & Retention ... Mr. Chris KRZAK
20 Assoc Provost Academic Pgm Devel ... Dr. Michael GROSS
124 Associate VP for Student Retention ... Ms. Kathleen BOODY
32 Dean of Students ... Dr. Amani JENNINGS
42 Director of Campus Ministry ... Mr. Jeff SCHAFFER
41 Director Athletics/Recreation ... Mr. Dan SEMPKOWSKI
50 Dean School of Business ... Dr. Jennifer EDMONDS
53 Dean of School of Education ... Dr. Kelly MCNEAL
49 Dean School of Arts & Sciences ... Dr. Mary CHINERY
09 Director of Institutional Research ... Mr. Wayne ARNDT
08 Director of Library Services ... Mr. Jeffrey DONNELLY
06 Registrar ... Ms. Kathleen BOODY
21 Controller ... Ms. Kristen NAGLE
15 Director of Human Resources ... Ms. Dianna SOFO
13 Chief Information Officer ... Mr. AJ LACOMBA
37 Director of Financial Aid ... Ms. Cynthia MCCARTHY
88 Dir Conferences & Special Events ... Ms. Allison LAGERQUIST
29 Director of Alumni/Donor Relations ... Ms. Alicia SMITH
36 Director Career Services ... Ms. Ceceilia O'CALLAGHAN
38 Director of Counseling ... Dr. Robin SOLBACH
23 Director of Health Services ... Ms. Robin SOLBACH
18 Director of Facilities ... Mr. Michael PUTNAM
19 Director of Security ... Mr. Charles TIGHE

123 Director Graduate Admissions ... Mr. Jerred THOMPSON
39 Director of Residence Life ... Mr. Seth RICHARDS
04 Executive Asst to President ... Ms. Stephanie TEDESCO
105 Web Administrator ... Mr. Richard BERARDI
108 Asst VP for University Assessment ... Sr. Janet THIEL
96 Purchasing Coordinator ... Ms. Julie PARLACOSKI
30 Asst Vice Pres for Development ... Mr. Frank MASCIA
102 Dir Foundation/Corporate Relations ... Ms. Lori THOMAS

Hackensack Meridian School of Medicine (C)

123 Metro Blvd, Nutley NJ 07110

County: Essex | FICE Identification: 042933 | Unit ID: 495314
Telephone: (973) 542-6500 | Carnegie Class: Not Classified
FAX Number: N/A | Calendar System: Other
URL: www.hmsom.org
Established: 2020 | Annual Undergrad Tuition & Fees: N/A
Enrollment: N/A | Coed
Affiliation or Control: Independent Non-Profit | IRS Status: 501(c)3
Highest Offering: First Professional Degree
Accreditation: @M, #MED

01 Founding Dean ... Dr. Bonita STANTON
05 Sr Assoc Dean Academic Affairs ... Dr. Miriam HOFFMAN

Hudson County Community College (D)

70 Sip Avenue, Jersey City NJ 07306

County: Hudson | FICE Identification: 012954 | Unit ID: 184995
Telephone: (201) 714-7100 | Carnegie Class: Assoc/MT-VT-High Trad
FAX Number: (201) 656-1799 | Calendar System: Semester
URL: www.hccc.edu
Established: 1974 | Annual Undergrad Tuition & Fees (In-District): $8,390
Enrollment: 7,039 | Coed
Affiliation or Control: State/Local | IRS Status: 501(c)3
Highest Offering: Associate Degree
Accreditation: M, ACFEI, ADNUR, EMT, MAC, RAD

01 President ... Dr. Christopher M. REBER
05 Vice President Academic Affairs ... Dr. Darryl JONES
10 Vice Pres Business/Finance & CFO ... Ms. Veronica ZEICHNER
111 Vice Pres Planning/Development ... Dr. Nicholas CHIARAVALLOTI
15 Vice President Human Resources ... Ms. Anna KRUPITSKIY
32 VP for Student Affairs/Enrollment ... Mrs. Lisa DOUGHERTY
50 Assoc Dean Business and Science ... Ms. Catherine SIRANGELO-ELBADAWY
37 Executive Director Financial Aid ... Ms. Sylvia F. MENDOZA
88 Assoc Dean English and ESL ... Ms. Jenny BOBEA
06 Registrar ... Ms. Victoria ORELLANA
13 Chief Information Officer ... Ms. Patricia CLAY
07 Director of Admissions ... Mr. Matthew FESSLER
81 Dean of Instruction/Sciences ... Mr. Burl YEARWOOD
88 Director Testing & Assessment ... Ms. Darlery FRANCO
88 Interim Assoc Dean Culinary Arts ... Mr. Ara KARAKASHIAN
51 Assoc VP Cont Educ & Workforce Dev ... Ms. Lori MARGOLIN
21 Controller ... Mr. Geoffrey SIMS
25 Director of Grants ... Mr. Sean KERWICK
08 Librarian ... Vacant
35 Asst Dean Student Life & Leadership ... Ms. Veronica GEROSIMO
26 Director of Communications ... Ms. Jennifer CHRISTOPHER
121 Associate Dean Student Success ... Dr. Sheila DYNAN
40 Manager HCCC Bookstore ... Mr. Jose ORTIZ
96 Dir of Contracts and Procurement ... Mr. Jeff ROBERSON
19 Director Security/Safety ... Mr. John QUIGLEY
04 Executive Admin Asst to President ... Ms. Alexa RIANO
18 Exec Dir Engineering Operations ... Mr. Ilya ASHMYAN
08 Interim Dean of College Libraries ... Mr. James COX
106 Exec Dir Center for Online Learning ... Mr. Matthew LABRAKE
45 Exec Dir Institutional Research ... Mr. John SCANLON
28 VP Diversity/Equity and Inclusion ... Mr. Yeurys PUJOLS
29 Alumni Manager ... Ms. Maria LITA SARMIENTO

Jersey College (E)

546 US Highway 46, Teterboro NJ 07608

County: Bergen | FICE Identification: 041341 | Unit ID: 455196
Telephone: (201) 489-5836 | Carnegie Class: Spec 2-yr-Health
FAX Number: (201) 525-0986 | Calendar System: Quarter
URL: jerseycollege.edu
Established: 2003 | Annual Undergrad Tuition & Fees: N/A
Enrollment: 3,514 | Coed
Affiliation or Control: Proprietary | IRS Status: Proprietary
Highest Offering: Associate Degree
Accreditation: COE, ADNUR

00 Chancellor ... Greg KARZHEVSKY
01 President ... Steven B. LITVACK
05 Provost ... Colette GARGIULO

Kean University (F)

1000 Morris Avenue, Union NJ 07083-0411

County: Union | FICE Identification: 002622 | Unit ID: 185262
Telephone: (908) 737-5326 | Carnegie Class: DU-Mod
FAX Number: (908) 737-4636 | Calendar System: Semester
URL: www.kean.edu
Established: 1855 | Annual Undergrad Tuition & Fees (In-State): $12,445
Enrollment: 14,064 | Coed
Affiliation or Control: State | IRS Status: 501(c)3
Highest Offering: Doctorate
Accreditation: M, #ARCPA, ART, CAATE, CACREP, CAEP, CIDA, MUS, NUR, OT, PSPSY, PTA, SP, SW, THEA

01 President ... Dr. Lamont REPOLLET
10 Chief Financial Officer ... Mr. Andrew BRANNEN
11 SVP of Administration ... Dr. Michael SALVATORE
111 SVP Transformational Lrng/Ext Affs ... Dr. Joseph YOUNGBLOOD
05 Provost/VP Academic Affairs ... Vacant
32 VP for Student Affairs ... Mr. Matthew CARUSO
26 VP University Relations ... Ms. Karen SMITH
100 Chief of Staff ... Ms. Audrey KELLY
45 SVP of Planning/Special Counsel ... Ms. Felice VAZQUEZ
12 Exec Vice Chancellor WKU ... Vacant
43 Assoc VP/Chief University Counsel ... Ms. Kristin GANLEY
84 VP Enrollment Services ... Ms. Marsha MCCARTHY
12 Assoc VP/Dean Kean Ocean ... Vacant
12 Acting Assoc VPAA Kean Wenzhou ... Ms. Felice VAZQUEZ
13 AVP Information Technology ... Mr. Joseph MARINELLO
20 Asst VP Academic Affairs ... Ms. Joy MOSKOVITZ
39 Asst VP Residential Stdnt Services ... Ms. Maximina RIVERA
18 Assoc VP Planning/Facilities ... Mr. Steve REMOTTI
08 Assoc VP University Library ... Mr. David BIRDSELL
37 Asst VP Student Financial Services ... Mr. Faruque CHOWDHURY
58 Dean Nathan Weiss Grad Col ... Dr. Christine THORPE
53 Dean Col Education ... Dr. Barbara RIDENER
79 Acting Dean Col Liberal Arts ... Dr. Jonathan MERCANTINI
50 Dean Col Business & Public Mgt ... Dr. Jin WANG
81 Dean Col Nat & Applied Hlth Sci ... Dr. George CHANG
48 Dean Michael Graves Col ... Dr. David MOHNEY
106 VP Transform Lrng/Chief Online Ofcr ... Mr. John O'CALLAGHAN
15 Exec Dir Human Services ... Ms. Jennifer PETERS
108 Assoc Dir Accredit & Assessment ... Mr. Mukul ACHARYA
09 Dir Institutional Research ... Vacant
114 Director Budget ... Ms. Jennifer STRAHAN
21 Dir General Accounting ... Mr. Joseph ANTONOWICZ
37 Dir Financial Aid ... Mr. Thomas FOGA
06 Registrar ... Mr. Scott SNOWDEN
25 Dir Research & Sponsored Pgms ... Vacant
27 Assoc Dir University Relations ... Ms. Margaret MCCORRY
96 Dir for Procurement/Business Svcs ... Mr. Faruque CHOWDHURY
38 Dir Counseling & Disability Svcs ... Mr. Vidal ANNAN
65 Director for Sustainability ... Ms. Suzanne KUPIEC
104 Dir Center International Studies ... Ms. Katsumi KISHIDA
35 Asst VP for Student Affairs ... Mr. Kerrin LYLES
19 Dir of Campus Police ... Mr. Anthony MONTICELLO
23 Dir for Health Services ... Dr. Geneque STANISLAUS
88 Dir Veterans Student Services ... Mr. Vito ZAJDA
22 Dir Affirmative Action ... Vacant
04 Admin Assistant to the President ... Ms. Maris HENSON
28 Exec Dir Diversity/Equity/Inclusion ... Dr. Alberta T. QUICK
41 Athletic Director ... Mr. David K. WILLIAMS
86 Chief Government Affairs Officer ... Ms. Kellie LEDET

Keser Torah-Mayan Hatalmud (G)

218 Joe Parker Road, Lakewood NJ 08701

County: Ocean | FICE Identification: 041803 | Unit ID: 461847
Telephone: (732) 367-4259 | Carnegie Class: Spec-4-yr-Faith
FAX Number: N/A | Calendar System: Semester
Established: 1991 | Annual Undergrad Tuition & Fees: N/A
Enrollment: N/A | Male
Affiliation or Control: Independent Non-Profit | IRS Status: 501(c)3
Highest Offering: Baccalaureate
Accreditation: AIJS

Mercer County Community College (H)

1200 Old Trenton Road, PO Box 17202, West Windsor NJ 08550

County: Mercer | FICE Identification: 004740 | Unit ID: 185509
Telephone: (609) 586-4800 | Carnegie Class: Assoc/MT-VT-High Trad
FAX Number: (609) 570-3870 | Calendar System: Semester
URL: www.mccc.edu
Established: 1966 | Annual Undergrad Tuition & Fees (In-District): $5,814
Enrollment: 6,342 | Coed
Affiliation or Control: State/Local | IRS Status: 501(c)3
Highest Offering: Associate Degree
Accreditation: M, AAB, ADNUR, FUSER, MACTE, MLTAD, PTAA, RAD

01 President ... Dr. Deborah PRESTON
111 Vice President College Advancement ... Mr. Joseph CLAFFEY
05 Vice President for Academic Affairs ... Dr. Robert SCHREYER
10 Vice President for Admin & Finance ... Ms. Laura SCHEPPS
32 Interim VP Student Affairs ... Dr. Tonia PERRY-CONLEY
15 Vice President for Human Resources ... Ms. Barbara BASEL
76 Dean Health Professions ... Mr. Kevin DUFFY
49 Dean of Liberal Arts ... Dr. Robert KLEINSCHMIDT
50 Dean Business/Technology ... Ms. Laura SOSA
12 Dean of James Kerney Campus ... Dr. Tonia PERRY-CONLEY
13 Chief Information Officer ... Mr. Inder SINGH
21 Exec Dir of Finance ... Mr. Mark BANYACSKI
26 Director Marketing ... Mr. Francis PAIXAO
06 Registrar ... Vacant
37 Director of Financial Aid ... Mr. Jonathan NG

09 Senior Dir Institutional Research ... Ms. Nina MAY
18 Chief Facilities/Physical Plant ... Mr. Bryon MARSHALL
96 Director of Purchasing ... Mr. Steven QUATTRO
84 Dean Student Enrollment Management .. Ms. Savita BAMBHROLIA
08 Director of Library Services ... Ms. Pam PRICE
101 Special Asst to the President/Board ... Ms. Beth BROWER
104 Coord of Global Education ... Dr. Andrea LYNCH
106 Dean Innov/Online Educ/Stdnt Suc ... Dr. Gonzalo PEREZ
25 Chief Contracts/Grants Admin ... Ms. Eileen SWIATKOWSKI
36 Director Transfer & Career Services ... Vacant
41 Athletic Director ... Mr. John SIMONE
108 Dean Inst Effectiveness ... Dr. Elizabeth ANDERSON
19 Exec Director Security/Safety ... Mr. Bryon MARSHALL

Middlesex College (A)

2600 Woodbridge Avenue, Edison NJ 08818-3050
County: Middlesex FICE Identification: 002615
Unit ID: 185536
Telephone: (732) 548-6000 Carnegie Class: Assoc/HT-Mix Trad/Non
FAX Number: (732) 906-4666 Calendar System: Semester
URL: www.middlesexcc.edu
Established: 1964 Annual Undergrad Tuition & Fees (In-District): $7,416
Enrollment: 10,084 Coed
Affiliation or Control: State/Local IRS Status: 501(c)3
Highest Offering: Associate Degree
Accreditation: M, ADNUR, DH, RAD

01 President ... Dr. Mark MCCORMICK
05 VP for Academic Affairs ... Dr. Linda SCHERR
10 Chief Financial Officer ... Mr. Frank MALTINO
111 VP for Institutional Advancement ... Dr. Michelle CAMPBELL
108 VP for Institutional Effectiveness ... Dr. Jeffrey HERRON
103 Exec Dir Workforce Dev/Lifelong Lrn ... Ms. Joananne COFFARO
18 Exec Director Facilities Management ... Mr. Wayne DEAK
84 Exec Dean Student & Enrollment Svcs ... Dr. José LAUREANO
13 Exec Director Information Tech ... Mr. John MATTALIANO
21 Controller ... Ms. Caryl CERQUA
07 Director Admissions & Recruitment ... Ms. Lisa RODRIGUEZ-GREGORY
06 Registrar ... Mr. Richard COLE
37 Financial Aid Director ... Dr. Taina MORALES
26 Acting Director Marketing and Comm ... Ms. Joselyn QUEZADA
96 Director of Purchasing ... Ms. Madeline CATERINICCHIO
09 Dean Inst Research/Assessment ... Dr. Meghan ALAI
25 Director Grants Development ... Ms. Yamillet FEBO-GOMEZ
29 Dir Development & Alumni Relations ... Ms. Lisa KELLY
04 Admin Assistant to President ... Ms. Bernadette ROA
15 Exec Director of Human Resources ... Mr. Joseph MORGAN
08 Director Library ... Ms. Marilyn OCHOA
49 Acting Dean Liberal Arts ... Dr. Theresa OROSZ
50 Acting Dean Business/STEM and HP ... Dr. Donna HOWELL

Monmouth University (B)

400 Cedar Avenue, West Long Branch NJ 07764-1898
County: Monmouth FICE Identification: 002616
Unit ID: 185572
Telephone: (732) 571-3400 Carnegie Class: Masters/L
FAX Number: (732) 571-3629 Calendar System: Semester
URL: www.monmouth.edu
Established: 1933 Annual Undergrad Tuition & Fees: $40,680
Enrollment: 5,674 Coed
Affiliation or Control: Independent Non-Profit IRS Status: 501(c)3
Highest Offering: Doctorate
Accreditation: M, ARCPA, CACREP, CAEP, NURSE, SP, SW

01 President ... Dr. Patrick F. LEAHY
04 Exec Asst to President & BOT ... Ms. Annette GOUGH
05 Provost/SVP Academic Affairs ... Dr. Pamela SCOTT-JOHNSON
104 Director of Global Education ... Ms. MyKellann MALONEY
45 AVP Inst Research & Effectiveness ... Ms. Christine BENOL
06 Registrar ... Ms. Gloria SCHOPF
79 Dean Sch Humanities/Soc Sci ... Dr. David H. GOLLAND
50 Dean Leon Hess Business Sch ... Dr. Raj DEVASAGAYAM
53 Interim Dean School of Education ... Dr. Wendy HARRIOTT
81 Interim Dean Sch of Science ... Dr. Joseph F. COYLE
66 Interim Dean Sch of Nurs/Heath Stds ... Dr. Sarah SHULTZ
70 Dean School of Social Work ... Dr. Robin MAMA
92 Dean Honors School ... Dr. Nancy MEZEY
08 University Librarian ... Mr. Kurt WAGNER
10 Vice President Finance ... Mr. William G. CRAIG
21 Assoc VP for Finance/Budgets ... Mr. Joseph A. PINGITORE
96 Director of Purchasing ... Mr. Mark MIRANDA
43 Acting VP & General Counsel ... Ms. Charlene DIANA
117 Dir of Compliance/Risk Mgr ... Mr. Michael WUNSCH
22 Director Equity and Diversity ... Ms. Nina ANDERSON
18 Acting Exec Dir Camp Plng & Fac ... Mr. Timothy ORR
19 Chief of Police ... Mr. Carlos ORTIZ
15 Assoc VP for Human Resources ... Ms. Robyn SALVO
32 VP Student Life & Ldrshp Engagement ... Mrs. Mary Anne NAGY
35 Assoc VP for Student Life ... Mr. James PILLAR
35 Dir Student Activities/Student Ctr ... Ms. Amy BELLINA
111 VP University Advancement ... Ms. Amanda KLAUS
26 Assoc VP Univ Mktg/Communications ... Ms. Tara PETERS
110 Assoc VP for Univ Advancement ... Mrs. Lucille FLYNN
84 Vice Pres Enrollment Management ... Dr. Robert MC CAIG
37 Assoc VP Enr Mgmt/Dir Fin Aid ... Ms. Claire ALASIO
07 Assoc VP for UG & GR Admission ... Ms. Lauren VENTO-CIFELLI
41 Director of Athletics ... Mr. Jeff STAPLETON
13 Vice Pres Information Management ... Dr. Edward CHRISTENSEN
36 Exec Director Career Development ... Ms. Beth M. RICCA
86 Dir of Government & Community Rels ... Mr. Paul DEMENT
27 Exec Director of Univ Communication ... Mr. Michael MAIDEN
39 Assoc Dir Res Life/Housing Ops ... Ms. Megan JONES
29 Sr Dir Alum Engage/Annual Giving ... Ms. Lindsay S. WOOD
38 Dir Counseling & Prevention Svcs . Mr. Christopher MCKITTRICK
100 Chief of Staff ... Ms. Emily B. MILLER-GONZALEZ
28 Director of Diversity and Inclusion ... Ms. Zaneta RAGO-CRAFT
44 Assoc Dir Rec Alumni & Student Pgms . Ms. Laura MACDONALD

Montclair State University (C)

1 Normal Avenue, Montclair NJ 07043-9987
County: Essex and Passaic FICE Identification: 002617
Unit ID: 185590
Telephone: (973) 655-4000 Carnegie Class: DU-Higher
FAX Number: N/A Calendar System: Semester
URL: www.montclair.edu
Established: 1908 Annual Undergrad Tuition & Fees (In-State): $13,073
Enrollment: 21,005 Coed
Affiliation or Control: State IRS Status: 501(c)3
Highest Offering: Doctorate
Accreditation: M, ART, AUD, CAATE, CACREP, CAEP, CLPSY, DANCE, DIETD, DIETI, MUS, NURSE, PH, SP, SW, THEA

01 President ... Dr. Jonathan KOPPELL
05 Provost/VP Academic Affairs ... Dr. Junius J. GONZALES
10 Int Vice Pres Finance & Treasurer ... Mr. Michael GAVIN
32 Vice Pres Student Devel/Campus Life ... Dr. Dawn M. SOUFLERIS
84 Vice Pres Enrollment Management ... Dr. Wendy LIN-COOK
18 Vice Pres Univ Facilities ... Mr. Shawn M. CONNOLLY
13 Vice Pres Info Technology/CIO ... Ms. Candace C. FLEMING
30 Vice Pres Development ... Ms. Colleen COPPLA
26 Vice Pres Communications/Marketing ... Dr. Joseph A. BRENNAN
15 Vice Pres Human Resources ... Mr. David VERNON
114 Exec Director Budget and Planning ... Mr. David JOSEPHSON
43 University Counsel ... Mr. Mark FLEMING
46 Vice Prov Research/Dean Grad School ... Dr. Scott HERNESS
89 Assoc Prov UG Ed/Dean Univ College ... Dr. David HOOD
79 Dean Col Humanities & Soc Sciences ... Dr. Peter KINGSTONE
81 Dean Col Science & Mathematics ... Dr. Lora BILLINGS
53 Acting Dean Col Educ & Human Svcs ... Dr. Katrina BULKLEY
57 Dean College of the Arts ... Mr. Daniel A. GURSKIS
50 Dean School of Business ... Dr. Kimberly HOLLISTER
66 Dean School of Nursing ... Dr. Janice SMOLOWITZ
60 Dir School of Communication & Media ... Dr. Keith STRUDLER
64 Director School of Music ... Mr. Anthony MAZZOCCHI
08 Dean Library Services ... Ms. Danianne MIZZY
35 Dean of Students ... Ms. Margaree COLEMAN-CARTER
20 Assoc Provost Academic Affairs ... Dr. Kenneth SUMNER
20 Assoc Provost Academic Affairs .. Dr. Joanne F. COTE-BONANNO
21 Associate VP Finance ... Mr. Michael GALVIN
121 Assoc VP Student Acad Services ... Vacant
88 Assoc VP Campus Planning/Proj Mgmt ... Mr. Michael ZANKO
14 Assoc VP Enterprise Tech Services ... Mr. Jeff GIACOBBE
14 Assoc VP Enterprise Application Svc ... Ms. Donna SADLON
88 Assoc VP Program Management Office ... Mr. Samir BAKANE
110 Assoc VP Development ... Ms. Lisa HOYT
109 Assoc VP Campus Business Services ... Mr. Ed MIDGLEY
102 Assoc VP Foundation Adm & Finance ... Mr. Jeffrey CAMPO
88 Assoc University Counsel ... Ms. Maria ANDERSON
07 Director Undergraduate Admissions ... Ms. Jordanna MAZIARZ
37 Director Financial Aid ... Mr. James T. ANDERSON
09 Asst VP Institutional Research ... Ms. Klavdiya HAMMOND
06 University Registrar ... Ms. Leslie SUTTON-SMITH
19 Chief of Police ... Mr. Paul M. CELL
41 Athletic Director ... Mr. Robert CHESNEY
100 Chief of Staff ... Mr. Keith D. BARRACK
86 Director Government Relations ... Vacant
04 Exec Asst to President ... Ms. Karen M. AIELLO

Mosdos Yaakov V'Yisroel (D)

1951 New Central Avenue, Lakewood NJ 08701
County: Ocean Identification: 667434
Telephone: (732) 905-2764 Carnegie Class: Not Classified
FAX Number: N/A Calendar System: Semester
URL: myy.edu
Established: Annual Undergrad Tuition & Fees: N/A
Enrollment: N/A Male
Affiliation or Control: Independent Non-Profit IRS Status: 501(c)3
Highest Offering: Baccalaureate
Accreditation: AIJS

New Brunswick Theological Seminary (E)

35 Seminary Place, New Brunswick NJ 08901
County: Middlesex FICE Identification: 002619
Unit ID: 185758
Telephone: (732) 247-5241 Carnegie Class: Spec-4-yr-Faith
FAX Number: (732) 249-5412 Calendar System: Semester
URL: www.nbts.edu
Established: 1784 Annual Graduate Tuition & Fees: N/A
Enrollment: 121 Coed
Affiliation or Control: Reformed Church In America IRS Status: 501(c)3
Highest Offering: Doctorate; No Undergraduates
Accreditation: M, THEOL

01 President ... Dr. Micah L. MCCREARY
100 Chief of Staff/HR Coordinator ... Ms. Amanda BRUEHL
10 Exec VP Operations/CFO ... Mr. Kenneth TERMOTT
13 Dir Communications/Technology ... Mr. Steve MANN
111 VP Seminary Advancement/Recruitment ... Ms. Cathy PROCTOR
05 Dean of Academic Affairs ... Dr. Beth LANEEL TANNER
21 Manager/Bursar ... Ms. Tara HAMILL
08 Director of the Library ... Mr. T. Patrick MILAS
06 Registrar ... Ms. Jeanette CARRILLO
32 Dean of Students/Title IX Coord ... Ms. Joan MARSHALL
108 Assoc Dean of Assessment ... Dr. Terry SMITH
07 Director of Admissions ... Vacant
18 Facilities Manager ... Mr. Paul KUHN
36 Director of Field Education ... Dr. Faye TAYLOR
37 Financial Aid Coordinator ... Ms. Rachel SEFCIK

New Jersey City University (F)

2039 Kennedy Boulevard, Jersey City NJ 07305-1597
County: Hudson FICE Identification: 002613
Unit ID: 185129
Telephone: (201) 200-2000 Carnegie Class: Masters/L
FAX Number: (201) 200-2352 Calendar System: Semester
URL: www.njcu.edu
Established: 1927 Annual Undergrad Tuition & Fees (In-State): $14,738
Enrollment: 7,550 Coed
Affiliation or Control: State IRS Status: 501(c)3
Highest Offering: Doctorate
Accreditation: M, ACBSP, ART, CACREP, CAEP, MUS, NURSE, @SW

01 Acting President ... Mr. Jason KROLL
05 Provost/Sr VP Academic Affairs ... Dr. Tamara JHASHI
11 Vice Pres & Chief Operating Officer ... Dr. Aaron ASKA
111 VP Advance/Chief Strategy Officer ... Vacant
10 Int VP/Chief Financial Officer ... Mr. Ben DURANT
32 Int Assoc VP Student Affairs ... Ms. Jodi BAILEY
84 Int VP Enrollment/Student Success ... Mr. Benjamin RHODIN
26 Assoc VP Marketing/Communications ... Ms. Faith JACKSON
15 Assoc VP Human Resources ... Ms. Alicia FRANQUI
20 Assoc Provost for Academic Affairs ... Dr. Nurdan S. DUZGOREN-AYDIN
13 Assoc VP Information Technology ... Ms. Phyllis SZANI
102 Chief Devel Officer/Exec Dir Found ... Mr. Kwi BRENNAN
85 Assoc VP Global Initiatives ... Ms. Tamara CUNNINGHAM
21 Controller ... Ms. Rosemary TAVARES
49 Dean College of Arts & Sciences ... Dr. Joao SEDYCIAS
53 Dean College of Education ... Dr. Donna BREAVLT
50 Dean School of Business ... Dr. Bernard MCSHERRY
107 Dean Col of Professional Studies ... Dr. Marvin WALKER
108 Assoc VP Inst Effectiveness ... Vacant
12 Exec Dir NJCU at Fort Monmouth ... Vacant
08 Director Library Services ... Mr. Frederick SMITH
07 Director Admissions ... Mr. Jose BALDA
06 Registrar ... Mr. Navin SAIBOO
36 Director Career Planning/Placement ... Vacant
19 Associate VP Public Safety ... Dr. Ronald HURLEY
41 Assoc VP & Director Athletics ... Mr. Robert COLE
18 Assoc VP Building Services ... Vacant
29 Director Donor/Alumni Engagement ... Vacant
38 Director Counseling & Wellness Svcs ... Vacant
96 Associate VP Business Services ... Ms. Edie DELVECCHIO
43 Exec VP and University Counsel ... Mr. Andre ACEBO, JR.
37 Director of Financial Aid ... Vacant
117 Budget Officer & Risk Manager ... Mr. David R. RIDER
39 Assistant Dean for Residence Life ... Ms. Jennifer K. LUCIANO
106 Director Online Learning ... Vacant
25 Executive Director Grants Office ... Mr. Todd REGN
04 Confidential Asst to the President ... Mr. Michael SIMS
104 Dir Intl Programs & Study Abroad ... Mr. Craig KATZ
28 Director EEO/AA/Diversity ... Ms. Lisa NORCIA MARSHALL
116 Internal Auditor ... Ms. Alice BLOUNT-FENNEY

New Jersey Institute of Technology (G)

University Heights, Newark NJ 07102-1982
County: Essex FICE Identification: 002621
Unit ID: 185828
Telephone: (973) 596-3000 Carnegie Class: DU-Highest
FAX Number: (973) 642-4380 Calendar System: Semester
URL: www.njit.edu
Established: 1881 Annual Undergrad Tuition & Fees (In-State): $17,674
Enrollment: 11,652 Coed
Affiliation or Control: State IRS Status: 501(c)3
Highest Offering: Doctorate
Accreditation: M, ART, CIDA

01 President ... Dr. Teik C. LIM
05 Provost and Senior Executive VP ... Dr. Atam P. DHAWAN
10 Sr VP Finance/CFO ... Ms. Catherine BRENNAN
88 Sr VP for Real Estate & Capital Dev ... Mr. Andrew P. CHRIST
30 VP Development & Alumni Relations ... Dr. Kenneth ALEXO, JR.
15 VP for Human Resources ... Mr. Dale A. MCLEOD
26 Chief Marketing & Comm Officer ... Dr. Matthew GOLDEN
88 VP/Chief Commercial Officer ... Mr. Simon NYNENS
43 General Counsel/VP Legal Affairs ... Ms. Holly C. STERN
20 Sr Vice Prov Acad Affs & Stdnt Svcs ... Dr. Basil BALTZIS
54 Dean Newark College of Engineering ... Dr. Moshe KAM
48 Dean Col Architecture & Design ... Dr. Gabrielle ESPERDY
49 Dean Col Science/Liberal Arts ... Dr. Kevin D. BELFIELD
50 Dean School of Management ... Dr. Oya I. TUKEL
92 Dean A Dorman Honors College ... Dr. Louis I. HAMILTON
77 Dean Ying Wu College of Computing ... Dr. Craig GOTSMAN
46 Sr Vice Provost for Research ... Dr. Atam P. DHAWAN
21 AVP Accounting & Treasury Mgmt ... Mr. Brian J. KIRKPATRICK
58 Vice Provost Graduate Studies ... Dr. Sotirios G. ZIAVRAS

13 Vice Provost & CIO .... Ms. Kamalika SANDELL
84 AVP Enrollment Mgmt/Academic Svcs .... Vacant
41 Assoc VP/Director of Athletics .... Mr. Leonard I. KAPLAN
32 VP/Dean of Students & Campus Life .... Dr. Marybeth BOGER
29 Assoc VP for Constituent Relations .... Mr. Michael A. WALL
04 Sr Assistant to President .... Ms. Renee WATKINS
88 Exec Dir Ctr for Pre-College Pgms ...... Dr. Jacqueline L. CUSACK
36 Exec Director Career Devel Svcs .... Mr. Gregory MASS
09 Exec Director Inst Effectiveness .... Dr. Eugene P. DEESS
08 University Librarian .... Ms. Ann D. HOANG
06 Registrar .... Dr. Jerry TROMBELLA
37 Exec Dir Student Financial Aid Svcs .... Ms. Ivon NUNEZ
22 Exec Director EOP .... Dr. Crystal SMITH
38 Dir Counseling & Psych Services .... Dr. Phyllis BOLLING
19 Chief of Police .... Mr. Kevin S. KESSELMAN
24 Dir Media & Technology Support Svcs .... Mr. Joseph BONCHI
85 Exec Director Global Initiatives .... Dr. Marieta CHEMISHANOVA
88 Sr Dir Events & Conference Svcs .... Ms. Lorie BROWN
96 Executive Director Purchasing .... Ms. Eugenia REGENCIO
86 Chief External Affairs Officer .... Dr. Angela R. GARRETSON
105 Director Web Services .... Mr. Ersal ASLAM
07 Exec Dir of University Admissions .... Mr. Stephen M. ECK
106 Assoc CIO Digital Lrng/Campus Supp .... Mr. Blake HAGGERTY
25 Exec Director Sponsored Research ... Dr. Eric D. HETHERINGTON
35 Assoc Dean of Students .... Mr. Sean R. DOWD
122 Assoc Dir Fraternity/Sorority Life .... Mr. Michael A. DAVIS

Ocean County College (A)

PO Box 2001, Toms River NJ 08754-2001

County: Ocean | FICE Identification: 002624
Unit ID: 185873
Telephone: (732) 255-0400 | Carnegie Class: Assoc/HT-High Non
FAX Number: (732) 255-0444 | Calendar System: Semester
URL: www.ocean.edu
Established: 1964 | Annual Undergrad Tuition & Fees (In-District): $5,790
Enrollment: 7,480 | Coed
Affiliation or Control: State/Local | IRS Status: 501(c)3
Highest Offering: Associate Degree
Accreditation: M, ADNUR

01 President .... Dr. Jon H. LARSON
10 Exec VP of Finance & Administration ..... Ms. Sara WINCHESTER
32 VP Student Affairs .... Dr. Gerald RACIOPPI
05 VP of Academic Affairs .... Dr. Joseph KONOPKA
90 VP e-Learning & Lrng Enterprises .... Dr. Eileen GARCIA
15 Assoc VP Human Resources .... Ms. Tracey DONALDSON
20 Asst VP for Academic Affairs .... Dr. Antoinette M. CLAY
18 Asst VP Facilities .... Mr. Matthew KENNEDY
57 Interim Dean Language and the Arts .. Dr. Samantha GLASSFORD
81 Dean Math/Science & Tech .... Dr. Sylvia RIVIELLO
66 Dean of Nursing .... Ms. Teresa WALSH
83 Dean of Social Science .... Ms. Rosann BAR
104 Assoc VP of Intl Programs Academic .... Dr. Maysa HAYWARD
102 Exec Dir OCC Foundation .... Mr. Kenneth MALAGIERE
103 Exec Dir Workforce & Prof Educ .... Ms. Kaitlin EVERETT
08 Director of Library Services .... Ms. Donna ROSINSKI-KAUS
13 Chief Information Officer .... Mr. James ROSS
37 Director of Financial Aid .... Ms. Yessica GARCIA-GUZMAN
06 Registrar .... Ms. Janine EMMA
121 Dir of Academic Advising Services .... Ms. Anna REGAN
19 Director of College Security .... Mr. Thomas DESIMONE
26 Exec Director of College Relations .... Ms. Jan KIRSTEN
93 Director of EOF & OMS .... Ms. Laura RICKARDS
18 Interim AVP Facilities & Construct .... Mr. James CALAMIA
41 Exec Dir of Athletics .... Ms. Ilene COHEN
45 Exec Dir of Institutional Planning .... Ms. Alexa BESHARA
35 Director of Student Life .... Ms. Jennifer FAZIO
29 Alumni & Advancement Director .... Ms. Kimberly MALONEY
38 Dir Counseling/Student Development .... Dr. Kathryn PANDOLPHO
84 Exec Director Enrollment Services .... Ms. Sheenah HARTIGAN
105 Assoc Director Web Services .... Ms. Maureen CONLON
25 Director Grant Administration .... Ms. Kayci CLAYTON
96 Exec Director Procure & Compliance .... Ms. Christine HEALEY
106 Dean of e-Learning .... Ms. Vivian LYNN

Passaic County Community College (B)

1 College Boulevard, Paterson NJ 07509-1179

County: Passaic | FICE Identification: 009994
Unit ID: 186034
Telephone: (973) 684-6868 | Carnegie Class: Assoc/MT-VT-High Trad
FAX Number: (973) 684-5843 | Calendar System: Semester
URL: www.pccc.edu
Established: 1968 | Annual Undergrad Tuition & Fees (In-District): $7,350
Enrollment: 5,549 | Coed
Affiliation or Control: State/Local | IRS Status: 501(c)3
Highest Offering: Associate Degree
Accreditation: M, ADNUR, MAC, RAD

01 President .... Dr. Steven ROSE
05 SVP Academic/Student Affairs .... Dr. Jacqueline KINEAVY
10 Vice Pres Finance/Adm Services .... Mr. Steven HARDY
13 Vice Pres Information Technology .... Mr. Bradley MORTON
15 Associate Vice Pres Human Resources ...... Mr. Jose FERNANDEZ
20 Sr Dean Academic Affairs .... Dr. Bassel STASSIS
08 Head Librarian .... Ms. Mibong LA
66 Dean Nurse Educ/Health Sciencess .... Dr. Donna STANKIEWICZ
121 Dean Academic Success Center .... Mr. Peter HYNES
09 Exec Dir Institutional Research .... Dr. Justin HULL
88 Ex Dir Cultural Affs/The Poetry Ctr .... Ms. Maria GILLAN
111 Vice President Inst Advancement .... Mr. Todd SORBER
84 AVP/Dean Enrollment Svcs .... Ms. Rebecca ROYAL
88 Dn Academic Initiative Policy Mgmt .... Ms. Betsy MARINACE
18 Assoc VP Facilities/Planning .... Mr. Brian EGAN
37 Director Financial Aid .... Ms. Linda GAYTON
06 Registrar .... Ms. Kathleen NELSON
19 Director Security .... Mr. Glenn BROWN
35 Director Student Activities .... Vacant
41 Athletic Director .... Mr. Wayne MARTIN
07 Director of Admissions .... Ms. Ashley CASTIGLIA
29 Director Alumni Relations .... Vacant
32 AVP/Dean of Student Affairs .... Dr. Sharon GOLDSTEIN
26 Chief Public Relations Officer .... Mr. Todd SORBER
96 Director of Purchasing .... Mr. Michael D'AGATI
101 Dir Board Affairs/Asst to President .... Ms. Evelyn DEFEIS
103 Exec Dir Workforce/Career Dev .... Ms. Janet ALBRECHT

Pillar College (C)

60 Park Place, Suite 701, Newark NJ 07102

County: Essex | FICE Identification: 036663
Unit ID: 440794
Telephone: (973) 803-5000 | Carnegie Class: Bac-A&S
FAX Number: (973) 242-3282 | Calendar System: Semester
URL: www.pillar.edu
Established: 1908 | Annual Undergrad Tuition & Fees: $22,756
Enrollment: 534 | Coed
Affiliation or Control: Other | IRS Status: 501(c)3
Highest Offering: Master's
Accreditation: M, BI

01 President .... Dr. Rupert A. HAYLES, JR.
00 Chancellor .... Dr. David E. SCHROEDER
30 Exec Dir Development/Operations .... Mr. Simao DASILVA
05 VP Academic Affairs/Dean of College .... Ms. Amy HUBER
11 Chf Operating Ofcr/Exec Vice Pres .... Vacant
88 VP Strategic Alliances .... Dr. Wayne R. DYER
58 VP Academic Development .... Dr. Ralph GRANT
06 Registrar .... Mr. Brian SCHROEDER
37 Director of Financial Aid .... Ms. Alexandra MADRIGAL
07 Assoc VP of Admissions .... Mr. Dominic DIGIOACCHINO
08 Assoc Dean Information Resources .... Ms. Vinell SPIED
26 VP Institutional Outreach & Mktg .... Ms. Erica OLIVER
32 Assoc Dean Student Development .... Mr. Nishanth THOMAS
04 Admin Assistant to the President .... Ms. Alexandra MADRIGAL
09 Director Institutional Research .... Mr. Brian SCHROEDER
13 Chief Information Technology Office .... Vacant
15 Director of Human Resources .... Ms. Samantha ARES

Princeton Theological Seminary (D)

PO Box 821, 64 Mercer Street, Princeton NJ 08542-0803

County: Mercer | FICE Identification: 002626
Unit ID: 186122
Telephone: (609) 497-7990 | Carnegie Class: Spec-4-yr-Faith
FAX Number: (609) 924-2973 | Calendar System: Semester
URL: www.ptsem.edu
Established: 1812 | Annual Graduate Tuition & Fees: N/A
Enrollment: 350 | Coed
Affiliation or Control: Presbyterian Church (U.S.A.) | IRS Status: 501(c)3
Highest Offering: Doctorate; No Undergraduates
Accreditation: M, THEOL

01 President .... Dr. M. Craig BARNES
111 EVP for External Relations .... Mr. Shane A. BERG
10 VP Finance/CFO/Treasurer .... Mr. Kurt A. GABBARD
26 VP for External Relations .... Ms. Anne WHITAKER STEWART
05 Dean and VP of Academic Affairs .... Dr. Jacqueline E. LAPSLEY
32 Dean Student Life & VP Stdnt Rels .... Rev. John E. WHITE
20 Senior Assoc Academic Dean .... Dr. Shawn OLIVER
78 Int Dir Vocational/Field Education .... RevDr. Catherine C. DAVIS
51 Assoc Dean of Continuing Educ .... Rev. Dayle G. ROUNDS
06 Registrar .... Ms. Brenda D. WILLIAMS
07 Dir Admissions/Enrollment Mgmt .... Mr. Joel David ESTES
08 Managing Dir of the Library .... Ms. Evelyn FRANGAKIS
110 Assoc VP for Advancement .... Vacant
15 Int Director of Human Resources .... Ms. Pamela WHITT
13 Director of Information Tech/CIO .... Mr. Jeffrey SIEBEN
18 Director of Facilities/Construction .... Mr. German MARTINEZ
09 Dir of Institutional Research .... Mr. Matthew WITKOWSKI
88 Business Office Consultant .... Mr. John W. GILMORE
96 Director Contracts/Procurement .... Mr. Stephen CARDONE
20 Assoc Dean for Academic Admin .... Dr. Rose Ellen DUNN
38 Director of Student Counseling .... Ms. Wanda Marie SEVEY
42 Minister of the Chapel .... Rev. Janice S. AMMON
28 Assoc Dean of Inst Diversity .... Rev. Victor ALOYO, JR.
04 Deputy to the President .... Ms. Catherine AHMAD
37 Assoc Director Financial Aid .... Mr. Michael D. LIVIO
44 Director of Annual Giving .... Ms. Cheryl ALI
112 Director of Planned Giving .... Vacant
29 Director of Alumni Relations .... Rev. Ann-Henley NICHOLSON

Princeton University (E)

Princeton NJ 08544-1098

County: Mercer | FICE Identification: 002627
Unit ID: 186131
Telephone: (609) 258-3000 | Carnegie Class: DU-Highest
FAX Number: N/A | Calendar System: Semester
URL: www.princeton.edu
Established: 1746 | Annual Undergrad Tuition & Fees: $48,502
Enrollment: 7,853 | Coed
Affiliation or Control: Independent Non-Profit | IRS Status: 501(c)3
Highest Offering: Doctorate
Accreditation: M, CAEP

01 President .... Cristopher L. EISGRUBER
03 Executive Vice President .... Treby WILLIAMS
05 Provost .... Deborah PRENTICE
04 Vice President & Secretary .... Hilary PARKER
10 Vice Pres for Finance & Treasurer .... Jim MATTEO
111 Vice President for Advancement .... Kevin B. HEANEY
26 Vice Pres Comm/Public Affairs .... Gadi DECHTER
32 Vice President of Campus Life .... Rochelle CALHOUN
18 Vice President for Facilities .... KyuJung E. WHANG
13 Vice President Info Technology/CIO .... Jay DOMINICK
15 Vice President for Human Resources .... Romy RIDDICK
109 Vice Pres for University Services .... Chad L. KLAUS
116 VP/Chief Audit & Compliance Officer .... Nilufer K. SHROFF
43 VP & General Counsel .... Ramona E. ROMERO
20 Vice Provost Academic/Budget Plng .... Richard MYERS
22 Vice Provost Inst Equity/Diversity .... Michelle MINTER
09 Vice Provost Institutional Research .... Jed MARSH
88 Vice Prov Space Programming/Plng .... Paul LAMARCHE
114 Budget Dir/Vice Provost Finance .... Steven GILL
85 Actg Vice Provost Intl Initiatives .... Aly KASSAM-REMTULLA
29 Deputy VP Alumni Engagement .... Alexandra H. DAY
44 AVP Annual Giving/Advancement .... Susan E. WALSH
88 AVP Capital Projects/Construction .... Jim KAZDA
88 Assoc Vice Pres University Services .... Andrew KANE
30 AVP for Development .... Kerstin LARSEN
39 AVP Univ Svcs/Housing .... Andrew KANE
46 Chair Univ Rsrch Bd/Dean Research .... Pablo DEBENEDETTI
88 President PRINCO .... Andrew K. GOLDEN
58 Dean of the Graduate School .... Rodney PRIESTLEY
20 Dean of the Faculty .... Gene Andrew JARRETT
49 Dean of the College .... Jill S. DOLAN
54 Dean School of Engineering .... Andrea J. GOLDSMITH
82 Int Dean Sch of Public/Intl Affairs .... Nolan MCCARTY
48 Dean of School of Architecture .... Monica PONCE DE LEON
42 Dean of Religious Life .... Alison BODEN
35 Dean of Undergraduate Students .... Kathleen DEIGNAN
07 Dean of Admission .... Karen RICHARDSON
17 Exec Director Health Services .... John KOLLIGIAN
08 University Librarian .... Anne JARVIS
06 Registrar .... Polly WINFREY GRIFFIN
37 Dir Undergraduate Financial Aid .... Robin A. MOSCATO
86 Director Government Affairs .... Joyce A. RECHTSCHAFFEN
31 Dir Community & Regional Affairs .... Kristin APPELGET
41 Director of Athletics .... Mollie D. MARCOUX
96 Director of Procurement Svcs .... Mohamed ELA
38 Dir of Counseling & Psych Services .... Calvin R. CHIN
16 Director Human Resources .... John J. MARTIN
85 Director Davis International Center .... Albert RIVERA
90 Assoc CIO/Dir Academic Services OIT .... Serge J. GOLDSTEIN
14 Assoc CIO/Dir Support Services OIT .... David MORREALE
91 Dir Enterprise Infrastructure OIT .... Donna E. TATRO
104 Sr Assoc Dean for Intl Pgms ... Rebecca GRAVES-BAYAZITOGLU
19 Executive Director Public Safety .... Paul OMINSKY
36 Exec Dir Center for Career Dev .... Kimberly BETZ

Rabbi Jacob Joseph School (F)

1 Plainfield Avenue, Edison NJ 08817-4494

County: Middlesex | FICE Identification: 030775
Unit ID: 384421
Telephone: (732) 985-6533 | Carnegie Class: Spec-4-yr-Faith
FAX Number: (732) 985-6553 | Calendar System: Semester
Established: 1982 | Annual Undergrad Tuition & Fees: $11,950
Enrollment: 73 | Male
Affiliation or Control: Independent Non-Profit | IRS Status: 501(c)3
Highest Offering: Baccalaureate
Accreditation: RABN

01 President .... Mr. Avi SCHICK
03 Rosh Yeshiva .... Rabbi Zalman BUSEL
05 Rosh Yeshiva .... Rabbi Joseph EICHENSTEIN
37 Financial Aid Director .... Rabbi Yitzchok WEINTRAUB

Rabbinical College of America (G)

226 Sussex Avenue, Morristown NJ 07960-3600

County: Morris | FICE Identification: 008609
Unit ID: 186186
Telephone: (973) 267-9404 | Carnegie Class: Spec-4-yr-Faith
FAX Number: (973) 553-6957 | Calendar System: Trimester
URL: www.rca.edu
Established: 1956 | Annual Undergrad Tuition & Fees: $12,000
Enrollment: 258 | Male
Affiliation or Control: Independent Non-Profit | IRS Status: 501(c)3
Highest Offering: Baccalaureate
Accreditation: RABN

01 Dean .... Rabbi Moshe HERSON
04 Admin Assistant to the Dean .... Rabbi Mendy HERSON
26 Public Relations Officer .... Mrs. Chana TUNK
06 Registrar .... Mrs. Shoshana SOLOMON
88 Director New Direction Program .... Rabbi Zalman DUBINSKY
10 Chief Business Officer .... Vacant
37 Director Student Financial Aid .... Rabbi Yisroel GOLDBERG
08 Chief Librarian .... Rabbi Sholom SPALTER
51 Dir Continuing Educ/Alumni Rels .... Rabbi Boruch HECHT
88 Director Semicha Program .... Rabbi Chaim SCHAPIRO
18 Director Building and Grounds .... Rabbi Hershel LIPSKIER

Rabbinical Seminary M'kor Chaim (A)

160 Locust Street, Lakewood NJ 08701
County: Ocean FICE Identification: 008617
Unit ID: 194718
Telephone: (718) 851-0183 Carnegie Class: Not Classified
FAX Number: (718) 853-2967 Calendar System: Semester
Established: 1965 Annual Undergrad Tuition & Fees: $8,300
Enrollment: 34 Male
Affiliation or Control: Independent Non-Profit IRS Status: 501(c)3
Highest Offering: Second Talmudic Degree
Accreditation: AIJS

Ramapo College of New Jersey (B)

505 Ramapo Valley Road, Mahwah NJ 07430-1680
County: Bergen FICE Identification: 009344
Unit ID: 186201
Telephone: (201) 684-7500 Carnegie Class: Masters/L
FAX Number: (201) 684-7508 Calendar System: Semester
URL: www.ramapo.edu
Established: 1969 Annual Undergrad Tuition & Fees (In-State): $14,952
Enrollment: 6,042 Coed
Affiliation or Control: State IRS Status: 501(c)3
Highest Offering: Doctorate
Accreditation: M, CAEP, NUR, SW

01 President .... Dr. Cindy R. JEBB
05 Interim Provost/VP Academic Affairs .... Dr. Susan GAULDEN
10 VP Admin & Fin/Chief of Operations . Ms. Kirsten LOEWRIGKEIT
43 VP and General Counsel .... Mr. Michael A. TRIPODI
111 Int VP Inst Advance/Dir Foundation .... Dr. Angela CRISTINI
84 VP Enrollment Mgmt/Student Affairs .... Mr. Christopher ROMANO
45 Chief Planning Officer .... Vacant
100 Chief of Staff/Board Liaison .... Dr. Brittany A. WILLIAMS-GOLDSTEIN
116 Director of Internal Audit .... Ms. Patricia CHAVEZ
20 Vice Prov Curriculum & Assessment .... Dr. Susan GAULDEN
88 Director of Capital Planning .... Mr. Daniel ROCHE
13 AVP/Chief Information Officer .... Mr. Robert DOSTER
86 Government Relations Officer .... Mr. Patrick W. O'CONNOR
105 Asst VP Mktg/Comm & Web Admin .... Ms. Melissa HORVATH-PLYMAN
08 Interim College Librarian/Dean .... Ms. Leigh-Cregan KELLER
06 Registrar .... Ms. Fernanda PAPALIA
07 Interim Director of Admissions .... Mr. Anthony DOVI
37 Director of Financial Aid .... Mr. F. Shawn O'NEILL
21 Controller .... Ms. Colleen O'KEEFE
15 Asst VP of HR & Benefits .... Ms. Viriginia GALDIERI
78 Dir Exper Learning/Career Svcs .... Ms. Beth RICCA
32 Dean of Students .... Ms. Melissa VAN DER WALL
41 Director of Athletics .... Mr. Harold CROCKER
18 Director of Facilities .... Mr. Michael CUNNINGHAM
19 Director Public Safety .... Vacant
88 Director Educ Opportunity Program .... Ms. Barbara HARMON-FRANCIS
50 Dean Anisfield School of Business .... Dr. Edward PETKUS
79 Int Dean Sch Humanities/Global Stds .... Dr. Susan HANGEN
57 Interim Dean Sch of Contemp Arts .... Mr. Peter CAMPBELL
83 Dean Sch Soc Science & Human Svc .... Dr. Aaron S. LORENZ
81 Int Dn Sch Theoretical/Applied Sci .... Dr. Edward SAIFF
53 Asst Dean for Teacher Education .... Dr. Brian CHINNI
38 Director Ctr for Health/Counseling .... Dr. Judith GREEN
29 Dir Alumni Relations .... Vacant
04 Executive Assistant to President .... Ms. Sara GAZZILLO
23 Coordinator Health Services .... Ms. Debbie LUKACSKO
09 Director of Institutional Research .... Dr. Gurvinder KHANEJA
22 Dir Affirmative Action/EEO .... Vacant
40 Bookstore Manager .... Ms. Theresa KING
85 Dir Intl Education/Study Abroad .... Mr. Ben LEVY
36 Asst Dir Career Dev & Placement .... Ms. Debra STARK
96 Director of Procurement .... Mr. Shawn LAIDLAW
103 Manager of Learning/Devel & Perf .... Mr. Roger JANS
25 Asst VP of Grants/Sponsor Programs .... Ms. Angela CRISTINI
28 Chief Diversity & Equity Officer .... Ms. Nicole MORGAN AGARD
35 Director of Student Conduct .... Ms. Kathleen HALLISSEY
121 Asst VP of Student Success .... Mr. Joseph CONNELL
114 Chief Budget Officer .... Ms. Beth WALKLEY
113 Director of Student Accounts .... Ms. Debra SCHULTES
118 Benefits Manager .... Vacant
119 Network Administrator .... Vacant
39 Dir Resident Life/Student Housing .... Ms. Lisa GONSISKO
110 Asst Dir of Institutional Advance .... Mr. David TERDIMAN
102 Sr Director Constituent Relations .... Mr. Peter RICE
112 Director Major Gifts .... Vacant
122 Asst Dir Stdnt Involve-Greek Life .... Ms. Amanda RIEHL

Raritan Valley Community College (C)

118 Lamington Road, Branchburg NJ 08876
County: Somerset FICE Identification: 007731
Unit ID: 186645
Telephone: (908) 526-1200 Carnegie Class: Assoc/MT-VT-Mix Trad/Non
FAX Number: (908) 526-0253 Calendar System: Semester
URL: www.raritanval.edu
Established: 1966 Annual Undergrad Tuition & Fees (In-District): $6,672
Enrollment: 7,080 Coed
Affiliation or Control: State/Local IRS Status: 501(c)3
Highest Offering: Associate Degree
Accreditation: M, ADNUR, CAHIIM, MAC, OPD, OTA

01 President .... Dr. Michael MCDONOUGH
05 Provost & VP Academic Affairs .... Vacant
10 Vice President Finance/Facilities .... Mr. John TROJAN
15 Exec Dir HR & Labor Relations .... Ms. Cheryl WALLACE
32 VP for Student Affairs & Outreach .... Ms. Jacki BELIN
49 Dean Liberal/Fine Arts/Bus/Pub Svc .... Dr. Patrice MARKS
81 Dean STEM & Health Science .... Dr. Sarah IMBRIGLIO
121 Dean Academic Support & Ed Partners .... Dr. Audrey LOERA
18 Exec Director Facilities/Grounds .... Mr. Brian O'ROURKE
92 Dir Honors Pgm & Alumni Outreach .... Mr. Greg DESANCTIS
24 Director Media Relations .... Ms. Donna STOLZER
102 Executive Director Foundation .... Mr. Michael MARION
14 Exec Dir Technology Services .... Mr. Robert PESCINSKI
21 Controller/Exec Dir of Finance .... Ms. Violet J. WILLENSKY
09 Dir of Inst Research/Assessment .... Ms. Sarah DONNELLY
88 Director of Planetarium .... Ms. Amie GALLAGHER
88 Director of Child Care Center .... Ms. Gwendolyn WRIGHT
37 Director of Financial Aid .... Mr. Lenny MESONAS
06 Registrar .... Mr. John WHEELER
96 Director of Purchasing .... Mr. Michael DEPINTO
35 Director of Student Life .... Mr. Russell BAREFOOT
84 Exec Dir Enrollment Management .... Ms. Carolyn WHITE
35 Dean of Student Affairs .... Mr. Jason FREDERICKS
19 Director Security/Safety .... Mr. Robert SZKODNEY
106 Dir Online Educ/Distance Learning .... Mr. Brett COUP
101 Secretary to the Board of Trustees .... Ms. Sheri PONTAROLLO
28 Dir Diversity/Equity & Inclusion .... Dr. Windy PAZ-AMOR
41 Athletic Director .... Mr. Joseph PAVLOW

Rider University (D)

2083 Lawrenceville Road, Lawrenceville NJ 08648-3099
County: Mercer FICE Identification: 002628
Unit ID: 186283
Telephone: (609) 896-5000 Carnegie Class: Masters/L
FAX Number: (609) 895-5681 Calendar System: Semester
URL: www.rider.edu
Established: 1865 Annual Undergrad Tuition & Fees: $45,860
Enrollment: 4,636 Coed
Affiliation or Control: Independent Non-Profit IRS Status: 501(c)3
Highest Offering: Doctorate
Accreditation: M, CACREP, CAEP, CAEPN, MUS, NURSE

01 President .... Dr. Gregory DELL'OMO
05 Provost/Vice Pres Academic Affairs .... Dr. DonnaJean A. FREDEEN
10 Vice President Finance/Treasurer .... Mr. James HARTMAN
111 Vice Pres University Advancement .... Ms. Karin KLIM
32 Vice President Student Affairs .... Dr. Leanna FENNEBERG
84 Vice Pres Enrollment Management .... Mr. Drew C. AROMANDO
43 VP Legal Affs/General Counsel .... Mr. Mark SOLOMON
18 VP Facilities/Auxiliary Services .... Mr. Michael F. RECA
15 VP Human Resources .... Mr. Robert STOTO
28 VP for DEI/Chief Diversity Officer .... Dr. Barbara J. LAWRENCE
45 VP Strategic Initiatives & Planning .... Ms. Debbie STASOLLA
13 CIO & Assoc VP Info Tech .... Mr. Douglas MCCREA
26 Assoc VP for Univ Mktg/Comm .... Ms. Kristine A. BROWN
20 Associate Provost/Legal Counsel .... Dr. Matt STIEGLITZ
49 Dean Col Arts & Sciences .... Dr. Kelly BIDLE
53 Dean Col of Educ & Human Svcs .... Dr. Jason BARR
50 Dean Norm Brodsky Col of Business .... Dr. Gene KUTCHER
09 Director Institutional Research .... Vacant
121 Asst VP AA & Student Success .... Mr. Jim CONLON
06 Registrar .... Ms. Susan A. STEFANICK
19 Director of Public Safety .... Mr. James WALDON
29 Director of Alumni Relations .... Ms. Natalie M. POLLARD
41 Director of Athletics .... Mr. Donald P. HARNUM
36 Exec Director Career Dev & Success .... Ms. Kim BARBERICH
28 Exec Director Diversity & Inclusion .... Dr. Pamela PRUITT
38 Director of Counseling .... Dr. Anissa MOODY
96 Director of Procurement .... Ms. Ann Marie MEAD
07 Director for UG & Transfer Adm .... Ms. Susan MAKOWSKI
40 Manager College Store .... Ms. Catherine RUSSOMANNO
124 Asst Dir Student Involvement .... Ms. Kadi DIALLO

Rowan College at Burlington County (E)

900 College Circle, Mt. Laurel NJ 08054
County: Burlington FICE Identification: 007730
Unit ID: 183877
Telephone: (856) 222-9311 Carnegie Class: Assoc/HT-Mix Trad/Non
FAX Number: (609) 894-0183 Calendar System: Semester
URL: www.rcbc.edu
Established: 1966 Annual Undergrad Tuition & Fees (In-District): $5,159
Enrollment: 7,316 Coed
Affiliation or Control: State/Local IRS Status: 501(c)3
Highest Offering: Associate Degree
Accreditation: M, ADNUR, CAHIIM, DH, DMS, EMT, NAIT, RAD

01 President .... Dr. Michael A. CIOCE
04 Exec Asst to the President .... Ms. Lynne Marie DEVERICKS
05 Sr Vice President/Provost .... Dr. David SPANG
10 Sr VP Admin and Operations .... Mr. Thomas J. CZERNIECKI
103 VP WFD/Lifelong Learning .... Ms. Anna PAYANZO COTTON
84 VP Enroll Mgmt and Student Success .... Dr. Karen ARCHAMBAULT
13 Chief Information Officer .... Mr. Mark MEARA
15 Exec Dir Finance/Human Resources .... Mr. Harry METZINGER
11 Chief Operations Officer .... Mr. Matthew FARR
102 Exec Director of RCBC Foundation .... Ms. Lindsey DANIELLO
26 Exec Dir Marketing/Communications .... Mr. Greg VOLPE
16 Asst Director of HR .... Ms. Michelle RUSSELL
49 Dean of Liberal Arts .... Dr. Donna VANDERGRIFT
81 Dean of STEM .... Dr. Edem TETTEH
76 Dean of Health Sciences .... Dr. Karen MONTALTO
106 Dean of Learning Resources .... Dr. Martin A. HOFFMAN, SR.
07 Dean of Enrollment Mgmt .... Mr. Jarrett KEALEY
32 Dean of Student Success .... Dr. Catherine R. BRIGGS
06 Registrar .... Ms. LacyJane RYMAN-MESCAL
41 Director of Athletics .... Ms. Heather CONGER
88 Director of Culinary Arts .... Mr. James BRUDNICKI
88 Director of EOF Program .... Ms. Edith CORBIN
19 Director of Public Safety .... Mr. Andrew EATON

Rowan College of South Jersey (F)

1400 Tanyard Road, Sewell NJ 08080-9518
County: Gloucester FICE Identification: 006901
Unit ID: 184791
Telephone: (856) 468-5000 Carnegie Class: Assoc/HT-High Trad
FAX Number: N/A Calendar System: 4/1/4
URL: https://www.rcsj.edu/
Established: 1966 Annual Undergrad Tuition & Fees (In-District): $5,400
Enrollment: 6,369 Coed
Affiliation or Control: State/Local IRS Status: 501(c)3
Highest Offering: Associate Degree
Accreditation: M, ACBSP, ADNUR, DMS, NMT, PTAA

01 President .... Dr. Frederick KEATING
05 VP Academic Services/Provost .... Dr. Brenden RICKARDS
11 Vice President & COO .... Mr. Dominick BURZICHELLI
32 Vice President Student Svcs .... Ms. Judith ATKINSON
13 Vice President/CIO .... Mr. Josh R. PIDDINGTON
10 Exec Director Financial Services .... Ms. Cheryl LEWIS
15 Exec Director Human Resource .... Ms. Coryndi MCFADDEN
04 Sr Exec Assistant to the President .... Ms. Meg RESUE
28 Exec Dir Diversity and Equity .... Mrs. Almarie JONES
09 Dean Inst Research & Assessment .... Ms. Karen DURKIN
66 Dean Nursing & Allied Health .... Dr. Susan HALL
49 Dean Liberal Arts .... Dr. Paul RUFINO
81 Dean STEM .... Dr. Christina NASE
20 Dean Academic Compliance .. Dr. Danielle ZIMECKI-FENNIMORE
61 Dean Law and Justice .... Mr. Fred H. MADDEN
50 Dean Business Studies .... Ms. Patricia CLAGHORN
07 Exec Director Admissions/Registrar .... Ms. Sandra HOFFMAN
36 Director Career & Academic Planning .... Ms. Megan RUTTLER
35 Exec Director Student Engagement .... Ms. Samantha VAN KOOY
08 Director Library Services .... Mrs. Jane S. CROCKER
19 Director Security/Safety .... Mr. Joseph GETSINGER
37 Exec Dir Financial Aid & Admission .... Mr. Michael CHANDO
96 Controller/Purchasing .... Mr. Mark ZORZI

Rowan College of South Jersey Cumberland Campus (G)

3322 College Drive, PO Box 1500,
Vineland NJ 08362-1500
Telephone: (856) 691-8600 FICE Identification: 002601
Accreditation: &M, RAD

Rowan University (H)

201 Mullica Hill Road, Glassboro NJ 08028-1700
County: Gloucester FICE Identification: 002609
Unit ID: 184782
Telephone: (856) 256-4000 Carnegie Class: DU-Higher
FAX Number: (856) 256-4929 Calendar System: Semester
URL: www.rowan.edu
Established: 1923 Annual Undergrad Tuition & Fees (In-State): $12,939
Enrollment: 19,678 Coed
Affiliation or Control: State IRS Status: 501(c)3
Highest Offering: Doctorate
Accreditation: M, ART, CAATE, CACREP, CAEPN, CLPSY, DIETC, EXSC, MED, MUS, NURSE, OSTEO, THEA

01 President .... Dr. Ali HOUSHMAND
05 Provost/Sr VP for Academic Affairs .... Dr. Anthony LOWMAN
10 Senior Vice Pres of Finance/CFO .... Mr. Joseph F. SCULLY
32 SVP for Student Affairs .... Dr. Jeffrey HAND
111 VP Univ Advance/Exec Dir Fndn .... Mr. Jesse R. SHAFER
35 VP Student Life/Dean Students .... Dr. Kevin S. KOETT
86 VP Govt Rels/External Relationships .... Mr. Sean KENNEDY
18 VP for Facilities & Operations .... Dr. Joseph CAMPBELL
15 VP Human Resources/CHRO .... Ms. Theresa DRYE
44 Chief of Staff .... Mr. Ronald J. TALLARIDA
20 VP Academic Affairs .... Dr. Roberta HARVEY
13 VP Information Resources/CIO .... Dr. Mira LALOVIC-HAND
14 VP Info/Resources & Tech .... Mr. Mark SEDLOCK
26 VP for University Relations .... Dr. Joe CARDONA
46 Vice President for Research .... Dr. Tabbetha DOBBINS
43 General Counsel/Board Liaison .... Ms. Melissa WHEATCROFT
88 Chief Audit/Compliance/Privacy Ofcr .... Mr. Ray BRAEUNIG
84 VP for Strategic Enrollment Mgmt .... Mr. Darren WAGNER
88 VP for Student Affairs .... Ms. Rory MCELWEE
20 Vice Provost for Faculty Affairs .... Dr. Mariano SAVELSKI
28 VP Diversity/Equity & Inclusion .... Dr. Penny MCPHERSON MYERS
19 Asst VP Public Safety/Emerg Mgmt .... Mr. Michael KANTNER
63 Dean of Cooper Medical School of RU .... Dr. Annette REBOLI
50 Dean Rohrer College of Business .... Dr. Susan LEHRMAN
81 Dean College of Science/Mathematics . Dr. Vojislava POPHRISTIC
53 Dean of the College of Education .... Dr. Gaetane JEAN-MARIE
57 Dean of College of Performing Arts .... Dr. Rick DAMMERS
88 VP Strategic Ventures/Initiatives .... Dr. Horacio SOSA
54 Dean of the College of Engineering ..... Dr. Giuseppe R. PALMESE

60 Dean of Col of Comm & Creat Arts .... Dr. Sanford M. TWEEDIE
83 Dean of the Col of Hum & Soc Sci .... Dr. Nawal H. AMMAR
63 Dean School of Osteopathic Medicine ...... Dr. Thomas CAVALIERI
22 SVP Diversity/Equity/Inclusion .... Dr. Monika SHEALEY
41 Dean of the Honors College .... Dr. Lee TALLEY
88 Dean of the School of Vet Medicine .... Dr. Matthew EDSON
66 Dean School of Nurs & Health Prof .... Dr. Peter RATTIGAN
65 Dean School of Earth & Environment .... Dr. Kenneth LACOVARA
08 Assoc Provost of Library Info Serv .... Dr. Robert HILLIKER
16 Assoc VP HR/Talent & Employee Mgmt .... Mr. Henry OH
14 Assoc VP Info/Resources & Tech .... Ms. Jackie RING

Rutgers University - Camden (A)

303 Cooper Street, Camden NJ 08102
County: Camden FICE Identification: 004741
Unit ID: 186371
Telephone: (856) 225-6095 Carnegie Class: DU-Higher
FAX Number: (856) 225-6495 Calendar System: Semester
URL: www.camden.rutgers.edu
Established: 1926 Annual Undergrad Tuition & Fees (In-State): $14,877
Enrollment: 7,076 Coed
Affiliation or Control: State IRS Status: 501(c)3
Highest Offering: Doctorate
Accreditation: &M, CAEPT, LAW, NURSE, PTA, SPAA

00 President Rutgers University .... Dr. Jonathan HOLLOWAY
88 Chief of Staff to Pres/SVP Admin .... Dr. Andrea CONKLIN BUESCHEL
02 Chancellor Rutgers Camden .... Dr. Antonio TILLIS
100 Chief of Staff Rutgers Camden .... Mr. Michael J. SEPANIC
05 Provost .... Dr. Michael PALIS
11 Sr Vice Chancellor Admin & Finance .... Mr. Larry GAINES
03 Sr Vice Chancellor .... Dr. Daniel HART
20 Int Vice Chancellor Student Success .... Dr. Marsha BESONG
32 Vice Chancellor Student Affairs .... Ms. Mary Beth DAISEY
46 Vice Chancellor Research .... Dr. Benedetto PICCOLI
84 Vice Chancellor Enrollment Mgmt .... Dr. Craig WESTMAN
111 Acting Vice Chancellor Advancement .... Mr. Scott D. OWENS
28 Assoc Chancellor Diversity .... Dr. Nyemma WATSON
06 Assoc Registrar .... Ms. Diana KEOUGH
50 Dean School of Business .... Dr. Monica ADYA
61 Int Co-Dean Rutgers Law School .. Ms. Rose CUISON-VILLAZOR
61 Co-Dean Rutgers Law School .... Ms. Kimberly MUTCHERSON
35 Dean of Students .... Mr. Thomas J. DIVALERIO
49 Dean Fac Arts & Sciences .... Dr. Howard MARCHITELLO
66 Dean School of Nursing .... Dr. Donna NICKITAS
58 Assoc Dean Grad School .... Dr. Michelle MELOY
39 Assoc Dean Students .... Ms. Allison WISNIEWSKI
85 Asst Dean International Students .... Ms. Elizabeth A. ATKINS
36 Asst Dean Career Center .... Ms. Cheryl A. HALLMAN
37 Exec Director Financial Aid .... Ms. Danielle BARBEE
18 Exec Director Space Management .... Mr. Christopher PYE
30 Sr Director Development .... Ms. Kate BRENNAN
105 Sr Director Office of Creative Svcs ... Ms. Joanne DUS-ZASTROW
110 Director of Development .... Ms. Akua ASIAMAH-ANDRADE
53 Director MA Teaching Program .... Dr. Sara M. BECKER
41 Director Athletics & Recreation .... Mr. Jeffrey L. DEAN
103 Director Economic Development .... Mr. Gregory GAMBLE
08 Director Paul Robeson Library .... Ms. Regina KOURY
25 Director Sponsored Research .... Ms. Cammie MORRISON
106 Director Instructional Design .... Mr. William PAGAN
10 Director Finance and Administration .... Ms. Rosa M. RIVERA
07 Director Enrollment Communications .... Dr. Yosmeriz ROMAN
13 Director Information Technology .... Mr. Thomas J. RYAN
23 Director Student Wellness Center .... Dr. Neuza SERRA
94 Director Gender Studies .... Dr. Shauna SHAMES
92 Director Honors College .... Dr. Lee Ann WESTMAN
104 Assoc Director International Stdnts .... Ms. Elizabeth ATKINS
90 Assoc Director IT .... Mr. Timothy DIVITO
22 Asst Director EOF .... Ms. Randi FERGUSON
51 Asst Director Continuing Studies .... Ms. Dalynn KNIGGE
29 Asst Director Alumni Engagement .... Ms. Mary Clare VENUTO
88 Chair Economic Department .... Dr. I-Ming CHIU
82 Chair Political Science Department .... Dr. Maureen DONAGHY
57 Chair Fine Arts Department .... Dr. Kenneth ELLIOTT
88 Chair English Department .... Dr. Richard EPSTEIN
81 Chair Mathematics Department .... Dr. Siqi FU
81 Chair Chemistry Department .... Dr. Catherine GRGICAK
79 Chair World Languages & Cultures .... Dr. Tyler HOFFMAN
73 Chair Philosophy and Religion Dept .... Dr. Nicole KARAPANAGIOTIS
80 Chair Public Policy Department .... Dr. Lorraine MINNITE
81 Chair Physics .... Dr. Sean M. O'MALLEY
77 Chair Computer Science Department ... Dr. Suneeta RAMASWAMI
81 Chair Biology Department .... Dr. Daniel SHAIN
88 Chair Childhood Studies Department .... Dr. Lynne VALLONE
83 Chair Psychology Department .... Dr. Bill WHITLOW
83 Chair Sociology/Anthro Department .... Dr. Wojtek WOLFE
88 Chair History Department .... Dr. Wendy WOLOSON
19 Chief Campus Police .... Mr. Richard DINAN
39 Manager Housing & Residence Life .... Mr. Brandon CHANDLER
15 Manager Human Resources .... Ms. Roxanne HUERTAS
96 Sr Analyst University Procurement .... Mr. Christian AHA
09 Research Analyst .... Ms. Emily WOOD
38 Staff Psychologist .... Dr. Rachel THUER
101 Secretary of the University .... Ms. Kimberlee PASTVA
122 Asst Dir Campus Ctr-Greek Life .... Mr. Patrick WALLACE

† Regional accreditation is carried under Rutgers the State University of New Jersey New Brunswick.

Rutgers University - New Brunswick (B)

57 US Highway 1, New Brunswick NJ 08901-8554
County: Middlesex FICE Identification: 002629
Unit ID: 186380
Telephone: (848) 932-7821 Carnegie Class: DU-Highest
FAX Number: (732) 932-5532 Calendar System: Semester
URL: https://newbrunswick.rutgers.edu/
Established: 1766 Annual Undergrad Tuition & Fees (In-State): $15,003
Enrollment: 50,411 Coed
Affiliation or Control: State IRS Status: 501(c)3
Highest Offering: Doctorate
Accreditation: M, ART, CACREP, CAEP, CEA, CLPSY, DANCE, DIETD, HSA, IPSY, LIB, LSAR, MUS, PCSAS, PH, PHAR, PLNG, SCPSY, SPAA, SW

00 President Rutgers University .... Dr. Jonathan HOLLOWAY
88 Chief of Staff to Pres & SVP Admin .... Dr. Andrea CONKLIN BUESCHEL
02 Chancellor/Provost New Brunswick .... Dr. Francine CONWAY
17 Chancellor Rutgers RBHS .... Dr. Brian J. STROM
100 Chief of Staff Rutgers RBHS .... Mr. Steven ANDREASSEN
76 Provost Rutgers RBHS .... Dr. Jeffrey CARSON
76 Provost Rutgers RBHS ...... Dr. Patricia FITZGERALD-BOCARSLY
88 CEO Univ Behavioral Health Care .... Dr. Frank GHINASSI
28 Senior VP Equity .... Dr. Enobong (Anna) BRANCH
15 Sr Vice Pres Human Resources .... Ms. Vivian FERNANDEZ
30 Sr Assoc VP Development .... Ms. Andrianni VOLLAS VISCARIELLO
111 Vice Provost Faculty Advancement .... Dr. Ingrid FULMER
46 Vice Provost Research .... Dr. Denise HIEN
20 Vice Provost UG Education .... Dr. Carolyn MOEHLING
20 Vice Provost Academic Affairs .... Dr. Saundra TOMLINSON-CLARKE
10 Sr Vice Chancellor Fin & Admin RBHS .... Ms. Kathleen BRAMWELL
23 Sr Vice Chanc Clinical Affs RBHS .... Dr. Vicente H. GRACIAS
20 Sr Vice Chancellor Acad Affs RBHS .... Dr. M. Bishr OMARY
21 Vice Chancellor Finance .... Ms. Romayne BOTTI
26 Vice Chancellor Comm & Marketing .... Ms. Jennifer HOLLINGSHEAD
88 Vice Chancellor Grad Medical Educ .... Dr. Sherry HUANG
88 Vice Chanc Diversity & Inclusion .... Dr. Sangeeta LAMBA
88 Vice Chancellor Cancer Pgms RBHS .... Dr. Steven K. LIBUTTI
84 Vice Chancellor Enroll Management .... Mr. Courtney MCANUFF
32 Vice Chancellor Student Affairs .... Dr. Salvador MENA
88 Vice Chancellor Faculty Development .... Dr. Maral MOURADIAN
88 Vice Chanc Translational Med RBHS ..... Dr. Reynold PANETTIERI
88 Vice Chanc Interprofessional Pgm .... Dr. Denise V. RODGERS
88 Assoc Vice Chanc Technology & Instr .... Dr. Paul HAMMOND
27 Assoc Vice Chanc Comm & Marketing .... Mr. Zach HOSSEINI
88 Assoc Vice Chanc Admin & Engagement .... Ms. Keisha DABROWSKI
35 Assoc Vice Chanc Student Affairs .... Dr. Anne NEWMAN
06 University Registrar .... Ms. Kelley BRENNAN-SOKOLOWSKI
47 Int Exec Dean Agri & Nat Resources .... Dr. Laura LAWSON
49 Exec Dean School Arts & Sciences .... Dr. Peter MARCH
67 Dean Ernest Mario Sch Pharm .... Dr. Joseph BARONE
53 Dean Graduate School of Educ .... Dr. Wanda BLANCHETT
88 Dean Life Sciences SAS .... Dr. Lori COVEY
88 Dean Sch Mgmt Labor Relations .... Dr. Adrienne EATON
54 Dean School of Engineering .... Dr. Thomas N. FARRIS
52 Dean Rutgers School of Dental Med .... Dr. Cecile FELDMAN
66 Dean Division of Nursing Science .... Dr. Linda FLYNN
57 Dean Mason Gross School of Art .... Dr. Jason GEARY
92 Admn Dean New Brunswick Honors Col .... Dr. Paul GILMORE
69 Dean School of Public Health .... Dr. Perry N. HALKITIS
63 Dean New Jersey Medical School .... Dr. Robert JOHNSON
88 Int Dean Grad Sch App & Prof Psych .... Dr. Ryan J. KETTLER
50 Dean Sch of Business Newark/NB .... Dr. Lei LEI
97 Dean Douglass Residential College .... Dr. Jacquelyn S. LITT
76 Dean School of Health Professions ..... Dr. Gwendolyn M. MAHON
92 Academic Dean Honors College .... Dr. Matt MATSUDA
58 Int Dean School of Grad Studies .... Dr. Henrik PEDERSEN
70 Dean School of Social Work .... Dr. Cathryn C. POTTER
62 Dean Sch Communication & Info .... Dr. Jonathan POTTER
80 Dean EJB Sch Plng/Public Policy .... Dr. Piyushimita THAKURIAH
12 Asst Dean College Avenue Campus .... Ms. Cynthia SANCHEZ GÓMEZ
12 Asst Dean Livingston Campus .... Dr. Mahasti HASHEMI
12 Asst Dean Busch Campus .... Dr. Jennifer KIM-LEE
88 Vice Dean School of Graduate Stds .... Dr. Kathleen SCOTTO
19 Exec Director Police Services/Chief .... Mr. Kenneth B. COP
39 Exec Director of Residence Life .... Mr. Dan MORRISON
109 Exec Director Student Centers .... Mr. William O'BRIEN
18 Exec Director Space Management .... Mr. Christopher PYE
88 Exec Director Center for Org Leader .... Dr. Brent D. RUBEN
105 Sr Director Office of Creative Svcs ... Ms. Joanne DUS-ZASTROW
31 Sr Director Community Affairs .... Ms. Melissa SELESKY
122 Dir Fraternity & Sorority Affairs .... Ms. JoAnn ARNHOLT
88 Dir Advanced Biotech/Medicine .... Dr. Martin J. BLASER
07 Director Undergrad Admissions .... Ms. Kate BRITTAIN
123 Director Graduate Admissions .... Ms. Linda J. COSTA
88 Director Inst Health/Health Policy .... Dr. XinQi DONG
88 Dir Center Org Dev & Leadership .... Dr. Ralph GIGLIOTTI
09 Director Data Analytics & Mgmt .... Ms. Tina GRYCENKOV
41 Director Intercollegiate Athletics .... Mr. Patrick E. HOBBS
13 Director IT .... Mr. Brian LUPER
08 Director New Brunswick Libraries .... Ms. Dee MAGNONI
60 Director UG Studies Journalism .... Mr. Steven MILLER
85 Dir International Student Services .... Ms. Mohini MUKHERJEE
25 Director Research Financial Service .... Mr. Lamar OGLESBY
96 Director Strategic Sourcing .... Ms. Susan PANACEK
106 Director Instructional Design .... Mr. William PAGAN
22 Director SAS Equal Opp Fund Program .. Dr. Michelle SHOSTACK
38 Director of CAPS Counseling .... Dr. Steven SOHNLE
104 Director Study Abroad .... Dr. Dan WAITE
37 Director Financial Aid .... Ms. Sherrell WATSON-HALL
75 Dir Occupational Hlth Sciences Inst .... Dr. Helmut ZARBL
74 Program Director UG Animal Sciences .... Dr. Aparna M. ZAMA
36 Int Director Career Exploration .... Mr. William JONES
64 Int Director Music Education .... Dr. Steven KEMPER
103 Asst Director Continuing Studies .... Ms. Dalynn KNIGGE
87 Asst Director NB Summer Session .... Ms. Barbara RUSEN
94 Chair Dept Women's/Gender Studies .... Dr. Ethel BROOKS
65 Chair Dept of Ecol/Evol/Natural Res .... Dr. Julie LOCKWOOD
73 Chair Dept of Religion .... Dr. Tao JIANG
82 Chair Political Sciences Dept .... Dr. Daniel KELEMAN
81 Chair Math Department .... Dr. Michael SAKS
29 Sr Alumni Engagement Associate .... Mr. Elijah ROSENTHAL
101 Secretary of the University .... Ms. Kimberlee PASTVA

Rutgers University - Newark (C)

123 Washington St., Newark NJ 07102
County: Essex FICE Identification: 002631
Unit ID: 186399
Telephone: (973) 353-5541 Carnegie Class: DU-Higher
FAX Number: (973) 353-1048 Calendar System: Semester
URL: https://www.newark.rutgers.edu/
Established: 1908 Annual Undergrad Tuition & Fees (In-State): $14,502
Enrollment: 13,231 Coed
Affiliation or Control: State IRS Status: 501(c)3
Highest Offering: Doctorate
Accreditation: &M, ANEST, CAEPT, IPSY, LAW, NURSE, @SP, SPAA, SW

00 President Rutgers University .... Dr. Jonathan HOLLOWAY
88 Chief of Staff Pres & SVP Admin .... Dr. Andrea CONKLIN BUESCHEL
02 Chancellor Rutgers Newark .... Dr. Nancy E. CANTOR
05 Exec Vice Chancellor & Provost .... Dr. Ashwani MONGA
03 Exec Vice Chancellor .... Dr. Sherri-Ann P. BUTTERFIELD
26 Sr Vice Chancellor Public Affairs .... Mr. Peter ENGLOT
46 Sr Vice Chancellor Research .... Dr. Piotr PIOTROWIAK
10 Sr Vice Chancellor Admin & CFO .... Ms. Amber RANDOLPH
32 Sr Vice Chancellor Student Affairs .... Dr. Corlisse THOMAS
86 Vice Chanc External & Govt Rels .... Dr. Marcia W. BROWN
20 Vice Chancellor Acad Pgms/Strategy .... Dr. John GUNKEL
30 Vice Chancellor for Development .... Dr. Irene O'BRIEN
84 Assoc VC Enroll Svcs & Experience .... Dr. Bil LEIPOLD
31 Asst Chancellor Cmty Partnerships .... Dr. Diane HILL
84 Asst Chancellor Enroll Management .... Ms. LaToya BATTLE-BROWN
114 Asst Provost Budget Admin .... Dr. Mary TAMASCO
06 Registrar .... Ms. Marie DIAZ-TORRES
61 Int Co-Dean Rutgers Law School .. Ms. Rose CUISON-VILLAZOR
61 Co-Dean Rutgers Law School .... Ms. Kimberly MUTCHERSON
66 Dean Division of Nursing Science .... Dr. Linda FLYNN
58 Dean Graduate School Newark .... Dr. Taja-Nia HENDERSON
50 Dean Business Newark/New Bruns .... Dr. Lei LEI
49 Dean Arts & Science .... Dr. Jacqueline MATTIS
80 Dean Sch Public Affairs & Admin .... Dr. Charles MENIFIELD
88 Dean School Criminal Justice .... Dr. William MCCARTHY
39 Assoc Dean Housing & Residence Life .... Dr. Angelita BONILLA
88 Exec Director Newark Learn Collabor ..... Ms. Robyn BRADY INCE
18 Exec Director Space Management .... Mr. Christopher PYE
36 Exec Director Career Services .... Ms. Bernadette SO
38 Exec Dir Student Health & Wellness .... Dr. Anice THOMAS
85 Exec Dir Global Engage/Exp Lrng .... Dr. Clayton WALTON
45 Director Admin & Strategic Dev .... Dr. Margaret BRENNAN-TONETTA
13 Director IT .... Ms. Shelley COUSINS
88 Director Express Newark .... Dr. Frances BARTKOWSKI
94 Director Women's & Gender Studies .. Dr. Catherine FITZPATRICK
60 Director Journalism Program .... Ms. Robin GABY FISHER
41 Director of Athletics & Recreation .... Mr. Mark GRIFFIN
29 Director Alumni Relations .... Mr. Terranze GRIFFIN
64 Director RU Chorus .... Mr. Brian HARLOW
19 Director Public Safety Newark .... Mr. Carmelo V. HUERTAS
15 Director Human Resources .... Ms. Candace JOSEPH
90 Director Acad Technology Services .... Ms. Joy MCDONALD
37 Director Financial Aid .... Ms. Natalia MORISSEAU
25 Director Research Financial Svcs .... Mr. Lamar OGLESBY
106 Director Instructional Design .... Mr. William PAGAN
87 Director Summer Session .... Ms. Carmen PARDO
88 Director Center for Metro Research .... Dr. Charles M. PAYNE
81 Director UG Mathematics .... Dr. Robert PUHAK
23 Director Health Services .... Dr. Sandra SAMUELS
92 Director Honors College .... Dr. Laura TROIANO
104 Director Study Abroad .... Mr. Dan WAITE
27 Dir Communications/Marketing .... Ms. Kimberlee S. WILLIAMS
09 Director Inst Effectiveness .... Mr. Chengbo YIN
96 Assoc Director Univ Procurement .... Mr. Wes COLEMAN
103 Asst Director Continuing Studies .... Ms. Dalynn KNIGGE
08 Int Assoc Univ Librarian Newark .... Ms. Rhonda MARKER
21 Manager Business Office .... Ms. Rosann RICHARDS
57 Chair Arts/Culture/Media .... Mr. Ned DREW
83 Chair Sociology Department .... Dr. Christopher DUNCAN
82 Chair Political Science Department .... Dr. Elizabeth HULL
88 Chair African American Studies .... Mr. John KEENE
53 Chair Urban Education Program .... Dr. Arthur B. POWELL
22 Program Coordinator EOF .... Mr. Amir MALCOLM
04 Sr Exec Associate to Chancellor .... Ms. Carla HAILEY PENN
101 Secretary of the University .... Ms. Kimberlee PASTVA

† Regional accreditation is carried under Rutgers the State University of New Jersey New Brunswick.

Rutgers New Jersey Medical School (A)
185 South Orange Avenue, Newark NJ 07103
Telephone: (973) 972-4538 FICE Identification: 002620
Accreditation: &M, MED

Rutgers - Robert Wood Johnson Medical School (B)
675 Hoes Lane West, Piscataway NJ 08854
Telephone: (732) 235-6300 FICE Identification: 024549
Accreditation: &M, CAMPEP, IPSY, MED, PAST

Rutgers School of Dental Medicine (C)
110 Bergen Street, Suite B812, Newark NJ 07103
Telephone: (973) 972-4440 FICE Identification: 024635
Accreditation: &M, DENT

Rutgers School of Health Professions (D)
65 Bergen Street, Room 149, Newark NJ 07107
Telephone: (973) 972-4276 FICE Identification: 020668
Accreditation: &M, ARCPA, CACREP, CAHIIM, CYTO, DIET, DIETI, DMS, MLS, OTA, PTA

Rutgers School of Nursing (E)
180 University Avenue, Newark NJ 07102
Telephone: (973) 353-5293 Identification: 666970
Accreditation: &M, MIDWF, NURSE

Rutgers School of Public Health (F)
683 Hoes Lane West, Piscataway NJ 08854
Telephone: (732) 235-9700 Identification: 666991
Accreditation: &M, PH

Saint Elizabeth University (G)
2 Convent Road, Morristown NJ 07960-6989
County: Morris FICE Identification: 002600
Unit ID: 186618
Telephone: (973) 290-4000 Carnegie Class: Masters/M
FAX Number: N/A Calendar System: Semester
URL: www.steu.edu
Established: 1899 Annual Undergrad Tuition & Fees: $34,876
Enrollment: 1,272 Coed
Affiliation or Control: Roman Catholic IRS Status: 501(c)3
Highest Offering: Doctorate
Accreditation: M, #ARCPA, COPSY, DIETD, DIETI, NUR, SW

01 President ... Dr. Gary B. CROSBY
05 VP for Academic Affairs ... Dr. Anne BARTLETT
32 VP Student Life ... Ms. Katherine BUCK
10 VP Finance Admin/Treasurer ... Mr. Michael FESCOE
111 VP Institutional Advancement ... Mr. Joseph ERCKERT
84 VP Enrollment Management ... Ms. Joanne LANDERS
21 Controller ... Ms. Julia PEREZ
06 Registrar ... Ms. Marybeth OBRYCKI
09 Dir Inst Research & Acad Assessment ... Dr. Michele YURECKO
08 Director Mahoney Library ... Mr. Mark FERGUSON
42 Campus Minister ... Ms. Clare ETTENSOHN
18 Director of Facilities & Security ... Mr. James GERRISH
37 Director of Financial Aid ... Ms. Rebecca E. REES
26 Director Marketing/ Communications ... Ms. Denise G. PANYIK-DALE
22 Director EOF Program ... Mr. David HILL
78 Coord Experiential Lrng & Mentoring ... Ms. Mayelin TORRES
38 Director of Counseling ... Ms. Zsuzsanna NAGY
88 Dir Volunteerism & Svc Learning ... Ms. Jayne I. MURPHY-MORRIS
35 Director of Student Engagement ... Ms. Naima K. RICKS
41 Director of Athletics ... Mr. Thomas WAGENBLAST
29 Dir Alumni Engagement/Alumni Assoc ... Ms. Jennifer SANCHEZ
15 Director Human Resources ... Ms. MaryAnn MAIKISCH
109 C-Store/Dining Services ... Mr. Dean PIACENTINI
110 Asst VP Institutional Advancement ... Vacant
105 Director IT-Web ... Mr. David B. RABINOWITZ
13 Chief Info Technology Officer ... Ms. Margie ROHR
107 Dean of Professional Studies ... Dr. Patricia HEINDEL
49 Dean of Arts and Sciences ... Dr. Anthony SANTAMARIA
19 Director Bi-Campus Security ... Mr. Richard WALL
39 Director Residence Life ... Ms. Deborah J. PAWLIKOWSKI
04 Exec Asst to President ... Mrs. Meghan AITKEN
07 Director of Admissions ... Ms. Nadine HAWKINS
108 Director Institutional Assessment ... Ms. Michele YURECKO
86 Director Government Relations ... Vacant
90 Director Academic Computing ... Dr. Jeffrey GUTKIN
91 Director Administrative Computing ... Ms. Angela IANNELLI

Saint Peter's University (H)
2641 Kennedy Boulevard, Jersey City NJ 07306-5997
County: Hudson FICE Identification: 002638
Unit ID: 186432
Telephone: (201) 761-6000 Carnegie Class: Masters/L
FAX Number: (201) 761-7801 Calendar System: Semester
URL: www.saintpeters.edu
Established: 1872 Annual Undergrad Tuition & Fees: $38,760
Enrollment: 3,197 Coed
Affiliation or Control: Roman Catholic IRS Status: 501(c)3
Highest Offering: Doctorate
Accreditation: M, IACBE, NURSE

01 President ... Dr. Eugene J. CORNACCHIA
45 Spec Asst to Pres for Inst Plng ... Dr. Virginia BENDER
100 Special Assistant to the President ... Dr. Eileen POIANI
04 Exec Admin Asst to President ... Ms. Jane HALMA
05 Provost/VP Academic Affairs ... Dr. Frederick BONATO
10 VP of Finance & Business ... Mr. Paul CIRAULO
32 VP Stdnt Life & Development ... Ms. Erin MCCANN
42 Vice Pres for Mission & Ministry ... Fr. Andrew DOWNING, SJ
84 VP Enrollment Mgmt & Marketing ... Ms. Elizabeth SULLIVAN
13 CIO of Information Technology/Ops ... Mr. Michael DE VARTI
111 Vice President Advancement ... Ms. Leah LETO
20 Assoc VP Academic Affairs ... Dr. Nicole DECAPUA-RINCK
66 Dean of Nursing ... Dr. Lauren O'HARE
50 KPMG Dean School of Business ... Dr. Mary Kate NAATUS
53 Dean Caufield School of Education ... Dr. Stephanie SQUIRES
49 Dean College of Arts & Sciences ... Dr. WeiDong ZHU
78 Exec Dir Career Engagement/Exp Lrng ... Ms. Taina CUTLER
123 Exec Dir Admission Graduate ... Vacant
26 Exec Dir University Communications ... Ms. Sarah MALINOWSKI-FERRARY
37 Director of Student Fin Aid ... Ms. Jennifer RAGSDALE
08 Director of the Library ... Ms. Daisy DECOSTER
09 Executive Director of IR ... Mr. Ben SCHOLZ
19 Director of Campus Safety ... Mr. Scott TORRE
15 Director of Human Resources ... Ms. Elena SERRA
29 Director Alumni Engagement ... Ms. Claudia POPE-BAYNE
44 Director of Annual Giving ... Mr. Scott DONOVAN
38 Dir of Counseling & Psyc Service ... Ms. Colleen SZEFINSKI
39 Director of Residence Life ... Mr. Christopher AMBROSE
41 Director of Athletics ... Ms. Rachelle PAUL
14 Director of Network Services ... Mr. Bert VABRE
51 Director of Center Global Learning ... Mr. Scott KELLER
18 Dir of Facility & Univ Services ... Ms. Anna DE PAULA
102 Dir Foundation/Corp & Govt Rels ... Mr. Emory EDWARDS
105 Dir of Web Strategies & Comm ... Vacant
36 Director of Student Placement ... Ms. Laura PAKHMANOV
06 Registrar ... Ms. Kamla SINGH
43 General Counsel ... Mr. Eugene T. PAOLINO

Salem Community College (I)
460 Hollywood Avenue, Carneys Point NJ 08069-2799
County: Salem FICE Identification: 005461
Unit ID: 186469
Telephone: (856) 299-2100 Carnegie Class: Assoc/HVT-High Non
FAX Number: (856) 351-2634 Calendar System: Semester
URL: www.salemcc.edu
Established: 1972 Annual Undergrad Tuition & Fees (In-District): $6,360
Enrollment: 865 Coed
Affiliation or Control: State/Local IRS Status: 501(c)3
Highest Offering: Associate Degree
Accreditation: M, ADNUR

01 President ... Dr. Michael GORMAN
05 Dean of Academic Affairs ... Mr. Kenneth ROBEL
10 Chief Financial/Business Ofcr ... Mr. Rod JEFFERSON
04 Exec Asst to the President ... Ms. Maria FANTINI
20 Assoc Dean of Academic Affairs ... Mrs. Maura CAVANAGH-DICK
84 Dean of Enrollment/Admissions ... Mrs. Kelly SCHIMPF
06 Registrar ... Ms. Jill JAMES
108 Dir of Institutional Effectiveness ... Mr. Marc ROY
19 Director of Public Safety ... Mr. Chuck WEIGLE
09 Asst Dean Inst Research & Planning ... Mr. Ronald BURKHARDT
30 Dir of Inst Advancement/Alumni ... Mr. William CLARK
37 Director of Financial Aid ... Mrs. Heather STITH
66 Dir of Nursing/Allied Health ... Mrs. Terri COVELLO
88 Director of Academic & Info Svcs ... Ms. Jennifer PIERCE
13 Director of Information Technology ... Mr. Larry MCKEE
102 Executive Director SCC Foundation ... Ms. Ceil SMITH
21 Manager of Finance ... Ms. Lynn MCCOSKER
121 Dir of Advisement/Student Support ... Mrs. Laura GREEN
88 Accounts Manager ... Ms. Adrienne MUSUMECI
07 Director of Admissions ... Ms. Amy BENNIS-KIMBALL
15 Manager Human Resources ... Ms. Barbara QUAILE
41 Athletic Director ... Mr. Bob BUNNELL

Seminary Bnos Chaim (J)
388 Chestnut Street, Lakewood NJ 08701
County: Ocean FICE Identification: 042712
Telephone: (732) 730-7589 Carnegie Class: Not Classified
FAX Number: N/A Calendar System: Semester
URL: www.seminarybnoschaim.com
Established: Annual Undergrad Tuition & Fees: N/A
Enrollment: N/A Male
Affiliation or Control: Independent Non-Profit IRS Status: 501(c)3
Highest Offering: Associate Degree
Accreditation: AIJS

Seton Hall University (K)
400 S Orange Avenue, South Orange NJ 07079-2697
County: Essex FICE Identification: 002632
Unit ID: 186584
Telephone: (973) 761-9000 Carnegie Class: DU-Higher
FAX Number: N/A Calendar System: Semester
URL: www.shu.edu
Established: 1856 Annual Undergrad Tuition & Fees: $45,290
Enrollment: 9,814 Coed
Affiliation or Control: Roman Catholic IRS Status: 501(c)3
Highest Offering: Doctorate
Accreditation: M, ARCPA, CAATE, CAEP, COPSY, HSA, LAW, NURSE, OT, PTA, SP, SPAA, SW, THEOL

01 President ... Dr. Joseph E. NYRE
05 Provost & Executive Vice President ... Dr. Katia PASSERINI
11 EVP Operations & Chief of Staff ... Mr. Patrick G. LYONS
10 Vice Pres for Finance/CFO ... Ms. Donna M. MCMONAGLE
111 Vice Pres for University Relations ... Mr. Matthew BOROWICK
32 VP for Student Services ... Dr. Monica BURNETTE
43 General Counsel ... Ms. Kimberly A. CAPADONA
42 Vice Pres for Mission & Ministry ... Rev. Colin KAY
101 VP for Board Affairs/Univ Strategy ... Dr. Michele NELSON
84 Sr Vice Pres for Enrollment Mgmt ... Dr. Alyssa MCCLOUD
110 Vice Pres for Advancement ... Mr. Jon PAPARSENOS
21 Assoc Provost for Strategy/Finance ... Mr. Erik LILLQUIST
20 Assoc Provost for Academic Affairs ... Dr. Christopher CUCCIA
108 Assoc Prov Undergrad Ed/Assessment ... Dr. Peter SHOEMAKER
88 Assistant Provost Faculty Affairs ... Ms. Amy NEWCOMBE
61 Dean of Law School ... Ms. Kathleen BOOZANG
08 Dean of University Libraries ... Dr. John E. BUSCHMAN
66 Dean of Nursing ... Dr. Marie FOLEY
49 Dean of Arts & Sciences ... Dr. Georita FRIERSON
53 Interim Dean Education/Human Svcs ... Dr. Joseph MARTINELLI
73 Interim Rector/Dean Sch of Theology ... Msgr. Gerard MCCARREN
51 Dean Cont Educ/Professional Studies ... Ms. Karen PASSARO
60 Interim Dean Comm & the Arts ... Dr. Renee ROBINSON
63 Dean School of Health & Med Science ... Dr. Brian SHULMAN
82 Dean Diplomacy/Intl Relations ... Dr. Courtney SMITH
50 Dean School of Business ... Dr. Joyce A. STRAWSER
35 Assoc VP/Dean of Students ... Ms. Karen VAN NORMAN
88 Special Advisor to Provost ... Dr. Jonathan FARINA
88 Special Advisor to Provost ... Rev. Forrest PRITCHETT
88 Special Advisor to Provost ... Dr. Kurt ROTTHOFF
88 Director Core Curriculum ... Dr. Nancy ENRIGHT
09 Dir Plng/Inst Research & Assessment ... Ms. Connie L. BEALE
88 Director of Business Intelligence ... Ms. Bonnie BURKHARDT
45 Dir Advising Tech Integration ... Dr. Anna CALKA
88 Director Academic Events/Planning ... Ms. Bernadette MCVEY
88 Exec Asst Provost/Spec Proj Coord ... Ms. Christine YARWOOD
88 Special Projects Coordinator ... Ms. Kaerielle LARSEN
13 Chief Information Officer ... Dr. Stephen LANDRY
15 Assoc Vice Pres Human Resources ... Mr. Michael SILVESTRO
28 Chief Equity/Diversity/Compliance ... Ms. Lori A. BROWN
18 Assoc VP for Facilities & Operation ... Mr. John SIGNORELLO
102 Sr Dir Found/Corporate Relations ... Ms. Kelly MESSINA
19 Asst VP Security ... Mr. Patrick LINFANTE
88 Asst VP/Dean ... Dr. Majid WHITNEY
29 Assoc VP Alum Rel/Annual Giving ... Mr. Anthony D. BELLUCCI
41 Dir Athletics/Recreational Services ... Mr. Bryan FELT
07 Dir of Undergraduate Admissions ... Ms. Katherine FAINER
38 Director of Counseling ... Dr. Dianne AGUERO-TROTTER
88 Director Administrative Svcs ... Mr. Peter TRUNK
37 Director of Financial Aid ... Ms. Javonda ASANTE
06 University Registrar ... Ms. Autumn BUCIOR
96 Director of Procurement ... Mr. Martin E. KOELLER
22 Director of EOP ... Mr. Jason G. OLIVEIRA
88 Minister to Priest Community ... Fr. Gerald BUONOPANE
112 Exec Dir Princ Gifts/Strategic ... Ms. Sheila S. WOLFINGER
88 Sr Dir Gift Plng/Princ Gifts Office ... Ms. Nora RAHAIM
88 Director of Facilities Engineering ... Mr. Leon VANDEMEULEBROEKE
88 Director of Upward Bound ... Ms. Marva COLE-FRIDAY
58 Director Graduate Affairs/Info Svcs ... Mr. Israel CHIA
36 Director of the Career Center ... Mr. Jorge RIVERA
23 Director Health Services ... Dr. Diane LYNCH
104 Director International Programs ... Ms. Maria BOUZAS
39 Director of Housing/Res Life ... Ms. Jessica PROANO
88 Asst Director Intl Programs ... Mr. Douglas CANTELMO
30 Assoc VP Development ... Mr. Brian RUARK
04 Executive Asst to the President ... Ms. Lisa B. METZ

Stevens Institute of Technology (L)
1 Castle Point Terrace, Hoboken NJ 07030
County: Hudson FICE Identification: 002639
Unit ID: 186867
Telephone: (201) 216-5000 Carnegie Class: DU-Higher
FAX Number: (201) 216-8341 Calendar System: Semester
URL: www.stevens.edu
Established: 1870 Annual Undergrad Tuition & Fees: $55,952
Enrollment: 7,257 Coed
Affiliation or Control: Independent Non-Profit IRS Status: 501(c)3
Highest Offering: Doctorate
Accreditation: M

01 President ... Dr. Nariman FARVARDIN
04 Exec Assistant to the President ... Ms. Phyllis RUIZ
05 Provost/SVP for Academic Affairs ... Dr. Jianmin QU
30 VP Development/Alumni Engagement ... Ms. Laura ROSE
10 CFO/VP for Finance/Treasurer ... Dr. Louis MAYER
15 Vice President Human Resources ... Mr. Warren PETTY
43 Vice President General Counsel ... Ms. Kathy L. SCHULZ
13 VP for Information Technology & CIO ... Mr. Tej PATEL
26 VP University Relations ... Ms. Beth MCGRATH
18 VP for Facilities/Campus Operations ... Mr. Robert MAFFIA
32 Assistant VP Student Affairs ... Ms. Sara KLEIN
84 AVP Enrollment Management ... Ms. Susan GROSS
21 AVP Fin Planning/Budgeting/Analysis ... Ms. Theresa PASCOE
35 Dean of Students ... Mr. Kenneth NILSEN
39 Dean for Residential & Dining Svcs ... Ms. Trina BALLANTYNE
20 Assoc Dean Undergraduate Academics ... Dr. Erol CESMEBASI
29 AVP Alumni Engagement & ED/SAA ... Ms. Megan STEVENS
36 Exec Director of Stevens Career Ctr ... Ms. Cherena WALKER
19 Chief of Campus Police ... Mr. Timothy GRIFFIN

41 Athletic Director — Mr. Russell ROGERS
85 Director Intl Student/Scholar Svcs — Ms. Jean LEE
38 Director of Student Counseling — Dr. Eric D. ROSE
25 Exec Director Sponsored Research — Ms. Barbara DEHAVEN
54 Dean Schaefer Sch of Engr & Science — Dr. Jean ZU
50 Dean School of Business — Dr. Gregory PRASTACOS
49 Dean College of Arts & Letters — Dr. Kelland THOMAS
77 Interim Sch of Systems & Enterprise — Dr. Anthony BARRESE
07 Dean of UG Admissions — Vacant
09 Exec Dir of Institutional Research — Ms. Minghui WANG
28 Exec Dir Diversity/Equity/Inclusion — Ms. Susan METZ
58 Sr Vice Provost Graduate Education — Dr. Constantin CHASSAPIS
20 Vice Prov Acad Innov & Faculty Affs — Dr. Xiangwu ZENG
46 Vice Provost Research/Innovation — Dr. Dilhan KALYON
06 University Registrar — Ms. Anna-Lize HARRIS
08 Library Director — Ms. Linda BENINGHOVE
104 Director International Programs — Ms. Susan RACHOUH
106 Assistant Dean WebCampus — Mr. Robert ZOTTI
96 Director of Procurement — Mr. Brian SEABOLD
108 Asst Director for Assessment — Vacant
102 Director Corporate/Foundation Rels — Ms. Jenna NIMAR
105 Sr Dir Clt Supt/Learning Tech Svcs — Mr. Michael SCALERO
88 Dean of Academic Administration — Mr. Siva THANGAM
86 Dir Corp/Govt/Community Relations — Mr. Gregory TOWNSEND

Stockton University (A)

101 Vera King Farris Drive, Galloway NJ 08205-9441
County: Atlantic　FICE Identification: 009345
Unit ID: 186876
Telephone: (609) 652-1776　Carnegie Class: DU-Mod
FAX Number: N/A　Calendar System: Semester
URL: www.stockton.edu
Established: 1969　Annual Undergrad Tuition & Fees (In-State): $14,329
Enrollment: 9,893　Coed
Affiliation or Control: State　IRS Status: 501(c)3
Highest Offering: Doctorate
Accreditation: M, ART, CAEP, NURSE, OT, PTA, SP, SW

01 President — Dr. Harvey KESSELMAN
05 Provost & VP for Academic Affairs — Dr. Leamor KAHANOV
03 Exec VP and Chief of Staff — Dr. Susan C. DAVENPORT
10 Vice Pres Admin/Finance & CFO — Ms. Jennifer POTTER
32 Vice President Student Affairs — Dr. Christopher C. CATCHING
15 VP Personnel/Labor/Govt Relations — Mr. Michael ANGULO
20 Assoc Provost for Academic Success — Dr. Ariane HUTCHINS-NEWMAN
20 Assoc Provost for Academic Affairs — Ms. AmyBeth GLASS
96 Interim Dir Procurement/Contract — Mr. Robert YUFER
13 Chief Information Officer — Mr. Scott HUSTON
18 Sr VP Facilities & Operations — Mr. Donald M. HUDSON
28 Chief Ofcr Inst Diversity/Inclusion — Dr. Valerie HAYES
88 Exec Dir WJ Hughes Ctr Pub Policy — Mr. John FROONJIAN
30 Chief Dev Ofcr/Exec Dir Found — Mr. Daniel P. NUGENT
26 Exec Dir Univ Relations/Marketing — Mr. Geoffrey PETTIFER
84 Chief Enrollment Management Officer — Mr. Robert HEINRICH
07 Director of Admissions — Ms. Heather MEDINA
06 Registrar — Mr. Joseph LOSASSO
53 Dean School of Education — Dr. Claudine KEENAN
97 Dean School of General Studies — Dr. Robert S. GREGG
79 Dean School Arts & Humanities — Dr. Lisa HONAKER
50 Interim Dean School of Business — Dr. Warren KLEINSMITH
81 Dean School of Natural Sci/Math — Dr. Peter STRAUB
83 Dean Sch Social/Behav Sciences — Dr. Marissa LEVY
76 Dean School of Health Sciences — Dr. Brent ARNOLD
09 Director Institutional Research — Ms. Jessica KAY
08 Director of Library Services — Vacant
88 Director SRI & ETTC — Ms. Patricia WEEKS
37 Director of Financial Aid — Mr. Christopher CONNORS
19 Director of Campus Public Safety — Mr. Adrian WIGGINS
88 Interim Dir Performing Arts Center — Ms. Anjanette CHRISTY
41 Interim Dir Athletics & Recreation — Mr. Anthony BERICH
39 Executive Director Residential Life — Mr. Steven E. RADWANSKI
124 Asst VP Transitions & Retention — Mr. Walter L. TARVER, III
43 General Counsel — Mr. Brian KOWALSKI
121 Dir Ctr for Academic Advising — Mr. Elvis GYAN
114 Exec Dir Budget/Fin Plng/Camp Svcs — Ms. Diane GARRISON
29 Director Alumni Relations — Ms. Sara FAUROT
110 Assoc Chf Devel Ofcr/Campaign Mgr — Ms. Cindy CRAGER
12 COO Atlantic City Campus — Mr. Brian K. JACKSON
04 Admin Assistant to the President — Ms. Kathryn MASON
25 Exec Dir Research & Spons Programs — Ms. Jennifer KOSAKOWSKI
45 Chief Plng Ofcr/Dep Chief of Staff — Mr. Peter BARATTA
38 Asst VP Student Health & Wellness — Dr. Zupenda DAVIS-SHINE
104 Director Global Engagement — Dr. Jiangyuan ZHOU
22 Director Title IX/EEO — Vacant
35 Dir Ofc Student Development — Mr. Joseph THOMPSON

Sussex County Community College (B)

One College Hill Road, Newton NJ 07860-1146
County: Sussex　FICE Identification: 025688
Unit ID: 247603
Telephone: (973) 300-2100　Carnegie Class: Assoc/HT-Mix Trad/Non
FAX Number: (973) 579-9351　Calendar System: Semester
URL: www.sussex.edu
Established: 1982　Annual Undergrad Tuition & Fees (In-District): $7,080
Enrollment: 2,190　Coed
Affiliation or Control: State/Local　IRS Status: 501(c)3
Highest Offering: Associate Degree
Accreditation: M, MAC

01 President — Dr. Jon H. CONNOLLY
45 Chief Budget Officer — Karen UNRATH
05 SVP of Academic & Student Affairs — Dr. Kathleen OKAY
15 Chief Operating & HR Officer — James GADDY
26 Dir of Marketing/Public Info — Kathleen PETERSON
88 Asst Dean Library/Learning Resource — Dr. Kathleen CARR
09 VP Student Success/Inst Effective — Dr. Cory HOMER
41 Dir of Athletics/Dean Student Affs — John KUNTZ
10 Institutional Comptroller — Manal MESEHA
19 Director Campus Safety & Security — Fred MAMAY
113 Dir of Bursar/Financial Services — Kimberly RYAN
08 Director of College Library — Stephanie COOPER
07 Director of Admissions — Todd POLTERSDORF
37 Director of Financial Aid — Diane PIENTA-LETT
06 Registrar — Solweig DIMINO
100 Chief of Staff/EA to the BOT — Wendy FULLEM
04 President's Office Assistant — Melissa DEJOSEPH
102 Exec Director of Foundation — Stan KULA
13 Director Information Technology — Judy LOVAS
38 Director Student Counseling — Kathy GALLICHIO
18 Chf Facilities/Physical Plant Ofcr — Charlene PETERSON
107 Dean of Prof Studies/SS & STEM — Nancy GALLO
49 Assoc VPAA/Dean Liberal Arts — Sherry FITZGERALD
88 Dean of Technical Occupations — Jason FRUGE
96 Director of Purchasing — Heather GALLAGHER

Talmudical Academy of New Jersey (C)

Route 524, Adelphia NJ 07710-9999
County: Monmouth　FICE Identification: 011989
Unit ID: 186900
Telephone: (732) 431-1600　Carnegie Class: Spec-4-yr-Faith
FAX Number: (732) 431-3951　Calendar System: Semester
URL: https://talmudicalacademynj.com/
Established: 1971　Annual Undergrad Tuition & Fees: $13,900
Enrollment: 63　Male
Affiliation or Control: Independent Non-Profit　IRS Status: 501(c)3
Highest Offering: Baccalaureate
Accreditation: RABN

01 President — Mr. Charles SEMAH
05 Dean/Registrar — Rabbi Yeruchim SHAIN
10 Chief Financial/Business Officer — Mr. Neal GOTTLIEB

Thomas Edison State University (D)

111 W State Street, Trenton NJ 08608-1176
County: Mercer　FICE Identification: 021922
Unit ID: 187046
Telephone: (609) 984-1100　Carnegie Class: Masters/M
FAX Number: (609) 292-9000　Calendar System: Other
URL: www.tesu.edu
Established: 1972　Annual Undergrad Tuition & Fees (In-State): $7,182
Enrollment: 10,495　Coed
Affiliation or Control: State　IRS Status: 501(c)3
Highest Offering: Doctorate
Accreditation: M, ACBSP, CAEPT, NURSE, POLYT

01 President — Dr. Merodie A. HANCOCK
05 Provost/SVP Academic Affairs — Dr. Cynthia BAUM
10 Senior Vice President & CFO — Mr. Christopher STRINGER
111 VP for Advancement/Foundation Board — Ms. Mary HEAGLEY
28 Chief Student Success/Equity & Incl — Dr. Jasmeial JACKSON
86 Vice Pres Cmty & Govt Affairs — Ms. Marcela MAZIARZ
84 VP Enrollment Management — Dr. Dennis DEVERY
45 Vice Prov Strategic Initiatives — Dr. Jeff HARMON
51 Vice Prov/Dean Watson Sch Cont Stds — Dr. Malcom K. OLIVER
09 Assoc VP for Planning & Research — Dr. Ann Marie SENIOR
26 Senior Director of Communications — Ms. Victoria A. MONAGHAN
88 Assoc VP Organizational Learn/CTO — Mr. Matthew COOPER
21 Treasurer — Mr. Steve D. ALBANO
100 Chief of Staff — Mr. Michael MANCINI
88 Director Market Research/Assessment — Ms. Marie R. POWER-BARNES
43 General Counsel — Ms. Jennifer HOFF
66 Dean School of Nursing — Dr. Filomela MARSHALL
49 Dean Heavin Sch of Arts & Sciences — Dr. John AJE
50 Dean School of Business & Mgmt — Dr. Michael WILLIAMS
06 Assoc Vice Pres/Univ Registrar — Ms. Cathy PUNCHELLO
15 Chief Human Resources Officer — Ms. Heather BROOKS
21 Controller — Mr. John SCHAIBLE
13 Director of MIS — Mr. Seth ARONSON
88 Senior Dir of Prof Development — Mr. Maureen WOODRUFF
29 Director of Alumni Affairs — Ms. Meg FRANTZ
37 Director of Financial Aid — Mr. James OWENS
18 Director Facilities & Operations — Ms. Mary C. HACK
88 Assoc VP for Strategic Initiatives — Ms. Misty ISAK
08 State Librarian — Ms. Mary CHUTE
105 Dir Website/Multimedia Productivity — Mr. Jeffery LUSHBAUGH
30 Dir Development Operations — Ms. Jennifer GUERRERO
22 ADA Coordinator — Ms. Laura BRENNER-SCOTTI
88 Sr Fellow/Dir Ctr Leadership/Govt — Ms. Melissa A. MASZCZAK
04 Executiv Assistant to the President — Ms. Jamie ADAMS
101 Secretary of the Institution/Board — Mr. Michael MANCINI

† The Thomas Edison State University 12-month enrollment is 17,511.

Union College (E)

1033 Springfield Avenue, Cranford NJ 07016-1598
County: Union　FICE Identification: 002643
Unit ID: 187198
Telephone: (908) 709-7000　Carnegie Class: Assoc/MT-VT-High Trad
FAX Number: (908) 709-0527　Calendar System: Semester
URL: www.ucc.edu
Established: 1933　Annual Undergrad Tuition & Fees (In-District): $10,562
Enrollment: 8,298　Coed
Affiliation or Control: State/Local　IRS Status: 501(c)3
Highest Offering: Associate Degree
Accreditation: M, PTAA

01 President — Dr. Margaret M. MCMENAMIN
05 Vice President Academic Affairs — Dr. Maris LOWN
10 Vice President Finance & Operations — Dr. Lori A. WILKIN
32 Vice President Student Development — Dr. Demond T. HARGROVE
11 Vice President Admin Services — Dr. Bernard A. POLNARIEV
88 Associate VP Operations — Mr. Vincent LOTANO
21 Assistant VP Finance — Ms. Marlene M. SOUSA
20 Assoc VP Academic Affairs — Vacant
09 Exec Dir of Institutional Research — Dr. Andrew S. ZINER
102 Exec Director Foundation — Mr. Douglas ROUSE
51 Exec Dir Cont Educ & Workforce Dev — Dr. Lisa HISCANO
26 Exec Dir Col Relations & Board Sec — Dr. Jaime M. SEGAL
43 Assc Gen Couns/Exec Dir Procurement — Dr. Marlene WHITE
12 Dean Plainfield Campus — Dr. Victoria UKACHUKWU
12 Dean Elizabeth Campus — Dr. Elizabeth RAMOS
88 Dean of Curriculum & Accreditation — Dr. Sara N. LACAGNINO
79 Dean of Humanities — Dr. Melissa SANDE
81 Interim Dean of STEM — Mr. William DUNSCOMBE
83 Dean Social Sciences & Business — Dr. Melinda C. NORELLI
12 Assoc Dean Scotch Plains Campus — Dr. Nicole D. CIPPOLETTI
116 Dir Financial Reporting & Grants — Ms. Jane KANE
96 Director of Purchasing — Mr. Mark ANDERSON
13 Chief Information Officer — Mr. Eric WINCH
18 Director Facilities — Mr. Christopher SAPARA-GRANT
19 Director Public Safety — Mr. Joseph HINES
25 Director of Grants — Ms. Cheryl SHIBER
15 Assoc Director of Human Resources — Vacant
35 Dean of Students — Dr. Takeem L. DEAN
121 Dean of Student Success — Ms. Heather KEITH
88 Asst Dean of Students — Ms. Beatriz RODRIGUEZ
88 Assistant Director of College Life — Ms. Zulema CHEEK
06 Registrar — Vacant
37 Director of Financial Aid — Mr. Dayne CHANCE
113 Director of Student Accounts — Ms. Kathryn VELLIOS
07 Director of Admissions — Mr. Gregory BENEDICT, JR.
28 Director EOF — Mr. Samuel CASIMIR
41 Assistant Director of Athletics — Ms. Marbely MONTAS
24 Director Media Services — Mr. Patrick GALLAGHER
106 Director of Instructional Design — Vacant
08 Director of Libraries — Ms. Jane JIANG
88 Dir Acad Learning Center — Mr. Jose PAEZ-FIGUEROA
14 Technical Director — Mr. Kevin TSAKONAS
91 Enterprise Applications Director — Mr. Wisam SHAHIN
04 Executive Assistant to President — Ms. Susan MATIKA
40 Manager Bookstore — Ms. Christine SALZMAN

Union County College Elizabeth Campus (F)

40 W Jersey Street, Elizabeth NJ 07202-2314
Telephone: (908) 965-6000　Identification: 770134
Accreditation: &M, DNUR, EMT

Union County College Plainfield Campus (G)

232 E 2nd Street, Plainfield NJ 07060
Telephone: (908) 412-3599　Identification: 770135
Accreditation: &M, CNEA, #COARC

Warren County Community College (H)

475 Route 57 W, Washington NJ 07882-4343
County: Warren　FICE Identification: 025039
Unit ID: 245625
Telephone: (908) 835-9222　Carnegie Class: Assoc/HT-High Non
FAX Number: (908) 689-9262　Calendar System: Semester
URL: www.warren.edu
Established: 1981　Annual Undergrad Tuition & Fees (In-District): $5,490
Enrollment: 3,251　Coed
Affiliation or Control: State/Local　IRS Status: 501(c)3
Highest Offering: Associate Degree
Accreditation: M, ADNUR, MAC

01 President — Dr. William AUSTIN
10 Vice Pres Finance & Operations — Ms. Barbara PRATT
51 Vice Pres Corporate/Continuing Educ — Ms. Eve AZAR
11 Dean of Administration — Mr. Dennis FLORENTINE
07 VP of Student Services — Mr. Jeremy BEELER
05 VP of Academics — Dr. Marianne VANDEURSEN
37 Director of Financial Aid — Ms. Jacqueline DALY
15 Director Human Resources — Ms. Sharon HINTZ
04 Administrative Asst to President — Ms. Genevieve VASKO
08 Head Librarian — Ms. Lisa STOLL
09 Director of Institutional Research — Ms. Nikki DADARRIA
102 Dir Foundation/Corporate Relations — Ms. Samir ELBASSIOUNY

William Paterson University of New Jersey (I)

300 Pompton Road, Wayne NJ 07470-2152
County: Passaic　FICE Identification: 002625
Unit ID: 187444
Telephone: (973) 720-2000　Carnegie Class: Masters/L
FAX Number: N/A　Calendar System: Semester
URL: www.wpunj.edu

Established: 1855   Annual Undergrad Tuition & Fees (In-State): $13,770
Enrollment: 9,635   Coed
Affiliation or Control: State   IRS Status: 501(c)3
Highest Offering: Doctorate
Accreditation: **M**, ART, CAATE, CACREP, CAEP, CLPSY, MPCAC, MUS, NURSE, PH, #SP

01	President	Dr. Richard HELLDOBLER
05	Senior Vice President/Provost	Dr. Joshua POWERS
100	Chief of Staff to President/ BOT	Ms. Loretta MCLAUGHLIN VIGNIER
10	Sr VP Administration/Finance	Vacant
111	Vice Pres Institutional Advancement	Ms. Pamela FERGUSON
32	Vice President Student Development	Dr. Miki CAMMARATA
84	VP of Enrollment Management	Dr. Reginald ROSS
20	Assoc Provost Academic Development	Ms. Danielle LIAUTAUD
114	Director of University Budgets	Mr. Timothy LEVER
11	Assoc VP for Administration	Mr. Kevin GARVEY
26	VP Marketing & Public Relations	Mr. Stuart GOLDSTEIN
15	Vice Pres Human Resources	Ms. Allison BOUCHER-JARVIS
19	Dir Public Safety & Univ Police	Mr. Charles LOWE
35	Assoc VP for Student Development	Mr. Francisco DIAZ
35	Assoc VP/Dean Student Development	Dr. Glen SHERMAN
60	Interim Dean Col Arts/ Comm	Dr. Loretta C. MCLAUGHLIN VIGNIER
53	Dean College of Education	Dr. Amy GINSBERG
66	Dean College of Science & Health	Dr. Venkatanarayanan SHARMA
79	Dean Col of Arts/Humanities/Soc Sci	Dr. Wartyna DAVIS
50	Dean College of Business	Dr. Anthony BOWRIN
08	Dean D & L Cheng Library	Dr. Edward OWUSU-ANSAH
21	Assoc VP Finance & Controller	Ms. Samantha GREEN
28	Dir Empl Rels/Ethics/Title IX Coord	Ms. Regina A. TINDALL
51	Exec Dir Cont Educ/Distance Lrng	Dr. Bernadette TIERNAN
20	Associate Provost	Ms. Kara M. RABBITT
20	Associate Provost Academic Affairs	Dr. Sandra B. HILL
20	Assoc Prov for Curriculum & Intl Ed	Dr. Jonathan LINCOLN
86	Assoc VP Govt & External Relations	Mr. Guillermo DE VEYGA
27	Sr Director Public Relations	Ms. Mary Beth ZEMAN
29	Executive Director Alumni	Ms. Jenna VILLANI
108	Exec Dir Inst Research & ASMT	Dr. Sesime ADANU
13	Chief Information Officer	Mr. Eric ROSENBERG
43	General Counsel	Ms. Melissa REARDON HENRY
16	Director of Human Resources	Ms. Denise ROBINSON-LEWIS
07	Assoc Vice President Admissions	Mr. Ken SCHNEIDER
37	Director Financial Aid	Mr. Michael CORSO
06	Registrar	Ms. Susan ASTARITA
88	Director Athletic Communications	Ms. Heather BROCIOUS
36	Director of Career Dev & Advisement	Ms. Sharon ROSENGART
39	Director of Residence Life	Ms. Rebecca BAIRD
23	Dir Counseling/Health & Wellness	Dr. Jill GUZMAN
40	Director Bookstore	Mr. Scott DUNLAP
85	Director International Student Svcs	Ms. Cinzia RICHARDSON
94	Director of Women's Center	Dr. Librada SANCHEZ
96	Director of Purchasing	Mr. Stephen SONDEY
89	Director of New Student Programs	Ms. Amanda VASQUEZ
92	Dean of Honors College	Dr. Barbara ANDREW
35	Dir Campus Activ/Svc & Leadership	Ms. Donna MINNICH SPUHLER
88	Assoc Dir Instruction/Research Tech	Mr. Patrick RYAN
04	Exec Assistant to President	Ms. Sherry WASHINGTON
88	Director of Communications	Mr. Gregory CANNON

Yeshiva Bais Aharon (A)
905 Park Avenue, Lakewood NJ 08701
County: Ocean   Identification: 667291
   Unit ID: 490319
Telephone: (732) 367-7604   Carnegie Class: Spec-4-yr-Faith
FAX Number: (732) 367-1777   Calendar System: Semester
Established: 2012   Annual Undergrad Tuition & Fees: $9,250
Enrollment: 24   Male
Affiliation or Control: Independent Non-Profit   IRS Status: 501(c)3
Highest Offering: Baccalaureate
Accreditation: **AIJS**

Yeshiva Chemdas Hatorah (B)
950 Massachusetts Avenue, Lakewood NJ 08701
County: Ocean   Identification: 667281
   Unit ID: 491622
Telephone: (732) 363-7110   Carnegie Class: Spec-4-yr-Faith
FAX Number: (732) 961-5220   Calendar System: Other
URL: https://yeshivachemdashatorah.com/
Established: Annual Undergrad Tuition & Fees: N/A
Enrollment: N/A   Male
Affiliation or Control: Independent Non-Profit   IRS Status: 501(c)3
Highest Offering: Baccalaureate
Accreditation: **AIJS**

01	Dean	Rabbi Aron PRUZANSKY

Yeshiva Gedola Tiferes Yaakov Yitzchok (C)
65 Cross Street, Lakewood NJ 08701
County: Ocean   FICE Identification: 042801
   Unit ID: 493716
Telephone: (732) 901-6703   Carnegie Class: Spec-4-yr-Faith
FAX Number: N/A   Calendar System: Semester
URL: yeshivatyy.com
Established: Annual Undergrad Tuition & Fees: N/A
Enrollment: N/A   Male

Affiliation or Control: Independent Non-Profit   IRS Status: 501(c)3
Highest Offering: Baccalaureate
Accreditation: **AIJS**

Yeshiva Gedola Tiferes Yerachmiel (D)
911 Somerset Avenue, Lakewood NJ 08701
County: Ocean   FICE Identification: 042738
   Unit ID: 491914
Telephone: (732) 676-1790   Carnegie Class: Spec 2-yr-Other
FAX Number: N/A   Calendar System: Semester
URL: yeshivagedolatiferesyerachmiel.com
Established: Annual Undergrad Tuition & Fees: N/A
Enrollment: N/A   Male
Affiliation or Control: Independent Non-Profit   IRS Status: 501(c)3
Highest Offering: Baccalaureate
Accreditation: **AIJS**

Yeshiva Gedolah of Cliffwood (E)
200 Center Street, Keyport NJ 07735
County: Monmouth   Identification: 667322
   Unit ID: 491710
Telephone: (732) 765-9126   Carnegie Class: Spec-4-yr-Faith
FAX Number: (732) 865-7247   Calendar System: Semester
Established: 2004   Annual Undergrad Tuition & Fees: N/A
Enrollment: N/A   Male
Affiliation or Control: Independent Non-Profit   IRS Status: 501(c)3
Highest Offering: First Talmudic Degree
Accreditation: **RABN**

01	CEO	Samuel ALSTER
06	Registrar	Baruch SEGEL
10	CFO	Shimon ALSTER
37	Financial Aid Administrator	Aryeh BRODSKY

Yeshiva Gedolah Keren Hatorah (F)
1083 Brook Road, Lakewood NJ 08701
County: Ocean   Identification: 667282
   Unit ID: 491640
Telephone: (732) 942-1811   Carnegie Class: Spec 2-yr-Other
FAX Number: (732) 994-4222   Calendar System: Other
URL: yeshivagedolahkerenhatorah.com
Established: 2009   Annual Undergrad Tuition & Fees: N/A
Enrollment: N/A   Male
Affiliation or Control: Independent Non-Profit   IRS Status: 501(c)3
Highest Offering: Baccalaureate
Accreditation: **AIJS**

Yeshiva Gedolah Shaarei Shmuel (G)
511 Ocean Ave, Lakewood NJ 08701
County: Ocean   Identification: 667260
   Unit ID: 488350
Telephone: (732) 363-2164   Carnegie Class: Spec-4-yr-Faith
FAX Number: (732) 364-3331   Calendar System: Other
URL: https://yeshivagedolahshaareishmuel.com/
Established: 2008   Annual Undergrad Tuition & Fees: $8,800
Enrollment: 77   Male
Affiliation or Control: Independent Non-Profit   IRS Status: 501(c)3
Highest Offering: First Talmudic Degree
Accreditation: **@RABN**

Yeshiva Gedolah Tiferes Boruch (H)
21 Rockview Avenue, North Plainfield NJ 07060
County: Union   Identification: 667283
Telephone: (908) 753-2600   Carnegie Class: Not Classified
FAX Number: (908) 753-4243   Calendar System: Semester
URL: yeshivagedolahtiferesboruch.com
Established: 1989   Annual Undergrad Tuition & Fees: N/A
Enrollment: N/A   Male
Affiliation or Control: Independent Non-Profit   IRS Status: 501(c)3
Highest Offering: Baccalaureate
Accreditation: **AIJS**

05	Rosh Yeshiva	Vacant

Yeshiva Gedolah Zichron Leyma (I)
2035 Vauxhall Road, Union NJ 07083
County: Union   FICE Identification: 041924
   Unit ID: 476692
Telephone: (908) 587-0502   Carnegie Class: Spec-4-yr-Faith
FAX Number: (908) 349-3111   Calendar System: Semester
URL: www.yzl.edu
Established: 1999   Annual Undergrad Tuition & Fees: $10,750
Enrollment: 34   Male
Affiliation or Control: Independent Non-Profit   IRS Status: 501(c)3
Highest Offering: First Talmudic Degree
Accreditation: **RABN**

Yeshiva Ohr Zechariah (J)
199 Joe Parker Road, Lakewood NJ 08701
County: Ocean   FICE Identification: 042796
Telephone: (732) 730-2808   Carnegie Class: Not Classified
FAX Number: N/A   Calendar System: Semester
URL: yeshivaohrzechariah.com

Established: Annual Undergrad Tuition & Fees: N/A
Enrollment: N/A   Male
Affiliation or Control: Independent Non-Profit   IRS Status: 501(c)3
Highest Offering: Baccalaureate
Accreditation: **AIJS**

Yeshiva Toras Chaim (K)
999 Ridge Avenue, Lakewood NJ 08701-2120
County: Ocean   FICE Identification: 041311
   Unit ID: 451398
Telephone: (732) 414-2834   Carnegie Class: Spec-4-yr-Faith
FAX Number: (732) 414-2838   Calendar System: Semester
Established: 2000   Annual Undergrad Tuition & Fees: $12,250
Enrollment: 218   Male
Affiliation or Control: Independent Non-Profit   IRS Status: 501(c)3
Highest Offering: Baccalaureate
Accreditation: **RABN**

05	Chief Academic Officer	Rabbi Mendel SLOMOVITS
06	Registrar	Mrs. Devoiry DURST
10	Bookkeeper	Mrs. Michal GROSSMAN

Yeshiva Yesodei Hatorah (L)
2 Yesodei Court, Lakewood NJ 08701
County: Ocean   Identification: 667109
   Unit ID: 481438
Telephone: (732) 370-3360   Carnegie Class: Spec-4-yr-Faith
FAX Number: (732) 886-2659   Calendar System: Semester
Established: 1995   Annual Undergrad Tuition & Fees: $12,500
Enrollment: 52   Male
Affiliation or Control: Independent Non-Profit   IRS Status: 501(c)3
Highest Offering: First Talmudic Degree
Accreditation: **RABN**

05	Dean	Rabbi Shaya TREFF
10	Chief Financial/Business Officer	Rabbi Yanky ENGLAUDER
20	Associate Academic Officer	Rabbi Yisroel Meir TREFF

Yeshivas Be'er Yitzchok (M)
1391 North Avenue, Elizabeth NJ 07208
County: Union   FICE Identification: 041234
   Unit ID: 451370
Telephone: (908) 354-6057   Carnegie Class: Spec-4-yr-Faith
FAX Number: (908) 820-0431   Calendar System: Semester
URL: https://yeshivasbeeryitzchok.org/
Established: 1999   Annual Undergrad Tuition & Fees: $10,900
Enrollment: 57   Male
Affiliation or Control: Independent Non-Profit   IRS Status: 501(c)3
Highest Offering: Baccalaureate
Accreditation: **AIJS**

01	Chief Executive Officer	Rabbi Avrohom SCHULMAN
37	Director of Student Financial Aid	Mrs. Chana MILLER

Yeshivas Emek Hatorah (N)
395 Kent Road, Howell NJ 07731
County: Monmouth   FICE Identification: 042703
Telephone: (732) 367-1289   Carnegie Class: Not Classified
FAX Number: N/A   Calendar System: Semester
URL: yeshivasemekhatorah.com
Established: Annual Undergrad Tuition & Fees: N/A
Enrollment: N/A   Male
Affiliation or Control: Independent Non-Profit   IRS Status: 501(c)3
Highest Offering: Baccalaureate
Accreditation: **AIJS**

NEW MEXICO

Brookline College (O)
4201 Central Avenue NW Ste J, Albuquerque NM 87015
Telephone: (505) 880-2877   Identification: 666724
Accreditation: **ABHES**

† Branch campus of Brookline College, Phoenix, AZ

Burrell College of Osteopathic Medicine (P)
3501 Arrowhead Drive, Las Cruces NM 88001
County: Dona Ana   Identification: 667248
   Unit ID: 488554
Telephone: (575) 674-2266   Carnegie Class: Spec-4-yr-Med
FAX Number: (575) 674-2267   Calendar System: Semester
URL: www.burrell.edu
Established: 2013   Annual Graduate Tuition & Fees: N/A
Enrollment: 645   Coed
Affiliation or Control: Other   IRS Status: Proprietary
Highest Offering: Doctorate; No Undergraduates
Accreditation: **OSTEO**

01	President	Mr. John L. HUMMER
05	Dean & Chief Academic Officer	Dr. William PIERATT
10	CFO/VP Admin & Finance	Ms. Jennifer TAYLOR

13 Chief Information Officer/AVP Admin .... Mr. Jeff HARRIS
84 AVP Enroll Svcs/Inst Effectiveness .... Ms. Nina NUNEZ
06 Registrar .... Mr. Eric SANDOVAL
07 Director of Admissions .... Ms. Natalie DAVIS
37 Director of Financial Aid .... Dr. Marlene MELENDEZ
32 Exec Dir of Student Affairs .... Ms. Vanessa RICHARDSON
15 Director of Human Resources .... Ms. Dawn M. LEAKE
111 VP of Institutional Advancement .... Ms. Victoria PINEDA
26 Dir Communications & Marketing .... Ms. Karla WALTON
28 Interim Diversity Officer .... Ms. Miley GRANDJEAN
09 Asst Dean for Research .... Dr. Joseph BENOIT
08 Library Director .... Ms. Norice LEE
04 Admin Assistant to the President .... Ms. Linda KUTINAC

Carrington College - Albuquerque (A)

1001 Menaul Boulevard NE, Albuquerque NM 87107
Telephone: (505) 254-7777 Identification: 666014
Accreditation: &WJ, ADNUR, MAC

† Regional accreditation is carried under the parent institution in Sacramento, CA.

Central New Mexico Community College (B)

900 University Boulevard SE, Albuquerque NM 87106
County: Bernalillo FICE Identification: 004742
Unit ID: 187532
Telephone: (505) 224-3000 Carnegie Class: Assoc/HT-Mix Trad/Non
FAX Number: N/A Calendar System: Semester
URL: www.cnm.edu
Established: 1965 Annual Undergrad Tuition & Fees (In-District): $1,650
Enrollment: 21,398 Coed
Affiliation or Control: State/Local IRS Status: 501(c)3
Highest Offering: Associate Degree
Accreditation: HLC, ACBSP, ACFEI, ADNUR, CAHIIM, COARC, CONST, DA, DMS, EMT, MLTAD, NDT, PTAA, RAD, SURGT

01 President .... Ms. Tracy HARTZLER
05 Vice President for Academic Affairs ... Dr. Sydney D. GUNTHORPE
32 Vice President for Student Services .... Ms. Nireata SEALS
10 Vice Pres for Finance & Operations .... Mrs. Olivia PADILLA JACKSON
35 Dean of Students .... Mr. Christopher CAVAZOS
08 Director Learning Resources ...... Ms. Poppy JOHNSON RENVALL
13 Chief Information Officer .... Mr. Victor LEON
103 Sr Director of Programs .... Ms. Mary GALLIVAN
36 Career Job Placement Services .... Ms. Stacey COOLEY
30 Exec Director of Development .... Mr. Clinton WELLS
21 Exec Dir Fiscal Ops/Comptroller .... Ms. Christine DUNCAN
07 Director of Admissions .... Ms. Andrea GURROLA
26 Exec Dir Mktg & Public Relations .... Mrs. Angela SIMS
27 Dir Communications/Media Relations .... Mr. Brad MOORE
37 Sr Director Student Financial Aid .... Ms. Krystle MONTOYA
15 Executive Director Human Resources .... Vacant
81 Dean Sch of Math/Sci/Engr .... Mr. Philip LISTER
50 Dean Sch Business/Hos & Technology .... Ms. Kalynn PIRKL
72 Dean Sch of Skilled Trades & Arts .... Ms. Amy BALLARD
53 Dean Sch of Education .... Ms. LouAnne LUNDGREN
49 Dean Sch of Liberal Arts .... Ms. Melanie VIRAMONTES
76 Dean Health/Wellness/Public/Safety .... Ms. Carol ASH
06 Registrar .... Ms. Rosenda MINELLA
18 Exec Dir Physical Plant .... Mr. Marvin MARTINEZ
35 Director of Student Life .... Ms. Brittany KARNEZIS
96 Director of Purchasing .... Mr. Marcos MENDIOLA
19 Chief of Safety & Security .... Mr. John CORVINO
04 Exec Asst to President .... Ms. Janet HURULA
09 Dir Assess/Institutional Research .... Ms. Linda MARTIN
29 Director Alumni Relations .... Vacant
43 Dir Legal Svcs/General Counsel .... Mr. Michael ANAYA

Clovis Community College (C)

417 Schepps Boulevard, Clovis NM 88101-8381
County: Curry FICE Identification: 004743
Unit ID: 187639
Telephone: (575) 769-2811 Carnegie Class: Assoc/MT-VT-High Non
FAX Number: (575) 769-4190 Calendar System: Semester
URL: www.clovis.edu
Established: 1971 Annual Undergrad Tuition & Fees (In-State): $1,616
Enrollment: 2,321 Coed
Affiliation or Control: State IRS Status: 501(c)3
Highest Offering: Associate Degree
Accreditation: HLC, ADNUR, PTAA, RAD

01 President .... Dr. Charles NWANKWO
05 EVP Academic Affairs/Student Svcs .... Dr. Robin JONES
10 Chief Financial Officer .... Ms. Heather LOVATO
13 VP of IT and Operations .... Mr. Norman KIA
21 Comptroller .... Ms. Katrina WALLEY
07 Dir Admissions/Records/Registrar .... Ms. Kari SMITH
37 Director of Financial Aid .... Ms. April CHAVEZ
08 Director Library/Learning Resources .... Mr. Paul MOORE
121 Dir Center for Student Success .... Ms. Emily GLIKAS
86 Dir of Advising & Govt Relations .... Mr. Marcus SMITH
15 Director of Human Resource Services .... Ms. Regina DART
88 Director Small Business Development .... Ms. Sandra TAYLOR-SAWYER
91 Administrative Info Systems Manager .... Mr. Ronald WILDER
84 AVP Enrollment Mgmt/Student Affs .... Dr. Robin KUYKENDALL
36 Director Student Placement .... Vacant

111 Dir of Institutional Advancement .... Ms. Kolby RAINS
18 Director of Physical Plant .... Mr. Paul ARAGON
76 Div Chair Allied Health Programs .... Ms. Shawna MCGILL
79 Div Chair Languages/History/Theater .... Mr. Gregory RAPP
50 Div Chair Business Admin/Accounting .... Ms. Monica TURNER
81 Div Chair Math/Science/Hum/HPE .... Mr. Don SCROGGINS
77 Div Chair CIS/Art/Comm .... Mr. Ray WALKER
04 Executive Asst to President .... Ms. Beverly ARAGON
09 Director of Institutional Research .... Ms. Courtney TEMPEL
19 Director of Campus Security .... Mr. Freddie SALAZAR
105 Marketing & Website Manager .... Vacant
25 Exec Dir Plng/Sponsored Projects .... Dr. Mindy WATSON
36 Career & Development Coordinator .... Ms. Sarah FULMER
90 Director of User Services .... Mr. Ricky FUENTES
96 Director of Purchasing .... Mr. Steve BROOKS

Dine College Shiprock Branch (D)

1228 Yucca St., PO Box 580, Shiprock NM 87420
Telephone: (505) 368-3500 Identification: 770007
Accreditation: &HLC

† Branch campus of Dine College, Tsaile, AZ

Eastern New Mexico University Main Campus (E)

1500 S Avenue K, Portales NM 88130-7400
County: Roosevelt FICE Identification: 002651
Unit ID: 187648
Telephone: (575) 562-1011 Carnegie Class: Masters/L
FAX Number: (575) 562-2980 Calendar System: Semester
URL: www.enmu.edu
Established: 1927 Annual Undergrad Tuition & Fees (In-State): $6,648
Enrollment: 5,266 Coed
Affiliation or Control: State IRS Status: 501(c)3
Highest Offering: Master's
Accreditation: HLC, ACBSP, MUS, NUR, SP, SW

01 President/System Chancellor .... Dr. Patrice CALDWELL
05 Vice President Academic Affairs .... Dr. Jamie LAURENZ
10 Vice Prest Business Affairs/CFO .... Vacant
32 Vice President for Student Affairs .... Dr. Jeff LONG
13 VP of Technology/CIO .... Mr. Clark ELSWICK
45 VP Planning/Analysis/Inst Research .... Vacant
20 Asst Vice Pres for Academic Affairs .... Dr. Suzanne BALCH-LINDSAY
58 Asst VP Research/Graduate Dean .... Dr. John MONTGOMERY
111 AVP Advancement/Exec Dir Foundation .... Ms. Noelle BARTL
26 Asst Vice Pres of Communications .... Mr. John HOUSER
21 Comptroller .... Mrs. Carol FLETCHER
53 Dean Education/Technology .... Dr. Lee HURREN
50 Dean Business .... Dr. Herbert SNYDER
57 Dean Fine Arts .... Dr. Jeff GENTRY
49 Dean Liberal Arts & Science .... Dr. Mary AYALA
22 Affirmative Action Officer .... Ms. Jessica SMALL
08 Director of Library .... Vacant
06 Registrar .... Ms. DeLynn BARGAS
37 Director Student Financial Aid .... Mr. Brent SMALL
84 Director Enrollment Services .... Mr. Cody SPITZ
15 Exec Director of Human Resources .... Mr. Benito GONZALES
88 Director of Broadcasting .... Mr. Duane RYAN
18 Director Physical Plant .... Mr. John KANMORE
41 Athletic Director .... Mr. Paul WEIR
19 Chief of University Police .... Mr. Brad MAULDIN
36 Dir Counseling Center/Career Svcs .... Ms. Susan LARSEN
39 Director Student Housing .... Mr. Steven ESTOCK
09 Director Institutional Research .... Mr. Brendan HENNESSEY
96 Director of Purchasing .... Mr. Scott DAVIS
29 Coordinator of Alumni .... Ms. Annamaria SHORT
106 Dir of Distance Learning/Outreach .... Mr. Ryan ROARK
35 Director Campus Life .... Mr. Reydecel COSS

Eastern New Mexico University-Roswell (F)

52 University Blvd., Roswell NM 88203
County: Chaves FICE Identification: 002661
Unit ID: 187666
Telephone: (575) 624-7000 Carnegie Class: Assoc/HVT-Mix Trad/Non
FAX Number: (575) 624-7342 Calendar System: Semester
URL: www.roswell.enmu.edu
Established: 1958 Annual Undergrad Tuition & Fees (In-State): $2,424
Enrollment: 1,698 Coed
Affiliation or Control: State IRS Status: 501(c)3
Highest Offering: Associate Degree
Accreditation: HLC, ADNUR, COARC, EMT, MAC, #OTA

01 President .... Dr. Shawn POWELL
05 VP of Academic & Student Affairs .... Ms. Annemarie OLDFIELD
10 VP Business Operations .... Mrs. Rosie DURAN
08 Director Learning Resource Center .... Mrs. Veronica MUNOZ
32 Director of Student Affairs .... Mr. Devin STROMAN
06 Registrar .... Mr. Chris MEEKS
30 Director College Development .... Mrs. Donna ORACION
07 Director Admissions and Records .... Ms. Griselda AUBERT
13 Dir of Information Technology .... Mr. Jacob PUCKETT
15 Director of Human Resources .... Ms. Teresa CASAREZ
18 Director of Physical Plant .... Mr. Jim RICHARDSON
19 Director of Security .... Mr. Brad MCFADIN
96 Purchasing Agent .... Ms. Charlee MERCHANT
09 Exec Dir Inst Effectiveness .... Mr. Todd DEKAY

04 Executive Admin Asst to President ..... Ms. Dina GARIBAY JENKS
49 AVP of Arts & Science Education .... Mr. Robert MOORE
76 Interim AVP of Health Education .... Ms. Mavis WILLIAMS
72 AVP of Technical Education .... Mr. Ron FLURY
22 Dir Affirmative Action/Equal Opp .... Ms. Jessica SMALL
28 Director of Diversity .... Vacant
25 Director Accounting & Grants .... Ms. Traci DIXON
37 Director Student Financial Aid .... Ms. Destinee SALAYANDIA
84 Director Enrollment Services .... Ms. Angie BERSANE

EC-Council University (G)

101C Sun Avenue NE, Albuquerque NM 87109
County: Bernalillo Identification: 667232
Telephone: (505) 922-2889 Carnegie Class: Not Classified
FAX Number: (505) 856-8267 Calendar System: Other
URL: www.eccu.edu
Established: 2003 Annual Undergrad Tuition & Fees: N/A
Enrollment: N/A Coed
Affiliation or Control: Proprietary IRS Status: Proprietary
Highest Offering: Master's
Accreditation: DEAC

00 CEO/Chairman .... Sanjay BAVISI
01 President .... Lata BAVISI
05 Dean .... Venus FISHER
06 Registrar .... Bunny MARTINEZ
32 Student Support Executive .... David VALDEZ

Institute of American Indian Arts (H)

83 Avan Nu Po Road, Santa Fe NM 87508-1300
County: Santa Fe FICE Identification: 021464
Unit ID: 187745
Telephone: (505) 424-2300 Carnegie Class: Tribal
FAX Number: (505) 424-4500 Calendar System: Semester
URL: www.iaia.edu
Established: 1962 Annual Undergrad Tuition & Fees: $4,726
Enrollment: 693 Coed
Affiliation or Control: Federal IRS Status: Exempt
Highest Offering: Master's
Accreditation: HLC

01 President .... Robert MARTIN
10 Vice President of Operations .... Lawrence MIRABAL
05 Academic Dean .... Felipe COLON
15 Director of Human Resources .... Todd SPILMAN
04 Admin Assistant to the President .... Renee WHITE
06 Registrar .... Melanie BUCHLEITER
07 Assoc Dean Admissions & Retention .... Mary SILENTWALKER
08 Library Director .... Sara QUIMBY
09 Director of Institutional Research .... Mary Beth WORLEY
13 Diretor of Information Technology .... Anthony COCA
18 Director of Facilities .... Henry MIGNARDOT
25 Director of Sponsored Programs .... Laurie LOGAN BRAYSHAW
26 Director of Communications .... Jason ORDAZ
111 Director of Inst Advancement .... Suzette SHERMAN
37 Director of Financial Aid .... Scott WHITAKER

Luna Community College (I)

366 Luna Drive, Las Vegas NM 87701-1510
County: San Miguel FICE Identification: 009962
Unit ID: 363633
Telephone: (505) 454-2500 Carnegie Class: Assoc/MT-VT-Mix Trad/Non
FAX Number: (505) 454-2519 Calendar System: Semester
URL: www.luna.edu
Established: 1970 Annual Undergrad Tuition & Fees (In-District): $1,370
Enrollment: 720 Coed
Affiliation or Control: State/Local IRS Status: 501(c)3
Highest Offering: Associate Degree
Accreditation: #HLC, ACBSP, ADNUR, DA

01 President .... Mr. Edward MARTINEZ
05 VP of Instruction/Student Services .... Dr. Dani DAY
10 Vice Pres of Finance/CFO .... Vacant
09 Institutional Research Admin .... Ms. Denise GIBSON
07 Director of Admissions .... Mr. David LUCERO
06 Registrar .... Ms. Alicia CHACON
18 Manager Physical Plant .... Mr. Matthew CORDOVA
37 Director Student Financial Aid .... Ms. Gayle MARTINEZ
15 Director Human Resources .... Ms. Carolyn CHAVEZ
08 Learning Resource Center Manager .... Ms. Linda SALAZAR
13 Director IE&R/IT .... Mr. Greg SALAZAR
04 Admin Assistant to the President .... Ms. Anna GARDUÑO
121 Director of Academic & Career Plng .... Ms. Inca GARDUÑO-CRESPIN
41 Athletic Director .... Mr. Carl VIGIL
96 Director of Purchasing .... Ms. Jessica FLORES

Mesalands Community College (J)

911 S 10th Street, Tucumcari NM 88401-3352
County: Quay FICE Identification: 032063
Unit ID: 188261
Telephone: (575) 461-4413 Carnegie Class: Assoc/MT-VT-High Non
FAX Number: (575) 461-1901 Calendar System: Semester
URL: www.mesalands.edu
Established: 1980 Annual Undergrad Tuition & Fees (In-District): $2,136
Enrollment: 709 Coed
Affiliation or Control: State/Local IRS Status: 501(c)3
Highest Offering: Associate Degree

Accreditation: HLC

01 President ... Dr. Gregory T. BUSCH
04 Executive Asst to President ... Ms. Margaret RAGLAND
32 Vice President Student Affairs ... Dr. Aaron KENNEDY
05 Vice President of Academic Affairs ... Ms. Natalie GILLARD
26 Vice President Public Relations ... Mr. Josh MCVEY
11 Vice President of Campus Affairs ... Mr. Jim MORGAN
121 Vice President of Student Success ... Ms. Hazel ROUNTREE
06 Registrar ... Dr. Forrest KAATZ

National College of Midwifery (A)

1041 Reed Street, Suite C, Taos NM 87571
County: Taos Identification: 666251
Telephone: (575) 758-8914 Carnegie Class: Not Classified
FAX Number: N/A Calendar System: Trimester
URL: www.midwiferycollege.edu
Established: 1989 Annual Undergrad Tuition & Fees: N/A
Enrollment: N/A Coed
Affiliation or Control: Independent Non-Profit IRS Status: 501(c)3
Highest Offering: Baccalaureate
Accreditation: MEAC

01 CEO/President ... Marcy ANDREW
11 Chief Operations Officer ... Clorinda ROMERO
05 Provost ... Cassaundra JAH
07 Director of Admissions ... Renee DOTSON COX
30 Development Officer ... Han LUU

Navajo Technical University (B)

PO Box 849, Crownpoint NM 87313-0849
County: McKinley FICE Identification: 023576
Unit ID: 187596
Telephone: (505) 387-7401 Carnegie Class: Tribal
FAX Number: (505) 786-5644 Calendar System: Semester
URL: www.navajotech.edu
Established: 1979 Annual Undergrad Tuition & Fees: $4,070
Enrollment: 1,350 Coed
Affiliation or Control: Tribal Control IRS Status: 501(c)3
Highest Offering: Master's
Accreditation: HLC, ACFEI

01 President ... Dr. Elmer GUY
32 Dean of Student Services ... Ms. Jerlynn HENRY
10 Finance Director ... Ms. Cheryl THOMPSON
05 Dean of Undergraduate Studies ... Dr. Casmir AGBARAJI
06 Registrar/Director of Admissions ... Mr. Kelly CHIQUITO
37 Student Financial Aid Officer ... Mr. Gary SEGAY
04 Executive Assistant ... Ms. Tonilee BECENTI
13 IT Director ... Mr. Jared RIBBLE
41 Athletic Director ... Mr. George LAFRANCE
15 Human Resource Director ... Ms. Wanda COOKE

† Tuition figure is for a student enrolled in a federally recognized Indian tribe.

New Mexico Highlands University (C)

Box 9000, Las Vegas NM 87701-9000
County: San Miguel FICE Identification: 002653
Unit ID: 187897
Telephone: (877) 850-9064 Carnegie Class: Masters/L
FAX Number: N/A Calendar System: Semester
URL: www.nmhu.edu
Established: 1893 Annual Undergrad Tuition & Fees (In-State): $6,558
Enrollment: 2,777 Coed
Affiliation or Control: State IRS Status: 501(c)3
Highest Offering: Master's
Accreditation: HLC, ACBSP, CACREP, CAEP, MPCAC, NURSE, SW

01 President ... Dr. Sam MINNER
05 Provost/VP for Academic Affairs ... Dr. Roxanne GONZALES
10 VP Finance & Admin ... Mr. Max BACA
32 Dean of Students ... Dr. Kimberly BLEA
36 Director Center Prof Development ... Mr. Reynaldo MAESTAS
06 Registrar ... Ms. Henrietta ROMERO
09 Dir Inst Effectiveness & Research ... Dr. Heather TILSON
13 Director of Information Technology ... Mr. Joe GIERI
15 Director Human Resources ... Mr. Faron VALENCIA
18 Director of Facilities Mgmt ... Ms. Sylvia BACA
19 Chief Police/Security ... Mr. Clarence ROMERO
26 Director of University Relations ... Mr. Sean WEAVER
29 Alumni Director ... Ms. Juli SALMAN
111 Vice President for Advancement ... Dr. Theresa LAW
70 Dean School of Social Work ... Dr. Cristina DURAN
49 Dean College of Arts & Science ... Dr. Brandon KEMPNER
37 Director of Financial Aid ... Ms. Susan CHAVEZ
40 Bookstore Manager ... Ms. Naomi VILLANUEVA
50 Dean School of Business ... Dr. Veena PARBOTEEAH
53 Dean School of Education ... Dr. Mary EARICK
39 Director Student Housing ... Ms. Yvette WILKES
04 Sr Exec Admin to President ... Ms. Maria SENA
08 Chief Library Officer ... Mr. Ruben ARAGON
106 Director Online/Extended Learning ... Dr. Patrick WILSON
41 Athletic Director ... Mr. Andrew EHLING
96 Director of Purchasing ... Mr. Adam BUSTOS
84 Dir of Strategic Enrollment Mgmt ... Mr. Benito PACHECO
25 Chief Contract/Grants Administrator ... Dr. Ian WILLIAMSON
100 Special Assistant to the President ... Mr. Leon BUSTOS
86 Assoc VP for Govt Relations ... Dr. Denise MONTOYA

New Mexico Institute of Mining and Technology (D)

801 Leroy Place, Socorro NM 87801-4796
County: Socorro FICE Identification: 002654
Unit ID: 187967
Telephone: (575) 835-5434 Carnegie Class: Masters/S
FAX Number: (575) 835-6329 Calendar System: Semester
URL: www.nmt.edu
Established: 1889 Annual Undergrad Tuition & Fees (In-State): $8,361
Enrollment: 1,686 Coed
Affiliation or Control: State IRS Status: 501(c)3
Highest Offering: Doctorate
Accreditation: HLC

01 President ... Dr. Stephen G. WELLS
04 Executive Asst to the President ... Ms. Vanessa M. GRAIN
10 Vice Pres Administration & Finance ... Mr. Cleve MCDANIEL
05 Vice President Academic Affairs ... Dr. Doug WELLS
46 Interim Vice Pres Research ... Dr. Nelia D. DUNBAR
32 Acting Vice Pres of Student Life ... Dr. David GREENE
20 Assoc Vice Pres Academic Affairs ... Dr. Peter MOZLEY
88 Assoc VP Research ... Mr. Carlos REY ROMERO
86 Director of Government Affairs ... Mr. David MANZANO
15 Director of Human Resources ... Ms. JoAnn SALOME
22 Director Affirm Action & Compliance ... Mr. Randy SAAVEDRA
111 Director Office for Advancement ... Ms. Colleen FOSTER
26 Communications/Marketing Director ... Ms. Kathryn BAUER
30 Director of OIC ... Ms. Myrriah TOMAR
65 Int Dir Bur Geology & Mineral Res ... Dr. J Michael TIMMONS
12 Director Petro Recovery Res Ctr ... Dr. Robert BALCH
13 Director of Information Services ... Mr. Daniel LUNCEFORD
58 Dean of Graduate Studies ... Dr. Aly EL-OSERY
35 Dir Student Learning & Engagement ... Mr. Michael VOEGERL
06 Associate Registrar ... Ms. Heather JUAREZ
07 Director of Admission ... Mr. Gregory STRINGER
37 Director of Financial Aid ... Mr. Kenneth AERTS
109 Dir Auxiliary Services ... Ms. Nowka GUTIERREZ
38 Dir Counseling/Disabilities Svcs ... Ms. Angela GAUTIER
08 Director Library ... Mr. David COX
19 Director of Campus Police ... Mr. Scott SCARBOROUGH
88 Dir Physical Recreation ... Ms. Melissa BEGAY
18 Director Facilities Management ... Mr. Robby MONTGOMERY
96 Chief Procurement Officer ... Ms. Kimela MILLER

New Mexico Junior College (E)

1 Thunderbird Circle, Hobbs NM 88240-9123
County: Lea FICE Identification: 002655
Unit ID: 187903
Telephone: (575) 392-4510 Carnegie Class: Assoc/Mt-VT-High Trad
FAX Number: (575) 492-2732 Calendar System: Semester
URL: www.nmjc.edu
Established: 1965 Annual Undergrad Tuition & Fees (In-District): $2,072
Enrollment: 1,406 Coed
Affiliation or Control: Local IRS Status: 501(c)3
Highest Offering: Associate Degree
Accreditation: HLC, ADNUR

01 President ... Dr. Derek MOORE
05 Vice President Instruction ... Jeff MCCOOL
10 Vice President Finance ... Joshua MORGAN
32 Vice President Student Services ... Cathy MITCHELL
103 Vice President Training & Outreach ... Steve SAUCEDA
43 General Counsel/Admin Services ... Scotty HOLLOMAN
13 Dir Computer Information System ... Bill KUNKO
26 Director of Communications ... Valerie ONSUREZ GAUNA
04 Executive Asst to the President ... Norma FAUGHT
37 Director Financial Aid ... Kerrie MITCHELL
66 Director of Allied Health/Nursing ... Cammie ARMSTRONG
18 VP for Operations/Special Projects ... Dr. Charley CARROLL
81 Dean Applied Sciences/Learning Tech ... Dr. Stephanie FERGUSON
49 Dean Arts/Sciences/Learning Support ... Dianne MARQUEZ
84 Dean of Students ... Sarah PATTERSON
40 Director of Bookstore Services ... Julie BUCHANAN
19 Director of Public Safety ... Walter COBURN
08 Director of Library Services ... Vacant
96 Coordinator of Purchasing ... JoeMike GOMEZ
41 Director of Athletics ... Deron CLARK
102 Acct/Controller-NMJC Foundation ... Tina KUNKO
21 Controller ... Stacey WYNN
39 Director of Resident Life ... Eric GARCIA
88 Dir Western Heritage Museum/LCCHF ... Erin ANDERSON
88 Dir NMJC Research Foundation ... Dennis HOLMBERG
06 Registrar ... Angela MARMOLEJO GOMEZ
19 Director of Campus Security/Safety ... Dennis KELLEY
30 Director of Development ... Vacant
15 Director of Human Resources ... Amy COOMBES

New Mexico Military Institute (F)

101 W College, Roswell NM 88201-5173
County: Chaves FICE Identification: 002656
Unit ID: 187912
Telephone: (575) 622-6250 Carnegie Class: Assoc/HT-Mix Trad/Non
FAX Number: (575) 624-8058 Calendar System: Semester
URL: www.nmmi.edu
Established: 1891 Annual Undergrad Tuition & Fees (In-State): $6,616
Enrollment: 493 Coed
Affiliation or Control: State IRS Status: 501(c)3
Highest Offering: Associate Degree
Accreditation: HLC

01 Superintendent/President ... MGen. Jerry W. GRIZZLE
32 Commandant ... Col. Thomas TATE
100 Chief of Staff ... Col. David WEST
10 Chief Financial Officer ... Col. Deana CURNUTT
05 Dean ... Dr. Orlando GRIEGO
41 Athletic Director/Dir Physical Educ ... Col. Jose BARRON
116 Internal Auditor ... Vacant
88 Professor of Military Science ... LtCol. Ryan L. EISENHAUER
20 Vice Dean & High School Princ ... Col. Jose PORRAS
15 Human Resources/Title IX Director ... Ms. Dori CAMERON
50 Assoc Dean Social Science/Business ... LtCol. Cody NORTHRUP
81 Assoc Dean Science/Mathematics ... Dr. Mia YANG
79 Assoc Dean Humanities ... LtCol. Patricia MATCHIN
64 Director of Music ... Mr. Matthew BRADY
08 Director of the Library ... Vacant
18 Chief Facilities/Physical Plant ... Mr. Kent TAYLOR
06 Registrar ... Maj. Chris WRIGHT
37 Director of Financial Aid ... Maj. Monica L. GARCIA
88 Mil Services Academies Prep Dir ... Vacant
19 Chief of Campus Police ... Mr. Jerrold LONOWSKI
38 Director of Cadet Counseling Center ... Mrs. Teresa GRAY
29 Director Alumni Relations ... LtCol. Danny ARMIJO
04 Executive Secretary to President ... Ms. Bernadette BEATTY
09 Director of Institutional Research ... Ms. Michele BATES
102 Dir Foundation/Corporate Relations ... Mr. Jimmy BARNES
13 Chief Info Technology Officer ... Mr. Todd LUPIEN
07 Director of Admissions ... LtCol. Kris WARD

New Mexico State University Main Campus (G)

Box 30001, 3Z, Las Cruces NM 88003-8001
County: Dona Ana FICE Identification: 002657
Unit ID: 188030
Telephone: (575) 646-2035 Carnegie Class: DU-Higher
FAX Number: (575) 646-6334 Calendar System: Semester
URL: www.nmsu.edu
Established: 1888 Annual Undergrad Tuition & Fees (In-State): $7,301
Enrollment: 14,227 Coed
Affiliation or Control: State IRS Status: 501(c)3
Highest Offering: Doctorate
Accreditation: HLC, CAATE, CAEP, COPSY, DIETD, DIETI, IPSY, MUS, NURSE, PH, SP, SPAA, SW

01 President ... Dr. John FLOROS
00 Chancellor ... Dr. Dan ARVIZU
11 Vice Chancellor ... Dr. Ruth JOHNSTON
05 Interim Provost/Chief Academic Ofcr ... Dr. Dorothy CAMPBELL
10 Sr VP Administration/Finance ... Dr. Andrew BURKE
111 VP Univ Advance/Pres NMSU Found ... Mr. Derek DICTSON
32 VP Student Success/Enroll Mgmt ... Dr. Renay SCOTT
26 Assoc VP Marketing/Communications ... Mr. Justin BANNISTER
21 Assoc VP Admin & Finance ... Ms. D'Anne STUART
15 Asst VP Human Resources Svcs ... Ms. Gena W. JONES
20 Assoc VP/Deputy Provost ... Ms. Rebecca CAMPBELL
09 Int Asst VP Institutional Analysis ... Mr. Calixto MELERO
86 Asst VP Government Relations ... Mr. Ricardo REL
49 Dean College of Arts & Sciences ... Dr. Enrico PONTELLI
50 Dean Business College ... Dr. James HOFFMAN
53 Dean College of Education ... Dr. Henrietta PICHON
54 Dean College of Engineering ... Dr. Lakshmi REDDI
58 Dean Graduate School ... Dr. Luis CIFUENTES
76 Int Dean Col Health & Social Svcs ... Vacant
35 Dean of Students ... Dr. Ann GOODMAN
13 Interim Chief Information Officer ... Mr. Chris KIELT
06 University Registrar ... Ms. Dacia SEDILLO
43 General Counsel ... Mr. Roy COLLINS
08 Dean University Library ... Ms. Katherine TERPIS
29 AVP Marketing & Strat Initiatives ... Mrs. Lynn SCHLEMEYER
21 University Controller ... Ms. Norma NOEL
39 Acting Director Student Housing ... Ms. Ophelia WATKINS
23 Exec Director Health & Wellness ... Ms. Lori MCKEE
41 Director Athletics ... Mr. Mario MOCCIA
35 Asst VP Student Affairs ... Dr. Anthony S. MARIN
96 Dir Procurement Services ... Ms. Javier CORDERO
22 Dir Institutional Equity/EEO ... Ms. Laura CASTILLE
07 Director Admissions ... Ms. Seth MINER
18 Assoc VP Facilities Services ... Mr. Luis CAMPOS
27 Dir of Marketing/Creative Svcs ... Dr. Melissa CHAVIRA
47 Dean College of Agriculture ... Dr. Rolando FLORES
92 Dean Honors College ... Dr. Phame CAMARENA
12 President NMSU-DACC ... Dr. Monica TORRES
12 Branch Executive Director ... Dr. Ken VAN WINKLE
100 Chief of Staff ... Mrs. Leslie CERVANTES
37 Director Student Financial Aid ... Dr. Vandeen MCKENZIE
102 Dir Foundation/Corporate Relations ... Vacant
28 Director of Diversity ... Dr. Teresa Maria Linda SCHOLZ
122 Fraternity/Sorority Life Advisor ... Ms. Abby HOWARD

New Mexico State University at Alamogordo (H)

2400 N Scenic Drive, Alamogordo NM 88310-4239
County: Otero FICE Identification: 002658
Unit ID: 187994
Telephone: (575) 439-3600 Carnegie Class: Assoc/HT-High Non
FAX Number: (575) 439-3643 Calendar System: Semester
URL: www.nmsua.edu
Established: 1958 Annual Undergrad Tuition & Fees (In-State): $2,424
Enrollment: 941 Coed
Affiliation or Control: State IRS Status: 501(c)3
Highest Offering: Associate Degree

Accreditation: HLC

12 Branch Exec Director .... Dr. Ken VAN WINKLE
05 Vice President for Academic Affairs .... Dr. Mark CAL
32 Vice President for Student Services ...... Mrs. Anne RICKSECKEER
10 Vice President for Business/Finance .... Mr. Antonio SALINAS
08 Librarian .... Ms. Emily ANDERSON
37 Financial Aid Representative .... Vacant
09 Director of Institutional Research .... Mr. Greg HILLIS
15 Director Human Resources .... Vacant
96 Senior Buyer .... Mr. Lee M. KINNEY
106 Dir Online Education/E-learning .... Mrs. Sherrell WHEELER
108 Director Institutional Assessment .... Dr. Joyce HILL

New Mexico State University Dona Ana Community College (A)

2800 Sonoma Ranch Boulevard, Las Cruces NM 88011
County: Dona Ana Identification: 666649
Unit ID: 187620
Telephone: (575) 527-7500 Carnegie Class: Assoc/MT-VT-Mix Trad/Non
FAX Number: (575) 528-7300 Calendar System: Semester
URL: dacc.nmsu.edu
Established: 1973 Annual Undergrad Tuition & Fees (In-State): $2,160
Enrollment: 7,028 Coed
Affiliation or Control: State IRS Status: 501(c)3
Highest Offering: Associate Degree
Accreditation: HLC, ACBSP, ADNUR, COARC, DA, DH, DMS, EMT, IFSAC, RAD

01 President .... Dr. Monica TORRES
05 VP Academic Affairs .... Dr. Xeturah WOODLEY
10 VP Business & Finance .... Ms. Kelly BROOKS
32 VP Student Services .... Mr. Amadeo LEDESMA
26 VP External Relations .... Vacant
20 AVP Acad Affairs/Assessment & Accr .... Dr. Jennifer HODGES
84 Assoc VP Acad Affairs/Enroll Mgt .... Vacant
49 Division Dean Arts/Hum/Social Sci .... Ms. Shannon BRADLEY
50 Division Dean Business/Public Svcs .... Mr. Jonathan M. NUNLEY
76 Division Dean Health Sciences .... Ms. Josefina CARMONA
72 Division Dean Advanced Technologies .... Mr. Chipper MOORE
103 Exec Director Workforce Dev/Trng .... Dr. Fred OWENSBY
08 Director Library Services .... Ms. Terese DESIMIO
121 Director Academic Advising .... Mr. Brad MAZDRA
09 Director Institutional Analysis .... Vacant
55 Director Adult Education .... Dr. Patricia BRAINARD
31 Director Community Education .... Dr. Mary ULRICH
21 Manager Business Office .... Ms. Debra PEEL
15 Manager Human Resources Operation .... Ms. Yvette BENITIZ
90 Director Computer Support .... Vacant
18 Manager Facilities Services .... Mr. Michael LUCHAU
07 Director Admissions .... Ms. Geraldine MARTINEZ
37 Director Financial Aid .... Ms. Michelle LOPEZ
22 Director Student Accessibility Svcs .... Dr. Jesse HAAS

New Mexico State University Grants (B)

1500 Third Street, Grants NM 87020-2025
Telephone: (505) 287-6678 FICE Identification: 008854
Accreditation: &HLC

† Regional accreditation is carried under the parent institution in Las Cruces, NM.

Northern New Mexico College (C)

921 N Paseo de Onate, Espa´ola NM 87532-2649
County: Rio Arriba FICE Identification: 020839
Unit ID: 188058
Telephone: (505) 747-2100 Carnegie Class: Bac/Assoc-Mixed
FAX Number: (505) 747-2170 Calendar System: Semester
URL: www.nnmc.edu
Established: 1909 Annual Undergrad Tuition & Fees (In-State): $4,952
Enrollment: 1,234 Coed
Affiliation or Control: State IRS Status: 501(c)3
Highest Offering: Baccalaureate
Accreditation: HLC, ACBSP, ADNUR, CAEPN, NURSE

01 Interim President .... Dr. Barbara M. MEDINA
10 Vice President Finance & Admin .... Mr. C. Vince LITHGOW
05 Provost/VP Academic Affairs .... Dr. Ivan LOPEZ-HURTADO
32 Int Asst Provost Student Affairs .... Dr. Don APPIARIUS
06 Registrar .... Ms. Janice BACA
08 Head Librarian .... Ms. Courtney BRUCH
07 Acting Director Admissions .... Ms. Emma HASHMAN
37 Director of Financial Aid .... Ms. Kathy LEVINE
13 Director Information Technologies .... Mr. Jimi MONTOYA
15 Director of Human Resources .... Mr. Kenneth LUCERO
102 Dir Foundation/Corporate Relations .... Dr. Barbara M. MEDINA
28 Director of Equity & Diversity .... Vacant
18 Director of Facilities/Security .... Mr. Shawn P. MADRID
09 Director of Institutional Research .... Ms. Carmella SANCHEZ
21 Dir Small Business Development .... Ms. Julianna BARBEE
121 Director Institutional Advisement .... Ms. Dulce MARTI
41 Athletic Director/Coach .... Mr. Ryan CORDOVA
101 Executive Office Director .... Ms. Amy F. PEÑA
51 Coordinator Continuing Education .... Ms. Cecilia ROMERO
53 Chair Dept of Education .... Dr. Sandra RODRIGUEZ
76 Chair Dept of Nursing/Health Sci .... Ms. Ellen TRABKA
50 Chair Dept Business Administration .... Dr. Lori BACA
54 Chair Dept Engineering/Technology .... Dr. Sadia AHMED
26 Creative Dir Communications/Mktg .... Ms. Sandy KROLICK
96 Chief Procurement Officer .... Ms. Josephine VELASQUEZ

Pima Medical Institute-Albuquerque (D)

4400 Cutler Avenue NE, Albuquerque NM 87110-3935
Telephone: (505) 881-1234 FICE Identification: 036783
Accreditation: ABHES, CNEA, COARC, DH, PTAA

† Branch campus of Pima Medical Institute-Tucson, Tucson, AZ

Ruidoso Branch Community College (E)

709 Mechem Drive, Ruidoso NM 88345
Telephone: (575) 315-1120 Identification: 770345
Accreditation: &HLC

St. John's College (F)

1160 Camino de la Cruz Blanca,
Santa Fe NM 87505-4599
County: Santa Fe FICE Identification: 002093
Unit ID: 245652
Telephone: (505) 984-6000 Carnegie Class: Bac-A&S
FAX Number: (505) 984-6003 Calendar System: Semester
URL: www.sjc.edu
Established: 1964 Annual Undergrad Tuition & Fees: $35,760
Enrollment: 355 Coed
Affiliation or Control: Independent Non-Profit IRS Status: 501(c)3
Highest Offering: Master's
Accreditation: HLC

01 President .... Mr. Mark ROOSEVELT
05 Dean of the College .... Mr. J. Walter STERLING
30 Vice Pres for Dev/Alumni Affairs .... Ms. Phelosha COLLAROS
10 Treasurer/Finance Officer .... Mr. Michael S. DURAN
58 Assoc Dean Graduate Programs .... Mr. Edward WALPIN
06 Registrar .... Ms. Julie ROMERO
08 Library Director .... Ms. Jennifer SPRAGUE
07 Director of Admissions .... Ms. Caroline RANDALL
09 Director of Institutional Research .... Ms. Alethea SCALLY
15 Director of Human Resources .... Mr. Aaron YOUNG
18 Chief Facilities/Physical Plant .... Mr. Phillip KANIATOBE
29 VP of Development/Alumni Relations .... Ms. Phelosha COLLAROS
36 Director Career Services .... Mr. Charles BERGMAN
37 Director Student Financial Aid .... Ms. Darlene SANDOVAL
13 Chief Information Technology Office .... Mr. Mehmet GORGULU

† Affiliated with St. John's College, Maryland.

San Juan College (G)

4601 College Boulevard, Farmington NM 87402-4699
County: San Juan FICE Identification: 002660
Unit ID: 188100
Telephone: (505) 326-3311 Carnegie Class: Assoc/HVT-Mix Trad/Non
FAX Number: (505) 566-3385 Calendar System: Semester
URL: www.sanjuancollege.edu
Established: 1956 Annual Undergrad Tuition & Fees (In-District): $1,618
Enrollment: 5,240 Coed
Affiliation or Control: Local IRS Status: 501(c)3
Highest Offering: Associate Degree
Accreditation: HLC, ADNUR, CAHIIM, COARC, DH, EMT, OTA, PTAA, SURGA, SURGT

01 President .... Dr. Toni PENDERGRASS
03 Executive Vice President .... Mr. Edward DESPLAS
05 Vice Pres for Learning .... Dr. Adrienne FORGETTE
32 Vice Pres for Student Services .... Dr. Boomer APPLEMAN
04 Executive Asst to President .... Ms. Donna ELLIS
20 Associate VP for Learning .... Ms. Sandy GILPIN
15 VP of Human Resources/Legal Action .... Ms. Kerri LANGONI
102 Executive Director Foundation .... Ms. Gayle DEAN
21 Controller .... Mr. Kristie ELLIS
26 Director Marketing/Public Relations .... Ms. Rhonda SCHAEFER
124 Director of Retention .... Dr. Jenniffer VALORA
84 Sr Dir Enrollment Management .... Vacant
50 Dean School of Business & IT .... Mr. Eddy RAWLINSON
79 Dean School of Humanities .... Ms. Lisa SNYDER
76 Dean School of Health Sciences .... Ms. Sherrie PAXSON
65 Dean School of Energy .... Ms. Alicia CORBELL
72 Dean School Trades & Technology .... Mr. Ruben JOHNSON
81 Dean Math/Science & Engineering .... Dr. Michael OTTINGER
16 Asst Dir HR Equity/Diversity .... Ms. Stacey ALLEN
28 Director Native American Programs .... Mr. Byron TSABETSAYE
08 Director Library Services .... Ms. Samanthi HEWAKAPUGE
37 Sr Director of Financial Aid .... Ms. Mindi-Kim SCHRUM
18 Director Physical Plant .... Mr. Chris HARRELSON
19 Director Security/Safety .... Mr. Kenneth HIBNER
35 Director Student Activities .... Ms. Amanda ROBLES
96 Director Purchasing .... Mr. Frank COLE
38 Director Student Advising Center .... Ms. Christy FERRATO
74 Director Vet-Tech Program .... Ms. Laura BLACK
06 Registrar .... Ms. Sherri SCHAAF
09 Sr Dir of Institutional Research .... Mr. Ron JERNIGAN
13 Chief Info Technology Officer (CIO) .... Mr. Roy LYTLE
103 AVP of Workforce & Economic Devel .... Dr. Lorenzo REYES

Santa Fe Community College (H)

6401 Richards Avenue, Santa Fe NM 87508-4887
County: Santa Fe FICE Identification: 022781
Unit ID: 188137
Telephone: (505) 428-1000 Carnegie Class: Assoc/MT-VT-High Non
FAX Number: (505) 428-1296 Calendar System: Semester
URL: www.sfcc.edu
Established: 1983 Annual Undergrad Tuition & Fees (In-State): $2,505
Enrollment: 3,459 Coed
Affiliation or Control: State IRS Status: 501(c)3
Highest Offering: Associate Degree
Accreditation: HLC, ADNUR, COARC, DA, EMT, MAC

01 President .... Dr. Becky ROWLEY
05 Vice Pres Academic Affairs .... Ms. Margaret PETERS
10 Vice Pres Finance/CFO .... Mr. Nick TELLES
32 Vice President for Student Affairs .... Ms. Margaret PETERS
09 VP Planning/Inst Effectiveness .... Mr. Yash MORIMOTO
121 Assoc VP for Student Success .... Ms. Thomasinia ORTIZ-GALLEGOS
51 Dir Cont Educ/Contract Training .... Ms. Kris SWEDIN
26 Exec Dir Marketing/Public Rels .... Mr. Todd LOVATO
102 Exec Dir SFCC Foundation .... Ms. Deborah BOLDT
06 Registrar .... Ms. Diana BACA
13 Chief Information Officer .... Ms. Cori BERGEN
37 Financial Aid Director .... Ms. Kelly DURBIN
66 Director of Nursing Education .... Ms. Terri TEWART
08 Library Director .... Ms. Valerie NYE
15 Human Resources Manager .... Ms. Michelle HARDING
88 Director Small Business Development .... Mr. Brian DUBOFF
18 Director of Facilities .... Mr. Dobby SCHMIDT
12 Executive Director HEC .... Ms. Rebecca ESTRADA
101 Executive Asst to the President .... Ms. Patricia NEWMAN
96 Director of Purchasing .... Mr. John APODACA
25 Director of Grants .... Ms. Ann BLACK
49 Dean School of Liberal Arts .... Dr. James WYSONG
54 Dean Sch Health/Engineering & Math .... Dr. Terri TEWART
76 Dean School of Fitness Education .... Dr. Jenny LANDEN
57 Dean Sch Arts/Design & Media Arts .... Dr. James WYSONG
75 Int Dean Trades/Tech/Sustainability .... Ms. Julia DEISLER
50 Dean School of Business & Educ .... Dr. Joseph COOKE

Southeast New Mexico College (I)

1500 University Drive, Carlsbad NM 88220-3598
County: Eddy FICE Identification: 002659
Unit ID: 188003
Telephone: (575) 234-9200 Carnegie Class: Assoc/HT-High Non
FAX Number: (575) 885-4951 Calendar System: Semester
URL: senmc.edu
Established: 1950 Annual Undergrad Tuition & Fees (In-State): $2,068
Enrollment: 1,203 Coed
Affiliation or Control: State IRS Status: 501(c)3
Highest Offering: Associate Degree
Accreditation: HLC, ADNUR

01 Interim President .... Dr. Andrew NWANNE
05 Int VP Academic Affairs .... Dr. Monty HARRIS
32 Vice Pres Student Services .... Juanita GARCIA
10 VP Business & Finance .... Dr. Karla VOLPI
37 Director Financial Aid .... Diana CAMPOS
15 Human Resources Specialist .... Vacant
26 Director Marketing & Publications .... Sky KLAUS
04 Administrative Asst to President .... Merdia THERAGOOD
18 Chief Facilities/Physical Plant .... Gary ROPER
09 Director of Institutional Research .... Vacant
06 Registrar .... Amy DEWEY
08 Chief Library Officer .... Samantha VILLA
101 Secretary of the Institution/Board .... Michelle SAPIEN
103 Director Workforce Development .... Mike MCNAIR
13 Chief Information Technology Office .... Corey BARELA-EUBANK
96 Director of Purchasing .... Rebecca SILVA

Southwest Acupuncture College (J)

2100 Calle de la Vuelta, Santa Fe NM 87505-6351
County: Santa Fe FICE Identification: 026220
Unit ID: 366605
Telephone: (505) 438-8884 Carnegie Class: Spec-4-yr-Other Health
FAX Number: (505) 438-8883 Calendar System: Semester
URL: www.acupuncturecollege.edu
Established: 1980 Annual Undergrad Tuition & Fees: N/A
Enrollment: 33 Coed
Affiliation or Control: Proprietary IRS Status: Proprietary
Highest Offering: Master's; No Lower Division
Accreditation: ACUP

01 CEO .... Dr. Anthony ABBATE
03 Executive Director .... Dr. Skya ABBATE
10 Chief Fiscal Officer .... Ms. Piper KING
12 Campus Director Santa Fe .... Dr. Paul ROSSIGNOL
17 Clinical Director Santa Fe .... Dr. Pamela BARRETT
05 Academic Dean Santa Fe .... Ms. Susan CHANEY
37 Financial Aid Director .... Ms. Angela ANAYA
07 Director of Admissions & Alumni .... Ms. Sophia BUNGAY
08 Chief Library Officer .... Ms. Elizabeth MARTINEZ
04 Administrative Assistant .... Ms. Sandy SZABAT

Southwest University of Naprapathic Medicine (K)

2006 Botulph Road, Ste A, Sante Fe NM 87505
County: Santa Fe Identification: 667420
Telephone: (505) 467-8777 Carnegie Class: Not Classified
FAX Number: N/A Calendar System: Quarter
URL: sunm.edu
Established: 2006 Annual Graduate Tuition & Fees: N/A
Enrollment: N/A Coed
Affiliation or Control: Proprietary IRS Status: Proprietary
Highest Offering: Doctorate; No Undergraduates

Accreditation: DEAC

01 President .... Dr. Patrick NUZZO

Southwestern College (A)

3960 San Felipe Road, Santa Fe NM 87507
County: Santa Fe FICE Identification: 030761
Unit ID: 188207
Telephone: (505) 471-5756 Carnegie Class: Spec-4-yr-Other Health
FAX Number: (505) 471-4071 Calendar System: Quarter
URL: www.swc.edu
Established: 1977 Annual Graduate Tuition & Fees: N/A
Enrollment: 164 Coed
Affiliation or Control: Independent Non-Profit IRS Status: 501(c)3
Highest Offering: Master's; No Undergraduates
Accreditation: HLC, ACATE

01 President .... Dr. Ann FILEMYR
03 Exec VP/Dir New Earth Institute SWC .... Ms. Katherine NINOS
05 Dean of the College .... Dr. Virginia P. VIGIL
84 Director of Enrollment Services .... Ms. Dru PHOENIX
06 Registrar .... Ms. Andrea PACHECO
10 Chief Finance Officer .... Ms. Allison FRANK
13 Chief Technology Officer .... Ms. Donna HARRINGTON
32 Director of Student & Career Svcs .... Ms. Lily GUTIERREZ
08 Chief Library Officer .... Mr. Larry HARKCOM
11 Chief of Operations/ Administration .... Ms. Dianne DELOREN
15 Chief Human Resources Officer .... Ms. Esperanza GRIEGO
37 Director Student Financial Aid .... Ms. Lara BARELA

Southwestern Indian Polytechnic Institute (B)

9169 Coors Boulevard, NW, Albuquerque NM 87120
County: Bernalillo FICE Identification: 025110
Unit ID: 188216
Telephone: (505) 346-2348 Carnegie Class: Tribal
FAX Number: (505) 346-2343 Calendar System: Trimester
URL: www.sipi.edu
Established: 1971 Annual Undergrad Tuition & Fees: $1,095
Enrollment: 450 Coed
Affiliation or Control: Federal IRS Status: 501(c)3
Highest Offering: Associate Degree
Accreditation: HLC, OPD

01 President .... Dr. Sherry ALLISON
10 Vice Pres College Operations .... Mr. Eric CHRISTENSEN
05 Vice President Academic Programs .... Ms. Valerie MONTOYA
09 Dir Institutional Rsch/Effect/Plng .... Mr. Edward HUMMINGBIRD
32 Director Student Services .... Dr. Cecelia COMETSEVAH
07 Director Admissions/Registrar .... Vacant
15 Human Resources Specialist .... Ms. Dawn AMI
18 Facilities Director .... Ms. Renee ALLEN
37 Financial Aid Specialist .... Ms. Melynda MITCHELL

University of New Mexico Main Campus (C)

1 University of New Mexico, Albuquerque NM 87131-0001
County: Bernalillo FICE Identification: 002663
Unit ID: 187985
Telephone: (505) 277-0111 Carnegie Class: DU-Highest
FAX Number: (505) 277-6019 Calendar System: Semester
URL: www.unm.edu
Established: 1889 Annual Undergrad Tuition & Fees (In-State): $8,161
Enrollment: 22,311 Coed
Affiliation or Control: State IRS Status: 501(c)3
Highest Offering: Doctorate
Accreditation: HLC, ARCPA, CAATE, CACREP, CAEPN, CAMPEP, CLPSY, DANCE, DENT, DH, DIETD, DIETI, EMT, IPSY, LAW, LSAR, MED, MIDWF, MLS, MUS, NMT, NURSE, OT, PCSAS, PH, PHAR, PLNG, PTA, SP, SPAA, THEA

01 President .... Garnett S. STOKES
05 Provost .... Dr. James HOLLOWAY
17 Vice Chancellor of Clinical Affairs .... Dr. Michael RICHARDS
10 SVP Finance & Administration .... Dr. Teresa COSTANTINIDIS
100 Chief of Staff .... Dr. Terry BABBITT
20 Sr Vice Prov for Academic Affairs .... Dr. Barbara L. RODRIGUEZ
46 Vice President Research .... Dr. Ellen FISHER
25 AVP Research Administration .... Patricia HENNING
32 Vice President Student Affairs .... Dr. Eliseo S. TORRES
28 Vice Chancellor HSC Diversity .... Dr. John Paul SANCHEZ
84 Vice Prov Enrollment & Analytics .... Dan GARCIA
15 Vice President Human Resources .... Dorothy ANDERSON
21 University Controller .... Elizabeth METZGER
13 Chief Information Officer .... Duane ARRUTI
14 Int Deputy Chief Information Ofcr .... Brian PIETREWICZ
43 Chief Legal Counsel .... Loretta MARTINEZ
29 Int AVP Alumni Relations .... Connie BEIMER
20 Dir Financial Ops Academic Affairs .... Nicole DOPSON
35 AVP Student Life .... Vacant
35 AVP Student Services .... Dr. Tim GUTIERREZ
50 Dean Anderson School of Mgmt .... Dr. Mitzi MONTOYA
48 Dean Sch of Architecture & Planning .... Robert A. GONZALEZ
49 Dean College of Arts & Sciences .... Dr. Mark PECENY
53 Dean College of Education .... Hansel E. BURLEY
54 Dean School of Engineering .... Dr. Christos CHRISTODOULOU
57 Dean College of Fine Arts .... Dr. Harris SMITH
61 Dean School of Law .... Sergio PAREJA
63 Exec Vice Dean School of Medicine .... Dr. Martha MCGREW
66 Dean College of Nursing .... Dr. Christine KASPER
67 Dean College of Pharmacy .... Dr. Donald A. GODWIN
80 Dir School of Public Admin .... Dr. Bruce J. PERLMAN
97 Dean University College .... Dr. Eric LAU
58 Dean Office of Graduate Studies .... Dr. Julie COONROD
51 Exec Director Continuing Education .... Audrey ARNOLD
08 Dean University Libraries .... Dr. Richard CLEMENT
26 Chief Univ Marketing & Comm Officer .... Cinnamon BLAIR
27 HSC Comm/Marketing/Public Info Ofcr .... Alex SANCHEZ
27 University Media Relations Officer .... Daniel JIRON
105 Mgr University Web Communications .... Matt CARTER
86 Director Government Affairs .... Dr. Barbara DAMRON
09 Director Institutional Analytics .... Dr. Heather S. MECHLER
88 University Architect .... Amy COBURN
18 Director Facilities Management .... Al SENA
19 Interim Chief of Police .... Joseph SILVA
96 Chief Procurement Officer .... Bruce E. CHERRIN
23 Exec Dir Student Health/Counseling .... Dr. James WILTERDING
22 Chief Compliance Officer .... Francie CORDOVA
56 Director Extended Learning .... Debby KNOTTS
35 Dean of Students .... Nasha TORREZ
07 Director Admissions and Recruitment .... Matt HULETT
06 Registrar .... Sheila JURNAK
37 Director Student Financial Aid .... Brian MALONE
36 Director Career Services .... Dr. Jenna S. CRABB
39 Int Dir Res Life & Student Housing .... Megan CHIBANGA
40 Interim Director Bookstore .... Lisa WALDEN
108 Director of Assessment .... Julie SANCHEZ
102 UNM Foundation President and CEO .... Jeff TODD
30 VP for Development .... Larry RYAN
30 VP Development Health Sciences Ctr .... Bill UHER
88 CEO UNM Hospital .... Kate BECKER
04 Administrative Asst to President .... Mitch GARRITY
101 Special Asst to Board of Regents .... Mallory REVIERE

University of New Mexico-Gallup (D)

705 Gurley Avenue, Gallup NM 87301
Telephone: (505) 863-7500 FICE Identification: 006881
Accreditation: &HLC, ADNUR, CAHIIM, DA, MLTAD

† Regional accreditation is carried under the parent institution in Albuquerque, NM.

University of New Mexico-Los Alamos (E)

4000 University Drive, Los Alamos NM 87544-2233
Telephone: (505) 662-5919 Identification: 666742
Accreditation: &HLC

† Regional accreditation is carried under the parent institution in Albuquerque, NM.

University of New Mexico-Taos (F)

1157 Country Road 110, Ranchos de Taos NM 87557
Telephone: (575) 737-6215 Identification: 666743
Accreditation: &HLC, ADNUR

† Regional accreditation is carried under the parent institution in Albuquerque, NM.

University of New Mexico-Valencia (G)

280 La Entrada Road, Los Lunas NM 87031-7633
Telephone: (505) 925-8500 Identification: 666741
Accreditation: &HLC, ADNUR

† Regional accreditation is carried under the parent institution in Albuquerque, NM.

University of St. Francis (H)

1500 N. Renaissance Blvd, NE, Ste C, Albuquerque NM 87107
Telephone: (505) 266-5565 Identification: 770099
Accreditation: &HLC, ARCPA

† Branch campus of University of St. Francis, Joliet, IL

University of the Southwest (I)

6610 Lovington Highway, Hobbs NM 88240-9129
County: Lea FICE Identification: 002650
Unit ID: 188182
Telephone: (575) 392-6561 Carnegie Class: Masters/L
FAX Number: N/A Calendar System: Semester
URL: www.usw.edu
Established: 1962 Annual Undergrad Tuition & Fees: $16,200
Enrollment: 904 Coed
Affiliation or Control: Independent Non-Profit IRS Status: 501(c)3
Highest Offering: Doctorate
Accreditation: HLC, CACREP

01 President/CEO .... Dr. Ryan TIPTON
10 Executive VP/CFO .... Ms. Paula SMITH
18 Assoc VP Facilities & Athletics .... Mr. Steve APPEL
32 Assoc VP Campus Life/Stdnt Affairs .... Ms. Amanda GUZMAN
15 Asst VP HR & Regulatory Compliance .... Ms. Veronica TORREZ
05 Dean Faculty & Instruction/CAO .... Dr. Brianna LOPEZ
53 Dean College of Education .... Dr. Laura HUNT
37 Executive Director of Financial Aid .... Ms. Sandy WILKINSON
84 Director of Enrollment .... Dr. Ryan TIPTON
06 University Registrar .... Ms. Lissete TERRAZAS
13 Dir Enterprise Resource Systems .... Mr. Josh FORD
38 University Counselor .... Mr. Brian ARNOLD
105 Instructional Design Technician .... Mr. David WILLIS
26 Dir of Mktg/Stakeholder Rels Coord .... Ms. Maria DUARTE
04 Administrative Asst to President .... Ms. Linda WOODFIN
88 Dir Operations Academic Affairs .... Ms. Andrea DODSON
42 Campus Pastor/Christian Ministry .... Mr. David BLACKWOOD
39 Asst to Director of Student Affairs .... Ms. Yasmeen SANCHEZ

Western New Mexico University (J)

PO Box 680, Silver City NM 88062-0680
County: Grant FICE Identification: 002664
Unit ID: 188304
Telephone: (575) 538-6238 Carnegie Class: Masters/L
FAX Number: (575) 538-6364 Calendar System: Semester
URL: wnmu.edu
Established: 1893 Annual Undergrad Tuition & Fees (In-State): $6,574
Enrollment: 2,896 Coed
Affiliation or Control: State IRS Status: 501(c)3
Highest Offering: Beyond Master's But Less Than Doctorate
Accreditation: HLC, ACBSP, CAEP, NAEYC, NURSE, SW

01 President .... Dr. Joseph SHEPARD
05 Provost/Vice Pres Academic Affairs .... Dr. Jack CROCKER
32 Interim VP Student Affairs .... Ms. Betsy MILLER
10 VP Business Affairs .... Ms. Kelley RIDDLE
30 VP External Affairs .... Dr. Magdaleno MANZANAREZ
26 VP Compliance & Communications .... Ms. Julia MORALES
20 Assoc VP Academic Affairs .... Dr. Patricia WEST-OKIRI
06 Registrar .... Ms. Susan RUSSELL
08 University Librarian .... Dr. Gilda BAEZA-ORTEGO
37 Director Student Financial Aid .... Ms. Debra REYES
07 Director Admissions & Recruitment .... Mr. Andrew LUNT
09 Director of Institutional Research .... Vacant
15 Director of Human Resources .... Ms. Michelle HALT
18 Asst VP of Facilities .... Mr. Kevin MATTHES
26 Director of Marketing .... Mr. Mario SANCHEZ
29 Director of Alumni Development .... Ms. Kacie PETERSON
36 Career Services Coordinator .... Ms. Rhonda MCCALL
35 Asst Dean of Student Life & Develop .... Ms. Jessica MORALES
96 Director Materials/Resources .... Ms. Amy BACA
19 Director Campus Police .... Mr. Eddie FLORES
41 Athletic Director .... Mr. Scott NOBLE
53 Dean of Education .... Dr. Debra DIRKSEN
04 Exec Admin to the President .... Ms. Mary Rae MCDONALD
22 Affirmative Action/Equal Oppty .... Ms. Debra NOBLE
102 Executive Director Foundation .... Ms. Jodi EDENS-CROCKER
13 Chief Information Officer .... Mr. Jason COLLET
50 Dean of Business .... Dr. Steven CHAVEZ

NEW YORK

Academy for Jewish Religion (K)

28 Wells Avenue, Yonkers NY 10701
County: Westchester Identification: 667403
Telephone: (914) 709-0900 Carnegie Class: Not Classified
FAX Number: N/A Calendar System: Trimester
URL: www.ajr.edu
Established: 1956 Annual Graduate Tuition & Fees: N/A
Enrollment: N/A Coed
Affiliation or Control: Jewish IRS Status: 501(c)3
Highest Offering: Master's; No Undergraduates
Accreditation: THEOL

01 CEO & Academic Dean .... Dr. Ora HORN PROUSER
20 Associate Academic Officer .... Matthew GOLDSTONE
06 Registrar .... Linda RIPPS
07 Director of Admissions .... Lisa KLINGER-KANTOR
08 Chief Library Officer .... Ellie SHEMTOV
11 Chief of Operations/Administration .... Suli FASSLER
32 Chief Student Affairs/Life Officer .... Michael KASPER
36 Director Student Placement .... Beth KRAMER-MAZER
37 Director Student Financial Aid .... David CAVILL

Adelphi University (L)

One South Avenue, PO Box 701, Garden City NY 11530-0701
County: Nassau FICE Identification: 002666
Unit ID: 188429
Telephone: (516) 877-3000 Carnegie Class: DU-Mod
FAX Number: (516) 877-3545 Calendar System: Semester
URL: www.adelphi.edu
Established: 1896 Annual Undergrad Tuition & Fees: $41,435
Enrollment: 7,584 Coed
Affiliation or Control: Independent Non-Profit IRS Status: 501(c)3
Highest Offering: Doctorate
Accreditation: M, AUD, CAEP, CEA, CLPSY, IPSY, NURSE, SP, SW

01 President .... Dr. Christine M. RIORDAN
05 Provost/Executive VP .... Dr. Chris K. STORM, JR.
10 EVP of Finance & Operations .... Mr. James J. PERRINO
28 VP of Diversity/Equity/Inclusion .... Ms. Jacqueline JONES LAMON
111 AVP Advancement/External Relations .... Ms. Maggie YOON GRAFER
84 VP Enrollment Mgmt/Communications .... Ms. Kristen CAPEZZA
26 AVP Branding Strategy & Univ Comm .... Ms. Joanna TEMPLETON
100 Chief of Staff .... Ms. Maggie YOON GRAFER

20 Deputy Provost ... Vacant
32 Assoc Provost for Student Success ... Dr. R. Sentwali BAKARI
20 Assoc Provost Fac Adv & Research ... Vacant
21 CFO & Assoc VP ... Vacant
13 Chief Information Officer ... Ms. Carol Ann BOYLE
15 Chief Human Resource Officer ... Ms. Lucinda J. DONNELLY
11 VP Wellness/Safety/Administration ... Mr. Eugene PALMA
09 Assistant Provost for IR ... Dr. Nava LERER
18 Asst VP for Facilities Management ... Mr. Robert J. SHIPLEY
37 Asst VP Student Financial Services ... Ms. Sheryl L. MIHOPULOS
49 Dean College of Arts & Sciences ... Dr. Vincent WANG
53 Dean Col of Educ & Health Sciences ... Dr. Xiao-lei WANG
66 Dean Col of Nursing & Public Health ... Dr. Elaine L. SMITH
70 Dean School of Social Work ... Mr. Manoj PARDASONI
83 Dean GF Derner Sch of Psychology ... Dr. Jacques BARBER
50 Dean RB Willumstad Sch of Business ... Dr. Rajib N. SANYAL
92 Dean Honors College ... Dr. Susan DINAN
107 Dean Col of Prof & Cont Studies ... Mr. Andy ATZERT
08 Interim Dean University Libraries ... Ms. Debbi SMITH
35 Dean of Student Affairs/Asst VP ... Vacant
22 Exec Dir Diversity/Equity/Inclusion ... Ms. Chotsani WEST
16 Dir Talent Mgmt & Labor Relations ... Ms. Jane FISHER
41 Director of Athletics ... Mr. Daniel MCCABE
36 Exec Dir Center Career & Prof Dev ... Mr. Thomas J. WARD, JR.
06 University Registrar ... Mr. Steven E. SMITH
104 Director International Education ... Ms. Shannon HARRISON
23 Director Health Services ... Ms. Jacqueline JOHNSTON
38 Director Counseling & Support Svcs ... Dr. Carol A. LUCAS
39 Director Residential Life/Housing ... Mr. Guy SENEQUE
29 Exec Director Alumni Relations ... Ms. Jodie SPERICO
114 Dir of Financial Ops & Assoc VP ... Mr. Michael J. MCLEOD
96 Director of Procurement ... Ms. Elizabeth F. KASH
108 Director Institutional Assessment ... Vacant
105 Director of Web Development ... Ms. Tara A. COYLE
101 Director of Board Relations ... Ms. Mary ALDRIDGE
91 Director of Postmodern ERP ... Mr. Michael DICRESCIO
44 Director of Participation ... Ms. Jennifer WALSH
88 Spec Asst to Provost for Strat Init ... Dr. Sam GROGG
46 Director Research & Sponsored Pgms ... Ms. Mary CORTINA
88 Dir Faculty Ctr for Prof Excellence ... Ms. Nathalie ZARISFI

Albany College of Pharmacy and Health Sciences (A)

106 New Scotland Avenue, Albany NY 12208-3492
County: Albany FICE Identification: 002885
Unit ID: 188526
Telephone: (518) 694-7200 Carnegie Class: Spec-4-yr-Other Health
FAX Number: (518) 694-7202 Calendar System: Semester
URL: www.acphs.edu
Established: 1881 Annual Undergrad Tuition & Fees: $36,745
Enrollment: 1,118 Coed
Affiliation or Control: Independent Non-Profit IRS Status: 501(c)3
Highest Offering: Doctorate
Accreditation: M, CYTO, MLS, PH, PHAR

01 President ... Toyin TOFADE
05 Dean/VP of Academic Affairs ... Anuja GHORPADE
46 Director of Research ... Martha HASS
12 Interim Regional Dean for VT Campus ... Abby BOIRE
32 VP of Student Affairs ... John FELIO
10 VP of Finance ... Michele VIEN
111 VP of Institutional Advancement ... Vicki DILORENZO
84 VP of Enrollment Management ... Tiffany GUTIERREZ
13 Chief Information Officer ... Joshua SINGLETARY
11 VP of Administrative Operations ... Packy MCGRAW
07 Director of Admissions ... Kevin RIVENBURG
06 Registrar ... Al SACCO
26 Director of Public Relations ... Diane O'CONNOR
41 Director of Athletics & Rec ... Robert COLEMAN
15 VP of Human Resources ... Susan KARAVOLAS
30 AVP of Development ... Jackie MAHONEY
37 Director of Financial Aid ... Justin WELLIVER

Albany Law School (B)

80 New Scotland Avenue, Albany NY 12208-3494
County: Albany FICE Identification: 002886
Unit ID: 188535
Telephone: (518) 445-2311 Carnegie Class: Spec-4-yr-Law
FAX Number: (518) 445-2315 Calendar System: Semester
URL: www.albanylaw.edu
Established: 1851 Annual Undergrad Tuition & Fees: N/A
Enrollment: 566 Coed
Affiliation or Control: Independent Non-Profit IRS Status: 501(c)3
Highest Offering: First Professional Degree
Accreditation: @M, LAW

01 President & Dean ... Dean Alicia OUELLETTE
05 Assoc Dean Academic Affairs ... Dean Connie MAYER
10 Vice President Finance & Business ... Mr. Victor E. RAUSCHER
08 Director of Library ... Mr. David WALKER
111 Vice President Inst Advancement ... Dr. Jeffrey SCHANZ
32 Associate Dean for Student Affairs ... Prof. Rosemary QUEENAN
06 Assistant Dean and Registrar ... Ms. Joanne FITZSIMMONS
36 Asst Dean Career Center ... Ms. Mary WALSH FITZPATRICK
26 Director Communications ... Mr. Tom TORELLO
04 Executive Assistant to the Dean ... Ms. Barbara JORDAN-SMITH
07 Assistant Dean of Admissions ... Ms. Amy MANGIONE
88 Director Clinical Program ... Prof. Connie MAYER
29 Director Alumni Engage/Inst Events ... Mr. Geoffrey SEBER
15 Director Human Resources ... Ms. Sherri DONNELLY
37 Director Student Financial Aid ... Ms. Andrea WEDLER
18 Director of Facilities & Admin Svcs ... Mr. Brian LAPLANTE
36 Director of Career Services ... Ms. Joanne CASEY
108 Director Institutional Assessment ... Mr. Will TREVOR

Albany Medical College (C)

47 New Scotland Avenue, Mail #34,
Albany NY 12208-3479
County: Albany FICE Identification: 002887
Unit ID: 188580
Telephone: (518) 262-6008 Carnegie Class: Spec-4-yr-Med
FAX Number: (518) 262-6515 Calendar System: Semester
URL: www.amc.edu
Established: 1839 Annual Graduate Tuition & Fees: N/A
Enrollment: 835 Coed
Affiliation or Control: Independent Non-Profit IRS Status: 501(c)3
Highest Offering: Doctorate; No Undergraduates
Accreditation: M, ANEST, ARCPA, IPSY, MED, PAST

01 Dean ... Dr. Alan S. BOULOS
10 EVP/COO/Chief Financial Officer ... Ms. Frances SPREER-ALBERT
05 Vice Dean for Academic Admin ... Dr. Ellen COSGROVE
17 Hospital General Director ... Dr. Peter PAIGE
32 Assoc Dean for Acad & Student Affs ... Vacant
63 Assoc Dean Graduate Medical Educ ... Dr. Joel BARTFIELD
22 Assoc Dean Cmty Outreach/Medical Ed ... Dr. Ingrid M. ALLARD
08 Asc Dn Info Resrcs/Tech/Dir Library ... Ms. Enid GEYER
88 Asst Dean Medical Education ... Dr. Rebecca KELLER
58 Assoc Dean for Graduate Studies ... Dr. Peter VINCENT
06 Registrar ... Ms. Krista REYNOLDS-STUMP
58 Director Graduate Medical Education ... Ms. Catherine RIDDLE
76 Director Physician Asst Program ... Dr. Nathan GARDNER
29 Executive Director Alumni Relations ... Ms. Sandra DINOTO
26 Director Communications ... Ms. Sue FORD
30 Chief Development ... Vacant
51 Director Cont Medical Education ... Ms. Jennifer PRICE
15 Director Human Resources ... Ms. Sandra CASTILLA
37 Director Student Financial Aid ... Ms. Ann LOUGHMAN
28 Chief Diversity Officer ... Dr. Angela ANTONIKOWSKI
96 Director of Purchasing ... Ms. Ann CRISLIP
27 Marketing Manager ... Mr. Eli FANNING
03 Executive Assoc Dean ... Mr. John DEPAOLA
09 Director of Institutional Research ... Dr. Paul FEUSTEL
85 Director Foreign Students ... Ms. Marianne R. WILLIAMS
13 Chief Info Technology Officer (CIO) ... Mr. George HICKMAN
18 Chief Facilities Physical Plant ... Mr. Donald STICHTER
19 Director Security/Safety ... Mr. Charles DAY
38 Director Student Counseling ... Dr. Jeffrey WINSEMAN
43 Dir Legal Services/General Counsel ... Mr. Lee HESSBERG
45 Chief Institutional Planning ... Ms. Courtney BURKE
76 Director Nurse Anesthesia Pgm ... Dr. Jodi DELLA ROCCA
07 Director of Admissions ... Ms. Julia SALTANOVICH

Albert Einstein College of Medicine (D)

1300 Morris Park Avenue, Bronx NY 10461
FICE Identification: 042797
Unit ID: 385415
Telephone: (718) 430-2000 Carnegie Class: Spec-4-yr-Eng
FAX Number: N/A Calendar System: Semester
URL: www.einsteinmed.edu
Established: 1953 Annual Undergrad Tuition & Fees: N/A
Enrollment: N/A Coed
Affiliation or Control: Independent Non-Profit IRS Status: 501(c)3
Highest Offering: First Professional Degree
Accreditation: M, MED

01 Dean/EVP/CAO ... Dr. Gordon F. TOMASELLI
63 Executive Dean ... Dr. Edward R. BURNS
15 Vice Pres Human Resources ... Ms. Yvonne RAMIREZ
10 CFO & Assoc Vice President ... Mr. James GERAGHTY
32 Assoc Dean for Student Affairs ... Dr. Allison LUDWIG
07 Associate Dean of Admissions ... Ms. Noreen KERRIGAN

Alfred University (E)

One Saxon Drive, Alfred NY 14802-1205
County: Allegany FICE Identification: 002668
Unit ID: 188641
Telephone: (607) 871-2111 Carnegie Class: Masters/L
FAX Number: (607) 871-2339 Calendar System: Semester
URL: www.alfred.edu
Established: 1836 Annual Undergrad Tuition & Fees: $34,960
Enrollment: 2,187 Coed
Affiliation or Control: Independent Non-Profit IRS Status: 501(c)3
Highest Offering: Doctorate
Accreditation: M, AAQEP, ART, CAATE, CACREP, NASP, SCPSY

01 President ... Dr. Mark A. ZUPAN
05 Int Provost/VP for Academic Affairs ... Dr. Elizabeth A. DOBIE
10 VP for Business & Finance/Treasurer ... Ms. Giovina LLOYD
30 Interim VP for University Relations ... Mr. Mark H. RIORDAN
84 VP for Enrollment Management ... Mr. Jonathan KENT
32 VP for Student Affairs ... Vacant
57 Dean School of Art & Design ... Ms. Lauren LAKE
49 Dean Col of Lib Arts & Sciences ... Dr. Robert STEIN
107 Dean College of Business ... Mr. Mark LEWIS
54 Dean School of Engineering ... Dr. Gabrielle G. GAUSTAD
35 Dean Student Wellbeing ... Dr. Tamara KENNEY
29 Alumni Engagement Officer ... Ms. Janet MARBLE
37 Exec Dir Student Financial Aid Svcs ... Ms. Jane A. GILLILAND
07 Director of Admissions ... Ms. Kristen VARGASON
06 Interim Registrar ... Ms. Tammy JURSZA-WILLIAMS
19 Chief of Public Safety ... Ms. Jessica M. MIDDAUGH
26 Exec Dir of Mktg & Communication ... Mr. Michael KOZLOWSKI
39 Dir Residence Communities ... Mr. Max KOSKOFF
13 Director Information Tech Svcs ... Mr. Gary O. ROBERTS
36 Int Director Career Development Ctr ... Ms. Jill CRANDALL
41 Athletic Director ... Mr. Paul VECCHIO
23 Dir Counseling & Wellness Center ... Vacant
08 Dean of Libraries ... Mr. Brian T. SULLIVAN
15 Director of Human Resources ... Mr. Mark A. GUINAN
21 Controller ... Ms. Amanda R. AZZI
92 Director of the Honors Program ... Dr. Julianna R. GRAY
94 Dir of Women's Leadership Center ... Vacant
18 Dir Facilities/Capital Projects ... Mr. Jamie T. BABCOCK
101 Secretary to the Corporation ... Ms. Mary C. MCALLISTER
104 Dir Study Abroad Programs ... Vacant
40 Bookstore Manager ... Mrs. Marcy K. BRADLEY
87 Dir of Summer/Parent Programs ... Vacant
09 Director of Institutional Research ... Mr. Frederick B. RODGERS
28 Chief Diversity Officer ... Dr. Brian SALTSMAN
102 Dir Foundation/Corporate Relations ... Mr. Brian SHANAHAN
96 Director of Procurement ... Mrs. Melissa BADEAU

Alliance University (F)

2 Washington Street, New York NY 10004
County: Manhattan FICE Identification: 002790
Unit ID: 194161
Telephone: (646) 378-6100 Carnegie Class: Masters/L
FAX Number: N/A Calendar System: Semester
URL: www.nyack.edu
Established: 1882 Annual Undergrad Tuition & Fees: $25,500
Enrollment: 2,063 Coed
Affiliation or Control: The Christian And Missionary Alliance
IRS Status: 501(c)3
Highest Offering: Doctorate
Accreditation: #M, CAEP, MFCD, MUS, NURSE, SW, THEOL

01 President ... Mr. Rajan G. MATHEWS
04 Exec Assistant to the President ... Ms. Autumn-Carol NOVA
05 Provost/VP for Academic Affairs ... Dr. David F. TURK
88 Exec Assistant to the Provost ... Mrs. Bonita R. D'AMIL
73 VP/Dean Alliance Seminary ... Dr. Ronald WALBORN
50 Dean School of Business & Ldrshp ... Dr. Anita UNDERWOOD
64 Assistant Dean School of Music ... Dr. Peter HOLSBERG
53 Acting Dean School of Education ... Dr. Peter HOLSBERG
66 Dean School of Nursing ... Dr. Elizabeth SIMON
121 Dean Student Success ... Dr. Gwen PARKER AMES
49 Assoc Dean of School of Arts & Sci ... Dr. Jeffrey DUECK
32 Vice Pres of Student Development ... Mrs. Wanda VELEZ
42 Vice President of Church Relations ... Dr. Charles HAMMOND
06 Institutional Registrar ... Mrs. Tracy WALKER
37 Dir of Fin Svcs Undergrad ... Mr. Isaac FOSTER
41 Director of Athletics ... Mr. Keith A. DAVIE
15 Vice President of Human Resources ... Mrs. Karen DAVIE
13 Director of Information Technology ... Mr. Kevin A. BUEL
09 Director of Institutional Research ... Dr. Greg BEEMAN
18 Director of Operations/Aramark ... Mr. Doug WALKER
26 Dir of Public & Media Relations ... Mrs. Deborah WALKER
105 Webmaster ... Mr. Joshua WAY
108 Director Institutional Assessment ... Ms. Kristen LUBA
07 Director of Admissions ... Dr. David JENNINGS
29 Manager of Alumni Relations ... Mr. Christopher SMITH

American Academy of Dramatic Arts (G)

120 Madison Avenue, New York NY 10016-7089
County: New York FICE Identification: 007465
Unit ID: 188678
Telephone: (212) 686-9244 Carnegie Class: Spec 2-yr-A&S
FAX Number: (212) 545-7934 Calendar System: Other
URL: www.aada.edu
Established: 1884 Annual Undergrad Tuition & Fees: $37,230
Enrollment: 159 Coed
Affiliation or Control: Independent Non-Profit IRS Status: 501(c)3
Highest Offering: Associate Degree
Accreditation: M, THEA

01 President ... Ms. Susan ZECH
111 Sr VP Institutional Advancement ... Vacant
10 Chief Financial Officer ... Mr. Joel BLOCK
05 Director of Instruction ... Ms. Julia SMELIANSKY
07 Director of Admissions ... Ms. Kerin REILLY
27 Sr Director of Marketing ... Mr. James LUBIN
08 Librarian ... Ms. Deborah PICONE
21 Controller ... Ms. Linda VIALA
11 Senior Director of Operations ... Mr. Peter TUFEL
26 Director External Affairs ... Vacant
37 Director of Financial Aid ... Ms. Lisa SHAHEEN
04 Exec Assistant to the President ... Ms. Cecily HALL

American Academy McAllister Institute of Funeral Service (H)

1501 Broadway, STE 1102, New York NY 10036
County: New York FICE Identification: 010813
Unit ID: 188687
Telephone: (212) 757-1190 Carnegie Class: Spec 2-yr-A&S
FAX Number: (212) 765-5923 Calendar System: Semester

URL: www.funeraleducation.org
Established: 1926 Annual Undergrad Tuition & Fees: $18,292
Enrollment: 463 Coed
Affiliation or Control: Independent Non-Profit IRS Status: 501(c)3
Highest Offering: Associate Degree
Accreditation: #FUSER

01 President .... Dr. Donald CYMBOR
05 VP/Int Academic Dean .... Rev. John FRASER
10 Bursar .... Mr. Jay TSO
37 Financial Aid Officer .... Ms. Natalie GIVAN
06 Registrar .... Mr. Andre RAMPAUL
07 Dir of Admissions/Enrollment Mgmt .... Ms. Tracy LENTZ
20 Academic Advisor .... Ms. Charlotte RERRICK
20 Academic Advisor .... Ms. Karen CARR
43 Legal Counsel .... Mr. Charles MAURER

Arnot Ogden Medical Center (A)

600 Roe Avenue, Elmira NY 14905
County: Chemung FICE Identification: 006435
Telephone: (607) 737-4153 Carnegie Class: Not Classified
FAX Number: (607) 737-4116 Calendar System: Semester
URL: arnothealth.org
Established: Annual Undergrad Tuition & Fees: N/A
Enrollment: N/A Coed
Affiliation or Control: Independent Non-Profit IRS Status: 501(c)3
Highest Offering: Associate Degree
Accreditation: ADNUR, RAD

ASA College (B)

151 Lawrence Street, Brooklyn NY 11201
County: Kings FICE Identification: 030955
Unit ID: 404994
Telephone: (718) 522-9073 Carnegie Class: Bac/Assoc-Assoc Dom
FAX Number: (718) 532-1433 Calendar System: Semester
URL: www.asa.edu
Established: 1985 Annual Undergrad Tuition & Fees: $12,528
Enrollment: 2,965 Coed
Affiliation or Control: Proprietary IRS Status: Proprietary
Highest Offering: Baccalaureate
Accreditation: M, MAC

01 Interim President .... Mr. Alex SHCHEGOL
05 Provost .... Dr. Shanthi KONKOTH
26 Vice President Marketing/Admissions .. Ms. Victoria KOSTYUKOV
29 VP Placement/Alumni Services .... Ms. Lesia WILLIS
37 VP Financial Aid Services .... Ms. Victoriya SHTAMLER
11 VP Planning & Operations .... Ms. Maritza MERCADO
86 VP Govt & Community Relations .... Mr. Roberto DUMAUAL
10 Controller .... Mr. Mark MIRENBERG
20 Academic Dean .... Dr. Edward KUFUOR
106 Director of Distance Learning .... Mr. Joel ALMORADIE
08 Head Librarian .... Mr. Brook STOWE
06 Registrar .... Ms. Mariana ZINDER
13 IT Director .... Mr. David ESTRIN
108 Director Institutional Assessment .... Ms. Ksenia KASIMOVA
09 Director Institutional Research .... Ms. Anna BOUKHMAN
15 Director of Human Resources .... Vacant
18 Chief Facilities/Physical Plant .... Mr. Walter KRUMER
50 Dean of Business .... Ms. Bridget UDEH
61 Dean of Legal Studies .... Vacant
49 Dean of Arts and Sciences .... Mr. Lizhi (Frank) ZHU
79 Director for Language Studies .... Ms. Ludmilla DRAGUSHANSKAYA
36 Director College/Career Prep .... Ms. Denise DUBRON
76 Dean of Health Disciplines .... Dr. Nasser SEDHOM
66 Dean of Nursing .... Ms. Donna M. REID
54 Dean Div Engineering & Technology .... Vacant
20 Dean Academic & Program Development ... Ms. Deborah HUGHES
88 Ombudsperson .... Dr. Jennifer ROSS
32 Asst Dean for Student Success .... Ms. Lillian GRANILLO
16 Title IX Coordinator .... Dr. Jayne WEINBERGER
38 Director Student Counseling ..... Ms. Tatyana KRYZHANOVSKAYA
41 Athletic Director .... Dr. Jody KING
39 Director Student Housing .... Vacant

Bais Binyomin Academy, Inc (C)

51 Carlton Road, Monsey NY 10952
County: Rockland FICE Identification: 029120
Unit ID: 128586
Telephone: (845) 207-0330 Carnegie Class: Not Classified
FAX Number: N/A Calendar System: Semester
Established: 1976 Annual Undergrad Tuition & Fees: $9,650
Enrollment: 35 Male
Affiliation or Control: Independent Non-Profit IRS Status: 501(c)3
Highest Offering: First Talmudic Degree
Accreditation: RABN

01 Rosh Hayeshiva .... Rabbi Meyer HERSHKOWITZ
04 Associate Rosh Hayeshiva .... Rabbi Yeruchom ZEILBERGER

Bais Medrash Ateres Shlomo (D)

220 Bennett Avenue, New York NY 10040
County: New York Identification: 667321
Telephone: (212) 419-5758 Carnegie Class: Not Classified
FAX Number: (914) 736-1055 Calendar System: Semester
URL: baismedrashateresshlomo.com
Established: 2016 Annual Undergrad Tuition & Fees: N/A
Enrollment: N/A Male
Affiliation or Control: Jewish IRS Status: 501(c)3
Highest Offering: First Talmudic Degree
Accreditation: AIJS

Bais Medrash of Dexter Park (E)

445 South Pascack Road, Chestnut Ridge NY 10977
County: Rockland FICE Identification: 042846
Unit ID: 495031
Telephone: (845) 735-2807 Carnegie Class: Spec-4-yr-Faith
FAX Number: N/A Calendar System: Semester
URL: bmdpark.com
Established: Annual Undergrad Tuition & Fees: N/A
Enrollment: N/A Male
Affiliation or Control: Independent Non-Profit IRS Status: 501(c)3
Highest Offering: First Talmudic Degree
Accreditation: AIJS

Bank Street College of Education (F)

610 W 112 Street, New York NY 10025-1898
County: New York FICE Identification: 002669
Unit ID: 189015
Telephone: (212) 875-4400 Carnegie Class: Spec-4-yr-Other
FAX Number: (212) 875-4759 Calendar System: Semester
URL: www.bankstreet.edu
Established: 1916 Annual Graduate Tuition & Fees: N/A
Enrollment: 599 Coed
Affiliation or Control: Independent Non-Profit IRS Status: 501(c)3
Highest Offering: Master's; No Undergraduates
Accreditation: M, AAQEP

01 President .... Shael POLAKOW-SURANSKY
100 Chief of Staff .... Katherine CONNELLY
11 Chief Operating Officer .... Justin TYACK
10 Chief Financial Officer .... Aparna MURALIDHARAN
30 VP Development .... Marcela HAHN
05 VP Bank Street Education Center .... Tracy FRAY-OLIVER
28 VP Governance/Social Justice/Equity .... Akilah ROSADO
58 Dean of the Graduate School .... Cecelia TRAUGH
88 Dean of Children's Programs .... Doug KNECHT
123 Director of Graduate Admissions .... Stephen OSTENDORFF
06 Registrar .... Meghan CHVIRKO
37 Director of Student Financial Aid .... Emmett COOPER
29 Director of Alumni Relations .... Eric GUTIERREZ
15 Chief Human Resources Officer .... Elyse MATTHEWS
13 Chief Information Officer .... Judith JOHNSON
18 Dir of Facilities/Security/Safety .... Carlos ESQUIVEL
08 Director of Library Services .... Kristin FREDA
36 Director of Student Placement .... Susan LEVINE
04 Executive Assistant to President .... Regina WRIGHT

Bard College (G)

PO Box 5000, Annandale-On-Hudson NY 12504-5000
County: Dutchess FICE Identification: 002671
Unit ID: 189088
Telephone: (845) 758-6822 Carnegie Class: Bac-A&S
FAX Number: (845) 758-4294 Calendar System: Semester
URL: www.bard.edu
Established: 1860 Annual Undergrad Tuition & Fees: $56,036
Enrollment: 2,465 Coed
Affiliation or Control: Independent Non-Profit IRS Status: 501(c)3
Highest Offering: Doctorate
Accreditation: M

01 President .... Dr. Leon BOTSTEIN
03 Executive Vice President of College .... Vacant
05 EVP/VP Acad Affs/Dir Civic Engage .... Dr. Jonathan BECKER
10 SVP/Chief Financial Officer .... Mr. Taun TOAY
30 VP Alumni/ae Affairs/Development .... Ms. Debra R. PEMSTEIN
11 Vice President for Administration .... Ms. Coleen MURPHY ALEXANDER
20 Associate VP for Academic Affairs .... Dr. David SHEIN
100 Chief of Staff .... Ms. Malia DU MONT
32 VP for Student Affairs .... Ms. Erin CANNAN
09 VP for Institutional Research .... Dr. Mark D. HALSEY
35 Dean of Student Affairs .... Ms. Bethany NOHLGREN
20 Associate Dean of the College .... Ms. Deirdre D'ALBERTIS
57 Dir Milton Avery Grad Sch of Arts .... Mr. Arthur GIBBONS
88 Dir Bard Grad Ctr Decorative Arts .... Dr. Susan WEBER
88 Exec Dir Ctr Curatorial Studies .... Mr. Tom ECCLES
110 Asst VP Dir of Inst Support .... Ms. Karen UNGER
88 Director Ctr Environmental Policy .... Dr. Eban GOODSTEIN
37 Director Financial Aid .... Ms. Denise ACKERMAN
06 Registrar .... Mr. Peter GADSBY
26 Associate VP of Communications .... Mr. Mark PRIMOFF
15 Director of Human Resources .... Ms. Kimberly ALEXANDER
21 Associate VP for Finance .... Vacant
88 Director Inst Writing/Thinking .... Ms. Erica KAUFMAN
18 Director of Buildings & Grounds .... Mr. Randy CLUM
13 Director Mgmt Info Systems .... Mr. Michael TOMPKINS
29 Director Alumni/ae Affairs .... Ms. Jane BRIEN
36 Assoc Director Career Development ... Ms. Maureen AURIGEMMA
19 Director Safety & Security .... Mr. John GOMEZ
88 Director of Institutional Research .... Mr. Joseph F. AHERN
24 Director of Audio/Video Services .... Mr. Paul LABARBERA
28 Director of Multicultural Affairs .... Dr. Ann SEATON
41 Director of Athletics .... Ms. Kristin E. HALL
40 Bookstore Manager .... Ms. Merry MEYER
23 Director Student Health Services .... Ms. Barbara BRISKEY
38 Director Student Counseling .... Ms. Tamara TELBERG
07 Director of Admission .... Ms. Mackie SIEBENS
39 Director of Housing .... Ms. Nancy W. SMITH
90 Chief Information Officer .... Mr. David BRANGAITIS

Barnard College (H)

3009 Broadway, New York NY 10027-6598
County: New York FICE Identification: 002708
Unit ID: 189097
Telephone: (212) 854-5262 Carnegie Class: Bac-A&S
FAX Number: (212) 854-6220 Calendar System: Semester
URL: www.barnard.edu
Established: 1889 Annual Undergrad Tuition & Fees: $57,479
Enrollment: 2,744 Female
Affiliation or Control: Independent Non-Profit IRS Status: 501(c)3
Highest Offering: Baccalaureate
Accreditation: M

01 President .... Sian L. BEILOCK
43 VP Legal Affairs/Chief of Staff .... Jomysha STEPHEN
05 Provost & Dean of Faculty .... Linda BELL
100 EVP of College/General Counsel .... Jomysha STEPHEN
11 VP Campus Svcs/Int VP Operations .... Roger MOSIER
30 Vice President for Development .... Lisa YEH
10 CFO & Vice Pres for Finance .... Eileen M. DI BENEDETTO
13 Int Exec Dir Info Technology .... Victoria SWANN
15 Exec Director Human Resources .... Kathleen VETERI
84 VP for Enrollment & Communications .... Jennifer FONDILLER
28 VP Diversity/Equity & Inclusion .... Ariana GONZÁLEZ STOKAS
32 Dean of the College .... Leslie GRINAGE
20 Interim Dean of Studies .... Christina KUAN TSU
06 Registrar .... Vacant
37 Director of Financial Aid .... Nanette DILAURO
35 Associate Dean for Student Life .... Emy CARDOZA
39 Interim Exec Dir Res Life & Housing .... Lizeth JARAMILLO
23 Exec Director of Student Health Svc .... Mary Joan MURPHY
36 Dean Beyond Barnard .... A-J ARONSTEIN
36 Dean Beyond Barnard .... Nikki YOUNGBLOOD GILES
29 Exec Director of Alumnae Relations .... Karen SENDLER
08 Interim Co-Dean Library .... Melanie HIBBERT
08 Interim Co-Dean Library .... Kristen HOGAN
08 Interim Co-Dean Library .... Miriam NEPTUNE
101 Secretary to the Board of Trustees .... Virginia RYAN
19 Interim Exec Director Public Safety .... Amy ZAVADIL
109 Director of Business Operations .... Douglas MAGET
18 Director Facilities Services .... Daniel DAVIS
09 Exec Dir Institutional Assessment .... Nikisha WILLIAMS
88 Spec Asst to Pres/Dir Family Engage .... Katelyn DUTTON
102 Asst VP for Development .... Kate MARTINEZ
104 Assoc Provost Inst Initiatives .... Giorgio DIMAURO
38 Director Student Counseling .... Mary COMMERFORD
44 Director Annual Giving .... Sally VALLIMARESCU
96 Director of Purchasing .... Douglas MAGET
07 Dean of Admissions/Enrollment .... Christina LOPEZ
22 Dir Ctr Access Res/Disability Svcs .... Holly TEDDER

† Affiliated with Columbia University in the City of New York.

Be'er Yaakov Talmudic Seminary (I)

12 Truman Avenue, Spring Valley NY 10977
County: Rockland FICE Identification: 041928
Unit ID: 476717
Telephone: (845) 362-3053 Carnegie Class: Spec-4-yr-Faith
FAX Number: (845) 406-9699 Calendar System: Semester
URL: www.byts.edu
Established: 1995 Annual Undergrad Tuition & Fees: $10,460
Enrollment: 565 Male
Affiliation or Control: Independent Non-Profit IRS Status: 501(c)3
Highest Offering: Special 5-year Faith
Accreditation: RABN

01 CEO .... Mr. Jacob UNGER
05 Dean .... Rabbi Israel EISENBERGER
06 Registrar/Administrator .... Rabbi Yitzchok SOIFER
37 Financial Aid Administrator .... Mrs. Chana NOTIS

Beis Medrash Heichal Dovid (J)

211 Beach 17th Street, Far Rockaway NY 11691-4433
County: Queens FICE Identification: 037133
Unit ID: 444413
Telephone: (718) 868-2300 Carnegie Class: Spec-4-yr-Faith
FAX Number: (718) 868-0517 Calendar System: Semester
URL: heichaldovid.org
Established: 1999 Annual Undergrad Tuition & Fees: $10,000
Enrollment: 183 Male
Affiliation or Control: Independent Non-Profit IRS Status: 501(c)3
Highest Offering: Second Talmudic Degree
Accreditation: RABN

01 Dean .... Rabbi Yaakov BENDER
05 Rosh Yeshiva .... Rabbi Shlomo Avidgor ALTUSKY
37 Financial Aid Officer .... Rabbi Aaron STEINBERG

The Belanger School of Nursing (K)

650 McClellan Street, Schenectady NY 12304
County: Schenectady FICE Identification: 006448
Unit ID: 190956
Telephone: (518) 243-4471 Carnegie Class: Spec 2-yr-Health
FAX Number: (518) 243-4470 Calendar System: Semester
URL: www.ellisbelangerschoolofnursing.org

Established: 1903 Annual Undergrad Tuition & Fees: $10,664
Enrollment: 143 Coed
Affiliation or Control: Independent Non-Profit IRS Status: 501(c)3
Highest Offering: Associate Degree
Accreditation: ADNUR

01 Director Ms. Michele HEWITT
05 Dean Ms. Dawne DEVOE OLBRYCH
37 Financial Aid Coordinator/Registrar Ms. Patricia BRUNDIGE
22 ADA Coordinator/Stdnt Svcs Mngr Ms. Carolyn LANSING
08 Head Librarian Ms. Emily SPINNER
07 Director of Admissions Ms. Cathy BIESTY
19 Director Security/Safety Mr. Keith EDWARDS
26 Sr Dir Marketing/Communications Mr. Philip SCHWARTZ

Berkeley College (A)

3 East 43rd Street, New York NY 10017-4604
County: New York FICE Identification: 007394
Unit ID: 189228
Telephone: (212) 986-4343 Carnegie Class: Bac-Diverse
FAX Number: (212) 818-1169 Calendar System: Semester
URL: www.berkeleycollege.edu
Established: 1931 Annual Undergrad Tuition & Fees: $27,000
Enrollment: 2,376 Coed
Affiliation or Control: Proprietary IRS Status: Proprietary
Highest Offering: Master's
Accreditation: M, IACBE

00 Chairman of the Board Mr. Kevin L. LUING
01 President Dr. Diane RECINOS
03 Executive Vice President Mr. Tim LUING
05 Interim Provost Dr. Marianne VAKALIS
10 Vice President & Controller Mr. Stephen RUTKOWSKI
121 VP Academic Advisement Mr. Brian MAHER
32 VP Student Development/Campus Life Dr. Sherrille SHABAZZ
36 Vice President Career Services Ms. Amy SORICELLI
113 VP Student Finance & Inst Effect Mr. Will MOYA
13 Senior VP/Chief Information Officer Mr. Leonard DE BOTTON
88 VP Financial Aid Compliance Mr. Howard LESLIE
20 Asst Provost Teaching and Learning Ms. Dana HEIMLICH
50 Dean School of Business Dr. Joseph SCURALLI
76 Dean School Health Studies Vacant
107 Dean School of Professional Studies Dr. Marianne VAKALIS
106 Dean Online Dr. Joseph SCURALLI
58 Director MBA Program Dr. David GLAZER
97 Director General Education Dr. Gregory HOTCHKISS
11 Campus Operating Officer Ms. Linda MAURO
37 Associate VP Financial Aid Mr. Alejandro GUIRAL
15 VP Human Resources Ms. Karen J. CARPENTIERI
84 VP Graduate & Undergrad Enrollment Mr. David J. BERTONE
26 Dir Communications & Ext Relations Ms. Kelly DEPSEE
06 Registrar Ms. Deborah PALICIA
29 AVP Alumni Relation & Career Svcs Mr. Michael IRIS
22 Director Accessibility Services Ms. Katherine WU
88 Asst VP Military & Veterans Affairs Mr. Edward J. DENNIS
38 Sr Director Personal Counseling Dr. Sandra E. COPPOLA
85 VP International Operations Dr. Nori JAFFER
123 Director Graduate Admissions Mr. Michael LINCOLN
18 Senior Vice President Operations Mr. Thomas ALESSANDRELLO
19 Asst VP Pub Safety/Emergency Mgmt Mr. Robert MAGUIRE
109 Senior Director Auxiliary Services Mr. Luis COLLAZO
119 Director of Information Security Mr. Dana KILCREASE
09 Director Institutional Research Ms. Rebecca J. DRENNEN

Bet Medrash Gadol Ateret Torah (B)

901 Quentin Road, Brooklyn NY 11223
County: Kings Identification: 667146
Unit ID: 485999
Telephone: (347) 394-1036 Carnegie Class: Spec-4-yr-Faith
FAX Number: (347) 394-1096 Calendar System: Semester
Established: 1992 Annual Undergrad Tuition & Fees: $10,050
Enrollment: 142 Male
Affiliation or Control: Independent Non-Profit IRS Status: 501(c)3
Highest Offering: Second Talmudic Degree
Accreditation: @RABN

01 President/CEO Rabbi Joseph HARARI-RAFUL
05 Executive Director Irwin SHAMAH
06 Registrar Mrs. Ruchana MANSOUR
11 Chief of Operations/Administration Zev KLEINER

Beth Hamedrash Shaarei Yosher Institute (C)

4102-10 16th Avenue, Brooklyn NY 11204-1099
County: Kings FICE Identification: 011192
Unit ID: 189273
Telephone: (718) 854-2290 Carnegie Class: Not Classified
FAX Number: (718) 854-2292 Calendar System: Semester
Established: 1962 Annual Undergrad Tuition & Fees: $10,350
Enrollment: 97 Male
Affiliation or Control: Independent Non-Profit IRS Status: 501(c)3
Highest Offering: Second Talmudic Degree
Accreditation: RABN

01 Chief Executive Officer Rabbi Pinches KAFF
05 Chief Academic Officer Rabbi Chaim ROSENBERG
29 Director Alumni Association Rabbi Eliyohu ROSENBLUM
37 Director Student Financial Aid Rabbi Aaron ROTTENBERG
06 Registrar Rabbi Sol ROSENBERG

Beth Medrash Meor Yitzchok (D)

65 Dykstra's Way East, Monsey NY 10952
County: Rockland Identification: 667111
Unit ID: 486196
Telephone: (845) 426-3488 Carnegie Class: Spec-4-yr-Faith
FAX Number: (845) 425-5415 Calendar System: Semester
Established: 2007 Annual Undergrad Tuition & Fees: $10,400
Enrollment: 187 Male
Affiliation or Control: Independent Non-Profit IRS Status: 501(c)3
Highest Offering: First Talmudic Degree
Accreditation: RABN

37 Financial Aid Administrator Isreal WEINGARTEN

Bill and Sandra Pomeroy College of Nursing at Crouse Hospital (E)

736 Irving Avenue, Syracuse NY 13210
County: Onondaga FICE Identification: 006445
Unit ID: 190451
Telephone: (315) 470-7481 Carnegie Class: Spec 2-yr-Health
FAX Number: (315) 470-5774 Calendar System: Semester
URL: www.crouse.org/nursing
Established: 1913 Annual Undergrad Tuition & Fees: $17,148
Enrollment: 245 Coed
Affiliation or Control: Independent Non-Profit IRS Status: 501(c)3
Highest Offering: Associate Degree
Accreditation: ADNUR

05 Dean Patricia MORGAN
20 Assistant Dean for Faculty David FALCI
07 Assistant Dean for Enrollment Amy GRAHAM
32 Assistant Dean for Students Ryan BARKER
06 Registrar/Bursar Jeanne CELSO
37 Financial Affairs Officer Kenny KENDALL
88 Instruction/Technology Coordinator Kelly DUFFY
08 Head Librarian Ellen OWENS

Boricua College (F)

3755 Broadway, New York NY 10032-1599
County: New York FICE Identification: 013029
Unit ID: 189413
Telephone: (212) 694-1000 Carnegie Class: Bac-Diverse
FAX Number: (212) 694-1015 Calendar System: Semester
URL: www.boricuacollege.edu
Established: 1974 Annual Undergrad Tuition & Fees: $11,025
Enrollment: 588 Coed
Affiliation or Control: Independent Non-Profit IRS Status: 501(c)3
Highest Offering: Master's
Accreditation: M

01 President Dr. Victor G. ALICEA
04 Exec Assistant to the President Ms. Sandra BELLAMY
05 VP Academic Affairs Dr. Shivaji SENGUPTA
13 VP Information & Tech/Facil Mgmt Mr. Irving RAMIREZ
20 VP Academic Planning & Programming Dr. John GUZMAN
15 VP Personnel/Human Resources Ms. Francia L. CASTRO
43 Legal Counsel Mr. Jorge BATISTA
10 Director Finance Mr. Elias OYOLA
113 Director Bursar Office Mr. Jose R. MANSO
07 Dir Admissions Bronx Campus Ctr Mr. Teofilo SANTIAGO
07 Dir Admissions Manhattan Campus Mr. Ismael SANCHEZ
07 Dir Admissions Brooklyn Cam Ctr Ms. Aurea MORALES
06 Director Registration & Assessments Ms. Beatriz AHORRIO
37 Director Financial Aid Ms. Rosalia CRUZ
08 Director Library/Learning Resources Ms. Liza RIVERA
18 Dir Environment Svcs Manhattan Camp Mr. Carlos ANDUJAR
18 Dir Environment Svcs Brooklyn Mr. Juan RIVERA PAGAN
18 Dir Environment Svcs Bronx Camp Mr. Jose VAZQUEZ
30 Director of Development Vacant
20 Dean Acad Affairs Manhattan Campus Mr. Moises PEREYRA
20 Dean Academic Affairs Bronx Campus Vacant

Brooklyn Law School (G)

250 Joralemon Street, Brooklyn NY 11201-3798
County: Kings FICE Identification: 002677
Unit ID: 189501
Telephone: (718) 625-2200 Carnegie Class: Spec-4-yr-Law
FAX Number: (718) 780-0393 Calendar System: Semester
URL: www.brooklaw.edu
Established: 1901 Annual Graduate Tuition & Fees: N/A
Enrollment: 1,162 Coed
Affiliation or Control: Independent Non-Profit IRS Status: 501(c)3
Highest Offering: First Professional Degree; No Undergraduates
Accreditation: LAW

01 President/Dean Dean Michael T. CAHILL
00 Dean and President Emerita Dean Joan G. WEXLER
05 Vice Dean of Academic Affairs Dean Miriam BAER
20 Assoc Dean for Experiential Educ Dean Stacy CAPLOW
20 Assoc Dn Faculty/Rsrch/Scholarship Dean Jocelyn SIMONSON
32 Dean of Students Dean Jennifer R. LANG
10 Assoc Dean Admin/Finance Dean Michael GERBER
21 Treasurer Ms. Shoshanna M. CAMPBELL
07 Dean of Admissions Dean Eulas BOYD, JR.
36 Dean of Career Development Dean Karen EISEN
08 Director of Library Prof. Brittany PERSSON
111 Chief Advancement Officer Ms. Annie NIENABER
29 Director of Alumni Relations Ms. Caitlin MONCK
06 Registrar Ms. Julie BROWN
37 Director of Financial Aid Ms. Nancy L. ZAHZAM
11 VP of Operations Ms. Colette RODGERS
18 Director of Facilities Mr. Steven OLEKSIW
15 Director of Human Resources Ms. Danielle STEFANIA
43 Gen Counsel/Chf Compliance Officer Ms. Stephanie VULLO

*Bryant & Stratton College System Office (H)

200 Redtail Rd., Orchard Park NY 14127
County: Erie Identification: 666828
Telephone: (716) 250-7500 Carnegie Class: N/A
FAX Number: (716) 250-7510
URL: www.bryantstratton.edu

01 President & CEO Dr. Francis J. FELSER
11 VP/Chief Operating Officer Mr. David VADEN
10 VP/Chief Financial Officer Mr. Christopher GERACE
13 VP/Online Division and CIO Ms. Doreen JUSTINGER
84 VP/Chief Enrollment Officer Ms. Tracy NANNERY
108 VP Research/Planning & Assessment Ms. Anne LORIA

*Bryant & Stratton College (I)

110 Broadway, 2nd Floor, Buffalo NY 14203
County: Erie FICE Identification: 002678
Unit ID: 189583
Telephone: (716) 884-9120 Carnegie Class: Bac/Assoc-Mixed
FAX Number: (716) 884-0091 Calendar System: Semester
URL: www.bryantstratton.edu
Established: 1854 Annual Undergrad Tuition & Fees: $17,833
Enrollment: 855 Coed
Affiliation or Control: Proprietary IRS Status: Proprietary
Highest Offering: Baccalaureate
Accreditation: M, MAC, NURSE

02 Director of WNY Campuses Mr. Jeffrey P. TREDO
05 WNY Dean of Instruction Dr. Christian BLUM
07 Director of Admissions Mr. Kevin MUSE
36 Director of Career Services Mrs. Diane CZAPLICKI
10 WNY Business Office Director Ms. Kathleen OWCZARCZAK

*Bryant & Stratton College (J)

1259 Central Avenue, Albany NY 12205-5230
Telephone: (518) 437-1802 FICE Identification: 004749
Accreditation: &M, MAC

*Bryant & Stratton College (K)

854 Long Pond Road, Rochester NY 14612-3049
Telephone: (585) 720-0660 FICE Identification: 012470
Accreditation: &M, MAC, OTA

*Bryant & Stratton College (L)

953 James Street, Syracuse NY 13203-2502
Telephone: (315) 472-6603 FICE Identification: 008276
Accreditation: &M, MAC, OTA, PTAA

Canisius College (M)

2001 Main Street, Buffalo NY 14208-1098
County: Erie FICE Identification: 002681
Unit ID: 189705
Telephone: (716) 883-7000 Carnegie Class: Masters/L
FAX Number: (716) 888-2525 Calendar System: Semester
URL: www.canisius.edu
Established: 1870 Annual Undergrad Tuition & Fees: $30,230
Enrollment: 2,820 Coed
Affiliation or Control: Roman Catholic IRS Status: 501(c)3
Highest Offering: Master's
Accreditation: M, #ARCPA, CACREP

01 President Mr. Steve K. STOUTE
05 VP Academic Affairs Dr. Sara R. MORRIS
10 Vice Pres Business/Finance Mr. Timothy P. BALKIN
32 VP for Student Affairs Dr. Harold O. FIELDS
111 VP Institutional Advancement Ms. Kimberly A. VENTI
84 VP for Enrollment Management Dr. Danielle D. IANNI
04 AVP/Assistant to the President Ms. Erica C. SAMMARCO
20 Assoc VP for Academic Affairs Dr. Jennifer LODI SMITH
20 Assoc VP for Academic Affairs Dr. Jeff R. LINDAUER
113 Asst VP/Dir Stdnt Rec & Fin Svcs Mr. Kevin M. SMITH
07 Asst Dir Enrollment Operations Mr. Travis M. DAWSON
35 AVP Student Dev & Success/HESA Dir Dr. Mark R. HARRINGTON
08 Director of Library Ms. Kristine E. KASBOHM
112 Director of Principal Gifts Mr. J. Patrick GREENWALD
21 Controller Mr. Ronald J. HABERER
50 Dean School of Business Dr. Denise M. ROTONDO
37 Assoc Dir of Stdnt Records/Fin Svcs Ms. Mary A. KOEHNEKE
06 Registrar/Asst Dir Stdnt Rec & FA Ms. Lisa C. FISCHER
26 Chief Communications Officer Ms. Eileen C. HERBERT
15 Assoc VP for HR and Compliance Ms. Linda M. WALLESHAUSER

53 Interim Dean School Educ/Human Svcs ... Dr. Nancy WALLACE
25 Director of Sponsored Programs ... Ms. Mary Ann LANGLOIS
18 Director Facilities Management ... Mr. Thomas E. CIMINELLI
23 Director Student Health Center ... Ms. Patricia H. CREAHAN
38 Director Counseling Center ... Ms. Eileen A. NILAND
39 Assoc Dean of Stdnts/Dir Resid Life ... Mr. Matthew H. MULVILLE
104 Director Study Abroad ... Mr. Brian SMITH
40 Bookstore Manager ... Mr. Joseph ZOMERI
41 Director Athletics ... Mr. William J. MAHER
42 Director Campus Ministry ... Mr. Spencer LIECHTY
90 Director of User Services ... Mr. Scott D. CLARK
94 Dir of Women's Business Center ... Ms. Sara L. VESCIO
92 Director of All College Honors Pgm ... Dr. Janet M. MCNALLY
24 Director Media Center ... Mr. Daniel J. DREW
91 Director Administrative Computing ... Ms. Michele FOLSOM
108 Dir Inst & Research Effectiveness ... Ms. Lauren YOUNG
102 Dir Foundation/Corp/Govt Relations ... Mrs. Sandy A. MILLER
19 Director Public Safety ... Mrs. Kimberly L. BEATY
29 Director Alumni Engagement ... Ms. Cece R. GOTHAM
44 Director Canisius Fund ... Ms. Erin M. ZACK
28 Assoc Dean for Diversity/Inclusion ... Ms. Fatima L. RODRIGUEZ JOHNSON
106 Online Learning & Innovation Dir ... Dr. Mark K. GALLIMORE

Cayuga Community College (A)

197 Franklin Street, Auburn NY 13021-3099
County: Cayuga
FICE Identification: 002861
Unit ID: 189839
Telephone: (315) 255-1743
Carnegie Class: Assoc/HT-High Non
FAX Number: (315) 255-2117
Calendar System: Semester
URL: www.cayuga-cc.edu
Established: 1953
Annual Undergrad Tuition & Fees (In-District): $5,884
Enrollment: 2,906
Coed
Affiliation or Control: State/Local
IRS Status: 501(c)3
Highest Offering: Associate Degree
Accreditation: M, ADNUR, OTA

01 President ... Mr. Brian M. DURANT
04 Assistant to President/Board ... Ms. Annette M. LEFEVER
05 Provost/Vice Pres Academic Affairs ... Dr. Ronald G. CANTOR
32 Vice President Student Affairs ... Vacant
10 Chief Financial Officer ... Ms. Kelly ALBRECHT
102 Executive Director Foundation ... Mr. Guy T. COSENTINO
07 Director of Admissions ... Mr. Bruce M. BLODGETT
09 Director Institutional Research ... Ms. Virginia RUDNICK
08 Library Director ... Ms. Sara DAVENPORT
41 Director of Athletics ... Mr. DJ BEVIVINO
15 Director Human Resources ... Ms. Lindsey SUPPES
35 Director Student Activities ... Mr. Norman LEE
19 Director Public Safety ... Mr. Doug KINNEY

Cazenovia College (B)

22 Sullivan Street, Cazenovia NY 13035
County: Madison
FICE Identification: 002685
Unit ID: 189848
Telephone: (800) 654-3210
Carnegie Class: Bac-Diverse
FAX Number: (315) 655-4143
Calendar System: Semester
URL: www.cazenovia.edu
Established: 1824
Annual Undergrad Tuition & Fees: $36,668
Enrollment: 800
Coed
Affiliation or Control: Independent Non-Profit
IRS Status: 501(c)3
Highest Offering: Baccalaureate
Accreditation: M, AAQEP, ART, IACBE

01 President ... Dr. David BERGH
03 Executive Vice President ... Vacant
05 VP Academic Affs/Dean of Faculty ... Dr. Sharon A. DETTMER
32 Vice Pres for Student Affairs ... Dr. Karey PINE
10 VP Financial Affs/Chief Fin Officer ... Mr. Mark H. EDWARDS
26 Director Marketing/Communications ... Mr. Timothy D. GREENE
07 Sr Assoc Director of Admissions ... Ms. Kristen BOWERS
15 Director Human Resources ... Ms. Janice ROMAGNOLI
111 Int Dir Institutional Advancement ... Ms. Samantha HARMON
89 Dean First Year Program ... Mr. Jesse LOTT
08 Director of Library Services ... Ms. Heather C. WHALEN-SMITH
37 Financial Aid Coordinator ... Mr. Nicholas M. KORDEK
06 Registrar ... Ms. Sherri J. BENEDICT
23 Director Health Services ... Ms. Deborah FRANK
36 Dir Career/Extended Learning Svcs ... Ms. Katherine GEORGE
41 Director Intercollegiate Athletics ... Mr. Pete WAY
13 Director of Technology Development ... Mr. David PALMER
09 Dir Institutional Rsrch/Assessment ... Dr. Jon C. DALY
18 Dir of Physical Plant Operations ... Mr. Jeff SLOCUM
29 Director Alumni Relations ... Ms. Shari WHITAKER
04 Exec Assistant to the President ... Ms. Judy L. PAPAYANAKOS
51 Dir for Adult/Continuing Educ ... Ms. Carla M. DESHAW
58 Assoc Dir for Graduate & Intl Pgms ... Mr. Charles F. HARCOURT
19 Director of Campus Safety ... Ms. Roberta COMERFORD
28 Director for Multicultural Affairs ... Ms. Katiuzca LOAIZA-ESPINOZA
96 Payroll & Purchasing Coordinator ... Ms. Kelli GRAHAM
44 Director Annual Giving ... Ms. Cary RUEPPEL
113 Bursar ... Ms. Abby BERRY

Central Yeshiva Beth Joseph (C)

1502 Avenue N, Brooklyn NY 11230
County: Kings
Identification: 667157
Unit ID: 488004
Telephone: (718) 269-4080
Carnegie Class: Spec-4-yr-Faith
FAX Number: (718) 269-4080
Calendar System: Semester
Established: 1942
Annual Undergrad Tuition & Fees: $11,000
Enrollment: 23
Male
Affiliation or Control: Independent Non-Profit
IRS Status: 501(c)3
Highest Offering: First Talmudic Degree
Accreditation: RABN

01 Chief Executive Officer ... Rabbi Moshe JOFEN
05 Dean ... Rabbi Mordechai JOFEN
37 Director Student Financial Aid ... Rabbi Yechezkel MOSCOVITZ
06 Registrar ... Rabbi Baruch MILLER

Central Yeshiva Tomchei Tmimim Lubavitch America (D)

841-853 Ocean Parkway, Brooklyn NY 11230-2798
County: Kings
FICE Identification: 004776
Unit ID: 189857
Telephone: (718) 774-3430
Carnegie Class: Spec-4-yr-Faith
FAX Number: N/A
Calendar System: Semester
URL: centralyeshiva.com/registration/choose-yeshiva
Established: 1941
Annual Undergrad Tuition & Fees: $7,700
Enrollment: 594
Male
Affiliation or Control: Independent Non-Profit
IRS Status: 501(c)3
Highest Offering: Second Talmudic Degree
Accreditation: AIJS

01 Principal and Director ... Rabbi Mendel BLAU
05 Dean ... Rabbi Zalman LABKOWSKI

*The City University of New York (E)

205 E. 42nd Street, New York NY 10017
County: New York
FICE Identification: 025061
Unit ID: 190035
Telephone: (646) 664-9100
Carnegie Class: N/A
FAX Number: (646) 664-3868
URL: https://www.cuny.edu/

01 Chancellor ... Dr. Felix V. MATOS RODRIGUEZ
05 Exec VC/University Provost ... Dr. Wendyl F. HENSEL
10 Interim Vice Chancellor/CFO ... Ms. Christina CHIAPPA
101 Secretary of the Board of Trustees ... Ms. Gayle HORWITZ
43 General Counsel/SVC Legal Affs ... Mr. Derek DAVIS
86 SVC Inst Affairs/Special Counsel ... Ms. Glenda G. GRACE
11 Exec VC/Chief Operating Officer ... Mr. Hector BATISTA
18 VC Facility Plng/Construction Mgmt ... Mr. Mohamed ATTALLA
13 VC/Chief Information Officer ... Mr. Eusebio (Seb) FORMOSO
32 VC Student Affairs/Enrollment ... Dr. Denise B. MAYBANK
88 Sr Vice Chanc for Labor Relations ... Ms. Pamela S. SILVERBLATT
09 Assoc VC/Vice Provost for Research ... Dr. Tamera SCHNEIDER
15 Vice Chanc for Human Resources Mgmt ... Ms. Doriane K. GLORIA
111 Vice Chanc for Univ Advancement ... Mr. James D. GALLO
26 Vice Chanc Communications/Marketing ... Ms. Maite JUNCO

*Baruch College/City University of New York (F)

One Bernard Baruch Way, New York NY 10010-5526
County: New York
FICE Identification: 007273
Unit ID: 190512
Telephone: (646) 312-1000
Carnegie Class: Masters/L
FAX Number: N/A
Calendar System: Semester
URL: www.baruch.cuny.edu
Established: 1968
Annual Undergrad Tuition & Fees (In-District): $7,462
Enrollment: 19,740
Coed
Affiliation or Control: State/Local
IRS Status: 501(c)3
Highest Offering: Doctorate
Accreditation: M, IPSY, SPAA

02 President ... Dr. S. David WU
05 Provost/SVP Academic Affairs ... Dr. Linda ESSIG
10 Vice Pres Administration/Finance ... Ms. Katharine COBB
84 VP Enroll Mgmt/Strategic Init ... Ms. Mary GORMAN
111 VP for College Advancement ... Mr. David SHANTON
13 VP for Information Services ... Mr. Arthur DOWNING
26 VP for Comm/Ext Rels & Econ Dev ... Ms. Christina LATOUF
32 VP Student Affairs/Dean of Students ... Dr. Art KING
21 Asst Vice President Finance ... Ms. Mary FINNEN
43 Asst VP Legal Counsel ... Ms. Olga DAIS
20 Assoc Provost ... Dr. Dennis SLAVIN
102 President Baruch College Fund ... Vacant
50 Dean Zicklin School of Business ... Dr. Fenwick HUSS
49 Int Dean Weissman School ... Dr. Jessica LANG
80 Int Dean School Public/Intl Affairs ... Dr. Nancy ARIES
08 Dean of Library ... Mr. Arthur DOWNING
100 Chief of Staff ... Ms. Kenya N. LEE
25 Director of Sponsored Programs ... Ms. Zolicia ABOTSI
15 Exec Dir of Human Resources ... Ms. Andrea CAVINESS
36 Director Career Development Center ... Ms. Ellen STEIN
90 Asst Dir Client Svcs/Fac Liaison ... Vacant
85 Director Intl Student Office ... Ms. Rosa KELLEY
19 Director Public Safety ... Mr. Robert CURRY
09 Dir Institutional Rsrch/Pgm Assess ... Mr. John CHOONOO
29 Director Alumni Relations ... Ms. Janet ROSSBACH
96 Director of Purchasing ... Dr. Diane OQUENDO
28 Exec Chief Diversity Officer ... Mr. Elliott DAWES
41 Athletic Director ... Ms. Heather MACCULLOCH
86 Dir of Govt and Community Relations ... Mr. Eric LUGO
06 Senior Registrar ... Mr. Edward ADAMS
104 Director Study Abroad ... Dr. Richard MITTEN
37 Director of Financial Aid Services ... Ms. Elizabeth RIQUEZ
07 Dir of Undergraduate Admissions ... Ms. Marisa DELACRUZ
108 Asst Provost for Assessment/Accred ... Dr. Rachel FESTER

*City University of New York Borough of Manhattan Community College (G)

199 Chambers Street, New York NY 10007-1047
County: New York
FICE Identification: 002691
Unit ID: 190521
Telephone: (212) 220-1230
Carnegie Class: Assoc/HT-High Trad
FAX Number: (212) 220-1244
Calendar System: Semester
URL: www.bmcc.cuny.edu
Established: 1963
Annual Undergrad Tuition & Fees (In-District): $5,170
Enrollment: 22,496
Coed
Affiliation or Control: State/Local
IRS Status: 501(c)3
Highest Offering: Associate Degree
Accreditation: M, ADNUR, CAHIIM, COARC, EMT

02 President ... Dr. Anthony MUNROE
05 Acting Provost/SVP Academic Affairs ... Dr. Erwin WONG
11 Vice President Administration/Plng ... Vacant
43 Spec Legal Counsel/Labor Designee ... Ms. Meryl R. KAYNARD
32 Vice President of Student Affairs ... Dr. Marva CRAIG
111 Vice Pres of Inst Advancement ... Ms. Lorna A. MALCOLM
84 Vice Pres Enrollment Management ... Dr. Sanjay RAMDATH
10 Asst Vice Pres of Finance ... Ms. Elena SAMUELS
51 Dean Ctr for Cont Ed/Workforce Dev ... Mr. Anthony WATSON
25 Dean Office of Sponsored Programs ... Ms. Aleksandra CATARUZOLO
20 Dean for Instruction/Curriculum ... Vacant
20 Assoc Dean of Faculty ... Dr. David BARNET
121 Asst Dean Academic Support ... Ms. Janice ZUMMO
37 Director Financial Aid ... Ms. Albina KHASIDOVA
15 Director Human Resources ... Ms. Gloria CHAO
07 Director of Admissions ... Ms. Lisa KASPER
06 Senior Registrar ... Mr. Mohammad ALAM
08 Dir Learning Resource Center ... Mr. Gregory FARRELL
09 Dean Inst Effective/Strategic Plng ... Dr. Christopher SHULTS
28 Chief Diversity Officer ... Ms. Odelia LEVY
18 Asst VP Planning/Facilities ... Mr. Jorge YAFAR
26 Exec Director Public Affairs ... Mr. Manuel ROMERO
41 Director of Athletics ... Vacant
102 Dir Foundation/Corporate Relations ... Mr. Brian HALLER
36 Dir Academic Advise/Transfer Center ... Ms. Carei THOMAS
38 Director Counseling Center ... Vacant
96 Director of Procurement ... Ms. Leonore GONZALEZ
86 Director Government Relations ... Mr. Douglas ISRAEL

*City University of New York Bronx Community College (H)

2155 University Avenue, Bronx NY 10453-2895
County: Bronx
FICE Identification: 002692
Unit ID: 190530
Telephone: (718) 289-5100
Carnegie Class: Assoc/HT-High Trad
FAX Number: (718) 289-6011
Calendar System: Semester
URL: www.bcc.cuny.edu
Established: 1957
Annual Undergrad Tuition & Fees (In-District): $5,206
Enrollment: 8,370
Coed
Affiliation or Control: State/Local
IRS Status: 501(c)3
Highest Offering: Associate Degree
Accreditation: M, ACBSP, ADNUR, MLTAD, NMT, RAD

02 President ... Dr. Thomas A. ISEKENEGBE
05 Provost/VP Academic Affairs ... Dr. Lester RAPALO
86 Government Rels and Ext Affairs Dir ... Mr. David W. LEVERS
32 VP for Student Affairs ... Ms. Irene R. DELGADO
111 VP for Advance/Comm & Ext Rels ... Dr. Eddy BAYARDELLE
26 Asst VP Comm & Marketing ... Mr. Richard GINSBERG
84 Vice President for Enrollment Mgmt ... Dr. Bernard GANTT
11 AVP for Campus Operations ... Mr. David A. TAYLOR
30 Asst VP for Development ... Vacant
103 Dean for Workforce & Econ Dev ... Vacant
45 Dean for Research/Plng & Assessment ... Vacant
20 Assoc Dean AA for Curr & Fac Dev ... Dr. Alexander OTT
10 Dir for Financial & Business Svcs ... Ms. Gina UGARTE
06 Registrar/Dir Enrollment ... Ms. Karen THOMAS
13 Interim Chief Information Officer ... Ms. Luisa MARTICH
37 Financial Aid Director ... Ms. Margaret NELSON
07 Director for Admission/Recruitment ... Mr. Joshua A. PEREZ
15 Interim Human Resources Director ... Ms. Elizabeth RIVERA
08 Chief Librarian ... Prof. Michael J. MILLER
19 Public Safety Director ... Mr. Saul FRAGUADA
41 Student Athletics Director ... Vacant
18 Chief Super Physical Plant Svcs ... Vacant
29 Director of Alumni Relations ... Mr. Robert WHELAN
88 Mgr of College Discovery ... Ms. Cynthia SUAREZ-ESPINAL
43 Exec Counsel & Deputy to Pres ... Ms. Susan FIORE
96 Director of Purchasing ... Ms. Kelema K. BRADFORD
28 Chief Diversity/Affirm Act Ofcr ... Ms. Jessenia PAOLI
14 Deputy Chief Technology Officer ... Ms. Luisa MARTICH
108 Academic Assessment Manager ... Dr. Richard LAMANNA
20 Dean for Academic Affairs ... Dr. Luis MONTENEGRO
90 Dir for Academic Comp Svcs Desk ... Ms. Wanda SANTIAGO
91 Manager of Admin Systems & Svcs ... Mr. Rolly WILTSHIRE
51 Manager Continuing/Prof Education ... Vacant
25 Dir of Grants Development ... Ms. Judith EISENBERG
22 Affirmative Action Specialist ... Mr. Oluwafemi AKINSANYA
102 Dev Corp and Foundation Rel Mgmt ... Ms. Julia OLIVA
104 Dir Intl Educ and Study Abroad Pgm ... Vacant
09 OIR Inst Research Specialist ... Mrs. Chelsea RAMOS
46 Director of Research & Testing ... Mr. Chris EFTHIMIOU
106 Dir IT Academic App/CTLT ... Mr. Mark LENNERTON

36 Dir Transfer and Job Placement ... Mr. Alan FUENTES
04 Administrative Asst to President ... Ms. Amirah COUSINS
100 Chief of Staff ... Ms. Susan FIORE
38 Director Student Counseling ... Vacant

*City University of New York Brooklyn College (A)

2900 Bedford Avenue, Brooklyn NY 11210-2889
County: Kings FICE Identification: 002687
Unit ID: 190549
Telephone: (718) 951-5000 Carnegie Class: Masters/L
FAX Number: N/A Calendar System: Semester
URL: www.brooklyn.cuny.edu
Established: 1930 Annual Undergrad Tuition & Fees (In-District): $7,440
Enrollment: 17,735 Coed
Affiliation or Control: State/Local IRS Status: 170(c)1
Highest Offering: Master's
Accreditation: M, AUD, CACREP, DIETD, DIETI, SP

02 President ... Ms. Michelle J. ANDERSON
05 Provost/Sr Vice Pres Acad Affairs ... Dr. Anne LOPES
10 Sr VP for Finance & Administration ... Mr. Alan GILBERT
111 Vice Pres Institutional Advancement ... Mr. Todd GALITZ
32 Vice President for Student Affairs ... Dr. Ronald JACKSON
84 VP Enroll Management and Retention ... Ms. Lillian O'REILLY
100 Chief of Staff to Pres & Exec Dir ... Vacant
43 Chief Legal/Labor Relations Officer ... Mr. Tony THOMAS
108 Assoc Prov & AVP Inst Effectiveness ... Dr. Tammie CUMMING
20 Assoc Provost for Faculty & Admin ... Dr. Tammy LEWIS
53 Dean School of Education ... Dr. April BEDFORD
57 Dean Schl Visual Media & Perf Arts ... Dr. Maria A. CONELLI
83 Int Dean Sch Humanities & Soc Sci ... Dr. Kenneth GOULD
81 Dean Schl Natural & Behav Sciences ... Dr. Kleanthis PSARRIS
50 Dean Koppelman Sch Business ... Dr. Susanne SCOTT
13 Asst VP Info Technology Services ... Vacant
08 Assoc Dn Lib/Ex Dir Acad Info Tech ... Dr. Mary MALLERY
88 Assoc Dean Sch of Business ... Dr. Herve QUENEAU
88 Asst Dean Academic Programs ... Dr. Lucas RUBIN
35 Assistant Dean for Student Services ... Mr. Dave BRYAN
35 Assistant Dean for Student Life ... Ms. Moraima SMITH
28 Chief Diversity Officer ... Mr. Anthony BROWN
113 Exec Dir Student Fin Svcs & Bursar ... Ms. Yasmin ALI
07 Exec Director Enrollment Services ... Ms. Natalie COOMBS
45 Exec Director Budget & Planning ... Mr. Emir GANIC
121 Exec Dir Student Success Center ... Ms. Tracy NEWTON
18 Executive Director of Operations ... Vacant
21 Comptroller ... Ms. Beatrice GILLING RAYNOR
15 Exec Dir Human Resource Services ... Ms. Renita W. SIMMONS
26 Assoc Dir Communications/Marketing ... Ms. Anita BULAN
112 Managing Dir Campaign & Leader Gift ... Ms. Emily MOQTADERI
09 Sr Dir Inst Rsrch & Data Analysis ... Dr. Michael AYERS
25 Dir Research & Sponsored Programs ... Ms. Robin NESBY
96 Dir Procurement & Support Services ... Ms. Madonna CHARLES
29 Director of Alumni Affairs ... Ms. Lisa DICCE
06 Interim Registrar ... Ms. Natalie COOMBS
41 Dir Rec Intramurals/Intercol Athl ... Mr. Bruce FILOSA
36 Dir Magner Ctr/Career Dev & Interns ... Ms. Natalia GUARIN-KLEIN
38 Director Personal Counseling ... Dr. Gregory KUHLMAN
114 Director of Budget ... Mr. Michael LANZA
37 Director Financial Aid ... Mr. Antonio MARRERO
88 Testing & Transfer Evaluation Ofcr ... Ms. Monica RIVERA
92 Dir Scholars Pgm & Honors Academy ... Dr. Lisa SCHWEBEL
90 Dir Acad Information Technologies ... Mr. Howard SPIVAK
19 Director Safety & Security ... Mr. Donald A. WENZ

*City University of New York The City College (B)

160 Convent Avenue, New York NY 10031-9198
County: New York FICE Identification: 002688
Unit ID: 190567
Telephone: (212) 650-7000 Carnegie Class: DU-Higher
FAX Number: (212) 650-7680 Calendar System: Semester
URL: www.ccny.cuny.edu
Established: 1847 Annual Undergrad Tuition & Fees (In-District): $7,340
Enrollment: 15,227 Coed
Affiliation or Control: State/Local IRS Status: 501(c)3
Highest Offering: Doctorate
Accreditation: M, ARCPA, CLPSY, LSAR, #MED

02 President ... Dr. Vincent G. BOUDREAU
05 Provost/Sr VP Academic Affairs ... Mr. Tony LISS
102 VP & Exec Dir Fndn/Comms/Sr Advisor ... Ms. Dee Dee MOZELESKI
10 Vice Pres Finance & CFO ... Mr. Felix LAM
84 VP Student Affairs/Enrollment Mgmt ... Ms. Celia P. LLOYD
18 AVP Facilities Mgmt ... Mr. David ROBINSON
86 VP Governmental/Community Affairs ... Vacant
11 VP Operations/Chief Info Officer ... Mr. Kenneth IHRER
63 Dean CUNY Sch of Medicine ... Ms. Carmen R. GREEN
54 Dean of Engineering ... Dr. Alex COUZIS
53 Dean School of Education ... Mr. Edwin LAMBOY
47 Dean School of Architecture ... Ms. Marta GUTMAN
88 Dean of CWE-Div of Interdiscip Stds . Dr. Juan Carlos MERCADO
81 Dean of Science ... Dr. Susan L. PERKINS
82 Dean School of Civic/Global Ldrshp ... Dr. Andrew RICH
79 Int Dean of Humanities & The Arts ... Ms. Renata MILLER
43 Executive Counsel to the President ... Mr. Paul F. OCCHIOGROSSO
15 Asst Vice Pres of Human Resources ... Vacant
23 Exec Director Health and Wellness ... Vacant
06 Senior Registrar ... Mr. Thomas CASTIGLIONE
35 Exec Dir of Student Affairs at CWE ... Ms. Sophia DEMETRIOU
08 Interim Chief Librarian ... Mr. Loren MENDELSOHN
25 Dir for Grants & Sponsored Pgms ... Ms. Candice BAPTISTE-SEXTON
09 Exec Dir Institutional Research ... Ms. Nikisha P. WILLIAMS
37 Director of Financial Aid ... Ms. Arshaw RAMKARAN
27 Public Relations Coordinator ... Ms. Ashley AROCHO
28 Chief Diversity Officer ... Ms. Diana COUZZO
36 Director of Career Services ... Ms. Katie NAILLER
19 Exec Dir Public Safety/Security ... Mr. Pat MORENA
24 Director of Instructional Media ... Mr. Nana ABEYIE
07 Dir of Undergraduate Admissions ... Ms. Joanna KUCHARSKI
96 Director of Business Services ... Vacant
104 Director Study Abroad ... Dr. Juan Carlos MERCADO
105 Director Web Services ... Mr. Juan BAEZ
29 Director Alumni Affairs ... Mr. David COVINGTON
39 Dir Resident Life/Student Housing ... Ms. Meera RAMSOONDAR-CUEVAS
41 Interim Athletic Director ... Mr. Steve MACIAS

*College of Staten Island CUNY (C)

2800 Victory Boulevard, Staten Island NY 10314-6600
County: Richmond FICE Identification: 002698
Unit ID: 190558
Telephone: (718) 982-2000 Carnegie Class: Masters/L
FAX Number: N/A Calendar System: Semester
URL: www.csi.cuny.edu
Established: 1976 Annual Undergrad Tuition & Fees (In-District): $7,490
Enrollment: 12,797 Coed
Affiliation or Control: State/Local IRS Status: 501(c)3
Highest Offering: Doctorate
Accreditation: M, ADNUR, CAEP, MLS, MPCAC, NUR, PTA, SW

02 President ... Dr. Timothy G. LYNCH
05 Sr VP Acad Affairs/Provost ... Dr. J. Michael PARRISH
32 VP Student Affairs ... Ms. Jennifer S. BORRERO
111 Int AVP Institutional Advancement ... Ms. Kim A. WILLIAMS
10 AVP for Finance & Budget/CFO ... Mr. Carlos A. SERRANO
18 VP Campus Planning/Facilities ... Ms. Hope BERTE
84 AVP Enrollment Svcs/Dean Admissions ... Mr. Alexander SCOTT
20 Assoc Provost Undergrad Studies ... Dr. Ralf PEETZ
13 AVP & CIO Info Technology Services ... Dr. Patricia KAHN
81 Dean of Science & Technology ... Dr. Michael J. CAVAGNERO
79 Dean Humanities & Social Sci ... Dr. Sarolta A. TAKACS
08 Associate Dean & Chief Librarian ... Ms. Amy STEMPLER
86 Int VP Econ Dev/Cont Stds/Govt Rels ... Mr. Robert WALLACE
35 Executive Dir Student Svcs ... Ms. Danielle E. DIMITROV
50 Dean School of Business ... Dr. Susan L. HOLAK
76 Dean School of Health Sciences ... Vacant
53 Dean School of Education ... Dr. Burnett JOINER
28 Chief Diversity Officer/Title IX ... Vacant
100 Int Chief of Staff/Dir Employee Rel ... Ms. Jessica COLLURA
88 Int Assoc Provost Grad Stds Rsrch ... Dr. Dante TAWFEEQ

*City University of New York Graduate Center (D)

365 Fifth Avenue, New York NY 10016-4309
County: New York FICE Identification: 004765
Unit ID: 190576
Telephone: (212) 817-7000 Carnegie Class: DU-Highest
FAX Number: N/A Calendar System: Semester
URL: www.gc.cuny.edu
Established: 1961 Annual Undergrad Tuition & Fees (In-District): N/A
Enrollment: 9,300 Coed
Affiliation or Control: State/Local IRS Status: 501(c)3
Highest Offering: Doctorate
Accreditation: M, AUD, CAHIIM, CLPSY, DIETI, JOUR, NURSE, PH

02 President ... Dr. Robin L. GARRELL
05 Provost & SVP Graduate Center ... Dr. Steve EVERETT
10 SVP Finance & Administration ... Mr. Brian A. PETERSON
13 AVP Information Technology/CIO ... Ms. Elaine MONTILLA
111 Int VP Institutional Advancement ... Ms. Wendy DEMARCO FUENTES
26 VP Communications ... Ms. Wendy DEMARCO FUENTES
32 VP Student Affairs ... Mr. Matthew G. SCHOENGOOD
21 Deputy to SVP Finance & Admin ... Mr. Ken TIRINO
81 Dean for Science ... Dr. Joshua BRUMBERG
20 Assoc Provost & Dean Academic Affs ... Dr. David OLAN
08 Chief Librarian ... Dr. Maura A. SMALE
19 Exec Dir Security & Public Safety ... Mr. John FLAHERTY
15 Exec Dir of Human Resources ... Mr. David BOXILL
37 Exec Dir Fellowships/Financial Aid ... Ms. Phyllis SCHULZ
20 Exec Director of Academic Affairs ... Ms. Patti MYATT
06 Dir Stdnt Services/Senior Registrar ... Mr. Vincent J. DELUCA
85 Director International Students ... Ms. Linda ASARO
43 Legal Counsel & Labor Designee ... Ms. Lynette M. PHILLIPS
18 Director Facilities ... Mr. Charles SCOTT
07 Director Admissions ... Mr. Les GRIBBEN
25 Director Sponsored Research ... Ms. Huyuni SURATT
38 Dir Well Ctr/Psy Coun Svc/Adult Dev ... Dr. Robert HATCHER
04 Administrative Asst to President ... Ms. Alexandra ROBINSON

*City University of New York Herbert H. Lehman College (E)

250 Bedford Park Boulevard W, Bronx NY 10468-1589
County: Bronx FICE Identification: 007022
Unit ID: 190637
Telephone: (718) 960-8000 Carnegie Class: Masters/L
FAX Number: N/A Calendar System: Semester
URL: www.lehman.edu
Established: 1968 Annual Undergrad Tuition & Fees (In-District): $7,410
Enrollment: 15,091 Coed
Affiliation or Control: State/Local IRS Status: 501(c)3
Highest Offering: Doctorate
Accreditation: M, CACREP, CAEP, DIETD, DIETI, NURSE, SP, SW

02 President ... Dr. Fernando DELGADO
100 Deputy to Pres for Operations/Comm ... Vacant
05 Provost/SVP Academic Affairs ... Dr. Peter O. NWOSU
84 VP Enrollment Mgmt/Assoc Provost ... Mr. Richard FINGER
10 VP Administration/Finance ... Ms. Rene M. ROTOLO
111 Vice Pres Institutional Advancement ... Ms. Susan EBERSOLE
32 Vice President Student Affairs ... Dr. Jermaine A. WRIGHT
13 Vice Pres/Chief Info Officer ... Ms. Ediltrudys RUIZ
28 VP Diversity/Human Resources ... Ms. Dawn EWING-MORGAN
79 Dean School of Arts/Humanities ... Dr. James MAHON
83 Int Dean School of Nat & Soc Sci ... Dr. Pamela MILLS
20 Assoc Provost for Academic Affairs ... Dr. Victor BROWN
76 Dean Sch Hlth Sci/Hum Svc/Nurs ... Dr. Elgloria HARRISON
51 Dean School Cont Educ/Prof Studies ... Dr. Jane MACKILLOP
53 Int Assoc Dean School of Education ... Ms. Rene PARMAR
08 Chief Librarian ... Dr. Kenneth SCHLESINGER
43 Exec Counsel to Pres/Labor Designee ... Ms. Bridget BARBERA
18 Dir Campus Planning/Facilities ... Ms. Robin AUCHINCLOSS
45 AVP Strategy/Policy & Analytics ... Vacant
26 AVP for Marketing & Communications ... Vacant
35 AVP of Student Affairs ... Mr. Conrad WALKER
21 Asst VP for Financial Operations ... Ms. Gina HARWOOD
14 Asst VP Information Technology ... Vacant
06 Senior Registrar ... Ms. Yvette ROSARIO
07 Director of Admissions/Recruitment ... Ms. Laurie AUSTIN
29 Assoc Director of Alumni Relations ... Mr. Robert PAGAN
88 Director of the Art Gallery ... Mr. Bartholomew F. BLAND
36 Director of Career Services ... Ms. Bascilla TOUSSAINT
38 Director Counseling Center ... Ms. Karen SMITH MOORE
37 Dir Financial Aid/Enroll Mgmt ... Ms. Vera SENESE
89 Director Freshman Year Initiative ... Dr. Steven WYCKOFF
46 Assoc Dir Research & Sponsored Pgm ... Ms. Valerie LURIA
92 Director of Honors College Program ... Dr. Gary SCHWARTZ
15 Director of Human Resources ... Mr. Eric WASHINGTON
09 Director of Institutional Research ... Vacant
121 Sr Dir Acad Pgms/SEEK Pgm ... Ms. Althea FORDE
27 Int Asst VP Media Rels/Publications ... Vacant
88 Exec Dir Performing Arts Center ... Ms. Eva BORNSTEIN
19 Director of Public Safety ... Mr. Fausto RAMIREZ
109 Director of Auxiliary Services ... Ms. Luz ANDUJAR
41 Athletic Director ... Mr. Ryan MCCARTHY
40 Bookstore Manager ... Mr. Dominique WEST
120 Dir Online Education/E-learning ... Dr. Olena ZHADKO
114 Director of Budget ... Ms. Bethania ORTEGA
44 Director Advancement Initiatives .. Ms. Tara REGIST TOMLINSON

*Hostos Community College-City University of New York (F)

500 Grand Concourse, Bronx NY 10451-5323
County: Bronx FICE Identification: 008611
Unit ID: 190585
Telephone: (718) 518-4300 Carnegie Class: Assoc/HT-High Trad
FAX Number: (718) 518-4294 Calendar System: Semester
URL: www.hostos.cuny.edu
Established: 1970 Annual Undergrad Tuition & Fees (In-District): $5,208
Enrollment: 6,136 Coed
Affiliation or Control: State/Local IRS Status: 501(c)3
Highest Offering: Associate Degree
Accreditation: M, DH, RAD

02 President ... Dr. Daisy COCCO DE FILIPPIS
05 Provost/VP Academic Affairs ... Dr. Shiang-Kwei WANG
10 Senior Vice Pres for Admin/Finance ... Ms. Esther RODRIGUEZ-CHARDAVOYNE
32 VP Student Development/Enroll Mgmt ... Dr. La Toro YATES
100 Executive Chief of Staff ... Ms. Diana KREYMER
111 Vice Pres Institutional Advancement ... Ms. Colette ATKINS
103 VP Cont Educ & Workforce Dev ... Dr. Evelyn FERNÁNDEZ-KETCHAM
13 Asst Vice Pres Info Technology ... Vacant
114 Finance/Budget Director ... Ms. Fanny DUMANCELA
18 Exec Dir Facil Plng Des Mgmt ... Ms. Elizabeth FRIEDMAN
31 Dean for Community Rels ... Ms. Ana I. GARCIA-REYES
20 Asst Dean of Academic Affairs ... Dr. Andrea FABRIZIO
84 Asst Dean of Enrollment Management ... Vacant
35 Assistant Dean of Student Life ... Ms. Johanna GOMEZ
43 Exec Counsel & Labor Designee ... Mr. Eugene SOHN
26 Director of Communication ... Vacant
38 Director of Counseling ... Ms. Linda ALEXANDER-WALLACE
15 Exec Director Human Resources ... Ms. Christine DIAS-SINGH
86 Dir Government/External Affairs ... Vacant
06 Registrar ... Mr. David PRIMAK
07 Dir of Admissions & Recruitment ... Mr. Carlos RIVERA
37 Director of Financial Aid ... Ms. Leslie KING
19 Director of Campus Security ... Mr. Arnaldo BERNABE
25 Director Grants & Contracts ... Ms. Kelba SOSA
09 Director Institutional Research ... Mr. Piotr KOCIK
08 Head Librarian ... Ms. Madeline FORD
28 Chief Diversity Officer ... Ms. Latoya JEFFERS
29 Development/Alumni Relations Mgr ... Mr. Felix SANCHEZ
36 Director Student Career Programs ... Ms. Lisanette ROSARIO
35 Director Student Activities ... Mr. Jerry ROSA
96 Director of Procurement ... Mr. Devon HARIPRASHAD

108	Dn Inst Eff/Strat Plng/Assess & OAA	Dr. Babette AUDANT
21	Exec Director Business & Finance	Mr. Ken ACQUAH

*City University of New York Hunter College (A)

695 Park Avenue, New York NY 10065

County: New York   FICE Identification: 002689
Unit ID: 190594
Telephone: (212) 772-4000   Carnegie Class: Masters/L
FAX Number: N/A   Calendar System: Semester
URL: www.hunter.cuny.edu
Established: 1870   Annual Undergrad Tuition & Fees (In-District): $7,382
Enrollment: 24,052   Coed
Affiliation or Control: State/Local   IRS Status: 501(c)3
Highest Offering: Doctorate
Accreditation: **M**, AUD, CACREP, CAEPN, CYTO, DIET, DIETD, DIETI, NURSE, PLNG, PTA, #SP, SPAA, SW

02	President	Ms. Jennifer J. RAAB
100	Chief of Staff	Ms. Anne LYTLE
10	VP Finance/HR & Business Dev	Ms. Livia CANGEMI
05	Acting Provost/VP Academic Affairs	Mr. Majoj PARDASANI
32	VP Student Affs/Dean of Stdnts	Ms. Eija AYRAVAINEN
43	General Counsel/Dean of Faculty	Ms. Suzanne PIPER
26	Asst VP & Dir Communication	Vacant
28	Dean Diversity and Compliance	Mr. John ROSE
49	Dean School of Arts & Sciences	Dr. Andrew POLSKY
70	Acting Dean School of Social Work	Ms. Mary CAVANAUGH
53	Dean School of Education	Mr. Michael MIDDLETON
66	Dean School of Nursing	Dr. Elizabeth CAPEZUTI
08	Acting Chief Librarian	Mr. John PELL
06	Registrar	Vacant
09	Director of Institutional Research	Mr. Andrew WALLACE
15	AVP Human Resources	Ms. Galia GALANSKY
121	Assistant Dean for Academic Support	Mr. Brian MAASJO
29	Director Alumni Relations	Vacant
19	College Security Director	Mr. Joseph FOELSCH
35	Assistant Dean for Student Affairs	Ms. Lori JANOWSKI
41	Athletic Director	Ms. Terry WANSART
07	Sr Dir Recruitment & Admissions	Mr. Joseph FANTOZZI

*City University of New York John Jay College of Criminal Justice (B)

524 West 59th Street, New York NY 10019-1093

County: New York   FICE Identification: 002693
Unit ID: 190600
Telephone: (212) 237-8000   Carnegie Class: Masters/L
FAX Number: (212) 237-8607   Calendar System: Semester
URL: www.jjay.cuny.edu
Established: 1964   Annual Undergrad Tuition & Fees (In-District): $7,470
Enrollment: 15,766   Coed
Affiliation or Control: State/Local   IRS Status: 501(c)3
Highest Offering: Master's
Accreditation: **M**, CLPSY, FEPAC, SPAA

02	President	Ms. Karol V. MASON
05	Provost	Dr. Yi LI
32	Vice Pres Student Affairs	Vacant
111	Vice Pres Institutional Advancement	Ms. Robin MERLE
84	VP Enrollment Management	Mr. Brian KERR
04	Executive Assoc to President	Ms. Raeanne DAVIS
46	Associate Provost/Dean of Research	Dr. Anthony CARPI
10	Vice Pres & COO	Mr. Mark FLOWER
20	Assoc Prov & Dean of Undergrad Stds	Dr. Dara BYRNE
37	Director of Financial Aid	Mr. Vincent PIZZUTI
35	Director Student Activities	Ms. Danielle OFFICER
25	Director of Funded Research	Ms. Susy MENDES
09	Director of Institutional Research	Mr. Ricardo ANZALDUA
89	Director of First Year Experience	Ms. Katalin SZUR
06	Registrar	Mr. Daniel MATOS
88	Director of CRJ Research & Eval	Dr. Jeffrey BUTTS
07	Director of Admissions	Mr. Vincent PAPANDREA
13	Chief Information Officer	Mr. Joe LAUB
19	Director of Public Safety	Mr. Diego REDONDO
26	Director of Media Relations	Mr. Richard RELKIN
27	Chief Communications Officer	Ms. Kira POPLOWSKI
36	Dir of Career Development Svcs	Ms. Chantelle WRIGHT
38	Director of Counseling	Dr. Gerard BRYANT
41	Athletic Director	Ms. Catherine ALVES
21	Associate Business Officer	Ms. Emily KARP
29	Dir Alumni Relations/Annual Giving	Mr. Steve DERCOLE
96	Director of Purchasing	Mr. Daniel DOLAN
18	Director Facilities/Physical Plant	Mr. Anthony BRACCO
43	Vice President & Exec Counsel	Mr. Tony BALKISSOON
86	Exec Dir of External Relations	Ms. Mindy BOCKSTEIN
121	Dir of Academic Advisement	Ms. Katherine MUNET-PABON
22	Int Dir of Accessibility Services	Ms. Malaine CLARKE
104	Director Study Abroad	Mr. Kenneth YANES
28	Director Diversity/Compliance	Ms. Gabriela LEAL
39	Director Student Housing	Ms. Jessica CARSON
102	Dir Foundation/Corporate Relations	Ms. Rona LANE
106	Dir Online Education/E-learning	Ms. Judith CAHN
15	Exec Director of Human Resources	Vacant

† The Clinical Psychology PhD is awarded through the CUNY Graduate Center.

*City University of New York Kingsborough Community College (C)

2001 Oriental Boulevard, Brooklyn NY 11235-2333

County: Kings   FICE Identification: 002694
Unit ID: 190619
Telephone: (718) 368-5109   Carnegie Class: Assoc/HT-Mix Trad/Non
FAX Number: (718) 368-5003   Calendar System: Other
URL: www.kbcc.cuny.edu
Established: 1963   Annual Undergrad Tuition & Fees (In-District): $5,252
Enrollment: 15,116   Coed
Affiliation or Control: State/Local   IRS Status: 501(c)3
Highest Offering: Associate Degree
Accreditation: **M**, ADNUR, EMT, POLYT, PTAA, SURGT

02	President	Dr. Claudia V. SCHRADER
05	Vice Pres Academic Affs/Provost	Dr. Joanne RUSSELL
10	Vice Pres Finance/Administration	Mr. Eduardo RIOS
100	Executive Chief of Staff	Ms. Nadine BROWNE
32	Vice Pres of Student Affairs	Vacant
51	Dean Continuing Education	Ms. Christine ZAGARI-LOPORTO
35	Director of Student Life	Ms. Helen NASSER
84	Vice Pres Enrollment Management	Dr. Johana RIVERA
09	Vice Pres Inst Effectiveness	Vacant
111	Vice Pres Institutional Advancement	Vacant
15	Director of Human Resources	Ms. Micheline DRISCOLL
22	Dir Affirmative Action/EO Officer	Mr. Michael VALENTE
19	Director of Security & Safety	Mr. Kenneth GREENE
08	Chief Librarian	Ms. Tina KOPEL
06	Registrar	Mr. Avery MULLEN
18	Campus Facilities Officer	Vacant
37	Financial Aid Officer	Mr. Sinu JACOB
13	Chief Information Officer	Mr. Asif HUSSAIN
36	Director Career Services	Ms. Marisa JOSEPH
24	Director of Educational Media	Mr. Michael ROSSON
41	Director of Athletics	Mr. Robert ALLISON
96	Director of Purchasing	Ms. Kiesha STEWART
29	Director Alumni Relations	Ms. Aba AGOLLI
38	Director Student Counseling	Ms. Althea MADURAMENTE
07	Director of Admissions	Ms. Erica LEVY

*LaGuardia Community College/ City University of New York (D)

31-10 Thomson Avenue, Long Island City NY 11101-3083

County: Queens   FICE Identification: 010051
Unit ID: 190628
Telephone: (718) 482-7200   Carnegie Class: Assoc/HT-High Trad
FAX Number: (718) 609-2000   Calendar System: Semester
URL: www.lagcc.cuny.edu
Established: 1971   Annual Undergrad Tuition & Fees (In-District): $5,218
Enrollment: 16,971   Coed
Affiliation or Control: State/Local   IRS Status: 501(c)3
Highest Offering: Associate Degree
Accreditation: **M**, ADNUR, EMT, OTA, PTAA

02	President	Mr. Kenneth ADAMS
05	Provost/Senior Vice President	Dr. Paul ARCARIO
04	Senior Advisor to President	Vacant
11	Vice President of Administration	Mr. Shahir ERFAN
111	VP of Institutional Advancement	Vacant
13	Vice Pres Information Technology	Mr. Henry SALTIEL
32	Vice President Student Affairs	Vacant
51	Vice Pres Continuing Education	Mr. Sunil B. GUPTA
20	Assoc Dean for Academic Affairs	Ms. Dion MILLER
121	Int Assoc Dean for Student Success	Dr. Fay BUTLER
84	Int Assoc Dean Enrollment Mgmt	Dr. Gail BAKSH-JARRETT
103	Int Asst Dean of Workforce Dev	Dr. Assuanta HOWARD
18	Exec Dir Facilities Mgmt/Planning	Mr. Kenneth CAMPANELLI
15	Int Exec Dir of Human Resources	Ms. Marta CLARK
10	Exec Director Finance & Business	Vacant
08	Acting Chief Librarian	Mr. Steve OVADIA
37	Director Student Financial Services	Vacant
07	Director of Admissions	Ms. LaVora DESVIGNE
26	Dir Marketing/Communications	Ms. Georgina TARASKEWICH
21	Associate Business Manager	Ms. Carmen LUONG
36	Director Employment/Career Svc Ctr	Ms. Claudia BALDONEDO
96	Director Procurement/Contracts	Ms. Tawanikka SMITH
86	Government Relations Manager	Ms. Claudia CHAN
30	Int Exec Director of Development	Ms. Laura BARTOVICS
100	Chief of Staff	Ms. Nayelli VALENCIA TURRENT
19	Director Security/Safety	Ms. Yvonne GAUL
28	Executive Director of Diversity	Ms. Wendy NICHOLSON

*City University of New York Medgar Evers College (E)

1650 Bedford Avenue, Brooklyn NY 11225-2010

County: Kings   FICE Identification: 010097
Unit ID: 190646
Telephone: (718) 270-4900   Carnegie Class: Bac-A&S
FAX Number: (718) 270-5126   Calendar System: Semester
URL: www.mec.cuny.edu
Established: 1970   Annual Undergrad Tuition & Fees (In-District): $7,352
Enrollment: 5,237   Coed
Affiliation or Control: State/Local   IRS Status: 501(c)3
Highest Offering: Baccalaureate
Accreditation: **M**, ACBSP, ADNUR, CAEP, NUR, SW

02	President	Dr. Patricia RAMSEY

11	Chief Operating Officer	Ms. Jacqueline CLARK
05	Provost/SVP for Academic Affairs	Dr. Antoinette COLEMAN
10	VP Finance & Administration	Ms. Jacqueline CLARK
20	Asst VP & Assoc Provost	Vacant
18	Asst Vice President of Facilities	Vacant
32	SVP for Student Success	Mr. Jesse KANE
20	Dean of Academic Affairs	Vacant
51	Dean Sch Professional & Comm Dev	Dr. Evelyn CASTRO
50	Dean of the School of Business	Dr. Jo-Ann ROLLE
49	Dean of the School of Liberal Arts	Dr. Ethan GOLOGAR
53	Dean School of Education	Dr. Sheilah PAUL
72	Dean School of Science/Health/Tech	Dr. Mohsin PATWARY
100	SVP for Strategy/Chief of Staff	Dr. Kimberly WHITEHEAD
43	Interim Special Counsel to the Pres	Ms. Shirley IRICK
04	Exec Assistant to the President	Mrs. Lisa ANDERSON
22	Director of Affirmative Action	Vacant
06	Registrar	Vacant
86	Exec Dir Govt Affs/Comm & Mktg	Vacant
13	Asst VP/CIO	Mr. Xavier BARRETO
37	Director of Financial Aid	Vacant
38	Director of Counseling	Dr. JoAnn JOYNER-GRAHAM
19	Director of Security	Mr. Jerry HOFFMAN
41	Director of Athletics	Ms. Chetara MURPHY
25	Grants Officer	Mr. Chi KOON
89	Dir Freshman Year Program	Ms. Deborah CHARLES
55	Director Evening/Weekend Programs	Ms. Yvette WALL
36	Sr Director of Career Development	Ms. Antoinette ROBERSON
30	Director of Development	Dr. Michael G. FLANIGAN
84	Exec Dir Enrollment Management	Mrs. Shannon CLARKE-ANDERSON
29	Director of Alumni Relations	Ms. Marsha ESCAGY
07	Director Admissions	Ms. Jo-Ann JACOBS
09	Director of Institutional Research	Dr. Eva CHAN
08	Interim Chief Librarian	Dr. Judith SCHWARTZ
66	Chair Dept of Nursing	Dr. Shirley DANIELS
50	Chair Dept of Business Admin	Ms. Evelyn MAGGIO
70	Chair Department of Social Work	Dr. Edward HERNANDEZ
88	Chair Multi-Early Child & Elem Educ	Dr. Rupam SARAN
60	Chair Dept of Mass Comm	Dr. Clinton CRAWFORD
88	Chair Department Accounting	Dr. Rosemary WILLIAMS
81	Chair Department of Mathematics	Dr. Jean M. JEAN MICHEL
77	Chair Dept Physics/Computer Sci	Dr. Armando HOWARD
81	Chair Department of Biology	Dr. Chiyedza SMALL
83	Chair Dept of Social/Behavioral Sci	Dr. Maria DELONGORIA
83	Chair Department of Psychology	Dr. Maudry LASHLEY
80	Chair Dept of Public Administration	Dr. Zulema BLAIR
77	Chair Computer Info Systems	Dr. David AHN
88	Chair Department Economics/Finance	Dr. Emmanuel EGBE
79	Chair Department of English	Dr. Tonya HEGAMIN
73	Chair Dept of Philosophy & Religion	Dr. Vivaldi JEAN MARIE
88	Chair Dept World Language/Culture	Dr. Sheldon HUGGINS
81	Chair Chemistry/Environmental Sci	Dr. Alicia REID
88	Chair Dev & Special Education	Dr. Ken HOYTE
35	Director of Student Life	Ms. Amani REECE
15	Human Resources Manager	Ms. Janis GRANT
113	Director Office of the Bursar	Ms. Thais PILIERI

*New York City College of Technology/City University of New York (F)

300 Jay Street, Brooklyn NY 11201-1909

County: Kings   FICE Identification: 002696
Unit ID: 190655
Telephone: (718) 260-5000   Carnegie Class: Bac-Diverse
FAX Number: (718) 260-5198   Calendar System: Semester
URL: www.citytech.cuny.edu
Established: 1946   Annual Undergrad Tuition & Fees (In-District): $7,320
Enrollment: 15,513   Coed
Affiliation or Control: State/Local   IRS Status: 501(c)3
Highest Offering: Baccalaureate
Accreditation: **M**, ACPHA, ADNUR, ART, CSHSE, DH, DT, NUR, OPD, RAD

02	President	Dr. Russell K. HOTZLER
05	Provost/VP Academic Affairs	Dr. Pamela BROWN
10	Vice Pres Finance/Administration	Dr. Miguel CAIROL
84	Int VP Enrollment/Student Affairs	Dr. Marling SONE
20	Associate Provost Academic Affairs	Dr. Reginald BLAKE
43	General Counsel/Affirmative Action	Ms. Katherine M. RAYMOND
07	Director of Admissions	Ms. Alexis CHACONIS
06	Registrar	Vacant
37	Director of Financial Aid	Ms. Sandra HIGGINS
08	Interim Librarian	Ms. Anne LEONARD
13	AVP/Chief Information Officer	Ms. Rita UDDIN
107	Dean of Professional Studies	Ms. Maureen ARCHER
72	Int Dean of Technology/Design	Dr. Gerarda M. SHIELDS
49	Dean of Arts & Science	Mr. Justin VASQUEZ-PORITZ
51	Dean Continuing Education	Dr. Carol SONNENBLICK
55	Director Evening Session	Vacant
15	OFSR Exec Dir/Labor Designee/HR	Ms. Sandra GORDON
25	Grants Officer	Ms. Melissa EMANUS
24	Director of Inst Tech/Media Svcs	Ms. Nathalie ZARISFI
09	Director of Assessment	Ms. Yongchao (Yimi) ZHAO
26	AVP Public Relations	Ms. Faith CORBETT
29	Director Alumni Relations	Ms. Trang LE-CHAN
38	Director Student Counseling	Ms. Cynthia BINK
96	Director of Purchasing	Mr. Wayne ROBINSON
18	Chief Facilities/Physical Plant	Mr. Brendan STACK
30	Chief Development/Spec Asst to Pres	Dr. Caroline HELLMAN
21	Executive Dir of Business Mgmt	Mr. Wayne ROBINSON

*City University of New York Queens College (A)

65-30 Kissena Boulevard, Flushing NY 11367-1597
County: Queens FICE Identification: 002690
Unit ID: 190664
Telephone: (718) 997-5000 Carnegie Class: Masters/L
FAX Number: (718) 997-5598 Calendar System: Semester
URL: www.qc.cuny.edu
Established: 1937 Annual Undergrad Tuition & Fees (In-District): $7,538
Enrollment: 19,700 Coed
Affiliation or Control: State/Local IRS Status: 501(c)3
Highest Offering: Master's
Accreditation: M, CACREP, CAEP, CLPSY, DIETD, DIETI, LAW, LIB, MUS, SP

02 President ... Mr. Frank H. WU
05 Int Provost/VP Academic Affairs ... Dr. Patricia PRICE
10 VP Finance/Administration ... Vacant
32 VP for Student Affs/Enrollment Mgmt ... Ms. Jennifer JARVIS
26 VP Comm/Mktg/Sr Advisor to Pres ... Mr. Jay HERSHENSON
84 VP Enrollment & Student Retention ... Vacant
111 VP Inst Advancement/Alumni Rels ... Ms. Laurie DORF
43 Int Exec Counsel to the President ... Ms. Judith MASSIS-SANCHEZ
100 Chief of Staff ... Vacant
27 Director of Communications ... Ms. Leslie JAY
13 AVP/CIO Information Tech ... Mr. Troy HAHN
20 Int Assoc Provost Acad/Fac Affairs ... Dr. Meghan HEALEY
20 Assoc Provost Res and Intl Programs ... Vacant
21 AVP Budget and Finance ... Mr. Joseph LOUGHREN
35 Int Asst VP for Student Affairs ... Mr. Sean PIERCE
121 Int Assoc Prov Innov/Stdnt Success ... Dr. Nathalia HOLTZMAN
57 Dean of Arts & Humanities ... Dr. William MCCLURE
81 Dean of Math & Natural Sciences ... Dr. Daniel WEINSTEIN
53 Interim Dean of Education ... Dr. Bobbie KABUTO
58 Dean of Graduate Studies ... Vacant
83 Dean of Social Sciences ... Dr. Ekaterina PECHENKINA
15 AVP Human Resources ... Ms. Lee KELLY
41 Director of Athletics ... Mr. Robert TWIBLE
88 Director of Events ... Ms. Sylvia HERNANDEZ
18 AVP Facilities ... Mr. Zeco KRCIC
07 Executive Director for the QC Hub ... Vacant
38 Director of Counseling & Advisement ... Vacant
06 Director QC Hub/Registrar ... Mr. James CURRY
09 Dean of Inst Effectiveness ... Vacant
08 Interim Assoc Dean/Chief Librarian ... Ms. Simone YEARWOOD
37 Co-Director QC Hub/Financial Aid ... Mr. Clifford COULOUTE
29 Manager Alumni Affairs ... Ms. Laura ABRAMS
19 Interim Director of Security/Safety ... Ms. Deborah HUGGINS
28 Chief Diversity Officer ... Ms. Jerima DEWESE
96 Director of Purchasing ... Mr. Surinder VIRK
86 AVP Ext Affairs & Govt Relations ... Mr. Jeffrey ROSENSTOCK
26 Director of Marketing ... Ms. Lillian ZEPEDA
104 Director of Study Abroad ... Vacant
25 Chief Contract/Grants Administrator ... Ms. Poline PAPOULIS

† The Clinical Psychology PhD is awarded through the CUNY Graduate Center.

*City University of New York Queensborough Community College (B)

222-05 56th Avenue, Bayside NY 11364-1497
County: Queens FICE Identification: 002697
Unit ID: 190673
Telephone: (718) 631-6262 Carnegie Class: Assoc/HT-High Trad
FAX Number: N/A Calendar System: Semester
URL: www.qcc.cuny.edu
Established: 1958 Annual Undergrad Tuition & Fees (In-District): $5,210
Enrollment: 12,405 Coed
Affiliation or Control: State/Local IRS Status: 501(c)3
Highest Offering: Associate Degree
Accreditation: M, ACBSP, ADNUR, ART, DANCE, THEA

02 President ... Dr. Christine MANGINO
05 Sr Vice Pres Academic Affs/Provost ... Dr. Timothy LYNCH
10 Vice Pres Finance & Admin ... Mr. William FAULKNER
111 Vice Pres Institutional Advancement ... Vacant
32 Vice President Student Affairs ... Dr. Brian KERR
20 Dean of Faculty ... Dr. Sandra PALMER
15 Dean Human Resource/Labor Rels ... Ms. Liza LARIOS
108 VP Strategic Plng/Assessment ... Vacant
51 VP Continuing Ed/Workforce Dev ... Vacant
88 Dean Accred Assessment ... Dr. Arthur CORRADETTI
26 VP/Chief Communications/Mktg Ofcr ... Mr. Stephen DI DIO
13 Chief Information Technology Ofcr ... Mr. Ralph ROMANELLI
06 Registrar ... Ms. Emiko SANCHEZ
08 Chief Librarian ... Ms. Jeanne GALVIN
07 Asst Dean of New Student Enrollment ... Ms. Patricia RAMOS
09 Director of Institutional Research ... Ms. Elisabeth LACKNER
16 Director of Human Resources ... Ms. Sangeeta NOEL
19 Director of Safety & Security ... Mr. John TRIOLO
22 Chief Diversity Officer ... Ms. Josephine PANTALEO
04 Executive Asst to President ... Ms. Elaine IOANNOU
104 Dir Ctr for Intl Stds/Study Abroad ... Ms. Lampeto (Betty) EFTHYMIOU
84 Dean of Enrollment Management ... Ms. Veronica LUKAS
36 Director of Career Services ... Ms. Constance PELUSO
18 Chief Admin Superintendent ... Mr. Joseph CARTOLANO
30 Development Officer ... Ms. Saji SHEERAZI
21 Exec Dir Finance/Admin Operations ... Mr. David WASSERMAN
114 Exec Dir Budget/Resource Planning ... Mr. Mark CARPENTIER
35 Asst Dean of Student Dev/Conduct ... Ms. Tikola RUSSELL
103 Dean Continuing Educ/Workforce Dev ... Ms. Hui-Yin HSU

*City University of New York Stella and Charles Guttman Community College (C)

50 West 40th Street, New York NY 10018
County: New York Identification: 667126
Unit ID: 475565
Telephone: (646) 313-8000 Carnegie Class: Assoc/HT-High Trad
FAX Number: N/A Calendar System: Semester
URL: www.guttman.cuny.edu
Established: 2011 Annual Undergrad Tuition & Fees (In-District): $5,194
Enrollment: 1,021 Coed
Affiliation or Control: State/Local IRS Status: 501(c)3
Highest Offering: Associate Degree
Accreditation: M

02 President ... Larry JOHNSON
05 Provost and Vice President ... Vacant
10 Vice Pres Admin & Finance ... Mary COLEMAN
32 VP Student Engagement ... Charles PRYOR
09 Director of Institutional Research ... Elisa HERTZ
100 Chief of Staff ... Linda MERIANS
13 Chief Info Technology Officer (CIO) ... John STROUD
15 Director Human Resources ... Nila BHAUMIK
18 Director Facilities Planning ... Shirley LAW
19 Director Public Safety ... Vacant
37 Director Student Financial Aid ... Cristina ORTIZ-HARVEY
06 Registrar ... Cortes MARISOL
07 Director of Admissions ... So SOPHEA
86 Director Government Relations ... Vacant
04 Administrative Asst to President ... Brady GALAN
29 Director Alumni Relations ... LaToya JACKSON
08 Chief Library Officer ... Vacant
28 Chief Diversity Officer ... Jaclyn HELMS
38 Director Student Counseling ... Courtney STEVENSON
43 Director Legal Services ... Lori FOX

*City University of New York York College (D)

94-20 Guy Brewer Boulevard, Jamaica NY 11451-0001
County: Queens FICE Identification: 004759
Unit ID: 190691
Telephone: (718) 262-2000 Carnegie Class: Masters/S
FAX Number: (718) 262-2352 Calendar System: Semester
URL: www.york.cuny.edu
Established: 1966 Annual Undergrad Tuition & Fees (In-District): $7,358
Enrollment: 7,784 Coed
Affiliation or Control: State/Local IRS Status: 501(c)3
Highest Offering: Master's
Accreditation: M, ARCPA, CAEP, EXSC, MLS, NUR, OT, SW

02 President ... Dr. Berenecea J. EANES
05 Interim Sr VP & Provost ... Dr. Derrick BRAZILL
10 VP of Administration & Finance/COO ... Mr. Charles BOZIAN
32 Int VP Enroll Mgmt & Student Aff ... Dr. Karen WILLIAMS
111 Int VP Institutional Advancement ... Ms. Dana TRIMBOLI
49 Interim Dean Sch of Arts & Sciences ... Dr. George WHITE
50 Int Dean Sch of Bus & Info Systems ... Dr. Maureen BECKER
83 Dean Sch of Health Sci & Prof Pgms ... Dr. Maureen BECKER
43 Labor & Legal Affairs ... Mr. Russell PLATZEK
15 Interim Exec Director HR ... Mr. Elgin FORD
19 Exec Dir Facilities & Planning ... Mr. Kachi AKOMA
21 Exec Dir Bus Oper & Compliance ... Ms. Vivian FEBUS
13 Chief Information Officer ... Mr. Claudio LINDOW
09 AVP Inst Effective/Strategic Plng ... Dr. Lori HOEFFNER
100 Chief of Staff ... Ms. Dana TRIMBOLI
06 Registrar ... Ms. Sharon DAVIDSON
08 Chief Librarian ... Ms. Njoki KINYATTI
90 Director of Academic Computing ... Dr. Che-Tsao HUANG
86 Exec Dir Govt/Strategic Initiative ... Dr. Earl G. SIMONS
19 Director of Public Safety ... Mr. James ASSMANN
37 Director of Financial Aid ... Ms. Beverly BROWN
18 Director Campus Planning ... Mr. Noel GAMBOA
35 Director Student Activities ... Dr. Jean PHELPS
36 Director Career Services ... Ms. Linda H. CHESNEY
25 Dir Research/Sponsored Programs ... Ms. Dawn HEWITT
38 Director of Counseling Cntr ... Dr. Jayoung CHOI
41 Director of Athletics ... Mr. Carl CHRISTIAN
04 Executive Asst to the President ... Ms. Veronica MARIANI
28 Director of Diversity ... Vacant
96 Director of Purchasing ... Ms. Christine WEITHERS
07 Director of Admissions ... Mr. Anthony DAVIS
103 Director Workforce Development ... Vacant

Clarkson University (E)

8 Clarkson Ave, Potsdam NY 13699
County: St. Lawrence FICE Identification: 002699
Unit ID: 190044
Telephone: (315) 268-6400 Carnegie Class: DU-Higher
FAX Number: (315) 268-7647 Calendar System: Semester
URL: www.clarkson.edu
Established: 1896 Annual Undergrad Tuition & Fees: $52,724
Enrollment: 4,025 Coed
Affiliation or Control: Independent Non-Profit IRS Status: 501(c)3
Highest Offering: Doctorate
Accreditation: M, AAQEP, ARCPA, HSA, OT, PTA

01 President ... Dr. Marc P. CHRISTENSEN
05 Interim Provost ... Dr. Goodarz AHMADI
111 VP External Relations ... Dr. Kelly O. CHEZUM
10 Chief Financial Officer ... Mr. Kenneth KLINE
32 VP Student Affairs ... Mr. Brian T. GRANT
30 VP Development & Alumni Relations ... Mr. Matthew DRAPER
15 Chief Human Resources Officer ... Ms. Amy MCGAHERAN
28 Chief Inclusion Officer ... Dr. Jennifer BALL
41 Athletics Director ... Mr. Scott J. SMALLING
13 Chief Information Officer ... Mr. Joshua A. FISKE
04 Assistant to the President ... Ms. Carrie CAPELLA
16 Asst Dir Human Resources ... Ms. Diana LETOURNEAU
45 Int Vice Provost Research & Tech ... Dr. Michelle L. CRIMI
88 Assoc Provost Faculty Achievement ... Dr. Christopher ROBINSON
20 Assoc Vice Provost Acad Affairs ... Ms. Amanda PICKERING
88 Dir Academic Affairs Operations ... Ms. Suzanne E. DAVIS
49 Dean of Arts & Sciences ... Dr. Darryl SCRIVEN
50 Dean of Business ... Dr. Diego NOCETTI
88 Sr Adv to the Pres on Anti-Racism ... Dr. Augustine LADO
54 Dean of Engineering ... Dr. William JEMISON
76 Founding Dean of Health Sciences ... Dr. Lennart JOHNS
08 Dean of Libraries ... Ms. Michelle L. YOUNG
65 Dir Inst for a Sustainable Environ ... Dr. Susan POWERS
58 Dean of Graduate School ... Dr. Michelle CRIMI
53 Chair of Education ... Dr. Catherine SNYDER
12 Exec Dir Beacon Institute ... Mr. Michael WALSH
88 Head of The Clarkson School ... Dr. Benjamin GALLUZZO
88 Dir of Inst for STEM Education ... Dr. Kathleen KAVANAGH
92 Director Honors Program ... Dr. Kate KRUEGER
88 Director Clarkson Ignite ... Ms. Ashley SWEENEY
09 Dir Institutional Research ... Ms. Jenna STONE
21 Controller ... Mr. Keith ROSSER
88 Dir Facilities Planning & Constr ... Ms. Anastasia THOMAS
18 Director Facilities & Services ... Mr. Michael TREMPER
117 Dir Legal Affairs/Compliance/Risk ... Ms. Debra DRESCHER
06 Registrar ... Ms. Jen J. STOKES
07 Director of Admissions ... Mr. Matthew RUTHERFORD
37 Director Financial Aid ... Ms. Kara PITTS
88 Int Dir Clarkson School Admission ... Ms. Carrie LABARR
121 Assoc Vice Provost Academic Support ... Ms. Cathy MCNAMARA
35 Interim Dean of Students ... Ms. Kelsey PEARSON
35 AVP Student Affairs & Global Init ... Vacant
19 Director Campus Safety & Security ... Ms. Marlene W. HALL
23 Director Student Health Center ... Ms. Amanda ROSS
36 Director Career Center ... Ms. Heather DIFINO
104 Study Abroad Coordinator ... Ms. Christine BAILEY
38 Director of Counseling ... Ms. Coreen BOHL
85 Director Intl Students & Scholars ... Ms. Tess C. CASLER
29 Assoc VP Engagement & Operations ... Ms. Teresa PLANTY
110 Assoc VP Development ... Mr. Steven SMALLING
102 Dir Donor Engmnt/Stwrdshp/Found Rel ... Ms. Erin LONDRAVILLE
44 Director Annual Giving Programs ... Ms. Nichole THOMAS
91 Director Administrative Computing ... Mr. Chris CUTLER
119 Dir Net Services & Info Security ... Mr. Brian HUNTLEY
90 Dir Academic Technology & Support ... Ms. Laura PERRY
105 Director Web Development ... Ms. Julie DAVIS
26 Director of Media Relations ... Ms. Melissa M. LINDELL
27 Director of Interactive Marketing ... Ms. Jessica CARISTA
88 Dir of Creative Services & Proj Mgt ... Mr. David HOMSEY
40 Bookstore Manager ... Mr. Evan HITCHMAN

Clinton Community College (F)

136 Clinton Point Drive, Plattsburgh NY 12901-9573
County: Clinton FICE Identification: 006787
Unit ID: 190053
Telephone: (518) 562-4200 Carnegie Class: Assoc/HT-Mix Trad/Non
FAX Number: (518) 561-4890 Calendar System: Semester
URL: www.clinton.edu
Established: 1966 Annual Undergrad Tuition & Fees (In-District): $6,831
Enrollment: 1,060 Coed
Affiliation or Control: State/Local IRS Status: 501(c)3
Highest Offering: Associate Degree
Accreditation: M

01 President ... Dr. John KOWAL
05 Int Vice President Academic Affairs ... Ms. Carey GOYETTE
10 Vice Pres for Admin/Business Affs ... Vacant
32 Dean of Student Affairs ... Mr. John BORNER
111 Exec Dir Institutional Advancement ... Mr. Chris CHAMARS
20 Assoc Vice Pres Academic Affairs ... Vacant
37 Director of Financial Aid ... Ms. Mary LA PIERRE
84 Dean of Enrollment Management .. Mrs. Anna MIARKA-GRZELAK
06 Registrar ... Mr. Jonathan REID
13 Director Information Technology ... Vacant
15 Director of Human Resources ... Vacant
18 Director of Buildings/Grounds ... Mr. Robert TROMBLEY
04 Administrative Asst to President .... Mrs. Tammy M. VILLANUEVA
21 Controller ... Mr. Ronald GRAHAM

Cochran School of Nursing (G)

967 North Broadway, Yonkers NY 10701-1399
County: Westchester FICE Identification: 006443
Unit ID: 190071
Telephone: (914) 964-4282 Carnegie Class: Spec 2-yr-Health
FAX Number: (914) 964-4266 Calendar System: Semester
URL: www.cochranschoolofnursing.us
Established: 1894 Annual Undergrad Tuition & Fees: N/A
Enrollment: 94 Coed
Affiliation or Control: Independent Non-Profit IRS Status: 501(c)3
Highest Offering: Associate Degree

Accreditation: ADNUR

01 Dean ... Dr. Patrick REINHARD
08 Director of CSN Learning Resource ... Ms. Andria CLEGHORN
32 Director Student Services/Finances ... Ms. Alphonsa ITTOOP
06 Registrar ... Ms. Lisa PEGUES
07 Admissions Counselor ... Ms. Haaneen EL JAMAL
88 Information Literacy Officer ... Ms. Diana KRPIC
37 Financial Aid Officer ... Ms. Maria GONCALVES

Cold Spring Harbor Laboratory, School of Biological Sciences (A)

PO Box 100, One Bungtown Road,
Cold Spring Harbor NY 11724-0100
County: Suffolk FICE Identification: 034563
Unit ID: 436377
Telephone: (516) 367-6890 Carnegie Class: Not Classified
FAX Number: (516) 367-6919 Calendar System: Other
URL: www.cshl.edu
Established: 1890 Annual Graduate Tuition & Fees: N/A
Enrollment: N/A Coed
Affiliation or Control: Independent Non-Profit IRS Status: 501(c)3
Highest Offering: Doctorate; No Undergraduates
Accreditation: NY

01 President ... Dr. Bruce STILLMAN
05 Dean of Academic Affairs ... Dr. Terri I. GRODZICKER
10 Chief Financial Officer ... Mr. Scott QUEHL
30 VP Development/Cmty Relations ... Mr. Charles V. PRIZZI
13 VP Information Technology/CIO ... Mr. Douglas TORRE
15 Vice Pres Human Resources ... Ms. Katherine G. RAFTERY
26 Vice Pres Communications ... Ms. Dagnia ZEIDLICKIS
43 Vice Pres General Counsel ... Ms. Debra ARENARE
81 Dean ... Dr. Alexander GANN
06 Registrar ... Dr. Alyson KASS-EISLER
25 Chief Contract/Grants Administrator ... Mr. Walter GOLDSCHMIDTS
28 Director of Diversity ... Ms. Charla LAMBERT
07 Director of Admissions ... Ms. Kimberly CRETEUR

Colgate Rochester Crozer Divinity School (B)

320 North Goodman Street, Ste 207, Rochester NY 14607
County: Monroe FICE Identification: 002700
Unit ID: 190080
Telephone: (585) 271-1320 Carnegie Class: Spec-4-yr-Faith
FAX Number: (585) 271-8013 Calendar System: Semester
URL: www.crcds.edu
Established: 1817 Annual Graduate Tuition & Fees: N/A
Enrollment: 46 Coed
Affiliation or Control: Independent Non-Profit IRS Status: 501(c)3
Highest Offering: Doctorate; No Undergraduates
Accreditation: THEOL

01 President ... Dr. Angela D. SIMS
11 VP Institutional Effectivenss/COO ... Rev. Paula B. BLUE
10 VP Finance/Administration ... Ms. Barbara BRELAND
05 VP Academic Affairs ... Dr. Deborah ROGERS
111 VP Institutional Advancement ... Dr. Courtney WILEY-HARRIS
94 Dean of Women & Gender Studies ... Dr. Hilary J. SCARSELLA
07 Director of Admissions ... Ms. Polly BUSH
30 Director of Development ... Ms. Lisa BORS
06 Registrar/Coord Financial Aid ... Ms. Qhamora KIMBROUGH
04 Executive Administrator ... Ms. Lydia CRIM

Colgate University (C)

13 Oak Drive, Hamilton NY 13346-1386
County: Madison FICE Identification: 002701
Unit ID: 190099
Telephone: (315) 228-1000 Carnegie Class: Bac-A&S
FAX Number: (315) 228-7798 Calendar System: Semester
URL: www.colgate.edu
Established: 1819 Annual Undergrad Tuition & Fees: $60,015
Enrollment: 3,054 Coed
Affiliation or Control: Independent Non-Profit IRS Status: 501(c)3
Highest Offering: Master's
Accreditation: M, AAQEP

01 President ... Brian W. CASEY
05 Provost & Dean of Faculty ... Lesleigh CUSHING
10 Sr VP for Finance & Admin ... Joseph S. HOPE
100 Chief of Staff/Sec to the BOT ... Hanna RODRIGUEZ-FARRAR
11 VP for Administration ... Christopher WELLS
32 VP & Dean of the College ... Paul J. MCLOUGHLIN, II
41 VP & Director of Athletics ... Nicki MOORE
101 VP/Sr Philanthropic Advisor ... Robert L. TYBURSKI
07 VP of Admission & Fin Aid ... Gary L. ROSS
26 VP Communications & Univ Events ... L. H. JACK
111 VP for Advancement ... Karl W. CLAUSS
15 Assoc VP Human Resources ... Lori CHLAD
04 Assistant to the President ... Susan LIGHT
21 Associate Vice Pres/Controller ... Brittany PLUMLEY
114 Assoc VP Budget & Financial Plg ... John COLLINS
21 Asst VP Finance & Administration ... Dan PARTIGIANONI
18 Assoc VP for Facilities/Cap Proj ... Stephen HUGHES
20 Associate Dean of the Faculty ... Doug JOHNSON
20 Associate Dean of the Faculty ... Krista INGRAM
20 Associate Dean of the Faculty ... April BAPTISTE
45 Vice Provost Admin & Planning ... Trish ST. LEGER
28 VP for Equity & Inclusion ... Renee MADISON
06 Assoc Prov Inst Analysis/Registrar ... Neil ALBERT
35 Dean of Students ... Dorsey SPENCER
07 Dean of Admission ... Tara BUBBLE
08 University Librarian ... Courtney YOUNG
13 Chief Information Officer ... Niranjan DAVRAY
112 AVP Advancement/Planned Giving ... Andrew CODDINGTON
110 Assoc VP Advancement Admin Planning ... Thirza MORREALE
88 Assoc VP Advancement/Dir Prof Net ... Jennifer STONE
29 Director of Alumni Relations ... Jillian COLE
37 Sr Assoc Dean & Dir Financial Aid ... Gina M. SOLIZ
109 Assoc VP Cmty Affairs/Aux Services ... Joanne BORFITZ
19 Assoc VP for Campus Safety ... Joseph HERNON
40 Sr Retail Insignia ... Craig WILSON
42 University Chaplain/Campus Rabbi ... Barry BARON
38 Asst VP Counseling/Psych Services ... Dawn LAFRANCE
96 Director of Purchasing ... Molly OGDEN
23 Director Student Health Services ... Ellen LARSON
94 Director Women's Studies ... Susan THOMSON
88 Director Relationship Development ... Sara GROH
88 Director Advancement Operations ... Lindsey HOHAM
44 Director Annual Giving ... Catherine MARHENKE
39 Asst VP Residential Planning/Prog ... Terra PECKSKAMP
22 Title IX Coord/Equity & Diversity ... Tamala FLACK
102 Dir Univ Grants & Sponsored Rsrch ... Laura FESTINE
104 Director of Off-Campus Study ... Joanna HOLVEY BOWLES
43 Asst VP Risk & Strategic Analysis ... Andrew FAGON

College of Mount Saint Vincent (D)

6301 Riverdale Avenue, Riverdale NY 10471-1093
County: Bronx FICE Identification: 002703
Unit ID: 193399
Telephone: (718) 405-3200 Carnegie Class: Bac-Diverse
FAX Number: (718) 601-6392 Calendar System: Semester
URL: www.mountsaintvincent.edu
Established: 1847 Annual Undergrad Tuition & Fees: $40,980
Enrollment: 2,663 Coed
Affiliation or Control: Independent Non-Profit IRS Status: 501(c)3
Highest Offering: Master's
Accreditation: M, ACBSP, #ARCPA, NURSE

01 President ... Dr. Susan R. BURNS
05 Provost/Dean of Faculty ... Vacant
20 Vice Provost & Dean of the College ... Dr. Lynne BONGIOVANNI
07 Sr VP for Admission/External Rels ... Ms. Madeleine MELKONIAN
10 Executive VP/Treasurer/CFO ... Mr. Abed ELKESHK
11 VP for Operations ... Mr. Kevin DEGROAT
13 VP Information Technology/CIO ... Mr. W. Adam WICHERN, III
32 Vice President for Student Affairs ... Ms. Kelli SMITH
88 Director Mission Integration ... Mr. Matthew SHIELDS
06 Registrar ... Mrs. Jeannette PICHARDO
08 Director of Library ... Mr. Joseph LEVIS
09 Director of Institutional Research ... Sr. Carol M. FINEGAN, SC
36 Director Career Education ... Mr. Robson CHERETTA
37 Director of Financial Aid ... Vacant
42 Dir Campus Ministry/Act Dir Mission ... Mr. Mathew SHIELDS
35 Dir of Student Affairs/Assoc Dean ... Dr. Gabrielle OCCHIOGROSSO
41 Dir Athletics & Recreation ... Mr. Phil STERN
38 Director Counseling Services ... Ms. Rebecca HALPERIN
23 Director of Health Services ... Mrs. Eileen MCCABE
26 Director for Public Relations/Mktg ... Ms. Leah MUNCH
19 Dir Campus Safety/Security ... Mr. Thomas VASSALLO
66 Dean College of Nursing ... Ms. Annemarie MCALLISTER
44 Assoc Dir Alumnae Rels/Annual Giv ... Ms. Kristin YANNIELLO
15 Director of Human Resources ... Vacant
21 Controller ... Mr. James WONG
04 Assistant to the President ... Ms. Mary BAUER
18 Director of Facilities ... Mr. Ryan ANDERSON
07 Director of Admissions ... Vacant
92 Director of Honors Program ... Dr. Rosita VILLAGOMEZ
97 Director of Core Curriculum ... Dr. Robert JACKLOSKY

The College of Saint Rose (E)

432 Western Avenue, Albany NY 12203-1490
County: Albany FICE Identification: 002705
Unit ID: 195234
Telephone: (518) 454-5111 Carnegie Class: Masters/L
FAX Number: (518) 438-3293 Calendar System: Semester
URL: www.strose.edu
Established: 1920 Annual Undergrad Tuition & Fees: $34,354
Enrollment: 3,863 Coed
Affiliation or Control: Independent Non-Profit IRS Status: 501(c)3
Highest Offering: Master's
Accreditation: M, ACBSP, CACREP, MUS, NASP, SP, SW

01 President ... Ms. Marcia J. WHITE
100 Chief of Staff ... Ms. Lisa HALEY-THOMSON
05 Provost/VP Academic Affairs ... Dr. Margaret MCLANE
58 Assoc Provost for Grad & Prof Study ... Vacant
32 VP for Student Development ... Vacant
10 VP for Finance & Administration ... Ms. Debra L. POLLEY
111 Interim VP Inst Advancement ... Mr. Robert DIVITO
15 Assoc Vice Pres Human Res/Risk Mgt ... Mr. Jeffrey KNAPP
21 AVP Financial Reporting/Comptroller ... Ms. Valerie MYERS
114 Assistant VP for Financial Planning ... Ms. Christina BARBER
07 Interim Assoc VP for Admissions ... Mr. Daniel GALLAGHER
37 Asst VP of Financial Aid ... Mr. Steven W. DWIRE
42 Dir Spiritual Life/Interfaith Init ... Ms. Joan HORGAN
13 Associate Vice President for IT ... Vacant
35 AVP Stdnt Devel/Compliance/Wellness ... Ms. Jennifer RICHARDSON
18 Assoc VP for Facilities Operations ... Mr. Gary GOSS
06 Registrar ... Mr. Craig TYNAN
08 Director of Library Services ... Vacant
39 Director Residence Life ... Ms. Phylicia COLEY
36 Assistant Director Career Center ... Ms. Emily NICHOLSON
41 Assoc VP & Director of Athletics ... Ms. Lori ANCTIL
19 Director of Safety/Security ... Mr. Steven STELLA
121 Director of Academic Advisement ... Ms. Jennifer HANKIN
109 Director Purchasing/Auxiliary Svcs ... Ms. Patricia BUCKLEY
09 Assoc VP of Institutional Effective ... Mrs. Lisa KEATING
40 Manager of Campus Store ... Mr. Austin ANTLE
24 Technology Support Services Manager ... Ms. Rachel RAMSEY
04 Exec Admin Asst to the President ... Ms. Maria RUSSO
50 Dean School of Business ... Dr. Rajarshi AROSKAR
79 Dean Arts & Humanities ... Dr. Gerald LORENTZ
81 Dean Math & Sciences ... Dr. Ian MACDONALD
53 Interim Dean School of Education ... Dr. Theresa WARD
112 Director of Major Gifts ... Ms. Therese STILLMAN
29 Director of Alumni Engagement ... Ms. Frances VORSKY
26 AVP of Marketing & Communications ... Ms. Jennifer GISH
28 Chief Diversity Ofcr/Dir Leadership ... Ms. Yolanda CALDWELL
23 Dir of Counseling/Health Services ... Mr. Mark PARISI
113 Bursar ... Ms. Deana BIZZARRO
27 Dir of Marketing & Communications ... Mr. Michael HICKLING
44 Director Annual Giving ... Ms. Colleen KEATING

The College of Westchester (F)

325 Central Avenue, White Plains NY 10606
County: Westchester FICE Identification: 005208
Unit ID: 197285
Telephone: (914) 948-4442 Carnegie Class: Bac-Diverse
FAX Number: (914) 948-5441 Calendar System: Semester
URL: www.cw.edu
Established: 1915 Annual Undergrad Tuition & Fees: $22,410
Enrollment: 934 Coed
Affiliation or Control: Proprietary IRS Status: Proprietary
Highest Offering: Baccalaureate
Accreditation: M

01 President & CEO ... Mrs. Mary Beth DEL BALZO
05 Provost/VP Academic Affairs ... Dr. Warren ROSENBERG
88 Vice President Special Projects ... Mr. Dale T. SMITH
84 VP of Enrollment Management ... Mr. Matt CURTIS
36 Director of Career Services ... Ms. Joann SONDEY
32 VP of Student Services & Retention ... Ms. Maria GANGI
37 Dir of Student Financial Services ... Mrs. Dianne PEPITONE

Columbia-Greene Community College (G)

4400 Route 23, Hudson NY 12534-9543
County: Columbia FICE Identification: 006789
Unit ID: 190169
Telephone: (518) 828-4181 Carnegie Class: Assoc/HT-Mix Trad/Non
FAX Number: (518) 822-2015 Calendar System: Semester
URL: www.sunycgcc.edu
Established: 1966 Annual Undergrad Tuition & Fees (In-District): $5,616
Enrollment: 1,445 Coed
Affiliation or Control: State/Local IRS Status: 501(c)3
Highest Offering: Associate Degree
Accreditation: M, ADNUR

00 Chairman of the Board ... Dr. Edward SCHNEIER, JR.
01 President ... Dr. Carlee DRUMMER
05 Provost/VP Acad & Student Affairs ... Dr. George TIMMONS
10 VP Administration/Chief Fin Ofcr ... Ms. Dianne TOPPLE
20 Dean of Academic Affairs ... Dr. Casey O'BRIEN
18 Director Building & Grounds ... Ms. Alison MURPHY
26 Director Marketing & Communications ... Ms. Jaclyn STEVENSON
37 Director of Financial Aid ... Ms. Joel PHELPS
06 Registrar ... Ms. Ann BRUNO
13 Director Information Systems ... Mr. Gino RIZZI
15 Director of Human Resources ... Ms. Melissa FANDOZZI
22 Affirmative Action Officer ... Ms. Melissa FANDOZZI
31 Director of Community Services ... Ms. Amanda KARCH
41 Athletic Director ... Mr. Nicolas DYER
121 Director Academic Support Center ... Vacant
103 Director of Workforce Development ... Ms. Christopher NARDONE
07 Asst Director of Admissions ... Mr. Kevin KROPP
102 Exec Dir of CG Community Foundation ... Ms. Joan KOWEEK
113 Bursar ... Ms. Christy WARD
19 Director of Security ... Mr. John LEONE
96 Purchasing Officer ... Ms. Patricia DAY
04 Assistant to the President ... Ms. Mary GARAFALO
29 Director Alumni Relations ... Ms. Christine PERRY
84 Assistant Dean of Enrollment Mgmt ... Mr. Matthew GREEN

Columbia University in the City of New York (H)

615 West 131st Street, New York NY 10027-6902
County: New York FICE Identification: 002707
Unit ID: 190150
Telephone: (212) 854-1754 Carnegie Class: DU-Highest
FAX Number: (212) 851-7022 Calendar System: Semester
URL: www.columbia.edu
Established: 1754 Annual Undergrad Tuition & Fees: $61,671
Enrollment: 30,135 Coed
Affiliation or Control: Independent Non-Profit IRS Status: 501(c)3
Highest Offering: Doctorate

Accreditation: M, ANEST, CAMPEP, CEA, DENT, HSA, IPSY, JOUR, LAW, MED, MIDWF, NASP, NURSE, OT, PH, PLNG, PTA, SPAA, SW

01 President .... Mr. Lee C. BOLLINGER
05 Provost .... Dr. Mary C. BOYCE
03 Senior Exec Vice President .... Mr. Gerald M. ROSBERG
49 EVP/Dean Arts & Sciences .... Dr. Amy HUNGERFORD
76 Exec VP Health/Biomed Sciences .... Dr. Lee GOLDMAN
09 Exec Vice President Research .... Dr. Jeanette M. WING
43 General Counsel .... Ms. Jane E. BOOTH
26 EVP Public Affairs/Communications .... Ms. Shailagh J. MURRAY
101 Secretary of the University .... Mr. Jerome DAVIS
10 EVP for Finance/Info Tech .... Ms. Anne R. SULLIVAN
18 Exec Vice President Facilities .... Mr. David GREENBERG
85 Exec Vice President Global Dev .... Mr. Safwan M. MASRI
30 Exec Vice Pres Development & Alumni .... Ms. Amelia J. ALVERSON
32 Exec Vice President University Life .... Mr. Dennis A. MITCHELL
41 Athletic Director .... Mr. Peter E. PILLING
88 Ombuds Officer .... Ms. Joan WATERS
100 Chief of Staff to President .... Ms. Susan K. GLANCY
20 Vice Provost Academic Programs .... Dr. Julie KORNFELD
20 Vice Provost Faculty Affairs .... Ms. Latha VENKATARAMAN
11 Vice Provost Administration .... Mr. Troy EGGERS
88 Vice Provost Teaching & Learning .... Mr. Soulaymane KACHANI
28 Vice Provost Diversity & Inclusion .... Dr. Dennis MITCHELL
08 Vice Provost & Univ Librarian .... Ms. Ann D. THORNTON
48 Dean Grad School Arch/Plng/Preserv .... Ms. Amale ANDRAOS
57 Dean School of the Arts .... Dr. Carol BECKER
58 Dean Grad School of Arts & Science .... Dr. Carlos J. ALONSO
50 Dean Graduate School of Business . Dr. Constantinos MAGLARAS
49 Dean Columbia College/VP UG Educ .... Dr. James J. VALENTINI
107 Dean School of Professional Studies .... Mr. Jason M. WINGARD
54 Dean Sch Engr/Applied Science .... Vacant
82 Dean School Intl/Public Affairs .... Ms. Merit E. JANOW
97 Dean School General Studies .... Dr. Lisa ROSEN-METSCH
60 Dean Graduate School Journalism .... Mr. Stephen W. COLL
61 Dean School of Law .... Ms. Gillian LESTER
70 Dean School of Social Work .... Dr. Melissa BEGG
63 Int EVP/Dean Faculty of Medicine .... Dr. Anil RUSTGI
52 Dean Sch Dental & Oral Surgery .... Dr. Christian S. STOHLER
66 Dean School of Nursing .... Dr. Bobbie BERKOWITZ
69 Dean School of Public Health .... Dr. Linda P. FRIED
38 Exec Director Student Counseling .... Dr. Richard EICHLER
113 Assoc VP Student Financial Svcs .... Dr. Jane HOJAN-CLARK
06 Assoc Vice Pres & Registrar .... Mr. Barry S. KANE
07 Dean Undergrad Admissions/Fin Aid .... Ms. Jessica MARINACCIO

† Parent institution of Barnard College and Teachers College, Columbia University.

Congregation Talmidei Mesivta Tiferes Schmiel Aleksander (A)

1535 63rd Street, Brooklyn NY 11219

County: Kings FICE Identification: 042769
Unit ID: 493600
Telephone: (718) 435-2105 Carnegie Class: Spec-4-yr-Faith
FAX Number: (917) 410-7477 Calendar System: Semester
Established: Annual Undergrad Tuition & Fees: $19,000
Enrollment: 173 Male
Affiliation or Control: Independent Non-Profit IRS Status: 501(c)3
Highest Offering: First Talmudic Degree
Accreditation: @RABN

01 CEO .... Rabbi Abraham SINGER

Congregation YMH (B)

1368 39th Street, Brooklyn NY 11218

County: Queens Identification: 667428
Telephone: (718) 972-3772 Carnegie Class: Not Classified
FAX Number: (718) 972-3773 Calendar System: Semester
URL: www.congymh.org
Established: 2015 Annual Undergrad Tuition & Fees: N/A
Enrollment: N/A Male
Affiliation or Control: Independent Non-Profit IRS Status: 501(c)3
Highest Offering: First Talmudic Degree
Accreditation: RABN

11 Administrator .... Moshe FISHMAN

Cooper Union (C)

30 Cooper Square, New York NY 10003-7120

County: New York FICE Identification: 002710
Unit ID: 190372
Telephone: (212) 353-4100 Carnegie Class: Bac-Diverse
FAX Number: (212) 353-4244 Calendar System: Semester
URL: www.cooper.edu
Established: 1859 Annual Undergrad Tuition & Fees: $46,820
Enrollment: 887 Coed
Affiliation or Control: Independent Non-Profit IRS Status: 501(c)3
Highest Offering: Master's
Accreditation: M, ART

01 President .... Laura SPARKS
05 Assoc Dean Academic Affairs .... Ruben SAVIZKY
10 Vice President Finance and Admin .... John RUTH
84 Vice President for Enrollment .... Mark CAMPBELL
111 VP for Development/Alumni Affairs .... Terri COPPERSMITH
07 Assoc Dir of Admissions .... Hilary FERNANDEZ
57 Dean School of Art .... Michael (Mike) ESSL
88 Associate Dean School of Art .... Adriana FARMIGA
48 Dean School of Architecture .... Nader TEHRANI
54 Dean School of Engineering .... Barry SHOOP
32 Dean of Students .... Christopher CHAMBERLIN
88 Asst Dean School of Architecture .... Hayley EBER
79 Assoc Dean Humanities/Social Sci .... Nada AYAD
15 Chief Talent Officer .... Natalie BROOKS
88 Creative Director .... Mindy LANG
45 VP Strategic Initiatives/Effective .... Antoinette (Toni) TORRES
27 Media Relations Manager .... Kim NEWMAN
88 Assoc Dean Educational Innovation .... Lisa SHAY
101 Secretary of the Institution/Board .... Charlotte WESSELL
06 Assoc Registrar .... David CHENKIN
19 Dir Campus Safety/Security .... Thomas TRESSELT
29 Deputy Dir of Alumni Affairs .... Jennifer DURST
30 Development Associate .... Adam D'ALEXANDER
37 Sr Dir Student Financial Svcs .... Charlie XU
15 Dir of Human Resources .... Mary Ann NISSEN

† Every student receives a full-tuition scholarship.

Cornell University (D)

Day Hall, Ithaca NY 14850

County: Tompkins FICE Identification: 002711
Unit ID: 190415
Telephone: (607) 255-2000 Carnegie Class: DU-Highest
FAX Number: (607) 255-5396 Calendar System: Semester
URL: www.cornell.edu
Established: 1865 Annual Undergrad Tuition & Fees: $59,282
Enrollment: 23,620 Coed
Affiliation or Control: Independent Non-Profit IRS Status: 501(c)3
Highest Offering: Doctorate
Accreditation: M, CIDA, DIETD, DIETI, HSA, LAW, LSAR, PH, PLNG, VET

01 President .... Martha E. POLLACK
05 Provost .... Michael I. KOTLIKOFF
63 Prov Medical Affairs/Dean Med Col .... Augustine M.K CHOI
43 VP and General Counsel .... Donica T. VARNER
20 Vice Prov Academic Affairs .... Avery AUGUST
18 VP for Facilities and Campus Svcs .... Rick BURGESS
100 Chief of Staff .... Kelly E. CUNNINGHAM
10 Executive Vice President/CFO .... Joanne M. DESTEFANO
46 VP for Research and Innovation .... Emmanuel P. GIANNELLIS
13 VP & CIO for Info Technology .... David LIFKA
32 VP Student & Campus Life .... Ryan T. LOMBARDI
26 VP for University Relations .... Joel M. MALINA
115 Chief Investment Officer .... Kenneth M. MIRANDA
116 Chief Auditor .... Aidtya V. MISRA
15 VP and Chief Human Resources .... Mary OPPERMAN
88 Chief Compliance Officer .... Christine STALLMAN
114 Vice Pres Budget & Planning .... Laura E. SYER
29 VP Alumni Affairs/Development .... Fred VAN SICKLE
54 Dean College of Engineering .... Lynden A. ARCHER
77 Dean of Computing and Info Science .... Kavita BALA
80 Dean Brooks School Public Policy .... Colleen BARRY
08 University Librarian .... Gerald R. BEASLEY
58 Vice Prov & Dean Grad School .... Kathryn J. BOOR
88 Dean Industrial/Labor Relations .... Alexander J. COLVIN
20 Dean of Faculty .... Eve DE ROSA
59 Dean College Human Ecology .... Rachel DUNIFON
47 Dean Col Agriculture/Life Sciences .... Benjamin Z. HOULTON
49 Dean College Arts & Sciences .... Ray JAYAWARDHANA
51 Dean Cont Education/Summer Session .... Charles W. JERMY
80 Dean Johnson Grad School of Mgmt .... Andrew KAROLYI
72 Dean/Vice Prov Cornell NYC Tech .... J. Gregory MORRISETT
50 Dean SC Johnson College of Business .... Mark NELSON
61 Dean Law School .... Jens D. OHLIN
88 Dean Nolan School Hotel Admin .... Kate D. WALSH
74 Dean College Veterinary Medicine .... Lorin D. WARNICK
48 Dean College Arch/Art/Planning .... J. Meejin YOON
50 Dean Dyson School Applied Economics .... Jinhua ZHAO
50 Dean of the Weill Graduate School .... Barbara L. HEMPSTEAD
84 Vice Provost Enrollment .... Jonathan BURDICK
20 Vice Provost Academic Integration .... Gary KORETZKY
120 VP for External Educ/eCornell .... Paul A. KRAUSE
88 Vice Prov Engagement/Land Grant .... Katherine MCCOMAS
97 Vice Provost Undergrad Educ .... Lisa NISHII
20 Deputy Provost .... John A. SILICIANO
88 Vice Prov for Academic Innovation .... Julia THOM-LEVY
85 Vice Prov for International Affairs .... Wendy WOLFORD
21 Assoc Vice President/Treasurer .... Michelle BENEDICT-JONES
09 Assoc Vice Prov Inst Research .... Marin E. CLARKBERG
114 Asst Vice Pres/Director of Budget .... Davina A. DESNOES
19 Associate VP Public Safety .... David HONAN
86 Associate VP for Govt Relations .... Charles KRUZANSKY
28 Assoc Vice Prov Faculty Diversity .... Yael LEVITTE
21 Assoc VP and University Controller .... William SIBERT
07 Dir Undergraduate Admissions .... Shawn FELTON
42 Dir Cornell United Religious Works .... Oliver GOODRICH
37 Director Financial Aid .... Kevin JENSEN
06 University Registrar .... Rhonda K. KITCH
104 Dir Office of Global Learning .... Brandon LANNERS
35 Dean of Students .... Marla LOVE
41 Director Athletics/Physical Educ .... J. Andrew NOEL, JR.
36 Interim Exec Director Career Svcs .... Jessamyn PERLUS
25 Sr Director Sponsored Fin Svcs .... Jeffrey A. SILBER

† Parent institution of Weill Medical College of Cornell University.

The Culinary Institute of America (E)

1946 Campus Drive, Hyde Park NY 12538-1499

County: Dutchess FICE Identification: 007304
Unit ID: 190503
Telephone: (845) 905-4288 Carnegie Class: Spec-4-yr-Arts
FAX Number: (845) 452-0165 Calendar System: Semester
URL: www.ciachef.edu
Established: 1946 Annual Undergrad Tuition & Fees: $34,650
Enrollment: 3,231 Coed
Affiliation or Control: Independent Non-Profit IRS Status: 501(c)3
Highest Offering: Master's
Accreditation: M

01 President .... Dr. Tim RYAN
10 VP Finance and Administration .... Ms. Maria KRUPIN
111 VP Advancement .... Mr. Kevin ALLAN
05 Provost .... Mr. Mark ERICKSON
20 VP Academic Affairs .... Dr. Michael SPERLING
26 VP Mktg & Communications .... Mr. Dan VINH
45 Sr Advisor/Industry Leadership .... Mr. Greg DRESCHER
32 VP & Dean of Student Affairs .... Dr. Kathleen MERGET
12 VP Strat Init & Branch Campuses .... Ms. Susan CUSSEN
84 Assoc VP Enrollment Management .... Ms. Rachel BIRCHWOOD
100 VP/Chief of Staff .... Mr. Rick TIETJEN
35 Assistant Director Student Life .... Ms. Kristina FLETCHER
38 Director Counseling & Psych Svcs .... Ms. Mueller CHRISTIANE
09 Dir Inst Research & Effectiveness .... Ms. Betsy CARROLL
23 Director Health Services .... Ms. Mary Ann SWEENEY
21 Director Finance .... Mr. Steven STROM
96 Director Purchasing & Storeroom .... Mr. Gower LANE
19 Director Campus Safety .... Mr. William CAREY
37 Director Student Financial Planning .... Ms. Jeanine GEMMEL
88 Dean Academic Engagement & Admin .... Ms. Carolyn TRAGNI
88 Dean School of Culinary Arts .... Mr. Brendan WALSH
49 Dean School of Lib Arts & Food Std .... Ms. Denise BAUER
108 Dir Accreditation and Assessment .... Mr. Matthew RUANE
06 Registrar .... Mr. Chet KOULIK
36 Director Career & Academic Advising .... Ms. Crystal DECAROLIS
08 Ref & Info Sys Litc Librarian .... Ms. Raven FONFA
15 Senior Director Human Resources .... Ms. Shay GARRIOCH
04 Executive Asst to President .... Ms. Shannon CAMPER
110 Senior Advancement Officer .... Mr. Brad WHITMORE
50 Dean School of Business & Mgmt Stds .... Ms. Annette GRAHAM
88 Acting Dean School of Cul Science .... Mr. Ted RUSSIN
88 Asst Director Faculty Relations .... Ms. Danielle GLENDENNING
88 Director Creative Services .... Ms. Terri TOTTEN
39 Assoc Dean Campus Life/Stdnt Dev .... Mr. James MANLEY
41 Asst Dir Recreation & Wellness .... Mr. Serge NALYWAYKO

Daemen College (F)

4380 Main Street, Amherst NY 14226-3592

County: Erie FICE Identification: 002808
Unit ID: 190725
Telephone: (716) 839-3600 Carnegie Class: DU-Mod
FAX Number: (716) 839-8516 Calendar System: Semester
URL: www.daemen.edu
Established: 1947 Annual Undergrad Tuition & Fees: $30,360
Enrollment: 2,536 Coed
Affiliation or Control: Independent Non-Profit IRS Status: 501(c)3
Highest Offering: Doctorate
Accreditation: M, ARCPA, CAATE, CYTO, IACBE, NUR, PTA, SW

01 President .... Dr. Gary A. OLSON
05 SVP Academic Affs/Dean of College .... Dr. Michael S. BROGAN
10 VP for Business Affairs & Treasurer .... Dr. Robert ROOD
111 VP Institutional Advancement .... Ms. Emily BURNS PERRYMAN
32 VP Student Affairs .... Dr. Greg J. NAYOR
20 Assoc VP Academic Affairs .... Ms. Doris MURPHY
21 VP for Business Affairs/Comptroller .... Ms. Lisa A. ARIDA
13 VP & Chief Information Officer .... Ms. Melaine KENYON
09 Director of Institutional Research .... Mr. Lee ALLARD
35 Dean of Students .... Ms. Kerry SPICER
108 Assoc VP of Inst Effectiveness .... Ms. Irene HOLOHAN-MOYER
08 Director of RIC & Library Service .... Ms. Melissa PETERSON
06 Registrar .... Ms. Tiffany SHADDEN
100 Chief of Staff .... Ms. Amanda R. GROSS
121 Asst Dean for Academic Advisement .... Ms. Sabrina FENNELL
37 Director of Financial Aid .... Mr. Jeffrey M. PAGANO
15 Director of Human Resources .... Ms. Tracy MASSE
26 Dir of Institutional Communications .... Mr. Daniel ROBISON
39 Dir of Housing & Residence Life .... Ms. Emilee YORMICK
35 Director of Student Activities .... Mr. Michael PAGLICCI
18 Director of Facilities .... Mr. Don PHILLIPS
19 Director of Campus Safety .... Mr. Douglas SMITH
41 Director of Athletics .... Ms. Traci MURPHY
96 Dir of Purchasing/Central Services .... Ms. Mary HARTNETT
92 Director of Honors Program .... Mr. Jay WENDLAND
29 Director Alumni Relations .... Ms. Kathryn HAMMER
40 Bookstore Manager .... Ms. Jaclyn HERNE
88 Dir of New Program Development .... Ms. Susan M. MARCHIONE
04 Admin Assoc Office of the President .... Ms. Sarah PORZUCEK
104 Director Study Abroad .... Ms. Ann ROBINSON
106 Exec Dir of Web Communications .... Mr. Thomas WOJCIECHOWSKI
38 Clinical Director of Counseling .... Ms. Danielle EADIE
84 Dean of Enrollment .... Ms. Julie ZULEWSKI

Davis College (G)

400 Riverside Drive, Johnson City NY 13790-2714

County: Broome FICE Identification: 021691
Unit ID: 194569
Telephone: (607) 729-1581 Carnegie Class: Spec-4-yr-Faith
FAX Number: (607) 729-2962 Calendar System: Semester
URL: www.davisny.edu
Established: 1900 Annual Undergrad Tuition & Fees: $17,150
Enrollment: 79 Coed

Affiliation or Control: Independent Non-Profit IRS Status: 501(c)3
Highest Offering: Baccalaureate
Accreditation: M, BI

01 President Dr. Doug BLANC
05 Academic Dean Dr. JoAnna OSTER
32 Vice Pres of Student Affairs Vacant
10 Director of Finance Mr. Larry ELLIS
11 Director of Operations Ms. Naomi SARAVANAPAVAN
06 Registrar/Dir Financial Aid Ms. Naomi SARAVANAPAVAN
08 Librarian Mrs. Shelley BYRON
108 Dir Institutional Effectiveness Ms. Shelley BYRON
18 Chief Facilities/Physical Plant Vacant
41 Athletic Director Vacant

Dominican University New York (A)

470 Western Highway, Orangeburg NY 10962-1210
County: Rockland FICE Identification: 002713
Unit ID: 190761
Telephone: (845) 848-7800 Carnegie Class: DU-Mod
FAX Number: (845) 359-2313 Calendar System: Semester
URL: www.dc.edu
Established: 1952 Annual Undergrad Tuition & Fees: $30,720
Enrollment: 1,724 Coed
Affiliation or Control: Independent Non-Profit IRS Status: 501(c)3
Highest Offering: Doctorate
Accreditation: M, IACBE, NURSE, OT, PTA, SW

00 Chancellor Sr. Kathleen SULLIVAN
01 President Sr. Mary Eileen O'BRIEN
100 Special Asst to the President Ms. Denise MCLAUGHLIN
04 Exec Assistant to the President Dr. Elena MURPHY
05 Vice Pres Academic Affairs Dr. Thomas S. NOWAK
84 Vice Pres Enrollment Management Mr. Brian FERNANDES
10 Vice Pres Financial Affairs/CFO Mr. Anthony CIPOLLA
111 Vice Pres Inst Advancement Mr. Joseph VALENTI
32 Vice Pres Student Development Mr. John BURKE
09 Dir Inst Research/Plng/Assessment Mr. Fredric COHEN
20 Assistant Academic Dean Dr. Kevin HERMBERG
20 Assistant Academic Dean Dr. Daphne ESTWICK
76 Division Dir Allied Health Dr. Pamela STORY
50 Division Dir Business Admin Mr. Ivan RUDOLPH-SHABINSKY
79 Division Dir Humanities Dr. Kathleen HICKEY
81 Division Dir Math & Sciences Dr. Jennifer SASSANO
66 Division Dir Nursing Dr. Nancy DIDONA
83 Division Dir Social Sciences Dr. Christopher LIBERTINI
53 Division Dir Teacher Education Dr. Diane DISPAGNA
08 Head Librarian Ms. Mary-Elizabeth SCHAUB
07 Director of Admissions Ms. Emma FORTUNATO
06 Registrar Ms. Mary MCFADDEN
37 Director Financial Aid Ms. Stacy SALINAS
21 Controller Mr. Kenneth FLUG
113 Bursar Ms. Elizabeth FONTES
15 Director Human Resources Ms. Lisa KAYAL
96 Director of Purchasing Mr. Peter PABON
13 Exec Dir Info Technology/CIO Mr. Russell DIAZ
19 Director Public Safety/Security Mr. John LENNON
18 Manager Facilities/Physical Plant Mr. Agron GASHI
30 Dir Annual Giv/Parent & Alumni Rels Ms. Joanne SORACE
41 Athletic Director Mr. Joseph CLINTON
42 Director Campus Ministry Sr. Barbara MCENEANY
36 Director Career Development Vacant
26 Director Communications Ms. Susan CERRA
27 Dir Marketing/Communications Svcs Mr. Brett BEKRITSKY
31 Dir Cmty Engagemt/Ldrship Devel Ms. Dana MCSTOWE
38 Director Counseling Ms. Alise COHEN
39 Director Residential Life Mr. Joseph DRATCH
35 Director Student Activities Ms. Rachel MCGINTY

Dutchess Community College (B)

53 Pendell Road, Poughkeepsie NY 12601-1595
County: Dutchess FICE Identification: 002864
Unit ID: 190840
Telephone: (845) 431-8000 Carnegie Class: Assoc/HT-Mix Trad/Non
FAX Number: (845) 431-8984 Calendar System: Semester
URL: www.sunydutchess.edu
Established: 1957 Annual Undergrad Tuition & Fees (In-District): $4,896
Enrollment: 8,034 Coed
Affiliation or Control: State/Local IRS Status: 501(c)3
Highest Offering: Associate Degree
Accreditation: M, ADNUR, EMT, MLTAD

01 President Dr. Peter G. JORDAN
32 Dean of Student Services Dr. Colleen M. TROGISCH
10 VP & Dean of Administration Dr. Ellen M. GAMBINO
05 Dean of Academic Affairs Ms. Maria F. BOADA
20 Associate Dean of Academic Affairs Dr. Susan ROGERS
20 Acting Assoc Dean of Academic Affs Dr. Angela L. RIOS
31 Assoc VP & Dean Comm Svcs Spec Pgms Vacant
21 Associate VP Administration Ms. Donna ROCAP
06 Registrar Ms. Angela ROMANO
84 Assoc Dean Stdnt Svcs/Enrollment Mr. Michael ROE
08 Director of the Library Ms. Bonnie GALLAGHER
111 Exec Dir Institutional Advancement Ms. Diana POLLARD
09 Director Planning/Inst Research Mr. Scott SCHNACKENBERG
37 Director Financial Aid Mr. Robert ZASSO
38 Director Counseling Dr. Mark BALABAN
15 Interim Director of Human Resources Ms. Ruth SPENCER
18 Assoc VP of Admin Facilities Mgmt Ms. Bridgette ANDERSON
19 Chief of Campus Safety & Security Ms. Nilda HOFFMAN
13 Acting Assoc Dean Admin Info Tech Mr. Michael SOLTISH
35 Director of Student Life Vacant
26 Director of Marketing/Social Media Ms. Gail GLOVER
106 Dir of Instrctional Tech/e-Learning Ms. Chrisie MITCHELL
88 Director of Scheduling Ms. Danielle WILLIAMS
12 Director DCC Fishkill Branch Mr. Timothy DECKER
04 Exec Assistant to the President Ms. AnneMarie ANDREWS
101 Exec Asst to the Board of Trustees Ms. Linda M. BEASIMER
39 Director Residence Life Ms. Kaitlin YOUNG
25 Chief Contract/Grants Administrator Mr. Martin SCHNEIDER
28 Chief Diversity Officer Ms. Jackie GOFFE-MCNISH
96 Director of Purchasing Mr. Thomas DUFFY

D'Youville College (C)

320 Porter Avenue, Buffalo NY 14201-1084
County: Erie FICE Identification: 002712
Unit ID: 190716
Telephone: (716) 829-8000 Carnegie Class: DU-Mod
FAX Number: (716) 829-7820 Calendar System: Semester
URL: www.dyc.edu
Established: 1908 Annual Undergrad Tuition & Fees: $28,886
Enrollment: 2,785 Coed
Affiliation or Control: Independent Non-Profit IRS Status: 501(c)3
Highest Offering: Doctorate
Accreditation: M, ARCPA, CHIRO, DIETC, IACBE, NURSE, OT, PHAR, PTA

01 President Dr. Lorrie CLEMO
00 Chair of Board Mr. Joe COZZO
100 Chief of Staff Dr. Jason MACLEOD
05 VP for Academic Affairs Dr. Natalia BLANK
10 Chief Financial Officer Ms. Karen COSTA
84 VP Enrollment Management Mr. Shabeer H. AMIRALI
45 VP Inst Effectiveness & Planning Mr. Joggeshwar DAS
18 VP of Operations Mr. Nathan MARTON
111 VP of Institutional Advancement Ms. Kimberly PIETRO
88 Chief Mission Officer Dr. Denise DIRIENZO
66 Dean School of Nursing Dr. Deborah GARRISON
32 Chief Student Affairs Officer Mr. Benjamin GRANT
67 Dean School of Pharmacy Dr. Canio MARASCO
76 Dean School of Health Professions Dr. Lisa RAFALSON
106 Dean of Online Learning Dr. Jeremiah GRABOWSKI
21 Controller Ms. Taylor PARKER
88 Executive Director Kavinoky Theatre Ms. Loraine O'DONNELL
13 Director Information Technology Mr. Joseph GUNNELLS
06 Registrar Mr. Daryl SMITH
09 Dir Inst Rsrch/Assessment Support Dr. Henry BOATENG
121 Dir of Stdnt Success/Academic Advis Ms. Stephanie ATTI
124 Director of Student Retention Mr. Ryan MILLER
35 Assoc Student Affairs Officer Ms. Danielle NESSELBUSH
41 Director Athletics Ms. Ona HALLADAY
36 Director Career Services Center Ms. Christine DEMCIE
15 Director of Human Resources Ms. Tammy MASTON
88 Dir of HEOP & Transfer Services Ms. Christina SPINK-FORMANSKI
08 Director of the Library Mr. Rand BELLAVIA
26 Director of Marketing Ms. Jamie ADAMS
19 Director Security Mr. Keith BOVA
37 Director Financial Aid Ms. Nitasha SETH
88 Director of Veteran Affairs Mr. Mark MARTINEZ
96 Director of Purchasing Ms. Tammy DISTEFANO

Eisek HaTorah D'Rachmistrivka (D)

60 Sunset Avenue, Staten Island NY 10314
County: Richmond Identification: 667435
Telephone: (718) 438-5040 Carnegie Class: Not Classified
FAX Number: N/A Calendar System: Semester
URL: eisek.org
Established: Annual Undergrad Tuition & Fees: N/A
Enrollment: N/A Male
Affiliation or Control: Independent Non-Profit IRS Status: 501(c)3
Highest Offering: First Talmudic Degree
Accreditation: AIJS

Elim Bible Institute and College (E)

7245 College Street, Lima NY 14485
County: Livingston Identification: 667245
Unit ID: 488305
Telephone: (585) 582-1230 Carnegie Class: Spec 2-yr-Other
FAX Number: (585) 582-8130 Calendar System: Semester
URL: www.elim.edu
Established: 1924 Annual Undergrad Tuition & Fees: $9,980
Enrollment: 103 Coed
Affiliation or Control: Independent Non-Profit IRS Status: 501(c)3
Highest Offering: Baccalaureate
Accreditation: TRACS

01 President Dr. Fred ANTONELLI
03 Executive Vice President & Provost Dr. Danuta CASE
10 Chief Financial Officer Shaun FOWLER
11 VP of Business Affairs Andrew WEILER
07 Admissions Director Lisa WALDMAN
37 Financial Aid Director Shannon NGUYEN
06 Registrar Cana FUEST
108 IE Director Ashley ALLEN
35 Associate Dean of Students Cassandra WILHELM
73 Program Chair Dr. Daniel KAUTU
50 Program Chair Emily SANDERS
13 IT Director Jackson DAY
26 Marketing Director Leah WILSON
08 Head Librarian Rev. Brenda COLLIER
88 Campus Life Director Gabriel CEPEDA

The Elmezzi Graduate School of Molecular Medicine (F)

350 Community Drive, Manhasset NY 11030-3828
County: Nassau Identification: 666671
Unit ID: 486080
Telephone: (516) 562-3405 Carnegie Class: Spec-4-yr-Other Health
FAX Number: (516) 562-1022 Calendar System: Other
URL: https://www.northwell.edu/
Established: 1999 Annual Graduate Tuition & Fees: N/A
Enrollment: 9 Coed
Affiliation or Control: Independent Non-Profit IRS Status: 501(c)3
Highest Offering: Doctorate; No Undergraduates
Accreditation: NY

01 President Dr. Kevin J. TRACEY
03 Provost Dr. Bettie M. STEINBERG
05 Dean Dr. Annette LEE
20 Associate Dean Dr. Christine METZ
10 Chief Financial Officer Ms. Michele FRANKEL
11 Chief of Administration Ms. Emilia HRISTIS
19 Director Security/Safety Mr. Robert KIKEL
25 Director Contracts/Grants Admin Ms. Diane MARBURY

Elmira College (G)

One Park Place, Elmira NY 14901-2099
County: Chemung FICE Identification: 002718
Unit ID: 190983
Telephone: (607) 735-1800 Carnegie Class: Bac-Diverse
FAX Number: (607) 735-1758 Calendar System: Other
URL: www.elmira.edu
Established: 1855 Annual Undergrad Tuition & Fees: $36,228
Enrollment: 768 Coed
Affiliation or Control: Independent Non-Profit IRS Status: 501(c)3
Highest Offering: Master's
Accreditation: M, NUR

01 President Dr. Charles W. LINDSAY
10 VP of Finance and Administration Ms. Kathleen MCDERMOTT
05 Provost Dr. Patricia IRELAND
111 Vice Pres of Advancement Mr. Wade HART
32 VP Campus Life/Chief Retention Ofcr Dr. Elizabeth LAMBERT
09 Director of Institutional Research Vacant
26 VP of Communications & Marketing Ms. Jennifer L. SWAIN
84 VP of Enrollment Mr. W. Eric SYKES
20 Dean of Academic Affairs Vacant
37 Director of Financial Aid Mrs. Lorraine MOTHERSHED
06 Registrar Mr. Michael HALPERIN
58 Director of Graduate Studies Mr. Andrew STAGE
08 Dir of the Gannett-Tripp Library Ms. Margaret KAPPANADZE
41 Director of Athletics Ms. Rhonda FAUNCE
36 Career Svcs/Cmty Engagement Coord Ms. Melanie MOON
50 Chair of Business/Economics Dr. Alison WOLFE
79 Chair of Creative Arts/Humanities Dr. Mitchell R. LEWIS
81 Chair of Math/Natural Sciences Dr. Corey STILTS
83 Chair of Soc/Behavioral Science Dr. Christopher TERRY
53 Director of Teacher Education Dr. Stephanie JOHNSON
88 Dir of Comm Sciences/Disorders Dr. James BAER
66 Director of Nurse Education Dr. Milissa VOLINO
29 Director of Alumni Relations Ms. Ellen HIMMELREICH
39 Director of Residence Life Ms. Jaime PANOS
40 Operations Clerk Mr. David RUNDLE
15 AVP of Human Resources Ms. Jessica CARPENTER
13 Director of IT Mr. Thomas STEFFES
19 Director of Campus Safety Mr. Joseph KANE
112 Director of Major and Planned Gifts Vacant
44 Director of Annual Giving Ms. Lindsay BAKER
102 Director of Grants Mrs. Valerie R. ROSPLOCK
23 Director of Health Services Ms. Rachel MCEVOY
04 Exec Assistant to the President Mrs. Mary C. BARRETT
38 Director of Counseling Dr. Kevin MURPHY
90 Dir of Help Desk/User Services Ms. Charlotte ECHEVARRIA
96 Finance/Accounting Assistant Ms. Pat HUGHES
110 Director of Advancement Services Ms. Bailey KNAPSACK
30 Director of Development Ms. Angela FLEMING
121 Director of CAPE/Career Services Ms. Rachel REDMOND
07 Director of Admissions Mr. Patrick GILLETTE
18 Director of Campus Facilities Mr. Joshua CAMPBELL
21 Comptroller Mr. Kyle GILBERT
28 Dir of Diversity/Equity/Inclusion Mr. Larry PARKER
35 Assistant Dean of Students Ms. Jaime PANOS

Elyon College (H)

1400 West 6th Street, Brooklyn NY 11204
County: Kings Identification: 667290
Unit ID: 490346
Telephone: (718) 259-5600 Carnegie Class: Spec 2-yr-Other
FAX Number: (218) 259-8024 Calendar System: Trimester
URL: elyoncollege.org
Established: Annual Undergrad Tuition & Fees: $14,020
Enrollment: 47 Coed
Affiliation or Control: Independent Non-Profit IRS Status: 501(c)3
Highest Offering: Associate Degree
Accreditation: CNCE

01 President Rabbi Chaim A. WALDMAN
05 Dean Academic &Student Affairs Rabbi Samuel KOHN

Erie Community College (A)

121 Ellicott Street, Buffalo NY 14203-2698
County: Erie FICE Identification: 010684
Unit ID: 191083
Telephone: (716) 842-2770 Carnegie Class: Assoc/MT-VT-Mix Trad/Non
FAX Number: (716) 851-1129 Calendar System: Semester
URL: www.ecc.edu
Established: 1971 Annual Undergrad Tuition & Fees (In-District): $5,722
Enrollment: 8,364 Coed
Affiliation or Control: State/Local IRS Status: 501(c)3
Highest Offering: Associate Degree
Accreditation: M, ACFEI, ADNUR, CAHIIM, COARC, DH, DIETT, DT, EMT, MAC, MLTAD, OPD, OTA, RTT

01 President .... Dr. David BALKIN
111 EVP Inst Advancement & Efficiency .... Vacant
11 EVP Administration & Finance .... Vacant
05 Int Provost/EVP Academic Affs .... Dr. Adiam TSEGAI
84 Vice President Enrollment Mgmt .... Vacant
32 VP Student Affairs .... Vacant
35 Dean of Students City .... Ms. Petrina HILL-CHEATOM
35 Dean of Students North .... Mr. Jason PERRI
35 Dean of Students South .... Ms. Amy YODER
13 Interim Chief Information Officer .... Mr. Scott ERMER
76 Vice Provost Health Sciences .... Vacant
14 Director of ERP Sys & Info Svcs .... Mr. David L. ARLINGTON
18 Vice President Facilities/Security .... Mr. Mark PACHOLEC
109 Coordinator Institutional Services .... Mr. Joel J. DAMIANI
15 Associate Vice Pres Human Resources ... Ms. Tracey CLEVELAND
16 Employee Relations Manager .... Vacant
49 Dean Liberal Arts & Science North .... Vacant
49 Dean Liberal Arts & Science South .... Ms. Joanne COLMERAUER
50 Dean Business/Public Service .... Mr. Juan MARTINEZ
56 Dir Dist Learning/Alternative Pgms .... Mr. Patrick RYAN
72 Dean Engineering/Technology .... Ms. Adiam TSEGAI
28 Chief Diversity Officer .... Ms. Tracey ARCHIE
06 Director of Registration .... Vacant
07 Director of Admissions .... Mr. Philip STRUEBEL
08 Librarian City .... Ms. Kathleen POWERS
08 Librarian North .... Mr. Matthew BEST
08 Librarian South .... Ms. Taheera SHAHEED-SONUBI
40 Bookstore Manager City .... Ms. Susan SCHMITTENDORF
40 Bookstore Manager North .... Ms. Teresa KALINOWSKI
40 Bookstore Manager South .... Mr. Michael FOX
23 Health Services Nurse South .... Ms. Frances WILLIAMS
23 Health Services Nurse North .... Ms. Lisa GRAZIANO
23 Health Services Nurse City .... Ms. Kelly ROCKWELL
36 Career Resource Center Director .... Ms. Katherine MARSHALL
09 Director Institutional Research .... Ms. Marlene ARNO
45 Vice Provost .... Dr. Fabio ESCOBAR
27 Exec Dir of Marketing/Communication .... Ms. Paula SANDY
41 Director of Athletics .... Mr. Steven MULLEN
37 Director of Financial Aid .... Mr. Scott WELTJEN
21 Business Manager .... Mr. Paul F. DANIEU
24 Audio Visual Coordinator City .... Mr. Mark DZIELSKI
24 Audio Visual Coordinator North .... Mr. Ryan NOGLE
24 Audio Visual Coordinator North .... Mr. Nicholas SONRICKER
24 Audio Visual Coordinator South .... Mr. David SEIFERT
103 Coordinator of Corporate Training .... Vacant
25 Grants Coordinator .... Mr. Michael J. BIGGANE
29 Coordinator of Alumni Affairs .... Ms. Sarah LASKY
22 Dir of Student Access/Veteran Affs .... Mr. Daniel FRONTERA
88 Advanced Studies Coordinator .... Ms. Deborah F. SCHMITT

Excelsior College (B)

7 Columbia Circle, Albany NY 12203-5159
County: Albany FICE Identification: 002834
Unit ID: 196680
Telephone: (518) 464-8500 Carnegie Class: Masters/L
FAX Number: (518) 464-8777 Calendar System: Other
URL: www.excelsior.edu
Established: 1971 Annual Undergrad Tuition & Fees: N/A
Enrollment: 21,974 Coed
Affiliation or Control: Independent Non-Profit IRS Status: 501(c)3
Highest Offering: Master's
Accreditation: M, ADNUR, IACBE, NUR

01 President .... Dr. David SCHEJBAL
43 Deputy Counsel .... Mr. Michael DISIENA
05 Provost/VP Academic Affairs .... Dr. John CARON
10 VP Finance/CFO .... Mr. Richard HANNMANN
11 Chief Operating Officer .... Mr. James LETTKO
117 Exec Dir of Risk Management .... Ms. Holly ROGERS
13 Chief Technology Officer .... Mr. Saul MORSE
15 VP Human Resources .... Mr. Mark HOWE
46 AVP Analytics/Decision Support .... Dr. Lisa DANIELS
108 Exec Dir Outcomes Assessment .... Mr. Andre FOISY
21 Controller .... Ms. Hillary KOLDIN
97 Dean of Undergraduate Studies .... Dr. Catherine SEAVER
66 Dean of Nursing .... Dr. Mary Lee POLLARD
58 Dean of Graduate Studies .... Dr. Scott DOLAN
88 Ombudsperson .... Ms. Kathy MORAN
88 Exec Dir of Test Development .... Ms. Mika HOFFMAN
26 Chief Marketing/Bus Dev Officer .... Ms. Dawn GERRAIN
91 Deputy CIO of Enterprise Systems .... Mr. Donn AIKEN
88 Exec Dir Enterprise Ops .... Mr. Dan MERKT
88 Director of Creative Services .... Ms. Maria SPARKS
28 Diversity Coordinator .... Ms. Toby HAMLIN
37 Exec Dir Financial Aid .... Ms. Susan MERCHANT
14 Chief Operations Officer for IT .... Ms. Andrea LALA
88 Exec Dir of Enterprise Apps Support .... Mr. Jim WALL
88 Exec Director Transcript Analysis .... Ms. Kat MCGRATH
07 Exec Director of Admissions .... Ms. Patti HOEG
101 Asst to Pres for Trustee .... Ms. Laurie KEENAN

Fashion Institute of Technology (C)

Seventh Avenue at 27 Street, New York NY 10001-5992
County: New York FICE Identification: 002866
Unit ID: 191126
Telephone: (212) 217-7999 Carnegie Class: Masters/S
FAX Number: N/A Calendar System: Semester
URL: www.fitnyc.edu
Established: 1944 Annual Undergrad Tuition & Fees (In-District): $5,913
Enrollment: 8,191 Coed
Affiliation or Control: State/Local IRS Status: 501(c)3
Highest Offering: Master's
Accreditation: M, ACBSP, ART, CIDA

01 President .... Dr. Joyce F. BROWN
10 Treasurer/VP Finance/Administration .... Ms. Sherry F. BRABHAM
101 Secy of College/General Counsel .... Mr. Stephen P. TUTTLE
05 Interim Vice Pres, Academic Affairs .... Dr. Yasemin JONES
26 Vice Pres Comm/External Rels ... Ms. Loretta LAWRENCE KEANE
84 VP Enrollment/Student Success .... Ms. Catherine O'ROURKE
15 VP Human Res Mgmt/Labor Rels .... Dr. Cynthia M. GLASS
30 VP Advancement/Exec Dir FIT Fdn .... Mr. Philips R. MCCARTY
13 Acting VP of Information Technology .... Mr. Laurence A. BAACH
88 Deputy to Pres Industry/Partnership .... Ms. Joanne ARBUCKLE
100 Deputy to the President .... Ms. Jennifer LOTURCO
28 Chief Diversity Officer .... Dr. Ronald A. MILON
45 Acting Exec Dir Strategic Planning .... Ms. Jacqueline JENKINS
88 Associate General Counsel .... Mr. Eric ODIN
20 Assoc VP, Acad Affairs Operations .... Mr. Sidney A. GRIMES
20 Interim Assoc VP Academic Affairs .... Dr. Deborah KLESENSKI-RISPOLI
21 Assoc Vice Pres, Finance & Admin .... Mr. Bayard KING
27 Assistant VP Comm/External Rels .... Ms. Carol LEVEN
14 AVP Business Intelligence .... Doris BERGER
88 Asst VP Enrollment Management .... Mr. Terence PEAVY
32 Asst VP Student Success/Dean Stdnts .... Dr. Shadia A. SACHEDINA
119 AVP & Chief Info Security Officer .... Mr. Walter KERNER
58 Interim Dean, Graduate Studies .... Dr. Brooke CARLSON
50 Dean School Business & Technology .... Ms. Shannon MAHER
49 Dean School of Liberal Arts .... Dr. Patrick KNISLEY
104 Dean for International Education .... Dr. Deirdre C. SATO
51 Exec Dir Continuing & Prof Studies .... Mr. Daniel GERGER
57 Dean School of Art & Design .... Mr. Troy RICHARDS
121 Assoc Dean Student Acad Support .... Dr. Tardis JOHNSON
88 Acting Associate Dean Art & Design .... Ms. Melanie REIM
09 Asst Dean Inst Research & Effect .... Dr. Darrell GLENN
20 Asst Dean Curriculum & Instruction .... Ms. Deborah KLESENSKI-RISPOLI
35 Assistant Dean of Students .... Ms. Suzanne MCGILLICUDDY
88 Assistant Dean for International Ed .... Dr. Helen GAUDETTE
08 Acting Director G Marcus Library .... Ms. Greta EARNEST
88 Director of The Museum at FIT .... Dr. Valerie STEELE
88 Exec Dir FIT/Infor DTech Lab .... Mr. Michael FERRARO
18 Executive Director of Facilities .... Mr. George JEFREMOW
108 Exec Dir Management Analysis .... Mr. Joseph IANNINI
07 Director of Admissions .... Mr. Richard S. SUNDAY
22 Affirmative Action Officer .... Ms. Deliwe KEKANE
38 Director Counseling Center .... Dr. Susan BRETON
39 Director of Residential Life .... Ms. Christina DIGGS
37 Acting Director of Financial Aid .... Mr. Barry FISCHER
06 Director of Registration & Records .... Ms. Rita CAMMARATA
36 Director Career & Internship Svcs .... Mr. Frantz L. ALCINDOR
35 Director of Student Life .... Ms. Michelle VAN-ESS
19 Director of Public Safety .... Mr. Mario CABRERA
86 Director Govt & Community Relations .... Ms. Lisa WAGER
41 Director Athletics & Recreation .... Mr. Keith HERON
96 Director of Budget .... Ms. Nancy SU
88 Dir of Educational Opportunity Pgms .... Ms. Taur D. ORANGE
21 Controller .... Ms. Shelci GRAHAM
88 Dir Envir Health/Safety Compliance .... Mr. Paul DEBIASE
29 Dir Alumni Engagement/Giving/Fndn .... Ms. Amy GARAWITZ
105 Manager Digital Strategy .... Ms. Taryn REJHOLEC
55 Dir Evening/Weekend/Pre-College Pgm .... Ms. Michele NAGEL
96 Director of Procurement Services .... Mr. Walter WINTER
85 Acting Director, Intl Student Svcs .... Ms. Marie MEKARI
90 Director Educ Tech/Desktop Svcs .... Ms. Meredith PERKINS
106 Director Online Learning .... Ms. Tamara CUPPLES
16 Director, Employee & Labor Relns .... Ms. Esther OLIVERAS
92 Exec Dir President'l Scholars Pgm .... Ms. Yasemin C. LEVINE
88 Director of Policy and Compliance .... Ms. Griselda GONZALEZ
116 Internal Auditor .... Mr. Harold LEDERMAN
04 Assistant to the President .... Ms. Beverly SOLOCHEK
04 Special Assistant to the President ..... Ms. Alin BABASOLOUKIAN

Fei Tian College (D)

140 Galley Hill Road, Cuddebackville NY 12729
County: Orange Identification: 667205
Telephone: (845) 672-0550 Carnegie Class: Not Classified
FAX Number: (845) 977-0481 Calendar System: Semester
URL: www.feitian.edu
Established: Annual Undergrad Tuition & Fees: N/A
Enrollment: N/A Coed
Affiliation or Control: Independent Non-Profit IRS Status: 501(c)3
Highest Offering: Baccalaureate
Accreditation: NY

01 President .... Ms. Vina LEE

Finger Lakes Community College (E)

3325 Marvin Sands Drive, Canandaigua NY 14424-8405
County: Ontario FICE Identification: 007532
Unit ID: 191199
Telephone: (585) 394-3522 Carnegie Class: Assoc/HT-High Non
FAX Number: (585) 394-5005 Calendar System: Semester
URL: www.flcc.edu
Established: 1965 Annual Undergrad Tuition & Fees (In-District): $5,534
Enrollment: 5,640 Coed
Affiliation or Control: State/Local IRS Status: 501(c)3
Highest Offering: Associate Degree
Accreditation: M, ADNUR

01 President .... Dr. Robert NYE
05 Provost/VP Academic & Student Affs .... Ms. Cassy KENT
10 Vice President of Admin/Finance .... Mr. Ken MOSTENBOCKER
84 Vice Pres Enrollment Management .... Ms. Carol S. URBAITIS
32 Assoc Vice Pres of Student Affairs .... Ms. Sarah WHIFFEN
108 VP Strategic Init/Assessment .... Ms. Debora ORTLOFF
20 Assoc VP Instruction & Assessment .... Dr. Beth JOHNSON
15 Chief Human Resources Officer .... Ms. Michelle POLOWCHAK
111 Chief Advancement Officer .... Mr. Louis NOCE
19 Dir Campus Security Ops/Act Chf Pol ..... Mr. Matthew MCGRATH
21 Controller .... Ms. Christine PALACE-NEININGER
18 Director of Facilities & Grounds .... Ms. Catherine AHERN
07 Director of Admissions .... Mr. Matthew STEVER
06 Registrar/AVP Enrollment Mgmt .... Mr. Michael FISHER
37 Director of Financial Aid .... Ms. Megan KENNERKNECHT
35 Director of Student Life .... Ms. Jennie ERDLE
13 Chief Information Officer .... Mr. Edward KELTY
38 Dir Educ Planning/Career Services .... Ms. Mehegan MURPHY
36 Career Services Coordinator .... Ms. Tammie WOODY
08 Director Library Learning Resources .... Ms. Sarah MOON
26 Director of Marketing .... Ms. Christen ACCARDI
23 Director of Student Health Services .... Ms. Janette ARUCK
24 Dir Instructional Technology .... Vacant
29 Director of Alumni Relations .... Mr. Justin KUCZMA
72 Chair Science & Technology .... Ms. Jennifer CARNEY
50 Chair Business .... Mr. Patrick RAE
65 Chair Environment Conservation Hort .... Mr. John FOUST
57 Chair Visual/Performing Arts .... Mr. Richard COOK
66 Chair Nursing .... Ms. Heather REECE-TILLACK
68 Chair Physical Education .... Mr. Eric MARSH
81 Chair Computer Science .... Mr. William MCLAUGHLIN
79 Chair Humanities .... Ms. Maureen MASS-FEARY
83 Chair Social Science .... Mr. Joshua W. HELLER
81 Chair Mathematics .... Ms. Theresa GAUTHIER
09 Director of Institutional Research .... Ms. Debora ORTLOFF
103 Director Workforce Development .... Mr. Todd SLOANE
106 Director of Online Learning .... Mr. Ryan MCCABE
28 Chief Diversity Officer .... Mr. Sim COVINGTON
04 Admin Assistant to the President .... Ms. Penny HAMILTON
30 Director of Development .... Ms. Brie CHUPALIO
41 Athletic Director .... Ms. Samantha BOCCACINO

Finger Lakes Health College of Nursing and Health Sciences (F)

196 North Street, Geneva NY 14456
County: Ontario Identification: 667154
Unit ID: 475422
Telephone: (315) 787-4005 Carnegie Class: Spec 2-yr-Health
FAX Number: (313) 787-4275 Calendar System: Semester
URL: www.flhcon.edu
Established: 2008 Annual Undergrad Tuition & Fees: $12,690
Enrollment: 115 Coed
Affiliation or Control: Independent Non-Profit IRS Status: 501(c)3
Highest Offering: Associate Degree
Accreditation: ABHES, ADNUR, PNUR

01 Interim Dean .... Kathy MILLS
32 Student Services Coordinator .... Ann SPAYD

Five Towns College (G)

305 North Service Road, Dix Hills NY 11746-6055
County: Suffolk FICE Identification: 012561
Unit ID: 191205
Telephone: (631) 656-2157 Carnegie Class: Spec-4-yr-Arts
FAX Number: (631) 656-2172 Calendar System: Semester
URL: www.ftc.edu
Established: 1972 Annual Undergrad Tuition & Fees: $25,595
Enrollment: 632 Coed
Affiliation or Control: Proprietary IRS Status: Proprietary
Highest Offering: Doctorate
Accreditation: M, CAEPN, MUS, THEA

01 President .... Dr. David COHEN
05 Provost .... Ms. Carolann MILLER
10 Vice Pres Finance/Administration .... Mr. Hubert STACHURA
32 Dean of Students .... Ms. Angela JASUR
06 Registrar .... Mr. Eric FARAHANI
37 Director of Financial Aid .... Mr. Jason LABONTE
08 Library Director .... Mr. John VANSTEEN
38 College Counselor .... Mr. Randy GEIBEL
64 Chair of Music Division .... Dr. Jill MILLER-THORN
50 Chair of Business Division .... Ms. Kate KIMMEL
49 Chair of Liberal Arts Division .... Dr. Jennifer DARDZINSKI
53 Chair of Music Education Department .... Dr. Margaret THIELE
57 Chair of Theatre Arts .... Dr. David KRASNER

36 Director Student Placement .... Ms. Krysti O'ROURKE
18 Interim Director of Facilities .... Mr. Russell ROXBURGH
19 Interim Director of Public Safety .... Mr. Brandon MORAN
39 Director of Residential Life .... Mr. Thomas O'BOYLE
07 Interim Director of Admissions .... Ms. Maureen WALTON
09 Director of Institutional Research .... Dr. Joshua DINSMAN
13 Chief Information Technology Office .... Mr. Craig HEALY
41 Athletic Director .... Mr. Matthew GUERCIO

Fordham University (A)

441 East Fordham Road, Bronx NY 10458-9993
County: Bronx FICE Identification: 002722
Unit ID: 191241
Telephone: (718) 817-1000 Carnegie Class: DU-Higher
FAX Number: (718) 817-4925 Calendar System: Semester
URL: www.fordham.edu
Established: 1841 Annual Undergrad Tuition & Fees: $56,161
Enrollment: 16,364 Coed
Affiliation or Control: Independent Non-Profit IRS Status: 501(c)3
Highest Offering: Doctorate
Accreditation: M, CLPSY, COPSY, LAW, MPCAC, SCPSY, SW

01 President .... Ms. Tania TETLOW
100 Assoc VP Pres Operations .... Mrs. Dorothy MARINUCCI
04 Asst Univ Sec/Spec Asst to Pres .... Dr. Michael R. TREROTOLA
05 Provost/SVP .... Dr. Dennis C. JACOBS
10 SVP/CFO and Treasurer .... Ms. Martha K. HIRST
32 Sr Vice President Student Affairs .... Mr. Jeffrey L. GRAY
84 Vice Pres Enrollment .... Mr. John W. BUCKLEY
21 Vice President for Finance .... Mr. Nicholas B. MILOWSKI
13 Vice President and CIO .... Mr. Anand PADMANABHAN
12 Vice President for Lincoln Center .... Mr. Frank SIMIO
30 Vice President for Development .... Mr. Roger A. MILICI, JR.
88 Vice President for Mission .... Rev. John CECERO, S.J.
11 Vice President for Administration .... Mr. Marco VALERA
15 Vice President for HR .... Ms. Kay TURNER
43 General Counsel/Sec of University .... Ms. Margaret T. BALL
20 Vice Provost .... Dr. Jonathan CRYSTAL
20 Assoc Vice Pres Academic Affairs .... Dr. Benjamin CROOKER
20 Assoc Vice Pres Academic Affairs .... Dr. Ellen FAHEY-SMITH
28 CDO/AVP Academic Affairs .... Mr. Rafael ZAPATA
20 Assoc Vice Pres Academic Affairs .... Dr. Ron JACOBSON
29 AVP/Director of Alumni Relations .... Mr. Michael GRIFFIN
06 Asst Vice Pres Enrollment/Registrar .... Dr. Gene FEIN
86 Assoc Vice Pres for Government Rels .... Ms. Lesley A. MASSIAH-ARTHUR
35 Assoc VP Student Affairs .... Ms. Michele BURRIS
35 Asst VP and Dean of Students .... Mr. Christopher RODGERS
35 Asst VP/Dean of Student Services .... Mr. Keith ELDREDGE
35 Dean of Students LC .... Dr. Jenifer CAMPBELL
12 Dean Fordham College at Rose Hill .... Dr. Maura B. MAST
49 AVP Arts & Sci Educ/Dean A&S Fac .... Dr. Eva BADOWSKA
58 Dean Grad Arts and Sciences .... Vacant
73 Interim Dean Religious Education .... Rev. Francis X. MCALOON, S.J.
50 Int Dean Gabelli School Business .... Dr. Lerzan AKSOY
107 Dean Sch of Prof and Cont Studies .... Dr. Anthony R. DAVIDSON
12 Dean Fordham College LC .... Dr. Laura AURICCHIO
53 Dean Graduate Education LC .... Dr. Jose Luis ALVARADO
61 Dean School of Law LC .... Mr. Matthew DILLER
70 Dean Graduate Social Service LC .... Dr. Debra MCPHEE
09 Director Institutional Research .... Dr. Jeannine PINTO
42 Executive Director Campus Ministry .... Rev. Jose-Luis SALAZAR, S.J.
21 Assoc Vice Pres/Controller .... Mr. Anthony GRONO
19 AVP Public Safety .... Mr. Robert FITZER
22 Title IX Coordinator .... Mr. Kareem PEAT
46 Chief Research Officer/AVP .... Dr. Z. George HONG
08 Director of University Libraries .... Ms. Linda LOSCHIAVO
23 Director of Health Center .... Ms. Maureen KEOWN
88 Asst Dean Student Involvement .... Dr. Catharine A. MCGLADE
88 AVP of Athletic Alumni Relations .... Mr. Francis X. MCLAUGHLIN
96 Director of Strategic Sourcing .... Vacant
38 Director of Psychological Svcs .... Dr. Jeffrey NG
28 Asst Dean/Dir Multicultural Affairs .... Mr. Juan Carlos MATOS
36 Director Career Services .... Ms. Annette MCLAUGHLIN
39 Asst Dean/Dir Residential Life .... Mr. Charles R. CLENCY
07 Dean of Admission .... Dr. Patricia PEEK
41 Interim Athletic Director .... Mr. Edward KULL
26 Asst VP Communications .... Mr. Bob HOWE

Fulton-Montgomery Community College (B)

2805 State Highway 67, Johnstown NY 12095-3790
County: Montgomery FICE Identification: 002867
Unit ID: 191302
Telephone: (518) 736-3622 Carnegie Class: Assoc/HT-High Trad
FAX Number: (518) 762-5693 Calendar System: Semester
URL: www.fmcc.edu
Established: 1963 Annual Undergrad Tuition & Fees (In-District): $5,718
Enrollment: 1,946 Coed
Affiliation or Control: State/Local IRS Status: 501(c)3
Highest Offering: Associate Degree
Accreditation: M, ADNUR, RAD

01 President .... Dr. Greg TRUCKENMILLER
05 Provost/VP Acad/Stdnt Affairs .... Ms. Diana PUTNAM
32 Assoc Provost Acad/Stdnt Affairs .... Dr. Jacqueline SNYDER
20 Associate Dean of Acad/Stdnt Affs .... Mr. Daniel FOGARTY
35 Associate Dean .... Ms. Arlene SPENCER
18 Director of Facilities .... Mr. Paul MARSHALL
07 Associate Dean for Admissions .... Ms. Laura LAPORTE
113 Bursar .... Mr. Jared DEMAGISTRIS
15 Human Resources Manager .... Ms. Connie GRANT
06 Registrar .... Mr. Scott COLLINS
08 Librarian .... Mr. Daniel TOWNE
36 Director of Career Planning .... Ms. Andrea SCRIBNER
121 Director of Advisement .... Ms. Mary-Jo FERRAUILO-DAVIS
30 Chief Development .... Ms. Lesley LANZI
37 Coordinator Financial Aid .... Ms. Rebecca COZZOCREA
04 Administrative Asst to President .... Ms. Diane BOSLET
19 Director of Public Safety .... Mr. Mark PIERCE
41 Athletic Director .... Mr. Kevin JONES
13 Chief Information Officer .... Mr. Romeyn PRESCOTT
10 Chief Financial/Business Officer .... Ms. Chasity HULSAVER

General Theological Seminary (C)

440 West 21st Street, New York NY 10011-2981
County: New York FICE Identification: 002726
Unit ID: 191320
Telephone: (212) 243-5150 Carnegie Class: Spec-4-yr-Faith
FAX Number: (212) 727-3907 Calendar System: Semester
URL: www.gts.edu
Established: 1817 Annual Graduate Tuition & Fees: N/A
Enrollment: 56 Coed
Affiliation or Control: Protestant Episcopal IRS Status: 501(c)3
Highest Offering: Master's; No Undergraduates
Accreditation: THEOL

01 Acting Dean and President .... Rev Dr. Michael DELASHMUTT
111 VP for Institutional Advancement .... Ms. Donna ASHLEY
05 Asst Dean of Acad Adm & Registrar .... Ms. Jamie TAN
15 Director of HR & Financial Aid .... Ms. Trecia O'SULLIVAN
30 Director of Development .... Mr. Jonathan SILVER

† Affiliated with Virginia Theological Seminary, Alexandria VA.

Genesee Community College (D)

One College Road, Batavia NY 14020-9704
County: Genesee FICE Identification: 006782
Unit ID: 191339
Telephone: (585) 343-0055 Carnegie Class: Assoc/MT-VT-Mix Trad/Non
FAX Number: (585) 343-4541 Calendar System: Semester
URL: www.genesee.edu
Established: 1966 Annual Undergrad Tuition & Fees (In-District): $5,040
Enrollment: 4,735 Coed
Affiliation or Control: State/Local IRS Status: 501(c)3
Highest Offering: Associate Degree
Accreditation: M, ADNUR, COARC, PTAA

01 President .... Dr. James SUNSER
05 Provost/VP Academic Affairs .... Dr. Craig LAMB
81 Dean Math/Science/Career Education .... Dr. Rafael ALICEA-MALDONADO
83 Dean Human Communication/Behavior .... Mr. Timothy TOMCZAK
56 Dean of Distributed Learning .... Mr. Ed LEVINSTEIN
20 Director Accelerated Col Enrol Pgms .... Ms. Ann VALENTO
06 Registrar .... Ms. Karlyn BACKUS
57 Director Fine & Performing Arts .... Ms. Maryanne ARENA
68 Director of Health & Physical Educ .... Ms. Rebecca DZIEKAN
10 VP for Finance & Operations .... Ms. Gina WEAVER
09 Assoc VP Inst Rsrch & Assessment .... Ms. Carol MARRIOTT
15 Executive Director Human Resources .... Ms. Christa ALDRICH
88 Director Business Skills Training .... Mr. John MCGOWAN
21 Controller .... Ms. Kristin L. YUNKER
13 VP/Chief Information Officer .... Mr. Nikolas VARRONE
18 Director of Buildings & Grounds .... Mr. Levi OLSEN
32 VP for Student & Enrollment Svcs .... Dr. Shelitha WILLIAMS
35 Dean of Students .... Ms. Patricia CHAYA
07 Assistant Dean of Admissions .... Ms. Lyndsay GERHARDT
37 Director of Financial Aid .... Mr. Joseph A. BAILEY
124 Dir of Student Engagement & Inclus .... Ms. Kelly STARCHOK
41 Director of Athletics .... Ms. Kristen SCHUTH
30 VP Devel & External Affairs .... Mr. Justin JOHNSTON
04 Administrative Asst to President .... Ms. Bethany ARADINE
19 Director Security/Safety .... Mr. Stephen WISE
08 Chief Library Officer .... Ms. Jessica HIBBARD

Glasgow Caledonian New York College (E)

64 Wooster Street, New York NY 10012
County: New York Identification: 667340
Telephone: (646) 768-5300 Carnegie Class: Not Classified
FAX Number: N/A Calendar System: Semester
URL: www.gcnyc.com
Established: 2017 Annual Graduate Tuition & Fees: N/A
Enrollment: N/A Coed
Affiliation or Control: Independent Non-Profit IRS Status: 501(c)3
Highest Offering: Master's; No Undergraduates
Accreditation: M

01 President/Vice Chancellor .... Dr. Pamela GILLIES
05 Vice President/Provost .... Dr. Jacqueline LEBLANC
06 Registrar .... Mr. Stephen LOPEZ
11 Dir of Operations/Title IX Coord .... Ms. Jessica CHANG-RUSSELL
07 Dir Admissions/Recruitment .... Ms. Dominique STUDER

Hamilton College (F)

198 College Hill Road, Clinton NY 13323-1218
County: Oneida FICE Identification: 002728
Unit ID: 191515
Telephone: (315) 859-4011 Carnegie Class: Bac-A&S
FAX Number: (315) 859-4991 Calendar System: Semester
URL: www.hamilton.edu
Established: 1812 Annual Undergrad Tuition & Fees: $58,510
Enrollment: 1,902 Coed
Affiliation or Control: Independent Non-Profit IRS Status: 501(c)3
Highest Offering: Baccalaureate
Accreditation: M

01 President .... David WIPPMAN
05 VPAA/Dean of Faculty .... Suzanne KEEN
11 Vice Pres Administration/Finance .... Karen L. LEACH
111 Vice Pres Advancement .... Lori R. DENNISON
13 Vice Pres Information Technology .... Joseph SHELLEY
07 VP/Dean Admission & Financial Aid .... Monica C. INZER
32 Vice Pres/Dean of Students .... Terry MARTINEZ
26 VP Communications/Marketing .... Melissa RICHARDS
20 Associate Dean of Faculty .... Nathan GOODALE
20 Associate Dean of Faculty .... Penny YEE
41 Athletic Director .... Jonathan T. HIND
39 Director Residential Life .... Travis R. HILL
10 AVP of Finance and Controller .... Carol GABLE
08 Dir of Library/Info Technology .... Joe SHELLLEY
27 Sr Director Content Communications .... Stacey J. HIMMELBERGER
37 Director of Financial Aid .... K. Cameron FEIST
36 Exec Director of the Career Center .... Sam WELCH
06 Registrar .... Kristin M. FRIEDEL
15 Director of Human Resources .... Stephen STEMKOSKI
18 Associate VP for Facilities .... Roger F. WAKEMAN
19 Director of Campus Safety .... Frank COOTS
38 Director Counseling/Psych Services .... David WALDEN
42 Catholic Chaplain .... Peter EL HACHEM
24 Director Audiovisual Services .... Timothy J. HICKS
09 Director of Institutional Research .... Jasmine X. YANG
26 Associate VP of Communications .... Michael J. DEBRAGGIO
28 Chief Diversity Officer .... Terry M. MARTINEZ
29 Director Alumni Relations .... Sharon T. RIPPEY
96 Director of Procurement/Admin .... Lucy BURKE
40 Manager College Store .... Jennifer PHILLIPS
100 Chief of Staff .... Gillian M. KING

Hartwick College (G)

One Hartwick Drive, Oneonta NY 13820-1790
County: Otsego FICE Identification: 002729
Unit ID: 191533
Telephone: (607) 431-4000 Carnegie Class: Bac-A&S
FAX Number: (607) 431-4206 Calendar System: 4/1/4
URL: www.hartwick.edu
Established: 1797 Annual Undergrad Tuition & Fees: $48,364
Enrollment: 1,209 Coed
Affiliation or Control: Independent Non-Profit IRS Status: 501(c)3
Highest Offering: Master's
Accreditation: M, AAQEP, ART, MUS, NURSE

01 President .... Mr. Darren R. REISBERG
10 Vice President Finance/CFO .... Ms. Karen ZUILL
111 VP for College Advancement .... Ms. Paula Lee HOBSON
84 VP Enrollment Mgmt & Student Exper .... Ms. Karen MCGRATH
26 VP for Strategic Communications .... Mrs. Gail GLOVER
04 Exec Assistant to the President .... Ms. Lisa CORBETT
15 VP for HR/Inclusion & Compliance .... Ms. Suzanne JANITZ
29 Asst VP for Alumni Relations .... Ms. Megan GRAY
07 Int Asst VP for Admissions .... Mr. Ray TATUM
20 Asst Dean of Faculty .... Dr. Cherilyn LACY
39 Director Residence Life & Housing .... Dr. Colleen BUNN
06 Registrar .... Mr. Matthew SANFORD
08 Interim Director of Libraries .... Mr. David HEYDUK
13 Director Inst Info Systems Services .... Ms. Deb B. HILTS
91 Director Technologies Services .... Mr. Bryan DEL BENE
18 Director of Facilities Services .... Mr. Joseph MACK
41 Director of Athletics .... Mr. John CZARNECKI
38 Director of Counseling Services .... Mr. Gary ROBINSON
23 Director of Student Health Center .... Ms. Amy GARDNER
27 Marketing Communications Manager .... Mr. David LUBELL
12 Director Pine Lake Campus .... Ms. Erin TOAL
21 Asst VP for Finance/Controller .... Ms. Petrea DELBERTA
09 Director of Institutional Research .... Mr. J. R BJERKLIE
19 Director of Campus Safety .... Mr. Donald DEPASS
40 Manager of B&N Bookstore .... Mr. Frank WERDANN
102 Dir Foundation/Corporate Relations .... Ms. Lisa IANNELLO
105 Assoc Dir Comm for Web Services .... Ms. Stephanie BRUNETTA
108 Director Institutional Assessment .... Mr. Joseph BJERKLIE
37 Director of Financial Aid .... Mr. Brian BIRCH
44 Leadership Annual Giving Officer .... Mr. Tim RAIMY
112 Director of Planned Giving .... Ms. Patricia DOPAZO

Hebrew Union College-Jewish Institute of Religion (H)

1 West 4th Street, New York NY 10012-1186
County: New York FICE Identification: 004054
Unit ID: 203067
Telephone: (212) 674-5300 Carnegie Class: Spec-4-yr-Faith
FAX Number: (212) 388-1720 Calendar System: Semester
URL: www.huc.edu
Established: 1875 Annual Graduate Tuition & Fees: N/A
Enrollment: 335 Coed

Affiliation or Control: Jewish IRS Status: 501(c)3
Highest Offering: Doctorate; No Undergraduates
Accreditation: M, PAST

01 President ... Dr. Andrew REHFELD
05 Provost/Dean ... Rabbi Andrea WEISS
10 Chief Financial Officer ... Ms. Amy GOLDBERG
101 Exec Sec to Board of Governors ... Ms. Andrea KANN
26 AVP National Dir Public Affs/Comm ... Ms. Jean B. ROSENSAFT
44 Director of Institutional Giving ... Ms. Cheryl SLAVIN
08 Librarian ... Mr. Yoram BITTON
07 Director Recruitment/Admission ... Rabbi Adam ALLENBERG
13 Director of Information Systems ... Vacant
37 National Director of Financial Aid ... Ms. Roseanne ACKERLEY

Helene Fuld College of Nursing (A)

24 East 120th Street, New York NY 10035
County: New York FICE Identification: 010153
Unit ID: 191597
Telephone: (212) 616-7200 Carnegie Class: Spec-4-yr-Other Health
FAX Number: (212) 616-7299 Calendar System: Quarter
URL: www.helenefuld.edu
Established: 1945 Annual Undergrad Tuition & Fees: N/A
Enrollment: 525 Coed
Affiliation or Control: Independent Non-Profit IRS Status: 501(c)3
Highest Offering: Baccalaureate
Accreditation: M, ADNUR, NURSE

01 President ... Dr. Joyce P. GRIFFIN-SOBEL
05 Exec Vice President/Provost ... Dr. Sandy CAROLLO
10 Chief Financial Officer ... Mrs. Galina VILKINA
100 Chief of Staff ... Ms. Leslie FOUNTAIN WILLIAMS
32 Director of Student Affairs ... Ms. Joanna OJADA
08 Director of Library ... Mr. Indrajeet SINGH CHAUHAN
35 Assoc Director of Student Services ... Ms. Gladys PINEDA
26 Assistant Dean of External Affairs ... Ms. Cathy DOLAN
15 Director Human Resources ... Jamar WILSON
38 Student Wellness Counselor ... Ms. Dana GOLIN
04 Executive Assistant ... Ms. Kadia DARBY
13 Director Information Technology ... Mr. Eickel ORTIZ
07 Director of Admissions ... Mr. Brian GARRETT
29 Director Alumni Relations ... Vacant

Herkimer County Community College (B)

100 Reservoir Road, Herkimer NY 13350-1598
County: Herkimer FICE Identification: 004788
Unit ID: 191612
Telephone: (315) 866-0300 Carnegie Class: Assoc/MT-VT-Mix Trad/Non
FAX Number: (315) 866-5539 Calendar System: Semester
URL: www.herkimer.edu
Established: 1966 Annual Undergrad Tuition & Fees (In-District): $5,706
Enrollment: 2,224 Coed
Affiliation or Control: State/Local IRS Status: 501(c)3
Highest Offering: Associate Degree
Accreditation: M, PTAA

01 President ... Dr. Cathleen C. MCCOLGIN
10 Sr VP for Admin & Finance ... Mr. Nicholas LAINO
05 Provost ... Mr. Michael ORIOLO
32 Dean of Students ... Mr. Donald DUTCHER
20 Associate Dean Academic Affairs BH ... Mr. William MCDONALD
83 Assoc Dean Academic Affs Social Sci ... Dr. Robin RIECKER
20 Assoc Dean of Academic Affairs ... Mrs. Linda LAMB
15 Director of Human Resources ... Mr. James SALAMY
41 Director of Athletics ... Mr. Donald DUTCHER
08 Director of Library Services ... Mr. Alfred BEROWSKI
09 Director Institutional Research ... Ms. Karen AYOUCH
100 Assistant to the President ... Mr. Daniel SARGENT
18 Director Facilities Operations ... Mr. Robert WOUDENBERG
37 Director Student Financial Aid ... Ms. Maureen BOUFAS
26 Director of Public Relations ... Ms. Rebecca RUFFING
36 Career Services Counselor ... Mrs. Suzanne PADDOCK
96 Purchasing Agent ... Mr. Nicholas LAINO
102 Dir Foundation/Corporate Relations ... Mr. Robert FOWLER
19 Director of Campus Safety ... Mr. Timothy ROGERS
39 Director Residence Life ... Mr. Jason RATHBUN
04 Admin Assistant to the President ... Ms. Shari HUNT
07 Director of Admissions ... Dr. Denver STICKROD
38 Director Student Counseling ... Ms. Wendy MARCHESE
06 Registrar ... Ms. Jaclyn HARRINGTON
13 Chief Information Technology Ofcr ... Mr. Edris NOORI
104 Director Study Abroad ... Vacant
108 Assoc Dean Institution Assessment ... Ms. Mary Ann CARROLL

Hilbert College (C)

5200 South Park Avenue, Hamburg NY 14075-1597
County: Erie FICE Identification: 002735
Unit ID: 191621
Telephone: (716) 649-7900 Carnegie Class: Bac-Diverse
FAX Number: (716) 649-0702 Calendar System: Semester
URL: www.hilbert.edu
Established: 1957 Annual Undergrad Tuition & Fees: $24,530
Enrollment: 801 Coed
Affiliation or Control: Independent Non-Profit IRS Status: 501(c)3
Highest Offering: Master's
Accreditation: M

01 President ... Dr. Michael S. BROPHY
05 Provost/Vice Pres Academic Affs ... Dr. Ann RIVERA
111 Vice Pres Inst Advancement ... Ms. Kathleen CHRISTY
10 Vice Pres for Finance and Admin ... Mr. Ryan CASTER
84 Dean of Admissions and Fin Aid ... Ms. Meghan HARMON
32 Vice President & Dean of Stdnts ... Mr. Gregory ROBERTS
42 VP Mission and Equity ... Dr. Diedre DEBOSE
26 Dir Marketing & Communications ... Mr. Matthew HEIDT
92 Director Honors Program ... Dr. Amy E. SMITH
39 Dir Res Life & Community Stds ... Ms. Grace ADAMS
41 Athletic Director ... Mr. Tim SEIL
19 Director Security/Safety ... Mr. Joe LAROSA
29 Dir Annual Fund/Alumni Engagement ... Ms. LeeAnn PETRONSKY
08 Director of McGrath Library ... Ms. Chloe SANTANGELO
36 Director of Career Development ... Ms. Rachel WOZNIAK
37 Director Financial Aid ... Ms. Nicole GRIFFO
108 Asst Provost Inst Effectiveness ... Dr. Katelyn LETIZIA
38 Director Student Counseling ... Mr. Chris SIUTA
09 Director of Institutional Research ... Dr. John WISE
15 Director of Human Resources ... Ms. Maura FLYNN
35 Director of Student Involvement ... Mr. Alexander GILL
96 Director of Purchasing ... Mr. Gary DILLSWORTH
21 Asst Vice Pres Business/Finance ... Mr. Anthony WIERTEL
18 Chief Facilities/Physical Plant ... Mr. Gary DILLSWORTH
04 Administrative Asst to President ... Vacant
13 Chief Information Officer ... Dr. Dennis GENDRON

Hobart and William Smith Colleges (D)

300 Pulteney Street, Geneva NY 14456-3397
County: Ontario FICE Identification: 002731
Unit ID: 191630
Telephone: (315) 781-3000 Carnegie Class: Bac-A&S
FAX Number: (315) 781-3654 Calendar System: Semester
URL: www.hws.edu
Established: 1822 Annual Undergrad Tuition & Fees: $58,650
Enrollment: 1,833 Coordinate
Affiliation or Control: Independent Non-Profit IRS Status: 501(c)3
Highest Offering: Master's
Accreditation: M

01 President ... Mr. Mark D. GEARAN
100 Chief of Staff ... Vacant
111 Vice President for Advancement ... Mr. Robert O'CONNOR
30 Associate VP for Development ... Mr. Stephen CARAHER
04 Assistant to the President ... Ms. Amanda BLOWERS
10 VP for Finance & Administration/CFO ... Mr. Mark EDWARDS
32 VP Campus Life & Dean of Students ... Ms. Becca BARILE
26 VP for Marketing & Communications ... Ms. Cathy WILLIAMS
27 Associate VP of Communications ... Ms. Mary LECLAIR
110 Associate VP for Advancement ... Mr. Jared WEEDEN
43 Vice President and General Counsel ... Mr. Louis GUARD
19 Associate VP of Campus Safety ... Mr. Martin CORBETT
39 Associate VP for Student Wellness ... Ms. Shelle BASILIO
122 Asst Dean of Students ... Ms. Kristen TOBEY
21 Controller ... Ms. Carol GROVER
28 Interim VP for DEI/Title IX Coord ... Mr. Bill BOERNER
05 Provost & Dean of Faculty ... Dr. Sarah KIRK
13 VP for Strategic Initiatives/CIO ... Mr. Fred DAMIANO
15 Director of Human Resources ... Ms. Deborah DRAIN
06 Registrar ... Vacant
08 Interim College Librarian ... Ms. Sara GREENLEAF
104 Dean of Global Education ... Dr. Thomas D'AGOSTINO
41 Director of Athletics ... Mr. Brian MILLER
33 Dean of Hobart College ... Dr. Scott BROPHY
34 Dean of William Smith College ... Ms. Lisa KAENZIG
20 Sr Associate Provost ... Dr. Jamie MAKINSTER
20 Assoc Provost for Faculty Affairs ... Dr. Nick METZ
108 Associate Provost ... Dr. Susan PLINER
84 VP of Admissions and Financial Aid ... Ms. Kathleen REGAN
07 Dean of Admissions ... Mr. John YOUNG
113 Director of Student Accounts ... Ms. Rebecca BARNES
85 Director of International Students ... Ms. Marilyn O'HORA UHNAK
37 Director of Financial Aid ... Ms. Dawn LANGDON
29 Dir of Alumni & Alumnae Relations ... Ms. Chevy DEVANEY
88 Director Advancement Services ... Ms. Karen REUSCHER
88 Director of Parent Program ... Ms. Jennifer MURRAY
112 Director of Planned Giving ... Ms. Angela TALLO
88 Sr Dir Development for Athletics ... Mr. Michael CRAGG
88 Director Stewardship Programs ... Ms. Kelly YOUNG
102 Dir Corp/Foundation Rels/Legal Affs ... Mr. Gerard BUCKLEY
44 Director Annual & Athletic Giving ... Ms. Dulcie MEYER
27 Director of Marketing ... Ms. Gina KANE
105 Director Web Development ... Mr. Michael DIMAURO
88 Dir of Community Values & Conflict ... Mr. Joshua BISHOP
88 Director of Admissions ... Mr. Alan PAYNTER
96 Director Procurement/Auxiliary Svcs ... Ms. Claudette STERN
88 Director of Intercultural Affairs ... Dr. Alejandra MOLINA
88 Director Academic Opportunity Pgm ... Ms. Renee GRANT
42 Chaplain ... Rev. Nita BYRD
88 Director Athletic Communications ... Mr. Ken DEBOLT
31 Dir Community Engagement ... Ms. Kathleen FLOWERS
36 Director Center for Career Services ... Ms. Brandi FERRARA
38 Director Counseling Center ... Ms. Jennifer HOGAN
12 Director Finger Lakes Institute ... Dr. Lisa CLECKNER
25 Director of Sponsored Programs ... Ms. Roberta TRUSCELLO
09 Interim Director of IR ... Dr. Alden GASSERT
88 Director Conferences/Events ... Ms. Stephanie YEARSLEY
101 Secretary of the Institution/Board ... Ms. Robin LORD

Hofstra University (E)

100 Hofstra University, Hempstead NY 11549-1000
County: Nassau FICE Identification: 002732
Unit ID: 191649
Telephone: (516) 463-6600 Carnegie Class: DU-Mod
FAX Number: (516) 463-4848 Calendar System: Semester
URL: www.hofstra.edu
Established: 1935 Annual Undergrad Tuition & Fees: $49,410
Enrollment: 10,444 Coed
Affiliation or Control: Independent Non-Profit IRS Status: 501(c)3
Highest Offering: Doctorate
Accreditation: M, ACATE, ANEST, ARCPA, AUD, CAATE, CACREP, CAMPEP, CLPSY, HSA, IPSY, JOUR, LAW, MED, NURSE, OT, PERF, PH, SCPSY, SP

01 President ... Dr. Susan POSER
05 Provost ... Dr. Charles RIORDAN
20 Special Advisor to the Provost ... Vacant
43 VP Legal Affairs/General Counsel ... Ms. Jennifer MONE
10 Sr VP Financial Affairs/Treasurer ... Ms. Catherine HENNESSY
18 VP for Facilities and Operations ... Mr. Joseph BARKWILL
41 VP & Director of Athletics ... Mr. Rick COLE, JR.
26 Vice President University Relations ... Ms. Melissa A. CONNOLLY
84 VP Enrollment & Student Affairs ... Ms. Jessica L. EADS
13 VP Digital Innovation & Technology ... Vacant
30 Vice President for Development ... Mr. Alan J. KELLY
28 Chief Diversity & Inclusion Officer ... Mr. Cornell CRAIG
92 Dean Honors College ... Dr. Warren FRISINA
66 Dean Sch Nursing & Health Prof ... Dr. Kathleen GALLO
60 Dean School of Communication ... Mr. Mark LUKASIEWICZ
61 Dean Law School ... Hon. A. Gail PRUDENTI
54 Dean School of Engineering ... Dr. Sina Y. RABBANY
49 Int Dean Col Liberal Arts/Science ... Dr. Daniel E. SEABOLD
88 Dean Health Prof & Human Services ... Vacant
63 Dean Medical School ... Dr. David BATTINELLI
50 Dean Zarb School of Business ... Dr. Janet A. LENAGHAN
09 Sr Assoc Provost Inst Rsrch ... Ms. Cynthia P. LANGIN
114 Vice Provost Budget & Planning ... Mr. Richard M. APOLLO
25 Vice Provost Rsrch/Sponsored Pgms ... Ms. Sofia KAKOULIDIS
08 Director Library & Info Services ... Mr. Howard E. GRAVES
35 AVP & Dean of Students ... Ms. Michelle VAN-ESS-GRANT
36 Exec Dir Career Center ... Ms. Michelle KYRIAKIDES
38 Dir Student Counseling Services ... Dr. John C. GUTHMAN
39 Dir Residential Operations ... Ms. Novia P. WHYTE
23 Dir Health & Wellness Center ... Dr. Robert STAHL
29 Exec Director Alumni Affairs ... Ms. Amy R. REICH
40 Manager Bookstore ... Mr. Will GILER
06 Registrar/Dir of Academic Records ... Mr. Evan S. KOEGL
121 Dean for University Advisement ... Mr. Marc E. OPPENHEIM
15 Chief Human Resources Officer ... Ms. Denise S. CUNNINGHAM
19 Director Public Safety ... Ms. Geraldine HART
96 Director of Purchasing Contracts ... Mr. David DALE
37 Director Student Financial Aid ... Ms. Sandra MERVIUS
04 Exec Assistant to the President ... Ms. Laura A. MASON
100 Chief of Staff ... Dr. Jean PEDEN CHRISTODOULOU
44 Director Annual Giving ... Ms. Lauren R. DIPRETA

Holy Trinity Orthodox Seminary (F)

PO Box 36, Jordanville NY 13361-0036
County: Herkimer FICE Identification: 002733
Telephone: (315) 858-0945 Carnegie Class: Not Classified
FAX Number: (315) 858-0945 Calendar System: Semester
URL: www.hts.edu
Established: 1948 Annual Undergrad Tuition & Fees: N/A
Enrollment: N/A Male
Affiliation or Control: Russian Orthodox IRS Status: 501(c)3
Highest Offering: Baccalaureate
Accreditation: NY

01 Rector/CEO ... M.Rev. Luke MURIANKA
05 Dean/COO ... Dr. Nicholas SCHIDLOVSKY
10 Financial Manager ... V.Rev. Archimandrite HARDING
30 Director of Development ... R.Deac. Michael PAVUK
07 Director of Admissions/Registrar ... Rev. Ephraim WILLMARTH
08 Librarian ... Mr. Michael PEREKRESTOV
13 Information Technology Manager ... Mr. Benjamin MARQUARDT

Houghton University (G)

One Willard Avenue, Houghton NY 14744-0128
County: Allegany FICE Identification: 002734
Unit ID: 191676
Telephone: (585) 567-9200 Carnegie Class: Bac-A&S
FAX Number: (585) 567-9572 Calendar System: Semester
URL: www.houghton.edu
Established: 1883 Annual Undergrad Tuition & Fees: $34,466
Enrollment: 902 Coed
Affiliation or Control: Wesleyan Church IRS Status: 501(c)3
Highest Offering: Master's
Accreditation: M, AAQEP, MUS

01 President ... Dr. Wayne D. LEWIS, JR.
05 Chief Academic Ofcr/Dean of Faculty ... Dr. David DAVIES
32 Dean of Student Life ... Mr. Marc SMITHERS
10 Vice President for Finance ... Mr. Dale WRIGHT
111 Vice President for Advancement ... Mr. Karl SISSON
84 Vice President for Enrollment ... Mr. Jason TOWERS
06 Registrar ... Mr. Kevin KETTINGER
37 Director of Financial Aid ... Ms. Marianne LOPER
08 Director of the Library ... Mr. David STEVICK
29 Dir Alumni & Community Relations ... Ms. Phyllis GAERTE
42 Dean of the Chapel ... Dr. Michael JORDAN
09 Director of Data Management ... Mr. Kurt HABECKER
36 Director of VOCA ... Ms. Rachel WRIGHT
15 Director of Human Resources ... Ms. Nancy STANLEY
26 Dir Marketing & Communications ... Mr. Michael BLANKENSHIP

13 Director of Technology ... Mr. Donald HAINGRAY
18 Director of Facilities ... Mr. Chad PLYMALE
19 Chief Security Officer ... Mr. Ray M. PARLETT
23 Director of Health Services ... Dr. David BRUBAKER
41 Executive Director of Athletics ... Mr. Matthew WEBB
21 Controller ... Ms. Danae FORREST
39 Director Residence Life ... Ms. Katie BREITIGAN
38 Director Counseling Services ... Dr. William BURRICHTER
92 Director of Honors Program ... Dr. Benjamin LIPSCOMB
30 Director of Advancement Services ... Mr. John ODEN
100 Chief of Staff ... Dr. Gregory BISH

Hudson Valley Community College (A)

80 Vandenburgh Avenue, Troy NY 12180-6096
County: Rensselaer FICE Identification: 002868
Unit ID: 191719
Telephone: (518) 629-4822 Carnegie Class: Assoc/MT-VT-Mix Trad/Non
FAX Number: (518) 629-4576 Calendar System: Semester
URL: www.hvcc.edu
Established: 1953 Annual Undergrad Tuition & Fees (In-District): $5,964
Enrollment: 8,933 Coed
Affiliation or Control: State/Local IRS Status: 501(c)3
Highest Offering: Associate Degree
Accreditation: M, ADNUR, COARC, DH, DMS, EMT, FUSER, NAEYC, POLYT, RAD, SURGT

01 President ... Dr. Roger A. RAMSAMMY
04 Executive Asst to the President ... Ms. Suzanne K. KALKBRENNER
10 VP for Administration & CFO ... Mr. Donal CHRISTIAN
05 Vice President for Academic Affairs ... Ms. Judith DILORENZO
32 Vice President for Student Affairs ... Mr. Louis COPLIN
50 Acting Dean Business/Liberal Arts ... Ms. Ronalyn WILSON
81 Dean of STEM ... Dr. Jonathan ASHDOWN
103 Dean Econ/Workforce Development ... Ms. Penny HILL
76 Dean School of Health Sciences ... Dr. Patricia KLIMKEWICZ
08 Dir of College Learning Centers ... Ms. Marcy PENDERGAST
07 Director of Admissions ... Ms. Julie PANZANARO
06 Registrar ... Mr. Ian LACHANCE
13 Chief Information Officer ... Mr. Jonathan BRENNAN
18 Director Physical Plant ... Vacant
45 Exec Dir Institutional Effective ... Ms. Kathleen PETLEY
37 Interim Director of Financial Aid ... Ms. Heather HENRY
36 Dir Center For Careers & Transfer ... Dr. Gayle HEALY
15 Exec Director of Human Resources ... Ms. Karen PAQUETTE
19 Director of Public Safety ... Mr. Fred ALIBERTI
23 Coordinator Health Services ... Ms. Claudine POTVIN-GIORDANO
22 Director of Disability Resources ... Ms. DeAnne MARTOCCI
09 Director Planning & Research ... Ms. Vaidehi AGASHE
35 Director of Student Life ... Mr. Alfredo BALARIN
85 International Student Advisor ... Dr. Jay DEITCHMAN
40 Bookstore Manager ... Ms. Stephanie DANZ
41 Director of Athletics ... Mr. Justin HOYT
20 Asst VP of Academics ... Ms. Ronalyn WILSON
96 Dir Business Services/Purchasing ... Ms. Patricia GASTON
21 Comptroller ... Mr. John BRAUNGARD
26 Exec Dir Communications/Marketing ... Mr. Dennis KENNEDY
86 Exec Dir External & Govt Affairs ... Ms. Regina LAGATTA
25 Director of Grants ... Ms. Cheryl L. BEAUCHAMP
29 Alumni Relations/Annual Giving ... Ms. Jana PUTZIG
106 Interim Dir of Distance Learning ... Ms. Elissa BAKER
108 Dean Institutional Assessment ... Dr. Margaret GEEHAN
105 Web Coordinator ... Ms. Sandra EYERMAN
28 Chief Diversity Officer ... Mr. Ainsley THOMAS
30 Dir of Development/Donor Relations ... Ms. Angela D. O'NEAL
16 Director of Human Resources ... Ms. Deborah RICHEY

Icahn School of Medicine at Mount Sinai (B)

One Gustave L. Levy Place, New York NY 10029-6500
County: New York FICE Identification: 007026
Unit ID: 193405
Telephone: (212) 241-6500 Carnegie Class: Spec-4-yr-Eng
FAX Number: (212) 241-7146 Calendar System: Other
URL: www.icahn.mssm.edu
Established: 1963 Annual Graduate Tuition & Fees: N/A
Enrollment: 1,298 Coed
Affiliation or Control: Independent Non-Profit IRS Status: 501(c)3
Highest Offering: Doctorate; No Undergraduates
Accreditation: M, CAMPEP, DENT, IPSY, MED, PH

01 President & CEO ... Dr. Kenneth L. DAVIS
05 Exec Vice Pres/Dean Sch of Medicine ... Dr. Dennis S. CHARNEY
10 Sr Vice Pres for Finance ... Mr. Stephen HARVEY
63 Dean for Medical Education ... Dr. David MULLER
11 Dean for Operations ... Mr. Jeffrey SILBERSTEIN
13 Dean for Information Technology ... Ms. Kristin MYERS
28 Director of Diversity ... Dr. Gary BUTTS

Iona University (C)

715 North Avenue, New Rochelle NY 10801-1890
County: Westchester FICE Identification: 002737
Unit ID: 191931
Telephone: (914) 633-2000 Carnegie Class: Masters/L
FAX Number: (914) 633-2642 Calendar System: Semester
URL: www.iona.edu
Established: 1940 Annual Undergrad Tuition & Fees: $41,580
Enrollment: 3,590 Coed
Affiliation or Control: Independent Non-Profit IRS Status: 501(c)3
Highest Offering: Master's
Accreditation: M, MFCD, NASP, OT, SP, SW

01 President ... Dr. Seamus CAREY
05 Interim Provost/SVP Academic Affs ... Dr. Tricia MULLIGAN
10 SVP Finance & Administration ... Vacant
111 Sr VP Advancement/External Affairs ... Ms. Laura DOHERTY
100 VP Strat Initiatives & Board Secy ... Ms. MaryEllen CALLAGHAN
84 VP Enrollment Mgmt/Stdnt Affairs ... Mr. Kevin O'SULLIVAN
13 Vice Provost Info Technology/CIO ... Ms. Joanne STEELE
37 Assoc VP Student Financial Services ... Ms. Eileen DOYLE
14 Asst Vice Provost for Info Tech ... Mr. Dimitris HALARIS
20 Assistant Provost ... Dr. Nadine COSBY
32 Associate Dean of Students ... Ms. Elizabeth OLIVIERI-LENAHAN
49 Dean School Arts & Sciences ... Dr. Joseph STABILE
50 Dean School of Business ... Dr. Lynne RICHARDSON
43 General Counsel ... Ms. Sandy CURKO
18 Director of Facilities Management ... Mr. Richard MURRAY
39 Director Residential Life ... Mr. Aaron HARMAN
15 Director of HR & Title IX Coord ... Ms. Denise SMITH
38 Director of Counseling Center ... Dr. Brielle STARK-ADLER
36 Asst VP Enrollment Mgmt/Career Init ... Mr. Matthew CARDIN
08 Director of Libraries ... Mr. Richard PALLADINO
42 Director of Campus Ministries ... Dr. Sean D'ALFONSO
06 Registrar ... Mr. Daniel ARNDT
41 Director of Athletics ... Mr. Matthew T. GLOVASKI
86 Director of Govt Relations/Grants ... Vacant
09 Dir of Inst Effectiveness/Planning ... Mr. Jason DIFFENDERFER
21 Director of Business Services ... Ms. Nancy MORANO
26 VP for Marketing & Communications ... Ms. Mary Clare REILLEY
19 Dir of Campus Safety & Security ... Mr. Adrian NAVARRETE
23 Director of Health Services ... Ms. Patty FURLONG
96 Business Services Senior Specialist ... Ms. Casey DELLICARPINI
92 Director of Honors Program ... Dr. Kim PAFFENROTH
123 Director of Graduate Admissions ... Vacant
04 Executive Asst to President ... Ms. Laura PROSTANO
105 Webpage Designer/Developer ... Mr. Peter MACELI
29 Director Alumni Relations ... Vacant
11 Chief Operating Officer ... Vacant
28 Chief Diversity Officer ... Dr. Sumita FURLONG
30 Sr Director of Development ... Ms. Christine M. DOWNES

Island Drafting and Technical Institute (D)

128 Broadway, Amityville NY 11701-2704
County: Suffolk FICE Identification: 007375
Unit ID: 191959
Telephone: (631) 691-8733 Carnegie Class: Spec 2-yr-Tech
FAX Number: (631) 691-8738 Calendar System: Semester
URL: www.idti.edu
Established: 1957 Annual Undergrad Tuition & Fees: $16,950
Enrollment: 68 Coed
Affiliation or Control: Proprietary IRS Status: Proprietary
Highest Offering: Associate Degree
Accreditation: ACCSC

01 President ... Mr. James G. DI LIBERTO
03 Vice President ... Mr. John G. DI LIBERTO
05 Dean ... Ms. Patricia HAUSFELD
37 Director Student Financial Aid ... Mr. Daniel GREENER

Ithaca College (E)

953 Danby Road, Ithaca NY 14850-7001
County: Tompkins FICE Identification: 002739
Unit ID: 191968
Telephone: (607) 274-3011 Carnegie Class: Masters/L
FAX Number: N/A Calendar System: Semester
URL: www.ithaca.edu
Established: 1892 Annual Undergrad Tuition & Fees: $46,610
Enrollment: 5,354 Coed
Affiliation or Control: Independent Non-Profit IRS Status: 501(c)3
Highest Offering: Doctorate
Accreditation: M, AAQEP, #ARCPA, CAATE, CAPRT, MUS, OT, PTA, SP, THEA

01 President ... Dr. La Jerne T. CORNISH
100 Chief of Staff ... Ms. Odalys DIAZ PINEIRO
05 Provost/SVP for Academic Affairs ... Ms. Melanie STEIN
10 VP of Finance & Administration ... Mr. Timothy DOWNS
43 General Counsel ... Ms. Emily ROCKETT
84 VP Marketing & Enrollment Strategy ... Ms. Laurie KOEHLER
111 Interim VP Philanthropy/Engagement ... Mr. Quincy DAVIDSON
15 VP Human Resources/Planning ... Ms. Hayley HARRIS
32 VP Student Affairs/Campus Life ... Ms. Bonnie S. PRUNTY
26 Chief Communications Officer ... Mr. Robert WAGNER
13 Chief Information Officer ... Mr. David WEIL
18 Assoc VP for Facilities Management ... Vacant
21 Assoc VP for Business & Finance ... Mr. Marc ISRAEL
20 Associate Provost Academic Programs ... Ms. Stacia ZABUSKY
20 Assoc Provost Faculty Affairs ... Mr. Brendan MURDAY
58 Assoc Provost Grad & Prof Studies ... Ms. Christina MOYLAN
79 Dean School of Humanities/Science ... Dr. Claire GLEITMAN
64 Dean School of Music/Theatre/Dance ... Dr. Anne HOGAN
76 Dean Sch Health Sciences/Human Perf ... Dr. Linda PETROSINO
50 Dean School of Business ... Dr. Michael JOHNSON-CRAMER
60 Dean School of Communication ... Ms. Amy FALKNER
06 Registrar ... Ms. Vikki LEVINE
09 Director Analytics & Inst Research ... Ms. Claire BORCH
07 Director of Admission ... Ms. Nicole EVERSLEY BRADWELL
12 Director London Center ... Ms. Meghan CALLAHAN
38 Director Counseling/Health/Wellness ... Dr. Jennifer METZGAR
37 Exec Dir Student Financial Services ... Ms. Shana GORE
35 Dean of Students ... Ms. Marsha DAWSON
08 College Librarian ... Ms. Michelle MILLET
41 AVP & Dir Intercollegiate Athletics ... Ms. Susan BASSETT
114 Director of Budget ... Ms. Beth REYNOLDS
27 Director of Public Relations ... Mr. David C. MALEY
40 Director of College Stores ... Vacant
28 Exec Dir Student Equity & Belonging ... Mr. Luca MAURER
85 Dir International Student Services ... Ms. Diana DIMITROVA
88 Dir Center for Faculty Excellence ... Ms. Aimee GERMAIN
04 Exec Assistant to the President ... Ms. MaryAnn TAYLOR
96 Director Procurement & Compliance ... Mr. Bernie MURTHA
101 Secretary & Legal Counsel to Board ... Ms. Nancy PRINGLE
104 Director Study Abroad ... Ms. Rachel GOULD
19 Exec Dir Public Safety & Emer Mgmt ... Mr. Bill KERRY
39 Dir Resident Life/Judicial Affairs ... Ms. Laura DAVIS

Jamestown Business College (F)

7 Fairmount Avenue, Box 429, Jamestown NY 14702-0429
County: Chautauqua FICE Identification: 008495
Unit ID: 192004
Telephone: (716) 664-5100 Carnegie Class: Spec-4-yr-Bus
FAX Number: (716) 664-3144 Calendar System: Quarter
URL: www.jbc.edu
Established: 1886 Annual Undergrad Tuition & Fees: $12,645
Enrollment: 284 Coed
Affiliation or Control: Proprietary IRS Status: Proprietary
Highest Offering: Baccalaureate
Accreditation: M

01 President ... Mr. David CONKLIN
05 Dean ... Ms. Pamela REESE
07 Director Admissions ... Ms. Christina CONKLIN
06 Registrar ... Ms. Erica SHEESLEY
37 Director of Financial Aid ... Ms. Victoria BARAN

Jamestown Community College (G)

525 Falconer Street, Jamestown NY 14701
County: Chautauqua FICE Identification: 002869
Unit ID: 191986
Telephone: (716) 338-1000 Carnegie Class: Assoc/HT-Mix Trad/Non
FAX Number: (716) 338-1466 Calendar System: Semester
URL: www.sunyjcc.edu
Established: 1950 Annual Undergrad Tuition & Fees (In-District): $6,336
Enrollment: 3,430 Coed
Affiliation or Control: State/Local IRS Status: 501(c)3
Highest Offering: Associate Degree
Accreditation: M, ADNUR, OTA

01 President ... Dr. Daniel T. DEMARTE
05 Vice Pres of Academic Affairs ... Dr. Marilyn A. ZAGORA
11 Vice Pres of Administration ... Mr. Michael MARTELLO
32 Vice Pres of Student Affairs ... Dr. Kirk YOUNG
103 Vice Pres of Workforce Readiness ... Mr. Holger EKANGER
12 Exec Dir of Catt County Campus ... Ms. Paula SNYDER
09 Chief Inst Research/Planning Ofcr ... Ms. Katie CARPEN
06 Registrar ... Ms. Tracy KELLY
07 Director Admission ... Ms. Corrine CASE
08 Library Director ... Mr. Timothy ARNOLD
37 Exec Dir Student Finance/Records ... Ms. Michelle SCHRAM
15 Exec Director Human Resources ... Ms. Nicolette RICZKER
41 Athletic Director ... Mr. George SISSON
43 Legal Counsel ... Vacant
18 Director Facilities/Physical Plant ... Mr. David JOHNSON
04 Administrative Asst to President ... Ms. Marsha L. HERN
19 Director Security/Safety ... Mr. Barry SWANSON
30 Chief Development/Advancement ... Vacant
39 Director Student Housing ... Mr. Tyler SILAGYI
105 Director Web Services ... Ms. Karli CHAMP
13 Int Exec Dir of Technology ... Mr. Kyle BROWN
29 Director Alumni Relations ... Ms. Heather MORRIS
21 Exec Director Administrative Svcs ... Ms. Karen FULLER
96 Financial Analyst/Business Office ... Ms. Jennifer BEEBE
36 Director Student Placement ... Vacant
38 Director Student Counseling ... Ms. Tammy SMITH
102 Exec Dir Foundation/Corporate Rels ... Ms. Maria KINDBERG
22 Dir Affirmative Action/Equal Opp ... Ms. Nickey RICZKER
25 Chief Contract & Grants Admin ... Ms. Katrina JONES
44 Director Annual Giving ... Ms. Maria KINDBERG

Jamestown Community College Cattaraugus County Campus (H)

260 North Union Street, PO Box 5901, Olean NY 14760-5901
Telephone: (716) 376-7504 Identification: 770138
Accreditation: &M

Jefferson Community College (I)

1220 Coffeen Street, Watertown NY 13601-1897
County: Jefferson FICE Identification: 002870
Unit ID: 192022
Telephone: (315) 786-2200 Carnegie Class: Assoc/HT-Mix Trad/Non
FAX Number: (315) 786-0158 Calendar System: Semester
URL: www.sunyjefferson.edu
Established: 1961 Annual Undergrad Tuition & Fees (In-District): $5,688
Enrollment: 2,658 Coed
Affiliation or Control: State/Local IRS Status: 501(c)3
Highest Offering: Associate Degree
Accreditation: M, ADNUR

01 Administrator-in-Charge .... Dr. Dan J. DUPEE, II
05 Interim Vice Pres Academic Affairs .... Ms. Jerilyn FAIRMAN
10 Interim VP Admin/Finance .... Mr. Willliam EMM
32 VP for Student Engagement/Retention .... Dr. Corey A. CAMPBELL
49 Assoc VP for Liberal Arts .... Vacant
81 Associate VP for STEM .... Dr. Scott SCHAEFFER
04 Special Assistant to the President .... Ms. Karen FREEMAN
08 Library Director .... Mr. John THOMAS
84 Dean of Enrollment Services .... Vacant
37 Director Financial Aid .... Ms. Robyn RHYNER
06 Registrar .... Ms. Jessica EMERSON
88 Director Small Business Center .... Ms. Elizabeth LONERGAN
09 Associate VP Strategic Initiatives .... Dr. Megan STADLER
18 Chief Facilities/Physical Plant .... Mr. Joseph MOORE
29 Alumni Development Officer .... Ms. Edie ROGGIE
35 Dir of Student Activities/Inclusion .... Ms. Margaret TAYLOR
36 Coord Career Planning/Placement .... Ms. Michele D. GEFELL
88 Dir of Educ Planning/Veteran Svcs .... Ms. Rebecca SMALL KELLOGG
26 Dir of Marketing/Communications .... Ms. Gillian MAITLAND
15 Associate VP for Human Resources .... Ms. Kerry A. YOUNG
30 College Development Officer .... Mr. Ben FOSTER
119 Chief Security Information Officer .... Mr. Donald HORTON
19 Director Security/Safety .... Mr. Wesley HISSONG
41 Athletic Director .... Mr. Jeffrey WILEY
88 Director Opportunity Programs .... Ms. Gabrielle THOMPSON
07 Director of Admissions .... Ms. Chelsea MARRA
13 Director Institutional Technology .... Ms. Monica J. PAPAGNI
39 Dir Resident Life/Student Housing .... Ms. Jacquelyn THURMAN

Jewish Theological Seminary of America (A)

3080 Broadway, New York NY 10027-4649
County: New York FICE Identification: 002740
Unit ID: 192040
Telephone: (212) 678-8000 Carnegie Class: Spec-4-yr-Faith
FAX Number: (212) 678-8947 Calendar System: Semester
URL: www.jtsa.edu
Established: 1886 Annual Undergrad Tuition & Fees: $58,703
Enrollment: 360 Coed
Affiliation or Control: Independent Non-Profit IRS Status: 501(c)3
Highest Offering: Doctorate
Accreditation: M, PAST

01 Chancellor .... Dr. Shuly SCHWARTZ
10 Vice Chanc Finance/Administration .... Ms. Clare PEETERS
30 Vice Chanc/Chief Development Ofcr .... Ms. Linda ZISK
05 Provost .... Dr. Jeffrey KRESS
10 Chief Financial Officer .... Ms. Barbara CALISSI
43 General Counsel .... Mr. Keath BLATT
49 Dean List College Jewish Studies .... Dr. Amy KALMANOFSKY
53 Dean Davidson School of Education .... Dr. Shira EPSTEIN
58 Dean of The Graduate School .... Dr. Amy KALMANOFSKY
64 Director Miller Cantorial School .... Cantor Nancy ABRAMSON
73 Dean of Religious Leadership .... Rabbi Ayelet COHEN
32 Dean of Student Life .... Ms. Sara HOROWITZ
08 Librarian .... Dr. David KRAEMER
15 Director of Human Resources .... Ms. Diana TORRES-PETRILLI
18 Director of Operations .... Mr. James ESPOSITO
13 Director Information Technology .... Mr. Ray MORALES
06 Registrar/Director Financial Aid .... Ms. Amy S. FEINFELD
39 Director of Residence Life .... Mr. Bradley MOOT
84 Director of Enrollment Management .... Ms. Melissa PRESENT
38 Director Student Counseling .... Dr. David DAVAR
29 Director of Alumni Affairs .... Mrs. Melissa FRIEDMAN
31 Director of Community Engagement .... Rabbi Julia ANDELMAN
04 Executive Asst to Chancellor .... Ms. Chava BLUMENTHAL
19 Director Security/Safety .... Chief Anthony VAUGHAN

The Juilliard School (B)

60 Lincoln Center Plaza, New York NY 10023-6588
County: New York FICE Identification: 002742
Unit ID: 192110
Telephone: (212) 799-5000 Carnegie Class: Spec-4-yr-Arts
FAX Number: (212) 724-0263 Calendar System: Semester
URL: www.juilliard.edu
Established: 1905 Annual Undergrad Tuition & Fees: $49,260
Enrollment: 961 Coed
Affiliation or Control: Independent Non-Profit IRS Status: 501(c)3
Highest Offering: Doctorate
Accreditation: M

01 President .... Mr. Damian WOETZEL
05 Provost & Dean .... Mr. Adam MEYER
10 Vice Pres/Chief Financial Officer .... Ms. Christine TODD
08 VP for Library/Info Resources .... Ms. Jane GOTTLIEB
111 VP & Chief Advancement Officer .... Ms. Alexandra WHEELER
18 AVP for Facilities Management .... Mr. Cameron CHRISTENSEN
84 VP Enrollment Mgmt/Student Dev .... Ms. Joan D. WARREN
43 Vice Pres Admin/General Counsel .... Mr. Maurice F. EDELSON
100 Vice President & Chief of Staff .... Ms. Ciaran ESCOFFERY
26 Vice Pres for Public Affairs .... Ms. Rosalie CONTRERAS
32 Dean for Student Development .... Mr. Barrett HIPES
20 Dean of Academic Affairs .... Mr. Jose GARCIA-LEON
64 Deputy Dean/Director Music Division .... Vacant
64 Asst Dean/Dir of Chamber Music .... Ms. Barli NUGENT
35 Asst Dean of Student Affairs .... Ms. Sabrina TANBARA
57 Dir Richard Rodgers Drama Div .... Mr. Evan YIONOULIS
57 Artistic Director of Dance Division .... Ms. Alicia Graf MACK
57 Artistic Director of Vocal Arts .... Mr. Brian ZEGER
88 Director of Performance Activities .... Ms. Anna ROYZMAN
88 Artistic Dir Pre-College Division .... Ms. Yoheved KAPLINSKY
06 Registrar .... Ms. Katherine GERTSON
07 Assoc Dean Enrollment Management .... Dr. Kathleen TESAR
112 Director of Major Gifts .... Ms. Katie MURTHA
15 Director of Human Resources .... Ms. Katie GERMANA
38 Director of Counseling Services .... Mr. William BUSE
37 Director Student Financial Aid .... Ms. Tina GONZALEZ
88 Director of Juilliard Jazz .... Mr. Wynton MARSALIS
36 Director Career Services .... Ms. Rachel CHRISTENSEN
13 Chief Information Officer .... Mr. Carl YOUNG
14 Chief Technology Officer .... Mr. Steve DOTY
19 Director Security/Safety .... Mr. Adam GAGAN
29 Director Alumni Relations .... Ms. Rebecca VACCARELLI
39 Director of Residence Life .... Mr. Todd PORTER

Kehilath Yakov Rabbinical Seminary (C)

638 Bedford Avenue, Brooklyn NY 11211-8007
County: Kings FICE Identification: 010549
Unit ID: 192165
Telephone: (718) 963-1212 Carnegie Class: Spec-4-yr-Faith
FAX Number: (718) 387-8586 Calendar System: Semester
Established: 1948 Annual Undergrad Tuition & Fees: $10,300
Enrollment: 158 Male
Affiliation or Control: Independent Non-Profit IRS Status: 501(c)3
Highest Offering: First Talmudic Degree
Accreditation: RABN

01 President .... Mr. Sandor SCHWARTZ

Keuka College (D)

141 Central Avenue, Keuka Park NY 14478
County: Yates FICE Identification: 002744
Unit ID: 192192
Telephone: (315) 279-5000 Carnegie Class: Masters/M
FAX Number: (315) 279-5216 Calendar System: Semester
URL: www.keuka.edu
Established: 1890 Annual Undergrad Tuition & Fees: $34,032
Enrollment: 1,535 Coed
Affiliation or Control: Independent Non-Profit IRS Status: 501(c)3
Highest Offering: Master's
Accreditation: M, AAQEP, IACBE, NURSE, OT, SW

01 President .... Mrs. Amy STOREY
05 Provost/VP for Academic Affairs .... Dr. Bradley FUSTER
10 VP for Finance/Administration .... Mr. Robert BAUMET
13 VP of Technology & Continuing Educ .... Dr. Timothy SELLERS
26 VP of Marketing and Enrollment Mgmt .... Mr. Peter BEKISZ
32 VP for Student Development .... Dr. Heather MALDONADO
20 Associate Provost .... Mr. Kenneth SANDERS
20 Assistant Provost .... Dr. Margaret SPOFFORD XAVIER
08 Director of Library .... Ms. Linda PARK
29 Sr Dir Alumni Relations/Advancement .... Mrs. Billy Jo JAYNE
15 AVP of Human Resources .... Ms. Colleen BERTRAND
21 Controller .... Mr. Philip CATALANO
19 Director of Campus Safety .... Mr. James CUNNINGHAM
41 AVP/Director of Athletics .... Mr. Jon ACCARDI
42 College Chaplain .... Mr. Eric DETAR
06 Registrar .... Ms. Katelyn CHEPLICK
26 Sr Director of Marketing .... Ms. Tammy SWALES
96 Purchasing Supervisor .... Mr. Trevor THILLMAN
88 Div Chair Applied Health & Wellness .... Dr. Kristen BACON
76 Founding Dean Applied Hlth & Well .... Dr. Christopher ALTERIO
50 Div Chair Business & Management .... Dr. Mark MCNANEY
53 Div Chair of Education .... Dr. Klaudia LORINCZOVA
79 Div Chair Humanities/Fine Arts .... Dr. Jennie JOINER
81 Div Chair Natural Sciences/Math .... Dr. Michael KECK
66 Div Chair Nursing .... Dr. Elizabeth RUSSO
70 Div Chair Social Work .... Dr. Jason MCKINNEY
44 Director of Annual Giving .... Ms. Kaitlyn CARHART
88 Senior Dir of Conference Services .... Ms. Abigail DINAN
104 Assoc Director Intercultural Affs .... Mr. Brenden NAVARRO
85 Director of Global Affairs .... Ms. Jennifer ALESSI
85 Dean of International Program/Asia .... Mr. Gary GISS
119 Director of Info Systems & Security .... Mr. Dharmen PATEL
27 Director of Comm & Media Relations .... Mr. Kevin FRISCH
31 Dir of Community Relations/Events .... Ms. Katharine WAYE
88 Dir of Field Period Pgm/Internships .... Ms. Ann EMO
88 Senior Accountant .... Ms. Kayla ROBINSON
08 Director of HEOP .... Ms. Lisa THOMPSON
113 Director of Student Accounts .... Ms. Mary Ellen GRIFFITHS
37 Director of Financial Aid .... Ms. Stacia DALABA
07 Director of Admissions .... Ms. Ashley LARIMORE
23 Director of Health Services .... Ms. Kristen BRAY

The King's College (E)

56 Broadway, New York NY 10004-1613
County: New York FICE Identification: 040953
Unit ID: 454184
Telephone: (212) 659-7200 Carnegie Class: Bac-A&S
FAX Number: (212) 659-7210 Calendar System: Semester
URL: www.tkc.edu
Established: 1938 Annual Undergrad Tuition & Fees: $37,690
Enrollment: 442 Coed
Affiliation or Control: Independent Non-Profit IRS Status: 501(c)3
Highest Offering: Baccalaureate
Accreditation: M

00 Chairman of the Board of Trustees .... Mr. Timothy DUNN
01 President .... Dr. Tim GIBSON
03 Executive Vice President .... Mr. Brian BRENBERG
05 Interim Provost .... Dr. Matthew PARKS
10 Chief Financial Officer .... Mr. Frank TORINO
32 Vice President Student Development .... Mr. David LEEDY
07 Vice Pres Admissions .... Mr. Mat MARQUEZ
35 Dean of Students .... Mr. David LEEDY
21 Asst VP & Controller .... Ms. Judy BARRINGER
84 Assoc VP Enrollment Management .... Ms. Whitney CLARK
06 Registrar .... Mr. Paul MIDDLEKAUFF
37 Director of Financial Aid .... Ms. Anna PETERS
100 Chief of Staff .... Ms. Megan DISHMAN
09 Director of Institutional Research .... Dr. Kimberly THORNBURY
26 Dir Strategic Communication .... Ms. Rebecca AU-MULLANEY
29 Exec Director of Alumni Affairs .... Ms. Sophia COSTON
18 Director Facilities .... Mr. Rich SWITZER
30 Chief Development Officer .... Ms. Bridget ROGERS
36 Director Career Development .... Mr. Matthew PERMAN
38 Director Student Counseling .... Ms. Esther JHUN
08 Director Library Services .... Ms. Christina ROGERS
39 Director Resident Life .... Ms. Leticia MOSQUEDA
41 Athletic Director .... Mr. Bryan FINLEY
15 Director Human Resources .... Ms. Grace GLEASON
102 Director Grants and Foundation .... Mr. Michael TOSCANO
13 Director of Information Technology .... Mr. Bracey FUENZALIDA

Le Moyne College (F)

1419 Salt Springs Road, Syracuse NY 13214-1301
County: Onondaga FICE Identification: 002748
Unit ID: 192323
Telephone: (315) 445-4100 Carnegie Class: Masters/L
FAX Number: (315) 445-4540 Calendar System: Semester
URL: www.lemoyne.edu
Established: 1946 Annual Undergrad Tuition & Fees: $35,910
Enrollment: 3,409 Coed
Affiliation or Control: Independent Non-Profit IRS Status: 501(c)3
Highest Offering: Doctorate
Accreditation: M, AAQEP, ARCPA, NURSE, OT

01 President .... Dr. Linda M. LEMURA
05 Prov/VP Acad Affs & Stdnt Dev .... Dr. James HANNAN
10 VP Finance/Administration .... Mr. Joseph E. GRASSO
111 Vice Pres Advancement .... Mr. Bill BROWER
84 Vice Pres of Enrollment .... Dr. Timothy LEE
88 Vice Pres Mission Integration & DEI .... Rev. Charles ODUKE, SJ
88 Rector of the Jesuit Community .... Rev. Donald KIRBY, SJ
49 Interim Dean of Arts & Sciences .... Dr. Beth MITCHELL
50 Dean School of Business .... Mr. James E. JOSEPH
58 Dean of Graduate & Prof Studies .... Dr. Meega WELLS
20 Assoc Provost .... Dr. Mary K. COLLINS
21 Controller .... Ms. Nicole BROWN
15 Sr Dir HR Operations .... Ms. Tara BUNCH
41 Director of Athletics .... Mr. Bob BERETTA
18 Asst VP Facilities Mgmt & Planning .... Mr. Jed S. SCHNEIDER
32 Assoc Provost for Student Devel .... Mr. Shaun CRISLER
35 Asst Dean for Student Development .... Mr. Mark G. GODLESKI
121 Asst Dean for Academic Advising .... Ms. Allison FARRELL
88 Asst Dean/Dir CSTEP & STEP .... Ms. Darshini ROOPNARINE
07 Senior Director of Admission .... Ms. Mary CHANDLER
51 Director of Continuing Education .... Vacant
88 Dir of Transfer Admission .... Ms. Cathy ANDERSON
13 Director of Info Technology .... Mr. Shaun C. BLACK
09 Director of Institutional Research .... Dr. Daniel L. SKIDMORE
22 EEO/Affirmative Action Officer .... Vacant
06 Registrar .... Ms. Natasha FARRELL
08 Director of the Library .... Ms. Inga BARNELLO
42 Director of Campus Ministry .... Mr. Thomas ANDINO
27 Director of Communications .... Mr. Joseph B. DELLA POSTA
88 Director Campus Life & Leadership .... Mr. John R. HALEY
19 Int Director of Security .... Mr. Jack LAWTON
39 Dir of Campus Life & Leadership .... Mr. John HALEY
36 Dir Career Advising/Development .... Ms. Meredith TORNABENE
100 Chief of Staff .... Ms. Carly J. COLBERT
28 Asst to the Provost for Diversity .... Dr. Tabor FISHER
86 Director Govt/Foundation Relations .... Mr. Steven W. KULICK
29 Director of Alumni Engagement .... Ms. Kasha GODLESKI
23 Dir Wellness Ctr for Health & Couns .... Ms. Maria RANDAZZO
88 Director of HEOP and AHANA .... Ms. Kelsi-Leandra LANE
40 Bookstore Manager .... Vacant

LIM College (G)

545 5th Avenue, 7th Floor, New York NY 10017
County: New York FICE Identification: 007466
Unit ID: 192271
Telephone: (212) 752-1530 Carnegie Class: Spec-4-yr-Bus
FAX Number: (212) 832-6109 Calendar System: Semester
URL: www.limcollege.edu
Established: 1939 Annual Undergrad Tuition & Fees: $28,756
Enrollment: 1,681 Coed
Affiliation or Control: Proprietary IRS Status: Proprietary
Highest Offering: Master's
Accreditation: M, ACBSP

01 President .... Elizabeth S. MARCUSE
05 Provost .... Lisa SPRINGER
10 EVP Finance & Operations/Treasurer .... Michael T. DONOHUE
30 Sr VP of External Relations .... Gail NARDIN
26 VP of Marketing and Communications .... Danielle YANNOTTA
84 VP of Enrollment Services .... Kristina ORTIZ
86 VP of Govt Relations/Cmty Affairs .... Christopher E. BARTO

21 VP of Finance and Controller .... Erik PAULSON
32 Vice President of Student Affairs .... Curtis HOOVER
58 Chair of Graduate Studies .... Vacant
20 Assoc Dean of Academic Affairs .... Patricia FITZMAURICE
35 AVP of Student Affairs .... Erica MONNIN
08 Director of Library Services .... Lou ACIERNO
06 College Registrar .... Carolyn DISNEW
36 AVP of Career and Internship Svcs .... Nina FIDDIAN-GREEN
38 Dir of Counseling Services .... Heather S. O'LEARY
07 Director of Admissions .... Laura HEALY
09 Director of Institutional Research .... Eugene MULLER
21 Accounting Manager .... Svetlana KANEVSKAYA
96 Purchasing Director .... Eric MARTIN
27 Director of Communications .... Meredith FINNIN
27 Director of Marketing .... Laura CIOFFI
13 Chief Technology Officer .... Maurice MORENCY
14 Director of Information Technology .... Nelson LEON
18 Manager of Facilities .... Kwamina AFFUL
88 Dean of Academic Administration .... Gilbert STACK
121 Director of Academic Advising .... Jackie CORAGGIO
15 Dir of Human Resources .... Carolyn MCINTOSH
104 Study Abroad Coordinator .... Indigo GOODSON
106 Director of Online Innovation .... Deepa RAO-SISARIO
123 Assoc Dir of Grad Admiss/Advising .... George TOLEDO
04 Assistant to the President .... Doris PETTI
28 Asst Director of Diversity .... Focrun NAHAR
39 Resident Community Coordinator .... Joshua LEWIS
88 Instructional Designer .... Chu CHEUNG
88 Assistant to the Provost .... Schuyler OSGOOD

Long Island Business Institute (A)

6500 Jericho Turnpike, Commack NY 11725
Telephone: (631) 499-7100 Identification: 770746
Accreditation: NY

Long Island Business Institute (B)

136-18 39th Avenue 5th Floor, Flushing NY 11354
County: Queens FICE Identification: 020937
Unit ID: 192509
Telephone: (718) 939-5100 Carnegie Class: Spec 2-yr-Other
FAX Number: (718) 939-9235 Calendar System: Semester
URL: www.libi.edu
Established: 1968 Annual Undergrad Tuition & Fees: $10,416
Enrollment: 1,186 Coed
Affiliation or Control: Proprietary IRS Status: Proprietary
Highest Offering: Associate Degree
Accreditation: NY

01 President .... Ms. Monica W. FOOTE
05 Provost .... Ms. Stacey JOHNSON
11 Dir Operations/Inst Effectiveness .... Ms. Michelle HOUSTON
10 Assoc Dir Administration/Fin Aid .... Mr. Li ZHU
37 Financial Aid Specialist .... Ms. Yun Lin (Cynthia) LIU
08 Sr Librarian Flushing Campus .... Ms. Adrianna ARGUELLES
06 Registrar .... Ms. Connie ZHENG

*Long Island University (C)

700 Northern Boulevard, Brookville NY 11548-1327
County: Nassau FICE Identification: 002751
Unit ID: 192457
Telephone: (516) 299-2501 Carnegie Class: N/A
FAX Number: N/A
URL: www.liu.edu

01 President .... Dr. Kimberly R. CLINE
05 VP for Academic Programs .... Mr. Mohammed CHERKAOUI
13 VP for Information Technology & CIO .... Mr. George BAROUDI
10 Vice President Finance & Treasurer .... Mr. Christopher N. FEVOLA
32 VP of Student Affairs .... Mr. Michael BERTHEL
111 Vice President of Univ Advancement .... Ms. Kerry KRUCKEL
18 VP for Facilities .... Mr. Roy FERGUS
43 University Counsel .... Ms. Elizabeth GAFFNEY
45 Chief of Strategic Planning .... Mr. Andy PERSON
05 Senior VP for Academic Affairs .... Dr. Randy BURD
11 Chief Operating Officer .... Mr. Joseph SCHAEFER
19 Director Security/Safety .... Mr. Michael FEVOLA
29 Chief of Alumni Engagement .... Ms. Jodie SPERICO
41 Athletic Director .... Dr. William MARTINOV

*Long Island University - LIU Post (D)

720 Northern Boulevard, Brookville NY 11548
County: Nassau FICE Identification: 002754
Unit ID: 192448
Telephone: (516) 299-2900 Carnegie Class: DU-Higher
FAX Number: (516) 299-2137 Calendar System: Semester
URL: www.liu.edu/post
Established: 1954 Annual Undergrad Tuition & Fees: $39,136
Enrollment: 15,066 Coed
Affiliation or Control: Independent Non-Profit IRS Status: 501(c)3
Highest Offering: Doctorate
Accreditation: M, ACATE, CACREP, CLPSY, DIET, DIETD, DIETI, LIB, MLS, NURSE, RAD, SP, SPAA, SW, #VET

02 President .... Dr. Kimberly R. CLINE
05 Vice President for Academic Affairs .... Dr. Ed WEIS
49 Dean College Liberal Arts .... Dr. Paul GILMORE
66 Dean Sch Health Prof/Nursing .... Vacant
50 Dean College of Management .... Ms. Graziela FUSARO
53 Dean College of Educ/Info & Tech .... Dr. Laura SEINFELD
81 Dean College of Science .... Dr. Michael KINCH
74 Dean College of Veterinary Med .... Dr. Carmen FUENTEALBA
88 Dean of School of Comm & Design .... Vacant
32 Dean of Students/LIU Promise .... Ms. Ashley JOHN
92 Director Honors College .... Dr. Andy PERSON
88 Dir Tilles Ctr for Performing Arts .... Mr. Tom DUNN

Long Island University - LIU Brooklyn (E)

1 University Plaza, Brooklyn NY 11201
Telephone: (718) 488-1011 FICE Identification: 004779
Accreditation: &M, ARCPA, CLPSY, COARC, DMS, NURSE, OT, PH, PHAR, PTA, SP, SPAA, SW

Long Island University - LIU Hudson (F)

735 Anderson Hill Road, Purchase NY 10577
Telephone: (914) 831-2700 Identification: 666078
Accreditation: &M

Long Island University - LIU Riverhead (G)

121 Speonk Riverhead Road, Riverhead NY 11901-3499
Telephone: (631) 287-8010 Identification: 666174
Accreditation: &M

Louis V. Gerstner Jr. Graduate School of Biomedical Sciences, Memorial Sloan Kettering Cancer Center (H)

1275 York Avenue, P.O. Box 441, New York NY 10065
County: New York Identification: 666643
Telephone: (646) 888-6639 Carnegie Class: Not Classified
FAX Number: (646) 422-2351 Calendar System: Semester
URL: www.sloankettering.edu
Established: 2004 Annual Graduate Tuition & Fees: N/A
Enrollment: N/A Coed
Affiliation or Control: Independent Non-Profit IRS Status: 501(c)3
Highest Offering: Doctorate; No Undergraduates
Accreditation: NY

01 President .... Dr. Craig B. THOMPSON
05 Provost .... Dr. Joan MASSAGUE
20 Dean .... Dr. Michael H. OVERHOLTZER
88 Associate Dean .... Ms. Linda BURNLEY
81 VP Scientific Education & Training .... Dr. Ushma S. NEILL
06 Registrar .... Mr. David L. MCDONAGH
08 Director of Library Services .... Ms. Donna S. GIBSON
88 Assistant Dean .... Dr. Thomas G. MAGALDI
28 Assoc Dir Trainee Diversity Init .... Dr. Yaihara M. FORTIS SANTIAGO
22 Title IX Coordinator .... Ms. Lindsay CORNACCHIA
22 Title IX Coordinator .... Ms. Leslie M. BALLANTYNE

Machzikei Hadath Rabbinical College (I)

5407 16th Avenue, Brooklyn NY 11204-1805
County: Kings FICE Identification: 013026
Unit ID: 192624
Telephone: (718) 854-8777 Carnegie Class: Spec-4-yr-Faith
FAX Number: (718) 851-1265 Calendar System: Semester
URL: mhrc.edu
Established: 1956 Annual Undergrad Tuition & Fees: $11,650
Enrollment: 158 Male
Affiliation or Control: Independent Non-Profit IRS Status: 501(c)3
Highest Offering: Special 5-year Faith
Accreditation: RABN

01 President .... Mr. Alexander SCHAECHTER

Mandl School - The College of Allied Health (J)

254 W 54th Street, 9th Floor, New York NY 10019
County: New York FICE Identification: 007401
Unit ID: 192688
Telephone: (212) 247-3434 Carnegie Class: Spec 2-yr-Health
FAX Number: (212) 247-3617 Calendar System: Semester
URL: www.mandl.edu
Established: 1924 Annual Undergrad Tuition & Fees: $14,600
Enrollment: 493 Coed
Affiliation or Control: Proprietary IRS Status: Proprietary
Highest Offering: Associate Degree
Accreditation: ABHES, COARC, SURTEC

01 President .... Mr. Melvyn P. WEINER
05 Vice President of Academic Affairs .... Dr. Orsete DIAS
11 VP Operations/Dir Financial Aid .... Mr. Stuart WEINER
36 Vice President of Career Services .... Mr. James FLANAGAN
06 Vice Pres Records & Registration .... Mr. Marc WEINER
84 Vice Pres Enrollment Management .... Ms. Randie SENSER
10 Chief Financial Officer .... Mrs. Nettie WEINER
07 Director of Recruitment .... Ms. Racquel GARCIA

Manhattan College (K)

Manhattan College Parkway, Bronx NY 10471-4099
County: Bronx FICE Identification: 002758
Unit ID: 192703
Telephone: (718) 862-8000 Carnegie Class: Masters/L
FAX Number: (718) 862-8014 Calendar System: Semester
URL: www.manhattan.edu
Established: 1853 Annual Undergrad Tuition & Fees: $45,880
Enrollment: 3,965 Coed
Affiliation or Control: Independent Non-Profit IRS Status: 501(c)3
Highest Offering: Master's
Accreditation: M, AAQEP

01 Interim President .... Br. Daniel GARDNER
05 Provost & VP Academic Affairs .... Dr. Steven SCHREINER
10 VP for Finance & CFO .... Mr. Matthew S. MCMANNESS
32 Vice President Student Life .... Dr. Ronald GRAY
111 Vice President College Advancement .... Mr. Thomas MAURIELLO
15 Vice President for Human Resources .... Ms. Barbara A. FABE
18 Vice President for Facilities .... Vacant
84 Vice President Enrollment Mgmt .... Dr. Colette GEARY
88 Vice President for Mission .... Br. Jack CURRAN
20 Associate Provost .... Dr. Rani ROY
35 Assistant VP of Student Life .... Dr. Emmanuel AGO
35 Dean of Students .... Dr. Esmilda ABREU-HORNBOSTEL
06 Registrar .... Mr. Carlos TONCHE
07 Dir of Undergraduate Admissions .... Ms. Tara FAY-REILLY
08 Director of Libraries .... Dr. William WALTERS
13 Interim Chief Info Officer .... Mr. Robert MORAN
19 Director of Public Safety .... Mr. Peter DECARO
29 Director of Alumni Relations .... Mr. Louis CALVELLI
26 Assistant VP Marketing & Comm .... Mrs. Lydia E. GRAY
36 Director Ctr Career Development .... Ms. Rachel CIRELLI
38 Dir of Counseling & Health Services .... Ms. Jennifer MCARDLE
39 Director of Residence Life .... Mr. Charles CLENCY
41 Director of Athletics .... Ms. Marianne REILLY
42 Director of Campus Ministry .... Fr. Thomas FRANKS
30 Director of Development/Advancement .... Mr. Stephen WHITE
78 Director Opportunity Pgms .... Mr. Andrew BURNS
40 Director of Campus Bookstore .... Mr. Henry CASTILLO
22 Dir of Personnel/Affirm Action Ofcr .... Ms. Vickie M. COWAN
09 Dir Institutional Research .... Dr. Thomas KIRNBAUER
21 Controller .... Mr. Dennis LONERGAN
21 Business Manager .... Mr. Kenneth WALDHOF
85 International Student Advisor .... Ms. Debra L. DAMICO
37 Director of Financial Aid Admin .... Ms. Denise SCALZO
49 Dean of Liberal Arts .... Dr. Cory BLAD
50 Dean of O'Malley School of Business .... Dr. Donald GIBSON
53 Dean of Education & Health .... Dr. Karen NICHOLSON
54 Dean of Engineering .... Dr. Tim WARD
51 Dean of Sch Cont & Prof Studies .... Dr. Steven GOSS
121 Director Ctr for Academic Success .... Ms. Marisa PASSAFIUME
81 Dean of Science .... Dr. Marcy PETEROY-KELLY
88 Dir of Specialized Resource Center .... Ms. Anne VACCARO
123 Director of Graduate Admissions .... Mr. Kevin TAYLOR
88 Dir Acad Support Svcs/HE Opp Pgm .... Ms. Marilyn CARTER-STEVENS
104 Director Study Abroad .... Dr. Ricardo DELLO BUONO
43 VP External/Legal Affs/Chf of Staff .... Vacant
28 Director Equity/Diversity/Title IX .... Vacant
108 Director of Assessment .... Dr. Edward DEE
88 Compliance Officer .... Mr. Goldie ADELE

Manhattan School of Music (L)

130 Claremont Avenue, New York NY 10027-4631
County: New York FICE Identification: 002759
Unit ID: 192712
Telephone: (212) 749-2802 Carnegie Class: Spec-4-yr-Arts
FAX Number: (212) 749-5471 Calendar System: Semester
URL: www.msmnyc.edu
Established: 1918 Annual Undergrad Tuition & Fees: $49,270
Enrollment: 939 Coed
Affiliation or Control: Independent Non-Profit IRS Status: 501(c)3
Highest Offering: Doctorate
Accreditation: M

01 President .... Dr. James GANDRE
05 Executive VP and Provost .... Dr. Joyce GRIGGS
10 Sr VP and CFO .... Ms. Tangella MADDOX
111 VP for Advancement .... Ms. Susan MADDEN
84 VP/Dean of Enrollment Management .... Ms. Melissa COCCO
26 VP for Media and Communications .... Mr. Jeff BREITHAUPT
15 VP for Human Relations & Admin .... Ms. Carol MATOS
20 Dean of Academic Affairs .... Ms. Kelly SAWATSKY
32 Dean of Students .... Dr. Monica CHRISTENSEN
88 Dean of Performance/Production Ops .... Ms. Madeline TOLLIVER
100 Chief of Staff .... Ms. Alexa SMITH
18 Dir of Facilities & Campus Safety .... Mr. Bryan GREANEY
13 Chief Information Officer .... Mr. Neeraj KUMAR
21 Assoc VP of Finance & Controller .... Mr. Anthony CAMMARANO
06 Registrar .... Ms. Christy PASTORE
106 Dir of Distance Learning & Rec Arts .... Mr. Chris SHADE
37 Director of Financial Aid .... Ms. Anna CHRISSOTIMOS
84 Director of Enrollment .... Mr. Jonathan HERBERT
35 Director of Student Engagement .... Ms. Melanie DORSEY
39 Director of Residence Life .... Ms. April JENKINS
31 Director of Community Partnerships .... Ms. Rebecca CHARNOW
29 Assoc Dir for Alumni Engagement .... Vacant
08 Director of Library Services .... Mr. Peter CALEB
44 Assoc Dir of Annual Giving .... Ms. Julie WALLIN
40 Campus Store Manager .... Ms. Katherine COPLAND

85 Director of Intl Student Services .... Mr. Michael LOCKHART
88 Ctr for Music Entrepreneurship .... Mr. Chris VAUGHN
21 Assoc VP of Finance and Controller .... Mr. Hector PAREDES
04 Admin Asst Office of the President ....Ms. Nicole WEIGELT

Manhattanville College (A)

2900 Purchase Street, Purchase NY 10577-2132
County: Westchester FICE Identification: 002760
Unit ID: 192749
Telephone: (914) 694-2200 Carnegie Class: Masters/L
FAX Number: (914) 694-6234 Calendar System: Semester
URL: www.mville.edu
Established: 1841 Annual Undergrad Tuition & Fees: $40,330
Enrollment: 2,408 Coed
Affiliation or Control: Independent Non-Profit IRS Status: 501(c)3
Highest Offering: Doctorate
Accreditation: M, CAEP, NURSE, RAD

01 Interim President .... Dr. Louise H. FEROE
04 Exec Admin Asst to the President ....Ms. Deborah A. FALLONE
05 Provost/VP of Academic Affairs ....Ms. Christine DEHNE
10 VP Finance/Operations ....Ms. Jean HALL
07 Vice Pres Admissions & Marketing .... Mr. Troy COGBURN
111 Vice Pres Inst Advancement .... Ms. Sarah E. KELLY
18 Director of Physical Plant ....Mr. Michael WENZ
32 VP Student Affairs/Chief Div Ofcr ....Dr. Cindy L. PORTER
49 Dean School of Arts & Sciences ....Dr. Rebecca LAFLEUR
13 CIO/VP Digital Strategy & Planning ....Mr. Jim RUSSELL
107 Assoc Dean School of Prof Studies ....Ms. Laura PERSKY
53 Dean School of Education ....Dr. Shelley WEPNER
26 AVP for Communications & Marketing .... Ms. Cara CEA
06 Registrar ....Ms. Jeneen KELLY
08 Director of the Library .... Mr. Jeff ROSEDALE
37 Director of Financial Aid ....Ms. Cecilia GRANDA
38 Assoc Dean Stdnt Health/Counseling ....Ms. Melissa BOSTON
35 Dean of Students ....Vacant
41 Director of Athletics ....Ms. Julene CAULFIELD
36 Director Center for Career Devel ....Vacant
19 Director of Security ....Mr. Anthony HERRMANN
15 Director of Human Resources ....Mr. Rich SHEEHY
96 Director of Purchasing ....Mr. Matthew HYLAND
104 Int Dir Intl Stdnt Svcs/Stdy Abroad ....Ms. Katherine PALMER
23 Assoc Dn Student Health/Counseling ....Ms. Melissa BOSTON
100 Special Assistant to the President ....Ms. Loren MCDERMOTT
30 Dir of Advance Svcs & Prospect Mgmt ....Ms. Elizabeth FIORE
39 Asst Dean of Student Engagement ....Ms. Susan BOYD
44 Director Annual Giving ....Ms. Meghan CASEY
29 Director Alumni Relations ....Ms. Polly SCHMITZ

Maria College (B)

700 New Scotland Avenue, Albany NY 12208-1798
County: Albany FICE Identification: 002763
Unit ID: 192785
Telephone: (518) 438-3111 Carnegie Class: Spec-4-yr-Other Health
FAX Number: (518) 438-7170 Calendar System: 4/1/4
URL: www.mariacollege.edu
Established: 1958 Annual Undergrad Tuition & Fees: $15,610
Enrollment: 864 Coed
Affiliation or Control: Independent Non-Profit IRS Status: 501(c)3
Highest Offering: Master's
Accreditation: M, ADNUR, NUR, OT, OTA

01 President ....Dr. Lynn ORTALE
05 VP for Academic Affairs ....Dr. Anne S. JUNG
10 Vice Pres Finance/Enrollment Mgmt ...Dr. Joseph M. MCDONALD
11 VP for Administration ....Mr. Joel D. NUDI
111 Sr VP Inst Advance/Marketing/Comm .....Ms. Victoria L. BATTELL
110 Assoc VP Advancement ....Vacant
37 Director Financial Aid ....Mr. Richard F. SABBIA
06 Registrar ....Ms. Karen CONRAD
07 AVP Enroll Mgmt/Dir of Admissions ....Ms. Katie LESKO
08 Librarian ....Ms. Krista ROBBIN
13 Director of Information Technology ....Ms. Robin DELORENZO
18 Superintendent Physical Plant ....Mr. Andrew PEREZ
36 Director Career Services ....Dr. Jason COLEY
15 Manager of Human Resources ....Ms. Rosalyn VAZQUEZ
20 Dean of College ....Dr. Anne S. JUNG
09 AVP of Institutional Research ....Dr. Kim SPEERSCHNEIDER
04 Admin Assistant to the President ....Mrs. Sandra K. GRADY
30 Director of Development ....Ms. Katelyn PAULY
32 AVP Student Affairs/Dean of Stdnts ......Ms. Barbara RUSLANDER

Marist College (C)

3399 North Road, Poughkeepsie NY 12601-1387
County: Dutchess FICE Identification: 002765
Unit ID: 192819
Telephone: (845) 575-3000 Carnegie Class: Masters/L
FAX Number: (845) 471-6213 Calendar System: Semester
URL: www.marist.edu
Established: 1929 Annual Undergrad Tuition & Fees: $42,290
Enrollment: 6,600 Coed
Affiliation or Control: Independent Non-Profit IRS Status: 501(c)3
Highest Offering: Doctorate
Accreditation: M, ARCPA, CAATE, MLS, PTA, SPAA, SW

01 President ....Dr. Dennis J. MURRAY
03 EVP/Chief Strategy/Innovation Ofcr ......Dr. Geoffrey L. BRACKETT
05 Vice President for Academic Affairs ......Dr. Thomas S. WERMUTH
84 VP Enrollment/Mktg & Communications ...... Mr. Sean P. KAYLOR
111 Vice President College Advancement ....Mr. Christopher M. DELGIORNO
13 VP Information Technology/CIO ....Mr. Michael CAPUTO
32 VP/Dean for Student Affairs ....Mrs. Deborah A. DICAPRIO
10 Vice President Business Affairs/CFO .... Mr. John P. PECCHIA
15 VP for Human Resources ....Mrs. Christina DANIELE
20 Assoc VP/Dean Academic Affairs ....Dr. John RITSCHDORFF
07 Asst VP Enroll Mgmt/Dean UG Admiss ...Mr. Kent W. RINEHART
123 Dean Graduate Admission ....Mrs. Kelly HOLMES
35 Assoc Dean of Student Affairs ....Mr. Steve SANSOLA
43 College Counsel ....Ms. Sima Saran AHUJA
29 Executive Director Alumni Relations ....Ms. Amy K. WOODS
09 Director Inst Research & Planning ....Vacant
06 Assoc Dean Stdnt Acad Aff/Registrar ....Mrs. Judith IVANKOVIC
37 Exec Dir Student Financial Services ....Mr. Joseph R. WEGLARZ
08 Director of Library .... Ms. Becky ALBITZ
18 Director of Physical Plant ....Mr. Justin BUTWELL
26 Asst VP Marketing & Communications .... Mrs. Elisabeth W. TAVAREZ
96 Director of Purchasing ....Mr. Stephen J. KOCHIS
36 Director Career Services ....Dr. Mary O. JONES
19 Director of Safety & Security ....Mr. John BLAISDELL
39 Director of Housing & Resident Life ....Mrs. Sarah H. ENGLISH
41 Director of Athletics ....Mr. Timothy S. MURRAY
24 Director of Media & Instruct Tech ....Ms. Joey WALL
23 Director of Health Services ....Dr. Claudia ZEGANS
38 Director of Counseling ....Dr. Naomi A. FERLEGER
42 Director Campus Ministry .... Bro. Francis E. KELLY
44 Director of Annual Giving ....Ms. Hannah ALLEY-KELLER
105 Director Web Services ....Vacant
50 Dean School of Management ....Vacant
60 Dean School of Communication/Arts .... Dr. Jacqueline REICH
77 Dean School of Comp Sci/Mathematics ......Dr. Roger L. NORTON
49 Dean School of Liberal Arts ....Dr. Martin B. SHAFFER
81 Dean School of Science .... Dr. Alicia SLATER
107 Dean School of Professional Pgms ....Vacant
83 Dean Sch of Social/Behavioral Sci .... Dr. Deborah GATINS
104 Dean International Programs ....Mr. John PETERS
101 Chief of Staff & Secy to Board ....Mrs. Emily V. SALAND
25 Director of Academic Grants ....Mrs. Donna S. BERGER
28 Diversity/Inclusion/Engagement Ofcr ....Vacant

Marymount Manhattan College (D)

221 E 71st Street, New York NY 10021-4597
County: New York FICE Identification: 002769
Unit ID: 192864
Telephone: (212) 517-0400 Carnegie Class: Bac-A&S
FAX Number: (212) 517-0541 Calendar System: Semester
URL: www.mmm.edu
Established: 1936 Annual Undergrad Tuition & Fees: $37,410
Enrollment: 1,722 Coed
Affiliation or Control: Independent Non-Profit IRS Status: 501(c)3
Highest Offering: Master's
Accreditation: M

01 President .... Dr. Kerry WALK
10 Executive VP Finance & Admin/CFO ....Ms. Maisha WILLIAMS
05 VP Acad Affairs/Dean of Faculty ....Dr. Peter NACCARATO
111 VP Institutional Advancement ....Mr. Graham CIRAULO
84 VP for Student Enroll/Engagement ....Vacant
32 AVP Stdnt Success/Engage/Dn Stdnts ...... Ms. Emmalyn YAMRICK
15 Associate VP for Human Resources .... Ms. Bree BULLINGHAM
45 Associate VP Strategic Initiatives .... Dr. Kathleen LEBESCO
21 AVP Finance & Admin/Controller ....Mr. John RAGNO
20 AVP for Academic Administration ....Mr. Richard SHELDON
13 AVP for IT ....Mr. Kurt JN MARIE
28 Chief EDI Officer ....Vacant
36 Exec Dir of Career Svcs ....Ms. Robin E. NACKMAN
88 Associate Controller & Dir Finance ....Ms. Sun YOON
07 Dean of Admissions .... Mr. Christian ANDRADE
121 Associate VP/Dean Acad Excellence .... Mr. Michael G. SALMON
88 Associate VP Enrollment Management ....Ms. Christine SNEVA
06 Registrar ....Ms. Regina CHAN
09 Dir Institutional Research ....Vacant
35 Assoc Dir Student Dev & Activities .... Ms. Stephanie TOVAR
124 Dean of Student Success Advising ....Ms. Melissa WEEKES-STOUTE
08 Director of the Library ....Mr. Brian ROCCO
22 Dir of Acad Access/Disability Svcs .... Ms. Lauren KILIAN
38 Dir Counseling & Wellness Center .... Ms. Deborah GUORDANO
12 Dir of Bedford Hills College Prog .... Ms. Aileen BAUMGARTNER
96 Director of Administrative Services ....Vacant
114 Asst Controller for Recon/Reporting ....Vacant
19 Director of EM & Campus Safety ....Mr. Jason BALSAN
26 Sr Director of Strategic Comm ....Mr. Stephen EICHINGER
35 Dean of Students ....Dr. Dayne HUTCHINSON
109 Exec Dir of Business Operations .... Ms. Diana ZAMBROTTA-SHEETZ
102 Sr Dir Inst Giving/Advance Svcs ....Vacant
44 Sr Dir Indiv Giving/Donor Rel ....Vacant
112 Director of Major Gifts/Parent Prog ....Ms. Rita MURRAY
04 Special Assistant to the President ....Ms. Tunisia WRAGG

Mechon L'Hoyroa (E)

168 Maple Avenue, Monsey NY 10952
County: Rockland FICE Identification: 042615
Unit ID: 490328
Telephone: (845) 425-9565 Carnegie Class: Spec-4-yr-Faith
FAX Number: (845) 425-2094 Calendar System: Other
Established: 1990 Annual Undergrad Tuition & Fees: N/A
Enrollment: 57 Male
Affiliation or Control: Jewish IRS Status: 501(c)3
Highest Offering: First Talmudic Degree
Accreditation: AIJS

01 Rosh Kollel ....Reb. Yitzchok M. TAUBER

Medaille University (F)

18 Agassiz Circle, Buffalo NY 14214-2695
County: Erie FICE Identification: 002777
Unit ID: 192925
Telephone: (716) 880-2000 Carnegie Class: Masters/L
FAX Number: (716) 884-0291 Calendar System: Semester
URL: www.medaille.edu
Established: 1875 Annual Undergrad Tuition & Fees: $31,500
Enrollment: 2,076 Coed
Affiliation or Control: Independent Non-Profit IRS Status: 501(c)3
Highest Offering: Doctorate
Accreditation: M, CACREP, CAHIIM, CLPSY, IACBE

01 President ....Dr. Kenneth M. MACUR
05 Vice President Academic Affairs .... Ms. Carmen R. WILSON
10 Vice President Business/Finance ....Mr. Robert MCDOW
111 Vice Pres for Inst Advancement .... Mr. David GREENMAN
09 AVP for Researach/Grants/Assessment ....Dr. Mary M. TODD
32 VP for Student Development .... Ms. Amy M. DEKAY
41 Athletic Director ....Ms. Susan M. ROARKE
36 Director Career Planning/Placement ....Ms. Carol CULLINAN
13 Chief Information Officer ....Mr. Robert D. CHYKA
06 Registrar ....Ms. Tracey KONGATS
07 Director Undergrad Admissions .... Ms. Brooke URBAN
08 Int Library Director ....Mr. Thomas ORANGE
37 Director Financial Aid ....Mr. James P. AYERS
15 Director of Human Resources ....Ms. Bobbie J. BILOTTA
35 Dir Student Conduct/Residence Life .... Ms. Candice CADENA
38 Director Counseling Services ....Ms. Rosalina B. RIZZO
19 Director of Campus Public Safety ....Ms. Debra D. KELLY

Medaille University Rochester Campus (G)

1880 S Winton Road, Suite 1, Rochester NY 14618
Telephone: (585) 272-0030 Identification: 770140
Accreditation: &M

Mercy College (H)

555 Broadway, Dobbs Ferry NY 10522-1189
County: Westchester FICE Identification: 002772
Unit ID: 193016
Telephone: (800) 637-2969 Carnegie Class: Masters/L
FAX Number: (914) 674-5978 Calendar System: Semester
URL: www.mercy.edu
Established: 1950 Annual Undergrad Tuition & Fees: $20,558
Enrollment: 9,547 Coed
Affiliation or Control: Independent Non-Profit IRS Status: 501(c)3
Highest Offering: Doctorate
Accreditation: M, ARCPA, CAEP, EXSC, MLS, NURSE, OT, OTA, PTA, SP, SW

01 President ....Mr. Timothy HALL
05 Provost ....Dr. Eva FERNANDEZ
20 Assoc Provost for Academic Affairs .... Dr. Dena WHIPPLE
32 Vice President of Student Affairs .... Mr. Kevin JOYCE
50 Dean School of Business ....Dr. Lloyd GIBSON
53 Interim Dean School of Education ....Dr. Eric MARTONE
83 Dean School Soc/Behav Sci ....Dr. Stuart SIDLE
81 Int Dean School Health/Natural Sci .... Dr. Kathleen GOLISZ
66 Associate Dean of Nursing ....Dr. Miriam FORD
49 Dean School of Liberal Arts ....Dr. Peter WEST
15 Director of Human Resources .... Ms. Annette PIECORA
11 VP Operations & Facilities ....Mr. Thomas SIMMONDS
10 VP Finance & Chief Financial Ofcr ....Mr. Brett CARROLL
84 VP for Enrollment Management ....Mr. Adam CASTRO
111 Chief Advancement Officer ....Ms. Bernadette WADE
100 Chief of Staff ....Ms. Jessica HABER
04 Exec Assistant Office of President .... Ms. Grace CREIGHTON
108 Director of Learning Assessment ....Ms. Victoria FERRARA
43 General Counsel ....Ms. Kristen BOWES
37 Director of Financial Aid .... Mr. Paul LORENZONI
07 Executive Director of Admissions ....Mrs. Allison GURDINEER
09 Dir Institutional Research ....Ms. Joanne DEMARCO
121 Exec Dir Student Success .... Mr. Rajesh KUMAR
39 Interim Dir Residence Life ....Ms. Brittnay CROCCO
13 Chief Information Officer ....Ms. Camille SHELLEY
14 Director of Information Technology .... Mr. Todd PRATTELLA
06 Registrar ....Mrs. Danielle QUILLIGAN
45 Exec Dir Inst Planning & Assessment .... Mr. Matthew PRESSER
113 Exec Director of Student Accounts .... Ms. Felicia BRANDON
21 Controller ....Ms. Narda ROMERO
19 Exec Dir Safety & Emergency Mgmt ....Mr. Konrad MOTYKA
114 Director Budget & Planning .... Ms. Claire HOWARD-COSTER
18 Director of Operations ....Ms. Orla FITZSIMONS
96 Director of Purchasing ....Ms. Patricia SABATINO
08 Interim Director of Libraries ....Dr. Moddie BRELAND
41 Director of Athletics ....Mr. Matt KILCULLEN
26 AVP Marketing & Analytics ....Mr. Christian CONNELLY
27 Director of Communications ....Ms. Jessica BAILY
30 Exec Director of Development ....Ms. Katherine COPPINGER
29 Director of Alumni Relations ....Ms. Alexis MCGRATH-ROTHENBERG
25 Dir Sponsored Programs .... Ms. Janet PARTENZA
85 Sr Dir International Student Svcs ....Ms. Bogdana VLADESCU
104 Sr Dir International Student Svcs ....Ms. Bogdana VLADESCU
106 Director Online Learning ....Dr. Mary LOZINA
103 Director of Career Education ....Ms. Lyn LEIS
101 Secretary of the Institution/Board .... Ms. Jessica HABER

112 Assoc Dir Donor Rels/Annual Giving ..... Ms. Heather APOLLONIO
23 Director Health & Wellness .... Ms. Colleen POWERS
38 Director Student Counseling Center .... Dr. Ori SHINAR

Mesivta of Eastern Parkway Rabbinical Seminary (A)

510 Dahill Road, Brooklyn NY 11218-5559
County: Kings FICE Identification: 009335
Unit ID: 193061
Telephone: (718) 438-1002 Carnegie Class: Spec 2-yr-Other
FAX Number: (718) 438-2591 Calendar System: Semester
Established: 1947 Annual Undergrad Tuition & Fees: $9,450
Enrollment: 45 Male
Affiliation or Control: Independent Non-Profit IRS Status: 501(c)3
Highest Offering: Second Talmudic Degree
Accreditation: RABN

01 President .... Rabbi Issac HEIMOVITZ
32 Dean of Students .... Rabbi Shlomo Z. EPSTEIN
37 Director of Student Financial Aid .... Rabbi Ira LIBERMAN
46 Director of Research .... Rabbi Hersch BASCH
10 Chief Fiscal Officer .... Rabbi Joseph HALBERSTADT

Mesivtha Tifereth Jerusalem of America (B)

145 E Broadway, New York NY 10002-6301
County: New York FICE Identification: 003974
Unit ID: 193070
Telephone: (212) 964-2830 Carnegie Class: Spec-4-yr-Faith
FAX Number: (212) 349-5213 Calendar System: Semester
Established: 1907 Annual Undergrad Tuition & Fees: $12,000
Enrollment: 62 Male
Affiliation or Control: Independent Non-Profit IRS Status: 501(c)3
Highest Offering: Second Talmudic Degree
Accreditation: RABN

01 President & Dean Faculties .... Rabbi David BEREL
06 Registrar .... Chana YAMPOLSKY
37 Director Student Financial Aid .... E. GOLD

Metropolitan College of New York (C)

60 West Street, New York NY 10006
County: New York FICE Identification: 009769
Unit ID: 190114
Telephone: (212) 343-1234 Carnegie Class: Masters/M
FAX Number: (212) 343-7399 Calendar System: Semester
URL: www.metropolitan.edu
Established: 1964 Annual Undergrad Tuition & Fees: $20,188
Enrollment: 856 Coed
Affiliation or Control: Independent Non-Profit IRS Status: 501(c)3
Highest Offering: Master's
Accreditation: M, ACBSP

01 President .... Dr. Joanne PASSARO
10 VP Finance & Admin/CFO .... Ms. Michelle BLANKENSHIP
05 VP for Academic Affairs .... Mr. Humphrey CROOKENDALE
84 VP Enrollment Mgmt/Student Svcs .... Ms. Joy COLELLI
13 VP Technology/CIO .... Mr. Adrian SMITH
15 Director Human Resources .... Ms. Elaine ROBLES
30 Chief Development Officer .... Ms. Kristin CURRY
80 Dean Human Svcs & Public Admin .... Vacant
32 Dean of Students .... Ms. Clotilde IBARRA
07 Director of Admissions .... Vacant
06 Registrar .... Ms. Joanna BOSTON
37 Dir of Financial Aid/Scholarships .... Vacant
36 Dir of Career/Professional Dev .... Mr. Philip MEADE
08 Director of Library Services .... Ms. Kate ADLER
09 Dir Institutional Rsrch/Assessment .... Ms. Tamara NOECKER
26 Director Public/Alumni Relations .... Ms. Tina GEORGIOU
113 Bursar .... Mr. Taurean KENNEDY
04 Exec Assistant to the President .... Ms. Isabel CABRERA

Mildred Elley (D)

855 Central Avenue, Albany NY 12206
County: Albany FICE Identification: 022195
Unit ID: 193201
Telephone: (518) 786-0855 Carnegie Class: Assoc/HVT-High Non
FAX Number: (518) 786-0898 Calendar System: Semester
URL: www.mildred-elley.edu
Established: 1917 Annual Undergrad Tuition & Fees: $13,509
Enrollment: 466 Coed
Affiliation or Control: Proprietary IRS Status: Proprietary
Highest Offering: Associate Degree
Accreditation: ABHES

00 Chairwoman of the Board .... Ms. Faith A. TAKES
01 President .... Dr. John J. MCGRATH

Mildred Elley-New York City (E)

25 Broadway, 16th Floor, New York NY 10004
Telephone: (212) 380-9004 Identification: 770747
Accreditation: ABHES

Mirrer Yeshiva Central Institute (F)

1795 Ocean Parkway, Brooklyn NY 11223-2010
County: Kings FICE Identification: 004798
Unit ID: 193247
Telephone: (718) 645-0536 Carnegie Class: Spec-4-yr-Faith
FAX Number: (718) 645-9251 Calendar System: Semester
Established: 1947 Annual Undergrad Tuition & Fees: $10,170
Enrollment: 156 Male
Affiliation or Control: Independent Non-Profit IRS Status: 501(c)3
Highest Offering: Second Talmudic Degree
Accreditation: RABN

00 Chancellor .... Rabbi Avrohom Yaakov NELKENBAUM
01 President and Dean .... Rabbi Osher KALMANOWITZ
05 Vice President & Dean .... Rabbi Asher BERENBAUM
33 Dean of Men .... Rabbi Esrael ERLANGER
03 Executive Director .... Rabbi Pinchas HECHT
06 Registrar-Administrator .... Rabbi Eli ADLIN
08 Director of the Library .... Rabbi Aaron SAPOZNICK
38 Director of Guidance .... Rabbi Yisroel FISHMAN
37 Financial Aid Director .... Mrs. Devorah BERENBAUM

Mohawk Valley Community College (G)

1101 Sherman Drive, Utica NY 13501-5394
County: Oneida FICE Identification: 002871
Unit ID: 193283
Telephone: (315) 792-5400 Carnegie Class: Assoc/HT-High Non
FAX Number: (315) 792-5666 Calendar System: Semester
URL: www.mvcc.edu
Established: 1946 Annual Undergrad Tuition & Fees (In-District): $5,500
Enrollment: 5,704 Coed
Affiliation or Control: State/Local IRS Status: 501(c)3
Highest Offering: Associate Degree
Accreditation: M, ADNUR, CAHIIM, COARC, RAD, SURTEC

01 President .... Dr. Randall J. VAN WAGONER
04 Assistant to the President .... Ms. Gloria KAROL
88 Exec Dir Org Culture & Wellness .... Ms. Jill HEINTZ
09 Dir Institutional Research/Analysis .... Ms. Marie MIKNAVICH
05 Vice Pres Learning/Academic Affairs .... Dr. Lewis J. KAHLER
32 Vice Pres Student Affairs .... Ms. Stephanie C. REYNOLDS
10 Vice Pres Administrative Services .... Mr. Thomas SQUIRES
111 VP Cmty Devel/Exec Dir MVCC Found .... Mr. Frank DUROSS
20 Asst VP Learning/Academic Affairs .... Mr. James LYNCH
108 Dean Curriculum/Assessment .... Ms. Julie DEWAN
20 Asst VP Learning/Academic Affairs .... Mr. Timothy THOMAS
81 Dean School of STEM Transfer .... Mr. Jake MIHEVC
57 Dean School of Art .... Mr. Todd BEHRENDT
50 Dean School of Business/Hospitality .... Ms. Christine VANNAMEE
54 Dean School of STEM Career .... Dr. Robert WOODROW
79 Dean School of Humanities .... Mr. Jim ROBERTS
76 Dean School of Health Sciences ..... Ms. Melissa COPPERWHEAT
83 Dean School of Public/Human Service .... Vacant
08 Director College Libraries .... Mr. Stephen FRISBEE
84 Dean Enrollment .... Mrs. Jennifer DEWEERTH
121 Dean Student Support .... Mr. James MAIO
39 Dean Student & Residence Life .... Mr. Dennis GIBBONS
103 Assoc VP of Workforce Development ... Ms. Franca ARMSTRONG
30 Dir of Development .... Ms. Deanna FERRO-AURIENCE
96 Coord Expend/Fixed Asset Procure .... Ms. Joyce PALMER
13 Exec Dir of Information Technology .... Ms. Mary Jane PARRY
88 Dir Ctr Community/Economic Dev .... Ms. Sarah LAM
15 Exec Director of Human Resources .... Mrs. Crystal MARCEAU
26 Director Marketing/Communications .... Mr. Alen SMAJIC
07 Director of Admissions .... Mr. Daniel IANNO
37 Director of Financial Aid .... Mr. Michael PEDE
06 Dir of Student Records/Registrar .... Mrs. Rosemary V. SPETKA
18 Dir of Facilities and Operations .... Mr. Michael MCHARRIS
19 Exec Dir Pub Safety/Emergency Mgmt .... Mr. David AMICO
21 Business Office Controller .... Mr. Brian MOLINARO
41 Dean of Athletics .... Mr. Gary BROADHURST
28 Director of Diversity .... Dr. Todd MARSHALL

Mohawk Valley Community College Rome Campus (H)

1101 Floyd Avenue, Rome NY 13440
Telephone: (315) 339-3470 Identification: 770141
Accreditation: &M

Molloy University (I)

1000 Hempstead Avenue, PO Box 5002,
Rockville Centre NY 11571-5002
County: Nassau FICE Identification: 002775
Unit ID: 193292
Telephone: (516) 323-3000 Carnegie Class: Masters/L
FAX Number: N/A Calendar System: 4/1/4
URL: www.molloy.edu
Established: 1955 Annual Undergrad Tuition & Fees: $32,550
Enrollment: 5,115 Coed
Affiliation or Control: Independent Non-Profit IRS Status: 501(c)3
Highest Offering: Doctorate
Accreditation: M, CACREP, COARC, CVT, IACBE, MUS, NMT, NURSE, SP, SW

01 President .... Dr. James P. LENTINI
05 Provost/VP Academic Affairs .... Dr. Michelle PISKULICH
10 Vice Pres for Finance & Treasurer .... Dr. Susan WILLIAMS
84 Vice Pres Enrollment Management .... Ms. Linda ALBANESE
111 VP for Advancement .... Mr. Edward J. THOMPSON
32 VP for Student Affairs[1] .... Dr. Janine BISCARI
42 VP for Mission & Ministry .... Ms. Catherine MUSCENTE
30 Dir Development & Special Projects .... Ms. Angela ZIMMERMAN
113 Director Student Financial Services .... Ms. Debra O'CONNOR
36 Asst Director of Career Services .... Ms. Cristen D'ACCORDO
41 Director of Athletics .... Ms. Susan CASSIDY
07 Dean of Admissions .... Mr. Stephen OSTENDORFF
37 Director of Financial Aid .... Mrs. Ana C. LOCKWARD
06 Registrar .... Ms. Susan FORTMAN
09 Assoc Dir Inst Effectiveness .... Ms. Kristie CONROY
15 Asst VP for Human Resources .... Ms. Lisa MILLER
18 Asst VP for Facilities .... Mr. James MULTARI
26 Asst VP of Marketing & Public RelsR .... Mr. Ken YOUNG
19 Director of Public Safety .... Mr. Brian CONNORS
85 Director of International Education ... Ms. Kimberly LANGENMAYR
105 Director of Web Technologies .... Vacant
20 Assoc Provost for Academic Affairs .... Dr. Barbara T. SCHMIDT
13 VP Technology/Inst Effectiveness .... Mr. Michael TORRES
91 Dir Networking/Infrastructure .... Mr. Sean LAURIE
08 Head Librarian .... Ms. Judith BRINK-DRESCHER
100 Chief of Staff .... Ms. Diane K. FORNIERI
106 Dean Innovative Delivery Methods .... Ms. Amy GAIMARO
04 Executive Asst to the President .... Ms. Ann Marie LUONGO

Monroe College (J)

2501 Jerome Avenue, Bronx NY 10468-5407
County: Bronx FICE Identification: 004799
Unit ID: 193308
Telephone: (718) 933-6700 Carnegie Class: Masters/L
FAX Number: (718) 295-5861 Calendar System: Semester
URL: www.monroecollege.edu
Established: 1933 Annual Undergrad Tuition & Fees: $16,536
Enrollment: 6,541 Coed
Affiliation or Control: Proprietary IRS Status: Proprietary
Highest Offering: Master's
Accreditation: M, ACBSP, ACFEI, ADNUR, CAEP, NUR, PNUR

01 President .... Marc M. JEROME
05 SVP of Academic/Student Affairs .... Dr. Karenann CARTY
21 Controller .... Olesia TIAGI
12 SVP/Bronx Campus Dean .... Anthony ALLEN
12 SVP/New Rochelle Campus Dean .... David DIMOND
26 Executive Director Public Affairs .... Jacqueline RUEGGER
58 SVP King Graduate School .... Alex EPHREM
32 VP Academic/Student Affairs .... Carol GENESE
86 Asst Vice Pres Governmental Affairs .... Dr. Donald E. SIMON
108 Asst VP Inst Research & Effective .... Dr. Edward S. SCHNEIDERMAN
27 Executive Director of Marketing .... Lauren ROSENTHAL
06 Registrar .... Abigail THORPE
09 Dir Institutional Research .... Peter NWAKEZE
07 Dean Admissions NR Campus .... Michael NIEDZWIECKI
21 AVP Student Financial Services .... Daniel SHARON
113 Bursar .... Scott STERN
35 Dean of Intl Student Services .... Mark SONNENSTEIN
07 Dean of International Admissions .... Gersom LOPEZ
07 Vice President Online Admissions .... Craig PATRICK
37 Director Student Financial Aid .... Calette FAGAN-MURDOCK
36 VP Corporate & Community Outreach .... Pamela DELLAPORTA
08 Director of Library Services BX .... Christine ARTIS
08 Director of Library Services NR .... Tom GORDON
39 Director of Residential Life .... Romario DACOSTA
29 Director of Alumni Relations .... Leslie JEROME
13 Chief Info Technology Officer (CIO) .... Michael MCGOVERN
04 Executive Assistant to President .... Jennifer NACCARI
15 Director of Human Resources .... Kerry MCLAUGHLIN
19 Director of Public Safety .... Clifford HOLLINGSWORTH
41 Athletic Director .... Luis MELENDEZ

Monroe Community College (K)

1000 E Henrietta Road, Rochester NY 14623-5780
County: Monroe FICE Identification: 002872
Unit ID: 193326
Telephone: (585) 292-2000 Carnegie Class: Assoc/MT-VT-High Non
FAX Number: (585) 427-2749 Calendar System: Semester
URL: https://www.monroecc.edu/
Established: 1961 Annual Undergrad Tuition & Fees (In-District): $5,662
Enrollment: 10,161 Coed
Affiliation or Control: State/Local IRS Status: 501(c)3
Highest Offering: Associate Degree
Accreditation: M, ADNUR, DH, EMT, MLTAD, RAD, SURGT

01 President .... Dr. DeAnna R. BURT-NANNA
10 CFO & VP Admin Svcs .... Mr. Gregory T. HINTON
05 Actg Provost/VP Academic/Stdnt Svcs .... Dr. Kimberly MCKINSEY-MABRY
04 Executive Asst to President .... Ms. Marra GREEN
28 VP/Chief Diversity Officer .... Dr. Calvin J. GANTT
103 VP Econ Dev/Workforce Svc .... Dr. Robin COLE, JR.
102 VP Advancement/Dir MCC Foundation ...... Ms. Gretchen D. WOOD
19 Interim Director Public Safety .... Mr. Christopher J. PIRO
15 Director Human Resources .... Ms. Kristen M. LOWE
20 Assoc ViP Instructional Svcs .... Dr. Terrance KEYS
20 Assoc Vice Pres Academic Services .... Ms. Kimberley COLLINS
32 Assoc Vice Pres Student Services .... Vacant
84 Assoc VP Enrollment Mgmt .... Ms. Christine CASALINUOVO-ADAMS
11 Assoc Vice President Admin Svcs .... Mr. Darrell K. JACHIM-MOORE

13 AVP Technology Svcs/CIO ... Ms. Eileen M. WIRLEY
18 Assoc Vice Pres Facilities ... Mr. Quent RHODES
86 Asst to the Pres Govt/Cmty Rels ... Vacant
30 Assoc Vice Pres of Development ... Mr. Mark J. PASTORELLA
79 Dean Humanities & Social Services ... Dr. Michael JACOBS
81 Dean STEM and Health ... Ms. Margaret I. KAMINSKY
97 Dean Academic Foundations ... Dr. Medea RAMBISH
72 Academic Director Applied Tech ... Dr. Daniel RAIMONDO
88 Dean Public Safety Training Ctr ... Mr. Michael S. KARNES
21 Controller ... Mr. Michael G. QUINN
37 Director Financial Aid ... Mr. Jerome S. ST. CROIX
41 Director Athletics ... Mr. Aaron M. BOUYEA
35 Director Student Svcs DC ... Ms. Kimberly F. DELARGE
07 Acting Director of Admissions ... Ms. Julie SLATE
06 Director Registrar & Records ... Ms. Sarah HAGREEN
121 Director Advise/Transfer Services ... Ms. Holly WYNN-PREISCHE
08 Director ETS Libraries ... Ms. Katherine E. GHIDIU
38 Dir Counseling/Health & Disability ... Ms. Aubrey ZAMIARA
88 Director of Curriculum & Pgm Devel ... Mr. Andrew FREEMAN
108 Assistant Director Assessment ... Dr. Susan L. HALL
39 Director Housing/Residence Life ... Ms. Jamia DANZY
36 Director Career Services ... Ms. Michelle P. MAYO
88 Director Educ Opportunity Program ... Ms. Charlene A. LINZY
09 Director Institutional Research ... Mr. William DIXON
96 Director of Purchasing ... Mr. Michael M. BATES
91 Assoc Dir Comm and Network Services ... Mr. James F. CLEMENT
40 Manager Bookstore ... Ms. Charlene SUTER
25 Dir Strategic Resources & Grants ... Ms. Carolyn W. HUNT
45 Director Institutional Planning ... Ms. Valarie L. AVALONE
44 Coord Alumni & Annual Giving ... Ms. Karen A. SHAW
101 Secy to the Board of Trustees/Pres ... Ms. Linda M. HALL
23 Director of Health Services ... Vacant
12 Exec Dean Downtown Campus ... Vacant
43 Legal Counsel ... Vacant

Montefiore School of Nursing (A)

53 Valentine Street, Mount Vernon NY 10550
County: Westchester — FICE Identification: 022178
Unit ID: 193380
Telephone: (914) 361-6221 — Carnegie Class: Spec 2-yr-Health
FAX Number: (914) 665-7047 — Calendar System: Semester
URL: www.montefioreschoolofnursing.org
Established: 2014 — Annual Undergrad Tuition & Fees: $12,067
Enrollment: 88 — Coed
Affiliation or Control: Independent Non-Profit — IRS Status: 501(c)3
Highest Offering: Associate Degree
Accreditation: ADNUR

05 Dean ... Dr. Rebecca GREER
20 Assistant Dean ... Susan JOSEPH
32 Coordinator of Student Services ... Chanelle HYDE

Mount Saint Mary College (B)

330 Powell Avenue, Newburgh NY 12550-3412
County: Orange — FICE Identification: 002778
Unit ID: 193353
Telephone: (845) 561-0800 — Carnegie Class: Masters/M
FAX Number: (845) 562-6762 — Calendar System: Semester
URL: www.msmc.edu
Established: 1959 — Annual Undergrad Tuition & Fees: $34,412
Enrollment: 2,125 — Coed
Affiliation or Control: Independent Non-Profit — IRS Status: 501(c)3
Highest Offering: Master's
Accreditation: M, IACBE, NURSE

01 President ... Dr. Jason N. ADSIT
05 Vice President for Academic Affairs ... Dr. George ABAUNZA
10 Vice Pres Finance & Admin/Treasurer ... Mr. Art GLASS
111 Vice Pres for College Advancement ... Mrs. Nikki KHURANA-BAUGH
32 Vice President for Students ... Mrs. Elaine O'GRADY
20 Assistant VP for Academic Affairs ... Mrs. Barbara W. PETRUZZELLI
84 Dean of Admissions ... Mrs. Susana BRISCOE-ALBA
38 Asst Dean of Support Services ... Vacant
06 Registrar ... Ms. Jannelle HAUG
07 Director of Admissions ... Ms. Eileen BARDNEY
08 Director of the Library ... Ms. Vivian MILCZARSKI
37 Director of Financial Aid ... Ms. Thalia MCFARLANE
09 Asst VP of Inst Research/CDO ... Mr. Ryan WILLIAMS
15 Director of Human Resources ... Mrs. Sharnie CANARY
42 Chaplain ... Fr. Gregoire J. FLUET
35 Director of Student Activities ... Ms. Barbara MULLIGAN
29 Director of Alumni Affairs ... Ms. Michelle A. IACUESSA
41 Director of Athletics & Recreation ... Ms. Jessica MUSHEL
36 Director of the Career Center ... Ms. Ellen BOURHIS NOLAN
13 Chief Information Officer ... Mr. Dennis RUSH
96 Purchasing Manager ... Mr. Brian MOORE
106 Director of Online Learning ... Ms. Kristen DELLASALA
39 Director of Residence Life ... Ms. Amy R. WEIT
18 Exec Director of Facilities & Space ... Ms. Maryann PILON
26 Exec Dir of Marketing/Communication ... Mr. Dean DIMARZO
04 Executive Asst to the President ... Ms. Barbara CONNOLLY
19 Director Security/Safety ... Mr. Richard J. ALGARIN
44 Director Annual Giving ... Ms. Margaret TREACY
50 Dean School of Business ... Ms. Tiffany N. GAGLIANO
66 Dean School of Nursing ... Vacant
88 Asst to Pres Mission Integration ... Dr. Charles ZOLA

Nassau Community College (C)

1 Education Drive, Garden City NY 11530-6793
County: Nassau — FICE Identification: 002873
Unit ID: 193478
Telephone: (516) 572-7501 — Carnegie Class: Assoc/HT-High Trad
FAX Number: (516) 572-7750 — Calendar System: Semester
URL: www.ncc.edu
Established: 1959 — Annual Undergrad Tuition & Fees (In-District): $6,330
Enrollment: 13,864 — Coed
Affiliation or Control: State/Local — IRS Status: 501(c)3
Highest Offering: Associate Degree
Accreditation: M, ADNUR, CAHIIM, COARC, FUSER, MLTAD, PTAA, RTT, SURGT

01 Interim President ... Dr. Maria P. CONZATTI
05 Acting VP Academic Affairs ... Dr. Genette ALVAREZ-ORTIZ
18 AVP Facilities Management ... Mr. Phillip CAPPELLO
10 Interim VP Finance/CFO ... Ms. Lisa HAHN
21 Asst Dir Finance ... Mr. Abel CANTILLO
32 Interim VP Academic/Stdnt Svcs ... Dr. Charmian SMITH
35 Asst VP Academic/Student Services ... Dr. David FOLLICK
111 VP Institutional Advancement ... Mr. Adrian KERRIGAN
22 Assoc VP Equity/Inclusion & AA/CDO ... Dr. Craig J. WRIGHT
28 Dir Affirm Action & Compliance ... Ms. Nardos HAMILTON
86 VP Government & Community Relations ... Dr. Jerry KORNBLUTH
43 General Counsel ... Ms. Donna M. HAUGEN
88 Asst VP Labor Relations ... Dr. Laurie PEZZULLO
15 Associate VP Human Resources ... Ms. Dorlena DUNBAR
16 Asst VP HR Operations ... Ms. Deborah REED-SEGRETI
88 Dir Human Resources ... Ms. Kathryn AUSTIN
113 Assoc VP Student Financial Affairs ... Ms. Sandra V. FRIEDMAN
113 Dir Student Financial Affairs ... Ms. Annmarie WELCH
37 Director Financial Aid ... Ms. Patricia NOREN
25 Asst VP Sponsored Programs ... Mr. Edmund KOEPPEL
96 Director Procurement ... Vacant
18 Dir Design & Construction ... Mr. Robert JAROCKI
88 Dir Environmental Health & Safety ... Mr. Robert RAMIREZ
88 Coord Hazardous Materials/Waste ... Mr. Christopher ENRIGHT
18 Project Mgr Capital Construction ... Mr. Christopher ROTELLA
114 Budget Supervisor ... Mr. Charles SOFTY
116 Fiscal Affairs Accounting Exec ... Mr. Edward GUTMAN
88 Supervisor Payroll/Time & Leave ... Ms. Marie A. FEDE
20 Acting Dean of Academic Affairs ... Dr. Denise DEAL
20 Acting Dean of Academic Affairs ... Dr. Elizabeth A. WOOD
20 Acting Dean of Academic Affairs ... Dr. Elizabeth A. GAUDINO-GOERING
51 Assoc Vice Pres Lifelong Learning ... Vacant
103 Asst Dir Workforce Development ... Ms. Katherine WAGNER
88 Asst Dir Community Pgms/Testing ... Ms. Maureen RAMERT
09 Asst Dir Institutional Effectivenes ... Ms. Tina S. WYNDER
106 Asst VP Distance Education ... Dr. Deborah SPIRO
108 Asst VP Acad Assess Program Review ... Vacant
26 Dir Marketing/Communications ... Ms. Lindsey ANGIOLETTI
06 Registrar ... Mr. Chester BARKAN
41 Director Athletics/PED ... Ms. Kerri-Ann MCTIERNAN
08 Chairperson Library ... Ms. Christine FARADAY
19 Asst Director Public Safety ... Mr. Robert CHAMPNESS
23 Director Student Health Services ... Dr. Neil SINGHANI
121 Director Academic Advisement ... Ms. Amanda FOX
13 Assoc VP/CIO ... Ms. Mary FLORATOS
91 IT Manager Network Services ... Vacant
102 Executive Dir NCC Foundation ... Ms. Joy DEDONATO
04 Exec Asst to Pres/Board of Trustees ... Ms. Anne E. BRANDI
45 AVP Inst Effectiveness & Strat Plng ... Vacant
36 Dir Placement Testing ... Ms. Noreen WADE
88 Asst Dean Judicial Affairs ... Ms. Jacqueline CUFFEY
93 Director EOP ... Mr. William CLYDE, JR.
85 Dean International Education ... Vacant

Nazareth College of Rochester (D)

4245 East Avenue, Rochester NY 14618-3790
County: Monroe — FICE Identification: 002779
Unit ID: 193584
Telephone: (585) 389-2525 — Carnegie Class: Masters/L
FAX Number: (585) 586-2452 — Calendar System: Semester
URL: www.naz.edu
Established: 1924 — Annual Undergrad Tuition & Fees: $36,735
Enrollment: 2,791 — Coed
Affiliation or Control: Independent Non-Profit — IRS Status: 501(c)3
Highest Offering: Doctorate
Accreditation: M, AAQEP, ACATE, ART, MLS, MUS, NURSE, OT, PTA, SP, SW, THEA

01 President ... Dr. Elizabeth L. PAUL
04 Executive Assistant to President ... Ms. Cathleen M. STEVENS
05 Vice President Academic Affairs ... Dr. Andrea TALENTINO
111 Vice Pres Institutional Advancement ... Mr. Darrell BELL
10 Vice President Finance & Admin ... Mr. Patrick RICHEY
84 Vice Pres Enrollment & Student Exp ... Mr. Frank WILLIAMS
28 Vice President Diversity/Inclusion ... Dr. Lisa DURANT-JONES
26 VP Marketing & Communications ... Ms. Elizabeth CRONIN
15 Assoc VP Human Resources ... Ms. Deborah J. WINSLOW-SCHABER
32 Assoc VP Student Engagement ... Ms. Kim HARVEY
20 Asst VP Academic Affairs ... Dr. Mary Ellen VORE
06 Registrar ... Vacant
37 Director Student Financial Aid ... Ms. Renee SWIFT
13 Director Information Tech Svcs ... Ms. Karen KUPPINGER
08 Director of Library ... Ms. Catherine DOYLE
19 Director of Security ... Mr. Raymond CRUZ
29 Director of Alumni Relations ... Ms. Caroline TOLBERT
41 Director of Athletics ... Mr. Peter G. BOTHNER
42 Director Center for Spirituality ... Mr. Jamie FAZIO
36 Director of Career Services ... Vacant
18 Director Buildings/Grounds ... Mr. Peter LANA
09 Director of Institutional Research ... Vacant
23 Director of Health Services ... Ms. Susan QUINN
121 Director of Academic Advisement ... Ms. Linda SEARING
113 Bursar ... Mr. John GARBE
49 Dean of Col of Arts and Sciences ... Dr. Thomas LAPPAS
76 Dean School of Health & Human Svcs ... Dr. Catherine RASMUSSIN
53 Dean School of Education ... Dr. Kathleen DABOLL-LAVOIE
50 Dean Sch of Business & Leadership ... Dr. Kenneth RHEA
88 Exec Dir of Ctr International Educ ... Dr. Nevan FISHER
88 Dir of Center for Service Learning ... Ms. Shirley SOMMERS
89 Dir Stdnt Transition/First Year Ctr ... Mr. Andrew MORRIS
96 Director of Purchasing ... Ms. Joanne FITZGERALD
123 Dir Graduate Admissions/Transfer ... Mr. John MORDACI
86 Director Government Relations ... Mr. Brian SHANAHAN

The New School (E)

66 W 12th Street, New York NY 10011-8603
County: New York — FICE Identification: 020662
Unit ID: 193654
Telephone: (212) 229-5600 — Carnegie Class: DU-Higher
FAX Number: N/A — Calendar System: Semester
URL: www.newschool.edu
Established: 1919 — Annual Undergrad Tuition & Fees: $51,022
Enrollment: 9,047 — Coed
Affiliation or Control: Independent Non-Profit — IRS Status: 501(c)3
Highest Offering: Doctorate
Accreditation: M, CLPSY, SPAA

01 President ... Dr. Dwight A. MCBRIDE
101 Sr VP Admin/Univ Sec/Chief of Staff ... Dr. Jennifer HOBBS
04 Executive Assistant to President ... Ms. Mary KARMELEK
05 Exec VP Academic Affairs/Provost ... Dr. Renée T. WHITE
88 Sr Director/Chief of Strategy ... Ms. Jane MCNAMARA
10 Exec VP Business & Operations ... Mr. Tokumbo SHOBOWALE
11 Asst VP Business & Operations/COS ... Ms. Lisa BONNER
48 Exec Dean Parsons School for Design ... Dr. Rachel SCHREIBER
82 Exec Dean Pub Engage & Dean Milano ... Dr. Mary WATSON
64 Exec Dean Perf Arts and Dean Mannes ... Mr. Richard KESSLER
83 Dean New School for Social Research ... Dr. William MILBERG
49 Dean Eugene Lang College ... Dr. Jennifer WILSON
12 Dean Parsons Paris ... Ms. Florence LECLERC-DICKLER
30 Sr VP Development/Alumni Engagement ... Mr. Jonah NIGH
26 Sr VP Marketing and Business Dev ... Ms. Anne ADRIANCE
43 Int Sr VP and General Counsel ... Ms. Junea WILLIAMS-EDMUND
28 Sr VP EISJ/Chief Diversity Officer ... Ms. Melanie HART
20 Sr Vice Prov for Faculty Affairs ... Dr. Michael SCHOBER
20 Dep Prov Academic Planning & Admin ... Ms. Jin KIM
84 Sr Vice Prov Enrollment Management ... Ms. Carol KIM
20 Vice Provost Curriculum & Learning ... Ms. Maggie KOOZER
46 Vice Provost Research ... Dr. Adam BROWN
09 Vice Prov Inst Rsrch Decison Sup ... Dr. Paula MAAS
32 Interim Vice Prov Student Success ... Ms. Xenia MARKOWITT
88 Assoc Dean/Dean Fashion ... Dr. Ben BARRY
88 Assc Dn/Dean Art/Design Hist/Theory ... Dr. Rhonda GARELICK
88 Assoc Dean/Dean Art/Media & Tech ... Dr. Shana AGID
88 Assoc Dean/Dean Constructed Envir ... Mr. David LEWIS
88 Assoc Dean/Dean Media Studies ... Mr. Vladan NIKOLIC
48 Assoc Dean/Dean Design Strategies ... Ms. Cynthia LAWSON
88 Assoc Dean/Dean Undergrad Stds ... Ms. Erin CHO
88 Assoc Dean/Dean School of Drama ... Mr. Pippin PARKER
64 Assoc Dean/Dean School of Jazz ... Mr. Keller COKER
88 Director Creative Writing ... Mr. Luis JARAMILLO
06 VP & University Registrar ... Ms. Rebecca HUNTER
20 Assoc Provost Faculty Affairs ... Dr. Eleni LITT
08 Assoc Prov Libraries/Archives & Ac ... Mr. Ed SCARCELLE
35 Assoc Prov for Student Life ... Ms. Susan AUSTIN
121 Assoc Prov Acad Advising/Career Dev ... Ms. Lorenley BAEZ
88 Assoc VP Community Engagement ... Ms. Deborah BOGOSIAN
88 Sr VP Corporate Partnerships ... Ms. Deborah GIBB
15 VP Human Resources ... Ms. Sonya WILLIAMS
27 VP University Marketing ... Ms. Lisa PRESTON
31 Asst VP Cmty and Public Affairs ... Ms. Amy MALSIN
86 Sr Dir Government and Ext Affairs ... Vacant
13 Sr VP & Chief Information Officer ... Mr. Lin ZHOU
14 Assoc VP Foundation Technology ... Mr. Chris BREZIL
91 Asst VP Enterprise Applications/BI ... Mr. Shawn OGIBA
90 Sr Director Academic Technology ... Mr. Marcus LONGMUIR
14 Sr Director Operations (IT) ... Ms. Jennifer SMITH
119 Director Info Security and Privacy ... Vacant
21 Asst VP Finance & Controller ... Ms. Natalie PRESSEY
114 Asst VP Budget & Planning ... Ms. Loretta FERRARI
96 Director of Business Operations ... Mr. Gregory HERRERA
22 VP EEO/Affirmative Action ... Ms. Rhonnie JAUS
16 Asst VP Human Resources ... Mr. Irwin KROOT
118 Asst VP Benefits ... Ms. Andrea YENCO
18 Asst VP Facilities Management ... Mr. Thomas WHALEN
88 Asst VP Design & Construction ... Ms. Jo GOLDBERGER
19 Director Security ... Mr. Thomas ILICETO
102 Asst VP Inst Giving/Acad Initiative ... Ms. Laura CRONIN
112 Asst VP of Development Parsons ... Mr. André ALLAIRE
112 Asst VP of Development NSSR ... Ms. Meg KAUFMAN
23 Assoc Provost Student Health Svcs ... Ms. Tracy ROBIN
38 Sr Director Counseling Services ... Dr. Jerry FINKELSTEIN
124 Asst Prov for Student Engagement ... Mr. Zach HARRELL
93 Asst Prov for Student Advocacy ... Ms. Shondrika MERRITT
25 Asst Provost Research Support ... Dr. Cheryl GREEN

37 Sr Director Financial Aid .... Ms. Deirdre BAIRSTOW-ALLEN
22 Director Student Disability Svcs .... Mr. Nicholas FARANDA

New York Academy of Art (A)

111 Franklin Street, New York NY 10013
County: New York FICE Identification: 026001
Unit ID: 366368
Telephone: (212) 966-0300 Carnegie Class: Spec-4-yr-Arts
FAX Number: N/A Calendar System: Semester
URL: www.nyaa.edu
Established: 1982 Annual Graduate Tuition & Fees: N/A
Enrollment: 97 Coed
Affiliation or Control: Independent Non-Profit IRS Status: 501(c)3
Highest Offering: Master's; No Undergraduates
Accreditation: M, ART

01 President .... Mr. David KRATZ
05 Provost .... Mr. Peter DRAKE
30 Vice Pres of Development ....Mr. Gregory THORNBURY
32 Director of Student Services ....Ms. Noelle TIMMONS
11 Director of Operations .... Mr. Michael SMITH
06 Registrar/Director of Admissions ....Ms. Katie HEMMER
15 Director of Human Resources .... Mr. Stephan KORSAKOV

New York Automotive and Diesel Institute (B)

178-18 Liberty Avenue, Jamaica NY 11433
County: Queens FICE Identification: 035373
Unit ID: 440262
Telephone: (718) 658-0006 Carnegie Class: Spec 2-yr-Tech
FAX Number: (718) 658-4044 Calendar System: Semester
URL: nyadi.edu
Established: Annual Undergrad Tuition & Fees: N/A
Enrollment: N/A Coed
Affiliation or Control: Proprietary IRS Status: Proprietary
Highest Offering: Associate Degree
Accreditation: ACCSC

01 College President .... Patrick HART
05 Dean of Academic Affairs ....Joseph SANTORA

New York College of Health Professions (C)

6801 Jericho Turnpike, Syosset NY 11791-4413
County: Nassau FICE Identification: 025994
Unit ID: 418126
Telephone: (516) 364-0808 Carnegie Class: Spec-4-yr-Other Health
FAX Number: (516) 364-6645 Calendar System: Trimester
URL: www.nycollege.edu
Established: 1981 Annual Undergrad Tuition & Fees: $14,226
Enrollment: 367 Coed
Affiliation or Control: Independent Non-Profit IRS Status: 501(c)3
Highest Offering: Master's
Accreditation: NY, #ACUP

01 President .... Dr. A Li SONG
10 Chief Financial Officer .... Mr. Errol VIRASAWMI
63 Dean Grad Sch Oriental Medicine .... Dr. Qi (Helen) ZHANG
05 Dean of Academic Affairs .... Vacant
06 Registrar .... Ms. Amy KOTOWSKI
08 Dir Library/Information Services .... Ms. Cynthia CAYEA
113 Bursar .... Ms. Jacqueline MCINTYRE
13 Manager Information Technology .... Mr. Peter WANG
32 Student Services Administrator ....Mr. Brian ALVAREZ
88 Dean Sch of Massage Therapy .... Dr. Steven HAFFNER

New York College of Podiatric Medicine (D)

53 E 124th Street, New York NY 10035-1815
County: New York FICE Identification: 002749
Unit ID: 194073
Telephone: (212) 410-8000 Carnegie Class: Spec-4-yr-Other Health
FAX Number: (212) 876-7670 Calendar System: Semester
URL: www.nycpm.edu
Established: 1911 Annual Undergrad Tuition & Fees: N/A
Enrollment: 337 Coed
Affiliation or Control: Independent Non-Profit IRS Status: 501(c)3
Highest Offering: First Professional Degree
Accreditation: POD

01 President ....Mr. Louis L. LEVINE
05 Vice Pres Academic Affairs/Dean ....Dr. Michael J. TREPAL
11 Chief Operating Ofcr/VP Admin ....Mr. Joel STURM
10 Sr Director of Finance .... Mr. Avi COHEN
13 Vice Pres Info Systems & Technology ....Mr. Aman SAFAEI
63 VP Medical Education/Medical Dir ....Dr. Mark SWARTZ
20 Dean Clinical Educ/Dir Res Pgms .... Dr. Ronald SOAVE
09 Dean Institutional Research ....Dr. Eileen CHUSID
32 Dean Student Affairs .... Ms. Lisa LEE
07 Asst Dean Academic Administration .... Mr. Alain SILVERIO
88 Asst Clinical Clerkships/Affairs .... Ms. Maxiel MEDINA
26 Director Public Affairs/Development ....Ms. Ellen LUBELL
08 Director of Library .... Mr. Paul TREMBLAY
06 Registrar .... Ms. Doreen D'AMICO
19 Director Security/Safety ....Ms. Lydia PEREZ
39 Housing Manager ....Mr. Adrian RICE
15 Chief Human Resources Officer .... Ms. Sandra DANIELS

New York College of Traditional Chinese Medicine (E)

200 Old Country Road, Suite 500, Mineola NY 11501-4204
County: Nassau FICE Identification: 034433
Unit ID: 439783
Telephone: (516) 739-1545 Carnegie Class: Spec-4-yr-Other Health
FAX Number: (516) 873-9622 Calendar System: Trimester
URL: www.nyctcm.edu
Established: 1996 Annual Undergrad Tuition & Fees: N/A
Enrollment: 213 Coed
Affiliation or Control: Independent Non-Profit IRS Status: 501(c)3
Highest Offering: Master's
Accreditation: ACUP

01 President ....Dr. Yemeng CHEN
11 Administrative Dean ....Dr. Dong-Hua YANG
05 Academic Dean ....Dr. Megan HAUNGS
10 Financial Director .... Ms. Kathy ZHOU
07 Admissions Manager ....Ms. Lynn BAI
23 Clinic Director ....Ms. Mona LEE-YUAN
88 Clinic Manager .... Ms. Yiping ZHAO
06 Records Manager .... Ms. Susan SU
37 Financial Aid/Admin Coordinator .... Ms. Marianne RENOIS
21 Financial Manager .... Ms. Lily ZOU
08 Operations Manager ....Ms. Ling Ling CHANG
32 Student Services Coordinator ....Ms. Lois GROSS
04 Administrative Coordinator .... Ms. Elise MA
13 Educational Technology Manager .... Mr. Xudong FU

The New York Conservatory for Dramatic Arts (F)

39 West 19th Street, New York NY 10011
County: New York FICE Identification: 031207
Unit ID: 421841
Telephone: (212) 645-0030 Carnegie Class: Spec 2-yr-A&S
FAX Number: (212) 645-0039 Calendar System: Semester
URL: www.nycda.edu
Established: 1980 Annual Undergrad Tuition & Fees: $34,400
Enrollment: 257 Coed
Affiliation or Control: Proprietary IRS Status: Proprietary
Highest Offering: Associate Degree
Accreditation: THEA

01 Chief Executive Officer .... Mike Vishol DABIDAT
05 Head of School ....Jay GOLDENBERG
06 Registrar ....Nazig TCHAKARIAN
08 Head Librarian .... Martha REPPETTO
07 Director of Admissions .... Bryce RUSSELL
10 Chief Financial Officer .... Emily CHOU
37 Director Student Financial Aid .... Alexander VO
18 Director of Operations .... Christiaan KOOP
32 Student Services Manager .... Kim SOSA

New York Graduate School of Psychoanalysis (G)

16 West Tenth Street, New York NY 10011
Telephone: (212) 260-7050 Identification: 770116
Accreditation: &EH

† Branch campus of Boston Graduate School of Psychoanalysis, Brookline, MA

New York Institute of Technology (H)

Northern Boulevard, Old Westbury NY 11568-8000
County: Nassau FICE Identification: 004804
Unit ID: 194091
Telephone: (516) 686-7516 Carnegie Class: Masters/L
FAX Number: (516) 686-7613 Calendar System: Semester
URL: www.nyit.edu
Established: 1955 Annual Undergrad Tuition & Fees: $39,760
Enrollment: 6,851 Coed
Affiliation or Control: Independent Non-Profit IRS Status: 501(c)3
Highest Offering: Doctorate
Accreditation: M, ARCPA, CACREP, CAEP, CIDA, NURSE, OSTEO, OT, PTA

01 President ....Dr. Henry FOLEY
05 Int Provost/VP Academic Affairs ....Dr. Jerry BALENTINE
11 EVP & COO .... Dr. Jerry BALENTINE
20 Int Associate Provost ....Dr. Francesca FIORE
30 VP Development & Alumni Relations ....Mr. Patrick MINSON
26 Int VP Strategic Communications .... Dr. Joseph POSILLICO
10 VP Financial Affs/CFO & Treasurer .... Ms. Barbara HOLAHAN
21 Controller ....Ms. Eileen VALERIO
43 General Counsel .... Ms. Catherine FLICKINGER
13 CIO & VP Information Tech ....Ms. Pennie TURGEON
84 VP Enrollment Management .... Dr. Joseph POSILLICO
18 Chief Arch/VP RE & Sus Cap Plng ....Ms. Suzanne MUSHO
06 Registrar .... Mr. Ian K. WHITE
76 Dean School of Health Professions .... Dr. Gordon SCHMIDT
48 Dean Sch Architecture & Design .... Ms. Maria PERBELLINI
54 Dean School of Engr/Computer Sci ....Dr. Babak DASTGHEIB-BEHESHTI
49 Dean School Arts & Sciences .... Dr. Daniel QUIGLEY
50 Int Dean School of Management ....Dr. Deborah COHN
32 Dean of Students/Student Life ....Mr. Felipe HENAO
36 Senior Director Career Success .... Ms. Amy BRAVO
09 Int Director Rsrch/Assess/Dec Supp ....Dr. Francesca FIORE
22 Equity Officer & Title IX Coord ....Mr. Christopher CAROZZA
07 Dean Admissions & Financial Aid ....Ms. Karen VAHEY
27 Exec Dir of Strategic Comm ....Ms. Bobbie DELL'AQUILO
29 Director of Alumni Relations ....Ms. Sabrina POLIDORO
88 Dir Operations RE & Sus Cap ....Mr. Spiros DANDOURAS
19 Assoc Director Safety & Security ....Mr. Michael ZALESKI
25 Sr Dir Sponsored Pgm & Research ....Ms. Dawn GRZAN
121 Assoc Dean Undergrad Stdnt Success ....Ms. Monika ROHDE
15 Executive Director Human Resources ....Ms. Katherine ZULIANI
14 Director Academic Tech Svcs .... Ms. Laurie HARVEY
91 Director Information Tech Services .... Mr. Brian MAROLDO
04 Special Assistant to President .... Mr. Michael SCHIAVETTA
105 Director Mobile & Web Dev Services ....Mr. Bobby SAHA
96 Assistant Director of Purchasing .... Ms. Kelly CASTILLO
28 VP Equity/Inclusion & CMO .... Dr. Brian HARPER
37 Director Financial Aid .... Ms. Tricia BOWMAN

New York Law School (I)

185 West Broadway, New York NY 10013-2959
County: New York FICE Identification: 002783
Unit ID: 193821
Telephone: (212) 431-2100 Carnegie Class: Spec-4-yr-Law
FAX Number: (212) 965-8838 Calendar System: Semester
URL: www.nyls.edu
Established: 1891 Annual Graduate Tuition & Fees: N/A
Enrollment: 1,076 Coed
Affiliation or Control: Independent Non-Profit IRS Status: 501(c)3
Highest Offering: Doctorate; No Undergraduates
Accreditation: LAW

01 Dean and President ....Dean Anthony CROWELL
05 Assoc Dean Academic/Student Engage . Dean William P. LAPIANA
10 Sr Vice President & CFO ....Mr. Plachikkat (PV) ANANTHARAM
26 Asst VP of Marketing/Communications .... Ms. Regina CHUNG
08 Director of Law Library/Assoc Dean ... Prof. Camille BROUSSARD
111 Assoc Dean Institutional Advancemnt ....Mr. Jeffery BECHERER
07 Asst Dean Admissions/Financial Aid ....Ms. Ella Mae ESTRADA
36 Assoc Dean Acad Plng and Career Dev ....Ms. Erin BOND
21 Vice Pres Financial Plng & Mgmt .... Mr. Shin MOON
18 Chief Maintenance/Operations/Secur ....Mr. Paul REPETTO
19 Manager of Security & Life Safety ....Mr. Sean FRETT
15 Vice President Human Resources .... Ms. Jody PARIANTE
16 Executive Director of HR .... Ms. Jennifer KHUU
121 Exec Director of Academic Success ....Ms. Megan MONTCALM
88 Assistant Dean for Bar Success .... Ms. Preyal SHAH
32 Associate Dean for Student Life .... Ms. Sally HARDING
11 Chief of Bus Ops & Events .... Mr. Kraig BEAUDOIN
30 Director of Development .... Vacant
06 Associate Dean and Registrar .... Mr. Oral HOPE
13 Chief Information Officer .... Mr. Thomas SOCASH
35 Assistant Dean of Student Life ....Ms. Shani DARBY
96 Purchasing Coordinator .... Mr. Norman DAWKINS
104 Director Study Abroad ....Mr. Michael RHEE
86 Director Government Relations .... Mr. Ariel DVORKIN
37 Director Student Financial Aid .... Vacant
04 Exec Assistant to the President ....Mr. Frank CHIAPPETTA
43 Assoc Dean & General Counsel .... Mr. Matthew GEWOLB
09 Sr Dir Institutional Research .... Ms. Jill BEZEL

New York Medical College (J)

40 Sunshine Cottage Road, Valhalla NY 10595-1690
County: Westchester FICE Identification: 002784
Unit ID: 193830
Telephone: (914) 594-4900 Carnegie Class: Spec-4-yr-Med
FAX Number: (914) 594-4145 Calendar System: Other
URL: www.nymc.edu
Established: 1860 Annual Graduate Tuition & Fees: N/A
Enrollment: 1,604 Coed
Affiliation or Control: Jewish IRS Status: 501(c)3
Highest Offering: Doctorate; No Undergraduates
Accreditation: M, DENT, MED, MLS, PAST, PH, PTA, SP

00 President ....Dr. Alan H. KADISH
01 Chancellor and CEO ....Dr. Edward C. HALPERIN
100 Chief of Staff .... Ms. Vilma BORDONARO
63 Dean School of Medicine ....Dr. Jerry NADLER
10 Vice Pres Financial Operations ....Mr. Adam D. HAMMERMAN
26 Vice Pres Communications .... Ms. Jennifer RIEKERT
46 Vice President for Research .... Dr. Salomon AMAR
43 Vice Pres/Chief Counsel .... Mr. Nicholas JANIGA
58 Dean Grad Sch Basic Medical Science ....Dr. Marina HOLZ
76 Dean Sch Health Sciences & Practice ....Dr. Robert W. AMLER
30 Chief Development Officer ....Ms. Bess CHAZHUR
86 Vice President Government Affairs ....Dr. Robert W. AMLER
21 Controller ....Ms. Irene CRASTRO-BOLIN
13 Dir Information Tech Services .... Mr. James CURRAN
32 VC Stdnt Svcs/Vice Dean Grad Med Ed ....Dr. Richard G. MCCARRICK
35 Sr Assoc Dean Student Affairs .... Dr. Jane PONTERIO
37 Asc Dn Stdnt Affs/Dir Finan Plng ....Mr. Anthony M. SOZZO
08 Assoc Dean/Dir Health Sci Library .... Ms. Marie ASCHER
07 Director of Admissions ....Ms. Karen MURRAY
06 College Registrar .... Ms. Eileen ROMERO
39 Director Student Housing ....Ms. Katherine E. DILLON
18 Dir Capital Planning/Facilities .... Ms. Sarah COTTET
19 Director of Security ....Mr. William ALLISON
85 Intl Student/Scholar Advisor ....Ms. Elizabeth WARD
23 Director Health Services ....Ms. Marisa MONTECALVO
38 Director Student Counseling .... Dr. Mark SINGER
105 Director Web Communications ....Mr. Kevin R. CUMMINGS
24 Head Educational Media ....Mr. Michael COTTER

14 Coord of Instruct Computing Tech .... Mr. Jason DI NARDI
04 Admin Assistant to the President .... Ms. Ashley MCCARRICK
22 Dir Affirm Action/Equal Opportunity .... Ms. Lisa TRONAZANO
29 Director Alumni Affairs .... Ms. Tara ALFANO
96 Director of Purchasing .... Ms. Maribel GIRALDO
15 Human Resources Officer .... Ms. Lisa M. TRONZANO

The New York School for Medical and Dental Assistants (A)

33-10 Queens Blvd, Long Island City NY 11101-2327
County: Queens FICE Identification: 010551
Unit ID: 193858
Telephone: (718) 793-2330 Carnegie Class: Spec 2-yr-Health
FAX Number: (718) 793-0619 Calendar System: Semester
URL: nysmda.com
Established: 1967 Annual Undergrad Tuition & Fees: N/A
Enrollment: 381 Coed
Affiliation or Control: Proprietary IRS Status: Proprietary
Highest Offering: Associate Degree
Accreditation: ACCSC

01 Campus Co-Director .... D. Clinton ARNABOLDI
10 Campus Co-Director/CFO .... Douglas K. JORDAN
05 Vice President of Academic Affairs .... Dr. Rafeeque AHMAD
06 Director/Registrar .... Rotanetta HIGHSMITH

New York School of Interior Design (B)

170 East 70th Street, New York NY 10021-5110
County: New York FICE Identification: 020690
Unit ID: 194116
Telephone: (212) 472-1500 Carnegie Class: Spec-4-yr-Arts
FAX Number: (212) 472-3800 Calendar System: 4/1/4
URL: www.nysid.edu
Established: 1916 Annual Undergrad Tuition & Fees: $26,322
Enrollment: 621 Coed
Affiliation or Control: Independent Non-Profit IRS Status: 501(c)3
Highest Offering: Master's
Accreditation: M, ART, CIDA

01 President .... Mr. David SPROULS
05 VP Academic Affairs/Dean .... Dr. Ellen FISHER
10 VP for Finance & Administration .... Ms. Jane CHEN
26 Dir External Rels/Chief of Staff .... Ms. Laura CATLAN
15 Assistant VP of Administration .... Ms. Yvonne MORAY
20 Associate Dean .... Mr. Daniel HARPER
32 Dean of Students .... Ms. Karen HIGGINBOTHAM
07 Director of Admissions .... Mr. Emmanuel CRUZ
18 Director of Facilities .... Mr. Zeke KOLENOVIC
30 Director of Development .... Ms. Joy COOPER
08 Director of the Library .... Mr. Billy KWAN
06 Registrar .... Ms. Jennifer MELENDEZ
37 Financial Aid Manager .... Ms. Antoinette ESPOSITO
113 Bursar .... Mr. Joseph FANTOZZI
13 Dir of Network & Tech Support Svcs .... Mr. Dan TRUONG
38 Director of Counseling Services .... Dr. Penni MORGANSTEIN
09 Director of Institutional Research .... Mr. Christopher VINGER
04 Admin Assistant to the President .... Ms. Jeanne KO

New York Theological Seminary (C)

475 Riverside Drive, Suite 500, New York NY 10115-0083
County: New York FICE Identification: 002674
Unit ID: 193894
Telephone: (212) 870-1211 Carnegie Class: Spec-4-yr-Faith
FAX Number: (212) 870-1236 Calendar System: Semester
URL: www.nyts.edu
Established: 1900 Annual Graduate Tuition & Fees: N/A
Enrollment: 272 Coed
Affiliation or Control: Independent Non-Profit IRS Status: 501(c)3
Highest Offering: Doctorate; No Undergraduates
Accreditation: #THEOL

01 President .... Dr. LaKeesha WALROND
30 VP Inst Advancement & Research .... Vacant
05 VP Academic Affairs/Dean .... Dr. Tamara HENRY
10 Chief Financial Officer/Controller .... Mr. Craig KING
08 Librarian .... Dr. Rafael REYES
06 Registrar .... Ms. Gina L. GREEN
37 Director Financial Aid .... Ms. Tamisia WHITE
105 Director Web Services .... Mr. Ahsan RAZA
108 Director Institutional Assessment .... Vacant
29 Director Alumni Relations .... Mr. Cassius RUDOLPH
38 Director of Student Counseling .... Vacant
07 Director Admissions/Student Svcs .... Dr. Adriane HILL
11 Chief Operations Officer .... Ms. Lenier THOMAS
106 Dean of Online Education/E-learning .... Dr. Jin HAN

New York University (D)

70 Washington Square South, New York NY 10012-1092
County: New York FICE Identification: 002785
Unit ID: 193900
Telephone: (212) 998-1212 Carnegie Class: DU-Highest
FAX Number: N/A Calendar System: Semester
URL: www.nyu.edu
Established: 1831 Annual Undergrad Tuition & Fees: $54,880
Enrollment: 52,775 Coed
Affiliation or Control: Independent Non-Profit IRS Status: 501(c)3
Highest Offering: Doctorate
Accreditation: M, AAQEP, ACATE, ART, CAMPEP, COPSY, DENT, DH, DIETD, DIETI, HSA, IPSY, JOUR, LAW, MED, MIDWF, MPCAC, NURSE, OT, PAST, PH, PLNG, PTA, SP, SPAA, SURGT, SW

01 President .... Dr. Andrew HAMILTON
100 Chief of Staff to President .... Mr. Richard BAUM
05 Provost .... Dr. Katherine FLEMING
03 Executive Vice President .... Dr. Martin DORPH
26 SVP Univ Relations/Public Affairs .... Dr. Lynne BROWN
30 Sr VP Development/Alumni Relations .... Mr. Robert CASHION
32 VP Univ Life/Global Engagement .... Mr. Jason PINA
28 SVP Global Inclusion/Diversity Ofcr .... Dr. Lisa COLEMAN
10 SVP Finance and Budget/CFO .... Ms. Stephanie PIANKA
43 SVP/General Counsel & Secretary .. Ms. Aisha OLIVER-STANLEY
46 Vice Provost for Research .... Dr. Stacie GROSSMAN BLOOM
35 AVP/Dean of Students .... Mr. Rafael RODRIGUEZ
18 VP Capital Projects/Facilities .... Ms. Linda CHIARELLI
27 SVP Public Affairs/Strategic Comm .... Mr. John H. BECKMAN
84 Sr Vice Pres Enrollment .... Ms. MJ KNOLL-FINN
15 Vice Pres Human Resources .... Ms. Sabrina ELLIS
13 VP and Chief Information Officer .... Mr. Len PETERS
45 Vice Provost for Resource Planning .... Mr. Anthony JIGA
19 VP Global Campus Safety .... Mr. Fountain WALKER
06 University Registrar .... Ms. Elizabeth A. KIENLE-GRANZO
20 Deputy Provost .... Dr. C. Cybele RAVER
104 VP for Global Programs .... Dr. Nancy J. MORRISON
07 AVP for Undergrad Admissions .... Mr. Jonathan WILLIAMS
20 Asst Provost Academic Pgm Review .... Dr. Diana L. KARAFIN
41 Asst VP Stdnt Affairs/Dir Athletics .... Mr. Christopher BLEDSOE
23 Assoc VP Stdnt Hlth/Exec Dir SHC .... Dr. Carlo CIOTOLI
37 Asst VP Financial Aid .... Ms. Lynn E. HIGINBOTHAM
22 AVP Ofc of Equal Opportunity .... Ms. Mary SIGNOR
08 Dean of Libraries .... Mr. H. Austin BOOTH
39 Sr Director Housing Services .... Mr. Neil S. HANRAHAN
09 Exec Dir of Institutional Research .... Mr. David P. VINTINNER

Niagara County Community College (E)

3111 Saunders Settlement Road, Sanborn NY 14132-9460
County: Niagara FICE Identification: 002874
Unit ID: 193946
Telephone: (716) 614-6200 Carnegie Class: Assoc/MT-VT-High Trad
FAX Number: (716) 614-6700 Calendar System: Semester
URL: www.niagaracc.suny.edu
Established: 1962 Annual Undergrad Tuition & Fees (In-District): $5,501
Enrollment: 4,389 Coed
Affiliation or Control: State/Local IRS Status: 501(c)3
Highest Offering: Associate Degree
Accreditation: M, ACFEI, ADNUR, MAC, PTAA, RAD, SURGT

01 President .... Dr. William MURABITO
05 Vice President Academic Affairs .... Ms. Lydia ULATOWSKI
103 Asst VP of Acad Affairs/Econ Devel .... Mr. Brian MICHEL
10 Dir of Financial Acct & Reporting .... Ms. Patrice ELNICKI
32 Vice President of Student Services .... Ms. Julia PITMAN
11 Vice President of Administration .... Mr. Wayne LYNCH
09 Director of Planning Research .... Ms. Akie YANAGI
15 Asst VP of Human Resources .... Ms. Catherine BROWN
84 Asst VP Student Svcs/Stdnt Engage .... Mr. Robert MCKEOWN
21 Director of Business Services .... Mr. John EICHNER
04 Assistant to President .... Ms. Barbara WALCK
06 Registrar .... Ms. Julie SCHUCKER
35 Director of Student Development .... Vacant
37 Director of Financial Aid .... Mr. James TRIMBOLI
26 Director Public Relations .... Ms. Barbara DESIMONE
18 Assistant Director of Facilities .... Mr. Donald SAPH
08 Head Librarian .... Ms. Jean LINN
105 Director Web Services .... Vacant
106 Dir Online Education/E-learning .... Ms. Lisa DUBUC
13 Asst VP of Information Technology .... Mr. Jesse GOLDBERG
19 Director Security/Safety .... Mr. Ross ANNABLE
102 Foundation Director .... Ms. Deborah BREWER
39 Executive Director Student Housing .... Mr. Richard JOHNSON
41 Athletic Director .... Ms. Amanda HASELEY
91 Dir User & Administrative Tech .... Mr. Matt MACKEY
29 Alumni Development Specialist .... Vacant
25 Director of Grants .... Vacant
36 Dir Career and Transitional Svcs .... Ms. Alissa SHUGATS-CUMMINGS

Niagara University (F)

5795 Lewiston Road, Niagara University NY 14109
County: Niagara FICE Identification: 002788
Unit ID: 193973
Telephone: (716) 285-1212 Carnegie Class: Masters/L
FAX Number: (716) 286-8710 Calendar System: Semester
URL: www.niagara.edu
Established: 1856 Annual Undergrad Tuition & Fees: $35,240
Enrollment: 3,544 Coed
Affiliation or Control: Roman Catholic IRS Status: 501(c)3
Highest Offering: Doctorate
Accreditation: M, ACPHA, CACREP, CAEP, NURSE, SW

01 President .... Rev. James MAHER, CM
03 Executive Vice President .... Dr. Debra COLLEY
05 Provost/VP for Academic Affairs .... Dr. Timothy IRELAND
12 VP Ontario Administration .... Vacant
32 VP Student Affairs .... Mr. Christopher R. SHEFFIELD
85 VP for International Relations .... Dr. Duleep DEOSTHALE
111 VP Institutional Advancement .... Ms. Jaclyn ROSSI
42 VP Mission Integration .... Rev. Gregory SEMENIUK, CM
84 VP Undergrad Enrollment & Mktg .... Mr. Michael J. FREEDMAN
15 VP Human Resources .... Ms. Lisa ARNET
28 VP Diversity/Equity & Inclusion .... Dr. Tamra MINOR
26 AVP of Public/External/Govt Rels .... Mr. Thomas BURNS
102 Asst VP Spons Pgms & Found Rels .... Ms. Adrienne STANFILL
20 Associate Provost .... Dr. Henrik C. BORGSTROM
41 Director of Athletics .... Mr. Simon GRAY
43 General Counsel .... Mr. Jeremy COLBY
10 Chief Financial/Innovation Ofcr .... Mr. Robert MORREALE
35 Dean of Student Affairs .... Mrs. Averl HARBIN
49 Dean Col of Arts & Science .... Dr. Peter BUTERA
66 Dean Col of Nursing .... Dr. Christine VERNI
50 Dean Col of Business Admin .... Dr. Mark FRASCATORE
53 Dean Col of Education .... Dr. Chandra FOOTE
88 Dean Col of Hosp/Sport/Tourism Mgt .... Ms. Bridget NILAND
20 Dean of Academic Services .... Ms. Antonia KNIGHT
108 Exec Dir Inst Effect & Assessment .... Dr. Vennessa L. WALKER
09 Director of Institutional Research .... Mr. Daniel LYMAN
18 Director of Facility Services .... Mr. Daniel MCMANN
88 Campus Superintendent .... Mr. Keith SARGENT
88 Director of Transfer Enrollment .... Mr. Mark E. WOJNOWSKI
07 Director of Admissions .... Ms. Stephanie BUCZKOWSKI
08 Director of Libraries .... Mr. David SCHOEN
19 Director of Campus Safety .... Mr. John F. BARKER
37 Director of Financial Aid .... Ms. Katie L. KOCSIS
39 Director of Residence Life .... Ms. Kimberly FENTON
35 Director of Campus Activities .... Mrs. Mati ORTIZ
13 Chief Information Officer .... Mr. Richard P. KERNIN
23 Dir of Student Health & Wellness .... Ms. Carter WANAMAKER
121 Director Academic Success Center .... Mrs. Diane STOELTING
88 Exec Dir Inst for Civic Engagement .... Dr. Karen KWANDRANS
35 Dir Rec & Intramurals/Kiernan Ctr .... Mr. Derek PUFF
21 Controller .... Ms. Christina HOVEN
123 Dir of Strategic Enrollment Oper .... Mr. Evan F. PIERCE
92 Honors Program Coordinator .... Dr. Michael BARNWELL
93 Assoc Dir Multicultural Affairs .... Vacant
22 Title IX Coordinator .... Mrs. Megan ALTMAN-COSGROVE
06 University Registrar .... Mr. Harry GONG
113 Director of Student Accounts .... Mr. Jacob KOPERA
25 Dir Sponsored Pgms & Fndn Rels .... Ms. Jill SHUEY
36 Director of Career Services .... Ms. Stephanie MORRIS
88 Veterans Services Program Director ..... Mr. Karl HINTERBERGER
04 Executive Asst to President .... Ms. Maritza MULREADY

North Country Community College (G)

23 Santanoni Avenue, PO Box 89,
Saranac Lake NY 12983-0089
County: Essex FICE Identification: 007111
Unit ID: 194028
Telephone: (518) 891-2915 Carnegie Class: Assoc/HVT-Mix Trad/Non
FAX Number: (518) 891-2915 Calendar System: Semester
URL: www.nccc.edu
Established: 1967 Annual Undergrad Tuition & Fees (In-District): $6,562
Enrollment: 1,602 Coed
Affiliation or Control: State/Local IRS Status: 501(c)3
Highest Offering: Associate Degree
Accreditation: M

01 President .... Mr. Joe KEEGAN
05 Vice Pres of Academic Affairs .... Mrs. Sarah MAROUN
10 Chief Financial Officer .... Mr. Erik HARVEY
21 Director of Financial Operations .... Mrs. Lisa SYMONDS
84 VP of Marketing & Enrollment .... Mr. Kyle JOHNSTON
06 Registrar/Records Officer .... Mrs. Shelly ST. LOUIS
09 Asst Dean Inst Research/Support .... Mr. Scott HARWOOD
32 Dean of Campus & Student Life .... Ms. Kim IRLAND
29 Director Alumni Relations .... Mrs. Diana FORTUNE
04 Executive Asst to the President .... Mrs. Stacie HURWITCH
37 Director of Financial Aid .... Mrs. MaryEllen CHAMBERLAIN
41 Athletic Director .... Mr. Chad LADUE

Northeast College of Health Sciences (H)

2360 State Route 89, Seneca Falls NY 13148-0800
County: Seneca FICE Identification: 012277
Unit ID: 193751
Telephone: (315) 568-3000 Carnegie Class: Spec-4-yr-Other Health
FAX Number: (315) 568-3012 Calendar System: Trimester
URL: www.northeastcollege.edu
Established: 1919 Annual Undergrad Tuition & Fees: N/A
Enrollment: 676 Coed
Affiliation or Control: Independent Non-Profit IRS Status: 501(c)3
Highest Offering: First Professional Degree
Accreditation: M, CHIRO

01 President .... Dr. Michael MESTAN
05 Exec VP of Academic Affairs .... Dr. Anne KILLEN
10 VP of Finance .... Mr. Sean ANGLIM
111 VP Stakeholder Engagement .... Dr. J. Todd KNUDSEN
84 VP Enrollment & Planning .... Dr. Jennifer SESSLER
11 VP of Administrative Services .... Mr. Christopher MCQUEENEY
20 Asst VP of Academic Affairs .... Dr. J. Nicolas POIRIER
07 Asst VP of Enrollment & Admissions .... Mr. Scott BOOTH
06 Registrar .... Mr. Kevin MCCARTHY
37 Director Financial Aid .... Mr. Darrin ROOKER
106 Dean of Online Education .... Dr. Peter NICKLESS
46 Dean of Faculty & Research .... Dr. Jeanmarie BURKE
12 Depew Health Center Administrator .... Dr. Ana STEARNS
12 Levittown Health Ctr Chief of Staff .... Vacant

88 Director of Clinical Education ... Dr. Wendy MANERI
51 Director Post Grad & Cont Educ ... Dr. Owen PAPUGUA
08 Director of the Library ... Dr. Fantasia THORNE-ORTIZ
108 Dir of Ed Effectiveness/ Compliance ... Dr. Suellen CHRISTOPOULUS-NUTTING
09 Quality Engineer Enrollment & Plng ... Ms. Patricia MERKLE
15 Human Resources Manager ... Ms. Christine MCDERMOTT
13 Information Tech Administrator ... Mr. Shane SHOWERS
19 Director Facilities/Security ... Mr. William WAYNE
88 Dir MS Diagnostic Imaging Program ... Dr. Chad WARSHEL
90 Sr Systems Administrator ... Mr. Miles SINICROPI
24 Educational Tech Administrator ... Mr. Bernard CECCHINI
23 Director of Clinical Operations ... Mrs. Melissa BAXTER
21 Controller ... Ms. Karen QUEST
04 Executive Asst to the President ... Ms. Beth GRUMMONS

Northeastern Seminary (A)

2265 Westside Drive, Rochester NY 14624-1932
County: Monroe — FICE Identification: 034194
Unit ID: 439817
Telephone: (585) 594-6800 — Carnegie Class: Spec-4-yr-Faith
FAX Number: (585) 594-6801 — Calendar System: Semester
URL: www.nes.edu
Established: 1998 — Annual Graduate Tuition & Fees: N/A
Enrollment: 206 — Coed
Affiliation or Control: Independent Non-Profit — IRS Status: 501(c)3
Highest Offering: Doctorate; No Undergraduates
Accreditation: M, THEOL

01 President ... Dr. Deana L. PORTERFIELD
05 Academic Vice President ... Dr. Benjamin ESPINOZA
32 VP Student/Organizational Dev ... Ms. Kristen BROWN
07 AVP for Seminary Enrollment ... Mr. JP ANDERSON
04 Administrative Asst to President ... Mrs. Mimi WHEELER
06 Registrar ... Ms. Lesa KOHR
10 VP Finance/Chief Financial Officer ... Ms. Laurie LEO
111 VP for Institutional Advancement ... Mr. Alexander JONES
13 AVP Information Technology ... Mr. Peter SAXENA
11 Dean ... Dr. Elizabeth GERHARDT
111 Director of Inst Advancement ... Mr. William MOSIER-PETERSON

† The Seminary is affiliated with Roberts Wesleyan College.

Ohr Hameir Theological Seminary (B)

141 Furnace Woods Road,
Cortlandt Manor NY 10567-6112
County: Westchester — FICE Identification: 011984
Unit ID: 194189
Telephone: (914) 736-1500 — Carnegie Class: Not Classified
FAX Number: (914) 736-1055 — Calendar System: Semester
Established: 1962 — Annual Undergrad Tuition & Fees: $12,250
Enrollment: 92 — Male
Affiliation or Control: Independent Non-Profit — IRS Status: 501(c)3
Highest Offering: Second Talmudic Degree
Accreditation: RABN

01 President ... Rabbi E. KANAREK
30 Chief Devel Ofcr/Dir Financial Aid ... Rabbi Jacob ROTHBERG
06 Registrar ... Rabbi Berel KANAREK

Onondaga Community College (C)

4585 West Seneca Turnpike, Syracuse NY 13215-4585
County: Onondaga — FICE Identification: 002875
Unit ID: 194222
Telephone: (315) 498-2622 — Carnegie Class: Assoc/HT-Mix Trad/Non
FAX Number: (315) 492-9208 — Calendar System: Semester
URL: www.sunyocc.edu
Established: 1962 — Annual Undergrad Tuition & Fees (In-District): $5,754
Enrollment: 8,545 — Coed
Affiliation or Control: State/Local — IRS Status: 501(c)3
Highest Offering: Associate Degree
Accreditation: M, ADNUR, CAHIIM, NAEYC, PTAA, SURGT

01 President ... Dr. Warren HILTON
05 Provost/SVP Academic Affairs ... Dr. Anastasia URTZ
10 SVP/Chief Financial Officer ... Mr. Mark MANNING
03 VP Governance and Compliance ... Vacant
30 Vice President Development ... Vacant
84 VP Enrollment/Development & Comm ... Vacant
09 VP Inst Plng/Assessment/Research ... Dr. Agatha AWUAH
15 VP Human Resources ... Ms. Bridget SCHOLL
13 Asst VP Information Tech Svcs ... Mr. Steven WILEY
20 Asst Provost Academic Affairs ... Mr. Christopher THUOT
28 VP/Chief Diversity Officer ... Ms. Eunice WILLIAMS
37 Director Financial Aid ... Mr. Kevin SAPIO
41 Athletic Director ... Mr. Michael BORSZ
08 Chair Library ... Dr. Fantasia THORNE-ORTIZ
19 Director Campus Safety & Security ... Dr. Andrea MOUREY
22 Director Disability Services ... Ms. Nancy CARR
06 Registrar ... Mr. Christopher WOLFS
113 Assistant Director Student Accounts ... Ms. Sally LUTON
96 Assistant VP Management Services ... Mr. Michael MCMULLEN
88 Director of Sustainability ... Dr. Sean VORMWALD
04 Assistant to the President ... Ms. Julie HART
25 AVP Research & Grants ... Ms. Nicole SCHLATER
29 Assistant Director Alumni Comm ... Mr. Russ CORBIN
45 AVP Inst Effectiveness & Planning ... Ms. Wendy TARBY
26 AVP Advancement Communications ... Ms. Susan TORMEY
44 Director Annual Giving ... Ms. Steffani WILLIAMS
39 Director Resident Life/Student Hous ... Mr. Shawn EDIE

Orange County Community College (D)

115 South Street, Middletown NY 10940-6437
County: Orange — FICE Identification: 002876
Unit ID: 194240
Telephone: (845) 344-6222 — Carnegie Class: Assoc/HT-High Trad
FAX Number: (845) 343-1228 — Calendar System: Semester
URL: www.sunyorange.edu
Established: 1950 — Annual Undergrad Tuition & Fees (In-District): $6,094
Enrollment: 5,862 — Coed
Affiliation or Control: State/Local — IRS Status: 501(c)3
Highest Offering: Associate Degree
Accreditation: M, ACBSP, ADNUR, DH, MLTAD, OTA, PTAA, RAD

01 President ... Dr. Kristine M. YOUNG
05 Vice Pres Academic Affairs ... Ms. Erika HACKMAN
32 Vice Pres Student Services ... Ms. Gerianne BRUSATI
10 VP Administration/Finance ... Mr. Paul MARTLAND
111 Vice Pres Institutional Advancement ... Vacant
13 Chief Information Officer ... Mr. Leland J. HACH
84 Assoc VP for Enrollment Management ... Vacant
76 Assoc VP Health Professions ... Dr. Michael GAWRONSKI, JR.
102 Int Executive Director Foundation ... Ms. Dawn ANSBRO
50 Int Assoc VP Business/Math/Sci/Tech ... Mr. Josh LAVORGNA
35 Assoc Vice Pres Stdnt Engagemt/ Comp ... Ms. Madeline TORRES-DIAZ
15 Assoc Vice Pres Human Resources ... Ms. Iris MARTINEZ-DAVIS
08 Library Director ... Mr. Andrew HEIZ
51 Dir Continuing/Professional Educ ... Mr. David KOHN
19 Int Director Campus Security/Safety ... Mr. Anthony JACKLITSCH
09 Inst Plng/Assessment/Research Ofcr ... Ms. Christine WORK
18 Director Administrative Services ... Mr. Michael WORDEN
37 Director of Financial Aid ... Mr. Raymond TORRES
06 Registrar ... Ms. Darlene BENZENBERG
26 Communications Officer ... Mr. Mike ALBRIGHT
121 Director Academic Advising ... Ms. Talia LLOSA
07 Director of Admissions ... Mr. Maynard SCHMIDT
35 Director Student Activities ... Mr. Steve HARPST
04 Exec Asst to President ... Ms. Charissa GONZALEZ
41 Athletic Director ... Mr. Wayne SMITH
28 Chief Diversity Officer ... Mr. Willie WILLIAMS
29 Dir Alumni Engagement/Cmty Rels ... Ms. Jennifer D'ANDREA

Orange County Community College Newburgh Branch Campus (E)

1 Washington Center, Newburgh NY 12550
Telephone: (845) 562-2454 — Identification: 770144
Accreditation: &M

Pace University (F)

1 Pace Plaza, New York NY 10038-1598
County: New York — FICE Identification: 002791
Unit ID: 194310
Telephone: (212) 346-1200 — Carnegie Class: DU-Mod
FAX Number: (212) 346-1933 — Calendar System: Semester
URL: www.pace.edu
Established: 1906 — Annual Undergrad Tuition & Fees: $47,684
Enrollment: 12,835 — Coed
Affiliation or Control: Independent Non-Profit — IRS Status: 501(c)3
Highest Offering: Doctorate
Accreditation: M, #ARCPA, CACREP, DIETC, IPSY, LAW, NURSE, OT, PSPSY, @SP, SPAA

01 President ... Mr. Marvin KRISLOV
10 Exec Vice President/CFO ... Mr. Robert C. ALMON
05 Interim Provost ... Dr. Joseph R. FRANCO
84 Vice Pres Enrollment/Placement ... Ms. Robina C. SCHEPP
30 VP Development/Alumni Relations ... Mr. Gary LAERMER
13 VP Information Tech/Int CIO ... Dr. Beth GORDON
26 VP/Chief Marketing Ofcr Univ Rels ... Ms. Mary BAGLIVO
15 Int Assoc VP Human Resources ... Ms. Susan DONAHUE
09 Asst Vice Pres Plng/Assess/Inst Res ... Ms. Nancy DERIGGI
19 Associate VP General Services ... Mr. Frank MCDONALD
50 Dean Lubin School of Business ... Mr. Lawrence SINGLETON
49 Dean Dyson College Arts/Sci ... Vacant
53 Dean School of Education ... Vacant
76 Dean College Health Professions ... Dr. Marcus TYE
77 Dean School of CSIS ... Dr. Jonathan H. HILL
32 Dean of Students New York ... Ms. Rachel CARPENTER
32 Dean of Students Westchester ... Vacant
61 Dean School of Law ... Mr. Horace E. ANDERSON, JR.
107 Asst VP Continuing/Professional Ed ... Dr. Christine SHAKESPEARE
06 Graduate Registrar ... Ms. Margaret JONES
06 Law School Registrar ... Ms. Nilda RODRIGUEZ
06 Associate University Registrar ... Ms. Barbara MCCARTHY
88 Asst Director Adult Education NY ... Ms. Nicola FOSTER
21 Interim Comptroller ... Mr. William VOLL
43 University Counsel ... Mr. Stephen BRODSKY
113 University Bursar ... Ms. Susan WEYGANT
07 Dir of Admissions NY/Westchester ... Ms. Joanna BRODA
22 Affirmative Action Officer ... Ms. Arletha MILES
14 Asst VP Information Technology Svcs ... Mr. Chris ELARDE
84 Director Adult Enroll Svcs/New York ... Ms. Janet KIRTMAN
38 Director Counseling Services ... Dr. Richard SHADICK
39 Director of Residential Life ... Mr. A. Patrick ROGER-GORDON
40 Executive Director Bookstore ... Ms. Mary LIETO
85 Assoc Dir Intl Pgms & Services ... Mr. Kraig WALKUP
96 Director of Purchasing - Contracts ... Ms. Alice SEIFERT

18 Director Facilities/Physical Plant ... Mr. Abdul JABAR
28 Director of Diversity ... Ms. Shanelle HENRY ROBINSON

Paul Smith's College (G)

PO Box 265, Paul Smiths NY 12970-0265
County: Franklin — FICE Identification: 002795
Unit ID: 194392
Telephone: (518) 327-6000 — Carnegie Class: Bac-Diverse
FAX Number: N/A — Calendar System: Semester
URL: www.paulsmiths.edu
Established: 1937 — Annual Undergrad Tuition & Fees: $30,194
Enrollment: 681 — Coed
Affiliation or Control: Independent Non-Profit — IRS Status: 501(c)3
Highest Offering: Master's
Accreditation: M

01 Interim President ... Dr. Nicholas HUNT-BULL
05 Provost ... Dr. Catherine LALONDE
30 VP Development/Alumni Relations ... Mr. Steven FREDERICK
84 VP Enrollment Management ... Mr. Robert HERR
32 VP Student Affairs ... Ms. Courtney BRINGLEY
29 Director of Alumni Relations ... Ms. Heather TUTTLE
13 Director Information Technology ... Mr. Michael MAGURK
06 Registrar ... Dr. Jeffrey WALTON
19 Lead Campus Safety Officer ... Mr. Gary LEWIS
09 Director Institutional Research ... Dr. Jeffrey WALTON
22 Director HEOP ... Ms. Kate MULLEN
41 Director of Athletics ... Mr. James TUCKER
10 Controller ... Ms. Lauren POEHLMAN
40 Manager of College Store ... Ms. Courtney TEMPLE
96 Purchasing Agent ... Ms. Cynthia LEMERY
36 Career Services Coordinator ... Ms. Lydia WRIGHT
20 Assoc Academic Officer/Provost ... Vacant
04 Exec Assistant to the President ... Ms. Kathleen KECK
15 Director of Human Resources ... Ms. Gwen GOODMAN
26 Dir Marketing/Communications ... Ms. Sarah WHEELER
37 Director Student Financial Aid ... Ms. Sonya STEIN
38 Director Student Counseling ... Ms. Najla HRUSTANOVIC
39 Director Student Life & Housing ... Mr. Lou KAMINSKI
18 Director of Facilities ... Mr. Jeremy ASMUS
08 Director of Library Services ... Mr. Andrew KELLY
07 Director of Admissions ... Ms. Hannah ACKERMAN

Phillips School of Nursing at Mount Sinai Beth Israel (H)

148 East 126th Street, New York NY 10035
County: New York — FICE Identification: 006438
Unit ID: 189282
Telephone: (212) 614-6110 — Carnegie Class: Spec-4-yr-Other Health
FAX Number: (212) 614-6109 — Calendar System: Semester
URL: https://www.mountsinai.org/locations/beth-israel/pson
Established: 1904 — Annual Undergrad Tuition & Fees: N/A
Enrollment: 254 — Coed
Affiliation or Control: Independent Non-Profit — IRS Status: 501(c)3
Highest Offering: Baccalaureate
Accreditation: NY, ADNUR, NURSE

01 Dean ... Dr. Todd AMBROSIA
05 Sr Associate Dean ... Dr. Laly JOSEPH
09 Asst Dean Inst Effectiveness ... Vacant
32 Director Student Services ... Ms. Ashni PATEL
30 Dir Development/Communications ... Ms. Linda FABRIZIO
15 Chief Human Resources Officer ... Ms. Jane MAKSOUD

Plaza College (I)

118-33 Queens Boulevard, Forest Hills NY 11375
County: Queens — FICE Identification: 012358
Unit ID: 194499
Telephone: (718) 779-1430 — Carnegie Class: Bac/Assoc-Mixed
FAX Number: (718) 779-7423 — Calendar System: Semester
URL: www.plazacollege.edu
Established: 1916 — Annual Undergrad Tuition & Fees: $13,450
Enrollment: 914 — Coed
Affiliation or Control: Proprietary — IRS Status: Proprietary
Highest Offering: Baccalaureate
Accreditation: M, CAHIIM, DH, MAC

01 President ... Charles E. CALLAHAN, III
10 Vice Pres of Financial Services ... Vacant
11 Chief Operating Officer ... Charles E. CALLAHAN, IV
05 Dean of Academic Affairs ... Marie DOLLA
06 Registrar ... Carol GARCIA
21 Comptroller ... Linda ROCKHILL
07 Director of Admissions ... Vanessa LOPEZ
20 Dean Curriculum Development ... Marianne C. ZIPF
08 College Librarian ... Eva BABALIS
23 Director Health Services ... Candice CALLAHAN
37 Director Financial Aid ... Peggy CHUNG
32 Dean of Students ... Dawn VETRANO
35 Dean of Student Activities ... Jonathan HOWLE
15 Director of HR/HR Officer ... Correne CAVALIERI
09 Assoc Dean Institutional Research ... Edward DEE
13 Chief Technology Officer ... David COLUCCI
88 Director of ARC/Library ... Allison KRAMPF
14 Manager Information Technology ... Norman ALVARADO
76 Program Director Medical Assisting ... Daryl ANDERSON
26 Director of Communications ... Brittany TRAVIS
38 Freshman Counseling ... Caroline CALLAHAN
36 Director of Career Services ... Regina POKIDAYLO

Pratt Institute (A)

200 Willoughby Avenue, Brooklyn NY 11205-3899

County: Kings | FICE Identification: 002798 | Unit ID: 194578
Telephone: (718) 636-3600 | Carnegie Class: Spec-4-yr-Arts
FAX Number: (718) 636-3670 | Calendar System: Semester
URL: www.pratt.edu
Established: 1887 | Annual Undergrad Tuition & Fees: $53,814
Enrollment: 4,353 | Coed
Affiliation or Control: Independent Non-Profit | IRS Status: 501(c)3
Highest Offering: Master's
Accreditation: M, AAQEP, CIDA, LIB, PLNG

01 President ... Ms. Frances BRONET
05 Provost ... Dr. Donna HEILAND
100 Chief of Staff ... Ms. Nicole HAAS
32 Vice President for Student Life ... Ms. Delmy LENDOF
10 Vice Pres Finance/Administration ... Ms. Cathleen KENNY
111 Vice Pres for Inst Advancement ... Ms. Daphne HALPERN
84 Vice President for Enrollment ... Mr. Rick LONGO
28 VP for Diversity/Equity/Inclusion ... Ms. Nsombi B. RICKETTS
26 Vice Pres Communications/Marketing ... Mr. James KEMPSTER
13 Chief Info Technology Officer (CIO) ... Mr. Joseph HEMWAY
11 Assistant to Pres Administration ... Ms. Josie CAPORUSCIO
88 Assoc Provost Strat Partnerships ... Dr. Allison DRUIN
08 Director of the Library ... Mr. Russ ABELL
15 Assistant VP of Human Resources ... Mr. Steve RICCOBONO
51 Dean Continuing Education ... Ms. Maira SEARA
57 Dean of Art ... Mr. Jorge OLIVER
48 Dean School of Architecture ... Dr. Harriet HARRISS
88 Dean of Design ... Ms. Anita COONEY
49 Interim Dean Liberal Arts/Science ... Dr. Helio TAKAI
62 Dean Information/Library Sci ... Dr. Anthony COCCIOLO
35 Asst VP for Student Affairs ... Ms. Rhonda SCHALLER
37 Exec Director Student Financial Svc ... Mr. Nedzad GOGA
06 Registrar ... Mr. Luke PHILLIPS
18 Chief Facilities Officer ... Mr. Christopher GAVLICK
19 Asst VP for Campus Safety ... Mr. Dennis MAZONE
39 Director Housing Operations ... Mr. Tuan VU
39 Director of Residential Life ... Ms. Katie HALE
14 Asst VP of Information Tech ... Ms. Diana RUSSO
43 Director of Legal Affairs ... Mr. Thomas GREENE
09 Chief Strategy Officer ... Mr. Adam FRIEDMAN
110 Assoc VP Inst Advancement ... Ms. Jessica TALLMAN
41 Athletic Director ... Mr. Walter RICKARD

Rabbinical Academy Mesivta Rabbi Chaim Berlin (B)

1605 Coney Island Avenue, Brooklyn NY 11230-4715

County: Kings | FICE Identification: 003976 | Unit ID: 194657
Telephone: (718) 377-0777 | Carnegie Class: Spec-4-yr-Faith
FAX Number: (718) 338-5578 | Calendar System: Semester
Established: 1939 | Annual Undergrad Tuition & Fees: $12,450
Enrollment: 336 | Male
Affiliation or Control: Independent Non-Profit | IRS Status: 501(c)3
Highest Offering: Second Talmudic Degree
Accreditation: RABN

01 Provost ... Rabbi Abraham H. FRUCHTHANDLER
05 President of the Faculty ... Rabbi Aaron M. SCHECHTER
03 Executive Director ... Rabbi Y. Mayer LASKER
29 Director of Alumni Association ... Mendel SCHECHTER
45 Chief Planning Officer ... Rabbi Tuvia M. OBERMEISTER
20 Associate Director ... Eli RABINOWITZ
37 Financial Aid Administrator ... Michael A. REISS

Rabbinical College Beth Shraga (C)

28 Saddle River Road, Monsey NY 10952-3035

County: Rockland | FICE Identification: 010943 | Unit ID: 194693
Telephone: (845) 356-1980 | Carnegie Class: Spec 2-yr-Other
FAX Number: (845) 425-2604 | Calendar System: Semester
Established: 1965 | Annual Undergrad Tuition & Fees: $14,250
Enrollment: 40 | Male
Affiliation or Control: Independent Non-Profit | IRS Status: 501(c)3
Highest Offering: Second Talmudic Degree
Accreditation: RABN

01 President ... Rabbi Emanuel SCHIFF

Rabbinical College Bobover Yeshiva B'nei Zion (D)

1577 48th Street, Brooklyn NY 11219-3293

County: Kings | FICE Identification: 008614 | Unit ID: 194666
Telephone: (718) 438-2018 | Carnegie Class: Spec-4-yr-Faith
FAX Number: (718) 871-9031 | Calendar System: Semester
Established: 1947 | Annual Undergrad Tuition & Fees: $8,500
Enrollment: 418 | Male
Affiliation or Control: Independent Non-Profit | IRS Status: 501(c)3
Highest Offering: First Talmudic Degree
Accreditation: RABN

01 President ... Rabbi Boruch Avrohom HOROWITZ

Rabbinical College of Long Island (E)

205 W Beech Street, Long Beach NY 11561-0630

County: Nassau | FICE Identification: 010378 | Unit ID: 194736
Telephone: (516) 255-4700 | Carnegie Class: Spec-4-yr-Faith
FAX Number: (516) 255-4701 | Calendar System: Semester
Established: 1965 | Annual Undergrad Tuition & Fees: $9,100
Enrollment: 160 | Male
Affiliation or Control: Independent Non-Profit | IRS Status: 501(c)3
Highest Offering: First Talmudic Degree
Accreditation: RABN

01 President ... Vacant
06 Registrar ... Rabbi Dovid N. ROTHSCHILD
32 Dean of Students ... Rabbi Yeruchem PITTER
07 CEO and Director of Admissions ... Rabbi Chaim HOBERMAN
37 Financial Aid Administrator ... Rabbi Shlomo TEICHMAN
06 Assistant Registrar ... Mrs. Toni TURNER

Rabbinical College Ohr Shimon Yisroel (F)

215-217 Hewes Street, Brooklyn NY 11211-8102

County: Kings | FICE Identification: 031292 | Unit ID: 405854
Telephone: (718) 855-4092 | Carnegie Class: Spec-4-yr-Faith
FAX Number: (646) 448-2272 | Calendar System: Semester
Established: | Annual Undergrad Tuition & Fees: $14,600
Enrollment: 211 | Male
Affiliation or Control: Independent Non-Profit | IRS Status: 501(c)3
Highest Offering: First Talmudic Degree
Accreditation: RABN

01 President ... Rabbi Shulem WALTER

Rabbinical College Ohr Yisroel (G)

8800 Seaview Avenue, Brooklyn NY 11236

County: Kings | Identification: 667145 | Unit ID: 484871
Telephone: (718) 633-4715 | Carnegie Class: Spec-4-yr-Faith
FAX Number: (347) 702-5436 | Calendar System: Semester
Established: 2009 | Annual Undergrad Tuition & Fees: $9,000
Enrollment: 115 | Male
Affiliation or Control: Independent Non-Profit | IRS Status: 501(c)3
Highest Offering: First Talmudic Degree
Accreditation: @RABN

01 President ... Rabbi Daniel GELDZAHLER

Rabbinical Seminary of America (H)

76-01 147th Street, Flushing NY 11367-3148

County: Queens | FICE Identification: 003978 | Unit ID: 194763
Telephone: (718) 268-4700 | Carnegie Class: Spec-4-yr-Faith
FAX Number: (718) 268-4684 | Calendar System: Semester
Established: 1933 | Annual Undergrad Tuition & Fees: $9,900
Enrollment: 502 | Male
Affiliation or Control: Independent Non-Profit | IRS Status: 501(c)3
Highest Offering: Second Talmudic Degree
Accreditation: RABN

01 President ... Rabbi David HARRIS
01 President ... Rabbi Akiva GRUNBLATT
01 President ... Rabbi Shaul OPOCZYNSKI
03 Executive Vice President ... Rabbi Hayim SCHWARTZ
11 Director of Operation ... Rabbi Meir GLAZER
06 Registrar ... Rabbi Abraham SEMMEL
05 Executive Director ... Rabbi Yehuda JEGER
30 Director Development ... Rabbi Yossi SINGER
37 Director of Financial Aid ... Mrs. Laya EISENSTEIN
18 Chief Physical Plant ... Mr. Michoel KESSLER
88 Director of Special Projects ... Vacant
91 Director of Admin Computing ... Mr. Yechiel WALDMAN
39 Director Student Housing ... Rabbi Elisha FEINBERG
111 Associate Director Development ... Mr. Raphael ADLER

Relay Graduate School of Education (I)

25 Broadway, 3rd Floor, New York NY 10004

County: New York | Identification: 667117 | Unit ID: 475033
Telephone: (212) 228-1888 | Carnegie Class: Spec-4-yr-Other
FAX Number: (212) 228-1855 | Calendar System: Other
URL: www.relay.edu
Established: 2011 | Annual Graduate Tuition & Fees: N/A
Enrollment: 3,790 | Coed
Affiliation or Control: Independent Non-Profit | IRS Status: 501(c)3
Highest Offering: Master's; No Undergraduates
Accreditation: M, CAEP

01 President ... Dr. Mayme HOSTETTER
05 Provost ... Ms. Kari FEINBERG
11 Executive Vice President ... Vacant
10 Chief Financial/Operating Officer ... Mr. Julian ROBERTS
32 Chief Student Services Officer ... Ms. Kelly BOUCHER MORRIS
20 Senior Dean ... Dr. Therese ZOSEL-HARPER
15 Chief People Person ... Ms. Jessica SMITH

Rensselaer Polytechnic Institute (J)

110 8th Street, Troy NY 12180-3590

County: Rensselaer | FICE Identification: 002803 | Unit ID: 194824
Telephone: (518) 276-6000 | Carnegie Class: DU-Highest
FAX Number: N/A | Calendar System: Semester
URL: www.rpi.edu
Established: 1824 | Annual Undergrad Tuition & Fees: $57,012
Enrollment: 7,501 | Coed
Affiliation or Control: Independent Non-Profit | IRS Status: 501(c)3
Highest Offering: Doctorate
Accreditation: M

01 President ... Dr. Martin A. SCHMIDT
05 Provost ... Dr. Prabhat HAJELA
11 Acting Vice Pres for Administration ... Mr. Ernie J. KATZWINKEL
26 Int VP Strategic Comm/External Rels ... Mr. Gary ZARR
10 Vice President for Finance/CFO ... Ms. Eileen MCLOUGHLIN
45 Acting Vice Pres for Research ... Dr. Robert HULL
111 Vice Pres Institutional Advancement ... Mr. Graig R. EASTIN
32 Vice President Student Life ... Dr. Peter KONWERSKI
15 Vice Pres Human Resources ... Mr. Curtis N. POWELL
13 Vice Pres for Info Services & CIO ... Mr. John E. KOLB
84 Vice Pres Enrollment Management ... Dr. Jonathan D. WEXLER
43 Secretary of Inst/General Counsel ... Mr. Craig A. COOK
27 Assoc VP Marketing/Communications ... Ms. Pamela S. SMITH
41 Assoc Vice Pres/Director Athletics ... Dr. Lee MCELROY
19 AVP Public Safety/Emergency Mgmt ... Mr. Vadim THOMAS
21 Asst Vice Pres for Administration ... Mr. Paul W. MARTIN
29 Asst Vice Pres Alumni Relations ... Vacant
35 Asst Vice Pres & Dean of Students ... Mr. Travis APGAR
121 Asst Vice Pres of Student Success ... Ms. Lisa TRAHAN
54 Dean School of Engineering ... Dr. Shekhar GARDE
81 Dean School of Science ... Dr. Curt BRENEMAN
79 Dean Sch of Humanities/Arts/Soc Sci ... Dr. Mary SIMONI
50 Acting Dean Lally School Management ... Dr. Chanaka EDIRISINGHE
48 Dean School of Architecture ... Mr. Evan DOUGLIS
107 Dean Acad & Admin Affs Hartford ... Dr. Aric KRAUSE
58 Vice Provost/Dean Graduate Educ ... Dr. Stanley DUNN
20 Vice Provost/Dean Undergrad Educ ... Dr. Keith MOO-YOUNG
06 Registrar ... Ms. Rajni Etka SOHARU
37 Director Financial Aid ... Mr. Martin C. DANIELS
09 Director of Institutional Research ... Dr. Judith STODDARD
08 Director of Libraries ... Mr. Andrew C. WHITE
25 Director of Research Finance ... Mr. John BRAUNGARD
36 Director Career Development Center ... Mr. Philip BRUCE
07 Director Undergrad Admissions ... Ms. Karen S. LONG
123 Director Graduate Admissions ... Mr. Jarron P. DECKER
18 Director Physical Plant ... Mr. Ernest J. KATZWINKEL
23 Exec Director Student Health Center ... Dr. Leslie LAWRENCE
38 Director Counseling Center ... Ms. Anita CHU
96 Director Procurement Services ... Ms. Rachael CAPO
105 Director Web Services ... Mr. Andrew C. WHITE
90 Director Client Info Services ... Ms. Jacqueline B. STAMPALIA
91 Director Enterprise Info Services ... Ms. Mary Alice O'BRIEN
39 Dean Student Living & Learning ... Mr. John LAWLER
30 Assoc VP Development & Fundraising ... Mr. Joel B. KINCART

Richard Gilder Graduate School at the American Museum of Natural History (K)

200 Central Park West, New York NY 10024

County: New York | Identification: 667003 | Unit ID: 458548
Telephone: (212) 769-5055 | Carnegie Class: Not Classified
FAX Number: (212) 769-5257 | Calendar System: Other
URL: www.amnh.org/our-research/richard-gilder-graduate-school
Established: 2006 | Annual Graduate Tuition & Fees: N/A
Enrollment: N/A | Coed
Affiliation or Control: Independent Non-Profit | IRS Status: 501(c)3
Highest Offering: Doctorate; No Undergraduates
Accreditation: NY, CAEP

01 Dean ... Dr. John J. FLYNN

Roberts Wesleyan University (L)

2301 Westside Drive, Rochester NY 14624-1997

County: Monroe | FICE Identification: 002805 | Unit ID: 194958
Telephone: (585) 594-6000 | Carnegie Class: Masters/L
FAX Number: (585) 594-6371 | Calendar System: Semester
URL: www.roberts.edu
Established: 1866 | Annual Undergrad Tuition & Fees: $33,500
Enrollment: 1,706 | Coed
Affiliation or Control: Independent Non-Profit | IRS Status: 501(c)3
Highest Offering: Doctorate
Accreditation: M, AAQEP, IACBE, MUS, NURSE, PSPSY, SW

01 President ... Dr. Deana L. PORTERFIELD
05 Sr VP & Chief Academic Officer ... Dr. David BASINGER
10 Sr Vice President & Treasurer ... Ms. Laurie LEO
32 VP for Student & Org Development ... Ms. Kristen BROWN
111 VP Institutional Advancement ... Mr. Alexander JONES
84 VP for Enrollment Management ... Mrs. Kimberley WIEDEFELD
07 Exec Director of UG Admissions ... Ms. Mary SASSO
26 AVP for Brand/Marketing Comm ... Ms. Donna MCLAREN
13 Assoc VP for Information Technology ... Mr. Pradeep SAXENA

40 Director of Bookstore Services .... Mr. Ben KNEELAND
41 Director of Athletics .... Mr. Robert SEGAVE
37 Director of Student Financial Svcs .... Ms. Amy SCHMALFUSS
09 Dir Institutional Research/Assess .... Dr. Paul W. KENNEDY
42 Chaplain .... Rev. Gerald COLEMAN
06 Registrar .... Mrs. Lesa J. KOHR
04 Administrative Asst to President .... Mrs. Mimi WHEELER
15 Director Personnel Services .... Ms. Pamela SIMMONS
18 Chief Facilities/Physical Plant .... Mr. T. Richard GREER
19 Director Security/Safety .... Mr. Rick BILLITIER
25 Chief Contracts/Grants Admin .... Mr. Kirk KETTINGER
29 Director Alumni Relations .... Ms. Michelle BLAAKMAN
103 Dir Workforce/Career Development .... Ms. Mary FLAHERTY
104 Director International Engagement .... Vacant
50 Dean School of Business .... Ms. Laura FALCO
28 Interim Dir Multicultural Affairs .... Mrs. Jessica COLEMAN
53 Dean of Education .... Dr. Kristen DRISKILL

† Parent institution of Northeastern Seminary.

Rochester Institute of Technology (A)

2 Lomb Memorial Drive, Rochester NY 14623-5604
County: Monroe — FICE Identification: 002806
Unit ID: 195003
Telephone: (585) 475-2411 — Carnegie Class: DU-Higher
FAX Number: (585) 475-7049 — Calendar System: Quarter
URL: www.rit.edu
Established: 1829 — Annual Undergrad Tuition & Fees: $51,240
Enrollment: 16,158 — Coed
Affiliation or Control: Independent Non-Profit — IRS Status: 501(c)3
Highest Offering: Doctorate
Accreditation: M, ARCPA, ART, CAEP, CEA, CIDA, DIETD, DMS, HSA, IPSY, MIL, #NASP

01 President .... Dr. David C. MUNSON, JR.
05 Provost/SVP Academic Affairs .... Dr. Ellen GRANBERG
100 Chief of Staff .... Mrs. Karen A. BARROWS
10 Sr Vice Pres Finance/Administration .... Dr. James H. WATTERS
84 VP Enrollment Management .... Mr. Ian MORTIMER
32 Sr Vice President Student Affairs .... Dr. Sandra S. JOHNSON
12 President NTID/RIT Vice Pres & Dean .... Dr. Gerard J. BUCKLEY
12 President RIT Kosovo .... Dr. Kamal SHAHRABI
12 President RIT Croatia .... Mr. Donald HUDSPETH
12 President RIT Dubai .... Dr. Yousef AL-ASSAF
111 VP for University Advancement .... Mr. Phillip CASTLEBERRY
26 VP/Chief Marketing Officer .... Mr. John K. TRIERWEILER
86 Vice President Govt/Cmty Relations .... Ms. Vanessa HERMAN
46 Vice President Research .... Dr. Ryne RAFFAELLE
28 VP/Provost Diversity/Inclusion .... Dr. Keith JENKINS
76 Dean Col Health Sciences/Tech .... Dr. Yong Tai WANG
20 Vice Provost Academic Affairs .... Dr. Christine M. LICATA
36 Director Coop Educ/Career Svcs .... Ms. Maria RICHART
27 AVP University Communications .... Mr. Bob FINNERTY
110 Assoc VP Univ Advancement .... Ms. Cathy HAIN
20 Assoc Provost AA & Director GIS .... Dr. Nabil NASR
08 Director of RIT Libraries .... Ms. Marcia TRAVERNICHT
29 Exec Director Alumni/Const Engage .... Mr. Jon RODIBAUGH
21 Assoc VP/Controller/Asst Treasurer .... Ms. Milagros CONCEPCION
18 Assoc VP Facilities Management Svcs .... Mr. John MOORE
06 Assoc VP/Registrar .... Mr. Joe LOFFREDO
07 Asst VP/Dean of Admissions .... Ms. Marian NICOLETTI
37 Exec Dir Fin Aid & Scholarship .... Ms. Meaghan M. DRUMM
88 Exec Director Corp Relations .... Ms. Tara DELEO
123 Sr AVP/Dir Grad/PT Enroll Svcs .... Ms. Diane ELLISON
112 Exec Dir Planned Giving/Major Gifts .... Mr. Hallett BURRALL
09 Asst VP Inst Research .... Dr. Joan E. GRAHAM
15 Assoc VP/Chief Human Resources Ofcr .... Ms. Jo Ellen PINKHAM
44 Executive Director Annual Giving .... Ms. Marisa PSAILA
35 Assoc VP Student Development .... Dr. Heath BOICE-PARDEE
85 Director International Student Svcs .... Mr. Jeffrey W. COX
96 Exec Director Procurement Services .... Ms. Joann BODENSTEINER
102 Exec Director Foundation Relations .... Ms. Sara VINCH
107 Dean/Director Univ Studies .... Dr. James HALL
50 Dean Saunders Col of Business .... Dr. Jacqueline MOZRALL
54 Dean Gleason Col of Engineering .... Dr. Doreen EDWARDS
72 Dean of Engineering Technology .... Dr. S. Manian RAMKUMAR
49 Dean College of Liberal Arts .... Dr. Anna WESTERSTAHL STENPORT
81 Interim Dean College of Science .... Andre HUDSON
57 Dean College of Art & Design .... Dr. Todd JOKL
77 Interim Dean Computer/Info Science .... Matt HUENERFAUTH
58 Dean/Assoc Provost Graduate Educ .... Dr. Diane SLUSARSKI
04 Exec Admin Asst to President .... Ms. Sonia RODRIGUEZ
11 Chief of Administration .... Mrs. Karen A. BARROWS
13 Interim Chief Info Tech Officer .... Ms. Joan GRAHAM
41 Exec Dir Intercollegiate Athletics .... Ms. Jacqueline NICHOLSON
103 Direcctor of Talent Management .... Vacant
104 Assoc Provost Intl Educ/Global Pgms .... Dr. James A. MYERS
105 AVP Univeristy Web Services .... Mr. Raman S. BHALLA
106 Exec Dir Innovative Learning Inst .... Dr. Neil F. HAIR
108 Asst Prov Assessment/Accreditation .... Vacant
19 Director Public Safety .... Mr. Gary D. MOXLEY
38 Director Counseling & Psych Svcs .... Dr. David R. REETZ
39 AVP Student Auxiliary Svcs .... Mr. Kory SAMUELS

Rockefeller University (B)

1230 York Avenue, New York NY 10065-6399
County: New York — FICE Identification: 002807
Unit ID: 195049
Telephone: (212) 327-8000 — Carnegie Class: Spec-4-yr-Eng
FAX Number: (212) 327-8699 — Calendar System: Trimester
URL: www.rockefeller.edu
Established: 1901 — Annual Graduate Tuition & Fees: N/A
Enrollment: 255 — Coed
Affiliation or Control: Independent Non-Profit — IRS Status: 501(c)3
Highest Offering: Doctorate; No Undergraduates
Accreditation: NY

01 President .... Dr. Richard P. LIFTON
03 Executive Vice President .... Dr. Timothy O'CONNOR
43 Vice President & General Counsel .... Ms. Deborah YEOH
05 Vice President Academic Affairs .... Mr. Michael W. YOUNG
10 Vice President Finance .... Mr. James H. LAPPLE
30 Sr Vice President Development .... Ms. Maren E. IMHOFF
17 Vice President for Medical Affairs .... Dr. Barry S. COLLER
20 Dean & Vice Pres of Educ Affairs .... Dr. Sidney STRICKLAND
18 Assoc Vice Pres Plant Operations .... Mr. Alexander KOGAN
45 Assoc Vice Pres Plng & Constr .... Mr. George B. CANDLER
13 Chief Information Officer .... Mr. Anthony CARVALLOZA
25 Dir Pgm Dev & Sponsored Research .... Ms. Collette L. RYDER
08 University Librarian .... Dr. Matthew V. COVEY
19 Director Security .... Mr. James ROGERS
26 Assoc VP Communications/Public Affs .... Mr. Franklin HOKE

Rockland Community College (C)

145 College Road, Suffern NY 10901-3699
County: Rockland — FICE Identification: 002877
Unit ID: 195058
Telephone: (845) 574-4000 — Carnegie Class: Assoc/HT-High Trad
FAX Number: (845) 574-4463 — Calendar System: Semester
URL: www.sunyrockland.edu
Established: 1959 — Annual Undergrad Tuition & Fees (In-District): $5,618
Enrollment: 5,735 — Coed
Affiliation or Control: State/Local — IRS Status: 501(c)3
Highest Offering: Associate Degree
Accreditation: M, ADNUR, OTA

01 Officer in Charge .... Dr. Susan DEER
10 Int Chief Financial Officer .... Dr. Daniel DOBELL
05 Officer in Charge of Academic Affs .... Dr. Katherine LYNCH
84 VP Enrollment & Student Affairs .... Dr. Bart GRACHAN
13 Chief Information Officer .... Mr. Gary HOLEMAN
32 Dean Student Development .... Vacant
15 Exec Dir Human Resources .... Ms. Natalie SCOTT
37 Director Financial Aid .... Ms. Madelene APONTE
06 Registrar .... Ms. Robin CONKLIN
28 Dir Equity/Compliance/Affirm Act .... Ms. Melissa ROY
09 Director of Institutional Research .... Dr. Jim ROBERTSON
20 Asst to Vice Pres Academic Affairs .... Ms. Patricia KOBES
100 Chief of Staff/Sec to the Board .... Mr. Ben NAYLOR
106 Dir Online Education/E-learning .... Ms. Lilia JUELE
11 Dir Administrative Services .... Mr. Dennis CALLINAN
19 Director Public Safety .... Mr. William MURPHY
07 Director of Admissions .... Mr. Brian SONDEY

Russell Sage College (D)

65 First Street, Troy NY 12180-4199
County: Rensselaer — FICE Identification: 002810
Unit ID: 195128
Telephone: (518) 244-2000 — Carnegie Class: DU-Mod
FAX Number: (518) 244-2460 — Calendar System: Semester
URL: www.sage.edu
Established: 1916 — Annual Undergrad Tuition & Fees: $32,950
Enrollment: 2,389 — Coed
Affiliation or Control: Independent Non-Profit — IRS Status: 501(c)3
Highest Offering: Doctorate
Accreditation: M, AAQEP, ART, DIETD, DIETI, IACBE, MPCAC, NURSE, OT, PTA

01 President .... Dr. Christopher AMES
05 Provost .... Dr. Theresa HAND
111 VP for Institutional Advancement .... Ms. Kate ADAMS
84 VP Marketing/Enroll Mgmt .... Mr. Thomas NESBITT
20 Dean Russell Sage College .... Dr. Andrea REHN
10 VP for Finance & Treasurer .... Mr. Rick BARTHELMAS
32 Vice Pres for Campus Life .... Ms. Patricia CELLEMME
35 Dean of Students Troy Campus .... Ms. Stacy GONZALEZ
35 Dean of Students Albany Campus .... Ms. Sharon MURRAY
76 Dean of Health Sciences .... Dr. Kathleen KELLY
06 Registrar .... Ms. Kathy SCOVILLE
94 Exec Dir of Women's Institute-RSC .... Ms. Shelly CALABRESE
26 Sr Dir of Marketing/Communications .... Mr. Douglas GRUSE
07 Director of UG Admission .... Ms. Sarah BARRETT
50 Dean School of Management .... Dr. John PELIZZA
53 Dean School of Education .... Dr. John PELIZZA
29 Sr Director Alumnae/i Relations .... Ms. Joan CLIFFORD
123 Dir of Graduate & Adult Admissions .... Mr. Michael JONES
37 Director of Financial Aid .... Ms. Kelley ROBINSON
15 Director of Human Resources .... Ms. Laura D'AGOSTINO
09 Director of Institutional Research .... Ms. Lori PIZER
18 Director Facilities Management .... Mr. John ZAJACESKOWSKI
121 Sr Dir of Academic Advisement .... Ms. Karen SCHELL
121 Dir of Academic Advisement-RSC .... Ms. Beth MANEY
92 Director of Honors Programs .... Dr. Tonya MOUTRAY
04 Exec Admin Asst to President .... Ms. Janet RONDEAU
08 Head Librarian .... Mr. Christopher WHITE
105 Webmaster .... Mr. Sean DUFFY
108 Dir Institutional Effectiveness .... Mr. Kirk ROBINSON
19 Associate Director Public Safety .... Mr. Charles MCDONALD
39 Director of Residence Life .... Ms. Grace GIANCOLA
41 Athletic Director .... Ms. Sandy AUGESTINE-COLLINS
44 Sr Director of Annual Giving .... Ms. Kathleen DANICA
91 Director of IT/Network Services .... Mr. John HARRIS
106 Director of Online Education .... Ms. Kimberly TAYLOR
28 Director of Diversity & Inclusion .... Ms. Barbara COCKFIELD
25 Asst Provost for Grants & Community .... Dr. Kimberly FREDERICKS

Saint Bernard's School of Theology & Ministry (E)

120 French Road, Rochester NY 14618-3822
County: Monroe — FICE Identification: 002815
Unit ID: 195155
Telephone: (585) 271-3657 — Carnegie Class: Spec-4-yr-Faith
FAX Number: (585) 271-2045 — Calendar System: Semester
URL: www.stbernards.edu
Established: 1893 — Annual Graduate Tuition & Fees: N/A
Enrollment: 91 — Coed
Affiliation or Control: Roman Catholic — IRS Status: 501(c)3
Highest Offering: Master's; No Undergraduates
Accreditation: THEOL

01 President .... Dr. Stephen J. LOUGHLIN
05 Academic Dean .... Dr. Matthew KUHNER
04 Exec Asst to the President .... Mrs. Kelly BRUNACINI
10 Finance Manager .... Mr. Tom KUBUS
07 Director of Admissions/Fin Aid .... Mr. Matthew BROWN
18 Chief Facilities/Physical Plant Ofc .... Mr. Patrick SWEENEY
30 Development Coordinator & Registrar .... Mrs. Sophia ZDANOWSKI

St. Bonaventure University (F)

P.O. Box A, St. Bonaventure NY 14778
County: Cattaraugus — FICE Identification: 002817
Unit ID: 195164
Telephone: (716) 375-2000 — Carnegie Class: Masters/M
FAX Number: N/A — Calendar System: Semester
URL: www.sbu.edu
Established: 1858 — Annual Undergrad Tuition & Fees: $36,515
Enrollment: 2,540 — Coed
Affiliation or Control: Roman Catholic — IRS Status: 501(c)3
Highest Offering: Master's
Accreditation: M, #ARCPA, CACREP, CAEPN, JOUR, NURSE

01 President .... Dr. Jeff GINGERICH
05 Provost and VP for Academic Affairs .... Dr. Joseph E. ZIMMER
32 Vice Pres for Student Affairs .... Ms. Kathryn O'BRIEN
10 VP Finance & Administration/CFO .... Mr. H. Daniel HUNGERFORD
26 Chief Communications Officer .... Mr. Thomas MISSEL
111 Vice Pres for Advancement .... Mr. Robert VAN WICKLIN
84 Vice President for Enrollment .... Mr. Bernard VALENTO
57 Exec Dir of Q Arts Center .... Mr. Ludwig BRUNNER
100 Assoc VP & Chief of Staff .... Ms. Ann LEHMAN
15 Director of Human Resources .... Ms. Kyle LESLIE
07 Director of Recruitment .... Mr. Douglas BRADY
37 Director of Financial Aid .... Mr. Christopher CARTMILL
06 Registrar .... Mr. George B. SWINDOLL
13 Assoc Provost/Chief Info Officer .... Dr. Michael HOFFMAN
08 Director Friedsam Memorial Library .... Ms. Ann TENGLUND
101 Director of Board/Govt/Cmty Rels .... Mr. Thomas BUTTAFARRO, JR.
29 Director of Alumni Services .... Mr. Joseph FLANAGAN
36 Director of Career Services .... Ms. Pamela FERMAN
43 University Counsel .... Mr. Jeff REISNER
23 Assoc Dean Stdnt & Cmty Wellbeing .... Ms. Del Rey HONEYCUTT
18 Director of Facilities Operations .... Mr. Jared SMITH
21 Controller .... Ms. Nancy K. TAYLOR
19 Director of Safety and Security .... Mr. Gary SEGRUE
40 Manager Bookstore .... Ms. Annette DONAVON
44 Director Annual Giving Program .... Mr. Alan RIDDLE
92 Director of Honors Program .... Dr. Megan WALSH
49 Dean School of Arts & Sci .... Dr. David HILMEY
50 Dean School of Business .... Dr. Matricia JAMES
58 Dean School of Graduate Studies .... Dr. Michael HOFFMAN
53 Interim Dean School of Education .... Dr. Latoya PIERCE
60 Dean Jandoli Sch of Communication .... Mr. Aaron CHIMBLE
76 Dean School of Health Professions .... Dr. Douglas PISANO
26 Director Marketing and Promotions .... Mr. Seth JOHNSON
41 Acting Director of Athletics .... Ms. Barb QUESTA

St. Elizabeth College of Nursing (G)

2215 Genesee Street, Utica NY 13501-5998
County: Oneida — FICE Identification: 006461
Unit ID: 195702
Telephone: (315) 801-8253 — Carnegie Class: Spec 2-yr-Health
FAX Number: (315) 801-8271 — Calendar System: Semester
URL: www.secon.edu
Established: 1904 — Annual Undergrad Tuition & Fees: $18,570
Enrollment: 155 — Coed
Affiliation or Control: Independent Non-Profit — IRS Status: 501(c)3
Highest Offering: Associate Degree
Accreditation: M, ADNUR

01 President .... Dr. Kimberly PANKO
32 Dean of Student/Faculty Devel .... Mrs. Julie WELLS-TSIATSOS
06 Registrar & Bursar .... Mr. Joseph CASCELLA
10 Director of Finance & Enrollment .... Ms. Sherry WOJNAS

St. Francis College (H)

180 Remsen Street, Brooklyn NY 11201-4398
County: Kings — FICE Identification: 002820
Unit ID: 195173
Telephone: (718) 522-2300 — Carnegie Class: Bac-Diverse
FAX Number: (718) 522-1274 — Calendar System: Semester
URL: www.sfc.edu
Established: 1859 — Annual Undergrad Tuition & Fees: $26,798
Enrollment: 2,735 — Coed
Affiliation or Control: Independent Non-Profit — IRS Status: 501(c)3

Highest Offering: Master's
Accreditation: M, NURSE

01	President	Dr. Miguel MARTINEZ-SAENZ
10	Chief Financial Officer	Ms. Maureen LAWRENCE
86	Vice Pres Govt/Community Relations	Ms. Linda WERBEL DASHEFSKY
30	Vice President of Development	Mr. Thomas FLOOD
84	Asst VP Enrollment Mgmt/Dir Admiss	Mr. Robert OLIVA
18	VP Facilities Mgmt/Capital Projects	Mr. Kevin O'ROURKE
104	VP Internationalization Initiative	Mr. Reza FAKHARI
05	VP Academic Affairs/Academic Dean	Dr. Jennifer LANCASTER
20	AVP Academic Affs/Dean Curriculum	Dr. Kathleen GRAY
58	Assoc Dean Grad Pgms/Adult Educ	Vacant
121	Assoc Dean for Student Success	Ms. Monica MICHALSKI
15	Exec Director of Human Resources	Mr. Richard GRASSO
13	Exec Dir Information Technology	Mr. Matthew HOGAN
06	Registrar	Ms. Susan E. WEISMAN
32	Dean of Students	Dr. Jose RODRIGUEZ
08	Director Library Services	Ms. Mona WASSERMAN
36	Director of Career Development	Ms. Naomi KINLEY
29	Director of Alumni Relations	Vacant
41	Director of Athletics	Ms. Irma GARCIA
42	Director Campus Ministry	Dr. Joel WARDEN
09	Director of Institutional Research	Mr. Steven CATALANO
100	Chief of Staff	Ms. Monique PRYOR
26	Exec Dir Marketing/Communications	Ms. Tearanny STREET
106	AVP of Online Learning & Program	Dr. Gale GIBSON-GAYLE
19	Asst Director of Campus Security	Mr. Edward EVANS
25	Chief Contract/Grants Administrator	Ms. Emily WARD
23	Director of Student Health Services	Ms. Natasha EDWARDS
39	Dir Student Engagement/Resid Life	Ms. Anilsa NUNEZ

St. John Fisher University (A)

3690 East Avenue, Rochester NY 14618-3597
County: Monroe
FICE Identification: 002821
Unit ID: 195720
Telephone: (585) 385-8000
Carnegie Class: DU-Mod
FAX Number: (585) 899-3870
Calendar System: Semester
URL: www.sjfc.edu
Established: 1948
Annual Undergrad Tuition & Fees: $35,150
Enrollment: 3,610
Coed
Affiliation or Control: Independent Non-Profit
IRS Status: 501(c)3
Highest Offering: Doctorate
Accreditation: M, CACREP, CAEP, COSMA, NURSE, PHAR

01	President	Dr. Gerard J. ROONEY
04	Senior Executive Assistant	Ms. Mary M. MCGOWAN
05	Provost/VP for Academic Affairs	Dr. Kevin RAILEY
84	VP Enrollment Management	Mr. Jose J. PERALES
10	VP Finance/CFO	Mr. Hezekiah SIMMONS
32	VP Student Affairs/Dean of Students	Dr. Matha THORNTON
111	VP Institutional Advancement	Mr. Christopher M. BIEHN
49	Dean School of Arts/Sciences	Dr. Ann Marie FALLON
50	Interim Dean School of Business	Dr. Carol WITTMEYER
53	Dean School of Education	Dr. Joellen MAPLES
66	Dean School of Nursing	Dr. Patricia GATLIN
67	Dean School of Pharmacy	Dr. Christine R. BIRNIE
28	Director Multicultural Affairs	Mr. Yantee SLOBERT
06	Registrar	Mr. Jason WELCH
15	Asst Vice Pres Human Resources	Ms. Valerie C. BENJAMIN
28	Senior Diversity Officer	Dr. Marlowe WASHINGTON
26	Director Marketing & Communications	Ms. Kate M. TOROK
08	Director of the Library	Ms. Melissa JADLOS
13	Chief Information/Computing Officer	Mr. Stacy S. SLOCUM
16	Director of Payroll & Accts Payable	Ms. Mary R. POWLEY
37	Director Student Financial Aid	Ms. Marie FICO
42	Director Campus Ministry	Fr. Kevin MANNARA
19	Interim Director Safety & Security	Mr. Russell REYNOLDS
41	Athletic Director	Mr. Robert A. WARD
18	Director of Facilities Services	Mr. Kenneth WIDANKA
21	Controller	Ms. Diane MARTZ
23	Dir of Health & Wellness Center	Ms. Rebecca KIEFFER
104	Director of Global Education	Ms. Maria S. PLUTINO
07	Director of Freshman Admissions	Ms. Stacy A. LEDERMANN
123	Dir of Transfer/Grad Admissions	Ms. Michelle GOSIER
09	Director Institutional Research	Ms. Elizabeth A. LACHANCE
35	Director Student Affairs	Ms. Amanda METZGER
36	Director Career Services	Dr. Julia OVERTON-HEALY
105	Webmaster	Ms. Jody C. BENEDICT
96	Director of Purchasing	Ms. Susan WISNIEWSKI
101	Secretary to the Board	Ms. Stephanie WILLIAMS
29	Director Alumni Affairs	Ms. Teah TERRANCE
30	Asst VP for Development	Mr. Adam PARE
39	Director Residential Life	Mr. Derick WIGLE

St. John's University (B)

8000 Utopia Parkway, Queens NY 11439-0001
County: Queens
FICE Identification: 002823
Unit ID: 195809
Telephone: (718) 990-6161
Carnegie Class: DU-Mod
FAX Number: (718) 990-2314
Calendar System: Semester
URL: www.stjohns.edu
Established: 1870
Annual Undergrad Tuition & Fees: $44,760
Enrollment: 20,143
Coed
Affiliation or Control: Roman Catholic
IRS Status: 501(c)3
Highest Offering: Doctorate
Accreditation: M, ARCPA, ART, AUD, CACREP, CLPSY, EMT, LAW, LIB, MLS, NASP, PHAR, @PTA, RAD, SCPSY, SP

01	President	Rev. Brian J. SHANLEY, OP
03	Executive VP Mission	Rev. Aidan ROONEY, CM
05	Provost/VP Academic Affairs	Dr. Simon MOLLER
10	VP Business Affairs/CFO/ Treasurer	Ms. Sharon HEWITT WATKINS
11	VP Admin/Secretary & Gen Counsel	Mr. Joseph E. OLIVA
111	VP University Advancement/Relations	Dr. Christian P. VAUPEL
28	VP Equity & Inclusion	Dr. Rachel PEREIRA
100	VP/Chief of Staff	Ms. Nunziatina A. MANULI
124	VP Student Success/Retention Strat	Ms. Sarah J. KELLY
32	VP Student Affairs	Dr. Kathryn T. HUTCHINSON
15	Assoc VP for Human Resources	Ms. Keaton WONG
13	Chief Information Officer	Ms. Anne R. PACIONE
41	Director of Athletics	Mr. Michael CRAGG
49	Dean St John's College	Dr. Teresa DELGADO
53	Dean The School of Education	Dr. James WOLFINGER
61	Dean School of Law	Mr. Michael A. SIMONS
50	Dean The Tobin College of Business	Dr. Norean R. SHARPE
67	Dean Pharmacy/Health Sciences	Dr. Anne Y. LIN
107	Int Dean Collins Col Prof Studies	Dr. Luca IANDOLI
12	Interim Vice Provost - SI	Mr. David GACHIGO
08	University Librarian	Ms. Caroline FUCHS
20	Vice Provost & Chief of Staff	Ms. Linda A. SHANNON
20	Vice Provost	Dr. Andre MCKENZIE
46	Vice Provost Grad Ed/Clin Op&Resrch	Dr. Marc E. GILLESPIE
31	VP Community Relations	Mr. Joseph A. SCIAME
88	Chief Data Officer	Mr. Dallas MADDOX
115	Chief Investment Officer	Mr. Steven KEATING
114	Assoc VP for Budget and Planning	Mr. Michael MCLEOD
18	Assoc VP Campus Facilities/Services	Mr. Brian BAUMER
91	Assoc VP Bus Process & Applications	Ms. Maura A. WOODS
26	Assoc VP Univ Comms & Public Affs	Mr. Brian BROWNE
42	Assoc VP University Ministry	Ms. Victoria R. SANTANGELO
27	Asst VP Marketing & Brand	Ms. Linda ROMANO
30	Asst VP Inst Advancement/Alumni Rel	Mr. Scott VANDEUSEN
93	Asst VP Office of Equity/Inclusion	Ms. Monique JERNIGAN
20	Assoc Provost Acad Plng & Res Mgmt	Ms. Victoria BALKON
121	Assoc Provost Student Success	Dr. Jacqueline H. GROGAN
07	Asst Provost for Enrollment Mgmt	Mrs. Samantha R. WRIGHT
04	Presidential Asst Administration	Ms. Carolyn MADAIO
88	Administrative Assistant	Ms. Maureen A. O'BRIEN
106	Exec Dir CTL/Online Learning	Dr. Cynthia R. PHILLIPS
09	Exec Dir Institutional Research	Dr. Christine M. GOODWIN
90	Exec Dir Operations/ Infrastructure	Mr. Kenneth J. MAHLMEISTER
88	Exec Director for Mission	Ms. Lucy A. PESCE
19	Exec Dir Public Safety	Ms. Denise VENCAK
36	Exec Dir University Career Services	Ms. Paulette B. GONZALEZ
88	Exec Director Vincentian Center	Rev. Patrick J. GRIFFIN, CM
88	Exec Dir Center Equity & Inclusion	Dr. Manouchkathe CASSAGNOL
06	University Registrar	Ms. Joanne A. LLERANDI
43	Deputy General Counsel	Mr. Joshua S. HURWIT
21	Controller	Ms. Jankie D. BEHARRY
113	Bursar	Ms. Dorota A. MANTEL
29	Director Alumni Relations	Mr. Mark A. ANDREWS
38	Director Counseling Center	Vacant
39	Director Residence Life	Mr. Eric M. FINKELSTEIN
105	Director Digital Communications	Ms. Patricia A. WATTS
37	Director Student Financial Services	Ms. Eileen M. FLOOD
37	Director Financial Aid/Research	Ms. Maryanne H. TWOMEY
25	Dir Grants & Sponsored Research	Vacant
92	Director Honors Program	Dr. Robert J. FORMAN
16	Director Human Resources Services	Ms. Cynthia F. SIMPSON
22	Dir EEO/Compliance & Title IX	Ms. Danielle HAYNES
88	Dir CRES Institute	Dr. Natalie BYFIELD
116	Director Internal Audit	Mr. Jorge J. OSORIO
85	Dir Int Students/Scholar Svcs	Ms. Amy R. SCHOENFELD
112	Director of Gift Planning	Ms. Susan M. DAMIANI
23	Director Student Health Services	Ms. Sharon MACARTHUR
104	Director Outbound Program-Global	Mr. Gregory BRUHN
88	Dir University Events	Ms. Sandy MOROCHO
88	Co-Dir LGBTQ+ Center	Dr. Candice D. ROBERTS
88	Co-Dir LGBTQ+ Center	Dr. Shanté P. SMALLS
07	Sr Asst Director Admissions - SI	Mr. David A. PIERRE
37	Asst Director Financial Aid - SI	Mr. Thomas J. MARLOW
40	Manager of Bookstore	Ms. Dominique WEST

Saint Joseph's College, New York (C)

245 Clinton Avenue, Brooklyn NY 11205-3688
County: Kings
FICE Identification: 002825
Unit ID: 195544
Telephone: (718) 940-5300
Carnegie Class: Masters/L
FAX Number: (718) 636-7245
Calendar System: Semester
URL: www.sjcny.edu
Established: 1916
Annual Undergrad Tuition & Fees: $29,200
Enrollment: 5,012
Coed
Affiliation or Control: Independent Non-Profit
IRS Status: 501(c)3
Highest Offering: Master's
Accreditation: M, AAQEP, ADNUR, CAPRT, NUR

01	President	Dr. Donald R. BOOMGAARDEN
05	Interim Provost/VP Academic Affairs	Dr. Heather BARRY
26	VP of Marketing &d Communications	Ms. Jessica MCALEER
10	Chief Financial Officer	Mr. John C. ROTH
20	Executive Dean - BK	Dr. Phillip DEHNE
13	VP IT and Chief Information Officer	Ms. Michelle PAPAJOHN
32	VP for Student Life & Campus Svcs	Ms. Shantey HILL-HANNA
111	VP for Institutional Advancement	Ms. Rory SHAFFER-WALSH
84	VP for Enrollment Management	Ms. Christine MURPHY
41	VP for Athletics	Ms. Shantey HILL-HANNA
19	Director Security/Safety	Mr. Michael MCGRANN
88	Director of Child Study Center	Dr. Susan STRAUT COLLARD
90	Exec Director Client Services	Ms. Lichele ABEAR
37	Director of Financial Aid	Ms. Amy THOMPSON
36	Exec Director Career Development	Vacant
15	Exec Director of Human Resources	Ms. D'adra CRUMP
18	Director Physical Plant	Ms. Linda VIGNATO
21	Controller	Ms. Marion KOWALSKI
14	Exec Director Network Operations	Mr. Ted DEC
06	College Registrar	Mr. Robert PERGOLIS
08	Director of Library	Dr. Elizabeth POLLICINO MURPHY
27	Director of Public Affairs	Mr. Michael BANACH
28	Coordinator of Diversity	Vacant
112	Planned Giving Officer	Ms. Susan LOUCKS
38	Director of Counseling	Dr. Cynthia CABRAL
29	Director of Alumni Engagement	Ms. Paulina MELIN
09	Director of Institutional Research	Ms. Allison LIST
102	Asst Director Foundation Relations	Ms. Katherine CORWIN
86	Director Government Relations	Mr. Michael BANACH
04	Executive Admin Asst to President	Ms. Kimberly MAILLEY
108	Director Institutional Assessment	Ms. Heather BARRY

St. Joseph's College of Nursing (D)

206 Prospect Avenue, Syracuse NY 13203-1806
County: Onondaga
FICE Identification: 006467
Unit ID: 195191
Telephone: (315) 448-5040
Carnegie Class: Spec 2-yr-Health
FAX Number: (315) 448-5745
Calendar System: Semester
URL: www.sjhcon.org
Established: 1898
Annual Undergrad Tuition & Fees: $22,156
Enrollment: 383
Coed
Affiliation or Control: Independent Non-Profit
IRS Status: 501(c)3
Highest Offering: Associate Degree
Accreditation: M

01	Dean	Dr. Lenore L. BORIS
05	Associate Dean for Academic Affairs	Dr. Nancy POOLE

Saint Joseph's Seminary (E)

201 Seminary Avenue, Yonkers NY 10704-1852
County: Westchester
FICE Identification: 002826
Telephone: (914) 968-6200
Carnegie Class: Not Classified
FAX Number: (914) 376-2019
Calendar System: Semester
URL: www.dunwoodie.edu
Established: 1896
Annual Graduate Tuition & Fees: N/A
Enrollment: N/A
Coed
Affiliation or Control: Roman Catholic
IRS Status: 501(c)3
Highest Offering: Master's; No Undergraduates
Accreditation: M, THEOL

01	Rector	Bishop James MASSA
03	Vice Rector	Rev. William CLEARY
05	Academic Dean	Rev. Matthew S. ERNEST
32	Dean of Seminarians	Rev. Michael BRUNO
07	Director of Admissions	Rev. Thomas BERG
06	Registrar	Ms. Roenice GONZALEZ
08	Director of Library Services	Mr. Connor FLATZ
26	Dir of Communications/Technology	Ms. Cynthia F. HARRISON
108	Dir of Assessment/Accreditation	Ms. Diane LAMA
18	Director of Buildings & Grounds	Mr. Joseph DI LELLO

St. Lawrence University (F)

23 Romoda Drive, Canton NY 13617-1423
County: St. Lawrence
FICE Identification: 002829
Unit ID: 195216
Telephone: (315) 229-5011
Carnegie Class: Bac-A&S
FAX Number: (315) 229-5502
Calendar System: Other
URL: www.stlawu.edu
Established: 1856
Annual Undergrad Tuition & Fees: $58,750
Enrollment: 2,319
Coed
Affiliation or Control: Independent Non-Profit
IRS Status: 501(c)3
Highest Offering: Master's
Accreditation: M, CAEPT

01	President	Dr. Kathryn A. MORRIS
05	Vice Pres/Dean Academic Affairs	Dr. Karl K. SCHONBERG
111	Vice Pres University Advancement	Mr. Thomas PYNCHON
10	VP Finance/Administration & Treas	Mr. Stephen HIETSCH
32	Vice Pres/Dean Student Life	Mr. Earlhagi BRADLEY
07	VP & Dean for Admissions/Fin Aid	Ms. Florence HINES
26	VP University Communications	Mr. Paul REDFERN
89	Associate Dean of the First-Year	Dr. Sarah BARBER
35	Associate Dean of Student Life	Mr. Rance DAVIS
06	Registrar	Ms. Lorie MACKENZIE
37	Director of Financial Aid	Mrs. Patricia J B. FARMER
36	Director of Career Services	Ms. Jillian MCKERNAN-WALLEY
09	Director of Institutional Research	Ms. Christine ZIMMERMAN
18	Chief Facilities/Physical Plant	Mr. Daniel B. SEAMAN
20	Assoc Dean of Academic Admin	Ms. Lorie R. MACKENZIE
29	Director Alumni Relations	Mr. Joseph C. KENISTON
39	Director Residence Life	Mr. Christopher MARQUARDT
23	Director of Health & Counseling	Mr. Timothy CORBITT
84	Exec Director Enrollment Management	Mr. Jeremy FREEMAN
96	Director of Purchasing	Mr. Nickolas ORMASEN
15	Director Personnel Services	Mrs. Colleen MANLEY
38	Director Student Counseling	Mr. Timothy CORBITT
04	Exec Assistant to the President	Ms. Cheryl CASEY-ROSE
19	Director Security/Safety	Mr. Patrick GAGNON
28	Director of Diversity	Dr. Kimberly FLINT-HAMILTON
41	Athletic Director	Mr. Robert DUROCHER
13	Exec Dir Enterprise/Infrastructure	Mr. Darrin GOODROW
14	Exec Dir Campus Svcs & Outreach IT	Ms. Rene THATCHER

Saint Paul's School of Nursing-Queens (A)

97-77 Queens Boulevard, Queens NY 11374

County: Queens FICE Identification: 012364
Unit ID: 189811
Telephone: (718) 357-0500 Carnegie Class: Spec 2-yr-Health
FAX Number: (718) 357-4683 Calendar System: Semester
URL: www.stpaulsschoolofnursing.edu
Established: 1969 Annual Undergrad Tuition & Fees: $20,871
Enrollment: 747 Coed
Affiliation or Control: Proprietary IRS Status: Proprietary
Highest Offering: Associate Degree
Accreditation: ABHES

01 Campus President .... Paul FERRISE

Saint Paul's School of Nursing-Staten Island (B)

2 Teleport Dr Ste 203, Corp Comm 2,
Staten Island NY 10311

County: Richmond FICE Identification: 009479
Unit ID: 195784
Telephone: (718) 818-6470 Carnegie Class: Spec 2-yr-Health
FAX Number: (718) 818-6020 Calendar System: Semester
URL: www.stpaulsschoolofnursing.edu
Established: 1904 Annual Undergrad Tuition & Fees: $17,731
Enrollment: 746 Coed
Affiliation or Control: Proprietary IRS Status: Proprietary
Highest Offering: Associate Degree
Accreditation: ABHES

01 Campus President .... Mr. Anthony A. STANZIANI
05 Dean of Education .... Dr. Lynne HARTMAN
66 Dean of Nursing .... Dr. Tamara BROWN
06 Registrar .... Ms. Mintu PHILIP
10 Business Office Manager .... Ms. Mary Ellen ELIAS
07 Director of Admissions .... Mr. Douglas YOUNG
36 Director of Career Services .... Ms. Lynn SALVAGE
37 Director of Financial Aid .... Mr. Charles JOHNSON, III
08 LRC Manager .... Ms. Judy LEE

St. Peter's Hospital College of Nursing (C)

714 New Scotland, 111 Marian Hall, Albany NY 12208

County: Albany FICE Identification: 012203
Unit ID: 192961
Telephone: (518) 525-6850 Carnegie Class: Spec 2-yr-Health
FAX Number: (518) 525-6852 Calendar System: Semester
URL: www.sphp.com/memorial-college-of-nursing
Established: 1901 Annual Undergrad Tuition & Fees: $13,911
Enrollment: 135 Coed
Affiliation or Control: Independent Non-Profit IRS Status: 501(c)3
Highest Offering: Associate Degree
Accreditation: ADNUR

01 Dean .... Dr. Caroline MOSCA
32 Dean of Student Services .... Ms. Angela COX

† Relocated to Maria College of Albany Campus

St. Thomas Aquinas College (D)

125 Route 340, Sparkill NY 10976-1050

County: Rockland FICE Identification: 002832
Unit ID: 195243
Telephone: (845) 398-4000 Carnegie Class: Masters/S
FAX Number: (845) 359-8136 Calendar System: 4/1/4
URL: www.stac.edu
Established: 1952 Annual Undergrad Tuition & Fees: $34,200
Enrollment: 1,779 Coed
Affiliation or Control: Independent Non-Profit IRS Status: 501(c)3
Highest Offering: Master's
Accreditation: M, IACBE

01 President .... Dr. Kenneth D. DALY
10 SVP/VP Administration & Finance .... Mr. Joseph DONINI
05 Provost/Vice Pres Academic Affairs .... Dr. Robert MURRAY
32 Vice Pres/Dean Student Development .... Mrs. Denise HOPKINS-POSELLE
15 Director Human Resources .... Mrs. Maria COUPE
07 Director Admissions .... Ms. Samantha BAZILE
09 Dir Inst Research/Program Develop .... Dr. Renee QUINTYNE
21 Controller .... Ms. Jennifer MAZZA
44 Dir Annual Giving & Alumni Affairs .... Mr. James ERRICO
35 Director Student Activities .... Mr. Nicholas MIGLIORINO
38 Director Student Counseling .... Dr. Louis MUGGEO
06 Registrar .... Ms. Eileen MURPHY
36 Director Career Development .... Mrs. Maureen MULHERN
37 Director Financial Aid .... Mrs. Joanne SULLIVAN
13 Director of Computing Services .... Mr. Sunny ANTHWAL
18 Dir Facilities & Construction .... Mr. James DOYLE
26 Dir Campus Communications/Enr Mktg .... Ms. Annie LOMBARDI
50 Dean School of Business .... Mr. Michael MURPHY
53 Dean School of Education .... Dr. Meenakshi GAJRIA
49 Dean School of Arts & Sciences .... Dr. Heath BOWEN
81 Dean School of STEM .... Dr. Bianca WENTZEL
04 Executive Asst to President .... Ms. Lee TAUSSI
41 Athletic Director .... Mrs. Nicole RYAN

Saint Vladimir's Orthodox Theological Seminary (E)

575 Scarsdale Road, Yonkers NY 10707

County: Westchester FICE Identification: 002833
Unit ID: 195580
Telephone: (914) 961-8313 Carnegie Class: Spec-4-yr-Faith
FAX Number: (914) 961-4507 Calendar System: Semester
URL: www.svots.edu
Established: 1938 Annual Graduate Tuition & Fees: N/A
Enrollment: 79 Coed
Affiliation or Control: Independent Non-Profit IRS Status: 501(c)3
Highest Offering: Doctorate; No Undergraduates
Accreditation: THEOL

01 President .... V.Rev. Chad HATFIELD
05 Academic Dean .... Dr. Ionut Alexandru TUDORIE
10 Chief Financial Officer .... Ms. Carmen MUNOZ
13 Chief Technology Officer .... Mr. Georgios KOKONAS
42 Director of Spiritual Formation .... Rev. Vincent TEMIROV
06 Registrar .... Mrs. Gabrielle RUSSIN
08 Librarian .... Mrs. Danielle EARL
32 Student Affairs Administrator .... Mrs. Gabrielle RUSSIN
108 Dir Institutional Assessment .... Dr. Ionut Alexandru TUDORIE
88 Sr Advisor Advancement .... Mr. Ted BAZIL
26 Director of Marketing .... Ms. Sarah WERNER
111 Dir of Institutional Advancement .... Ms. Sharon ROSS
04 Admin Assistant to President .... Mrs. Ann SANCHEZ
07 Director of Admissions .... Mr. Alexandru POPOVICI
18 Chf Facilities/Physical Plant Ofcr .... Mr. Rafael RIVERA

Salvation Army College for Officer Training (F)

201 Lafayette Avenue, Suffern NY 10901-4707

County: Rockland Identification: 666020
Telephone: (845) 368-7200 Carnegie Class: Not Classified
FAX Number: (845) 357-6644 Calendar System: Other
URL: https://easternusa.salvationarmy.org/cfot/
Established: 1905 Annual Undergrad Tuition & Fees: N/A
Enrollment: N/A Coed
Affiliation or Control: Independent Non-Profit IRS Status: 501(c)3
Highest Offering: Associate Degree
Accreditation: NY

01 Principal .... LtCol. James LABOSSIERE
11 Asst Principal for Administration .... Major Ron STARNES
05 Director of Curriculum .... Major Sun-Kyung SIMPSON
09 Coord Inst Research/Accred Liaison .... Dr. Dennis A. VANDER WEELE
10 Chief Business Officer .... Major Paul CORNELL
15 Director Personnel Services .... Major Jorge MARZAN
20 Associate Academic Officer .... Capt. Sheila WILLIAMS-GAGE
72 Education Tech Coordinator .... Mr. Marcos A. LOPEZ
13 Director of IT & Communications .... Mr. Daniel MACHADO

Samaritan Hospital School of Nursing (G)

1300 Massachusetts Avenue, Troy NY 12180

County: Rensselaer FICE Identification: 009248
Unit ID: 195289
Telephone: (518) 268-5010 Carnegie Class: Spec 2-yr-Health
FAX Number: (518) 268-5040 Calendar System: Semester
URL: https://www.sphp.com/careers/schools-of-nursing/samaritan-ho
Established: 1903 Annual Undergrad Tuition & Fees: $14,292
Enrollment: 152 Coed
Affiliation or Control: Independent Non-Profit IRS Status: 501(c)3
Highest Offering: Associate Degree
Accreditation: ADNUR, PNUR

01 Dean/Director .... Ms. Patti CANNISTRACI

Sarah Lawrence College (H)

1 Meadway, Bronxville NY 10708-5999

County: Westchester FICE Identification: 002813
Unit ID: 195304
Telephone: (914) 337-0700 Carnegie Class: Bac-A&S
FAX Number: N/A Calendar System: Semester
URL: www.slc.edu
Established: 1926 Annual Undergrad Tuition & Fees: $57,520
Enrollment: 1,506 Coed
Affiliation or Control: Independent Non-Profit IRS Status: 501(c)3
Highest Offering: Master's
Accreditation: M, AAQEP

01 President .... Dr. Cristle COLLINS JUDD
05 Provost and Dean of Faculty .... Dr. Kanwal SINGH
10 Vice Pres Finance/Operations .... Vacant
111 VP for Advancement/External Rels .... Patricia GOLDMAN
09 AVP Inst Research & Govt Relations .... Thomas L. BLUM
84 VP Enrollment & Dean of Admission .... Kevin MCKENNA
20 Associate Dean of the College .... Melissa FRAZIER
32 Dean of Studies & Student Life .... Daniel TRUJILLO
35 Dean of Student Affairs .... Vacant
58 Dean Graduate Studies .... Kim FERGUSON
06 Registrar .... Daniel LICHT
08 Director of Libraries .... Bobbie SMOLOW
13 Chief Technology Officer .... Sean JAMESON
29 Director of Alumni .... Christina CAMARDELLA
36 Director Career Counseling .... Angela CHERUBINI
44 Individual Giving Officer .... Elisa BALESTRA
28 Assoc Dean Engage/Div/EquityInclus .... Amada SANDOVAL
18 Asst Vice President of Facilities .... Maureen GALLAGHER
19 Director of Campus Safety .... James VERDICCHIO
04 Executive Asst to President .... Donna WATSON
104 Asst Dean Study Abroad .... Prema SAMUEL
37 Director Student Financial Aid .... Nick SALINAS
102 Director Foundation/Corporate Rels .... Vacant
15 VP for Human Resources .... Danielle COSCIA
41 Athletic Director .... Kristin MAILE
96 Director of Purchasing .... Jennifer MELENDEZ
101 Secretary of the Institution/Board .... Thomas BLUM

School of Visual Arts (I)

209 E 23rd Street, New York NY 10010-3994

County: New York FICE Identification: 007468
Unit ID: 197151
Telephone: (212) 592-2000 Carnegie Class: Masters/L
FAX Number: (212) 725-3587 Calendar System: Semester
URL: www.sva.edu
Established: 1947 Annual Undergrad Tuition & Fees: $43,400
Enrollment: 3,692 Coed
Affiliation or Control: Proprietary IRS Status: Proprietary
Highest Offering: Master's
Accreditation: M, ACATE, CIDA

01 President .... David J. RHODES
03 Executive Vice President .... Anthony P. RHODES
05 Provost .... Christopher J. CYPHERS
10 Chief Financial Officer .... Gary SHILLET
32 Exec Dir of Student Affairs/Admiss .... Javier VEGA
26 Exec Director of External Relations .... Angelia WOJAK
13 Chief Information Officer .... Cosmin TOMESCU
06 Registrar .... Jason KOTH
07 Director Admission .... Matthew R. FARINA
35 Director of Student Affairs .... Bill MARTINO
08 Director Visual Arts Library .... Caitlin KILGALLEN
37 Director Financial Aid .... William BERRIOS
36 Director Career Development .... Patricia ROMEU
30 Director Development/Alumni Affairs .... Jane NUZZO
19 Director Security .... Nick AGJMURATI
15 Exec Director of Human Resources .... Vennette JONES
09 Director of Institutional Research .... Jerold DAVIS
26 Director of Communication .... Joyce KAYE
106 Director Office of Learning Tech .... Jennifer PHILLIPS
22 Associate Director/Title IX Coord .... Laurel CHRISTY
28 Director of Diversity .... Jarvis WATSON
39 Associate Director Residence Life .... Stefanie JOSHUA
91 Director Administrative Computing .... Elena VASILENKO-BLANK

Sh'or Yoshuv Rabbinical College (J)

1 Cedarlawn Avenue, Lawrence NY 11559-1714

County: Nassau FICE Identification: 025059
Unit ID: 195438
Telephone: (516) 239-9002 Carnegie Class: Spec-4-yr-Faith
FAX Number: (516) 239-9003 Calendar System: Semester
URL: www.shoryoshuv.org
Established: 1963 Annual Undergrad Tuition & Fees: $10,560
Enrollment: 183 Male
Affiliation or Control: Independent Non-Profit IRS Status: 501(c)3
Highest Offering: Second Talmudic Degree
Accreditation: RABN

01 Dean .... Rabbi Naftali JAEGER
05 Executive Director .... Mr. Moshe RUBIN
32 Director of Student Affairs .... Rabbi Elysha SANDLER
04 Executive Assistant .... Mrs. Hindie FRIED
06 Registrar .... Mrs. Elynn ROSENBERG
11 FAA .... Mr. Mendel M. JAROSLAWICZ

Siena College (K)

515 Loudon Road, Loudonville NY 12211-1462

County: Albany FICE Identification: 002816
Unit ID: 195474
Telephone: (518) 783-2302 Carnegie Class: Masters/S
FAX Number: (518) 783-4280 Calendar System: Semester
URL: www.siena.edu
Established: 1937 Annual Undergrad Tuition & Fees: $40,175
Enrollment: 3,425 Coed
Affiliation or Control: Independent Non-Profit IRS Status: 501(c)3
Highest Offering: Master's
Accreditation: M, NURSE, SW

01 President .... Dr. Christoper P. GIBSON
05 Provost & Senior VP .... Dr. Margaret MADDEN
32 VP for Student Life .... Dr. Maryellen GILROY
10 VP for Finance & Admin .... Ms. Mary STRUNK
84 VP for Enrollment Management .... Mr. Ned JONES
30 VP for Development & Ext Affairs .... Mr. David SMITH
100 Chief of Staff/VP .... Mr. Jason RICH
88 VP for Mission .... Fr. Mark REAMER, OFM
41 VP & Dir of Athletics .... Mr. John D'ARGENIO
13 Chief Information Officer .... Mr. Mark BERMAN
49 Dean of Liberal Arts .... Dr. Christiane FARNAN
50 Interim Dean of Business .... Dr. Katherine SILVESTER
81 Dean of Science .... Dr. John CUMMINGS
20 Assoc VP for Academic Affairs .... Dr. Glenn BRADDOCK

88	Assoc VP for Enrollment Mgmt	Ms. Mary LAWYER
35	Assoc VP Student Life	Mr. Michael PAPADOPOULOS
15	Assoc VP for Human Resources	Ms. Cynthia KING-LEROY
18	Asst VP for Facilities Management	Mr. Mark FROST
19	Asst VP Stdnt Life/Dir Public Safe	Mr. Ron MATOS
20	Assoc VP Academic Affairs Admin	Ms. Laurie FAY
06	Registrar	Ms. Kari BENNETT
07	Dir of Admissions	Ms. Katie SZALDA
08	Dir of Library	Ms. Vicki PARSONS
92	Dir of Honors Program	Dr. Wendy POJMANN
39	Asst Dean of Students	Mr. Adam CASLER
36	Dir of the Career Center	Ms. Debra DELBELSO
26	Chief Information Officer	Ms. Mary PARLETT-SWEENEY
42	Chaplain of the College	Fr. Lawrence ANDERSON, OFM
38	Dir of Counseling Center	Dr. Nicole MULLER
29	Dir Alumni Engage/Grants/Spons	Ms. Cherisse YOUNG
09	Dir of Institutional Research	Ms. Tara COPE
94	Dir Sr Thea Bowman Ctr for Women	Ms. Beth DEANGELIS
23	Dir of Health Services	Ms. Carrie HOGAN
110	AVP for Devel & External Affairs	Mr. Brad BODMER
28	Dir of Damietta Cross-Cultural Ctr	Br. George CAMACHO
104	Dir of Study Abroad/Intl Pgms	Br. Brian BELANGER, OFM
109	Dir of Auxiliary Svcs & Procurement	Ms. Laura ZOCCO
43	Legal Services/General Counsel	Ms. Rose SEGGOS
20	Dir of Academic Programs	Ms. Lynn ROGERS
121	Dir of Siena Enhanced Edu Dev/SEED	Ms. Holly CHEVERTON
88	Dir HEOP	Ms. Yasmin FISHER
25	Dir Grants & Sponsored Pgms	Ms. Sally SOUTHWICK
22	Title IX Coord/EEO Specialist	Ms. Lois GOLAND
88	Dir Office of Accessibility	Ms. Lindsay GREEN
88	Assoc Dir for Strat/Comm & Exp	Mr. Zachary BRIMMER
101	Asst Dir of Board/Cabinet Rels	Mrs. Kathleen KIERNAN
108	Assoc VPAA/Inst Effectiveness	Dr. Mohua BOSE
88	Presidential Actions Officer	Mr. George CHRISTIAN
88	Asst Dir for Exp & Exec Asst	Ms. Kiley M. PENDERGAST
45	Chief Institutional Planning Ofcr	Mr. Michael UTZIG

Skidmore College (A)

815 N Broadway, Saratoga Springs NY 12866-1632

County: Saratoga — FICE Identification: 002814
Unit ID: 195526
Telephone: (518) 580-5000 — Carnegie Class: Bac-A&S
FAX Number: (518) 580-5936 — Calendar System: Semester
URL: www.skidmore.edu
Established: 1911 — Annual Undergrad Tuition & Fees: $58,278
Enrollment: 2,582 — Coed
Affiliation or Control: Independent Non-Profit — IRS Status: 501(c)3
Highest Offering: Baccalaureate
Accreditation: M, ART, SW

01	President	Dr. Marc C. CONNER
05	VP Academic Affairs/Dean of Faculty	Dr. Michael T. ORR
10	Vice Pres Finance/Admin/Treasurer	Ms. Donna NG
111	Vice President for Advancement	Ms. Carey Anne ZUCCA
15	Interim Director for HR	Ms. Sarah DELANEY VERO
32	Vice President/Dean of Students	Dr. Adrian BAUTISTA
35	Assistant VP for Student Affairs	Ms. Gail L. CUMMINGS-DANSON
07	VP & Dean of Admiss & Fin Aid	Ms. Mary Lou W. BATES
88	Managing Dir of Special Programs	Dr. Auden THOMAS
06	Registrar	Mr. David DECONNO
20	Assoc Dean for Stdnt Acad Affairs	Dr. Michael F. ARNUSH
28	Assoc Dn for Diversity/Faculty Affs	Dr. Janet G. CASEY
88	Assoc Dean Infrastructure/Fac Affs	Dr. Patricia FEHLING
89	Dir of First Year Experience	Dr. Amon EMEKA
39	Assoc Dean Res Life/Student Conduct	Ms. Ann Marie PRZYWARA
88	Dir Student Academic Services	Mr. Jamin TOTINO
45	VP Strategic Plng & Inst Diversity	Dr. Joshua C. WOODFORK
26	VP Communications & Mktg	Ms. Jacqueline CONRAD
09	Director of Institutional Research	Mr. Joseph STANKOVICH
102	Dir Foundation & Corporate Rels	Mr. Barry PRITZKER
46	Director of Sponsored Research	Ms. Mary HOEHN
13	Chief Technology Officer	Mr. Dwane M. STERLING
27	Director of Marketing & Engagement	Mr. Luke MEYERS
88	Dir Acad Pgm/Resid/Inst & Cmty Pgms	Dr. Auden THOMAS
22	Asst Dir EEO & Workforce Diversity	Ms. Jude KLEIN
91	Director IT-Enterprise Systems	Mr. Kevin L. CRIDER
104	Dir of Off-Campus Study & Exchanges	Ms. Cori FILSON
44	Sr Assoc Dir Donor Engagement	Ms. Barb CASEY
30	Assoc VP Advancement & Campaign Dir	Ms. Lori EASTMAN
29	Exec Dir Alumni Rels/Col Events	Mr. Michael SPOSILI
36	Assoc Dean Stdnt Affs/Career Dev	Vacant
37	Director of Financial Aid	Ms. Beth POST
38	Assoc Dn Stdnt Affs/Health/Wellness	Dr. Julia C. ROUTBORT
21	Asst VP for Finance & Controller	Mr. Kyle BERNARD
109	Asst VP for Fin Planning & Aux Svcs	Ms. Kelley A. PATTON-OSTRANDER
23	Director of Health Services	Ms. Patricia BOSEN
18	Director of Facilities Services	Mr. Daniel RODECKER
19	Director of Campus Safety	Mr. Timothy J. MUNRO
08	College Librarian	Ms. Marta BRUNNER
96	Director of Purchasing	Mrs. Carol N. SCHNITZER
42	Dir Religious & Spiritual Life	Ms. Parker DIGGORY
24	Asst Director Media Services	Mr. DJ WALKER
40	Skidmore Shop Sales Manager	Ms. Dawn J. ARIA
88	Special Assistant to the President	Ms. Jeanne M. SISSON
101	Board Coordinator	Ms. Kathleen A. GRIMES
41	Assoc Dean Stdnt Affs/Athletics Dir	Ms. Gail L. CUMMINGS-DANSON
108	Inst Effectiveness Specialist	Dr. Amy J. TWEEDY

Sotheby's Institute of Art (B)

570 Lexington Ave, 6th Floor, New York NY 10022

County: New York — Identification: 667007
Unit ID: 481094
Telephone: (212) 517-3929 — Carnegie Class: Spec-4-yr-Arts
FAX Number: (212) 517-6568 — Calendar System: Semester
URL: www.sothebysinstitute.com
Established: 2006 — Annual Graduate Tuition & Fees: N/A
Enrollment: 135 — Coed
Affiliation or Control: Proprietary — IRS Status: Proprietary
Highest Offering: First Professional Degree; No Undergraduates
Accreditation: ART

01	Director/CEO	Ms. Ann-Marie RICHARD
10	Jr Accountant	Mr. Philip LAM
08	Head Librarian	Mr. Eric WOLF
32	Chief Student Affairs/Student Life	Ms. Sara MOORE
06	Registrar	Mr. Giovanni PALOMO

*State University of New York System Office (C)

State University Plaza, Albany NY 12246-0001

County: Albany — FICE Identification: 008788
Unit ID: 195827
Telephone: (518) 320-1100 — Carnegie Class: N/A
FAX Number: (518) 320-1561
URL: www.suny.edu

01	Interim Chancellor	Ms. Deborah F. STANLEY
15	SVP/Chief Human Resources Officer	Ms. Julie PETTI
28	Interim Chief Diversity Officer	Ms. Valerie DENT
05	Provost in Charge	Dr. Shadi SHAHEDIPOUR-SANDVIK
11	Chief Operating Officer	Ms. Beth BERLIN
46	Sr VC Research/Innov/Econ Devel	Dr. Shadi SHAHEDIPOUR-SANDVIK
43	SVC Legal Affairs/General Counsel	Ms. Anta CISSE-GREEN
22	System Affirmative Action Officer	Ms. Jennie Marie DURAN
18	SVC for Cap Facil/GM Constr Fund	Mr. Robert HAELEN
17	SVC Acad Health & Univ Hospital	Ms. Valerie GREY
88	Sr VC for Cmty Col & Educ Pipeline	Ms. Johanna DUNCAN-POITIER
88	University Faculty Senate President	Ms. Gwen KAY
20	Sr Assoc VC and Vice Prov Acad Affs	Vacant
10	Interim CFO	Mr. Robert L. MEGNA
84	Assoc VC for Enrollment Management	Vacant

*University at Albany, SUNY (D)

1400 Washington Avenue, Albany NY 12222-1000

County: Albany — FICE Identification: 002835
Unit ID: 196060
Telephone: (518) 442-3300 — Carnegie Class: DU-Highest
FAX Number: N/A — Calendar System: Semester
URL: www.albany.edu
Established: 1844 — Annual Undergrad Tuition & Fees (In-State): $10,160
Enrollment: 17,688 — Coed
Affiliation or Control: State — IRS Status: 501(c)3
Highest Offering: Doctorate
Accreditation: M, AAQEP, CLPSY, COPSY, IPSY, LIB, MPCAC, NASP, PH, PLNG, SCPSY, SPAA, SW

02	President	Havidán RODRÍGUEZ
05	Provost/Sr VP Academic Affairs	Carol KIM
46	Vice President for Research	Thenkurussi KESAVADAS
10	Vice Pres Finance & Administration	Todd FOREMAN
30	VP Univ Dev & Exec Dir UA Found	Fardin SANAI
32	Vice President Student Affairs	Michael N. CHRISTAKIS
41	Director of Athletics	Mark BENSON
43	Chief Campus Counsel	Amanda MALESZWESKI
86	VP Govt & Community Relations	Sheila SEERY
28	Chief Diversity Officer & Assoc VP	Samuel CALDWELL
21	Assoc VP Office of Risk Mgmt	Kevin WILCOX
35	Assoc VP Enrollment Mgmt	Ed ENGELBRIDE
100	Chief of Staff	Bruce SZELEST
49	Dean College of Arts & Sciences	Jeanette ALTARRIBA
53	Interim Dean School of Education	Virginia GOATELY
50	Dean School of Business	Sen NILANJAN
69	Int Dean School of Public Health	Mary GALLANT
77	Dean Col Emer Prep/Homeland/Cyber	Robert GRIFFIN
80	Interim Dean Rockefeller College	Julie NOVKOV
70	Dean School of Social Welfare	Lynn WARNER
54	Dean Engineering & Applied Sci	Kim L. BOYER
58	Vice Provost & Dean Grad Educ	Kevin WILLIAMS
08	Dean of Libraries	Rebecca MUGRIDGE
06	College Registrar	Karen CHICO HURST
29	Exec Director Alumni Association	Lee SERRAVILLO, JR.
38	Dir Counsel/Psych Svcs/Asst VP SA	Estela RIVERO
104	Int VP Ctr for Intl Ed/Global Strat	Gilbert VALVERDE
106	Assoc Provost for Online Learning	Vacant
20	Assoc Vice Prov AA & Chief of Staff	Steve GALIME
07	Director of Admissions	Michael MCKEON
09	Int Dir of Institutional Research	Jeffrey GERKEN

*State University of New York at Binghamton (E)

4400 Vestal Parkway E, Binghamton NY 13902

County: Broome — FICE Identification: 002836
Unit ID: 196079
Telephone: (607) 777-2000 — Carnegie Class: DU-Highest
FAX Number: (607) 777-4000 — Calendar System: Semester
URL: www.binghamton.edu
Established: 1946 — Annual Undergrad Tuition & Fees (In-State): $10,014
Enrollment: 18,148 — Coed
Affiliation or Control: State — IRS Status: 501(c)3
Highest Offering: Doctorate
Accreditation: M, AAQEP, CLPSY, MUS, NURSE, PCSAS, PHAR, SPAA, SW

02	President	Dr. Harvey G. STENGER, JR.
100	Chief of Staff	Ms. Darcy FAUCI
05	Exec VP for Academic Affs/Provost	Dr. Donald E. HALL
11	Vice President Operations	Ms. JoAnn NAVARRO
26	Vice Pres Univ Comm/Mktg	Mr. Gregory DELVISCIO
32	Vice President Student Affairs	Vacant
46	Vice President for Research	Dr. Bahgat SAMMAKIA
22	VP Diversity/Equity/Inclusion	Dr. Karen JONES
111	Vice President Advancement	Mr. John C. KOCH
104	Exec Vice Prov Intl Initiatives	Dr. Hari SRIHARI
20	Senior Vice Provost	Dr. Michael F. MCGOFF
58	Interim Dean of Graduate School	Dr. Donald NIEMAN
35	Assistant VP for Students	Dr. Randall EDOUARD
102	Exec Dir of Bing Foundation	Ms. Sheila DOYLE
13	AVP/Chief Information Officer	Dr. Niyazi BODUR
04	Exec Assistant to the President	Ms. Laura L. O'NEIL
15	Assoc Vice Pres for Human Resources	Mr. Joseph P. SCHULTZ
07	Director of Admissions/Student Svcs	Ms. Margaret A. GATES
08	Dean of Libraries	Dr. Curtis KENDRICK
85	Director Intl Students/Scholar Svcs	Ms. Patricia MARRAPESE
37	Dir Financial Aid/Stdnt Records	Ms. Amber STALLMAN
38	Director Health & Counseling	Ms. Johann FIORE CONTE
36	Director Career Development Center	Ms. Kelli SMITH
19	Director Public Safety	Mr. Timothy FAUGHANAN
41	Director Athletics	Mr. Patrick ELLIOTT
88	Director Educ Opportunities Pgm	Mr. Calvin GANTT
28	Asst Vice Pres for Diversity	Ms. Nicole SIRJU-JOHNSON
92	Director Binghamton Univ Scholars	Dr. William ZIEGLER
94	Exec Director of Women's Studies	Ms. Dara J. SILBERSTEIN
96	Director of Procurement	Mr. Matthew SCHOFIELD
09	Asst Provost Institutional Research	Ms. Nasrin FATIMA
49	Int Dean Arts & Science Harpur Col	Dr. Celia KLIN
50	Dean School of Management	Dr. Upinder S. DHILLON
54	Dn Watson Sch Engr/Applied Science	Dr. Hari SRIHARI
66	Dean Decker School of Nursing	Dr. Mario ORTIZ
31	Dean Community & Public Affairs	Dr. Laura BRONSTEIN
43	Campus Atty/General Counsel	Ms. Barbara SCARLETT

*University at Buffalo-SUNY (F)

3435 Main Street, Buffalo NY 14214

County: Erie — FICE Identification: 002837
Unit ID: 196088
Telephone: (716) 645-2000 — Carnegie Class: DU-Highest
FAX Number: N/A — Calendar System: Semester
URL: www.buffalo.edu
Established: 1846 — Annual Undergrad Tuition & Fees (In-State): $10,526
Enrollment: 32,347 — Coed
Affiliation or Control: State — IRS Status: 501(c)3
Highest Offering: Doctorate
Accreditation: M, AAQEP, ANEST, AUD, CAATE, CACREP, CAMPEP, CLPSY, DA, DENT, DIET, DIETI, IPSY, LAW, LIB, MED, MLS, MPCAC, NASP, NMT, NURSE, OT, PCSAS, PH, PHAR, PLNG, PSPSY, PTA, SP, SW

02	President	Dr. Satish K. TRIPATHI
05	Provost/Exec VP Academic Affs	Dr. A. Scott WEBER
10	Vice Pres Finance & Administration	Ms. Laura E. HUBBARD
32	Vice President Student Life	Dr. Brian F. HAMLUK
17	Vice President Health Sciences	Dr. Allison BRASHEAR
111	Vice Pres Univ Advancement	Mr. Rodney M. GRABOWSKI
46	Vice Pres for Research/Econ Develop	Dr. Venugopal GOVINDARAJU
84	Vice Provost of Enrollment	Mr. Lee H. MELVIN
15	Assoc VP Human Resources	Mr. Mark COLDREN
58	Vice Provost Educational Affairs	Dr. Graham L. HAMMILL
20	Vice Provost for Faculty Affairs	Dr. Robert GRANFIELD
104	Vice Provost for International Educ	Dr. Nojin KWAK
08	Vice Provost for Univ Libraries	Ms. Evviva LAJOIE
13	VP & Chief Information Officer	Mr. Brice J. BIBLE
37	Director Financial Aid	Mr. John GOTTARDY
09	Vice Provost Inst Analysis & Plng	Mr. Craig W. ABBEY
88	Assoc VP Academic Planning	Mr. William J. MCDONNELL
96	Asst Vice Pres Procurement Services	Vacant
26	VP Univ Communications	Mr. John DELLACONTRADA
22	Vice Provost Inclusive Excellence	Dr. Despina M. STRATIGAKOS
28	Dir Equity/Diversity/Inclusion	Ms. Sharon E. NOLAN-WEISS
41	Vice President & Dir of Athletics	Mr. Mark M. ALNUTT
91	Int Dir Enterprise Application Svcs	Ms. Kelly KENLINE
07	Director of UG Admissions	Vacant
19	Chief of Police	Mr. Chris J. BARTOLOMEI
39	Director of Campus Living	Mr. Tom R. TIBERI
38	Director of Counseling Services	Dr. Sharon L. MITCHELL
23	Director Health Services	Ms. Susan M. SNYDER
36	Director Career Design Center	Ms. Arlene F. KAUKUS
85	Director Intl Students/Scholar Svc	Ms. Kathryn E. TUDINI
40	Manager University Bookstores	Mr. Gregory NEUMANN
92	Director Univ Honors College	Dr. Dalia A. MULLER
29	Assoc VP Alumni Eng & Annual Giving	Ms. Cynthia KHOO-ROBINSON
27	Assoc VP Marketing & Digital Comm	Mr. Jeffrey N. SMITH
18	Assoc Vice Pres Univ Facilities	Ms. Tonga PHAM
48	Dean School Arch & Planning	Dr. Robert G. SHIBLEY
49	Dean College of Arts/Sciences	Dr. Robin G. SCHULZE
52	Dean School Dental Medicine	Dr. Joseph J. ZAMBON
53	Dean Graduate Sch of Education	Dr. Suzane N. ROSENBLITH
54	Dean School Engr/Applied Science	Dr. Kemper E. LEWIS

61 Dean School of Law ... Ms. Aviva ABRAMOVSKY
50 Dean School of Management ... Dr. Ananth IYER
63 Dean School Medicine/Biomed Sci ... Dr. Allison BRASHEAR
66 Dean School of Nursing ... Dr. Annette B. WYSOCKI
67 Dean School Pharmacy/Pharm Sciences ... Dr. Gary M. POLLACK
76 Dean Sch Public Hlth/Hlth Prof ... Dr. Jean WACTAWSKI-WENDE
70 Dean School of Social Work ... Dr. Keith A. ALFORD
97 Dean Undergraduate Education ... Dr. Ann M. BISANTZ
06 Registrar ... Dr. Kara C. SAUNDERS
88 Exec Dir Educ Opportunity Ctr ... Dr. Julius G. ADAMS
100 Chief of Staff ... Dr. Beth DEL GENIO
103 Dir Workforce Plng & Recruitment ... Ms. Jamie L. BLUHM
108 Assoc Vice Prov/Dir Inst Assessment ... Dr. Carol M. VANZILE-TAMSEN
86 Director Government Relations ... Ms. Megan TOOHEY

*State University of New York at Fredonia (A)

280 Central Avenue, Fredonia NY 14063-1136
County: Chautauqua FICE Identification: 002844
Unit ID: 196158
Telephone: (716) 673-3111 Carnegie Class: Masters/S
FAX Number: N/A Calendar System: Semester
URL: www.fredonia.edu
Established: 1826 Annual Undergrad Tuition & Fees (In-State): $8,492
Enrollment: 4,055 Coed
Affiliation or Control: State IRS Status: 501(c)3
Highest Offering: Master's
Accreditation: M, ART, MUS, SP, SW, THEA

02 President ... Dr. Stephen KOLISON
100 Chief of Staff and Exec Asst ... Dr. Naomi BALDWIN
05 Exec VP and Provost ... Dr. David STARRETT
10 VP for Finance & Admin ... Mr. Michael D. METZGER
32 Interim VP for Student Affairs ... Dr. Tracy STENGER
111 Interim VP Univ Adv & Exec Dir FCF ... Ms. Betty GOSSETT
21 Assoc VP Finance & Admin ... Dr. Judy LANGWORTHY
20 Vice Provost ... Dr. Judith HOROWITZ
124 Interim AVP Ret & Acad Success ... Ms. Erin MROCZKA
49 Dean College of Liberal Arts & Sci ... Dr. Andy KARAFA
64 Interim Dean School of Music ... Dr. Laura KOEPKE
50 Interim Dean School of Business ... Dr. Mojtaba SEYEDIAN
53 Interim Dean College of Education ... Dr. Janeil REY
06 Registrar ... Mr. Scott D. SAUNDERS
84 Exec Dir of Enrollment ... Mr. Cory BEZEK
07 Director of Admissions ... Ms. Dana BEARER
37 Director of Financial Aid ... Mr. Brandon M. GILLILAND
08 Director Library Services ... Ms. Kerrie WILKES
09 Dir Institutional Research/Planning ... Dr. Xiao Y. ZHANG
106 Online Learning Coordinator ... Ms. Lisa MELOHUSKY
51 Director of Extended Learning ... Mr. Eric SKOWRONSKI
36 Assoc Dir of Career Development ... Mr. Chris LAGROW
19 Chief University Police ... Mr. Brent ISAACSON
93 Exec Dir of Student Engagement ... Ms. Khristian J. KING
39 Director Residence Life ... Mrs. Kathy FORSTER
41 Athletic Director ... Mr. Gerald FISK
23 Director of Student Health ... Ms. Deborah A. DIBBLE
38 Clinical Dir Mental Health Srvcs ... Mr. Jeffrey JANICKI
13 Chief Information Officer ... Mr. Benjamin HARTUNG
15 Director of Human Resources ... Ms. Maria CARROLL
26 Director of Marketing & Comm ... Mr. Jeffrey WOODARD
92 Director of Honors Program ... Dr. Natalie GERBER
18 Director Facilities Services ... Mr. Kevin P. CLOOS
121 Director of Acad Advising ... Ms. Amy MARSHALL
96 Director of Purchasing ... Mrs. Shari K. MILLER
28 Chief Diversity Officer ... Dr. Vicki T. SAPP
29 Director Alumni Affairs ... Ms. Patricia A. FERALDI
104 Director Office International Educ ... Vacant
105 Web Content Manager ... Mr. Jonathan WOOLSON
85 Asst Dir International Student Svcs ... Mr. Jacob CZELUSTA
25 Director University Services ... Mr. Soteris TZITZIS
114 Director of Budget ... Ms. Ann ALDRICH
113 Director Student Accounts ... Ms. Lynn BOWERS
116 Director of Internal Control ... Amy BEERS

*State University of New York at New Paltz (B)

1 Hawk Drive, New Paltz NY 12561-2443
County: Ulster FICE Identification: 002846
Unit ID: 196176
Telephone: (845) 257-7869 Carnegie Class: Masters/L
FAX Number: (845) 257-3009 Calendar System: Semester
URL: www.newpaltz.edu
Established: 1823 Annual Undergrad Tuition & Fees (In-State): $8,416
Enrollment: 7,489 Coed
Affiliation or Control: State IRS Status: 501(c)3
Highest Offering: Beyond Master's But Less Than Doctorate
Accreditation: M, AAQEP, ART, CACREP, MUS, SP, THEA

02 President ... Dr. Donald P. CHRISTIAN
100 Chief of Staff/VP Communication ... Ms. Shelly A. WRIGHT
05 Interim Provost ... Dr. Barbara G. LYMAN
10 Vice Pres Administration & Finance ... Ms. Michele HALSTEAD
30 VP Development/Alumni Relations ... Ms. Erica MARKS
32 Student Affairs Vice President ... Dr. Stephanie BLAISDELL
84 Vice Pres Enrollment Management ... Mr. Jeffrey D. GANT
20 Assoc Provost ... Dr. Laurel GARRICK DUHANEY
13 Asst Vice Pres Tech/Info Systems ... Mr. John REINA
21 Asst Vice President Administration ... Ms. Julieta MAJAK
114 Asst VP Budget ... Ms. Julie WALSH
09 Asst VP Inst Research/Planning ... Ms. Lucy WALKER
18 Asst VP Facilities Management ... Mr. John SHUPE
58 Assistant VP Grad & Ext Learning ... Ms. Shala MILLS
53 Dean of Education ... Dr. René ANTROP-GONZÁLEZ
57 Dean Fine & Performing Arts ... Dr. Jennifer MOKREN
49 Dean Liberal Arts & Sciences ... Dr. Laura BARRETT
50 Dean School of Business ... Dr. Kristin BACKHAUS
54 Dean Science & Engineering ... Dr. Daniel FREEDMAN
07 Dean of Admissions ... Ms. Lisa JONES
08 Dean Sojourner Truth Library ... Mr. W. Mark COLVSON
86 Ex Dir Compliance/Camp Clm/Title IX ... Ms. Tanhena PACHECO DUNN
07 Assoc Dean/Dir Freshmen Admissions ... Ms. Kimberly STRANO
15 Director Human Resources ... Ms. Tanhena PACHECO DUNN
37 Director of Financial Aid ... Ms. Maureen LOHAN-BREMER
06 Registrar ... Ms. Stella TURK
29 Director Alumni Relations ... Mr. Chris BROWN
38 Director Student Counseling ... Dr. Gweneth LLOYD
26 Media Relations Manager ... Ms. Melissa KACZMAREK
96 Director of Purchasing/Procurement ... Mr. David FARBANIEC
19 Chief of Police ... Ms. Mary RITAYIK
41 Interim Athletic Director ... Mr. Matt GIUFRE
39 Dir Resident Life/Student Housing ... Ms. Corinna CARACCI

*State University of New York at Oneonta (C)

108 Ravine Parkway, Oneonta NY 13820-4015
County: Otsego FICE Identification: 002847
Unit ID: 196185
Telephone: (607) 436-3500 Carnegie Class: Masters/M
FAX Number: N/A Calendar System: Semester
URL: www.oneonta.edu
Established: 1889 Annual Undergrad Tuition & Fees (In-State): $8,740
Enrollment: 6,718 Coed
Affiliation or Control: State IRS Status: 501(c)3
Highest Offering: Master's
Accreditation: M, AAFCS, DIET, DIETD, IPSY, MUS, THEA

02 Acting President ... Mr. Dennis CRAIG
100 Chief of Staff ... Ms. Danielle MCMULLEN
05 Interim Provost/VP Academic Affairs ... Dr. Richard LEE
10 VP Finance/Administration ... Ms. Julie PISCITELLO
32 Interim VP Student Development ... Dr. Bernadette TIAPO
111 Vice President College Advancement ... Mr. Paul J. ADAMO
26 VP External Affairs ... Dr. Franklin D. CHAMBERS
20 Assoc Provost Academic Programs ... Dr. Eileen MORGAN-ZAYACHEK
83 Dean School of Liberal Arts ... Dr. Elizabeth DUNN
50 Int Dean Sch of Economics/Business ... Dr. Elizabeth DUNN
53 Dean School of Educ & Human Ecology ... Dr. Mark DAVIES
81 Dean School of Sciences ... Dr. Tracy ALLEN
58 Director of Graduate Studies ... Vacant
35 Assoc Vice Pres Student Development ... Ms. Amanda FINCH
18 Chief Facilities/Safety Officer ... Mr. Lachlan SQUAIR
19 Chief of Police ... Ms. Jennifer FILA
15 Chief Human Resources Officer ... Ms. Dia M. CARLETON
26 Chief Communication/Mktg Officer ... Mr. Hal S. LEGG
28 AVP/Chief Diversity Officer ... Ms. Bernadette TIAPO
07 Exec Director of Admissions ... Ms. Karen A. BROWN
29 Director of Alumni Engagement ... Ms. Laura MADELONE LINCOLN
110 Director Advancement Services ... Mr. Benjamin WENDROW
44 Director Fund for Oneonta ... Ms. Kim NOSTROM
41 Associate Athletic Director ... Mr. Ryan HOOPER
114 Budget Control Officer/Director ... Ms. Kimberly DEVLIN
25 Director Business Services ... Ms. Betty M. TIRADO
36 Director Career Development ... Vacant
13 Chief Information Officer ... Mr. Steven MANISCALCO
23 Dir Health & Counseling Services . Dr. Melissa A. FALLON-KORB
24 Director Creative Media Services ... Mr. David W. GEASEY
37 Associate Director Financial Aid ... Ms. Barbara PLEDGER
09 Dir Institutional Research ... Ms. Caitlin ALLEN
85 Director International Education ... Ms. Katherine STANLEY
89 Director Orientation/First Year Exp ... Ms. Monica C. GRAU
96 Procurement/Travel Office Manager ... Ms. Terri THOMAS
06 College Registrar ... Ms. Maureen P. ARTALE
93 Director Access/Opportunity Pgms ... Ms. Pathy LEIVA
22 Affirmative Action Officer ... Mr. Andrew STAMMEL
04 Assistant to the President ... Ms. Kathleen WEBSTER
08 Chief Library Officer ... Mr. Darren CHASE

*Stony Brook University (D)

310 Administration Building, Stony Brook NY 11794-0701
County: Suffolk FICE Identification: 002838
Unit ID: 196097
Telephone: (631) 632-6265 Carnegie Class: DU-Highest
FAX Number: (631) 632-6621 Calendar System: Semester
URL: www.stonybrook.edu
Established: 1957 Annual Undergrad Tuition & Fees (In-State): $10,091
Enrollment: 26,782 Coed
Affiliation or Control: State IRS Status: 501(c)3
Highest Offering: Doctorate
Accreditation: M, ARCPA, AT, CAATE, CAMPEP, CLPSY, COARC, COARCP, DENT, @DIET, DIETI, EMT, HSA, IPSY, JOUR, MED, MIDWF, MLS, NURSE, OT, PCSAS, PH, PTA, RADDOS, RTT, @SP, SW

02 President/CEO ... Dr. Maurie MCINNIS
03 EVP/Provost ... Dr. Carl LEJUEZ
63 Sr VP HSC/CEO SBU Medicine ... Dr. Harold PAZ
11 Sr VP for Finance & Administration ... Mr. Jed SHIVERS
46 Vice President Research ... Dr. Richard REEDER
32 VP Student Affairs ... Dr. Richard GATTEAU
10 VP Finance ... Mr. Lyle GOMES
111 VP University Advancement ... Mr. Justin FINCHER
86 SVP Government & Community Rels ... Ms. Judith GREIMAN
100 Chief Deputy ... Ms. Judith GREIMAN
26 VP Communications & Marketing ... Mr. William WARREN
28 VP for Equity and Inclusion ... Dr. Judith B. CLARKE
17 CEO University Hospital ... Ms. Carol GOMES
13 Int SVP of Info Techonolgy & CIO ... Mr. Charlie MCMAHON
43 Int Counsel in Charge ... Ms. Suzanne SHANE
49 Dean College of Arts & Sciences ... Dr. Nicole SAMPSON
81 Dean Sch of Marine/Atmospheric Sci ... Dr. Paul SHEPSON
52 Dean School of Dental Medicine ... Dr. Patrick LLOYD
41 Athletic Director ... Mr. Shawn R. HEILBRON
58 Int Dean Grad Sch/VProv Grad Stds ... Dr. Celia MARSCHIK
76 Dean School Health Tech & Mgmt ... Dr. Stacy JAFFE GROPACK
66 Int Dean School of Nursing ... Dr. Patricia BRUCKENTHAL
70 Dean School of Social Welfare ... Dr. Shari MILLER
50 Dean College of Business ... Dr. Manuel LONDON
60 Dean School of Journalism ... Ms. Laura LINDENFELD
08 Dean of Libraries ... Mr. Karim BOUGHIDA
88 Exec Dir LI State Vets Home ... Mr. Fred SGANGA
19 Chief of Police ... Ms. Dawn SMALLWOOD
15 VP Human Resource Svcs ... Ms. Lynn JOHNSON
28 Dir Diversity/AA/Equal Employ Oppty ... Ms. Marjolie LEONARD
09 VP Inst Rsrch/Plng/Effectiveness ... Dr. Braden J. HOSCH
85 Int Dean International Programs ... Ms. Lindsi WALKER
23 Director University Health Services ... Dr. Rachel BERGESON
38 Dir Counseling/Psych Services ... Dr. Julian PESSIER
36 Director Career Placement Center ... Ms. Marianna SAVOCA
06 Registrar ... Ms. Diane BELLO
96 Director of Purchasing/Procurement ... Ms. Carmen GONZALEZ
04 Sr Executive Asst to President ... Ms. Lorraine RUBINO

*SUNY Downstate Health Sciences University (E)

450 Clarkson Avenue, Brooklyn NY 11203-2098
County: Kings FICE Identification: 002839
Unit ID: 196255
Telephone: (718) 270-1000 Carnegie Class: Spec-4-yr-Med
FAX Number: (718) 270-4092 Calendar System: Semester
URL: www.downstate.edu
Established: 1860 Annual Undergrad Tuition & Fees (In-State): N/A
Enrollment: 2,118 Coed
Affiliation or Control: State IRS Status: 501(c)3
Highest Offering: Doctorate
Accreditation: M, ARCPA, DMS, MED, MIDWF, NURSE, OT, PH, PTA

02 President ... Dr. Wayne J. RILEY
100 SVP/Chief of Staff ... Dr. Keydron GUINN
10 VP/Chief Financial Officer ... Dr. Richard MILLER
11 SVP Administration/Chief Admin Ofcr ... Ms. Heidi J. ARONIN
05 Sr Vice Pres for Academic Affairs ... Dr. Pascal IMPERATO
63 SVP/Dean College of Medicine ... Dr. F. Charles BRUNICARDI
32 VP Academic & Student Affairs ... Dr. Jeffrey S. PUTMAN
26 AVP Communications & Marketing . Ms. Dawn SKEETE-WALKER
13 VP/Chief Information Officer ... Vacant
121 AVP Academic Support Services ... Dr. Seth LANGLEY
07 Director of Admissions ... Dr. Shushawna DEOLIVEIRA
06 Registrar ... Ms. Anne SHONBRUN
37 Director Student Financial Aid ... Ms. Farah BURNETT
27 Dir Media & Public Relations ... Mr. John GILLESPIE
04 Executive Asst to President ... Ms. Reina ALFRED
08 Interim Librarian ... Dr. Mohamed HUSSAIN
09 Director of Institutional Research ... Ms. Charis NG
15 VP Human Resources ... Ms. Judith DORSEY
18 VP Facilities Mgmt/Development ... Mr. James MINTO
19 Interim Chief University Police ... Mr. Israel MALDONADO
28 AVP Diversity & Inclusion ... Ms. Victoria AJIBADE
25 Chief Contracts/Grants Admin ... Ms. Maureen CRYSTAL
39 Director Student Housing ... Ms. Margaret O'SULLIVAN
43 Dir Legal Services/General Counsel ... Mr. Kevin O'MARA
45 Chief Institutional Planning ... Vacant
53 Dean College of Nursing ... Dr. Lori A. ESCALLIER
76 Dean School of Health Professions ... Dr. Allen LEWIS
69 Dean School of Public Health ... Dr. Kitaw DEMISSIE
58 Dean School of Graduate Studies ... Dr. Mark STEWART
86 Director Government Relations ... Mr. Jelanie DESHONG
90 Asst Director Academic Computing ... Dr. Jim NEILL
96 Exec Dir of Contracts & Purchasing ... Mr. Raul TOSADO
113 Interim Director Bursar ... Ms. De Anne KENNEDY-LORDE
108 Director Institutional Assessment ... Dr. Bonnie GRANAT
36 Director Student Placement ... Vacant

*State University of New York Upstate Medical University (F)

750 E Adams Street, Syracuse NY 13210-2375
County: Onondaga FICE Identification: 002840
Unit ID: 196307
Telephone: (315) 464-5540 Carnegie Class: Spec-4-yr-Med
FAX Number: (315) 464-8823 Calendar System: Semester
URL: https://www.upstate.edu
Established: 1834 Annual Undergrad Tuition & Fees (In-State): N/A
Enrollment: 1,528 Coed
Affiliation or Control: State IRS Status: 501(c)3
Highest Offering: Doctorate
Accreditation: M, ARCPA, COARC, DENT, DMOLS, EMT, IPSY, MED, MLS, NURSE, PAST, PERF, PH, PTA, RAD, RTT

02 President Dr. Mantosh DEWAN
63 Dean College of Medicine Dr. Lawrence CHIN
17 CEO University Hospital Dr. Robert CORONA
10 Vice President Finance & Management Mr. Eric SMITH
05 Vice President Academic Affairs Dr. Lynn CLEARY
46 Vice President for Research Dr. David AMBERG
58 Dean College Graduate Studies Dr. Mark SCHMITT
66 Dean College of Nursing Dr. Tammy AUSTIN-KETCH
76 Dean College of Health Professions Dr. Katherine BEISSNER
102 Exec Director HSC Foundation Ms. Eileen PEZZI
100 Interim Chief of Staff Ms. Linda VEIT
32 Dean Student Affairs Dr. Julie R. WHITE
43 Senior Managing Counsel Ms. Lisa ALEXANDER
29 Director of Medical Alumni Affairs Mr. Paul W. NORCROSS
15 VP Human Resources Mr. Jeffrey STEVENS
13 Chief Information Officer Mr. Mark ZEMAN
28 Chief Diversity Officer Dr. Daryll DYKES
108 Director Evaluation/Assessment Dr. Lauren GERMAIN
06 Registrar/Dir Inst Research Ms. Jennifer MARTIN TSE
08 Director of Libraries Ms. Christina POPE
07 Assoc Dean Admissions/Financial Aid Ms. Jennifer C. WELCH
106 Director E-Learning Dr. Pamela YOUNGS-MAHER
18 Chief Facilities/Physical Plant Mr. Timothy O'HARA
21 Assistant Vice President Finance Mr. David ANTHONY
37 Director Student Financial Aid Ms. Nicole MORGANTE

*SUNY Broome Community College (A)

PO Box 1017, Binghamton NY 13902-1017

County: Broome | FICE Identification: 002862 | Unit ID: 189547
Telephone: (607) 778-5000 | Carnegie Class: Assoc/HT-Mix Trad/Non
FAX Number: (607) 778-5310 | Calendar System: Semester
URL: www.sunybroome.edu
Established: 1946 | Annual Undergrad Tuition & Fees (In-District): $6,136
Enrollment: 5,386 | Coed
Affiliation or Control: State/Local | IRS Status: 501(c)3
Highest Offering: Associate Degree
Accreditation: M, ADNUR, CAHIIM, DH, MAC, MLTAD, #PTAA, RAD

02 President Dr. Kevin DRUMM
05 VP/Academic Officer Dr. Penny HAYNES
11 Vice Pres Admin/Financial Affairs Mr. Michael SULLIVAN
32 VP Student Development & CDO Dr. Carol ROSS-SCOTT
10 Associate Vice Pres & Controller Ms. Jeanette TILLOTSON
49 Assoc VP & Dean of LA & Bus Dr. Jeffrey ANDERSON
51 Dir Continuing Education Ms. Danielle BRITTON
76 Interim Dean Health Sciences Dr. Kimberly MCLAIN
35 Assoc VP & Dean of Students Mr. Marquis BENNETT
102 Executive Director BCC Foundation Ms. Catherine R. WILLIAMS
08 Director Learning Resource Center Ms. Robin PETRUS
07 Director of Admissions Ms. Maja SZOSTAK
15 Human Resources Officer Ms. Lynn FEDORCHAK
06 Registrar Mr. Martin GUZZI
36 Director of Placement Services Vacant
108 Dean Inst Effectiveness Dr. Kimberly MCLAIN
18 Director Facilities Management Mr. David LIGEIKIS
37 Director of Financial Aid Ms. Laura HODEL
13 Dir IT Services Mr. Conal LARKIN
19 Director of Public Safety Mr. Nick BREY
25 Director of Sponsored Programs Ms. Shelli CORDISCO
41 Director of Athletics Ms. Colleen CASHMAN
40 Bookstore Manager Ms. Teresa CONTESSA
88 Dir Educational Opportunity Pgm Ms. Venessa RODRIGUEZ
96 Director of Purchasing Mr. Randy CAMPBELL
26 Dir of Marketing/Communications Mr. Jesse WELLS
85 Ast Dir Intl Admiss/Intl Stdnt Stds Ms. Susan WELLINGTON
104 Coordinator Study Abroad Program Ms. Maria BASUALDO
38 Student Counseling Ms. Melissa MARTIN
22 Dir Affirmative Action/EEO Ms. Paige SEDLACEK
39 Director Student Housing Mr. Evan BIGAM
04 Assistant to the President Ms. Diana D. LENZO
84 Exec Enrollment Management Officer Mr. Jesse WELLS
103 Director Workforce Development Ms. Danielle BRITTON
30 Director Development & Alumni Ms. Lisa SCHAPPERT
106 Asst Dean of Distance Learning Dr. Stephanie MALMBERG
105 Web Developer Ms. Ciara CABLE

*State University of New York, The College at Brockport (B)

350 New Campus Drive, Brockport NY 14420-2914

County: Monroe | FICE Identification: 002841 | Unit ID: 196121
Telephone: (585) 395-2211 | Carnegie Class: Masters/L
FAX Number: N/A | Calendar System: Semester
URL: www.brockport.edu
Established: 1835 | Annual Undergrad Tuition & Fees (In-State): $8,624
Enrollment: 7,592 | Coed
Affiliation or Control: State | IRS Status: 501(c)3
Highest Offering: Doctorate
Accreditation: M, CAATE, CACREP, CAEP, CAPRT, DANCE, EXSC, NURSE, SPAA, SW, THEA

02 President Dr. Heidi R. MACPHERSON
05 Provost & VP Academic Affairs Dr. Martin ABRAHAM
10 VP Administration & Finance Mr. James WALL
84 VP Enrollment Mgmt/Student Affairs Dr. Kathryn WILSON
111 VP Advancement Mr. Michael ANDRIATCH
20 Vice Provost Dr. Eileen DANIEL
28 Chief Diversity Officer Ms. Damita A. DAVIS
18 Director of Physical Plant Mr. Kevin RICE
32 AVP EMSA - Student Affairs Dr. Lorraine ACKER
21 AVP Finance & Management Ms. Karen M. RIOTTO
13 CIO Mr. Robert CUSHMAN
49 Dean Arts and Sciences Dr. Jose MALIEKAL
50 Dean Business and Management Dr. Dan GOEBEL
53 Dean Educ/Health & Hum Svcs Dr. Thomas J. HERNANDEZ
14 Director of Info Tech System Mr. Stephen COOK
07 Dir of Undergrad Admissions Mr. Robert WYANT
58 Dir Center for Grad Studies Mr. Michael HARRISON
104 Dir Global Educ and Engagement Ms. Lindsay CRANE
37 Dir Financial Aid Daily Ops Dr. Kimberley WILLIS
36 Int Director of Career Services Ms. Stephanie LEARN
19 Chief of University Police Mr. Daniel VASILE
06 College Registrar Mr. Peter DOWE
15 AVP for Human Resources Ms. Tammy GOUGER
22 Affirmative Action Officer Ms. Christiana ORTIZ
124 AVP EMSA - Plng/Assess/Retention Dr. Sara KELLY
23 Director Student Health/Counseling Ms. Michelle KULESZO
39 Dir Residential Life Ms. Monique REW-BIGELOW
41 Director of Athletics Mr. Erick HART
25 Director of Grants Development Ms. Justine BRIGGS
92 Director of Honors Program Dr. Austin BUSCH
09 Int Dir Inst Research & Analysis Ms. Taneika THOMPSON
96 Director of Procurement & Payment Mr. Mark W. STACY
94 Chair Women and Gender Studies Dr. Milo OBOURN
29 Director Alumni Relations Mr. Kerry GOTHAM
04 Senior Assistant to the President Ms. Julie A. PRUSS
08 Director of Library Services Ms. Bonnie SWOGER
88 Title IX & College Compliance Ofcr Ms. Denine CARR

*State University of New York College at Buffalo (C)

1300 Elmwood Avenue, Buffalo NY 14222-1091

County: Erie | FICE Identification: 002842 | Unit ID: 196130
Telephone: (716) 878-4000 | Carnegie Class: Masters/L
FAX Number: (716) 878-3039 | Calendar System: Semester
URL: www.buffalostate.edu
Established: 1871 | Annual Undergrad Tuition & Fees (In-State): $8,428
Enrollment: 8,339 | Coed
Affiliation or Control: State | IRS Status: 501(c)3
Highest Offering: Master's
Accreditation: M, ART, ACPHA, CAEPN, CIDA, DIET, DIETC, DIETD, FEPAC, JOUR, MUS, NAIT, SP, SW, THEA

02 President Dr. Katherine S. CONWAY-TURNER
100 Chief of Staff Vacant
05 Provost/VP Academic Affairs Dr. James MAYROSE
10 Vice President Finance & Management Ms. Laura J. BARNUM
32 Vice President Student Affairs Dr. Timothy W. GORDON
111 VP Inst Advance & FNDN Exec Dir Dr. James M. FINNERTY
84 VP Enrollment Management Dr. Randyll BOWEN
19 Chief University Police Mr. James MAYORAL
21 Assoc Vice President & Comptroller Mr. James A. THOR
15 Interim AVP for HRMO Mrs. Jamie E. WARNES
09 AVP Inst Effectiveness Ms. Kim M. BARRON
13 Associate VP for IT Mr. Khaleel M. GATHERS
108 Associate Provost Dr. Amitra A. WALL
30 Assoc VP Development Mr. R. Scott BURNS
110 AVP Institutional Advancement Mr. William J. BENFANTI
51 Dir Continuing Prof Studies Ms. Kristin E. FIELDS
53 Dean School of Education Dr. Wendy A. PATERSON
49 Dean School of Arts and Sciences Dr. Brian C. CRONK
107 Dean School of the Professions Dr. Carol A. DENYSSCHEN
58 Dean Graduate School Dr. Kevin J. MILLER
88 Resident Manager Chartwells Mr. Glenn R. BUCELLO
88 Director Liberty Partnership Ms. Patrice A. CATHEY
88 Director STEP Mr. Darryl CARTER
88 Director Upward Bound Mr. Donald A. PATTERSON
36 Director of Career Development Ms. Denise M. HARRIS
26 Interim Exec Dir Marketing/Comm Mr. Jerod T. DAHLGREN
07 Director Undergraduate Admissions Mr. David P. LORETO
06 Registrar Dr. Nigel R. MARRINER
37 Director of Financial Aid Ms. Connie F. COOKE
39 Asst Dean Residence Life Dr. Philip BADASZEWSKI
113 Dir Student Accounts Mrs. Jayme S. RITER
41 Director Intercollegiate Athletics Ms. Renee M. CARLINEO
23 AVP Weigel Wellness Center Dr. Rock D. DOYLE
35 Dean of Students Ms. Sarah M. YOUNG
85 Int Dir Student Global Engagement Ms. Joy A. GUARINO
25 AVP for Sponsored Program Admis Mrs. Donna L. SCUTO
124 Asst Dean Student Ldrshp/Engagement Mr. David W. COX
09 Director Institutional Research Mr. Yves M. GACHETTE
29 Interim Dir of Alumni Engagement Ms. Katelyn M. BRICKHOUSE
96 Director of Contract Management Mr. Steven M. OLSEN
40 Manager College Bookstore Ms. Lynn M. PUMA
88 Assoc Director Student Leadership Ms. Kristen E. MRUK
22 Int Dir Student Accessibility Svcs Ms. Sumana SILVERHEELS
28 Interim Chief Diversity Officer Ms. Lisa T. MORRISON-FRONCKOWIAK
88 Asst Dean Stdnt Conduct/Cmty Stand Ms. Janelle BROOKS
18 Officer in Charge Facilities Mr. Kris A. KAUFMAN
88 Design & Construction Manager Mr. Brian D. WITTMER
38 Clinical Manager Student Counseling Dr. Charlene J. VETTER
88 Assoc Director Student Leadership Mr. Luke C. HAUMESSER
08 Chief Library Officer Mr. Charles F. LYONS

*State University of New York College at Cortland (D)

PO Box 2000, Cortland NY 13045-0900

County: Cortland | FICE Identification: 002843 | Unit ID: 196149
Telephone: (607) 753-2011 | Carnegie Class: Masters/M
FAX Number: (607) 753-5999 | Calendar System: Semester
URL: www.cortland.edu
Established: 1868 | Annual Undergrad Tuition & Fees (In-State): $8,677
Enrollment: 6,832 | Coed
Affiliation or Control: State | IRS Status: 501(c)3
Highest Offering: Master's
Accreditation: M, CAATE, CAEP, CAPRT, PH, SP

02 President Dr. Erik J. BITTERBAUM
05 Provost Dr. Mark PRUS
32 Vice Pres Student Affairs Mr. C. Gregory SHARER
111 Vice Pres Inst Advancement Mr. Peter PERKINS
10 Vice Pres for Finance & Mgmt Mr. Mark YACAVONE
18 Assoc VP Facilities Management Mr. Zach NEWSWANGER
20 Assoc Prov for Academic Affairs Dr. Carol VAN DER KARR
84 Asst Vice Pres Enrollment Mgmt Mr. Jose FELICIANO
09 Director Inst Research/Assessment Mr. Stephen CUNNINGHAM
08 Director of Libraries Ms. Jennifer KRONENBITTER
06 Registrar Vacant
36 Director of Career Services Ms. Nanette PASQUARELLO
15 Assoc VP Human Resources Mr. Gary EVANS
29 Exec Director Alumni Engagement Ms. Erin BOYLAN
38 Dir Counseling/Student Devel Dr. Carolyn BERSHAD
37 Dir of Student Financial Aid Ms. Karen GALLAGHER
19 Chief of University Police Mr. Mark DEPAULL
28 Chief Diversity/Equity/Incl Ofcr Ms. Lorraine LOPEZ-JANOVE
91 Director Admin Computing Svcs Vacant
13 Assoc VP and Chief Info Officer Ms. Lisa KAHLE
107 Dean Professional Studies Dr. John COTTONE
49 Dean Arts & Sciences Dr. Bruce MATTINGLY
26 Director of Communications Mr. Frederic PIERCE
53 Dean of Education Dr. Andrea LACHANCE
93 Dir Educational Opportunity Program Dr. Lewis ROSENGARTEN
92 Director of Honors Program Dr. Sebastian PURCELL
94 Coord Women/Gender/Sexual Studies Dr. Jena CURTIS
96 Director of Purchasing Ms. Melissa FOX
22 Affirmative Action Officer Ms. Melanie WOODWARD
88 Director Multicult Life/Diversity Ms. AnnaMaria CIRRINCIONE
41 Athletic Director Mr. Mike URTZ
104 Director International Programs Dr. Mary SCHLARB
25 Assoc Dir Research & Sponsored Pgms Mr. Thomas FRANK
39 Director Student Housing Vacant
07 Director of Admissions Mr. Jose FELICIANO
04 Admin Assistant to the President Ms. Lori PORTER
100 Chief of Staff Dr. April THOMPSON
122 Asc Dir Campus Act-Greek Affairs Ms. Sandra WOHLLEBER

*State University of New York College at Geneseo (E)

1 College Circle, Geneseo NY 14454-1401

County: Livingston | FICE Identification: 002845 | Unit ID: 196167
Telephone: (585) 245-5000 | Carnegie Class: Masters/S
FAX Number: (585) 245-5005 | Calendar System: Semester
URL: www.geneseo.edu
Established: 1871 | Annual Undergrad Tuition & Fees (In-State): $8,856
Enrollment: 4,911 | Coed
Affiliation or Control: State | IRS Status: 501(c)3
Highest Offering: Master's
Accreditation: M, CAEP

02 President Dr. Denise A. BATTLES
05 Interim Provost Dr. Joe COPE
20 Vice Provost for Academic Affairs Dr. Glenn GEISER-GETZ
11 Vice President for Finance & Admin Ms. Julie BUEHLER
32 Vice Pres for Student & Campus Life Mr. Michael TABERSKI
111 VP College Advancement/Geneseo Fndn Ms. Ellen LEVERICH
84 Vice Pres Enrollment Mgmt Dr. Costas SOLOMOU
10 Asst VP Administration/Controller Ms. Tracy MARSHALL
26 Chief Comm & Marketing Officer Ms. Kerri HOWELL
100 Chief of Staff Ms. Wendi KINNEY
15 Asst Vice Pres Human Resources Ms. Julie A. BRIGGS
29 Director Alumni Relations Ms. Amanda MCCARTHY
20 Asst Prov Curriculum/Assessment Dr. Melanie BLOOD
35 Dean of Students Dr. Leonard SANCILIO
07 Director of Admissions Ms. Christie SMITH
08 Library Director Mr. Corey HA
13 Director Computing/Info Technology Ms. Susan E. CHICHESTER
37 Director of Financial Aid Ms. Susan ROMANO
25 Director of Sponsored Research Dr. Anne E. BALDWIN
09 Int Dir of Institutional Research Dr. Matthew PASTIZZO
06 Registrar Ms. Keely BIELAT SOLTOW
36 Director of Career Development Ms. Jessie STACK LOMBARDO
28 Chief Diversity Officer robbie ROUTENBERG
88 Int Dir Multicultural Pgms & Svcs Ms. Natalie WEATHERS-GREEN
19 Chief of University Police Mr. Scott EWANOW
18 Asst VP Facilities & Planning Mr. Robert M. AMES
114 Dir of Acct & Budgeting Services Mr. Jeffrey NORDLAND
38 Director of Counseling Services Dr. Jaime CASTILLO
38 Asst Director of Counseling Svcs Dr. Beth K. CHOLETTE
96 Director of Purchasing Ms. Rebecca E. ANCHOR
04 Asst to President Ms. Susan MOORE
121 Dean of Acad Planning & Advising Dr. Celia A. EASTON
41 Dir of Intercollegiate Athletics Ms. Dani DREWS
50 Dean of School of Business Dr. Mary Ellen ZUCKERMAN
53 Dean of School of Education Dr. Jolanda WESTERHOF
90 Director Educational Technology Ms. Laurie FOX
14 Assoc Director & Manager Info Sys Mr. Paul JACKSON
104 Director Study Abroad Mr. Samuel CARDAMONE
39 Director of Residence Life Ms. Sarah FRANK
30 Director of Development Ms. Miglena CHARPIED

*State University of New York College at Old Westbury (A)

P.O. Box 210, 223 Store Hill Road,
Old Westbury NY 11568-0210

County: Nassau | FICE Identification: 007109 | Unit ID: 196237
Telephone: (516) 876-3000 | Carnegie Class: Masters/M
FAX Number: (516) 876-3209 | Calendar System: Semester
URL: www.oldwestbury.edu
Established: 1965 | Annual Undergrad Tuition & Fees (In-State): $8,122
Enrollment: 5,007 | Coed
Affiliation or Control: State | IRS Status: 501(c)3
Highest Offering: Master's
Accreditation: M, AAQEP, PH

02	President	Dr. Timothy E. SAMS
100	EVP/Chief of Staff	Dr. Jo-Ann ROBINSON
05	Provost/Sr VP Acad Affairs	Dr. Duncan QUARLESS
84	Int VP for Enrollment Services	Mr. Jeffrey HANDLER
32	Int VP of Student Affairs	Dr. Gail DISABATINO
10	VP for Business & Finance/CFO	Ms. Martha M. SANTANA
15	Int Director Human Resources	Dr. David TOMANIO
111	VP Inst Advance/Exec Dir Foundation	Dr. Wayne EDWARDS
26	VP Communications/College Relations	Mr. Michael G. KINANE
21	Assoc VP Business Affs/Controller	Mr. Pat LETTINI
20	Acting Associate Provost	Dr. Barbara HILLERY
21	Assoc VP of Business Compliance	Mr. Arthur H. ANGST, JR.
20	Asst Vice Pres Academic Affairs	Mr. Anthony BARBERA
09	Asst VP Inst Effectiveness & Admin	Dr. Jacob HELLER
49	Dean Sch of Arts & Sciences	Dr. Cheryl A. WILSON
50	Acting Dean School of Business	Dr. Shalei SIMMS
35	Dean of Students	Ms. Claudia L. MARIN ANDRADE
53	Acting Dean School of Education	Dr. Diana P. SUKHRAM
107	Director School of Prof Studies	Dr. Edward BEVER
19	Chief of Police	Mr. Steven SIENA
13	Chief Information Officer	Vacant
06	Acting Registrar	Ms. Regina SCARBROUGH
89	Director First-Year Experience	Dr. Laura M. ANKER
31	Director of Community Relations	Ms. Carolyn BENNETT
29	Director of Alumni Affairs	Ms. Penny J. CHIN
22	Dir Ofc Svcs for Stdnts/Disability	Ms. Stacey DEFELICE
92	Director Honors College	Dr. Anthony L. DELUCA
08	Library Director	Ms. Antonia DIGREGORIO
88	Coordinator of Scholarships	Ms. Pritpal KAINTH
108	Dir Inst Research & Assessment	Ms. Sandra KAUFMANN
109	Exec Dir Auxiliary Svc Corp	Ms. Carol KAUNITZ
88	Dir Ofc of Student Conduct	Ms. Kathleen LIEBLICH
88	Director of Capital Planning	Mr. Ray MAGGIORE
88	Dir Spec Programs Acad Affairs	Mr. Yves M. MAGLOIRE
36	Dir Career Plng & Development	Ms. Jerilyn MARINAN
18	Director of Facilities	Mr. Timothy MCGARRY
35	Director of Student Activities	Ms. Suzanne MCLOUGHLIN
25	Director of Sponsored Programs	Mr. Thomas MURPHY
96	Director of Purchasing	Mr. James MWAURA
37	Director Financial Aid	Ms. Mildred O'KEEFE
88	Dir Educational Opportunity Program	Dr. Jerrell W. ROBINSON
38	Dir Counseling/Psych Wellness Svcs	Dr. Oren SHEFET
39	Director Residential Life	Mr. Gareth SHUMACK
23	Dir Student Health Services	Ms. Cristine TESORIERO
89	Dir Orientation & Special Events	Ms. Jaclyn VENTO
41	Director of Athletics	Ms. Lenore J. WALSH
07	Director of Admissions	Mr. Frank PIZZARDI
122	Asst Dir Stdnt Ldrshp-Greek Life	Ms. Kya SIMMONS

*State University of New York College at Oswego (B)

7060 State Route 104, Oswego NY 13126-3501

County: Oswego | FICE Identification: 002848 | Unit ID: 196194
Telephone: (315) 312-2500 | Carnegie Class: Masters/L
FAX Number: (315) 312-5799 | Calendar System: Semester
URL: www.oswego.edu
Established: 1861 | Annual Undergrad Tuition & Fees (In-State): $8,651
Enrollment: 7,636 | Coed
Affiliation or Control: State | IRS Status: 501(c)3
Highest Offering: Master's
Accreditation: M, ART, CACREP, CAEPN, MUS, THEA

02	Officer in Charge	Dr. Mary C. TOALE
05	Provost/VP Academic Affairs	Dr. Scott R. FURLONG
10	VP Admin/Finance	Ms. Victoria L. FURLONG
32	VP Student Affairs	Dr. Kathleen KERR
30	VP Devel/Alumni Engagement	Ms. Mary CANALE
100	Chief of Staff	Ms. Kristi ECK
04	Int Exec to Pres/Affirm Action Ofcr	Mr. Reginald T. BRAGGS
26	Chief Communication Officer	Mr. Wayne WESTERVELT
84	Dir of Enrollment Mgmt	Dr. Scott R. FURLONG
18	Asst VP for Facilities Services	Mr. Mitch FIELDS
20	Associate Provost	Dr. Rameen MOHAMMADI
25	Assoc Provost Research Dev & Admin	Mr. William BOWERS
35	Assoc VP Student Affairs	Mr. Gabriel MARSHALL
35	Dean of Students	Ms. Christy HUYNH
94	Director Gender & Women's Studies	Dr. Joanna GOPLEN
06	Registrar	Mr. Jerret LEMAY
08	Director of Library	Ms. Sarah CONRAD WEISMAN
91	Assoc Dir Campus Tech Services	Mr. Michael C. PISA
37	Director Admissions/Financial Aid	Mr. Rodrick ANDREWS
09	Director Inst Research & Assessment	Dr. Deborah FURLONG
36	Director Career Services	Mr. Gary MORRIS
38	Director Counseling Services	Ms. Katherine WOLFE-LYGA
15	Director Human Resources	Ms. Amy PLOTNER
19	University Police Chief	Mr. Kevin VELZY
23	Director of Health Services	Ms. Angela BROWN
39	Int Dir Residence Life & Housing	Ms. Sara REBEOR
41	Director of Athletics	Ms. Wendy MCMANUS
96	Purchasing Associate	Ms. Karen HURD
13	Chief Technology Officer	Mr. Sean MORIARTY
29	Director of Alumni Engagement	Ms. Laura KELLY
40	College Store Manager	Ms. Susan RABY
49	Dean Col Lib Arts & Science	Dr. Kristin CROYLE
53	Dean School of Education	Dr. Laura SPENCELEY
58	Dean Grad Studies	Dr. Kristen C. EICHHORN
50	Dean School of Business	Dr. Prabakar KOTHANDARAMAN
51	Dean of Extended Learning	Ms. Jill PIPPIN
60	Int Dean of Comm/Media & the Arts	Dr. Jennifer KNAPP
121	Asst VP Student Support	Dr. Kathleen EVANS
109	Executive Director Auxiliary Svcs	Mr. Stephen MCAFEE
104	Assoc Provost Intl Educ Programs	Dr. Joshua S. MCKEOWN
28	Int Chief Diversity/Inclusion Ofcr	Ms. Kendra CADOGAN

*State University of New York College at Plattsburgh (C)

101 Broad Street, Plattsburgh NY 12901-2637

County: Clinton | FICE Identification: 002849 | Unit ID: 196246
Telephone: (518) 564-2000 | Carnegie Class: Masters/M
FAX Number: (518) 564-3932 | Calendar System: Semester
URL: www.plattsburgh.edu
Established: 1889 | Annual Undergrad Tuition & Fees (In-State): $8,574
Enrollment: 5,109 | Coed
Affiliation or Control: State | IRS Status: 501(c)3
Highest Offering: Master's
Accreditation: M, AAQEP, CACREP, DIETD, NASP, NURSE, SP, SW

02	President	Dr. Alexander ENYEDI
05	Provost/VP Academic Affairs	Dr. Anne HERZOG
10	Int VP Administration/Finance	Mr. Todd MORAVEC
111	Vice Pres Institutional Advancement	Ms. Anne W. HANSEN
32	Int VP Student Success/Enrollment	Ms. Cori JACKSON
35	Int Dean of Students	Mr. Stephen MATTHEWS
49	Dean of Arts & Sciences	Dr. Meg PEARSON
53	Dean Educ/Health/Human Svcs	Dr. Denise SIMARD
50	Int Dean of Business/Economics	Dr. Brian NEUREUTHER
08	Library Director	Ms. Elin O'HARA
28	VP Diversity/Equity/Inclusion	Ms. Allison HEAD
20	AVP Academic Affairs	Dr. JoAnn GLEESON-KREIG
96	Asst VP Regional Procurement Svcs	Mr. Sean B. DERMODY
15	Director of Human Resources	Ms. Sarah REYELL
110	Director of Advancement Services	Mr. David P. GREGOIRE
06	Registrar	Ms. Pamela MUNSON
114	Dir Budget/Financial Reporting	Ms. Magen M. RENADETTE
19	Chief University Police	Mr. Patrick RASCOE
07	Director or Admissions	Ms. Carrie WOODWARD
109	Exec Dir College Auxiliary Services	Ms. Catherine KELEHER
100	Chief of Staff	Mr. Kennith KNELLY
121	Director of Academic Advising	Ms. Elizabeth BERNOT
29	Director of Alumni Relations	Ms. Kerry CHAPIN-LAVIGNE
41	Director of Athletics	Mr. Michael P. HOWARD
36	Director of Career Development Ctr	Ms. Tobi HAY
40	College Store Manager	Ms. Susan BROWN
30	Director for Development	Ms. Faith M. LEACH
18	Asst VP of Facilities	Mr. Tyson MOULTON
37	Director of Student Financial Svcs	Mr. Todd A. MORAVEC
39	Int Dir Campus Housing/Cmty Living	Mr. James SHERMAN
09	Dir of Institutional Effectiveness	Ms. Sara PHILLIPS
25	Dir of Contracts/Purchasing Svcs	Ms. Jenna BEAUREGARD
46	Dir Sponsored Research/Programs	Mr. Michael E. SIMPSON
88	Director of Student Conduct	Mr. Larry K. ALLEN
23	Dir Ctr for Stdnt Hlth & Psych Svcs	Dr. Kathleen M. CAMELO
04	Executive Asst to the President	Ms. Cherice GRANGER
13	CIO/Information Technology Svcs	Mr. TJ MYERS

*State University of New York College at Potsdam (D)

44 Pierrepont Avenue, Potsdam NY 13676-2294

County: Saint Lawrence | FICE Identification: 002850 | Unit ID: 196200
Telephone: (315) 267-2000 | Carnegie Class: Masters/M
FAX Number: (315) 267-2496 | Calendar System: Semester
URL: www.potsdam.edu
Established: 1816 | Annual Undergrad Tuition & Fees (In-State): $8,554
Enrollment: 3,084 | Coed
Affiliation or Control: State | IRS Status: 501(c)3
Highest Offering: Master's
Accreditation: M, CAEP, MUS, THEA

02	President	Dr. Kristin G. ESTERBERG
05	Provost	Dr. Bette S. BERGERON
10	Interim VP for Business Affairs	Mr. Keith B. KAPLAN
111	VP College Advancement	Mr. Sal CANIA
84	Vice President for Enrollment	Mr. Patrick A. QUINN
100	Chief of Staff	Ms. Nicole A. FEML
11	Asst VP for Administration & HR	Mrs. Melissa E. PROULX
18	Asst Vice Pres for Facilities	Vacant
13	Chief Information Officer	Vacant
53	Dean Educ & Prof Studies	Dr. Allen C. GRANT
49	Dean of Arts and Sciences	Dr. Gretchen GALBRAITH
64	Dean of Music	Dr. William GIBBONS
08	Director of Libraries	Ms. Lauren A. JACKSON-BECK
06	Registrar	Ms. Stephanie L. CLAXTON
37	Director of Financial Aid	Ms. Tommiann R. RUSSELL
36	Director of Career Planning	Vacant
38	Director of Counseling Center	Mrs. Gena C. NELSON
15	Director of Human Resources Opers	Ms. Jennifer MURRAY
19	Chief of University Police	Mr. Tim M. ASHLEY
29	Director of Alumni Relations	Ms. Mona O. VROMAN
109	Executive Dir of Auxiliary Corp	Mr. Daniel J. HAYES
23	Director of Health Services	Ms. Tracy J. HARCOURT
32	Interim Dean of Students	Mr. Eric D. DUCHSCHERER
40	Director of College Bookstore	Mr. Lyndon J. LAKE
41	Interim Athletic Director	Mr. Mark J. MISIAK
25	Director Research & Sponsored Pgms	Mr. Jack MCGUIRE
92	Director of Honors Program	Dr. Thomas N. BAKER
94	Director of Women's Studies	Dr. Christine M. DORAN
27	Asst VP Marketing/Communications	Mrs. Mindy E. THOMPSON
58	Director of Graduate and Cont Educ	Dr. Alan L. HERSKER
28	Interim Chief Diversity Officer	Dr. Claudia J. FORD
09	Director of Institutional Research	Mrs. Judith R. SINGH
104	Director Study Abroad	Vacant
96	Director of Purchasing	Vacant
39	Director of Residence Life	Ms. Julie DOLD
44	Director Annual Giving	Ms. Rebecca WEISSMAN
26	Director of Public Relations	Ms. Alexandra JACOBS WILKE

*Purchase College, State University of New York (E)

735 Anderson Hill Road, Purchase NY 10577-1402

County: Westchester | FICE Identification: 006791 | Unit ID: 196219
Telephone: (914) 251-6000 | Carnegie Class: Bac-A&S
FAX Number: (914) 251-6014 | Calendar System: Semester
URL: www.purchase.edu
Established: 1967 | Annual Undergrad Tuition & Fees (In-State): $8,953
Enrollment: 3,685 | Coed
Affiliation or Control: State | IRS Status: 501(c)3
Highest Offering: Master's
Accreditation: M, ART

02	President	Dr. Milly PENA
10	CFO/VP Operations	Ms. Judy NOLAN
05	Provost/VP Academic Affairs	Mr. Barry PEARSON
32	Int VP Student Affs & Enroll Mgmt	Ms. Patricia BICE
111	VP of Institutional Advancement	Vacant
19	Chief of University Police	Mr. Dayton TUCKER
57	Director Conservatory Theatre Arts	Vacant
81	Dean Sch Natural/Social Sciences	Dr. Linda BASTONE
79	Chair School of Humanities	Dr. Aviva TAUBENFELD
20	Assoc Provost Academic Affairs	Dr. Gregory TAYLOR
88	Dir Performing Arts Center	Mr. Seth SOLOWAY
88	Director Neuberger Museum of Art	Dr. Tracy FITZPATRICK
08	Interim Director of the Library	Mr. Keith LANDA
64	Dir Conservatory of Music	Dr. Jennifer UNDERCOFLER
13	Director Campus Technology Services	Mr. Bill JUNOR
37	Director Student Financial Services	Corey YORK
38	Director of Counseling Center	Dr. Cathie CHESTER
36	Director Career Development	Ms. Wendy MOROSOFF
15	Director of Human Resources	Ms. Kathleen FARRELL
41	Athletic Director	Mr. Chris BISIGNANO
35	Dean of Student Affairs	Ms. Patricia BICE
09	Director of Institutional Research	Ms. Barbara MOORE
18	Sr Dir Capital Facilities Planning	Mr. Michael KOPAS
22	Title IX Officer/Affirm Action Ofcr	Ms. Jerima DEWESE
88	Environmental Health/Safety Officer	Mr. Edward MUSAL
44	Director Annual Giving	Ms. Carla WEILAND-ZALEZNAK

*State University of New York College of Agriculture and Technology at Cobleskill (F)

106 Suffolk Circle, Cobleskill NY 12043

County: Schoharie | FICE Identification: 002856 | Unit ID: 196033
Telephone: (518) 255-5011 | Carnegie Class: Bac-Diverse
FAX Number: (518) 255-5333 | Calendar System: Semester
URL: www.cobleskill.edu
Established: 1911 | Annual Undergrad Tuition & Fees (In-State): $8,591
Enrollment: 2,079 | Coed
Affiliation or Control: State | IRS Status: 501(c)3
Highest Offering: Baccalaureate
Accreditation: M, ACFEI, EMT, HT

02	President	Dr. Marion TERENZIO
05	Provost & Vice Pres Academic Affs	Dr. Susan ZIMMERMANN
100	Chief of Staff	Ms. Amy HEALY
32	VP for Student Development	Dr. Anne HOPKINS-GROSS
10	Vice Pres Business & Finance	Ms. Wendy GILMAN
11	Int Vice Pres Operations	Mr. Caleb GRANT
30	Vice Pres for Development	Mr. John J. ZACHAREK
47	Dean Agriculture/Natural Res	Dr. Timothy MOORE
49	Dean Liberal Arts & Sciences	Dr. Gail WENTWORTH
08	Dean Library/Information Svcs	Vacant
26	Assoc Dir Strategic Communications	Mr. Jason POLITI
06	Registrar	Vacant
21	Interim Chief Business Officer	Ms. Laura GROSS
29	Finance & Alumni Engagement Coord	Ms. Shannon M. MANCHESTER
84	AVP Enroll/Marketing/Communications	Mr. Caleb GRANT
39	Asst Vice Pres for Student Dev	Dr. Matthew LALONDE
36	Director of Student Success Ctr	Ms. Donna PESTA

23 Interim Co-Director Wellness Center .... Ms. Cheryl PEROG
23 Co-Director Wellness Center .... Ms. Lynn ONTL
37 Director of Financial Aid .... Ms. Louise BIRON
41 Director of Athletics .... Ms. Marie CURRAN-HEADLEY
13 Director Information Tech Services .... Vacant
19 Chief University Police Dept .... Mr. Richard BIALKOWSKI
09 Chief Strat Plng/Inst Effectiveness .... Dr. Tara WINTER
15 Human Resource Manager .... Ms. Nicole FIELD
18 Director Facilities/Physical Plant .... Mr. Joseph BATCHELDER
40 Manager Bookstore .... Ms. Jeri USATCH
85 Director of International Programs .... Dr. Susan JAGENDORF
25 Dir of Grants and Sponsored Program .... Mr. Barry GELL
22 Asc Dir Campus Outreach/Programming .... Mr. Jeffrey C. FOOTE
113 Dir of Student Accounts .... Ms. Sarah LEDERMANN
105 Web/Social/New Media Coordinator .... Mr. Mohamed BALIGH

*State University of New York College of Environmental Science and Forestry (A)

1 Forestry Drive, Syracuse NY 13210-2778
County: Onondaga FICE Identification: 002851
Unit ID: 196103
Telephone: (315) 470-6500 Carnegie Class: DU-Higher
FAX Number: (315) 470-6779 Calendar System: Semester
URL: www.esf.edu
Established: 1911 Annual Undergrad Tuition & Fees (In-State): $9,130
Enrollment: 2,127 Coed
Affiliation or Control: State IRS Status: 501(c)3
Highest Offering: Doctorate
Accreditation: M, CONST, LSAR

02 President .... Ms. Joanie MAHONEY
05 Int Provost/VP for Academic Affairs .... Dr. David NEWMAN
10 CFO/Vice Pres for Administration .... Mr. Joseph RUFO
11 Executive Operating Officer .... Mr. Mark LICHTENSTEIN
100 Chief of Staff/Chief Sust Officer .... Mr. Mark LICHTENSTEIN
04 Asst to the President .... Ms. Ragan A. SQUIER
86 VP for Govt & External Relations .... Vacant
45 Exec Dir for Strategic Initiatives .... Mr. Matthew J. MILLEA
30 Asst VP for Development .... Ms. Brenda T. GREENFIELD
46 Vice President for Research .... Dr. John STELLA
58 Assoc Prov & Dean Grad School .... Mr. S. Scott SHANNON
32 Vice Provost/Dean Student Affairs .... Dr. Anne E. LOMBARD
21 Director Business Affairs .... Mr. David R. DZWONKOWSKI
13 Chief Information Officer .... Vacant
15 Director Human Resources .... Mr. Timothy BLEHAR
26 AVP Communications/Marketing .... Vacant
19 Acting Chief of University Police .... Mr. Robert DUGAN
28 Chief Diversity Officer .... Dr. Malika CARTER
08 Director of College Libraries .... Mr. Matthew R. SMITH
07 Director of Admissions .... Mrs. Susan H. SANFORD
37 Director of Financial Aid .... Mr. Mark J. HILL
29 Director of Alumni Affairs .... Ms. Debbie J. CAVINESS
18 Dir Facil Planning/Design & Constr .... Mr. Gary S. PEDEN
36 Dir of Career Services .... Mr. John TURBEVILLE
38 Dir of Counseling Services .... Ms. Ruth LARSON
35 Dir Stdnt Involvement & Leadership .... Mrs. Laura CRANDALL
41 Dir of Intercollegiate Athletics .... Mr. Daniel RAMIN
43 Associate Counsel .... Ms. Kelly BERGER
104 Dir of International Education .... Mr. Thomas E. CARTER
44 Development Officer - Annual Giving .... Ms. Tammy SCHLAFER
91 Manager of Information Systems .... Mr. Kenneth J. STVAN
06 Registrar .... Ms. Leslie A. RUTKOWSKI
09 Asst Dir Assessment & Inst Research .... Dr. Sophie A. GUBLO-JANTZEN
22 Title IX Coord & Affirm Action Ofcr .... Ms. Rebecca A. HODA-KEARSE
84 Asst Provost for Enrollment Mgmt . Ms. Katherine M. MCCARTHY
106 Director ESF Open Academy .... Dr. Tondelaya K. GEORGE

*State University of New York College of Optometry (B)

33 W 42nd Street, New York NY 10036-8003
County: New York FICE Identification: 009929
Unit ID: 196228
Telephone: (212) 938-4000 Carnegie Class: Spec-4-yr-Other Health
FAX Number: (212) 938-5696 Calendar System: Semester
URL: www.sunyopt.edu
Established: 1971 Annual Graduate Tuition & Fees: N/A
Enrollment: 402 Coed
Affiliation or Control: State IRS Status: 501(c)3
Highest Offering: Doctorate; No Undergraduates
Accreditation: M, OPT, OPTR

02 President .... Dr. David A. HEATH
05 Dean/VP Academic Affairs .... Dr. David TROILO
10 VP For Administration and Finance .... David A. BOWERS
32 Vice Pres Student Affairs .... Dr. Guilherme ALBIERI
17 Vice Pres for Clinical Admin ..... Liduvina MARTINEZ-GONZALEZ
111 Vice Pres Institutional Advancement .... Dawn RIGNEY
43 Senior Counsel .... Wendy L. RAVITZ
28 Dir of Diversity/Equity/Inclusion .... Dr. Joy HAREWOOD
04 Assistant to the President .... Carolina GOMEZ-JONES
09 Dir Institutional Research/Planning ..... Dr. Suresh VISWANATHAN
08 Director Library Services .... Elaine WELLS
15 Asst Vice Pres of Human Resources .... Guerda FILS
06 Registrar .... Jacqueline MARTINEZ
58 Assoc Dean Rsrch/Graduate Studies ...... Dr. Stewart BLOOMFIELD
37 Financial Aid Officer .... Vito CAVALLARO
13 Chief Info Technology Officer .... Robert PELLOT
84 Director Enrollment Management .... Dr. Guilherme ALBIERI
96 Director of Purchasing .... Ying Ting WAN LEESHUE
07 Director of Admissions .... Christian ALBERTO
29 Assoc Vice Pres of Alumni Affairs .... Jennifer Kelly CAMPBELL

*Alfred State College (C)

10 Upper College Drive, Alfred NY 14802-1196
County: Allegany FICE Identification: 002854
Unit ID: 196006
Telephone: (607) 587-4215 Carnegie Class: Bac/Assoc-Mixed
FAX Number: N/A Calendar System: Semester
URL: www.alfredstate.edu
Established: 1908 Annual Undergrad Tuition & Fees (In-State): $8,726
Enrollment: 3,667 Coed
Affiliation or Control: State IRS Status: 501(c)3
Highest Offering: Baccalaureate
Accreditation: M, ADNUR, CAHIIM, CONST, FEPAC, IACBE, NURSE, RAD

02 President .... Dr. Steven A. MAURO
05 Provost .... Dr. Kristin POPPO
32 Vice President Student Affairs .... Dr. Gregory S. SAMMONS
111 Exec Dir Institutional Advancement .... Ms. Danielle M. WHITE
09 Dir Inst Research/Planning/Effect .... Mr. Daniel D. JARDINE
84 VP for Enrollment Mgmt .... Ms. Betsy PENROSE
13 Director Computer Services .... Mr. Michael A. CASE
100 Chief of Staff .... Ms. Wendy DRESSER-RECKTENWALD
37 Sr Dir Student Financial Services .... Mrs. Julie ROSE
29 Int Director Alumni Relations .... Ms. Roxana SAMMONS
18 Director of Facilities .... Mr. Jon NICKERSON
14 Asst Director of Computing Services .... Mr. Carl H. RAHR, JR.
23 Sr Director Health Svcs/Wellness .... Ms. Hollie M. HALL
121 Assoc VP of Academic Services .... Ms. Kathleen CASEY
19 Chief of University Police .... Mr. Scott RICHARDSON
96 Director of Purchasing .... Mrs. Michelle MCCARTHY
10 Chief Financial Officer .... Mr. Joseph T. GREENTHAL
36 Director of Career Planning .... Ms. Elaine MORSMAN
49 Dean School of Arts & Sciences .... Mr. Dan KATZ
54 Dean School of Mgmt & Engr Tech .... Dr. John WILLIAMS
75 Int Dean Sch Applied Technology .... Mr. Jeff STEVENS
41 Athletic Director .... Mr. Jason DOVIAK
04 Executive Assistant to President .... Ms. Trish HAGGERTY

*SUNY Adirondack (D)

640 Bay Road, Queensbury NY 12804-1498
County: Warren FICE Identification: 002860
Unit ID: 188438
Telephone: (518) 743-2200 Carnegie Class: Assoc/HT-High Trad
FAX Number: (518) 745-1433 Calendar System: Semester
URL: www.sunyacc.edu
Established: 1960 Annual Undergrad Tuition & Fees (In-District): $5,832
Enrollment: 2,994 Coed
Affiliation or Control: State/Local IRS Status: 501(c)3
Highest Offering: Associate Degree
Accreditation: M, ADNUR

02 President .... Dr. Kristine DUFFY
05 Vice Pres Academic Affairs .... Mr. John JABLONSKI
10 Vice Pres Admin Services .... Ms. Ann Marie SCHEIDEGGER
84 VP for Enrollment & Student Affairs .... Mr. John DELATE
20 AVP Academic Affairs .... Ms. Diane WILDEY
32 Dean of Student Affairs .... Ms. Kathryn O'SICK
09 Director of Inst Research/Planning .... Vacant
13 Chief Information Officer .... Ms. Mary HAND
15 AVP of Human Resources .... Ms. Mindy WILSON
51 Dean Continuing Educ & Workforce .... Mrs. Caelynn PRYLO
40 Director Bookstore .... Mr. Tom KENT
21 Dir of Business/Financial Affairs .... Ms. Lisa DESTER
18 Director of Facilities .... Mr. Marc MORIN
37 Director Financial Aid .... Ms. Colleen WISE
06 Registrar .... Ms. Mary ALDOUS
07 Asst Director of Registration .... Mr. Ryan THOMAS
08 Library Chair .... Ms. Emily GOODSPEED
35 Dir of Student Engagement/Diversity .... Mr. Taylor TESTA
04 Executive Assistant to President .... Ms. Brooke TOMA
19 Director of Public Safety .... Mr. Joseph MCDADE

*SUNY Canton-College of Technology (E)

34 Cornell Drive, Canton NY 13617-1098
County: Saint Lawrence FICE Identification: 002855
Unit ID: 196015
Telephone: (315) 386-7011 Carnegie Class: Bac-Diverse
FAX Number: (315) 386-7930 Calendar System: Semester
URL: www.canton.edu
Established: 1906 Annual Undergrad Tuition & Fees (In-State): $8,689
Enrollment: 3,135 Coed
Affiliation or Control: State IRS Status: 501(c)3
Highest Offering: Baccalaureate
Accreditation: M, ADNUR, COSMA, FUSER, IACBE, NUR, PNUR, PTAA

02 President .... Dr. Zvi SZAFRAN
05 Provost .... Dr. Peggy A. DE COOKE
11 Vice Pres for Administration .... Ms. Shawn MILLER
10 Chief Financial Officer .... Ms. Shawn MILLER
111 Vice Pres for Advancement .... Ms. Tracey THOMPSON
32 Vice President for Student Affairs .... Ms. Courtney D. BISH
35 Dean of Students .... Ms. Courtney D. BISH
72 Dean Canino Sch Eng Tech .... Mr. Michael J. NEWTOWN
76 Dean Sch Sci/Health/Crim Justice .... Dr. Michele SNYDER
50 Dean Sch Business/Liberal Arts .... Dr. Kirk JONES
20 Associate Provost .... Dr. Molly MOTT
41 Director of Athletics .... Mr. Randy B. SIEMINSKI
100 Exec Dir for University Relations .... Dr. Lenore VANDERZEE
101 College Council Secretary .... Ms. Michaela J. YOUNG
04 Exec Assistant to the President .... Ms. Michaela J. YOUNG
35 Director Student Activities .... Ms. Priscilla LEGGETTE COLLINS
28 Co-Chief Diversity Officer/AAO .... Ms. Lashawanda T. INGRAM
28 Co-Chief Diversity Officer/AAO ..... Ms. Emily HAMILTON-HONEY
96 Director of Purchasing .... Ms. Bethany A. MARTIN
37 Director of Financial Aid .... Ms. Heather M. ADNER
21 Dir OHS/College Accountant .... Ms. Amanda CRUMP
15 Director of Human Resources .... Ms. Amanda DECKERT
36 Director of Career Services .... Ms. Julie PARKMAN
06 Registrar .... Ms. Sharon TAVERNIER
08 Executive Director Learning Commons .... Ms. Johanna LEE
18 Director of Physical Plant .... Mr. Martin AVERY
19 Chief of University Police .... Mr. Timothy ASHLEY, II
23 Director of Health Services .... Ms. Amanda PERSONS
26 Dir Public Rels/Web Coord .... Mr. Travis SMITH
40 Manager Campus Store .... Mr. Corey JORDAN
39 Director of Residence Life .... Mr. John M. KENNEDY
09 Dir of Inst Research/Assessment .... Ms. Sarah E. TODD
13 Assistant VP IT/CIO .... Mr. Kyle BROWN
29 Director of Alumni Engagement .... Ms. Jamie BURGESS
38 Director of Counseling .... Ms. Melinda A. MILLER
84 Executive Director of Enrollment .... Ms. Melissa EVANS
88 Executive Director of Facilities .... Mr. Michael R. MCCORMICK
30 Dir Development & Planned Giving .... Mr. Geoffrey VANDERWOUDE
90 Help Desk Manager .... Mr. Benjamin MATOTT
104 Director Intl Programs .... Ms. Erin LASSIAL
88 Dir CREST Center/Veterans Coord .... Mr. Patrick MASSARO
25 Dir Sponsored Programs & Research .... Ms. Betsy ROHR ADAMS

*SUNY Corning Community College (F)

One Academic Drive, Corning NY 14830-3297
County: Steuben FICE Identification: 002863
Unit ID: 190442
Telephone: (607) 962-9000 Carnegie Class: Assoc/HT-High Non
FAX Number: (607) 962-9456 Calendar System: Semester
URL: www.corning-cc.edu
Established: 1956 Annual Undergrad Tuition & Fees (In-District): $5,824
Enrollment: 4,063 Coed
Affiliation or Control: State/Local IRS Status: 501(c)3
Highest Offering: Associate Degree
Accreditation: M, ADNUR

01 President .... Dr. William P. MULLANEY
10 Executive Director of Finance/CFO .... Ms. Susan CHANDLER
05 Provost .... Dr. Barbara CANFIELD
30 Exec Dir CCC Development Foundation ...... Mr. John MARCHESE
06 Registrar .... Ms. Loretta HENDRICKSON
84 Director of Enrollment Operations .... Mr. Christian KULL
15 Exec Dir of HR and Ch Div Officer .... Ms. Connie PARK
18 Exec Dir Aux/Campus Services .... Mr. David BURDICK
37 Director Student Financial Aid .... Ms. Shalena CLARY
32 Assoc Dean Student Services .... Mr. Paul ANDREWS
04 Exec Assistant to the President .... Ms. Nogaye KA-TANDIA
103 Exec Dir Workforce Development .... Ms. Jeanne ESCHBACH
19 Director Public Safety .... Mr. Michael FRIEBIS
13 Chief Information Officer .... Ms. Denise BURBEY
09 Director of Library .... Ms. Rejoice SCHERRY
09 Dir Inst Research/Effectiveness .... Mr. Zachary DUNBAR

*SUNY Schenectady County Community College (G)

78 Washington Avenue, Schenectady NY 12305
County: Schenectady FICE Identification: 006785
Unit ID: 195322
Telephone: (518) 381-1200 Carnegie Class: Assoc/HT-High Non
FAX Number: (518) 346-0379 Calendar System: Semester
URL: www.sunysccc.edu
Established: 1967 Annual Undergrad Tuition & Fees (In-District): $5,524
Enrollment: 4,015 Coed
Affiliation or Control: State/Local IRS Status: 501(c)3
Highest Offering: Associate Degree
Accreditation: M, ACFEI, MUS

01 President .... Dr. Steady MOONO
05 Vice Pres for Academic Affairs .... Dr. Cheryl GOOCH
10 Vice President of Administration .... Mr. Patrick RYAN
30 Vice Pres Development/External Affs .... Ms. Stacy MCILDUFF
45 Vice Pres for Strategic Initiatives .... Dr. David CLICKNER
103 Exec Dir Workforce Dev/Cmty Educ .... Ms. Sarah WILSON-SPARROW
13 Chief Information Officer .... Mr. Jeffrey SNOW
20 Dean of Academic Affairs .... Vacant
32 Dean of Student Affairs .... Mr. Stephen FRAGALE
37 Asst Dean of Financial Aid .... Mr. Mark BESSETTE
06 Registrar .... Dr. Kristy BERG
07 Director of Admissions .... Ms. Laura SPRAGUE
08 Director Library Services .... Ms. Jacqueline KELEHER-HUGHES
18 Director of Facilities .... Mr. Anthony SCHWARTZ
36 Exec Dir Sche Col/Career Outreach ..... Dr. DeShawn MCGARRITY
15 Human Resources Specialist .... Ms. Leah RYE
09 Director Institutional Research .... Mr. Dale MILLER
22 Dir Educ Opp Pgms/Access .... Ms. Tiombe FARLEY

10 Controller ... Ms. Aimee S. WARFIELD
100 Chief of Staff ... Dr. Hamin SHABAZZ
26 Exec Director of Marketing & PR ... Ms. Karen TANSKI
27 Public Rels/Publications Specialist ... Ms. Heather L. MEANEY
19 Director Security/Safety ... Mr. Eric FLUTY

*State University of New York College of Technology at Delhi (A)

454 Delhi Drive, Delhi NY 13753-4454
County: Delaware FICE Identification: 002857
Unit ID: 196024
Telephone: (607) 746-4000 Carnegie Class: Bac-Diverse
FAX Number: (607) 746-4208 Calendar System: Semester
URL: www.delhi.edu
Established: 1913 Annual Undergrad Tuition & Fees (In-State): $8,640
Enrollment: 3,077 Coed
Affiliation or Control: State IRS Status: 501(c)3
Highest Offering: Master's
Accreditation: M, ACFEI, ADNUR, CONST, NUR, NURSE

02 Officer-in-Charge ... Dr. Mary H. BONDEROFF
05 Provost ... Dr. Thomas T. JORDAN
32 VP for Student Life ... Mr. Tomas A. AGUIRRE
111 Vice Pres for College Advancement ... Mr. Michael A. SULLIVAN
36 Career Planning & Devel Associate ... Ms. Kristin A. DEFOREST
13 Chief Information Officer ... Mr. Shawn P. BRISLIN
19 Chief of University Police ... Mr. Martin A. PETTIT
39 Asst VP Housing/Aux Svcs/Enrol Svcs ... Mr. John J. PADOVANI
08 Director of the Resnick Library ... Ms. Carrie J. FISHNER
31 Sr Staff Assoc Ctr for Cmty Engage ... Ms. Michele T. DEFREECE
18 Director of Physical Plant ... Mr. David A. LOVELAND
41 Director of Athletics ... Mr. Robert H. BACKUS
06 Interim Registrar ... Ms. Cynthia R. HEALEY
37 Director of Financial Aid ... Ms. Elizabeth D. BERRY
23 Director of Health Services ... Ms. Tanyia A. HYNES
29 Director of Alumni/Annual Giving ... Ms. Lucinda C. BRYDON
21 Controller ... Ms. Amy L. BROWN
26 Vice Pres Communications/Marketing ... Mr. Mark J. SULLIVAN
04 Administrative Asst to President ... Mr. George L. SPIELMAN
102 Exec Director College Foundation ... Mr. Joel SMITH
22 Dir Human Resources/Affirm Action ... Ms. Diane R. HANNA
25 Grants Specialist ... Ms. Ellen A. LIBERATORI

*State University of New York Empire State College (B)

2 Union Avenue, Saratoga Springs NY 12866-4390
County: Saratoga FICE Identification: 010286
Unit ID: 196264
Telephone: (518) 587-2100 Carnegie Class: Masters/L
FAX Number: (518) 587-2886 Calendar System: Other
URL: www.esc.edu
Established: 1971 Annual Undergrad Tuition & Fees (In-State): $7,630
Enrollment: 10,724 Coed
Affiliation or Control: State IRS Status: 501(c)3
Highest Offering: Doctorate
Accreditation: M, AAQEP, IACBE, NURSE

02 President ... Dr. Lisa VOLLENDORF
100 Chief of Staff ... Dr. Leigh YANNUZZI
11 Interim Chief Operating Officer ... Ms. Alexandra BONITATIBUS
05 Acting Provost ... Dr. Nathan E. GONYEA
111 Int AVP of Advancement ... Dr. Sue EPSTEIN
84 VP for Enrollment Management ... Dr. Clayton STEEN
10 Chief Financial Officer/AVP Admin ... Ms. Alexandra BONITATIBUS
13 Chief Information Officer ... Mr. Todd MYLES
26 AVP for Communications/Marketing ... Mr. Solomon SYED
15 Asst VP for Human Resources ... Ms. Tracey MEEK
20 Dean Academic/Instructional Svcs ... Dr. Lisa D'ADAMO-WEINSTEIN
20 Vice Prov Academic Administration ... Dr. Tai ARNOLD
20 Int Vice Provost Academic Affairs ... Dr. Frank VANDER VALK
32 Acting Vice Prov Student Success ... Ms. Seana LOGSDON
70 Associate Dean Social Science ... Dr. Frank VANDER VALK
50 Associate Dean Business ... Dr. Julie GEDRO
79 Associate Dean Humanities ... Dr. Megan MULLEN
58 Assoc Dean School for Grad Studies ... Dr. Nathan GONYEA
66 Dean School of Nursing ... Dr. Kim STOTE
28 Int Chief Diversity Officer ... Dr. Audeliz MATIAS
12 Co-Int Exec Director Metro Center ... Dr. Christopher WHANN
91 Director Admin Applications ... Mr. Mark CLAVERIE
110 Director Advancement Services ... Ms. Vicki SCHAAKE
29 Dir Alumni and Student Relations ... Ms. Maureen WINNEY
44 Director of the Fund ... Ms. Stephanie CORP
21 Director Business Office ... Ms. Becky PALMIERI
108 Dir Collegewide Academic Review ... Dr. Nan TRAVERS
27 Director of Communications ... Mr. David HENAHAN
88 Director of Academic Development ... Mr. Brian GOODALE
88 Dir Compliance/Environment Sustain ... Ms. Sadie ROSS
18 Senior Director of Facilities ... Mr. Rick REIMANN
30 Director of Development ... Mr. Toby TOBROCKE
88 Director College Project Management ... Mr. Walter LEWIS
96 Director Procurement ... Mr. Charley SUMMERSELL
24 Director Publications ... Mr. Kirk STARCZEWSKI
19 Director of Safety & Security ... Mr. Mark JANKOWSKI
113 Director Student Accounts ... Ms. Pamela MALONE
88 Int Dir Veteran & Military Educ ... Ms. Desiree DRINDAK
06 Registrar ... Ms. Pamela ENSER
07 Sr Director Admissions ... Ms. Jennifer D'AGOSTINO

*Farmingdale State College (C)

2350 Broadhollow Road, Farmingdale NY 11735-1021
County: Suffolk FICE Identification: 002858
Unit ID: 196042
Telephone: (934) 420-2000 Carnegie Class: Bac-Diverse
FAX Number: N/A Calendar System: Semester
URL: www.farmingdale.edu
Established: 1912 Annual Undergrad Tuition & Fees (In-State): $8,395
Enrollment: 10,018 Coed
Affiliation or Control: State IRS Status: 501(c)3
Highest Offering: Master's
Accreditation: M, AAB, ART, DH, MLS, NURSE

02 President ... Dr. John S. NADER
05 Provost/SVP for Academic Affairs ... Dr. Laura JOSEPH
10 Executive VP & CFO ... Mr. Gregory O'CONNOR
28 VP DEI Excellence ... Dr. Kevin JORDAN
111 VP Inst Advancement/Enrollment Mgmt ... Vacant
30 VP Development & Communications ... Mr. Matthew COLSON
20 Associate Provost ... Dr. Christopher MALONE
21 Asst VP Administration & Finance ... Ms. Dorothy HUGHES
35 Acting Dean of Students & Title IX ... Mr. Frank RAMPELLO
19 Chief University Police ... Mr. Daniel DAUGHERTY
18 Acting Dir Physical Plant Operation ... Mr. Mark ORLICH
26 Sr Director of Communications ... Vacant
06 Registrar ... Ms. Cindy MCCUE
07 Director of Admissions ... Ms. Jeanne SOTO
08 Head Librarian ... Ms. Karen GELLES
15 Asst VP Human Resources ... Ms. Marybeth MCCLOSKEY
14 Director of Information Technology ... Mr. Jeffrey BORAH
36 Director Career Development Center ... Ms. Dolores CIACCIO
37 Director Student Financial Services ... Ms. Diane KAZANECKI-KEMPTER
09 Chf Off Inst Research Effectiveness ... Ms. Patricia LIND-GONZALEZ
23 Director of Campus Heath & Wellness ... Mr. Kevin MURPHY
41 Dir Athletics Admin & Ext Affairs ... Vacant
41 Dir of Athletics Comp & Operations ... Mr. Thomas AZZARA
39 Dir Student Activities/Campus Ctr ... Ms. Eunice RO
102 President Farmingdale Foundation ... Mr. Robert VAN NOSTRAND
24 Dir Instructional Tech Support Ctr ... Mr. Martin BRANDT
29 Dir Alum Engagement & Stewardship ... Ms. Michelle JOHNSON
40 Manager Bookstore ... Mr. Matthew DAVID
21 Asst VP for Finance & Controller ... Ms. Keri FRANKLIN
96 Acting Dir of Procurement ... Ms. Lisa BRUNS
75 Executive Director LIEOC ... Mr. Charles MIRANDA
50 Dean School of Business ... Dr. Richard VOGEL
76 Dean School of Health Sciences ... Dr. Denny RYMAN
49 Dean School of Arts & Sciences ... Dr. Charles ADAIR
54 Dean School of Engineering Tech ... Dr. Barbara CHRISTIE
104 Study Abroad Specialist ... Ms. Elizabeth HAMBERGER
105 Director Web Program & Developement ... Ms. Sylvia NAVARRO-NICOSIA
85 Acting Dir International Education ... Mr. James HALL
04 Executive Assistant to President ... Ms. Carolyn FEDDER
122 Coord Stdnt Act-Frat/Sorority Life ... Mr. Lukas MIEDREICH
13 Chief IO and Chief ISO ... Mr. Pete GRIZZAFFI
38 Director Campus Mental Health Svcs ... Dr. Andrew BERGER
39 Residence Hall Director ... Ms. Danielle CHAPMAN
121 Dir Academic Advisement & Info Ctr ... Dr. Alexander CAVIEDES

*State University of New York Maritime College (D)

6 Pennyfield Avenue, Throggs Neck NY 10465-4198
County: Bronx FICE Identification: 002853
Unit ID: 196291
Telephone: (718) 409-7200 Carnegie Class: Masters/S
FAX Number: (718) 409-7392 Calendar System: Semester
URL: www.sunymaritime.edu
Established: 1874 Annual Undergrad Tuition & Fees (In-State): $8,522
Enrollment: 1,671 Coed
Affiliation or Control: State IRS Status: 501(c)3
Highest Offering: Master's
Accreditation: M, IACBE

02 President ... Dr. Michael A. ALFULTIS
05 Provost/Vice Pres Academic Affairs ... Dr. Jennifer K. WATERS
10 Vice Pres Finance/Admin ... Mr. Scott DIETERICH
111 Vice President Advancement ... Mr. Douglas HASBROUCK
20 Academic Dean ... Vacant
100 Chief of Staff ... CAPT. Mark WOOLLEY
07 Dean of Admissions ... Mr. Rohan HOWELL
32 Assoc Provost/Dean of Students ... Mr. William IMBRIALE
27 Director of External Affairs ... CAPT. Mark WOOLLEY
15 AVP Human Resources/Chief Div Ofcr ... Ms. Lu-Ann AUGUSTINE-PLAISANCE
19 University Police Chief ... Mr. Myron PRYJMAK
37 Director Financial Aid ... Ms. Andrea DAMAR
41 Interim Director of Athletics ... Mr. Mike BERKUN
06 Registrar ... Ms. Sarah GRADY
09 Dir Inst Research/Assessment ... CAPT. Mark WOOLLEY
08 Library Director ... Ms. Jillian KEHOE
88 Dean Maritime Educ/Training ... CAPT. Ernest FINK
54 Dean School of Engineering ... Dr. Carl DELO
50 Dean Sch of Business/Sci/Humanities ... Dr. Joseph HOFFMAN

*SUNY Morrisville (E)

PO Box 901, Morrisville NY 13408-0901
County: Madison FICE Identification: 002859
Unit ID: 196051
Telephone: (315) 684-6000 Carnegie Class: Bac/Assoc-Mixed
FAX Number: (315) 684-6116 Calendar System: Semester
URL: www.morrisville.edu
Established: 1908 Annual Undergrad Tuition & Fees (In-State): $8,740
Enrollment: 2,486 Coed
Affiliation or Control: State IRS Status: 501(c)3
Highest Offering: Master's
Accreditation: M, ACBSP, ADNUR, NUR

02 President ... Dr. David E. ROGERS
05 Interim Academic Officer ... Dr. Jason ZBOCK
10 Chief Financial Officer ... Mr. Jamie CYR
84 Chief Enrollment Officer ... Dr. Robert C. BLANCHET
32 VP Student Affairs ... Vacant
47 Dean School Agric/Business/Tech ... Dr. Anthony CONTENTO
49 Dean Liberal Arts/Sciences/Society ... Dr. jason ZBOCK
111 VP for Inst Advancement ... Ms. Theresa R. KEVORKIAN
07 Director of Admission ... Ms. Devyn THOMAS
37 Director of Financial Aid ... Ms. Dacia L. BANKS
09 Director of Institutional Research ... Ms. Marian D. WHITNEY
08 Director of Library ... Ms. Christine A. RUDECOFF
23 Director Student Health Center ... Ms. Debra P. BABOWICZ
15 Director Human Resources ... Ms. Amy MCLAUGHLIN
29 Alumni Engagement Coordinator ... Ms. Rhiannon L. DACUNHA
26 Exec Dir Communications/Marketing ... Mr. Jeff MACHARYAS
06 Registrar ... Ms. Marian D. WHITNEY
13 Director of Technology Svcs ... Mr. Kyle A. CAMPANARO
18 Exec Director of Facilities ... Mr. Christopher S. MARONEY
19 Chief of Police ... Mr. Paul G. FIELD
36 Career Planning/Development Ofcr ... Ms. Barbara A. ROBACK
39 Director Student Housing ... Ms. Elizabeth R. ACKMAN
41 Athletic Director ... Mr. Matt GRAWROCK
108 Associate Provost of Assessment ... Vacant
28 Director of Diversity ... Vacant
04 Admin Assistant to the President ... Ms. Jennifer JONES
25 Chief Contract and Grants Administr ... Mr. Miguel PEREIRA

*SUNY Polytechnic Institute (F)

100 Seymour Road, Utica NY 13502
County: Oneida FICE Identification: 011678
Unit ID: 196112
Telephone: (315) 792-7100 Carnegie Class: Masters/L
FAX Number: (315) 792-7222 Calendar System: Semester
URL: www.sunypoly.edu
Established: 1966 Annual Undergrad Tuition & Fees (In-State): $8,427
Enrollment: 3,044 Coed
Affiliation or Control: State IRS Status: 501(c)3
Highest Offering: Doctorate
Accreditation: M, CAHIIM, NURSE

02 Acting President ... Dr. Tod LAURSEN
11 Chief Operating Officer ... Mr. Michael FRAME
04 Assistant to the President ... Ms. Laurie HARTMAN
46 Int VP for Research Advancement ... Dr. Shadi SHAHEDIPOUR-SANDVIK
15 VP for Human Resources ... Ms. Rhonda HAINES
32 VP for Student Affairs ... Ms. Marybeth LYONS
30 AVP for Development ... Mrs. Andrea LAGATTA
05 Provost ... Dr. Steven SCHNEIDER
84 AVP for Enrollment Mgmt ... Ms. Maryrose RAAB
49 Dean Arts & Sciences ... Dr. Andrew RUSSELL
50 Dean Business ... Dr. Arthur LU
54 Dean Engineering ... Dr. Michael CARPENTER
81 Dean Nanoscale Science & Engr ... Dr. Andre MELENDEZ
76 Dean Health Professions ... Dr. Joanne JOSEPH
19 Chief of Police ... Mr. Gary BEAN
18 Director of Facilities ... Mr. Matt PUTNAM
41 Director Athletics ... Mr. Kevin M. GRIMMER
21 Associate VP of Business Affairs ... Ms. Susan HEAD
88 Director of Student Conduct ... Ms. Megan WYETT
36 Director Career Services ... Mr. Jose Miguel LONGO
23 Director Health & Wellness Center ... Ms. Jo RUFFRAGE
09 Assistant VP Institutional Research ... Ms. Valerie FUSCO
35 AVP Student Affairs ... Mrs. Jennifer ADAMS
37 Director Student Financial Aid ... Mr. Michael ALSHEIMER
06 Registrar ... Mrs. Meghan GETMAN
123 Coordinator Graduate Center ... Ms. Alicia FOSTER
43 Associate Counsel ... Mr. Mark LEMIRE
13 Chief Information Officer ... Mr. Andrew BELLINGER
28 Chief Diversity Officer ... Dr. Mark MONTGOMERY
07 Director of Admissions ... Ms. Gina LISCIO
08 Director of Library Services ... Ms. Rebecca HEWITT
120 Dir Online Education/E-learning ... Mr. Rick SHELTON
29 Director Alumni Relations ... Vacant
96 Director of Purchasing ... Mr. David MANORE

*Suffolk County Community College Central Administration (G)

533 College Road, Selden NY 11784-2899
County: Suffolk Identification: 666658
Unit ID: 366395
Telephone: (631) 451-4000 Carnegie Class: N/A
FAX Number: (631) 451-4715
URL: www.sunysuffolk.edu

01 President ... Mr. Edward BONAHUE
27 College Communications Director ... Mr. Drew BIONDO
43 College General Counsel ... Mr. Louis J. PETRIZZO
05 VP Academic Affairs ... Dr. Paul M. BEAUDIN
10 VP Business/Financial Affairs ... Mr. Mark HARRIS

30 Vice Pres Institutional Advancement .... Ms. Mary Lou ARANEO
45 VP Planning/Inst Effectiveness .... Ms. Kaliah GREENE
32 Int Asst VP of Student Affairs .... Dr. Patty MUNSCH
13 VP Computer Information Systems ..... Mr. Shady AZZAM-GOMEZ
103 Assoc VP Workforce/Econ Development ..... Mr. John LOMBARDO
84 College Dean Enrollment Management ... Ms. Joanne E. BRAXTON
06 Assoc Dean Master Sched/Registrar .... Ms. Anna FLACK
35 Assistant Dean Student Services .... Ms. Katherine AGUIRRE
37 College Director of Financial Aid .... Ms. Nancy A. BREWER
28 Col Coord Multicultural Affairs .... Mr. James W. BANKS
102 Executive Director Foundation .... Dr. Sylvia DIAZ
30 Col Assoc Dean Inst Advancement .... Mr. Andrew FAWCETT
104 Col Assoc Dean Spec Prog & Ext Part .... Dr. Iaroslava BABENCHUK
106 Asst Dean Instructional Technology .... Mr. Douglas KAHN
14 Assoc Dean Computer Info Systems .... Vacant
19 Director Fire/Public Safety .... Mr. Baycan FIDELI
22 Chief Diversity Officer/Title IX .... Ms. Christina VARGAS
25 Assoc Dean Grants Development .... Dr. William T. TUCKER
26 Dir College Relations/Publications .... Ms. Mary M. FEDER
29 Director Alumni Relations .... Mr. Russell MALBROUGH
41 College Assoc Director of Athletics .... Mr. Joseph KOSINA
86 Col Director Legislative Affairs .... Mr. Benjamin ZWIRN
96 Admin Director Business Operations .... Ms. Beatriz CASTANO
36 Director Career Services .... Ms. Tania VELAZQUEZ
18 Executive Director Facilities .... Mr. Paul COOPER

*Suffolk County Community College (A)

533 College Road, Selden NY 11784-2899

County: Suffolk — FICE Identification: 002878
Telephone: (631) 451-4000 — Carnegie Class: Not Classified
FAX Number: (631) 451-4015 — Calendar System: Semester
URL: www.sunysuffolk.edu
Established: 1959 — Annual Undergrad Tuition & Fees (In-District): N/A
Enrollment: N/A — Coed
Affiliation or Control: State/Local — IRS Status: 501(c)3
Highest Offering: Associate Degree
Accreditation: M, ADNUR, CAHIIM, DIETT, EMT, OTA, PNUR, PTAA

02 Campus CEO/Executive Dean .... Dr. Irene RIOS
05 Assoc Dean of Academic Affairs .... Dr. Sandra SPROWS
05 Assoc Dean of Academic Affairs .... Dr. Fara AFSHAR
32 Assoc Dean of Student Affairs .... Dr. Edward MARTINEZ
37 Director of Financial Aid .... Ms. Renee NUNZIATO
35 Assistant Dean of Student Affairs .... Dr. Katherine AGUIRRE
08 Interim Head Librarian .... Ms. Dana ANTONUCCI-DURGAN
13 Director of Enterprise Applications .... Mr. Christopher T. BLAKE
18 Director Facilities/Physical Plant .... Mr. Steve HARTMANN
36 Asst Dean Stdnt Affs/Dir Career Svc .... Ms. Tania VELAZQUEZ
92 Coordinator Honors Program .... Mr. Albin COFONE
10 Admin Director of Business Affairs .... Mr. John CIENSKI
90 Coord of Instructional Technology .... Vacant
91 Assoc Director Data Center .... Mr. John GANNON

Sullivan County Community College (B)

112 College Road, Loch Sheldrake NY 12759-5721

County: Sullivan — FICE Identification: 002879
Unit ID: 195988
Telephone: (845) 434-5750 — Carnegie Class: Assoc/MT-VT-Mix Trad/Non
FAX Number: (845) 434-4806 — Calendar System: Semester
URL: www.sunysullivan.edu
Established: 1962 — Annual Undergrad Tuition & Fees (In-District): $6,310
Enrollment: 1,701 — Coed
Affiliation or Control: State/Local — IRS Status: 501(c)3
Highest Offering: Associate Degree
Accreditation: M, ACBSP, COARC

01 President .... Mr. John (Jay) QUAINTANCE
05 Int VP Academic & Student Affs .... Mr. Lawrence WEILL
10 Chief Financial Officer/Controller .... Ms. Faith DEMING
32 Dean Student Development Services .... Mr. Chris DEPEW
49 Dean of Liberal Arts & Sciences .... Ms. Rosemarie HANOFEE
31 Dean of Community Outreach .... Vacant
07 Director Admissions & Recruiting .... Ms. Christina BUCKLER
84 Student Enrollment Specialist .... Mr. Frank SINIGAGLIA
41 Director of Athletics .... Mr. Chris DEPEW
15 Director of Human Resources .... Ms. Stephanie GREENO
09 Director Institutional Research .... Dr. Jeffrey KEEFER
38 Director Student Counseling .... Vacant
13 Director Institutional Technology .... Mr. Quazi RAHMAN
19 Director Public Safety .... Mr. Matt LASPISA
06 Dir Registration Services/Registrar .... Ms. Anne MARCHAL
26 Dean of Communications .... Ms. Eleanor DAVIS
04 Dir Executive Operations/AA to BOT .... Ms. Maura CAYCHO
37 Director Student Financial Aid .... Ms. Keri WHITEHEAD

Swedish Institute-College of Health Sciences (C)

151 W 26th Street, New York NY 10001

County: New York — FICE Identification: 021700
Unit ID: 196389
Telephone: (212) 924-5900 — Carnegie Class: Spec 2-yr-Health
FAX Number: (212) 924-7600 — Calendar System: Semester
URL: www.swedishinstitute.edu
Established: 1916 — Annual Undergrad Tuition & Fees: $24,040
Enrollment: 765 — Coed
Affiliation or Control: Proprietary — IRS Status: Proprietary
Highest Offering: Associate Degree
Accreditation: ACCSC, SURGT

01 President and CEO .... Mr. Michael S. BOTTRILL
10 Director of Finance .... Mr. Nathan FIELDS
05 Chief Academic Officer .... Dr. Joseph BALATBAT
07 Director of Admissions/COO .... Mr. Derrick RUFFIN
88 VP for Program Development .... Mr. John KATOMSKI
88 Dean of Advanced Personal Training .... Mr. Vincent METZO
88 Dean for Massage Therapy .... Ms. Ericka CLINTON
66 Dean of Nursing .... Ms. Hillory THORPE
13 Director of Information Technology .... Vacant
32 Director of Student Services .... Ms. Kathlyn GUEST
26 Director of Public Relations .... Vacant
37 Financial Aid Director .... Ms. Anuvita PARBHU
08 Director of Library Services .... Mr. Nicholas LONG
06 Registrar .... Ms. Qiana HORTON
113 Bursar .... Ms. Beatriz ACEVEDO
51 Director of Continuing Education .... Ms. Tania OGULLUKIAN
40 Bookstore Manager .... Mr. Dan YUEN
36 Director of Career Services .... Mr. Richard GARDNER

Syracuse University (D)

900 South Crouse Avenue, Syracuse NY 13244

County: Onondaga — FICE Identification: 002882
Unit ID: 196413
Telephone: (315) 443-1870 — Carnegie Class: DU-Highest
FAX Number: (315) 443-3503 — Calendar System: Semester
URL: www.syr.edu
Established: 1870 — Annual Undergrad Tuition & Fees: $55,926
Enrollment: 21,322 — Coed
Affiliation or Control: Independent Non-Profit — IRS Status: 501(c)3
Highest Offering: Doctorate
Accreditation: M, AAQEP, ART, AUD, CACREP, CIDA, CLPSY, DIETD, DIETI, FEPAC, JOUR, LAW, LIB, MFCD, MUS, PH, SCPSY, SP, SPAA, SW

01 Chancellor & President .... Mr. Kent SYVERUD
05 Vice Chancellor/Provost/CAO .... Dr. Gretchen RITTER
10 Int Sr Vice President & CFO .... Ms. Gwenn JUDGE
43 Sr VP and General Counsel .... Mr. Daniel J. FRENCH
100 Sr VP and Chief of Staff .... Ms. Candace CAMPBELL JACKSON
111 Chief Advancement Officer/SVP .... Mr. Matthew TER MOLEN
32 Sr VP Student Experience .... Mr. Allen GROVES
101 SVP/Secretary Board of Trustees .... Ms. Lisa A. DOLAK
88 SVP for Academic Operations .... Mr. Steve BENNETT
41 Athletic Director .... Mr. John WILDHACK
26 SVP & Chief Marketing Officer .... Ms. Dara J. ROYER
21 Comptroller .... Ms. Jean B. GALLIPEAU
15 Sr VP/Chief Human Resources Officer .... Mr. Andrew GORDON
20 Assoc Provost Faculty Affairs .... Ms. LaVonda REED
20 Assoc Prov for Academic Affairs .... Dr. Chris JOHNSON
13 VP Information Technology/CIO .... Mr. Samuel SCOZZAFAVA
46 Vice Pres for Research .... Dr. Ramesh RAINA
48 Dean School of Architecture .... Dr. Michael A. SPEAKS
49 Dean College of Arts & Sciences .... Dr. Karin RUHLANDT
58 Assoc Prov Grad Stds/Dean Grad Sch .... Dr. Peter VANABLE
08 Dean of University Libraries .... Mr. David SEAMAN
53 Dean School of Education .... Dr. Joanna O. MASINGILA
76 Dean Col of Sport & Human Dynamics .... Dr. Diane LYDEN MURPHY
54 Dean Col Engineering/Computer Sci .... Dr. J. Cole SMITH
62 Dean iSchool .... Mr. Rajiv DEWAN
61 Dean College of Law .... Dr. Craig M. BOISE
50 Dean Whitman School of Management .... Dr. Eugene ANDERSON
60 Dean Newhouse Sch Public Comm .... Mr. Mark LODATO
57 Dean Col Visual & Performing Arts .... Dr. Michael TICK
51 Dean University College .... Dr. Michael FRASCIELLO
07 Dean of Admissions .... Dr. Maurice A. HARRIS
42 Dean Hendricks Chapel .... Rev. Brian KONKOL
88 Vice Chancellor Strat Init & Innov .... Dr. Michael HAYNIE
18 VP and Chief Facilities Officer .... Mr. Pete SALA
19 SVP Safety/Chief Law Enforce Ofcr .... Mr. Anthony CALLISTO
28 Chief Diversity Officer .... Dr. Keith ALFORD
122 Asst Dean Fraternity/Sorority Affs .... Ms. Pam PETER

Talmudical Institute of Upstate New York (E)

769 Park Avenue, Rochester NY 14607-3046

County: Monroe — FICE Identification: 025506
Unit ID: 196440
Telephone: (585) 473-2810 — Carnegie Class: Not Classified
FAX Number: (585) 442-0417 — Calendar System: Semester
URL: tiuny.org
Established: 1974 — Annual Undergrad Tuition & Fees: $6,150
Enrollment: 8 — Male
Affiliation or Control: Independent Non-Profit — IRS Status: 501(c)3
Highest Offering: Second Talmudic Degree
Accreditation: RABN

01 Dean .... Rabbi Menachem DAVIDOWITZ
03 Executive Vice President .... Rabbi Shlomo NOBLE

Talmudical Seminary of Bobov (F)

5120 New Utrecht Avenue, Brooklyn NY 11204-1108

County: Kings — FICE Identification: 041155
Unit ID: 451404
Telephone: (718) 854-8700 — Carnegie Class: Spec-4-yr-Faith
FAX Number: (718) 854-8707 — Calendar System: Semester
Established: 2005 — Annual Undergrad Tuition & Fees: $10,200
Enrollment: 423 — Male
Affiliation or Control: Independent Non-Profit — IRS Status: 501(c)3
Highest Offering: First Talmudic Degree
Accreditation: RABN

01 Dean .... Rabbi Joshua RUBIN
37 Director Student Financial Aid .... Josef DEUTSCH
06 Registrar .... Solomon GORDON

Talmudical Seminary Oholei Torah (G)

667 Eastern Parkway, Brooklyn NY 11213-3397

County: Kings — FICE Identification: 012011
Unit ID: 196431
Telephone: (718) 774-5050 — Carnegie Class: Spec-4-yr-Faith
FAX Number: (718) 778-0784 — Calendar System: Semester
URL: tsot.edu/
Established: 1956 — Annual Undergrad Tuition & Fees: $10,300
Enrollment: 331 — Male
Affiliation or Control: Independent Non-Profit — IRS Status: 501(c)3
Highest Offering: First Talmudic Degree
Accreditation: RABN

01 President .... Mr. Zalman CHEIN
05 Dean .... Elchonon LESCHES
10 Business Officer .... Dov KLYNE
37 Financial Aid Officer .... Sholom ROSENFELD

Teachers College, Columbia University (H)

525 West 120th Street, New York NY 10027

County: New York — FICE Identification: 003979
Unit ID: 196468
Telephone: (212) 678-3000 — Carnegie Class: DU-Higher
FAX Number: (212) 678-4048 — Calendar System: Semester
URL: www.tc.columbia.edu
Established: 1887 — Annual Graduate Tuition & Fees: N/A
Enrollment: 4,547 — Coed
Affiliation or Control: Independent Non-Profit — IRS Status: 501(c)3
Highest Offering: Doctorate; No Undergraduates
Accreditation: M, AAQEP, ABAI, CLPSY, COPSY, DIET, DIETI, MPCAC, PH, SCPSY, SP

01 President .... Dr. Thomas R. BAILEY
05 Provost & VP for Academic Affairs .... Vacant
111 Vice Pres for Inst Advancement .... Ms. Kelly MOODY
10 Vice Pres Finance & Operations .... Mr. Henry PERKOWSKI
11 Vice Pres for Administration .... Ms. Lisa SEALES
22 Vice Pres for Diversity/Cmty Affs .... Ms. Janice S. ROBINSON
88 VP Sch/Cmty Prtnrshp/Spec Adviser .... Vacant
21 Assoc Vice Pres/Controller .... Ms. Elisha RODRIGUEZ
15 Asst VP Human Res/Chief HR Officer .... Ms. Robyn DAVIS-MAHONEY
18 Asst VP Facilities .... Mr. Brian ALFORD
100 Chief of Staff .... Dr. Catherine EMBREE
13 Chief Information Officer .... Mr. Dan ARACENA
08 Library Director .... Ms. Jennifer GOVAN
19 Director Public Safety .... Mr. John DEANGELIS
43 General Counsel .... Mr. Michael FEIERMAN
29 Director Alumni Relations .... Vacant
32 Vice Provost for Student Affairs .... Dr. Thomas ROCK
84 Chief Enrollment Officer .... Dr. Tania CASTAÑEDA
04 Admin Assistant to the President .... Ms. Crystal WILSON
06 Registrar .... Ms. Megan MASSARO
07 AVP for Admission & Enrollment .... Ms. Kate BRITTAIN
37 Director of Financial Aid .... Mr. Thomas ZARKOS
86 Director Government Relations .... Mr. Matthew CAMP

† Affiliated with Columbia University in the City of New York.

Tompkins Cortland Community College (I)

170 North Street, PO Box 139, Dryden NY 13053-8504

County: Tompkins — FICE Identification: 006788
Unit ID: 196565
Telephone: (607) 844-8211 — Carnegie Class: Assoc/HT-High Non
FAX Number: (607) 844-9665 — Calendar System: Semester
URL: www.TompkinsCortland.edu
Established: 1968 — Annual Undergrad Tuition & Fees (In-District): $6,547
Enrollment: 4,764 — Coed
Affiliation or Control: State/Local — IRS Status: 501(c)3
Highest Offering: Associate Degree
Accreditation: M, ADNUR

01 Administrator in Charge .... Dr. Paul REIFENHEISER
05 Provost and VP of Academic Affairs .... Dr. Paul REIFENHEISER
10 VP for Finance and Administration .... Mr. Bill TALBOT
32 Vice President for Student Services .... Mr. Greg MCCALLEY
15 VP for Human Resources .... Ms. Sharon CLARK
31 Asst VP for College Relations .... Ms. Deb MOHLENHOFF
20 Associate Provost .... Dr. Malvika TALWAR
21 Comptroller .... Ms. Kathleen MCCONNELL
08 Library Director .... Mr. Gregg KIEHL
84 Associate Dean for Enrollment Mgmt .... Ms. LaSonya GRIGGS
121 Director of Student Success Service . Ms. Michelle NIGHTINGALE
37 Director of Financial Aid .... Ms. Tamara OLIVER
26 Director of Communications .... Mr. Bryan CHAMBALA
07 Assoc Director of Admissions .... Mr. Kar-Leam TOXEY
13 Chief Information Officer .... Mr. Timothy DENSMORE
19 Director of Safety & Security .... Mr. John GEBO
41 Athletic Director .... Mr. Mick R. MCDANIEL

39 Director of Residence Life .... Vacant
18 Director of Facilities .... Vacant
28 Chief Diversity Officer/Dir ODESS .... Mr. Seth THOMPSON
04 Exec Assistant to the President .... Ms. Jan BRHEL
102 Exec Director Foundation .... Ms. Julie GERG

Torah Temimah Talmudical Seminary (A)

3323 Richmond Avenue, Staten Island NY 10312
County: Kings FICE Identification: 021916
Unit ID: 196583
Telephone: (718) 853-8500 Carnegie Class: Spec-4-yr-Faith
FAX Number: (718) 854-0872 Calendar System: Semester
Established: 1978 Annual Undergrad Tuition & Fees: $11,050
Enrollment: 45 Male
Affiliation or Control: Independent Non-Profit IRS Status: 501(c)3
Highest Offering: Second Talmudic Degree
Accreditation: RABN

01 President & Dean .... Rabbi Tzvi MARGULIES
06 Registrar .... Rabbi Moshe SCHACHAR
37 Financial Aid Administrator .... Mr. Martin WALDMAN
11 Administrator .... Rabbi Betzalel BUSEL

*Touro University - Executive Offices (B)

50 West 47th Street, Fl 14, New York NY 10036
County: New York Identification: 667405
Unit ID: 196592
Telephone: (646) 565-6000 Carnegie Class: N/A
FAX Number: N/A
URL: www.touro.edu

01 President/Chief Executive Officer .... Dr. Alan KADISH
03 Executive Vice President .... Rabbi Moshe D. KRUPKA
10 Senior Vice President & CFO .... Mr. Melvin M. NESS
05 Senior Vice President and Provost .... Dr. Patricia E. SALKIN
43 Senior VP of Legal Affairs .... Mr. Michael NEWMAN
11 Senior Vice President of Operations .. Mr. Jeffrey ROSENGARTEN
13 VP/Chief Information Officer .... Dr. Franklin STEEN
20 Touro Provost for Biomedical Affair .... Dr. Edward HALPERIN
116 Chief Internal Auditor .... Dr. Sabine CHARLES
46 Sr VP Rsrch Affs/Chf Biomed Rsrch .... Dr. Salomon AMAR
88 VP Student Administrative Services .... Mr. Matthew F. BONILLA
20 VP Undergrad Educ/Dean of Faculty .... Dr. Stanley L. BOYLAN
32 VP Plng & Assessment/Dean of Stdnts .... Mr. Robert GOLDSCHMIDT
106 VP Online Ed & Dean Landers Women .... Dr. Marian STOLTZ-LOIKE
88 Liaison European Branch Campuses .... Dr. Simcha FISHBANE
85 VP for International Affairs .... Dr. Israel SINGER
86 Assoc VP of Govt Relations .... Mr. Clifford METH
56 Vice President IPE/Dean NYSCAS .... Dr. Judah WEINBERGER
88 Vice Pres of Community Engagement .... Rabbi Alan G. CINER
31 VP of Community Affairs .... Dr. Martin KATZENSTEIN
111 Vice Pres Institutional Advancement .... Mr. Paul GLASSER
110 AVP Institutional Advancement .... Ms. Beth GORIN
26 Dir of Communication/External Rels .... Ms. Elisheva SCHLAM
105 Director Web Services .... Ms. Lisa HALBERSTAM
21 Controller .... Mr. Stuart LIPPMAN
114 Director of Budget & Planning .... Mr. David BELL
20 Assoc Provost for Acad Afrs GR/PR .... Dr. Nelly LEJTER MORALES
88 Asso Provost for Special Projects .... Dr. Louis PRIMAVERA
53 Sp Asst Provost for New Initiatives .... Dr. Jacob EASLEY, II
09 AVP Inst Research & Effectiveness .... Mr. Evan HOBERMAN
88 Asst Provost Accreditation/Faculty .... Ms. Denise VANDERSAL
88 Dir Strat Initiative/Dir CETL .... Dr. Rima ARANHA
88 Dir Reg Compliance/Title IX Coord .... Mr. Matthew LIEBERMAN
88 Assoc Gen Counsel/Reg Compliance .... Mrs. Nicole BARNETT
96 Director of Purchasing .... Ms. Wanda HERNANDEZ
18 Dir of Facilities/Real Estate .... Mr. Mark GOODMAN
15 Chief Human Resources Officer .... Mr. Thomas MODERO
16 Sr Dir of HR Policies & Operations .... Mr. Elan BARAM
19 Director of Security .... Ms. Lydia PEREZ
19 Dir of Emergency Preparedness .... Ms. Shoshana YEHUDAH
91 Chief Info Security Officer .... Ms. Patricia CIUFFO
14 Deputy CIO .... Ms. Renate LAINE
14 Deputy CIO .... Mr. Charles MATTIELLO
35 AVP Student Administrative Services .... Mr. Matthew CONNELL
06 University Registrar .... Ms. Lidia MEINDL
113 Bursar & Exec Dir Student Finances .... Ms. Inbal HAIMOVICH
37 Director Financial Aid Operations .... Ms. Yelena VOLIS
07 Director of Admissions .... Dr. Benjamin ENOMA
88 Dir Strat Plng/Analysis & Report .... Mr. Tzvi ELEFF
88 VP PA Pgm Dev & Operations .... Dr. Joseph TOMMASINO
08 Director of Libraries .... Ms. Bashe SIMON
108 Dir of Assessment and Evaluation .... Dr. Eric LINDEN
04 Executive Asst to President .... Ms. Elaine GOLDBERG
88 Asst to Exec Vice President .... Ms. Amy JACOBS
88 Exec Asst to SVP Acad Affs and Prov .... Mrs. Chana YURMAN
41 Athletic Director .... Mr. Irv BADER

*Touro University - Main Campus (C)

320 West 31st St, New York NY 10001
County: New York FICE Identification: 010142
Telephone: (212) 463-0400 Carnegie Class: Not Classified
FAX Number: N/A Calendar System: Semester
URL: www.touro.edu
Established: 1971 Annual Undergrad Tuition & Fees: N/A
Enrollment: N/A Coed
Affiliation or Control: Independent Non-Profit IRS Status: 501(c)3
Highest Offering: Doctorate
Accreditation: M, ARCPA, CAEP, NURSE, OT, PTA, RAD, SP, SW

01 President/Chief Executive Officer .... Dr. Alan KADISH
03 Executive Vice President .... Rabbi Moshe D. KRUPKA
35 VP Student Admin Services .... Mr. Matthew F. BONILLA
66 Dir Sch of Hlth Science .... Prof. Sandra RUSSO
07 Director of Admissions .... Mr. Brian DIELE
85 Vice Pres International Affairs .... Dr. Israel SINGER
53 Dean Graduate Sch of Education .... Dr. Jacob EASLEY, II
58 Dean Graduate Sch of Jewish Studies .... Dr. Michael A. SHMIDMAN
72 Dean Grad Sch of Tech .... Dr. Issac HERSKOWITZ
06 University Registrar .... Ms. Lidia MEINDL
08 Director of Libraries .... Ms. Bashe SIMON
88 Assoc Dean Grad Sch Jewish Studies .... Dr. Moshe SHERMAN
88 Assoc Dean Grad Sch of Education .... Dr. Charity DACEY
88 Assoc Dean Sch of Health Sciences .... Dr. Rivka MOLINSKY
88 Assoc Dean Grad Sch of Education .... Dr. Yuriy KARPOV
88 Associate Dean NYSCAS .... Mr. Lenin ORTEGA
88 Associate Dean NYSCAS .... Ms. Elvira TSIRULNIK
88 Assoc Dean Acad Afrs SHS, Dir PsyD .... Dr. Frank GARDENER
07 Director Undergraduate Admissions .... Mr. Arthur WIGFALL
123 Director Graduate Admissions .... Dr. Benjamin ENOMA
88 Asst Dean Grad Sch Ed/Chair/Lead .... Dr. Nilda SOTO-RUIZ
88 Chair Grad Sch Ed Disabilities .... Dr. Laurie BOBLEY
88 Interim Chair Grad Sch Ed Sch Cnsli .... Dr. Yair MAMAN
88 Dir Grad Sch Ed Lander Center .... Dr. Velma L. COBB
53 Chair Grad Sch Ed Instruc Tech .... Mr. Isaac HERSKOWITZ
88 Chair Grad Sch Ed Early Child/Sp Ed .... Dr. Susan COUREY
88 Chair Grad Sch Ed Child Ed/Sp Ed . Dr. Elina LAMPERT-SHEPEL
88 Chair Grad Sch Ed Jewish Chld/Sp Ed .... Dr. Jeffrey LICHTMAN
88 Chair Grad Sch Ed Literacy .... Dr. Elaine NIKOLAKAKOS
76 Chair Sch Hlth Sci Physical Therapy .... Dr. Jill HORBACEWICZ
88 Chair Grad Sch Ed TESOL .... Dr. Olga DEJESUS
88 Chair Grad Sch Ed Math Ed .... Dr. Brenda STRASSFELD
75 Chairperson OT Sch Hlth Sci .... Dr. Stephanie DAPICE-WONG
88 Dir Grad Sch Ed Clinical Practice .... Dr. Ruth BEST
88 Director Physician Assistant .... Ms. Paula BOYLE
106 VP Online Educ/Dean Womens Division .... Dr. Marian STOLTZ-LOIKE
10 Senior Vice President & CFO .... Mr. Mevin M. NESS
05 Senior Vice President and Provost .... Dr. Patricia SALKIN
43 Senior Vice President Legal Affairs .... Mr. Michael NEWMAN
11 Senior Vice President of Operations .. Mr. Jeffrey ROSENGARTEN
13 VP, Chief Information Officer .... Dr. Franklin STEEN
86 Assoc VP of Govt Affairs .... Mr. Clifford METH
116 Director of Internal Audit .... Dr. Sabine CHARLES
05 Provost for Biomedical Research .... Dr. Salomon AMAR
20 VP Undergrad Ed/Dean Facilities .... Dr. Stanley BOYLAN
32 VP Plng Assessment/Dean Students ... Dr. Robert GOLDSCHMIDT
05 Touro Provost Biomedical Affairs .... Dr. Edward HALPERIN
31 VP Community Engagement .... Rabbi Alan CINER
88 Liaison European Branch Campuses .... Dr. Simcha FISHBANE
31 VP Community Affairs .... Mr. Martin KATZENSTEIN
56 Vice President IPE/Dean NYSCAS .... Dr. Judah WEINBERGER
111 VP Institutional Advancement .... Mr. Paul GLASSER
09 AVP Insti. Research & Effectiveness .... Mr. Evan HOBERMAN
52 Dean College of Dental Medicine .... Dr. Ronnie MYERS
63 Dean College Osteopathic Medicine .... Dr. Kenneth STEIER
61 Dean Touro Law Center .... Ms. Elena LANGAN
67 Dean College of Pharmacy .... Dr. Henry COHEN
76 Dean School of Health Sciences .... Dr. Steven LORENZET
70 Dean Grad Sch of Social Work .... Dr. Nancy GALLINA
12 Dean Lander College for Men .... Dr. Moshe SOKOL
49 Dean Lander College Arts & Sciences .... Dr. Henry ABRAMSON
38 Dean Advising & Counseling .... Dr. Avery HOROWITZ
50 Dean Grad School Business .... Dr. Mary LO RE
51 Asst Dean School Lifelong Education .... Dr. Briendy STERN
37 Dir Reg Compliance/Financial Aid .... Mr. Matthew LIEBERMAN
17 VP, PA Prg Dev & Oper, Chr, PA Prg ... Dr. Joseph TOMMASINO
88 Chair SHS Speech Language Pathology .... Ms. Hindy LUBINSKY
83 Chr Sch Hlth Sci Behavioral Science .... Dr. Faye FRIED-WALKENFELD
110 AVP Institutional Advancement .... Ms. Beth GORIN
110 Asst Dean-Institutional Advancement .... Ms. Anastasia HAGAN
91 Chief Info Security Officer .... Ms. Patricia CIUFFO
19 Director of Security .... Ms. Lydia PEREZ
117 Director Emergency Preparedness .... Ms. Shoshana YEHUDAH
15 Director of Human Resources .... Mr. Thomas MODERO
96 Director of Purchasing .... Ms. Wanda HERNANDEZ
18 Director Facilities/Real Estate .... Mr. Mark GOODMAN
21 Controller .... Mr. Stuart LIPPMAN
26 Dir Communications/External Rels .... Ms. Elisheva SCHLAM
36 Director of Student Placement .... Ms. Jodi SMOLEN
04 Executive Asst to President .... Ms. Elaine GOLDBERG
88 Asst to Exec VP .... Ms. Amy JACOBS
104 Director Study Abroad .... Ms. Chana SOSEVSKY
105 Director Web Services .... Ms. Lisa HALBERSTAM
41 Athletic Director .... Mr. Irv BADER
114 Director Budget & Planning .... Mr. David BELL

*Touro University - Flatbush (D)

1602 Avenue J, Brooklyn NY 11230
Telephone: (718) 252-7800 Identification: 770146
Accreditation: &M, CAEP, SP

*Touro University - Harlem (E)

230 West 125th Street, New York NY 10027
Telephone: (646) 981-4500 Identification: 770989
Accreditation: &M, OSTEO, PHAR

*Touro University - Long Island (F)

225 Eastview Drive, Central Islip NY 11722
Telephone: (631) 665-1600 Identification: 770148
Accreditation: &M, ARCPA, CAEP, LAW

*Touro University - Kew Gardens Hills (G)

75-31 150th Street, Kew Gardens Hills NY 11367
Telephone: (718) 820-4800 Identification: 770992
Accreditation: &M

*Touro University, Touro College of Dental Medicine - Westchester New York (H)

19 Skyline Dr, Hawthorne NY 10532
Telephone: (914) 594-3865 Identification: 770991
Accreditation: &M, DENT

*Touro University - Middletown Campus (I)

60 Prospect Avenue, Middletown NY 10940
Telephone: (845) 648-1100 Identification: 770990
Accreditation: &M, #ARCPA, &OSTEO

Trocaire College (J)

360 Choate Avenue, Buffalo NY 14220-2094
County: Erie FICE Identification: 002812
Unit ID: 196653
Telephone: (716) 826-1200 Carnegie Class: Spec-4-yr-Other Health
FAX Number: (716) 828-6109 Calendar System: Semester
URL: www.trocaire.edu
Established: 1958 Annual Undergrad Tuition & Fees: $18,340
Enrollment: 1,376 Coed
Affiliation or Control: Independent Non-Profit IRS Status: 501(c)3
Highest Offering: Baccalaureate
Accreditation: M, ADNUR, CAHIIM, NUR, RAD, SURGT

01 President .... Dr. Bassam M. DEEB
10 VP for Finance .... Mr. Michael CUCINOTTA
05 Vice President for Academic Affairs .... Dr. Richard T. LINN
84 VP for Enrollment & Student Affairs .... Ms. Kathleen SAUNDERS
111 Director of Advancement .... Ms. Colleen STEFFEN
13 Chief Information Officer .... Mr. Kamu PINDIPROLU
88 Special Asst to Pres External Affs .... Ms. Jacqueline MATHENY
66 Dean McAuley School Nursing .... Dr. Linda J. KERWIN
15 Chief Human Resources Officer .... Ms. Janet PETERS
07 Dean of Admissions .... Mr. Mark PETRIE
37 Director of Financial Aid .... Mr. Jonathan HUDACK
25 Grant Coordinator .... Dr. Deidre O'ROURKE
06 Registrar .... Ms. Dorothy WORRALL
121 Dir Advisement & Student Support .... Dr. Christine RYAN
88 Director Learning Center .... Mr. Derrick GUNTER
124 Director of Student Engagement .... Ms. Lauren RECZEK
18 Facilities Director .... Mr. Richard MCGILVRAY
40 Manager Bookstore .... Mr. Brent MERRILL
76 Dean of Allied Health & Professions .... Dr. Linda KERWIN
108 Coordinator of Assessment/Research .... Ms. Kate LEVY
103 VP for Innovation and Advancement .... Dr. Gary SMITH
36 Coord of Career Services .... Mr. David FERRIS, JR.
04 Admin Assistant to the President .... Ms. Michelle PHILLIPS
08 Director of Library Services .... Ms. Michele BRANCATO
38 Director Wellness Center .... Ms. Genevieve KRULY

Ulster County Community College (K)

491 Cottekill Road, PO Box 557, Stone Ridge NY 12484
County: Ulster FICE Identification: 002880
Unit ID: 196699
Telephone: (845) 687-5000 Carnegie Class: Assoc/HT-High Non
FAX Number: (845) 687-5083 Calendar System: Semester
URL: www.sunyulster.edu
Established: 1961 Annual Undergrad Tuition & Fees (In-District): $5,740
Enrollment: 3,089 Coed
Affiliation or Control: State/Local IRS Status: 501(c)3
Highest Offering: Associate Degree
Accreditation: M, ADNUR

01 President .... Dr. Alison BUCKLEY
100 Chief of Staff .... Ms. Jennifer ZELL
84 Dean of Enroll Mgmt & Student Affs .... Ms. Megan SHEELEY
05 VP for Academic Affairs .... Mr. Kevin STONER
51 VP of Continuing & Prof Educ .... Mr. Christopher MARX
10 VP for Administrative Services .... Ms. Jamie CAPUANO
13 Chief Info Technology Officer .... Mr. Dennis MICHAELS
28 Chief Diversity Officer .... Ms. Candice VANDYKE
111 Exec Dir of Inst Advance & Ext Rels .... Ms. Lorraine SALMON
88 Director of Accessibility Services .... Mr. Eric FORTUNE-READER
08 Director of Library Services .... Ms. Kari MACK
37 Director of Financial Aid .... Mr. Christopher CHANG
06 Registrar .... Ms. Sarah FAJARDO
41 Asst Dean Students/Athletic Dir .... Mr. Matthew BRENNIE
19 Acting Dir of Safety & Security .... Mr. John SCHATZEL
26 Director of Marketing & Media .... Ms. Deborah KAUFMAN
36 Dir Student Place/Acad Support Svcs .... Ms. Jane KITHCART
18 Director of Plant Operations .... Mr. Donald STEWARD, III
09 Director of Institutional Research .... Ms. Laura FOSS
103 AVP Workforce Development .... Mr. Christopher MARX
15 Director of Personnel Services .... Mrs. Debra DELANOY
11 Dean of Admin Services - Finance .... Ms. Amy WINTERS

16 Dean for Admin Op/Payroll & HR .... Mr. CJ RIOUX
38 Crisis Counselor/Student Affairs .... Ms. Ashley BROWN
96 Coord Procurement/General Services .... Vacant
101 Secretary of the Institution/Board .... Ms. Jennifer ZELL
121 Assistant Dean of Student Success .... Ms. Wendy BEESLEY
78 Asst Dean Workforce/Career/Apprent .... Mrs. Barbara REER
22 Dir Affirm Act/Equal Oppty/Title IX .... Ms. Jamie CAPUANO

Unification Theological Seminary (A)

4 West 43rd Street 2nd Floor, New York NY 10036
County: Manhattan FICE Identification: 032163
Unit ID: 246789
Telephone: (212) 563-6647 Carnegie Class: Spec-4-yr-Faith
FAX Number: (212) 563-6431 Calendar System: Semester
URL: www.uts.edu
Established: 1975 Annual Undergrad Tuition & Fees: N/A
Enrollment: 130 Coed
Affiliation or Control: Unification Church IRS Status: 501(c)3
Highest Offering: Doctorate
Accreditation: M

01 President .... Dr. Thomas WARD
05 Academic Dean .... Dr. Keisuke NODA
11 Vice President .... Dr. Michael MICKLER
88 Director of Field Education .... Dr. Thomas WARD
10 Director of Finances .... Mr. Frank ZOCHOL
06 Registrar .... Mrs. Ute DELANEY
08 Librarian .... Mr. Robert WAGNER
37 Student Financial Aid Director .... Mr. Henry CHRISTOPHER
18 Plant Director .... Mr. Carl VERDERBER
84 Dean of Enrollment Management .... Mr. Steven BOYD
32 Chief Student Affairs/Student Life .... Mr. Steven BOYD
13 Chief Info Technology Officer .... Mr. Robert PUMPHREY
04 Admin Assistant to the President .... Ms. Christina MIYAKE

Union College (B)

807 Union Street, Schenectady NY 12308-3181
County: Schenectady FICE Identification: 002889
Unit ID: 196866
Telephone: (518) 388-6000 Carnegie Class: Bac-A&S
FAX Number: (518) 388-6800 Calendar System: Trimester
URL: www.union.edu
Established: 1795 Annual Undergrad Tuition & Fees: $59,502
Enrollment: 2,047 Coed
Affiliation or Control: Independent Non-Profit IRS Status: 501(c)3
Highest Offering: Baccalaureate
Accreditation: M

01 President .... Dr. David R. HARRIS
05 Vice Pres Academic Affairs .... Dr. Michele P. ANGRIST
111 Vice President College Relations .... Dr. Robert J. PARKER, JR.
10 AVP for Finance & Administration .... Ms. Marsha R. ANDERSON-BEWERSDORF
07 VP Admissions/Fin Aid/Enrollment ... Mr. Matthew J. MALATESTA
100 Chief of Staff .... Ms. Darcy CZAJKA
22 Chief Diversity Officer .... Vacant
32 VP Student Affairs/Dean of Students .... Mr. Ryan KEYTACK
20 Dean of Studies .... Vacant
13 Chief Information Officer .... Ms. Ellen YU
06 Senior Registrar .... Ms. Sarah FARSAD
08 College Librarian .... Ms. Frances J. MALOY
26 Director of Media and Public Rels .... Mr. Phillip J. WAJDA
37 Director of Financial Aid .... Ms. Linda M. PARKER
38 Director of Student Counseling .... Mr. Marcus S. HOTALING
36 Assoc Director of Career Center .... Mr. Peter A. FOWLER
15 Chief Human Resources Officer .... Mr. Tye A. DIENES
41 Assoc Director of Athletics .... Ms. Beth TIFFANY
19 Director Campus Safety .... Mr. Thomas CONSTANTINE
39 Director Residence Life .... Ms. Amanda J. IVERSON
09 Director of Institutional Research .... Mr. Len SCHLEGEL
108 Director Institutional Assessment .... Mr. Ashok RAMASUBRAMANIAN

† Tuition figure is a comprehensive fees figure.

Union Theological Seminary (C)

3041 Broadway, New York NY 10027-5792
County: New York FICE Identification: 002890
Unit ID: 196884
Telephone: (212) 662-7100 Carnegie Class: Spec-4-yr-Faith
FAX Number: (212) 280-1416 Calendar System: Semester
URL: www.utsnyc.edu
Established: 1836 Annual Graduate Tuition & Fees: N/A
Enrollment: 226 Coed
Affiliation or Control: Independent Non-Profit IRS Status: 501(c)3
Highest Offering: Doctorate; No Undergraduates
Accreditation: M, THEOL

01 President .... Dr. Serene JONES
88 Senior Strategic Advisor .... Mr. Fred DAVIE
10 VP Finance & Operations .... Ms. Nina WONG
30 VP for Development .... Ms. Rita WALTERS
05 VP of Academic Affairs and Dean .... Dr. Su YON PAK
32 Dean of Students .... Ms. Abigail ASGARALLI
78 Senior Director of Integrative Educ .... Dr. Su Y. PAK
07 VP for Admissions and Financial Aid .... Ms. Vanessa HUTCHINSON
06 Registrar .... Ms. Anjali MONCRIEFFE
18 Assoc Vice Pres Building/Grounds .... Vacant
39 Director Housing/Campus Services . Mr. Michael ORZECHOWSKI
15 Chief Human Resources Officer ..... Ms. Diana TORRES-PETRILLI
100 Chief of Staff .... Mr. Jody WEST
13 Chief Info Technology Officer (CIO) .... Mr. Donald JOSHUA
29 Asst Dir Alumni Relations .... Mr. Kevin BENTLEY
37 Director Student Financial Aid .... Ms. Melissa DESRAVINES
04 Admin Assistant to the President .... Mr. Thomas ARBUCKLE, II
28 Director of Diversity .... Rev. Karmen SMITH

United Talmudical Seminary (D)

191 Rodney Street, Brooklyn NY 11211-7900
County: Kings FICE Identification: 011189
Unit ID: 197018
Telephone: (718) 963-9770 Carnegie Class: Spec-4-yr-Faith
FAX Number: (718) 963-9775 Calendar System: Semester
Established: 1949 Annual Undergrad Tuition & Fees: $15,300
Enrollment: 3,118 Male
Affiliation or Control: Independent Non-Profit IRS Status: 501(c)3
Highest Offering: Second Talmudic Degree
Accreditation: RABN

01 Dean .... Rabbi Zalman TEITLBAUM
05 Assoc Dean Scholastic Services .... Rabbi Yeruchem DEUTSCH
37 Financial Aid Administrator .... Mr. Bernard KATZ
10 Administrator .... Mr. Solomon GREENFELD

University of Rochester (E)

500 Joseph C. Wilson Boulevard, Rochester NY 14627
County: Monroe FICE Identification: 002894
Unit ID: 195030
Telephone: (585) 275-2121 Carnegie Class: DU-Highest
FAX Number: (585) 275-0359 Calendar System: Semester
URL: www.rochester.edu
Established: 1850 Annual Undergrad Tuition & Fees: $58,241
Enrollment: 11,741 Coed
Affiliation or Control: Independent Non-Profit IRS Status: 501(c)3
Highest Offering: Doctorate
Accreditation: M, CACREP, CAMPEP, CLPSY, DENT, IPSY, MED, MFCD, MLS, MUS, NNPR, NURSE, PAST, PDPSY, PH

01 President .... Mrs. Sarah C. MANGELSDORF
05 Provost .... Mr. David FIGLIO
10 EVP Administration & Finance/CFO .... Ms. Elizabeth MILAVEC
17 Sr Vice Pres Health Sci/Med Ctr CEO .... Dr. Mark B. TAUBMAN
115 Sr Vice Pres/Chief Investment Ofcr .... Mr. Douglas PHILLIPS
111 SVP & Chief Advancement Officer .... Mr. Thomas FARRELL
43 Vice Pres & General Counsel .... Ms. Donna G. PAYNE
28 Int Vice Pres Equity/Inclusion/CDO .... Ms. Adrienne MORGAN
26 Vice Pres Communications .... Ms. Elizabeth STAUDERMAN
13 Vice Pres/CIO for the University .... Vacant
58 Vice Provost/Univ Dean of Grad Ed .... Ms. Melissa STURGE-APPLE
100 Pres Chief of Staff/Board Secretary .... Mr. Tony GREEN
32 Dean of Students .... Mr. Matthew BURNS
08 Dean River Campus Libraries .... Ms. Mary Ann MAVRINAC
49 Dean of School of Arts & Sciences .... Ms. Gloria CULVER
88 Dean of Arts/Sci & Engr Faculty .... Mr. Donald HALL
54 Dean of Hajim Engineering School .... Ms. Wendi HEINZELMAN
07 Dir of AS&E Undergrad Admissions .... Mr. Jason NEVINGER
37 Director of Financial Aid .... Ms. Samantha VEEDER
108 Assoc Provost Academic Admin .... Ms. Jane Marie SOUZA
114 Sr Assoc VP Budgets & Planning .... Mr. Michael W. ANDREWS
63 Dean School of Medicine & Dentistry .... Dr. Mark B. TAUBMAN
64 Dean of Eastman School of Music .... Mr. Jamal ROSSI
66 Dean of School of Nursing .... Ms. Kathy RIDEOUT
50 Dean of Simon Business School .... Mr. Andrew AINSLIE
53 Dean Warner Grad Sch Educ & Hum Dev .... Vacant
35 Assoc Dean Students Arts/Sci & Engr .... Ms. Anne-Marie ALGIER
23 Chief Medical Officer .... Dr. Michael J. APOSTOLAKOS
52 Dir Eastman Institute Oral Health .... Dr. Eli ELIAV
25 Assoc VP Research & Project Admin .... Ms. Gunta LIDERS
18 Sr AVP Facilities & Services .... Mr. Michael CHIHOSKI
29 AVP Alumni & Constituent Relations .... Dr. Karen CHANCE MERCURIUS
86 Vice Pres Govt/Community Relations .... Mr. Peter J. ROBINSON
96 Assoc Vice Pres Purchasing & Supply .... Mr. Carl TIETJEN
04 Executive Asst to the President .... Ms. Deb DALE
06 University Registrar .... Ms. Tina STURGIS
19 Director of Public Safety .... Mr. Mark T. FISCHER
15 VP/Chief Human Resources Officer .... Ms. Kathleen GALLUCCI
88 Dir of the Memorial Art Gallery .... Mr. Jonathan BINSTOCK
41 Director of Athletics & Recreation .... Mr. George VANDERZWAAG
39 Exec Dir Res Life & Housing Svcs .. Ms. Laurel CONTOMANOLIS
36 Assoc Vice Provost Career Education .... Mr. Joe TESTANI
101 Administrator to Board of Trustees .... Mr. Jack S. BAILEY
42 Director Religious & Spiritual Life .... Rev. Denise YARBROUGH
104 Director Study Abroad .... Ms. Tynelle STEWART
22 AVP Equity & Inclusion .... Ms. Adrienne MORGAN
09 Sr Univ Dir Institutional Research .... Mr. John PODVIN

U.T.A. Mesivta of Kiryas Joel (F)

PO Box 2009, Monroe NY 10949-8509
County: Orange FICE Identification: 038023
Unit ID: 446604
Telephone: (845) 783-9901 Carnegie Class: Spec-4-yr-Faith
FAX Number: (845) 782-3620 Calendar System: Semester
Established: 1999 Annual Undergrad Tuition & Fees: $13,500
Enrollment: 2,268 Male
Affiliation or Control: Independent Non-Profit IRS Status: 501(c)3
Highest Offering: First Talmudic Degree
Accreditation: RABN

00 Chief Executive Officer .... David GOLDBERGER
01 President .... Elias HOROWITZ
05 Rosh Yeshiva .... Rabbi Aharon TEITELBAUM
37 Financial Aid Director .... David SCHWARTZ

Utica University (G)

1600 Burrstone Road, Utica NY 13502-4892
County: Oneida FICE Identification: 002883
Unit ID: 197045
Telephone: (315) 792-3111 Carnegie Class: Masters/L
FAX Number: (315) 792-3292 Calendar System: Semester
URL: www.utica.edu
Established: 1946 Annual Undergrad Tuition & Fees: $22,110
Enrollment: 4,613 Coed
Affiliation or Control: Independent Non-Profit IRS Status: 501(c)3
Highest Offering: Doctorate
Accreditation: M, ACBSP, CONST, DIETC, NURSE, OT, PTA, @SW

01 President .... Dr. Laura CASAMENTO
05 Provost & Vice Pres Academic Aff .... Dr. Todd PFANNESTIEL
10 Vice Pres Financial Affs/Treasurer .... Ms. Pamela SALMON
32 SVP Student Life & Enrollment .... Dr. Jeffrey GATES
04 Special Assistant to the President .... Mr. Anthony VILLANTI
111 AVP of Advancement .... Ms. Amy LINDNER
13 VP for Infrastructure and CIO .... Mr. Matthew S. CARR
28 VP DEI Chief Diversity Officer .... Dr. Anthony M. BAIRD
117 VP for Emergency Management .... Mr. Shad M. CROWE
20 Associate Provost .... Dr. Robert M. HALLIDAY
26 Asst VP Marketing/Communication .... Mr. Kelly L. ADAMS
76 Dean for Health Professions/Educ .... Dr. Ahmed Y. RADWAN
49 Dean for Arts & Sciences .... Dr. Sharon H. WISE
50 Dean for Business & Justice Studies ....Dr. Stephanie R. NESBITT
35 Interim Dean of Students .... Ms. Karen FERRER-MUNIZ
113 Dir of Student Accounting .... Ms. Susan BOUCHER
36 Director Career Readiness .... Ms. Kailea MURRAY
37 Director of Financial Aid .... Ms. Karolina HOLL
06 Registrar .... Mr. Craig DEWAN
30 Director of Development .... Ms. Ashlea SCHAD
41 Director of Physical Educ/Athletics .... Mr. David FONTAINE
39 Director of Student Living .... Ms. Marissa FINCH
13 Dir College Info & Application Svcs .... Mr. Scott HUMPHREY
15 Director of Human Resources .... Ms. Lisa GREEN
107 Exec Dir Corp/Professional Pgms .... Ms. Joni L. PULLIAM
85 Dean of International Education .... Ms. Deborah WILSON-ALLAM
18 Director Facilities Management .... Mr. Daniel C. BOLLANA
19 Director of Campus Safety .... Mr. Musco MILLNER
92 Director Honors Program .... Dr. Lawrence DAY
28 Dir Office of Opportunity Programs .... Mr. John OSSOWSKI
96 Manager of Purchasing .... Ms. Bobbi H. SMOROL
108 Dean of Academic Assessment .... Dr. Ann DAMIANO
08 Head Librarian .... Mr. James K. TELIHA
106 Assoc Prov/VP E-learning .... Dr. Polly SMITH
43 Dir Legal Services/General Counsel ..... Mr. Andrew W. BEAKMAN
09 Assoc Director of Inst Research .... Ms. Brandy GRAY
122 Dir of Col Engagement-Greek Life .... Ms. Lauryn MOORE

Vassar College (H)

124 Raymond Avenue, Poughkeepsie NY 12604-0001
County: Dutchess FICE Identification: 002895
Unit ID: 197133
Telephone: (845) 437-7000 Carnegie Class: Bac-A&S
FAX Number: (845) 437-7187 Calendar System: Semester
URL: www.vassar.edu
Established: 1861 Annual Undergrad Tuition & Fees: $60,930
Enrollment: 2,435 Coed
Affiliation or Control: Independent Non-Profit IRS Status: 501(c)3
Highest Offering: Master's
Accreditation: M

01 President .... Dr. Elizabeth BRADLEY
05 Dean of the Faculty .... Mr. William HOYNES
20 Dean of the College .... Mr. Carlos ALAMO
10 Vice Pres Finance & Administration .... Mr. Bryan SWARTHOUT
13 VP CIS/Chief Information Officer .... Mr. Carlos GARCIA
07 Dean Admission/Financial Aid .... Ms. Sonya SMITH
49 Dean of Studies .... Dr. Benjamin LOTTO
20 Sr Assoc Dean College Prof Dev .... Mr. Edward L. PITTMAN
35 Assoc Dean Col/Dir Campus Activit .... Ms. Teresa QUINN
06 Registrar .... Ms. Colleen MALLET
08 Director of the Libraries .... Mr. Andrew ASHTON
36 Director Career Development Center .... Ms. Stacy Lee SCHNEIDER BINGHAM
15 AVP Human Resources .... Ms. Sarah BAKKE
18 Exec Dir of Facilities Operations .... Mr. William PEABODY
38 Director of Psychological Services .... Dr. Wendy A. FREEDMAN
96 Director of Purchasing .... Ms. Rosaleen CARDILLO
04 Exec Asst to President .... Ms. Veronica PECCIA
104 Director Study Abroad .... Dr. Tracey HOLLAND
19 Director Security/Safety .... Ms. Arlene SABO
29 VP Alumni Relations/Exe Dir AAVC .... Ms. Lisa TESSLER
41 Athletic Director .... Ms. Michelle WALSH

Vaughn College of Aeronautics and Technology (I)

86-01 23rd Avenue, Flushing NY 11369
County: Queens FICE Identification: 002665
Unit ID: 188340
Telephone: (718) 429-6600 Carnegie Class: Bac-Diverse
FAX Number: (718) 429-0671 Calendar System: Semester

URL: www.vaughn.edu
Established: 1932 Annual Undergrad Tuition & Fees: $26,150
Enrollment: 1,442 Coed
Affiliation or Control: Independent Non-Profit IRS Status: 501(c)3
Highest Offering: Master's
Accreditation: M, AAB, IACBE

01 President ... Dr. Sharon B. DEVIVO
10 Vice Pres for Business & Finance ... Mr. Robert G. WALDMANN
84 Vice President Enrollment Services ... Vacant
15 Asst VP College Svcs/Human Resource ... Mr. Michael HARRINGTON
05 Vice Pres of Academic Affairs ... Dr. Paul LAVERGNE
32 VP Student Affairs ... Ms. Kelli SMITH
35 Assoc VP/Dean Student Affairs ... Ms. Elaine T. WHITE
30 Asst VP Development/Alumni Rels ... Mr. Stephen DESALVO
37 Director of Financial Aid ... Ms. Tameika BENNETT
06 Registrar/Assoc VP Enrollment ... Mrs. Beatriz CRUZ
08 Director of Library Services ... Ms. Pamela SOOKRALLI
26 Assoc VP of Public Affairs ... Ms. Maureen KIGGINS
96 Coordinator of Purchasing ... Mr. Manuel ADRIANZEN
09 Manager Institutional Effectiveness ... Mr. Christopher PILEGGI
07 Assoc VP Enrollment ... Mr. Celso ALVAREZ
18 Director of Facilities ... Mr. Justin BURMEISTER
38 Dir Student Counseling/Wellness ... Ms. Stacey DUTIL
13 Asst Director Computer Operations ... Mr. Hamwant (Neil) SINGH
88 Vice Pres Training ... Mr. Domenic PROSCIA
04 Administrative Asst to President ... Ms. Barbara LOCKE
103 Dir Workforce/Career Development ... Ms. Chaundra DANIELS
106 Dir Online Education/E-learning ... Ms. Yelena RUDINSKAYER
41 Athletic Director ... Mr. Ricky MCCOLLUM
19 Director Security/Safety ... Mr. Martin CAPUNAY
101 Secretary of the Institution/Board ... Ms. Barbara LOCKE
39 Dir Resident Life/Student Housing ... Ms. Becky FALTO

Villa Maria College of Buffalo (A)

240 Pine Ridge Road, Buffalo NY 14225-3999
County: Erie FICE Identification: 002896
Unit ID: 197142
Telephone: (716) 896-0700 Carnegie Class: Bac-Diverse
FAX Number: (716) 896-0705 Calendar System: Semester
URL: www.villa.edu
Established: 1960 Annual Undergrad Tuition & Fees: $25,400
Enrollment: 508 Coed
Affiliation or Control: Independent Non-Profit IRS Status: 501(c)3
Highest Offering: Baccalaureate
Accreditation: M, CIDA, MUS, OTA, PTAA

01 President ... Dr. Matthew GIORDANO
05 Vice President for Academic Affairs ... Dr. Ryan HARTNETT
10 Vice President for Finance ... Mr. Richard PINKOWSKI
30 Vice President for Development ... Mrs. Mary ROBINSON
84 VP for Enrollment Mgmt & Operations ... Mr. Brian EMERSON
88 Vice President for Mission ... Dr. Donald MONNIN
20 Dean of Faculty ... Dr. Ann RIVERA
06 Registrar ... Mrs. Erin PAWLAK
07 Director of Admissions ... Ms. Becky STRATHEARN
08 Director of Library Services ... Ms. Lucy WAITE
37 Director of Financial Aid ... Ms. Aimee MURCH
09 Director of Institutional Research ... Sr. Mary Albertine STACHOWSKI
38 Director of the Care Center ... Ms. Karen ZGODA
13 Director of Computer Services ... Vacant
18 Plant & Grounds Manager ... Mr. David WISNER
25 Director of Grants ... Mrs. Mary ROBINSON
88 Instructional Design & Program Dev ... Dr. Ryan HARTNETT
36 Dir Career Svcs & Internships ... Mrs. Judith PISKUN
42 Campus Minister ... Vacant
85 Director of Foreign Students ... Vacant
26 Dir Communications & Marketing ... Ms. Kristen SCHOBER
32 Director of Student Affairs ... Mr. DJ (Donald) SCHIER
22 Affirmative Action Officer ... Ms. Diane M. HANDZLIK
29 Director of Alumni Relations ... Ms. Rachel TABAK
121 Director Student Success Center ... Mrs. Elizabeth KERR
57 Art Department Chair ... Mr. Robert GRIZANTI
76 Health Sciences Chair ... Dr. Kim KOTZ
79 Humanities & Social Sci Chair ... Dr. Will MEYERS
64 Music Department Chair ... Mr. Anthony CASUCCIO
81 Natural Sciences/Prof Studies Chair ... Vacant
108 Director Institutional Assessment ... Dr. Matthew GIORDANO
04 Administrative Asst to President ... Ms. Michaelene KARPINSKI
103 Dir Workforce/Career Development ... Dr. Ryan HARTNETT
41 Director of Athletics ... Ms. Amanda JANOSKY
15 Director of Human Resources ... Dr. Carleen FLOREA
88 Director of Achieve ... Mrs. Jennifer CORNACCHIO
21 Accounting Manager ... Ms. Mary DETTELIS
88 Special Events Coordinator ... Mrs. Tracy ROZLER

Wagner College (B)

1 Campus Road, Staten Island NY 10301-4479
County: Richmond FICE Identification: 002899
Unit ID: 197197
Telephone: (718) 390-3100 Carnegie Class: Masters/M
FAX Number: (718) 390-3467 Calendar System: Semester
URL: www.wagner.edu
Established: 1883 Annual Undergrad Tuition & Fees: $50,010
Enrollment: 2,070 Coed
Affiliation or Control: Independent Non-Profit IRS Status: 501(c)3
Highest Offering: Doctorate
Accreditation: M, AAQEP, ACBSP, ARCPA, NUR

01 Interim President ... Mr. Angelo G. ARAIMO
05 Provost/VP Academic Affairs ... Dr. Tarshia L. STANLEY
84 Sr VP for Planning & Enrollment ... Mr. Angelo G. ARAIMO
11 VP Administration ... Vacant
04 Assistant to the President ... Ms. Ria CARNAVAS
32 VP Internationalization/Campus Life ... Ms. Ruta SHAH-GORDON
10 CFO/VP for Finance & Administration ... Mr. John CARRESCIA, JR.
108 Assoc Provost for Assessment ... Vacant
20 Assoc Provost for Academic Affairs ... Dr. Nicholas RICHARDSON
06 Registrar ... Ms. Athena TURNER-FREDERICK
13 Chief Information Officer ... Mr. Frank CAFASSO
42 Chaplain ... Ms. Elaine SCHENK
29 Director Alumni Relations ... Ms. Nicolina ASTORINA
39 Director Residential Educ ... Mr. Thomas TRESSLER-GELOK
30 Exec Director Development ... Ms. Kaitlin GIRTON
18 Director of Campus Operations ... Mr. Daniel SWITZER
41 Director of Athletics ... Mr. Walter HAMELINE
23 Dean of Health & Wellness ... Ms. Kathleen OBERFELDT
19 Security Supervisor ... Mr. Robert LARSON
15 Chief HR/Diversity Officer ... Ms. Jazzmine CLARKE-GLOVER
37 Director of Financial Aid ... Ms. Theresa WEIMER
58 Director of Graduate Studies ... Ms. Kathleen AHERN
09 IR Director/Asst Dir of Enrollment ... Ms. Patricia CLANCY
35 Assistant Dean Campus Life ... Ms. Ange CONCEPCION
36 Dean & Director CACE ... Dr. Matthew KUBACKI
08 Director of the Horrman Library ... Mr. Dennis SCHAUB
101 Secretary to BOT/Dir Planned Giving ... Mr. David MARTIN
122 Asst Dean Campus Life-Greek Life ... Mr. Thomas TRESSLER-GELOK

Webb Institute (C)

298 Crescent Beach Road, Glen Cove NY 11542-1398
County: Nassau FICE Identification: 002900
Unit ID: 197221
Telephone: (516) 671-2213 Carnegie Class: Spec-4-yr-Other Tech
FAX Number: (516) 674-9838 Calendar System: Semester
URL: www.webb.edu
Established: 1889 Annual Undergrad Tuition & Fees: $52,880
Enrollment: 101 Coed
Affiliation or Control: Independent Non-Profit IRS Status: 501(c)3
Highest Offering: Baccalaureate
Accreditation: M

01 President ... Mr. Mark F. MARTECCHINI
05 Director Academic Services ... Ms. Jocelyn WILSON
20 Assistant Dean ... Prof. Richard C. HARRIS
08 Librarian ... Ms. Patricia M. PRESCOTT
30 Director of Development ... Mr. Anthony ZIC
10 Director of Financial Affairs ... Ms. Rhonda LIGHTCAP
09 Director of Institutional Research ... Prof. Richard A. ROYCE
32 Director of Student Affairs ... Ms. Lauren CARBALLO
18 Director of Facilities ... Mr. John FERRANTE
84 Director of Admissions ... Ms. Lauren CARBALLO
29 Director of Alumni Relations ... Ms. Gailmarie SUJECKI
26 Chief Public Relations Officer ... Mr. Kyle KOLEDA
13 Director of Information Tech ... Mr. Peter MILLER
06 Registrar ... Ms. Jocelyn M. WILSON
04 Administrative Asst to President ... Ms. Gailmarie SUJECKI
15 Director Personnel Services ... Ms. Svetlana MILLER
37 Director of Financial Aid ... Ms. Jocelyn M. WILSON

Weill Cornell Medicine (D)

1300 York Avenue, New York NY 10065-4805
Telephone: (212) 746-5454 FICE Identification: 004762
Accreditation: &M, ARCPA, DENT, IPSY, MED

† Regional accreditation is carried under the parent institution Cornell University, Ithaca, NY.

Wells College (E)

170 Main Street, Aurora NY 13026-0500
County: Cayuga FICE Identification: 002901
Unit ID: 197230
Telephone: (315) 364-3266 Carnegie Class: Bac-A&S
FAX Number: (315) 364-3227 Calendar System: Semester
URL: www.wells.edu
Established: 1868 Annual Undergrad Tuition & Fees: $31,800
Enrollment: 357 Coed
Affiliation or Control: Independent Non-Profit IRS Status: 501(c)3
Highest Offering: Baccalaureate
Accreditation: M, AAQEP

01 President ... Dr. Jonathan GIBRALTER
05 VP for Academic/Student Affairs ... Dr. Susan E. HENKING
10 Vice President and CFO ... Mr. Robert A. CREE
21 Controller ... Ms. Susan WEATHERBY
111 Vice President for Advancement ... Mr. Larry JEROME
84 Vice President for Enrollment Svcs ... Mr. Gerard TURBIDE
06 Assistant Registrar ... Ms. Melanie CULLEN
08 Acting Library Director ... Ms. Tiffany RAYMOND
37 Director Financial Aid ... Ms. Laura BURNS
44 Director of Annual Giving ... Ms. Mary WEBBER
26 Dir of Communications/Marketing ... Mr. Christopher POLLOCK
112 Dir Planned/Leadership Giving ... Ms. Pamela SHERADIN
19 Supervisor of Campus Safety ... Mr. Dave HEWITT
18 Dir of Facilities/Physical Plant ... Mr. Brian BROWN
15 Manager of Human Resources ... Ms. Kit VAN ORMAN

Westchester Community College (F)

75 Grasslands Road, Valhalla NY 10595-1636
County: Westchester FICE Identification: 002881
Unit ID: 197294
Telephone: (914) 606-6600 Carnegie Class: Assoc/HT-Mix Trad/Non
FAX Number: (914) 606-6780 Calendar System: Semester
URL: www.sunywcc.edu
Established: 1946 Annual Undergrad Tuition & Fees (In-District): $5,036
Enrollment: 10,072 Coed
Affiliation or Control: State/Local IRS Status: 501(c)3
Highest Offering: Associate Degree
Accreditation: M, ADNUR, COARC, EMT, RAD

01 President ... Dr. Belinda S. MILES
05 Provost & VP Academic Affairs ... Dr. Vanessa MOREST
32 VP Stdnt Access/Involve/Success ... Vacant
10 VP/Dean Administrative Svcs/CFO ... Mr. Brian MURPHY
111 VP Ext Affairs/Exec Dir Foundation ... Ms. Dolores SWIRIN-YAO
103 VP Workforce Dev & Cmty Education ... Ms. Teresita WISELL
100 VP Strategic Opers/Chief of Staff ... Dr. Shawn BROWN
81 Dean School of Math/Science/Engr ... Dr. Raymond HOUSTON
76 Dean School of Health Careers/Tech ... Vacant
50 Dean School of Bus & Prof Careers ... Dr. Carmen Leonor MARTINEZ-LOPEZ
79 Dean School Arts/Hum/Soc Science ... Vacant
22 Associate Dean & Director of EOC ... Dr. Gina GAINES
35 Assoc Dean Student Personnel Svcs ... Ms. Ellen ZENDMAN
08 Asc Dn Lrng Res/Dist Lrng/Inst Tech ... Ms. Pamela POLLARD
26 Director of College/Cmty Relations ... Mr. Mark STOLLAR
06 Registrar ... Mr. Christopher WESTBY
37 Dir of Student Financial Assistance ... Mr. Jason FRANKY
13 Vice President of IT ... Mr. Anthony SCORDINO
07 Director of Admissions ... Ms. Gloria DE LA PAZ
84 Assoc Dean Enrollment Management ... Dr. Ruben BARATO
15 Director Human Resources ... Ms. Aurora WORKMAN
88 Dir Faculty Student Assoc ... Mr. Joseph POPPA
45 Asst Dean Planning and Inst Effect ... Ms. Yelizaveta ADAMS
19 Director of Security ... Mr. Scott SULLIVAN
24 Director Media Services ... Mr. Gennaro MASELLI
41 Athletic Director ... Mr. Michael BELFIORE
21 Assoc Business Officer/Controller ... Ms. Dawn GILLINS
18 Director Physical Plant ... Mr. Robert CIRILLO
96 Deputy Purchasing Agent ... Mr. Stewart GLASS
27 Publications Manager ... Mr. Edward TATTON
23 Coordinator Student Health Services ... Ms. Janice GILROY
88 Coord of Transfer Services ... Ms. Robin GRAFF
101 Secretary of the Institution/Board ... Ms. Yolanda HOWELL
105 Director Web Services ... Mr. Patrick DANNENHOFFER
25 Chief Contract/Grants Administrator ... Dr. Laurie MILLER-MCNEILL
28 Director of Diversity ... Dr. Rinardo REDDICK
29 Director Alumni Affairs ... Ms. Michelle SCHLEIBAUM
44 Director Annual Giving ... Ms. Jessica DENARO

Yeshiva Aish Torah Dushinsky (G)

1623 44th Street, Brooklyn NY 11204
County: Kings Identification: 667429
Telephone: (718) 873-2252 Carnegie Class: Not Classified
FAX Number: (718) 310-3333 Calendar System: Semester
Established: 1988 Annual Undergrad Tuition & Fees: N/A
Enrollment: N/A Male
Affiliation or Control: Independent Non-Profit IRS Status: 501(c)3
Highest Offering: First Talmudic Degree
Accreditation: RABN

Yeshiva Derech Chaim (H)

1573 39th Street, Brooklyn NY 11218-4413
County: Kings FICE Identification: 022651
Unit ID: 197647
Telephone: (718) 438-5476 Carnegie Class: Spec-4-yr-Faith
FAX Number: (718) 435-9285 Calendar System: Semester
URL: https://ydc.edu/
Established: 1975 Annual Undergrad Tuition & Fees: $12,100
Enrollment: 127 Male
Affiliation or Control: Independent Non-Profit IRS Status: 501(c)3
Highest Offering: Second Talmudic Degree
Accreditation: RABN

01 President ... Rabbi Chaim RENNERT
01 President ... Rabbi Moshe PLUTCHOK

Yeshiva D'Monsey Rabbinical College (I)

2 Roman Boulevard, Monsey NY 10952-3106
County: Rockland FICE Identification: 031473
Unit ID: 420325
Telephone: (845) 426-3276 Carnegie Class: Spec-4-yr-Faith
FAX Number: (845) 352-1119 Calendar System: Semester
Established: 1984 Annual Undergrad Tuition & Fees: $7,500
Enrollment: 71 Male
Affiliation or Control: Independent Non-Profit IRS Status: 501(c)3
Highest Offering: Second Talmudic Degree
Accreditation: RABN

01 Rosh Yeshiva ... Rabbi Sholom GREEN
05 Rosh Yeshiva ... Rabbi Ruvain GREEN
37 Financial Aid Director ... Rabbi Aron BERGER

Yeshiva of Far Rockaway   (A)
802 Hicksville Road, Far Rockaway NY 11691-5219
County: Queens   FICE Identification: 041196
   Unit ID: 190752
Telephone: (718) 327-7600   Carnegie Class: Spec-4-yr-Faith
FAX Number: (718) 327-1430   Calendar System: Semester
URL: https://www.yofr.org/
Established: 1969   Annual Undergrad Tuition & Fees: $13,750
Enrollment: 43   Male
Affiliation or Control: Independent Non-Profit   IRS Status: 501(c)3
Highest Offering: First Talmudic Degree
Accreditation: **RABN**

01   President .... Rabbi Yechiel I. PERR
03   Executive Director .... Rabbi Shayeh KOHN
32   Dean of Students .... Rabbi Dovid KLEINKAUFMAN
06   Registrar .... Mrs. Tamara MASLOW

Yeshiva Gedolah Imrei Yosef   (B)
D'Spinka
1466 56th Street, Brooklyn NY 11219-4696
County: Kings   FICE Identification: 030001
   Unit ID: 375230
Telephone: (718) 851-8721   Carnegie Class: Spec-4-yr-Faith
FAX Number: (718) 686-8849   Calendar System: Semester
Established: 1987   Annual Undergrad Tuition & Fees: $9,500
Enrollment: 187   Male
Affiliation or Control: Independent Non-Profit   IRS Status: 501(c)3
Highest Offering: First Talmudic Degree
Accreditation: **RABN**

01   President .... Joseph SALAMON

Yeshiva Gedolah Kesser Torah   (C)
50 Cedar Lane, Monsey NY 10952
County: Rockland   Identification: 667112
   Unit ID: 481410
Telephone: (845) 406-4308   Carnegie Class: Spec-4-yr-Faith
FAX Number: (845) 406-4199   Calendar System: Semester
Established: 2004   Annual Undergrad Tuition & Fees: $11,300
Enrollment: 85   Male
Affiliation or Control: Independent Non-Profit   IRS Status: 501(c)3
Highest Offering: First Talmudic Degree
Accreditation: **RABN**

00   CEO .... Rabbi David FISHMAN
01   President .... David BERNSTEIN
06   Registrar .... Rabbi Ephraim SALB
37   Director Student Financial Aid .... Yaakov BERGER

Yeshiva Karlin Stolin Beth Aaron   (D)
V'Israel Rabbinical Institute
1818 54th Street, Brooklyn NY 11204-1545
County: Kings   FICE Identification: 025058
   Unit ID: 197601
Telephone: (718) 232-7800   Carnegie Class: Spec-4-yr-Faith
FAX Number: (718) 331-4833   Calendar System: Semester
Established: 1948   Annual Undergrad Tuition & Fees: $11,800
Enrollment: 132   Male
Affiliation or Control: Independent Non-Profit   IRS Status: 501(c)3
Highest Offering: First Talmudic Degree
Accreditation: **RABN**

01   Chief Executive Officer .... Rabbi Yochanan PILCHICK
05   Dean Theology/Chief Acad
     Officer .... Rabbi Gedalyah MACHLIS, OBM
06   Registrar .... Rabbi Aryeh WOLPIN
08   Librarian .... Rabbi Yochanan GOLDHABER
10   Fiscal Officer .... Rabbi Irving PERRES
37   Financial Aid Director .... Rabbi David STEIN
33   Dean of Men .... Rabbi Gedelyah MACHLIS

Yeshiva of Kasho   (E)
944 East 84th Street, Brooklyn NY 11236
County: Kings   FICE Identification: 043017
Telephone: (718) 522-6646   Carnegie Class: Not Classified
FAX Number: (718) 310-3333   Calendar System: Semester
Established: 1995   Annual Undergrad Tuition & Fees: N/A
Enrollment: N/A   Male
Affiliation or Control: Independent Non-Profit   IRS Status: 501(c)3
Highest Offering: First Talmudic Degree
Accreditation: **RABN**

01   Director .... Aron BLUM
37   Financial Aid Administrator .... Vacant

Yeshiva and Kolel Bais Medrash   (F)
Elyon
73 Main Street, Monsey NY 10952-3013
County: Rockland   FICE Identification: 026229
   Unit ID: 245777
Telephone: (845) 356-7065   Carnegie Class: Spec-4-yr-Faith
FAX Number: N/A   Calendar System: Semester
Established: 1945   Annual Undergrad Tuition & Fees: N/A
Enrollment: N/A   Male

Affiliation or Control: Independent Non-Profit   IRS Status: 501(c)3
Highest Offering: First Talmudic Degree
Accreditation: **AIJS**

Yeshiva Kollel Tifereth Elizer   (G)
1227 47th Street, Brooklyn NY 11219
County: Kings   Identification: 667367
   Unit ID: 491057
Telephone: (718) 600-8897   Carnegie Class: Spec-4-yr-Faith
FAX Number: (718) 889-7033   Calendar System: Semester
URL: https://yeshivakolleltifereethelizer.com/
Established: 1987   Annual Undergrad Tuition & Fees: N/A
Enrollment: N/A   Male
Affiliation or Control: Independent Non-Profit   IRS Status: 501(c)3
Highest Offering: First Talmudic Degree
Accreditation: **RABN**

01   Chief Executive Officer .... Rabbi Avrum Yehuda LOW
10   Chief Financial Officer .... Rabbi Hershel LOW
37   Financial Aid Administrator .... Rabbi Yesoscher MEISELS
06   Registrar .... Mrs. Rochel LOW

Yeshiva of Machzikai Hadas   (H)
1301 47th Street, Brooklyn NY 11219
County: Kings   FICE Identification: 041381
   Unit ID: 455257
Telephone: (718) 853-2442   Carnegie Class: Spec-4-yr-Faith
FAX Number: (718) 853-2504   Calendar System: Semester
Established: 2001   Annual Undergrad Tuition & Fees: $10,100
Enrollment: 457   Male
Affiliation or Control: Independent Non-Profit   IRS Status: 501(c)3
Highest Offering: First Talmudic Degree
Accreditation: **RABN**

01   Rosh Yeshiva .... Rabbi Yidel MONHEIT

Yeshiva of Nitra Rabbinical College   (I)
194 Division Avenue, Brooklyn NY 11211-7199
County: Kings   FICE Identification: 011670
   Unit ID: 197674
Telephone: (718) 387-0422   Carnegie Class: Spec-4-yr-Faith
FAX Number: (718) 387-9400   Calendar System: Semester
URL: yeshivaofnitra.org/
Established: 1946   Annual Undergrad Tuition & Fees: $12,750
Enrollment: 197   Male
Affiliation or Control: Independent Non-Profit   IRS Status: 501(c)3
Highest Offering: Second Talmudic Degree
Accreditation: **RABN**

01   President .... Mr. Mendel KLEIN
05   Dean .... Rabbi Samuel D. UNGAR
11   Administrative Officer .... Mr. Ernest SCHWARTZ

Yeshiva of Ocean   (J)
7120 Highway 52, Greenfield Park NY 12435
County: Ulster   FICE Identification: 042766
   Unit ID: 493594
Telephone: (845) 647-2607   Carnegie Class: Spec-4-yr-Faith
FAX Number: N/A   Calendar System: Semester
URL: yeshivaofocean.com
Established: Annual Undergrad Tuition & Fees: N/A
Enrollment: N/A   Male
Affiliation or Control: Independent Non-Profit   IRS Status: 501(c)3
Highest Offering: First Talmudic Degree
Accreditation: **AIJS**

Yeshiva Ohr Naftoli   (K)
701 Blooming Grove Turnpike, New Windsor NY 12553
County: Orange   Identification: 667284
   Unit ID: 490504
Telephone: (845) 784-4020   Carnegie Class: Spec-4-yr-Faith
FAX Number: (845) 784-2028   Calendar System: Other
URL: www.ohrnaftoli.org
Established: Annual Undergrad Tuition & Fees: $9,926
Enrollment: 37   Male
Affiliation or Control: Independent Non-Profit   IRS Status: 501(c)3
Highest Offering: First Talmudic Degree
Accreditation: **AIJS**

01   Executive Director .... Rabbi Yitzchok KRAUSZ

Yeshiva Ohr Yisrael   (L)
2899 Nostrand Avenue, Brooklyn NY 11229
County: Kings   Identification: 667077
   Unit ID: 486017
Telephone: (718) 382-8702   Carnegie Class: Spec-4-yr-Faith
FAX Number: (718) 382-8703   Calendar System: Semester
URL: www.yoy.edu
Established: 1999   Annual Undergrad Tuition & Fees: $8,250
Enrollment: 36   Male
Affiliation or Control: Independent Non-Profit   IRS Status: 501(c)3
Highest Offering: First Talmudic Degree
Accreditation: **RABN**

01   Rosh Yeshiva .... Avraham ZUCKER
10   Treasurer .... Avi KAHN

Yeshiva Shaar Ephraim   (M)
178 Maple Avenue, Monsey NY 10952
County: Rockland   FICE Identification: 042590
   Unit ID: 490276
Telephone: (845) 426-3110   Carnegie Class: Spec-4-yr-Faith
FAX Number: (845) 425-4721   Calendar System: Semester
URL: shaarephraim.org
Established: 2012   Annual Undergrad Tuition & Fees: $14,175
Enrollment: 83   Male
Affiliation or Control: Independent Non-Profit   IRS Status: 501(c)3
Highest Offering: First Talmudic Degree
Accreditation: **RABN**

01   President .... Rabbi Yehuda OSHRY
33   Dean of Men .... Rabbi Moshe GREENBERG
37   Director of Financial Aid .... Mr. Dov KRESCH

Yeshiva Shaar HaTorah-Grodno   (N)
83-96 117th Street, Kew Gardens NY 11415
County: Queens   FICE Identification: 021520
   Unit ID: 197692
Telephone: (718) 846-1940   Carnegie Class: Spec-4-yr-Faith
FAX Number: (718) 850-7916   Calendar System: Semester
URL: shaarhatorah.edu/
Established: 1976   Annual Undergrad Tuition & Fees: $17,160
Enrollment: 106   Male
Affiliation or Control: Independent Non-Profit   IRS Status: 501(c)3
Highest Offering: Second Talmudic Degree
Accreditation: **RABN**

01   Administrator .... Rabbi Yoel YANKELEWITZ

Yeshiva Shaarei Torah of   (O)
Rockland
91 W Carlton Road, Suffern NY 10901-4013
County: Rockland   FICE Identification: 034963
   Unit ID: 441609
Telephone: (845) 352-3431   Carnegie Class: Spec-4-yr-Faith
FAX Number: (845) 352-3433   Calendar System: Semester
URL: https://www.yst.edu
Established: 1977   Annual Undergrad Tuition & Fees: $13,750
Enrollment: 90   Male
Affiliation or Control: Independent Non-Profit   IRS Status: 501(c)3
Highest Offering: First Talmudic Degree
Accreditation: **AIJS**

01   President .... Dr. Don ZWICKLER
05   Rosh Hayeshiva .... Rabbi Mordechai WOLMARK
37   Financial Aid Administrator ...... Mr. Elimelech SCHWARTZ
06   Registrar .... Mrs. Rachel CELNIK

Yeshiva Sholom Shachna   (P)
401 Elmwood Avenue, Brooklyn NY 11230
County: Kings   Identification: 667147
   Unit ID: 486026
Telephone: (718) 252-6333   Carnegie Class: Spec-4-yr-Faith
FAX Number: (718) 338-2536   Calendar System: Semester
URL: yeshivasholomshachna.com
Established: 2005   Annual Undergrad Tuition & Fees: $10,750
Enrollment: 106   Male
Affiliation or Control: Independent Non-Profit   IRS Status: 501(c)3
Highest Offering: First Talmudic Degree
Accreditation: **@RABN**

01   Chief Executive Officer .... Rabbi Meir Chaim GUTFREUND
10   Chief Financial/Business Officer ..... Mrs. Dina GUTFREUND
05   Chief Academic Officer/Registrar ..... Rabbi Simcha OLEN
37   Director for Financial Aid .... Mrs. Esther FARKAS

Yeshiva of the Telshe Alumni   (Q)
4904 Independence Avenue, Riverdale NY 10471
County: Bronx   FICE Identification: 025463
   Unit ID: 431983
Telephone: (718) 601-3523   Carnegie Class: Spec-4-yr-Faith
FAX Number: (718) 601-2141   Calendar System: Semester
URL: https://yeshivatelshealumni.com/
Established: 1981   Annual Undergrad Tuition & Fees: $10,700
Enrollment: 75   Male
Affiliation or Control: Independent Non-Profit   IRS Status: 501(c)3
Highest Offering: First Talmudic Degree
Accreditation: **RABN**

01   President .... Rabbi Avrohom AUSBAND
03   Executive Director .... Rabbi Noson JOSEPH
29   Administrator .... Rabbi Moshe FERBER

Yeshiva University   (R)
500 W 185th Street, New York NY 10033-3201
County: New York   FICE Identification: 002903
   Unit ID: 197708
Telephone: (212) 960-5400   Carnegie Class: DU-Mod
FAX Number: (212) 960-0055   Calendar System: Semester

URL: www.yu.edu
Established: 1886 Annual Undergrad Tuition & Fees: $46,475
Enrollment: 5,524 Coordinate
Affiliation or Control: Independent Non-Profit IRS Status: 501(c)3
Highest Offering: Doctorate
Accreditation: M, #ARCPA, CLPSY, IPSY, LAW, OT, PSPSY, SP, SW

01 President ... Dr. Ari BERMAN
05 Provost/Sr VP Academic Affairs ... Dr. Selma BOTMAN
20 Deputy Provost ... Dr. Timothy STEVENS
100 Chief of Staff to the President ... Ms. Julie SCHREIER
10 Vice Pres/Chief Financial Officer ... Mr. Michael SCHREIBER
111 Vice Pres Institutional Advancement ... Ms. Ellen FINKELSTEIN
11 Vice President University Affairs ... Dr. Herbert C. DOBRINSKY
13 Chief Information Officer ... Ms. Suzett SOLER-MCDINE
43 VP Legal Affs/Secretary/Gen Counsel ... Mr. Andrew J. LAUER
11 Vice Pres Administrative Services ... Mr. Patrick GALLAGHER
26 Exec Dir Communications/Public Affs ... Mr. Doron STERN
04 Exec Assistant to President ... Ms. Ilana LEHRER
08 Director of University Libraries ... Mr. Paul GLASSMAN
32 Vice Provost/Univ Dean of Students ... Dr. Chaim NISSEL
73 Dn Undergrad Torah Stds/REITS ... Rabbi Yosef KALINSKY
49 Dean YU Undergrad Fac Arts Sci ... Dr. Karen BACON
50 Dean Sy Syms School of Business ... Dr. Noam WASSERMAN
58 Dean Ferkauf Graduate School Psych ... Dr. Leslie F. HALPERN
58 Dean Bernard Revel Graduate School ... Dr. Daniel RHYNHOLD
58 Dean Azrieli Grad Sch Jewish Educ ... Dr. Rona NOVICK
70 Dean Wurzweiler School Social Work ... Vacant
81 Dean Katz School of Sci & Health ... Dr. Paul RUSSO
37 Director of Student Finances ... Mr. Robert FRIEDMAN
07 Dir Undergraduate Recruitment ... Mr. Marc ZHARNEST
29 Director of Alumni Engagement ... Ms. Aliza ABRAMS KONIG
06 University Registrar ... Ms. Jennifer SPIEGEL
09 Director of Institutional Research ... Mr. Yuxiang LIU
96 Director of Procurement ... Mr. Thomas CANNON
15 Chief Human Resources Officer ... Ms. Julie AUSTER
38 Director Student Counseling ... Dr. Yael MUSKAT
22 Dir Affirmative Action/EEO ... Ms. Renee COKER
41 Athletic Director ... Mr. Joe BENDARSH
19 Director Security/Safety ... Mr. Donald SOMMERS
36 Executive Director Career Center ... Ms. Susan BAUER
18 Chief Facilities & Admin Officer ... Mr. Randy APFELBAUM
84 Assistant VP Enrollment ... Ms. Geri MANSDORF
86 Director Government Relations ... Mr. Jon GREENFIELD

Yeshiva Yesoda Hatorah Vetz Chaim (A)

505 Bedford Avenue, Brooklyn NY 11211
County: Kings Identification: 667368
Unit ID: 494737
Telephone: (718) 302-7500 Carnegie Class: Spec-4-yr-Faith
FAX Number: N/A Calendar System: Semester
Established: 2013 Annual Undergrad Tuition & Fees: N/A
Enrollment: N/A Male
Affiliation or Control: Independent Non-Profit IRS Status: 501(c)3
Highest Offering: First Talmudic Degree
Accreditation: RABN

01 President ... Mr. Alfred SCHONBERGER
11 Administrator ... Mr. Samuel FISCHER
37 Director of Financial Aid ... Mr. Getzel FALKOWITZ

Yeshiva Zichron Aryeh (B)

1213 Bay 25th Street, Far Rockaway NY 11691
County: Queens Identification: 667110
Unit ID: 487746
Telephone: (347) 619-9074 Carnegie Class: Spec-4-yr-Faith
FAX Number: (516) 295-5737 Calendar System: Semester
Established: 1992 Annual Undergrad Tuition & Fees: $8,750
Enrollment: 28 Male
Affiliation or Control: Independent Non-Profit IRS Status: 501(c)3
Highest Offering: First Talmudic Degree
Accreditation: RABN

03 Executive Vice President ... Rabbi Shaya COHEN
10 Controller ... Rabbi Ari DERDIK
06 Registrar/Dir of Admissions ... Rabbi Yehuda COHEN
37 Financial Aid Admin ... Mr. Yaakov JAFFE
18 Chief Facilities ... Mr. Danny SCHUSTER

Yeshivas Maharit D'Satmar (C)

475 County Rt. 105, Monroe NY 10950
County: Orange Identification: 667204
Unit ID: 488101
Telephone: (845) 782-1380 Carnegie Class: Spec-4-yr-Faith
FAX Number: (845) 302-1093 Calendar System: Semester
URL: yeshivasmaharit.org/
Established: 2011 Annual Undergrad Tuition & Fees: $11,500
Enrollment: 143 Male
Affiliation or Control: Independent Non-Profit IRS Status: 501(c)3
Highest Offering: First Talmudic Degree
Accreditation: @RABN

01 CEO ... Yitzchok TYRNAUER
06 Registrar ... Joel BRAVER
10 Associate Business Officer ... Libi WITRIOL
37 Director of Financial Aid ... Yoel KESTENBAUM

Yeshivas Novominsk (D)

1690 60th Street, Brooklyn NY 11204-2138
County: Kings FICE Identification: 031271
Unit ID: 405058
Telephone: (718) 438-2727 Carnegie Class: Not Classified
FAX Number: (718) 438-2472 Calendar System: Semester
URL: https://yeshivasnovominsk.com/
Established: 1988 Annual Undergrad Tuition & Fees: $10,300
Enrollment: 165 Male
Affiliation or Control: Independent Non-Profit IRS Status: 501(c)3
Highest Offering: First Talmudic Degree
Accreditation: RABN

01 Executive Director ... Rabbi Lipa BRENNAN
32 Dean of Students ... Rabbi Yehoshua PERLOW
32 Dean of Students ... Rabbi Yisroel PERLOW
11 Administrator ... Rabbi Boruch TWERSKI

Yeshivat Hechal Shemuel (E)

1532 East Tenth Street, Brooklyn NY 11230
County: Kings FICE Identification: 042785
Unit ID: 493664
Telephone: (718) 336-2702 Carnegie Class: Spec-4-yr-Faith
FAX Number: N/A Calendar System: Semester
URL: hechalshemuel.com
Established: Annual Undergrad Tuition & Fees: N/A
Enrollment: N/A Male
Affiliation or Control: Independent Non-Profit IRS Status: 501(c)3
Highest Offering: First Talmudic Degree
Accreditation: AIJS

Yeshivath Viznitz (F)

PO Box 446, Monsey NY 10952-0446
County: Rockland FICE Identification: 013027
Unit ID: 197735
Telephone: (845) 731-3700 Carnegie Class: Spec-4-yr-Faith
FAX Number: (845) 356-7359 Calendar System: Semester
Established: 1946 Annual Undergrad Tuition & Fees: $8,640
Enrollment: 842 Male
Affiliation or Control: Independent Non-Profit IRS Status: 501(c)3
Highest Offering: Second Talmudic Degree
Accreditation: RABN

01 President ... Rabbi David ROSENBERG
10 Chief Executive/FiscalOfficer ... Rabbi Chaim ROSENFELD

Yeshivath Zichron Moshe (G)

PO Box 580, South Fallsburg NY 12779-0580
County: Sullivan FICE Identification: 011821
Unit ID: 197744
Telephone: (845) 434-5240 Carnegie Class: Spec-4-yr-Faith
FAX Number: (845) 434-1009 Calendar System: Semester
URL: https://yeshivathzichronmoshe.com/
Established: 1969 Annual Undergrad Tuition & Fees: $13,450
Enrollment: 240 Male
Affiliation or Control: Independent Non-Profit IRS Status: 501(c)3
Highest Offering: First Talmudic Degree
Accreditation: AIJS

01 President ... Rabbi Ephraim Y. SHER
37 Director Student Financial Aid ... Rabbi Dov PERECMAN
06 Registrar ... Mrs. Miryom R. MILLER

NORTH CAROLINA

Barton College (H)

400 Atlantic Christian College Dr, Wilson NC 27893
County: Wilson FICE Identification: 002908
Unit ID: 197911
Telephone: (252) 399-6300 Carnegie Class: Bac-Diverse
FAX Number: (252) 399-6374 Calendar System: Semester
URL: www.barton.edu
Established: 1902 Annual Undergrad Tuition & Fees: $32,590
Enrollment: 1,177 Coed
Affiliation or Control: Christian Church (Disciples Of Christ)
IRS Status: 501(c)3
Highest Offering: Master's
Accreditation: SC, NURSE, SW

01 President ... Dr. Douglas N. SEARCY
05 Provost/VP Acad Affs/Stdnt Engage ... Dr. Kevin PENNINGTON
10 Vice Pres Finance & Administration ... Mr. Chris MCKENZIE
111 Vice President Inst Advancement ... Vacant
84 Vice President for Enrollment Mgmt ... Mr. Dennis T. MATTHEWS
32 VP Student Engagement/Success ... Ms. Amanda METTS
07 Executive Dir of Admissions ... Ms. Krystal ALICES
30 Asst VP for Leadership Giving ... Mr. Tom MAZE
20 Assistant Provost Integrative Lrng ... Ms. Blythe TAYLOR
50 Dean School of Business ... Mr. Ron EGGERS
66 Dean School of Nursing ... Dr. Sharon SARVEY
53 Dean School of Education ... Dr. Jackie ENNIS
79 Dean School of Humanities ... Dr. Liz KISER
35 Dean of Students ... Ms. Laura NEWHOUSE
81 Dean School of Sciences ... Dr. Tamara AVANT
76 Dean Allied Health & Sport Studies ... Dr. Steve FULKS
70 Director of Social Work Program ... Ms. Trinette B. LANGLEY
57 Dean Visual/Performing & Comm Arts ... Ms. Susan FECHO
58 Dean Graduate/Professional Studies ... Vacant
21 Controller ... Mr. Ronnie RAPER
41 Athletic Director ... Mr. Todd WILKINSON
106 Dir Online Education/E-learning ... Ms. Lorraine RAPER
36 Asst Provost Academic/Career Plng ... Ms. Angie WALSTON
06 Registrar ... Ms. Sheila MILNE
37 Director Student Financial Aid ... Mr. Thomas WELCH
26 Director of Public Relations ... Mrs. Kathy DAUGHETY
08 Director of the Library ... Mr. Robert CAGNA
15 VP for People & Support ... Mrs. Vicky MORRIS
23 Exec Director of Health Services ... Mrs. Jennifer HIGH
110 Exec Director of Inst Advancement ... Mr. Archer BANE
13 Sr Director Technology Services ... Mr. David GRAYBEAL
18 Director of Facilities Services ... Mr. Mark A. TERRELL
42 Chaplain ... Rev. Alysun SKINNER
40 Bookstore Manager ... Ms. Latisha FAISON
04 Executive Asst to President ... Ms. Luann CLARK
88 Director of Publications ... Mr. Keith TEW
105 Director Web Services ... Vacant
09 Director of Institutional Research ... Ms. Lorie A. DALOLA
28 Director of Diversity ... Ms. Vicky A. MORRIS
122 Coord Campus Life-Frat/Sor Life ... Vacant

Belmont Abbey College (I)

100 Belmont Mount Holly Road, Belmont NC 28012-1802
County: Gaston FICE Identification: 002910
Unit ID: 197984
Telephone: (704) 461-6701 Carnegie Class: Bac-Diverse
FAX Number: (704) 461-6670 Calendar System: Semester
URL: belmontabbeycollege.edu/
Established: 1876 Annual Undergrad Tuition & Fees: $18,500
Enrollment: 1,467 Coed
Affiliation or Control: Roman Catholic IRS Status: 501(c)3
Highest Offering: Master's
Accreditation: SC

01 President ... Dr. William K. THIERFELDER
10 SVP Finance/Admin/Operations ... Mr. Allan MARK
05 Provost ... Dr. Travis FEEZELL
20 Vice Provost for Academic Affairs ... Dr. David WILLIAMS
26 VP College Relations ... Mr. Philip BRACH
92 Dean of the Honors College ... Dr. Joseph WYSOCKI
08 Director of the Library ... Mr. Donald BEAGLE
06 Registrar ... Ms. Margot RHOADES
09 Vice Prov Assessment/Rsrch/Accred ... Ms. Karen PRICE
36 Director Career Counseling/Placemnt ... Vacant
27 Exec Dir Marketing/Communications ... Mr. Rolando RIVAS
37 Dir Student Financial Services ... Mrs. Julie HODGE
38 Director of Wellness Center ... Mrs. Melanie ECKSTEIN
41 Athletic Director ... Mr. Stephen MISS
21 Controller ... Ms. Beth RUNSER
19 Chief of Campus Police ... Mr. Andy LEONARD
42 Director of Campus Ministry ... Mr. Wesley NELSON
15 Exec Director of Human Resources ... Ms. Cheryl TROTTER
07 Vice Provost and Dean of Admissions ... Mr. Martin C. AUCOIN
13 Chief Info Technology Officer (CIO) ... Mr. Nash HASAN
32 Vice President and Dean of Students ... Mr. Tom MACALESTER
04 Sr Executive Assistant to the Pres ... Ms. Maria DIMURA
11 Assoc VP Administration Development .. Ms. Samantha DONOHUE

Bennett College (J)

900 E Washington Street, Greensboro NC 27401-3239
County: Guilford FICE Identification: 002911
Unit ID: 197993
Telephone: (336) 273-4431 Carnegie Class: Bac-A&S
FAX Number: (336) 370-8688 Calendar System: Semester
URL: www.bennett.edu
Established: 1873 Annual Undergrad Tuition & Fees: $18,513
Enrollment: 232 Female
Affiliation or Control: United Methodist IRS Status: 501(c)3
Highest Offering: Baccalaureate
Accreditation: @TRACS, SW

01 President ... Ms. Suzanne E. WALSH
05 Vice Pres Academic Affairs ... Dr. Laura COLSON
10 Vice President for Business Ops ... Mr. Greg HODGES
111 Vice Pres Inst Advancement ... Mr. Franklin MCCAIN, JR.
84 VP Enrollment Mgmt/Stdnt Svcs ... Vacant
32 Exec Dir Student Affairs ... Vacant
26 Dir Strategic Communications ... Ms. Phanalphie RHUE
09 Dir Inst Plng/Assess/Effect/Rsrch ... Mr. Brian AURITI
08 Director of Holgate Library ... Ms. Joan WILLIAMS
07 Director of Admissions ... Mr. James CRAWFORD
37 Interim Director of Financial Aid ... Mr. Justin PICHEY
29 Sr Dir Alumnae Rels & Annual Giving ... Ms. Deborah LOVE
38 Director Counseling ... Ms. Aishia GRIFFIN
15 Director of Human Resources ... Ms. Ebony KENDRICK
42 Chaplain ... Rev Dr. Natalie MCLEAN
88 Faculty Lead Asst Professor ... Mr. Franklin WARREN
79 Faculty Lead Assoc Professor ... Dr. Sara WRENN
19 Executive Director Campus Safety ... Mr. Jermaine THOMAS
13 Dir MIS/IPAER Crd Spec Initiatives ... Dr. Mondrail MYRICK
04 Virtual Asst to Pres/Proj Coord ... Ms. Elizabeth HARTWIG
104 Exec Dir Global & Interdisc Studies ... Dr. Anne HAYES
25 Dir Title III & Sponsored Programs ... Ms. Sylvia NICHOLSON
39 Dir Campus Life/Student Activities ... Ms. Rachel PRIDGEN
121 Director Student Success ... Ms. Tonya DOANE
88 Dir Wellness & Accesibility Svcs ... Dr. Lucheia GRAVES

21 Controller ..... Ms. Elizabeth WAUGH
06 Registrar ..... Mr. Sam GROGG
18 Exec Dir Campus Operations ..... Mr. Thomas GRIFFIS, JR.

Brevard College (A)

One Brevard College Drive, Brevard NC 28712-3306
County: Transylvania FICE Identification: 002912
Unit ID: 198066
Telephone: (828) 641-0641 Carnegie Class: Bac-Diverse
FAX Number: N/A Calendar System: Semester
URL: www.brevard.edu
Established: 1853 Annual Undergrad Tuition & Fees: $30,250
Enrollment: 828 Coed
Affiliation or Control: United Methodist IRS Status: 501(c)3
Highest Offering: Master's
Accreditation: SC, MUS

01 President ..... Dr. Bradley J. ANDREWS
05 VP Academic Affairs/Dean of Faculty ..... Dr. Jennifer FRICK-RUPPER
10 VP for Finance & Operations ..... Mr. Juan C. MASCARO
30 VP for Alumni Affairs & Development ..... Mr. Patrick WAGNER
07 Vice Pres Admissions/Financial Aid ..... Dr. Ryan C. HOLT
32 VP Student Life/Dean of Students ..... Dr. Debora D'ANNA
04 Executive Asst to the President ..... Ms. Katherine T. PARNELL
13 Dir of Information Technology ..... Mr. William DEWITT
06 Registrar ..... Mr. Quintin OVEROCKER
21 Associate VP Finance/Controller ..... Mr. Mitchell RADFORD
08 Director of Library ..... Dr. Marie JONES
30 Director of Development ..... Vacant
19 Dir of Safety/Security/Risk Mgmt ..... Mr. Stan JACOBSEN
41 Director of Athletics ..... Ms. Myranda NASH
18 Director of Facilities/Grounds ..... Mr. Burke ULREY
121 Assoc Dean Student Support/Advising ..... Ms. Shirley E. ARNOLD
36 Assoc Dir of Career Exploration/Dev ..... Ms. Nacole POTTS
92 Director of Honors Program ..... Dr. Robert J. CABIN
38 Assoc Dean/Dir of Counseling ..... Mr. Kevin GEORGE
57 Chair Division of Fine Arts ..... Dr. Kathryn GRESHAM
79 Chair Division of Humanities ..... Dr. Uzzie CANNON
83 Chair Div of Social Sciences ..... Dr. Laura VANCE
81 Chair Div Env Stds/Math/Nat Science ..... Dr. Sarah MAVEETY
88 Chair Division of WLEE ..... Dr. Jennifer L. KAFSKY
26 Director of Public Information ..... Ms. Christie CAUBLE
108 Dir of Institutional Effectiveness ..... Mr. Michael COHEN
37 Dir of Admissions & Financial Aid ..... Mr. David VOLRATH
15 Director of Human Resources ..... Ms. Kelly KEARNAN
09 Director of Institutional Research ..... Vacant
29 Director Alumni Affairs ..... Ms. Megan SHINA
39 Dir of Housing & Student Conduct ..... Mr. Christopher CENTER

Cabarrus College of Health Sciences (B)

401 Medical Park Drive, Concord NC 28025-3959
County: Cabarrus FICE Identification: 006477
Unit ID: 198109
Telephone: (704) 403-1555 Carnegie Class: Spec-4-yr-Other Health
FAX Number: (704) 403-1764 Calendar System: Semester
URL: www.cabarruscollege.edu
Established: 1942 Annual Undergrad Tuition & Fees: $13,966
Enrollment: 526 Coed
Affiliation or Control: Independent Non-Profit IRS Status: 501(c)3
Highest Offering: Master's
Accreditation: SC, ADNUR, MAC, NURSE, OT, OTA, SURGT

01 President ..... Dr. Cam CRUICKSHANK
05 Interim Provost ..... Dr. Jon BELLUM
32 Dean Student Affs/Enrollment Mgmt ..... Ms. Christine CORSELLO
10 Chief Financial Officer ..... Mrs. Sandra HARVEY
66 Dean of Nursing ..... Dr. Cristine EUDY
88 OT Assistant Program Chair ..... Ms. Nancy GREEN
88 Master OT Program Chair ..... Dr. Jacqueline MAYO
88 Medical Assisting Program Chair ..... Ms. Rachel HOUSTON
88 Surgical Technology Program Chair ..... Ms. Michelle GAY
88 Medical Imaging Program Chair ..... Mrs. Rhonda WEAVER
97 General Education Program Chair ..... Mrs. Zinat HASSANPOUR
88 Respiratory Therapy Program Chair ..... Mr. Lanny INABNIT
88 Cmty Hlth & Wellness Program Chair ..... Ms. Rachel HOUSTON
88 Hlth Sci & LDR Dev Program Chair ..... Ms. Rhonda WEAVER
26 Manager Marketing & Events ..... Vacant
37 Director of Financial Aid ..... Mrs. Valerie RICHARD
06 Dir Student Records & Info Mgmt ..... Mrs. Mary ELMORE
07 Dir of Admissions & Recruitment ..... Mr. Britt ELLIS
04 Administrative Asst to President ..... Mrs. Heather PENINGER
08 Head Librarian ..... Mrs. Cassie DIXON
09 Dir Inst Research & Effectiveness ..... Mrs. Tripti DEVKOTA

Campbell University (C)

PO Box 127, Buies Creek NC 27506-0097
County: Harnett FICE Identification: 002913
Unit ID: 198136
Telephone: (910) 893-1200 Carnegie Class: DU-Mod
FAX Number: (910) 893-1424 Calendar System: Semester
URL: www.campbell.edu
Established: 1887 Annual Undergrad Tuition & Fees: $36,740
Enrollment: 5,964 Coed
Affiliation or Control: Baptist IRS Status: 501(c)3
Highest Offering: Doctorate
Accreditation: SC, ACBSP, ARCPA, CACREP, LAW, NURSE, OSTEO, PH, PHAR, PTA, SW, THEOL

00 Chancellor ..... Dr. Jerry WALLACE
01 President ..... Dr. J. Bradley CREED
03 Executive Vice President ..... Dr. John ROBERSON
05 Vice Pres Academic Affs & Provost ..... Dr. Mark HAMMOND
111 Vice President for Advancement ..... Dr. Britt DAVIS
32 Vice President for Student Life ..... Rev. Faithe BEAM
84 Vice Pres Enrollment Management ..... Dr. David MEE
10 VP for Business/CFO ..... Ms. Sandra CONNOLLY
49 Dean of College of Arts & Science ..... Dr. Michael WELLS
61 Dean of the Law School ..... Mr. J. Rich LEONARD
50 Dean Lundy-Fetterman Sch Business ..... Dr. Kevin O'MARA
53 Dean School of Education ..... Dr. Alfred BRYANT
67 Dean College of Pharmacy/Health Sci ..... Dr. Michael ADAMS
63 Dean of Osteopathic Medical School ..... Dr. Brian KESSLER
54 Dean School of Engineering ..... Dr. Jenna CARPENTER
35 Dean of Campus Life ..... Ms. Kellie NOTHSTINE
06 Registrar ..... Ms. Karen PORE
29 AVP of Alumni Engagement ..... Ms. Sarah SWAIN
08 Dean of Library ..... Ms. Sarah STEELE
37 Director of Financial Aid ..... Mr. Preston DODSON
13 CIO/Assoc VP for IT ..... Ms. Sherri YERK-ZWICKL
26 AVP Communications/Marketing ..... Ms. Haven HOTTEL
15 Director Human Resources ..... Mr. Trent ELMORE
18 Director Facilities Management ..... Mr. Andy SNEAD
38 Director Student Counseling ..... Mrs. Laura RICH
96 Director of Procurement ..... Mr. Thomas PHAM
92 Director of Honors Program ..... Dr. Sherry TRUFFIN
09 Asst Provost for Inst Effectiveness ..... Mrs. Maren HESS
106 Dean of Adult & Online Education ..... Dr. Beth RUBIN
41 Acting Athletic Director ..... Mrs. Hannah BAZEMORE
43 Dir Legal Services/General Counsel ..... Ms. Gina CALABRO
04 Exec Assistant to the President ..... Ms. Suzanne CREWS
07 Director of Admissions ..... Vacant
104 Dean of Global Engagement ..... Dr. Donna WALDRON
19 Director Security/Safety ..... Mr. Chase BANKER
44 Director Annual Giving ..... Ms. Robin GORDON
122 Dir Fraternity/Sorority Life ..... Ms. Alexis BONAMASSA
39 Dir Resident Life/Student Housing ..... Ms. Chloe JONES

Carolina Christian College (D)

PO Box 777, 4209 Indiana Avenue, Winston-Salem NC 27105
County: Forsyth FICE Identification: 035703
Unit ID: 199971
Telephone: (336) 744-0900 Carnegie Class: Spec-4-yr-Faith
FAX Number: (336) 744-0901 Calendar System: Semester
URL: www.carolina.edu
Established: 1945 Annual Undergrad Tuition & Fees: $8,930
Enrollment: 74 Coed
Affiliation or Control: Independent Non-Profit IRS Status: 501(c)3
Highest Offering: Doctorate
Accreditation: BI

01 President ..... Dr. LaTanya V. TYSON
05 VP of Academics/Graduate Studies ..... Dr. Derrick THORPE
32 Dean of Students ..... Mr. Tyrone TYSON
10 Chief Business Officer ..... Ms. Jennifer CLAVER
08 Library Director ..... Ms. Sarah TAYLOR
37 Financial Aid Director ..... Ms. Garriell LUCAS
06 Registrar ..... Ms. Daneisha DESMOND
09 Director of Institutional Research ..... Ms. Nneka FORSMAN
07 Director of Admissions ..... Ms. Qiana Anngel BAZEMORE

Carolina College of Biblical Studies (E)

817 S. McPherson Church Road, Fayetteville NC 28303
County: Cumberland FICE Identification: 041542
Unit ID: 461032
Telephone: (910) 323-5614 Carnegie Class: Spec-4-yr-Faith
FAX Number: (910) 323-0425 Calendar System: Semester
URL: www.ccbs.edu
Established: 1973 Annual Undergrad Tuition & Fees: $5,964
Enrollment: 167 Coed
Affiliation or Control: Non-denominational IRS Status: 501(c)3
Highest Offering: Master's
Accreditation: BI

01 President ..... Dr. Bill KORVER
05 Provost ..... Dr. Chris DICKERSON
30 Vice Pres Strategic Development ..... Mr. Gary BARRETT
10 Vice Pres of Finance ..... Mr. Richard HOVATER
84 VP Enrollment/Student Services ..... Dr. Rodney PHILLIPS

Carolinas College of Health Sciences (F)

2110 Water Ridge Parkway, Charlotte NC 28217
County: Mecklenburg FICE Identification: 031042
Unit ID: 433174
Telephone: (704) 355-5043 Carnegie Class: Spec-4-yr-Other Health
FAX Number: (704) 355-9336 Calendar System: Semester
URL: www.CarolinasCollege.edu
Established: 1990 Annual Undergrad Tuition & Fees (In-District): $15,424
Enrollment: 514 Coed
Affiliation or Control: State/Local IRS Status: 501(c)3
Highest Offering: Baccalaureate
Accreditation: SC, ADNUR, HT, MLS, NURSE, RAD, RTT

01 President ..... Dr. T. Hampton HOPKINS

05 Provost ..... Dr. Jodie HUFFSTETLER
10 Dean Administrative/Financial Svcs ..... Ms. Sandra HARVEY
32 Dean Student Affs/Enrollment Mgmt ..... Mr. Anthony BROOKS
06 Registrar ..... Ms. Paige LEVESQUE
30 Dir Development/Alumni Relations ..... Ms. Ruthie MIHAL
07 Director Admissions & Recruitment ..... Vacant
37 Director Financial Aid ..... Mr. Justin PICHY
90 Director Teaching/Learning & Tech ..... Dr. Jared SMITH
09 Institutional Research Coordinator ..... Ms. Cheryl PULLIAM
04 Admin Assistant to President ..... Ms. Pat LEWIS

Carolina University (G)

420 S Broad Street, Winston-Salem NC 27101-5197
County: Forsyth FICE Identification: 002956
Unit ID: 489937
Telephone: (336) 725-8344 Carnegie Class: Masters/S
FAX Number: (336) 725-5522 Calendar System: Semester
URL: www.carolinau.edu
Established: 1945 Annual Undergrad Tuition & Fees: $14,580
Enrollment: 951 Coed
Affiliation or Control: Independent Non-Profit IRS Status: 501(c)3
Highest Offering: Doctorate
Accreditation: TRACS

01 President ..... Dr. Charles W. PETITT
32 Chancellor/Dean of Students ..... Dr. Steve CONDON
05 Exec Vice President Academic Affs ..... Dr. Sandeep GOPALAN
73 VP/Dir of Ministry Program ..... Dr. Byron EDENS
10 Chief Financial Officer ..... Dr. Chris RONK
13 Chief Info Technology Officer ..... Vacant
37 Financial Aid Director ..... Mrs. Mandy MCLAIN
41 Athletic Director ..... Dr. Steve CONDON
108 Dir Inst Effectiveness/Registrar ..... Vacant
30 Asst to Chanc Univ Advancement ..... Ms. Shealynn MILLER
18 Chf Facilities/Physical Plant Ofcr ..... Vacant

Catawba College (H)

2300 W Innes Street, Salisbury NC 28144-2488
County: Rowan FICE Identification: 002914
Unit ID: 198215
Telephone: (704) 637-4111 Carnegie Class: Bac-Diverse
FAX Number: (704) 637-4444 Calendar System: Semester
URL: www.catawba.edu
Established: 1851 Annual Undergrad Tuition & Fees: $31,436
Enrollment: 1,371 Coed
Affiliation or Control: United Church Of Christ IRS Status: 501(c)3
Highest Offering: Master's
Accreditation: SC, ACBSP, NURSE

01 President ..... Dr. David NELSON
42 Senior Vice President/Chaplain ..... Dr. Kenneth W. CLAPP
05 Provost ..... Dr. Constance ROGERS-LOWERY
30 VP of Development ..... Ms. Meg K. DEES
07 Vice Pres for Admissions ..... Vacant
04 Assistant to President ..... Mrs. Amy H. WILLIAMS
09 Dir Institutional Research ..... Dr. Sharon SULLIVAN
10 Chief Financial Officer ..... Ms. Lauren COX
15 Chief Human Resources Officer ..... Mr. Drew DAVIS
13 Chief Information Tech Officer ..... Vacant
32 Senior VP/Dean of Students ..... Dr. Jared TICE
88 Director of Student Conduct ..... Ms. Laura GILLAND
08 Library Director ..... Mr. Earl GIVENS
06 Registrar ..... Ms. Chrisanne RANCATI
37 Director of Financial Assistance ..... Ms. Kelli HAND
36 Director of Placement ..... Vacant
88 Director Sports Info & Promotion ..... Mr. Jim D. LEWIS
40 Director Bookstore ..... Mrs. Stephanie TAYLOR
41 Athletic Director ..... Vacant
18 Chief Facilities/Physical Plant ..... Mr. Billy WHITE
29 Director Alumni Relations ..... Ms. Savannah SHAVER
19 Director Security/Safety ..... Mr. David NAJARIAN
44 Director Annual Giving ..... Ms. Mindy MILLER
101 Secretary of the Institution/Board ..... Mrs. Amy H. WILLIAMS
106 Dean of Distance & Online Education ..... Vacant
39 Director Housing & Residence Life ..... Mr. Marcus WASHINGTON
50 Dean of Business ..... Dr. Eric HAKE
26 Chief Public Relations Officer ..... Ms. Jodi BAILEY

Chamberlain University-Charlotte (I)

2015 Aysley Town Blvd, Ste 204, Charlotte NC 28273
Telephone: (980) 939-6241 Identification: 770979
Accreditation: &HLC, NURSE

† Branch campus of Chamberlain University-Addison, Addison, IL

Charlotte Christian College and Theological Seminary (J)

PO Box 790106, Charlotte NC 28227-9446
County: Mecklenburg FICE Identification: 038273
Unit ID: 444778
Telephone: (704) 334-6882 Carnegie Class: Spec-4-yr-Faith
FAX Number: (704) 334-6885 Calendar System: Semester
URL: www.charlottechristian.edu
Established: 1996 Annual Undergrad Tuition & Fees: N/A
Enrollment: 182 Coed
Affiliation or Control: Independent Non-Profit IRS Status: 501(c)3
Highest Offering: Doctorate
Accreditation: TRACS

01 President ..... Dr. Eddie G. GRIGG
05 VP of Academic/Student Affairs ..... Dr. Adiaha STRANGE
10 Business Office Manager/CFO ..... Mr. Al WITT
111 Director of Advancement ..... Vacant
06 Registrar/Dir International Student ..... Ms. Nancy RAY
08 Head Librarian ..... Dr. Gwendolyn PEART
07 Director of Admissions ..... Mr. George SHEARS, III
37 Financial Aid Officer ..... Mr. Kenneth ROACH
04 Admin Assistant to the President ..... Mr. Matt RUSSELL

Chowan University (A)

One University Place, Murfreesboro NC 27855-1844
County: Hertford FICE Identification: 002916
Unit ID: 198303
Telephone: (252) 398-6500 Carnegie Class: Bac-Diverse
FAX Number: (252) 398-1190 Calendar System: Semester
URL: www.chowan.edu
Established: 1848 Annual Undergrad Tuition & Fees: $25,880
Enrollment: 1,100 Coed
Affiliation or Control: Baptist IRS Status: 501(c)3
Highest Offering: Master's
Accreditation: SC, MUS

01 President ..... Dr. Kirk E. PETERSON
05 Vice President Academic Affairs ..... Dr. Danny B. MOORE
20 Associate Provost Academic Affairs ..... Dr. John DILUSTRO
20 Assoc Provost External Relations ..... Dr. Brenda S. TINKHAM
10 Vice President Business Affairs ..... Mr. Danny R. DAVIS
32 Vice President Student Affairs ..... Dr. Montrose STREETER
111 Vice President for Advancement ..... Mr. Andy WILSON
07 Vice President Admissions ..... Dr. Daniel WILSON
41 Vice Pres/Director for Athletics ..... Mr. Patrick M. MASHUDA
13 Assistant VP Information Technology ..... Mr. James R. HOWELL
112 Executive Director of Major Gifts ..... Mr. John TAYLOE
15 Director of Human Resources ..... Mrs. Emily TERRY
06 Registrar ..... Mr. Richard TODD
26 Dir of Univ Rels/Communications ..... Mrs. Kimberly BAILEY
08 Head Librarian ..... Mrs. Georgia E. WILLIAMS
37 Director of Financial Aid ..... Ms. Ruth CASPER
42 Campus Minister ..... Ms. Mari E. WILES
18 Director Physical Plant ..... Mr. Alex CHAPPELL
19 Chief of Security ..... Mr. Derek A. BURKE
35 Director Student Life ..... Mr. Bradley CASH
36 Director Counseling/Career Services ..... Ms. Yolanda MAJETTE
39 Director Housing & Residence Life ..... Ms. Sher-Ron LAUD
09 Director Institutional Research ..... Vacant
88 Director Upward Bound ..... Mr. E. Frank STEPHENSON
21 Director Business Services ..... Mrs. Julie W. EMORY
29 Director Alumni Services ..... Mrs. Kay M. THOMAS
122 Director Greek Life ..... Mr. Bradley CASH
49 Dean School of Arts/Sciences ..... Dr. Jennifer PLACE
50 Dean School of Business and Design ..... Dr. Hunter TAYLOR
53 Dean School of Educ & Profess Stds ..... Dr. Ella E. BENSON
88 Dean School Accessibility Services ..... Vacant
58 Dean School of Graduate Studies ..... Dr. John DILUSTRO
40 Bookstore Manager ..... Vacant

Daoist Traditions College of Chinese Medical Arts (B)

382 Montford Avenue, Asheville NC 28801
County: Buncombe FICE Identification: 041464
Unit ID: 455178
Telephone: (828) 225-3993 Carnegie Class: Spec-4-yr-Other Health
FAX Number: (828) 255-3306 Calendar System: Semester
URL: www.daoisttraditions.edu
Established: 2003 Annual Graduate Tuition & Fees: N/A
Enrollment: 110 Coed
Affiliation or Control: Proprietary IRS Status: Proprietary
Highest Offering: Doctorate; No Undergraduates
Accreditation: ACUP

01 President/Financial Director ..... Dr. Mary Cissy MAJEBE
04 Administrative Asst to President ..... Jennifer MOORE
05 Academic Dean ..... Megan BURNS
07 Director of Admissions ..... Juliet DANIEL
08 Librarian ..... Emily FADER

Davidson College (C)

PO Box 5000, Davidson NC 28035-5000
County: Mecklenburg FICE Identification: 002918
Unit ID: 198385
Telephone: (704) 894-2000 Carnegie Class: Bac-A&S
FAX Number: (704) 894-2005 Calendar System: Semester
URL: www.davidson.edu
Established: 1837 Annual Undergrad Tuition & Fees: $55,175
Enrollment: 1,983 Coed
Affiliation or Control: Independent Non-Profit IRS Status: 501(c)3
Highest Offering: Baccalaureate
Accreditation: SC

01 President ..... Dr. Carol E. QUILLEN
05 Vice Pres Acad Affs/Dean of Faculty ..... Dr. Philip N. JEFFERSON
26 Vice President College Relations ..... Ms. Eileen M. KEELEY
10 Vice Pres Finance & Administration ..... Ms. Ann MCCORVEY
32 VP Student Life/Dean of Students ..... Dr. Byron P. MCCRAE
07 VP & Dean Admissions/Financial Aid ..... Mr. Christopher J. GRUBER
09 VP Planning/Institutional Research ..... Ms. Linda M. LEFAUVE
43 VP and General Counsel ..... Ms. Sarah L. PHILLIPS
111 Exec Dir of Advancement Opers ..... Vacant
20 Assoc Dean Academic Administration ..... Vacant
45 VP for Strategic Initiatives ..... Vacant
20 Assoc Dean of Faculty ..... Dr. Fuji P. LOZADA
30 Assoc VP of Development ..... Mr. Brad MARTIN
31 Assoc VP Campus/Community Relations ..... Ms. Stephanie GLASER
06 Registrar ..... Ms. Angela B. DEWBERRY
13 Chief Information Officer ..... Mr. Kevin DAVIS
37 Director Financial Aid ..... Mr. Chad A. SPENCER
15 Director of Human Resources ..... Dr. Kim BALL
41 Director of Athletics ..... Mr. Chris CLUNIE
08 Director of the Library ..... Ms. Lisa FORREST
29 Director Alumni Relations ..... Ms. Marya L. HOWELL
21 Controller/Director Business Svcs ..... Ms. Lori GASTON
18 Director Facilities & Engineering ..... Mr. David M. HOLTHOUSER
19 Chief of Campus Police ..... Mr. Julian COAXUM
36 Exec Dir Career Development ..... Mr. Jamie STAMEY
35 Director of College Union ..... Mr. Mike GOODE
39 Dir Resid Life/Assoc Dean Students ..... Mr. Jason S. SHAFFER
42 College Chaplain ..... Dr. Robert C. SPACH
88 Dir Ctr for Interdisciplinary Stds ..... Dr. Jane MANGAN
82 Assoc Dean Intl Programs/Studies ..... Dr. Jonathan BERKEY
25 Director of Grants & Contracts ..... Dr. Mary W. MUCHANE
24 Director of Digital Innovation ..... Ms. Kristen ESHLEMAN
38 Director Student Counseling ..... Mr. David GRAHAM
44 Exec Dir of Engagement ..... Ms. Lisa H. COMBS
96 Director of Purchasing ..... Vacant
40 College Store General Manager ..... Mr. William T. REILLY
04 Executive Asst to President ..... Mrs. Traci L. RUSS-WILSON
27 Chief Comm & Marketing Officer ..... Mr. Mark JOHNSON

Duke University (D)

Durham NC 27706-8001
County: Durham FICE Identification: 002920
Unit ID: 198419
Telephone: (919) 684-8111 Carnegie Class: DU-Highest
FAX Number: (919) 684-3200 Calendar System: Semester
URL: www.duke.edu
Established: 1838 Annual Undergrad Tuition & Fees: $57,633
Enrollment: 16,172 Coed
Affiliation or Control: Independent Non-Profit IRS Status: 501(c)3
Highest Offering: Doctorate
Accreditation: SC, ANEST, ARCPA, CAEP, CAMPEP, CLPSY, CVT, DIET, DIETI, IPSY, LAW, MED, NURSE, PA, PAST, PCSAS, PTA, SPAA, THEOL

01 President ..... Vincent PRICE
03 Executive Vice President ..... Daniel ENNIS
05 Provost ..... Sally KORNBLUTH
17 Chancellor for Health Affairs ..... A. Eugene WASHINGTON
10 Vice Pres Financial Svcs ..... Rachel SATTERFIELD
11 Vice President for Administration ..... Kyle CAVANAUGH
07 Dean Undergraduate Admissions ..... Christoph O. GUTTENTAG
21 Exec Vice Provost Finance & Admin ..... Jennifer FRANCIS
13 Vice Prov Information Technology ..... Tracy FUTHEY
88 Vice Prov Interdisciplinary Studies ..... Edward BALLEISEN
88 Vice Provost Faculty Advancement ..... Abbas BENMAMOUN
46 Int Vice Pres Research/Innovation ..... R. Sanders WILLIAMS
08 Librarian/Vice Prov Library Affairs ..... Joseph SALEM
37 Asst Vice Provost/Dir Financial Aid ..... Miranda MCCALL
65 Dean Sch of the Environment ..... Toddi R. STEELMAN
61 Dean of Law School ..... Kerry ABRAMS
63 Dn Sch Med/Sr Vice Chanc Acad Affs ..... Mary E. KLOTMAN
50 Dean Fuqua School of Business ..... William BOULDING
73 Dean of the Divinity School ..... Edgardo COLON-EMERIC
58 Dean Grad Sch/Vice Prov Grad Educ ..... Vacant
49 Dean Faculty Arts/Science ..... Mohamed NOOR
66 Dean School of Nursing ..... Vincent GUILAMO-RAMOS
54 Interim Dean of Engineering ..... Jeff GLASS
80 Dean Sanford Sch of Public Policy ..... Judith KELLEY
88 Director Duke University Press ..... Dean SMITH
18 Vice President for Facilities ..... John NOONAN
06 Registrar ..... Frank BLALARK
09 Director of Institutional Research ..... David JAMIESON-DRAKE
04 Executive Asst to the President ..... Sarah BRAMAN
101 VP & University Secretary ..... Margaret W. EPPS
102 Asst VP Foundation Relations ..... Beth EASTLICK
105 Senior Manager Web Services ..... Ryn NASSER
22 Vice President Institutional Equity ..... Kimberly HEWITT
26 Chief Public Relations/Marketing ..... Michael SCHOENFELD
29 Director Alumni Relations ..... Sterly WILDER
32 Vice President Student Affairs ..... Mary Pat MCMAHON
36 Executive Director Career Center ..... Gregory J. VICTORY
41 VP and Director Athletics ..... Nina E. KING
43 Vice President and General Counsel ..... Pamela BERNARD
44 Asst VP Annual Giving ..... Jennifer SPISAK-CAMERON
20 Vice Provost Undergrad Education ..... Gary BENNETT
57 Vice Provost for the Arts ..... John V. BROWN
86 Assoc VP Federal Relations ..... Christopher SIMMONS
96 VP Supply Chain ..... Jim CHURCHMAN
104 Executive Director Global Education ..... Amanda KELSO
30 VP Alumni Affairs/Development ..... David KENNEDY
88 Vice President Durham Affairs ..... Stelfanie WILLIAMS
19 Chief of Police ..... John DAILEY
39 Interim Dir Residential Life ..... Deb LOBIONDO

ECPI University-Charlotte (E)

4800 Airport Center Pkwy #100, Charlotte NC 28208
Telephone: (704) 399-1010 Identification: 770951
Accreditation: &SC, MAAB

† Branch campus of ECPI University, Virginia Beach, VA

ECPI University-Greensboro (F)

7802 Airport Center Drive, Greensboro NC 27409
Telephone: (336) 792-7594 Identification: 770952
Accreditation: &SC, MAAB

† Branch campus of ECPI University, Virginia Beach, VA

ECPI University-Raleigh (G)

4101 Doie Cope Road, Raleigh NC 27613
Telephone: (919) 283-5748 Identification: 770953
Accreditation: &SC, MAAB

† Branch campus of ECPI University, Virginia Beach, VA

Elon University (H)

2700 Campus Box, Elon NC 27244-2010
County: Alamance FICE Identification: 002927
Unit ID: 198516
Telephone: (336) 278-2000 Carnegie Class: DU-Mod
FAX Number: N/A Calendar System: 4/1/4
URL: www.elon.edu
Established: 1889 Annual Undergrad Tuition & Fees: $37,921
Enrollment: 7,117 Coed
Affiliation or Control: Independent Non-Profit IRS Status: 501(c)3
Highest Offering: Doctorate
Accreditation: SC, ARCPA, CAEPN, JOUR, LAW, PTA

01 President ..... Dr. Connie LEDOUX BOOK
05 Int Provost/EVP Academic Affairs ..... Dr. Raghu TADEPALLI
45 VP for Strategic Initiatives ..... Mr. Jeff STEIN
100 Chief of Staff/Sec to Bd Trustees ..... Mr. Patrick NOLTEMEYER
04 Special Assistant to the President ..... Mr. Dan ANDERSON
04 Special Assistant to the President ..... Vacant
04 Special Assistant to President ..... Mr. Gerald O. WHITTINGTON
88 VP Emeritus for Student Life ..... Dr. Smith JACKSON
84 VP for Enrollment Management ..... Mr. Greg ZAISER
32 Vice Pres for Student Life ..... Dr. Jon DOOLEY
26 Vice Pres University Communications ..... Mr. Mike HASKINS
22 VP/Assoc Prov Inclusive Excellence ..... Dr. Randy WILLIAMS
111 Vice Pres University Advancement ..... Mr. James B. PIATT
41 Director of Athletics ..... Mr. Dave L. BLANK
88 Exec Director for Access & Success ..... Dr. Travella FREE
20 Sr Assoc Provost for Faculty Affs ..... Dr. Tim PEEPLES
20 Assoc Prov Acad Excellence/Opers ..... Dr. Paul MILLER
20 Assoc Provost for Academic Affairs ..... Dr. Jennifer PLATANIA
10 VP for Finance & Administration ..... Mrs. Janet WILLIAMS
21 AVP Finance & Administration ..... Ms. Susan M. KIRKLAND
49 Dean College of Arts & Sciences ..... Dr. Gabie SMITH
50 Dean Love School of Business ..... Dr. Raghu TADEPALLI
60 Interim Dean School Communications ..... Dr. Kenn GAITHER
53 Dean of School of Education ..... Dr. Ann BULLOCK
61 Interim Dean School of Law ..... Mr. Alan WOODLIEF
76 Interim Dean School Health Sciences ..... Dr. Stephen FOLGER
85 Dean of Global Studies ..... Dr. Nick GOZIK
35 Associate VP of Student Life ..... Mrs. Jana Lynn F. PATTERSON
08 Dean and University Librarian ..... Ms. Joan RUELLE
06 Registrar ..... Dr. Rodney PARKS
42 University Chaplain ..... Rev. Kirstin BOSWELL
37 Asst VP for Financial Aid ..... Dr. M. Patrick MURPHY
110 Assoc VP University Advancement ..... Mr. John BARNHILL
30 Assoc VP/Dir Principal Gifts ..... Mr. Brian BAKER
29 Asst VP Annual Giv/Alum Engagement ..... Mr. Brian FEELEY
110 Asst VP Univ Advancemt Parent Engmt ..... Ms. Jozi SNOWBERGER
121 Interim Dir of Academic Advising ..... Ms. Kathy ZIGA
36 Director of Student Prof Dev Ctr ..... Ms. Brooke BUFFINGTON
88 Dir of Planning/Design/Construction ..... Mr. Brad D. MOORE
18 Asst VP of Physical Plant ..... Mr. Tom FLOOD
15 Assoc VP Human Resources ..... Ms. Kelli SHUMAN
109 Asst VP for Auxiliary Services ..... Ms. Carrie RYAN
19 Chief of Campus Safety/Police ..... Mr. Joe LEMIRE
23 Dir Student Health/Univ Physician ..... Dr. Ginette ARCHINAL
38 Director Counseling Services ..... Ms. Anita HODNETT
11 Asst VP for Admin Services ..... Mr. Christopher D. FULKERSON
108 Dir Accreditation and Assessment ..... Dr. Maurice LEVESQUE
09 Exec Director Institutional Rsrch ..... Dr. Robert I. SPRINGER
13 Assoc VP for InfoTechnology and CIO ..... Mr. Christopher C. WATERS
25 Director of Sponsored Programs ..... Ms. Bonnie BRUNO
92 Director of Honors Program ..... Dr. Lynn HUBER
94 Director Women's/Gender Studies ..... Ms. Shayna MEHAS
96 Director of Purchasing ..... Mr. Jeff HENDRICKS
88 Director of Sustainability ..... Ms. Elaine DURR
104 Exec Dir of Global Engagement ..... Ms. Rhonda WALLER
28 Dir Inclusive Excellence/Educ/Dev ..... Ms. Carla FULLWOOD
39 Assoc Director of Residence Life ..... Ms. Aneshia JERRALDS
102 Director Foundation/Corporate Rels ..... Ms. Chris ESTERS
44 Director Annual Giving ..... Ms. Chandler BOYLE
122 Asst Director Greek Life ..... Ms. Alexis SWIDER

Gardner-Webb University (I)

PO Box 897 (110 South Main Street), Boiling Springs NC 28017-0897
County: Cleveland FICE Identification: 002929
Unit ID: 198561
Telephone: (704) 406-2361 Carnegie Class: DU-Mod
FAX Number: (704) 406-4329 Calendar System: Semester
URL: www.gardner-webb.edu
Established: 1905 Annual Undergrad Tuition & Fees: $32,180
Enrollment: 3,536 Coed
Affiliation or Control: Baptist IRS Status: 501(c)3

Highest Offering: Doctorate
Accreditation: SC, ACBSP, ADNUR, ARCPA, CACREP, CAEP, EXSC, MUS, NUR, THEOL

01 President .... Dr. William M. DOWNS
05 Provost & VP for Academic Affairs .... Dr. Karen AUBREY
04 Exec Assistant to the President .... Mrs. Stephanie L. STEARNS
10 Vice President of Finance & Admin .... Mr. Timothy SHUEY
26 VP of Marketing .... Mr. Richard K. MCDEVITT
111 VP for External Affairs/Advancement .... Mr. Nate EVANS
32 Vice Pres Student Development .... Mrs. Lesley VILLAROSE
84 Interim VP Enrollment Management .... Ms. Julie FLEMING
41 Vice President for Athletics .... Mr. Chuck S. BURCH
45 VP Planning & Inst Effectiveness .... Dr. Jeffrey L. TUBBS
18 Director of Operations .... Mr. David WACASTER
13 Asst VP for Technology Services .... Ms. Didi LEDBETTER
20 Assoc Provost Prof/Graduate Studies .... Dr. Bruce BOYLES
21 Assoc VP for Business & Finance .... Ms. Robin G. HAMRICK
37 Asst VP for Financial Planning .... Ms. Anita ELLIOTT
06 Registrar .... Mrs. LouAnn P. SCATES
20 Assoc Provost Academic Development .... Ms. Carmen BUTLER
19 Chief of University Police .... Mr. Barry JOHNSON
27 Assoc VP for Marketing/Comm .... Mr. Noel T. MANNING
08 Director of the Library .... Ms. Pam DENNIS
38 Director of Counseling Services .... Ms. Stephanie ALLEN
58 Dean of Graduate School .... Dr. Sydney BROWN
73 Dean of Divinity School .... Dr. Robert W. CANOY
76 Dean of College of Health Sci .... Dr. Nicole WATERS
92 Director of Honors Program .... Dr. Wilson HAWKINS
88 Director Program for Blind/Deaf .... Mrs. Cheryl J. POTTER
21 Comptroller .... Ms. Haley KENDRICK
35 Assistant Dean of Students .... Mr. Brian ARNOLD
42 Interim VP for Christian Life .... Mr. Neal PAYNE
39 Assoc Director of Housing .... Ms. Shelbilynn BOELSCHE
50 Dean of College of Business .... Dr. Mischia TAYLOR
15 Interim AVP of Human Resources .... Ms. Esther PORTER
09 Director of Institutional Research .... Ms. Lisa KINDLER
29 Director Alumni Relations .... Mrs. Leah CLEVENGER
44 Asst VP of Advancement .... Ms. Sara MCCALL
109 Director of Operations Support .... Mr. Brian SPEER
110 Assoc VP of Advancement .... Mr. Aaron HINTON
103 Director Professional Development .... Mr. Micah MARTIN
106 Director of Digital Learning .... Dr. Emily ROBERTSON
108 Director Institutional Assessment .... Dr. Lucas STERN
28 Director of Diversity .... Mr. Lawrence BRINSON
53 Dean School of Education .... Dr. Prince BULL
105 AVP Web & Digital Communications .. Ms. Theandra THOMPSON
43 University Counsel .... Mr. Steve SERCK

Grace Communion Seminary (A)

3120 Whitehall Park Drive, Charlotte NC 28273-3335
County: Mecklenburg — Identification: 667115
Telephone: (980) 495-3978 — Carnegie Class: Not Classified
FAX Number: (844) 350-3419 — Calendar System: Semester
URL: www.gcs.edu
Established: 2008 — Annual Graduate Tuition & Fees: N/A
Enrollment: N/A — Coed
Affiliation or Control: Independent Non-Profit — IRS Status: 501(c)3
Highest Offering: Master's; No Undergraduates
Accreditation: DEAC

01 President/CEO .... Dr. Gary DEDDO
05 Dean of Faculty .... Dr. Michael MORRISON
06 Registrar .... Ms. Georgia MCKINNON
10 CFO/Liaison Officer .... Vacant

Greensboro College (B)

815 W Market Street, Greensboro NC 27401-1875
County: Guilford — FICE Identification: 002930
Unit ID: 198598
Telephone: (336) 272-7102 — Carnegie Class: Masters/S
FAX Number: (336) 217-6634 — Calendar System: Semester
URL: www.greensboro.edu
Established: 1838 — Annual Undergrad Tuition & Fees: $18,960
Enrollment: 944 — Coed
Affiliation or Control: United Methodist — IRS Status: 501(c)3
Highest Offering: Master's
Accreditation: SC, ACBSP, MUS

00 Chairman of the Board .... Mr. Martha BRADBERRY
01 President .... Dr. Lawrence D. CZARDA
101 Clerk to the Board of Trustees .... Ms. Susan J. BARRINGER
04 Exec Asst to President .... Ms. Lindsay ALTHAUS
100 Chief of Staff .... Ms. Emily M. SCOTT
05 VP Academic Affairs .... Dr. Daniel MALOTKY
10 VP Business & Finance .... Mr. Chris ELMORE
111 VP Advancement & Admissions .... Ms. Anne J. HURD
20 Assoc VP Academic Admin .... Ms. Martha M. BUNCH
20 Dean of the Faculty .... Dr. Jessica SHARPE
57 Dean School of Arts .... Prof. Jo HALL
50 Dean School of Business .... Dr. Karen KNOCH
53 Dean School of Soc Sci & Education .... Dr. Natasha VEALE
79 Dean School of Humanities .... Dr. Michelle PLAISANCE
81 Dean School of Science & Mathematic .... Dr. Stuart DAVIDSON
07 Dean of Admissions .... Ms. Julianne SCHATZ
13 Chief Information Officer .... Mr. Gregg CHOTTINER
14 Network Support Supervisor .... Ms. Stephanie FULLER
37 Financial Aid Director .... Ms. Lindsay S. LATHAM
113 Student Accounts Director .... Ms. Marilyn WOODS
26 Sr Dir Marketing & Communications .... Mr. Tom SAITTA
06 Registrar .... Mr. Travis MICKEY
32 Dean of Students .... Ms. Shana PLASTERS
39 Director Residence Life .... Mr. John FELTON
89 First Year Experience Director .... Ms. Jenna AVENT
36 Career Services Director .... Ms. Caryn ATWATER
104 Study Abroad Director .... Dr. Jason MYERS
09 Institutional Research Director .... Dr. Jeff ANKROM
108 Director Institutional Assessment .... Dr. Dana L. DALTON
121 Academic Success Director .... Ms. Tica D. GREEN
124 Student Retention Director .... Vacant
28 Diversity Equity Inclusion Director .... Ms. Tasha M. MYERS
15 Human Resources Director .... Ms. Sonia HOFFMAN
18 Facilities Director .... Mr. Joseph TISCH
19 Security Director .... Mr. Calvin L. GILMORE
23 Student Health Director .... Ms. Lauren T. CHILDREY
38 Counseling Services Director .... Ms. Bernette JONES
92 George Ctr/Honors Studies Director .... Prof. Brittany SONDBERG
30 Asst VP Development .... Ms. Ellie P. YEARNS
29 Alumni Giving & Programs Director .... Ms. Hannah SOOTS
08 Library Director .... Mr. Will RITTER
41 Athletic Director .... Mr. Kim STRABLE
42 Campus Chaplain .... Rev. Robert W. BREWER
40 Bookstore Manager .... Mr. Cliff BRALY, JR.
21 Controller .... Ms. Michelle STILES
88 Title IX Coordinator .... Ms. Emily SCOTT

Guilford College (C)

5800 W Friendly Avenue, Greensboro NC 27410-4173
County: Guilford — FICE Identification: 002931
Unit ID: 198613
Telephone: (336) 316-2000 — Carnegie Class: Bac-A&S
FAX Number: (336) 316-2950 — Calendar System: Other
URL: www.guilford.edu
Established: 1837 — Annual Undergrad Tuition & Fees: $40,120
Enrollment: 1,429 — Coed
Affiliation or Control: Friends — IRS Status: 501(c)3
Highest Offering: Master's
Accreditation: SC, ACBSP

01 President .... Dr. Jim W. HOOD
05 Interim Provost .... Dr. Rob WHITNELL
04 Exec Administrator to Pres & CFO .... Dr. Meredeth D. SUMMERS
10 CFO/VP Administration & Finance .... Mr. John WILKINSON
26 Vice Pres Marketing/Enrollment .... Mr. Roger DEGERMAN
111 Vice Pres Advancement .... Dr. Ara SERJOIE
22 VP Diversity/Equity/Inclusion .... Dr. Barbara LAWRENCE
29 Assoc VP Alumni/Constituent Rels .... Mr. R. Ty BUCKNER
28 Assoc VP Diversity/Equity/Inclusion .... Dr. Krishauna HINES-GAITHER
32 Dean of Students .... Dr. Steven MENCARINI
20 Associate Academic Dean .... Dr. Kathryn SHIELDS
20 Interim Academic Dean .... Dr. Kyle DELL
37 Director of Financial Aid .... Ms. Char BEDILLION
06 Registrar .... Dr. Alfred MOORE
08 Director of the Library .... Ms. Suzanne M. BARTELS
41 Director of Athletics .... Dr. Bill FOTI
19 Director of Public Safety .... Mr. Jermaine THOMAS
15 Director Human Resources .... Ms. Janet GOULD
09 Dir Inst Research/Assessment .... Dr. Stephanie HARGRAVE
13 Director Info Technology & Services .... Ms. Gloria THORNTON
42 WR Rogers Dir of Friends Center .... Dr. C. Wess DANIELS
38 Director Student Counseling .... Ms. Taleisha BOWEN
92 Director Honors Program .... Dr. Heather HAYTON
96 Director of Purchasing .... Ms. Tracy A. HALL
104 Director Study Abroad .... Mr. Daniel DIAZ
88 Exec Coordinator to the Provost .... Ms. Lisa DEMERS
44 Director Annual Giving .... Vacant
07 Director of Admissions .... Mr. Kyle WOODEN

Heritage Bible College (D)

PO Box 1628, Dunn NC 28335-1628
County: Harnett — FICE Identification: 030893
Unit ID: 198677
Telephone: (910) 892-3178 — Carnegie Class: Spec-4-yr-Faith
FAX Number: (910) 491-9790 — Calendar System: Semester
URL: www.heritagebiblecollege.edu
Established: 1971 — Annual Undergrad Tuition & Fees: $8,328
Enrollment: 43 — Coed
Affiliation or Control: Other — IRS Status: 501(c)3
Highest Offering: Baccalaureate
Accreditation: @BI, TRACS

01 President .... Mr. Stephen RZONCA
05 Academic Dean .... Mrs. Dana SCHAEFER
10 Business Administrator .... Mrs. LeAnne PAGE
09 Dir Inst Effectiveness/Dir Library .... Ms. Janet PARKER
13 Chief Info Technology Officer (CIO) .... Mr. Wesley JOHNSON
07 Director Admissions/Financial Aid .... Mr. Sterling THARRINGTON
06 Registrar .... Mr. Matt CLARK

High Point University (E)

One University Parkway, High Point NC 27268-0001
County: Guilford — FICE Identification: 002933
Unit ID: 198695
Telephone: (336) 841-9000 — Carnegie Class: Bac-Diverse
FAX Number: (336) 841-4599 — Calendar System: Semester
URL: www.highpoint.edu
Established: 1924 — Annual Undergrad Tuition & Fees: $38,080
Enrollment: 5,617 — Coed
Affiliation or Control: United Methodist — IRS Status: 501(c)3
Highest Offering: Doctorate
Accreditation: SC, ARCPA, ART, CAATE, CAEP, CIDA, PHAR, PTA

01 President .... Dr. Nido R. QUBEIN
05 SVP for Academic Affairs/Provost .... Dr. Daniel E. ERB
10 Sr VP for Business Affairs .... Mr. Brad CALLOWAY
84 Sr VP for Graduate Enrollment .... Mr. Andy BILLS
26 Sr VP for Communications .... Mr. Roger D. CLODFELTER, JR.
32 SVP Student Life/Health/Wellness .... Vacant
30 Sr VP for Development .... Mr. Christopher H. DUDLEY
07 SVP for Undergrad Admissions .... Mr. Kerr C. RAMSAY
46 VP for Research and Planning .... Dr. Jeffrey M. ADAMS
18 VP for Facilities & Auxiliary Svcs .... Mr. Barry S. KITLEY
21 VP for Financial Affairs .... Ms. Debi SHUTTERS
88 VP for Exp Learning & Career Dev .....Dr. Stephanie O. CROFTON
13 VP for Enterprise IT .... Mr. Curtis BARKER
41 VP for Athletics and AD .... Mr. Dan HAUSER
123 Assoc VP of Graduate Admissions .... Mr. Andrew S. MODLIN
35 Asst VP for Student Life .... Dr. Tara K. SHOLLENBERGER
35 Asst VP for Student Life .... Mr. Scott WOJCIECHOWSKI
35 Asst VP for Student Life .... Ms. Erica D. LEWIS
88 Asst VP for Graduate Admissions .... Mr. Lars C. FARABEE
27 Asst VP for Communication Mgt .... Ms. Hillary C. KOKAJKO
27 Asst VP for Communications .... Ms. Pamela J. HAYNES
110 Asst VP for Development .... Mr. McKennon SHEA
88 Asst VP for Facility Operations .... Mr. Troy J. THOMPSON
49 Dean of College of Arts & Science .... Mr. Ken D. ELSTON
57 Dean of School of Art and Design .... Dr. John C. TURPIN
50 Dean of School of Business .... Dr. James B. WEHRLEY
60 Dean of School of Communication . Dr. Virginia M. MCDERMOTT
53 Dean of School of Education .... Dr. Kristy P. DAVIS
54 Dean of the School of Engineering ....Dr. Michael OUDSHOORN
76 Dean of School of Health Sciences .... Dr. Daniel E. ERB
81 Dean of School of Natural Sciences .... Dr. Angela C. BAUER
67 Dean of School of Pharmacy .... Dr. Earl W. LINGLE
20 Assistant Dean Academic Services .... Ms. Karen C. NAYLON
08 Director of Library Services .... Mr. David L. BRYDEN
23 Medical Director .... Dr. Marnie S. MARLETTE
19 Chief of Security .... Mr. Derek S. STAFFORD
06 Registrar .... Mr. Danny K. BROOKS
15 AVP of Human Resources .... Mr. Marc SEARS
88 Sr Director of University Events .... Ms. Melissa L. ANDERSON
29 Director of Alumni Engagement .... Mr. Bradley G. TAYLOR
37 Sr Dir Student Financial Services .... Mr. Jonathan M. MADOR
25 Director of Sponsored Programs .... Ms. Leanna NICKS
38 Director of Counseling Services .... Dr. M.J RALEIGH
09 Dir of Inst Research & Assessment .... Mr. James S. LOWREY
113 Assoc Director of Student Accounts .... Ms. Megan INCH
96 Mgr Contracts & Procurement .... Mr. Gene BUNTING
40 Manager Bookstore .... Mr. William HOLSTON
85 Director of International Students .... Ms. Marjorie R. CHURCH
36 Director of Career Development .... Dr. William A. GENTRY
104 Director of Global Education .... Dr. Jeffrey M. PALIS
88 Director of Service Learning .... Dr. Joseph D. BLOSSER
88 Director of Undergraduate Research .... Dr. Joanne D. ALTMAN
04 Admin Assistant to President .... Ms. Judy K. RAY
88 Manager of University Mail Center .... Mr. Michael R. HALL
20 VP for Academic Affairs .... Dr. Angela C. BAUER

Hood Theological Seminary (F)

1810 Lutheran Synod Drive, Salisbury NC 28144-5768
County: Rowan — FICE Identification: 036633
Unit ID: 443076
Telephone: (704) 636-7611 — Carnegie Class: Spec-4-yr-Faith
FAX Number: (704) 636-7685 — Calendar System: Semester
URL: www.hoodseminary.edu
Established: 1904 — Annual Undergrad Tuition & Fees: N/A
Enrollment: 142 — Coed
Affiliation or Control: African Methodist Episcopal Zion Church — IRS Status: 501(c)3
Highest Offering: Doctorate
Accreditation: THEOL

01 President .... Dr. Vergel L. LATTIMORE
05 Academic Dean .... Dr. Trevor EPPEHIMER
32 Dean of Students .... Dr. Dora R. MBUWAYESANGO
10 Chief Financial Officer .... RevDr. Regina M. DANCY
26 Dir Communication/Info/Pub .... Ms. Kelly BRYANT
111 Dir Institutional Advancement .... Mr. John C. EVERETT
06 Registrar .... Ms. Nancy BAKER
19 Chief of Security .... Mr. James MILTON
07 Director of Admissions .... RevDr. Reginald BOYD, JR.
08 Director of the Library .... Ms. Patricia COMMANDER
37 Director Student Financial Aid .... Ms. Angela DAVIS-BAXTER
15 Director of Human Resources .... RevDr. Regina M. DANCY

Johnson & Wales University-Charlotte (G)

801 W Trade Street, Charlotte NC 28202-1122
Telephone: (980) 598-1000 — Identification: 666375
Accreditation: &EH

† Regional accreditation is carried under the parent institution in Providence, RI.

Johnson C. Smith University (H)

100 Beatties Ford Road, Charlotte NC 28216-5398
County: Mecklenburg — FICE Identification: 002936
Unit ID: 198756
Telephone: (704) 378-1000 — Carnegie Class: Bac-A&S
FAX Number: (704) 372-1242 — Calendar System: Semester
URL: www.jcsu.edu
Established: 1867 — Annual Undergrad Tuition & Fees: $18,784
Enrollment: 1,306 — Coed

Affiliation or Control: Independent Non-Profit IRS Status: 501(c)3
Highest Offering: Master's
Accreditation: SC, LC, SW

01 President .... Mr. Clarence (Clay) D. ARMBRISTER
05 Sr VP for Academic Affairs .... Dr. Karen MORGAN
10 Sr Vice Pres for Finance/Admin .... Mr. Greg PETZKE
111 Vice President for Inst Advancement .... Ms. Tami SIMMONS
86 VP Government Sponsored Pgms .... Dr. Diane BOWLES
15 VP Admin Svcs/Chief HR Officer ..... Ms. Latrelle P. MCALLISTER
32 Vice Pres Student Affairs .... Dr. Davida HAYWOOD
84 AVP Enrollment Management .... Dr. Rhonda MOSES
81 Dean College of STEM .... Dr. Vijaya L. GOMPA
49 Interim Dean of Arts and Letters .... Dr. Matthew DEFORREST
70 Dean of School of Social Work .... Dr. Helen CALDWELL
35 Dean of Students .... Mr. Takeem DEAN
89 Assoc Dean of First-Year Experience .... Dr. Cathy JONES
97 Dean of the University College .... Dr. Antonio HENLEY
107 Int Dean Metro College Prof Studies .Dr. Melita POPE MITCHELL
121 Dean of Academic Support Services .... Mr. John NORRIS
08 Director of the Library .... Ms. Monika RHUE
13 Chief Information Officer .... Mr. John NORRIS
09 Dir Assessment/Effect/Inst Rsrch .... Mrs. Sharell CANNADY
26 Director of Comm and Marketing .... Ms. Sherri BELFIELD
29 Director Alumni Affairs .... Mrs. Wanda FOY-BURROUGHS
37 Director Financial Aid .... Ms. Rochelle D. KING
41 Athletic Director .... Mr. Stephen JOYNER, SR.
06 Registrar .... Mrs. Keisha WILSON
40 Manager of Bookstore .... Ms. Kathy DEVLIN
117 Manager Risk Management .... Mrs. Debra HOLLIS
39 Coordinator of Housing Services .... Ms. Ashley SMITH
23 Health Center Coordinator .... Ms. Marian JONES
19 Dir Security/Safety/Chief Police .... Mr. Jermaine CHERRY
18 Director Facilities .... Ms. Erna JONES

Lees-McRae College (A)

191 Main Street, Banner Elk NC 28604-0128
County: Avery FICE Identification: 002939
Unit ID: 198808
Telephone: (828) 898-5241 Carnegie Class: Bac-Diverse
FAX Number: (828) 898-8814 Calendar System: Semester
URL: www.lmc.edu
Established: 1900 Annual Undergrad Tuition & Fees: $27,390
Enrollment: 838 Coed
Affiliation or Control: Presbyterian Church (U.S.A.) IRS Status: 501(c)3
Highest Offering: Master's
Accreditation: SC, NURSE

01 President .... Dr. Herbert L. KING
04 Exec Assistant to the President .... Ms. Michelle TAIT
05 Provost & Dean of Faculty .... Dr. Alyson GILL
45 VP Planning & External Relations .... Mr. Blaine J. HANSEN
10 VP Finance/Business Affairs .... Mr. Jon KOKOS
84 VP Enrollment Management .... Mr. Kevin PHILLIPS
111 VP for Institutional Advancement .... Mr. Edward ROBERTS
41 VP Athletics/Club Sports .... Mr. Craig MCPHAIL
32 VP for Student Affairs .... Dr. Melanie HULBERT
66 Dean Nursing/Health Sciences .... Dr. Kimberly S. PRIODE
79 Dean Arts/Humanities/Education .... Dr. Pamela VESELY
81 Dean Natural & Behavioral Sciences .... Vacant
50 Dean Business & Management .... Ms. Amy ANDERSON
111 Director of Advancement Services .... Ms. Mary TAYLOR
121 Dir Burton Ctr for Student Success .... Ms. Beth BEGGS
08 Director Libraries .... Ms. Jess BELLEMER
06 Registrar .... Ms. Lynn HINSHAW
19 Director Security/Safety .... Mr. H.D STEWART
13 Director Technology Services .... Vacant
15 Director Human Resources .... Ms. Mary FURST
21 Controller .... Ms. Susan STEPHENSON
35 Associate Dean of Students .... Vacant
26 Director Marketing & Design .... Ms. Lauren FOSTER
07 Director Admissions .... Ms. Amanda MERRITT
37 Director Financial Aid .... Ms. Karen KING
36 Director Career Services .... Ms. Grace CHAMPION
38 Director Counseling Services .... Ms. Marla GENTILE
113 Bursar .... Ms. Denise DYER
23 Director of Health Services .... Mr. Carl GRIEWISCH
121 Director of Tutoring Services .... Ms. Sue MCGUIRE
112 Major Gifts Officer .... Mr. Samuel STEPHENSON
09 Director of Institutional Research .... Ms. Taylor BARRY
18 Chief Facilities/Physical Plnt Ofcr .... Mr. James LEENHOUTS
29 Director Alumni Affairs .... Dr. Katie TALBERT
106 Dean of Online Education/E-learning .... Dr. Jennifer LOPES
28 Director of Diversity .... Vacant
39 Dir Resident Life/Student Housing .... Ms. Erin SMITH

Lenoir-Rhyne University (B)

625 7th Avenue NE, Hickory NC 28601-3984
County: Catawba FICE Identification: 002941
Unit ID: 198835
Telephone: (828) 328-1741 Carnegie Class: Masters/L
FAX Number: (828) 328-7368 Calendar System: Semester
URL: www.lr.edu
Established: 1891 Annual Undergrad Tuition & Fees: $39,900
Enrollment: 2,686 Coed
Affiliation or Control: Evangelical Lutheran Church In America
IRS Status: 501(c)3
Highest Offering: Doctorate
Accreditation: SC, ACBSP, CACREP, DIETI, NURSE, OT, PH, THEOL

01 President .... Dr. Fred WHITT
05 Provost .... Dr. Jennifer BURRIS
10 Sr Vice President Finance/Admin .... Mr. Jeremy SHREVE
111 Vice Pres Institutional Advancement .... Mrs. Catherine NIEKRO
45 VP Mission/Engagement/Innovation .... Dr. Laura CRAWLEY
32 Asst Provost/Dean of Students .... Dr. Katie FISHER
28 Vice President for DEI .... Mr. Avery STALEY
58 Dean Grad Studies/Lifelong Learning .... Dr. Amy WOOD
06 Registrar .... Mr. Stacey BRACKETT
08 Librarian .... Mr. Frank QUINN
15 Director of Human Resources .... Ms. Angelene FORTUNE
40 Director of Bookstore .... Ms. Dondi JOYNER
18 Director of Facilities/Plant .... Mr. Jesse CHILDERS
41 Athletic Director .... Ms. Kim PATE
42 Campus Pastor .... Rev. Todd CUTTER
19 Director of Security .... Mr. Norris YODER
92 Director of Honors Program .... Dr. Joshua RING
13 Chief Information Officer .... Ms. Cherie WHIPPLE
26 Dir of Marketing/Athletics .... Mr. Nick ROBINSON
88 Director of Conferences & Events .... Mr. Scott WOODARD
07 Director of Enrollment Services .... Mr. Eric BRANDON
09 Dir of Inst Research/Assess .... Vacant
37 Director Student Financial Aid .... Ms. Courtney THOMPSON-BALLARD
38 Dir Student Counseling/Placement .... Mr. Todd CUTTER
88 Dir Liberal Arts/Visiting Writers .... Dr. Rand BRANDES
28 Director Multicultural Affairs .... Mr. Terry PHILLIPS
88 Director Solmaz Institute .... Ms. Kimberly PENNINGTON
65 Co-Director Reese Institute .... Dr. John BRZORAD
85 Dir of International Programs .... Ms. Brittany MARINELLI
53 Dean Col of Education/Human Svcs .... Dr. Hank WEDDINGTON
76 Dean College of Health Sciences .... Dr. Michael MCGEE
49 Dean College of Arts & Sciences .... Dr. Jennifer HELLER
81 Dean Col of Profess/Math Studies .... Dr. Mary LESSER
36 Director Student Placement .... Ms. Katie WOHLMAN
39 Director Student Housing .... Ms. Kelli MEDLEY
43 Dir of Compliance/Title IX .... Ms. Dawn FLOYD
04 Exec Assistant to the President .... Ms. Cameron WOMACK
29 Director Alumni Affairs .... Ms. Mary Ellen SHERRILL
44 Director Annual Giving .... Ms. Tatum POTTENGER
122 Dir Stdnt Orientation-Greek Life .... Ms. Carla FOWLER

Living Arts College @ School of Communication Arts (C)

3000 Wakefield Crossing Drive, Raleigh NC 27614-7076
County: Wake FICE Identification: 031090
Unit ID: 421832
Telephone: (919) 488-8500 Carnegie Class: Bac-Diverse
FAX Number: (919) 488-8490 Calendar System: Quarter
URL: www.living-arts-college.edu
Established: 1992 Annual Undergrad Tuition & Fees: $16,600
Enrollment: 171 Coed
Affiliation or Control: Proprietary IRS Status: Proprietary
Highest Offering: Baccalaureate
Accreditation: ACICS

01 Campus President .... James RAMSEY, III

Livingstone College (D)

701 W Monroe Street, Salisbury NC 28144-5298
County: Rowan FICE Identification: 002942
Unit ID: 198862
Telephone: (704) 216-6000 Carnegie Class: Bac-Diverse
FAX Number: (704) 216-6217 Calendar System: Semester
URL: www.livingstone.edu
Established: 1879 Annual Undergrad Tuition & Fees: $18,296
Enrollment: 845 Coed
Affiliation or Control: African Methodist Episcopal Zion Church
IRS Status: 501(c)3
Highest Offering: Master's
Accreditation: SC, IACBE, SW

01 President .... Dr. Anthony J. DAVIS
04 Exec Admin Asst to the President .... Ms. Tracy JOHNSON
05 Vice Pres Academic Affairs .... Dr. Kelli V. RANDALL
10 Vice Pres Business & Finance/Ops .... Mr. Reginald DICKENS
32 Vice President Student Affairs .... Dr. Orlando LEWIS
111 AVP Inst Advancement/Dir Title III .... Ms. Leslie JONES DAVIDSON
35 Assoc Vice Pres of Student Affairs .... Ms. Terri STEVENSON
20 Asst Vice Pres Academic Affairs .... Vacant
38 Dean of Counseling Services .... Dr. Rhonda FLOWERS-CORPENING
06 Registrar .... Mrs. Wendy JACKSON
08 Director Library Services .... Ms. Laura JOHNSON
26 Vice Pres Comm/PR/Exec Asst to Pres .Dr. State W. ALEXANDER
37 Director of Financial Aid .... Ms. Stephanie MCNEIL
36 Director of Career Services .... Ms. Brenda MITCHELL
13 Director of Computer Info Systems .... Mr. Chong DAN
15 Director of Human Resources .... Dr. Jacqueline MILLER
29 Director Alumni Affairs .... Ms. Vincia MILLER
09 Director of Institutional Research .... Mr. Robert L. MCINNIS
07 Director of Admissions .... Vacant
40 Bookstore & Retail Coordinator .... Mr. Timothy GRAY
41 Athletic Director .... Mr. Lamonte J. MASSEY-SAMPSON
27 Director Public Relations .... Ms. Kimberly HARRINGTON

Louisburg College (E)

501 N. Main Street, Louisburg NC 27549-7705
County: Franklin FICE Identification: 002943
Unit ID: 198871
Telephone: (919) 496-2521 Carnegie Class: Assoc/HT-High Trad
FAX Number: (919) 496-7141 Calendar System: Semester
URL: www.louisburg.edu
Established: 1787 Annual Undergrad Tuition & Fees: $19,795
Enrollment: 490 Coed
Affiliation or Control: United Methodist IRS Status: 501(c)3
Highest Offering: Associate Degree
Accreditation: SC

01 President .... Dr. Gary M. BROWN
05 VP of Academic Life .... Dr. Calandra LOCKHART
10 Chief Financial Officer .... Ms. Anna FAATILIGA
84 VP of Enrollment Management .... Vacant
32 VP of Student Life .... Mr. Justin JANAK
111 VP of Institutional Advancement .... Ms. Alitha PALICH
20 Dean of Academic Operations .... Ms. Maleeka T. LOVE
06 Registrar .... Ms. Tanya BARNES-JONES
41 Athletic Director .... Mr. Mike HOLLOMAN
07 Director of Admissions .... Mr. Hunter KIRBY
39 Asst Dean of Students/Choices Coord .... Ms. Toni COCHIS
37 Director of Financial Aid .... Ms. Karen OVERTON
18 Director of Facilities/Maintenance .... Mr. John CLARK
13 Director of Information Tech .... Mr. Adam SNELL
15 Director of Human Resources .... Ms. Terry WRIGHT
04 Administrative Asst to President .... Ms. Larraine ABBOTT
29 Alumni Engagement Officer .... Ms. Kathryn O'LEARY
09 Director of Institutional Research .... Vacant
19 Chief of Campus Safety .... Mr. Ron GUARDINO, JR.
08 Librarian .... Ms. Kristine JONES

Lumbee River Christian College (F)

PO Box 248, Shannon NC 28386
County: Hoke Identification: 667092
Telephone: (910) 843-5304 Carnegie Class: Not Classified
FAX Number: N/A Calendar System: Semester
URL: lumbeeriver.edu
Established: 1968 Annual Undergrad Tuition & Fees: N/A
Enrollment: N/A Coed
Affiliation or Control: Assemblies Of God Church IRS Status: 501(c)3
Highest Offering: Baccalaureate
Accreditation: BI

01 President .... James A. KEYS
05 Acting Academic Dean .... Tony BUCHANAN
11 Vice Pres Administration .... Vacant
32 Vice Pres Student Life .... John DAVIS
08 Chief Librarian .... Liisa KELLY
06 Registrar/Dir Financial Aid .... Carolee NICHOLS
108 Director Institutional Assessment .... Gay DAVIS
10 Chief Financial Officer .... Tracy KEYS
07 Director of Admissions .... Vacant
21 Associate Financial Officer .... Cassidy CUMMINGS

Manna University (G)

5117 Cliffdale Road, Fayetteville NC 28314
County: Cumberland FICE Identification: 041737
Unit ID: 461528
Telephone: (910) 221-2224 Carnegie Class: Bac-Diverse
FAX Number: N/A Calendar System: Semester
URL: https://manna.edu/
Established: 2000 Annual Undergrad Tuition & Fees: $6,200
Enrollment: 247 Coed
Affiliation or Control: Other Protestant IRS Status: 501(c)3
Highest Offering: Doctorate
Accreditation: BI

01 President .... Dr. Steven CROWTHER
11 Vice President of Administration .... Ms. Cathy LUCAS
05 Academic Dean .... Mr. Ron MCBRIDE
84 Dean of Enrollment Management .... Mr. Frank BRAZELL
32 Dean of Students .... Mr. John MCINTYRE
106 Dean of Online Education/E-Learning .... Ms. Stefanie ERTEL
10 Chief Financial Officer .... Ms. Omayra COON
30 Director of Development .... Dr. Diane AXON
08 Librarian .... Ms. Elsa MCBRIDE
108 Director of Assessment & Planning .... Ms. Sharyn J. TEAGUE
06 Registrar .... Ms. Dahly ALLUP

Mars Hill University (H)

PO Box 370, Mars Hill NC 28754-0370
County: Madison FICE Identification: 002944
Unit ID: 198899
Telephone: (828) 689-1307 Carnegie Class: Bac-Diverse
FAX Number: (828) 689-1478 Calendar System: Semester
URL: www.mhu.edu
Established: 1856 Annual Undergrad Tuition & Fees: $35,052
Enrollment: 1,049 Coed
Affiliation or Control: Independent Non-Profit IRS Status: 501(c)3
Highest Offering: Master's
Accreditation: SC, AAQEP, MUS, NURSE, SW

01 President .... Dr. Tony FLOYD
111 Vice President for Inst Advancement .... Mr. Harold (Bud) G. CHRISTMAN
05 Provost & VP of Enrollment Mgmt .... Dr. Tracy PARKINSON
10 Vice President for Finance .... Mr. Roger SLAGLE
32 VP for Student Life .... Dr. David ROZEBOOM
07 Director of Admissions .... Ms. Kristie VANCE
06 University Registrar .... Ms. Marie NICHOLSON
08 Director of Library Services .... Vacant

26 Sr Dir of Marketing/Communications .... Ms. Samantha FENDER
11 Sr Director of Planning & Strategy .... Dr. Grainger CAUDLE
42 University Chaplain .... Rev. Stephanie MCLESKEY
41 Athletic Director ....Mr. Rick BAKER
37 Director of Financial Aid .... Ms. Nichole BUCKNER
85 Director International Education .... Dr. Greg CLEMMONS
09 Director Institutional Research ....Dr. Kim REIGLE
38 Director of Counseling ....Vacant
13 Chief Information Officer ....Mr. Ted BRUNER
18 Director of Facilities ....Vacant
109 Director of Auxiliary Services ....Vacant
19 Director of Security/Safety ....Mr. Kevin WEST
28 Dir of Diversity/Equity/Inclusion ....Mr. Jonathan MCCOY
29 Ex Dir of Alumni & Board Relations .... Dr. Joy KISH
112 Director of Donor Relations .... Mr. John CHASTAIN
44 Director of the Mars Hill Fund ....Ms. Erin MAENNLE
102 Foundations Engagement ....Ms. Stacey SPARKS
04 Admin Assistant to the President ....Ms. Danielle HAGERMAN
108 Dir Inst Effectiveness/Assessment ....Vacant
36 Director of Career Services ....Mr. James KNIGHT
15 Director of Human Resources .... Ms. Jennie MATTHEWS

Meredith College (A)

3800 Hillsborough Street, Raleigh NC 27607-5298
County: Wake FICE Identification: 002945
Unit ID: 198950
Telephone: (919) 760-8600 Carnegie Class: Bac-A&S
FAX Number: (919) 760-2828 Calendar System: Semester
URL: www.meredith.edu
Established: 1891 Annual Undergrad Tuition & Fees: $39,952
Enrollment: 1,802 Female
Affiliation or Control: Independent Non-Profit IRS Status: 501(c)3
Highest Offering: Master's
Accreditation: SC, CIDA, DIETD, DIETI, MUS, SW

01 President ....Dr. Jo ALLEN
05 Sr Vice Pres and Provost .... Dr. Matthew POSLUSNY
111 Vice Pres Institutional Advancement ....Dr. Charles (Lennie) BARTON
10 Vice Pres for Business & Finance .... Dr. Tammi JACKSON
32 Vice President for College Programs ....Dr. Jean JACKSON
26 Vice President of Marketing .... Ms. Kristi EAVES-MCLENNAN
35 Dean of Students ....Ms. Ann C. GLEASON
58 Director of Graduate Programs ....Dr. Monica MCKINNEY
06 Registrar .... Ms. Shelly MCMAHON
09 Dir Research/Planning & Assessment .... Dr. C. Dianne RAUBENHEIMER
08 Director Library Info Services .... Ms. Laura DAVIDSON
07 Director of Admissions ....Ms. Shery BOYLES
37 Director of Financial Assistance ....Mr. Kevin MICHAELSEN
35 Dir Student Activ/Leadership Devel ....Ms. Cheryl S. JENKINS
36 Director Office of Career Planning .... Ms. Dana SUMNER
29 Dir of Alumnae & Parent Relations .... Ms. Hilary ALLEN
38 Director of Counseling Center ....Ms. Beth A. MEIER
121 Director of Student Success Center ....Dr. Tina ROMANELLI
31 Director Campus Events .... Mr. Bill BROWN
23 Director Health Services .... Dr. Mary JOHNSON
42 Campus Minister ....Rev. Stacy PARDUE
13 Chief Information Officer .... Mr. Jeffrey HOWLETT
19 Chief Campus Police ....Mr. Al WHITE
15 Director of Human Resources ....Ms. Pamela GALLOWAY
18 Chief Facilities/Physical Plant ....Mr. Todd LECHNER
21 Director of Accounting .... Ms. Susan WILLIAMS
104 Director of International Programs ....Dr. Brooke SHURER
88 Director of Strong Points ....Ms. Beth HWANG

Methodist University (B)

5400 Ramsey Street, Fayetteville NC 28311-1498
County: Cumberland FICE Identification: 002946
Unit ID: 198969
Telephone: (910) 630-7005 Carnegie Class: Masters/S
FAX Number: (910) 630-7317 Calendar System: Semester
URL: www.methodist.edu
Established: 1956 Annual Undergrad Tuition & Fees: $36,076
Enrollment: 1,773 Coed
Affiliation or Control: United Methodist IRS Status: 501(c)3
Highest Offering: Doctorate
Accreditation: SC, ACBSP, ARCPA, CAATE, NURSE, OT, PTA, SW

01 President ....Dr. Stanley T. WEARDEN
05 Provost ....Dr. Suzanne BLUM MALLEY
11 VP Planning and Administration ....Ms. Sheila C. KINSEY
10 VP Business Affairs/Controller .... Ms. Dawn AUSBORN
32 VP for Student Affairs ....Mr. William WALKER
84 VP Enrollment Management .... Mr. Rick D. LOWE
111 VP Institutional Advancement .... Mr. Greg SWANSON
42 VP Campus Ministry/Cmty Engagement ......Rev. Kelli W. TAYLOR
41 VP/Director of Athletics .... Mr. Dave EAVENSON
106 Vice Prov Online/Extended Learning ....Dr. Beth CARTER
13 Chief Information Officer .... Dr. Mary LEARY MCCANTS
28 Chief Diversity Officer ....Dr. Quincy MALLOY, SR.
07 Dean of Admissions ....Mr. Jamie W. LEGG
35 Assoc Dean Student Services ....Mr. Todd D. HARRIS
36 Assoc Dean Student/Career Services . Ms. Antoinette P. BELLAMY
29 Director Alumni Affairs .... Ms. Taylor MURPHY
26 Director Marketing/Communication ....Mr. Brad JOHNSON
88 Director of Accreditation ....Dr. Donald L. LASSITER
37 Director of Financial Aid ....Ms. Bonnie J. ADAMSON
06 Registrar ....Ms. Jasmin K. BROWN
08 Head Librarian .... Ms. Tracey PEARSON
104 Dir Intl Programs/Study Abroad .... Ms. Minnu PAUL

19 Director Police/Public Safety .... Mr. Mark BREWINGTON
15 Director Human Resources ....Mrs. Debra YEATTS
18 Director of Facilities ....Mr. Bill YOUNG
38 Director Student Counseling ....Dr. Deirdre JACKSON
96 Director of Purchasing .... Ms. Mckenzie JACKSON
04 Exec Assistant to the President .... Ms. Jessica W. HOBBS
105 Director Web Services ....Mr. Michael MOLTER
25 Chief Contract/Grants Administrator .... Ms. Wendy HUSTWIT
39 Director Housing & Residence Life .... Ms. Barb MORGAN
90 Director Academic Computing ....Mr. Bruce MORGAN
122 Dir Stdnt Involve Ctr-Greek Life ....Ms. Aly MAGRAS

Mid-Atlantic Christian University (C)

715 N Poindexter, Elizabeth City NC 27909-4054
County: Pasquotank FICE Identification: 022809
Unit ID: 199458
Telephone: (252) 334-2000 Carnegie Class: Bac-Diverse
FAX Number: (252) 334-2071 Calendar System: Semester
URL: www.macuniversity.edu
Established: 1948 Annual Undergrad Tuition & Fees: $16,490
Enrollment: 165 Coed
Affiliation or Control: Churches Of Christ IRS Status: 501(c)3
Highest Offering: Baccalaureate
Accreditation: SC

01 President ....Mr. John W. MAURICE, JR.
05 Vice President Academic Affairs .... Dr. Kevin W. LARSEN
32 Vice President Student Life .... Mr. Bryan WISDOM
07 Asst Director of Admissions ....Mrs. Rebekah LANGLEY
111 Director Institutional Advancement ....Chris BELL
10 Vice President Finance ....Mrs. Sara SHEPHERD
09 Director of Institutional Research .... Dr. Kevin W. LARSEN
06 Registrar ....Miss Yolanda K. TESKE
08 Director of Library ....Mr. Rodney WOOTEN
38 Counselor ....Dr. David S. KING
37 Financial Aid Administrator ....Mrs. Emily MENEELY
49 Chair of Arts and Sciences ....Dr. Robert W. SMITH
42 Chair of Bible & Christian Ministry ....Dr. Claudio F. DIVINO
88 Chair of Marketplace Ministry ....Dr. David S. KING
41 Athletic Director .... Mr. J. Andy MENEELY

Miller-Motte College (D)

3725 Ramsey Street, Fayetteville NC 28311
Telephone: (910) 354-1900 Identification: 770728
Accreditation: ACCSC

† Branch campus of Miller-Motte College, Chattanooga, TN.

Miller-Motte College (E)

105 New Frontier Way, Jacksonville NC 28546
Telephone: (910) 478-4300 Identification: 770729
Accreditation: ACCSC

† Branch campus of Miller-Motte College, Chattanooga, TN.

Miller-Motte College (F)

3901 Capital Boulevard, Suite 151, Raleigh NC 27604
Telephone: (919) 723-2820 Identification: 770727
Accreditation: ACCSC, DA, MAC

† Branch campus of Miller-Motte College, Chattanooga, TN.

Miller-Motte College (G)

5000 Market Street, Wilmington NC 28405-3430
Telephone: (910) 392-4660 FICE Identification: 030632
Accreditation: ACCSC, DA

† Branch campus of Miller-Motte College, Chattanooga, TN.

Montreat College (H)

PO Box 1267, 310 Gaither Circle,
Montreat NC 28757-1267
County: Buncombe FICE Identification: 002948
Unit ID: 199032
Telephone: (828) 669-8012 Carnegie Class: Bac-Diverse
FAX Number: (828) 669-9554 Calendar System: Semester
URL: www.montreat.edu
Established: 1916 Annual Undergrad Tuition & Fees: $28,750
Enrollment: 950 Coed
Affiliation or Control: Non-denominational IRS Status: 501(c)3
Highest Offering: Master's
Accreditation: SC, CACREP

01 President ....Dr. Paul J. MAURER
10 VP for Finance and Administration .... Mr. John BEAGHAN
58 VP and Dean for Adult/Grad Studies .... Dr. Dave POOLE
05 VP and Dean for Academic Affairs ....Dr. Mark HIJLEH
84 VP for Enrollment Mgmt & Athletics ....Mr. Jose LARIOS
32 VP & Dean for Student Services ....Dr. Daniel BENNETT
111 Chief Advancement Officer ....Mr. Brian GUENGERICH
26 VP Marketing/Communications .... Ms. Sara BAUGHMAN
29 Director Alumni Parent Relations ....Vacant
37 Director of Student Financial Svcs ....Mr. Jeremy HURSE
38 Director of Counseling .... Mr. Wesley DAVIS
110 Director for Advancement Services .... Ms. Kristine BUCKWALTER
08 Library Director ....Mr. Nathan KING
21 Controller ....Ms. Rhonda DEVAN

20 Associate Dean for Academic Affairs ....Dr. Mark HUNTER
04 Executive Assistant to President ....Mrs. Jenna HUNTER
42 Dean of Spiritual Formation ....Rev. Rachel TOONE
06 Registrar ....Mr. Fred MILLER
40 Bookstore Manager .... Mrs. Carly LEE
19 Director of Campus Security ....Mr. Bill HENSLEY
18 Chief Facilities/Physical Plant .... Mr. Tommy HENDRIX
13 Chief Information Technology Office .... Mr. Paul HAWKINSON
07 Director of Admissions ....Mrs. Erin CHAPMAN
15 Human Resources Officer .... Ms. Mickie KELLY
36 Director Student Placement .... Ms. Karen EILERS

*North Carolina Community College System (I)

200 W Jones Street, 5001 MSC, Raleigh NC 27699-5001
County: Wake FICE Identification: 033445
Telephone: (919) 807-7100 Carnegie Class: N/A
FAX Number: (919) 807-7166
URL: www.nccommunitycolleges.edu

01 President .... Mr. Thomas STITH, III
05 Sr Vice Pres/Chief Academic Officer .... Dr. Kimberly GOLD
100 Chief of Staff/EVP .... Ms. Jennifer HAYGOOD
10 Vice Pres/Chief Financial Officer .....Ms. Elizabeth GROVENSTEIN
13 Chief Information Officer .... Mr. Patrick FLEMING
46 Assoc VP for STEM Innovation .... Dr. Matthew MEYER
101 Exec Director State Board Affairs .... Mr. Bryan JENKINS
04 Exec Assistant to the President ....Ms. Kelly BARRETTO

*Alamance Community College (J)

1247 Jimmie Kerr Road/PO Box 8000,
Graham NC 27253-8000
County: Alamance FICE Identification: 005463
Unit ID: 199786
Telephone: (336) 578-2002 Carnegie Class: Assoc/MT-VT-High Non
FAX Number: (336) 578-1987 Calendar System: Semester
URL: www.alamancecc.edu
Established: 1958 Annual Undergrad Tuition & Fees (In-District): $2,492
Enrollment: 4,037 Coed
Affiliation or Control: State/Local IRS Status: 501(c)3
Highest Offering: Associate Degree
Accreditation: SC, ACFEI, DA, EMT, HT, MAC, MLTAD

02 President ....Dr. Algie C. GATEWOOD
03 Executive Vice President ....Dr. Constance WOLFE
10 VP Admin & Fiscal Svcs .... Mr. Christopher D. CREPPS
111 VP Institutional Advancement ....Ms. Carolyn RHODE
05 VP of Instruction ....Dr. Lisa JOHNSON
103 VP Workforce Development ....Mr. Gary SAUNDERS
32 VP Student Success ....Dr. Carol DISQUE
50 Dean Business/Arts & Sciences ....Ms. Sonya MCCOOK
72 Dean Industrial Technologies ....Mr. Justin SNYDER
69 Dean Health & Public Svcs ....Mr. David FRAZEE
21 Controller .... Ms. Steffanie VAUGHAN
06 Registrar ....Mr. Kenneth DOBBINS
11 AVP Administrative Services .... Mr. Thomas HARTMAN
15 Interim Director Human Resources .....Ms. Valerie FEARRINGTON
13 Director Information Services ....Mr. Shawn O'HARA
08 Director Learning Resources Center ....Ms. Sara THYNNE
26 Director Public Information/Mktg ....Ms. Sarah HARDIN
56 Director Occupational Ext Program ....Vacant
84 Director Enrollment Management ....Ms. Elizabeth BREHLER
37 Director Financial Aid ....Ms. Sabrina DEGAIN
36 Director Counseling & Career Svcs ....Ms. Ilona OWENS
38 Special Needs/Counseling Svcs Coord ....Ms. Monica ISBELL
121 Academic Support Specialist ....Ms. Jennifer BROWNELL
09 Institutional Researcher ....Dr. Jessica HARRELL
19 Director Security/Safety ....Vacant
04 Admin Assistant to the President .... Ms. Darian RADER
28 Director of Diversity & Inclusion ....Mr. Josefvon JONES

*Asheville - Buncombe Technical Community College (K)

340 Victoria Road, Asheville NC 28801-4897
County: Buncombe FICE Identification: 004033
Unit ID: 197887
Telephone: (828) 398-7900 Carnegie Class: Assoc/MT-VT-High Non
FAX Number: (828) 281-9696 Calendar System: Semester
URL: www.abtech.edu
Established: 1959 Annual Undergrad Tuition & Fees (In-District): $2,632
Enrollment: 6,601 Coed
Affiliation or Control: State/Local IRS Status: 501(c)3
Highest Offering: Associate Degree
Accreditation: SC, ACFEI, CNEA, DA, DH, DMS, EMT, MAC, MLTAD, OTA, RAD, SURGT

02 President ....Dr. John GOSSETT
10 VP Business & Finance/CFO ....Dr. Dirk WILMOTH
13 Vice Pres Information Technology ....Mr. Brian WILLIS
05 VP Instructional Services ....Dr. Beth STEWART
20 Associate VP Instructional Services ....Dr. Gene LOFLIN
32 VP Student Services ....Dr. Terry BRASIER
15 VP Human Resources & OD .... Ms. Shanna CHAMBERS
103 VP Econ/Workforce Dev/Cont Educ ....Ms. Deborah WRIGHT
04 Exec Administrative Assistant ....Ms. Carolyn RICE
111 Exec Director College Advancement .... Ms. Amanda EDWARDS
49 Dean Arts & Sciences ....Mr. Kenet ADAMSON
50 Dean Business & Hospitality Educ ....Ms. Brenda MCFARLAND

54 Dean Engineering & Applied Tech .....Mr. Vernon D. DAUGHERTY
35 Director Student Life/Development .... Ms. Michele HATHCOCK
21 Exec Director Business Services ....Ms. Melissa VALKO
37 Director of Financial Aid ....Vacant
06 Associate Registrar ....Mr. Jason HECHT
84 Director Enrollment Services ....Ms. Lisa F. BUSH
24 Director Library Services ....Mr. Russell TAYLOR
12 Director Madison County Campus ....Ms. Sherri DAVIS
18 Director Plant Operations ....Mr. Lee PACK
19 Chief of Police/Security ....Ms. Kara WALKER
31 Director Community Services Program ....Ms. Brinda W. CALDWELL
08 Librarian ....Mr. Russell TAYLOR
09 Exec Director Research & Planning ....Ms. Anne OXENREIDER
26 Exec Dir Community Rels/Marketing ....Ms. Kerri GLOVER
28 Director of Diversity ....Ms. Erika L. LETT
40 Bookstore Manager ....Mr. Taylor NORRIS
96 Purchasing Agent ....Ms. Carmalita FORTENBERRY
72 Dir Cust Rels/Technology Services ....Mr. Cris HARSHMAN

*Beaufort County Community College (A)

5337 US Hwy 264 East, Washington NC 27889-7889

County: Beaufort FICE Identification: 008558
Unit ID: 197966

Telephone: (252) 946-6194 Carnegie Class: Assoc/HT-Mix Trad/Non
FAX Number: (252) 940-6234 Calendar System: Semester
URL: www.beaufortccc.edu
Established: 1967 Annual Undergrad Tuition & Fees (In-District): $2,518
Enrollment: 1,382 Coed
Affiliation or Control: State/Local IRS Status: 501(c)3
Highest Offering: Associate Degree
Accreditation: SC, MLTAD

02 President ....Dr. David LOOPE
05 VP of Academic Affairs ....Dr. Lisa HILL
10 VP of Administrative Services ....Mr. Mark NELSON
32 VP of Student Services ....Dr. LaTonya NIXON
51 VP of Continuing Education ....Mrs. Stacey GERARD
111 VP of Institutional Advancement ....Ms. Serena SULLIVAN
09 Dean Inst Effectiveness ....Mrs. Kimberly MULLIS
26 Mktg & PR Coordinator ....Mr. Attila NEMECZ
31 Dir of Community Partnerships ....Mr. Clay CARTER
66 Dean of Nursing & Allied Health ....Mr. Kent DICKERSON
49 Dean Arts & Sciences ....Ms. Samantha SPENCER
50 Dean of Business & Industrial Tech ....Mr. Ben MORRIS
08 Director of Library ....Mrs. Paula HOPPER
14 Network Administrator ....Mr. Tony MOORE
91 System Administrator ....Mr. Patrick ROHRMAN
15 Director of Human Resources ....Ms. Nicole HAM
19 Chief of Campus Police ....Mr. William CHRISMON
37 Director of Financial Aid ....Ms. Patricia WINDLEY
06 Registrar ....Ms. Melissa A. FRANCIS
07 Director of Admissions ....Mrs. Shelby PHILLIPS
103 Dir of Business & Industry Svcs ....Mr. Lentz STOWE
04 Executive Asst to President & Board ...... Mrs. Jennie SINGLETON
96 Purchasing Coordinator ....Ms. Rebecca ADAMS
38 Director of Counseling ....Mrs. Kimberly JACKSON
105 Webmaster ....Mr. Justin MCKEITHAN
18 Dir Campus Operations ....Mr. Jason SQUIRES
13 Chief Technology Officer/Info Tech ....Mr. David LOONEY
21 Controller ....Ms. Gay EDWARDS

*Bladen Community College (B)

PO Box 266, Dublin NC 28332-0266

County: Bladen FICE Identification: 007987
Unit ID: 198011

Telephone: (910) 879-5500 Carnegie Class: Assoc/HVT-High Non
FAX Number: (910) 879-5564 Calendar System: Semester
URL: www.bladencc.edu
Established: 1967 Annual Undergrad Tuition & Fees (In-State): $2,558
Enrollment: 1,057 Coed
Affiliation or Control: State IRS Status: 501(c)3
Highest Offering: Associate Degree
Accreditation: SC, @CNEA

02 President ....Dr. Amanda LEE
04 Exec Admin Asst to the President .... Ms. Melissa HESTER
05 VP and Chief Academic Officer ....Ms. Cynthia MCKOY
111 VP for Institutional Advancement ....Ms. Sondra GUYTON
32 Vice President for Student Services ....Mr. Barry PRIEST
10 Vice President for Finance ....Mr. Jay STANLEY
21 Controller ....Mr. Roy THOMPSON
08 Director Student Resource Center ....Ms. Sherwin RICE
09 Dir Institutional Effect & Planning ....Ms. Lisa DEVANE
37 Director of Financial Aid ....Ms. Samantha BENSON
106 Director of Distance Learning ....Mr. Ray SHEPPARD
15 Director of Human Resources ....Ms. Tiina MUNDY
18 Director of Facilities ....Mr. Junior RIDEOUT
26 POI/Marketing Coordinator ....Vacant
102 Foundation Director ....Ms. Linda BURNEY
06 Registrar ....Ms. Andrea CARTER-FISHER

*Blue Ridge Community College (C)

180 W Campus Drive, Flat Rock NC 28731-4728

County: Henderson FICE Identification: 009684
Unit ID: 198039

Telephone: (828) 694-1700 Carnegie Class: Assoc/HT-High Non
FAX Number: (828) 694-1690 Calendar System: Semester
URL: www.blueridge.edu
Established: 1969 Annual Undergrad Tuition & Fees (In-District): $2,651
Enrollment: 2,399 Coed
Affiliation or Control: State/Local IRS Status: 501(c)3
Highest Offering: Associate Degree
Accreditation: SC, EMT, NAEYC, SURGT

02 President ....Dr. Laura B. LEATHERWOOD
05 VP for Instruction ....Ms. Katherine ALLEN
32 VP for Student Services ....Ms. Kirsten BUNCH
103 VP Economic/Workforce Development ....Dr. Scott QUEEN
10 AVP for Finance/CFO ....Ms. Carolyn W. ALLEY
11 Vice Pres General Administration ....Dr. Chad MERRILL
111 VP Institutional Advancement ....Ms. Lisa ADKINS
49 Dean for Arts and Sciences ....Ms. Deborah DEWITT
72 Dean for Advanced Technology ....Mr. Joe SHOOK
76 Dean for Health Sciences ....Ms. Leigh ANGEL
97 Dean for Basic Skills ....Ms. Robin NORRIS-PAULISON
50 Dean for Business/Service Careers .... Ms. Brenda BLACKBURN
44 Institutional Advance/Rsrch Coord ....Dr. Jessica HARRELL
06 Registrar ....Ms. Sara SCHUMACHER
08 Director for Library Services ....Mr. Anthony BALTIERO
37 Director Financial Aid ....Ms. Amanda BUCHANAN
13 Assoc Vice Pres Technology/CIO ....Mr. Steven YOUNG
18 Director of Facilities ....Mr. Peter HEMANS
26 Dir of Marketing & Communications ....Mr. Benjamin RICKERT
84 Director of Enrollment Management ....Ms. Laura SIMMONS
15 Director of Human Resources ....Ms. Lorri ALLISON
19 Director of Police & Public Safety ....Mr. Philip HOSMER
04 Admin Assistant to the President ....Ms. Tammy L. PRYOR

*Brunswick Community College (D)

50 College Road, Bolivia NC 28422

County: Brunswick FICE Identification: 021707
Unit ID: 198084

Telephone: (910) 755-7300 Carnegie Class: Assoc/HT-Mix Trad/Non
FAX Number: (910) 754-9609 Calendar System: Semester
URL: www.brunswickcc.edu
Established: 1979 Annual Undergrad Tuition & Fees (In-State): $2,532
Enrollment: 1,553 Coed
Affiliation or Control: State IRS Status: 501(c)3
Highest Offering: Associate Degree
Accreditation: SC, CAHIIM, MAC

02 President ....Dr. Gene SMITH
05 Exec Vice Pres/Chief Academic Ofcr ....Dr. Lois SMITH
10 Vice President Budget and Finance .... Ms. Sheila GALLOWAY
32 Vice Pres of Student Affairs .. Dr. Denise A. HOUCHEN-CLAGETT
09 Director of Institutional Planning ....Dr. Tracy L. SOMERLAD
08 Dir Learning Resources/Acad Support .... Mrs. Carmen ELLIS
06 Registrar/Dir Enrollment ....Vacant
15 Director Human Resources ....Ms. Nancy DISBROW
18 AVP/Physical Plant Director ....Mr. Jack LUCIANO
102 Director Resource Development ....Ms. Elizabeth WASSUM
26 Director of Marketing & Public Rels ....Ms. Julia STUART
37 Financial Aid/Veterans Affs Coord ....Ms. Tracy SOMERLAD
72 Dean Professional Technical Service .... Mr. Eric HOLLOMAN
49 Dean Arts & Sciences ....Dr. Kim JONES
04 Executive Assist to President ....Ms. Cynthia STERLING
13 Chief Info Officer ....Mr. Dave SORENSON
41 Athletic Director ....Mr. Robert ALLEN
36 Career Counselor ....Ms. Leslie WILDER

*Caldwell Community College and Technical Institute (E)

2855 Hickory Boulevard, Hudson NC 28638-1399

County: Caldwell FICE Identification: 004835
Unit ID: 198118

Telephone: (828) 726-2200 Carnegie Class: Assoc/HT-Mix Trad/Non
FAX Number: (828) 726-2216 Calendar System: Semester
URL: www.cccti.edu
Established: 1964 Annual Undergrad Tuition & Fees (In-District): $2,528
Enrollment: 3,845 Coed
Affiliation or Control: State/Local IRS Status: 501(c)3
Highest Offering: Associate Degree
Accreditation: SC, ADNUR, DMS, EMT, MAC, PTAA, RAD

02 President ....Dr. Mark POARCH
32 Vice President Student Services ....Mrs. Dena HOLMAN
103 Dean Cont Ed/Workforce Development ....Ms. Brandy DUNLAP
11 Vice President of Operations ....Mr. Donnie BASSINGER
12 Executive Director Watauga Campus ....Mr. Steve MELTON
05 Vice President of Instruction ....Vacant
84 Dir Enrollment Mgmt Services ....Mr. Dennis SEAGLE
08 Director Learning Resources Center ....Ms. Alison BEARD
37 Director Financial Aid ....Mrs. Ann WRIGHT
36 Dir Custom Training/Work Based Lrng ....Mr. Rick SHEW
15 Director Human Resources ....Mrs. Rose MOON
10 Controller ....Mrs. Rashelle PENLEY
09 Dir Inst Effectiveness/Research ....Mrs. Liz SILVERS
26 Public Relations Officer ....Mr. Edward TERRY
102 Director Foundation Office ....Ms. Marla CHRISTIE
38 Director Student Counseling ....Mr. Shannon BROWN
96 Purchasing Agent ....Mrs. Barbara DAY
40 Director of College Stores ....Mrs. Trina CURTIS
04 Exec Assistant to the Pres/Board ....Mrs. Donna CHURCH
18 Director Facility Services ....Mr. Jeff HERMAN
06 Registrar ....Ms. Beth HOLLAND
13 Chief Info Technology Officer (CIO) .... Ms. Susan WOOTEN
105 Director Web Services ....Mr. Gary WILSON
28 Director of Diversity ....Mr. Jimmy GRIFFITH
41 Athletic Director ....Mr. Jeff LINK
100 Chief of Staff ....Dr. Jason CHAFFIN

*Cape Fear Community College (F)

411 N Front Street, Wilmington NC 28401-3993

County: New Hanover FICE Identification: 005320
Unit ID: 198154

Telephone: (910) 362-7000 Carnegie Class: Assoc/HT-High Trad
FAX Number: (910) 763-2279 Calendar System: Semester
URL: www.cfcc.edu
Established: 1958 Annual Undergrad Tuition & Fees (In-District): $2,748
Enrollment: 8,680 Coed
Affiliation or Control: State/Local IRS Status: 501(c)3
Highest Offering: Associate Degree
Accreditation: SC, ADNUR, DA, DH, DMS, MAC, NAEYC, OTA, RAD, SURGT

02 President ....Mr. James P. MORTON
32 VP Student Svcs & Enrollment Mgmt ....Ms. Sabrina TERRY
05 Vice Pres Academic Affairs ....Dr. Jason CHAFFIN
10 Vice President Business Services .... Ms. Christina GREENE
111 VP Advancement & Arts ....Mr. Lionel FERNANDO
103 VP Economic & Workforce Development ....Mr. John DOWNING
06 Registrar ....Ms. Angela MURPHY
102 Director Philanthropy & Foundation .... Mr. Logan THOMPSON
26 VP Marketing & Community Relations .... Ms. Sonja JOHNSON
84 Dean of Enrollment Management ....Ms. Jackie FOSTER
08 Dean Learning Resources Center ....Ms. Catherine LEE
37 Sr Director of Financial Aid ....Ms. Rachel CAVANUAGH
13 Exec Dir Information Tech Svcs ....Mr. Jakim FRIANT
15 VP Human Resources & College Safety .... Ms. Anne SMITH
35 Dean of Student Affairs ....Mr. Robby MCGEE
75 Dean Career/Technical Education ....Mr. Mark COUNCIL
49 Dean Arts & Sciences ....Ms. Lynn CRISWELL
96 Director of Purchasing/Inventory ....Ms. Liz MANTOOTH
76 Dean Health & Human Services ....Dr. Mary NAYLOR
105 Web Services Analyst ....Ms. Christina HEIKKILA
100 Exec Dir Pres Office/Board Liaison ....Ms. Michelle LEE
19 Director Campus Safety/Training ....Ms. Lynn SYLVIA
25 Director of Grant Development ....Ms. Val CLEMMONS
22 Dir of Disability Support Services ....Ms. Aimee HELMUS
41 Dir Student Activities/Athletics ....Mr. Ryan MANTLO
18 Exec Dir Capital Projects & Maint ....Mr. David KANOY
88 Director Customized Training ....Ms. Jan YOKELEY
07 Sr Dir Admissions/Recruitment ....Mr. Jeremy GIBBONS
09 VP of Institutional Effectiveness ....Mr. Michael COBB

*Carteret Community College (G)

3505 Arendell Street, Morehead City NC 28557-2989

County: Carteret FICE Identification: 008081
Unit ID: 198206

Telephone: (252) 222-6000 Carnegie Class: Assoc/MT-VT-High Trad
FAX Number: (252) 222-2514 Calendar System: Semester
URL: www.carteret.edu
Established: 1963 Annual Undergrad Tuition & Fees (In-District): $2,640
Enrollment: 1,347 Coed
Affiliation or Control: State/Local IRS Status: 501(c)3
Highest Offering: Associate Degree
Accreditation: SC, ADNUR, COARC, MAC, RAD

02 President ....Dr. Tracy MANCINI
05 VP for Instruction/Student Support ....Dr. Maggie BROWN
103 VP Corp/Community Education ....Mr. Perry L. HARKER
10 VP Finance/Administrative Services ....Mr. Matthew BANKO
18 VP of Plant Operations/Facilities ....Mr. Steve SPARKS
102 Exec Director of the Foundation ....Ms. Brenda REASH
49 Dean Arts & Sciences ....Ms. Doree HILL
88 Dean of Applied Science ....Ms. Nicole THOMPSON
76 Dean of Health Sciences ....Ms. Laurie A. FRESHWATER
32 Dean of Student Services ....Mr. Lewis STROUD
13 Dir Network/Info Systems/Security ....Mr. John GREEN
15 Director of Human Resources ....Ms. Amanda BRYANT
26 Director Marketing/Public Affairs ....Ms. Logan OKUN
96 Director of Business Operations .... Ms. Donna L. CUMBIE
37 Director/Financial Aid Officer ....Ms. Brenda J. LONG
06 Director Enrollment Svcs/Registrar ....Ms. Jennifer FOX
09 Dir Inst Rsrch/Effectiveness ....Mr. Jonathan TYNDALL
106 Dir of Instruct Support/Dist Lrng ....Mr. Ed LADENBURGER
08 Director of the Library ....Ms. Elizabeth BAKER
84 Director Admissions & Enrollment ....Ms. Elizabeth NEW
04 Exec Assistant to the President ....Vacant
19 Director Security/Safety ....Mr. Richard ABELL

*Catawba Valley Community College (H)

2550 Highway 70, SE, Hickory NC 28602-9699

County: Catawba FICE Identification: 005318
Unit ID: 198233

Telephone: (828) 327-7000 Carnegie Class: Assoc/HT-Mix Trad/Non
FAX Number: (828) 327-7276 Calendar System: Semester
URL: www.cvcc.edu
Established: 1960 Annual Undergrad Tuition & Fees (In-District): $2,367
Enrollment: 4,328 Coed
Affiliation or Control: State/Local IRS Status: 501(c)3
Highest Offering: Associate Degree
Accreditation: SC, ADNUR, CAHIIM, COARC, DH, EMT, NDT, POLYT, RAD, SURGT

02 President ....Dr. Garrett D. HINSHAW

03 Executive Vice President .... Dr. Larry PUTNAM
05 Chief Academic Officer .... Ms. Brice MELTON
10 Sr VP Business Affairs/Operations .... Mr. Wes BUNCH
32 Dean of Student Access/Development .... Mrs. Cindy COULTER
15 Chief Human Resources Officer .... Mr. Roger IRVIN
07 Director of Admissions .... Ms. Laurie WEGNER
21 Chief Business Administrator .... Ms. Jennifer HAMM
37 Director Scholarships/Financial Aid .... Ms. Carolyn BRANDON
09 Chief Ofcr Accountability/Research .... Mr. Kevin ROUSE
88 Associate Dean .... Ms. Crystal GLENN
88 Sr Director Small Business Center .... Mr. Jeff NEUVILLE
50 Director Business/Technology Ext .... Ms. Susan BLAKE
88 Director Manufacturing Sol Center .... Ms. Jodi GEIS
13 Chief Technology Officer .... Mr. Daniel CLANTON
19 Chief of Staff/Safety/Security .... Mr. Steve HUNT
51 Associate Dean .... Dr. Chanell MORELLO
103 Exec Dir Strat Business Partnership .... Ms. Tammy MULLER
76 Dean Sch of Health & Public Service .... Ms. Robin ROSS
04 Special Asst to Pres/Board Liaison .... Mr. John WATTS
29 Director Events/Tours/Alumni .... Ms. Melanie ZIMMERMAN
41 Director of Athletics .... Mr. Nick SCHROEDER
26 Public Information Officer .... Mr. Cody DALTON
30 Exec Director of Development .... Ms. Jennifer JONES

*Central Carolina Community College (A)

1105 Kelly Drive, Sanford NC 27330-9000
County: Lee FICE Identification: 005449
Unit ID: 198251
Telephone: (919) 775-5401 Carnegie Class: Assoc/MT-VT-High Non
FAX Number: (919) 718-7380 Calendar System: Semester
URL: www.cccc.edu
Established: 1958 Annual Undergrad Tuition & Fees (In-District): $2,554
Enrollment: 5,154 Coed
Affiliation or Control: State/Local IRS Status: 501(c)3
Highest Offering: Associate Degree
Accreditation: SC, CAHIIM, DA, DH, DMS, EMT, MAC

02 President .... Dr. Lisa M. CHAPMAN
05 VP/Chief Academic Officer .... Dr. Kristi SHORT
10 Exec Vice Pres/Chief Financial Ofcr .... Dr. Philip PRICE
32 Vice President Student Services .... Mr. Ken R. HOYLE
09 VP Assessment/Planning/Research .... Dr. Linda SCUILETTI
26 Assoc VP Marketing/External Rels .... Dr. Marcie DISHMAN
12 Provost Chatham Campus .... Dr. Mark HALL
35 Dean of Student Support Svcs .... Ms. Heather WILLETT
04 Exec Asst to Pres/Secretary to BOT .... Ms. Lorraine WHITAKER
08 Assoc Director Learning Resources .... Ms. B. J THOMPSON
102 Exec Director of CCCC Foundation .... Dr. Emily HARE
06 Dean of Enrollment/Registrar .... Ms. Jamie TYSON-CHILDRESS
15 Director Human Resources .... Ms. Trinity FAUCETT
07 Director of Admissions .... Mr. Adam WADE
37 Director Financial Aid .... Ms. Amber WERKHEISER
18 Physical Plant Manager .... Mr. Ronnie MEASAMER
75 Dean Career/Technical Programs .... Mr. Drew GOODSON
76 Dean Health Sciences/Human Services .... Ms. Denise MARTIN
121 AVP Onboarding & Advising .... Mr. Scott BYINGTON
49 Dean Arts & STEM .... Dr. Cristy HOLMES

*Central Piedmont Community College (B)

PO Box 35009, Charlotte NC 28235-5009
County: Mecklenburg FICE Identification: 002915
Unit ID: 198260
Telephone: (704) 330-2722 Carnegie Class: Assoc/HT-Mix Trad/Non
FAX Number: N/A Calendar System: Semester
URL: www.cpcc.edu
Established: 1963 Annual Undergrad Tuition & Fees (In-District): $2,792
Enrollment: 16,668 Coed
Affiliation or Control: State/Local IRS Status: 501(c)3
Highest Offering: Associate Degree
Accreditation: SC, ACFEI, ADNUR, COARC, CSHSE, CVT, CYTO, DA, DH, EMT, MAC, MLTAD, NAEYC, OTA, POLYT, PTAA, SURGT

02 President .... Dr. Kandi W. DEITEMEYER
111 EVP Institutional Advancement .... Dr. Kevin MCCARTHY
05 VP Academic Affairs .... Dr. Heather HILL
32 VP Student Affairs .... Dr. Chris CATHCART
45 VP Strategy/Org Excellence .... Dr. Tracie CLARK
10 VP Finance & Admin Services .... Mr. Mike WHITEMAN
15 VP Talent & Org Engagement/COS .... Mr. Mark SHORT
26 VP Comm/Marketing/Public Relations .... Mr. Jeff LOWRANCE
13 VP for Info Technology & CIO .... Mr. Rick FOGERTY
21 AVP Finance/Admin Services .... Ms. Jessica BOYCE
20 AVP Academic Affairs .... Dr. Edith MCELROY
102 AVP Foundation/Inst Advancement .... Ms. Katie JONES
20 AVP Academic Affairs .... Mr. George HENDERSON
25 Assoc VP Government Rels & Grants .... Mr. Michael HORN
18 Assoc VP Facilities & Construction .... Ms. Vicki SAVILLE
04 Admin Assistant to the President .... Vacant
116 Exec Director Compliance/Audit .... Ms. Kelley HORTON
19 Exec Dir College Security .... Mr. Charles WRIGHT
22 Executive Director Institution/EEO .... Mr. Leon MATTHEWS
88 Dean Educational Partnership .... Mr. Chris PAYNTER
124 Dean Retention Services .... Dr. Clint MCELROY
35 Dean Student Life/Service Learning .... Mr. Mark HELMS
84 Dean Enrollment Management .... Dr. Daniel (JJ) MCEACHERN
08 Dean Libraries .... Ms. Gloria KELLEY
121 Dean College & Career Readiness .... Ms. Karen PAULY
07 Dean Admissions & Registration .... Mr. Greg STANLEY
76 Dean Health Professions/Human Svcs .... Ms. Karen SUMMERS

*Cleveland Community College (C)

137 S Post Road, Shelby NC 28152-6296
County: Cleveland FICE Identification: 008082
Unit ID: 198321
Telephone: (704) 669-6000 Carnegie Class: Assoc/MT-VT-Mix Trad/Non
FAX Number: (704) 669-4202 Calendar System: Semester
URL: www.clevelandcc.edu
Established: 1965 Annual Undergrad Tuition & Fees (In-District): $2,602
Enrollment: 2,269 Coed
Affiliation or Control: State/Local IRS Status: 501(c)3
Highest Offering: Associate Degree
Accreditation: SC, EMT, IFSAC, MAC, RAD, SURGT

02 President .... Dr. Jason HURST
05 Vice President of Academic Affairs .... Dr. Becky SAIN
32 Vice President of Student Affairs .... Dr. Andy GARDNER
10 Vice Pres Business Operations/CFO .... Mr. Bruce COLE
102 Executive Director CCC Foundation .... Dr. Mary CARLSON
09 Dean of Plng & Institutional Effect .... Dr. Laura BOWEN
121 Dean of Equity & Student Support .... Ms. Nedra MADDOX
84 Dean of Enrollment .... Dr. Emily HURDT
08 Director of Library Services .... Ms. Lisa TREXLER
96 Purchasing Officer .... Mr. Lance ASHLEY
18 Director of Physical Plant .... Mr. Mark FOX
19 Campus Security Supervisor .... Mr. Michael HAWKINS
15 Director Human Resources/Safety .... Mr. Allen KNICELEY
13 Chief Information Officer .... Mr. Jonathan DAVIS
14 Network Administrator .... Mr. Robin DYER
24 Audiovisual Coordinator .... Mr. Rodger PERRY
26 Public Relations & Comm Coordinator .... Mrs. Paula VESS
88 Dean of College Transfer .... Dr. Starr CAMPER
103 VP Econ/Workforce Development .... Mr. Tony FOGLEMAN
41 Athletic Director/Dean of CCR .... Dr. Chris NANNEY
100 Chief of Staff .... Mrs. Kristin BLANTON
106 Director of E-learning .... Dr. Chance WITHERSPOON
76 Dean Health Sciences & Public Svcs .... Dr. Christina HILL
103 Dean of Workforce Development .... Ms. Amy DULIN
27 Marketing Coordinator .... Mrs. Kendra HANELINE

*Coastal Carolina Community College (D)

444 Western Boulevard, Jacksonville NC 28546-6816
County: Onslow FICE Identification: 005316
Unit ID: 198330
Telephone: (910) 455-1221 Carnegie Class: Assoc/MT-VT-High Trad
FAX Number: (910) 455-7027 Calendar System: Semester
URL: www.coastalcarolina.edu
Established: 1963 Annual Undergrad Tuition & Fees (In-District): $2,462
Enrollment: 3,571 Coed
Affiliation or Control: State/Local IRS Status: 501(c)3
Highest Offering: Associate Degree
Accreditation: SC, ADNUR, DA, DH, EMT, MLTAD, PNUR, SURGT

02 President .... Mr. David L. HEATHERLY
05 VP for Instruction .... Vacant
09 VP Inst Effective & Student Success .... Ms. Sharon R. MCGINNIS
11 VP Administrative Support Svcs .... Dr. Annette HARPINE
32 Division Chair for Student Services .... Mr. Matthew HERRMANN
15 Personnel Officer .... Ms. Cindy BURKHART
26 Pub Info Ofcr/Ex Dir Col Foundation .... Ms. Emily ELLIS
07 Director for Admissions .... Ms. Heather CALIHAN
18 Dir Physical Plant/Auxiliary Svcs .... Ms. Carol LURZ
37 Director for Financial Aid Services .... Ms. Christina WALLACE
88 Director for Veterans Services .... Mr. Devere P. MICHEAU
103 Director Economic Development .... Ms. Anne C. SHAW
04 Assistant to the President and BOT .... Ms. Lora TAYLOR
06 Registrar .... Ms. Mishelle DUPUIS

*College of the Albemarle (E)

1208 North Road Street, Elizabeth City NC 27906-2327
County: Pasquotank FICE Identification: 002917
Unit ID: 197814
Telephone: (252) 335-0821 Carnegie Class: Assoc/HT-High Non
FAX Number: (252) 335-2011 Calendar System: Semester
URL: www.albemarle.edu
Established: 1960 Annual Undergrad Tuition & Fees (In-District): $2,270
Enrollment: 2,508 Coed
Affiliation or Control: State/Local IRS Status: 501(c)3
Highest Offering: Associate Degree
Accreditation: SC, ADNUR, MAC, MLTAD, SURGT

02 President .... Dr. Jack BAGWELL
10 Chief Financial Officer .... Mrs. Susan GENTRY
05 Vice President for Learning .... Dr. Evonne CARTER
11 VP Business & Admin Services .... Vacant
32 VP Student Success & Enroll Mgmt .... Ms. Kris BURRIS
12 Dean Dare County Campus .... Mr. Timothy SWEENEY
102 Executive Director Foundation .... Dr. Catherine DEHART
37 Director Admissions & Financial Aid .... Ms. Angela R. GODFREY-DAWSON
35 Coord Student Life & Leadership .... Ms. Dawn ALLEN
06 Registrar .... Ms. Andrea DANCE
88 Director Small Business Center .... Ms. Ginger H. O'NEAL
78 Work-Based Learning Liaison .... Mrs. Lynn JENNINGS
04 Exec Assistant to the President .... Mrs. Valerie MUELLER
08 Director Library .... Mr. Rodney WOOTEN
12 Campus Admin Edenton-Chowan Campus .... Mrs. Robin ZINSMEISTER

13 Director Mgmt Information Services .... Mr. Wayman WHITE
15 Director Human Resources .... Ms. Ella BUNCH
18 Director Physical Facilities .... Mr. James DAVISON
23 Dean Health & Wellness .... Ms. Robin HARRIS
40 Administrative Services Manager .... Mr. William DEFEO
09 Dir IR/Planning/Effectiveness/Tech .... Dr. Dean ROUGHTON
88 Coord Prison Education Programs .... Mr. Andre WILLIAMS
88 Coordinator Secondary Education .... Mr. Derek MEREDITH
49 Dean Arts and Sciences .... Mr. Dean ROUGHTON
50 Dean Business & Applied Tech .... Mrs. Michelle WATERS
81 Dept Chair Sciences .... Mr. Todd KRUEGER
83 Department Chair Social Sciences .... Mr. Brian EDWARDS
60 Dept Chair English & Comm .... Mrs. Laura MORRISON
54 Dept Chair Math and Engineering .... Mrs. Lisa MEADS
76 Dept Chair Allied Health .... Mr. Jeffrey CARTER
77 Dept Chair Bus & Computer Sys Tech .... Ms. Sharon BROWN
57 Department Chair Human & Fine Arts .... Ms. Christina WEISNER
66 Dept Chair ADN .... Mrs. Katie MILLER
19 Dir Public Safety & Preparedness .... Mr. Dennis SMITH
36 Dir College and Career Readiness .... Mrs. Kimberly GREGORY
121 Director Advising & Student Success .... Mrs. Eushekia HEWITT
103 Dean Workforce Dev/Pub Svc/Career .... Mrs. Robin ZINSMEISTER
106 Coordinator Distance Education .... Dr. Susan PECK

*Craven Community College (F)

800 College Court, New Bern NC 28562-4984
County: Craven FICE Identification: 006799
Unit ID: 198367
Telephone: (252) 638-7200 Carnegie Class: Assoc/HT-Mix Trad/Non
FAX Number: (252) 638-4232 Calendar System: Semester
URL: www.cravencc.edu
Established: 1965 Annual Undergrad Tuition & Fees (In-District): $2,114
Enrollment: 2,629 Coed
Affiliation or Control: State/Local IRS Status: 501(c)3
Highest Offering: Associate Degree
Accreditation: SC, ACBSP, CAHIIM, @CNEA, MAC, NAEYC, PTAA

02 President .... Dr. Raymond STAATS
05 VP for Instruction .... Dr. Kathleen GALLMAN
11 VP for Administration .... Mr. Jim MILLARD
32 VP for Students .... Mr. Gery BOUCHER
12 Dean Havelock-Cherry Point Campus .... Ms. Tanya MCGHEE
49 Dean Liberal Arts & Univ Transfer .... Dr. Betty HATCHER
36 Dean Career Programs .... Mr. Ricky MEADOWS
76 Dean Health Programs .... Dr. J. Alec NEWTON
13 Dean Technology Services .... Mr. Timothy HALL
88 Dean Teaching & Learning .... Ms. Jenifer MARQUIS
84 Dean Enrollment Management .... Ms. Zomar PETER
103 Dean Workforce Development .... Mr. Robin MATTHEWS
88 Dean Volt Center .... Mr. Eddie FOSTER
09 Exec Director Inst Effectiveness .... Ms. Erin BINGHAM
111 Executive Director Inst Advancement .... Mr. Charles WETHINGTON
10 Exec Dir Financial Services .... Vacant
15 Exec Director Human Resources .... Ms. Denise SALERNO
37 Executive Director Financial Aid .... Ms. Susie GAMES
18 Executive Director Facilities .... Mr. John MELVILLE
07 Director Admissions & Records .... Ms. Donna MARSHALL
113 Director of Student Accounts .... Ms. Kisha SIMPSON
08 Director Library Services .... Mrs. Wendy WHITE
88 Director Educational Partnerships .... Ms. Jennifer BUMGARNER
19 Director Security & Emergency Mgmt .... Mr. Dendray BALLARD
26 Director Communications .... Mr. Craig RAMEY
31 Director Cmty Workforce Relations .... Vacant
88 Director TRIO Student Support Svcs .... Ms. Sandra HUNTER
88 Director Basic Skills Programs .... Ms. Sandy BAYLISS-CARR
96 Procurement & Fixed Assets Officer .... Mr. Hiram Todd MURPHREY
06 Registrar .... Ms. Yuko BOYD
04 Exec Asst to Pres/Board of Trustees .... Ms. Amber SMITH

*Davidson-Davie Community College (G)

PO Box 1287, Lexington NC 27293-1287
County: Davidson FICE Identification: 002919
Unit ID: 198376
Telephone: (336) 249-8186 Carnegie Class: Assoc/MT-VT-Mix Trad/Non
FAX Number: (336) 249-0379 Calendar System: Semester
URL: www.davidsondavie.edu
Established: 1958 Annual Undergrad Tuition & Fees (In-District): $2,588
Enrollment: 3,765 Coed
Affiliation or Control: State/Local IRS Status: 501(c)3
Highest Offering: Associate Degree
Accreditation: SC, ADNUR, CAHIIM, DA, EMT, MAC, MLTAD, NAEYC, SURGT

02 President .... Dr. Darrin L. HARTNESS
05 EVP Academic & Student Affairs .... Dr. Susan D. BURLESON
10 VP Financial/Administrative Svcs .... Ms. Laura L. YARBROUGH
102 VP Ext Affairs/Exec Dir Foundation .... Ms. Jenny M. VARNER
76 Dean Health Sciences .... Ms. Holly MYERS
20 AVP Academic Programs/Studies .... Dr. Christy FORREST
103 AVP Workforce Dev & Cmty Engagement .... Dr. Jonathan BROWN
35 Director Student Support Services .... Ms. Shareka BROWN
108 Dean IE & Innovations .... Ms. Cameron SHIRLEY
07 Director Recruitment & Admissions .... Ms. Cailin ASIP
36 Director Career Development .... Mr. Charles MAYER
18 Director Physical Plant Services .... Mr. Keith RAKER
15 Director Human Resources .... Ms. Adrienne FRIDDLE
04 Executive Asst to President .... Ms. Elle KING
08 Head Librarian .... Mr. Jason SETZER
37 Director Student Financial Aid .... Mr. Brian DE YOUNG

41	Athletic Director	Mr. Matthew RIDGE
09	Director of Institutional Research	Mr. Mark PUTERBAUGH
111	Dir Development/Advancement	Ms. Kristin BRIGGS
124	Dean Student Engagement/Completion	Ms. Keisha JONES
13	Director Information Technology	Mr. Donald BECK

*Durham Technical Community College　　(A)

1637 East Lawson Street, Durham NC 27703-5023

County: Durham　　FICE Identification: 005448
Unit ID: 198455

Telephone: (919) 536-7200　　Carnegie Class: Assoc/MT-VT-High Non
FAX Number: (919) 536-7296　　Calendar System: Semester
URL: www.durhamtech.edu
Established: 1961　Annual Undergrad Tuition & Fees (In-District): $1,958
Enrollment: 4,672　　Coed
Affiliation or Control: State/Local　　IRS Status: 501(c)3
Highest Offering: Associate Degree
Accreditation: SC, ADNUR, CAHIIM, CEA, COARC, CR, DT, EMT, MAC, NAEYC, OPD, OTA, PNUR, SURGT

02	President	Mr. John B. BUXTON
05	Int VP/Chief Academic Officer	Ms. Kara BATTLE
11	VP/Chief Campus Ops	Dr. Susan BOWEN
10	VP Finance/Administration	Mr. Andrew KLEITSCH, II
32	VP/Chief Student Services Ofcr	Mr. Abraham DONES
35	Dean Student Svcs Officer	Mr. Greg BELLAMY
100	Chief of Staff	Ms. Tina B. RUFF
04	Executive Asst to the President	Ms. Toni BROWN
13	Information Tech Svcs	Mr. Earl STENLUND
09	Dir Institutional Research/Eval	Dr. Melanie RIESTER
15	VP/Chief Talent & Equity Officer	Ms. Angela DAVIS
08	Director Library	Ms. Julie HUMPHREY
37	Dir Financial Aid/Veteran Svcs	Ms. Nadine FORD
109	Director Auxiliary Services	Ms. Yolanda V. MOORE-JONES
18	Director Facility Services	Mr. Marshall R. FULLER
26	Dir Marketing/Comm/Public Info Ofcr	Mr. Nathan HARDIN

*Edgecombe Community College　　(B)

2009 W Wilson Street, Tarboro NC 27886-9399

County: Edgecombe　　FICE Identification: 008855
Unit ID: 198491

Telephone: (252) 823-5166　　Carnegie Class: Assoc/HVT-Mix Trad/Non
FAX Number: N/A　　Calendar System: Semester
URL: www.edgecombe.edu
Established: 1967　Annual Undergrad Tuition & Fees (In-District): $2,640
Enrollment: 1,459　　Coed
Affiliation or Control: State/Local　　IRS Status: 501(c)3
Highest Offering: Associate Degree
Accreditation: SC, ADNUR, CAHIIM, COARC, MAC, PNUR, RAD, SURGT

02	President	Dr. Gregory MCLEOD
05	Vice President of Instruction	Dr. Bruce PANNETON
11	Vice Pres Administrative Services	Ms. Debbie BATTEN
32	Vice President Student Services	Ms. Samanthia PHILLIPS
84	Dean Enrollment and Financial Aid	Mr. Sherlock MCDOUGALD
35	Dean of Students	Mr. Tony ROOK
108	Director of Inst Effectiveness	Ms. Reinishia GONZALEZ
26	Director of Public Information	Ms. Mary T. BASS
08	Director of Library Services	Ms. Deborah PARISHER
06	Registrar	Ms. Kienesha EBRON
15	Director Personnel Services	Ms. Jessica BALAZSI
18	Chief Facilities/Physical Plant	Mr. John BUTTS
13	Director Computer Services	Mr. Brad HILL
30	Director of Development	Mr. Lynwood ROBERSON

*Fayetteville Technical Community College　　(C)

PO Box 35236, 2201 Hull Road, Fayetteville NC 28303-0236

County: Cumberland　　FICE Identification: 007640
Unit ID: 198534

Telephone: (910) 678-8400　　Carnegie Class: Assoc/MT-VT-Mix Trad/Non
FAX Number: (910) 678-8269　　Calendar System: Semester
URL: www.faytechcc.edu
Established: 1961　Annual Undergrad Tuition & Fees (In-State): $2,544
Enrollment: 10,932　　Coed
Affiliation or Control: State　　IRS Status: 501(c)3
Highest Offering: Associate Degree
Accreditation: SC, ADNUR, COARC, DA, DH, EMT, FUSER, PTAA, RAD, SURGA, SURGT

02	President	Dr. Larry KEEN
05	Sr VP Academic/Student Svcs	Dr. Mark SORRELLS
10	Sr VP Business and Finance	Mrs. Robin DEAVER
15	VP Human Res/Inst Effect/Assessment	Mr. Carl MITCHELL
11	VP for Administrative Services	Vacant
13	VP Learning Technologies	Vacant
43	VP for Legal Services	Mr. David SULLIVAN
18	VP for Facilities Support Services	Mr. Richard LEE
26	Exec Dir Marketing/Public Relations	Ms. Catherine PRITCHARD
102	Executive Director of Foundation	Ms. Sandy AMMONS
84	Dean Enrollment Mgmt/Financial Aid	Mr. Oscar RODRIGUEZ
51	Assoc Vice Pres for Cont Educ	Dr. Jolee MARSH
32	Assoc Vice Pres Student Services	Dr. Rosemary KELLY
06	Registrar	Ms. Melissa A. JONES
21	Assoc Vice Pres Business & Finance	Mr. Charles SMITH

07	Director of Admissions	Ms. Carla WASHINGTON
20	Assoc Vice Pres of Academic Support	Ms. DeSandra WASHINGTON
14	AVP of Mgmt Information Svcs	Mrs. Pamela SCULLY
18	Director of Facility Services	Mr. Gregory Quinten KIGHT
96	Procurement Manager Business/Financ	Mr. Todd DUNN
50	Dean of Business Programs	Vacant
66	Dean of Nursing	Dr. Murtis WORTH
49	Dean of Arts/Humanities	Dr. Kenjuana MCCRAY
76	Dean of Allied Health Programs	Ms. Michelle WALDEN
54	Dean Engr/Applied Tech Pgms	Mrs. Pamela GIBSON
81	Dean of Sciences & Mathematics	Dr. Melissa HARMON
80	Dean of Public Service	Mrs. Linda NOVAK
77	Dean of Computer Technologies	Mrs. Tenette PREVATTE
08	Director of Library Services	Ms. Mary DIRISIO
09	Dean of Institutional Effectiveness	Dr. Vincent CASTANO
19	Director Security/Safety	Mr. Joseph BAILER
37	Director Student Financial Aid	Mrs. Regina MAHONEY
41	Athletic Director	Dr. Shannon YATES

*Forsyth Technical Community College　　(D)

2100 Silas Creek Parkway, Winston-Salem NC 27103-5197

County: Forsyth　　FICE Identification: 005317
Unit ID: 198552

Telephone: (336) 723-0371　　Carnegie Class: Assoc/MT-VT-High Trad
FAX Number: (336) 761-2399　　Calendar System: Semester
URL: www.forsythtech.edu
Established: 1960　Annual Undergrad Tuition & Fees (In-State): $2,152
Enrollment: 7,587　　Coed
Affiliation or Control: State　　IRS Status: 501(c)3
Highest Offering: Associate Degree
Accreditation: SC, CAHIIM, CNEA, COARC, CVT, DA, DH, DMS, MAC, NMT, RAD, RTT

02	President	Dr. Janet N. SPRIGGS
05	VP Student Academic Success/CAO	Dr. Jacob SURRATT
103	VP Economic & Workforce Development	Mr. Alan K. MURDOCK
10	VP Business Services & CFO	Ms. Kizzy LEA
22	VP Incl Excellence & Employee Supp	Vacant
13	VP Information Technology & CIO	Mr. Chris PEARCE
45	VP for Strategic Innovation	Mr. Kevin OSBORNE
32	VP Student Success Services	Ms. Masonne SAWYER
84	VP for Strategy & Outreach	Ms. Paula DIBLEY
15	Assoc VP Human Resources	Ms. Rachel SCHROEDER
102	Exec Director Foundation	Mr. William GREEN
50	Dean Business & Info Tech	Ms. Pamela SHORTT
49	Dean Arts & Sciences	Dr. Torry REYNOLDS
53	Dean Education & Human Services	Ms. Anu WILLIAMS
54	Dean of Engineering Tech Div	Mr. John CARSTENS
76	Dean of Health Technologies	Ms. Linda LATHAM
88	Dean Cmty & Workforce Development	Mr. Joshua BURCHAM
08	Dean of Learning Resources	Mr. J. Randel CANDELARIA
88	Dean College and Career Readiness	Dr. Sydney RICHARDSON
66	Dept Chair Practical Nursing	Ms. Angie LUNDGREN
66	Dept Chair Assoc Degree Nursing	Ms. Renee HARRISON
07	Director of Admissions & Records	Ms. Heather AZZU
21	Exec Director Financial Services	Ms. Demetria BURTON
37	Director Student Financial Services	Ms. Adina LONG
06	Registrar	Ms. Gwen D. WHITAKER
18	Executive Director Facilities	Mr. Scott BOOTH
19	Chief of Police	Ms. Carolyn MCMACKIN
88	Director Small Business Center	Mr. Allan YOUNGER
35	Director Student Life & Engagement	Ms. Beverly N. LEWIS
96	Exec Director Purchasing/Aux Svcs	Mr. Keith BLYTHE
109	Director Auxiliary Services	Mr. Brian A. HICKS
88	Exec Director National Ctr Biotech	Mr. Russel READ
88	Exec Dir Div Operations/Support	Ms. Michelle DANCHO
12	Director Stokes County Center	Ms. Sally ELLIOTT
88	AVP Business Partnerships	Ms. Jennifer B. COULOMBE
88	Dean of Public Safety	Mr. Konrad WALSH
88	Dir Transportation Technology Ctr	Ms. Kirsten SEAMSTER
88	AVP Transformative Learning Center	Dr. James COOK
29	Director Donor Relations	Ms. Angela COOK
25	Director Grant Writing & Dev	Mr. Mike MASSOGLIA
44	Director Development & Annual Fund	Ms. Patricia VAUGHN
34	Director Shugarts Women's Center	Ms. Kenyetta RICHMOND
36	Director Career Services	Ms. Jessica LONG
26	Director College Relations	Mr. Devin PURGASON
121	Exec Director Student Support Svcs	Dr. Stacy WATERS-BAILEY

*Gaston College　　(E)

201 Highway 321 South, Dallas NC 28034-1499

County: Gaston　　FICE Identification: 002973
Unit ID: 198570

Telephone: (704) 922-6200　　Carnegie Class: Assoc/MT-VT-High Trad
FAX Number: (704) 922-2323　　Calendar System: Semester
URL: www.gaston.edu
Established: 1964　Annual Undergrad Tuition & Fees (In-District): $2,704
Enrollment: 5,345　　Coed
Affiliation or Control: State/Local　　IRS Status: 501(c)3
Highest Offering: Associate Degree
Accreditation: SC, ACBSP, ADNUR, EMT, IFSAC, MAC, NAEYC, PNUR

02	President	Dr. John HAUSER
03	EVP Academic/Student Affairs	Dr. Dewey DELLINGER
103	Int VP Econ & Workforce Development	Mr. Greg SMITH
10	VP Finance/Operations & Facilities	Ms. Shelly ALMAN
102	Chief Dev Ofcr/Dir Foundation	Mr. Luke UPCHURCH

04	Exec Admin Assistant to Pres	Ms. Mary Ellen DILLON
11	VP Admin Services/CHRO	Mr. Todd BANEY
88	VP/GM Man & Textiles Innov Network	Mr. Sam BUFF
05	VP Academic Affairs	Dr. Heather WOODSON
32	VP Student Affairs/Enrollment Mgmt	Dr. Audrey SHERRILL
88	VP Educational Partnerships	Dr. Jennifer NICHOLS
21	Controller	Ms. Tracy BARRETT
26	Exec Dir Marketing/Communication	Ms. Julie OSTROWSKI
103	Dean Career & Tech Education	Dr. Lisa ALBRIGHT-JURS
49	Dean Arts & Sciences	Ms. Tonia BROOME
76	Dean Health & Human Services	Dr. Allison ABERNATHY
12	Dean Lincoln/Kimbrell Campus	Dr. John MCHUGH
35	Dean Student Development	Ms. Renita JOHNSON
88	Dean Learning Resources	Mr. Calvin CRAIG
06	Dir Registration & Records	Ms. Alisa ROY
18	Dir Facilities Management	Mr. Russell SMYRE
37	Dir Financial Aid/Veterans Affairs	Ms. Ungina PERKINS
25	Dir Grants/Special Projects	Mr. Luke UPCHURCH
09	Dir Institutional Effectiveness	Vacant
124	Dir Student Success & Retention	Mr. Damon MURRAY
08	Dir Libraries	Dr. Harry COOKE
121	Dir Advising/Testing	Mr. Zach KENDRA-DILL
07	Dir Admissions	Ms. Tanisha WILLIAMS
40	Dir Bookstore/Vending Services	Mr. Charles WILSON
75	Dir Textile Technology Ctr	Mr. Dan RUSCH
19	Chief Campus Police & Security	Mr. Talmadge MCINNIS
13	Chief Technology Services Officer	Ms. Savonne MCNEILL
15	Dir Human Resources	Ms. Carol DENTON
88	Dir Customized Training	Ms. Emily HANSLEY
51	Dir Cont Educ & Bus/Industry Trng	Ms. Jodi HUFFMAN
88	Dir Life Skills	Ms. Rebecca MCLAIN
78	Dir Apprentice/Work-Based Learning	Ms. Jill HENDRIX
66	Dir of Nursing	Ms. Leslie PRESSLEY
88	Dir Fire Rescue	Mr. Josh CRISP

*Guilford Technical Community College　　(F)

PO Box 309, Jamestown NC 27282-0309

County: Guilford　　FICE Identification: 004838
Unit ID: 198622

Telephone: (336) 334-4822　　Carnegie Class: Assoc/MT-VT-High Trad
FAX Number: (336) 454-2745　　Calendar System: Semester
URL: www.gtcc.edu
Established: 1958　Annual Undergrad Tuition & Fees (In-State): $2,319
Enrollment: 10,821　　Coed
Affiliation or Control: State　　IRS Status: 501(c)3
Highest Offering: Associate Degree
Accreditation: SC, ACFEI, CAHIIM, DA, DH, EMT, IFSAC, MAC, NAEYC, PTAA, RAD, SURGT

02	President	Dr. Anthony CLARKE
05	Sr Vice Pres Instruction	Dr. Beth PITONZO
32	VP Student Services	Dr. James EDWARDS
11	VP Operations & Facilities	Mr. Mitchell JOHNSON
10	VP of Business & Finance/CFO	Ms. Nancy B. SOLLOSI
121	AVP Student Services	Mr. Kirby MOORE
103	VP Workforce & Continuing Educ	Dr. Manuel DUDLEY
50	Dir Business & Industry Training	Mr. Stephen CASTELLOE
15	AVP Human Resources/CHRO	Ms. Cheryl BRYANT-SHANKS
13	Chief Information Officer	Mr. Ron HORN
18	Director of Construction	Mr. Charles YOUNG
09	Director of Institutional Research	Dr. Kristen CORBELL
07	Director of Admissions	Mr. Jesse CROSS
35	Director of Student Life	Ms. Berri V. CROSS
37	Director Financial Aid	Ms. Lisa A. KORETOFF
19	Chief of Campus Police	Mr. Gene SAPINO
06	Registrar	Mr. Keith KARRIKER
21	AVP Business & Finance/Controller	Ms. Angela M. CARTER
40	Bookstore Manager	Mr. Shawn G. DEE
36	Coordinator Career Services	Vacant
38	Director Counseling & Assessment	Dr. Ernest LAWSON
26	AVP Mktg/Comm & Foundation	Ms. Jan KNOX
08	Dir of Library Services	Ms. Monica YOUNG
41	Athletic Director	Mr. Kirk CHANDLER
96	Director of Purchasing	Mr. Michael STOUT
04	Sr Admin Assistant to the President	Ms. April SANDOVAL

*Halifax Community College　　(G)

PO Drawer 809, Weldon NC 27890-0809

County: Halifax　　FICE Identification: 007986
Unit ID: 198640

Telephone: (252) 536-2551　　Carnegie Class: Assoc/MT-VT-High Non
FAX Number: (252) 536-4144　　Calendar System: Semester
URL: www.halifaxcc.edu
Established: 1967　Annual Undergrad Tuition & Fees (In-District): $2,608
Enrollment: 988　　Coed
Affiliation or Control: State/Local　　IRS Status: 501(c)3
Highest Offering: Associate Degree
Accreditation: SC, DH, MLTAD, NAEYC

02	Acting President	Dr. David L. FORESTER
04	Exec Assistant to the President	Ms. Lisa C. BARKLEY
05	Vice Pres Academic Affairs	Dr. Jeffery B. FIELDS
10	Vice President Admin Services	Mr. David FORESTER
111	VP Inst Effectiveness/Advancement	Dr. Edwin IMASUEN
32	VP Student Svcs & Enrollment Mgmt	Dr. Barbara BRADLEY-HASTY
20	Dean of Curriculum Programs	Ms. Allisha HICKS
06	Registrar	Ms. Dawn VELIKY
07	Director of Admissions/Enrol Mgmt	Vacant

08	Director Learning Resources	Dr. Deana GUIDO
09	Dir of Institutional Research	Mr. Marcus LEWIS
26	Dir Public Relations & Marketing	Vacant
38	Director Counseling Services	Ms. Charice ROSSER
18	Director Facilities/Physical Plant	Vacant
36	Director Career/College Promise	Ms. Sonya ROBINSON
37	Director of Financial Aid	Mrs. Tara KEETER
96	Purchasing Agent	Ms. Nicole BOONE
15	Director Human Resources	Mrs. Margaret MURGA
13	Information Systems Manager	Ms. Caroline HARRIS
49	Div Chair Arts & Sciences/Business	Mr. Eugene TINKLEPAUGH
76	Div Chr Health Sciences/Humanities	Ms. Allisha HICKS
75	Div Chair Vocation/Industrial Tech	Vacant
106	Director of Distance Learning	Ms. Nichole PITCHFORD
19	Chief Campus Security	Lt. Emmett SMITH
25	Chief Contracts/Grants Admin	Vacant
102	Exec Director of HCC Foundation	Vacant
103	Dean of Workforce & Economic Dev	Mr. Dale FEY
29	Director Alumni Affairs	Ms. Kimberly MACK

*Haywood Community College (A)

185 Freedlander Drive, Clyde NC 28721-9453

County: Haywood	FICE Identification: 008083
	Unit ID: 198668
Telephone: (828) 627-2821	Carnegie Class: Assoc/MT-VT-Mix Trad/Non
FAX Number: (828) 627-3606	Calendar System: Semester
URL: www.haywood.edu	
Established: 1965	Annual Undergrad Tuition & Fees (In-State): $2,580
Enrollment: 1,440	Coed
Affiliation or Control: State	IRS Status: 501(c)3
Highest Offering: Associate Degree	
Accreditation: SC, MAC, NAEYC	

02	President	Dr. Shelley Y. WHITE
05	Vice President of Instruction	Mrs. Wendy HINES
32	Vice President Student Services	Dr. Michael COLEMAN
10	Vice President Business Operations	Mrs. Karen DENNEY
18	Director of Campus Development	Mr. Brek LANNING
111	Exec Dir College Advancement	Ms. Hylah BIRENBAUM
26	Director Marketing & Communications	Mrs. Michelle HARRIS
15	Director of Human Resources	Mrs. Sara J. PHILLIPS
84	Dir of Enrollment Mgmt/Registrar	Mrs. Danielle HARRIS
37	Sr Dir Student Enrollment/Fin Aid	Mrs. Tracy RAPP
09	Dir Inst Excellence/Research/Grants	Mr. David ONDER
103	Dean of Workforce & Industry	Mr. Doug BURCHFIELD

*Isothermal Community College (B)

PO Box 804, Spindale NC 28160-0804

County: Rutherford	FICE Identification: 002934
	Unit ID: 198710
Telephone: (828) 395-1292	Carnegie Class: Assoc/HT-Mix Trad/Non
FAX Number: (828) 286-1120	Calendar System: Semester
URL: www.isothermal.edu	
Established: 1964	Annual Undergrad Tuition & Fees (In-District): $1,994
Enrollment: 2,042	Coed
Affiliation or Control: State/Local	IRS Status: 501(c)3
Highest Offering: Associate Degree	
Accreditation: SC	

02	President	Dr. Margaret H. ANNUNZIATA
11	COO & Vice Pres	Mr. Stephen MATHENY
05	Vice Pres Academic & Student Affs	Dr. Greg THOMAS
103	Vice Pres Cmty/Workforce Educ	Dr. Thad HARRILL
32	Dean of Student Affairs	Ms. Sandra LACKNER
49	Dean of Arts & Sciences	Dr. Kathy ACKERMAN
51	Dean of Continuing Education	Ms. Donna HOOD
12	Director of Polk Campus & HRD	Ms. Karen MARSHALL
08	Director Library Services	Mr. Charles WIGGINS
10	Controller	Ms. Amy M. PENSON
37	Financial Aid Officer	Ms. Pamela ELLIS
26	Dir Marketing/Community Relations	Mr. Mike GAVIN
18	Dir Plant Operations/Maintenance	Mr. Bill DOLL
84	Director of Enrollment Management	Ms. Diane DICKERSON
06	Registrar	Ms. Rachel MERCANTINI
96	Director of Purchasing	Ms. Trish HUNTSINGER
13	Director of Information Technology	Mr. Robby WALTERS
40	Bookstore Manager	Ms. Danielle ALEY
04	Executive Asst to President	Ms. DeeDee BARNARD
09	Director of Institutional Research	Mr. Adam PETIT

*James Sprunt Community College (C)

PO Box 398, Kenansville NC 28349-0398

County: Duplin	FICE Identification: 007687
	Unit ID: 198729
Telephone: (910) 296-2400	Carnegie Class: Assoc/HT-Mix Trad/Non
FAX Number: (910) 296-1636	Calendar System: Semester
URL: www.jamessprunt.edu	
Established: 1964	Annual Undergrad Tuition & Fees (In-State): $2,570
Enrollment: 1,202	Coed
Affiliation or Control: State	IRS Status: 501(c)3
Highest Offering: Associate Degree	
Accreditation: SC	

02	President	Dr. Jay CARRAWAY
05	VP of Curriculum Services	Dr. Dustin WALSTON
103	AVP Workforce Development/Cont Ed	Ms. Gloria WIGGINS
10	VP Admin & Fiscal Services	Ms. Jessica MCMAHON
32	Associate VP of Student Services	Dr. Shakeena WHITE
13	Assoc VP of Information Technology	Mr. Jeff TAYLOR

100	Chief of Staff	Mrs. Renee SUTTON
06	Registrar	Ms. Kelly ENGLISH
07	Admissions Specialist	Ms. Wanda EDWARDS
37	Director Financial Aid/Vet Affairs	Ms. Tracy WARD
38	Director of Student Counseling	Ms. Amber FERRELL
08	Director Library Services	Mrs. Colleen R. KEHOE-ROBINSON
15	Dir Human Resources/Title IX Coord	Ms. Tonya KENAN
97	Director of General Education	Mr. Andy CAVENAUGH
09	Dir Research/Plng/Inst Effective	Mrs. Norma Jean HATCHER
26	Director of Public Info/Print Media	Vacant
18	Chief Facilities/Physical Plant	Mr. Dennis SUTTON
96	Director of Purchasing	Mrs. Amanda FARINA
55	Instr/Coord Evening/Weekend Svcs	Vacant
19	Director Security/Safety	Mr. Richard WHITMAN
04	Admin Assistant to the President	Ms. Jeanette RACKLEY

*Johnston Community College (D)

PO Box 2350, 245 College Road,
Smithfield NC 27577-2350

County: Johnston	FICE Identification: 009336
	Unit ID: 198774
Telephone: (919) 934-3051	Carnegie Class: Assoc/MT-VT-Mix Trad/Non
FAX Number: (919) 209-2142	Calendar System: Semester
URL: www.johnstoncc.edu	
Established: 1969	Annual Undergrad Tuition & Fees (In-District): $2,657
Enrollment: 4,182	Coed
Affiliation or Control: State/Local	IRS Status: 501(c)3
Highest Offering: Associate Degree	
Accreditation: SC, ADNUR, DMS, EMT, MAC, NAEYC, RAD	

02	Interim President	Dr. Kenneth A. BOHAM
10	VP Facilities & Finance	Mr. Michael BARALDI
05	Interim Vice Pres of Instruction	Ms. Dee Dee DAUGHTRY
32	Vice Pres of Student Services	Dr. Pamela J. HARRELL
09	VP of IE & Strategic Initiatives	Dr. Terri S. LEE
111	VP Advancement/Community Rels	Dr. Twyla C. WELLS
13	Assoc VP/Chief Information Officer	Mr. Jeff PICKERING
08	Library Administrator	Mrs. Jennifer SEAGRAVES
105	Dir of Digital Comm & Webmaster	Mr. Dustin H. GURLEY
06	Registrar	Ms. Deena H. HENRY
37	Director Financial Aid	Mrs. Betty C. WOODALL
109	Assoc VP of Auxiliary Services	Mr. Ken H. MITCHELL
15	Interim Assoc VP of Human Resources	Mr. David SHEHDAN
07	Dir of Admissions/Student Success	Mrs. Megan L. SHANER
103	Exec Dir Econ Dev & Corp Partners	Mrs. Danielle T. KROEGER
76	AVP Health/Wellness & Human Svcs	Mrs. Angela P. SWANK
49	AVP of University Studies/Educ Tech	Mrs. Dawn S. DIXON
50	AVP Business/Applied Tech	Dr. Jennifer SERVI-ROBERTS
26	Sr Dir Comminications & Marketing	Ms. Carrie DENSMORE
18	Director of Facility Services	Mr. Michael MASSEY
96	Director of Purchasing	Mrs. Brandi MITCHELL
88	Director Campus Police & Security	Ms. Sarah GIBBS
04	Exec Asst to the President	Mrs. Sandy MILLARD

*Lenoir Community College (E)

231 Highway 58 South, Kinston NC 28502-0188

County: Lenoir	FICE Identification: 002940
	Unit ID: 198817
Telephone: (252) 527-6223	Carnegie Class: Assoc/MT-VT-High Non
FAX Number: (252) 233-6879	Calendar System: Semester
URL: www.lenoircc.edu	
Established: 1958	Annual Undergrad Tuition & Fees (In-District): $2,568
Enrollment: 2,361	Coed
Affiliation or Control: State/Local	IRS Status: 501(c)3
Highest Offering: Associate Degree	
Accreditation: SC, @CNEA, EMT, MAC, POLYT, RAD, SURGT	

02	President	Dr. Rusty HUNT
11	Senior VP Administrative Services	Ms. Deborah SUTTON
05	VP of Instruction	Dr. John Paul BLACK
32	VP of Student Services & IE	Dr. Stanley ELLIOTT
37	Director of Financial Aid	Mrs. Shelia WIGGINS
84	Director Enrollment Mgmt/Admissions	Dr. Dusk STROUD
35	Dean of Student Services	Mrs. Kimberly HILL
10	Controller	Mr. J. D GIBBS
13	Chief Info Ofcr/Dean Admin Svcs	Mr. Lee WETHERINGTON
09	Director Innovation & Effectiveness	Ms. Nikki PROCTOR
15	Director Human Resources	Mrs. Tasha JOHNSON
18	Maintenance Supervisor	Mr. Karl JOHNSON
41	Athletic Director	Mrs. Shelly BARNES
06	Registrar	Ms. Kamesha WILSON
96	Purchasing Agent	Ms. Cindy JONES
26	Director of Mktg/Recruiting/Comm	Ms. Richy HUNEYCUTT
111	Director Institutional Advancement	Mrs. Jeanne KENNEDY
36	Career Connections Coordinator	Mrs. Sherry IRSIK
08	Director of Library Services	Mr. Rich GARAFOLO
50	Dean of Business & Industry	Mr. Warren MOORE
20	Associate VP of Instruction	Dr. Timothy MADDOX
76	Dean of Health Sciences & Nursing	Dr. Alexis WELCH
103	Dean of Workforce Dev & Pub Safety	Dr. Justin TILGHMAN
35	Director Student Support	Mrs. Shelly BARNES

*Martin Community College (F)

1161 Kehukee Park Road, Williamston NC 27892-9988

County: Martin	FICE Identification: 007988
	Unit ID: 198905
Telephone: (252) 792-1521	Carnegie Class: Assoc/HT-High Non
FAX Number: (252) 792-0826	Calendar System: Semester
URL: www.martincc.edu	
Established: 1967	Annual Undergrad Tuition & Fees (In-State): $1,915
Enrollment: 944	Coed

Affiliation or Control: State	IRS Status: 501(c)3
Highest Offering: Associate Degree	
Accreditation: SC, MAC, PTAA	

02	President	Mr. Wesley BEDDARD
03	Executive Vice President	Dr. Brian BUSCH
05	AVP of Academic Affairs	Dr. Tabitha MILLER
10	Chief Financial Officer	Ms. Tammy BAILEY
11	AVP of Operations	Mr. Billy BARBER
37	Financial Aid Director	Ms. Terri LEGGETT
07	Counselor and Admissions	Ms. Vanessa TRIPP
06	Registrar	Ms. Eileen JARMUL
51	AVP Continuing Education	Mr. Nathan MIZELL
18	Director of Facilities	Mr. Walter WHEELER
15	Human Resource Director	Ms. Morgan ROBERSON
13	Director of IT	Mr. Jason FREEMAN
09	Director of Institutional Research	Ms. Maureen GREEN
96	Director of Purchasing	Ms. Jennifer CHERRY
12	Director of Bertie Campus	Ms. Deborah THOMPSON
08	Library Director	Ms. Mary Anne CAUDLE
04	Assistant to President	Ms. Blair MAJOR
26	Dir Communications/PIO	Ms. Judy JENNETTE
106	Director Online Education	Ms. Kim BARBER
102	Director Foundation/Corporate Rels	Ms. Kismet MATTHEWS

*Mayland Community College (G)

PO Box 547, Spruce Pine NC 28777-0547

County: Mitchell	FICE Identification: 011197
	Unit ID: 198914
Telephone: (828) 765-7351	Carnegie Class: Assoc/MT-VT-High Non
FAX Number: (828) 765-0728	Calendar System: Semester
URL: www.mayland.edu	
Established: 1971	Annual Undergrad Tuition & Fees (In-District): $2,558
Enrollment: 441	Coed
Affiliation or Control: State/Local	IRS Status: 501(c)3
Highest Offering: Associate Degree	
Accreditation: SC, MAC	

02	President	Dr. John C. BOYD
04	Assistant to the President	Ms. Brooke BURLESON
10	Vice President Administrative Svcs	Mrs. Amanda BUCHANAN
05	Vice Pres Academics & Workforce Dev	Mrs. Rita EARLEY
32	Dean of Students	Ms. Michelle MUSICH
76	Dean of Health Sciences Programs	Mrs. Kim BURR
49	Dean of Arts & Sciences	Ms. Sherry SHERMAN
72	Dean of Career Technologies	Ms. Brenda MCFEE
08	Director Learning Resources Center	Mr. Jon WILMESHERR
09	Dir Institutional Effectiveness	Ms. Debbie MITCHELL
06	Registrar	Vacant
88	Dean of Basic Skills Programs	Mr. Steve GUNTER
12	Dean Avery County EWD	Mrs. Melissa C. PHILLIPS
12	Dean Mitchell County EWD	Mr. Chris HELMS
103	Associate VP Workforce Dev & CE	Dr. Monica S. CARPENTER
37	Director Student Financial Aid	Ms. Sonja PETERSON
18	Director Facilities/Physical Plant	Mr. Lee WHITTINGTON
13	Dir Management Information Systems	Mr. Tommy R. LEDFORD
15	Director Personnel Services	Mr. Judy MCCLURE
96	Coordinator of Purchasing/Equipment	Mr. William ELLIS

*McDowell Technical Community College (H)

54 College Drive, Marion NC 28752-8728

County: McDowell	FICE Identification: 008085
	Unit ID: 198923
Telephone: (828) 652-6021	Carnegie Class: Assoc/MT-VT-High Non
FAX Number: (828) 652-1014	Calendar System: Semester
URL: www.mcdowelltech.edu	
Established: 1964	Annual Undergrad Tuition & Fees (In-District): $1,926
Enrollment: 1,048	Coed
Affiliation or Control: State/Local	IRS Status: 501(c)3
Highest Offering: Associate Degree	
Accreditation: SC, CAHIIM	

02	President	Dr. Brian S. MERRITT
05	Vice Pres for Learning/Student Svcs	Dr. Penny CROSS
10	Vice Pres Finance/Administration	Mr. Ryan GARRISON
20	Dean Curriculum Programs	Dr. James BENTON
09	Director of Inst Effectiveness	Mr. Ladelle HARMON
26	Director of External Relations	Mr. Michael K. LAVENDER
13	Director of Technology/Info Systems	Mr. Elmer R. MACOPSON
08	Director of Library Services	Ms. Ramona DEANGELUS
88	Director of Industrial Training	Mr. Eddie SHUFORD
49	Dean Arts & Sciences	Mrs. Judy MELTON
06	Registrar	Ms. Aprille BAILEY
37	Director Student Financial Aid	Vacant
36	Director of Student Enrichment Ctr	Mr. Wingate CAIN
97	Director College/Career Readiness	Mrs. Teresa VALENTINO
22	Director VA & Disability Services	Vacant
51	Director of Continuing Education	Vacant
88	Director Law Enforcement Trng	Mr. Alan MOORE
15	Director of Human Resources	Ms. Breanna ROSE
102	Foundation Director	Mr. Chip CROSS
88	Director MTCC Small Business Center	Mr. Frank SILVER
04	Exec Assistant to the President	Ms. Madalyn GAITO

*Mitchell Community College (I)

500 W Broad Street, Statesville NC 28677-5293

County: Iredell	FICE Identification: 002947
	Unit ID: 198987
Telephone: (704) 878-3200	Carnegie Class: Assoc/HT-High Non
FAX Number: (704) 878-0872	Calendar System: Semester

URL: www.mitchellcc.edu
Established: 1852 Annual Undergrad Tuition & Fees (In-State): $2,651
Enrollment: 3,373 Coed
Affiliation or Control: State IRS Status: 501(c)3
Highest Offering: Associate Degree
Accreditation: SC, ADNUR, MAC, MUS

02 President ... Dr. Tim BREWER
05 Vice President for Instruction ... Vacant
10 Vice Pres of Finance/Administration ... Mr. Gerald HYDE
103 Vice Pres Workforce Development/CEC ... Ms. Carol JOHNSON
111 Executive Director for Advancement ... Mrs. Molly NICHOLSON
32 Vice President for Student Services ... Dr. JJ MCEACHERN
12 Dean of Mooresville Campus ... Mrs. Marla HARRIS
09 Exec Director Research & Planning ... Ms. Eva GIFFORD
37 Director of Financial Aid ... Ms. Candace COOPER
18 Director of Facilities ... Mr. Chad LACKEY
88 Director of Educational Partnership ... Ms. Amanda RHEA
06 Registrar ... Ms. Betsy PATTERSON
19 Director of Public Safety ... Mr. David BULLINS
121 Director of Academic Advising ... Ms. Myra LEWIS
15 Director of Human Resources ... Mr. Paul SANTOS
97 Dean of College Transfer ... Ms. Tia COLEMAN
50 Dean of Bus/Agriculture/Public Svc ... Vacant
66 Dean of Nursing and Sciences ... Ms. Linda WIERSCH
04 Admin Assistant to the President ... Ms. Vicki HOLLAND
07 Director of Admissions ... Ms. T'Sha HARRISON
08 Chief Library Officer ... Dr. Beverly RUFTY
26 Chief Public Relations Officer ... Ms. Haley JONES
28 Director of Diversity ... Dr. Beverly BROWN
96 Purchasing Officer ... Ms. Tammy RACKLEY

*Montgomery Community College (A)

1011 Page Street, Troy NC 27371-0787
County: Montgomery FICE Identification: 008087
Unit ID: 199023
Telephone: (910) 898-9600 Carnegie Class: Assoc/MT-VT-High Non
FAX Number: (910) 576-2176 Calendar System: Semester
URL: www.montgomery.edu
Established: 1967 Annual Undergrad Tuition & Fees (In-District): $2,537
Enrollment: 679 Coed
Affiliation or Control: State/Local IRS Status: 501(c)3
Highest Offering: Associate Degree
Accreditation: SC, DA, MAC

02 President ... Dr. Chad A. BLEDSOE
05 VP of Instruction/Student Services ... Lee PROCTOR
11 VP of Administrative Services ... Jeanette MCBRIDE
32 Dean of Student Services ... Dr. Michelle AHERON
51 Dean of Continuing Education ... Andrew GARDNER
102 Executive Director Foundation/Grant ... Korrie ERVIN
26 Dir of Communications/Marketing ... Kelly MORGAN
09 Dir Institutional Effectiveness ... Greg TAYLOR
13 Dir of Information Technology ... Stephanie WEISHNER
04 Assistant to the President ... Courtney B. ATKINS
06 Director of Records ... Karen FRYE
37 Director of Financial Aid ... Doni S. HATCHEL
15 Director Of Human Resources ... Melinda HILL
10 Accountant ... Tonya LUCK
18 Director of Facilities ... Wanda FRICK
07 Admissions Counselor/Recruiter ... Jessica LATHAM
08 Head Librarian ... Touger VANG

*Nash Community College (B)

522 N Old Carriage Road, Rocky Mount NC 27804-0488
County: Nash FICE Identification: 008557
Unit ID: 199087
Telephone: (252) 443-4011 Carnegie Class: Assoc/MT-VT-High Non
FAX Number: (252) 451-8201 Calendar System: Semester
URL: www.nashcc.edu
Established: 1967 Annual Undergrad Tuition & Fees (In-District): $2,666
Enrollment: 2,623 Coed
Affiliation or Control: State/Local IRS Status: 501(c)3
Highest Offering: Associate Degree
Accreditation: SC, MAC, NAEYC, PTAA

02 President ... Dr. Lew K. HUNNICUTT
04 Executive Assistant to President ... Mrs. Odell P. HOLLIDAY
103 VP Corporate/Economic Dev ... Mrs. Wendy C. MARLOWE
111 VP Institutional Advancement ... Ms. Pamela H. BALLEW
05 Vice President for Instruction ... Dr. Tammie L. CLARK
10 Vice President of Finance ... Mrs. Adrienne S. COVINGTON
13 Vice President Technology & CIO ... Dr. Jonathan S. VESTER
32 Vice President Student Services ... Mr. Mike LATHAM
26 Dean of Marketing/Strategic Engage ... Mrs. Kelley P. DEAL
09 Assoc Dean Institutional Effective ... Mrs. Farley A. PHILLIPS
88 Director Small Business Center ... Ms. Tierra NORWOOD
07 Director of Admissions/Recruitment ... Mrs. Tammie WEBB
37 Director of Financial Aid ... Ms. Tammy LESTER
15 Director Human Resources ... Ms. Morgan H. ROBERSON
18 Director of Facilities ... Mr. Greg DEANS
06 Registrar/Director of Records ... Mrs. Kathy S. ADCOX
08 Chief Library Officer ... Mr. Robert JAMES
19 Director Security/Safety ... Ms. Sara WIGGINS
25 Chief Contract/Grants Administrator ... Ms. Lucrecia A. HIGH
29 Director Alumni Affairs ... Mrs. Denise BEAMER
38 Director Student Counseling ... Ms. Sonya SMALL

*Pamlico Community College (C)

PO Box 185, Grantsboro NC 28529-0185
County: Pamlico FICE Identification: 007031
Unit ID: 199263
Telephone: (252) 249-1851 Carnegie Class: Assoc/MT-VT-High Non
FAX Number: (252) 249-2377 Calendar System: Semester
URL: www.pamlicocc.edu
Established: 1962 Annual Undergrad Tuition & Fees (In-District): $1,867
Enrollment: 362 Coed
Affiliation or Control: State/Local IRS Status: 501(c)3
Highest Offering: Associate Degree
Accreditation: SC, #MAC

02 President ... Dr. Jim ROSS
10 CFO ... Ms. Sherry RABY
05 Vice Pres Instructional Svcs ... Ms. Michelle WILLIS KRAUSS
32 Vice Pres of Student Services ... Mr. Jamie GIBBS
13 CIO ... Mr. Scott FRAZER
09 Dir of Institutional Effectiveness ... Dr. Rebecca PESKO
06 Registrar ... Ms. Gretchen STEIGER
37 Director of Financial Aid ... Ms. Meredith BEEMAN
21 Controller ... Ms. Karan SMITH
26 Director of Public Affairs ... Mr. Sandy WALL
04 Executive Asst to President ... Ms. Michelle NOEVERE
106 Coordinator of Distance Learning ... Ms. Kathy MAYO
08 Chief Library Officer ... Mr. Paul GOODSON
18 Chf Facilities/Physical Plant Ofcr ... Mr. George WILLEY
96 Director of Purchasing ... Ms. Sue FORE

*Piedmont Community College (D)

1715 College Dr, Roxboro NC 27573-1197
County: Person FICE Identification: 009646
Unit ID: 199324
Telephone: (336) 599-1181 Carnegie Class: Assoc/MT-VT-High Non
FAX Number: (336) 597-3817 Calendar System: Semester
URL: www.piedmontcc.edu
Established: 1970 Annual Undergrad Tuition & Fees (In-District): $2,546
Enrollment: 1,329 Coed
Affiliation or Control: State/Local IRS Status: 501(c)3
Highest Offering: Associate Degree
Accreditation: SC, EMT, MAC

02 President ... Dr. Pamela G. SENEGAL
05 Vice Pres Instruction/CAO ... Dr. Barbara BUCHANAN
11 Vice Pres Administrative Services ... Ms. Beverly J. MURPHY
32 Vice President Student Development ... Ms. Shelly T. STONE-MOYE
111 Vice Pres Advancement & Comm ... Ms. Elizabeth R. TOWNSEND
76 Dean Health & Wellness ... Ms. Alisa L. MONTGOMERY
106 Dean Distance Lrng/Learning Commons ... Dr. Don M. MILLER
50 Dean Business Studies/Emerging Tech ... Ms. Melissa G. ROBBINS
72 Dean Technical & Manufacturing ... Mr. Walter C. MONTGOMERY
84 Dean Enrollment Services ... Ms. Paulita N. WILLIAMS
97 Dean Univ Transfer & Gen Educ ... Dr. David TOWNSEND
13 Chief Information Officer ... Mr. Jim TAGLIARENI
06 Registrar ... Ms. Swanita FULLER
18 Director Facility Services ... Mr. Ed MORRAH
15 Director Human Resources & Org Dev ... Vacant
09 Dir Research/Inst Effectiveness ... Ms. Michele W. MATHIS
19 Dir College Safety/Title IX Coord ... Mr. Adam W. IRBY
04 Executive Asst to President ... Ms. Felicia P. HOLT
10 Controller ... Ms. Laurie CLAYTON
12 Dir Caswell Co Campus Operations ... Ms. Emily B. BUCHANAN
07 Director Admissions & Recruitment ... Vacant

*Pitt Community College (E)

PO Drawer 7007, Greenville NC 27835-7007
County: Pitt FICE Identification: 004062
Unit ID: 199333
Telephone: (252) 493-7200 Carnegie Class: Assoc/MT-VT-High Non
FAX Number: (252) 321-4458 Calendar System: Semester
URL: www.pittcc.edu
Established: 1961 Annual Undergrad Tuition & Fees (In-State): $1,940
Enrollment: 7,688 Coed
Affiliation or Control: State IRS Status: 501(c)3
Highest Offering: Associate Degree
Accreditation: SC, CAHIIM, CNEA, COARC, DA, DMS, EMT, MAC, OTA, POLYT, RAD, RADDOS, RTT

02 President ... Dr. Lawrence L. ROUSE
05 EVP Academic Affairs & Student Svcs ... Dr. Thomas GOULD
26 VP Strat Initiatives/Cmty Engage ... Dr. Johnny SMITH
111 Vice Pres Institutional Advancement ... Mrs. Marianne COX
20 Asst Vice Pres Academic Affairs ... Ms. Lori PREAST
13 AVP Information Technology/Services ... Mr. Ernest SIMONS
10 VP of Finance/Budget/Facility Svcs ... Mr. Ricky BROWN
04 Executive Admin Asst to President ... Ms. Linda KING
08 Director Library ... Ms. Leigh RUSSELL
09 VP of Planning & Research ... Dr. Brian MILLER
15 Vice President of HR/OITS/Safety ... Dr. Ina RAWLINSON
91 Director of Admin Computing ... Mr. Wes WOOTEN
06 Registrar ... Ms. Anita R. TYRE
38 Director of Counseling ... Dr. Kimberly WILLIAMSON
88 Director Basic Skills Program ... Ms. Melissa MORLOCK
18 Director of Facilities ... Mr. Timothy STRICKLAND
41 Athletic Director ... Ms. Dawn MANNING
29 Director of Alumni Relations ... Mr. John BACON
96 Director of Purchasing ... Ms. Jane ALLIGOOD
19 Chief Public Safety/Campus Police ... Mr. Tyrone TURNAGE
88 Director Small Business Svcs ... Mr. Jerry ENSOR
104 Director Study Abroad ... Vacant
37 Director Financial Aid ... Ms. Lee BRAY
40 Manager of College Store ... Ms. Holly BARBEE
106 Coord Instructional Tech/Dist Educ ... Mr. Mike CLENDENEN
88 Director of High School Programs ... Ms. Natasha WORTHINGTON
50 Division Dean of Business ... Ms. Katherine CLYDE
76 Division Dean Health Sciences ... Ms. Donna V. NEAL
49 Division Dean of Art & Sciences ... Dr. Stephanie MANLEY-ROOK
75 Div Dean Construct/Ind Tech ... Vacant
61 Div Dean Legal Sci/Public Svc ... Dr. Dan MAYO
07 Director of Admissions ... Ms. Rhonda W. JONES
102 Dir Foundation/Corporate Relations ... Ms. Georgia SIGMON
105 Director Web Services ... Vacant
25 Director Grants Management ... Ms. Jaymi MITCHELL
27 Marketing Director ... Ms. Jane POWER
84 Asst VP Enrollment Management ... Mr. Brian JONES

*Randolph Community College (F)

629 Industrial Park Avenue, Asheboro NC 27205
County: Randolph FICE Identification: 005447
Unit ID: 199421
Telephone: (336) 633-0200 Carnegie Class: Assoc/HT-Mix Trad/Non
FAX Number: (336) 629-4695 Calendar System: Semester
URL: www.randolph.edu
Established: 1962 Annual Undergrad Tuition & Fees (In-District): $2,386
Enrollment: 2,548 Coed
Affiliation or Control: State/Local IRS Status: 501(c)3
Highest Offering: Associate Degree
Accreditation: SC, EMT, MAC, RAD

02 President ... Dr. Robert S. SHACKLEFORD, JR.
10 Vice Pres Administrative Services ... Ms. Daffie H. GARRIS
05 Vice Pres Instructional Services ... Ms. Suzanne Y. ROHRBAUGH
32 Vice President Student Services ... Mr. Chad WILLIAMS
103 VP Workforce Development/Cont Educ ... Mr. Elbert J. LASSITER
111 VP Institutional Advancement ... Ms. Shelley W. GREENE
08 Dean Library Services ... Ms. Deborah S. LUCK
12 Director Archdale Center ... Ms. Tonya C. MONROE
26 Director Marketing ... Ms. Felicia R. BARLOW
18 Director Facilities Operations ... Ms. Cindi J. GOODWIN
13 Director Information Tech Svcs ... Ms. Tara A. WILLIAMS
09 Planning & Assessment Specialist ... Ms. Stacy C. SCHMITT
15 Director of Human Resources ... Ms. Melanie AVELINO
37 Director Financial Aid & Veteran Af ... Mr. Joel TROGDON
07 Dir Admissions/Records & Registrar ... Ms. Hillary D. PRITCHARD
88 Director of ABE and AHS ... Ms. Jordan H. WILLIAMSON
88 Director Public Safety Programs ... Ms. Regina L. BREWER
96 Purchasing Agent ... Mr. Christopher G. HUSSEY
04 Exec Asst to Pres/Board of Trustees ... Ms. Heather O. CLOUSTON
19 Dir Safety/Emergency Preparedness ... Mr. Matthew R. NEEDHAM
30 Director of Development ... Ms. Lorie L. MCCROSKEY

*Richmond Community College (G)

Box 1189, Hamlet NC 28345-1189
County: Richmond FICE Identification: 005464
Unit ID: 199449
Telephone: (910) 410-1700 Carnegie Class: Assoc/MT-VT-Mix Trad/Non
FAX Number: (910) 582-7028 Calendar System: Semester
URL: www.richmondcc.edu
Established: 1964 Annual Undergrad Tuition & Fees (In-District): $2,536
Enrollment: 2,226 Coed
Affiliation or Control: State/Local IRS Status: 501(c)3
Highest Offering: Associate Degree
Accreditation: SC, MAC

02 President ... Dr. W. Dale MCINNIS
32 Vice President for Student Services ... Ms. Lisa INMAN
05 Vice President for Instruction/CAO ... Mr. Kevin PARSONS
10 Executive VP and CFO ... Mr. Brent BARBEE
26 VP of Mktg & Strategic Plng ... Ms. Sheri DUNN-RAMSAY
30 Assoc VP for Development ... Dr. Hal SHULER
11 Assoc VP for Administrative Svcs ... Ms. Katina BROWN
09 Director of Institutional Research ... Ms. Chihoko TERRY
15 Director of Human Resources ... Ms. Gaye CLARK
27 Dir of Marketing & Communications ... Ms. Wylie BELL
21 Controller ... Ms. Debbie CASHWELL
36 Director of Career and Transfer Svc ... Ms. Patsy STANLEY
37 Director of Student Financial Aid ... Ms. Emily JARRELL
96 Purchasing Officer ... Mr. Martin BRIDGES
18 Director of Facility Services ... Mr. Scotty MABE
38 Director Student Counseling ... Mr. Chris GARDNER
04 Executive Asst to President ... Ms. Teena PARSONS
06 Registrar ... Ms. Cayce HOLMES
106 Director of Distance Learning ... Ms. Katelynn ARNER
13 Chief Information Officer ... Mr. Lee MONTROSE
54 Dean of Engineering & Tech/Trades ... Mr. Ryan COBB
49 Dean of Arts & Sciences ... Vacant
88 Dean Adult Education & Immured Pgm ... Mr. John KESTER
76 Dean Allied Health & Human Services ... Ms. Janet SIMS
50 Dean of Business/Tech/Public Svc ... Dr. Miriam HUNTLEY

*Roanoke-Chowan Community College (H)

109 Community College Road, Ahoskie NC 27910
County: Hertford FICE Identification: 008613
Unit ID: 199467
Telephone: (252) 862-1200 Carnegie Class: Assoc/HT-High Trad
FAX Number: (252) 862-1358 Calendar System: Semester
URL: www.roanokechowan.edu

Established: 1967 Annual Undergrad Tuition & Fees (In-District): $2,642
Enrollment: 525 Coed
Affiliation or Control: State/Local IRS Status: 501(c)3
Highest Offering: Associate Degree
Accreditation: SC

02 President .... Dr. Murray J. WILLIAMS
05 VP of Instruction/Student Services .... Ms. Jami WOODS
10 VP of Administration/Fiscal Svcs .... Ms. Latoya J. WILEY
20 Assoc VP of Instruction .... Ms. Kim HARRELL
21 Assoc VP of Admin/Fiscal Svcs .... Mr. Tracy E. PEELE
51 Assoc Dean Continuing Education .... Ms. Wendy VANN
76 Director Allied Health Programs .... Ms. Jamie BURNS
32 AVP of Student Services .... Dr. Tanya W. OLIVER
21 Controller .... Vacant
18 Dir of Facil/Campus Police .... Mr. Timothy LASSITER
106 Director Distance Learning .... Ms. Melanie TEMPLE
37 Director Financial Aid .... Mrs. Ruchelle RICKS
13 Director of Information Systems .... Mr. Clarence E. HALL
13 Director of Information Systems .... Vacant
08 Director of Library Services .... Ms. Carol A. HANKINSON
84 College Registrar .... Mrs. Amy F. WIGGINS
121 Director Student Support Services .... Vacant
15 Director Human Resources .... Vacant
06 Registrar/Continuing Educ/Workforce .... Ms. Sharda D. BRITT
102 Director R-CCC Foundation .... Ms. Stephanie BENSON
102 Director R-CCC Foundation .... Vacant
09 Director of Institutional Research .... Vacant
88 Director of Small Business Center .... Mr. Derrick ARMSTEAD
30 Vice President External Affairs .... Mrs. Wendy P. VANN
96 Purchasing Agent/Equipment Coord .... Ms. Susan B. MELTON
04 Exec Assistant to the President .... Ms. Kim SANDERS
19 Director Security/Safety .... Mr. Timothy LASSITER
07 Director Admission/Student Life .... Ms. Rushelle D. SAXBY

*Robeson Community College (A)

5160 Fayetteville Road, Lumberton NC 28360
County: Robeson FICE Identification: 008612
Unit ID: 199476
Telephone: (910) 272-3700 Carnegie Class: Assoc/HVT-High Trad
FAX Number: (910) 272-3546 Calendar System: Semester
URL: www.robeson.edu
Established: 1965 Annual Undergrad Tuition & Fees (In-District): $2,563
Enrollment: 1,828 Coed
Affiliation or Control: State/Local IRS Status: 501(c)3
Highest Offering: Associate Degree
Accreditation: SC, @CNEA, COARC, RAD, SURGT

02 President .... Ms. Melissa SINGLER
05 VP Instruction/Sppt Svcs/CAO .... Ms. Patrena ELLIOTT
103 VP Workforce Devel/Continuing Educ .... Mr. Eric FREEMAN
10 VP Business/Institutional Services .... Ms. Tami GEORGE
13 VP Information Sys/Chief Info Ofcr .... Mr. Dustin LONG
76 Asst VP Univ Transfer/Hlth Sci Pgms .... Ms. LaRonda LOWERY
32 Asst VP Student Services .... Mr. Ronnie LOCKLEAR
07 Director of Admissions/Enroll Svcs .... Ms. Patricia LOCKLEAR
08 Director of Learning Resource Svcs .... Ms. Maryellen O'BRIEN
06 Dir Records/Registration/Registrar .... Ms. Sherry MARTIN
37 Director of Financial Aid .... Ms. Zilma LOPES
18 Director of Facilities .... Mr. Jamie COLLINS
102 Director Foundation & Development .... Vacant
36 Counseling & Career Services .... Ms. Susan MOORE
15 Director of Human Resources .... Ms. Sally CARR
96 Purchasing Specialist .... Ms. Jamie WILKINS
04 Executive Assistant to President .... Ms. Courtney JACOBS
09 Dir of Institutional Effectiveness .... Dr. Kenneth BOWEN
19 Director of Security .... Ms. Patricia CLARK
26 Chief Public Relations Officer .... Ms. Cheryl HEMRIC

*Rockingham Community College (B)

215 Wrenn Memorial Road, Wentworth NC 27375
County: Rockingham FICE Identification: 002958
Unit ID: 199485
Telephone: (336) 342-4261 Carnegie Class: Assoc/MT-VT-Mix Trad/Non
FAX Number: (336) 349-9986 Calendar System: Semester
URL: www.rockinghamcc.edu
Established: 1963 Annual Undergrad Tuition & Fees (In-District): $1,966
Enrollment: 1,922 Coed
Affiliation or Control: State/Local IRS Status: 501(c)3
Highest Offering: Associate Degree
Accreditation: SC, COARC, SURGT

02 President .... Dr. Mark O. KINLAW
05 Vice President for Academic Affairs .... Ms. Sheila REGAN
11 VP of Administrative Services .... Mr. Steven W. WOODRUFF
32 Vice Pres for Student Development .. Dr. Robert S. LOWDERMILK
18 AVP Facilities/External Affairs .... Dr. E. Anthony GUNN
103 Dean Workforce Development .... Mr. Christopher BROOKS
49 Dean of Arts & Sciences .... Ms. Celeste H. ALLIS
76 Dean of Health & Public Services .... Ms. Vickie CHITWOOD
88 Director Testing Services .... Ms. Kimberly SHIREMAN
13 AVP Technology/Inst Effectiveness .... Ms. Gretchen PARRISH
06 Registrar .... Vacant
08 Director Library Services/Archivist .... Ms. Mary GOMEZ
30 Dir Development/Exec Dir Foundation .... Ms. Kim PRYOR
37 Director of Financial Aid .... Ms. Carol PERRY
84 Director of Enrollment Services .... Mr. Derick SATTERFIELD
35 Director Student Life .... Ms. Maggie MURRAY
40 Bookstore Manager .... Ms. Angie PURGASON
15 Director Human Resources .... Ms. Joy G. CHAPPELL
26 Director Public Information .... Ms. Gerri HUNT
96 Purchasing Ofcr/Capital Projects .... Mr. Caleb RORRER

*Rowan-Cabarrus Community College (C)

1333 Jake Alexander Blvd., South, Salisbury NC 28145
County: Rowan FICE Identification: 005754
Unit ID: 199494
Telephone: (704) 216-7222 Carnegie Class: Assoc/MT-VT-High Non
FAX Number: N/A Calendar System: Semester
URL: www.rccc.edu
Established: 1963 Annual Undergrad Tuition & Fees (In-State): $2,632
Enrollment: 7,109 Coed
Affiliation or Control: State IRS Status: 501(c)3
Highest Offering: Associate Degree
Accreditation: SC, ADNUR, DA, EMT, OTA, PNUR, PTAA, RAD

02 President .... Dr. Carol SPALDING
18 Chief Officer Civility/Environment ... Mr. Jonathan CHAMBERLAIN
100 Chief Ofcr Govt/Advance/Cmty Rels .... Ms. Sarah DEVLIN
15 Chief Officer Human Resources .... Mrs. Nekita EUBANKS
13 Chief Officer Information Svcs .... Mr. Kenneth INGLE, III
10 Chief Financial/Business Officer .... Ms. Kelly KLUTTZ
51 VP Corporate & Continuing Education .... Mr. Craig LAMB
32 Vice President Student Success .... Ms. Natasha LIPSCOMB
05 Vice President Academic Programs .... Dr. Michael QUILLEN
20 Assoc Academic Vice President .... Ms. Debra NEESMITH
20 Assoc Academic Vice President ..... Dr. Angelo MARKANTONAKIS
76 Dean Health & Education .... Dr. Wendy BARNHARDT
49 Dean Arts and Sciences .... Ms. Carol SCHERCZINGER
72 Dean Technical Programs .... Mr. Zackary HUBBARD
69 Dean Public Services .... Dr. Chris NESBITT
36 Exec Dir College & Career Readiness .... Mr. Jay TAYLOR
08 Director Library Services .... Mr. Timothy HUNTER
25 Director Grants .... Ms. Rebecca HOOKS
121 Exec Dir Students Success Svc .... Ms. Crystal RYERSON
96 Director of Procurement .... Mr. Steve CHILDRESS
37 Director of Student Financial Aid .... Ms. Allison SCOTT
06 Registrar/Dir Admission & Records .... Mr. Phillip LOPP
35 Director Student Life .... Mrs. Barb MEIDL
09 Exec Dir Inst Effectiveness & Rsch .... Vacant
19 Director Campus Safety & Security .... Mr. Paul DUPREE
124 Director Recruitment & Retention .... Dr. A'Lelianne WARREN
102 Foundation Director .... Ms. Connie RHEINECKER
119 Dir Info Security/IT Const & Comp .... Mr. Steven SAINE
38 Director TRIO/Wellness & Access Svc .... Mrs. Misty MOLER

*Sampson Community College (D)

P.O. Box 318, Clinton NC 28329-0318
County: Sampson FICE Identification: 007892
Unit ID: 199625
Telephone: (910) 592-8081 Carnegie Class: Assoc/MT-VT-High Non
FAX Number: (910) 592-8048 Calendar System: Semester
URL: www.sampsoncc.edu
Established: 1967 Annual Undergrad Tuition & Fees (In-District): $2,830
Enrollment: 1,492 Coed
Affiliation or Control: State/Local IRS Status: 501(c)3
Highest Offering: Associate Degree
Accreditation: SC, ADNUR, MAC, PNUR

02 President .... Dr. Bill STARLING
05 Vice Pres Academic & Student Affs .... Mrs. Blair HAIRR
10 Vice Pres Finance & Administration .... Mrs. Kelly JACKSON
32 Dean of Student Services .... Dr. Marvin RONDON
111 Dean of Advance/Exec Dir Foundation .... Mrs. Lisa TURLINGTON
103 Dean of Wkfc Dev/Continuing Educ .... Mrs. Amanda BRADSHAW
84 Director of Enrollment .... Ms. Amelia ELMORE
121 Dir Institutional & Student Success .... Ms. Emily BROWN
13 Dir IT/Chief Information Officer .... Mr. Michael BLANKENSHIP
06 Registrar .... Ms. Billie Jo PITTMAN
19 Director of Security .... Mr. Darryl GRADY
37 Dir Financial Aid/Veteran Services .... Ms. Marleen POWELL
08 Dir Learning Resource Ctr .... Ms. Michelle MILLIKEN
106 Director of Distance Learning .... Ms. Marion POPE
15 Director of Personnel .... Mrs. Frankie SUTTER

*Sandhills Community College (E)

3395 Airport Road, Pinehurst NC 28374-8283
County: Moore FICE Identification: 002961
Unit ID: 199634
Telephone: (910) 692-6185 Carnegie Class: Assoc/MT-VT-High Trad
FAX Number: (910) 695-1823 Calendar System: Semester
URL: www.sandhills.edu
Established: 1963 Annual Undergrad Tuition & Fees (In-State): $2,764
Enrollment: 3,990 Coed
Affiliation or Control: State IRS Status: 501(c)3
Highest Offering: Associate Degree
Accreditation: SC, CNEA, COARC, EMT, MAC, MLTAD, RAD, SURGT

02 President .... Dr. John R. DEMPSEY
11 EVP/Chief Operating Officer .... Ms. Brenda JACKSON
05 SVP of Academic Affairs .... Dr. Rebecca ROUSH
32 VP of Student Services .... Mrs. Kellie SHOEMAKE
35 AVP for Student Services .... Dr. David FARMER
51 VP Continuing Education/WF Dev .... Ms. Andrea KORTE
45 VP College Initiatives .... Mr. Ron LAYNE
15 Assoc VP Human Resources .... Ms. Wendy B. DODSON
04 Exec Assistant to the President .... Ms. Heather LYONS
20 Dean of Instruction .... Dr. Julie VOIGT
09 Dean of Planning & Research .... Ms. Lindsey FARMER
111 VP of Institutional Advancement .... Ms. Germaine ELKINS
08 Dean of Learning Resources .... Vacant
06 Director of Records & Registration .... Ms. Jean BLUE
37 Director of Financial Aid .... Ms. Shenika WARD
106 Dean of Academic Support .... Ms. Wendy KAUFFMAN
13 Chief Information Officer .... Mr. Roderick BROWER
19 Director of Security/Safety .... Mr. Dwight THREET
18 Director of Facilities .... Mr. Doug SMITH
57 Exec Dir Bradshaw Perform Arts Ctr .... Mr. Joseph BROWN
26 Director Marketing/Public Relations .... Ms. Karen MANNING
40 Bookstore Manager .... Ms. Sandra DALES
07 Director of Admissions .... Ms. Cary GREENE

*South Piedmont Community College (F)

PO Box 126, Polkton NC 28135-0126
County: Anson/Union FICE Identification: 007985
Unit ID: 197850
Telephone: (704) 272-5300 Carnegie Class: Assoc/HT-High Non
FAX Number: (704) 272-5350 Calendar System: Semester
URL: www.spcc.edu
Established: 1999 Annual Undergrad Tuition & Fees (In-District): $2,015
Enrollment: 3,019 Coed
Affiliation or Control: State/Local IRS Status: 501(c)3
Highest Offering: Associate Degree
Accreditation: SC, DMS, EMT, MAC, NAEYC

02 President .... Dr. Maria PHARR
05 Vice Pres Acad & Stdnt Affs/CAO .... Mr. Carl BISHOP
10 VP Finance/Administrative Svcs/CFO .... Ms. Michelle BROCK
04 Exec Assistant to President .... Mrs. Elizabeth HAMRICK
15 Assoc VP Human Res/Payroll/Org Dev .... Ms. Lauren SELLERS
21 Assoc Vice Pres Finance/Admin Svcs .... Mr. Richard ASHLEY
13 Assoc VP Info Tech Svcs/CIO .... Ms. Natisha GIVENS
20 Assoc VP of Academic Affairs .... Dr. Makena STEWART
35 Assoc VP of Student Affairs .... Mr. Brandon DYER
18 Executive Director of Facilities .... Mr. Thomas SUGGS
108 Assoc VP Planning/IE .... Ms. Jill MILLARD
49 Dean School of Arts & Science .... Dr. Diane PAIGE
76 Dean Health & Public Services .... Mr. Ryan ANTHONY
72 Dean Applied Science & Technology .... Dr. Mark LITTLE
36 Dean College & Career Readiness .... Ms. Kelly STEGALL
06 Registrar .... Ms. Cathy HORNE
121 Director Academic Advising .... Ms. Laura SIMMONS
84 Director of Recruitment/Enrollment .... Ms. Lauren MESEROLL
96 Director of Purchasing .... Mr. Anthony BARBOUR
88 Director Learning Commons .... Ms. Kamisha KIRBY
19 Director Safety & Security .... Mr. William KILGO

*Southeastern Community College (G)

4564 Chadbourn Highway, PO Box 151,
Whiteville NC 28472-0151
County: Columbus FICE Identification: 002964
Unit ID: 199722
Telephone: (910) 642-7141 Carnegie Class: Assoc/MT-VT-Mix Trad/Non
FAX Number: (910) 642-5658 Calendar System: Semester
URL: www.sccnc.edu
Established: 1964 Annual Undergrad Tuition & Fees (In-State): $2,600
Enrollment: 1,271 Coed
Affiliation or Control: State IRS Status: 501(c)3
Highest Offering: Associate Degree
Accreditation: SC, MLTAD

02 President .... Dr. Chris ENGLISH
05 Exec VP & Chief Academic Officer .... Dr. Sylvia COX
11 VP Administrative Services/COO .... Ms. Lacie JACOBS
32 Dean of Student Services .... Ms. Colene FAULK
76 Dean of Healthcare & Public Safety .... Ms. Kimberly FINE
20 Dean of Student Lrng & Innovation .... Ms. Elizabeth HIGH
103 Dean Careers & Technical Training .... Ms. Angela RANSOM
09 Dean of Inst Effectiveness .... Dr. Natalie HINSON
08 Librarian .... Ms. Kay HOUSER
102 SCC Foundation Director .... Ms. Terrie H. PRIEST
15 Director Human Resources .... Mr. Bill MAULTSBY
21 Controller .... Ms. Donna TURBEVILLE
26 Dir Marketing & Communications .... Ms. Haylee DAMATO
13 Director of Information Technology .... Mr. Jason STRICKLAND
37 Director of Financial Aid .... Ms. Sheila DOCKERY
06 Dir of Student Records/Registrar .... Vacant
36 Director of Counseling .... Ms. Julia ROBERTS
04 Admin Assistant to the President .... Ms. Jennie M. SIMMONS

*Southwestern Community College (H)

447 College Drive, Sylva NC 28779-8581
County: Jackson FICE Identification: 008466
Unit ID: 199731
Telephone: (828) 339-4000 Carnegie Class: Assoc/MT-VT-Mix Trad/Non
FAX Number: (828) 586-3129 Calendar System: Semester
URL: www.southwesterncc.edu
Established: 1964 Annual Undergrad Tuition & Fees (In-District): $2,337
Enrollment: 2,259 Coed
Affiliation or Control: State/Local IRS Status: 501(c)3
Highest Offering: Associate Degree
Accreditation: SC, CAHIIM, COARC, DMS, EMT, MAC, MLTAD, OTA, PTAA, RAD

02 President .... Dr. Don L. TOMAS
05 Exec VP Instruction/Student Svcs .... Dr. Thom R. BROOKS
10 VP for Financial & Admin Services .... Vacant
13 VP Information Technology .... Mr. Scott BAKER

103 Dean of Workforce/Cont Education ... Mr. Scott SUTTON
12 Dean Macon Campus ... Dr. Cheryl DAVIDS
06 Dir Student Records/Registrar ... Ms. Clyanne HYDE
08 Library Director ... Ms. Tina ADAMS
09 Director Inst Research & Planning ... Mr. Jonathan E. DEAN
26 Director of Public Relations ... Mr. Tyler GOODE
102 Director of SCC Foundation ... Mr. Brett L. WOODS
84 Director of Enrollment Management ... Dr. Mark ELLISON
18 Director of Human Resources ... Ms. Lisa SIZEMORE

*Stanly Community College (A)

141 College Drive, Albemarle NC 28001-7458
County: Stanly — FICE Identification: 011194
Unit ID: 199740
Telephone: (704) 982-0121 — Carnegie Class: Assoc/MT-VT-High Non
FAX Number: (704) 982-0819 — Calendar System: Semester
URL: www.stanly.edu
Established: 1971 — Annual Undergrad Tuition & Fees (In-District): $2,674
Enrollment: 2,432 — Coed
Affiliation or Control: State/Local — IRS Status: 501(c)3
Highest Offering: Associate Degree
Accreditation: SC, CNEA, COARC, EMT, MAC, MLTAD, RAD

02 President ... Dr. John ENAMAIT
45 VP of Strategic Planning/Compliance ... Mrs. Carmen NUNALEE
05 VP of Academic Affairs/CAO ... Mr. Jeff PARSONS
32 VP Student Success ... Dr. Myra FURR
10 VP Administrative Services/CFO ... Mrs. Kimberly BRADSHAW
76 Assoc VP Health & Public Svcs ... Mrs. Christie HONEYCUTT
50 Assoc VP Transfer & Business ... Mrs. Tammi MCILWAINE
75 Assoc VP AMIT ... Mr. Devin BAUCOM
13 Chief Technical Officer ... Mr. Heath LUQUIRE
14 Director of Enterprise Applications ... Mr. Joel ALLEN
119 Director of Network Services ... Mr. Terry MCMANUS
120 Dean of Center for Teaching & Lrng ... Mr. Joe POLLARD
04 Exec Aide to President ... Mrs. Abby ELKINS
103 Director of Econ/Workforce Dev ... Mrs. Krista BOWERS
37 Dean Financial Aid Management ... Ms. Petra FIELDS
84 Dean of Enrollment Management ... Mr. Patrick HOLYFIELD
35 Dean of Students ... Mr. Marcus PRYOR
121 Dean of Advising ... Mrs. Jennifer HATLEY
06 Curriculum Associate Registrar ... Ms. Michelle POPLIN
38 Director Counseling/Special Svcs ... Mrs. Tracie CARPENTER
26 Director Marketing & Communications ... Mrs. Nicole WILLIAMS
07 Director of Admissions ... Mrs. Heather BURNETTE
21 Dean of Business Services ... Mr. Michael SPERLING
18 Administrative & Facilities Service ... Mr. Blake BOSTIC
102 Exec Director of SCC Foundation ... Ms. Jeania MARTIN
15 Director of Human Resources ... Mrs. Lori POPLIN
08 LRC Director ... Mr. Joel FERDON
24 Director of Media Services ... Mr. Mark SAMPLE
109 Dean of Auxiliary Services ... Mrs. Shelley OSBORNE
19 Director of Security ... Mr. Michael HINSON
09 Director Inst Research/Planning ... Dr. Cindy DEAN

*Surry Community College (B)

630 S Main Street, Dobson NC 27017-0304
County: Surry — FICE Identification: 002970
Unit ID: 199768
Telephone: (336) 386-8121 — Carnegie Class: Assoc/MT-VT-High Non
FAX Number: (336) 386-8951 — Calendar System: Semester
URL: www.surry.edu
Established: 1964 — Annual Undergrad Tuition & Fees (In-State): $2,663
Enrollment: 3,103 — Coed
Affiliation or Control: State — IRS Status: 501(c)3
Highest Offering: Associate Degree
Accreditation: SC, EMT, MAC, PTAA

02 President ... Dr. David R. SHOCKLEY
10 Chief of Finance ... Mr. Tony L. MARTIN
05 Chief Academic/Tech Officer ... Dr. Candace HOLDER
09 Exec Dir of Analytics & Research ... Mr. Michael FAULKNER
15 Director of Human Resources ... Ms. Melonie WEATHERS
18 Chief Facilities/Physical Plant ... Mr. Randy ROGERS
19 Chief of Police/Safety Director ... Mr. Marty SHROPSHIRE
26 Director of Mktg/PIO ... Ms. Julie PHARR
41 Athletic Director ... Mr. Mark TUCKER

*Tri-County Community College (C)

21 Campus Circle, Murphy NC 28906-7919
County: Cherokee — FICE Identification: 009430
Unit ID: 199795
Telephone: (828) 837-6810 — Carnegie Class: Assoc/HT-High Non
FAX Number: (828) 837-0028 — Calendar System: Semester
URL: www.tricountycc.edu
Established: 1964 — Annual Undergrad Tuition & Fees (In-State): $2,363
Enrollment: 991 — Coed
Affiliation or Control: State — IRS Status: 501(c)3
Highest Offering: Associate Degree
Accreditation: SC, EMT

02 President ... Dr. Donna TIPTON-ROGERS
05 VP for Teaching & Learning ... Dr. Steve WOOD
10 VP for Business & Finance/CFO ... Mr. Bill VESPASIAN
13 Dir of Computing & Information Mgt ... Mr. Jason OUTEN
124 Coordinator Advising/Career Center ... Ms. Samantha Major JONES
103 Exec Dir Workforce/Govt Relations ... Mr. Paul WORLEY
09 Dean Planning & Research/EC Liaison ... Dr. Jason CHAMBERS
15 Director of Human Resources ... Ms. Connie IVEY

91 Systems Administrator/Data Base Mgr ... Mr. Randy GUYETTE
106 Learning Mgt Systems Administrator ... Mr. Donnie MORROW
108 Dean Institutional Effectiveness ... Mr. Roarke ARROWOOD
06 Registrar Curriculum ... Ms. Holly HYDE
37 Director of Financial Aid ... Ms. Diane OWL
96 Director of Purchasing ... Ms. Joy KEPHART
32 Director of Student Services ... Ms. Kelly HEMBREE
18 Director of Facilities ... Mr. Tim NICHOLSON
04 Senior Assistant to the President ... Ms. Helen KILPATRICK
26 Director of Communications ... Ms. Grace CHESHIRE
08 Director of Learning Resources ... Ms. Rachel WHITENER

*Vance-Granville Community College (D)

PO Box 917, Henderson NC 27536-0917
County: Vance — FICE Identification: 009903
Unit ID: 199838
Telephone: (252) 492-2061 — Carnegie Class: Assoc/MT-VT-High Non
FAX Number: (252) 430-0460 — Calendar System: Semester
URL: www.vgcc.edu
Established: 1969 — Annual Undergrad Tuition & Fees (In-State): $1,948
Enrollment: 2,963 — Coed
Affiliation or Control: State Related — IRS Status: 501(c)3
Highest Offering: Associate Degree
Accreditation: SC, CSHSE, HT, MAC, RAD

02 President ... Dr. Rachel M. DESMARAIS
05 VP Learning/Engagement/Success ... Dr. Levy BROWN
10 VP for Finance & Operations ... Mr. Steve GRAHAM
103 VP Workforce & Cmty Engagement ... Dr. Jerry EDMONDS, II
09 VP of Institutional Research & Tech ... Dr. Kenneth A. LEWIS, JR.
88 Dean of Corp Learning & Prof Dev ... Ms. Cherrelle LAWRENCE
50 Dean of Bus & Industry Solutions ... Ms. Tanya WEARY
88 Dean K12 Partnerships/Warren Campus ... Mr. Lyndon HALL
26 Director of Marketing ... Mr. Chris LA ROCCA
37 Director of Financial Aid ... Mr. Robert LEONARD
15 Director of Human Resources ... Mr. Kevin TOMPKINS
08 Director Learning Resources Center ... Ms. Elaine STEM
09 Director of Planning & Research ... Ms. Julie HICKS
18 Director of Plant Operations ... Mr. Ashley ROBERSON
121 Dir of Advising & College Success ... Ms. Amy O'GEARY
36 Director of Career Services ... Ms. Linda FLETCHER
06 Registrar ... Ms. Kathy KTUL
84 Dean Student Access/Support ... Ms. Kali BROWN

*Wake Technical Community College (E)

9101 Fayetteville Road, Raleigh NC 27603-5696
County: Wake — FICE Identification: 004844
Unit ID: 199856
Telephone: (919) 866-5000 — Carnegie Class: Assoc/HT-High Trad
FAX Number: (919) 779-3360 — Calendar System: Semester
URL: www.waketech.edu
Established: 1958 — Annual Undergrad Tuition & Fees (In-District): $2,432
Enrollment: 21,760 — Coed
Affiliation or Control: State/Local — IRS Status: 501(c)3
Highest Offering: Associate Degree
Accreditation: SC, ACFEI, ADNUR, DA, DH, EMT, MAC, MLTAD, NDT, RAD

02 President ... Dr. Scott RALLS
03 Executive Vice President ... Dr. Gayle GREENE
03 Executive Vice President ... Dr. Nicole REAVES
30 VP of Devel & Strategic Partnership ... Mr. Matthew B. SMITH
05 VP Curriculum Education Svcs ... Mrs. Sandra L. DIETRICH
103 VP Workforce Continuing Education ... Mr. Anthony CAISON
10 VP of Financial & Business Svcs ... Mrs. Marla L. TART
26 VP Communications/Public Relations ... Mrs. Laurie C. CLOWERS
15 VP Human Resources/College Safety ... Ms. Benita I. CLARK
84 VP Enrollment and Student Services ... Dr. Brian GANN
18 Vice Pres Facilities ... Mr. Jeffrey J. CARTER
13 VP Information Technology Svcs ... Dr. Ryan SCHWIEBERT
88 AVP Enrollment Services ... Mr. John W. SAPARILAS
35 AVP Student Services ... Mr. Kevin A. BROWN
88 AVP Military Veteran Spec Program ... Mrs. Scarlet EDWARDS
88 AVP CE Operations/CCO Assessment ... Mrs. Monica P. GEMPERLEIN
103 Provost Career Programs/CCO ... Mr. Walter MARTIN
76 Provost Health Sci Campus ... Dr. Angela BALLENTINE
04 Strategic Projects Coord/Exec Asst ... Mrs. Savannah VINCE
19 Chief of Police ... Mr. Michael A. PENRY
81 Dean Mathematics and Sciences ... Dr. John BAKKEN
14 Dean Information Technology ... Ms. Cindy LUTTRELL
76 Dean Health Sciences ... Ms. Angela WASHINGTON
88 Dean Student Life/Student Conduct ... Dr. Jonathan WIRT
88 Dean of Enrollment/Student Services ... Ms. Wendy COOK
75 Dean Occup Svcs/Chf Campus Ofcr ... Ms. Lonette MIMS
88 Dean of Professional Services ... Ms. Pamela LITTLE
124 Dean of Student Engagement & Impact ... Mr. Michael COLEMAN
08 Dean of Library Services ... Dr. Carenado DAVIS
07 Dean Admissions and Outreach ... Ms. Santrell CAISON
30 COO/Sr Dir Foundation Rels/Admin ... Mrs. Stephanie S. LAKE
25 Dean Sponsored Programs ... Mrs. Amy MACDONALD
06 Sr Dean Curriculum/Registrar ... Ms. Holly Elaine SWART
72 Dean Tech Training & Career Dev ... Mr. Jeffrey MERRITT
37 Dean Financial Aid/Veterans Affairs ... Mrs. Regina M. HUGGINS
88 Sr Dean Strat Innovations/Spec Proj ... Mrs. Karen B. PHINAZEE
88 Associate Dean Admissions ... Ms. Tina P. CARTER
27 Dir Communications Ops/Brand Mgmt ... Mrs. Francie W. SANDERSON
36 Dean Career & Employment Resources ... Mrs. Lynn E. KAVCSAK
121 Associate Dean of Academic Advising ... Mr. Davis SMITH
88 Dean Public Safety Education Campus ... Mr. Jeffrey B. ROBINSON
50 Dean Business & Public Svcs Tech ... Ms. Catherine LASSITER
75 Dean Applied Engr & Technologies ... Ms. Lora EDDINGTON
88 Dean Transportation ... Mr. David FAVRE
77 Dean/Provost Computer Technologies ... Dr. Keith BABUSZCZAK
88 Sr Dean Strategic Innovations ... Dr. Kai WANG

*Wayne Community College (F)

3000 Wayne Memorial Drive Box 8002,
Goldsboro NC 27533-8002
County: Wayne — FICE Identification: 002980
Unit ID: 199892
Telephone: (919) 735-5151 — Carnegie Class: Assoc/MT-VT-High Trad
FAX Number: (919) 739-7137 — Calendar System: Semester
URL: www.waynecc.edu
Established: 1957 — Annual Undergrad Tuition & Fees (In-District): $2,524
Enrollment: 2,701 — Coed
Affiliation or Control: State/Local — IRS Status: 501(c)3
Highest Offering: Associate Degree
Accreditation: SC, ADNUR, DA, DH, MAC, MLTAD, NAEYC, PNUR

02 President ... Dr. Patricia A. PFEIFFER
05 VP Academic/Student Services ... Dr. Brandon M. JENKINS
10 VP Finance/Chief Financial Officer ... Mrs. Joy KORNEGAY
11 VP of Operations ... Mr. Derek HUNTER
09 AVP Inst Effectiveness/Chf of Staff ... Mrs. Dorothy MOORE
32 AVP Academic and Student Services ... Ms. Joanna MORRISETTE
51 VP of Workforce/Continuing Educ ... Ms. Renita DAWSON
15 AVP Human Res/Safety/Compliance ... Mr. Charles GAYLOR, IV
72 Division Dean Applied Technologies ... Dr. Ernie WHITE
49 Division Dean Arts & Sciences ... Mrs. Laura BUDDIN
50 Div Dean Business & Computer Tech ... Dr. Tracy SCHMELTZER
76 Div Dean Allied Health/Public Svc ... Mrs. Janeil MARAK
88 Division Dean Public Safety ... Mrs. Angie BLIZZARD
08 Director Library Services ... Dr. Ruth Aletha ANDREW
12 Coordinator Seymour Johnson AFB ... Mrs. Dori FRASER
92 Honors Program Coordinator ... Mrs. Deniz TUCK
106 Distance Education Specialist ... Mr. Randall SHEARON
26 Director Office of Communications ... Mr. Ken JONES
13 Director Information Technology ... Mr. Matt BAUER
18 Facility Operations Superintendent ... Mr. Chris SCHOTT
19 Chief Campus Police & Security ... Chief Willie L. BRINSON
40 Manager Bookstore ... Ms. DiAnna BARBER
103 Ex Dir Wayne Bus/Indus Ctr & WORKS ... Mr. Craig FOUCHT
07 Director Admissions & Records ... Ms. Jennifer MAYO
37 Director Student Financial Aid ... Ms. Katrina LEE
78 Director College & Career Promise ... Mrs. Lorie WALLER
35 Student Activities Coordinator ... Ms. Paige HAM
96 Director of Purchasing ... Mr. Wade QUINN
102 Executive Director of Foundation ... Mrs. Adrienne NORTHINGTON
27 Public Information Officer ... Ms. Tara HUMPHRIES
16 Director Human Resources ... Ms. Melanie BELL
04 Senior Executive Asst to President ... Mrs. Amber TYLER
38 Director of Counseling ... Mrs. Melanie JENKINS
88 Director of Inventory Management ... Mr. Wade QUINN
124 Director College Transfer Advising ... Ms. Peyton OVERBEE
25 Chief Contract/Grants Administrator ... Mrs. Tiffany I. CREECH

*Western Piedmont Community College (G)

1001 Burkemont Avenue, Morganton NC 28655-4504
County: Burke — FICE Identification: 002982
Unit ID: 199908
Telephone: (828) 448-3500 — Carnegie Class: Assoc/MT-VT-High Non
FAX Number: (828) 438-6015 — Calendar System: Semester
URL: www.wpcc.edu
Established: 1964 — Annual Undergrad Tuition & Fees (In-State): $2,577
Enrollment: 1,792 — Coed
Affiliation or Control: State — IRS Status: 501(c)3
Highest Offering: Associate Degree
Accreditation: SC, ADNUR, DA, MAC, MLTAD

02 President ... Dr. Joel D. WELCH
05 VP Academic Affairs & Workforce Dev ... Ms. Cindy DAVIES
10 VP Admin Svcs/Chief Financial Ofcr ... Ms. Sandra K. HOILMAN
121 VP Stdnt Success/Support Svcs ... Ms. Susan A. BERLEY
32 Dean of Student Services ... Ms. Susan WILLIAMS
08 Library Director ... Ms. Nancy DANIEL
54 Dean Applied Technologies ... Mr. Michael DANIELS
49 Dean Arts & Sciences ... Ms. Ann Marie MCNEELY
06 Director Records & Registration ... Mr. Tou VANG
15 Director Human Resources ... Ms. Lisa H. SESSIONS
84 Director Enrollment Management ... Mrs. Jennifer PROPST
37 Director Student Financial Aid ... Ms. Dori BARRON
13 Director Management Info Systems ... Ms. Nancy E. NORRIS
96 Director of Purchasing ... Ms. Robin HALL
18 Director Facility Services ... Mr. Ronald GRAY
04 Exec Asst to President ... Ms. Stacey SHOLAR
19 Director Security/Safety ... Mr. Zebedee GRAHAM

*Wilkes Community College (H)

1328 S Collegiate Drive, Wilkesboro NC 28697-0120
County: Wilkes — FICE Identification: 002983
Unit ID: 199926
Telephone: (336) 838-6100 — Carnegie Class: Assoc/MT-VT-Mix Trad/Non
FAX Number: (336) 903-3219 — Calendar System: Semester
URL: www.wilkescc.edu
Established: 1965 — Annual Undergrad Tuition & Fees (In-State): $2,572
Enrollment: 2,435 — Coed

Affiliation or Control: State IRS Status: 501(c)3
Highest Offering: Associate Degree
Accreditation: SC, @CNEA, COARC, DA, MAC, RAD

02 President ... Dr. Jeff A. COX
05 VP of Instruction ... Dr. Yolanda WILSON
10 Senior VP of Administration ... Mr. D. Morgan FRANCIS, JR.
32 VP of Instr Support/Student Svcs ... Ms. Kim E. FAW
13 VP Information Technology/CIO ... Mr. Mike WINGLER
103 VP WDCE/Ashe Campus ... Mr. Christopher D. ROBINSON
12 Director Alleghany Center ... Ms. Wanda BECK
09 Inst Effectiveness Exec Director ... Ms. Nicole FOGLE
72 Dean Applied Career Technologies ... Mr. Ronald DOLLYHITE
50 Dean Business/Public Svc Tech Div ... Mrs. Kristen MACEMORE
76 Dean Health Sciences Division ... Ms. Tamara BECK
18 Exec Director/Facilities Services ... Mr. Morgan FRANCIS
111 VP Inst Advance/Exec Dir Found ... Ms. Allison PHILLIPS
15 Exec Director of Human Resources ... Ms. Sherry P. COX
06 Registrar ... Mr. Michael WARD
35 Dean of Student Services ... Mr. Scott JOHNSON
37 Director of Financial Aid ... Ms. Roberta HARLESS
38 Director Counseling & Career Svcs ... Dr. Lynda K. BLACK
36 Coord Occup/Business/Spec Careers ... Ms. Marina BRANNOCK
08 Director Learning Resources ... Ms. Christy EARP
38 Director SAGE ... Mr. Bruce HOLLAR
40 Bookstore Manager ... Ms. Kelly CHURCH
26 Public Info & Relations Officer ... Ms. Patty PARSONS
19 Chief of Police/Campus Police Dept ... Mr. Jamie MCGUIRE
04 Executive Asst to President ... Ms. Cynthia ALFORD
96 Purchasing Agent ... Ms. Amber BLACKBURN
07 Assoc Dean of Admissions ... Ms. Elisabeth BLEVINS

*Wilson Community College (A)

PO Box 4305, Wilson NC 27893-0305
County: Wilson FICE Identification: 004845
Unit ID: 199953
Telephone: (252) 291-1195 Carnegie Class: Assoc/MT-VT-High Non
FAX Number: (252) 243-7148 Calendar System: Semester
URL: www.wilsoncc.edu
Established: 1958 Annual Undergrad Tuition & Fees (In-State): $2,642
Enrollment: 1,862 Coed
Affiliation or Control: State IRS Status: 501(c)3
Highest Offering: Associate Degree
Accreditation: SC, SURGT

02 President ... Dr. Tim WRIGHT
05 Vice Pres for Academic Affairs ... Mr. Robert HOLSTEN
10 Vice Pres for Finance & Admin Svcs ... Ms. Jessica JONES
09 Director of Institutional Research ... Vacant
32 Vice Pres of Student Development ... Ms. Amy NOEL
76 Dean of Allied Health & Sciences ... Ms. Miranda YELVERTON
50 Dean of Business & Applied Tech ... Vacant
72 Dean of Industrial Technologies ... Mr. Travis FLEWELLING
15 Director of Human Resources ... Ms. Cindy ALLEN
08 Head Librarian ... Mr. Terrence MARTIN
21 Controller ... Ms. Deborah WHITE
06 Dir of Enrollment Svcs/Registrar ... Ms. Jennifer GONYEA
07 Dir of Admissions/Student Success ... Mr. Gregg MASSENBURG
18 Director of Facilities ... Mr. Ray OWENS
37 Dir of Financial Aid/Vet Affairs ... Ms. Lisa BAKER
111 Director Institutional Advancement ... Ms. Jessica GRIFFIN
13 Director of IT ... Ms. Susan WEEKLEY
96 Purchasing & Capital Projects Mgr ... Ms. Donna A. TURNER
40 Bookstore Manager ... Ms. Kaschia SPELLS
04 Exec Asst to the President ... Ms. Tracy LANE
106 Director of Inst Support Svcs ... Ms. Angela HERRING

North Carolina Wesleyan College (B)

3400 N Wesleyan Boulevard,
Rocky Mount NC 27804-8630
County: Nash FICE Identification: 002951
Unit ID: 199209
Telephone: (252) 985-5100 Carnegie Class: Bac-Diverse
FAX Number: (252) 985-5231 Calendar System: 4/1/4
URL: www.ncwc.edu
Established: 1956 Annual Undergrad Tuition & Fees: $32,750
Enrollment: 1,720 Coed
Affiliation or Control: United Methodist IRS Status: 501(c)3
Highest Offering: Master's
Accreditation: SC, AAQEP, EXSC, NURSE

01 President ... Dr. Evan DUFF
05 Interim Provost ... Dr. Molly WYATT
11 Vice President of Administration ... Ms. Suzanne BRACKETT
84 Vice President of Enrollment ... Mr. Michael DREW
32 Dean of Stdnts/Stdnt Affairs Admin ... Mr. Jason MODLIN
88 Dean of Accreditation ... Mr. Jarrod KELLY
06 Registrar ... Mrs. Candace CASHWELL
08 Director of Library ... Ms. Rachel MCWILLIAMS
26 Director Marketing Communications ... Ms. Crystal HILL
23 Director Health Services ... Ms. Jessica BRYS-WILSON
36 Associate Dean of Career Services ... Mrs. Jessie LANGLEY
19 Director of Campus Security ... Mr. J. W. SEARS
41 Director of Athletics ... Mr. Aaron DENTON
10 Controller ... Mr. Andrew VOTIPKA
37 Director of Financial Aid ... Ms. Leah HILL
15 Director of Human Resources ... Mr. Darrell S. WHITLEY
18 Director of Facilities ... Mr. David FRYAR
38 Director of Counseling Services ... Ms. Quenetta JOHNSON
40 Manager College Store ... Mr. Marcus RICH
20 Associate Academic Officer ... Dr. Molly WYATT

85 Director International Services ... Ms. Dawn TURNER
13 Chief Info Technology Officer (CIO) ... Mr. Gregory BOYKIN
39 Director of Residence Life ... Mr. Steve BURRELL
50 Chair Business ... Dr. Jackie LEWIS

Pfeiffer University (C)

48380 US Highway 52 N / PO Box 960,
Misenheimer NC 28109-0960
County: Stanly FICE Identification: 002955
Unit ID: 199306
Telephone: (704) 463-1360 Carnegie Class: Masters/M
FAX Number: (704) 463-1363 Calendar System: Semester
URL: www.pfeiffer.edu
Established: 1885 Annual Undergrad Tuition & Fees: $31,840
Enrollment: 1,185 Coed
Affiliation or Control: United Methodist IRS Status: 501(c)3
Highest Offering: Master's
Accreditation: SC, ACBSP, #ARCPA, CAEP, MUS, NURSE

01 President ... Dr. Scott W. BULLARD
04 Executive Assistant to President ... Ms. Teena P. MAULDIN
13 CIO ... Vacant
10 Vice President for Finance/CFO ... Mrs. Robin LESLIE
05 Provost/VP Academic Affairs ... Dr. Daniel MYNATT
32 VP Student Affairs/Dean of Students ... Mr. Ron LAFFITTE
84 VP for Enrollment ... Ms. Emily CARELLA
15 Director of Human Resources ... Ms. Ramanda MEDLIN
41 Director of Athletics ... Ms. Danielle LAFFERTY
06 Registrar ... Ms. Robin LISTERMAN
09 Exec Director IR/Plng & Research ... Mrs. Julia KENNEDY
26 Director of Inst Communications ... Mr. Casey HABICH
38 Director of Counseling ... Vacant
08 Director of the Library ... Ms. Lara LITTLE
37 Director of Financial Aid ... Ms. Amy BROWN
121 Dir of Academic Support Services ... Dr. Jim E. GULLEDGE
19 Dir of Campus Safety & Security ... Mr. Erik MCGINNIS
18 Director of Facilities ... Ms. Sharon K. BARD
42 University Chaplain ... Rev. Maegan HABICH
36 Director of Career Development ... Ms. Caroline SAWYER
39 Director of Residence Life ... Ms. Regina SIMMONS
58 Director of MCE Program ... Vacant
111 Exec Dir of Inst Advancement ... Ms. JoEllen NEWSOME
29 Director of Alumni Affairs ... Vacant
40 Bookstore Manager ... Ms. Dechelle ELLIS
104 Coord of Intl Studies/Study Abroad ... Ms. Rebecca HRACZO
50 Dean of the Undergraduate College ... Dr. Michael THOMPSON
53 Dean of the Graduate College ... Dr. Chris BOE

Queens University of Charlotte (D)

1900 Selwyn Avenue, Charlotte NC 28274-0001
County: Mecklenburg FICE Identification: 002957
Unit ID: 199412
Telephone: (704) 337-2200 Carnegie Class: Masters/L
FAX Number: (704) 337-2517 Calendar System: Semester
URL: www.queens.edu
Established: 1857 Annual Undergrad Tuition & Fees: $37,332
Enrollment: 2,338 Coed
Affiliation or Control: Presbyterian Church (U.S.A.) IRS Status: 501(c)3
Highest Offering: Master's
Accreditation: SC, CAEPN, CIDA, MUS, NURSE

01 President ... Dr. Daniel G. LUGO
05 VP Academic Affairs & Provost ... Dr. Sarah FATHERLY
30 VP Univ Advancement & Athletics ... Ms. Jennifer ERIKSEN
26 VP Stdnt Engagement/Dean of Stdnts . Ms. Maria FLORES-MILLS
10 CFO & VP for Administration ... Ms. Mary Alice BOYD
13 AVP/Chief Information Officer ... Mr. Brian BAUTE
49 Int Dean Col A & S/Cato School Educ ... Dr. Jeremiah WILLS
50 Dean of McColl School of Business ... Dr. Rick MATHIEU
60 Dean Knight School of Communication ... Vacant
76 Dean Blair College of Health ... Dr. Tama MORRIS
06 Registrar ... Ms. Linda FLEISCHMAN
15 Director of Human Resources ... Ms. Teri ORSINI, SPHR

Reformed Theological Seminary (E)

2101 Carmel Road, Charlotte NC 28226-6399
Telephone: (704) 366-5066 Identification: 666785
Accreditation: &SC, THEOL

† Regional accreditation is carried under the parent institution in Jackson, MS.

St. Andrews University (F)

1700 Dogwood Mile, Laurinburg NC 28352-5598
Telephone: (910) 277-5555 FICE Identification: 002967
Accreditation: &SC

† Regional accreditation is carried under the parent institution, Webber International University, Babson Park, FL.

Saint Augustine's University (G)

1315 Oakwood Avenue, Raleigh NC 27610-2298
County: Wake FICE Identification: 002968
Unit ID: 199582
Telephone: (919) 516-4000 Carnegie Class: Bac-Diverse
FAX Number: (919) 828-0817 Calendar System: Semester
URL: www.st-aug.edu
Established: 1867 Annual Undergrad Tuition & Fees: $16,884
Enrollment: 1,110 Coed
Affiliation or Control: Protestant Episcopal IRS Status: 501(c)3
Highest Offering: Baccalaureate
Accreditation: SC

01 President ... Dr. Christine MCPHAIL
111 VP Inst Advancement & External Affs ... Ms. Caroline CARTER
100 VP & Chief of Staff ... Mr. Bernardo I. DARGAN
05 Provost/VP Academic Affairs ... Dr. Josiah SAMPSON, III
10 SVP for Business & Administration ... Mr. Edward PATRICK
20 Vice Provost for Academic Services ... Dr. Orlando E. HANKINS
88 VP for Special Projects ... Mr. Eugene NICHOLSON
30 VP of Development ... Ms. Veronica CREECH
32 AVP Student Affairs ... Dr. Cindy LOVE
22 ADA Coordinator ... Ms. Tiffany TUMA
15 Director Human Resources ... Ms. Norma P. SMITH
35 Dean of Students ... Ms. Ann BROWN
42 Chaplain ... Rev. Hershey M. STEPHENS
13 Chief Information Officer ... Mr. Farooq AGHA
41 Interim Director Athletics ... Mr. David BOWSER
06 Registrar ... Ms. Martarash TORAIN
50 Dean Business/Mgmt & Technology ... Mr. Van SAPP
83 Dean Social and Behavioral Sciences ... Vacant
81 Dean Sciences/Math/Public Health ... Dr. Mark A. MELTON
79 Dean Humanities/Educ/Soc Sci ... Dr. Wanda B. CONEAL
97 Dean General College ... Dr. Kengie R. BASS
37 Director Financial Aid ... Ms. Sharon R. GRIFFIN
08 Director of Library Service ... Ms. Tiawanna S. NEVELS
19 Director of Public Safety ... Mr. Charles L. SIMPSON, JR.
18 Director Physical Plant ... Vacant
29 Director Alumni Affairs ... Ms. Sheryl H. XIMINES
39 Dir Student Life/Housing ... Mr. Jarron MORTIMER
90 Director Academic Computing ... Ms. Carlene J. MORGAN
07 Dean of Enroll Mgmt/Admissions ... Mr. Paul VANDERGRIFT
106 Director Online Education ... Vacant
25 Chief Contract/Grants Administrator ... Ms. Linda GUNN-JONES
26 Int Chief Marketing Officer ... Mr. Demarcus WILLIAMS

Salem College (H)

601 South Church Street, Winston-Salem NC 27101
County: Forsyth FICE Identification: 002960
Unit ID: 199607
Telephone: (336) 721-2600 Carnegie Class: Bac-A&S
FAX Number: (336) 917-5339 Calendar System: Semester
URL: www.salem.edu
Established: 1772 Annual Undergrad Tuition & Fees: $31,016
Enrollment: 636 Female
Affiliation or Control: Moravian Church IRS Status: 501(c)3
Highest Offering: Master's
Accreditation: SC, MUS

01 President ... Dr. Summer MCGEE
100 Chief of Staff ... Ms. Renee GARCIA-PRAJER
84 Vice President for Enrollment Mgmt ... Mr. James MCCOY
05 VP Acad/Stdnt Affs/Dean of Col ... Dr. Gary DAYNES
111 VP for Inst Advancement ... Ms. Kathryn M. BARNES
45 VP for Strategic Planning ... Ms. Katherine K. WATTS
10 VP Finance & Admin/CFO ... Mr. David BROWNING
32 Interim Dean of Students ... Ms. Victoria BURGOS
58 Dean of Graduate Studies ... Dr. Sheryl LONG
20 Dean of Undergraduate Studies ... Dr. Jenna SHEFFIELD
08 Director of Libraries ... Ms. Elizabeth NOVICKI
13 Chief Information Officer ... Mr. David HINSON
15 Director of Payroll & Benefits ... Ms. Debbie SULLIVAN
38 Director Counseling Services ... Ms. Robin CAMPBELL
21 Asst VP for Finance & Controller ... Mr. Scott MORIN
37 Asst VP Student Financial Aid ... Mr. Paul COSCIA
36 Exec Dir Career Innovation ... Ms. Collier LUMPKIN
41 Athletic Director ... Ms. Patricia HUGHES
19 Director Security/Safety ... Ms. Karen BOYD
15 Director of Human Resources ... Ms. Orielle HOPE
07 Dean of Admissions ... Dr. Glenn MCGEE
18 Executive Director of Operations ... Mr. Stephen PRAJER
06 Registrar ... Ms. Susan BRAWLEY
23 Health and Wellness Coordinator .. Ms. Jennifer PYRTLE-HORAN
28 VP for Equity Diversity Inclusion ... Dr. AJ MAZARIS

Shaw University (I)

118 East South Street, Raleigh NC 27601
County: Wake FICE Identification: 002962
Unit ID: 199643
Telephone: (919) 546-8300 Carnegie Class: Bac-Diverse
FAX Number: (919) 546-8301 Calendar System: Semester
URL: www.shawu.edu
Established: 1865 Annual Undergrad Tuition & Fees: $16,480
Enrollment: 1,283 Coed
Affiliation or Control: Baptist IRS Status: 501(c)3
Highest Offering: Master's
Accreditation: SC, CAEP, SW, THEOL

01 President ... Dr. Paulette DILLARD
05 VP for Academic Affairs ... Dr. Renata DUSENBURY
10 VP for Finance & Administration ... Mr. David BYRD
111 VP for Institutional Advancement ... Ms. Marilyn RICHARDS
32 VP for Student Affairs ... Dr. Ashton CLEVELAND
84 VP Enrollment Mgmt/Student Success ... Mr. Terrance DIXON
88 VP Real Estate/Strat Development ... Mr. Kevin SULLIVAN
15 Assoc VP Human Resources ... Mr. Richard BARNES
13 Chief Information Officer ... Mr. Joel FAISON
73 Dean Divinity School ... Dr. Gregory HOWARD
07 Director Admissions ... Mr. Joshua LOWE
06 Registrar ... Ms. Jody HAMILTON

51 Assoc Director Adult Degree Pgms .... Ms. Christal PINCHBACK
08 Director of Library Services ... Dr. Keyunda MILLER-MCCOLLUM
41 Director of Athletics .... Mr. George KNOX
39 Director Housing/Residence Life .... Dr. Vonda EASTERLING
38 Director Counseling Center .... Ms. Jerelene CARVER
88 Director Judicial Services .... Ms. Agnes BAXTER
36 Director of Experiential Learning .... Ms. Morgan RAY
50 Dean Business & Prof Studies .... Dr. Lynette WOOD
49 Dean Arts/Sciences & Humanities .... Dr. Valerie JOHNSON
121 Dean Academic Support .... Dr. Vanessa RAYNOR
35 Dean of Students .... Dr. Tobias MORGAN
53 Dept Head Education & Child Develop .... Dr. Lucy WILSON
81 Dept Head General/Interdisciplinary .... Mr. Jason MORGAN
76 Dept Head Health/Human/Life Science .... Dr. Kimberly RAIFORD
60 Dept Head Mass Comm & Digital Tech .... Mr. Titus BURRELL
83 Dept Head Social & Justice Studies .... Dr. MaNina MCNEILL
19 Chief Campus Police & Security .... Mr. Steven LESANE
26 Director Public Relations .... Vacant
30 Senior Director Development .... Ms. Melodie CARTER
105 Digital Media Manager .... Mr. Jamal FEATHERSTONE
25 Dir Sponsored Programs/Title III .... Ms. Tori WILLIS
124 Director Student Retention .... Ms. Jalesa SUTTON
29 Director Alumni Relations .... Vacant
92 Director Honors Program .... Dr. Paul-Arthur PIERRRE-LOUIS
37 Director Student Financial Aid .... Mr. Ibrahim BAH
106 Dir Digital Teaching & Learning .... Ms. Jillian JACKSON

Shepherds Theological Seminary (A)

6051 Tryon Road, Cary NC 27518-9316
County: Wake — FICE Identification: 041730
Unit ID: 461485
Telephone: (919) 573-5350 — Carnegie Class: Spec-4-yr-Faith
FAX Number: (919) 573-1438 — Calendar System: Semester
URL: www.shepherds.edu
Established: 2003 — Annual Graduate Tuition & Fees: N/A
Enrollment: 136 — Coed
Affiliation or Control: Non-denominational — IRS Status: 501(c)3
Highest Offering: Doctorate; No Undergraduates
Accreditation: THEOL

01 President .... Dr. Stephen DAVEY
05 Provost/Dean .... Dr. Tim M. SIGLER
20 Vice Pres Academic Affairs/CAO .... Mr. Thomas PITTMAN
10 Chief Financial Officer .... Mr. Ewart HODGINS
32 Dean of Students .... Dr. Peter GOEMAN
06 Registrar .... Mrs. Lucy BURGGRAFF
26 Director of Church Relations .... Dr. Les LOFQUIST
56 Director of The West Institute .... Dr. Clayton SCHULTZ
56 Director of Texas Teaching Site .... Dr. Thomas BABER
27 Director of Communications .... Mrs. Marilyn FITCH
108 Director of Assessment .... Mr. Edward GELB
111 Director of Advancement .... Mr. Brett INGALLS
56 Director of Shepherds Institute .... Mr. Jimmy CARTER
88 Director of Tampa Bay Teaching Site .... Mr. Anthony DEROSSE

Southeastern Baptist Theological Seminary (B)

120 S. Wingate St, Wake Forest NC 27588-1889
County: Wake — FICE Identification: 002963
Unit ID: 199759
Telephone: (919) 761-2100 — Carnegie Class: DU-Mod
FAX Number: N/A — Calendar System: Semester
URL: www.sebts.edu
Established: 1950 — Annual Undergrad Tuition & Fees: $9,562
Enrollment: 3,343 — Coed
Affiliation or Control: Southern Baptist — IRS Status: 501(c)3
Highest Offering: Doctorate
Accreditation: SC, THEOL

01 President .... Dr. Daniel L. AKIN
05 Provost/Dean of Faculty/CAO .... Dr. Keith WHITFIELD
03 Executive Vice President (COO) .... Mr. Ryan HUTCHINSON
20 VP Academic Administration .... Mr. Chris THOMPSON
111 Vice Pres Institutional Advancement .... Dr. Jonathan SIX
32 VP Student Services/Dean Students .... Dr. Mark LIEDERBACH
10 Chief Financial/Business Officer .... Mr. Chris HLAVACEK
18 Chief Facilities/Physical Plnt Ofcr .... Mr. Travis WILLIAMS
04 Administrative Asst to President .... Mrs. Kim HUMPHREY
06 Registrar .... Dr. Trevor KING
07 Director of Admissions .... Mr. Jonathan GOFORTH
29 Dir Financial/Alumni Development .... Mr. Drew DAVIS
37 Director of Financial Aid .... Dr. David PHILLIPS
08 Director Library Services .... Mr. Jason FOWLER
106 Dir Online Education .... Mr. Jerry LASSETTER
09 Institutional Researcher .... Mr. Will JOHNSTON
13 Director Information Technologies .... Mr. Wayne JENKS
15 Director Human Resources .... Mrs. Dawn SATTERWHITE
39 Director Student Housing .... Mr. Bradley BOAK
43 General Counsel .... Mr. George HARVEY
19 Director Security/Safety .... Dr. Michael S. LAWSON
30 Director of Development .... Mr. Drew DAVIS
108 Director Institutional Assessment .... Ms. Liani WILKINSON
26 Chief Public Relations Officer .... Ms. Rebecca PATE

Southeastern Free Will Baptist College (C)

532 Eagle Rock Rd, Box 1960, Wendell NC 27591
County: Wake — Identification: 667309
Telephone: (919) 365-7711 — Carnegie Class: Not Classified
FAX Number: (919) 365-4940 — Calendar System: Semester
URL: sfwbc.edu
Established: 1983 — Annual Undergrad Tuition & Fees: N/A
Enrollment: N/A — Coed
Affiliation or Control: Free Will Baptist — IRS Status: 501(c)3
Highest Offering: Baccalaureate
Accreditation: TRACS

01 President .... Rev. Nate ANGE
05 College Dean .... Dr. Russ MOOTS
30 Director of Development/Donor Rels .... Rev. Steve BERRY
32 Dean of Students .... Mr. Timothy GAYNOR
05 Academic Dean .... Mr. Marc HOLLOMAN
10 Business Manager .... Mr. Daniel OSBORNE
04 Admin Assistant to the President .... Mrs. Lynnette GAYNOR
08 Chief Library Officer .... Mrs. Catherine PENDLEY
37 Director Student Financial Aid .... Mr. Jeremy HOPKINS

Southern Evangelical Seminary (D)

15009 Lancaster Hwy, Charlotte NC 28277
County: Mecklenburg — FICE Identification: 036115
Telephone: (704) 847-5600 — Carnegie Class: Not Classified
FAX Number: (704) 845-1747 — Calendar System: Semester
URL: www.ses.edu
Established: 1992 — Annual Undergrad Tuition & Fees: N/A
Enrollment: N/A — Coed
Affiliation or Control: Independent Non-Profit — IRS Status: 501(c)3
Highest Offering: Doctorate
Accreditation: TRACS

01 President of the Seminary .... Dr. Phill GINN
05 Academic Dean .... Dr. J. Thomas BRIDGES
07 Dir Recruiting and Admissions .... Mr. Adam TUCKER
10 Chief Operating Officer/CFO .... Mr. Scott WOODS
32 Dean of Students .... Dr. Mel WINSTEAD
08 Dir Library Services .... Dr. Rob MAYER
06 Registrar .... Dr. Douglas E. POTTER
04 Executive Asst to President .... Mrs. Christina S. WOODSIDE
106 Dir Online Education/E-learning .... Mr. Alex JOSEPH
12 Director of Bible College .... Dr. Timothy BROWN

University of Mount Olive (E)

634 Henderson Street, Mount Olive NC 28365-1263
County: Wayne — FICE Identification: 002949
Unit ID: 199069
Telephone: (919) 658-2502 — Carnegie Class: Masters/S
FAX Number: (919) 658-7180 — Calendar System: Semester
URL: www.umo.edu
Established: 1951 — Annual Undergrad Tuition & Fees: $22,194
Enrollment: 2,536 — Coed
Affiliation or Control: Original Free Will Baptist Church — IRS Status: 501(c)3
Highest Offering: Master's
Accreditation: SC, ACBSP, NURSE

01 President .... Dr. H. Edward CROOM
03 Executive Vice President .... Dr. Carol G. CARRERE
05 Interim VP for Academic Affairs .... Dr. Kenneth D. HINES
10 Senior VP for Business & Finance .... Mr. Jeremy SHREVE
84 VP for Enrollment .... Mr. Tim WOODARD
32 Senior VP for Student Affairs .... Dr. Dan SULLIVAN
111 VP for Institutional Advancement .... Mr. Jason GIPE
20 Associate VP for Academic Admin .... Dr. David DOMMER
49 Dean School of Arts and Sciences .... Dr. Gerald SEATON
50 Dean Tillman School of Business .... Dr. Kathy BEST
88 Dean of Learning Commons .... Dr. Delight YOKLEY
123 AVP for Adult & Graduate Enrollment .... Dr. Lisa M. NUESELL
08 Director of Library Services .... Ms. Pamela R. WOOD
09 Director Inst Research & Planning .... Dr. Juliane SANTIAGO
06 Registrar .... Ms. Vicky WARRICK
35 Director of Campus Life .... Ms. Nicole L. GARRETT
36 Director of Career Center .... Ms. Laurica YANCEY
26 Director of Public Relations .... Ms. Rhonda E. JESSUP
102 Dir Foundation & Sponsored Programs ... Mr. Dustin BANNISTER
37 Director of Financial Aid .... Mr. Brian BLACKBURN
15 Director of Human Resources .... Ms. Cordelia A. WILCOX
18 Director Building & Grounds .... Mr. Jeff D. BROGDEN
13 Director Technology Services .... Mr. Kenneth M. DAVIS, JR.
14 Director Technology Support .... Mr. Robert R. PRUETT
41 VP for Athletics .... Mr. Jeffrey M. EISEN

*University of North Carolina General Administration (F)

Box 2688, 910 Raleigh Road, Chapel Hill NC 27515-2688
County: Orange — FICE Identification: 002971
Unit ID: 199175
Telephone: (919) 962-1000 — Carnegie Class: N/A
FAX Number: (919) 962-2751
URL: www.northcarolina.edu

01 President .... Mr. Peter HANS
05 Sr Vice Pres Academic Affairs/CAO ...... Dr. Kimberly VAN NOORT
10 SVP Finance/CFO .... Ms. Jennifer HAYGOOD
100 Chief of Staff .... Ms. Norma HOUSTON
11 Chief Operating Officer .... Mr. Jonathan PRUITT
20 VP Academic Affairs .... Mr. David J. ENGLISH
13 VP for Information Tech & CIO .... Mr. Keith E. WERNER
32 VP Student Affairs .... Ms. Bethany MEIGHEN
111 Vice Pres for Advancement .... Mr. Timothy A. MINOR
14 Assoc Vice Pres Data & Analytics .... Ms. Diane E. MARIAN
43 SVP Legal Affs & General Counsel .... Mr. Andrew TRIPP
101 Asst VP/Sec of the University .... Ms. Meredith STEADMAN
86 Vice Pres Federal Relations .... Ms. Elizabeth MORRA
26 Vice President for Communications .... Ms. Jane STANCILL
15 SVP for Human Resources/CHRO .... Mr. Matthew BRODY
86 SVP for Govt/External Affairs .... Mr. Bart GOODSON

*Appalachian State University (G)

287 Rivers Street, Boone NC 28608-0001
County: Watauga — FICE Identification: 002906
Unit ID: 197869
Telephone: (828) 262-2000 — Carnegie Class: Masters/L
FAX Number: (828) 262-2347 — Calendar System: Semester
URL: www.appstate.edu
Established: 1899 — Annual Undergrad Tuition & Fees (In-State): $7,410
Enrollment: 20,023 — Coed
Affiliation or Control: State — IRS Status: 501(c)3
Highest Offering: Doctorate
Accreditation: SC, ART, CAATE, CACREP, CAEP, CAPRT, CIDA, DANCE, DIETD, DIETI, IPSY, MFCD, MUS, NURSE, PH, SP, SPAA, SW, THEA

02 Chancellor .... Dr. Sheri EVERTS
100 Chief of Staff/Vice Chancellor .... Mr. Hank T. FOREMAN
05 Provost/Exec Vice Chancellor .... Dr. Heather NORRIS
10 Vice Chanc Business Affairs .... Mr. Paul D. FORTE
32 Vice Chanc Student Development .... Mr. J.J BROWN
111 Vice Chanc Univ Advancement .... Ms. Jane BARGHOTHI
20 Vice Provost for Undergrad Educ .... Dr. Mark GINN
46 Interim Vice Provost for Research .... Dr. Ece KARATAN
26 Assc VC Advance/Chief Comm Ofcr .... Mrs. Megan HAYES
84 Assoc VC for Enrollment Management .... Ms. Cindy BARR
29 Exec Director of Alumni Affairs .... Mrs. Stephanie L. BILLINGS
43 General Counsel .... Mr. Paul MEGGETT
13 Interim Chief Information Officer .... Mr. Tom VAN GILDER
06 University Registrar .... Ms. Debbie RACE
38 Dir Counseling/Psychological Svcs .... Dr. Christopher J. HOGAN
37 Director of Financial Aid .... Mr. Wesley ARMSTRONG
15 Director of Human Resources .... Mr. Mark BACHMEIER
09 Exec Dir Inst Research/Planning .... Mrs. Heather H. LANGDON
51 Exec Director of Distance Education .... Dr. Terry RAWLS
41 Director of Athletics .... Mr. Douglas P. GILLIN
49 Dean for College of Arts & Sciences .... Dr. Neva J. SPECHT
50 Acting Dean for College of Business .... Dr. Sandra VANNOY
53 Dean for College of Education .... Dr. Melba C. SPOONER
57 Dean for College Fine/Applied Arts .... Dr. Janice POPE
64 Dean for the School of Music .... Dr. James DOUTHIT
58 Dean of Graduate School .... Dr. Michael MCKENZIE
08 Interim Dean of Libraries .... Mr. Paul ORKISZEWSKI
18 Dir of the Physical Plant .... Mr. Jeff PIERCE
114 Budget Director .... Mr. John E. ADAMS
96 Director of Materials Management .... Mr. John WALL
28 Dir Multicultural Student Devel .... Vacant

*East Carolina University (H)

1000 East Fifth Street, Greenville NC 27858-4353
County: Pitt — FICE Identification: 002923
Unit ID: 198464
Telephone: (252) 328-6212 — Carnegie Class: DU-Higher
FAX Number: (252) 328-4155 — Calendar System: Semester
URL: www.ecu.edu
Established: 1907 — Annual Undergrad Tuition & Fees (In-State): $7,239
Enrollment: 28,798 — Coed
Affiliation or Control: State — IRS Status: 501(c)3
Highest Offering: Doctorate
Accreditation: SC, AAFCS, ANEST, ARCPA, ART, AUD, CAATE, CACREP, CAEPN, CAHIIM, CAMPEP, CAPRT, CARTE, CEA, CIDA, CLPSY, CONST, DENT, DIETD, DIETI, LIB, MED, MFCD, MIDWF, MLS, MUS, NAIT, NURSE, OT, PH, PLNG, PTA, SCPSY, SP, SPAA, SW, THEA

02 Chancellor .... Dr. Philip ROGERS
100 Chief of Staff .... Dr. Chris LOCKLEAR
05 Provost & Sr VC Academic Affairs .... Dr. Robin N. COGER
32 Vice Chancellor for Student Affairs .... Dr. Virginia HARDY
10 VC Administration & Finance .... Ms. Stephanie COLEMAN
111 Vice Chanc Univ Advancement .... Mr. Christopher DYBA
46 Acting Chief Research/Engagement .... Dr. Sharon PAYNTER
39 Assoc VC Campus Living/Dining .... Mr. Peter C. GROENENDYK
35 Assoc Vice Chanc & Dean of Stdnts .... Dr. Lynn M. ROEDER
22 Assoc Provost Equity/Diversity .... Dr. Lakesha ALSTON FORBES
43 Vice Chancellor for Legal Affairs .... Mr. Paul ZIGAS
09 Associate Provost IPAR .... Dr. Ying ZHOU
41 Athletic Director .... Mr. Jon GILBERT
13 CIO & Assoc Vice Chanc ITCS .... Mr. Zach LOCH
15 Assoc VC Human Resources .... Ms. Kitty WETHERINGTON
18 Assoc VC for Campus Opers .... Mr. William BAGNELL
88 Assoc VC Environ Health & Safety .... Mr. Bill KOCH
88 Assistant VC of Global Affairs .... Dr. Jon REZEK
45 Dir of Institutional Plng & Accred .... Dr. Cynthia BELLACERO
88 Dir of Campus Rec & Wellness .... Mr. William EHLING
26 Exec Dir Comm/Public Affs/Mktg .... Ms. Jeannine HUTSON
07 Assistant VC/Director of Admissions .... Ms. Stephanie WHALEY
06 Registrar .... Ms. Angela R. ANDERSON
08 Director JY Joyner Library .... Ms. Jan LEWIS
88 Dir Health Sciences Library .... Ms. Beth KETTERMAN
101 Asst Secretary to Board of Trustees .... Ms. Megan AYERS
37 Director of Financial Aid .... Ms. Julie POORMAN
19 Chief of Police .... Mr. Jon R. BARNWELL
51 Int Exec Dir Acad Out/Cont/Dist Ed .... Ms. Jennifer M. BAYSDEN
27 Director of Marketing Strategy .... Mr. Clint BAILEY
27 Project Manager Vendor Relations .... Mr. Jimmy ROSTAR
96 Director of Purchasing/Real Estate .... Mr. Kevin CARRAWAY

36 Director Career Services ... Mr. Tom HALASZ
116 Chief Audit Officer ... Mr. Wayne B. POOLE
21 AVC for Financial Services ... Mr. Vincent FALVO
49 Dean College of Arts & Sciences ... Dr. Allison DANELL
76 Dean College of Allied Health ... Dr. Robert ORLIKOFF
68 Int Dean Col Health/Human Perform ... Dr. Stacey ALTMAN
63 Dean BSOM ... Dr. Michael WALDRUM
66 Dean College of Nursing ... Dr. Bimbola F. AKINTADE
50 Int Dean College of Business ... Dr. Michael HARRIS
57 Dean Col Fine Arts/Comm ... Dr. Linda KEAN
53 Int Dean College of Education ... Dr. Art ROUSE
72 Dean Col of Engineering and Tech ... Dr. Harry PLOEHN
58 Int Dean Graduate School ... Dr. Kathleen COX
92 Int Dean Honors College ... Dr. Todd FRALEY
63 Executive Dean BSOM ... Dr. Jason HIGGINSON
52 Dean School of Dental Medicine ... Dr. Gregory CHADWICK
88 Dean Integrated Coastal Programs ... Dr. Reide CORBETT
04 Assistant to Chancellor ... Ms. Christy DANIELS
25 Dir of Grants and Contracts ... Ms. Julie COLE
86 Director of Strategic Initiatives ... Ms. Karson NELSON
102 President/CEO ECU Foundation ... Mr. Chris DYBA
54 Chairperson Engineering ... Dr. Barbara MULLER-BORER
108 Director Institutional Assessment ... Dr. Kristen DREYFUS
122 Coord Fraternity/Sorority Life ... Mr. Christopher COOPER

*Elizabeth City State University (A)

1704 Weeksville Road, Elizabeth City NC 27909-7806
County: Pasquotank FICE Identification: 002926
Unit ID: 198507
Telephone: (252) 335-3400 Carnegie Class: Bac-Diverse
FAX Number: (252) 335-3731 Calendar System: Semester
URL: www.ecsu.edu
Established: 1891 Annual Undergrad Tuition & Fees (In-State): $3,260
Enrollment: 2,002 Coed
Affiliation or Control: State IRS Status: 501(c)3
Highest Offering: Master's
Accreditation: SC, AAB, CAEP, MUS, SW

02 Chancellor ... Dr. Karrie G. DIXON
05 Provost/VC Acad Affairs ... Dr. Farrah J. WARD
03 Vice Chanc/Chief of Staff ... Dr. Derrick L. WILKINS
11 VC for Operations/General Counsel ... Mr. Alyn GOODSON
10 VC for Business & Finance/CFO ... Ms. Lisa R. MCCLINTON
32 Vice Chancellor for Student Affairs ... Mr. Gary L. BROWN
111 VC for University Advancement ... Ms. Anita B. WALTON
116 Director of Internal Audit ... Ms. Sharnita I. WILSON-PARKER
86 Special Asst Government Relations ... Mr. Carson D. RICH
100 Deputy Chief of Staff ... Ms. Gwendolyn SANDERS
04 Executive Asst to Chancellor ... Ms. Sandra F. POWERS
13 Int Chief Information Officer ... Mr. Eric ZARGHAMI
41 Athletic Director ... Mr. James DUBOSE, JR.
15 Chief Human Resources Officer ... Ms. Shamica LANE
26 Int Assoc VP Strat Communications ... Ms. Ayana HERNANDEZ
20 Interim Assoc VC Academic Affairs ... Dr. Gloria E. PAYNE
20 Interim Assoc VC Academic Affairs ... Dr. Melinda R. ANDERSON
06 Assoc VC Academic Affairs/Registrar ... Dr. Althea A. RIDDICK
21 Controller ... Ms. Gina R. KNIGHT
96 Director of Business Services ... Vacant
114 Director of Budget ... Mr. Robert J. THIBEAULT
109 Director of Auxiliary Services ... Ms. Sherron D. WHITE
113 Accountant/Bursar ... Ms. Thelma R. WILLIAMS
14 Deputy Chief Information Officer ... Mr. Eric V. ZARGHAMI
90 IT Client Services Manager ... Vacant
91 IT Systems Administrator ... Ms. Angela W. BAILEY
09 Dir Institutional Effectiveness ... Dr. Fred M. OKANDA
35 Assoc Vice Chanc Student Affairs ... Mr. Kevin J. WADE
08 Director of Library Services ... Dr. Juanita M. SPENCE
121 Exec Dir Student Success/Retention ... Vacant
07 Interim Director of Admissions ... Mr. Darius D. EURE
38 Director Counseling Center ... Ms. Jody GRANDY
36 Interim Director of Career Services ... Ms. Yolanda S. CARCANA
37 Director Student Financial Aid ... Mr. Jeremi WATKINS
102 Dir Foundation and Corp Relations ... Vacant
29 Dir Alumni Relations and Engagement ... Mr. Enoch D. BOND
112 Major and Planned Gifts Officer ... Ms. Teresa C. LASSITER
18 Interim Dir of Facilities/Planning ... Mr. Harley G. GRIMES
26 Director of Marketing ... Ms. Rhonda HAYES
87 Director of Summer School ... Dr. Chyna N. CRAWFORD
104 Director of International Programs ... Dr. Andre P. STEVENSON
58 Director of Graduate Education ... Dr. Timothy A. GOODALE
106 Dir Distance/Continuing Educ ... Dr. Kimberley N. STEVENSON
19 Director of Public Safety ... Mr. John MANLEY
39 Director Housing/Resident Life ... Ms. Sabrina R. WILLIAMS
88 Chair of University Studies ... Dr. Tarsha M. ROGERS
23 Director of Student Health Services ... Ms. Gloria M. BROWN
25 Director of Sponsored Programs ... Ms. AnneMarie DELGADO

*Fayetteville State University (B)

1200 Murchison Road, Fayetteville NC 28301-4298
County: Cumberland FICE Identification: 002928
Unit ID: 198543
Telephone: (910) 672-1111 Carnegie Class: Masters/M
FAX Number: (910) 672-1769 Calendar System: Semester
URL: https://www.uncfsu.edu/
Established: 1867 Annual Undergrad Tuition & Fees (In-State): $5,309
Enrollment: 6,726 Coed
Affiliation or Control: State IRS Status: 501(c)3
Highest Offering: Doctorate
Accreditation: SC, ART, CAEPN, FEPAC, MUS, NAEYC, NURSE, SW

02 Chancellor ... Mr. Darrell T. ALLISON
100 Chief of Staff ... Ms. Samantha HOLMES
05 Provost/Vice Chanc Academic Affs ... Dr. Monica TERRELL LEACH
10 Int Vice Chanc Business/Finance ... Mr. Greg LOVINS
32 Vice Chancellor Student Affairs ... Dr. Juanette COUNCIL
111 Interim Vice Chancellor Advancement ... Mr. Chris DAVIS
13 Vice Chanc Info Technology/CIO ... Dr. Hector MOLINA
18 Assoc Vice Chanc Facilities Mgmt ... Mr. Jon PARSONS
15 Assoc Vice Chanc Human Resources ... Mr. Carl DEAN
20 Interim AVC Academic Affairs ... Dr. Samuel ADU-MIREKU
45 Assoc VC Pgms/Plng/Assessment ... Vacant
92 Acting Program Director Honors ... Dr. Erin WHITE
06 Registrar ... Ms. Sarah BAKER
26 AVC Communications/Public Relations ... Mr. Jeff WOMBLE
08 Director of Library Services ... Vacant
07 Exec Director of Admissions ... Vacant
39 Director of Residence Life ... Ms. Adrina RUSSELL
37 Exec Director Student Financial Aid ... Mrs. Kamesia HOUSE
43 General Counsel ... Mrs. Wanda LESSANE JENKINS
41 Athletic Director ... Mr. Anthony T. BENNETT
96 Purchasing Manager ... Ms. Victoria MCALLISTER
28 Director of Diversity ... Vacant
89 Asst Dean University College ... Ms. Mary HOGAN
66 Associate Dean Nursing ... Dr. Afua ARHIN
50 Dean School Business/Economics ... Dr. Ulysses TAYLOR
53 Interim Dean School of Education ... Dr. Chandrika JOHNSON
79 Int Dean Col Humanities/Social Sci ... Dr. Sharon WILLIAMS
04 Executive Asst to Chancellor ... Ms. Treva BENTLEY
86 VC External Affairs/Military Rels ... Mr. Wesley FOUNTAIN
25 Chief Contracts/Grants Admin ... Ms. Chrystal COOPER-JOHNSON
84 AVC Enrollment Management ... Vacant
29 Director of Alumni Affairs ... Vacant

*North Carolina Agricultural and Technical State University (C)

1601 East Market Street, Greensboro NC 27411-0001
County: Guilford FICE Identification: 002905
Unit ID: 199102
Telephone: (336) 334-7500 Carnegie Class: DU-Higher
FAX Number: (336) 334-7136 Calendar System: Semester
URL: www.ncat.edu
Established: 1891 Annual Undergrad Tuition & Fees (In-State): $6,657
Enrollment: 12,753 Coed
Affiliation or Control: State IRS Status: 501(c)3
Highest Offering: Doctorate
Accreditation: SC, AAFCS, CACREP, CAEPN, CONST, JOUR, LC, LSAR, MUS, NAIT, NUR, SW, THEA

02 Chancellor ... Dr. Harold L. MARTIN, SR.
05 Provost/Exec VC Academic Affairs ... Dr. Tonya SMITH-JACKSON
10 VC Business & Finance ... Mr. Robert POMPEY
100 Chief of Staff ... Ms. Erin HART
46 VC Research ... Mr. Eric MUTH
32 VC Student Affairs ... Dr. Melody C. PIERCE
15 Chief HR Officer ... Dr. Veronica SILLS
13 VC ITS & CIO ... Mr. Tom JACKSON
43 General Counsel ... Ms. Melissa HOLLOWAY
111 VC University Advancement ... Mr. Kenneth E. SIGMON, JR.
20 AVP Academic Budget/Operations ... Vacant
26 AVC University Relations ... Mr. Todd H. SIMMONS
114 AVC for Budget & Planning ... Mrs. Chartarra JOYNER
58 VP Grad Research/Dean Grad College ... Dr. Clay GLOSTER
45 VP Strategic Planning & Inst Effect ... Vacant
18 AVC for Bus/Finance/Facilities ... Mr. Andrew M. PERKINS, JR.
19 AVC Police/Public Safety ... Mr. Jermaine CHERRY
08 Dean Library Services ... Ms. Vicki COLEMAN
47 Dean Agriculture/Environmental Sci ... Dr. Mohamed AHMEDNA
49 Dean Arts/Human/Soc Sciences ... Dr. Frances WARD-JOHNSON
53 Dean College of Education ... Dr. Paula PRICE
54 Interim Dean College of Engineering ... Dr. Stephanie LUSTER-TEASLEY
66 Dean College Health & Hum Sci ... Dr. Elimelda ONGERI
50 Int Dean College of Business/Econ ... Dr. Lisa OWENS-JACKSON
72 Dean College Science and Technology ... Dr. Abdellah AHMIDOUCH
54 Dean Joint Sch Nanosci/Nanoeng ... Dr. Sherine O. OBARE
06 Int VProv Stdnt Success/Registrar ... Ms. Regina DAVIS
84 Int AVP for Enrollment Management ... Dr. Dawn NAIL
37 Director Financial Aid ... Mr. Travis RICHARD
36 Exec Director Career Services ... Ms. Cynthia DOWNING
29 AVC for Alumni Relations ... Ms. Teresa DAVIS
85 Dir International Student Affairs ... Ms. Loreatha D. GRAVES
88 Dir Multicultural Student Center ... Mr. Gerald SPATES
41 Director of Athletics ... Mr. Earl M. HILTON, III
39 Exec Dir Housing/Residence Life ... Mr. John LOWNEY
23 Dir Student Health Services ... Dr. David H. WAGNER
38 Director of Counseling Service ... Dr. Vivian D. BARNETTE
25 Director of Contracts/Grants ... Ms. Natalie TEAGLE
92 Director of Honors Program ... Dr. Margaret KANIPES
96 Director of Procurement Services ... Ms. Martinique WILLIAMS
27 Director of Media Relations ... Vacant
40 Bookstore Manager ... Ms. Michaele WIGGINS
106 Dir of ITS/Distance Education ... Dr. Tracie O. LEWIS
108 Int Dir of Assessment ... Ms. Thelma WOODARD
22 Director Affirmative Action/EEO ... Ms. Linda MANGUM
112 AVC for Major Gifts/Annual Giving ... Vacant
86 Director External Affairs ... Mr. Oliver THOMAS
07 Director of Admissions ... Ms. Jameia TENNIE
101 Secretary to the Board ... Ms. Shannon BENNETT

*North Carolina Central University (D)

1801 Fayetteville Street, Durham NC 27707-3129
County: Durham FICE Identification: 002950
Unit ID: 199157
Telephone: (919) 530-6100 Carnegie Class: Masters/L
FAX Number: (919) 530-5014 Calendar System: Semester
URL: www.nccu.edu
Established: 1910 Annual Undergrad Tuition & Fees (In-State): $6,629
Enrollment: 8,078 Coed
Affiliation or Control: State IRS Status: 501(c)3
Highest Offering: Doctorate
Accreditation: SC, ACPHA, CACREP, CAEPN, CAPRT, DIET, DIETD, DIETI, LAW, LIB, MUS, NUR, SP, SPAA, SW, THEA

02 Chancellor ... Dr. Johnson O. AKINLEYE
05 Provost & VCAA ... Dr. David H. JACKSON, JR.
100 Chief of Staff ... Dr. Catherine EDMONDS
43 General Counsel ... Mrs. Fenita T. MORRIS-SHEPARD
10 VC Admin & Finance ... Ms. Akua J. JOHNSON MATHERSON
32 VC for Student Affairs ... Dr. Angela COLEMAN
111 Vice Chanc Inst Advancement ... Dr. Gia SOUBLET
20 Assoc Provost for Academic Programs ... Dr. Michelle L. MAYO
11 Assoc VC Administration/Finance ... Mr. Antonio MCDANIEL
15 Chief Human Resources Officer ... Mr. Michael E. HILL
85 AVC Innovative/Engaged/Global Educ ... Vacant
45 Assoc VC Strategic Planning ... Mr. Johnnie SOUTHERLAND
35 Assistant VC of Student Affairs ... Mr. William CLEMM, II
13 Chief Information Officer ... Mrs. Leah KRAUS
07 Director Undergraduate Admissions ... Mr. Michael A. BAILEY
30 Director of External Affairs ... Dr. Michael PAGE
06 Registrar ... Dr. Jerome GOODWIN
91 Interim Student Systems Manager ... Mr. Damond L. NOLLAN
29 Director of Alumni Relations ... Mrs. LaMisa M. FOXX
26 Assoc VC for Public Relations ... Vacant
37 Director of Financial Aid ... Ms. Sharon J. OLIVER
08 Director Library Services ... Dr. Theodosia T. SHIELDS
19 Chief of University Police ... Mr. Damon WILLIAMS
121 Exec Dir Student Academic Success ... Vacant
88 Director Art Museum ... Ms. Brenda FAISON
39 Director Residential Life ... Mr. Jeremi CHEEKS
41 Director Athletics ... Dr. Louis PERKINS
111 Assoc VC Inst Advancement ... Ms. Susan HESTER
96 Director of Purchasing ... Mr. James TANZOSCH
92 Director of Honors Program ... Dr. Karen K. JACKSON
38 Director of Counseling Center ... Ms. Charnequa KENNEDY
22 Director of EEO & Employee Relation ... Ms. Delores R. HARRIS
84 Assoc VC Enrollment Management ... Dr. Damon R. WADE
109 Dir Auxiliaries/Business Services ... Mr. Derrick N. MAGEE
40 Manager Bookstore ... Ms. Jacqueline MCDOWELL
58 Dean Sch Grad Stds/Asc VC Grad Rsch ... Dr. Jaleh REZAIE
61 Dean of the Law School ... Ms. Browne C. LEWIS
62 Dean School of Library/Info Science ... Dr. Jon P. GANT
50 Dean School of Business ... Dr. Anthony C. NELSON
97 Dean of University College ... Dr. William R. MOULTRIE
49 Dean College of Arts and Sciences ... Dr. Carlton E. WILSON
83 Dean College Behavioral/Social Sci ... Dr. La Verne M. REID
53 Dean School of Education ... Dr. Audrey W. BEARD
04 Executive Asst to Chancellor ... Ms. Deborah MCQUEEN
102 Executive Director NCCU Foundation ... Mr. Ernest JENKINS
104 Asst Director International Affairs ... Dr. Olivia JONES
105 Director Web Services ... Mr. Damond NOLLAN
106 Director Division Extended Studies ... Mrs. Kimberly C. PHIFER-MCGHEE
108 Director of Surveys & Evaluations ... Ms. Tia M. DOXEY
25 Director Contracts/Grants Admin ... Vacant
36 Director Career Services ... Mr. Charles JENNINGS
44 Director Annual Giving ... Ms. Asma MAHMOOD

*North Carolina State University (E)

20 Watauga Club Drive, Raleigh NC 27695
County: Wake FICE Identification: 002972
Unit ID: 199193
Telephone: (919) 515-2191 Carnegie Class: DU-Highest
FAX Number: (919) 515-7740 Calendar System: Semester
URL: www.ncsu.edu
Established: 1887 Annual Undergrad Tuition & Fees (In-State): $9,101
Enrollment: 36,042 Coed
Affiliation or Control: State IRS Status: 501(c)3
Highest Offering: Doctorate
Accreditation: SC, ART, CACREP, CAEP, CAPRT, IPSY, LSAR, SCPSY, SPAA, SW, VET

02 Chancellor ... Dr. William Randy WOODSON
05 Provost/Exec Vice Chancellor ... Dr. Warwick A. ARDEN
43 Vice Chanc & General Counsel ... Ms. Allison NEWHART
10 Vice Chanc Finance & Admin ... Mr. Charles MAIMONE
46 Vice Chanc Research & Innovation ... Dr. Mladen VOUK
32 Vice Chanc/Dn Div Acad & Stdnt Affs ... Dr. Doneka SCOTT
111 Vice Chanc Univ Advancement ... Mr. Brian C. SISCHO
13 Vice Chanc Information Technology ... Dr. Marc I. HOIT
86 VC Ext Affs/Partnerships/Econ Dev ... Mr. Kevin D. HOWELL
100 Chief of Staff/Sec of University ... Ms. Paula GENTIUS
106 Sr Vice Prov Acad Outreach/Entrepre ... Vacant
08 Vice Provost/Director of Libraries ... Mr. Greg RASCHKE
22 VP Inst Equity & Diversity ... Ms. Sheri SCHWAB
18 Assoc Vice Chanc Facilities ... Mr. Doug MORTON
39 Assoc Vice Chanc Housing and Living ... Dr. Barry OLSON
26 Assoc Vice Chanc Univ Communication ... Mr. Brad BOHLANDER
29 Assoc Vice Chanc Alumni Relations ... Mr. Benny SUGGS
15 Assoc Vice Chanc Human Resources ... Mr. Tim J. DANIELSON
19 Chief of Police ... Mr. Dan HOUSE
09 Sr Vice Prov Inst Rsrch & Planning ... Ms. Mary K. LELIK
07 AVP & Director Admissions ... Mr. Jon WESTOVER
06 Sr Vice Provost for EMAS ... Dr. Don HUNT
25 Director of Contracts & Grants ... Mr. Justo TORRES
37 Director of Financial Aid ... Ms. Krista RINGLER

38 Director of Counseling Center ... Dr. Monica OSBURN
41 Director of Athletics ... Mr. Boo CORRIGAN
21 Assoc Vice Chancellor & Treasurer ... Ms. Mary T. PELOQUIN-DODD
96 Dir Procurement & Business Svcs ... Mrs. Sharon LOOSMAN
79 Dean Col of Humanities & Social Sci ... Dr. Deanna P. DANNELS
48 Dean College of Design ... Dr. Mark HOVERSTEN
54 Dean College of Engineering ... Dr. Louis A. MARTIN-VEGA
47 Interim Dean CALS ... Dr. John M. DOLE
65 Dean College of Natural Resources ... Dr. Myron FLOYD
53 Dean College of Education ... Dr. Paola SZTAJN
50 Dean Poole College of Management ... Dr. Frank BUCKLESS
81 Dean College of Sciences ... Dr. Chris MCGAHAN
88 Dean Wilson College of Textiles ... Dr. David HINKS
74 Dean College of Vet Medicine ... Dr. Kate MEURS
58 Dean The Graduate School ... Dr. Peter J. HARRIES

*University of North Carolina at Asheville (A)

1 University Heights, Asheville NC 28804-8503

County: Buncombe | FICE Identification: 002907 | Unit ID: 199111
Telephone: (828) 251-6500 | Carnegie Class: Bac-A&S
FAX Number: (828) 251-6495 | Calendar System: Semester
URL: www.unca.edu
Established: 1927 | Annual Undergrad Tuition & Fees (In-State): $7,244
Enrollment: 3,363 | Coed
Affiliation or Control: State | IRS Status: 501(c)3
Highest Offering: Master's
Accreditation: SC, CAEP

02 Chancellor ... Dr. Nancy J. CABLE
100 Interim Chief of Staff ... Mr. Brian HART
05 Provost/VC Academic Affairs ... Dr. Kai CAMPBELL
10 Vice Chancellor Admin & Finance ... Mr. John PIERCE
111 Vice Chancellor Advancement ... Mr. Kirk I. SWENSON
32 Vice Chanc for Student Affairs ... Dr. Meghan HARTE WEYANT
15 Interim Director of Human Resources ... Ms. Christy WILLIAMS
41 Director of Athletics ... Ms. Janet R. CONE
09 Dir IR/Effectiveness/Planning ... Mr. Deaver TRAYWICK
81 Dean Natural Science ... Dr. Herman HOLT
79 Dean Humanities ... Dr. Tracey RIZZO
83 Dean Social Science ... Dr. Agya BOAKYE-BOATEN
08 University Librarian ... Ms. Brandy BOURNE
13 Chief Information Officer ... Mr. Scott COWDREY
07 VC Admissions/Financial Aid ... Ms. Kortni R. CAMPBELL
06 Registrar ... Ms. Lynne HORGAN
21 Assoc VC of Finance/Controller ... Ms. Mary HALL
19 Asst VC for Public Safety ... Vacant
96 Purchasing Officer ... Mr. Joel KNISLEY
26 Chief Communication/Mktg Ofcr ... Ms. Sarah BROBERG
27 Media and Public Relations Spec ... Ms. Crissa SINKOVIC
23 Dir Student Health/Counseling ... Mr. John CUTSPEC
88 AVC of Student Affairs ... Dr. Melanie FOX
39 Dir of Housing/Student Life Opers ... Mr. Vollie BARNWELL
36 Director of Career Center ... Ms. Lisa MANN
35 Interim Dean of Students ... Ms. Megan PUGH
04 Exec Asst to Chancellor ... Vacant
86 Exec Dir Govt and Cmty Relations ... Ms. Lakesha MCDAY

*University of North Carolina at Chapel Hill (B)

Chapel Hill NC 27599-0001

County: Orange | FICE Identification: 002974 | Unit ID: 199120
Telephone: (919) 962-2211 | Carnegie Class: DU-Highest
FAX Number: (919) 962-5604 | Calendar System: Semester
URL: www.unc.edu
Established: 1789 | Annual Undergrad Tuition & Fees (In-State): $8,980
Enrollment: 30,092 | Coed
Affiliation or Control: State | IRS Status: 501(c)3
Highest Offering: Doctorate
Accreditation: SC, ACAE, ARCPA, AUD, CAATE, CACREP, CAEP, CAMPEP, CLPSY, DENT, DH, DIET, DMOLS, HSA, IPSY, #JOUR, LAW, LC, LIB, MED, MLS, NMT, NURSE, OT, PAST, PCSAS, PH, PHAR, PLNG, PTA, RAD, RADDOS, RTT, SCPSY, SP, SPAA, SW

02 Chancellor/CEO ... Dr. Kevin M. GUSKIEWICZ
05 Provost & Exec Vice Chancellor ... Dr. Chris CLEMENS
20 Exec Vice Provost ... Ms. Amy LOCKLEAR HERTEL
10 Vice Chancellor Finance/Operations ... Mr. Nathan KNUFFMAN
32 Vice Chancellor Student Affairs ... Dr. Amy JOHNSON
13 VC Info Technology/Chief Info Ofcr ... Dr. Michael BARKER
46 Int Vice Chancellor for Research ... Dr. Penny GORDON-LARSEN
17 CEO UNC Health Care/VC Medical Affs ... Dr. A. Wesley BURKS
106 Vice Prov Digital/Lifelong Learning ... Mr. Todd NICOLET
08 Vice Provost/University Librarian ... Ms. Elaine WESTBROOKS
114 Assoc Vice Chanc Finance/Budget ... Mr. Stephen AGOSTINI
21 Asst Provost Finance ... Mr. Barron MATHERLY
20 Vice Prov Acad/Cmty Engagement ... Mr. Joseph JORDAN
88 Assoc Prov Strategy/Spec Projects ... Ms. Debbi CLARKE
18 Assoc Vice Chanc Facilities Svcs ... Ms. Anna WU
88 Asst Prov/Dir Acad Support Athletes ... Ms. Michelle BROWN
22 Vice Provost Equity & Inclusion ... Dr. Leah COX
09 Asst Prov/Dir Inst Rsch/Assessment ... Dr. Lynn E. WILLIFORD
39 Exec Dir Carolina Housing ... Mr. Allan BLATTNER
41 Director of Athletics ... Mr. Lawrence (Bubba) R. CUNNINGHAM
06 Asst Prov/Univ Registrar ... Ms. Lauren DIGRAZIA
07 Vice Prov Enroll/Ugrad Admiss ... Ms. Rachelle FELDMAN
29 President General Alumni Assoc ... Mr. Douglas S. DIBBERT
37 Assoc Provost Student Aid ... Ms. Jackie COPELAND
88 Assoc Provost Rural Innovation ... Ms. Giselle CORBIE
27 Assoc Vice Chanc Communications ... Ms. Beth KEITH
27 Assoc Vice Chanc Communications ... Ms. Tanya MOORE
16 Int Asst Provost Academic Personnel ... Mr. Linc BUTLER
88 Asst Prov Interprofessional Educ ... Ms. Meg ZOMORODI
36 Exec Dir University Career Svcs ... Dr. Tierney BATES
19 Asst Vice Chanc/Chief of Police ... Chief Brian JAMES
27 Director University Relations ... Mr. Mike MCFARLAND
88 Chief Sustainability Officer ... Dr. Michael PIEHLER
96 Chief Ofcr/Exec Dir Procurement ... Mr. Beau JIMMERSON
100 Chief of Staff ... Ms. Christi HURT
11 Sr Vice Prov Business Operations ... Mr. Rick WERNOSKI
87 Dean of the Summer School ... Vacant
49 Dean College Arts & Sciences ... Mr. James W. WHITE
85 Vice Prov Global Affairs ... Ms. Barbara STEPHENSON
61 Dean School of Law ... Mr. Martin BRINKLEY
63 Dean School of Medicine ... Dr. A. Wesley BURKS
52 Interim Dean School of Dentistry ... Dr. Edward J. SWIFT
66 Dean School of Nursing ... Dr. Valerie HOWARD
58 Dean of Graduate School ... Dr. Suzanne W. BARBOUR
50 Dean Kenan-Flagler Business School ... Dr. Douglas SHACKLEFORD
70 Dean School of Social Work ... Ms. Ramona DENBY-BRINSON
67 Dean School of Pharmacy ... Dr. Angela KASHUBA
60 Int Dean School of Journalism ... Ms. Heidi HENNICK-KAMINSKI
62 Dean School of Info/Library Science ... Dr. Gary MARCHIONINI
69 Dean School of Public Health ... Dr. Barbara K. RIMER
53 Dean School of Education ... Dr. Fouad ABD-EL-KHALICK
80 Dean School of Government ... Dr. Michael R. SMITH
23 Exec Dir Campus Health Services ... Mr. Keith PITTMAN
104 Assoc Provost Global Affairs ... Ms. Heather WARD
116 Chief Audit Officer ... Mr. Dean WEBER
15 Vice Chancellor Human Resources/EEO ... Ms. Becci MENGHINI
88 Assoc Vice Provost Innovation ... Ms. Michelle BOLAS
00 Chair Board of Trustees ... Mr. Davis I. BOLIEK
86 Vice Chancellor Public Affairs ... Mr. Clayton SOMERS
30 Vice Chancellor Univ Development ... Mr. David ROUTH
117 Vice Chancellor Risk Management ... Mr. George BATTLE, III
43 Vice Chancellor & General Counsel ... Mr. Charles MARSHALL

*University of North Carolina at Charlotte (C)

9201 University City Boulevard, Charlotte NC 28223-0001

County: Mecklenburg | FICE Identification: 002975 | Unit ID: 199139
Telephone: (704) 687-8622 | Carnegie Class: DU-Higher
FAX Number: N/A | Calendar System: Semester
URL: https://www.uncc.edu/
Established: 1946 | Annual Undergrad Tuition & Fees (In-State): $7,096
Enrollment: 30,146 | Coed
Affiliation or Control: State | IRS Status: 501(c)3
Highest Offering: Doctorate
Accreditation: SC, ANEST, ART, CAATE, CACREP, CAEP, CEA, CLPSY, #COARC, DANCE, EXSC, HSA, IPSY, MUS, NURSE, PH, POLYT, SPAA, SW, THEA

02 Chancellor ... Dr. Sharon L. GABER
100 Chief of Staff ... Ms. Kim S. BRADLEY
05 Provost/Vice Chanc Academic Affairs ... Dr. Joan F. LORDEN
20 Interim Sr Associate Provost ... Dr. Lee GRAY
88 Assoc Prov Urban Rsrch/Cmty Engage ... Mr. Byron WHITE
10 Vice Chancellor Business Affairs ... Mr. Richard AMON
111 Interim VC Univ Advancement ... Ms. Beth CRIGLER
86 Spec Asst for Constituent Relations ... Ms. Betty DOSTER
32 Vice Chancellor Student Affairs ... Dr. Kevin BAILEY
46 Vice Chanc Research/Econ Dev ... Dr. Richard A. TANKERSLEY
13 Vice Chanc Info Tech Svcs/CIO ... Dr. Michael CARLIN
18 Assoc Vice Chanc Facilities Mgmt ... Mr. Rich STEELE
08 Dean Atkins Library ... Dr. Anne C. MOORE
114 Assoc Prov Budget & Personnel ... Ms. Lori MCMAHON
82 Asst Provost for Intl Programs ... Mr. Joel A. GALLEGOS
88 Assistant Provost ... Dr. Leslie ZENK
26 Assoc VC for Univ Communications ... Dr. Jennifer AMES-STUART
117 Chief Risk Officer ... Mr. Steven DUNHAM
107 Assoc Provost School of Prof Stds ... Mr. Asher HAINES
31 Sr Dir Community Relations ... Ms. Joy P. SPRINGS
39 Assoc VC/Dir Residence Life ... Dr. Casey TULLOS
21 Assoc Vice Chancellor for Finance ... Ms. Anne BROWN
21 Int Assoc VC Business Svcs ... Ms. Bonnie MURPHY
58 Assoc Provost/Dean Graduate School ... Dr. Thomas L. REYNOLDS
84 Assoc Provost Enrollment Mgmt ... Ms. Claire KIRBY
43 VC for Inst Integrity/Gen Counsel ... Mr. James E. HUMPHREY, IV
07 Director Undergraduate Admissions ... Ms. Sarah HUMPHRIES NAZIONALE
35 Dean of Students/Assoc VC Stdnt Aff ... Ms. Christine REED DAVIS
37 Director of Financial Aid ... Mr. Bruce BLACKMON
38 Int Assoc VC Health & Wellbeing ... Dr. Dennis WIESE
36 Assoc Provost Univ Career Center ... Dr. Patrick MADSEN
40 Bookstore & Licensing Program Mngr ... Ms. Rachel SKIPWORTH
29 Exec Director Alumni Affairs ... Ms. Sallie HUTTON SISTARE
88 Assoc VC Safety and Security ... Mr. John BOGDAN
19 Chief/Dir Police & Public Safety ... Mr. Jeffrey A. BAKER
09 Assoc Prov Inst Effective/Analytic ... Mr. Stephen A. COPPOLA
108 Asst Provost Assessment/Accred ... Dr. Christine ROBINSON
41 Director of Athletics ... Mr. Mike HILL
96 Director of Materials Mgmt ... Mr. Scott BRECHTEL
93 Dir Acad Diversity/Inclusion ... Mrs. Regena BROWN
23 Assoc VC Health & Wellbeing ... Dr. Mari ROSS
15 Assoc Vice Chanc Human Res/Aff Act ... Mr. Gary W. STINNETT
85 Dir Intl Student/Scholar Svcs ... Mr. Tarek A. ELSHAYEB
104 Director Study Abroad ... Mr. Brad SEKULICH
48 Dean College of Arts/Architecture ... Mr. Brook MULLER
50 Dean College of Business ... Dr. Jennifer TROYER
54 Dean College of Engineering ... Dr. Robert S. KEYNTON
53 Dean College of Education ... Dr. Malcolm B. BUTLER
49 Int Dean Col of Lib Arts & Sciences ... Dr. John SMAIL
76 Dean Col of Health & Human Svcs ... Dr. Catrine TUDOR-LOCKE
72 Int Dean Col of Computing/Inform ... Dr. Bojan CUKIC
97 Dean Univ Col/Assoc Prov UG Pgm ... Dr. Lisa WALKER
121 Asst Dean for UG Educ/Advising ... Dr. David DEARDEN
92 Dean Honors College ... Dr. Malin PEREIRA
06 University Registrar ... Mr. Jonathan REECE
44 Director of Planning Giving ... Ms. Amy SHEHEE
44 Director of Annual Giving ... Ms. Stacie G. YOUNG
04 Executive Asst to President ... Ms. Shari DUNN
25 Exec Dir Contracts/Grants Admin ... Ms. Valerie CRICKARD
28 Director Faculty Affairs/Diversity ... Dr. Yvette HUET
14 Deputy CIO/AVC for Ent Infra ... Mr. Jesse BEAUMAN

*University of North Carolina at Greensboro (D)

PO Box 26170, Greensboro NC 27402-6170

County: Guilford | FICE Identification: 002976 | Unit ID: 199148
Telephone: (336) 334-5000 | Carnegie Class: DU-Higher
FAX Number: (336) 256-0408 | Calendar System: Semester
URL: www.uncg.edu
Established: 1891 | Annual Undergrad Tuition & Fees (In-State): $7,403
Enrollment: 19,764 | Coed
Affiliation or Control: State | IRS Status: 501(c)3
Highest Offering: Doctorate
Accreditation: SC, ANEST, ART, CAATE, CACREP, CAEP, CAPRT, CIDA, CLPSY, DANCE, DIETD, DIETI, LIB, MUS, NURSE, PH, SP, SPAA, SW, THEA

02 Chancellor ... Dr. Franklin D. GILLIAM
100 Chief of Staff ... Ms. Waiyi TSE
88 Associate Chief of Staff ... Ms. Kelly HARRIS
88 Associate Vice Chancellor ... Ms. Adrienne M. CRAIG
04 Assistant to the Chancellor ... Ms. Nikki M. BAKER
88 Chancellor's Fellow Campus Climate ... Dr. Andrea HUNTER
86 Dir State & External Affairs ... Mr. Andrew R. CAGLE
32 Vice Chanc for Student Affairs ... Dr. Cathy AKENS
41 Director Intercollegiate Athletics ... Mr. Brian MACKIN
05 Provost/Executive Vice Chancellor ... Dr. Debbie STORRS
20 Senior Vice Provost ... Dr. Alan J. BOYETTE
08 Int Dean of University Libraries ... Mr. Michael A. CRUMPTON
58 Int Dean Graduate School ... Dr. Gregory BELL
49 Dean of Arts & Sciences ... Dr. John Z. KISS
50 Dean of Business & Economics ... Dr. McRae BANKS
53 Dean of Education ... Dr. Randall D. PENFIELD
68 Dean of Health & Human Sciences ... Dr. Carl G. MATTACOLA
64 Dean of Visual & Performing Arts ... Dr. bruce d. MCCLUNG
66 Dean of Nursing ... Dr. Debra J. BARKSDALE
54 Dean Joint Sch NanoScience/Engineer ... Dr. Sherine O. OBARE
106 Dean UNCG Online ... Dr. Karen BULL
92 Dean Lloyd International Honors Col ... Mr. Omar ALI
111 VC University Advancement ... Dr. Beth FISCHER
29 Dir Alumni Relations ... Ms. Mary G. LANDERS
44 Asst Dir Annual Giving ... Ms. Rie INGOLD
26 VC Strategic Communications ... Mr. Richard CAMPBELL
27 Assoc VC Int Mktg/Communications ... Ms. Kimberly OSBORN
10 VC Finance and Administrative Div ... Mr. Bob SHEA
21 Int Assoc VC Finance ... Mr. Paul FORTE
25 Dir Contracts and Grants ... Mr. William D. WALTERS
113 Mgr Cashiers & Student Accounts ... Mr. Todd MITCHELL
96 Director Purchasing ... Mr. Michael F. LOGAN
40 University Bookstore Manager ... Mr. Brad LIGHT
15 Assoc VC Human Resources ... Ms. Jeanne MADORIN
118 Benefits Manager ... Ms. Emily FOUST
09 Dir Inst Rsch & Enterpr Data Mgt ... Ms. Karen BLACKWELL
46 Vice Chanc Research & Engagement ... Dr. Terri L. SHELTON
108 AVP/Dir Assess & Accred Pgm Plng ... Dr. Jodi E. PETTAZZONI
22 Dir Affirm Action/Equal Opportunity ... Ms. Patricia LYNCH
43 University General Counsel ... Mr. Jerry D. BLAKEMORE
19 Director Safety/Emergency Mgmt ... Mr. Zachary SMITH
18 Associate Vice Chanc for Facilities ... Mr. Sameer KAPILESHWARI
13 Vice Chanc Info Tech Services ... Ms. Donna R. HEATH
14 Assoc VC Learning Tech Client Svcs ... Mr. Todd SUTTON
90 Learning Technology Sr Mgr ... Mr. David KIRKLAND
105 Int Dir Admin Tech & Digital Engage ... Mr. Chris WATERS
119 Chief Information Security Officer ... Dr. Casey FORREST
35 Assoc VC/Dean Students ... Dr. Brett CARTER
84 Vice Chancellor Enrollment Mgmt ... Ms. Tina MCENTIRE
07 AVC Enroll Mgmt/Int Dir UG Admiss ... Mr. Joel LEE
123 Grad Recruit/Admissions/Retention ... Ms. Kelly MERIS
06 University Registrar ... Mr. Chris PARTRIDGE
37 Int Dir Financial Aid ... Mr. John LUCAS
39 Director Housing & Residence Life ... Mr. Timothy JOHNSON
36 Director Career & Prof Development ... Ms. Nicole HALL
38 Director Counseling Center ... Dr. Jennifer M. WHITNEY
121 AVP Stdnt Succ/Dean Undergrad Stds ... Dr. Andrew HAMILTON
124 AVP Stdnt Success Strat & Innov ... Dr. Samantha RAYNOR
89 Dir New Stdnt Transitions/First Yr ... Dr. Kim SOUSA-PEOPLES
28 Director Intercultural Engagement ... Mr. Agusto E. PENA
23 Director Student Health Services ... Ms. Kathleen BABER
104 Assoc Provost Intl Programs ... Dr. Maria ANASTASIOU
88 AVP Academic Resources ... Ms. Mitzi W. BURCHINAL
88 AVP Faculty Personnel Svs ... Ms. Andrea WHITLEY
97 AVP Univ Teaching/Learning Commons ... Dr. David J. TEACHOUT
88 Director of Recreation and Wellness ... Dr. Jill BEVILLE
88 Dir Faculty Personnel Svcs ... Mrs. Anjanie MOSCATELLO

*University of North Carolina at Pembroke (A)

One University Drive, PO Box 1510,
Pembroke NC 28372-1510

County: Robeson | FICE Identification: 002954
Unit ID: 199281
Telephone: (910) 521-6000 | Carnegie Class: Masters/L
FAX Number: (910) 521-6176 | Calendar System: Semester
URL: www.uncp.edu
Established: 1887 | Annual Undergrad Tuition & Fees (In-State): $3,456
Enrollment: 8,262 | Coed
Affiliation or Control: State | IRS Status: 501(c)3
Highest Offering: Master's
Accreditation: SC, ART, CAATE, CACREP, CAEPN, MUS, NURSE, SW

02 Chancellor .... Dr. Robin G. CUMMINGS
43 General Counsel .... Mr. Kelvin JACOBS
05 Provost/VC Academic Affairs .... Dr. Marsha POLLARD
100 Chief of Staff .... Mr. Mark GOGAL
10 Vice Chanc Finance & Admin .... Mr. Gabriel ESZTERHAS
116 Chief Audit Officer .... Ms. Kelley HORTON
32 Vice Chanc Student Affairs .... Dr. Jeff HOWARD
41 Director of Athletics .... Mr. Dick CHRISTY
111 Vice Chanc for Advancement .... Mr. Steve VARLEY
26 Chief Univ Communications/Mktg Ofcr .... Ms. Jodi PHELPS
22 Dir Title IX/Clery Act Compliance .Ms. Ronette SUTTON GERBER
88 Asst to Chancellor Rsrch/Comm .... Ms. Tabi CAIN
04 Executive Asst to the Chancellor .... Ms. Jocelyn GRAHAM
20 Assoc Vice Chanc Academic Affs .... Dr. Scott BILLINGSLEY
85 Assoc VC Global Engagement .... Ms. Cathy Lee ARCUINO
84 Assoc Vice Chanc for Enrollment Mgt .... Dr. Melissa SCHAUB
45 Assoc VC for Planning/Accreditation .... Dr. Elizabeth NORMANDY
25 Assoc VC Research and Sponsored .... Vacant
53 Interim Dean of School of Education .... Dr. Zoe LOCKLEAR
50 Dean of School of Business .... Dr. Barry O'BRIEN
49 Dean of Arts & Sciences .... Dr. Jeff FREDERICK
08 Dean of Library Services .... Dr. Dennis SWANSON
58 Dean of The Graduate School .... Dr. Irene AIKEN
89 Dean of University College .... Ms. Beth HOLDER
92 Dean of Honors College .... Dr. Mark MILEWICZ
76 Dean College of Health Sciences .... Vacant
88 Director for Academic Resources .... Ms. Leslie T. BELL
09 Director Institutional Research .... Dr. Chunmei YAO
06 Registrar .... Ms. Natricia DRAKE
07 Assoc Dir of Undergrad Admissions .... Ms. Ashley PRYER
37 Director Financial Aid .... Ms. Jenelle HANDCOX
121 Dir Center for Student Success .... Dr. Derek OXENDINE
88 Director Accessibility Resource .... Dr. Nicolette CAMPOS
106 Dir Online/Distance Education .... Dr. Charles TITA
25 Dir Sponsored Research/Grant .... Ms. Lisa HUNT
21 Assoc Vice Chancellor for Finance .... Vacant
13 Assoc VC Info Resources/CIO .... Dr. Katina BLUE
15 Asst Vice Chanc for Human Resources .... Ms. Angela REVELS
18 Asst VC for Facilities .... Vacant
16 Deputy Chief Human Resources Ofcr .... Ms. Donna STRICKLAND
103 Dir Employee Rels/Workforce Dev .... Ms. Nicolette S. CAMPOS
88 Facilities Superintendent .... Mr. Mark VESELY
119 Chief Information Security Officer .... Mr. Don BRYANT
14 Dir of Infrastructure/CISO .... Mr. Kevin PAIT
14 Deputy CIO/Dir IT Support Services .... Ms. Liz CUMMINGS
96 Director of Business Services .... Ms. Karen SWINEY
21 Controller .... Ms. Jennifer ADDISON
113 Bursar .... Ms. Cynthia REVELS
114 Director Budget & Planning .... Ms. Kristy NANCE
35 Asst Vice Chanc Student Affairs .... Vacant
38 Director Counseling/Testing Center .... Ms. LynnDee HORNE
35 Dir of Campus Engagement/Leadership .... Mr. Abdul GHAFFAR
39 Director Housing and Resident Life .... Mr. Paul POSENER
28 Dir Office of Diversity/Inclusion .... Dr. Lawrence LOCKLEAR
36 Director Career Services Center .... Mr. Bradley MERRITT
88 Sports Information Director .... Mr. Todd ANDERSON
80 Director Public Administration Pgm .... Dr. Emily NEFF-SHARUM
23 Director of Student Health Services .... Ms. Cora BULLARD
44 Assistant Director of Annual Fund .... Mr. Paris ROEBUCK
110 Dir Advancement Services .... Vacant
27 Director of Creative Services .... Mr. David YBARRA
31 Director of Community Relations .... Mr. Paul JOLICOEUR
19 Director Security/Safety .... Mr. McDuffie CUMMINGS, JR.
88 Faculty Senate Chair .... Dr. Mitu ASHRAF
104 Director Study Abroad .... Mr. Alexander BRANDT

*University of North Carolina Wilmington (B)

601 S College Road, Wilmington NC 28403-5931

County: New Hanover | FICE Identification: 002984
Unit ID: 199218
Telephone: (910) 962-3030 | Carnegie Class: DU-Higher
FAX Number: N/A | Calendar System: Semester
URL: www.uncw.edu
Established: 1947 | Annual Undergrad Tuition & Fees (In-State): $7,181
Enrollment: 17,915 | Coed
Affiliation or Control: State | IRS Status: 501(c)3
Highest Offering: Doctorate
Accreditation: SC, CAATE, CAEPN, CARTE, CEA, CLPSY, #COARC, MUS, NURSE, PH, SPAA, SW

02 Chancellor .... Dr. Aswani K. VOLETY
05 Provost/Vice Chanc Academic Affairs .... Dr. James WINEBRAKE
10 Vice Chancellor Business Affairs .... Mr. Miles LACKEY
32 Vice Chanc for Student Affairs .... Dr. Lowell DAVIS
111 Vice Chanc University Advancement .... Mr. Eddie STUART
110 Assoc Vice Chanc Univ Advancement .... Ms. Missy KENNEDY
21 Assoc Vice Chanc Business Services .... Vacant
21 Assoc VC Business Affs/Facilities .... Mr. Mark D. MORGAN
31 Assoc Vice Chanc Cmty Engagement .... Ms. Jeanine MINGE
106 Assoc VC for Distance Education .... Dr. Jeremy DICKERSON
46 Assoc Provost for Research .... Dr. Stuart BORRETT
28 Chief Diversity Officer .... Dr. Donyell ROSEBORO
26 Chief Mktg/Communications Officer .... Ms. Andrea WEAVER
09 Assoc Provost Inst Research/Plng .... Dr. Andy MAUK
35 Assoc VC/Dean of Students .... Dr. Michael A. WALKER
85 Assoc VC International Programs .... Dr. Michael WILHELM
15 Assoc VC Human Resources .... Ms. Lori PREISS
100 Chief of Staff .... Mr. Bradley BALLOU
06 University Registrar .... Ms. Amanda FLEMING
08 University Librarian .... Ms. Lucy HOLMAN
37 Director Financial Aid/Scholarships .... Mr. Frederick HOLDING
18 Director of Physical Plant .... Mr. David OLSON
19 Assoc Dir Envir Health & Safety .... Mr. Jeffrey CAMPBELL
23 Dir Student Health/Wellness Center .... Ms. Katrin WESNER
109 Director of Auxiliary Services .... Mr. Brian DAILEY
41 Director of Athletics .... Mr. Jimmy BASS
36 Director of the Career Center .... Ms. Nadirah PIPPEN
29 Director of Alumni Relations .... Mrs. Lindsay LEROY
96 Director of Purchasing .... Mr. John ROBINSON
38 Dir Counseling Center/Univ Testing .... Dr. Mark PEREZ-LOPEZ
40 Manager Bookstore .... Ms. Mee So YIM
49 Interim Dean Col Arts & Sciences .... Dr. Michelle SCATTON-TESSIER
50 Dean Cameron School of Business .... Dr. Robert BURRUS
53 Dean Watson School of Education .... Dr. Van O. DEMPSEY
66 Director School of Nursing .... Dr. Linda HADDAD
58 Dean of Graduate School .... Dr. Chris FINELLI
76 Dean Col Health & Human Svcs .... Dr. Justine REEL
04 Executive Assistant to the Chanc .... Ms. Carolyn S. HARTMAN
07 Director Admissions .... Dr. Lauren FRANKLIN
13 Chief Info Technology Officer (CIO) .... Ms. Sharyne MILLER
25 Dir Sponsored Pgms/Rsrch/Compliance .... Ms. Kati CHIPPS
43 General Counsel .... Mr. John SCHERER
54 Director Engineering .... Dr. Amy REAMER
90 Consulting Services Support Dir .... Ms. Beverly VAGNERINI
101 Asst to the Chancellor/Trustees .... Mr. Mark LANIER
39 Director of Housing .... Mr. Kevin MEANEY
108 Dir Office of Inst Effectiveness .... Dr. Andy MAUK
30 Director of Development .... Ms. Dawn CARTER
102 Dir Foundation/Corporate Relations .... Ms. Megan GORHAM
122 Asst Dir Fraternity/Sorority Life .... Ms. Lindsey TRIONE

*University of North Carolina School of the Arts (C)

1533 S Main Street, Winston-Salem NC 27127-2738

County: Forsyth | FICE Identification: 003981
Unit ID: 199184
Telephone: (336) 770-3399 | Carnegie Class: Spec-4-yr-Arts
FAX Number: (336) 770-3375 | Calendar System: Semester
URL: www.uncsa.edu
Established: 1963 | Annual Undergrad Tuition & Fees (In-State): $9,358
Enrollment: 1,070 | Coed
Affiliation or Control: State | IRS Status: 501(c)3
Highest Offering: Master's
Accreditation: SC

02 Chancellor .... Mr. Brian COLE
05 Provost & Exec Vice Chancellor .... Mr. Patrick SIMS
10 Vice Chanc for Finance & Admin .... Mr. Michael SMITH
111 Int Vice Chanc for Advancement .... Mr. Rich WHITTINGTON
26 Vice Chanc Strategic Communication .... Ms. Claire MACHAMER
43 Vice Chanc/General Counsel .... Mr. David HARRISON
32 Vice Provost & Dean Student Affairs .... Dr. Tracey FORD
88 Vice Chanc Economic Development .... Mr. Jim DECRISTO
18 Assoc Vice Chancellor Facilities .... Mr. Steve MARTIN
09 Director of Institutional Research .... Mr. Jeff PATON
07 Director of Admissions .... Mr. Paul RAZZA
08 University Librarian .... Ms. Sarah FALLS
27 Director of Communications .... Ms. Marla CARPENTER
06 Registrar .... Vacant
15 AVC/Chief Human Resources .... Ms. Angela MAHONEY
37 Director of Financial Aid .... Mrs. Jane KAMIAB
49 Interim Dean of Liberal Arts .. Ms. Martine Kei GRREEN-ROGERS
64 Dean School of Music .... Mr. Saxton ROSE
57 Dean School of Dance .... Ms. Endalyn TAYLOR
48 Dean Sch of Design/Production .... Mr. Michael KELLEY
88 Dean School of Drama .... Mr. Scott ZIGLER
13 Chief Technology Officer .... Mr. Terrence HARMON
19 Chief of Police .... Mr. Frank BRINKLEY
38 Dir of Counseling & Testing Svcs .... Vacant
96 Director of Purchasing .... Ms. Jeanette VALENTINE
57 Exec Dir Kenan Inst for the Arts .... Mr. Kevin BITTERMAN
88 Dean School of Filmmaking .... Ms. Deborah LAVINE
88 Headmaster/Dean HS Academic Program .... Mr. Martin FERRELL
35 Director of Student Engagement .... Mr. Steve GALLAGHER
87 Dir Educ Outreach & Summer Programs .... Ms. Suzanna WATKINS
23 Director of Health Services .... Ms. Sharon SUMMER
100 Chief of Staff .... Mr. James DECRISTO
102 Foundation Director .... Ms. Cynthia LIBERTY
108 Director of Inst Effectiveness .... Mr. Jeff PATON

*Western Carolina University (D)

One University Drive, HFR 501,
Cullowhee NC 28723-9646

County: Jackson | FICE Identification: 002981
Unit ID: 200004
Telephone: (828) 227-7100 | Carnegie Class: DU-Mod
FAX Number: (828) 227-7176 | Calendar System: Semester
URL: www.wcu.edu
Established: 1889 | Annual Undergrad Tuition & Fees (In-State): $4,285
Enrollment: 12,243 | Coed
Affiliation or Control: State | IRS Status: 501(c)3
Highest Offering: Doctorate
Accreditation: SC, ANEST, ART, CAATE, CACREP, CAEP, CAPRT, CARTE, CIDA, DIETD, DIETI, EMT, IPSY, MUS, NURSE, PSPSY, PTA, SP, SPAA, SW, THEA

02 Chancellor .... Dr. Kelli R. BROWN
05 Provost/Vice Chanc Academic Affs .... Dr. Richard STARNES
20 Vice Provost for Academic Affairs .... Dr. Carol BURTON
10 Vice Chanc Admin & Finance .... Mr. Mike BYERS
32 Vice Chancellor/Student Affairs .... Dr. H. Samuel MILLER, JR.
121 Assoc Vice Chanc Student Success .... Mr. William MOULTRIE
35 Asst Vice Chanc/Student Affairs .... Ms. Kellie MONTEITH
111 Vice Chancellor Advancement .... Mrs. Jamie RAYNOR
18 Assoc VC for Facilities Management .... Mr. Joe WALKER
100 Chief of Staff .... Dr. Melissa WARGO
04 Assistant to the Chancellor .... Ms. Jessica WOODS
43 General Counsel .... Mr. Shea BROWNING
38 Director of Counseling Services .... Dr. Kimberly GORMAN
06 Registrar .... Mr. Larry HAMMER
84 Asst Vice Chanc/Undergrad Enrollmnt .... Mr. Phil CAULEY
09 Asst Vice Chancellor of OIPE .... Mr. Tim METZ
37 Director of Financial Aid .... Ms. Trina ORR
15 Assoc VC of Human Resources .... Dr. Cory CAUSBY
13 Chief Information Officer .... Mr. Craig FOWLER
29 Director of Alumni Affairs .... Mr. Marty RAMSEY
08 Dean of Library Services .... Dr. Chuck THOMAS
88 Exec Director Education Outreach .... Dr. Carolyn CALLAGHAN
109 Director Campus Services .... Mr. Bryant BARNETT
41 Athletic Director .... Mr. Alex GARY
23 Director University Health Services .... Ms. Pamela BUCHANAN
96 Director of Business Operations .... Mr. Bruce BARKER
40 Director Book & Supply Store .... Ms. Jennifer THOMAS
38 Director of Advising Center .... Mr. Travis BULLUCK
36 Director of Career Services .... Ms. Theresa C. PAUL
26 Exec Dir Communications/Marketing .... Mr. Benny SMITH
50 Dean College of Business .... Dr. AJ GRUBE
57 Dean of Fine & Performing Arts .... Dr. George H. BROWN
58 Dean Grad School & Research .... Dr. Brian KLOEPPEL
49 Dean Arts & Sciences .... Dr. David KINNER
72 Dean Kimmel School Constr Mgmt/Tech .... Dr. Randy COLLINS
53 Dean Educ & Allied Professions .... Dr. Kim WINTER
76 Dean Health & Human Sciences .... Dr. Lori ANDERSON
92 Dean of Honors College .... Dr. Jill GRANGER
88 Exec Director Creative Services .... Ms. Tiffany WYSOCKI
86 Deputy COS/Dir of External Rels .... Ms. Christy AGNER
88 Chief Marketing & Comm Officer .... Mr. Travis JORDAN
28 Chief Diversity Officer .... Dr. Ricardo NAZARIO-COLON

*Winston-Salem State University (E)

601 MLK Jr. Drive, 200 Blair Hall,
Winston-Salem NC 27110-0001

County: Forsyth | FICE Identification: 002986
Unit ID: 199999
Telephone: (336) 750-2000 | Carnegie Class: DU-Mod
FAX Number: (336) 750-2049 | Calendar System: Semester
URL: www.wssu.edu
Established: 1892 | Annual Undergrad Tuition & Fees (In-State): $5,941
Enrollment: 5,169 | Coed
Affiliation or Control: State | IRS Status: 501(c)3
Highest Offering: Doctorate
Accreditation: SC, CACREP, CAEPN, CAPRT, COSMA, MLS, MUS, NURSE, OT, PTA, SW

02 Chancellor .... Dr. Elwood L. ROBINSON
05 Provost/VC Academic Affairs .... Dr. Anthony GRAHAM
32 Assoc Prov/VC Student Development .... Dr. Melvin NORWOOD
20 Associate Provost .... Vacant
45 Assoc Prov Administration/Plng .... Mrs. Letitia C. WALL
10 Vice Chanc Finance & Admin .... Mrs. Constance MALLETTE
111 Vice Chanc Univ Advancement .... Mrs. LaTanya D. AFOLAYAN
100 Int Vice Chancellor/Chief of Staff .... Ms. Letitia WALL
18 Assoc Vice Chanc Facilities Mgmt .... Mr. Timothy MCMULLEN
13 Assoc Prov/Chief Information Ofcr .... Mrs. Raisha COBB
116 Int Dir Internal Audit/Compliance .... Mr. Santonius R. ISOM
19 Dir of Police/Campus Safety .... Chief Amir HENRY
08 Director of Library Services .... Ms. Wanda BROWN
39 Director Housing/Residence Life .... Dr. Shawn ODOM
37 Int Director of Financial Aid .... Ms. Jill POWELL
15 Assoc Vice Chanc Human Resources .... Dr. Tracy A. WORTHEY
26 Dir of Public Relations .... Ms. Haley N. GINGLES
84 Dir Enrollment Communications .... Vacant
102 Exec Director Univ Donor Events .... Ms. Kimberly REESE
35 Asst Dean of Students .... Mr. Mitch MITCHELL
23 Dir of Student Health Center .. Dr. Karen THOMPSON-WILLIAMS
41 Athletic Director .... Ms. Etienne M. THOMAS
07 Director of Admissions .... Dr. Kerwin GRAHAM
43 Chief Legal Counsel .... Dr. Ivey BROWN
96 Director Purchasing .... Mr. Alan G. IRELAND
90 Director Academic Computer Center .... Mr. Cuthrell JOHNSON

79 Dean University College LLL ....Dr. Manju BHAT
76 Int Dean School of Health Science ....Dr. Leslee S. BATTLE
88 Director of Title III ....Dr. Everette L. WITHERSPOON
06 Registrar ....Ms. Marquita J. GRAVES
108 Director Institutional Assessment . Dr. Becky MUSSAT-WHITLOW
122 Coord Student Orgs-Greek Life ....Ms. Katrina MCCOY

Wake Forest University (A)

1834 Wake Forest Road, Winston-Salem NC 27109-8758
County: Forsyth FICE Identification: 002978
Unit ID: 199847
Telephone: (336) 758-5000 Carnegie Class: DU-Higher
FAX Number: (336) 758-6074 Calendar System: Semester
URL: www.wfu.edu
Established: 1834 Annual Undergrad Tuition & Fees: $57,760
Enrollment: 8,789 Coed
Affiliation or Control: Independent Non-Profit IRS Status: 501(c)3
Highest Offering: Doctorate
Accreditation: SC, ANEST, ARCPA, CACREP, DENT, IPSY, LAW, MED, THEOL

01 President ....Dr. Susan R. WENTE
43 SVP/General Counsel/Sec BOT ....Mr. J. Reid MORGAN
10 Exec Vice Pres/Chief Financial Ofcr ....Mr. B. Hofler MILAM
05 Provost ....Mr. Rogan KERSH
11 Vice President for Administration ....Mr. John SHENETTE
111 Vice Pres University Advancement ....Mr. Mark A. PETERSEN
32 Vice Pres Campus Life ....Dr. Penny RUE
115 Vice Pres/Chief Investment Officer ....Mr. James J. DUNN
100 Chief of Staff ....Ms. Mary E. PUGEL
35 Assoc Vice Pres/Dean of Students ....Mr. Adam GOLDSTEIN
44 Asst VP/Dir Parent & Donor Rels ....Ms. Minta A. MCNALLY
30 Sr AVP of Development ....Mr. Robert T. BAKER
13 Vice Pres Info Tech/CIO ....Mr. Mur MUCHANE
46 Assoc Provost for Research ....Dr. Keith BONIN
49 Dean of the College ....Dr. Michele K. GILLESPIE
61 Dean School of Law ....Ms. Jane AIKEN
50 Int Dean of Business ....Ms. Michelle ROEHM
73 Dean of Divinity ....Dr. Jonathan L. WALTON
107 Dean School of Professional Studies ....Dr. Charles L. IACOVOU
09 Assist Provost Inst Research ....Mr. Phil HANDWERK
08 Dir of the Z Smith Reynolds Library ....Mr. Tim PYATT
07 Dean of Admissions ....Ms. Karen VARGAS
37 Director of Financial Aid ....Mr. William T. WELLS
36 VP Innovation & Career Dev ....Mr. Andy CHAN
06 Registrar ....Mr. Harold PACE
41 Director of Athletics ....Mr. John D. CURRIE
15 VP Human Resources ....Ms. Dedee I. DELONGPRE JOHNSTON
18 Director Facilities Management ....Mr. John SHENETTE
38 Dir University Counseling Center ....Dr. Marianne A. SCHUBERT
23 Director Student Health Service ....Dr. Cecil D. PRICE
42 Chaplain ....Rev. Timothy L. AUMAN
19 Chief University Police ....Ms. Regina G. LAWSON
22 EEO Mgr/Diversity & Compliance Dir ....Ms. Angela CULLER
94 Director Women's & Gender Studies ....Dr. Wanda BALZANO
26 Sr AVP Comm/External Relations ....Mr. Brett EATON
104 Director Study Abroad ....Mr. David F. TAYLOR
29 Director Alumni Engagement ....Mrs. Kelly MCCONNICO
122 Asst Dean Ldrshp-Frat/Sorority Life ....Ms. Betsy ADAMS

Warren Wilson College (B)

PO Box 9000, Asheville NC 28815-9000
County: Buncombe FICE Identification: 002979
Unit ID: 199865
Telephone: (828) 771-2000 Carnegie Class: Bac-A&S
FAX Number: (828) 771-7097 Calendar System: Semester
URL: www.warren-wilson.edu
Established: 1894 Annual Undergrad Tuition & Fees: $38,350
Enrollment: 703 Coed
Affiliation or Control: Presbyterian Church (U.S.A.) IRS Status: 501(c)3
Highest Offering: Master's
Accreditation: SC, SW

01 Interim President ....Mr. William H. CHRISTY
05 Provost/Dean of Faculty ....Dr. Jay ROBERTS
10 VP Administration & Finance/CFO ....Ms. Belinda BURKE
30 Sr Dir of Development/Advancement ....Ms. Renee DANGER-JAMES
32 Director of Student Life ....Ms. Tacci SMITH
84 Vice Pres Enrollment/Marketing ....Mr. Brian LIECHTI
37 Director Financial Aid ....Mr. Derrick EVERHART
44 Sr Dir Constituent Relations/Comm ....Ms. Mary HAY
26 Director of Marketing/Operations ....Mr. Morgan DAVIS
38 Dir of Counseling/Student Wellbeing ....Ms. Mariel EPSTEIN-OLSEN
121 Asst Dean of Advising/Career Dev ....Ms. Lindsey KASS-GREEN
42 Dir of Spiritual Life & Chaplain ....Rev. Shannon SPENCER
07 Director of Admission ....Mr. Nathan WYRICK
19 Director Public Safety ....Mr. Jonathan DAVIDSON
06 Registrar/Dean Acad Administration ....Ms. Brooke MILLSAPS
15 Director of Human Resources ....Ms. Heather SCHALK

Watts School of Nursing (C)

2828 Croasdaile Drive, Ste 200, Durham NC 27705
County: Durham FICE Identification: 006483
Unit ID: 199883
Telephone: (919) 470-7349 Carnegie Class: Not Classified
FAX Number: (919) 383-4014 Calendar System: Semester
URL: www.wattsschoolofnursing.org
Established: 1895 Annual Undergrad Tuition & Fees: N/A
Enrollment: N/A Coed
Affiliation or Control: Independent Non-Profit IRS Status: 501(c)3
Highest Offering: Baccalaureate
Accreditation: ABHES

William Peace University (D)

15 E Peace Street, Raleigh NC 27604-1194
County: Wake FICE Identification: 002953
Unit ID: 199272
Telephone: (919) 508-2000 Carnegie Class: Bac-Diverse
FAX Number: (919) 508-2326 Calendar System: Semester
URL: www.peace.edu
Established: 1857 Annual Undergrad Tuition & Fees: $32,450
Enrollment: 830 Coed
Affiliation or Control: Presbyterian Church (U.S.A.) IRS Status: 501(c)3
Highest Offering: Baccalaureate
Accreditation: SC, NURSE

01 President ....Dr. Brian C. RALPH
100 Dir of Presidential Operations ....Ms. Kelley DIETZ
05 Vice President for Academic Affairs ....Dr. Charles DUNCAN
111 Vice Pres University Advancement ....Ms. Jodi STAMEY
32 Vice President for Student Life ....Mr. Frank RIZZO
10 Vice Pres Administration/CFO ....Mr. George (Rocky) A. YEARWOOD
84 VP Enrollment Mgmt/Marketing ....Ms. Colleen MURPHY
20 Assoc VP Academic Affairs ....Ms. Carolyn BLATTNER
15 Assoc Vice Pres for Human Resources ....Ms. Kathy LAMBERT
18 Assoc VP for Buildings and Grounds ....Mr. John B. CRANHAM
13 Chief Information Officer ....Mr. Darryl MCGRAW
06 Registrar ....Ms. Melanie FULLER
37 Director of Financial Aid ....Ms. Valerie CLEM-BROWN
41 Director of Athletics ....Mr. Thomas CURLE
29 Director Alumni Relations ....Ms. Ellie BARKER
07 Interim Director of Admissions ....Ms. Ashley MURRAY
19 Director of Public Safety ....Mr. Michael Andrew JOHN
26 Dir Communications/Donor Relations ....Ms. Elizabeth EDWARDS
28 Director of Diversity/Equity ....Ms. Leah YOUNG

Wingate University (E)

220 N. Camden Road, Wingate NC 28174-0159
County: Union FICE Identification: 002985
Unit ID: 199962
Telephone: (704) 233-8000 Carnegie Class: DU-Mod
FAX Number: (704) 233-8014 Calendar System: Semester
URL: www.wingate.edu
Established: 1896 Annual Undergrad Tuition & Fees: $38,896
Enrollment: 3,653 Coed
Affiliation or Control: Southern Baptist IRS Status: 501(c)3
Highest Offering: Doctorate
Accreditation: SC, ACBSP, ARCPA, MUS, NUR, OT, PHAR, PTA

01 President ....Dr. T. Rhett BROWN
05 Provost ....Dr. Jeffrey J. FREDERICK
41 Athletic Director ....Ms. Kelley KISH
10 CFO ....Ms. Melissa PERDUE
100 SVP/Chief of Staff ....Dr. Heather C. MILLER
111 SVP for University Advancement ....Mr. James R. BULLOCK
32 VP Campus Life & Operations ....Dr. D. Patrick BIGGERSTAFF
88 VP of Student Services ....Mr. James AMBROSE
15 VP for Human Resources ....Ms. Sherri SATTERFIELD
88 VP Strategic Partnerships ....Mr. Vincent TILSON
21 VP Business ....Mr. William H. DURHAM
88 VP Business Intelligence ....Mr. J. Samuel PETOSKEY
20 Vice Provost of Academic Affairs ....Dr. Travis TEAGUE
121 Vice Provost of Academic Success ....Dr. Brooke MITCHELL
110 Vice President Capital Investments ....Mr. Scott E. HUNSUCKER
108 Vice Provost Institutional Effect ....Dr. Eric F. SCHNEIDER
109 AVP for Auxiliary Services ....Vacant
88 AVP Project Coordinator ....Ms. Becca PAYLOR
18 Associate VP of Campus Operations ....Ms. Glenda H. BEBBER
67 Dean School of Pharmacy ....Dr. Susan BRUCE
49 Dean School Arts & Sciences ....Dr. Carrie HOEFFERLE
50 Dean School of Business ....Dr. Sergio CASTELLO
53 Dean School of Education ....Dr. Charlesa HANN
68 Dean School of Sport Sciences ....Dr. Brandy CLEMMER
08 Director of Library ....Mr. Keith LASSITER
39 Assoc Dean Res Life & Involvement ....Ms. Jessica HEAD
37 Director Student Financial Planning ....Ms. Jenn P. HALL
91 Director Administrative Computing ....Mr. Timothy D. HERRIN
42 Minister to Students ....Rev. A. Dane JORDAN
40 Director of Campus Store ....Ms. Sherri SHANK
19 Campus Safety Chief ....Mr. Mike EASLEY
38 Director of Counseling Services ....Ms. Melinda FREDERICK
14 Director of Information Technology ....Ms. Jeanette K. BUJAK
35 AVP and Dean of Campus Life ....Mr. Michael REYNOLDS
06 Registrar ....Ms. Maria TAYLOR
36 AVP New Stdnt Orient/Career Svcs ..Ms. Elizabeth BIGGERSTAFF
04 Executive Assistant to President ....Ms. Tammy T. BRITT
13 CIO ....Mr. Steve SHANK
88 VP Institutional Integrity ....Dr. Nancy RANDALL
84 VP Enrollment Management ....Dr. Eva BAUCOM
43 SVP General Counsel ....Mr. Ben SIDBURY
26 Chief Public Relations Officer ....Ms. Kristen YOST
96 Director of Purchasing ....Ms. Amy YOW
88 Exec Dir Collaborative Common Good ....Dr. Cathy WRIGHT
27 AVP Marketing & Events ....Ms. Stacey HARRIS

NORTH DAKOTA

Cankdeska Cikana Community College (F)

PO Box 269, 214 First Avenue,
Fort Totten ND 58335-0269
County: Benson FICE Identification: 022365
Unit ID: 200208
Telephone: (701) 766-4415 Carnegie Class: Tribal
FAX Number: (701) 766-4077 Calendar System: Semester
URL: www.littlehoop.edu
Established: 1974 Annual Undergrad Tuition & Fees: $3,300
Enrollment: 182 Coed
Affiliation or Control: Independent Non-Profit IRS Status: 501(c)3
Highest Offering: Associate Degree
Accreditation: HLC

01 President ....Dr. Cynthia A. LINDQUIST
05 CO-Academic Dean ....Ms. Jackie LAMPERT
05 Co-Academic Dean ....Ms. Kim KREBSBACH
10 CFO ....Mrs. Chelly MERKEL-VEER
11 Dean of Administration ....Mr. Stuart YOUNG
06 Registrar ....Ms. Samantha GOURD
15 Human Resources Director ....Ms. Vanessa THOMAS
37 Director Financial Aid ....Ms. Lindsay ONEBEAR

*North Dakota University System Office (G)

600 E Boulevard Avenue, Dept. 215,
Bismarck ND 58505-0230
County: Burleigh FICE Identification: 033434
Telephone: (701) 328-2960 Carnegie Class: N/A
FAX Number: (701) 328-2961
URL: www.ndus.edu

01 Chancellor ....Mark HAGEROTT
100 Chief of Staff ....Terry MEYER
05 VC Acad/Student Affairs ....Lisa JOHNSON
10 VC Administrative Affairs/CFO ....David KREBSBACH
13 VC IT/Chief Information Officer ....Darin KING
45 VC Strategy/Strategic Engagement ....Jerry ROSTAD
37 Director of Financial Aid ....Brenda ZASTOUPIL
09 Dir of Institutional Research ....Jennifer WEBER
26 Dir of Communications & Media Rels ....Billie Jo LORIUS
88 Director of Financial Reporting ....Robin PUTNAM
20 Dir Acad Affs/Workforce Innovation ....Claire GUNWALL
32 Director of Student Affairs ....Katie FITZSIMMONS
18 Director Facilities Planning ....Rick TONDER
21 Director of Finance ....Jamie WILKE
15 Director of Human Resources ....Jane GRINDE
101 Secretary of the Institution/Board ....Kristie HETZLER

*University of North Dakota (H)

264 Centennial Drive, Grand Forks ND 58202
County: Grand Forks FICE Identification: 003005
Unit ID: 200280
Telephone: (701) 777-3000 Carnegie Class: DU-Higher
FAX Number: (701) 777-2696 Calendar System: Semester
URL: www.und.edu
Established: 1883 Annual Undergrad Tuition & Fees (In-State): $10,276
Enrollment: 13,615 Coed
Affiliation or Control: State IRS Status: 501(c)3
Highest Offering: Doctorate
Accreditation: HLC, AAB, ANEST, ARCPA, ART, CAATE, CAEPN, CLPSY, COPSY, DIETC, HT, LAW, MED, MLS, MUS, NURSE, OT, PH, PTA, SP, SPAA, SW, THEA

02 President ....Dr. Andrew ARMACOST
100 Chief of Staff ....Mr. Robert CAROLIN
05 VP Academic Affairs/Provost ....Dr. Eric LINK
10 Vice Pres Finance/Operations & CFO ....Ms. Karla STEWART
32 Int Vice Pres Student Affairs ....Ms. Beth HELLWIG
17 Vice President Health Affairs ....Dr. Joshua WYNNE
46 Int VP Research/Economic Devel ....Dr. John MIHELICH
26 VP Marketing/Communications ....Ms. Meloney LINDER
27 Director of Communications ....Mr. David L. DODDS
27 Dir of Marketing & Creative Svcs ....Ms. Jennifer SWANGLER
21 Assoc VP Finance ....Vacant
18 Assoc VP Facilities ....Mr. Michael PIEPER
84 Vice Provost/Enrollment Management ....Ms. Janelle KILGORE
13 Chief Information Officer ....Dr. Madhavi MARASINGHE
08 Dean of Libraries & Info Res ....Vacant
06 Registrar ....Mr. Scott CORRELL
15 AVP Human Resources/Payroll Svcs ....Ms. Peggy VARBERG
19 AVP Public Safety/Police Chief ....Mr. Rodney CLARK
38 Director Univ Counseling Center ....Mr. Thomas SOLEM
20 Director Faculty Development ....Dr. Anne KELSCH
22 AVP EEO & Title IX ....Ms. Donna SMITH
37 Director Student Finance ....Mr. Matt LUKACH
39 Director Housing ....Mr. Troy NOELDNER
23 Director of Student Health ....Ms. Jessica DOTY
43 General Counsel ....Mr. Jason JENKINS
41 Director Athletics ....Mr. William CHAVES
21 Controller ....Ms. Sharon LOILAND
35 Dean of Students ....Mr. Alex POKORNOWSKI
92 Director Honors Program ....Dr. A. Rebecca ROZELLE-STONE
114 Assoc Dir Resource Plng/Alloc ....Ms. Cindy FETSCH

49 Dean of Arts & Sciences — Dr. Brad RUNDQUIST
58 Dean School of Graduate Studies — Mr. Chris NELSON
61 Dean School of Law — Mr. Brian PAPPAS
66 Int Dn Col Nursing/Prof Discipline — Dr. Maridee SHOGREN
50 Dean Business/Public Admin — Dr. Amy HENLEY
54 Dean College of Engr/Mines — Dr. Brian TANDE
53 Dean Col Education/Human Devel — Dr. Cindy JUNTUNEN
88 Dean of Aerospace Sciences — Dr. Robert KRAUS
63 Dean Sch Medicine/Health Science — Dr. Joshua WYNNE
35 Assoc Vice Pres for Student Affairs — Ms. Cassie GERHARDT
88 Director Memorial Union — Ms. Cheryl GREW-GILLEN
109 Director Dining Services — Mr. Orlynn ROSAASEN
88 Director TRIO Programs — Mr. Derek SPORBERT
07 Director Admissions — Ms. Jennifer AAMODT
09 Dir University Analytics/Planning — Ms. Amanda MOSKE
105 Director Web/Multimedia Mktg — Ms. Tera BUCKLEY
106 Vice Prov Online Educ/Strat Plng — Dr. Jeffrey HOLM
25 Director Rsrch & Spons Pgm Dev — Ms. Michael SADLER

*Dickinson State University (A)

291 Campus Drive, Dickinson ND 58601-4896
County: Stark — FICE Identification: 002989
Unit ID: 200059
Telephone: (701) 483-2507 — Carnegie Class: Bac-Diverse
FAX Number: (701) 483-2006 — Calendar System: Semester
URL: www.dickinsonstate.edu
Established: 1918 — Annual Undergrad Tuition & Fees (In-State): $8,122
Enrollment: 1,441 — Coed
Affiliation or Control: State — IRS Status: 501(c)3
Highest Offering: Master's
Accreditation: HLC, CAEP, IACBE, MUS, NUR, PNUR

02 President — Dr. Stephen D. EASTON
05 Provost/Vice President — Dr. Debora DRAGSETH
10 Chief Financial Officer — Mr. Kent ANDERSON
32 Dean of Students — Ms. Kayla NOAH
29 Exec Dir Alumni Assoc/Foundation — Mr. Ty ORTON
41 Director of Intercollege Athletics — Mr. Pete STANTON
12 Programming Specialist DSU Bismarck — Ms. Nicky KADRMAS
06 Director of Academic Records — Ms. Kathy MEYER
08 Acting Director of Library Services — Ms. Monica STRUCK
13 Director of Information Technology — Mr. Todd HAUF
37 Director of Financial Aid — Mr. Christopher MEEK
121 Tutoring Center Specialist/Advisor — Ms. Monica WATSON
109 Director of Food Service — Ms. Victoria BURGOS
85 Director of International Programs — Mr. Rus KISER
39 Housing/Director of Student Life — Mr. Eric HOLBROOK
15 Director of Human Resources — Ms. Krissy KILWEIN
18 Director of Facility Operations — Mr. Trent MYRAN
19 Director of Public Safety — Mr. Ed STRIEFEL
04 Executive Asst to President — Vacant
22 Title IX Coordinator — Dr. Kathleen GEISEN
07 Director of Admissions — Ms. Stephanie OSBORNE
09 Data Analyst — Mr. Ruizhe JIANG
36 Career Services Specialist — Mr. Sagan OSBORNE

*Mayville State University (B)

330 3rd Street, NE, Mayville ND 58257-1299
County: Traill — FICE Identification: 002993
Unit ID: 200226
Telephone: (701) 788-2301 — Carnegie Class: Bac-Diverse
FAX Number: (701) 788-4748 — Calendar System: Semester
URL: www.mayvillestate.edu
Established: 1889 — Annual Undergrad Tuition & Fees (In-State): $7,381
Enrollment: 1,168 — Coed
Affiliation or Control: State — IRS Status: 501(c)3
Highest Offering: Master's
Accreditation: HLC, CAEP, NURSE

02 President — Dr. Brian VAN HORN
05 Interim VPAA/Dean of Nursing — Ms. Tami SUCH
10 Interim VP for Business Affairs — Mr. Steven BENSEN
32 VP Student Affairs & Inst Research — Dr. Andrew J. PFLIPSEN
102 Executive Foundation Director — Mr. Lon JORGENSEN
41 Athletic Director — Vacant
04 Exec Assistant to the President — Ms. Mary L. TRUDEAU
26 Dir Public Relations & Marketing — Ms. Beth I. SWENSON
07 Director Recruitment/Outreach — Mr. James R. MOROWSKI
06 Dir Academic Records/Registrar — Ms. Heather HOYT
106 Director of Extended Learning — Ms. Misti L. WUORI
37 Director of Financial Aid — Ms. Susan CORDAHL
08 Director of Library Services — Ms. Kelly J. KORNKVEN
35 Director of Student Life — Dr. Jeffrey A. POWELL
40 Director of Bookstore — Ms. Pam B. SOHOLT
18 Director of Physical Plant — Mr. Dan P. LORENZ
18 Director of Facilities Services — Mr. Bob J. KOZOJED
15 Director of Human Resources — Ms. Sarah GASEVIC
13 Chief Information Officer — Mr. Robert R. FREDERICK
21 Controller — Ms. Courtney PETERSON
38 Director of Counseling Services — Ms. Hanna KASTER
121 Dir Student Success/Disability Svc — Ms. Katie J. RICHARDS
28 Dir Diversity/Inclusion — Ms. Bella HETTICH
36 Director of Career Services — Ms. Megan VIG
25 Director Grants & Research — Dr. Robert D. MIESS
108 Int Dir Inst Accred/Assessment — Dr. Erin KUNZ
50 Division Chair Business — Ms. Rhonda L. NELSON
53 Dean/Div Chair Education — Dr. Pamela L. JOHNSON
68 Division Chair Physical Education — Mr. Scott B. PARKER
81 Division Chair Science/Math — Dr. Joseph MEHUS
66 Interim Div Chair Nursing — Dr. Collette CHRISTOFFERS
49 Division Chair Liberal Arts — Dr. Erin KUNZ

*Minot State University (C)

500 University Avenue W, Minot ND 58707-0001
County: Ward — FICE Identification: 002994
Unit ID: 200253
Telephone: (701) 858-3000 — Carnegie Class: Masters/M
FAX Number: (701) 839-6933 — Calendar System: Semester
URL: www.minotstateu.edu
Established: 1913 — Annual Undergrad Tuition & Fees (In-State): $7,896
Enrollment: 2,920 — Coed
Affiliation or Control: State — IRS Status: 501(c)3
Highest Offering: Beyond Master's But Less Than Doctorate
Accreditation: HLC, CAEP, IACBE, MUS, NURSE, SP, SW

02 President — Dr. Steven SHIRLEY
05 VP for Academic Affairs — Dr. Laurie GELLER
10 Vice President for Finance/Admin — Mr. Brent WINIGER
111 Vice President for Advancement — Mr. Rick HEDBERG
32 Vice President for Student Affairs — Mr. Kevin HARMON
21 AVP Business Services/Controller — Ms. Jonelle WATSON
84 Assoc VP Enrollment/Grad/Marketing — Dr. Jacek MROZIK
07 Director Enrollment Services — Ms. Michelle SAYLER
18 Facilities Management — Mr. Brian SMITH
06 Registrar — Ms. Rebecca RINGHAM
08 Chair of Library Services — Ms. Jane LAPLANTE
23 Director of Student Wellness — Mr. Paul BREKKE
37 Director of Financial Aid — Ms. Laurie WEBER
29 Director Alumni Relations — Ms. Janna MCKECHNIE
13 Director Computer Services — Mr. George WITHUS
40 Director Bookstore — Ms. Tiffany HETH
41 Athletic Director — Mr. Kevin FORDE
26 Director University Communications — Mr. Michael LINNELL
15 Director of Human Resources — Ms. Sara ABRAHAMSON
12 Dean of Dakota College at Bottineau — Dr. Carmen SIMONE
36 Director of Campus Career Services — Ms. Lynda BERTSCH
25 Grants & Contracts Accountant — Ms. Sheila LATHAM
09 Director of Institutional Research — Ms. Cari OLSON
04 Executive Asst to President — Ms. Deb WENTZ
39 Director Student Housing — Ms. Karina STANDER
27 Director of Marketing — Mr. Cole KRUEGER
104 Director International Programs — Ms. Libby CLAERBOUT
19 Director Security/Safety — Mr. Gary ORLUCK
88 Director of Military Resource Ctr — Mr. Andrew HEITKAMP
22 Title IX Coordinator — Ms. Lisa DOOLEY
56 Director of CEL — Dr. Robert NORMAN
108 Director Institutional Assessment — Dr. Nathan ANDERSON

*North Dakota State University Main Campus (D)

P.O. Box 6050, Fargo ND 58108-6050
County: Cass — FICE Identification: 002997
Unit ID: 200332
Telephone: (701) 231-8011 — Carnegie Class: DU-Highest
FAX Number: (701) 231-8722 — Calendar System: Semester
URL: www.ndsu.edu
Established: 1890 — Annual Undergrad Tuition & Fees (In-State): $10,168
Enrollment: 12,846 — Coed
Affiliation or Control: State — IRS Status: 501(c)3
Highest Offering: Doctorate
Accreditation: HLC, ACPHA, ART, CAATE, CACREP, CAEP, CAEPN, CIDA, COARC, CONST, DIETC, DIETD, EXSC, LSAR, MUS, NURSE, PH, PHAR, THEA

02 President — Dr. David COOK
05 Provost — Dr. Margaret FITZGERALD
10 Vice President Business & Finance — Mr. Bruce BOLLINGER
46 Vice Pres Research & Creative Act — Dr. Jane SCHUH
56 Vice President Ag/Univ Extension — Mr. Greg LARDY
102 Pres/CEO Fdn/Alumni Assn — Mr. John GLOVER
13 VP IT/Chief Information Officer — Mr. Marc WALLMAN
84 Vice Prov Student Affs/Enroll Mgmt — Ms. Laura OSTER-AALAND
20 Vice Provost Faculty/Title IX — Ms. Canan BILEN-GREEN
25 Assoc VP Sponsored Programs Admin — Ms. Valrey V. KETTNER
26 Assoc VP University Relations — Ms. Laura MCDANIEL
06 University Registrar — Mr. Philip HUNT
91 Director Administrative Systems — Mr. Joel BESELER THOMPSON
08 Dean of Libraries — Dr. Jolie GRAYBILL
51 Int Dir Distance/Continuing Educ — Dr. Stacy DUFFIELD
37 Director Financial Aid/Scholarships — Dr. Matt SANCHEZ
36 Director Career Center — Ms. Rebecca BAHE
50 Interim Dean Business — Dr. Alan KALLMEYER
54 Dean Engineering/Architecture — Dr. Michael KESSLER
53 College of Human Sciences & Educ — Mr. Ron WERNER-WILSON
49 Dean Arts/Humanities/Social Science — Dr. David BERTOLINI
81 Dean of Science & Mathematics — Dr. Kimberly WALLIN
67 Dean of Pharmacy/Nursing/Allied Sci — Dr. Charles D. PETERSON
47 Dean of Agric/Food Sys & Nat Res — Dr. Greg LARDY
58 Dean Graduate School — Ms. Susan SELL
114 Director of Budget — Ms. Cynthia ROTT
18 Director Facilities Management — Mr. Mike ELLINGSON
19 Dir of Univ Police/Safety Officer — Mr. Mike BORR
38 Director Counseling Center — Dr. William BURNS
23 Director Wellness Center — Mr. Jobey LICHTBLAU
39 Director of Residence Life — Mr. Rian NOSTRUM
40 Director Bookstore — Ms. Kimberly ANVINSON
41 Director of Athletics — Mr. Matt LARSEN
57 Director Fine Arts — Dr. E. John MILLER
09 Dir Institutional Research/Analysis — Ms. Emily BERG
96 Director of Purchasing — Ms. Stacey O. WINTER
07 Interim Director of Admissions — Ms. Seinquis LEINEN
04 Executive Asst to President — Ms. Stephanie WAWERS

15 Director HR/Payroll — Mr. Mark GENKINGER
88 Dir Grant & Contract Accounting — Ms. Ann YOUNG
100 Chief of Staff — Mr. Christopher WILSON
104 Director Study Abroad — Ms. Alicia KAUFFMAN
04 Assoc Executive Asst to President — Ms. La Donna K. DE GELDERE
122 Coord Fraternity/Sorority Life — Ms. Jordan DIPALMA

*Valley City State University (E)

101 College Street, SW, Valley City ND 58072-4098
County: Barnes — FICE Identification: 003008
Unit ID: 200572
Telephone: (701) 845-7122 — Carnegie Class: Bac-Diverse
FAX Number: (701) 845-7104 — Calendar System: Semester
URL: www.vcsu.edu
Established: 1889 — Annual Undergrad Tuition & Fees (In-State): $7,942
Enrollment: 1,676 — Coed
Affiliation or Control: State — IRS Status: 501(c)3
Highest Offering: Master's
Accreditation: HLC, CAEPN, MUS

02 President — Dr. Alan LAFAVE
05 Vice President for Academic Affairs — Mr. Larry BROOKS
10 Interim VP Business Affairs — Ms. Erica BUCHHOLZ
32 Vice President for Student Affairs — Dr. Erin KLINGENBERG
53 Dean Sch of Education/Graduate Stds — Dr. Allen BURGAD
08 Library Director — Ms. Jennier JENNESS
20 Director Student Academic Services — Ms. Kaleen PETERSON
37 Director Student Financial Aid — Ms. Marcia PRITCHERT
13 Chief Information Officer — Mr. Joseph TYKWINSKI
41 Interim Athletic Director — Mr. Dennis MCCULLOCH
84 Director of Enrollment Services — Ms. Erin HEIDE
111 Exec Dir of University Advancement — Mr. Corey ANDERSON
18 Director Facilities Services — Vacant
15 Human Resources Director — Ms. Jennifer LARSON
29 Asst Dir Univ Advance/Alumni Rels — Ms. Kim HESCH
38 Director of Student Counseling — Dr. Erin KLINGENBERG
26 Director Marketing/Communications — Ms. Tamara Jo TAFT
40 Director Bookstore — Mr. Todd ROGELSTAD
06 Registrar — Ms. Shannon HONE
09 Director Inst Effectiveness/Plng — Dr. Kerry GREGORYK
36 Career Services Coordinator — Ms. Janna KOHLER
19 Director Security/Safety — Ms. Jessica GORTMAKER
28 Director for Diversity & Inclusion — Dr. Kelly LAFRAMBOISE
39 Dir Resident Life/Student Housing — Ms. Erin EDINGER

*Bismarck State College (F)

PO Box 5587, Bismarck ND 58506-5587
County: Burleigh — FICE Identification: 002988
Unit ID: 200022
Telephone: (701) 224-5400 — Carnegie Class: Bac/Assoc-Assoc Dom
FAX Number: (701) 224-5550 — Calendar System: Semester
URL: bismarckstate.edu
Established: 1939 — Annual Undergrad Tuition & Fees (In-State): $4,731
Enrollment: 3,716 — Coed
Affiliation or Control: State — IRS Status: 501(c)3
Highest Offering: Baccalaureate
Accreditation: HLC, ADNUR, EMT, MLTAD, SURGT

02 President — Dr. Douglas J. JENSEN
03 Executive Vice President — Ms. Rebecca COLLINS
05 VP Academic Affairs — Mr. Dan LEINGANG
111 VP College Advance/Exec Dir Found — Ms. Kari KNUDSON
32 VP Student Affairs — Ms. Kaylyn BONDY
88 Dean Nat Energy Ctr of Excell — Mr. Bruce EMMIL
84 Dean of Enrollment Management — Ms. Karen ERICKSON
72 Dean Current & Emerging Technology — Ms. Mari VOLK
13 Chief Information Officer — Ms. Carol FLAA
15 Chief Human Resources Officer — Ms. Nicole MIKKELSEN
10 Chief Financial Officer — Ms. Sonya KOBLE
106 Chief Dist Learning/Military Affs — Vacant
26 Public Relations Manager — Ms. Juanita LEE
51 Dean Continuing Education — Ms. Sara VOLLMER
08 Director of Library Services — Ms. Marlene ANDERSON
18 Chief Buildings/Grounds Officer — Mr. Don ROETHLER
41 Director of Athletics — Mr. Myron SCHULTZ
37 Director of Financial Aid — Mr. Scott LINGEN
39 Director Student & Residence Life — Ms. Heather SHEEHAN
06 Director Academic Records/Registrar — Ms. Sandy FRIED
121 Director of Student Success — Ms. Kate MILLNER
108 Director IE & Strategic Planning — Dr. John CARROLL
88 Program Manager NECE — Mr. Dan SCHMIDT
88 Program Manager NECE — Mr. Kyren MILLER
88 Polytechnic Program Outreach Dir — Ms. Alicia UHDE
40 Bookstore Manager/Purchasing Coord — Ms. Debra SANDNESS
04 Executive Assistant to President — Ms. Janell CAMPBELL
19 Campus Safety & Security Manager — Mr. Matthew GIDDINGS
07 Director of Admissions — Ms. Retha MATTERN

*Dakota College at Bottineau (G)

105 Simrall Boulevard, Bottineau ND 58318-1198
County: Bottineau — FICE Identification: 002995
Unit ID: 200314
Telephone: (701) 228-2277 — Carnegie Class: Assoc/HVT-High Non
FAX Number: (701) 228-5468 — Calendar System: Semester
URL: www.dakotacollege.edu
Established: 1906 — Annual Undergrad Tuition & Fees (In-State): $5,106
Enrollment: 1,060 — Coed
Affiliation or Control: State — IRS Status: 501(c)3
Highest Offering: Associate Degree

Accreditation: **HLC**, @CNEA, EMT

02 Campus Dean .... Dr. Jerry MIGLER
10 Director of Business Affairs .... Ms. Lisa MOCK
05 Assoc Dean Academic/Student Affairs .... Vacant
08 Librarian .... Ms. Hattie ALBERTSON
06 Registrar .... Ms. Heidi KIPPENHAN
37 Director Financial Aid .... Ms. April ABRAHAMSON
41 Athletic Director .... Mr. Corey GORDER
30 Director of Development .... Ms. Leslie STEVENS
39 Housing Director .... Ms. Bridget GUSTAFSON
28 Director of Diversity .... Vacant
40 Bookstore Manager .... Ms. Christina ENNA
18 Chief Facilities/Physical Plant .... Mr. Christopher NERO
38 Director Student Counseling .... Ms. Corey GORDER
04 Administrative Asst to President .... Ms. Sandy HAGENESS
106 Dir Online Education/E-learning .... Ms. Kayla O'TOOLE
25 Chief Contracts/Grants Admin .... Vacant
07 Director of Admissions .... Ms. Beth MACDONALD
13 Chief Information Technology Ofcr .... Mr. Brad GANGL

*Lake Region State College (A)

1801 College Drive N, Devils Lake ND 58301-1598
County: Ramsey — FICE Identification: 002991
Unit ID: 200192
Telephone: (701) 662-1600 — Carnegie Class: Assoc/MT-VT-High Non
FAX Number: (701) 662-1570 — Calendar System: Semester
URL: www.lrsc.edu
Established: 1941 — Annual Undergrad Tuition & Fees (In-State): $4,843
Enrollment: 1,771 — Coed
Affiliation or Control: State — IRS Status: 501(c)3
Highest Offering: Associate Degree
Accreditation: **HLC**, ADNUR

02 President .... Dr. Douglas D. DARLING
05 VP Academic/Student Affairs .... Mr. Lloyd HALVORSON
10 VP Administrative Affairs .... Mrs. Joann KITCHENS
12 Director of GFAFB Branch Campus .... Mr. John COWGER
102 Executive Director Foundation .... Ms. Elonda NORD
32 Assistant VP Student Affairs .... Mr. Daniel DRIESSEN
37 Dir Financial Aid/Placemnt Svcs .... Ms. Kelsey WALTERS
109 Director Food Service .... Ms. Rosalie SEIBEL
18 Director Physical Plant .... Mr. Chad ESTENSON
08 Librarian .... Mrs. Jolie JOHNSTON
41 Director Athletics .... Mr. Jared MARSHALL
13 Director of Information Technology .... Mr. Gary HAUGLAND
15 HR Risk Mgmt/Placement Svcs .... Mrs. Sandi LILLEHAUGEN
40 Director of Campus Store .... Mrs. Karen HANSON
06 Registrar .... Mr. Daniel JOHNSON
26 Director of College Relations/Mktg .... Ms. Erin WOOD
31 Dir Distance Educ/Outreach Svcs .... Vacant
20 Director of Academic Affairs .... Mrs. Jade ERICKSTAD
28 Director of Diversity .... Mr. Scott DUNBAR
38 Counseling Services .... Ms. Jessica DIMITCH
21 Controller .... Ms. Brandi NELSON
04 Administrative Asst to President .... Ms. Bobbi J. LUNDAY
29 Director Alumni Relations .... Ms. Elonda NORD
39 Director Student Housing .... Mr. Scott DUNBAR

*North Dakota State College of Science (B)

800 N Sixth Street, Wahpeton ND 58076-0002
County: Richland — FICE Identification: 002996
Unit ID: 200305
Telephone: (800) 342-4325 — Carnegie Class: Assoc/HVT-High Trad
FAX Number: (701) 671-2145 — Calendar System: Semester
URL: www.ndscs.edu
Established: 1903 — Annual Undergrad Tuition & Fees (In-State): $5,450
Enrollment: 2,829 — Coed
Affiliation or Control: State — IRS Status: 501(c)3
Highest Offering: Associate Degree
Accreditation: **HLC**, ADNUR, CAHIIM, DA, DH, EMT, OTA, PNUR

02 President .... Dr. Rod FLANIGAN
05 Vice Pres for Instruction .... Dr. Lisa KARCH
32 Vice Pres Student Affairs .... Dr. Jane VANGSNESS FRISCH
103 Vice Pres Workforce Development .... Vacant
10 Chief Financial Officer .... Mr. Keith JOHNSON
13 Chief Information Officer .... Mr. Cloy TOBOLA
37 Director Financial Aid .... Mrs. Shelley BLOME
29 Exec Dir of Alumni Foundation .... Mrs. Kim NELSON
41 Athletic Director .... Mr. Stuart ENGEN
15 Exec Dir Human Resources .... Mrs. Sandi GILBERTSON
18 Director Facilities/Physical Plant .... Mr. Andrew PEDERSEN
39 Exec Director of Residence Life .... Mrs. Melissa JOHNSON
49 Dean Arts Sciences/Business .... Vacant
64 Director of Music .... Mr. Bryan POYZER
04 Exec Assistant to the President .... Mrs. Kijia HOMES
08 Chief Library Officer .... Vacant
19 Director Security/Safety .... Mrs. Whitney LINK
26 Communications Manager .... Dr. Jane VANGNESS FRISCH
06 Registrar .... Mr. Mike PAOLINI

*Williston State College (C)

1410 University Avenue, Williston ND 58801-1326
County: Williams — FICE Identification: 003007
Unit ID: 200341
Telephone: (701) 774-4200 — Carnegie Class: Assoc/MT-VT-High Trad
FAX Number: (701) 774-4211 — Calendar System: Semester
URL: www.willistonstate.edu
Established: 1961 — Annual Undergrad Tuition & Fees (In-State): $5,528
Enrollment: 959 — Coed
Affiliation or Control: State — IRS Status: 501(c)3
Highest Offering: Associate Degree
Accreditation: **HLC**, @CNEA

02 President .... Dr. Bernell HIRNING
05 Vice President Academic Affairs .... Kimberli WRAY
10 Chief Financial Officer .... Riley YADON
32 Dean of Students .... Megan KASNER
102 Exec Director WSC Foundation .... Hunter BERG
103 Regional Director for Technical Pgm .... Kenley NEBEKER
37 Coord for Student Financial Aid .... Andrea CARVER
06 Registrar .... Jennifer NEBEKER
41 Athletic Director .... Jayden OLSON

Nueta Hidatsa Sahnish College (D)

PO Box 490, New Town ND 58763-0490
County: Mountrail — FICE Identification: 025537
Unit ID: 200086
Telephone: (701) 627-4738 — Carnegie Class: Tribal
FAX Number: (701) 627-3609 — Calendar System: Semester
URL: www.nhsc.edu
Established: 1973 — Annual Undergrad Tuition & Fees: $3,870
Enrollment: 179 — Coed
Affiliation or Control: Independent Non-Profit — IRS Status: 501(c)3
Highest Offering: Baccalaureate
Accreditation: **HLC**

01 President .... Dr. Twyla BAKER-DEMARAY
05 Vice Pres Academic Affairs .... Mr. Robert RAINBOW
32 Vice Pres Student Services .... Dr. Connie KING GOTTSCHALL
10 Comptroller .... Mr. Jeremy LEWIS
20 Academic Dean .... Dr. Kerry HARTMAN
25 Director Grants/Accreditation .... Dr. Stacey MORTENSEN
06 Registrar .... Ms. Joetta MCLEOD
37 Director Financial Aid .... Ms. Jacquelyn ZELTINGER
08 Director Library Services .... Ms. Amy SOLIS
124 Student Devel Retention Counselor .... Ms. Deanna RAINBOW
40 Bookstore Manager .... Ms. Iona LITTLE WHITEMAN

Rasmussen University - Fargo/Moorhead (E)

4012 19th Avenue South, Fargo ND 58103-7196
Telephone: (701) 277-3889 — FICE Identification: 004846
Accreditation: **&HLC**

† Regional acreditation is carried under parent institution in Saint Cloud, MN. The tuition figure is an average, actual tuition may vary.

Sitting Bull College (F)

9299 Highway 24, Fort Yates ND 58538-9706
County: Sioux — FICE Identification: 021882
Unit ID: 200466
Telephone: (701) 854-8000 — Carnegie Class: Tribal
FAX Number: (701) 854-8197 — Calendar System: Semester
URL: www.sittingbull.edu
Established: 1973 — Annual Undergrad Tuition & Fees: $4,010
Enrollment: 229 — Coed
Affiliation or Control: Tribal Control — IRS Status: 501(c)3
Highest Offering: Master's
Accreditation: **HLC**, @SW

01 President .... Dr. Laurel VERMILLION
11 Vice President Operations .... Dr. Koreen RESSLER
05 Academic Dean .... Dr. Shawn HOLTZ
37 Director Financial Student Aid .... Ms. Jazalyn CORLEY
06 Registrar .... Ms. Lisa MCLAUGHLIN
08 Librarian .... Ms. Jodi THUNDER HAWK
40 Director of Bookstore .... Mrs. Tracy MAHER
15 Human Resources Manager .... Ms. Elisabeth HERTEL

Trinity Bible College & Graduate School (G)

50 S 6th Avenue, Ellendale ND 58436-7150
County: Dickey — FICE Identification: 012059
Unit ID: 200484
Telephone: (701) 349-3621 — Carnegie Class: Spec-4-yr-Faith
FAX Number: (701) 349-5786 — Calendar System: Semester
URL: www.trinitybiblecollege.edu
Established: 1948 — Annual Undergrad Tuition & Fees: $17,340
Enrollment: 231 — Coed
Affiliation or Control: Assemblies Of God Church — IRS Status: 501(c)3
Highest Offering: Doctorate
Accreditation: **BI**

01 President .... Dr. Paul ALEXANDER
03 Executive Vice President .... Vacant
05 Vice President of Academic Affairs .... Dr. Bill HENNESSY
32 Vice Pres of Student Development .... Ms. Twyla KUNTZ
84 Director of Enrollment .... Rev. Matthew PAYNE
58 Dean of Graduate School .... Dr. Carol ALEXANDER
06 Academic Registrar .... Ms. Sara BEST
08 Librarian .... Mrs. Phyllis KUNO
18 Director of Facility Services .... Mr. Mike FERGEL
41 Athletic Director .... Mr. Jordan NOWELL
04 Admin Assistant to the President .... Mrs. Jessica M. SAYLOR
26 Director of Marketing .... Mrs. Maggie PAYNE
38 Director Student Counseling .... Ms. Amanda BELMONT
29 Director Alumni Affairs .... Mr. Bryan JACOBSON

Turtle Mountain Community College (H)

Box 340, Belcourt ND 58316-0340
County: Rolette — FICE Identification: 023011
Unit ID: 200527
Telephone: (701) 477-7862 — Carnegie Class: Tribal
FAX Number: (701) 477-7870 — Calendar System: Semester
URL: www.tm.edu
Established: 1972 — Annual Undergrad Tuition & Fees: $2,250
Enrollment: 586 — Coed
Affiliation or Control: Independent Non-Profit — IRS Status: 501(c)3
Highest Offering: Baccalaureate
Accreditation: **HLC**, MLTAD

01 Interim President .... Dr. Donna BROWN
03 Vice President .... Dr. Kellie M. HALL
05 Academic Dean .... Dr. Terri MARTIN PARISIEN
32 Dean of Student Affairs .... Wanda LADUCER
10 Comptroller .... Tracy AZURE
75 Director Vocational/Education .... Sheila TROTTIER
06 Registrar .... Angel GLADUE
51 Dir of Community/Adult Education .... Sandra LAROCQUE
07 Admissions Records Officer .... Joni LAFONTAINE
37 Financial Aid Director .... Sheila MORIN
40 Director of Bookstore .... Shirley MORIN
22 Title III Director .... Dave RIPLEY
04 Executive Assistant to President .... Vacant
101 Secretary of the Institution/Board .... Candace LONGIE
38 Director Student Counseling .... Dr. Andrea LAVERDURE
41 Athletic Director .... Pete DAVIS
09 Director of Institutional Research .... Ace CHARETTE
19 Safety/Compliance Officer .... Chris PARISIEN
08 Library Director .... Laisee ALLERY
13 IT Director .... Chad DAVIS
36 Placement Center Coordinator .... Mike VANDAL
53 Director of Teacher Education .... Dr. Teresa DELORME
15 Human Resources Manager .... Holly CAHILL
18 Facilities/Physical Plant Manager .... Wesley DAVIS

United Tribes Technical College (I)

3315 University Drive, Bismarck ND 58504-7596
County: Burleigh — FICE Identification: 022429
Unit ID: 200554
Telephone: (701) 255-3285 — Carnegie Class: Tribal
FAX Number: (701) 530-0605 — Calendar System: Semester
URL: www.uttc.edu
Established: 1969 — Annual Undergrad Tuition & Fees: $4,252
Enrollment: 326 — Coed
Affiliation or Control: Independent Non-Profit — IRS Status: 501(c)3
Highest Offering: Baccalaureate
Accreditation: **HLC**

01 President .... Dr. Leander MCDONALD
05 Vice Pres Academic Affairs .... Dr. Lisa AZURE
11 Vice Pres Campus Services .... Ms. Jolene DECOTEAU
10 Chief Financial Officer .... Mrs. Katina DECOTEAU
84 Dean of Enrollment Management .... Mr. Darko DRAGANIC
06 Registrar .... Ms. Aja BAKER
15 Human Resources Director .... Mrs. Rae GUNN
41 Athletic Director .... Mr. Pete CONWAY
19 Safety and Security Director .... Mr. Joely HEAVY RUNNER
04 Exec Assistant to the President .... Ms. Courtney LAWRENCE
08 Librarian .... Mrs. Charlene WEIS
20 Dean of Instruction .... Ms. Sheridan MCNEIL
37 Financial Aid Director .... Mr. Scott SKARRO
106 Director Distance Education .... Vacant
09 Director Institutional Research .... Ms. Leah WOODKE
39 Director Student Housing .... Ms. Melissa PLENTY CHIEF
18 Campus Planner .... Mr. Melvin MINER
26 College Relations Director .... Mr. Brent KLEINJAN
13 Information Technology Supervisor .... Mr. Brian DECOTEAU

University of Jamestown (J)

6000 College Lane, Jamestown ND 58405-0001
County: Stutsman — FICE Identification: 002990
Unit ID: 200156
Telephone: (701) 252-3467 — Carnegie Class: Masters/S
FAX Number: (701) 253-4318 — Calendar System: Semester
URL: www.uj.edu
Established: 1883 — Annual Undergrad Tuition & Fees: $23,498
Enrollment: 1,147 — Coed
Affiliation or Control: Presbyterian Church (U.S.A.) — IRS Status: 501(c)3
Highest Offering: Doctorate
Accreditation: **HLC**, NURSE, PTA

01 President .... Dr. Polly PETERSON
05 Provost .... Dr. Paul OLSON
32 VP Student Affairs .... Mr. Dustin JENSEN
20 Assoc Prov/Dean Undergraduate Col .. Dr. Christopher REDFEARN
84 Vice President of Enrollment Mgmt .... Mr. Greg ULLAND
30 VP Development and Alumni Relations .... Mr. Brett MOSER
26 Executive VP .... Ms. Tena LAWRENCE
101 Asst to Pres/Secy to Bd of Trustees .... Ms. Erin KLEIN
06 Registrar .... Mr. Michael P. WOODLEY
37 Director of Financial Aid .... Ms. Judy HAGER
08 Librarian .... Mrs. Tuya DUTTON
78 Director Experiential Education .... Dr. Heidi LARSON
27 Director of Design & Publications .... Ms. Donna SCHMITZ

41 Athletic Director .... Mr. Sean JOHNSON
13 Chief Information Officer .... Mr. Chris HOKE
18 Chief Facilities/Physical Plant .... Mr. Ramone GUNKE
105 Director Web Services .... Vacant
19 Director Security/Safety .... Ms. Nicole HEINLE
22 Dir Affirmative Action/EEO .... Ms. Becky KNODEL
39 Director Student Housing .... Vacant
108 Director of Assessment .... Ms. Anna ENGDAHL
29 Director of Alumni Relations .... Ms. Setareh CAMPION
44 Director Annual Giving .... Mr. Jim KLEMANN
88 Executive VP UJAccelerated .... Mr. Scott MEYER
10 Chief Financial/Business Officer .... Ms. Kresha WIEST
15 Director of Human Resources .... Ms. Becky L. KNODEL

University of Mary (A)

7500 University Drive, Bismarck ND 58504-9652
County: Burleigh
FICE Identification: 002992
Unit ID: 200217
Telephone: (701) 255-7500
Carnegie Class: DU-Mod
FAX Number: (701) 255-7687
Calendar System: Semester
URL: www.umary.edu
Established: 1959
Annual Undergrad Tuition & Fees: $19,830
Enrollment: 3,799
Coed
Affiliation or Control: Roman Catholic
IRS Status: 501(c)3
Highest Offering: Doctorate
Accreditation: **HLC**, CAATE, COARC, EXSC, IACBE, MUS, NURSE, OT, PTA, SP, SW

01 President .... Msgr. James P. SHEA
03 Executive Vice President .... Mr. Jerome J. RICHTER
05 Vice President for Academic Affairs .... Dr. Diane FLADELAND
10 Vice President Financial Affairs .... Mrs. Christi SCHAEFBAUER
32 Vice President Student Development .... Mr. Reed RUGGLES
26 Vice President for Public Affairs .... Mrs. Brenda K. NAGEL
30 Director of Mission Advancement .... Mr. Paul KEENEY
06 Registrar .... Ms. Melissa MCDOWALL
08 Librarian .... Ms. Nicole ECKROTH
37 Director of Financial Aid .... Mrs. Karrie K. HUBER
07 Director of Admissions .... Mrs. Alexis TIBOR
09 Director of Institutional Research .... Mr. James SORENSON
15 Director Human Resources .... Mrs. Tonya LINK
18 Chief Facilities/Physical Plant .... Mr. Luke SEIDLING
20 Associate Academic Officer .... Vacant
04 Assistant to the President .... Mr. Austin J. HOLGARD
50 Dean of Business .... Dr. Karel SOVAK
53 Dean of Education .... Dr. Rod JONAS
54 Dean of Engineering .... Dr. Terry PILLING

OHIO

Allegheny Wesleyan College (B)

2161 Woodsdale Road, Salem OH 44460-8920
County: Columbiana
FICE Identification: 034573
Unit ID: 200873
Telephone: (330) 337-6403
Carnegie Class: Spec-4-yr-Faith
FAX Number: (424) 228-3006
Calendar System: Semester
URL: www.awc.edu
Established: 1956
Annual Undergrad Tuition & Fees: $6,800
Enrollment: 67
Coed
Affiliation or Control: Wesleyan Church
IRS Status: 501(c)3
Highest Offering: Baccalaureate
Accreditation: **BI**

01 President .... Rev. Daniel R. HARDY, SR.
05 Academic Dean .... Mrs. Jeanne W. ZVARITCH
10 Business Manager .... Miss Katrina KAUFMAN
32 Dean of Students .... Rev. Timothy FORRIDER
30 Director of Development .... Mr. Tom SANDERS
06 Registrar & Director Admissions .... Mr. James DENTLER
08 Head Librarian .... Mrs. Crystal WHITHAM
37 Financial Aid Administrator .... Mrs. Esther PHELPS
09 Dir of Institutional Effectiveness .... Mrs. Jeanne ZVARITCH
40 Bookstore Manager .... Rev. Daniel GILES
33 Dean of Men .... Mr. Timothy HARTLEY
34 Dean of Women .... Miss Bethany PETERS
07 Director of Admissions .... Mr. James DENTLER
18 Chief Facilities/Physical Plant .... Mr. Darrin PATTERSON
29 Director Alumni Relations .... Rev. Douglas STRAWN
38 Director Student Counseling .... Mrs. Kimberly FORD
04 Admin Assistant to the President .... Mr. Paul DUNCAN
13 Chief Information Tech Officer .... Mr. Matt DAVIS
84 Director Enrollment Management .... Mr. Tom SANDERS
15 Chief Human Resources Officer .... Miss Katrina KAUFMAN

American Institute of Alternative Medicine (C)

6685 Doubletree Avenue, Columbus OH 43229-1113
County: Franklin
FICE Identification: 035344
Unit ID: 441636
Telephone: (614) 825-6255
Carnegie Class: Spec-4-yr-Other Health
FAX Number: (614) 825-6279
Calendar System: Quarter
URL: www.aiam.edu
Established: 1994
Annual Undergrad Tuition & Fees: $14,338
Enrollment: 341
Coed
Affiliation or Control: Proprietary
IRS Status: Proprietary
Highest Offering: Master's
Accreditation: **ACCSC**, ACUP

00 Chief Executive Officer .... Diane SATER-WEE
01 Campus President .... Dr. Ralynn ERNEST
05 Academic Dean .... Dr. Elaine HIATT
32 Asst Director of Educ/Student Svcs .... Melissa FISCHER
21 Controller .... Barry COOK
37 Director of Financial Aid .... Debbie BREWER
06 Registrar .... James BROOKS
66 Director of Nursing .... Pamela FROST
08 Library Manager .... Melissa FISCHER

American Winds College of Aeronautics (D)

1600 B Triplett Boulevard, Akron OH 44306
County: Summit
Identification: 667401
Telephone: (330) 733-2500
Carnegie Class: Not Classified
FAX Number: (330) 733-2501
Calendar System: Quarter
URL: www.americanwinds.edu
Established:
Annual Undergrad Tuition & Fees: N/A
Enrollment: N/A
Coed
Affiliation or Control: Proprietary
IRS Status: Proprietary
Highest Offering: Associate Degree
Accreditation: **CNCE**

01 President .... Denise HOBART
121 VP Student of Success/Admissions .... Kelly SIZEMORE

Antioch College (E)

One Morgan Place, Yellow Springs OH 45387
County: Greene
Identification: 667214
Unit ID: 483018
Telephone: (937) 767-1286
Carnegie Class: Bac-A&S
FAX Number: N/A
Calendar System: Quarter
URL: www.antiochcollege.edu
Established: 1853
Annual Undergrad Tuition & Fees: $37,143
Enrollment: 116
Coed
Affiliation or Control: Independent Non-Profit
IRS Status: 501(c)3
Highest Offering: Baccalaureate
Accreditation: **HLC**

01 President .... Dr. Jane FERNANDES
05 Vice Pres Academic Affairs .... Dr. David KAMMLER
111 Acting VP Advancement/Dir Alum Rels .... Ms. April WOLFORD
32 Vice Pres Student Affairs/Diversity .... Ms. Mila COOPER
84 Vice Pres Enrollment/Stdnt Success .... Dr. Gariot LOUIMA
06 Registrar .... Ms. Donna EVANS
10 Vice Pres Operations & Business .... Ms. Hannah SPIRRISON MONTGOMERY
13 Dir Information Technology .... Mr. Kevin STOKES
37 Director of Financial Aid .... Mr. Matthew DEC
15 Director of Human Resources .... Ms. Mindi HIXSON
04 Exec Asst to President/BOT .... Ms. Anita BROWN

Antioch University (F)

900 Dayton Street, Yellow Springs OH 45387-1635
County: Greene
FICE Identification: 003010
Unit ID: 442392
Telephone: (937) 769-1800
Carnegie Class: Spec-4-yr-Bus
FAX Number: (937) 769-1806
Calendar System: Semester
URL: www.antioch.edu
Established:
Annual Undergrad Tuition & Fees: N/A
Enrollment: 157
Coed
Affiliation or Control: Independent Non-Profit
IRS Status: 501(c)3
Highest Offering: Doctorate
Accreditation: **HLC**, ACATE, CACREP, CLPSY, MFCD

01 Chancellor .... Mr. William GROVES
05 Vice Chancellor Academic Affairs .... Dr. Chet HASKELL
10 Vice Chancellor/CFO .... Dr. Allan GOZUM
15 Vice Chancellor Human Resources .... Ms. Maria-Judith RODRIGUEZ
13 Director IT/Chief Information Ofcr .... Mr. Rodney FOWLKES
04 Exec Asst to the Executive Team .... Ms. Judy OWENS
06 Registrar .... Ms. Maureen HEACOCK
08 Head Librarian .... Ms. Dana KNOTT
101 Exec Asst to Chancellor & Board .... Ms. Leslie BATES
111 Director Institutional Advancement .... Ms. Laura ANDREWS
37 Director Student Financial Aid .... Mr. Donald RONAN
26 Dir Mktg Content/Communications .... Ms. Karen HAMILTON

† Parent institution of Antioch University Midwest in OH; Antioch University Seattle in WA; Antioch University New England in NH; and Antioch University Los Angeles and Antioch University Santa Barbara in CA.

Art Academy of Cincinnati (G)

1212 Jackson Street, Cincinnati OH 45202-7106
County: Hamilton
FICE Identification: 003011
Unit ID: 201061
Telephone: (513) 562-6262
Carnegie Class: Spec-4-yr-Arts
FAX Number: (513) 562-8778
Calendar System: Semester
URL: www.artacademy.edu
Established: 1869
Annual Undergrad Tuition & Fees: $34,854
Enrollment: 235
Coed
Affiliation or Control: Independent Non-Profit
IRS Status: 501(c)3
Highest Offering: Master's
Accreditation: **HLC**, ART

01 President .... Mr. Joe GIRANDOLA
05 VP for Academic Affairs/CAO .... Ms. Paige WILLIAMS
11 VP Administration and Finance .... Mrs. Lea WAGNER
07 VP Admissions and Retention .... Dr. Chris BRIDGES
37 Director of Financial Aid .... Mr. Jeff ALBERS
06 Director of Registrar Services .... Mr. Alex SIEBERT
21 Accounting Specialist .... Mrs. Rose EMORY
15 Human Resources Generalist .... Ms. Linda KOLLMANN
32 Director of Student Services .... Mr. Rickie PLEASANT
113 Student Accounts Specialist .... Vacant
04 Executive Assistant to President .... Ms. Lacey HASLAM
105 Website Manager .... Mr. Jimmy BAKER
13 Director of IT .... Mr. Stewart HEMMERT
88 Office Manager .... Ms. Wendy TAYLOR-REIDY
26 Director of Marketing .... Mr. Nicholas KORN
28 Associate Director of Diversity .... Ms. Anissa LEWIS
29 Alumni Coordinator .... Ms. Jacquelyn SOMMER
36 Assoc Director of Professional Dev .... Ms. Audrey BERTAUX
38 Mental Health Counselor .... Ms. Casey RIORDAN

Ashland University (H)

401 College Avenue, Ashland OH 44805
County: Ashland
FICE Identification: 003012
Unit ID: 201104
Telephone: (419) 289-4142
Carnegie Class: Masters/L
FAX Number: (419) 289-5099
Calendar System: Semester
URL: www.ashland.edu
Established: 1878
Annual Undergrad Tuition & Fees: $23,060
Enrollment: 4,447
Coed
Affiliation or Control: Brethren Church
IRS Status: 501(c)3
Highest Offering: Doctorate
Accreditation: **HLC**, ACBSP, #ARCPA, CAATE, CACREP, CAEP, DIETD, MUS, NURSE, SW, THEOL

01 President .... Dr. Carlos CAMPO
73 Dean of the Seminary .... Dr. John BYRON
05 Provost .... Dr. Amiel JARSTFER
32 Vice President Student Affairs .... Dr. Robert POOL
111 Vice President Inst Advancement .... Mrs. Margaret POMFRET
84 Vice President Enrollment Mgmt/Mktg .... Mr. Keith RAMSDELL
18 Vice Pres Facilities/Mgmt & Plng .... Mr. Rick M. EWING, II
88 Vice President of Correctional Educ .... Dr. Todd MARSHALL
10 CFO .... Mr. Marc PASTERIS
13 Chief Tech & Info Officer .... Vacant
42 Director Religious Life .... Dr. Charles NEFF
37 Director Student Financial Aid .... Mr. Stephen C. HOWELL
29 Director Alumni Engagement .... Mr. Jeff ALIX
26 Director Marketing/Communications .... Ms. Karen MARTIN
15 Director of Human Resources/Legal .... Mr. Joshua A. HUGHES
36 Director Career Services .... Vacant
26 Director Public Relations .... Vacant
41 Director Athletics .... Mr. Albert KING
88 Exec Director Ashbrook Center .... Dr. Jeff SIKKENGA
09 Director Inst Research & Assessment .... Dr. Larry BUNCE
07 Director Admissions .... Mr. Wray BLAIR
123 Director Graduate Admissions .... Mr. Bernard BANNIN
49 Dean College Arts & Sciences .... Dr. Dawn WEBER
106 Interim Dean Online & Adult Studies .... Ms. Shawn ORR
50 Dean College Business/Econ .... Dr. Elad GRANOT
53 Interim Dean College Education .... Mr. Steve DENNEY
66 Dean Col Nursing & Health Sci .... Dr. Carrie KEIB
51 Exec Director Prof Development .... Dr. James POWELL
19 Director Security/Safety .... Mr. David B. MCLAUGHLIN
38 Director Counseling .... Dr. Oscar MCKNIGHT
112 Associate Director Planned Giving .... Mrs. Amy CLARK
39 Director Residence Life .... Mrs. Christy GRUNDY
102 Chief Corporate Relations Officer .... Dr. Dan LAWSON
104 Director Study Abroad .... Ms. Rebecca PARILLO
122 Assistant Director Greek Life .... Mr. Dustin HARGIS
25 Dir Univ Grants & Foundation Rels .... Mrs. Sharon LOWE
06 Registrar .... Mr. Mark BRITTON
08 Director Library .... Mr. Scott SAVAGE
109 Director Auxiliary Services .... Mr. Matthew PORTNER
40 Bookstore Manager .... Ms. Amanda BROWN
85 Director Foreign Students .... Mr. Scott PARILLO
121 Director Academic Support .... Ms. Megan SHERAR
04 Director Office of the President .... Mr. Aaron ROSS
28 Director Diversity .... Vacant
30 Associate VP Development .... Mr. Jason MILLER
44 Interim Director Annual Giving .... Ms. Allison GOURNIAK

ATA College (I)

225 Pictoria Drive Suite 200, Cincinnati OH 45246
Telephone: (513) 671-1920
Identification: 666673
Accreditation: **ABHES**

† Branch campus of ATA College, Louisville, KY.

Athena Career Academy (J)

5203 Airport Highway, Toledo OH 43615
County: Lucas
FICE Identification: 041922
Unit ID: 476683
Telephone: (419) 329-4075
Carnegie Class: Spec 2-yr-Other
FAX Number: N/A
Calendar System: Quarter
URL: athenacareers.edu
Established:
Annual Undergrad Tuition & Fees: N/A
Enrollment: N/A
Coed
Affiliation or Control: Proprietary
IRS Status: Proprietary
Highest Offering: Associate Degree
Accreditation: **COE**

Athenaeum of Ohio (A)

6616 Beechmont Avenue, Cincinnati OH 45230-5900
County: Hamilton FICE Identification: 003013
Unit ID: 201140
Telephone: (513) 231-2223 Carnegie Class: Spec-4-yr-Faith
FAX Number: (513) 231-3254 Calendar System: Semester
URL: www.athenaeum.edu
Established: 1829 Annual Graduate Tuition & Fees: N/A
Enrollment: 160 Coed
Affiliation or Control: Roman Catholic IRS Status: 501(c)3
Highest Offering: Master's; No Undergraduates
Accreditation: HLC, THEOL

01 President & Rector ... V.Rev. Anthony R. BRAUSCH
05 Academic Dean ... Rev. David ENDRES
10 Business Manager ... Mr. Martin DORSEY
73 Dean of the School of Theology ... Rev. Ryan RUIZ
111 VP Development/Advancement ... Dr. Lori RASSATI
32 Dean of Students ... Rev. Daniel HESS
08 Head Librarian ... Mrs. Connie SONG
13 Chief Information Technology Ofcr ... Mr. Ken BIRCK
44 Director of the Annual Fund ... Mr. Justin HANKS
06 Registrar & Director of Assessment ... Mr. Jeffrey ROYER

Aultman College of Nursing and Health Sciences (B)

2600 Sixth Street SW, Canton OH 44710-1799
County: Stark FICE Identification: 006487
Unit ID: 201177
Telephone: (330) 363-6347 Carnegie Class: Spec-4-yr-Other Health
FAX Number: (330) 580-6654 Calendar System: Semester
URL: www.aultmancollege.edu
Established: 2004 Annual Undergrad Tuition & Fees: $18,950
Enrollment: 355 Coed
Affiliation or Control: Independent Non-Profit IRS Status: 501(c)3
Highest Offering: Baccalaureate
Accreditation: HLC, ADNUR, NURSE, RAD, @SW

01 President ... Dr. Jean PADDOCK
10 VP Business & Student Affairs ... Jeannine SHAMBAUGH
05 VP Academic Affairs ... Dr. Brock REIMAN
06 Registrar and Data Management ... Christine COURT
13 Director of Information Technology ... Jacqui KRUMPELMAN
121 Dean of Student Success ... Sue SHEPHERD
37 Director Finance and Financial Aid ... Wendy DAVIS
49 Dean Foundational Educ & Profession ... Dr. Theresa BENZEL
66 Dean of Nursing ... Dr. Joann DONNENWIRTH

Baldwin Wallace University (C)

275 Eastland Road, Berea OH 44017-2088
County: Cuyahoga FICE Identification: 003014
Unit ID: 201195
Telephone: (440) 826-2900 Carnegie Class: Masters/L
FAX Number: (440) 826-3777 Calendar System: Semester
URL: www.bw.edu/
Established: 1845 Annual Undergrad Tuition & Fees: $34,504
Enrollment: 3,399 Coed
Affiliation or Control: Independent Non-Profit IRS Status: 501(c)3
Highest Offering: Master's
Accreditation: HLC, ARCPA, CAEP, EXSC, MUS, NURSE, SP

01 President ... Dr. Robert C. HELMER
05 Provost ... Dr. Stephen D. STAHL
10 Vice President for Finance & Admin ... Mr. William M. RENIFF
32 Vice Pres of Student Affairs ... Dr. Timeka RASHID
84 Vice Pres of Enrollment Management ... Dr. Scott SCHULZ
111 Interim Vice Pres for Advancement ... Mrs. Ellen ZEGARRA
26 Asst VP/Director College Relations ... Mr. Dan KARP
20 Associate Provost ... Dr. Lisa HENDERSON
89 Dean of First Year Students ... Mr. Marc WEST
51 Director of Adult Learning ... Ms. Nancy JIROUSEK
08 Director of Ritter Library ... Mr. Charles VESEI
13 Chief Information Officer ... Mr. Greg G. FLANIK
44 Director Annual Giving ... Ms. Ann MILLER
29 Assoc Director Alumni Relations ... Ms. Lisa JUDGE
30 Senior Advancement Officer ... Mrs. Ellen ZEGARRA
37 Director of Financial Aid ... Mr. William MCGINLEY
15 Chief Talent Officer ... Mr. Jeremy SHORT
38 Director of Counseling Services ... Ms. Sophia D. KALLERGIS
121 Coordinator of Academic Advising ... Ms. Dianna SPYCHER
06 Registrar ... Mr. Tim SEITZ
07 Director UG Enrollment ... Ms. Joyce CENDROSKI
123 Assoc Dir Tr/Adult & Grad Admission ... Ms. Katelyn GLASER
18 Director of Buildings & Grounds ... Mr. Randy HUDAK
88 Director of Intercultural Education ... Dr. Javier MORALES-ORTIZ
96 Director of Purchasing ... Ms. Karen STENGER
28 Director Campus Diversity Affairs ... Vacant
04 Administrative Asst to President ... Ms. Kimberlee A. KUHAJDA
09 Director of Institutional Research ... Ms. Susan T. WARNER
104 Director Study Abroad ... Ms. Christy L. SHREFLER
39 Director Student Housing ... Mr. Robin W. GAGNOW
102 Dir Foundation/Corporate Relations ... Ms. Ellen ZEGARRA
19 Director Security/Safety ... Mr. Gary BLACK
41 Athletic Director ... Mr. Steve THOMPSON
50 Dean of School of Business ... Dr. Frank BRAUN
53 Dean of School of Education ... Dr. Michael SMITH
36 Director Career Services ... Mr. Patrick KEEBLER
122 Dir Student Life/Involve-Greek Life ... Mr. Marc WEST

Belmont College (D)

68094 Hammond Road, Saint Clairsville OH 43950-9766
County: Belmont FICE Identification: 009941
Unit ID: 201283
Telephone: (740) 695-9500 Carnegie Class: Assoc/HVT-Mix Trad/Non
FAX Number: (740) 695-2247 Calendar System: Semester
URL: www.belmontcollege.edu
Established: 1969 Annual Undergrad Tuition & Fees (In-State): $4,218
Enrollment: 802 Coed
Affiliation or Control: State IRS Status: 501(c)3
Highest Offering: Associate Degree
Accreditation: HLC, EMT, MAC, RAD

01 President & CEEO ... Dr. Paul F. GASPARRO
05 Provost ... Dr. Jeremy VITTEK
11 Vice Pres of Administrative Affairs ... Vacant
15 VP Organizational Effectiveness ... Mrs. Judi MCMULLEN
26 Mgr of Marketing & Strategic Comm ... Mrs. Julie L. KECK
32 Dean of Student Affairs ... Mrs. Bridgette DAWSON
20 Dean of Academic Affairs ... Dr. Jesse GIPKO
09 Institutional Research/Plng Analyst ... Dr. Matthew WILLIAMSON
06 Registrar ... Ms. Jennifer NIPPERT
37 Director of Financial Aid ... Ms. Danielle MOORE
121 Transfer/Articulat/Academic Advisor ... Vacant
13 Exec Dir of Info Svcs & Security ... Mr. Troy CALDWELL
04 Exec Asst to President ... Ms. Kristy KOSKY
11 Director of Operations ... Vacant

Bluffton University (E)

1 University Drive, Bluffton OH 45817-2104
County: Allen FICE Identification: 003016
Unit ID: 201371
Telephone: (419) 358-3000 Carnegie Class: Bac-Diverse
FAX Number: (419) 358-3323 Calendar System: Semester
URL: www.bluffton.edu
Established: 1899 Annual Undergrad Tuition & Fees: $34,502
Enrollment: 750 Coed
Affiliation or Control: Mennonite Church IRS Status: 501(c)3
Highest Offering: Master's
Accreditation: HLC, CAEP, @DIET, DIETD, MUS, SW

01 President ... Dr. Jane WOOD
10 Interim VP Fiscal Affairs ... Mr. John BURKHART
111 Vice Pres Advancement & Enroll Mgmt ... Ms. Robin BOWLUS
05 Vice Pres & Dean Academic Affairs ... Dr. Lamar NISLY
32 VP Student Life & Athletics ... Mr. Phillip TALAVINIA
08 Director of Libraries ... Ms. Carrie PHILLIPS
06 Registrar ... Ms. Iris NEUFELD
26 Dir PR & Advancement Operations ... Ms. Claire CLAY
18 Director Building/Grounds ... Mr. Steven HEINZE
15 Director Human Resources ... Ms. Tracey JORDAN
04 Director of President's Office ... Ms. Karen BONTRAGER
13 Chief Info Technology Officer (CIO) ... Vacant
36 Director Student Placement ... Vacant
39 Director of Residence Life ... Mr. Steve BURRELL
44 Annual Fund Coordinator ... Vacant
105 Director Web Services ... Ms. Sara KISSEBERTH
37 Director of Financial Aid ... Mr. Lawrence MATTHEWS

Bowling Green State University (F)

220 McFall Center, Bowling Green OH 43403-0001
County: Wood FICE Identification: 003018
Unit ID: 201441
Telephone: (419) 372-2211 Carnegie Class: DU-Higher
FAX Number: (419) 372-6050 Calendar System: Semester
URL: www.bgsu.edu
Established: 1910 Annual Undergrad Tuition & Fees (In-State): $11,573
Enrollment: 18,142 Coed
Affiliation or Control: State IRS Status: 501(c)3
Highest Offering: Doctorate
Accreditation: HLC, AAB, ART, CAATE, CACREP, CAEPN, CLPSY, CONST, COSMA, DIETD, DIETI, EXSC, FEPAC, IPSY, JOUR, MLS, MUS, NAIT, NURSE, @PTA, SP, SPAA, SW, THEA

01 President ... Dr. Rodney K. ROGERS
05 Sr VP Academic Affairs/Provost ... Dr. Joe B. WHITEHEAD, JR.
10 CFO/VP Finance & Admin ... Ms. Sherideen S. STOLL
100 VP Partnerships/Chief of Staff ... Dr. Sue HOUSTON
32 Vice President Student Affairs ... Vacant
04 Executive Asst to President ... Ms. Laurel E. ZAWODNY
111 VP Univ Advancement ... Ms. Pam CONLIN
84 VP Enrollment Management ... Ms. Cecilia CASTELLANO
20 Vice Provost Academic Affairs ... Dr. Glenn DAVIS
35 Dean of Students ... Mr. Chris BULLINS
11 Asst VP for Campus Operations ... Dr. Andrea DEPINET
26 Asst VP for Mktg & Brand Stratgy ... Ms. Amy WEST
30 Exec Dir Donor Rels & Stewardship ... Ms. Laura J. MOORE
46 VP Research & Econ Engagement ... Vacant
88 Dir Recreation and Wellness ... Mr. David HOLLINGER
41 Director of Athletics ... Vacant
15 Chief Human Resources Officer ... Ms. Viva MCCARVER
39 Director of Residence Life ... Mr. Joshua LAWRIE
45 VP Capital Planning/Campus Ops ... Ms. April SMUCKER
13 Chief Information Officer ... Mr. John M. ELLINGER
43 General Counsel ... Ms. Natalie JACKSON
58 Dean Graduate College ... Dr. Jennifer J. WALDRON
49 Dean College Arts/Sciences ... Dr. Ellen SCHENDEL
50 Dean College Business Admin ... Dr. Jennifer PERCIVAL
88 Director Service Learning ... Dr. Virginia J. ROSSER
53 Dean Col of Educ & Human Dev ... Dr. Dawn SHINEW
12 Dean Firelands College ... Dr. Andrew KURTZ
69 Dean College Hlth/Human Svcs ... Dr. James CIESLA
08 Dean University Libraries ... Ms. Sara BUSHONG
64 Dean College of Musical Arts ... Dr. William MATHIS
72 Dean College of TAAE ... Dr. Jennie GALLIMORE
57 Director of School of Art ... Mr. Charlie KANWISCHER
60 Dir Sch of Media & Communication ... Dr. Laura STAFFORD
88 Dir Sch Human Move/Sport/Leisure ... Dr. Ray SCHNEIDER
88 Dir Sch Family & Consumer Sciences ... Dr. Deborah G. WOOLDRIDGE
88 Dir Sch Educ Fnds/Leadership/Policy ... Dr. Patrick PAUKEN
53 Dir Sch of Teaching & Learning ... Dr. Mark SEALS
92 Dean Honors College ... Dr. Simon MORGAN-RUSSELL
106 Assoc Director eCampus ... Dr. Sheri ORWICK OGDEN
85 Exec Dir International Student Svcs ... Dr. Marcia SALAZAR-VALENTINE
21 Exec Dir of Business Operations ... Mr. Bradley K. LEIGH
07 Director Admissions ... Ms. Adrea SPOON
114 Dir Budgeting & Resource Planning ... Ms. Sharon SWARTZ
06 University Registrar ... Ms. Michelle RABLE
40 Retail Sales/Cust Svc Mgr Bookstore ... Ms. Lori NAUGLE
19 Director Public Safety ... Mr. Michael A. CAMPBELL
36 Director Career Center ... Ms. Danielle DIMOFF
38 Int Director/Training Director ... Dr. Denise LITTERER
37 Dir Student Financial Aid ... Dr. Betsy JOHNSON
23 Asst Director Center for Health ... Ms. Marlene REYNOLDS
44 Director of Annual Giving ... Vacant
101 Secretary to the Board ... Dr. Patrick PAUKEN
88 Co-Gen Manager WBGU Public Media ... Vacant
88 Co-Gen Manager WBGU Public Media ... Ms. Tina L. SIMON
88 Director Trio Programs ... Ms. Victoria AMPIAW
116 Internal Auditing & Adv Svcs ... Mr. James LAMBERT
88 Director Women's Center ... Vacant
22 Director Accessibility Svcs ... Ms. Peggy DENNIS
88 Director Marvin Center/Leadership ... Dr. Jacob E. CLEMENS
109 Director Dining Services ... Mr. Richard ROLDAN
96 Director of Business Operations ... Mr. Phillip WORLEY
88 Director Student Employment ... Ms. Dawn FRIESON
88 Director Learning Commons ... Mr. Travis BROWN
121 Director Advising Services ... Mr. Dermot M. FORDE
88 Asst VP Non-Trad & Transfer Svcs ... Dr. Barbara L. HENRY
09 Director Institutional Research ... Dr. Oyebanjo A. LAJUBUTU
65 Dir Sch Earth/Environ & Society ... Dr. Jeffrey SNYDER
112 AVP for Development ... Ms. Robin STOCK
28 AVP Equity/Div/Incl/Title IX Coord ... Ms. Jennifer Q. MCCARY
35 Assoc VP Student Affairs ... Ms. Jodi WEBB
122 Coord Fraternity/Sorority Life ... Ms. Courtney TAYLOR

Bowling Green State University Firelands College (G)

One University Drive, Huron OH 44839-9719
Telephone: (419) 433-5560 FICE Identification: 007856
Accreditation: &HLC, COARC, DMS

† Regional accreditation is carried under the parent institution in Bowling Green, OH.

Bryant & Stratton College (H)

12955 Snow Road, Parma OH 44130-1013
Telephone: (216) 265-3151 FICE Identification: 022744
Accreditation: &M, ADNUR, MAC, NURSE, PNUR, PTAA

† Regional accreditation is carried under the parent institution (corporate office) in Buffalo, NY.

Capital University (I)

1 College and Main Street, Columbus OH 43209-2394
County: Franklin FICE Identification: 003023
Unit ID: 201548
Telephone: (614) 236-6011 Carnegie Class: Masters/L
FAX Number: N/A Calendar System: Semester
URL: www.capital.edu
Established: 1850 Annual Undergrad Tuition & Fees: $38,298
Enrollment: 3,020 Coed
Affiliation or Control: Evangelical Lutheran Church In America
IRS Status: 501(c)3
Highest Offering: First Professional Degree
Accreditation: HLC, ACBSP, CAATE, CAEP, LAW, MUS, NURSE, SW, THEOL

01 President ... Mr. David L. KAUFMAN
05 Provost & VP for Learning ... Dr. Jody FOURNIER
10 Vice President Business & Finance ... Mr. William MEA
43 University Counsel & Vice President ... Dr. Tanya J. POTEET
84 VP Strategic Enrollment Mgmt & Mktg ... Mr. Jean-Paul SPAGNOLO
111 Vice Pres Inst Advancement ... Ms. Jennifer PATTERSON
04 Exec Assistant to President ... Ms. Melissa LUNG
20 Sr Assoc Provost ... Dr. Terry D. LAHM
21 Asst VP Business & Finance ... Mr. Erin DELFFS
30 Assoc Vice President Development ... Ms. April NOVOTNY
26 Dir of Communications/Media Rels ... Ms. Denise RUSSELL
09 Director of Institutional Research ... Dr. Larry T. HUNTER
06 Associate Registrar ... Ms. Cindy LAH
07 Assoc Director of Admissions ... Ms. Deanna BOND
29 Assoc Director of Alumni Engagement ... Ms. Kyrsten ROBINETTE
36 Director of Career Services ... Mr. Eric R. ANDERSON
08 Head of Library ... Mr. Matt COOK
121 Director Academic Success ... Mr. Bruce EPPS
41 Assoc Athletic Director ... Ms. Dixie JEFFERS

13 Assoc Director Client Services ..... Mr. Rob AHERN
85 Director Intl Education & ESL ..... Ms. Jennifer ADAMS
32 Dean Engagement & Success ..... Ms. Deanna WAGNER
18 Director Facilities Management ..... Mr. Paul MATTHEWS
15 Director Human Resources ..... Mr. Mark PRINGLE
38 Dir Univ Counseling/Health Svcs ..... Dr. Cathy MCDANIELS WILSON
28 Director Diversity and Inclusion ..... Mr. Ralph COCHRAN
40 Manager Bookstore ..... Ms. Cassandra STRALEY
42 University Pastor ..... Mr. Andrew TUCKER
61 Dean of Law School ..... Mr. Reynaldo VALENCIA
64 Interim Dean of the Conservatory ..... Dr. Tom ZUGGER
53 Chair Department of Education ..... Dr. James WIGHTMAN
66 Dean School of Nursing ..... Dr. Renee DUNNINGTON
102 Dir Foundation/Corporate Relations ..... Mr. Gregory WINSLOW
108 Assoc Provost Accred & Analytics ..... Dr. Jens HEMMINGSEN
22 Asst Provost/Title IX Coordinator ..... Ms. Jennifer SPEAKMAN
19 Director Security/Safety ..... Mr. Frank FERNANDEZ
105 Assoc Director Web & Digital Svcs ..... Mr. Russel PEPPER
39 Director Residential & Comm Life ..... Mr. Jon GEYER
50 Dean School of Management & Ldrshp ..... Dr. Sherry PECK
37 Director Financial Aid ..... Mr. John BROWN
122 Assoc Dir Fraternity/Sorority Life ..... Mr. Matt RHYAND

Capital University Law School (A)

303 East Broad Street, Columbus OH 43215
Telephone: (614) 236-6500 Identification: 770347
Accreditation: &HLC

Case Western Reserve University (B)

10900 Euclid Avenue, Cleveland OH 44106-7001
County: Cuyahoga FICE Identification: 003024
Unit ID: 201645
Telephone: (216) 368-2000 Carnegie Class: DU-Highest
FAX Number: N/A Calendar System: Semester
URL: www.case.edu
Established: 1826 Annual Undergrad Tuition & Fees: $52,948
Enrollment: 11,465 Coed
Affiliation or Control: Independent Non-Profit IRS Status: 501(c)3
Highest Offering: Doctorate
Accreditation: HLC, AA, ANEST, ARCPA, CAEP, CAMPEP, CLPSY, DENT, DIETD, DIETI, IPSY, LAW, MED, MIDWF, MUS, NURSE, PH, SP, SW

01 President ..... Dr. Eric W. KALER
100 VP & Chief of Staff ..... Ms. Katie M. BRANCATO
05 Provost/Executive Vice President ..... Dr. Ben VINSON, III
10 Exec VP for Finance & CFO ..... Mr. John F. SIDERAS
30 Sr VP Univ Relations & Development ..... Ms. Carol L. MOSS
17 Sr VP Medical Affairs/Dean Medicine ..... Dr. Stanton L. GERSON
46 Int Vice President for Research ... Dr. James MCGUFFIN CAWLEY
13 Interim VP Utech/CIO ..... Mr. Miro HUMER
84 Vice Pres for Enrollment ..... Mr. Richard W. BISCHOFF
32 Vice President for Student Affairs ..... Mr. Louis W. STARK
18 Int VP Campus Plng/Facility Mgmt ..... Mr. Chris PANICHI
15 Vice President for Human Resources ..... Ms. Carolyn GREGORY
43 General Counsel/Secretary ..... Mr. Peter G. POULOS
19 Vice President for Campus Services ..... Mr. Richard J. JAMIESON
26 VP Univ Marketing & Communications ..... Ms. Chris SHERIDAN
86 Asst VP Government Relations ..... Ms. Jennifer RUGGLES
31 Asst VP Local Govt/Community Rels ..... Mr. Julian ROGERS
29 Sr Exec Director Alumni Relations ..... Mr. Bradford CREWS
45 Assoc VP Univ Plng & Administration ..... Ms. Victoria WRIGHT
28 VP Inclusion/Diversity/Equal Oppty ..... Mr. Robert L. SOLOMON
22 Asst Vice Pres & Director of Equity ..... Vacant
27 Dir Media Relations/Communications ..... Mr. Bill LUBINGER
21 Treasurer ..... Mr. Michael J. LEE
115 Deputy Chief Investment Officer ..... Mr. Timothy R. MILANICH
20 Vice Provost Undergrad Education ..... Dr. Donald L. FEKE
82 Vice Prov International Affairs ..... Mr. David FLESHLER
97 Dean of Undergraduate Studies ..... Dr. Jeffrey WOLCOWITZ
21 Controller ..... Ms. Patricia L. KOST
06 Registrar ..... Ms. Amy S. HAMMETT
37 Director of Financial Aid ..... Ms. Venus PULIAFICO
07 Director Undergraduate Admissions ..... Mr. Robert R. MCCULLOUGH
08 University Librarian & Vice Prov ..... Ms. Yolanda COOPER
121 Vice Provost of Student Success ..... Dr. Thomas MATTHEWS
85 Dir International Student Svcs ..... Ms. Marielena MAGGIO
38 Exec Dir Univ Health & Counsel Svcs ..... Dr. Sara LEE
09 Int Dir of Institutional Research ..... Dr. Edward BOLDEN
96 Interim Procurement Mgr ..... Mr. Simon FRITZ
41 Athletic Director ..... Mr. TJ SHELTON
61 Co-Dean of Law ..... Mr. Michael P. SCHARF
61 Co-Dean of Law ..... Ms. Jessica W. BERG
49 Dean of Arts & Sciences ..... Ms. Joy K. WARD
66 Dean of Nursing ..... Dr. Carol M. MUSIL
52 Dean of Dental Medicine ..... Dr. Kenneth B. CHANCE
50 Dean of Management ..... Dr. Manoj MALHOTRA
70 Dean Applied Social Science ..... Dr. Dexter VOISIN
54 Dean of Engineering ..... Dr. Venkataramanan BALAKRISHNAN
58 Dean of Graduate Studies ..... Dr. Charles E. ROZEK
04 Executive Asst to President ..... Ms. Jane M. VONDRAK
102 Asst VP Corporate Rels ..... Ms. Anne M. BORCHERT
25 Associate VP for Research ..... Ms. Stephanie ENDY

Cedarville University (C)

251 N Main Street, Cedarville OH 45314-0601
County: Greene FICE Identification: 003025
Unit ID: 201654
Telephone: (937) 766-2211 Carnegie Class: Masters/M
FAX Number: (937) 766-2760 Calendar System: Semester
URL: www.cedarville.edu
Established: 1887 Annual Undergrad Tuition & Fees: $32,564
Enrollment: 4,461 Coed
Affiliation or Control: Baptist IRS Status: 501(c)3
Highest Offering: Doctorate
Accreditation: HLC, ACBSP, CAATE, CAEP, MUS, NURSE, PHAR, SW

01 President ..... Dr. Thomas WHITE
05 Vice President for Academics ..... Dr. Thomas MACH
10 Vice President for Business/CFO ..... Mr. Christopher SOHN
111 Vice President for Advancement ..... Dr. Will SMALLWOOD
32 VP Stdnt Life/Christian Ministries ..... Dr. Jon WOOD
26 VP for Marketing and Communications ..... Dr. Janice SUPPLEE
84 Vice President for Enrollment Mgmt ..... Dr. Scott VAN LOO
41 Athletic Director ..... Dr. Alan GEIST
43 General Counsel ..... Mr. John HART
20 Assistant VP for Academics ..... Dr. Randall MCKINION
15 VP for Human Resources ..... Mr. John DAVIS
21 Associate VP for Finance/Controller ..... Mr. Phillip GRAFTON
18 Associate VP for Operations ..... Mr. Rodney JOHNSON
13 Associate VP for Technology/CIO ..... Mr. Micah COOPER
42 Associate VP Christian Ministries ..... Mr. Jim CATO
06 University Registrar ..... Mrs. Fran CAMPBELL
97 Dean Undergraduate Programs ..... Dr. Pamela D. JOHNSON
08 Dean Library Services ..... Mr. Josh MICHAEL
73 Dean School of Biblical/Theological ..... Dr. Jason LEE
53 Dean School of Education ..... Vacant
50 Dean School of Business ..... Dr. Jeffrey HAYMOND
67 Dean School of Pharmacy ..... Dr. Marc SWEENEY
66 Dean School of Nursing ..... Mrs. Angelia MICKLE
54 Dean School Engineering/Comp Sci ..... Dr. Robert CHASNOV
34 Dir Stdt Development/Dean of Women ..... Miss Mindy MAY
33 Assc Dean Stdnt Devel/Dean of Men ..... Mr. Brad D. SMITH
26 Exec Director of Public Relations ..... Mr. Mark WEINSTEIN
37 Exec Director of Financial Aid ..... Mr. Kim JENERETTE
29 Exec Director Alumni ..... Mr. Jeff BESTE
19 Director of Campus Safety ..... Mr. Douglas W. CHISHOLM
105 Director Web Services ..... Mr. Mark MAZELIN
108 Director Assessment & Accreditation ..... Mr. Tom BETCHER
36 Director Career Services ..... Mr. Jeff REEP
40 Manager of Retail Services ..... Mrs. Tammy L. SLONE
04 Executive Asst to the President ..... Dr. Zach BOWDEN
101 Admin Assoc to Pres/Asst Secy BOT ..... Mrs. Angela MCINTOSH

Central Ohio Technical College (D)

1179 University Drive, Newark OH 43055-1767
County: Licking FICE Identification: 011046
Unit ID: 201672
Telephone: (740) 366-1351 Carnegie Class: Assoc/HVT-High Non
FAX Number: (740) 366-5047 Calendar System: Semester
URL: www.cotc.edu
Established: 1971 Annual Undergrad Tuition & Fees (In-State): $4,776
Enrollment: 3,029 Coed
Affiliation or Control: State IRS Status: 501(c)3
Highest Offering: Associate Degree
Accreditation: HLC, ACBSP, ACFEI, ADNUR, CSHSE, DMS, IFSAC, NAEYC, RAD, SURGT

01 President ..... Dr. John BERRY
10 Vice President Business & Finance ..... Mr. David BRILLHART
05 Provost ..... Dr. Eric HEISER
97 Dean for General Educ/Transfer Pgms ..... Dr. Chad WEIRICK
32 Dean of Students ..... Ms. Holly MASON
100 Vice President & Chief of Staff ..... Dr. Jacqueline PARRILL
103 VP Econ Dev/Workforce Solutions ..... Vacant
08 Director of Library ..... Ms. Katie BLOCKSIDGE
06 Records Manager/Registrar ..... Ms. Veronica RINE
26 Director Marketing/Public Relations ..... Ms. Suzanne BRESSOUD
15 Director of Human Resources ..... Ms. Sue WADLEY
37 Director Student Financial Services ..... Ms. Faith PHILLIPS
19 Director Public Safety ..... Mr. Adam FEATHERLING
111 Director of Advancement ..... Ms. Kim MANNO
35 Asst Dean of Students ..... Ms. Hannah BARNEY
13 Chief Information Officer ..... Vacant
22 Program Mgr Learn Asst Ctr Disabled ..... Ms. Connie ZANG
96 Manager of Purchasing ..... Ms. Kimberley SIBERT
18 Facilities Superintendent ..... Mr. Brian BOEHMER
51 Coord of Community Svc/Learning ..... Ms. Vorley TAYLOR
36 Dir Career Dev & Experiential Lrng ..... Mr. Derek THATCHER
04 Assistant to the President ..... Ms. Jan TOMLINSON
09 Director of Institutional Research ..... Mr. Christopher DOLL
50 Dean for Business/Engineering/IT ..... Vacant
84 Dean of Enrollment Management ..... Ms. Sarah MORRISON
101 Secretary of the Institution/Board ..... Ms. Jan TOMLINSON

Central Ohio Technical College Coshocton Campus (E)

200 North Whitewoman Street, Coshocton OH 43812
Telephone: (740) 622-1408 Identification: 770348
Accreditation: &HLC

Central Ohio Technical College Knox Campus (F)

236 South Main Street, Mount Vernon OH 43050
Telephone: (740) 392-2526 Identification: 770350
Accreditation: &HLC

Central Ohio Technical College Pataskala Campus (G)

8660 East Broad Street, Reynoldsburg OH 43068
Telephone: (740) 755-7090 Identification: 770351
Accreditation: &HLC

Central State University (H)

PO Box 1004, 1400 Brush Row Road, Wilberforce OH 45384-1004
County: Greene FICE Identification: 003026
Unit ID: 201690
Telephone: (937) 376-6332 Carnegie Class: Bac-Diverse
FAX Number: (937) 376-6138 Calendar System: Semester
URL: www.centralstate.edu
Established: 1887 Annual Undergrad Tuition & Fees (In-State): $6,726
Enrollment: 4,021 Coed
Affiliation or Control: State IRS Status: 501(c)3
Highest Offering: Master's
Accreditation: HLC, ACBSP, ART, CAEP, MUS, SW

01 President ..... Dr. Jack THOMAS
100 Chief of Staff ..... Mr. Charles SHAHID
05 Provost/VP Academic Affairs ..... Dr. F. Erik BROOKS
10 Vice President Admin & Finance ..... Mr. Curtis PETTIS
111 Vice Pres Institutional Advancement ..... Mr. Jahan CULBREATH
32 Vice President Student Affairs ..... Mrs. Wendy HAYES
13 Director/Chief Information Officer ..... Vacant
20 Assoc Vice Pres Academic Affairs ..... Vacant
06 Interim University Registrar ..... Ms. Amanda PAYTON
08 Director of Hallie Q Brown Library ..... Ms. Carolin STERLING
89 Exec Director of University College ..... Dr. Gene MOORE
12 Director of CSU Dayton ..... Mrs. Lesa DEVOND
09 Director Assessment/Inst Research ..... Mr. Mohammad ALI
19 Chief of Police ..... Chief Stephanie HILL
26 Director Public Relations ..... Vacant
23 Medical Director ..... Dr. Karen MATHEWS
29 Director Alumni Relations ..... Mr. Keith PERKINS
36 Director Career Services ..... Ms. Karla HARPER
37 Director Student Financial Aid ..... Mrs. Demarus CRAWFORD-WHITE
39 Director of Residence Life ..... Mr. Justyn FRY
41 Athletic Director ..... Ms. Tara OWENS
42 Director Campus Ministry ..... Rev. Kima CUNNINGHAM
46 Director Sponsored Pgms/Research ..... Mr. Morakinyo KUTI
49 Dean Coll Humanities/Arts & Sci ..... Dr. George ARASIMOWICZ
50 Dean College of Business ..... Dr. Gurupdesh PANDHER
53 Dean College of Education ..... Dr. Zaki SHARIF
54 Dean Col of Science and Engineering ..... Dr. Michelle CORLEY
15 Director of Human Resources ..... Ms. Tonya TURNER
21 Director Business Svcs/Capital Dev ..... Ms. Cynthia MICHAEL
25 Director Grants Accounting ..... Vacant
92 Exec Director Honors College ..... Dr. Paul A. SCHLAG
21 Controller ..... Ms. Candy CARR
114 Budget Director ..... Ms. Sheila BROWN
38 Director of Counseling Services ..... Ms. Sonia HUNT
104 Director of Global Education ..... Dr. Fahmi ABBOUSHI
106 Dir Online Learning ..... Dr. Jean-Jacques MEDASTIN
18 Director Facilities Management ..... Mr. Milton THOMPSON
43 General Counsel ..... Ms. Laura WILSON
86 Chief Ofcr of Government Relations ..... Mr. Charles SHAHID
07 Director of Admissions ..... Vacant
108 Director Institutional Assessment ..... Dr. Rebecca ERTEL

Chamberlain University-Cleveland (I)

6700 Euclid Avenue, Suite 201, Cleveland OH 44103
Telephone: (216) 361-6005 Identification: 770505
Accreditation: &HLC, NURSE

† Branch campus of Chamberlain University-Addison, Addison, IL

Chamberlain University-Columbus (J)

4111 Worth Avenue, Columbus OH 43219
Telephone: (614) 252-8890 Identification: 770499
Accreditation: &HLC, NURSE

† Branch campus of Chamberlain University-Addison, Addison, IL

Chatfield College (K)

20918 State Route 251, Saint Martin OH 45118-9059
County: Brown FICE Identification: 010880
Unit ID: 201751
Telephone: (513) 875-3344 Carnegie Class: Assoc/HT-High Non
FAX Number: (513) 875-3912 Calendar System: Semester
URL: www.chatfield.edu
Established: 1971 Annual Undergrad Tuition & Fees: $14,957
Enrollment: 170 Coed
Affiliation or Control: Independent Non-Profit IRS Status: 501(c)3
Highest Offering: Associate Degree
Accreditation: HLC

01 President ..... Mr. Robert ELMORE
11 Vice President/COO ..... Ms. Kelly GRAMLING
05 Chief Academic Officer/Dean ..... Dr. Peter HANSON
10 Director of Finance ..... Ms. Mary R. JACOBS
111 Director of Advancement ..... Mrs. Kelly WATSON
07 Director of Admissions & Marketing ..... Ms. Christina MULLIS
20 Assoc Dean/Cinci Site Director ..... Ms. Tausha ROSS

04 Executive Asst to President .... Ms. Kimberly A. MONACO
06 Registrar .... Ms. Shelia YATES-MATTINGLY
08 Head Librarian .... Ms. Emilia KNISLEY
37 Financial Aid Manager .... Ms. Amy ROTH

The Christ College of Nursing and Health Sciences (A)

2139 Auburn Avenue, Cincinnati OH 45219
County: Hamilton FICE Identification: 006489
Unit ID: 201821
Telephone: (513) 585-2401 Carnegie Class: Spec-4-yr-Other Health
FAX Number: (513) 585-3540 Calendar System: Semester
URL: www.thechristcollege.edu
Established: 2006 Annual Undergrad Tuition & Fees: $15,381
Enrollment: 1,015 Coed
Affiliation or Control: Independent Non-Profit IRS Status: 501(c)3
Highest Offering: Baccalaureate
Accreditation: HLC, NURSE

01 President .... Dr. Gail E. KIST-KLINE
05 VP of Academic Affairs .... Dr. Connie MCFADDEN CHASE
10 VP of Strategy & Business Affairs .... Mr. Bradley A. JACKSON
32 Dean Student Affairs .... Dr. Meghan E. HOLLOWELL
04 Executive Assistant to President .... Ms. Alison L. MCLAREN
37 Director of Financial Aid .... Mr. Tim RING
06 Registrar .... Ms. Susan MACK
07 Director Admissions & Recruitment .... Mr. Ryan BOYD
66 Associate Dean of Nursing .... Mrs. Elizabeth HAGER
76 Associate Dean of Health Sciences .... Ms. Edna D. BROWN

Cincinnati College of Mortuary Science (B)

645 W North Bend Road, Cincinnati OH 45224-1462
County: Hamilton FICE Identification: 010906
Unit ID: 201867
Telephone: (513) 761-2020 Carnegie Class: Spec-4-yr-Arts
FAX Number: (513) 761-3333 Calendar System: Semester
URL: www.ccms.edu
Established: 1882 Annual Undergrad Tuition & Fees: N/A
Enrollment: 84 Coed
Affiliation or Control: Independent Non-Profit IRS Status: 501(c)3
Highest Offering: Baccalaureate
Accreditation: HLC, FUSER

01 President & CEO .... Mr. Jack E. LECHNER, JR.
11 Vice President & COO .... Mr. Mark D. IVEY
84 Dean of Enrollment Management .... Mr. Kevin BRINKMAN
37 Financial Aid Director .... Mr. Russ ROMANDINI
108 Dir Institutional Effectiveness .... Mrs. Beth WILLIAMS
05 Academic Chair .... Ms. Teresa DUTKO
08 Director Library/IT .... Ms. Molly JONES
88 Office Manager .... Mr. Randy ANDERSON
06 Registrar .... Ms. Brooke BOLTON
30 Director of Development .... Mr. Ken COGGESHALL

Cincinnati State Technical and Community College (C)

3520 Central Parkway, Cincinnati OH 45223-2690
County: Hamilton FICE Identification: 010345
Unit ID: 201928
Telephone: (513) 569-1500 Carnegie Class: Assoc/HVT-Mix Trad/Non
FAX Number: (513) 569-1495 Calendar System: Other
URL: www.cincinnatistate.edu
Established: 1966 Annual Undergrad Tuition & Fees (In-State): $5,040
Enrollment: 6,873 Coed
Affiliation or Control: State IRS Status: 501(c)3
Highest Offering: Baccalaureate
Accreditation: HLC, ACFEI, ADNUR, CAHIIM, COARC, CONST, DIETT, DMS, EMT, MAC, MLTAD, NAEYC, OTA, SURGT

01 President .... Dr. Monica POSEY
05 Provost .... Mr. Robbin HOOPES
13 Vice Pres for Technology/CIO .... Mr. Frankie BAKER
103 Vice Pres Workforce Development .... Ms. Amy WALDBILLIG
84 VP Enrollment/Student Development .... Ms. Amy WALDBILLIG
72 Dean of Innovative Technology .... Mr. Doug BOWLING
50 Dean of Business Technologies .... Ms. Yvonne BAKER
81 Dean Humanities/Sciences .... Mr. Geoff WOOLF
06 Registrar .... Mr. Jason A. MOORE
08 Library Director .... Mrs. Crissy ROSS
35 Director Student Activities .... Vacant
15 Director of Human Resources .... Ms. Falonda ROGERS
102 Executive Director CS Foundation .... Mr. Elliott RUTHER
04 Executive Administrative Associate .... Ms. Angelica KENNEDY
19 Dean Health & Public Safety .... Dr. Denise ROHR
101 Secretary to the Board of Trustees .... Ms. Angelica KENNEDY
07 Director of Admissions .... Ms. Deborah POWELEIT
111 Chief Inst Advancement/Development .... Mr. Elliott V. RUTHER
10 Chief Financial Officer .... Mr. Christopher CALVERT
37 Director Student Financial Aid .... Ms. Penny PARSONS
09 Director of Institutional Research .... Ms. Mollie MILLER
18 Chief Facilities/ Physical Plant Of .... Ms. Kim VASKO
20 Associate Academic Officer .... Dr. Denise ROHR
26 Chief Public Relations Officer .... Mr. Elliott RUTHER
29 Director Alumni Affairs .... Mrs. Kim TAYLOR
121 Sr Dir Student Success/Development .... Mrs. Soni HILL
36 Director Student Placement .... Mrs. Kelly HARPER
96 Director of Purchasing .... Mr. Tony COWDEN

Clark State College (D)

570 E Leffel Lane, PO Box 570,
Springfield OH 45501-0570
County: Clark FICE Identification: 004852
Unit ID: 201973
Telephone: (937) 325-0691 Carnegie Class: Assoc/HVT-High Non
FAX Number: (937) 328-6142 Calendar System: Semester
URL: www.clarkstate.edu
Established: 1966 Annual Undergrad Tuition & Fees (In-State): $4,032
Enrollment: 5,396 Coed
Affiliation or Control: State IRS Status: 501(c)3
Highest Offering: Baccalaureate
Accreditation: HLC, ADNUR, EMT, MAC, MLTAD, PTAA

01 President .... Dr. Jo A. BLONDIN
05 Provost/Vice Pres Academic Affairs .... Dr. Tiffany HUNTER
10 VP for Business Affairs .... Doug SCHANTZ
32 VP of Student Affairs .... Dr. Dawayne KIRKMAN
102 Foundation Director .... Toni OVERHOLSER
21 Controller .... Kathy NELSON
07 Dean Enrollment Services .... Dr. Ronald GORDON
124 Dean Student Engagemt/Support Svcs .... Nina WILEY
49 Dean Arts & Sciences .... Naomi LOUIS
50 Dean Business/Applied Technologies .... Dr. Sharon BOMMER
76 Dean Health/Human/Public Services .... Dr. Rhoda SOMMERS
37 Financial Aid Director .... Victoria OWENS
06 Registrar .... Diane SEAMAN
13 Senior VP IT/Safety/Strategic Init .... Dr. Matt FRANZ
15 Director of Human Resources .... Laura WHETSTONE
57 Exec Dir Performing Arts Center .... Adele ADKINS
08 Director Library Services .... Dr. Sterling J. COLEMAN, JR.
18 Dir Facilities/Oper/Maint .... Daniel AYARS
41 Dir Athletics and Student Life .... Justin MCCULLA
103 Dir Workforce & Business Solutions .... Gerritt SMITH
88 Dir Commercial Trans Training Ctr .... Duane HODGE
106 Interim Dir Ctr Teaching/Learning .... Brittany BRIGGS
26 VP Marketing/Diversity/Community .... Crystal JONES
04 Executive Asst to the President .... Mellanie TOLES
09 Institutional Research Technician .... Kelly NERIANI

Cleveland Institute of Art (E)

11610 Euclid Avenue, Cleveland OH 44106-1710
County: Cuyahoga FICE Identification: 003982
Unit ID: 202046
Telephone: (216) 421-7000 Carnegie Class: Spec-4-yr-Arts
FAX Number: (216) 421-7438 Calendar System: Semester
URL: www.cia.edu
Established: 1882 Annual Undergrad Tuition & Fees: $44,385
Enrollment: 599 Coed
Affiliation or Control: Independent Non-Profit IRS Status: 501(c)3
Highest Offering: Baccalaureate
Accreditation: HLC, ART

01 President & CEO .... Ms. Kathryn HEIDEMANN
04 Exec Assistant to CEO & VP IA .... Vacant
05 VP Academic/Dean Fac Affairs/CAO .... Mr. Greg WATTS
84 VP Enrollment & Marketing .... Ms. Yvette SOBKY SHAFFER
111 VP Institutional Advancement .... Ms. Malou MONAGO
10 VP Business Affairs & CFO .... Mr. John TORTELLI
15 VP Human Resources & Inclusion .... Ms. Charise REID
13 Assoc VP of Info Systems & Tech .... Mr. Matthew MCKENNA
32 Assoc VP Stdnt Affs/Dean of Stdnts .... Mr. Jesse GRANT
06 Registrar .... Ms. Stephanie MORTSON
121 Director of Academic Services .... Ms. Elisaida MENDEZ
39 Assistant Dean of Students .... Mr. Matthew SMITH
36 Director of Career Center .... Ms. Lauren RYAN
08 Director of Library .... Ms. Laura PONIKVAR
51 Dir Continuing Ed & Community .... Ms. Gabrielle BURRAGE
07 Assoc Director of Admissions .... Mr. Tom GREEN
37 Director of Financial Aid .... Mr. Marlon JONES
44 Dir of Annual Giving & Stewardship .... Ms. Bethany GRESH
102 Director of Foundation Relations .... Ms. Kate MACEK
29 Director Alumni & Scholarships .... Ms. Alexandra BURRAGE
26 Director of Communications .... Mr. Michael BUTZ
27 Director of Enrollment Marketing .... Mr. Richard SARIAN
21 Controller .... Ms. Sally PALMER
19 Chief of Public Safety .... Mr. Steve HAMMETT
18 Director Facilities Mgmt & Safety .... Mr. Joe FERRITTO
119 Assoc Dir of Network Administration .... Mr. Greg SLABY
120 Assoc Dir of Online Services .... Mr. Matthew MINNICH
16 Assoc Director of HR .... Ms. Lisa SCHUMANN
88 Dir of Admissions Systems .... Mr. Eric REITZ
09 Dir of Inst Rsrch & Effectiveness .... Ms. Ambreen HASAN

Cleveland Institute of Music (F)

11021 East Boulevard, Cleveland OH 44106-1776
County: Cuyahoga FICE Identification: 003031
Unit ID: 202073
Telephone: (216) 791-5000 Carnegie Class: Spec-4-yr-Arts
FAX Number: (216) 791-3063 Calendar System: Semester
URL: www.cim.edu
Established: 1920 Annual Undergrad Tuition & Fees: $42,040
Enrollment: 381 Coed
Affiliation or Control: Independent Non-Profit IRS Status: 501(c)3
Highest Offering: Doctorate
Accreditation: HLC, MUS

01 President/CEO .... Mr. Paul HOGLE
05 Exec VP and Provost .... Mr. Scott HARRISON
11 Senior Vice President .... Mr. Eric BOWER
20 Vice President of Academic Affairs .... Dr. Dean SOUTHERN
10 Controller .... Ms. Kathleen GUSTAFSON
13 Asst Vice President of Technology .... Mr. Michael BRATANOV
84 Dean of Enrollment Management .... Mr. Fred PETERBARK
32 Int Assoc Dean of Student Affairs .... Ms. Cicely SCHONBERG
37 Director Financial Aid .... Ms. Kristine GRIPP
06 Assoc Dean Acad Affs/Registrar .... Mrs. Hallie MOORE
15 Vice Pres of People & Culture .... Mrs. Tammie BELTON
08 Director of the Library .... Dr. Kevin MCLAUGHLIN
04 Executive Admin Asst to President .... Ms. Nancy SNELL
88 Dean of Artistic Admin .... Ms. Donna YOO
07 Director of Admissions .... Ms. Rachel KUNCE

Cleveland State University (G)

2121 Euclid Avenue, Cleveland OH 44115-2214
County: Cuyahoga FICE Identification: 003032
Unit ID: 202134
Telephone: (216) 687-2000 Carnegie Class: DU-Higher
FAX Number: (216) 687-9366 Calendar System: Semester
URL: www.csuohio.edu
Established: 1964 Annual Undergrad Tuition & Fees (In-State): $11,185
Enrollment: 15,247 Coed
Affiliation or Control: State IRS Status: 501(c)3
Highest Offering: Doctorate
Accreditation: HLC, CACREP, CAEP, CAMPEP, CEA, COPSY, IPSY, LAW, MUS, NURSE, OT, PH, PLNG, PTA, SP, SPAA, SW

01 President .... Dr. Laura J. BLOOMBERG
05 Int Provost/SVP Academic Affairs .... Dr. Nigamanth SRIDHAR
10 SVP Business Affairs/CFO .... Mr. David N. JEWELL
84 VP Enrollment & Student Svcs .... Mr. Jonathan D. WEHNER
100 Chief of Staff/VP Administration .... Ms. Jeanell N. HUGHES
46 Int VP Research .... Ms. Meredith BOND
111 VP Univ Advanc/Exec Dir Foundation .... Dr. Julie REHM
32 AVP Campus Engage/Dean of Students .... Ms. Ali MARTIN SCOUFIELD
28 VP Campus Engagement/DEI .... Dr. Phillip A. COCKRELL
20 Vice Provost for Academic Planning .... Dr. Marius BOBOC
20 Vice Provost Academic Programs .... Dr. John HOLCOMB
26 Assoc VP University Mktg .... Vacant
15 Assoc VP Human Resources .... Mr. Douglas DYKES
35 Assoc VP Student Affairs .... Vacant
21 Controller/Asst VP Finance .... Ms. Nicole ADDINGTON
49 Dean College of Arts/Sciences .... Mr. Andrew KERSTEN
50 Dean College of Business .... Dr. Kenneth B. KAHN
53 Dean College Education/Public Affs .... Mr. Roland ANGLIN
54 Dean Washkewicz Col Engineering .... Mr. Richard SCHOEPHOERSTER
58 Int Dean College Graduate Studies .... Dr. Meredith BOND
61 Dean of College of Law .... Mr. Lee FISHER
80 Dean College Urban Affairs .... Dr. Roland ANGLIN
92 Dean Honors College .... Dr. Elizabeth LEHFELDT
43 General Counsel .... Ms. Sonali B. WILSON
08 Director of Libraries .... Mr. David LODWICK
22 Dir Office of Institutional Equity .... Ms. Rachel LUTNER
07 Director Undergraduate Admissions .... Ms. Cristina WAYTON
09 Director Institutional Research .... Mr. Tom GEAGHAN
85 Director International Programs .... Dr. Joshladd KWAI
38 Director Counseling Center .... Dr. Brittany SOMMERS
37 Director Student Financial Aid .... Ms. Rachel SCHMIDT
06 Asst Vice President/Registrar .... Ms. Janet STIMPLE
41 Director of Athletics .... Mr. Scott GARRETT
29 Asst VP Alumni Relations .... Ms. Anne-Marie E. CONNORS
18 Exec Dir Facilities Services .... Vacant
96 Purchasing Manager .... Mr. Michael EAMES
04 Director Office of the President .... Vacant
114 Exec Dir Budget & Operations .... Ms. Bonnie KALNASY
106 Director Center for E-learning .... Ms. Caryn LANZO
13 Chief Info Technology Ofcr (CIO) .... Vacant
39 Dir Resident Life/Student Housing .... Ms. Allison HEURING
86 Pres Advisor Government Relations .... Vacant
19 Director Security/Safety .... Mr. Anthony TRASKA

The College of Wooster (H)

1189 Beall Avenue, Wooster OH 44691-2363
County: Wayne FICE Identification: 003037
Unit ID: 206589
Telephone: (330) 263-2000 Carnegie Class: Bac-A&S
FAX Number: (330) 263-2427 Calendar System: Semester
URL: www.wooster.edu
Established: 1866 Annual Undergrad Tuition & Fees: $54,000
Enrollment: 1,924 Coed
Affiliation or Control: Independent Non-Profit IRS Status: 501(c)3
Highest Offering: Baccalaureate
Accreditation: HLC, CAEP, MUS

01 President .... Dr. Sarah BOLTON
05 Provost .... Dr. Lisa PERFETTI
10 Vice Pres Finance/Bus/Treasurer .... Mr. James PRINCE
111 Vice President for Advancement .... Mr. Wayne WEBSTER
84 Vice Pres Enrollment/College Rels .... Ms. Jennifer WINGE
32 VP Student Affairs/Dean of Students ...... Ms. Myrna HERNANDEZ
04 Executive Asst to President .... Ms. Sally WHITMAN
15 Assoc Vice Pres Human Resources .... Ms. Gail PHOENIX
18 Assoc VP Facilities Mgmt & Planning .... Mr. Mike TAYLOR
109 Assoc VP Auxiliaries .... Ms. Sheila WILSON
20 Dean Curriculum/Academic Engagement .... Dr. Jennifer BOWEN
20 Dean for Faculty Development .... Dr. Christa CRAVEN
28 VP Diversity/Equity/Inclusion .... Ms. Cheryl NUNEZ

13 Chief Information Planning Officer ... Dr. Ellen FALDUTO
06 Registrar ... Mr. Nicholas SZYMANSKI
08 Librarian of the College ... Vacant
37 Director of Financial Aid ... Ms. Dana KENNEDY
27 Chief Comm/Marketing Officer ... Ms. Melissa ANDERSON
29 Dir of Alumni Rels & Wooster Fund ... Mr. Thomas MCARTHUR
36 Director Career Services ... Ms. Lisa KASTOR
19 Director Security/Protective Svcs ... Mr. Joe KIRK
101 Secretary of College/Chief Staff ... Ms. Angela JOHNSTON

Columbus College of Art & Design (A)

60 Cleveland Avenue, Columbus OH 43215-1758
County: Franklin | FICE Identification: 003039
Unit ID: 202170
Telephone: (614) 224-9101 | Carnegie Class: Spec-4-yr-Arts
FAX Number: N/A | Calendar System: Semester
URL: www.ccad.edu
Established: 1879 | Annual Undergrad Tuition & Fees: $37,370
Enrollment: 1,009 | Coed
Affiliation or Control: Independent Non-Profit | IRS Status: 501(c)3
Highest Offering: Master's
Accreditation: HLC

01 President ... Dr. Melanie CORN
04 Exec Assistant to the President ... Ms. Sheri LUCAS
05 Provost ... Ms. Julie TAGGART
10 Chief Fiscal Officer ... Mr. Tom DOTSON
11 VP Planning & Administration ... Vacant
30 VP for Institutional Engagement ... Mr. Chris MUNDELL
84 VP for Enrollment Management ... Ms. D. Jean HESTER
32 AVP for Student Affairs ... Ms. Athena SANDERS
20 Dean of Undergraduate Studies ... Mr. Tom GATTIS
26 VP Marketing & Communications ... Ms. Jill MOORHEAD
58 Dean of Graduate Studies ... Ms. Jennifer SCHLUETER
06 Registrar ... Ms. Michele KIBLER
13 Chief Information Officer ... Mr. Matt GARDZINA
15 Director of Human Resources ... Ms. Beverly THOMAS
08 Director of Library Services ... Ms. Leslie JANKOWSKI NIEMCZURA
19 Director of Safety & Security ... Mr. Wallace TANKSLEY
18 Director of Facilities ... Mr. Dan PARRA
38 Director of Counseling & Wellness ... Ms. Erin VLACH
37 AVP of Financial Aid & Registration ... Ms. Susan KANNENWISCHER
36 Director Career Resources ... Ms. Tiffany SPERRING
21 Controller ... Mr. Roger ESCOLAS
51 Director of Career Education ... Ms. Jessi WALKER
39 Director of Residence Life ... Ms. Liz GORDON-CANLAS
109 AVP for Operations ... Ms. Richelle SIMONSON

Columbus State Community College (B)

PO Box 1609, Columbus OH 43216-1609
County: Franklin | FICE Identification: 006867
Unit ID: 202222
Telephone: (614) 287-5353 | Carnegie Class: Assoc/MT-VT-High Non
FAX Number: (614) 287-5113 | Calendar System: Semester
URL: www.cscc.edu
Established: 1963 | Annual Undergrad Tuition & Fees (In-State): $4,888
Enrollment: 27,621 | Coed
Affiliation or Control: State | IRS Status: 501(c)3
Highest Offering: Associate Degree
Accreditation: HLC, ACBSP, ACFEI, ACPHA, ADNUR, CAHIIM, COARC, CONST, CSHSE, DH, DIETT, EMT, MAC, MLTAD, RAD, SURGT

01 President ... Dr. David T. HARRISON
05 Sr VP/CAO Academic Affairs ... Dr. Martin MALIWESKY
10 Sr VP Business Services/CFO ... Ms. Aletha SHIPLEY
26 VP Enrollment Svcs & Marketing ... Mr. Allen KRAUS
13 VP Information Technology ... Dr. Michael BABB
11 VP Administration ... Mr. Richard HATCHER
32 VP Student Affairs ... Dr. Desiree POLK-BLAND
111 VP Office of Advancement ... Ms. Kathryn TROMBITAS
20 Associate VP Academic Affairs ... Vacant
03 Executive Vice President ... Dr. Rebecca BUTLER
12 Dean of Delaware Campus ... Dr. Tina DIGGS
49 Dean of Arts & Sciences ... Dr. Allysen TODD
76 Dean Health and Human Services ... Mr. Kirk DICKERSON
50 Dean Business & Engineering Tech ... Ms. Carmen DANIELS
35 Sr Director Student Life ... Mr. Terrence BROOKS
91 Director IT Budget/Planning ... Mr. Etienne MARTIN
21 Director II Controller ... Ms. Jan ELLIS
06 Director Office of the Registrar ... Dr. Regina RANDALL
37 Director Financial Aid ... Ms. Deneene MERCHANT
19 Chief of Police ... Chief Sean ASBURY
18 Senior Director Facilities Mgmt ... Mr. Mark DUDGEON
28 VP DEI/Chief Diversity Officer ... Mr. Almar WALTER
09 Associate VP Inst Effectiveness ... Dr. Jennifer ANDERSON
08 Director Library ... Ms. Dana KNOTT
15 Exec Dir Human Resources ... Ms. Kristen TREADWAY
07 Director of Admissions ... Vacant
40 Director Operations/Bookstore ... Mr. Phillip SANDERS
96 Director Procurement/College Svcs ... Mr. Bradley FARMER
43 General Counsel ... Mr. Charles NOBLE, III
04 Exec Assistant to the President ... Ms. Vickie HUNTER
106 Dean Digital Educ & Instruct Svcs ... Dr. Thomas ERNEY

Columbus State Community College-Delaware (C)

5100 Cornerstone Drive, Delaware OH 43015
Telephone: (740) 203-8345 | Identification: 770353
Accreditation: &HLC

Cuyahoga Community College (D)

700 Carnegie Avenue, Cleveland OH 44115-2878
County: Cuyahoga | FICE Identification: 003040
Unit ID: 202356
Telephone: (216) 987-4000 | Carnegie Class: Assoc/MT-VT-High Non
FAX Number: (216) 566-5977 | Calendar System: Semester
Established: 1963 | Annual Undergrad Tuition & Fees (In-District): $4,322
Enrollment: 18,754 | Coed
Affiliation or Control: State/Local | IRS Status: 501(c)3
Highest Offering: Associate Degree
Accreditation: HLC, ACBSP, ACFEI, ACPHA, ADNUR, CAHIIM, COARC, DH, DIETT, DMS, EMT, MAC, MLTAD, NDT, NMT, OTA, PTAA, RAD, SURGT

01 President ... Dr. Michael A. BASTON
05 Exec VP & Provost ... Dr. Karen MILLER
10 Exec VP Administration & Finance ... Mr. David KUNTZ
103 Exec VP Workforce/Comm & Econ Dev ... Mr. William GARY
12 Campus President East Campus ... Mr. Todd KITCHEN
12 President/CEO Corporate College ... Vacant
12 Int Campus President Metro Campus ... Dr. Denise MCCORY
12 Int Campus Pres Westshore Campus ... Ms. Janice TAYLOR HEARD
12 Campus President West Campus ... Dr. Donna IMHOFF
21 Vice Pres Finance & Business Svcs ... Ms. Jennifer DEMMERLE
15 Vice Pres/Chief Human Res Officer ... Ms. Lillian WELCH
30 Vice Pres Development/Foundation ... Ms. Megan O'BRYAN
27 Chief Innovation/Strategy Ofcr ... Mr. Standish STEWART
86 Vice Pres Govt Affs/Comm Outreach ... Ms. Claire ROSACCO
84 VP Inst Research/Enrollment Mgmt ... Ms. Angela JOHNSON
26 Vice Pres Integrated Communications ... Ms. Jenny FEBBO
43 Vice Pres Legal Services ... Ms. Renee RICHARD
20 VP/Asst Provost Learning Engagement ... Ms. Lindsay ENGLISH
108 AVP Program Accreditation ... Ms. Chandra ARTHUR
88 VP/Dean Pub Safety/Criminal Justice ... Chief Clayton HARRIS
88 Vice Pres Manufacturing ... Ms. Alicia BOOKER
22 Assoc VP Access & Cmty Engagement ... Dr. JaNice MARSHALL
88 Exec Dir Access Learning & Success ... Dr. Sandra MCKNIGHT
88 Deputy Gen Counsel & Exec Dir ... Mr. Jason CARTER
88 Exec Director Media Engineering ... Mr. Robert (Bob) BRYAN
13 Exec Director EIS ... Mr. Jon DOLINAR
18 Exec Director Plant Operations ... Mr. Shehadeh ABDELKARIM
88 Exec Dir Veteran Services/Programs ... Ms. Marjorie MORRISON
88 Exec Dir College Services & Retail ... Mr. Chris MOIR
88 Exec Dir Supplier Managed Services ... Mr. Stephen HILBERT
96 VP Capital Const & Supply Mgmt ... Ms. Cynthia LEITSON
88 Dean GM Hospitality Management ... Mr. Michael HUFF
88 Exec Director Talent Management ... Mr. Barry ROYKO
20 Dean Learning & Engagement East ... Ms. Holly CRAIDER
20 Dean Learning & Engagement West ... Dr. Janice TAYLOR HEARD
20 Dean Learning & Engagement Metro ... Ms. Amy PARKS
20 Dean Lrng & Engagement Westshore ... Vacant
32 Dean of Student Affairs ... Ms. Ralonda ELLIS-HILL
35 Dean Access & Completion West ... Dr. Tim DORSEY
35 Dean Access & Completion East ... Mr. Andrew CRAWFORD
35 Dean Access & Completion Westshore ... Dr. Kristine WALZ
66 Dean Nursing ... Dr. Vivian YATES
88 Program Director Dietary Technology ... Ms. Judith KAPLAN
76 Assoc Dean Health Careers & Science ... Mr. Gregory MALONE
81 Assoc Dean STEM West ... Mr. Ormond BRATHWAITE
83 Assoc Dean Social Sciences West ... Ms. Courtney CLARKE
49 Assoc Dean Liberal Arts East ... Dr. William CUNION
49 Assoc Dean Creative Arts ... Ms. Amy PARKS
49 Assoc Dean Liberal Arts West ... Dr. Felisa EAFFORD
50 Assoc Dean Bus/Math & Tech East ... Dr. Ann CONRAD
72 Assoc Dean Bus IT Applied Tech West ... Ms. Pamela GRANT
54 Dean Manufacturing Engineer ... Mr. Lam WONG
88 Assoc Dean Hospitality Management ... Ms. Karen MONATH
88 Assoc Dean Nursing ... Ms. Ebony DRUMMER
100 Chief of Staff/Exec Asst to Pres ... Ms. Ronna MCNAIR
23 Assoc Dean Public Safety & EMT ... Dr. James PLOSKONKA
28 Exec Dir of Diversity & Inclusion ... Ms. Magda GOMEZ
110 Exec Director Development ... Ms. Sharon COON
09 Exec Director Evidence Inquiry ... Mr. G. Rob STUART
38 Dean Access Completion ... Mrs. Ralonda ELLIS-HILL
38 Assistant Dean Counseling-East ... Ms. Kate VODICKA
38 Assistant Dean Counseling-West ... Mr. Christopher JOHNSTON
04 Executive Admin Associate ... Ms. Barbara BELL
102 Exec Director Development Office ... Ms. Kate MCDADE
41 Athletic Director West ... Mr. Mark RODRIGUEZ
88 Mgr Transfer Res Ctr Metro Campus ... Ms. Melissa SWAFFORD
41 Dir Student Life/Athletics/Rec ... Ms. Jennifer DAVIS
88 Dean Creative Arts ... Dr. G. Paul COX
14 Int VP Workforce Innov/Dean IT ... Ms. Standish STEWART
91 Director Network Services ... Mr. Peter ANDERSON

Cuyahoga Community College Eastern Campus (E)

4250 Richmond Road, Highland Hills OH 44122
Telephone: (216) 987-6000 | Identification: 770355
Accreditation: &HLC

Cuyahoga Community College Metropolitan Campus (F)

2900 Community College Avenue, Cleveland OH 44115
Telephone: (800) 954-8742 | Identification: 770354
Accreditation: &HLC

Cuyahoga Community College Western Campus (G)

11000 Pleasant Valley Road, Parma OH 44130
Telephone: (800) 954-8742 | Identification: 770356
Accreditation: &HLC

Cuyahoga Community College Westshore (H)

31001 Clemens Road, Westlake OH 44145
Telephone: (800) 954-8742 | Identification: 770357
Accreditation: &HLC

Davis College (I)

433 North Summit Street, Suite 202, Toledo OH 43604
County: Lucas | FICE Identification: 004855
Unit ID: 202435
Telephone: (419) 473-2700 | Carnegie Class: Assoc/HVT-High Non
FAX Number: (419) 473-2472 | Calendar System: Quarter
URL: www.daviscollege.edu
Established: 1858 | Annual Undergrad Tuition & Fees: $14,130
Enrollment: 109 | Coed
Affiliation or Control: Proprietary | IRS Status: Proprietary
Highest Offering: Associate Degree
Accreditation: HLC

01 President ... Diane BRUNNER
05 VP Academic & Student Services ... Mary RYAN BULONE
84 VP of Enrollment Management ... Tim BRUNNER
37 Director Student Financial Aid ... Nancy POWERS
07 Director of Admissions ... Amy BERG
113 Bursar ... Brittany GUNNETT
36 Career Services Coordinator ... Brittany GUNNETT

The Defiance College (J)

701 N Clinton Street, Defiance OH 43512-1695
County: Defiance | FICE Identification: 003041
Unit ID: 202514
Telephone: (419) 784-4010 | Carnegie Class: Bac-Diverse
FAX Number: (419) 784-4101 | Calendar System: Semester
URL: www.defiance.edu
Established: 1850 | Annual Undergrad Tuition & Fees: $33,910
Enrollment: 607 | Coed
Affiliation or Control: United Church Of Christ | IRS Status: 501(c)3
Highest Offering: Master's
Accreditation: HLC, CAEP, IACBE, NURSE, SW

01 President ... Dr. Richanne C. MANKEY
05 VP for Academic Affairs ... Dr. Agnes CALDWELL
10 Vice Pres for Finance & Management ... Mr. Timothy PRUETT
32 VP Student Affs/Dean of Students ... Mrs. Lisa MARSALEK
84 Vice President for Enrollment Mgmt ... Mrs. Tracey D. FORD
88 Dean McMaster Sch Adv Hum ... Mrs. Mary Ann STUDER
15 Director of Human Resources ... Mrs. Mary E. BURKHOLDER
08 Dir of Library and Instr Resource ... Mrs. Lisa CRUMIT-HANCOCK
26 Director Public Relations/Marketing ... Mr. Ryan IMBROCK
13 Director of Computer Services ... Mr. Ryan NUNN
06 Registrar ... Vacant
37 Director of Financial Aid ... Vacant
41 Athletic Director ... Mr. Derek WOODLEY
28 Director Intercultural Relations ... Ms. Mercedes CLAY
39 Director of Residence Life ... Ms. Jennifer WALTON
18 Director of Physical Plant ... Mr. Ted CZARTOSKI
21 Director of Accounting ... Mrs. Kristine BOLAND
04 Administrative Asst to President ... Mrs. Judy LYMANSTALL
103 Dir Workforce/Career Development ... Ms. Sally BISSELL
50 Dean of Business ... Mr. William SHOLL
53 Dean of Education ... Dr. Carla HIGGINS
38 Director Student Counseling ... Ms. Lynn BRAUN
44 Director of Annual Giving ... Vacant
30 Exec Director of Development ... Mrs. Brittanie KUHR
122 Dir Stdnt Activities-Greek Life ... Mr. Sidney FAINE

Denison University (K)

100 W College Street, Granville OH 43023-1359
County: Licking | FICE Identification: 003042
Unit ID: 202523
Telephone: (740) 587-0810 | Carnegie Class: Bac-A&S
FAX Number: (740) 587-6417 | Calendar System: Semester
URL: www.denison.edu
Established: 1831 | Annual Undergrad Tuition & Fees: $56,680
Enrollment: 2,258 | Coed
Affiliation or Control: Independent Non-Profit | IRS Status: 501(c)3
Highest Offering: Baccalaureate
Accreditation: HLC

01 President ... Dr. Adam S. WEINBERG
05 Provost ... Dr. Kimberly A. COPLIN
100 VP/Chief of Staff ... Dr. Rajesh BELLANI
10 VP Finance & Management/CFO ... Mr. David A. ENGLISH
111 VP Institutional Advancement ... Mr. Greg BADER

32 VP of Student Life ... Mr. Alexander MILLER
84 VP Enrollment Management ... Mr. Gregory W. SNEED
89 Dean of First-Year Students ... Dr. Mark MOLLER
88 Special Asst to Pres & Provost ... Dr. Joyce MEREDITH
41 Assoc VP of Athletics ... Ms. Nan CARNEY-DEBORD
115 Chief Investment Officer ... Ms. Kathleen BROWNE
04 Executive Asst to President ... Ms. Nancy BERG
122 Director Fraternity/Sorority Life ... Ms. Dana PURSLEY
15 Director Human Resources/Operations ... Mr. Jim ABLES

East Ohio College (A)

15258 State Route 170, East Liverpool OH 43920
County: Columbiana FICE Identification: 023014
Unit ID: 204884
Telephone: (330) 385-1070 Carnegie Class: Spec 2-yr-Health
FAX Number: (330) 385-4606 Calendar System: Semester
URL: www.ovct.edu
Established: 1886 Annual Undergrad Tuition & Fees: $14,497
Enrollment: 170 Coed
Affiliation or Control: Proprietary IRS Status: Proprietary
Highest Offering: Associate Degree
Accreditation: ABHES

01 President ... Mrs. Courtney E. MARTIN
37 Financial Aid Officer ... Mrs. Jenason DALRYMPLE
36 Director Career Management ... Mr. Craig MONTE

Eastern Gateway Community College - Jefferson County Campus (B)

110 John Scott Hwy, Steubenville OH 43952
County: Jefferson FICE Identification: 007275
Unit ID: 203331
Telephone: (740) 264-5591 Carnegie Class: Assoc/HT-Mix Trad/Non
FAX Number: N/A Calendar System: Semester
URL: www.egcc.edu
Established: 1966 Annual Undergrad Tuition & Fees (In-District): $4,026
Enrollment: 40,036 Coed
Affiliation or Control: State/Local IRS Status: 501(c)3
Highest Offering: Associate Degree
Accreditation: #HLC, CAHIIM, COARC, DA, EMT, RAD

01 President ... Mr. Michael GEOGHEGAN
05 Sr VP of Academic Affairs ... Dr. John CROOKS
11 SVP & Chief Operations Officer .. Mr. Robert ROESCHENTHALER
32 SVP/Chief Student Affairs Ofcr ... Ms. Christina WANAT
12 Sr VP of Youngstown Campus ... Mr. Arthur DALY
09 VP Institutional Research/Reporting ... Mr. Christopher BIRD
28 Sr VP of Inst Diversity & Aspire ... Ms. Karla MARTIN
20 Dean of Academics ... Dr. Thomas GRAHAM
37 Director of Financial Aid ... Mr. Kurt PAWLAK
15 VP of Human Resources ... Mr. Joshua MARTIN
88 Compliance Officer ... Ms. Stephanie SEVERIN
10 Controller ... Mr. Robert SEMICH
76 Dean Health Science/Public Service ... Ms. Gina AUGUSTINE
18 Director Building & Grounds ... Mr. Julius J. DZIEWATKOSKI
06 Registrar ... Ms. Marlise SIPES
21 Deputy CFO ... Ms. Jennifer REED
108 VP Institutional Effectiveness ... Ms. Vanessa BIRNEY

Eastern Gateway Community College - Youngstown Campus (C)

101 East Federal Street, Youngstown OH 44503
Telephone: (800) 682-6553 Identification: 770987
Accreditation: &HLC

† Branch campus of Eastern Gateway Community College in Steubenville, OH.

Edison State Community College (D)

1973 Edison Drive, Piqua OH 45356-9239
County: Miami FICE Identification: 012750
Unit ID: 202648
Telephone: (937) 778-8600 Carnegie Class: Assoc/MT-VT-High Non
FAX Number: (937) 778-1920 Calendar System: Semester
URL: www.edisonohio.edu
Established: 1973 Annual Undergrad Tuition & Fees (In-State): $5,050
Enrollment: 4,202 Coed
Affiliation or Control: State IRS Status: 501(c)3
Highest Offering: Associate Degree
Accreditation: HLC, ADNUR, MAC, MLTAD, PTAA

01 President ... Dr. Doreen LARSON
04 Executive Asst to the President ... Ms. Heather LANHAM
05 Provost ... Mr. Chris SPRADLIN
10 VP of Administration & Finance ... Mr. James LEHMKUHL
32 Dean of Student Affairs ... Ms. Jessica CHAMBERS
31 VP Business/Cmty Partnerships ... Mr. Rick HANES
13 Chief Information Officer ... Ms. Amy CROW
15 Exec Director Human Resources ... Ms. Kara MYERS
35 Director of Student Services ... Ms. Loleta COLLINS
49 Dean of Arts & Sciences ... Dr. Paul HEINTZ
09 Assoc Prov Planning/Effectiveness ... Ms. Mona WALTERS
21 Controller ... Mr. James LEHMKUHL
41 Director Athletics ... Mr. Nathan COLE
37 Director of Financial Aid ... Ms. Chris CUMMINGS
26 Dir of Marketing & Communications ... Mr. Bruce MCKENZIE

84 Enrollment Manager ... Ms. Stacey BEAN
06 Registrar ... Ms. Mary BORNHORST
08 Director of Library/Learning Center ... Ms. Lisa HOOPS
18 Dir of Physical Plant/Facilities ... Mr. Harold HITCHCOCK

ETI Technical College of Niles (E)

2076-86 Youngstown-Warren Road, Niles OH 44446-4398
County: Trumbull FICE Identification: 030790
Unit ID: 200590
Telephone: (330) 652-9919 Carnegie Class: Assoc/HVT-High Trad
FAX Number: (330) 652-4399 Calendar System: Semester
URL: www.eticollege.edu
Established: 1989 Annual Undergrad Tuition & Fees: $10,460
Enrollment: 121 Coed
Affiliation or Control: Proprietary IRS Status: Proprietary
Highest Offering: Associate Degree
Accreditation: ACCSC

01 Director ... Mrs. Renee ZUZOLO
07 Director of Admissions ... Mrs. Diane MARSTELLER
37 Director Financial Aid ... Ms. Kay MADIGAN

Felbry College School of Nursing (F)

6055 Cleveland Avenue, Columbus OH 43231
County: Franklin FICE Identification: 042350
Unit ID: 487861
Telephone: (614) 781-1085 Carnegie Class: Spec 2-yr-Health
FAX Number: (614) 929-3816 Calendar System: Semester
URL: felbrycollege.edu
Established: 2007 Annual Undergrad Tuition & Fees: $30,315
Enrollment: 288 Coed
Affiliation or Control: Proprietary IRS Status: Proprietary
Highest Offering: Baccalaureate
Accreditation: ABHES

01 CEO/On Site Administrator ... Feyi TOLANI
05 Dean/Dir of Nursing ... Dr. Cathryn BAACK
88 Compliance ... Vanessa STAFFORD
06 Registrar ... Vacant
18 Chf Facilities/Physical Plant Ofcr ... Brains BANDA

Fortis College (G)

555 E Alex-Bell Road, Centerville OH 45459-6120
County: Montgomery FICE Identification: 021907
Unit ID: 205179
Telephone: (937) 433-3410 Carnegie Class: Spec 2-yr-Health
FAX Number: (937) 435-6516 Calendar System: Semester
URL: https://www.fortis.edu/campuses/ohio/centerville.html
Established: 1970 Annual Undergrad Tuition & Fees: $14,543
Enrollment: 559 Coed
Affiliation or Control: Proprietary IRS Status: Proprietary
Highest Offering: Associate Degree
Accreditation: ACCSC, ADNUR

01 College President ... Christopher NICKELL
05 Dean of Education ... Lisa MAYS
09 Registrar ... Andrea BEHR
07 Director Admissions ... Vacant
37 Sr Director Financial Aid ... Rachel KARMON

Fortis College (H)

2545 Bailey Road, Cuyahoga Falls OH 44221-2949
County: Summit FICE Identification: 009412
Unit ID: 487302
Telephone: (330) 923-9959 Carnegie Class: Spec 2-yr-Health
FAX Number: (330) 923-0886 Calendar System: Other
URL: www.fortis.edu
Established: 1922 Annual Undergrad Tuition & Fees: N/A
Enrollment: N/A Coed
Affiliation or Control: Proprietary IRS Status: Proprietary
Highest Offering: Associate Degree
Accreditation: ACCSC

01 Campus President ... Mr. Brian PARKER
05 Academic Dean ... Ms. Shannon MCMANAMON

Franciscan University of Steubenville (I)

1235 University Boulevard, Steubenville OH 43952-1763
County: Jefferson FICE Identification: 003036
Unit ID: 205957
Telephone: (740) 283-3771 Carnegie Class: Masters/M
FAX Number: (740) 283-6472 Calendar System: Semester
URL: www.franciscan.edu
Established: 1946 Annual Undergrad Tuition & Fees: $30,180
Enrollment: 3,304 Coed
Affiliation or Control: Roman Catholic IRS Status: 501(c)3
Highest Offering: Master's
Accreditation: HLC, CACREP, CAEP, IACBE, NURSE, SW

01 President ... Rev. Dave PIVONKA, TOR
88 VP of Franciscan Life ... Rev. Jonathan ST. ANDRE, TOR
10 VP of Finance ... Mr. Robert DOUGHERTY
05 VP for Academic Affairs ... Dr. Daniel KEMPTON
31 Director of Community Relations ... Mr. Joseph WALLACE

45 Exec Dir of Institutional Effect ... Dr. James MELLO
11 Vice Pres of Operations ... Mr. Brenan PERGI
15 Director of Human Resources ... Ms. Holly J. MCILWAIN
32 Vice President of Student Life ... Dr. Daniel DENTINO
84 Vice Pres of Enrollment Management ... Mr. Joel S. RECZNIK
111 VP for Advancement ... Mr. Bob HICKEY
88 Local Minister ... Rev. Jonathan MCELHONE, TOR
42 University Chaplain ... Rev. Shawn ROBERSON, TOR
79 Dean of Humanities & Soc Sciences ... Dr. Regina BOERIO
107 Dean of Professional Programs ... Dr. Christin JUNGERS
81 Dean of Natural & Applied Science ... Dr. Daniel KUEBLER
73 Dean of Philosophy and Theology ... Dr. Stephen HILDEBRAND
121 Dean of Advising & Acad Operations ... Ms. Ann DULANY
105 Director Infrastructure Services ... Mr. Dennis BREEN
08 Director of Library ... Ms. Amy LEONI
88 VP of Center for Evangelization ... Mr. Mark JOSEPH
29 Dir of Alumni & Constituent Rels ... Mr. Timothy J. DELANEY
26 Dir Marketing & Communications ... Ms. Lisa M. FERGUSON
07 Dean of Admissions ... Mr. Mark HANRAHAN
06 Registrar ... Ms. Kelli BEATTY
84 Exec Dir of Enrollment Services ... Mr. John L. HERRMANN
09 Director of Institutional Research ... Dcn. Mark A. ERSTE, SR.
21 Controller ... Mr. David LYLE
40 Director of Bookstore ... Ms. Dreama THOMPSON
18 Director Physical Plant Services ... Mr. Joseph P. MCGURN
88 Director of Missionary Outreach ... Mr. Rhett YOUNG
88 Director of Chapel Ministries ... Mr. Robert PALLADINO
38 Director of Wellness Center ... Mr. Matthew BURRISS
19 Director Campus Security ... Vacant
106 Dean of Online Programs ... Dr. Cory MALONEY
108 Director Institutional Assessment ... Vacant
37 Director of Financial Aid ... Mr. Jody PEELER
26 Exec Dir Marketing & Communications ... Ms. Kimberly SPONSELLER
101 Corporate Secretary of University ... Ms. Janine MURDOCK
117 Dir of Risk Mgmt & Compliance ... Mr. John PIZZUTI
41 Director of Athletics ... Mr. Scott GREVE
35 Dean of Students ... Mr. Matthew SCHAEFER
88 Director of Academic Effectiveness ... Ms. Alicia BOYLE
44 Director Annual Giving ... Mr. Benjamin GESSLER
23 Assoc Dir of Wellness Ctr ... Ms. Charlotte JONES
30 Exec Dir Philanthropic Giving ... Mr. Michael ANDREOLA
106 Director of Franciscan Life Online ... Ms. Lindsey SCHROCK
88 Dean of Personal Vocation ... Mr. David SCHMIEISING
20 Director of Teaching Excellence ... Dr. Matthew BREUNINGER

Franklin University (J)

201 S Grant Avenue, Columbus OH 43215-5399
County: Franklin FICE Identification: 003046
Unit ID: 202806
Telephone: (614) 797-4700 Carnegie Class: Masters/L
FAX Number: N/A Calendar System: Trimester
URL: www.franklin.edu
Established: 1902 Annual Undergrad Tuition & Fees: $9,577
Enrollment: 5,926 Coed
Affiliation or Control: Independent Non-Profit IRS Status: 501(c)3
Highest Offering: Doctorate
Accreditation: HLC, CAEP, CAHIIM, IACBE, NURSE

01 President ... Dr. David R. DECKER
11 Sr VP Administration/Chief of Staff ... Ms. Christi L. CABUNGCAL
05 SVP/Provost Academic Affairs ... Dr. Christopher WASHINGTON
26 VP Marketing ... Ms. Linda M. STEELE
111 VP University Advancement ... Vacant
32 SVP Student Affs & Enrollment Mgmt ... Dr. Lynne HULL
108 Exec Director Accreditation & Auth ... Ms. Kelly EVANS WILSON
10 SVP/Chief Financial Officer ... Dr. Marvin BRISKEY
45 VP Planning & University Services ... Vacant
04 Executive Assistant to President ... Ms. Bonnie MCCANN
35 Dean of Students ... Dr. Blake RENNER
13 SVP/Chief Information Officer ... Mr. Rick SUNDERMAN
88 Dir of Accreditation & Inst Effect ... Ms. Susanne SMITH
09 Director Inst Effectiveness ... Mr. Kristopher COBLE
06 Registrar ... Mr. Frank YANCHAK
08 Director of Library Services ... Ms. Alyssa DARDEN
37 Director of Financial Aid ... Vacant
121 Exec Dir Student Affairs Operations ... Ms. Wendi ROBINSON
88 Dean/VP Acad Quality & Planning ... Dr. Patrick BENNETT
88 SVP/Exec Dir Domestic Partnership ... Mr. Bill CHAN
18 Director of Facilities ... Mr. Carl BROWN
26 Director of Public Relations ... Ms. Sherry MERCURIO
29 Director of Alumni Engagement & Dev ... Ms. Sherry MERCURIO
96 Director of Purchasing ... Mr. Bob DONAHUE
118 Director of Benefits ... Ms. Brenda LISTON
88 Director Teaching Excellence ... Dr. Meghan RAEHLL
49 Dean Arts/Science & Technology ... Dr. Kody KUEHNL
50 Dean College of Business ... Dr. Alyncia BOWEN
69 Dean College of Health & Public Adm ... Dr. Jonathan MCCOMBS
53 Dean School of Education ... Dr. Patrick BENNETT
85 SVP Global Programs ... Dr. Godfrey MENDES
15 Director of Human Resources ... Ms. Molly MILLER
88 Director of Accounting ... Mr. Sean HUNTER
21 Exec Dir of Financial Services ... Mr. Randolph SNYDER
19 Director Security/Safety ... Mr. Clifton SPINNER

Galen College of Nursing (K)

100 E Business Way, Suite 200, Cincinnati OH 45241
Telephone: (513) 475-3600 Identification: 770537
Accreditation: &SC, ADNUR, NURSE

† Branch campus of Galen College of Nursing, Louisville, KY

Global Tech College (A)

4346 Secor Rd, Toledo OH 43623

County: Lucas | Identification: 667346
Telephone: (567) 200-6829 | Carnegie Class: Not Classified
FAX Number: (567) 200-6841 | Calendar System: Quarter
URL: www.globaltech.edu
Established: 2012 | Annual Undergrad Tuition & Fees: N/A
Enrollment: N/A | Coed
Affiliation or Control: Proprietary | IRS Status: Proprietary
Highest Offering: Associate Degree
Accreditation: CNCE

01 President .... Dr. Joseph G. HOSNY
11 Dir Admin & Financial Affs .... Dr. Ramsey ATIEH
05 Dir Academic Affs & Student Svcs .... Dr. Michelle CHEASTY
07 Dir of Admissions & Marketing .... John REESE

God's Bible School and College (B)

1810 Young Street, Cincinnati OH 45202-6838

County: Hamilton | FICE Identification: 022205
Unit ID: 202903
Telephone: (513) 721-7944 | Carnegie Class: Bac-Diverse
FAX Number: (513) 763-6649 | Calendar System: Semester
URL: www.gbs.edu
Established: 1900 | Annual Undergrad Tuition & Fees: $7,150
Enrollment: 335 | Coed
Affiliation or Control: Interdenominational | IRS Status: 501(c)3
Highest Offering: Master's
Accreditation: HLC, BI, CAEP

01 President .... Rodney S. LOPER
05 Vice President for Academic Affairs .... Aaron PROFITT
32 Vice President for Student Affairs .... Sonja VERNON
30 Vice President for Donor Relations .... Vacant
06 Registrar .... Kent STETLER
08 Head Librarian .... Stephanie OWENS
10 Vice President for Finance .... David FREDERICK
13 Dir of UX and Digital Strategies .... Jason WEED
84 Vice Pres for Enrollment Services .... Matt HALLAM
37 Financial Aid Coordinator .... Valorie QUESENBERRY

Good Samaritan College of Nursing and Health Science (C)

375 Dixmyth Avenue, Cincinnati OH 45220-2489

County: Hamilton | FICE Identification: 006494
Unit ID: 202912
Telephone: (513) 862-2743 | Carnegie Class: Spec-4-yr-Other Health
FAX Number: (513) 862-3572 | Calendar System: Semester
URL: www.gscollege.edu
Established: 2001 | Annual Undergrad Tuition & Fees: $15,470
Enrollment: 372 | Coed
Affiliation or Control: Independent Non-Profit | IRS Status: 501(c)3
Highest Offering: Baccalaureate
Accreditation: HLC, ADNUR, NUR

01 President .... Dr. Judy KRONENBERGER
05 Dean Academic Affairs/Allied Health .... Dr. Pryze SMITH
66 Academic Dean of Nursing .... Dr. Michelle ROA
10 College Business Administator .... Vacant
11 Associate Dean of Campus Operations .... Dr. Beth MOORE
09 Dir of Inst Assessment/Educ Tech .... Dr. Terri PULLEN
84 Dean of Enrollment .... Dr. Trent HAYES
06 Registrar .... Ms. Isabelle CAYO SANDERS

Heidelberg University (D)

310 E Market Street, Tiffin OH 44883-2462

County: Seneca | FICE Identification: 003048
Unit ID: 203085
Telephone: (419) 448-2000 | Carnegie Class: Masters/S
FAX Number: (419) 448-2124 | Calendar System: Semester
URL: www.heidelberg.edu
Established: 1850 | Annual Undergrad Tuition & Fees: $32,300
Enrollment: 1,230 | Coed
Affiliation or Control: United Church Of Christ | IRS Status: 501(c)3
Highest Offering: Master's
Accreditation: HLC, ACBSP, CAATE, CACREP, CAEP, MUS, NURSE

01 President .... Dr. Robert HUNTINGTON
05 Int VP for Academic Affairs/Provost .... Dr. Bryan SMITH
10 VP for Admin & Business Affairs .... Mr. Hoa NGUYEN
84 VP for Enrollment Mgmt & Marketing .... Dr. Anthony BOURNE
111 VP Univ Advancement & Alumni Affs .... Mr. Phil NESS
29 Exec Dir Alumni Engage/Major Gifts ..Ms. Ashley HELMSTETTER
13 Assoc VP for Information Resources .... Mr. Kurt HUENEMANN
18 Assoc VP for Facilities & Engr .... Mr. Rod MORRISON
06 Registrar .... Mr. Leroy MORGAN
50 Dean of Business & Technology .... Dr. Scott JOHNSON
108 Dir of Acad Assessment & Effect .... Ms. Jordan KAUFMAN
104 Director Intl Affairs & Studies .... Ms. Julie ARNOLD
26 Dir of Marketing & Communications .... Mr. Rick SHERLOCK
36 Exec Dir of HYPE & Placement .... Mr. Mark MCKEE
121 Exec Dir of Owen Center .... Dr. Courtney DEMAYO PUGNO
08 Director of Library .... Ms. Laurie REPP
41 Athletic Director .... Mr. Matt PALM
21 Business Officer .... Ms. Barb GABEL
30 Exec Dir for Development .... Mr. James MINEHART
32 Dean of Student Affairs .... Dr. Chris ABRAMS
39 Asst Dn Stdnt Affs for Campus Life .... Mr. Mark ZENO
124 Dir Student Engagement .... Ms. Jacqueline SIRONEN
15 Chief Human Resources Officer .... Ms. Leslie ERWIN
22 Title IX Coord & HR Generalist .... Ms. Monica VERHOFF
21 Controller .... Mr. Joel WILKINS
04 Exec Asst to President & Provost .... Ms. April RUSSELL
42 Director of Campus Ministry .... Rev. Paul STARK
19 Director Security/Safety .... Mr. Jeff RHOADES
28 Coord of Multicultural Student Affs .... Mr. Shaun GUNNELL
105 Director Web Services .... Mr. Neil CARRIER
37 Director of Financial Aid .... Ms. Cathy BELFIORE

Herzing University-Akron (E)

1600 S Arlington Street, 100, Akron OH 44306-3958

Telephone: (330) 724-1600 | FICE Identification: 020695
Accreditation: &HLC, ADNUR, NURSE

† Regional accreditation is carried under the parent institution in Madison, WI.

Hiram College (F)

Box 67, Hiram OH 44234-0067

County: Portage | FICE Identification: 003049
Unit ID: 203128
Telephone: (330) 569-3211 | Carnegie Class: Bac-Diverse
FAX Number: (330) 569-5494 | Calendar System: Other
URL: www.hiram.edu
Established: 1850 | Annual Undergrad Tuition & Fees: $24,500
Enrollment: 1,110 | Coed
Affiliation or Control: Independent Non-Profit | IRS Status: 501(c)3
Highest Offering: Master's
Accreditation: HLC, CAEP, NURSE

01 President .... Dr. David P. HANEY
05 VP Academic Affairs/Dean of College .... Dr. Robert BOHRER
10 CFO/VP Business and Finance .... Ms. Nancy G. RUBIN
30 VP Development & Alumni Relations .... Mr. Walter C. WILLIAMS
32 Interim Dean of Students .... Ms. Detra WEST
84 VP of Enrollment Management .... Dr. Andrea D. WELCH
20 Associate Dean Academic Affairs .... Dr. Jeffrey C. SWENSON
06 Registrar .... Ms. Mary BLAND
08 Director Library .... Ms. Janet VOGEL
102 Dir Foundation/Corp/Govt Relations .... Ms. Mary K. LANG
29 Exec Dir Development/Alumni Rels .... Ms. Lynne DEWYRE
07 Director of Admission .... Ms. Jana N. WILLAN
112 Director of Planned Giving .... Ms. Peggy A. PAINLEY
37 Director Financial Services .... Ms. Andrea L. LEHMAN
36 Director of Career Services .... Ms. Marijean BENEDIK
121 Coordinator of Academic Development .... Ms. Stephanie A. SIMPSON
13 Executive Director IT .... Mr. Peter E. MAHONEY
108 Director of Institutional Research .... Dr. Laura A. VAN WORMER
23 Director of Health Services .... Ms. Asha L. GOODNER
41 Director of Athletics .... Mr. Scott A. POHLMAN
15 Director Human Resources .... Ms. Karen HOLLAND
18 Director of the Physical Plant .... Mr. Ryan OLSZEWSKI
21 Interim Controller .... Ms. Linda MUREN
35 Director of Campus Involvement .... Vacant
38 Director Student Counseling .... Dr. Kevin P. FEISTHAMEL
28 Assoc Dean/Dir Diversity & Inclus .... Ms. Detra E. WEST
96 Director of Purchasing .... Ms. Martha A. SCHETTLER
26 Dir Strategic Marketing/Media Rels .... Ms. Jenelle BAYUS
27 Internal Communications .... Ms. Elise PITKIN
105 Website Administrator .... Mr. Adam M. KALCIC
04 Executive Asst to President .... Ms. Candice K. PAINLEY
104 Study Away Coordinator .... Dr. Matthew F. NOTARIAN
19 Director Security/Safety .... Mr. Daniel FYNES
39 Assistant Dean of Students .... Mr. Mick STEINER
42 Chaplain .... Rev. Christopher J. MCCREIGHT

Hocking College (G)

3301 Hocking Parkway, Nelsonville OH 45764-9704

County: Athens | FICE Identification: 007598
Unit ID: 203155
Telephone: (740) 753-3591 | Carnegie Class: Assoc/HVT-High Trad
FAX Number: (740) 753-7005 | Calendar System: Semester
URL: www.hocking.edu
Established: 1968 | Annual Undergrad Tuition & Fees (In-State): $5,180
Enrollment: 2,431 | Coed
Affiliation or Control: State | IRS Status: 501(c)3
Highest Offering: Associate Degree
Accreditation: HLC, ACBSP, ACFEI, ADNUR, DH, EMT, MAC, MLTAD, PTAA

01 President .... Dr. Betty YOUNG
10 Exec Director Finance/Treasurer .... Mr. Mark FULLER
05 VP Academics/Workforce Development .... Ms. Jacqueline HAGEROTT
32 VP Student Affs/Chief Div/Incl Ofcr .... Ms. Hannah GUADA
15 Director Human Resources .... Ms. Chrystal MARCUM
04 Exec Assistant to the President .... Mr. Kyle FULLER
37 Exec Director Financial Aid .... Mr. Stephen POWELL
26 Exec Dir Mktg/Public Rels/Enrol Mgt .... Mr. Joshua MOORE
19 Chief Hocking College Police .... Ms. Tiffany TIMS
06 Registrar .... Ms. Diane WOLF
18 Exec Dir Facilities/Skill Trades .... Mr. Bryan LUTZ
102 Director Foundation .... Mr. Douglas WELLS
100 Exec VP & Chief of Staff .... Mr. Jeff DAUBENMIRE
45 Exec Dir Strat Init/Sp Asst to Pres .... Dr. Shah HASAN

Hocking College Perry Campus (H)

5454 State Route 37, New Lexington OH 43764

Telephone: (740) 342-3337 | Identification: 770359
Accreditation: &HLC

Hondros College of Business (I)

4140 Executive Pkwy, Ste 222, Westerville OH 43081

County: Franklin | Identification: 667426
Telephone: (614) 350-5748 | Carnegie Class: Not Classified
FAX Number: (614) 413-3914 | Calendar System: Quarter
URL: hondroscollegeofbusiness.com
Established: 2009 | Annual Undergrad Tuition & Fees: N/A
Enrollment: N/A | Coed
Affiliation or Control: Proprietary | IRS Status: Proprietary
Highest Offering: Associate Degree
Accreditation: DEAC

01 President .... Tina LAPP

Hondros College of Nursing (J)

1810 Successful Drive, Fairborn OH 45324

Telephone: (937) 879-1940 | Identification: 770751
Accreditation: ABHES, CNEA

Hondros College of Nursing (K)

5005 Rockside Road, Suite 130, Independence OH 44131

Telephone: (216) 524-1143 | Identification: 770750
Accreditation: ABHES, CNEA

Hondros College of Nursing (L)

7600 Tyler's Place Boulevard, West Chester OH 45069

Telephone: (513) 508-3005 | Identification: 770749
Accreditation: ABHES, CNEA

Hondros College of Nursing (M)

4140 Executive Parkway, Westerville OH 43081-3855

County: Franklin | FICE Identification: 040743
Unit ID: 203386
Telephone: (614) 508-7277 | Carnegie Class: Spec-4-yr-Other Health
FAX Number: (614) 508-7280 | Calendar System: Quarter
URL: www.hondros.edu
Established: 1981 | Annual Undergrad Tuition & Fees: $18,847
Enrollment: 2,159 | Coed
Affiliation or Control: Proprietary | IRS Status: Proprietary
Highest Offering: Associate Degree
Accreditation: ABHES, CNEA

00 CEO .... Harry WILKINS
01 Campus Executive Director .... Kelly CAVANAGH
66 Dean/Director of Nursing .... Dr. Carole SULLIVAN
07 Director of Admission .... Robert MINTO
37 Financial Aid Manger .... Amy BULL

International College of Broadcasting (N)

6 S Smithville Road, Dayton OH 45431-1898

County: Montgomery | FICE Identification: 013132
Unit ID: 203289
Telephone: (937) 258-8251 | Carnegie Class: Assoc/HT-High Trad
FAX Number: (937) 258-8714 | Calendar System: Semester
URL: www.icb.edu
Established: 1968 | Annual Undergrad Tuition & Fees: $15,520
Enrollment: 60 | Coed
Affiliation or Control: Proprietary | IRS Status: Proprietary
Highest Offering: Associate Degree
Accreditation: ACCSC

01 President/School Director .... J. Michael LEMASTER
05 Director of Education .... Ronda DOSTER
36 Dir Career Student Services .... Kenny PYLES
07 Director of Admissions .... J. Michael LEMASTER

John Carroll University (O)

1 John Carroll Boulevard, University Heights OH 44118

County: Cuyahoga | FICE Identification: 003050
Unit ID: 203368
Telephone: (216) 397-1886 | Carnegie Class: Masters/L
FAX Number: (216) 397-4256 | Calendar System: Semester
URL: www.jcu.edu
Established: 1886 | Annual Undergrad Tuition & Fees: $44,406
Enrollment: 3,278 | Coed
Affiliation or Control: Roman Catholic | IRS Status: 501(c)3
Highest Offering: Beyond Master's But Less Than Doctorate
Accreditation: HLC, CACREP, CAEP

01 President .... Dr. Alan MICIAK
04 Exec Assistant to the President .... Maura JOCHUM
88 VP for Univ Mission & Identity .... Dr. Edward PECK
43 General Counsel .... Colleen TREML
05 Provost & Academic Vice President .... Dr. Steven HERBERT
10 VP Finance & Administration .... Robert CONNORS

32	Vice President for Student Affairs	Dr. Sherri CRAHEN
84	VP for Enrollment Management	Ray BROWN
26	AVP for Integrated Marketing & Comm	Michael SCANLAN
18	Associate VP for Facilities	Jeremiah SWETEL
20	Vice Provost Academic Affairs	Dr. James KRUKONES
108	Asst Provost Assessment & IE	Dr. R. Todd BRUCE
121	Asst Provost Academic Advising	Laura ATKINS
37	Asst VP Enrollment/Financial Svcs	Claudia WENZEL
30	AVP for Development	Richard DAY
15	AVP Human Resources	Jennifer RICK
84	AVP Enrollment Operations	Steve VITATOE
08	Director of the Library	Vacant
13	Chief Information Officer	James BURKE
50	Dean Boler College	Dr. Elad GRANOT
49	Dean College of Arts & Sciences	Dr. Bonnie GUNZENHAUSER
58	Dean of Graduate Studies	Dr. Rebecca DRENOVSKY
83	Assoc Dean Humanities & Soc Sci	Dr. Rodney HESSINGER
81	Assoc Dean Sciences & Mathematics	Dr. Michael MARTIN
109	Director of Auxiliary Services	Rory HILL
21	Controller	John CLIFFORD
25	Director of Sponsored Research	Erica KENNEDY
114	Dir of Budget & Financial Analysis	Jennifer DILLON
112	Senior Director of Major Gifts	Mary RYCYNA
29	Exec Dir of Alumni Rel & Annual Giv	David VITATOE
31	Dir Ctr for Service & Social Action	Katherine FEELY, SND
102	Dir Foundation Rels & Grant Writing	Pamela GEORGE-MERRILL
19	Director & Chief of JCUPD	Brian HURD
09	Director of Institutional Research	Maria O'CONNOR
117	Dir Regulatory Affairs & Risk Mgmt	Garry HOMANY
22	Affirm Action Officer for Faculty	Dr. James KRUKONES
91	Director Enterprise Applications	John SULLY
24	Center Digital Media Fac Liaison	Dr. Jay TARBY
119	Data Security Engineer	James SPITZNAGEL
93	Dir Ctr for Student Div & Inclusion	Selen ZARRELLI
23	Dir of Student Health & Wellness	Janet KREVH
92	Director Honors Program	Dr. Angela CANDA
06	Registrar	Michelle REYNARD
38	Director Univ Counseling Services	Dr. Mark ONUSKO
39	Director of Residence Life	Lisa BROWN CORNELIUS
41	Sr Director Athletics & Recreation	Michelle MORGAN
42	Director of Campus Ministry	John SCARANO
122	Mgr Stdnt Life Pgms-Greek Life	Mary Ann HANICAK

Kent State University Kent Campus (A)

PO Box 5190, Kent OH 44242-0001

County: Portage — FICE Identification: 003051 — Unit ID: 203517

Telephone: (330) 672-3000 — Carnegie Class: DU-Highest

FAX Number: (330) 672-2190 — Calendar System: Semester

URL: www.kent.edu

Established: 1910 — Annual Undergrad Tuition & Fees (In-State): $11,009

Enrollment: 26,822 — Coed

Affiliation or Control: State — IRS Status: 501(c)3

Highest Offering: Doctorate

Accreditation: HLC, AAB, ACPHA, ART, AUD, CAATE, CACREP, CAEPN, CAPRT, CIDA, CLPSY, CONST, DANCE, DIETD, DIETI, EXSC, #JOUR, LIB, LSAR, MUS, NAIT, NURSE, PH, POD, SCPSY, SP, SPAA, THEA

01	President	Dr. Todd DIACON
05	Senior Vice President/Provost	Dr. Melody TANKERSLEY
10	Senior Vice Pres Finance & Admin	Dr. Mark M. POLATAJKO
15	Vice Pres Human Resources	Mr. Jack WITT
111	VP Inst Advancement	Ms. Valoree VARGO
32	Vice Pres Student Affairs	Dr. Lamar R. HYLTON
84	VP Enrollment Management	Dr. Sean BROGHAMMER
26	VP University Relations	Mr. Stephen WARD
46	VP Research	Dr. Doug DELAHANTY
13	Vice Pres Information Services/CIO	Mr. John M. RATHJE
28	VP Diversity/Equity/Inclusion	Dr. Amoaba GOODEN
20	Dean Undergraduate Studies	Dr. Eboni PRINGLE
35	Student Ombuds	Ms. Amy QUILLIN
124	Assoc VP Univ Outreach & Engagement	Dr. Dana LAWLESS-ANDRIC
20	Assoc Provost Faculty Affairs	Mr. Kevin WEST
29	AVP Donor & Volunteer Engagement	Mr. Scott MCKINNEY
16	Human Resources Director-CPM	Mr. David DIXON
06	Registrar	Mr. Chris DORSTEN
43	Vice Pres General Counsel	Mr. Willis WALKER
100	VP and University Secretary	Ms. Charlene K. REED
41	Director Intercollegiate Athletics	Mr. Randale RICHMOND
118	Director of Compliance & Benefits	Vacant
37	AVP Enroll Mgmt/Student Fin Aid	Ms. Brenda BURKE
07	Assoc VP Enroll Mgmt/Admissions	Vacant
19	Director of Public Safety	Mr. Dean TONDIGLIA
12	Dean Trumbull Campus	Dr. Bill AYRES
96	Director of Procurement	Mr. Timothy J. KONCZAL
49	Dean Arts & Sciences	Dr. Mandy MUNRO-STASIUK
50	Dean of Business Administration	Dr. Deborah F. SPAKE
53	Dean EHHS	Dr. James HANNON
57	Dean of the Arts	Dr. John R. CRAWFORD-SPINELLI
66	Dean College of Nursing	Dr. Versie JOHNSON-MALLARD
51	Asst VP Continuing & Distance Educ	Ms. Valerie I. KELLY
92	Dean Honors College	Dr. Alison SMITH
08	Dean of University Libraries	Mr. Kenneth BURHANNA
48	Dean Architecture/Environ Design	Mr. Mark MISTUR
60	Dean Col of Comm & Information	Dr. Amy REYNOLDS
54	Dean Aeronautics & Engineering	Dr. Christina BLOEBAUM
88	Dean College of Podiatric Medicine	Dr. Allan BOIKE
21	Director Business Admin Svcs	Mr. Mark M. MATEJCIK
08	Library Director-CPM	Mrs. Donna M. PERZESKI
18	Dir Opers Satellite Facilities CPM	Mr. Dan RIDGWAY
04	Sr Assistant to the President	Ms. Diana BOLDON
101	Board Ops Mgr/Asst to EO	Ms. Charlene NICHOL
86	Director Government Relations	Mr. Nicholas GATTOZZI
122	Asst Dir Fraternity/Sorority Life	Mr. Dennis CAMPBELL

Kent State University at Ashtabula (B)

3300 Lake Road W, Ashtabula OH 44004-2299

Telephone: (440) 964-3322 — FICE Identification: 003052

Accreditation: &HLC, ADNUR, COARC, OTA, PTAA, RAD

† Regional accreditation is carried under the parent institution in Kent, OH.

Kent State University East Liverpool Campus (C)

400 E Fourth Street, East Liverpool OH 43920-3497

Telephone: (330) 385-3805 — FICE Identification: 003056

Accreditation: &HLC, ADNUR, OTA, PTAA

† Regional accreditation is carried under the parent institution in Kent, OH.

Kent State University Geauga Campus (D)

14111 Claridon-Troy Road, Burton Township OH 44021-9500

Telephone: (440) 834-4187 — FICE Identification: 003059

Accreditation: &HLC, ADNUR

† Regional accreditation is carried under the parent institution in Kent, OH.

Kent State University Salem Campus (E)

2491 State Route 45 South, Salem OH 44460-9412

Telephone: (330) 332-0361 — FICE Identification: 003061

Accreditation: &HLC, RAD, RTT

† Regional accreditation is carried under the parent institution in Kent, OH.

Kent State University Stark Campus (F)

6000 Frank Avenue NW, North Canton OH 44720-9988

Telephone: (330) 499-9600 — FICE Identification: 003054

Accreditation: &HLC

† Regional accreditation is carried under the parent institution in Kent, OH.

Kent State University Trumbull Campus (G)

4314 Mahoning Avenue, NW, Warren OH 44483-1998

Telephone: (330) 847-0571 — FICE Identification: 003064

Accreditation: &HLC

† Regional accreditation is carried under the parent institution in Kent, OH.

Kent State University Tuscarawas Campus (H)

330 University Drive, NE, New Philadelphia OH 44663-9403

Telephone: (330) 339-3391 — FICE Identification: 003062

Accreditation: &HLC, ADNUR

† Regional accreditation is carried under the parent institution in Kent, OH.

Kenyon College (I)

106 College-Park Street, Gambier OH 43022-9623

County: Knox — FICE Identification: 003065 — Unit ID: 203535

Telephone: (740) 427-5000 — Carnegie Class: Bac-A&S

FAX Number: (740) 427-3077 — Calendar System: Semester

URL: www.kenyon.edu

Established: 1824 — Annual Undergrad Tuition & Fees: $55,020

Enrollment: 1,615 — Coed

Affiliation or Control: Independent Non-Profit — IRS Status: 501(c)3

Highest Offering: Baccalaureate

Accreditation: HLC

01	President	Dr. Sean DECATUR
05	Provost	Dr. Jeff BOWMAN
111	Vice President Advancement	Ms. Colleen GARLAND
10	Vice President for Finance	Mr. Todd E. BURSON
08	Vice Pres Library & Info Svcs	Mr. Ronald K. GRIGGS
100	Chief of Staff	Ms. Susan MORSE
112	Assoc VP for Planned Giving	Mr. Kyle W. HENDERSON
32	Dean of Students	Ms. Robin HART RUTHENBECK
07	Dean of Admissions/Fin Aid	Ms. Diane ANCI
20	Associate Provost	Dr. Sheryl HEMKIN
06	Registrar/Dean Academic Support	Ms. Ellen K. HARBOURT
26	Vice President for Communications	Ms. Janet MARSDEN
29	Assoc VP Alumni & Parent Engagement	Mr. Shawn DAILEY
37	Director of Financial Aid	Mr. Craig SLAUGHTER
38	Dir Cox Health & Counseling Center	Mr. Christopher SMITH
15	Director of Human Resources	Ms. Jennifer G. CABRAL
42	Director of Religious/Spiritual	Rabbi Marc BRAGIN
18	VP Facility/Planning/Sustainability	Mr. Ian SMITH
22	Civil Rights/Title IX Coordinator	Ms. Samantha HUGHES
19	Director of Campus Safety	Mr. Michael SWEAZEY
09	Director of Institutional Research	Ms. Erika M. FARFAN
21	Manager of Business Services	Mr. Frederick S. LINGER
28	Director Diversity/Equity/Inclusion	Mr. A. Chris KENNERLY
101	Director of Board Relations	Ms. Kathryn LAKE
04	Executive Asst to President	Ms. Mary Ellen O'MEARA
41	Athletic Director	Ms. Jill MCCARTNEY

Kettering College (J)

3737 Southern Boulevard, Kettering OH 45429-1299

County: Montgomery — FICE Identification: 007035 — Unit ID: 203544

Telephone: (937) 395-8601 — Carnegie Class: Spec-4-yr-Other Health

FAX Number: (937) 395-8106 — Calendar System: Semester

URL: www.kc.edu

Established: 1967 — Annual Undergrad Tuition & Fees: $13,824

Enrollment: 763 — Coed

Affiliation or Control: Seventh-day Adventist — IRS Status: 501(c)3

Highest Offering: Doctorate

Accreditation: HLC, ARCPA, COARC, DMS, NUR, OT, RAD

00	Chairman of the Board	Mr. Walter SACKETT
01	President	Dr. Nate BRANDSTATER
15	Vice President Human Resources	Mr. Timothy DUTTON
05	Dean for Academic Affairs	Dr. Rafael CANIZALES
32	Dean of Student Success	Mr. Adam BROWN
102	President of Foundation	Mr. Rick THIE, II
84	Assoc Dean Enrollment Mgmt	Mrs. Jessica BEANS
121	Assoc Dean Student Success	Mr. Ben HOTELLING
10	Chief Business Officer	Mrs. Wendi BARBER
21	Director of Finance/Administration	Mr. Nicholas HENSON
06	Registrar	Mrs. Robin VANDERBILT
37	Director Student Financial Aid	Mrs. Kim RAWLINS
40	Manager Bookstore	Mrs. Jessica OLDFIELD
42	Campus Chaplain	Mr. Steve CARLSON
32	Director Student Life	Mr. Kris HARTER
26	Public Relations Officer	Ms. Lauren BROOKS
08	Director of Library	Ms. Pamela STEVENS
07	Director of Admissions	Mrs. Katrina HILL
36	Director Career Services	Mr. Benjamin HOTELLING
13	Senior Information Officer	Mr. Jim NESBIT

Lake Erie College (K)

391 W Washington Street, Painesville OH 44077-3389

County: Lake — FICE Identification: 003066 — Unit ID: 203580

Telephone: (440) 375-7000 — Carnegie Class: Masters/S

FAX Number: (440) 375-7005 — Calendar System: Semester

URL: www.lec.edu

Established: 1856 — Annual Undergrad Tuition & Fees: $33,172

Enrollment: 949 — Coed

Affiliation or Control: Independent Non-Profit — IRS Status: 501(c)3

Highest Offering: Master's

Accreditation: HLC, ARCPA, CAEPT, IACBE

01	President	Dr. Brian POSLER
05	Provost	Bryan DEPOY
10	Vice Pres Administration & Finance	Brian DIRK
111	VP for Institutional Advancement	Jennifer SCHULLER
84	Vice President for Enrollment	Chauncey JACKSON
53	Dean School of Educ & Prof Studies	Dr. Katharine DELAVAN
32	Associate VP for Student Affairs	Kimberly ROBARE
50	Dean School of Business	Dr. Jennifer KINNAIRD
88	Dean School of Equine Studies	Dr. Pam HESS
79	Dean School of Arts/Human & SS	Dr. Jennifer SWARTZ-LEVINE
81	Dean School of Nat Sci & Math	Dr. Jonathan TEDESCO
06	Registrar	Amanda FORDYCE
88	Director Physician Assistant Pgm	Sean KRAMER
36	Dir Career Dev/Experiential Lrng	Eric EVANS
13	Director of Information Technology	Brad LUHTA
15	Director of Human Resources	Rachel HANNI
38	Director Student Success Center	Dr. John SPIESMAN
18	Director Physical Plant	Joe BALLENTINE
29	Executive Dir of Alumni Relations	Kelsey HUKILL
41	Director of Athletics	Molly HOFFMAN
08	Director Lincoln Library	Jeanna PURSES
19	Director Security	Richard KLINE
88	Director Professional Development	Jennifer MILLER
04	Executive Assistant	Leah JACKSON
88	Associate Dir of Alumni Relations	Catherine BEISEL
37	Director Student Financial Aid	Tricia PANGONIS
26	Exec Dir Public Relations/Marketing	Angela DELPRETE
101	Secretary of the Institution/Board	Leah JACKSON
106	Dean of Online Education/E-learning	Eric OESTMANN
44	Director Annual Giving	Vacant

Lakeland Community College (L)

7700 Clocktower Drive, Kirtland OH 44094-5198

County: Lake — FICE Identification: 006804 — Unit ID: 203599

Telephone: (440) 525-7000 — Carnegie Class: Assoc/HT-Mix Trad/Non

FAX Number: (440) 525-7651 — Calendar System: Semester

URL: www.lakelandcc.edu

Established: 1967 — Annual Undergrad Tuition & Fees (In-District): $4,347

Enrollment: 5,331 — Coed

Affiliation or Control: State/Local — IRS Status: 501(c)3

Highest Offering: Associate Degree

Accreditation: HLC, ADNUR, CAHIIM, COARC, DH, EMT, HT, MAC, MLTAD, NAEYC, OTA, POLYT, @PTAA, RAD, SURGT

01	President	Dr. Morris W. BEVERAGE, JR.
05	Exec VP & Provost	Dr. Laura BARNARD
10	Exec Vice Pres/Treasurer	Mr. Michael E. MAYHER

100 Chief of Staff/SVP Inst Effective ...Ms. Catherine BUSH
26 Chief Commun Ofcr/VP College Rels ...Ms. Dawn M. PLANTE
20 Assoc Provost Teach & Learn ...Dr. Deborah L. HARDY
32 Assoc VP/Dean of Students ...Mr. Mario D. PETITTI, JR.
81 Dean of Arts and Sciences ...Mr. Adam CLOUTIER
76 Dean of Health Technologies ...Dr. Deborah L. HARDY
88 Int Dir for Articulation & Transfer ...Ms. Barbara FRIEDT
21 Deputy Treasurer & Dir for Budget ...Mr. Thomas REYNOLDS
13 CIO Administrative Technologies ...Mr. Rick PENNY
21 Controller ...Mr. Michael GRAFF
18 Director for Facilities Management ...Mr. Bert DIEHL
19 Chief of Police ...Mr. Stephen GAGLIARDI
124 Asst Provost Strategic Retention ...Ms. Stephanie BROWN
84 Senior Dir Enrollment Operations ...Ms. Melissa A. AMSPAUGH
35 Director of Student Activities ...Mr. Mario PETITTI
30 Dir Development/Alumni Relations ...Mr. Gregory SANDERS
96 Director of Purchasing ...Mr. Tom A. KIRCHNER
43 General Legal Counsel ...Mr. Michael FISHER
86 Director Government Relations ...Ms. Amy SABATH

Lakewood University (A)

2231 North Taylor Road, Cleveland Heights OH 44112
County: Cuyahoga Identification: 666715
Telephone: (800) 517-0857 Carnegie Class: Not Classified
FAX Number: (216) 803-9899 Calendar System: Other
URL: www.lakewood.edu
Established: 1998 Annual Undergrad Tuition & Fees: N/A
Enrollment: N/A Coed
Affiliation or Control: Independent Non-Profit IRS Status: 501(c)3
Highest Offering: Master's
Accreditation: DEAC

00 President and Founder ...Ms. Tanya HAGGINS
05 Academic Dean ...Mr. James GEPPERTH
30 Vice President of Business Develop ...Mr. Isaac HAGGINS
11 Vice President of Operations ...Mr. Tommy SUTTON-LOVETT

Lorain County Community College (B)

1005 N Abbe Road, Elyria OH 44035-1691
County: Lorain FICE Identification: 003068
Unit ID: 203748
Telephone: (440) 365-5222 Carnegie Class: Assoc/HT-Mix Trad/Non
FAX Number: (440) 365-6519 Calendar System: Semester
URL: www.lorainccc.edu
Established: 1963 Annual Undergrad Tuition & Fees (In-District): $4,400
Enrollment: 10,138 Coed
Affiliation or Control: State/Local IRS Status: 501(c)3
Highest Offering: Baccalaureate
Accreditation: HLC, ADNUR, ART, DH, DMS, EMT, MAC, MLTAD, OTA, PNUR, PTAA, RAD, SURGT

01 President ...Dr. Marcia J. BALLINGER
46 VP Strategic & Institutional Devel ...Ms. Tracy A. GREEN
05 Provost/VP Acad Affairs & UP ...Dr. Jonathan N. DRYDEN
10 Vice President Admin Svcs/Treasurer ...Mr. Jonathan VOLPE
88 Assoc Prov University Partnership ...Vacant
08 Dean Teaching & Learner Support ...Dr. Danielle BUDZICK
84 Assoc Prov Enroll/Fin Career Svcs ..Ms. Marisa VERNON WHITE
13 Chief Information Tech Officer ...Mr. Donald HUFFMAN
15 Director Human Resources ...Mr. Keith BROWN
88 Dir Talent and Business Innovation ...Ms. Terri B. SANDU
18 Director of Physical Plant ...Mr. Leo MAHONEY
57 Dir Stocker Humanit/Fine Arts Ctr .Ms. Janet HERMAN-BARLOW
54 Dean Engr/Business & Info Tech ...Ms. Kelly ZELESNIK
76 Dean Health & Wellness ...Dr. Christopher HIRSCHLER
79 Dean Arts/Humanities ...Dr. Brenda PONGRACZ
81 Dean Science/Mathematics ...Mr. Aaron WEISS
83 Dean Social Science/Human Svc ...Dr. Denise DOUGLAS
06 Registrar ...Ms. Sun Kyong JAMERSON
101 Executive Assoc Board Liaison ...Ms. Jocelyn WIESER
19 Director of Campus Security ...Mr. Ken COLLINS
26 Dir School & Community Partnership ...Ms. Cynthia KUSHNER
102 LCC Foundation Exec Director ...Ms. Lisa BROWN
31 Director Strategic Cmty Engagement ...Ms. Alison MUSSER

Lourdes University (C)

6832 Convent Boulevard, Sylvania OH 43560-2898
County: Lucas FICE Identification: 003069
Unit ID: 203757
Telephone: (419) 885-3211 Carnegie Class: Masters/S
FAX Number: (419) 882-3987 Calendar System: Semester
URL: www.lourdes.edu
Established: 1958 Annual Undergrad Tuition & Fees: $25,644
Enrollment: 1,253 Coed
Affiliation or Control: Roman Catholic IRS Status: 501(c)3
Highest Offering: Doctorate
Accreditation: HLC, ANEST, CAEPT, IACBE, NURSE, SW

01 President ...Dr. Mary Ann GAWELEK
00 President Emerita ...Sr. Ann Francis KLIMKOWSKI
04 Exec Admin Asst to the President ...Ms. Theresa HOLUP
05 Provost ...Dr. Terry KELLER
10 Vice President of Finance ...Vacant
42 VP for Mission & Ministry ...Sr. Barbara VANO, OSF
111 Vice President for Inst Advancement ...Ms. Mary SABIN
84 VP of Enrollment Management ...Mr. Jeffrey LILES
49 Dean College of Arts & Sciences ...Dr. Kate BEUTEL
53 Dean College of Social Services ...Dr. Jami CURLEY
66 Dean College of Nursing ...Dr. Christina SILKA

50 Dean Col Business & Leadership ...Dr. David BURKITT
32 VP Student Affairs/Dean of Students ...Mr. Greg KNESER
39 Asst Dean of Residence Life ...Mr. Noah FOX
37 Director of Financial Aid ...Ms. Callie ZAKE
26 Director of University Relations ...Ms. Helene SHEETS
08 Director of Library Services ...Sr. Sandra RUTKOWSKI
06 Registrar ...Ms. Anya MARCERO
13 Chief Information Officer ...Mr. Michael MCCORMICK
15 Director of Human Resources ...Mr. Michael WISNIEWSKI
36 Director of Career Services ...Mr. Thomas AVERY
21 Director of Finance ...Ms. Kimberly SHEEHAN
30 Director of Donor Relations ...Ms. Brittany TELANDER
18 Director of Facilities & Grounds ...Mr. Michael CRAVENS
22 Title IX Coordinator ...Mr. Greg KNESER
19 Director of Campus Security ...Mr. Benjamin TUCKER
07 Director of Undergrad Admissions ...Ms. Callie ZAKE
41 VP of Athletics ...Ms. Janet EATON-SMITH
121 Dean of Student Success ...Ms. Alisa SMITH
102 Grants and Strategic Initiatives ...Ms. Cindy MILLER
28 Director of Diversity ...Vacant
29 Director Alumni Affairs ...Ms. Alissa HUNT

Malone University (D)

2600 Cleveland Avenue NW, Canton OH 44709-3308
County: Stark FICE Identification: 003072
Unit ID: 203775
Telephone: (330) 471-8100 Carnegie Class: Masters/M
FAX Number: (330) 471-8478 Calendar System: Semester
URL: www.malone.edu
Established: 1892 Annual Undergrad Tuition & Fees: $32,416
Enrollment: 1,463 Coed
Affiliation or Control: Friends IRS Status: 501(c)3
Highest Offering: Master's
Accreditation: HLC, ACBSP, CACREP, CAEP, MUS, NURSE, SW

01 President ...Dr. Gregory J. MILLER
10 Vice Pres for Finance/CFO ...Mrs. Katie A. ROBBINS
05 Interim Provost ...Dr. Christina M. SCHNYDERS
32 Chief Student Development Officer ...Ms. Melody K. SCOTT
111 Vice Pres for Advancement ...Dr. Patrick S. ROBERTS
26 Vice Pres for Marketing & Comm ...Mr. Timothy A. BRYAN
84 Vice Pres for Enrollment Management ...Dr. Jason R. MOYER
66 Chair of Nursing/Chief Nurse Admin ...Dr. Carrie D. STROUP
21 Controller ...Ms. Shari A. APPEL
06 Registrar ...Mr. Gary L. PHELPS
07 Director of Admissions ...Ms. Ann O. LAWSON
29 Dir Alumni/Constituent Engagement ...Ms. Megan J. MAUCK
110 Dir of Adv Rsrch/Foundation Grants ...Mrs. Paula M. CALHOUN
37 Director of Financial Aid ...Mrs. Pamela S. PUSTAY
41 Athletic Director ...Ms. Tanya C. HOCKMAN
08 Director of Library ...Ms. Rebecca L. FORT
106 Exec Director of Distance Learning ...Mr. John W. KOSHMIDER, III
93 Director of Multicultural Services ...Ms. Andrea B. RAMSEY
104 Dir Ctr for Intercultural Studies ...Dr. Elizabeth P. ROE
19 Director Security/Safety ...Mr. Jack O. ANGELO
13 Chief Information Officer ...Mr. M. Adam KLEMANN
90 Senior Network Engineer ...Mr. James M. SHAFFER
42 Director of Spiritual Formation ...Rev Dr. Linda J. LEON
105 Webmaster/Photo/Videographer ...Mr. Joshua C. MCMANAWAY
40 Bookstore Manager ...Mrs. Kathy L. SECREST
04 Exec Asst to Pres/Asst to Board ...Mrs. Teresa L. PITTINGER
88 Dir of Inst Reporting & Data Mgmt ...Mrs. Sara K. BURKE
92 Director of Honors Program ...Dr. Steven M. JENSEN
89 Dir of the College Experience Pgm ...Dr. Marcia K. EVERETT
38 Director of Counseling Center ...Mr. Timothy T. MORBER
23 Health Center Director ...Ms. Rebecca K. RODAK
15 Director of Human Resources ...Ms. Patrice D. YACKO
108 Director Institutional Assessment ...Dr. Kyle D. CALDERHEAD

Marietta College (E)

215 Fifth Street, Marietta OH 45750-4033
County: Washington FICE Identification: 003073
Unit ID: 203845
Telephone: (740) 376-4000 Carnegie Class: Bac-Diverse
FAX Number: (800) 331-7896 Calendar System: Semester
URL: www.marietta.edu
Established: 1835 Annual Undergrad Tuition & Fees: $36,764
Enrollment: 1,254 Coed
Affiliation or Control: Independent Non-Profit IRS Status: 501(c)3
Highest Offering: Master's
Accreditation: HLC, ARCPA, CAATE, CAEP, MUS

01 President ...Dr. William N. RUUD
05 Provost/Dean of Faculty ...Dr. Janet L. BLAND
10 VP for Administration & Finance ...Ms. Michele L. MARRA
111 VP for Advancement ...Dr. Joshua JACOBS
32 VP Student Life/Chf Diversity Ofcr ...Dr. Richard K. DANFORD
84 VP for Enrollment Mgmt ...Mr. Scot SCHAEFER
88 Dean McDonough Ctr for Leadership ...Dr. Robert MCMANUS
101 Secretary to the Board of Trustees ...Dr. Mark MILLER
08 Director of Library ...Dr. N. Douglas ANDERSON
07 Director of Admissions ...Ms. Katie FENNELL
18 Director of Physical Plant ...Mr. Rodney WOOD
06 Registrar ...Ms. Tina K. PERDUE
15 Director of Human Resources ...Ms. Caprice HUDSON
19 Chief of Campus Police ...Mr. James S. WEAVER
26 Exec Dir of Strategic Comm & Mktg ...Mr. Thomas D. PERRY
09 Institutional Researcher ...Mr. William (Bill) CLARK
36 Director of the Career Center ...Ms. Betsy KNOTT
41 Director of Athletics ...Mr. Larry R. HISER

13 Director of Information Technology ...Mr. Aaron COWDERY
63 PA Program Director ...Mr. David SAMS
104 Director of Education Abroad ...Ms. Christy BURKE
25 Grants Officer ...Ms. Chantal CENTOFANTI-FIELDS
51 Continuing Education ...Ms. Tina K. HICKMAN
35 Associate Dean of Students ...Ms. KJ MCCONNELL
04 Executive Coordinator to President ...Ms. Paula LEWIS
29 Alumni Relations ...Dr. Joshua JACOBS
28 Assoc Dean of Stdnts/Chief Div Ofcr ...Mr. Tony MAYLE
30 Director of Development ...Mr. Josh JACOBS
37 Assistant VP for Student Enrollment ...Ms. Emily SCHUCK
44 Senior Director Annual Giving ...Ms. Kathryn GLOOR
38 Director Student Counseling ...Ms. Andrea EUSER
39 Dir Resident Life/Student Housing ...Ms. KJ MCCONNELL
86 Director Government Relations ...Mr. Tom PERRY

Marion Technical College (F)

1467 Mount Vernon Avenue, Marion OH 43302-5694
County: Marion FICE Identification: 010736
Unit ID: 203881
Telephone: (740) 389-4636 Carnegie Class: Assoc/HVT-High Non
FAX Number: (740) 389-6136 Calendar System: Semester
URL: www.mtc.edu
Established: 1971 Annual Undergrad Tuition & Fees (In-State): $5,565
Enrollment: 2,147 Coed
Affiliation or Control: State IRS Status: 501(c)3
Highest Offering: Associate Degree
Accreditation: HLC, ADNUR, CAHIIM, DMS, MAC, MLTAD, OTA, PTAA, RAD, SURGT

01 President ...Dr. Ryan MCCALL
111 Vice Pres Planning & Advancement ...Dr. Amy ADAMS
10 VP Business Affairs & CFO ...Ms. Rhonda WARD
05 VP Academic & Student Affairs/CSO ...Dr. Bob HAAS
100 Chief of Staff & Govt Relations ...Ms. Laura WOUGHTER
13 Executive Director IT Operations ...Mr. Steve DUVALL
26 Director of Marketing ...Mr. Justin DEAN
06 Registrar ...Ms. Kristy TAYLOR
37 Director Student Financial Aid ...Ms. Deb LANGDON
07 Director of Admissions ...Mr. Tony BOX
36 Director of Career Services ...Ms. Kristi BUTLER
102 Director of Foundation ...Mr. Mike STUCKEY
88 Director of College Credit Plus ...Ms. Callum MORRIS
121 Director of Student Advising ...Ms. Laura EMERICK
15 Director of Human Resources ...Ms. Cretia JOHNSON
22 Director of Disability Svcs ...Dr. Jenifer MONTAG
103 Director of Workforce Solutions ...Mr. Mike AUGENSTEIN
18 Coord Facil Improvements/Operations ...Ms. Leeann GRAU
88 Director Student Support Programs ...Ms. Kathy RICE
72 Assoc Dean Technical Programs ...Mr. Mike WHITE
76 Assoc Dean Health Programs ...Ms. Debra MYERS
76 Assoc Dean Health Programs ...Mr. Chad HENSEL
28 Director of Diversity ...Ms. Primrose IGONOR

Mercy College of Ohio (G)

2221 Madison Avenue, Toledo OH 43604
County: Lucas FICE Identification: 030970
Unit ID: 203960
Telephone: (419) 251-1313 Carnegie Class: Spec-4-yr-Other Health
FAX Number: N/A Calendar System: Semester
URL: www.mercycollege.edu
Established: 1992 Annual Undergrad Tuition & Fees: $18,950
Enrollment: 1,561 Coed
Affiliation or Control: Roman Catholic IRS Status: 501(c)3
Highest Offering: Master's
Accreditation: HLC, ADNUR, #ARCPA, CAHIIM, EMT, NURSE, POLYT, RAD

01 President ...Dr. Susan WAJERT
05 VP Acad Affs/Dean of Faculty ...Vacant
32 VP Student Affs/Dean of Students ...Mr. Marc ADKINS
84 VP Enrollment Mgmt & Partnerships ...Ms. Lori EDGEWORTH
66 Dean Nursing and Allied Hlth ...Dr. Elizabeth SPRUNK
76 Dean of Arts and Sciences ...Dr. Barbara STOOS
58 Dean of Graduate Studies ...Dr. Kim WATSON
117 Dir of Compliance/Risk Mgmt ...Ms. Stacey BROWN
13 Dir of College Information Tech ...Mr. Jeff METZGER
10 Chief Financial Officer ...Ms. Andrea FLEMING
111 Int Director College Advancement ...Ms. Sandy SNYDER
08 Director Library/Resource Services ...Ms. Rebecca DANIELS
09 Dir Inst Research/Registrar ...Mr. Mark MCKELLIP
37 Financial Aid Director ...Ms. Julie LESLIE
26 Director of Communication ...Ms. Denise HUDGIN
42 Dir Campus Ministry & Svcs Learning ...Rev. Gerald CAMERON
21 Business Manager ...Ms. Diane RAHN
18 Coordinator of Operations ...Ms. Sherri WEBSTER
29 Coordinator Alumni Relations ...Ms. Hannah BOHN
121 Assistant Dean of Student Success ...Ms. Lisa SANCRANT
36 Dir of Career/Prof Dev & Retention ...Ms. Melanie ROCKHILL
106 Dir of Distance Education ...Dr. Dan FRENCH
28 Dir of Diversity & Inclusion ...Mr. Javier SOLORZANO PARADA
04 Administrative Asst to President ...Ms. Andrea RAFTERY
07 Director of Admissions ...Vacant

Methodist Theological School in Ohio (H)

3081 Columbus Pike, Delaware OH 43015-3211
County: Delaware FICE Identification: 003075
Unit ID: 203997
Telephone: (740) 363-1146 Carnegie Class: Spec-4-yr-Faith
FAX Number: (740) 362-3135 Calendar System: 4/1/4

URL: www.mtso.edu
Established: 1958 Annual Graduate Tuition & Fees: N/A
Enrollment: 139 Coed
Affiliation or Control: United Methodist IRS Status: 501(c)3
Highest Offering: Doctorate; No Undergraduates
Accreditation: HLC, THEOL

01 President .... Rev. Jay A. RUNDELL
05 Dean and VP for Academic Affairs .... Dr. Valerie BRIDGEMAN
20 Associate Dean .... Dr. Yvonne ZIMMERMAN
11 Dir Strategic Init & Operations .... Ms. Leigh PRECISE
10 Controller .... Ms. Sarah MOUCH
26 Director of Communications .... Mr. Danny RUSSELL
84 Director of Enrollment Management .... Rev. Benjamin HALL
30 Director of Development .... Rev. Claudine LEARY
08 Director of the Library .... Ms. Elonda CLAY
06 Registrar .... Mr. Lee RICHARDS
37 Director of Financial Aid .... Ms. Molly HOFFMAN
32 Director of Student Services .... Ms. Kristin LOFRUMENTO
13 Director Information Technology .... Mr. Matthew REHM
18 Facilities Manager .... Mr. Keith HUFFMAN
15 Coordinator of Human Resources .... Ms. Erin WIGGINS

Miami University (A)

501 E High Street, Oxford OH 45056-1846
County: Butler FICE Identification: 003077
Unit ID: 204024
Telephone: (513) 529-1809 Carnegie Class: DU-Higher
FAX Number: (513) 529-3841 Calendar System: Semester
URL: www.miamioh.edu
Established: 1809 Annual Undergrad Tuition & Fees (In-State): $16,223
Enrollment: 18,880 Coed
Affiliation or Control: State IRS Status: 501(c)3
Highest Offering: Doctorate
Accreditation: HLC, ART, CAEP, CIDA, CLPSY, DIETD, DIETI, IPSY, MUS, NURSE, SP, SW, THEA

01 President .... Dr. Gregory P. CRAWFORD
05 Provost/VP Academic Affairs .... Dr. Elizabeth R. MULLENIX
10 Sr VP Finance & Bus Svcs/Treasurer .... Dr. David K. CREAMER
32 Vice President Student Affairs .... Dr. Jayne E. BROWNELL
111 VP University Advancement .... Mr. Brad M. BUNDY
13 VP Information Technology/CIO .... Mr. David A. SEIDL
15 Assoc VP Academic Personnel .... Ms. Ruth GROOM
20 Sr Associate Provost .... Dr. Carolyn A. HAYNES
20 Assoc Prov & Dean of Undergrad Educ .... Ms. Amy A. BERGERSON
35 Dean of Students .... Dr. Kimberly MOORE
26 VP/Chief Mktg & Communications Ofcr .... Ms. Jessica RIVINIUS
45 VP Research & Innovation .... Dr. Susan A. MCDOWELL
18 Assoc VP Facilities Planning & Op .... Mr. Cody J. POWELL
84 VP Enroll Mgmt/Student Success .... Mr. Brent L. SHOCK
28 VP Inst Diversity & Inclusion .... Dr. Cristina ALCALDE
09 Assoc VP Institutional Research .... Dr. Padma PATIL
29 Assoc Vice Pres Alumni Relations .... Mrs. Kim TAVARES
88 VP Institutional Relations .... Mr. Randi Malcolm THOMAS
100 Chief of Staff & Sec to Board .... Mr. Ted O. PICKERILL
49 Dean College Arts & Science .... Dr. Christopher A. MAKAROFF, JR.
53 Dean Education/Health & Society .... Dr. Jason E. LANE
50 Dean Farmer Sch of Business .... Dr. Jenny DARROCH
57 Int Dean College of Creative Arts .... Mr. John B. WEIGAND
54 Dean College of Engr & Computing .... Dr. Beena SUKUMARAN
08 Dean University Libraries .... Mr. Jerome CONLEY
58 Dean Graduate School .... Dr. Michael W. CROWDER
49 Dean Col of Lib Arts & Applied Sci .... Dr. Ande DUROJAIYE
07 AVP Strat Enroll Mgmt/Marketing .... Vacant
51 Assoc VP Global Initiatives .... Dr. Cheryl D. YOUNG
108 Dir Center for Teaching Excellence .... Dr. Ellen J. YEZIERSKI
88 Univ Dir Liberal Educ/ Assessment .... Dr. Shelly JARRETT BROMBERG
92 Univ Dir Honors & Scholars Program .... Dr. Zeb BAKER
16 Assoc VP Human Resources .... Ms. Dawn FAHNER
23 Medical Director Student Health Svc .... Vacant
104 Dir Intl Student & Scholar .... Ms. Molly HEIDEMANN
06 University Registrar .... Ms. Mandy L. EUEN
36 Asst VP Career Exploration/Success .... Ms. Jen FRANCHAK
38 Director Student Counseling Service .... Dr. John A. WARD
19 Chief of Police .... Mr. Stephen VANWINKLE
96 Chief Procurement Officer .... Mr. Mark TAYLOR
43 VP & University General Counsel .... Ms. Amy E. SHOEMAKER
22 Assoc VP Equity & Equal Opportunity .... Ms. Kenya D. ASH
41 Director Intercollegiate Athletics .... Mr. David A. SAYLER
17 Director Student Wellness .... Ms. Rebecca BAUDRY YOUNG
04 Exec Assistant to the President .... Ms. Dawn TSIRELIS
37 Student Financial Aid Director .... Vacant
102 Asst Dir Corporate/Foundation Rels .... Mr. Ryan GILLEY
109 Assoc VP Auxiliaries .... Vacant
44 Asst VP Dev Ind/Annual Giving .... Ms. Emily BERRY
114 Assoc VP Budgeting & Analysis .... Dr. David A. ELLIS
105 Director of Web Marketing .... Ms. Jessica REA
25 Dir Research & Sponsored Pgms .... Ms. Anne P. SCHAUER
39 Director of Residence Life .... Dr. Vicka BELL-ROBINSON

Miami University Middletown (B)

4200 N University Boulevard, Middletown OH 45042-3497
Telephone: (513) 727-3200 FICE Identification: 003080
Accreditation: &HLC

† Regional accreditation is carried under the parent institution in Oxford, OH.

Miami University Regionals (C)

1601 University Boulevard, Hamilton OH 45011-3399
Telephone: (513) 785-3000 FICE Identification: 003079
Accreditation: &HLC

† Regional accreditation is carried under the parent institution in Oxford, OH.

The Modern College of Design (D)

1725 E David Road, Dayton OH 45440-1612
County: Montgomery FICE Identification: 025530
Unit ID: 205391
Telephone: (877) 300-9866 Carnegie Class: Spec 2-yr-A&S
FAX Number: (937) 294-5869 Calendar System: Semester
URL: https://themodern.edu
Established: 1983 Annual Undergrad Tuition & Fees: $33,164
Enrollment: 190 Coed
Affiliation or Control: Proprietary IRS Status: Proprietary
Highest Offering: Baccalaureate
Accreditation: ACCSC

01 Owner/President/Creative Director .... Ms. Jessica BARRY
26 Vice Pres of Industry Relations .... Mr. Matt FLICK
32 Vice President of Student Affairs .... Ms. Melissa FERGUSON
05 Chief Academic Officer .... Ms. Korrine TOADVINE
36 Director of Career Services .... Mr. Rick WILLITS
37 Director of Financial Aid .... Ms. Veronica DAVIDSON
07 Director of Admissions .... Ms. Samira ZACHARIAS

Mount Carmel College of Nursing (E)

127 S Davis Avenue, Columbus OH 43222-1504
County: Franklin FICE Identification: 030719
Unit ID: 204176
Telephone: (614) 234-5800 Carnegie Class: Spec-4-yr-Other Health
FAX Number: (614) 234-2875 Calendar System: Semester
URL: www.mccn.edu
Established: 1990 Annual Undergrad Tuition & Fees: $14,675
Enrollment: 903 Coed
Affiliation or Control: Roman Catholic IRS Status: 501(c)3
Highest Offering: Doctorate
Accreditation: HLC, NURSE

01 President .... Dr. Kathleen WILLIAMSON
05 Assoc Dean Academic Affairs .... Dr. Jami NININGER
88 Assoc Dean Innovation/Partnerships .... Dr. Scott DOLAN
103 Assoc Dean Ldrshp-Clinical Practice .... Dr. Jerry MANSFIELD
32 Assoc Dean Student Svcs .... Dr. Todd EVERETT
12 Asst Dean Regional Campus .... Ms. Cora ARLEDGE
04 Senior Executive Assistant .... Ms. Colleen MURPHY
107 Dir Doctor-Nurse Practice Pgm .... Dr. Thelma PATRICK
58 Director Graduate Programs .... Dr. Roxanne OLIVER
66 Director Accelerated Programs .... Dr. Folorunso LADIPO
88 Director Compliance & Safety .... Mr. Mitch JOSEPH-KEMPLIN
10 Deputy Chief Financial Officer .... Ms. Libby MELZER
21 Director Business Affairs .... Ms. Kathy SMITH
15 Chief Human Resources Officer .... Ms. Amanda MCCULLOUCH
06 Director Records & Registration .... Ms. Michelle LIVINGSTON
07 Director Admissions & Recruitment .... Dr. Kim CAMPBELL
108 Dir Institutional Effectiveness .... Ms. Susannah TOWNSEND
30 Director of Development .... Ms. Alyssa FRY
37 Senior Financial Aid Advisor .... Mr. Steve WETZ
08 Regional Director Library Services .... Mr. Stevo ROKSANDIC
26 Marketing/Communication Strategist .... Ms. Alexandra REESE
121 Student Success Coordinator .... Ms. Nancy HANN

Mount St. Joseph University (F)

5701 Delhi Road, Cincinnati OH 45233-1670
County: Hamilton FICE Identification: 003033
Unit ID: 204200
Telephone: (513) 244-4200 Carnegie Class: DU-Mod
FAX Number: (513) 244-4654 Calendar System: Semester
URL: www.msj.edu
Established: 1920 Annual Undergrad Tuition & Fees: $32,200
Enrollment: 2,031 Coed
Affiliation or Control: Roman Catholic IRS Status: 501(c)3
Highest Offering: Doctorate
Accreditation: HLC, #ACBSP, ARCPA, CAEP, NURSE, PTA, SW

01 President .... Dr. H. James WILLIAMS
111 VP of Institutional Advancement .... Ms. Sydney PROCHAZKA
26 VP of Marketing & Communications .... Mr. Jeff WAMPLER
05 Provost .... Dr. Diana DAVIS
10 Chief Financial Officer .... Mr. Jeffrey C. BRIGGS
43 VP Compliance Risk/General Counsel .... Ms. Paige L. ELLERMAN
20 Assoc Provost for Academic Support .... Ms. Heather CRABBE
20 Associate Provost Academic Affairs .... Dr. Christa CURRY
13 AVP Campus Technology .... Mr. Alex NAKONECHNYI
15 Director of Human Resources .... Ms. Teri COMPTON
32 Dean of Students .... Ms. Janet COX
06 Registrar .... Ms. Ginny TAYLOR
37 Director Student Admin Services .... Ms. Kathy KELLY
36 Director Career/Exper Educ .... Ms. Amanda MEEKER
102 Dir of Corp & Foundation Relations .... Ms. Shannon ZOZ
110 Director of Advancement .... Ms. Sydney PROCHAZKA
44 Senior Philanthropy Officer .... Mr. Dan EMSICKE
29 Director of Alumni Engagement .... Ms. Morgan CARPENTER
110 Director of Advancement Services .... Ms. Colleen PFEIFFENBERGER
18 Director Buildings & Grounds .... Mr. Stacy DECKER
09 Director Institutional Research .... Ms. Madalyn WHITE
07 VP for Recruitment & Admissions .... Dr. Christopher POWERS
21 Controller .... Ms. Kristi BENGEL
38 Director Wellness Center .... Ms. Patsy SCHWAIGER
08 Director Library .... Mr. Scott LLOYD
13 Director Instructional Technology .... Ms. Jacqueline ROBERTS
19 Director of Campus Police .... Mr. Kevin KOO
41 Director of Athletics .... Ms. Melanee WAGENER
88 Dir Learning Center/Disability Svcs .... Ms. Stacy MUELLER
42 Director of Mission Integration .... Sr. Karen ELLIOTT, CPPS
109 Director of Auxiliary Services .... Ms. Katrina KENTON
76 Dean of Health Sciences .... Dr. Darla VALE
79 Dean of Arts & Humanities .... Dr. Michael SONTAG
50 Dean of Business .... Dr. Sharon WAGNER
53 Dean of Education .... Dr. Laura SAYLOR
83 Dean Behavioral & Natural Sciences .... Dr. Gene KRITSKY
91 Director Administrative Computing .... Mr. Dan LUKAC
105 Webmaster .... Mr. Dan FIELDS
23 Coordinator Health Services .... Ms. Amy DEMKO
04 Exec Asst to the President .... Ms. Jacque MEYER
28 Chief Diversity & Inclusion Officer .... Mr. Rayshawn EASTMAN
121 Director Academic Advising .... Ms. Mary E. MAZUK

Mount Vernon Nazarene University (G)

800 Martinsburg Road, Mount Vernon OH 43050-9500
County: Knox FICE Identification: 007085
Unit ID: 204194
Telephone: (740) 392-6868 Carnegie Class: Masters/M
FAX Number: (740) 397-2769 Calendar System: Semester
URL: www.mvnu.edu
Established: 1968 Annual Undergrad Tuition & Fees: $31,610
Enrollment: 2,140 Coed
Affiliation or Control: Church Of The Nazarene IRS Status: 501(c)3
Highest Offering: Master's
Accreditation: HLC, ACBSP, CAEPN, MUS, NURSE, SW

01 President/CEO .... Dr. Henry W. SPAULDING, II
10 Vice Pres for Finance/CFO .... Mr. Scott L. CAMPBELL
05 Vice Pres for Academic Affairs/CAO .... Dr. Amy KOVACH
26 VP for University Relations .... Rev. James SMITH
32 Vice President Student Life .... Vacant
58 VP for Graduate and Prof Studies .... Dr. Eric STETLER
42 Campus Pastor .... Rev. Stephanie LOBDELL
21 Director of Business Services .... Mr. Steven JENKINS
84 VP for Enrollment Management .... Mr. Justin NOWICKI
88 Director of Faculty Services GPS .... Mr. Kevin CHANEY
06 University Registrar .... Mr. Mel SEVERNS
15 Director of Human Resources .... Mr. Alan SHAFFER
38 Director Counseling and Wellness .... Dr. Eric BROWNING
13 Director of Information Tech .... Mr. John WALCHLE
29 Director of Alumni Relations .... Rev. Brad A. KOCHIS
40 Director of the Bookstore .... Mrs. Gina A. BLANCHARD
27 Coord Communications & Pub Rels .... Ms. Samantha SCOLES
53 Dir Teacher Education/Certification .... Dr. Jessica GRUBAUGH
37 Dir of Student Fin Services .... Ms. Vickie WILLIAMS
18 Director of Facilities Operations .... Mr. Ben COOK
21 Controller .... Ms. Debra DEVORE
35 Director of Campus Life .... Ms. Tiffany VAN DAME
28 Director Intercultural Affairs .... Mr. Tavaris TAYLOR
04 Assistant to President .... Mrs. Lisa L. VAN NEST
08 Director of the Library .... Mr. Timothy RADCLIFFE
105 Director Web Services .... Mr. Carlos SERRAO
106 Dir Online Education/E-learning .... Vacant
50 Dean of the School of Business .... Dr. Melanie TIMMERMAN
81 Dean School of Natural & Social Sci .... Dr. LeeAnn COUTS
09 Director of Institutional Research .... Mrs. Krissta HADSELL
07 Director of Admissions .... Mrs. Crystal GOEHRING
104 Director Study Abroad .... Ms. Krissta HADSELL
41 Athletic Director .... Mr. Chip WILSON
54 Dept Chair Engineering .... Dr. Jose OOMMEN
30 Executive Director for Development .... Mr. Darrel GEORGE
39 Dir Resident Life/Student Housing .... Vacant
108 AVP of Institutional Effectiveness .... Dr. Melanie TIMMERMAN
124 AVP for Student Success & Retention .... Mrs. Joy STRICKLAND
121 Director of Student Success .... Dr. Lee CHAMBERS
79 Dean of School of Arts & Humanities .... Dr. Yvonne SCHULTZ
66 Dean of School of Nursing .... Dr. Judy GREGG
73 Dean School of Christian Ministry .... Dr. Douglas VAN NEST
88 Director of Civil Rights .... Dr. Christina JONES
85 Dir Center for Global Engagement .... Dr. Brenita NICHOLAS-EDWARDS
19 Director Security/Safety .... Mrs. Jaimi DENNISON
44 Director Annual Giving .... Mr. Justin BROWN

Muskingum University (H)

260 Stadium Drive, New Concord OH 43762-1199
County: Muskingum FICE Identification: 003084
Unit ID: 204264
Telephone: (740) 826-8211 Carnegie Class: Masters/S
FAX Number: (740) 826-8404 Calendar System: Semester
URL: www.muskingum.edu
Established: 1837 Annual Undergrad Tuition & Fees: $29,490
Enrollment: 2,231 Coed
Affiliation or Control: Presbyterian Church (U.S.A.) IRS Status: 501(c)3
Highest Offering: Beyond Master's But Less Than Doctorate
Accreditation: HLC, CAATE, CAEP, MUS, NURSE, OT

01 President .... Dr. Susan SCHNEIDER HASSELER

05 Provost ... Dr. Nancy J. EVANGELISTA
10 VP Business/Finance & Treasurer ... Mr. Philip LAUBE
30 Vice Pres of Inst Advancement ... Mr. Paul MCCLELLAND
84 VP for Enrollment ... Mrs. Marcy RITZERT
32 Assoc VP for Student Affairs ... Mr. Michael MALONE
08 Director of Library ... Dr. Nainsi HOUSTON
06 Registrar ... Mrs. Heather PRITCHARD
36 Assistant Director Career Services ... Mrs. Jacquelyn L. VASCURA
13 Director of Computer Services ... Mr. Ryan D. HARVEY
26 Exec Dir Strategic Comm/Marketing ... Ms. Michelle BALL
07 Director of Admission ... Mr. Jake BURNETT
19 Director of Public Safety ... Mr. Danny E. VINCENT
42 College Minister ... Vacant
18 Supt of Building & Grounds ... Mr. Kevin J. WAGNER
41 Director of Athletics ... Mrs. Kari WINTERS
37 Director of Student Financial Aid ... Mrs. Amber GUMP
38 Director of Student Counseling ... Vacant
04 Admin Assistant to the President ... Mrs. Amanda HUBER

MyComputerCareer (A)

380 Polaris Pkwy Suite 110, Westerville OH 43082

County: Delaware | FICE Identification: 041245
Telephone: (866) 606-6922 | Carnegie Class: Not Classified
FAX Number: N/A | Calendar System: Quarter
URL: mycomputercareer.edu
Established: 2007 | Annual Undergrad Tuition & Fees: N/A
Enrollment: N/A | Coed
Affiliation or Control: Proprietary | IRS Status: Proprietary
Highest Offering: Associate Degree
Accreditation: CNCE

01 Campus Director ... Teresa GARY
07 Admissions Director ... Michael BROWN
37 Financial Aid Director ... Susan BORGESI
36 Sr Career Services Director ... Tricia MOSHER

North Central State College (B)

2441 Kenwood Circle, Mansfield OH 44906

County: Richland | FICE Identification: 005313
Unit ID: 204422
Telephone: (419) 755-4800 | Carnegie Class: Assoc/HVT-High Non
FAX Number: (419) 755-4750 | Calendar System: Semester
URL: www.ncstatecollege.edu
Established: 1961 | Annual Undergrad Tuition & Fees (In-State): $4,468
Enrollment: 2,729 | Coed
Affiliation or Control: State | IRS Status: 501(c)3
Highest Offering: Baccalaureate
Accreditation: HLC, ACBSP, ADNUR, COARC, EMT, #PTAA, RAD

01 President ... Dr. Dorey DIAB
04 Exec Assistant to the President ... Mr. Stephen R. WILLIAMS
05 Vice President Academic Services ... Dr. Kelly A. GRAY
32 Vice President Student Svcs & IE ... Mr. Thomas PRENDERGAST
10 VP/CFO of Business Services ... Ms. Lori L. MCKEE
26 Exec Dir Marketing & Public Rels ... Mr. Keith STONER
07 Director of Admissions ... Ms. Amanda SHEETS
15 Exec Director of Human Resources ... Mr. R. Douglas HANUSCIN
37 Director of Financial Aid ... Ms. Amanda KALTENBAUGH
08 Head Librarian ... Ms. Andrea WITTMER
22 Coord Disability Services ... Mr. Doug HESTAND
20 Dean Academic Services ... Dr. Toni JOHNSON
49 Dean of Liberal Arts ... Dr. Howard WALTERS
88 Asst Dean Liberal Arts ... Dr. Steven HAYNES
50 Dean of Business Ind & Technology ... Mr. Daniel WAGNER
51 Asst Dean of Business Ind & Tech ... Dr. Vincent PALOMBO
54 Dir/Chair Engineering BSMET ... Mr. Daniel O. WAGNER
76 Dean Health Sciences/Dir Nursing ... Ms. Melinda ROEPKE
66 Asst Dean Health Sciences ... Ms. Leesa COX
13 Director of IT ... Mr. Paul ALLEN
06 Registrar ... Mr. Brad DUNMIRE
18 Manager of Facilities ... Mr. Kevin KLINE
88 Director Accounting Services ... Ms. Michele SCHAAD
102 Vice President College Foundation ... Ms. Christine COPPER
121 Dir of Student Success & Transition ... Ms. Monica DURHAM
88 Phi Theta Kappa Advisor ... Ms. Barb KEENER
40 Campus Bookstore Manager ... Ms. Carla BUTDORFF
21 Controller ... Ms. Lori L. MCKEE
105 Web Master ... Vacant
41 Athletics & Student Engagement ... Ms. Jennifer RACER
29 Coord of Alumni/Employer Relations ... Mr. Randy BLANKENSHIP
36 Career Development Counselor ... Ms. Paula WALDRUFF
108 Director Institutional Assessment ... Dr. Gina KAMWITHI
19 Director Public Safety ... Sgt. Don WALLIS
28 Director of Diversity ... Dr. Toni JOHNSON

The North Coast College (C)

11724 Detroit Avenue, Lakewood OH 44107-3002

County: Cuyahoga | FICE Identification: 012896
Unit ID: 206394
Telephone: (216) 221-8584 | Carnegie Class: Bac-Diverse
FAX Number: (216) 221-2311 | Calendar System: Semester
URL: www.thencc.edu
Established: 1966 | Annual Undergrad Tuition & Fees: $22,800
Enrollment: 48 | Coed
Affiliation or Control: Proprietary | IRS Status: Proprietary
Highest Offering: Baccalaureate
Accreditation: #ACCSC

01 President ... Dr. Milan MILASINOVIC
05 Dean of Academic Affairs ... Mr. Patrick MELNICK
37 Director of Student Financial Svcs ... Ms. Martha SNODGRASS
06 Registrar ... Ms. Margery SPONSLER
07 Director of Admissions ... Ms. Yolanda COLLINS-TAYLOR
08 Chief Library Officer ... Ms. Laura JENSEN
106 Dean of Online Education/E-learning ... Ms. Jasmine ROCCO
15 Chief Human Resources Officer ... Ms. Karen MADIGAN

Northeast Ohio Medical University (D)

4209 State Route 44, PO Box 95,
Rootstown OH 44272-0095

County: Portage | FICE Identification: 024544
Unit ID: 204477
Telephone: (330) 325-2511 | Carnegie Class: Spec-4-yr-Med
FAX Number: (330) 325-7943 | Calendar System: Other
URL: www.neomed.edu
Established: 1973 | Annual Graduate Tuition & Fees: N/A
Enrollment: 985 | Coed
Affiliation or Control: State | IRS Status: 501(c)3
Highest Offering: First Professional Degree; No Undergraduates
Accreditation: HLC, AA, MED, PH, PHAR

01 President ... Dr. John LANGELL
100 Chief of Staff ... Ms. Michelle M. MULHERN
26 VP Govt & External Affairs ... Mr. John J. STILLIANA
46 VP Research/Sponsored Programs ... Dr. Steven P. SCHMIDT
05 VP Academic Affairs ... Dr. Richard J. KASMER
17 VP Health Affairs ... Dr. Elisabeth H. YOUNG
10 VP Operations & Finance ... Ms. Mary TAYLOR
111 VP Advancement ... Vacant
28 VP HR & Diversity ... Mr. Andre L. BURTON
26 VP Comm/Chief Marketing Officer . Mr. Roderick L. INGRAM, SR.
63 Dean College of Medicine ... Dr. Elisabeth H. YOUNG
58 Dean College of Graduate Studies ... Dr. Steven P. SCHMIDT
67 Dean College of Pharmacy ... Dr. Richard J. KASMER
43 General Counsel ... Ms. Maria R. SCHIMER
32 Sr Exec Dir Acad Affs & Stdnt Svcs ... Dr. Sandra M. EMERICK
88 Sr Ex Dir Wasson Ctr & Interprof Ed ... Dr. Holly A. GERZINA
25 Exec Dir Research & Sponsored Pgms ... Ms. Rebecca L. HAYES
09 Exec Dir Institutional Research ... Dr. Deborah LOYET
84 Sr Exec Dir Strategic Enroll Init ... Mr. James F. BARRETT
88 Dir Comparative Medicine Unit ... Dr. Stanley D. DANNEMILLER
29 Dir Alumni Rels & Annual Giving ... Mr. Craig S. EYNON
38 Dir Counseling Services ... Dr. Jennifer L. DOUGALL
13 Sr Ex Dir Information Technology ... Mr. Ronald L. MCGRADY
15 Dir Human Resources ... Ms. Charity DAVIS
18 Dir Campus Operations ... Mr. Dale A. HLUCH
24 Dir Academic Technology Services ... Mr. Michael G. WRIGHT
08 Dir Learning Center ... Mr. Craig R. THEISSEN
19 Dir Public Safety/Police Chief ... Ms. Kali A. MEONSKE
124 Exec Dir Academic Services ... Dr. Terri E. ROBINSON
114 Dir of Budget & Accounting ... Ms. Jacalyn E. KOVACH
40 Supervisor Bookstore ... Ms. Christine L. KOVACICH
06 Registrar ... Ms. Katherine M. MIRANDA
37 Dir Financial Aid ... Mr. Michael A. KEMPE

Northwest State Community College (E)

22-600 State Route 34, Archbold OH 43502-9542

County: Henry | FICE Identification: 008677
Unit ID: 204440
Telephone: (419) 267-5511 | Carnegie Class: Assoc/HVT-High Non
FAX Number: (419) 267-3688 | Calendar System: Semester
URL: www.northweststate.edu
Established: 1968 | Annual Undergrad Tuition & Fees (In-State): $4,338
Enrollment: 3,736 | Coed
Affiliation or Control: State | IRS Status: 501(c)3
Highest Offering: Associate Degree
Accreditation: HLC, ACBSP, ADNUR, MAC

01 President ... Dr. Todd HERNANDEZ
03 Executive Vice President ... Mr. Albert LEWIS, JR.
05 VP for Academics ... Dr. Daniel BURKLO
84 VP Enrollment Mgmt/Student Affairs ... Ms. Lana SNIDER
49 Dean of Arts & Sciences ... Ms. Jamilah TUCKER
66 Dean of Nursing & Allied Health ... Dr. Kathy KEISTER
50 Dean Business & Public Services ... Mr. Jason RICKENBERG
54 Dean STEM & IND Technologies ... Dr. Ryan HAMILTON
06 Registrar ... Ms. Connie KLINGSHIRN
18 Director of Plant Operations ... Mr. Kevin GERKEN
15 VP Human Resources ... Ms. Kathryn MCKELVEY
10 Chief Fiscal & Admin Officer ... Ms. Jennifer THOME
21 Director of Accounting & Finance ... Vacant
07 Director of Admissions ... Mr. Austin FLORES
102 Executive Director Foundation ... Ms. Robbin WILCOX
37 Director Student Financial Aid ... Ms. Amber YOCOM
26 Marketing & Communications ... Mr. James BELLAMY
40 Bookstore Manager ... Mr. Kemp STAPLETON
08 Director Library ... Ms. Kristi ROTROFF
121 Dean of Learner Services ... Ms. Cassie RICKENBERG
103 VP Workforce Development ... Mr. James DREWES
14 Dir Network Systems/Tech Support ... Mr. Robert DUNCAN
13 Exec Dir Information Technology ... Vacant
88 Director CTS/AMTC ... Mr. David CONOVER
04 Executive Assistant ... Ms. Megan BATT

Notre Dame College (F)

4545 College Road, South Euclid OH 44121-4293

County: Cuyahoga | FICE Identification: 003085
Unit ID: 204468
Telephone: (216) 381-1680 | Carnegie Class: Bac-Diverse
FAX Number: (216) 381-3802 | Calendar System: Semester
URL: www.notredamecollege.edu
Established: 1922 | Annual Undergrad Tuition & Fees: $30,750
Enrollment: 1,585 | Coed
Affiliation or Control: Roman Catholic | IRS Status: 501(c)3
Highest Offering: Master's
Accreditation: HLC, CAEP, NURSE

01 President ... Dr. J. Michael PRESSIMONE
10 Vice Pres Finance and CFO ... Vacant
111 Vice Pres for Advancement ... Ms. Culeen CAREY
05 Interim Provost and Dean of Faculty ... Dr. David OROSZ
124 Dean of Retention & Acad Support ... Ms. Sandy GRASSMAN
88 Chief Mission Officer ... Mr. Ted STEINER
66 Nursing Division Chair ... Dr. Colleen SWEENEY
53 Education Division Chair ... Dr. Sue CORBIN
81 Math & Science Division Chair ... Dr. Sharon BALCHAK
50 Business Division Chair ... Ms. Natalie STROUSE
79 Arts and Humanities Division Chair ... Mr. Kenneth PALKO
84 Vice Pres for Enrollment ... Ms. Beth FORD
07 Asst Dean for Enrollment ... Ms. Amanda MEANS
06 Registrar ... Ms. Tracy SABRANSKY
37 Director of Financial Aid ... Ms. Allison MCBRADY
113 Director of Student Accounts ... Vacant
19 Director of Security/Safety ... Mr. Joseph GRECOL
18 Director of Physical Plant ... Mr. Tom MEEKS
13 Director of Information Technology ... Mr. Michael KIEC
15 Director of Human Resources ... Ms. Judy WEST
08 Director of Library ... Ms. Karen ZOLLER
42 Director of Campus Ministry ... Mr. Ted STEINER
38 Director of Counseling Center ... Mr. Jerry HAYES
32 Dean of Students ... Dr. D. Chris GILL
39 Director of Residence Life ... Mr. Shane YOUNG
29 Director Alumni Relations ... Ms. Nakeysha HAMILTON
04 Assistant to the President ... Sr. Carol ZIEGLER, SND
106 Dean Adult/Online/Graduate Educ ... Dr. Florentine HOELKER
41 Athletic Director ... Mr. Scott SWAIN

Oberlin College (G)

173 West Lorain Street, Oberlin OH 44074-1057

County: Lorain | FICE Identification: 003086
Unit ID: 204501
Telephone: (440) 775-8121 | Carnegie Class: Bac-A&S
FAX Number: (440) 775-8886 | Calendar System: 4/1/4
URL: www.oberlin.edu
Established: 1833 | Annual Undergrad Tuition & Fees: $58,554
Enrollment: 2,658 | Coed
Affiliation or Control: Independent Non-Profit | IRS Status: 501(c)3
Highest Offering: Master's
Accreditation: HLC

01 President ... Ms. Carmen T. AMBAR
10 VP for Finance & Admin ... Ms. Rebecca VASQUEZ-SKILLINGS
111 VP for Advancement ... Mr. Michael GRZESIAK
26 Vice President for Communications ... Mr. Josh JENSEN
64 Dean of the Conservatory ... Dr. William QUILLEN
49 Dean of Arts & Sciences ... Dr. David KAMITSUKA
32 VP & Dean of Students ... Ms. Karen GOFF
07 Dean Admissions/Financial Aid ... Dr. Manuel CARBALLO
43 VP/General Counsel & Secretary ... Mr. Matthew LAHEY
21 Assoc Vice President Finance ... Ms. Julienne MELVIN
29 Exec Director Alumni Assoc ... Mr. Terry KURTZ
88 Assoc Dean of College of Arts & Sci ... Dr. Michael PARKIN
13 Chief Information Tech Officer ... Mr. Ben HOCKENHULL
08 Azariah Smith Root Dir of Libraries ... Ms. Valerie HOTCHKISS
07 Int Dir Admissions Conservatory ... Ms. Beth WEISS
38 Director of Counseling Center ... Dr. John HARSHBARGER
57 Director of Allen Art Museums ... Dr. Andria DERSTINE
06 Registrar ... Dr. Trecia POTTINGER
37 Director of Financial Aid ... Ms. Michele KOSBOTH
09 Director of Institutional Research ... Mr. Ross PEACOCK
18 Chief Facilities Operator ... Mr. Kevin BROWN
36 Exec Dir Career Development Center ... Mr. Anthony PERNELL-MCGEE
42 Director Religious and Spiritual Li ... Rev. David F. DORSEY
39 Asst VP & Dean Res Educ/Campus Life ... Dr. Mark ZENO
41 Director of Physical Educ/Athletics ... Ms. Natalie WINKELFOOS
19 Exec Dir Student Safety & Wellbeing ... Dr. Andrew ONI
28 Asst VP/Dean Intercultural Engage ... Dr. Mark SAPARA
96 Institutional Buyer ... Mr. Rick SNODGRASS
15 Chief Human Resources Officer ... Mr. Joseph VITALE, JR.
04 Assistant to President ... Mrs. Jennifer S. BRADFIELD
100 Chief of Staff ... Mr. David HERTZ
102 Exec Dir Office of Foundations ... Ms. Pamela SNYDER
112 AVP Leadership & Planned Giving ... Ms. Maria MILLER
115 Chief Investment Officer ... Mr. Jun YANG
16 Deputy Human Resources Officer ... Ms. Maggie NIEVES
118 Director of Compensation & Benefits ... Mr. Thomas SCHILTZ
35 Assoc Dean of Students ... Mr. Thom JULIAN

Ohio Business College (H)

5202 Timber Commons Drive, Sandusky OH 44870-5894

Telephone: (419) 627-8345 | Identification: 666467
Accreditation: COE

† Branch campus of Ohio Business College, Sheffield Village, OH.

Ohio Business College (I)

5095 Waterford Drive, Sheffield Village OH 44035

County: Lorain | FICE Identification: 021585
Unit ID: 203720
Telephone: (440) 934-3101 | Carnegie Class: Spec 2-yr-Other

FAX Number: (440) 934-3105 Calendar System: Quarter
URL: www.ohiobusinesscollege.edu
Established: 1903 Annual Undergrad Tuition & Fees: $9,385
Enrollment: 184 Coed
Affiliation or Control: Proprietary IRS Status: Proprietary
Highest Offering: Associate Degree
Accreditation: COE, MAC

01 Campus Director ... Mr. Scott BEHMER
05 Director of Education ... Mr. Greg SCHULTZ
07 Master Admissions Rep ... Ms. Nicole SMITH
37 Lead Financial Aid Administrator ... Mr. Jeston THOMAS
36 Career Services Director ... Mr. Roy SMITH
06 Registrar ... Ms. Rhonda HIGGINS

Ohio Christian University (A)

1476 Lancaster Pike, Circleville OH 43113-0458
County: Pickaway FICE Identification: 003030
Unit ID: 201964
Telephone: (740) 474-8896 Carnegie Class: Masters/M
FAX Number: (740) 477-7755 Calendar System: Semester
URL: www.ohiochristian.edu
Established: 1948 Annual Undergrad Tuition & Fees: $21,990
Enrollment: 2,186 Coed
Affiliation or Control: Other Protestant IRS Status: 501(c)3
Highest Offering: Master's
Accreditation: HLC, CAEPT

01 President ... Dr. Jon KULAGA
05 Vice President of Academics ... Vacant
10 Vice President of Finance ... Mr. Ted PERRY
111 Vice President for Advancement ... Mr. Matt HUNNELL
84 Vice President for Enrollment ... Mr. Phil HOOKS
13 Executive Director of IT ... Mr. Jerad BADER
09 AVP for Institutional Effectiveness ... Dr. Cynthia TWEEDELL
50 Dean of Business ... Dr. Jon TOMLINSON
53 Dean of Education ... Dr. Jeanne BRUCE
49 Dean of School of Arts and Sciences ... Dr. Krista STONEROCK
83 Dean of Social and Behavioral Scien ... Dr. Sylvia MCDONALD
06 Registrar ... Mr. Dustin EPPERLY
35 Director of Student Engagement ... Mr. Eric FEHR
42 Director of Spiritual Formation ... Mr. Kevin BENNIE
121 Director of Advising ... Ms. Michelle SAMPLE
08 Director of Library Services ... Ms. Tina CRAFT
37 Director Student Financial Services ... Mr. Brandon RITCHEY
41 Athletic Director ... Mr. George ARROYO
15 Director for Human Resources ... Ms. Allison BROWNING
26 Chief Marketing Officer ... Mr. Dave HIRSCHLER
106 PSEO Director ... Mrs. Beth ASH
18 Director of Physical Plant ... Mr. Jerry SPARKS
19 Director of Security ... Mr. Anthony DILLARD
04 Executive Asst to President ... Ms. Lois J. TAYLOR
29 Director Alumni Affairs ... Ms. Michelle BLANTON
07 Director of Admissions ... Ms. Alana BRADLEY
30 Director of Development ... Ms. Kathleen KEHL

Ohio Dominican University (B)

1216 Sunbury Road, Columbus OH 43219-2099
County: Franklin FICE Identification: 003035
Unit ID: 204617
Telephone: (614) 251-4500 Carnegie Class: Masters/M
FAX Number: (614) 251-4634 Calendar System: Semester
URL: www.ohiodominican.edu
Established: 1911 Annual Undergrad Tuition & Fees: $32,880
Enrollment: 1,415 Coed
Affiliation or Control: Roman Catholic IRS Status: 501(c)3
Highest Offering: Doctorate
Accreditation: HLC, ACBSP, ARCPA, CAEPN, SW

01 President ... Ms. Connie GALLAHER
05 Vice President Academic Affairs ... Dr. Manuel MARTINEZ
10 Vice Pres Finance & Admin/CFO ... Mr. Alvin RODACK
84 Vice Pres Enrollment Management ... Mr. John NAUGHTON
111 VP for Advancement & External Rels ... Mr. Mark COOPER
04 Exec Asst to President/Vice Pres ... Ms. Heather MORRIS
32 Assoc Vice Pres Student Success ... Ms. Sharon REED
26 AVP Marketing/Public Relations ... Mr. Tom BROCKMAN
123 Assoc VP of Grad & Adult Admissions ... Mr. John NAUGHTON
110 Assoc VP for Advancement ... Ms. Christie FLOOD-WEINER
121 Dir of Advising & Student Success ... Mr. Adam HIRSCHFELD
07 Director Undergraduate Admissions ... Ms. Alecia DENNIS
114 Controller ... Ms. Vicki STEELE
13 Chief Information Officer ... Mr. Chris THEVE
37 Director of Financial Aid ... Ms. Tara SCHNEIDER
08 Director of the Library ... Ms. Michelle SARFF
36 Director Career Services ... Ms. Jessica HALL
15 Director of Human Resources ... Ms. Amy THOMAS
42 Director of Campus Ministry ... Fr. Paul COLLOTON
39 Director of Resident Life ... Ms. Lara CONRAD
41 Athletic Director ... Mr. Jeff BLAIR
19 Director of Safety ... Mr. Robin OLSON
06 Registrar ... Ms. Happiness MAPIRA
29 Director Alumni Relations ... Ms. Christie FLOOD-WEINER

Ohio Institute of Allied Health (C)

6245 Old Troy Pike, Huber Heights OH 45424
County: Montgomery FICE Identification: 035833
Unit ID: 483647
Telephone: (937) 237-1010 Carnegie Class: Not Classified
FAX Number: (937) 237-0506 Calendar System: Quarter
URL: oiah.edu
Established: 2010 Annual Undergrad Tuition & Fees: N/A
Enrollment: N/A Coed
Affiliation or Control: Independent Non-Profit IRS Status: 501(c)3
Highest Offering: Associate Degree
Accreditation: COE

Ohio Northern University (D)

525 S Main Street, Ada OH 45810-1599
County: Hardin FICE Identification: 003089
Unit ID: 204635
Telephone: (419) 772-2000 Carnegie Class: Bac-Diverse
FAX Number: (419) 772-1932 Calendar System: Semester
URL: www.onu.edu
Established: 1871 Annual Undergrad Tuition & Fees: $34,440
Enrollment: 2,817 Coed
Affiliation or Control: United Methodist IRS Status: 501(c)3
Highest Offering: First Professional Degree
Accreditation: HLC, CAEP, EXSC, LAW, MLS, MUS, NAIT, NURSE, PHAR

01 President ... Dr. Daniel A. DIBIASIO
05 Interim Provost/VP Academic Affs ... Dr. Julie K. HURTIG
10 Vice President Financial Affairs ... Mr. Jason M. BROGE
111 Vice Pres of University Advancement . Ms. Shannon M. SPENCER
84 Vice Pres Enrollment Management ... Dr. William T. EILOLA
32 VP Student Affairs/Dean of Students ... Dr. Adriane L. THOMPSON-BRADSHAW
43 Vice President & General Counsel ... Mr. Andrew C. HUGHEY
49 Dean of Arts & Sciences ... Dr. Chris BOWERS
54 Dean of Engineering ... Dr. John-David S. YODER
67 Dean of Pharmacy ... Dr. Steven J. MARTIN
50 Dean Business Administration ... Dr. John C. NAVIN
61 Dean of the College of Law ... Dr. Charles H. ROSE, III
110 Assistant VP for Advancement ... Ms. Kelly LAWRIE
08 Director of Heterick Library ... Ms. Kathleen T. BARIL
39 Director of Residence Life ... Ms. Jedda DECKER
38 Director of Counseling ... Mr. Anthony C. RIVERA
29 Director of Alumni Relations ... Mr. Dylan WOOD
08 Director of the Law Library ... Vacant
42 University Chaplain ... Rev Dr. David E. MACDONALD
18 General Manager of Physical Plant ... Mr. Marc E. STALEY
13 Chief of Information Officer ... Mr. Jeff A. RIEMAN
09 Director of Institutional Research ... Mr. Joshua W. DEANS
15 Associate VP of Human Resources ... Ms. Tonya D. PAUL
20 Assoc VP for Academic Affairs ... Dr. Julie HURTIG
37 Asst VP for Enroll Mgt/Dir Fin Aid ... Mrs. Melanie K. WEAVER
114 Exec Budget Dir/Univ Controller ... Mr. Mark A. RUSSELL
26 Exec Dir Communications & Marketing ... Mrs. Amy M. PRIGGE
07 Director of Admissions ... Ms. Deborah L. MILLER
06 University Registrar ... Mr. Wilson J. TURNER
28 Int Dir Multicultural Development ... Dr. Albertina L. WALKER
41 Director of Athletics ... Mr. Thomas E. SIMMONS
44 Director of Planned Giving ... Ms. Ellie F. BECKWITH-MCMANUS
96 Director of Business Services ... Ms. Vicki J. NIESE
101 Secretary to the Board ... Ms. Jennifer L. ROBY
19 Director of Public Safety ... Mr. Greg R. HORNE

The Ohio State University Main Campus (E)

281 W. Lane Ave., Columbus OH 43210-1358
County: Franklin FICE Identification: 003090
Unit ID: 204796
Telephone: (614) 292-6446 Carnegie Class: DU-Highest
FAX Number: (614) 292-9180 Calendar System: Semester
URL: www.osu.edu
Established: 1870 Annual Undergrad Tuition & Fees (In-State): $11,518
Enrollment: 61,369 Coed
Affiliation or Control: State IRS Status: 501(c)3
Highest Offering: Doctorate
Accreditation: HLC, AAB, ABAI, ACAE, ART, AUD, CAATE, CACREP, CAEP, CAHIIM, CAMPEP, CIDA, CLPSY, COARC, CONST, DANCE, DENT, DH, DIET, DIETC, DIETD, DIETI, DMS, HSA, IPSY, LAW, LSAR, MED, MFCD, MIDWF, MLS, MUS, NURSE, OPT, OPTR, OT, PAST, PCSAS, PH, PHAR, PLNG, PTA, RAD, RTT, SCPSY, SP, SPAA, SW, THEA, VET

01 President ... Dr. Kristina M. JOHNSON
05 Executive Vice Pres/Provost ... Dr. Melissa L. GILLIAM
121 Sr VProv Stdnt Acad Excellence ... Dr. Charlene GILBERT
20 Sr Vice Provost ... Dr. Kay WOLF
124 Vice Prov Outreach/Engagement ... Dr. Ryan SCHMIESING
10 Sr VP Business & Finance/CFO ... Mr. Michael PAPADAKIS
43 Sr VP & General Counsel ... Ms. Anne GARCIA
32 Vice President for Student Life ... Dr. Melissa SHIVERS
20 Vice Provost for Academic Programs ... Mr. W. Randy SMITH
20 Vice Prov Acad Policy & Faculty Res ... Dr. Helen MALONE
26 Sr VP Marketing & Communications .. Ms. Elizabeth PARKINSON
46 EVP Research Innovation & Knowledge ... Dr. Grace WANG
86 Vice Pres of Govt Affairs ... Ms. Stacy RASTAUKAS
23 Int Co-Leader/CFO ... Mr. Mark LARMORE
23 Int Co-Leader/Chief Clinical Ofcr ... Dr. Andrew THOMAS
47 Vice Pres Ag Admin & Dean FAES ... Dr. Cathann KRESS
111 Sr VP for Advance/Pres OSU Found ... Mr. Michael EICHER
28 Vice Prov Diversity & Inclusion ... Dr. James L. MOORE
58 Vice Provost/Dean Grad School ... Dr. Alicia L. BERTONE
41 Sr VP/Athletics Director ... Mr. Gene D. SMITH
18 Assoc VP Facilities Op/Dev ... Mr. Mark E. CONSELYEA
84 Assoc VP Strategic Enroll Planning ... Vacant
13 Vice President & CIO ... Ms. Cindy LEAVITT
15 SVP Talent Culture & HR ... Dr. Jeff RISINGER
08 Vice Provost/Director of Libraries ... Mr. Damon E. JAGGARS
100 Chief of Staff ... Mr. JR BLACKBURN
101 Secretary Board of Trustees ... Ms. Jessica A. EVELAND
17 COO Medical Center ... Mr. Jay ANDERSON
85 Vice Prov Glob Strat/Intl Affs ... Dr. Gil I. LATZ, II
90 Exec Dir Ohio Supercomp Ctr ... Mr. David HUDAK
29 President/CEO Alumni Assoc ... Ms. Molly RANZ CALHOUN
12 Exec Dean of Reg Campuses ... Dr. Gregory S. ROSE
49 Int Vice Prov/Exec Dean Arts & Sci ... Dr. David HORN
50 Dean Fisher Col of Business ... Dr. Anil K. MAKHIJA
52 Dean College of Dentistry ... Dr. Carroll A. TROTMAN
53 Dean College of Educ & Hum Ecology ... Dr. Donald L. POPE-DAVIS
54 Dean College of Engineering ... Dr. Ayanna HOWARD
61 Dean College of Law ... Dr. Lincoln L. DAVIES
63 Dean College of Medicine ... Dr. Carol R. BRADFORD
66 Dean College of Nursing ... Dr. Bernadette MELNYK
88 Dean College of Optometry ... Dr. Karla S. ZADNIK
67 Dean College of Pharmacy ... Dr. Henry J. MANN
80 Dean JG College of Public Affairs ... Dr. Trevor L. BROWN
69 Dean College of Public Health ... Dr. Amy L. FAIRCHILD
70 Dean College of Social Work ... Dr. Tom GREGOIRE
74 Dean Col Veterinary Medicine ... Dr. Rustin MOORE
09 Asst VP Inst Research/Planning ... Vacant
37 Exec Dir Student Financial Aid ... Ms. Amy J. WHEELER
06 University Registrar ... Ms. Adrienne BRICKER
88 Exec Dir OSAS Analysis & Reporting ... Ms. Linda S. KATUNICH
11 Sr Vice Pres Admin & Planning ... Mr. Jay D. KASEY
19 Director of Public Safety ... Ms. Monica MOLL
39 Dir STEP Ops Housing Administration ... Ms. Toni GREENSLADE-SMITH

The Ohio State University Agricultural Technical Institute (F)

1328 Dover Road, Wooster OH 44691-4000
Telephone: (330) 264-3911 FICE Identification: 010687
Accreditation: &HLC

† Regional accreditation is carried under the parent institution in Columbus, OH.

The Ohio State University at Lima Campus (G)

4240 Campus Drive, Lima OH 45804-3597
Telephone: (419) 995-8600 FICE Identification: 003092
Accreditation: &HLC

† Regional accreditation is carried under the parent institution in Columbus, OH.

The Ohio State University Mansfield Campus (H)

1760 University Drive, Mansfield OH 44906-1599
Telephone: (419) 755-4011 FICE Identification: 003093
Accreditation: &HLC

† Regional accreditation is carried under the parent institution in Columbus, OH.

The Ohio State University at Marion (I)

1465 Mount Vernon Avenue, Marion OH 43302-5628
Telephone: (740) 389-6786 FICE Identification: 003094
Accreditation: &HLC

† Regional accreditation is carried under the parent institution in Columbus, OH.

The Ohio State University Newark Campus (J)

1179 University Drive, Newark OH 43055-9990
Telephone: (740) 366-3321 FICE Identification: 003095
Accreditation: &HLC

† Regional accreditation is carried under the parent institution in Columbus, OH.

Ohio Technical College (K)

1374 E 51st Street, Cleveland OH 44103-1269
County: Cuyahoga FICE Identification: 011745
Unit ID: 204608
Telephone: (216) 881-1700 Carnegie Class: Spec 2-yr-Tech
FAX Number: (216) 881-9145 Calendar System: Quarter
URL: www.ohiotech.edu
Established: 1969 Annual Undergrad Tuition & Fees: N/A
Enrollment: 426 Coed
Affiliation or Control: Proprietary IRS Status: Proprietary
Highest Offering: Associate Degree
Accreditation: ACCSC

01 President ... Mr. Bill HANTL
32 VP of Student Engagement ... Ms. Bonnie LACORTE
19 Director Security/Safety ... Mr. Glenn BODIFORD
37 Director Student Financial Aid ... Mr. Michael CAMPBELL
06 Registrar ... Ms. Sarah MANCINI
07 Director of Admissions ... Mr. Jordan BRENNER

Ohio University Main Campus (L)

1 Ohio University, Athens OH 45701-2979
County: Athens FICE Identification: 003100
Unit ID: 204857
Telephone: (740) 593-1000 Carnegie Class: DU-Highest

FAX Number: N/A Calendar System: Semester
URL: www.ohio.edu
Established: 1804 Annual Undergrad Tuition & Fees (In-State): $12,612
Enrollment: 25,714 Coed
Affiliation or Control: State IRS Status: 501(c)3
Highest Offering: Doctorate
Accreditation: HLC, AAFCS, ADNUR, ARCPA, AUD, CAATE, CACREP, CAEP, CAPRT, CEA, CIDA, CLPSY, COSMA, DANCE, DIETD, DIETI, FEPAC, IPSY, JOUR, MUS, NAIT, NURSE, OSTEO, PH, PTA, SP, SW, THEA

01 President .... Dr. Hugh SHERMAN
100 Chief of Staff .... Vacant
05 Executive VP & Provost .... Dr. Elizabeth SAYRS
10 VP for Finance & Administration .... Vacant
32 Interim VP for Student Affairs .... Dr. Bill SCHAFER
111 VP for University Advancement .... Mr. Nico KARAGOSIAN
13 Chief Information Officer .... Mr. Christopher AMENT
46 Interim VP Research & Dean Grad Col .... Dr. David KOONCE
84 Vice Pres Enrollment Management .... Ms. Candace BOENINGER
102 CEO University Foundation .... Mr. Nico KARAGOSIAN
43 General Counsel .... Ms. Stacey BENNETT
26 VP Univ Communications/Marketing .... Ms. Robin OLIVER
89 Interim Dean University College .... Dr. David NGUYEN
49 Dean College of Arts & Sciences .... Dr. Florenz PLASSMANN
50 Dean College of Business .... Dr. Jackie REESE-ULMER
60 Dean Scripps Col Communication .... Dr. Scott TITSWORTH
53 Int Dn Patton College of Education .... Dr. Sarah HELFRICH
54 Interim Dean Russ Col Eng/Tech .... Dr. Maj MIRMIRANI
57 Dean College of Fine Arts .... Dr. Matthew SHAFTEL
69 Int Dean Col Health/Human Services .... Dr. John MCCARTHY
92 Dean Honors Tutorial College .... Dr. Donal SKINNER
63 Dean Heritage Col Osteopathic Med .... Dr. Kenneth JOHNSON
62 Dean University Libraries .... Dr. Neil ROMANOSKY
35 Interim AVP/Dean of Students .... Dr. Kathy FAHL
12 Dean Campus/Cmty Relations Eastern .... Dr. David ROHALL
12 Dean Southern Campus .... Dr. Deborah MARINSKI
12 Dean Campus/Cmty Rels Chillicothe .... Dr. Roberta MILLIKEN
12 Dean Campus/Cmty Rels Lancaster .... Dr. Jarrod TUDOR
12 Dean Campus/Cmty Rels Zanesville .... Dr. Hannah NISSEN
20 Vice Provost for Faculty Devel .... Dr. Katie HARTMAN
58 Asst Dean Graduate College .... Dr. Katherine TADLOCK
09 Assoc Prov Inst Effectiveness .... Dr. Loralyn TAYLOR
41 Director of Athletics .... Ms. Julie CROMER
06 University Registrar .... Mrs. Debra M. BENTON
15 Chief Human Resources Officer .... Ms. Colleen BENDL
29 Asst Vice Pres Alumni Relations .... Vacant
35 Assistant VP Student Affairs .... Mr. Imants JAUNARAJS
07 Asst VProv/Dir Undergrad Admission .... Dr. Mateo REMSBURG
38 Dir Counseling/Psychological Svcs .... Dr. Paul CASTELINO
112 Assistant VP Gift Planning .... Ms. Kelli KOTOWSKI
37 Dir Student Fin Aid/Scholarships .... Ms. Valerie MILLER
19 Chief of Police .... Chief Andrew POWERS
85 Dir International Svcs/Operations .... Dr. Diane CAHILL
39 Executive Dir Residential Housing .... Ms. Jneanne HACKER
28 Interim VP Diversity & Inclusion .... Dr. Salome NNOROMELE
24 Media Library Manager .... Ms. Robin WOOTEN
113 Bursar .... Ms. Sherry ROSSITER
101 Secretary to Board of Trustees .... Dr. David MOORE
86 Director of Government Relations .... Mr. Eric BURCHARD
88 Ombudsman .... Mr. Mac STRICKLEN
04 Presidential Assistant .... Ms. Joanna STOLTZFUS

Ohio University Chillicothe Campus (A)

101 University Drive, Chillicothe OH 45601-0629
Telephone: (740) 774-7200 FICE Identification: 003102
Accreditation: &HLC

† Regional accreditation is carried under the parent institution in Athens, OH.

Ohio University Eastern Campus (B)

45425 National Road, Saint Clairsville OH 43950-9724
Telephone: (740) 695-1720 FICE Identification: 003101
Accreditation: &HLC

† Regional accreditation is carried under the parent institution in Athens, OH.

Ohio University Lancaster Campus (C)

1570 Granville Pike, Lancaster OH 43130-1097
Telephone: (740) 654-6711 FICE Identification: 003104
Accreditation: &HLC, MAC

† Regional accreditation is carried under the parent institution in Athens, OH.

Ohio University Southern Campus (D)

1804 Liberty Avenue, Ironton OH 45638-2279
Telephone: (740) 533-4600 Identification: 666000
Accreditation: &HLC

† Regional accreditation is carried under the parent institution in Athens, OH.

Ohio University Zanesville (E)

1425 Newark Road, Zanesville OH 43701-2695
Telephone: (740) 453-0762 FICE Identification: 003108
Accreditation: &HLC

† Regional accreditation is carried under the parent institution in Athens, OH.

Ohio Wesleyan University (F)

61 S Sandusky Street, Delaware OH 43015-2398
County: Delaware FICE Identification: 003109
Unit ID: 204909
Telephone: (740) 368-2000 Carnegie Class: Bac-A&S
FAX Number: (740) 368-3299 Calendar System: Semester
URL: www.owu.edu
Established: 1842 Annual Undergrad Tuition & Fees: $47,130
Enrollment: 1,426 Coed
Affiliation or Control: United Methodist IRS Status: 501(c)3
Highest Offering: Baccalaureate
Accreditation: HLC, CAEP, MUS

01 President .... Dr. Rockwell F. JONES
05 Provost .... Dr. Karlyn A. CROWLEY
10 VP for Finance/Admin/Treasurer .... Ms. Maura S. DONAHUE
111 VP for University Advancement .... Ms. Natalie MILBURN DOAN
84 Vice President for Enrollment .... Dr. Stefanie D. NILES
32 VP for Student Engagement/Success .... Dr. Dwayne K. TODD
26 Chief Communications Officer .... Mr. Will E. KOPP
09 Assoc Provost for Inst Research .... Dr. Dale E. SWARTZENTRUBER
108 Asst Prov Assessment/Accreditation .... Dr. Barbara S. ANDERECK
28 Interim Chief Diversity Officer .... Dr. Dawn M. CHISEBE
37 Director Student Financial Aid .... Mr. Kevin F. PASKVAN
36 Director of Career Services .... Ms. Leslie J. MELTON
06 Int Registrar .... Ms. Jaime E. MILBURN
13 Assoc Provost Academic Support .... Dr. Brian A. RELLINGER
19 Director of Public Safety .... Mr. Sean R. BOLENDER
29 Director Alumni Relations .... Ms. Katie P. WEBSTER
124 Admin Director OWU Connections .... Mr. Darrell J. ALBON
18 Director Physical Plant .... Mr. Jay E. SCHEFFEL
15 Director of Human Resources .... Ms. Imogene G. JOHNSON
31 Director Community Svc Learning .... Ms. Sally S. LEBER
04 Exec Asst to President/Board Secy .... Ms. Tammy A. LOWKS
23 Director Wellness Center .... Ms. Marsha A. TILDEN
39 Director Residential Life .... Mr. Brian J. EMERICK
41 Director of Athletics .... Mr. Doug W. ZIPP
42 Int Chaplain .... Rev. Chad E. JOHNS
35 Dean of Student Services .... Mr. Brad T. PULCINI
92 Honors Program Director .... Dr. Mark A. ALLISON
102 Foundation Relations Manager .... Ms. Sue E. HAIDLE
07 Director of Admission .... Ms. Laurie S. PATTON
96 Director of Purchasing .... Ms. Melanie T. KALB

Otterbein University (G)

1 South Grove Street, Westerville OH 43081-2006
County: Franklin FICE Identification: 003110
Unit ID: 204936
Telephone: (614) 890-3000 Carnegie Class: Masters/M
FAX Number: (614) 823-3114 Calendar System: Semester
URL: www.otterbein.edu
Established: 1847 Annual Undergrad Tuition & Fees: $33,074
Enrollment: 2,652 Coed
Affiliation or Control: United Methodist IRS Status: 501(c)3
Highest Offering: Doctorate
Accreditation: HLC, ANEST, CAATE, CAEPN, MUS, NURSE, THEA

01 President .... Dr. John L. COMERFORD
05 Provost/VPAA .... Dr. Wendy R. SHERMAN HECKLER
32 Vice President Student Affairs .... Ms. Dawn STEWART
10 VP for Business Affairs/CFO .... Ms. Susan BOLT
111 VP Institutional Advancement .... Mr. Michael MCGREEVEY
84 Vice President for Enrollment .... Mr. Jefferson BLACKBURN-SMITH
08 Director of the Library .... Ms. Tiffany LIPSTREU
06 Registrar .... Mr. David SCHNEIDER
36 Director Career Planning/Placement .... Mr. Paul NEWELL
37 Director of Financial Aid .... Mrs. Kirsten CROTTE
41 Athletic Director .... Ms. Dawn STEWART
42 Chaplain .... Dr. Judy GUION-UTSLER
07 Executive Director of Admissions .... Mr. Mark MOFFITT
15 Director Human Resources .... Vacant
18 Director Physical Plant .... Mr. Patrick SINCONOLFI
29 Director Alumni Relations .... Mr. Steve CRAWFORD
28 Director of Diversity .... Vacant
21 Assistant Controller .... Mr. Christopher A. HAYTER
09 Director of Institutional Research .... Dr. Sean M. MCLAUGHLIN
19 Director of Security .... Mr. Larry BANASZAK
04 Executive Assistant to President .... Ms. Becky SMITH
39 Director Student Housing .... Ms. Tracy BENNER
38 Director Student Counseling .... Dr. Kathleen RYAN
44 Director Annual Giving .... Ms. Raeceen DUKEHART
25 Chief Contract/Grants Administrator .... Ms. Janelle M. HALLETT
30 Director of Development .... Ms. Kathleen M. BONTE

Owens Community College (H)

30335 Oregon, PO Box 10000, Toledo OH 43699-1947
County: Wood FICE Identification: 005753
Unit ID: 204945
Telephone: (567) 661-6000 Carnegie Class: Assoc/MT-VT-High Non
FAX Number: N/A Calendar System: Semester
URL: www.owens.edu
Established: 1965 Annual Undergrad Tuition & Fees (In-State): $5,702
Enrollment: 7,536 Coed
Affiliation or Control: State IRS Status: 501(c)3
Highest Offering: Associate Degree
Accreditation: HLC, ACBSP, ACFEI, ADNUR, CAHIIM, DH, DMS, EMT, MAC, NAEYC, NAIT, OTA, PTAA, RAD, RADMAG, SURGT

01 President .... Dr. Dione SOMERVILLE
101 Secretary to the Board of Trustees .... Ms. Patricia JEZAK
04 Executive Assistant to President .... Ms. Tiffany WHITLOW
05 VP Academic Affairs/Provost .... Dr. Denise SMITH
10 Treasurer .... Mr. Jeff GANUES
11 VP Administration .... Ms. Lisa NAGEL
84 VP Enrollment Mgmt/Student Svcs .... Vacant
103 Dean Workforce/Comm Service .... Mr. Quinton ROBERTS
12 Dean Findlay Campus .... Vacant
21 Controller .... Ms. Katie FEHER
13 Chief Information Officer .... Mr. Brian LAUBER
19 Chief of Police .... Chief Steven HARRISON
37 Director Financial Aid .... Ms. Andrea MORROW
26 Director Mktg & Communications .... Vacant
15 Exec Director Human Resources .... Mr. Jason MORRIS
18 Executive Director Operations .... Ms. Danielle TRACY
09 Director Inst Research .... Mr. Jason CROWLEY
81 Dean School of STEM .... Vacant
66 Dean School of Nursing/Health Prof .... Ms. Cathy FORD
50 Dean Sch Business/Info/Public Svc .... Dr. Michael PFAHL
57 Dean School of Liberal Arts .... Mr. Michael SANDER
08 Director Library Services .... Ms. Jane BERGER
106 Director eLearning .... Mr. Gary SEFTON
32 Exec Dir Student Services .... Mr. David SHAFFER
102 Exec Dir Found/Govt & Cmty Rels .... Vacant
35 Director Student Life/Stdnt Conduct .... Dr. Danielle FILIPCHUK
109 Director Business Operations .... Mr. David WAHR
85 Manager Intl Stdnt Services .... Ms. Annette SWANSON
43 General Counsel .... Ms. Lisa NAGEL
41 Director Athletics .... Ms. Shelley WHITAKER
06 Registrar .... Ms. Jill GENTRY

Owens Community College Findlay Campus (I)

3200 Bright Road, Findlay OH 45840
Telephone: (567) 429-3500 Identification: 770360
Accreditation: &HLC

Payne Theological Seminary (J)

PO Box 474, Wilberforce OH 45384-0474
County: Greene FICE Identification: 010017
Unit ID: 204990
Telephone: (937) 376-2946 Carnegie Class: Spec-4-yr-Faith
FAX Number: (937) 250-7956 Calendar System: 4/1/4
URL: www.payneseminary.edu
Established: 1849 Annual Graduate Tuition & Fees: N/A
Enrollment: 177 Coed
Affiliation or Control: African Methodist Episcopal IRS Status: 501(c)3
Highest Offering: Doctorate; No Undergraduates
Accreditation: THEOL

01 President .... Dr. Michael BROWN
05 Academic Dean .... Dr. Betty HOLLEY
30 Director of Development .... Vacant
10 Director of Finance .... Mr. Raymond INGRAM
06 Registrar .... Ms. Maryjo LEWIS
07 Admissions Officer .... Ms. Althea SMOOT

Pontifical College Josephinum (K)

7625 N High Street, Columbus OH 43235-1498
County: Franklin FICE Identification: 003113
Unit ID: 205027
Telephone: (614) 885-5585 Carnegie Class: Bac-A&S
FAX Number: (614) 885-2307 Calendar System: Semester
URL: www.pcj.edu
Established: 1888 Annual Undergrad Tuition & Fees: $25,262
Enrollment: 86 Male
Affiliation or Control: Roman Catholic IRS Status: 501(c)3
Highest Offering: Master's
Accreditation: #HLC, THEOL

01 Rector/President .... V.Rev. Steven P. BESEAU
10 VP for Administration/Treasurer .... Mr. John O. ERWIN
111 Vice President for Advancement .... Mr. Douglas H. STEIN
73 Vice Rec Sch Theology/Dn of Men .... Rev. Kenneth BRIGHENTI
49 Vice Rector College Liberal Arts .... Rev. Stash DAILEY
05 Chief Academic Officer .... Dr. Perry CAHALL
06 Registrar/Dir of Financial Aid .... Mr. Samuel J. DEAN
08 Director Library Services .... Mrs. Beverly LANE
108 Dir of Inst Plng/Assessment/Accred .... Mr. Eric S. GRAFF
26 Director of Communications .... Ms. Carolyn DINOVO
07 Admissions Coordinator .... Ms. Arminda CRAWFORD
105 Web Developer .... Ms. Tracy BROCKMAN
04 Admin Assistant to the President .... Ms. Barb CHEEK
18 Chief Facilities/Physical Plant Ofc .... Mr. Gary SHOTTS
38 Director Student Counseling .... Dr. Timothy LUIS
41 Athletic Director .... Mr. Joe GERNETZKE

Professional Skills Institute (L)

1505 Holland Road, Maumee OH 43537
County: Lucas FICE Identification: 023377
Unit ID: 205054
Telephone: (419) 720-6670 Carnegie Class: Spec 2-yr-Health
FAX Number: (419) 720-6674 Calendar System: Quarter
URL: www.proskills.edu
Established: 1984 Annual Undergrad Tuition & Fees: $12,767
Enrollment: 350 Coed
Affiliation or Control: Proprietary IRS Status: Proprietary
Highest Offering: Baccalaureate

Accreditation: ABHES, PTAA

00 CEO Michael MARINO
01 Campus President Elizabeth FOGLE
05 Dean of Education Susan LIPPENS
07 Director of Admissions Vacant

Rabbinical College of Telshe (A)

28400 Euclid Avenue, Wickliffe OH 44092-2584
County: Lake FICE Identification: 003115
Unit ID: 205124
Telephone: (440) 943-5300 Carnegie Class: Spec-4-yr-Faith
FAX Number: (440) 943-5303 Calendar System: Quarter
Established: 1941 Annual Undergrad Tuition & Fees: $13,400
Enrollment: 59 Male
Affiliation or Control: Independent Non-Profit IRS Status: 501(c)3
Highest Offering: Doctorate
Accreditation: RABN

01 President Rabbi Dovid GOLDBERG
06 Registrar Rabbi Abraham MATITIA

Rhodes State College (B)

4240 Campus Drive, Lima OH 45804-3597
County: Allen FICE Identification: 010027
Unit ID: 203678
Telephone: (419) 995-8200 Carnegie Class: Assoc/HVT-High Non
FAX Number: (419) 221-0450 Calendar System: Semester
URL: www.rhodesstate.edu
Established: 1971 Annual Undergrad Tuition & Fees (In-State): $4,325
Enrollment: 3,324 Coed
Affiliation or Control: State IRS Status: 501(c)3
Highest Offering: Associate Degree
Accreditation: HLC, ACBSP, ADNUR, COARC, COARCP, CSHSE, DH, EMT, MAC, MAC, OTA, PTAA, RAD

01 President Dr. Cynthia E. SPIERS
10 Vice President Business & Finance Mr. Russ LITKE
05 SVP for Academic/Student Affairs Dr. Antoinette BALDIN
111 VP for Institutional Advancement Mr. Kevin L. REEKS
103 SVP Workforce Development Dr. Antoinette BALDIN
84 VP Enrollment Management Dr. Brendan GREANEY
45 Exec Dir Inst Effectiveness/Plng Dr. Nanette SMITH
20 Dean of Academic Affairs Dr. Eric MASON
32 Dean of Student Affairs Dr. Jeannette PASSMORE
21 Controller/Asst Treasurer Mr. David BRUNS
37 Director Financial Aid Ms. Pamela HUGHES
09 Coordinator Institutional Research Ms. Lindsey BALLIET
36 Director of Career Development Ms. Krista RICHARDSON
08 Head Librarian Ms. Tina SCHNEIDER
15 Exec Director Human Resources Ms. Andrea GOINGS
49 Dean Technology & Liberal Studies Dr. Andrea FABER
76 Dean Health Sciences & Public Svc Ms. Angela HEATON
18 Chief Facilities/Physical Plant Vacant
26 Dir Mktg & Public Relations Ms. Paula SIEBENECK
04 Exec Admin Asst to the President Ms. Sandy KORTOKRAX
06 Registrar Ms. Alissa ZIMMERMAN
07 Director of Admissions Mr. Chad TEMAN
13 Director Information Technology Mr. Tony JACKSON
19 Director Security/Safety Mr. Mark MATHEWS
28 Director of DEI Dr. Renee BRADLEY
29 Director Alumni Affairs Ms. Kim MILLER

Rosedale Bible College (C)

2270 Rosedale Road, Irwin OH 43029-9517
County: Madison FICE Identification: 034253
Unit ID: 439899
Telephone: (740) 857-1311 Carnegie Class: Spec 2-yr-Other
FAX Number: (877) 857-1312 Calendar System: Semester
URL: www.rosedale.edu
Established: 1952 Annual Undergrad Tuition & Fees: $8,756
Enrollment: 71 Coed
Affiliation or Control: Mennonite Church IRS Status: 501(c)3
Highest Offering: Associate Degree
Accreditation: BI

01 President Mr. Jeremy MILLER
05 Academic Dean Mr. Phil WEBER
32 Dean of Students Mr. Matthew SHOWALTER
84 Director of Enrollment Services Mr. Hans SHENK
08 Director of Library Services Mr. Reuben SAIRS
06 Registrar Ms. Heather MAUST
10 Chief Financial Officer Mr. Lynford SCHROCK
26 Chief Public Relations Officer Mr. Kenneth MILLER
04 Administrative Asst to President Vacant
18 Chief Facilities/Physical Plant Mr. Darnell BRENNEMAN
37 Financial Aid Coordinator Mrs. Twila WEBER
30 Director of Development Ms. Jewel SHOWALTER

Saint Mary Seminary and Graduate School of Theology (D)

28700 Euclid Avenue, Wickliffe OH 44092-2585
County: Lake FICE Identification: 004061
Telephone: (440) 943-7600 Carnegie Class: Not Classified
FAX Number: (440) 943-7577 Calendar System: Semester
URL: www.stmarysem.edu
Established: 1848 Annual Graduate Tuition & Fees: N/A
Enrollment: N/A Coed
Affiliation or Control: Roman Catholic IRS Status: 501(c)3
Highest Offering: Doctorate; No Undergraduates
Accreditation: HLC, THEOL

01 President/Rector Rev. Mark A. LATCOVICH
03 Vice President/Vice Rector Rev. Joseph KOOPMAN
05 Academic Dean Sr. Mary MCCORMICK, OSU
32 Student Dean Rev. Michael G. WOOST
42 Spiritual Director Rev. David BLINE
06 Registrar/Assistant Dean Sr. Brendon ZAJAC, SND
08 Librarian Mr. Alan K. ROME
10 CFO/Treasurer Mr. Philip GUBAN
04 Administrative Asst to President Mrs. Angie PAVLIK
90 Director Academic Computing Sr. Brendon ZAJAC
18 Chief Facilities/Physical Plant Mr. Philip GUBAN
108 Director Institutional Assessment Sr. Brendon ZAJAC, SND
13 Chief Info Technology Officer (CIO) Mr. Alan K. ROME
19 Director Security/Safety Mr. Philip GUBAN
105 Director Web Services Vacant

Shawnee State University (E)

940 Second Street, Portsmouth OH 45662-4344
County: Scioto FICE Identification: 009942
Unit ID: 205443
Telephone: (740) 351-3205 Carnegie Class: Masters/S
FAX Number: (740) 351-3470 Calendar System: Semester
URL: www.shawnee.edu
Established: 1975 Annual Undergrad Tuition & Fees (In-State): $8,604
Enrollment: 3,485 Coed
Affiliation or Control: State IRS Status: 501(c)3
Highest Offering: Doctorate
Accreditation: HLC, ADNUR, CAEPN, COARC, DH, EMT, MLTAD, NUR, OT, OTA, PTAA, RAD

01 President Dr. Jeffrey BAUER
05 Provost/VP Academic & Student Affs Dr. Sunil AHUJA
20 Associate Provost Dr. Jennifer PAULEY
10 Vice President for Finance & Admin Dr. Jonica BURKE
111 VP for Advancement & Enrollment Mgt Dr. Eric BRAUN
43 General Counsel Mr. Michael MCPHILLIPS
26 Director Communications Ms. Elizabeth BLEVINS
107 Dean College Professional Studies Dr. Paul MADDEN
49 Int Dean College Arts & Sciences Dr. Kimberly INMAN
08 Director of Library Services Ms. Suzanne JOHNSON-VARNEY
13 Director Univ Information Systems Mr. Charles WARNER
30 Executive Director of Development Mr. Chris MOORE
07 Director of Admissions Mr. James FARMER
06 Registrar Ms. Tamara SHEETS
32 Dean of Students Ms. Marcie SIMMS
15 Director of Human Resources Ms. Malonda JOHNSON
41 Athletic Director Mr. Jeff HAMILTON
37 Director of Financial Aid Ms. Nicole NEAL
36 Director Career Svcs & Workforce Ms. Angie DUDUIT
38 Director of Counseling & Psych Svcs Dr. Linda KOENIG
85 Director for International Pgms Mr. Ryan WARNER
18 Director of Facilities Mr. Butch KOTCAMP
97 Director General Education Program Dr. Michael BARNHART
09 Dir Institutional Research Mr. Matthew CRAWFORD
21 Controller Mr. Greg BALLENGEE
19 Chief of Police Mr. Jon PETERS
04 Executive Asst to President Ms. Pamela OTWORTH
25 Chief Grants Administrator Mr. Chris SHAFFER
108 Director Institutional Assessment Dr. Marc SCOTT
103 Director Workforce Development Ms. Angie DUDUIT
28 Dir of Diversity/Equity/Inclusion Ms. Malonda JOHNSON

Sinclair Community College (F)

444 W Third Street, Dayton OH 45402-1460
County: Montgomery FICE Identification: 003119
Unit ID: 205470
Telephone: (937) 512-3000 Carnegie Class: Assoc/MT-VT-High Non
FAX Number: (937) 512-4596 Calendar System: Semester
URL: www.sinclair.edu
Established: 1887 Annual Undergrad Tuition & Fees (In-District): $4,329
Enrollment: 18,687 Coed
Affiliation or Control: State/Local IRS Status: 501(c)3
Highest Offering: Baccalaureate
Accreditation: HLC, ACBSP, ACFEI, ACPHA, ADNUR, ART, CAHIIM, COARC, DH, DIETT, EMT, MAC, MLTAD, MUS, NDT, OTA, PTAA, RAD, SURGT, THEA

01 President Dr. Steven L. JOHNSON
22 VP Equity/Anti-Racism/Title IX Ms. Janet JONES
05 Provost Dr. Anthony PONDER
10 VP & Chief Financial Officer Mr. Michael D. BARHORST
103 SVP for Workforce Development Dr. Dave COLLINS
15 Chief Human Resources Officer Mr. Nathaniel NEWMAN
32 SVP Student Development Dr. Scott MARKLAND
111 SVP for Advancement Ms. Madeline ISELI
100 VP External Affairs/Chief of Staff Mr. Adam MURKA
13 Chief Information Officer Mr. Scott MCCOLLUM
88 Chief School Partnership Officer Dr. Melissa TOLLE
106 Dean of eLearning Dr. Christina AMATO
20 Interim Director Student Completion Ms. Carol BONNER
20 Associate Provost Dr. Jennifer KOSTIC
81 Dean Science/Math/Engineering Mr. Karl HESS
76 Dean Health Sciences Dr. Rena SEBOR
50 Dean Business/Public Svc Ms. Angela FERNANDEZ
83 Interim Dean Arts/Comm & Social Sci Ms. Phyllis ADAMS
43 General Counsel Ms. Lauren ROSS
06 Registrar Dr. Tina HUMMONS
84 AVP for Enrollment Operations Mr. Matthew MOORE
104 Director International Education Ms. Deborah GAVLIK
121 Director Academic Advising Ms. Karla KNEPPER
04 Admin Assistant to the President Ms. Angela MILLER
08 Chief Library Officer Ms. Debra OSWALD
18 Chf Facilities/Physical Plant Ofcr Ms. Yolanda JUNIOR
19 Dir Public Safety/Chief of Police Mr. Thomas THOMPSON
25 Director Grants Development Mr. Steve BRIGHT
28 Director of Diversity Mr. Michael CARTER
30 Director of Development Dr. Zach BECK
35 Director of Student Affairs Ms. Alicia SCHROEDER
41 Athletic Director Vacant
96 Director of Purchasing Mr. Paul MURPHY
07 Director of Admissions & Marketing Dr. Korrin ZISWILER
09 Director of Research and Analytics Mr. Karl KONSDORF
11 Chief of Operations/Administration Mr. Jeff MILLER
29 Director Alumni Affairs Mr. Mike ORR

Southern State Community College (G)

100 Hobart Drive, Hillsboro OH 45133-9488
County: Highland FICE Identification: 012870
Unit ID: 205966
Telephone: (937) 393-3431 Carnegie Class: Assoc/MT-VT-High Non
FAX Number: (937) 393-9370 Calendar System: Semester
URL: www.sscc.edu
Established: 1975 Annual Undergrad Tuition & Fees (In-State): $5,312
Enrollment: 2,018 Coed
Affiliation or Control: State IRS Status: 501(c)3
Highest Offering: Associate Degree
Accreditation: HLC, ADNUR, MAC

01 President Dr. Nicole ROADES
05 Vice President Academic Affairs Dr. Erica GOODWIN
10 Chief Financial Officer Dr. Steven HINSHAW
32 Vice Pres Student Svcs/Enroll Mgmt Mr. James BLAND
12 Director of Central Campus Dr. Jessica WISE
72 Dean of Core & Technical Studies Mr. Jeff MONTGOMERY
12 Director of Brown County Campus Ms. Amy MCCLELLAN
103 Dean Workforce Dev/Community Svcs Ms. Amy MCCLELLAN
15 Vice President of Human Resources Ms. Mindy MARKEY-GRABILL
55 Director Adult Opportunity Center Ms. Susan ARMSTRONG
91 Information Systems Coordinator Ms. Katy MARKEY
06 Registrar Ms. Amanda THOMPSON
66 Director of Nursing Dr. Julianne KREBS
08 Librarian Ms. Angel MOOTISPAW
37 Director of Financial Aid Ms. Suzanne HARMON
07 Director Recruitment & Admissions Vacant
13 VP of Technology and Infrastructure Mr. Brian RICE
04 Executive Asst to President Ms. Robin THOLEN

† Enrollment figure encompasses all 4 campuses.

Southern State Community College Brown County Campus (H)

351 Brooks-Malott Rd, Mt Orab OH 45154
Telephone: (937) 444-7722 Identification: 770361
Accreditation: &HLC

Stark State College (I)

6200 Frank Avenue, NW, North Canton OH 44720-7299
County: Stark FICE Identification: 010881
Unit ID: 205841
Telephone: (330) 494-6170 Carnegie Class: Assoc/HVT-Mix Trad/Non
FAX Number: (330) 497-6313 Calendar System: Semester
URL: www.starkstate.edu
Established: 1960 Annual Undergrad Tuition & Fees (In-District): $4,310
Enrollment: 10,772 Coed
Affiliation or Control: State/Local IRS Status: 501(c)3
Highest Offering: Associate Degree
Accreditation: HLC, ACBSP, ACFEI, ADNUR, CAHIIM, COARC, DH, DIETT, EMT, MAC, MLTAD, OTA, PTAA, SURGA, SURGT

01 President Dr. Para M. JONES
05 Provost and Chief Academic Officer Dr. Lada GIBSON-SHREVE
10 CFO/VP of Business Mr. Kevin D. GARDNER
84 VP for Enrollment Management Dr. Stephanie SUTTON
15 Director of Human Resources Ms. Melissa A. GLANZ
53 Dean Ed/Liberal Arts/Math/Science Mr. Andrew STEPHAN
76 Dean Health/Human Services Ms. Kelly REINSEL
50 Dean Business/Engr & IT Dr. Donald BALL
21 Comptroller Mr. Joe RICHARDS
37 Dir Financial Aid & Scholarships Mr. Matthew KIRKSEY
18 Dir Physical Plant/Construction Mr. Steve SPRADLING
40 Bookstore Manager Ms. Kathryn FEICHTER
06 Registrar Ms. Pam ARRINGTON
111 Exec Dir Advance & SSC Foundation Ms. Marisa ROHN
114 Director of Budget Mr. Bruce WYDER
09 Director of Institutional Research Mr. Peter TRUMPOWER
54 Dean Engineering Technologies Dr. Don BALL
106 Director eStarkState Ms. Linda MOROSKO
08 Head Librarian Ms. Marcia ADDISON
04 Exec Admin Asst to President Ms. Teri ROSS
07 Exec Director of Admissions Mr. J.P COONEY
26 Director of Marketing Ms. Robyn STEINMETZ
19 Director Security/Safety Mr. Gregory BOUDREAUX

Stautzenberger College (J)

8001 Katherine Boulevard, Brecksville OH 44141
Telephone: (440) 838-1999 Identification: 770760

Accreditation: **ACCSC**, DMS, SURTEC

Stautzenberger College　　　　　　　　(A)
1796 Indian Wood Circle, Maumee OH 43537-4007
County: Lucas　　　　　　　　　　　FICE Identification: 004866
　　　　　　　　　　　　　　　　　　　Unit ID: 205887
Telephone: (419) 866-0261　　　　Carnegie Class: Assoc/HVT-High Non
FAX Number: (419) 867-9821　　　　　Calendar System: Other
URL: https://www.sctoday.edu
Established: 1926　　　Annual Undergrad Tuition & Fees: $16,699
Enrollment: 551　　　　　　　　　　　　　　　　　　　　Coed
Affiliation or Control: Proprietary　　　IRS Status: Proprietary
Highest Offering: Associate Degree
Accreditation: **ACCSC**, SURTEC

01	Campus President	Ms. Amy BEAUREGARD
05	Academic Dean	Mr. Carlton ELLIS, III
37	Financial Aid Director	Mrs. Mari L. HUFFMAN
36	Career Services Director	Mr. Robert A. GARVER
06	Registrar	Ms. Terri KINDER
08	Head Librarian	Ms. Lori VAN LIERE
32	Director of Sstudent Services	Mr. Cameron MILLER

Terra State Community College　　　(B)
2830 Napoleon Road, Fremont OH 43420-9670
County: Sandusky　　　　　　　　FICE Identification: 008278
　　　　　　　　　　　　　　　　　　　Unit ID: 206011
Telephone: (419) 334-8400　　Carnegie Class: Assoc/HVT-Mix Trad/Non
FAX Number: (419) 355-1247　　　　Calendar System: Semester
URL: www.terra.edu
Established: 1968　Annual Undergrad Tuition & Fees (In-State): $5,338
Enrollment: 2,057　　　　　　　　　　　　　　　　　　　Coed
Affiliation or Control: State　　　　　IRS Status: 501(c)3
Highest Offering: Associate Degree
Accreditation: **HLC**, ADNUR, CAHIIM, MAC, PTAA

01	President	Dr. Ron SCHUMACHER
111	VP Inst Advancement/Exec Dir Fdn	Dr. Cory STINE
10	VP Financial Affairs	Ms. Jacque FOOS
05	VP Academic Affairs	Mr. William TAYLOR
32	VP Student Affairs/Enrollment Svcs	Dr. Garien HUDSON
49	Dean Lib Arts/Bus/Hlthcare/Nursing	Ms. Ann SERGENT
72	Dean Technology/Skilled Trades	Mr. Andrew SHELLA
41	Athletic Director	Mr. Gregory HEDDEN
09	Dir Planning/Inst Effectiveness	Ms. Ellen WARDZALA
06	Registrar	Mr. Eric STEINBERGER
13	Manager Information Technology	Mr. Wayne YERDON
08	Librarian	Ms. Amy KREILICK
04	Executive Assistant to President	Ms. Lisa SHUEY
106	Instructional Technologist	Ms. Melinda YERDON
35	Associate Dean of Students	Mr. Todd LONG
19	Director Security/Safety	Ms. Jen KIN
15	Human Resources Manager	Mr. Scott KNEESKERN

Tiffin University　　　　　　　　　　　(C)
155 Miami Street, Tiffin OH 44883-2161
County: Seneca　　　　　　　　　FICE Identification: 003121
　　　　　　　　　　　　　　　　　　　Unit ID: 206048
Telephone: (419) 447-6442　　　　Carnegie Class: Masters/L
FAX Number: N/A　　　　　　　　　Calendar System: Semester
URL: www.tiffin.edu
Established: 1888　　Annual Undergrad Tuition & Fees: $27,610
Enrollment: 2,933　　　　　　　　　　　　　　　　　　　Coed
Affiliation or Control: Independent Non-Profit　　IRS Status: 501(c)3
Highest Offering: Doctorate
Accreditation: **HLC**, ACBSP

01	President	Dr. Lillian SCHUMACHER
05	Provost & Chief Academic Ofcr	Dr. Peter HOLBROOK
84	VP Enrollment Management	Dr. Amy WOOD
111	VP University Advancement	Mr. Mitchell BLONDE
10	VP Finance/Administration	Mr. Devin FRANK
15	VP Human Resources	Ms. Nadia LEWIS
108	VP Inst Planning & Effectiveness	Dr. Teresa SHAFER
26	Exec Dir PR/Mktg/Communications	Ms. Deborah ROSZMAN
04	Exec Assistant to the President	Ms. Ellen LUCIUS
32	Dean of Students	Mr. Jacob SIMON
13	Chief Information Officer	Mr. Jason MARSON
07	Exec Director Undergrad Admissions	Ms. Sarah JOHNSON
06	Registrar & Assoc Provost	Ms. Melissa WEININGER
41	VP/Director Athletics	Mr. Lonny ALLEN
21	AVP Finance/Controller	Mr. Owen HOSKINS
08	Head Librarian	Ms. Luanne EDWARDS
29	Director Alumni Relations	Ms. Vickie WILKINS
36	Exec Director of Career Services	Ms. Amanda HUMMEL
18	Director of Physical Plant	Mr. John WANK
35	Assistant Dean of Student Life	Mr. Stephen SANNEY
44	Director of Annual Giving	Ms. Mikki KING
28	AVP Intercultural & Cmty Engagement	Mr. Jacob SIMON
37	Director Student Financial Aid	Ms. Tangi RITCHIE
49	Dean of Arts & Sciences	Vacant
50	Dean of Business	Dr. Terry SULLIVAN
83	Dean Criminal Justice/Social Sci	Dr. Peter PIRAINO
09	Director of Institutional Research	Ms. Holly ALLGOOD
88	Dir Faculty Advising & Mentoring	Mr. Jonathan BEARD
19	Director Campus Safety & Security	Mr. Jason DENNIS
106	Vice Provost/Online & Extended Lrng	Dr. Daniel CLARK

Tri-State Bible College　　　　　　　(D)
506 Margaret Street, PO Box 445,
South Point OH 45680-8402
County: Lawrence　　　　　　　　FICE Identification: 034754
　　　　　　　　　　　　　　　　　　　Unit ID: 206154
Telephone: (740) 377-2520　　　Carnegie Class: Spec-4-yr-Faith
FAX Number: (740) 377-0001　　　　Calendar System: Semester
URL: www.tsbc.edu
Established: 1970　　Annual Undergrad Tuition & Fees: $9,100
Enrollment: 20　　　　　　　　　　　　　　　　　　　　Coed
Affiliation or Control: Independent Non-Profit　　IRS Status: 501(c)3
Highest Offering: Master's
Accreditation: **BI**

01	President	Mr. Rex HOWE
05	VP Academic Affairs	Vacant
10	Director of Finance	Ms. Jeana GRAVES
11	VP Admin/Fin Aid Dir/Reg/Chief HR	Ms. Roberta MERCER
32	Vice Pres Student Affairs	Mr. Leroy FULFORD
18	Vice President Operations	Mr. Manfred LANGER
20	Academic Dean Online Programs	Mr. David LAMBERT

Union Institute & University　　　　(E)
2090 Florence Avenue, Cincinnati OH 45206-1947
County: Hamilton　　　　　　　　FICE Identification: 010923
　　　　　　　　　　　　　　　　　　　Unit ID: 206279
Telephone: (513) 861-6400　　　Carnegie Class: Masters/S
FAX Number: (513) 861-0779　　　　Calendar System: Semester
URL: www.myunion.edu
Established: 1964　　Annual Undergrad Tuition & Fees: $15,686
Enrollment: 809　　　　　　　　　　　　　　　　　　　Coed
Affiliation or Control: Independent Non-Profit　　IRS Status: 501(c)3
Highest Offering: Doctorate
Accreditation: **HLC**, CACREP, @DIET, LC, SW

01	President	Dr. Karen SCHUSTER-WEBB
05	Vice President Academic Affairs	Dr. Nelson SOTO
04	Executive Assistant to President	Ms. Susan GRACE
10	Chief Financial Officer	Ms. Sandra MILLS
15	Vice President Human Resources	Ms. Patty BURKE
111	VP Inst Innovation/Economic Dev	Dr. Shanda GORE
20	Associate VP of Academic Affairs	Dr. Arlene SACKS
06	Registrar	Ms. Lew Rita MOORE
13	Director Information Technology	Mr. Anthony KENDALL
18	Director Facilities Management	Mr. Ray BOLIN
88	Special Assistant to the President	Dr. Rhonda BRINKLEY-KENNEDY
108	AVP for Institutional Effectiveness	Dr. Peter CACCAVERI
08	Director Library Services	Mr. Matthew PAPPATHAN
37	Director Financial Aid	Ms. Jean POHLMAN
29	Director Alumni Relations	Ms. Carolyn KRAUSE
32	Director Student Success	Dr. Jay KEEHN
106	Dir Center for Teaching & Learning	Dr. Bob COTTER
30	Director of Development	Vacant

United Theological Seminary　　　　(F)
4501 Denlinger Road, Dayton OH 45426-2308
County: Montgomery　　　　　　　FICE Identification: 003122
　　　　　　　　　　　　　　　　　　　Unit ID: 206288
Telephone: (937) 529-2201　　　Carnegie Class: Spec-4-yr-Faith
FAX Number: N/A　　　　　　　　　Calendar System: Trimester
URL: www.united.edu
Established: 1871　　Annual Graduate Tuition & Fees: N/A
Enrollment: 412　　　　　　　　　　　　　　　　　　　Coed
Affiliation or Control: United Methodist　　IRS Status: 501(c)3
Highest Offering: Doctorate; No Undergraduates
Accreditation: **HLC**, THEOL

01	President	Dr. Kent MILLARD
05	Vice Pres Academic Affairs & Dean	Dr. David WATSON
10	Vice Pres Finance/Treasurer	Mr. Steven SWALLOW
84	Vice Pres for Enrollment	Dr. Bridget WEATHERSPOON
30	Vice Pres Development	Ms. Callie PICARDO
101	Exec Asst to President/Corp Secy	Ms. Laura WEBER
20	Assoc Dean Academic Affairs	Dr. Vivian JOHNSON
26	Chf Marketing & Accreditation Ofcr	Ms. Karen E. PAYNE
06	Registrar	Ms. Karen CLARK
13	Director of Information Technology	Vacant
08	Librarian	Mr. Ken S. COCHRANE
42	Dean of the Chapel	Dr. Tesia MALLORY
27	Director of Communications	Ms. Rachel HURLEY
37	Director Financial Aid	Ms. Marcia BYRD
29	Director of Alumni/ae Relations	Mrs. Harriet WATSON
18	Facility Manager	Mr. Steve SWALLOW
07	Senior Dir Admissions	Dr. Bridget WEATHERSPOON
32	Asst Dean of Student Success	Rev. Chad CLARK
106	Director of Distance Learning	Ms. Heather SHELLABARGER

The University of Akron, Main Campus　　　　　　　　　　　　　　　　(G)
302 Buchtel Common, Akron OH 44325
County: Summit　　　　　　　　　FICE Identification: 003123
　　　　　　　　　　　　　　　　　　　Unit ID: 200800
Telephone: (330) 972-7111　　　Carnegie Class: DU-Higher
FAX Number: (330) 972-6990　　　　Calendar System: Semester
URL: www.uakron.edu
Established: 1870　Annual Undergrad Tuition & Fees (In-State): $11,881
Enrollment: 16,094　　　　　　　　　　　　　　　　　　Coed

Affiliation or Control: State　　　　　IRS Status: 501(c)3
Highest Offering: Doctorate
Accreditation: **HLC**, ANEST, ART, AUD, CACREP, CAEP, COARC, COPSY,
DANCE, DIETC, EXSC, IFSAC, IPSY, LAW, MFCD, MUS, NURSE, PH, SP, SW

01	President	Dr. Gary L. MILLER
05	Exec Vice President & Provost	Dr. John WIENCEK
100	VP/Chief of Staff	Dr. Paul E. LEVY
20	Sr Vice Provost	Vacant
10	Sr VP Finance & Administration/CFO	Mr. Dallas A. GRUNDY
43	Vice President & General Counsel	Ms. M. Celeste COOK
32	VP for Student Affairs	Dr. John A. MESSINA
13	Chief Information Officer	Mr. John T. CORBY
32	Dean of Students	Mr. Michael A. STRONG
30	Vice President of Development	Mrs. Kimberly M. COLE
18	Chief Planning & Facilities	Mr. Stephen L. MYERS
88	Communications & Content Mgr	Mrs. Jessica WHITEHILL
21	Interim Controller	Mr. Douglas BRUMBAUGH
46	Actg VP Research & Business Engmt	Dr. Philip A. ALLEN
22	VP Inclusion/Equity & CDO	Dr. Sheldon B. WRICE
15	Assoc VP Talent Dev/Human Resources	Mrs. Sarah J. KELLY
26	VP/Chief Comm and Marketing Officer	Mrs. Tammy EWIN
19	Chief of Police & Campus Safety	Chief Dale E. GOODING, JR.
43	Assoc VP & Deputy General Counsel	Mr. John J. REILLY
06	Registrar	Mr. Ronald L. BOWMAN, JR.
07	Director of Admissions	Ms. Kim GENTILE
09	Lead Inst Research Info Officer	Vacant
09	VP Research & Business Engagement	Dr. Suzanne BAUSCH
14	Acting Director Technology Transfer	Ms. Kelly A. BIALEK
08	Dean University Libraries	Dr. Aimee L. DECHAMBEAU
49	Dean Buchtel College Arts & Sci	Dr. Mitchell S. MCKINNEY
54	Dean College of Engineering	Dr. Craig C. MENZEMER
12	Director of Regional Campuses	Dr. Heather A. HOWLEY
50	Dean College of Business	Dr. Robert J. NEMER
76	Acting Dean Health Professions	Dr. Timothy M. MCCARRAGHER
61	Dean School of Law	Mrs. Emily M. JANOSKI-HAEHLEN
58	Dean Graduate School	Dr. Suzanne BAUSCH
37	Director Student Financial Aid	Mrs. Jennifer E. HARPHAM
29	Asst VP Alumni Relations	Mr. Willy KOLLMAN
96	Director of Purchasing	Ms. Shandra L. IRISH
88	Senior Director Digital Comm	Mr. Jermel WILKERSON, SR.
105	Director of Web Services	Mr. Anthony W. SERPETTE
92	Dean Honors College	Dr. Fedearia A. NICHOLSON-SWEVAL
88	Director UA Adult Focus	Mrs. Laura H. CONLEY
41	Director Athletics	Mr. Charles D. GUTHRIE, JR.
36	Ex Dir Counseling/Test/Career Ctr	Dr. Juanita K. MARTIN
39	Dir of Residence Life and Housing	Dr. Melinda F. GROVE
25	Assoc Dir IRB Administration	Vacant
85	Exec Dir Center for Intl Stds & Sch	Ms. Nicola KILLE
23	Director Health Services	Ms. Lisa L. RITENOUR
86	Spec Asst Gov Rels/Assoc Dir RCBIAP	Dr. Matthew P. AKERS
91	Director IT Support Services	Mr. Neal L'AMOREAUX
27	Sr Director External Communications	Ms. Cristine BOYD
104	Exec Dir Global Engagement	Ms. Robyn K. BROWN
04	Admin Assistant to the President	Mrs. Kristin A. BRUMMOND
53	Interim Director Education	Dr. Lisa LENHART

The University of Akron-Wayne College　　　　　　　　　　　　　　　(H)
1901 Smucker Road, Orrville OH 44667-9758
Telephone: (330) 683-2010　　　FICE Identification: 010818
Accreditation: &HLC

† Regional accreditation is carried under the parent institution in Akron, OH.

University of Cincinnati Main Campus　　　　　　　　　　　　　　　　(I)
2624 Clifton Avenue, Cincinnati OH 45221-0001
County: Hamilton　　　　　　　　FICE Identification: 003125
　　　　　　　　　　　　　　　　　　　Unit ID: 201885
Telephone: (513) 556-6000　　　Carnegie Class: DU-Highest
FAX Number: (513) 556-3237　　　　Calendar System: Semester
URL: www.uc.edu
Established: 1819　Annual Undergrad Tuition & Fees (In-State): $12,138
Enrollment: 40,826　　　　　　　　　　　　　　　　　　Coed
Affiliation or Control: State　　　　　IRS Status: 501(c)3
Highest Offering: Doctorate
Accreditation: **HLC**, ANEST, ART, #AUD, CACREP, CAEP, CAHIIM, CAMPEP,
CIDA, CLPSY, COARC, CONST, DANCE, DENT, DIETC, DIETD, IPSY, LAW, MED,
MIDWF, MLS, MUS, NMT, NURSE, OT, PH, PHAR, PLNG, PTA, #RADMAG,
SCPSY, SP, SW, THEA

01	President	Dr. Neville G. PINTO
05	Exec VP/Provost Academic Affairs	Dr. Valerio FERME
11	Sr VP for Administration & Finance	Mr. Patrick KOWALSKI
03	Executive VP	Dr. Ryan HAYS
46	Vice President for Research	Dr. Patrick A. LIMBACH
63	Dean Med/Sr VP Health Affairs	Dr. Andrew FILAK
111	VP Univ Advancement/Alumni Rels	Mr. Peter LANDGREN
86	Chief Marketing Officer	Ms. Nicola ZIADY
32	Vice Pres Student Affairs & Svcs	Ms. Debra S. MERCHANT
10	Vice President for Finance	Ms. Carol METZGER
13	Chief Digital Officer	Mr. Bharath PRABHAKARAN
43	General Counsel	Ms. Lori A. ROSS
15	Sr Assoc VP/Chief HR Officer	Ms. Tamie L. GRUNOW
84	Vice Provost Enrollment	Mr. Jack D. MINER
31	Director Community Development	Ms. Megan SMITH
26	Exec Dir/Spokesperson Public Rels	Ms. M. B REILLY
07	Asst Vice Prov Admissions	Ms. Yosmeriz ROMAN
110	Vice Pres for Development	Mr. Stephen ROSFELD
76	Dean Allied Health Sciences	Dr. Tina WHALEN

49 Int Dean Arts & Sciences ... Dr. Margaret HANSON
50 Dean Business ... Dr. Marianne W. LEWIS
64 Dean Col Conservatory of Music ... Vacant
48 Dean Design/Architecture/Art & Plng ... Dr. Timothy J. JACHNA
53 Dean Education/Crim Justice & HS ... Dr. Lawrence J. JOHNSON
54 Dean Engineering & Applied Sci ... Dr. John W. WEIDNER
61 Dean Law ... Ms. Verna L. WILLIAMS
66 Interim Dean Nursing ... Dr. Denice GORMLEY
67 Dean Pharmacy ... Dr. Christopher SURRATT
58 Dean Graduate School ... Dr. Rose Marie WARD
70 Director School Social Work ... Dr. Ruth Anne VAN LOON
08 Dean Library ... Mr. Xuemao WANG
29 VP Alumni Affairs ... Ms. Jennifer HEISEY
28 VP Equity/Inclusion/Cmty Impact ... Dr. Bleuzette MARSHALL
41 Director Athletics ... Mr. John A. CUNNINGHAM
40 Regional Manager of the Bookstore ... Mr. Shane ZALESKI
38 Director Counseling Center ... Dr. Tara H. SCARBOROUGH
39 Sr Assoc VP Campus Services ... Mr. Todd DUNCAN
37 Director Student Financial Aid ... Mr. Randy ULSES
09 Director Institutional Research ... Mrs. Suzana H. LUZURIAGA VOIGHT
19 Director Public Safety/Police Chief ... Mr. Eliott ISAAC
06 Registrar ... Vacant
96 Assoc VP Purchasing ... Mr. Thomas B. GUERIN
45 Co-Dir Institute for Policy Rsrch ... Dr. Eric RADEMACHER
45 Co-Dir Institute for Policy Rsrch ... Dr. Kimberly DOWNING
104 Vice Provost International Affs ... Dr. Raj MEHTA
18 Chief Facilities/Physical Plant ... Mr. Joseph H. HARRELL
101 Exec Director Board of Trustees ... Ms. Nicole BLOUNT
88 Chief Innovation Officer ... Mr. David J. ADAMS
25 Assoc VP Sponsored Research ... Mr. Patrick E. CLARK
88 Asst VP eLearning ... Mr. Paul C. FOSTER
04 Administrative Asst to President ... Mr. Lawrence P. LAMPE
100 Chief of Staff ... Dr. Ryan HAYS
106 Vice Prov/Dean Cincinnati Online ... Dr. Jason E. LEMON
102 Dir Foundation/Corporate Relations ... Ms. Carol G. RUSSELL
105 Director Web Services ... Mr. Jeremy A. MARTIN

University of Cincinnati Blue Ash College (A)

9555 Plainfield Road, Blue Ash OH 45236-1096
County: Hamilton FICE Identification: 004868
Unit ID: 201955
Telephone: (513) 745-5600 Carnegie Class: Bac/Assoc-Assoc Dom
FAX Number: (513) 745-5780 Calendar System: Semester
URL: www.ucblueash.edu
Established: 1967 Annual Undergrad Tuition & Fees (In-State): $6,256
Enrollment: 7,239 Coed
Affiliation or Control: State IRS Status: 501(c)3
Highest Offering: Baccalaureate
Accreditation: HLC, ADNUR, ART, DH, MAC, RAD

01 Dean ... Dr. Robin LIGHTNER
05 Assoc Dean Academic Affairs ... Dr. Tracy HERRMANN
10 Director Business Affairs ... Ms. Diane WHITE
20 Asst Dean Academic Affairs ... Vacant
18 Director Facilities & Campus Plan ... Mr. Rob KNARR
13 Director Information Technology ... Mr. Dale HOFSTETTER
07 Director Admissions ... Mr. Brad TATE
09 Director Institutional Research ... Mr. Steve MILLER
30 Director Development ... Ms. Jennifer BERIGAN
08 Library Director ... Ms. Heather MALONEY
26 Director Mktg/Communication ... Mr. Pete GEMMER
32 Asst Dean Student Life ... Ms. Sarah WOLFE
121 Associate Dir of Academic Advising ... Ms. Laurie MALONE
35 Director One Stop Student Services ... Ms. Martha GEIGER
15 HR Manager ... Ms. Amy SMITH
22 Director Accessibility Resources ... Ms. Pamela GOINES

University of Cincinnati-Clermont College (B)

4200 Clermont College Drive, Batavia OH 45103-1785
County: Clermont FICE Identification: 010805
Unit ID: 201946
Telephone: (513) 556-5400 Carnegie Class: Bac/Assoc-Assoc Dom
FAX Number: (513) 732-5275 Calendar System: Semester
URL: www.ucclermont.edu
Established: 1972 Annual Undergrad Tuition & Fees (In-State): $5,864
Enrollment: 7,504 Coed
Affiliation or Control: State IRS Status: 501(c)3
Highest Offering: Baccalaureate
Accreditation: HLC, CAHIIM, PTAA, SURGT

01 Dean ... Dr. Jeffrey C. BAUER
05 Assoc Dean Academic Affairs ... Ms. Lisa MAHLE-GRISEZ
20 Sr Assistant Dean Academic Affairs ... Mr. Richard STACKPOLE
32 Sr Asst Dean Student Services ... Ms. Mae HANNA
08 Director Library ... Ms. Catherine CARLSON
09 Asst Dean Acad Init/Inst Effective ... Ms. Susan RILEY
10 Business Officer ... Mr. Daniel SOLAZZO
35 Assistant Dean of Student Affairs ... Ms. Jennifer RADT
07 Assoc Director Admissions ... Mr. Blaine KELLEY
22 Director Accessibility & Testing ... Ms. Meghann LITTRELL
41 Athletic Director ... Mr. Brian SULLIVAN
36 Asst Dean Career Services ... Ms. Dana PARKER
84 Assoc Director of Enrollmnt Svcs ... Vacant
106 Dir Online Learning ... Ms. Karen LANKISCH
28 Chief Diversity Officer ... Ms. Jennifer RADT
30 Director of Development ... Ms. Jeannie HELSEL

University of Dayton (C)

300 College Park, Dayton OH 45469-0001
County: Montgomery FICE Identification: 003127
Unit ID: 202480
Telephone: (937) 229-1000 Carnegie Class: DU-Higher
FAX Number: (937) 229-4000 Calendar System: Semester
URL: www.udayton.edu
Established: 1850 Annual Undergrad Tuition & Fees: $44,890
Enrollment: 11,650 Coed
Affiliation or Control: Roman Catholic IRS Status: 501(c)3
Highest Offering: Doctorate
Accreditation: HLC, ARCPA, ART, CACREP, CAEP, CEA, DIETD, LAW, MUS, PTA, SPAA

01 President ... Dr. Eric F. SPINA
05 Provost/EVP Academic Affairs ... Dr. Paul H. BENSON
32 VP Student Development ... Mr. William M. FISCHER
10 EVP Finance & Admin Services ... Mr. Andrew E. HORNER
111 VP Univ Advancement ... Mr. Chris MORRISON
26 VP Marketing & Communications ... Ms. Molly WILSON
41 VP/Director of Athletics ... Mr. Neil G. SULLIVAN
15 VP Human Resources ... Mr. Troy W. WASHINGTON
28 VP Diversity & Inclusion ... Dr. Lawrence A. BURNLEY
84 VP for Strategic Enrollment Mgmt ... Dr. Jason K. REINOEHL
42 VP for Mission and Rector ... Rev. James F. FITZ, SM
46 VP for Research ... Dr. John E. LELAND
30 Sr Dir Development/Principal Gifts ... Mr. James F. BROTHERS
42 Exec Director Campus Ministry ... Ms. Crystal C. SULLIVAN
31 Dir Ctr for Ldrshp in Cmty ... Ms. Hunter P. GOODMAN
20 Assoc Provost Faculty & Admin Affs ... Dr. Carolyn ROECKER-PHELPS
88 Asc Prov Lrng Spprt/Dir Rch Tch Ctr .. Dr. Deborah J. BICKFORD
06 Registrar ... Ms. Jennifer M. CREECH
07 Dir of Admission/Recruitment ... Mr. Nate PERRY
19 Exec Director/Chief of Police ... Mr. Savalas KIDD
09 Director Institutional Studies ... Ms. Susan K. SEXTON
21 Comptroller ... Ms. Angela K. BUECHELE
35 Assoc VP/Dean of Students ... Ms. Christine M. SCHRAMM
36 Director Career Services ... Mr. Jason C. ECKERT
38 Asst VP Student Dev/Dir Counseling ... Vacant
18 VP for Facilities/Management/Plng ... Mr. Richard KRYSIAK, JR.
23 Medical Director Univ Health Ctr ... Dr. Mary P. BUCHWALDER
08 Dean University Libraries ... Ms. Kathleen M. WEBB
49 Dean College A&S ... Dr. Jason L. PIERCE
61 Dean School of Law ... Mr. Andrew L. STRAUSS
50 Dean Sch of Business Admin ... Dr. John MITTELSTAEDT
58 Assoc Prov Graduate Acad Affairs ... Dr. Paul M. VANDERBURGH
13 Assoc Provost & Chief Info Officer ... Dr. Thomas D. SKILL
53 Interim Dean SOE & Health Sci ... Dr. Corinne DAPRANO
54 Dean School of Engineering ... Dr. Eddy M. ROJAS
29 Alumni Engagement Officer ... Ms. Catherine GRADY
35 Dir Student Life & Kennedy Union ... Ms. Amy L. LOPEZ-MATTHEWS
39 Asst Dean Students & Dir Res Life ... Mr. Steven T. HERNDON
40 Manager UD Bookstore ... Ms. Julie M. BANKS
43 Univ Counsel/Dir Legal Affairs ... Ms. Mary A. RECKER
96 Dir Univ Purchases/Business Service ... Vacant
92 Dir University Honors/Scholars Pgm ... Dr. John P. MCCOMBE
94 Chair Women's/Gender Studies ... Vacant
22 Dir Affirmative Action & Compliance ... Ms. Patricia BERNAL-OLSON
86 Exec Dir Govt/Regional Relations ... Mr. S. Ted BUCARO
27 Dir Marketing & Creative Services ... Ms. Kim B. LALLY
04 Asst to President ... Ms. Annette MITCHELL
100 Executive Director ... Mr. Thomas U. WECKESSER
101 Secretary of the Board of Trustees ... Ms. Lisa S. RISMILLER

The University of Findlay (D)

1000 North Main Street, Findlay OH 45840-3653
County: Hancock FICE Identification: 003045
Unit ID: 202763
Telephone: (419) 422-8313 Carnegie Class: DU-Mod
FAX Number: (419) 434-4822 Calendar System: Semester
URL: www.findlay.edu
Established: 1882 Annual Undergrad Tuition & Fees: $36,484
Enrollment: 4,829 Coed
Affiliation or Control: Church Of God IRS Status: 501(c)3
Highest Offering: Doctorate
Accreditation: HLC, ACBSP, ARCPA, CAEP, CEA, NMT, NURSE, OT, PHAR, PTA, SW

01 President ... Dr. Katherine R. FELL
05 Vice President for Academic Affairs ... Dr. Darin E. FIELDS
10 VP Business Affairs/Treasurer ... Ms. Kimberly WILLIAMS
84 Interim VP Enrollment Management ... Mr. Mike FRANTZ
111 Vice Pres University Advancement ... Dr. Marcia SLOAN LATTA
32 Vice President for Student Affairs ... Ms. Brandi LAURITA
20 Assoc VP Academic Affairs ... Dr. C. Damon OSBORNE
04 Assistant to the President ... Ms. Liz DITTO
81 Dean College of Sciences ... Dr. Jeffrey FRYE
50 Dean College of Business ... Dr. Kirby OVERTON
49 Dean Col of Arts/Hum & Social Sci ... Dr. Ronald TULLEY
76 Dean College Health Professions ... Dr. Richard STATES
67 Dean College of Pharmacy ... Dr. Debra PARKER
53 Dean College of Education ... Dr. Julie MCINTOSH
18 Director of Physical Plant ... Mr. Orion JONES
06 Registrar ... Mr. Anthony SILECCHIA
41 Athletic Director ... Ms. Brandi LAURITA
08 Interim Director of Shafer Library ... Ms. Rebecca QUINTUS
37 Director of Financial Aid ... Mr. Joseph F. SPENCER

13 VP of Information Tech Services ... Dr. Raymond MCCANDLESS
26 Interim Director of Marketing/Comm ... Ms. Amy DEPUY
36 Dir Career/Professional Development ... Mr. Bradley C. HAMMER
15 Director of Human Resources ... Mr. Robert LINK
23 Director of Health Services ... Ms. Tara SMITH
38 Director of Counseling Services ... Ms. Jodi FIRSDON
40 University Stores Manager ... Mr. Jay CANTERBURY
42 Director Christian Ministries ... Mr. Matthew GINTER
19 Chief of Police/Dir of Security ... Mr. William SPRAW
104 Assoc VP Student Engagement ... Mr. Christopher SIPPEL
101 Secretary to the Board of Trustees ... Ms. Liz DITTO
25 Grants Manager ... Dr. Juliann REINEKE
88 Int Dir International Admissions ... Ms. Debbie VANATTA
21 Controller/ Assistant Treasurer ... Ms. Megan SCHULTE
39 Director of Housing ... Ms. Shari HELLMAN
35 Assoc VP for Student Life ... Mr. Johnathan FERRARO
44 Director Annual Giving ... Ms. Amanda NICOL
110 Assoc VP for Advancement ... Mr. Tyson PINION
07 Director of Admissions Operations ... Ms. Kelli E. WAGES
88 Director of Admissions/Events ... Ms. DeeDee SPRAW
09 Director of IR and Assessment ... Dr. Kristen R. LINDSAY

University of Mount Union (E)

1972 Clark Avenue, Alliance OH 44601-3993
County: Stark FICE Identification: 003083
Unit ID: 204185
Telephone: (330) 821-5320 Carnegie Class: Masters/S
FAX Number: (330) 829-2811 Calendar System: Semester
URL: www.mountunion.edu
Established: 1846 Annual Undergrad Tuition & Fees: $32,600
Enrollment: 2,178 Coed
Affiliation or Control: Independent Non-Profit IRS Status: 501(c)3
Highest Offering: Doctorate
Accreditation: HLC, ACBSP, ARCPA, CAEP, COSMA, MUS, NURSE, PTA

01 President ... Dr. Thomas J. BOTZMAN
05 Vice Pres Acad Affs/Provost ... Dr. Jeffrey R. BREESE
10 Vice Pres Business Affs/Treasurer ... Mr. Patrick D. HEDDLESTON
111 Vice President Univ Advancement ... Mr. Gregory KING
32 Vice Pres Student Affs/Dean Stdnts ... Mr. John FRAZIER
84 Vice President for Enrollment Mgmt ... Ms. Lindajean WESTERN
26 Vice President for Marketing ... Ms. Melissa GARDNER
08 Librarian ... Ms. Carla SARRAT
06 University Registrar ... Dr. Bryan BOATRIGHT
07 Director of Admission ... Dr. Eric YOUNG
112 Director of Planned Giving ... Ms. Bethany LESLIE
13 Director of Information Technology ... Ms. Tina STUCHELL
110 Director of Advancement ... Mr. Joseph D. MONTGOMERY
29 Director Alumni/College Activities ... Ms. Audra YOUNGEN
85 Director Center for Global Educ ... Dr. Jennifer HALL
18 Director of Physical Plant ... Mr. Lee SMITH
15 Director of Human Resources ... Ms. Marci CRAIG
39 Director of Residence Life ... Ms. Sara SHERER
42 Interim University Chaplain ... Mr. Stephen DAGES
36 Assistant Dean for Student Success ... Ms. Jessica CUNION
40 Manager of University Store ... Ms. Aimee SCHULLER
41 Interim Athletic Director ... Mr. Michael PARNELL
04 Exec Assistant to the President ... Ms. Heather HICKMAN
45 Assoc VP Planning Implementation ... Mr. Ronald CROWL
35 Associate Dean of Students ... Ms. Michelle GAFFNEY
96 Purchasing and Risk Manager ... Mr. Shawn BAGLEY
19 Director Security/Safety ... Mr. William KETJEN
28 Director of Diversity & Inclusion ... Mr. Ronald HOLDEN
38 Director of Counseling Services ... Ms. Francine PACKARD
44 Director of the Mount Union Fund ... Ms. Bethany LESLIE
37 Director Student Financial Aid ... Ms. Kathleen THOMAS
79 Dean of Arts & Humanities ... Dr. Heather DUDA
76 Dean of Natural & Health Sciences ... Dr. Sandra MADAR
83 Dean of Applied & Social Sciences ... Dr. Kristine STILL
09 Director of Institutional Research ... Ms. Suzette BURLINGAME

University of Northwestern Ohio (F)

1441 N Cable Road, Lima OH 45805-1498
County: Allen FICE Identification: 004861
Unit ID: 204486
Telephone: (419) 227-3141 Carnegie Class: Bac/Assoc-Mixed
FAX Number: (419) 229-6926 Calendar System: Quarter
URL: www.unoh.edu
Established: 1920 Annual Undergrad Tuition & Fees: $11,550
Enrollment: 3,009 Coed
Affiliation or Control: Independent Non-Profit IRS Status: 501(c)3
Highest Offering: Master's
Accreditation: HLC, ACBSP, CAHIIM, MAC

01 President ... Dr. Jeffrey A. JARVIS
05 Vice Pres Academic Affairs/Provost ... Dr. Dean HOBLER
10 Vice President Finance ... Mrs. Marcia EICKHOLT
07 Dir of Admissions-Coll of Business ... Mr. Tony AZZARELLO
18 Vice Pres of Property Management ... Vacant
26 VP Public Relations/Marketing ... Mrs. Stephanie MALLOY
15 Exec Director of Human Resources ... Ms. Geri MORRIS
21 Controller ... Mr. James S. BRONDER
37 Director of Financial Aid ... Ms. Kimberly CLEVENGER
04 Executive Assistant to President ... Mrs. Jennifer BENDELE
72 Dean of Applied Technologies ... Mr. Kevin MEAGER
06 Director of Registration ... Ms. Traci WELLS

University of Rio Grande (A)

218 N College Avenue, PO BOX 500,
Rio Grande OH 45674-3100

County: Gallia — FICE Identification: 003116
Unit ID: 205203
Telephone: (740) 245-5353 — Carnegie Class: Bac/Assoc-Mixed
FAX Number: (740) 245-5266 — Calendar System: Semester
URL: www.rio.edu
Established: 1876 — Annual Undergrad Tuition & Fees: $27,481
Enrollment: 1,551 — Coed
Affiliation or Control: Independent Non-Profit — IRS Status: 501(c)3
Highest Offering: Master's
Accreditation: HLC, ADNUR, CAEP, COARC, DMS, IACBE, NUR, RAD, SW

01 President .... Mr. Ryan SMITH
05 Provost/VP of Academic Affairs .... Dr. Kellie BEAN
10 CFO/VP of Finance .... Mrs. Meghann FRALEY
32 COO/VP Student & Admin Affairs .... Mrs. Rebecca LONG
45 Associate Provost Inst Effective .... Dr. David A. LAWRENCE
15 Director of Human Resources .... Mr. Chris NOURSE
26 Director of Marketing .... Ms. Renee DELAWDER
49 Dean College of Arts & Science .... Ms. Lynley CAREY
107 Dean College Prof/Tech Studies .... Dr. Donna MITCHELL
06 Registrar .... Ms. Olivia BEVAN
07 Director of Recruitment .... Ms. Kristie RUSSELL
88 Interim Director of Student Success .... Mrs. Amanda EHMAN
111 Exec Dir Institutional Advancement .... Ms. Annette WARD
41 Athletic Director .... Mr. Jeff LANHAM
08 Interim Director of Davis Library .... Ms. Carrie GIRTON
13 Chief Information Officer .... Mr. Allen HUDSON
14 Management Information Systems Adm .... Mr. Eric LOLLATHIN
29 Director of Alumni Relations .... Vacant
04 Exec Admin Assist to President .... Ms. Diane CLARK
19 Interim Campus Police Chief .... Mr. Sean MCINTYRE
37 Director Financial Aid .... Mr. Chad CURLEY
36 Director of Career Services .... Mrs. Susan HAFT
121 Dir Acad Support/Stdnt Access .... Dr. Stephanie ALEXANDER
35 Interim Dean of Students .... Mr. Seth LAWRENCE

University of Toledo (B)

2801 W Bancroft, Toledo OH 43606-3390

County: Lucas — FICE Identification: 003131
Unit ID: 206084
Telephone: (419) 530-4636 — Carnegie Class: DU-Higher
FAX Number: (419) 530-4984 — Calendar System: Semester
URL: www.utoledo.edu
Established: 1872 — Annual Undergrad Tuition & Fees (In-State): $11,082
Enrollment: 18,319 — Coed
Affiliation or Control: State — IRS Status: 501(c)3
Highest Offering: Doctorate
Accreditation: HLC, ARCPA, ART, CAATE, CACREP, CAEP, CAHIIM, CAMPEP, CAPRT, CEA, CLPSY, COARC, DENT, EMT, LAW, MED, MLS, MUS, NURSE, OT, PA, PH, PHAR, PTA, SP, SW, THEA

01 President .... Dr. Gregory C. POSTEL
100 Chief of Staff .... Ms. Diane MILLER
05 Int EVP Academic Affairs/Provost .... Dr. Risa DICKSON
63 EVP for Clin Affs/Dean COMLS .... Dr. Christopher COOPER
10 EVP Finance & Admin/CFO .... Mr. Matt SCHROEDER
43 Vice President/General Counsel .... Mr. Charles JAKE
32 VP for Student Affairs/Dean Stdnts .... Dr. Sammy SPANN
111 VP for Advancement .... Mr. Floyd AKINS
84 VP Enrollment Management .... Mr. David MEREDITH
46 Vice President Research .... Dr. Frank J. CALZONETTI
13 Vice President CIO/CTO .... Dr. William MCCREARY
41 VP and Director of Athletics .... Mr. Bryan BLAIR
28 VP for Diversity and Inclusion .... Dr. Dilip DAS
17 CEO Univ Toledo Med Ctr .... Mr. Richard SWAINE
86 VP Government Relations .... Ms. Diane MILLER
26 VP Marketing/Communications .... Dr. Adrienne KING
06 University Registrar .... Ms. Julie R. QUINONEZ
58 Int Dean Graduate Studies .... Dr. Scott MOLITOR
50 Dean Neff Business & Innovation .... Dr. Anne BALASZ
53 Dean J Herb College of Educ .... Dr. Raymond WITTE
54 Dean Engineering .... Dr. Michael TOOLE
76 Dean Health & Human Services .... Dr. Mark MERRICK
79 Int Dean Arts & Letters .... Dr. Melissa GREGORY
61 Dean Law .... Mr. Ben BARROS
81 Dean NSM .... Dr. Marc SEIGAR
66 Dean Nursing .... Dr. Linda LEWANDOWSKI
67 Dean Pharmacy & Pharm Sciences .... Dr. Pamela HEATON
92 Dean Jesup Scott Honors College .... Dr. Heidi APPEL
89 Dean University College .... Dr. Barbara KOPP-MILLER
37 AVP Financial Aid/Enrollment Svcs .... Mr. Gina ROBERTS
15 Sr AVP/Chief Human Res Officer .... Mr. John ELLIOTT
102 President Foundation .... Ms. Brenda LEE
29 AVP Alumni Engagement .... Mr. William PIERCE
36 Dir Exp Lrng and Career Svcs .... Ms. Shelly DROUILLARD
85 Director Ctr for Intl Studies .... Ms. Sara CLARK
116 Director Internal Audit .... Mr. David CUTRI
19 Chief of Police .... Mr. Rod THEIS
40 General Manager Bookstore SU .... Ms. Colleen STRAYER
18 AVP Facilities/Physical Plant .... Mr. Jason TOTH
08 Director University Libraries .... Mr. Thomas ATWOOD
04 Sr Dir of Admin Operations .... Ms. Katie DEBENEDICTIS
07 Director of Admissions .... Mr. Collin PALMER
101 Secretary of the Institution/Board .... Ms. Katie DEBENEDICTIS
96 Director of Supply Chain Management .... Ms. Jennifer PASTOREK

Ursuline College (C)

2550 Lander Road, Cleveland OH 44124-4398

County: Cuyahoga — FICE Identification: 003134
Unit ID: 206349
Telephone: (440) 449-4200 — Carnegie Class: Masters/M
FAX Number: (440) 646-8318 — Calendar System: Semester
URL: www.ursuline.edu
Established: 1871 — Annual Undergrad Tuition & Fees: $34,630
Enrollment: 1,100 — Female
Affiliation or Control: Roman Catholic — IRS Status: 501(c)3
Highest Offering: Doctorate
Accreditation: HLC, ACATE, CACREP, CAEP, IACBE, NURSE, SW

01 President .... Sr. Christine DEVINNE
05 Vice President Academic Affairs .... Dr. Kathryn LAFONTANA
10 Vice Pres & Chief Financial Officer .... Mr. Timothy CLYMER
111 Vice Pres Institutional Advancement .... Mr. Richard KONISIEWICZ
32 Vice President of Student Affairs .... Ms. Deanne HURLEY
84 Vice Pres of Enrollment Management .... Mr. Mike BROWN
49 Dean Arts/Sciences & Prof Studies .... Dr. Jenise SNYDER
66 Dean College of Nursing .... Dr. Patricia SHARPNACK
88 Exec Dir Prof Dev/Degree Completion .... Ms. Brooke SCHARLOTT
08 Director of Library & Acad Support .... Ms. Suzanna SCHROEDER-GREEN
06 Registrar & Dir Academic Ops .... Ms. Barbara HELMS
21 Controller .... Ms. Kimberly LAKOTA
30 Director of Development .... Ms. Kathleen WILDMAN
37 Director of Financial Aid .... Ms. Mary Lynn PERRI
29 Dir Alumnae Relations/Annual Fund .... Ms. Mary GYGLI
26 Dir of Marketing/Communications .... Ms. Ann MCGUIRE
15 Director of Human Resources .... Ms. Kelli KNAUS
13 Dir of Information Technology .... Mr. Matt BOOS
39 Director of Residence Life .... Ms. Gina DEMART-KRAUS
42 Director Campus Ministry .... Ms. Paula FITZGERALD
28 Asst Dean of Diversity .... Ms. Yolanda KING
106 Dir Online Education/E-learning .... Vacant
41 Athletic Director .... Ms. Cynthia MCKNIGHT
04 Sr Executive Asst to President .... Ms. Julie HERBERT
19 Director Security/Safety .... Mr. Richard THOMPSON
22 Dir Compliance/Title IX/Disability .... Ms. Deborah KAMAT
07 Director of Admissions .... Ms. Emily HAGGERTY
09 Coordinator Institutional Research .... Ms. Lynn LUCAS
38 Coordinator Student Counseling .... Dr. Anita CULBERTSON

Valor Christian College (D)

PO Box 800, Columbus OH 43216

County: Franklin — Identification: 667093
Unit ID: 486257
Telephone: (614) 837-4088 — Carnegie Class: Spec 2-yr-Other
FAX Number: (614) 837-6904 — Calendar System: Semester
URL: www.valorcollege.edu
Established: 1990 — Annual Undergrad Tuition & Fees: $8,410
Enrollment: 289 — Coed
Affiliation or Control: Independent Non-Profit — IRS Status: 501(c)3
Highest Offering: Baccalaureate
Accreditation: BI

01 President .... Ken GRUNDEN
05 Vice Pres Academic Affairs .... Laquetta CORTNER
32 Dean of Students .... Horace SIMONS
42 Campus Pastor .... Ashton PARSLEY
04 Exec Asst to VP Academic Affairs .... Vonnetta KING
37 Director of Financial Aid .... Norm STOPPENBRINK

Walsh University (E)

2020 East Maple Street, North Canton OH 44720

County: Stark — FICE Identification: 003135
Unit ID: 206437
Telephone: (330) 490-7090 — Carnegie Class: DU-Mod
FAX Number: (330) 499-7165 — Calendar System: Other
URL: www.walsh.edu
Established: 1958 — Annual Undergrad Tuition & Fees: $31,725
Enrollment: 2,651 — Coed
Affiliation or Control: Roman Catholic — IRS Status: 501(c)3
Highest Offering: Doctorate
Accreditation: HLC, CACREP, CAEP, NURSE, OT, PTA

01 President .... Dr. Tim COLLINS
10 Vice Pres Finance/Business Affairs .... Ms. Laurel LUSK
05 Vice Pres Academic Affairs .... Dr. Michael DUNPHY
111 Vice Pres of Advancement .... Mr. Eric BELDEN
41 Interim Vice Pres for Athletics .... Mr. Jason FAUTAS
26 VP for Marketing/Communications .... Ms. Teresa FOX
13 VP of Administration/CIO .... Dr. Brian GREENWELL
07 Vice Pres for Enrollment .... Ms. Rebecca CONEGLIO
20 Assoc VP of Academic Admin .... Ms. Edna MCCULLOH
09 Dean Inst Effectiveness .... Dr. Ute LAHAIE
32 Vice Pres Student Affairs .... Mr. Bryan BADAR
18 Director of Facilities & Grounds .... Mr. John SCHISSLER
91 Database Administrator .... Ms. Hope STANCIU
100 Chief of Staff .... Dr. Rachel HOSLER
42 Senior Chaplain .... Fr. Thomas CEBULA
38 Director Counseling Services .... Ms. Frances MORROW
42 Director of Campus Ministry .... Mr. Ben WALTHER
31 Dir Campus & Community Programs .... Ms. Jacqueline M. MANSER
37 Director Financial Aid .... Mrs. Holly VAN GILDER
15 Director of Human Resources .... Ms. Kristin HANNON
29 Director of Alumni Relations .... Ms. Stephanie KOONTZ
25 Director of Grants .... Dr. Rachel HAMMEL
19 Chief of Campus Police .... Mr. Ron PERDUE
08 Director of Library Services .... Ms. LuAnn BORIS
83 Dean School of Behav/Health Science .... Dr. Pamela RITZLINE
49 Dean School of Arts & Science .... Vacant
66 Dean Byers School of Nursing .... Ms. Judy KREYE
04 Executive Asst to President .... Ms. Christine SCHEETZ
06 Registrar .... Vacant
50 Int Dean DeVille School of Business .... Dr. Michael PETROCHUK
53 Chair Div of Education .... Mr. Gary JACOBS
104 Director of Global Learning .... Mr. Michael CINSON
35 Dean of Students .... Ms. Tiffany KINNARD-PAYTON
96 Director of Purchasing .... Ms. Rebecca MIMA
27 Director of University Relations .... Ms. Kimberly GRAVES

Washington State Community College (F)

710 Colegate Drive, Marietta OH 45750-9225

County: Washington — FICE Identification: 010453
Unit ID: 206446
Telephone: (740) 374-8716 — Carnegie Class: Assoc/HVT-High Non
FAX Number: (740) 374-9562 — Calendar System: Semester
URL: www.wscc.edu
Established: 1971 — Annual Undergrad Tuition & Fees (In-State): $3,960
Enrollment: 1,809 — Coed
Affiliation or Control: State — IRS Status: 501(c)3
Highest Offering: Associate Degree
Accreditation: HLC, COARC, MLTAD

01 President .... Dr. Vicky WOOD
10 Chief Financial Officer .... Ms. Angela LANG
111 VP of Institutional Advancement .... Ms. Amanda K. HERB
05 VP for Academic Affairs .... Ms. Sarah PARKER
03 VP of Organizational Effectiveness .... Mr. Gary BARBER
102 Exec Dir Foundation & Grants Dev .... Vacant
76 Dean of Health Sciences/Sciences .... Dr. Heather KINCAID
49 Dean of Public Services & Transfer .... Dr. Jona HALL
54 Dean of Engineering .... Mr. George BILOKONSKY
06 Registrar .... Ms. Dustin TAYLOR
07 Director of Admissions .... Ms. Carrie THRASH
26 Dir of Marketing & Communications .... Vacant
37 Director of Financial Aid .... Ms. Reba BARTRUG
08 Director Library Services .... Mr. Jeffrey GRAFFIUS
22 Director of College Access and ETS .... Ms. Donna MUNTZ
04 Admin Assistant to the President .... Ms. Cecily B. FYFFE
103 Director Workforce Development .... Vacant
18 Chief Facilities/Physical Plant Ofc .... Mr. Brandon HERB

Wilberforce University (G)

PO Box 1001, Wilberforce OH 45384-1001

County: Greene — FICE Identification: 003141
Unit ID: 206491
Telephone: (937) 376-2911 — Carnegie Class: Bac-Diverse
FAX Number: (937) 376-2627 — Calendar System: Semester
URL: www.wilberforce.edu
Established: 1856 — Annual Undergrad Tuition & Fees: $13,250
Enrollment: 453 — Coed
Affiliation or Control: African Methodist Episcopal — IRS Status: 501(c)3
Highest Offering: Master's
Accreditation: HLC

01 President .... Dr. Elfred A. PINKARD
84 SVP of Enrollment/Student Affairs .... Dr. Tashia BRADLEY
10 Sr VP of Administration & Finance .... Mr. William WOODSON
15 VP of Administration and HR . Mrs. Anita R. JEFFERSON-GOMEZ
05 Int Provost/VP Academic Affairs .... Dr. Johnny JONES
111 VP of Institutional Advancement .... Mrs. Natalie COLES
32 VP Student Engagement & Success .... Mr. Parris CARTER
49 Dean of Arts & Sciences .... Dr. Sharon TIPPINS
107 Int Dean of Professional Studies .... Dr. Anuradha VENKATESWARAN
07 Director of Admissions .... Ms. Jocelyn NEELY
06 Registrar .... Mrs. Rudell MOORE
113 Bursar .... Ms. Debra OLIVER
41 Athletic Director .... Mr. Dereck WILLIAMS
51 Director of CLIMB Program .... Ms. Kimberly HARDY-PORTER
25 Director Title III/Sponsored Pgms .... Mrs. Mary MORALE
19 Chief of Campus Police & Safety .... Mr. Jon CROSS
04 Executive Asst to the President .... Mrs. Danita PEARL
18 Director of Plant Logistics .... Mr. Kevin FRYE
37 Director Student Financial Aid .... Mrs. Andrea SANDERS
08 Director of Library Services .... Ms. Stephanie ROSTRON
13 Director of IT .... Mr. Andrew MONCE
29 Director Alumni Affairs .... Mr. Albert BAILEY
21 Controller .... Mr. Jason COOK
09 Director of Institutional Research .... Dr. Michael ROBINSON

Wilmington College (H)

1870 Quaker Way, Wilmington OH 45177-2499

County: Clinton — FICE Identification: 003142
Unit ID: 206507
Telephone: (937) 382-6661 — Carnegie Class: Bac-Diverse
FAX Number: (937) 383-8574 — Calendar System: Semester
URL: www.wilmington.edu
Established: 1870 — Annual Undergrad Tuition & Fees: $27,400
Enrollment: 1,165 — Coed
Affiliation or Control: Friends — IRS Status: 501(c)3
Highest Offering: Master's
Accreditation: HLC, CAATE, CAEP, COSMA

01 President .... Dr. Trevor M. BATES
04 Assistant to the President .... Ms. Annie BENNER-IIAMES
100 Chief of Staff .... Vacant
05 VP/Chief Academic Ofcr/Dean Faculty ... Dr. Kenneth PATTERSON
10 CBO/VP Business/Finance .... Ms. Beatriz IBANEZ
111 VP/Chief Advancement Officer .... Mr. Joe BULL
88 Vice President External Programs .... Ms. Sylvia STEVENS
32 VP/Chief Student Affs/Dean Stdnts .... Ms. Sigrid B. SOLOMON
41 Senior Director of Athletics .... Mr. William WILSON
84 Chief Enrollment Officer/Admissions .... Mr. Dennis KELLY
124 AVP of Student Retention/Success .... Ms. Deanna VATAN
09 Dir Institutional Effectiveness .... Mr. Daniel MCCAMISH
26 Sr Dir of Pub Relations/Admissions .... Mr. Randall F. SARVIS
06 Registrar/Academic Records .... Ms. Sue HUTCHENS
08 Director of Watson Library .... Mr. Michael WELLS
15 Senior Director of Human Resources .... Ms. Libby HAYES
36 Director of Career Services .... Dr. Nina TALLEY
18 Director of Physical Plant .... Mr. Randy GERBER
29 Director of Alumni Engagement .... Mr. John SCHRANTZ
37 Sr Dir Fin Aid/One Stop Center .... Ms. Cheryl LOUALLEN
07 Sr Director of Admission .... Mr. Adam LOHREY
21 Controller .... Mr. Brian COBB
102 Director Leadership Giving .... Vacant
105 Assoc Director Digital Marketing .... Ms. Ashleigh WELLMAN
13 Director of Information Technology .... Mr. George DIMIDIK
28 Sr Director Diversity/Inclusion .... Mr. Chip MURDOCK
38 Director of Counseling .... Ms. Kazi MCDOWELL
39 Dir Resident Life/Student Housing .... Mr. Nick HOOVER
44 Annual Fund Coordinator .... Ms. Sarah HOLTSCLAW
114 Budget Director .... Ms. Sara SCOTT

Wilmington College Cincinnati (A)

3520 Central Pkwy, 181 Main Bldg, Cincinnati OH 45223
Telephone: (513) 569-4580 Identification: 770364
Accreditation: &HLC

Winebrenner Theological Seminary (B)

950 N. Main Street, Second Floor, Findlay OH 45840
County: Hancock FICE Identification: 004060
Unit ID: 206516
Telephone: (419) 434-4200 Carnegie Class: Spec-4-yr-Faith
FAX Number: N/A Calendar System: Trimester
URL: winebrenner.edu
Established: 1942 Annual Graduate Tuition & Fees: N/A
Enrollment: 67 Coed
Affiliation or Control: Independent Non-Profit IRS Status: 501(c)3
Highest Offering: Doctorate; No Undergraduates
Accreditation: HLC, CACREP, THEOL

01 President/CEO .... Dr. Brent C. SLEASMAN
05 VP of Academic Advancement/Dean .... Dr. Bruce COATS
10 Director of Finance .... Mr. Tom WEAVER
06 Records Coordinator/Student Success .... Mr. Kevin RISNER
04 Assistant to the President .... Vacant
108 Director Institutional Assessment .... Dr. Kathryn HELLEMAN
84 Director Enrollment Management .... Mrs. Amy J. KINNEY

Wittenberg University (C)

PO Box 720, Springfield OH 45501-0720
County: Clark FICE Identification: 003143
Unit ID: 206525
Telephone: (937) 327-6231 Carnegie Class: Bac-A&S
FAX Number: (937) 327-6340 Calendar System: Semester
URL: www.wittenberg.edu
Established: 1845 Annual Undergrad Tuition & Fees: $41,476
Enrollment: 1,488 Coed
Affiliation or Control: Evangelical Lutheran Church In America
IRS Status: 501(c)3
Highest Offering: Master's
Accreditation: HLC, CAEPN, MUS, NURSE

01 President .... Dr. Michael FRANDSEN
05 Provost .... Dr. Michelle MATTSON
10 Vice Pres Finance/Administration .... Mr. Rob YOUNG
84 Vice Pres Enrollment Management .... Ms. Carola THORSON
111 VP University Advancement .... Ms. Rebecca KOCHER
26 Vice Pres Marketing/Communications .... Ms. Karen GERBOTH
41 VP/Director Athletics/Recreation .... Mr. Brian AGLER
35 Vice Pres/Dean of Students .... Ms. Casey GILL
09 Assoc Prov Acad Affs/Inst Research .... Dr. Darby L. HILLER-FREUND
124 Sr Assoc Dean Stdnt Success/Retent .... Mr. Jonathan DURAJ
85 Director International Education .... Ms. JoAnn BENNETT
20 Director of Academic Services .... Ms. Grace WHITELEY SEVER
42 Pastor to the University .... Rev. Rachel SANDUM TUNE
08 Interim Library Director .... Ms. Kristin PETERS
13 Chief Information Officer .... Mr. Richard MICKOOL
31 Director Community Service .... Ms. Kristen L. COLLIER
06 Registrar .... Ms. Debra LOVELESS
07 Sr Assoc Dir of Admissions .... Ms. Linda BEALS
58 Director Graduate Studies in Educ .... Dr. Amy MCGUFFEY
94 Director of Women's Studies .... Dr. Heather H. WRIGHT
29 Dir of Alumni/Lifelong Engagement .... Ms. Holly GERSBACHER
27 Sports Information Director .... Mr. AJ MEYER
105 Sr Writer/Web Communications Spec .... Mr. Ryan MAURER
39 Associate Dean for Residence Life .... Ms. Sherri SADOWSKI
38 Director Student Counseling .... Mr. Matthew WEST
88 Director Student Involvement .... Ms. Liz ARTZ
28 Assoc Dean Students/Dir Diversity .. Ms. Corrine WITHERSPOON
37 Exec Director of Financial Aid .... Ms. Amy BARNHART
15 Director Human Resources .... Ms. Mary Beth WALTER
19 Chief of Police .... Mr. Jim HUTCHINS
40 Manager of Bookstore .... Ms. Amy GARNER

Wright State University Main Campus (D)

3640 Colonel Glenn Highway, Dayton OH 45435-0001
County: Greene FICE Identification: 003078
Unit ID: 206604
Telephone: (937) 775-3333 Carnegie Class: DU-Higher
FAX Number: (937) 775-3301 Calendar System: Semester
URL: www.wright.edu
Established: 1964 Annual Undergrad Tuition & Fees (In-State): $10,012
Enrollment: 10,936 Coed
Affiliation or Control: State IRS Status: 501(c)3
Highest Offering: Doctorate
Accreditation: HLC, CAATE, CACREP, CAEPN, CLPSY, EXSC, MED, MLS, MUS, NURSE, PH, SPAA, SW

01 President .... Dr. Susan L. EDWARDS
05 Provost/SVP for Academic Affairs .... Dr. Amy THOMPSON
11 Chief Operating Officer/EVP .... Mr. Gregory P. SAMPLE
32 Dean of Students .... Dr. Chris TAYLOR
46 Vice Prov Research & Innovation .... Dr. Madhavi KADAKIA
111 Int Vice Pres Univ Advancement .... Mr. Bill BIGHAM
84 Vice Pres Enrollment Management/CRO ... Ms. Susan SCHAURER
20 Vice Prov Acad Aff/Dean Grad School .... Dr. Barry MILLIGAN
10 Assoc Vice Pres Financial Operation .... Mr. Burhan KAWOSA
08 University Librarian .... Ms. Karen WILHOIT
15 Assoc Vice Pres for Human Resources .... Ms. Emily HAMMAN
50 Dean Raj Soin Col of Business .... Dr. Thomas L. TRAYNOR
53 Dean Health/Education/Human Svcs .... Dr. James DENNISTON
54 Dean Engr/Computer Science .... Dr. Brian RIGLING
12 Vice Provost/CAO Lake Campus .... Dr. Andrea FABER
49 Dean Liberal Arts .... Dr. Gary SCHMIDT
66 Chair Sch Nursing & Health .... Dr. Ann M. STALTER
63 Dean Boonshoft School of Medicine .... Dr. Valerie WEBER
83 Chair Sch of Prof Psychology .... Dr. Michelle SCHULTZ
81 Dean Science/Mathematics .... Dr. Ayse SAHIN
06 Registrar .... Dr. Lisa RUNYAN
13 Chief Information Officer .... Mr. Michael STANKAS
36 Director Career Services .... Ms. Cheryl STUART
37 Director of Financial Aid .... Ms. Kim EVERHART
38 Director Counsel/Wellness Svcs .... Dr. Robert A. RANDO
29 Exec Director Alumni Relations .... Mr. Gregory SCHARER
28 Vice Pres Inclusive Excellence .... Dr. Matthew C. CHANEY
22 Director Disability Services .... Mr. Tom WEBB
41 Director of Athletics .... Mr. Bob GRANT
85 Director Univ Center for Intl Educ .... Ms. Michelle STREETER-FERRARI
39 Director Residence Services .... Vacant
19 Director of Public Safety .... Mr. Kurt A. HOLDEN
92 Director Honors Program .... Dr. Susan CARRAFIELLO
09 Director Institutional Research .... Dr. Aaron SKIRA
04 Executive Asst to President .... Ms. Rebecca TRAXLER
102 CFO WSU Foundation .... Mr. Robert BATSON
44 Director Annual Giving .... Ms. Amy N. SHOPE JONES
101 Secretary to the Board .... Mr. Daniel PALMER
26 Director Communications .... Mr. Seth BAUGUESS
27 Director Marketing .... Mr. Mark D. ANDERSON
43 General Counsel .... Mr. Sean CULLEY

Wright State University Lake Campus (E)

7600 Lake Campus Drive, Celina OH 45822-2952
Telephone: (419) 586-0300 FICE Identification: 009169
Accreditation: &HLC

† Regional accreditation is carried under the parent institution in Dayton, OH.

Xavier University (F)

3800 Victory Parkway, Cincinnati OH 45207-1096
County: Hamilton FICE Identification: 003144
Unit ID: 206622
Telephone: (513) 745-3000 Carnegie Class: DU-Mod
FAX Number: (513) 745-4223 Calendar System: Semester
URL: www.xavier.edu
Established: 1831 Annual Undergrad Tuition & Fees: $42,460
Enrollment: 7,061 Coed
Affiliation or Control: Roman Catholic IRS Status: 501(c)3
Highest Offering: Doctorate
Accreditation: HLC, CAATE, CACREP, CAEP, CLPSY, HSA, MACTE, MUS, NURSE, OT, RAD, SW

01 President .... Dr. Colleen M. HANYCZ
05 Provost/Chief Academic Officer .... Dr. Rachel CHRASTIL
100 Chief of Staff .... Dr. Kelley L. MILLS
10 VP Financial Admin/CBO .... Mr. Phil CHICK
26 Vice Pres for University Relations .... Mr. Gary R. MASSA
88 Vice Pres Mission & Identity/CMO .... Dr. Debra MOONEY
13 Exec Dir Information Technologies .... Mr. Mark BROCKMAN
28 VP Inst Diversity/Inclusion & CDIO .... Dr. Ivy K. BANKS
30 Assoc VP for University Relations .... Ms. Susan ABEL
32 Assoc Prov/Chief Student Affs Ofcr .... Dr. David J. JOHNSON
20 Associate Provost Academic Affairs .... Dr. Rashmi ASSUDANI
20 Assoc Prov Strategic Initiatives .... Dr. Gary LEWANDOWSKI
20 Associate Provost & CIO .... Vacant
18 Vice President for Facilities .... Mr. Robert M. SHEERAN
11 VP for Admin/Director Athletics .... Mr. Greg CHRISTOPHER
15 Assoc Vice Pres for Human Resources .... Ms. Jenni DRAMIS
84 Vice Pres Enrollment Management .... Mr. Aaron MEIS
44 Exec Dir Gifts & Estate Planning .... Mr. Mark MCLAUGHLIN
42 Dir Center for Mission/Identity .... Mr. Joseph P. SHADLE
06 Registrar .... Dr. Andrea WAWRZUSIN
121 Exec Dir of Student Support Svcs .... Ms. Lea MINNITI
27 Assoc VP Marketing & Communications .. Mr. Doug RUSCHMAN
39 Sr Dir Student Affairs/Ofc Res Life .... Ms. Lori A. LAMBERT
40 Director of Bookstore .... Ms. Lucy JONES
86 Director of Government Relations .... Mr. Sean COMER
83 Dean College Prof Sciences .... Dr. Cynthia GEER
07 Dir Enr Prospect Mgmt/Parent Rels .... Ms. Mary KNIFFIN
35 Sr Dir Student Affairs/ Involvement .... Ms. Leah BUSAM KLENOWSKI
49 Dean College Arts & Sciences .... Dr. David MENGEL
66 Dean College of Nursing .... Dr. Nezam AL-NSAIR
19 Dir Public Safety/Chief of Police .... Chief Robert WARFEL
37 Director of Financial Aid .... Ms. Adrienne MONTGOMERY
43 General Counsel/Sec of the Board .... Ms. Becky CULL
29 Dir Alumni Rels/Ex Dir Athletic Dev .... Mr. Brian MALEY
09 Dir Office Institutional Research .... Mrs. Emily SHIPLEY
50 Dean Williams College of Business .... Dr. Thomas HAYES
51 Dir Adult & Prof Educ at Xavier .... Ms. Patricia MEYER
96 Dir Purchasing & Supply Management .... Mr. John MERCER
88 Dir TRIO Student Support Services .... Dr. Daniel L. MCSPADDEN
36 Director Career Development Office .... Vacant
04 Admin Assistant to the President .... Ms. Nancy DOWNING
38 Director Counseling Services .... Ms. Jamie BAXTER

Youngstown State University (G)

One University Plaza, Youngstown OH 44555-0001
County: Mahoning FICE Identification: 003145
Unit ID: 206695
Telephone: (330) 941-3001 Carnegie Class: Masters/L
FAX Number: (330) 941-7169 Calendar System: Semester
URL: www.ysu.edu
Established: 1908 Annual Undergrad Tuition & Fees (In-State): $9,656
Enrollment: 11,835 Coed
Affiliation or Control: State IRS Status: 501(c)3
Highest Offering: Doctorate
Accreditation: HLC, ANEST, ART, CAATE, CACREP, CAEP, COARC, DH, DIET, DIETD, EMT, EXSC, MLS, MLTAD, MUS, NUR, NURSE, PH, PTA, SW

01 President .... Mr. James P. TRESSEL
05 Provost/VP Academic Affairs .... Dr. Brien N. SMITH
10 Vice Pres Finance & Business Op .... Mr. Neal P. MCNALLY
09 Vice Pres for Institutional Effect .... Dr. Mike SHERMAN
32 Assoc VP for Student Experience .... Mrs. Joy POLKABLA BYERS
43 Vice President and General Counsel .... Ms. Holly A. JACOBS
26 Assoc VP for University Relations .... Ms. Shannon TIRONE
13 AVP/Chief Information Officer .... Mr. James YUKECH
50 Dean of Business Administration .... Dr. Kelly L. WILKINSON
53 Dean of Education .... Dr. Charles HOWELL
81 Dean of Science/Tech/Eng/Math .... Dr. Wim F. STEELANT
57 Dean Creative Arts & Communication .... Dr. Phyllis M. PAUL
76 Dean Health & Human Services .... Dr. Jeffery ALLEN
58 Dean College of Graduate Studies .... Dr. Salvatore A. SANDERS
20 Assoc Provost Acad Pgms/Planning .... Dr. Kevin BALL
41 Exec Director of Athletics .... Mr. Ronald A. STROLLO
08 Manager Library Operations .... Ms. Anna TORRES
29 Dir University Events & Protocol .... Ms. Jacquelyn LEVISEUR
07 Director Admissions .... Ms. Christine HUBERT
06 Registrar .... Ms. Jeanne HERMAN
19 Chief of University Police .... Mr. Shawn V. VARSO
18 Associate Vice President Facilities .... Mr. John P. HYDEN
23 Dir Environ/Occup Health & Safety .... Ms. Julie GENTILE
84 AVP Enrollment & Business Services .... Ms. Elaine RUSE
21 AVP Finance and Controller .... Ms. Katrena J. DAVIDSON
88 Cash Management Officer .... Mr. David EDWARDS
88 Director Support Services .... Mr. Danny J. O'CONNELL
90 Director Media/Acad Computing .... Mr. Michael S. HRISHENKO
88 Director WYSU-FM .... Mr. Gary SEXTON
04 Exec Assistant to President .... Ms. Cynthia M. BELL
106 Dir Online Education/E-learning .... Ms. Jessica CHILL
104 Assoc Provost Intl Programs .... Dr. Nathan MYERS
108 Director Institutional Assessment .... Ms. Hillary FUHRMAN
22 Director EEO and Policy .... Ms. Dana LANTZ
38 Director Student Counseling .... Dr. Ann JARONSKI
15 Chief Human Resources Officer .... Ms. Cynthia KRAVITZ
103 Exec Director Workforce Development .... Mrs. Jennifer ODDO
28 Assoc Provost Diversity & Inclusion .... Ms. Carol BENNETT

Zane State College (H)

1555 Newark Road, Zanesville OH 43701-2626
County: Muskingum FICE Identification: 008133
Unit ID: 204255
Telephone: (740) 454-2501 Carnegie Class: Assoc/MT-VT-High Non
FAX Number: (740) 454-0035 Calendar System: Semester
URL: www.zanestate.edu
Established: 1969 Annual Undergrad Tuition & Fees (In-State): $5,456
Enrollment: 2,223 Coed
Affiliation or Control: State IRS Status: 501(c)3
Highest Offering: Associate Degree
Accreditation: HLC, ACBSP, ACFEI, CAHIIM, MAC, MLTAD, OTA, PTAA, RAD

01 President .... Dr. Chad M. BROWN
111 Director of Advancement .... Mrs. Katlyn PORTER
05 Chief Academic Officer .... Dr. Larisa HARPER

10	Chief Financial Officer	Ms. Terri BALDWIN
84	Chief Enrollment Officer	Mr. Justin GROTE
50	Dean of Business/Engineering & Tech	Mrs. Marcie MOORE
103	Dean Workforce Development	Ms. Tracey HOOPER-PORTER
13	Dir of ITS Operations	Mr. Bryan BAKER
09	Dir of Institutional Research	Mr. Andrew MORRISON
25	Director of Grants & Contracts	Vacant
26	Director of Marketing	Ms. Murphie RAMBO
27	Dir of Strat Comm & College Rels	Mrs. Jennifer FOLDEN
32	Chief Student Affairs Officer	Dr. Elizabeth KLINE
21	Comptroller	Ms. Tammy S. HUFFMAN
40	Director of Bookstore Operations	Ms. Vicki MITCHELL
76	Dean Health/Public Svc	Mrs. Shelley ZIMMERMAN
06	Asst Dean Curriculum/Registrar	Ms. Theresa KOLK-CONNER
18	Director of Facilities	Mr. Joseph KEATING
04	Exec Asst to Pres/Coord Annual Giv	Mrs. Julie A. MACLAINE
49	Dean of Arts and Sciences	Dr. Elizabeth KLINE

OKLAHOMA

ATA College   (A)
10820 East 45th St., Ste 100, Tulsa OK 74146

County: Tulsa
FICE Identification: 040603
Unit ID: 449728
Telephone: (918) 496-0800
Carnegie Class: Not Classified
FAX Number: N/A
Calendar System: Quarter
URL: www.ata.edu
Established:
Annual Undergrad Tuition & Fees: N/A
Enrollment: N/A
Coed
Affiliation or Control: Proprietary
IRS Status: Proprietary
Highest Offering: Associate Degree
Accreditation: **ABHES**

Bacone College   (B)
2299 Old Bacone Road, Muskogee OK 74403-1568

County: Muskogee
FICE Identification: 003147
Unit ID: 206817
Telephone: (918) 683-4581
Carnegie Class: Bac-Diverse
FAX Number: (918) 781-7422
Calendar System: Semester
URL: www.bacone.edu
Established: 1880
Annual Undergrad Tuition & Fees: $14,700
Enrollment: 321
Coed
Affiliation or Control: American Baptist
IRS Status: 501(c)3
Highest Offering: Baccalaureate
Accreditation: **HLC**, IACBE, RAD

01	President	Dr. Ferlin CLARK
05	VP of Academic Affairs	Ms. Wambli SINA WIN
32	VP of Student Affairs	Dr. Kelly LACHANCE
10	VP Finance/CFO	Ms. Mary Jo PRATT
45	VP Strategic Initiatives & Projects	Dr. Nicole BEEN
30	VP of Development	Vacant
15	Director Human Resources	Mr. William LOWE
57	Director School of Indian Art	Mr. Gerald COURNOYER
88	Director Ctr for American Indians	Mr. Aaron ADSON
41	Athletic Director	Mr. Mike GONZALES
26	Director of College Relations/Tech	Ms. Wendy BURTON
04	Assistant to President	Ms. Marcia TAYLOR
06	Registrar	Mrs. Linda MILAM
07	Director of Admissions	Vacant
08	Director/Head Librarian	Mr. David MCMILLIAN
13	Director of Network Systems	Mr. Chris EHLERS
37	Director of Financial Aid	Mr. Josh CHAPMAN
19	Chief of Campus Police	Mr. John LINDSEY
40	Bookstore Manager	Ms. Elizabeth KALER
88	Executive Director Indigenous Study	Dr. Nicky MICHAEL
76	Director Radiography Program	Ms. Shawn DIXON
68	Interim Chair Exercise Sciences	Dr. Jyoti ABRAHAM
61	Dean Tribal Law & Criminal Justice	Ms. Wambli WIN
50	Chair School of Business & Finance	Dr. John WINTERS
121	Director Student Support Services	Ms. Patricia FARRELL
107	Chair of Professional Studies	Dr. Rebecca TRUELOVE
49	Chair of Liberal Arts	Ms. Linda JORDAN
88	Director Ctr for Christian Ministry	Dr. Stephen WILEY
59	Chair of Family Studies	Dr. Donna SHARP
88	Assistant to VP Student Affairs	Ms. Jana TAYLOR
39	Director of Campus Housing	Mr. Kendall SCOTT

Cameron University   (C)
2800 W Gore Boulevard, Lawton OK 73505-6377

County: Comanche
FICE Identification: 003150
Unit ID: 206914
Telephone: (580) 581-2200
Carnegie Class: Masters/S
FAX Number: (580) 581-2867
Calendar System: Semester
URL: www.cameron.edu
Established: 1908
Annual Undergrad Tuition & Fees (In-State): $6,450
Enrollment: 3,771
Coed
Affiliation or Control: State
IRS Status: 501(c)3
Highest Offering: Master's
Accreditation: **HLC**, ACBSP, CAEPN, COARC, MUS, RAD

01	President	Dr. John M. MCARTHUR
05	Vice President for Academic Affairs	Dr. Ronna J. VANDERSLICE
10	Vice Pres for Business & Finance	Dr. Scott SCHNEIDER
111	Vice Pres University Advancement	Mr. Albert D. JOHNSON, JR.
84	VP for Enroll Mgmt & Stdnt Success	Dr. Jerrett PHILLIPS
20	Assoc Vice Pres Academic Affairs	Dr. Margery KINGSLEY

20	Asst Vice Pres Academic Affairs	Ms. Susan CAMP
49	Dean School of Arts and Sciences	Vacant
58	Dean School of Grad & Prof Studies	Dr. Jennifer DENNIS
21	Controller	Ms. Amanda KOLL
26	Senior Director of Public Affairs	Mr. Keith MITCHELL
30	Director of Development	Ms. Tiffany SMITH
29	Director of Alumni Relations	Ms. Jonna TURNER
41	Director Athletic Administration	Mr. Jim C. JACKSON
07	Director of Admissions	Ms. Brenda DALLY
06	Registrar	Ms. Renee ROACH
09	Dir Inst Rsrch/Assess/Accountabilty	Dr. Karla OTY
37	Director of Financial Assistance	Ms. Caryn PACHECO
13	Director Information Tech Services	Mr. Kelly MCCLURE
15	Director of Human Resources	Vacant
36	Director of Student Development	Dr. Jennifer PRUCHNICKI
19	Director Public Safety	Mr. John DEBOARD
18	Director Physical Facilities	Mr. Robert HANEFIELD
96	Purchasing Agent	Ms. Laura KANE
22	EEO Officer/Title IX Coordinator	Ms. Christi WILLIAMS

Carl Albert State College   (D)
1507 S McKenna, Poteau OK 74953-5208

County: LeFlore
FICE Identification: 003176
Unit ID: 206923
Telephone: (918) 647-1200
Carnegie Class: Not Classified
FAX Number: (918) 647-1201
Calendar System: Semester
URL: www.carlalbert.edu
Established: 1933
Annual Undergrad Tuition & Fees (In-State): N/A
Enrollment: N/A
Coed
Affiliation or Control: State
IRS Status: 501(c)3
Highest Offering: Associate Degree
Accreditation: **HLC**, ADNUR, PTAA

01	President	Dr. Jay FALKNER
32	VP for Student Affairs	Mr. Bill NOWLIN
05	Vice President of Academic Affairs	Dr. Marc WILLIS
10	Chief Financial Officer	Mr. Brian ROBERTS
84	VP of Enrollment Management	Mr. Bill NOWLIN
13	Director Information Technology	Mr. Jerry ELLIS
101	Admin Assistant to Pres Office	Ms. Cortney SMITH
26	Dir Marketing/Community Relations	Ms. Holly BORMANN
06	Registrar/VA Coordinator	Ms. Dee Ann DICKERSON
37	Director of Financial Aid	Mr. Jeremy MINOR
88	TRIO Director	Ms. Michelle WHITE
18	Director of Physical Plant	Mr. Chuck LEWIS
15	Human Resources Director	Mr. Will HIGGINS
21	Business Office Manager	Ms. Amanda SABATUCCI
108	Inst Effect/Assessment Officer	Ms. Kelly KELLOGG
102	Exec Dir of CASC Dev Foundation	Ms. Mandy ROBERTS
106	Coord for Virtual Campus/English	Ms. Sarah BROWN
19	Instructor/Campus Police Coord	Mr. Chad BROWN

Carl Albert State College Sequoyah County Campus   (E)
1601 S. Opdyke St, Sallisaw OK 74955

Telephone: (918) 775-6977
Identification: 770366
Accreditation: **&HLC**

Central Oklahoma College   (F)
14820 Serenita Ave, Oklahoma City OK 73134

County: Oklahoma
FICE Identification: 022385
Unit ID: 206932
Telephone: (405) 609-6622
Carnegie Class: Not Classified
FAX Number: N/A
Calendar System: Quarter
URL: www.centraloc.edu
Established: 1975
Annual Undergrad Tuition & Fees: $7,817
Enrollment: 14,132
Coed
Affiliation or Control: Proprietary
IRS Status: Proprietary
Highest Offering: Associate Degree
Accreditation: **ACCSC**, SURGT

00	President	Michael PUGLIESE
01	Chief Executive Officer	Carol FISHER

College of the Muscogee Nation   (G)
PO Box 917, 2170 Raven Circle, Okmulgee OK 74447

County: Okmulgee
Identification: 667122
Unit ID: 480967
Telephone: (918) 549-2800
Carnegie Class: Tribal
FAX Number: (918) 759-6930
Calendar System: Trimester
URL: www.CMN.edu
Established: 1994
Annual Undergrad Tuition & Fees: $6,600
Enrollment: 252
Coed
Affiliation or Control: Tribal Control
IRS Status: 501(c)3
Highest Offering: Associate Degree
Accreditation: **HLC**

01	President	Dr. Monte RANDALL
05	Dean of Academic Affairs	Mr. Mekko TYNER
10	Director of Business Affairs	Mrs. Jan HART

Community Care College   (H)
4242 S Sheridan Road, Tulsa OK 74145-1119

County: Tulsa
FICE Identification: 033674
Unit ID: 439570
Telephone: (918) 610-0027
Carnegie Class: Assoc/HVT-Mix Trad/Non
FAX Number: (918) 610-0029
Calendar System: Other
URL: www.communitycarecollege.edu

Established: 1995
Annual Undergrad Tuition & Fees: N/A
Enrollment: 658
Coed
Affiliation or Control: Independent Non-Profit
IRS Status: 501(c)3
Highest Offering: Associate Degree
Accreditation: **ACCSC**, MAAB, SURGT

01	President	Dr. Raye MAHLBERG
04	Exec Assistant to the President	Brandi PACKARD
06	Registrar	Brigitte KURR
07	Director of Admissions	Vacant
10	Chief Financial/Business Officer	Pallavi AGARWAL
15	Chief Human Resources Officer	Brenda KNOX
36	Director Career Services	Linda DEWITT
37	Director Student Financial Aid	Karissa MARCANGELI

Connors State College   (I)
700 College Road, Warner OK 74469-9700

County: Muskogee
FICE Identification: 003153
Unit ID: 206996
Telephone: (918) 463-2931
Carnegie Class: Assoc/MT-VT-High Trad
FAX Number: (918) 203-3775
Calendar System: Semester
URL: www.connorsstate.edu
Established: 1908
Annual Undergrad Tuition & Fees (In-State): $3,672
Enrollment: 2,069
Coed
Affiliation or Control: State
IRS Status: 501(c)3
Highest Offering: Associate Degree
Accreditation: **HLC**, ADNUR, OTA, PTAA

01	President	Dr. Ronald S. RAMMING
05	VP for Academic Affairs	Dr. Makenna GARRISON
10	VP for Fiscal Services	Mr. Mike LEWIS
26	Assoc VP for External Affairs	Vacant
37	Director of Financial Aid	Ms. Mattie KEYS
08	Director of Learning Center	Ms. Ona BRITTON-SPEARS
13	Director of Information Technology	Mr. Heath HODGES
06	Registrar	Mr. John NORWOOD
07	Director of Recruitment	Ms. Jessica LANGSTON
15	Director of Human Resources	Ms. Nicole MOTE
09	Director of Institutional Research	Vacant
41	Athletic Director	Mr. Bill MUSE
32	Dean of Students	Mr. Jake LAWSON
35	Asst Dean of Students	Vacant
19	Chief of Police	Mr. James MENDENHALL
04	Executive Asst to the President	Ms. Derotha RIVENBARK
20	Asst VP Acad/Stdt Affs/Acad Support	Ms. Robin O'QUINN
102	Director of Development Foundation	Dr. Krystle LANE

East Central University   (J)
1100 E 14th Street, Ada OK 74820-6899

County: Pontotoc
FICE Identification: 003154
Unit ID: 207041
Telephone: (580) 332-8000
Carnegie Class: Masters/L
FAX Number: (580) 332-1623
Calendar System: Semester
URL: www.ecok.edu
Established: 1909
Annual Undergrad Tuition & Fees (In-State): $7,052
Enrollment: 3,608
Coed
Affiliation or Control: State
IRS Status: 501(c)3
Highest Offering: Master's
Accreditation: **HLC**, ACBSP, CACREP, CAEP, CAEPN, MUS, NUR, SW

01	President	Mr. Wendell GODWIN
05	Provost/VP Academic Affairs	Dr. Jeffrey GIBSON
10	Exec VP Administration/Finance	Ms. Jessica KILBY
32	VP Student Development	Dr. Brandon HILL
111	VP Institutional Advancement	Ms. Amy FORD
41	Interim Director Athletics	Mr. Matt COLE
20	Assoc Provost/Graduate School Dean	Dr. Sarah PETERS
11	Asst VP Administration/Finance	Mr. Ty ANDERSON
20	Dir Curriculum & Faculty Affairs	Ms. Haley VICKERS
06	Registrar	Dr. Elwyn MARTIN
50	Interim Dean School of Business	Dr. Michael SCOTT
53	Dean College of Educ & Psych	Dr. Jerry MIHELIC
49	Dean College of Lib Arts & Soc Sci	Dr. Katherine LANG
81	Dean College of Health & Sciences	Dr. Kenneth ANDREWS
35	Dean of Students	Mr. Nicholas BUCKLEY
09	Director Inst Effectiveness	Ms. Meredith JONES
25	Director Grants & Research	Ms. Leah LYON
121	Dir Academic Success Center	Dr. Haley MATLOCK
08	Director Library	Ms. Dana BELCHER
18	Director Facilities Mgmt	Mr. Darryl OVERSTREET
07	Director Admissions	Ms. Ashlee HECK
96	Director Purchasing	Ms. Chandra MILLER
37	Director Financial Aid	Ms. Becky ISAACS
21	Controller	Ms. Kelly DICKEY
113	Bursar	Ms. Amy SCHLUP
13	Interim Director IT	Ms. Mary LAMACK
29	Director Alumni Relations	Ms. Ashia TODD
23	Director Stdnt Health Services	Ms. Lisa LETELLIER
38	Director Stdnt Counseling Ctr	Ms. Jennifer COX
85	Director Intl Student Pgms & Svcs	Ms. Jessika BAILEY
22	Dir Testing & Accessibility Svcs	Ms. Kim ROGERS
19	Chief of University Police	Mr. Bert MILLER
108	Assessment Coordinator	Dr. Robin ROBERSON
39	Director Residence Life	Ms. Leena RUDOLPH

Eastern Oklahoma State College   (K)
1301 W Main Street, Wilburton OK 74578-4999

County: Latimer
FICE Identification: 003155
Unit ID: 207050
Telephone: (918) 465-2361
Carnegie Class: Assoc/HT-High Trad
FAX Number: (918) 465-2431
Calendar System: Semester

URL: www.eosc.edu
Established: 1909 Annual Undergrad Tuition & Fees (In-State): $4,767
Enrollment: 1,342 Coed
Affiliation or Control: State IRS Status: 501(c)3
Highest Offering: Associate Degree
Accreditation: HLC, ADNUR, #COARC

01 President Dr. Janet WANSICK
05 VP of Academic Affairs Vacant
32 VP for Student/External Affairs Ms. Trish MCBEATH
12 Dean of McAlester Campus Ms. Anne BROOKS
35 Director of Student Life Ms. London WHITE
41 Athletic Director Mr. Alfred DAVIS
26 Dir Marketing/Communications Ms. Trish MCBEATH
13 Chief Technical Officer Mr. George LARSON
08 Director Library & Media Services Ms. Maria MARTINEZ
15 Chief Human Resources Officer Ms. Nicole MOTE
06 Registrar/Admissions Ms. Jennifer LABOR
18 Director Physical Plant Operations Mr. Randy LIVINGSTON
37 Financial Aid Director Ms. Mimi KELLEY
19 Campus Police Chief Mr. Alton JONES
04 Exec Assistant to the President Ms. Candace RANEY
10 Interim VP of Business Affairs Ms. Trisha WHITE
102 Exec Dir EOSC Found & Alumni Rels Ms. Teresa BRADY

Family of Faith Christian University (A)

PO Box 1805, Shawnee OK 74802-1805
County: Pottawatomie FICE Identification: 036763
Unit ID: 443058
Telephone: (405) 695-5533 Carnegie Class: Spec-4-yr-Faith
FAX Number: (405) 273-8535 Calendar System: Semester
URL: https://familyoffaith.edu/
Established: 1992 Annual Undergrad Tuition & Fees: $7,920
Enrollment: 148 Coed
Affiliation or Control: Independent Non-Profit IRS Status: 501(c)3
Highest Offering: Doctorate
Accreditation: BI

01 President Dr. Samuel W. MATTHEWS
05 Provost Mrs. Elaine W. PHILLIPS
10 Vice Pres Operations/Finance Mr. Daniel MATTHEWS
32 Vice Pres Student Affairs Mrs. Dara GILLIAM
42 Director of Spiritual Life Mr. Chris BERNARD
108 Dir of Accreditation/Assessment Mrs. Elaine W. PHILLIPS
104 Director of International Studies Mrs. Dara GILLIAM

Langston University (B)

PO Box 1500, Langston OK 73050
County: Logan FICE Identification: 003157
Unit ID: 207209
Telephone: (405) 466-2231 Carnegie Class: Masters/S
FAX Number: N/A Calendar System: Semester
URL: www.langston.edu
Established: 1897 Annual Undergrad Tuition & Fees (In-State): $6,509
Enrollment: 2,038 Coed
Affiliation or Control: State IRS Status: 501(c)3
Highest Offering: Doctorate
Accreditation: HLC, ACBSP, CACREP, CAEPN, NUR, PTA

01 President Dr. Kent J. SMITH, JR.
11 VP for Operations Mrs. Theresa D. POWELL
10 VP Fiscal/Admin Affairs Vacant
111 VP Inst Advancement/Development Ms. LaTonya R. ANDERSON
05 Vice President Academic Affairs Dr. Ruth JACKSON
13 Chief Information Officer Mr. Pritchard MONCRIFFE
20 Executive Director of LU-Tulsa Dr. Dytisha DAVIS
21 Comptroller Mrs. Karlon JAMES
32 Dean of Students Mr. Joshua BUSBY
29 Director Alumni Affairs Mrs. Vonnie WARE-ROBERTS
26 Director Public Relations Vacant
07 Director of Admissions Mr. Carlos ROBINSON
37 Director Financial Aid Ms. Shelia R. MCGILL
15 Director of Human Resources Mrs. Cynthia S. BUCKLEY
09 Director Inst Research & Planning Dr. Sheilynda STEWART
06 Registrar Vacant
41 Athletic Director Mrs. Donnita ROGERS
19 Chief of Police Mr. Mario HOLLAND
96 Purchasing Manager Ms. Chaste COPPAGE
49 Dean School of Arts & Sciences Dr. Alonzo F. PETERSON
50 Dean School of Business Dr. Joshua M. SNAVELY
47 Dean School Agric/Applied Science Dr. Wesley L. WHITTAKER
66 Dean School of Nursing/Hlth Profess Dr. Teressa HUNTER
53 Dean School of Education/Behav Sci Dr. Emily PATTERSON HARRIS
88 Dean School of Physical Therapy Dr. Elicia L. POLLARD
84 Exec Director Enrollment Mgmt Mrs. Sheila MCGILL
04 Executive Asst to President Ms. Elaine C. PRESTON
39 Director Student Housing Mr. Kavaris SIMS
44 Annual Giving Officer Ms. Jillian B. WHITAKER
38 Director Student Counseling Dr. Eartha W. COLLIER
08 Chief Library Officer Dr. Lynne SIMPSON
122 Asst Dn Stdnt Engage-Greek Life Mr. Kavaris SIMS

Mid-America Christian University (C)

3500 SW 119th Street, Oklahoma City OK 73170-4500
County: Cleveland FICE Identification: 006942
Unit ID: 245953
Telephone: (405) 691-3800 Carnegie Class: Masters/M
FAX Number: N/A Calendar System: Semester
URL: www.macu.edu
Established: 1953 Annual Undergrad Tuition & Fees: $18,838
Enrollment: 2,083 Coed
Affiliation or Control: Church Of God IRS Status: 501(c)3
Highest Offering: Master's
Accreditation: HLC

01 President Rev. Phil GREENWALD
03 Executive VP Dr. Bobbie SPURGEON-HARRIS
05 Vice Pres for Academic Affairs Dr. Sharon LEASE
32 VP Student Engagement/Success Ms. Morgan THOMPSON
45 VP for University Advancement Mr. Steve SEATON
13 Chief Information Officer Mr. Jody ALLEN
15 Director of Human Resources Ms. Shauntae SOURIE
108 Dir Institutional Effectiveness Mr. Ray DILLMAN
06 Registrar Ms. Stephanie DAVIDSON
37 Director Office of Financial Aid Ms. Rita CASTLEBERRY
07 Asst VP of Enrollment Services Vacant
18 Director of Facilities Ms. Connie GALL
29 Director Alumni Relations Ms. Ashley GOTCHER
04 Executive Asst to President Ms. Carrie GREEN
08 Director of Library Services Ms. Marsha KENDRICK
10 Chief Financial Officer Ms. Kristin JASPER
19 Director of Public Safety Mr. Tim GIBSON
41 Athletic Director Mr. Marcus MOELLER

Miller-Motte College (D)

3801 S. Sheridan, Tulsa OK 74145
Telephone: (918) 663-9000 Identification: 770781
Accreditation: ACCSC

† Branch campus of Miller-Motte College, Chattanooga, TN.

Murray State College (E)

One Murray Campus, Tishomingo OK 73460-3130
County: Johnston FICE Identification: 003158
Unit ID: 207236
Telephone: (580) 387-7000 Carnegie Class: Assoc/HT-High Trad
FAX Number: (580) 371-9844 Calendar System: Semester
URL: www.mscok.edu
Established: 1908 Annual Undergrad Tuition & Fees (In-State): $6,231
Enrollment: 2,172 Coed
Affiliation or Control: State IRS Status: 501(c)3
Highest Offering: Associate Degree
Accreditation: HLC, ADNUR, OTA, PTAA

01 President Dr. Tim FALTYN
05 VP Acad Affs/Institutional Effect Ms. Becky HENTHORN
04 Exec Assistant to President/Board Mrs. Amy CASKEY
10 VP Finance/Administration/CFO Mr. Justin CELLUM
32 Exec Dir for Student Affairs Mr. Quinton JONES
20 Dean of Instruction Ms. Ginger COTHRAN
18 AVP Facilities/Safety Mr. Sam HOLT
102 Exec Director MSC Foundation Vacant
37 Dir Financial Aid Ms. Traci FRANKS
08 Director of Library Mr. Stephen FINLAY
74 Veterinary Tech Program Director Ms. Laura SANDMANN
66 Director of Nursing Ms. Robin COPPEDGE
06 Registrar Vacant
15 Director of Human Resources Ms. Maeleesa HARRELL
35 Director Student Support Services Ms. Ronda PICKENS
21 Comptroller Ms. Sherry GRAY-DEVINE

Northeastern Oklahoma Agricultural and Mechanical College (F)

200 I Street, NE, Miami OK 74354-6434
County: Ottawa FICE Identification: 003160
Unit ID: 207290
Telephone: (918) 542-8441 Carnegie Class: Assoc/MT-VT-High Trad
FAX Number: (918) 542-9759 Calendar System: Semester
URL: www.neo.edu
Established: 1919 Annual Undergrad Tuition & Fees (In-State): $4,913
Enrollment: 1,769 Coed
Affiliation or Control: State IRS Status: 501(c)3
Highest Offering: Associate Degree
Accreditation: HLC, ADNUR, MLTAD, PTAA

01 President Dr. Kyle STAFFORD
05 Vice President Academic Affairs Mr. Dustin GROVER
10 Vice President for Fiscal Affairs Mr. Micah MUNDELL
32 VP Student Affairs/Enrollment Svcs Mrs. Amy ISHMAEL
20 Asst VP for Academic Affairs Vacant
37 Director of Financial Aid Mr. David FISHER
26 Coordinator of Public Information Ms. Shelby SAUL
15 Human Resources Generalist Ms. Hollie SNYDER
18 Director Facilities/Physical Plant Mr. Jeff BOMAN
13 Coord Instructional Technology Mr. Zach LAWSON
30 Exec Dir Development Foundation Mr. David CARTER OWENS
121 Director Academic Advising Center Mrs. Rachel LLOYD
41 Athletic Director Mr. Joe RENFRO
105 Webmaster Mr. Trey DAWSON
06 Registrar Mrs. Shay CLAPP
21 AVP for Fiscal Affairs/Controller Mrs. Cheryl MOUDY
40 Bookstore Manager Mrs. Kathryn VANOVER
08 Director Library Services Ms. Leslie HAYES
47 Department Chair Agriculture Dr. Mary BOOTH
83 Department Chair Social Science Dr. Jeff BIRDSONG
81 Dept Chair Mathematics/Science Mr. Steve DIXON
66 Dept Chr Nurs/Allied Hlth/Phys Educ Mrs. Kathleen NORMAN
50 Dept Chair Business and Technology Mrs. Joy BAUER
04 Executive Asst to President Mrs. Kendra CUMMINS
19 Director Security/Safety Mr. Buddy LAMBERT
39 Director Student Housing Mr. Jim ROWLAND
96 Coordinator of Purchasing Mr. Charlie WILMONTH

Northeastern State University (G)

600 N Grand Avenue, Tahlequah OK 74464-2399
County: Cherokee FICE Identification: 003161
Unit ID: 207263
Telephone: (918) 456-5511 Carnegie Class: Masters/L
FAX Number: (918) 458-2015 Calendar System: Semester
URL: www.nsuok.edu
Established: 1909 Annual Undergrad Tuition & Fees (In-State): $6,915
Enrollment: 7,349 Coed
Affiliation or Control: State IRS Status: 501(c)3
Highest Offering: First Professional Degree
Accreditation: HLC, ACBSP, #ARCPA, CACREP, CAEP, DIETD, EXSC, MLS, MUS, NUR, OPT, OPTR, SP, SW

01 President Dr. Steve TURNER
10 Chief Financial/Business Officer Mrs. Christy LANDSAW
05 Provost & VP Academic Affairs Dr. Debborah LANDRY
11 VP for Administration/Finance Ms. Christy LANDSAW
86 Dir Community/Government Relations Vacant
26 VP University Relations Mr. Dan MABERY
32 Vice President Student Affairs Dr. Jerrid FREEMAN
21 Director Business Affairs Mr. Austin ROSENTHAL
20 Asst VP Academic Affairs Dr. Carla SWEARINGEN
20 Asst VP Academic Affairs Admin Dr. Pam FLY
12 Dean Broken Arrow Campus Vacant
12 Dean Muskogee Campus Dr. Kimberly WILLIAMS
49 Dean College of Liberal Arts Dr. Mike CHANSLOR
50 Dean College of Business/Technology Dr. Janet BUZZARD
53 Dean College of Education Dr. Vanessa ANTON
81 Dean Science & Health Professions Dr. Pamela HATHORN
88 Dean Optometry Dr. Douglas PENISTEN
08 Exec Director of NSU Libraries Dr. Michael JONES
108 Exec Director Inst Effectiveness Dr. Julie SAWYER
30 Director of Development Ms. Peggy GLENN
15 Director of Human Resources Mrs. Jean LOGUE
37 Director Student Financial Services Mrs. Cynthia BENDABOUT
06 Registrar Ms. Janet KELLEY
07 Director Admissions/Recruitment Mr. Brandon MILLER
84 Asst VP Enrollment Management Dr. Kelly Jo LARSEN
18 Assistant VP Facilities Mr. Richard COPELAND
41 Director of Athletics Mr. Matt COCHRAN
19 Director of Public Safety Mr. James BELL
22 Sr Coord Stdnt Disability Svcs Mrs. Donna AGEE
29 Director Alumni Services Mr. Daniel JOHNSON
109 Asst VP of Auxiliary Services Mr. Chris ADNEY
39 Director of Housing Mrs. Whitney ARBAUGH
35 Asst VP Student Affairs Admin Ms. Sheila SELF
96 Director Purchasing Contr Payments Mr. Austin ROSENTHAL
44 Stewards/Annual Giving Coordinator Ms. Cami HIGHERS
04 Administrative Asst to President Ms. Robin HUTCHINS
13 Chief Info Tech Officer/Director IT Dr. Richard REIF
28 Diversity and Inclusion Coord Vacant
38 Director Student Counseling Svcs Mrs. Leigh-Anna MILLER

Northeastern State University (H)

3100 East New Orleans St, Broken Arrow OK 74014
Telephone: (918) 449-6000 Identification: 770372
Accreditation: &HLC

Northeastern State University at Muskogee (I)

2400 W Shawnee, Muskogee OK 74401
Telephone: (918) 683-0040 Identification: 770373
Accreditation: &HLC, OT

Northern Oklahoma College (J)

1220 E Grand Avenue, PO Box 310,
Tonkawa OK 74653-0310
County: Kay FICE Identification: 003162
Unit ID: 207281
Telephone: (580) 628-6200 Carnegie Class: Assoc/MT-VT-Mix Trad/Non
FAX Number: (580) 628-6209 Calendar System: Semester
URL: www.noc.edu
Established: 1901 Annual Undergrad Tuition & Fees (In-State): $3,648
Enrollment: 3,374 Coed
Affiliation or Control: State IRS Status: 501(c)3
Highest Offering: Associate Degree
Accreditation: HLC, ACBSP, ADNUR, COARC

01 President Dr. Clark HARRIS
05 Vice Pres for Academic Affairs Ms. Diana WATKINS
10 Vice President Financial Affairs Mrs. Anita SIMPSON
12 Vice President for NOC Enid Mr. Jeremy HISE
12 Vice President for NOC Stillwater Vacant
32 Vice President for Student Affairs Mr. Jason JOHNSON
30 VP for Development/Community Rels Mrs. Sheri SNYDER
13 Director Information Technology Mr. Michael MACHIA
15 Director Human Resources Ms. Shannon CRANFORD
84 VP Enrollment Management/Registrar Dr. Rick EDGINGTON
08 Director of Library Services Mr. Benjamin HAINLINE
18 Assoc Vice Pres of Physical Plant Mr. Larry DYE

41 Athletic Director .... Mr. Alan FOSTER
37 Director Student Financial Aid .... Ms. Holly LEE
40 Manager Student Bookstore .... Mrs. Jimilea JANSSON

Northwestern Oklahoma State University (A)

709 Oklahoma Boulevard, Alva OK 73717-2799
County: Woods   FICE Identification: 003163
Unit ID: 207306
Telephone: (580) 327-1700   Carnegie Class: Masters/S
FAX Number: (580) 327-1881   Calendar System: Semester
URL: www.nwosu.edu
Established: 1897   Annual Undergrad Tuition & Fees (In-State): $8,173
Enrollment: 1,833   Coed
Affiliation or Control: State   IRS Status: 501(c)3
Highest Offering: Doctorate
Accreditation: HLC, ACBSP, CAEP, NUR, NURSE, SW

01 President .... Dr. Bo S. HANNAFORD
03 Executive Vice President .... Dr. David M. PECHA
05 VP for Academic Affairs .... Dr. James BELL
26 Director Marketing/Univ Relations .... Ms. Kelsey A. MARTIN
32 Dean of Student Affairs .... Mr. Calleb N. MOSBURG
41 Athletic Director .... Mr. Brad FRANZ
06 Registrar .... Ms. Sheri K. LAHR
37 Director Financial Aid .... Ms. Tara HANNAFORD
113 Bursar .... Ms. Paige FISCHER
07 Asst Dean of Students & Recruitment .... Mr. Matt ADAIR
18 Chief Facilities/Physical Plant .... Mr. Doug CHAFFIN
15 Human Resource Director .... Ms. Cheryl ELLIS
29 Director Alumni Relations .... Mr. John W. ALLEN
58 Assoc Dean of Graduate Studies .... Dr. Shawn P. HOLLIDAY
08 Director of Libraries .... Mrs. Shannon LEAPER
09 Institutional Research Specialist .... Ms. Ashley FISCHER

Oklahoma Baptist University (B)

500 W University, Shawnee OK 74804-2590
County: Pottawatomie   FICE Identification: 003164
Unit ID: 207403
Telephone: (405) 585-4000   Carnegie Class: Masters/S
FAX Number: N/A   Calendar System: Semester
URL: www.okbu.edu
Established: 1910   Annual Undergrad Tuition & Fees: $31,352
Enrollment: 1,763   Coed
Affiliation or Control: Southern Baptist   IRS Status: 501(c)3
Highest Offering: Master's
Accreditation: HLC, ACBSP, CAEP, MUS, NURSE

01 President .... Dr. Heath THOMAS
05 Provost .... Vacant
10 Exec VP Business Affs/Admin Svcs .... Mr. Randy SMITH
111 VP for Advancement .... Mr. Tim RASNIC
32 VP of Campus Life/Dean of Students .... Mr. Brandon PETERSEN
28 Interim VP for University Culture .... Ms. B.J GLOVER
84 VP for Enrollment Management .... Mr. Will BRANTLEY
41 Athletic Director .... Mr. Robert DAVENPORT
13 VP of Tech/Digital Innovation/CTO .... Vacant
26 Assoc VP Marketing & Communication .... Ms. Paula GOWER
21 Asst VP Finance/Admin Svcs .... Mr. Lester KASTERKE
37 Director Student Financial Services .... Ms. Danielle WELLMAN
06 Dir Academic Records/Registrar .... Ms. Marcia MCQUERRY
21 Controller .... Ms. Shannon HESTER
15 Director of Human Resources .... Vacant
19 Chief of University Police .... Mr. David SHANNON
18 Mgr of Facility Services .... Mr. Robert MARQUARDT
36 Dir of Career Services & Alumni Eng .... Ms. Lori HAGANS
73 Dean of Theology/Arts/Humanities .... Dr. Matthew EMERSON
50 Dean Business/Health Sci/Educ .... Dr. Larinee DENNIS
88 Chair School of Business .... Dr. David HOUGHTON
66 Chair School of Nursing .... Vacant
73 Chair School of Theology/Ministry .... Dr. Luke STAMPS
53 Chair School of Education .... Dr. Elizabeth JUSTICE
09 Dir of Institutional Research .... Mr. Marcus BREWER
07 Director of Admissions .... Ms. Kalyn FULLBRIGHT
04 Exec Assistant to the President .... Ms. Sydnie DAVIDSON
39 Director Student Housing .... Ms. Erin GULESERIAN
88 Dir of Community Experiences .... Ms. Allison CADE
08 Chief Library Officer .... Ms. Julie RANKIN
29 Director Alumni Association .... Ms. Lea Ann QUIRK

Oklahoma Christian University (C)

PO Box 11000, Oklahoma City OK 73136-1100
County: Oklahoma   FICE Identification: 003165
Unit ID: 207324
Telephone: (405) 425-5000   Carnegie Class: Masters/M
FAX Number: (405) 425-5090   Calendar System: Semester
URL: www.oc.edu
Established: 1950   Annual Undergrad Tuition & Fees: $25,090
Enrollment: 2,055   Coed
Affiliation or Control: Independent Non-Profit   IRS Status: 501(c)3
Highest Offering: Master's
Accreditation: HLC, ACBSP, CAEP, CIDA, MLS, MUS, NURSE

01 President .... Mr. John DESTEIGUER
00 Chancellor .... Dr. Ken JONES
13 Chief Information Officer .... Mr. John HERMES
05 Chief Academic Officer .... Dr. Jeff MCCORMACK
111 Chief Advancement Officer .... Ms. Christine MERIDETH
43 Chief Legal Officer .... Mr. Stephen ECK
32 Chief Student Life Officer & Dean .... Mr. Neil ARTER
76 Chair Div Natural/Health Sciences .... Dr. Jennifer GRAY
49 Dean The New College .... Dr. Sada KNOWLES
06 Interim Registrar .... Mrs. Karen DRISKILL
19 Chief of Police Dept .... Mr. Greg GILTNER
41 Athletic Director .... Mr. David LYNN
18 Director of Physical Plant Services .... Mr. Cary FALLING
37 Exec Dir Financial Svcs & Budgets .... Mr. Clint LARUE
104 Director of International Programs .... Mr. John OSBORNE
89 Dir of Freshman Experience .... Mr. Trent DOBBS
85 International Student Advisor .... Mrs. Makenna ESTES
38 Director of Counseling Services .... Mr. Sheldon ADKINS
121 Director of Student Success .... Mrs. Hannah LEFTWICH
35 Assistant Dean of Students .... Mr. Gary JONES
04 Executive Assistant to President .... Mrs. Teri MUELLER
39 Director Student Housing .... Mrs. Candace BASS
10 Chief Financial Officer .... Mrs. Jennifer RAY

Oklahoma City Community College (D)

7777 S May Avenue, Oklahoma City OK 73159-4444
County: Oklahoma   FICE Identification: 010391
Unit ID: 207449
Telephone: (405) 682-1611   Carnegie Class: Assoc/HT-High Trad
FAX Number: (405) 682-7585   Calendar System: Semester
URL: www.occc.edu
Established: 1972   Annual Undergrad Tuition & Fees (In-District): $4,059
Enrollment: 12,227   Coed
Affiliation or Control: State/Local   IRS Status: 501(c)3
Highest Offering: Associate Degree
Accreditation: HLC, ACBSP, ADNUR, AT, EMT, NAEYC, OTA, PTAA

01 President .... Dr. Mautra JONES
03 Executive Vice President .... Dr. M. Scott FERN
04 Exec Assistant to the President .... Ms. Janice STALLWORTH
101 Exec Asst to the Board of Regents .... Ms. Kim VELLECA
05 Provost .... Dr. Jeremy THOMAS
05 Vice President Academic Affairs .... Dr. Vincent BRIDGES
32 VP Student Affairs .... Dr. Jason JOHNSON
10 Chief Financial Officer .... Ms. Cynthia GARY
88 Director of Cultural Programs .... Mr. Lemuel BARDEGUEZ
15 Vice Pres/Dir Human Resources .... Dr. Regina SWITZER
13 VP of IT Infrastructure .... Mr. Tim WHISENHUNT
20 Associate VP Academic Affairs .... Dr. Glenne WHISENHUNT
35 Associate VP Student Affairs .... Mr. Chris SNODDY
18 Exec Dir of Facilities Management .... Mr. Chris SNOW
79 Dean of Arts English/Humanities .... Vacant
76 Dean of Health Professions .... Dr. Kathy WHEAT
81 Dean Math/Engineering/Phys Science .... Dr. Max SIMMONS
83 Dean of Social Sciences .... Vacant
50 Dean of Bus & Information Tech .... Mr. John CLAYBON
30 Chief Development Officer .... Mr. Von ALLEN
26 Exec Director of Marketing & PR .... Ms. Kim TERRY
25 Director of Grants & Contracts .... Mr. Von ALLEN
09 Dir Institutional Effectiveness .... Mr. Matt EASTWOOD
37 Director of Student Financial Aid .... Ms. Sonya GORE
21 Director of Financial Accounting .... Ms. Billie Jo BERGERON
114 Dir of Budgeting/Fiscal Planning .... Mr. David CHURCHILL
19 Chief of Police .... Mr. Daniel PIAZZA
113 Bursar .... Mr. David PRICE
40 Director of Bookstore .... Mr. Woodie COLEMAN
117 Emergency Manager .... Mr. Patrick SOLINSKI
96 Director of Purchasing .... Mr. Craig SISCO
88 Dir Recreation and Fitness .... Mr. Michael SHUGART
36 Director Career Transitions Program .... Ms. Lisa BROWN
22 Director of Equity and Compliance .... Mr. Jade CARTER
91 Dir Enterprise Resource Planning .... Ms. Jill LINDBLAD
08 Director of Library Services .... Ms. Ann RAIA
88 Dir of Ctr for Learning/Teaching .... Vacant
07 Dir of Recruitment & Admiss .... Mr. Michael HOGGATT
121 Director of Academic Advising .... Ms. Stephanie MILLER
06 Registrar .... Ms. Amanda WILLIAMS-MIZE

Oklahoma City University (E)

2501 N Blackwelder, Oklahoma City OK 73106-1493
County: Oklahoma   FICE Identification: 003166
Unit ID: 207458
Telephone: (405) 208-5000   Carnegie Class: DU-Mod
FAX Number: (405) 208-5916   Calendar System: Semester
URL: www.okcu.edu
Established: 1904   Annual Undergrad Tuition & Fees: $32,744
Enrollment: 2,617   Coed
Affiliation or Control: United Methodist   IRS Status: 501(c)3
Highest Offering: Doctorate
Accreditation: HLC, ARCPA, CAEP, LAW, MUS, NUR, @PTA

01 President .... Dr. Kenneth R. EVANS
05 Provost/VPAA .... Dr. Michelle KIEC
111 VP University Advancement .... Ms. Lynann STERK-BROOKS
10 Chief Financial Officer .... Mr. Kevan BUCK
32 VP Student Affairs/Dean of Students .... Dr. Amy AYRES
15 VP for Human Resources .... Ms. Joey CROSLIN
28 VP Diversity/Equity & Inclusion .... Dr. Talia CARROLL
84 Asst VP/Dean Enrollment Services .... Mr. Kevin WINDHOLZ
41 Director of Athletics .... Mr. Corey BRAY
19 Chief of Police .... Mr. Dexter NELSON
13 Chief Info Officer (CIO) .... Mr. Gerry HUNT
06 Registrar .... Mr. Charles MONNOT
09 Director of Institutional Research .... Mr. Mark MCCLENDON
08 Director Dulaney-Browne Library .... Dr. Victoria SWINNEY
37 Director of Financial Aid .... Mr. Christopher DAY
26 S Director of Comm & Marketing .... Mr. Nick TROUGAKOS
92 Director of Honors Program .... Dr. Karen YOUMANS
07 Director of Undergrad Admissions . Ms. Tasha CASEY-LOVELESS
18 Chief Facilities/Physical Plant .... Mr. Mark CLOUSE
29 Exec Director Alumni Engagement .... Ms. Megan HORNBEEK ALLEN
36 Director of Career Services .... Ms. Kanika BROWN
49 Dean of Arts & Sciences .... Dr. Amy E. CATALDI
50 Dean School of Business .... Dr. Sri BELDONA
61 Dean School of Law .... Mr. James ROTH
64 Dean School of Music .... Mr. Mark PARKER
66 Interim Dean of School of Nursing .... Dr. Gina CRAWFORD
73 Director School of Religion .... Dr. Sharon BETSWORTH
88 Int Dean Sch of AmDance/Arts Mgmt .... Ms. Melanie SHELLEY
104 Coordinator Study Abroad .... Vacant
38 Director of Counseling Services .... Ms. Mindy WINDHOLZ
39 Director University Housing .... Mr. Gregory STEWART
43 University General Counsel .... Ms. Casey ROSS
44 Director Annual Giving .... Ms. Emily BENDICK
04 Executive Asst to President .... Ms. Sarah POWERS
105 Web Services Manager .... Mr. Brian BYRNE

Oklahoma Panhandle State University (F)

Box 430, Goodwell OK 73939-0430
County: Texas   FICE Identification: 003174
Unit ID: 207351
Telephone: (580) 349-2611   Carnegie Class: Bac-Diverse
FAX Number: (580) 349-2302   Calendar System: Semester
URL: www.opsu.edu
Established: 1909   Annual Undergrad Tuition & Fees (In-State): $7,384
Enrollment: 1,337   Coed
Affiliation or Control: State   IRS Status: 501(c)3
Highest Offering: Baccalaureate
Accreditation: HLC, CAEP, NUR

01 President .... Dr. Tim FALTYN
05 Provost .... Dr. Julie DINGER
10 AVP of Fiscal Affairs .... Ms. Elizabeth MCMURPHY
111 Vice President of Operations .... Dr. Ryan BLANTON
20 AVP of Academic Affairs .... Dr. Brad DUREN
47 Dean Agriculture/Science/Nursing .... Ms. Shawna TUCKER
50 Dean Business & Technology .... Mr. Davin WINGER
32 Dean of Student Services .... Ms. Amber GLASS
06 Int Registrar/Dir of Admissions .... Ms. Olivia ROBINSON
37 Director Student Financial Aid .... Ms. Erin MOORE
09 Director Institutional Research .... Mr. Dillon SCHOENHALS
13 Director of Technology .... Mr. Howard HENDERSON
15 Director Human Resources .... Ms. Dana COLLINS
08 Director of Library .... Mr. Alton (Tony) HARDMAN
21 Comptroller .... Ms. Tiffany MURLEY
38 Director Counseling/Career Services .... Ms. Deanna Rene RAMON
26 Director Campus Communications .... Ms. Natasha EIDSON
41 Athletic Officer .... Mr. Victor ESPARZA
40 Bookstore Manager .... Ms. Heather UTT
18 Director Physical Plant .... Mr. Robby JOHNSON
29 Director Alumni Relations/Webmaster .... Mr. Nick TUTTLE
96 Director of Purchasing .... Ms. Carol HILL
04 Administrative Asst to President .... Ms. Calandra ROSE

Oklahoma State University (G)

219 PIO Building, Stillwater OK 74078
County: Payne   FICE Identification: 003170
Unit ID: 207388
Telephone: (405) 744-5000   Carnegie Class: DU-Highest
FAX Number: N/A   Calendar System: Semester
URL: osu.okstate.edu/
Established: 1890   Annual Undergrad Tuition & Fees (In-State): $9,019
Enrollment: 24,535   Coed
Affiliation or Control: State   IRS Status: 501(c)3
Highest Offering: Doctorate
Accreditation: HLC, CAATE, CACREP, CAEPN, CARTE, CIDA, CLPSY, COPSY, DIETD, DIETI, JOUR, LSAR, MFCD, MUS, NURSE, PCSAS, SCPSY, SP, THEA, VET

01 President .... Dr. Kayse SHRUM
04 Exec Assistant to the President .... Ms. Melissa WADLEY
102 President & CEO OSU Foundation .... Ms. Blaire ATKINSON
05 Provost & Sr Vice President .... Dr. Jeanette MENDEZ
03 Sr Vice Pres Executive Affairs .... Mr. Kyle WRAY
10 Sr Vice Pres Admin & Finance .... Mr. Joseph B. WEAVER, JR.
47 VP/Dean Ag/Sci & Natural Resources .... Dr. Thomas COON
41 Vice President Athletic Programs .... Mr. Chad WEIBERG
84 Vice Pres Enrollment Mgmt .... Ms. Karen CHEN
46 Vice President for Research .... Dr. Kenneth SEWELL
32 Vice President Student Affairs .... Dr. Doug HALLENBECK
09 Assoc VP/Dir Inst Res & Analytics .... Dr. Christie HAWKINS
20 Prov/Sr VP Academic Affairs .... Mr. Chris FRANISCO
58 Assoc Provost/Dean Graduate College .... Dr. Sheryl TUCKER
21 Assoc Vice President & Controller .... Ms. Tammy ECK
28 VP Institutional Diversity .... Dr. Jason KIRKSEY
15 Asst VP Admin/Human Resources .... Ms. Christa LOUTHAN
24 Asst Prov/Dir Inst Tch/Lrng Excel .... Dr. Christine ORMSBEE
13 Chief Information Officer .... Dr. Raj MURTHY
18 Chief Facilities Officer .... Mr. Ron TARBUTTON
96 Chief Procurement Officer .... Mr. Scott SCHLOTTHAUER
19 Chief Public Safety Officer .... Mr. Michael ROBINSON
36 Director Career Services .... Ms. Kellie EBERT

26 Assoc VP of Brand Management ....Ms. Megan HORTON
25 Dir Grants/Contracts/Financial Admn ....Dr. Robert DIXON
37 Director Scholarships/Financial Aid ....Mr. Chad BLEW
39 Director of University Housing ....Dr. Leon MCCLINTON
108 Director Univ Assessment & Testing ....Mr. Ryan CHUNG
38 Dir Univ Counseling Svcs & UHS ....Mr. Jack HENNEHA
88 Assoc Dir Institutional Research ....Mr. Larry BURNS
40 Dir Student Union Bookstore ....Mr. Lance HINKLE
39 Asst Director Resident Life ....Mumbe KITHAKYE
85 Dir Intl Students & Scholars ....Mr. Tim T. HUFF
53 Dean College of Education ....Dr. Jon PEDERSEN
54 Dean Engineering ....Dr. Paul J. TIKALSKY
92 Dean Honors College ....Mr. Richard FROHOCK
49 Dean Arts & Sciences ....Dr. Keith GARBUTT
08 Dean Library ....Dr. Sheila G. JOHNSON
50 Dean Spears School of Business ....Dr. Ken EASTMAN
74 Dean Veterinary Medicine ....Dr. Carlos RISCO
06 Registrar ....Ms. Rita PEASTER

Oklahoma State University Center for Health Sciences (A)

1111 W 17th Street, Tulsa OK 74107-1898
Telephone: (918) 582-1972 FICE Identification: 011282
Accreditation: &HLC, #ARCPA, FEPAC, OSTEO

† Regional accreditation is carried under the parent institution in Stillwater, OK.

Oklahoma State University Institute of Technology-Okmulgee (B)

1801 E Fourth Street, Okmulgee OK 74447-3901
County: Okmulgee FICE Identification: 003172
Unit ID: 207564
Telephone: (918) 293-4678 Carnegie Class: Bac/Assoc-Mixed
FAX Number: (918) 293-4644 Calendar System: Trimester
URL: www.osuit.edu
Established: 1946 Annual Undergrad Tuition & Fees (In-State): $5,774
Enrollment: 2,349 Coed
Affiliation or Control: State IRS Status: 501(c)3
Highest Offering: Baccalaureate
Accreditation: HLC, ADNUR

01 President ....Dr. Bill PATH
10 VP Fiscal Services ....Mr. Jim SMITH
05 Provost/VP Academic Affairs ....Dr. Lisa WEIS
32 VP Student Services ....Dr. Ina AGNEW
20 Associate VP Academic Affairs ....Ms. Jody GRAMMER
103 Assoc VP Workforce & Econ Dev ....Mr. Charles HARRISON
49 Dean Arts/Sciences & Health Science ....Dr. Trey HILL
54 Dean Engineering/Construction Tech ....Mr. Steve OLMSTEAD
88 Dean Transportation & Heavy Equip ....Mr. Terryl LINDSEY
57 Dean Creative & Information Tech ....Mr. Christian BRADLEY
37 Dir Student Financial Services ....Mr. Matt SHORT
13 Associate VP Technology Services ....Mr. Kevin HULETT
07 Director of Admissions/ Registrar ....Ms. Crystal BOWLES PALACIOZ
15 Director of Human Resources ....Ms. Paula NORTH
09 Director of Institutional Research ....Ms. Michelle CANAN
18 Dir Physical Plant Services ....Mr. Mark PITCHER
35 Dean of Students ....Mr. Devin DEBOCK
109 Dir Student Union & Auxiliary Svcs ....Mr. James BYRD
35 Director of Student Life ....Ms. Kamie RASH
39 Director of Residential Life ....Mr. Bo HUDSON
08 Director of Library ....Ms. Jenny DUNCAN
96 Director of Purchasing ....Ms. Jalynda BAILEY
38 Counselor ....Ms. Kathy AVERY
40 Manager Bookstore ....Ms. Shayla KING
26 Director of Marketing ....Ms. Lindsay LYNCH
19 Campus Police Chief ....Mr. Matt WOOLIVER
04 Admin Asst to President ....Ms. Claudette BUTCHER
88 Dir Tutoring Ctr/Acad Accommodation ....Mr. Chad SPURLOCK
29 Director Alumni Relations ....Vacant

Oklahoma State University - Oklahoma City (C)

900 N Portland Ave, Oklahoma City OK 73107-6195
County: Oklahoma FICE Identification: 009647
Unit ID: 207397
Telephone: (405) 947-4421 Carnegie Class: Bac/Assoc-Assoc Dom
FAX Number: (405) 945-3289 Calendar System: Semester
URL: www.osuokc.edu
Established: 1961 Annual Undergrad Tuition & Fees (In-State): $5,070
Enrollment: 4,949 Coed
Affiliation or Control: State IRS Status: 501(c)3
Highest Offering: Baccalaureate
Accreditation: HLC, ADNUR, DMS, EMT

01 President ....Mr. Scott NEWMAN
04 Exec Assistant to the President ....Ms. Paige LANDRETH
05 Provost/Vice Pres Academic Affairs ....Dr. Pam STINSON
10 Vice President Budget & Finance ....Ms. Ronda REECE
20 Associate VP Academic Affairs ....Mr. Tracy EDWARDS
32 Int VP of Student Experience ....Dr. Joey FRONHEISER
30 Associate Dir Development ....Mr. Donovan WOODS
11 Vice Pres of Operations ....Mr. Mike WIDELL
08 Director Library Services ....Ms. Elaine REGIER
37 Sr Director Financial Aid ....Ms. Bessie CARTER
15 Sr Director Human Resources ....Ms. Melissa HERREN
18 Dir of Building Maint/Energy Mgr ....Mr. Mickey FULLER
26 Sr Dir Marketing/Communications ....Mr. Cordell JORDAN
121 Director Academic Advisement ....Ms. Krystle DICK
07 Dir Recruitment & Admissions ....Ms. Brandee MORGAN
96 Director of Purchasing ....Ms. Sharon FITZPATRICK
113 Director Business Services ....Ms. Kim BEAUCOURT
06 Registrar ....Mr. Kyle BROWN
25 Sr Director Institutional Grants ....Ms. Jackie WESTON
19 Sr Director Safety & Security ....Mr. Darvin GORE
108 Sr Dir Institutional Effectiveness ....Ms. Virginia SMITH
88 Sr Dir Community Engagement ....Dr. Lisa FISHER
13 Chief Information Officer ....Mr. Richard BARR
28 Director Disability Svcs//Inclusion ....Ms. Emily CHENG
93 Director Upward Bound ....Mr. Donovan KELSO

Oklahoma State University - Tulsa (D)

700 N Greenwood Avenue, Tulsa OK 74106-0702
Telephone: (918) 594-8000 Identification: 666053
Accreditation: &HLC

† Regional accreditation is carried under the parent institution in Stillwater, OK.

Oklahoma Wesleyan University (E)

2201 Silver Lake Road, Bartlesville OK 74006-6299
County: Washington FICE Identification: 003151
Unit ID: 206835
Telephone: (800) 468-6219 Carnegie Class: Masters/S
FAX Number: N/A Calendar System: Semester
URL: www.okwu.edu
Established: 1905 Annual Undergrad Tuition & Fees: $28,924
Enrollment: 934 Coed
Affiliation or Control: Wesleyan Church IRS Status: 501(c)3
Highest Offering: Doctorate
Accreditation: HLC, CAEPN, IACBE, NURSE

01 President ....Dr. Jim DUNN
05 Provost/VP for Academic Affairs ....Dr. Mark WEETER
10 Vice President for Business Affairs ....Dr. Kirk JACKSON
32 Vice Pres for Student Development ....Mr. Kyle WHITE
84 Vice President for Enrollment Svcs ....Dr. Kevin OSBORN
35 Assoc VP for Student Dev ....Rev. Ben ROTZ
53 Dean School of Educ & Exercise Sci ....Dr. Keri BOSTWICK
73 Dean Sch of Ministry/Christ Theol ....Dr. Jerome VAN KUIKEN
49 Dean of School of Arts & Sciences ....Dr. Dalene FISHER
50 Dean of School of Business ....Dr. Wendel WEAVER
66 Dean of School of Nursing ....Dr. Jessica JOHNSON
58 Dir of Grad & Professional Studies ....Dr. Brett ANDREWS
21 Director of Accounting ....Mrs. Tabitha BENBROOK
06 Exec Dir of Student Services ....Mrs. Kandi MOLDER
13 Director of Information Technology ....Mr. Alex JOHNSON
08 Head Librarian ....Mrs. Cheryl SALERNO
37 Director of Financial Aid ....Mrs. Tirzah KNIGHT
15 Director of Human Resources ....Mrs. Rachel GLASS-SHOWLER
41 Athletic Director ....Mr. Kirk KELLEY
04 Executive Assistant to President ....Ms. Leeann LITTLE
39 Director of Residential Life ....Mrs. Megan YOUNG
124 Dir of Student Engagement ....Mr. Aaron BUNKER
18 Director of Buildings and Grounds ....Mr. Dalton HIGGINS
19 Director of Campus Safety ....Mr. Stevan DJUKIC
101 Secretary of the Institution/Board ....Mr. Trevor SHAKIBA
26 VP of Creative Impact ....Mr. Kory PENCE
29 Dir of Alumni Rel & Grant Writing ....Ms. Charissa DUNN
43 General Counsel ....Dr. David PRESTON

Oral Roberts University (F)

7777 S Lewis Avenue, Tulsa OK 74171-0003
County: Tulsa FICE Identification: 003985
Unit ID: 207582
Telephone: (918) 495-6161 Carnegie Class: Masters/M
FAX Number: (918) 495-6033 Calendar System: Semester
URL: https://oru.edu/
Established: 1965 Annual Undergrad Tuition & Fees: $30,930
Enrollment: 4,317 Coed
Affiliation or Control: Independent Non-Profit IRS Status: 501(c)3
Highest Offering: Doctorate
Accreditation: HLC, ACBSP, CAEP, MUS, NURSE, SW, THEOL

01 President ....Dr. William M. WILSON
05 Provost ....Dr. Kathaleen REID-MARTINEZ
10 Chief Financial Officer ....Mr. Neal STENZEL
11 Chief Operations Officer ....Mr. Tim PHILLEY
111 VP of External Affairs ....Dr. Charles SCOTT
43 University Counsel ....Mr. Terry KOLLMORGEN
32 Vice President Student Life ....Dr. Clarence BOYD
13 VP of Technology & Innovation ....Mr. Michael MATHEWS
84 AVP Of Enrollment Management - Res ....Mrs. Alison VUJNOVIC
84 AVP of Enrollment Management-Online ....Mr. Nathan CARSON
14 AVP of Technology & Innovation ....Mr. Vinay MANDA
21 Controller ....Ms. Michelle MCMILLAN
08 Dean of the University Library ....Vacant
104 Director Study Abroad ....Mr. Filipe AZEVEDO
106 AD of Online & Lifelong Learning ....Dr. Jay GARY
54 Dean Col of Science & Engineering ....Dr. Kenneth WEED
49 Dean Col of Arts & Cultural Studies ....Dr. William C. ELLIS
73 Dean College Theology/Ministry ....Dr. Wonsuk MA
50 Dean College of Business ....Dr. Julie HUNTLEY
76 Dean College of Health Sciences ....Dr. Dean PRENTICE
53 Dean College of Education ....Dr. Kim BOYD
35 Dean of Student Development ....Mrs. Lori COOK
35 Director of Student Services ....Mrs. Juli ATKINSON
41 Director for Athletics ....Mr. Tim JOHNSON
25 Grants Facilitator ....Vacant
38 Director of Student Counseling ....Dr. Jonathan FORREST
92 Director of Honors Program ....Dr. Kenneth WEED
113 Director Student Accounts ....Mr. Steve THANNICKAL
96 Purchasing Manager ....Mrs. Jeanine NOWELL
06 University Registrar ....Dr. Connie SJOBERG
89 Director of New Student Relations ....Ms. Stephanie OTTMAN
07 Exec Director Intl Admissions ....Mrs. Jessica TENORIO
37 Director of Financial Aid ....Mrs. Emily ATKERSON
19 Director of Security/Safety ....Mr. Bill (William) HUNT
15 Director of Human Resources ....Dr. Kathryn LENTZ
04 Executive Asst to President ....Mrs. Lisa BOWMAN
101 Secretary of the Institution/BOT ....Ms. Alyssa SANDERS
30 VP Development & Alumni Relations ..Mr. Mike (Robert) CARTER
108 Director of University Assessment ....Mr. Trevor ELLIS
39 Dir Concierge/Residential Services ....Mrs. JaMeece BRISCO

Phillips Theological Seminary (G)

901 N Mingo Road, Tulsa OK 74116-5612
County: Tulsa FICE Identification: 025602
Unit ID: 414966
Telephone: (918) 610-8303 Carnegie Class: Spec-4-yr-Faith
FAX Number: (918) 610-8404 Calendar System: Semester
URL: www.ptstulsa.edu
Established: 1906 Annual Graduate Tuition & Fees: N/A
Enrollment: 170 Coed
Affiliation or Control: Christian Church (Disciples Of Christ)
IRS Status: 501(c)3
Highest Offering: Doctorate; No Undergraduates
Accreditation: PAST, THEOL

01 President ....Nancy C. PITTMAN
125 President Emeritus ....Gary PELUSO-VERDEND
05 VP Academic Affairs & Dean ....Lee H. BUTLER, JR.
10 Vice Pres Finance & Admin ....Karen MCMILLAN
111 Vice Pres Advancement ....Terry EWING
108 Assoc Dean Assessment & Faculty Dev ....Joseph A. BESSLER
20 Assoc Dn Contextual Ed/Church Rels ....Vacant
73 Director Doctor of Ministry Program ....Kathleen D. MCCALLIE
37 Financial Aid Officer ....Todd MANTOCK
08 Dean of Library ....Sandy SHAPOVAL
29 Sr Dir Stewardship & Alumni Rels ....Malisa PIERCE
26 Sr Director Seminary Relations ....Kurt GWARTNEY
06 Registrar ....Virginia THOMPSON
04 Executive Assistant to President ....Ashley M. GIBSON
15 Sr Director of Human Resources ....Torii RANSOME FREEMAN

Randall University (H)

3701 S. I-35 Service Road, Moore OK 73160
County: Cleveland FICE Identification: 010266
Unit ID: 207157
Telephone: (405) 912-9000 Carnegie Class: Bac-A&S
FAX Number: (405) 912-9050 Calendar System: Semester
URL: www.ru.edu
Established: 1959 Annual Undergrad Tuition & Fees: $16,547
Enrollment: 311 Coed
Affiliation or Control: Free Will Baptist IRS Status: 501(c)3
Highest Offering: Master's
Accreditation: TRACS

00 Chancellor ....Dr. Timothy W. EATON
01 President ....Rev. Robert G. THOMPSON
10 Chief Financial Officer ....Mr. Todd JENSON
05 Chief Academic Officer ....Dr. Brent SYKES
21 Chief Business Officer ....Ms. Pat MILLER
32 Dean of Students ....Ms. Jody BLACKWELL
42 Director of Church Engagement ....Rev. Mason POLK
07 Admissions Coordinator ....Mr. Evan ALDRIDGE
37 Financial Aid Coordinator ....Mr. Cliff BRISTOW
08 LRC Director ....Ms. Nancy J. DRAPER
13 Director of MIS ....Mr. Quentin C. LOOP
06 Registrar ....Ms. Patti ASHBY
41 Athletic Director ....Mr. Todd JENSON
106 Director of Online Learning ....Mrs. Michelle COFFMAN

Redlands Community College (I)

1300 S Country Club Road, El Reno OK 73036-5304
County: Canadian FICE Identification: 003156
Unit ID: 207069
Telephone: (405) 262-2552 Carnegie Class: Assoc/HT-High Non
FAX Number: (405) 422-1200 Calendar System: Semester
URL: www.redlandscc.edu
Established: 1938 Annual Undergrad Tuition & Fees (In-District): $5,360
Enrollment: 1,917 Coed
Affiliation or Control: State/Local IRS Status: 501(c)3
Highest Offering: Associate Degree
Accreditation: HLC, ADNUR

01 President ....Mr. Jack BRYANT
05 Chief Academic & Compliance Officer ....Ms. Rose Marie MOORE
100 Exec Vice Pres /Chief of Staff ....Ms. Jena MARR
47 Dept Head of Agriculture ....Ms. Annie PEARSON
18 Director Physical Plant ....Mr. Richard BUCHHOLZ
08 Director Learning Resource Center ....Vacant
06 Registrar/Director Student Records ....Ms. Holly AVILA
37 Director Financial Aid ....Ms. Paris PRZEKURAT
41 Athletic Director ....Mr. Eli ZUCKSWORTH

13 Director of Information Technology ... Mr. Jeff PEARCE
22 Director of Upward Bound ... Mrs. Kacey DANIELS
09 Coord of Institutional Research ... Mr. Troy MILLIGAN
32 Exec Director of Student Services ... Mrs. Tricia HOBSON
21 Business Office Supervisor ... Mrs. Brenda HARKINS
15 Coordinator Personnel/Payroll ... Mrs. Kim ANDRADE
26 Exec Director of External Affairs ... Mrs. Dayna ROWE
39 Coordinator of Resident Life ... Ms. Tina JACOBS

Rogers State University (A)

1701 W Will Rogers Boulevard,
Claremore OK 74017-3252

County: Rogers — FICE Identification: 003168
Unit ID: 207661
Telephone: (918) 343-7777 — Carnegie Class: Bac-Diverse
FAX Number: (918) 343-7898 — Calendar System: Semester
URL: www.rsu.edu
Established: 1909 — Annual Undergrad Tuition & Fees (In-State): $7,470
Enrollment: 3,400 — Coed
Affiliation or Control: State — IRS Status: 501(c)3
Highest Offering: Master's
Accreditation: HLC, NUR

01 President ... Dr. Larry RICE
05 Vice President for Academic Affairs ... Dr. Richard BECK
10 VP for Administration & Finance ... Dr. Mark RASOR
30 Vice President for Development ... Mr. Steve VALENCIA
32 Vice Pres for Student Affairs/Admin ... Dr. Robert GOLTRA
12 Director Bartlesville Campus ... Ms. Ronda RIDEN
20 Assoc VP for Academic Affairs ... Dr. Mary MILLIKIN
21 Comptroller/Asst Vice Pres Bus Affs ... Mr. Michael ALLGOOD
12 Director Pryor Campus ... Mr. Brett ROWH
107 Dean School of Professional Studies ... Dr. Susan WILLIS
49 Dean School of Arts and Sciences ... Dr. Keith MARTIN
35 Director of Student Development ... Ms. Jeana Rae CONN
08 Interim Director of the Library ... Ms. Kaitlin CROTTY
07 Director of Admissions ... Mr. Lee JOHNSON
29 Director of Alumni Engagement ... Mr. Travis PECK
04 Exec Assistant to the President ... Ms. Alyssa CRAVENS
18 Director Physical Plant ... Mr. Karl REYNOLDS
19 Campus Police Sergeant ... Mr. Joe BATT
26 Director of Marketing ... Mr. Brandon IRBY
37 Director of Financial Aid ... Vacant
91 Director Administrative Computing ... Ms. Cathy BURNS
13 Director Information Technology ... Mr. Brian REEVES
15 Director of Human Resources ... Ms. Jamil HAYNES
41 Director of Athletics ... Dr. Chris RATCLIFF
39 Director Residential Life ... Ms. Kyla SHORT
09 Director of Institutional Research ... Ms. Shelly BORGSTROM
06 Registrar ... Mr. Bradley HAMMOND

Rogers State University-Bartlesville (B)

401 South Dewey Avenue, Bartlesville OK 74003
Telephone: (918) 338-8000 — Identification: 770379
Accreditation: &HLC

Rogers State University-Pryor (C)

2155 Highway 69A, Pryor Creek OK 74361
Telephone: (918) 825-6117 — Identification: 770380
Accreditation: &HLC

Rose State College (D)

6420 SE 15th, Midwest City OK 73110-2799

County: Oklahoma — FICE Identification: 009185
Unit ID: 207670
Telephone: (405) 733-7673 — Carnegie Class: Assoc/MT-VT-High Trad
FAX Number: (405) 733-7399 — Calendar System: Semester
URL: www.rose.edu
Established: 1970 — Annual Undergrad Tuition & Fees (In-District): $4,754
Enrollment: 6,722 — Coed
Affiliation or Control: State/Local — IRS Status: 501(c)3
Highest Offering: Associate Degree
Accreditation: HLC, ADNUR, CAHIIM, COARC, DA, DH, MLTAD, NAEYC, RAD

01 President ... Dr. Jeanie WEBB
10 Exec Vice President and CFO ... Dr. Kent LASHLEY
05 Vice President for Academic Affairs ... Ms. Isabelle BILLEN
32 Vice President for Student Affairs ... Mr. Lance NEWBOLD
26 Exec Dir PR & Comm/Govt Liaison ... Dr. Bradley BARRICK
13 Vice President for Info Technology ... Mr. John PRIMO
41 Exec Dir Athletic Programs ... Mr. Coty COOPER
102 Vice Pres Foundation & Resource Dev ... Ms. Cindy MIKEMAN
20 AVP Acad Affs & Inst Effectiveness ... Mr. Travis HURST
35 Assoc Vice Pres for Student Life ... Ms. Kirby HARZMAN
21 Sr Dir Fiscal Operations ... Mr. Raymond BLANKE
15 AVP Human Res/Affirm Action Ofcr ... Ms. Alberta NUTTER
109 Assoc VP for Campus Operations ... Mr. Richard ANDREWS
84 Assoc VP Enrollment Mgmt/ Registrar ... Ms. Mechelle AITSON-ROESSLER
37 Director Financial Aid ... Mr. Steve DAFFER
18 Director Operations ... Mr. Ardie RODGERS
41 Dir Health & Wellness Activities ... Mr. Chris LELAND
88 Director Special Services ... Dr. Joanne STAFFORD
08 Dean Learning Resources Center ... Mr. Chris MEYER
50 Dean Business & Info Tech Division ... Dr. Mark TIPPIN
54 Dean Engineering & Science Division ... Dr. Ryan STODDARD
79 Dean Liberal Arts Division ... Ms. Toni CASTILLO
76 Dean Health Sciences Division ... Ms. Barbara BAUMEISTER
88 Exec Dir Faculty Staff Advancement ... Dr. Juanita ORTIZ
101 Exec Asst to the President & Board ... Ms. Michelle NUTTER
19 Coord of Safety/Security/Risk Mgmt ... Mr. Joedon HUGHES
39 Director of Residence Life ... Ms. Kim QUERI
28 Exec Dir Diversity & Cultural Affs ... Dr. Monique BRUNER
118 Director Payroll & Employee Benefit ... Ms. Krista NORTON
04 Sr Exec Admin Asst to the President ... Ms. Emily FISHER
88 Dir Student Union & Event Services ... Dr. Anita POOLE-ENDSLEY
103 Director Workforce Development ... Vacant
106 Dean of E-learning & Acad Outreach ... Ms. Dana LINDON-BURGETT
108 Director Data Research ... Mr. John CAIN

Seminole State College (E)

PO Box 351, Seminole OK 74818-0351

County: Seminole — FICE Identification: 003178
Unit ID: 207740
Telephone: (405) 382-9950 — Carnegie Class: Assoc/HT-High Trad
FAX Number: (405) 382-3122 — Calendar System: Semester
URL: www.sscok.edu
Established: 1931 — Annual Undergrad Tuition & Fees (In-District): $5,190
Enrollment: 1,476 — Coed
Affiliation or Control: State/Local — IRS Status: 501(c)3
Highest Offering: Associate Degree
Accreditation: HLC, ADNUR, MLTAD, PTAA

01 President ... Ms. Lana REYNOLDS
05 Vice President Academic Affairs ... Dr. Amanda ESTEY
10 Vice President Fiscal Affairs ... Vacant
32 Vice President of Student Affairs ... Dr. Bill KNOWLES
13 Director Mgmt Information Systems ... Mr. Marc HUNTER
66 Director of Nursing ... Ms. Crystal BRAY
06 Registrar ... Mrs. Sheila MORRIS
15 Director Human Resources ... Mrs. Holly WILSON-BYRD
26 Director of Public Relations ... Ms. Kim PRINGLE
04 Administrative Asst to President ... Ms. Mechell DOWNEY
37 Director Student Financial Aid ... Ms. Edie CATHEY
39 Director Student Housing ... Ms. Melinda SIMS
41 Athletic Director ... Mr. Mike ST. JOHN
08 Chief Library Officer ... Ms. Robin TYLER
18 Chief Facilities/Physical Plant Ofc ... Mr. Clint ROBERSTSON
19 Director Security/Safety ... Mr. Shane MARSHALL

Southeastern Oklahoma State University (F)

425 W University Blvd, Durant OK 74701-3330

County: Bryan — FICE Identification: 003179
Unit ID: 207847
Telephone: (580) 745-2000 — Carnegie Class: Masters/L
FAX Number: N/A — Calendar System: Semester
URL: www.se.edu
Established: 1909 — Annual Undergrad Tuition & Fees (In-State): $6,750
Enrollment: 5,607 — Coed
Affiliation or Control: State — IRS Status: 501(c)3
Highest Offering: Master's
Accreditation: HLC, AAB, CAEP, MUS

01 President ... Dr. Thomas NEWSOM
05 Vice Pres Academic Affairs ... Dr. Teresa GOLDEN
10 Vice Pres Business Affairs/CFO ... Mr. Dennis WESTMAN
32 Vice President of Student Affairs ... Ms. Liz MCCRAW
07 Assoc Dean Admissions/Registrar ... Ms. Kristie LUKE
58 Dean Graduate School ... Vacant
37 Director Student Financial Aid ... Mr. Tony LEHRLING
08 Library Director ... Ms. Sandra THOMAS
41 Director of Athletics ... Mr. Keith BAXTER
26 Dir Univ Comm/Spec Asst Pres ... Mr. Alan BURTON
21 Director Finance/Controller ... Ms. Crystal CHEEK
18 Director Facilities/Physical Plant ... Mr. Dan SIMMONS
28 Director of Compliance and Safety ... Mr. Mike DAVIS
96 Purchasing Agent ... Ms. Dana BELL
40 Book Store Manager ... Ms. Jackie CODNER
29 Director Alumni Rels & Univ Develop ... Mr. Mark WEBB
106 Dir Online Education/E-learning ... Ms. Christala SMITH
19 Chief of Police ... Mr. Durwood COOK
39 Director Student Housing ... Dr. Kelly D'ARCY
04 Exec Asst to President ... Ms. Terri ROGERS
06 Registrar ... Ms. Rachel TOEWS
15 Director of Human Resources ... Ms. Marjorie ROBERTSON

Southern Nazarene University (G)

6729 NW 39 Expressway, Bethany OK 73008-2694

County: Oklahoma — FICE Identification: 003149
Unit ID: 206862
Telephone: (405) 789-6400 — Carnegie Class: Masters/L
FAX Number: (405) 491-6381 — Calendar System: Semester
URL: www.snu.edu
Established: 1899 — Annual Undergrad Tuition & Fees: $26,000
Enrollment: 2,208 — Coed
Affiliation or Control: Church Of The Nazarene — IRS Status: 501(c)3
Highest Offering: Doctorate
Accreditation: HLC, ACBSP, CAEP, MUS, NURSE

01 President ... Dr. J. Keith NEWMAN
05 Provost & VP Academic Affairs ... Dr. Timothy EADES
03 Executive Vice President ... Dr. Mike REDWINE
10 Vice President Financial Affairs ... Dr. Scott STRAWN
88 VP Intercultural Lrng/Engagement ... Dr. Lena CROUSO
26 VP External Relations ... Rev. Larry MORRIS
84 VP for Trad Enrollment & Marketing ... Dr. Marian REDWINE
42 Univ Pastor/Dean of the Chapel ... Dr. Blair SPINDLE
21 Assoc VP for Financial Services ... Mr. Chris PETERSON
79 VP Acad Affairs Traditional ... Dr. Steve BETTS
58 VP Academic Affairs PGS ... Dr. Mark WINSLOW
06 Registrar ... Mr. Charles CHITWOOD
37 Director Student Financial Aid ... Mr. Perry DIEHM
37 Dir of Financial Aid/Traditional ... Mrs. Jamie SALAZAR
32 Dean of Students ... Mrs. Katy BRADLEY
38 Director Student Counseling ... Dr. Scott SECOR
36 Director Career Planning/Placement ... Mrs. Michelle MULLENS
08 Director Learning Resources Center ... Mr. Joshua ACHIPA
29 Exec Dir Alumni Relations ... Mr. Todd BRANT
13 Director Information Technology ... Mr. Keith CUMMINGS
121 Assoc VP for Student Success ... Dr. Twyler EARL
09 Director Institutional Research ... Mrs. Debra HERLIHY
84 VP for Enrollment/Marketing PGS ... Mrs. Johnna VANOVER
66 Director of Nursing ... Dr. Brittany CUMMINGS
15 Director Human Resources ... Mrs. Gail COLLIER
18 Director of Physical Plant ... Mr. Ron LESTER
24 Director Network ... Mr. Geoffrey FREELANDER
88 Social Media Coordinator ... Mrs. Hailee THOMPSON
40 Bookstore Manager ... Vacant
41 Athletic Director ... Mr. Daniel THOMASON
53 VP Strategy & Innovation ... Dr. Dennis WILLIAMS
04 Executive Asst to President ... Mrs. Tollya SPINDLE
19 Director Security/Safety ... Mr. Dan HANSEN
25 Chief Contracts/Grants Admin ... Dr. Gwen HACKLER
39 Director Student Housing ... Mrs. Katy BRADLEY
28 Director of Diversity ... Dr. Lena CROUSO

Southwestern Christian University (H)

PO Box 340, 7210 NW 39th Expressway,
Bethany OK 73008-0340

County: Oklahoma — FICE Identification: 003180
Unit ID: 207856
Telephone: (405) 789-7661 — Carnegie Class: Bac-Diverse
FAX Number: (405) 495-0078 — Calendar System: Semester
URL: www.swcu.edu
Established: 1946 — Annual Undergrad Tuition & Fees: $19,114
Enrollment: 486 — Coed
Affiliation or Control: Pentecostal Holiness Church — IRS Status: 501(c)3
Highest Offering: Master's
Accreditation: HLC

01 President ... Dr. Tom L. MURRAY
05 VP Academic Affairs ... Dr. Adrian HINKLE
10 VP for Business and Finance ... Mr. Kyle TAYLOR
32 Vice President for Student Services ... Mr. Brad DAVIS
41 Vice President of Athletics ... Mr. Mark ARTHUR
37 Director of Financial Aid ... Mrs. Rita PALMER
07 Vice President of Admissions ... Mr. Joe BLACKWELL
08 Director of Library Services ... Mr. Michael LOWDER
06 Registrar ... Ms. Ifeoma FAVOUR OKORO
58 Director of Graduate Studies ... Mrs. Shelley GROVES
35 Dean of Students ... Mr. Zach SHERRILL
20 Dean of Academics ... Vacant
30 Chief Development Officer ... Ms. April BLACK
18 Director of Plant/Property Mgmt ... Mr. Robert PALMER
26 Director of Sports Information/PR ... Mr. Philip YOUNTS
13 Director of Information Technology ... Mr. Scott KLEPPER
106 Director of Online Education ... Ms. Misty FOSTER
15 Director of Human Resources ... Mrs. Rita PALMER
04 Executive Asst to President ... Ms. Erin BROWN
19 Director Security/Safety ... Mr. Darin DAVIS
39 Director Student Life/Resident Dir ... Ms. Kaylee BISHOP
09 Director of Institutional Research ... Mr. Jesse HEATH
108 Director of Assessment ... Ms. Patty CLOUSE

Southwestern Oklahoma State University (I)

100 Campus Drive, Weatherford OK 73096-3098

County: Custer — FICE Identification: 003181
Unit ID: 207865
Telephone: (580) 772-6611 — Carnegie Class: Masters/L
FAX Number: (580) 774-3795 — Calendar System: Semester
URL: www.swosu.edu
Established: 1901 — Annual Undergrad Tuition & Fees (In-State): $7,913
Enrollment: 4,898 — Coed
Affiliation or Control: State — IRS Status: 501(c)3
Highest Offering: First Professional Degree
Accreditation: HLC, ACBSP, CAEP, CAHIIM, IACBE, MLTAD, MUS, NAIT, NUR, OTA, PHAR, PTAA, RAD

01 President ... Dr. Diana LOVELL
10 VP Business and Finance ... Ms. Brenda K. BURGESS
05 VP for Academic Affairs/Provost ... Dr. Joel KENDALL
32 VP Student Affairs ... Dr. Patsy PARKER
20 Assoc Provost Acad Affairs ... Vacant
26 VP for Marketing/Public Relations ... Mr. Brian D. ADLER
111 Asst Vice Pres Inst Advancement ... Mr. Garrett KING
35 Dean of Students ... Mr. Joshua ENGLE
21 Business Affairs Dir/Comptroller ... Mr. Steve JOHNSON
13 Information Technology Services Dir ... Ms. Dian RAY
06 Registrar ... Mr. Shamus MOORE
08 Library Dir ... Mr. Jason M. DUPREE
37 Student Financial Services Dir ... Mr. Jerome L. WICHERT
15 VP Human Resources/Affirm Action ... Mr. David MISAK
84 Enrollment Mgmt/Career Services Dir ... Mr. Todd BOYD

41 Athletics Director ... Mr. Todd HELTON
06 Registrar Sayre Campus ... Ms. Terry BILLEY
38 Counseling Services Dir ... Ms. Susan ELLIS
18 Physical Plant Dir ... Mr. James SKINNER
57 Facilities Dir FAC & PCEC ... Mr. Nate DOWNS
36 Career Exploration Coordinator ... Ms. Heather HUMMEL
58 Dean College of Prof/Grad Studies ... Dr. Chad L. KINDER
49 Dean College of Arts/Sciences ... Dr. Jason JOHNSON
67 Dean College of Pharmacy ... Dr. David RALPH
12 Dean College of Assoc/Applied Prog ... Mr. Bill SWARTWOOD
53 Assoc Dean Sch of Behavioral Sci ... Dr. Randy BARNETT
50 Assoc Dean Sch of Business/Tech ... Dr. Patsy PARKER
66 Assoc Dean Sch of Nursing ... Dr. Darryl BARNETT
04 Exec Assistant to the President ... Ms. Misty ZINK
105 Web Services Dir ... Ms. Susan MCELHANEY
106 CETL Dir ... Ms. Lisa FRIESSEN
108 Assessment & Testing Dir ... Ms. Jan KLIEWER
19 Public Safety Dir ... Ms. Kendra BROWN
25 Office of Sponsored Programs Dir ... Dr. Lori GWYN
39 Residence Life & Housing Dir ... Mr. Chad MARTIN
88 Univ Press Mgr ... Ms. Kandy HOUSE
88 Business Enterprise Center Dir ... Mr. Doug MISAK
40 Univ Bookstore Dir ... Ms. Ashley HANCOCK
88 Upward Bound Dir ... Ms. Jamie NOVEY
23 Wellness Center Dir ... Mr. Scott MILLER
88 Student Union Dir ... Ms. Jackie REAGAN
88 Food Services Dir ... Ms. Radonna SAWATZKY
104 International Student Affairs Dir ... Vacant
124 Retention Management Coordinator ... Dr. Wendy YODER
07 Director of Admissions ... Mr. Todd BOYD

† Campus at Sayre offers a two-year degree and is regionally accredited (NH) under parent institution.

Spartan College of Aeronautics and Technology (A)

8820 E Pine Street, Tulsa OK 74115
County: Tulsa FICE Identification: 007678
Unit ID: 207254
Telephone: (918) 836-6886 Carnegie Class: Bac/Assoc-Mixed
FAX Number: (918) 831-5287 Calendar System: Other
URL: www.spartan.edu
Established: 1928 Annual Undergrad Tuition & Fees: $21,915
Enrollment: 708 Coed
Affiliation or Control: Proprietary IRS Status: Proprietary
Highest Offering: Baccalaureate
Accreditation: ACCSC

00 CEO ... Mr. Rob POLSTON
01 President ... Ms. Kari PAHNO
05 Chief Academic & Operations Ofcr ... Dr. Todd CELLINI
10 CFO ... Vacant
11 Campus Director ... Mr. Marc SHERROD
32 Dean of Student Affairs ... Ms. Alessia CUMMINGS
18 Dean of Operations ... Mr. Damon BOWLING
04 Executive Asst to President ... Ms. Catherine LOEPER
07 Director of Admissions ... Mr. Jeff STOLTENBERG
37 Director Student Financial Aid ... Ms. Megan COKER
06 Registrar ... Ms. Kari CAGLE

Tulsa Community College (B)

6111 E Skelly Dr, Tulsa OK 74135
County: Tulsa FICE Identification: 009763
Unit ID: 207935
Telephone: (918) 595-7000 Carnegie Class: Assoc/MT-VT-High Trad
FAX Number: (918) 595-7092 Calendar System: Semester
URL: www.tulsacc.edu
Established: 1968 Annual Undergrad Tuition & Fees (In-State): $3,445
Enrollment: 15,568 Coed
Affiliation or Control: State IRS Status: 501(c)3
Highest Offering: Associate Degree
Accreditation: HLC, ADNUR, CAHIIM, COARC, CVT, DH, MLTAD, OTA, PTAA, #RAD

01 President/CEO ... Dr. Leigh GOODSON
05 Sr VP and Chief Academic Officer ... Dr. Angela SIVADON
111 VP Advancement & Found Pres ... Ms. Kari SHULTS
11 VP Administration and COO ... Mr. Sean A. WEINS
103 VP Workforce Development ... Mr. Pete SELDEN
43 General Counsel ... Ms. MacKenzie WILFONG
45 Chief Strategy Officer ... Dr. Lindsay WHITE
32 VP Student Success & Equity ... Dr. Eunice TARVER
20 AVP Academic & Campus Operations ... Dr. Greg STONE
20 AVP Academic Affairs ... Dr. Kristopher COPELAND
10 Chief Financial Officer ... Mr. Mark MCMULLEN
13 AVP Admin Operations & CTO ... Mr. Michael SIFTAR
15 Chief Human Resources Officer ... Mr. Evan JEWSBURY
84 Assoc VP Enrollment & Retention ... Ms. Eileen KENNEY
37 Assistant VP Financial Aid ... Ms. Norma NAVARRO-CASTELLANOS
26 Dir Marketing/Communications ... Ms. Laurie TILLEY
60 Dean Comm/English/World Lang ... Dr. Paula WILLYARD
08 Dean Libraries ... Ms. Paula SETTOON
49 Dean Liberal Arts & Public Service ... Dr. Brad DUREN
81 Dean Science & Aeronautics ... Ms. Julie PORTERFIELD
57 Dean Visual & Performing Arts ... Ms. Kelly CLARK
76 Dean Health Sciences ... Ms. Jenny FIELDS
54 Dean Mathematics & Engineering ... Ms. Sheila YOUNGBLOOD
88 Dean Center for Creativity ... Ms. Annina COLLIER
89 Dean Engaged Learning ... Ms. Cindy SHANKS
50 Dean Business & IT ... Mr. Travis WHITE
121 Dean Student Success ... Ms. Jennifer BEATIE
35 Dean Student Success & Equity ... Mr. Scott GOVE
124 Dean Retention/Engagement ... Ms. Corinice WILSON
18 Dir Physical Facilities Operations ... Mr. Steven COX
18 Dir Facilities Plng/Constr Mgmt ... Mr. Joel CARR
22 Dir Civil Rights Compl/Title IX ... Ms. Heather HANCOCK
96 Dir Purch & Inventory Control ... Mr. Bill CREECH
09 Director Institutional Research ... Ms. Kirstin KRUG
19 Chief of Police ... Mr. Melvin MURDOCK
25 Dir Sponsored Programs ... Dr. Barbara WAXMAN
104 Dir Fac Dev & Global Learning ... Dr. Douglas PRICE
106 Faculty Coord Online Learning ... Ms. Jennifer CAMPBELL
51 Dir Continuing Education ... Vacant
06 College Registrar ... Ms. Lindsay FIELDS
07 Dir Admissions/Prosp Stdnt Svcs ... Ms. Rachael ACHIVARE-HILL
36 Dir Career & Retention Programs ... Mr. Mark HAYS
112 Chief Development Officer ... Ms. Megan KORN
105 Web Manager ... Ms. Melissa CLOUD
92 Honors Program Coord ... Dr. Allen CULPEPPER
04 Exec Asst to President ... Ms. Carrie BATESON
108 Assessment Manager ... Dr. Allison TIFFT
38 Director Wellness Services ... Ms. Jessica HEAVIN

Tulsa Community College Metro Campus (C)

909 South Boston Avenue, Tulsa OK 74119
Telephone: (918) 595-7224 Identification: 770383
Accreditation: &HLC, DMS

Tulsa Community College Northeast Campus (D)

3727 East Apache Street, Tulsa OK 74115
Telephone: (918) 595-7524 Identification: 770384
Accreditation: &HLC, EMT

Tulsa Community College Southeast Campus (E)

10300 East 81st Street, Tulsa OK 74133
Telephone: (918) 595-7724 Identification: 770385
Accreditation: &HLC

Tulsa Community College West Campus (F)

7505 W 41st Street, Tulsa OK 74107-8633
Telephone: (918) 595-8060 Identification: 770386
Accreditation: &HLC

Tulsa Welding School (G)

2545 E 11th Street, Tulsa OK 74104-3909
County: Tulsa FICE Identification: 009618
Unit ID: 207962
Telephone: (918) 587-6789 Carnegie Class: Spec 2-yr-Tech
FAX Number: (918) 587-8170 Calendar System: Other
URL: www.tws.edu
Established: 1949 Annual Undergrad Tuition & Fees: N/A
Enrollment: 785 Coed
Affiliation or Control: Proprietary IRS Status: Proprietary
Highest Offering: Associate Degree
Accreditation: ACCSC

01 Campus President ... Mr. Carlton SMITH
05 Director of Student Outcomes ... Vacant
07 Director of Adult Admissions ... Vacant
37 Director of Financial Aid ... Vacant

University of Central Oklahoma (H)

100 N University Drive, Edmond OK 73034-5209
County: Oklahoma FICE Identification: 003152
Unit ID: 206941
Telephone: (405) 974-2000 Carnegie Class: Masters/L
FAX Number: (405) 359-5841 Calendar System: Semester
URL: www.uco.edu
Established: 1890 Annual Undergrad Tuition & Fees (In-State): N/A
Enrollment: N/A Coed
Affiliation or Control: State IRS Status: 501(c)3
Highest Offering: Master's
Accreditation: HLC, ART, CAATE, CAEPN, CIDA, DIETD, DIETI, EXSC, FEPAC, FUSER, MPCAC, MUS, NURSE, SP, SPAA

01 President ... Ms. Patti NEUHOLD-RAVIKUMAR
05 Provost ... Dr. Charlotte SIMMONS
11 Vice Pres for Operations ... Mr. Kevin FREEMAN
32 Vice President ESS ... Mr. Christopher LYNCH
13 Chief Information Officer ... Ms. Sonya WATKINS
26 Vice Pres University Relations ... Ms. Adrienne NOBLES
30 Vice Pres Development ... Mr. Art COTTON
06 Associate Vice President/Registrar ... Dr. Adam JOHNSON
20 Assoc VP Academic Affairs ... Vacant
108 Assoc VP Inst Effectiveness ... Dr. Gary STEWARD
21 Asst VP Financial Operations ... Mr. Frank TURBEVILLE
18 Asst Vice Pres Facilities Mgt ... Mr. Kevin TERO
35 Asst Vice Pres Student Affairs ... Mr. Cole STANLEY
88 Asst Vice Pres Operations ... Mr. Benjamin HASTINGS
41 Athletic Director ... Mr. Stan WAGNON
09 Director Institutional Research ... Mr. William SCHEIDELER
08 Exec Director University Libraries ... Dr. Habib TABATABAI
37 Director Student Financial Services ... Mr. Jason PRIDEAUX
29 Director Alumni Relations ... Ms. Lauri MONETTI
85 Exec Dir Global Affairs ... Dr. Dennis DUNHAM
19 Exec Dir Public Safety/Trans ... Mr. Jeff HARP
15 VP People & Culture ... Ms. Diane FEINBERG
88 Asst Director Leadership Central ... Ms. Claire PAINTER
07 Dir of Undergraduate Admissions ... Mr. Dallas CALDWELL
28 Director of Diversity & Inclusion .. Ms. Dene ROSEBURR-OLOTU
96 Director of Purchasing ... Mr. David YOUNG
50 Dean of Business Administration ... Dr. Jeremy OLLER
53 Dean College Education ... Dr. Donna COBB
49 Int Dean College of Liberal Arts ... Dr. David MACEY
81 Dean College Math/Science ... Dr. Gloria CADDELL
58 Dean Graduate Studies ... Dr. Jeanetta SIMS
57 Dean of College Fine Arts & Design ... Ms. Charleen WEIDELL

University of Oklahoma Health Sciences Center (I)

1100 N. Lindsay, Oklahoma City OK 73104
Telephone: (405) 271-4000 FICE Identification: 005889
Accreditation: &HLC, ARCPA, AUD, CAMPEP, DENT, DH, DIETC, DIETI, DMS, HSA, IPSY, MED, NMT, NURSE, OT, PDPSY, PH, PHAR, PTA, RAD, RTT, SP

† Regional accreditation is carried under the parent institution in Norman, OK.

University of Oklahoma Norman Campus (J)

660 Parrington Oval, Norman OK 73019-3070
County: Cleveland FICE Identification: 003184
Unit ID: 207500
Telephone: (405) 325-0311 Carnegie Class: DU-Highest
FAX Number: (405) 325-7605 Calendar System: Semester
URL: www.ou.edu
Established: 1890 Annual Undergrad Tuition & Fees (In-State): $11,688
Enrollment: 27,772 Coed
Affiliation or Control: State IRS Status: 501(c)3
Highest Offering: Doctorate
Accreditation: HLC, AAB, CAEP, CIDA, CONST, JOUR, LAW, LIB, LSAR, MUS, PLNG, SPAA, SW

01 President ... Mr. Joseph HARROZ, JR.
10 SVP & Chief Financial Officer ... Mr. Matthew D. BROCKWELL
11 Interim VP for Operations ... Mr. Brian E. HOLDERREAD
05 Sr Vice President/Provost ... Dr. Andre-Denis G. WRIGHT
43 Interim VP/General Counsel ... Ms. Susanna GATTONI
32 VP Student Affairs/Dean of Students ... Dr. David A. SURRATT
101 VP Univ Governance/Exec Sec ... Mr. Tim RHODES
100 VP Exec Affairs/Chief of Staff ... Mr. M. Sean BURRAGE
106 VP for Online Learning ... Dr. Gregg A. GARN
88 Sr Assoc VP Univ Outreach ... Dr. Belinda P. BISCOE
58 Dean Graduate College ... Dr. Randy S. HEWES
46 Int VP for Research & Partnrshps ... Dr. Tomas J. DIAZ DE LA RUBIA
26 VP for Marketing/Communications ... Vacant
15 VP & Chief Human Resources Ofcr ... Ms. Dorothy ANDERSON
13 Senior Associate VP and CIO ... Mr. David M. HORTON
86 Chief Government Affairs Officer ... Ms. Hollye HUNT
121 Assoc Prov for Acad Advising ... Dr. Kathleen S. SMITH
09 Assoc Provost/Dir Inst Research ... Ms. Susannah B. LIVINGOOD
18 Assoc VP Facilities Management ... Dr. Matthew C. ROM
109 Director of Food Services ... Mr. Frank M. HENRY
41 VP for Intercollegiate Athletics ... Mr. Joseph R. CASTIGLIONE
21 Assistant VP & Controller ... Ms. Karen S. SMITH
23 AVP for Student Affs/Health Svcs ... Dr. William R. WAYNE
36 Director Career Services ... Ms. Robin E. HUSTON
19 Chief of Police ... Mr. Nathaniel R. TARVER
22 Equal Opportunity Officer ... Ms. Christine H. TAYLOR
84 VP for Enrollment Management ... Mr. Jeffrey J. BLAHNIK
85 Dir International Student Services ... Ms. Robyn D. ROJAS
104 Director Education Abroad ... Ms. Shanna M. VINCENT
37 Dir of Financial Aid & Scholarships ... Mr. Bradley T. BURNETT
51 Dean College of PACS ... Vacant
48 Dean Col of Architecture ... Mr. Hans E. BUTZER
49 Dean Col of Arts & Sciences ... Dr. David M. WROBEL
53 Dean Jeannine Rainbolt Col of Educ ... Dr. Stacy L. REEDER
54 Dean Gallogly Col of Engineering ... Dr. John KLIER
57 Dean Weitzenhoffer Col Fine Arts ... Ms. Mary Margaret HOLT
61 Dean College of Law ... Ms. Katheleen G. GUZMAN
08 Dean University Libraries ... Ms. Denise STEPHENS
65 Dean Col Atmospheric/Geographic Sc ... Dr. Berrien MOORE, III
50 Dean Price Col of Business ... Dr. Corey C. PHELPS
92 Interim Dean Honors College ... Dr. R. Rich HAMERLA
60 Dean Gaylord Col Journal/Mass Comm ... Mr. C. Ed KELLEY
89 Dean University College ... Dr. Nicole J. CAMPBELL
65 Dean Mewborne Col of Earth & Energy ... Dr. J. Michael STICE
82 Assoc Prov/Dean Col Intl Studies ... Dr. Scott A. FRITZEN
20 Vice Provost for Instruction ... Dr. Mark C. MORVANT
28 VP Diversity/Equity & Inclusion ... Dr. Belinda H. HYPPOLITE
04 Administrative Asst to President ... Ms. Taylor J. AUSTIN
116 Chief Audit Executive ... Mr. Charles D. WRIGHT
35 Assoc Provost Fac & Student Affairs ... Mr. Christopher O. WALKER
14 Exec Dir of Technology Advancement ... Mr. Aaron A. BIGGS
88 Assoc Provost Academic Engagement ... Ms. Michelle A. EODICE
114 Assoc VP for Budget & Finance ... Mr. Stewart M. BERKINSHAW
122 Assoc Dir Fraternity/Sorority Pgms ... Ms. Kylie FRISBY
06 Registrar ... Ms. Kellie J. DYER

† Tuition is based on 30 credit hour per year.

University of Oklahoma Schusterman Center (A)
4502 E 41st Street, Tulsa OK 74135-2512
Telephone: (918) 660-3000 Identification: 770387
Accreditation: &HLC, ARCPA, OT

University of Science and Arts of Oklahoma (B)
1727 W Alabama, Chickasha OK 73018-5322
County: Grady FICE Identification: 003167
Unit ID: 207722
Telephone: (405) 224-3140 Carnegie Class: Bac-A&S
FAX Number: (405) 574-1220 Calendar System: Trimester
URL: www.usao.edu
Established: 1908 Annual Undergrad Tuition & Fees (In-State): $8,040
Enrollment: 733 Coed
Affiliation or Control: State IRS Status: 501(c)3
Highest Offering: Baccalaureate
Accreditation: HLC, CAEP, MUS

01 President ...Dr. John H. FEAVER
05 Vice President for Academic Affairs ...Dr. Donna MILES
10 Vice Pres for Business & Finance ...Mr. Mick D. COPONITI
32 VP Student Success/Human Resources ...Ms. Monica TREVINO
13 VP Univ Advancement/Info Technology ...Mr. Sid HUDSON
30 Vice President for Development ...Mr. JP AUDAS
08 Director of Library ...Ms. Nicole MCMONAGLE
06 Registrar/Dir of Enrollment/Records ...Ms. Chelsea PHILLIPS
26 Dir of Communications/Marketing ...Ms. Amy GODDARD
37 Director of Financial Aid ...Ms. Laura I. COPONITI
32 Dean of Students/Dir Student Svcs ...Ms. Nancy HUGHES
29 Director of Alumni Development ...Vacant
18 Director of Physical Plant ...Mr. Mike COPONITI
09 Institutional Research Analyst ...Ms. Kristi JOHN
15 Director Personnel Services ...Ms. Monica TREVINO
07 Dean of Admissions & Recruitment ...Mr. Sheppard MCCONNELL
38 Director Student Counseling ...Dr. Misty STEELE
49 Chair Div of Arts & Humanities ...Dr. Stephen WEBER
50 Chair Div of Social Sci & Business ...Dr. James VAUGHN
53 Chair Division of Education ...Dr. Sarah LAYMAN
81 Chair Div of Science/Physical Educ ...Dr. J.C SANDERS
88 Chair Interdisciplinary Studies ...Dr. Shelley REES
41 Athletic Director ...Mr. Brisco MCPHERSON
19 Emergency Preparedness/Security ...Mr. Russell POOL

University of Tulsa (C)
800 S Tucker, Tulsa OK 74104
County: Tulsa FICE Identification: 003185
Unit ID: 207971
Telephone: (918) 631-2000 Carnegie Class: DU-Higher
FAX Number: (918) 631-2033 Calendar System: Semester
URL: www.utulsa.edu
Established: 1894 Annual Undergrad Tuition & Fees: $43,985
Enrollment: 3,960 Coed
Affiliation or Control: Independent Non-Profit IRS Status: 501(c)3
Highest Offering: Doctorate
Accreditation: HLC, ANEST, CAATE, CLPSY, LAW, MUS, NUR, SP

01 President ...Mr. Brad CARSON
04 Exec Assistant to the President ...Mrs. Doreen GRIFFITHS
41 Director of Athletics ...Mr. Rick DICKSON
05 Vice Prov Faculty Affs/Acad Init ...Ms. Jennifer L. AIREY
08 Int Ida McFarlin Dean of Library ...Mr. Bob PICKERING
58 Int Dean of Graduate School ...Ms. Jennifer L. AIREY
49 Dean Arts & Sciences ...Dr. Karen PETERSEN
50 Dean of the Collins Col of Business ...Ms. Kathy TAYLOR
54 Dean Engineering/Natural Sciences ...Dr. James R. SOREM, JR.
61 Dean of Law ...Mr. Oren GRIFFIN
29 Exec Director Alumni Relations ...Ms. Amy M. FREIBERGER
26 Sr Exec Dir Marketing/Communication ...Ms. Mona CHAMBERLIN
88 Dir Public Affairs/Economic Dept ...Ms. Melissa ABDO
10 Interim Chief Financial Officer ...Mr. Eric SCHICK
21 Assoc VP & Controller ...Mr. Michael D. THESENVITZ
114 Dir of Univ Budgets for Exec VP ...Ms. Mindi FUSER
113 Bursar ...Ms. Teresa FUSELIER
96 Director Purchasing ...Ms. Stephanie EYLER
15 VP & Chief Human Resources Officer ...Ms. Barbara ABERCROMBIE
118 Employee Benefits Coordinator ...Ms. Brittany COLE
09 VP of Institutional Research ...Mr. Victor SOE
108 Director Institutional Assessment ...Ms. Monica VARNER
22 Accessibility Officer/ADA ...Ms. Tawny RIGSBY
28 VP Diversity/Equity & Inclusion ...Ms. Kelli MCLOUD-SCHINGEN
43 Deputy General Counsel ...Ms. Cheryl DIXON
19 Director Campus Security ...Mr. Clayton STATON
18 Assoc VP Operations & Facilities ...Mr. John HOLDERMAN
13 Vice Pres Information Services ...Ms. Angela KOUPLEN
90 Dir of Academic & Learning Tech ...Ms. Janet CAIRNS
91 Dir ERP Operations ...Mr. Chris FARWELL
105 Director of Web Systems ...Mr. Matthew CASTEEL
35 Dean of Students ...Mr. Michael MCCLENDON
84 Sr Vice Provost for Enroll Mgmt ...Ms. Casey REED
07 Dean of Admission ...Ms. Patricia DEBOLT
06 Registrar ...Ms. Hope GEIGER
37 Director Student Financial Svcs ...Ms. Vicki A. HENDRICKSON
39 Assoc VP for Campus Student Housing ...Ms. Melissa H. FRANCE
36 Exec Director Career Services ...Ms. Christy CAVES
38 Director Counseling & Psych Svcs ...Ms. Stephanie O'NEAL
121 Director Student Success Coach ...Ms. Christina CARTER
42 University Chaplain ...Dr. Jeffrey FRANCIS
111 VP Univ Advance/Alumni Engagement ...Ms. Kayla HALE
88 Assistant Director of Purchasing ...Ms. Natalie GILBERT
119 Chief Information Security Officer ...Mr. Jonathan KIMMITT
117 Vice Pres for Risk Mgmt ...Mr. Matt WARREN
76 Int Dean Oxley Col of Health Sci ...Mr. Ron WALKER
100 Chief of Staff ...Mrs. Jen BENNETT
88 VP Bus Continuity/Sustainability ...Ms. Robin PLOEGER
88 VP of Innovation ...Mr. Tom ADELSON

Western Oklahoma State College (D)
2801 N Main Street, Altus OK 73521-1397
County: Jackson FICE Identification: 003146
Unit ID: 208035
Telephone: (580) 477-2000 Carnegie Class: Assoc/MT-VT-High Trad
FAX Number: (580) 477-7777 Calendar System: Semester
URL: www.wosc.edu
Established: 1926 Annual Undergrad Tuition & Fees (In-State): $4,978
Enrollment: 1,353 Coed
Affiliation or Control: State IRS Status: 501(c)3
Highest Offering: Associate Degree
Accreditation: HLC, CNEA, NAEYC

01 President ...Dr. Chad WIGINTON
05 VP for Academic Affairs ...Ms. Chrystal OVERTON
10 Vice President for Business Affairs ...Ms. Melissa MCMAHON
32 Vice Pres Student Support Services ...Ms. Terri PEARSON
09 Assist Dir of Inst Effectiveness ...Ms. Anita MILLER
26 Director of Public Relations ...Ms. Maegan MARTIN
07 Director of Admissions & Registrar ...Ms. Lana SCOTT
37 Director of Financial Aid ...Ms. SaVana DENTON
30 Dir Development/Alumni Relations ...Ms. Debbie VALERIO
41 Director Athletics ...Vacant
08 Director of Learning Resources ...Ms. Suzanne ROOKER
15 Director Personnel Services ...Ms. April NELSON
18 Director Physical Plant ...Mr. Doyle JENCKS
38 Counselor ...Ms. Cheryl ORR

OREGON

American College of Healthcare Sciences (E)
5005 S Macadam, Portland OR 97239
County: Multnomah FICE Identification: 041944
Unit ID: 443599
Telephone: (503) 244-0726 Carnegie Class: Spec-4-yr-Other Health
FAX Number: (503) 244-0727 Calendar System: Semester
URL: www.achs.edu
Established: 1978 Annual Undergrad Tuition & Fees: $11,640
Enrollment: 856 Coed
Affiliation or Control: Proprietary IRS Status: Proprietary
Highest Offering: Master's
Accreditation: DEAC

01 President/CEO ...Tracey ABELL
05 Chief Academic Officer ...Dr. Tiffany RODRIGUEZ
11 Chief Operating Officer ...Brooke PILLSBURY
07 Interim Dean of Admissions ...Amanda HELLER
29 Director of Alumni & Career Svcs ...Amy SWINEHART
06 Registrar ...Jennifer MORRISON
26 Chief Marketing Officer ...Kate HARMON
37 Director of Financial Aid ...Stephanie NORTH
08 Director of Library Services ...Ashley EHMIG
22 Title IX Coordinator ...Brooke PILLSBURY

American Denturist College (F)
145 E. 12th Alley, Eugene OR 97401
County: Lane Identification: 667421
Telephone: (541) 654-5885 Carnegie Class: Not Classified
FAX Number: N/A Calendar System: Other
URL: adc.edu
Established: 2011 Annual Undergrad Tuition & Fees: N/A
Enrollment: N/A Coed
Affiliation or Control: Proprietary IRS Status: Proprietary
Highest Offering: Baccalaureate
Accreditation: DEAC

05 Director of Education ...Todd YOUNG

Blue Mountain Community College (G)
PO Box 100, Pendleton OR 97801-0100
County: Umatilla/Morrow/Baker FICE Identification: 003186
Unit ID: 208275
Telephone: (541) 276-1260 Carnegie Class: Assoc/HT-High Non
FAX Number: (541) 278-5886 Calendar System: Quarter
URL: www.bluecc.edu
Established: 1962 Annual Undergrad Tuition & Fees (In-District): $6,300
Enrollment: 1,292 Coed
Affiliation or Control: State/Local IRS Status: 501(c)3
Highest Offering: Associate Degree
Accreditation: NW

01 President ...Mr. Mark BROWNING
05 Vice President of Instruction ...Mr. John FIELDS
32 Vice Pres Student Affairs ...Vacant
11 Chief Operating Officer ...Mr. David SHELLBERG
08 Director of Library & Media Svcs ...Ms. Brittany YOUNG
102 Executive Director Foundation ...Mr. Ken DANIEL
37 Director of Student Financial Aid ...Ms. Danielle HODGEN
04 Administrative Asst to President ...Ms. Shannon FRANKLIN
10 Chief Financial Officer ...Ms. Celeste TATE
106 Dir Online Education/E-learning ...Vacant
13 Chief Info Technology Officer (CIO) ...Mr. Brad HOLDEN
38 Director Student Counseling ...Vacant
15 Chief Human Resources Officer ...Ms. Norma JAIME-SANCHEZ
41 Athletic Director ...Ms. Dawn MCCLENDON
103 Dean Workforce Development ...Ms. Tammy KRAWCZYK
124 Dean Student Retention ...Mr. Wade MULLER
84 Director Enrollment Svcs/Registrar ...Ms. Theresa BOSWORTH
18 Chief Facilities/Physical Plant ...Mr. Dwayne WILLIAMS
20 Dean Student Learning & Success ...Mr. Daniel G. ANDERSON
44 Director Annual Giving ...Mr. Ken DANIEL

Bushnell University (H)
828 E. 11th Ave., Eugene OR 97401-3745
County: Lane FICE Identification: 003208
Unit ID: 209409
Telephone: (541) 343-1641 Carnegie Class: Masters/S
FAX Number: (541) 343-9159 Calendar System: Semester
URL: www.bushnell.edu
Established: 1895 Annual Undergrad Tuition & Fees: $32,320
Enrollment: 717 Coed
Affiliation or Control: Christian Church (Disciples Of Christ)
IRS Status: 501(c)3
Highest Offering: Master's
Accreditation: NW, CACREP, IACBE, NURSE

01 President ...Dr. Joseph WOMACK
04 Exec Admin Asst to President ...Ms. Jennifer BOX
05 VP Academic Affairs/Dean of Faculty ...Dr. Dennis LINDSAY
10 VP Finance & Administration ...Mr. Gene DE YOUNG
32 VP Student Development/Enrollment ...Mr. Michael FULLER
111 VP Advancement ...Dr. Keith POTTER
26 Senior Director of Public Affairs ...Mr. Patrick WALSH
07 Dean of Admission ...Ms. Kacie GERDRUM
21 Asst VP for Financial Services ...Ms. Jocelyn HUBBS
41 Athletic Director ...Mr. Corey ANDERSON
42 Campus Pastor ...Mr. Troy DEAN
39 Director of Residence Life ...Ms. Jennifer LITTLE
35 Director Student Programs ...Mr. Paul WRIGHT
121 Dean of Career & Academic Resources ...Ms. Angela DOTY
06 Registrar ...Dr. John D'AGUANNO
108 Director of Assessment ...Mr. Brian MILLS
44 Director of Annual Giving ...Ms. Bethany DILLA
30 Director of Development ...Ms. Corynn GILBERT
107 Assoc Dean of Professional Studies ...Vacant
50 Dean Business/Leadership/Tech ...Vacant
73 Assoc Dean Bible/World Christianity ...Mr. Agametochukwu IHEANYI-IGWE
49 Assoc Dean of Arts & Sciences ...Ms. Constance WILMARTH
64 Assoc Dean Music & Performing Arts ...Mr. Kelly BALLARD
83 Dean of Psychology and Counseling ...Dr. Ryan MELTON
53 Associate Dean of Education ...Ms. Suzanne PRICE
66 Associate Dean of Nursing ...Dr. Linda VELTRI
13 Director Tech & Physical Operations ...Mr. Stead HALSTEAD
37 Director of Financial Aid ...Mr. Nathan ICENHOWER

Central Oregon Community College (I)
2600 NW College Way, Bend OR 97703
County: Deschutes FICE Identification: 003188
Unit ID: 208318
Telephone: (541) 383-7700 Carnegie Class: Assoc/HT-Mix Trad/Non
FAX Number: N/A Calendar System: Quarter
URL: www.cocc.edu
Established: 1949 Annual Undergrad Tuition & Fees (In-District): $6,111
Enrollment: 4,304 Coed
Affiliation or Control: Local IRS Status: 501(c)3
Highest Offering: Associate Degree
Accreditation: NW, ACFEI, ADNUR, CAHIIM, COMTA, DA, EMT, IFSAC, MAC

01 President ...Dr. Laurie CHESLEY
05 Vice President Academic Affairs ...Dr. Annemarie HAMLIN
10 Chief Financial Officer ...Mr. David DONA
20 Instructional Dean ...Dr. Julie DOWNING
20 Instructional Dean ...Dr. Annemarie HAMLIN
20 Instructional Dean ...Dr. Michael FISHER
32 Vice Pres Student Affairs ...Dr. Alicia MOORE
07 Director of Admissions/Registrar ...Mr. Tyler HAYES
08 Director of Library Services ...Dr. Tina HOVEKAMP
26 Director Marketing/Public Relations ...Ms. Jenn KOVITZ
18 Director Campus Services ...Mr. Joe VIOLA
15 Director Human Resources ...Ms. Naomi ROUNDTREE
35 Director of Student and Campus Life ...Mr. Andrew DAVIS
09 Dir Institutional Effectiveness ...Ms. Brynn PIERCE
38 Director Student Counseling ...Ms. Diane PRITCHARD
40 Director Bookstore/Auxiliary Svcs ...Ms. Lori BENEFIEL
108 Director Curriculum & Assessment ...Mr. Franklin CLARK
19 Director Security/Safety ...Vacant
25 Director Contracts/Risk Management ...Ms. Sharla ANDRESEN
102 Chief Advance Ofcr/Dir Foundation ...Mr. Zak BOONE
51 Director of Continuing Education ...Ms. Glenda LANTIS
04 Admin Assistant to the President ...Ms. Deena COOK
13 Chief Information Officer ...Dr. Laura BOEHME
106 Director of E-learning ...Ms. Kristine ROSHAU
28 Director of Diversity ...Ms. Christy WALKER
37 Director Student Financial Aid ...Ms. Breana SYLWESTER

Chemeketa Community College (A)

PO Box 14007, Salem OR 97309-7070
County: Marion FICE Identification: 003218
Unit ID: 208390
Telephone: (503) 399-5000 Carnegie Class: Assoc/HT-Mix Trad/Non
FAX Number: (503) 399-5214 Calendar System: Quarter
URL: www.chemeketa.edu
Established: 1962 Annual Undergrad Tuition & Fees (In-District): $5,670
Enrollment: 8,328 Coed
Affiliation or Control: Local IRS Status: 501(c)3
Highest Offering: Associate Degree
Accreditation: NW, ADNUR, CAHIIM, DA, EMT, IFSAC

01	President/Chief Executive Officer	Dr. Jessica HOWARD
05	VP Academic Officer	Dr. Michael VARGO
11	VP Governance & Administration	Mr. David HALLETT
32	VP Student Affairs	Dr. Bruce CLEMETSEN
13	Associate VP/CIO	Mr. Michael KINKADE
10	AVP/CFO	Mr. Aaron HUNTER
107	Exec Dean Gen Educ/Transfer Studies	Mr. Don BRASE
75	Interim Exec Dean CTE	Mr. Marshall ROACH
121	Exec Dean Student Dev/Learning Res	Mr. Manuel GUERRA
88	Exec Dean Regional Ed & Acad Dev	Ms. Holly NELSON
83	Dean Liberal Arts & Social Sciences	Dr. Keith RUSSELL
76	Dean Health Services	Ms. Sandra KELLOGG
37	Director Financial Aid	Mr. Ryan WEST
38	Dean Counseling/Career Services	Mr. Christopher POTTS
81	Dean Science/Eng/Math/Comp Science	Mr. Timor SAFFARY
50	Dn Bus/Tech/Early Chld Ed/Vis Comm	Dr. R. TAYLOR
111	Exec Dir Institutional Advancement	Dr. Marie HULETT
88	Interim Dean Curric Instr/Accred	Ms. Julie PETERS
47	Dir Agric Innov/Prod Tech	Mr. Larry CHEYNE
08	Director Library/Learning Resources	Ms. Natalie BEACH
10	Interim Chief Financial Officer	Mr. Rich MCDONALD
18	Dir Capital Projects/Facilities	Mr. Rory ALVAREZ
15	Associate VP Human Resources	Ms. Alice SPRAGUE
19	Director Public Safety	Mr. Tony MOORE
109	Director Auxiliary/Contracted Svcs	Ms. Meredith SCHREIBER
88	Coordinator Prof Tech Educ	Mr. Ed WOODS
28	Chief Diversity & Equity Officer	Ms. Vivi CALEFFI-PRICHARD
124	Dean Student Retention/College Life	Mr. Mike EVANS
06	Registrar/Dir Enrollment Services	Ms. Melissa FREY
09	Director of Institutional Research	Vacant
43	General Counsel/Legal Resources	Ms. Rebecca HILLYER
12	Dean Woodburn Center	Mr. Elias VILLEGAS
12	Director Polk Center	Mr. Glen MILLER
12	Director Yamhill Valley Campus	Ms. Danielle HOFFMAN
04	Exec Coord to the President/Board	Ms. Julie DEUCHARS

Clackamas Community College (B)

19600 Molalla Avenue, Oregon City OR 97045-7998
County: Clackamas FICE Identification: 004878
Unit ID: 208406
Telephone: (503) 594-6000 Carnegie Class: Assoc/HT-High Non
FAX Number: N/A Calendar System: Quarter
URL: www.clackamas.edu
Established: 1966 Annual Undergrad Tuition & Fees (In-District): $5,334
Enrollment: 5,555 Coed
Affiliation or Control: Local IRS Status: 501(c)3
Highest Offering: Associate Degree
Accreditation: NW, MAC, NAEYC

01	President	Dr. Tim COOK
05	VP Instruct & Stdnt Svcs/Provost	Dr. David PLOTKIN
11	Vice Pres College Services	Ms. Alissa MAHAR
04	Executive Asst to the President	Ms. Kattie RIGGS
102	Executive Director Foundation	Ms. Debra MASON
26	Public Information Officer	Ms. Lori HALL
06	Registrar/Enrol Svcs/Operations Mgr	Mr. Chris SWEET
32	Assoc Dean Acad Found/Connect Div	Ms. Jennifer ANDERSON
13	Dean/CIO Information Technology	Mr. Saby WARAICH
49	Dean Arts & Sciences	Ms. Sue GOFF
46	Dean Inst Effectiveness & Planning	Mr. Jason KOVAC
72	Assoc Dn Tech/Hlth Occup/Wrkfc Div	Ms. Shalee HODGSON
15	Dean Human Resources	Ms. Melissa RICHARDSON
88	Dir Office Education Partnerships	Ms. Ni'Cole SIMS
10	Dean Business Services	Mr. Jeff SHAFFER
11	Dean Campus Services	Mr. Bob COCHRAN
18	Director Campus Services	Vacant
41	Director Health/PE/Athletics	Mr. Jim MARTINEAU
13	Director IT Operations	Vacant
09	Director of Institutional Research	Ms. Ashley SEARS
37	Director Student Financial Aid	Vacant
19	Director Security/Safety	Mr. Thomas SONOFF
28	Director of Diversity	Ms. Casey LAYTON

Clatsop Community College (C)

1651 Lexington Avenue, Astoria OR 97103
County: Clatsop FICE Identification: 003189
Unit ID: 208415
Telephone: (503) 325-0910 Carnegie Class: Assoc/HT-High Non
FAX Number: (503) 325-5738 Calendar System: Quarter
URL: www.clatsopcc.edu
Established: 1958 Annual Undergrad Tuition & Fees (In-District): $4,230
Enrollment: 754 Coed
Affiliation or Control: State/Local IRS Status: 501(c)3
Highest Offering: Associate Degree
Accreditation: NW

01	President	Mr. Chris BREITMEYER
05	Vice President Academic Affairs	Dr. Peter WILLIAMS
10	Vice President Finance & Operations	Ms. JoAnn ZAHN
32	Vice President of Student Success	Mr. Jerad SORBER
06	Registrar	Ms. Jiang Fei KOCH
26	Director Communication & Marketing	Ms. Julie KOVATCH
13	Director Computer Services	Mr. Greg RIEHL
15	Director Human Resources	Ms. Desiree NOAH
37	Director Student Financial Aid	Mr. Lloyd MUELLER
09	Director of Institutional Research	Vacant
18	Dir Physical Plant/Sr Project Mgr	Mr. Shaun MARTIN
21	Interim Director Accounting Svcs	Ms. Stephanie HOMER
102	Director College Foundation	Ms. Angela HUNT
08	Director of Library	Mr. Dan MCCLURE
04	Executive Coordinator to President	Ms. Patricia SCHULTE
106	Distance Education Coordinator	Mrs. Kirsten HORNING
103	Dean Workforce Educ & Training	Ms. Kristen WILKIN
88	Dean Transfer Education	Ms. Teena TOYAS

College of Emergency Services (D)

12438 SE Capps Road, Clackamas OR 97015
County: Clackamas Identification: 667128
Telephone: (971) 236-9231 Carnegie Class: Not Classified
FAX Number: (971) 653-9239 Calendar System: Semester
URL: www.collegeofems.com
Established: 1995 Annual Undergrad Tuition & Fees: N/A
Enrollment: N/A Coed
Affiliation or Control: Proprietary IRS Status: Proprietary
Highest Offering: Associate Degree
Accreditation: ABHES, EMT

01	Program Medical Director	Dr. David LEHRFELD
05	Lead Instructor	Lauren ENRIGHT

Columbia Gorge Community College (E)

400 East Scenic Drive, The Dalles OR 97058
County: Wasco FICE Identification: 041519
Unit ID: 420556
Telephone: (541) 506-6000 Carnegie Class: Assoc/HT-High Non
FAX Number: N/A Calendar System: Quarter
URL: www.cgcc.edu
Established: 1977 Annual Undergrad Tuition & Fees (In-District): $4,752
Enrollment: 825 Coed
Affiliation or Control: State/Local IRS Status: 501(c)3
Highest Offering: Associate Degree
Accreditation: NW, MAC

01	President	Dr. Marta CRONIN
05	VP of Instructional Services	Jarett GILBERT
10	VP of Finance	Dr. Lorelle DAVIES
32	Vice Pres Student Services	Michael ESPINOZA
26	Manager Marketing & Cmty Outreach	Dan SPATZ
13	Exec Director of Infrastructure	Danny DEHAZE
06	Registrar/Veteran Svcs	Mary MARTIN
07	Director of Admissions	Vacant
08	Dean of Library & Learning Commons	Dylan MCMANUS
108	Dir Curriculum & Assessment	Susan LEWIS
15	Director Human Resources	Courtney JUDAH
18	Director of Facilities Services	Vacant
37	Director Financial Aid	Axel FERNANDEZ
102	Exec Director Foundation	Wendy PATTON
39	Dir of Housing/Student Life	Tiffany PRINCE

Concorde Career College (F)

1425 NE Irving Street, Portland OR 97232
County: Multnomah FICE Identification: 008887
Unit ID: 208479
Telephone: (503) 281-4181 Carnegie Class: Spec 2-yr-Health
FAX Number: (503) 281-6739 Calendar System: Other
URL: www.concorde.edu/campus/portland
Established: 1996 Annual Undergrad Tuition & Fees: N/A
Enrollment: 466 Coed
Affiliation or Control: Proprietary IRS Status: Proprietary
Highest Offering: Associate Degree
Accreditation: ACCSC, COARC, MAC, POLYT, SURGT

01	Campus President	Siri DIXON
05	Academic Dean	Dennis KELLEY
07	Director of Admissions	Richard BALDISSERI

Corban University (G)

5000 Deer Park Drive SE, Salem OR 97317
County: Marion FICE Identification: 001339
Unit ID: 210331
Telephone: (503) 375-7585 Carnegie Class: Masters/S
FAX Number: (503) 585-4316 Calendar System: Semester
URL: www.corban.edu
Established: 1935 Annual Undergrad Tuition & Fees: $34,188
Enrollment: 1,160 Coed
Affiliation or Control: Independent Non-Profit IRS Status: 501(c)3
Highest Offering: Master's
Accreditation: NW, AAQEP, CACREP

01	Interim President	Dr. Thomas CORNMAN
05	Interim Provost	Dr. Christopher VETTER
10	Vice President for Business & CFO	Ms. Patricia SHELTON

32	Vice President for Student Life	Dr. Brian JAWORSKI
111	Vice President for Advancement	Ms. Shannon JOHNSON
28	Chief Diversity Officer	Ms. Mechelle GARRETT
84	Assoc Provost for Enrollment	Mr. Jordan LINDSEY
20	Assoc Provost & Dean of Faculty	Dr. Felicia SQUIRES
106	Assoc Provost for E-Learning	Dr. Richard WEBER
06	Interim Registrar	Ms. Allison SORENSEN
35	Dean of Student Engagement	Mr. Eugene EDWARDS
21	Controller	Ms. Ellen ZARFAS
00	Chair of the Board of Trustees	Mr. Rod HOFF
100	EA & Chief of Staff	Mr. Jeremy HALE
101	Secretary of the Board of Trustees	Dr. James GLEASON
50	Dean of the Hoff School of Business	Dr. Bryce BERNARD
53	Dean of the School of Education	Dr. Aaron IMIG
73	Dean of the School of Ministry	Dr. Gregory TRULL
79	Chair Department of Humanities	Dr. Ryan STARK
47	Director of Agriculture Science	Dr. Susie NELSON
64	Director of Music	Dr. Mark STANEK
66	Director of Nursing	Dr. Kathleen KENNEDY
19	Director of Campus Safety	Mr. Mike ROTH
13	Director Information Services	Ms. Brenda GIBSON
41	Athletic Director	Mr. Marty ZIESEMER
26	Director of MARCOM	Ms. Rebekah BENHAM
18	Director of Facilities	Mr. Chris ROWLEY
29	Director of Alumni Relations	Ms. Shirley TURNER
38	Director of Corban Counseling	Dr. Lori SCHELSKE
92	Director of the Honors Program	Prof. Evan HEDLUND
08	Librarian	Dr. Garrett TROTT
39	Director of Residence Life	Mr. Conner LOCKE
37	Director of Financial Aid	Ms. Jennifer BRUCE
56	Director of the OSCI Extension	Dr. Amit BHATIA
121	Assoc Director of Student Support	Ms. Janet SYVERSON
14	Asst Director of IS	Mr. Matthew SPEARS
27	Asst Director of MARCOM	Mr. Joshua TRAMMELL
15	Senior Human Resources Generalist	Ms. Bethany BIGELOW
110	Senior Development Officer	Mr. Scott SHERMAN
110	Senior Development Officer	Mr. Darrel WHITE
114	Financial Project Manager	Ms. Marla Kay TRAHAN
120	Online Program Manager	Dr. Kristine MEDYANIK
118	Payroll Business Partner	Ms. Debi NISSEN

Eastern Oregon University (H)

One University Boulevard, La Grande OR 97850-2807
County: Union FICE Identification: 003193
Unit ID: 208646
Telephone: (541) 962-3672 Carnegie Class: Masters/S
FAX Number: (541) 962-3493 Calendar System: Quarter
URL: www.eou.edu
Established: 1929 Annual Undergrad Tuition & Fees (In-State): $9,405
Enrollment: 2,853 Coed
Affiliation or Control: State IRS Status: 501(c)3
Highest Offering: Master's
Accreditation: NW, AAQEP, IACBE

01	Interim Co-President	Ms. Lara MOORE
01	Interim Co-President	Mr. Richard CHAVES
05	Interim Provost/VP Academic Affairs	Dr. Matt SEIMEARS
32	Vice President for Student Affairs	Dr. Lacy KARPILO
10	Vice President Finance & Admin	Ms. Lara MOORE
111	VP University Advancement	Mr. Tim SEYDEL
101	General Counsel/Board Secretary	Mr. Chris BURFORD
49	Dean Col Arts/Humanities/Social Sci	Mr. Nathan LOWE
50	Dean College of Business	Dr. Ed HENNINGER
53	Interim Dean College of Education	Dr. Rae Ette NEWMAN
81	Dean College of STM Health Science	Dr. Peter GEISSINGER
08	Library Assistant Director	Ms. Sarah RALSTON
84	Assoc VP Enrollment Management	Ms. Holly CHASON
09	Director of Institutional Research	Ms. Holly CHASON
41	Director of Athletics	Ms. Anji WEISSENFLUH
15	Director of Human Resources	Mr. Chris MCLAUGHLIN
28	Assoc VP Diversity & Equity	Vacant
06	Registrar	Ms. Emily SHARRATT
37	Interim Director of Financial Aid	Mr. Jason HIBBERT
30	Exec Director of Philanthropy	Ms. Emily ADAMS
07	Director of Admissions	Ms. Genesis MEADERDS
39	Director of Residence Life	Mr. Jeremy JONES
19	Director Campus Safety/Security	Mr. Jim HOFFMAN
13	Dir Computing & Telecommunications	Mr. Jeff CARMAN
26	Director of Marketing	Mr. Justin MONTGOMERY
18	Director of Facilities & Planning	Mr. John GARLITZ
35	Dir of Student Relations/Title IX	Ms. Colleen DUNNE-CASCIO
38	Director Counseling Center	Dr. Marianne WEAVER
04	Exec Assistant to the President	Ms. Kimberly NEWMAN

George Fox University (I)

414 N Meridian, Newberg OR 97132-2697
County: Yamhill FICE Identification: 003194
Unit ID: 208822
Telephone: (503) 538-8383 Carnegie Class: DU-Mod
FAX Number: (503) 554-3880 Calendar System: Semester
URL: www.georgefox.edu
Established: 1891 Annual Undergrad Tuition & Fees: $38,370
Enrollment: 4,106 Coed
Affiliation or Control: Friends IRS Status: 501(c)3
Highest Offering: Doctorate
Accreditation: NW, AAQEP, ACBSP, #ARCPA, CAATE, CACREP, CLPSY, IPSY, MUS, NURSE, PTA, SW, THEOL

01	President	Dr. Robin E. BAKER
05	Provost	Dr. Andrea SCOTT

10 Exec VP Finance/CFO ... Ms. Vicki PIERSALL
111 Int Vice President for Advancement ... Mr. Kyle DICKINSON
32 Vice President Student Life ... Dr. Bradley A. LAU
84 VP Enrollment & Marketing ... Ms. Lindsay KNOX
28 AVP Intercultural Engagement ... Dr. Rebecca HERNANDEZ
21 Asst VP of Finance/Controller ... Ms. Cris BANTON
100 Chief of Staff ... Ms. Melissa D. TERRY
08 Dean of Libraries ... Mr. Alexander ROLFE
07 Director of Undergrad Admissions ... Ms. Lindsay KNOX
06 Registrar ... Ms. Melissa THOMAS
36 Dir of Career Services/IDEA Center ... Ms. Wendy FLINT
18 Director of Plant Services ... Mr. Jeremiah HORTON
37 Director of Financial Aid ... Ms. Johanna KAYE
96 Director Purchasing/Admin Services ... Mr. Matt HAMMAR
41 Director of Athletics ... Mr. Adam PUCKETT
105 Director of Web Development ... Mr. Peter CRACKENBERG
15 Exec Dir Human Res/Title IX Coord ... Ms. Nichole DREW
42 Univ Pastor/Dean of Spiritual Life ... Ms. Jamie NOLING-AUTH
26 Director of Executive Communication ... Mr. Rob FELTON
13 Chief Information Officer ... Mr. Tim GOODFELLOW
19 Director Security Services ... Mr. Ed GIEROK
35 Dean Stdnt Svcs/Dir Hlth/Counseling ... Dr. William C. BUHROW
73 Dean of Portland Seminary ... Dr. MaryKate MORSE
83 Dean Sch Behavioral/Health Sci ... Dr. David CIMBORA
53 Dean School of Education ... Mr. Marc SHELTON
54 Dean of Engineering ... Dr. Robert HARDER
09 Chief Data Officer ... Mr. Tyler SUSMILCH
04 Executive Asst to the President ... Ms. Jennifer MCCOLLUM
103 Recruiting and Training Manager ... Ms. Kara HOLCOMBE
104 Director Study Abroad ... Dr. David J. MARTÍNEZ
108 Director Institutional Assessment ... Mr. Rob BOHALL
29 Director Alumni Affairs ... Ms. Sara REAMY
30 Executive Director of Development ... Mr. Kyle DICKINSON
39 Director University Housing ... Ms. Kayin GRIFFITH
44 Director Annual Giving ... Mr. Gene CHRISTIAN
90 Director Academic Computing ... Mr. Josh NAUMAN

Gutenberg College (A)

1883 University Street, Eugene OR 97403-1368
County: Lane   FICE Identification: 039324
Telephone: (541) 683-5141   Carnegie Class: Not Classified
FAX Number: (541) 683-6997   Calendar System: Quarter
URL: www.gutenberg.edu
Established: 1994   Annual Undergrad Tuition & Fees: N/A
Enrollment: N/A   Coed
Affiliation or Control: Independent Non-Profit   IRS Status: 501(c)3
Highest Offering: Baccalaureate
Accreditation: TRACS

01 President ... Chris SWANSON
10 Vice President Finance ... Mark BRAISHER
05 Dean ... Thomas DEWBERRY
07 Vice President ... Eliot GRASSO
06 Registrar ... Chris SWANSON
39 Dir Resident Life/Student Housing ... Gil GRECO

Klamath Community College (B)

7390 S 6th Street, Klamath Falls OR 97603-7121
County: Klamath   FICE Identification: 034283
Unit ID: 428392
Telephone: (541) 882-3521   Carnegie Class: Assoc/HT-High Non
FAX Number: (541) 885-7758   Calendar System: Quarter
URL: www.klamathcc.edu
Established: 1996   Annual Undergrad Tuition & Fees (In-District): $4,497
Enrollment: 1,492   Coed
Affiliation or Control: State/Local   IRS Status: 501(c)3
Highest Offering: Associate Degree
Accreditation: NW

01 President ... Dr. Roberto GUTIERREZ
11 Vice Pres Administrative Svcs ... Mr. Geoffrey LAHAIE
05 Vice Pres Academic Affairs ... Ms. Jamie JENNINGS
32 Vice Pres Student Affairs ... Ms. Gail SCHULL
26 Vice Pres External Programs ... Mr. Charles MASSIE
15 Exec Dir HR & General Counsel ... Mr. Joshua GUEST
20 Dean of Instruction ... Dr. Jeanne LAHAIE
66 Dean of Nursing/Health/Science ... Ms. Allison SANSOM
75 Dean of Career Technical Education ... Mr. Christopher STICKLES
13 Director Information Services ... Mr. Paul BREEDLOVE
06 Registrar ... Mr. M. SHABBIR
18 Facilities Director ... Mr. Mike HOMFELDT
10 Director Business Svcs/Controller ... Vacant
37 Financial Aid Director ... Mr. Nathan HENDRICKSON
04 Executive Admin Asst to President ... Ms. Shannon CHILDS
09 Institutional Researcher ... Mr. Bill JENNINGS
25 Grants Program Manager ... Mr. Peter LAWSON

Lane Community College (C)

4000 E 30th Avenue, Eugene OR 97405-0640
County: Lane   FICE Identification: 003196
Unit ID: 209038
Telephone: (541) 463-3000   Carnegie Class: Assoc/HT-High Non
FAX Number: (541) 463-5201   Calendar System: Quarter
URL: www.lanecc.edu
Established: 1964   Annual Undergrad Tuition & Fees (In-District): $5,153
Enrollment: 7,702   Coed
Affiliation or Control: Local   IRS Status: 501(c)3
Highest Offering: Associate Degree
Accreditation: NW, ACFEI, CAHIIM, DA, DH, EMT, MAC, PTAA

01 President ... Dr. Stephanie BULGER
05 Int VP of Academic Affairs ... Mr. Grant MATTHEWS
10 VP Finance & College Operations ... Dr. George STALLIARD, SR.
49 AVP Academic & Student Affairs ... Dr. Jennifer FREI
103 AVP CTE/Workforce Development ... Mr. Grant MATTHEWS
28 AVP Diversity/Equity/Inclusion ... Mr. Greg EVANS
32 Int Sr VP Student Affairs/Registrar ... Ms. Dawn WHITING
15 Chief Human Resources Officer ... Mr. Shane TURNER
18 Director Facilities Mgmt & Planning ... Ms. Jennifer HAYWARD
19 Director Public Safety ... Ms. Lisa RUPP
08 Library Dean ... Mr. Ian CORONADO
26 Public Information Officer ... Vacant
102 Foundation Director ... Ms. Wendy JETT
04 Executive Asst to President/Board ... Ms. Tami HILL
104 Interim Dir International Programs ... Ms. Mandie PRICHARD
45 Chief Strategy & Planning Officer ... Vacant
100 Chief of Staff ... Vacant
43 Director Legal Services ... Mr. Michael BLADE

Lewis and Clark College (D)

615 S. Palatine Hill Road, Portland OR 97219-7899
County: Multnomah   FICE Identification: 003197
Unit ID: 209056
Telephone: (503) 768-7000   Carnegie Class: Bac-A&S
FAX Number: (503) 768-7055   Calendar System: Semester
URL: www.lclark.edu
Established: 1867   Annual Undergrad Tuition & Fees: $55,266
Enrollment: 3,157   Coed
Affiliation or Control: Independent Non-Profit   IRS Status: 501(c)3
Highest Offering: Doctorate
Accreditation: NW, ACATE, CACREP, CAEP, LAW, MFCD

01 President ... Dr. Robin HOLMES-SULLIVAN
43 VP/COS/General Counsel ... Mr. David REESE
07 Vice Pres Admiss & Financial Aid ... Mr. Eric STAAB
05 Chief Academic Officer/Dean ... Dr. Bruce SUTTMEIER
58 Dean Grad Sch Education/Counseling ... Dr. Scott FLETCHER
61 Dean of the Law School ... Ms. Jennifer JOHNSON
28 Dean of Diversity and Inclusion ... Dr. Danille TORRES
10 VP Opers/Chief Financial Ofcr ... Ms. Andrea DOOLEY
111 Vice Pres Institutional Advancement ... Mr. Josh WALTER
32 Vice President of Student Life ... Dr. Evette CASTILLO CLARK
09 Asst VP of Research & Planning ... Dr. Renee ORLICK
26 Assoc VP of Communications ... Ms. Stacey KIM
13 Assoc VP & Chief Information Ofcr ... Mr. Adam BUCHWALD
15 Assoc VP/Director Human Resources ... Mrs. Heyke KIRKENDALL-BAKER
18 Assoc Vice Pres Facilities Services ... Mr. David ERNEVAD
06 Registrar College of Arts/Sciences ... Ms. Judy FINCH
06 Registrar Law School ... Ms. Tiffany HENNING
06 Registrar Graduate School ... Ms. Courtney WHETSTINE
37 Assoc VP for Financial Aid ... Ms. Anastacia DILLON
08 Director of Watzek Library ... Mr. Mark DAHL
85 Assoc Dean Intl Stdnts & Scholars ... Mr. Brian WHITE
30 Assoc VP & Director of Development ... Mr. Aaron WHITEFORD
29 Senior Director Alumni/Parent Pgms ... Mr. Andrew MCPHEETERS
19 Interim Director of Campus Safety ... Mr. Bill CURTIS
42 Dir of Religious & Spiritual Life ... Dr. Mark DUNTLEY
41 Director of PE & Athletics ... Mr. Mark PIETROK
39 Asst Dean for Campus LIfe ... Mr. Ben MEOZ
14 Director of IT Operations ... Mr. Patrick RYALL
23 Assoc Dean Stdnt Health & Wellness ... Vacant
101 Executive Asst Board Relations ... Ms. Leslie THOMAS
04 Executive Asst to the President ... Ms. Rachel MARTINEZ
102 Director Corp/Foundation Relations ... Mr. David JOHNSON
104 Director Overseas & Off Campus Pgms ... Ms. Blythe KNOTT

Linfield University (E)

900 SE Baker Street, McMinnville OR 97128-6894
County: Yamhill   FICE Identification: 003198
Unit ID: 209065
Telephone: (503) 883-2200   Carnegie Class: Bac-A&S
FAX Number: (503) 883-2472   Calendar System: 4/1/4
URL: www.linfield.edu
Established: 1858   Annual Undergrad Tuition & Fees: $45,132
Enrollment: 1,392   Coed
Affiliation or Control: American Baptist   IRS Status: 501(c)3
Highest Offering: Master's
Accreditation: NW, CAEP, MUS, NURSE

01 President ... Dr. Miles DAVIS
05 Interim VP Academic Affairs/Provost ... Dr. Mark MCPHAIL
10 Vice Pres Finance/Admin/CFO ... Dr. Mike WENZ
111 Vice Pres University Advancement ... Mr. Joseph HUNTER
32 Interim VP Student Affairs ... Mr. Jeff MACKAY
84 VP Enrollment Mgt & Student Success ... Mr. Gerardo OCHOA
66 Interim Dean of Nursing ... Dr. Paul SMITH
35 Dean of Students ... Mr. Jeff MACKAY
15 Director of Human Resources ... Ms. Lynn JOHNSON
21 AVP Finance & Administration ... Ms. Allison HORN
85 Associate Director Intl Programs ... Ms. Michelle TOMSETH
06 Registrar ... Ms. Diane CRABTREE
07 Director of Admission ... Ms. Lisa KNODLE-BRAGIEL
08 Library Director ... Ms. Ginny BLACKSON
09 Director of Institutional Research ... Ms. Jennifer BALLARD
37 Director of Financial Aid ... Ms. Keri BURKE
13 Chief Information Officer ... Mr. Sam WILLIAMS
105 Webmaster ... Mr. Jonathan PIERCE
51 Director of Continuing Education ... Vacant
19 Director of Public Safety ... Mr. Dennis MARKS
38 Director of Student Health ... Ms. Patricia HADDELAND

26 AVP Strat Comm/Chief Mktg Officer ... Mr. Scott Bernard NELSON
44 Director of Annual Giving ... Ms. Ellen BRAZIEL
30 Sr Dir of Devel & Campaign Dir ... Mr. Craig HAISCH
29 Dir of Alumni & Parent Engagement ... Ms. Debbie HARMON FERRY
36 Director of Career Development ... Mr. Michael HAMPTON
42 Chaplain ... Mr. Jeremy RICHARDS
41 Athletic Director ... Mr. Garry KILLGORE
40 Bookstore Manager ... Mr. Aaron SLOPER
04 Exec Assistant to the President ... Ms. Allison XAVIER
39 Asst Director of Housing Operations ... Mr. Geoffrey RATH
50 Dean of Business ... Ms. Jennifer MADDEN
49 Int Dean Col of Arts & Sciences ... Ms. Gennie VANBEEK
88 Dir Learning Support Services ... Mr. Jeff LARSON
110 Dir of Prospect Devel & Strategy ... Ms. Diana HUNT
88 Dir of Adv Data Systems ... Ms. Miranda LUNA

Linn-Benton Community College (F)

6500 Pacific Boulevard, SW, Albany OR 97321-3774
County: Linn   FICE Identification: 006938
Unit ID: 209074
Telephone: (541) 917-4999   Carnegie Class: Assoc/MT-VT-Mix Trad/Non
FAX Number: (541) 917-4445   Calendar System: Quarter
URL: www.linnbenton.edu
Established: 1966   Annual Undergrad Tuition & Fees (In-District): $5,487
Enrollment: 4,956   Coed
Affiliation or Control: State/Local   IRS Status: 501(c)3
Highest Offering: Associate Degree
Accreditation: NW, DA, MAC, OTA, POLYT, SURGT

01 President ... Dr. Lisa AVERY
05 Vice Pres Academic Affs/Wrkfce Dev ... Dr. Ann BUCHELE
10 Vice Pres Finance & Operations ... Mr. Sheldon FLOM
12 Regional Director Benton County ... Mr. Jeff DAVIS
15 Dir Human Resources/Affirm Act Ofcr ... Mr. Scott ROLEN
41 Director of Athletics ... Mr. Mark MAJESKI
81 Dean Science/Engr & Math ... Ms. Kristina HOLTON
49 Dean Arts/Soc Sci/Humanities Div ... Ms. Meg ROLAND
20 Dean of Instruction ... Ms. Katie WINDER
111 Exec Dir Institutional Advancement ... Ms. Jennifer BOEHMER
04 Executive Asst to President ... Ms. Amanda KLIEVER
06 Assoc Dean Registrar/Admissions ... Mr. Danny AYNES
13 Chief Info Technology Officer (CIO) ... Mr. Michael QUINER
18 Chief Facilities/Physical Plant ... Mr. Terrell LANGLEY
28 Dir Equity/Diversity/Inclusion ... Mr. Jason DORSETTE
09 Director of Institutional Research ... Mr. Justin SMITH
37 Dir Financial Aid/Veterans Affairs ... Ms. Karen ASH

Mount Angel Abbey & Seminary (G)

1 Abbey Drive, Saint Benedict OR 97373-0505
County: Marion   FICE Identification: 003203
Unit ID: 209241
Telephone: (503) 845-3951   Carnegie Class: Spec-4-yr-Faith
FAX Number: (503) 845-3128   Calendar System: Semester
URL: www.mountangelabbey.org
Established: 1889   Annual Undergrad Tuition & Fees: $24,770
Enrollment: 127   Coed
Affiliation or Control: Roman Catholic   IRS Status: 501(c)3
Highest Offering: Doctorate
Accreditation: NW, THEOL

01 President-Rector ... Msgr. Joseph V. BETSCHART
05 Academic Dean ... Dr. Shawn KEOUGH
11 VP of Admin/Dir Human Formation ... Rev. Stephen CLOVIS
20 Associate Dean ... Dr. Andrew CUMMINGS
06 Registrar/Director of Financial Aid ... Mr. Terence MERRITT
07 Director of Admissions ... Fr. Teresio CALDWELL, OSB
04 Exec Asst to the President-Rector ... Mrs. Nancy BROSTROM
10 Procurator ... Fr. Martin GRASSEL, OSB
30 Director of Development ... Ms. Jodi KILCUP
26 Communications Manager ... Ms. Theresa MYERS
08 Librarian ... Dr. Brian MORIN
29 Alumni Relations ... Ms. Maurissa FISHER
112 Director of Planned Giving ... Ms. Susan GALLAGHER
44 Director of Annual Giving ... Ms. Melissa EDDINGS
15 Chief Human Resources Officer ... Ms. Colette BLAKELY
108 Director Institutional Assessment ... Dr. Liam DE LOS REYES

Mt. Hood Community College (H)

26000 SE Stark, Gresham OR 97030-3300
County: Multnomah   FICE Identification: 003204
Unit ID: 209250
Telephone: (503) 491-6422   Carnegie Class: Assoc/HT-High Non
FAX Number: (503) 491-7389   Calendar System: Quarter
URL: www.mhcc.edu
Established: 1965   Annual Undergrad Tuition & Fees (In-District): $5,286
Enrollment: 6,812   Coed
Affiliation or Control: Local   IRS Status: 501(c)3
Highest Offering: Associate Degree
Accreditation: NW, COARC, FUSER, PTAA, SURGT

01 President ... Dr. Lisa SKARI
05 Vice President of Instruction ... Mr. Alfred MCQUARTERS
15 Associate VP of Human Resources ... Vacant
10 VP of Finance and Administration ... Ms. Jennifer DEMENT
09 Associate VP Institutional Research ... Mr. Sergey SHEPELOV
35 Dir Student Development/Tech ... Ms. Christi HART
32 Vice President of Student Services ... Mr. John HAMBLIN
13 Associate VP Information Technology ... Ms. Linda VIGESAA

111 Vice Pres of College Advancement ... Mr. Al SIGALA
76 Dean Allied Health & Nursing ... Dr. Carri CLAYCOMB
81 Dean of Mathematics/Science ... Mr. Peter SZUCS
79 Dean Humanities/Math/Social Science ... Ms. Sara RIVARA
50 Dean Business/Engr/Applied Tech ... Ms. Kristin LIMA
103 Exec Dean Workforce/CTE/Partner ... Mr. Douglas SAMUELS
04 Executive Asst to the President ... Vacant
101 Executive Asst to the Board ... Vacant
106 Director Online Learning ... Ms. Cat SCHLEICHERT
41 Athletic Director ... Dr. Kim HYATT
84 Director of Enrollment Services ... Ms. Dawn SALLEE-JUSTESEN
18 Associate Vice Pres Facilities ... Mr. Charles GEORGE
19 Manager of Public Safety ... Mr. Wayne FEAGLE
28 Associate VP of DEI ... Ms. Traci SIMMONS
37 Director of Financial Aid ... Mr. Christopher NATELBORG

Multnomah University (A)

8435 NE Glisan Street, Portland OR 97220-5898
County: Multnomah FICE Identification: 003206
Unit ID: 209287
Telephone: (503) 255-0332 Carnegie Class: Masters/S
FAX Number: (503) 254-1268 Calendar System: Semester
URL: www.multnomah.edu
Established: 1936 Annual Undergrad Tuition & Fees: $28,000
Enrollment: 623 Coed
Affiliation or Control: Independent Non-Profit IRS Status: 501(c)3
Highest Offering: Doctorate
Accreditation: NW, THEOL

01 President ... Dr. Eric Anthony JOSEPH
84 VP Enrollment and Athletics ... Mr. Mike ANDERSON
11 Executive Vice President/COO ... Mr. Ted ALLEN
111 Vice President of Advancement ... Dr. Robert LARSON
28 VP Diversity/Inclusive Development ... Dr. Jessica L. TAYLOR
05 Chief Academic Officer ... Mr. Alin VRANCILA
49 Dean School of Arts and Sciences ... Dr. Daniel SCALBERG
73 Dean School of Bible & Theology ... Dr. Derek CHINN
107 Dean School of Prof Studies ... Dr. Steven HOLLER
32 Dean of Students & Athletics ... Dr. Joseph SLAVENS
42 Director of Spiritual Life & Campus ... Ms. Chelsea HOSTETLER
35 Associate Dean of Student Success ... Mrs. Christy MARTIN
108 Dir of Institutional Effectiveness ... Mrs. Lydia GILLESPIE
06 Registrar ... Ms. Amy M. STEPHENS
21 Controller ... Mrs. Debbie WHITEHEAD
08 Library Director ... Ms. Suzanne SMITH
37 Director Student Financial Aid ... Mrs. Deborah REZENE
13 Director Information Technology ... Mr. Sudha PEETHALA
15 Director of Human Resources ... Ms. Tracy L. MORESCHI
41 Athletic Director ... Mr. Mike ANDERSON
26 Director of Marketing/Communication ... Mr. Brenn BORROR
18 Executive Director of Operations ... Mr. Eric LINMAN
04 Assistant to the President ... Mrs. Denise STONE
19 Director of Campus Safety ... Mr. Josh HARPER
38 Director Student Counseling ... Mrs. Rebecca JONES
121 Associate Dean of Student Success ... Mrs. Christy MARTIN
106 Learning Mgmt Systems Specialist ... Ms. Alyssa CHARLES

National University of Natural Medicine (B)

49 South Porter Street, Portland OR 97201-4878
County: Multnomah FICE Identification: 025340
Unit ID: 209296
Telephone: (503) 552-1555 Carnegie Class: Spec-4-yr-Other Health
FAX Number: (503) 499-0022 Calendar System: Quarter
URL: nunm.edu
Established: 1956 Annual Undergrad Tuition & Fees: N/A
Enrollment: 485 Coed
Affiliation or Control: Independent Non-Profit IRS Status: 501(c)3
Highest Offering: Doctorate
Accreditation: NW, ACUP, NATUR

01 President ... Dr. Melanie HENRIKSEN
10 EVP/Chief Finance Officer ... Mr. Gerald BORES
05 Chief Academics/VP Inst Effective ... Ms. Cheryl MILLER
32 VP Student Engagement & Innovation ... Dr. Glenn C. SMITH
15 VP of Human Resources ... Ms. Kathy STANFORD
84 VP of Enrollment Management ... Ms. Beth WOODWARD
88 VP Health Centers & Aux Ops ... Ms. Nora SANDE
88 Director Helfgott Research Inst ... Dr. Ryan BRADLEY
11 Administrative Dean ... Dr. Charles KUNERT
63 Int Dir Naturopathic Medicine ... Dr. Kelly BALTAZAR
88 Director of Curriculum Innovation ... Dr. Shehab EL-HASHEMY
58 Director Graduate Medical Education ... Dr. Dee SAUNDERS
88 Interim Director CCM ... Mr. Andrew MCINTYRE
20 Director Undergrad & Grad Studies ... Dr. Tim IRVING
88 Department Chair Nutrition ... Dr. Erlandsen ANDREW
76 Department Chair Health Sciences ... Dr. Heather ZWICKEY
35 Dean of Students ... Ms. Rachael ALLEN
08 University Librarian ... Ms. Noelle STELLO
23 Director of Health Centers ... Dr. Brooke LINN
28 Director of Equity & Inclusion ... Ms. Ayasha SHAMSUD-DIN
06 Registrar ... Ms. Kelly GAREY
07 Director of Admissions ... Vacant
26 Director Marketing & Communication ... Ms. Sherrie MARTEL
37 Director of Financial Aid ... Ms. Sally KALSTROM
121 Director of Student Success ... Ms. Morgan CHICARELLI
120 Director Instructional Design/Tech ... Mr. Justin FOWLER
13 IT Manager ... Mr. Steve FONG
19 Chief of Campus Security ... Mr. Mike HALE

100 Chief of Staff & Strategic Engage ... Mr. Jeremy ANDERSON-SLOAN
88 Associate Dean Administration ... Ms. Heather SCHIFFKE
38 Interim Director Counseling Service ... Dr. Jason RIBNER
88 Laboratory Director ... Dr. Sonia KAPUR
18 Manager of Facilities ... Mr. Dave MCALLISTER
17 Chief Medical Officer/Dean Clinics ... Dr. Jessica NAGELKIRK

New Hope Christian College (C)

2155 Bailey Hill Road, Eugene OR 97405-1194
County: Lane FICE Identification: 021597
Unit ID: 208725
Telephone: (541) 485-1780 Carnegie Class: Spec-4-yr-Faith
FAX Number: (541) 343-5801 Calendar System: Semester
URL: www.newhope.edu
Established: 1925 Annual Undergrad Tuition & Fees: $15,700
Enrollment: 52 Coed
Affiliation or Control: Other IRS Status: 501(c)3
Highest Offering: Baccalaureate
Accreditation: BI

01 President ... Dr. Wayne CORDEIRO
05 Academic Dean ... Mr. Donald GRAFTON
11 Vice President of Operations ... Mr. Thomas KIRST
04 Executive Assistant to President ... Mrs. Lori HIGASHI
13 Chief Technology Officer ... Mr. Peter THOURSON
32 Dean of Student Services ... Mr. Aaron CORDEIRO
35 Director of Student Life ... Mr. Paul WRIGHT
29 Director of Alumni Relations ... Vacant
84 Enrollment Management ... Mr. Christopher KIRIAKOS
37 Director of Financial Aid ... Ms. Sayaka MEARIG
06 Registrar ... Mrs. Floria GRAFTON
10 Director Financial Services ... Ms. Elaine NAULU
08 Librarian ... Mrs. Uilani CORDEIRO
07 Admissions Assistant ... Ms. Leslie KIRIAKOS

Oregon Coast Community College (D)

400 SE College Way, Newport OR 97366
County: Lincoln FICE Identification: 032132
Unit ID: 423652
Telephone: (541) 867-8501 Carnegie Class: Assoc/MT-VT-High Non
FAX Number: (541) 265-3820 Calendar System: Quarter
URL: www.oregoncoast.edu
Established: 1987 Annual Undergrad Tuition & Fees (In-District): $5,148
Enrollment: 417 Coed
Affiliation or Control: State/Local IRS Status: 501(c)3
Highest Offering: Associate Degree
Accreditation: NW

01 President ... Dr. Birgitte RYSLINGE
05 VP of Academic Affairs ... Dan LARA
32 VP Student Affairs ... Dr. Andres OROZ
11 VP Administrative Services ... Robin GINTNER
26 VP Engagement & Entrepreneurship ... Dave PRICE
04 Exec Assistant to the President ... Kathleen ANDREWS
06 Registrar ... Ann HOVEY
08 Director of Library and Media Svcs ... Darci ADOLF
15 Director of Human Resources ... Joy GUTKNECHT
18 Director of Facilities ... Chris ROGERS

Oregon College of Oriental Medicine (E)

75 NW Couch Street, Portland OR 97209-4018
County: Multnomah FICE Identification: 026037
Unit ID: 369659
Telephone: (503) 253-3443 Carnegie Class: Spec-4-yr-Other Health
FAX Number: (503) 253-2701 Calendar System: Quarter
URL: www.ocom.edu
Established: 1983 Annual Graduate Tuition & Fees: N/A
Enrollment: 236 Coed
Affiliation or Control: Independent Non-Profit IRS Status: 501(c)3
Highest Offering: Doctorate; No Undergraduates
Accreditation: ACUP

01 President/CEO ... Dr. Sherri GREEN
10 CFO/VP of Finance ... Neville WELLMAN
05 Vice President of Academic Affairs ... Dr. Valerie HOBBS
11 Vice Pres Planning & Operations ... Dr. Phil LUNDBERG
58 Dean of Postgraduate Studies ... Dr. Beth BURCH
88 Associate Dean of Doctoral Studies ... Dr. Zhaoxue LU
46 Interim Director of Research ... Vacant
15 Director of Human Resources ... Amber APPLETON
06 Registrar ... Carol ACHESON
07 Director of Admissions ... Anna GRACE
37 Director Student Financial Aid ... Katrina HITZEMAN
44 Director of Annual Giving ... Vacant
08 Director of Library Services ... Candise BRANUM
13 Director of Facilities and IT ... Chris LANGFORD
38 Director Student Counseling ... Elizabeth MILES
32 Dir of Student and Alumni Affairs ... Mike LAW

Oregon Health & Science University (F)

3181 SW Sam Jackson Park Road, Portland OR 97239-3098
County: Multnomah FICE Identification: 004882
Unit ID: 209490
Telephone: (503) 494-8311 Carnegie Class: Spec-4-yr-Eng
FAX Number: (503) 494-5738 Calendar System: Quarter
URL: www.ohsu.edu
Established: 1887 Annual Undergrad Tuition & Fees (In-State): N/A
Enrollment: 3,035 Coed
Affiliation or Control: State IRS Status: 501(c)3
Highest Offering: Doctorate
Accreditation: NW, ANEST, ARCPA, CAHIIM, CAMPEP, DENT, DIETI, EMT, IPSY, MED, MIDWF, MLS, NURSE, PH, RTT

01 President ... Dr. Danny O. JACOBS
03 Executive Vice Provost ... Dr. David W. ROBINSON
05 Provost Education & Research ... Dr. Marie CHISHOLM-BURNS
18 Assoc VP Facilities/Physical Plant ... Mr. Scott PAGE
84 Vice Prov Enroll & Academic Program ... Ms. Cherie HONNELL
46 Chief Research Officer ... Dr. Peter BARR-GILLESPIE
63 Dean School of Medicine ... Dr. David JACOBY
52 Dean School of Dentistry ... Dr. Ron SAKAGUCHI
69 Dean Joint School of Public Health ... Dr. Richard JOHNSON
66 Dean School of Nursing ... Dr. Susan BAKEWELL-SACHS
06 Registrar ... Ms. Gwen HYATT
17 Director University Hospital ... Mr. Peter RAPP
88 Director Vollum Inst Adv Biomed Res ... Dr. Richard H. GOODMAN
15 Chief People Officer ... Vacant
08 University Librarian ... Ms. Kristine ALPI
26 VP and Chief Marketing Officer ... Ms. Kimberly OVITT
88 Director Child Devel/Rehab Center ... Dr. Brian ROGERS
37 Director Student Financial Aid ... Ms. Rachel DURBIN
28 Vice Pres for Equity & Inclusion ... Dr. Derick DU VIVIER
108 Vice Prov Educ Improve/Innovation ... Dr. Constance TUCKER

Oregon Institute of Technology (G)

3201 Campus Drive, Klamath Falls OR 97601-8801
County: Klamath FICE Identification: 003211
Unit ID: 209506
Telephone: (541) 885-1000 Carnegie Class: Bac-Diverse
FAX Number: (541) 885-1101 Calendar System: Quarter
URL: www.oit.edu
Established: 1947 Annual Undergrad Tuition & Fees (In-State): $11,269
Enrollment: 5,323 Coed
Affiliation or Control: State IRS Status: 501(c)3
Highest Offering: Master's
Accreditation: NW, COARC, DH, DMS, EMT, IACBE, MLS, POLYT

01 President ... Dr. Nagi G. NAGANATHAN
05 Provost/Vice Pres Academic Affairs ... Ms. Joanna MOTT
10 VP Finance/Administration ... Mr. John HARMAN
32 VP Student Affairs/Dean of Students ... Dr. Erin FOLEY
37 Director of Financial Aid ... Ms. Tracey A. LEHMAN
15 Int AVP Human Resources ... Ms. Sandi HANAN
07 Director of Admissions ... Mr. Erik JOHNSON
06 Registrar ... Ms. Wendy IVIE
21 Assistant VP Financial Operations ... Vacant
13 Assoc VP/Chief Information Officer ... Ms. Connie ATCHLEY
26 Executive Director of Marketing ... Mr. Marcus POPIOLEK
23 Director Student Health Services ... Mrs. Gaylyn MAURER
18 Director Facilities Svcs ... Mr. Thom DARRAH
41 Athletic Director ... Mr. John VANDYKE
35 Director Campus Life ... Ms. Holly ANDERSON
88 Assoc Director Campus Life ... Ms. Josie HUDSPETH
36 Assoc Director of Career Services ... Ms. Sarah MOORE
09 Institutional Research Analyst ... Mr. Farooq SULTAN
30 VP Institutional Advanc/Development ... Mr. Ken FINCHER
04 Sr Exec Assistant to the President ... Mrs. Adria D. PASCHAL
19 Director Security/Safety ... Mr. Edward DANIELS
39 Dir Resident Life/Student Housing ... Ms. Mandi CLARK
43 Director of Legal Services ... Mr. David GROFF
84 Assoc VP Strategic Enrollment ... Vacant
96 Director of Procurement Contracts ... Ms. Vivian CHEN
100 Senior Advisor to the President ... Ms. Sandra FOX
49 Dean of Health/Arts & Sciences ... Mr. Dan PETERSON
54 Dean of Engineering ... Dr. Tom KEYSER

Oregon State University (H)

1500 SW Jefferson Avenue, Corvallis OR 97331-8507
County: Benton FICE Identification: 003210
Unit ID: 209542
Telephone: (541) 737-0123 Carnegie Class: DU-Highest
FAX Number: N/A Calendar System: Quarter
URL: www.oregonstate.edu
Established: 1868 Annual Undergrad Tuition & Fees (In-State): $11,858
Enrollment: 32,312 Coed
Affiliation or Control: State IRS Status: 501(c)3
Highest Offering: Doctorate
Accreditation: NW, CAATE, CACREP, CAEPN, CEA, CONST, DIETD, DIETI, IPSY, PH, PHAR, SPAA, VET

01 President ... Dr. Jayathi MURTHY
05 Provost/Exec Vice President ... Dr. Ed FESER
10 Vice Pres Finance/Admin ... Mr. Mike GREEN
111 Vice Pres University Advancement ... Mr. Steve CLARK
46 Vice President for Research ... Dr. Irem TUMER
20 Vice Provost for Faculty Affairs ... Dr. Richard SETTERSTEN
32 Assoc Vice Provost Student Affairs ... Mr. Dan LARSON
12 V Prov/Campus Ex Ofcr OSU-Cascades ... Dr. Andrew KETSDEVER
102 President & CEO OSU Foundation ... Mr. Shawn SCOVILLE
11 Sr Assoc VP for Administration ... Mr. Paul ODENTHAL
106 Assoc Provost for Ecampus ... Ms. Lisa TEMPLETON
47 Dean of Agricultural Sciences ... Dr. Staci SIMONICH
50 Dean of Business ... Dr. Tim CARROLL
54 Dean of Engineering ... Dr. Scott ASHFORD

65 Dean of Forestry .... Dr. Thomas DELUCA
68 Dean of Health & Human Sciences .... Dr. Brian PRIMACK
65 Dean of Earth/Ocean/Atmospheric Sci .. Dr. Tuba OZKAN-HALLER
67 Interim Dean of Pharmacy .... Dr. David BEARDEN
81 Interim Dean of Science .... Dr. Vrushali BOKIL
74 Dean of Veterinary Medicine .... Dr. Susan TORNQUIST
51 Assoc Provost Extended Campus .... Ms. Lisa TEMPLETON
35 Dean of Student Life .... Dr. Kevin DOUGHERTY
92 Dean University Honors College .... Dr. Toni DOOLEN
53 Dean of Education .... Dr. Susan GARDNER
08 University Librarian .... Ms. Anne-Marie DEITERING
22 Interim Director Equity & Inclusion .... Mr. Scott VIGNOS
43 General Counsel .... Ms. Becca GOSE
41 Director Intercollegiate Athletics .... Mr. Scott BARNES
37 Dir of Financial Aid/Scholarship .... Mr. Keith RAAB
23 Dir Student Health Services .... Ms. Jenny HAUBENREISER
38 Dir Univ Counseling/Psych Svcs .... Dr. Ian KELLEMS
39 Director Univ Housing/Dining Svcs .... Mr. Stephen JENKINS
06 Registrar .... Ms. Rebecca MATHERN
07 Director of Admissions .... Mr. Noah BUCKLEY
24 Director Media & Outreach Services .... Mr. John GREYDANUS
14 Dir of Enterprise Computing Service .... Mr. Kent KUO
15 AVP Chief Human Resources Officer .... Ms. Heather HORN
19 Chief of Police .... Ms. Shanon ANDERSON
29 Exec Dir of Alumni Association .... Mr. John VALVA
86 Director Government Relations .... Ms. Katie FAST
27 Dir News/Comm Svcs/Asst Vice Pres .... Ms. Annie HECK
26 Director of University Marketing .... Ms. Melody K. OLDFIELD
105 Asst Director Web Communications .... Mr. David A. BAKER
28 Chief Diversity Officer .... Mr. Scott VIGNOS
09 Director of Institutional Research .... Mr. Salvador CASTILLO
84 Director Enrollment Management .... Mr. Jon BOECKENSTEDT
40 General Mgr & CEO OSU Bookstores .... Mr. Steve E. ECKRICH
96 Manager Procurement/Contract Svcs .... Ms. Kelly L. KOZISEK
101 Secretary of the Institution/Board .... Ms. Jackie BANGS
45 Chief Institutional Planning Office .... Dr. Sherm BLOOMER
122 Coordinator Greek Life .... Ms. Kelsey ELAM-GEUTING

Pacific Bible College (A)

28 S. Fir St., Suite 212, Medford OR 97501

County: Jackson
Identification: 667252
Unit ID: 407610
Telephone: (541) 776-9942
Carnegie Class: Spec 2-yr-Other
FAX Number: (541) 770-9065
Calendar System: Semester
URL: https://pacificbible.edu/
Established: 1991
Annual Undergrad Tuition & Fees: $4,370
Enrollment: 47
Coed
Affiliation or Control: Non-denominational
IRS Status: 501(c)3
Highest Offering: Baccalaureate
Accreditation: BI

01 President .... Mr. Mike ROBINSON
05 Chief Academic Officer .... Mr. Matthew MCAULIFFE
37 Student Financial Aid Coordinator .... Ms. Amy STONEHILL
04 Administrative Assistant .... Ms. Kathy CURRAN
06 Registrar .... Mr. Elijah THOMAS

Pacific University (B)

2043 College Way, Forest Grove OR 97116-1797

County: Washington
FICE Identification: 003212
Unit ID: 209612
Telephone: (503) 357-6151
Carnegie Class: DU-Mod
FAX Number: (503) 352-2242
Calendar System: Semester
URL: www.pacificu.edu
Established: 1849
Annual Undergrad Tuition & Fees: $48,095
Enrollment: 3,808
Coed
Affiliation or Control: Independent Non-Profit
IRS Status: 501(c)3
Highest Offering: Doctorate
Accreditation: NW, AAQEP, #ACBSP, ARCPA, AUD, CAATE, CLPSY, DH, IPSY, MPCAC, MUS, OPT, OPTR, OT, PHAR, PTA, SP, SW

01 President .... Dr. Jennifer L. COYLE
05 Vice Pres Academic Affairs/Provost .... Dr. Ann BARR-GILLESPIE
10 Vice Pres Finance & Administration .... Mr. Jim LANGSTRAAT
111 Int Vice Pres Univ Advancement .... Mr. Zachary WALLACE
84 Vice Pres Enrollment Management .... Ms. Sarah PHILLIPS
50 Dean of Col of Business/Gen Counsel .... Ms. Jennifer YRUEGAS
32 Vice Pres Student Affairs .... Mr. Narce RODRIGUEZ
26 Assoc VP of Marketing/Comm .... Ms. Jenni LUCKETT
110 Sr AVP for University Advancement .... Ms. Jan STRICKLIN
21 Assoc VP for Finance/Controller .... Ms. Karen RASMUSSEN
07 Assoc Vice Pres of Admissions .... Ms. Karen DUNSTON
123 AVP Grad & Prof Admiss/Enroll .... Mr. Jon-Erik LARSEN
29 AVP Engagement Ops/Advancement .... Ms. Martha CALUS-MCLAIN
20 Vice Provost Academic Affairs .... Dr. Lisa CARSTENS
20 Vice Provost/Exec Dean .... Dr. Mary VON
06 Registrar .... Ms. Nikol ROUBIDOUX
18 Director of Facilities .... Ms. Cindy SCHUPPERT
37 Director Financial Aid .... Ms. Leslie LIMPER
13 Chief Information Officer .... Mr. Brandon GATKE
76 Exec Dean Col of Health Professions .... Dr. Mary VON
49 Dean of Arts & Sciences .... Dr. Sarah PHILLIPS
63 Dean College of Optometry .... Dr. Fraser C. HORN
67 Dean School of Pharmacy .... Dr. Marketa MARVANOVA
53 Dean College of Education .... Dr. Leif GUSTAVSON
83 Interim Dean School of Grad Psych .... Dr. Peter VIK
08 Dean of University Libraries .... Mr. Isaac GILMAN
41 Dir of Intercollegiate Athletics .... Mr. Keith BUCKLEY
75 Dir Sch Physical/Occup Therapy .... Dr. Jennifer PITONYAK
23 Director of Health Services .... Ms. Perla ANDRADE
15 Director of Human Resources .... Ms. Helen HOWELL
35 Dir Univ Center/Student Activities .... Mr. Steve KLEIN
52 Director Dental Hygiene Studies .... Ms. Amy COPLEN
40 Manager Bookstore .... Ms. Stacie SHOOK
38 Director of the Counseling Center .... Ms. Laura STALLINGS
09 Director of Institutional Research .... Mr. William O'SHEA
04 Executive Asst to President .... Ms. Rebeka ANDRADE
100 Chief of Staff .... Ms. Karla STAIHAR
112 Major Gift Ofcr Found/Corp Rels .... Mr. Orhan K. BELDING
104 Director International Programs .... Dr. Shpresa HALIMI
28 Director Equity/Diversity/Inclusion .... Ms. Narcedalia RODRIGUEZ

Portland Community College (C)

PO Box 19000, Portland OR 97280-0990

County: Multnomah
FICE Identification: 003213
Unit ID: 209746
Telephone: (971) 722-6111
Carnegie Class: Assoc/HT-Mix Trad/Non
FAX Number: (971) 722-4960
Calendar System: Quarter
URL: www.pcc.edu/
Established: 1961
Annual Undergrad Tuition & Fees (In-District): $4,810
Enrollment: 22,904
Coed
Affiliation or Control: Local
IRS Status: 501(c)3
Highest Offering: Associate Degree
Accreditation: NW, ADNUR, CAHIIM, DA, DH, EMT, IFSAC, MAC, MLTAD, NAEYC, RAD

01 President .... Dr. Adrien BENNINGS
03 Executive Vice President .... Vacant
100 Program Administrator .... Dr. Traci FORDHAM
05 Vice President of Academic Affairs .... Ms. Katy W. HO
32 Interim Vice Pres Student Affairs .... Dr. Heather LANG
10 Vice Pres Finance/Administration .... Mr. Eric BLUMENTHAL
21 Assoc VP Financial Services .... Ms. Dina FARRELL
15 Int Associate VP Human Resources .... Ms. Jennifer DELAIX
13 Chief Information Officer .... Mr. Michael NORTHOVER
20 Assoc VP Academic/Career Pathways .... Mr. Jeremy ESTRELLA
20 Assoc VP Academic/Career Pathways .... Dr. Karen PAEZ
20 Dean Academic/Stdnt Affs Operations .... Mr. Kurt SIMONDS
20 Dean Instruction Southeast Campus .... Vacant
88 Dean of K-12/Community Partnerships .... Ms. Vicky LOPEZ-SANCHEZ
35 Dean of Student Life & Engagement .... Mr. Josh PETERS-MCBRIDE
121 Dean Acad/Career Pathway Guidance .... Ms. Sonya BEDIENT
35 Dean of Student Belonging/Wellbeing .... Ms. Lauren SMITH
84 Dean Enrollment Strategy/Services .... Mr. Ryan CLARK
18 Director Facilities Management Svcs .... Mr. Brad ORTMAN
08 Dean Library Services .... Ms. Michelle M. BAGLEY
09 Dir Institutional Effectiveness .... Ms. Laura MASSEY
19 Director Public Safety .... Mr. Derrick FOXWORTH
37 Director Financial Aid/Veteran Svcs .... Mr. Peter GOSS
28 Interim Chief Diversity Officer .... Ms. Traci FORDHAM
102 Executive Director of Foundation .... Ms. Christina KLINE
07 Manager of Enrollment Services .... Ms. Darilis GARCIA
31 Director of Community Engagement .... Ms. Kate CHESTER
96 Manager Purchasing .... Mr. Mike MATHEWS
22 Dir Accessible Educ/Disability Res .... Ms. Kaela PARKS
20 Exec Dean Instruction/SA Innov/Tech .... Ms. Loraine SCHMITT

Portland State University (D)

PO Box 751, Portland OR 97207-0751

County: Multnomah
FICE Identification: 003216
Unit ID: 209807
Telephone: (503) 725-3000
Carnegie Class: DU-Higher
FAX Number: (503) 725-4882
Calendar System: Quarter
URL: www.pdx.edu
Established: 1946
Annual Undergrad Tuition & Fees (In-State): $10,112
Enrollment: 23,640
Coed
Affiliation or Control: State
IRS Status: 501(c)3
Highest Offering: Doctorate
Accreditation: NW, CACREP, CAEP, CEA, HSA, LC, MUS, PH, PLNG, SP, SPAA, SW, THEA

01 President .... Dr. Stephen PERCY
43 General Counsel & Board Secretary .... Ms. Cindy STARKE
05 Provost & VP Academic Affairs .... Dr. Susan JEFFORDS
10 Vice President Finance/Admin .... Dr. Kevin REYNOLDS
102 CEO PSU Foundation .... Ms. Sarah SCHWARZ
100 Chief of Staff .... Ms. Clair C. PINKERTON
84 Vice Pres Enrollment Mgmt .... Dr. Chuck KNEPFLE
46 Interim VP Research & Grad Studies .... Dr. Kelly CLIFTON
28 VP Global Diversity & Inclusion .... Dr. Ame LAMBERT
32 VProv Stdnt Affs/Dean Stdnt Life .... Dr. Michele TOPPE
20 Vice Provost Acad Pers Ldrshp & Dev .... Dr. Shelly CHABON
26 AVP Communications/Dir Marketing .... Ms. Julie SMITH
15 AVP for Human Resources .... Mr. Nathan KLINKHAMMER
09 Director Inst Research/Planning .... Dr. Kathi A. KETCHESON
19 Director Campus Public Safety .... Mr. Willie HALIBURTON
13 VP & Chief Information Officer .... Mr. Kirk KELLY
86 VP for Public Affairs .... Mr. Kevin NEELY
08 Interim Dean University Library .... Dr. Michael BOWMAN
41 Athletics Director .... Ms. Valerie CLEARY
49 Dean of CLAS .... Dr. Todd ROSENSTIEL
50 Dean School of Business .... Mr. Clifford ALLEN
53 Dean Graduate Sch of Education .... Dr. Marvin LYNN
54 Dean Col Engr/Computer Science .... Dr. Richard CORSI
57 Dean College of the Arts .... Dr. Leroy BYNUM
70 Dean School of Social Work .... Dr. Jose COLL
80 Int Dean Col Urban/Public Affairs .... Dr. Sy ADLER
06 AVP & University Registrar .... Ms. Cindy BACCAR
23 Exec Dir Stdnt Health & Counseling .... Dr. Dana TASSON
58 Dean Graduate Studies .... Ms. Rossitza WOOSTER
122 Coord Stdnt Advising-Greek Life .... Ms. Madeline FRISK

Process Work Institute (E)

2049 NW Hoyt Street, Portland OR 97209

County: Multnomah
Identification: 667297
Telephone: (503) 223-8188
Carnegie Class: Not Classified
FAX Number: (503) 227-7003
Calendar System: Quarter
URL: www.processwork.edu
Established: 1989
Annual Graduate Tuition & Fees: N/A
Enrollment: N/A
Coed
Affiliation or Control: Independent Non-Profit
IRS Status: 501(c)3
Highest Offering: Master's; No Undergraduates
Accreditation: ACICS

01 Executive Director/Dean .... Dr. Hellene GRONDA

Reed College (F)

3203 SE Woodstock Boulevard, Portland OR 97202-8199

County: Multnomah
FICE Identification: 003217
Unit ID: 209922
Telephone: (503) 771-1112
Carnegie Class: Bac-A&S
FAX Number: (503) 777-7769
Calendar System: Semester
URL: www.reed.edu
Established: 1908
Annual Undergrad Tuition & Fees: $60,620
Enrollment: 1,385
Coed
Affiliation or Control: Independent Non-Profit
IRS Status: 501(c)3
Highest Offering: Master's
Accreditation: NW

01 President .... Dr. Audrey BILGER
111 Vice Pres College Relations/Plng .... Mr. Hugh E. PORTER
05 Dean of the Faculty .... Dr. Kathryn C. OLESON
10 Vice President Finance & Treasurer .... Ms. Lynn VALENTER
32 Vice President for Student Life .... Dr. Karnell MCCONNELL-BLACK
04 Exec Asst to the President .... Ms. Dawn G. THOMPSON
28 Dean for Institutional Diversity .... Dr. Phyllis ESPOSITO
35 Dean of Students .... Ms. Tawana PARKS
23 Director Health & Counseling .... Dr. Johanna WORKMAN
07 Vice Pres/Dean Admission & Fin Aid .... Mr. Milyon TRULOVE
06 Registrar .... Mr. Jason MAHER
08 College Librarian .... Ms. Dena HUTTO
30 Executive Director of Development .... Ms. Sarah PANETTA
37 Director of Financial Aid .... Ms. Sandy SUNDSTROM
09 Director of Institutional Research .... Mr. Mike TAMADA
26 Exec Dir Comm & Public Affairs .... Vacant
13 Chief Information Officer .... Ms. Valerie MORENO
14 Deputy Chief Information Officer .... Ms. Marianne M. COLGROVE
91 Director Administrative Computing .... Ms. Kerri A. CREAGER
21 Associate Treasurer & Controller .... Mr. Rob TUST
15 Director of Human Resources .... Ms. Heather QUINN-BARRON
29 Sr Dir Alumni Pgms & Annual Fund .... Vacant
102 Dir Corporate/Foundation Support .... Mr. Jeremy NICULESCU
104 Director International Programs .... Dr. Alberto DEL RIO MALO
36 Dean of Stdnts/Dir Life Beyond Reed .... Ms. Alice HARRA
58 Assoc Dean Graduate & Special Pgms .... Ms. Ashley HUDSON
18 Director Facilities Operations .... Mr. Steven W. YEADON
19 Director Community Safety .... Mr. Gary GRANGER
41 Director of Athletics/Fitness .... Mr. Michael LOMBARDO
40 Director Bookstore & Auxiliary Svcs .... Ms. Jessica VALESKE
39 Asst Dean of Students for Res Life .... Vacant

Rogue Community College (G)

3345 Redwood Highway, Grants Pass OR 97527-9298

County: Josephine
FICE Identification: 010182
Unit ID: 209940
Telephone: (541) 956-7500
Carnegie Class: Assoc/MT-VT-Mix Trad/Non
FAX Number: (541) 471-3591
Calendar System: Quarter
URL: www.roguecc.edu
Established: 1970
Annual Undergrad Tuition & Fees (In-District): $5,040
Enrollment: 3,765
Coed
Affiliation or Control: Local
IRS Status: 501(c)3
Highest Offering: Associate Degree
Accreditation: NW, EMT

01 College President .... Dr. Randy WEBER
05 VP Student Learning & Success .... Ms. Juliet LONG
10 VP Operations & Finance/CFO .... Ms. Lisa STANTON
76 Director SOHOPE .... Ms. Lisa PARKS
88 Director Small Bus Dev Center .... Ms. Ruth SWAIN
81 Dean of Instuction Art/Science/Tech .... Ms. Kimberly FREEZE
08 Head Librarian .... Mr. Robert FELTHOUSEN
102 Executive Director Foundation .... Vacant
15 VP People/Culture & Safety .... Ms. Jamee HARRINGTON
117 Director Risk Mgmt/Title IX .... Mr. Sean TAGGART
13 Director Information Technology .... Mr. Josh OGLE
109 Director Auxiliary Svcs/Ship/Rec .... Ms. Laura HAGA-DUFFY
26 Dir Marketing/Call Center .... Vacant
37 Dir Student Financial Aid .... Ms. Frankie EVERETT
14 Director IT Network Services .... Mr. Mike MCCLURE
88 Director TRiO-EOC/ETS .... Ms. Hollie ADAIR
88 Director TRiO-SSS Programs .... Ms. Colletta YOUNG
09 Director of Institutional Research .... Ms. Laurie ROE
88 Director Apprenticeship .... Ms. Andrea ANDERSON
96 Dir Contract and Procurement .... Ms. Jodie FULTON
91 Director of IT Programming & QA .... Mr. Al SHELDON
18 Director of Facilities/Operations .... Mr. Grant LAGORIO
20 Data Mgmt Specialist Curriculum/Sch .... Ms. Marita WILDER

124	Director of Student Engagement	Dr. Rene MCKENZIE
06	Director Enrollment Svcs/Registrar	Ms. Dani CROUCH
07	Director Admissions & Recruitment	Ms. Nicole SAKRAIDA
04	Assistant to the Pres Operationss	Ms. Vicki MCCRARY
121	Dean of Student Success	Ms. April HAMLIN
22	Dir of Advising & Comp/Title IX	Ms. April HAMLIN
108	Outcomes & Assessment Coordinator	Ms. Terrie SANDLIN
28	Coord Equity/Diversity & Inclusion	Mr. Marco VASQUEZ
38	Faculty/Chair Student Counseling	Ms. Michelle GRAY
50	Faculty/Dept Chair Bus Tech	Ms. Melissa POLEN
51	Director of Continuing Educ	Ms. Diane HOOVER
76	Director Allied Health Occupations	Vacant
41	Athletic Director	Mr. Darren VAN LEHN
101	Secretary of the Institution/Board	Ms. Rachelle BROWN
97	Dean of General Education & Trans	Mr. Navarro CHANDLER
21	Director Business Office	Ms. Mariane BERRY
88	Director Advising & Military Svcs	Ms. Nikki JOHNSON
16	Human Resources Director	Ms. Kati AVERYT
114	Coordinator Budget	Ms. Natalie HERKLOTZ
86	Community & Governmental Relations	Ms. Julie RAEFIELD

Southern Oregon University (A)

1250 Siskiyou Boulevard, Ashland OR 97520-5001

County: Jackson — FICE Identification: 003219
Unit ID: 210146
Telephone: (541) 552-7672 — Carnegie Class: Masters/L
FAX Number: (541) 552-6329 — Calendar System: Quarter
URL: www.sou.edu
Established: 1872 — Annual Undergrad Tuition & Fees (In-State): $10,710
Enrollment: 5,140 — Coed
Affiliation or Control: State — IRS Status: 501(c)3
Highest Offering: Master's
Accreditation: NW, ACBSP, CACREP, MUS

01	President	Dr. Richard J. BAILEY, JR.
05	Provost/VP Academic Affairs	Dr. Susan WALSH
10	VP for Finance & Administration	Mr. Greg PERKINSON
111	VP Advancement/Dir Foundation	Ms. Janet FRATELLA
86	Vice Pres Government Relations	Ms. Jeanne STALLMAN
32	VP Student Affairs/Enrollment	Mr. Neil WOOLF
15	Director of Human Resources	Ms. Alana LARDIZABAL
26	Ex Dir Interactive Mktg/Media Rels	Ms. Nicolle ALEMAN
18	Assoc Dir Facilities Mgmt/Planning	Mr. Leon CROUCH
21	Director of Business Services	Vacant
08	University Librarian	Vacant
19	Director of Campus Public Safety	Mr. Robert GIBSON
29	Director of Alumni Affairs	Mr. Mike BEAGLE
88	Director of Schneider Museum of Art	Mr. Scott MALBAURN
28	Director of Diversity & Inclusion	Ms. Sabrina PRUD'HOMME
57	Director Center for the Arts	Dr. David HUMPHREY
83	Director Social Sciences	Dr. Dan DENEUI
97	Director Undergraduate Studies	Dr. Lee AYERS
81	Director STEM	Dr. Sherry ETTLICH
50	Dir Business Comm & Environment	Mr. Vincent SMITH
79	Director Humanities & Culture	Dr. Scott REX
88	Director Educ Health & Leadership	Dr. John KING
06	Registrar	Dr. Matt STILLMAN
07	Director of Admissions	Mr. Zac OLSON
09	Director of Institutional Research	Mr. Chris STANEK
41	Athletic Director	Mr. Matt SAYRE
101	University Board Secretary	Ms. Sabrina PRUD'HOMME
39	Director Student Housing	Ms. Staci BUCHWALD
35	Director of Student Life	Ms. Carrie VATH

Southwestern Oregon Community College (B)

1988 Newmark Avenue, Coos Bay OR 97420-2911

County: Coos — FICE Identification: 003220
Unit ID: 210155
Telephone: (541) 888-2525 — Carnegie Class: Assoc/HT-Mix Trad/Non
FAX Number: (541) 888-7285 — Calendar System: Quarter
URL: www.socc.edu
Established: 1961 — Annual Undergrad Tuition & Fees (In-District): $6,260
Enrollment: 1,537 — Coed
Affiliation or Control: Local — IRS Status: 501(c)3
Highest Offering: Associate Degree
Accreditation: NW, ACFEI, EMT, NAEYC

01	President	Dr. Patty SCOTT
11	VP Administrative Services	Mr. Jeff WHITEY
05	VP Instructional Services	Dr. Ali MAGEEHON
84	VP Enrollment & Student Services	Ms. Meredith STONE
12	Executive Dean Curry Campus	Vacant
72	Dean of Career and Technical Educ	Mr. Daniel KOOPMAN
20	Dean of LDC	Vacant
111	Dean of Advancement/Alumni Rels	Ms. Elise HAMNER
37	Dean Financial Aid/Registration	Ms. Avena SINGH
121	Dean Student Success/Transfer	Mr. Jared GARDNER
13	Exec Director Integrated Technology	Mr. John TAYLOR
88	Exec Director OCCI (Culinary)	Mr. Randy TORRES
41	Athletic Director	Dr. Mike HERBERT
117	Director of Security/Risk/Emergency	Mr. Rob ATON
18	Director Facilities Services	Mr. Ron BUFORD
06	Registrar	Ms. Avena SINGH
15	Chief Human Resources Officer	Ms. Rachele LYON
10	Executive Director Business Service	Ms. Leigh FITZHENRY
66	Director Nursing	Ms. Joannie MILLER
39	Director Residence Life	Mr. Joe BELTER
88	Director SOCC Business Dev Center	Mr. Derek TONN
38	Director Student Support Services	Ms. Michele BENOIT

40	Manager Bookstore	Ms. Clarissa RICKELS
09	Dir Institutional Effectiveness	Ms. Alisha LUND
04	Exec Asst to the Pres/Board of Educ	Ms. Dina LASKEY
26	Graphic Designer and Communication	Ms. Anne MATTHEWS

Sumner College (C)

8338 NE Alderwood Road, Ste 100, Portland OR 97220

County: Multnomah — FICE Identification: 021049
Unit ID: 208512
Telephone: (503) 972-6230 — Carnegie Class: Spec 2-yr-Health
FAX Number: (503) 952-0010 — Calendar System: Other
URL: www.sumnercollege.edu
Established: 1974 — Annual Undergrad Tuition & Fees: N/A
Enrollment: 464 — Coed
Affiliation or Control: Proprietary — IRS Status: Proprietary
Highest Offering: Baccalaureate
Accreditation: ABHES, NURSE

01	President	Joanna S. RUSSELL

Tillamook Bay Community College (D)

4301 3rd Street, Tillamook OR 97141

County: Tillamook — Identification: 666647
Unit ID: 420723
Telephone: (503) 842-8222 — Carnegie Class: Assoc/HT-High Non
FAX Number: (503) 842-8336 — Calendar System: Quarter
URL: www.tillamookbaycc.edu
Established: 1981 — Annual Undergrad Tuition & Fees (In-District): $4,176
Enrollment: 497 — Coed
Affiliation or Control: State/Local — IRS Status: 501(c)3
Highest Offering: Associate Degree
Accreditation: NW

01	President	Dr. Ross L. TOMLIN
05	VP of Instruction/Student Services	Dr. Paul JARRELL
10	Chief Finance Officer	Vacant
30	VP Admin/College Relations	Mrs. Heidi LUQUETTE
32	VP of Student Services	Mrs. Rhoda HANSON
15	Dir Hum Resources/Facilities/Safety	Mr. Pat RYAN
09	Dir of Institutional Effectiveness	Ms. Erin MCCARLEY

Treasure Valley Community College (E)

650 College Boulevard, Ontario OR 97914-3423

County: Malheur — FICE Identification: 003221
Unit ID: 210234
Telephone: (541) 881-8822 — Carnegie Class: Assoc/MT-VT-High Non
FAX Number: (541) 881-5510 — Calendar System: Quarter
URL: www.tvcc.cc
Established: 1961 — Annual Undergrad Tuition & Fees (In-District): $5,760
Enrollment: 1,470 — Coed
Affiliation or Control: Local — IRS Status: 501(c)3
Highest Offering: Associate Degree
Accreditation: NW, ADNUR, MAC

01	President	Dr. Dana YOUNG
05	Vice President of Academic Affairs	Mr. Eddie ALVES
11	Vice Pres Admin Services	Ms. Shirley HAIDLE
32	Vice President of Student Services	Mr. Travis MCFETRIDGE
08	Librarian	Ms. Tara DOMINICK
26	Assoc VP College/Public Relations	Ms. Abby LEE
37	Financial Aid Director	Ms. Diahann DERRICK
13	Director Information Technology	Mr. Scott CARPENTER
07	Director of Admissions	Ms. Stephanie OESTER
15	Director of Human Resources	Ms. Anne-Marie KELSO
51	Director of Continuing Education	Ms. Andrea TESTI
41	Athletic Director	Mr. Levi DAY
09	Dir of Institutional Effectiveness	Ms. Nino KALATOZI
102	TVCC Foundation Exec Dir	Ms. Cathy YASUDA
40	Bookstore Manager	Mr. Kjetil ROM
04	Executive Asst to President	Ms. Gina ROPER
39	Director Student Housing	Ms. Theigha COOPERRIDER-FRYMAN
07	Director Admissions/Student Success	Mr. Travis MCFETRIDGE

Umpqua Community College (F)

1140 Umpqua College Road, Roseburg OR 97470

County: Douglas — FICE Identification: 003222
Unit ID: 210270
Telephone: (541) 440-4600 — Carnegie Class: Assoc/HT-Mix Trad/Non
FAX Number: (541) 440-4637 — Calendar System: Quarter
URL: www.umpqua.edu
Established: 1964 — Annual Undergrad Tuition & Fees (In-District): $5,297
Enrollment: 2,140 — Coed
Affiliation or Control: Local — IRS Status: 501(c)3
Highest Offering: Associate Degree
Accreditation: NW, DA, EMT

01	President	Dr. Rachel POKRANDT
05	Vice President of Instruction	Dr. Teresa RIVENES
32	Vice President of Student Services	Mr. Jim PITTMAN
10	CFO	Ms. Natalya BROWN
20	Dean of Learning & Support Services	Ms. Danielle HASKETT
84	Asst VP Enrollment/Student Services	Ms. Missy OLSON
37	Director of Financial Aid	Ms. Michelle BERGMANN
13	Director Informational Technology	Mr. Tim HILL
08	Director of Library Services	Vacant

103	Dean Community Educ & Partnership	Ms. Robin VAN WINKLE
09	Director Institutional Research	Mr. Steve ROGERS
15	Director of Human Resources	Ms. Kelley PLUEARD
04	Executive Asst to President & Board	Ms. Robynne WILGUS
06	Director of Registration & Records	Ms. Brenna HOBBS
18	Director of Facilities & Security	Vacant
41	Athletic Director	Mr. Craig JACKSON
96	Purchasing Manager	Ms. Joy YORI
19	Chief of Security	Mr. Scott FRAY
26	Dir Communications & Marketing	Ms. Suzi PRITCHARD
102	CEO UCC Foundation	Ms. Jessica PAUGH
108	Dir Institutional Effectiveness	Ms. Jana PIERCE

University of Oregon (G)

1585 E. 13th Avenue, Eugene OR 97403

County: Lane — FICE Identification: 003223
Unit ID: 209551
Telephone: (541) 346-1000 — Carnegie Class: DU-Highest
FAX Number: N/A — Calendar System: Quarter
URL: www.uoregon.edu
Established: 1876 — Annual Undergrad Tuition & Fees (In-State): $13,857
Enrollment: 21,752 — Coed
Affiliation or Control: State — IRS Status: 501(c)3
Highest Offering: Doctorate
Accreditation: NW, AAQEP, ART, CEA, CIDA, CLPSY, COPSY, IPSY, JOUR, LAW, LSAR, MFCD, MUS, NASP, PCSAS, PLNG, SCPSY, SP, SPAA

01	Interim President	Dr. Patrick PHILLIPS
100	Sr Advisor/Chief of Staff to Pres	Mr. Greg J. STRIPP
05	Acting Provost/Senior Vice Pres	Ms. Janet WOODRUFF-BORDEN
10	VP Finance & Admin & CFO	Ms. Jamie H. MOFFITT
32	VP Student Life	Dr. Kevin MARBURY
111	VP University Advancement	Mr. Michael C. ANDREASEN
46	VP Research & Innovation	Dr. Anshuman (AR) RAZDAN
26	VP University Communications	Ms. Richie HUNTER
43	Vice President and General Counsel	Mr. Kevin REED
20	VProv Undergrad Educ/Stdnt Success	Dr. Kimberly JOHNSON
28	VP Equity & Inclusion	Dr. Yvette M. ALEX-ASSENSOH
84	VP Student Svcs & Enrollment Mgmt	Dr. Roger J. THOMPSON
13	Vice Prov Information Services/CIO	Mr. Abhijit PANDIT
85	Dean/Vice Provost Global Engagement	Dr. Dennis C. GALVAN
86	Assoc Vice Pres Federal Affairs	Ms. Betsy A. BOYD
86	Senior Director State Affairs	Ms. Jenna ADAMS-KALLOCH
29	AVP Alumni Affairs/Exec Dir UOAA	Mr. Raphe BECK
06	University Registrar	Ms. Julia POMERENK
07	Interim AVP/Dir of Admissions	Dr. Lisa HARRIS
08	Vice Provost & University Librarian	Ms. Alicia SALAZ
21	Dir Business Affairs and Controller	Mr. Kelly B. WOLF
37	Director Student Financial Aid	Mr. Jim J. BROOKS
36	Director of Career Center	Mr. Paul TIMMINS
15	Chief Human Resources Officer	Mr. Mark SCHMELZ
18	Assoc VP Planning & Facilities Mgmt	Mr. Mike HARWOOD
22	AVP/Chief Civil Rights & Title IX	Ms. Nicole COMMISSIONG
41	Director Intercollegiate Athletics	Mr. Rob A. MULLENS
56	Executive Dir UO Academic Extension	Ms. Sandra K. GLADNEY
49	Dean College Arts & Science	Dr. Bruce BLONIGEN
48	Dean College of Design	Dr. Adrian PARR
50	Dean College of Business	Vacant
53	Interim Dean College of Education	Dr. Laura Lee MCINTYRE
60	Dean School of Journalism/Comm	Dr. Juan-Carlos MOLLEDA
58	Vice Provost for Graduate Studies	Ms. Krista CHRONISTER
61	Dean School of Law	Ms. Marcilynn BURKE
64	Dean School of Music & Dance	Dr. Sabrina MADISON-CANNON
92	Interim Dean Clark Honors College	Ms. Carol STABILE
09	Director of Institutional Research	Dr. JP MONROE
38	Dir Counseling & Testing Center	Dr. Shelly K. KERR
96	Chief Procurement Officer	Mr. Greg SHABRAM
101	Secretary of the University/Board	Mr. Tim INMAN
19	Chief of Police	Mr. Jason WADE
39	Director Student Housing	Mr. Michael M. GRIFFEL
114	Vice Provost Budget & Planning	Dr. Brad SHELTON
90	Director Academic Technology	Vacant
106	Assoc VP Online & Distance Educ	Ms. Carol GERING
30	Senior Assoc VP for Development	Mr. Paul ELSTONE

University of Portland (H)

5000 N Willamette Boulevard, Portland OR 97203-5798

County: Multnomah — FICE Identification: 003224
Unit ID: 209825
Telephone: (503) 943-8000 — Carnegie Class: Masters/M
FAX Number: (503) 943-7491 — Calendar System: Semester
URL: www.up.edu
Established: 1901 — Annual Undergrad Tuition & Fees: $49,644
Enrollment: 3,999 — Coed
Affiliation or Control: Independent Non-Profit — IRS Status: 501(c)3
Highest Offering: Doctorate
Accreditation: NW, CAEP, MUS, NURSE, SW, THEA

01	President	Dr. Robert D. KELLY
05	Provost	Dr. Herbert A. MEDINA
41	Vice President for Athletics	Mr. Scott R. LEYKAM
10	Vice Pres for Financial Affairs	Mr. Eric C. BARGER
43	Vice Pres & General Counsel	Ms. Andrea M. BARTON
15	Vice President for Human Resources	Ms. Dana LOPEZ
26	Vice Pres for Mktg & Communications	Mr. Michael E. LEWELLEN
32	Vice President for Student Affairs	Rev. John J. DONATO, CSC
11	Vice Pres for University Operations	Vacant

111 Int Vice Pres for Univ Relations .... Rev. Edwin H. OBERMILLER
20 Associate Provost .... Ms. Elise M. MOENTMANN
85 Assoc Prov Intl Educ/Diver/Inclus .... Dr. Eduardo R. CONTRERAS
35 Assoc VP for Student Development .... Dr. Tamara HERDENER
07 Assoc Provost for Admissions .... Mr. Gerardo CIFUENTES
49 Dean of Arts & Sciences .... Dr. Valerie BANSCHBACH
50 Dean of Business .... Dr. Michael DEVAUGHN
53 Dean of Education .... Dr. John L. WATZKE
54 Dean of Engineering .... Dr. Brian FABIEN
08 Dean of Library .... Ms. Xan ARCH
66 Dean of Nursing .... Dr. Casey R. SHILLAM
18 Assoc VP Const & Facilities .... Mr. David HOBBS
30 Assoc VP for Development .... Ms. Amy EATON
88 Assoc VP for Land Use & Planning .... Ms. Jennie CAMBIER
29 Director Alumni Relations .... Ms. Gina AMATO YAZZOLINO
40 Director Bookstore .... Ms. Melanie KELLAR
42 Director Campus Ministry .... Rev. Peter WALSH, CSC
36 Director Career Services .... Ms. Amy E. CAVANAUGH
112 Dir Gift Planning & Major Gifts .... Vacant
09 Director Institutional Research .... Dr. Michael JOHNSON
19 Director Public Safety .... Ms. Sara WESTBROOK
39 Director Residence Life .... Mr. Andrew WEINGARTEN
37 Director Student Financial Aid .... Ms. Janet K. TURNER
104 Director of Studies Abroad .... Ms. Maraina MONTGOMERY
35 Director Student Activities .... Mr. Jeromy A. KOFFLER
88 Director University Events .... Mr. Joe D. KALEEL
23 Director University Health Center .... Ms. Kaylin SOLDAT
25 Associate Director of Grants .... Ms. Megan MOSMAN
21 Controller .... Mr. Kenneth PIFER
06 Registrar .... Ms. Roberta D. LINDAHL
04 Executive Asst to President .... Ms. Jordan PARKS
100 Chief of Staff .... Mr. Evan LEADEM

University of Western States (A)

8000 NE Tillamook Street, Portland OR 97213

County: Multnomah | FICE Identification: 012309 | Unit ID: 210438

Telephone: (503) 256-3180 | Carnegie Class: DU-Mod

FAX Number: (503) 251-5723 | Calendar System: Quarter

URL: www.uws.edu

Established: 1904 | Annual Undergrad Tuition & Fees: N/A

Enrollment: 1,195 | Coed

Affiliation or Control: Independent Non-Profit | IRS Status: 501(c)3

Highest Offering: Doctorate

Accreditation: NW, CHIRO

01 President .... Dr. Joseph BRIMHALL
03 Executive Vice President .... Dr. Rosalia MESSINA
11 Sr VP of Finance and Administration .... Mr. Glenn FORD
10 Chief Business Officer .... Ms. Lisa LOPEZ
05 Provost/VP Academic Affairs .... Dr. Dana SIMS
88 Special Assistant to the President .... Dr. Patrick BROWNE
23 Chief Medical Officer .... Dr. Bill MOREAU
45 VP Innovation/Strategic Initiative .... Dr. Sara MATHOV
88 Associate Dean Clinical Internship .... Dr. Stanley EWALD
13 Interim Chief Technology Officer .... Mr. Mark STALEY
20 Dean of Teaching and Learning .... Dr. Denise DALLMANN
32 Assoc Vice Pres of Student Affairs .... Ms. Elena HOWELLS
26 AVP University Comm & Marketing .... Ms. Megan NUGENT
15 Director Human Resources .... Ms. Kathleen CANNON
06 Registrar .... Ms. Michelle DODGE
08 University Librarian .... Ms. Stephanie DEBNER
63 Dean College of Chiropractic .... Dr. Kathleen GALLIGAN
58 Dean College of Graduate Studies .... Dr. Alisa BATES
108 Director Academic Assessment .... Dr. Cecelia MARTIN
10 Exec Dir Clinic Business Operation .... Ms. Monika MAJCHRZAK
07 Executive Director of Admissions .... Mr. Joshua CIVIELLO
117 Executive Director of Emergency Mgt .... Mr. Sean SPELLECY
114 Exec Dir of Budget & Resource Plng .... Ms. Tonja HODGKINSON
88 Director of Capital Planning/Devel .... Mr. Chris ADAMS
37 Director Financial Aid .... Ms. Kim LAMBORN
31 Director Community Engagement .... Ms. Alisa FAIRWEATHER
26 Director of Marketing .... Ms. Jennifer ROSENBERGER
30 Development Officer .... Ms. Amy LODHOLZ
29 Alumni Relations Manager .... Ms. Chelsea NORDBY
09 AVP Institutional Effectiveness .... Dr. Rachael PANDZIK
108 Dir Inst Appraisal and Accred .... Dr. Susan DONOFF
38 Dir Clinical Mental Hlth Counseling .... Dr. Michelle COX
28 Dir of Diversity/Equity & Inclusion ..... Ms. Abolade MAJEKOBAJE
35 Director of Student Svcs Online .... Ms. Rachel HASSE
117 Director of Risk Management .... Mr. David MUSIAL
35 Director of Student Svcs On-Campus ..... Ms. Jenna GERACITANO
109 Director of Auxiliary Services .... Ms. Amber LYSIAK
04 Exec Assistant Office of the Pres .... Ms. Miranda HOLTMANN
25 Research/Inst Review Board Admin .... Ms. Leslie TAKAKI

Warner Pacific University (B)

2219 SE 68th Avenue, Portland OR 97215

County: Multnomah | FICE Identification: 003225 | Unit ID: 210304

Telephone: (503) 517-1020 | Carnegie Class: Bac-Diverse

FAX Number: (503) 517-1350 | Calendar System: Semester

URL: www.warnerpacific.edu

Established: 1937 | Annual Undergrad Tuition & Fees: $19,860

Enrollment: 466 | Coed

Affiliation or Control: Church Of God | IRS Status: 501(c)3

Highest Offering: Master's

Accreditation: NW, AAQEP, NURSE, SW

01 President .... Dr. Brian L. JOHNSON
05 Vice Pres Acad Affs/Dean of Faculty .... Dr. Miriam CHITIGA
10 EVP/CFO .... Mr. Doug WADE
111 VP for University Advancement .... Ms. Wendy MARSH
32 VP for Student Success & Engagement .... Dr. Ashlee SPEARMAN
84 VP for Enrollment Management .... Mr. Dwight SANCHEZ
37 Assistant Director of Financial Aid .... Ms. Nancy DRUMMOND
07 Associate Director of Admissions .... Ms. Yolanda ROSEBY
41 Interim Director of Athletics .... Mr. Matt GREGG
08 Director of Library Services .... Dr. Lishi KWASITSU
06 Registrar .... Dr. Marlo WATERS
13 Director Information Technology .... Dr. Max SIGANDER
29 Alumni & Events Officer .... Ms. Mary CLAYTON
42 Interim Student Chaplain .... Mr. Lorenzo PETERSON
35 Associate Dean of Students .... Ms. Felita SINGLETON
15 Director of Human Resources .... Mrs. Rachel LEA
09 Dir of Assessment/Inst Research .... Mr. Gary RAILSBACK
26 Chief of Staff/VP Strategic Comm .... Ms. Jennifer BOEHMER
38 Director Student Counseling .... Mr. Gene HALL
21 Controller .... Mrs. Cheryl ANDERSON
121 AVP for Student Success/Engagement .... Mrs. Araceli CRUZ
04 Exec Assistant to the President .... Ms. Lyne BACON
19 Exec Dir Facilities/Campus Safety .... Mr. Daniel ROBLES
88 Sr Asst Director for Admissions .... Ms. Deepika KAPIL

Western Oregon University (C)

345 N Monmouth Avenue, Monmouth OR 97361-1394

County: Polk | FICE Identification: 003209 | Unit ID: 210429

Telephone: (503) 838-8000 | Carnegie Class: Masters/L

FAX Number: (503) 838-8474 | Calendar System: Quarter

URL: www.wou.edu

Established: 1856 | Annual Undergrad Tuition & Fees (In-State): $10,194

Enrollment: 4,554 | Coed

Affiliation or Control: State | IRS Status: 501(c)3

Highest Offering: Beyond Master's But Less Than Doctorate

Accreditation: NW, CACREP, CAEPN

01 Interim President .... Dr. Jay KENTON
03 Vice President & General Counsel .... Mr. Ryan HAGEMANN
05 Provost/VP Academic Affairs .... Dr. Rob WINNINGHAM
32 Vice President Student Affairs .... Dr. Gary DUKES
10 VP Finance & Administration .... Dr. Ana KARAMAN
20 Interim Assoc VP Academic Programs .. Dr. Erin BAUMGARTNER
121 Asst VP Student Engagement .... Vacant
86 Associate VP for Public Affairs .... Mr. Dave MCDONALD
108 Assoc Provost Program Development .... Ms. Sue MONAHAN
35 Dean of Students .... Ms. Tina M. FUCHS
49 Dean Col Liberal Arts & Sciences .... Dr. Kathy CASSITY
53 Dean College of Education .... Dr. Mark GIROD
43 Deputy General Counsel .... Mr. Carson CAMPBELL
06 Registrar .... Ms. Amy CLARK
15 Int Exec Director Human Resources .... Ms. Heather MERCER
111 Executive Director of Advancement .... Ms. Erin MCDONOUGH
08 Dean Hamersly Library/Acad Innov .... Chelle BATCHELOR
13 Dir University Computing Solutions .... Vacant
18 Director Facilities Services .... Mr. Michael SMITH
19 Director University Public Safety .... Ms. Rebecca CHILES
23 Dir Student Health/Counseling Ctr .... Ms. Beth SCROGGINS
26 Dir Public Relations/Communications .... Ms. Denise VISUANO
37 Director Financial Aid .... Ms. Kella HELYER
41 Athletic Director .... Ms. Randi LYDUM
46 Dir of Teaching Research Institute .... Vacant
28 Asst Dir Multicultural Student Svcs .... Ms. Luanne CARRILLO
04 Executive Asst to President .... Mrs. LouAnn VICKERS
21 Controller/Business Services .... Mr. Gabe DOUGHERTY
07 Director of Admissions .... Ms. Anna HERNANDEZ HUNTER
09 Director of Institutional Research .... Dr. Abdus SHAHID
122 Asst Dir Stdnt Engage-Greek Life .... Ms. Alyssa ROLLINS

Western Seminary (D)

5511 SE Hawthorne Boulevard, Portland OR 97215-3399

County: Multnomah | FICE Identification: 007178 | Unit ID: 210368

Telephone: (503) 517-1800 | Carnegie Class: Spec-4-yr-Faith

FAX Number: (503) 517-1801 | Calendar System: Semester

URL: https://www.westernseminary.edu/

Established: 1927 | Annual Graduate Tuition & Fees: N/A

Enrollment: 826 | Coed

Affiliation or Control: Independent Non-Profit | IRS Status: 501(c)3

Highest Offering: Doctorate; No Undergraduates

Accreditation: NW, CACREP, THEOL

01 President .... Dr. Charles CONNIRY
10 Interim COO .... Mr. Robert GEBHARDT
05 VP Academic Affairs/Dean of Faculty .... Dr. Josh MATHEWS
111 VP of Advancement .... Mr. Robert JONES
32 Chief Student Affairs/Life Officer .... Ms. Rebekah BUCHTERKIRCHEN
20 Associate Academic Dean .... Ms. Julia MAYO
06 Registrar .... Ms. Cynthia MATHAI
21 Controller .... Mr. Jonathan GIBSON
35 Director of Student Services .... Mr. Andy PELOQUIN
13 Director of Information Services .... Mr. Sean GORDON
37 Financial Aid Director .... Mr. Spencer REED
106 Asst Director of Distance Education .... Mr. Jon RAIBLEY
15 Human Resources Director .... Ms. Ashley MITCHELL
08 Library Director .... Mr. Matthew THIESEN
26 Director of Marketing .... Mr. Ben HOFFMAN
18 Chief Facilities/Physical Plant .... Mr. Noah BROWN
106 Director of Distance Education .... Mr. Andrew PACK
07 Director of Admissions .... Mr. Andrew HEDINGER
04 Admin Assistant to the President .... Ms. Kelly BORROR

Willamette University (E)

900 State Street, Salem OR 97301-3930

County: Marion | FICE Identification: 003227 | Unit ID: 210401

Telephone: (503) 370-6300 | Carnegie Class: Bac-A&S

FAX Number: (503) 370-6148 | Calendar System: Semester

URL: www.willamette.edu

Established: 1842 | Annual Undergrad Tuition & Fees: $53,834

Enrollment: 1,866 | Coed

Affiliation or Control: Independent Non-Profit | IRS Status: 501(c)3

Highest Offering: Doctorate

Accreditation: NW, CEA, LAW, MUS, SPAA

01 President .... Dr. Stephen THORSETT
05 Sr VP for Academic/Student Affairs .... Dr. Carol LONG
10 VP for Finance and Treasurer .... Mr. Dan VALLES
111 Vice President for Advancement .... Ms. Shelby RADCLIFFE
07 VP & Dean of Admission .... Ms. Mary RANDERS
13 Vice President and CIO .... Ms. Jacqueline BARRETTA
32 VP Student Affairs/Dean of Students .... Ms. Lisa LANDREMAN
49 Dean of the College Liberal Arts .... Dr. Ruth P. FEINGOLD
61 Dean of the College of Law .... Mr. Brian GALLINI
50 Dean Graduate School Management .... Dr. Orn BODVARSSON
42 Chaplain .... Rev. Ineda ADENSANYA
23 Director of Bishop Wellness Center .... Mr. Donald A. THOMSON
88 Director Center Dispute Resolution .... Dr. Aaron SIMOWITZ
91 Director Administrative Computing .. Mr. Harvey J. PRUDHOMME
37 Director Student Financial Aid .... Ms. Patricia K. HOBAN
09 Director of Institutional Research .... Dr. Kelley STRAWN
06 University Registrar .... Ms. Laura JACOBS ANDERSON
08 University Librarian .... Mr. Craig MILBERG
21 Controller .... Mr. Kenneth PIFER
40 Bookstore Manager .... Mr. Dan C. VALLES
104 Director of International Education .... Mr. Kris LOU
41 Athletic Director .... Mr. Rob PASSAGE
29 Assoc VP Alumni & Parent Relations .... Mr. Tyler REICH
112 Assoc Dir of Dev for Gift Planning .... Ms. Cathy M. GASKIN
15 VP Human Resources/Risk Management .... Ms. Shana SECHRIST
35 Assoc Dean Stdnts/Stdnt Activities .... Ms. Lisa C. HOLLIDAY
36 Director Career Development .... Ms. Mandy DEVEREUX
28 Director of Multicultural Affairs .... Mr. Gordon K. TOYAMA
18 Director Facilities Management .... Mr. Gary GRIMM
26 Chief Communications Officer .... Mr. Tim COBB
19 Director Security/Safety .... Mr. Ross STOUT
04 Executive Assistant to President .... Ms. Elizabeth GARLAND
100 Chief of Staff .... Ms. Colleen KAWAHARA
22 Title IX Coordinator .... Ms. Darci HEROY
39 Director of Housing & Conferences .... Mr. Scott ETHERTON
43 General Counsel .... Ms. Yvonne TAMAYO
122 Dir Student Engage-Greek Life .... Ms. Lisa HOLLIDAY

PENNSYLVANIA

Albright College (F)

N 13th & Bern Streets, PO Box 15234, Reading PA 19612-5234

County: Berks | FICE Identification: 003229 | Unit ID: 210571

Telephone: (610) 921-2381 | Carnegie Class: Bac-A&S

FAX Number: (610) 921-7530 | Calendar System: 4/1/4

URL: www.albright.edu

Established: 1856 | Annual Undergrad Tuition & Fees: $26,688

Enrollment: 1,584 | Coed

Affiliation or Control: United Methodist | IRS Status: 501(c)3

Highest Offering: Master's

Accreditation: M

01 President .... Dr. Jacquelyn S. FETROW
05 Provost/SVP Academic Affairs .... Dr. Karen CAMPBELL
10 Vice Pres Administration/Finance .... Mr. Gregory L. FULMER
111 Vice President Advancement .... Ms. Wendy PARSONS
32 SVP Student & Campus Life/CHO .... Ms. Samantha WESNER
26 Vice President for Communications .... Ms. Jennifer STOUDT
13 VP DSI & Chief Information Officer .... Mr. Jason HOERR
89 Assoc Dean First Yr Exp/Acad Affs .... Dr. Robert SEESENGOOD
08 Interim Director Library Services .... Ms. Sandy STUMP
102 Dir of The Fund for Albright/ADV .... Ms. Caitlin KAMERER
21 AVP & Controller/F&SP .... Mr. Rick W. MELCHER
37 Director of Financial Aid .... Ms. Chris HANLON
35 Actg Dean of Stdnts/Title IX Coord .... Ms. Becky ACHEY
06 Associate Registrar .... Ms. Debra BAVER
36 Director Career Development/AA .... Ms. Laura KLINE
39 Director of Residential Life/SCL ..... Ms. Amanda HIGGINBOTHAM
38 Director of Counseling/SCL .... Dr. Brenda J. INGRAM-WALLACE
18 Director Facilities/Svcs/Opers .... Mr. Chuck MURPHY
41 Co-Athletic Director .... Mr. Richard E. FERRY
41 Co-Athletic Director .... Ms. Janice J. LUCK
19 Director of Public Safety .... Mr. Michael L. GROSS
40 Book Store Manager .... Ms. Heather SHERMAN
42 Chaplain/SCL .... RevDr. Sudha ALLITT
42 Chaplin/SCL .... Rev. Melvin SENSENIG
42 Chaplain/SCL .... Rev. Ibrahim BANGURA
15 Director of Human Resources .... Ms. Kim HUBRIC
85 Dir of OSIL/Coord Multicultural .... Mr. Keith WALLS
09 Director of Institutional Research .... Vacant
25 Dir of Grants & Sponsored Programs .... Ms. Julie SWEITZER
92 Director Honors Program .... Dr. Julia F. HEBERLE
92 Director Honors Program .... Mr. Christopher J. CATONE
07 Director of Admission/EM .... Ms. Jennifer WILLIAMSON

88 Dir of Conferences/Pres Office .... Ms. Lois A. KUBINAK
100 Chief of Staff/President's Office .... Ms. Kathy L. CAFONCELLI
88 Director of Schumo Center/SCL ....Ms. Alison BURKE
22 Dir of Stdnt Accessibility/Advocacy ....Ms. Sherry YOUNG
109 General Manager Dining Services/SCL ... Mr. Heath MCCORMICK
106 Dir Digital Learning & Innovation ....Vacant
112 Sr Dir Prospect Rsrch/Stewardship .... Ms. Jessica MORRIS
108 Dir Assessment/Inst Effectiveness .... Ms. Maria QUEERY

Allegheny College (A)

520 N Main Street, Meadville PA 16335-3902
County: Crawford FICE Identification: 003230
Unit ID: 210669
Telephone: (814) 332-3100 Carnegie Class: Bac-A&S
FAX Number: (814) 332-2796 Calendar System: Semester
URL: www.allegheny.edu
Established: 1815 Annual Undergrad Tuition & Fees: $50,980
Enrollment: 1,667 Coed
Affiliation or Control: United Methodist IRS Status: 501(c)3
Highest Offering: Baccalaureate
Accreditation: M

01 Acting President .... Dr. Ronald B. COLE
03 Exec Vice President and COO ....Vacant
05 Provost & Dean of the College .... Ms. Angela T. HADDAD
111 Vice Pres Institutional Advancement ...... Mr. Matthew P. STINSON
84 Vice Pres for Enrollment Mgmt ....Ms. Ellen V. JOHNSON
32 VP Student Life/Dean of Students .... Ms. April THOMPSON
10 VP Finance & Administration/CFO ....Ms. Linda S. WETSELL
04 Assistant to the President ....Ms. Pamela S. HIGHAM
110 AVP Development & Alumni Affairs ....Mr. Philip R. FOXMAN
26 Vice President College Relations ....Ms. Susan SALTON
28 Dean for Institutional Diversity .Ms. Heather MOORE ROBERSON
20 Associate Provost .... Dr. Terry BENSEL
37 Senior Assoc Dir Financial Aid .... Ms. Natasha ECKART
108 VP for Info Svcs & Assessment .... Dr. Richard A. HOLMGREN
06 Assoc Provost/Int Registrar ....Ms. Jennifer DEARDEN
08 Director of the Library .... Dr. Richard A. HOLMGREN
15 Director of Human Resources ....Ms. Jennifer PADLAN
19 Director of Public Safety ....Mr. Jim BASINGER
44 Director of Annual Giving ....Ms. Sara PINEO
18 Director Physical Plant ....Vacant
13 Director of Enterprise Services ....Mr. Jason M. RAMSEY
41 Director of Athletics ....Mr. William ROSS
31 Director of Civic Engagement .... Dr. David RONCOLATO
38 Director of Counseling Center .... Dr. Trae YECKLEY
09 Director of Institutional Research ....Vacant
36 Director Career Education .... Mr. James FITCH
88 Associate Dean for Wellness Educ ....Ms. Gretchen BECK
42 Chaplain ....Dr. Jane Ellen NICKELL
88 Dir Center Political Participation ....Dr. Brian HARWARD
22 Director of Disability Services .... Mr. John J. MANGINE
57 Director of Art & Publications .... Ms. Penny M. DREXEL
27 Assoc Dir Marketing & Communication ...... Mr. Jason ANDRACKI
40 Manager of Bookstore ....Vacant
96 Purchasing & Student Services Coord .... Ms. Kathleen M. CONAWAY

Allegany College of Maryland Bedford County Campus (B)

18 North River Lane, Everett PA 15537-1410
Telephone: (814) 652-9528 Identification: 770124
Accreditation: &M

† Branch campus of Allegany College of Maryland, Cumberland, MD

Alvernia University (C)

400 Saint Bernardine Street, Reading PA 19607-1799
County: Berks FICE Identification: 003233
Unit ID: 210775
Telephone: (610) 796-8200 Carnegie Class: DU-Mod
FAX Number: (610) 777-6632 Calendar System: Semester
URL: www.alvernia.edu
Established: 1958 Annual Undergrad Tuition & Fees: $38,030
Enrollment: 2,560 Coed
Affiliation or Control: Roman Catholic IRS Status: 501(c)3
Highest Offering: Doctorate
Accreditation: M, ACBSP, CAATE, CACREP, NURSE, OT, PTA, SW

01 President ....Mr. John R. LOYACK
05 SVP & Provost ....Dr. Glynis FITZGERALD
10 VP/Chief Financial Officer .... Mr. Larry SHAUB
111 VP for Institutional Advancement ....Mr. Thomas MINICK
84 SVP Enrollmt Managemt/Student Affs ....Ms. Mary-Alice OZECHOSKI
100 SVP & Chief of Staff ....Dr. John R. MCCLOSKEY, JR.
42 VP Mission & Ministry .... Dr. Darryl MACE
26 Director of Marketing & Comm ....Mr. Kristopher NOLT
13 CIO .... Mr. Robert IANNELLI
32 Dean of Students ....Ms. Karolina DREHER
35 Associate Dean of Students .... Ms. Abby SWATCHICK
06 Registrar ....Ms. Beki STEIN
21 Assistant Controller ....Mr. Troy HIGH
92 Director Honors Program .... Dr. Victoria WILLIAMS
41 Director Athletics & Recreation ....Mr. Bill STILES
09 Dean of Institutional Research ....Dr. Evelina PANAYOTOVA
15 Executive Director Human Resources ....Mrs. Allyson MULLIN
18 Dir of Facilities Operations ....Mr. Daniel NATAL
88 Dir of Facility Plng/Construction .... Mr. Matthew BOARDER
36 Career Development Director .... Mrs. Megan ADUKAITIS
37 Sr Dir of Student Financial Svcs ....Ms. Christine SAADI
96 Procurement Manager .... Ms. Ann NAWROCKI
58 VP Graduate & Adult Education .... Dr. Gaetan GIANNINI
49 Dean College of HESS ....Dr. Elizabeth MATTEO
04 Executive Admin Assistant ....Ms. Kelly STORTI
19 Director of Public Safety ....Mr. Edward HEIM
08 Director of Library ....Ms. Christina STEFFY
25 Director of Grants ....Ms. Laurel RADZIESKI
104 Director Intl Student Recruitment ....Dr. Sibel AHI
108 Assoc Director Inst Assessment ....Mr. Scott PAVONE
39 Dir Resident Life/Student Housing ....Ms. Shannon MERKEY
50 Dean Business/Comm/Leadership ....Dr. Travis BERGER
54 Dean of STEAM .... Dr. Rodney RIDLEY

The American College of Financial Services (D)

630 Allendale Rd, King of Prussia PA 19406
County: Montgomery FICE Identification: 033173
Unit ID: 210809
Telephone: (610) 526-1000 Carnegie Class: Spec-4-yr-Bus
FAX Number: (610) 526-1310 Calendar System: Other
URL: www.theamericancollege.edu
Established: 1927 Annual Undergrad Tuition & Fees: N/A
Enrollment: 5,723 Coed
Affiliation or Control: Independent Non-Profit IRS Status: 501(c)3
Highest Offering: Doctorate
Accreditation: M

01 President & CEO ....Mr. George NICHOLS, III
05 Executive Vice President & Provost .... Dr. Gwen HALL
20 Assoc Provost Faculty & Curriculum ....Dr. Kathleen IRWIN
111 VP Advancement/Alumni Rel ....Mr. Stephen J. GROURKE
15 VP Admin & Chief HR Officer ....Ms. Deborah GLENN
45 VP Organizational Effectiveness ....Mr. Bryan JOHNSON
32 Assoc VP Student Experience .... Mr. Rob HUGHES
04 Assistant to the President .... Ms. Jean C. MEYER
117 Chief Financial and Risk Officer .... Mr. Mark MONTGOMERY
26 Chief Marketing Officer ....Vacant
13 Chief Technology Officer .... Mr. Ed M. MCEVOY
88 AVP Accreditation .... Dr. Lynn WALLACE
06 Registrar ....Mr. Will JACOBS
08 Library Services .... Ms. Shiloa THOMAS
88 AVP/Director Assessments & Exams ..Ms. Diane M. HAMMONDS

Arcadia University (E)

450 S Easton Road, Glenside PA 19038-3295
County: Montgomery FICE Identification: 003235
Unit ID: 211088
Telephone: (215) 572-2900 Carnegie Class: Masters/L
FAX Number: (215) 572-0240 Calendar System: Semester
URL: www.arcadia.edu
Established: 1853 Annual Undergrad Tuition & Fees: $45,340
Enrollment: 3,300 Coed
Affiliation or Control: Independent Non-Profit IRS Status: 501(c)3
Highest Offering: Doctorate
Accreditation: M, ACBSP, ARCPA, ART, FEPAC, MPCAC, PH, PTA

01 President ....Dr. Ajay NAIR
05 Provost & VP Academic Affairs ....Dr. Jeff RUTENBECK
84 VP Enrollment Management ....Mr. Rakin HALL
10 VP of Finance and CFO .... Ms. Joan SINGLETON
43 General Counsel ....Ms. Margaret CALLAHAN
13 VP and Chief Information Officer .Ms. Rashmi RADHAKRISHNAN
30 VP Development/Alumni Engagement .... Ms. Brigette BRYANT
26 VP for Marketing and Communications ....Ms. Laura BALDWIN
32 Dean of Students ....Mr. Andrew GORETSKY
18 Assoc VP Facilities/Capital Plng .... Mr. Thomas J. MACCHI
88 VP/Exec Dir Col of Global Studies ....Ms. Lorna STERN
21 Assoc VP Finance & COO TCGS ....Ms. Colleen BURKE
15 Assoc VP Human Resources .... Ms. Mary SWEENEY
20 Deputy Provost ....Dr. Thomas EGAN
06 Registrar .... Mr. William ELNICK
88 Sr Associate Registrar ....Mrs. Nicole M. ZUCKER
49 Dean College Arts & Sciences ....Dr. Rebecca KOHN
76 Dean College of Health Sciences ....Dr. Rebecca L. CRAIK
51 Coord Office of Continuing Studies ....Ms. Kathryn PHILLIPS
50 Dean School of Global Business ...Mr. Thomas M. BRINKER, JR.
58 Dean Graduate & Undergrad Studies .... Dr. Nancy ROSOFF
82 Dean International Affairs ....Dr. Warren HAFFAR
28 Assoc Dean Institutional Diversity ....Ms. Judith DALTON
35 Dean of Students ....Dr. Andrew GORETZKY
20 Assoc Dean Undergraduate Studies ....Mr. Bruce KELLER
88 Asst Dean Graduate Studies ....Ms. Mary Kate MCNULTY
109 Director Auxiliary Services .... Ms. Mimi BASSETTI
29 Director Alumni Relations ....Vacant
88 Director University Art Gallery ....Mr. Richard TORCHIA
41 Director Athletics & Recreation ....Mr. Brian GRANATA
88 Director Campus Visits and EM ....Ms. Kathleen BEARDSLEY
36 Director Career Education ....Ms. Marissa DEITCH
38 Director Counseling Services ....Ms. Amy HENNING
37 Exec Dir Financial Aid & Enroll Mgt . Ms. Holly R. KIRKPATRICK
25 Director Sponsored Research ....Ms. Natalia SHABLIA
88 Director of Academic Administration ....Ms. Kristin O. JUDGE
96 Purchasing Coordinator ....Ms. Jennifer SUDLOW
88 Payroll Manager .... Ms. Heather MAJOR
19 Director of Public Safety ....Ms. Ruth EVANS
88 Title IX Coordinator ....Ms. Nora NELLE
101 Executive Dir Board of Trustees ....Mr. Kevin MULDOON
88 Assoc Dean International Affairs ....Ms. Janice FINN
45 Director of Strategic Initiatives ....Mr. Joseph S. SUN
07 Asst Vice Pres of Admissions ....Ms. Collene PERNICELLO
04 Exec Assistant to the President ....Ms. April WANSER
09 Director of Institutional Research ....Ms. Bridget MILLER

Aspira City College (F)

4322 North 5th Street, Philadelphia PA 19140
County: Philadelphia FICE Identification: 031091
Unit ID: 214023
Telephone: (215) 455-2300 Carnegie Class: Not Classified
FAX Number: N/A Calendar System: Semester
URL: www.aspiracitycollege.edu
Established: 1974 Annual Undergrad Tuition & Fees: $12,097
Enrollment: 5 Coed
Affiliation or Control: Independent Non-Profit IRS Status: 501(c)3
Highest Offering: Associate Degree
Accreditation: ACCSC

01 President ....Mr. Alfredo B. CALDERON
11 Int Campus Director .... Ms. Nerissa CONN
10 Chief Operating Officer ....Mr. Thomas DARDEN
90 Director of Education - IT ....Vacant
21 Controller ....Mr. Xinyan YI
37 Financial Aid Director .... Ms. Madeline SARGENT
07 Admissions Representative ....Mr. Karl ARNEY
36 Career Manager ....Vacant

Berks Technical Institute (G)

2205 Ridgewood Road, Wyomissing PA 19610-1168
Telephone: (610) 372-1722 FICE Identification: 022539
Accreditation: ACCSC

† Branch campus of Miller-Motte College, Chattanooga, TN.

Bidwell Training Center (H)

1815 Metropolitan Street, Pittsburgh PA 15233-2200
County: Allegheny FICE Identification: 031015
Unit ID: 211149
Telephone: (412) 323-4000 Carnegie Class: Not Classified
FAX Number: (412) 325-7378 Calendar System: Quarter
URL: bidwelltraining.edu
Established: 1968 Annual Undergrad Tuition & Fees: N/A
Enrollment: N/A Coed
Affiliation or Control: Independent Non-Profit IRS Status: 501(c)3
Highest Offering: Associate Degree
Accreditation: ACCSC, MAC

01 Executive Director .... Dr. Kimberly RASSAU
11 Sr Dir Operations/Financial Aid ....Mr. Ken HUSELTON
06 Registrar ....Ms. Patricia THOMAS

Bryn Athyn College of the New Church (I)

PO Box 717, Bryn Athyn PA 19009-0717
County: Montgomery FICE Identification: 003228
Unit ID: 210492
Telephone: (267) 502-2400 Carnegie Class: Bac-A&S
FAX Number: (215) 938-2658 Calendar System: Trimester
URL: www.brynathyn.edu
Established: 1876 Annual Undergrad Tuition & Fees: $25,449
Enrollment: 287 Coed
Affiliation or Control: Church of New Jerusalem IRS Status: 501(c)3
Highest Offering: Master's
Accreditation: M

01 President ....Mr. Brian BLAIR
10 Chief Financial Officer ....Mr. Daniel T. ALLEN
05 Dean of Academics/Faculty ....Dr. Wendy CLOSTERMAN
73 Dean of Theological School ....Rev. Andrew M T. DIBB
32 Dean of Student Affairs .... Dr. Suzanne NELSON
84 VP Enrollment Management/ Admissions ....Mr. William LARROUSSE
08 Director of Swedenborg Library ....Mrs. Carol TRAVENY
41 Director of Athletics ....Dr. Suzanne NELSON
13 Chief Information Officer ....Ms. Lelia HOWARD
15 Director of Human Resources ....Ms. Melissa GAMBA
19 Director of Public Safety ....Mr. James KALAVIK
42 Chaplain ....Rev. Grant SCHNARR
04 Executive Asst to President ....Ms. Melodie GREER
14 Director Information Technology ....Mr. Richard DAUM
06 Registrar ....Ms. Casey SCHAUDER
37 Asst Director of Financial Aid ....Ms. Ashley MCCARRIE

Bryn Mawr College (J)

101 N Merion Avenue, Bryn Mawr PA 19010-2899
County: Montgomery FICE Identification: 003237
Unit ID: 211273
Telephone: (610) 526-5000 Carnegie Class: Bac-A&S
FAX Number: (610) 526-7450 Calendar System: Semester
URL: www.brynmawr.edu
Established: 1885 Annual Undergrad Tuition & Fees: $54,440
Enrollment: 1,634 Female
Affiliation or Control: Independent Non-Profit IRS Status: 501(c)3
Highest Offering: Doctorate
Accreditation: M, SW

01 President ... Kimberly CASSIDY
05 Provost ... Tim HARTE
49 Dean Undergraduate College ... Jennifer WALTERS
10 Chief Financial/Admin Officer ... Kari FAZIO
30 Chief Development Officer ... Bob MILLER
84 Chief Enrollment Officer ... Cheryl Lynn HORSEY
26 Chief Communications Officer ... Jesse GALE
08 Director Libraries/Chief Info Ofcr ... Gina SIESING
58 Dean of Graduate Studies ... Sharon BURGMAYER
28 Asst Dean Col of Access/Cmty Devel ... Vanessa CHRISTMAN
06 Registrar ... Kirsten O'BEIRNE
37 Director of Financial Aid ... Susan CHADWICK
19 Director of Public Safety ... Tom KING
41 Dir Athletics & Physical Education ... Kathleen TIERNEY
21 Controller ... Tijana STEFANOVIC
09 Director of Institutional Research ... Richard BARRY
18 Director of Facilities ... Nina BISBEE
07 Director of Admissions ... Marissa TURCHI
15 Director of Human Resources ... Martin MASTASCUSA
29 Director of Alumnae Relations ... Millie BOND
101 Secretary of the Institution/Board ... Ruth LINDEBORG

Bucknell University (A)

1 Dent Drive, Lewisburg PA 17837
County: Union FICE Identification: 003238
Unit ID: 211291
Telephone: (570) 577-2000 Carnegie Class: Bac-A&S
FAX Number: (570) 577-3760 Calendar System: Semester
URL: www.bucknell.edu
Established: 1846 Annual Undergrad Tuition & Fees: $58,202
Enrollment: 3,726 Coed
Affiliation or Control: Independent Non-Profit IRS Status: 501(c)3
Highest Offering: Master's
Accreditation: M, MUS

01 President ... Dr. John C. BRAVMAN
100 Chief of Staff ... Ms. Karin RILLEY
43 General Counsel ... Ms. Karin RILLEY
04 Exec Director President Office ... Ms. Carol M. KENNEDY
41 Director Athletics & Recreation ... Mr. Jermaine M. TRUAX
05 Provost ... Dr. Elisabeth MERMANN-JOZWIAK
45 VP for Strategic Initiatives ... Dr. Robert MIDKIFF
20 Assoc Provost ... Dr. Ghislaine MCDAYTER
20 Assoc Provost ... Dr. Angele KINGUE
49 Dean of Arts & Sciences ... Dr. Karl VOSS
50 Dean Freemen College of Management ... Vacant
54 Dean College of Engineering ... Dr. Brad PUTMAN
92 Honors Council Chair ... Dr. Robert W. JACOB
88 Dir Acad Finance & Operations ... Ms. Pamela A. BENFER
88 Dir Small Business Development Ctr ... Mr. Steven V. STUMBRIS
57 Exec Dir Weis Ctr Performing Arts ... Ms. Kathryn L. MAGUET
111 VP University Advancement ... Dr. Scott G. ROSEVEAR
30 Assoc VP University Advancement ... Mr. Joshua L. GRILL
30 Assoc VP University Advancement ... Ms. Kathleen GRAHAM
112 Executive Dir Leadership Gifts ... Ms. Michelle L. ROBERTSON
110 Senior Development Adviser ... Mr. Mark ELLIOTT
88 Exec Dir People Success Operations ... Ms. Lucille TARIN
30 Director Development ... Ms. Abbey SCHECKTER
30 Director Development ... Mr. Mark SHARER
30 Director Development ... Ms. Barbara MARTIN
88 Dir Prospect Research & Mgmt ... Ms. Cynthia D. JANESCH
88 Exec Dir Adv Mktg/Research/Strategy ... Ms. Natasha WILLIAMS
29 Executive Director Alumni/Family ... Ms. Kristin STETLER
44 Dir Annual Fund Individual Giving ... Ms. Mary Ann STANTON
112 Dir Estate Trust and Gift Planning ... Ms. Melissa M. DIEHL
26 VP for Communications ... Ms. Heather JOHNS
27 Director of Media Relations ... Mr. Mike FERLAZZO
10 VP Finance & Administration ... Ms. Eileen E. PETULA
21 Assoc VP/Treasurer and Controller ... Ms. Elizabeth D. STEWART
115 Dir of Investments ... Ms. Angela MOTTO
25 Executive Dir Sponsored Projects ... Mr. Robert GUTIERREZ
88 Assoc Controller Financial Services . Mr. Ronald E. STAUFFER, II
109 Director of Business Services ... Ms. Lori J. WILSON
88 Asst Controller ... Ms. Michelle M. HENDRICKS
88 Assoc Controller Accounting Svcs ... Mr. William D. GEORGE
88 Dir Financial Information Systems ... Ms. Pamela K. NOONE
113 Director of Disbursement Services ... Mr. Jody D. GRAYBILL
88 Bursar Services Manager ... Ms. Carol YOST
96 Director of Procurement Services ... Vacant
88 Exec Dir Events Management Office ... Ms. Dana M. MIMS
116 Director of Internal Audit ... Mr. Robert L. HOSTER
117 Dir Risk Management & Insurance ... Mr. Gregg ROKAVEC
15 VP Human Resources ... Dr. Nicole WHITEHEAD
16 Dir of Recruitment & Compensation ... Vacant
118 Director of HRIS & Benefits ... Vacant
09 Asst Prov Inst Research/Assessment ... Mr. Kevork T. HORISSIAN
28 Interim Assoc Provost Diversity ... Dr. Anjalee HUTCHINSON
19 Chief of Public Safety ... Mr. Anthony M. MORGAN
18 AVP Facilities & Sustainability ... Mr. Jeffrey LOSS
88 Dir of Construction & Design ... Mr. Dominic SILVERS
13 VP Library & Information Technology ... Mr. Param S. BEDI
14 Exec Dir Enterprise Technologies ... Mr. Kevin WILLEY
119 Info Security Program Manager ... Mr. Brandon SEYMORE
32 Dean of Students ... Ms. Amy A. BADAL
35 Associate Dean of Students ... Ms. Lena CRAIN
35 Associate Dean of Students ... Ms. Denelle BROWN
35 Associate Dean of Students ... Ms. Kari M. CONRAD
35 Associate Dean of Students ... Ms. Jane GRASSADONIA
84 VP Enrollment Management ... Ms. Lisa KEEGAN
07 Dean of Admissions ... Mr. Kevin MATHES
37 Interim Director Financial Aid ... Ms. Erin WOLFE
39 Dir of Housing Services ... Mr. Stephen J. APANEL
36 Exec Director Career Services ... Ms. Pamela G. KEISER
38 Dir Counseling & Stdnt Dev Ctr ... Dr. Kelly KETTLEWELL
22 Dir Accessibility Resources ... Lakeisha MEYER
122 Dir Fraternity/Sorority Affairs ... Ms. Olivia LIBBY
42 University Chaplain ... Rev. Kurt D. NELSON
85 Dir International Student Services ... Ms. Jennifer E. FIGUEROA
104 Dir Global & Off-Campus Education ... Mr. Stephen K. APPIAH-PADI
88 Dir Inst Equity/Title IX Coord ... Ms. Samatha HART
88 Interim Dir of Civic Engagement ... Ms. Lynn PIERSON
88 Dir Gender and Sexuality Resources ... Mr. William K. MCCOY
88 Director of Writing Center ... Ms. Deirdre M. O'CONNOR

Bucks County Community College (B)

275 Swamp Road, Newtown PA 18940-4106
County: Bucks FICE Identification: 003239
Unit ID: 211307
Telephone: (215) 968-8000 Carnegie Class: Assoc/HT-Mix Trad/Non
FAX Number: (215) 968-8129 Calendar System: Semester
URL: www.bucks.edu
Established: 1964 Annual Undergrad Tuition & Fees (In-District): $9,098
Enrollment: 6,988 Coed
Affiliation or Control: Local IRS Status: 501(c)3
Highest Offering: Associate Degree
Accreditation: M, ACBSP, ADNUR, ART, IFSAC, MLTAD, MUS, RAD

01 President ... Dr. Felicia L. GANTHER
05 Provost ... Ms. Lisa ANGELO
10 VP for Administrative Affairs & CFO .. Mr. Dennis W. MATTHEWS
121 VP Student Success ... Dr. Kelly KELLEWAY
13 VP Tech & Innovation/CIO ... Mr. Brant STEEN
21 Assoc VP Finance ... Mr. David JERDAN
88 Int Assoc VP Strategic Partnership ... Ms. Tracy TIMBY
28 Assoc VP Govt Rels & CDO ... Mr. Kevin ANTOINE
114 Exec Dir Budget & Internal Audit ... Ms. Loren HERBERT
09 Exec Dir Research/Assess/Analytics ... Dr. Maureen MCCARTHY
103 Exec Dir Workforce Development ... Ms. Susan HERRING
18 Exec Director Physical Plant ... Mr. Martin SNYDER
26 Exec Dir Marketing/Public Relations ... Ms. Megan SMITH
100 Chief of Staff & Board Liaison ... Ms. Kathleen C. FEDORKO
15 Exec Director Human Resources ... Dr. Patricia BRINING
96 Director of Purchasing ... Mr. Eric GULI
106 Associate Dean Bucks Online ... Ms. Susan DARLINGTON
37 Director Financial Aid ... Ms. Donna M. WILKOSKI
36 Director Career Services ... Ms. Sharon STEPHENS
32 Director Student Life & Athletics ... Mr. Matt J. CIPRIANO
19 Exec Dir Security & Safety ... Mr. Dennis MCCAULEY
08 Director Library Services ... Ms. Monica KUNA
07 Director of Admissions ... Ms. Joyce WHEATLEY
06 Registrar ... Ms. Rebecca BREUNINGER
102 Executive Director Foundation ... Ms. Christina MCGINLEY
68 Dean Kinesiology & Sport Studies ... Dr. Priscilla RICE
81 Dean STEM ... Dr. Shawn WILD
50 Interim Dean Business & Innovation ... Mr. Greg LUCE
57 Dean Arts ... Mr. John MATHEWS
83 Dean Social & Behavioral Sci ... Dr. Lynn DELLAPIETRA
76 Dean Health Sciences ... Dr. Constance CORRIGAN
79 Dean Language & Literature ... Ms. Nicole TRACEY
88 Dean Learning Resources ... Mr. Bill HEMMIG

Butler County Community College (C)

107 College Drive, Butler PA 16002
County: Butler FICE Identification: 003240
Unit ID: 211343
Telephone: (724) 287-8711 Carnegie Class: Assoc/MT-VT-High Trad
FAX Number: (724) 285-6047 Calendar System: Semester
URL: www.bc3.edu
Established: 1965 Annual Undergrad Tuition & Fees (In-District): $8,250
Enrollment: 2,984 Coed
Affiliation or Control: Local IRS Status: 501(c)3
Highest Offering: Associate Degree
Accreditation: M, ACBSP, ADNUR, MAC, PTAA

01 President ... Dr. Nicholas C. NEUPAUER
05 VP for Academic Affairs ... Dr. Belinda M. RICHARDSON
11 VP for Administration & Finance ... Mr. James A. HRABOSKY
32 VP Student Affairs/Enrollment Mgt ... Dr. G. Case WILLOUGHBY
10 Chief Business Officer ... Mr. Wm. Jake FRIEL
50 Interim Dean of Business ... Ms. Sherri MACK
79 Dean of Liberal Arts ... Mr. Stephen M. JOSEPH
83 Dean of Educ & Behavioral Sciences ... Dr. Nichol ZAGINAYLO
66 Dean of Nursing/Allied Health ... Dr. Patricia T. ANNEAR
72 Dean of Nat Science/Tech ... Mr. Matt KOVAC
106 Dean of Education Technology ... Ms. Ann MCCANDLESS
08 Dean of Library Services ... Mr. Martin J. MILLER
35 Dean of Student Development ... Dr. Joshua NOVAK
103 Dean of Workforce Development ... Ms. Lisa M. CAMPBELL
09 Asst Dean of Institutional Research ... Ms. Sharla M. ANKE
15 Exec Director Human Resources ... Ms. Christina M. FLEEGER
26 Exec Director of Comm & Marketing .. Ms. Jessica M. MATONAK
18 Exec Director of Operations ... Mr. Brian R. OPITZ
102 Exec Director of the Foundation ... Ms. Megan M. COVAL
51 Director of Lifelong Learning ... Mr. Paul M. LUCAS
07 Dean of Admissions ... Ms. Amy PIGNATORE
13 Director of Information Technology ... Mr. Matt MILLER
32 Director of Student Life ... Mr. Rob A. SNYDER
88 Director of Records/Registration ... Ms. Rebecca A. SMITH
12 Director of BC3 at Armstrong ... Ms. Karen ZAPP
12 Dir of BC3 at Lawrence Crossing ... Mr. Sean M. CARROLL
12 Director of BC3 at Cranberry ... Dr. Ryan KOCIELA
12 Director of BC3 at LindenPointe ... Ms. Lauren A. BUCHANAN
12 Director of BC3 at Brockway ... Dr. Jill MARTIN-REND
37 Director of Financial Aid ... Ms. Julianne E. LOUTTIT
88 Director of Admissions ... Ms. Morgan M. RIZZARDI
41 Athletic Director ... Mr. Rob A. SNYDER
19 Director of Campus Police/Security ... Mr. K. Scott RICHARDSON
22 Dir Affirmative Action/EEO ... Ms. Christina M. FLEEGER
88 Director of Children's Center ... Ms. Gina RAJCHEL
40 Bookstore Manager ... Mr. Richard A. BENKO
06 Registrar ... Ms. Amy PIGNATORE
75 Coord of Business/Industry Trng ... Ms. Kathy STROBEL
96 College Services/Purchasing Agent ... Ms. Nicole BARNES
105 Web Manager ... Vacant
30 Int Assoc Dir of the Foundation ... Ms. Lynn ISMAIL
29 Director Alumni Affairs ... Ms. Bobbi Jo CORNETTI
04 Administrative Asst to President ... Ms. Juliann SHEPTAK

Byzantine Catholic Seminary of Ss. Cyril and Methodius (D)

3605 Perrysville Avenue, Pittsburgh PA 15214-2229
County: Allegheny FICE Identification: 041180
Unit ID: 444103
Telephone: (412) 321-8383 Carnegie Class: Spec-4-yr-Faith
FAX Number: N/A Calendar System: Semester
URL: www.bcs.edu
Established: 1950 Annual Graduate Tuition & Fees: N/A
Enrollment: 47 Coed
Affiliation or Control: Other IRS Status: 501(c)3
Highest Offering: Master's; No Undergraduates
Accreditation: THEOL

01 Rector ... V.Rev. Robert M. PIPTA
32 Director of Human Formation ... Rev. Ronald BARUSEFSKI
05 Academic Dean ... Rev. Christiaan KAPPES
08 Director of Information Services ... Dr. Sandra COLLINS
11 Registrar/Dir of Seminary Opers ... Ms. Carol PRZYBORSKI
108 Director of Assessment ... Dr. Matthew K. MINERD
10 Chief Financial Officer ... Dcn. Robert SHALHOUB
15 Human Resources Administrator ... Ms. Helen KENNEDY

Cabrini University (E)

610 King of Prussia Road, Radnor PA 19087-3698
County: Delaware FICE Identification: 003241
Unit ID: 211352
Telephone: (610) 902-8200 Carnegie Class: Masters/M
FAX Number: (610) 902-8204 Calendar System: Semester
URL: www.cabrini.edu
Established: 1957 Annual Undergrad Tuition & Fees: $33,845
Enrollment: 2,009 Coed
Affiliation or Control: Roman Catholic IRS Status: 501(c)3
Highest Offering: Doctorate
Accreditation: M, ACBSP, SW

01 Interim President ... Mrs. Helen DRINAN
05 Provost/SVP Academic Affairs ... Dr. Chioma UGOCHUKWU
10 VP Finance & Treasurer ... Mr. Jim COOPER
111 VP Advancement & External Rels ... Mr. Stephen HIGHSMITH
32 VP Mission/DEI/Student Engagement ... Dr. Angela CAMPBELL
100 Chief of Staff/SVP Strat Initiative ... Mr. Brian EURY
26 Dir Inst Comm & Web Strategy ... Ms. Trish BRADLEY
35 Dean of Students ... Dr. Stephen RUPPRECHT
50 Dean School Business/Prof Studies ... Dr. Tim MANTZ
53 Dean School of Education ... Dr. Beverly BRYDE
49 Dean School of Arts & Sciences ... Dr. Richard THOMPSON
04 Exec Asst to the President & VPIA ... Ms. Claire CLUTE
06 Registrar ... Mr. Gerard DONAHUE
08 Library Director ... Ms. Anne SCHWELM
19 Director Public Safety ... Mr. Joseph FUSCO
18 Director of Facilities ... Ms. Patty SMITH
37 Director of Financial Aid ... Vacant
36 Dir of Career & Professional Dev ... Ms. Erin GABRIELE
41 Director of Athletics & Recreation ... Ms. Kate CORCORAN
15 Director Human Resources ... Ms. Nikki GILLUM-CLEMONS
21 Controller ... Vacant
24 Dir Center for UDL/Ed Tech/Resource ... Ms. Mary BUDZILOWICZ
40 Bookstore Manager ... Ms. Tiffany REED
105 Director of Content Marketing ... Ms. Molly HARTY
20 Associate Provost ... Dr. Michelle FILLING-BROWN
35 Dean Student Engage/Leadership ... Dr. Anne FILIPPONE
92 Director of the Honors Program ... Dr. Thomas CONWAY
28 Director Office of Diversity ... Ms. Lailah DUNBAR
38 Director Counseling/Psych Service ... Dr. Alissa BROWN
39 Director of Residence Life ... Mr. Brett BUCKRIDGE
07 Dean Univ Admissions & Fin Aid ... Ms. Kimberley LEWIS
101 Dir Trustee Admin & Pres Initiative ... Mrs. Nancy OLLINGER
102 Exec Dir Grants & Foundation Rels ... Dr. Laura CHISHOLM
88 Creative Director ... Mr. Kevin HAUGH
96 Procurement Manager ... Ms. Elizabeth KANARAS

Cairn University (F)

200 Manor Avenue, Langhorne Manor PA 19047-2990
County: Bucks FICE Identification: 003351
Unit ID: 215114
Telephone: (215) 752-5800 Carnegie Class: Masters/M
FAX Number: (215) 702-4341 Calendar System: Semester
URL: www.cairn.edu
Established: 1913 Annual Undergrad Tuition & Fees: $29,853
Enrollment: 1,229 Coed
Affiliation or Control: Independent Non-Profit IRS Status: 501(c)3
Highest Offering: Master's

Accreditation: M, BI, IACBE, MUS, SW

01 President Dr. Todd J. WILLIAMS
32 Sr VP Student Affairs & Admin Mr. J. Scott CAWOOD
05 Sr VP/Provost Dr. Adam PORCELLA
111 Sr VP Stewardship and Development Mr. Graham THORPE
10 Sr VP Finance Mr. Yunn KANG
15 Sr VP Human Resources Ms. Mary BOYER
06 Registrar Dr. Steven SCHLENKER
35 VP/Dean of Students Mr. Rick SWIFT
73 Dean School of Divinity Dr. Keith PLUMMER
49 Dean School of Liberal Arts & Sci Dr. Aneesh KHUSHMAN
50 Dean School of Business Mr. Yunn KANG
53 Dean School of Education Dr. Stacey BOSE
64 Dean School of Music Dr. Benjamin HARDING
08 Dean Educational Resources Ms. Stephanie KACELI
106 Dir Educ Tech & Distance Learning Mr. Sali KACELI
29 VP Alumni/Community Affairs Mr. Nathan WAMBOLD
84 VP Enrollment Mr. Thomas SHERF
41 Director Athletics Vacant
18 VP Campus Operations Mr. Andrew NORTON
39 Associate Dean of Students Mr. Andrew GORDON
38 Director Counseling Services Ms. Kim JETTER
37 Director Financial Aid Mr. Stephen CASSEL
23 Director Health Services Ms. Robyn BROGAN
09 Research & Analytics Specialist Mr. Rick HOUSEKNECHT
19 Director Safety & Security Mr. Kevin CORNETTO
13 Director Tech Svcs/Data Governance Mr. David HUI
21 Director Business Services Mr. Andrew ALLERS
26 Director Marketing Mr. John MULVANEY
04 Administrative Asst to President Ms. Lori MILLER
108 VP Institutional Effectiveness Mr. Emir RUIZ ESPARZA

Carlow University (A)

3333 Fifth Avenue, Pittsburgh PA 15213-3165
County: Allegheny FICE Identification: 003303
Unit ID: 211431
Telephone: (800) 333-2275 Carnegie Class: Masters/L
FAX Number: (412) 578-6668 Calendar System: Semester
URL: www.carlow.edu
Established: 1929 Annual Undergrad Tuition & Fees: $31,446
Enrollment: 1,976 Coed
Affiliation or Control: Roman Catholic IRS Status: 501(c)3
Highest Offering: Doctorate
Accreditation: M, #ARCPA, CACREP, #COARC, COPSY, IACBE, NURSE, @SP, SW

01 President Dr. Kathy W. HUMPHREY
05 Provost/VP Academic Affairs Dr. Sibdas GHOSH
10 CFO/SVP Finance & Admin Services Mr. David J. MEADOWS
84 VP Enrollment Mgmt & Mktg Ms. Mollie E. CECERE
111 VP Advancement Ms. Caralynn A. KASSABOV
32 VP Student Affairs/Dean of Students Dr. Timothy P. PHILLIPS
101 Chief of Staff/Secretary of Board Dr. Bridgette N. COFIELD
88 Special Asst to Pres/Mercy Heritage Sr. Sheila A. CARNEY, RSM
106 Asst Prov Online & Acad Operations Mr. Jason KRALL
15 VP Human Res/Diversity/Inclusion Dr. Mary Anne S. KOLENY
66 Dean Health and Wellness Dr. Rhonda E. MANEVAL
49 Dean Arts & Science Dr. Matthew E. GORDLEY
13 Chief Information Officer Vacant
26 Exec Dir Marketing/Comm & Brand Ms. Beth M. FAZZINI
21 Controller Ms. Nancy DEGENHARDT
09 Sr Dir Inst Research/Effect/Plng Dr. Edith L. COOK
103 Int Pgm Dir Innov & Workforce Dev Dr. Howard A. STERN
06 Registrar Ms. Elizabeth A. MCCLINTOCK
88 Interim Head of Campus Lab School Ms. Sarah POSTI
84 Director Enrollment Management Mr. Joel W. MULLNER
123 Dir Adult/Grad/Regional Admissions Ms. Wendy S. PHILLIPS
36 Director Career Development Ms. Jennifer A. O'TOOLE
113 Manager Student Accounts Mr. Logan D. BANNON
08 Exec Dir Library & Lrng Commons Ms. Alexius SMITH-MACKLIN
35 Asst Dean of Students Ms. Erin I. BOYLES
39 Director Residence Life Vacant
23 Director Health Services Ms. Carla R. BERGAMASCO
41 Director Athletics Mr. Lou ZADECKY
88 Director Wellness & Fitness Svcs Ms. Julie M. GAUL
18 Manager of Facility Services Mr. Dan J. HALL
19 Chief of Police Ms. Corrin M. CULHANE
37 Director Financial Aid Ms. Natalie L. WILSON
112 Major Gifts Officer Ms. Jane W. BINLEY
102 Dir Corp/Found Rels/Advancement Vacant
27 Director Media & Public Rels Mr. Sean MCFARLAND
42 Campus Ministry Ms. Siobhan K. DEWITT
04 Exec Asst to the President Ms. Angelica L. BONDY
28 Director of Equity and Inclusion Dr. Maleea D. JOHNSON
43 Director of Annual Giving Ms. Regan GIBNEY

Carnegie Mellon University (B)

5000 Forbes Avenue, Pittsburgh PA 15213-3890
County: Allegheny FICE Identification: 003242
Unit ID: 211440
Telephone: (412) 268-2000 Carnegie Class: DU-Highest
FAX Number: (412) 268-2330 Calendar System: Semester
URL: www.cmu.edu
Established: 1900 Annual Undergrad Tuition & Fees: $58,810
Enrollment: 13,519 Coed
Affiliation or Control: Independent Non-Profit IRS Status: 501(c)3
Highest Offering: Doctorate
Accreditation: M, MUS

01 President Dr. Farnam JAHANIAN
05 Provost/Chief Academic Officer Dr. James H. GARRETT, JR.
10 Vice President and CFO Ms. Angela BLANTON
115 Chief Investment Officer Mr. Charles A. KENNEDY
111 VP for University Advancement Mr. Scott M. MORY
46 Int VP for Research Mr. Daryl WEINERT
43 Vice President/General Counsel Ms. Mary Jo DIVELY
26 VP Marketing & Communications Mr. Nicholas SCIBETTA
101 Secretary of the Corporation Ms. Mary Jo DIVELY
20 Vice Provost for Education Dr. Amy L. BURKERT
20 Vice Provost for Faculty Ms. Molly STEENSON
09 Vice Provost for Inst Effect & Plng Mr. Henry ZHENG
11 Vice President for Operations Mr. Daryl WEINERT
100 Chief of Staff Mr. Rick SIGER
32 VP Student Affairs/Dean of Students Ms. Gina CASALEGNO
13 VP Info Tech/Chief Information Ofcr Mr. Stan M. WADDELL
15 AVP & Chief Human Resources Officer Mrs. Michelle PIEKUTOWSKI
28 Vice Provost for Diversity Ms. Wanda HEADING-GRANT
84 AVP & Dir of Enrollment Services Ms. Lisa M. KRIEG
14 Director Software Engr Inst Dr. Paul D. NIELSEN
07 Dean of Admissions Mr. Michael STEIDEL
08 Dean of University Libraries Mr. Keith WEBSTER
06 Registrar Mr. John R. PAPINCHAK
54 Dean Carnegie Inst of Technology Dr. William H. SANDERS
12 Dean at the Qatar Campus Mr. Michael TRICK
57 Dean College Fine Arts Dr. Mary Ellen POOLE
49 Dean Dietrich College Dr. Richard SCHEINES
50 Dean Tepper School of Business Dr. Isabelle BAJEUX-BESNAINOU
81 Dean Mellon College of Science Dr. Rebecca W. DOERGE
80 Dean Heinz Sch Publ Policy/Mgmt Dr. Ramayya KRISHNAN
77 Dean School of Computer Sciences Dr. Martial H. HEBERT
86 Assoc VP Government Relations Mr. Timothy MCNULTY

Cedar Crest College (C)

100 College Drive, Allentown PA 18104-6196
County: Lehigh FICE Identification: 003243
Unit ID: 211468
Telephone: (610) 437-4471 Carnegie Class: Masters/S
FAX Number: (610) 437-5955 Calendar System: Semester
URL: www.cedarcrest.edu
Established: 1867 Annual Undergrad Tuition & Fees: $41,567
Enrollment: 1,433 Female
Affiliation or Control: Non-denominational IRS Status: 501(c)3
Highest Offering: Doctorate
Accreditation: M, ACBSP, ANEST, DIETD, DIETI, FEPAC, NUR, NURSE, SW

01 President Dr. Elizabeth MEADE
05 Provost Dr. Robert A. WILSON
10 Chief Financial Officer/Treasurer Ms. Audra J. KAHR
111 VP Institutional Advancement Ms. Valerie DOWNING
84 VP Enrollment Mgmt/Student Affairs Dr. Lisa BUNDERS
06 Registrar Mr. Gregory GOLETZ
29 Exec Director for Alumnae Affairs Ms. Mary NEUENSCHWANDER
19 Chief of Campus Safety and Security Mr. Mark VITALOS
18 Director of Facilities Mr. Michael STANTON
08 Library Director Dr. Stephani GOMEZ
13 Director Information Technology Mr. Bruce SARTE
09 Dir of Institutional Research Ms. Lyn WILLIAMS
04 Assistant to the President Ms. Erin FENSTERMACHER
37 Dir Student Financial Services Ms. Valerie KREISER
22 Director Health/Counseling Services Ms. Nancy ROBERTS
26 Dir Marketing/Communication Ms. Kristen LAUDENSLAGER
40 Manager Bookstore Ms. Breanna GANTHER
28 Director of Diversity Dr. Leon JOHN
41 Interim Athletic Director Ms. Kimberly BEGLEY
101 Secretary of the Institution/Board Ms. Meghan GRADY
104 Director Study Abroad Dr. Kelly HALL
15 Chief Human Resources Officer Ms. Lisa GARBACIK
32 Dean of Students Dr. Calley STEVENS TAYLOR

Central Penn College (D)

600 Valley Road, Summerdale PA 17093-0309
County: Cumberland FICE Identification: 004890
Unit ID: 211477
Telephone: (800) 759-2727 Carnegie Class: Bac-Diverse
FAX Number: (717) 732-5254 Calendar System: Quarter
URL: www.centralpenn.edu
Established: 1881 Annual Undergrad Tuition & Fees: $18,714
Enrollment: 963 Coed
Affiliation or Control: Proprietary IRS Status: Proprietary
Highest Offering: Master's
Accreditation: M, MAC, OTA, #PTAA

01 President Dr. Linda FEDRIZZI-WILLIAMS
05 VPAA/Provost Dr. Krista WOLFE
10 Assistant VP of Finance Ms. Jennifer MARIARCHER
111 VP of Advncmnt & Strat Initiatives Mr. Michael FEDOR
15 VP of People & Culture Ms. Maggie LEBO
26 AVP Advncmnt & Strategic Initiative Mrs. Mary E. WETZEL
06 Registrar Mrs. Jen CORRELL
18 Facilities Director Mr. Christopher SHERIFF
37 Financial Aid Director Ms. Kathy J. SHEPARD
41 Athletic Director Ms. Kasey HICKS
36 Dean of Career Services & Devel Mr. Steven HASSINGER
39 Dir of Student Housing & Res Life Ms. Lindsay GARBER
108 Dir of Institutional Assessment Ms. Laura R. DIMINO

Central Pennsylvania Institute of Science and Technology (E)

540 North Harrison Rd, Pleasant Gap PA 16823
County: Centre FICE Identification: 005335
Unit ID: 369668
Telephone: (814) 359-2793 Carnegie Class: Spec 2-yr-Tech
FAX Number: (814) 359-3489 Calendar System: Quarter
URL: www.cpi.edu
Established: 1969 Annual Undergrad Tuition & Fees (In-District): N/A
Enrollment: 113 Coed
Affiliation or Control: State/Local IRS Status: 501(c)3
Highest Offering: Associate Degree
Accreditation: ACCSC

01 President Dr. Richard C. MAKIN

Chatham University (F)

Woodland Road, Pittsburgh PA 15232-2826
County: Allegheny FICE Identification: 003244
Unit ID: 211556
Telephone: (412) 365-1100 Carnegie Class: DU-Mod
FAX Number: (412) 365-1505 Calendar System: Semester
URL: www.chatham.edu
Established: 1869 Annual Undergrad Tuition & Fees: $39,902
Enrollment: 2,353 Coed
Affiliation or Control: Independent Non-Profit IRS Status: 501(c)3
Highest Offering: Doctorate
Accreditation: M, ARCPA, CAATE, CIDA, COPSY, IACBE, MPCAC, NURSE, OT, PTA, SW

01 President Dr. David FINEGOLD
10 Vice Pres Finance/Administration Mr. Walter B. FOWLER
05 Vice President Academic Affairs Dr. Jenna TEMPLETON
84 Vice Pres Enrollment Management Ms. Amy BECHER
26 Vice Pres for Mktg & Communications Mr. Bill CAMPBELL
111 Vice Pres University Advancement Ms. Carey MILLER
106 Director Chatham Online Mr. Mark KASSEL
88 Dn Falk Sch Sustainability/Environ Mr. Lou LEONARD
21 Assoc VP Finance/Admin Ms. Jennifer HOERSTER
45 Vice Pres of Planning Mr. Sean COLEMAN
09 Director of IR & Effectiveness Mr. Giovanni GAROFALO
06 Registrar Ms. Maria KRONISER
37 Asst Vice Pres Financial Aid Ms. Jennifer A. BURNS
08 Director of Library Ms. Jill AUSEL
29 Director of Alumni Engagement Ms. Lauren TUDOR
44 Asst Director of Annual Giving Mr. Kyle GLASER
30 Associate VP of Development Ms. Amanda KILE
15 Asst VP of Human Resources Mr. Frank M. GRECO
18 Asst VP of Facilities Management Mr. Robert R. DUBRAY
19 Chief of Police Ms. Donna GROSSI
41 Director of Athletics Mr. Leonard TREVINO
32 Dean of Students Mr. Chris PURCELL
38 Director of Student Counseling Dr. Elsa M. ARCE
35 Asst Dean of Students Mr. Colvin GEORGES, JR.
49 Dean School Arts/Science/Business Dr. Edith BARRETT
76 Dean School of Health Sciences Dr. Salvador BONDOC
04 Exec Assistant to the President Ms. Brittany TYLER
13 CIO/Director of Info Technology Mr. Paul STEINHAUS
35 Asst Dean of Students Mr. Shawn A. MCQUILLAN
88 Dir University Sustainability Ms. Mary WHITNEY
102 Dir of Institutional Partnerships Ms. Emily WILMORE
104 Study Abroad Coordinator Ms. Karin CHIPMAN
28 Asst VP Diversity/Inclusion Dr. Kristin DUKES
50 Chair/Director Business Mr. James PIERSON
53 Director of Education Dr. Kristin HARTY
105 Web Content Manager Ms. Sara POLETTI

Chestnut Hill College (G)

9601 Germantown Avenue, Philadelphia PA 19118-2693
County: Philadelphia FICE Identification: 003245
Unit ID: 211583
Telephone: (215) 248-7000 Carnegie Class: Masters/M
FAX Number: (215) 248-7155 Calendar System: Semester
URL: www.chc.edu
Established: 1924 Annual Undergrad Tuition & Fees: $38,200
Enrollment: 1,528 Coed
Affiliation or Control: Roman Catholic IRS Status: 501(c)3
Highest Offering: Doctorate
Accreditation: M, CLPSY, IPSY, MACTE, MPCAC

01 President Dr. William LATIMER
05 VP Academic Affairs/Dean of Faculty Dr. Christopher DOUGHERTY
10 Int Vice Pres for Financial Affairs Mr. Robert WALLETT
30 Vice President for Inst Advancement Ms. Erin WOOLEY
32 Vice President for Student Life Dr. Lynn ORTALE
84 Vice Pres Enrollment Management Mr. Troy MILLER
11 Asst to Pres for Administration Sr. Kathryn MILLER, SSJ
58 Dean School of Graduate Studies Dr. William CUNNINGHAM
97 Int Dean School Undergrad Studies Dr. Jacqueline REICH
51 Dean Continuing/Professional Stds Dr. Elaine GREEN
08 Dean Library/Information Resources Sr. Mary Josephine LARKIN, SSJ
28 Chief Officer for Diversity/Equity Dr. LaKeisha THORPE
26 Chief Communications Officer Mr. Chris SPANGLER
42 Director of Campus Ministry Ms. Anna RYAN-BENDER
35 Dean of Student Life Dr. Krista BAILEY MURPHY
20 Director Campus Life Operations Ms. Chelsea FARREN

06 Registrar Mr. Michael REIG
38 Director Counseling Center Sr. Sheila KENNEDY, SSJ
85 Int Coord of Global Education Dr. Walter PERRY
13 Director of IT Services Mr. Rich MACINTYRE
23 Director Health Services Ms. Deirdre HORAN
36 Director of Career Development Ms. Nancy DACHILLE
07 Dir Admission/Sch Graduate Studies Ms. Ariel EDWARDS
07 Director Accelerated Admissions Ms. April FOWLKES
21 Controller Mr. Mitch BILKER
37 Director Financial Aid Ms. Yolanda COLE
09 Director of Institutional Research Sr. Patricia O'DONNELL, SSJ
102 Dir Corporate/Found/Govt Relations Ms. Rebecca POWERS
29 Director of Alumnae/i Affairs Ms. Maureen MCLAUGHLIN
41 Director of Athletics Mr. Jesse BALCER
15 Director Human Resources Ms. Sharon DOUGHERTY
19 Dir Security/Safety/Bldgs/Grounds Ms. Polly TETI
18 Director of Facilities Mr. Mark MCGRATH
88 Financial Systems Analyst Ms. Meg O'BRIEN
39 Director Residence Life Mr. William WHITE
04 Administrative Asst to President Ms. Bianca HART
40 Manager of Campus Store Ms. Jennifer WARING

Clarks Summit University (A)

538 Venard Road, S. Abington Twp. PA 18411-1297
County: Lackawanna FICE Identification: 002670
Unit ID: 211024
Telephone: (570) 586-2400 Carnegie Class: Masters/S
FAX Number: (570) 585-9226 Calendar System: Semester
URL: www.clarkssummitu.edu
Established: 1932 Annual Undergrad Tuition & Fees: $26,082
Enrollment: 768 Coed
Affiliation or Control: Baptist IRS Status: 501(c)3
Highest Offering: Doctorate
Accreditation: M, BI

01 President Dr. James R. LYTLE
04 Executive Assistant to President Ms. Darlene CATLETT
05 VP of Academics Dr. William J. HIGLEY
32 VP of Student Development Mr. Ted BOYKIN
34 Associate Dean of Women Mrs. Faye MOORE
11 Exec Dir of Administrative Svcs Mr. Allen R. DREYER
37 Director of Financial Aid Mr. Larry ELLIS
84 Exec Dir On-Campus Enrollment Mgmt Mr. Frank JUDSON
13 Director of Information Technology Mr. David BOSKET
06 Registrar Mr. Chris WELMAN
09 Director of Institutional Research Mr. Robert PLANTZ
29 Exec Dir Alumni & Development Mr. Paul GOLDEN
73 Assoc Dean of School of Theology Mr. James BUCHANAN
53 Dean of School of Education Dr. Ritch KELLEY
49 Dean of School of Arts & Sciences Dr. Janet K. HICKS
106 Exec Dir Online Learning Ms. Erica YOUNG
10 Controller Mr. Daniel KING
26 Exec Dir Marketing/Communications Ms. Dena CAMBRA

Commonwealth Technical Institute at the Hiram G. Andrews Center (B)

727 Goucher Street, Johnstown PA 15905-3092
County: Cambria FICE Identification: 025366
Unit ID: 212975
Telephone: (814) 255-8200 Carnegie Class: Assoc/HVT-Mix Trad/Non
FAX Number: (814) 255-5709 Calendar System: Semester
URL: www.dli.pa.gov/Individuals/Disability-Services/hgac/
Established: 1959 Annual Undergrad Tuition & Fees: $7,664
Enrollment: 133 Coed
Affiliation or Control: Proprietary IRS Status: Proprietary
Highest Offering: Associate Degree
Accreditation: ACCSC

01 Center Director Jill MORICONI
11 Center Deputy Director James MARKER
05 Director of Education James THOMAS
07 Director of Admissions Martin TRAN
32 Chief Student Life Officer Stacie ANDREWS
37 Director Student Financial Aid Chris ZAKRAYSEK

Community College of Allegheny County (C)

800 Allegheny Avenue, Pittsburgh PA 15233-1895
County: Allegheny FICE Identification: 003231
Unit ID: 210605
Telephone: (412) 237-4413 Carnegie Class: Assoc/HVT-Mix Trad/Non
FAX Number: (412) 237-4420 Calendar System: Semester
URL: www.ccac.edu
Established: 1966 Annual Undergrad Tuition & Fees (In-District): $8,323
Enrollment: 13,217 Coed
Affiliation or Control: State/Local IRS Status: 501(c)3
Highest Offering: Associate Degree
Accreditation: M, ADNUR, CAHIIM, COARC, DIETT, DMS, EMT, MAC, MLTAD, NAEYC, NMT, OTA, PTAA, RTT, SURGT

01 President Dr. Quintin B. BULLOCK
05 Provost/Exec Vice Pres Acad Affairs Dr. Stuart BLACKLAW
10 Vice President Finance Dr. Brian MCKLOSKEY
43 Vice President and General Counsel Mr. Anthony DITOMMSO
84 VP Enrollment Management Dr. Brian SAJKO
12 Northwest Regional President Dr. Evon WALTERS
12 Southeast Regional President Ms. Charlene NEWKIRK
103 Interim VP Workforce Development Ms. Deborah KILLMYER
15 VP Human Resources Ms. Kimberly MANIGAULT
102 CEO Educational Foundation Mr. James MCMAHON
13 VP & Chief Information Officer Mr. Chuck GRAHAM
06 Registrar Dr. Diane JACOBS
18 VP & Chief Facilities Management Mr. Carlo VAZQUEZ
21 Controller Mr. James FLYNN
25 Executive Director Grants Ms. Natasha WALTON
96 Director Purchasing/Contracts Admin Mr. Mike CVETIC
28 Chief Diversity/Equity/Inclusion Dr. Angelica PEREZ-JOHNSTON
26 Executive Director Public Relations Ms. Elizabeth JOHNSTON
04 Exec Asst to the President & BoT Ms. Bonita L RICHARDSON
100 Chief of Staff Dr. Frank SARGENT
19 Exec Director Security/Safety Mr. Andre HENDERSON

Community College of Allegheny County Boyce Campus (D)

595 Beatty Road, Monroeville PA 15146-1396
Telephone: (724) 327-1327 Identification: 770150
Accreditation: &M, AT

Community College of Allegheny County North Campus (E)

8701 Perry Highway, Pittsburgh PA 15237-5353
Telephone: (412) 366-7000 Identification: 770151
Accreditation: &M

Community College of Allegheny County, South Campus (F)

1750 Clairton Road, West Mifflin PA 15122-3029
Telephone: (412) 237-2222 Identification: 770152
Accreditation: &M

Community College of Beaver County (G)

1 Campus Drive, Monaca PA 15061-2588
County: Beaver FICE Identification: 006807
Unit ID: 211079
Telephone: (724) 480-2222 Carnegie Class: Assoc/HVT-High Trad
FAX Number: (724) 480-3573 Calendar System: Semester
URL: www.ccbc.edu
Established: 1966 Annual Undergrad Tuition & Fees (In-District): $12,630
Enrollment: 1,713 Coed
Affiliation or Control: State/Local IRS Status: 501(c)3
Highest Offering: Associate Degree
Accreditation: M, ADNUR

01 President Dr. Roger W. DAVIS
05 Executive Vice President & Provost Dr. Shelly MOORE
10 VP Finance/Operations and IT Mr. Glenn NATALI
15 VP Human Resources Ms. Sally MERCER
32 VP Student Affairs & Enrollment Dr. Sutonia BOYKIN
13 AVP of IT Mr. Brandon BERG
26 Assoc VP Communications Ms. Leslie A. TENNANT
35 Assoc VP of Student Affairs Ms. Angela M. HAMILTON
103 Dean Workforce & Continuing Educ Mr. John S. GOBERISH
37 Director Student Financial Services Mr. Steve PLANEY
04 Assistant to the President & Board Ms. Roni GILES
76 Dean Nursing & Allied Health Ms. Elaine STROUSS
49 Senior Dean Dr. John HIGGS
88 Dean Aviation Sciences Dr. John HIGGS
88 Dean HS Academies & Dual Enroll Ms. Joyce CIRELLI
111 Exec Dir Advance & Sponsored Pgms Mr. Kolton CODNER
35 Director of Student Life Mr. Colin SISK
88 Associate Dean Dr. Katie THOMAS
88 Associate Dean Dr. Chet THOMPSON
06 Registrar Ms. Rose WHELPLEY
08 Chief Library Officer Ms. Terri GALLAGHER
09 Exec Dir of Plng/Assessment/Imp Ms. Sara LEIGH
21 Director of Financial Operations Mr. Matthew ZELEZNIK

Community College of Philadelphia (H)

1700 Spring Garden Street, Philadelphia PA 19130-3991
County: Philadelphia FICE Identification: 003249
Unit ID: 215239
Telephone: (215) 751-8000 Carnegie Class: Assoc/HT-High Trad
FAX Number: (215) 751-8762 Calendar System: Semester
URL: www.ccp.edu
Established: 1965 Annual Undergrad Tuition & Fees (In-District): $8,592
Enrollment: 13,672 Coed
Affiliation or Control: State/Local IRS Status: 501(c)3
Highest Offering: Associate Degree
Accreditation: M, ADNUR, COARC, DH, MLTAD, NAEYC, RAD

01 President Dr. Donald GENERALS
10 Vice President Business & Finance Mr. Jacob EAPEN
45 VP Strat Initiative/Cmty Engagement Vacant
111 Vice Pres Institutional Advancement Ms. Mellissia ZANJANI
05 VP Academic and Student Success Dr. Alycia MARSHALL
103 VP Workforce Dev & Economic Innova Ms. Carol DE FRIES
43 General Counsel Ms. Victoria ZELLERS
13 Associate VP for IT Mr. Vijay SONTY
15 Assoc VP Human Resources Ms. Lisa HUTCHERSON
32 Interim Dean of Students Mr. Richard KOPP
84 Associate VP Enrollment Mgmt Dr. Darren LIPSCOMB
49 Dean Liberal Studies Dr. Chae SWEET
51 Dean Div Adult/Community Education Dr. David E. THOMAS
72 Div Dean of Business/Technology Dr. Arielle NORMENT
09 Director Institutional Research Dr. Sesime ADANU
06 Director Stdnt Records/Registration Vacant
18 Int AVP Facilities/Construction Mgt Mr. John WIGGINS
28 Diversity Compliance Officer Ms. Leila LAWRENCE
07 Director of Recruitment/Admissions Mr. Jason HAND
37 Director Financial Aid Mr. Robert FORREST
96 Director of Purchasing Ms. Marsia HENLEY
38 Dept Head Student Counseling Ms. Carmen COLON
36 Coord Career Info/Placement Svcs Ms. Tracy HANTON
29 Coord Alumni Rels/Annual Giving Ms. Lyvette BROOKS
25 Coord Grants/Prospect Research Ms. Anne GRECO
86 Government Relations Officer Ms. Mikecia WITHERSPOON
03 Special Assistant to the President Ms. Danielle LIAUTAUDWATKINS

Curtis Institute of Music (I)

1726 Locust Street, Philadelphia PA 19103-6187
County: Philadelphia FICE Identification: 003251
Unit ID: 211893
Telephone: (215) 893-5252 Carnegie Class: Spec-4-yr-Arts
FAX Number: (215) 893-9065 Calendar System: Semester
URL: www.curtis.edu
Established: 1924 Annual Undergrad Tuition & Fees: $3,015
Enrollment: 145 Coed
Affiliation or Control: Independent Non-Profit IRS Status: 501(c)3
Highest Offering: Master's
Accreditation: M, MUS

01 President & Chief Executive Officer Mr. Roberto DIAZ
11 Sr Vice Pres Administration Mr. Larry BOMBACK
111 Vice President Inst Advancement Mr. Christopher MOSSEY
05 Dean of Academics/Students Mr. Paul BRYAN
13 Chief Technology Officer Mr. Matt MORGAN
06 Registrar Mr. Darin KELLY
07 Admissions/Recruitment Manager Ms. Belmary LORCAS
08 Library Director Ms. Michelle OSWELL
15 Managing Director Human Resources Ms. Kimberly GOULD

Delaware County Community College (J)

901 S Media Line Road, Media PA 19063-1094
County: Delaware FICE Identification: 007110
Unit ID: 211927
Telephone: (610) 359-5000 Carnegie Class: Assoc/MT-VT-High Trad
FAX Number: (610) 359-5343 Calendar System: Semester
URL: www.dccc.edu
Established: 1967 Annual Undergrad Tuition & Fees (In-District): $9,710
Enrollment: 9,989 Coed
Affiliation or Control: State/Local IRS Status: 501(c)3
Highest Offering: Associate Degree
Accreditation: M, ADNUR, ART, COARC, EMT, MAC, NAEYC, SURGT

01 President Dr. L. Joy GATES BLACK
10 VP Finance/Admin & Treasurer Dr. Patricia BENSON
05 Vice Pres Academic Affairs Dr. Marian MCGORRY
111 Vice President for Advancement Ms. Rachel MCCAUSLAND
12 Vice Provost & Vice Pres Chester Co Dr. Mary Jo BOYER
84 Vice President of Enrollment Mgmt Dr. Mitch MURTHA
15 VP Human Resources Ms. Sara EVANS
103 VP Workforce Dev & Cmty Educ Ms. Karen KOZACHYN
13 CIO Information Technology Ms. Bianca VALENTE
32 VP Student Affairs Dr. Justin Tyler OWENS
88 Director Municipal Police Academy Mr. William DAVIS
106 Dean Distance Learning Services Dr. Alexandra SALAS
37 Director of Financial Aid Mr. Raymond L. TOOLE
06 Registrar Ms. Hope L. DIEHL
09 Assoc Vice Prov Inst Effectiveness Dr. Christopher TOKPAH
91 Director Admin Computing Mr. Bob HARDCASTLE
29 Director Alumni Programs Mr. Douglas J. FERGUSON
89 Director of First Year Experience Dr. Kendrick MICKENS
25 Grant Manager Ms. Bernadette WALSH
31 Director Community Education Ms. Patricia S. SCEPANSKY
41 Dir Athletics/Campus Engagement Ms. Allyson GLEASON
19 Director Safety & Security Mr. Matthew BRENNER
12 Director Southeast Center Vacant
108 Director Assessment Center Mr. Christos THEODOROPULOS
18 Director Facilities Mr. Nate SIMCOX
81 Dean STEM Dr. Umadevi GARIMELLA
50 Dean Business & Social Science Dr. Richard MCFADDEN
79 Dean Comm/Arts & Humanities Dr. Terri AMLONG
76 Dean Health/Nursing/EMS Dr. Genny CAVANAUGH
04 Executive Assistant to President Ms. Diane FOSTER
26 Executive Dir of Marketing & Comm Mr. Daniel KANAK
100 Chief of Staff Mr. Harry COSTIGAN
86 Director Govt Relations/Comm Mr. Anthony TWYMAN
28 Chief Diversity & Inclusion Officer Ms. Simmuelle MEYERS

Delaware Valley University (K)

700 E Butler Avenue, Doylestown PA 18901-2697
County: Bucks FICE Identification: 003252
Unit ID: 211981
Telephone: (215) 345-1500 Carnegie Class: Masters/S
FAX Number: (215) 345-5277 Calendar System: Semester
URL: www.delval.edu
Established: 1896 Annual Undergrad Tuition & Fees: $40,620
Enrollment: 2,303 Coed
Affiliation or Control: Independent Non-Profit IRS Status: 501(c)3

Highest Offering: Doctorate
Accreditation: M, ACBSP, #ARCPA, LSAR, MPCAC

01 President ... Dr. Benjamin RUSILOSKI
04 Executive Asst to the President ... Ms. Kristen OLSZEWSKI
100 Chief of Staff ... Vacant
05 VP Academic Affairs/Dean of Faculty ... Dr. Gloria OIKELOME
32 VP Campus Life & Inclusive Excel ... Dr. April VARI
10 VP for Finance & Admin/CFO ... Mr. Curt TOPPER
30 VP for Development & Alumni Affairs ... Mr. Joe FIOCHETTA
09 Director of Institutional Research ... Mr. Jim SLIZEWSKI
84 VP for Enrollment Management ... Ms. Kathy PAYNE
81 Dean of Life & Physical Sciences ... Dr. Jean SMOLEN
47 Dean Agriculture & Environ Science ... Dr. Broc SANDELIN
50 Dean Business & Humanities ... Dr. Tanya CASAS
58 Dean of Graduate & Prof Studies ... Ms. Danielle PEDROTTY
06 Registrar ... Mr. James SLIZEWSKI
41 Athletic Director ... Mr. David DUDA
26 VP Marketing & Communications ... Ms. Kathy HOWELL
21 Asst VP Finance & Administration ... Ms. Jennifer LISING
07 Executive Director of Admission ... Dr. Thomas SPEAKMAN
13 CIO ... Mr. Steve RIEKS
36 Assistant Director Career Education ... Ms. Katherine MARTUCCI
08 Librarian ... Mr. Peter A. KUPERSMITH
37 Director Student Financial Aid ... Mrs. Melissa WALSH
107 Dir Graduate & Professional Studies ... Ms. Yolonda UDVARDY
38 Director Counseling/Learn Support ... Ms. Sharon DONNELLY
23 Director Health Services ... Ms. Meredyth VANVREEDE
119 Information Security Officer ... Mr. Michael PILCH
35 Asst Dean of Stdnts/Dir Stdnt Inv ... Mr. Andrew MOYER
19 Director Security/Public Safety ... Mr. Tim POIRIER
15 Director of Human Resources ... Mr. Robert CONNELLY
18 Director of Facilities & Grounds ... Mr. Jeff BROWN
44 Director Annual Giving & Adv Svcs ... Mr. Kevin LADDEN
96 Director of Purchasing ... Mr. Craig NORCROSS
88 Associate VP for Business Dev ... Ms. Julia KELLY
88 Assistant Director E360 Program ... Ms. Emmaline ARMSTRONG
104 Director Study Abroad ... Vacant
106 Dir Online Education/E-learning ... Ms. Cynthia RENNER
29 Director Alumni Engagement ... Ms. Rachel MAUER
28 Asst Dean Stdnt Dev/Div & Incl ... Ms. Evie HUNTER
39 Dir Resident Life/Student Housing ... Ms. Carey HADDOCK
88 Coordinator of Student Activities ... Mr. Justin BROUSE

DeSales University (A)

2755 Station Avenue, Center Valley PA 18034-9568
County: Lehigh — FICE Identification: 003986
Unit ID: 210739
Telephone: (610) 282-1100 — Carnegie Class: DU-Mod
FAX Number: N/A — Calendar System: Semester
URL: www.desales.edu
Established: 1965 — Annual Undergrad Tuition & Fees: $39,500
Enrollment: 3,302 — Coed
Affiliation or Control: Roman Catholic — IRS Status: 501(c)3
Highest Offering: Doctorate
Accreditation: M, ACBSP, ARCPA, NURSE, PTA, @SP

01 President ... V.Rev. James J. GREENFIELD, OSFS
04 Executive Asst President's Office ... Ms. Nancy SEIER
03 Executive Vice President ... Dr. Gerard JOYCE
88 Vice President for Mission ... Rev. Kevin NADOLSKI, OSFS
10 VP for Admin & Finance ... Mr. Robert SNYDER
05 Provost & VP for Academic Affairs ... Bro. Daniel WISNIEWSKI, OSFS
111 Vice Pres Institutional Advancement ... Ms. Cheryl MURPHY
32 Vice President for Student Life ... Mrs. Linda ZERBE
88 VP for Campus Environment ... Mr. Marc ALBANESE
28 AVP Diversity/Equity/ Inclusion ... Vacant
84 Assoc VP for Enrollment Management ... Mr. Derrick WETZEL
26 AVP of Marketing & Communications ... Ms. Carolyn STEIGLEMAN
13 AVP for Information Technology ... Mr. Mark ALBERT
20 Assoc Provost of Academic Pgm ... Dr. Robert BLUMENSTEIN
58 Dean Graduate & Adult Education ... Mr. Ronald NORDONE
108 Asst Prov for Curr Assessment ... Dr. Sue MCGORRY
88 Asst Provost for Special Programs ... Dr. Katherine RAMSLAND
106 Dean of Online Education ... Dr. Eric HAGAN
55 Asst Dean Adult & Continuing Educ ... Mr. Michael YERGEY
42 University Chaplain ... Rev. Daniel LANNEN
15 Exec Dir of Human Resources ... Ms. Margie GRANDINETTI
27 Exec Dir of Communications ... Mr. Tom MCNAMARA
06 Registrar ... Mr. Thomas MANTONI
36 Exec Dir of Career Development ... Ms. Kristin EICHOLTZ
09 Dir of Institutional Rsrch/Analysis ... Ms. Lisa PLUMMER
11 Assoc VP for Admininistration ... Mr. Peter RAUTZHAN
44 Assoc VP for Annual Giving ... Vacant
35 Assoc Dean of Students for Engage ... Mr. Nicholas LUCHKO
38 Assoc Dean of Students for Wellness ... Ms. Wendy KALAMAR
21 Director of Finance & Treasurer ... Mr. Michael SWEETANA
113 Bursar ... Ms. Hollie KNAUSS
116 Comptroller ... Ms. Deanne FENSTERMACHER
19 Interim Chief of Police ... Chief Richard WILLIAMS
08 Director of Trexler Library ... Mr. Ed ZIMMERMAN
102 Director Corp/Foundation Relations ... Mrs. Kathy DIAMANDOPOULOS
112 Senior Major Gift Officer ... Mr. Michael RITCHIE
29 Director of Alumni Relations ... Mr. Daniel VILLANTI
07 Director of Admissions ... Ms. Kate MCNALLY
37 Director of Financial Aid ... Mrs. Joyce FARMER
41 Director of Athletics ... Mr. Scott COVAL
18 Director of Facilities ... Mr. Jim MOLCHANY
109 Director of Campus Environment ... Mr. Jeffrey RICHTER
120 Dir of Instr Design & Technology ... Mr. Jim HOLTON
104 Director of International Learning ... Mr. Brian MACDONALD
105 Interim Director of Web Strategy ... Mr. David OBLAS
91 Infrastructure Team Leader ... Mr. Paul BENNER
24 Campus Media Engineer ... Mr. Michael YORGEY
39 Assoc Director of Campus Life ... Ms. Joanne CARR
22 Title IX Coordinator ... Mr. Thomas JOHNSON
16 Asst Director of Human Resources ... Ms. Donna MIKOL
124 Assoc Dean of Academic Life ... Dr. Scott MATTINGLY
123 Dir of Admissions Adult & Grad Stds ... Ms. Leslie BARTHOLOMEW
121 Dir of the Academic Resource Ctr ... Ms. Ann KOEFER
23 Director of the Health Center ... Ms. Tammy LIPPINCOTT
88 Dir of Student Accessibility ... Ms. Carolyn TIGER
40 Campus Store Manager ... Mr. Joseph JUDGE
50 Division Head of Business ... Dr. Christopher COCOZZA
79 Div Head of Liberal Arts & Soc Sci ... Dr. Sarah NYTROE
66 Div Head of Nursing ... Dr. MaryElizabeth DOYLE-TADDUNI
81 Div Head of Sciences & Mathematics ... Dr. Joshua SLEE
57 Div Head of Performing Arts ... Ms. Anne LEWIS

Dickinson College (B)

Box 1773, College & Louther Street,
Carlisle PA 17013-2896
County: Cumberland — FICE Identification: 003253
Unit ID: 212009
Telephone: (800) 644-1773 — Carnegie Class: Bac-A&S
FAX Number: N/A — Calendar System: Semester
URL: www.dickinson.edu
Established: 1783 — Annual Undergrad Tuition & Fees: $56,523
Enrollment: 1,932 — Coed
Affiliation or Control: Independent Non-Profit — IRS Status: 501(c)3
Highest Offering: Master's
Accreditation: M

01 President ... Mr. John E. JONES, III
05 Provost/Dean of the College ... Dr. Neil B. WEISSMAN
84 VP Enrollment Mgmt/Dean Admissions ... Ms. Catherine M. DAVENPORT
10 VP for Finance/Admin & CFO ... Mr. David WALKER
111 VP College Advancement ... Mr. Carlo ROBUSTELLI
32 VP Student Life ... Dr. George H. STROUD
13 CIO/VP Information Services ... Ms. Jill M. FORRESTER
15 Assoc VP Human Resource Services ... Ms. Debra HARGROVE
43 Vice President & General Counsel ... Mr. Vincent CHAMPION
100 Chief of Staff/Secretary of College ... Ms. Karen N. FARYNIAK
18 Assoc VP Sustain & Facilities Plng ... Mr. Kenneth E. SHULTES
20 Sr Assoc Provost Academic Affairs ... Dr. Catrina HAMILTON-DRAGER
20 Asst Provost for Curriculum ... Ms. Deb L. BOLEN
110 Assoc VP College Advancement ... Ms. Jessica J. WILSON
109 Assoc VP Auxil Svcs & Budget Mgmt ... Vacant
26 VP Marketing & Communications ... Ms. Connie MCNAMARA
06 Registrar ... Ms. Elizabeth WHITE-HURST
41 Athletic Director ... Mr. Joel M. QUATTRONE
09 Dir Institutional Effectiveness ... Mr. Lester D. KO
37 Director of Financial Aid ... Vacant
104 Assoc Provost/Exec Dir Global Stdy ... Ms. Samantha C. BRANDAUER
31 Assoc Provost/Exec Dir CCLA ... Dr. Gary R. KIRK
88 Asc Prov/Dir Ctr Sustainability Ed ... Dr. Neil A. LEARY
36 Dean/Dir Career Development ... Ms. Annie KONDAS
23 Exec Dir Wellness Center ... Ms. Lauren STRUNK
21 Assoc VP Fin Ops & Controller ... Mr. Sean WITTE
27 Director of Media Relations ... Ms. Christine BAKSI
29 Director of Alumni Relations ... Ms. Liz TOTH
114 Director Planning & Budget ... Vacant
90 Director Academic Tech ... Vacant
08 Assoc Director Library Resources ... Ms. Theresa ARNDT
40 Dir of College Bookstore ... Ms. Katie CRANE
19 Asst VP Compliance/Campus Safety ... Ms. Dolores A. DANSER
102 Dir Academic & Foundation Relations ... Ms. Cheryl E. KREMER
39 Assoc Dean/Dir Res Life & Housing ... Vacant
35 Assoc VP Student Life ... Ms. Angie HARRIS
112 Asst VP College Advancement ... Ms. Tara C. RENAULT
113 Bursar Financial Operations ... Ms. Sally HECKENDORN
105 Director Online Marketing ... Ms. Sarah M. SHERIFF
42 Director Cmty Svcs/Religious Life ... Dr. Cody NIELSEN
28 Title IX Coordinator ... Ms. Katharina MATIC

Douglas Education Center (C)

130 Seventh Street, Monessen PA 15062-1097
County: Westmoreland — FICE Identification: 020683
Unit ID: 212045
Telephone: (724) 684-3684 — Carnegie Class: Spec 2-yr-A&S
FAX Number: (724) 684-7463 — Calendar System: Semester
URL: www.dec.edu
Established: 1904 — Annual Undergrad Tuition & Fees: $17,750
Enrollment: 207 — Coed
Affiliation or Control: Proprietary — IRS Status: Proprietary
Highest Offering: Associate Degree
Accreditation: ACCSC

01 President & CEO ... Mr. Jeffrey D. IMBRESCIA
05 Chief Academic Officer ... Mr. Julian IMBRESCIA
10 Director of Financial Services ... Mr. Jeffrey FEDOREK
20 Senior Academic Affairs Coordinator ... Ms. N. Renee MCDOWELL
07 Executive Director of Admissions ... Mr. Tony BAEZ MILAN
11 Executive Director of Operations ... Ms. Amanda PHILLIPS
26 Chief Marketing Officer ... Mr. Kevin G. FEAR
88 Supervisor of Cosmetology ... Ms. Karen NELSON
36 Director of Career Services ... Ms. Dana MELVIN
13 Exec Dir of Information Technology ... Mr. John SECHRIST

Drexel University (D)

3141 Chestnut Street, Philadelphia PA 19104-2875
County: Philadelphia — FICE Identification: 003256
Unit ID: 212054
Telephone: (215) 895-2000 — Carnegie Class: DU-Highest
FAX Number: (215) 895-1414 — Calendar System: Quarter
URL: www.drexel.edu
Established: 1891 — Annual Undergrad Tuition & Fees: $56,238
Enrollment: 23,589 — Coed
Affiliation or Control: Independent Non-Profit — IRS Status: 501(c)3
Highest Offering: Doctorate
Accreditation: M, ACATE, ANEST, ARCPA, ART, CAEP, CAHIIM, CEA, CIDA, CLPSY, CONST, DIET, DIETD, HT, IPSY, LAW, LC, LIB, MED, MFCD, NURSE, PA, PH, PTA

01 President ... Mr. John A. FRY
05 Provost/Executive Vice President ... Dr. Paul E. JENSEN
111 SVP Inst Advancement ... Mr. David L. UNRUH
10 Exec Vice Pres/Treasurer/COO ... Mrs. Helen Y. BOWMAN
84 SVP Enrollment Mgmt/Student Success ... Ms. Evelyn THIMBA
26 AVP Communications/Marketing ... Mr. Craig KAMPES
43 Sr VP & General Counsel ... Mr. Michael J. EXLER
86 Sr VP Govt & Community Relations ... Mr. Brian T. KEECH
20 Vice Prov Undergraduate Education ... Dr. Shivanthi ANANDAN
13 Vice Pres IT & CIO ... Mr. Thomas DECHIARO
28 VP Diversity & Inclusion ... Dr. Leslie ASHBURN-NARDO
88 Exec Dir/VProv Cultural Partnership ... Dr. Rosalind REMER
88 VP & Exec Dir Applied Innovation ... Mr. Shintaro KAIDO
46 Sr Vice Provost for Research ... Dr. Aleister SAUNDERS
32 SVP Stdnt Success/Dean Student Life ... Dr. Subir SAHU
09 Vice Provost Institutional Research ... Dr. Sujoy DAS
108 VP Compliance/Privacy & IA ... Ms. Kim P. GUNTER
115 Vice President Investments ... Ms. Catherine B. ULOZAS
88 Sr Vice Provost Partnerships ... Dr. Lucy E. KERMAN
15 Vice Pres Human Resources & PMOE ... Ms. Megan E. WEYLER
49 Int Dean College Arts & Sciences ... Dr. Kelly JOYCE
50 Dean LeBow College of Business ... Dr. Vibhas MADAN
54 Dean College of Engineering ... Dr. Sharon WALKER
77 Dean Col of Computing & Informatics ... Dr. Yi DENG
92 Dean of Pennoni Honors College ... Dr. Paula COHEN
81 SVP/CSO/Dean Grad Sch of Biomed Sci ... Dr. Elisabeth VANBOCKSTAELE
62 Dean of Libraries ... Dr. Danuta A. NITECKI
88 Dean Close Sch of Entrepreneurship ... Dr. Donna M. DECAROLIS
61 Dean Kline School of Law ... Mr. Daniel M. FILLER
60 Dean Col of Media Arts & Design ... Mr. Jason SCHUPBACH
53 Dean School of Education ... Dr. Penny HAMMRICH
63 Sr VP & Dean College of Medicine ... Dr. Charles B. CAIRNS
66 Dean Col Nursing/Health Prof ... Dr. Laura N. GITLIN
69 Dean Dornsife Sch of Public Health ... Dr. Ana V. DIEZ ROUX
81 Dean School Biomed Engineering ... Dr. Paul BRANDT-RAUF
19 Interim VP Public Safety ... Mr. Robert LIS
41 Athletic Director ... Ms. Maisha KELLY
36 Vice Prov Career Development Ctr ... Mr. Ian SLADEN
22 Title IX Coordinator ... Mr. Paul APIÇELLA
85 Vice Provost Global Engagement ... Dr. Rogelio MIÑANA
88 Chair Faculty Senate ... Dr. Kevin G. OWENS
83 Director AJ Drexel Autism Institute ... Dr. Diana ROBINS
06 Registrar ... Dr. Giuseppe SALOMONE
104 Senior Director Education Abroad ... Ms. Ahaji SCHREFFLER
18 VP Real Estate & Facilities ... Mr. Alan GREENBERGER
28 AVP HR/Chief Diversity Officer ... Ms. Kim GHOLSTON
39 Senior Exec Director Resident Life ... Dr. Melissa DEPRETTO-BEHAN
96 VP/Chief Procurement Officer ... Ms. Julie JONES
123 Assistant VP Graduate Admissions ... Dr. Angela L. MONTGOMERY
07 Dean of Undergraduate Admissions ... Mr. Michael KEATON
101 Assoc VP & Board Secretary ... Mr. Darin PFEIFER
102 Exec Director Found/Corp Rels ... Ms. Brenna MCBRIDE
29 Director Alumni Affairs ... Mr. Christopher BERTONE
30 Executive Director of Development ... Mr. Nik KOZEL
37 Executive Director Financial Aid ... Ms. Cindy DE LONE
38 Executive Director of Counseling ... Dr. Tania CZARNECKI

Duquesne University (E)

600 Forbes Avenue, Pittsburgh PA 15282-0001
County: Allegheny — FICE Identification: 003258
Unit ID: 212106
Telephone: (412) 396-6000 — Carnegie Class: DU-Higher
FAX Number: (412) 396-4186 — Calendar System: Semester
URL: www.duq.edu
Established: 1878 — Annual Undergrad Tuition & Fees: $41,892
Enrollment: 8,830 — Coed
Affiliation or Control: Roman Catholic — IRS Status: 501(c)3
Highest Offering: Doctorate
Accreditation: M, ANEST, ARCPA, CAATE, CACREP, CAEP, CEA, CLPSY, FEPAC, LAW, MUS, NURSE, OT, PHAR, PTA, SCPSY, SP

01 President ... Mr. Kenneth G. GORMLEY
04 Assistant to the President ... Ms. Margaret EISEMAN
05 Provost/Exec Vice Pres ... Dr. David J. DAUSEY
10 Sr Vice Pres for Finance & Business ... Dr. Matthew J. FRIST
32 Sr Vice Pres for Student Life ... Dr. Douglas FRIZZELL
111 Sr VP for University Advancement ... Mr. Jim MILLER
88 Sr Vice Pres Mission/Identity ... Rev. Raymond FRENCH, CSSP
43 SVP Legal Affairs/General Counsel ... Ms. Pamela W. CONNELLY
26 VP Marketing and Communications ... Mr. Gabriel WELSCH
41 Vice Pres of Athletics ... Mr. David HARPER
20 Assoc Academic Vice President ... Dr. Darlene WEAVER
20 Assoc Academic Vice President ... Dr. Jeffrey A. MILLER

13 Vice Pres Information Tech/CIO ....Dr. Charles R. BARTEL
84 Vice Pres Enrollment Management ....Mr. Joel BAUMAN
109 Director Auxiliary Services ....Mr. Scott RICHARDS
85 Exec Dir International Programs ....Dr. Joseph DECROSTRA
06 Registrar ....Dr. Kimberly HOERITZ
08 Librarian ....Dr. Sara BARON
29 Asst Vice Pres Alumni Relations ....Ms. Sarah SPERRY
09 Director of Institutional Research ....Mr. Matthew NORTH
37 AVP for Financial Aid ....Mr. Richard C. ESPOSITO
15 Asst Vice Pres/CHRO ....Mr. John G. GREENO
19 Director of Security ....Mr. Thomas HART
88 Dir Environmental Health/Safety ....Ms. Paula D. SWEITZER
18 Asst VP/Chief Facilities Officer ....Mr. Rodney W. DOBISH
36 Director of Career Services ....Ms. Nicole FELDHUES
22 Dir Anti-discrimination/Risk Mgmt ....Mr. Sean F. WEAVER
23 Director Health Service ....Ms. Dessa MRVOS
38 Dir University Counseling Center ....Dr. Ian C. EDWARDS
39 Director Residence Life ....Mrs. Sharon G. OELSCHLAGER
42 Director Campus Ministry ....Rev. William CHRISTY
28 Chief Diversity Officer ....Ms. Crystal MCCORMICK WARE
50 Dean Business & Administration ....Dr. Dean B. MCFARLIN
63 Dean Col of Osteopathic Medicine ....Dr. John M. KAUFFMAN
66 Dean of Nursing ....Dr. Mary Ellen S. GLASGOW
67 Interim Dean of Pharmacy ....Dr. James K. DRENNEN, III
64 Interim Dean of Music ....Dr. David Allen WEHR
53 Dean of Education ....Dr. Cindy M. WALKER
76 Dean of Health Sciences ....Dr. Fevzi AKINCI
61 Dean of Law ....Ms. April BARTON
49 Dean of Liberal Arts/Graduate ....Dr. Kristine BLAIR
65 Dean of Natural/Environment Sci ....Dr. Philip P. REEDER
40 Bookstore Manager ....Mr. John KACHUR
07 AVP Undergraduate Admissions ....Ms. Debra A. ZUGATES
100 Chief of Staff/Sr Advisor to Pres ....Mr. Daniel GILMAN
30 Asst VP for External Relations ....Ms. Mary Beth FORD
106 Dir Online Education/E-learning ....Dr. Michael W. BRIDGES
122 Admin Assistant Ofc of Greek Life ....Ms. Deborah A. WILLSON

Eastern University (A)

1300 Eagle Road, Saint Davids PA 19087-3696
County: Delaware   FICE Identification: 003259
Unit ID: 212133
Telephone: (610) 341-5800   Carnegie Class: Masters/L
FAX Number: N/A   Calendar System: Semester
URL: www.eastern.edu
Established: 1925   Annual Undergrad Tuition & Fees: $34,706
Enrollment: 3,504   Coed
Affiliation or Control: American Baptist   IRS Status: 501(c)3
Highest Offering: Doctorate
Accreditation: M, #ACBSP, EXSC, MPCAC, NURSE, SW, THEOL

01 President ....Dr. Ronald A. MATTHEWS
10 Vice Pres for Finance/Operations ....Vacant
05 Provost/VP Academic Affairs ....Dr. Kenton SPARKS
06 Registrar ....Ms. Sarah ROCHE
32 Asst Vice Pres for Student Develop ....Dr. Jacqueline IRVING
45 VP for Inst Planning/Effectiveness ....Dr. Christine P. MAHAN
111 Vice President Advancement ....Ms. Luisa WILSMAN
110 Associate VP Advancement ....Ms. Natissa KULTAN-PFAUTZ
15 Chief Human Resources Officer ....Ms. Kacey BERNARD
118 Sr Dir of Benefits Admin & Trng ....Ms. Patti MCHUGH
04 Exec Asst to the President ....Ms. Heather NORCINI
12 Executive Dean Esperanza College ....Ms. Marilyn MARSH
76 Int Dean Col of Health & Science ....Dr. Eloise MENESES
73 Int Dean Palmer Theological Sem ....Ms. K-lee JOHNSON
50 Int Dean Col of Business Leadership . Ms. Christa LEE-CHUVALA
92 Dean College Arts/Humanities/Honors ....Dr. Brian WILLIAMS
53 Dean College of Education ....Dr. Susan EDGAR-SMITH
18 Exec Dir Facilities Services ....Mr. Jeffrey GROMIS
105 Senior Web Manager ....Ms. Allison MARSHALECK
09 Asst Vice Pres for Inst Effect ....Mr. Thomas A. DAHLSTROM
26 Assoc VP Marketing/Enroll & Comm ....Ms. Kelly GODDARD
113 Senior Director Student Accounts ....Ms. Lisa WELLER
08 Director of University Library ....Ms. Joy DLUGOSZ
42 University Chaplain ....Rev Dr. Joseph B. MODICA
37 Director of Financial Aid ....Ms. Andrea RUTH
13 Chief Information Officer ....Mr. Eric MCCLOY
24 Supervisor ITSC Resources ....Mr. Paul THORPE
36 Director of Talent & Career Dev ....Ms. Sarah TODD
41 Director of Athletics ....Mr. Eric MCNELLEY
19 Director of Public Safety ....Mr. Michael BICKING
88 Exec Dir Conferences/Spec Events ....Ms. Meggin CAPERS
38 Dir Counseling/Academic Support ....Dr. Lisa M. HEMLICK
85 Dir Intl Student & Scholar Services ....Ms. Augusta ALLEN
39 Dir of Student Conduct & Comm Stand ....Mr. Christopher WRIGHT
40 Follett Bookstore Manager ....Mr. Christopher HOAGLAND
93 Int Dir Multicultural Student Init ....Ms. Theresa NOYE
109 Director Auxiliary Services ....Mr. Byron MCMILLAN
120 Mgr Instruct Design & Lrng Tech ....Ms. Susan YAVOR
104 Sr Assc Reg/Coord Off-Campus Pgm ....Mr. Brian MINSTER
106 Asst Provost for Acad Ops/Dir CTLT ....Dr. Rebecca GIDJUNIS
96 Financial Asst/Purchasing Mgr ....Ms. Heather SYKES
07 Dir of Undergraduate Admissions ....Ms. Claire GOWEN
101 Asst to the Office of the BOT ....Ms. Amanda KELLY
28 Spec Asst to the Pres for Diversity ....Mr. Randolph WALTERS
29 Assoc VP for Alumni & Family Engage ..Mr. Timothy WORTHAM
30 Dir Alumni & Fam Philanthropic Eng ....Ms. Rebecca CHARUK
90 Director Technology Services ....Mr. Carlos GONZALEZ

† Parent institution of Palmer Theological Seminary.

Elizabethtown College (B)

1 Alpha Drive, Elizabethtown PA 17022-2298
County: Lancaster   FICE Identification: 003262
Unit ID: 212197
Telephone: (717) 361-1000   Carnegie Class: Masters/S
FAX Number: (717) 361-1207   Calendar System: Semester
URL: www.etown.edu
Established: 1899   Annual Undergrad Tuition & Fees: $32,960
Enrollment: 1,881   Coed
Affiliation or Control: Other   IRS Status: 501(c)3
Highest Offering: Doctorate
Accreditation: M, ACBSP, ARCPA, MUS, OT, SW

01 President ....Dr. Elizabeth A. RIDER
05 Provost & VP Academic Affairs ....Dr. Kristi A. KNEAS
10 Sr Vice President Admin & Finance ....Mr. Gerald L. SILBERMAN
111 VP Institutional Advancement ....Mr. Brian G. FALCK
84 Vice Pres Enrollment Management ....Mr. John F. CHAMPOLI
32 Vice Pres Student Life ....Ms. Nichole J. GONZALEZ
11 VP Operations & Aux Services ....Mr. Robert J. KERIN
28 Senior Advisor DEB ....Dr. Kesha M. WILLIAMS
107 Dean of SGPS & School of Business ....Dr. Najiba BENABESS
07 Assistant VP Enrollement Mgmt ....Mr. Adam D. SMITH
35 Asst Dean of Students & Dir of CSS ....Ms. Stephanie A. RANKIN
26 Exec Dir Marketing/Communications ....Ms. Keri B. STRAUB
102 Exec Dir Foundation/Govt Relations ....Ms. Lesley M. FINNEY
09 Director Institutional Research ....Ms. Debra K. SHEESLEY
37 Director of Financial Aid ....Ms. Melodie R. JACKSON
08 Director The High Library ....Ms. Sarah PENNIMAN
29 Exec Director Alumni Devel/Programs ....Mr. Mark A. CLAPPER
19 Asst Director of Campus Security ....Mr. Gerald KELLEY
41 Director of Athletics ....Mr. Chris MORGAN
42 Chaplain/Director Religious Life . Ms. Amy SHORNER-JOHNSON
15 Director of Human Resources ....Ms. Ann M. THOMPSON
04 Exc Assistant to the President ....Ms. Peggy H. STAUFFER
06 Registrar ....Ms. Beverly SCHMALHOFER
101 Liaison to Board of Trustees ....Ms. Keri B. STRAUB
13 Chief Information Technology Ofcr ....Mr. Brian C. HELM
38 Assoc Dean Student Counseling ....Dr. Bruce G. LYNCH
44 Director Annual Giving ....Mr. Benjamin R. OSTERHOUT

Erie Institute of Technology (C)

940 Millcreek Mall, Erie PA 16565-1002
County: Erie   FICE Identification: 022039
Unit ID: 212434
Telephone: (814) 868-9900   Carnegie Class: Spec 2-yr-Tech
FAX Number: (814) 868-9977   Calendar System: Semester
URL: www.erieit.edu
Established: 1958   Annual Undergrad Tuition & Fees: $14,839
Enrollment: 282   Coed
Affiliation or Control: Proprietary   IRS Status: Proprietary
Highest Offering: Associate Degree
Accreditation: ACCSC

01 Director ....Mr. Paul FITZGERALD
05 Director of Education ....Ms. Kate HUSHON
07 Admissions Director ....Ms. Barb BOLT

Esperanza College (D)

4261 North 5th Street, Philadelphia PA 19140
Telephone: (215) 324-0746   Identification: 770153
Accreditation: &M

† Branch campus of Eastern University, Saint Davids, PA

Fortis Institute (E)

166 Slocum Street, Forty Fort PA 18704-2347
County: Luzerne   FICE Identification: 030115
Unit ID: 249609
Telephone: (570) 288-8400   Carnegie Class: Spec 2-yr-Health
FAX Number: (570) 287-7936   Calendar System: Other
URL: www.fortis.edu
Established: 1984   Annual Undergrad Tuition & Fees: $13,921
Enrollment: 182   Coed
Affiliation or Control: Proprietary   IRS Status: Proprietary
Highest Offering: Associate Degree
Accreditation: ACCSC

01 Campus President ....Vacant
05 Director of Education ....Christopher JONES
07 Asst Director of Admissions ....Vacant
37 Director Financial Aid ....Stacie TAROLI

Fortis Institute (F)

517 Ash Street, Scranton PA 18509
County: Lackawanna   FICE Identification: 030116
Unit ID: 385503
Telephone: (570) 558-1818   Carnegie Class: Spec 2-yr-Health
FAX Number: (570) 342-4537   Calendar System: Other
URL: www.fortis.edu/scranton-pennsylvania.php
Established: 1986   Annual Undergrad Tuition & Fees: $28,087
Enrollment: 279   Coed
Affiliation or Control: Proprietary   IRS Status: Proprietary
Highest Offering: Associate Degree
Accreditation: ACCSC, DH

01 Campus President ....Ms. Madeline LEVY CRUZ
06 Registrar ....Mr. Art BOBBOUINE
07 Asst Director of Admissions ....Mr. Eric ROGERS
36 Director Career/Student Services ....Ms. Heather CONTARDI
37 Director Student Financial Aid ....Ms. Stacie TAROLI

† Tuition varies by degree program.

Franklin & Marshall College (G)

PO Box 3003, Lancaster PA 17604-3003
County: Lancaster   FICE Identification: 003265
Unit ID: 212577
Telephone: (717) 358-3971   Carnegie Class: Bac-A&S
FAX Number: (717) 358-4183   Calendar System: Semester
URL: www.fandm.edu
Established: 1787   Annual Undergrad Tuition & Fees: $61,062
Enrollment: 2,254   Coed
Affiliation or Control: Independent Non-Profit   IRS Status: 501(c)3
Highest Offering: Baccalaureate
Accreditation: M

01 President ....Dr. Barbara K. ALTMANN
10 VP for Finance/Admin & Treasurer ....Mr. Michael TODD
111 Vice Pres for College Advancement ....Mr. Matthew EYNON
84 VP for Enrollment Management ....Mr. Jimmie FOSTER
26 Vice Pres for College Communication . Ms. Barbara STAMBAUGH
05 Provost/Dean of Faculty ....Dr. Cameron WESSON
32 VP and Dean of Student Affairs ....Ms. Margaret HAZLETT
88 Acting Director of the Klehr Center ....Ms. Amy ZYLBERMAN
11 Associate VP for Administration ....Mr. Barry BOSLEY
45 VP for Strategic Initiatives ....Dr. Alan S. CANIGLIA
100 Interim Dir Ofc of the President ....Dr. Deb MORIARTY
08 College Librarian ....Mr. Scott VINE
85 Assoc Dean International Programs ....Ms. Sue MENNICKE
20 Associate Dean of Faculty ....Dr. Annalisa CRANNELL
20 Associate Dean of Faculty ....Dr. Amelia RAUSER
28 Assoc Dir of Multicultural Affairs ....Ms. Xay CHONGTUA
88 Assistant Dean/College House Dean ....Ms. Melissa GIESS
88 Assistant Dean/College House Dean ....Ms. Courtnee N. JORDAN-COX
88 Assistant Dean/College House Dean ....Dr. Beth PROFFITT
88 Assistant Dean/College House Dean ....Mr. Todd DEKAY
88 Assistant Dean/College House Dean ....Mr. Jedrek DINEROS
21 Asst VP for Treasury & Controller ....Mr. Sean GALLOWAY
15 Assoc VP Human Resources/CHRO ....Mr. Johnson EAPEN
18 Associate VP/Facilities Management ....Mr. Mike WETZEL
19 Assoc VP Public Safety ....Mr. William MCHALE, JR.
23 Managing Physician Student Wellness ....Dr. Amy A. MYERS
13 VP and Chief Information Officer ....Ms. Carrie RAMPP
37 Director Financial Aid ....Mr. Clarke C. PAINE
38 Head of Counseling Services ....Dr. Lauren A. FIRESTONE
90 Dir Instruct/Emerging Technology ....Mr. Teb LOCKE
06 College Registrar ....Ms. Laura A. MEDVIC
29 Asst VP/Alumni Engagement ....Ms. Amy T. LAYMAN
07 Dean of Admission ....Vacant
41 Athletic Director ....Ms. Lauren PACKER
43 VP and General Counsel ....Vacant
101 Secretary of the Board ....Dr. Deb MORIARTY
102 Dir Corp/Found/Cmty Partners ....Vacant
44 Director Annual Giving ....Mr. Ramy RAHAL
39 Dir Resident Life/Student Housing ....Ms. Lori N. FOUST
09 Director of Institutional Research ....Ms. Chris D. ALEXANDER

Gannon University (H)

University Square, Erie PA 16541-0001
County: Erie   FICE Identification: 003266
Unit ID: 212601
Telephone: (814) 871-7000   Carnegie Class: DU-Mod
FAX Number: (814) 871-7338   Calendar System: Other
URL: www.gannon.edu
Established: 1925   Annual Undergrad Tuition & Fees: $34,526
Enrollment: 4,251   Coed
Affiliation or Control: Roman Catholic   IRS Status: 501(c)3
Highest Offering: Doctorate
Accreditation: M, ACBSP, ANEST, ARCPA, CAATE, CACREP, CEA, COARC, COARCP, EXSC, NURSE, OT, PTA, RAD, @SP, SW

01 President ....Dr. Keith TAYLOR
05 Provost & VP Student Experience ....Dr. Walter IWANENKO, JR.
45 Chief Institutional Planning Ofcr ....Ms. Valerie BACIK
111 Vice Pres University Advancement ....Ms. Barbara BEUSCHER
88 Assoc Vice President for Mission ....Rev. Michael KESICKI
84 Vice President for Enrollment ....Mr. William EDMONDSON
32 VP Student Development & Engagement ....Vacant
10 VP Finance & Campus Operations ....Ms. Jennifer R. LUNDY
04 Assistant to the President ....Ms. Darlene A. MCMICHAEL
79 Dean Col Humanities/Educ/Soc Sci ....Dr. Lori LINDLEY
54 Dean Col Engineering/Business ....Dr. Karinna VERNAZA
76 Dean Morosky Col Health Prof/Sci ....Dr. Sarah EWING
49 Director of Liberal Studies ....Dr. Megan WOLLER
08 Director Nash Library ....Mr. Ken BRUNDAGE
37 Director of Financial Aid ....Mr. Andrew TEETS
06 Registrar ....Mr. Zachary HOPKINS
36 Assoc Dir Career Dev/Employment Svc ....Ms. Erin HART
39 Director of Residence Life ....Ms. Denise GOLDEN
88 Dir Stdnt Org/Leadership Dev ....Ms. Jaime MCCASLIN
30 Associate VP for Development ....Ms. Almi CLERKIN
100 Chief of Staff/Dir Marketing/Comm ....Mr. Douglas OATHOUT
102 Dir of Research/Foundation Rels ....Vacant
21 Controller ....Mr. Jeffrey TAYLOR
114 Assoc Vice President Budget ....Ms. Mary Kathleen LEONARD

15 Exec Director of Human Resources .... Mr. Frederick KENDRICK
41 Director of Athletics ....Ms. Lisa GODDARD MCGUIRK
19 Director Campus Police & Safety ....Mr. Les FETTERMAN
13 Chief Information Officer ....Mr. Mark JORDANO
42 University Chaplain .... Rev. Michael KESICKI
07 Director of Admissions ....Mr. Thomas P. CAMILLO
09 Director of Institutional Research ....Mr. Dana BAGWELL
18 Director Physical Plant/Maintenance ....Ms. Ashley SPEARS
38 Director Student Counseling ....Dr. Jodi GIACOMELLI
86 Dir Community/Government Relations ......Ms. Erika A. RAMALHO
96 Director of Purchasing ....Ms. Bridget SETH
40 Bookstore Manager ....Ms. Amber COOK
29 Director Alumni Affairs ....Vacant

Geisinger Commonwealth School of Medicine (A)

525 Pine Street, Scranton PA 18509
County: Lackawanna FICE Identification: 041672
Unit ID: 456542
Telephone: (570) 504-7000 Carnegie Class: Spec-4-yr-Med
FAX Number: (570) 504-9660 Calendar System: Semester
URL: https://www.geisinger.edu/education
Established: 2009 Annual Graduate Tuition & Fees: N/A
Enrollment: 607 Coed
Affiliation or Control: Independent Non-Profit IRS Status: 501(c)3
Highest Offering: Doctorate; No Undergraduates
Accreditation: M, MED

01 President and Dean ....Dr. Julie BYERLEY
10 VP for Finance & Admin/CFO ....Ms. Anna ARVAY
05 Provost/Vice Dean for Education ....Dr. William JEFFRIES
28 Vice Dean for DEI ....Vacant
32 Dean Student Affairs ....Dr. Tanja ADONIZIO
20 Assoc Dean Academic Administration .... Dr. Andrea DIMATTIA
20 Assoc Dean Academic Administration .... Ms. Rebecca SLANGAN
07 Assoc Dean Admission/Enrol/Fin Aid .... Dr. Michelle SCHMUDE
58 Associate Dean Graduate Education .... Dr. Jennifer BOARDMAN
66 Assoc Dean Nursing Student Educ .... Dr. Rebecca STOUDT
35 Asst Dean of Students .... Ms. Jacquelyn GHORMOZ
06 Registrar .... Mr. Edward LAHART
37 Director of Financial Aid ....Ms. Sue MCNAMARA
29 Director of Alumni Relations ....Mr. Chris BOLAND
08 Associate Dean Library Services ....Ms. Amy ALLISON
77 Associate Dean for Educational IT ... Mr. James FRANCESCHELLI
18 Director of Facilities ....Mr. John GORCZYK
19 Manager of Public Safety ....Mr. Steven JARBOLA
26 Director of Media and PR ....Ms. Elizabeth ZYGMUNT

Geneva College (B)

3200 College Avenue, Beaver Falls PA 15010-3557
County: Beaver FICE Identification: 003267
Unit ID: 212656
Telephone: (724) 846-5100 Carnegie Class: Masters/S
FAX Number: (724) 847-6687 Calendar System: Semester
URL: www.geneva.edu
Established: 1848 Annual Undergrad Tuition & Fees: $29,040
Enrollment: 1,349 Coed
Affiliation or Control: Reformed Presbyterian Church IRS Status: 501(c)3
Highest Offering: Master's
Accreditation: M, ACBSP, CACREP, CNEA

01 President ....Dr. Calvin L. TROUP
05 Provost ....Dr. Melinda R. STEPHENS
111 Vice Pres of Advancement ....Dr. Marvin L. DEWEY
10 VP Business/Finance ....Mr. Timothy R. BAIRD
84 VP Enrollment & Marketing ....Mr. Willem M. DE RUIJTER
13 CIO & VP Information Technology ....Mr. Chris A. TREIB
21 Controller ....Mrs. Kami S. GREENE
07 Assoc VP for Enrollment ....Mr. Dave B. LAYTON
32 VP of Student Dev/Title IX Coord ....Ms. Jamie R. SWANK
124 Director of Student Engagement .... Ms. Rebekah CASE
58 Dean Grad/Adult & Online Programs ....Mr. John D. GALLO
06 Registrar ....Mr. William M. STARKE
37 Director of Student Financial Svcs .... Ms. Tara M. VERRICO
08 Librarian ....Mr. Steve P. KENNEALLY
26 Director Public Relations ....Mrs. Lindsay M. COURTEAU
29 Director Alumni Relations ....Ms. Kelly J. SANZARI
41 Chief Athletic Officer ....Mr. Van G. ZANIC
18 Director of Physical Plant ....Mr. Dan D. KIGER
36 Director of Career Development ....Ms. Krista M. AUTREY
85 International Admissions Counselor ....Ms. Bridget E. FOX
40 Campus Store Manager ....Vacant
19 Director of Security ....Mr. David A. WARGO
28 Interim Coordinator of Diversity ....Mrs. Kristie A. MARTEL
92 Director of Honors Program ....Dr. Eric MILLER
39 Director of Residence Life ....Mrs. Kelsey L. MURPHY
23 Health Services Director ....Mrs. Beth L. CARLSON
96 Purchasing Coordinator ....Ms. Heidi J. SRAY
88 Accounting and Payroll Manager .... Mr. William NICHOLS
121 Director of Student Success ....Mr. Thomas C. PYLE
04 Executive Asst to President .... Mrs. Andrea KAMICKER
09 Director of Institutional Research .... Mr. Jordan BOUSCHER
50 Business Dept Chair ....Dr. Christen S. ADELS
53 Education Dept Chair ....Dr. Deana MACK
54 Engineering Dept Chair ....Dr. Anthony C. COMER
90 Director of Technology Services ....Mr. Jeremy T. YERSE
104 Dir Crossroads/Ctr Special Programs ....Dr. Jeffrey S. COLE
105 Online Marketing/Webmaster ....Mr. Michael W. DUNCAN
106 Dean Grad/Adult/Online Programs ....Mr. John D. GALLO
15 Chief Human Resources Officer ....Mr. Jerry L. MILLER

30 Director of Development ....Ms. Kelli J. MCKEE
38 Director Student Counseling ....Ms. Amy L. SOLMAN

Gettysburg College (C)

300 N Washington Street, Gettysburg PA 17325-1486
County: Adams FICE Identification: 003268
Unit ID: 212674
Telephone: (717) 337-6000 Carnegie Class: Bac-A&S
FAX Number: (717) 337-6008 Calendar System: Semester
URL: www.gettysburg.edu
Established: 1832 Annual Undergrad Tuition & Fees: $58,500
Enrollment: 2,507 Coed
Affiliation or Control: Evangelical Lutheran Church In America
IRS Status: 501(c)3
Highest Offering: Master's
Accreditation: M, MUS

01 President ....Mr. Robert IULIANO
05 Provost ....Dr. Christopher ZAPPE
30 Vice Pres Dev/Alumni/Parent Rels .....Mr. Clarence (Tres) MULLIS
10 Vice President Finance/Treasurer ....Mr. Daniel T. KONSTALID
32 Vice President for College Life ....Ms. Anne EHRLICH
84 Vice Pres Enrollment/Education Svcs ....Mr. Carey THOMPSON
13 Vice President Information Tech ....Dr. Rod TOSTEN
45 Assoc Provost for Plng/Fac & Tech ....Vacant
28 Chief Diversity Officer .... Ms. Eloisa GORDON-MORA
100 Chief of Staff/Strat Adv to Pres ....Ms. Kristin J. STUEMPFLE
21 Associate Vice President/Treasurer .... Mr. Christopher DELANEY
26 Exec Dir Communications/Marketing ....Ms. Jamie YATES
35 Associate Dean of College Life ....Mr. James P. DUFFY
85 Dir International Student Services .... Mr. Brad LANCASTER
06 Registrar ....Mr. Brian REESE
37 Director of Financial Aid ....Ms. Kathryn F. ADAMS
07 Dean of Admissions ....Ms. Gail M. SWEEZEY
42 Chaplain ....Vacant
09 Director for Institutional Analysis ....Ms. Suhua DONG
38 Exec Dir of Counseling & Wellness ....Ms. Krista DHRUV
08 Dean of the Library ....Ms. Robin WAGNER
29 Exec Director of Alumni Relations ....Mr. Joe LYNCH
41 Exec Director for Athletics ....Mr. Mike M. MATIIA
19 Executive Director of Campus Safety ....Mr. Alex WILTZ
18 Exec Dir Facilities Plng & Mgmt .... Mr. James BIESECKER
21 Sr Dir of Financial Svcs/Controller .... Ms. Sharon S. DAYHOFF
80 Director Center for Public Service .... Ms. Gretchen NATTER
39 Dir Res Life & First Yr Programs .... Ms. Danielle PHILLIPS
121 Dean Center for Student Success ....Ms. Keira KANT
122 Dir Student Activities & Greek Life ....Mr. Jonathan ALLEN
40 Director of College Bookstore .... Mr. Michael J. KOTLINSKI
15 Exec Director Human Resources ....Ms. Jennifer R. LUCAS
16 Asst Director Human Resources .... Ms. Cassandra FOCKLER
102 Dir Foundation/Govt & FAC Grants ....Vacant
104 Dir Global Init/Ctr Global Educ ....Ms. Rebecca A. BERGREN
04 Administrative Asst to President ....Ms. Pamela EISENHART
109 Exec Dir Aux Svcs/Life Safety Mgr ....Vacant
36 Exec Dir Ctr for Career Engagement ....Mr. Marc GOLDMAN

Gratz College (D)

7605 Old York Road, Melrose Park PA 19027-3010
County: Montgomery FICE Identification: 004058
Unit ID: 212771
Telephone: (215) 635-7300 Carnegie Class: Masters/S
FAX Number: (215) 635-1046 Calendar System: Trimester
URL: www.gratz.edu
Established: 1895 Annual Undergrad Tuition & Fees: N/A
Enrollment: 454 Coed
Affiliation or Control: Independent Non-Profit IRS Status: 501(c)3
Highest Offering: Doctorate
Accreditation: M

01 President ....Dr. Zev ELEFF
05 Dean of Gratz College ....Dr. Honour MOORE
26 Chief Public Relations Officer ....Ms. Dodi KLIMOFF
84 Director of Enrollment Management .... Mr. Dave MALTER
06 Registrar .... Mr. Scott MINKOFF
13 Manager Information Technoloy ....Ms. Suzette QUILES
15 Personnel Services ....Ms. Yaffa HOWARD
111 Dir Institutional Advancement ....Ms. Naomi HOUSMAN
07 Assoc Director of Enroll Mgmt .... Ms. Mindy BLECHMAN
88 Director of Gratz Advance .... Ms. Deborah LEON
37 Student Financial Services Advisor ....Vacant
106 Online Education/E-learning ....Dr. Philip MOORE
08 Dir of Library/Info Tech Svcs ....Ms. Donna GUERIN
18 Chief Facilities/Physical Plant ....Mr. Ernest COLLINS
04 Administrative Asst to President ....Ms. Dodi KLIMOFF
10 Mgr Business Operations/Facilities ...Mr. Thomas CIPRIANO, JR.
101 Secretary of the Institution/Board .... Ms. Sharon LIEBHABER
19 Director Security/Safety ....Ms. Suzette QUILES

Great Lakes Institute of Technology (E)

5100 Peach Street, Erie PA 16509
County: Erie FICE Identification: 021122
Unit ID: 213181
Telephone: (814) 864-6666 Carnegie Class: Spec 2-yr-Health
FAX Number: (814) 868-1717 Calendar System: Other
URL: www.glit.edu
Established: 1965 Annual Undergrad Tuition & Fees: N/A
Enrollment: 429 Coed
Affiliation or Control: Proprietary IRS Status: Proprietary
Highest Offering: Associate Degree
Accreditation: ACCSC, DMS, SURGT

01 Director/CEO ....Eric BERRIOS
07 Director of Admissions ....Mark STOTTS
37 Director Student Financial Aid ....Andrew DICK
05 Director of Education/Compliance ....Vickie CLEMENTS
10 Director of Finance ....Andrea CAMPBELL
36 Director Career Services ....Carl ROZENEK

Grove City College (F)

100 Campus Drive, Grove City PA 16127-2104
County: Mercer FICE Identification: 003269
Unit ID: 212805
Telephone: (724) 458-2000 Carnegie Class: Bac-Diverse
FAX Number: (724) 458-2190 Calendar System: Semester
URL: www.gcc.edu
Established: 1876 Annual Undergrad Tuition & Fees: $18,930
Enrollment: 2,277 Coed
Affiliation or Control: Non-denominational IRS Status: 501(c)3
Highest Offering: Master's
Accreditation: M, ACBSP, EXSC, NUR, SW

01 President .... Hon. Paul J. MCNULTY
05 Provost and VP Academic Affairs ....Dr. Peter M. FRANK
10 Vice Pres for Business & Finance ....Mr. Michael R. BUCKMAN
32 Vice Pres For Student Life/Learning .... Mr. Larry E. HARDESTY
111 Vice President for Inst Advancement .. Mr. Jeffrey D. PROKOVICH
11 Vice President for Operations ....Mr. James M. LOPRESTI
13 Vice Pres/Chief Information Officer ....Dr. Vincent F. DISTASI
84 VP of Enrollment Svcs & Registrar .... Dr. John G. INMAN
88 Vice Pres for Student Recruitment .... Mr. Lee S. WISHING, III
100 Assistant to the President ....Ms. Betty L. TALLERICO
49 Dean Sch of Arts/Letters ....Dr. Paul C. KEMENY
81 Dean Sch of Sci/Engr/Math ....Dr. Richard N. SAVAGE
66 Director of Nursing ....Dr. Janey A. ROACH
21 Director of Financial Services ....Mrs. Michelle M. WILLIAMS
15 Director of Human Resources ....Mrs. Marci K. WAGNER
35 Assistant Dean of Students ....Dr. John M. COYNE
07 Director of Admissions ....Vacant
36 Director of Career Services ....Ms. Amanda L. SPOSATO
08 Librarian ....Mrs. Barbra M. MUNNELL
37 Director of Financial Aid ....Vacant
88 Dir Stdnt Rec/Club Sports/Frat Life ... Mr. Andrew A. TONCIC, JR.
35 Director Stdnt Activities/Programs ....Mr. T. Scott GORDON
19 Director of Campus Safety ....Mr. Seth J. VAN TIL
23 Director of Health & Wellness Ctr ....Mrs. Amy E. PAGANO
40 Bookstore Manager ....Mrs. Carrie J. ROSE
41 Athletic Director ....Mr. Todd D. GIBSON
42 Chaplain ....Rev Dr. Donald D. OPITZ
29 Sr Dir Alumni & College Relations ......Ms. Melissa A. MACLEOD
30 Sr Director of Development ....Mr. Brian M. POWELL
26 Sr Director of Communications ....Mrs. Jacquelyn P. MULLER
38 Director of College Counseling ....Dr. Suzanne N. HOUK
39 Director of Residence Life ....Mr. Jonathan J. DIBENEDETTO

Gwynedd Mercy University (G)

1325 Sumneytown Pike, PO Box 901,
Gwynedd Valley PA 19437-0901
County: Montgomery FICE Identification: 003270
Unit ID: 212832
Telephone: (215) 646-7300 Carnegie Class: DU-Mod
FAX Number: (215) 641-5596 Calendar System: Semester
URL: www.gmercyu.edu
Established: 1948 Annual Undergrad Tuition & Fees: $35,430
Enrollment: 2,737 Coed
Affiliation or Control: Roman Catholic IRS Status: 501(c)3
Highest Offering: Doctorate
Accreditation: M, COARC, IACBE, NURSE, OT, RTT, SW

01 President ....Ms. Deanne H. D'EMILIO
05 Provost & VP Academic Affairs ....Dr. Mary H. VAN BRUNT
10 Vice Pres Finance/Administration ....Mr. James E. TRUSDELL
111 Vice Pres University Advancement ....Mr. Keith RICHARDSON
32 VP Stdnt Svcs/Dean of Students .... Mr. Joshua STERN
42 VP Mission/Planning & Effectiveness .... Dr. James GALLO
84 VP for Mktg & Enrollment Mgmt ....Ms. Kelly STATMORE
108 AVP for Assessment & Compliance ....Vacant
110 AVP University Advancement ....Ms. Christina RISO
06 Registrar ....Ms. Joanna RAUDENBUSH
08 Director of Library ....Ms. Jing Feng XIA
37 Director of Student Financial Aid ....Mr. Joseph ALAIMO
13 AVP & Chief Information Officer ....Mr. Gregg CHOTTINER
29 Director Alumni Relations ....Ms. Gianna QUINN
09 Director of Institutional Research ....Dr. Jing GAO
15 AVP Human Resources ....Vacant
21 Controller ....Ms. Jennifer GINNETTI
38 Director Counseling ....Ms. Pamela MOORE
07 AVP of Undergrad Admissions ....Ms. Aimee HUFFSTETLER
96 Director of Procurement ....Mr. Frank PETKA
102 Dir Foundation/Corporate Relations ....Ms. Josephina BANNER
19 Director Campus Safety/Security ....Ms. Joanna GALLAGHER
41 Athletic Dir/Head Women's Bsktbl ....Mr. Keith MONDILLO
39 Director Student Housing ....Ms. Michelle MURRAY
18 Dir Facilities/Physical Plant Ofcr ....Mr. Andrew SEAMAN
28 AVP Diversity/Equity & Inclusion ....Ms. Tatiana DIAZ
36 Director Career Development ....Mr. Nicholas SCHAEFFER
44 Director Annual Giving ....Ms. Mia MCGLYNN
49 Dean of Arts and Sciences ....Dr. Lisa MCGARRY
50 Dean of Business and Education ....Dr. Mary SORTINO
121 Dean of Student Success ....Dr. Meredith HOCH
66 Dean of Nursing ....Dr. Ann PHALEN

HACC, Central Pennsylvania's Community College (A)

1 HACC Drive, Harrisburg PA 17110-2999

County: Dauphin FICE Identification: 003273
Unit ID: 212878
Telephone: (800) 222-4222 Carnegie Class: Assoc/HVT-Mix Trad/Non
FAX Number: (717) 909-1491 Calendar System: Semester
URL: www.hacc.edu
Established: 1964 Annual Undergrad Tuition & Fees (In-District): $8,160
Enrollment: 15,376 Coed
Affiliation or Control: State/Local IRS Status: 501(c)3
Highest Offering: Associate Degree
Accreditation: M, ACBSP, ACFEI, ADNUR, ART, COARC, CSHSE, CVT, DA, DH, DMS, EMT, MLTAD, NAEYC, PNUR, RAD, SURGT

01 President/CEO .... Dr. John J. SYGIELSKI
05 VP Academic Affairs .... Dr. Al GRISWOLD
32 VP Student Affairs/Enroll Mgmt .... Dr. Chrissy DAVIS JONES
10 Vice Pres Finance/CFO .... Mr. Timothy SANDOE
111 VP College Advancement .... Dr. Linnie S. CARTER
20 Assoc Provost Academic Affairs .... Dr. Kathleen T. DOHERTY
103 Assoc Provost Workforce Development .... Mr. Victor RODGERS
15 Int VP Human Resources .... Ms. Ellen HORSCH
28 Chief Inclusion/Diversity Officer .... Dr. Armenta HINTON
106 Associate Provost Virtual Learning .... Ms. Doreen FISHER-BAMMER
06 Registrar .... Dr. Genita D. MANGUM
13 VP Information Technology/CIO .... Mr. Robert H. MESSNER
96 Director Procurement and Contracts .... Mr. Lee W. HAYES
19 Director Safety and Security .... Vacant
40 Director College Bookstores .... Mr. Kyle J. DIBRITO
21 Controller .... Mr. Rich CARDAMONE
09 Exec Dir Inst Effectiveness .... Mr. Bob MESSNER
37 Director Financial Aid .... Vacant
102 Executive Director HACC Foundation .... Dr. Linnie S. CARTER
04 Executive Asst to the President .... Mrs. Kristin GRAESER

HACC Gettysburg Campus (B)

731 Old Harrisburg Road, Gettysburg PA 17325
Telephone: (717) 337-3855 Identification: 770156
Accreditation: &M

HACC Lancaster Campus (C)

1641 Old Philadelphia Pike, Lancaster PA 17602
Telephone: (717) 293-5000 Identification: 770157
Accreditation: &M

HACC Lebanon Campus (D)

735 Cumberland Street, Lebanon PA 17042
Telephone: (717) 270-4222 Identification: 770158
Accreditation: &M

HACC York Campus (E)

2010 Pennsylvania Avenue, York PA 17404
Telephone: (717) 718-0328 Identification: 770159
Accreditation: &M

Harcum College (F)

750 Montgomery Avenue, Bryn Mawr PA 19010-3476

County: Montgomery FICE Identification: 003272
Unit ID: 212869
Telephone: (610) 525-4100 Carnegie Class: Assoc/HVT-High Trad
FAX Number: (610) 526-6009 Calendar System: Semester
URL: www.harcum.edu
Established: 1915 Annual Undergrad Tuition & Fees: $26,000
Enrollment: 1,150 Coed
Affiliation or Control: Independent Non-Profit IRS Status: 501(c)3
Highest Offering: Associate Degree
Accreditation: M, ADNUR, DA, DH, HT, MLTAD, NAEYC, OTA, PTAA, RAD

01 President .... Dr. Jon Jay DETEMPLE
05 Executive VP/CAO/Legal Officer .... Dr. Julia INGERSOLL
10 SVP/Chief Financial Officer .... Mr. Dario BELLOT
32 Dean of Student Life .... Dr. Edward KOVACS
84 VP of Enrollment Management .... Ms. Rachel BOWEN
111 VP of Institutional Advancement .... Ms. Brooke WALKER
15 Assoc VP HR/CHRO .... Mr. Hunt BARTINE
20 Asst VP Academic Support Services .... Vacant
37 Asst VP Financial Aid .... Ms. Paula LEHRBERGER
51 Exec Dir of Partnership Sites .... Dr. Evelyn SANTANA
18 Facilities Manager .... Mr. Nikolay KARPALO
06 Registrar .... Ms. Beth MCMICHAEL
08 Director of Library Services .... Ms. Katie MCGOWAN
85 Director of International Programs .... Ms. Michelle STANZIANO
26 Exec Dir of Communications & Mktg .... Ms. Gale MARTIN
29 Director of Alumni Relations .... Ms. Melissa SAMANGO
38 Director of Counseling Services .... Ms. Kathy ANTHONY
36 Interim Dir Career & Transfer Svcs .... Ms. Claire WILLIAMS
39 Assistant Dean of Student Life .... Mr. Jameel TUCKER
35 Director of Campus Activities .... Mr. Trevor GULLEDGE
21 Director of Business Services .... Mr. Stephen KLEPONIS
19 Director of Campus Safety .... Mr. Rick SANFILIPPO
41 Associate VP for Athletics .... Mr. Drew KELLY
04 Dir President's Office Operations .... Ms. Tricia FLEMING
09 Exec Dir of Inst Rsrch/Strat Plng .... Mr. Tim ELY
106 Dir Online Education/E-learning .... Mr. Stephen PIPITONE
108 Director Institutional Assessment .... Mr. Tim ELY
86 External Affairs .... Dr. Jon Jay DETEMPLE

Harrisburg University of Science and Technology (G)

326 Market Street, Harrisburg PA 17101-2116

County: Dauphin FICE Identification: 039483
Unit ID: 446640
Telephone: (717) 901-5100 Carnegie Class: Masters/L
FAX Number: (717) 901-3152 Calendar System: Trimester
URL: www.harrisburgu.edu
Established: 2001 Annual Undergrad Tuition & Fees: $23,900
Enrollment: 3,997 Coed
Affiliation or Control: Independent Non-Profit IRS Status: 501(c)3
Highest Offering: Doctorate
Accreditation: M, NURSE

01 President/CEO .... Dr. Eric D. DARR
05 Provost/Chief Academic Officer .... Dr. Bilita S. MATTES
10 COO/Chief Financial Officer .... Mr. Duane F. MAUN
103 VP Strategic Workforce Dev/Univ Ctr .... Ms. Kelly POWELL LOGAN
26 Assoc VP Comm/Marketing/Alum Rels .... Mr. Steven M. INFANTI
13 Assoc VP/Chief Information Officer .... Mr. Alex C. PITZNER
15 Assoc VP Human Resources .... Ms. Ellyn GARCIA
108 Director of Assessment .... Ms. Penny L. WEIDNER
37 Director Financial Aid Svcs .... Mr. Christopher MOWL
06 Registrar/Assoc Provost .... Ms. Sandra NELSON
07 Director of Admissions .... Ms. Laurie BARROW
08 University Librarian .... Mr. David RUNYON
32 AVP of Student Services .... Ms. Melissa MORGAN

Haverford College (H)

370 Lancaster Avenue, Haverford PA 19041-1392

County: Delaware & Montgomery FICE Identification: 003274
Unit ID: 212911
Telephone: (610) 896-1000 Carnegie Class: Bac-A&S
FAX Number: (610) 896-4202 Calendar System: Semester
URL: www.haverford.edu
Established: 1833 Annual Undergrad Tuition & Fees: $59,162
Enrollment: 1,307 Coed
Affiliation or Control: Independent Non-Profit IRS Status: 501(c)3
Highest Offering: Master's
Accreditation: M

01 President .... Dr. Wendy E. RAYMOND
05 Provost .... Dr. Linda STRONG-LEEK
10 SVP Finance/Chief Admin Officer .... Mitchell L. WEIN
111 Acting VP for Inst Advancement .... Deborah STRECKER
32 Dean of the College .... Dr. John MCKNIGHT
07 VP & Dean of Admission .... Jess LORD
104 Director of Intl Academic Programs .... Rebecca AVERY
115 Chief Investment Officer .... Michael CASEL
110 Asst VP Institutional Advancement .... Diane WILDER
100 VP & Chief of Staff .... Dr. Jesse LYTLE
41 Director of Athletics .... Wendall SMITH
26 Asst VP College Communications .... Chris MILLS
09 Director of Institutional Research .... Catherine FENNELL
08 Librarian .... Dr. Terry SNYDER
15 Director of Human Resources .... T. Muriel BRISBON
21 Asst VP & Controller .... Terri ALBERTSON
96 Director of Purchasing .... Nikoletta MILLAS
18 Director of Physical Plant .... Donald CAMPBELL
19 Director of Safety & Security .... Thomas KING
88 Director Conferences/Dir Campus Ctr .... Geoffey LABE
109 Assoc Director of Dining Services .... Vacant
40 Bookstore Manager .... Lydia WHITELAW
39 Director of Student Housing .... Nathan DIEHL
23 Director of Health Services .... Kathy MCGOVERN
38 Director Counseling/Disability Svcs .... Dr. Philip ROSENBAUM
36 Dean of Career/Prof Advising .... Amy FEIFER
06 Registrar .... James KEANE
37 Director of Financial Aid .... Michael COLAHAN
29 Director of Alumni & Parent Rels .... Lauren PORTNOY
44 Director of Gift Planning .... Olga BRIKER
20 Director for Academic Resources .... Brian CUZZOLINA
35 Asst Dean of Student Activities .... Michael ELIAS
13 Chief Information Officer .... Megan FITCH
04 Administrative Asst to President .... Joan WANKMILLER

Holy Family University (I)

9801 Frankford Avenue, Philadelphia PA 19114-2009

County: Philadelphia FICE Identification: 003275
Unit ID: 212984
Telephone: (215) 637-7700 Carnegie Class: Masters/L
FAX Number: (215) 637-3787 Calendar System: Semester
URL: www.holyfamily.edu
Established: 1954 Annual Undergrad Tuition & Fees: $31,640
Enrollment: 3,087 Coed
Affiliation or Control: Roman Catholic IRS Status: 501(c)3
Highest Offering: Doctorate
Accreditation: M, ACBSP, CLPSY, IFSAC, NURSE, RAD

01 President .... Dr. Anne PRISCO
10 VP for Finance/Administration/CFO .... Mr. Eric NELSON
05 VP for Academic Affairs .... Dr. Illana R. LANE
28 VP for Mission/Diversity .... Sr. Rita FANNING, CSFN
13 Chief Information Officer .... Ms. Leslie MARGOLIS
84 VP Enrollment Mgmt .... Dr. Abigail WERNICKI
32 Interim VP of Student Life .... Mr. Michael MCNULTY
111 Int VP for University Advancement .... Mr. Joshua E. LISS
26 VP Marketing/Communications .... Ms. Sherrie MADIA
06 Assoc VP Academic Svcs/Registrar .... Vacant
35 Dean of Students/Title IX Coord .... Ms. Marianne PRICE
37 Director Student Financial Aid .... Ms. Janice HETRICK
21 Assoc VP/Controller .... Ms. Anne MCMAHON
15 Assoc VP for Human Resources .... Ms. Jennifer LULING
30 Asst VP for Development .... Mr. Joshua LISS
102 Asst VP Corp Foundation & Govt Rels .... Ms. Kim CAULFIELD
08 Exec Director Library Services .... Ms. Shannon BROWN
38 Director Counseling Services .... Ms. Lisa SPATAFORE
42 Director of Campus Ministry .... Rev. James MACNEW
07 Director Undergraduate Admissions .... Ms. Lauren CAMPBELL
41 Director of Athletics .... Mr. Timothy HAMILL
66 Dean of Nursing/Allied Health Prof .... Dr. Margaret HARKINS
49 Dean of School of Arts & Sciences .... Dr. Rochelle ROBBINS
50 Dean of Business/Professional Stds .... Dr. Krisit RINGEN
29 Asst Dir Alumni & Parent Relations .... Ms. Julie REMPFER
09 Director of Institutional Research .... Mr. Mark GREEN
18 Director Campus Operations .... Mr. Edward MCLAUGHLIN
39 Director Residence Life .... Mr. Troy YOUNG
101 Board Liaison & Special Asst .... Ms. Kate BRESLIN
19 Director Security/Safety-Allied .... Mr. Dave NEUMAN
85 Dir International Student Affairs .... Vacant
108 Dir Institutional Assessment .... Vacant
44 Director of Development .... Ms. Christina BENDER
23 Director of Health Services .... Dr. Tracy BOYLE
105 Website Manager .... Mr. Christopher LAMBERT
04 Admin Assistant to the President .... Ms. Patricia TOWNSEND
100 Chief of Staff .... Dr. Sylvia MCGEARY

Hussian College (J)

1500 Spring Garden Street, Philadelphia PA 19130

County: Philadelphia FICE Identification: 007469
Unit ID: 212993
Telephone: (215) 574-9600 Carnegie Class: Spec-4-yr-Arts
FAX Number: (267) 831-6054 Calendar System: Semester
URL: www.hussiancollege.edu
Established: 1946 Annual Undergrad Tuition & Fees: $21,428
Enrollment: 101 Coed
Affiliation or Control: Proprietary IRS Status: Proprietary
Highest Offering: Baccalaureate
Accreditation: ACCSC

01 President .... Dr. Jeremiah STAROPOLI
05 Dean of Academic Affairs .... Sylvia MCCRAY
07 Director of Admissions .... Vacant
37 Director of Financial Aid .... Vacant

Immaculata University (K)

1145 King Road, Immaculata PA 19345-0654

County: Chester FICE Identification: 003276
Unit ID: 213011
Telephone: (610) 647-4400 Carnegie Class: DU-Mod
FAX Number: (610) 251-1668 Calendar System: Semester
URL: www.immaculata.edu
Established: 1920 Annual Undergrad Tuition & Fees: $27,750
Enrollment: 2,563 Coed
Affiliation or Control: Roman Catholic IRS Status: 501(c)3
Highest Offering: Doctorate
Accreditation: M, ACBSP, CACREP, CLPSY, DIETD, DIETI, IPSY, MUS, NURSE

01 President .... Ms. Barbara LETTIERE
05 VP Academic Affairs & Provost .... Dr. Angela TEKELY
10 VP Finance/Administration .... Ms. Amy BOSIO
111 VP Institutional Advancement .... Ms. Susan ARNOLD
32 VP Student Development & UG Admiss .... Ms. Patricia CANTERINO
26 VP Marketing & Communications .... Vacant
42 VP Mission and Ministry .... Sr. Antoine LAWLOR, IHM
06 Registrar .... Ms. Avery TURNER
26 Director of Communications .... Mr. Gary BALAKOFF
15 Exec Director of Human Resources .... Ms. Claudine VITA
08 Executive Director of Library .... Dr. Jeffrey ROLLISON
13 Chief Information Officer .... Mr. Bryan STEINBERG
07 Director of Admissions .... Ms. Christine RHINE
37 Director Student Financial Aid .... Ms. Dina STERN
88 Director Curriculum & Instruction .... Ms. Dorothy (Darcy) DOYLE
29 Director Alumni Relations .... Ms. Karen MATWEYCHUK
36 Director Career & Prof Development .... Ms. Heidi HARRISON
104 Director Study Abroad .... Vacant
85 International Student Services .... Sr. Janet WALTERS, IHM
20 Dean of Academic Affairs .... Ms. Mary Kate BOLAND
58 Dean College of Graduate Studies .... Dr. Marcia PARRIS
88 Dean College of Undergrad Studies .... Dr. Jean SHINGLE
107 Dean College of Adult Prof Studies .... Dr. Jean SHINGLE
21 Director of Finance/Controller .... Ms. Joanne CRISTINZIO
19 Director Campus Safety & Protection .... Mr. Dennis DOUGHERTY
22 Title IX Coordinator .... Ms. Janelle CRONMILLER
38 Director Counseling Services .... Ms. Jessica GILPERT
18 Director of Facilities .... Mr. Kevin CONVERY
25 Director of Sponsored Research .... Vacant
45 Director of Strategic Initiatives .... Sr. M. Carroll ISSELMANN, IHM
110 Director of Advancement Services .... Ms. Martha BORRACCINI
39 Director Res Life & Student Housing .... Ms. Jenny LINDSAY
09 Office Inst Research/Effectiveness .... Ms. Cecelia OSWALD
04 Executive Admin Asst to President .... Ms. Patricia DONOGHUE
106 Online Education/E-learning .... Dr. Angela TEKELY
121 Exec Dir of Learning Support .... Ms. Jennifer PERUSO
28 Director of Diversity & Inclusion .... Vacant

Institute of Medical and Business Careers (A)

133 Jefferson Rd, Ste 101, Pittsburgh PA 15235
County: Allegheny FICE Identification: 041551
Telephone: (412) 244-3240 Carnegie Class: Not Classified
FAX Number: (412) 244-3241 Calendar System: Other
URL: www.imbc.edu
Established: Annual Undergrad Tuition & Fees: N/A
Enrollment: N/A Coed
Affiliation or Control: Proprietary IRS Status: Proprietary
Highest Offering: Associate Degree
Accreditation: ABHES

01 Director ... Ms. Sherri STEELE

International Institute for Restorative Practices (B)

531 Main Street, Bethlehem PA 18018
County: Northampton FICE Identification: 042061
Unit ID: 448691
Telephone: (610) 807-9221 Carnegie Class: Spec-4-yr-Other
FAX Number: (610) 807-0423 Calendar System: Trimester
URL: www.iirp.edu
Established: 2005 Annual Graduate Tuition & Fees: N/A
Enrollment: 185 Coed
Affiliation or Control: Independent Non-Profit IRS Status: 501(c)3
Highest Offering: Master's; No Undergraduates
Accreditation: M

01 Interim President ... Ms. Linda KLIGMAN
05 Provost ... Dr. Craig ADAMSON
11 Vice President for Administration ... Ms. Linda B. KLIGMAN
10 Chief Financial Officer ... Ms. Robin BELL
32 Dean of Student Services ... Ms. Jamie KAINTZ

JNA Institute of Culinary Arts (C)

1212 S Broad Street, Philadelphia PA 19146-3119
County: Philadelphia FICE Identification: 031033
Unit ID: 419341
Telephone: (215) 468-8800 Carnegie Class: Spec 2-yr-A&S
FAX Number: (215) 468-8838 Calendar System: Quarter
URL: www.culinaryarts.edu
Established: 1988 Annual Undergrad Tuition & Fees: $14,575
Enrollment: 14 Coed
Affiliation or Control: Proprietary IRS Status: Proprietary
Highest Offering: Associate Degree
Accreditation: ACCSC

01 School Director ... Mr. Joseph DIGIRONIMO
05 Director of Academics ... Dr. Nicole DIGIRONIMO

Johnson College (D)

3427 North Main Avenue, Scranton PA 18508-1495
County: Lackawanna FICE Identification: 021142
Unit ID: 213233
Telephone: (570) 702-8856 Carnegie Class: Assoc/HVT-High Trad
FAX Number: (570) 348-2181 Calendar System: Semester
URL: www.johnson.edu
Established: 1912 Annual Undergrad Tuition & Fees: $20,025
Enrollment: 497 Coed
Affiliation or Control: Independent Non-Profit IRS Status: 501(c)3
Highest Offering: Associate Degree
Accreditation: M, PTAA, RAD

01 President & CEO ... Dr. Katie LEONARD
10 Chief Financial Officer ... Ms. Liz RENDA
15 VP of Human Resources & Sr Advisor ... Ms. Stephenie VERGNETTI
32 VP of Student & Academic Affairs ... Mr. William BURKE
11 Chief Administrative Officer ... Mr. Mike NOVAK
88 Associate VP of Faculty ... Ms. Barb BYRNE
05 Chief Academic Officer ... Dr. Kellyn WILLIAMS
09 Director of Inst Effectiveness ... Dr. Laura LITTLE
04 Exec Assistant to President ... Ms. Ann SPARACINO
21 Associate Director of Finance ... Ms. Kristin MASCI
16 Asst Director of Human Resources ... Ms. Heather BUCK
08 Resource Officer ... Ms. Ashley HASSENBEIN
32 Director of Student Engagement ... Mr. Nolan RENZ
38 Counselor/Manager Disability Svcs ... Ms. Melissa SAXON-PRICE
13 Director of Information Technology ... Mr. Jerry MARSH
18 Director of Facilities ... Mr. Joseph MUSHENO
26 Sr Dir of Marketing/Communications ... Mr. Doug COOK
111 Sr Director of Advancement ... Ms. Karen BAKER
36 Career Services Manager ... Ms. Dana HEALEY
37 Director of Financial Aid ... Vacant
124 Associate Dir of Student Success ... Mr. Mike MCGURL
06 Registrar ... Vacant
103 Manager of Continuing Education ... Ms. Felicia ENNES
84 Director Enrollment Management ... Vacant

Juniata College (E)

1700 Moore Street, Huntingdon PA 16652-2119
County: Huntingdon FICE Identification: 003279
Unit ID: 213251
Telephone: (814) 641-3000 Carnegie Class: Bac-A&S
FAX Number: (814) 641-3199 Calendar System: Semester
URL: www.juniata.edu
Established: 1876 Annual Undergrad Tuition & Fees: $49,175
Enrollment: 1,356 Coed
Affiliation or Control: Independent Non-Profit IRS Status: 501(c)3
Highest Offering: Master's
Accreditation: M, IACBE, SW

01 President ... Dr. James A. TROHA
05 Provost ... Dr. Lauren BOWEN
84 VP Enrollment ... Mr. Jason E. MORAN
32 VP Student Life & Dean of Students ... Dr. Matthew DAMSCHRODER
111 VP for Advancement ... Mr. James R. WATT
13 Asst VP/Chief Information Officer ... Ms. Anne WOOD
10 Controller/Chief Financial Officer ... Ms. Karla D. WISER
28 Dean Equity/Diversity & Inclusion . Dr. Crystal SELLERS BATTLE
85 Acting Dean International Programs ... Ms. Caitlin MURPHY
06 Registrar ... Ms. Dawn SCIALABBA
37 Dir Student Financial Plng ... Ms. Tracie M. PATRICK
15 Director of Human Resources ... Ms. Tracy L. GRAJEWSKI
18 Director of Facilities Services ... Mr. Tristan S. DEL GIUDICE
35 Assistant Dean of Students ... Mr. Jesse W. LEONARD
41 Athletic Director ... Mr. Greg M. CURLEY
90 Dir Technology Solutions Center ... Mr. Joel C. PHEASANT
113 Bursar ... Ms. Lauren A. PEROW
114 Assistant Controller ... Mr. Jeremy M. KOLLER
124 Asst Dean of Students Campus Life ... Ms. Erin PASCHAL
88 Director of Conferences & Events ... Ms. Lorri P. SHIDELER
07 Senior Associate Dean of Admission ... Ms. Terri L. BOLLMAN-DALANSKY
36 Executive Director of Career Devel ... Mr. David D. MEADOWS
04 Executive Asst to President ... Mrs. Bethany D. SHEFFIELD
43 College Counsel ... Mr. David P. ANDREWS
19 Director of Public Safety ... Mr. Timothy LAUNTZ

Keystone College (F)

One College Green, P.O. Box 50, La Plume PA 18440-0200
County: Lackawanna FICE Identification: 003280
Unit ID: 213303
Telephone: (570) 945-8000 Carnegie Class: Bac-Diverse
FAX Number: (570) 945-8962 Calendar System: Semester
URL: www.keystone.edu
Established: 1868 Annual Undergrad Tuition & Fees: $17,000
Enrollment: 1,386 Coed
Affiliation or Control: Independent Non-Profit IRS Status: 501(c)3
Highest Offering: Master's
Accreditation: M, IACBE

01 Interim President ... Mr. John F. PULLO, SR.
05 Provost/VP Academic Affairs ... Dr. Andra BASU
10 Vice Pres Finance & Administration ... Mr. Stuart RENDA
111 Vice President for Advancement ... Ms. Frances LANGAN
84 Vice Pres Enrollment Management ... Mr. David RHODES
32 Vice President Student Life ... Dr. Nicole LANGAN
08 Associate Dean of Miller Library ... Ms. Mari FLYNN
07 Director of Admissions ... Ms. Maureen CRAVATH
06 Associate Dean/Registrar ... Ms. Kate OWENS
37 Director Financial Aid ... Vacant
13 Chief Information Officer ... Mr. Charles L. PROTHERO
15 Director of Human Resources ... Vacant
26 Senior Director College Relations ... Mr. Fran CALPIN
09 Director Institutional Research ... Ms. Robyn DICKINSON
41 Director of Athletics ... Mr. Scott GOWER

King's College (G)

133 N River Street, Wilkes-Barre PA 18711-0801
County: Luzerne FICE Identification: 003282
Unit ID: 213321
Telephone: (570) 208-5900 Carnegie Class: Masters/M
FAX Number: (570) 825-9049 Calendar System: Semester
URL: www.kings.edu
Established: 1946 Annual Undergrad Tuition & Fees: $40,080
Enrollment: 2,320 Coed
Affiliation or Control: Roman Catholic IRS Status: 501(c)3
Highest Offering: Doctorate
Accreditation: M, ARCPA, CAATE, @DIET, NURSE

01 President ... Rev. Thomas P. LOONEY, CSC
05 Provost & VP for Academic Affairs ... Dr. Joseph EVAN
10 Exec VP for Business Affairs ... Ms. Janet KOBYLSKI
111 Vice President for Inst Advancement ... Mr. Frederick PETTIT
32 Vice President for Student Affairs ... Vacant
84 Vice President for Enrollment Mgmt ... Mr. Christopher DEARTH
04 Exec Assistant to the President ... Ms. Jacqueline GRANT
13 Associate VP/Chief Info Officer ... Mr. Paul MORAN
26 Exec Dir College Marketing/Comm ... Ms. Wendy HINTON
08 Director of Library ... Mr. David SCHAPPERT
35 Assoc Vice Pres Student Affairs ... Mr. Robert MCGONIGLE
50 Dean Wm G McGowan Sch Business ... Dr. Barry WILLIAMS
06 Registrar ... Mr. Daniel CEBRICK
37 Director of Financial Aid ... Ms. Barbara SCHMITT
42 Chaplain/Director Campus Ministry ... Rev. Brogan RYAN, CSC
36 Director Career Planning & Placemnt ... Mr. Christopher SUTZKO
15 Associate VP Human Resources ... Ms. Regina CORCHADO
29 Director of Engagement ... Ms. Rose GRYSKEVICZ
18 Executive Director of Facilities ... Mr. Thomas GILGALLON
19 Director of Security/Safety ... Mr. James GILGALLON
41 Dir of Intercollegiate Athletics ... Ms. Cheryl ISH
21 Associate VP Finance ... Ms. Holly KULP
39 Assoc Dean of Students Res Life ... Ms. Megan CASEY
09 Director of Institutional Research ... Ms. Marian PALMERI
28 Director of College Diversity ... Ms. Jasmine TABRON-GIDDINGS
90 Managing Dir of User Services ... Mr. Raymond PRYOR
91 Managing Director for MIS ... Mr. William CORCORAN
104 Director Study Abroad ... Ms. Margaret KOWALSKY
25 Dir of Inst and Academic Grants ... Ms. Michelle GIOVAGNOLI
44 Director Annual Giving ... Ms. Desiree VOITEK

La Roche University (H)

9000 Babcock Boulevard, Pittsburgh PA 15237-5898
County: Allegheny FICE Identification: 003987
Unit ID: 213358
Telephone: (412) 367-9300 Carnegie Class: Masters/S
FAX Number: (412) 536-1062 Calendar System: Semester
URL: www.laroche.edu
Established: 1963 Annual Undergrad Tuition & Fees: $30,320
Enrollment: 1,292 Coed
Affiliation or Control: Roman Catholic IRS Status: 501(c)3
Highest Offering: Doctorate
Accreditation: M, ACBSP, ADNUR, ANEST, ART, CIDA, NUR

01 President ... Sr. Candace INTROCASO, CDP
04 Exec Asst to the President ... Ms. Karen P. WILLOUGHBY
05 Provost & SVP for Academic Affairs ... Dr. Howard J. ISHIYAMA
84 VP for Enrollment Mgmt ... Dr. James (Chip) E. WEISGERBER
10 VP for Finance & Administration ... Mr. Stephen LIPPIELLO
32 VP for Student Life/Dean Stdnts ... Ms. Colleen RUEFLE
111 VP for University Advancement ... Ms. Michele A. HUFNAGEL
20 Associate Provost & Academic Dean ... Dr. Rosemary MCCARTHY
121 Dean of Academic Support Services ... Ms. Marie DEEM
35 Asst Dean of Students ... Mr. David DAY
83 Div Chair Natural & Behavioral Sci ... Dr. Rebecca BOZYM
79 Div Chair Humanities ... Dr. Edward BOBINCHOCK
50 Div Co-Chair Management ... Dr. Lynn ARCHER
50 Div Co-Chair Management ... Ms. Shelia MUELLER
57 Div Chair Design ... Ms. Lisa KAMPHAUS
53 Div Co-Chair Education & Nursing ... Dr. Kathryn SILVIS
66 Div Co-Chair Education & Nursing ... Dr. Terri LIBERTO
06 Registrar ... Ms. Katie ELVERSON
08 Director Library ... Ms. Alecia KERR
07 Executive Director for Enrollment ... Ms. Hope SCHIFFGENS
26 Assoc VP Mktg & Media Relations ... Mr. Brady BUTLER
37 Director of Financial Aid ... Mr. Robert CLEMENS
41 Director of Athletics ... Mr. Jim TINKEY
42 Director of Mission & Ministry ... Fr. Peter HORTON
39 Director Residence Life ... Ms. Ashley TESTA
13 Chief Information Officer ... Ms. Terri BALLARD
85 Director International Student Svcs ... Dr. Natasha GARRETT
29 Exec Dir Alumni Rels/Annual Giving ... Ms. Melissa KEEBLER
09 Director of Institutional Research ... Mr. John INGRAM
18 Assoc VP of Facilities Management ... Mr. J.R YOUNG
38 Dir Counseling & Health Services ... Ms. Erin DORSCH
19 Director Public Safety ... Mr. Mark WILCOX
15 Assoc VP of Human Resources ... Ms. Eileen PETRONE
40 Bookstore Manager ... Ms. Michelle JAMES
113 Director of Student Accounts ... Ms. Danya TINKEY
104 Coordinator Study Abroad ... Ms. Casey BAKER
110 Director of Advancement Svcs ... Ms. Kim CORRADO
105 Director Web Services ... Mr. David SIROKI
28 Dir Diversity/Equity & Inclusion ... Ms. Sarah WHITE

La Salle University (I)

1900 W Olney Avenue, Philadelphia PA 19141-1199
County: Philadelphia FICE Identification: 003287
Unit ID: 213367
Telephone: (215) 951-1000 Carnegie Class: DU-Mod
FAX Number: N/A Calendar System: Semester
URL: www.lasalle.edu
Established: 1863 Annual Undergrad Tuition & Fees: $32,425
Enrollment: 4,624 Coed
Affiliation or Control: Roman Catholic IRS Status: 501(c)3
Highest Offering: Doctorate
Accreditation: M, ANEST, CACREP, CLPSY, DIETC, DIETD, MFCD, NURSE, PH, SP, SW

01 President ... Dr. Daniel J. ALLEN
05 Int Provost/VP Academic Affairs ... Dr. Lynne TEXTER
10 VP Finance and Administration ... Mr. Thomas SIBSON
32 VP Student Affairs & Enrollment Mgt ... Dr. Gabrielle ST. LEGER
43 Vice President and General Counsel ... Mr. Sean CORGAN
20 Associate Provost ... Dr. David CICHOWICZ
20 Assistant Provost ... Ms. Teri CERASO
111 Asst VP University Advancement ... Mr. Daniel JOYCE
49 Dean School of Arts & Sciences ... Dr. Pamela BARNETT
50 Dean School of Business Admin ... Dr. Yusuf UGRAS
66 Dean School of Nursing/Health Sci ... Dr. Kathleen CZEKANSKI
22 Affirmative Action Officer/Title IX ... Ms. Rose Lee PAULINE
26 AVP Marketing and Communication ... Dr. Angela M. POLEC
29 Sr Dir Alumni Engage/Annual Giving ... Ms. Mary Kay MCGETTIGAN
58 Dir Grad Ctr/East European Studies ... Vacant
77 Director MS/CIS ... Ms. Margaret MCCOEY
53 Director Grad Education Program ... Dr. Greer RICHARDSON
60 Dir Grad Communication ... Dr. Michael SMITH
66 Director Undergraduate Nursing ... Vacant
66 Dir Grad Nursing RN-MSN Pgm ... Dr. Patricia DILLON
69 Dir Master Public Health Program ... Dr. Candace ROBERTSON-JAMES
88 Dir Grad Econ Crime Forensics ... Ms. Margaret MCCOEY
58 Dir Grad Pgm Nonprofit Leadership ... Dr. Laura OTTEN

39 Asst VP Res Life Community Dev .... Mr. Alan B. WENDELL
35 Asst VP for Campus Life .... Vacant
42 Director Univ Ministry & Service .... Bro. Robert J. KINZLER
92 Dir University Honors Program .... Bro. Michael MCGINNISS
13 Chief Information Officer .... Vacant
08 Director of the Library .... Ms. Sarah CLARK
18 Asst VP Facilities Mgmt .... Mr. Dennis SHORES, JR.
19 Asst VP Public Safety .... Ms. Amanda GUTHORN
15 Asst VP Human Resources .... Ms. Kristin HEASLEY
41 Vice Pres Intercollegiate Athletics .... Mr. Brian BAPTISTE
30 Director of Development .... Mr. John PRENDERGAST
07 Int Executive Director of Admission .... Ms. Molly WALSH
37 Director Financial Aid .... Ms. Jennifer HOUSEMAN
06 Registrar .... Vacant
83 Dir Doctorate in Psych Program .... Dr. Megan SPOKAS
88 Dir Academic Partnerships .... Vacant
72 Graduate Director Instruct Tech Mgt .... Ms. Margaret MCCOEY
88 Director Full-time MBA Program .... Ms. Elizabeth SCOFIELD
28 Multicultural Education Coordinator .... Ms. Cherylyn L. RUSH
105 Sr Dir of Marketing/Tech/Analytics .... Mr. Gregory FALA
66 Dir Doctor of Nursing Practice Pgm .... Dr. Patricia BICKNELL
88 Director Graduate History .... Vacant
88 Sr Dir Athletic Dev/Assoc Athl Dir .... Mr. Brian FRANKOWSKI
100 Chief of Staff/Dir of Gov Affairs .... Dr. Mark ENGBERG
101 Sec of Inst/Board & Asst to Pres .... Ms. Lisa WILLIE
106 Dir Distributed Learning/Educ Tech .... Mr. David LEES
102 Dir of Foundation/Government Grants .... Ms. Theresa MALANDRA
38 Director Student Counseling .... Ms. Jessica BRANNAN
122 Asst Dir Campus Prgmg-Greek Life .... Ms. Mina KOLLER

Lackawanna College (A)

501 Vine Street, Scranton PA 18509-3206

County: Lackawanna FICE Identification: 003283
Unit ID: 213376
Telephone: (570) 961-7810 Carnegie Class: Bac/Assoc-Mixed
FAX Number: (570) 961-7858 Calendar System: 4/1/4
URL: www.lackawanna.edu
Established: 1894 Annual Undergrad Tuition & Fees: $16,130
Enrollment: 2,043 Coed
Affiliation or Control: Independent Non-Profit IRS Status: 501(c)3
Highest Offering: Baccalaureate
Accreditation: M, CNEA, DMS, MAC, OTA, PTAA, SURGT

01 President .... Dr. Jill A. MURRAY
11 Chief Operating Officer .... Mr. TJ ELTRINGHAM
10 Vice President of Finance/Admin .... Mr. John RISBOSKIN
05 Provost/Chief Academic Officer .... Dr. Erica PRICCI
32 Associate VP for Student Engagement .... Mr. Dan LAMAGNA
07 Regional Director of Admissions .... Mr. Tom BOGUSH
111 Vice Pres for College Advancement .... Mr. Brian COSTANZO
15 VP for Human Resources .... Ms. Renee MUNDY
35 Dean of Students .... Mr. Kris LIEBEGOTT
20 Associate Dean of Faculty Affairs .... Mrs. Adrienne ASBURY
29 Mgr of Special Events/Alumni Rels .... Ms. Megan MOULD
113 Director of Student Financial Svcs .... Ms. Joya WHITTINGTON
26 Director of External Relations .... Vacant
41 Director of Athletics .... Mr. Erik LARSON
121 Director of Advising & Transfer Svc . Mrs. Barbara NOWOGORSKI
06 Registrar .... Mrs. Theresa SCOPELLITI
19 Director of Public Safety .... Mr. Carl GRAZIANO
116 Audit Officer .... Vacant
25 Grant Administrator .... Ms. Laurel RADZIESKI
39 Director Housing & Residence Life .... Mr. Jeff KRISIAK
18 Director of Facilities .... Mr. Derek GREGORY
37 Director of Financial Aid .... Mr. Matthew PETERS
13 Director of MIS .... Mrs. Melanie KOWALSKI
124 Director of Student Retention .... Mrs. Denise LARSON
04 Executive Asst to President .... Ms. Mary A. OLIVERI
106 Dir Online Education/E-learning .... Mr. Gopu KIRON
101 Assistant Secretary for the Board .... Ms. Mary A. OLIVERI
86 Director Government Relations .... Mrs. Cathy WECHSLER

Lafayette College (B)

730 High Street, Markle Hall Suite, Easton PA 18042-1798

County: Northampton FICE Identification: 003284
Unit ID: 213385
Telephone: (610) 330-5000 Carnegie Class: Bac-A&S
FAX Number: (610) 330-5127 Calendar System: Semester
URL: www.lafayette.edu
Established: 1826 Annual Undergrad Tuition & Fees: $55,742
Enrollment: 2,514 Coed
Affiliation or Control: Independent Non-Profit IRS Status: 501(c)3
Highest Offering: Baccalaureate
Accreditation: M

01 President .... Ms. Nicole HURD
05 Provost .... Dr. John MEIER
30 Vice Pres Dev/College Relations .... Ms. Kimberly SPANG
32 VP Campus Life .... Dr. Annette DIORIO
15 Vice President Human Resources ..... Ms. Leslie F. MUHLFELDER
26 VP Marketing/Communications .... Mr. Mark EYERLY
13 VP and Chief Information Officer .... Mr. John L. O'KEEFE
10 VP Finance & Administration .... Mr. Roger DEMARESKI
54 Director of Engineering .... Dr. Scott R. HUMMEL
100 VP & Liaison to Board of Trustees .... Dr. Melissa STARACE
84 Vice Pres for Enrollment Management .... Mr. Gregory MACDONALD
121 Dean Advising & Co-Curricular Pgms .... Dr. Mike OLIN
08 Dean of Libraries .... Ms. Anne HOUSTON
35 Dean of Students .... Mr. Brian SAMBLE
07 Dean of Admissions/AVP Enroll Mgmt .... Mr. Matthew HYDE

37 Assoc VP of Financial Aid .... Dr. Forrest STUART
09 Director of Institutional Research .... Dr. Simon T. TONEV
06 Registrar .... Ms. Kara HOWE
41 Director of Athletics .... Ms. Sherryta FREEMAN
36 AVP of Career Services .... Mr. Mike SUMMERS
23 Director Health Services .... Dr. Jeffrey E. GOLDSTEIN
38 Director Counseling Center .... Dr. Melissa GARRISON
19 Director of Public Safety .... Mr. Jeffrey E. TROXELL
18 Exec Director of Facilities .... Mr. Bruce S. FERRETTI
29 Executive Director Alumni Relations .... Ms. Rachel NELSON MOELLER
16 Director of HR/Employment .... Ms. Lisa Youngkin REX
96 Manager of Procurement .... Ms. Patricia REICH
88 Title IX Coordinator .... Ms. Amanda HANINCIK
20 Dean of Faculty .... Dr. Jamila BOOKWALA
115 Chief Investment Officer .... Ms. Krishna K. MEMANI
04 Executive Assistant to President .... Ms. Katherine D. KANEPS
122 Dir Stdnt Involvement-Greek Life .... Ms. Vanessa PEARSON

Lake Erie College of Osteopathic Medicine (C)

1858 W Grandview Boulevard, Erie PA 16509-1025

County: Erie FICE Identification: 030908
Unit ID: 407629
Telephone: (814) 866-6641 Carnegie Class: Spec-4-yr-Med
FAX Number: (814) 866-8123 Calendar System: Semester
URL: www.lecom.edu
Established: 1992 Annual Graduate Tuition & Fees: N/A
Enrollment: 4,336 Coed
Affiliation or Control: Independent Non-Profit IRS Status: 501(c)3
Highest Offering: First Professional Degree; No Undergraduates
Accreditation: M, OSTEO, PHAR

01 President/CEO .... Dr. John M. FERRETTI
05 Provost/Sr Vice Pres/Dean Acad Affs .... Dr. Silvia M. FERRETTI
10 Vice Pres of Fiscal Affairs/CFO .... Mr. Steve G. INMAN
52 Dean School of Dental Medicine .... Dr. Thomas YOON
20 Assoc Dean Acad Affairs Bradenton .... Dr. Mark KAUFFMAN
63 Asst Dean Clinical Educ Bradenton .... Dr. Steven MA
63 Assoc Dean of Clinical Education .... Dr. Michael ROWANE
63 Asst Dean of Plans/Ops/Train Safety .... Dr. Regan SHABLOSKI
63 Asst Dean Preclinical Ed Bradenton .... Dr. James GNARRA
63 Assoc Dean Preclinical Educ Erie .... Dr. Jon KALMEY
81 Assoc Dean Biomedical Sciences .... Dr. Randy KULESZA
58 Dean of SHSA .... Dr. Timothy NOVAK
67 Dean School of Pharmacy .... Dr. Rachel OGDEN
88 Asst Dean of Florida Pathway .... Dr. Tatiana YERO
88 Vice Dean SDM .... Dr. Katie DINH
88 Asst Dean of Pre-Clinical Educ .... Dr. Todd NOLAN
26 VP of External Affairs .... Msgr. David RUBINO
32 Director of Student Affairs .... Ms. Shari GOULD
09 Inst Dir Plng/Assess/Accred/Rsrch .... Dr. Mathew BATEMAN
43 Dir Legal Services/General Counsel .... Mr. Richard E. FERRETTI
08 Inst Dir of Learning Resources .... Mr. Dan WELCH
38 Director of Behavioral Health .... Dr. Melanie DUNBAR
13 Director of Information Technology .... Mr. Randy HARRIS
46 Asst Dean of Research .... Dr. Bertalan DUDAS
88 Director of Research Medical Col .... Dr. Diana SPEELMAN
15 Inst Dir of HR/EEO and Title IX .... Mr. Aaron E. SUSMARSKI
19 Inst Dir of Police & Security .... Mr. Kevin GOODE
88 Asst Dean Med Educ/Fac Dev .... Dr. Mark TERRELL
18 Facilities Director .... Mr. Brian KING
37 Asst Director of Financial Aid .... Ms. Elise LEE
06 Institutional Registrar .... Mr. Jeremy SIVILLO
96 Inst Director of Purchasing .... Ms. Naz KROL
04 Exec Assistant to the President .... Ms. Helen R. MCKENZIE

Lancaster Bible College|Capital Seminary & Graduate School (D)

901 Eden Road, Lancaster PA 17601-5036

County: Lancaster FICE Identification: 003285
Unit ID: 213400
Telephone: (717) 569-7071 Carnegie Class: Masters/S
FAX Number: (717) 560-8260 Calendar System: Semester
URL: www.lbc.edu
Established: 1933 Annual Undergrad Tuition & Fees: $27,370
Enrollment: 2,038 Coed
Affiliation or Control: Independent Non-Profit IRS Status: 501(c)3
Highest Offering: Doctorate
Accreditation: M, BI, COSMA, MUS, SW

01 President .... Dr. Thomas L. KIEDIS
04 Assistant to the President .... Mrs. Judith M. HECKAMAN
05 Provost .... Mrs. Tricia WILSON
111 VP of Advancement .... Mr. Scott KEATING
10 VP of Finance .... Mr. Matthew MASON
88 VP of Institutional Alignment .... Rev. Zachary RITVALSKY
88 VP of Global Education .... Dr. Beau WALKER
32 VP of TUD Education .... Mr. Peter BEERS

Lancaster County Career and Technology Center (E)

1730 Hans Herr Drive, Willow Street PA 17584

County: Lancaster FICE Identification: 023108
Unit ID: 418533
Telephone: (717) 464-7050 Carnegie Class: Spec 2-yr-Other
FAX Number: (717) 464-9518 Calendar System: Semester
URL: www.lancasterctc.edu
Established: 1970 Annual Undergrad Tuition & Fees (In-District): N/A
Enrollment: 348 Coed
Affiliation or Control: State/Local IRS Status: 501(c)3
Highest Offering: Associate Degree
Accreditation: COE, DH

01 Superintendent of Record .... Dr. Michele BALLIET
11 Administrative Director .... Dr. Stuart SAVIN
05 Supervisor of Curriculum .... Mike MOELLER
32 Supervisor of Student Services .... Darla GETTLE
15 Human Resources Director .... Catherine DOUGHTY
10 Business Manager .... Dr. Michael DELPRIORE

Lancaster Theological Seminary (F)

555 W James Street, Lancaster PA 17603-2812

County: Lancaster FICE Identification: 003286
Unit ID: 213446
Telephone: (717) 393-0654 Carnegie Class: Spec-4-yr-Faith
FAX Number: (717) 393-4254 Calendar System: Trimester
URL: www.lancasterseminary.edu
Established: 1825 Annual Graduate Tuition & Fees: N/A
Enrollment: 99 Coed
Affiliation or Control: United Church Of Christ IRS Status: 501(c)3
Highest Offering: Doctorate; No Undergraduates
Accreditation: M, THEOL

01 President .... Dr. Bryon GRIGSBY
10 VP for Finance & Administration .... Mr. Mark REED
15 VP & Chief Human Resource Officer .... Mr. Jon CONRAD
73 Dean/CEO .... RevDr. Heather H. VACEK
05 Associate Dean/CAO .... Rev Dr. Vanessa LOVELACE
30 Vice Pres of Development/Alumni .... Ms. Jill ANDERSON
07 Dir of Admissions & Financial Aid .... Rev. Diane A. BOGUES
08 Seminary Librarian .... Mrs. Myka K. STEPHENS
06 Registrar .... Mrs. Teresa BENNEIAN
13 Director Computing/Information Mgmt ...... Mr. Augustine APPREY
88 Admin Asst to Academic Affairs .... Ms. Carter FARMER

Lansdale School of Business (G)

290 Wissahickon Ave, North Wales PA 19454-4114

County: Montgomery FICE Identification: 007779
Unit ID: 213473
Telephone: (215) 699-5700 Carnegie Class: Assoc/HVT-High Trad
FAX Number: (215) 699-8770 Calendar System: Semester
URL: www.LSB.edu
Established: 1918 Annual Undergrad Tuition & Fees: $11,850
Enrollment: 119 Coed
Affiliation or Control: Proprietary IRS Status: Proprietary
Highest Offering: Associate Degree
Accreditation: ACCSC

01 President .... Mr. Marlon D. KELLER
03 Executive Director .... Mrs. Marianne H. JOHNSON
32 Student Services Coordinator .... Ms. Jacklyn G. WHEELER
08 Librarian .... Mrs. Marie B. WALCROFT
37 Financial Aid Coordinator .... Mr. David E. SOUZA
36 Career Services Coord/Dean Students .... Ms. Kellyann R. GERIA

Laurel Business Institute (H)

11 East Penn Street, Uniontown PA 15401-3453

County: Fayette FICE Identification: 025462
Unit ID: 250027
Telephone: (724) 439-4900 Carnegie Class: Assoc/HVT-High Trad
FAX Number: (724) 439-3607 Calendar System: Semester
URL: www.laurel.edu
Established: 1985 Annual Undergrad Tuition & Fees: $10,912
Enrollment: 238 Coed
Affiliation or Control: Proprietary IRS Status: Proprietary
Highest Offering: Associate Degree
Accreditation: ACCSC, COARC

01 President .... Mrs. Nancy M. DECKER
11 Executive Director .... Mrs. Bonnie MARSH
10 Vice President of Finance .... Ms. Vicki M. JOLLIFFE
15 Vice President of Human Resources ..... Mr. Chuck SANTORE, JR.
13 Director of IT .... Mr. Ken LAPIKAS
37 Vice President of Financial Aid .... Ms. Stephanie M. MIGYANKO
07 Director of Admission .... Ms. Kelly RUSSO
20 Academic Coordinator .... Ms. Sandi FIELD

Laurel Technical Institute (I)

2370 Broadway Avenue, Hermitage PA 16148

County: Mercer FICE Identification: 020925
Unit ID: 215992
Telephone: (724) 983-0700 Carnegie Class: Assoc/HVT-High Trad
FAX Number: (724) 983-8355 Calendar System: Semester
URL: www.laurel.edu
Established: 1925 Annual Undergrad Tuition & Fees: $10,912
Enrollment: 122 Coed
Affiliation or Control: Proprietary IRS Status: Proprietary
Highest Offering: Associate Degree
Accreditation: ACCSC, COARC

01 President .... Ms. Nancy DECKER
11 Director/Exec VP of Operations .... Mr. Douglas DECKER
07 Director of Admission .... Ms. Kelly RUSSO
05 Director of Education .... Ms. Michele TOTA

Lebanon Valley College (A)

101 N College Avenue, Annville PA 17003-1400
County: Lebanon FICE Identification: 003288
Unit ID: 213507
Telephone: (717) 867-6161 Carnegie Class: Masters/S
FAX Number: (717) 867-6124 Calendar System: Semester
URL: www.lvc.edu
Established: 1866 Annual Undergrad Tuition & Fees: $46,030
Enrollment: 1,959 Coed
Affiliation or Control: United Methodist IRS Status: 501(c)3
Highest Offering: Doctorate
Accreditation: M, ACBSP, CAATE, EXSC, MUS, PTA, @SP

01 President .... Dr. James M. MACLAREN
05 Provost/Vice Pres Academic Affairs .... Dr. Susan TAMMARO
111 Vice President of Advancement .... Mr. Matthew WEAVER
10 Vice Pres Finance/Administration .... Mr. Shawn P. CURTIN
84 Vice President of Enrollment .... Mr. Edwin R. WRIGHT
32 VP Stdnt Affs/Dean of Students .... Dr. Robert L. MIKUS
26 VP of Marketing/ Communications .... Mrs. Molly O'BRIEN-FOELSCH
13 Senior Director of Information Tech .... Mr. David W. SHAPIRO
15 Sr Dir of Human Res/TitleIX Coord .... Mrs. Ann C. HAYES
58 Assoc Prov Grad & Prof Studies .... Vacant
06 Assistant Dean and Registrar .... Mr. Jeremy A. MAISTO
41 Director of Athletics .... Mr. Richard L. BEARD
114 Dir of Finance/Chief Budget Officer .... Ms. Wendy ALBERT
21 Controller .... Mr. Gabriel PAZ
37 Director of Financial Aid .... Mrs. Kendra M. FEIGERT
36 Exec Director of the Breen Center .... Dr. Tomomi M. HORNING
28 VP of Diversity/Equity & Inclusion .... Dr. Felicia BROWN-HAYWOOD
19 Public Safety Supervisor .... Mr. Brian BOYER
104 Director of Global Education .... Mrs. Jill T. RUSSELL
39 Director of Residential Life .... Ms. Caitlin LENKER
22 Director of Accessibility Resources .... Mrs. Erin E. HANNAFORD
50 Director of the MBA Program .... Dr. Treva CLARK
08 Director of the Bishop Library .... Mrs. Maureen A. BENTZ
30 Director of Individual Giving .... Ms. Jordan EVANGELISTA
18 Director of Facilities Management .... Mr. Michael MUMPER
35 Assoc Dean Student Affairs .... Mr. Jeremy MUNSON
42 Chaplain .... Mrs. Andrea HALDEMAN
27 Director Campus Communications .... Dr. Thomas M. HANRAHAN
91 Dir Enterprise Information Systems .... Mr. Jason GAMBLE
24 Director of Audiovisual Technology .... Mr. Andrew S. GREENE
38 Director of Counseling Services .... Mr. James FELTY
88 Director of Student Activities .... Mrs. Jennifer M. EVANS
88 Assistant Controller .... Mr. Todd M. LATSHAW
29 Director Alumni & Parent Engagement .... Mrs. Susan SARISKY JONES
04 Admin Assistant to the President .... Mrs. Heather L. WHITMAN

Lehigh Carbon Community College (B)

4525 Education Park Drive, Schnecksville PA 18078-2598
County: Lehigh FICE Identification: 006810
Unit ID: 213525
Telephone: (610) 799-2121 Carnegie Class: Assoc/MT-VT-Mix Trad/Non
FAX Number: (610) 799-1527 Calendar System: Semester
URL: www.lccc.edu
Established: 1966 Annual Undergrad Tuition & Fees (In-District): $8,070
Enrollment: 6,205 Coed
Affiliation or Control: Local IRS Status: 501(c)3
Highest Offering: Associate Degree
Accreditation: M, ACBSP, ADNUR, CAHIIM, CSHSE, NAEYC, PNUR, PTAA

01 President .... Dr. Ann D. BIEBER
05 VP Academic/Student Dev .... Ms. Larissa M. VERTA
10 VP Finance & Admin Svcs .... Ms. Stefanie E. NESTER
84 VP Enrollment Management .... Dr. Cindy M. HANEY
04 Exec Asst to President and Board .... Ms. Tracy BEAN
32 Dean of Student Development/Equity .... Ms. Peggy M. HEIM
106 Dean Educ/Comp Sci & Online Lrng .... Dr. Kelly TRAHAN
13 Chief Information Security Officer .... Mr. Joshua MITCHELL
79 Int Dean Humanities/Arts/Social Sci .... Dr. Eike REICHARDT
76 Dean Healthcare Sci/Aviatn/Math/Sci .... Mr. Craig A. KOLLER
103 Dean Workfrc/Cmty Educ/Tech Ed .... Dr. Andrea K. GRANNUM-MOSLEY
26 Exec Dir College Relations .... Ms. Linda BAKER
09 Exec Dir Inst Research & Effectiv .... Vacant
114 Dir Budgets & Purchasing .... Ms. Shannon HELMER
102 Executive Director Foundation .... Ms. Silvia VARGAS
07 Exec Dir Recruitment & Enroll .... Ms. Ellia SABLAN-ZEBEDY
36 Dir Career Development .... Ms. Christina L. MOYER
108 Dn Accred/Compliance/Curric/Assess .... Mr. Scott W. AQUILA
88 Exec Dir of High School Connections .... Mr. Brandon KWIATEK
15 Dir HR/Title IX/Equity Coord .... Ms. Donna M. WILLIAMS
88 Dir Org & Faculty Development .... Vacant
66 Director Nursing Programs .... Dr. Tina VANBUREN
35 Director Student Life .... Ms. Gene F. EDEN
14 Asst Dir Technical Architect .... Mr. Ervin J. MEASE
18 Dir Facilities Mgmt & Public Safety .... Mr. George CALABA
37 Exec Dir Fin Aid & Scholarship .... Ms. Tracey RICHARDS
88 Dir Academic Grants .... Mr. Greg BOTT
41 Director Athletics .... Ms. MaryAnn RUSH-WALLACE
88 Grant Writer .... Ms. Mary KOVALCHICK
74 Dir Veterinary Tech Program .... Ms. Lisa A. MARTINI-JOHNSON
27 Dir Marketing & Publications .... Ms. Jill YAPSUGA
06 Dir Registration/Student Records .... Ms. Fae SCHRACK
40 Bookstore Manager .... Ms. Rachel FRAME
38 Dir Counseling & Cmty Standards .... Mr. Brian C. DELONG
19 Public Safety Supervisor .... Mr. Gary D. OLEWINE
113 Dir Student Accounts .... Ms. Ann L. BOYLE
121 Int Dean Acad Support & Success .... Dr. Jodi ROWLANDS
21 Controller .... Ms. Stacey BETZ

Lehigh University (C)

27 Memorial Drive W, Bethlehem PA 18015-3094
County: Northampton FICE Identification: 003289
Unit ID: 213543
Telephone: (610) 758-3000 Carnegie Class: DU-Higher
FAX Number: (610) 691-5420 Calendar System: Semester
URL: www.lehigh.edu
Established: 1865 Annual Undergrad Tuition & Fees: $55,260
Enrollment: 7,067 Coed
Affiliation or Control: Independent Non-Profit IRS Status: 501(c)3
Highest Offering: Doctorate
Accreditation: M, COPSY, IPSY, MPCAC, SCPSY, THEA

01 President .... Dr. Joseph J. HELBLE
05 Provost/SVP for Academic Affairs .... Dr. Nathan N. URBAN
10 Vice Pres Finance & Administration .... Ms. Patricia A. JOHNSON
88 VP for International Affairs .... Dr. Cheryl A. MATHERLY
30 VP Development and Alumni Relations .... Mr. Joseph E. BUCK
46 VP/Assoc Prov Research/Grad Studies .... Dr. Alan J. SNYDER
26 Interim VP Comm & Public Affairs .... Mr. Ira L. RUBIEN
28 VP Diversity/Inclusion & Equity .... Dr. Donald A. OUTING
115 Chief Investment Officer .... Ms. Kristin AGATONE
09 Vice Provost Institutional Research .... Dr. Yenny ANDERSON
32 Vice Provost Student Affairs .... Dr. Ricardo HALL
13 Vice Provost Library & Tech Svcs .... Dr. Greg REIHMAN
88 Vice Provost for Academic Diversity .... Mr. Henry U. ODI
86 Assoc VP for Govt Relations .... Mr. Christopher C. CARTER
21 Assoc VP Finance/Asst Secy Board .... Vacant
15 Assoc VP for Human Resource .... Mr. Chris HALLADAY
18 Interim AVP Facilities Svcs/Archit .... Mr. Don J. PASDA
20 Deputy Provost Academic Affairs .... Ms. Jennifer M. JENSEN
35 Dean of Students .... Ms. Katherine W. LAVINDER
29 Asst VP of Alumni Engagement .... Ms. Jennifer L. CUNNINGHAM
31 Asst VP Community & Regional Affs .... Ms. Adrienne J. WASHINGTON
54 Dean Engr & Applied Science .... Dr. Stephen P. DEWEERTH
49 Dean of Arts & Sciences .... Dr. Robert FLOWERS
50 Dean of Business/Economics .... Dr. Georgette C. PHILLIPS
53 Dean of Education .... Dr. William GAUDELLI
69 Interim Dean College of Health .... Dr. Elizabeth DOLAN
07 Vice Provost Admiss/Financial Aid .... Mr. Dan WARNER
41 Murray H Goodman Dean of Athletics .... Mr. Joseph D. STERRETT
06 Registrar .... Mr. Steven H. WILSON
37 Director Financial Aid .... Ms. Jennifer L. MERTZ
106 Director Distance Education .... Ms. Margaret A. PORTZ
36 Director Career Services .... Ms. Lori B. KENNEDY
23 Medical Dir Health Center .... Mr. Steven BOWERS
39 Director Residential Services .... Mr. Ozzie BREINER
40 Director Bookstore .... Ms. Renee LUTZ
19 Chief University Police .... Mr. Jason D. SCHIFFER
38 Interim Dir of Counseling Svcs .... Dr. Aaron STERBA
42 Chaplain .... Rev. Lloyd H. STEFFEN
43 General Counsel .... Mr. Frank A. ROTH
114 Director of Budget .... Mr. Stephen J. GUTTMAN
96 Manager Strategic Sourcing .... Ms. Jane ALTEMOSE
84 Director Enrollment Management .... Ms. Jennifer E. O'BRIEN-KNOTTS
100 Chief of Staff .... Mr. Erik J. WALKER
04 Executive Asst to the President .... Ms. Donna L. FEIST
104 Director Study Abroad .... Ms. Katie W. RADANDE
122 Dir Special Projects-Greek Life .... Ms. Madalyn EADLINE
102 Director Foundation/Corporate Rels .... Mr. Ed CLARKE

Lincoln Technical Institute (D)

5151 Tilghman Street, Allentown PA 18104-3298
County: Lehigh FICE Identification: 007759
Unit ID: 213570
Telephone: (610) 398-5300 Carnegie Class: Assoc/HVT-High Trad
FAX Number: (610) 395-2706 Calendar System: Semester
URL: www.lincolntech.edu
Established: 1946 Annual Undergrad Tuition & Fees: N/A
Enrollment: 599 Coed
Affiliation or Control: Proprietary IRS Status: Proprietary
Highest Offering: Associate Degree
Accreditation: ACCSC

01 Campus President .... Mrs. Angela REPPERT
05 Director of Education .... Ms. Hollie ESTES
66 Director of Nursing .... Mrs. Michelle DAVIS
11 Director of Administrative Services .... Mrs. Rebecca DRAYTON
07 Director of Admissions .... Mr. Vincent SALVATORIELLO
36 Director of Career Services .... Mrs. Charmain BRODY
37 Financial Aid Manager .... Ms. Erica BRANDI

Lincoln Technical Institute (E)

9191 Torresdale Avenue, Philadelphia PA 19136-1595
County: Philadelphia FICE Identification: 007832
Unit ID: 213589
Telephone: (215) 335-0800 Carnegie Class: Spec 2-yr-Tech
FAX Number: (215) 335-1443 Calendar System: Other
URL: www.lincolntech.com
Established: 1946 Annual Undergrad Tuition & Fees: N/A
Enrollment: 389 Coed
Affiliation or Control: Proprietary IRS Status: Proprietary
Highest Offering: Associate Degree
Accreditation: ACCSC

01 Campus President .... Mr. Jim KUNTZ
32 Director of Admissions .... Ms. Michele GRANT
05 Director of Education .... Mrs. Jennifer MCLAUGHLIN
11 Director Administration .... Ms. Gina ALTSHULER
36 Director of Career Services .... Ms. Emily MATTHEWS

Lincoln University (F)

1570 Baltimore Pike, Lincoln University PA 19352-0999
County: Chester FICE Identification: 003290
Unit ID: 213598
Telephone: (484) 365-8000 Carnegie Class: Masters/M
FAX Number: (484) 365-7316 Calendar System: Semester
URL: www.lincoln.edu
Established: 1854 Annual Undergrad Tuition & Fees (In-State): $11,266
Enrollment: 2,077 Coed
Affiliation or Control: State Related IRS Status: 501(c)3
Highest Offering: Master's
Accreditation: M, NURSE

01 President .... Dr. Brenda A. ALLEN
111 AVP for Institutional Advancement .... Ms. Samira MALIK
100 Chief of Staff/Mgr Board Trustees .... Ms. Diane M. BROWN
05 Provost and VP for Academic Affairs .... Vacant
10 Vice Pres Fiscal Affairs/Treasurer .... Mr. Charles GRADOWSKI
32 VP Student Success/Dean of College .... Dr. Lenetta LEE
15 Vice President Human Resources .... Mr. Jake TANKSLEY
13 Chief Information Officer .... Mr. Justin MCKENZIE
42 Chaplain .... Rev Dr. Frederick FAISON
09 Asst Prov Inst Effect/Research/Plng .... Ms. Tiffany LEE
08 Int Director of Library .... Ms. Sophia SOTILLEO
35 Assoc Dean of College/Students .... Rev Dr. Frederick FAISON
84 Assoc Provost Enrollment Management .... Dr. Kimberly TAYLOR-BENNS
26 Manager of Comm & Public Relations .... Mr. Terrance J. YOUNG
29 Assoc VP of Alumni Relations .... Ms. Deborah JOHNSON
35 AVP Stdnt Success/Dean of Students .... Mr. Brian DUBENION
06 Registrar .... Ms. Catherine RUTLEDGE
36 Director Career Development .... Vacant
41 Director of Athletics .... Mr. Harry STINSON
21 Controller .... Mr. Jay SIMMONS
85 Director of International Services .... Ms. Dafina BLACKSHER DIABATE
23 Director Health Services .... Ms. Velva GREENE-RAINEY
123 Dir Graduate Student Svcs/Admission .... Ms. Jernice LEA
37 Director Financial Aid .... Ms. Kim ANDERSON
96 Director of Purchasing .... Ms. Lynn POWELL
20 Dean of the Faculty .... Dr. Patricia JOSEPH
121 Assoc VP Academic Support .... Ms. Evelyn POE
07 Director of Admissions .... Mrs. Nokoia FORDE
19 Director Security/Safety .... Mr. Marc PARTEE
22 Director Title III .... Ms. Marion BERNARD-AMOS
38 Director Student Counseling .... Ms. Rachel MANSON
44 Director Annual Giving .... Mr. Rich LANCASTER
90 Proj Manager Academic Computing .... Ms. Nancy EVANS

Luzerne County Community College (G)

521 Trailblazer Drive, Nanticoke PA 18634-3899
County: Luzerne FICE Identification: 006811
Unit ID: 213659
Telephone: (570) 740-0200 Carnegie Class: Assoc/HVT-Mix Trad/Non
FAX Number: (570) 740-0750 Calendar System: Semester
URL: www.luzerne.edu
Established: 1966 Annual Undergrad Tuition & Fees (In-District): $10,020
Enrollment: 4,454 Coed
Affiliation or Control: Local IRS Status: 501(c)3
Highest Offering: Associate Degree
Accreditation: M, ACBSP, ADNUR, COARC, DH, EMT, NAEYC, SURGT

01 President .... Mr. Thomas P. LEARY
101 Executive Asst to President/BOT .... Ms. Paula LABENSKI
05 Vice Pres Academic Affairs .... Vacant
32 VP of Enrollment Mgmt/Student Affs .... Ms. Rosana REYES
103 VP of Applied Tech/Workforce Devel .... Ms. Susan SPRY
15 Dean Human Resources .... Mr. John SEDLAK
66 Dean of Nursing/Health Sciences .... Ms. Deborah VILEGI PAYNE
13 Chief Information Officer .... Ms. Patricia YENCHA
10 VP of Finance .... Ms. Cheryl BAUR
07 Assistant Director Admissions .... Mr. Ed HENNIGAN
37 Director of Student Financial Aid .... Mr. Mark CARPENTIER
08 Director of Library .... Ms. Katherine CUMMINGS
38 Dir Counseling/Stdnt Support Svcs .... Mrs. Janine KELLEY
35 Dir Student Life/Athletics .... Ms. Kristen CORCORAN
09 Director Inst Research/Planning .... Ms. Graceann PLATUKUS
18 Director of Physical Plant .... Mr. Keith GRAHAM
30 Exec Dir Institutional Advancement .... Ms. Rebecca BROMINSKI
84 Director Enrollment Management .... Mr. Jim DOMZALSKI
26 Director of College Relations .... Ms. Lisa NELSON
29 Director Alumni Relations .... Ms. Bonnie LAUER
28 Diversity Coordinator .... Ms. Judi MYERS
19 Director of Public Safety/Security .... Mr. Douglas FAWBUSH

Lycoming College (H)

700 College Place, Williamsport PA 17701-5192
County: Lycoming FICE Identification: 003293
Unit ID: 213668
Telephone: (570) 321-4000 Carnegie Class: Bac-A&S
FAX Number: (570) 321-4337 Calendar System: Semester
URL: www.lycoming.edu

Established: 1812 Annual Undergrad Tuition & Fees: $42,939
Enrollment: 1,065 Coed
Affiliation or Control: United Methodist IRS Status: 501(c)3
Highest Offering: Baccalaureate
Accreditation: M

01 President .... Dr. Kent C. TRACHTE
05 Provost and Dean of the Faculty .... Dr. Philip W. SPRUNGER
10 VP for Finance and Admin/Treasurer .... Mr. Jeffrey L. BENNETT
111 Executive Vice President .... Dr. Charles W. EDMONDS
84 VP for Enrollment Management .... Mr. Michael J. KONOPSKI
21 Controller .... Ms. Dawn HENDRICKS
32 Vice President for Student Life .... Dr. Daniel P. MILLER
20 Vice Provost .... Dr. Susan ROSS
89 Assistant Dean First Year Students .... Dr. Theresa A. SPANELLA
08 Director of Snowden Library .... Ms. Rebecca DONALD
06 Registrar .... Ms. Jilliane BOLT-MICHEWICZ
37 Director of Financial Aid .... Mr. James LAKIS
13 Chief Information Officer .... Mr. Robert L. DUNKLEBERGER
29 Asst VP Alumni Relations .... Ms. Amy S. REYES
112 Sr Dir for Major Planned Gifts .... Mr. Robb DIETRICH
39 Assoc Dean of Students .... Ms. Kate HUMMEL
41 Director of Athletics .... Mr. Michael CLARK
110 Assoc Dir of Major Gifts .... Ms. Nicole GARCIA
44 Director of Annual Giving .... Vacant
15 Assoc VP of Human Resources .... Ms. Kacy HAGAN
18 Chief Facilities/Physical Plant .... Mr. F. Douglas KUNTZ
23 Director of Health Services .... Vacant
38 Director Student Counseling .... Mr. Townsend VELKOFF
40 Campus Store Manager .... Ms. Patricia E. BAUSINGER
92 Lycoming Scholars .... Dr. Cullen CHANDLER
94 Women's Studies .... Dr. Kerry RICHMOND
118 Human Resources Benefits Coord .... Ms. Cathleen A. LUTZ
04 Assistant to the President .... Ms. Diane CARL
09 Director of Institutional Research .... Dr. Chiaki KOTORI
108 Associate Provost .... Dr. Amy ROGERS
90 Dir of IT Core Services .... Ms. Nicole KUNTZ
91 Director Administrative Computing .... Ms. Janet PAYNE
07 Director of Admissions .... Ms. Jessica A. QUINTANA HESS
102 Foundations Relations Officer .... Ms. Melanie TAORMINA
104 Coordinator of Study Abroad .... Ms. Allison HOLLADAY
105 Director Web Services .... Mr. Robert BROWN
19 Director Security/Safety .... Ms. Holly BLEAM
26 Sr Dir of Marketing & Comm .... Ms. Marla KRAMER
122 Dir Stdnt Involvement-Greek Life .... Ms. Tara LEIGH

Manor College (A)

700 Fox Chase Road, Jenkintown PA 19046-3399
County: Montgomery FICE Identification: 003294
Unit ID: 213774
Telephone: (215) 885-2360 Carnegie Class: Bac/Assoc-Assoc Dom
FAX Number: (215) 576-6564 Calendar System: Semester
URL: www.manor.edu
Established: 1947 Annual Undergrad Tuition & Fees: $18,530
Enrollment: 834 Coed
Affiliation or Control: Independent Non-Profit IRS Status: 501(c)3
Highest Offering: Baccalaureate
Accreditation: M, ACBSP, DA, DH

01 President .... Dr. Jonathan PERI
05 Interim Provost and VPAA .... Dr. Gerard O'SULLIVAN
06 Registrar .... Ms. Dianne I. SARIDAKIS
13 Manager of IT and Plant .... Mr. Joseph VINGLESS
15 Director of Human Resources .... Ms. Christine COLELLA
111 VP of Institutional Advancement .... Ms. Kelly PEIFFER
10 VP of Finance & Facilities .... Ms. Janice SALERNO
19 Manager of Public Safety .... Mr. David CARISTO
26 VP of Marketing/Communications .... Ms. Kelly PEIFFER
32 VP and Dean of Student Affairs .... Ms. Allison C. MOOTZ
84 VP of Enrollment Management .... Dr. Joseph GILLESPIE
37 Director Financial Aid .... Mr. Chris T. HARTMAN
38 Director Counseling .... Ms. Christine B. PRINCE
39 Assistant Director Residence Life .... Ms. Shamika FORD
41 Director Athletics .... Mr. John DEMPSTER
79 Humanities and Social Science Chair .... Dr. Matthew SMALARZ
08 Head Librarian .... Mr. Richard JUTKIEWICZ
09 Director of Institutional Research .... Mr. John T. KREBS
04 Exec Assistant to the President .... Mrs. Katharina M. KILMER
76 Dean of Allied Health Sciences .... Mrs. Jaime SIMPSON
50 Dean Business/Educ & Prof Studies .... Dr. Cherie CROSBY-WEEKS
06 Director of Student Records .... Mr. Nick RUDNYTZKY
105 Creative Services Manager .... Ms. Allison MEYERS
108 Director Institutional Assessment .... Mr. John KREBS
96 Director of Purchasing .... Mrs. Janice SALERNO
110 Executive Dir of Advancement .... Mr. Tom SIMS

Marywood University (B)

2300 Adams Avenue, Scranton PA 18509-1598
County: Lackawanna FICE Identification: 003296
Unit ID: 213826
Telephone: (570) 348-6211 Carnegie Class: Masters/L
FAX Number: (570) 961-4769 Calendar System: Semester
URL: www.marywood.edu
Established: 1915 Annual Undergrad Tuition & Fees: $36,928
Enrollment: 2,613 Coed
Affiliation or Control: Roman Catholic IRS Status: 501(c)3
Highest Offering: Doctorate
Accreditation: M, ACATE, ACBSP, ARCPA, ART, CACREP, CLPSY, COARC, DIETD, DIETI, MUS, NURSE, SP, SW

01 President .... Sr. Mary PERSICO, IHM
05 Provost .... Dr. Christina A. CLARK
10 VP for Finance/Administration .... Mr. William MCDONALD
111 Vice Pres University Advancement .... Dr. Renee G. ZEHEL
84 VP Enrollment Svcs/Student Success .... Mr. Robert C. PIUROWSKI
15 Exec Director of Human Resources .... Ms. Molly BARON
26 Exec Dir Marketing/Communication .... Mr. James M. BROWN
18 VP of Operations .... Ms. Wendy YANKELITIS
49 Dean College of Arts/Science .... Dr. Jeffrey JOHNSON
76 Interim Dean Col Health/Human Svcs .... Ms. Shelby W. YEAGER
107 Dean Col of Prof Studies .... Mr. James J. SULLIVAN
70 Director School of Social Work .... Sr. Angela KIM
08 University Librarian .... Dr. Susan M. FREY
06 Interim Registrar .... Mr. William J. MANLEY
07 Dir of UG Admissions .... Ms. Rachel HARTZ
37 Director of Financial Aid .... Vacant
113 Student Accounts Receivable .... Ms. Darlene J. SEDLAK
44 Leadership Annual Giving Officer .... Ms. Patricia H. ROSETTI
20 Associate Provost .... Ms. Leslie W. CHRISTIANSON
30 Sr Dir Development & Annual Giving .... Ms. Christina M. MACE
121 Asst Provost for Student Success .... Dr. Paul J. BALLARD
27 Public Relations Director .... Ms. Juneann GRECO
41 Exec Director Athletics/Recreation .... Mr. Patrick MURPHY
36 Director of Career Development .... Dr. Christina BRUNDAGE
42 VP for Mission Services .... Sr. Catherine LUXNER
88 Dir of Dining Services .... Ms. Jinny SAVAGE
13 Chief Information Officer .... Mr. James DUTCHER
19 Chief Campus Safety .... Mr. Michael C. PASQUALICCHIO
23 Director of Student Health Services .... Ms. Maura K. SMITH
38 Director Counseling & Student Devel .... Dr. Robert S. SHAW
110 Dir Advancement Services .... Ms. Elizabeth M. STIRES
29 Director of Alumni Engagement .... Mr. Kevin FARRELL
35 Dean of Students .... Mr. Ross NOVAK
22 Dir of Student Equity/Inclusion .... Ms. Keshia A. VILCHERT
09 Asst Dir for Research & Spons Pgms .... Ms. Tabbi L. MILLER-SCANDLE
109 Exec Dir Confer/Events/Auxil Svcs .... Mr. John J. COVAL
04 Exec Secretary to the President .... Ms. Robyn M. KRUKOVITZ
43 Secretary Univ & General Counsel .... Ms. Mary T. GARDIER PATERSON
28 Exec Dir Equity & Inclus/Title IX .... Dr. Yerodin LUCAS
21 Assoc VP for Finance/ Administration .... Ms. Ashton J. VOGELSANG
32 Asst VP for Student Services .... Sr. Elizabeth A. MCGILL
88 Accounting Supervisor .... Ms. Dina M. KORNISH
104 Associate Provost for Global Educ .Dr. Seong-Yoon (David) KANG

McCann School of Business & Technology (C)

2200 North Irving Street, Allentown PA 18109
Telephone: (484) 223-4600 Identification: 770768
Accreditation: ACCSC

† Branch campus of Miller-Motte College, Chattanooga, TN.

McCann School of Business & Technology (D)

7495 Westbranch Highway, Lewisburg PA 17837
Telephone: (570) 497-8014 Identification: 666485
Accreditation: ACCSC, SURGT

† Branch campus of Miller-Motte College, Chattanooga, TN.

Mercyhurst University (E)

501 E 38th Street, Erie PA 16546-0001
County: Erie FICE Identification: 003297
Unit ID: 213987
Telephone: (814) 824-2000 Carnegie Class: Masters/M
FAX Number: (814) 824-2438 Calendar System: Semester
URL: www.mercyhurst.edu
Established: 1926 Annual Undergrad Tuition & Fees: $41,350
Enrollment: 2,790 Coed
Affiliation or Control: Roman Catholic IRS Status: 501(c)3
Highest Offering: Doctorate
Accreditation: M, ACPHA, ADNUR, ARCPA, CAATE, @CNEA, COARC, DANCE, IACBE, MUS, PTAA, SW

01 President .... Dr. Kathleen GETZ
05 Vice President for Academic Affairs .... Dr. Joanne M. HOSEY-MCGURK
10 Vice Pres Finance & Administration .... Mr. Michael HELLER
30 Vice Pres University Development .... Vacant
32 Vice Pres of Student Life .... Dr. Laura ZIRKEL
84 VP for Enrollment .... Ms. Dionne VEITCH
13 Chief Information Officer .... Ms. Jeanette BRITT
18 Director Facilities/Physical Plant .... Ms. Jeanette BRITT
38 Director Student Counseling Service .... Ms. Judy SMITH
07 Director Undergraduate Admissions .... Mr. Christian BEYER
06 Registrar .... Ms. Michele WHEATON
08 Dir Univ Libraries/Online Learning .... Ms. Darci JONES
39 Dir Residential Life/Stdnt Conduct .... Vacant
19 Director of Public Safety Programs .... Mr. Donald J. FUHRMANN
29 Dir Alumni Engagement .... Ms. Lindsay FRANK
42 Director of Campus Ministry .... Fr. James PISZKER
37 Director of Student Financial Svcs .... Ms. Carrie NEWMAN
41 Director of Athletics .... Mr. Bradley DAVIS
09 Director of Institutional Research .... Mrs. Sheila W. RICHTER
15 Director Human Resources .... Ms. Corry MILLER
93 Coordinator Multicultural Affairs .... Vacant
04 Administrative Asst to President .... Ms. Stacey WILEY
104 Director Study Abroad .... Dr. Heidi HOSEY
26 Chief Public Relations/Marketing .... Mr. Sean P. CUNEO
43 Dir Legal Services/General Counsel .Mrs. Meredith BOLLHEIMER

Messiah University (F)

One University Avenue, Mechanicsburg PA 17055
County: Cumberland FICE Identification: 003298
Unit ID: 213996
Telephone: (717) 766-2511 Carnegie Class: Masters/L
FAX Number: (717) 691-6025 Calendar System: Semester
URL: www.messiah.edu
Established: 1909 Annual Undergrad Tuition & Fees: $37,180
Enrollment: 3,370 Coed
Affiliation or Control: Interdenominational IRS Status: 501(c)3
Highest Offering: Doctorate
Accreditation: M, ACBSP, ART, CAATE, CACREP, DIETD, DIETI, MUS, NURSE, OT, PTA, SW, THEA

01 President .... Dr. Kim S. PHIPPS
05 Provost .... Dr. Randall G. BASINGER
10 Vice Pres for Finance & Planning .... Mr. David S. WALKER
11 Vice President for Operations .... Mrs. Kathrynne G. SHAFER
111 Vice President for Advancement .... Mr. Barry G. GOODLING
84 Vice Pres for Enrollment Management .... Mr. John A. CHOPKA
15 VP for Human Res & Compliance .... Ms. Amanda A. COFFEY
28 VP for Diversity Affairs .... Dr. Todd ALLEN
121 Vice Provost for Student Success .... Dr. Kristin M. HANSEN-KIEFFER
58 Asst Provost/Dean of Grad Studies .... Dr. Robert PEPPER
79 Dean School of Humanities .... Dr. Peter K. POWERS
81 Dean School of Science/Engr/Health .... Dr. Angela HARE
32 Dean of Students .... Mr. Kevin VILLEGAS
35 Associate Dean of Students .... Mr. Douglas M. WOOD
30 Exec Director of Development .... Dr. Jon C. STUCKEY
93 Dir of Intercultural Office .... Vacant
07 Director of Admissions .... Mrs. Dana J. BRITTON
37 Director of Financial Aid .... Mr. Gregory L. GEARHART
39 Asst Dir of Residence Life/Housing .... Mr. Bryce WATKINS
21 Dir Financial Operations/Controller .... Mrs. Christine HARTMAN
06 Registrar .... Ms. Carrie WIDDOWSON
08 Director of the Murray Library .... Ms. Linda POSTON
91 Director Information Services .... Mr. John P. LUFT
90 Dir Learning Technology Services .... Mrs. Susan K. SHANNON
09 Director of Institutional Research .... Ms. Laura M. MILLER
42 Campus Pastor .... Vacant
26 Exec Director Communications .... Mrs. Carla E. GROSS
29 Director Alumni & Parent Relations .... Mr. Jay W. MCCLYMONT
38 Director of the Engle Center .... Ms. Eleanor MUIR
41 Athletics Director .... Ms. Sarah GUSTIN HAMROCK
92 Dir of the College Honors Program .... Dr. James LAGRAND
18 Director of Facility Services .... Mr. Bradley A. MARKLEY
36 Dir Career/Profess Development .... Mrs. Christina R. HANSON
40 Campus Store Manager .... Vacant
19 Director Safety/Dispatch Services .... Ms. Cindy L. BURGER
04 Executive Coordinator for President .... Mrs. Karin BISBEE
96 Purchasing Manager .... Mrs. Daisy ANDERSON
23 Coordinator of Health Services .... Mrs. Michelle LUCAS
105 Web Services Manager .... Ms. Ramona FRITSCHI
108 Director of Assessment .... Ms. Kate WILKINS
20 Associate Provost .... Dr. Alison NOBLE

Missio Seminary (G)

421 N. 7th St., Philadelphia PA 19123
County: Philadelphia FICE Identification: 023230
Unit ID: 211130
Telephone: (215) 368-5000 Carnegie Class: Spec-4-yr-Faith
FAX Number: (215) 368-2301 Calendar System: Semester
URL: www.missio.edu
Established: 1971 Annual Graduate Tuition & Fees: N/A
Enrollment: 223 Coed
Affiliation or Control: Independent Non-Profit IRS Status: 501(c)3
Highest Offering: Doctorate; No Undergraduates
Accreditation: M, THEOL

01 President .... Dr. Frank JAMES, III
30 VP Strategic Init/Development .... Mr. Charles BLACHFORD
05 Dean of the Faculty .... Dr. David LAMB
05 Academic Dean .... Dr. Todd MANGUM
04 Executive Assistant to the Pres .... Mrs. Beatrice L. BARKLEY
10 Business Office Director .... Ms. Kim BILLUPS
73 Director of DMin Program .... Dr. Kyuboem LEE
37 Director Student Financial Aid .... Mr. Jermaine HARRINGTON
08 Director of Library Services .... Ms. Shaelagh MARTIN
06 Registrar/Dir of Academic Services .... Dr. Colleen WILLENBRING
07 Interim Director of Admissions .... Mr. Brian BAE
13 Chief Info Technology Officer .... Mr. Gregg ALDERFER
29 Director of Strategic Relations .... Ms. Wendy WALTERS

Misericordia University (H)

301 Lake Street, Dallas PA 18612-1098
County: Luzerne FICE Identification: 003247
Unit ID: 214069
Telephone: (570) 674-6400 Carnegie Class: DU-Mod
FAX Number: (570) 675-2441 Calendar System: Semester
URL: www.misericordia.edu
Established: 1924 Annual Undergrad Tuition & Fees: $35,940
Enrollment: 2,374 Coed
Affiliation or Control: Roman Catholic IRS Status: 501(c)3
Highest Offering: Doctorate
Accreditation: M, #ARCPA, DMS, IACBE, NURSE, OT, PTA, RAD, SP, SW

01 President .... Dr. Daniel J. MYERS
10 Vice Pres Finance & Administration .... Mr. Mark VAN ETTEN, JR.

05 Vice President Academic Affairs .... Dr. David REHM
111 VP of Institutional Advancement .... Ms. Tanya EASTON
32 Vice Pres of Mission & Student Life .... Ms. Amy LAHART
84 Vice President of Enrollment Mgmt .... Mr. Glenn BOZINSKI
21 Assoc Vice Pres of Finance .... Mr. Ronald S. HROMISIN
102 AVP of Advancement .... Mr. Larry PELLEGRINI
100 Chief of Staff .... Mr. James ROBERTS
06 Registrar .... Mr. Joseph REDINGTON
35 Dean of Students .... Ms. Callie RIMPFEL
29 Director Alumni Relations .... Ms. Lailani AUGUSTINE
08 Librarian .... Ms. Jennifer LUKSA
04 Exec Assistant to the President .... Ms. Lisa BORCHERT
96 Director of Purchasing .... Vacant
121 Director of Student Success Center .... Ms. Amy KLINE
42 Director Campus Ministry .... Ms. Christine SOMERS
41 Director of Athletics .... Mr. Charles EDKINS
39 Director of Residence Life .... Mr. Angelo NUDO
14 Manager Applications Development .... Mr. Matt MIHAL
13 Director of Information Technology .... Mr. Val APANOVICH
88 Director of Student Engagement .... Ms. Darcy BRODMERKEL
36 Dir Insalaco Ctr Career Development ... Ms. Bernadette RUSHMER
51 Director of Adult Education/CACE .... Mr. Paul NARDONE
15 Director of Human Resources .... Ms. Pamela PARSNIK
37 Assoc Director of Financial Aid .... Ms. Karen COLE
19 Director Security/Safety .... Ms. Ruth ANDERIKA
18 Director of Facilities .... Mr. Taras MIHALKO
09 Director of Institutional Research .... Vacant
90 Manager of User Services .... Mr. David A. JOHNDROW
07 Director of Admissions .... Mr. Stephen SECORA
104 Director Study Abroad .... Vacant

Montgomery County Community College (A)

340 Dekalb Pike, Blue Bell PA 19422-1400
County: Montgomery FICE Identification: 004452
Unit ID: 214111
Telephone: (215) 641-6300 Carnegie Class: Assoc/MT-VT-Mix Trad/Non
FAX Number: (215) 461-1460 Calendar System: Semester
URL: www.mc3.edu
Established: 1964 Annual Undergrad Tuition & Fees (In-District): $10,350
Enrollment: 9,827 Coed
Affiliation or Control: State/Local IRS Status: 501(c)3
Highest Offering: Associate Degree
Accreditation: M, ADNUR, CSHSE, DH, MLTAD, NAEYC, PTAA, RAD, SURGT

01 President .... Dr. Victoria BASTECKI-PEREZ
88 Admin Director Ofc of the President .... Ms. Tiffany BREGOVI
05 VP for Academic Affairs .... Dr. Gloria OIKELOME
103 Dean of Workforce Development .... Mr. Kyle LONGACRE
13 VP for Info Tech & Inst Effective .... Dr. Celeste M. SCHWARTZ
10 VP of Finance .... Mr. Charles SOMERS
102 Exec Director of Foundation .... Mr. Jay BROWNING
32 VP of Engage & Stdnt Experience .... Mr. Philip NEEDLES
06 Dir of Records & Registrar .... Ms. Sherry PHILLIPS
11 VP Admin Services .... Ms. Diane O'CONNOR
21 Controller .... Vacant
30 Dir of Dev/Major & Planned Gifts .... Ms. Traci CONNELLY GOIDAS
19 Director of Campus Safety .... Mr. Lee ALLAN
37 Director of Financial Aid .... Ms. Christal CHATMAN
09 Exec Dir of Inst Effectiveness .... Ms. Bridget HAINES-FRANK
28 Dir Equity/Diversity & Belonging .... Vacant
29 Dir of Career & Alumni Engagement .... Ms. Takisha MUNDY
26 Director of Strategic Communication .... Ms. Diane VANDYKE
08 Director of Libraries .... Ms. Robin BOWLES
18 Director of Facilities Mgmt .... Mr. Michael BILLETTA
88 Assoc Dir of Foundation Relations .... Mr. Donald SMITH
35 AVP of Student Services .... Mr. Matthew SWATCHICK
96 Director of Procurement .... Ms. Jenny RARIG
50 Dean of Business/Prof Studies .... Mr. Terence LYNN
86 Director Government Relations .... Mr. Michael BETTINGER
41 Dir Athletics & Campus Recreation .... Ms. Kelly DUNBAR
84 Exec Dir of Enrollment Svcs .... Ms. Natalie PALMER
100 Special Assistant to the President .... Dr. Jenna MEEHAN
07 Dir of Admissions/Recruitment .... Mr. Michael HARCUM
108 Dir Educational Effectiveness .... Ms. Tracy KAISER-GOEBEL
15 Director of Human Resources .... Ms. Shannon SCHMIDT
20 Assoc VP of Academic Affairs .... Dr. Lianne HARTMAN
25 Chief Contract and Grants Administr .... Vacant
12 VP Potts Campus/Educ Partnerships .... Ms. Therol J. DIX
38 Director Wellness Center .... Dr. Nichole KANG
54 Dean of STEM .... Dr. James BRETZ

Montgomery County Community College Pottstown Campus (B)

101 College Drive, Pottstown PA 19464
Telephone: (610) 718-1800 Identification: 770162
Accreditation: &M

Moore College of Art and Design (C)

1916 Race Street, Philadelphia PA 19103-1179
County: Philadelphia FICE Identification: 003300
Unit ID: 214148
Telephone: (215) 965-4000 Carnegie Class: Spec-4-yr-Arts
FAX Number: (215) 568-8017 Calendar System: Semester
URL: www.moore.edu
Established: 1848 Annual Undergrad Tuition & Fees: $44,806
Enrollment: 389 Female
Affiliation or Control: Independent Non-Profit IRS Status: 501(c)3
Highest Offering: Master's
Accreditation: M, CIDA

01 President .... Ms. Cecelia FITZGIBBON
10 SVP Finance & Administration .... Mr. William L. HILL, II
111 VP Institutional Advancement .... Ms. Elizabeth CAHILL
05 Academic Dean/CAO .... Ms. Lynn TOMASZEWSKI
32 Dean of Students .... Mr. Joshua WILKIN
09 Assoc Dean/Director Inst Research .... Ms. Claudine THOMAS
39 Director Residence Life/Housing .... Ms. Kimberley FOX
88 Director of Galleries .... Ms. Gabrielle LAVIN
51 Assoc Dean Cont Educ/Grad Studies .... Dr. Joanna JENKINS
26 Chief Mktg & Communications Ofcr .... Ms. Nicole STEINBERG
110 Assoc Director of Advancement .... Ms. Patricia MA
29 Assoc Dir Alumnae Affs/Annual Fund .... Ms. Laura KOCHMAN
08 Library Director .... Ms. Kimberly LESLEY
07 Dean of Admissions .... Mr. Jonathan SQUIRE
37 Director of Financial Aid .... Ms. Ashley SLOWE
06 Registrar .... Mr. Michael MCHUGH
15 Director Human Resources .... Ms. Rachel PHILLIPS
36 Director Career Center .... Ms. Belena CHAPP
90 Academic Computing Manager .... Mr. Dennis DAWTON
100 Chief of Staff .... Ms. Alysson CWYK

Moravian University (D)

1200 Main St., Bethlehem PA 18018-6650
County: Northampton FICE Identification: 003301
Unit ID: 214157
Telephone: (610) 861-1300 Carnegie Class: Masters/S
FAX Number: (610) 625-7918 Calendar System: Semester
URL: www.moravian.edu
Established: 1742 Annual Undergrad Tuition & Fees: $47,367
Enrollment: 2,605 Coed
Affiliation or Control: Moravian Church IRS Status: 501(c)3
Highest Offering: Doctorate
Accreditation: M, ACBSP, CAATE, MUS, NURSE, OT, @PTA, SP, THEOL

01 President .... Dr. Bryon L. GRIGSBY
05 Provost/Dean of Faculty .... Dr. Carol TRAUPMAN-CARR
10 VP Finance & Administration .... Mr. Mark F. REED
15 VP Human Resources .... Mr. Jon B. CONRAD
30 VP Development and Alumni .... Ms. Jill C. ANDERSON
32 Exec VP Student Affairs/COO .... Dr. Nicole L. LOYD
84 VP for Enrollment and Marketing .... Mr. Scott DAMS
13 VP and Chief Information Officer .... Mr. David BRANDES
100 Chief of Staff .... Mrs. Elaine C. DEITCH
121 Dean of Student Success .... Dr. Kevin HARTSHORN
76 Dean of Natural & Health Sci .... Dr. Diane HUSIC
79 Dean of Arts/Humanities/SS .... Dr. Daniel JASPER
73 VP and Dean of the Seminary .... Dr. Heather VACEK
35 Asst VP Student Affairs .... Ms. Amy SAUL
21 Director of Finance .... Mr. Wilson GONZALEZ
39 Assoc Dean of Students .... Ms. Liz YATES SEAMAN
113 Director of Student Accounts .... Ms. Dawn SNOOK
06 Institutional Registrar .... Ms. Monique DAVIS
88 Dir Business/Financial Operations .... Ms. Rachel LYALL
18 Dir Facilities Mgt Plng/Construct .... Ms. Yasmin BUGAIGHIS
19 Chief of Police .... Mr. V. Harrison DILLARD
26 Dir of Marketing & Communications .... Mr. Michael CORR
08 Library Director .... Ms. Janet OHLES
37 Director of Financial Aid .... Mrs. Naree SIMMONS
41 Director of Athletics .... Ms. Mary Beth SPIRK
42 Chaplain .... Rev. Jennika BORGER
88 Director of the Payne Gallery .... Dr. David LEIDICH
23 Nurse Coordinator .... Mrs. Stephanie C. DILLMAN
105 Webmaster .... Ms. Christie JACOBSEN
09 Adv to Pres for Data Analytics/IR .... Mrs. Grace SUN
28 VP and Dean for Equity & Inclusion .... Mr. Christopher HUNT
122 Assoc Director Greek Life .... Ms. Meghan SANTAMARIA
07 Director of Admissions .... Ms. Evelynne BLATT
101 Assistant Secretary to Board .... Mrs. Elaine DEITCH
104 Assoc Dean for Study Abroad .... Dr. Anize APPEL
110 Asst VP of Development .... Dr. Robert BRECKINRIDGE
29 Exec Dir Alumni & Family Engagement .... Mrs. Amanda MAENZA
38 Director of the Counseling Center ... Ms. Allison BLECHSCHMIDT
44 Director Annual & Affinity Giving .... Ms. Julie KULP

Mount Aloysius College (E)

7373 Admiral Peary Highway, Cresson PA 16630-1999
County: Cambria FICE Identification: 003302
Unit ID: 214166
Telephone: (814) 886-6383 Carnegie Class: Bac-Diverse
FAX Number: (814) 886-2978 Calendar System: Semester
URL: www.mtaloy.edu
Established: 1853 Annual Undergrad Tuition & Fees: $24,370
Enrollment: 2,806 Coed
Affiliation or Control: Independent Non-Profit IRS Status: 501(c)3
Highest Offering: Master's
Accreditation: M, ACBSP, ADNUR, DMS, NUR, PTAA, SURGT

01 President .... Mr. John N. MCKEEGAN
05 VP Academic Affairs .... Dr. David HASCHAK
32 VP Student Affairs .... Dr. Robin GORE
84 VP for Enrollment Management .... Mr. Jacob YALE
07 Dean of Admissions .... Mr. Andrew D. CLOUSE
111 VP Institutional Advancement .... Dr. John FARKAS
10 SVP Administration & Strategy/CFO .... Mr. Michael BAKER
06 Registrar .... Vacant
08 Director of Library .... Vacant
37 Director of Financial Aid .... Ms. Stacy L. SCHENK
15 VP People & Mission/CHRO .... Ms. Tonia J. GORDON
26 VP Marketing & Comm .... Mr. Sam WAGNER
13 Director of Information Technology .... Mr. Rich J. SHEA
23 Director of Health Services .... Ms. Shannon D. GROVE
40 Bookstore Manager .... Ms. Christine M. CLINTON
41 Director of Athletics .... Mr. Kevin KIME
19 Chief of Police .... Mr. Troy WRIGHT
18 Director of Physical Plant .... Mr. Gerald RUBRITZ
09 Institutional Researcher .... Mr. Bryan J. PEARSON
121 Dir Student Success & Persistence . Ms. Kimberly WASHINGTON
38 Dir Student Counseling/Disabilities .... Vacant
39 Director of Residence Life .... Vacant
42 Director Campus Ministry .... Ms. Amy KANICH
44 Manager of Annual Giving .... Ms. Sally GORDON
04 Administrative Asst to President .... Ms. Carla NELEN

Muhlenberg College (F)

2400 West Chew Street, Allentown PA 18104-5586
County: Lehigh FICE Identification: 003304
Unit ID: 214175
Telephone: (484) 664-3100 Carnegie Class: Bac-A&S
FAX Number: (484) 664-3234 Calendar System: Semester
URL: www.muhlenberg.edu
Established: 1848 Annual Undergrad Tuition & Fees: $54,600
Enrollment: 2,067 Coed
Affiliation or Control: Evangelical Lutheran Church In America
IRS Status: 501(c)3
Highest Offering: Master's
Accreditation: M

01 President .... Dr. Kathleen HARRING
05 Provost .... Dr. Laura FURGE
10 Treasurer & Chief Finance Officer .... Mr. Kent DYER
26 Vice President Communications .... Vacant
111 Vice President of Advancement .... Ms. Rebekkah L. BROWN
15 Vice President for Human Resources .... Dr. Jill WALSH
32 Vice President of Student Affairs .... Ms. Allison WILLIAMS
58 VP/Exec Dir Grad Continuing Educ .... Dr. A.J LEMHENEY
04 Exec Asst to the President & BoT .... Ms. Sonya CONRAD
30 Senior Assoc VP for Development .... Mr. Mike GARDNER
20 Dean of Academic Life .... Dr. Michele DEEGAN
104 Dean of Global Education .... Vacant
37 Assoc Dean Admission/Dir Finan Aid .... Mr. Gregory S. MITTON
22 Asst Dean Acad Res/Disability Svcs .... Mr. David HALLOWELL
29 Asst VP Alumni Affairs/Career Svc .... Ms. Natalie HAND
51 Dean Continuing Studies/CGE .... Dr. Michael MILLER
84 VP of Enrollment Management .... Ms. Megan RYAN
08 Director of Trexler Library .... Ms. Tina L. HERTEL
06 Registrar .... Ms. Ginger YAVORSKI
13 Chief Information Officer .... Mr. Jose DIEUDONNE
19 Dir/Chief of Campus Safety/Security .... Mr. Brian FIDATI
124 Assoc Dean Stdnts/Dir Stdnt Engage .... Ms. Ellen LENTINE
36 Executive Director Career Svcs .... Mr. Sean SCHOFIELD
114 Chief Budget/Accting Ofcr .... Ms. Eleanor LEWIS
23 Exec Dir Health/Counseling Svcs .... Ms. Brynnmarie DORSEY
38 Director Counseling Services .... Dr. Timothy SILVESTRI
42 Chaplain .... Rev. Janelle NEUBAUER
09 Dir Institutional Research/Records .... Vacant
18 Director Plant Operations .... Mr. James BOLTON
96 Director of Business Svcs .... Mr. Brian BLENIS
40 Bookstore Manager .... Ms. Karen R. NORMANN
122 Asst Dir Stdnt Orgs-Greek Life .... Ms. Ellen LENTINE

Neumann University (G)

One Neumann Drive, Aston PA 19014-1298
County: Delaware FICE Identification: 003988
Unit ID: 214272
Telephone: (610) 459-0905 Carnegie Class: Masters/M
FAX Number: (610) 459-1370 Calendar System: Semester
URL: www.neumann.edu
Established: 1965 Annual Undergrad Tuition & Fees: $32,960
Enrollment: 2,506 Coed
Affiliation or Control: Roman Catholic IRS Status: 501(c)3
Highest Offering: Doctorate
Accreditation: M, ACBSP, CAATE, CACREP, MLS, NUR, PTA, SW

01 President .... Dr. Chris E. DOMES
05 Vice President Academic Affairs .... Dr. Lawrence DIPAOLO
100 Chief of Staff .... Mr. Brad BAKER
32 Vice Pres Student Affairs .... Dr. Christopher HAUG
10 Vice Pres Finance/Administration .... Mr. Gene MCWILLIAMS
88 Vice President Mission/Ministry .... Sr. Kathy DOUGHERTY, OSF
111 Vice Pres University Advancement .... Ms. Carrie SNYDER
84 VP of Enrollment Mgmt & Marketing .... Ms. Francesca REED
15 Vice President HR & Risk Management .... Mr. David W. BROWNLEE
13 CIO & Assoc VP of IR and Planning .. Dr. Richard H. HARTWELL
49 Dean School of Arts & Science .... Dr. Alfred G. MUELLER, II
50 Dean School of Business .... Dr. Eric R. WELLINGTON
53 Dean School of Educ/Human Svcs .... Dr. Amy HOYLE
66 Dean School Nursing/Health Sciences .... Dr. Kathleen HOOVER
35 Dean of Students .... Ms. Stephanie JONES
04 Assistant to President .... Ms. Connie GALLAGHER
06 Registrar .... Mr. Joel A. NATALE
18 Facilities Director .... Mr. William J. LEONARD
19 Director Safety & Security .... Mr. Leon J. FRANCIS
08 Director Library .... Ms. Tiffany MCGREGOR
26 Director Media Relations .... Mr. Stephen T. BELL
42 Chaplain .... Rev. Akolla ETUGE, OFM CAP
51 Exec Dir of Adult Continuing Educ .... Dr. Jilian DONNELLY
29 Asst VP Alumni & Community Outreach .... Ms. Judi STANAITIS
38 Director Counseling .... Vacant

39 Director Housing & Residence Life .... Ms. Alexandria L. THOMAS
112 Dir Major Gifts & Planned Giving .... Mr. Fran WALMSLEY
44 Director Donor Impact .... Ms. Brandi BURGESS
41 Director Athletics .... Mr. Chuck SACK
36 Dir Career & Personal Development .... Ms. Preeti SINGH
121 Dean Academic Support Services .... Mr. Michael MULLEN
88 Director Child Development Center .... Mr. John SPERDUTO
21 Controller .... Mr. John YOUHOUSE
37 Director Financial Assistance .... Ms. Eileen TUCKER
23 Director Health Services .... Ms. Faith CELLA
07 Dir of Undergraduate Admissions .... Mr. Edward WRIGHT
31 Coordinator of Cultural Programming ..... Mr. Nicholas DIMARINO
88 Director Conference/Scheduling Svcs .... Ms. Jess WEBSTER
40 Director University Bookstore .... Ms. Natalie VAN WYK
88 Director Developmental Education .... Ms. Lori BLOUNT
124 Dir Student Engagement & Ldrshp .... Mr. Matt FULLMER
105 Director Web Services .... Ms. Rachel SPINA

New Castle School of Trades (A)

4117 Pulaski Road, New Castle PA 16101

County: Lawrence FICE Identification: 007780
Unit ID: 214290
Telephone: (724) 964-8811 Carnegie Class: Assoc/HVT-High Trad
FAX Number: (724) 202-6147 Calendar System: Other
URL: www.ncstrades.edu
Established: 1945 Annual Undergrad Tuition & Fees: N/A
Enrollment: 606 Coed
Affiliation or Control: Proprietary IRS Status: Proprietary
Highest Offering: Associate Degree
Accreditation: ACCSC

01 President .... Mr. Rex SPALDING
05 Director of Education .... Mr. Tony GIOVANNELLI
07 Director of Admissions .... Mr. John MEISSNER
88 Veteran Affairs Director .... Mr. Jim CATHELINE
10 Fiscal Director .... Mrs. Donna DAVIS
36 Director Student Placement .... Mrs. Carrie KRAYNAK
37 Director Student Financial Aid .... Mrs. Trudy SOTTER

Northampton Community College (B)

3835 Green Pond Road, Bethlehem PA 18020-7599

County: Northampton FICE Identification: 007191
Unit ID: 214379
Telephone: (610) 861-5300 Carnegie Class: Assoc/MT-VT-High Trad
FAX Number: (610) 861-5070 Calendar System: Semester
URL: www.northampton.edu
Established: 1967 Annual Undergrad Tuition & Fees (In-District): $10,080
Enrollment: 8,951 Coed
Affiliation or Control: State/Local IRS Status: 170(c)1
Highest Offering: Associate Degree
Accreditation: M, ACBSP, ACPHA, ADNUR, DH, DMS, FUSER, NAEYC, PNUR, RAD

01 President .... Dr. Dave A. RUTH
05 Interim VP Academic Affairs .... Dr. Karen BEARCE
10 Vice President Finance & Operations .... Mr. James F. DUNLEAVY
111 Vice Pres Institutional Advancement .... Ms. Sharon BEALES
32 Vice Pres Enroll/Student Affairs .... Mr. Sedwick HARRIS
31 Vice President Community Education .... Ms. Lauren LOEFFLER
12 Dean Monroe Campus .... Vacant
79 Dean Humanities & Social Sciences .... Dr. Christine PENSE
53 Dean Education/Academic Success .... Dr. Elizabeth BUGAIGHIS
50 Dean Business & Technology .... Dr. Denise FRANCOIS-SEENY
76 Dean Allied Health & Sciences .... Dr. Judith REX
13 Assoc VP/Chief Information Officer .... Mr. Brian GARDNER
26 Exec Dir Marketing & Communications .... Mr. Brad DREXLER
06 Registrar .... Ms. Mary SINIBALDI MANCINO
84 Asst VP Enrollment Mgmt/Retention .... Mr. Robert MCGANN
37 Director Financial Aid .... Ms. Sarah FEVIG
108 Dir of Institutional Effectiveness .... Ms. Dorothy SCHRAMM
15 Exec Dir Human Resources/Title IX .... Ms. Karen ANGENY
09 Director of Institutional Research .... Mr. Marco ANGLESIO
18 Director Buildings & Grounds .... Mr. William SMITH
29 Dir Alumni Engagement/Annual Fund .... Ms. Karen GLOSE
36 Director Career Services .... Ms. Karen VERES
35 Dean of Students .... Mr. Eric ROSENTHAL
07 Senior Assoc Dir of Enrollment Svcs .... Ms. Mary S. MANCINO
28 VP Diversity/Equity/Inclusion .... Dr. Robert ROBINSON
19 Director Security/Safety .... Mr. Keith MORRIS

Northampton Community College Monroe Campus (C)

2411 Route 715, Tannersville PA 18372

Telephone: (570) 369-1800 Identification: 770164
Accreditation: &M

Peirce College (D)

1420 Pine Street, Philadelphia PA 19102-4699

County: Philadelphia FICE Identification: 003309
Unit ID: 214883
Telephone: (215) 545-6400 Carnegie Class: Bac-Diverse
FAX Number: (215) 670-9366 Calendar System: Semester
URL: www.peirce.edu
Established: 1865 Annual Undergrad Tuition & Fees: $15,060
Enrollment: 1,046 Coed
Affiliation or Control: Independent Non-Profit IRS Status: 501(c)3
Highest Offering: Master's
Accreditation: M, ACBSP, CAHIIM

01 President & CEO .... Dr. Mary Ellen CARO
10 VP Finance/Administration .... Ms. Elizabeth M. KRAPP
05 VP Academic Affairs/Provost .... Dr. Rita J. TOLIVER-ROBERTS
103 VP Workforce Dev & Career Partnrshp ...... Mr. Hassan CHARLES
26 VP Integrated Marketing/Comm .... Mr. Joseph GUZZARDO
84 VP Enrollment Mgmt/Student Services .... Mr. Brad K. HODGE
15 VP Human Res/Chief Diversity Ofcr .... Ms. Carrie ROBINSON
108 Asst VP Institutional Assessment .... Ms. Debra S. SCHRAMMEL
13 Chief Information Officer .... Mr. James T. BURNS
08 Chief Library Officer .... Ms. Kristin INCIARDI
109 Chief Auxiliary Services Officer .... Mr. Vito R. CHIMENTI
04 Director Office of the President .... Ms. Tara E. MCBRIDE
06 Registrar/Dean Academic Advising .... Dr. Shannon BEGLEY
07 Director of Admissions .... Vacant
37 Director Student Financial Aid .... Ms. Ruthann WYATT
86 Director Government Relations .... Ms. Amanda HILL

Penn Commercial Business/ Technical School (E)

242 Oak Spring Road, Washington PA 15301-6822

County: Washington FICE Identification: 004902
Unit ID: 214892
Telephone: (724) 222-5330 Carnegie Class: Assoc/HVT-High Non
FAX Number: (724) 222-4722 Calendar System: Quarter
URL: www.penncommercial.edu
Established: 1929 Annual Undergrad Tuition & Fees: $17,313
Enrollment: 238 Coed
Affiliation or Control: Proprietary IRS Status: Proprietary
Highest Offering: Associate Degree
Accreditation: ACCSC

01 President/Owner .... Mr. Robert S. BAZANT
11 Vice President of Operations .... Ms. Marianne ALBERT
04 Assistant to the President .... Vacant
07 Asst Director of Admissions .... Mr. Michael BERRY
32 Director of Student Services .... Ms. Kristine GORBY
37 Director of Financial Aid .... Ms. Jayme TUITE
05 Director of Education .... Ms. Anita ROSSELL
09 Director of Reports & Statistics .... Mrs. Melissa PAPSON
36 Director of Career Services .... Mr. Jeff MANUKIN

Penn State University Park (F)

201 Old Main, University Park PA 16802-1503

County: Centre FICE Identification: 003329
Unit ID: 214777
Telephone: (814) 865-4700 Carnegie Class: Not Classified
FAX Number: (814) 863-7590 Calendar System: Semester
URL: www.psu.edu
Established: 1855 Annual Undergrad Tuition & Fees (In-State): N/A
Enrollment: N/A Coed
Affiliation or Control: State Related IRS Status: 501(c)3
Highest Offering: Doctorate
Accreditation: M, ART, CAATE, CACREP, CAEP, CAEPN, CEA, CLPSY, DIET, DIETD, FEPAC, HSA, IPSY, JOUR, LAW, LSAR, MUS, NURSE, PCSAS, SCPSY, SP, THEA

01 President .... Dr. Neeli BENDAPUDI
05 Executive Vice President & Provost .... Dr. Nicholas P. JONES
100 SVP/Chief of Staff .... Mr. Michael WADE SMITH
46 Vice President for Research .... Dr. Lora G. WEISS
32 Vice President for Student Affairs .... Dr. Damon R. SIMS
26 Vice Pres Strategic Communications .... Mr. Lawrence H. LOKMAN
30 Vice Pres Devel/Alumni Relations .... Mr. O. Richard BUNDY, III
10 Sr Vice Pres Finance & Bus/Treas .... Dr. Sara F. THORNDIKE
106 Vice President for Outreach .... Ms. Tracey D. HUSTON
11 Vice President for Administration .... Mr. Frank GUADAGNINO
104 Vice Provost for Global Programs .... Dr. Roger N. BRINDLEY
43 Vice President & General Counsel .... Dr. Stephen S. DUNHAM
49 Vice Pres & Dean Undergrad Educ .... Dr. Yvonne GAUDELIUS
20 Vice Provost Faculty Affairs .... Dr. Kathleen BIESCHKE
28 Vice Provost Educational Equity ...... Dr. Marcus A. WHITEHURST
12 Vice Pres Commonwealth Campuses .... Dr. Madlyn L. HANES
13 Vice Pres Info Tech/CIO .... Mr. Donald J. WELCH
45 Vice Provost Plng/Assessment/ IR .... Dr. Lance C. KENNEDY-PHILLIPS
09 Asst VP Institutional Research .... Dr. Karen VANCE
108 Director of Assessment .... Dr. Geoff MAMEROW
45 Asst VP for Strategic Planning .... Dr. Daniel NEWHART
22 Assoc Vice Pres Affirmative Action .... Dr. Suzanne C. ADAIR
114 University Budget Officer .... Ms. Mary Lou D. ORTIZ
21 Assoc Vice Pres Finance/Corp Cont ..... Mr. Joseph J. DONCSECZ
21 Assoc Vice Pres Finance & Business .... Vacant
15 Vice Pres Human Resources .... Ms. Lorraine GOFFE
18 Assoc Vice President Physical Plant .... Mr. William E. SITZABEE, JR.
109 Assoc VP Auxiliary & Business Svcs ...... Mr. John PAPAZOGLOU
106 Vice Prov Online Education .... Dr. Renata S. ENGEL
27 Director News/Media Relations .... Ms. Lisa M. POWERS
39 Asst VP for Housing & Food Svcs .... Ms. Cheryl FABRIZI
37 Asst VP UG Ed/Exec Dir Stdnt Aid .... Ms. Melissa J. KUNES
29 AVP Alumni Rels/CEO PS Alum Assoc .... Mr. Paul J. CLIFFORD
115 Exec Director Office of Investment .... Mr. Joseph M. CULLEN
07 Asst VP UG Admissions .... Mr. Rob SPRINGALL
38 Director Counseling/Psych Services .... Dr. Benjamin D. LOCKE
41 Athletic Director .... Ms. A. Sandy BARBOUR
86 Vice Pres for Govt & Cmty Rels .... Mr. Zachery MOORE
06 University Registrar .... Mr. Robert A. KUBAT
36 Senior Director Career Services .... Dr. Robert M. ORNDORFF
17 CEO Penn State Health .... Mr. Stephen M. MASSINI
08 Dean Univ Libraries/Scholar Comm .... Ms. Faye A. CHADWELL
47 Dean Agricultural Sciences .... Dr. Richard T. ROUSH
48 Dean Arts & Architecture .... Dr. B. Stephen CARPENTER
50 Dean Business .... Dr. Charles H. WHITEMAN
60 Dean Communications .... Dr. Marie HARDIN
65 Dean Earth & Mineral Sciences .... Dr. Lee KUMP
53 Dean Education .... Dr. Kimberly LAWLESS
54 Dean Engineering .... Dr. Justin SCHWARTZ
58 V Prov Grad Educ/Dean Grad School .... Dr. Regina VASILATOS-YOUNKEN
76 Dean Health & Human Dev .... Dr. Craig J. NEWSCHAFFER
66 Dean School of Nursing .... Ms. Laurie A. BADZEK
56 Assoc Dean/Dir Coop Extension .... Dr. Brent HALES
81 Dean Science .... Dr. Tracy LANGKILDE
72 Dean Info Sciences and Technology .... Dr. Andrew L. SEARS
92 Dean Honors College .... Dr. Peggy A. JOHNSON
61 Dean Penn State Law .... Dr. Hari M. OSOFSKY
63 Dean College of Medicine .... Dr. Kevin BLACK
75 Chief Penn College of Technology .... Dr. Davie J. GILMOUR
88 Assoc Vice President for Research .... Dr. John W. HANOLD
19 Chief Op Univ Police/Public Safety .... Mr. Joseph MILEK
23 Director University Health Services .... Dr. Robin E. OLIVER-VERONESI
96 Director Procurement Services .... Mr. R. Duane ELMORE
04 Exec Admin Assistant to President .... Ms. Carmella MULROY-DEGENHART
116 Director of Internal Audit .... Mr. Daniel P. HEIST
119 Chief Information Security Officer .... Mr. Donald J. WELCH, JR.
101 Secretary of the Institution/Board .... Ms. Shannon S. HARVEY

† The legal name of Penn State and all its campuses is The Pennsylvania State University. For communication purposes, the name is shortened to Penn State followed by the name of the campus.

Penn State Abington (G)

1600 Woodland Road, Abington PA 19001-3918

Telephone: (215) 881-7300 FICE Identification: 003342
Accreditation: &M, ART

† Regional accreditation is carried under the parent institution in University Park, PA.

Penn State Altoona (H)

3000 Ivyside Park, Altoona PA 16601-3777

Telephone: (814) 949-5000 FICE Identification: 003331
Accreditation: &M

† Regional accreditation is carried under the parent institution in University Park, PA.

Penn State Beaver (I)

100 University Drive, Monaca PA 15061-2764

Telephone: (724) 773-3800 FICE Identification: 003332
Accreditation: &M

† Regional accreditation is carried under the parent institution in University Park, PA.

Penn State Berks (J)

Tulpehocken Road, PO Box 7009,
Reading PA 19610-1016

Telephone: (610) 396-6000 FICE Identification: 003334
Accreditation: &M, OTA

† Regional accreditation is carried under the parent institution in University Park, PA.

Penn State Brandywine (K)

25 Yearsley Mill Road, Media PA 19063-5522

Telephone: (610) 892-1200 FICE Identification: 006922
Accreditation: &M

† Regional accreditation is carried under the parent institution in University Park, PA.

Penn State Dickinson Law (L)

150 South College Street, Carlisle PA 17013-2861

Telephone: (717) 240-5000 FICE Identification: 003254
Accreditation: &M, LAW

† Part of Penn State University. Regional accreditation is carried under the parent institution in University Park, PA.

Penn State DuBois (M)

One College Place, DuBois PA 15801-2549

Telephone: (814) 375-4700 FICE Identification: 003335
Accreditation: &M, OTA, #PTAA

† Regional accreditation is carried under the parent institution in University Park, PA.

Penn State Erie, The Behrend College (N)

4701 College Drive, Erie PA 16563-0001

Telephone: (814) 898-6000 FICE Identification: 003333
Accreditation: &M

† Regional accreditation is carried under the parent institution in University Park, PA.

Penn State Fayette, The Eberly Campus (A)
2201 University Drive, Lemont Furnace PA 15456-1025
Telephone: (724) 430-4100   FICE Identification: 003336
Accreditation: &M, EMT, PTAA

† Regional accreditation is carried under the parent institution in University Park, PA.

Penn State Great Valley School of Graduate (B) Professional Studies
30 E Swedesford Road, Malvern PA 19355-1488
Telephone: (610) 648-3200   FICE Identification: 003348
Accreditation: &M

† Regional accreditation is carried under the parent institution in University Park, PA.

Penn State Greater Allegheny (C)
4000 University Drive, McKeesport PA 15132-7644
Telephone: (412) 675-9000   FICE Identification: 003339
Accreditation: &M

† Regional accreditation is carried under the parent institution in University Park, PA.

Penn State Harrisburg (D)
777 West Harrisburg Pike, Middletown PA 17057-4846
Telephone: (717) 948-6250   FICE Identification: 006814
Accreditation: &M, SPAA

† Regional accreditation is carried under the parent institution in University Park, PA.

Penn State Hazleton (E)
76 University Drive, Hazleton PA 18202-8025
Telephone: (570) 450-3000   FICE Identification: 003338
Accreditation: &M, MLTAD, PTAA

† Regional accreditation is carried under the parent institution in University Park, PA.

Penn State Lehigh Valley (F)
2809 Saucon Valley Road, Center Valley PA 18034-8447
Telephone: (610) 285-5000   FICE Identification: 003330
Accreditation: &M

† Regional accreditation is carried under the parent institution in University Park, PA.

Penn State Milton S. Hershey Medical (G) Center College of Medicine
500 University Drive, Hershey PA 17033-2360
Telephone: (717) 531-8563   FICE Identification: 006813
Accreditation: &M, ARCPA, IPSY, MED, MLS, PAST, PH

† Regional accreditation is carried under the parent institution in University Park, PA.

Penn State Mont Alto (H)
One Campus Drive, Mont Alto PA 17237-9700
Telephone: (717) 749-6000   FICE Identification: 003340
Accreditation: &M, OTA, PTAA

† Regional accreditation is carried under the parent institution in University Park, PA.

Penn State New Kensington (I)
3550 Seventh Street Road, Route 780,
New Kensington PA 15068-1765
Telephone: (724) 334-5466   FICE Identification: 003341
Accreditation: &M, RAD

† Regional accreditation is carried under the parent institution in University Park, PA.

Penn State Schuylkill (J)
200 University Drive, Schuylkill Haven PA 17972-2202
Telephone: (570) 385-6000   FICE Identification: 003343
Accreditation: &M, RAD

† Regional accreditation is carried under the parent institution in University Park, PA.

Penn State Scranton (K)
120 Ridge View Drive, Dunmore PA 18512-1602
Telephone: (570) 963-2500   FICE Identification: 003344
Accreditation: &M

† Regional accreditation is carried under the parent institution in University Park, PA.

Penn State Shenango (L)
147 Shenango Avenue, Sharon PA 16146-1537
Telephone: (724) 983-2803   FICE Identification: 003345
Accreditation: &M, OTA, PTAA

† Regional accreditation is carried under the parent institution in University Park, PA.

Penn State Wilkes-Barre (M)
44 University Drive, Dallas PA 18612
Telephone: (570) 675-2171   FICE Identification: 003346
Accreditation: &M

† Regional accreditation is carried under the parent institution in University Park, PA.

Penn State York (N)
1031 Edgecomb Avenue, York PA 17403-3326
Telephone: (717) 771-4000   FICE Identification: 003347
Accreditation: &M

† Regional accreditation is carried under the parent institution in University Park, PA.

Pennco Tech (O)
3815 Otter Street, Bristol PA 19007-3696
County: Bucks   FICE Identification: 009449
   Unit ID: 214944
Telephone: (215) 785-0111   Carnegie Class: Spec 2-yr-Tech
FAX Number: (215) 785-1945   Calendar System: Other
URL: www.penncotech.edu
Established: 1973   Annual Undergrad Tuition & Fees: N/A
Enrollment: 511   Coed
Affiliation or Control: Proprietary   IRS Status: Proprietary
Highest Offering: Associate Degree
Accreditation: ACCSC

01	CEO	Michael S. HOBYAK
05	Director of Education/School Dir	Fred PARCELLS
07	Director of Admissions	Karl MANCUSO
06	Supervisor of Registrars	Sondra KOOB
32	Director Student Services	sean COSTELLO
37	Director Student Financial Aid	Debbie KEILFRIDER
36	Director Career Services	Teresa SCHEERER

Pennsylvania Academy of the Fine (P) Arts
128 N Broad Street, Philadelphia PA 19102-1424
County: Philadelphia   FICE Identification: 021073
   Unit ID: 214971
Telephone: (215) 972-7600   Carnegie Class: Spec-4-yr-Arts
FAX Number: (215) 569-0153   Calendar System: Semester
URL: www.pafa.edu
Established: 1805   Annual Undergrad Tuition & Fees: $40,376
Enrollment: 188   Coed
Affiliation or Control: Independent Non-Profit   IRS Status: 501(c)3
Highest Offering: Master's
Accreditation: M, ART

01	Interim President & CEO	Ms. Elizabeth B. WARSHAWER
10	Chief Financial Officer	Ms. Maryanne MURPHY
84	SVP Enrollment Mgmt	Mr. Ryan BURTON-ROMERO
15	SVP Human Res/Int Chief of Staff	Ms. Lisa BIAGAS
05	Exec Dean School of Fine Arts	Mr. Clint A. JUKKALA
32	Dean of Students	Mr. Ryan BURTON-ROMERO
35	Director of Student Services	Ms. Morgan HOBBS
37	Director of Financial Aid	Ms. Celeste FRANKLIN
36	Director of Career Services	Mr. Gregory MARTINO
08	Director of Library Services	Mr. Brian DUFFY
06	Registrar	Mr. Peter MEDWICK
18	Director of Facilities Management	Mr. Ed POLETTI
19	Director of Security and Safety	Mr. Jimmie GREENO
13	Director of Information Technology	Mr. Kevin MARTIN
04	Exec Assistant to President and CEO	Ms. Sheryl KESSLER
58	Director of Grad Program Services	Mr. Steven CONNELL
20	Academic Services Coordinator	Mr. C.J STAHL
38	Student Care Coordinator	Ms. Juliana FOMENKO
88	Executive Assistant to the Dean	Ms. Katharine S. PEPPLE

Pennsylvania College of Art & (Q) Design
204 N Prince Street, Box 59, Lancaster PA 17608-0059
County: Lancaster   FICE Identification: 022699
   Unit ID: 215053
Telephone: (717) 396-7833   Carnegie Class: Spec-4-yr-Arts
FAX Number: (717) 396-1339   Calendar System: Semester
URL: www.pcad.edu
Established: 1982   Annual Undergrad Tuition & Fees: $27,650
Enrollment: 242   Coed
Affiliation or Control: Independent Non-Profit   IRS Status: 501(c)3
Highest Offering: Master's
Accreditation: M, ART

01	President	Mr. Michael MOLLA
05	Provost	Ms. Carissa MASSEY

10	VP of Finance and Administration	Ms. Elizabeth P. BENNETT
32	Dean of Students	Ms. Jessica EDONICK
28	Dean Diversity/Equity & Inclusion	Ms. Debbie BAZARSKY
28	Dir Development/Strat Initiatives	Mr. Todd SNOVEL
26	Director Strategic Communications	Ms. Daina SAVAGE
07	Director of Enrollment/Admissions	Ms. Jenn RENKO
35	Director Student Life	Mr. Jeff BINGEMAN
18	Director of Facilities	Mr. Dan FREILER
113	Bursar	Ms. Lisa GOOD
04	Exec Asst to the President	Ms. Amy GASTON
37	Director of Financial Aid	Mr. J. David HERSHEY
51	Director of Continuing Education	Ms. Natalie LASCEK
13	Director of IT	Mr. Alex LEONHART
88	Dir Institute Entrepreneurship	Vacant
06	Registrar	Mr. Christopher WAGENHEIM
08	Dir Ctr for Teaching/Learning	Ms. Mariah POSTLEWAIT
90	Director Academic Computing	Mr. Hylon PLUMB
15	Human Resources Manager	Ms. Michele WHERLEY

Pennsylvania College of Health (R) Sciences
850 Greenfield Road, Lancaster PA 17601
County: Lancaster   FICE Identification: 009863
   Unit ID: 442356
Telephone: (800) 622-5443   Carnegie Class: Spec-4-yr-Other Health
FAX Number: (717) 947-6250   Calendar System: Semester
URL: www.pacollege.edu
Established: 1903   Annual Undergrad Tuition & Fees: $29,922
Enrollment: 2,011   Coed
Affiliation or Control: Independent Non-Profit   IRS Status: 501(c)3
Highest Offering: Doctorate
Accreditation: M, ADNUR, COARC, CVT, DMS, MLS, NMT, NURSE, RAD, SURGT

01	President	Dr. Mary Grace SIMCOX
05	VP Academic Affairs	Dr. Jean HERSHEY
108	VP Institutional Effectiveness	Dr. Penni LONGENECKER
10	VP Finance & Administration	Mr. Thomas HULSTINE
111	VP Advancement	Ms. Ellen WILEY
15	VP Human Resources	Vacant
13	Chief Information Officer	Mr. Kevin BALSBAUGH
84	VP Enrollment Management	Dr. Erika WILKINSON
04	Administrative Asst to President	Ms. Susan GARDINA
06	Registrar	Mr. Edwin ADDIS
109	Director of Campus & Auxiliary Svcs	Mr. Kyle MOORE
07	Director of Admissions	Mr. William RHINIER

Pennsylvania College of (S) Technology
One College Avenue, Williamsport PA 17701-5799
County: Lycoming   FICE Identification: 003395
   Unit ID: 366252
Telephone: (570) 326-3761   Carnegie Class: Bac/Assoc-Mixed
FAX Number: (570) 327-4503   Calendar System: Semester
URL: www.pct.edu
Established: 1989   Annual Undergrad Tuition & Fees (In-State): $17,610
Enrollment: 4,565   Coed
Affiliation or Control: State   IRS Status: 501(c)3
Highest Offering: Master's
Accreditation: M, ACBSP, ACFEI, ADNUR, ARCPA, CAHIIM, CONST, DH, EMT, NAIT, NUR, PNUR, PTAA, RAD, SURGT

01	President	Dr. Michael J. REED
05	VP for Academic Affairs/Provost	Dr. Nesli ALP
10	Senior VP for Finance/CFO	Ms. Suzanne T. STOPPER
111	Vice Pres Institutional Advancement	Ms. Loni N. KLINE
84	VP Enrollment Mgmt & Assoc Provost	Dr. Carolyn R. STRICKLAND
32	VP for Student Affairs	Mr. Elliott STRICKLAND, JR.
103	VP for Workforce Development	Ms. Shannon M. MUNRO
15	VP for Human Resources	Ms. Hillary E. HOFSTROM
20	Dean of Curriculum & Instruction	Ms. Joanna K. FLYNN
88	Dean of Academic Operations	Mr. Anthony J. PACE
04	Administrative Asst to President	Mrs. Valerie A. BAIER
66	Dean of Nursing & Health Sciences	Dr. Valerie MYERS
54	Dean of Engineering Technologies	Dr. Bradley M. WEBB
50	Dean of Business/Arts & Sciences	Dr. Sue A. KELLEY
102	Exec Dir of Penn College Foundation	Mr. Kyle A. SMITH
109	Dir Gen General Services	Mr. Timothy O. RISSEL
88	Director of Construction & Planning	Mr. Jason K. BOGLE
18	Director of Facilities Operations	Mr. Don J. LUKE
08	Director of the Madigan Library	Ms. Tracey AMEY
14	Dir of Educational Technologies	Mr. Walter J. SHULTZ, JR.
09	Exec Dir Assessment/Research/Plng	Dr. Brian L. CYGAN
06	Registrar	Ms. Maria N. PISELLI
35	Associate Dean of Student Affairs	Dr. Jennifer MCLEAN
39	Dir Residence Life/Student Conduct	Mr. Jon D. WESCOTT
19	Chief of Police	Mr. Chris E. MILLER
26	Assoc VP Public Rels & Marketing	Mr. Joseph S. YODER
29	Director Alumni Relations	Ms. Kimberly R. CASSEL
102	Director of Corporate Relations	Ms. Elizabeth A. BIDDLE
88	Director Children Learning Center	Ms. Linda A. REICHERT
41	Director of Athletics	Mr. Scott KENNELL
124	Director of Student Engagement	Ms. Allison A. GROVE
22	Director of Disability Services	Ms. Dawn M. DICKEY
96	Director/Procurement Services	Ms. Karen P. FESSLER
07	Director of Admissions	Ms. Audriana L. EMPET
89	Director of College Transitions	Ms. Tanya BERFIELD
38	Director of Counseling	Dr. Kathy W. ZAKARIAN

100 Chief of Staff .... Mr. Patrick MARTY
30 Director of Development .... Ms. Heather M. SHUEY
124 Dean Col Transitions/Stdnt Success .... Mr. Randy ZANGARA
37 Director Student Financial Aid .... Ms. Jessica S. HUNTER
90 Director Academic Computing .... Mr. Brad MILLER
13 Chief Information Technology Ofcr .... Mr. Jeff BROWN
28 Director of Diversity .... Dr. Nate WOODS, JR.

† Affiliate of Pennsylvania State University.

Pennsylvania Highlands Community College (A)

101 Community College Way, Johnstown PA 15904-2949
County: Cambria FICE Identification: 031804
Unit ID: 414911
Telephone: (814) 262-6400 Carnegie Class: Assoc/MT-VT-High Non
FAX Number: (814) 269-9700 Calendar System: Semester
URL: www.pennhighlands.edu
Established: 1994 Annual Undergrad Tuition & Fees (In-District): $8,640
Enrollment: 2,456 Coed
Affiliation or Control: State/Local IRS Status: 501(c)3
Highest Offering: Associate Degree
Accreditation: M, MAC

01 President .... Dr. Steve NUNEZ
32 VP of Student Services .... Trish CORLE
10 VP of Finance/Administration .... Lorraine DONAHUE
05 VP of Academic Affairs .... Robert FARINELLI
15 Assistant VP of Human Resources .... Susan FISHER
09 Asst VP of Inst Effectiveness .... Gary BOAST
13 Chief Information Officer .... Matthew HOFFMAN
12 Regional Center Director .... Robert SEKERAK
12 Director Blair Center .... Chris FARRELL
12 Director Huntingdon Center .... Marissa DAVIS
12 Director Somerset Center .... Landon LOYA
08 Dean Library Svcs/Special Projects .... Dr. Barbara ZABOROWSKI
06 Dean Enrollment Services/Registrar .... Michelle STUMPF
20 Dean of Faculty .... Erica REIGHARD
111 Exec Dir of Inst Advancement .... Kathleen MORRELL
18 Director of Facilities Operation .... Reb BROWNLEE
07 Director Admissions and Recruiting .... Matthew BODENSCHATZ
21 Director of Finance/Administration .... Christopher PRIBULSKY
37 Director of Student Financial Svcs .... Ashley KRINJECK
26 Director of Marketing/Communication .... Raymond WEIBLE, JR.
19 Director of Security and Safety .... Cregg DIBERT
35 Dir of Student Activities/Athletics .... Suzanne BRUGH
121 Director of Student Success Center .... Mindy NITCH
04 Assistant to the President .... Nicole ROBSON

Pennsylvania Institute of Technology (B)

800 Manchester Avenue, Media PA 19063-4098
County: Delaware FICE Identification: 010998
Unit ID: 214582
Telephone: (610) 892-1500 Carnegie Class: Spec 2-yr-Health
FAX Number: (610) 892-1510 Calendar System: Quarter
URL: www.pit.edu
Established: 1953 Annual Undergrad Tuition & Fees: $13,905
Enrollment: 454 Coed
Affiliation or Control: Independent Non-Profit IRS Status: 501(c)3
Highest Offering: Baccalaureate
Accreditation: M, PTAA

01 Executive Vice President/CEO .... Mr. Harry (Matt) M. MEYERS
05 Dean of Academic Affairs .... Dr. Heather PFLEGER
10 Chief Financial Officer .... Ms. Annamarie CASSIDY
32 Director of Student Services .... Ms. Kamira EVANS
06 Dir of Inst Research/Registrar .... Mr. Craig M. JACOBS
07 Director of Admissions .... Ms. Laura BLOMGREN
37 Financial Aid Director .... Ms. Laura BLOMGREN
18 Director of Facilities .... Mr. Frederick FIVECOAT
13 Dir of Information Technology .... Mr. Michael TESTA
08 Director of the Library .... Vacant
20 Assoc Dean of Academic Affairs .... Ms. Rachelle CHAYKIN

*Pennsylvania's State System of Higher Education, Office of the Chancellor (C)

2300 Vartan Way, STE 207, Harrisburg PA 17110
County: Dauphin FICE Identification: 029371
Unit ID: 214661
Telephone: (717) 720-4000 Carnegie Class: N/A
FAX Number: (717) 720-4011
URL: www.passhe.edu

01 Chancellor .... Dr. Daniel GREENSTEIN
03 Deputy Chancellor .... Mr. Randy GOIN, JR.
10 Exec Vice Chancellor Admin/Finance .... Ms. Sharon MINNICH
05 Vice Chancellor/CAO .... Dr. Donna WILSON
26 Chief Strategic Relations Officer .... Mr. Cody JONES
43 Chief Legal Counsel .... Mr. Andrew LEHMAN
88 System Redesign Project Manager .... Ms. Rosa LARA

*Cheyney University of Pennsylvania (D)

1837 University Circle PO Box 200, Cheyney PA 19319-0200
County: Delaware FICE Identification: 003317
Unit ID: 211608
Telephone: (610) 399-2000 Carnegie Class: Bac-A&S
FAX Number: (610) 399-2415 Calendar System: Semester
URL: www.cheyney.edu
Established: 1837 Annual Undergrad Tuition & Fees (In-State): $10,904
Enrollment: 623 Coed
Affiliation or Control: State IRS Status: 501(c)3
Highest Offering: Master's
Accreditation: M, ACPHA

02 President .... Mr. Aaron A. WALTON
05 Provost .... Ms. Kizzy MORRIS
10 Exec Dir Finance & Admin .... Ms. Cynthia MOULTRIE
21 Controller .... Ms. Victoria ATKINS
38 Chairperson Guidance & Counseling .... Ms. Jolly MALICKEL
06 Interim Registrar .... Ms. Stephanie STEVENS
37 Director Student Financial Services .... Ms. Tonya WILLIAMS
09 Exec Dir Institutional Research .... Dr. Erika SHEHATA
18 Exec Director of Operations .... Mr. James LEWIS
19 Dir of Campus & Public Safety .... Mr. Mark CORBIN
41 Athletic Director .... Ms. Tammy A. BAGBY
17 College Physician .... Dr. Manijeh BAHREMAND
43 University Legal Counsel .... Ms. Cathleen MCCORMICK
32 Interim Exec Dir Student Affairs .... Mr. Gregory SMITH
39 Director of Housing .... Ms. Ramona DIXON
103 Dir Title III/Grants Administration .... Ms. Mamie STEPHENS
113 Bursar .... Ms. Lauronda FLETCHER
92 Director of Keystone Honors Academy .... Dr. Eric SCHUMACHER
84 Exec Dir Enrollment Management .... Mr. Jeffrey JONES
25 Grant and Contract Accountant .... Mr. George JONES
04 Executive Associate to President .... Vacant
15 Exec Director of Human Resources .... Mr. John GRUENWALD
07 Interim Director of Admissions .... Ms. Jacqueline GOODE

*Commonwealth University of Pennsylvania (E)

400 E Second Street, Bloomsburg PA 17815-1399
County: Columbia FICE Identification: 003315
Unit ID: 211158
Telephone: (570) 389-4000 Carnegie Class: Masters/L
FAX Number: (570) 389-3700 Calendar System: Semester
URL: www.bloomu.edu
Established: 1839 Annual Undergrad Tuition & Fees (In-State): $10,958
Enrollment: 8,427 Coed
Affiliation or Control: State IRS Status: 501(c)3
Highest Offering: Doctorate
Accreditation: M, ANEST, ART, AUD, CAEP, EXSC, MUS, NURSE, RAD, SP, SW, THEA

02 President .... Dr. Bashar W. HANNA
05 Sr VP & Provost Acad Affairs .... Dr. Diana ROGERS-ADKINSON
10 Interim VP Finance/Administration .... Mr. Eric NESS
32 VP of Student Success & Campus Life .... Dr. Martha WYGMANS
111 Vice Pres University Advancement .... Mr. Erik EVANS
84 Vice Pres Stdnt Success/Enroll Mgmt .... Dr. Stephen LEE
86 Director External & Govt Relations .... Mr. Dan KNORR
28 Chief DEI Officer .... Mr. Albert JONES
100 Interim Chief of Staff .... Mr. Eric NESS
20 Interim Vice Provost/Dean UG Educ .... Dr. Kara SHULTZ
58 Int Assoc Vice Prov/Dean Grad Stds .... Dr. Heather FELDHAUS
13 Interim AVP for Technology .... Dr. Edward KELLER
18 Asst VP for Facilities Management .... Mr. Eric NESS
35 Dean of Students .... Mr. George RUSCZYK
26 AVP Marketing/Communications .... Ms. Jennifer UMBERGER
29 AVP Alumni/Professional Engagement .... Dr. Lynda MICHAELS
07 AVP for Undergraduate Admissions .... Mr. Christopher LAPOS
09 AVP of Institutional Research .... Dr. Cori MYERS
49 Dean College of Liberal Arts .... Dr. James BROWN
50 Dean Zeigler College of Business .... Dr. Todd SHAWVER
81 Dean College of Science/Tech .... Dr. Latha RAMAKRISHNAN
53 Interim Dean College of Education .... Dr. Amy EITZEN
15 Senior AVP of Human Resources .... Ms. Deana HILL
16 Assoc VP Human Resources .... Ms. Tena MAURER
06 Registrar/Dir Enrollment Services .... Ms. Linda L. SWISHER
22 Executive Director of DEI .... Ms. Madelyn RODRIQUEZ
37 Director of Financial Aid .... Ms. Pam KATHCART
103 Exec Director of Workforce Devel .... Ms. Hope LINEMAN
41 Director of Athletics .... Dr. Michael S. MCFARLAND
42 Director Protestant Campus Ministry .... Rev. Jill YOUNG
42 Director Catholic Campus Ministry .... Fr. Richard MOWERY
19 Dir Bloomsburg University Police .... Mr. Leo SOKOLOSKI
92 Director University Honors Program .... Vacant
96 Dir Regional Procurement Office .... Mr. Jeffrey MANDEL
08 Director Library Services .... Mr. Scott DIMARCO
102 Executive Director BU Foundation .... Mr. Jerome DVORAK
90 Manager Technology Support Services .... Mr. David S. CELLI
40 Manager University Store .... Ms. Laura HEGER

*East Stroudsburg University of Pennsylvania (F)

200 Prospect Street, East Stroudsburg PA 18301-2999
County: Monroe FICE Identification: 003320
Unit ID: 212115
Telephone: (570) 422-3211 Carnegie Class: Masters/L
FAX Number: (570) 422-3777 Calendar System: Semester
URL: www.esu.edu
Established: 1893 Annual Undergrad Tuition & Fees (In-State): $11,559
Enrollment: 5,835 Coed
Affiliation or Control: State IRS Status: 501(c)3
Highest Offering: Doctorate
Accreditation: M, ACPHA, CAATE, CAEPN, COSMA, EXSC, NUR, PH, SP, SW

02 Interim President .... Mr. Kenneth A. LONG
05 Int Provost Academic Affairs .... Dr. Margaret BALL
32 VP Camp Life/Inclulsive Excellence .... Dr. Santiago SOLIS
10 Vice Pres Administration & Finance .... Vacant
46 VP Economic Devel/ Entrepreneurship .... Ms. Mary Frances POSTUPACK
84 Vice Pres Enrollment Management .... Ms. Karen E. LUCAS
58 Director Graduate/Extended Studies .... Dr. William BAJOR
49 Dean of Arts & Sciences .... Dr. Nieves GRUNEIRO-ROADCAP
76 Dean of Health Sciences .... Dr. Denise SEIGART
53 Dean of Education .... Dr. Brooke LANGAN
50 Dean of Business & Management .... Dr. Sylvester WILLIAMS
35 Dean of Student Life .... Ms. Jennie SMITH
100 Chief of Staff & Governmental Rels .... Mr. Miguel BARBOSA
07 Director of Admissions .... Mr. Alexander SPERRAZZA
06 Registrar/Dir Enrollment Services .... Ms. Geryl KINSEL
37 Director Financial Aid .... Ms. Kary TEJEDA
36 Dir Career Dev/Workforce Plng .... Ms. Breanna BETARIE
38 Director Counseling Center .... Ms. Jennifer YOUNG
41 Director of Athletics .... Dr. Allen SNOOK
39 Int Dir Residential/Dining Services .... Dr. Jennie SMITH
88 Dir of Student Activity Association .... Mr. Joe AKOB
21 Chief Financial Officer .... Ms. Donna R. BULZONI
13 Chief Information Officer .... Dr. Robert SMITH
18 Director of Facilities Management .... Mr. John BLOSHINSKI
96 Asst Dir of Procurement/Contracting .... Ms. Denise AYLWARD
29 Director of Alumni Engagement .... Vacant
26 Asst Director University Relations .... Ms. Elizabeth RICHARDSON
09 Dir Inst Effect/Planning/Assessment .... Vacant
28 Ctr for Multicul Affs/Inclusive Ed .... Ms. Lyesha J. FLEMING
09 Int Exec Dir Institutional Research .... Ms. Joseline KRAEMER
15 Director of Human Resources .... Dr. Yvonne CATINO
29 Director of Alumni Affairs .... Ms. Nancy BOYER

*Indiana University of Pennsylvania (G)

1011 South Drive, Indiana PA 15705-0001
County: Indiana FICE Identification: 003277
Unit ID: 213020
Telephone: (724) 357-2100 Carnegie Class: DU-Higher
FAX Number: (724) 357-6213 Calendar System: Semester
URL: www.iup.edu
Established: 1875 Annual Undergrad Tuition & Fees (In-State): $13,144
Enrollment: 10,037 Coed
Affiliation or Control: State IRS Status: 501(c)3
Highest Offering: Doctorate
Accreditation: M, ACFEI, ACPHA, ART, CACREP, CAEP, CLPSY, COARC, DIET, DIETD, EMT, EXSC, MUS, NURSE, PLNG, SP, THEA

02 President .... Dr. Michael A. DRISCOLL
05 Provost & VP Academic Affairs .... Dr. Lara LUETKEHANS
11 Vice Pres Administration/Finance .... Dr. Debra L. FITZSIMMONS
32 Vice President Student Affairs .... Dr. Thomas SEGAR
84 VP Enrollment Management .... Ms. Patricia MCCARTHY
111 Vice Pres University Advancement .... Dr. Khatmeh OSSEIRAN-HANNA
10 Assoc Vice President for Finance .... Mr. William BUTTZ
20 Assoc VP Academic Administration .... Dr. John N. KILMARX
58 Dean Grad Studies & Research .... Dr. Hilliary CREELY
15 Assoc Vice Pres Human Resources .... Mr. Craig BICKLEY
50 Int Dean Eberly Col of Business .... Dr. Prashanth BHARADWAJ
53 Int Dean Col Educ & Communication .... Dr. Sue RIEG
81 Dean Col Natural Science & Math .... Dr. Steve HOVAN
57 Dean College of Arts & Humanities .... Dr. Curt SCHEIB
66 Dean College Health & Human Svcs .... Dr. Sylvia GAIKO
08 Dean of Libraries & University Col .... Dr. Yaw ASAMOAH
06 Registrar .... Dr. Michael POWELL
13 Chief Information Officer .... Mr. William S. BALINT
45 Exec Dir IR/Planning/Assessment .... Mr. Chris KITAS
14 Exec Dir of Technology Services Ctr .... Mr. Todd D. CUNNINGHAM
26 Exec Dir of Marketing/Communication .... Dr. Michael POWERS
19 Interim Dir Public Safety & Police .... Mr. Douglas CAMPBELL
36 Director Career Development Ctr .... Dr. Tammy P. MANKO
29 Director Alumni Engagement .... Mr. Zach HILLIARD
44 Dir Annual Giving & Advance Svcs .... Mr. Nathan BISH
85 Asst VP Intl Education & Global .... Dr. Michele L. PETRUCCI
46 Assistant Dean for Research .... Vacant
39 Director Housing/Residential Living .... Ms. Valerie BARONI
40 Co-op Store Director .... Mr. Tim L. SHARBAUGH
41 Athletic Director .... Mr. Todd GARZARELLI
23 Nurse Director .... Ms. Melissa L. DICK
12 Director of Regional Campuses .... Mr. Richard J. MUTH
43 Staff Attorney .... Ms. Cathleen MCCORMACK
27 Exec Director of Media Relations .... Ms. Michelle S. FRYLING
96 Procurement Svcs PASSHE -Western .... Ms. Jennifer LEWIS
37 Director of Financial Aid .... Ms. Tiffany POTTS
07 Executive Director of UG Admissions .... Ms. Stacy HOPKINS
26 Chief Marketing Officer .... Mr. Chris NOAH
18 Director of Facilities Operations .... Mr. Laurence MILLER
28 Diversity/Inclusion/Title IX Coord .... Ms. Elise GLENN
38 Director Student Counseling .... Dr. Jessica MILLER
122 Asst Dir Fraternity/Sorority Life .... Ms. Betsy SARNESO

*Kutztown University of Pennsylvania (A)

15200 Kutztown Road, Kutztown PA 19530-0730
County: Berks FICE Identification: 003322
Unit ID: 213349
Telephone: (610) 683-4000 Carnegie Class: Masters/L
FAX Number: (610) 683-4693 Calendar System: Semester
URL: www.kutztown.edu
Established: 1866 Annual Undergrad Tuition & Fees (In-State): $11,156
Enrollment: 7,890 Coed
Affiliation or Control: State IRS Status: 501(c)3
Highest Offering: Doctorate
Accreditation: M, ART, CACREP, COSMA, MUS, SW

02 President .... Dr. Kenneth S. HAWKINSON
05 Provost/VP Academic Affairs .... Dr. Lorin BASDEN ARNOLD
10 VP Finance & Facilities .... Mr. Matt DELANY
84 Int VP Enrollment Mgmt/Stdnt Affs .... Dr. Donavan MCCARGO
22 VP Compliance/Equity .... Mr. Jesus PENA
102 Executive Director KU Foundation .... Mr. Alex OGEKA
26 VP University Relations & Athletics .... Mr. Matt SANTOS
20 Int VProv Acad Affs/Dean Grad Stds .... Dr. Michelle KIEC
21 Asst VP Finance & Business Services .... Mr. Matthew DELANEY
32 Asst VP/Dean of Students .... Dr. Donavan MCCARGO
13 Asst VP Information Technology .... Mr. Troy VINGOM
15 Director of Human Resources .... Ms. Jennifer S. WEIDMAN
57 Int Dean College Visual/Perf Arts .... Dr. Bradley SHOPE
49 Dean College Liberal Arts/Sci .... Dr. David BEOUGHER
50 Dean College of Business .... Dr. Anne CARROLL
53 Dean College Education .... Dr. John WARD
62 Director of Library Services .... Ms. Martha STEVENSON
09 Director Institutional Research .... Dr. Fawad RAFI
06 Interim Registrar .... Mr. Benjamin TROUT
37 Director of Financial Aid .... Mr. Bernard L. MCCREE
38 Director Counseling & Psych Svcs .... Dr. Lisa COULTER
96 Purchasing Manager .... Vacant
07 Director Undergraduate Admissions .... Ms. Krista D. EVANS
19 Chief of Police .... Mr. John DILLON
36 Director Career/Community Services .... Ms. Kerri GARDI
04 Sr Executive Assoc to President .... Ms. Toyia HEYWARD
108 Assoc Prov Accreditation/Acad Affs .... Dr. Karen RAUCH
106 Dir Online Education/E-learning .... Mr. Douglas SCOTT

*Millersville University of Pennsylvania (B)

PO Box 1002, Millersville PA 17551-0302
County: Lancaster FICE Identification: 003325
Unit ID: 214041
Telephone: (717) 871-4636 Carnegie Class: Masters/L
FAX Number: N/A Calendar System: 4/1/4
URL: www.millersville.edu
Established: 1855 Annual Undergrad Tuition & Fees (In-State): $11,665
Enrollment: 7,456 Coed
Affiliation or Control: State IRS Status: 501(c)3
Highest Offering: Doctorate
Accreditation: M, ACBSP, ART, CAEP, CEA, @CNEA, COARC, MUS, NAIT, NURSE, SW

02 President .... Dr. Daniel A. WUBAH
05 Vice Pres Academic Affs/Provost .... Dr. Gail GASPARICH
10 Interim VP Finance & Administration .... Mrs. Debbie NEWSOM
111 Vice Pres for Advancement .... Mr. Victor RAMOS
32 Vice Pres for Student Affairs .... Dr. Mary Beth WILLIAMS
28 Chief Diversity Officer .... Mr. Carlos WILEY
100 VP External Affs & Chief of Staff .... Dr. Victor DESANTIS
20 Associate Provost Academic Admin .... Dr. James A. DELLE
108 Asst VP Inst Assessment & Planning .... Dr. Carol RUNGE
13 Interim Chief Technology Officer .... Mr. Joshua HARTRANFT
15 Exec Director of Human Resources .. Ms. Diane L. COPENHAVER
37 Director of Financial Aid .... Ms. Emiyaril ALVAREZ
35 AVP Student Affs/Enrollment Mgmt .... Vacant
84 Assoc VP SA & Enrollment Mgmt .. Mr. Thomas J. RICHARDSON
26 Asst VP Communications/Marketing . Mr. Gregory E. FREEDLAND
18 Assistant VP Facilities .... Mr. Thomas A. WALTZ, JR.
53 Dean Education & Human Services .... Dr. Lara WILLOX
79 Dean Arts/Human & Social Sci .... Dr. Ieva ZAKE
81 Dean Science & Technology .... Dr. Marc HARRIS
58 Dean Col of Grad Stds & Adult Lrng .... Dr. James DELLE
86 VP External Rels/Chief of Staff .... Dr. Victor S. DESANTIS
06 Registrar .... Ms. Alison M. HUTCHINSON
07 Director of Admissions .... Ms. Katy A. CHARLES
121 Dir Student Access/Support Services .... Ms. Darlene R. NEWMAN
36 Dir Exp Learn & Career Mgmt .... Ms. Melissa WARDWELL
38 Director Counseling/Human Devel .... Dr. Joseph LYNCH
19 Chief of University Police .... Mr. Peter J. ANDERS
41 Dir of Intercollegiate Athletics .... Mr. Miles P. GALLAGHER
40 University Store Manager .... Mr. Michael NITROY
42 Campus Minister .... Rev. Trip BEANS
110 Assoc VP for Advancement .... Ms. Alice R. MCMURRY
09 Int AVP Inst Assessment/Planning .... Dr. Kyle W. VERBOSH
112 Major Gift Officer .... Mr. Robert BENTLEY
102 Dir Sponsored Pgms & Research Admin .... Mr. Jeffry PORTER
96 Procurement Manager .... Ms. Ruth SHEETZ
57 Director Visual & Performing Arts .... Ms. Robin D. ZAREMSKI
27 Director of Communications .... Ms. Janet E. KACSKOS
106 Director of Online Programs .... Ms. Janice R. MOORE
29 Director Alumni Engagement .... Ms. Kristin SCHAB
43 Dir Legal Services/General Counsel .... Mr. Cliff KELLY
04 Executive Assoc to the President .... Ms. Pietra JAMISON
08 Chief Library Officer .... Mr. Andrew WELAISH
101 Secretary of the Institution/Board .... Mrs. Jennifer HART
104 Director Study Abroad .... Dr. Patreice CAMPBELL
50 Dean Lombardo College of Business .... Dr. Marc I. TOMLJANOVICH
122 Asst Dir Stdnt Orgs-Greek Life .... Ms. Jackie ALIOTTA

*Pennsylvania Western University (C)

250 University Avenue, California PA 15419-1394
County: Washington FICE Identification: 003316
Unit ID: 211361
Telephone: (724) 938-4000 Carnegie Class: Masters/L
FAX Number: (724) 938-4138 Calendar System: Semester
URL: www.calu.edu
Established: 1852 Annual Undergrad Tuition & Fees (In-State): $11,108
Enrollment: 6,885 Coed
Affiliation or Control: State IRS Status: 501(c)3
Highest Offering: Doctorate
Accreditation: M, ACBSP, ART, CACREP, CAEP, CAPRT, NURSE, PTAA, RAD, SP, SW, THEA

02 President .... Dr. Dale-Elizabeth PEHRSSON
100 Chief of Staff to the President .... Ms. Kelly MORAN-REPINSKI
04 Exec Asst to the President .... Mrs. Anna STEWART
05 Provost/Sr VP for Academic Affairs .... Dr. Scott MILLER
10 VP Administration & Finance .... Ms. Fawn PETROSKY
84 SVP Enrol Mgmt/Global Online Advanc .... Dr. Errin LAKE
09 Director of Institutional Research .... Mr. Steve ZIDEK
58 Dean of Graduate Studies .... Dr. Yugo IKACH
121 Int Director of Academic Success .... Ms. Jill LOOP
30 VP for Development & Alumni Rels .... Mr. Anthony MAURO
32 SVP for Student Affairs/Inst Effect .... Dr. Susanne FENSKE
13 Assoc VP and Chief Info Officer .... Mr. Paul ALLISON
72 Dean Eberly College of Sci & Tech .... Dr. Brenda FREDETTE
49 Dean College of Educ & Liberal Arts .... Dr. Kristen MAJOCHA
08 Dean Library Svcs & UG Researc .... Mr. Douglas HOOVER
07 Dean of Admissions .... Ms. Tracey SHEETZ
123 Director Graduate Admissions .... Mr. Ben BRUDNOCK
37 Director of Financial Aid .... Mr. Jeff DERUBBO
06 Registrar .... Mr. Shayne GERVAIS
36 Dir Career & Prof Dev Center .... Ms. Rhonda GIFFORD
92 Director Honors Program .... Mr. Mark AUNE
29 Director of Alumni Relations .... Dr. Ryan BARNHART
39 Facilities & Occupancy Manager .... Mrs. Jackie THORN
94 Director Women's Studies .... Dr. Marta MCCLINTOCK-COMEAUX
104 Study Abroad/Asst Dir Admissions .... Ms. Kristen LOUTTIT
41 Athletic Director .... Dr. Karen HJERPE
15 Director Human Resources .... Mr. Eric GUISER
22 Dir Equity/Compliance & Title IX .... Dr. John BURNETT
19 Chief of Police .... Mr. Ed MCSHEFFERY
18 Director of Facilities Mgmt .... Mr. Mike KANALIS
26 VP for Communications & Marketing .... Mrs. Christine KINDL
27 Director of Marketing .... Mrs. Keli HENDERSON
88 Director of Creative Services .... Mr. Greg SOFRANKO
40 Bookstore Manager .... Ms. Amy NASH
96 Purchasing Agent Supervisor .... Ms. Melissa WALKER
108 Assoc Prov for Assessment & Accred .... Dr. Leonard COLELLI
28 VP Diversity/Equity/Inclusion .... Dr. Terrence MITCHELL
113 Acting Director of Student Accounts .... Mr. Jack ROGERS
85 Intl Stdnt Advis/Asst Dir Welc Ctr .... Mr. Kevin EGGLESTON

*Shippensburg University of Pennsylvania (D)

1871 Old Main Drive, Shippensburg PA 17257-2200
County: Cumberland FICE Identification: 003326
Unit ID: 216010
Telephone: (717) 477-7447 Carnegie Class: Masters/L
FAX Number: (717) 477-1273 Calendar System: Semester
URL: www.ship.edu
Established: 1871 Annual Undergrad Tuition & Fees (In-State): $13,544
Enrollment: 6,130 Coed
Affiliation or Control: State IRS Status: 501(c)3
Highest Offering: Doctorate
Accreditation: M, CACREP, CAEPN, JOUR, SW

02 President .... Dr. Charles E. PATTERSON
05 Interim Provost and Vice President .... Dr. Nicole HILL
10 Sr VP Administration & Finance .... Vacant
84 Sr Associate VP for Enrollment Mgmt .... Ms. JoEllen LINDNER
15 Director Human Resources .... Vacant
102 Pres Shippensburg Univ Foundation .... Dr. Leslie CLINTON
21 Assoc VP for A&F/CFO .... Ms. Melinda D. FAWKS
13 Chief Information Officer .... Dr. Justin SENTZ
35 Dean of Students .... Ms. Lorie DAVIS
20 Assoc Provost & Interim Dean .... Dr. Tracy SCHOOLCRAFT
124 AVP for Retention & Student Success .... Dr. Jennifer A. HAUGHIE
09 Exec Dir Research/Assessment/Plng .... Dr. Eric J. ZEGLEN
51 Exec Dir CMDPC .... Ms. Lorelee ISBELL
06 Registrar .... Ms. Cathy J. SPRENGER
32 Interim VP of Student Affairs .... Ms. Lorie DAVIS
07 Exec Dir of Admissions .... Dr. Megan LUFT
36 Sr Dir Career/Mentoring & Prof Dev .... Ms. Victoria BUCHBAUER
37 Director Financial Aid .... Ms. Trina SNYDER
29 Dir Alumni Outreach & Data Mgmt .... Ms. Lori SMITH
39 Dir Housing & Residence Life .... Ms. Jen MILBURN
08 Dean of Libraries .... Ms. Michelle FOREMAN
28 AVP Inclusion/Belonging/Dir Social .... Dr. Manuel RUIZ
88 Dir Pride & Gender Equity Center .... Vacant
25 Interim Dir Public Svcs & Spons Pgm .... Ms. Antonia PRICE
38 Director of Counseling Center .... Dr. Christopher CARLTON
88 Director of Conference Services .... Ms. Lauren AHLQUIST
53 Dean College Education & Human Svcs .... Dr. Nicole R. HILL
49 Dean College Arts & Science .... Dr. Leslie BROWN
50 Dean College of Business .... Dr. John KOOTI
26 Dir Communications and Marketing .... Mr. Ken BACH
92 Dir of Honors College .... Dr. Kim KLEIN
121 AVP & Dean for Student Success .... Vacant
93 Dir Multicultural Student Affairs .... Ms. Diane JEFFERSON
116 Dir of Accounting .... Mr. Michael FELICE
18 Chief Facilities/Physical Plant .... Mr. Jeffrey KUGLER
96 Director of Purchasing/Contracting .... Mr. Wesley LIGHT
19 Director Public Safety .... Mr. Michael LEE
41 Athletic Director .... Mr. Jeff A. MICHAELS
04 Exec Associate to the President .... Mr. Scott BROWN
104 Dir International Programs .... Ms. Mary BURNETT
100 Chief of Staff .... Vacant
113 Interim Bursar .... Ms. Merisa HARBAUGH
122 Dir of Fraternity and Sorority Life .... Ms. Brigette ALLEN

*Slippery Rock University of Pennsylvania (E)

1 Morrow Way, Slippery Rock PA 16057-1326
County: Butler FICE Identification: 003327
Unit ID: 216038
Telephone: (724) 738-9000 Carnegie Class: Masters/L
FAX Number: (724) 738-2169 Calendar System: Semester
URL: www.sru.edu
Established: 1889 Annual Undergrad Tuition & Fees (In-State): $9,984
Enrollment: 8,860 Coed
Affiliation or Control: State IRS Status: 501(c)3
Highest Offering: Doctorate
Accreditation: M, ART, ARCPA, CAATE, CACREP, CAEPN, CAHIIM, CARTE, COSMA, DANCE, EXSC, MUS, NURSE, OT, PTA, SW, THEA

02 President .... Dr. William BEHRE
05 Provost/VP Acad & Student Affs .... Dr. Abbey ZINK
11 Sr VP for Admin & Economic Devel .... Dr. Amir MOHAMMADI
111 Vice Pres for Univ Advancement .... Dr. Dennis WASHINGTON
18 Asst Vice Pres for Facilities/Plng .... Mr. Scott ALBERT
15 Chief Human Resources Officer .... Ms. Lynne M. MOTYL
28 Asst VP Div & Compliance/Title IX .... Ms. Holly M. MCCOY
100 Chief of Staff .... Ms. Tina L. MOSER
10 Chief Financial & Data Officer .... Ms. Carrie J. BIRCKBICHLER
84 Chief Enrollment Mgmt Officer .... Dr. Amanda A. YALE
32 Chief Student Affairs Officer .... Mr. David WILMES
13 Assoc Provost Info Technology .... Dr. John ZIEGLER
102 Exec Director SRU Foundation Inc .... Dr. Edward BUCHA
26 Chief Comm/Public Affairs Officer .... Mr. Robert KING
37 Director Student Financial Aid .... Ms. Alyssa DOBSON
19 Director Public Safety .... Mr. Paul NOVAK
19 Director University Police .... Mr. Kevin SHARKEY
08 Manager of Library Operations .... Ms. Jennifer J. BARTEK
14 Director of Info & Adm Tech Svcs .... Mr. Henry MAGUSIAK
06 Director Acad Records & Registrar .... Ms. Connie EDWARDS
07 Director Undergraduate Admissions .... Mr. Michael MAY
23 Director Health Services .... Ms. Kristina BENKESER
36 Assistant Director Career Services .... Ms. Renee COYNE
29 Director Alumni Affairs .... Ms. Kelly BAILEY
76 Interim Dean Col Health/Engr/Sci .... Dr. Michael ZIEG
123 Director Graduate Admissions ... Ms. Brandi WEBER-MORTIMER
41 Athletic Director .... Ms. Roberta PAGE
39 Director of Residence Life .... Mr. Patrick T. BESWICK
25 Director Grants & Sponsored Rsrch .... Ms. Casey HYATT
38 Director of Student Counseling .... Dr. Chris CUBERO
93 Director of Inclusive Excellence .... Vacant
96 Int Dir of Contracts & Purchasing .... Ms. Terri LEASE
88 Assoc Provost Trans Exper .... Dr. Bradley WILSON
49 Dean College Liberal Arts .... Dr. Dan BAUER
50 Dean College of Business .... Dr. Lawrence SHAO
53 Dean College of Education .... Dr. Keith DILS
04 Admin Assistant to the President .... Ms. Kelli RENSEL

*West Chester University of Pennsylvania (F)

700 South High Street, West Chester PA 19383-0001
County: Chester FICE Identification: 003328
Unit ID: 216764
Telephone: (610) 436-1000 Carnegie Class: DU-Higher
FAX Number: (610) 436-3115 Calendar System: Semester
URL: www.wcupa.edu
Established: 1871 Annual Undergrad Tuition & Fees (In-State): $10,471
Enrollment: 17,719 Coed
Affiliation or Control: State IRS Status: 501(c)3
Highest Offering: Doctorate
Accreditation: M, #ARCPA, ART, CAATE, CACREP, CAEPN, CLPSY, COARC, DIETD, @DIETI, EXSC, FEPAC, MUS, NURSE, PH, PLNG, SP, SPAA, SW, THEA

02 President .... Dr. Chris FIORENTINO
100 VP UA & Chief of Staff .... Mr. Andrew LEHMAN
04 Sr Assoc to the President .... Ms. Megan FAHEY
28 VP & Chief Diversity Officer .... Dr. Tracey RAY
05 Executive VP & Provost .... Dr. R. Lorraine BERNOTSKY
10 Vice President Admin/Finance .... Mr. Todd MURPHY
13 Sr Assoc VP Info Svcs/Tech & CIO .... Mr. Jatinder SINGH
119 Information Security Officer .... Vacant
111 VP Advancement & External Affairs .... Dr. Zebulun DAVENPORT
32 VP for Student Affairs .... Dr. Tabetha ADKINS
35 Interim AVP of Student Development .... Dr. Diane D'ARCANGELO
49 Dean College Arts & Humanities .... Dr. Jen BACON
20 VP Academic Ops & Deputy Provost .... Dr. Jeffery OSGOOD

07 Asst VP Admissions .... Ms. Sarah FREED
53 Dean College of Educ & Social Work .... Dr. Desha WILLIAMS
50 Dean College Business/Public Mgmt .... Dr. Evan LEACH
81 Dean College Science & Math .... Dr. Radha PYATI
76 Dean College Health Science .... Dr. Scott HEINERICHS
64 Dean School of Music .... Dr. Chris HANNING
25 VProv Rsrch & Creat Act Fac Dev .... Dr. Nicole BENNETT
23 Director Student Health Center .... Vacant
15 Chief Human Resources Officer .... Mr. William HELZLSOUER
124 Asst VP for Student Engagement .... Ms. Sara HINKLE
122 Director of Fraternity & Sorority .... Ms. Denine ROCCO
85 Dir International Programs .... Dr. Angela HOWARD
102 Chief Exec Officer WCU Foundation .... Mr. Christopher MOMINEY
18 Assoc Vice President for Facilities .... Mr. Gary BIXBY
88 Dir Facilities Finance/Support Svcs .... Ms. Susan MILLER
21 Controller .... Ms. Catherine KLEPONIS
09 AVP Inst Effectiveness & Planning .... Ms. Lisa YANNICK
113 Asst VP Stdnt Financial Svcs/Bursar .... Ms. Colleen CORRADO
114 Assoc VP Budget & Financial Plng .... Ms. Ilene MATES
26 Sr Assoc VP for Univ Comm & Mktg .... Ms. Nancy GAINER
24 Director Publications/Printing Svcs .... Mr. Matthew BORN
31 Director Cultural/Community Affairs .... Mr. John RHEIN
88 Director Conference Services .... Ms. Mary Beth KURIMAY
08 University Librarian .... Vacant
88 Director Teacher Education Center .... Dr. James B. PRICE
36 Director Career Devel Center .... Ms. Jennifer ROSSI-LONG
97 Interim Dean University College .... Dr. John CRAIG
88 Dir Learning Asst/Resource .... Dr. Jocelyn MANIGO
37 Director Financial Aid .... Mr. Daniel MCILHENNEY
38 Director Counseling Center .... Dr. Rachel DALTRY
29 Director Alumni Relations .... Ms. Jenna BIRCH
41 Director Athletics .... Dr. Terry BEATTIE
88 Director Sports Information .... Mr. James ZUHLKE
93 Dir Multicultural Affairs .... Dr. Dametraus JAGGERS
88 Sr Director Women & Gender Equity .... Ms. Sendy ALCIDONIS
19 Chief of Public Safety .... Mr. Raymond STEVENSON
96 Director Business Services .... Mr. Jeff BAUN
14 Exec Dir Deputy CIO/IT Infra Svcs .... Mr. Kevin PARTRIDGE
88 Asst Dir Sourcing/Planning/Project .... Ms. Chaw-ye CHANG
105 Exec Dir Application Development .... Vacant
89 Director New Student Programs .... Dr. Kristin AUSTIN
88 Asst Dean of Students .... Mr. Peter GALLOWAY
39 Residence Life & Housing Director .... Vacant
88 Asst Dean of Student Conduct .... Ms. Christina BRENNER
88 Dir Student Leadership/Involve .... Dr. Leah TOBIN
109 Senior Director Sykes Student Union .... Dr. Clayton KOLB
122 Senior Dir Fraternity & Sorority .... Ms. Cara JENKINS
121 Sr Vice Provost Student Success .... Ms. Kathleen HOWLEY
88 Dir Pre-major Academic Advising .... Dr. Ann COLGAN
92 Director Honors College .... Dr. Kevin DEAN
104 Asst VP for International Programs .... Vacant
106 Exec Director Distance Educ Svcs .... Dr. Rui LI
88 Exec Dir Student Service Inc .... Ms. Donna SNYDER
40 Student Svcs Inc Bookstore Manager ..... Mr. Stephen MANNELLA
06 Sr AVP Acad Systems/Univ Registrar .... Ms. Megan JERABEK

Philadelphia College of Osteopathic Medicine (A)

4170 City Avenue, Philadelphia PA 19131-1694
County: Philadelphia FICE Identification: 003352
Unit ID: 215123
Telephone: (215) 871-6100 Carnegie Class: Spec-4-yr-Med
FAX Number: (215) 871-6719 Calendar System: Trimester
URL: www.pcom.edu
Established: 1899 Annual Graduate Tuition & Fees: N/A
Enrollment: 3,133 Coed
Affiliation or Control: Independent Non-Profit IRS Status: 501(c)3
Highest Offering: Doctorate; No Undergraduates
Accreditation: M, ARCPA, CLPSY, IPSY, NASP, OSTEO, SCPSY

01 President & CEO .... Dr. Jay S. FELDSTEIN
05 Provost/Sr VP Academic Affairs/Dean .... Dr. Kenneth J. VEIT
10 Vice Pres Finance/Treasurer/CFO .... Mr. Peter DOULIS
17 Chief Acad Ofcr-PCOM Mednet-Opti .... Dr. David KUO
43 Chief Legal Affairs Officer .... Mr. David F. SIMON
63 Dean Osteopathic Med Pgm-SGA Campus .... Dr. William CRAVER, III
67 Dean School of Pharmacy .... Dr. Shawn SPENCER
20 Assoc Dean Graduate Medical Educ .... Dr. David KUO
20 Dean/Chief Academic Ofcr-GA Campus .... Dr. Andrea MANN
12 Chief Campus Officer-Georgia Campus .... Mr. Bryan GINN
46 Chief Science Officer .... Dr. Mindy GEORGE-WEINSTEIN
32 Chief Student Affairs Officer .... Ms. Patience MASON
26 Chief Marketing/Communications Ofcr ... Ms. Wendy W. ROMANO
37 Chief Student Financial Aid Officer .... Mr. Samuel MATHENY
15 Chief Human Resources Officer .... Ms. Christina MAZZELLA
07 Chief Admissions Officer .... Ms. Adrianne JONES
28 Chief Diversity/Cmty Relations Ofcr .... Dr. Marcine PICKRON-DAVIS
13 Chief Technology Officer .... Mr. Richard SMITH
88 Chief Compliance Officer .... Ms. Margaret MCKEON
18 Chief Facilities/Plant Operations .... Mr. Frank H. WINDLE
111 Chief Advancement Officer .... Ms. Carrie COLLINS
08 Chair of Library/Exec Director .... Mr. Oliver CHEN
06 Registrar .... Ms. Maureen O'MARA CARVER
19 Director Security .... Ms. Terri ALLEN
117 Director Risk Management .... Mr. Isaiah LOPEZ
96 Purchasing Manager .... Ms. LaVerne MAYES
04 Executive Asst to the President .... Ms. Lynn A. KUSH
19 Chief Occ & Envir Safety Officer .... Mr. Patrick WOLF
17 Chief Practice Operations Officer .... Mr. Stephen CASTELLANO

PITC Institute (B)

827 Glenside Ave, Wyncote PA 19095
County: Montgomery FICE Identification: 037813
Unit ID: 444811
Telephone: (215) 392-2938 Carnegie Class: Not Classified
FAX Number: (215) 576-5652 Calendar System: Semester
URL: www.pitc.edu
Established: 1998 Annual Undergrad Tuition & Fees: N/A
Enrollment: 347 Coed
Affiliation or Control: Proprietary IRS Status: Proprietary
Highest Offering: Associate Degree
Accreditation: ABHES

01 President .... Dr. Shahid AHMED
06 Registrar .... Lourdes GUILLEN
07 Director of Admissions .... Alice BRUNDAGE
10 Chief Financial/Business Officer .... Mark GEORGE
108 Director Institutional Assessment .... Michele LONG
11 Chief of Operations/Administration .... Yamaris RIVERA
36 Director Student Placement .... Elina ANN
37 Director Student Financial Aid .... Lana RYBALOV

Pittsburgh Career Institute (C)

421 Seventh Avenue, Pittsburgh PA 15219-1907
County: Allegheny FICE Identification: 022023
Unit ID: 216782
Telephone: (412) 281-2600 Carnegie Class: Spec 2-yr-Health
FAX Number: (412) 209-0419 Calendar System: Other
URL: www.pci.edu
Established: 2014 Annual Undergrad Tuition & Fees: $15,064
Enrollment: 217 Coed
Affiliation or Control: Proprietary IRS Status: Proprietary
Highest Offering: Associate Degree
Accreditation: ACICS, COARC, DMS, SURGT

01 Campus President .... Patti L. YAKSHE
05 Chief Academic Officer .... Jill ARGALL
09 Director of Institutional Research .... Cindy SMITH
36 Director Student Placement .... Patty O'ROURKE

Pittsburgh Institute of Aeronautics (D)

PO Box 10897, Pittsburgh PA 15236-0897
County: Allegheny FICE Identification: 005310
Unit ID: 215381
Telephone: (412) 346-2100 Carnegie Class: Spec 2-yr-Tech
FAX Number: (412) 466-0513 Calendar System: Quarter
URL: www.pia.edu
Established: 1929 Annual Undergrad Tuition & Fees: $16,650
Enrollment: 567 Coed
Affiliation or Control: Independent Non-Profit IRS Status: 501(c)3
Highest Offering: Associate Degree
Accreditation: ACCSC

01 President/CEO .... Ms. Suzanne L. MARKLE
05 Exec Dir Academic & Student Affairs .... Mr. Jason S. MONGAN
37 Director of Financial Aid .... Ms. Donata CLARK
11 Vice President of Operations .... Mr. Steven D. SABOLD
07 Director of Admissions and Outreach .... Ms. Roxanne OBER
18 Director of Campus Operations .... Mr. Gary E. HOYLE
19 Director of Safety and Development .... Mr. John KOVAC

Pittsburgh Institute of Mortuary Science (E)

5808 Baum Boulevard, Pittsburgh PA 15206-3706
County: Allegheny FICE Identification: 010814
Unit ID: 215390
Telephone: (412) 362-8500 Carnegie Class: Spec 2-yr-A&S
FAX Number: (412) 362-1684 Calendar System: Trimester
URL: www.pims.edu
Established: 1939 Annual Undergrad Tuition & Fees: N/A
Enrollment: 191 Coed
Affiliation or Control: Independent Non-Profit IRS Status: 501(c)3
Highest Offering: Associate Degree
Accreditation: FUSER

01 President/CEO/Dean of Admin .... Mr. Eugene C. OGRODNIK
05 Program Director/COO .... Dr. Barry T. LEASE
32 Dean of Faculty/Students .... Mr. Michael BURNS
06 Registrar/Dir Admin Services .... Ms. Nicole ELACHKO
07 Admissions Advisor .... Ms. Maria SPROULL
113 Bursar/Financial Aid .... Ms. Karen S. ROCCO

Pittsburgh Technical College (F)

1111 McKee Road, Oakdale PA 15071-3205
County: Allegheny FICE Identification: 007437
Unit ID: 215415
Telephone: (412) 809-5100 Carnegie Class: Bac/Assoc-Assoc Dom
FAX Number: (412) 809-5320 Calendar System: Quarter
URL: www.ptcollege.edu
Established: 1946 Annual Undergrad Tuition & Fees: $16,460
Enrollment: 1,559 Coed
Affiliation or Control: Independent Non-Profit IRS Status: 501(c)3
Highest Offering: Baccalaureate
Accreditation: M, ACFEI, PNUR, SURGT

01 President .... Dr. Alicia B. HARVEY-SMITH
04 Executive Assistant .... Vacant
111 Chief of Staff/Exec Dir Advancement .... Brenda PSOTKA
28 Chief DEI Officer .... Marsha N. LINDSAY
43 General Counsel .... Gretchen GARDNER
14 Supervisor of Network Operations .... Jon BUHAGIAR
102 Exec Director Corporate College .... Sunjay BALI
13 Chief Information Officer .... William SHOWERS
21 Vice President Financial Services .... Connie VANCAMP
10 VP of Administration/CFO .... Jay CLAYTON
50 Dean of Business/Online .... Dr. Melissa WERTZ
06 Registrar .... Samantha BYCURA
66 Dean of Nursing/Health Professions .... Teresa DUCSAY
53 Dean of Education Services .... Dr. Bonnie ORDONEZ
09 Exec. Director Inst. Research .... Nancy FEATHER
25 Grants Mgr/Foundation Relations .... Julie THROCKMORTON
26 VP of Marketing/Communication .... Barry SHEPARD
27 Digital Marketing Manager .... Shiantal FERGUSON
101 Executive Assistant/Sec to Board .... Jayme HOLLOWAY
05 Vice President of Academic Affairs .... Dr. Eileen STEFFAN
36 Director of Career Services .... Kristy SWEGMAN
32 Vice President of Student Affairs .... Vacant
29 Alumni Coordinator .... Christine IOLI
15 Director of HR/Title IX Coordinator .... Lindsay SEAL
19 Director of Public Safety .... Gregory BOLYARD
39 Director of Resident Life .... Gloria RITCHIE
18 Director of Facilities Services .... Tom VUCELICH
37 Assoc VP Student Financial Aid .... Jill BITTEL
86 Manager of Compliance .... Melissa BROWN
40 Campus Store Manager .... Cynthia KLEIN
84 AVP Enrollment & Student Success .... Dr. Rebecca DUNCAN-RAMIREZ

Pittsburgh Theological Seminary (G)

616 N. Highland Avenue, Pittsburgh PA 15206-2596
County: Allegheny FICE Identification: 003356
Unit ID: 215424
Telephone: (412) 362-5610 Carnegie Class: Spec-4-yr-Faith
FAX Number: N/A Calendar System: Semester
URL: www.pts.edu
Established: 1794 Annual Graduate Tuition & Fees: N/A
Enrollment: 209 Coed
Affiliation or Control: Presbyterian Church (U.S.A.) IRS Status: 501(c)3
Highest Offering: Doctorate; No Undergraduates
Accreditation: M, THEOL

01 President .... Dr. Asa J. LEE
05 Int Dean of Faculty/VP Acad Affairs .... Dr. Leanna FULLER
111 VP Seminary Advancement .... Mr. Charles FISCHER, III
32 Assoc Dean of Students & Formation .... Rev. Ayana TETER
10 Vice Pres Finance & Administration .... Mr. Thomas HINDS
06 Registrar .... Ms. Anne B. MALONE
08 Director of the Library .... Ms. Michelle SPOMER
78 Assoc Dean Acad Pgms/Field Educ .... Dr. Barbara BLODGETT
29 Director of Alumni/ae Services .... Rev. Carolyn CRANSTON
73 Int Dir Doctor of Ministry Program .... Dr. Denise THORPE
51 Director Continuing Education .... Dr. Helen BLIER
37 Associate Director of Financial Aid .... Mr. Ryan JENSEMA
84 Sr Dir of Enrollment Services .... Ms. Tracy RIGGLE YOUNG
04 Exec Asst to President/Sec to BOD .... Rev. Andrew GREENHOW
13 Director of Information Technology .... Mr. David MIDDLETON
15 Human Resources Manager .... Ms. Kathleen GREEN
18 Facilities Director .... Mr. Tom FULTON
30 Director of Development .... Mr. Dominick OLIVER
26 Sr Director of Communications .... Ms. Melissa LOGAN

Point Park University (H)

201 Wood Street, Pittsburgh PA 15222-1984
County: Allegheny FICE Identification: 003357
Unit ID: 215442
Telephone: (412) 391-4100 Carnegie Class: DU-Mod
FAX Number: (412) 392-3998 Calendar System: Semester
URL: www.pointpark.edu
Established: 1960 Annual Undergrad Tuition & Fees: $34,200
Enrollment: 3,591 Coed
Affiliation or Control: Independent Non-Profit IRS Status: 501(c)3
Highest Offering: Doctorate
Accreditation: M, CLPSY, DANCE, IACBE

01 President .... Dr. Don GREEN
05 Provost .... Dr. Michael SOTO
20 Associate Provost .... Dr. Jonas PRIDA
10 Sr VP Finance and Operations .... Ms. Bridget MANCOSH
43 Sr VP and General Counsel .... Vacant
26 VP of External Affairs .... Ms. Mariann K. GEYER
84 VP Enrollment Management .... Ms. Trudy WILLIAMS
30 Asst VP Development/Alumni Rels ...... Ms. Stephanie ADAMCZYK
32 VP of Student Affs/Dean of Stdnts .... Mr. Keith PAYLO
15 VP of Human Resources .... Ms. Lisa STEFANKO
18 Vice President of Operations .... Mr. Christopher J. HILL
19 AVP Public Safety/Chief Police .... Mr. Jeffrey D. BESONG
09 Assoc VP Institutional Research ...... Mr. Christopher E. CHONCEK
21 AVP of Finance .... Mr. Jim HARDT
20 Asst VP Academic Affairs .... Mr. Nelson CHIPMAN
13 Asst Vice Pres Info Technology .... Mr. Tim WILSON
50 Dean Rowland School of Business .... Dr. Steve TANZILLI
53 Dean Sch of Education .... Dr. Darlene MARNICH
79 Chair Psychology .... Dr. Matthew ALLEN
54 Chair Natural Science/Engr Tech .... Dr. Gregg JOHNSON
88 Chair Criminal Justice/Intell Stds .... Mr. Michael BOTTA
88 Chair Business Management .... Mr. Patrick MULVIHILL

88 Chair Accounting/Econ/Finance/IT ... Ms. Margaret GILFILLAN
88 Chair Theatre ... Ms. April DARAS
88 Chair Dance ... Vacant
88 Dean Conservatory Performing Arts ... Mr. Garfield LEMONIUS
88 Chair Literary Arts ... Dr. Sarah PERRIER
60 Dean School of Communication ... Dr. Raymond ANCKNEY
88 Chair Sport Art Entertain Mgmt ... Mr. Bob DERDA
83 Chair Humanities/Social Science ... Dr. Channa NEWMAN
88 Chair Community Engagement ... Dr. Heather STARR FIEDLER
06 University Registrar ... Mr. Scott SPENCER
08 Director/Librarian/Academic Svcs ... Ms. Liz EVANS
27 Mng Dir Marketing/Public Relations ... Mr. Louis CORSARO
39 Director of Campus Life ... Ms. Janet D. EVANS
07 Director of Admissions ... Ms. Joell MINFORD
41 Director of Athletics ... Mr. John ASHAOLU
88 Dir Conference & Event Services ... Ms. Christina MORTON
38 Director of Counseling Services ... Dr. Kurt KUMLER
106 AVP Online Education/E-learning ... Mr. Nelson CHIPMAN
29 Director Alumni Relations ... Vacant
37 Director Student Financial Aid ... Mr. George SANTUCCI
44 Director Annual Fund Pgms/Indiv Giv ... Vacant
88 Dir Center for Media Innovation ... Mr. Andrew CONTE
28 AVP of Title IX & Diversity ... Ms. Vanessa LOVE

Reading Area Community College (A)

PO Box 1706, Reading PA 19603-1706
County: Berks FICE Identification: 010388
Unit ID: 215585
Telephone: (610) 372-4721 Carnegie Class: Assoc/MT-VT-Mix Trad/Non
FAX Number: (610) 372-4264 Calendar System: Semester
URL: www.racc.edu
Established: 1971 Annual Undergrad Tuition & Fees (In-District): $9,990
Enrollment: 3,924 Coed
Affiliation or Control: State/Local IRS Status: 501(c)3
Highest Offering: Associate Degree
Accreditation: M, ADNUR, COARC, MLTAD, PNUR

01 President ... Dr. Susan D. LOONEY
05 SVP Academic Affairs/Provost ... Ms. Cynthia SEAMAN
10 Sr VP Fin & Admin Svcs/Treasurer ... Mr. Kenneth DEARSTYNE
111 VP Col Advance/Exec Dir Foundation ... Mr. Anthony DEMARCO
32 Dean of Student Affairs ... Ms. Maria MITCHELL
15 VP of Fiscal & Human Services ... Ms. Dolores PETERSON
84 Dean of Enrollment Management ... Ms. Kay LITMAN
09 Dir Assessment/Research/Planning ... Mr. David SWEELEY
81 Assoc Dean STEM ... Ms. Patricia MEJABI
62 Assoc Dean Library Svcs/Lrng Res ... Ms. Mary Ellen HECKMAN
50 Assoc Dean of Business Division ... Ms. Linda BELL
79 Assoc Dean Comm/Arts & Humanities ... Mr. Brian SCHELL
83 Assoc Dean Soc Sci/Human Svc/Fnd St ... Dr. Robin ECKERT
103 Exec Dir Workforce Dev/Cmty Educ ... Vacant
26 Director Marketing/Communications ... Mr. David HESSEN
13 Director Information Technology ... Mr. Anderson FORREST
37 Director Financial Aid/Registrar ... Mr. Benjamin ROSENBERGER
96 Director of Purchasing ... Ms. Cindy URICK
18 Director of Facilities/Safety ... Mr. Alberto OTHUON
04 Exec Admin Asst to the President ... Ms. Sandra STRAUSE
20 Dean of Instruction ... Mr. Kevin COOTS
07 Dir Admiss & Enrollment Svcs ... Ms. Kathy CUNNINGHAM
35 Coordinator of Student Life ... Ms. Jamica ANDREWS
76 Assoc Dean of Health Prof ... Dr. Stacia VISGARDA
28 Director of Diversity ... Ms. Lizette FLOWERS

Reconstructionist Rabbinical College (B)

1299 Church Road, Wyncote PA 19095-1898
County: Montgomery FICE Identification: 022734
Unit ID: 215619
Telephone: (215) 576-0800 Carnegie Class: Spec-4-yr-Faith
FAX Number: (215) 576-6143 Calendar System: Semester
URL: www.rrc.edu
Established: 1968 Annual Graduate Tuition & Fees: N/A
Enrollment: 43 Coed
Affiliation or Control: Jewish IRS Status: 501(c)3
Highest Offering: Doctorate; No Undergraduates
Accreditation: M

01 President ... Rabbi Deborah WAXMAN
05 Vice Pres Academic Affairs ... Dr. Amanda BECKENSTEIN MBUVI
03 Executive Vice President ... Rabbi Amber POWERS
26 Asst Vice Pres Communications ... Vacant
11 Director of Operations ... Mr. Robert CHAVEZ
08 Library Director ... Rabbi Alan LAPAYOVER
15 Director of Human Resources ... Ms. Cheryl TYSON

Reformed Episcopal Seminary (C)

826 Second Avenue, Blue Bell PA 19422-1257
County: Montgomery Identification: 667050
Unit ID: 216348
Telephone: (610) 292-9852 Carnegie Class: Spec-4-yr-Faith
FAX Number: (610) 292-9853 Calendar System: Quarter
URL: www.reseminary.edu
Established: 1887 Annual Graduate Tuition & Fees: N/A
Enrollment: 18 Coed
Affiliation or Control: Reformed Episcopal Church IRS Status: 501(c)3
Highest Offering: Master's; No Undergraduates
Accreditation: THEOL

01 President and Dean ... Rev Dr. Jonathan S. RICHES
05 Associate Dean of Faculty ... Rev Dr. Derek COOPER
07 Associate Dean of Admissions & Aid ... Dr. Robert ARNER
13 Dir Information Technology/Web Dev ... Rev. Vic BROBERG
18 Assoc Dean of Facilities/Finance ... Rev. Shawn D. RILEY
32 Chief Student Affairs/Life Officer ... Mr. John MAZZAMUTO

Reformed Presbyterian Theological Seminary (D)

7418 Penn Avenue, Pittsburgh PA 15208-2594
County: Allegheny FICE Identification: 003358
Unit ID: 215628
Telephone: (412) 731-6000 Carnegie Class: Not Classified
FAX Number: N/A Calendar System: Quarter
URL: www.rpts.edu
Established: 1810 Annual Graduate Tuition & Fees: N/A
Enrollment: N/A Coed
Affiliation or Control: Reformed Presbyterian Church IRS Status: 501(c)3
Highest Offering: Doctorate; No Undergraduates
Accreditation: THEOL

01 President ... Dr. Barry J. YORK
08 Library Director ... Mr. Jordan FEAGLEY
10 Treasurer ... Mr. James MCFARLAND
06 Registrar/Dir Admiss & Stdnt Svcs ... Mr. Edwin BLACKWOOD
37 Director of Financial Aid ... Mr. Josh MENEELY
111 Director of Inst Advancement ... Mr. Mark SAMPSON
11 Director of Operations ... Mr. Joshua NYE

Robert Morris University (E)

6001 University Boulevard,
Moon Township PA 15108-1189
County: Allegheny FICE Identification: 003359
Unit ID: 215655
Telephone: (412) 397-6400 Carnegie Class: DU-Mod
FAX Number: N/A Calendar System: Semester
URL: www.rmu.edu
Established: 1921 Annual Undergrad Tuition & Fees: $32,130
Enrollment: 4,134 Coed
Affiliation or Control: Independent Non-Profit IRS Status: 501(c)3
Highest Offering: Doctorate
Accreditation: M, CAEP, HSA, MPCAC, NAEYC, NMT, NURSE

01 President ... Dr. Michelle L. PATRICK
10 SVP Business Affairs/Treasurer ... Mr. Jeffrey A. LISTWAK
05 Provost ... Vacant
43 General Counsel & VP Legal Affairs ... Ms. Renee T. CAVALOVITCH
103 SVP Corporate Rels & Strategic Init ... Dr. Derya A. JACOBS
84 Vice Pres Enrollment Management ... Dr. Kevin HEARN
32 Vice President for Student Life ... Mr. John A. MICHALENKO
30 Vice President Development ... Mr. Matthew B. MILLET
18 Vice Pres for Facilities ... Mr. Perry F. ROOFNER
26 Vice Pres Public Rels/Marketing ... Mr. Jonathan E. POTTS
100 VP Planning & Admin/Chief of Staff ... Dr. David R. MAJKA
41 VP & Director of Athletics ... Mr. Chris A. KING
50 Acting Dean School of Business ... Dr. Prasad VEMALA
54 Dean School of Engr/Math/Science ... Dr. Maria V. KALEVITCH
79 Dean Sch Informatics/Humanities/SS ... Dr. Amjad ALI
66 Dean School of Nursing/Educ ... Dr. Mark M. MEYERS
88 Dir Univ/Athletic Sponsorship ... Mr. Matt F. O'BRIEN
84 Assoc VP Enrollment Management ... Ms. Kellie L. LAURENZI
31 AVP Cmty Engage/Leadership Devel ... Ms. Peggy M. OUTON
46 Assoc Provost Research/Graduate ... Dr. Sushil ACHARYA
20 Assoc Provost Academic Alliances ... Dr. Tim M. SCHLAK
35 Assistant Dean of Students ... Mrs. Maureen H. KEEFER
08 University Librarian ... Ms. Chloe P. MILLS
21 Chief Acctg/Financial Planning Ofcr ... Ms. Melissa A. MICCO
06 University Registrar ... Ms. Daniell C. MATTHEWS
19 Chief of Police ... Mr. Jeff JAMES
36 Senior Director Career Center ... Mr. David J. AUSMAN
39 Director Residence Life ... Mrs. Anne L. LAHODA
28 Chief Diversity/Inclusion Officer ... Dr. Anthony G. ROBINS
27 Sr Dir Marketing & Public Relations ... Mr. Brian J. EDWARDS
37 Sr Director Financial Aid ... Ms. Stephanie N. HENDERSHOT
44 Director Alumni Engagement ... Ms. Jennifer C. YOUNG
04 Exec Assistant to the President ... Ms. Valerie M. MURRAY
101 Board Liaison & Asst Secretary ... Ms. Jill M. KRIEGER
13 Chief Information Technology Ofcr ... Mr. Phillip G. MILLER
15 Chief Human Resources Officer ... Ms. Lisa H. HERNANDEZ

Rosedale Technical College (F)

215 Beecham Drive, Suite 2, Pittsburgh PA 15205-9791
County: Allegheny FICE Identification: 012050
Unit ID: 215682
Telephone: (412) 521-6200 Carnegie Class: Spec 2-yr-Tech
FAX Number: (412) 521-2520 Calendar System: Semester
URL: www.rosedaletech.org
Established: 1949 Annual Undergrad Tuition & Fees: $15,125
Enrollment: 385 Coed
Affiliation or Control: Independent Non-Profit IRS Status: 501(c)3
Highest Offering: Associate Degree
Accreditation: ACCSC

01 President ... Dennis F. WILKE
05 Director of Education ... Kara CHAN
30 VP College Development/Comm ... Debbie BIER
84 Dir Student Enrollment & Outreach ... Kim BELL

Rosemont College (G)

1400 Montgomery Avenue, Rosemont PA 19010-1699
County: Montgomery FICE Identification: 003360
Unit ID: 215691
Telephone: (610) 527-0200 Carnegie Class: Masters/M
FAX Number: (610) 527-0341 Calendar System: Semester
URL: www.rosemont.edu
Established: 1921 Annual Undergrad Tuition & Fees: $20,650
Enrollment: 777 Coed
Affiliation or Control: Roman Catholic IRS Status: 501(c)3
Highest Offering: Master's
Accreditation: M, CACREP

01 Interim President ... Mr. Jim CAWLEY
05 Provost/VP Academic/Student Affairs ... Dr. Mika NASH
10 VP for Finance & Administration ... Mr. Marty MEHRINGER
111 VP of Institutional Advancement ... Mrs. Jen TUBEROSA
32 Dean Student Success & Engagement ... Dr. Karen GEIGER
84 VP of Enrollment & Marketing ... Mrs. Meghan HALEY
110 Asst VP of Development ... Ms. Mary REINETTE ANDREWS
08 Exec Director of Library & Learning ... Mr. Brice PETERSON
58 Dean Schools Graduate/Prof Studies ... Mr. Jay KOLICK
20 Academic Dean Undergrad College ... Mrs. Paulette HUTCHINSON
07 Dir Enrollment Information Systems ... Vacant
29 Asst VP for Alumni Relations ... Mrs. Julie HYLAND
26 Director of External Relations ... Mrs. Katie DUBOFF
41 Director of Athletics ... Dr. Phillip MILLER
15 Director of Human Resources ... Mrs. Andrea BYRON
42 VP of Mission & Ministry ... Sr. Peg DOYLE, SHCJ
38 Director of Counseling Cntr ... Vacant
39 Director of Residence Life ... Mr. Malek STEWART
19 Co-Director of Public Safety ... Mr. Ilir CONI
19 Co-Director of Public Safety ... Ms. Esmeralda JEAN-BAPTISTE
21 Controller ... Mr. Charles STEINMETZ
37 Director of Financial Aid ... Vacant
06 Registrar ... Ms. Maureen MALONE
28 VP Diversity & Belonging ... Vacant
04 Admin Assistant to the President ... Ms. Jen EAST
13 Chief Information Technology Ofcr ... Mr. Dan MASON

Saint Charles Borromeo Seminary (H)

100 E Wynnewood Road, Wynnewood PA 19096-3099
County: Montgomery FICE Identification: 003364
Unit ID: 216047
Telephone: (610) 667-3394 Carnegie Class: Spec-4-yr-Faith
FAX Number: (610) 667-7635 Calendar System: Semester
URL: www.scs.edu
Established: 1832 Annual Undergrad Tuition & Fees: $22,570
Enrollment: 180 Male
Affiliation or Control: Roman Catholic IRS Status: 501(c)3
Highest Offering: Master's
Accreditation: M, THEOL

01 Rector & President ... M.Rev. Timothy C. SENIOR
05 Vice President for Academic Affairs ... Rev. Robert A. PESARCHICK
03 Vice Rector ... Rev. Patrick BRADY
10 Chief Financial Officer/COO ... Mr. Mark MCLAUGHLIN
108 VP Info Services & Assessment ... Mrs. Cait KOKOLUS
33 Dean of Men Theology ... Rev. Brian KANE
33 Dean of Men College ... Rev. George SZPARAGOWSKI
08 Director of Library Services ... Mr. James HUMBLE
06 Registrar ... Mr. Todd CHIARAVALLOTI
42 Dir Spiritual Formation Theology ... Fr. Herb SPERGER
42 Dir Spiritual Formation College ... Fr. Dennis CARBONARO
88 Director Pastoral/Apostolic Form ... Rev. George SZPARAGOWSKI
73 Dean School of Theological Studies ... Msgr. Michael MAGEE
21 Director of Financial Services ... Ms. Barbara COADY
37 Director Student Financial Aid ... Ms. Nora DOWNEY
29 Director Alumni Affairs ... Ms. Aileen KAIN

Saint Francis University (I)

PO Box 600, Loretto PA 15940-0600
County: Cambria FICE Identification: 003366
Unit ID: 215743
Telephone: (814) 472-3000 Carnegie Class: Masters/L
FAX Number: (814) 472-3003 Calendar System: Semester
URL: www.francis.edu
Established: 1847 Annual Undergrad Tuition & Fees: $39,278
Enrollment: 2,769 Coed
Affiliation or Control: Roman Catholic IRS Status: 501(c)3
Highest Offering: Doctorate
Accreditation: M, ARCPA, EXSC, IACBE, NURSE, OT, PTA, SW

01 President ... Rev. Malachi VAN TASSELL, TOR
05 Vice President for Academic Affairs ... Dr. Michael MCGINNIS
10 Vice President for Finance ... Mr. Jeffrey SAVINO
32 Vice Pres for Student Development ... Dr. Frank MONTECALVO
42 Director of Mission Integration ... Fr. Matthew SIMONS, TOR
111 Vice President for Advancement ... Mr. Robert CRUSCIEL
84 Vice Pres for Enrollment Management ... Mr. Steven SOBA
86 Asst VP Govt Rels/Grants/Found ... Mr. Robert YOUNG
08 Dean of Library Services ... Ms. Sandra A. BALOUGH
97 Dean of General Education ... Dr. Irene WOLF
06 Registrar ... Mr. Jacob TAYLOR
09 Director of Institutional Research ... Ms. Tammy GRAESSLE
37 Financial Aid Director ... Vacant
26 VP for Communications & Marketing ... Ms. Erin MCCLOSKEY
30 Director of Development ... Ms. Marie B. MELUSKY
38 Director of Counseling Center ... Vacant

13 Director Computer Services ... Mr. Jason NAIRN
29 Director of Alumni Relations ... Mr. Eric HORELL
51 Dean Francis Worldwide ... Dr. Trisha MCFADDEN
18 Director of Physical Plant ... Mr. David WILLIAMS
21 Controller ... Mr. Thomas R. FRITZ
41 Director of Athletics ... Mr. James DOWNER
88 Dir Small Business Devel Center ... Mr. Jeff BOLDIZAR
19 University Police ... Capt. Eric ALLEN
39 Director of Residence Life ... Mr. Donald MILES
42 Director of Campus Ministry ... Rev. Stephen WARUSZEWSKI
121 Dean of Student Academic Success ... Dr. Renee BERNARD
124 Dir of Student Engagement ... Ms. Kristen CORCORAN
15 Director of Human Resources ... Ms. Marian BENDER
28 Director of Multicultural Affairs ... Ms. Lynne BANKS
96 Director of Purchasing ... Mr. Michael KUTCHMAN
20 Associate Provost ... Dr. Peter R. SKONER
40 Manager of Bookstore ... Ms. Barbara SHINGLE
04 Admin Assistant to the President ... Ms. Vickie SOYKA
07 Director of Admissions ... Dr. Bobby ANDERSON
104 Director Study Abroad ... Ms. Leona HORNER

Saint Joseph's University (A)

5600 City Avenue, Philadelphia PA 19131-1376
County: Philadelphia FICE Identification: 003367
Unit ID: 215770
Telephone: (610) 660-1000 Carnegie Class: Masters/L
FAX Number: (610) 660-1201 Calendar System: Semester
URL: www.sju.edu
Established: 1851 Annual Undergrad Tuition & Fees: $47,940
Enrollment: 6,779 Coed
Affiliation or Control: Roman Catholic IRS Status: 501(c)3
Highest Offering: Doctorate
Accreditation: M, ACBSP, #ARCPA, OT, PHAR, PTA

01 President ... Dr. Mark C. REED
05 Provost ... Dr. Cheryl A. MCCONNELL
10 VP Financial Affairs ... Mr. David R. BEAUPRE
26 VP University Relations ... Mr. Joseph P. KENDER
88 Executive Director of Mission ... Rev. Daniel R. JOYCE, SJ
49 Dean College of Arts & Sciences ... Vacant
50 Dean Haub School of Business ... Dr. Joseph A. DIANGELO, JR.
32 VP Student Life ... Dr. Cary M. ANDERSON
41 VP Director of Athletics ... Ms. Jill R. BODENSTEINER
84 VP Enrollment Management ... Ms. Karen PELLEGRINO
27 Chief Marketing/Communications Ofcr ... Ms. Elizabeth K. WALSH
18 AVP Administrative Services ... Mr. Timothy MCGURIMAN
43 General Counsel ... Ms. Tracey PACHMAN
100 AVP Chief of Staff ... Ms. Sarah F. QUINN
84 AVP Enrollment Management ... Mr. Robert J. MCBRIDE
13 Chief Information Officer ... Mr. Francis J. DISANTI
04 Admin Assistant to the President ... Ms. Jennifer L. FALCON
06 Registrar ... Vacant
07 Director of Admissions ... Ms. Maureen MATHIS
08 Chief Library Officer ... Ms. Anne Z. KRAKOW
09 Director of Institutional Research ... Mr. James F. GRASELL
101 Secretary of the Institution/Board ... Ms. Sarah F. QUINN
104 Director Study Abroad ... Mr. Thomas KESARIS
15 Chief Human Resources Officer ... Ms. Zenobia HARGUST
19 Director Security/Safety ... Mr. Arthur G. GROVER
28 Director of Diversity ... Dr. Nicole R. STOKES
37 Director Student Financial Aid ... Ms. Elizabeth A. RIHL LEWINSKY
38 Director Student Counseling ... Dr. Gregory K. NICHOLLS
44 Director Annual Giving ... Mr. Michael A. RATH
86 Director Government Relations ... Mr. Wadell RIDLEY
96 Director of Purchasing ... Ms. Deborah T. TAVERA
102 Director Foundation/Corporate Rels ... Ms. Janet Y. SCHULZE
53 Dean Health Studies/Education ... Dr. Angela R. MCDONALD

St. Tikhon's Orthodox Theological Seminary (B)

PO Box 130, South Canaan PA 18459-0130
County: Wayne FICE Identification: 039193
Telephone: (570) 561-1818 Carnegie Class: Not Classified
FAX Number: N/A Calendar System: Semester
URL: www.stots.edu
Established: 1938 Annual Undergrad Tuition & Fees: N/A
Enrollment: N/A Coed
Affiliation or Control: Other IRS Status: 501(c)3
Highest Offering: First Professional Degree
Accreditation: THEOL

01 President ... Metr. Tikhon MOLLARD
03 Rector/CEO ... Abp. Michael DAHULICH
05 Seminary Dean/COO ... V.Rev. John PARKER
10 Chief Financial Officer ... Ms. Janet A. VANDUYN
04 Administrative Asst to Dean/COO ... Ms. Marina HITCHCOCK
08 Librarian ... Vacant
06 Registrar/Assoc Dean Academic Affs ... Dr. Paul J. WITEK
30 Dir Office of Mission Development ... Dr. David FOX
32 Director Student Life ... Fr. Ignatius GAUVAIN

Saint Vincent College (C)

300 Fraser Purchase Road, Latrobe PA 15650-2690
County: Westmoreland FICE Identification: 003368
Unit ID: 215798
Telephone: (724) 805-2500 Carnegie Class: Bac-A&S
FAX Number: (724) 805-2019 Calendar System: Semester
URL: www.stvincent.edu
Established: 1846 Annual Undergrad Tuition & Fees: $37,604
Enrollment: 1,634 Coed
Affiliation or Control: Roman Catholic IRS Status: 501(c)3
Highest Offering: Doctorate
Accreditation: M, ACBSP, ANEST

01 President ... Fr. Paul TAYLOR, OSB
05 VP Academic Affairs ... Dr. John DELANEY
03 Executive Vice President/COO ... Dr. Jeffrie MALLORY
10 VP Finance/Treasurer ... Mr. Joshua GUISER
111 VP Institutional Advancement ... Mr. David HOLLENBAUGH
32 VP Student Affairs ... Vacant
07 Dean of Admissions ... Ms. Heather KABALA
13 Chief Information Officer ... Mr. Justin FABIN
50 Dean McKenna Sch Bus/Econ/Govt ... Dr. Michael URICK
81 Dean Science/Math & Computing ... Dr. Stephen M. JODIS
49 Dean Arts/Humanities/Social Science ... Dr. Elaine BENNETT
06 Registrar ... Ms. Celine R. BRUDNOK
08 Librarian ... Bro. David KELLY, OSB
29 Director of Alumni Relations ... Mr. Brian NIEMIEC
36 Director Career Services ... Ms. Kimberly WOODLEY
121 AVP Student Success and Retention ... Fr. Francois DIOUF, OSB
15 AVP for HR and Talent Acquisition ... Ms. Nicole SIGMUND
42 Director of Campus Ministry ... Rev. Maximilian MAXWELL, OSB
23 Director Wellness Center ... Ms. Gretchen FLOCK
19 Director Public Safety ... Ms. Stephanie FAGO
41 Athletic Director ... Rev. Myron KIRSCH, OSB
35 Dean of Students ... Vacant
96 Director of Purchasing ... Vacant
18 Director of Facility Management ... Mr. Douglas EPPLEY
40 Manager Book Center ... Rev. Anthony GROSSI, OSB
58 Coord of Graduate Studies ... Ms. Amanda GUNTHER
04 Executive Asst to President ... Ms. Lisa POOLE
104 Director Study Abroad ... Vacant
37 AVP Financial Aid ... Ms. Mary GAZAL
102 AVP Foundation/Govt/Corporate Rels ... Ms. Christine FOSCHIA
43 Dir Legal Services/General Counsel ... Mr. Bruce ANTKOWIAK
108 Director Assessment & IR ... Vacant
26 Dir Marketing/Communications ... Mr. Zachary FLOCK
39 Dir Res Life and Student Conduct ... Mr. Ishmael SOLOMON

Saint Vincent Seminary (D)

300 Fraser Purchase Road, Latrobe PA 15650-2690
County: Westmoreland Identification: 666018
Unit ID: 215813
Telephone: (724) 805-2592 Carnegie Class: Spec-4-yr-Faith
FAX Number: (724) 532-5052 Calendar System: Semester
URL: www.saintvincentseminary.edu
Established: 1846 Annual Undergrad Tuition & Fees: N/A
Enrollment: 54 Coed
Affiliation or Control: Roman Catholic IRS Status: 501(c)3
Highest Offering: Master's
Accreditation: THEOL

01 Rector ... V.Rev. Edward M. MAZICH, OSB
00 Chancellor ... Rt Rev. Martin BARTEL, OSB
88 Director of Spiritual Formation ... Rev. Boniface N. HICKS, OSB
05 Academic Dean ... Rev. Patrick T. CRONAUER, OSB
03 Vice-Rector ... Rev. John-Mary TOMPKINS, OSB
42 Director of Liturgy ... Rev. Cyprian G. CONSTANTINE, OSB
88 Director of Pastoral Formation ... Rev. Jude BRADY
32 Dean of Students ... Rev. Emmanuel O. AFUNUGO
38 Dir of Pre-Theologian Formation ... Dr. Lawrence SUTTON
04 Administrative Asst to President ... Ms. Lisa POOLE
11 EVP/Chief Operating Officer ... Mr. Jeffrie MALLORY
06 Registrar ... Ms. Celine BRUDNOK
07 Dean of Admissions ... Ms. Heather KABALA
08 Director of Libraries ... Br. David KELLY, OSB
10 VP for Finance & Treasury/CFO ... Mr. Joshua GUISER
101 Secretary of the Institution/Board ... Rev. Warren MURRMAN, OSB
26 Director Marketing/Communication ... Mr. Zach FLOCK
13 Chief Info Technology Officer (CIO) ... Mr. Justin FABIN
118 Dir Ben/Staff Conduct/Asst Counsel ... Mrs. Judith MAHER
18 Dir of Facilities/Capital Mgmt/Plng ... Mr. Douglas EPPLEY
15 AVP Human Res/Talent Acquisition ... Ms. Nicole SIGMUND
19 Director of Public Safety ... Sgt. Stephanie FAGO
22 Asst Gen Counsel/Title 9 Coord ... Miss Eileen FLINN
102 Asst VP Found/Govt & Corp Relations ... Ms. Christine L. FOSCHIA
29 Director of Alumni Relations ... Mr. Brian NIEMIEC
30 Director of Mission Advancement ... Mr. Shannon JORDAN
37 Asst VP for Financial Aid ... Ms. Mary GAZAL
41 Athletic Director ... Rev. Myron KIRSCH, OSB
43 Counsel to College/Archabbey ... Mr. Bruce ANTKOWIAK
111 VP Inst Advancement/Campaign Dir ... Mr. David HOLLENBAUGH
108 Coordinator of Assessment ... Ms. Kelly SHRUM
27 Dir of PR - Archabbey & Seminary ... Ms. Kim METZGAR
104 Asst Dean Studies/Dir Acad Accom ... Vacant
106 Director Application Services ... Mr. Roberto WISNESCK
91 Dir Enterprise/Application Services ... Mr. Doug CARNS
36 Dir Career/Professional Development ... Ms. Kimberly WOODLY
39 Asst Director Resident Life ... Mr. Tristin GREER
21 Accounting & Finance Manager ... Mr. Ricardo EZZI
50 Dean of School of Business ... Dr. Mike URICK
86 Assistant to President/Mission ... Br. Norman HIPPS, OSB
117 Dir Technical/Cybersecurity Svcs ... Vacant

Salus University (E)

8360 Old York Road, Elkins Park PA 19027-1516
County: Philadelphia FICE Identification: 003311
Unit ID: 214564
Telephone: (215) 780-1400 Carnegie Class: Spec-4-yr-Other Health
FAX Number: (215) 780-1325 Calendar System: Quarter
URL: www.salus.edu
Established: 1919 Annual Undergrad Tuition & Fees: N/A
Enrollment: 1,280 Coed
Affiliation or Control: Independent Non-Profit IRS Status: 501(c)3
Highest Offering: Doctorate
Accreditation: M, ARCPA, AUD, OPT, OPTR, OT, SP

01 President ... Dr. Michael H. MITTLEMAN
05 Provost & VP Academic Affairs ... Dr. Barry ECKERT
10 Vice Pres Finance/Business Affairs ... Mr. Donald KATES
17 Vice Pres Clinical Operations ... Dr. John GAAL
32 Dean Student Affairs ... Dr. James CALDWELL
116 Research Compliance Coordinator ... Mr. Nicholaus JONES
06 Registrar ... Ms. Shannon BOSS
13 Int VP Tech/Learning Resources Svcs ... Mr. Christopher ESPOSITO
37 Director Student Financial Affairs ... Ms. Jamie SCHULANG
18 Assoc VP Facilities Mgmt/Inst Svcs ... Mr. Richard ECHEVARRI
111 VP Inst Advancement/Community Rels ... Ms. Jackie PATTERSON
26 Director of Communications ... Ms. Alexis ABATE
29 Director Alumni Relations/Giving ... Vacant
51 Dean Intl/Continuing Education ... Mrs. Melissa VITEK
40 Bookstore Manager ... Mr. Joe NOCE
24 Director Instructional Media ... Mr. Glenn ROEDEL
36 Dir Student Placement/Student Affs ... Mr. Ryan HOLLISTER
84 Director Enrollment Management ... Dr. Jim CALDWELL
88 Exec Dir Inst Visually Impaired ... Dr. Brooke KRUEMMLING
08 Director Learning Resource Center ... Ms. Marietta DOOLEY
19 Director of Security ... Mr. Carlos RODRIGUEZ
15 Dir Human Res/Affirm Action/Facil ... Ms. Maura KEENAN
96 Director of Purchasing ... Ms. Lydia FRIEL
28 Director of Diversity ... Dr. Juliana WILLIAMS

Seton Hill University (F)

1 Seton Hill Drive, Greensburg PA 15601-1599
County: Westmoreland FICE Identification: 003362
Unit ID: 215947
Telephone: (724) 834-2200 Carnegie Class: Masters/M
FAX Number: N/A Calendar System: Semester
URL: www.setonhill.edu
Established: 1883 Annual Undergrad Tuition & Fees: $37,946
Enrollment: 1,935 Coed
Affiliation or Control: Roman Catholic IRS Status: 501(c)3
Highest Offering: Doctorate
Accreditation: M, ARCPA, DENT, DIET, DIETC, EXSC, IACBE, MUS, NURSE, @PTA, SW

01 President ... Dr. Mary FINGER
88 VP Mission ... Sr. Maureen O'BRIEN, SC
05 Provost ... Sr. Susan YOCHUM, SC
10 Vice Pres Finance/Admin & CFO ... Ms. Jennifer LUNDY
43 VP/General Counsel ... Ms. Imogene CATHEY
111 Vice Pres Institutional Advancement ... Ms. Molly ROBB SHIMKO
13 Chief Information Officer ... Ms. Melissa ALSING
84 Vice Pres Enrollment Management ... Mr. Brett FRESHOUR
21 Controller ... Mr. Brent JACKSON
32 Vice President for Student Affairs ... Dr. Rosalie CARPENTER
07 Director Undergraduate Admissions ... Ms. Amanda GODULA
08 Director of Library ... Mr. David STANLEY
29 Director of Alumni Relations ... Ms. Ashley ZWIERZELEWSKI
37 Director of Financial Aid ... Ms. Tracey DE BAEZ SNYDER
36 Director of Career Development ... Ms. Renee STAREK
15 Asst VP Human Resources ... Mrs. Darlene SAUERS
18 Director Facilities ... Mr. Cale GEARY
41 Executive Athletic Director ... Mr. Chris SNYDER
42 Director Campus Ministry ... Mr. Tony KRZMARZICK
06 Registrar ... Ms. Constance BECKEL
38 Director Student Counseling ... Ms. Teresa BASSI-COOK
09 Director of Institutional Research ... Dr. Jason DRAPER
26 Chief Public Relations Officer ... Ms. Jennifer REEGER
96 Director of Purchasing ... Mr. Charles O'NEILL
19 Director Public Safety/Police Chief ... Ms. Michele PROCTOR
22 Dir Affirmative Action/EEO ... Ms. Darlene SAUERS
25 Dir Grants & Government Support ... Ms. Cynthia FERRARI
39 Director Student Housing ... Mr. Cory CAMPBELL
04 Exec Asst to the President/Provost ... Ms. Jennifer ZEMBA
100 Chief of Staff ... Ms. Carol BILLMAN
28 Director of Diversity ... Dr. Adriel HILTON

South Hills School of Business and Technology (G)

508 58th Street, Altoona PA 16602
Telephone: (814) 944-6134 Identification: 770772
Accreditation: ACCSC, CAHIIM, MAAB

South Hills School of Business and Technology (H)

480 Waupelani Drive, State College PA 16801-4516
County: Centre FICE Identification: 013263
Unit ID: 216083
Telephone: (814) 234-7755 Carnegie Class: Assoc/HT-High Trad
FAX Number: (814) 234-0926 Calendar System: Quarter
URL: www.southhills.edu
Established: 1970 Annual Undergrad Tuition & Fees: $18,475
Enrollment: 307 Coed
Affiliation or Control: Proprietary IRS Status: Proprietary
Highest Offering: Associate Degree
Accreditation: ACCSC, CAHIIM, DMS, MAAB

00 Owner ... Mrs. Maralyn MAZZA
01 President/Director ... Mr. S. Paul MAZZA, III
05 Academic Affairs Officer ... Ms. Ingrid THOMPSON
07 Director of Admissions/Marketing ... Mr. Glenn SLATER

37 Director Student Financial Aid .... Mr. LeRoy SPICER
20 Director of Education/Reg Affairs ....Ms. Natalie LOMBARDO-BEAVER

Susquehanna University (A)

514 University Avenue, Selinsgrove PA 17870-1164
County: Snyder FICE Identification: 003369
Unit ID: 216278
Telephone: (570) 374-0101 Carnegie Class: Bac-A&S
FAX Number: (570) 372-4040 Calendar System: Semester
URL: www.susqu.edu
Established: 1858 Annual Undergrad Tuition & Fees: $51,140
Enrollment: 2,241 Coed
Affiliation or Control: Evangelical Lutheran Church In America
IRS Status: 501(c)3
Highest Offering: Master's
Accreditation: M, MUS

01 President ....Dr. Jonathan GREEN
100 Chief of Staff ....Mr. Malcolm DERK
05 Provost/Dean of Faculty ....Dr. Dave RAMSARAN
11 VP for Operations .... Ms. Jennifer BUCHER
10 VP for Finance ....Mr. Jeffrey LISTWAK
111 Vice President for Advancement .... Ms. Melissa KOMORA
84 VP for Enrollment & Student Fin Svc ...Mr. Delorean J. MENIFEE
32 VP Student Life/Dean of Students ....Dr. Francy MAGEE
81 Dean Natural and Social Sciences ....Dr. Katherine H. STRAUB
79 Dean Arts and Humanities ....Dr. Laurie J. CARTER
50 Dean Weis School of Business ....Dr. Matthew ROUSU
26 VP for Marketing & Communications ....Mr. Aaron MARTIN
15 Senior Director of Human Resources .... Ms. Grace LOWRY
04 Senior Admin Asst to the President .... Ms. Sharon POPE
38 Dean Health & Wellness .... Dr. Stacey PEARSON-WHARTON
89 Director of First Year Experience .... Ms. Samantha PROFFITT
28 Sr Dir of Inclusion & Diversity ....Ms. Dena SALERNO
07 Assistant VP of Admission .... Ms. Jessica SULLIVAN
08 Director of the Library .... Mr. Robert SIECZKIEWICZ
37 Asst VP Student Financial Svcs ....Mr. Justin RUMMEL
06 Registrar ....Ms. Jeannette RORK
42 University Chaplain ....Rev. Scott M. KERSHNER
13 Chief Information Officer ....Ms. Jennifer SERVIDIO
41 Director of Athletics ....Mr. Sharief HASHIM
36 Asst Provost/Dir Career Development ... Ms. Michaeline SHUMAN
88 Director of Event Management .... Ms. Michelle HARMAN
110 Associate VP for Advancement ....Ms. Rebecca TOTH
108 Asst Prov of Inst Effectiveness .... Ms. Danielle BROWN
25 Director of Grants & Foundation Rel ..Mr. Christopher WONDERS
104 Dean of Global Programs .... Dr. Scott MANNING
18 AVP for Facilities & Campus Safety .... Mr. Christopher BAILEY
92 Director of Honors Program .... Dr. Marcos KRIEGER
122 Asst Dir Engagement-Greek Life ....Vacant

Swarthmore College (B)

500 College Avenue, Swarthmore PA 19081-1390
County: Delaware FICE Identification: 003370
Unit ID: 216287
Telephone: (610) 328-8000 Carnegie Class: Bac-A&S
FAX Number: (610) 328-8000 Calendar System: Semester
URL: www.swarthmore.edu
Established: 1864 Annual Undergrad Tuition & Fees: $54,456
Enrollment: 1,437 Coed
Affiliation or Control: Independent Non-Profit IRS Status: 501(c)3
Highest Offering: Master's
Accreditation: M

01 President ....Valerie A. SMITH
05 Provost & Dean of the Faculty ....Sarah WILLIE LEBRETON
10 Vice President Finance & Admin ....Robert GOLDBERG
111 Vice President for Advancement ....Elizabeth BOLUCH WOOD
15 Vice Pres for Human Resources ....Beth GLASSMAN
26 VP Communications .... Andy HIRSCH
07 Vice Pres & Dean of Admissions ....Jim BOCK
18 Assoc VP Sustainable Fac Op/Cap Pln ....Andrew FEICK
21 Asst Vice Pres Finance & Controller .... Alice TURBIVILLE
32 Vice President for Student Affairs .... James TERHUNE
28 Asst Dean of Diversity/Inclusion ....Imaani EL-BURKI
06 Registrar ....Kristen SMITH
08 College Librarian .... Peggy SEIDEN
108 Asst VP Inst Effective/Assessment .... Robin H. SHORES
29 Asst VP Alumni & Family Programs ....Vacant
37 Director of Financial Aid .... Varo L. DUFFINS
36 AVP/Executive Dir Career Services ....Claire KLIEGER
19 Director of Public Safety ....Michael HILL
43 General Counsel ....Sharmaine LAMAR
23 Director Worth Health Center .... Casey ANDERSON
38 Director Psychological Services ....Simone COLLINS
41 Director Physical Educ/Athletics .... Brad KOCH
13 Chief Info Technology Officer ....Vacant
35 Director Student Engagement .... Rachel HEAD
104 Director Off-Campus Study ....Pat MARTIN
39 Director of Residential Communities ....Estrellita LONGORIA
105 Web Developer .... Les LEACH
16 AVP/HR and Equal Opportunity .... Paula MCDONALD
96 Sr Manager Strategic Sourcing .... Chris KANE
102 Director Institutional Relations .... David FOREMAN
04 Executive Asst to the President ....Jen GIFFORD
100 Chief of Staff ....Erin BROWNLEE DELL

Talmudical Yeshiva of Philadelphia (C)

6063 Drexel Road, Philadelphia PA 19131-1296
County: Philadelphia FICE Identification: 012523
Unit ID: 216311
Telephone: (215) 477-1000 Carnegie Class: Spec-4-yr-Faith
FAX Number: (215) 477-5065 Calendar System: Semester
Established: 1953 Annual Undergrad Tuition & Fees: $9,725
Enrollment: 132 Male
Affiliation or Control: Independent Non-Profit IRS Status: 501(c)3
Highest Offering: First Talmudic Degree
Accreditation: RABN

01 Chief Executive Officer (President) .... Mr. Alexander TAUB
05 Dean ....Rabbi Shmuel KAMENETSKY
05 Dean ....Rabbi Yehuda SVEI
05 Dean ....Rabbi Sholom KAMENETSKY

Temple University (D)

1801 N Broad Street, Philadelphia PA 19122
County: Philadelphia FICE Identification: 003371
Unit ID: 216339
Telephone: (215) 204-7405 Carnegie Class: DU-Highest
FAX Number: (215) 204-5600 Calendar System: Semester
URL: www.temple.edu
Established: 1884 Annual Undergrad Tuition & Fees (In-State): $16,970
Enrollment: 37,236 Coed
Affiliation or Control: State Related IRS Status: 501(c)3
Highest Offering: Doctorate
Accreditation: M, ARCPA, ART, CAATE, CAHIIM, CARTE, CLPSY, DANCE, DENT, @DIET, IPSY, JOUR, LAW, LSAR, MED, MUS, NURSE, OT, PCSAS, PH, PHAR, PLNG, POD, PTA, SCPSY, SP, SW, THEA

01 President ....Dr. Jason WINGARD
28 VP Diversity/Equity & Inclusion ....Dr. Valerie I. HARRISON
05 Provost ....Mr. Gregory M. MANDEL
43 VP & University Counsel ....Mr. Cameron ETEZADY
32 VP for Student Affairs ....Dr. Theresa A. POWELL
13 Interim VP Information Technology .... Mr. Larry BRANDOLPH
17 President/CEO Health Sys/Hospitals .... Mr. Michael A. YOUNG
26 Int AVP Strategic Univ Events ....Dr. Elizabeth LEEBRON TUTELMAN
10 Chief Operating Officer ....Mr. Kenneth H. KAISER
85 Int Vice Prov Global Engagement .... Dr. Emilia ZANKINA
35 Assoc VP/Dean of Students .... Dr. Stephanie IVES
111 VP Inst Advancement ....Ms. Mary E. BURKE
46 VP for Research ....Dr. Michele M. MASUCCI
18 VP Planning & Capital Projects ....Mr. Gennaro J. LEVA
21 Sr Assoc VP Finance ....Mr. William J. WILKINSON
109 Assoc VP Business Services ....Mr. Michael D. SCALES
15 VP Human Resources ....Ms. Sharon I. BOYLE
21 VP Finance & Treasurer .... Mr. David MARINO
22 Assoc VP/Chief Inclusion Officer .... Dr. Tiffenia ARCHIE
100 Asst VP Fin/Admin & Chief of Staff .....Ms. Kathryn P. D'ANGELO
20 Vice Provost for Faculty Affairs .... Dr. Jeremy S. JORDAN
20 Vice Provost Undergrad Studies .... Dr. Daniel BERMAN
108 Vice Provost Assessment ....Dr. Jodi LEVINE LAUFGRABEN
08 Dean for University Libraries ....Mr. Joseph P. LUCIA
06 Registrar .... Mr. Bhavesh BAMBHROLIA
41 Vice President/Athletics Director ....Mr. Arthur JOHNSON
35 Assoc Director Student Affairs ....Dr. Daniel DENGEL
36 Exec Director Career Services ....Ms. Kristen GALLO
88 Chief Compliance Officer .... Mr. Alejandro J. DIAZ
09 Director IR/Assessment ....Ms. Gina L. CALZAFERRI
104 Director Educ Abroad & Overseas .... Ms. Maureen GORDON
23 Sr Admin Student & Employee Health ....Dr. Mark DENYS
37 Director Student Financial Svcs .... Ms. Emilie VANTRIESTE
97 Vice Provost University College .... Dr. Vicki Lewis MCGARVEY
96 Director Purchasing ....Ms. Donna L. SCHWEIBENZ
113 Associate VP/Bursar ....Mr. Conrad MUTH
20 Assoc Vice Provost Undergrad ....Mr. Michael LAWLOR
84 Vice Provost Enroll Mgmt ....Vacant
40 Bookstore General Manager ....Mr. James HANLEY
49 Dean College of Liberal Arts ....Dr. Richard DEEG
53 Int Dean Col of Educ & Human Dev ....Dr. James E. DAVIS
61 Dean Beasley School of Law .... Ms. Rachel REBOUCHE'
64 Dean Boyer College of Music .... Dr. Robert T. STROKER
57 Dean Tyler School of Art ....Ms. Susan CAHAN
50 Dean Fox School of Business & Mgmt .....Dr. Ronald ANDERSON
52 Dean Kornberg School of Dentistry .... Dr. Amid ISMAIL
63 Int Dean Lewis Katz Sch of Medicine ....Dr. Amy J. GOLDBERG
67 Dean School of Pharmacy .... Dr. Jayanth PANYAM
54 Dean College of Engineering ....Dr. Keya SADEGHIPOUR
88 Dean School of Podiatric Medicine ....Dr. John A. MATTIACCI
72 Dean College of Science & Tech .... Dr. Michael KLEIN
60 Dean Klein College of Media & Comm ..... Mr. David BOARDMAN
69 Interim Dean College Public Health ....Dr. Jennifer IBRAHIM
88 Dean Sch Sport/Tourism/Hosp Mgmt ....Dr. Ronald ANDERSON
12 Dean Temple Japan Campus ....Mr. Matthew WILSON
12 Dean Temple Rome .... Dr. Emilia ZANKINA
07 Director of Admissions .... Ms. Karin W. MORMANDO
101 VP/University Secretary ....Mr. Michael B. GEBHARDT
19 VP Public Safety .... Ms. Jennifer GRIFFIN

Thaddeus Stevens College of Technology (E)

750 E King Street, Lancaster PA 17602-3198
County: Lancaster FICE Identification: 007912
Unit ID: 216296
Telephone: (717) 299-7731 Carnegie Class: Assoc/HVT-High Trad
FAX Number: (717) 299-7748 Calendar System: Semester
URL: www.stevenscollege.edu
Established: 1905 Annual Undergrad Tuition & Fees (In-State): $8,450
Enrollment: 1,227 Coed
Affiliation or Control: State IRS Status: 501(c)3
Highest Offering: Associate Degree
Accreditation: M

01 President ....Mr. Pedro RIVERA
03 Vice President/Spec Asst to Pres .... Dr. Timothy BIANCHI
05 Vice Pres Academic Affairs ....Dr. Antonio JACKSON
10 Vice President Finance and Admin .... Mr. George LONGRIDGE
20 Dean of Academic Affairs ....Mr. Michael DEGROFT
32 VP of Student Services/Athletic Dir ....Dr. Christopher METZLER
84 Dean of Enrollment Services .... Ms. Melissa WISNIEWSKI
08 Director of the Library .... Ms. Katherine PENNAVARIA
108 Dir Plng/Assess/Accountability/IR ....Dr. Adrienne FLACK
15 Dir Employee Engage/HR Specialist .... Ms. Heather BURKY
26 Exec Dir Strategy/Marketing & Comm ....Ms. Ann VALUCH
111 Exec Dir of College Advancement ....Ms. Pam SMITH
36 Director of Career Services ....Ms. Laurie GROVE
38 Coordinator of Student Counseling .... Ms. Debra SCHUCH
38 Mental Health Counselor ....Ms. Michelle MARMO
39 Director Residence Life/Registrar .... Mr. Jason KUNTZ
18 Facilities Maintenance Manager ....Mr. Gene DUNCAN
13 Director of Information Technology .... Mr. Andrew CARSON
37 Director of Financial Aid .... Ms. Emily SMOKER
07 Assoc Director of Admissions .... Ms. Megan WYSOCK
04 Exec Asst to President ....Ms. Stacy THORNWALL-ROGERS
06 Registrar ....Ms. Amber DUH
28 Chief Diversity/Equity & Inclusion .... Dr. Marian WILSON
30 Director of Development ....Mr. Warren TAYLOR

† Qualified individuals are eligible for full scholarships based on family/financial status.

Thiel College (F)

75 College Avenue, Greenville PA 16125-2181
County: Mercer FICE Identification: 003376
Unit ID: 216357
Telephone: (724) 589-2000 Carnegie Class: Bac-Diverse
FAX Number: (724) 589-2850 Calendar System: Semester
URL: www.thiel.edu
Established: 1866 Annual Undergrad Tuition & Fees: $33,520
Enrollment: 768 Coed
Affiliation or Control: Evangelical Lutheran Church In America
IRS Status: 501(c)3
Highest Offering: Master's
Accreditation: M, #ARCPA, @SP

01 President ....Dr. Susan TRAVERSO
05 VP Academic Affairs/Dean of College ....Vacant
111 Vice Pres for College Advancement .... Ms. Roberta LEONARD
10 VP Finance & Administration ....Ms. Amy ARBOGAST
13 Director IT Services ....Vacant
04 Executive Asst to President .... Mrs. Amy TACZANOWSKY
32 VP of Student Life & Athletics .... Mr. Michael MCKINNEY
84 VP Enrollment Management ....Mrs. Ashley ZULLO
20 Assoc Academic Dean .... Dr. Greg BUTCHER
26 VP Communications/Marketing ....Mr. Richard ORR
41 Director of Athletics ....Vacant
112 Dir of Advancement ....Mr. Mark BATT
29 Director of Alumni Relations ....Mr. David HUMMEL
18 Director of Facilities Operations .... Ms. Kimberly M. BRADEN
08 Director Library ....Ms. Tressa A. SNYDER
15 Director Human Resources ....Mrs. Jennifer CLARK
36 Director of Career Development ....Ms. Liza SCHAEF
19 Chief of Police/Dir Public Safety ....Mr. Dennis BISH
06 Registrar ....Mrs. Laura PICKENS
42 Campus Pastor ....Rev. Brian T. RIDDLE
07 Director of Admissions ....Mrs. Sonya L. LAPIKAS
37 Director Financial Aid .... Ms. Michelle WORK
28 Dir Diversity/Equity & Inclusion ....Vacant
38 Director Counseling Center .... Ms. Melanie R. BROADWATER

Thomas Jefferson University (G)

925 Chestnut Street, Suite #110, Philadelphia PA 19107
County: Philadelphia FICE Identification: 012393
Unit ID: 216366
Telephone: (215) 955-6000 Carnegie Class: DU-Higher
FAX Number: (215) 955-1122 Calendar System: Quarter
URL: www.jefferson.edu
Established: 1824 Annual Undergrad Tuition & Fees: $41,866
Enrollment: 8,286 Coed
Affiliation or Control: Independent Non-Profit IRS Status: 501(c)3
Highest Offering: Doctorate
Accreditation: M, ACBSP, ANEST, ARCPA, ART, CAATE, CACREP, CAMPEP, CIDA, CYTO, DENT, @DIET, DMS, EMT, LSAR, MED, MFCD, MIDWF, MLS, NURSE, OT, OTA, PAST, PERF, PH, PHAR, PTA, RAD, RADDOS, RADMAG, RTT, @SP

01 President/CEO Jefferson Health ....Dr. Joseph G. CACCHIONE
11 EVP & Chief Operating Officer .... Ms. Kathleen GALLAGHER
100 EVP/Chief of Staff ....Mr. John EKARIUS
05 Provost/EVP Academic Affairs .... Dr. Mark L. TYKOCINSKI
26 EVP Univ Marketing/Relations ....Mr. Charles LEWIS
10 Exec VP/Chief Financial Officer ......Mr. Peter L. DEANGELIS, JR.
111 EVP Institutional Advancement ....Dr. Elizabeth DALE
43 EVP & Chief Legal Counsel .... Ms. Cristina G. CAVALIERI
46 Assoc Provost Clinical Research .... Dr. David WHELLAN

18 Sr Vice Pres for Facilities Mgmt .... Mr. Clayton MITCHELL
15 EVP/Chief Human Resources Ofcr .... Mr. Clayton FITZHUGH
28 EVP/Chief Diversity/Inclusion Ofcr ....Ms. Lisette MARTINEZ
58 Dean Jeff College of Life Sciences .... Dr. Gerald GRUNWALD
63 Dean Sidney Kimmel Medical College .. Dr. Mark L. TYKOCINSKI
66 Dean Jeff Col of Nursing .... Dr. Marie MARINO
67 Dean Jefferson College of Pharmacy ....Dr. Rebecca FINLEY
76 Dean Jeff Col Health Professions ....Dr. Michael DRYER
69 Interim Dean Jeff Sch of Pop Health .... Dr. Willie OGLESBY
32 Assoc Provost Student Affairs ....Ms. Jennifer FOGERTY
35 Dean of Student & Admissions SKMC .....Dr. Clara A. CALLAHAN
07 Director of Admissions ....Ms. Erin FINN
06 University Registrar .... Mr. Kris PELUSZAK
29 Exec Director of Alumni Assoc SKMC .... Ms. Cristina GESO
08 University Librarian ....Mr. Anthony FRISBY
23 Medical Director Univ Health Svcs .... Dr. Ellen M. O'CONNOR
24 Director Medical Media Services ....Mr. Pejman MAKARECHI
39 Manager Housing/Residence Life .... Ms. Laurie YUNKE
37 Univ Director Student Financial Aid ....Ms. Susan MCFADDEN
40 Director Bookstore .... Mr. Travis HARLEY
13 Chief Information Officer ....Mr. Nassar NIZAMI
19 Director of Security ....Mr. Joseph BYHAM
85 Dir International Exchange Services ....Ms. Janice M. BOGEN
123 Dir Admission/Recruitment/Grad Stds .... Mr. Marc STEARNS
22 Assoc Dean Diversity/Minority Affs .... Dr. Bernard LOPEZ
96 Director of Purchasing ....Mr. Robert C. BURKHOLDER
35 Associate Provost Student Affairs ....Dr. Charles A. POHL
04 Executive Associate to President ....Ms. Grace L. HARDESKI
09 Interim Dir of Inst Research ....Dr. Raelynn COOTER
101 Secretary of the Institution/Board .....Ms. Michele R. DOUGHERTY
102 Dir Foundation/Corporate Relations .... Ms. Molly GERBER
103 Dir Workforce/Career Development ......Ms. Jennifer M. GRONSKY
105 Director Web Services ....Ms. Chris MCNAMEE-SMITH
25 Dir Grants/Research Admin ....Mr. Timothy SCHAILEY
36 Director Student Placement .... Ms. Jennifer GRONSKY
38 Director Student Counseling ....Dr. Deanna NOBLEZA
44 Director Annual or Planned Giving .... Ms. Lisa REPKO
45 Chief Institutional Planning ....Vacant
84 Director Enrollment Management ....Ms. Erin M. FINN
86 Director Government Relations ....Mr. Hugh J. LAVERY
90 Director Academic Computing .... Mr. Michael DEVENNEY
104 Director Study Abroad .... Ms. Madeleine WILCOX
106 Dean Online Education/E-learning .... Dr. Anthony FRISBY
41 Athletic Director .... Mr. Thomas SHIRLEY
50 Dean of Business Administration ....Dr. Philip RUSSEL
53 Dean School of Education .... Dr. Matt D. BAKER
54 Dean School of Engineering ....Dr. Ron KANDER
79 Dean Col of Humanities and Science ....Dr. Barbara KIMMELMAN
48 Dean Architecture/Built Environment .... Dr. Barbara KLINKHAMMER

Triangle Tech, Bethlehem (A)

3184 Airport Road, Bethlehem PA 18017
Telephone: (610) 266-2910 Identification: 770587
Accreditation: ACCSC

Triangle Tech, DuBois (B)

225 Tannery Row Rd, Falls Creek PA 15840
County: Clearfield FICE Identification: 021744
Unit ID: 216454
Telephone: (814) 371-2090 Carnegie Class: Assoc/HVT-High Trad
FAX Number: (814) 371-9227 Calendar System: Semester
URL: www.triangle-tech.edu
Established: 1982 Annual Undergrad Tuition & Fees: $17,800
Enrollment: 132 Coed
Affiliation or Control: Proprietary IRS Status: Proprietary
Highest Offering: Associate Degree
Accreditation: ACCSC

01 Director ....Mr. Jarred HETRICK
05 Academic Affairs Advisor .... Mrs. Joan HOCKMAN
07 Admiss/Recruiting/Training Coord .... Mrs. Joy BURKE
36 Career Advisor ....Ms. Erica HAND
37 Financial Aid Administrator ....Ms. Michelle L. JASHINSKI

Triangle Tech, Greensburg (C)

222 E Pittsburgh Street, Suite A,
Greensburg PA 15601-3304
County: Westmoreland FICE Identification: 021290
Unit ID: 216445
Telephone: (724) 832-1050 Carnegie Class: Assoc/HVT-High Trad
FAX Number: (724) 834-0325 Calendar System: Semester
URL: www.triangle-tech.edu
Established: 1944 Annual Undergrad Tuition & Fees: $17,758
Enrollment: 127 Coed
Affiliation or Control: Proprietary IRS Status: Proprietary
Highest Offering: Associate Degree
Accreditation: ACCSC

02 Director of Branch Campus/CEO .... Ariel MCKNIGHT
05 Exec Dir of Compliance & Education .... Deborah G. HEPBURN

Triangle Tech, Pittsburgh (D)

1940 Perrysville Avenue, Pittsburgh PA 15214-3897
County: Allegheny FICE Identification: 007839
Unit ID: 216436
Telephone: (412) 359-1000 Carnegie Class: Assoc/HVT-High Trad
FAX Number: (412) 359-1012 Calendar System: Semester
URL: www.triangle-tech.edu
Established: 1944 Annual Undergrad Tuition & Fees: $17,792
Enrollment: 109 Coed
Affiliation or Control: Proprietary IRS Status: Proprietary
Highest Offering: Associate Degree
Accreditation: ACCSC

00 Chairman/Chief Executive Officer .... James R. AGRAS
01 President ....Timothy J. MCMAHON
13 Exec Vice Pres of IT/Facilities ....Rudy AGRAS
15 Vice President of Human Resources .... Sofia A. JANIS
12 School Director/Title IX Coord ....Christopher LUND
05 Exec Dir of Compliance & Education .... Deborah G. HEPBURN
07 Executive Director of Admissions .... Terry KUCIC
37 Executive Director of Financial Aid .... Catherine A. WAXTER

Triangle Tech, Sunbury (E)

191 Performance Road, Sunbury PA 17801
Telephone: (570) 988-0700 Identification: 770586
Accreditation: ACCSC

Trinity Episcopal School for Ministry (F)

311 11th Street, Ambridge PA 15003-2397
County: Beaver FICE Identification: 022993
Unit ID: 216463
Telephone: (724) 266-3838 Carnegie Class: Spec-4-yr-Faith
FAX Number: (724) 266-4617 Calendar System: Semester
URL: www.tsm.edu
Established: 1976 Annual Graduate Tuition & Fees: N/A
Enrollment: 160 Coed
Affiliation or Control: Protestant Episcopal IRS Status: 501(c)3
Highest Offering: Doctorate; No Undergraduates
Accreditation: THEOL

05 Academic Dean ....Dr. Erika MOORE
32 Dean of Students/Director of Chapel .... Mr. Geoffrey MACKEY
07 Director of Admissions/Recruitment .... Mrs. Janessa FISK
11 Dean of Administration/Registrar .... Mrs. Stacey WILLIARD
30 Director of Development ....Vacant
26 Director of Communications ....Vacant
15 Human Resources Administrator ....Mrs. Elaine LUCCI
13 Information Technology Manager ....Mr. Steve SIMS
08 Chief Library Officer ....Mrs. Susanah HANSON
106 Director of Online Education ....Mr. Russ WARREN
18 Director of Facilities .... Mr. Justin FISK
29 Director Alumni Affairs .... Mr. Jack WALSH
10 Director of Accounting ....Mr. John MCCOY
04 Admin Assistant to the President ....Ms. Allyson MARTIN
36 Director Student Placement .... Rev. Karen STEVENSON
44 Director Annual Giving ....Ms. Carrie SHREWSBURY

United Career Institute (G)

PO Box 278 1015 Mount Braddock Road,
Mount Braddock PA 15465-0278
Telephone: (724) 437-4600 Identification: 666035
Accreditation: ABHES

† Branch campus of West Virginia Junior College, Morgantown, WV.

United Lutheran Seminary (H)

61 Seminary Ridge, Gettysburg PA 17325-1795
County: Adams FICE Identification: 003291
Unit ID: 213631
Telephone: (717) 338-3000 Carnegie Class: Spec-4-yr-Faith
FAX Number: N/A Calendar System: 4/1/4
URL: www.unitedlutheranseminary.edu
Established: 1826 Annual Graduate Tuition & Fees: N/A
Enrollment: 390 Coed
Affiliation or Control: Evangelical Lutheran Church In America
IRS Status: 501(c)3
Highest Offering: Doctorate; No Undergraduates
Accreditation: M, THEOL

01 President .... Dr. R. Guy ERWIN
05 Dean /VP Student Svcs ....Dr. J. Jayakiran SEBASTIAN
111 Interim VP Advancement .... Mr. Conor BROOKS
15 VP Human Resources/DEI ....Mr. Ed HENRY
10 Chief Financial Officer/CFO ....Mr. Buff CARLSON
26 Dir Strategic Marketing & Comm ....Ms. Linda FIORE
08 Library Director and Archivist ....Mr. Evan E. BOYD
37 Director of Financial Aid .... Mr. Tyrone GADSON
06 Registrar ....Ms. Julie RITTER
13 Director of IT Systems/Ed Tech ....Mr. Donald L. REDMAN
28 Dir of Diversity/Equity/Inclusion ....Vacant

The University of the Arts (I)

320 S Broad Street, Philadelphia PA 19102-4944
County: Philadelphia FICE Identification: 003350
Unit ID: 215105
Telephone: (215) 717-6380 Carnegie Class: Spec-4-yr-Arts
FAX Number: (215) 717-6520 Calendar System: Semester
URL: www.uarts.edu
Established: 1876 Annual Undergrad Tuition & Fees: $46,680
Enrollment: 1,530 Coed
Affiliation or Control: Independent Non-Profit IRS Status: 501(c)3
Highest Offering: Doctorate
Accreditation: M, MUS

01 President .... Mr. David YAGER
100 Chief of Staff ....Mr. Franklyn CANTOR
04 Admin Assistant to the President ....Ms. Melanie ROMAY
32 VP Enroll Mgmt & Student Affairs ....Vacant
05 Vice President for Academic Affairs .... Ms. Carol GRANEY
10 Vice Pres Finance/Administration .... Mr. Stephen LIGHTCAP
111 Vice Pres Advancement .... Mr. Andrew PACK
13 AVP Information Technology .... Mr. Len LIPKIN
07 AVP of Admissions ....Ms. Angela JONES-O'BRIEN
15 AVP for Human Resources ....Ms. Christine SCHAEFER
26 AVP for Enrollment Marketing .... Ms. Maria RAHA
37 AVP for Student Financial Aid ....Ms. Mariann CARDONICK
28 Dir Diversity/Equity/Inclusion ....Mr. Stephen CIRINO
09 Dir of Inst Rsrch & Effectiveness ....Dr. Deborah DUFFY
06 Registrar .... Mr. Jeffrey KISLER

University of Pennsylvania (J)

1 College Hall, Room 100, Philadelphia PA 19104-6830
County: Philadelphia FICE Identification: 003378
Unit ID: 215062
Telephone: (215) 898-5000 Carnegie Class: DU-Highest
FAX Number: (215) 898-5756 Calendar System: Semester
URL: www.upenn.edu
Established: 1740 Annual Undergrad Tuition & Fees: $60,042
Enrollment: 26,552 Coed
Affiliation or Control: Independent Non-Profit IRS Status: 501(c)3
Highest Offering: Doctorate
Accreditation: M, ANEST, CAMPEP, CEA, CLPSY, DENT, IPSY, LAW, LSAR, MED, MIDWF, NURSE, PAST, PCSAS, PH, PLNG, SW, VET

01 President .... Ms. M. Elizabeth MAGILL
03 Executive Vice President .... Mr. Craig CARNAROLI
05 Provost ....Vacant
20 Vice Provost for Education .... Dr. Karen DETLEFSEN
06 Registrar .... Ms. Margaret KIP
07 Dean of Admissions .... Ms. Whitney SOULE
32 Vice Provost University Life ....Vacant
10 Vice Pres Finance & Treasurer ....Vacant
18 Vice Pres Facil/Real Est Svcs ....Ms. Anne PAPAGEORGE
17 CEO Univ of PA Health System ....Mr. Kevin B. MAHONEY
08 Vice Provost/Dir of Libraries ......Ms. Constantia CONSTANTINOU
13 Vice Pres Info Technology/CIO ....Mr. Thomas H. MURPHY
100 VP & Chief of Staff .... Mr. Michael CITRO
28 SVP Inst Affs/Chief Diversity Ofcr ....Ms. Joann MITCHELL
30 SVP Development/Alumni Relations ....Vacant
15 Sr Vice Pres Human Resources .... Dr. John J. HEUER
86 Vice Pres Govt & Cmty Affairs .... Mr. Jeffrey COOPER
19 Vice President Public Safety .... Ms. Kathleen SHIELDS ANDERSON
26 Vice Pres for Univ Communications .... Mr. Stephen J. MACCARTHY
21 Vice Pres Business Services .... Ms. Marie D. WITT
114 Vice Pres Budget Mgmt Analysis .... Mr. Trevor C. LEWIS
43 Senior Vice Pres/General Counsel ....Ms. Wendy S. WHITE
101 VP & University Secretary .... Ms. Medha NARVEKAR
31 VP Social Equity & Community ....Rev. Charles L. HOWARD
09 VP Inst Rsrch/Sr Adv to Pres .... Dr. Stacey J. LOPEZ
20 Interim Provost .... Dr. Beth A. WINKELSTEIN
20 Vice Provost Faculty Affairs .... Dr. Laura PERNA
29 Assoc VP Alumni Relations ....Mr. Fredrick H. WAMPLER
46 Sr Vice Provost for Research ....Dr. Dawn A. BONNELL
88 Assoc Vice Pres Rsrch Svcs ....Ms. Elizabeth D. PELOSO
116 VP Audit/Compliance & Privacy .... Mr. Gregory J. PELLICANO
31 Assoc VP/Dir Ctr Gmty Partnerships ....Dr. Ira HARKAVY
28 Assoc Vice Prov Equity & Access .... Rev. William GIPSON
21 Comptroller ....Mr. Russell DI LEO
63 Exec Vice Pres/Dean Sch of Medicine .... Dr. J. L. JAMESON
49 Dean School Arts & Sciences .... Dr. Steven J. FLUHARTY
54 Dean School of Engr/Applied Science .... Dr. Vijay KUMAR
66 Dean School of Nursing .... Dr. Antonia VILLARRUEL
50 Dean Wharton School .... Dr. Erika H. JAMES
60 Dean Annenberg Sch Communications ....Dr. John L. JACKSON, JR.
52 Dean School of Dental Medicine .... Dr. Mark S. WOLFF
48 Dean Weitzman School of Design .... Dr. Frederick STEINER
53 Dean Graduate School Education ....Dr. Pam GROSSMAN
61 Dean School of Law .... Dr. Theodore W. RUGER
70 Dean School Social Policy/Practice ....Dr. Sara BACHMAN
74 Dean School of Veterinary Medicine ....Dr. Andrew HOFFMAN
107 Vice Dean Liberal & Prof Studies ....Ms. Nora E. LEWIS
85 Dir Intl Student & Scholar Svcs ......Dr. Rodolfo R. ALTAMIRANO
36 Exec Dir of Career Services .... Dr. Barbara HEWITT
37 Dir Student Financial Aid ....Ms. Elaine P. VARAS
35 Int Vice Provost/Sr AVP Stdnt Affs ....Ms. Tamara KING
38 Dir Counseling/Psych Services ....Vacant
102 Exec Dir Corp & Found Rels .... Dr. Diana B. ALTEGOER
28 Exec Dir Affirm Action & Equal Opp .... Mr. Sam B. STARKS
23 Sr Dir Student Health Services ....Vacant
57 Exec Art Dir Annenberg Ctr Per Arts ...Mr. Christopher A. GRUITS
88 Exec Dir Morris Arboretum ....Mr. William CULLINA
88 Dir Institute of Contemporary Art .... Ms. Zoe RYAN
88 Dir Museum of Archeology/Anthrplgy .....Mr. Christopher WOODS
41 Dir Intercollegiate Athletics ....Ms. Alanna SHANAHAN
14 IT Director .... Mr. James F. JOHNSON
91 IT Exec Dir Admin Info Tech ....Ms. Jeanne F. CURTIS
39 Exec Dir Col Houses & Acad Svcs ....Dr. Hikaru KOZUMA
104 Exec Director Study Abroad .... Mr. Nigel COSSAR
106 Exec Director Online Learning Init ....Dr. Rebecca STEIN
04 Executive Asst to President .... Ms. Jodi SARKISIAN
105 Sr Dir Web Strategy & Visual Comm ....Mr. Steven MINICOLA
44 Exec Dir Gift Plng/Assoc Gen Couns ....Ms. Marcie L. MERZ

96 Chief Procurement Officer .... Mr. Mark MILLS
122 Dir of F&S Leadership Community .... Ms. Jessica Nicole RYAN
88 Chief Wellness Officer .... Dr. Benoit DUBE

University of Pittsburgh (A)

4200 Fifth Avenue, Pittsburgh PA 15260-3583
County: Allegheny FICE Identification: 003379
Unit ID: 215293
Telephone: (412) 624-4141 Carnegie Class: DU-Highest
FAX Number: N/A Calendar System: Semester
URL: www.pitt.edu
Established: 1787 Annual Undergrad Tuition & Fees (In-State): $19,679
Enrollment: 32,277 Coed
Affiliation or Control: State Related IRS Status: 501(c)3
Highest Offering: Doctorate
Accreditation: M, ADNUR, ANEST, ARCPA, ATECH, AUD, CAATE, CACREP, CAHIIM, CAMPEP, CEA, CLPSY, COARC, DENT, DH, DIET, EMT, HSA, HT, IPSY, LAW, LIB, MED, MIDWF, NUR, NURSE, OPE, OT, PCSAS, PH, PHAR, PTA, SP, SPAA, SW, THEA

01 Chancellor and Chief Exec Officer .... Dr. Patrick GALLAGHER
05 Sr Vice Chancellor & Provost .... Dr. Ann E. CUDD
63 Sr VC Health Sci/Dean Sch of Med .... Dr. Anantha SHEKHAR
101 Sr VC Engagement/Secy BOT .... Vacant
10 Senior Vice Chancellor and CFO .... Mr. Hari SASTRY
115 Chief Investment Officer .... Mr. Jeffer CHOUDHRY
46 Sr Vice Chancellor for Research .... Dr. Rob A. RUTENBAR
43 Sr Vice Chanc & Chief Legal Officer .... Ms. Geovette E. WASHINGTON
111 SVC Philanthropic & Alumn Engage .... Ms. Kristin DAVITT
13 VC/Chief Information Officer .... Mr. Mark HENDERSON
26 Vice Chanc for Communications .... Ms. Ellen L. MORAN
101 Secretary of the Board of Trustees .... Ms. Rosalyn JONES
11 Sr VC Business & Operations .... Mr. David N. DEJONG
28 VC Diversity & Inclusion .... Dr. Clyde WILSON PICKETT
41 Director of Athletics .... Ms. Heather R. LYKE
86 VC Community & Govt Relations .... Mr. Paul A. SUPOWITZ
86 VC Gov Relations and Advocacy .... Mr. David BROWN
100 Chief of Staff .... Mr. Kevin WASHO
20 Vice Provost Undergraduate Studies .... Dr. Joseph J. MCCARTHY
58 Vice Provost Graduate Studies .... Dr. Amanda J. GODLEY
32 Vice Provost Student Affairs .... Mr. Kenyon R. BONNER
88 Vice Provost for Budget & Analytics .... Mr. Stephen R. WISNIEWSKI
88 Vice Provost Faculty Affairs .... Ms. Lu-in WANG
88 Vice Prov Faculty Diversity & Dev .... Mr. John M. WALLACE
88 Treasurer .... Mr. Paul LAWRENCE
21 Controller .... Mr. Thurman D. WINGROVE
21 Assoc VC Financial Operations .... Ms. Maureen BEAL
102 VC Corporate & Foundation Relations .... Mr. Thomas P. CRAWFORD
19 Assoc VC Public Safety & Emer Mgmt .... Mr. Ted P. FRITZ
109 VC Hospitality & Auxil Services .... Mr. Matthew STERNE
31 VC Engagement and Community Affairs .... Ms. Lina DOSTILIO
29 Vice Chancellor Alumni Relations .... Ms. Nancy MERRIT
15 VC Human Resources .... Mr. James GALLAHER
16 Asst VC Consulting Services .... Mr. Mark D. BURDSALL
18 VC Facilities Management .... Mr. Scott C. BERNOTAS
118 Asst VC Benefits .... Mr. John KOZAR
88 VC Planning Design & Construction .... Ms. Mary Beth MCGREW
88 VC Real Estate .... Mr. Anish KUMAR
27 University Spokesperson .... Mr. Kevin ZWICK
06 University Registrar .... Mr. Jonathan C. HELM
92 Dean Honors College .... Dr. Nicola FOOTE
35 Dean of Students .... Dr. Carla PANZELLA
07 Chief Enrollment Officer .... Mr. Marc L. HARDING
49 Dean Deitrich Sch Arts & Sci/CGS .... Dr. Kathleen M. BLEE
50 Dean Jos M Katz Gr Sch Bus .... Dr. Arjang A. ASSAD
54 Dean Swanson School of Engineering .... Mr. James R. MARTIN, II
52 Dean School of Dental Medicine .... Dr. Bernard J. COSTELLO
61 Dean School of Law .... Ms. Amy J. WILDERMUTH
80 Dean Grad Sch Public/Intl Affs .... Dr. Carissa SLOTTERBACK
70 Dean School of Social Work .... Ms. Elizabeth M. FARMER
76 Dean Sch of Health & Rehabilitation .... Dr. Anthony DELITTO
67 Dean School of Pharmacy .... Dr. Patricia D. KROBOTH
66 Dean School of Nursing .... Dr. Jacqueline DUNBAR-JACOB
69 Dean Grad School Public Health .... Dr. Maureen LICHTVELD
62 Dean School of Computing and Inform .... Mr. Bruce CHILDERS
53 Dean School of Education .... Dr. Valerie KINLOCH
12 President Johnstown Campus .... Dr. Jem M. SPECTAR
12 President Greensburg Campus .... Dr. Robert G. GREGERSON
12 Interim Pres Bradford & Titusville .... Mr. Richard T. ESCH
104 Vice Provost Global Affairs .... Dr. Ariel ARMONY
39 Assoc Dean of Stdnts/Stdnt Exper .... Mr. Steven L. ANDERSON
36 Assoc Dean Stdnt Ldrshp/Career Svcs .... Vacant
35 Assoc Dean of Students/Stdnt Engage .... Ms. Linda WILLIAMS-MOORE
23 Assoc Dean of Students/Wellness .... Mr. Jay E. DARR
24 Assoc Prov Univ Ctr Teach & Learn .... Ms. Cynthia GOLDEN
19 Chief University Police .... Mr. James K. LOFTUS
04 Exec Asst to the Chancellor .... Ms. Sue MESICK
96 Manager Purchasing Services .... Mr. Thomas E. YOUNGS, JR.
08 Dir Univ Library System .... Ms. Kornelia TANCHEVA
106 Dir Online Programs .... Mr. Stephen M. BUTLER
37 Director Financial Aid .... Dr. Randall MCCREADY
116 Director Internal Audit .... Mr. John P. ELLIOTT
09 Director Institutional Research .... Mr. Rob G. RODGERS
88 Director University Press .... Mr. Peter KRACHT
88 Int Dir Univ Ctr Soc & Urban Res .... Mr. Scott R. BEACH
88 Dir Ctr for Philosophy of Science .... Mr. Edouard MACHERY
88 Dir Learning Research & Dev Center .... Mr. Charles A. PERFETTI
40 Exec Dir Univ Store & Strat Initiat .... Ms. Monica D. RATTIGAN
88 Director Sustainability .... Ms. Aurora SHARRARD

University of the Sciences in Philadelphia (B)

600 S 43rd Street, Philadelphia PA 19104-4495
County: Philadelphia FICE Identification: 003353
Unit ID: 215132
Telephone: (215) 596-8800 Carnegie Class: DU-Mod
FAX Number: (215) 895-1100 Calendar System: Semester
URL: www.usciences.edu
Established: 1821 Annual Undergrad Tuition & Fees: $27,500
Enrollment: 2,375 Coed
Affiliation or Control: Independent Non-Profit IRS Status: 501(c)3
Highest Offering: Doctorate
Accreditation: M, ACBSP, OT, PHAR, PTA

01 Interim President .... Dr. Valerie P. WEIL
05 Provost/VP Academic Affairs .... Ms. Jill BAREN
106 VP USciences Online .... Mr. Ron KISHEN
111 VP Institutional Advancement .... Mr. Robert RUDD
10 Int Chief Financial/Operating Ofcr .... Ms. Brigid K. ISACKMAN
102 Dir of Corporate/Foundation Rels .... Ms. Madalina VERES
13 Associate VP & CIO .... Dr. Mark NESTOR
110 AVP Institutional Advancement .... Ms. Kim BARKHAMER
14 Exec Dir Information Technology .... Mr. John MASCIANTONIO
37 Director of Financial Aid .... Ms. Pamela RAMANATHAN
06 Registrar .... Ms. Therese ANDERSON
29 Director of Alumni Relations .... Mr. Casey J. RYAN
32 VP Student Affairs/Dean of Students .... Mr. Ross RADISH
49 Int Dean Misher Col Arts/Sciences .... Dr. Vojislava POPHRISTIC
76 Dean Samson Col of Health Sciences .... Dr. Sinclair SMITH
15 Director Human Resources .... Ms. Ruth ROBERTS
19 Director Public Safety/Security .... Mr. Michael LAPOTASKY
41 Director of Athletics .... Dr. Mark CASERIO
21 Controller/Asst VP Finance .... Ms. Brigid K. ISACKMAN
96 Director Purchasing/Auxiliary Svcs .... Mr. Vincent HORN
20 Associate Provost Academic Affairs .... Dr. John CONNORS
04 Executive Asst to President .... Ms. Beth PILIPZECK
90 Exec Director Academic Technology .... Dr. Rodney B. MURRAY
07 Executive Director of Admissions .... Mr. Augustine DISTEFANO, JR.

The University of Scranton (C)

800 Linden St, Scranton PA 18510-4622
County: Lackawanna FICE Identification: 003384
Unit ID: 215929
Telephone: (570) 941-7400 Carnegie Class: Masters/L
FAX Number: (570) 941-6369 Calendar System: Semester
URL: www.scranton.edu
Established: 1888 Annual Undergrad Tuition & Fees: $47,084
Enrollment: 4,957 Coed
Affiliation or Control: Roman Catholic IRS Status: 501(c)3
Highest Offering: Doctorate
Accreditation: M, ANEST, CACREP, CAHIIM, CSHSE, EXSC, HSA, NURSE, OT, PTA

01 President .... Rev. Joseph G. MARINA, SJ
05 Sr VP Academic Affairs & Provost .... Dr. Michelle MALDONADO
10 Sr VP Finance & Administration .... Mr. Edward J. STEINMETZ, JR.
111 VP for University Advancement .... Mr. Thomas MACKINNON
84 VP for Enrollment Mgmt .... Ms. Shannon ZOTTOLA
03 Sr VP to President/External Affairs .... Mr. Gerald C. ZABOSKI
114 Asst VP Budget/Financial Planning .... Mr. Patrick R. DONOHUE
13 CIO .... Dr. Carl HURST
15 Assoc Vice Pres Human Resources .... Ms. Patricia L. TETREAULT
42 Exec Dir of the Jesuit Center .... Mr. Ryan SHEEHAN
43 General Counsel .... Mr. Robert B. FARRELL
49 Dean Arts & Sciences .... Dr. David DZUREC
50 Dean Kania School of Management .... Dr. Mark HIGGINS
107 Dean Panuska Col of Prof Studies .... Dr. Victoria CASTELLANOS
08 Dean of Library/Info Fluency .... Prof. George AULISIO
51 Asst Dir for OL/Off-Campus Programs .... Dr. Lisa M. LOBASSO
32 Vice President for Student Life .... Dr. Robert W. DAVIS, JR.
20 Assoc Provost Academic Affs .... Dr. David MARX
07 Assoc VP Admiss & Undergrad Enroll .... Mr. Joseph M. ROBACK
37 Assoc VP Financial Aid & Enrollment .... Ms. Mary Kay ASTON
18 Assoc VP Facilities Operations .... Mr. James L. CAFFREY
29 Int Exec Dir Alumni/Donor Engagemnt .... Ms. Frani MANCUSO
06 Registrar .... Ms. Julie FERGUSON
36 Director of Career Services .... Ms. Chris WHITNEY
28 Exec Dir of Equity/Diversity Office .... Ms. Elizabeth GARCIA
38 Director of Counseling Center .... Dr. Bob LISKOWICZ
96 Director of Purchasing .... Mr. Mark CRUCIANI
04 Admin Assistant to the President .... Ms. Maribeth A. SMITH
101 Secretary of the Institution/Board .... Mrs. Tara M. SEELY
104 Assoc Director Global Education .... Ms. Kara BISHOP
108 Director Institutional Assessment .... Dr. Mary Jane K. DIMATTIO
19 Director Security/Safety .... Mr. Donald J. BERGMANN
41 Athletic Director .... Mr. David L. MARTIN
39 Dir Resident Life/Student Housing .... Mr. Bradley TROY
44 Director Annual Giving .... Ms. Bridget CHOMKO

University of Valley Forge (D)

1401 Charlestown Road, Phoenixville PA 19460-2373
County: Chester FICE Identification: 003306
Unit ID: 216542
Telephone: (610) 935-0450 Carnegie Class: Bac-Diverse
FAX Number: (610) 935-9353 Calendar System: Semester
URL: www.valleyforge.edu
Established: 1939 Annual Undergrad Tuition & Fees: $22,606
Enrollment: 557 Coed
Affiliation or Control: Assemblies Of God Church IRS Status: 501(c)3
Highest Offering: Master's
Accreditation: M, SW

01 President .... Rev. David J. KIM
32 VP of Student Life .... Rev. Jennifer D. GALE
05 VP of Academic Affairs .... Dr. Jerome N. DOUGLAS
09 VP of Institutional Effectiveness .... Dr. Todd G. GUEVIN
43 University Counsel .... Rev. Shahan G. TEBERIAN
10 VP of Finance and Operations .... Dr. Stacy R. SAUCHUK
13 Director of Information Technology .... Mr. Paul VAN RIJN
21 Accountant .... Mr. Tom STILWELL
18 Director of Facilities Operations .... Ms. Mindy S. ROWE
07 Director of Admissions .... Mrs. Charity J. SCHNEEBERGER
30 VP of Development .... Rev. Steven R. DEFRAIN
41 Director of Athletics .... Ms. Gretchen L. LEVAN
37 Asst Director of Financial Aid .... Mr. Jared M. SIDDALL
19 Director of Security .... Vacant
15 Director Human Resources .... Mrs. Veronica A. BIRD
96 Director of Purchasing .... Mrs. Rebekah LEE
08 Librarian/Dir Storms Research Ctr .... Ms. Melanie R. OESTREICH
121 Director of Student Success .... Ms. Claire EILER
11 Director of Operations .... Mrs. Julia G. PATTON
26 Director of Marketing .... Vacant
06 Registrar .... Mr. Chris J. ADDICKS
23 Director of Health Services .... Mrs. Lauren E. BORN
39 Housing Coordinator .... Vacant
04 Administrative Asst to President .... Ms. Samantha L. DAVID
29 Director of Alumni Affairs .... Ms. Kari L. MAUERMAN

Ursinus College (E)

PO Box 1000, 601 East Main Street, Collegeville PA 19426-1000
County: Montgomery FICE Identification: 003385
Unit ID: 216524
Telephone: (610) 409-3000 Carnegie Class: Bac-A&S
FAX Number: (610) 489-0627 Calendar System: Semester
URL: www.ursinus.edu
Established: 1869 Annual Undergrad Tuition & Fees: $55,210
Enrollment: 1,493 Coed
Affiliation or Control: Independent Non-Profit IRS Status: 501(c)3
Highest Offering: Baccalaureate
Accreditation: M

01 President .... Dr. Robyn E. HANNIGAN
05 Vice Pres Academic Affairs/Dean .... Dr. Mark SCHNEIDER
111 Vice Pres for Advancement .... Mr. Mark GADSON
43 Vice Pres and General Counsel .... Mr. Robert CLOTHIER
84 Vice President/Dean for Enrollment .... Ms. Shannon ZOTTOLA
32 VP for Student Affairs .... Ms. Missy BRYANT
31 VP for College/Cmty Engagement .... Dr. Heather LOBBAN-VIRAVONG
21 Assoc Vice President Finance/Admin .... Ms. Mary CORRELL
15 Assoc Vice Pres Human Resources .... Ms. Kelley WILLIAMS
13 Chief Info Technology Officer (CIO) .... Mr. Gene SPENCER
45 Chief Strat/Innovation Officer .... Dr. Meredith GOLDSMITH
08 Manager Library Operations .... Ms. Maureen DAMIANO
36 Director of Career & Post-Grad Dev .... Ms. Sue SLADEN
18 Director of Facilities .... Mr. Steve GEHRINGER
23 VP for Health and Wellness .... Mrs. Laura MOLIKEN
26 VP Comm & Strategic Partnerships .... Mr. Thomas YENCHO
37 Director Student Financial Services .... Mrs. Ellen CURCIO
06 Registrar .... Ms. Barbara A. BORIS
29 Exec Director of Alumni Relations .... Ms. Pamela PANARELLA
09 Director of Institutional Research .... Mr. Jack LAFAYETTE
28 Dir of Institute for Incl & Equity .... Ms. Ashley HENDERSON
07 Director of Admission .... Ms. Diane GREENWOOD

Valley Forge Military College (F)

1001 Eagle Road, Wayne PA 19087-3695
County: Delaware FICE Identification: 003386
Unit ID: 216551
Telephone: (610) 989-1200 Carnegie Class: Assoc/HT-High Trad
FAX Number: (610) 975-9642 Calendar System: Semester
URL: www.vfmac.edu
Established: 1935 Annual Undergrad Tuition & Fees: $30,975
Enrollment: 110 Coed
Affiliation or Control: Independent Non-Profit IRS Status: 501(c)3
Highest Offering: Associate Degree
Accreditation: M

00 Chairman of the Board .... Mr. John ENGLISH
01 President/CEO .... Col. Stu HELGESON
03 Commandant of Cadets .... Col. Julian J. RIVERA
05 Provost .... Dr. Robert F. SMITH
32 Dean of Student Services .... Dr. Jesse PHILLIPS
10 Director of Finance and Operations .... Mr. D. Eric SAUL
06 Registrar .... LtCol. Tracey HARTLEY
07 Director of Admissions .... Ms. Anna BRENNAN
13 Director Information Technology .... Mr. Michael G. BROCK
18 Director of Facilities .... Mr. George ELSE
23 Director of Health Services .... Ms. Debbie HAMMER
08 Director of Library Services .... Ms. Dana KERRIGAN
15 Director of Human Resources .... Ms. Lauren GUARDINO
26 Chief Public Relations/Marketing .... Ms. Mary HELLER
111 Dir of Institutional Advancement .... Ms. Kathleen ELSMORE
29 Director Alumni Relations .... Mr. Tom GOLDBLUM
09 Director of Institutional Research .... Ms. Deepa RAMAKRISHNAN

Vet Tech Institute (A)

125 Seventh Street, Pittsburgh PA 15222-3400
County: Allegheny FICE Identification: 008568
Unit ID: 213914
Telephone: (412) 391-7021 Carnegie Class: Spec 2-yr-Health
FAX Number: (412) 232-4348 Calendar System: Semester
URL: www.vti.edu
Established: 1958 Annual Undergrad Tuition & Fees: $15,140
Enrollment: 292 Coed
Affiliation or Control: Proprietary IRS Status: Proprietary
Highest Offering: Associate Degree
Accreditation: ACCSC

01 President ... Ms. Jackie FLYNN
05 Director of Education ... Ms. Lynn SLACK
32 Director of Student Services ... Ms. Deborah SPOZARSKI

Villanova University (B)

800 Lancaster Avenue, Villanova PA 19085-1699
County: Delaware FICE Identification: 003388
Unit ID: 216597
Telephone: (610) 519-4500 Carnegie Class: DU-Higher
FAX Number: (610) 519-5000 Calendar System: Semester
URL: www.villanova.edu
Established: 1842 Annual Undergrad Tuition & Fees: $57,460
Enrollment: 11,032 Coed
Affiliation or Control: Roman Catholic IRS Status: 501(c)3
Highest Offering: Doctorate
Accreditation: M, ANEST, CACREP, LAW, NURSE, SPAA, THEOL

01 President ... RevDr. Peter M. DONOHUE, OSA
43 Vice President & General Counsel ... Mr. E. Michael ZUBEY, JR.
05 Provost ... Dr. Patrick G. MAGGITTI
111 Sr Vice Pres University Advancement ... Vacant
11 EVP Administration/Operations ... Mr. Roger DEMARESKI
13 Chief Information Officer ... Ms. Kelly DONEY
32 Vice President for Student Life ... Rev. Kathy J. BYRNES
26 Vice Pres University Communication ... Ms. Ann DIEBOLD
42 Vice Pres for Mission & Ministry ... Rev. Kevin DEPRINZIO, OSA
10 Vice President for Finance ... Mr. Neil J. HORGAN
20 Vice Provost for Academics ... Dr. Craig WHEELAND
41 Vice Pres/Director of Athletics ... Mr. Mark JACKSON
35 Assoc Vice Pres for Student Life ... Mr. Thomas DEMARCO
15 AVP Human Res/Affirm Action Ofcr ... Mr. Raymond DUFFY
109 Assoc Vice Pres for Auxiliary Svcs ... Mr. Anthony ALFANO
29 Assoc Vice Pres Alumni Relations ... Vacant
46 Assoc Vice Provost for Research ... Dr. Amanda GRANNAS
28 Assoc Vice Prov Diversity/Inclusion ... Dr. Teresa A. NANCE
84 Dean Enrollment Management ... Mr. J. Leon WASHINGTON
09 Exec Dir Planning/Inst Research ... Dr. James F. TRAINER
18 Vice Pres Facilities Management ... Mr. Robert MORRO
07 Director University Admission ... Mr. Michael M. GAYNOR
08 Librarian & Dir of Falvey Library ... Ms. Millicent GASKELL
49 Dean Liberal Arts & Sciences ... Dr. Adele LINDENMEYR
50 Dean Villanova Sch of Business ... Dr. Joyce RUSSELL
58 Dean Graduate Studies LA&S ... Dr. Emory WOODARD
61 Dean Widger School of Law ... Mr. Mark ALEXANDER
66 Dean of Nursing ... Dr. Donna HAVENS
54 Dean of Engineering ... Dr. Michele MARCOLONGO
88 Dir Ctr Service/Social Justice ... Ms. Kate GIANCATARINO
88 Dir Ctr Grad Pastoral Ministry Educ ... Dr. John P. EDWARDS
107 Dean Col of Professional Studies ... Dr. Christine PALUS
85 Dir Intl Students & Human Services ... Mr. Stephen T. MCWILLIAMS
37 Director Financial Assistance ... Ms. Amanda CONSTABLE
19 Director of Public Safety ... Mr. David TEDJESKE
36 Executive Director Career Services ... Mr. Kevin GRUBB
92 Director of the Honors Program ... Dr. Anna MORELAND
38 Director of Univ Counseling Center ... Dr. Joan G. WHITNEY
94 Dir Gender & Women's Studies ... Dr. Shauna M. MACDONALD
39 Director for Housing Services ... Mr. Skylor MORTON
96 Director of Procurement ... Mr. John R. DURHAM
27 Director of Media Relations ... Mr. Jonathan GUST
23 Director Student Health Center ... Dr. Mary MCGONIGLE
23 Medical Director Student Health Ctr ... Dr. Brian BULLOCK
06 Registrar ... Ms. Pamela BRAXTON
88 University Compliance Officer ... Ms. Leyda L. BENITEZ
100 Executive Assistant to President ... Ms. Erin BUCKLEY
106 Exec Dir Online Programs ... Ms. Kristy IRWIN
53 AVP Teaching/Learning ... Dr. Matthew KERBEL
86 AVP Government Relations ... Mr. Chris KOVOLSKI

Walnut Hill College (C)

4207 Walnut Street, Philadelphia PA 19104-3518
County: Philadelphia FICE Identification: 021928
Unit ID: 215637
Telephone: (215) 222-4200 Carnegie Class: Spec-4-yr-Arts
FAX Number: (215) 222-4219 Calendar System: Other
URL: www.walnuthillcollege.edu
Established: 1974 Annual Undergrad Tuition & Fees: $23,550
Enrollment: 159 Coed
Affiliation or Control: Proprietary IRS Status: Proprietary
Highest Offering: Baccalaureate
Accreditation: ACCSC

01 President ... Mr. Daniel LIBERATOSCIOLI
03 Executive Vice President ... Mr. David MORROW
11 Vice President Administrative Svcs ... Ms. Peggy LIBERATOSCIOLI
10 Vice President of Operations ... Mr. Dennis LIBERATI
88 VP of Culinary/Pastry Arts ... Chef Todd BRALEY
05 Assoc Dean Teaching/Learning ... Dr. Joshua SEERY
07 Director of Admissions ... Vacant
32 Dir Student/Community Engagement ... Vacant
26 Director of Marketing ... Vacant
04 Admin Assistant to the President ... Ms. Gabrielle WESTRAADT
09 Director of Institutional Research ... Ms. Molly WILSON
13 Chief Information Technology Ofcr ... Mr. Paul MILLER
19 Director Security/Safety ... Mr. Joseph GEIGER

Washington & Jefferson College (D)

60 S Lincoln Street, Washington PA 15301-4801
County: Washington FICE Identification: 003389
Unit ID: 216667
Telephone: (724) 503-1001 Carnegie Class: Bac-A&S
FAX Number: (724) 223-6534 Calendar System: 4/1/4
URL: www.washjeff.edu
Established: 1781 Annual Undergrad Tuition & Fees: $50,169
Enrollment: 1,167 Coed
Affiliation or Control: Independent Non-Profit IRS Status: 501(c)3
Highest Offering: Master's
Accreditation: M

01 President ... Dr. John KNAPP
05 VP Academic Affairs/Dean of College ... Dr. Jeffrey FRICK
10 CFO/VP Business/Finance ... Mr. Jim IRWIN
30 VP Development/Alumni Relations ... Dr. Carolyn CAMPBELL-GOLDEN
84 VP for Enrollment ... Ms. Tracey SHEETZ
21 Assoc VP for Business & Finance ... Mr. Thomas SZEJKO
32 VP Student Life/Dean of Students ... Ms. Eva CHATTERJEE-SUTTON
20 Associate Dean for Academic Affairs ... Dr. Dana SHILLER
20 Associate Dean for Academic Affairs ... Dr. Steven MALINAK
18 Director of Facilities ... Mr. Jeffrey PLETA
26 VP Marketing/Communications ... Vacant
06 Registrar ... Ms. Kara CLARK
29 Asst VP Alumni Engagement ... Ms. Kerri LACOCK
07 Dean of Admission ... Mr. Robert ADKINS
37 Director of Financial Aid ... Ms. Bethany BOWMAN
13 Dir of Information/Technology Svcs ... Vacant
15 Director Human Resources ... Ms. Sharon KOLESAR
19 Dir Campus & Public Safety ... Mr. Jonathan ROSNICK
36 Assoc Dean/Dir of Career Pathways ... Ms. Vivienne FELIX
40 Bookstore Manager ... Ms. Cynthia BRICELAND
41 Director of Athletics ... Mr. Scott MCGUINNESS
08 Director of Library Services ... Ms. Ronalee CIOCCO
102 Foundation & Corp Relations Officer ... Mr. James ORLICK
91 Director for Admin Computing ... Mr. Michael A. TIMKO
104 Asst Dir International Programs ... Ms. Michaela CULLEY
108 Dir of Institutional Effectiveness ... Ms. Theresa FORD
121 Director of Academic Advising ... Mr. Richard BARBER
88 Director Conferences and Events ... Ms. Maureen VALENTINE
38 Director of Counseling Services ... Ms. Shelly LEAR
39 Director of Residence Life ... Mr. Justin SWANK
88 Ethics & Compliance Officer ... Ms. Carrie HOWARD

Waynesburg University (E)

51 W College Street, Waynesburg PA 15370-1222
County: Greene FICE Identification: 003391
Unit ID: 216694
Telephone: (724) 627-8191 Carnegie Class: Masters/M
FAX Number: N/A Calendar System: Semester
URL: www.waynesburg.edu
Established: 1849 Annual Undergrad Tuition & Fees: $26,500
Enrollment: 1,576 Coed
Affiliation or Control: Presbyterian Church (U.S.A.) IRS Status: 501(c)3
Highest Offering: Doctorate
Accreditation: M, CAATE, CACREP, IACBE, NURSE

00 Chancellor ... Dr. Timothy R. THYREEN
01 President ... Mr. Doug LEE
05 Provost ... Dr. Dana BAER
10 Chief Financial Officer ... Mrs. Laura COSS
32 Int Dean of Students ... Ms. Patricia BRISTOR
06 Registrar ... Mrs. Vicki WILSON
41 Athletic Director ... Mr. Adam JACK
13 VP Information Technology Services ... Mr. William DUMIRE
08 Director Eberly Library ... Mr. Rea REDD
26 Communication Specialist ... Ms. Ashley WISE
36 Career Development Specialist ... Ms. Sarah BELL
38 Student Counselor ... Mrs. Jane S. OWEN
21 Business Ofc Supervisor/Controller ... Mrs. Laura COSS
23 Director of Student Health Services ... Ms. Sherry PARSONS
15 Director Human Resources ... Mr. Tom HELMICK
37 Director Student Financial Aid ... Mr. Matthew STOKAN

Westminster College (F)

319 South Market Street, New Wilmington PA 16172-0001
County: Lawrence FICE Identification: 003392
Unit ID: 216807
Telephone: (724) 946-8761 Carnegie Class: Bac-A&S
FAX Number: (724) 946-7132 Calendar System: Semester
URL: www.westminster.edu
Established: 1852 Annual Undergrad Tuition & Fees: $37,675
Enrollment: 1,228 Coed
Affiliation or Control: Presbyterian Church (U.S.A.) IRS Status: 501(c)3
Highest Offering: Master's
Accreditation: M, MUS, NURSE

01 President ... Dr. Kathy B. RICHARDSON
05 Vice Pres Academic Affairs ... Dr. Jamie G. MCMINN
111 VP Institutional Advancement ... Dr. Jean M. HALE
10 Vice Pres Finance/Mgmt Services ... Mr. Kenneth J. ROMIG
84 Vice President for Enrollment ... Dr. Karen H. SCHEDIN
32 VP Student Affs/Dean Student Affs ... Ms. Gina M. VANCE
42 College Chaplain ... Rev. James R. MOHR
35 Assoc Dean of Student Affairs ... Ms. Candace C. OKELLO
13 CIO ... Ms. Erin T. SMITH
37 Director Student Financial Aid ... Ms. Cheryl GERBER
06 Interim Registrar ... Dr. Rose REINHART
36 Director of Professional Dev Center ... Mr. Chad A. SERFASS
29 Sr Director of Alumni Engagement ... Ms. Kara H. MONTGOMERY
41 Athletic Director ... Mr. Jason A. LENER
18 Director of Physical Plant ... Mr. Jason R. JANUSZIEWICZ
21 Business Manager ... Ms. Janet M. SMITH
19 Director of Public Safety ... Mr. Phillip R. LENZ
23 Director of the Wellness Center ... Ms. Melissa M. BARON
40 Bookstore Manager ... Ms. Kay A. GALANSKI
15 Director of Human Resources ... Ms. Kimberlee K. CHRISTOFFERSON
38 Counselor ... Ms. Sarah M. GELLMAN

Westminster Theological Seminary (G)

2960 Church Road, Glenside PA 19038
County: Montgomery FICE Identification: 003393
Unit ID: 216816
Telephone: (215) 887-5511 Carnegie Class: Spec-4-yr-Faith
FAX Number: (215) 887-5404 Calendar System: Semester
URL: www.wts.edu
Established: 1929 Annual Graduate Tuition & Fees: N/A
Enrollment: 854 Coed
Affiliation or Control: Independent Non-Profit IRS Status: 501(c)3
Highest Offering: Doctorate; No Undergraduates
Accreditation: M, THEOL

01 President ... Dr. Peter A. LILLBACK
05 Chief Academic Officer ... Dr. David B. GARNER
32 VP for Campus Life/Dean of Students ... Rev. Steven J. CARTER
111 Vice Pres Stewardship ... Mr. Jerry TIMMIS
11 Chief Operations Officer ... Mr. Chun LAI
106 Dean of Online Learning ... Dr. Iain DUGUID
37 Admissions Coord & Fin Aid Officer ... Mrs. Cyndi MYERS
07 Director of Admissions ... Dr. Nathan SHANNON
08 Director of Library Services ... Mr. Alexander (Sandy) FINLAYSON
73 Dean of Pastoral Theology ... Dr. John CURRIE
13 Director of Technology ... Mr. Sam IM
18 Director of Physical Plant ... Mr. Richard W. MAIENSHEIN
29 Director Alumni Affairs ... Dr. David FILSON
121 Associate Director Student Success ... Ms. Jaclyn GOBER
10 Director of Finance ... Ms. Pau Ping SZE TO
101 Secretary of the Board ... Mr. Lee AUGSBURGER

Westmoreland County Community College (H)

145 Pavilion Lane, Youngwood PA 15697-1895
County: Westmoreland FICE Identification: 010176
Unit ID: 216825
Telephone: (724) 925-4000 Carnegie Class: Assoc/HVT-High Non
FAX Number: (724) 925-1150 Calendar System: Semester
URL: www.westmoreland.edu
Established: 1970 Annual Undergrad Tuition & Fees (In-District): $9,732
Enrollment: 4,369 Coed
Affiliation or Control: Local IRS Status: 501(c)3
Highest Offering: Associate Degree
Accreditation: M, ACFEI, ADNUR, DA, DH, DMS, MAC

01 President ... Dr. Tuesday STANLEY
05 Vice Pres Acad Affs/Stdnt Svcs ... Dr. Kristy BISHOP
11 Vice Pres Administrative Services ... Mr. Gregory ROSE
103 VP Workforce & Cmty Devel/Cont Educ ... Vacant
25 Director of Grants ... Ms. Debra J. WILLIAMS
15 Director Human Resources ... Ms. Lauren M. FARRELL
106 Dean Dist Educ/Learning Resources ... Ms. Annette BOYER
50 Dean Business/Math/Science/Engineer ... Ms. Cynthia PROCTOR
76 Dean Health Professions/Nursing ... Ms. Sue SNYDER
72 Dean Technology ... Dr. Byron KOHUT
79 Dean Public Svc/Human/Soc Science ... Dr. Andrew BARNETTE
84 Vice Pres Enrollment Mgmt ... Dr. Sydney BEELER
102 Exec Director Education Foundation ... Ms. Debra D. WOODS
37 Director Financial Aid ... Ms. Janet DAVIDSON
18 Director Facilities ... Mr. Stephen MARKIEWICZ
13 Director Information Technology ... Mr. Steve BUDNY
26 Exec Dir Marketing/Communications ... Ms. Janet K. CORRINNE-HARVEY
07 Director Admissions/Registrar ... Vacant
41 Director Student Life/Athletics ... Vacant
45 Dean Planning/Assessment & IE ... Ms. Lindsay HERROD
96 Director of Purchasing ... Ms. Jill BUDNY

Widener University (I)

One University Place, Chester PA 19013-5792
County: Delaware FICE Identification: 003313
Unit ID: 216852
Telephone: (610) 499-4000 Carnegie Class: DU-Mod
FAX Number: N/A Calendar System: Semester
URL: www.widener.edu
Established: 1821 Annual Undergrad Tuition & Fees: $48,575
Enrollment: 6,150 Coed

Affiliation or Control: Independent Non-Profit IRS Status: 501(c)3
Highest Offering: Doctorate
Accreditation: M, ACPHA, CLPSY, @DIET, HSA, IPSY, LAW, NURSE, OT, PTA, @SP, SW

01 President ... Dr. Stacey M. ROBERTSON
05 Provost ... Dr. Andrew A. WORKMAN
10 Vice Pres Administration/Finance ... Ms. Linda K. GILBERT
111 Vice Pres University Advancement ... Ms. Theresa TRAVIS
13 VP Library & Info Systems ... Mr. Eric BEHRENS
84 VP for Enrollment Services ... Mr. Joseph E. HOWARD
21 Associate VP & Controller ... Mr. William LOCKARD, III
15 Assoc VP for Human Resources ... Ms. Keesha CHAVIS
20 Interim Vice Provost Acad Affairs ... Dr. Mark A. NICOSIA
121 Associate Provost Student Success .. Dr. Geraldine A. BLOEMKER
32 Dean of Students ... Dr. John P. DOWNEY
54 Dean School of Engineering ... Dr. Fred A. AKL
49 Dean College Arts & Sciences ... Dr. David E. LEAMAN
50 Dean School of Business Admin ... Dr. Anthony WHEELER
66 Dean School of Nursing ... Dr. Anne M. KROUSE
76 Dean Col Health/Human Services ... Dr. Robin L. DOLE
113 Bursar ... Ms. Diana BARRACLOUGH
08 Interim Director Wolfgram Library ... Ms. Molly M. WOLF
06 Registrar ... Ms. Kristen CHANDO
09 Dir of Inst Res & Effectiveness ... Dr. Stephen W. THORPE
36 Exec Dir Career Services ... Dr. Janet R. LONG
41 Director of Athletics ... Mr. Jack L. SHAFER
85 Interim Dir Intl Student Svcs ... Ms. Kimberly GENTILE
19 Executive Director of Campus Safety ... Mr. Anthony PLURETTI
40 Manager Campus Bookstore ... Vacant
91 Assoc VP Digital Transformation ... Ms. Linda TAYLOR
88 Director Technical Resources ... Mr. Perry M. DRAYFAHL
96 Director of Purchasing ... Ms. Michelle SHELTON
121 Dir Student Success/Retention ... Mr. Timothy J. CAIRY
92 Dir Honors Program in General Educ ... Dr. Mark S. GRAYBILL
94 Director of Women's Studies ... Dr. Annalisa CASTALDO
100 Chief of Staff ... Dr. Kathryn J. HERSCHEDE
26 Director of Communications ... Ms. Mary ALLEN
39 Assoc Dean of Students ... Ms. Catherine A. FEMINELLA
07 Exec Director of Admissions ... Ms. Courtney KELLY
105 Digital Experience Manager ... Ms. Heather N. ASTORGA
28 Chief Diversity Officer ... Ms. Micki DAVIS
37 Director Student Financial Aid ... Ms. Paula LEHRBERGER
18 Chief Facilities/Physical Plant Ofc ... Mr. Kevin M. KANE

† See Delaware listing of Widener University School of Law.

Widener University Commonwealth Law School (A)

3800 Vartan Way, PO Box 69380,
Harrisburg PA 17106-9380
Telephone: (717) 541-3900 Identification: 667244
Accreditation: &M, LAW

† Branch campus of Widener University, Chester, PA.

Wilkes University (B)

84 W South Street, Wilkes-Barre PA 18766-0001
County: Luzerne FICE Identification: 003394
Unit ID: 216931
Telephone: (570) 408-4000 Carnegie Class: DU-Mod
FAX Number: (570) 408-2934 Calendar System: Semester
URL: www.wilkes.edu
Established: 1933 Annual Undergrad Tuition & Fees: $38,752
Enrollment: 4,781 Coed
Affiliation or Control: Independent Non-Profit IRS Status: 501(c)3
Highest Offering: Doctorate
Accreditation: M, ACBSP, CEA, NURSE, PHAR

01 President ... Dr. Greg CANT
05 Provost & Sr Vice President ... Dr. David WARD
10 Vice Pres Finance & COO ... Ms. Ellen GALLAGHER
84 VP for Enrollment Mgmt & Marketing ... Ms. Kishan ZUBER
32 Int Vice President Student Affairs ... Mr. Mark ALLEN
111 VP for Advancement ... Mr. Kevin BOYLE
21 Controller ... Ms. Courtney LOMAX
20 Associate Provost for Academics ... Dr. Jonathan D. FERENCE
15 AVP/Human Resource Officer ... Mr. Joseph HOUSENICK
35 Dean of Students ... Dr. Mark R. ALLEN
49 Dean College Arts & Sciences ... Dr. Paul RIGGS
67 Int Dean Nesbitt School of Pharmacy ... Ms. Michelle HOLT MACEY
50 Dean School of Business/Engineering ... Dr. Abel ADEKOLA
88 Asst to President External Affairs ... Mr. Michael WOOD
66 Dean College of Nursing & Education .. Dr. Deborah A. ZBEGNER
09 Exec Director Info/Analysis/Plng ... Mr. Brian BOGERT
29 Director of Alumni Relations ... Ms. Mary SIMMONS
41 Director of Athletics ... Ms. Addy MALATESTA
23 Director Health Services ... Ms. Diane E. O'BRIEN
36 Director Career Services ... Mrs. Carol A. BOSACK-KOSEK
39 Director Residence Life ... Mr. Amin RASHID
58 Director Graduate Teacher Education ... Dr. Karim MEDICO
06 Registrar ... Mrs. Susan A. HRITZAK
37 Executive Director of Financial Aid ... Mr. Jared MENGHINI
26 AVP Marketing & Communications ... Ms. Gabrielle D'AMICO
18 Director Facilities Services ... Mr. Charles CARY
07 Exec Dir Undergraduate Enrollment ... Mr. Christopher MAYERSKI
28 Director of Diversity Initiatives ... Ms. Erica ACOSTA
96 Dir Procurement & Financial Svcs ... Ms. Alicia BOND
25 Director of Sponsored Programs ... Ms. Amanda MODROVSKY
27 Director of Communications ... Ms. Gabrielle D'AMICO

04 Executive Assistant to President ... Ms. Bridget GIUNTA
19 Director Security/Safety ... Mr. Michael KRZYWICKI

Williamson College of the Trades (C)

106 S New Middletown Road, Media PA 19063-5299
County: Delaware FICE Identification: 041238
Unit ID: 216940
Telephone: (610) 566-1776 Carnegie Class: Assoc/HVT-High Trad
FAX Number: (610) 566-6502 Calendar System: Semester
URL: www.williamson.edu
Established: 1888 Annual Undergrad Tuition & Fees: $28,320
Enrollment: 249 Male
Affiliation or Control: Independent Non-Profit IRS Status: 501(c)3
Highest Offering: Associate Degree
Accreditation: @M, ACCSC

01 President ... Mr. Michael J. ROUNDS
03 Executive Vice President ... Dr. Todd M. ZACHARY
05 Chief Academic Officer ... Dr. Michelle H. WILLIAMS
10 Chief Financial Officer ... Ms. Nancy M. CATANIA
111 VP Institutional Advancement ... Ms. Arlene A. SNYDER
11 VP of Operations ... Mr. Corey A. JACKSON
108 VP Research and Assessment ... Mr. Thomas E. WISNESKI
32 Dean of Students ... Mr. Thomas J. MOFFITT
84 VP Enrollment Management ... Mr. Jason C. MERILLAT
41 Athletic Director ... Mr. Dale H. PLUMMER
38 Chaplain/Counselor ... Rev. Mark A. SPECHT
06 Registrar ... Ms. Stephanie C. BOON
04 Executive Assistant/President ... Ms. Joan E. BERRY
36 Director Student Placement ... Ms. Margret T. KINGHAM
39 Director Residence Life ... Mr. John J. TULLY
20 Associate CAO ... Ms. Olivia MARTINEZ

Wilson College (D)

1015 Philadelphia Avenue, Chambersburg PA 17201-1285
County: Franklin FICE Identification: 003396
Unit ID: 217013
Telephone: (717) 264-4141 Carnegie Class: Masters/M
FAX Number: (717) 264-1578 Calendar System: 4/1/4
URL: www.wilson.edu
Established: 1869 Annual Undergrad Tuition & Fees: $26,090
Enrollment: 1,535 Coed
Affiliation or Control: Presbyterian Church (U.S.A.) IRS Status: 501(c)3
Highest Offering: Master's
Accreditation: M, CNEA

01 President ... Dr. Wesley R. FUGATE
05 VP for Academic Affairs/Dean of Fac ... Dr. Elissa HEIL
111 VP for Institutional Advancement ... Dr. Angela ZIMMANN
10 VP for Finance & Administration ... Mr. Brian ECKER
84 VP for Enrollment Management ... Mr. William SOMMERS
32 VP for Student Dev/Dean of Students ... Dr. Mary Beth WILLIAMS
100 Chief of Staff ... Ms. Melissa J. IMES
06 Registrar ... Ms. Jean B. HOOVER
37 Dean of Financial Aid ... Ms. Linda D. BRITTAIN
09 Director of Institutional Effective ... Ms. Cynthia M. EMORY
18 Director of Physical Plant ... Mr. Jason WARRENFELTZ
26 VP of Marketing & Communications . Ms. Cassandra H. LATIMER
40 College Store Coordinator ... Ms. Robin HERRING
41 Director of Athletics ... Ms. Tina HILL
88 Director of Conferences ... Ms. Kelsey YOUNG
29 Director of Alumnae Programs ... Ms. Marybeth FAMULARE
15 Director of Human Resources ... Ms. Crystal COLLIER-WALKER
121 Assoc Dean of Academic Advising ... Dr. Deborah AUSTIN
21 Assoc VP for Finance/Admin ... Ms. Lori A. TOSTEN
36 Director of Career Development ... Ms. Linda A. BOECKMAN
38 Director of Counseling ... Ms. Angela BAKER
88 Dir of Single Parent Scholars Pgm ... Ms. Katherine KOUGH
28 Dir Justice/Equity/Diversity/Incl ... Dr. Erica JOHNSON
42 Chaplain ... Rev. Derek WADLINGTON
39 Director of Residence Life ... Mr. Ryan COLL
102 Dir of Strategic Relationship Dev ... Ms. Dianna HEIM
07 Director of Admissions ... Mr. Michael MONTANA
30 Director of Development ... Ms. Denise MCDOWELL
13 Chief Info Technology Officer ... Dr. Amy DIEHL

Won Institute of Graduate Studies (E)

137 S Easton Road, Glenside PA 19038
County: Montgomery FICE Identification: 039493
Unit ID: 442064
Telephone: (215) 884-8942 Carnegie Class: Spec-4-yr-Other Health
FAX Number: (215) 884-9002 Calendar System: Trimester
URL: www.woninstitute.edu
Established: 2002 Annual Graduate Tuition & Fees: N/A
Enrollment: 124 Coed
Affiliation or Control: Independent Non-Profit IRS Status: 501(c)3
Highest Offering: Doctorate; No Undergraduates
Accreditation: M, ACUP

01 President ... Dr. Bokin KIM
11 Chief Administrative Officer ... Ms. Colleen O'CONNELL
10 Chief Financial Officer ... Ms. Maria PERRY
05 Chief Academic Officer ... Dr. Gerry O'SULLIVAN
06 Registrar ... Mr. Max FINKEL
08 Librarian ... Vacant
85 International Student Advisor ... Dr. Hojin PARK
13 Chief Info Technology Officer ... Ms. Elizabeth REED
04 Admin Assistant to the President ... Mr. Frederick RANALLO-HIGGINS
18 Chief Facilities/Phys Plant Ofcr ... Mr. Youngbin KIM

Yeshiva Beth Moshe (F)

930 Hickory Street, Scranton PA 18505-2196
County: Lackawanna FICE Identification: 013134
Unit ID: 217040
Telephone: (570) 346-1747 Carnegie Class: Spec-4-yr-Faith
FAX Number: (570) 346-2251 Calendar System: Semester
Established: 1965 Annual Undergrad Tuition & Fees: $9,800
Enrollment: 42 Male
Affiliation or Control: Independent Non-Profit IRS Status: 501(c)3
Highest Offering: Second Talmudic Degree
Accreditation: RABN

01 Chief Executive Officer ... Rabbi Yaakov SCHNAIDMAN
03 Executive Director ... Rabbi Avrohom PRESSMAN

York College of Pennsylvania (G)

441 Country Club Road, York PA 17403-3651
County: York FICE Identification: 003399
Unit ID: 217059
Telephone: (717) 846-7788 Carnegie Class: Masters/S
FAX Number: (717) 849-1607 Calendar System: Semester
URL: www.ycp.edu
Established: 1787 Annual Undergrad Tuition & Fees: $21,700
Enrollment: 4,039 Coed
Affiliation or Control: Independent Non-Profit IRS Status: 501(c)3
Highest Offering: Doctorate
Accreditation: M, ACBSP, ANEST, CAPRT, COARC, COSMA, MUS, NURSE

01 President ... Dr. Pamela J. GUNTER-SMITH
05 Provost & Dean Academic Affairs ... Vacant
10 VP Finance & Campus Operations ... Mr. Anthony DECOCINIS
20 Assoc Dean Academic Affairs ... Dr. Carl SEAQUIST
121 Associate Provost ... Dr. Joshua LANDAU
32 Dean of Student Dev/Campus Life ... Dr. Richard SATTERLEE
18 Asst to President Capital Projects ... Dr. Kenneth M. MARTIN
111 VP of Development ... Mr. Troy MILLER
41 Asst Dean Athletics & Recreation ... Mr. Paul SAIKIA
84 Vice Pres Enrollment Management ... Mr. Brian HAZLETT
26 Chief Communication Officer ... Ms. Mary E. DOLHEIMER
07 Director of Admissions ... Mr. Michael THORP
06 Registrar ... Ms. Tonaya SHAFFER
08 Librarian ... Mr. Jim KAPOUN
37 Director of Financial Aid ... Mr. Eric DINSMORE
13 CIO ... Dr. Ilya YAKOVLEV
29 Director Alumni Relations ... Mrs. Kristin SCHAB
36 Asst Dean Career Development ... Ms. Beverly A. EVANS
06 Assistant Registrar ... Mr. Matthew ROSS
19 Director of Public Safety ... Mr. Edward C. BRUDER
39 Director of Residence Life ... Mr. Robbie BACON
15 Director Human Resources ... Mrs. Vicki L. STEWART
38 Director Counseling Services ... Mr. Darrell WILT
23 Director Health Services ... Mrs. Amy DOWNS
40 Director Bookstore ... Mrs. Lynn P. FERRO
88 Director Campus & Special Events ... Ms. Sherry HEFLIN
102 Dir Corporate/Foundation/Govt Rels ... Mr. Jeffrey VERMEULEN
27 College Editor ... Mrs. Gail HUGANIR
42 Coordinator Religious Activities ... Mrs. Louise WORLEY
31 Dean Ctr for Community Engagement ... Dr. Dominic F. DELLICARPINI
09 Director of Institutional Research ... Dr. Sarah GALLIMORE
20 Director of Faculty Development ... Ms. Holly SYPNIEWSKI
04 Sr Executive Asst to President ... Mrs. Cynthia E. REISINGER
35 Assc Dir Stdnt Activity/Orientation ... Ms. Tamah AMROM
35 Asst Dean Stdnt Affs/New Stdnt Pgmg ... Ms. Sara GOODWIN
35 Asst Dean Student Dev/Campus Life ... Mr. Robbie BACON

YTI Career Institute (H)

2900 Fairway Drive, Altoona PA 16602
County: Blair FICE Identification: 030819
Unit ID: 375939
Telephone: (814) 944-5643 Carnegie Class: Spec 2-yr-Health
FAX Number: (959) 282-5093 Calendar System: Quarter
URL: www.yti.edu
Established: 2006 Annual Undergrad Tuition & Fees: N/A
Enrollment: 59 Coed
Affiliation or Control: Proprietary IRS Status: Proprietary
Highest Offering: Associate Degree
Accreditation: ACCSC, #COARC

02 Campus Dir of Operations/Education ... Mr. Carl KENYON

† Effective February 12, 2018, Altoona Campus has ceased recruiting new students

YTI Career Institute / Lancaster (I)

3050 Hempland Road, Lancaster PA 17601
Telephone: (717) 295-1100 Identification: 770588
Accreditation: ACCSC, CAHIIM

YTI Career Institute (J)

1405 Williams Road, York PA 17402-9017
County: York FICE Identification: 021274
Unit ID: 217077
Telephone: (717) 757-1100 Carnegie Class: Assoc/HVT-High Trad
FAX Number: (717) 757-4964 Calendar System: Quarter
URL: https://yti.edu
Established: 1967 Annual Undergrad Tuition & Fees: N/A
Enrollment: 708 Coed

Affiliation or Control: Proprietary IRS Status: Proprietary
Highest Offering: Associate Degree
Accreditation: ACCSC, ACFEI

00 President and CEO ... Mr. James BOLOGA
02 Campus Dir Operations/Education ... Dr. Thomas BANKS
05 VP Academics ... Ms. Vicki KANE
07 Asst Dir of Admissions ... Ms. Angie JONES
06 Registrar ... Ms. JoElle HEINBAUGH

RHODE ISLAND

Brown University (A)

One Prospect Street, Providence RI 02912
County: Providence FICE Identification: 003401
Unit ID: 217156
Telephone: (401) 863-1000 Carnegie Class: DU-Highest
FAX Number: (401) 863-3700 Calendar System: Semester
URL: www.brown.edu
Established: 1764 Annual Undergrad Tuition & Fees: $60,696
Enrollment: 9,948 Coed
Affiliation or Control: Independent Non-Profit IRS Status: 501(c)3
Highest Offering: Doctorate
Accreditation: EH, CAMPEP, IPSY, MED, PDPSY, PH

01 President ... Christina H. PAXSON
05 Provost ... Richard LOCKE
45 Exec VP Planning & Policy ... Russell CAREY
11 Exec VP Finance/Administration ... Sarah LATHAM
111 Senior VP for Advancement ... Sergio GONZALEZ
10 VP Finance/Chief Financial Officer ... Michael WHITE
26 VP Communications ... Cass CLIATT
28 VP Institutional Equity & Diversity ... Sylvia CAREY-BUTLER
32 VP Campus Life & Student Services ... Eric ESTES
15 VP Human Resources ... Marie WILLIAMS
43 VP & General Counsel ... Eileen GOLDGEIER
69 Int Dean School of Public Health ... Ronald AUBERT
100 Chief of Staff/Asst to President ... Marguerite JOUTZ
58 Dean of Graduate School ... Vacant
115 VP & Chief Investment Officer ... Jane DIETZE
63 Dean of Medicine/Biological Science ... Mukesh JAIN
54 Dean of Engineering ... Vacant
107 Dean School Professional Studies ... Shankar PRASAD
20 Dean of the Faculty ... Leah VANWEY
46 VP for Research ... Jill PIPHER
13 Chief Digital & Information Officer ... William THIRSK
20 Dean of the College ... Rashid ZIA
09 Director of Institutional Research ... Katharine BARNES
23 Assoc VP Health & Wellness ... Vanessa BRITTO
86 Asst VP Govt & Community Relations ... Albert DAHLBERG
20 Deputy Provost for Academic Affairs ... Elizabeth DOHERTY
06 University Registrar ... Robert FITZGERALD
18 VP for Facilities Management ... Michael GUGLIELMO, JR.
41 Director of Athletics ... Grace CALHOUN
38 Dir Counseling & Psychological Svcs ... Bryant FORD
08 University Librarian ... Joseph MEISEL
19 Exec Dir & Chief of Public Safety ... Rodney CHATMAN
07 Dean of Admission ... Logan POWELL
29 Vice President Alumni Relations ... Zach LANGWAY
21 Assoc VP & University Controller ... Charlene SWEENEY
37 Dean of Financial Aid ... James TILTON

Bryant University (B)

1150 Douglas Pike, Smithfield RI 02917-1291
County: Providence FICE Identification: 003402
Unit ID: 217165
Telephone: (401) 232-6000 Carnegie Class: Masters/L
FAX Number: (401) 232-6319 Calendar System: Semester
URL: www.bryant.edu
Established: 1863 Annual Undergrad Tuition & Fees: $46,863
Enrollment: 3,674 Coed
Affiliation or Control: Independent Non-Profit IRS Status: 501(c)3
Highest Offering: Beyond Master's But Less Than Doctorate
Accreditation: EH, ARCPA

00 Chairman Board of Trustees ... Mr. David BEIRNE
01 President ... Dr. Ross GITTELL
05 Provost/Chief Academic Officer ... Dr. Rupendra PALIWAL
32 VP Student Affairs/Dean of Students ... Dr. Inge-Lise AMEER
82 VP International Affairs ... Dr. Hong YANG
10 VP Business Affairs ... Ms. Donna NG
111 VP University Advancement ... Mr. David WEGRZYN
13 VP Information Services/CIO ... Mr. Chuck LOCURTO
84 VP Enrollment Management ... Ms. Michelle CLOUTIER
26 Chief Marketing and Communications ... Ms. Lorraine DAIGNAULT
15 AVP Human Resources ... Mr. Timothy PAIGE
22 AVP Diversity/Equity & Inclusion ... Dr. Kevin MARTINS
18 Assoc VP Facilities Opers ... Mr. Andrew DEMELIA
21 Assoc VP Business & Controller ... Mr. Farokh BHADA
20 Associate Provost ... Dr. Wendy SAMTER
45 Exec Dir Inst Effect & Strategy ... Dr. Edinaldo TEBALDI
49 Dean College of Arts & Sciences ... Dr. Veronica MCCOMB
50 Dean College of Business ... Dr. Madan ANNAVARJULA
51 Dir Exec Development Center ... Vacant
88 Dir RI Export Assistance Center ... Mr. Andrew GELFUSO
121 Asst Dean for Student Success ... Dr. Laurie L. HAZARD
88 Int Director Center for Teaching ... Ms. Ilisabeth BORNSTEIN
06 Interim Registrar ... Ms. Laura HAYWARD
28 Asst VP Student Engagement ... Dr. Mailee KUE
35 Asst VP for Student Affairs ... Mr. John DENIO
36 Dir Career Services ... Dr. Kevin GAW
38 Dir Counseling/Rel/Spiritual Life ... Dr. Noelle HARRIS
19 Dir Public Safety ... Mr. Stephen BANNON
88 Dir Capital Projects ... Mr. Thomas MANN
88 Asst Dir Women's Center ... Ms. Kelly BOUTIN
37 Dir Financial Aid ... Mr. John B. CANNING
88 Dir Conference Services ... Ms. Nicole BEAUREGARD
30 Exec Dir Development ... Mr. Edward MAGRO
29 Dir Alumni Relations ... Ms. Robin T. WARDE
90 Dir Acad Computing & Media Svcs ... Mr. Phillip LOMBARDI
91 Dir Admin Systems ... Ms. Christine BIGWOOD
14 Dir Campus Technology ... Mr. David GANNON
16 Assoc Dir Human Resources ... Ms. Catherine CURRIE
41 Dir Athletics ... Mr. Bill SMITH
09 Dir Inst Effect & Strategy ... Mr. Robert JONES
88 Exec Dir US-China Institute ... Dr. Hong YANG
105 Chief Library Officer ... Ms. Laura KOHL
104 Director Study Abroad ... Ms. Cindi LEWIS
102 Dir Foundation/Corporate Relations ... Ms. Robin RICHARDSON
113 Director of Business Svcs/Bursar ... Ms. Michelle MARCANO
40 Manager Bookstore ... Mr. Stanley STOWIK
04 Admin Assistant to the President ... Ms. Vicky ATKINS
39 Dir Resident Life ... Ms. Jana VALENTINE

College Unbound (C)

325 Public Street, Providence RI 02905
County: Providence Identification: 667355
Unit ID: 493822
Telephone: (401) 752-2640 Carnegie Class: Spec-4-yr-Other
FAX Number: N/A Calendar System: Semester
URL: www.collegeunbound.edu
Established: 2009 Annual Undergrad Tuition & Fees: N/A
Enrollment: N/A Coed
Affiliation or Control: Independent Non-Profit IRS Status: 501(c)3
Highest Offering: Baccalaureate
Accreditation: EH

01 President ... Dennis LITTKY
05 VP Academic Affairs/Provost ... Adam BUSH
03 Executive Vice President ... Robert CAROTHERS
04 Exec Assistant to the President ... Tara HAGOPIAN

Community College of Rhode Island (D)

400 East Avenue, Warwick RI 02886-1807
County: Kent FICE Identification: 003408
Unit ID: 217475
Telephone: (401) 825-1000 Carnegie Class: Assoc/HT-High Trad
FAX Number: (401) 825-2166 Calendar System: Semester
URL: www.ccri.edu
Established: 1964 Annual Undergrad Tuition & Fees (In-State): $4,806
Enrollment: 13,684 Coed
Affiliation or Control: State IRS Status: 501(c)3
Highest Offering: Associate Degree
Accreditation: EH, ACBSP, ADNUR, ART, COARC, COMTA, DA, DH, DMS, HT, MLTAD, MUS, NAEYC, OTA, PNUR, PTAA, RAD

01 President ... Dr. Meghan HUGHES
05 Vice President for Academic Affairs ... Dr. Rosemary COSTIGAN
10 Vice President Finance/Strategy ... Ms. Kristen ALBRITTON
32 VP Stdnt Affs & Chf Outcomes Ofcr ... Ms. Sara ENRIGHT
111 AVP Institutional Advancement/Col ... Mr. Robert (Bobby) G. GONDOLA, JR.
18 Interim Director of Physical Plant ... Mr. David A. SNOW
79 Interim Dean, Arts/Humanities/SoSc ... Mr. John COLE
76 Dean Health & Rehab Service ... Dr. Suzanne M. CARR
50 Interim Dean Bus/Sci/Tech & Math ... Ms. Barbara NAUMAN
103 Vice President of Workforce Develop ... Vacant
08 Dean of Library & Academic Innovati ... Mr. George K. HART
35 Dean of Students ... Mr. Michael J. CUNNINGHAM, II
21 Controller ... Mr. David J. RAWLINSON
35 Assoc Dean Student Life/Svc Lrng ... Dr. Rebecca H. YOUNT
15 Director of Human Resources ... Ms. Sybil F. BAILEY
13 Director Information Technology ... Ms. Pamela J. CHRISTMAN
19 Chief of Police ... Mr. Sean COLLINS
26 Director Marketing & Communications ... Ms. Amy P. KEMPE
41 Interim Director of Athletics ... Mr. Kevin S. SALISBURY
09 Interim Dir Inst Research/Planning ... Mr. Phillip S. GORDON
113 Bursar ... Vacant
88 Director Access to Opportunity ... Ms. Tracy KARASINSKI
109 Auxiliary Svcs Business Director ... Dr. Raymond N. KARASEK, III
22 Dir AA/EEO/Div/Incl/Title IX Coord ... Vacant
96 Director of Purchasing ... Ms. Lisa M. CONSIDINE-FONTES
36 Coordinator Career Services ... Ms. Camille NUMRICH
37 Director of Financial Aid ... Ms. Kelly A. MORRISSEY
04 Assistant to the President ... Ms. Deborah M. ZIELINSKI
06 Registrar ... Ms. Cathy L. PICARD-TESSIER
07 Director of Admissions ... Ms. Teresa M. KLESS
11 AVP for Administration ... Ms. Alix R. OGDEN
14 Director of Operations (IS) ... Mr. William R. FERLAND
38 Dean Student Dev/Assessment ... Mr. Robert D. CIPOLLA
43 Dir Legal Services/General Counsel ... Mr. Ronald A. CAVALLARO

Johnson & Wales University (E)

8 Abbott Park Place, Providence RI 02903-3703
County: Providence FICE Identification: 003404
Unit ID: 217235
Telephone: (401) 598-1000 Carnegie Class: Masters/L
FAX Number: (401) 598-2880 Calendar System: Semester
URL: https://www.jwu.edu/
Established: 1914 Annual Undergrad Tuition & Fees: $34,736
Enrollment: 5,676 Coed
Affiliation or Control: Independent Non-Profit IRS Status: 501(c)3
Highest Offering: Doctorate
Accreditation: EH, ARCPA, DIETD, OT

01 Chancellor ... Ms. Mim L. RUNEY
02 President Providence Campus ... Ms. Marie BERNARDO-SOUSA
05 Provost ... Dr. Richard WISCOTT
10 Vice Chancellor of Finance & Admin ... Mr. Joseph J. GREENE
88 Vice Chancellor Acad Administration ... Dr. Sandra AFFENITO
86 VP Comm & Government Relations ... Ms. Lisa PELOSI
84 VP of Enrollment Management ... Mr. Akhil GUPTA
15 Vice President of Human Resources ... Ms. Diane D'AMBRA
13 VP of Information Technology ... Mr. Dave SOUZA
88 VP Col Professional Studies ... Ms. Cindy PARKER
111 VP of Advancement & Univ Relations ... Ms. Maureen DUMAS
21 Vice President of Finance ... Ms. Danielle SANTAMARIA
43 Vice President & General Counsel ... Ms. Luba SHUR
101 University Secretary ... Ms. Emily GILCREAST
08 Dean of Libraries ... Ms. Rosita HOPPER
76 Dean College of Health & Wellness ... Ms. Laura GALLIGAN
49 Dean College of Arts & Sciences ... Mr. Michael R. FEIN
50 Dean College of Business ... Ms. Mary MEIXELL
107 Dean Col of Professional Studies ... Mr. David R. CARTWRIGHT
88 Assoc Dean Col of Culinary Arts ... Dr. Susan MARSHALL
54 Dean College of Engr & Design ... Mr. Frank TWEEDIE
88 Dean Col of Food Innov & Tech ... Mr. Jason EVANS
88 Interim Dean Col Hospitality Mgmt ... Ms. Jennifer GALIPEAU
06 Interim University Registrar ... Ms. Kimberly BUXTON
27 Director University Marketing ... Mr. Joe MAGENNIS
109 Vice President of Auxiliary Service ... Mr. Michael DOWNING
114 University Budget Director ... Ms. Eileen T. HASKINS
21 Director of Accounting Services ... Ms. Laurie O'KEEFE
116 Dir of Financial Plng & Analysis ... Ms. Michele VON HEIN
37 Dir Student Financial Svcs ... Ms. Dawn BLANCHETTE
121 Dir of Academic Success Center ... Vacant
16 Director of Human Resources ... Ms. Rebecca TONDREAU
118 Director of Benefits ... Ms. Christine OLIVER
09 Exec Dir Inst Research & Analysis ... Ms. Kristen SULLIVAN
29 Dir of Alumni Relations ... Ms. Lori ZABATTA
19 Exec Dir of Campus Safety/Security ... Mr. LeRoy ROSE, JR.
18 VP of Facilities Management ... Mr. Jason WITHAM
119 Director of Information Security ... Mr. Nicholas TELLA
32 VP of Stdnt Affairs/Dean of Stdnts ... Vacant
38 Assoc Dean Counsel/Health/Wellness ... Mr. Joseph BARRESI, JR.
35 Assoc Dean of Students ... Ms. Mel GRAF
07 Director of Admissions ... Ms. Amy OCONNELL
39 Director of Residential Life ... Mr. Nev KRAGULJEVIC
36 Director of Career Services ... Ms. Donna REMINGTON
85 Dir International Student Services ... Mr. Wesley ROY
104 Asst Director of Study Abroad ... Ms. Amy EWEN
44 Director Annual Giving ... Ms. Maureen MACLURE
96 Dir of Culinary Purchasing & Ops ... Mr. Erik GOELLNER
122 Assc Dir Stdnt Engage-Greek Life ... Ms. Elizabeth ZMARLICKI
04 Exec Asst to Senior Administration ... Ms. Tara MCGEE
41 Director of Athletics ... Ms. Dana GARFIELD

New England Institute of Technology (F)

One New England Tech Blvd., East Greenwich RI 02818
County: Kent FICE Identification: 007845
Unit ID: 217305
Telephone: (800) 736-7744 Carnegie Class: Masters/S
FAX Number: (401) 886-0859 Calendar System: Quarter
URL: www.neit.edu
Established: 1940 Annual Undergrad Tuition & Fees: $31,827
Enrollment: 2,031 Coed
Affiliation or Control: Independent Non-Profit IRS Status: 501(c)3
Highest Offering: Doctorate
Accreditation: EH, ADNUR, COARC, MLTAD, NUR, OT, OTA, PTAA, SURGT

01 President ... Mr. Richard I. GOUSE
03 Executive Vice President ... Mr. Scott A. FREUND
05 Senior Vice President and Provost ... Dr. Douglas H. SHERMAN
10 Sr VP Financial Affs & Endowment ... Ms. Cheryl C. CONNORS
32 Vice Pres Student Support Services ... Ms. Catherine B. KENNEDY
21 VP of Finance & Business Admin ... Mr. Kenneth JALBERT
103 VP Corporate Educ & Training ... Mr. Steven H. KITCHIN
20 Associate Provost ... Dr. Henry YOUNG
84 VP of Enrollment Mgt & Marketing ... Mr. Tim REARDON
37 Director Financial Aid ... Ms. Anna KELLY
08 Director Library ... Mr. Joseph HOLLAND
36 Director of Career Services ... Ms. Patricia BLAKEMORE
109 Director Auxiliary Services ... Mr. Patrick TRACEY
06 Registrar ... Mr. Erik VAN RENSELAAR
35 Director of Student Support Service ... Ms. Lee PEEBLES
13 Chief Info Technology Officer (CIO) ... Mr. Jacques LAFLAMME
19 Director Security/Safety ... Ms. Pamela MOFFATT-LIMOGES
43 Dir Legal Services/General Counsel ... Mr. Philip PARSONS
96 Director of Purchasing ... Mr. William MENARD
39 Director Student Housing ... Ms. Danielly JAMOUS

Providence College (G)

1 Cunningham Square, Providence RI 02918-0001
County: Providence FICE Identification: 003406
Unit ID: 217402
Telephone: (401) 865-1000 Carnegie Class: Masters/L
FAX Number: (401) 865-2057 Calendar System: Semester
URL: www.providence.edu
Established: 1917 Annual Undergrad Tuition & Fees: $54,388
Enrollment: 4,821 Coed

Affiliation or Control: Roman Catholic IRS Status: 501(c)3
Highest Offering: Master's
Accreditation: EH, SW

01 President ... Rev. Kenneth SICARD, OP
03 Executive Vice President/ Treasurer ... Ms. Ann MANCHESTER-MOLAK
04 Asst to Pres & Exec Vice President ... Vacant
05 Sr VP Academic Affairs/Provost ... Dr. Sean F. REID
10 Sr VP for Finance & Business/CFO ... Mr. John M. SWEENEY
111 Sr VP for Institutional Advancement ... Mr. Gregory T. WALDRON
43 Vice President/General Counsel ... Mr. Christopher NERONHA
42 Vice Pres for Mission & Ministry ... Rev. James CUDDY, OP
21 Assoc VP for Finance/Asst Treasurer ... Ms. Lori A. COTE
32 Assoc VP for Student Affairs ... Dr. Steven A. SEARS
20 Assoc VP for Academic Affairs ... Dr. Brian J. BARTOLINI
41 Assoc VP for Athletics/Athletic Dir ... Mr. Steven R. NAPOLILLO
15 Sr AVP for Human Resources ... Ms. Mirlen A. MAL
28 Assoc VP/Chief Diversity Officer ... Vacant
26 Assoc VP Public Affairs/Cmty Rels ... Mr. Steven J. MAURANO
20 Assoc VP for Academic Affairs ... Mr. Charles J. HABERLE
07 Assoc VP Admissions/Financial Aid ... Mr. Raul A. FONTS
29 Asst Vice Pres for Alumni Relations ... Ms. Sarah R. OSOWA
30 Asst Vice Pres for Development ... Ms. Andrea B. KEEFE
45 Asst VP Capital Projects & Fac Plng ... Mr. Mark F. RAPOZA
58 Dean of Undergrad & Grad Studies ... Vacant
49 Interim Dean School Arts & Sciences ... Dr. Joan R. BRANHAM
107 Dean School of Professional Studies ... Vacant
50 Dean School of Business ... Dr. Sylvia MAXFIELD
51 Actg Dean Sch Continuing Education ... Ms. Carmen AGUILAR
66 Inaugural Dean Nursing/Health Sci ... Dr. Kyle J. MCINNIS
35 AVP Stdnt Affs/Asst Dean of Stdnts ... Ms. Tiffany D. GAFFNEY
06 Registrar ... Ms. Yvonne D. ARRUDA
104 Dean of Global Education ... Vacant
88 Director of Student Activities ... Ms. Sharon L. HAY
84 Associate Dean of Enrollment Svcs ... Vacant
37 Exec Director of Financial Aid ... Ms. Sandra J. OLIVEIRA
19 Exec Director Safety & Security ... Vacant
18 Exec Director of Physical Plant ... Mr. Andrew J. SULLIVAN
08 Director of Library ... Dr. Mark J. CAPRIO
09 Director of Institutional Research ... Ms. Melanie R. SULLIVAN
90 Dir Enterprise Infrastructure & Ops ... Mr. John R. MATTESON
92 Director Liberal Arts Honors ... Dr. Stephen J. LYNCH
96 Exec Director of Business Services ... Mr. Gene R. ROBBINS
121 AVP/Dean of Student Success Center ... Mr. Bryan D. MARINELLI
88 VP Student Development & Compliance ... Vacant
13 Chief Information Officer/CIO ... Mr. Paul V. FONTAINE
102 Dir Foundation/Corporate Relations ... Ms. Marilyn E. DESCHENES
105 Director Web Services ... Mr. Daniel C. DEMMONS
108 Director Institutional Assessment ... Ms. Cathy A. GAGNE
39 Dir Resident Life/Student Housing ... Mr. Nedzer C. ERILUS

Rhode Island College (A)

600 Mount Pleasant Avenue, Providence RI 02908-1991
County: Providence FICE Identification: 003407
Unit ID: 217420
Telephone: (401) 456-8000 Carnegie Class: Masters/L
FAX Number: (401) 456-8379 Calendar System: Semester
URL: www.ric.edu
Established: 1854 Annual Undergrad Tuition & Fees (In-State): $10,260
Enrollment: 7,072 Coed
Affiliation or Control: State IRS Status: 501(c)3
Highest Offering: Doctorate
Accreditation: EH, ANEST, ART, CACREP, IACBE, MUS, NURSE, SW

01 President ... Dr. Jack R. WARNER
05 Provost/VP Academic Affairs ... Dr. Helen TATE
10 VP/Chief Financial Officer ... Mr. Stephen NEDDER
32 AVP for Student Services ... Dr. Ducha HANG
111 VP for Advancement ... Ms. Kimberly C. DUMPSON
45 Exec Dir Strategic Initiative ... Mr. Clark M. GREENE
107 Assoc VP Prof Studies & Cont Educ ... Ms. Jenifer GIROUX
28 Assoc VP Equity/Diversity/ Inclusion ... Ms. Anna M. CANO-MORALES
102 Executive Director RIC Foundation ... Mr. Edwin R. PACHECO
20 Vice Prov Undergraduate Affairs ... Dr. Holly L. SHADOIAN
35 Int Assoc Dean of Student Life ... Ms. Pegah RAHMANIAN
13 Asst VP Information Services/CIO ... Mr. Jon BARTELSON
84 Dean of Enrollment Management ... Mr. James TWEED
11 Int Asst VP Administration/Finance ... Mr. Kevin J. FITTA
58 Int Dean of Graduate Studies ... Dr. Leslie SCHUSTER
49 Dean Faculty Arts & Sciences ... Dr. Earl L. SIMSON
53 Dean Sch Education & Human Dev ... Dr. Jeannine DINGUS-EASON
50 Int Dean School of Business ... Dr. Alema KARIM
66 Dean School of Nursing ... Dr. Carolynn MASTERS
70 Int Dean School of Social Work ... Dr. Jayashree NIMMAGADDA
15 Director of Human Resources ... Ms. Maggie SULLIVAN
22 Dir Institutional Equity ... Ms. Margaret A. LYNCH GADALETA
19 Director of Security & Safety ... Mr. James MENDONCA
09 Dir Inst Research & Planning ... Dr. Christopher P. HOURIGAN
114 Director of Budget & Fin Plng ... Mr. Robert EATON
18 Director Facilities & Operations ... Mr. James M. JERUE
18 Director Capital Projects ... Mr. Kevin J. FITTA
96 Director of Purchasing ... Ms. Jessica L. SILVA
08 Director of the Library ... Ms. Carissa DELIZIO
07 Director of Admissions ... Mr. Jason S. ANTHONY
121 Director of Academic Advising ... Mr. Christopher DACOSTA
06 Director of Records ... Ms. Tamecka C. HARDMON
37 Sr Assoc Director Financial Aid ... Ms. Nancy A. BESSETTE
41 Dir of Athletics ... Mr. Donald E. TENCHER
90 Director User Support Services ... Mr. David E. TOMS
91 Director Management Info Sys ... Dr. Bin YU

119 Director of Information Security ... Mr. Henk E. SONDER
39 Director Res Life/Housing ... Ms. Darcy DUBOIS
36 Director Career Dev Center ... Ms. Demetria MORAN
23 Int Dir College Health Services ... Ms. Christie RISHWORTH
38 Int Director Counseling Center ... Dr. Ryan PORELL
29 Director Alumni Affairs ... Ms. Suzanna ALBA
104 Director of Study Abroad ... Ms. Gersende CHANFRAU
88 Director of Unity Center ... Ms. Pegah RAHMANIAN
113 Bursar ... Ms. Charlene L. SZCZEPANEK
105 Director Web Services ... Ms. Karen M. RUBINO
26 Dir of College Comm & Marketing ... Vacant

Rhode Island School of Design (B)

2 College Street, Providence RI 02903-2784
County: Providence FICE Identification: 003409
Unit ID: 217493
Telephone: (401) 454-6100 Carnegie Class: Masters/L
FAX Number: (401) 454-6320 Calendar System: 4/1/4
URL: www.risd.edu
Established: 1877 Annual Undergrad Tuition & Fees: $54,890
Enrollment: 2,227 Coed
Affiliation or Control: Independent Non-Profit IRS Status: 501(c)3
Highest Offering: Master's
Accreditation: EH, LSAR

01 President ... Ms. Crystal WILLIAMS
100 Chief of Staff and Communications ... Ms. Taylor SCOTT
05 Provost ... Dr. Kent KLEINMAN
10 Sr VP Finance and Administration ... Mr. Dave PROULX
84 VP Enrollment & Student Affairs ... Mr. Jamie O'HARA
88 Interim Director RISD Museum of Art ... Ms. Sarah GANZ BLYTHE
111 VP Institutional Engagement ... Mr. O'Neil OUTAR
26 Chief Marketing/Communcation Ofcr ... Ms. Kerci M. STROUD
20 Vice Provost ... Dr. Dan CAVICCHI
28 Assoc Prov Social Equity/Inclusion ... Mr. Matthew SHENODA
20 Assoc Prov Rsrch/Strtgic Prtnrships ... Ms. Sarah CUNNINGHAM
15 VP Human Resources ... Ms. Candace BAER
18 VP Campus Services ... Mr. Jack SILVA
43 General Counsel ... Ms. Renee BYAS
32 Assoc VP Student Affairs ... Ms. Barbara LOMONACO
20 Dean of Faculty ... Dr. Patricia BARBEITO
48 Dean Architecture & Design ... Ms. Scheri FULTINEER
57 Dean of Fine Arts ... Mr. Brooks HAGAN
88 Dean Experimental/Foundation Stds ... Ms. Joanne STRYKER
49 Dean of Liberal Arts ... Dr. Damian WHITE
08 Dean of Libraries ... Ms. Margot NISHIMURA
37 Asst VP for Enrollment Services ... Mr. Anthony GALLONIO
13 CIO ... Mr. Rick MICKOOL
06 Registrar ... Ms. Alison SHERMAN

Roger Williams University (C)

One Old Ferry Road, Bristol RI 02809-2921
County: Bristol FICE Identification: 003410
Unit ID: 217518
Telephone: (401) 253-1040 Carnegie Class: Masters/M
FAX Number: N/A Calendar System: Semester
URL: www.rwu.edu
Established: 1956 Annual Undergrad Tuition & Fees: $38,274
Enrollment: 4,702 Coed
Affiliation or Control: Independent Non-Profit IRS Status: 501(c)3
Highest Offering: First Professional Degree
Accreditation: EH, CONST, LAW

01 President ... Dr. Ioannis MIAOULIS
05 Provost ... Dr. Margaret EVERETT
10 EVP Finance/Administration ... Mr. Marc LEONETTI
100 Chief of Staff ... Mr. Brian WILLIAMS
21 VP for Accounting/Treasury Mgmt ... Ms. Nicole TURNER
32 Vice President for Student Life ... Mr. John J. KING
111 VP Institutional Advancement ... Ms. Amy BERKELEY
28 Vice President/Chief Diversity Ofcr ... Dr. Stephanie AKUNVABEY
08 Dean University Library ... Ms. Betsy P. LEARNED
26 Assoc VP Enrollment Mgmt/Marketing ... Ms. Tracy M. DACOSTA
84 VP & Dean Enrollment Mgmt ... Ms. Amy TIBERIO
15 Asst Vice Pres of Human Resources ... Mr. Thomas MCDONOUGH
09 AVP for Institutional Research ... Ms. Jennifer DUNSEATH
51 Dean of University College ... Ms. Gena BIANCO
27 AVP of Marketing/Communications ... Ms. Lynne MELLO
110 AVP of Institutional Advancement ... Mr. Aaron BUZAY
28 Dir Inst Diversity/Equity/Inclusion ... Vacant
61 Dean RWU School of Law ... Mr. Gregory BOWMAN
48 Dean Cummings Sch of Architechture ... Mr. Stephen E. WHITE
50 Dean Gabelli School of Business ... Dr. Susan MCTIERNAN
54 Dean Sch Engrng/Comput/Constr Mgmt ... Dr. Robert GRIFFIN
88 Dean School of Justice Studies ... Dr. Eric BRONSON
123 Director Graduate Admissions ... Mr. Marcus HANSCOM
49 Dean Sch Social/Natural Sciences ... Dr. Benjamin GREENSTEIN
13 Chief Information Officer ... Mr. Daryl FORD
07 Dean of Admissions ... Ms. Amanda MARSILI
37 Director of Financial Aid ... Ms. Diane USHER
96 Director of Purchasing ... Ms. Kathy KANTERMAN
88 Director of Special Events ... Ms. Heidi DAGWAN
06 Registrar ... Mr. Daniel O'DRISCOLL
19 Director of Public Safety ... Mr. Mark PORTER
41 Director of Athletics ... Ms. Kristen JACOBS
18 Asst VP Facilities/Capital Projects ... Mr. John AMITRANO
38 Dir Counseling/Student Devel ... Mr. Christopher BAILEY
23 Director of Health Services ... Ms. Anne M. MITCHELL
39 Director of Residence Life/Housing ... Vacant
88 Director of Prospect Research ... Ms. Nancy L. RAMOS
22 Title IX Coord/Associate Dean ... Ms. Jennifer STANLEY
40 Manager Bookstore ... Ms. Stephanie ROSE

Salve Regina University (D)

100 Ochre Point Avenue, Newport RI 02840-4192
County: Newport FICE Identification: 003411
Unit ID: 217536
Telephone: (401) 847-6650 Carnegie Class: Masters/L
FAX Number: (401) 341-2925 Calendar System: Semester
URL: www.salve.edu
Established: 1947 Annual Undergrad Tuition & Fees: $42,920
Enrollment: 2,771 Coed
Affiliation or Control: Roman Catholic IRS Status: 501(c)3
Highest Offering: Doctorate
Accreditation: EH, ART, CACREP, IACBE, NURSE, SW

00 Chair of the Board of Trustees ... Ms. Cheryl MROZOWSKI
01 President ... Dr. Kelli ARMSTRONG
05 Vice Pres Academic Affairs/Provost ... Dr. Nancy SCHREIBER
32 Vice President Student Affairs ... Dr. Letizia GAMBRELL-BOONE
111 VP University Relations ... Mr. Michael L. SEMENZA
10 Chief of Finance/VP for Operations ... Mr. Michael N. GRANDCHAMP
84 Vice Pres Enrollment Management ... Mr. James R. FOWLER
45 Vice Pres Strategic Initiatives ... Dr. James LUDES
88 Vice Pres for Mission Integration ... Dr. Theresa LADRIGAN-WHELPLEY
100 Chief of Staff ... Mr. Michael V. PIMENTAL
26 Sr Assoc VP/Chief Comm Officer ... Ms. Kristine HENDRICKSON
15 Assoc VP and Chief HR Officer ... Ms. Nancy ESCHER
13 AVP Info Technology/CIO and CISO ... Mr. Irving BRUCKSTEIN
21 Asst VP Finance/Controller ... Mrs. Michele G. WOOD
20 Associate Provost ... Dr. Donna M. COOK
20 Director of Academic Operations ... Ms. Stefanie PICARD
18 Asst VP for Facilities Management ... Mr. Eric MILNER
28 Asst VP Diversity and Retention ... Dr. Sami NASSIM
110 Asst VP for Advancement ... Ms. Katherine HOROSCHAK
112 Asst VP Development /Planned Giving ... Ms. Sandra ANTHOINE
07 Dean of Undergraduate Admissions ... Ms. Colleen EMERSON
58 Vice Provost Grad & Prof Studies ... Dr. David ALTOUNIAN
88 Dean of Undergraduate Studies ... Dr. Steven RODENBORN
44 Sr Director of Annual Giving Pgm ... Ms. Victoria DUCLOS
14 Sr Dir of Enterprise Applications ... Ms. Christine DUMONT
41 Athletic Director ... Ms. Jody MOORADIAN
09 Dir Inst Research/Effectiveness ... Ms. Annemarie BARTLETT
32 Assoc VP/Dean of Students ... Ms. Kathleen FARLEY
06 Registrar ... Ms. Alissa BERTRAM
37 Director of Financial Aid ... Ms. Anne MCDERMOTT
29 Director Alumni & Parent Pgms ... Vacant
08 Director of Library Services ... Ms. Dawn EMSELLEM
39 Director of Residence Life ... Mr. Jim MOURNIGHAN
90 Director of Tech Services Center ... Mr. Brian A. MCDONNELL
19 Director of Security/Safety ... Mr. Michael CARUOLO
40 Director of Bookstore ... Mr. Michael LEDDY
23 Director Health Services ... Ms. Elizabeth GALVIN
36 Director of Career Development ... Mr. Michael WISNEWSKI
104 Director of International Programs ... Ms. Erin FITZGERALD
38 Director of Counseling Services ... Ms. Meghan M. DECARVALHO
30 Chief Advancement Officer ... Ms. MaeLynn PATTEN
31 Dir Community Engagement/Service ... Ms. Kelly POWERS
112 Director of Major Gifts ... Mr. Christopher PINAULT
35 Associate Dean of Students ... Ms. Jennifer JENSEN
124 Director of Student Engagement ... Ms. Dyanna MOREIRA
96 Purchasing Manager ... Ms. Samantha ANGEL
04 Exec Assistant to the President ... Ms. Robyn GREENE

University of Rhode Island (E)

45 Upper College Road, Kingston RI 02881
County: Washington FICE Identification: 003414
Unit ID: 217484
Telephone: (401) 874-1000 Carnegie Class: DU-Higher
FAX Number: (401) 874-7149 Calendar System: Semester
URL: www.uri.edu
Established: 1892 Annual Undergrad Tuition & Fees (In-State): $15,004
Enrollment: 17,649 Coed
Affiliation or Control: State IRS Status: 501(c)3
Highest Offering: Doctorate
Accreditation: EH, AAQEP, CAMPEP, CLPSY, @DIET, DIETD, DIETI, EXSC, LIB, LSAR, MFCD, MUS, NURSE, PHAR, PTA, SP

01 President ... Dr. Marc PARLANGE
100 Chief of Staff/Sec to Board ... Ms. Michelle CURRERI
05 Int Provost/VP Academic Affairs ... Ms. Laura BEAUVAIS
46 Vice Pres Research/Economic Devel ... Dr. Peter SNYDER
10 Vice Pres for Admin & Finance ... Ms. Abigail RIDER
88 Assoc VP Res/Int Prop Mgmt/Comm ... Mr. Michael KATZ
88 Dir Univ Res External Relations ... Ms. Melissa MCCARTHY
88 Dir Research Development ... Ms. Karen MARKIN
46 Assoc VP Research Admin ... Dr. Theodore A. MYATT
29 Exec Dir Alumni Relations/Secy Assn ... Ms. Michele NOTA
26 Int Exec Dir Ext Relations/Comm ... Ms. Linda A. ACCIARDO
114 Dir Budget & Financial Planning ... Ms. Linda BARRETT
21 Controller ... Vacant
15 Asst Vice Pres Human Resource Admin ... Ms. Anne Marie COLEMAN
16 Director Personnel Services ... Ms. Laura KENERSON
19 Director Public Safety ... Mr. Stephen N. BAKER
12 Dir W.A. Jones Campus ... Ms. Maria DISANO
88 Assoc Dean Business Administration ... Dr. Shaw CHEN
88 Dir Capital Projects ... Mr. Paul DEPACE
88 Dir Planning & Real Estate Dev ... Mr. Ryan CARILLO
88 Dir Property & Support Svc ... Mrs. Vicki DUBE
96 Director Purchasing & Univ Stores ... Ms. Tracey ANGELL
28 AVP/Chief Diversity Officer ... Ms. Mary Grace ALMANDREZ

43 General Counsel ... Ms. Alyssa BOSS
32 Vice President Student Affairs ... Ms. Ellen M. REYNOLDS
109 Dir Dining Services ... Mr. Pierre ST-GERMAIN
41 Director of Athletics ... Mr. Thorr D. BJORN
103 Dir Career and Experiential Edu ... Ms. Kim STACK
38 Int Director Counseling Center ... Dr. Cory CLARK
88 Dir Recreational Services ... Ms. Jodi HAWKINS
35 Dean of Students ... Mr. Daniel GRANEY
88 Dir Special Pgms/Talent Devel ... Mr. Gerald WILLIAMS
88 Int Mgr Conf & Spec Pgm ... Ms. Sheri DAVIS
35 Asst VP Student Affs & Dir HRL ... Mr. Frankie MINOR
39 Assoc Dir Housing & Res Life ... Dr. Jeffrey PLOUFFE
23 Director Health Services ... Ms. Ellen REYNOLDS
40 Administrator Bookstore ... Mr. Paul WHITNEY
88 Spec Asst to the Prov for Acad Plng ... Ms. Ann M. MORRISSEY
88 Vice Prov Acad Finance/Personnel ... Dr. Matthew H. BODAH
84 AVP Enrollment Mgmt/Stdnt Success ... Mr. Dean LIBUTTI
07 Dean of Admissions ... Ms. Cynthia L. BONN
06 Dir Enrollment Services/Registrar ... Dr. Carnell JONES, JR.
20 Vice Provost for Acad & Fac Init ... Dr. Anne VEEGER
13 Int Chief Information Officer ... Mr. Karlis KAUGARS
90 Dir Media & Technology Services ... Mr. David S. PORTER
91 Dir University Computing Systems ... Ms. Donna BELDEN
51 Dean Col Educ & Prof Studies ... Dr. Anthony ROLLE
49 Dean of Arts & Sciences ... Dr. Jeanette E. RILEY
50 Dean Business Administration ... Dr. Maling EBRAHIMPOUR
54 Dean of Engineering ... Dr. Raymond M. WRIGHT
89 Dean Univ Col & Spec Acad Pgms ... Dr. Jayne E. RICHMOND
58 Dean of Graduate School ... Dr. Nasser H. ZAWIA
66 Dean of Nursing ... Dr. Barbara E. WOLFE
67 Dean of Pharmacy ... Dr. Paul LARRAT
69 Dean Col of Health Sciences ... Dr. Gary LIGUORI
53 Director School of Education ... Dr. David BYRD
88 Dean Grad School Oceanography ... Dr. Bruce CORLISS
88 Dean of Environment & Life Sciences ... Dr. John KIRBY
08 Dean University Libraries ... Mr. Karim B. BOUGHIDA
22 Director Affirm Act/Equal Oppty/Div ... Ms. Roxanne GOMES
37 Assoc Dir Enrol Svcs/Fin Aid ... Mr. Kenneth S. FERUS
92 Director Honors Program ... Dr. Lynne DERBYSHIRE
102 President URI Foundation ... Ms. Elizabeth O'ROURKE
85 Vice Provost for Global Initiatives ... Ms. Gifty AKO-ADOUNVO
106 Dir Learning/Assessment & Online ... Dr. Diane GOLDSMITH
94 Dir Gender and Women Studies ... Dr. Rosaria PISA
105 Manager Web Services ... Ms. Lisa CHEN
111 Sr Dir Advancement Services ... Mr. Scott BURDICK
44 Dir of Annual & Parent Giving ... Mr. John GARCIA

University of Rhode Island Feinstein Providence Campus (A)

80 Washington Street, Providence RI 02903
Telephone: (401) 277-5000 Identification: 770118
Accreditation: &EH

University of Rhode Island Narragansett Bay Campus (B)

215 South Ferry Road, Narragansett RI 02882-1197
Telephone: (401) 874-6222 Identification: 770129
Accreditation: &EH

SOUTH CAROLINA

Aiken Technical College (C)

PO Drawer 696, Aiken SC 29802-0696
County: Aiken FICE Identification: 010056
Unit ID: 217615
Telephone: (803) 508-7263 Carnegie Class: Assoc/MT-VT-High Trad
FAX Number: N/A Calendar System: Semester
URL: www.atc.edu
Established: 1972 Annual Undergrad Tuition & Fees (In-District): $5,306
Enrollment: 1,925 Coed
Affiliation or Control: State/Local IRS Status: 501(c)3
Highest Offering: Associate Degree
Accreditation: SC, ACBSP, ADNUR, DA, MAC, NAEYC, PNUR, RAD, SURGT

01 President ... Dr. Forest E. MAHAN
04 Executive Assistant to President ... Ms. Jill UHLER
05 VP Academic & Student Affairs ... Dr. Vinson BURDETTE
111 VP Advancement/Inst Effectiveness ... Ms. Mechelle ENGLISH
76 Dean of Health Sciences ... Dr. Brian LOGAN
51 Dean of Continuing Education ... Dr. Steve SIMMONS
97 Dean of General Education ... Fr. Frederick ROGERS
10 Vice Pres Administrative Services ... Mr. Andy JORDAN
37 Director of Financial Aid ... Ms. Erynn BLACK
13 Director of Info Systems Mgmt ... Mr. Walter BUSBEE
15 Director of Human Resources ... Ms. Sylvia BYRD
21 Controller ... Ms. Betsy CLINE
96 Director of Purchasing ... Vacant
18 Director Facilities & Operations ... Mr. Kevin MCCARTHY
84 Director of Enrollment Services ... Mrs. Dawn BUTTS
38 Director Counseling/Disabilities ... Mr. Rich WELDON
26 Director Marketing & PR ... Ms. Nikasha DICKS
30 Director Foundation & Alumni ... Dr. Elizabeth LACLAIR

Allen University (D)

1530 Harden Street, Columbia SC 29204-1085
County: Richland FICE Identification: 003417
Unit ID: 217624
Telephone: (803) 376-5700 Carnegie Class: Bac-A&S
FAX Number: N/A Calendar System: Semester
URL: www.allenuniversity.edu
Established: 1870 Annual Undergrad Tuition & Fees: $13,340
Enrollment: 705 Coed
Affiliation or Control: African Methodist Episcopal IRS Status: 501(c)3
Highest Offering: Master's
Accreditation: SC

01 President ... Dr. Ernest MCNEALEY
05 VP Academic Affairs ... Dr. Toni MUHAMMAD
81 Dean Mathematics/Natural Sciences ... Vacant
79 Dean Arts and Humanities ... Dr. Kevin TRUMPETER
73 Dean D.G. Theological Seminary ... Dr. Jamal-Dominique HOPKINS
50 Dean Business/Soc Sci & Education ... Vacant
32 VP Student Affairs ... Dr. John Michael HARPE
10 VP Fiscal Affairs ... Ms. Ruby FIELDING
111 VP Institutional Advancement ... Mr. Dub TAYLOR
30 AVP Inst Advance/Dir Development ... Mr. Ti BARNES
26 Dir Marketing & Communications ... Ms. Anika V. COBB
15 Chief Human Resources Officer ... Ms. Andraea HERRIN
41 Athletic Director ... Mr. Theodore KEATON
09 Director Institutional Research ... Vacant
08 Director of Library Services ... Ms. Carol BOWERS
90 Director of IT Services ... Mr. Samuel PASCHAL
36 Director Counseling/Placement ... Dr. Flavia ELDEMIRE
39 Director Residential Life & Health ... Ms. Oveta GLOVER
35 Director of Student Activities ... Ms. Lisa REEVES
19 Chief of Police ... Chief Kelvin DAVIS
84 Dean Enrollment Mgmt/Registrar ... Ms. Marilyn DEBERRY
07 Director of Admissions ... Mrs. Heather TURNER
37 Director of Financial Aid ... Ms. Lola KENNEDY
21 Asst VP Fiscal Affairs/Comptroller ... Mr. John SAMPSON
113 Bursar ... Ms. Sharon DAVIS
18 Director of Operations ... Mr. Robert RILEY
29 Director of Alumni Affairs ... Vacant
25 Director of Sponsored Programs ... Ms. Sunya YOUNG
88 Director of Bands ... Mr. Eddie ELLIS
04 Executive Assistant ... Ms. Violet HARRISON

American College of the Building Arts (E)

649 Meeting St, Charleston SC 29403
County: Charleston FICE Identification: 042830
Unit ID: 485698
Telephone: (843) 577-5245 Carnegie Class: Spec-4-yr-Other
FAX Number: (843) 764-9832 Calendar System: Semester
URL: acba.edu
Established: 2004 Annual Undergrad Tuition & Fees: $20,572
Enrollment: 93 Coed
Affiliation or Control: Independent Non-Profit IRS Status: 501(c)3
Highest Offering: Baccalaureate
Accreditation: ACCSC

01 President ... Lt.Gen. Colby M. BROADWATER, III
05 Chief Academic Officer ... Dr. A. Wade RAZZI
10 Chief Financial Officer ... Mr. Chad H. URBAN

Anderson University (F)

316 Boulevard, Anderson SC 29621-4035
County: Anderson FICE Identification: 003418
Unit ID: 217633
Telephone: (864) 231-2000 Carnegie Class: Masters/L
FAX Number: (864) 231-2004 Calendar System: Semester
URL: www.andersonuniversity.edu
Established: 1911 Annual Undergrad Tuition & Fees: $29,980
Enrollment: 3,848 Coed
Affiliation or Control: Other IRS Status: 501(c)3
Highest Offering: Doctorate
Accreditation: SC, ACBSP, ART, CAEPN, MUS, NURSE, PTA, THEA

01 President ... Dr. Evans P. WHITAKER
20 Provost ... Dr. Ryan NEAL
11 Sr VP Administration & Brand ... Mr. David RASHED
30 SVP Development/Pres Affairs ... Mr. James LANDRITH
32 Sr VP Student Development ... Dr. James FEREIRA
13 Chief Information Officer ... Mr. Ron OPPATT
10 VP Finance/Chief Financial Officer ... Ms. Kristie COLE
28 VP Diversity and Inclusion ... Dr. James NOBLE
41 VP Athletics ... Mr. Bert EPTING
42 VP Church Rel/Sr Campus Pastor ... Mr. Mayson EASTERLING
42 VP Christian Life/Campus Min ... Vacant
84 VP Enrollment Management ... Ms. Pam ROSS
106 VP Tech/Online Learning/Innovation ... Dr. Benjamin DEATON
26 VP Marketing & Communications ... Vacant
27 Exec Dir Public Relations ... Mr. Andrew BECKNER
20 Asst Provost ... Mr. Nathan COX
29 AVP for Alumni/Parent Relations ... Mr. Jason RUTLAND
73 Dean COCS & Clamp Div Sch ... Mr. James DUDUIT
66 Dean School of Nursing ... Vacant
49 Dean College of Arts/Sciences ... Dr. Wayne COX
57 Dean SC School of the Arts ... Dr. David LARSON
88 Dean School Int Design ... Ms. Anne MARTIN
50 Dean College of Business ... Mr. Steven NAIL
76 Dean College of Health Professions ... Dr. Donald PEACE
82 Dean School Pub Svc/Admin ... Dr. Clarence WILLIAMSON
53 Dean College of Education ... Dr. Mark BUTLER
88 Assoc Dean College of Business ... Dr. Evie MAXEY
121 Dean Student Success ... Dr. Dianne KING
06 University Registrar ... Mrs. Elizabeth CRANFORD
35 Dean Student Life ... Mr. Jonathan GROPP
35 Dean Student Development ... Ms. Robyn SANDERSON
100 Chief of Staff ... Mr. John DON
88 Exec Dir Conf Svcs/Univ Events ... Mrs. Jody BRYANT
07 Dir Admission ... Mr. William MONTS
08 Dir Thrift Library ... Mr. Kent MILLWOOD
09 Dir External Reporting ... Mr. Daryl A. IVERSON
15 Dir Human Resources ... Mrs. Amy PORPILIA
18 Dir Facilities ... Mr. Charles DICKERSON
19 Dir Campus Safety ... Mr. Edward AMAN
21 Controller ... Mrs. Victoria PIERCE
88 Dir Sports Med/Asst Dir Ath ... Mr. William DUVALL
23 Dir Health Services/Nurse ... Mrs. Debbie TAYLOR
35 Dir Student Activities ... Ms. Brenna MORRIS
36 Dir Career Services ... Vacant
37 Dir Financial Aid & Scholarships ... Mr. Mike SAPIENZA
39 Dr Resident Life/Student Housing ... Ms. Anne PATTERSON
38 Dir Counseling ... Ms. Erin MAURER
104 Dir International Programs ... Dr. Ann-Margaret THEMISTOCLEOUS
04 Exec Assistant to the President ... Mrs. Alana DEAN PRICE

Benedict College (G)

1600 Harden Street, Columbia SC 29204-1086
County: Richland FICE Identification: 003420
Unit ID: 217721
Telephone: (803) 253-5000 Carnegie Class: Bac-Diverse
FAX Number: (803) 253-5059 Calendar System: Semester
URL: www.benedict.edu
Established: 1870 Annual Undergrad Tuition & Fees: $17,200
Enrollment: 1,731 Coed
Affiliation or Control: Independent Non-Profit IRS Status: 501(c)3
Highest Offering: Master's
Accreditation: SC, ACBSP, ART, CAEPN, SW

01 President ... Dr. Roslyn C. ARTIS
05 Vice Pres for Academic Affairs ... Dr. Janeen WITTY
100 Chief of Staff ... Dr. Verna F. ORR
10 Vice President Business/Finance ... Mr. Chris THOMPSON
108 Assoc VP for Academic Assessment ... Dr. Kimberly HAYNES STEPHENS
32 Vice President Student Affairs ... Mr. Gary E. KNIGHT
111 Vice Pres Institutional Advancement ... Mrs. Leandra H. BURGESS
20 Assoc Vice Pres Academic Affairs ... Dr. George A. DEVLIN
21 Asst VP for Business & Finance ... Ms. Jackie BROWN
26 Asst VP for Comm & Marketing ... Ms. Kymm HUNTER
07 Director of Admissions ... Ms. Keisha MONTGOMERY
29 Assistant VP for Alumni Relations ... Ms. Ada A. BELTON
13 Chief Information Officer ... Mr. Anthony CALDWELL
84 Assoc VP for Enrollment Management ... Dr. Vareva HARRIS
15 Exec Director of Human Resources ... Ms. Martha SMITH
06 Registrar/Director Student Records ... Mrs. Roberta DAVIS
41 Athletics Director ... Mr. Willie WASHINGTON
38 Exec Dir Career Pathways Initiative ... Mr. Brian LOVE
42 Campus Minister ... RevDr. Lillie A. BURGESS
19 Director Campus Safety ... Mr. Kevin PORTEE
36 Career Development Coordinator ... Ms. Sonya JOHNSON
37 Director Financial Aid ... Ms. Monique RICKENBAKER
08 Director of Library ... Mrs. Darlene ZINNERMAN-BETHEA
88 Assessment Coordinator ... Dr. Chasisity SPRINGS
25 Coordinator Title III ... Ms. Deborah MCKENZIE
49 Dean Sch Human/Arts/Soc Sci ... Vacant
50 Dean TAB School of Bus/Econ ... Dr. Tracy DUNN
53 Dean Educ/Health Human Svcs ... Dr. Akilah CARTER-FRANCIQUE
54 Dean Sch Science/Engineering ... Dr. Fouzi ARAMMASH
92 Dean School of Honors ... Dr. Shaneen CORUJO
57 Chair Communications and Arts ... Ms. Gina MOORE
50 Chair Business Admin/Mgmt/Mktg ... Mr. Melvin MILLER
59 Chair Education and Family Studies ... Dr. Tracy MIDDLETON
70 Chair Social Work ... Dr. Eunika SIMONS
81 Chair Bio/Chem/Environment Hlth Sci ... Dr. Larry LOWE
68 Chair Health and Sport Management ... Dr. Paula SHELBY
88 Chair Accounting and Finance ... Dr. Tracy WASHINGTON

Bob Jones University (H)

1700 Wade Hampton Boulevard, Greenville SC 29614-0001
County: Greenville FICE Identification: 003421
Unit ID: 217749
Telephone: (864) 242-5100 Carnegie Class: Masters/S
FAX Number: (864) 235-6661 Calendar System: Semester
URL: www.bju.edu
Established: 1927 Annual Undergrad Tuition & Fees: $20,890
Enrollment: 3,029 Coed
Affiliation or Control: Independent Non-Profit IRS Status: 501(c)3
Highest Offering: Doctorate
Accreditation: SC, NURSE, TRACS

00 Chancellor ... Dr. Bob JONES, III
01 President ... Dr. Stephen D. PETTIT
05 Exec Vice Pres for Academic Affairs ... Dr. Gary M. WEIER
111 VP Advancement & Alumni Relations ... Mr. John D. MATTHEWS
26 Chief Communication Officer ... Ms. Carol A. KEIRSTEAD
11 Vice Provost for Academic Admin ... Dr. David A. FISHER
45 Vice Provost Strategic Initiatives ... Dr. Beverly CORMICAN
10 VP for Business and Finance ... Mr. Steve DICKINSON
32 EVP Student Dev/Ministry Advance ... Dr. Alan T. BENSON
84 VP for Enrollment and Marketing ... Dr. Bobby WOOD
15 Chief Human Resources Officer ... Mr. Kevin L. TAYLOR
13 Chief Information Officer ... Mr. Brian W. BURCH
49 Dean College of Arts and Science ... Dr. Renae WENTWORTH
73 Dean School of Religion ... Dr. Kevin OBERLIN

73 Dean BJU Seminary ... Dr. Neal CUSHMAN
57 Dean Sch Fine Arts & Communication ... Dr. Darren P. LAWSON
53 Dean School of Educ & Human Svcs ... Dr. Brian A. CARRUTHERS
50 Dean School of Business ... Vacant
76 Dean School of Health Professions ... Dr. Jessica MINOR
06 Registrar ... Dr. Daniel SMITH
35 Director of Student Life ... Mr. Jonathan G. DAULTON
34 Women's Director of Student Life ... Ms. Deneen LAWSON
07 Director of Admission ... Rev. Stephen L. BRADLEY
88 Director of Ministry Training ... Dr. Nathan G. CROCKETT
41 Athletic Director ... Dr. Neal RING
37 Director of Financial Aid ... Mrs. Susan YOUNG
08 Dean of Libraries ... Vacant
09 Sr Dir Planning/Rsrch/Assessment ... Rev. Phil GERARD
100 Chief of Staff ... Mr. Randy PAGE

Central Carolina Technical College (A)

506 N Guignard Drive, Sumter SC 29150-2499
County: Sumter FICE Identification: 003995
Unit ID: 218858
Telephone: (803) 778-1961 Carnegie Class: Assoc/MT-VT-Mix Trad/Non
FAX Number: (803) 778-7880 Calendar System: Semester
URL: www.cctech.edu
Established: 1962 Annual Undergrad Tuition & Fees (In-State): $6,594
Enrollment: 2,885 Coed
Affiliation or Control: State IRS Status: 501(c)3
Highest Offering: Associate Degree
Accreditation: SC, ADNUR, CSHSE, MAC, NAEYC, SURGT

01 President ... Dr. Kevin POLLOCK
05 Vice President for Academic Affairs ... Dr. Jeffery THOMAS
10 Vice President for Business Affairs ... Ms. Beth YOUNG
32 Vice President for Student Affairs ... Ms. Lisa BRACKEN
111 Vice Pres Institutional Advancement ... Ms. Misty HATFIELD
04 Assistant to the President ... Ms. Diana REARDON
103 Dean Workforce Development/ SCETC ... Mr. Joshua CASTLEBERRY
08 Dean of Learning Resources ... Ms. Nancy BISHOP
26 Director Public Relations ... Ms. Nicole OUELLETTE
15 Director Human Resources ... Mrs. Ronalda S. STOVER
13 Director Information/Learning Tech ... Mr. David RIBELIN
06 Registrar ... Ms. Jennifer SZUPKA
07 Dir Recruitment & Admissions ... Dr. A. Sierra NEAL
37 Director Student Financial Aid ... Mr. Ken BERNARD
09 Dir Research/Institutional Effect ... Mr. Bryan MAY
121 Dir TRIO/SSS/VUB ... Mr. Jim OREE
54 Dean of Industrial and Engineering ... Mr. Bert HANCOCK
76 Dean of Health Sciences ... Dr. Vicki MARTIN
97 Dean of General Education ... Mr. Jason TISDEL
38 Dir Counseling & Student Life ... Ms. Renee PATCHIN
19 Director Security/Safety ... Ms. Emily BROADWAY

Charleston School of Law (B)

81 Mary Street, PO Box 535, Charleston SC 29402
County: Charleston FICE Identification: 040963
Unit ID: 451510
Telephone: (843) 329-1000 Carnegie Class: Spec-4-yr-Law
FAX Number: (843) 720-7899 Calendar System: Semester
URL: www.charlestonlaw.edu
Established: 2003 Annual Graduate Tuition & Fees: N/A
Enrollment: 558 Coed
Affiliation or Control: Proprietary IRS Status: Proprietary
Highest Offering: First Professional Degree; No Undergraduates
Accreditation: LAW

01 President ... Mr. J. Edward BELL, III
05 Provost and Dean ... Mr. Larry CUNNINGHAM
20 Associate Dean Academic Affairs ... Ms. Margaret M. LAWTON
07 Assoc Dean Admission/Financial Aid ... Ms. Jacqueline B. BELL
32 Assoc Dean of Students ... Mr. Nicholas SANDERS
13 Assoc Dean of Info Services ... Ms. Katie BROWN
10 Chief Financial Officer ... Mr. Robert J. QUILLINAN
06 Registrar ... Ms. Emma BAKER
15 Director Human Resources ... Ms. Shera L. SILVIS
08 Director of Library ... Ms. Katie BROWN
88 Exec Assist to the Provost & Dean ... Ms. Diane REXROAD
18 Chief Fac/Physical Plant Ofcr ... Mr. Victor SILVIS
28 Director of Diversity ... Ms. Debra J. GAMMONS
37 Director of Financial Aid ... Mr. Bobby GREER

Charleston Southern University (C)

PO Box 118087, Charleston SC 29423-8087
County: Charleston FICE Identification: 003419
Unit ID: 217688
Telephone: (843) 863-7000 Carnegie Class: Masters/M
FAX Number: (843) 863-8074 Calendar System: Semester
URL: www.csuniv.edu
Established: 1964 Annual Undergrad Tuition & Fees: $28,100
Enrollment: 3,350 Coed
Affiliation or Control: Southern Baptist IRS Status: 501(c)3
Highest Offering: Doctorate
Accreditation: SC, ARCPA, CAATE, CAEPN, IACBE, MUS, NUR, @PTA

01 President ... Dr. Dondi E. COSTIN
46 Vice Pres for Strategic Planning ... Dr. Michael BRYANT
05 Vice President Academic Affairs ... Dr. Jacqueline FISH
10 VP for Business Affairs ... Mr. Luke BLACKMON
04 Exec Assistant to the President ... Mrs. Faye WOOD
07 Director of Admissions ... Mrs. Kimberly FORD
84 Vice Pres Enrollment Management ... Dr. Tony TURNER
30 Vice Pres Development ... Mr. David BAGGS
20 Asst VP for Academic Affairs ... Dr. Scott YARBROUGH
32 VP for Student Affs/Dean of Stdnts ... Mr. Clark CARTER
13 Chief Information Officer ... Mr. Shannon PHILLIPS
08 Director of the Library ... Mr. Eric KISTLER
06 Registrar ... Mrs. Amanda BARON
21 Controller ... Mrs. Janelle FOX
26 Director of Integrated Marketing ... Mr. Richard ESPOSITO
09 Dir of Institutional Effectiveness ... Mr. Jeffrey BABETZ
58 Dir of Graduate Business Program ... Dr. Maxwell ROLLINS
41 Athletic Director ... Mr. Jeff BARBER
42 Asst Dean Campus Ministries ... Mr. Jon DAVIS
19 Director of Security ... Mr. John WILSON
90 Director of Computer Science ... Dr. Sean HAYES
18 Director of Facility Services ... Mr. Nick CIMORELLI
07 Director of Enrollment Services ... Mr. Nick BALLENGER
15 Director of Human Resources ... Mrs. Lindsey WALKE
36 Assistant Dean for Career Center ... Dr. Nina GRANT
38 Director of Student Counseling ... Mrs. Kimberly PERKINS
96 Director of Purchasing ... Mrs. Lisa OROZCO
37 Director Student Financial Aid ... Mrs. Teri KARGES
39 Assistant Dean of Residence Life ... Ms. Casey BOLDUC
50 Dean College of Business ... Dr. David PALMER
83 Dean Humanities/Social Sciences ... Dr. John KUYKENDALL
81 Dean Science & Mathematics ... Dr. Todd ASHBY
66 Dean of Nursing/Health Sciences ... Dr. Andreea MEIER
53 Dean College of Education ... Dr. Julie FERNANDEZ
104 Director International Programs ... Mrs. Stephanie LEVAN
108 Director Institutional Assessment ... Mr. Jeff BABETZ
106 Assoc VP for CSU Online ... Dr. Marc EMBLER
28 Director of Diversity ... Rev. Tim GRANT
29 Director Alumni Affairs ... Mr. Hunter MIZELL

The Citadel, The Military College of South Carolina (D)

171 Moultrie Street, Charleston SC 29409-0001
County: Charleston FICE Identification: 003423
Unit ID: 217864
Telephone: (843) 225-3294 Carnegie Class: Masters/L
FAX Number: (843) 953-5287 Calendar System: Semester
URL: www.citadel.edu
Established: 1842 Annual Undergrad Tuition & Fees (In-State): $12,620
Enrollment: 3,740 Coed
Affiliation or Control: State IRS Status: 501(c)3
Highest Offering: Beyond Master's But Less Than Doctorate
Accreditation: SC, CACREP, CAEP, MPCAC, NURSE

01 President ... Gen. Glenn M. WALTERS, RET.
00 Chairman of the Board ... Col. Dylan W. GOLF
05 Provost/Dean ... BGen. Sally SELDEN
11 Senior Vice Pres for Operations ... Col. Cardon CRAWFORD, RET.
10 Vice President of Finance ... Col. Charles CANSLER
32 Commandant of Cadets ... Col. Thomas J. GORDON
26 Vice President for Comm & Marketing ... Vacant
41 Dir Intercollegiate Athletics ... Mr. Mike CAPACCIO
102 Chief Exec Officer of Foundation ... Dr. Jay DOWD
04 Executive Assistant to President ... Cdr. William LIND
18 Vice Pres Facilities/Engineering ... Cdr. Jeffrey LAMBERSON
43 General Counsel ... Mr. Mark C. BRANDENBURG
20 Assoc Provost Academic Affairs ... Col. Kevin BOWER
108 Dir Accreditation and Assessment ... Dr. Karin ROOF
07 Director of Admissions ... Vacant
06 Registrar ... Maj. Keith GAUVIN
113 Treasurer ... Ms. Lindsey M. NETTLES
29 Exec Dir Alumni Affairs ... Mr. Tom MCALISTER
08 Director of Library ... Mr. Aaron WIMER
13 Chief Information Officer ... Vacant
109 Director of Auxiliary Services ... Mrs. Amy ORR
37 Director Financial Aid/ Scholarships ... LtCol. Henry M. FULLER, JR.
15 Chief Human Resources Officer ... Maj. Leah S. SCHONFELD
36 Director of Career Services ... Ms. Page TISDALE
38 Director of Citadel Counseling Ctr ... Dr. Suzanne BUFANO
84 Assoc Provost for Enrollment Mgmt ... Dr. Kelly BRENNAN
09 Director of Institutional Research ... Ms. Lisa L. PACE
19 Director of Public Safety ... Chief Michael TURNER
23 College Physician ... Dr. Carey M. CAPELL
40 Director of the Cadet Store ... Ms. Linda MATTINGLY
42 Chaplain/Dir Religious Activities ... Mr. Aaron MEADOWS
92 Director Honors Program ... Dr. Deirdre RAGAN
86 Director Govt & Community Affairs ... Col. Cardon B. CRAWFORD
96 Director of Purchasing ... Vacant
22 Dir Affirmative Action/Equal Oppty ... Dr. Shawn EDWARDS
50 Dean of the School of Business ... Col. Michael WEEKS
53 Dean of the School of Education ... Col. Evan T. ORTLIEB
54 Dean of the School of Engineering ... Col. Andrew WILLIAMS
81 Dean School of Science/Math ... Col. Darin T. ZIMMERMAN
79 Dean Sch Humanities/Social Sciences ... Col. Brian M. JONES
101 Spec Asst to President/Brd Matters ... Ms. Lori HEDSTROM
93 Director Multicultural Affairs ... LtCol. Robert P. PICKERING
16 Deputy Director of Human Resources ... Mr. Wesley S. SAMS
114 Chief Budget Administrator ... Maj. Michael S. KEENEY
121 Director of Student Success ... LtCol. Robert P. PICKERING
116 Audit Officer ... Mr. Gary MALLOY
28 Asst Provost for Diversity ... Vacant
21 Controller ... Vacant
105 College Web Designer ... Mr. John STABINGER
119 IT Security Manager ... Mr. Justin CONSOLVO
58 Asst Dean of Graduate College ... Vacant
44 Sr Director of Legacy Giving ... Mr. Bill YAEGER
112 VP Legacy/Annual Reunion Giving ... Mr. Jonathan KRESKEN
27 Director of Marketing ... Mr. Phil REICHNER
104 Director Study Abroad ... Maj. Zane SEGLE
120 Director Teaching Innovation ... Dr. Diana CHESHIRE

Claflin University (E)

400 Magnolia Street, Orangeburg SC 29115-4477
County: Orangeburg FICE Identification: 003424
Unit ID: 217873
Telephone: (800) 922-1276 Carnegie Class: Bac-A&S
FAX Number: (803) 531-2860 Calendar System: Semester
URL: www.claflin.edu
Established: 1869 Annual Undergrad Tuition & Fees: $17,046
Enrollment: 2,048 Coed
Affiliation or Control: United Methodist IRS Status: 501(c)3
Highest Offering: Master's
Accreditation: SC, ACBSP, CAEP, MUS, NURSE

01 President ... Dr. Dwaun J. WARMACK
05 Provost/Chief Academic Officer ... Dr. Karl S. WRIGHT
10 Vice President for Fiscal Affairs ... Mrs. Tijuana R. HUDSON
111 Int VP Institutional Advancement ... Mr. Marcus H. BURGESS
32 Vice Pres Student Devel & Services ... Dr. Leroy A. DURANT
45 VP Plng/Assessment/Information Svcs ... Dr. Zia HASAN
20 Int Vice Provost Academic Programs ... Dr. Verlie A. TISDALE
26 AVP Communications & Marketing ... Mr. George W. JOHNSON
108 AVP Institutional Effectiveness ... Dr. Bridget P. DEWEES
15 Assoc Vice Pres Human Resources ... Ms. Shirley A. BIGGS
39 Exec Dir Housing & Residence Life ... Mr. Dillon BECKFORD
07 Director of Admissions ... Mr. Michael ZEIGLER
79 Dean Sch Humanities & Soc Science ... Dr. Isaiah R. MCGEE
50 Dean School of Business ... Dr. Nicholas HILL
53 Dean School of Education ... Dr. Anthony PITTMAN
81 Dean Sch Natural Sciences & Math ... Dr. Verlie A. TISDALE
13 Assoc VP Information Tech Svcs ... Mr. James E. BRENN
51 Exec Dir Prof/Continuing Studies ... Vacant
08 Library Director ... Mrs. Marilyn GIBBS DRAYTON
37 Director of Financial Aid ... Ms. Terria C. WILLIAMS
36 Director of Career Development ... Mrs. Carolyn R. SNELL
41 Athletic Director ... Mr. Robert O'NEAL
06 Registrar ... Mrs. Tanika L. BEARD
29 Director Alumni Affairs/Annual Fund ... Mrs. Zelda LEE
19 Int Exec Director of Public Safety ... Mr. Melvin WILLIAMS
46 Asst Vice Provost for Research ... Vacant
04 Executive Admin Asst to President ... Ms. Melvenia WILLIAMS
09 Director of Institutional Research ... Vacant
84 Int Vice Pres Enrollment Management ... Mr. Reynolda BROWN

Clemson University (F)

201 Sikes Hall, Clemson SC 29634-0001
County: Pickens FICE Identification: 003425
Unit ID: 217882
Telephone: (864) 656-3311 Carnegie Class: DU-Highest
FAX Number: (864) 656-4040 Calendar System: Semester
URL: www.clemson.edu
Established: 1889 Annual Undergrad Tuition & Fees (In-State): $15,558
Enrollment: 26,406 Coed
Affiliation or Control: State IRS Status: 501(c)3
Highest Offering: Doctorate
Accreditation: SC, ART, CACREP, CAEP, CAPRT, CARTE, CONST, CVT, DIETD, IPSY, LSAR, NURSE, PH, PLNG

01 President ... Dr. James P. CLEMENTS
05 Provost ... Dr. Robert H. JONES
43 General Counsel/Sec to Board ... Mr. W.C. (Chip) HOOD
10 Exec VP for Finance & Operations ... Mr. Anthony E. WAGNER
32 VP Student Affairs ... Dr. Chris MILLER
86 VP Governmental Affairs ... Ms. Angela LEIDINGER
111 Vice President for Advancement ... Mr. A. Neill CAMERON, JR.
86 Vice Pres Public Services ... Dr. George R. ASKEW
46 Vice President for Research ... Dr. Tanju KARANFIL
103 Vice Pres for Economic Development ... Dr. John M. BALLATO
13 Vice Pres & Chief Info Officer ... Mr. Brian VOSS
85 Vice Provost for International Affs ... Ms. Sharon NAGY
100 Chief of Staff ... Mr. Max ALLEN
29 VP Development/Alumni Relations ... Mr. Brian J. O'ROURKE
18 AVP/Chief Facilities Officer ... Mr. Todd BARNETTE
35 Sr Assoc Dean of Students ... Ms. Kimberly M. POOLE
20 Assoc Provost Faculty Development ... Ms. Amy L. LAWTON-RAUH
22 AVP Access & Equity ... Mr. Lewis J. KNIGHTON, JR.
26 AVP Strategic Comm/Univ Relations ... Mr. Joseph P. GALBRAITH
28 Chief Inclusion/Equity Officer ... Mr. Lee A. GILL
08 Dean of Libraries ... Mr. Christopher N. COX
84 AVP Enrollment Management ... Mr. David KUSKOWSKI
06 Registrar ... Mrs. Debra SPARACINO
37 Director of Financial Aid ... Mrs. Elizabeth MILAM
36 Exec Director of Career Center ... Mr. O'Neil BURTON
38 Director of Counseling ... Dr. Birma GAINOR
47 Dean Col Agric/Forestry/Life Sci ... Dr. Keith L. BELLI
58 Dean Graduate School/Vice Provost ... Dr. John M. LOPES
48 Dean Col Arch/Arts/Humanities ... Dr. Nicholas VAZSONYI
54 Dean Col Engr/Sciences ... Dr. Anand GRAMOPADHYE
83 Dean Col of Behavioral/Social Sci ... Dr. Leslie HOSSFELD
50 Dean College of Business ... Ms. Wendy YORK
53 Acting Dean College of Education ... Dr. Jeff C. MARSHALL
81 Dean of Science ... Dr. Cynthia YOUNG
09 Director Institutional Research ... Dr. Juan XU
39 Executive Director of Housing ... Ms. Kathy B. HOBGOOD
41 Director of Athletics ... Mr. Graham NEFF
112 AVP of Estate & Planned Giving ... Ms. Jovanna J. KING

23	Director Student Health Services	Mr. George W. CLAY
15	Human Resources Director	Ms. Alejandra S. KENNEDY
91	Exec Dir Enterprise Applications	Mr. Barrett KENDJORIA
25	Director Sponsored Programs	Ms. Sheila T. LISCHWE
19	AVP Public Safety/Police Chief	Chief Greg MULLEN
96	Director of Purchasing	Mr. Michael NEBESKY
04	Exec Assistant to the President	Ms. Donna Jean (DJ) LAWS
88	Exec Dir Teaching Effect/Innovation	Ms. Taimi OLSEN
121	Director of Academic Success Center	Ms. Susan WHORTON
104	Director Study Abroad	Ms. Meredith F. WILSON
07	Director of Admissions	Mr. Richard BARTH
122	Asst Dean Stdnts/Dir Greek Life	Mr. Gary WISER
108	Director Institutional Assessment	Mr. Radek OSTROWSKI

Clinton College (A)

1029 Crawford Road, Rock Hill SC 29730-5152

County: York   FICE Identification: 004923
  Unit ID: 217891

Telephone: (803) 327-7402   Carnegie Class: Bac/Assoc-Mixed
FAX Number: (803) 327-3261   Calendar System: Semester
URL: www.clintoncollege.edu
Established: 1894   Annual Undergrad Tuition & Fees: $10,020
Enrollment: 119   Coed
Affiliation or Control: African Methodist Episcopal Zion Church
  IRS Status: 501(c)3

Highest Offering: Baccalaureate
Accreditation: **TRACS**

01	President	Dr. Lester A. MCCORN
04	Exec Assistant to the President	Ms. Cheryl J. MCCULLOUGH
05	VP Academic Affairs/Dean	Dr. Alvin MCLAMB
111	VP Institutional Advancement	Mr. Adrian SCOTT
32	VP for Student Affairs	Dr. Angelyne BROWN
10	VP for Business & Finance	Ms. Archinya INGRAM
06	Registrar	Ms. Laveria WYNN
37	Financial Aid	Ms. Pamela WHITE
08	Director Library Services	Ms. Nina ISHOKIR
41	Athletic Director	Mr. Alfonzo DUNCAN
18	Superintendent Buildings/Grounds	Mr. Donnie INGRAM
07	Director of Admissions	Mr. Sedrick SINGLETARY
35	Director Student Support Services	Ms. Judith COWAN

Coastal Carolina University (B)

PO Box 261954, Conway SC 29528-6054

County: Horry   FICE Identification: 003451
  Unit ID: 218724

Telephone: (843) 347-3161   Carnegie Class: Masters/L
FAX Number: (843) 349-2990   Calendar System: Semester
URL: www.coastal.edu
Established: 1954   Annual Undergrad Tuition & Fees (In-State): $11,640
Enrollment: 10,118   Coed
Affiliation or Control: State   IRS Status: 501(c)3
Highest Offering: Doctorate
Accreditation: **SC**, ART, CAEP, MUS, NUR, PH, THEA

01	President	Dr. Michael T. BENSON
05	Provost and EVP Academic Affairs	Dr. Daniel J. ENNIS
10	Vice President Finance/CFO	Mr. David FROST
30	Interim Vice Pres Philanthropy	Mr. Bryan STEROS
32	VP Student Affairs/Enroll	
	Mgmt	Ms. Yvonne HERNANDEZ FRIEDMAN
26	Vice Pres Univ Communications	Vacant
15	VP Human Resources/Equal Opp	Mr. Thomas S. KOCZARA
41	Vice Pres of Athletics	Mr. Matthew L. HOGUE
50	Int Dean Business Administration	Dr. Erika E. SMALL
53	Dean of Education	Dr. Edward JADALLAH
79	Dean of Humanities & Fine Arts	Dr. Claudia BORNHOLDT
81	Dean of Science	Dr. Michael H. ROBERTS
97	Dean of University College	Dr. Sara HOTTINGER
13	AVP Information Tech Svcs	Mr. Fadi BAROODY
29	Int VP Advancement/Alumni Relations	Ms. Diane F. SANDERS
108	Assoc Provost Strategy & Devel	Dr. Holley TANKERSLEY
20	Asc Prov Curriculum/Stdnt Progress	Dr. James SOLAZZO
58	Interim Dean Graduate Studies	Dr. Robert F. YOUNG
104	Assoc Provost Global Initiatives	Dr. Darla J. DOMKE-DAMONTE
09	Exec Dir of Planning and Research	Ms. Christine L. MEE
06	University Registrar	Ms. Stacy A. WYETH
19	Director Public Safety	Mr. David ROPER
21	Controller	Mr. Gregory T. THOMPSON
28	VP for Diversity/Equity & Inclusion	Dr. Atiya STOKES-BROWN
39	Sr Director of Housing	Ms. Kathy A. DALEY
37	Associate Director of Client Svcs	Ms. Samantha HICKS
37	Associate Director of Operations	Ms. Sarah WEAVER
92	Director Honors Program	Dr. Louis E. KEINER
36	Director Career Services	Dr. Verne W. WALKER
96	Dir Procurement/Business Services	Mr. Dean P. HUDSON
18	Director of Facilities Planning	Mr. T. Rein MUNGO
27	Assoc VP for Univ Communications	Ms. Martha S. HUNN
84	AVP Enrollment Mgmt	Ms. Amanda E. CRADDOCK
22	Assoc VP Human Resources/EEO	Ms. Kimberly B. SHERFESEE
43	Sr VP/University Counsel	Mr. Carlos JOHNSON
08	University Librarian	Dr. Melvin D. DAVIS
100	Chief of Staff/VP Exec Initiatives	Mr. Travis E. OVERTON

Coker University (C)

300 E College Avenue, Hartsville SC 29550-3797

County: Darlington   FICE Identification: 003427
  Unit ID: 217907

Telephone: (843) 383-8000   Carnegie Class: Masters/S
FAX Number: (843) 383-8319   Calendar System: Semester
URL: www.coker.edu

Established: 1908   Annual Undergrad Tuition & Fees: $31,524
Enrollment: 1,087   Coed
Affiliation or Control: Independent Non-Profit   IRS Status: 501(c)3
Highest Offering: Master's
Accreditation: **SC**, ART, DANCE, MUS

01	President	Dr. Natalie HARDER
05	Provost & Dean of Faculty	Dr. Susan HENDERSON
28	Dir of Diversity/Interfaith/Inclus	Ms. Darlene SMALL
13	Director of IT	Dr. Cathy CUPPETT
41	VP Athletics & Athletic Facilities	Dr. Lynn GRIFFIN
108	VP of Institutional Effectiveness	Dr. Kathryn FLAHERTY
111	Interim VP for Advancement	Mr. Grady JONES
10	VP for Finance & Administration	Mr. Dan BURYJ
32	VP for Student Services	Mr. Tyson BEALE
35	AVP for Resource Development	Ms. Brianna DOUGLAS
09	Dir of Institutional Research	Ms. Lynn RAWLS
21	Chief Financial Officer	Ms. Robin A. PERDUE
37	Director of Student Financial Svcs	Vacant
29	Director of Alumni Engagement	Mr. Evan VAUGHN
08	Director of the Library	Mr. Todd RIX
19	Director of Campus Safety	Mr. Michael WILLIAMSON
04	Executive Asst to President	Ms. Heather NORMENT
15	Director of Human Resources	Ms. Ella MARSHALL
39	Dir Resident Life/Student Housing	Mr. Cole HEATHERLY
53	Dean of Education	Dr. Karen CARPENTER
06	Registrar	Ms. Shannon FLOWERS

College of Charleston (D)

66 George Street, Charleston SC 29424-0100

County: Charleston   FICE Identification: 003428
  Unit ID: 217819

Telephone: (843) 805-5507   Carnegie Class: Masters/M
FAX Number: (843) 953-5811   Calendar System: Semester
URL: www.cofc.edu
Established: 1770   Annual Undergrad Tuition & Fees (In-State): $12,978
Enrollment: 10,384   Coed
Affiliation or Control: State   IRS Status: 501(c)3
Highest Offering: Master's
Accreditation: **SC**, CAEP, MUS, SPAA, THEA

01	President	Dr. Andrew T. HSU
05	Provost & Exec Vice Pres	Dr. Suzanne AUSTIN
100	Chief of Staff	Mr. Paul D. PATRICK
101	Vice Pres Col Events/Exec Sec	
	BOT	Ms. Elizabeth W. KASSEBAUM
04	Exec Admin to the President	Ms. Michelle MCGREW
10	EVP for Business Affairs	Mr. John LOONAN
18	VP for Facilities Management	Mr. John P. MORRIS
26	VP Marketing/Enrollment Plng	Ms. Amy TAKAYAMA-PEREZ
111	Int Exec VP Instl Advancement	Ms. Cathy MAHON
32	Exec Vice President Student Affairs	Ms. Alicia D. CAUDILL
35	AVP Student Well-Being/Dean Stdnts	Ms. Ann ALMASI-BUSH
43	General Counsel Legal Affairs	Ms. Angela B. MULHOLLAND
19	Chief of Police/AVP Public Safety	Chief Chip SEARSON
20	Associate Provost	Dr. Deanna M. CAVENY
121	Assoc Provost Student Success	Dr. Christopher A. KOREY
104	Assoc Provost Academic/Intl Pgms	Dr. Mark P. DEL MASTRO
13	Senior VP/Chief Information Officer	Mr. Mark STAPLES
102	Internal Auditor/Fin Dir of Found	Mr. J. R BARNHART
109	Dir Business & Auxiliary Services	Ms. Ashleigh F. PARR
96	Chief Procurement Officer	Ms. Wendy E. WILLIAMS
15	VP for Human Resources	Mr. Edward POPE
22	Dir Equal Opportunity Programs	Ms. Kimberly A. GERTNER
84	VP Univ Mktg/Enrollment	
	Planning	Mrs. Amy A. TAKAYAMA-PEREZ
09	Director of Institutional Research	Ms. Michelle L. SMITH
28	VP Institutional Diversity	Dr. Renard HARRIS
89	Asst VP New Student Programs	Ms. Melinda MILEY
06	Registrar	Ms. Aimee PFEIFER
21	Treasurer	Mr. David G. KATZ
58	Dean of the Graduate School	Dr. Kameelah L. MARTIN
57	Dean School of the Arts	Mr. Edward HART
50	Dean School of Business	Dr. Paul H. SCHWAGER
53	Dean School of Education	Dr. Frances C. WELCH
79	Dean School of Languages	Dr. Timothy JOHNSON
81	Dean School Science & Math	Dr. Sebastian VAN DELDEN
83	Dean Sch of Human/Soc Sci	Dr. Gibbs KNOTTS
62	Dean of Libraries	Dr. John WHITE
92	Dean Honors College	Dr. Elizabeth MEYER-BERNSTEIN
41	Director Athletics	Mr. Matt ROBERTS
25	Director Research and Grants	Ms. Susan A. RIVALEAU
37	Exec Dir Fin Assist/Vet Affairs	Mr. Robert N. KERSEY
29	Vice President Alumni Affairs	Ms. Ann PRYOR
121	Dir Center for Academic Advising	Ms. Karen HAUSCHILD
88	Dir Center for Student Learning	Ms. Melinda L. COLEMAN
108	AVP Inst Effectiveness	Dr. Divya BHATI
22	Dir Ctr for Disabilities Services	Ms. Anne OSOWSKI
35	Int Exec Dir Student Involvement	Ms. Deronda WASHINGTON
36	Director Career Services	Mr. Jim ALLISON, JR.
38	Director Counseling Center	Dr. Marcie WISEMAN
23	Student Health Svcs Practice Mgr	Ms. Lee PENNY
39	Director Residence Life	Ms. Melantha ARDREY
88	Dir Environmental Health and Safety	Mr. Cliff HAMILTON
88	Director of ECDC	Ms. Katie HOUSER
88	Sustainability Director	Ms. Darcy EVERETT
31	Ombudsperson	Ms. Evelyn H. NADEL
122	Asst Dir Fraternity/Sorority Life	Mr. Anthony MOWER

Columbia College (E)

1301 Columbia College Drive, Columbia SC 29203-5998

County: Richland   FICE Identification: 003430
  Unit ID: 217934

Telephone: (803) 786-3012   Carnegie Class: Masters/S
FAX Number: (803) 786-3752   Calendar System: Semester
URL: www.columbiasc.edu
Established: 1854   Annual Undergrad Tuition & Fees: $20,690
Enrollment: 1,218   Coed
Affiliation or Control: United Methodist   IRS Status: 501(c)3
Highest Offering: Master's
Accreditation: **SC**, CAEPN, DANCE, NURSE, SW

01	President	Dr. William T. BOGART
05	Provost	Dr. Kristine BARNETTE
10	Vice President for Finance	Ms. Wilma ALLEN
111	VP for Advancement	Mr. Francis G. SCHODOWSKI
32	VP for Student Affairs	Ms. LaNae R. BUDDEN
29	Exec Director of Alumnae Relations	Ms. Julie KING
09	Director Institutional Research	Dr. Scott A. SMITH
08	Director of Library	Vacant
19	Chief of Police	Mr. Windell HARRIS
37	Director of Financial Aid	Vacant
36	Director of Ctr for Career Coaching	Mr. Brian DYE
13	Dir of Info Technology Services	Vacant
18	Director of Facilities Management	Mr. Matthew ROMANO
26	Dir of Marketing & Communication	Ms. Emily WILSON
41	Director of Athletics	Ms. Debra WARDLAW
40	Director Bookstore	Ms. Cory CORP
38	Director Counseling Services	Ms. Hiluv JOHNSON
04	Executive Assistant to President	Ms. Joye G. HIPP
84	Director of Enrollment Management	Mr. Vinnie MALONEY
92	Director Honors Program/Faculty Dev	Dr. Marlee MARSH
06	Registrar	Ms. Sharon HOFFMAN
15	Chief Human Resources Officer	Ms. Beverly JAMES
28	Director of Diversity	Ms. Melissia BRANNEN
39	Director Residence Life	Ms. Shade' HOLMES
44	Director Annual Giving	Ms. Hope WATSON

Columbia International University (F)

7435 Monticello Road, Columbia SC 29203

County: Richland   FICE Identification: 003429
  Unit ID: 217925

Telephone: (803) 754-4100   Carnegie Class: Masters/M
FAX Number: (803) 786-4209   Calendar System: Semester
URL: www.ciu.edu
Established: 1923   Annual Undergrad Tuition & Fees: $24,650
Enrollment: 2,098   Coed
Affiliation or Control: Independent Non-Profit   IRS Status: 501(c)3
Highest Offering: Doctorate
Accreditation: **SC**, BI, CACREP, THEOL

01	President	Dr. Mark A. SMITH
00	Chancellor	Dr. Bill H. JONES
05	Senior Vice President/Provost	Dr. Jim LANPHER
111	VP of Institutional Advancement	Mrs. Diane MULL
32	VP Student Svcs & Online Studies	Dr. Rick CHRISTMAN
73	Dean Seminary & School of Ministry	Dr. David CROTEAU
49	Dean College of Arts & Sciences	Dr. Jim LANPHER
53	Dean College of Education	Dr. Connie MITCHELL
104	Dean College Intercultural Studies	Dr. Edward SMITHER
50	Dean Sch of Business & Prof Studies	Dr. Scott ADAMS
09	Dir Institutional Research/Assessmt	Dr. Roxianne SNODGRASS
101	Assoc Provost Online Studies	Dr. Brian SIMMONS
08	Director of Library	Mrs. Cynthia SNELL
06	University Registrar	Dr. Jennifer BOOTH
15	Director Human Resources	Mr. Donald E. JONES
32	Dean of Students	Dr. Andre ROGERS
13	VP Information Technology	Mr. Tirrell HOWELL
18	Director Physical Plant	Mr. Phil MILLER
10	Chief Financial Officer	Mr. Rob HARTMAN
37	Director Financial Aid	Mrs. Patty HIX
04	Executive Asst to President	Mrs. Debbie GERMANY
19	Director Security/Safety	Mr. Scott DEAL
41	Athletic Director	Mr. Darren RICHIE
106	Dean of Online Education/E-learning	Dr. Kevin JONES

Converse University (G)

580 E Main, Spartanburg SC 29302-0006

County: Spartanburg   FICE Identification: 003431
  Unit ID: 217961

Telephone: (864) 596-9000   Carnegie Class: Masters/S
FAX Number: (864) 596-9158   Calendar System: 4/1/4
URL: www.converse.edu
Established: 1889   Annual Undergrad Tuition & Fees: $20,500
Enrollment: 1,377   Coed
Affiliation or Control: Independent Non-Profit   IRS Status: 501(c)3
Highest Offering: Doctorate
Accreditation: **SC**, ART, CIDA, MFCD, MUS

01	President	Dr. Boone J. HOPKINS
05	Interim Provost	Dr. Lienne F. MEDFORD
10	Vice Pres for Finance and Business	Ms. Dianne CROCKER
11	VP Operations and Strategic Plng	Ms. Kristin LACEY
111	Interim VP for Philanthropy	Mr. Mike KENNEDY
79	Dean Humanities/Sciences/Business	Dr. Erin TEMPLETON
57	Dean School of the Arts	Dr. Christopher VANEMAN
53	Dean of Education/Grad Studies	Dr. Lienne MEDFORD
32	Dean of Students	Ms. Rhonda MINGO
08	Librarian	Mr. Wade WOODWARD
37	Director of Financial Planning	Mr. James KELLAM
06	Registrar	Vacant
15	Human Resources Director	Dr. Claire GREGG
13	Chief Information Officer	Mr. Zach CORBITT

26 Director of Media/Communications ... Ms. Holly DUNCAN
04 Exec Assistant to the President ... Mrs. Pamela GREENWAY
38 Director of Counseling Services ... Ms. Bethany GARR
09 Director Institutional Research ... Vacant
84 Vice Pres of Enrollment Management ... Ms. Jamie GRANT
18 Chief Facilities/Physical Plant ... Mr. Gladden SMOKE
29 Director Alumni Affairs ... Ms. Jessica EGGIMAN

Denmark Technical College (A)

PO Box 327, Denmark SC 29042-0327
County: Bamberg FICE Identification: 005363
Unit ID: 217989
Telephone: (803) 793-5176 Carnegie Class: Assoc/HVT-High Non
FAX Number: (803) 793-5942 Calendar System: Semester
URL: www.denmarktech.edu
Established: 1948 Annual Undergrad Tuition & Fees (In-State): $5,648
Enrollment: 491 Coed
Affiliation or Control: State IRS Status: 501(c)3
Highest Offering: Associate Degree
Accreditation: SC, ACBSP, NAEYC

01 President ... Dr. Willie L. TODD, JR.
03 Executive Vice President ... Dr. A. Clifton MYLES
05 VP for Academic Affairs/CAO ... Ms. Tia WRIGHT-RICHARDS
32 VP for Student Affairs ... Dr. Lamar J. WHITE
10 VP for Fiscal Affairs/CFO ... Mr. Clarence BONNETTE
35 Dean of Students ... Dr. Samuel HINTON
111 VP Institutional Advancement ... Dr. Sasha JOHNSON-COLEMAN
08 Dean of Learning Resources Ctr ... Ms. Carolyn FORTSON
13 Director of Information Technology ... Dr. Sid EMORY
19 Chief of Public Safety ... Mr. Rodney BONDS
15 Director of Human Resources ... Mr. Thomas MAYER
36 Dir Career Plng/PLC/Student Success ... Ms. Leslie HOLMAN-BROOKS
37 Director of Financial Aid ... Ms. Vanessa CHILDS
49 Dean of Arts & Sciences ... Ms. Rosaland KENNER
66 Dean of Nursing ... Ms. Karen MYERS
50 Dean Business/Computer/Related Tech ... Dr. Danny SWILLEY
84 Director of Admissions & Recruitmnt ... Dr. Stacey ROBERSON
103 Dean/Industrial Related Technology ... Dr. Hadi HAMID
39 Director of Residence Life ... Mr. Patrick SCIPIO
06 Registrar ... Ms. Renee SPELLS
88 Special Assistant to the President ... Mr. Kenneth CRAWFORD
41 Athletic Director ... Mr. Andre PAYNE
09 Statistical/Research Analyst ... Ms. Diane V. JACKSON
26 Chief Public Relations Officer ... Ms. Amy ROPER

ECPI University-Charleston (B)

3800 Paramount Drive, North Charleston SC 29405
Telephone: (843) 606-5902 Identification: 770955
Accreditation: &SC, MAAB

† Branch campus of ECPI University, Virginia Beach, VA

ECPI University-Columbia (C)

250 Berryhill Road, Ste 300, Columbia SC 29210-6467
Telephone: (803) 772-3333 Identification: 770956
Accreditation: &SC, MAAB

† Branch campus of ECPI University, Virginia Beach, VA

ECPI University-Greenville (D)

1001 Keys Drive, Ste 100, Greenville SC 29615
Telephone: (864) 288-2828 Identification: 770954
Accreditation: &SC, MAAB

† Branch campus of ECPI University, Virginia Beach, VA

Edward Via College of Osteopathic Medicine-Carolinas Campus (E)

350 Howard Street, Sparntanburg SC 29303
Telephone: (864) 327-9800 Identification: 770941
Accreditation: &OSTEO

† Branch campus of Edward Via College of Osteopathic Medicine, Blacksburg, VA.

Erskine College (F)

PO Box 338, 2 Washington Street,
Due West SC 29639-0338
County: Abbeville FICE Identification: 003432
Unit ID: 217998
Telephone: (864) 379-2131 Carnegie Class: DU-Mod
FAX Number: (864) 379-2167 Calendar System: Semester
URL: www.erskine.edu
Established: 1837 Annual Undergrad Tuition & Fees: $36,510
Enrollment: 943 Coed
Affiliation or Control: Other IRS Status: 501(c)3
Highest Offering: Doctorate
Accreditation: SC, CAEP, THEOL

01 President ... Dr. Steven C. ADAMSON
10 VP for Finance & Operations ... Mr. Christian HABEGER
111 VP for Advancement ... Mr. J. Paul BELL
41 Vice President for Athletics ... Mr. Mark L. PEELER
32 VP for Student Success ... Dr. Wendi SANTEE
29 Vice Pres of Alumni Affairs ... Mr. Paul BELL
05 Dean of College ... Mr. Shane BRADLEY
05 Dean of Seminary ... Mr. Seth NELSON
08 Assoc Dean of Library & Inst Effect ... Mr. John F. KENNERLY, JR.
06 Registrar ... Mrs. Tracy M. SPIRES
26 Director of Marketing ... Ms. Brianne HOLMES
37 Director of Student Financial Aid ... Mrs. Amanda TAYLOR
13 Director of Information Technology ... Mrs. Stephanie HUDSON
09 Director of Institutional Research ... Mr. Buck F. BROWN, JR.
42 Interim Chaplain ... Mr. Joshua CHILES
21 Accounting Manager ... Mrs. Kelly MCALHANEY
15 Director Human Resources ... Ms. Kathy ROLLINS
19 Chief of Erskine Police ... Mr. Matthew BUSBY
04 Administrative Asst to President ... Mrs. Polly JONES
07 Director of Admissions ... Ms. Kasey MCNAIR
27 Director Communications/Media Rels ... Mrs. Joyce GUYETTE
84 Dean of Enrollment ... Dr. Tim REES
18 Chief Facilities/Physical Plant ... Mr. Michael LEWIS

Florence - Darlington Technical College (G)

PO Box 100548, Florence SC 29502-0548
County: Florence FICE Identification: 003990
Unit ID: 218025
Telephone: (843) 661-8324 Carnegie Class: Assoc/HVT-High Trad
FAX Number: (843) 661-8011 Calendar System: Semester
URL: www.fdtc.edu
Established: 1964 Annual Undergrad Tuition & Fees (In-District): $5,030
Enrollment: 3,315 Coed
Affiliation or Control: State/Local IRS Status: 501(c)3
Highest Offering: Associate Degree
Accreditation: SC, ADNUR, CAHIIM, COARC, CSHSE, DA, DH, MLTAD, RAD, SURGT

01 President ... Dr. Jermaine M. FORD
05 Vice President Academic Affairs ... Dr. Marc DAVID
10 Int Vice Pres Business Affairs ... Dr. Debbie CHEEK
111 Director Institutional Advancement ... Vacant
13 Assoc VP Information Technologies ... Mr. Tyron JONES
12 VP of the SiMT ... Vacant
76 Assoc VP Allied Health ... Vacant
15 Assoc VP Internal Relations/EEO ... Mr. Terry DINGLE
09 Director Institutional Research ... Mr. Gary ANCHETA
06 Registrar ... Ms. Genell GAUSE
37 Director Financial Aid ... Ms. Monica STARR
96 Director of Purchasing ... Ms. Sierra FLYNN
07 Director of Admissions ... Ms. Lauren DORTON
18 Director of Facilities ... Mr. Christopher TAYLOR
04 Exec Assistant to the President ... Ms. Kimberley LUTZ

Francis Marion University (H)

PO Box 100547, Florence SC 29501-0547
County: Florence FICE Identification: 009226
Unit ID: 218061
Telephone: (843) 661-1362 Carnegie Class: Masters/M
FAX Number: (843) 661-1202 Calendar System: Semester
URL: www.fmarion.edu
Established: 1970 Annual Undergrad Tuition & Fees (In-State): $11,160
Enrollment: 4,148 Coed
Affiliation or Control: State IRS Status: Exempt
Highest Offering: Doctorate
Accreditation: SC, ART, CAEP, MPCAC, NURSE, @SP, THEA

01 President ... Dr. Luther F. CARTER
05 Provost/Dean Col of Liberal Arts ... Dr. Peter D. KING
10 VP Finance and Facilities ... Mr. Darryl BRIDGES
11 VP Administration/Planning ... Dr. Charlene WAGES
111 VP Institutional Advancement ... Mrs. Lauren STANTON
26 VP University Communications ... Mr. John SWEENEY
32 VP for Student Life ... Dr. Christopher M. KENNEDY
41 Athletic Director ... Mr. Murray G. HARTZLER
58 Assoc Provost/Dir of Grad Programs ... Mrs. Allison STEADMAN
84 VP of Enrollment Mgmt ... Dr. Alissa WARTERS
121 Assoc Provost for Advising ... Dr. Jennifer KUNKA
21 Asst VP for Accounting ... Mrs. Cathy SWARTZ
21 Assoc VP Financial Services ... Mr. Eric GARRIS
50 Dean School of Business ... Dr. Hari K. RAJAGOPALAN
53 Dean School of Education ... Dr. Courtney CLAYTON
76 Dean School of Health Sciences ... Dr. Karen GITTINGS
08 Dean of the Library ... Mrs. Demetra T. WALKER
37 Financial Assistance Director ... Ms. Kimberly M. ELLISOR
06 Registrar ... Mrs. Ann WILLIAMS
38 Director Counseling and Testing ... Dr. Will HUNTER
18 Assoc VP of Facilities ... Mr. Ralph U. DAVIS
36 Director Career Development ... Dr. Will CARSWELL
07 Director of Admissions ... Mr. Doug BRADY
35 Dean of Students ... Ms. LaTasha BRAND
29 Dir Alumni Affairs & Annual Giving ... Mr. D. Lee DAUGHERTY
96 Director of Purchasing ... Mrs. Leslie SHUPP
92 Director of Honors Program ... Dr. Jon W. TUTTLE
13 Chief Information Officer ... Mr. John DIXON
04 Administrative Asst to President ... Mrs. Elizabeth SHEFTON
105 Director of Multimedia Services ... Mr. Larry B. FALCK
19 Chief of Campus Police ... Mr. Donald R. TARBELL
39 Director Student Housing ... Mr. Kevin SHUPP
96 AVP of Purchasing/Contractual Svcs ... Mr. Paul MACDONALD
15 Assoc Director of Human Resources ... Mrs. Danagene RAZICK
09 Director of Institutional Research ... Ms. Emily J. GRAHAM

Furman University (I)

3300 Poinsett Highway, Greenville SC 29613-0001
County: Greenville FICE Identification: 003434
Unit ID: 218070
Telephone: (864) 294-2000 Carnegie Class: Bac-A&S
FAX Number: (864) 294-3001 Calendar System: Semester
URL: www.furman.edu
Established: 1826 Annual Undergrad Tuition & Fees: $52,092
Enrollment: 2,567 Coed
Affiliation or Control: Independent Non-Profit IRS Status: 501(c)3
Highest Offering: Master's
Accreditation: SC, CAEP, MUS

01 President ... Dr. Elizabeth DAVIS
05 VP Academic Affairs & Provost ... Dr. Beth PONTARI
10 VP for Finance & Administration ... Ms. Susan MADDUX
07 Vice President for Enrollment ... Vacant
32 Vice President for Student Life ... Ms. Connie L. CARSON
30 Vice President for Development ... Ms. Heidi H. MCCRORY
26 VP University Communications ... Mr. Tom EVELYN
20 Associate Academic Dean ... Vacant
100 Chief of Staff ... Ms. Elizabeth SEMAN
06 University Registrar ... Dr. Jason ABREU
58 Director Graduate Studies ... Vacant
08 Director Libraries ... Dr. Caroline MILLS
19 Chief of Police ... Mr. John MILBY
108 Asst Vice President Assessment ... Dr. David EUBANKS
37 Director of Financial Aid ... Ms. Andrea BYRD
29 Director of Alumni Association ... Ms. Allsion FOY
07 Assoc Vice President of Admissions ... Mr. Brad POCHARD
44 Director of Annual Giving ... Ms. Gloria GOOSBY
112 Director of Planned & Major Gifts ... Mr. John KEMP
25 Grants Administrator ... Vacant
94 Dir Women's/Gender/Sexuality Study ... Dr. Gretchen BRAUN
15 Asst VP Human Resources/AAO ... Ms. Sharen BEAULIEU
13 Chief Information Officer ... Mr. Danny TANG
36 Director Career Services ... Dr. John D. BARKER
109 Auxiliary Services Director ... Mr. Tony MCGUIRT
18 Asst VP for Facilities Services ... Mr. Jeff P. REDDERSON
51 Director Continuing Education ... Vacant
41 Director of Athletics ... Mr. Jason DONNELLY
46 Director UG Research ... Dr. Erik CHING
88 Director CTL ... Dr. Min-Ken LIAO
17 Director Student Health Services ... Dr. Ann KNOWLES
38 Director Counseling Center ... Dr. Thomas BAEZ
39 Director University Housing ... Mr. Ronald C. THOMPSON
88 Director Accessibility Resources ... Ms. Judy BAGLEY
42 Chaplain ... Dr. Vaughn CROWETIPTON
40 Director Bookstore ... Ms. Crystal JARROUGE
04 Executive Asst to President ... Vacant
114 Assoc VP Finance Budget Director ... Ms. Amy BLACKWELL
96 Director of Purchasing ... Ms. Jannie CHOICE
35 Director Student Activities ... Ms. Jessica BERKEY
104 Director Study Abroad ... Ms. Nancy GEORGIEV
43 Dir Legal Services/General Counsel ... Ms. Meredith GREEN
28 Director of Diversity ... Dr. Michael E. JENNINGS
09 Director of Institutional Research ... Ms. Katlyn SEPSEY
122 Assc Dir Fraternity/Sorority Life ... Ms. Ashley BAUDOUIN

Greenville Technical College (J)

PO Box 5616, Greenville SC 29606-5616
County: Greenville FICE Identification: 003991
Unit ID: 218113
Telephone: (864) 250-8000 Carnegie Class: Assoc/HVT-High Trad
FAX Number: N/A Calendar System: Semester
URL: www.gvltec.edu
Established: 1962 Annual Undergrad Tuition & Fees (In-State): $5,186
Enrollment: 10,536 Coed
Affiliation or Control: State IRS Status: 501(c)3
Highest Offering: Baccalaureate
Accreditation: SC, ACBSP, ACFEI, ADNUR, CAHIIM, COARC, DA, DH, DMS, EMT, MAC, MLTAD, NAEYC, OTA, PTAA, RAD, SURGT

01 President ... Dr. Keith MILLER
05 VP Learning/Workforce Devel ... Dr. Larry MILLER
10 Vice President Business/Finance ... Mrs. Jacqueline DIMAGGIO
32 Vice President Student Services ... Dr. Matteel KNOWLES
111 VP Advancement ... Ms. Ann WRIGHT
103 AVP Econ Dev/Corp Training ... Ms. Jennifer MOOREFIELD
45 VP Institutional Effectiveness ... Mrs. Lauren SIMER
04 Administrative Asst to President ... Ms. Rita SNYDER
06 Registrar ... Mrs. Gloria CARDEN
84 Dean Enrollment Services ... Ms. Tanisha LATIMER
15 VP Human Resources ... Ms. Susan M. JONES
18 Director Facilities ... Vacant
19 Chief of Police ... Mr. Terence BROOKS
25 Director Research and Grants ... Ms. Elizabeth VARGA
26 Director Marketing/Communications ... Mr. Joshua FRIESEN
28 AVP Executive Affairs ... Ms. Wendy WALDEN
37 Director Financial Aid ... Mr. Marty CARNEY
50 Dean School of Business & Comp Tech ... Mrs. Michelle E. BYRD
13 Chief Information Officer ... Vacant
86 Director Governmental Relations ... Mr. Eric BEDINGFIELD
21 AVP Finance ... Ms. Lisa MANGIONE
09 Director of Institutional Research ... Vacant
104 Director of Global Education ... Vacant
96 Procurement Manager ... Ms. Kristal DOHERTY
08 Chief Library Officer ... Ms. Stephanie BROKER
100 Chief of Staff ... Mrs. Julie A. EDDY
101 Secretary of the Institution/Board ... Ms. Rita SNYDER
30 Director of Development ... Mrs. Judy WILSON

38 Director Student Counseling ....Ms. Gina TERRY
54 Dean School of Engineering ....Mr. William BROTHERS

Horry-Georgetown Technical College (A)

2050 Highway 501 E, Conway SC 29526-9521
County: Horry FICE Identification: 004925
Unit ID: 218140
Telephone: (843) 347-3186 Carnegie Class: Assoc/MT-VT-High Trad
FAX Number: (843) 347-4207 Calendar System: Semester
URL: www.hgtc.edu
Established: 1966 Annual Undergrad Tuition & Fees (In-District): $5,356
Enrollment: 6,409 Coed
Affiliation or Control: State/Local IRS Status: 501(c)3
Highest Offering: Associate Degree
Accreditation: SC, ACFEI, ADNUR, #COARC, DA, DH, DMS, EMT, PNUR, PTAA, RAD, SURGT

01 President ....Dr. Marilyn J. FORE
05 EVP Academics/Workforce Development ..Dr. Jennifer WILBANKS
10 VP Finance and Administration ....Mr. Harold HAWLEY
13 VP for Technology Solutions ....Mr. John DOVE
84 Registrar ....Dr. Heather HOPPE
32 VP for Student Affairs ....Dr. Melissa BATTEN
20 AVP for Accreditation/Inst Support ....Dr. Becky BOONE
49 AVP Acad Affs Arts and Sciences ....Dr. Candace HOWELL
66 AVP Acad Affairs Nursing/Health Sci ....Mrs. Ann DANIELS
15 VP Human Resources ....Mrs. Jacquelyne SNYDER
08 Director of Library Services ....Dr. Richard MONIZ
21 AVP/Controller ....Ms. Ellen BLACK
84 AVP Student Enrollment Services ....Dr. Cynthia JOHNSTON
18 Superintendent Buildings & Grounds ....Mr. Kevin BROWN
37 Int Dir Financial Aid/Veterans Affs ....Mr. Scott CALLAHAN
36 Career Resource Ctr Coordinator ....Vacant
09 VP Inst Effectiveness & Development ....Ms. Lori HEAFNER
96 Procurement Manager ....Ms. Dianna CECALA
105 Web Services Coordinator ....Mr. Kevin ENGELMAN
19 Director Security/Safety ....Mr. Barry MARSH
26 Director of Public Relations ....Ms. Nicole HYMAN
27 Director of Marketing ....Ms. Lari ROPER

Lander University (B)

320 Stanley Avenue, Greenwood SC 29649-2099
County: Greenwood FICE Identification: 003435
Unit ID: 218229
Telephone: (864) 388-8000 Carnegie Class: Bac-Diverse
FAX Number: (864) 388-8890 Calendar System: Semester
URL: www.lander.edu
Established: 1872 Annual Undergrad Tuition & Fees (In-State): $11,700
Enrollment: 3,513 Coed
Affiliation or Control: State IRS Status: 501(c)3
Highest Offering: Master's
Accreditation: SC, ART, CAEP, MACTE, MUS, NURSE

01 President ....Dr. Richard E. COSENTINO
05 Provost/Vice Pres Academic Affairs ....Dr. Scott JONES
10 Vice Pres Business/Administration ....Mr. Joe GREENTHAL
32 Vice President for Student Affairs ....Mr. Boyd YARBROUGH
111 Vice President for Univ Advancement ....Vacant
100 Chief of Staff/VP Strategic Init ....Mr. Adam TAYLOR
84 VP for Enrollment & Access Mgmt ....Mr. Todd GAMBILL
08 Librarian ....Ms. Lisa WIECKI
38 Director Counseling ....Ms. Kim SHANNON
41 Director of Athletics ....Mr. Brian REESE
15 Director Human Resources ....Ms. London THOMAS
19 Director University Police ....Mr. Greg ALLEN
26 AVP Univ Relations/Publications ....Mrs. Megan PRICE
37 Director of Financial Aid ....Ms. Michelle LODATO
36 Director of Career Services ....Mrs. Amanda MORGAN
21 Controller ....Vacant
40 Dir Bookstore/Procurement/Print Svc ....Mr. Scott PILGRIM
13 Chief Info & Technology Officer ....Mr. Abdallah P. HADDAD
07 Director of Admissions ....Mrs. Jennifer M. MATHIS
18 Director Physical Plant/Engr Svcs ....Mr. Jeff S. BEAVER
06 Registrar ....Mr. Brandon FELDER
29 Director Alumni Relations ....Ms. Suzann COUTS
09 Director of Institutional Research ....Mr. Mac KIRKPATRICK
122 Exec Dir Stdnt Life-Greek Life ....Mr. Matthew GILSTRAP

Limestone University (C)

1115 College Drive, Gaffney SC 29340-3799
County: Cherokee FICE Identification: 003436
Unit ID: 218238
Telephone: (864) 489-7151 Carnegie Class: Bac-Diverse
FAX Number: (864) 487-8706 Calendar System: Semester
URL: www.limestone.edu
Established: 1845 Annual Undergrad Tuition & Fees: $26,300
Enrollment: 1,943 Coed
Affiliation or Control: Independent Non-Profit IRS Status: 501(c)3
Highest Offering: Master's
Accreditation: SC, ACBSP, CAATE, CAEPN, MUS, NURSE, SW

01 President ....Dr. Darrell PARKER
05 Provost ....Dr. Monica BALOGA
10 VP Finance/Operations & Admin ....Mr. Reggie BROWNING
111 VP Institutional Advancement ....Ms. Kelly T. CURTIS
84 Vice President Enrollment Services .Mr. Christopher N. PHENICIE
13 Chief Information Officer ....Mr. Terry MCKINNY
41 Vice Pres Intercollegiate Athletics ....Mr. Michael H. CERINO
53 Dean Education & Health Professions ....Dr. Shelly MEYERS
32 Assoc Provost of Student Success ....Mrs. Stacey W. MASON
04 Executive Asst to the President ....Mrs. Brandi P. HARTMAN
35 Dir of Recruitment & Student Svcs ....Mr. Kip ALTMAN
06 Registrar ....Ms. Pennie D. HUGHES
37 Director Financial Aid ....Ms. Summer NANCE
08 Director Library ....Ms. Lizah ISMAIL
26 Vice Pres Communications/Marketing ....Mr. Charles W. WYATT
36 Dir Center for Professional Dev ....Ms. Lindsay BATHOLOMEW
18 Director Physical Plant ....Mr. Hayden HUTCHINGS
92 Director Academic Honors Program ....Dr. Jonathan SARNOFF
70 Director & Chair of Social Work ....Mr. Henry HIOTT
19 Chief Campus Security ....Mr. William J. PETTY
21 Controller ....Vacant
23 Campus Nurse ....Mrs. Sandy B. GREEN
121 Director Academic Advising ....Ms. Pennie D. HUGHES
30 Assoc VP for Development ....Ms. Candace R. WATERS
109 Director Food Services ....Mr. Joe FIELDS
42 College Chaplain ....Dr. Tom LEGRAND
53 Dir of Teacher Education ....Dr. Jimmie HALE
28 Dir of Equity/Inclusion/Diversity ....Ms. Selena S. BLAIR
15 Dir Human Resources/AAEEO Officer ....Ms. Janie CORRY
123 Dir Grad Studies/Admiss & Enroll ....Ms. Adair HUDSON
88 Sr Assoc Athletics Dir Compliance ....Mr. Dennis L. BLOOMER
07 Director Admissions/Recruiting ....Mr. John BLALOCK
40 Campus Store Manager ....Mrs. Patti H. MCCRAW
38 College Counselor ....Mrs. Mary B. CAMPBELL
50 Dean Business ....Dr. Paul R. LEFRANCOIS
49 Dean Liberal Arts & Sciences ....Dr. Brian F. AMELING
57 Chair Dept Visual & Performing Arts ....Dr. Gena E. POOVEY
58 Dean of Graduate Education ....Dr. Betsy A. WITT
22 Dir Affirm Action/Equal Opportunity ....Ms. Janie CORRY
39 Director Residential Life & Housing ....Ms. Jessica D. GOINS
09 Dir Inst Research & Effectiveness ....Mr. Andrew ENGLISH
101 Secretary of the Institution/Board ....Mrs. Brandi P. HARTMAN

Medical University of South Carolina (D)

179 Ashley Avenue, Charleston SC 29425
County: Charleston FICE Identification: 003438
Unit ID: 218335
Telephone: (843) 792-2300 Carnegie Class: Spec-4-yr-Eng
FAX Number: N/A Calendar System: Semester
URL: www.musc.edu
Established: 1824 Annual Undergrad Tuition & Fees (In-State): N/A
Enrollment: 3,083 Coed
Affiliation or Control: State IRS Status: Exempt
Highest Offering: Doctorate
Accreditation: SC, ANEST, ARCPA, CAHIIM, CAMPEP, DENT, HSA, IPSY, MED, NURSE, OT, PERF, PH, PHAR, PTA, @SP

01 President ....Dr. David J. COLE
05 EVP Academic Affairs & Provost ....Dr. Lisa SALADIN
63 Interim Dean College of Medicine ....Dr. Terrence STEYER
10 Exec Vice Pres Finance & Operations ....Mr. Rick ANDERSON
30 VP Institutional Advancement ....Ms. Kate AZIZI
12 CEO MUSC Charleston Division ....Dr. David ZAAS
13 MUSC Information Solutions ....Mr. Mark MCMATH
20 Assoc Prov Educ Innov/Student Life ....Dr. Gigi SMITH
46 VP Research ....Dr. Lori MCMAHON
108 Assoc Prov Educ Plng/Effectiveness ....Dr. Suzanne THOMAS
52 Dean of Dental Medicine ....Dr. Sarandeep HUJA
76 Dean of Health Professions ....Dr. Zoher F. KAPASI
58 Dean of Graduate Studies ....Dr. Paula TRAKTMAN
66 Dean of Nursing ....Dr. Linda WEGLICKI
67 Dean of Pharmacy ....Dr. Philip D. HALL
08 Director of Libraries ....Ms. Shannon JONES
84 Director Enrollment Management ....Ms. Melissa FREELAND
23 Director Student Wellness Programs ....Mr. Kevin SMUNIEWSKI
43 General Counsel ....Ms. Annette R. DRACHMAN
26 Int Chief Comm/Marketing Officer ....Ms. Lisa MONTGOMERY
22 Dir Equity/EEO/Accessibility Svcs ....Ms. Stephanie T. PRICE
07 Director of Admissions ....Ms. Lyla HUDSON
18 Interim Chief Facilities Officer ....Mr. Greg WEIGLE
06 Registrar ....Mr. Patrick CASSANO
15 Director University Human Resources ....Ms. Susan H. CARULLO
38 Dir Counseling/Psych Services CAPS ....Dr. Alice Q. LIBET
29 Director Alumni Affairs ....Ms. Linda COX
37 Director Student Financial Aid ....Ms. Tami WYNDHAM-COOKE
96 Director of Purchasing ....Ms. Margaret WITT
03 EVP for Health Affairs ....Dr. Patrick CAWLEY
04 Admin Assistant to the President ....Ms. Tina KELLEY
100 Chief of Staff ....Ms. Dawn HARTSELL
101 Secretary of the Board ....Ms. Katherine HALTIWANGER
28 Chief Equity Officer ....Dr. Willette BURNHAM-WILLIAMS
86 Chief Governmental Affairs ....Mr. Mark SWEATMAN

† Tuition varies by degree program.

Midlands Technical College (E)

PO Box 2408, Columbia SC 29202-2408
County: Lexington, Richland, Fairfiel FICE Identification: 003993
Unit ID: 218353
Telephone: (803) 738-8324 Carnegie Class: Assoc/MT-VT-High Trad
FAX Number: (803) 738-7784 Calendar System: Semester
URL: www.midlandstech.edu
Established: 1974 Annual Undergrad Tuition & Fees (In-District): $5,916
Enrollment: 8,794 Coed
Affiliation or Control: State/Local IRS Status: 501(c)3
Highest Offering: Associate Degree
Accreditation: SC, ACBSP, ADNUR, COARC, CSHSE, DA, DH, MAC, MLTAD, NAEYC, NMT, PNUR, PTAA, RAD, SURGT

01 President ....Dr. Ronald RHAMES
03 Provost ....Dr. Barrie KIRK
05 Vice Provost Academics ....Dr. Diane CARR
51 Vice Provost Corp & Continuing Ed ....Ms. Amy SCULLY
10 Vice President for Business Affairs ....Ms. Debbie WALKER
32 Vice Pres Student Development Svcs ....Dr. Mary HOLLOWAY
30 VP for Institutional Support ....Ms. Starnell BATES
26 Asst Vice President for Marketing ....Ms. Stefanie GOEBELER
43 General Counsel ....Mr. Joseph BIAS
102 Associate VP for Philanthropy ....Ms. Nancy MCKINNEY
06 Registrar ....Ms. Carla KAISER
13 Director Information Resource Mgmt ....Mr. Tony HOUGH
37 Director of Student Financial Aid ....Ms. Angela WILLIAMS
84 AVP Enrollment Management Services ....Ms. Sylvia LITTLEJOHN
26 Director of Public Information ....Mr. Kevin FLOYD
15 Human Resource Director ....Ms. Faye GOWANS
07 Director of Admissions ....Mr. Derrah CASSIDY
124 Director of Student Retention ....Mr. Shickre SABBAGHA
04 Executive Asst to the President ....Ms. Kim BOATWRIGHT
08 Chief Library Officer ....Ms. Florence MAYS
09 Dir of Assessment/Research & Plng ....Mr. Kevin BRAY
106 Director of Distance Learning ....Ms. Mary Helen HENDRIX
108 Asst Dir Assessment/Research & Plng ....Mr. Chris LOWNES
18 Chief Facilities/Physical Plant Ofc ....Ms. Teresa COOK
19 Director Security/Safety ....Mr. Myron CHAMBLISS
25 Chief Contract/Grants Administrator ....Ms. Alice APPLEBY
29 Director Alumni Affairs ....Mr. Allen SHARPE
96 Director of Purchasing ....Ms. Latitia TREZEVANT
121 Director Academic & Career Advising ....Mr. Andrew NEWTON

Miller-Motte College (F)

2451 Highway 501, Conway SC 29526
Telephone: (843) 591-1100 Identification: 770778
Accreditation: ACCSC, MAC

† Branch campus of Miller-Motte College, Chattanooga, TN.

Miller-Motte College (G)

8085 Rivers Avenue, North Charleston SC 29406
Telephone: (843) 574-0101 Identification: 666256
Accreditation: ACCSC

† Branch campus of Miller-Motte College, Chattanooga, TN.

Morris College (H)

100 W College Street, Sumter SC 29150-3599
County: Sumter FICE Identification: 003439
Unit ID: 218399
Telephone: (803) 934-3200 Carnegie Class: Bac-Diverse
FAX Number: (803) 773-3687 Calendar System: Semester
URL: www.morris.edu
Established: 1908 Annual Undergrad Tuition & Fees: $14,980
Enrollment: 395 Coed
Affiliation or Control: Baptist IRS Status: 501(c)3
Highest Offering: Baccalaureate
Accreditation: SC, ACBSP, CAEP

01 President ....Dr. Leroy STAGGERS
00 Chairperson of the Board ....Dr. Lucy J. REUBEN
05 Interim Academic Dean ....Dr. Lewis P. GRAHAM, JR.
10 Director of Business Affairs ....Mr. Robert EAVES
45 Dir Planning/Govt Relations/IT ....Ms. Dorothy S. CHEAGLE
32 Dean Student Affairs ....Dr. Juana DAVIS-FREEMAN
15 Dir Human Resources ....Mrs. Abby LAWSON
111 Dir Inst Advancement/Church Rels ....Dr. Gloria SEABROOK-WRIGHT
42 College Minister ....Dr. Charles M. PEE
84 Int Dir Enrollment Mgmt & Records ....Dr. Christopher HALL
37 Director of Financial Aid ....Ms. Sul BLACK
06 Registrar ....Ms. Gloria SCRIVEN
108 Director of Assessment ....Dr. Lewis P. GRAHAM, JR.
13 Director MIS/Computer Center ....Mr. Monterrio JONES
21 Chief Accountant ....Mrs. Bernice IRBY
29 Director Alumni Affairs ....Vacant
26 Director Public Relations ....Vacant
24 Director Learning Resources Ctr ....Ms. Margaret N. MUKOOZA
08 Head Librarian ....Ms. Margaret N. MUKOOZA
36 Director Career Services ....Vacant
38 Director Counseling ....Ms. Quanda D. SIMS
39 Director Residential Life ....Mrs. Tonia T. WASHINGTON
41 Director of Athletics ....Mr. Christopher P. BROWN
23 Director of Health Services ....Ms. Felicia HEYWARD
40 Bookstore Manager ....Ms. Andrea JUNIOUS
18 Chief Facilities/Physical Plant Off ....Mr. Lonnie J. MCCOY
19 Director of Security/Safety ....Mr. Alvin S. ALSTON
81 Chairperson Mathematics/Science ....Dr. Radman ALI
53 Chairperson Education ....Dr. Carol M. MCCLAIN
83 Chairperson Rel/Human/Social Sci ....Ms. Karen HEBERT
97 Chairperson General Studies ....Dr. Evelyn COHENS
04 Exec Assistant to the President ....Ms. Kimberly A. WATSON

Newberry College (I)

2100 College Street, Newberry SC 29108-2126
County: Newberry FICE Identification: 003440
Unit ID: 218414
Telephone: (800) 845-4955 Carnegie Class: Bac-Diverse
FAX Number: (803) 321-5627 Calendar System: Semester
URL: www.newberry.edu

Established: 1856 Annual Undergrad Tuition & Fees: $28,150
Enrollment: 1,256 Coed
Affiliation or Control: Evangelical Lutheran Church In America
IRS Status: 501(c)3
Highest Offering: Master's
Accreditation: SC, CAEP, MUS, NURSE

01 President ... Dr. Maurice W. SCHERRENS
05 VP for Academic Affairs ... Dr. Sid PARRISH
10 VP for Administrative Affairs & CFO ... Mr. David SAYERS
111 VP for Institutional Advancement ... Ms. Lori Ann SUMMERS
20 Assoc VP Academic Affairs ... Dr. Timothy G. ELSTON
07 Director of Admissions ... Mr. Bill KUEHL
32 VP Student Affairs/Dean of Students ... Mr. Barry MCCLANAHAN
41 Director of Athletics ... Mr. Sean JOHNSON
15 Director of Human Resources ... Mrs. Nikki BROOKS
06 Registrar ... Ms. Whitney MERINAR
08 Librarian ... Mr. Austin REID
18 Assoc Director of Facilities ... Mr. Bobby LONG
42 Chaplain ... Rev. David W. COFFMAN
21 Director of Accounting ... Ms. Landee BUZHARDT
38 Dir Health & Counseling Services ... Mrs. Martha DORRELL
26 Director of Marketing & PR ... Mr. Russell RIVERS
19 Director Security/Safety ... Mr. Paul WHITMAN
37 Director of Financial Aid ... Ms. Lola KENNEDY
100 Chief of Staff ... Ms. Bobbie SIDES
88 Assoc Dir of Financial Aid ... Mrs. Danielle DELATORRE

North Greenville University (A)

PO Box 1892, Tigerville SC 29688-1892
County: Greenville FICE Identification: 003441
Unit ID: 218441
Telephone: (864) 977-7000 Carnegie Class: Masters/S
FAX Number: (864) 977-7021 Calendar System: Semester
URL: www.ngu.edu
Established: 1892 Annual Undergrad Tuition & Fees: $22,050
Enrollment: 2,280 Coed
Affiliation or Control: Southern Baptist IRS Status: 501(c)3
Highest Offering: Doctorate
Accreditation: SC, #ARCPA, CAEP, COSMA, MUS

01 President/CEO ... Dr. Gene C. FANT, JR.
04 Admin Assistant for President ... Ms. Angie WATSON
03 Executive Vice President ... Mr. Rich GRIMM
05 Provost & Dean of Univ Faculty ... Dr. Nathan FINN
32 Vice President Student Services ... Ms. Rachael RUSSIAKY
10 Senior Vice President for Finance ... Mr. Michael STOWELL
07 Director for Traditional Admissions ... Ms. Katie Lynn MARSHALL
111 Vice President for Advancement ... Mr. Marty O'GWYNN
42 Senior Campus Pastor ... Dr. Steve CROUSE
102 Director of Dev & Foundation Giving ... Dr. Phil GARDNER
13 VP Information Technology Svcs/CIO ... Mr. Tim HUGGINS
109 Senior AVP Tigerville Operations ... Mr. Billy WATSON
108 Assoc Prov Admin & Accreditation ... Dr. Jan FOSTER
06 Registrar ... Vacant
18 VP Campus Enhancement Services ... Mr. Mick DANIEL
41 Athletic Director ... Ms. Jan MCDONALD
08 Director of Hester Library ... Ms. Carla MCMAHAN
19 Director Campus Safety & Security ... Vacant
88 Assoc Prov for Acad Engagement ... Dr. Tawana SCOTT
35 VP Campus Ministries/Student Engage ... Mr. Jody JENNINGS
26 Director of Communications ... Mr. LaVerne B. HOWELL
43 University General Counsel ... Ms. Jill RAYBURN
15 Director of Personnel Services ... Mrs. Michelle L. SABOU
16 Human Resource Manager ... Mrs. Beth HOUCK
38 Personal Counselor Men ... Mr. Steve BIELBY
38 Personal Counselor Women ... Miss Sara BLACK
36 Director of Career Planning ... Mr. Stuart FLOYD
102 Dir of Dev & Corporate Relations ... Mr. Jason ROSS
14 AVP for Network & Desktop Services ... Mr. Tim PATTERSON
37 Director Financial Aid ... Mrs. Cindi PATTERSON
53 Dean Education ... Dr. Constance WRIGHT
79 Dean Humanities & Sciences ... Dr. H. Paul THOMPSON
57 Dean Communication & Fine Arts ... Dr. Web DRAKE
73 Dean Christian Studies ... Dr. Walter JOHNSON
50 Dean Business & Entrepreneurship ... Dr. John DUNCAN
106 Director of the eLearning Center ... Dr. Lena MASLENNIKOVA
35 Assoc VP for Student Engagement ... Dr. Jared THOMAS
29 AVP Advancement & Alumni Engagement . Mr. Lamont SULLIVAN
31 Sr Dir of Church & Cmty Engagement ... Dr. Tony BEAM

Northeastern Technical College (B)

1201 Chesterfield Hwy, Cheraw SC 29520
County: Chesterfield FICE Identification: 007602
Unit ID: 217837
Telephone: (843) 921-6900 Carnegie Class: Assoc/HVT-High Non
FAX Number: (843) 537-6148 Calendar System: Semester
URL: www.netc.edu
Established: 1969 Annual Undergrad Tuition & Fees (In-State): $5,186
Enrollment: 1,465 Coed
Affiliation or Control: State IRS Status: 501(c)3
Highest Offering: Associate Degree
Accreditation: SC

01 President ... Dr. Kyle WAGNER
05 Vice President of Instruction ... Vacant
32 Vice President of Student Affairs ... Ms. Mamie HARRIS
10 Director of Finance ... Vacant
111 VP Institutional Advancement ... Mrs. Erin FANN
15 Director for Human Resources ... Mrs. Christi MEGGS
06 Registrar ... Ms. Anne JONES
26 Coordinator for Public Relations ... Ms. Shannon JUSTICE
35 Dean of Student Life ... Mr. Darin COLEMAN
08 Head Librarian ... Mr. Ronnie STAFFORD
09 Director of Institutional Research ... Vacant
04 Executive Assistant ... Mrs. Lauren ODOMS
101 Secretary of the Board ... Ms. Lib NORTON
13 Information Technology Manager ... Mr. Josh BRITT
07 Dean of Admissions ... Ms. Danielle PACE
37 Director Student Financial Aid ... Ms. Lisa PRINCE
103 Dean Workforce Development ... Dr. Robert TAYLOR
25 Grants Manager ... Ms. Sharekka BRIDGES
49 Dean of Arts & Sciences ... Dr. Melisa JOHNSON

Orangeburg-Calhoun Technical College (C)

3250 Saint Matthews Road, Orangeburg SC 29118-8299
County: Orangeburg FICE Identification: 006815
Unit ID: 218487
Telephone: (803) 536-0311 Carnegie Class: Assoc/HVT-Mix Trad/Non
FAX Number: (803) 535-1388 Calendar System: Semester
URL: www.octech.edu
Established: 1966 Annual Undergrad Tuition & Fees (In-State): $5,714
Enrollment: 2,257 Coed
Affiliation or Control: State IRS Status: 501(c)3
Highest Offering: Associate Degree
Accreditation: SC, ACBSP, ADNUR, MAC, NAEYC, PNUR, PTAA, RAD

01 President ... Dr. Walt TOBIN
05 Vice Pres Academic Affairs ... Ms. Williette WARING BERRY
10 Vice President Business Affairs ... Mr. Kim HUFF
32 Vice President of Student Services ... Dr. Sandra S. DAVIS
11 Dean of Administration ... Vacant
36 Training/Econ Development Director ... Mrs. Sandra MOORE
06 Registrar ... Ms. Amy OTT
46 Dean Planning/Research/Development ... Ms. Faith MCCURRY
13 Director Information Technology ... Mr. John MCCASKILL
08 Dean Learning Resource Ctr/Library ... Mr. Jason REED
18 Physical Plant Director ... Mr. James S. BRYANT, III
37 Director Student Financial Aid ... Ms. Connie WILLIAMS
07 Director of Admissions ... Vacant
19 Chief of Safety/Security ... Mr. Jermaine MCFADDEN
09 Dir Acad Support/Inst Effectiveness ... Mr. Cleveland WILSON
15 Human Resource Director ... Ms. Marie HOWELL
96 Procurement Manager ... Mrs. Scarlet GEDDINGS
84 Director of Enrollment ... Ms. Tracy DIBBLE

Piedmont Technical College (D)

620 N. Emerald Road, Greenwood SC 29646
County: Greenwood FICE Identification: 003992
Unit ID: 218520
Telephone: (864) 941-8324 Carnegie Class: Assoc/HVT-High Trad
FAX Number: (864) 941-8555 Calendar System: Semester
URL: www.ptc.edu
Established: 1966 Annual Undergrad Tuition & Fees (In-District): $5,315
Enrollment: 4,712 Coed
Affiliation or Control: State/Local IRS Status: 501(c)3
Highest Offering: Associate Degree
Accreditation: SC, ADNUR, COARC, CVT, FUSER, MAC, OTA, RAD, SURGT

01 President ... Dr. Hope E. RIVERS
10 VP Business & Finance ... Ms. K. Paige CHILDS
05 VP Academic Affairs ... Dr. Keli FEWOX
32 VP Student Affairs/Communications ... Mr. Joshua BLACK
102 Asst VP Development/PTC Foundation ... Ms. Fran K. WILEY
51 Assoc VP Econ Dev & Cont Educ ... Mr. Rusty DENNING
108 Assoc VP Assessment & Compliance ... Dr. Donna FOSTER
15 Assoc VP Human Resources ... Ms. Alesia BROWN
13 Asst VP Information Tech ... Mr. Joel GRIFFIN
49 Dean Arts & Science ... Dr. Lisa MARTIN
76 Dean Health Care ... Ms. Tara GONCE
54 Dean Engr/Industrial Technology ... Mr. Alvie COES
106 Dean Curriculum/Online Learning ... Ms. Karla GILLIAM
35 Dean of Student Services ... Ms. Tamatha SELLS
07 Dean of Admissions ... Ms. Renae FRAZIER
26 Director Marketing/PR ... Mr. Russell MARTIN
88 Director Genesis Initiatives ... Mr. Steve B. COLEMAN
18 Director Facilities Management ... Vacant
08 Head Librarian ... Ms. Meredith DANIEL
19 Director Campus Police/Security ... Mr. Jeffrey CRISP
37 Director of Financial Aid ... Ms. Missy PERRY
06 Registrar ... Ms. Jalissa ALGER
21 Controller ... Ms. Wendy HUGHES
21 Sr Accountant ... Ms. Crystal PITTMAN
04 Exec Asst to the President ... Ms. Sally M. COOKE
25 Chief Contract and Grants Administr ... Ms. Caroline CHAPPELL
96 Director of Purchasing ... Mr. Brian MCKENNA

Presbyterian College (E)

503 S Broad Street, Clinton SC 29325-2865
County: Laurens FICE Identification: 003445
Unit ID: 218539
Telephone: (864) 833-2820 Carnegie Class: Bac-A&S
FAX Number: (864) 833-8481 Calendar System: Semester
URL: www.presby.edu
Established: 1880 Annual Undergrad Tuition & Fees: $40,260
Enrollment: 1,309 Coed
Affiliation or Control: Presbyterian Church (U.S.A.) IRS Status: 501(c)3
Highest Offering: Doctorate
Accreditation: SC, #ARCPA, CAEPN, PHAR

01 President ... Dr. Matthew P. VANDENBERG
04 Executive Asst to the President ... Mrs. Leah S. HUCKS
05 Provost/VP Academic Affairs ... Dr. Kerry PANNELL
84 VP of Enrollment Management ... Mr. Woody O'CAIN
07 Director of Admissions ... Vacant
20 Dean of Academic Programs ... Dr. J. Alicia ASKEW
09 Director of Institutional Research ... Dr. Sylvia J. SIEVERS
08 Director of Thomason Library ... Vacant
24 Director of Media Services ... Mr. Douglas J. WALLACE
104 Director of International Programs ... Mr. Viet X. HA
85 Asst Dir of International Programs ... Ms. Adriana K. SMITH
06 Registrar & Director of Records ... Mrs. Vicky W. WILSON
67 Dean School of Pharmacy ... Vacant
07 Dir of Admissions Pharmacy School ... Ms. Katherine J. KANE
10 VP Finance/Administration ... Mr. Jeff P. SCACCIA
21 Controller ... Mrs. Libby SHULL
18 Exec Director of Campus Services ... Mr. Michael D. CRISP
37 Director of Financial Aid ... Vacant
13 Director of Information Technology ... Vacant
90 Academic Computing Services Coord ... Dr. Robert W. HOWILER
91 Desktop Support/Aux Systems Sr Tech ... Ms. Nellie R. SHELTON
109 Manager of Auxiliary Services ... Mr. Jason T. KOENIG
32 Dean of Students ... Dr. Andrew PETERSON
39 Director of Residence Life ... Vacant
36 Assoc Dean Students/Career Dev ... Ms. Kimberly A. LANE
42 Director of Campus Ministries .. Ms. Rachel E. PARSONS-WELLS
19 Director of Safety & Risk Mgmt ... Mr. Lawrence P. MULHALL
38 Director Counseling Services ... Ms. Susan C. GENTRY-WRIGHT
111 VP for Advancement ... Vacant
29 Director Alumni Relations ... Ms. Ashtin LIZANICH
41 Director of Athletics ... Mr. Rob L. ACUNTO
15 VP of Human Resources/Title IX ... Ms. Terri TIBBS

Professional Golfers Career College (F)

4454 Bluffton Pk Crescent, Ste 200, Bluffton SC 29910
Telephone: (843) 757-9611 Identification: 770779
Accreditation: CNCE

† Branch campus of Professional Golfers Career College, Temecula, CA

Sherman College of Chiropractic (G)

PO Box 1452, Spartanburg SC 29304-1452
County: Spartanburg FICE Identification: 020637
Unit ID: 218751
Telephone: (864) 578-8770 Carnegie Class: Spec-4-yr-Other Health
FAX Number: (864) 599-4860 Calendar System: Quarter
URL: www.sherman.edu
Established: 1973 Annual Graduate Tuition & Fees: N/A
Enrollment: 423 Coed
Affiliation or Control: Independent Non-Profit IRS Status: 501(c)3
Highest Offering: Doctorate; No Undergraduates
Accreditation: SC, CHIRO

01 President ... Dr. Edwin CORDERO
03 Exec Asst to President/Sr VP ... Ms. Roberta THOMAS-WOOD
11 Senior Vice President ... Dr. Neil COHEN
05 Provost ... Dr. Robert IRWIN
20 Vice Pres of Academic Affairs ... Dr. Joseph DONOFRIO
10 COO/Chief Financial Officer ... Mrs. Karen CANUP
32 Vice Pres for Student Affairs ... Mrs. LaShanda HUTTO-HARRIS
84 Assoc VP for Enrollment Services ... Ms. Kendra STRANGE
111 Assoc VP for Inst Advancement ... Dr. Jillian FARRELL
21 Assoc VP for Finance ... Mr. David BEDFORD
45 AVP for Institutional Effectivenes ... Mrs. Crissy LEWIS
06 Registrar ... Ms. Melody SABIN
08 Director of Learning Resouces ... Mrs. Chandra PLACER
37 Director of Financial Aid ... Mr. Chris ROBERSON
26 Sr Director for Marketing & Comm ... Mrs. Karen RHODES
88 Director for Scholarly Activity ... Dr. Christopher KENT
88 Dir for Teaching & Learning ... Dr. Billie HARRINGTON
15 Director Personnel Services ... Mrs. Mandy SMITH

South Carolina State University (H)

300 College Street, NE, Orangeburg SC 29117-0001
County: Orangeburg FICE Identification: 003446
Unit ID: 218733
Telephone: (803) 536-7000 Carnegie Class: Masters/S
FAX Number: (803) 533-3622 Calendar System: Semester
URL: www.scsu.edu
Established: 1896 Annual Undergrad Tuition & Fees (In-State): $11,060
Enrollment: 2,339 Coed
Affiliation or Control: State IRS Status: 501(c)3
Highest Offering: Doctorate
Accreditation: SC, AAFCS, ART, CACREP, CAEP, CAEPN, DIETD, MUS, SP, SW

00 Chairman Board of Trustees ... Mr. Rodney C. JENKINS
01 President ... Mr. Alexander CONYERS
100 Chief of Staff ... Ms. Shondra F. ABRAHAM
05 Acting Provost ... Dr. Frederick EVANS
03 VP Strategic Alliances/Initiatives ... Vacant
10 Acting Vice Pres for Finance/Mgmt ... Mrs. Brenda WALKER
32 Vice Pres for Student Affairs ... Dr. Tamara JEFFRIES-JACKSON
88 VP/Executive Dir 1890 Programs ... Dr. Louis D. WHITESIDES
84 VP for Enrollment Management ... Dr. Manicia J. FINCH
43 General Counsel ... Vacant
20 Acting Associate Provost ... Dr. David STATEN
111 VP Inst Advancement/External Rels ... Ms. Sonja A. BELLAMY-BENNETT

46 Assoc Provost/Sponsored Program .... Mr. Elbert R. MALONE
07 Director of Admissions .... Mr. Davion L. PETTY
23 Director Brooks Health Center .... Ms. Pinkey CARTER
81 Dean Col Sci/Math/Engineering Tech . Dr. Stanley N. IHEKWEAZU
53 Actg Dean Col Educ/Human & Soc Sci .... Dr. Evelyn FIELDS
58 Acting Dean Col of Graduate Studies .... Dr. Lakeisha TUCKER
47 Acting Dean Col of Agriculture .... Dr. William H. WHITAKER
50 Dean College of Business .... Dr. Barbara L. ADAMS
54 Dean of Engineering .... Dr. Stanley N. IHEKWEAZU
08 Interim Dean Library Services .... Dr. Ruth A. HODGES
124 Actg Dir Student Success/Retention .... Mr. Tyron CLINTON
06 Acting Registrar .... Ms. Felicia L. MCMILLAN
13 Director UCITS .... Mr. Travis T. JOHNSON
37 Director of Financial Aid .... Ms. Tangar YOUNG
38 Director Counseling/Student Dev .... Dr. Cherilyn Y. TAYLOR-MINNIEFIELD
26 Director of Marketing .... Ms. Kay E. SNIDER
36 Director of Career Placement .... Mr. Joseph THOMAS
15 Director Human Resource Mgmt .... Mr. Ronald S. YORK
41 Director Athletics .... Mr. Stacy L. DANLEY
18 Director of Facilities Mgmt .... Mr. Ken DAVIS
96 Director Procurement Services .... Ms. Stacy GREGG
39 Director of Residential Life .... Ms. Stacey D. SOWELL
19 Chief of Campus Police .... Mr. Timothy TAYLOR
92 Dean Honors College .... Dr. Harriet A. ROLAND
88 Director Athletic Media Relations .... Mr. Kendrick D. LEWIS
25 Dir Grants & Contract .... Ms. Gwendolyn F. MITCHELL
22 Director of Title III .... Ms. Gloria D. PYLES
28 Director of Multicultural Affairs .... Ms. Carolyn G. FREE
88 Station Manager WSSB-FM .... Mr. Carlito D. A'SEE
88 Director of Compliance .... Vacant
101 Secretary/Board of Trustees .... Ms. Eartha J. MOSLEY
104 Dir International/National Exchange .... Dr. Learie B. LUKE
105 Web Services .... Vacant
29 Interim Director Alumni Relations .... Mrs. Iva L. GARDNER
108 Dir of Institutional Effectiveness .... Ms. Valerie GOODWIN
88 Director IP Stanback Museum/Planet .... Dr. Frank C. MARTIN
106 Exe Dir Teach/Learning/Ext Studies .... Ms. Bettina MOZIE
09 Director Institutional Research .... Mrs. Cammie S. BERRY
84 Director Enrollment Management .... Ms. Betty R. BOATWRIGHT
27 Public Information Officer .... Mr. Samuel WATSON
102 Executive Director of SCII .... Dr. Gwynth R. NELSON
88 Director of Bands .... Dr. Patrick MOORE
88 Director Child Dev Learning Center .... Mrs. Stephanie FELKS
114 Account Fiscal Manager III .... Mrs. Donna C. HANTON
30 Chief Development Office .... Mr. Adrian L. SCOTT

South University Columbia Campus (A)

9 Science Court, Columbia SC 29203-6400
Telephone: (803) 799-9082 FICE Identification: 004922
Accreditation: &SC, ACBSP, CACREP, MAC, NURSE, OTA, PTAA

† Regional accreditation is carried under the parent institution in Savannah, GA.

Southeastern College (B)

581 Columbia Mall Blvd, Columbia SC 29223
County: Richland FICE Identification: 037464
Unit ID: 444866
Telephone: (803) 798-8800 Carnegie Class: Spec 2-yr-Health
FAX Number: (803) 798-0003 Calendar System: Semester
URL: https://www.sec.edu
Established: 1997 Annual Undergrad Tuition & Fees: N/A
Enrollment: 193 Coed
Affiliation or Control: Proprietary IRS Status: Proprietary
Highest Offering: Associate Degree
Accreditation: ACCSC, MAAB

01 Campus President .... Janet CLARK

Southeastern College (C)

2431 Aviation Ave., Ste 703, North Charleston SC 29406
County: Charleston FICE Identification: 035554
Unit ID: 443261
Telephone: (843) 747-1279 Carnegie Class: Spec 2-yr-Health
FAX Number: (843) 747-7159 Calendar System: Semester
URL: https://www.sec.edu/
Established: 1997 Annual Undergrad Tuition & Fees: N/A
Enrollment: N/A Coed
Affiliation or Control: Proprietary IRS Status: Proprietary
Highest Offering: Associate Degree
Accreditation: ACCSC, MAAB

02 Campus President .... Tim VAN HORN
05 Dean of Academic Affairs .... Samantha POFF
06 Registrar .... Ashley MARQUES

Southern Wesleyan University (D)

907 Wesleyan Drive, PO Box 1020,
Central SC 29630-1020
County: Pickens FICE Identification: 003422
Unit ID: 217776
Telephone: (864) 644-5550 Carnegie Class: Masters/S
FAX Number: N/A Calendar System: Semester
URL: www.swu.edu
Established: 1906 Annual Undergrad Tuition & Fees: $25,676
Enrollment: 1,345 Coed
Affiliation or Control: Wesleyan Church IRS Status: 501(c)3
Highest Offering: Doctorate
Accreditation: SC, CAEPN, MUS

01 Interim President .... Dr. Bill S. CROTHERS
05 Provost .... Dr. April WHITE PUGH
10 Chief Financial Officer .... Mr. Ken WHITENER
32 Vice President for Student Life .... Dr. Chris CONFER
111 Vice President for Advancement .... Mr. Scott DRURY
41 Athletic Director .... Mrs. Julia REININGA
20 Vice Provost of Academic Strategy .... Dr. Sandra MCLENDON
37 Director of Financial Aid .... Mrs. Tasha MORGAN
15 Director of Human Resources .... Mrs. Dana L. FROST
08 Director of Library Services .... Mrs. Joni ADDIS
06 Registrar .... Ms. Regina BOLDING
29 Alumni Director .... Mr. Heath MULLIKIN
38 Director Student Counseling .... Ms. Monica PEREZ
124 Director of Retention .... Mr. Caleb SOUTHERN
07 AVP of Admissions .... Mr. David SLABAUGH
19 Director of Campus Safety .... Mr. Brad BOWEN
39 AVP for Residence Life .... Mr. Matthew THORPE
36 AVP for Student Wellness and Career .... Mrs. Ellen PATE
42 AVP Spiritual Life/Univ Chaplain .... Rev. Ken DILL
04 Executive Asst to President .... Mrs. Martha ERVIN
09 Director of Institutional Planning .... Mrs. Lisa CORBIN
13 Executive Director of IT .... Mr. Gregory R. DENLEA

Spartanburg Community College (E)

107 Community College Drive, Spartanburg SC 29303
County: Spartanburg FICE Identification: 003994
Unit ID: 218830
Telephone: (864) 592-4600 Carnegie Class: Assoc/MT-VT-High Trad
FAX Number: (864) 592-4642 Calendar System: Semester
URL: www.sccsc.edu
Established: 1963 Annual Undergrad Tuition & Fees (In-State): $6,030
Enrollment: 4,108 Coed
Affiliation or Control: State IRS Status: 501(c)3
Highest Offering: Associate Degree
Accreditation: SC, ACFEI, ADNUR, COARC, DA, EMT, MAC, MLTAD, NAEYC, RAD, SURGT

01 President .... Dr. G. Michael MIKOTA
03 Vice President Strategic Innovation .... Dr. Stacey L. OBI
111 Exec Dir Advancement/SCC Foundation .... Mr. John JARACZEWSKI
88 Vice Pres Economic Advancement .... Mr. Ethan BURROUGHS
12 Executive Director Cherokee Campus .... Ms. Amanda PAINTER
12 Exec Director Tyger River Campus .... Ms. Rhonda JOHNS
32 Dean Student Services .... Ms. Witney FISHER
88 Dean of CCE .... Ms. Rhonda JOHNS
08 Dean of Learning Resources .... Mr. Mark ROSEVEARE
76 Dean Health & Human Services .... Dr. Benita YOWE
49 Dean of Arts & Sciences .... Ms. Jenny WILLIAMS
07 Director Admissions Services .... Ms. Kimbraly PATTERSON
09 Director of Institutional Research .... Dr. Amanda ADAMS
26 Director Marketing/Public Relations .... Mrs. Cheri ANDERSON-HUCKS
29 Alumni Relations Coordinator .... Ms. Charm LOWE
38 Director Advising/Early Alert Svcs .... Mr. Michael HARVEY
13 Interim Director Information Tech .... Mr. David AUGHINBAUGH
18 Director Campus Operations .... Mr. Winston ANDERSON
19 Director Security/Safety .... Mr. Richard POWERS
06 Registrar .... Ms. Celia N. BAUSS
96 Director Procurement .... Mr. Michael D. CLARDY
21 Director of Finance .... Ms. Melissa P. HUGHES
37 Director of Financial Aid .... Mr. Jeffery BOYLE
106 Dir Online Education/E-learning .... Mr. Neil GRIFFIN
25 Director of Contracts & Grants .... Ms. Caroline SEXTON
04 Executive Asst to President .... Mrs. Donna WALKER
90 Director Academic Computing .... Mr. Roy SMITH
103 Director Workforce Development .... Mrs. Latokia TRIGG
27 Director Strategic Communications .... Mr. Colton GRACE

Spartanburg Methodist College (F)

885 Darryl Windham Dr, Spartanburg SC 29301-5899
County: Spartanburg FICE Identification: 003447
Unit ID: 218821
Telephone: (864) 587-4000 Carnegie Class: Assoc/HT-High Trad
FAX Number: (864) 587-4355 Calendar System: Semester
URL: www.smcsc.edu
Established: 1911 Annual Undergrad Tuition & Fees: $17,540
Enrollment: 1,051 Coed
Affiliation or Control: United Methodist IRS Status: 501(c)3
Highest Offering: Baccalaureate
Accreditation: SC

01 President .... Mr. W. Scott COCHRAN
05 Exec VP Acad Affairs/Student Dev .... Dr. Curt LAIRD
10 Executive VP for Business Affairs .... Mr. Eric MCDONALD
111 Vice Pres Institutional Advancement ..... Mrs. Jennifer DILLENGER
84 Vice Pres Enrollment Management .... Mr. Ben MAXWELL
26 Vice President for Marketing .... Mrs. Lisa WARE
32 VP for Student Development .... Ms. Courtney SHELTON
13 Vice Pres for Operations Info Tech .... Mr. Jason WOMICK
09 VP for Analytics & Improvement .... Mr. Jason WOMICK
11 Dean of Admin & Family Services .... Mr. DeAndre HOWARD
06 Registrar .... Ms. Jill R. JOHNSON
08 Library Director .... Ms. Lori HETRICK
04 Admin Assistant to the President .... Vacant
44 Director of Planned Giving .... Mr. Don TATE
37 Director of Financial Aid .... Mr. Kyle WADE
38 Director of Counseling Services .... Mr. Ronnie MCCARRELL
42 Chaplain/Director Church Relations .... Rev. Tim DRUM

41 Director of Athletics .... Ms. Megan AIELLO
18 Director Facilities Management .... Mr. Marty WOODS
29 Director of Alumni Relations .... Mrs. Leah L. PRUITT
15 Exec Director of Human Resources .... Mrs. Courtney DOBBINS
19 Chief of Campus Safety .... Mr. Chris CARTER
31 Director Community Life .... Mr. Corey BELL
108 Director Institutional Assessment .... Ms. Jessica HARWOOD
07 Executive Director of Admissions .... Ms. Julie LANFORD

Technical College of the Lowcountry (G)

921 S Ribaut Road, PO Box 1288,
Beaufort SC 29901-1288
County: Beaufort FICE Identification: 009910
Unit ID: 217712
Telephone: (843) 525-8211 Carnegie Class: Assoc/HVT-High Trad
FAX Number: (843) 525-8330 Calendar System: Semester
URL: www.tcl.edu
Established: 1969 Annual Undergrad Tuition & Fees (In-State): $5,740
Enrollment: 2,119 Coed
Affiliation or Control: State IRS Status: 501(c)3
Highest Offering: Associate Degree
Accreditation: SC, ADNUR, COMTA, PNUR, PTAA, RAD, SURGT

01 President .... Dr. Richard J. GOUGH
11 Vice Pres Administrative Services .... Ms. Janis HOFFMAN
05 Vice President for Academic Affairs .... Ms. Nancy WEBER
32 Vice President for Student Affairs .... Ms. Nancy WEBER
35 AVP for Student Affairs .... Mr. Rodney ADAMS
09 Director for Research/Planning .... Ms. Camille MYERS
15 Human Resources Director .... Ms. Sharon O'NEAL
20 Director for Learning Resources .... Ms. Sasha BISHOP
50 Div Dean Business Technologies .... Ms. Shunda WARE
49 Div Dean Arts & Sciences .... Dr. Fredrick COOPER
76 Dean Health Sciences .... Dr. Glenn LEVICKI
13 Director of Information Technology .... Mr. Hayes WISER
37 Director Financial Aid .... Ms. Georgeann WILLIAMS
111 VP for Inst Advancement .... Ms. Mary Lee CARNS
26 AVP for Public Relations .... Ms. Leigh COPELAND
109 Director for Auxiliary Services .... Ms. Louise RENNIX
18 Director of Facility Management .... Mr. Larry BECKLER
96 Procurement Manager .... Ms. Randee JOHNSON
06 Registrar .... Ms. Jillian KIRKLAND
103 Director for Workforce Solutions .... Ms. Melanie GALLION
04 Administrative Asst to President .... Ms. Ann CULLEN

Tri-County Technical College (H)

PO Box 587, Pendleton SC 29670-0587
County: Anderson FICE Identification: 004926
Unit ID: 218885
Telephone: (864) 646-8361 Carnegie Class: Assoc/HVT-High Trad
FAX Number: (864) 646-1889 Calendar System: Semester
URL: www.tctc.edu
Established: 1962 Annual Undergrad Tuition & Fees (In-District): $5,792
Enrollment: 5,582 Coed
Affiliation or Control: State/Local IRS Status: 501(c)3
Highest Offering: Associate Degree
Accreditation: SC, ACBSP, ADNUR, DA, MAC, MLTAD, NAEYC, PNUR, SURGT

01 President .... Dr. Galen DEHAY
05 Chief Academic Officer .... Dr. Anthony GUISEPPI-ELIE
10 Vice Pres Business Affairs .... Ms. Cara HAMILTON
111 VP Inst Advancement/Business Rels .... Mr. Grayson KELLY
15 VP Human Resources .... Ms. Marcia LEAKE
32 VP Student Support/Engagement .... Ms. Linda JAMEISON
51 Dean of Continuing Education .... Mr. Rick COTHRAN
84 AVP Enroll Mgmt/Educ Partnership .... Ms. Jenni CREAMER
35 Dean of Student Development .... Mr. Mark DOUGHERTY
49 Dean Arts & Sciences Division .... Mr. Tom LAWRENCE
72 Dean Engineering Technology Div .... Ms. Amanda ELMORE
50 Dean Business/Human Services Div .... Mrs. Jacquelyn BLAKLEY
76 Dean Health Education Division .... Mr. Ahmad CHAUDHRY
37 Student Financial Aid Director .... Ms. Melanie GILLESPIE
13 CIO/Information Technology Dir .... Mr. Luke VANWINGERDEN
26 Dir Public Relations/Communication .... Mrs. Karen POTTER
30 Director of Development .... Mrs. Courtney WHITE
07 Director of Admissions .... Ms. Tiffiny BLACKWELL
06 Registrar .... Mr. Scott HARVEY
09 Director of Institutional Research .... Mr. Chris MARINO
18 Chief Facilities/Physical Plant .... Mr. Ken KOPERA
21 Director of Fiscal Affairs .... Ms. Tracy WACTOR
96 Director of Purchasing .... Mr. Matthew WHITTEN
38 Director of Student Life/Counseling .... Ms. Croslena JOHNSON
04 Admin Assistant to the President .... Ms. Kathleen C. BRAND
100 Chief of Staff .... Mr. Dan COOPER
36 Student Placement .... Mr. Edward Adam PAIGE
84 Enrollment Management .... Mr. Adam GHILONI
103 Dean Integrated Workforce Solutions .... Mr. Bryan MANUEL
19 Director Security/Safety .... Mr. Marcus GUESS

Trident Technical College (I)

PO Box 118067, Charleston SC 29423-8067
County: Charleston FICE Identification: 004920
Unit ID: 218894
Telephone: (843) 574-6111 Carnegie Class: Assoc/MT-VT-Mix Trad/Non
FAX Number: N/A Calendar System: Semester
URL: www.tridenttech.edu
Established: 1964 Annual Undergrad Tuition & Fees (In-District): $5,143
Enrollment: 11,650 Coed
Affiliation or Control: State/Local IRS Status: 501(c)3

Highest Offering: Associate Degree
Accreditation: SC, ACBSP, ACFEI, ACPHA, ADNUR, CAHIIM, COARC, CSHSE, DA, DH, EMT, MAC, MLTAD, NAEYC, OTA, PNUR, PTAA, RAD

01 President .... Dr. Mary THORNLEY
10 Sr Vice President Business Affairs .... Mr. Scott POELKER
05 Vice President Education .... Dr. Cathy ALMQUIST
32 Vice President Student Services .... Dr. Patrice DAVIS
111 Vice President Advancement .... Ms. Meg HOWLE
13 Vice Pres Information Technology .... Mr. M.G MITCHUM
45 Assoc VP Planning/Accreditation .... Ms. Samantha RICHARDS
20 Asst Vice Pres Instruction .... Mr. David HARRIS
20 Asst VP Academic Programs .... Dr. Tim BROWN
35 Asst VP for Student Development .... Ms. Pam BROWN
15 Associate VP Human Resources .... Ms. DeVetta HUGHES
96 Dir Procurement/Risk Management .... Ms. Carol BELCHER
109 Dir Auxiliary Enterprises/Bookstore .... Ms. Jloundia PINCKNEY
18 Director Facilities .... Mr. Eric HAMILTON
21 Director Finance .... Ms. Gamellia DAVIS
26 Director Marketing .... Ms. Tina AHLEMANN
27 Director Public Info .... Mr. David HANSEN
88 Assistant VP Community Partnerships .... Ms. Melissa STOWASSER
30 Vice President Development .... Ms. Lisa PICCOLO
119 Information Security Officer .... Mr. Joseph GIBSON
124 Dean of Student Engagement .... Mr. Brian ALMQUIST
81 Dean Science & Mathematics .... Dr. Shakitha BARNER
79 Dean Humanities & Social Sciences .... Ms. Michelle CAYA
50 Dean Business Technology .... Dr. Laurie BOEDING
54 Dean Engineering & Construction .... Mr. Tim FULFORD
76 Dean Health Sciences .... Ms. Krista HARRINGTON
57 Dean Film Media and Visual Arts .... Mr. Glenn SEALE
88 Dean Manufacturing & Maintenance .... Mr. Robert ELLIOTT
88 Dean Culinary Inst of Charleston .... Mr. Mike SABOE
66 Dean Nursing .... Ms. Nancy HILBURN
75 Dean Aeronautical Studies .... Dr. Barry FRANCO
12 Dean Berkeley Campus .... Dr. Karen WRIGHTEN
12 Dean Mount Pleasant Campus .... Dr. Darren FELTY
12 Dean Palmer Campus .... Dr. Amy HUDOCK
19 Director Public Safety .... Mr. Mario EVANS
06 Registrar .... Mr. Evan REICH
07 Director of Admissions .... Mr. Ronald JOHNSON
09 Director of Institutional Research .... Ms. Samantha RICHARDS
37 Director Student Financial Aid .... Ms. Sarah DOWD
04 Executive Asst to President .... Ms. Helen SUGHRUE

University of South Carolina Columbia (A)

Columbia SC 29208-0001
County: Richland — FICE Identification: 003448
Unit ID: 218663
Telephone: (803) 777-7000 — Carnegie Class: DU-Highest
FAX Number: (803) 777-0101 — Calendar System: Semester
URL: www.sc.edu
Established: 1801 — Annual Undergrad Tuition & Fees (In-State): $12,688
Enrollment: 35,470 — Coed
Affiliation or Control: State — IRS Status: 501(c)3
Highest Offering: Doctorate
Accreditation: SC, ACPHA, ANEST, ARCPA, ART, CAATE, CACREP, CAEP, CAHIIM, CEA, CLPSY, DANCE, HSA, IPSY, JOUR, LAW, LIB, MED, MUS, NURSE, PH, PHAR, PTA, SCPSY, SP, SPAA, SW, THEA

01 President .... Dr. Michael AMIRIDIS
100 Chief of Staff .... Vacant
13 Vice President for IT & CIO .... Mr. Doug FOSTER
10 University Treasurer .... Mr. Patrick LARDNER
116 Exec Dir of Audit & Advisory Svcs .... Vacant
05 Interim Provost .... Dr. Stephen CUTLER
20 Vice Prov/Dean Undergrad Studies .... Dr. Sandra KELLY
11 Exec VP for Administration & CFO .... Mr. Edward I. WALTON
32 Dean of Students/Title IX Dir .... Mr. Marc SHOOK
15 Vice President Human Resources .... Ms. Caroline AGARDY
30 Vice President for Development .... Vacant
46 Vice President for Research .... Dr. Julius FRIDRIKSSON
26 Asst VP Univ Rels/Public Affairs .... Mr. Jeff STENSLAND
101 Univ Secretary & Sec to Board .... Mr. Cantey HEATH
20 Vice Prov & Dean of Faculty .... Dr. Cheryl ADDY
85 Vice Provost & Dir Global Carolina .... Dr. Sandra J. KELLY
84 Asst V Prov Enrl Mgmt & Dean UG Adm .... Mr. Scott VERZYL
63 Exec Dean School of Medicine .... Dr. Les HALL
08 Dean of University Libraries .... Dr. Tom MCNALLY
43 Gen Counsel & Exec Dir Compliance .... Mr. Walter H. PARHAM
09 Exec Dir Inst Rsch/Assess/Analytics .... Vacant
18 VP for Facilities & Transportation .... Mr. Derrick E. HUGGINS
19 AVP Law Enforce & Chief of Police .... Mr. Christopher L. WUCHENICH
37 Dir Student Fin Aid & Scholarship .... Mr. Joey DERRICK
36 Director Career Center .... Ms. Helen POWERS
06 University Registrar .... Mr. Aaron C. MARTERER
22 Asst VP Civil Rights & Title IX .... Ms. Molly PEIRANO
07 Director of Admissions .... Dr. Mary WAGNER
39 Exec Director of Student Housing .... Ms. April BARNES
23 Interim VP of Health & Chief Ofcr .... Dr. Jason STACY
41 Athletic Director .... Mr. Ray TANNER
45 Exec Dir Strategic Initiatives/Dev .... Mr. Jerry T. BREWER
27 Director News & Internal Relations .... Vacant
96 Director of Purchasing .... Mrs. Venis MANIGO
29 CEO USC Alumni Association .... Mr. Wes HICKMAN
12 Chancellor Palmetto College .... Dr. Susan ELKINS
88 Interim Dean Hosp/Retail/Sport HMgt .... Mr. Matt BROWN
50 Dean Moore School of Business .... Dr. Peter J. BREWS
53 Dean College of Education .... Vacant
54 Dean Col Engineering & Computing .... Dr. Hossein HAJ-HARIRI
69 Dean Arnold School of Public Health .... Dr. G. Thomas CHANDLER
60 Dean Col of Info & Communications .... Dr. Tom REICHERT
61 Dean School of Law .... Mr. William C. HUBBARD
63 Dean Greenville School of Medicine .... Dr. Marjorie JENKINS
67 Interim Dean Col of Pharmacy .... Dr. Julie M. SEASE
49 Dean Col of Arts & Sciences .... Dr. Joel H. SAMUELS
64 Dean School of Music .... Dr. Tayloe HARDING
92 Dean SC Honors College .... Dr. Steve LYNN
66 Dean College of Nursing .... Dr. Jeannette ANDREWS
70 Interim Dean College of Social Work .... Dr. Teri BROWNE
88 Director for Academic Programs .... Ms. Trena HOUP
28 VP of Diversity/Equity & Inclusion .... Mr. Julian R. WILLIAMS
103 Exe Dir Ofc of Economic Engagement .... Mr. William B. KIRKLAND
86 Director of State Govt Relations .... Mr. Derrick MEGGIE

University of South Carolina Aiken (B)

471 University Parkway, Aiken SC 29801-6399
County: Aiken — FICE Identification: 003449
Unit ID: 218645
Telephone: (803) 648-6851 — Carnegie Class: Masters/S
FAX Number: (803) 641-3362 — Calendar System: Semester
URL: www.usca.edu
Established: 1961 — Annual Undergrad Tuition & Fees (In-State): $10,760
Enrollment: 3,944 — Coed
Affiliation or Control: State — IRS Status: 501(c)3
Highest Offering: Master's
Accreditation: SC, CAEP, MPCAC, MUS, NURSE

01 Chancellor .... Dr. Daniel HEIMMERMANN
111 Vice Chanc Advance & External Rels .... Ms. Mary DRISCOLL
05 Provost & EVC of Academic Affairs .... Dr. Daren TIMMONS
32 VC Student Engagement/Inclusion .... Mr. Ahmed SAMAHA
13 Vice Chancellor Information Tech .... Mr. Ernest PRINGLE
10 VC for Admin and Finance/CFO .... Mr. Cam REAGIN
20 Asst Vice Chanc Academic Affairs .... Dr. Tim LINTNER
84 Assoc Vice Chanc Enrollment Mgmt .... Mr. Daniel J. ROBB
50 Int Dean School of Business Admin .... Dr. Sanela PORCA
53 Dean of the School of Education .... Dr. Judy BECK
66 Dean of the School of Nursing .... Dr. Thayer MCGAHEE
09 Dir Inst Effect/Research/Compliance .... Ms. Nicole SPENSLEY
08 Library Director .... Mr. Rodney LIPPARD
40 Purchasing Manager .... Ms. Heidi DIFRANCO
21 Controller .... Mr. Kevin CRAWFORD
15 Director of Human Resources .... Ms. Carla HAYES
88 Dir Campus Recreation & Wellness .... Ms. Mila PADGETT
07 Director of Admissions .... Mr. Andrew HENDRIX
36 Director of Career Services .... Mr. Corey FERALDI
37 Director Financial Aid .... Mr. Jack EDWARDS
06 Registrar .... Mr. Brock GILLIAM
41 Director of Athletics .... Mr. Jim HERLIHY
39 Assoc Director of Housing .... Ms. Hope SMITH-DUNBAR
19 Chief of Police .... Mr. Jason ZIKE
112 Major Gifts Officer .... Ms. Robin CALLICOTT
26 Dir Marketing & Community Relations .... Mr. James RABY

University of South Carolina Beaufort (C)

1 University Boulevard, Bluffton SC 29909-6085
County: Beaufort — FICE Identification: 003450
Unit ID: 218654
Telephone: (843) 208-8000 — Carnegie Class: Bac-Diverse
FAX Number: (843) 208-8299 — Calendar System: Semester
URL: www.uscb.edu
Established: 1959 — Annual Undergrad Tuition & Fees (In-State): $10,730
Enrollment: 2,006 — Coed
Affiliation or Control: State — IRS Status: 501(c)3
Highest Offering: Baccalaureate
Accreditation: SC, CAEPN, CSHSE, NURSE

01 Chancellor .... Dr. Al M. PANU
05 Provost & Exec VC for Acad Affairs .... Dr. Eric SKIPPER
111 Vice Chanc Advancement & Ext Rels .... Dr. Anna PONDER
84 Vice Chanc for Enrollment Mgmt .... Mr. Mack PALMOUR
10 Vice Chanc Finance/IT .... Ms. Beth G. PATRICK
32 Vice Chanc Student Development .... Dr. Angela D. SIMMONS
41 Athletic Director .... Mr. Quin MONAHAN
13 Chief Information Officer .... Vacant
20 Assoc Vice Chanc for Acad Affairs .... Dr. Martha MORIARTY
35 Asst Vice Chanc Student Development .... Ms. Deonne YEAGER
08 Librarian .... Ms. Melanie HANES-RAMOS
15 Director of Human Resources .... Dr. Sue GOLABEK
37 Director of Financial Aid .... Ms. Patricia GREENE
09 Dir Inst Effectiveness/Research .... Mr. Brian MALLORY
18 Director of Facilities .... Mr. Mike PARROTT
36 Director of Career Services .... Ms. Allison REYNOLDS
06 Registrar .... Mr. Gary SUTTON
88 Director of Military Program .... Mr. Michael WEISS
114 Budget Director .... Ms. Mary CORDRAY

University of South Carolina Lancaster (D)

PO Box 889, Lancaster SC 29721-0889
Telephone: (803) 313-7000 — FICE Identification: 003453
Accreditation: &SC, ACBSP, PNUR

† Regional accreditation is carried under University of South Carolina - Columbia.

University of South Carolina Salkehatchie (E)

PO Box 617, Allendale SC 29810-0617
County: Allendale — FICE Identification: 003454
Unit ID: 218681
Telephone: (803) 584-3446 — Carnegie Class: Assoc/HT-Mix Trad/Non
FAX Number: (803) 584-5038 — Calendar System: Semester
URL: uscsalkehatchie.sc.edu
Established: 1965 — Annual Undergrad Tuition & Fees (In-State): $7,558
Enrollment: 878 — Coed
Affiliation or Control: State — IRS Status: 501(c)3
Highest Offering: Associate Degree
Accreditation: &SC

01 Dean .... Dr. April CONE
32 Int Assoc Dean Acad & Stdnt Affs .... Dr. Sarah MILLER
08 Head Librarian .... Mr. Daniel JOHNSON
11 Director of Finance .... Ms. Jessica ALL
37 Director of Financial Aid .... Ms. Georgeann WILLIAMS
18 Dir Facilities/Safety/HR Director .... Dr. William A. SANDIFER
40 Business Office/Bookstore Manager .... Mr. Lamar HEWETT
07 Director of Admissions/Registrar .... Ms. Carmen BROWN
30 Chief Development .... Vacant
84 Exec Director Enrollment Mgmt Svcs .... Vacant
88 Director Leadership Institute .... Mr. Alexander JACKSON
15 Human Resource Manager .... Vacant
13 Director of Information Technology .... Ms. Gayle WALSH

† Regional accreditation is carried under University of South Carolina - Columbia.

University of South Carolina School of Medicine Greenville (F)

607 Grove Road, Greenville SC 29605
County: Greenville — Identification: 667114
Telephone: (864) 455-7992 — Carnegie Class: Not Classified
FAX Number: (864) 455-8404 — Calendar System: Semester
URL: greenvillemed.sc.edu
Established: 2010 — Annual Graduate Tuition & Fees: N/A
Enrollment: N/A — Coed
Affiliation or Control: State — IRS Status: 501(c)3
Highest Offering: Doctorate; No Undergraduates
Accreditation: MED

01 Dean .... Dr. Marjorie JENKINS
05 Assoc Dean Clinical Faculty Affairs .... Dr. Alyson J. MCGREGOR
20 Sr Assoc Dean Academic Affairs .... Dr. Phyllis MACGILVRAY
10 Assoc Dean Finance & Business Opers .... Eboni L. MARTEZ
30 Sr Director of Development .... Vacant
13 Director of IT and Facilities .... Vacant
15 Director of HR and Faculty Affairs .... Vacant
37 Sr Asst Dir Financial Aid .... Casey WILEY
07 Mgr of Admissions & Registration .... Gail HARDAWAY
32 Int Assoc Dean for Student Affairs .... Dr. Tom PACE

University of South Carolina Sumter (G)

200 Miller Road, Sumter SC 29150-2498
County: Sumter — FICE Identification: 003426
Unit ID: 218690
Telephone: (803) 775-8727 — Carnegie Class: Assoc/HT-High Non
FAX Number: (803) 775-2180 — Calendar System: Semester
URL: www.uscsumter.edu
Established: 1966 — Annual Undergrad Tuition & Fees (In-State): $7,558
Enrollment: 1,387 — Coed
Affiliation or Control: State — IRS Status: 501(c)3
Highest Offering: Associate Degree
Accreditation: &SC

01 Dean USC Sumter .... Mr. Michael SONNTAG
05 Exec Assoc Dean Acad/Stdnt Affairs .... Mr. Eric REISENAUER
32 Dir of Student Life and eSports .... Mr. Kristopher E. WEISSMANN
09 Institutional Research Analyst .... Mr. Chuck W. WRIGHT
08 Head Librarian .... Ms. Sharon H. CHAPMAN
07 Director of Admissions Services .... Mr. Keith E. BRITTON
51 Dir of Educational Partnerships .... Ms. Lara K. RICHARDSON
26 Dir of Marketing/Public Relations .... Ms. Alethia HUMMEL
40 Bookstore Manager .... Ms. Julie MCCOY
15 Human Resources Officer .... Ms. Marchetta L. WILLIAMS
88 Director Opportunity Scholars .... Ms. Lisa ROSDAIL
87 Director Shaw AFB Programs .... Mr. Rick BOYD
41 Athletic Director .... Ms. Adrienne CATALDO
13 Director of Info Technology .... Mr. Brian SMITH
37 Dir of Fin Aid & Veterans Affairs .... Ms. Nada MORANT-WILSON
06 Registrar .... Vacant

† Regional accreditation is carried under University of South Carolina - Columbia.

University of South Carolina Union (H)

PO Drawer 729, Union SC 29379-0729
County: Union — FICE Identification: 004927
Unit ID: 218706
Telephone: (864) 429-8728 — Carnegie Class: Assoc/HT-High Non
FAX Number: (864) 427-3682 — Calendar System: Semester
URL: uscunion.sc.edu
Established: 1965 — Annual Undergrad Tuition & Fees (In-State): $7,558
Enrollment: 1,071 — Coed

Affiliation or Control: State IRS Status: 501(c)3
Highest Offering: Associate Degree
Accreditation: &SC

01 Interim Campus Dean ....Dr. Randy LOWELL
05 Interim Assoc Dean Acad Affairs ....Dr. Majdouline AZIZ
84 Enrollment Director ....Mr. Bradley GREER
37 Director Financial Aid ....Mr. Bobby HOLCOMBE
15 Human Resource Manager ....Ms. Susan P. JETT
40 Bookstore Manager ....Ms. Tanja BLACK
13 Director of Information Technology ....Mr. Jeremy BLACK
30 Director of Marketing & Development ....Ms. Annie SMITH
08 Library Manager ....Ms. Sharon L. RUPP
121 Coord Academic Success Center ....Vacant
10 Director of Budget and Business Ops ....Ms. Michele LEE
12 USC Laurens Location Director ....Mr. Matt DEAN
19 Health and Safety/Security Director ....Mr. Tony GREGORY
18 Maintenance Director ....Mr. Donald LAWSON
06 Registrar ....Mr. Blake WILSON

† Regional accreditation is carried under University of South Carolina - Columbia.

University of South Carolina Upstate (A)

800 University Way, Spartanburg SC 29303-4996
County: Spartanburg FICE Identification: 006951
Unit ID: 218742
Telephone: (864) 503-5000 Carnegie Class: Bac-Diverse
FAX Number: (864) 503-5375 Calendar System: Semester
URL: www.uscupstate.edu
Established: 1967 Annual Undergrad Tuition & Fees (In-State): $11,583
Enrollment: 6,038 Coed
Affiliation or Control: State IRS Status: 501(c)3
Highest Offering: Master's
Accreditation: SC, ART, CAEP, CAHIIM, NURSE

01 Chancellor ....Dr. Bennie L. HARRIS
05 Prov/Sr Vice Chanc Academic Affairs ....Dr. David SCHECTER
13 Chief Information Officer ....Mr. Adam LONG
10 Vice Chanc for Finance and Admin . Ms. Sheryl TURNER-WATTS
111 Int VC Advance/Upstate Foundation ....Ms. Kim JOLLEY
12 Dir Acad Engagement Greenville Ctr ....Dr. Judith PRINCE
32 Interim Dean of Students ....Dr. Britton KATZ
06 Registrar ....Ms. Mary David FOX
84 Vice Chanc Enrollment Services ....Ms. Donette STEWART
28 Chief Diversity Officer ....Vacant
08 Dean Library ....Ms. Frieda M. DAVISON
37 Director Financial Aid ....Ms. Bonnie C. CARSON
29 Director of Alumni Relations ....Mr. Joshua JONES
102 Director Dev & Found Scholarships ....Vacant
40 Director Bookstore ....Mr. Jerry CARROLL
41 Athletic Director ....Mr. Daniel FEIG
18 Director Custodial Services ....Mr. Paul SCHMIDT
19 Dir Public Safety & Chief of Police ....Mr. Klay PETERSON
35 Assoc Vice Chanc Student Engagement ....Ms. Khrystal SMITH
39 Dir Housing Residential Life ....Ms. Julie MCMAHON
23 Director Health Services ....Ms. Mary BUCHER
09 Director of Planning and Research ....Ms. Sammara EVANS
88 Dir for Fitness and Campus Rec ....Mr. Mark RITTER
22 Dir Disability Services ....Ms. Wendy WOODSBY
114 Budget Director ....Ms. Vintress BROWN
22 Dir Equal Opp & Employee Relations ....Vacant
104 Dir Center for International Stds ....Dr. Deryle HOPE
106 Dir Distance Education ....Dr. David MCCURRY
88 Dir Ctr Teaching Excellence ....Dr. June CARTER
108 Dir Inst Effectiveness & Compliance ....Vacant
15 Director of Human Resources ....Ms. Dagmara BRUCE
88 Int Dir of African American Studies ....Dr. Warren CARSON

Voorhees College (B)

PO Box 678, Denmark SC 29042-0678
County: Bamberg FICE Identification: 003455
Unit ID: 218919
Telephone: (803) 780-1234 Carnegie Class: Bac-Diverse
FAX Number: (803) 780-1015 Calendar System: Semester
URL: www.voorhees.edu
Established: 1897 Annual Undergrad Tuition & Fees: $12,630
Enrollment: 368 Coed
Affiliation or Control: Protestant Episcopal IRS Status: 501(c)3
Highest Offering: Master's
Accreditation: SC, ACBSP

01 President ....Dr. Ronnie HOPKINS
05 Int Provost/VP Academic Affairs ....Dr. Damara HIGHTOWER-MITCHELL
10 VP Fiscal/Business Affairs ....Mrs. V. Diane O'BERRY
111 VP Inst Advancement & Development ....Dr. Prince BROWN
32 Vice President Student Affairs ....Ms. Charlene JOHNSON
84 VP Enrollment Management ....Ms. Phyllis THOMPSON
13 Interim Chief Technology Officer ....Mr. John STEWART
100 Interim Chief of Staff ....Ms. Karen COUNTZ
06 Registrar ....Ms. Felicia MASON-GARNER
32 Dean of Students ....Mr. Adrian WEST
37 Director of Financial Aid ....Mr. Augusta KITCHEN
35 Director Student Support Services ....Ms. Lynda JEFFERSON
08 Director of Library Services ....Mr. Herman MASON, JR.
18 Int Director Facilities Management ....Mr. George ELMORE
29 Director Alumni Affairs/ Development ....Ms. Stephanie RIVERS-KLUTTZ
88 Spec Asst to Pres Innov/Spec Init ....Mr. Kimoni HICKMAN

31 Director Community Relations ....Mr. Willie JEFFERSON
19 Director of Campus Safety/Security ....Mr. Shawn HALE
23 Director of Health Services ....Ms. Suzanne WILLIAMS
41 Director of Athletics ....Ms. Charlene JOHNSON
07 Director of Admissions/Recruitment ....Mr. Ricky SYNDAB
15 Director of Human Resources ....Mrs. Constance COLTER-BRABHAM
39 Director Housing & Residential Life ....Ms. Allison CLARK
40 Campus Store Clerk ....Mr. Travis FREDRICK

Williamsburg Technical College (C)

601 Martin Luther King, Jr. Avenue, Kingstree SC 29556-4103
County: Williamsburg FICE Identification: 009322
Unit ID: 218955
Telephone: (843) 355-4110 Carnegie Class: Assoc/HVT-High Non
FAX Number: (843) 355-4296 Calendar System: Semester
URL: www.wiltech.edu
Established: 1969 Annual Undergrad Tuition & Fees (In-District): $4,800
Enrollment: 635 Coed
Affiliation or Control: State/Local IRS Status: 501(c)3
Highest Offering: Associate Degree
Accreditation: SC, NAEYC

01 President ....Dr. Patricia A. LEE
10 VP Administration & Finance ....Ms. Melissa A. COKER
05 VP for Academic/Student Affairs ....Dr. Clifton R. ELLIOTT
09 Director of Planning and Research ....Ms. Veronica G. JACKSON
18 Assoc VP for Facilities Management ....Mr. Tyrone THOMAS
32 Assoc VP for Student Affairs ....Dr. Alexis W. DUBOSE
20 Assoc VP for Academic Affairs ....Dr. Gayle TREMBLE
103 Dir of Workforce Dev/Cont Education ....Vacant
08 Library Director ....Dr. Brandolyn LOVE
37 Director of Financial Aid ....Mrs. Jean BOOS
13 Director MIS ....Mr. Strong ROBERT
07 Director of Admissions/Advisement ....Ms. Cheryl DUBOSE
26 Director of Public Relations ....Ms. Rebecca BRADFORD
21 Comptroller ....Ms. Suzanna PUSHIA
15 Human Resources Manager ....Mrs. Jennifer STRONG
40 Bookstore Manager/Purchasing Agent ....Mrs. Monica ELLIOTT

Winthrop University (D)

Oakland Avenue, Rock Hill SC 29733-0001
County: York FICE Identification: 003456
Unit ID: 218964
Telephone: (803) 323-2211 Carnegie Class: Masters/L
FAX Number: N/A Calendar System: Semester
URL: www.winthrop.edu
Established: 1886 Annual Undergrad Tuition & Fees (In-State): $15,836
Enrollment: 5,576 Coed
Affiliation or Control: State IRS Status: 501(c)3
Highest Offering: Beyond Master's But Less Than Doctorate
Accreditation: SC, ART, CAATE, CACREP, CAEP, CIDA, COSMA, DANCE, DIETD, DIETI, EXSC, JOUR, MUS, SW, THEA

01 President ....Dr. Edward A. SERNA
05 Interim Provost ....Dr. Peter J. JUDGE
10 Vice Pres Finance & Business/CFO ....Mr. Justin T. OATES
111 Interim VP Inst Advancement ....Dr. Jack DEROCHI
32 Vice President for Student Affairs ....Ms. Sheila BURKHALTER
84 VP Enrollment Management/Marketing ....Mr. Joseph C. MILLER
100 VP/Chief of Staff ....Dr. Kimberly A. FAUST
19 Interim Chief Campus Police ....Mr. Charles S. YEARTA
20 Vice Prov Acad Quality/Innovation ....Dr. Meg WEBBER
88 Asst VP Curriculum/Program Support ....Mr. Tim DRUEKE
13 Asst VP Computing/Information Tech ....Mr. Patrice BRUNEAU
21 Assistant VP Finance ....Mr. Jeremy C. WHITAKER
18 Associate VP Facilities Management ....Mr. James J. GRIGG
15 VP Human Res/Empl Div & Wellness ....Ms. Lisa COWART
26 Assoc VP Univ Comm/Marketing ....Ms. Ellen M. WILDER-BYRD
58 Acting Dean Graduate School ....Dr. Greg OAKES
49 Dean College Arts & Science ....Dr. Takita SUMTER
50 Dean College Business Admin ....Dr. P.N SAKSENA
53 Dean College of Education ....Dr. Beth COSTNER
64 Interim Dean Col Visual/Perf Arts ....Ms. Karen OREMUS
08 Dean Library Services ....Ms. Kaetrena D. KENDRICK
97 Interim Dean University College ....Dr. Leigh POOLE
35 Dean of Students ....Vacant
41 Athletic Director ....Mr. Chuck REY
06 Registrar ....Ms. Gina G. JONES
07 Director Admissions Ops & Systems ....Mr. David ROLLINGS
37 Director of Financial Aid ....Ms. Michelle HARE
39 Interim Director Residence Life ....Mr. Howard SEIDLER
36 Director Career Dev & Internships ....Dr. Nina GRANT
96 Senior Procurement Officer ....Ms. Melissa O. MIMS
23 Director Health/Counseling Services ....Ms. Jackie CONCODORA
85 Director International Center ....Dr. Leigh POOLE
29 Exec Dir Alumni Rels/Annual Giving ....Ms. Lori TUTTLE
110 Advancement Services Manager ....Ms. Katherine LANGER
105 Director Web Development ....Mr. James U. RAY
106 Director of Online Learning ....Dr. Kimarie WHETSTONE
104 Study Abroad Advisor ....Ms. Taylor EVANS
108 Exec Dir Inst Effective/Dir Assess ....Dr. Noreen GAUBATZ
28 Assoc VP HR & Director of Diversity ....Ms. Zantrell Y. JONES
04 Assistant to the President ....Ms. Tammie C. PHILLIPS
102 Dir Foundation/Corporate Relations ....Ms. Robin EMBRY
09 Director Institutional Research ....Ms. Maria LINN

Wofford College (E)

429 N Church Street, Spartanburg SC 29303-3663
County: Spartanburg FICE Identification: 003457
Unit ID: 218973
Telephone: (864) 597-4000 Carnegie Class: Bac-A&S
FAX Number: (864) 597-4018 Calendar System: 4/1/4
URL: www.wofford.edu
Established: 1854 Annual Undergrad Tuition & Fees: $47,650
Enrollment: 1,764 Coed
Affiliation or Control: United Methodist IRS Status: 501(c)3
Highest Offering: Baccalaureate
Accreditation: SC

01 President ....Dr. Nayef H. SAMHAT
10 Chief Financial Officer ....Mr. Christopher L. GARDNER
05 Interim Provost ....Dr. Timothy J. SCHMITZ
111 Int Sr Vice Pres for Advancement ....Mr. Calhoun L. KENNEDY
11 Sr Vice Pres for Administration ....Mr. David M. BEACHAM
32 VP for Student Affairs/Dean Stdnts ....Ms. Roberta HURLEY
13 CIO/Assoc VP Information Services ....Dr. Baz ABOUDENEIN
84 Vice President for Enrollment ....Mr. Brand R. STILLE
18 Assoc VP Facilities/Cap Projects ....Mr. Jason H. BURR
21 Assoc VP for Finance and Controller ....Mr. Chris L. GARDNER
37 AVP Enrollment/Dir Financial Aid ....Ms. Carolyn B. SPARKS
08 Dean of Library ....Ms. Elizabeth ROBERTS
82 Dean of International Programs ....Ms. Amy E. LANCASTER
23 Assoc Dean Students/Dir Health Svcs ....Ms. Beth D. WALLACE
20 Associate Academic Officer ....Dr. Dan B. MATHEWSON
04 Exec Admin Asst to President ....Ms. Tonya K. BRYSON
41 Director of Athletics ....Mr. Richard A. JOHNSON
06 College Registrar ....Ms. Jennifer R. ALLISON
42 Chaplain ....Rev.Dr. Ronald R. ROBINSON
26 Dir for Marketing/Communications ....Ms. Crystal CRAWFORD
15 Director of Human Resources ....Ms. Chee J. LEE
07 Director of Admissions ....Ms. Megan TYLER
09 Director of Institutional Research ....Mr. Raymond H. RUFF, III
101 Secretary to the Board of Trustees ....Mr. David M. BEACHAM
108 Dir Institutional Effectiveness ....Dr. Ben J. BRYAN
38 Director Student Counseling ....Ms. Perry V. HENSON
19 Director Campus Safety ....Col. James R. HALL
28 Dir Diversity/Inclusion/Title IX ....Mr. Matthew K. HAMMETT
29 Director Alumni & Parents ....Mr. Thomas M. HENSON, JR.
36 Exec Dir The Space Career Center ....Mr. P. Curtis MCPHAIL
39 Asst Dean of Students for Res Life ....Mr. Brian J. LEMERE
44 Director Gift Planning ....Ms. Lisa H. DE FREITAS
96 Director Business Srvs/Risk Mgmt ....Mr. Daniel P. DEETER
22 Chief Equity Officer ....Dr. Dwain C. PRUITT

York Technical College (F)

452 S Anderson Road, Rock Hill SC 29730-3395
County: York FICE Identification: 003996
Unit ID: 218991
Telephone: (803) 327-8000 Carnegie Class: Assoc/MT-VT-High Trad
FAX Number: (803) 327-8059 Calendar System: Semester
URL: www.yorktech.edu
Established: 1964 Annual Undergrad Tuition & Fees (In-State): $5,395
Enrollment: 4,178 Coed
Affiliation or Control: State IRS Status: 501(c)3
Highest Offering: Associate Degree
Accreditation: SC, ACBSP, ADNUR, DA, DH, MLTAD, NAEYC, PNUR, RAD, SURGT

01 President ....Dr. Stacey MOORE
05 EVP Academic/Student Affairs ....Dr. Jamie COOPER
10 Interim VP Business Services ....Mr. Gary MCCOMBS
111 Vice President for Advancement ....Ms. Melanie E. JONES
50 Assoc VP Business/Computer/AA/AS ....Vacant
76 Assoc VP Health & Human Services ....Ms. Phoebe COQUEREL
54 Assoc Dean Industry/Engineer Tech ....Mr. Michael MCCLAIN
103 Asst VP Economic/Workforce Dev ....Ms. Sonia YOUNG
15 Asst Vice Pres of Human Resources ....Ms. Edwina ROSEBORO-BARNES
08 Head Librarian ....Ms. Esther BURGESS
35 Dean for Student Engagement ....Mr. James ROBSON
09 Director of Institutional Research ....Dr. Mary Beth SCHWARTZ
37 Director Compliance/Financial Aid ....Vacant
13 Information Services Director ....Mr. Richard PARTRIDGE
19 Chief Campus Security ....Mr. Bryan L. MCDOUGALD
18 Facilities Management Director ....Mr. Robert L. BROWN
06 Registrar ....Vacant
26 Director of Strategic Communication ....Vacant
07 Director Admissions ....Ms. Lydia HALL

SOUTH DAKOTA

Augustana University (G)

2001 S Summit, Sioux Falls SD 57197-0001
County: Minnehaha FICE Identification: 003458
Unit ID: 219000
Telephone: (605) 274-0770 Carnegie Class: Masters/M
FAX Number: (605) 274-5299 Calendar System: 4/1/4
URL: www.augie.edu
Established: 1860 Annual Undergrad Tuition & Fees: $35,884
Enrollment: 2,019 Coed
Affiliation or Control: Evangelical Lutheran Church In America
IRS Status: 501(c)3
Highest Offering: Doctorate
Accreditation: HLC, ART, CAATE, MUS, NURSE

01 President .... Ms. Stephanie HERSETH SANDLIN
05 Sr VP Academic Affairs/Provost .... Dr. Colin IRVINE
100 Chief of Staff .... Ms. Pamela MILLER
10 Vice Pres Finance/Administration .... Mr. Shannan NELSON
15 Vice President of Human Resources .... Ms. Deanna VERSTEEG
21 Assoc Vice President/Controller .... Ms. Carol SPILLUM
07 Assoc VP for Enrollment Mgmt .... Mr. Joel MUNZA
18 Assoc VP for University Services .... Mr. Rick TUPPER
32 Dean of Students .... Mr. Mark BLACKBURN
13 Director of IT .... Mr. Daniel D. DRENKOW
37 Director of Financial Aid .... Ms. Tresse EVENSON
08 Director of Library .... Ms. Ronelle THOMPSON
84 Asst Vice President for Enrollment .... Mr. Adam HEINITZ
30 Asst VP for Development .... Mr. Jon MAMMENGA
41 Athletic Director .... Mr. Josh MORTON
06 Registrar/Asst Dean of Instr Pgm .... Ms. Joni KRUEGER
121 Asst Vice Provost Student Success .... Ms. Billie STREUFERT
104 Director of Intl Pgm/Enrollment .... Mr. Ben IVERSON
20 Asst Vice Provost Acad Excellence .... Mr. Jay KAHL
28 Chief Diversity Officer .... Ms. Willette CAPERS
29 Sr Director Alumni Engagement .... Mr. Joel GACKLE
04 Exec Assistant to the President .... Ms. Teresa MOORE
53 Dean of Education .... Dr. Laurie DAILY
64 Dean of School of Music .... Dr. Peter FOLLIARD
09 Asst VP Enterprise Data Analytics .... Ms. Suzanne SMITH
45 Chief Strategy Officer & Exec VP .... Ms. Pamela HOMAN

Dakota Wesleyan University (A)

1200 W University, Mitchell SD 57301-4398
County: Davison FICE Identification: 003461
Unit ID: 219091
Telephone: (605) 995-2600 Carnegie Class: Bac-Diverse
FAX Number: (605) 995-2699 Calendar System: Semester
URL: www.dwu.edu
Established: 1885 Annual Undergrad Tuition & Fees: $29,770
Enrollment: 933 Coed
Affiliation or Control: United Methodist IRS Status: 501(c)3
Highest Offering: Master's
Accreditation: HLC, CAATE, IACBE, NURSE

01 President .... Dr. Daniel KITTLE
10 Executive Vice President/CFO .... Ms. Theresa KRIESE
05 Provost .... Dr. Joseph ROIDT
07 VP Admissions/Mktg/Communications .... Ms. Fredel THOMAS
111 VP for Institutional Advancement .... Ms. Kitty ALLEN
26 Dir of Marketing & Communications .... Ms. Jan LARSON
06 Registrar .... Mr. Stuart KEENAN
88 Dir Kelley Ctr for Entrepreneurship .... Ms. Rhonda POLE
88 Executive Director McGovern Center .... Dr. Joel ALLEN
08 Director of the McGovern Library .... Ms. Alexis BECKER
29 Director of Alumni Relations .... Mr. Jory HANSEN
37 Director of Financial Aid .... Ms. Mary ALEXANDER
15 Director of Human Resources .... Ms. Janet HAYEN
42 Campus Pastor .... Rev. Eric VAN METER
41 Director of Athletics .... Mr. Jon HART
18 Director of Physical Plant .... Mr. Louis SCHOENFELDER
32 Director of Student Life .... Mr. Tom HOEK
80 Dean Col Ldrshp & Pub Service .... Dr. Anne KELLY
20 Associate Provost .... Dr. Derek DRIEDGER
88 Director of PCL Program .... Dr. Alisha VINCENT
79 Dean College Arts & Humanities .... Dr. Vince REDDER
76 Dean Col Health/Fitness & Science .... Dr. Bethany MELROE LEHRMAN
04 Exec Admin Asst to Pres/Provost .... Ms. Emily GEORGE
50 Chair of Business .... Ms. Christine MAUSZYCKI
53 Chair of Education .... Dr. Ashley DIGMANN
13 Chief Info Technology Officer (CIO) .... Mr. Travis WALZ
50 Director of Business Grad Program .... Dr. Diana GOLDAMMER
53 Coord of Master of Arts in Educ .... Ms. Melissa WEBER
88 Co-Dir of Master of Ath Training .... Dr. Dan WAGNER
88 Co-Dir of Master of Ath Training .... Dr. Lana LOKEN
66 Administrative Chair of Nursing .... Dr. Penny TILTON
39 Dir Resident Life/Student Housing .... Mr. Dustin WHEELER

Institute of Lutheran Theology (B)

PO Box 833, Brookings SD 57006
County: Brookings Identification: 667318
Telephone: (605) 692-9337 Carnegie Class: Not Classified
FAX Number: N/A Calendar System: Semester
URL: www.ilt.edu
Established: 2009 Annual Undergrad Tuition & Fees: N/A
Enrollment: N/A Coed
Affiliation or Control: Independent Non-Profit IRS Status: 501(c)3
Highest Offering: Doctorate
Accreditation: BI

01 President .... Dr. Dennis BIELFELDT
03 Executive Vice President .... Mr. Leon MILES
84 Director of Enrollment Services .... Mr. Joel WILLIAMS
10 Director of Business Services .... Ms. Kelli ANAWSKI
08 Librarian .... Rev. David PATTERSON

John Witherspoon College (C)

4024 Sheridan Lake Road, Rapid City SD 57702
County: Pennington Identification: 667246
Telephone: (605) 342-0317 Carnegie Class: Not Classified
FAX Number: N/A Calendar System: Semester
URL: www.jwc.edu
Established: 2004 Annual Undergrad Tuition & Fees: N/A
Enrollment: N/A Coed
Affiliation or Control: Independent Non-Profit IRS Status: 501(c)3
Highest Offering: Baccalaureate
Accreditation: TRACS

01 President .... Dr. Ronald J. LEWIS
05 Chief Academic Officer .... Mr. Edwin C. EGBERT
00 Chairman of the Board .... Dr. Donald E. OLIVER
10 Chief Financial Officer .... Mrs. Carol B. HARRIS
08 Director of Learning Resources .... Mrs. Megan R. FERGUSON
88 Coordinator of Learning Resources .... Ms. Michelle C. PORTER
06 Registrar .... Mrs. Pamela S. RIDER
07 Director of Admissions .... Mrs. Rebecca E. PONTIOUS
125 President Emeritus/Chancellor .... Dr. C. Richard WELLS

Lake Area Technical College (D)

1201 Arrow Avenue, PO Box 730, Watertown SD 57201-2869
County: Codington FICE Identification: 005309
Unit ID: 219143
Telephone: (605) 882-5284 Carnegie Class: Assoc/HVT-High Trad
FAX Number: (605) 882-6299 Calendar System: Semester
URL: www.lakeareatech.edu
Established: 1965 Annual Undergrad Tuition & Fees (In-District): $6,862
Enrollment: 2,217 Coed
Affiliation or Control: Local IRS Status: Exempt
Highest Offering: Associate Degree
Accreditation: HLC, ADNUR, DA, EMT, MAC, MLTAD, OTA, PNUR, PTAA

01 President .... Mr. Michael D. CARTNEY
03 Vice President .... Ms. Diane STILES
32 Director of Student Services .... Ms. LuAnn STRAIT
84 Director of Enrollment .... Mr. Eric SCHULTZ
37 Director of Financial Aid .... Ms. Marlene SEEKLANDER
05 Dean of Academics .... Ms. Barb KLEINJAN
13 Director of Information Technology .... Ms. Christi CHANEY
30 Foundation Director .... Ms. Tracy BUISKER
108 Assessment Coordinator .... Ms. Jen HOWARD
103 Director of Corporate Education .... Ms. Terri CORDREY
88 Director of Outreach .... Mr. Shane SWENSON
25 Grant Writer & Compliance Manager .... Ms. Jennifer SEVERSON
08 Librarian .... Vacant
38 Counselor .... Ms. Jessi WHETSEL
121 Student Support & Equity Coord .... Ms. Stephanie TRAVERSIE
40 Interim Bookstore Manager .... Mr. Darrin CHRISTENSEN

Mitchell Technical College (E)

1800 E Spruce, Mitchell SD 57301-2002
County: Davison FICE Identification: 008284
Unit ID: 219189
Telephone: (605) 995-3025 Carnegie Class: Assoc/HVT-High Trad
FAX Number: (605) 995-3083 Calendar System: Semester
URL: www.mitchelltech.edu
Established: 1968 Annual Undergrad Tuition & Fees (In-District): $7,359
Enrollment: 1,162 Coed
Affiliation or Control: State/Local IRS Status: 501(c)3
Highest Offering: Associate Degree
Accreditation: HLC, ACFEI, MAC, MLTAD, RAD, RTT

01 President .... Mr. Mark WILSON
11 VP of Operations & Human Resources .... Mr. Scott FOSSUM
05 Vice President for Academics .... Dr. Carol GRODE-HANKS
84 Vice Pres for Enrollment Services .... Mr. Clayton DEUTER
13 Dean of Technology Systems .... Mr. David BOOS
10 Dean of Financial Operations .... Mr. Jared HOFER
121 Director of Student Success .... Ms. Danita LUCAS
09 Accred & Inst Effectiveness Dir .... Ms. Marla SMITH
18 Buildings & Grounds Director .... Mr. John SIEVERDING
102 Director of Foundation Relations .... Mr. Nick BAKHTIARI
06 Registrar .... Ms. Jill GREENWAY
37 Director Student Financial Aid .... Ms. Morgan HUBER
105 Marketing Director .... Mr. Bob KOBERNUSZ
07 Director of Enrollment .... Ms. Hillary VINING
36 Dir Career Svcs & Advising .... Ms. Janet GREENWAY

Mount Marty University (F)

1105 W 8th, Yankton SD 57078-3724
County: Yankton FICE Identification: 003465
Unit ID: 219198
Telephone: (605) 668-1545 Carnegie Class: Masters/S
FAX Number: N/A Calendar System: Semester
URL: www.mountmarty.edu
Established: 1936 Annual Undergrad Tuition & Fees: $29,136
Enrollment: 1,167 Coed
Affiliation or Control: Roman Catholic IRS Status: 501(c)3
Highest Offering: Doctorate
Accreditation: HLC, ANEST, NURSE

01 President .... Dr. Marcus LONG
101 Assistant to the President .... Ms. Joanna MUELLER
05 Provost/EVP for Academic Affairs .... Dr. William MILLER
10 VP for Finance & Administration .... Ms. Tabitha LIKNESS
111 VP for Mission & Advancement .... Ms. Barb REZAC
32 VP for Student Success .... Dr. Katie HARRELL
18 Vice President for Operations .... Mr. Chad ALTWINE
09 Director of Inst Effectiveness .... Ms. Kristen WELKER
66 Dean of Faculty/Nursing/Health Sci .... Dr. Kathy MAGORIAN
42 Director of Campus Ministry .... Ms. Jayne ARENS
12 Director of Watertown Location .... Ms. Kim BELLUM
37 Director Student Financial Aid .... Mr. Ken KOCER
06 Registrar .... Ms. Jonna SUPURGECI
13 AVP Information Technology .... Ms. Rebekah MCCUNE
08 Director of Library .... Ms. Sandra BROWN
40 Dir Bookstore/Central Scheduling .... Ms. Becky LUELLMAN
36 Dir of Career Services .... Mr. Todd SCHLIMGEN
41 Athletic Director .... Mr. Andy BERNATOW
15 Director of Human Resources .... Mr. Lane SPEIRS
44 Director of Annual Giving .... Ms. Abby KAISER
29 Director Alumni & Parent Relations .... Ms. Johanna JABLONOSKI
84 AVP for Enrollment/Dir Admission .... Mr. Greg FRANZ
88 Assistant to the EVP & Provost .... Ms. Joanna MUELLER
19 Dir of Campus Security .... Mr. Zachary HOOVER

National American University (G)

PO Box 677, Rapid City SD 57709
County: Pennington FICE Identification: 004057
Unit ID: 219204
Telephone: (605) 721-5200 Carnegie Class: DU-Mod
FAX Number: (605) 721-5241 Calendar System: Quarter
URL: www.national.edu
Established: 1941 Annual Undergrad Tuition & Fees: $14,985
Enrollment: 1,440 Coed
Affiliation or Control: Proprietary IRS Status: Proprietary
Highest Offering: Doctorate
Accreditation: HLC, CAHIIM, IACBE

01 Chief Executive Officer/President .... Dr. Ronald SHAPE
05 Provost & Chief Academic Officer .... Dr. Cindy MATHENA
10 Chief Financial Officer .... Mr. Thomas BICKART
11 COO .... Mr. Mark MENDOZA
37 Director Financial Aid .... Ms. Cheryl BULLINGER
08 Librarian .... Ms. Marsha STACEY
15 Director of Human Resources .... Mr. Gordon BROOKS

Oglala Lakota College (H)

Box 490, Kyle SD 57752-0490
County: Oglala Lakota FICE Identification: 014659
Unit ID: 219277
Telephone: (605) 455-6000 Carnegie Class: Tribal
FAX Number: (605) 455-2787 Calendar System: Semester
URL: www.olc.edu
Established: 1971 Annual Undergrad Tuition & Fees: $2,684
Enrollment: 1,251 Coed
Affiliation or Control: Tribal Control IRS Status: 501(c)3
Highest Offering: Master's
Accreditation: HLC, CNEA, SW

01 President .... Mr. Thomas H. SHORTBULL
05 Vice President for Instruction .... Dr. Dawn FRANK
10 Vice President for Business .... Ms. Julie JOHNSON
06 Registrar .... Ms. Leslie MESTETH
08 Director Learning Resources .... Ms. Sharon JANIS
15 Personnel Director .... Ms. Faith RICHARDS
37 Financial Aid Director .... Ms. Cheryce GULLIKSON
84 Director Enrollment Management .... Ms. Corey STOVER
07 Director of Admissions .... Ms. Leslie MESTETH
09 Director of Institutional Research .... Ms. Susanne AUER
29 Director Alumni Relations .... Ms. Marilyn POURIER
89 Director of Freshman Studies .... Ms. Susanne AUER
13 MIS Director .... Mr. Cliff DELONG
32 Director Student Affairs .... Mr. Don GIAGO
30 Director of Development .... Ms. Marilyn POURIER
51 Community/Cont Education Coord .... Ms. Kateri MONTILEAUX
81 Applied Science Department Chair .... Mr. David WHITE BULL
81 Math & Science Department Chair .... Ms. Karla WITT
49 Art & History Department Chair .... Ms. Kim BETTELYOUN
53 Education Department Chair .... Ms. Shannon AMIOTTE
66 Nursing Department Chair .... Ms. Michelle BRUNS
83 Social Work Department Chair .... Ms. Monique APPLE
88 LAKOTA Studies Department Chair .... Ms. Karen LONE HILL
18 Chief Facilities/Physical Plant .... Mr. Tony WARD

Presentation College (I)

1500 N Main Street, Aberdeen SD 57401-1280
County: Brown FICE Identification: 003467
Unit ID: 219295
Telephone: (605) 225-1634 Carnegie Class: Bac-Diverse
FAX Number: (605) 229-8330 Calendar System: Semester
URL: www.presentation.edu
Established: 1951 Annual Undergrad Tuition & Fees: $21,375
Enrollment: 625 Coed
Affiliation or Control: Roman Catholic IRS Status: 501(c)3
Highest Offering: Master's
Accreditation: HLC, IACBE, NURSE, RAD

01 President .... Dr. Paula LANGTEAU
05 Vice Pres for Academics .... Vacant
10 Vice Pres for Finance .... Dr. Daisy HALVORSON
84 Vice Pres for SAEM .... Dr. Marcus GARSTECKI
111 Vice President for Advancement .... Mr. Matthew BLAIR
06 Registrar .... Vacant
37 Director Student Financial Aid .... Ms. Amber BROCKEL
108 Assessment Coordinator .... Dr. Nancy VANDER HOEK
15 Director of Human Resources .... Dr. Jason PETTIGREW
04 Administrative Asst to President .... Ms. Stacy BAUER
26 Dir of Marketing/Public Relations .... Mr. Andy HANSEN
07 Director of Admissions .... Ms. India KLIPFEL
09 Director of Institutional Research .... Vacant
29 Director Alumni Relations .... Vacant
39 Director Student Housing .... Mr. DJ MOUNGA
41 Athletic Director .... Mr. Daniel GARRETT

Sinte Gleska University (A)

PO Box 105, Mission SD 57555-0105

County: Todd FICE Identification: 021437
Unit ID: 219374

Telephone: (605) 856-8100 Carnegie Class: Tribal
FAX Number: (605) 856-4135 Calendar System: Semester
URL: www.sintegleska.edu
Established: 1970 Annual Undergrad Tuition & Fees: $3,154
Enrollment: 438 Coed
Affiliation or Control: Independent Non-Profit IRS Status: 501(c)3
Highest Offering: Master's
Accreditation: HLC

01 President .... Mr. Lionel BORDEAUX
03 Executive Vice President .... Mr. Ted HAMILTON
111 Vice Pres Institutional Advancement .... Ms. Debra BORDEAUX
05 Vice Pres of Academic Affairs .... Ms. Cheryl MEDEARIS
11 Vice Pres General Administration .... Ms. Cheryl WHIRLWIND SOLDIER
10 CFO/VP Finance .... Ms. Carole GREGG
06 Registrar .... Mr. Jack HERMAN
08 Int Library Director .... Ms. Diana DILLON
37 Director Financial Aid/Admissions .... Mr. Midas GUNHAMMER
55 Director Adult Education .... Mr. Sherman MARSHALL, II
15 Director Human Resources .... Vacant

Sioux Falls Seminary (B)

2100 S Summit Avenue, Sioux Falls SD 57105-2729

County: Minnehaha FICE Identification: 004056
Unit ID: 219240

Telephone: (605) 336-6588 Carnegie Class: Spec-4-yr-Faith
FAX Number: (605) 335-9090 Calendar System: 4/1/4
URL: www.kairos.edu
Established: 1858 Annual Undergrad Tuition & Fees: $3,600
Enrollment: 508 Coed
Affiliation or Control: North American Baptist IRS Status: 501(c)3
Highest Offering: Doctorate
Accreditation: HLC, THEOL

01 President .... Mr. Gregory J. HENSON
05 Chief Academic Officer & Dean .... Dr. Larry W. CALDWELL
10 CFO and VP of Operations .... Mr. Nathan M. HELLING
26 Chief Creative Ofcr/VP Proj Design .... Ms. Shanda L. STRICHERZ
84 Kairos Enrollment Advisor .... Ms. LaNeil R. BARTELL
88 Dir of Luther House of Study .... Dr. Chris M. CROGHAN
88 Dir of Wesley House of Study .... Dr. Steve A. TREFZ
06 Registrar .... Ms. Brandi POHLMEIER
07 Enrollment Advisor .... Mr. Chad SMITH

Sisseton-Wahpeton College (C)

PO Box 689, Sisseton SD 57262-0689

County: Roberts FICE Identification: 022773
Unit ID: 219408

Telephone: (605) 698-3966 Carnegie Class: Tribal
FAX Number: (605) 698-3132 Calendar System: Semester
URL: https://www.swcollege.edu/
Established: 1979 Annual Undergrad Tuition & Fees (In-District): $4,510
Enrollment: 125 Coed
Affiliation or Control: Local IRS Status: 501(c)3
Highest Offering: Baccalaureate
Accreditation: HLC

01 President .... Dr. Lane AZURE
05 Dean of Academics .... Dr. Julie BUCKMAN
10 Comptroller .... Ms. Rhonda LABATTE
37 Financial Aid Director .... Mr. Sylvan FLUTE
07 Admissions Director .... Ms. Rachael FUENTES
66 Director Nursing .... Ms. Nola RAGAN
32 Dean of Students .... Mr. Vince OWEN
13 Director Information Technology .... Mr. Derrick LAWRENCE
18 Facilities Manager .... Mr. Russell EBERHARDT
06 Registrar .... Vacant
09 Director Institutional Research .... Mr. Scott MORGAN

*South Dakota State Board of Regents System Office (D)

306 E Capitol Avenue, Suite 200, Pierre SD 57501-2545

County: Hughes FICE Identification: 033438
Telephone: (605) 773-3455 Carnegie Class: N/A
FAX Number: (605) 773-5320
URL: www.sdbor.edu

01 Executive Director & CEO .... Dr. Brian MAHER
00 Board President .... Ms. Pamela ROBERTS
10 System VP Finance & Administration .... Ms. Heather FORNEY
05 System VP Academic Affairs .... Dr. Janice MINDER
100 Chief of Staff .... Mr. Nathan LUKKES
15 System Director of Human Resources .... Ms. Kayla BASTIAN
26 System Director of Communications .... Ms. Shuree MORTENSON
09 System Dir Institutional Research .... Ms. Wendy CAVENY
13 System CIO .... Mr. David HANSEN
20 System Assoc VP of Academic Affairs .... Dr. Pamela CARRIVEAU
116 System Internal Auditor .... Vacant

*The University of South Dakota (E)

414 E Clark, Vermillion SD 57069-2390

County: Clay FICE Identification: 003474
Unit ID: 219471

Telephone: (605) 677-5011 Carnegie Class: DU-Higher
FAX Number: (605) 677-5073 Calendar System: Semester
URL: www.usd.edu
Established: 1862 Annual Undergrad Tuition & Fees (In-State): $9,332
Enrollment: 9,459 Coed
Affiliation or Control: State IRS Status: 501(c)3
Highest Offering: Doctorate
Accreditation: HLC, ARCPA, ART, AUD, CACREP, CAEP, CLPSY, DH, EMT, JOUR, LAW, MED, MUS, NURSE, OT, PH, PTA, SP, SPAA, SW, THEA

02 President .... Ms. Sheila K. GESTRING
05 Provost/VP Academic Affairs .... Dr. Kurt HACKEMER
17 VP Health Affairs/Dean Med School .... Dr. Timothy RIDGWAY
10 Vice Pres Administration/Finance .... Ms. JoAnn KUNKEL
46 VP Research/Sponsored Programs .... Dr. Daniel ENGEBRETSON
26 VP Marketing/Enroll Svcs/Univ Rels .... Mr. Scott POHLSON
32 VP Student Svcs & Dean of Students .... Dr. Kimberly GRIEVE
15 Chief Human Resources Officer .... Mr. Warren TOLLEY
13 Chief Information Officer .... Ms. Cheryl TIAHRT
102 President/CEO Univ Foundation .... Mr. Steve BROWN
28 Int Associate VP of Diversity .... Mr. Travis LETELLIER
18 Asst VP Facilities Management .... Mr. Brian LIMOGES
09 AVP Inst Research/Plng/Assessment .... Mr. Daniel PALMER
20 Assoc Provost .... Dr. Lisa BONNEAU
12 Exec Dir University Ctr Sioux Falls .... Vacant
100 Chief of Staff .... Ms. Laura MCNAUGHTON
43 General Counsel .... Mr. AJ FRANKEN
96 Director of Auxiliary Services .... Mr. Darby GANSCHOW
08 Dean of Libraries .... Mr. Daniel R. DAILY
36 Dir Ctr for Academic & Career Plng .... Mr. Steve WARD
37 Director of Financial Aid .... Ms. Lindsay MILLER
41 Director Athletics .... Mr. David HERBSTER
19 Dir University Police Department .... Mr. Bryant JACKSON
06 Registrar .... Ms. Jennifer M. THOMPSON
84 Dean of Enrollment .... Mr. Mark PETTY
49 Int Dean College Arts & Sciences .... Dr. John DUDLEY
50 Dean School of Business .... Dr. Venky VENKATACHALAM
53 Dean School of Education .... Dr. Amy SCHWEINLE
57 Dean College Fine Arts .... Dr. Bruce KELLEY
61 Dean School of Law .... Mr. Neil FULTON
58 Dean Graduate School .... Dr. Beth FREEBURG
76 Dean School of Health Sciences .... Dr. Haifa ABOUSAMRA
04 Assistant to the President .... Ms. Niki SMIDT
22 Director EEO/Chief Title IX Officer .... Ms. Jean MERKLE

*Black Hills State University (F)

1200 University Street #9500, Spearfish SD 57799-9500

County: Lawrence FICE Identification: 003459
Unit ID: 219046

Telephone: (605) 642-6111 Carnegie Class: Masters/S
FAX Number: (605) 642-6763 Calendar System: Semester
URL: www.bhsu.edu
Established: 1883 Annual Undergrad Tuition & Fees (In-State): $8,672
Enrollment: 3,608 Coed
Affiliation or Control: State IRS Status: 501(c)3
Highest Offering: Master's
Accreditation: HLC, CAEP, MUS

02 President .... Dr. Laurie NICHOLS
05 Provost/Vice Pres Academic Affairs .... Dr. Jon KILPINEN
10 Vice President Finance/Admin .... Ms. Kathy J. JOHNSON
111 Vice Pres University Advancement .... Mr. Steve L. MEEKER
84 VP for Enrollment Management .... Dr. John ALLRED
26 Int Sr Director of Marketing .... Ms. Becca WALTERS
13 Data Processing Supervisor .... Ms. Roxy SCHMIT
37 Director Student Financial Aid .... Ms. Gail JOHNSON
38 Director Counseling Center .... Vacant
22 Title IX Coordinator .... Dr. Breon DERBY
32 Dean of Students .... Dr. Jane KLUG
15 Director of Human Resources .... Ms. Melissa HART
06 Registrar .... Ms. April M. MEEKER
07 Director of Admissions .... Mr. Joe RAINBOTH
21 Director of Business Services .... Mr. Rob HOUDEK
18 Director Facilities/Physical Plant .... Mr. Randy CULVER
29 Director Alumni Relations .... Mr. Tom WHEATON
09 Director of Institutional Research .... Mr. Rich LOOSE
08 Director Library Operations .... Mr. Scott AHOLA
104 Director International Studies .... Ms. Kaitlin PALMER
30 Director of Development .... Ms. Shauna JUNEK
19 Director Security/Safety .... Mr. Philip PESHECK
40 Director University Bookstore .... Mr. Michael JASTORFF
41 Director of Athletics .... Mr. Padriac MCMEEL
14 Director Network & Computer Svcs .... Mr. Fred NELSON
49 Dean College of Liberal Arts .... Dr. Amy FUQUA
50 Dean Col of Business & Natural Sci .... Dr. Cynthia ANDERSON
53 Int Dean Col of Educ/Behavioral Sci .... Dr. Betsy SILVA
04 Administrative Asst to President .... Ms. Nicole KIRSCH
25 Chief Contracts/Grants Admin .... Dr. Cate CALDWELL

*Dakota State University (G)

820 N Washington Avenue, Madison SD 57042-1799

County: Lake FICE Identification: 003463
Unit ID: 219082

Telephone: (888) 378-9988 Carnegie Class: Masters/M
FAX Number: N/A Calendar System: Semester
URL: www.dsu.edu
Established: 1881 Annual Undergrad Tuition & Fees (In-State): $9,536
Enrollment: 3,186 Coed
Affiliation or Control: State IRS Status: 501(c)3
Highest Offering: Doctorate
Accreditation: HLC, ACBSP, CAEP, CAHIIM, COARC

02 President .... Dr. José -Marie GRIFFITHS
04 Executive Assistant .... Ms. Miranda MORRIS
05 Provost & VP Academic Affairs .... Dr. Rebecca HOEY
10 Vice Pres for Business & Admin Svcs .... Mr. Stacy L. KRUSEMARK
32 Vice Pres Student Affairs .... Ms. Amy CRISSINGER
13 CIO .... Mr. Shawn JAACKS
15 Director of Human Resources .... Ms. Deb ROACH
46 VP Research/Economic Dev .... Dr. Ashley PODHRADSKY
41 Director of Athletics .... Mr. Jeff L. DITTMAN
26 Dir Communications & Marketing .... Ms. Kelli KOEPSELL
49 Dean Col of Arts and Sciences .... Dr. David KENLEY
50 Dean Col Business/Info Systems .... Dr. Dorine BENNETT
77 Dean Beacom College .... Dr. Pat ENGEBRETSON
53 Dean College of Education .... Dr. David DEJONG
58 Dean of Graduate Studies .... Dr. Mark HAWKES
108 Dir Institutional Effectiveness .... Dr. Jeanette MCGREEVY
09 Dir Institutional Research .... Ms. Laura CROSS
08 Director of Library .... Ms. Mary FRANCIS
106 Director Online Education .... Ms. Sarah RASMUSSEN
25 Director of Sponsored Programs .... Dr. Pete HOESING
06 Registrar .... Ms. Kathryn CALLIES
21 Controller .... Ms. Amy L. DOCKENDORF
18 Director Facilities Management .... Mr. Corey BRASKAMP
25 Director of Budget & Grants Admin .... Ms. Sara HARE
36 Director Career Services .... Ms. Kelli GREEN
121 Director Student Success .... Ms. Kristen UILK
40 Director of Bookstore .... Ms. Donna FAWBUSH
37 Director Financial Aid .... Ms. Denise R. GRAYSON
07 Director of Admissions .... Ms. Amber SCHMIDT
104 Dir International Programs .... Ms. Nicole CLAUSSEN
14 Chief Tech Officer .... Mr. Brent VAN AARTSEN
91 Dir Admin Computing Services .... Mrs. Stephanie BAATZ
119 Security Engineer .... Mr. Ben CABLE
24 Manager of Multimedia Services .... Mr. Tyler STEELE
111 VP for Institutional Advancement .... Mr. Jon SCHEMMEL
38 Dir Student Counseling .... Ms. Nicole BOWEN
39 Dir of Residence Life .... Ms. Wendi CARLSON-KENLEY

*Northern State University (H)

1200 S Jay Street, Aberdeen SD 57401-7198

County: Brown FICE Identification: 003466
Unit ID: 219259

Telephone: (605) 626-3011 Carnegie Class: Masters/S
FAX Number: (605) 626-3022 Calendar System: Semester
URL: www.northern.edu
Established: 1901 Annual Undergrad Tuition & Fees (In-State): $8,750
Enrollment: 3,431 Coed
Affiliation or Control: State IRS Status: 501(c)3
Highest Offering: Master's
Accreditation: HLC, ACBSP, ART, CACREP, CAEP, CAEPN, MUS

02 President .... Dr. Neal SCHNOOR
05 Provost/VP Academic Affairs .... Dr. Michael WANOUS
10 VP Finance/Administration .... Mrs. Veronica PAULSON
84 VP Enroll Mgmt/Comm/Mktg .... Mr. Justin FRAASE
20 Associate VP Academic Affairs .... Dr. Erin FOUBERG
13 VP Information Technologies/CIO .... Dr. Debbi BUMPOUS
102 President/CEO Foundation .... Mr. Zack FLAKUS
06 Registrar .... Mrs. Peggy HALLSTROM
08 Director Library .... Mr. Robert RUSSELL
38 Director Counseling Center .... Ms. Heather ALDENTALER
09 Dir Inst Research/Assessment .... Dr. Brenda MAMMENGA
37 Director Financial Aid .... Ms. Becky PRIBYL
39 Director Residence Life .... Mr. Martin SABOLO
21 Controller .... Ms. Kay FREDRICK
88 Assistant Controller .... Mr. David KNIGGE
15 Director Human Resources .... Ms. Susan BOSTIAN
18 Director Facilities Management .... Mr. Monte MEHLHOFF
49 Dean College Arts & Science .... Dr. Alyssa KIESOW
88 Assoc Dean College Arts & Sciences .... Dr. Ellizabeth HALLER
50 Dean School of Business .... Dr. Douglas OHMER
53 Dean School of Education .... Dr. Anna SCHWAN
57 Dean School of Fine Arts .... Dr. Kenneth BOULTON
58 Director Graduate Studies .... Dr. Erin FOUBERG
41 Director Athletics .... Mr. Nate DAVIS
96 Purchasing Agent .... Ms. Crystal JOSEPH
92 Director Honors Program .... Dr. Kristi BOCKORNY
85 Director International Programs .... Ms. Dominika BLUM
04 Executive Admin Asst to President .... Ms. Stacy BAUER
104 Coordinator Study Abroad .... Ms. Dominika BLUM
106 Director Online Education .... Mr. Ronald BROWNIE
121 Executive Director Student Success .... Ms. Britt LORENZ
36 Director Student Placement .... Ms. Maggie PENCE
88 Foundation Vice Pres .... Mr. Blake DAY
30 Director Development .... Ms. Aimee BURMESTER
26 Coordinator Marketing/Devel .... Ms. Lauren BITTNER
32 Dean of Students .... Mr. Sean BLACKBURN
07 Director Admissions .... Mr. Layton COOPER
88 Dir Student Involvement/Leadership .... Ms. Megan FREWALDT
88 Director Student Rights & Resp .... Ms. Krista BAU

*South Dakota School of Mines and Technology (I)

501 E Saint Joseph, Rapid City SD 57701-3995

County: Pennington FICE Identification: 003470
Unit ID: 219347

Telephone: (605) 394-2511 Carnegie Class: Masters/M
FAX Number: (605) 394-3388 Calendar System: Semester
URL: www.sdsmt.edu
Established: 1885 Annual Undergrad Tuition & Fees (In-State): $11,020
Enrollment: 2,475 Coed

Affiliation or Control: State IRS Status: 501(c)3
Highest Offering: Doctorate
Accreditation: HLC

02 President .... Dr. James RANKIN
05 Provost/VP Academic Affairs .... Dr. Lance ROBERTS
10 Vice Pres Finance/Admin/Controller .... Dr. Bill SPINDLE
46 Vice President of Research .... Dr. Ralph DAVIS
32 AVP Student Affs/Dean of Students .... Dr. Joseph DLUGOS
15 Vice President Human Resources .... Ms. Kelsey O'NEILL
20 AVP for Academic Affairs .... Ms. Darcy BRIGGS
84 AVP Enrollment Management .... Ms. Molly MOORE
96 Director of Business Services .... Ms. Barbara MUSTARD
26 Dir of Marketing & Communications . Ms. Ann M. BRENTLINGER
29 CEO Ctr for Alumni Rels/Advancement .... Mr. Paul R. KRUEGER
13 Director of Information Tech Svcs .... Mr. Bryan J. SCHUMACHER
08 Director of Devereaux Library .... Ms. Patricia M. ANDERSEN
36 Assistant VP for Student Dev .... Vacant
37 Director of Financial Aid .... Mr. David W. MARTIN
41 Director of Athletics .... Mr. Joel LUEKEN
102 President SDSM&T Foundation .... Vacant
18 AVP Facilities & Risk Mgmt .... Ms. Jerilyn C. ROBERTS
39 Dir of Housing & Operations .... Ms. Kathryn WAHLS
85 Director Ivanhoe International Ctr .... Ms. Susan R. AADLAND
58 Dean of Graduate Education .... Dr. Maribeth H. PRICE
38 Director Counseling/ADA Svcs .... Mr. Duane KAVANAUGH
06 Registrar .... Ms. Diana EASTMAN
40 Director of University Bookstore .... Mr. Marlin L. KINZER
35 Director of Student Engagement .... Mr. Cory L. HEADLEY
28 Director of Multicultural Affairs .... Vacant
122 Asst Dir Stdnt Engage-Greek Life .... Ms. Samantha HARKIN
121 Director of Student Success .... Ms. Lisa CARLSON

*South Dakota State University (A)

Campanile Avenue, Brookings SD 57007-2298
County: Brookings FICE Identification: 003471
Unit ID: 219356
Telephone: (605) 688-4111 Carnegie Class: DU-Higher
FAX Number: (605) 688-5822 Calendar System: Semester
URL: www.sdstate.edu
Established: 1881 Annual Undergrad Tuition & Fees (In-State): $9,200
Enrollment: 11,405 Coed
Affiliation or Control: State IRS Status: 501(c)3
Highest Offering: Doctorate
Accreditation: HLC, AAB, ACPHA, ART, CAATE, CACREP, CAEP, CIDA, DIET, DIETD, DIETI, EXSC, JOUR, LSAR, MLS, MUS, NURSE, PH, PHAR, THEA

01 President .... Dr. Barry H. DUNN
05 Provost/Vice Pres Acad Affairs .... Dr. Dennis HEDGE
32 VP Student Affs/Enrollment Mgmt .... Dr. Michaela WILLIS
46 VP for Research/Economic Dev .... Dr. Daniel SCHOLL
13 VP for Technology and Safety .... Mr. David OVERBY
10 Vice Pres Finance & Budget .... Mr. Michael HOLBECK
20 Vice Provost for Academic Affs .... Dr. Teresa SEEFELDT
88 Asst VP Intl Affairs .... Dr. Jon STAUFF
15 Vice Pres Human Resources .... Ms. Tracy GREENE
100 Chief of Staff .... Ms. Karyn WEBER
08 Dean of the Library .... Dr. Kristi TORNQUIST
07 Director of Admissions .... Mr. Shawn HELMBOLT
06 Registrar/Director .... Ms. Joyce KEPFORD
38 Dir of Student Health & Counseling .... Ms. Tammy LUNDAY
37 Director Financial Aid/Scholarships .... Ms. Beth VOLLAN
102 President & CEO of Foundation .... Mr. Steve ERPENBACH
29 President & CEO Alumni Association .... Ms. Andi FOUBERG
19 Chief of Safety & Security .... Mr. Tim HEATON
39 Dir of Housing & Res Life .... Ms. Rebecca PETERSON
40 Director of Bookstore/Aux Ops .... Mr. Derek PETERSON
41 Director of Athletics .... Mr. Justin SELL
28 Dir of Multicultural Affairs .... Dr. Michelle BAYER
56 Director of Extension .... Dr. Karla TRAUTMAN
26 Dir Marketing & Communications .... Mr. Michael LOCKREM
96 Business Manager .... Ms. Karen BRAVEK
43 Office of General Counsel .... Dr. Tracy GREENE
25 Director of Grants/Contracts .... Ms. Jill O'NEIL
24 Dir Instructional Design .... Dr. Shouhong ZHANG
85 Dir International Students/Scholars .... Vacant
47 Dean Col of Ag/Food/Environ Sci .... Dr. Joseph CASSADY
49 Dean Col of Arts/Hum & SS .... Dr. Lynn SARGEANT
54 Dean of Engineering .... Dr. Sanjeev KUMAR
53 Interim Dean Educ & Human Science .... Dr. Matthew VUKOVICH
66 Dean of Nursing .... Dr. Mary Anne KROGH
67 Dean of Pharmacy .... Dr. Dan HANSEN
58 Vice Provost for Graduate Education .... Dr. Victor TAYLOR
92 Dean Honors College .... Dr. Rebecca BOTT
81 Dean Col of Natural Science .... Dr. Charlene WOLF-HALL
09 Asst Dir Institutional Research .... Ms. Jennifer VANDER WAL
104 Director Study Abroad .... Ms. Sally GILLMAN
108 AVP Inst Research & Assessment .... Vacant
22 Director of EO/Title IX Coord .... Dr. Michelle JOHNSON

Southeast Technical College (B)

2320 N Career Avenue, Sioux Falls SD 57107-1302
County: Minnehaha FICE Identification: 007764
Unit ID: 219426
Telephone: (605) 367-7624 Carnegie Class: Assoc/HVT-High Trad
FAX Number: (605) 367-8305 Calendar System: Semester
URL: www.southeasttech.edu
Established: 1968 Annual Undergrad Tuition & Fees (In-District): $7,470
Enrollment: 2,330 Coed
Affiliation or Control: Local IRS Status: 501(c)3
Highest Offering: Associate Degree
Accreditation: HLC, ADNUR, CVT, DMS, MAC, NDT, SURGT

01 President .... Mr. Robert J. GRIGGS
05 Vice President of Academics .... Mr. Benjamin VALDEZ
10 Vice President Finance & Operations .... Mr. Richard KLUIN
84 VP for Enrollment Management .... Ms. Megan FISCHER
06 Director Student Success/Registrar .... Ms. Kristie VORTHERMS
13 Chief Information Officer .... Mr. Erik VANLAECKEN
15 Human Resources Director .... Ms. Heidi GEFROH
20 Dean of Curriculum/Instruction .... Dr. Fenecia HOMAN
20 Dean of Curriculum/Instruction .... Ms. Kristin POSSEHL
26 Marketing/Communications Coord .... Ms. Jennifer LAMBLEY
37 Financial Aid Director .... Mr. Micah HANSEN
102 Foundation Director .... Mr. Stephen WILLIAMSON
113 Director of Student Accounts .... Mr. James WESTCOTT
38 Student Personal Counselor .... Ms. Nicole MCMILLIN
04 Admin Assistant to the President .... Ms. Vicki OSWALD
07 Director of Admissions .... Ms. Mandy FREY
39 Director of Housing .... Mr. Andy VANZANTEN

University of Sioux Falls (C)

1101 W 22nd Street, Sioux Falls SD 57105-1699
County: Minnehaha FICE Identification: 003469
Unit ID: 219383
Telephone: (605) 331-5000 Carnegie Class: Masters/M
FAX Number: (605) 331-6615 Calendar System: 4/1/4
URL: www.usiouxfalls.edu
Established: 1883 Annual Undergrad Tuition & Fees: $19,520
Enrollment: 1,628 Coed
Affiliation or Control: American Baptist IRS Status: 501(c)3
Highest Offering: Doctorate
Accreditation: HLC, CAEP, IACBE, NURSE, SW

01 President .... Dr. Brett BRADFIELD
100 Dir Presidential and Bd Operations .... Ms. Karen BANGASSER
05 VP for Academic Affairs .... Mr. Joe OBERMUELLER
50 Chair School of Business .... Mr. Bradley VAN KALSBEEK
53 Chair School of Education .... Ms. Michelle HANSON
57 Chair Visual & Performing Arts .... Mr. Jonathan NEIDERHISER
65 Chair of Natural Sciences .... Dr. William SOEFFING
79 Chair of Humanities .... Ms. Jenny BANGSUND
83 Chair of Social Sciences .... Ms. Beth O'TOOLE
66 Director School of Nursing .... Ms. Jessica CHERENEGAR
88 Director of Degree Comp Program .... Ms. LuAnn GROSSMAN
06 Registrar .... Ms. Anna HECKENLAIBLE
10 VP for Business and Finance .... Vacant
21 Director for Business and Finance .... Ms. Staci ATTEMA
111 VP for Institutional Advancement .... Mr. Todd KNUTSON
112 VP for Principal Gifts .... Mr. Jon HIATT
26 Dir of Marketing and Communications . Ms. Whitney ALEXANDER
84 VP for Enrollment Management .... Ms. Aimee VANDER FEEN
07 Director of Admissions .... Mr. Kyle SIMONS
37 Director of Financial Aid .... Ms. Karrie MORGAN
15 VP of Human Resources .... Ms. Julie GEDNALSKE
09 AVP of Institutional Research .... Dr. Jason DOUMA
39 Director of Student Life & Housing .... Mr. Andrew PORTEOUS
58 Sr Dir of Grad & Continuing Studies .... Ms. Kama KONDA-VARILEK
42 Dean of the Chapel .... Rev. Dennis L. THUM
38 University Counselor .... Ms. Michelle DEHOOGH-KLIEWER
104 Director of International Education .... Mr. Randy NELSON
13 VP Info Technology and CIO .... Mr. William BARTELL
91 Dir Administrative Applications .... Mr. Rob HARRINGTON
106 Director of Online Education .... Ms. Tara JOHANNESON
08 Librarian .... Ms. Annie STERNBURG
41 Director of Athletics .... Ms. Pam GOHL
18 Director of Facilities .... Mr. Brad FLAYTON
19 Director of Campus Safety .... Mr. Kevin GREBIN
40 Dir of Cougar Central Bookstore .... Ms. Jennifer KNUTSON

Western Dakota Technical College (D)

800 Mickelson Drive, Rapid City SD 57703-4018
County: Pennington FICE Identification: 010170
Unit ID: 219480
Telephone: (605) 394-4034 Carnegie Class: Assoc/HVT-Mix Trad/Non
FAX Number: (605) 394-1789 Calendar System: Semester
URL: www.wdt.edu
Established: 1968 Annual Undergrad Tuition & Fees (In-District): $8,274
Enrollment: 1,324 Coed
Affiliation or Control: Local IRS Status: 501(c)3
Highest Offering: Associate Degree
Accreditation: HLC, EMT, MLTAD, SURGT

01 President .... Dr. Ann BOLMAN
05 VP for Teaching and Learning .... Ms. Tiffany HOWE
10 VP for Finance and Operations .... Ms. Christine GOLDSMITH
108 VP for Institutional Effectiveness .... Ms. Kelly OEHLERKING
15 Director of Human Resources .... Ms. Jade HOLLISTER
07 Admissions & Financial Aid Director .... Ms. Jill ELDER
06 Director Student Success/Registrar .... Ms. Debbie TOMS
18 Director of Facilities .... Mr. Bob GRIMSRUD
26 Director Strategic Communications .... Ms. Pam STILLMAN-ROKUSEK
111 Director Industry Relations/Grants .... Ms. Chandra CALVERT
04 Executive Assistant to President .... Ms. Kathi MAXSON
09 Reporting & Analysis Director .... Vacant
102 Foundation Director .... Ms. Danita SIMONS
13 Director of Information Systems .... Mr. Matthew GREENE

TENNESSEE

All Saints Bible College (E)

930 Mason Street, Memphis TN 38126
County: Shelby Identification: 667014
Telephone: (901) 322-0120 Carnegie Class: Not Classified
FAX Number: (901) 947-3504 Calendar System: Semester
URL: www.allsaintsonline.info
Established: 2002 Annual Undergrad Tuition & Fees: N/A
Enrollment: N/A Coed
Affiliation or Control: Church of God in Christ IRS Status: 501(c)3
Highest Offering: Baccalaureate
Accreditation: @BI

00 Chancellor .... Bishop Charles E. BLAKE
01 President .... Dr. Joseph E. FISHER

American Baptist College (F)

1800 Baptist World Center Drive, Nashville TN 37207
County: Davidson FICE Identification: 010460
Unit ID: 219505
Telephone: (615) 256-1463 Carnegie Class: Bac-Diverse
FAX Number: (615) 226-7855 Calendar System: Semester
URL: www.abcnash.edu
Established: 1924 Annual Undergrad Tuition & Fees: $12,474
Enrollment: 55 Coed
Affiliation or Control: Baptist IRS Status: 501(c)3
Highest Offering: Baccalaureate
Accreditation: BI

01 President .... Dr. Forrest E. HARRIS, SR.
05 Provost/Vice Pres Academic Affairs .... Dr. LaShante WALKER
10 EVP Admin/Finance/Legal Affairs .... Mr. Richard JACKSON
32 Vice Pres Campus Life .... Rev. Martin ESPINOSA
06 Registrar/Student Records .... Mr. Cedric AARON
21 Controller .... Ms. Brooke BELL
08 Director Library Services .... Vacant
04 Exec Asst to Pres/Title IX Coord .... Ms. Mary CARPENTER
25 Dir Proposal/Grant Research Devel .... Dr. Regina PRUDE
07 Dir Admissions/Public Relations .... Vacant

Aquinas College (G)

4210 Harding Pike, Nashville TN 37205-2005
County: Davidson FICE Identification: 003477
Unit ID: 219578
Telephone: (615) 297-7545 Carnegie Class: Not Classified
FAX Number: N/A Calendar System: Semester
URL: www.aquinascollege.edu
Established: 1961 Annual Undergrad Tuition & Fees: N/A
Enrollment: N/A Coed
Affiliation or Control: Roman Catholic IRS Status: 501(c)3
Highest Offering: Master's
Accreditation: SC

01 President .... Sr. Cecilia Anne WARNER, OP
05 Provost and Vice Pres for Academics .... Sr. Mary Edith HUMPHRIES, OP
20 Associate Provost .... Dr. William SMART
26 Dir of Communications/Marketing .... Vacant
07 Dir of Admiss & Registrar .... Sr. Gianna JUNKER, OP
08 Librarian .... Sr. Mary Esther POTTS, OP
53 Dean School of Education .... Sr. Marie Hannah SEILER, OP
21 Business Manager .... Mrs. Monica WARREN
09 Director of Institutional Research .... Dr. William SMART
18 Chief of Facilities/Physical Plant .... Mr. John WALL
88 Director of Catechetics .... Mr. Jason GALE
88 Dir Center for Catholic Education ... Sr. Elizabeth Anne ALLEN, OP
19 Director Security/Safety .... Mr. Andrew ATWOOD
101 Secretary of the Institution/Board ..... Sr. John Mary FLEMING, OP
13 Chief Info Technology Officer (CIO) .... Mrs. Joyce WALL
15 Chief Human Resources Officer .... Ms. Anne TARWATER
37 Director Student Financial Aid .... Mrs. Cynthia PIANA

Austin Peay State University (H)

601 College Street, Clarksville TN 37044-0002
County: Montgomery FICE Identification: 003478
Unit ID: 219602
Telephone: (931) 221-7011 Carnegie Class: Masters/L
FAX Number: (931) 221-7475 Calendar System: Semester
URL: www.apsu.edu
Established: 1927 Annual Undergrad Tuition & Fees (In-State): $8,303
Enrollment: 10,272 Coed
Affiliation or Control: State IRS Status: 501(c)3
Highest Offering: Doctorate
Accreditation: SC, ART, CACREP, CAEP, MLS, MUS, NURSE, RAD, RTT, @SP, SW

02 President .... Dr. Michael LICARI
05 Provost/VP Academic Affairs .... Dr. Maria CRONLEY
10 Vice President for Finance & Admin .... Mr. Shahrooz ROOHPARVAR
43 VP Legal Affairs & Org Strategy .... Ms. Dannelle WHITESIDE
32 Interim VP for Student Affairs .... Mr. Gregory SINGLETON
21 Assoc VP for Finance .... Mr. Benjamin HARMON
20 Vice Provost/Assoc VP Acad Affairs .... Dr. Lynne CROSBY
121 Vice Prov for Student Achievement .... Dr. Nancy KING SANDERS

111 Vice Pres Univ Advancement .... Mr. Kristopher PHILLIPS
86 Chief Cmty/Govt Relations/Board Sec .... Dr. Carol D. CLARK
26 Exec Dir Marketing/Public Rels .... Mr. Bill PERSINGER
12 Exec Dir APSU Fort Campbell .... Dr. Kristine NAKUTIS
29 Director of Alumni Relations .... Mr. Brad AVERITT
114 Assistant Vice President for Budget .... Ms. Sondra HAMILTON
08 Director Library .... Vacant
13 Assoc VP & Chief Info Officer .... Dr. David SANCHEZ
09 Dir Decision Support/Inst Effective .... Dr. Andrew LUNA
07 Director of Admissions .... Ms. Amy CORLEW
06 Registrar .... Vacant
18 Director of Plant Administration .... Mr. Thomas HUTCHINS
45 Dir University Design/Construction .... Mr. Marc BRUNNER
41 Athletic Director .... Mr. Gerald HARRISON
88 Athletics Communication Manager .... Mr. Cody BUSH
37 Director of Student Financial Aid .... Ms. Donna PRICE
121 AVP Student Success/Strategic Init .... Dr. Loretta GRIFFY
38 Dir of Student Counseling Services .... Vacant
35 Assoc Vice Pres & Dean of Students .... Mr. Gregory SINGLETON
88 Dir African Amer Cultural Ctr .... Mr. Harold WALLACE
15 Asst Vice President Human Resources .. Mrs. JaCenda ROBINSON
16 Director of Human Resources .... Ms. Fonda FIELDS
19 Assistant VP for Public Safety .... Mr. Michael KASITZ
39 Asst Vice President Student Affairs .... Mr. F. Joe MILLS
116 Director Internal Audit .... Mr. Blayne CLEMENTS
25 Dir Research & Sponsored Pgms .... Mr. Timothy ATKINSON
96 Director of Purchasing .... Ms. Judy BLAIN
22 Dir Equal Opportunity/Affirm Action .... Mrs. Sheila M. BRYANT
36 Director of Career Services .... Mr. Eric MORGAN
49 Dean College Arts & Letters .... Dr. William HOON
81 Dean College STEM .... Dr. Karen MEISCH
20 Sr Vice Provost & AVP Academic Affs .... Dr. Tucker BROWN
58 Assoc Provost/Dean Col Grad Stds .... Dr. Chad BROOKS
56 Exec Dir Extend/Intl Educ .... Dr. Tim HUDSON
106 Director of Distance Education .... Ms. Anna Carrie WEBB
104 Dir Study Abroad/Intl Exchange .... Dr. Marissa CHANDLER
50 Dean College of Business .... Dr. Mickey HEPNER
83 Int Dean Col of Behavioral Hlth Sci .... Dr. Marcy MAURER
53 Dean College of Education .... Dr. Prentice CHANDLER
28 Chief Diversity Officer/Title IX .... Ms. LaNeeca WILLIAMS
04 Executive Asst to the President .... Mrs. Lenora JACKSON
101 Secretary of the Institution/Board .... Mrs. Carol CLARK
44 Director Annual Giving .... Ms. Rebekah BISHOP

Baptist Health Sciences University (A)

1003 Monroe Avenue, Memphis TN 38104-3199
County: Shelby FICE Identification: 034403
Unit ID: 219639
Telephone: (901) 575-2268 Carnegie Class: Spec-4-yr-Other Health
FAX Number: (901) 572-2497 Calendar System: Trimester
URL: https://www.baptistu.edu/
Established: 1994 Annual Undergrad Tuition & Fees: $12,572
Enrollment: 890 Coed
Affiliation or Control: Independent Non-Profit IRS Status: 501(c)3
Highest Offering: Doctorate
Accreditation: SC, COARC, DMS, MLS, NDT, NMT, NURSE, RAD, RTT

01 President .... Dr. Betty Sue MCGARVEY
04 Administrative Asst to President .... Vacant
05 Provost/VP Academic Affairs .... Dr. Barry SCHULTZ
84 VP Enrollment Mgmt & Student Affs .... Dr. Tammy FOWLER
10 Vice President Financial & Business .... Ms. Leanne SMITH
11 Vice President Admin Svcs/HR .... Dr. Adonna CALDWELL
97 Dean General Educ & Health Studies .... Dr. Michelle MCDONALD
66 Dean Nursing .... Dr. Cathy STEPTER
76 Dean Allied Health .... Dr. Elizabeth WILLIAMS
32 Dean Student Life .... Dr. Brent OWENS
06 Registrar .... Mrs. Erica CHANDLER
07 Director of Admissions .... Ms. Erica JOHNSON
09 Dir Institutional Effectiveness/Pln .... Dr. Cameron A. CONN
29 Director Alumni Relations/Marketing .... Ms. Megan M. BURSI
35 Director Student Services .... Mr. Jeremy WILKES
37 Director Financial Aid .... Vacant

Belmont University (B)

1900 Belmont Boulevard, Nashville TN 37212-3757
County: Davidson FICE Identification: 003479
Unit ID: 219709
Telephone: (615) 460-6000 Carnegie Class: DU-Mod
FAX Number: (615) 460-6446 Calendar System: Semester
URL: www.belmont.edu
Established: 1890 Annual Undergrad Tuition & Fees: $37,030
Enrollment: 8,204 Coed
Affiliation or Control: Non-denominational IRS Status: 501(c)3
Highest Offering: Doctorate
Accreditation: SC, ART, CACREP, CAEP, CIDA, LAW, MUS, NURSE, OT, PHAR, PTA, SW, THEA

01 President .... Dr. Gregory JONES
05 Exec Vice President/Int Provost .... Dr. David GREGORY
100 Exec Vice President/Chief of Staff .... Dr. Susan H. WEST
43 EVP External Engage/Univ Counsel .... Dr. Jason ROGERS
09 VP for Institutional Effectiveness .... Dr. Paula GILL
30 VP Development .... Dr. Perry MOULDS
10 Vice President Finance & Operations .... Mr. Steven T. LASLEY
42 VP Faith Based Engagement .... Dr. Todd LAKE
45 VP for Strategic Initiatives .... Ms. Sarah CATES
88 VP for Transformative Innovation .... Dr. Amy CROOK
26 AVP Marketing & Public Relations .... Ms. April HEFNER
27 AVP Public Rels/Special Initiatives .... Ms. Hope BUCKNER
13 Assoc VP/Chief Information Officer .... Mr. William INGRAM
32 VP for Student Formation .... Dr. Tamika WILLIAMS
20 Vice Provost for Academic Affairs .... Dr. Phil JOHNSTON
84 VP for Enrollment .... Dr. Chris GAGE
35 Associate Dean of Students .... Dr. Anthony DONOVAN
108 Assoc Prov Assessment .... Ms. Patricia WHITE
85 Assoc Provost ISGE/Global Educ .... Dr. Mimi BARNARD
50 Dean College of Business .... Dr. Sarah FISHER GARDIAL
57 Dean College Music/Performing Arts .... Dr. Stephen EAVES
88 Dean College of Ent & Music Bus .... Mr. Doug HOWARD
49 Dean Col of Lib Arts & Soc Sci .... Dr. Bryce SULLIVAN
81 Dean Col of Sciences & Mathematics .... Dr. Thomas SPENCE
76 Dean Col Health Sciences/Nursing .... Dr. Cathy TAYLOR
73 Dean of Col Theol & Christian Min .... Dr. Darrell GWALTNEY
61 Dean College of Law .... Dr. Alberto GONZALES
67 Dean College of Pharmacy .... Dr. David GREGORY
53 Dean College of Education .... Dr. James MCINTYRE
06 University Registrar .... Dr. La Kiesha ARMSTRONG
35 Asst Dean of Student Support Svcs .... Ms. Angie BRYANT
39 Director of Residence Life .... Mr. Anthony DONOVAN
15 Sr Director of Human Resources .... Mrs. Leslie A. LENSER
37 Director of Financial Aid .... Mr. Charles HARPER
29 Assoc Director of Alumni Relations .... Ms. Julie THOMAS
18 Director of Facilities Management .... Mr. Robert CHAVEZ
19 Chief of Campus Security .... Mr. Pat CUNNINGHAM
90 Director Technology Services .... Mr. Randall REYNOLDS
08 Director of Library Services .... Ms. Sue MASZAROS
41 VP & Athletics Director .... Mr. Scott CORLEY
40 Manager Bookstore .... Ms. Shelley SARMIENTO
36 Dir Career & Professional Develop .... Ms. Mary Claire DISMUKES
38 Director Student Counseling .... Ms. Katherine CORNELIUS
104 Director of Global Education .... Dr. Witold WOLNY
07 Director of Admissions .... Ms. Brooke BRANNIN
28 Director of Diversity .... Dr. Susan WEST
88 Director of Data Collaborative .... Dr. Charles APIGIAN
88 Exec Dir of Transformational Hub .... Dr. Josh YATES

Bethel University (C)

325 Cherry Avenue, McKenzie TN 38201-1705
County: Carroll FICE Identification: 003480
Unit ID: 219718
Telephone: (731) 352-4000 Carnegie Class: Masters/L
FAX Number: (731) 352-4069 Calendar System: Semester
URL: www.bethelu.edu
Established: 1842 Annual Undergrad Tuition & Fees: $17,010
Enrollment: 4,001 Coed
Affiliation or Control: Cumberland Presbyterian IRS Status: 501(c)3
Highest Offering: Master's
Accreditation: #SC, ARCPA, NURSE

01 President .... Dr. Walter BUTLER
05 Chief Academic Officer .... Dr. Phyllis CAMPBELL
49 VP College of Arts and Sciences .... Ms. Cindy MALLARD
107 VP College of Professional Studies .... Mrs. Kimberly MARTIN
76 VP College of Health Sciences .... Dr. Joe HAMES
10 VP of Finance .... Mr. David HUSS
30 Vice President for Development .... Vacant
06 University Registrar .... Ms. Deborah NOBLE
07 Director Admissions/Recruitment .... Mrs. Tina HODGES
26 VP Strategic Initiatives .... Ms. Michelle MITCHELL
89 Director of College Orientation .... Mrs. Sandy LOUDEN
42 Senior Chaplain .... Rev. Anne HAMES
08 Library Director .... Ms. Jill WHITFILL
15 Human Resource Director .... Ms. Carolyn DOTSON
41 Athletic Director .... Mr. Dale KELLEY
09 Dir of Institutional Effectiveness .... Ms. Lisa TYLER
29 Director Alumni Relations .... Mrs. Myra CARLOCK
18 Chief Facilities/Physical Plant .... Mr. Randy TANAKA
04 Administrative Asst to President .... Ms. Vicky WILLIAMS
105 Director Web Services .... Mr. Jon MITCHELL
13 Chief Info Technology Officer (CIO) .... Mr. Jimmy BOMAR
19 Director Security/Safety .... Mr. Daniel THOMAS
39 Director Student Housing .... Ms. Peggy CARTER

Bryan College (D)

721 Bryan Drive, Dayton TN 37321-6275
County: Rhea FICE Identification: 003536
Unit ID: 219790
Telephone: (423) 775-2041 Carnegie Class: Masters/S
FAX Number: (423) 775-7330 Calendar System: Semester
URL: www.bryan.edu
Established: 1930 Annual Undergrad Tuition & Fees: $17,050
Enrollment: 1,412 Coed
Affiliation or Control: Independent Non-Profit IRS Status: 501(c)3
Highest Offering: Doctorate
Accreditation: SC, IACBE

01 President .... Dr. Douglas F. MANN
04 Exec Assistant to the President .... Vacant
05 Provost/VP of Academics .... Dr. David CALLAND
10 SVP of Business Operations/Finance .... Mr. Tim J. HOSTETLER
111 Vice Pres of Advancement/Athletics .... Mr. David HOLCOMB
32 VP Student Services/Ministries .... Mr. Nicholas PACURARI
58 Dir of the DBA & Graduate Programs .... Dr. Adina SCRUGGS
54 Dean School of Engineering .... Dr. Lyle C. SMITH
35 Dean of Students Support and Care .... Mr. Bruce A. MORGAN
37 Director of Financial Aid .... Mr. David L. HAGGARD
13 Director of Information Technology .... Mr. James SULLIVAN
06 Registrar .... Ms. Janet M. PIATT
08 Director of Library Services .... Dr. Gary N. FITSIMMONS
15 Director Personnel Services .... Mrs. Angie C. PRICE
41 Athletic Director .... Mrs. Jenny SWAFFORD
18 Director of Physical Plant .... Mr. David A. MORGAN
29 Director of Alumni Affairs .... Mrs. Paulakay HALL
07 Exec Director of Admissions .... Mr. Andrew SMITH
88 Accreditation Liaison .... Mr. Samuel J. YOUNGS
66 Dean Clara Ward School of Nursing .... Dr. Pamela A. GILES

Carson-Newman University (E)

1646 Russell Avenue, PO Box 557,
Jefferson City TN 37760-2204
County: Jefferson FICE Identification: 003481
Unit ID: 219806
Telephone: (865) 471-2000 Carnegie Class: DU-Mod
FAX Number: (865) 471-3502 Calendar System: Semester
URL: www.cn.edu
Established: 1851 Annual Undergrad Tuition & Fees: $29,500
Enrollment: 2,911 Coed
Affiliation or Control: Southern Baptist IRS Status: 501(c)3
Highest Offering: Doctorate
Accreditation: SC, AAFCS, ART, CACREP, CAEP, DIETD, MUS, NURSE

01 President .... Mr. Charles FOWLER
05 Provost .... Dr. Jeremy BUCKNER
111 Vice President University Relations .... Mr. Kevin TRIPLETT
32 Vice President Student Affairs .... Ms. Gloria WALKER
35 Asst Vice Pres of Student Affairs .... Mrs. Shelley BALL
08 Dean of Library Services .... Mr. Bruce KOCOUR
26 Exec Dir University Relations .... Mr. Kyle BENJAMIN
37 Director Financial Aid .... Vacant
15 Director of Human Resources .... Ms. Regenia FORD
38 Director Counseling Services .... Mrs. Jennifer CATLETT
13 Chief Information Officer .... Mr. David TUELL
18 Chief Facilities/Physical Plant .... Mr. Ondes WEBSTER
84 Vice Pres Enrollment Management .... Mrs. Danette SEALE
92 Director of Honors Program .... Dr. Andrew SMITH
10 Chief Business Officer .... Mrs. Elaine SMITH
41 Athletic Director .... Mr. Matthew POPE
85 Dean of Global Education .... Vacant
06 Registrar .... Mrs. Jessica SWINEY
04 Executive Assistant to President .... Mrs. Libby MILLER
19 Director Security/Safety .... Mr. Doug COCHRAN

Chattanooga College (F)

5600 Brainerd Road #B-38, Chattanooga TN 37411
County: Hamilton FICE Identification: 022042
Unit ID: 220118
Telephone: (423) 305-7783 Carnegie Class: Spec 2-yr-Health
FAX Number: (423) 624-1575 Calendar System: Quarter
URL: www.chattanoogacollege.edu
Established: 1968 Annual Undergrad Tuition & Fees: $10,690
Enrollment: 252 Coed
Affiliation or Control: Proprietary IRS Status: Proprietary
Highest Offering: Associate Degree
Accreditation: ACCSC

01 President .... Mr. William G. FAOUR
03 Vice President .... Mr. Toney C. MCFADDEN
05 Director of Education .... Ms. Karen WORLEY
37 Director Financial Aid .... Ms. Beth GASS

Christian Brothers University (G)

650 East Parkway South, Memphis TN 38104-5581
County: Shelby FICE Identification: 003482
Unit ID: 219833
Telephone: (901) 321-3000 Carnegie Class: Masters/M
FAX Number: (901) 321-3494 Calendar System: Semester
URL: www.cbu.edu
Established: 1871 Annual Undergrad Tuition & Fees: $34,880
Enrollment: 1,918 Coed
Affiliation or Control: Roman Catholic IRS Status: 501(c)3
Highest Offering: Master's
Accreditation: SC, ARCPA, CAEPN, NURSE

01 President .... Mr. David L. ARCHER
10 CFO & VP Administration .... Mr. Ronald BRANDON
05 VP Academics .... Dr. Paul HAUGHT
111 VP Advancement .... Mr. Mark BILLINGSLEY
84 VP Enrollment Mgmt .... Dr. Brian DALTON
32 VP Student Devel & Campus Life .... Ms. Beth GERL
13 VP ITS/Chief Info Officer .... Mr. Brett DOTY
26 VP Communications & Marketing .... Dr. Leslie GRAFF
88 VP Mission & Identity .... Br. Patrick CONWAY
28 VP Diversity/Equity & Inclusion .... Dr. Mary MCCONNER
11 VP Operations & Facilities .... Vacant
41 Director of Athletics .... Mr. Brian SUMMERS
100 Chief of Staff .... Ms. Susan ELLIOTT
88 Dir Cen Enterpreneurship & Innov .... Mr. Bryan BARRINGER
20 Assoc VP Acad & Strat Initiatives .... Dr. Jack HARGETT
85 Assoc VP Intl Initiatives .... Dr. Daniel S. HARPER
49 Dean School of Arts .... Dr. Benjamin R. JORDAN
50 Dean School of Business .... Dr. Lydia ROSENCRANTS
54 Dean School of Engineering .... Dr. Faris MALHAS
81 Dean School of Science .... Dr. James MCGUFFEE
55 Dean College Adult Prof Studies .... Dr. Divya CHOUDHARY
121 Dean Student Success .... Vacant
15 Assoc VP Human Resources .... Ms. Theresa JACQUES
21 Controller .... Ms. Lisa LUCAS
102 AVP Corp & Foundation Relations .. Ms. Kathleen TERRY-SHARP
110 Associate VP for Donor Relations .... Dr. Anne KENWORTHY

35 Associate VP for Student Life Dr. Timothy DOYLE
06 Registrar Mr. Scott SUMMERS
36 Director Career Services Ms. Amy WARE
31 Director Center Community Engage Dr. Leslie MCABEE
106 Director Center Digital Instruction Dr. Dale HALE
92 Director Honors Program Ms. Connie BECK
09 Dir Inst Research/Effectiveness Ms. Melissa S. ANDREWS
08 Director of Plough Library Ms. Kay CUNNINGHAM
18 Director Physical Plant Mr. Bill HECHT
29 Director Alumni Relations Ms. Torie MARION
44 Director Annual Giving Ms. Jennie DICKERSON
07 Director of Admissions Ms. Raquel SAULSBERRY
37 Director Student Financial Aid Ms. Elizabeth ROMAGNI
42 Director Campus Ministry Mr. Joseph PRESTON
19 Director Campus Police & Safety Mr. John D. LOTRIONTE
38 Director Counseling Center Ms. Beverly WORD
23 Director Health Resources Ms. Heather HARRINGTON
39 Director Residence Life Mr. Alton WADE
53 Dir Undergrad & Graduate Education Dr. Rosetta MAYFIELD-BURFORD
66 Director of Nursing Dr. Jennifer HITT-MAYO
96 Dir Procurement & Contract Services Ms. Susan BANNING
123 Director Graduate Admissions Ms. Erica MITCHELL
04 Executive Administrative Coord Ms. Chastity BLAIR
89 Coord 1st & 2nd Year Experience Vacant
40 Director Bookstore Ms. Melissa ROGERS

Concorde Career College (A)

5100 Poplar Avenue, Suite 132, Memphis TN 38137-0132
County: Shelby FICE Identification: 021571
Unit ID: 219903
Telephone: (901) 761-9494 Carnegie Class: Spec 2-yr-Health
FAX Number: (901) 761-3293 Calendar System: Semester
URL: https://www.concorde.edu/campus/memphis-tennessee
Established: 1967 Annual Undergrad Tuition & Fees: N/A
Enrollment: 1,367 Coed
Affiliation or Control: Proprietary IRS Status: Proprietary
Highest Offering: Associate Degree
Accreditation: **COE**, COARC, DH, MLTAD, NDT, OTA, POLYT, PTAA, RAD

01 Campus President Mr. Tommy STEWART
05 Academic Dean Dr. Kimberly NOVAK
05 Academic Dean Mrs. Terri KIMBLE

The Crown College of the Bible (B)

2307 W. Beaver Creek Drive, Powell TN 37849
County: Knox Identification: 667141
Telephone: (865) 938-8186 Carnegie Class: Not Classified
FAX Number: (865) 938-8188 Calendar System: Semester
URL: thecrowncollege.edu
Established: 1991 Annual Undergrad Tuition & Fees: N/A
Enrollment: N/A Coed
Affiliation or Control: Baptist IRS Status: 501(c)3
Highest Offering: Master's
Accreditation: **TRACS**

01 Founder & President Dr. Clarence SEXTON
03 Executive Vice President Mr. James ZENKER
05 Vice President of Academics Mr. Tim TOMLINSON
11 Vice President of Operations Mr. M. Shannon SEXTON
10 Vice President of Business/Finance Dr. Charles PRESCOTT
75 Vice President Trades Dr. Janice GILLIAM

Cumberland University (C)

1 Cumberland Square, Lebanon TN 37087-3554
County: Wilson FICE Identification: 003485
Unit ID: 219949
Telephone: (615) 444-2562 Carnegie Class: Masters/M
FAX Number: (615) 444-2569 Calendar System: Semester
URL: www.cumberland.edu
Established: 1842 Annual Undergrad Tuition & Fees: $25,386
Enrollment: 2,704 Coed
Affiliation or Control: Independent Non-Profit IRS Status: 501(c)3
Highest Offering: Master's
Accreditation: **SC**, ACBSP, CAATE, NURSE

01 President Dr. Paul STUMB, IV
05 Provost/Vice Pres Academic Affairs Dr. William MCKEE
10 Vice President of Finance Ms. Judy G. JORDAN
111 Vice President of Advancement Ms. Courtney WHEELER
32 AVP/Dean of Students Ms. Stephanie DAVIS
66 Dean Nursing and Health Sciences Dr. Mary GRIFFITH
100 Executive Coordinator to President Ms. Leslie STEELE
08 Director Library Services Ms. Bettina WARKENTIN
84 Exec Director Enrollment Services Dr. Eddie LOVIN
41 Director of Athletics Mr. Ron PAVAN
06 Registrar Ms. Tammi PAVAN
15 Director of Human Resources Ms. Tammy MARSHALL
13 Director of Information Technology Mr. Jerry ENGLAND
09 Director of Institutional Research Mr. Larry F. VAUGHAN
26 Exec Dir Communications/Marketing Ms. Caitlin VAUGHN
36 Dir of Career Services/Internships Ms. N. Leann BLEVINS
37 Director Student Financial Aid Ms. Beatrice LACHANCE
39 Director Student Housing Vacant
50 Dean Labry School of Business Dr. Chris FULLER
53 Dean of Humanities/Education & Art Dr. Eric CUMMINGS
27 Exec Dir Public Relations Mr. William "Rusty" RICHARDSON
39 Exec Director of Housing & Services Mr. Steve GIORDANO
108 Director Institutional Assessment Dr. Laurie DISHMAN
19 Director Security/Safety Mr. Mike THORNHILL

East Tennessee State University (D)

1276 Gilbreath Drive, Johnson City TN 37614-1700
County: Washington FICE Identification: 003487
Unit ID: 220075
Telephone: (423) 439-1000 Carnegie Class: DU-Higher
FAX Number: (423) 439-5770 Calendar System: Semester
URL: www.etsu.edu
Established: 1911 Annual Undergrad Tuition & Fees (In-State): $9,259
Enrollment: 13,713 Coed
Affiliation or Control: State IRS Status: 501(c)3
Highest Offering: Doctorate
Accreditation: **SC**, ART, AUD, CACREP, CAEP, CIDA, CLPSY, COARC, CSHSE, DH, DIETD, DIETI, MED, MUS, NAEYC, NURSE, PH, PHAR, PTA, RAD, SP, SW, THEA

02 President Dr. Brian E. NOLAND
00 Chairman Board of Trustees Dr. Linda LATIMER
100 Chief of Staff Dr. Adam S. GREEN
11 Chief Operating Officer Mr. Jeremy B. ROSS
10 Chief Financial Officer Dr. B.J KING
05 Sr VP for Academics/Provost Dr. Kimberly MCCORKLE
17 Vice President Clinical Affairs Dr. William A. BLOCK
111 VP University Advancement Ms. Pamela S. RITTER
32 VP for Student Life and Enrollment Dr. Joe H. SHERLIN
41 Director of Athletics Mr. Scott N. CARTER
28 VP of Equity and Inclusion Dr. Keith V. JOHNSON
116 Director of Internal Audit Ms. Rebecca B. LEWIS
43 University Counsel Dr. Mark A. FULKS
26 Chief Marketing/Communications Ofcr Ms. Jessica VODDEN
84 Asst VP Student Life & Enrollment Dr. Sam MAYHEW
07 Director of Admissions Ms. Heather A. LEVESQUE
35 Dean of Students Dr. T. Michelle BYRD
51 Dean Cont Studies & Acad Outreach Dr. Sharon MCGEE
20 Exec Vice Provost Dr. Robert PACK
46 VProv Research/Sponsored Pgms Mr. Nick HAGEMEILER
88 Assoc Vice Provost for Faculty Dr. Amy D. JOHNSON
88 Assoc Vice Prov Acad Initiatives Dr. William F. FLORA
35 Assoc VP Student Life & Engagement Dr. William G. KIRKWOOD
18 Assoc VP for Facilities Management Ms. Laura BAILEY
13 CIO/Sr Vice Provost for ITS Dr. Karen D. KING
112 Exec Director for Planned Giving Mr. Robert A. LANGE
29 Exec Director Alumni Association Ms. Whitney GOETZ
86 Assoc VP for Comm & Gov Relations Ms. Bridget R. BAIRD
66 Dean College of Nursing Dr. Leann HORSLEY
49 Dean College Arts & Science Dr. Joe BIDWELL
50 Dean College of Business/Technology Dr. Tony PITTARESE
76 Dean College of Clin/Rehab Sci Dr. Donald A. SAMPLES
53 Dean College of Education Dr. Janna L. SCARBOROUGH
92 Dean Honors College Dr. Christopher J. KELLER
63 Dean College of Medicine Dr. William A. BLOCK
67 Dean College of Pharmacy Dr. Debbie C. BYRD
69 Dean College of Public Health Dr. Randolph F. WYKOFF
58 Dean School of Graduate Studies Dr. Sharon J. MCGEE
08 Dean of Libraries Mr. David P. ATKINS
06 University Registrar Dr. Thomas N. DONOHOE
36 Director University Career Services Ms. Jenny LOCKMILLER
38 Director Counseling Center Dr. Dan L. JONES
37 Director of Financial Aid Ms. Catherine A. MORGAN
39 Director Student Housing Dr. Bonnie L. BURCHETT
93 Multicultural Director Ms. Laura C. TERRY
19 Police Chief/Public Safety Mr. Cesar GARCIA
25 Director of Sponsored Programs Ms. Wendy ECKERT
94 Director of Women's Studies Dr. Phyllis A. THOMPSON
15 Asst Vice Pres Human Resources Ms. Lori ERICKSON
108 Dir Institutional Effectiveness Dr. Cheri CLAVIER
45 Assoc VP/Chief Planning Officer Dr. Michael B. HOFF
09 Director of Institutional Research Dr. Joseph CHAPPELL

Fisk University (E)

1000 17th Avenue N, Nashville TN 37208-3051
County: Davidson FICE Identification: 003490
Unit ID: 220181
Telephone: (615) 329-8500 Carnegie Class: Bac-A&S
FAX Number: N/A Calendar System: Semester
URL: www.fisk.edu
Established: 1866 Annual Undergrad Tuition & Fees: $22,132
Enrollment: 911 Coed
Affiliation or Control: Independent Non-Profit IRS Status: 501(c)3
Highest Offering: Master's
Accreditation: **SC**, #ACBSP, MUS

01 Acting President Mr. Frank L. SIMS
03 Executive Vice President Dr. Jens FREDERIKSEN
05 Provost and VP of Academic Affairs Dr. Robert CARR, JR.
10 Vice President for Finance and CFO Mr. Norm E. JONES
88 Exec Director of Special Projects Dr. Kenneth E. JONES
88 Special Asst to the President Dr. Jason R. CURRY
20 Sr Vice Prov Faculty Initiatives Dr. Arnold BURGER
32 Associate Provost Student Affairs Dr. Natara GARVIN
108 Executive Director of Assessment Dr. Tdka M. KILIMANJARO
14 Director of Information Technology Mr. Brian GARNER
06 Registrar Mr. Edward ROSSER
08 Director of Library Services Mr. Brandon OWENS, SR.
81 Dean/Chair Math & Comp Sci Dr. Cathy MARTIN
106 Assoc Vice Prov Online Initiative Dr. Shirley BROWN
41 Dir of Athletics & Intramural Pgms Ms. Corrinne TARVER
25 Dir Sponsored Research & Programs Dr. Sajid HUSSAIN
111 Assoc VP Inst Advancement Ms. Sheila SMITH
18 Director of Facilities Mr. David COBB
19 Chief/Director of Campus Safety Mr. Mickey WEST
84 AVP Enroll Mgmt & Career Plng Ms. Latreace WELLS
15 Asst VP of Human Resources Ms. Carol COOPER
105 Web Administrator Mr. James DENNIS
39 Dean of Students Mr. Gary EDWARDS
43 Dir Legal Services/General Counsel Ms. Stacey GARRETT-KOJU
26 Director Marketing & Communication Ms. Maya BROWN
124 Director of AESP Mr. Jonas TELLIS
50 Chair of Business Admin Dr. Nicholas UMONTUEN
122 Dir Student Activities-Greek Life Mr. Nathaniel PERRY, III
29 Director Alumni Affairs Ms. Adrienne LATHAM

Fortis Institute (F)

1025 Highway 111, Cookeville TN 38501-4305
County: Putnam FICE Identification: 023263
Unit ID: 418870
Telephone: (931) 526-3660 Carnegie Class: Not Classified
FAX Number: (931) 372-2603 Calendar System: Quarter
URL: www.fortis.edu/cookeville-tennessee.php
Established: 1970 Annual Undergrad Tuition & Fees: N/A
Enrollment: N/A Coed
Affiliation or Control: Proprietary IRS Status: Proprietary
Highest Offering: Associate Degree
Accreditation: **ACCSC**, MLTAD, NUR, RAD, SURGT

01 Campus President Mr. James WILLIAMSON
06 Registrar Ms. Wendy BANDY
07 Director of Admissions Mr. David HANEY
10 Chief Business Officer Ms. Melissa LEWIS
36 Director Career Services Ms. Cindy GARRISON
37 Director Financial Aid Ms. Lisa WALLING

Fortis Institute-Nashville (G)

3354 Perimeter Hill Drive Suite 200, Nashville TN 37211
Telephone: (615) 320-5917 Identification: 770509
Accreditation: **ABHES**, CVT, MLTAD, RAD, SURGT, SURTEC

† Branch campus of Fortis Institute, Baton Rouge, LA.

Freed-Hardeman University (H)

158 E Main, Henderson TN 38340-2398
County: Chester FICE Identification: 003492
Unit ID: 220215
Telephone: (731) 989-6000 Carnegie Class: Masters/M
FAX Number: (731) 989-6023 Calendar System: Semester
URL: www.fhu.edu
Established: 1869 Annual Undergrad Tuition & Fees: $22,950
Enrollment: 2,188 Coed
Affiliation or Control: Churches Of Christ IRS Status: 501(c)3
Highest Offering: Doctorate
Accreditation: **SC**, ACBSP, CACREP, CAEP, NURSE, @PTAA, SW, THEOL

01 President Mr. David R. SHANNON
04 Executive Assistant to President Mrs. Donna STEELE
05 Provost and VP Academics Dr. Charles VIRES
10 Chief Financial Officer Dr. Jason BRASHIER
111 VP for Community Engagement Mr. Dave CLOUSE
32 VP Student Services Mr. TJ KIRK
110 Associate VP for Advancement Mr. Kyle LAMB
84 Associate VP Enrollment Management Mr. Joseph ASKEW
115 Chief Investment Officer Mr. Jay SATTERFIELD
41 Director of Athletics Mr. Jonathan ESTES
31 Associate VP Community Engagement Mr. Ryan MALECHA
07 Director of Admissions Mrs. Kaylan STEWART
29 Director of Alumni Engagement Mr. Chris RAMEY
35 Dean of Students Vacant
06 Registrar Mrs. Susan KIMPEL
37 Director Student Financial Services Mrs. Summer JUDD
15 Director of Human Resources Ms. LeVetta HUDSON
08 Library Director Mr. Wade OSBURN
70 Director of Social Work Program Dr. Nadine MCNEAL
24 A-V Supervisor Mrs. Gail NASH
21 Controller Mr. Ethan DARETY
108 Dir Institutional Effectiveness Mr. A.B WHITE
09 Director of Institutional Research Dr. Jim BARR
18 Director of Facilities and Grounds Mr. Shannon SEWELL
73 Dean College of Biblical Studies Dr. Mark A. BLACKWELDER
50 Dean College of Business Dr. Matt VEGA
53 Dean College of Educ & Behav Sci Dr. Sharen CYPRESS
49 Dean College of Arts & Sciences Dr. LeAnn SELF-DAVIS
92 Dean of Honors College Dr. Jenny JOHNSON
96 Purchasing Coordinator Mrs. Nina MIMS
40 University Book Store Manager Mrs. Katie THURMAN
19 Director of Campus Safety/Security Mr. Stewart BRACKIN
88 Dir of Emerging/Innovation Programs Dr. Jared GOTT
30 Assistant VP of Development Mr. David NEWBERRY
38 Director of Univ Counseling Center Mr. Jonathan HARRISON
39 Dir Resident Life/Student Housing Mrs. Missie ELLIS

Harding School of Theology (I)

1000 Cherry Road, Memphis TN 38117-5499
Telephone: (901) 761-1350 FICE Identification: 004081
Accreditation: **&HLC**, THEOL

† Regional accreditation is carried under Harding University, Searcy, AR.

Huntington University of Health Sciences (A)

118 Legacy View Way, Knoxville TN 37918
County: Knox Identification: 666971
Unit ID: 488068
Telephone: (865) 524-8079 Carnegie Class: Bac/Assoc-Mixed
FAX Number: (865) 524-8339 Calendar System: Semester
URL: www.huhs.edu
Established: 1985 Annual Undergrad Tuition & Fees: $6,610
Enrollment: 147 Coed
Affiliation or Control: Proprietary IRS Status: Proprietary
Highest Offering: Doctorate
Accreditation: DEAC

01 Chief Executive Officer/President ....Dr. Art PRESSER
05 Provost ....Mr. Gene BRUNO
10 Chief Financial Officer ....Mr. Robert SCHMAEFF
11 Director of Administration ....Ms. Amy STEWART
20 Assoc Director of Academic Affairs ....Vacant
07 Director of Admissions ....Mr. Gregory SCOTT
21 Director of Finance ....Vacant
37 Director of Financial Aid ....Ms. Heather MORRISON-MONGER
06 Registrar ....Ms. Amy STEWART
08 Head Librarian ....Ms. Pam WREN
58 Dean of Graduate Studies ....Mr. Chris NUTTING

Hussian College Clarksville (B)

2691 Trenton Road, Clarksville TN 37040-6718
Telephone: (931) 552-7600 Identification: 666492
Accreditation: ACCSC, PTAA

† Branch campus of Hussian College, Philadelphia, PA

The Institute for G.O.D. (C)

401 Center Street, Old Hickory TN 37188
County: Davidson Identification: 667419
Telephone: (615) 879-2022 Carnegie Class: Not Classified
FAX Number: N/A Calendar System: Semester
URL: instituteforgod.org
Established: 2004 Annual Undergrad Tuition & Fees: N/A
Enrollment: N/A Coed
Affiliation or Control: Independent Non-Profit IRS Status: 501(c)3
Highest Offering: Master's
Accreditation: @BI

01 Founder & President ....Gregg GARNER
05 Chief Academic Officer ....Jeffrey SHERROD
06 Registrar ....Shaun GALFORD
07 Director of Admissions ....Laurie KAGAY
08 Chief Library Officer ....Benjamin REESE
09 Director of Institutional Research ....Jeff SHERROD
37 Director Student Financial Aid ....Katherine DUNNING

John A. Gupton College (D)

1616 Church Street, Nashville TN 37203-2920
County: Davidson FICE Identification: 008859
Unit ID: 220464
Telephone: (615) 327-3927 Carnegie Class: Spec 2-yr-A&S
FAX Number: (615) 321-4518 Calendar System: Semester
URL: www.guptoncollege.edu
Established: 1946 Annual Undergrad Tuition & Fees: $11,583
Enrollment: 167 Coed
Affiliation or Control: Independent Non-Profit IRS Status: 501(c)3
Highest Offering: Associate Degree
Accreditation: SC, FUSER

01 President ....Mr. B. Steven SPANN
08 Dir Educational Support/Librarian ....Mr. William P. BRUCE
06 Registrar ....Ms. Lisa MOFFITT

Johnson University (E)

7900 Johnson Drive, Knoxville TN 37998-0001
County: Knox FICE Identification: 003495
Unit ID: 220473
Telephone: (865) 573-4517 Carnegie Class: Masters/M
FAX Number: (865) 251-2337 Calendar System: Semester
URL: www.johnsonu.edu
Established: 1893 Annual Undergrad Tuition & Fees: $18,290
Enrollment: 1,039 Coed
Affiliation or Control: Christian Churches And Churches of Christ
IRS Status: 501(c)3
Highest Offering: Doctorate
Accreditation: SC, BI, CACREP

01 President ....Dr. Thomas SMITH
05 Provost ....Dr. Greg LINTON
10 VP for Finance ....Cindy BARNARD
32 VP for Student Services ....Dr. Andrew FRAZIER
111 VP for Advancement ....Richard CLARK
11 VP for Campus Services ....Dr. Wilbur REID, III
07 Chief Admissions Officer ....Lisa TARWATER
26 Chief Communications Officer ....Jennifer JOHNSON
41 Athletic Director ....Brandon PERRY
44 Asst VP Planned Giving ....Philip EUBANKS
49 Dean Arts & Sciences ....Dr. Gary STRATTON
73 Dean Bible & Theology ....Dr. Steve COOK
50 Dean Business & Leadership ....Dr. Catherlyn BRIM
60 Dean Communication & Creative Arts ....Dr. Matthew BROADDUS
73 Dean Congregational Ministry ....Dr. Daniel OVERDORF
82 Dean Intercultural Studies ....Dr. Linda WHITMER
83 Dean Social & Behavioral Sciences ....Dr. Sean RIDGE
53 Dean Templar School of Education ....Dr. Roy MILLER
106 Assoc Provost for Online Education ....Dr. David EVELAND
35 Assoc Dean of Students ....Dr. Michael MOORE
35 Assoc Dean of Students ....Deborah LANE
13 Director of IT ....Luke EDWARDS
121 Director of Academic Support ....Kelly ESTES
06 Registrar ....Shawn SMITH
29 Director Alumni Relations ....Tyson CHASTAIN
38 Director Student Counseling ....Maria GRECO
30 Director of Church Relations ....Brian LAKIN
15 Director Human Resources ....Beverly DARNELL
18 Director of Facilities Services ....Ben LUTZ, JR.
37 Director of Financial Aid ....Rocky CHRISTENSEN
20 Director of Program Administration ....Tori SKOLOSH
09 Dir of Institutional Effectiveness ....Emili WILLIAMS
08 Library Director ....Carrie Beth LOWE
04 Admin Assistant to the President ....Jill BRANSON
39 Resident Life/Student Housing ....Weldon DAVIS
39 Resident Life/Student Housing ....Crystal HUSS

King University (F)

1350 King College Road, Bristol TN 37620-2699
County: Sullivan FICE Identification: 003496
Unit ID: 220516
Telephone: (423) 968-4861 Carnegie Class: Masters/L
FAX Number: (423) 968-4456 Calendar System: Other
URL: www.king.edu
Established: 1867 Annual Undergrad Tuition & Fees: $31,840
Enrollment: 1,746 Coed
Affiliation or Control: Presbyterian Church (U.S.A.) IRS Status: 501(c)3
Highest Offering: Doctorate
Accreditation: SC, NURSE, SW

01 President ....Mr. Alexander W. WHITAKER, IV
05 Provost ....Dr. Matthew ROBERTS
10 Vice President for Admin & Finance ....Mr. James P. DONAHUE
32 Vice President for Student Affairs ....Dr. Robert A. LITTLETON
84 Vice Pres of Enrollment Mgmt ....Dr. Jon HARR
111 Vice President for Advancement ....Vacant
08 Dean of Library Services ....Dr. Matt PELTIER
04 Executive Assistant to President ....Ms. Holly L. STEVENS
06 Registrar/Dir Regist & Records ....Mrs. Whitney CLELAND
110 Associate Director of Development ....Vacant
42 Chaplain ....Dr. Brian ALDERMAN
21 Director of Business Operations ....Mr. Thomas R. LARSON
41 Athletic Director ....Mr. J. David HICKS
38 Director of Counseling ....Ms. Heather C. BRADDOCK
88 Sports Information Director ....Mr. Travis L. CHELL
40 Bookstore Manager ....Vacant
37 Director Student Financial Aid ....Vacant
18 Chief Facilities/Physical Plant ....Mr. Todd THOMAS
92 Director of Honors Program ....Dr. Craig STREETMAN
27 Assoc Director of Communication ....Vacant
36 Director of Career Services ....Ms. Finley GREEN
29 Director Alumni & Cmty Engagement ....Mrs. Jenna M. CHRISTIE
13 Chief Information Officer ....Mr. Joel ROBERTSON
19 Director Safety & Security ....Mr. Benny BERRY
39 Dir Resident Life/Student Housing ....Mr. Chase ARNDT
104 Director Study Abroad ....Dr. Karen L. SHAW
108 Director Institutional Assessment ....Mr. Jason THEAD

Lane College (G)

545 Lane Avenue, Jackson TN 38301-4598
County: Madison FICE Identification: 003499
Unit ID: 220598
Telephone: (731) 426-7500 Carnegie Class: Bac-A&S
FAX Number: (731) 427-3987 Calendar System: Semester
URL: www.lanecollege.edu
Established: 1882 Annual Undergrad Tuition & Fees: $11,790
Enrollment: 1,095 Coed
Affiliation or Control: Christian Methodist Episcopal IRS Status: 501(c)3
Highest Offering: Baccalaureate
Accreditation: SC

01 President ....Dr. Logan C. HAMPTON
05 Acting VP Academic Affairs ....Mr. Daryll COLEMAN
11 Exec Vice Pres Administration ....Ms. Sherrill B. SCOTT
32 Vice President Student Affairs ....Mr. Darryl MCGEE
13 Assoc VP Information Technology ....Mr. Ernest L. MITCHELL, III
100 Chief of Staff/VP Inst Advancement ....Ms. Darlette C. SAMUELS
42 Head Chaplain ....Dr. Freeman MCKINDRA
37 Director of Financial Aid ....Ms. Regina ANDERSON
08 Librarian ....Ms. Lan WANG
06 Registrar ....Mr. Terry W. BLACKMON
20 Director Academic Assessment ....Vacant
19 Director of Safety/Security ....Mr. Steaven JOY
29 Director Alumni Relations ....Ms. Braylin LASTER
27 Chief Information Officer ....Vacant
86 Dir Gov Relations/Sr Adv to Pres ....Mr. Richard DONNELL, SR.
102 Director of Annual Fund ....Ms. Lisa PEOPLES

Lee University (H)

1120 N Ocoee St, Cleveland TN 37320-3450
County: Bradley FICE Identification: 003500
Unit ID: 220613
Telephone: (423) 614-8000 Carnegie Class: Masters/M
FAX Number: (423) 614-8083 Calendar System: Semester
URL: www.leeuniversity.edu
Established: 1918 Annual Undergrad Tuition & Fees: $19,540
Enrollment: 5,204 Coed
Affiliation or Control: Church Of God IRS Status: 501(c)3
Highest Offering: Doctorate
Accreditation: SC, ACBSP, CAATE, CAEP, MFCD, MUS, NURSE

01 President ....Dr. Mark L. WALKER
04 Executive Assistant to President ....Mrs. Andrea CAMPBELL-BROWN
10 Vice President Business & Finance ....Mr. Chris CONINE
05 Vice President for Academic Affairs ....Dr. Deborah MURRAY
32 VP for Student Development ....Vacant
26 VP for University Relations ....Dr. Brad MOFFETT
84 VP for Enrollment & Marketing ....Dr. Jayson VANHOOK
20 Asst VP Academic Affairs ....Dr. Jean ELEDGE
88 Assistant VP for Enrollment ....Dr. Shane GRIFFITH
21 Comptroller/Dir Accounting Services ....Mr. Duane PACE
37 Director of Financial Aid ....Mrs. Marian DILL
15 Director of Human Resources ....Vacant
13 Director of Information Technology ....Mr. Nate TUCKER
29 Director of Alumni Relations ....Vacant
39 Director of Residential Life ....Mr. Jarad RUSSELL
06 University Registrar ....Mrs. Erin LOONEY
113 Director Student Financial Services ....Ms. Kristy HARNER
08 Director Library Services ....Dr. Louis MORGAN
42 Director of Campus Ministries ....Dr. Rob FULTZ
25 Director of Grants/Foundation ....Mrs. Vanessa HAMMOND
19 Director of Campus Safety ....Mr. Matt BRINKMAN
23 Director of Health Services ....Ms. Rachel COFFEY
27 Director of Public Relations ....Mr. Brian CONN
73 Dean School of Religion ....Dr. Terry CROSS
49 Dean College of Arts & Sciences ....Dr. Matthew MELTON
53 Dean College of Education ....Dr. William ESTES
64 Dean School of Music ....Dr. William GREEN
66 Dean School of Nursing ....Dr. Sara CAMPBELL
106 Exec Dir of Div of Lee Online ....Dr. Joshua BLACK
50 Dean School of Business ....Dr. Dewayne THOMPSON
123 Director Grad & Online Enrollment ....Mr. Micah VORARITSKUL
38 Director of Counseling Center ....Dr. David QUAGLIANA
18 Dir Physical Plant/Building Svcs ....Mr. Larry BERRY
41 Athletic Director ....Mr. Larry CARPENTER
104 Director of Global Perspectives ....Mrs. Angeline MCMULLIN
36 Dir Center of Calling and Career ....Ms. Kristin POPE
07 Director Undergraduate Admissions ....Ms. Vanessa CAREY
09 Director of Institutional Research ....Ms. Elizabeth PACE

LeMoyne-Owen College (I)

807 Walker Avenue, Memphis TN 38126-6595
County: Shelby FICE Identification: 003501
Unit ID: 220604
Telephone: (901) 435-1477 Carnegie Class: Bac-Diverse
FAX Number: (901) 435-1699 Calendar System: Semester
URL: www.loc.edu
Established: 1862 Annual Undergrad Tuition & Fees: $12,076
Enrollment: 654 Coed
Affiliation or Control: Multiple Protestant Denominations
IRS Status: 501(c)3
Highest Offering: Baccalaureate
Accreditation: SC, ACBSP, #CAEP

01 President ....Dr. Vernell BENNETT-FAIRS
05 Provost/VP Academic Affairs ....Dr. Lisa LANG
10 VP Finance and Administration ....Mr. Stanley ROBINSON
32 Dean of Students ....Ms. Jean SAULSBERRY
111 VP Institutional Advancement ....Ms. Julie GRAVES
13 VP Information Technology ....Mr. Charles G. ELLIOTT
84 Exec Dir Strategic Enrollment Mgmt ....Vacant
15 Exec Dir Human Resources ....Ms. Shanta BROOKS
22 Director Title III Administration ....Mrs. Angela A. WOOTEN
08 Librarian ....Ms. Stacey SMITH
37 Director Student Financial Services ....Vacant
06 Registrar ....Ms. Mona WASHINGTON
100 Chief of Staff ....Dr. Cynthia SHELTON
29 Director of Alumni Relations ....Dr. June CHINN-JOINTER
09 Director Institutional Research ....Mr. Reongeneria MCFARLAND
92 Director Du Bois Honors Program ....Mr. Dorsey PATTERSON
50 Chair Business/Economic Development ....Dr. Katherine CAUSEY
53 Chair Education Division ....Dr. Ralph CALHOUN
57 Chair Div Fine Arts & Humanities ....Dr. Linda WHITE
65 Chair Div Natural & Math Science ....Dr. Sherry PAINTER
83 Chair Div Social & Behavioral Sci ....Mr. Michael ROBINSON
38 Director Student Counseling ....Mrs. Shalunda ASKEW-ELLIOTT
26 Exec Dir Communications ....Vacant
41 Director of Athletics ....Mr. William ANDERSON
11 Director Administrative Services ....Mr. Jesse CHATMAN
07 Director of Admissions ....Mrs. Wendy HARRIS
04 Administrative Asst to President ....Ms. Kimberly MONDAY
18 Chief Facilities/Physical Plant ....Mr. Anthony COWAN

Lincoln College of Technology Nashville (J)

1524 Gallatin Avenue, Nashville TN 37206-3298
County: Davidson FICE Identification: 007440
Unit ID: 221148
Telephone: (615) 226-3990 Carnegie Class: Spec 2-yr-Tech
FAX Number: (615) 262-8466 Calendar System: Other
URL: www.lincolncollegeoftechnology.com
Established: 1919 Annual Undergrad Tuition & Fees: N/A
Enrollment: 1,638 Coed
Affiliation or Control: Proprietary IRS Status: Proprietary

Highest Offering: Associate Degree
Accreditation: ACCSC

02 Campus President .... Mr. David WHITEFORD
05 Academic Dean .... Ms. Rachel OBPTANDE
07 Director of Admissions .... Mr. Shayne PULVER
37 Financial Aid Manager .... Ms. Wendy THOMPSON
36 Director of Career Services .... Ms. Sandra JORDAN

Lincoln Memorial University (A)

6965 Cumberland Gap Parkway,
Harrogate TN 37752-1901
County: Claiborne FICE Identification: 003502
Unit ID: 220631
Telephone: (423) 869-3611 Carnegie Class: DU-Mod
FAX Number: (423) 869-6250 Calendar System: Semester
URL: https://www.lmunet.edu/
Established: 1897 Annual Undergrad Tuition & Fees: $23,490
Enrollment: 4,885 Coed
Affiliation or Control: Independent Non-Profit IRS Status: 501(c)3
Highest Offering: Doctorate
Accreditation: SC, ACBSP, ADNUR, ANEST, ARCPA, CACREP, CAEP, LAW, MLS, NUR, OSTEO, @PTA, SW, VET

01 President .... Dr. E. Clayton HESS
111 VP University Advancement .... Ms. Cynthia L. WHITT
05 Executive VP Academic Affairs .... Dr. Jay STUBBLEFIELD
10 Exec VP Finance & Administration .... Ms. Christy GRAHAM
35 Assoc Dean Stdnts LMU-DCOM Knox .... Dr. Justina HYFANTIS
35 Assistant Dean of Students LMU-DCOM .... Dr. Kali WEAVER
61 VP/Dean School of Law .... Mr. Matthew LYON
11 Executive VP for Administration .... Dr. Jody GOINS
74 Dean College of Veterinary Med .... Dr. Stacy ANDERSON
63 Dean/CAO College of Osteopathic Med .... Dr. Christopher LOYKE
76 Dean Allied Health Sciences .... Dr. Elizabeth THOMPSON
89 Asst Dean Students/Dir 1st Yr Exp .... Ms. Elise SYOEN
53 Interim Dean of School of Education .... Dr. Teresa BICKNELL
81 Dean of Mathematics & Sciences .... Dr. Adam ROLLINS
66 Dean School of Nursing .... Dr. Tammy DEAN
50 Dean School of Business .... Dr. James MAXWELL
04 Exec Assistant to the President .... Mrs. Janet SMITH
37 Exec Dir Student Financial Services .... Ms. Tammy TOMFOHRDE
46 AVP Planning/Inst Effectiveness .... Dr. Kala PERKINS-HOLTSCLAW
108 Director of Assessment .... Dr. Carlton LARSEN
41 Athletic Director .... Mr. Jasher COX
18 Director Infrastructure Management .... Mr. David LAWS
15 Chief Human Resources Officer .... Ms. Amy EADS
96 Director Purchasing .... Ms. Aprile MASON
06 Registrar .... Ms. Helen BAILEY
42 University Chaplain .... Vacant
43 General Counsel .... Mr. Ryan BROWN
13 Chief Information Officer .... Mr. Jason MCCONNELL
26 Sr Dir Marketing/Public Relations .... Mrs. Katherine M. REAGAN
29 Sr Director Alumni Services .... Ms. Sheliah COSBY
40 Bookstore Manager (Barnes & Noble) .... Mr. Grey JANEWAY
49 Dean of Arts/Humanities/Social Sci .... Dr. Martin SELLERS
88 Special Assistant to the President .... Mr. Tommy THOMAS
63 VP/Dean School of Medical Sciences .... Dr. Mark MORAN
22 Title IX Coord/Ofc Inst Compliance .... Ms. Kelly HAWK
84 Executive Director for Enrollment .... Ms. Lindsay HAYWOOD
08 Director of the Library .... Ms. Rhonda ARMSTRONG
103 Director of Career Services .... Mr. Roger HOLTSCLAW
19 Chief of Campus Police & Security .... Mr. Patrick VAUGHT
25 Exec Director of Grants and Sponsor .... Ms. Carolyn GULLEY
28 Director for Inclusion & Diversity .... Ms. Wanda ELDAHAN
32 Assoc Dean of Student Affairs CVM .... Dr. Bess PIERCE
38 Director Mental Health Counseling .... Dr. Jason KISHPAUGH
44 Asst Dir of Alumni & Annual Giving .... Mr. Jared ZANET

Lipscomb University (B)

One University Park Dr., Nashville TN 37204-3951
County: Davidson FICE Identification: 003486
Unit ID: 219976
Telephone: (615) 966-1000 Carnegie Class: DU-Mod
FAX Number: (615) 966-1798 Calendar System: Semester
URL: www.lipscomb.edu
Established: 1891 Annual Undergrad Tuition & Fees: $34,744
Enrollment: 4,884 Coed
Affiliation or Control: Churches Of Christ IRS Status: 501(c)3
Highest Offering: Doctorate
Accreditation: SC, ACBSP, #ARCPA, CACREP, CAEP, DIETD, DIETI, EXSC, MFCD, MUS, NUR, PHAR, SW, THEOL

01 President .... Dr. Candice MCQUEEN
05 Provost .... Dr. W. Craig BLEDSOE
45 SVP for Strategy .... Dr. Susan C. GALBREATH
10 Senior VP Finance & Technology .... Mr. Jeffrey BAUGHN
111 SVP Advancement .... Dr. John LOWRY
32 SVP Enroll Mgmt/Student Engagement .... Dr. Matt PADEN
43 General Counsel .... Dr. David WILSON
23 Director of Health and Wellness .... Dr. Kevin EIDSON
26 VP Marketing .... Mr. Dave BRUNO
21 VP Finance .... Mr. Darrell DUNCAN
15 VP Human Resources .... Ms. Christy HOOPER
13 VP Information Technology .... Mr. Brett HINSON
41 Director of Athletics .... Mr. Philip HUTCHESON
27 VP University Relations .... Mr. Walt LEAVER
84 VP Enrollment Management .... Mr. Byron LEWIS
42 VP Church Services .... Dr. Scott SAGER
35 VP of Student Life .... Vacant
22 Spec Counsel for Diversity/Inclus .... Dr. William L. TURNER
20 Vice Provost for Academic Affairs .... Dr. Randy BOULDIN
17 Vice Provost of Health Affairs .... Dr. Quincy BYRDSONG
28 Assoc Prov Diversity & Inclusion .... Dr. Norma BURGESS
88 Vice Provost for Inst Effectiveness .... Dr. Elaine GRIFFIN
20 Associate Provost Academic Support .... Mr. Steve PREWITT
108 Assoc Provost Inst Effectiveness .... Dr. Catherine TERRY
06 Registrar .... Ms. Angel BEBOUT
73 Dean College of Bible & Ministry .... Dr. C. Leonard ALLEN
53 Dean Col of Education .... Dr. Trace HEBERT
49 Dean Col of Liberal Arts & Sciences .... Dr. David HOLMES
67 Dean College of Pharmacy .... Dr. Tom CAMPBELL
66 Executive Director Nursing .... Dr. Chelsia HARRIS
50 Dean College of Business .... Dr. Ray ELDRIDGE
54 Dean College of Engineering .... Mr. David ELROD
57 Dean Shinn Col Ent & Arts .... Mr. Mike FERNANDEZ
80 Dean Col Leadership & Public Svc .... Dr. Steve JOINER
77 Dean School of Computing/Technology .. Dr. Steve NORDSTROM
106 Int Exec Dir Col of Prof Studies .... Mr. Ted MEYER
08 Director of Library Services .... Ms. Julie HARSTON
88 Asst Dean Intercultural Development .... Mr. Prentice ASHFORD
73 Assoc Dean Hazelip Sch of Theology .... Dr. Frank GUERTIN
88 Dean Vocation/Spiritual Formation .... Mr. Deron SMITH
88 Director Academic Finance .... Ms. Carol LUSK
88 Found Dir Inst for Sustain Practice .... Mr. Dodd GALBREATH
88 Dir Inst for Law Justice & Society .... Ms. Kimberly MCCALL
88 Dir Inst for Civic Leadership .... Ms. Sara OESER
103 Director of Career Development Ctr .... Dr. Monica WENTWORTH
83 Chair Grad Studies in Psychology .... Dr. Shanna RAY
09 Director of Institutional Research .... Mr. Matt REHBEIN
38 Director Counseling Center .... Ms. Andrea MILLS
88 Dir Inst for Christian Spirituality .... Dr. Kris MILLER
19 ED of Campus Security & Safety .... Mr. Kyle DICKERSON
86 Director Community & Govt Relations .... Ms. Amanda MARTIN
07 Asst VP of Undergrad Admissions .... Mr. Johnathan AKIN
39 Dean of Housing and Residence Life .... Ms. Laurie SAIN
37 Assoc VP Student Financial Services .... Mr. Ron ANDERSON
44 Asst VP Annual Giving & Advanc Svcs .... Vacant
18 Director Campus Constr & Facilities .... Mr. Mike ENGELMAN
104 Director Global Learning .... Ms. Rebecca ZANOLINI
04 Admin Assistant to the President .... Ms. Leslie LANDISS

Maryville College (C)

502 E Lamar Alexander Parkway,
Maryville TN 37804-5907
County: Blount FICE Identification: 003505
Unit ID: 220710
Telephone: (865) 981-8000 Carnegie Class: Bac-A&S
FAX Number: (865) 981-8010 Calendar System: Semester
URL: www.maryvillecollege.edu
Established: 1819 Annual Undergrad Tuition & Fees: $36,292
Enrollment: 1,072 Coed
Affiliation or Control: Independent Non-Profit IRS Status: 501(c)3
Highest Offering: Master's
Accreditation: SC, MUS

01 President .... Dr. Bryan F. COKER
04 Assistant to President .... Ms. Suzette DONOVAN
00 Chairman of the Board .... Mr. Mike DAVIS
05 Vice Pres & Dean of College .... Dr. Dan KLINGENSMITH
32 Vice President & Dean of Students .... Dr. Melanie V. TUCKER
111 VP for Institutional Advancement .... Ms. Suzy BOOKER
07 VP for Admissions & Financial Aid .... Ms. Alayne BOWMAN
26 Exec Dir for Mktg & Communications .... Ms. Karen ELDRIDGE
45 Exec Director Strategic Initiatives .... Ms. Christy MCDONALD SLAVICK
20 Associate Dean & Director of IR .... Dr. Jerilyn SWANN
121 Asst Dean of Academic Success .... Dr. Heather MCMAHON
06 Interim Registrar .... Ms. Lisa VITALE
35 Assistant Dean of Students .... Ms. Desiree WASHINGTON
104 Director of International Education .... Ms. Kirsten SHEPPARD
36 Director of the Career Center .... Ms. Sarah TAYLOR-YEAPLE
37 Director of Financial Aid .... Ms. Erin JOHNSON
41 Athletic Director .... Ms. Sara QUATROCKY
08 Director of the Library .... Ms. Angela QUICK
18 Director of Physical Plant .... Mr. Larry MAY
42 Campus Minister .... Vacant
15 Director of Human Resources .... Ms. Keni LANAGAN
38 Director of Counseling .... Ms. Claudia WERNER
30 Director of Development .... Mr. Eric BELLAH
29 Director of Alumni Affairs .... Ms. Jennifer TRIPLETT
112 Director of Major Gifts .... Ms. Diana CANACARIS
40 Bookstore Manager .... Mr. Ryan LILLY
88 Gen Mgr Clayton Center for the Arts .... Mr. Blake SMITH
19 Director of Safety & Security .... Vacant
39 Asst Director Housing Operations .... Ms. Raeann REIHL
44 Director Annual Giving .... Ms. Meghan FAGG
09 Director of Institutional Research .... Dr. Jerilyn SWANN
10 Vice President of Finance .... Ms. Kelly LEONARD
101 Secretary of the Institution/Board .... Mr. Adriel MCCORD
11 Chief of Operations/Administration .... Mr. John K. BERRY

Meharry Medical College (D)

1005 Dr. D. B. Todd Jr. Boulevard,
Nashville TN 37208-3501
County: Davidson FICE Identification: 003506
Unit ID: 220792
Telephone: (615) 327-6111 Carnegie Class: Spec-4-yr-Med
FAX Number: (615) 327-6540 Calendar System: Semester
URL: www.mmc.edu
Established: 1876 Annual Graduate Tuition & Fees: N/A
Enrollment: 944 Coed
Affiliation or Control: Independent Non-Profit IRS Status: 501(c)3
Highest Offering: Doctorate; No Undergraduates
Accreditation: SC, ARCPA, DENT, MED, PH

01 President/Chief Executive Ofcr .... Dr. James E.K HILDRETH, SR.
05 Exec Vice Dean School .... Vacant
03 EVP for Administration .... Dr. Peter E. MILLET
63 Int Dean School of Medicine .... Dr. Digna FORBES
11 Sr Vice Pres for BOT Relations .... Dr. Saletta HOLLOWAY
26 VP Marketing/Communications .... Vacant
10 Sr Vice President Finance/CFO .... Mrs. LaMel BANDY-NEAL
32 Sr Vice Pres Student Affairs .... Dr. A. Dexter SAMUELS
58 Int Dean School of Graduate Studies .... Dr. Evangeline MOTLEY JOHNSON
20 Int VP Faculty Affairs .... Dr. Allysceaeioun BRITT
13 CIO/Ellucian Contract .... Mr. Dennis GENDRON
15 Assoc Vice Pres Human Resources .... Mr. Mark SMITH
21 Assoc Vice Pres Financial Systems .... Mr. Larry HOLDEN
111 SVP Institutional Advancement .... Mr. Patrick H. JOHNSON
25 Asst Controller Grants/Contracts .... Ms. Zulfat A. SUARA
43 SVP/General Counsel/Corp Sec .... Mrs. Ivanetta DAVIS-SAMUELS
46 SVP Research/Innovation .... Dr. Anil SHANKER
51 Director Lifelong Learning .... Dr. Allyson FLEMING
76 Dean Allied Health Professions .... Vacant
52 SVP & Dean School of Dentistry .... Dr. Cherae FARMER-DIXON
81 SVP/Dean Sch App Computational Sci .... Dr. Fortune MHLANGA
29 Executive Director Alumni Affairs .... Dr. Henry MOSES
07 Dir Admissions & Recruitment .... Ms. April E. CURRY-ROBERTS
08 Director of Library .... Vacant
19 Int Dir Campus Safety & Security .... Mr. Dontez HUSKEY
37 Director Student Financial Aid .... Ms. Barbara THARPE
09 Director Institutional Research .... Dr. Chau-Kuang CHEN
100 Chief of Staff/Dir Title III Adm .... Mrs. Sandra ANDERSON-WILLIAMS
18 Director Facilities .... Mr. Lewis ETHRIDGE
38 Director Counseling Center .... Ms. Sharda D. MISHRA
06 Registrar .... Ms. Miacia PORTER
04 Executive Assistant to the Pres .... Ms. Kimberly STEVENSON

Memphis Theological Seminary (E)

168 East Parkway S at Union, Memphis TN 38104-4395
County: Shelby FICE Identification: 010529
Unit ID: 220871
Telephone: (901) 458-8232 Carnegie Class: Spec-4-yr-Faith
FAX Number: (901) 452-4051 Calendar System: Semester
URL: www.memphisseminary.edu
Established: 1852 Annual Graduate Tuition & Fees: N/A
Enrollment: 183 Coed
Affiliation or Control: Cumberland Presbyterian IRS Status: 501(c)3
Highest Offering: Doctorate; No Undergraduates
Accreditation: SC, THEOL

01 President .... Dr. Jody HILL
05 Vice President Academic Affs & Dean .... Dr. Peter GATHJE
10 Vice President of Operations/CFO .... Cassandra F. PRICE-PERRY
84 VP Enrollment Services & IE .... Dr. Gail ROBINSON
08 Director of Library Services .... Ed HUGHES
32 Exec Director of Student Services .... Dr. Barry L. ANDERSON
37 Director of Financial Aid .... Fekecia GUNN
36 Director Student Placement .... Dr. Barry ANDERSON
90 Director Academic Computing .... Chris SMITH

Meridian Institute of Surgical Assisting (F)

1507 County Hospital Road, Nashville TN 37218
County: Davidson FICE Identification: 041650
Unit ID: 461324
Telephone: (877) 954-1500 Carnegie Class: Spec 2-yr-Health
FAX Number: (615) 746-6765 Calendar System: Semester
URL: www.meridian-institute.edu
Established: 1999 Annual Undergrad Tuition & Fees: N/A
Enrollment: 816 Coed
Affiliation or Control: Proprietary IRS Status: Proprietary
Highest Offering: Associate Degree
Accreditation: ABHES, SURGA, SURTEC

01 President .... Mr. Dennis STOVER
05 Dean of Academic Affairs .... Mr. Roy G. ZACHARIAS
10 CFO .... Ms. April WEST

Mid-America Baptist Theological Seminary (G)

2095 Appling Road, Cordova TN 38016-4911
County: Shelby FICE Identification: 029172
Telephone: (901) 751-8453 Carnegie Class: Not Classified
FAX Number: (901) 751-8454 Calendar System: Semester
URL: www.mabts.edu
Established: 1972 Annual Undergrad Tuition & Fees: N/A
Enrollment: N/A Coed
Affiliation or Control: Independent Non-Profit IRS Status: 501(c)3
Highest Offering: Doctorate
Accreditation: SC

01 President .... Dr. Michael R. SPRADLIN
05 Exec Vice Pres/Dean of the College .... Dr. Bradley THOMPSON
05 Vice Pres/Dean of the Seminary .... Dr. Lee BRAND, JR.
10 Vice Pres for Finance & Operations .... Dr. Randy REDD

30 Chief Development Offilcer ...Mr. Van GRAY
12 Director NE Branch ...Dr. Michael HAGGARD
06 Registrar ...Mrs. Rose MINK
08 Director of Library Services ...Mr. Terrence BROWN
04 Admin Assistant to the President ...Ms. Cary Beth DUFFEL
15 Director of Human Resources ...Ms. Karen NELSON

Mid-South Christian College (A)

PO Box 181056, Memphis TN 38181
County: Shelby
Identification: 667046
Unit ID: 481225
Telephone: (901) 375-4400
Carnegie Class: Spec-4-yr-Faith
FAX Number: N/A
Calendar System: Semester
URL: www.midsouthchristian.edu
Established: 1959
Annual Undergrad Tuition & Fees: $9,215
Enrollment: 22
Coed
Affiliation or Control: Independent Non-Profit
IRS Status: 501(c)3
Highest Offering: Baccalaureate
Accreditation: BI

01 President ...Mr. Larry GRIFFIN
05 Academic Dean ...Dr. Robert GRIFFIN
04 Executive Assistant ...Mrs. Jane GIBSON
06 Registrar ...Mr. Keith GRAHAM
08 Head Librarian ...Mrs. Judi HOMAN
10 Business Manager ...Mrs. Renae MASK
32 Director of Student Services ...Mr. John BLIFFEN

Middle Tennessee School of Anesthesia (B)

315 Hospital Drive, Madison TN 37115
County: Davidson
FICE Identification: 007783
Unit ID: 220996
Telephone: (615) 868-6503
Carnegie Class: Spec-4-yr-Other Health
FAX Number: (615) 868-9885
Calendar System: Quarter
URL: www.mtsa.edu
Established: 1950
Annual Graduate Tuition & Fees: N/A
Enrollment: 229
Coed
Affiliation or Control: Independent Non-Profit
IRS Status: 501(c)3
Highest Offering: Doctorate; No Undergraduates
Accreditation: SC, ANEST

01 President ...Dr. Christopher P. HULIN
05 VP Academics ...Dr. Mana OVERSTREET
10 VP for Finance & Administration ...Jon RONNING
111 VP for Advancement & Alumni ...James B. CLOSSER
20 Program Administrator ...Dr. Rusty GENTRY
09 Dir of Inst Effectiveness & LR ...Dr. Amy C. GIDEON
07 Coord Admissions/Recruitment ...Pam NIMMO
13 Director Information Technology ...Aaron HASTINGS
37 Director Financial Aid ...Jennifer SPEER
06 Registrar ...Jessica CREASON
15 Director of Human Resources ...Asia BYERS

Middle Tennessee State University (C)

1301 E Main Street, Murfreesboro TN 37132-0001
County: Rutherford
FICE Identification: 003510
Unit ID: 220978
Telephone: (615) 898-2300
Carnegie Class: DU-Higher
FAX Number: N/A
Calendar System: Semester
URL: www.mtsu.edu
Established: 1911
Annual Undergrad Tuition & Fees (In-State): $9,070
Enrollment: 22,080
Coed
Affiliation or Control: State
IRS Status: 501(c)3
Highest Offering: Doctorate
Accreditation: SC, AAB, AAFCS, #ARCPA, ART, CAATE, CACREP, CAEP, CAPRT, CIDA, DIETD, FEPAC, JOUR, MUS, NAIT, NURSE, SW, THEA

02 President ...Dr. Sidney A. MCPHEE
05 University Provost ...Dr. Mark E. BYRNES
10 VP Business & Finance ...Mr. Alan R. THOMAS
111 VP University Advancement ...Mr. William J. BALES
32 VP Student Affairs ...Dr. Debra K. SELLS
13 VP Info Tech/Chief Info Officer ...Ms. Yvette CLARK
26 VP Marketing/Communications ...Mr. Andrew J. OPPMANN
58 Vice Prov Research/Dean Grad Stds ...Dr. David L. BUTLER
121 Vice Prov Student Success ...Dr. Richard D. SLUDER
43 Univ Counsel & Board Secretary ...Mr. James C. FLOYD
116 Chief Audit Executive ...Ms. Diane SNODGRASS
100 Exec Asst to Pres & Chief of Staff ...Ms. Kimberly S. EDGAR
22 Asst to Pres for Equity/Compliance ...Ms. Christy SIGLER
28 Community Engagement & Inclusion ...Dr. Monica SMITH
20 Vice Provost Faculty Affairs ...Dr. Cheryl B. TORSNEY
20 Vice Provost for Academic Programs ...Dr. Amy ALDRIDGE SANFORD
20 Assoc Prov Academic Resources ...Ms. Rebecca COLE
45 Assoc Prov Strategic Planning ...Dr. Mary S. HOFFSCHWELLE
85 Vice Provost International Affairs ...Dr. Robert SUMMERS
07 Assoc Vice Prov Enrollment Svcs ...Dr. Laurie B. WITHEROW
14 Assoc Vice Pres Technical Svcs ...Mr. Chad MULLIS
21 Assoc Vice Pres Business Office ...Ms. Kathy THURMAN
35 Assoc Vice Pres/Dean Student Life ...Ms. Sarah SUDAK
15 Asst Vice Pres Human Resource Svcs ...Ms. Kathy I. MUSSELMAN
18 Asst Vice Pres Facilities Services ...Mr. Joe WHITEFIELD
11 Asst Vice Pres Admin/Business Svcs ...Vacant
117 Asst Vice Pres Compliance/ERM ...Mr. Drew HARPOOL
119 Asst Vice Pres/Chief Info Sec ...Ms. Deb ZSIGALOV
90 Asst Vice Pres Acad & Instruct Tech ...Dr. Albert C. WHITTENBERG
81 Dean Col Basic/Applied Sciences ...Dr. Paul G. VAN PATTEN
83 Dean College Behavioral & Hlth Sci ...Dr. Harold D. WHITESIDE
60 Dean College of Media/Entertainment ...Ms. Beverly KEEL
50 Dean College of Business ...Dr. David J. URBAN
53 Dean College of Education ...Dr. Frederick P. VANOSDALL
49 Dean College of Liberal Arts ...Dr. Leah T. LYONS
92 Dean University Honors College ...Dr. John R. VILE
08 Dean University Library ...Ms. Kathleen SCHMAND
106 Chief Online Learning Officer ...Dr. Trey MARTINDALE
09 Asst Vice Provost for IEPR ...Mr. Chris BREWER
06 Asst Vice Prov Regist/Stdnt Records ...Dr. Tyler HENSON
36 Dir Career & Development Center ...Ms. Beka CROCKET
37 Dir of Financial Aid & Scholarship ...Mr. Stephen F. WHITE
25 Dir Research & Sponsored Programs ...Dr. Dawn M. MCCORMACK
29 Director Alumni Relations ...Ms. Ginger C. FREEMAN
40 General Manager Bookstore ...Ms. Natalie KAROUSATOS
24 Dir Center for Educational Media ...Dr. Laura B. CLARK
38 Director Counseling Services ...Dr. Mary Kaye G. ANDERSON
30 Director Development Office ...Vacant
84 Dir Enrollment Technical Systems ...Ms. Teresa W. THOMAS
27 Director News & Media Relations ...Mr. Jimmy W. HART
41 Director of Athletics ...Mr. Chris J. MASSARO
23 Director of Student Health Services ...Mr. Richard L. CHAPMAN
19 Chief of Police/Dir Public Safety ...Mr. Kevin H. WILLIAMS
39 Dir Resident Life/Student Housing ...Ms. Michelle SAFEWRIGHT
96 Executive Director of Procurement ...Mr. Shirman THOMAS
44 Director Annual Giving ...Ms. Kristen KEENE

Miller-Motte College (D)

6397 Lee Highway, Suite 100, Chattanooga TN 37421
County: Hamilton
FICE Identification: 023068
Unit ID: 443650
Telephone: (423) 510-9675
Carnegie Class: Assoc/HVT-High Trad
FAX Number: (423) 510-1985
Calendar System: Other
URL: www.miller-motte.edu
Established: 1979
Annual Undergrad Tuition & Fees: N/A
Enrollment: 167
Coed
Affiliation or Control: Proprietary
IRS Status: Proprietary
Highest Offering: Associate Degree
Accreditation: ACCSC, SURGT

01 Executive Director ...Jay FRANK
07 Director of Admissions ...Danielle POTTER
05 Director of Education ...Amy HOAGLAND

Milligan University (E)

101 Neth Drive, Milligan TN 37682
County: Carter
FICE Identification: 003511
Unit ID: 486901
Telephone: (423) 461-8700
Carnegie Class: Masters/M
FAX Number: (423) 461-8755
Calendar System: Semester
URL: www.milligan.edu
Established: 1866
Annual Undergrad Tuition & Fees: $35,600
Enrollment: 1,338
Coed
Affiliation or Control: Independent Non-Profit
IRS Status: 501(c)3
Highest Offering: Doctorate
Accreditation: SC, ACBSP, ARCPA, CACREP, CAEP, NURSE, OT, THEOL

01 President ...Dr. William B. GREER
05 Vice Pres Academic Affairs/Dean ...Dr. Garland YOUNG
32 Dean of Students ...Mr. Tony JONES
111 Vice Pres Institutional Advancement ...Mrs. Rhajon SMITH
84 Vice Pres Enrollment Management ...Mrs. Lauren GULLETT
10 Vice Pres Business & Finance ...Mrs. Jacqui STEADMAN
06 Registrar ...Mrs. Stacy DAHLMAN
07 Director of Admissions ...Mr. Marty RILEY
08 Director of Library Services ...Mr. Gary DAUGHT
35 Director of Student Activities ...Mrs. Brealle DAVIS
29 Director of Alumni Rels/Development ...Ms. Theresa GARBE
15 Director Human Resources ...Ms. Leslie BEAN
09 Director of Institutional Research ...Ms. Brenda BOURN
37 Director of Financial Aid ...Mr. Gus MORGAN
88 Director of Church Relations ...Mr. Kit DOTSON
36 Director Student Placement ...Ms. Beth ANDERSON
18 Service Manager Facilities ...Mr. Ken BROYLES
28 Director Multicultural Engagement ...Ms. Gwen ELLIS
26 Director of Marketing ...Ms. Chandrea SHELL
19 Director Property & Risk Management ...Mr. Brent NIPPER
90 Director of Information Technology ...Mrs. Amanda BRISTOL
04 Admin Assistant to the President ...Ms. Kathy BARNES
38 Director Student Counseling ...Dr. Rebecca SAPP
41 Director of Athletics ...Mr. Christian POPE

New College Franklin (F)

136 3rd Ave South, PO Box 1575, Franklin TN 37064
County: Williamson
Identification: 667390
Telephone: (615) 815-8360
Carnegie Class: Not Classified
FAX Number: N/A
Calendar System: Semester
URL: www.newcollegefranklin.edu
Established: 2006
Annual Undergrad Tuition & Fees: N/A
Enrollment: N/A
Coed
Affiliation or Control: Independent Non-Profit
IRS Status: 501(c)3
Highest Offering: Baccalaureate
Accreditation: TRACS

01 President ...Gregory WILBUR
05 Dean of Academics ...Brandon SPUN
06 Dir Operations/Registrar/Bursar ...Tammy MCCOY
32 Dean of Students/Library Svcs ...Anneke SEELY

North Central Institute (G)

168 Jack Miller Boulevard, Clarksville TN 37042-4810
County: Montgomery
FICE Identification: 030791
Unit ID: 418889
Telephone: (931) 431-9700
Carnegie Class: Spec 2-yr-Tech
FAX Number: (931) 431-9771
Calendar System: Semester
URL: www.nci.edu
Established: 1988
Annual Undergrad Tuition & Fees: N/A
Enrollment: 62
Coed
Affiliation or Control: Proprietary
IRS Status: Proprietary
Highest Offering: Associate Degree
Accreditation: COE

01 President ...Tamela K. TALIENTO
06 Registrar ...Michelle HARTSON
07 Dean of Admissions ...Dale WOOD
37 Director of Financial Aid ...Michelle HARTSON
13 Director of Information Technology ...Leo JORDAN
10 Comptroller ...Patricia BELL

Nossi College of Art (H)

590 Creative Way, Nashville TN 37115
County: Davidson
FICE Identification: 025782
Unit ID: 368452
Telephone: (615) 514-2787
Carnegie Class: Spec-4-yr-Arts
FAX Number: (615) 514-2788
Calendar System: Trimester
URL: www.nossi.edu
Established: 1973
Annual Undergrad Tuition & Fees: $19,150
Enrollment: 289
Coed
Affiliation or Control: Proprietary
IRS Status: Proprietary
Highest Offering: Baccalaureate
Accreditation: ACCSC

01 President ...Mr. Cyrus VATANDOOST
00 Founder and Chairwoman ...Ms. Nossi VATANDOOST
05 Vice President for Academic Affairs ...Dr. Joseph LUCERO
07 Admissions Director ...Mrs. Mitzi HATFIELD
06 Registrar ...Mrs. Mindy GILBERT
08 Head Librarian ...Mrs. Kolleen LONGMIRE
26 Chief Public Relations/Marketing ...Mrs. Libby LUFF
10 Business Office Manager ...Mrs. Rachel DEWAAL
36 Director Student Placement ...Mr. Barry HOWARD

Omega Graduate School (I)

500 Oxford Drive, Dayton TN 37321-6736
County: Rhea
FICE Identification: 038403
Unit ID: 461120
Telephone: (423) 775-6596
Carnegie Class: Masters/S
FAX Number: (423) 775-6599
Calendar System: Semester
URL: www.ogs.edu
Established: 1981
Annual Graduate Tuition & Fees: N/A
Enrollment: 77
Coed
Affiliation or Control: Independent Non-Profit
IRS Status: 501(c)3
Highest Offering: Doctorate; No Undergraduates
Accreditation: TRACS

01 President ...Dr. Joshua REICHARD
00 Chancellor ...Dr. David ANDERSON
05 Dean of Faculty ...Dr. Cathie HUGHES
11 Vice President of Administration ...Vacant
32 Chief Student Success Officer ...Dr. Curtis MCCLANE
108 Director of Assessment ...Dr. Joshua REICHARD
10 Chief Finance & Operations Officer ...Ms. Sharlene DANIEL
29 Director Alumni Relations ...Vacant
62 Director of Library Science ...Dr. David WARD
06 Registrar ...Mr. Richard GAMBLE
08 Librarian ...Ms. Caroline GEER
84 Chief Academic/Enrollment Officer ...Dr. Brenda DAVIS
26 Dir Public Relations/Marketing ...Vacant

Pentecostal Theological Seminary (J)

900 Walker Street, NE, Cleveland TN 37311
County: Bradley
FICE Identification: 021883
Unit ID: 219842
Telephone: (423) 478-1131
Carnegie Class: Spec-4-yr-Faith
FAX Number: (423) 478-7711
Calendar System: 4/1/4
URL: www.ptseminary.edu
Established: 1975
Annual Graduate Tuition & Fees: N/A
Enrollment: 442
Coed
Affiliation or Control: Church Of God
IRS Status: 501(c)3
Highest Offering: Doctorate; No Undergraduates
Accreditation: SC, THEOL

01 President ...Dr. Michael L. BAKER
05 Dean of Faculty/VP for Academics ...Dr. David S. HAN
108 VP for Inst Effect/Accreditation ...Dr. Oliver L. MCMAHAN
10 Director of Finance ...Mr. Caleb PEACOCK
04 Exec Assistant to the President ...Mrs. Connie MERCER
06 Director of Acad Records/Registrar ...Mr. Garry FRASHER
15 Director of Human Resources ...Mrs. Joylita W. TERPSTRA
18 Dir of Facilities/Support Services ...Mr. Phillip WOOD
32 Sr Dir of Student Svcs & Cmty Life ...Dr. Welton WRISTON
37 Director of Financial Aid ...Mrs. Robin SLUDER

07 Director of Admissions .... Mr. Lee SEALS
106 Director Online Learning .... Ms. Priscilla HAN
29 Director of Alumni Relations .... Mrs. Sharon BAKER
13 Director of Information Technology .... Mr. Ken L. SMITH
36 Director Student Placement .... Dr. Daniel D. TOMBERLIN

Remington College (A)

2710 Nonconnah Boulevard, Memphis TN 38132-2110
Telephone: (901) 345-1000 Identification: 666062
Accreditation: ACCSC

† Branch campus of Remington College, Mobile, AL.

Remington College (B)

441 Donelson Pike, Suite 150, Nashville TN 37214-3558
Telephone: (615) 889-5520 Identification: 666307
Accreditation: ACCSC, DH

† Branch campus of Remington College, Mobile, AL.

Rhodes College (C)

2000 North Parkway, Memphis TN 38112-1690
County: Shelby FICE Identification: 003519
Unit ID: 221351
Telephone: (901) 843-3000 Carnegie Class: Bac-A&S
FAX Number: N/A Calendar System: Semester
URL: www.rhodes.edu
Established: 1848 Annual Undergrad Tuition & Fees: $50,910
Enrollment: 1,875 Coed
Affiliation or Control: Presbyterian Church (U.S.A.) IRS Status: 501(c)3
Highest Offering: Master's
Accreditation: SC, MUS

01 President .... Ms. Jennifer COLLINS
05 Provost .... Dr. Kathy BASSARD
10 VP for Finance & Business Affairs .... Mr. Kyle WEBB
30 Vice President for Development .... Ms. Jennifer G. WADE
84 Vice President for Enrollment .... Mr. Gil VILLANUEVA
26 VP for Marketing and Communications .... Ms. Linda BONNIN
45 Vice Pres of Strategic Initiatives .... Dr. Sherry TURNER
32 Interim VP for Student Life .... Dr. Alicia GOLSTON
35 Dean of Students .... Dr. Alicia GOLSTON
121 Assoc Dean of Students/Acad Support ..... Dr. Melissa CAMPBELL
20 Associate Provost .... Dr. Tim HUEBNER
06 Registrar .... Ms. Amanda MAXSON
37 Director of Financial Aid .... Mr. Michael MORGAN
08 Director of Barrett Library .... Ms. Darlene D. BROOKS
29 Director of Alumni Relations .... Ms. Tracy PATTERSON
15 Chief Human Resources Officer .... Ms. Claire R. SHAPIRO
14 Director of Info Services .... Mr. Richard TRENTHEM
19 Director of Campus Safety .... Mr. Ike SLOAS
41 Director of Athletics .... Mr. Jim DUNCAN
36 Director of Career Services .... Ms. Sandra G. TRACY
38 Director of Counseling Services .... Ms. Pam DETRIE
18 Director of Physical Plant .... Mr. Brian E. FOSHEE
27 Assoc Director of Communications .... Mr. Justin MCGREGOR
09 Director of Institutional Research .... Dr. Sherry TURNER
07 Director of Admission .... Ms. Megan STARLING
108 Director of Assessment .... Dr. Rashna RICHARDS
31 Director of Community Relations .... Ms. Kerri CAMPBELL
44 Director of Annual Giving .... Ms. Ellen CELOSKY
110 Senior Director of Development .... Ms. Amanda TAMBURRINO
112 Director of Golden Lynx Program .... Dr. Nichole SOULE
21 Senior Associate Comptroller .... Ms. Wanda JONES
25 Director of Grants .... Ms. Lydia SPENCER
04 Exec Admin Asst to the President .... Ms. Kristen H. HUNT
39 Director of Residence Life .... Ms. Aretha MILLIGAN

Richmont Graduate University (D)

1815 McCallie Avenue, Chattanooga TN 37404
County: Hamilton FICE Identification: 033554
Unit ID: 441104
Telephone: (423) 266-4574 Carnegie Class: Spec-4-yr-Other Health
FAX Number: (423) 265-7375 Calendar System: Semester
URL: www.richmont.edu
Established: 1933 Annual Graduate Tuition & Fees: N/A
Enrollment: 296 Coed
Affiliation or Control: Independent Non-Profit IRS Status: 501(c)3
Highest Offering: Doctorate; No Undergraduates
Accreditation: SC, CACREP

01 President .... Dr. Timothy QUINNAN
05 Acting Provost .... Dr. Josh RICE
10 VP of Finance .... Mr. Tim MCPHERSON
13 VP of Information Technology .... Mr. Darwin BLANDON
11 VP of Administration .... Ms. Roxanne SHELLABARGER
88 VP of Integration .... Dr. Dan SARTOR
32 Vice President of Student Affairs .... Dr. Amanda BLACKBURN
73 Dean School of Ministry .... Dr. Josh RICE
88 Dean School of Counseling .... Dr. Stephen BRADSHAW
88 Asst Dean of Clinical Affairs .... Ms. Jama WHITE
100 Chief of Staff .... Mr. Philip BURNS
08 Director of Libraries .... Mr. Ron BUNGER
09 Director of Institutional Research .... Dr. Mary PLISCO
108 Dir Institutional Effectiveness .... Mr. Peter BRINDLEY
18 Facilities & IT Manager .... Mr. Neil ANDERSON
26 Director of Communications .... Ms. Talia ASHLEY
29 Director Alumni Relations .... Ms. Martha BUSBY
30 Director of Development .... Ms. Amy ESTES

37 Director of Financial Aid .... Ms. Laura LILLARD
07 AVP Enrollment Mgmt .... Mr. Tyson FANT
15 Human Resources Officer .... Ms. Sara FERGUSON

SAE Institute Nashville (E)

7 Music Circle North, Nashville TN 37203
County: Davidson FICE Identification: 038303
Unit ID: 446525
Telephone: (615) 244-5848 Carnegie Class: Spec-4-yr-Arts
FAX Number: (615) 244-3192 Calendar System: Other
URL: nashville.sae.edu
Established: 1976 Annual Undergrad Tuition & Fees: $33,199
Enrollment: 211 Coed
Affiliation or Control: Proprietary IRS Status: Proprietary
Highest Offering: Baccalaureate
Accreditation: ACCSC

01 Campus Director .... Shannon MEGGERT
05 Director of Education .... Ryan GRIFFIN
06 Registrar .... Robin GARCIA
07 Director of Admissions .... Gail MUSSER
10 Chief Financial/Business Officer .... Luis MATA
11 Chief of Operations/Administration .... Jake ELSEN
36 Director Student Placement .... David ANDRIS
37 Director Student Financial Aid .... Shelly PICINICH
53 Dean of Education .... Gabriel JONES
84 Director Enrollment Management .... Sarah SIZEMORE

Sewanee: The University of the South (F)

735 University Avenue, Sewanee TN 37383-1000
County: Franklin FICE Identification: 003534
Unit ID: 221519
Telephone: (931) 598-1000 Carnegie Class: Bac-A&S
FAX Number: (931) 598-1145 Calendar System: Semester
URL: www.sewanee.edu
Established: 1857 Annual Undergrad Tuition & Fees: $47,980
Enrollment: 1,800 Coed
Affiliation or Control: Protestant Episcopal IRS Status: 501(c)3
Highest Offering: Doctorate
Accreditation: SC, THEOL

01 Acting Vice Chancellor & President .... Dr. Nancy J. BERNER
100 Chief of Staff .... Ms. Nicky HAMILTON
05 Acting Provost .... Dr. Scott WILSON
101 University Secretary .... Mr. Jay FISHER
88 Special Assistant to VC for SPI .... Ms. Karen PROCTOR
32 Vice Provost for Student Success .... Dr. Lisa STEPHENSON
28 Vice Provost for DEI .... Dr. Sibby ANDERSON-THOMPKINS
111 VP for University Relations .... Ms. Debbie VAUGHN
45 VP for Economic Development .... Mr. David SHIPPS
49 Vice Provost/Dean of College .... Dr. Terry L. PAPILLON
73 VP/Dean of the School of Theology .... Rev. James TURRELL
35 AProv Stdnt Life/Dean of Students .... Ms. Erica HOWARD
09 Asst Prov Academic Svcs/Inst Rsrch .... Dr. Paul G. WILEY
07 Assoc Prov/Dean of Admiss & Fin Aid .... Mr. Alan RAMIREZ
37 Assoc Dean Student Financial Aid .... Ms. Beth CRAGAR
20 Associate Dean for Academic Affairs .... Dr. Alex M. BRUCE
26 Assoc VP Marketing/Communications .... Mr. Parker OLIVER
88 AVP of Sewanee Dining .... Mr. Brent TATE
41 Director of Athletics .... Mr. John SHACKELFORD
29 Director of Alumni Relations .... Ms. Susan S. ASKEW
36 Director of Career Services .... Ms. Kim D. HEITZENRATER
38 Director of Wellness Commons .... Ms. Sarah RUNDLE
93 Dir of Multicultural Student Affs .... Ms. Rachel FREDERICKS
18 AVP Facilities Planning/Operations .... Ms. Karen SINGER
43 University Legal Counsel .... Ms. Marquitte STARKEY
19 Vice President for Public Safety .... Mr. Chip SCHANE
10 VP for Finance and Treasurer .... Dr. Douglass WILLIAMS
23 Director of Univ Health Services .... Ms. Karen THARP
24 Director of Media Services .... Mr. Michael OSTROWSKI
42 University Chaplain .... Rev. Peter W. GRAY
22 Assoc Dean Faculty Dev & Inclusion .... Dr. Betsy SANDLIN
39 Assistant Director of Resident Life .... Ms. Danielle VOSBURGH
44 Director Sewanee Fund .... Ms. Whitney FRANKLIN

South College (G)

3904 Lonas Drive, Knoxville TN 37909-3323
County: Knox FICE Identification: 004938
Unit ID: 220552
Telephone: (865) 251-1800 Carnegie Class: DU-Mod
FAX Number: (865) 584-7335 Calendar System: Quarter
URL: www.south.edu
Established: 1882 Annual Undergrad Tuition & Fees: $16,975
Enrollment: 5,171 Coed
Affiliation or Control: Proprietary IRS Status: Proprietary
Highest Offering: Doctorate
Accreditation: SC, ANEST, ARCPA, DMS, IACBE, MAC, NMT, NURSE, OTA, PHAR, PTA, PTAA, RAD

01 Chancellor .... Mr. Stephen A. SOUTH
111 VC Inst Advancement & Effectiveness .... Dr. Kim B. HALL
32 VC Student Services .... Ms. Gabriella FISCHER
05 Chief Academic Officer .... Dr. Ted RICHARDSON
11 Chief Operating Officer .... Mr. Brad ADAMS
10 Chief Financial Officer .... Mr. Matt CARR
84 Sr VP Enrollment Management .... Ms. Carrie MAJOR
04 Executive Assistant .... Ms. Angela BENNETT

37 Exec VP Financial Aid & Registrar .... Dr. Carol COLVIN
15 VP Talent & HR .... Mr. Randall CARR
13 VP Information Technology .... Mr. Jeremy UNDERWOOD
12 Campus President Orlando .... Mr. James MCCOY
12 Campus President Nashville .... Mr. Nick SOUTH
12 Campus President Pittsburgh/Online .... Dr. Amy HILBELINK
12 Campus President Asheville .... Dr. Lisa SATTERFIELD
12 Campus President Indianapolis .... Mr. Turner SOUTH
12 Campus President Atlanta .... Mr. Joshua HUFFAKER
21 Director of Administrative Services .... Mr. Ron HALL
13 Director Instructional Technology .... Mr. Jason PIETROPAULO
36 Career Services Coordinator .... Mr. Ben LANDERS
08 Head Librarian .... Ms. Anya MCKINNEY
06 Inst Registrar .... Ms. Michelle PRIDDY

Southern Adventist University (H)

4881 Taylor Cir, Collegedale TN 37315
County: Hamilton FICE Identification: 003518
Unit ID: 221661
Telephone: (423) 236-2000 Carnegie Class: Masters/M
FAX Number: (423) 236-1777 Calendar System: Semester
URL: www.southern.edu
Established: 1892 Annual Undergrad Tuition & Fees: $22,930
Enrollment: 2,730 Coed
Affiliation or Control: Seventh-day Adventist IRS Status: 501(c)3
Highest Offering: Doctorate
Accreditation: SC, ADNUR, CACREP, CAEP, IACBE, MUS, NUR, PTAA, SW

01 President .... Dr. Ken SHAW
05 Sr Vice Pres Academic Admin .... Dr. Robert YOUNG
10 Sr Vice Pres Financial Admin .... Mr. Tom VERRILL
32 Vice Pres Student Development .... Dr. Dennis NEGRÓN
111 Vice Pres Advancement .... Vacant
84 Vice Pres Enrollment Management .... Mr. Jason MERRYMAN
26 Vice Pres Marketing/University Rels .... Ms. Ingrid SKANTZ
20 Assoc VP Academic Admin .... Dr. Dionne FELIX
21 Assoc VP Financial Admin .... Mr. Marty HAMILTON
13 Assoc VP Information Systems .... Mr. Gary SEWELL
15 Assoc VP Human Resources .... Mrs. Brenda FLORES-LOPEZ
39 Dean of Students/Dir Residence Life .... Dr. Lisa HALL
50 Dean School of Business/Mgmt .... Dr. Stephanie SHEEHAN
53 Dean School of Education/Psych .... Dr. Tammie OVERSTREET
57 Dean School of Visual Art/Design .... Mr. Randy CRAVEN
60 Dean School of Journalism/ Comm .... Dr. Rachel WILLIAMS-SMITH
64 Dean School of Music .... Dr. Peter COOPER
66 Dean School of Nursing .... Dr. Holly GADD
68 Dean Sch of Phys Ed/Health/Wellness .... Dr. Robert BENGE
73 Dean School of Religion .... Dr. Greg KING
77 Dean School of Computing .... Dr. Rick HALTERMAN
70 Dean School Social Work/Family Studies .... Dr. Laura RACOVITA
72 Chair Technology .... Mr. Dale WALTERS
88 Chair Phys Therapist Asst Program .... Dr. Chris STEWART
81 Chair Mathematics .... Dr. Kevin BROWN
76 Chair Biology/Allied Health .... Dr. Keith SNYDER
88 Chair Chemistry .... Dr. Brent HAMSTRA
79 Chair English .... Dr. Keely TARY
82 Chair History & Political Studies .... Dr. Lisa DILLER
54 Chair Physics/Engineering .... Dr. Ken CAVINESS
18 Assoc Director Plant Services .... Mr. Bill CRUTTENDEN
35 Director Student Life/Activities .... Ms. Kari SHULTZ
37 Director Student Finance .... Mrs. Paula WALTERS
09 Director Inst Research/Planning .... Dr. Chris HANSEN
45 Director Strategic Initiatives .... Mrs. Barb EDENS
07 Director of Admissions .... Mr. Rick ANDERSON
08 Director of Libraries .... Mrs. Deyse BRAVO
06 Director Records & Advisement .... Ms. Karon POWELL
29 Director Alumni Relations .... Ms. Evonne CROOK
38 Director Student Success Center .... Dr. Jim WAMPLER
04 Administrative Asst to President .... Mrs. Joylynn SCOTT
28 Director of Diversity .... Mrs. Stephanie GUSTER

Southern College of Optometry (I)

1245 Madison Avenue, Memphis TN 38104-2222
County: Shelby FICE Identification: 003517
Unit ID: 221670
Telephone: (901) 722-3200 Carnegie Class: Spec-4-yr-Other Health
FAX Number: (901) 722-3279 Calendar System: Trimester
URL: www.sco.edu
Established: 1932 Annual Graduate Tuition & Fees: N/A
Enrollment: 538 Coed
Affiliation or Control: Independent Non-Profit IRS Status: 501(c)3
Highest Offering: Doctorate; No Undergraduates
Accreditation: SC, OPT, OPTR

01 President .... Dr. Lewis REICH
04 Executive Admin Assistant to Pres .... Ms. Sandra S. STEPHENS
101 Secretary to the Institution/Board .... Ms. Sandra STEPHENS
05 VP for Academic Affairs .... Dr. J. Bart CAMPBELL
09 Director of Institutional Research .... Dr. Michael CHRISTENSEN
108 Director Institutional Assessment .... Ms. Janelle ARJOON
51 Dir of Continuing Education .... Ms. Delores JOHNSON
20 Chair Optometric Education .... Dr. Lindsay ELKINS
121 Dir of Academic Support Services .... Dr. Carrie LEBOWITZ
17 Vice Pres for Clinical Programs .... Dr. James E. VENABLE
23 Director of Clinic Operations .... Mr. Gary SNUFFIN
32 Vice President for Student Services .... Mr. Joseph H. HAUSER
123 Dir of Admissions/Enrollment Svcs . Mr. Michael N. ROBERTSON
07 Asst Dir of Admissions .... Ms. Rebecca SMIETANA
88 Director of Student Recruitment .... Ms. Sunnie EWING
93 Coord of Minority Recruitment .... Dr. Jannette D. PEPPER

40 Campus Store Manager ....Ms. Denise HENSON
37 Director of Financial Aid ....Ms. LeChelle DAVENPORT
10 Vice President for Finance & Admin ....Mr. David L. WEST
21 Controller ....Ms. Carolyn WARREN
19 Manager of Security/Safety ....Mr. Don HENSON
18 Physical Plant Manager ....Mr. Trey ADAMS
13 Exec Dir of Information Services ....Mr. Dean SWICK
08 Director of Library ....Ms. Leslie HOLLAND
15 Executive Director Human Resources ....Ms. Tracy LINDOW
111 Vice President for Inst Advancement ....Mr. George C. MILLER
26 Dir of Strategic Communication/Mktg .... Mr. Jim HOLLIFIELD
29 Director of Alumni & Spec Events ....Ms. Beth FISHER
30 Director of Development ....Ms. Lauren TROWBRIDGE
36 Director of Hayes Center ....Dr. Lisa WADE
28 Coord Of Diversity & Inclusion ....Dr. Jannette D. PEPPER

*Tennessee Board of Regents Office (A)

1 Bridgestone Park, Nashville TN 37214
County: Davidson FICE Identification: 029031
Unit ID: 409379
Telephone: (615) 366-4400 Carnegie Class: N/A
FAX Number: N/A
URL: www.tbr.edu

01 Chancellor ....Dr. Flora W. TYDINGS
45 Exec Vice Chanc Policy & Strategy ....Dr. Russ DEATON
111 Vice Chanc External Affairs ....Dr. Kimberly MCCORMICK
10 Vice Chanc Business & Finance ....Mr. Danny GIBBS
43 General Counsel ....Mr. Brian LAPPS
108 VC Organizational Effectiveness ....Dr. Wendy J. THOMPSON
05 Vice Chancellor Academic Affairs ....Dr. Jothany BLACKWOOD
32 Vice Chanc Student Success ....Dr. Heidi LEMING
13 Chief Information Officer ....Mr. Stephen VIEIRA
15 Asst Vice Chanc for Human Resources ....Ms. April PRESTON
26 Communications Director ....Mr. Rick LOCKER

*Chattanooga State Community College (B)

4501 Amnicola Highway, Chattanooga TN 37406-1097
County: Hamilton FICE Identification: 003998
Unit ID: 219824
Telephone: (423) 697-4400 Carnegie Class: Assoc/MT-VT-High Trad
FAX Number: N/A Calendar System: Semester
URL: www.chattanoogastate.edu
Established: 1965 Annual Undergrad Tuition & Fees (In-State): $4,063
Enrollment: 7,452 Coed
Affiliation or Control: State IRS Status: 501(c)3
Highest Offering: Associate Degree
Accreditation: SC, ACBSP, ADNUR, COARC, DA, DH, DMS, EMT, MAC, NAEYC, NAIT, NMT, PTAA, RAD, RTT, SURGT

02 President ....Dr. Rebecca ASHFORD
05 Vice Pres Academic Affairs ....Ms. Beth NORTON
10 Exec Vice Pres Business & Finance ....Ms. Tammy SWENSON
32 Vice Pres Student Affairs ....Ms. Amanda BENNETT
72 Exec VP Technical College ....Dr. James BARROTT
13 Int VP Information Technology ....Mr. Brad MCCORMICK
111 Vice President College Adv & PR ....Ms. Nancy PATTERSON
21 Asst Vice Pres Business & Finance ....Ms. Susan JOSEPH
84 Asst Vice Pres Enrollment Services ....Mr. Brad MCCORMICK
45 Exec Director Inst Eff/Rsrch/Plng ....Dr. Traci WILLIAMS
18 Executive Director Plant Operations ....Mr. Guy DAVIS
20 Asst VP Academic Resources ....Ms. Judy LOWE
09 Director Institutional Research ....Ms. Bonnie RIGGS
26 Director Marketing ....Ms. Jennifer COOPER
37 Director Student Financial Aid ....Mr. Reed ALLISON
07 Dir of Admissions/Col Registrar ....Ms. Donna BETTIS
28 Director Multicultural Services ....Ms. Mary KNAFF
108 Dean Acad Assessment/Accred/Compl ....Mr. John HAWORTH
08 Dean Library Services ....Ms. Susan JENNINGS
76 Dean Allied Health & Nursing ....Dr. Mark KNUTSEN
79 Dean Humanities & Fine Arts ....Mr. Darrin HASSEVOORT
83 AVP Acad Affs/Dean Soc/Behav Sci ....Dr. Mosunmola GEORGE-TAYLOR
81 Interim Dean Math & Sciences ....Dr. Karen EASTMAN
50 Dean Business ....Mr. Barry JENNISON
35 Dean Student Engag/Support Svcs ....Ms. Sandy RUTTER
75 Dean Technical College ....Vacant
54 Dean Engineering & Info Technology .... Dr. Tremaine POWELL
88 Dir Welcome Center/Recruiting ....Ms. Kisha CALDWELL
15 Exec Dir HR/Affirm Action/Title I ....Mr. Brian EVANS
103 Director Economic & Workforce Dev ....Mr. Bo DRAKE
19 Interim Chief Security/Safety ....Mr. Donald COLEMAN
36 Director Student Placement ....Ms. Stephanie HOLLIS
124 Dir Educ Outreach Program/Retention .... Ms. Michelle KILGORE
110 Director College Advancement ....Ms. Tamberly SAWYERS
96 Director of Purchasing ....Ms. Kristie FARRIS

*Cleveland State Community College (C)

PO Box 3570, Cleveland TN 37320-3570
County: Bradley FICE Identification: 003999
Unit ID: 219879
Telephone: (423) 472-7141 Carnegie Class: Assoc/HT-High Trad
FAX Number: (423) 478-6255 Calendar System: Semester
URL: www.clevelandstatecc.edu
Established: 1967 Annual Undergrad Tuition & Fees (In-State): $4,338
Enrollment: 3,074 Coed
Affiliation or Control: State IRS Status: 501(c)3
Highest Offering: Associate Degree
Accreditation: SC, ACBSP, ADNUR, EMT, MAC, NAEYC, NAIT

02 President ....Dr. Ty STONE
05 VP for Academic Affairs ....Dr. Barsha PICKELL
32 VP for Student Services ....Dr. Michael STOKES
10 VP of Finance & Chief Op Officer ....Vacant
103 VP Workforce & Economic Dev ....Dr. Patricia WEAVER
111 Exec Dir of Advancement & Planning ....Dr. John SQUIRES
28 Asst to the Pres for Equity/Incl ....Mr. Willie THOMAS
50 Dean of Business & Healthcare ....Ms. Susan WEBB-CURTIS
92 Dean of Honors College & Acad Enh ....Vacant
79 Dean of Arts/Hum/Social Sci/Ed ....Dr. Ryan THOMPSON
81 Dean of STEM & Advanced Technology ....Mrs. Karen WYRICK
66 Director of Nursing ....Vacant
15 Director of Human Resources ....Mrs. Kellie FRANK
13 Director of Information Technology ....Mr. Chris MOWERY
103 Dir Workforce Development ....Ms. Heather BROWN
07 Director of Admissions & Records ....Mrs. Kelli ROACH
08 Director of the Library ....Ms. Gina CASH
19 Chief of Campus Police ....Mrs. Jennifer BLEDSOE
38 Dir of Counseling & Career Services ....Mr. Mark WILSON
41 Athletic Director ....Mr. Mike POLICASTRO
37 Director of Financial Aid ....Mrs. Jamie HAMBY
26 Director of Communications ....Ms. Holly TROTTER-VINCENT
29 Director of Development/ Alum ....Ms. Jill WOODRUFF

*Columbia State Community College (D)

1665 Hampshire Pike, Columbia TN 38401-5653
County: Maury FICE Identification: 003483
Unit ID: 219888
Telephone: (931) 540-2722 Carnegie Class: Assoc/HT-High Trad
FAX Number: (931) 540-2535 Calendar System: Semester
URL: www.columbiastate.edu
Established: 1966 Annual Undergrad Tuition & Fees (In-State): $4,582
Enrollment: 5,931 Coed
Affiliation or Control: State IRS Status: 501(c)3
Highest Offering: Associate Degree
Accreditation: SC, ACBSP, ADNUR, AT, COARC, EMT, MLTAD, NAIT, RAD

02 President ....Dr. Janet F. SMITH
05 VP for Academic Affairs ....Ms. Joni LENIG
10 VP for Finance & Administration ....Ms. Tammy S. BORREN
111 VP for Advancement ....Ms. Bethany LAY
20 Assoc VP Faculty/Curric & Programs ....Vacant
32 VP for Student Affairs ....Ms. Ruth Ann HOLT
13 Assoc VP for Info Technology ....Dr. Emily SICIENSKY
21 Assoc VP for Business Services ....Mr. Keith ISBELL
26 Director of Communications ....Ms. Amy SPEARS-BOYD
28 Asst to Pres for Access & Diversity ....Dr. Christa S. MARTIN
06 Director Records ....Vacant
15 Director Human Resources ....Ms. Laura JENT
08 Director Library ....Ms. Anne SCOTT
45 AVP Strat Plng/Effect/Retention ....Mr. Gary ROTHSTEIN
37 Director Financial Aid ....Mr. Matt LEWIS
41 Director Athletics ....Mr. Johnny LITTRELL
18 Director Facility Services & Safety ....Dr. Tim HALLMARK
12 VP for Williamson Campus & Ext Svcs ....Dr. Dearl LAMPLEY
96 Coordinator Purchasing ....Mr. Jon ARNOLD
84 Chief Enrollment Svcs Officer ....Ms. Jill RILEY
103 Dir Workforce/Career Development ....Vacant
104 Director Study Abroad ....Ms. Lacey BENNS
106 Dir Academic Engagement/Innovation ....Ms. Marla CARTWRIGHT
108 Director Institutional Assessment ....Mr. Harry DJUNAIDI
19 Director Security/Safety ....Mr. Randy CARROLL
04 Exec Assistant to the President ....Ms. Cheryl CASNER
07 Director of Admissions ....Ms. Jill RILEY
25 Development Officer/Grants Admin ....Mr. Patrick MCELHINEY
44 Director Annual Giving ....Ms. Shannon DAVIS

*Dyersburg State Community College (E)

1510 Lake Road, Dyersburg TN 38024-2450
County: Dyer FICE Identification: 006835
Unit ID: 220057
Telephone: (731) 286-3200 Carnegie Class: Assoc/HT-High Trad
FAX Number: (731) 286-3333 Calendar System: Semester
URL: www.dscc.edu
Established: 1967 Annual Undergrad Tuition & Fees (In-State): $4,338
Enrollment: 2,650 Coed
Affiliation or Control: State IRS Status: 501(c)3
Highest Offering: Associate Degree
Accreditation: SC, ACBSP, ADNUR, CAHIIM, EMT, NAEYC

02 President ....Dr. Scott COOK
05 Vice President for the College ....Dr. Jan REID-BUNCH
10 Vice Pres Finance/Admin Svcs .... Dr. Charlene WHITE
111 VP Advancement & External Affairs ....Dr. Amanda WALKER
13 Vice President of Technology ....Mr. Josh DUGGIN
32 Dean of Student Services ....Ms. Larenda FULTZ
08 Dean of Learning Resources Center ....Ms. Susan CHARLEY
37 Director of Financial Aid ....Mrs. Kacee HARDY
09 Dir Inst Effectiveness/Research ....Ms. Deica DISNEY
15 Director of Human Resources ....Vacant
103 Exec Director of Workforce Services ....Ms. Connie STEWART
121 Academic/Career Counselor ....Ms. Sherry BAKER
41 Director of Athletics ....Mr. Chad KLINE
18 Director of Physical Plant ....Mr. Mike SAMPLES
07 Director of Admissions & Records ....Vacant
96 Director of Administrative Services ....Ms. Beth MULLINS
21 Business & Student Fin Svcs Manager ....Ms. Donna MEALER
49 Dean of Arts & Sciences ....Mr. James BARHAM
72 Dean Career Tech/Distance Education ......Mr. Dennis ANDERSON
66 Dean of Nursing ....Ms. Amy JOHNSON
04 Administrative Asst to President ....Ms. Edith CARLTON

*Jackson State Community College (F)

2046 North Parkway, Jackson TN 38301-3797
County: Madison FICE Identification: 004937
Unit ID: 220400
Telephone: (731) 424-3520 Carnegie Class: Assoc/HT-Mix Trad/Non
FAX Number: (731) 425-2647 Calendar System: Semester
URL: www.jscc.edu
Established: 1965 Annual Undergrad Tuition & Fees (In-State): $4,324
Enrollment: 4,203 Coed
Affiliation or Control: State IRS Status: 501(c)3
Highest Offering: Associate Degree
Accreditation: SC, ACBSP, ADNUR, #COARC, EMT, MLTAD, NAIT, OTA, PTAA, RAD

02 President ....Dr. George PIMENTEL
05 Interim VP of Academic Affairs ....Dr. Tom PIGG
10 Vice Pres of Finance & Admin Affs ....Mr. Tim DELLINGER
30 Director of Development ....Ms. Lindsey TRITT
32 Interim VP of Student Services ....Ms. Robin MAREK
116 Internal Auditor ....Ms. Chrystal PITTMAN
15 Dir Human Resources/Affirm Action ....Ms. Amy WEST
09 Dir Inst Research & Accountability ....Mr. Don MYERS
13 Director of Information Technology ....Ms. Dana NAILS
21 Director of Business Services ....Mr. Adina KERFOOT
18 Director of Physical Plant ....Mr. Preston TURNER
96 Director of Purchasing.............................. Mr. Robert D. HEMRICK
12 Director Lexington Campus ....Ms. Sandy STANFILL
12 Director Savannah Campus ....Mrs. Meda FALLS
12 Director Humboldt Campus ....Ms. Lisa ROJAS
26 Director of PR and Marketing ....Mr. John MCCOMMON
37 Director Student Financial Aid ....Mr. John BRANDT
07 Director of Admissions and Records ....Ms. Robin MAREK
08 Head Librarian ....Mr. Scott COHEN
19 Director Security/Safety ....Mr. Shane YOUNG
41 Athletic Director ....Mr. Steve CORNELISON
04 Admin Assistant to the President .... Ms. Heather FREEMAN
22 Dir Affirmative Action/Equal Opp ....Ms. Amy WEST
103 Director Workforce Development .... Ms. Kimberly JOHNSON
106 Dean of Online Education/E-learning ....Dr. Patrick DAVIS, SR.

*Motlow State Community College (G)

PO Box 8500, Lynchburg TN 37352-8500
County: Moore FICE Identification: 006836
Unit ID: 221096
Telephone: (931) 393-1500 Carnegie Class: Assoc/HT-High Trad
FAX Number: (931) 393-1681 Calendar System: Semester
URL: www.mscc.edu
Established: 1969 Annual Undergrad Tuition & Fees (In-State): $4,330
Enrollment: 6,616 Coed
Affiliation or Control: State IRS Status: 501(c)3
Highest Offering: Associate Degree
Accreditation: SC, ACBSP, ADNUR, EMT, MLTAD, NAIT

02 President ....Dr. Michael TORRENCE
05 Exec VP for Academic Affairs ....Dr. Regina VERDIN
103 EVP Workforce and Cmty Development ....Dr. Tony MILLICAN
10 Exec VP for Finance & Admin ....Ms. Renee AUSTIN
26 VP External Affairs ....Ms. Terri BRYSON
13 Chief Information Officer ....Mr. Carlos PADILLA
32 Interim VP for Student Success ....Ms. Charlie COFFEY
72 Dean Career & Tech Programs ....Mr. Walter MCCORD
35 Dean of Students ....Ms. Yaritza GOTAY
66 Dean of Nursing and Allied Health ....Ms. Amy HOLDER
12 Asst Dean of McMinnville Campus ....Ms. Misty MAZZIE
12 Dean of Moore County Campus ....Dr. Pam HARRIS
12 Asst Dean Fayetteville Campus ....Ms. Lisa SANDERS
12 Dean of Smyrna Campus ....Dr. Gregory KILLOUGH
18 Director of Facilities ....Mr. Brian GAFFORD
31 Exec Dir of Community Relations ....Ms. Brenda CANNON
08 Director of Libraries ....Ms. Sharon EDWARDS
102 Asst Dir of the Foundation ....Ms. Sharon BATEMAN
37 Exec Dir of Financial Aid ....Mr. Joe MYERS, JR.
38 Director of Disability & Testing ....Ms. Belinda CHAMPION
07 Director of Admissions & Records ....Ms. Mae SANDERS
19 Director of Public Safety .... Mr. Ray HIGGINBOTHAM
41 Dean of Athletics ....Vacant
84 Director of Recruitment ....Vacant
15 Executive Dir of Human Resources .... Mr. Brian ROWE
21 Director of Fiscal Services ....Ms. Sandy SCHAFFER
121 Int Director of Student Success ....Mr. Kyle MACON
04 Executive Administrator ....Mrs. Alissa ROEBUCK
55 Director of Adult Initiatives ....Ms. Allison BARTON
27 Dir of Communications & Media Rels ....Vacant
90 Dean of Academic Technology ....Mr. Terry DURHAM
14 Director of Tech Operations ....Mr. Jeffery SHORT
88 Director of TN Promise ....Mr. Jonathan GRAHAM
108 Director of Quality Assurance ....Dr. Meagan MCMANUS
25 Director of Grants ....Ms. Tammy O'DELL
28 Compliance Officer ....Ms. Barbara SCALES
96 Purchasing and Contract Coordinator ....Ms. Kristin LUKE

*Nashville State Community College (A)

120 White Bridge Road, Nashville TN 37209-4515
County: Davidson FICE Identification: 008145
Unit ID: 221184
Telephone: (615) 353-3333 Carnegie Class: Assoc/HT-High Trad
FAX Number: (615) 353-3713 Calendar System: Semester
URL: www.nscc.edu
Established: 1969 Annual Undergrad Tuition & Fees (In-State): $4,294
Enrollment: 7,064 Coed
Affiliation or Control: State IRS Status: 501(c)3
Highest Offering: Associate Degree
Accreditation: SC, ACBSP, ACFEI, ADNUR, NAEYC, NAIT, OTA, SURGT

02 President .... Dr. Shanna L. JACKSON
10 VP Finance & Administration .... Ms. Mary M. CROSS
05 VP Academic Affairs & Workforce Dev .... Dr. Carol ROTHSTEIN
103 VP Economic & Community Dev .... Ms. Ginger HAUSSER
45 Assoc VP Planning/Research .... Mr. Charles CLARK
30 Exec Dir of Development .... Ms. Lauren P. BELL
32 VP Student Affairs & Enroll .... Dr. Carol J. MARTIN-OSORIO
20 Assoc VP Academic Affairs .... Dr. Sarah ROBERTS
116 Internal Auditor .... Mr. Henry HO
12 Director Clarksville Campus .... Ms. Kathleen AKERS
06 Int Dir of Records & Registration .... Mr. Kevin THOMAS
84 Interim Chief Enrollment Officer .... Ms. Laura P. MORAN
13 Director Technology Services .... Mr. Paul A. KAMINSKY
19 Director of Safety and Security .... Mr. Derrek G. SHEUCRAFT
37 Director of Financial Aid .... Ms. Jennifer D. BYRD
15 Director of Human Resources .... Ms. Jill FERRAND
18 Executive Director of Operations .... Mr. Christopher SAUNDERS
26 AVP Communications & Marketing .... Mr. Tom HAYDEN
106 Director of Online Learning .... Ms. Heather RIPPETOE
83 Dean of Social and Life Sciences .... Dr. Julie E. WILLIAMS
81 Dean Science/Tech/Eng/Math (STEM) .... Dr. Jennifer KNAPP
79 Dean English/Humanities & Arts .... Dr. Patricia J. ARMSTRONG
62 Dean Lrng Resources & Online Learn .... Dr. Faye M. JONES
50 Dean Business/Mgmt & Hospitality .... Ms. Karen L. STEVENSON
96 Director of Purchasing .... Mr. Mark HODGES
76 Director of Healthcare Professions .... Dr. Cynthia G. WALLER
22 Compliance & Diversity Officer .... Ms. Mia SNEED

*Northeast State Community College (B)

PO Box 246, 2425 Highway 75, Blountville TN 37617-0246
County: Sullivan FICE Identification: 005378
Unit ID: 221908
Telephone: (423) 323-3191 Carnegie Class: Assoc/MT-VT-High Trad
FAX Number: (423) 279-7636 Calendar System: Semester
URL: www.northeaststate.edu
Established: 1965 Annual Undergrad Tuition & Fees (In-State): $4,326
Enrollment: 5,397 Coed
Affiliation or Control: State IRS Status: 501(c)3
Highest Offering: Associate Degree
Accreditation: SC, ACBSP, ADNUR, CVT, DA, EMT, MLTAD, NAEYC, NAIT, SURGT

02 President .... Dr. Jeff MCCORD
100 Chief of Staff .... Dr. Stephanie BARHAM
05 Vice Pres Academic Affairs .... Dr. Connie MARSHALL
11 Vice Pres Administration .... Ms. Linda CALVERT
32 Vice President Student Success .... Dr. Susan GRAYBEAL
103 VP Economic & Workforce Development .... Dr. Sam ROWELL
10 Vice Pres Finance/Info Tech .... Mr. Chad BAILEY
56 Asst VP Multi-Campus Programs .... Dr. Pashia HOGAN
111 Director of Advancement .... Ms. Megan ALMAROAD
06 Registrar .... Ms. Deidra CLOSE
15 Director Human Resources .... Ms. Megan JONES
26 Dir Community Relations/Marketing .... Mr. Robert CARPENTER
45 Director Planning & Assessment .... Mr. John GRUBB
08 Dean Library .... Mr. Christopher DEMAS
79 Dean Humanities .... Ms. Elizabeth MCKNIGHT
81 Dean Mathematics .... Ms. Malissa TRENT
76 Dean Health Professions .... Mr. David BRYANT
72 Dean Technologies .... Ms. Donna FARRELL
83 Interim Dean Behavioral/Soc Science .... Ms. Trish CRAWFORD
81 Dean Science Division .... Mr. Chris HITECHEW
66 Director of Nursing .... Dr. Johanna NEUBRANDER
35 Dean of Students .... Mr. Brandon DOTSON
88 Veterans Affairs Specialist .... Mr. John ADCOX
18 Director of Plant Operations .... Mr. Pete MILLER
37 Director of Financial Aid .... Ms. Sarah DOHENY
96 Purchasing Coordinator .... Ms. Bernice HAGAMAN
04 Exec Assistant to the President .... Mr. Robert MILLER

*Pellissippi State Community College (C)

PO Box 22990, Knoxville TN 37933-0990
County: Knox FICE Identification: 012693
Unit ID: 221643
Telephone: (865) 694-6400 Carnegie Class: Assoc/HT-High Trad
FAX Number: (865) 539-7240 Calendar System: Semester
URL: www.pstcc.edu
Established: 1974 Annual Undergrad Tuition & Fees (In-State): $4,318
Enrollment: 9,334 Coed
Affiliation or Control: State IRS Status: 501(c)3
Highest Offering: Associate Degree
Accreditation: SC, ACBSP, ACFEI, ADNUR, NAEYC, NAIT

02 President .... Dr. L. Anthony WISE, JR.
05 VP of Academic Affairs .... Dr. Kellie TOON
13 Vice President Information Services .... Ms. Audrey J. WILLIAMS
10 Vice President Business & Finance .... Mr. Ronald L. KESTERSON
21 Asst VP Business Services .... Ms. Renee MOORE
102 Exec Director of Foundation .... Ms. Aneisa L. ROLEN
32 Vice President of Student Affairs .... Dr. Rushton W. JOHNSON, JR.
103 Exec Dir Business/Workforce Dev .... Ms. Teri T. BRAHAMS
12 Campus Dean Blount County Programs .... Ms. Priscilla DUENKEL
12 Campus Dean Strawberry Pl Program .... Dr. Mike NORTH
12 Campus Dean Magnolia Ave Programs .... Ms. Stella BRIDGEMAN
12 Campus Dean Division Street Program .... Ms. Esther L. DYER
35 Asst VP Student Aff/Dean of Student .... Mr. Travis C. LOVEDAY
88 Manager Student Transitions .... Mr. Barry SHUMPERT
35 Asst VP of Student Services .... Dr. Rachael C. CRAGLE
88 Manager Accounts Payable .... Ms. Debra CLARK
20 Asst VP of AA University Parallel .... Dr. Angela HUGHES
20 Asst VP AA Career & Technical Pgm .... Ms. Judy GOSCH
84 Asst VP Enrollment Services .... Ms. Leigh A. TOUZEAU
22 Exec Director Equity & Compliance .... Mr. George T. UNDERWOOD
35 Dir of Student Engagement & Leaders .... Ms. Matt SPRAKER
36 Director of Placement .... Vacant
88 Coordinator Disability Services .... Ms. Sarah E. MCMURRAY
26 Interim Dir Marketing/Communication .... Ms. Lesli BALES-SHERROD
07 Dir of Admiss & Records/Registrar .... Ms. Melanie M. PARADISE
08 Director of Library Services .... Dr. Mary Ellen SPENCER
24 Dir Educ Technology Svcs .... Vacant
37 Director of Financial Aid .... Ms. Jessica A. STREICH
108 Dir Inst Effective/Assessment/Plng .... Ms. Clarissa JACKSON
88 Asst Director Inst Effectiveness .... Ms. Olga EBERT-HOLBERG
18 Director of Facilities .... Ms. Regina MCNEW
19 Chief of Police .... Mr. Terry M. CROWE, JR.
114 Director Budget & Payroll .... Ms. Nancy DONAHUE
96 Director of Purchasing .... Mr. John S. CLARK
15 Interim Director Human Resources .... Ms. Elizabeth (Liz) ROSS
25 Director Grant Development .... Ms. Danette JOHNSON
104 Exec Dir TnCIS/International Educ .... Ms. Tracey BRADLEY
112 Director Major Gift Development .... Ms. Marilyn RODDY
44 Dir Annual Giving & Scholarships .... Vacant
29 Director Alumni & Donor Engagement .... Ms. Britney SINK
91 Dir Applications Programming Sup .... Mr. James (Dean) COPPLE
105 Dir of Network & Technical Services .... Mr. Larry BATES
28 Director of Access & Diversity .... Vacant
88 Director of Academic Testing .... Ms. Joan NEWMAN
88 Dir of Student Care & Advocacy .... Dr. Drema BOWERS
121 Director of Advising .... Dr. Rachael C. CRAGLE
88 Dir Academic Support Programs .... Ms. Jan T. SHARP
113 Bursar .... Ms. Mandy BENTZ
116 Director of Internal Audit .... Ms. Suzanne WALKER
88 Director of PACE .... Dr. Antija ALLEN
88 Director TRIO Student Support Svcs .... Ms. Venetia C. WILLLIAMS
88 Director Veteran Services .... Dr. Rachael C. CRAGLE
88 Director of Sales/Bus & Cmty Svcs .... Mr. Tim WILSON
88 Dir of Solution Mgmt/Bus & Cmty Svc .... Mr. Todd EVANS

*Roane State Community College (D)

276 Patton Lane, Harriman TN 37748-5011
County: Roane FICE Identification: 009914
Unit ID: 221397
Telephone: (865) 354-3000 Carnegie Class: Assoc/HT-High Trad
FAX Number: (865) 882-4585 Calendar System: Semester
URL: www.roanestate.edu
Established: 1971 Annual Undergrad Tuition & Fees (In-State): $4,552
Enrollment: 5,172 Coed
Affiliation or Control: State IRS Status: 501(c)3
Highest Offering: Associate Degree
Accreditation: SC, ACBSP, ADNUR, CAHIIM, COARC, COMTA, DH, EMT, NAEYC, NAIT, #OPD, OTA, POLYT, PTAA, RAD, SURGT

02 President .... Dr. Chris WHALEY
05 Vice Pres for Student Learning/CAO .... Dr. Diane WARD
10 Vice Pres Business & Finance .... Ms. Marsha MATHEWS
103 VP Workforce/Cmty Development .... Ms. Teresa S. DUNCAN
84 VP Stdnt Svcs/Enroll Mgt/Innovation .... Dr. Jamie STRINGER
12 Int Dir of Oak Ridge Branch Campus .... Mrs. Teresa S. DUNCAN
32 Dean of Students .... Dr. Lisa STEFFENSEN
108 VP Inst Effect/Plng/Stdnt Success .... Ms. Karen L. BRUNNER
21 Director of Financial Services .... Ms. Michelle PATTERSON
17 Dean of Health Sciences .... Dr. Patricia JENKINS
13 Computer Information Officer .... Ms. Keri PHILLIPS
09 Director Institutional Research .... Mr. Jeffrey J. TINLEY
22 Coordinator Affirmative Action .... Mr. Odell FEARN
08 Dir of Library Services .... Ms. Laura VAUGHN
18 Director Physical Plant & Expo Ctr .... Mr. Stan R. STARKEY
29 Director Alumni Relations .... Mr. Scott K. NIERMANN
96 Director of Purchasing & Contracts .... Ms. Dana WEST
36 Manager Workforce Trng & Placement .... Ms. Sonya PARKER
04 Assistant to President .... Ms. Sherry JACKSON
19 Director Safety/Chief of Police .... Mr. Danny R. WRIGHT
88 Special Assistant to President .... Ms. Tamsin MILLER
41 Athletic Director .... Mr. David LANE
104 Dir of International Education .... Mr. Charlie COBB
79 Interim Dean Humanities .... Dr. Geol GREENLEE
83 Int Dean Social/Behavioral Sciences .... Mr. Daniel C. HYDER
81 Dean Math & Science .... Dr. Susan MALEKPOUR
20 Int Dean of Student Academic Svcs .... Ms. Amy KEELING
121 Director of Student Success .... Ms. Kathryn R. BAKER
116 Director of Internal Audit .... Ms. Cynthia CORTESIO
119 Director IT Computing .... Mr. Peter SOUZA
88 Interim Dir Academic Advising .... Ms. Susan PEARSON
118 Manager Employee Benefits .... Ms. Joyce MARSALIS
06 Registrar .... Ms. Jessica HUNSAKER
102 Executive Director Foundation .... Mr. Scott K. NIERMANN
106 Dir Online Education/E-learning .... Dr. Susan R. SUTTON
15 Director Human Resources .... Mr. Odell FEARN
26 Dir Marketing & Public Relations .... Ms. Sarah SELF
37 Director Student Financial Aid .... Ms. Robin TOWNSON
38 Dir Stdnt Care Advoc/Disability Svc .... Mr. Randy S. WAGGONER
91 Director Administrative Computing .... Mr. Chris PANKRATZ
88 Dir Acad Pgm Initiatives & Grants .... Dr. Shelley ESQUIVEL
88 Director Middle College .... Mr. Aaron E. JONES

*Southwest Tennessee Community College (E)

PO Box 780, Memphis TN 38101-0780
County: Shelby FICE Identification: 010439
Unit ID: 221485
Telephone: (901) 333-5000 Carnegie Class: Assoc/HT-High Trad
FAX Number: (901) 333-4645 Calendar System: Semester
URL: www.southwest.tn.edu
Established: 2000 Annual Undergrad Tuition & Fees (In-State): $4,343
Enrollment: 7,371 Coed
Affiliation or Control: State IRS Status: 501(c)3
Highest Offering: Associate Degree
Accreditation: SC, ACBSP, ACFEI, ADNUR, EMT, MLTAD, NAEYC, PTAA, #RAD

02 President .... Dr. Tracy D. HALL
05 Vice President of Academic Affairs .... Vacant
86 Exec Dir Govt Rels/Dir Athletics .... Mr. Sherman D. GREER
111 Vice Pres Institutional Advancement .... Vacant
10 Chief Financial Officer .... Mrs. Jeannette SMITH
32 Vice Pres Student Affairs .... Mrs. Jacqueline A. FAULKNER
84 Assoc VP of Enrollment Services .... Ms. Shanita L. BROWN
103 Assoc Vice Pres of Workforce Dev .... Ms. Anita BRACKIN
26 Exec Director of Comm & Marketing .... Ms. Daphne J. THOMAS
13 Exec Dir Information Systems (CIO) .... Mr. Michael D. BOYD
18 Director Physical Plant .... Mr. Jonathan A. WELDON
19 Director Public Safety .... Mrs. Lezley A. WEBB
04 Exec Admin Assistant to President .... Ms. Mary CANO
15 Assoc VP Human Resources .... Ms. Iliana RICELLI
50 Dean of Business & Technology .... Mr. Robin COLE

*Volunteer State Community College (F)

1480 Nashville Pike, Gallatin TN 37066-3188
County: Sumner FICE Identification: 009912
Unit ID: 222053
Telephone: (615) 452-8600 Carnegie Class: Assoc/HT-High Trad
FAX Number: (615) 230-3577 Calendar System: Semester
URL: www.volstate.edu
Established: 1970 Annual Undergrad Tuition & Fees (In-State): $4,312
Enrollment: 8,832 Coed
Affiliation or Control: State IRS Status: 501(c)3
Highest Offering: Associate Degree
Accreditation: SC, ACBSP, CAHIIM, COARC, DA, DMS, EMT, MLTAD, POLYT, PTAA, RAD

02 President .... Dr. Orinthia MONTAGUE
05 Vice President Academic Affairs .... Dr. Jenniffer BREZINA
10 Vice President Business & Finance .... Ms. Beth CARPENTER
32 Vice President Student Services .... Dr. Emily SHORT
30 Vice Pres for Resource Development .... Ms. Karen MITCHELL
45 Vice Pres Inst Planning/Research .... Vacant
20 Asst VP of Academic Affairs .... Dr. Terri DAY
21 Asst Vice Pres Business & Finance .... Ms. Renee AUSTIN
51 Asst VP for Economic & Cmty Devel .... Vacant
76 Dean of Health .... Ms. Kim CHRISTMON
79 Dean Humanities .... Dr. Erin MANN
83 Dean Social Science/Education .... Mr. James BROWN
81 Dean Math & Science .... Dr. Everett Shane TALBOTT
50 Dean of Business .... Dr. Andy WHITE
15 Dir Personnel/Affirm Act/Human Res .... Ms. Lori CUTRELL
08 Director Library Services .... Ms. Rebecca FRANK
07 Dir Admissions & College Registrar .... Mr. Tim AMYX
13 Director Information Technology .... Mr. Kevin BLANKENSHIP
37 Director Student Financial Aid .... Ms. Tiffany SUMMERS
26 Director Public Relations .... Mrs. Tami WALLACE
18 Senior Director Physical Plant .... Mr. William NEWMAN
19 Chief Security & Safety .... Ms. Angela LAWSON
41 Director of Athletics .... Mr. Bobby HUDSON
121 Dean of Academic Support .... Ms. Rhonda GREGORY
88 Special Adult Programs/ADA Director .... Ms. Leslie SMITH
09 Director of Institutional Research .... Mrs. Ann Marie CALDERON
96 Director Purchasing .... Vacant
124 Director Retention Support Services .... Ms. Heather HARPER
36 Admin of Work-Based Learning .... Dr. Rick PARRENT
38 Director Counseling & Testing .... Mr. Terry BUBB
28 Manager of Diversity & Inclusion .... Mr. Jeff KING
88 Dir Health Sciences Ctr of Emphasis .... Ms. Kathryn MILLER
06 Registrar .... Mr. Tim AMYX
04 Executive Administrative Associate .... Ms. Karen WALLER
102 Foundation Development Officer .... Ms. Alison MUNCY

*Walters State Community College (G)

500 S Davy Crockett Parkway, Morristown TN 37813-6899
County: Hamblen FICE Identification: 008863
Unit ID: 222062
Telephone: (423) 585-2600 Carnegie Class: Assoc/HT-High Trad
FAX Number: (423) 585-6853 Calendar System: Semester
URL: www.ws.edu
Established: 1969 Annual Undergrad Tuition & Fees (In-State): $4,328

Enrollment: 5,742 Coed
Affiliation or Control: State IRS Status: 501(c)3
Highest Offering: Associate Degree
Accreditation: SC, ACBSP, ACFEI, ADNUR, CAHIIM, COARC, EMT, NAEYC, NAIT, OTA, PTAA, SURGT

02 President Dr. Anthony R. MIKSA
04 Exec Director to the President Ms. Leann LONG
05 Vice President Academic Affairs Dr. Donna SEAGLE
10 Vice President Business Affairs Dr. Mark HURST
32 Vice President Student Affairs Ms. Angi SMITH
111 Asst Vice Pres College Advancement Mr. Chris CATES
45 VP for Planning/Research/Assessment Vacant
20 VP for Educational Outreach Dr. John LAPRISE
18 Asst Vice Pres Facilities Mgmt Vacant
21 Asst Vice Pres Business Affairs Ms. Heather CARRIER
08 Dean of Library Dr. Jamie POSEY
103 Dean of Workforce Training Vacant
19 Dean of Public Safety Division Mr. Chad BRYANT
17 Dean Health Programs Ms. Marty K. RUCKER
12 Dean Greenville/Greene Co Center Mr. Mark WILLS
12 Dean Sevier County Campus Dr. Jama SUTTON
83 Dean of Behavioral/Social Sciences Dr. Whitney JARNAGIN
50 Dean of Business Vacant
79 Interim Dean of Humanities Dr. Rob PRATT
81 Dean of Mathematics Mr. John C. KNIGHT
65 Dean of Natural Science Dr. Matthew SMITH
75 Dean of Technical Education Mr. Thomas R. SEWELL
06 Dean Student Info System/Records Ms. Linda MASON
37 Director of Financial Aid Ms. Laura RODRIGUEZ
38 Exec Director Counseling/Testing Dr. Andy HALL
15 Exec Director of Human Resources Mr. Jarvis JENNINGS
26 Vice President Public Information Mr. James B. PECTOL
13 Chief Information Officer Mr. Stephen ANNIS
41 Director of Athletics Mr. Derek CREECH
07 Director of Admissions Ms. Avery SWINSON
19 Chief of Campus Police Vacant
89 Director Freshmen Studies Vacant
36 Director Student Placement Dr. Andy HALL
92 Director Honors Program Mr. David ATKINS
96 Asst Director of Purchasing Ms. Renee JARNIGAN
105 Director of Network Services Mr. Bill R. MOREFIELD
84 Director Enrollment Development Ms. Melanie REDDING
93 Coord Minority Student Recruit Ms. Roxanne BOWEN
108 Asst VP of Planning & Assessment Dr. Deanna GARMAN

Tennessee State University (A)

3500 John A Merritt Boulevard, Nashville TN 37209-1561
County: Davidson FICE Identification: 003522
Unit ID: 221838
Telephone: (615) 963-5000 Carnegie Class: DU-Higher
FAX Number: (615) 963-7412 Calendar System: Semester
URL: www.tnstate.edu
Established: 1912 Annual Undergrad Tuition & Fees (In-State): $9,012
Enrollment: 7,615 Coed
Affiliation or Control: State IRS Status: 501(c)3
Highest Offering: Doctorate
Accreditation: SC, AAFCS, ART, CAEP, CAHIIM, CEA, COARC, COPSY, DH, DIETD, MUS, NAIT, NUR, OT, PH, PTA, SP, SPAA, SW

02 President Dr. Glenda GLOVER
05 Int Provost/VP Academic Affairs Dr. Michael HARRIS
04 Senior Office Assistant Ms. Zanetta GOOCH
10 VP Business & Finance Mr. Douglas ALLEN, II
11 VP Administrative Affairs Vacant
32 Asst Vice Pres Student Affairs Mr. William HYTCHE
111 Dir Institutional Advancement Vacant
41 Athletic Director Mr. Michael ALLEN
43 University Legal Counsel Mr. Laurence PENDLETON
84 VP Enrollment Management Dr. John CADE
20 Assoc VP Academic Affairs Dr. Patricia CROOK
51 AVP Extended Education Center Dr. Evelyn NETTLES
15 Assoc VP Human Resources Ms. Linda C. SPEARS
21 Assoc VP Financial Services Mr. Bradley WHITE
37 Asst VP Financial Aid Ms. Amy B. WOOD
13 Chief Information Officer Mr. Timothy WARREN
26 Asst VP Public Rels/Communication Ms. Kelli SHARPE
09 Exec Director Inst Effectiveness Ms. Charlise ANDERSON
18 AVP Facilities Management Mr. Viron LYNCH
22 Director Equity & Inclusion Ms. Razel JONES
06 Registrar Vacant
19 AVP/Chief of Police Mr. Gregory RIBINSON
08 Int Exec Director Libraries Ms. Glenda ALVIN
49 Int Dean College of Liberal Arts Dr. Samantha MORGAN-CURTIS
50 Dean College of Business Dr. Millicent LOWNES-JACKSON
53 Int Dean College of Education Dr. Heraldo RICHARDS
54 Int Dean College of Engineering Dr. Lin LI
47 Dean Agriculture/Human/Natural Sci Dr. Carter CATLIN
76 Dean College of Health Sciences Dr. Ronald BARREDO

Tennessee Technological University (B)

1 William L. Jones Drive, Cookeville TN 38505
County: Putnam FICE Identification: 003523
Unit ID: 221847
Telephone: (931) 372-3101 Carnegie Class: DU-Higher
FAX Number: (931) 372-3898 Calendar System: Semester
URL: www.tntech.edu
Established: 1915 Annual Undergrad Tuition & Fees (In-State): $9,636
Enrollment: 10,177 Coed
Affiliation or Control: State IRS Status: 501(c)3
Highest Offering: Doctorate
Accreditation: SC, AAFCS, ART, CACREP, CAEP, @DIET, DIETD, MUS, NURSE

02 President Dr. Philip B. OLDHAM
05 Provost/Vice President Dr. Lori M. BRUCE
10 Vice Pres Planning & Finance Dr. Claire STINSON
84 Interim VP of Enrollment Management Ms. Karen LYKINS
32 Vice President of Student Affairs Dr. Cythnia POLK- JOHNSON
28 Chief Diversity Officer Dr. Robert OWENS
46 VP Research/Econ Development Dr. Jennifer TAYLOR
86 Chief Government Affairs Officer Dr. Terry SALTSMAN
100 Chief of Staff/Board Secretary Mr. Lee WRAY
88 Assoc VP for Research Vacant
111 Vice President Univ Advancement Dr. Kevin BRASWELL
41 Director of Athletics Mr. Mark WILSON
26 Chief Communication Officer Ms. Karen LYKINS
43 Director University Counsel Mr. Troy PERDUE
20 Sr Assoc VP Academic Affairs Dr. Mark STEPHENS
20 Assoc Provost/Vice Pres Acad Affs Dr. Xiaoming (Sharon) HUO
13 Assoc VP for Info Technlogy Dr. Brian SEILER
37 Dir Financial Aid & Veteran Affairs Ms. Mary MCCASKEY
45 Director of Strategic Planning Mr. Dewayne WRIGHT
15 Assoc VP Human Resources Mr. Kevin VEDDER
88 Compliance Ofcr/Clery Coordinator Mr. Greg HOLT
19 Director of University Police Mr. Tony NELSON
39 Exec Director of Residential Life Ms. Courtney THOMPSON
18 Assoc VP Physical Plant Mr. Chuck ROBERTS
38 Director Counseling Center Ms. Christina MICK
23 Director of Health Svcs Ms. Leigh A. RAY
36 Director Career Development Mr. Russ COUGHENOUR
85 Director International Education Mr. Charles WILKERSON
06 Registrar Ms. Brandi FLETCHER
92 Director Honors Program Dr. Rita BARNES
96 Director of Purchasing Ms. Donna WALLIS
21 Associate VP Business Ms. Emily WHEELER
29 Dir Alumni Engagement & Annual Giv Vacant
116 Director of Internal Audit Ms. Deanna METTS
07 Interim Director of Admissions Dr. Frank TITTLE
19 Dir Capital Project Administration Mr. James COBB
49 Interim Dean of Arts & Sciences Dr. Jeff ROBERTS
54 Dean of Engineering Dr. Joseph SLATER
47 Dean Agric & Human Ecology Dr. Darron SMITH
50 Dean of Business Admin Dr. Thomas PAYNE
53 Dean College of Education Dr. Lisa ZAGUMNY
57 Dean of College of Fine Arts Dr. Jennifer SHANK
66 Dean School of Nursing Dr. Kim HANNA
88 Dean Interdisciplinary Studies Dr. Mike GOTCHER
08 Dean Library & Learning Asst Dr. Doug BATES
58 Assoc Dean of Graduate Studies Dr. Alice CAMUTI
04 Asst to President/Asst Board Secy Ms. Diane SMITH
105 Director Web Services Mr. Cody BRYANT
108 Int Dir Inst Assess/Rsrch/Effective Dr. Kevin HARRIS
90 Director Academic Computing Mr. Will HOFFERT
91 Dir Enterprise Application System Vacant
110 Exec Dir of Univ Advancement Mr. John W. SMITH
104 Director Study Abroad Ms. Amy MILLER

Tennessee Wesleyan University (C)

204 East College St., Athens TN 37303
County: McMinn FICE Identification: 003525
Unit ID: 221731
Telephone: (423) 745-7504 Carnegie Class: Bac-Diverse
FAX Number: (423) 744-9968 Calendar System: Semester
URL: www.tnwesleyan.edu
Established: 1857 Annual Undergrad Tuition & Fees: $25,850
Enrollment: 1,116 Coed
Affiliation or Control: United Methodist IRS Status: 501(c)3
Highest Offering: Master's
Accreditation: SC, DH, NURSE, OT, SW

01 President Dr. Tyler FORREST
05 Vice President for Academic Affairs Dr. Grant WILLHITE
10 Vice Pres Financial/Business Affs Mrs. Gail HARRIS
32 Vice President for Student Life Dr. Scott MASHBURN
111 VP of Advancement/Alumni Affairs Mr. Blake MCCASLIN
37 Assoc VP Financial Aid Mrs. Lacey WEESE
108 VP for Inst Effectiveness Dr. Stephanie SMALLEN
07 Asst VP of Admissions Vacant
04 Executive Assistant to President Mrs. Gail ROGERS
08 Dir of Library & Info Svcs Ms. Julie ADAMS
06 Registrar Mrs. Julie MCCASLIN
41 Athletic Director Mr. Donny MAYFIELD
15 Human Resources Director Mr. Kyle FULBRIGHT
18 Chief of Facilities/Physical Plant Mr. Danny DUCKETT
26 Interim Asst VP Marketing/Comm Ms. J.J HULET
13 Assoc VP of Information Tech/CIO Mr. Brandon LAMBDIN

Trevecca Nazarene University (D)

333 Murfreesboro Road, Nashville TN 37210-2877
County: Davidson FICE Identification: 003526
Unit ID: 221892
Telephone: (615) 248-1200 Carnegie Class: DU-Mod
FAX Number: (615) 248-7728 Calendar System: Semester
URL: www.trevecca.edu
Established: 1901 Annual Undergrad Tuition & Fees: $26,898
Enrollment: 3,968 Coed
Affiliation or Control: Church Of The Nazarene IRS Status: 501(c)3
Highest Offering: Doctorate
Accreditation: SC, ARCPA, CACREP, CAEPN, MUS, NURSE, SW

01 President Dr. Dan BOONE
04 Assistant to the President Ms. Anne TWINING
05 Provost & Senior Vice President Dr. Tom MIDDENDORF
111 VP University Engagement Mrs. Peggy J. COONING
20 VP Academic Affairs and Accred Dr. Jonathan BARTLING
50 Assoc VP/Dean of Sch of Business Dr. Jim HIATT
26 Assoc Vice Pres Marketing & Comm Ms. Mollie YODER
32 VP/Dean of Student Development Ms. Jessica DYKES
84 VP Enrollment & Marketing Ms. Holly WHITBY
10 CFO Mr. Mariano MONZU
73 Dean School of Theol/Christian Min Dr. Timothy M. GREEN
88 Assoc Dn Acad Integrity/Innovation Dr. Heidi VENTURA
35 Asst Dean of Student Life Ms. Megan MCGHEE
39 Asc Dean Students Residential Life Mrs. Ronda LILIENTHAL
53 Dean of the School of Education Dr. Suzann HARRIS
49 Dean of School of Arts & Science Dr. Lena WELCH
64 Dean School of Music & Worship Arts Dr. David DIEHL
54 Dean School of STEM Dr. Stephen SILLIMAN
13 Chief Information Officer/ITS Dr. John EBERLE
06 Registrar Ms. Katrina CHAPMAN
19 Director of Security Mr. Greg DAWSON
07 VP Trad Undergrad Enrollment Ms. Melinda MILLER
41 Athletic Director Mr. Mark ELLIOTT
121 Assoc Dean of Student Success Ms. Michelle GAERTNER
38 Director Counseling Services Ms. Miller FOLK
85 Dir Global Engagement Ms. Katie MILLER
58 AVP & Dean of Graduate Studies Ms. LaMetrius DANIELS
21 Director of Financial Services Mr. Chuck SEAMAN
37 Dir of Student Financial Services Ms. Kylie PRUITT
15 Director Human Resources Mr. Steve SEXTON
76 Director Physician Asst Pgm Mr. Bret REEVES
29 Engagement Officer Alum Assoc Rev. Jennifer SHOWALTER
30 Engagement Officer Opers & Gifts Ms. Christy GRANT
27 Communications Director Mr. Brian BENNETT
124 Coordinator of Assessment/Retention Mr. Jeffrey SWINK
08 Chief Library Officer Dr. Andrea FOWLER
09 Director of Institutional Research Mr. Huey DAVIS
25 Engagement Officer Community & FE Ms. Janice LOVELL

Tusculum University (E)

60 Shiloh Road, Greeneville TN 37745-9997
County: Greene FICE Identification: 003527
Unit ID: 221953
Telephone: (423) 636-7300 Carnegie Class: Masters/M
FAX Number: (423) 638-7166 Calendar System: Semester
URL: https://home.tusculum.edu/
Established: 1794 Annual Undergrad Tuition & Fees: $25,500
Enrollment: 1,664 Coed
Affiliation or Control: Presbyterian Church (U.S.A.) IRS Status: 501(c)3
Highest Offering: Master's
Accreditation: SC, ACBSP, NURSE

01 President Dr. Scott HUMMEL
05 Provost & VP Academic Affairs Dr. Tricia HUNSADER
10 Vice Pres/Chief Financial Officer Ms. Benita BARE
84 VP Enrollment Mgmt & Financial Aid Dr. Jacob FAIT
41 VP Athletics & Univ Initiatives Mr. Doug JONES
32 AVP/Dean Student Affairs/Retention Ms. Claire HENSLEY
111 Assoc VP Inst Advancement Ms. Kimberly KIDWELL
06 Registrar Mr. Casey REAGAN
21 Controller Vacant
15 Chief Human Resource Officer Mr. Scott SMITH
08 Library Director Mrs. Kathy HIPPS
37 Director of Financial Aid Ms. Melissa WHITE
26 Director of Communications & Mktg Mr. Jim WOZNIAK
13 Director of Information Systems Mr. Chris SUMMEY
18 Director Facilities Management Mr. Chad GRINDSTAFF
92 Director of Honors Program Vacant
40 Bookstore Manager Vacant
19 Director of Campus Safety Mr. Shane MATTHEWS
49 Dean Col of Civic & Liberal Arts Mr. Wayne THOMAS
50 Interim Dean College of Business Dr. Kevin HILL
53 Dean College of Education Dr. Miriam STRODER
66 Dean of School of Nursing Vacant
09 Dir of Inst Research/Effectiveness Mr. Richard MILLER
121 Director of Student Success Mr. Chuck SUTTON

Union University (F)

1050 Union University Drive, Jackson TN 38305-3697
County: Madison FICE Identification: 003528
Unit ID: 221971
Telephone: (731) 668-1818 Carnegie Class: DU-Mod
FAX Number: (731) 661-5175 Calendar System: 4/1/4
URL: www.uu.edu
Established: 1823 Annual Undergrad Tuition & Fees: $34,630
Enrollment: 3,071 Coed
Affiliation or Control: Southern Baptist IRS Status: 501(c)3
Highest Offering: Doctorate
Accreditation: SC, ANEST, ART, CAATE, CAEP, MUS, NURSE, PHAR, SW

01 President Dr. Samuel (Dub) W. OLIVER
05 Provost/VP Academic Affairs Dr. John T. NETLAND
10 VP for Business Affairs Dr. Rick TAPHORN
111 Vice Pres Institutional Advancement Mrs. Catherine KWASIGROH
84 Vice Pres Enrollment Management Mr. Dan GRIFFIN
32 VP Student Life/Dean of Students Dr. Bryan CARRIER
42 Vice Pres for University Ministries Dr. Todd BRADY
108 Asst Provost Accred & Research Dr. Michele ATKINS
04 Exec Assistant to the President Mrs. Kristie KING
21 Assoc Vice Pres Business Svcs Mr. Hunter MARTIN
08 Director of the Library Services Ms. Melissa MOORE
26 Assoc VP University Communications Mr. Tim ELLSWORTH

13	Assoc VP Information Technology	Mr. James AVERY
15	AVP Human Resources/Business Ofc	Dr. John CARBONELL
07	Asst VP for Undergraduate Admiss	Mr. Robbie GRAVES
37	Director Student Financial Planning	Mr. Derek MOORE
49	Dean College Arts & Sciences	Dr. Hunter BAKER
50	Dean School of Business	Dr. Jason GARRETT
66	Dean School of Nursing	Dr. Kelly HARDEN
53	Dean College of Education	Dr. John FOUBERT
73	Dean Sch of Theology & Missions	Dr. Ray VANNESTE
67	Dean School of Pharmacy	Dr. Sheila MITCHELL
36	Dir Vocation Ctr/Life Call/Career	Mrs. Stephanie HAWLEY
06	Registrar	Mrs. Susan HOPPER
19	Director of Security/Safety	Mr. Johnny JINES
41	Director of Athletics	Mr. Tommy SADLER
18	Chief Facilities/Physical Plant	Mr. Stephen HOPPER
70	Dean School of Social Work	Mrs. Nita MEHR
51	Dean School Adult & Prof Studies	Dr. Renee DAUER

The University of Memphis (A)

Southern Avenue, Memphis TN 38152

County: Shelby — FICE Identification: 003509

Unit ID: 220862

Telephone: (901) 678-2000 — Carnegie Class: DU-Highest

FAX Number: N/A — Calendar System: Semester

URL: www.memphis.edu

Established: 1912 — Annual Undergrad Tuition & Fees (In-State): $9,912

Enrollment: 22,205 — Coed

Affiliation or Control: State — IRS Status: 501(c)3

Highest Offering: Doctorate

Accreditation: SC, ART, AUD, CACREP, CAEPN, CIDA, CLPSY, COPSY, DIETD, DIETI, HSA, IPSY, JOUR, LAW, MUS, NURSE, PH, PLNG, SCPSY, SP, SPAA, SW, THEA

02	President	Dr. Bill HARDGRAVE
05	Interim Provost	Dr. Abby PARRILL-BAKER
20	Vice Provost Academic Innovation	Dr. Richard IRWIN
10	EVP & Chief Financial Officer	Mr. Raaj KURAPATI
45	Chief University Planning Officer	Mr. Tony POTEET
18	VP Physical Plant	Mr. Ron BROOKS
19	Chief of Police	Mr. Derek MYERS
116	Chief Audit Executive	Ms. Vicki DEATON
111	Vice Pres Advancement	Ms. Joanna CURTIS
32	Vice Pres Student Academic Success	Dr. Karen WEDDLE-WEST
35	Asst VP Student Aff/Dev	Vacant
26	EVP External Relations	Ms. Tammy HEDGES
46	Exec VP Research & Innovation	Dr. Jasbir DHALIWAL
41	Director of Athletics	Mr. Laird VEATCH
43	University Counsel	Ms. Melanie MURRY
22	Interim Dir of Institutional Equity	Ms. Ceecy REED
13	CIO/Vice Provost for Info Tech	Dr. Robert JACKSON
84	Vice Provost Enrollment Services	Vacant
58	Dean Graduate School	Dr. Robin POSTON
21	Asst Vice Pres Business & Finance	Vacant
15	Asst Vice Pres Human Resources	Ms. Maria ALAM
08	Assoc Dean U of M Libraries	Mr. John EVANS
09	Director Institutional Research	Ms. Bridgette DECENT
36	Director Career & Employment Svcs	Ms. Alisha D. ROSE
06	Registrar	Ms. Darla KEEL
37	Int Exec Director of Student Aid	Mr. Andrew LINN
96	Executive Director Procurement Svcs	Mr. Nick PAPPAS
29	Director of Alumni Relations	Mr. Joshua JONES
92	Director University Honors Program	Dr. Melinda L. JONES
07	Assistant Vice Provost Admissions	Dr. Eric STOKES
28	Director of Diversity Initiatives	Dr. Karen WEDDLE-WEST
60	Dean Comm Sciences/Disorders	Dr. Linda D. JARMULOWICZ
49	Interim Dean of Arts & Sciences	Dr. Gary EMMERT
50	Interim Dean Business & Economics	Dr. Greg BOLLER
53	Dean of Education	Dr. Kandi HILL-CLARKE
54	Int Dean of Engineering	Dr. Russ J. DEATON
89	Dean University College	Dr. Richard IRWIN
57	Int Dean Communication & Fine Arts	Dr. Ryan FISHER
61	Dean School of Law	Ms. Kate SCHAFFZIN
66	Dean College of Nursing	Dr. Linda HADDAD
69	Dean School of Public Health	Dr. Joshi ASHISH
76	Dean College of Health Studies	Dr. Richard J. BLOOMER
104	Director Study Abroad	Ms. Rebecca DYCK-LAUMANN
108	Director Institutional Assessment	Dr. Colton COCKRUM
38	Director Student Counseling	Dr. Jane CLEMENT
112	Director of Planned Giving	Ms. Wesley LARUE
102	Dir Foundation/Corporate Relations	Ms. Kimberly GRANTHAM
106	Exe Dean Global/Academic Innovation	Dr. Richard L. IRWIN
44	Director of Annual Giving	Vacant
86	Director Government Relations	Ms. Katie VANLANDINHAM
39	Director of Residence Life	Mr. Brian ROCK
04	Admin Assistant to the President	Ms. LaTondra ARNETT
100	Chief of Staff	Ms. Stephanie BEASLEY
105	Director Web Services/Digital	Ms. Holly SNYDER
101	Secretary of the Institution/Board	Ms. Melanie MURRY
124	Dir Student Leadership/Involvement	Ms. MK TYLER

*University of Tennessee System Office (B)

505 Summer Place, UT Tower 12th FL, Knoxville TN 37902

County: Knox — FICE Identification: 008051

Telephone: (865) 974-1000 — Carnegie Class: N/A

FAX Number: (865) 974-3753

URL: www.tennessee.edu

01	President	Mr. Randy BOYD
10	Sr Vice President/CFO	Mr. David L. MILLER
05	VP Academic Affairs/Student Success	Dr. Linda C. MARTIN
30	UTFI President & CEO UT VP	Mr. Kerry WITCHER
86	VP for Government Rels/Advocacy	Ms. Carey WHITWORTH
45	VP Research/Outreach/Economic Dev	Dr. Stacey PATTERSON
43	General Counsel/Secretary	Mr. C. Ryan STINNETT
15	Chief Human Resources Officer	Mr. Brian DICKENS
86	Vice Pres Institute for Public Svc	Dr. Herb BYRD
26	VP Communications/Marketing	Ms. Tiffany CARPENTER
13	Chief Information Officer	Mr. Ramon PADILLA, JR.
21	Exec Dir Auditing/Consulting Svcs	Mr. Brian DANIELS

*University of Tennessee, Knoxville (C)

1331 Circle Park, Knoxville TN 37996

County: Knox — FICE Identification: 003530

Unit ID: 221759

Telephone: (865) 974-1000 — Carnegie Class: DU-Highest

FAX Number: (865) 974-1182 — Calendar System: Semester

URL: www.utk.edu

Established: 1794 — Annual Undergrad Tuition & Fees (In-State): $13,264

Enrollment: 30,559 — Coed

Affiliation or Control: State — IRS Status: 501(c)3

Highest Offering: Doctorate

Accreditation: SC, ANEST, ART, CACREP, CAEP, CAMPEP, CAPRT, CIDA, CLPSY, COPSY, DENT, DIET, DIETD, DIETI, IPSY, JOUR, LAW, LIB, LSAR, MLS, MUS, NURSE, PAST, PH, RAD, SCPSY, SW, THEA, VET

02	Chancellor	Dr. Donde PLOWMAN
100	Chancellor's Executive Assistant	Ms. Susan ENGLAND
100	Chief of Staff	Mr. Matthew SCOGGINS
05	Provost/Senior Vice Chancellor	Dr. John ZOMCHICK
32	Vice Chancellor for Student Life	Dr. Frank CUEVAS
46	Vice Chancellor for Research	Dr. Deborah CRAWFORD
10	Senior VC Finance & Administration	Mr. Chris CIMINO
28	VC for Diversity & Engagement	Mr. Tyvi SMALL
26	Vice Chancellor for Communications	Mrs. Tisha BENTON
30	Vice Chancellor for Development	Mr. Chip BRYANT
20	Vice Provost for Faculty Affairs	Dr. Diane KELLY
20	Vice Provost for Academic Affairs	Dr. RJ HINDE
58	Vice Provost/Dean Graduate School	Dr. Dixie THOMPSON
121	Vice Provost Student Success	Dr. Amber WILLIAMS
35	AVC Student Life/Dean of Students	Dr. Byron HUGHES
84	Vice Provost Enrollment Svcs	Ms. Kari ALLDREDGE
18	Assoc VC Facilities Svcs	Mr. Michael BRADY
41	Vice Chancellor/Dir Athletics	Dr. Daniel WHITE
22	Assoc VC Equity & Diversity	Ms. Katrice MORGAN
37	Director of Financial Aid	Mr. Jeffrey G. GERKIN
09	Dir Inst Research/Assessment	Ms. Denise GARDNER
38	Director of Student Counseling	Dr. Nicole SAYLOR
06	Registrar	Mr. Brian COLDREN
47	Dean Herbert College of Agriculture	Dr. Caula BEYL
48	Dean of Architecture and Design	Dr. Jason YOUNG
50	Dean Haslam College of Business	Dr. Steve MANGUM
60	Dean Communication/Information	Dr. Joe MAZER
53	Dean Educ/Health/Human Sciences	Dr. Ellen MCINTYRE
54	Dean Tickle College of Engineering	Dr. Matthew MENCH
61	Dean of Law	Prof. Lonnie T. BROWN
49	Dean of Arts & Sciences	Dr. Theresa LEE
66	Dean of Nursing	Dr. Victoria NIEDERHAUSER
70	Dean of Social Work	Dr. Lori MESSINGER
74	Dean of Veterinary Medicine	Dr. James P. THOMPSON
12	Sr Vice Chanc/SVP Inst of Agricul	Dr. Carrie CASTILLE
08	Dean of Libraries	Dr. Steve SMITH
12	Exec Dir of UT Space Institute	Dr. John SCHMISSEUR
07	Director of Undergrad Admissions	Mr. Fabrizio D'ALOISIO
13	Associate VC & CIO	Mr. Joel REEVES
29	Associate VC of Alumni Affairs	Mr. Duane WILES
104	Vice Provost Global Engagement	Dr. Gretchen NEISLER
15	Assoc Vice Chancellor HR	Dr. Mary LUCAL
19	Assoc Vice Chancellor Public Safety	Mr. Troy LANE
36	Exec Dir Career Development	Ms. Stephanie KIT

*University of Tennessee at Chattanooga (D)

615 McCallie Avenue, Chattanooga TN 37403-2504

County: Hamilton — FICE Identification: 003529

Unit ID: 221740

Telephone: (423) 425-4111 — Carnegie Class: DU-Mod

FAX Number: (423) 425-2200 — Calendar System: Semester

URL: www.utc.edu

Established: 1886 — Annual Undergrad Tuition & Fees (In-State): $9,656

Enrollment: 11,728 — Coed

Affiliation or Control: State — IRS Status: 501(c)3

Highest Offering: Doctorate

Accreditation: SC, ANEST, ART, CAATE, CACREP, CAEP, CIDA, @DIET, JOUR, MUS, NURSE, OT, PTA, SPAA, SW, THEA

02	Chancellor	Dr. Steven R. ANGLE
05	Provost & Sr VC Academic Affs	Dr. Jerold HALE
20	Vice Prov for Academic Affairs	Dr. Matt MATTHEWS
111	VC University Advancement	Ms. Kim WHITE
10	Interim VC Finance/Administration	Ms. Vicki FARNSWORTH
46	Vice Chancellor for Research	Dr. Joanne ROMAGNI
32	Vice Chanc Student Development	Vacant
28	Vice Chanc Diversity/Engagement	Ms. Stacy G. LIGHTFOOT
21	Assoc Vice Chanc Business/Fin Affs	Ms. Vanasia Conley PARKS
26	Vice Chanc Comm & Mktg	Ms. Cassie MATHES
41	Vice Chanc & AD	Mr. Mark WHARTON
26	Asst VC University Relations	Ms. Gina STAFFORD
18	Asst VC Operations/Fac Plng & Mgt	Mr. Tom M. ELLIS
13	VC for Communications and CIO	Ms. Vicki FARNSWORTH
100	Chief of Staff	Mr. David STEELE
08	Dean of UTC Library	Ms. Theresa LIEDTKA
35	Assoc Dean of Student Life	Mr. Jim HICKS
84	VC Enroll Mgmt/Student Success	Dr. Yancy FREEMAN
06	Director Records & Registrar	Mr. Joel WELLS
13	Manager Client Solutions/IT	Vacant
09	Dir of Planning/Eval/Inst Research	Ms. Eva LEWIS
36	Asst Dir Placement/Stdnt Employment	Mrs. Donna COOPER
15	Asst Vice Chanc Human Resources	Ms. Laure POU
38	Executive Director of Counseling	Dr. Elizabeth O'BRIEN
37	Director of Financial Aid	Ms. Jennifer BUCKLES
58	Dean of the Graduate School	Dr. Joanne ROMAGNI
49	Dean of Arts & Sciences	Dr. Pamela RIGGS-GELASCO
50	Dean of Business Administration	Dr. Robert DOOLEY
53	Dean of Health/Educ/Prof Studies	Dr. Valerie RUTLEDGE
54	Dean Engineering/Comp Science	Dr. Daniel PACK
66	Director of Nursing	Dr. Christine SMITH
22	Director of Equity & Inclusion	Ms. Rosite DELGADO
25	Director of Sponsored Programs	Ms. Meredith PERRY
29	Asst Vice Chanc Alumni Affairs	Mr. Jeff COGBURN
96	Procurement/Contracts (Purchasing)	Mr. Ken GUTHRIE
19	Chief of Police	Mr. Robert RATCHFORD
39	Director Student Housing	Ms. Valara SAMPLE
92	Dean Honors College	Dr. Linda FROST
88	Coordinator of Engagement	Mr. AJ DAVIS
104	Exec Director International Program	Mr. Takeo SUZUKI
43	Dir Legal Services/General Counsel	Mr. Yousef A. HAMADEH
04	Admin Assistant to the Chancellor	Ms. Teresa F. MCKINNEY
122	Coord Fraternity/Sorority Life	Ms. Laura PETRUS
07	Director of Admissions	Mr. Jason LYON

*University of Tennessee at Martin (E)

554 University Street, Martin TN 38238-0001

County: Weakley — FICE Identification: 003531

Unit ID: 221768

Telephone: (731) 881-7000 — Carnegie Class: Masters/M

FAX Number: (731) 881-7019 — Calendar System: Semester

URL: www.utm.edu

Established: 1900 — Annual Undergrad Tuition & Fees (In-State): $9,748

Enrollment: 7,117 — Coed

Affiliation or Control: State — IRS Status: 501(c)3

Highest Offering: Master's

Accreditation: SC, AAFCS, CAEP, DIETD, DIETI, MUS, NUR, SW

02	Chancellor	Dr. Keith S. CARVER, JR.
05	Provost & SVC for Academic Affairs	Dr. Philip A. CAVALIER
10	Sr Vice Chanc for Finance & Admin	Ms. Petra R. MCPHEARSON
32	Vice Chanc for Student Affairs	Dr. John A. LEWTER
111	Vice Chancellor Univ Advancement	Dr. Charles T. DEAL
20	Assoc Provost for Academic Affs	Dr. Victoria S. SENG
13	Chief Information Officer	Ms. Amy C. BELEW
28	Chief Diversity & Inclusion Officer	Dr. Mark MCCLOUD
114	Dir Budget & Mgmt Report	Ms. Carol WILLIAMS
35	Asst Vice Chanc for Student Affairs	Mr. John C. ABEL
30	Assoc VC Devel & Planned Giving	Ms. Jeanna C. SWAFFORD
04	Senior Advisor to the Chancellor	Ms. Edie B. GIBSON
29	Asst Vice Chanc Alumni Relations	Ms. Jacqueline JOHNSON
06	Dir of Acad Records & Registrar	Ms. Martha BARNETT
28	Equity & Diversity Ofcr AA/EEO	Ms. Dominique CROCKETT
15	Director of Human Resources	Mr. Michael WASHINGTON
09	Director Institutional Research	Dr. Rion MCDONALD
41	VC & Dir Intercollegiate Athletics	Mr. Kurt MCGUFFIN
08	Dean of Library	Dr. Erik NORDBERG
18	Int Dir of Physical Plant Opers	Mr. Brad BURKETT
19	Dir of Public Safety	Mr. Monte BELEW
96	Purchasing Agent	Ms. Lori A. DONAVANT
23	Dir Student Health & Counseling Svc	Ms. Shannon DEAL
39	Asst VC Student/Residential Life	Ms. Gina MCCLURE
26	VC Communications & Marketing	Mr. Robert (Bud) D. GRIMES
47	Dean Col Agri & App Sciences	Dr. Todd A. WINTERS
50	Dean Col Business & Global Affs	Dr. Ahmad TOOTOONCHI
53	Dean Col Educ/Health/Behav Sci	Ms. Cynthia L. WEST
79	Dean Col Humanities/Fine Arts	Dr. Lynn M. ALEXANDER
54	Int Dean Col Engr & Natural Sci	Dr. Nancy L. BUSCHHAUS
58	Dean of Graduate Studies	Dr. Joey MEHLHORN
105	Director Web Services	Mr. Brian C. INGRAM
25	Int Exec Dir Res Outreach/Econ Dev	Ms. Alisha M. MELTON
84	Exec Dir Enr Svcs/Stdnt Engagement	Dr. James D. MANTOOTH
07	Director of Admissions	Ms. Destin TUCKER
37	Dir Financial Aid/Scholarship	Ms. Jana COX
93	Asst Dir Multicultural Affairs	Vacant

*The University of Tennessee Southern (F)

433 W Madison Street, Pulaski TN 38478-2799

County: Giles — FICE Identification: 003504

Unit ID: 220701

Telephone: (931) 363-9800 — Carnegie Class: Bac-Diverse

FAX Number: (931) 363-9818 — Calendar System: Semester

URL: www.utsouthern.edu

Established: 1870 — Annual Undergrad Tuition & Fees (In-State): $25,850

Enrollment: 812 — Coed

Affiliation or Control: State — IRS Status: 170(c)1

Highest Offering: Master's

Accreditation: SC, NURSE

01	Interim Chancellor	Dr. Linda C. MARTIN
04	Exec Assistant to the Chancellor	Mrs. Kim W. HARRISON

05 Provost & VC of Academic Affairs ....Dr. Judy B. CHEATHAM
10 VC for Finance & Administration ....Mr. Robby SHELTON
32 Assoc VC for Student Affairs .... Dr. Daniel N. MCMASTERS
84 Assoc VC of Enrollment Management ....Mr. Tyler COX
111 Asst VC for Advancement Services ....Mrs. Edna G. LUNA
21 Asst VC of Finance ....Ms. Rhonda CLINARD
41 Athletic Director ....Mrs. Brandie PAUL
15 Chief Human Resources Officer ....Mr. James R. HLUBB
13 Chief Information Officer ....Mr. Cedrick NKULU
26 Chief Marketing & Comm Officer ....Mrs. Abby C. STANTON
35 Dean of Students .... Mrs. Sarah Catherine RICHARDSON
06 Registrar & Director of IR ....Dr. Chris MATTINGLY
37 Director of Financial Aid ....Mrs. Emma HLUBB
07 Director of Admissions ....Mrs. Alyssa SPANN
19 Director of Safety & Security ....Mrs. Josie B. TREVARTHEN
105 Director of Publications & Website ....Mrs. Susan CARLISLE
36 Director of Career Services ....Mrs. Julie SHELTON
40 Director of Bookstore ....Mrs. Margaret W. JACKSON
29 Alumni Affairs Director ....Mrs. Laura K. MCMASTERS
18 Facilities Director ....Mr. Rich BRICKER
08 Librarian ....Mr. Richard MADDEN
39 Residential Life Coordinator ....Ms. Kara WILLIAMS

*University of Tennessee Health Science Center (A)

875 Monroe Avenue, Memphis TN 38163
Telephone: (901) 448-5500 FICE Identification: 006725
Accreditation: SC, ANEST, ARCPA, AUD, CAHIIM, CAMPEP, CYTO, DENT, DH, HT, IPSY, MED, @MIDWF, MLS, NURSE, OT, PHAR, PTA, SP

Vanderbilt University (B)

2201 West End Avenue, Nashville TN 37235
County: Davidson FICE Identification: 003535
Unit ID: 221999
Telephone: (615) 322-7311 Carnegie Class: DU-Highest
FAX Number: (615) 343-7765 Calendar System: Semester
URL: www.vanderbilt.edu
Established: 1873 Annual Undergrad Tuition & Fees: $54,158
Enrollment: 13,537 Coed
Affiliation or Control: Independent Non-Profit IRS Status: 501(c)3
Highest Offering: Doctorate
Accreditation: SC, AUD, CACREP, CAEP, CAMPEP, CLPSY, DENT, DIETI, DMS, IPSY, LAW, MED, MIDWF, MLS, MUS, NMT, NURSE, PAST, PCSAS, PERF, PH, SP, THEOL

01 Chancellor ....Dr. Daniel DIERMEIER
05 Provost/Vice Chanc Academic Affairs ....Dr. C. Cybele RAVER
125 Chancellor Emeritus ....Dr. Nicholas ZEPPOS
63 Dean School of Medicine ....Dr. Jeffrey R. BALSER
10 Vice Chancellor Finance/CFO ....Mr. Brett SWEET
11 Vice Chanc Administration ....Mr. Eric KOPSTAIN
30 Vice Chanc Dev/Alumni Relations ....Mr. John M. LUTZ
46 Vice Provost for Research ....Dr. Padma RAGHAVAN
115 Vice Chanc for Investments ....Mr. Anders W. HALL
28 VC Equity/Diversity/Inclusion ....Dr. Andre L. CHURCHWELL
15 Chief Human Resources Ofcr ....Ms. Cleo RUCKER
41 Vice Chanc/Dir Athletics ....Dr. Candice STOREY LEE
112 Dir Trust and Estate Admin ....Ms. Susan HART
26 Vice Chancellor for Communications ....Mr. Steve ERTEL
13 Vice Chancellor Information Tech ....Mr. Brett C. SWEET
86 Vice Chanc Govt/Cmty Relations ....Mr. Nathan GREEN
43 Vice Chancellor/General Counsel ....Ms. Ruby Z. SHELLAWAY
09 Asst Provost/Exec Dir Inst Research ....Ms. Olivia KEW-FICKUS
20 Vice Provost Learning & Res Affairs ....Ms. Cynthia J. CYRUS
58 Int Dean of the Graduate School ....Dr. Bunmi OLATUNJI
08 University Librarian ....Dr. Valerie HOTCHKISS
27 Dean of Student Publications/Comm ....Mr. F. Clark WILLIAMS
21 Asst V Chanc for Finance/Controller ....Ms. Dalana ROBERTSON
06 Registrar ....Mr. Bart P. QUINET
84 Vice Provost Univ Enrollment Affs ....Vacant
07 Asst Dir Undergraduate Admissions ....Mr. Walt BIESCHKE
37 Director Student Financial Aid ....Mr. Brent B. TENER
38 Director Univ Counseling Center ....Dr. Todd WEINMAN
36 Exec Dir Career Center ....Dr. Katharine S. BROOKS
25 Director Sponsored Programs ....Mr. Andrew BUDELL
32 Assoc Provost/Dean of Students ....Mr. G.L BLACK
106 Assoc Provost for Educ Tech & Dev ....Dr. John M. SLOOP
49 Dean College of Arts & Science ....Dr. John G. GEER
54 Dean School of Engineering ....Dr. Philippe M. FAUCHET
66 Dean School of Nursing ....Dr. Linda NORMAN
53 Dean Education & Human Development ....Dr. Camilla P. BENBOW
64 Dean Blair School of Music ....Dr. Lorenzo CANDELARIA
73 Dean of the Divinity School ....Dr. Emilie M. TOWNES
61 Dean of the School of Law ....Dr. Chris GUTHRIE
50 Dean Owen Grad School of Mgmt ....Dr. M. Eric JOHNSON
45 Vice Prov Strategic Initiatives ....Vacant
20 Vice Prov Acad Affairs/Dean of Fac ....Dr. Vanessa BEASLEY
20 Vice Prov for Faculty Affairs ....Dr. Tracey GEORGE
42 University Chaplain ....Rev. Gretchen PERSON
19 AVC/Chief of Public Safety ....Mr. August J. WASHINGTON
22 Dir EO/AA & Disability Svcs ....Ms. Anita JENIOUS
88 Dir Sport Operations/Asst Vice Chan ....Mr. Brockton WILLIAMS
39 Sr Director Housing Operations ....Mr. James S. KRAMKA
44 Asst Vice Chancellor Annual Giving ....Mr. Kyle D. MCGOWAN
88 Asst Vice Chanc Federal Relations ....Ms. Christina D. WEST

Visible Music College (C)

200 Madison Avenue, Memphis TN 38103
County: Shelby FICE Identification: 039823
Unit ID: 449764
Telephone: (901) 381-3939 Carnegie Class: Spec-4-yr-Arts
FAX Number: (901) 377-0544 Calendar System: Semester
URL: www.visible.edu
Established: 2000 Annual Undergrad Tuition & Fees: $20,000
Enrollment: 209 Coed
Affiliation or Control: Independent Non-Profit IRS Status: 501(c)3
Highest Offering: Master's
Accreditation: TRACS

01 President ....Dr. Ken STEORTS
05 Vice President of Academics ....Dr. Cameron HARVEY
111 Vice President of Advancement ....Geordy WELLS
10 Vice President of Business ....Ben RAWLEY
32 Int Vice President of Students ....Dr. Ken STEORTS
06 Registrar ....Vacant
37 Financial Aid Manager ....Tonya WILLIAMS
15 Human Resources Coordinator ....Toni MELTON
18 Operations/IT Manager ....Heath BENSON
84 Enrollment Manager ....Vacant

Welch College (D)

1045 Bison Trail, Gallatin TN 37066
County: Sumner FICE Identification: 030018
Unit ID: 220206
Telephone: (615) 675-5255 Carnegie Class: Bac-Diverse
FAX Number: (615) 296-0400 Calendar System: Semester
URL: www.welch.edu
Established: 1942 Annual Undergrad Tuition & Fees: $19,582
Enrollment: 358 Coed
Affiliation or Control: Free Will Baptist IRS Status: 501(c)3
Highest Offering: Master's
Accreditation: SC, BI

01 President ....Dr. Matt PINSON
05 Provost ....Dr. Matthew J. MCAFFEE
45 Vice Pres for Strategic Initiatives ....Dr. P. Greg KETTEMAN
10 Vice President Financial Affairs ....Mr. Craig MAHLER
32 VP Student Svcs/Dean of Students ....Dr. Jon FORLINES
111 Vice Pres Institutional Advancement ....Mr. David WILLIFORD
108 Vice Pres for Inst Effectiveness ....Dr. Kevin HESTER
20 Vice Provost for Academic Admin ....Mr. Matthew BRACEY
34 Dean of Women ....Mrs. Susan FORLINES
55 Dean of Enriched Adult Studies ....Mr. William SLATER
08 Librarian ....Mrs. Christa THORNSBURY
09 Director of Institutional Research ....Mr. Wayne SPRUILL
84 Dir of Enrollment Services ....Mr. Daniel WEBSTER
26 Chief Public Relations/Marketing ....Mr. Josh OWENS
106 Dir of Online and Adult Studies ....Mr. William SLATER
44 Director of the Welch Fund ....Mr. Tim OWEN
18 Director of Plant Operations ....Mr. DeWayne WHITE
41 Athletic Director ....Mr. Greg FAWBUSH
37 Student Financial Aid Coordinator ....Mrs. Angie EDGMON
06 Registrar ....Mrs. Anna MCAFFEE
04 Exec Assistant to the President ....Ms. Martha FLETCHER

William Moore College of Technology (E)

1200 Poplar Avenue, Memphis TN 38104
County: Shelby FICE Identification: 011553
Unit ID: 222105
Telephone: (901) 726-1977 Carnegie Class: Assoc/HVT-High Non
FAX Number: (901) 726-1978 Calendar System: Trimester
URL: www.mooretech.edu
Established: 1909 Annual Undergrad Tuition & Fees: $8,848
Enrollment: 378 Coed
Affiliation or Control: Independent Non-Profit IRS Status: 501(c)3
Highest Offering: Associate Degree
Accreditation: COE

01 President ....Mr. Skip REDMOND
05 CAO/VP of Student Services ....Ms. Andrea BAIRD

Williamson College (F)

274 Mallory Station Road, Franklin TN 37067
County: Williamson FICE Identification: 035135
Unit ID: 443340
Telephone: (615) 771-7821 Carnegie Class: Spec-4-yr-Bus
FAX Number: (615) 771-7810 Calendar System: Other
URL: www.williamsoncc.edu
Established: 1996 Annual Undergrad Tuition & Fees: $14,350
Enrollment: 68 Coed
Affiliation or Control: Non-denominational IRS Status: 501(c)3
Highest Offering: Master's
Accreditation: BI

01 President ....Dr. Ed SMITH
05 Dir of Academic & Student Affairs ....Dr. Bryan THOMAS
11 Vice President for Operations ....Ms. Susan MAYS
32 Director of Student Services ....Ms. Robyn WOLLAS
06 Registrar ....Ms. Karen HUDSON
37 Dir Financial Aid/Veteran Affairs ....Ms. Cristina MAJORS
07 Admissions Department Manager ....Ms. Laura FLOWERS
26 Dir Marketing & Advancement ....Ms. Courtney STAFFORD
08 Chief Library Officer ....Ms. Alyxius YOUNG

TEXAS

Abilene Christian University (G)

ACU Box 29100, Abilene TX 79699-9100
County: Taylor FICE Identification: 003537
Unit ID: 222178
Telephone: (325) 674-2000 Carnegie Class: DU-Mod
FAX Number: (325) 674-2202 Calendar System: Semester
URL: www.acu.edu
Established: 1906 Annual Undergrad Tuition & Fees: $37,800
Enrollment: 5,291 Coed
Affiliation or Control: Churches Of Christ IRS Status: 501(c)3
Highest Offering: Doctorate
Accreditation: SC, AAQEP, CAATE, CIDA, DIETD, DIETI, JOUR, MFCD, MUS, NURSE, OT, SP, SW, THEOL

01 President ....Dr. Phil SCHUBERT
00 Chancellor ....Dr. Royce MONEY
100 Senior Advisor to the President ....Ms. Suzanne ALLMON
05 Provost ....Dr. Robert RHODES
111 VP for Advancement ....Mr. Dan MACALUSO
84 VP for Enrollment & Student Life ....Mrs. Tamara LONG
12 VP/Administrative Ofcr ACU Dallas ....Dr. Stephen JOHNSON
115 Chief Investment Ofcr/Pres ACIMCO ....Mr. Joe LEE
43 Vice President & General Counsel ....Mr. Slade SULLIVAN
102 ACU Foundation President ....Vacant
20 Vice Provost ....Dr. Susan LEWIS
84 Asst VP Enrollment Dallas ....Ms. Jessica MANNING
49 Dean College of Arts & Sciences ....Dr. Greg STRAUGHN
73 Dean College of Biblical Studies ....Dr. Ken R. CUKROWSKI
50 Dean College of Business Admin ....Dr. Brad CRISP
53 Dean College of Educ & Human Svcs ....Dr. Jennifer SHEWMAKER
92 Dean Honors College ....Dr. Jason MORRIS
58 Dean Graduate & Professional Stds ....Dr. Joey COPE
66 Dean School of Nursing ....Dr. Marcia STRAUGHN
08 Dean Library/Educational Technology ....Mr. James WISER
104 Director of the Ctr Intl Educ ....Dr. Stephen SHEWMAKER
32 Dean of Students ....Mr. Mark LEWIS
36 Director Career Center ....Mrs. Jill FORTSON
06 Registrar/Dir of Academic Dev ....Dr. Eric GUMM
11 Senior VP of Operations ....Mr. Kevin CAMPBELL
26 Int VP Marketing/Strategic Comm ....Mr. Blair SCHROEDER
39 Dir Residence Life/Stdnt Advocacy ....Ms. Shannon KACZMAREK
38 Director Univ Counseling Center ....Mr. Tyson ALEXANDER
18 Associate VP of Operations ....Mr. Corey RUFF
24 Exec Dir Teaching & Learning ....Dr. Laura CARROLL
29 Asst VP Alumni & Univ Relations ....Mr. Craig FISHER
19 Chief of Police ....Mr. Jason ELLIS
112 Dir Endowment Strategy/Sr Adv Ofcr ....Mr. Don GARRETT
41 Director of Athletics ....Mr. Allen WARD
15 Chief HR Officer/Title IX Coord ....Mrs. Wendy JONES
88 Director of Faculty Development ....Dr. Cliff BARBARICK
09 Asst Provost for Inst Effectiveness ....Dr. Chris RILEY
96 Director of Purchasing/Procurement ....Ms. Sandy HALL
101 Secretary to the Board of Trustees ....Mr. Slade SULLIVAN
04 Exec Assistant Office of President ....Mrs. Stephanie A. WOODLEE
46 Dir Research/Sponsored Programs ....Dr. Megan ROTH
07 Director of Enrollment Operations ....Mr. Garrett SUBLETTE
22 Title IX Deputy Coordinator ....Mrs. Sherita NICKERSON
28 Chief Diversity Officer ....Mr. Anthony WILLIAMS
13 Chief Information Officer ....Mr. Jon BRUNER
37 Director Student Financial Services ....Mr. Thomas RATLIFF

*Alamo Community College District Central Office (H)

2222 North Alamo Street, San Antonio TX 78215
County: Bexar FICE Identification: 003607
Unit ID: 222497
Telephone: (210) 485-0020 Carnegie Class: N/A
FAX Number: (210) 486-9166
URL: www.alamo.edu

01 Chancellor ....Dr. Mike FLORES
05 Vice Chanc for Academic Success ....Dr. George RAILEY, JR.
11 Vice Chanc for Finance & Admin ....Dr. Diane E. SNYDER
32 Vice Chancellor for Student Success ....Dr. Adelina SILVA
103 Vice Chanc Economic/Workforce Devel ....Mr. Robert MCKINLEY
13 VC Plng/Performance/Info Systems ....Dr. Thomas CLEARY
15 Assoc Vice Chanc Human Resources . Ms. Linda BOYER-OWENS
18 Assoc Vice Chanc Facilities ....Vacant
10 Assoc VC Finance & Fiscal Services ....Ms. Pamela ANSBOURY
04 Exec Assistant to the Chancellor ....Vacant
111 Int Exec Director Inst Advancement ....Dr. Marie KANE
116 Director of Internal Audit ....Mr. Bill WULLENJOHN
96 Director Acquisitions & Admin Svcs ....Mr. Gary O'BAR
19 Chief Department of Public Safety ....Vacant
21 Comptroller ....Vacant
12 President Northwest Vista College ....Dr. Ric BASER
12 President San Antonio College ....Dr. Robert VELA
12 President St Philip's College ....Dr. Adena WILLIAMS LOSTON
12 President Palo Alto College ....Dr. Robert GARZA
12 Pres Northeast Lakeview College ....Dr. Veronica GARCIA
37 Director Student Financial Aid ....Mr. Harold WHITIS
43 Dir Legal Services/General Counsel ....Mr. Ross LAUGHEAD
09 Dist Dir Inst Rsch/Effect/Planning ....Mr. Velda VILLARREAL

*Northeast Lakeview College (I)

1201 Kitty Hawk Road, Universal City TX 78148
County: Bexar Identification: 667278
Unit ID: 488730

Telephone: (210) 486-5000 Carnegie Class: Assoc/HT-Mix Trad/Non
FAX Number: N/A Calendar System: Semester
URL: www.alamo.edu/nlc
Established: 2007 Annual Undergrad Tuition & Fees (In-District): $6,592
Enrollment: 6,657 Coed
Affiliation or Control: Local IRS Status: 501(c)3
Highest Offering: Associate Degree
Accreditation: SC

02 President Dr. Veronica GARCIA
05 Vice Pres Academic Success Dr. Laura BOYER
32 Vice Pres Student Success Dr. Tangila DOVE

*Northwest Vista College (A)

3535 N Ellison Drive, San Antonio TX 78251-4217
County: Bexar FICE Identification: 033723
Unit ID: 420398
Telephone: (210) 486-4000 Carnegie Class: Assoc/HT-Mix Trad/Non
FAX Number: (210) 486-9105 Calendar System: Semester
URL: www.alamo.edu/nvc
Established: 1995 Annual Undergrad Tuition & Fees (In-District): $6,592
Enrollment: 18,542 Coed
Affiliation or Control: Local IRS Status: 501(c)3
Highest Offering: Associate Degree
Accreditation: SC

02 President Vacant
11 Vice President for College Services Mrs. Erin L. SHERMAN
05 Vice President for Academic Success Dr. Daniel POWELL
32 Vice President for Student Success Mrs. Deborah GAITAN
08 Director Learning Resources Center Mrs. Norma VELEZ-VENDRELL
38 Dean for Student Success Mrs. Jennifer COMEDY-HOLMES
26 Dir of Marketing & Strategic Comm Mrs. Renata SERAFIN
13 Director Info/Communications Tech Mr. Felix SALINAS
37 Associate Director of Financial Aid Mrs. Rosalinda ENCINA
113 Assistant Bursar Mrs. Patricia SANCHEZ
45 Director of Resources & College Dev Ms. Judy V. CAMARGO
18 Superintendent NVC Mr. Julian RODRIGUEZ
88 Dean for Academic Success/Support Mr. Patrick FONTENOT
20 Dean for Academic Success Dr. Russell FROHARDT
09 Director of Institutional Research Dr. Eliza HERNANDEZ
84 Director of Enrollment Management Dr. Yolanda REYES-GUEVARA
07 Associate Director of Admissions Mrs. Yvonne GUERRA
121 Dean for Student Success-Academic Mrs. Robin LUND

*Palo Alto College (B)

1400 W Villaret Boulevard, San Antonio TX 78224-2499
County: Bexar FICE Identification: 023413
Unit ID: 246354
Telephone: (210) 486-3000 Carnegie Class: Assoc/HT-High Non
FAX Number: (210) 921-5005 Calendar System: Semester
URL: www.alamo.edu
Established: 1985 Annual Undergrad Tuition & Fees (In-District): $6,592
Enrollment: 11,193 Coed
Affiliation or Control: Local IRS Status: 501(c)3
Highest Offering: Associate Degree
Accreditation: SC

02 President Dr. Robert GARZA
05 Vice President for Academic Success Ms. Elizabeth TANNER
10 Vice Pres of College Services Ms. Katherine DOSS
32 Vice President for Student Success Mr. Gilberto BECERRA
49 Dean Academic Success Mr. Patrick LEE
50 Dean Academic Success Dr. Raymond PFANG
08 Dean of Learning Resources Ms. Tina MESA
35 Dean of Student Success Ms. Monica AYALA-JIMENEZ
26 Director of Public Relations Mr. Jerry ARELLANO
113 Bursar Mr. Edward SANCHEZ
37 Assc Dir Student Financial Services Ms. Shirley LEIJA
41 Athletic Director Mr. Edward J. MORENO
18 Facilities Superintendnt/Phys Plant Mr. Sergio RIVERA
29 Coordinator Alumni Relations Ms. Priscilla AGUILAR
09 Dir Inst Rsrch/Plng/Effectiveness Ms. Caroline HARING
25 Director of Advancement & Grants Mr. Gaston CANTU
04 Administrative Asst to President Ms. Connie MARTINEZ
13 Chief Info Technology Director Mr. Nicolas BLAKENEY
84 Director Enrollment Management Ms. Elizabeth AGUILAR-VILLARREAL

*St. Philip's College (C)

1801 Martin Luther King, San Antonio TX 78203-2098
County: Bexar FICE Identification: 003608
Unit ID: 227854
Telephone: (210) 486-2000 Carnegie Class: Assoc/MT-VT-High Non
FAX Number: N/A Calendar System: Semester
URL: www.alamo.edu/spc/
Established: 1898 Annual Undergrad Tuition & Fees (In-District): $6,592
Enrollment: 12,696 Coed
Affiliation or Control: Local IRS Status: 501(c)3
Highest Offering: Associate Degree
Accreditation: SC, ACFEI, ACPHA, CAHIIM, COARC, CVT, DMS, HT, MLTAD, NAEYC, OTA, PTAA, RAD, SURGT

02 President Dr. Adena LOSTON WILLIAMS
05 Vice Pres of Academic Success Dr. Randall DAWSON
32 Int Vice Pres of Student Success Dr. Paul MACHEN
11 Int Vice Pres for College Svcs Dr. Vanessa ANDERSON
35 Int Dean for Student Success Ms. Destiny HARPER-LANE
84 Dean Student Success/Enroll Mgmt Ms. Christina CORTEZ
75 Dean Acad Success Appl Sci/Tech-SW Mr. Christopher BEARDSALL
75 Dean Acad Success Appl Sci/Tech-MLK Ms. Edith OROZCO
49 Dean for Acad Success Arts & Sci Mr. George JOHNSON
76 Dean for Acad Success Health Sci Ms. Jessica COOPER
37 Asst Director of Financial Aid Ms. Grace ZAPATA
45 Dir Planning/Research/Effectiveness Vacant
113 Assistant Bursar Ms. Sophia GONZALEZ
26 Director of Public Relations Ms. Adrian JACKSON
72 Director Instructional Technology Mr. John ORONA
18 Chief Facilities/Physical Plant Vacant
111 Director Institutional Advancement Dr. Sharon CROCKETT-BELL
114 Campus Budget Officer Mr. Jorge FLORES
106 Int Dean for Acad Success/Acad Svcs Dr. Diane GAVIN
25 Acad Pgm Dir/Title III/Grants Mgmt Dr. Tomeka WILSON
46 Director of Strategic Initiatives Mr. Jeffrey FRENCH
04 Executive Asst to President Ms. Marsha HALL

*San Antonio College (D)

1819 N Main, San Antonio TX 78212-4299
County: Bexar FICE Identification: 009163
Unit ID: 227924
Telephone: (210) 486-0000 Carnegie Class: Assoc/HT-Mix Trad/Non
FAX Number: N/A Calendar System: Semester
URL: www.alamo.edu/sac
Established: 1925 Annual Undergrad Tuition & Fees (In-District): $6,592
Enrollment: 19,231 Coed
Affiliation or Control: Local IRS Status: 501(c)3
Highest Offering: Baccalaureate
Accreditation: SC, ADNUR, CEA, DA, EMT, FUSER, MAC, NAEYC

02 President Dr. Robert H. VELA
32 Interim VP of Student Success Dr. Tiffany COX HERNANDEZ
11 Vice President of College Services Dr. Stella LOVATO
05 Interim VP of Academic Success Dr. Stella LOVATO
35 Interim Dean of Student Success Ms. Christina HORTON
72 Int Dean Acad Success Prof/Tech Dr. Jonathan LEE
106 Dean of Academic Success Online DC Dr. Sobia KHAN
49 Dean of Academic Success Art & Sci Dr. Conrad KRUEGER
88 Dean of Performance Excellence Dr. Francisco SOLIS
35 Dean of Student Success Dr. Maria DE LOS REYES
26 Director of Public Relations Mr. Ken SLAVIN
08 Director of Library Services Mr. LeBlanc LEE
84 Director of Enrollment Management Ms. Amy C. PENA
06 Dir of Student Success/Registrar Mr. J. Martin ORTEGA
85 Coordinator International Students Ms. Patrice BALLARD

Alvin Community College (E)

3110 Mustang Road, Alvin TX 77511-4898
County: Brazoria FICE Identification: 003539
Unit ID: 222567
Telephone: (281) 756-3500 Carnegie Class: Assoc/HVT-High Non
FAX Number: (281) 756-3854 Calendar System: Semester
URL: www.alvincollege.edu
Established: 1948 Annual Undergrad Tuition & Fees (In-District): $2,834
Enrollment: 5,737 Coed
Affiliation or Control: Local IRS Status: 501(c)3
Highest Offering: Associate Degree
Accreditation: SC, ADNUR, CAHIIM, COARC, DMS, EMT, NDT, POLYT

01 President Dr. Robert J. EXLEY
05 Vice President Instruction Vacant
10 VP Administrative Services Mr. Karl STAGER
32 VP Student Services Vacant
49 Dean of Arts & Sciences Mr. John MATULA
76 Dean Legal and Health Sciences Dr. Stacy EBERT
51 Dean Continued Educ/Wkforce Devel Vacant
97 Dean General Educ/Academic Support Dr. Nadezhda (Nadia) NAZARENKO
88 Dean Prof/Tech/Human Performance Mr. Jeffrey PARKS
06 Registrar Ms. Dana PENCE
08 Director of Library Services Mr. Greg REID
21 Director Fiscal Affairs/Controller Ms. Beth NELSON
13 Exec Dir Information Technology Mr. Kelly KLIMPT
37 Director Student Financial Aid Ms. Gabriela LEON
15 VP Human Resources Ms. Nichole ESLINGER
18 Director Physical Plant Ms. Hameedah MAJEED
29 Director Alumni Relations Ms. Wendy DEL BELLO
07 Dean Student Support Services Vacant
09 Exec Dir of Inst Effective/Research Vacant
30 VP Development & Outreach Ms. Wendy DEL BELLO
26 Chief Public Relations Officer Ms. Wendy DEL BELLO
88 Assistant Director Fiscal Affairs Ms. Laurel JOSEPH
35 Coordinator Student Activities Ms. Querencia JOSHUA
04 Sr Exec Asst to President/Board Mgr Ms. Tammy GIFFROW
19 Chief of Police Mr. Ronald PHILLIPS
96 Director of Purchasing Mr. Alan PHILLIPS

Amarillo College (F)

PO Box 447, Amarillo TX 79178-0001
County: Potter FICE Identification: 003540
Unit ID: 222576
Telephone: (806) 371-5000 Carnegie Class: Assoc/MT-VT-High Trad
FAX Number: (806) 371-5370 Calendar System: Semester
URL: www.actx.edu
Established: 1929 Annual Undergrad Tuition & Fees (In-District): $3,168
Enrollment: 9,079 Coed
Affiliation or Control: State/Local IRS Status: 501(c)3
Highest Offering: Associate Degree
Accreditation: SC, ADNUR, COARC, DH, EMT, MLTAD, MUS, NMT, OTA, PTAA, RAD, RTT, SURGT

01 President Dr. Russell D. LOWERY-HART
43 EVP/General Counsel Mr. Mark D. WHITE
05 VP of Academic Affairs Dr. Tamara T. CLUNIS
10 VP of Business Affairs Mr. Chris SHARP
26 VP Communications & Marketing Mr. Kevin J. BALL
84 VP of Enrollment Management Mr. Bob C. AUSTIN
32 VP of Student Affairs Ms. Denese SKINNER
15 VP for Human Resources Ms. Cheryl JONES
20 Assoc VP Academic Affairs Dr. Frank E. SOBEY
78 AVP Innovation & Work-Based Lrng Vacant
88 Associate VP Academic Services Ms. Becky K. BURTON
103 Exec Director Workforce Development Ms. Toni B. GRAY
76 Dean of Health Sciences Mrs. Kimberly A. CROWLEY
18 Manager Physical Plant Mr. Jim BACA
37 Director Financial Aid Ms. Kelly L. STEELMAN
08 Director AC Library Network Ms. Emily R. GILBERT
06 Registrar/Dir of Admissions Ms. Kristin D. MCDONALD-WILLEY
19 Chief of Police Mr. Scott ACKER
102 COO AC Foundation Mrs. Tracy D. DOUGHERTY
09 Exec Dir Decision Analytics & IR Mr. Collin C. WITHERSPOON
121 Director of Advising Mr. Ernesto F. OLMOS
88 Director Amarillo Museum of Art Mrs. Kim B. MAHAN
88 Director Criminal Justice Program Mr. Eric C. WALLACE
96 Director of Purchasing/Records Ret Ms. Kimberly L. CARLILE
81 Dean of STEM Ms. Edythe L. CARTER
72 Dean of Technical Education Dr. Linda MUNOZ
49 Dean of Liberal Arts Ms. Rebecca EASTON
46 Vice Pres Strategic Initiatives Ms. Cara J. CROWLEY
13 Chief Information Officer Mr. Shane E. HEPLER
04 Administrative Asst to President Ms. Toni J. VAN DYKE
106 Dir Online Education/E-learning Vacant
108 Director Inst Effectiveness Ms. Tina M. BABB
35 Director of Student Life Ms. Amber HAMILTON
28 Director of Outreach Services Ms. Cassie MONTGOMERY
12 Dean of Campus Ops Moore County Ms. Renee VINCENT
12 Dean of Campus Ops Hereford Mr. Daniel ESQUIVEL
112 Major Gifts Officer Ms. B. Peyton BIVINS

Amberton University (G)

1700 Eastgate Drive, Garland TX 75041
County: Dallas FICE Identification: 022594
Unit ID: 222628
Telephone: (972) 279-6511 Carnegie Class: Masters/L
FAX Number: (972) 279-9773 Calendar System: Semester
URL: www.amberton.edu
Established: 1971 Annual Undergrad Tuition & Fees: N/A
Enrollment: 1,103 Coed
Affiliation or Control: Independent Non-Profit IRS Status: 501(c)3
Highest Offering: Master's
Accreditation: SC, ACBSP

01 President Dr. Melinda REAGAN
05 Academic Dean Dr. Blair STEPHENSON
111 Dean Univ Advance/VP Strategic Svcs Dr. Jo Lynn LOYD
10 Chief Business Officer Mr. Brent BRADSHAW
06 Registrar Ms. Hannah GRAY
32 Dean for Student Services Vacant
84 Director for Recruiting Vacant
08 Head Librarian Ms. Jody PENDLETON

American College of Acupuncture and Oriental Medicine (H)

9100 Park West Drive, Houston TX 77063-4104
County: Harris FICE Identification: 031533
Unit ID: 429085
Telephone: (713) 780-9777 Carnegie Class: Spec-4-yr-Other Health
FAX Number: (713) 781-5781 Calendar System: Trimester
URL: www.acaom.edu
Established: 1991 Annual Graduate Tuition & Fees: N/A
Enrollment: 123 Coed
Affiliation or Control: Proprietary IRS Status: Proprietary
Highest Offering: Doctorate; No Undergraduates
Accreditation: SC, ACUP

01 President Dr. John Paul LIANG
11 Vice President of Operations Ms. Angel GUINARA
05 VP of Academic Affairs Dr. Wen HUANG
20 Dean of Clinical Training Dr. Baisong ZHONG
06 Registrar Ms. Vicki ROSMANN
09 Dir Inst Research/Effectiveness Mr. Michael Dale STAFFORD
37 Financial Aid Ofcr/Inst Compliance Ms. Theresa LIGON

American InterContinental University - Houston (I)

9999 Richmond Avenue, Houston TX 77042-4516
Telephone: (832) 201-3600 Identification: 666335
Accreditation: &HLC, ACBSP

† Regional accreditation is carried under the parent institution in Schaumburg, IL.

Ana G. Mendez University Dallas Campus (J)

3010 N. Stemmons Fwy, Dallas TX 75247
Telephone: (469) 341-7300 Identification: 770947
Accreditation: &M

† Branch campus of Universidad Ana G. Mendez, Rio Piedras, PR

Angelina College (A)

PO Box 1768, Lufkin TX 75902-1768
County: Angelina — FICE Identification: 006661
Unit ID: 222822
Telephone: (936) 639-1301 — Carnegie Class: Assoc/MT-VT-Mix Trad/Non
FAX Number: N/A — Calendar System: Semester
URL: www.angelina.edu
Established: 1966 — Annual Undergrad Tuition & Fees (In-District): $4,380
Enrollment: 4,195 — Coed
Affiliation or Control: State/Local — IRS Status: 501(c)3
Highest Offering: Associate Degree
Accreditation: **SC**, COARC, DMS, EMT, RAD, SURGT

01	President	Dr. Michael SIMON
05	Vice Pres Academic Affairs	Dr. Cynthia CASPARIS
10	Vice President Business Services	Mr. Chris SULLIVAN
31	Dean of Community Services	Dr. Tim DITORO
111	Exec Dir Inst Advancement	Mrs. Dana SMITHHART
84	Exec Dir Marketing & Enrollment	Mrs. Krista BROWN
13	Sr Dir Information Technology	Ms. Jennifer RAGSDALE
15	Sr Director Human Resources	Mrs. Tifini WHIDDON
18	Chief Facilities/Physical Plant	Mr. Steve CAPPS
21	Controller	Mr. Darin MURPHY
37	Dir Student Financial Aid	Mr. Glen GOFORTH
04	Manager of President's Office	Ms. Leigh Ann PYLE
108	Dir Institutional Effectiveness	Ms. Joy ROW
28	Spec Asst to Pres Div & Inclusion	Mr. Jamie HEREDIA

AOMA Graduate School of Integrative Medicine (B)

4701 West Gate Boulevard, Austin TX 78745
County: Travis — FICE Identification: 031564
Unit ID: 429094
Telephone: (512) 454-1188 — Carnegie Class: Spec-4-yr-Other Health
FAX Number: (512) 454-7001 — Calendar System: Quarter
URL: www.aoma.edu
Established: 1993 — Annual Graduate Tuition & Fees: N/A
Enrollment: 135 — Coed
Affiliation or Control: Proprietary — IRS Status: Proprietary
Highest Offering: Doctorate; No Undergraduates
Accreditation: **SC**, ACUP

01	President	Dr. Mary FARIA
05	Vice President of Faculty	Dr. Qianzhi (Jamie) WU
20	VP of Academics	Dr. Beth HOWLETT
32	Sr Dir Student Services & Diversity	Dr. Dami TOKOYA
10	Acting CFO	Ms. Linda FONTAINE
17	Sr Dir Doctoral Pgm/Clinical Excel	Dr. Violet SONG
11	Sr Director of Operations	Ms. Stephanee OWENBY
21	Sr Director of Finance	Ms. Kim MAGALDI
08	Head Librarian	Ms. Rita TERRELL
07	Dir of Admissions & Marketing	Mr. Brian BECKER
06	Registrar	Ms. Kenia SELVA
58	Dean of Academics	Dr. Yuxin HE
88	Dir Clinical Doctorate and IE	Dr. Diane STANLEY
88	Director Acupuncture	Dr. Yuxing LIU
106	Sr Dir Masters Pgm & Distance Educ	Dr. Phil GARRISION
88	Dir International Academic Research	Dr. Jing FAN
37	Director Student Financial Aid	Ms. Estella PROCTOR
81	Director of Biomedical Sciences	Vacant
88	Director of Clinical Readiness	Ms. Reagan TAYLOR

Arlington Baptist University (C)

3001 W Division, Arlington TX 76012-3497
County: Tarrant — FICE Identification: 020814
Unit ID: 222877
Telephone: (817) 461-8741 — Carnegie Class: Bac-Diverse
FAX Number: (817) 274-1138 — Calendar System: Semester
URL: www.ABU.edu
Established: 1939 — Annual Undergrad Tuition & Fees: $15,050
Enrollment: 160 — Coed
Affiliation or Control: Baptist — IRS Status: 501(c)3
Highest Offering: Master's
Accreditation: **BI**

01	President	Dr. Clifton MCDANIEL
05	Vice Pres Academic Affairs	Ms. Janie TAYLOR
32	Dean of Students	Vacant
10	Vice Pres Business Operations	Mr. David INGRAM
06	Registrar	Vacant
08	Head Librarian	Ms. Amy SCHAEFER
18	Director Physical Plant	Mr. Wes HRABAL
40	Director Bookstore	Mrs. Vickie BRYANT
111	Director Institutional Advancement	Vacant
41	Athletic Director	Vacant
106	Dir Online Education/E-learning	Vacant
37	Director of Financial Aid	Mr. John ROCHA
13	Chief Info Technology Officer (CIO)	Vacant

The Art Institute of Austin (D)

1204 Chestnut Street, Bastrop TX 78602
Telephone: (512) 691-1707 — Identification: 770973
Accreditation: **&SC**

Art Institute of Dallas (E)

8080 Park Lane, Suite 100, Dallas TX 75231-5993
Telephone: (214) 692-8080 — FICE Identification: 025396

Accreditation: **&SC**, CIDA

† Regional accreditation is carried under the parent institution, Miami International University, Miami, FL.

The Art Institute of Houston (F)

4140 Southwest Freeway, Houston TX 77027
County: Harris — FICE Identification: 021171
Unit ID: 222938
Telephone: (713) 623-2040 — Carnegie Class: Bac-Diverse
FAX Number: (713) 966-2700 — Calendar System: Quarter
URL: www.aih.aii.edu
Established: 1978 — Annual Undergrad Tuition & Fees: $19,354
Enrollment: 511 — Coed
Affiliation or Control: Independent Non-Profit — IRS Status: 501(c)3
Highest Offering: Baccalaureate
Accreditation: **SC**, CIDA

01	President	Harvey M. GIBLIN
05	Dean of Academic Affairs	Eric WATSON
32	Vice President of Student Affairs	LaToya WILLIAMS
07	Dean of Admissions	Pierre LAFAILLE
06	Registrar	Cynthia HOOPER
04	Executive Assistant to President	Tanya LITTLE-PALMER

The Art Institute of San Antonio (G)

10000 IH-10 W, Ste 200, San Antonio TX 78230
Telephone: (210) 338-7320 — Identification: 770974
Accreditation: **&SC**, CIDA

Auguste Escoffier School of Culinary Arts (H)

6020-B Dilliard Circle, Austin TX 78752-4438
County: Travis — FICE Identification: 037276
Unit ID: 444556
Telephone: (512) 451-5743 — Carnegie Class: Spec 2-yr-A&S
FAX Number: (512) 467-9120 — Calendar System: Quarter
URL: www.escoffier.edu
Established: 1997 — Annual Undergrad Tuition & Fees: N/A
Enrollment: 610 — Coed
Affiliation or Control: Proprietary — IRS Status: Proprietary
Highest Offering: Associate Degree
Accreditation: **COE**, ACFEI

01	Campus President	Mr. Marcus MCMELLON
07	Director of Admissions	Mr. David NORRIS
37	Director Student Financial Aid	Ms. Theresa BARGAS
36	Director of Career Services	Ms. Ann DERRICK
10	Director Business Operations	Ms. Mary REARDON

Austin College (I)

900 N Grand Avenue, Sherman TX 75090-4400
County: Grayson — FICE Identification: 003543
Unit ID: 222983
Telephone: (903) 813-2000 — Carnegie Class: Bac-A&S
FAX Number: (903) 813-3199 — Calendar System: 4/1/4
URL: www.austincollege.edu
Established: 1849 — Annual Undergrad Tuition & Fees: $42,590
Enrollment: 1,302 — Coed
Affiliation or Control: Presbyterian Church (U.S.A.) — IRS Status: 501(c)3
Highest Offering: Master's
Accreditation: **SC**

01	President	Mr. Steven P. O'DAY
05	VP Acad Aff & Dean of the Faculty	Dr. Beth GILL
32	VP Stdnt Affs/Chief Incl & Div Ofcr	Mr. Carllos LASSITER
111	Vice President for Institutional Ad	Ms. Gillian LOCKE
10	Vice President for Business Affairs	Mr. Pernell JONES
84	Vice President for Inst Enrollment	Ms. Baylee L. KOWERT
21	Assoc VP Business Affairs	Ms. Karen JOHNSON
110	Sr Assoc VP Inst Advancement	Ms. Suzanne CROUCH
29	Exec Dir Inst Events/Alumni Engmt	Ms. Kate CORE
37	AVP Enrollmt/Exec Dir Financial Aid	Ms. Laurie COULTER
07	AVP Enrollment/Dean of Admission	Ms. Mary RANDERS
42	Chaplain/Dir of Church Relations	Dr. John D. WILLIAMS
35	Dean of Students	Mr. Michael DEEN
06	Exec Dir Inst Research/Registrar	Dr. Eugenia HARRIS
08	College Librarian/Library Director	Ms. Barbara CORNELIUS
79	Dean of Humanities	Dr. Greg KINZER
81	Dean of Sciences	Dr. Michael HIGGS
83	Dean of Social Sciences	Dr. Lisa M. BROWN
15	Director of Human Resources	Ms. Melanie OELFKE
36	Director Career Services	Ms. Margie A. NORMAN
13	Director IT	Mr. Garrett HUBBARD
53	Chair of Education Dept	Dr. Sandy PHILIPOSE
104	International Education Coordinator	Ms. Cheryl MARCELO
26	Chief Mktg & Communications Ofcr	Dr. Lynn Z. WOMBLE
19	Dir of Public Safety/Police Chief	Chief Joe KEITZ
40	Manager of Campus Bookstore	Ms. Kelly JACKSON
27	Director of Communications	Ms. Vickie S. KIRBY
18	Exec Director of Facilities	Mr. David TURK
96	Purchasing & Accounts Payable Acct	Ms. Vicky MURPHY
102	Dir Corp/Foundation/Gov Relations	Ms. Lisa EMERY
41	Director of Athletics	Mr. David NORMAN
101	Asst to Pres/Asst Sec of Board	Ms. Genna BETHEL
38	Director of Counseling Services	Ms. Teresa MOORE
39	Director of Residence Life	Mr. Patrick MILLER
09	Director of Institutional Research	Mr. Amon SEAGULL

Austin Community College District (J)

6101 Highland Campus Drive, Austin TX 78752-4390
County: Travis — FICE Identification: 012015
Unit ID: 222992
Telephone: (512) 223-7598 — Carnegie Class: Bac/Assoc-Assoc Dom
FAX Number: (512) 223-7638 — Calendar System: Semester
URL: www.austincc.edu
Established: 1972 — Annual Undergrad Tuition & Fees (In-District): $10,830
Enrollment: 39,896 — Coed
Affiliation or Control: State/Local — IRS Status: 501(c)3
Highest Offering: Baccalaureate
Accreditation: **SC**, ACBSP, ACFEI, ADNUR, CAHIIM, DH, DMS, EMT, MLTAD, NAEYC, NUR, OTA, PNUR, PTAA, RAD, SURGT

01	Chancellor	Dr. Richard M. RHODES
05	Provost/EVP Academc/Student Affairs	Dr. Monique UMPHREY
10	EVP Finance & Administration	Mr. Neil W. VICKERS
11	EVP Campus Operation & Public Affs	Dr. Molly Beth MALCOLM
20	VP Instruction	Mr. Michael T. MIDGLEY
32	VP Student Affairs	Dr. Shasta BUCHANAN
15	VP Human Resources	Vacant
09	VP Effectiveness & Accountability	Dr. Jenna O. CULLINANE HEGE
21	VP Business Services	Ms. Angela HODGE
13	VP Information Technology	Mr. Jason MARSHALLL
45	VP Inst Planning/Develop & Eval	Dr. Mary E. HARRIS
18	Int VP Facilities & Construction	Mr. Aziz HUSSAINI
26	VP Communications & Marketing	Ms. Brette E. LEA
06	Registrar	Ms. Glynis MILLER
07	Executive Director of Admissions	Ms. Linda TERRY
08	Dean Library Services	Dr. Julie TODARO
19	Chief of Police	Mr. Lynn DIXON
37	Executive Director Financial Aid	Mr. Jason BRISENO
96	Director Procure to Pay	Mr. Robert HALL
29	Director Alumni Relations	Ms. Mary Ann CICALA
04	Special Assistant to the Chancellor	Ms. Pamela SUTTON
28	Director of Diversity	Mr. Larry DAVIS
30	Director of Development	Ms. Amy BAWCOM

Austin Presbyterian Theological Seminary (K)

100 E 27th Street, Austin TX 78705-5797
County: Travis — FICE Identification: 003544
Unit ID: 223001
Telephone: (512) 472-6736 — Carnegie Class: Spec-4-yr-Faith
FAX Number: (512) 479-0738 — Calendar System: Semester
URL: www.austinseminary.edu
Established: 1902 — Annual Graduate Tuition & Fees: N/A
Enrollment: 181 — Coed
Affiliation or Control: Presbyterian Church (U.S.A.) — IRS Status: 501(c)3
Highest Offering: Doctorate; No Undergraduates
Accreditation: **SC**, THEOL

01	President	Rev. Jose R. IRIZARRY
05	Academic Dean	Rev. Margaret AYMER
10	Vice Pres Finance/Administration	Ms. Heather ZDANCEWICZ
111	Vice Pres Institutional Advancement	Ms. Donna SCOTT
32	Dean of Students	Rev. Sarah GAVENTA
84	Vice Pres for Enrollment Management	Rev. Jorge D. HERRERA
51	VP Education Beyond the Walls	Ms. Melissa WIGINTON
08	Director of the Stitt Library	Dr. Timothy LINCOLN
06	Asst Dean Academic Affs/Registrar	Ms. Mary WALL
26	Director of Communications	Ms. Randal WHITTINGTON
100	Chief of Staff/President's Office	Ms. Mona SANTANDREA
13	Senior Director of Info Technology	Ms. Julie NEWTON
37	Director of Financial Aid	Mr. William WEST
18	Chief Facilities/Physical Plant	Mr. John EVERETT
30	Director of Development	Rev. Alan KRUMMENACHER
110	Director of Advancement Services	Mr. JR BARDEN
29	Director Alumni & Church Relations	Mr. Gary MATHEWS
21	Director of Financial Services	Mr. Mike CASTLEBERRY
14	Director of Network Services	Mr. Mike PENCE
88	Director of Latino/a Programs	Ms. Monica TORNOE
109	Director of Auxiliary Enterprises	Ms. Sarah GOMEZ
88	Director of Educational Design EBW	Rev. Erica KNISLEY
112	Associate for Donor Engagement	Ms. Judy MATETZSCHK-CAMPBELL
101	Secretary of the Institution/Board	Ms. Mona SANTANDREA

Bakke Graduate University (L)

8515 Greenville Ave, S206, Dallas TX 75243-7039
County: Dallas — FICE Identification: 031108
Unit ID: 420705
Telephone: (214) 329-4447 — Carnegie Class: Spec-4-yr-Faith
FAX Number: (214) 347-9367 — Calendar System: Semester
URL: www.bgu.edu
Established: 1990 — Annual Graduate Tuition & Fees: N/A
Enrollment: 159 — Coed
Affiliation or Control: Independent Non-Profit — IRS Status: 501(c)3
Highest Offering: Doctorate; No Undergraduates
Accreditation: **TRACS**

01	President	Dr. Brad SMITH
05	Academic Dean	Dr. Bryan MCCABE
10	Chief Operations/Financial Ofcr	Ms. Carolyn COCHRAN
06	Registrar	Ms. Judi MELTON
07	Director of Admissions	Ms. Kafi CARRASCO
08	Head Librarian	Ms. Jennifer ROMAN

106 Dir Online Education/E-learning ... Ms. Nathalia MIGHTY
37 Director Student Financial Aid ... Ms. Carolyn COCHRAN
09 Dir Institutional Effectiveness ... Dr. Judi MELTON

Baptist Health System School of Health Professions (A)

8400 Datapoint Drive, San Antonio TX 78229
County: Bexar FICE Identification: 006606
Unit ID: 223083
Telephone: (210) 297-9636 Carnegie Class: Spec-4-yr-Other Health
FAX Number: (210) 297-0075 Calendar System: Semester
URL: www.bshp.edu
Established: 1903 Annual Undergrad Tuition & Fees: N/A
Enrollment: 567 Coed
Affiliation or Control: Proprietary IRS Status: Proprietary
Highest Offering: Baccalaureate
Accreditation: ABHES, ADNUR, NUR, #RAD, SURGT, SURTEC

01 President and Dean ... Dr. Patricia E. ALVOET
06 Registrar ... Allison MCDANIEL

† Tuition varies by degree program.

Baptist Hospitals of Southeast Texas School of Radiologic Technology (B)

3030 Fannin Street, Ste A, Beaumont TX 77701
County: Jefferson Identification: 667153
Telephone: (409) 212-5724 Carnegie Class: Not Classified
FAX Number: N/A Calendar System: Semester
URL: https://www.bhset.net/our-services/school-of-radiologic-tech
Established: 1952 Annual Undergrad Tuition & Fees: N/A
Enrollment: N/A Coed
Affiliation or Control: Independent Non-Profit IRS Status: 501(c)3
Highest Offering: Associate Degree
Accreditation: ABHES, RAD

00 BHSET Chief of Administration ... Justin DOSS
01 Program Director ... Terre BREED

Baptist Missionary Association Theological Seminary (C)

P.O. Box 670/1530 East Pine Street,
Jacksonville TX 75766-5407
County: Cherokee FICE Identification: 023312
Unit ID: 223117
Telephone: (903) 586-2501 Carnegie Class: Spec-4-yr-Faith
FAX Number: (903) 586-0378 Calendar System: Semester
URL: www.bmats.edu
Established: 1957 Annual Undergrad Tuition & Fees: $6,900
Enrollment: 110 Coed
Affiliation or Control: Baptist IRS Status: 501(c)3
Highest Offering: Master's
Accreditation: SC, THEOL

01 President ... Dr. Charley HOLMES
05 Dean/Registrar ... Dr. Phillip ATTEBERY
04 Assistant to the President ... Keri SOUTHERN
32 Director of Student Services ... Dr. Ronnie J. JOHNSON
08 Library Director ... Jacob GUCKER
10 Chief Business Officer ... Chris PROCTOR

Baptist University of the Americas (D)

2418 W. Ansley Blvd., Bldg #3,
San Antonio TX 78224-1336
County: Bexar FICE Identification: 037333
Unit ID: 444398
Telephone: (210) 924-4338 Carnegie Class: Bac-Diverse
FAX Number: (210) 924-0888 Calendar System: Semester
URL: www.bua.edu
Established: 1947 Annual Undergrad Tuition & Fees: $6,480
Enrollment: 117 Coed
Affiliation or Control: Baptist IRS Status: 501(c)3
Highest Offering: Baccalaureate
Accreditation: BI

01 President/CEO ... Dr. Abraham JAQUEZ
100 Chief of Staff ... Dr. Gabriel CORTES
05 Dean Academic Affairs ... Dr. Sam GARCIA
10 CFO/Director for Admin/Finance ... Mr. Kevin RODRIGUEZ
37 Director of Financial Aid ... Mrs. Araceli ACOSTA
06 Registrar ... Ms. Maria DIAZ

Baylor College of Medicine (E)

One Baylor Plaza, Houston TX 77030-3411
County: Harris FICE Identification: 004949
Unit ID: 223223
Telephone: (713) 798-4951 Carnegie Class: Spec-4-yr-Eng
FAX Number: (713) 798-3692 Calendar System: Quarter
URL: www.bcm.edu
Established: 1900 Annual Graduate Tuition & Fees: N/A
Enrollment: 1,607 Coed
Affiliation or Control: Independent Non-Profit IRS Status: 501(c)3
Highest Offering: Doctorate; No Undergraduates
Accreditation: SC, ANEST, ARCPA, IPSY, MED, OPE

00 Chancellor ... Dr. Bert O'MALLEY
01 President and CEO ... Dr. Paul KLOTMAN
05 Provost/SVP Acad & Faculty Affairs ... Dr. Alicia MONROE
17 EVP/Dean of Clinical Affairs ... Dr. James MCDEAVITT
10 Sr VP/Chief Business Officer ... Mrs. Kimberly C. DAVID
111 Vice Pres Inst Advancement ... Ms. Stephanie YOUNG
43 Sr Vice Pres/General Counsel ... Mr. Robert F. CORRIGAN, JR.
26 VP Communications/Cmty Outreach ... Ms. Lori WILLIAMS
15 Vice President Human Resources ... Mr. Dane FRIEND
46 Sr Vice President/Dean Research ... Dr. Adam KUSPA
13 VP Information Technology ... Mr. Lee LEIBER
86 Vice Pres Government Relations ... Mr. Herb BUTRUM
88 Dean Natl Sch Tropical Medicine ... Dr. Peter J. HOTEZ
21 VP Finance/CFO ... Ms. Julie NICKELL
63 Dean School of Medicine ... Dr. Jennifer CHRISTNER
58 Dean Graduate Sch Biomed Sciences ... Dr. Carolyn SMITH
76 Dean School of Health Professions ... Dr. Robert MCLAUGHLIN
51 Sr Assoc Dean Cont Medical Educ ... Dr. C. Michael FORDIS, JR.
07 Assoc Dean for Admissions ... Dr. Karen JOHNSON
28 Assoc Dean Diversity/Equity/Admiss ... Dr. Jesus G. VALLEJO
32 Assoc Dean of Student Affairs ... Dr. Joseph KASS
35 Assistant Dean Student Affairs ... Dr. Andrea G. STOLAR
21 Controller ... Mr. Douglas R. SPADE
20 Assoc Provost Academic Affairs ... Ms. Lily SHIH
37 Director Student Financial Planning ... Ms. Hilda DELEON
88 Exec Director Environmental Safety ... Mr. Paul MURACA
75 Director Occupational Medicine ... Dr. James E. KELAHER
29 Director Alumni Affairs ... Mr. Alexander M. HOPKINS
96 Director Supply Chain Management ... Mr. Miguel MACHADO
06 Registrar ... Ms. Latoya R. WHITAKER
88 Asst Dean Graduate Medical Educ ... Dr. Nana E. COLEMAN
20 Associate Dean Curriculum ... Dr. Nadia ISMAIL
20 Associate Provost Faculty Affairs ... Dr. William THOMSON
09 Assoc Provost Fac Dev/Inst Research ... Dr. Nancy MORENO
28 Assoc Prov Inst Diversity/Stdnt Svc ... Dr. Toi HARRIS
04 Admin Assistant to the President ... Ms. Julie WOLKEN
100 Chief of Staff ... Ms. Lorie TABAK
101 Exec Dir Inst Gov/Board Rels ... Ms. Carolyn COCANOUGHER

Baylor University (F)

One Bear Place #97096, Waco TX 76798-7096
County: McLennan FICE Identification: 003545
Unit ID: 223232
Telephone: (254) 710-3555 Carnegie Class: DU-Highest
FAX Number: (254) 710-3557 Calendar System: Semester
URL: www.baylor.edu
Established: 1845 Annual Undergrad Tuition & Fees: $49,246
Enrollment: 19,297 Coed
Affiliation or Control: Baptist IRS Status: 501(c)3
Highest Offering: Doctorate
Accreditation: SC, CAATE, CIDA, CLPSY, DIET, DIETD, DIETI, HSA, IPSY, JOUR, LAW, MIDWF, MUS, NASP, NURSE, OT, PH, PTA, SCPSY, SP, SW, THEA, THEOL

01 President ... Dr. Linda A. LIVINGSTONE
05 Provost ... Dr. Nancy W. BRICKHOUSE
100 Chief of Staff to the President ... Ms. Tiffany HOGUE
10 Chief Business Officer ... Mr. Brett DALTON
117 Senior Director of Risk Management ... Mr. Paul FOX
111 VP for Advancement ... Mr. David ROSSELLI
32 Vice President Student Life ... Dr. Kevin P. JACKSON
26 VP Marketing & Comm/CMO ... Mr. Jason D. COOK
29 Assoc Vice Pres Alumni Engagement ... Ms. Amy ARMSTRONG
43 Gen Counsel/CLO & Corp Sec ... Mr. Christopher W. HOLMES
41 VP & Director of Athletics ... Mr. Mack RHOADES, IV
09 Director Inst Research/Testing ... Dr. Kathleen MORLEY
21 Assoc VP of Finance ... Mr. Brett POWELL
114 AVP of Budget & Planning ... Mr. Brian S. DENMAN
18 Asst VP for Facilities & Planning ... Mr. Don BAGBY
15 VP & Chief Human Resource Officer ... Mrs. Cheryl GOCHIS
13 VP Information Tech/Deputy CIO ... Mr. Jon ALLEN
08 Dean of Libraries ... Mr. Jeffry ARCHER
35 Vice Pres of Student Life ... Mr. Kevin P. JACKSON
06 Registrar ... Ms. Michelle JOHNSON
90 AVP Library/Academic Technology ... Mr. David BURNS
108 Dir of Inst Planning & Assessment ... Dr. J. Ben COX
97 Vice Provost Undergrad Education ... Dr. Wesley NULL
20 Vice Prov/Academic Affs & Policy ... Dr. James BENNIGHOFF
46 Vice Provost Research ... Dr. Kevin CHAMBLISS
84 Asst VP of Enrollment Mgmt ... Ms. Mary HERRIDGE
115 Chief Investment Officer ... Mr. David MOREHEAD
19 Chief of Police ... Mr. John KOLINEK, III
93 Dir Multicultural Affairs ... Ms. Pearlie BEVERLY
121 Assoc Dir Stdnt Success Initiative ... Ms. Amber THOMPSON
23 Medical Director Health Center ... Dr. Sharon STERN
51 Assoc Director of Professional Educ ... Ms. Jenna KINKEADE
25 Asst Vice Prov Rsrch/Dir Spons Pgm ... Ms. Lisa H. MCKETHAN
38 Exec Director Counseling Svcs ... Dr. James G. MARSH
40 Director Baylor Bookstore ... Ms. Larissa RUPLEY
86 Director Governmental Relations ... Ms. Rochonda FARMER-NEAL
96 Director of Procurement Services ... Mr. Richard WRIGHT
49 Dean College of Arts/Sciences ... Dr. Lee C. NORDT
50 Dean School of Business ... Dr. Sandeep MUZUMDER
53 Dean School of Education ... Dr. Shanna HAGAN-BURKE
61 Dean School of Law ... Mr. Bradley TOBEN
64 Dean School of Music ... Dr. Gary MORTENSON
66 Dean School of Nursing ... Dr. Linda PLANK
58 Vice Provost & Dean Graduate School ... Dr. Larry LYON
73 Dean Truett Theological Sem ... Dr. Todd D. STILL
54 Dean Engineering & Computer Science ... Dr. Dennis L. O'NEAL
92 Dean Honors College ... Dr. Douglas V. HENRY
85 Vice Provost for Global Engagement ... Dr. Jeffrey S. HAMILTON
35 Dean Student Development ... Vacant
89 Director of New Student Programs ... Dr. Nathan SHELBURNE
42 University Chaplain ... Dr. Burt BURLESON
88 Assoc Dean Student Conduct Admin ... Ms. Bethany J. MCCRAW
37 Sr Dir of Student Financial Aid ... Ms. Lisa MARTIN
88 Assoc VP Public Safety & Security ... Mr. Mark CHILDERS
04 Exec Assistant to the President ... Ms. Mia CASEY
101 Board Professional ... Ms. Kristy ORR
104 Director Study Abroad ... Mr. Bo WHITE
22 Affirmative Action & Equal Opp Mgr ... Ms. Shirl BROWN
39 Director Campus Living & Learning ... Ms. Tiffany P. LOWE
44 Director Leadership/Annual Giving ... Mr. Stephen SULLIVAN
07 Sr Director Undergrad Admissions ... Mr. Ross VANDYKE
122 Assoc Dir Fraternity/Sorority Life ... Ms. Erin ELLIS
28 Vice Provost for Faculty Diversity ... Dr. Steve REID

B.H. Carroll Theological Institute (G)

6500 N Belt Line Road, Suite 100, Irving TX 75063-6056
County: Tarrant Identification: 667089
Telephone: (972) 580-7600 Carnegie Class: Not Classified
FAX Number: (972) 756-0600 Calendar System: Semester
URL: www.bhcarroll.edu
Established: 2004 Annual Graduate Tuition & Fees: N/A
Enrollment: N/A Coed
Affiliation or Control: Southern Baptist IRS Status: 501(c)3
Highest Offering: Doctorate; No Undergraduates
Accreditation: BI, THEOL

01 President ... Dr. C. Gene WILKES
10 CFO/Director Business Affairs ... Ms. Debra HOLDER
07 Director of Admissions ... Ms. Michelle MARTIN
13 Director Information Technology ... Mr. Carl HEATH
30 Director of Development ... Mr. Stacey WHITT

The Bible Seminary (H)

2655 South Mason Rd, Katy TX 77450
County: Harris Identification: 667371
Telephone: (281) 646-1109 Carnegie Class: Not Classified
FAX Number: N/A Calendar System: Semester
URL: thebibleseminary.edu
Established: 2010 Annual Undergrad Tuition & Fees: N/A
Enrollment: N/A Coed
Affiliation or Control: Non-denominational IRS Status: 501(c)3
Highest Offering: Master's
Accreditation: TRACS

01 President and CEO ... Dr. K. Lynn LEWIS
05 Provost and CAO ... Dr. Scott STRIPLING
10 Vice Pres Finance & Admin/CFO ... Mr. Rick MCCALIP
06 Registrar ... Mrs. Carousel PIETERSE
08 Librarian ... Mrs. Janice HAMRIC
27 Communications Director ... Mr. Blake QUIMBY
21 Business Manager ... Mrs. Yamile SOTO
58 Dean of Graduate Programs ... Dr. Israel STEINMETZ
30 Director of Development ... Mrs. Angela MCCLINTON
26 Marketing Director ... Ms. Allison TAYLOR
32 Student Services Coordinator ... Mr. Clayton VAN HUSS

Blinn College (I)

902 College Avenue, Brenham TX 77833-4098
County: Washington FICE Identification: 003549
Unit ID: 223427
Telephone: (979) 830-4000 Carnegie Class: Assoc/HT-High Trad
FAX Number: (979) 830-4030 Calendar System: Semester
URL: www.blinn.edu
Established: 1883 Annual Undergrad Tuition & Fees (In-District): $5,700
Enrollment: 18,220 Coed
Affiliation or Control: State/Local IRS Status: 501(c)3
Highest Offering: Associate Degree
Accreditation: SC, ADNUR, CAHIIM, DH, EMT, PTAA, RAD, SURGT

01 Chancellor ... Dr. Mary HENSLEY
03 Exec Vice Chancellor ... Mr. Leighton SCHUBERT
101 Special Asst to BOT/Chancellor ... Ms. Laurie CLARK
05 Vice Chancellor Academic Affairs ... Dr. Marcelo BUSSIKI
17 VC Health Sci/Tech Ed & Cmty Pgms ... Mr. Jon (Jay) ANDERSON
32 Vice Chancellor Student Svcs ... Dr. Becky MCBRIDE
19 Chief College Police Department ... Mr. John CHANCELLOR
10 Vice Chanc Business/Finance/CFO ... Mr. Richard CERVANTES
15 Vice Chanc Human Resources ... Ms. Marie KIRBY
12 Executive Dean Brenham Campus ... Dr. John TURNER
12 Executive Dean Bryan Campus ... Dr. Jimmy BYRD
12 Executive Dean RELLIS Campus ... Mr. Chris MARRS
18 Asst VC Facilities/Planning/Constr ... Mr. Richard O'MALLEY
84 Dir Prosptv Stdnt Rels/Enroll Mgmt ... Ms. Elaine ABSHIRE
21 Asst VC Business & Finance ... Ms. Vicki WARD
09 Dir Inst Research/Effectiveness ... Mr. George GUARJARDO
88 Student Conduct Coord/Title IX Inv ... Ms. Sigrid WOODS
102 Exec Dir Foundation/Alumni Rel ... Ms. Susan MYERS
12 Exec Dean Schulenburg Campus ... Dr. Rebecca GARLICK
12 Exec Dean Sealy Campus ... Ms. Lisa CATON
13 Dir Administrative Computing Svcs ... Ms. Christine WIED
37 Dean Financial Aid/Scholarships ... Mr. Brent WILLIFORD
41 Athletic Dir/Mens Head Bsktbl Coach ... Mr. Scott SCHUMACHER
75 Dean Technology & Community Ed ... Ms. Karla FLANAGAN
96 Director Purchasing/Transportation ... Mr. Ross SCHROEDER
114 Director Budgets & Insurance ... Ms. Kristina BECKENDORF

103 Director Small Business Dev Center .... Mr. Matthew WEHRING
06 Registrar .... Ms. Kristi URBAN
26 Dir Comm/Media Relations/Marketing .... Mr. Rich BRAY
35 Dir Student Leadership/Activities .... Mr. Peter RIVERA
39 Dir Housing & Student Life .... Mr. Ryan MILLER
109 Dir Food Services .... Mr. James HARVILL
04 Exec Assistant to the Chancellor .... Ms. Sharon JOHNSTON
121 Exec Dir Academic Success .... Ms. Joyce LANGENEGGER
54 Academic Dean ECT&I .... Mr. Max HIBBS
81 Acad Dean Natural & Phys Science .... Dr. Elmer GODNEY
79 Acad Dean Humanities .... Dr. Patricia WESTERGAARD
50 Acad Dean Business & Mathematics .... Dr. Charles M. SMITH
83 Acad Dean Social Sciences .... Mr. Brandon FRANKE
57 Acad Dean Visual/Perf Arts & Kin .... Ms. Deborah VAVRA
106 Dean Distance Learning .... Dr. Mark WORKMAN
90 Dean Acad Tech Services .... Mr. Michael WELCH
76 Dean Health Sciences .... Ms. Michelle TRUBENSTEIN
28 Dean Title IX/Inst Divers/Equity .... Dr. Bennie GRAVES
38 Dir Disability Svcs & Counseling .... Ms. Samantha JOHNSON

Brazosport College (A)

500 College Drive, Lake Jackson TX 77566-3199
County: Brazoria FICE Identification: 007287
Unit ID: 223506
Telephone: (979) 230-3000 Carnegie Class: Bac/Assoc-Assoc Dom
FAX Number: (979) 230-3443 Calendar System: Semester
URL: www.brazosport.edu
Established: 1968 Annual Undergrad Tuition & Fees (In-District): $3,304
Enrollment: 3,852 Coed
Affiliation or Control: Local IRS Status: 501(c)3
Highest Offering: Baccalaureate
Accreditation: SC, EMT

01 President .... Dr. Vincent SOLIS
05 VP Academic & Student Affairs .... Dr. Shelley DIVINEY
103 VP Industry & Community Resources .... Ms. Anne BARTLETT
111 VP College Advancement .... Ms. Tracee WATTS
15 VP Human Resources .... Mr. Marshall CAMPBELL
10 VP Financial Services & CFO .... Ms. Lisa TEMPLER
32 Dean of Student Services .... Ms. Jo GREATHOUSE
20 Dean of Instruction .... Mr. Jeffrey DETRICK
45 Dean Plng/Inst Effectiv/Research .... Vacant
07 Director Admissions/Registrar .... Mr. Jerry MARTINEZ
38 Director Counseling and Testing .... Mr. Arnold RAMIREZ
26 Director Marketing & Communications .... Ms. Lauren MCCORMICK
13 Director Information Technology .... Mr. Ron PARKER
37 Director of Financial Aid .... Mr. Daniel YARRITU
08 Director Library & Learning Service .... Vacant
18 Director Facility Services .... Mr. John DITTO
88 Director Small Business Dev Center .... Ms. Jennifer FINNEY
31 Director Community Education .... Ms. Deborah EWING
88 Director Children's Center .... Ms. Christine WEBSTER
109 Director Business Services .... Ms. Ginger WOOSTER
116 Internal Auditor .... Ms. Evelyn CRUZ
09 Dir Planning/Inst Effectiv/Research .... Ms. Cindy ULLRICH
04 Admin Assistant to the President .... Ms. Kasie GUTHRIE
19 Director Security/Safety .... Mr. Chad LEVERITT
88 Dean School & College Partnerships .... Ms. Priscilla SANCHEZ

Brite Divinity School (B)

2925 Princeton Street, Fort Worth TX 76129-0001
County: Tarrant Identification: 666228
Unit ID: 450304
Telephone: (817) 257-7575 Carnegie Class: Spec-4-yr-Faith
FAX Number: (817) 257-6932 Calendar System: Semester
URL: www.brite.edu
Established: 1873 Annual Graduate Tuition & Fees: N/A
Enrollment: 142 Coed
Affiliation or Control: Independent Non-Profit IRS Status: 501(c)3
Highest Offering: Doctorate; No Undergraduates
Accreditation: SC, THEOL

01 President & Chief Executive Officer .... Dr. D. Newell WILLIAMS
05 Exec Vice President/Dean .... Dr. Michael MILLER
10 Vice President Business/Finance .... Mr. Jeffrey GUY
07 Director of Admissions .... Rev. Monica BRADLEY

Carrington College - Mesquite (C)

3733 West Emporium Circle, Mesquite TX 75150
Telephone: (972) 682-2800 Identification: 770967
Accreditation: &WJ

† Branch campus of Carrington College - Sacramento, Sacramento, CA

Center for Advanced Legal Studies (D)

800 W Sam Houston Pkwy, S Suite 100,
Houston TX 77042
County: Harris FICE Identification: 026047
Unit ID: 379782
Telephone: (713) 529-2778 Carnegie Class: Spec 2-yr-Other
FAX Number: (855) 422-4466 Calendar System: Other
URL: www.paralegal.edu
Established: 1987 Annual Undergrad Tuition & Fees: N/A
Enrollment: 243 Coed
Affiliation or Control: Proprietary IRS Status: Proprietary
Highest Offering: Associate Degree
Accreditation: ACCSC, COE

01 School Director/Co-Founder .... Mr. Doyle HAPPE
05 Dean .... Mr. Thomas SWANSON
07 Director of Admissions .... Mr. James SCHEFFER

Central Texas College (E)

PO Box 1800, Killeen TX 76540-9990
County: Bell FICE Identification: 004003
Unit ID: 223816
Telephone: (254) 526-7161 Carnegie Class: Assoc/MT-VT-High Non
FAX Number: N/A Calendar System: Semester
URL: www.ctcd.edu
Established: 1965 Annual Undergrad Tuition & Fees (In-District): $3,540
Enrollment: 10,173 Coed
Affiliation or Control: Local IRS Status: 501(c)3
Highest Offering: Associate Degree
Accreditation: SC, ADNUR, EMT, HT, MLTAD

01 Chancellor .... Mr. Jim YEONOPOLUS
103 Dep Chanc Inst Workforce Initiative .... Dr. Tina ADY
10 Deputy Chanc Finance & Admin .... Dr. Michele CARTER
05 Deputy Chanc Acad & Student Success .... Dr. Robin GARRETT
12 Dean Fort Hood .... Ms. Jacqueline HAIRE
20 Dean of Instruction .... Dr. Daniel FISCHER
32 Dean Student Services .... Dr. Johnelle WELSH
08 Dean Library Services .... Ms. Lori PURSER
84 Associate Dean Enrollment Services .... Ms. Eva HUTCHENS
06 Assoc Dean Admiss/Regist/Records .... Mr. Stephen O'DONOVAN
21 Assoc Dep Chanc Financial Mgmt .... Mr. Bob LIBERTY
15 Assoc Dep Chanc Human Res Mgmt .... Ms. Holly JORDAN
106 Dean Distance Educ/Curriculum Devel .... Ms. Sharon DAVIS
18 Assoc Dep Chanc Facilities & Const .... Mr. Mark HARMSEN
30 Director College Development .... Ms. Valerie PAYSON
09 Dir Institutional Effectiveness .... Dr. Marie VALENTIN
13 Assoc Dep Chanc Info Technology .... Mr. Cliff GAINES
07 Director Admissions/Recruitment .... Ms. Amy WILLIAMS
88 Director Testing .... Mr. Victor GATES
85 Director International Student Svcs .... Ms. Zeyra MONTEZ
22 Director Disability Support Svcs .... Dr. Christy SHANK
88 Director Substance Abuse Resource . Dr. Gerald MAHONE-LEIWS
36 Director Career Services .... Ms. Keisha HOLMAN
26 Int Director Marketing & Outreach .... Mr. Bruce VASBINDER
88 QA Liaison/C&I Campus Ops .... Ms. Diana CASTILLO
19 Chief Police/Security Services .... Chief Joseph BARRAGAN
40 Manager Bookstore .... Ms. Regina MARTINEZ-WOODRUFF
37 Assoc Dean Fin Aid/Veteran Svcs .... Ms. Lucette BRENDT
96 Assoc Dep Chanc Business Services .... Mr. Ted GONZALEZ
04 Administrative Asst to President .... Ms. Debra HAVENS
43 Dir Legal Services/General Counsel .... Ms. Traci BRIGGS
86 Director Government Relations .... Mr. Rudy SANDOVAL
25 Chief Contract/Grants Administrator .... Vacant
105 Web & Digital Media Manager .... Ms. Erica BURTON
28 Director of Diversity .... Dr. Michele CARTER

Chamberlain University-Houston (F)

11025 Equity Drive, Houston TX 77041
Telephone: (713) 277-9800 Identification: 770500
Accreditation: &HLC, NURSE

† Branch campus of Chamberlain University-Addison, Addison, IL

Chamberlain University-Irving (G)

4800 Regent Boulevard, Irving TX 75063
Telephone: (469) 706-6705 Identification: 770853
Accreditation: &HLC, NURSE

† Branch campus of Chamberlain University-Addison, Addison, IL

Chamberlain University-Pearland (H)

12000 Shadow Creek Pkwy, Pearland TX 77584
Telephone: (832) 664-7000 Identification: 770934
Accreditation: &HLC, NURSE

† Branch campus of Chamberlain College of Nursing-Addison, Addison, IL.

Christ Mission College (I)

10822 FM 1560, San Antonio TX 78254
County: Bexar Identification: 667320
Unit ID: 494630
Telephone: (210) 688-3101 Carnegie Class: Spec-4-yr-Faith
FAX Number: N/A Calendar System: Semester
URL: www.cmctx.org
Established: 1926 Annual Undergrad Tuition & Fees: N/A
Enrollment: N/A Coed
Affiliation or Control: Independent Non-Profit IRS Status: 501(c)3
Highest Offering: Baccalaureate
Accreditation: BI

01 President .... Dr. Monte MADSEN
05 VP of Academics .... Rev. Alicia CARRASCO
32 VP of Student Services .... Rev. Reva MADSEN
10 Sr Director of Finance .... Ms. Evelyn ARIAS
84 Enrollment Manager .... Rev. Yaritza ROMERO

Cisco College (J)

101 College Heights, Cisco TX 76437-1900
County: Eastland FICE Identification: 003553
Unit ID: 223898
Telephone: (254) 442-5000 Carnegie Class: Assoc/MT-VT-High Trad
FAX Number: (254) 442-5100 Calendar System: Semester
URL: www.cisco.edu
Established: 1940 Annual Undergrad Tuition & Fees (In-State): $4,860
Enrollment: 3,256 Coed
Affiliation or Control: State IRS Status: 501(c)3
Highest Offering: Associate Degree
Accreditation: SC, COARC, MAC, SURGT

01 President .... Dr. Thad ANGLIN
05 Vice President of Instruction .... Ms. Heather HICKS
32 Vice President for Student Services .... Dr. Jerry DODSON
10 VP of Business Services/CFO .... Ms. Audra TAYLOR
13 Exec Dir of Information Technology .... Dr. Tim MURPHY
30 Director of Development .... Ms. Martha MONTGOMERY
37 Director of Financial Aid .... Ms. Linda SELLERS
15 Director of Human Resources .... Ms. Laurie KINCANNON
08 Director of Library Services .... Ms. Donna CLARK
19 Director Campus Safety .... Mr. Roger TIGHE
84 Dir of Enrollment Svcs/Registrar .... Ms. Shirley DOVE
04 Executive Asst to President .... Ms. Sydni RABB
103 Dean Workforce/Economic Development .... Mr. Rick MARKS
106 Dir Online Education/E-learning .... Ms. Sheron CATON
35 Dean of Student Services .... Dr. Bryan COTTRELL
96 Dir of Operations and Procurement .... Ms. Beverly MASSEY

Clarendon College (K)

PO Box 968, Clarendon TX 79226-0968
County: Donley FICE Identification: 003554
Unit ID: 223922
Telephone: (806) 874-3571 Carnegie Class: Assoc/HVT-High Non
FAX Number: (806) 874-3201 Calendar System: Semester
URL: www.clarendoncollege.edu
Established: 1898 Annual Undergrad Tuition & Fees (In-District): $4,290
Enrollment: 1,334 Coed
Affiliation or Control: State/Local IRS Status: 501(c)3
Highest Offering: Associate Degree
Accreditation: SC

01 President .... Mr. Tex BUCKHAULTS
13 Vice Pres of Information Technology .... Mr. Will THOMPSON
05 Vice President of Academic Affairs .... Mr. Brad VANDEN BOOGAARD
10 Comptroller .... Ms. Kae HEWETT
04 Assistant to the President .... Mrs. Cindy LAMBERT
41 Athletic Director .... Mr. Mark JAMES
32 Director of Student Life .... Mr. Tadd ANDREWS
84 Assoc Dean of Enrollment Services .... Mrs. Janean REISH
37 Director of Financial Aid .... Mrs. Amanda SMITH
06 Registrar .... Mrs. Brandi HAVENS
08 Librarian .... Ms. Pamela REED
81 Division Chair Science/Health .... Mrs. Scarlet ESTLACK
49 Division Chair Liberal Arts .... Mrs. Kim JEFFREY
47 Division Chair Agriculture .... Mr. Johnny TREICHEL
76 Division Chair Allied Health .... Mrs. Jamie MEARS
75 Dean of CTE .... Mr. Mike DAVIS

Coastal Bend College (L)

3800 Charco Road, Beeville TX 78102-2197
County: Bee FICE Identification: 003546
Unit ID: 223320
Telephone: (361) 358-2838 Carnegie Class: Assoc/HVT-High Non
FAX Number: (361) 354-2333 Calendar System: Semester
URL: www.coastalbend.edu
Established: 1965 Annual Undergrad Tuition & Fees (In-District): $4,493
Enrollment: 4,105 Coed
Affiliation or Control: State/Local IRS Status: 501(c)3
Highest Offering: Associate Degree
Accreditation: SC, DH, RAD

01 President .... Dr. Justin HOGGARD
05 Provost/CAO .... Dr. Patricia REHAK
97 Dean of Transfer & General Studies .... Mr. Mark SECORD
32 Dean Student Svcs & Accessibility .... Dr. Kayla DEVORA-JONES
07 Director of Admissions/Registrar .... Ms. Candy FULLER
26 Int Director of Marketing & PR .... Ms. Amanda RAMIREZ
37 Director of Financial Aid .... Ms. Nora MORALES
12 Director of Alice Site .... Vacant
12 Director of Kingsville Site .... Mr. Keenan WOODS
12 Director of Pleasanton Site .... Vacant
10 Accounting Director/CFO .... Ms. Lajuana KASPRZYK
08 Director Library Services .... Vacant
15 Director Human Resources .... Ms. Dixie LYTLE
13 Director of IT/CIO .... Mr. Amador RAMIREZ
18 Director of Physical Plant .... Mr. Jacinto (JC) COLMENERO
04 Executive Asst to President .... Ms. Anna GARCIA
103 Dean of Career & Technical Educ .... Mr. Jarod BLEIBDREY
09 Exec Dir of Inst Effectiveness .... Dr. Michelle LANE
102 Exec Dir CBC Foundation .... Mr. Paul CANTRELL
19 Acting Police Chief/Safety .... Mr. Oscar RODRIGUEZ
41 Interim Athletic Director .... Mr. Vicente GARZA
66 Dean of Nursing & Allied Health .... Ms. Loana HERNANDEZ
84 Director of Dual Enrollment .... Ms. Susie GAITAN
39 Dir Resident Life/Student Housing .... Mr. Harold HILLYARD

College of Biblical Studies-Houston (M)

7000 Regency Square Boulevard, Houston TX 77036-3298
County: Harris FICE Identification: 034224
Unit ID: 388520

Telephone: (713) 785-5995 Carnegie Class: Spec-4-yr-Faith
FAX Number: (713) 785-5998 Calendar System: Semester
URL: www.cbshouston.edu
Established: 1976 Annual Undergrad Tuition & Fees: $6,801
Enrollment: 431 Coed
Affiliation or Control: Independent Non-Profit IRS Status: 501(c)3
Highest Offering: Baccalaureate
Accreditation: SC, BI

01 President Dr. Bill BLOCKER
04 Executive Assistant Mrs. Vicki PATTERSON
05 Provost Dr. Joseph D. PARLE
11 VP Administration/COO Mr. Paul KEITH
88 Vice President of Discipleship Dr. Lisa STEWART
10 Vice Pres/Chief Financial Officer Mr. Benjamin CHELLADURAI
84 VP Enrollment/Student Success Dr. Emmanuel LALANDE
26 Exec Dir Communications/PR Ms. Melinda MERILLAT
106 Dean Distance Educ Operations Mr. Shane BOOTHE
09 Dean Institutional Effectiveness Dr. Joel BADAL
18 Dir Real Estate Operations Mr. Terry BRYAN
15 Director of Human Resources Mr. Paul KEITH
06 Registrar Ms. Twyla GILLS
08 Director of Library Services Mr. Artis LOVELADY, III
32 Dean of Students Ms. Luzmar COBOS
20 Assoc Dean Faculty and Curr Dev Dr. Brittany BURNETTE
37 Senior Financial Aid Officer Vacant
111 Assoc VP Advancement Ms. Chelsea WHITE
88 Exec Director Grace Relations Dr. Charles WARE

College of Biomedical Equipment Technology (A)

11550 IH 10 West Suite 190, San Antonio TX 78230
County: Bexar Identification: 667323
Telephone: (210) 233-1102 Carnegie Class: Not Classified
FAX Number: N/A Calendar System: Other
URL: www.cbet.edu
Established: 2010 Annual Undergrad Tuition & Fees: N/A
Enrollment: N/A Coed
Affiliation or Control: Proprietary IRS Status: Proprietary
Highest Offering: Associate Degree
Accreditation: CNCE

01 President Dr. Richard (Monty) GONZALES
05 Director of Education Mr. Scott MCKNIGHT

The College of Health Care Professions (B)

6330 East Highway 290, Suite 180, Austin TX 78723
County: Travis FICE Identification: 034263
Unit ID: 437635
Telephone: (512) 617-5700 Carnegie Class: Spec 2-yr-Health
FAX Number: (512) 892-6643 Calendar System: Other
URL: www.chcp.edu
Established: 1988 Annual Undergrad Tuition & Fees: N/A
Enrollment: 666 Coed
Affiliation or Control: Proprietary IRS Status: Proprietary
Highest Offering: Associate Degree
Accreditation: ABHES, DMS, SURTEC

01 Campus President Ms. Monica JEFFS
05 Director of Education Mr. Kevin MCCARTY
07 Director of Admissions Ms. Ambrosia MMONU

The College of Health Care Professions (C)

240 Northwest Mall Boulevard, Houston TX 77092
County: Harris FICE Identification: 031281
Unit ID: 392257
Telephone: (713) 425-3100 Carnegie Class: Spec-4-yr-Other Health
FAX Number: (713) 425-3192 Calendar System: Other
URL: www.chcp.edu
Established: 1988 Annual Undergrad Tuition & Fees: N/A
Enrollment: 2,811 Coed
Affiliation or Control: Proprietary IRS Status: Proprietary
Highest Offering: Baccalaureate
Accreditation: ABHES, SURGT, SURTEC

01 Campus President Mr. Lee JONES
05 Director of Education Ms. Frances HESTER

The College of Health Care Professions-Dallas (D)

8585 N Stemmons Freeway, Ste N-300, Dallas TX 75247
Telephone: (214) 420-3400 Identification: 770531
Accreditation: ABHES

The College of Health Care Professions-Fort Worth (E)

4248 North Freeway, Fort Worth TX 76137
Telephone: (817) 632-5900 Identification: 770532
Accreditation: ABHES, DMS

The College of Health Care Professions-McAllen (F)

1917 Nolana Avenue, Ste 100, McAllen TX 78504
Telephone: (956) 800-1500 Identification: 770963
Accreditation: ABHES

The College of Health Care Professions-San Antonio (G)

4738 Northwest Loop 410, San Antonio TX 78229
Telephone: (210) 298-3600 Identification: 770964
Accreditation: ABHES, SURTEC

College of the Mainland (H)

1200 Amburn Road, Texas City TX 77591-2499
County: Galveston FICE Identification: 007096
Unit ID: 226408
Telephone: (409) 938-1211 Carnegie Class: Assoc/MT-VT-High Non
FAX Number: (409) 933-8010 Calendar System: Semester
URL: www.com.edu
Established: 1966 Annual Undergrad Tuition & Fees (In-District): $2,973
Enrollment: 4,335 Coed
Affiliation or Control: Local IRS Status: 501(c)3
Highest Offering: Baccalaureate
Accreditation: SC, ADNUR, CAHIIM, EMT, #MAC

01 President Dr. Warren NICHOLS
05 Vice President for Instruction Dr. Jerry FLIGER
10 Vice President for Fiscal Affairs Dr. Clen BURTON
32 Vice President for Student Services Dr. Helen BREWER
35 AVP Student Success/Dean of Stdnts Ms. Kris KIMBARK
07 Dir Admissions & Registrar Mr. Tomas GARCIA
15 Exec Dir of Human Resources Mr. Michael MCGEE
18 Director of Facility Services Mr. Bo BACON
08 Director Library Services Ms. Kathryn PARK
102 Exec Director of Foundation Dr. Lisa WATSON
28 Director of Institutional Equity Vacant
96 Director of Purchasing Ms. Sonja BLINKA
09 Research Specialist Ms. Lauren HARPER
04 Admin Assistant to the President Ms. Michelle GERAMI

Collin College (I)

3452 Spur 399, McKinney TX 75069
County: Collin FICE Identification: 023614
Unit ID: 247834
Telephone: (972) 758-3805 Carnegie Class: Bac/Assoc-Assoc Dom
FAX Number: (972) 758-3807 Calendar System: Semester
URL: www.collin.edu
Established: 1985 Annual Undergrad Tuition & Fees (In-District): $3,004
Enrollment: 35,390 Coed
Affiliation or Control: State/Local IRS Status: 501(c)3
Highest Offering: Baccalaureate
Accreditation: SC, ACFEI, ACPHA, ADNUR, CAHIIM, COARC, DH, DMS, EMT, MAC, NAEYC, NUR, POLYT, SURGA, SURGT

01 District President Dr. H. Neil MATKIN
04 Exec Asst to Pres/Board Secy Ms. Kristy HORKMAN
100 Chief of Staff Ms. Kimberly K. DAVISON
03 Interim Executive VP Dr. Bill L. KING
11 Sr VP Campus Operations Dr. Abe JOHNSON
10 Chief Financial Officer Ms. Melissa IRBY
26 Senior VP External Relations Mr. Steve M. MATTHEWS
15 Chief Human Resources Officer Mr. Floyd W. NICKERSON
43 General Counsel Ms. Monica A. VELAZQUEZ
111 VP Advancement Ms. Lisa R. VASQUEZ
18 VP Facilities & Construction Mr. Chris EYLE
116 Director Internal Audit Mr. Ali SUBHANI
19 Chief of Police Mr. D. Scott JENKINS
05 VP Academic Affairs Dr. Jon H. HARDESTY
12 VP/Provost-Frisco Mr. Craig C. LEVERETTE
12 Executive Dean-Celina Ms. Brenda C. CARTER
12 VP/Provost-McKinney Dr. Mark SMITH
12 Executive Dean-Farmersville Dr. Diana L. HOPES
12 VP/Provost-Plano Dr. Mary E. BARNES-TILLEY
12 Interim VP/Provost Allen Tech Dr. Brenden D. MESCH
12 VP/Provost Wylie Dr. Mary S. MCRAE
106 Exec Dean iCollin Virtual Campus Dr. Sarah K. LEE
121 Chief Student Success Officer Dr. Jay CORWIN
09 VP Institutional Research Dr. Thomas K. MARTIN
21 Assoc VP Financial Svcs & Rprtng Ms. Barbara A. JOHNSTON
21 Assoc VP/Controller Ms. Julie M. BRADLEY
32 VP Student & Enrollment Services Dr. Albert TEZENO
88 Assoc VP P-12 Partnerships Mr. Raul J. MARTINEZ
39 Dir Student Housing Operations Ms. Angela MCGILL
35 Assoc VP Student & Enrollment Svcs Dr. Alicia L. HUPPE
13 Chief Information Officer (IT) Dr. David STEPHENS
76 Dean Health Sci & Emergency Svcs Ms. Michelle L. MILLEN
66 Dean Nursing Dr. David PERUSKI
103 Dean Workforce Educ Frisco Vacant
97 Dean Academic Affairs Frisco Dr. Dawn J. RICHARDSON
97 Dean Academic Affairs McKinney Dr. Garry W. EVANS
79 Dean Bus/Languages & Math Plano Dr. Meredith L. WANG
57 Dean Arts & Educ Plano Dr. Lupita M. TINNEN
81 Dean Sciences Plano Dr. Kristen L. STREATER
97 Dean Academic Affairs Allen Tech Dr. Amy T. GAINER
103 Dean Workforce Educ Allen Tech Mr. Michael COFFMAN
20 Dean Academic & Workforce Wylie Ms. Daphne H. BABCOCK
55 Dean Evening & Weekend College Ms. Gaye M. COOKSEY
51 Exec Dean Cont Educ & Corp College Ms. Karen M. MUSA
51 COO Corporate College Dr. Roger H. WIDMER
07 Dean of Admissions Dr. Laura ISDELL
06 Registrar Ms. Jennifer WAITS
35 District Dean of Students Mr. Terrence P. BRENNAN
84 Dean Student & Enrol Svcs Frisco Ms. De'Aira M. HOLLOWAY
84 Dean Student & Enrol Svcs McKinney Ms. Traci RAMSEY
84 Dean Student & Enrol Svcs Plano Mr. Kirk D. LEE
84 Dean Student & Enrol Svcs Wylie Mr. Doug G. WILLIS
08 Exec Dir Library Frisco Ms. Vidya KRISHNASWAMY
08 Exec Dir Library McKinney Ms. Faye M. DAVIS
08 Exec Dir Library Plano Vacant
08 Exec Dir Library Wylie Ms. Nichole N. BOONE
37 Dir Financial Aid & Vet Affairs Mr. Alan D. PIXLEY
41 Director Athletics Dr. Albert TEZENO
96 Director Purchasing Ms. Cynthia L. WHITE
25 Dir Workforce & Econ Dev (Grants) Ms. Natalie G. GREENWELL

Commonwealth Institute of Funeral Service (J)

415 Barren Springs Drive, Houston TX 77090-5913
County: Harris FICE Identification: 003556
Unit ID: 366261
Telephone: (281) 873-0262 Carnegie Class: Spec 2-yr-A&S
FAX Number: (281) 873-5232 Calendar System: Quarter
URL: www.commonwealth.edu
Established: 1936 Annual Undergrad Tuition & Fees: $13,363
Enrollment: 256 Coed
Affiliation or Control: Independent Non-Profit IRS Status: 501(c)3
Highest Offering: Associate Degree
Accreditation: FUSER

01 President Mr. Cody LOPASKY
05 Dean of Academics Mr. James ROBINSON
32 Dean of Students Mr. Christopher LAYTON
37 Director Student Financial Aid Ms. Marlene PERRY
06 Registrar Ms. Patricia MORENO
08 Head Librarian Ms. Melissa DAVIS

Concorde Career College (K)

12606 Greenville Avenue, Suite 130, Dallas TX 75243
Telephone: (469) 221-3400 Identification: 770593
Accreditation: ACCSC, COARC, DH, PTAA, #SURGT

† Branch campus of Concorde Career College, Aurora, CO

Concorde Career College (L)

4803 NW Loop 410, Suite 200, San Antonio TX 78229
Telephone: (210) 428-2000 Identification: 770594
Accreditation: ACCSC, COARC, DH, PTAA, SURGT

† Branch campus of Concorde Career College, Kansas City, MO

Concorde Career Institute (M)

3015 West I-20, Grand Prairie TX 75052
County: Tarrant FICE Identification: 035423
Unit ID: 441742
Telephone: (469) 348-2500 Carnegie Class: Spec 2-yr-Health
FAX Number: (469) 348-2580 Calendar System: Semester
URL: https://www.concorde.edu/campus/grand-prairie-texas
Established: 1991 Annual Undergrad Tuition & Fees: N/A
Enrollment: 862 Coed
Affiliation or Control: Proprietary IRS Status: Proprietary
Highest Offering: Associate Degree
Accreditation: ACCSC, DH, NDT, POLYT, SURGT

01 Campus President Mr. Mike LOVEJOY

Concordia University Texas (N)

11400 Concordia University Drive, Austin TX 78726
County: Travis FICE Identification: 003557
Unit ID: 224004
Telephone: (512) 313-3000 Carnegie Class: Masters/L
FAX Number: (512) 313-3999 Calendar System: Semester
URL: www.concordia.edu
Established: 1926 Annual Undergrad Tuition & Fees: $33,800
Enrollment: 2,257 Coed
Affiliation or Control: Lutheran Church - Missouri Synod
IRS Status: 501(c)3
Highest Offering: Doctorate
Accreditation: SC, ACBSP, IACBE, NURSE

01 President/CEO Dr. Donald CHRISTIAN
04 Executive Asst to Pres/CEO Ms. Dana KORNFUEHRER
05 Provost & Executive VP Dr. Kristi KIRK
26 Sr VP External Affairs Ms. Beth ATHERTON
10 Chief Financial Officer Dr. Lynette GILLIS
45 Sr VP Planning & Quality Dr. Shane SOKOLL
84 VP of Enrollment Management Ms. Lara BAILIFF
11 VP of Administration Mr. Dan GREGORY
20 VP of Academic Operations Dr. KC POSPISIL
41 VP of Athletics Ms. Ronda SEAGRAVES
32 VP of Student Affairs Ms. Jennielle STROTHER
106 Assoc VP Digital Operations Dr. Alex HERRON
42 Campus Pastor Rev. Steve FICK
21 Controller Mr. Sairam PATHI
88 Dean of Teaching & Learning Dr. Sara SHIPPEY

66 Dean College of Nursing ... Dr. Jason SHUFFITT
79 Dir School of Humanities ... Dr. Ann SCHWARTZ
30 Director of Philanthropy ... Ms. Amanda KEETER
06 Dir Student Info Systems & Records ... Mr. Ricky ALLEN
15 Director Human Resources ... Mr. Sairam PATHI
37 Director Student Financial Services ... Mr. Russell JEFFREY
121 Director Student Success Center ... Ms. Ruth COOPER
36 Dir Vocation & Prof Development ... Ms. Randa SCOTT
35 Dean of Students ... Ms. Martha COMPTON
08 Director of Library Services ... Ms. Mikail MCINTOSH-DOTY
58 Director MBA Graduate Program ... Dr. Elise BRAZIER
19 Chief of Police ... Mr. Manuel JIMENEZ
29 Dir Donor & Alumni Relations ... Mr. Jeff FROSCH
102 Dir Found/Corp & Govt Relations ... Ms. Meghann BOLTON
112 Director of Major Gifts ... Ms. Tiffany JOHNSON
09 Dir Inst Research & Effectiveness ... Dr. Trey BUCHANAN
96 Director Support Services ... Mr. Eric SILBER
105 Web Administrator ... Mr. Bryan GILBERT

Criswell College (A)

4010 Gaston Avenue, Dallas TX 75246-1537
County: Dallas FICE Identification: 041218
Unit ID: 475608
Telephone: (214) 821-5433 Carnegie Class: Bac-Diverse
FAX Number: (214) 370-0497 Calendar System: Semester
URL: www.criswell.edu
Established: 1970 Annual Undergrad Tuition & Fees: $12,624
Enrollment: 209 Coed
Affiliation or Control: Independent Non-Profit IRS Status: 501(c)3
Highest Offering: Master's
Accreditation: SC

01 President ... Dr. Barry CREAMER
05 VP of Academic Affairs ... Dr. Christopher GRAHAM
10 VP of Finance ... Kevin STILLEY
32 VP of Student Affairs ... Luis JUÁREZ
111 VP of Advancement ... Dr. Joseph WOODDELL
04 Exec Assistant to President ... Daisy REYNOLDS
88 Assistant to Chief of Staff ... Judy FOWLER
06 Registrar ... Vacant
21 Controller ... Steve KEENER
07 Director of Admissions ... Vacant
08 Director of Library Services ... Valeri KNIGHTEN
100 Chief of Staff ... Winston HOTTMAN
13 Senior Director of Information Tech ... Dr. Scott SHIFFER
15 Director of Human Resources ... Martha BATTS
19 Chief of Police & Sr Dir Phys Plant ... Brad CORDER
28 Director African-American Relations ... Kendall LYONS
30 Director of Development ... Sharon MAXWELL
37 Director of Financial Aid ... Jimmy CRISWELL
09 Dir Acad Programmng & Inst Research ... Daniel HAGGERTY
29 Director of Alumni Affairs ... Rob COLLINGSWORTH
44 Director Annual Giving ... Cesia JUÁREZ

Culinary Institute LeNotre (B)

7070 Allensby Street, Houston TX 77022-4322
County: Harris FICE Identification: 037233
Unit ID: 444565
Telephone: (713) 692-0077 Carnegie Class: Spec 2-yr-A&S
FAX Number: (713) 692-7399 Calendar System: Other
URL: www.culinaryinstitute.edu
Established: 1998 Annual Undergrad Tuition & Fees: $17,782
Enrollment: 382 Coed
Affiliation or Control: Proprietary IRS Status: Proprietary
Highest Offering: Associate Degree
Accreditation: ACCSC, ACFEI

01 Chief Executive Officer ... Alain LENOTRE
06 Senior Registrar ... Flor RALDA
08 Chief Library Officer ... Connie PINE
106 Dean Online Education/E-learning ... Roberto HERNANDEZ
11 Chief of Operations/Administration ... Dr. Art CERVANTES
18 Chief Facilities/Physical Plant Ofc ... Elheme ELEZI
29 Director Alumni Affairs ... Patricia LOPEZ
84 Director Enrollment Management ... Alicia ORELLANA
96 Director of Purchasing ... Sam KELLEN

Culinary Institute of America San Antonio (C)

312 Pearl Parkway, Bldg 3,Ste 2102,
San Antonio TX 78215
Telephone: (210) 554-6400 Identification: 770131
Accreditation: &M

† Branch campus of The Culinary Institute of America, Hyde Park, NY

Dallas Baptist University (D)

3000 Mountain Creek Parkway, Dallas TX 75211-9299
County: Dallas FICE Identification: 003560
Unit ID: 224226
Telephone: (214) 333-7100 Carnegie Class: DU-Mod
FAX Number: (214) 333-5447 Calendar System: 4/1/4
URL: www.dbu.edu
Established: 1898 Annual Undergrad Tuition & Fees: $31,940
Enrollment: 4,247 Coed
Affiliation or Control: Baptist IRS Status: 501(c)3
Highest Offering: Doctorate
Accreditation: SC, ACBSP, CAEP, CEA, MUS

01 President ... Dr. Adam WRIGHT
02 Chancellor ... Dr. Gary COOK
100 Chief of Staff ... Mr. Dan GIBSON
10 Vice Pres for Financial Affairs ... Dr. Matt MURRAH
11 VP of Administration and Enrollment ... Mr. Jonathan TEAT
26 Vice President for Communications .. Dr. Blake KILLINGSWORTH
32 Vice President for Student Affairs ... Dr. Jay HARLEY
111 Vice President for Advancement ... Mr. Ryan HEFTON
85 Vice Pres for International Affairs ... Mr. Randy BYERS
13 VP for IT & Dean Online Education ... Dr. Matt WINN
27 Assistant VP for Communications ... Dr. Layna EVANS
88 Sr Advisor to Pres for Acad Affs ... Dr. Denny DOWD
05 Provost ... Dr. Norma HEDIN
20 Associate Provost ... Mrs. Deemie NAUGLE
20 Assistant Provost ... Dr. Mark HALE
108 Acad Dean/Accreditation Liaison ... Dr. Gail LINAM
06 Registrar ... Ms. Linda RONEY
35 Dean of Students ... Mrs. Tempress ASAGBA
84 Associate VP for Enrollment ... Mr. Jason WILLIAMS
07 Associate VP for UG Enrollment ... Dr. John BORUM
07 Director of UG Admissions ... Ms. Erin SMITH
58 Dean Cook School of Leadership ... Dr. Jack GOODYEAR
107 Dean Global Studies/Pre-Prof Pgms ... Dr. David COOK
50 Dean College of Business ... Dr. Jeff JOHNSON
81 Dean College Natural Science & Math ... Dr. Dionisio FLEITAS
53 Dean College of Education ... Dr. DeAnna JENKINS
57 Dean College of Fine Arts ... Dr. Wes MOORE
73 Dean College of Christian Faith ... Dr. Wayne DAVIS
79 Dean Col Humanities/Social Sciences ... Dr. Rob SULLIVAN
114 Asst VP for Financial Affairs ... Mr. Danny HASSETT
21 Controller ... Mrs. Mendi MCMAHAN
37 Director of Financial Aid ... Mrs. Shermain REED
113 Dir of Student Account Services ... Ms. Joy BONDURANT
105 Director of Web Services ... Mrs. Anu CHIVUKULA
29 Director of Alumni Affairs ... Mrs. Kathryn ROBNETT
08 Director of the Library ... Mr. Scott JEFFRIES
15 Director of Human Resources ... Mrs. Tamy ROGERS
43 General Counsel ... Ms. Christa POWERS
88 Director of Immigration ... Mr. Aaron PARISH
85 Director of Intl Student Services ... Mrs. Susie CASSEL
41 Director of Athletics ... Mr. Connor SMITH
35 Director of Student Life ... Mr. Wayne BRIGGS
121 Director of Student Success ... Mrs. Molly TAYLOR
36 Director of Career Development ... Mrs. Leoni MICHAEL
38 Dir Counseling & Spiritual Care ... Dr. Jordan DAVIS
39 Director of University Housing ... Ms. Allyson MILLER
24 Director of Media Services ... Mr. Rob LEWIS
19 Chief of Police ... Mr. Chris HAVENS
19 Director of Campus Security ... Mr. Donald KABETZKE
40 Manager Bookstore ... Vacant

Dallas Christian College (E)

2700 Christian Parkway, Dallas TX 75234-7299
County: Dallas FICE Identification: 006941
Unit ID: 224244
Telephone: (972) 241-3371 Carnegie Class: Bac-Diverse
FAX Number: (972) 241-8021 Calendar System: 4/1/4
URL: www.dallas.edu
Established: 1950 Annual Undergrad Tuition & Fees: $19,086
Enrollment: 246 Coed
Affiliation or Control: Christian Churches And Churches of Christ
IRS Status: 501(c)3
Highest Offering: Baccalaureate
Accreditation: BI

01 President ... Dr. Brian D. SMITH
05 VP for Academic Affairs ... Dr. John DERRY
84 VP for Enrollment Management ... Mr. Ken FAFFLER
111 VP for Institutional Advancement ... Mr. Mark WORLEY
10 VP of Finance & Operations ... Ms. Andrea SHORT
108 Dir Institutional Effectiveness ... Mr. Bruce LONG
06 Registrar ... Mrs. Crystal LAIDACKER
37 Dir of Student Financial Svcs ... Ms. Breanda WILLIAMS
18 Director of Facilities ... Mr. David LAGUNEZ
04 Exec Admin Assistant to the Pres ... Ms. Annette ESCLAVON

*Dallas College (F)

1601 South Lamar Street, Dallas TX 75215
County: Dallas FICE Identification: 009331
Unit ID: 224253
Telephone: (214) 378-1601 Carnegie Class: N/A
FAX Number: (214) 378-1810
URL: www.dcccd.edu

01 Chancellor ... Dr. Justin LONON
00 Chancellor Emeritus ... Dr. Joe D. MAY
86 EVC of Operations ... Vacant
05 District Provost ... Dr. Shawnda FLOYD
111 VC Advancement/Workforce ... Dr. Pyeper WILKINS
43 District General Counsel ... Mr. Robert WENDLAND
86 Chief Legislative Counsel ... Mr. Isaac FAZ
45 Chief Strategy Officer ... Ms. Mary BRUMBACH
10 Chief Financial Officer ... Mr. John ROBERTSON
13 Chief Innovations Officer (CIO) ... Mr. Tim MARSHALL
101 Board Relations Executive ... Mrs. Perla MOLINA
102 Chief Advancement Init/Foundation ... Dr. Pyeper WILKINS
100 Chief of Staff ... Mr. Juan GARCIA
11 Administrative Director ... Ms. Karen SETTLES-LEE

*Dallas College, Brookhaven Campus (G)

3939 Valley View, Dallas TX 75244-4997
County: Dallas FICE Identification: 021002
Unit ID: 223524
Telephone: (972) 860-4700 Carnegie Class: Not Classified
FAX Number: (972) 860-4897 Calendar System: Semester
URL: www.brookhavencollege.edu
Established: 1978 Annual Undergrad Tuition & Fees (In-District): N/A
Enrollment: N/A Coed
Affiliation or Control: State/Local IRS Status: 501(c)3
Highest Offering: Baccalaureate
Accreditation: &SC, ADNUR, ART, CAHIIM, EMT, NAEYC, RAD

02 President ... Dr. Linda BRADDY
103 Assoc VP Workforce/Continuing Educ ... Mr. Vernon L. HAWKINS
30 Assoc Vice Pres Development ... Ms. Marilyn K. LYNCH
50 Exec Dean Business Studies ... Dr. Giraud POLITE
45 Exec Dean Educational Resources ... Ms. Sarah FERGUSON
57 Exec Dean Fine Arts/Physical Educ ... Ms. Megan ABAJIAN
81 Exec Dean Science/Math ... Mr. Benjamin PEACOCK
76 Vice Provost of Health Sciences ... Dr. Juanita FLINT
13 Director Information Technology ... Mr. Michael DEASON
83 Exec Dean Social Sci/Distance Lrng ... Mr. Sam GOVEA
26 Executive Dean Communications ... Mrs. Kendra VAGLIENTI
38 Sr Exec Dean Guidance & Counseling ... Ms. Brenda DALTON
27 Dir Marketing/Public Information ... Ms. Meridith MCLARTY
06 Registrar ... Ms. Thoa Hoang VO
88 Sr Manager Intramural Sports ... Mr. Kevin HURST
21 Director of Business Operations ... Ms. Willadean MARTIN
36 Administrator of Placement ... Ms. Dominica MCCARTHY
18 Sr Director Physical Plant ... Mr. John WATSON
15 Chief Human Resources Officer ... Ms. Sherri ENRIGHT
35 Admin Office of Student Life ... Mr. Brian BORSKI
19 Commander of College Police ... Mr. Mark LOPEZ
88 Director of Sustainability ... Mr. Brandon MORTON

*Dallas College, Cedar Valley Campus (H)

3030 N Dallas Avenue, Lancaster TX 75134-3799
County: Dallas FICE Identification: 003561
Unit ID: 223773
Telephone: (972) 860-8201 Carnegie Class: Not Classified
FAX Number: (972) 682-7075 Calendar System: Semester
URL: www.cedarvalleycollege.edu
Established: 1974 Annual Undergrad Tuition & Fees (In-District): N/A
Enrollment: N/A Coed
Affiliation or Control: State/Local IRS Status: 501(c)3
Highest Offering: Baccalaureate
Accreditation: &SC

02 President ... Dr. Joseph SEABROOKS
05 Provost ... Dr. Shawnda NAVARRO FLOYD
32 VP Student Devel/Enrollment Mgmt ... Dr. Lisa COPPRUE
10 Int VP Business/Admin Services ... Mr. Jim JONES
81 Exec Dean Science/Tech/Engr/Math ... Mr. Eddy RAWLINSON
50 Exec Dean of Business/Technology ... Dr. Ruben JOHNSON
49 VProv Creative Arts/Design ... Dr. Solomon CROSS
51 Assoc Dean Open Enroll/Cont Educ ... Mr. Raymond RIVERA
88 Dir Sustainability/Advance Projects ... Dr. Maria BOCCALANDRO
35 Dean Student Support Services ... Ms. Grenna ROLLINGS
84 Sr Exec Dean Enrollment Mgmt ... Ms. Jarlene DECAY
08 Director Library Services ... Ms. Vidya KRISHNASWAMY
09 Dir Plng/Rsrch/Inst Effectiveness ... Ms. Nicole HAAN
18 Director Facilities Management ... Mrs. Cindy A. ROGERS
26 Chief Marketing Officer ... Vacant
15 Exec Director of Human Resources ... Mr. Warren DAVIS
13 Director Information Technology ... Mr. Michael WHITE
111 Exec Director of Advancement ... Ms. Patricia DAVIS
21 Director Business Services ... Mr. Jim JONES

*Dallas College, Eastfield Campus (I)

3737 Motley Drive, Mesquite TX 75150-2099
County: Dallas FICE Identification: 008510
Unit ID: 224572
Telephone: (972) 860-7100 Carnegie Class: Not Classified
FAX Number: (972) 860-8373 Calendar System: Semester
URL: www.eastfieldcollege.edu
Established: 1970 Annual Undergrad Tuition & Fees (In-District): N/A
Enrollment: N/A Coed
Affiliation or Control: State/Local IRS Status: 170(c)1
Highest Offering: Baccalaureate
Accreditation: &SC

02 President ... Dr. Eddie TEALER
05 Exec VP Academic Affairs ... Vacant
10 VP Business Services ... Mr. Jose C. RODRIGUEZ
45 Vice President Planning & Research ... Vacant
15 Senior Director Human Resources ... Mr. Andre JOHNSON
32 Assoc VP Student Svcs Admin ... Dr. Jose DELA CRUZ
111 AVP Advancement & Communication ... Ms. Sharon L. COOK
20 Assoc VP Academic Affairs ... Ms. Rachel B. WOLF
84 Exec Dean Access and Enrollment ... Dr. Patty R. YOUNG
12 Exec Dir Pleasant Grove Campus ... Dr. Javier E. OLGUIN
103 Senior Director Workforce Planning ... Ms. Tiffanie DOUGLAS
08 Executive Dean Library ... Ms. Karla J. GREER
72 Executive Dean of Career Tech ... Ms. Johnnie O. BELLAMY
81 Executive Dean STEM ... Dr. Jess P. KELLY

83 Exec Dean Social Sciences .... Ms. DeShaunta STEWART
57 Exec Dean Arts and Communications .... Ms. Courtney CARTER-HARBOUR
21 Exec Admin of Financial Affairs ....Ms. Heidi M. BASSETT
18 Director Facilities Management ....Mr. Michael BRANTLEY
28 Dir Ctr Equity/Inclusion/Diversity ....Ms. Ashmi PATEL
124 Dean Ofc Stdnt Engagement/Retention . Ms. Tania WITTGENFELD
46 Dean Resource Development ..... Dr. Tricia THOMAS-ANDERSON
51 Exec Dean Continuing Education ....Ms. Alisa JONES
26 Director of Marketing ....Ms. Donielle R. JOHNSON
106 Dean Inst Support & Distance Educ ....Mr. Abuzafar M. BASHET
88 Assoc Dean Educational Resources .... Ms. Lucinda A. GONZALES

*Dallas College, El Centro Campus (A)

801 Main Street, Dallas TX 75202-3604
County: Dallas FICE Identification: 004453
Unit ID: 224615
Telephone: (214) 860-2000 Carnegie Class: Assoc/MT-VT-High Non
FAX Number: (214) 860-2335 Calendar System: Semester
URL: www.elcentrocollege.edu
Established: 1966 Annual Undergrad Tuition & Fees (In-District): $4,050
Enrollment: 74,781 Coed
Affiliation or Control: State/Local IRS Status: 501(c)3
Highest Offering: Baccalaureate
Accreditation: &SC, ACFEI, ADNUR, COARC, CVT, DH, DMS, EMT, MAC, MLTAD, PNUR, RAD, SURGT

02 President ....Dr. Bradford WILLIAMS
05 SVP Academic Affairs ....Dr. Greg MORRIS
32 VP Student Svcs & Enrollment .... Ms. Karen STILLS
10 VP Business Services ....Ms. Lenora REECE
30 Manager of Development ....Vacant
76 Int Exec Dean Health Sciences ....Dr. Greg MORRIS
97 Exec Dean Academic Transfer .... Dr. Anthony MANSUETO
81 Exec Dean STEM ....Ms. Beth STALL
50 Exec Dean Business/Design/Pub Svc .... Dr. Sherry JONES
103 Dean of Instruct/CE/Workforce Educ ....Ms. Elizabeth GUERRA
106 Dean Instruct Innov/Acad Support .... Ms. Karla DAMRON
108 Int Dean Curriculum/Assessment ....Ms. Joselyn GONZALEZ
09 Assoc Dir Inst Effectiveness .... Ms. Nicosha PORTER
35 Dean Student Support Services ....Dr. Tracy JOHNSON
121 Dean Student Success .... Dr. Cornelius JOHNSON
89 Director College Programs ....Mr. Patrick VASQUEZ
08 Asst Dean Library ....Dr. Norman HOWDEN
84 Assoc Dean Enroll Services ....Ms. Rebecca J. GARZA
12 Exec Director West Campus ....Ms. Kathy ACOSTA
15 Exec Dir Human Resources ....Dr. Alfredo SANJUAN
19 College Police Captain ....Mr. James SMITH
26 Dir Marketing/Communications ....Ms. Priscilla A. STALEY
18 Col Director Facilities Services .... Mr. Jeremy MCCLELLAND
21 Dir Business Operations .... Ms. Keisha FARRINGTON
37 Dir Student Financial Aid ....Ms. Pam A. LUCAS
13 Sr Director Information Technology ...... Mr. Michael C. JOHNSON
85 Dir Col Pgms/International Center ....Mr. Robert G. REYES
36 Pgm Svcs Coord Career Services ....Ms. Christol JOHNSON
38 Licensed Psychologist ....Mr. David THOMPSON
23 Senior Manager Health Center .... Ms. LaJoyya JOHNSON
04 Executive Asst to President ....Ms. Ida KELLER
40 Manager Bookstore ....Ms. Venus MCGUIRE

*Dallas College, Mountain View Campus (B)

4849 W Illinois Avenue, Dallas TX 75211-6599
County: Dallas FICE Identification: 008503
Unit ID: 226930
Telephone: (214) 860-8680 Carnegie Class: Not Classified
FAX Number: (214) 860-8521 Calendar System: Semester
URL: www.mountainviewcollege.edu
Established: 1970 Annual Undergrad Tuition & Fees (In-District): N/A
Enrollment: N/A Coed
Affiliation or Control: State/Local IRS Status: 501(c)3
Highest Offering: Baccalaureate
Accreditation: &SC, ADNUR, OTA

01 College President ....Dr. Kenneth GONZALES
05 Vice President of Instruction ....Vacant
32 VP Student Svcs/Enrollment Mgmt .... Dr. Leonard GARRETT
10 Vice Pres of Business Services ....Vacant
84 Exec Dean Student Support Svcs .... Mr. Matthew SANCHEZ
90 Exec Dean Curriculum & Instruction ....Dr. Karen VALENCIA
06 Assoc Dean Lrng Sppt Svcs/Registrar ....Ms. Glenda GARRETT
18 Director Facilities Management ....Vacant
09 Dir of Planning/Research & IE .... Ms. Iva BERGERON
88 Administrator of Special Programs .... Ms. Cathy EDWARDS
103 Exec Dean of Workforce/Cont Educ ....Ms. Pat WEBB
26 Director Public Info/Marketing ....Ms. Jill LAIN
15 Exec Director Human Resources .... Mr. Warren DAVIS
36 Director Career Development ....Ms. Regina GARNER
45 Dean Resource Development ....Mr. Garth CLAYTON
04 Administrative Asst to President .... Mr. Michael ARREDONDO
08 Dir Library Services ....Ms. Jean BAKER
41 Athletic Director ....Mr. Manuel MANTRANA

*Dallas College, North Lake Campus (C)

5001 N MacArthur Boulevard, Irving TX 75038-3899
County: Dallas FICE Identification: 020774
Unit ID: 227191
Telephone: (972) 273-3000 Carnegie Class: Not Classified
FAX Number: (972) 273-3014 Calendar System: Semester
URL: www.dcccd.edu
Established: 1977 Annual Undergrad Tuition & Fees (In-District): N/A
Enrollment: N/A Coed
Affiliation or Control: State/Local IRS Status: 501(c)3
Highest Offering: Baccalaureate
Accreditation: &SC, ADNUR, CONST

02 President ....Dr. Christa SLEJKO
05 Vice Pres Academic Affairs/Provost .... Dr. Shawnda FLOYD
10 Vice Pres Business Services ....Vacant
32 VP Stdnt Success/Enrollment Mgmt .... Dr. Marisa PIERCE
84 Dean of Enrollment Mgmt/Stdnt Svcs .... Ms. Anabel JUAREZ
07 Dean Admissions/Registrar .... Ms. Francyenne MAYNARD
26 Director Marketing & Public Info ....Ms. Gina FEDERER
12 Exec Dean North & South Campus ....Mr. Arthur JAMES
12 Exec Dean West Campus ....Dr. Paul KELEMEN
09 Exec Dir Institutional Research ....Dr. Karen MONGO
18 Director Facilities Services ....Mr. John WATSON
19 Director Campus Police ....Mr. Randy REED
111 Dean of Advancement ....Dr. Kristine MASSEY
15 Exec Director Human Resources ....Vacant
21 Director Business Operations .... Ms. Elsy CARRANZA
35 Asst Dir Stdnt Pgms/Resources/Life ....Ms. Beth NIKOPOULOS
103 Exec Dean Workforce Dev/CE ....Mr. Tim SAMUELS
49 Executive Dean Liberal Arts ....Dr. Kenneth CHAPMAN
81 Exec Dean Math/Science ....Dr. Matthew DEMPSEY
50 Exec Dean Arts/Bus/Sports Sci Tech .... Dr. David EVANS
04 Administrative Asst to President .... Ms. Kari ANDREWS
41 Athletic Director ....Mr. Greg SOMMERS

*Dallas College, Richland Campus (D)

12800 Abrams Road, Dallas TX 75243-2199
County: Dallas FICE Identification: 008504
Unit ID: 227766
Telephone: (972) 238-6100 Carnegie Class: Not Classified
FAX Number: (972) 238-6957 Calendar System: Semester
URL: www.rlc.dcccd.edu
Established: 1972 Annual Undergrad Tuition & Fees (In-District): N/A
Enrollment: N/A Coed
Affiliation or Control: State/Local IRS Status: 501(c)3
Highest Offering: Baccalaureate
Accreditation: &SC

02 President ....Dr. Kathryn K. EGGLESTON
11 Sr Director Campus Administration ....Ms. Janet C. JAMES

Dallas Institute of Funeral Service (E)

3909 S Buckner Boulevard, Dallas TX 75227-4314
County: Dallas FICE Identification: 010761
Unit ID: 224271
Telephone: (214) 388-5466 Carnegie Class: Spec 2-yr-A&S
FAX Number: (214) 388-0316 Calendar System: Quarter
URL: www.dallasinstitute.edu
Established: 1945 Annual Undergrad Tuition & Fees: $12,790
Enrollment: 364 Coed
Affiliation or Control: Independent Non-Profit IRS Status: 501(c)3
Highest Offering: Associate Degree
Accreditation: FUSER

01 President .... Mr. Wayne CAVENDER
76 College Dean ....Ms. Erin WILSON
06 Registrar/Office Manager .... Ms. Tammy LEONARD
07 Director of Admissions .... Ms. Jan PERKINS
37 Director Financial Aid ....Ms. LaSonya BRYANT

Dallas International University (F)

7500 W Camp Wisdom Road, Dallas TX 75236-5629
County: Dallas FICE Identification: 038513
Telephone: (972) 708-7340 Carnegie Class: Not Classified
FAX Number: (972) 708-7292 Calendar System: Other
URL: www.diu.edu
Established: 1999 Annual Undergrad Tuition & Fees: N/A
Enrollment: N/A Coed
Affiliation or Control: Independent Non-Profit IRS Status: 501(c)3
Highest Offering: Doctorate
Accreditation: SC

01 President ....Dr. Doug TIFFIN
11 Vice President of Operations ....Mr. Jeff MINARD
15 Chief Human Resources Officer .... Mrs. Jodi EGAN
10 Vice President of Finance ....Mr. Rod JENKINS
32 Dean of Students .... Mrs. Meg TRIHUS
05 Dean of Academic Affairs ....Dr. Scott BERTHIAUME
42 Chaplain .... Mrs. Christine HARLAN
101 Secretary to the Board of Trustees ....Mr. Tad OLDENBURGER
30 Director of Development ....Vacant
04 Special Asst to President ....Ms. Valerie RHODES
09 Director of Inst Research/Svcs .... Mr. Richard LYNCH
21 Business Manager ....Mr. Paul SETTER
96 Lead Accountant ....Mr. Dan WALTON
35 Assistant Dean of Students .... Mr. Stephen PETERSON
20 Academic Dean Assistant .... Mr. Dan BOERGER
08 Library Director .... Ms. Brenda FLOWERS
84 Int Director of Recruiting ....Mr. John OH
07 Director of Admissions ....Mr. Stephen NASH
104 International Student Coordinator .... Mrs. Maggie JOHNSON
06 Registrar .... Mrs. Lynne LAMIMAN
37 Financial Aid Administrator ....Mr. Ken PRETTOL
29 Alumni Relations Coordinator .... Ms. Debbie MANTER
13 Director of Information Services ....Mr. Matt LONG
24 Director of Media Services ....Mr. Bill HARRIS
44 Development Assistant .... Mrs. Tricia REIMAN
26 Director of External Relationships ....Mr. John OH
125 President Emeritus ....Dr. David ROSS

† (f.k.a. Graduate Institute of Applied Linguistics)

Dallas Theological Seminary (G)

3909 Swiss Avenue, Dallas TX 75204-6493
County: Dallas FICE Identification: 003562
Unit ID: 224305
Telephone: (214) 887-5000 Carnegie Class: Spec-4-yr-Faith
FAX Number: (214) 887-5504 Calendar System: Semester
URL: www.dts.edu
Established: 1924 Annual Graduate Tuition & Fees: N/A
Enrollment: 2,447 Coed
Affiliation or Control: Independent Non-Profit IRS Status: 501(c)3
Highest Offering: Doctorate; No Undergraduates
Accreditation: SC, THEOL

01 President ....Dr. Mark M. YARBROUGH
05 Vice President for Education .... Dr. George HILLMAN
10 VP for Business & Finance/CFO .... Mr. David TARRANT
32 Dean of Student Life ....Rev. Herman BAXTER
111 Sr VP for Advancement ....Ms. Kimberly B. TILL
11 Sr VP for Operations/COO .... Mr. Robert F. RIGGS
26 VP for Communication and Community ....Mr. Joshua P. WINN
27 Exec Dir of Mktg and Communications ....Mr. Kraig MCNUTT
102 Exec Dir Dallas Seminary Found ....Mr. Scott TALBOT
20 Academic Dean ....Dr. James H. THAMES
12 Dean of DTS Houston ....Dr. Pierre CANNINGS
12 Dean DTS Washington DC ....Dr. Rodney ORR
58 Director of PhD Studies .... Dr. Vic A. ANDERSON
58 Director of DMin Studies .... Dr. D. Scott BARFOOT
09 Dir Inst Research & Effectiveness ....Dr. Jared AVERY
06 Registrar ....Ms. Sabrina HOPSON
88 Exec Dir of Leadership Center ....Mr. Bill HENDRICKS
88 Exec Dir of Cultural Engagement ....Dr. Darrell L. BOCK
07 Director of Admissions .... Mr. Luke BRYANT
08 Library Director .... Mr. Marvin T. HUNN, II
84 VP for Enrollment Svcs & Educ Tech ....Dr. John DYER
29 Director of Alumni Services .... Dr. Greg A. HATTEBERG
36 Director of Placement ....Dr. Paul E. PETTIT
42 Campus Pastor ....Dr. Joe M. ALLEN, JR.
35 Assistant Dean of Students .... Ms. Rebecca JOWERS
88 Dean of Academic Admin ....Mr. Nate MCKANNA
13 Director of Information Technology ....Mr. Kevin COX
19 Chief of Campus Police ....Mr. John S. BLOOM
10 VP for Global Ministries ....Dr. Michael ORTIZ
39 Manager of Housing .... Ms. Sarah CHAPELL
106 Director Online Education ....Mr. Martin MCKEE
88 Director of Chinese Studies ....Dr. Samuel CHIA
88 Director of DTS en Espanol ....Dr. Williams TRIGUEROS
38 Director of Counseling Services .... Mr. Robert C. DUCKWORTH
21 Controller ....Ms. Sonja FLORES
40 Director of Book Center .... Ms. Rachelle CERDA
85 Dir for Intl Stdnt Svcs/Disability ....Mr. Voltaire CACAL
04 Executive Asst to the President ....Ms. Michelle B. SCHIWIETZ
15 Director Human Resources ....Ms. Karen MCDONALD
88 Dir of Maintenance Operations ....Mr. Brian GERBERICH
18 Exec Dir of Facilities Operations ....Mr. Glenn MONRO
110 Executive Dir for Advancement .... Ms. Teri O'CONNOR
112 Director of Donor Management ....Mr. Jacob BECK
101 Communication and Board Coordinator .. Ms. Margaret TOLLIVER
37 Director Student Financial Aid ....Mrs. Jennifer MCCORMACK
96 Director of Purchasing ....Ms. Lisa REEVES

Del Mar College (H)

101 Baldwin Blvd., Corpus Christi TX 78404-3897
County: Nueces FICE Identification: 003563
Unit ID: 224350
Telephone: (361) 698-1200 Carnegie Class: Assoc/HVT-High Trad
FAX Number: (361) 698-1559 Calendar System: Semester
URL: www.delmar.edu
Established: 1935 Annual Undergrad Tuition & Fees (In-District): $4,820
Enrollment: 10,678 Coed
Affiliation or Control: Local IRS Status: 501(c)3
Highest Offering: Baccalaureate
Accreditation: SC, ACFEI, ADNUR, ART, CAHIIM, COARC, DA, DH, EMT, MLTAD, MUS, NAEYC, OTA, PTAA, RAD, SURGT, THEA

01 President & CEO ....Dr. Mark ESCAMILLA
43 General Counsel ....Mr. Augustin RIVERA, JR.
03 Exec Vice Pres/Chief Operating Ofcr ....Ms. Lenora KEAS
05 VP & Chief Academic Officer .... Dr. Jonda HALCOMB
10 VP & Chief Financial Officer ....Mr. Raul GARCIA
13 Vice Pres/Chief Information Ofcr .... Mr. Ali KOLAHDOUZ
11 VP Administration & Human Resources . Ms. Tammy MCDONALD
32 Vice President for Student Affairs ....Ms. Patricia BENAVIDES-DOMINGUEZ
18 VP/Chief Physical Facilities Ofcr .... Mr. John STRYBOS
108 AVP Planning & Inst Effectiveness .... Dr. Kristina WILSON
35 AVP for Student Affairs .... Ms. Cheryl SANDERS
101 Dir of CEO Office/Board Relations ....Ms. Delia PEREZ
19 Interim Chief of Police ....Ms. Lauren WHITE
26 Exec Dir Communication & Marketing ...... Ms. Lorette WILLIAMS
30 Exec Director of Development ....Ms. Mary MCQUEEN
88 Director Strategic Initiatives ....Ms. Kiwana DENSON
84 Dean Student Outreach/Enroll Svcs .... Ms. Graciela MARTINEZ
124 Dean Student Engagement & Retention ...... Ms. Rita HERNANDEZ

57 Dean Comm/Fine Arts & Soc Sciences ....Dr. Cynthia BRIDGES
50 Dean Business/Ent/Health Sciences ....Ms. Jennifer SRAMEK
88 Dean Industry & Public Service ....Mr. Davis MERRELL
81 Dean Sci/Tech/Eng/Math/Kin/Edu ....Dr. Jack SOUTHARD
51 Dean CE & Off Campus Programs ....Dr. Leonard RIVERA
103 Dean Workforce Pgms/Corporate Svcs ....Mr. Daniel KORUS
08 Dean of Learning Resources ....Mr. Cody GREGG
21 Comptroller/Revenue Budget Admin ....Mr. John J. JOHNSON
114 Dir Accounting/Budget Officer ....Dr. Cathy WEST
96 Director of Purchasing/Business Svc ....Mr. David DAVILA
88 Dir Environmental/Health/Safety ....Mr. Jack TWEDDLE
37 Director of Financial Aid ....Mr. Joseph RUIZ
06 Registrar ....Ms. Elizabeth ADAMSON
35 Dir Student Leadership/Campus Life ....Ms. Beverly CAGE
09 Director of Institutional Research ....Mr. Sushil PALLEMONI
15 Director of Human Resources ....Mr. Jerry W. HENRY
117 Director of Risk Management ....Ms. Jessica ALANIZ
88 Director of Payroll ....Ms. Katrina GARCIA
14 Deputy Chief Information Officer ....Ms. Jessica MONTALVO-CUMMINGS
119 Information Security Officer ....Mr. Gregory PALMER
30 Director of Development ....Mr. Matthew BUSBY
108 Dir Accreditation & Assessment ....Ms. Sydney SAUMBY

East Texas Baptist University (A)

One Tiger Drive, Marshall TX 75670-1498

County: Harrison — FICE Identification: 003564 — Unit ID: 224527
Telephone: (903) 935-7963 — Carnegie Class: Masters/S
FAX Number: (903) 938-7798 — Calendar System: Semester
URL: www.etbu.edu
Established: 1912 — Annual Undergrad Tuition & Fees: $27,640
Enrollment: 1,714 — Coed
Affiliation or Control: Baptist — IRS Status: 501(c)3
Highest Offering: Master's
Accreditation: SC, MLS, MUS, NURSE

01 President ....Dr. J. Blair BLACKBURN
05 Provost & Vice Pres Acad Affairs ....Dr. Thomas SANDERS
10 Vice Pres Financial Affairs ....Mr. Lee FERGUSON
111 Vice Pres University Advancement ....Dr. Scott BRYANT
41 Vice Pres Student Engage/Athletics ....Mr. Ryan ERWIN
26 Vice Pres Strat Initiatives & Comm ....Mrs. Sara BRAUN
84 Vice President for Enrollment ....Dr. Jeremy JOHNSTON
20 Asst Provost for Academic Affairs ....Mrs. Elizabeth PONDER
21 Asst Vice Pres for Financial Affs ....Mrs. Joanna HAMMOND
32 Asst Vice Pres Student Engagement ....Mrs. Holly EDWARDS
15 Assoc Vice Pres Human Resources ....Ms. Tara BACHTEL
11 Asst Vice Pres for Univ Operations ....Mr. Chris CRAWFORD
55 Asst Provost/Dir of Adult Ed & Grad ....Mr. Vince BLANKENSHIP
09 Dean Acad Services & Inst Research ....Dr. Marty WARREN
107 Dean School of Professional Studies ....Dr. Joseph BROWN
53 Dean School of Education ....Dr. Amber DAUB
73 Int Dean School of Christian Stds ....Dr. Sandy HOOVER
83 Dean Sch of Natural/Social Sci ....Dr. Laurie SMITH
50 Interim Dean School of Business ....Dr. Dale SIMS
79 Dean School of Humanities ....Dr. Sandy HOOVER
57 Dean School of Comm & Perf Arts ....Dr. Justin HODGES
106 Dean of Online Education ....Dr. Colleen HALUPA
66 Dean School of Nursing ....Dr. Rebekah GRIGSBY
13 Director of Inst Technology ....Mr. Barry HALE
08 Dean of Library Services ....Vacant
37 Director of Financial Aid ....Mrs. Linda SLAWSON
88 Director Baptist Student Ministry ....Mr. David GRIFFIN
40 Bookstore Manager ....Ms. Crystal HEBEBRAND
18 Director of Physical Operations ....Mr. Stephen RATCLIFF
85 Dir Great Commission Ctr/Global Ed ....Dr. Lisa SEELEY
121 Director of Academic Success ....Dr. Bryan MEAD
19 Director of Security & Compliance ....Mr. Larry NORTHCUTT
58 Director of Graduate Programs ....Ms. Viridiana JASSO DE LA GARZA
39 Director of Residence Life ....Mrs. Desirae' BRADLEY
35 Director of Student Activities ....Ms. Laura COURSEY
06 University Registrar ....Mr. Troy WHITE
42 Dean of Spiritual Life ....Dr. Scott STEVENS
29 Director of Alumni Relations ....Mrs. Cari JOHNSON
04 Assistant to the President ....Mr. Scott MCCURDY

El Paso Community College (B)

P.O. Box 20500, El Paso TX 79998

County: El Paso — FICE Identification: 010387 — Unit ID: 224642
Telephone: (915) 831-2000 — Carnegie Class: Assoc/HT-High Trad
FAX Number: N/A — Calendar System: Semester
URL: www.epcc.edu
Established: 1969 — Annual Undergrad Tuition & Fees (In-District): $3,274
Enrollment: 26,034 — Coed
Affiliation or Control: Local — IRS Status: 501(c)3
Highest Offering: Associate Degree
Accreditation: SC, ADNUR, CAHIIM, COARC, DA, DH, DMS, EMT, MAC, MLTAD, PTAA, RAD, SURGT

01 President ....Dr. William SERRATA
05 Vice Pres Instruction & WF Educ ....Dr. Steven SMITH
11 Vice Pres Financial and Admin Ops .Ms. Josette SHAUGHNESSY
13 Vice Pres Information Tech/CIO ....Vacant
32 Vice Pres Student & Enroll Svcs ....Dr. Amaya CARLOS
108 Vice Pres Rsrch/Accred & Planning ....Dr. Julie PENLEY
114 AVP Budget and Financial Svcs ....Mr. Fernando FLORES
26 AVP External Rels/Comm and Dev ....Ms. Keri L. MOE
14 Int AVP Information Tech ....Mr. Marco FERNANDEZ
20 AVP Instruction & Student Success ....Dr. Paula MITCHELL
103 AVP Workforce and CE ....Mr. Blayne J. PRIMOZICH
12 Campus Dean Valle Verde ....Dr. Myshie M. PAGEL
12 Campus Dean Instructional Pgms NW ....Dr. Lydia TENA
12 Campus Dean Mission del Paso ....Mr. Joshua I. VILLALOBOS
12 Campus Dean Rio Grande ....Dr. Souraya HAJJAR
12 Campus Dean Trans Mountain ....Mr. Ernest R. WEBB, II
12 Campus Dean Valle Verde ....Ms. Susana RODARTE
66 Dean Nursing RG ....Ms. Paula G. MEAGHER
76 Dean Hlth Career/TechEd/Math/Sci RG ....Dr. Souraya HAJJAR
81 Dean Math/Sci/Career Tech Educ TM ....Mr. Ernest R. WEBB, II
49 Int Dean Arch/Arts/Math/Science VV ....Dr. Allison BRUCE
57 Dean Comm/Performing Arts VV ....Mr. Daniel GUERRA
88 Dean Art Comm SS TM ....Ms. Terri L. MANN
88 Dean Arts Comm CTE SS ....Mr. Brian KIRBY
53 Dean Educ/Career/Tech VV ....Dr. Myshie M. PAGEL
88 Dean ATC VV ....Dr. Olga L. VALERIO
88 Dean Dual Credit & Early Col ....Ms. Maria Antonieta BADILLO
88 Exec Dir Empl Rel & Compliance ....Ms. Audry ORTEGON
15 Exec Dir Human Resources ....Dr. Andrew M. PENA
105 Exec Dir Net Sys & Support Svcs ....Mr. Marco A. FERNANDEZ
88 Exec Dir IT Soft A Analytics ....Mr. Abraham A. HUBAIL
37 Exec Dir Student Financial Aid ....Ms. Ines LOPEZ
18 Exec Director Physical Plant ....Mr. Richard L. LOBATO
07 Exec Director Admissions/Registrar ....Dr. Cassandra M. LACHICA-CHAVEZ
102 Exec Dir Resource Dev/Foundation ....Dr. Dolores GROSS
41 Athletic Director ....Mr. Felix HINOJOSA
25 Dir Grants Mgmt & Dev ....Mr. Robert T. ELLIOTT
45 Dir Institutional Effectiveness ....Vacant
84 Dir Recruitment Services ....Mr. Talamantes J. MICHAEL
88 Dir WF Strategic Initiatives .....Dr. Carmen AGUILERA-GOERNER
88 Dir Contract Opportunity Center ....Mr. Pablo ARMENDARIZ
23 Dir CE Health ....Ms. Cheryl L. STILES
88 Dir Small Business Dev Center ....Mr. Joseph C. FERGUSON
27 Int Dir Marketing/Cmty Rels ....Mr. James HEINEY
90 Dir Acad Computing Media Svc ....Mr. Sergio RAMOS
109 Dir Auxiliary Services ....Mr. Juan S. FLORES
45 Dir Institutional Planning ....Ms. Christina C. FRESCAS
88 Dir College Accred Compliance ....Ms. Mary Beth HAAN
88 Dir Curriculum Instruction Dev ....Ms. Yvette V. HUERTA
56 Dir Community Education Program ....Mr. Andres MURO
55 Dir Senior Adult Programs ....Ms. Mary A. YANEZ
51 Dir Dist Learning Support Svcs ....Ms. Luz E. CADENA
88 Dir Quality Enhancement Plan Assess ....Dr. Ondrea M. QUIROS
35 Int Dir Stdnt Ldrshp Campus Life ....Ms. Marlib GONZALEZ
36 Int Dir Career & Transfer Services ....Ms. Ines LOPEZ
88 Dir CE Bus Tech Ed Per ....Ms. Leticia GUERRA
96 Dir Purchasing & Contract Mgmt ....Mr. Ruben C. GALLARDO
09 Director Institutional Research ....Dr. Carol KAY
28 Int Dir Diversity & Inclusion Pgms ....Mr. Lee VASQUEZ
16 Dir Human Resources Development ...Mr. Alejandro HERNANDEZ
114 Director Budget ....Ms. Laura TELLEZ
22 Dir Ctr for Students w/Disabilities ....Ms. Maria LOPEZ
103 Director Workforce Development ....Vacant
121 Director Student Success ....Ms. Lucia M. RODRIGUEZ
88 Dir Law Enforcement Trng Academy ....Mr. Barry J. BOGLE
88 Dir Student Learning Outcomes ....Ms. Rebekah A. BELL
88 Project Dir Stemgrow Artic Program ....Vacant
19 Chief of Police ....Mr. Jose L. RAMIREZ
21 Comptroller ....Ms. Ana ZUNIGA
118 Assoc Dir Employee Benefits ....Ms. Victoria VIGGERS
04 Exec Asst to the President & BOT ....Ms. Pamela PAYNE

Fortis College (C)

1201 West Oaks Mall, Houston TX 77082

County: Harris — FICE Identification: 034244 — Unit ID: 392415
Telephone: (713) 266-6594 — Carnegie Class: Spec 2-yr-Health
FAX Number: (713) 782-5873 — Calendar System: Quarter
URL: https://www.fortis.edu/campuses/texas/houston-south.html
Established: — Annual Undergrad Tuition & Fees: N/A
Enrollment: 394 — Coed
Affiliation or Control: Proprietary — IRS Status: Proprietary
Highest Offering: Associate Degree
Accreditation: ACCSC, SURGT

01 Campus President ....Justin POND
05 Director of Education ....Lee Ann HIETT

Frank Phillips College (D)

PO Box 5118, Borger TX 79008-5118

County: Hutchinson — FICE Identification: 003568 — Unit ID: 224891
Telephone: (806) 457-4200 — Carnegie Class: Assoc/HT-High Non
FAX Number: (806) 457-4224 — Calendar System: Semester
URL: www.fpctx.edu
Established: 1948 — Annual Undergrad Tuition & Fees (In-District): $4,118
Enrollment: 1,575 — Coed
Affiliation or Control: Local — IRS Status: 501(c)3
Highest Offering: Associate Degree
Accreditation: SC

01 President ....Dr. Glendon FORGEY
05 EVP of Academic Affairs ....Dr. Shannon CARROLL
103 Dean of Workforce/CTE ....Ms. Taryn FRALEY
12 Provost of Allen Campus ....Ms. Cassi LAXTON
12 Provost of Rahll Campus ....Ms. Christy DOVAL
10 Chief Financial Officer ....Ms. Teri LANGWELL
111 VP Inst Advancement ....Ms. Jackie BRAND
26 Dir Marketing/Communications ....Vacant
38 Director Student Counseling/Testing ....Ms. Becky GREEN
09 AVP Institutional Research ....Ms. Michele STEVENS
08 Director of the Library ....Mr. Jason PRICE
37 Dir Student Financial Services ....Ms. Shannon CROSSLAND
18 Director Physical Plant ....Ms. Regina HANEY

Galen College of Nursing (E)

7411 John Smith Drive, Suite 1400, San Antonio TX 78229

Telephone: (210) 733-3056 — Identification: 770538
Accreditation: &SC, ADNUR, NURSE

† Branch campus of Galen College of Nursing, Louisville, KY

Galveston College (F)

4015 Avenue Q, Galveston TX 77550-7496

County: Galveston — FICE Identification: 004972 — Unit ID: 224961
Telephone: (409) 944-4242 — Carnegie Class: Assoc/HVT-Mix Trad/Non
FAX Number: (409) 944-1500 — Calendar System: Semester
URL: www.gc.edu
Established: 1966 — Annual Undergrad Tuition & Fees (In-District): $2,950
Enrollment: 2,060 — Coed
Affiliation or Control: State/Local — IRS Status: 501(c)3
Highest Offering: Baccalaureate
Accreditation: SC, ADNUR, DMS, EMT, NMT, RAD, RTT, SURGT

01 President ....Dr. Myles SHELTON
05 Vice President of Instruction ....Dr. Cissy MATTHEWS
11 VP for Admin/Student Services ....Dr. Van PATTERSON
32 Associate VP of Student Services ....Mr. Ron C. CRUMEDY
75 Dean of Tech & Prof Education ....Ms. Vera LEWIS-JASPER
30 Dir of Development/GC Foundation ....Ms. Kelly KENNEDY
10 Comptroller/CFO ....Mr. M. Jeff ENGBROCK
13 Director of Info Technology ....Mr. Jason SMITH
26 Director of Public Affairs ....Mr. Edgar CHRNKO
15 Dir Human Resources/Risk Management ....Dr. Mary Jan LANTZ
41 Athletic Director/Head Coach ....Ms. Kelly RAINES
07 Director Admissions/Registrar ....Mr. Scott BRANUM
66 Director of Nursing ....Ms. Donna CARLIN
09 Director Inst Effectiveness/Rsrch ....Ms. Carmen ALLEN
18 Director of Facilities ....Mr. Tracy MORGAN
08 Dir of Library/Learning Resources ....Ms. Telishia MICKENS
37 Director of Financial Aid ....Ms. Meghann NASH
04 Executive Assistant ....Ms. Breanne E. LOREFICE

Grace School of Theology (G)

3705 College Park Drive, The Woodlands TX 77384

County: Montgomery — Identification: 667100 — Unit ID: 481401
Telephone: (877) 476-8674 — Carnegie Class: Spec-4-yr-Faith
FAX Number: (877) 735-2867 — Calendar System: Semester
URL: www.gsot.edu
Established: 2002 — Annual Undergrad Tuition & Fees: $6,480
Enrollment: 590 — Coed
Affiliation or Control: Independent Non-Profit — IRS Status: 501(c)3
Highest Offering: Doctorate
Accreditation: THEOL, TRACS

01 President ....Dr. Dave ANDERSON
43 Exec Vice President/General Counsel ....Mr. Tom KRUPPSTADT
05 Provost/Chief Student Svcs Ofcr ....Mr. Mark HAYWOOD
111 Vice Pres Advancement/COO ....Mr. Daniel LABRY
32 Dean of Students ....Mr. Willie GAINES

Grayson College (H)

6101 Grayson Drive, Denison TX 75020-8299

County: Grayson — FICE Identification: 003570 — Unit ID: 225070
Telephone: (903) 465-6030 — Carnegie Class: Assoc/HVT-Mix Trad/Non
FAX Number: (903) 463-5284 — Calendar System: Semester
URL: www.grayson.edu
Established: 1963 — Annual Undergrad Tuition & Fees (In-District): $3,872
Enrollment: 4,066 — Coed
Affiliation or Control: State/Local — IRS Status: 501(c)3
Highest Offering: Baccalaureate
Accreditation: SC, ACFEI, ADNUR, DA, EMT, MLTAD, NAEYC, NUR

01 President ....Dr. Jeremy P. MCMILLEN
05 Vice President of Instruction ....Dr. Dava WASHBURN
32 Dean of Student Affairs ....Dr. Molly HARRIS
10 Vice President for Business Svcs ....Ms. Carolyn KASDORF
13 VP for Information Technology ....Mr. Gary PAIKOWSKI
04 Assistant to the President ....Mrs. Karen BOLLINGER
102 Exec Dir Grayson College Foundation ....Mr. Randy TRUXAL
07 Director of Admissions/Registrar ....Ms. Brandi FURR
37 Director of Financial Aid ....Ms. Stephanie MARTIN
14 Director of Network Services ....Mr. Mike BROWN
19 Director Public Safety ....Mr. Roger KISLOSKI
26 Director Marketing & Communications ....Ms. Rhea BERMEL
21 Director of Fiscal Services ....Mr. Danny HYATT
41 Director of Athletics ....Mr. Mike MCBRAYER
40 Bookstore Manager ....Ms. Helen BERGMAN
08 Director of Library ....Mrs. Lisa HEBERT
84 Dean of Strategic Enrollment ....Dr. Debbie SMARR
103 Exec Dir Ctr for Workforce Learning ....Dr. Djuna FORRESTER
15 Director Human Resources Office ....Mrs. Robyn VOIGHT

35 Dir Student Life & Development ... Ms. Shantee SIEBUHR
20 Dean of Academic Studies ... Dr. Chase MACHEN
12 Dean of South Campus ... Dr. Logan MAXWELL
101 Secretary of the Institution/Board ... Vacant
104 International Student Advisor ... Mr. Bradley MCCLENNY
18 Director of Maintenance ... Mr. Matt CORDER
25 Chief Grants Administrator ... Vacant
38 Dir Student Counseling/Social Svcs ... Mrs. Barbara MALONE

Hallmark University (A)

10401 IH-10 W, San Antonio TX 78230-1737
County: Bexar FICE Identification: 010509
Unit ID: 225201
Telephone: (210) 690-9000 Carnegie Class: Bac-Diverse
FAX Number: (210) 826-2876 Calendar System: Semester
URL: www.hallmarkuniversity.edu
Established: 1969 Annual Undergrad Tuition & Fees: N/A
Enrollment: 987 Coed
Affiliation or Control: Independent Non-Profit IRS Status: 501(c)3
Highest Offering: Master's
Accreditation: ACCSC

01 President/CEO ... Mr. Joseph B. FISHER
45 Sr VP of Institutional Strategy ... Mr. Taylor MERCIER
10 VP of Financial Affairs ... Ms. Roxanne DARTY
32 VP Student Affairs/Support Services ... Dr. Samuel (Lee) BEAUMONT
05 VP Academic Affairs/Workforce Dev ... Vacant
111 Vice President of Philanthropy ... Ms. Marion LEE
84 Vice President Enrollment ... Mr. Joshua POND

Hardin-Simmons University (B)

2200 Hickory, Abilene TX 79698-0001
County: Taylor FICE Identification: 003571
Unit ID: 225247
Telephone: (325) 670-1000 Carnegie Class: DU-Mod
FAX Number: (325) 670-1267 Calendar System: Semester
URL: www.hsutx.edu
Established: 1891 Annual Undergrad Tuition & Fees: $31,364
Enrollment: 2,128 Coed
Affiliation or Control: Baptist IRS Status: 501(c)3
Highest Offering: Doctorate
Accreditation: SC, ACBSP, ARCPA, CACREP, MUS, NURSE, PTA, @SP, SW, THEOL

01 President ... Mr. Eric I. BRUNTMYER
05 Provost & Chief Academic Officer ... Dr. Christopher L. MCNAIR
10 Vice President for Finance ... Dr. Jodie MCGAUGHEY
30 VP for Institutional Advancement ... Mr. Mike HAMMACK
84 VP for Enrollment Management ... Mrs. Vicki HOUSE
32 Vice President for Student Life ... Mrs. Stacey MARTIN
49 Dean College of Liberal Arts ... Dr. Stephen COOK
50 Dean Kelley College of Business ... Dr. Robert TUCKER
76 Dean College of Health Professions ... Dr. Janelle O'CONNELL
66 Dean School of Nursing ... Dr. Donalyn ALEXANDER
64 Assoc Dean School of Music ... Dr. Jeffrey COTTRELL
73 Assoc Dean Logsdon Sch of Theology ... Dr. Larry MCGRAW
53 Assoc Dean Irvin Sch of Education ... Dr. Renee COLLINS
13 Assoc Vice Pres Technical Services ... Mr. Travis P. SEEKINS
21 Asst VP for Finance and Controller ... Ms. Mary Beth KOUBA
38 Assoc VP Academic Advising/Retent ... Mrs. Gracie CARROLL
08 University Librarian ... Ms. Elizabeth NORMAN
06 Registrar ... Mrs. Kacey HIGGINS
29 Assoc VP for Alumni Engagement ... Ms. Heather HADLOCK
42 Chaplain ... Dr. Travis CRAVER
39 Director of Residence Life ... Vacant
15 Director of Human Resources ... Ms. Tera GIBSON
27 Dir of Univ Marketing ... Ms. Nikki SLATER
37 Dir Student Fin Aid & Scholarships ... Ms. Monica SMART
18 Facilities Services Director ... Mr. Tim MCCARRY
41 Athletic Director ... Mr. John M. NEESE
85 Director of International Studies ... Dr. Allan J. LANDWER

Hill College (C)

112 Lamar Drive, Hillsboro TX 76645-2711
County: Hill FICE Identification: 003573
Unit ID: 225371
Telephone: (254) 659-7500 Carnegie Class: Assoc/HT-High Non
FAX Number: (254) 582-7591 Calendar System: Semester
URL: www.hillcollege.edu
Established: 1923 Annual Undergrad Tuition & Fees (In-District): $2,982
Enrollment: 4,038 Coed
Affiliation or Control: Local IRS Status: 501(c)3
Highest Offering: Associate Degree
Accreditation: SC, CVT, EMT

01 President ... Dr. Pamela BOEHM
04 Executive Asst to the President ... Ms. Vonnie MORPHEW
05 Vice President Instruction ... Dr. Kerry SCHINDLER
25 Vice President External Affairs ... Ms. Jessyca BROWN
10 Vice Pres Administrative Services ... Mr. Billy D. CURBO
32 Vice President Student Services ... Ms. Lizza TRENKLE
13 Vice Pres Information Technology ... Mrs. Jessie WHITE
21 Dean Financial Services ... Mrs. Debbie GERIK
08 Librarian - Hill Campus ... Ms. Eve BOWEN
08 Library Services Director ... Mr. Kevin HENARD
15 Director Human Resources ... Mrs. Jamie JASKA
12 Exec Dir JCC/Dean of Students ... Mr. Craig BALCH
41 Athletic Director ... Mr. Paul BROWN

26 Coord Ext Affairs/Cmty Rels/Events ... Ms. Ashley TELLO
09 Dir of Institutional Effectiveness ... Ms. Sherry DAVIS
37 Director of Financial Aid ... Ms. Kathleen PUSTEJOVSKY
18 Director Physical Plant ... Vacant
30 Director Development ... Vacant

Houston Baptist University (D)

7502 Fondren Road, Houston TX 77074-3298
County: Harris FICE Identification: 003576
Unit ID: 225399
Telephone: (281) 649-3000 Carnegie Class: Masters/L
FAX Number: (281) 649-3012 Calendar System: Semester
URL: www.hbu.edu
Established: 1960 Annual Undergrad Tuition & Fees: $34,500
Enrollment: 3,963 Coed
Affiliation or Control: Southern Baptist IRS Status: 501(c)3
Highest Offering: Doctorate
Accreditation: SC, NUR, NURSE

01 President ... Dr. Robert SLOAN
05 Provost/VP Acad Affairs ... Dr. Stan NAPPER
10 CFO/COO ... Ms. Sandra MOONEY
111 VP Advancement & Univ Relations ... Ms. Sharon SAUNDERS
84 VP Enrollment Management ... Dr. James STEEN
26 VP Innovation & Strategic Mktg ... Dr. Jerome JOHNSTON
112 VP Major Gifts ... Mr. Charles BACARISSE
106 VP Online/Digital Learning/Pampell ... Dr. Steve PETERSON
20 Associate Provost ... Dr. Jeffrey GREEN
18 Assoc VP Facilities & Campus Opers ... Mr. John HOLMES
114 Assist VP Planning & Budget ... Ms. Valerie WADDLE
79 Dean College of Arts & Humanities ... Dr. Jodey HINZE
50 Dean Dunham College of Business ... Mr. Michael ROME
81 Dean Col of Science & Engineering ... Dr. Katie EVANS
92 Director Honors College ... Dr. Gary HARTENBURG
53 Dean College of Education & Beh Sci ... Dr. Kristie CERLING
57 Dean College of Arts & Humanities ... Dr. Jodey HINZE
66 Dean School Nursing & Allied Health ... Dr. Carol LAVENDER
41 Athletic Director ... Mr. Steve MONIACI
06 Director of Academic Records ... Mr. Jean TARRATS RIVERA
08 Director of Libraries ... Mr. Dean RILEY
42 Assoc University Minister ... Mr. Saleim KAHLEH
21 Assoc VP Financial Operations ... Ms. Loree WATSON
39 Int Dir Res Life /Dir Student Life ... Ms. MonSher SPENCER
13 Chief Information Officer (IT) ... Ms. Rosa BEAUGENE
09 Sr Dir Inst Rsrch & Effectiveness ... Mr. Todd COCKRELL
32 Assistant Provost ... Mr. Ed BORGES
88 SACS Liaison ... Ms. Lisa COVINGTON
04 Admin Asst to the President ... Ms. Karen FRANCIES
15 Director of Human Resources ... Ms. Jill STRUTTON
36 Dir of Career & Calling ... Mr. Aaron SWARTS
37 Dir Financial Aid & Scholarships ... Ms. Marisela MALDONADO
96 Cost Control Analyst ... Ms. Jody WILDING
07 Director Undergraduate Admissions ... Ms. Tiffany CHARLES
90 Director Academic Technology ... Ms. Tia CASTER
108 Sr Director Assessment & Compliance ... Ms. Lisa COVINGTON
19 Director Security/Safety ... Chief John KARSHNER
29 Asst VP Univ Relations/Events ... Ms. Candace DESROSIERS
30 Development Officer ... Ms. Sarah DENNIS
43 General Counsel ... Mr. Tyler BOYD
44 Director Annual Giving ... Ms. Page HERNANDEZ
91 Dir Enterprise Applications/ITS ... Ms. Linda PEREZ
73 Dean School Christian Thought ... Dr. Philip TALLON
101 Board Liaison ... Ms. Sharon SAUNDERS
105 Asst VP Recruitment Marketing ... Mr. Cary DELMARK
38 Director Counseling Ctr/Gideon Inst ... Dr. Diane LAMBERSON
104 Dir Spahr-Tan Center/Study Abroad ... Ms. Leslie SHELTON

Houston Community College (E)

3100 Main Street, Houston TX 77002
County: Harris FICE Identification: 010633
Unit ID: 225423
Telephone: (713) 718-2000 Carnegie Class: Assoc/HT-High Trad
FAX Number: N/A Calendar System: Semester
URL: www.hccs.edu
Established: 1971 Annual Undergrad Tuition & Fees (In-State): $4,344
Enrollment: 48,329 Coed
Affiliation or Control: State IRS Status: 501(c)3
Highest Offering: Associate Degree
Accreditation: SC, ACBSP, ACFEI, ACPHA, ART, CAHIIM, COARC, DA, DH, DMS, EMT, HT, MAC, MLTAD, NAEYC, NMT, OTA, PTAA, RAD, SURGT

01 Chancellor ... Dr. Cesar MALDONADO
04 Sr Exec Assistant to the Chancellor ... Ms. Keiana BLAKE
10 Sr VC Finance & Admin/CFO ... Mr. Marshall B. HEINS
43 General Counsel ... Mr. E. Ashley SMITH
05 VC Instructional Services/CAO ... Dr. Norma PEREZ
32 VC Student Services ... Dr. Shantay GRAYS
45 VC Plng & Inst Effect/Chf of Staff ... Dr. Kurt EWEN
26 VC Public Info/Comm & Ext Affairs ... Mr. Remmele YOUNG
103 VC Workforce Ed/Pres Southwest Col ... Dr. Madeline BURILLO-HOPKINS
12 President Central College ... Dr. Muddassir SIDDIQI
12 President Coleman College ... Dr. Phillip NICOTERA
12 President Northeast College ... Dr. Michael EDWARDS
12 President Northwest College ... Dr. Zachary HODGES
12 President Southeast College ... Dr. Frances VILLAGRAN-GLOVER
106 President Online College ... Dr. Margaret FORD FISHER
13 Chief Information Officer ... Ms. Fheryl J. PRESTAGE
15 Chief Human Resources Officer ... Ms. Izzy ANDERSON
18 Chief Facilities Officer ... Vacant

88 AVC College Readiness ... Dr. Desmond LEWIS
20 AVC Curriculum & Learning ... Mr. Miguel RAMOS
84 Int AVC Enrollment Management ... Dr. Betty FORTUNE
35 AVC Student Engagement/Success ... Dr. Debbie HAMILTON
20 AVC Instructional Services ... Dr. Jerome DRAIN
21 AVC Finance & Accounting ... Ms. Devi BALA
09 AVC Research Analytics & Support ... Dr. Andrea BURRIDGE
121 AVC Special Programs/Success ... Ms. Chassity HOLLIMAN-DOUGLAS
28 DEI Officer ... Dr. Donna DAVIS
102 Executive Director Foundation ... Ms. Karen SCHMIDT
114 Exec Director Budget & Treasury Ops ... Dr. Karla BENDER
37 Exec Director Student Financial Aid ... Ms. JoEllen PRICE
88 Exec Director Accounting ... Ms. Frederica WATSON
08 Exec Director Library Resources ... Mr. Michael STAFFORD
96 Exec Dir Procurement Operations ... Mr. Joseph GAVIN
22 Director EEO/Compliance ... Mr. David CROSS
07 Director of Admissions & Registrar ... Ms. Mary LEMBURG
113 Director Student Financial Svcs ... Ms. Paula STAPLETON
116 Director Internal Auditing ... Mr. Terrance CORRINGAN
101 Director Board Services ... Ms. Sharon WRIGHT
60 Dean English/Communications ... Ms. Amy TAN
65 Dean Earth/Life/Natural Science ... Dr. Tosha BARCLAY
49 Dean Liberal Arts & Humanities ... Ms. Helen GRAHAM
81 Dean Mathematics ... Mr. Timor SEVER
83 Dean Social & Behavioral Science ... Mr. Fabian VEGA
66 Dean Nursing ... Vacant
106 Dean Online College/Instruct Tech ... Vacant
50 COE Dean Business/Logistics ... Ms. Connie PORTER
46 COE Dean Arch/Design/Construction ... Mr. Kris ASPER
59 COE Dean Consumer Arts & Sci ... Ms. Suzette BRIMMER
72 COE Dean Digital & Info Tech ... Mr. Samir SABER
54 COE Dean Engineering ... Mr. John VASSELLI
88 COE Dean Global Energy ... Mr. Mehmet ARGIN
76 COE Dean Health Science ... Mr. Jeff GRICAR
88 COE Dean Material Science/Smart Mfg ... Mr. Urbina ALBERTO
88 COE Dean Public Safety ... Mr. Alvin COLLINS
57 COE Dean Visual & Performing Arts ... Ms. Colleen REILLY
88 COE Dean Automotive Technology ... Mr. David VOGEL
53 COE Dean Education Professions ... Vacant
88 COE Dean Resiliency ... Vacant

Houston Graduate School of Theology (F)

4300-C West Bellfort, Houston TX 77035
County: Harris FICE Identification: 023202
Unit ID: 246345
Telephone: (713) 942-9505 Carnegie Class: Spec-4-yr-Faith
FAX Number: (713) 942-9506 Calendar System: Semester
URL: www.hgst.edu
Established: 1983 Annual Graduate Tuition & Fees: N/A
Enrollment: 131 Coed
Affiliation or Control: Independent Non-Profit IRS Status: 501(c)3
Highest Offering: Doctorate; No Undergraduates
Accreditation: THEOL

01 President ... Dr. Becky L. TOWNE
04 Executive Assistant ... Dr. Rita H. JENKINS
37 Financial Aid Officer ... Ms. Linda LONG

Houston International College-Cardiotech Ultrasound School (G)

12135 Bissonnet, Ste E, Houston TX 77099
County: Harris FICE Identification: 041385
Unit ID: 458034
Telephone: (281) 495-0078 Carnegie Class: Spec 2-yr-Health
FAX Number: (281) 495-5618 Calendar System: Semester
URL: www.cardiotech.org
Established: 2003 Annual Undergrad Tuition & Fees: $11,868
Enrollment: 73 Coed
Affiliation or Control: Proprietary IRS Status: Proprietary
Highest Offering: Associate Degree
Accreditation: ABHES

01 CEO/Director ... Ms. Joan DOUGLAS
05 Director of Education ... Dr. Yasser SHERKAWY

Howard College (H)

1001 Birdwell Lane, Big Spring TX 79720-3799
County: Howard FICE Identification: 003574
Unit ID: 225520
Telephone: (432) 264-5000 Carnegie Class: Assoc/MT-VT-High Non
FAX Number: (432) 264-5623 Calendar System: Semester
URL: www.howardcollege.edu
Established: 1945 Annual Undergrad Tuition & Fees (In-District): $3,980
Enrollment: 3,674 Coed
Affiliation or Control: State/Local IRS Status: 501(c)3
Highest Offering: Associate Degree
Accreditation: SC, ADNUR, COARC, DH, EMT, RAD, SURGT

01 President ... Dr. Cheryl T. SPARKS
03 Executive Vice President ... Dr. Amy BURCHETT
10 Chief Business Ofcr/Internal Audit ... Mr. Steve SMITH
18 Chief Ops/Safety/Security Officer ... Mr. Fabian SERRANO
10 Chief Fiscal Officer/Controller ... Mrs. Brenda CLAXTON
08 Dean of Libraries/County Librarian ... Mrs. Mavour BRASWELL
13 Chief Tech/System/Data Sec Ofcr ... Mr. Eric HANSEN
106 Dean of eLearning & Instruction ... Ms. Jenee HIGGINS

37	Dean Financial Aid	Mrs. Candice MALDONADO
26	Director Information/Marketing	Mrs. Cindy SMITH
88	Special Projects Officer	Mr. Terry HANSEN
15	Chief Human Resources Officer	Mrs. Rhonda KERNICK
12	Executive Dean SWCD	Mr. Danny CAMPBELL
12	Executive Dean San Angelo	Mrs. Pam CALLAN
06	District Registrar	Mrs. TaNeal RICHARDSON
21	Director Student Accounting	Ms. Laura FITZPATRICK
30	Director Institutional Advancement	Mrs. Brenda MADORE
76	Dean Health Professions	Mrs. Luci GABEHART
09	Research and Reporting Officer	Mrs. Rebecca VILLANUEVA
21	Director Financial Accounting	Mrs. Jeannie CARROLL
108	Director Institutional Assessment	Mr. Bryan STOKES
121	Director Student Support	Ms. Tara LISLE
41	Athletic Director	Mr. Kyle COOPER
04	Executive Asst to the President	Mrs. Emma GARCIA

Howard Payne University (A)

1000 Fisk Street, Brownwood TX 76801-2715
County: Brown — FICE Identification: 003575
Unit ID: 225548
Telephone: (325) 649-8900 — Carnegie Class: Bac-Diverse
FAX Number: (325) 649-8975 — Calendar System: Semester
URL: www.hputx.edu
Established: 1889 — Annual Undergrad Tuition & Fees: $29,198
Enrollment: 1,060 — Coed
Affiliation or Control: Baptist — IRS Status: 501(c)3
Highest Offering: Master's
Accreditation: SC, MUS, NURSE, SW

01	President	Dr. Cory HINES
05	Vice President for Academic Affairs	Dr. Donnie AUVENSHINE
10	VP for Finance & Admin/CFO	Mr. Mike RODGERS
30	Vice President for Development	Dr. Dale MEINECKE
84	AVP for Enrollment Management	Dr. Ben MARTIN
18	Director of Facilities	Mr. Roger DEWELL
13	AVP for Info Tech Svcs/CIO	Dr. Jodi GOODE
06	AVP of Univ Records/Dean of Gen Ed	Dr. Wendy MCNEELEY
37	Director of Student Financial Aid	Mrs. Karen LAQUEY
07	Director of Admission	Mrs. P.J GRAMLING
26	AVP for University Communications	Mr. Kyle C. MIZE
20	AVP for Academic Affairs	Vacant
41	Director of Athletics	Mr. Hunter SIMS
91	Database Administrator	Vacant
90	Dir of Net & Infrastructure Svcs	Mr. Russell EZZELL
29	AVP for Alumni Relations	Dr. Kalie LOWRIE
04	Special Assistant to President	Mrs. Laura BENOIT
38	University Counselor	Vacant
08	Director of Library Services	Mrs. Deborah DILL
81	Dean School of Science & Math	Dr. Gerry CLARKSON
50	Dean School of Business	Dr. Brad LEMLER
53	Dean School of Education	Dr. Kylah CLARK-GOFF
64	Dean School of Music & Fine Arts	Dr. Richard FIESE
73	Dean School of Christian Studies	Dr. Gary GRAMLING
79	Dean School of Humanities	Dr. Millard KIMERY
78	Dir Experiential Learning/Prof Dev	Dr. Jennifer MCNIECE
19	Chief of Police	Chief Bob PACATTE
110	Director of Development	Dr. Shannon SIMS

Huston-Tillotson University (B)

900 Chicon Street, Austin TX 78702-2795
County: Travis — FICE Identification: 003577
Unit ID: 225575
Telephone: (512) 505-3000 — Carnegie Class: Bac-Diverse
FAX Number: (512) 505-3190 — Calendar System: Semester
URL: www.htu.edu
Established: 1875 — Annual Undergrad Tuition & Fees: $14,703
Enrollment: 1,058 — Coed
Affiliation or Control: Multiple Protestant Denominations
IRS Status: 501(c)3
Highest Offering: Master's
Accreditation: SC, ACBSP

01	President & CEO	Dr. Melva K. WILLIAMS
04	Executive Assistant to President	Ms. Mona BAKSHI
11	VP/COO/Clerk to Board	Mr. Wayne KNOX
10	VP of Business Admin & Finance	Mrs. Charlene ROLLINS
111	VP of Institutional Advancement	Mrs. Linda Y. JACKSON
05	Provost/VP Academic Affairs	Dr. Archibald W. VANDERPUYE
20	Associate Provost	Dr. Beverly L. DOWNING
32	Dean of Student Affairs	Dr. Courtney ROBINSON
84	Dean of Enrollment Management	Mr. Johannis JOB
15	Dir of Human Resources	Ms. Quinika QUALLS
08	Dir of Library & Media Svcs	Ms. Cynthia CHARLES
36	Dir of Career & Grad Development	Mr. Ralph SIMPSON
41	Director of Athletics	Dr. Monique CARROLL
13	Dir of Information Technology	Mr. Malcolm HARAWAY
26	Dir of Marketing & Public Relation	Dr. Autumn CAVINESS
18	Director of Facilities Operations	Mr. Elbert GORDON
29	Director of Alumni Affairs	Mr. Gilbert CUTKELVIN
39	Dir of Campus & Resident Life	Ms. Sarah GAINES
88	Dir of Ctr for Academic Excellence	Ms. Jennifer P. MILES
38	Dir Counseling & Consultation Ctr	Ms. Stephany COLEMAN
42	University Chaplain	Rev. Donald E. BREWINGTON
07	Dir of Recruitment & Admission	Ms. Asia HANEY
49	Dean of College of Arts & Sciences	Dr. Michael HIRSCH
50	Dean School of Business/Technology	Dr. Rohan THOMPSON
09	Dir of Institutional Research	Mr. Marcus JACKSON
19	Director Campus Safety	Mr. Leslie YORK
100	Chief of Staff	Dr. Karen MAGID

30	Dir of Development	Ms. Daphne MCDOLE
06	Registrar	Mrs. Earnestine STRICKLAND
35	Dir of Student Svcs ADP	Ms. Shakitha STINSON
55	Dir of Adult Degree Program	Ms. Debra DELLEY

Interactive College of Technology (C)

213 West Southmore, Ste 101, Pasadena TX 77502
County: Harris — FICE Identification: 023313
Unit ID: 440776
Telephone: (713) 920-1120 — Carnegie Class: Assoc/HVT-Mix Trad/Non
FAX Number: (713) 477-0348 — Calendar System: Semester
URL: https://www.ict.edu/campuses/tx/pasadena/
Established: — Annual Undergrad Tuition & Fees: $9,890
Enrollment: 45 — Coed
Affiliation or Control: Proprietary — IRS Status: Proprietary
Highest Offering: Associate Degree
Accreditation: COE

01	Campus Director	Mr. Greg WEAVER

Jacksonville College (D)

105 B. J. Albritton Drive, Jacksonville TX 75766-4759
County: Cherokee — FICE Identification: 003579
Unit ID: 225876
Telephone: (903) 586-2518 — Carnegie Class: Assoc/HT-High Non
FAX Number: (903) 586-0743 — Calendar System: Semester
URL: www.jacksonville-college.edu
Established: 1899 — Annual Undergrad Tuition & Fees: $8,000
Enrollment: 482 — Coed
Affiliation or Control: Baptist — IRS Status: 501(c)3
Highest Offering: Associate Degree
Accreditation: SC

01	President	Dr. Joseph LIGHTNER
05	Vice Pres/Academic Dean	Ms. Jodye JAY
32	Dean of Students	Mr. Jonathan BECKER
113	Director of Student Accounts	Ms. Jennifer HUGHES
41	Sr Director of Athletics	Mr. Kirby SHEPHERD
08	Director of Library/Learning Svcs	Ms. Victoria FINCK
07	Director of Admissions	Mr. Will CUMBEE
06	Registrar	Ms. Jodye JAY
18	Director of Maintenance/Transport	Mr. Todd CHANCEY
26	Director Public Relations	Dr. Jan MODISETTE
29	Director of Alumni Relations	Mr. Randy DECKER
37	Director of Financial Aid	Mr. Paul GALYEAN
39	Director of Housing	Mr. David WHITE
19	Chief of Security	Mr. Micael MORSE
13	Dir Information Technology	Mr. David ANDERSON
15	Director Human Resources	Ms. Esmeralda REYES
35	Director of Student Life	Mrs. Mirtha ECKLES
38	Director Student Counseling	Ms. Amber SANCHEZ
84	Sr Director Enrollment Management	Ms. Emily STURM
96	Director of Purchasing	Ms. Esmeralda REYES

Jarvis Christian College (E)

Highway 80 E., PR 7631, Hawkins TX 75765-1470
County: Wood — FICE Identification: 003637
Unit ID: 225885
Telephone: (903) 730-4890 — Carnegie Class: Bac-Diverse
FAX Number: (903) 769-4842 — Calendar System: Semester
URL: www.jarvis.edu
Established: 1912 — Annual Undergrad Tuition & Fees: $11,720
Enrollment: 719 — Coed
Affiliation or Control: Christian Church (Disciples Of Christ)
IRS Status: 501(c)3
Highest Offering: Master's
Accreditation: SC, ACBSP, SW

01	President	Dr. Lester C. NEWMAN
05	Provost/Vice Pres Academic Affairs	Dr. Glenell PRUITT
10	Vice Pres Administration & Finance	Ms. Paula LOVE
111	VP Institutional Advancement/Devel	Dr. Kenoye EKE
32	Vice Pres Student Services	Dr. Andre S. RICHARDSON
20	AVP Academic Affairs	Dr. Cynthia HESTER
110	AVP Institutional Advancement/Dev	Miss Gwendolyn WINTERS
09	AVP Inst Research & Effectiveness	Dr. Richard PLOTT
11	AVP Campus Opers & Emergency Mgmt	Mr. Cory GIPSON
13	Director Information Technology	Mr. Christopher WATSON
06	Registrar	Ms. Laura LANDER
39	Director Student Facilities/Housing	Ms. Courtney GRAY
84	Exec Director Enrollment Management	Dr. Darrin RANKIN
35	Exec Director Student Services	Ms. Yolanda JONES
26	Director of Public Relations	Ms. Janet RAGLAND
100	Chief of Staff/Director Title III	Mrs. Cynthia JACKSON
08	Head Librarian	Mr. Rodney ATKINS
38	Director Career Services	Mr. Chestley TALLEY
37	Director of Financial Aid	Ms. Cecelia JONES
41	Athletic Director	Mr. Bobby LADNER
42	Chaplain/Director of Religious Life	Mr. Sedaric DINKENS
15	Director Human Resources	Ms. Danielle DELINT
18	Chief Facilities/Physical Plant	Mr. Willie SANDIFER
04	Admin Assistant to the President	Mrs. Debra J. SIMMONS
19	Director Security/Safety	Chief Greg SINKFIELD
28	Coordinator of Diversity	Mrs. Linda HERNANDEZ
29	Executive Director Alumni Affairs	Mr. William HAMPTON
50	Dean of Business	Dr. Benson KARIUKI
53	Dean of Education	Dr. DeMesia STARLING
51	Dean Adult & Continuing Education	Dr. Dorothy LANGLEY
96	Purchasing Clerk	Vacant

12	Director of Jarvis-Dallas Site	Ms. Mavonee JEFFRIES
25	Assistant Dir Sponsored Programs	Ms. Drew ZOMALT
25	Assistant Dir Sponsored Programs	Dr. Barry HESTER
88	Director of Field Expereince	Ms. Shonna VANCE
88	Director of Academic Initiatives	Ms. Cleopatra ALLEN

KD Conservatory College of Film and Dramatic Arts (F)

2600 N Stemmons Fwy, Suite 117, Dallas TX 75207-2111
County: Dallas — FICE Identification: 023182
Unit ID: 225991
Telephone: (214) 638-0484 — Carnegie Class: Spec 2-yr-A&S
FAX Number: (214) 630-5140 — Calendar System: Semester
URL: www.kdstudio.com
Established: 1979 — Annual Undergrad Tuition & Fees: $17,187
Enrollment: 71 — Coed
Affiliation or Control: Proprietary — IRS Status: Proprietary
Highest Offering: Associate Degree
Accreditation: THEA

01	President/CEO	Ms. Kathy TYNER
05	Director/CAO	Mr. Michael SCHRAEDER
64	Program Chair - MT	Mr. Michael SERRECCHIA
88	Program Chair - Film Program	Mr. Robert COONROD
11	Head of Operations	Ms. Becky HARRIS
32	Head of Student Services	Ms. Jennifer LAUGHLIN
37	Student Financial Aid	Ms. Rikki WASHINGTON
08	Chief Library Officer	Ms. Judith HEAD

Kilgore College (G)

1100 Broadway, Kilgore TX 75662-3299
County: Gregg — FICE Identification: 003580
Unit ID: 226019
Telephone: (903) 984-8531 — Carnegie Class: Assoc/MT-VT-Mix Trad/Non
FAX Number: (903) 983-8600 — Calendar System: Semester
URL: www.kilgore.edu
Established: 1935 — Annual Undergrad Tuition & Fees (In-District): $4,056
Enrollment: 5,100 — Coed
Affiliation or Control: Local — IRS Status: 501(c)3
Highest Offering: Associate Degree
Accreditation: SC, ADNUR, EMT, PTAA

01	President	Dr. Brenda S. KAYS
05	Vice President of Instruction/CAO	Dr. Tracy SKOPEK
88	EVP Internal Collab/Strategic Init	Dr. Mike JENKINS
32	Vice Pres Student Services	Dr. Staci MARTIN
49	Div Dean Arts & Sciences	Mrs. Becky JOHNSON
76	Div Dean Health Sciences	Dr. Larry GUERRERO
80	Div Dean Public Svcs/Ind Technology	Mr. D'Wayne SHAW
50	Div Dean Business/Entrepr/Info Tech	Ms. Kristen STOVALL
78	Dir of Adult Vocational Education	Ms. Martha WOODRUFF
06	Registrar	Mr. Dennis CLIBORN
15	Director of Human Resources	Ms. Kara SHARMAN
13	Director of Information Technology	Mr. John COLVILLE
08	Director Library	Ms. Susan BLACK
40	Manager Retail Operations	Mr. Jason RUTHERFORD
19	Chief of Police	Chief William MCPHERSON
26	Director of Marketing	Mr. Manny ALMANZA
04	Executive Aide to the President	Mrs. Karen SCIBONA
37	Director of Financial Aid	Ms. Jackie KELLEY
85	Admissions/International Specialist	Ms. Jordan COLLARD
27	Asst Dir of Marketing & Public Info	Mr. Chris CRADDOCK
09	Coord of Institutional Research	Ms. Natalie BRYANT
38	Coord of Counseling & Accommodation	Ms. Melissa DOBBS
121	Coord Advising & Virtual Services	Ms. Stephanie ARRIOLA
39	Coord of Residential & Student Life	Mr. Terence MATHIS
07	Director of Admissions	Mr. Dennis CLIBORN
84	Dean of Enroll Mgmt/Student Success	Mr. Chris GORE
106	Distance Learning Specialist	Mr. William STOWE
18	Director of Facilities/Construction	Mr. Jeff WILLIAMS
41	Athletic Director	Ms. Courtney PRUITT
10	VP Admin Svcs/Chief Financial Ofcr	Mr. Terry HANSON
101	Secretary of the Institution/Board	Mrs. Karen SCIBONA
102	Exec Dir of Fndn/Community Rels	Mrs. Merlyn HOLMES
108	Dean Institutional Effectiveness	Ms. Ursula DYER
96	Director of Procurement Services	Ms. Betsy HANSARD

The King's University (H)

2121 E. Southlake Blvd., Southlake TX 76092-6507
County: Tarrant — FICE Identification: 035163
Unit ID: 439701
Telephone: (817) 722-1700 — Carnegie Class: Spec-4-yr-Faith
FAX Number: N/A — Calendar System: Semester
URL: tku.edu/
Established: 1997 — Annual Undergrad Tuition & Fees: $15,450
Enrollment: 666 — Coed
Affiliation or Control: Interdenominational — IRS Status: 501(c)3
Highest Offering: Doctorate
Accreditation: BI, THEOL, TRACS

01	President	Dr. Jon CHASTEEN
03	Exec Vice President	Dr. Rhonda DAVIS
05	VP-CAO	Dr. Robb BREWER
10	VP Business Admin/CFO	Ms. Ashley GREEN
111	Exec Director of Advancement	Mr. Bryan CHAMBERS
20	Exec Dean of Academics	Dr. Linda HOOVER
20	Exec Director of Academic Services	Mrs. Megan GRONDIN
84	Exec Director of Enrollment Mgmt	Mrs. Angela PRUIS

21 Exec Director of Finance ... Mrs. Pauline MOTTS
04 Senior Associate to the President ... Mrs. Barbara STORIE
120 Distance Education Coordinator ... Vacant
09 Director of Institutional Research ... Vacant
13 Director Information Technology ... Mr. Matt WILSON
06 Registrar ... Mr. Derek PRITCHETT
08 Director of Library Services ... Vacant
11 Director of Business Admin ... Mrs. Danielle CARRICO
121 Director Student Success ... Vacant
37 Director Student Financial Services ... Ms. Jennifer STEED
102 Dir Foundation/Corporate Relations ... Mr. Lee MIMMS
26 Dir of Marketing/Communications ... Mr. Michael KEITH
108 Director of Inst Effectiveness ... Mr. Allen GUTIERREZ
32 Chief Student Affairs/Life Officer ... Mrs. Julie COLE
19 Assoc Dir of Building & Security ... Mr. Todd STROYAN
113 Assoc Dir Student Accounts ... Mrs. LeAnne DOOLITTLE
18 Building and Facilities Coordinator ... Mr. Joshua SHERMAN

Laredo College (A)

West End Washington Street, Laredo TX 78040-4395
County: Webb FICE Identification: 003582
Unit ID: 226134
Telephone: (956) 722-0521 Carnegie Class: Bac/Assoc-Assoc Dom
FAX Number: (956) 721-5381 Calendar System: Semester
URL: www.laredo.edu
Established: 1946 Annual Undergrad Tuition & Fees (In-District): $4,480
Enrollment: 9,292 Coed
Affiliation or Control: Local IRS Status: 501(c)3
Highest Offering: Baccalaureate
Accreditation: SC, ADNUR, EMT, NUR, OTA, PTAA, RAD

01 President ... Dr. Minita RAMIREZ
05 Provost/VP of Academic Affairs ... Dr. Marisela RODRIGUEZ
84 VP of Student Success & Enrollment ... Dr. Federico SOLIS
111 Interim VP for Inst Advancement ... Dr. Diana Y. ORTIZ
10 VP of Finance ... Mr. Cesar VELA
117 VP of Compliance & Risk Mgmt ... Dr. David ARREAZOLA
103 Dean of Workforce Educ ... Mr. Heriberto HERNANDEZ
76 Dean of Health Sciences ... Dr. Dianna MILLER
51 Dean of Community Education ... Ms. Sandra CORTEZ
49 Dean of Arts & Sciences ... Dr. Horacio SALINAS
15 Sr Director of Human Resources ... Ms. Veronica CARDENAS

Lee College (B)

511 S Whiting, PO Box 818, Baytown TX 77522-0818
County: Harris FICE Identification: 003583
Unit ID: 226204
Telephone: (281) 427-5611 Carnegie Class: Assoc/HVT-High Trad
FAX Number: (281) 425-6555 Calendar System: Semester
URL: www.lee.edu
Established: 1934 Annual Undergrad Tuition & Fees (In-District): $3,762
Enrollment: 7,487 Coed
Affiliation or Control: State/Local IRS Status: 501(c)3
Highest Offering: Associate Degree
Accreditation: SC, ADNUR, CAHIIM

01 President ... Dr. Lynda VILLANUEVA
100 Chief of Staff/Dir Strategic Opers ... Ms. Leslie D. GALLAGHER
05 Provost/VP Academic & Student Affs ... Dr. Douglas WALCERZ
32 AVP Student Affairs & Enrollment ... Mr. Scott BENNETT
111 VP College Advancement ... Vacant
20 AVP Academic Affairs ... Dr. Dometrius HILL
10 VP Finance & Administration ... Ms. Annette FERGUSON
12 AVP Huntsville Center ... Ms. Donna P. ZUNIGA
13 Chief Information Officer ... Dr. Carolyn A. LIGHTFOOT
84 Exec Director Enrollment Svcs ... Mr. Scott BENNETT
102 ED Foundation/Resource Development ... Vacant
124 AVP Retention/Transition/Diversity ... Dr. Victoria MARRON
18 Exec Dir Facilities ... Mr. Terry ROYE
38 Director Advising & Counseling ... Ms. Sarah TIDWELL
31 Exec Dir School & Col Partnerships ... Dr. Marissa MORENO
86 Government Relations Liaison ... Ms. Leslie D. GALLAGHER
25 Director Grants Management ... Ms. Selah TACCONI
06 Registrar ... Dr. Carl HUSBAND
101 Board Liaison ... Ms. Leslie D. GALLAGHER
37 Director Financial Aid ... Mr. Felipe LEAL
96 Director Purchasing ... Ms. Keona ROBERTSON
26 Director Marketing & Public Affairs ... Mr. Brian WADDLE
15 Exec Director Human Resources ... Ms. Amanda SUMMERS
04 Coord of Executive Operations ... Ms. Vanessa CUBIDES

LeTourneau University (C)

PO Box 7001, 2100 S Mobberly Ave,
Longview TX 75607-7001
County: Gregg FICE Identification: 003584
Unit ID: 226231
Telephone: (903) 233-3000 Carnegie Class: Masters/M
FAX Number: (903) 233-3101 Calendar System: Semester
URL: www.letu.edu
Established: 1946 Annual Undergrad Tuition & Fees: $32,490
Enrollment: 3,122 Coed
Affiliation or Control: Independent Non-Profit IRS Status: 501(c)3
Highest Offering: Master's
Accreditation: SC, NURSE

01 President ... Dr. Steven D. MASON
05 Int Provost/VP for Academic Affairs ... Dr. Benjamin CALDWELL
30 VP for Development/Alumni Relations ... Dr. Terry ZEITLOW
10 VP Finance/Administration ... Mr. Mike HOOD
32 VP Student Affairs/Dean of Students ... Dr. Kristy MORGAN
84 VP Residential Enrollment Services ... Mr. Carl ARNOLD
26 VP Marketing & Communications ... Mr. Don EGLE
85 VP Global Initiatives Office ... Mr. Alan CLIPPERTON
20 Assoc Prov for Academic Admin ... Dr. Benjamin CALDWELL
88 VP for Global Operations ... Vacant
18 Asst VP of Facilities Services ... Mr. Chris CHAPMAN
53 Dean School of Education ... Dr. Larry FRAZIER
50 Dean School of Business ... Dr. Van GRAHAM
54 Dean Sch Engineering & Engr Tech ... Dr. Steve STARRETT
49 Dean School of Arts & Sciences ... Dr. Larry FRAZIER
88 Dean School of Aeronautical Science ... Mr. Fred L. RITCHEY
35 Dean of Students ... Mr. Steve CONN
08 Director Learning Resource Center ... Ms. Shelby WARE
41 Director of Athletics ... Ms. Terri DEIKE
25 Director Office of Sponsored Pgms ... Mr. Paul R. BOGGS
13 Chief Information Officer ... Mr. Ken JOHNSON
15 Director of Human Resources ... Mrs. Phyllis TURNER
23 Director Health Services ... Ms. Julie MOORE
19 Chief of Police ... Mr. Michael SCHULTZ
36 Director of Career Services ... Dr. Rachel OLSHINE FRASIER
06 University Registrar ... Dr. Texas RUEGG
84 Director of Enrollment Services ... Ms. Kristine SLATE
29 Director of Alumni & Parent Rels ... Vacant
27 Director of University Relations ... Ms. Janet RAGLAND
27 Director Marketing & Communication ... Ms. Kate GRONEWALD
21 Controller ... Ms. Vikki KEILERS
09 AVP for Accreditation & QA ... Dr. Karl PAYTON
88 Executive Dir Ctr for Faith & Work ... Mr. Bill PEEL
04 Administrative Asst to President ... Mrs. Denise BAILEY
106 Assoc VP for Global Student Success ... Mr. Carlton MITCHELL
37 Director Student Financial Aid ... Ms. Tracy WATKINS
38 Director Center for Counseling ... Mrs. Treva BARHAM
73 Dean School of Theology & Vocation ... Dr. Kelly LIEBENGOOD
66 Dean School of Nursing ... Dr. Kimberly QUIETT
101 Secretary of the Institution/Board ... Mr. Bud MCGUIRE
105 Director Web Services ... Mr. Mark ROEDEL
39 Director Student Housing ... Mr. Tony ZAPPASODI

Lincoln College of Technology (D)

2915 Alouette Drive, Grand Prairie TX 75052
County: Tarrant FICE Identification: 008353
Unit ID: 226277
Telephone: (972) 660-5701 Carnegie Class: Spec 2-yr-Tech
FAX Number: (972) 660-6148 Calendar System: Other
URL: www.lincolntech.com
Established: Annual Undergrad Tuition & Fees: N/A
Enrollment: 1,455 Coed
Affiliation or Control: Proprietary IRS Status: Proprietary
Highest Offering: Associate Degree
Accreditation: ACCSC

01 Campus President ... Mr. Mike COULING

Lone Star College System (E)

5000 Research Forest Drive,
The Woodlands TX 77381-4356
County: Harris FICE Identification: 011145
Unit ID: 227182
Telephone: (832) 813-6500 Carnegie Class: Assoc/HT-Mix Trad/Non
FAX Number: N/A Calendar System: Semester
URL: www.lonestar.edu
Established: 1972 Annual Undergrad Tuition & Fees (In-District): $4,680
Enrollment: 70,109 Coed
Affiliation or Control: State/Local IRS Status: 501(c)3
Highest Offering: Baccalaureate
Accreditation: SC, ADNUR, CAHIIM, COARC, DH, DMS, EMT, MAC, MUS, NUR, OTA, PTAA, RAD, SURGT

01 Chancellor ... Dr. Stephen C. HEAD
04 Executive Assistant to Chancellor ... Ms. Fatima BARNETT
100 Chief of Staff/Board Liaison ... Ms. Deseree PROBASCO
02 Exec VC/CEO of LSC-Online ... Dr. Seelpa H. KESHVALA
12 President of LSC-CyFair ... Dr. Valerie JONES
12 President of LSC-Houston North ... Dr. Quentin A. WRIGHT
12 President of LSC-Kingwood ... Dr. Melissa GONZALEZ
12 President of LSC-Montgomery ... Dr. Rebecca RILEY
12 President of LSC-North Harris ... Dr. Archie BLANSON
12 President of LSC-Tomball ... Dr. Lee Ann NUTT
12 President of LSC-University Park ... Dr. Shah ARDALAN
11 Chief Operating Officer/Gen Counsel ... Mr. Mario K. CASTILLO
119 Information Security Officer ... Mr. William DERWOSTYP
10 Chief Financial Officer ... Ms. Jennifer MOTT
32 VC Student Success/CEO of SO-UP ... Dr. Gerald F. NAPOLES
05 Vice Chancellor Academic Success ... Dr. Dwight SMITH, III
103 Senior AVC External/Employer Rels ... Ms. Linda L. HEAD
106 Senior Assoc VC LSC Online ... Dr. Laura MCMILLION
37 Senior Assoc VC Financial Aid ... Ms. Shannon VENEZIA
19 Senior Assoc VC & Chief of Police ... Mr. Paul WILLINGHAM
15 Senior Assoc VC Human Resources ... Ms. Patricia WOODS
20 Senior Assoc VC Academic Affairs ... Vacant
26 Chief Marketing Officer ... Ms. Elisa L. OLSEN
28 Chief Diversity Officer ... Ms. Carlecia WRIGHT
88 AVC Honors & International Educ ... Dr. Katharine H. CARUSO
114 Associate VC Budget & Treasury ... Ms. Tammy A. CORTES
09 Assoc VC Analytics & Inst Reporting ... Ms. Jacqueline A. GOFFNEY
91 Assoc VC Enterprise Applications ... Mr. Longin GOGU
88 AVC Governance/Audit & Compliance ... Ms. Sandra G. GREGERSON
109 Associate VC Supply Management ... Ms. Kathie GRIFFIS
35 Associate VC Student Services ... Mr. Garth E. HOWARD
13 Associate VC Campus Services ... Mr. Earl JUELG
21 AVC Fin Reporting & Ops/Controller ... Ms. Valerie A. KOT
14 Associate VC Technical Services ... Ms. Sherry MCINTYRE
18 Assoc VC Facilities & Construction ... Ms. Denise NEU
121 AVC Student Success & Completion ... Ms. Jamie C. POSEY
116 Exec Dir Audit & Consulting Svcs ... Ms. Leticia T. CHARBONNEAU
25 Int Exec Dir Resource Dev/Grants ... Ms. Cynthia DRUMMOND
06 Exec Dir Records/Enroll & Registrar ... Ms. Connie S. GARRICK
120 Exec Dir Online Instruct Dev/Supp ... Dr. Robert GREENE
88 Exec Dir Organizational/Prof Dev ... Ms. Melissa M. HINSHAW
105 Executive Director Digital Services ... Mr. John E. KING
51 Exec Director Continuing Education ... Mr. Connor O'SULLIVAN
102 Executive Director LSC Foundation ... Ms. Nicole ROBINSON GAUTHIER
25 Exec Dir Contracts Administration ... Ms. Elizabeth B. THOMPSON
108 Exec Dir Strategic Plng/Assessment ... Dr. Christopher T. TKACH
08 Director Library Technical Services ... Ms. Carol L. STEINMETZ

Lubbock Christian University (F)

5601 19th Street, Lubbock TX 79407-2099
County: Lubbock FICE Identification: 003586
Unit ID: 226383
Telephone: (806) 796-8800 Carnegie Class: Masters/M
FAX Number: (806) 720-7255 Calendar System: Semester
URL: www.lcu.edu
Established: 1957 Annual Undergrad Tuition & Fees: $24,260
Enrollment: 1,664 Coed
Affiliation or Control: Churches Of Christ IRS Status: 501(c)3
Highest Offering: Master's
Accreditation: SC, ACBSP, NUR, SW, @THEOL

01 President ... Dr. Scott MCDOWELL
05 Provost & Chief Academic Officer ... Dr. Kent GALLAHER
10 VP/Chief Financial Officer ... Mr. Andy BURCHAM
111 Vice Pres University Advancement ... Mr. Raymond RICHARDSON
21 Controller ... Mr. Brandon GOEN
13 Vice President for Technology ... Dr. Karl MAHAN
26 Sr Vice Pres University Relations ... Mr. John KING
27 VP of University Relations ... Mr. Warren MCNEILL
32 Vice Pres Student Life ... Mr. Randal DEMENT
84 Vice Pres Enrollment Management ... Ms. Lisa SHACKLETT
102 President University Foundation ... Mr. Bill BUNDY
107 Dean Col of Professional Studies ... Dr. Toby ROGERS
49 Dean Col Liberal Arts/Educ/Honors ... Dr. Stacy PATTY
73 Dean College of Biblical Studies ... Dr. Jeff CARY
50 Dean School of Business ... Mr. Toby ROGERS
09 VP for Institutional Effectiveness ... Ms. Yvonne HARWOOD
41 Athletic Director ... Mr. Scott LARSON
06 Registrar ... Ms. Sonja DIXON
37 Director of Financial Assistance ... Mrs. Amy HARDESTY
35 Dean of Students ... Mr. Josh STEPHENS
08 Director of Library Services ... Mrs. Amanda GUTHRIE
18 Director of Campus Facilities ... Mr. Kyle TURNER
38 Director Student Counseling ... Mr. John MAPLES
23 Director of Student Health Clinic ... Mrs. Darla STEWART
14 Sr Director of Technology Services ... Mr. Robert SMITH
22 Disability Services Coordinator ... Ms. Larinda CREEL
39 Director of Residential Life ... Mrs. Sunny PARK
07 Director Undergraduate Admissions ... Dr. Jody REDING
15 Human Resources Director/AVP ... Mrs. Brenda LOWE
19 Dir Public Safety/Chief Police ... Mr. Michael SMITH
40 Bookstore Manager ... Vacant
104 Director Global Campus ... Mrs. Heather HOWELL
53 Dean School of Education ... Dr. David BOYER
04 Assistant to the President ... Mr. Keegan STEWART

McLennan Community College (G)

1400 College Drive, Waco TX 76708-1498
County: McLennan FICE Identification: 003590
Unit ID: 226578
Telephone: (254) 299-8000 Carnegie Class: Assoc/HT-High Non
FAX Number: (254) 299-8654 Calendar System: Semester
URL: www.mclennan.edu
Established: 1965 Annual Undergrad Tuition & Fees (In-District): $4,200
Enrollment: 7,742 Coed
Affiliation or Control: State/Local IRS Status: 501(c)3
Highest Offering: Associate Degree
Accreditation: SC, ADNUR, CAHIIM, COARC, EMT, MAC, MLTAD, OTA, PTAA, RAD, SURGT

01 President ... Dr. Johnette MCKOWN
10 Vice Pres Finance & Administration ... Dr. Stephen BENSON
05 VP Instruction & Student Engagement ... Dr. Fred HILLS
22 Equal Employment Opportunity Ofcr ... Mr. Al POLLARD
32 Vice President Student Success ... Dr. Drew CANHAM
102 Exec Director MCC Foundation ... Ms. Kim PATTERSON
96 Director Purchasing & Auxil Svcs ... Ms. Jodi TINDELL
37 Director Financial Aid ... Ms. Sandi JONES
26 Director Marketing & Communication ... Dr. Lisa ELLIOTT
41 Director Athletics ... Mrs. Shawn TROCHIM
06 Director Records & Registration ... Ms. Holly SURGINER
07 Director Admissions & Recruitment ... Mrs. Karen CLARK
08 Director Library Services ... Mr. Kevin LIGHTFOOT
15 Director Human Resources ... Ms. Missy KITTNER
18 Director Physical Plant ... Mrs. Dianne E. FEYERHERM
21 Director Financial Services ... Mr. Grayson MEEK
76 Dean Health Professions ... Ms. Glynnis GAINES

49 Dean Arts & Sciences .... Mr. Brad CHRISTIAN
51 Dean Continuing Education .... Dr. Frank GRAVES
13 Chief Research/Effectiveness Ofcr .... Dr. Laura WICHMAN

McMurry University (A)

1400 Sayles Boulevard, Abilene TX 79697
County: Taylor FICE Identification: 003591
Unit ID: 226587
Telephone: (325) 793-3800 Carnegie Class: Bac-Diverse
FAX Number: (325) 793-4805 Calendar System: Semester
URL: www.mcm.edu
Established: 1923 Annual Undergrad Tuition & Fees: $28,830
Enrollment: 1,094 Coed
Affiliation or Control: United Methodist IRS Status: 501(c)3
Highest Offering: Master's
Accreditation: SC, NURSE

01 President .... Dr. Sandra HARPER
05 Vice Pres Academic Affairs .... Dr. Matt DRAUD
10 Vice Pres Finance & Administration .... Mrs. Lisa L. WILLIAMS
111 Vice Pres Institutional Advancement .... Mr. Mike HUTCHISON
26 Vice Pres Marketing/Communication .... Ms. Robin DANIELS
84 VP/Director Enrollment Management .... Mr. Grant GREENWOOD
105 Webmaster .... Mr. Abraham SALAZAR
13 Director of Administrative Systems .... Vacant
14 Director of Customer Services .... Vacant
06 Registrar .... Ms. Sarah DRISKILL
08 Director Jay-Rollins Library .... Ms. Terry YOUNG
32 Dean of Students & Campus Life .... Mr. Allen WITHERS
66 Dean School of Nursing .... Dr. Donalyn ALEXANDER
35 Director of Student Activities .... Mr. Jansen ROUILLARD
37 Director of Financial Aid .... Mr. Tim SECHRIST
21 Controller .... Ms. Tina SCHUELLER
15 Assoc Vice Pres HR & Compliance .... Ms. Lecia HUGHES
108 Dir of Institutional Effectiveness .... Dr. Jori SECHRIST
09 Director of Institutional Research .... Ms. Terry NIXON
29 Director Alumni Engagement .... Ms. Katelyn SCOTT
36 Director Counseling/Disability Svcs .... Mr. Jason SHAW
41 Vice Pres Athletics/Student Affairs .... Dr. Sam FERGUSON
42 Dir of Religious Life/Univ Chaplain .... Rev. Marty CASHBURLESS
19 Director of Campus Security/Safety .... Mr. Tim BUNDICK
23 Director of Health Services .... Ms. Brenda JOHNSON
39 Director of Residence Life .... Vacant
102 Director Donor Events/Stewardship .... Ms. Emily JACQUES
92 Director Honors Program .... Dr. Philip LE MASTERS
106 Director of Online Education .... Dr. Alicia WYATT
04 Executive Asst to President .... Ms. Renee SCOTT
50 Dean School of Business .... Dr. Paul MASON
18 Dir Facilities & Campus Projects .... Mr. Carl SCOTT
30 Executive Director for Development .... Mr. Josh POORMAN
102 Director of Foundation/Corporate .... Ms. Ashlee BRADFORD
44 Director Leadership Annual Giving .... Ms. Kenna HOGAN
100 Chief of Staff .... Ms. Lisa L. WILLIAMS

MediaTech Institute (B)

13300 Branch View Lane, Dallas TX 75234
County: Dallas FICE Identification: 041298
Unit ID: 455336
Telephone: (972) 869-1122 Carnegie Class: Spec 2-yr-A&S
FAX Number: N/A Calendar System: Other
URL: mediatech.edu
Established: 1999 Annual Undergrad Tuition & Fees: N/A
Enrollment: 217 Coed
Affiliation or Control: Proprietary IRS Status: Proprietary
Highest Offering: Associate Degree
Accreditation: ACCSC

01 President & CEO .... Russell WHITAKER
05 Director of Education .... Wes MARTIN
10 CFO .... Susan HANSEN

Messenger College (C)

2705 Brown Trail Ste 408, Bedford TX 76021
County: Tarrant FICE Identification: 030926
Unit ID: 417752
Telephone: (817) 554-5950 Carnegie Class: Spec-4-yr-Faith
FAX Number: (817) 391-4003 Calendar System: Semester
URL: www.messengercollege.edu
Established: 1987 Annual Undergrad Tuition & Fees: $9,180
Enrollment: 33 Coed
Affiliation or Control: Pentecostal Church of God IRS Status: 501(c)3
Highest Offering: Baccalaureate
Accreditation: TRACS

01 President .... Dr. James E. RAYBURN
05 VP of Academic Affairs .... Dr. Candace SCALF
08 Head Librarian .... Mary THOMASON
10 VP of Business Affairs .... Angela HEPPNER
32 Dir of Student Development .... Samuel KINNIN
37 Dir Student Financial Aid/Registrar .... Carolyn R. DOWD

MIAT College of Technology (D)

533 Northpark Central Drive, Houston TX 77073
Telephone: (713) 401-3399 Identification: 770972
Accreditation: ACCSC

† Branch campus of MIAT College of Technology, Canton, MI

Midland College (E)

3600 N Garfield, Midland TX 79705-6397
County: Midland FICE Identification: 009797
Unit ID: 226806
Telephone: (432) 685-4500 Carnegie Class: Bac/Assoc-Assoc Dom
FAX Number: (432) 685-4714 Calendar System: Semester
URL: www.midland.edu
Established: 1969 Annual Undergrad Tuition & Fees (In-District): $4,350
Enrollment: 4,737 Coed
Affiliation or Control: Local IRS Status: 501(c)3
Highest Offering: Baccalaureate
Accreditation: SC, CAHIIM, COARC, DMS, EMT

01 President .... Dr. Steve THOMAS
05 Vice President Instructional Svcs .... Dr. Damon KENNEDY
88 Special Advisor to President .... Dr. Deana SAVAGE
10 Vice Pres Administrative Services .... Mr. Rick BENDER
32 Vice President Student Services .... Mr. Michael DIXON
13 Vice Pres Info Tech/Facilities .... Mr. Shawn SHREVES
101 Exec Asst to President/Board .... Mrs. Leslie SHOEMAKER
51 Dean Adult & Continuing Educ .... Mr. Dale BEIKIRCH
57 Dean Engl/Humanities/FA/Comm .... Dr. William FEELER
72 Dean of Applied Technology .... Mr. Curt PERVIER
76 Dean of Health Sciences .... Ms. Carmen EDWARDS
81 Dean of Math/Natural Sciences .... Dr. Miranda POAGE
53 Dean of Education .... Dr. Denise MCKOWN
103 Associate VP of Workforce Educ .... Dr. Jennifer MYERS
111 Exec Dir Inst Advancement/MC Found .... Ms. Rebecca BELL
06 Registrar .... Mrs. Crystal VELASQUEZ
08 Head Librarian .... Vacant
15 Director of Human Resources/Payroll .... Mrs. Natasha MORGAN
18 Executive Director Facilities .... Mr. Joseph BUTTS
19 Interim Chief of Police .... Mr. Ashley BORGSTEDTE
35 Dean of Student Life .... Mrs. Wendy KANE
41 Athletic Director .... Mr. Forrest ALLEN
09 Dir Institutional Effect/Planning .... Mrs. Heather CHAVEZ
37 Director Student Financial Aid .... Ms. Yolanda RAMOS
96 Director Purchasing .... Ms. Barbara FENNELL
84 Dean of Enrollment Management .... Vacant
30 Dir Development & Alumni Relations .... Mrs. Erin CASEY RICHARDSON
26 Director Marketing & Communication .... Ms. Jaclynn TORRES
108 Dir Institutional Effectiveness .... Mrs. Kathryn ZIMMERHANZEL
20 Assoc VP of Instruction .... Vacant
39 Dir Resident Life/Student Housing .... Mr. Ty SOLIZ

Midwestern State University (F)

3410 Taft Boulevard, Wichita Falls TX 76308-2095
County: Wichita FICE Identification: 003592
Unit ID: 226833
Telephone: (940) 397-4000 Carnegie Class: Masters/L
FAX Number: (940) 397-4042 Calendar System: Semester
URL: www.msutexas.edu
Established: 1922 Annual Undergrad Tuition & Fees (In-State): $9,796
Enrollment: 5,860 Coed
Affiliation or Control: State IRS Status: 501(c)3
Highest Offering: Doctorate
Accreditation: SC, ART, CAATE, CACREP, CAEP, COARC, DH, MPCAC, MUS, NURSE, RAD, SW, THEA

01 President .... Dr. JuliAnn MAZACHEK
05 Provost/VP Academic Affairs .... Dr. James JOHNSTON
10 VP Business Affairs & Finance .... Dr. Beth REISSENWEBER
111 Int VP Univ Advance & Public Affs .... Rhonda MCCLUNG
32 VP Student Affairs .... Dr. Keith LAMB
84 VP Enrollment Management .... Fred DIETZ
18 Assoc VP Facilities Services .... Kyle OWEN
35 Assoc VP Student Affairs .... Matthew PARK
13 Chief Information Officer .... Paul CHAPPELL
06 Registrar .... Amanda RAINES
08 University Librarian .... Cortny BATES
37 Director of Financial Aid .... Donald PURVIS
38 Director of Counseling Center .... Dr. Pam MIDGETT
51 Dir Distance Educ/Acad Outreach .... Dr. Pamela MORGAN
07 Director of Admissions .... Gayonne BEAVERS
19 Chief of University Police .... Patrick COGGINS
26 Director Public Info/Marketing .... Julie GAYNOR
112 Dir Donor Services & Scholarships .... Laura PETERSON
36 Director Career Management Center .... Dirk WELCH
41 Director of Athletics .... Kyle WILLIAMS
15 Director of Human Resources .... Dawn FISHER
09 Director of Planning/Assessment .... Dr. Eboneigh HARRIS
21 Controller .... Chris STOVALL
23 Director Vinson Health Center .... Dr. Keith WILLIAMSON
20 Associate VP Academic Affairs .... Dr. Kristen GARRISON
50 Dean College Business Admin .... Dr. Jeff STAMBAUGH
53 Dean College of Education .... Dr. Leann CURRY
57 Interim Dean College of Fine Arts .... Dr. Leah GOSE
76 Dean Col Health Sci/Human Svcs .... Dr. Jeffrey KILLION
79 Dean College Humanities/Social Sci .. Dr. Samuel E. WATSON, III
81 Dean College of Science/Math & Engr .... Dr. Margaret BROWN MARSDEN
86 Director Board & Govt Relations .... Deborah L. BARROW
29 Liaison Alumni Engagement .... Leslee PONDER
121 Director of Academic Success Center .... Ashley HURST
105 Webmaster .... Jonathan SHIREY
96 Director of Purchasing .... Tracy NICHOLS
22 Dir Disability Support Services .... Debra HIGGINBOTHAM
39 Director Housing & Residence Life .... Kristi SCHULTE
30 Director University Development .... Steve SHIPP
104 Director Global Education Office .... Dr. Michael MILLS
88 Assoc Dir of Career Mgmt & Testing .... Lynn DUCIOAME
114 Dir Budget & Strat Fin Planning .... Anna DAUGHERTY
88 Dir Museum of Art at MSU Texas .... Tracee ROBERTSON
88 Director Student Support Services .... Lisa ESTRADA-HAMBY
88 Campus Postal Supervisor .... Jon LANE
92 Coordinator Honors Program .... Dr. Steve GARRISON
43 Dir Legal Services/General Counsel .... Barry MACHA
28 AVP Stdnt Affs for Equity & Inclus .... Cammie DEAN
04 Executive Assistant to the Pres .... Elizabeth TUCKER

Navarro College (G)

3200 W Seventh Avenue, Corsicana TX 75110-4899
County: Navarro FICE Identification: 003593
Unit ID: 227146
Telephone: (903) 874-6501 Carnegie Class: Assoc/MT-VT-High Trad
FAX Number: (903) 874-4636 Calendar System: Semester
URL: www.navarrocollege.edu
Established: 1946 Annual Undergrad Tuition & Fees (In-District): $4,508
Enrollment: 7,139 Coed
Affiliation or Control: Local IRS Status: 501(c)3
Highest Offering: Associate Degree
Accreditation: SC, ADNUR, EMT, MLTAD, OTA, PTAA

01 District President .... Dr. Kevin G. FEGAN
05 Vice Pres Academic Affairs .... Dr. Carol HANES
84 VP Enroll Mgmt/Inst Effect .... Ms. Sina RUIZ
10 Vice President Finance & Admin .... Ms. Teresa THOMAS
15 VP Human Resources .... Ms. Marcy BALLEW
111 VP Oper/Institutional Advancement .... Dr. Harold HOUSLEY
32 Vice President Student Services .... Ms. Maryann HAILEY
26 Director of Mktg/Public Relations .... Ms. Stacie SIPES
41 Athletic Director .... Mr. Michael LANDERS
20 Executive Dean of Acad Studies .... Dr. Jeanetta GROCE
103 Exec Dir Wrkfc/Career & Tech Educ .... Dr. Tara PETERS
106 Dean of Online Instruction .... Mr. Matthew MILLER
88 Dean of Midlothian Campus/Dual Cred .... Ms. Jeanette UNDERWOOD
76 Dean Waxahachie Campus/Health Prof ... Mr. Guy FEATHERSTON
12 Asst Dean of Mexia Campus .... Ms. Christina MIMS
51 Dean Wrkfrc Dev & Cont Educ .... Ms. Leslie HAYES
08 Dean of Libraries .... Mr. Tim KEVIL
07 Dir of Admissions/Registrar .... Ms. Tammy ADAMS
18 Exec Director of Facilities .... Mr. Todd HARRISON
13 Director of IT .... Mr. Barry SULLIVAN
37 Director Student Financial Aid .... Ms. Kristal NICHOLSON
39 Director of Residence Life .... Ms. Marisol ARENIVAS
104 Director of International Programs .... Ms. Elizabeth PILLANS
20 Dean Academic Studies .... Dr. Richard PHILLIPS
04 Exec Asst to District President .... Ms. Leslie SMITH

North American University (H)

11929 W. Airport Boulevard, Houston TX 77477
County: Fort Bend FICE Identification: 041795
Unit ID: 461795
Telephone: (832) 230-5555 Carnegie Class: Masters/M
FAX Number: N/A Calendar System: Semester
URL: www.na.edu
Established: 2010 Annual Undergrad Tuition & Fees: $9,900
Enrollment: 785 Coed
Affiliation or Control: Non-denominational IRS Status: 501(c)3
Highest Offering: Master's
Accreditation: ACCSC

01 President .... Dr. Serif A. TEKALAN
05 Provost/Vice Pres Academic Affairs .... Dr. Faruk TABAN
11 VP Administrative Affairs .... Dr. Kudbettin AKSOY
04 Administrative Asst to President .... Jill SELTZER
06 Registrar .... Edra EDWARDS
07 Senior Admissions Officer .... Anthony SORIANO
08 Head Librarian .... Gary CHAUFFEE
106 Dir Online Education/E-learning .... Mustafa MALDAR
13 Chief Info Technology Officer (CIO) .... Khudoyor S. ORTIKOV
32 Dean Student Affairs/Student Life .... Vacant
37 Assoc Dir Student Financial Aid .... Tia SIMON
10 Chief Financial Ofcr/Dir Bus Affs .... Dovran OVEZOV

North Central Texas College (I)

1525 W. California Street, Gainesville TX 76240-4699
County: Cooke FICE Identification: 003558
Unit ID: 224110
Telephone: (940) 668-7731 Carnegie Class: Assoc/MT-VT-High Non
FAX Number: (940) 668-6049 Calendar System: Semester
URL: www.nctc.edu
Established: 1924 Annual Undergrad Tuition & Fees (In-District): $4,560
Enrollment: 8,352 Coed
Affiliation or Control: State/Local IRS Status: 501(c)3
Highest Offering: Associate Degree
Accreditation: SC, ADNUR, EMT, SURGT

01 Chancellor .... Dr. G. Brent WALLACE
05 Vice Chanc Instruct Svcs/Provost .... Vacant
84 Vice Chanc Enrollment Mgmt .... Ms. Melinda CARROLL
10 Vice Chanc Fiscal Affairs .... Dr. Van MILLER
11 Vice Chanc Administrative Affairs .... Mr. Robbie BAUGH
30 Vice Chanc External Affairs .... Ms. Debbie SHARP
28 VC Equity/Diversity/Inclusion .... Dr. Bonita VINSON
108 Assoc VC Strategic Planning/IR .... Mr. David BROWN
13 AVC Information Technology/CIO .... Ms. Denise CASON
08 Dean of Libraries .... Ms. Diane ROETHER

32 Dean of Students/Dir Title IX ....Dr. Roxanne DEL RIO
15 Director Human Resources .... Ms. Kay SCHROEDER
37 Director Financial Aid ....Ms. Ashley TATUM
07 Sr Dir of Admissions/Recruiting ....Ms. Jennifer BEAL
38 Sr Director Advising/Counseling .... Ms. Tracey FLENIKEN
26 Sr Dir Marketing/Public Relations ....Vacant
41 Athletic Director .... Mr. Van HEDRICK
35 Director of Student Life .... Ms. Daisy GARCIA
76 Dean of Instruction Health Science ....Mr. Brandon HERNANDEZ
81 Dean Instruct Science/Teacher Ed .... Ms. Sara FLUSCHE
88 Dean of Instruction Dual Credit ....Dr. Larry GILBERT
49 Dean of Instruction Flower Mound .... Mrs. Sara ALFORD
19 Police Chief ....Ms. Nicole SHAW
12 Dir of Denton County Campuses ....Ms. Jessica DEROCHE
12 Director of Flower Mound Campus ....Ms. Jessica DEROCHE
12 Director of Bowie Campus .... Dr. Jose DASILVA
12 Director of Graham Campus .... Ms. Kim BIRDWELL

Northeast Texas Community College (A)

PO Box 1307, Mount Pleasant TX 75456-1307
County: Titus FICE Identification: 023154
Unit ID: 227225
Telephone: (903) 434-8100 Carnegie Class: Assoc/MT-VT-Mix Trad/Non
FAX Number: (903) 434-4402 Calendar System: Semester
URL: www.ntcc.edu
Established: 1984 Annual Undergrad Tuition & Fees (In-District): $5,009
Enrollment: 2,758 Coed
Affiliation or Control: Local IRS Status: 501(c)3
Highest Offering: Associate Degree
Accreditation: SC, EMT, FUSER, MAC, MLTAD, PTAA

01 President ....Dr. Ron CLINTON
04 Executive Asst to the President ....Ms. Shemetric T. WILLIAMS
32 Senior Vice Pres Student Success ....Dr. Kevin ROSE
11 Vice Pres Administrative Services .... Mr. Jeffrey CHAMBERS
111 Executive Vice Pres Advancement ....Dr. Jonathan W. MCCULLOUGH
05 Associate VP for Instruction ....Ms. Anna INGRAM
35 Associate VP for Student Services ....Ms. Kim IRVIN
84 Dean Enroll/Dir Student Fin Assist ....Ms. Kim IRVIN
76 Dean of Health Sciences .... Dr. Marta URDANETA
56 Associate Dean of Outreach Services ....Ms. Melody HENRY
18 Director of Plant Services .... Mr. Tom RAMLER
08 Director Learning Commons .... Mr. Ron BOWDEN
13 Director of Computer Services ....Mr. Sebastian BARRON
26 Director Marketing/Public Relations ....Ms. Jodi PACK
06 Registrar .... Ms. Betsy GOODING
15 Executive Director Human Resources .... Ms. Amy ADKINS
10 Controller ....Ms. Brandi M. CAVE
09 Dir Institutional Effectiveness ....Mr. Robert HUDSON
07 Admissions Coordinator ....Vacant
36 Career Development/Advisor ....Ms. Lynda WATSON
28 Director of Student Dev & Inclusion .... Mr. Kaymon FARMER
30 Director of Development ....Ms. Nita MAY
121 Advising Team Lead ....Ms. Katherine BELEW
106 Director Dual Credit/Distance Educ ....Dr. Miles YOUNG
19 Security Coordinator .... Mr. Russell TAYLOR
39 Director of Residential Life .... Mr. Scott WILHITE
41 Athletic Director .... Mr. Andrew MORGAN

Oblate School of Theology (B)

285 Oblate Drive, San Antonio TX 78216-6693
County: Bexar FICE Identification: 003595
Unit ID: 227289
Telephone: (210) 341-1366 Carnegie Class: Spec-4-yr-Faith
FAX Number: (210) 341-4519 Calendar System: Semester
URL: www.ost.edu
Established: 1903 Annual Graduate Tuition & Fees: N/A
Enrollment: 179 Coed
Affiliation or Control: Roman Catholic IRS Status: 501(c)3
Highest Offering: Doctorate; No Undergraduates
Accreditation: THEOL

01 President .... Dr. Scott WOODWARD
05 Vice Pres Academic Affairs/Dean ....Rev. Ken HANNON
10 Vice Pres Finance .... Mr. Rene ESPINOSA
111 Vice Pres Institutional Advancement .... Ms. Claudia GARCIA
20 Associate Dean .... Sr. Linda BOLINSKI
51 Director of Continuing Education .... Mrs. Victoria LUNA
18 Director of Physical Plant .... Mrs. K.T COCKERELL
08 Director of the Library .... Ms. Maria GARCIA
06 Registrar & Director of Admissions .... Mrs. Brenda REYNA
88 Director Theological Field Edu .... Mrs. Bonnie ABADIE
88 Director Ministry to Ministers Pgm ....Rev. Daniel RENAUD
88 Director DMin Program ....Rev. Wayne CAVALIER
88 Director PhD Program ....Rev. John MARKEY
26 Director Marketing/Communications ....Ms. Amy RUBIO
04 Admin Assistant to the President ....Mrs. Beth POCTA
13 Chief Information Technology Ofcr ....Sr. Sue PONTZ

Odessa College (C)

201 W University Boulevard, Odessa TX 79764-7127
County: Ector FICE Identification: 003596
Unit ID: 227304
Telephone: (432) 335-6400 Carnegie Class: Assoc/MT-VT-High Non
FAX Number: (432) 335-6860 Calendar System: Semester
URL: www.odessa.edu
Established: 1946 Annual Undergrad Tuition & Fees (In-District): $3,504
Enrollment: 7,019 Coed
Affiliation or Control: Local IRS Status: 501(c)3
Highest Offering: Baccalaureate
Accreditation: SC, ADNUR, EMT, MUS, PTAA, RAD, SURGT

01 President ....Dr. Gregory D. WILLIAMS
05 Vice President for Instruction ....Dr. Tramaine ANDERSON
20 Assoc VP Instruction/Operations ....Mr. Justin BATEMAN
20 Assoc VP Instruction/Efficacy ....Vacant
32 VP Student Svcs/Enrollment Mgmt ....Ms. Kimberly MCKAY
13 Vice Pres Information Technology ....Vacant
09 VP for Institutional Effectiveness ....Vacant
100 Chief of Staff .... Mr. Robert RIVAS
11 Vice President for Administration ....Mr. Ken ZARTNER
10 Chief Financial Officer ....Ms. Brandy HAM
49 Dean Liberal Arts & Educ w/STEM ....Mr. Pervis EVANS
81 Sr Dean School of STEM ....Vacant
50 Dean Business & Industry w/STEM ....Dr. Calvin FOGLE
76 Dean Health Sciences w/STEM ....Ms. Allisa CORNELIUS
111 VP Advance/Business & Govt Rels ....Ms. Jacqui GORE
84 Exec Director Enrollment Services ....Vacant
88 VP for Academic Partnerships ....Dr. Jonathan FUENTES
06 Registrar ....Vacant
41 Director Intercollegiate Athletics .... Mr. Wayne BAKER
37 Director Student Financial Svcs .... Ms. Daisy GARCIA
15 Director of Human Resources .... Ms. Lindsey BRYANT
18 Director Facilities & Construction .... Mr. Bryan HEIFNER
26 Exec Director of Marketing .... Mr. Frank RICH
96 Dir of Purchasing/Business Services ....Ms. Melanie ALLEN
04 Exec Assistant to the President .... Ms. Ashley WARREN

Our Lady of the Lake University (D)

411 SW 24th Street, San Antonio TX 78207-4689
County: Bexar FICE Identification: 003598
Unit ID: 227331
Telephone: (210) 434-6711 Carnegie Class: DU-Mod
FAX Number: (210) 431-3928 Calendar System: Semester
URL: www.ollusa.edu
Established: 1895 Annual Undergrad Tuition & Fees: $29,926
Enrollment: 2,771 Coed
Affiliation or Control: Roman Catholic IRS Status: 501(c)3
Highest Offering: Doctorate
Accreditation: SC, ACBSP, COPSY, MFCD, SP, SW

01 President ....Dr. Diane MELBY
10 Vice President Finance & Facilities .... Mr. Anthony TURRIETTA
05 Provost/Vice Pres Academic Affairs ....Dr. Lourdes ALVAREZ
11 Vice President Administration ....Ms. Rosalinda GARCIA
111 Vice President of Inst Advancement .... Ms. Georgina SCHMAHL
13 Vice Pres of Mission and Ministry .... Ms. Gloria URRABAZO
32 Vice President of Student Affairs ...Dr. George A. WILLIAMS, JR.
13 Chief Technology Officer .... Mr. Curtis L. SPEARS
26 Chief Communication Officer ....Ms. Anne GOMEZ
84 Chief Enrollment Officer .... Mr. Nelson DELGADO
09 Director of Institutional Research ....Mr. Humberto ESPINOZA-MOLINA
14 Director of Infrastructure Services ....Mr. Jeffrey ALLEN
37 Director of Financial Aid ....Ms. Esmarelda FLORES
18 Director Facilities Management ....Mr. Darrell R. GLASSCOCK
15 Director Human Resources .... Mr. Phillip VARGAS
19 Chief of Police/Dir Campus Safety .... Mr. Ramon ZERTUCHE
06 Registrar .... Ms. Betty GALVAN
42 University Chaplain ....Fr. Kevin FAUSZ
39 Director Residence Life .... Ms. Victor G. SALAZAR
36 Director Career Counsel/Placement ....Mr. Andres JAIME
23 Director of Health Services ....Ms. Julie KNEUPPER
41 Athletic Director ....Mr. Donald (Shane) HURLEY
44 Director Advancement Services .... Mr. Douglas SEAMAN
29 Dir Alumni/Family Relations .... Ms. Debora PEREZ
08 Director of the Library .... Ms. Maria CABANISS
04 Executive Asst to the President ....Ms. Ida PEREZ

Panola College (E)

1109 West Panola Street, Carthage TX 75633-2397
County: Panola FICE Identification: 003600
Unit ID: 227386
Telephone: (903) 693-2000 Carnegie Class: Assoc/MT-VT-Mix Trad/Non
FAX Number: (903) 693-1167 Calendar System: Semester
URL: www.panola.edu
Established: 1947 Annual Undergrad Tuition & Fees (In-District): $3,576
Enrollment: 2,513 Coed
Affiliation or Control: Local IRS Status: 501(c)3
Highest Offering: Associate Degree
Accreditation: SC, ADNUR, CAHIIM, EMT, MLTAD, OTA

01 President ....Dr. Gregory S. POWELL
05 Vice President of Instruction .... Dr. Billy W. ADAMS
32 Vice President of Student Services .... Mr. Don CLINTON
10 Vice President of Fiscal Services ....Mr. Alan HOWARD
49 Dean of Arts/Sciences/Technology .... Mrs. Natalie OSWALT
106 Dir of Distance/Digital Learning .... Mr. Texas REARDON
76 Dean of Health Sciences .... Mrs. Kelly REED-HIRSCH
15 Director of Human Resources ....Mr. Jeremy DORMAN
07 Director of Admissions/Registrar .... Mr. Joseph HARRIS
111 VP of Institutional Advancement ....Mrs. Jessica PACE
08 Director of Library ....Mr. Dale SAENZ
103 Dir of Workforce & Economic Devel .... Mrs. Whitney MCBEE
09 Director of Institutional Research ....Mrs. Tryphena WALKER
12 Director of Shelby County Operation .... Mrs. Cancee LESTER
12 Director of Marshall Operations ....Mrs. Laura WOOD
13 Director of IT Service .... Mrs. Tamisha CULBERSON
19 Campus Police Chief .... Mr. Jeff JONES
37 Director Student Financial Aid ....Mrs. Denise WELCH
18 Dir of Facilities/Physical Plant ....Mr. Alan MOON
04 Admin Assistant to the President ....Ms. Mary CHANCE
30 Director of Development ....Mrs. Jessica PACE

Paris Junior College (F)

2400 Clarksville Street, Paris TX 75460-6298
County: Lamar FICE Identification: 003601
Unit ID: 227401
Telephone: (903) 785-7661 Carnegie Class: Assoc/HT-High Non
FAX Number: (903) 782-0370 Calendar System: Semester
URL: www.parisjc.edu
Established: 1924 Annual Undergrad Tuition & Fees (In-District): $3,960
Enrollment: 4,421 Coed
Affiliation or Control: State/Local IRS Status: 501(c)3
Highest Offering: Associate Degree
Accreditation: SC, ADNUR, EMT, RAD, SURGT

01 President .... Dr. Pamela D. ANGLIN
05 Vice President of Academic Instruct ....Dr. Bryan RENFRO
103 Vice President Workforce Education .... Mr. John SPRADLING
32 VP Student Access/Success ....Mrs. Sheila REECE
76 Dean Health Occupations ....Dr. Greg FERENCHAK
06 Registrar ....Mrs. Amie CATO
10 Controller ....Vacant
37 Director Student Financial Aid ....Mrs. Kimberly HERRON
09 Director Institutional Research .... Dr. Jacque MESSINGER
111 Director Institutional Advancement ....Mrs. Baleigh MCCOIN
35 Director Student Life .... Mr. Kenneth WEBB
13 Director Information Technology .... Mr. Eddie MAHAR
26 Chief Public Relations Officer ....Ms. Margaret RUFF
18 Manager Plant Operations .... Mr. Jon EUBANKS
15 Director Personnel Services ....Mrs. Melanie HATCHER
04 Admin Assistant to the President ....Ms. Melissa SMITH
19 Director Security/Safety ....Mr. Shane BOATWRIGHT
41 Athletic Director ....Mr. William FOY

Parker University (G)

2540 Walnut Hill Lane, Dallas TX 75229-5609
County: Dallas FICE Identification: 023053
Unit ID: 243823
Telephone: (972) 438-6932 Carnegie Class: Masters/L
FAX Number: (214) 902-2496 Calendar System: Trimester
URL: www.parker.edu
Established: 1982 Annual Undergrad Tuition & Fees: $15,672
Enrollment: 1,697 Coed
Affiliation or Control: Independent Non-Profit IRS Status: 501(c)3
Highest Offering: Doctorate
Accreditation: SC, CAHIIM, CHIRO, COMTA, DMS, OTA

01 President .... Dr. William E. MORGAN
05 Provost .... Dr. Jayne MOSCHELLA
63 Dean College of Chiropractic ....Dr. Celia MAGUIRE
15 VP/Chief Human Resources Officer .. Vonetta FULLER-WILLIAMS
20 Associate Provost Academics ....Dr. Dana J. LAWRENCE
10 Vice Pres/CFO .... Clint GILCHRIST

Paul Quinn College (H)

3837 Simpson Stuart Road, Dallas TX 75241-4398
County: Dallas FICE Identification: 003602
Unit ID: 227429
Telephone: (214) 376-1000 Carnegie Class: Bac-Diverse
FAX Number: (214) 379-5559 Calendar System: Semester
URL: www.pqc.edu
Established: 1872 Annual Undergrad Tuition & Fees: $9,992
Enrollment: 468 Coed
Affiliation or Control: African Methodist Episcopal IRS Status: 501(c)3
Highest Offering: Master's
Accreditation: TRACS

01 President ....Dr. Michael J. SORRELL
05 Vice Pres Academic Affairs ....Dr. Chris DOWDY
10 Chief Financial Officer ....Mr. Bruce BRINSON
11 Chief Administrative Officer ....Dr. Kizuwanda GRANT
100 Chief of Staff .... Ms. Paola ESMIEU
06 Registrar .... Ms. Marquita MITCHELL
08 Director Library Services .... Ms. Clarice MEDLEY-WEEKS
13 Director of Technology ....Vacant
41 Athletic Director ....Mr. James (Zip) SUMMERS
30 Dir Corporate External Affairs ....Mr. Maurice WEST
37 Director of Financial Aid ....Ms. Natalie GONZALEZ
35 Dir Student Support Services ....Ms. Erica MARGUEZ
18 Facilities Manager ....Mr. Nahydiel MOLINA
26 Director External Affairs ....Ms. Kelsel THOMPSON
23 Campus Nurse ....Ms. Glenda DAVIS
84 Dir of Recruiting/Enrollment Mgmt ....Vacant

Peloton College (I)

8150 N. Central Expy, M-2240, Dallas TX 75206
County: Dallas FICE Identification: 041687
Unit ID: 459514
Telephone: (214) 777-6433 Carnegie Class: Assoc/HVT-High Trad
FAX Number: (214) 777-6477 Calendar System: Quarter
URL: pelotoncollege.edu
Established: 2005 Annual Undergrad Tuition & Fees: N/A
Enrollment: 131 Coed
Affiliation or Control: Proprietary IRS Status: Proprietary
Highest Offering: Associate Degree

Accreditation: COE

01 Campus President ..... Michelle O. ANDERSON
05 VP of Academic Operations ..... David PRICE
07 District Director of Admissions ..... Suzann MCDOWELL

Pima Medical Institute-El Paso (A)

6926 Gateway Blvd., E., El Paso TX 79915
Telephone: (915) 633-1133 Identification: 770962
Accreditation: ABHES, DMS, OTA, RAD

† Branch campus of Pima Medical Institute-Tucson, Tucson, AZ

Pima Medical Institute-Houston (B)

11125 Equity Drive, Suite 100, Houston TX 77041
Telephone: (713) 778-0778 Identification: 770510
Accreditation: ABHES, COARC, DH, DMS, OTA, PTAA, RAD

† Branch campus of Pima Medical Institute-Tucson, Tucson, AZ

Quest College (C)

5430 Fredericksburg Road, Ste 310,
San Antonio TX 78229
County: Bexar FICE Identification: 034003
Unit ID: 439507
Telephone: (210) 366-2701 Carnegie Class: Not Classified
FAX Number: (210) 366-0738 Calendar System: Semester
URL: www.questcollege.edu
Established: 1995 Annual Undergrad Tuition & Fees: N/A
Enrollment: 359 Coed
Affiliation or Control: Proprietary IRS Status: Proprietary
Highest Offering: Associate Degree
Accreditation: COE

00 President/CEO ..... Ms. Jeanne MARTIN
01 School Director ..... Ms. Christine URDIALEZ
06 Registrar ..... Mrs. Veronica PEREZ
07 Director of Admissions ..... Mrs. Denise SOSA
37 Director Student Financial Aid ..... Ms. Sandy CLAUSS
05 Dean of Education ..... Mrs. Veronica PAZ

Ranger College (D)

1240 College Circle, Ranger TX 76470-3298
County: Eastland FICE Identification: 003603
Unit ID: 227687
Telephone: (254) 647-3234 Carnegie Class: Assoc/HT-High Trad
FAX Number: N/A Calendar System: Semester
URL: www.rangercollege.edu
Established: 1926 Annual Undergrad Tuition & Fees (In-District): $4,510
Enrollment: 2,200 Coed
Affiliation or Control: Local IRS Status: 501(c)3
Highest Offering: Associate Degree
Accreditation: SC

01 President ..... Mr. Derrick WORRELS
12 SVP Brown/Erath Counties ..... Dr. Matt UNDERWOOD
05 Vice President of Instruction ..... Mrs. Dayna PROCHASKA
10 Vice President Business Service/CFO ..... Mrs. Gaylyn MENDOZA
103 Exec Vice President Workforce Devel ..... Mr. Dixon BAILEY
32 Vice President of Student Services ..... Mr. Ahmy ARCA
108 Vice President of Accreditation ..... Mrs. Debbie KARL
09 Director of Institutional Research ..... Mr. John SLAUGHTER
84 Dean of Enrollment Mgmt/Registrar ..... Ms. Christine PRUITT
18 Director of Physical Plant ..... Mr. Chuck LEMASTER
37 Director of Financial Aid ..... Mr. Don HILTON
38 Director of Counseling ..... Mr. Gabe LEWIS
15 Human Resources ..... Mrs. Lindy L. MATTHEWS
113 Bursar ..... Ms. Evonne CHERRY
41 Athletic Director ..... Mr. Scott NORWOOD
40 Director Bookstore ..... Miss Cindy STRINGER
08 Director of Library Services ..... Mr. Jon HALL
11 Vice President Administration ..... Mrs. Lindy L. MATTHEWS
13 VP of Technology ..... Mr. Robert CULVERHOUSE

Redeemed Christian Bible College and Seminary (E)

4320 Highway 380 Business, Greenville TX 75401
County: Hunt Identification: 667391
Telephone: (903) 303-7853 Carnegie Class: Not Classified
FAX Number: N/A Calendar System: Trimester
URL: www.rccgnaseminary.org
Established: 2012 Annual Undergrad Tuition & Fees: N/A
Enrollment: N/A Coed
Affiliation or Control: Independent Non-Profit IRS Status: 501(c)3
Highest Offering: Doctorate
Accreditation: @TRACS

01 President ..... Oluwasayo AJIBOYE

Regional Christian University (F)

510 E. Van Week Street, Edinburg TX 78541
County: Hidalgo Identification: 667394
Telephone: (956) 867-8721 Carnegie Class: Not Classified
FAX Number: (956) 378-9644 Calendar System: Semester
URL: regionalchristianuniversity.org
Established: 1998 Annual Undergrad Tuition & Fees: N/A
Enrollment: N/A Coed
Affiliation or Control: Non-denominational IRS Status: 501(c)3
Highest Offering: Baccalaureate
Accreditation: @BI

01 President/CEO ..... Dr. David J. HOYTE
05 Chief Academic Officer ..... Daynet PIEDRA

Remington College-Dallas Campus (G)

1800 Eastgate Drive, Garland TX 75041-5513
County: Dallas FICE Identification: 030265
Unit ID: 223463
Telephone: (972) 686-7878 Carnegie Class: Bac/Assoc-Assoc Dom
FAX Number: (972) 686-5116 Calendar System: Quarter
URL: www.remingtoncollege.edu
Established: 1987 Annual Undergrad Tuition & Fees: $16,075
Enrollment: 628 Coed
Affiliation or Control: Independent Non-Profit IRS Status: 501(c)3
Highest Offering: Baccalaureate
Accreditation: ACCSC

01 Director of Campus Administration ..... Diana MCWILLIAMS
05 Campus Dean ..... Lyvier LEFFLER
07 Director of Admissions ..... Andrea WADY
36 Director of Career Services ..... Christi KOEHLER
06 Registrar ..... Michael BELL

Remington College-Fort Worth Campus (H)

5555 Rufe Snow Drive, Suite 150,
North Richland Hills TX 76180
Telephone: (817) 451-0017 Identification: 666063
Accreditation: ACCSC

Remington College-Houston Southeast Campus (I)

20985 Interstate 45 South, Webster TX 77598
Telephone: (281) 554-1700 Identification: 770601
Accreditation: ACCSC

Remington College-North Houston Campus (J)

11310 Greens Crossing, Suite 300, Houston TX 77067
Telephone: (281) 885-4450 Identification: 770600
Accreditation: ACCSC

Rice University (K)

PO Box 1892, Houston TX 77251-1892
County: Harris FICE Identification: 003604
Unit ID: 227757
Telephone: (713) 348-0000 Carnegie Class: DU-Highest
FAX Number: N/A Calendar System: Semester
URL: www.rice.edu
Established: 1891 Annual Undergrad Tuition & Fees: $51,107
Enrollment: 7,643 Coed
Affiliation or Control: Independent Non-Profit IRS Status: 501(c)3
Highest Offering: Doctorate
Accreditation: SC

01 President ..... Dr. Reginald DESROCHES
101 Deputy Sec to Board of Trustees ..... Ms. Cynthia L. WILSON
05 Provost & Dean ..... Dr. Amy DITTMAR
10 Vice Pres Finance & Administration ..... Ms. Kelly FOX
30 Vice Pres Development/Alumni Rels ..... Ms. Kathi D. WARREN
115 Vice Pres Investments/Treasurer ..... Ms. Allison THACKER
84 Vice President for Enrollment ..... Ms. Yvonne DASILVA
26 Vice President for Public Affairs ..... Ms. Linda THRANE
13 Vice President IT/CIO ..... Mr. B. Paul PADLEY
46 Vice President Research ..... Dr. Ramamoorthy RAMESH
20 Vice Provost for Academic Affairs ..... Dr. Fred HIGGS
08 Vice Provost/University Librarian ..... Ms. Sara LOWMAN
45 Vice Pres Strategic Initiatives ..... Dr. Caroline LEVANDER
15 Associate Vice Pres Human Resources ..... Ms. Joan NELSON
43 VP & General Counsel ..... Mr. Omar SYED
06 Registrar ..... Mr. David TENNEY
29 Asst VP for Alumni Relations ..... Mr. James HURLEY
37 Director Student Financial Services ..... Ms. Anne E. WALKER
25 AVP Sponsored Proj/Res Compliance ..... Ms. Krystal TOUPS
41 Director of Athletics ..... Dr. Joseph KARLGAARD
85 Assoc Vice Provost Intl Education ..... Dr. Adria BAKER
39 Assoc Vice Pres Housing & Dining ..... Mr. Mark DITMAN
23 Director Student Health Services ..... Dr. Jessica MCKELVEY
09 Assoc VP Institutional Research ..... Dr. John M. CORNWELL
21 University Controller ..... Mr. Bradley FRALIC
116 Director of Internal Audit ..... Ms. Lisa LEE
19 Chief of Campus Police ..... Mr. Clemente RODRIGUEZ
22 Director of Inst Equity/EEO ..... Dr. Richard BAKER
27 Dir of News & Media Relations ..... Mr. Doug MILLER
21 Director Administrative Services ..... Mr. Eugen RADULESCU
28 Vice Provost ..... Dr. Alexander BYRD
38 Director of Student Counseling ..... Vacant
36 Dir Center for Career Development ..... Ms. Nicole VAN DEN HEUVEL
96 Director of Procurement ..... Vacant
79 Dean of School of Humanities ..... Dr. Kathleen CANNING
58 Dean Graduate/Postdoctoral Stds ..... Dr. Seiichi MATSUDA
97 Dean of Undergraduate Education ..... Dr. Bridget GORMAN
48 Dean of Architecture ..... Dr. Igor MARJANOVIC
64 Dean of Shepherd School of Music ..... Dr. Matthew LODEN
54 Dean Brown School Engineering ..... Dr. Luay NAKHLEH
50 Dean JH Jones Graduate Sch Business ..... Dr. Peter RODRIGUEZ
83 Dean of Social Sciences ..... Dr. Rachel KIMBRO
81 Dean of Wiess Sch Natural Science ..... Dr. Thomas KILLIAN
51 Dean Glasscock Sch Continuing Stds ..... Dr. Robert BRUCE
22 Director of Compliance ..... Ms. Chetna KOSHY
18 Chief Facilities/Physical Plant ..... Ms. Kathy JONES
04 Exec Asst to the President ..... Ms. Hope GATLIFF
102 Dir Foundation/Corporate Relations ..... Ms. Leah ASCHMANN
86 Director Government Relations ..... Mr. Nathan L. COOK

Rio Grande Bible Institute (L)

4300 South US Highway 281, Edinburg TX 78539-9650
County: Hidalgo Identification: 666395
Unit ID: 475185
Telephone: (956) 380-8100 Carnegie Class: Not Classified
FAX Number: (956) 380-8256 Calendar System: Semester
URL: www.riogrande.edu
Established: 1946 Annual Undergrad Tuition & Fees: N/A
Enrollment: N/A Coed
Affiliation or Control: Independent Non-Profit IRS Status: 501(c)3
Highest Offering: Baccalaureate
Accreditation: BI

01 President ..... Dr. Lawrence B. WINDLE
04 General Assistant ..... Mr. David LOYOLA
05 Vice Pres of Academic Division ..... Dr. Julio VARELA
30 Director of Ministerial Advancement ..... Mr. Bob ALLEN
06 Registrar ..... Mr. Keith SWARTZBAUGH
20 Academic Dean ..... Dr. Milton MOROCHO
07 Director of Admissions ..... Miss Maribel MENDONCA
10 Chief Financial/Business Officer ..... Mr. Jonathan WHITE

Rio Grande Valley College (M)

5419 N. Cage Blvd, Pharr TX 78577
County: Hidalgo FICE Identification: 041930
Unit ID: 476726
Telephone: (956) 781-6800 Carnegie Class: Spec 2-yr-Health
FAX Number: (956) 781-6807 Calendar System: Semester
URL: www.rgvcollege.edu
Established: 2008 Annual Undergrad Tuition & Fees: N/A
Enrollment: 614 Coed
Affiliation or Control: Proprietary IRS Status: Proprietary
Highest Offering: Associate Degree
Accreditation: ABHES

01 CEO/School Director ..... Dr. Annabelle RODRIGUEZ

St. Edward's University (N)

3001 S Congress Avenue, Austin TX 78704-6489
County: Travis FICE Identification: 003621
Unit ID: 227845
Telephone: (512) 448-8400 Carnegie Class: Masters/L
FAX Number: (512) 448-8492 Calendar System: Semester
URL: www.stedwards.edu
Established: 1885 Annual Undergrad Tuition & Fees: $49,076
Enrollment: 3,591 Coed
Affiliation or Control: Independent Non-Profit IRS Status: 501(c)3
Highest Offering: Doctorate
Accreditation: SC, CACREP, SW

00 Board Chair ..... Mr. Steve D. SHADOWEN
01 President ..... Dr. Montserrat FUENTES
05 Provost ..... Dr. Marianne WARD-PERADOZA
10 Interim Vice President Finance ..... Dr. Alicia BETSINGER
13 Vice President Information Tech ..... Mr. David E. WALDRON
45 VP Inst Effectiveness & Planning ..... Dr. Alicia BETSINGER
111 Vice President for Advancement ..... Mr. Joe DEMEDEIROS
84 Vice Pres for Enrollment Management ..... Ms. Tracy L. MANIER
32 Vice President for Student Affairs ..... Dr. Lisa L. KIRKPATRICK
26 Vice Pres Marketing & Communication ..... Ms. Christie CAMPBELL
42 Director of Campus Ministry ..... Fr. Ron RAAB
100 Chief of Staff/Sustainability Coord ..... Dr. David W. ABERCIA
20 Assoc VP Academic Affairs ..... Dr. Glenda BALLARD
124 Assoc VP Student Success ..... Dr. Nicole G. TREVINO
58 Dir Graduate/Professional Studies ..... Dr. Ellen C. MELTON
83 Dean Behavioral & Social Sciences ..... Dr. Catherine E. CAMPBELL
50 Interim Dean Munday Sch of Business ..... Dr. Louise E. SINGLE
79 Dean School of Arts & Humanities ..... Dr. Sharon D. NELL
81 Dean School of Natural Sciences ..... Dr. Jonathan HODGE
21 Assoc VP for Finance ..... Mr. Gary HUFF
11 Assoc VP Operations ..... Mr. James H. MORRIS
15 Assoc VP Human Resources ..... Dr. Melissa G. ESQUEDA
91 Assoc VP Digital Effectiveness ..... Ms. Angela M. SVOBODA
120 Assoc VP Digital Learning ..... Ms. Rebecca F. DAVIS
14 Assoc VP IT Resource Mgmt ..... Mr. Danny LORENTY
30 Assoc VP for Development ..... Mr. Gregory PERRIN
35 Assoc VP Student Affairs ..... Mr. Thomas B. SULLIVAN
41 Associate VP Athletics ..... Ms. Debora W. TAYLOR
86 Dir Govt & Community Relations ..... Ms. Liz JOHNSON
06 Registrar ..... Mr. Patrick W. FIELDS
35 Dean of Students/Title IX Deputy ..... Mr. Steven J. PINKENBURG
07 Interim Dir Freshman Admissions ..... Ms. Mallory B. MAZZARELLA
08 Interim Director Library ..... Mr. Robert C. GIBBS
109 Assoc VP for Business Services ..... Ms. Rebekah DESAI
37 Sr Director Student Financial Aid ..... Ms. Jennifer M. BECK
27 Director of Communications ..... Ms. Gwendollyn SCHULER
88 Director Master Planning ..... Mr. Steve D. RAMIREZ

113 Director of Student Accounts .... Mr. Peter J. BEILHARZ
114 Dir Budget & Resource Planning ....Ms. Lisa P. GRANTHAM
18 Director of Facilities Operations .... Mr. Bobby BULLARD
19 Chief/Director of Police Services ....Mr. Homer J. HUERTA
16 Director of Human Resources .... Ms. Jennifer CHARLES
97 Director of General Education ....Dr. Christie S. WILSON
121 Dir Academic Counseling & Support ...Ms. Kendall P. SWANSON
36 Int Dir Career & Professional Dev .... Dr. Nicole G. TREVINO
123 Dir Graduate and Transfer Admission ....Mr. David C. BRALOWER
85 Dir International Student Svcs .... Mr. Jacob HARRIS
104 Director of Study Abroad .... Ms. Eleanor EMERSON
119 Assoc Dir of Information Security ....Mr. Brant C. CHRISTIANSEN
39 Director for Housing Operations .... Ms. Ellisha D. ISOM
38 Interim Dir Health & Counseling Ctr ....Dr. Michael HERSHBERGER
89 Dir Student Activities/Transitions ....Mr. Carey J. MAYS
88 Assoc VP Faculty DEI ....Dr. Monique JIMENEZ-HERRERA
28 Dir Student Diversity & Inclusion ....Ms. Erica A. ZAMORA
110 Director of Development .... Ms. Anne E. WESTDYKE
102 Director Foundation Relations ....Ms. Jessica D. WILSON
44 Director Constituent Relations .... Ms. Sarah B. DICKENS
108 Director Institutional Assessment ....Dr. Jocelyn SHADFORTH
09 Director of Institutional Research ....Ms. Danica D. FRAMPTON
92 Director of Honors Program .... Dr. Emma WOELK
29 Assoc Dir Development & Alumni Ops ....Ms. Karin DICKS
96 Assistant Procurement Manager ....Mr. Tony ACEVEDO
04 Executive Assistant to President .... Ms. Laura LARGE
40 Campus Stores Manager ....Ms. Veronica LARA

St. Mary's University (A)

One Camino Santa Maria, San Antonio TX 78228-8572
County: Bexar FICE Identification: 003623
Unit ID: 228149
Telephone: (210) 436-3011 Carnegie Class: Masters/L
FAX Number: (210) 431-2226 Calendar System: Semester
URL: www.stmarytx.edu
Established: 1852 Annual Undergrad Tuition & Fees: $33,720
Enrollment: 3,458 Coed
Affiliation or Control: Roman Catholic IRS Status: 501(c)3
Highest Offering: Doctorate
Accreditation: SC, CACREP, LAW, MFCD, MUS

01 President .... Mr. Thomas M. MENGLER
05 Provost/VP Academic Affairs .... Dr. Jason PIERCE
10 Vice Pres for Admin & Finance ....Mr. Aaron HANNA
84 Vice Pres Enrollment Management ....Dr. Rosalind ALDERMAN
32 Vice Pres Stdnt Dev/Dean of Stdnts . Mr. Timothy (Tim) BESSLER
111 Vice Pres for Univ Advancement ....Mr. Joel LAUER
88 Vice President Mission ....Rev. John THOMPSON, SM
50 Dean Bill Greehey Sch of Business .... Dr. Rowena ORTIZ-WALTERS
79 Dean Humanities/Social Sciences .... Dr. Nancy LAGRECA
54 Int Dean Science/Engineering/Tech .... Dr. Ian MARTINES
61 Dean of Law ....Ms. Patricia ROBERTS
39 Director Residence Life ....Mr. James VILLARREAL
100 Chief of Staff/Office of President ....Ms. Dianne L. PIPES
06 Registrar ....Ms. Christina VILLANUEVA
08 Int Dir Louis J Blume Library .... Dr. Felicia CRUZ
37 Dir Financial Aid/Enrollment Ops ....Ms. Marivel OJEDA
90 Exec Dir Academic Tech Svcs ....Mr. Jeff SCHOMBURG
15 Exec Dir Human Res/Title IX Coord .....Ms. Janet GUADARRAMA
13 Vice Pres Information Services .... Mr. Curtis WHITE
119 Dir Ntwrk/Security Admin Info Svcs ...Mr. Robert STOOKSBERRY
14 Director Systems Support Services ....Mr. Frank NIEWIERSKI
42 Exec Director University Ministry ....Vacant
29 Executive Director Alumni Relations .... Mr. Peter HANSEN
26 Senior Director Communications ....Ms. Jennifer LLOYD
04 Sr Exec Assistant to the President ....Ms. Susie B. SALAZAR
102 Director Foundation/Corporate Rels ....Ms. Cecilia MACIAS
18 Exec Director Facilities Services ....Mr. Christopher VANSKIKE
28 VP of Diversity/Equity/Inclusion ....Dr. Shireen KING
41 Executive Director Athletics .... Mr. Robert COLEMAN

*San Jacinto College District (B)

4624 Fairmont Parkway, Pasadena TX 77504-3323
County: Harris FICE Identification: 029137
Telephone: (281) 998-6150 Carnegie Class: N/A
FAX Number: N/A
URL: www.sanjac.edu

01 Chancellor ....Dr. Brenda HELLYER
03 Deputy Chancellor and President .... Dr. Laurel WILLIAMSON
05 Chief Academic Officer ....Mr. Van WIGGINTON
10 Vice Chancellor Fiscal Affairs ....Mrs. Teri ZAMORA
15 Vice Chanc Human Resources ....Mrs. Sandra RAMIREZ
13 CIO ....Mr. Rob STANICIC
26 Vice Chanc Marketing/Govt Rels .... Mrs. Teri CRAWFORD
45 Vice Chanc Strategic Initiatives .... Dr. Allatia HARRIS
84 Dean Enroll Mgmt/College Registrar ....Mr. Kevin MCKISSON
09 Director of Research ....Mr. George GONZALEZ
37 Dean Financial Aid Services ....Mr. Robert MERINO
96 Director Contracts & Purchasing .... Ms. Ann KOKX-TEMPLET
04 Administrative Asst to President ....Ms. Mandi REILAND
19 Manager SHERM ....Mrs. Susana GONZALEZ
25 Director Grants Management ....Mrs. Tomoko OLSON
29 Director Alumni Relations ....Ms. Ruth KEENAN
32 Chief Student Affairs/Student Life ...... Ms. Joanna ZIMMERMANN
06 College Registrar ....Mr. Kevin MCKISSON

*San Jacinto College Central (C)

8060 Spencer Highway, Pasadena TX 77505-5903
County: Harris FICE Identification: 003609
Unit ID: 227979
Telephone: (281) 998-6150 Carnegie Class: Assoc/HVT-Mix Trad/Non
FAX Number: N/A Calendar System: Semester
URL: www.sanjac.edu
Established: 1960 Annual Undergrad Tuition & Fees (In-District): $3,240
Enrollment: 31,110 Coed
Affiliation or Control: Local IRS Status: 501(c)3
Highest Offering: Baccalaureate
Accreditation: &SC, ADNUR, COARC, DMS, MLTAD, NAEYC, NUR, RAD, SURGT

02 Deputy Chancellor and President .... Dr. Laurel WILLIAMSON
05 Provost .... Mr. Van A. WIGGINTON
32 Associate VC Student Services .... Ms. Joanna ZIMMERMANN
72 Assoc VC/SVP Ctr Petro/Energy/Tech .... Mr. James GRIFFIN
88 Director Petrochemical Technology ....Mr. Thomas STANG
06 Col Registrar/Dean of Records Mgmt ..... Mr. Kevin R. MCKISSON
50 Dean Business & Technology ....Dr. James RAGAISIS
49 Dean of Liberal Arts .... Dr. DeRhonda MCWAINE
76 Dean Health and Health Sciences ....Dr. Rhonda BELL
11 Dean of Administration ....Mr. Scott R. GERNANDER
35 Dean Student Development ....Vacant
88 Dean of Student Support Services ....Ms. Tanesha ANTOINE
84 Dean of Enrollment Services .... Mr. Jose DEJESUSGIL
37 Dean Financial Aid Services ....Mr. Robert MERINO
43 Dean Compliance & Judicial Affairs ....Dr. Kara KENNEBREW
92 Director Honors Program ....Dr. Eddie WELLER
08 Director Library ....Ms. Karen BLANKENSHIP
109 Director Campus Services ....Mr. Christopher CRUMLEY
121 Director Student Success Center ....Ms. Dawn SHEDD
88 Dir Educ Planning/Couns/Completion ...... Ms. Adriana ELIZONDO
88 Dual Credit Director ....Ms. Priscilla CULVER

† Regional accreditation is carried under the parent institution (district office) in Pasadena, TX.

*San Jacinto College North (D)

5800 Uvalde Road, Houston TX 77049-4599
County: Harris Identification: 666747
Unit ID: 22797901
Telephone: (281) 998-6150 Carnegie Class: Not Classified
FAX Number: (281) 459-7125 Calendar System: Semester
URL: www.sanjac.edu
Established: 1974 Annual Undergrad Tuition & Fees (In-District): N/A
Enrollment: N/A Coed
Affiliation or Control: Local IRS Status: 501(c)3
Highest Offering: Baccalaureate
Accreditation: &SC, ACFEI, CAHIIM, EMT, MAC

02 Deputy Chancellor and President .... Dr. Laurel WILLIAMSON
05 Provost ....Dr. William RAFFETTO
32 Associate VC Student Services ....Ms. Joanna ZIMMERMAN
07 College Registrar/Dean of Enroll ....Mr. Kevin MCKISSON
11 Dean Administration .... Ms. Minelia IZAGUIRRE
76 Dean Natural and Health Sciences ....Dr. Teddy FARIAS
50 Dean Business and Technology ....Ms. Heather RHODES
43 Dean Comp & Judicial Affairs ....Ms. Clare IANNELLI
62 Director Library ....Ms. Lyn GARNER
49 Dean Liberal Arts ....Mr. Shawn SILMAN
41 Athletic Director .... Mr. Tom ARRINGTON
92 Director Honors Program ....Dr. Eddie WELLER
88 Dual Credit Director .... Dr. Anne DICKENS
55 Director Evening/Weekend Services ....Mr. Don SPIES
121 Director Student Success Center ....Ms. Erika HERNANDEZ
37 Dean Financial Aid Services .... Mr. Robert MERINO
32 Dean Student Development ....Ms. Deborah SMITH
88 Dir Educational Planning & Counsel ....Ms. Sonia TOWNSEND

† Regional accreditation is carried under the parent institution (district office) in Pasadena, TX.

*San Jacinto College South (E)

13735 Beamer Road, Houston TX 77089-6099
County: Harris Identification: 666748
Unit ID: 22797902
Telephone: (281) 484-1900 Carnegie Class: Not Classified
FAX Number: (281) 922-3401 Calendar System: Semester
URL: www.sanjac.edu
Established: 1979 Annual Undergrad Tuition & Fees (In-District): N/A
Enrollment: N/A Coed
Affiliation or Control: Local IRS Status: 501(c)3
Highest Offering: Baccalaureate
Accreditation: &SC, ADNUR, OTA, PTAA

02 Deputy Chancellor and President .... Dr. Laurel WILLIAMSON
05 Provost .... Dr. Aaron KNIGHT
32 Assoc VC Student Services .... Ms. Joanna ZIMMERMANN
49 Dean of Liberal Arts & College Prep ....Dr. Kimberly DELAURO
50 Dean Business & Technology ....Mr. Kevin MORRIS
76 Dean Health and Natural Sciences .... Ms. Rhonda BILL
11 Dean Administration ....Mr. Joseph HEBERT
06 Registrar/Dean Records Mgmt ....Mr. Kevin MCKISSON
43 Dean Compliance & Judicial Affairs ....Ms. Kara KENNEBREW
92 Director Honors Program ....Dr. Eddie WELLER
55 Director Evening Division .... Mr. Ross KELSEY
08 Director Library .... Mr. Richard MCKAY
41 Director Athletics ....Ms. Kelly SAENZ
88 Dual Credit Director ....Ms. Kristen ROSS

35 Dean Student Development ....Ms. Tami KELLY
88 Dean Student Support Services ....Ms. Tanesha ANTOINE
121 Director Student Success Center ....Ms. Diana SHOKRALLA
37 Dean Financial Aid Services ....Mr. Robert MERINO

† Regional accreditation is carried under the parent institution (district office) in Pasadena, TX.

School of Automotive Machinists & Technology (F)

1911 Antoine Drive, Houston TX 77055
County: Harris FICE Identification: 030323
Unit ID: 377218
Telephone: (713) 683-3817 Carnegie Class: Spec 2-yr-Tech
FAX Number: (713) 683-7077 Calendar System: Semester
URL: www.samtech.edu
Established: 1985 Annual Undergrad Tuition & Fees: N/A
Enrollment: 152 Coed
Affiliation or Control: Proprietary IRS Status: Proprietary
Highest Offering: Associate Degree
Accreditation: ACCSC

01 President/Dir of Education ....Judson MASSINGILL
11 CEO/Sch Exec Director/Administrator ....Linda MASSINGILL
37 Financial Aid Director ....Susie FAERMAN

Schreiner University (G)

2100 Memorial Boulevard, Kerrville TX 78028-5611
County: Kerr FICE Identification: 003610
Unit ID: 228042
Telephone: (830) 896-5411 Carnegie Class: Masters/S
FAX Number: (830) 896-3232 Calendar System: Semester
URL: www.schreiner.edu
Established: 1923 Annual Undergrad Tuition & Fees: $31,938
Enrollment: 1,244 Coed
Affiliation or Control: Presbyterian Church (U.S.A.) IRS Status: 501(c)3
Highest Offering: Master's
Accreditation: SC, NURSE

01 President ....Dr. Charlie MCCORMICK
05 Provost/Vice Pres Academic Affairs .... Dr. Travis FRAMPTON
10 Vice Pres Planning & Finance .... Dr. Lucien COSTLEY
84 VP Stdnt Recruit/Ext Rels/Mktg/Comm .... Mr. Mark TUSCHAK
13 Vice Pres Infrastructure ....Mr. Rex QUICK
30 Director of Development ....Ms. Marta DIFFEN
07 Director of Admissions .... Ms. Danielle JENSCHKE
37 Director of Financial Aid ....Ms. Judy CUELLAR
06 Assistant Provost & Registrar ....Ms. Darlene BANNISTER
121 Dean Acad Support/Student Outcomes .... Dr. William WOODS
20 Dean of Faculty .... Dr. William DAVIS
21 Controller ....Ms. Elizabeth OEHLER
42 Campus Minister ....Vacant
32 Dean of Students .... Dr. Charlie HUEBER
27 University Relations Specialist .... Mr. Toby APPLETON
41 Athletic Director .... Mr. Bill RALEIGH
15 Director of Human Resource Services ....Vacant
18 Director Campus Operations ....Mr. Ed WINGARD
29 Alumni Relations Officer ....Mr. Micah WRASE
38 Director Student Counseling ....Ms. Kimberly J. WOODS
36 Director Advising & Career Devel ....Ms. Wendy BLAETTNER
04 Exec Assistant to the President .... Ms. Deborah SCOTT
08 Director Library .... Ms. Lisa MCCORMICK
19 Chief of Security .... Mr. Ken JACOBS
39 Director Residence Life .... Ms. Rachel CAVE
102 Foundation Relations Officer ....Mr. Roy BARTELS
104 Coordinator Multicultural Programs .... Mr. Thomas WOODS

Seminary of the Southwest (H)

501 E. 32nd St., Austin TX 78705
County: Travis FICE Identification: 003566
Unit ID: 224712
Telephone: (512) 472-4133 Carnegie Class: Spec-4-yr-Faith
FAX Number: (512) 472-3098 Calendar System: 4/1/4
URL: www.ssw.edu
Established: 1952 Annual Graduate Tuition & Fees: N/A
Enrollment: 135 Coed
Affiliation or Control: Protestant Episcopal IRS Status: 501(c)3
Highest Offering: Master's; No Undergraduates
Accreditation: SC, CACREP, THEOL

01 Dean & President ....V.Rev. Cynthia B. KITTREDGE
05 Academic Dean ....Dr. Scott BADER-SAYE
03 Executive Vice President .... Mr. Fred CLEMENT
111 VP of Institutional Advancement ......Mr. Charley SCARBOROUGH
07 Director of Admissions ....Rev. Hope BENKO
26 VP of Communications ....Mr. Eric SCOTT
10 Controller ....Ms. Susan VERSLUYS
06 Registrar/Director of Assessment .... Ms. Madelyn SNODGRASS
08 Director of the Booher Library ....Ms. Alison POAGE
18 Director of Facilities Management ....Mr. Tigh WALTERS
13 Director Information Technology .... Mr. Erik MORROW
100 Chief of Staff to Dean/President ....Ms. Lesley WILDER
30 Director of Development .... Ms. Donna EMERY
88 Director Loise Henderson Wessendorf .... Ms. Gena MINNIX
31 Dean of Community Life .... Rev. Dan JOSLYN-SIEMIATKOSKI

South Plains College (A)

1401 College Avenue, Levelland TX 79336-6595
County: Hockley FICE Identification: 003611
Unit ID: 228158
Telephone: (806) 894-9611 Carnegie Class: Assoc/HT-High Trad
FAX Number: N/A Calendar System: Semester
URL: www.southplainscollege.edu
Established: 1957 Annual Undergrad Tuition & Fees (In-State): $3,892
Enrollment: 8,880 Coed
Affiliation or Control: State IRS Status: 501(c)3
Highest Offering: Associate Degree
Accreditation: SC, ADNUR, COARC, EMT, PTAA, SURGT

01 President ... Dr. Robin SATTERWHITE
05 Vice President Academic Affairs ... Dr. Ryan GIBBS
10 Vice Pres Business Affairs ... Ms. Teresa GREEN
32 Vice President of Student Affairs ... Dr. Stan DEMERRITT
111 Vice Pres Institutional Advancement ... Ms. Julie S. GERSTENBERGER
49 Dean of Arts & Sciences ... Mr. Alan WORLEY
76 Dean of Health Occupations ... Mr. Jerry FINLEY
75 Dean of Technical Education ... Mr. Robbie M. BLAIR
51 Dean Continuing & Distance Educ ... Mr. Ryan FITZGERALD
11 Dean Administrative Services ... Mr. Ronnie WATKINS
07 Dean of Admissions & Records ... Ms. Kathryn PEREZ
12 Dean of Reese Center ... Ms. Kara MARTINEZ
09 Assoc Dean of Research & Reports ... Vacant
26 Assoc Dean of College Relations ... Mr. Dane DEWBRE
13 Assoc Dean Information Technology ... Mr. James HOWELL
103 Assoc Dean Workforce Development ... Vacant
35 Assoc Dean of Students ... Mr. Shane HILL
121 Director of Advising and Testing ... Mrs. Lola HERNANDEZ
37 Director of Financial Aid ... Ms. Susan NAZWORTH
08 Director of Libraries ... Mr. Mark GOTTSCHALK
30 Director of Development ... Mr. Jordan FLORES
15 Director of Human Resources ... Mrs. Jeri Ann DEWBRE
41 Director of Athletics ... Mr. Roger REDING
06 Registrar ... Mr. Andrew RUIZ
18 Director of Physical Plant ... Mr. Cary MARROW
40 Bookstore Manager ... Mr. Roger SHULL

South Texas College (B)

3201 W Pecan, McAllen TX 78501
County: Hidalgo FICE Identification: 031034
Unit ID: 409315
Telephone: (956) 872-5051 Carnegie Class: Bac/Assoc-Assoc Dom
FAX Number: (956) 971-3739 Calendar System: Semester
URL: www.southtexascollege.edu
Established: 1993 Annual Undergrad Tuition & Fees (In-District): $4,530
Enrollment: 28,233 Coed
Affiliation or Control: State/Local IRS Status: 501(c)3
Highest Offering: Baccalaureate
Accreditation: SC, ACBSP, ADNUR, CAHIIM, COARC, EMT, OTA, PTAA

01 President ... Mr. Ricardo J. SOLIS
05 Int Vice Pres Academic Affs/CAO ... Dr. Anahid PETROSIAN
10 VP Finance/Administrative Svcs ... Ms. Maria G. ELIZONDO
32 VP Student Affairs/Enroll Mgmt ... Mr. Matthew HEBBARD
88 VP Information Svcs and Planning ... Dr. David C. PLUMMER
111 Vice Pres Institutional Advancement ... Dr. Rodney RODRIGUEZ
103 Dean for Industry & Economy ... Mr. Carlos MARGO
49 Dean Liberal Arts ... Dr. Christopher NELSON
50 Dean Business/Public Safety/Tech ... Ms. Sara LOZANO
76 Dean Nursing/Allied Health ... Dr. Jayson VALERIO
81 Dean Math/Science/BA Programs ... Dr. Ali ESMAEILI
37 Director Student Financial Svcs ... Mr. Juan M. GALVAN
21 Comptroller ... Ms. Myriam LOPEZ
15 Director Human Resources ... Ms. Laura REQUENA
88 Special Assistant to the President ... Mr. Juan Carlos AGUIRRE
96 Director Purchasing ... Ms. Rebecca CAVAZOS
09 Dir Research/Analytical Svcs ... Mr. Serkan CELTEK
121 Dean Student Support Svcs ... Mr. Pablo HERNANDEZ, JR.
18 Director Operations/Maintenance ... Mr. George MCCALEB
18 Director Facilities Plng/Construct ... Mr. Ricardo DE LA GARZA
25 Assoc Dir Grants/Contracts Compl ... Ms. Samantha URIEGAS
12 Campus Administrator Starr Cty ... Dr. Arthuro MONTIEL
12 Campus Administrator Mid-Valley ... Mr. Daniel MONTEZ
16 Employee Relations Officer ... Mr. Jim NAVARRO
106 Dean Distance Learning ... Ms. Rachel SALE
26 Director Public Rels/Marketing ... Ms. Lynda LOPEZ
23 Dir of Student Activity/Wellness ... Mr. Elibariki NGUMA
06 Director Student Records/Registrar ... Ms. Cynthia BLANCO
20 Asst to VP Instructional Svcs ... Vacant
19 Director Regional Center for PSE ... Vacant
13 Chief Information Officer ... Ms. Alicia GOMEZ
08 Dean Library/Learning Support Svcs ... Mr. Jesus CAMPOS
88 Dir Centers for Lrng Excellence ... Ms. Lynell WILLIAMS
88 Dean Dual Credit Programs ... Dr. Rebecca DE LEON
90 Dir Info Commons Open Labs ... Dr. Lelia SALINAS
35 Dean Student Affairs ... Mr. Pablo HERNANDEZ, JR.
119 Chief Information Security Officer ... Mr. Victor GONZALEZ

South Texas College of Law Houston (C)

1303 San Jacinto Street, Houston TX 77002-7000
County: Harris FICE Identification: 004977
Unit ID: 228194
Telephone: (713) 659-8040 Carnegie Class: Spec-4-yr-Law
FAX Number: (713) 646-2909 Calendar System: Semester
URL: www.stcl.edu
Established: 1923 Annual Graduate Tuition & Fees: N/A
Enrollment: 999 Coed
Affiliation or Control: Independent Non-Profit IRS Status: 501(c)3
Highest Offering: First Professional Degree; No Undergraduates
Accreditation: LAW

01 President and Dean ... Mr. Michael F. BARRY
111 VP Advancement/Alumni Engagement ... Ms. Darcy DOUGLAS
32 Vice President Student Services ... Ms. Mandi GIBSON
05 Vice Pres & Assoc Dean Academics ... Ms. Cherie O. TAYLOR
04 Sr Exec Assistant to President/Dean ... Ms. Jennifer M. HUDSON
10 CFO ... Vacant
20 Vice Pres & Assoc Dean Faculty ... Mr. Ted FIELD
08 Director Library Services ... Ms. Colleen MANNING
88 Senior Director of Advocacy ... Mr. Robert GALLOWAY
78 VP & Assoc Dean Experiential Lrng ... Ms. Catherine G. BURNETT
13 Vice President Technology ... Mr. Randy MARAK
28 VP of Diversity/Equity & Inclusion ... Prof. Shelby MOORE
15 COO & General Counsel ... Mr. Steve ALDERMAN
26 Director Marketing/Communications ... Vacant
35 Assistant Dean Student Affairs ... Ms. Gena L. SINGLETON
36 Sr Director of Career Resources ... Ms. Nazleen JIWANI
07 Assistant Dean for Admissions ... Ms. Alicia CRAMER
21 Controller ... Ms. Kim GOODWIN
19 Director Security ... Mr. Kent BRAZELTON
24 Sr Director Instruct Technology ... Mr. Terry SMITH
14 Sr Director Information Services ... Mr. George MILZ
44 Dir Annual Giv & Alumni Engagement ... Ms. Kia WISSMILLER
102 Dir of Foundations & Corp Relations ... Ms. Julie BLAIR
18 Chief Facilities/Physical Plant ... Mr. William HILL
96 Sr Dir Purchasing & Office Services ... Ms. Dorrie RUSHING
26 Director of Public Relations ... Ms. Claire CATON
101 Secretary of the Institution/Board ... Ms. Jennifer M. HUDSON
104 Asst Dean Inst Compl & Intl Pgms ... Ms. Wanda MORROW
108 Director Institutional Assessment ... Ms. Francesca BONADUCE DE NIGRIS
121 Asst Dean Academic Success ... Ms. Lisa YARROW
15 Director of Human Resources ... Ms. Lauren DEVORE

South University-Austin (D)

1220 W. Louis Henna Boulevard, Round Rock TX 78681
Telephone: (512) 516-8800 Identification: 770917
Accreditation: &SC, ACBSP, NURSE, PTAA

† Branch campus of South University, Savannah, GA

Southern Bible Institute and College (E)

PO Box 763609, Dallas TX 75376
County: Dallas Identification: 667365
Telephone: (972) 224-5481 Carnegie Class: Not Classified
FAX Number: (972) 224-9517 Calendar System: Semester
URL: www.southernbible.org
Established: Annual Undergrad Tuition & Fees: N/A
Enrollment: N/A Coed
Affiliation or Control: Non-denominational IRS Status: 501(c)3
Highest Offering: Baccalaureate
Accreditation: @BI

01 President/CEO ... Rev. Terrance FORD
05 Vice Pres Academic Affairs ... Dr. Justin JACKSON

Southern Careers Institute (F)

1701 W. Ben White Blvd, Ste 100, Austin TX 78704
County: Travis FICE Identification: 030353
Unit ID: 226903
Telephone: (512) 432-1400 Carnegie Class: Spec 2-yr-Other
FAX Number: (512) 432-1401 Calendar System: Other
URL: scitexas.edu
Established: 1960 Annual Undergrad Tuition & Fees: N/A
Enrollment: 987 Coed
Affiliation or Control: Proprietary IRS Status: Proprietary
Highest Offering: Associate Degree
Accreditation: COE

01 Campus Director ... Lonnicia MAXWELL
05 Director of Education ... Raghunath NAIR

Southern Methodist University (G)

6425 Boaz Lane, Dallas TX 75205-0100
County: Dallas FICE Identification: 003613
Unit ID: 228246
Telephone: (214) 768-2000 Carnegie Class: DU-Higher
FAX Number: (214) 768-1001 Calendar System: Semester
URL: www.smu.edu
Established: 1911 Annual Undergrad Tuition & Fees: $58,540
Enrollment: 12,373 Coed
Affiliation or Control: Independent Non-Profit IRS Status: 501(c)3
Highest Offering: Doctorate
Accreditation: SC, ART, CACREP, CLPSY, DANCE, LAW, MUS, THEA, THEOL

01 President ... Dr. R. Gerald TURNER
11 VP Executive Affairs ... Dr. Harold W. STANLEY
05 Provost/VP Academic Affairs ... Dr. Elizabeth G. LOBOA
10 VP Business & Finance/Treasurer ... Ms. Chris C. REGIS
30 VP Devel & External Affairs ... Mr. Brad E. CHEVES
43 Gen Counsel/VP Leg Affs/Govt Rels ... Mr. Paul J. WARD
32 VP Student Affairs ... Dr. Kenechukwu (K.C.) MMEJE
41 Director of Athletics ... Mr. Richard L. HART
115 Chief Investment Officer ... Mr. Rakesh DAHIYA
13 Chief Information Officer ... Dr. Michael H. HITES
20 Assoc Provost for Faculty Success ... Dr. Paige WARE
121 Assoc Provost Stdnt Acad Success ... Dr. Sheri KUNOVICH
108 Assoc Prov Inst Plng/Effectiveness ... Dr. Dayna OSCHERWITZ
51 Asst Provost Global/Online/Cont Ed ... Dr. Michael J. ROBERTSON
46 Interim Assoc Provost Research ... Dr. Sukumaran NAIR
84 Assoc VP Enroll Management ... Mr. Wes K. WAGGONER
15 Assoc VP/Chief Human Res Officer ... Ms. Sheri STARKEY
117 Assoc VP/Chief Risk Officer ... Ms. Leigh Ann MOFFETT
114 Assoc VP Budgets/Finance ... Mr. Ernie BARRY
35 Assoc VP & Dean of Students ... Dr. Melinda SUTTON NOSS
109 Assoc VP of Campus Services ... Ms. Alison TWEEDY
18 Assoc VP Facilities Plng/Management ... Mr. Michael S. MOLINA
100 Asst Provost/Chief of Staff ... Mr. Daniel P. EADY
49 Dean Dedman College ... Dr. Thomas DIPIERO
50 Dean Cox School of Business ... Dr. Matthew B. MYERS
54 Interim Dean Lyle School of Engr ... Dr. Paul KRUEGER
57 Dean Meadows Sch of the Arts ... Dr. Sam HOLLAND
53 Dean Simmons Sch Educ/Human Dev ... Dr. Stephanie L. KNIGHT
61 Dean Dedman School of Law ... Dr. Jason P. NANCE
73 Dean Perkins School of Theology ... Dr. Craig C. HILL
58 Dean Moody Sch Grad/Advance Studies ... Dr. Robin POSTON
08 Dean of SMU Libraries ... Ms. Holly JEFFCOAT
07 Dean of Undergraduate Admissions ... Ms. Elena D. HICKS
26 Asst VP for Marketing/Comm ... Ms. Regina MOLDOVAN
112 Asst VP for Principal & Major Gifts ... Mr. Blake DAVIS
19 Chief of Police ... Mr. Jim L. WALTERS
06 Exec Dir Enroll Services/Registrar ... Mr. Robert L. LOTHRINGER
113 University Bursar ... Mr. Albert JABOUR
42 Chaplain/Minister to the University ... Rev. Lisa GARVIN
37 Exec Dir Student Financial Services ... Ms. Mary SAUCEDA
12 Director SMU-in-Taos ... Dr. Michael ADLER
27 Exec Dir of Creative Marketing ... Ms. Emily HUGHES ARMOUR
88 Exec Dir Program Services/Donor Rel ... Ms. Dana AYRES
44 Exec Dir Annual Giving/Alumni Rel ... Ms. Astria SMITH
23 Assoc Dean of Health Services ... Dr. Randy P. JONES
04 EA to Pres/Exec Dir Inst Acc/Eqty ... Ms. Samantha THOMAS
119 Chief Security Officer ... Mr. George FINNEY
116 Director of Internal Audit ... Ms. Chandra MCQUEEN
88 Sr Asst Dean of Graduate Studies ... Dr. Alan ITKIN
104 Director Study Abroad ... Ms. Christie PEARSON
96 Director of Procurement ... Ms. Shannon BROWN
25 Director of Sponsored Projects ... Ms. Ruth V. LOZANO
38 Director of Counseling Services ... Vacant
102 Dir Corp & Foundation Relations ... Mr. Rob STRAUSS
29 Dir Alumni Relations/Engagement ... Ms. Mary Margaret RANGEL
91 Assc CIO Data/Application Services ... Mr. Curt HERRIDGE
90 Assc CIO Academic/Tech Services ... Mr. Jason WARNER
09 Dir University Decision Support ... Dr. Michael D. TUMEO
39 Dean Res Life/Stdnt Housing ... Dr. Aramis WATSON
28 Director of Diversity ... Dr. Maria DIXON HALL

Southern Reformed College and Seminary (H)

26111 Beckendorff Rd, Katy TX 77493
County: Harris Identification: 667364
Telephone: (713) 467-4501 Carnegie Class: Not Classified
FAX Number: N/A Calendar System: Semester
URL: srsem.net
Established: Annual Undergrad Tuition & Fees: N/A
Enrollment: N/A Coed
Affiliation or Control: Independent Non-Profit IRS Status: 501(c)3
Highest Offering: Master's
Accreditation: @BI

01 President/CEO ... Dr. James A. LEE
32 Vice President for Student Affairs ... Dr. Steve W. HALL
05 Academic Dean ... Jong-Ho KIM
10 Business Office Manager ... Josiah DEARINGER

Southwest Texas Junior College (I)

2401 Garner Field Road, Uvalde TX 78801-6221
County: Uvalde FICE Identification: 003614
Unit ID: 228316
Telephone: (830) 278-4401 Carnegie Class: Assoc/HT-High Non
FAX Number: (830) 591-7354 Calendar System: Semester
URL: www.swtjc.edu
Established: 1946 Annual Undergrad Tuition & Fees (In-District): $4,062
Enrollment: 6,480 Coed
Affiliation or Control: Local IRS Status: 501(c)3
Highest Offering: Associate Degree
Accreditation: SC

01 President ... Dr. Hector GONZALES
11 Vice President Administrative Svcs ... Mr. Derek SANDOVAL
32 Vice President Student Services ... Mrs. Margot MATA
10 Vice President Finance ... Ms. Lisa ERMIS
05 Vice President Academic Services ... Dr. Mark UNDERWOOD
12 Vice President Del Rio ... Mrs. Connie BUCHANAN
12 Vice President Eagle Pass ... Mr. Gilbert S. BERMEA
103 Dean of Workforce Education ... Mr. Juan (Johnny) C. GUZMAN
49 Dean of College of Liberal Arts ... Dr. Cheryl L. SANCHEZ
121 Director of Academic Advising ... Vacant
37 Director of Financial Aid ... Ms. Yvette MIRELEZ
13 Director of Information Tech ... Mr. Frankie PANNELL
18 Physical Plant Director ... Mr. Kirk M. PALERMO
15 Human Resources Coordinator ... Mr. Oscar S. GARCIA
09 Director of Institutional Research ... Vacant

06 Registrar .... Mr. Steve MARTINEZ
08 Head Librarian .... Ms. Brenda CANTU
19 Director Security/Safety .... Mr. Jimmy CALLIHAM
96 Purchasing Manager .... Vacant
100 Chief of Staff .... Dr. Randa SCHELL

Southwest University at El Paso (A)

1414 Geronimo Drive, El Paso TX 79925
County: El Paso FICE Identification: 041317
Unit ID: 451556
Telephone: (915) 778-4001 Carnegie Class: Spec-4-yr-Other Health
FAX Number: (915) 778-1575 Calendar System: Other
URL: www.southwestuniversity.edu
Established: 2001 Annual Undergrad Tuition & Fees: $16,000
Enrollment: 1,558 Coed
Affiliation or Control: Proprietary IRS Status: Proprietary
Highest Offering: Baccalaureate
Accreditation: ABHES, IACBE, NURSE, #RAD

02 President .... Mr. Ben ARRIOLA, JR.
11 Vice President/School Director .... Ms. Marisol GUTIERREZ
05 Vice Pres/Academic Dean .... Mr. Jeremy BURCIAGA

Southwestern Adventist University (B)

100 W Hillcrest Street, Keene TX 76059-0567
County: Johnson FICE Identification: 003619
Unit ID: 228468
Telephone: (817) 645-3921 Carnegie Class: Bac-Diverse
FAX Number: (817) 202-6744 Calendar System: Semester
URL: www.swau.edu
Established: 1893 Annual Undergrad Tuition & Fees: $22,836
Enrollment: 754 Coed
Affiliation or Control: Seventh-day Adventist IRS Status: 501(c)3
Highest Offering: Master's
Accreditation: SC, IACBE, NURSE

01 President .... Mrs. Ana PATTERSON
05 VP for Academic Administration .... Dr. Donna BERKNER
10 VP for Financial Administration .... Dr. Carlos CHARNICHART
84 VP for Enrollment .... Ms. Rahneeka HAZELTON
32 VP for Student Services .... Mr. James THE
111 VP for Advancement .... Mr. Tony REYES
42 VP for Spiritual Development .... Mr. Russ LAUGHLIN
09 VP Institutional Rsrch/Effective .... Dr. Marcel SARGEANT
37 Asst VP for Student Finance .... Mr. Duane VALENCIA
21 Asst VP Financial Administration .... Dr. Satyanarayana RAMELLA
06 Registrar .... Mrs. Michelle KARMY
08 Librarian .... Ms. Cristina M. THOMSEN
34 Dean of Women .... Mrs. Janelle D. WILLIAMS
33 Dean of Men .... Mr. William IVERSON
13 Dir Information Technology Svcs .... Mr. E. Charles LEWIS
18 Plant Engineer .... Mr. Ken HANSON
26 Director of Marketing .... Mr. Josafat ZEMLEDUCH
30 Director for Development .... Vacant
29 Alumni/Communications Officer .... Mrs. Susan GRADY
38 Director of Counseling & Testing .... Dr. Marcel SARGEANT
22 Director of Disability Services .... Dr. Marcel SARGEANT
121 Dir Ctr for Acad Success/Advising .... Mrs. Renata OCAMPO
89 Project Director for HSI Grants .... Mr. Austen POWELL
07 Director of Admissions .... Ms. Rahneeka HAZELTON
15 Director of Human Resources .... Ms. Genelle MARTIN
19 Assoc Director of Security .... Mr. Matthew AGEE
25 Grant Writer .... Dr. Tom BUNCH
41 Athletic Director .... Mr. Tyler WOOLDRIDGE
50 Chair Business Dept .... Dr. Aaron MOSES
53 Chair Education Dept .... Dr. Cheryl THE
04 Special Assistant to the President .... Mr. Austen POWELL
66 Chair Nursing Dept .... Dr. Kerrie KIMBROW
81 Chair Biological Sciences .... Dr. Arthur SCHWARZ
60 Chair Communication Dept .... Ms. R. Brett HADLEY
88 Chair English Dept .... Dr. Renard DONESKEY
83 Chair History & Social Science .... Dr. Steve JONES
88 Chair Kinesiology Dept .... Dr. Paulino SANTOS-ANDINO
81 Chair Math & Physical Sci .... Dr. Nicholas MADHIRI
64 Chair Music .... Dr. Devon HOWARD
73 Chair Religion .... Dr. Jorge RICO

Southwestern Assemblies of God University (C)

1200 Sycamore, Waxahachie TX 75165-2397
County: Ellis FICE Identification: 003616
Unit ID: 228325
Telephone: (972) 937-4010 Carnegie Class: Masters/S
FAX Number: (972) 923-0488 Calendar System: Semester
URL: www.sagu.edu
Established: 1927 Annual Undergrad Tuition & Fees: $19,834
Enrollment: 1,985 Coed
Affiliation or Control: Assemblies Of God Church IRS Status: 501(c)3
Highest Offering: Doctorate
Accreditation: SC, IACBE, SW

01 President .... Dr. Kermit S. BRIDGES
05 Vice President for Academics .... Dr. Paul BROOKS
32 Vice President for Student Develop .... Dr. Lance MECHE
10 Vice Pres for Business & Finance .... Dr. Fred GORE
111 Vice President for Univ Advancement .... Rev. Rick BOWLES
20 Dean of Academic Services .... Rev. Donny LUTRICK
58 Dean of Graduate Studies .... Dr. Joseph HARTMAN
73 Dean Col Bible & Church Ministries .... Dr. Clancy HAYES
50 Dean Col of Business & Education .... Dr. Sue TAYLOR
09 VP Inst Effectiveness/Dn Col Music .... Dr. Kim JAMES
106 Dean for Distance Education .... Rev. Joseph HARTMAN
06 Registrar .... Ms. Shelly MCMULLIN
35 Dean of Students .... Vacant
88 Director of Learning Centers .... Mr. Aaron GUAJARDO
13 Sr Dir Information Technology .... Mr. Kirk PASCHALL
29 Director of Alumni Relations .... Mr. James CARNELL
08 Director of Learning Resources .... Ms. Radonna HOLMES
14 Director of Campus Software .... Mr. Mark WALKER
21 Dir of Business Services .... Ms. Katie WHITE
88 Senior Director of Accounting .... Ms. Alicia HAMILTON
37 Sr Director of Financial Aid .... Mr. Jeff FRANCIS
19 Director of Security .... Mr. Ron CRANE
07 Dean of Admissions .... Mr. Joshua MARTIN
24 Director of Media Services .... Mr. John COOKMAN
88 Director of Accounts Receivable .... Ms. Candace LUTRICK
36 Director of Career Development .... Ms. Beverly ROBINSON
41 Athletic Director .... Dr. Jesse GODDING
26 Director of University Marketing .... Rev. Rick BOWLES
15 Director of Human Resources .... Mrs. Ruth ROBERTS
88 Director of Admissions Info Systems .... Mr. Jarrod PACE
04 Executive Asst to President .... Ms. Patricia BROOKS
108 Director Institutional Assessment .... Rev. Jerry ROBERTS

Southwestern Baptist Theological Seminary (D)

PO Box 22370, Fort Worth TX 76122
County: Tarrant FICE Identification: 003617
Unit ID: 494603
Telephone: (817) 923-1921 Carnegie Class: Not Classified
FAX Number: (817) 921-8766 Calendar System: Semester
URL: www.swbts.edu
Established: 1908 Annual Undergrad Tuition & Fees: $8,980
Enrollment: N/A Coed
Affiliation or Control: Southern Baptist IRS Status: 501(c)3
Highest Offering: Doctorate
Accreditation: SC, MUS, THEOL

01 President .... Dr. Adam W. GREENWAY
05 Provost & VP for Academic Admin .... Dr. David S. DOCKERY
10 VP for Business Administration .... Mr. Clark LOGAN
111 VP for Institutional Advancement .... Dr. Ed UPTON
26 VP for Strategic Initiatives .... Mr. Colby T. ADAMS
20 Assoc Provost for Academic Svcs .... Dr. Travis H. TRAWICK
73 Dean School of Theology .... Dr. Jeffrey BINGHAM
53 Dean Sch of Educational Ministries .... Dr. Michael S. WILDER
64 Dean School of Church Music/Worship .... Dr. Joseph R. CRIDER
88 Dean School of Evangelism/Missions .... Dr. John D. MASSEY
12 Dean Texas Baptist College .... Dr. Benjamin M. SKAUG
32 Dean of Students .... Dr. Charles CARPENTER
34 Dean of Women .... Dr. Terri H. STOVALL

Southwestern Christian College (E)

Box 10, Terrell TX 75160-9002
County: Kaufman FICE Identification: 003618
Unit ID: 228486
Telephone: (972) 524-3341 Carnegie Class: Bac/Assoc-Assoc Dom
FAX Number: (972) 563-7133 Calendar System: Semester
URL: www.swcc.edu
Established: 1949 Annual Undergrad Tuition & Fees: $8,132
Enrollment: 84 Coed
Affiliation or Control: Churches Of Christ IRS Status: 501(c)3
Highest Offering: Baccalaureate
Accreditation: SC

01 President/CEO .... Dr. Ervin SEAMSTER, JR.
30 Vice President for Inst Expansion .... Dr. James MAXWELL
05 Chief Academic Officer .... Dr. Deborah HODRIDGE
10 Vice President Fiscal Affairs .... Mr. Douglas HOWIE
26 Vice President Public Relations .... Vacant
09 VP of Inst Research/Comptroller .... Ms. Joyce CATHEY
08 Librarian .... Ms. Shirley HUDSON
32 Interim Dean of Students .... Mr. Matthew L. TERRY, SR.
07 Director Admissions/Retention .... Mr. Shane MUSHONGA
37 Director of Financial Aid .... Mr. Eric KING
121 Director of Student Success .... Ms. Kecia BAKER
04 Admin Assistant to the President .... Dr. Stevie ROBERTS
06 Registrar .... Dr. Lisa JACKSON
19 Chief of Police .... Mr. Matthew L. TERRY, SR.
29 President Alumni Affairs .... Ms. Vernesha CATHEY
41 Athletic Director .... Mr. Bruce JOHNSON

Southwestern University (F)

1001 E University Avenue, Georgetown TX 78626-6144
County: Williamson FICE Identification: 003620
Unit ID: 228343
Telephone: (512) 863-6511 Carnegie Class: Bac-A&S
FAX Number: (512) 863-5788 Calendar System: Semester
URL: www.southwestern.edu
Established: 1840 Annual Undergrad Tuition & Fees: $45,120
Enrollment: 1,506 Coed
Affiliation or Control: United Methodist IRS Status: 501(c)3
Highest Offering: Baccalaureate
Accreditation: SC, MUS

01 President .... Dr. Laura TROMBLEY
42 Dir of Religious & Spiritual Life .... Ms. Emily ENTSMINGER
04 Exec Asst for Pres/Board Liaison .... Ms. Patricia WITT
05 Dean of Faculty .... Dr. Alisa GAUNDER
32 Vice President for Student Life .... Ms. Jaime WOODY
13 Assoc VP Information Technology .... Mr. Todd WATSON
10 VP for Finance and Administration .... Ms. Lenora CHAPMAN
30 Vice Pres for University Relations .... Mr. Paul SECORD
20 Assoc VP for Academic Affairs .... Ms. Julie A. COWLEY
26 VP Integrated Communications/CMO .... Mr. David OCHSNER
15 Assoc VP for Human Resources .... Ms. Elma F. BENAVIDES
35 Assistant VP of Student Life .... Ms. Lisa DELA CRUZ
35 Dean of Students .... Ms. Shelley STORY
29 Assoc VP for Alumni & Parents .... Ms. Megan FRISQUE
44 Director of Annual Giving .... Vacant
41 Assoc VP Intercollegiate Athletics .... Dr. Glenn SCHWAB
21 Assoc VP Finance Acct/Controller .... Ms. Brenda THOMPSON
19 Chief of Police .... Mr. Brad DUNN
84 Dean of Enrollment Services .... Ms. Christine BOWMAN
36 Dir Ctr Career & Prof Development .... Mr. Adrian RAMIREZ
121 Dir of Academic Success .... Mr. David SEILER
88 Dir Paideia Program/Assoc Professor .... Dr. Sergio COSTOLA
85 Director Intercultural Learning .... Ms. Monya LEMERY
09 Dir Inst Research & Effectiveness .... Ms. Natasha WILLIAMS
28 Dir of Student Inclusion/Diversity .... Ms. Malissa SANON
31 Sr Dir Community Engaged Learning .... Dr. Sarah BRACKMANN
08 Dir of Library Resources .... Ms. Amy ANDERSON
84 VP Recruitment & Enrollment .... Mr. Tom F. DELAHUNT
91 Director Administrative Computing .... Ms. Jennifer O'DANIEL
102 Senior Dir of Foundation Relations .... Ms. Sonya ROBINSON
105 Webmaster .... Mr. Ed HILLIS
18 Assoc VP Facilities Management .... Mr. Rick MARTINEZ

Stark College & Seminary (G)

7000 Ocean Drive, Corpus Christi TX 78412
County: Nueces Identification: 667345
Telephone: (361) 991-9403 Carnegie Class: Not Classified
FAX Number: (361) 991-8634 Calendar System: Semester
URL: www.stark.edu
Established: 1947 Annual Undergrad Tuition & Fees: N/A
Enrollment: N/A Coed
Affiliation or Control: Independent Non-Profit IRS Status: 501(c)3
Highest Offering: Master's
Accreditation: BI

01 President .... Dr. Anthony CELELLI
05 Provost .... Dr. Jena DUNN
10 Chief Financial/Business Officer .... Dr. Chris STAPPER
32 Chief Student Affairs/Life Officer .... Tina VILLARREAL
04 Admin Assistant to the President .... Rochelle ROOTS

Stephen F. Austin State University (H)

1936 North St., Nacogdoches TX 75962
County: Nacogdoches FICE Identification: 003624
Unit ID: 228431
Telephone: (936) 468-3401 Carnegie Class: Masters/L
FAX Number: N/A Calendar System: Semester
URL: www.sfasu.edu
Established: 1923 Annual Undergrad Tuition & Fees (In-State): $10,600
Enrollment: 12,620 Coed
Affiliation or Control: State IRS Status: 501(c)3
Highest Offering: Doctorate
Accreditation: SC, AAFCS, ART, CAATE, CACREP, CAEP, CIDA, DIETD, DIETI, IPSY, MUS, NUR, SP, SW, THEA

01 Interim President .... Dr. Steve WESTBROOK
05 Provost/EVP Academic Affairs .... Dr. Lorenzo SMITH
10 VP Finance/Administration .... Ms. Gina OGLESBEE
32 VP of Student Affairs .... Dr. Brandon FRYE
111 Vice Pres University Advancement .... Ms. Jill STILL
29 Exec Director Alumni .... Mr. Craig A. TURNAGE
20 Assoc Provost Academic Affairs .... Dr. Marc GUIDRY
84 Int Exec Dir of Enrollment Mgmt .... Ms. Rachele GARRETT
26 Chief Mktg/Comm Officer .... Mr. Graham GARNER
43 General Counsel .... Mr. Damon DERRICK
06 Registrar .... Mr. Mickey DIEZ
09 Director Institutional Research .... Ms. Karyn HALL
08 Library Director .... Mr. Jonathan HELMKE
39 Assoc Director of Residence Edu. .... Mr. Carl MACKEY
18 Interim Director of Physical Plant .... Mr. John BRANCH
37 Director of Financial Aid .... Ms. Rachele GARRETT
22 Director Affirmative Action .... Vacant
13 Chief Information Officer .... Mr. Anthony ESPINOZA
15 Interim Director of Human Resources .... Mr. John WYATT
19 Chief of University Police .... Mr. John FIELDS
23 Director Health Services Operations .... Ms. Marcie SHOEMAKER
41 Director of Athletics .... Mr. Ryan IVEY
35 Exec Director of Student Life .... Dr. Hollie GAMMEL-SMITH
38 Director of Counseling .... Ms. Clare FITE
96 Exec Dir of Finance & Admin Svcs .... Ms. Kay JOHNSON
46 Dir Research/Sponsored Programs .... Vacant
58 Int Dean Research & Grad Studies .... Dr. Sheryll JEREZ
49 Dean College Liberal/Applied Arts .... Dr. M. Dustin KNEPP
47 Dean College Forestry/Agriculture .... Dr. Hans M. WILLIAMS
53 Dean of College of Education .... Dr. Judy A. ABBOTT
57 Dean College Fine Arts .... Dr. Gary WURTZ
50 Dean College of Business .... Dr. Timothy BISPING
81 Dean College Sciences & Math .... Dr. Kimberly M. CHILDS
04 Asst to the President .... Ms. Joann BLACK
101 Coordinator of Board Affairs .... Ms. April SMITH
30 Exec Director of Development .... Dr. Trey TURNER
104 Director International Programs .... Ms. Heather CATTON

105 Director Web Services ....Mr. Jason L. JOHNSTONE
106 Int Dir Ctr for Teaching & Learning ....Ms. Alison REED
108 Dir Institutional Effectiveness ....Mr. John CALAHAN
28 Chief Diversity Officer ....Dr. Michara DELANEY-FIELDS
07 Associate Director of Admissions ....Mr. Kevin L. DAVIS
44 Director Advancement Services ....Ms. Sarah SARGENT

Tarrant County College District (A)

300 Trinity Campus Circle, Fort Worth TX 76102-6599
County: Tarrant FICE Identification: 003626
Unit ID: 228547
Telephone: (817) 515-5100 Carnegie Class: Assoc/HT-High Trad
FAX Number: (817) 515-5350 Calendar System: Semester
URL: www.tccd.edu
Established: 1965 Annual Undergrad Tuition & Fees (In-District): $3,402
Enrollment: 43,000 Coed
Affiliation or Control: State/Local IRS Status: 501(c)3
Highest Offering: Associate Degree
Accreditation: SC, ACFEI, ADNUR, CAHIIM, COARC, CONST, DH, DIETT, DMS, EMT, NMT, PTAA, RAD, SURGT

01 Acting Chancellor ....Dr. Elva C. LEBLANC
11 Chief Operating Officer ....Ms. Susan ALANIS
13 Chief Technology Officer ....Mr. Robert PACHECO
05 Exec Vice Chancellor & Provost ....Dr. Elva C. LEBLANC
103 EVP Corp Solutions/Economic Dev ....Ms. Shannon BRYANT
26 VC Communications/External Affairs ....Mr. Reginald GATES
20 VP Academic Affairs SO ....Dr. Shannon YDOYAGA
20 VP Academic Affairs NE ....Dr. Ritu RAJU
20 VP Academic Affairs NW ....Dr. Thomas SOSA
20 VP Academic Affairs SE ....Dr. Zena JACKSON
20 VP Academic Affairs TR ....Dr. Thomas MILLS
20 VP Academic Affairs TCC Connect ....Dr. Shelley PEARSON
32 VP Student Affairs NE ....Vacant
32 VP Student Affairs SE ....Dr. Michael DUPONT
32 VP Student Affairs SO ....Dr. Stephanie HILL
32 VP Student Affairs TR ....Dr. Julie AMON
32 VP Student Affairs NW ....Dr. Jan CLAYTON
12 President South Campus ....Dr. Daniel LUFKIN
12 President Northwest Campus ....Dr. Zarina BLANKENBAKER
12 President Northeast Campus ....Dr. Kenya AYERS
12 President Southeast Campus ....Dr. William COPPOLA
12 President Trinity River Campus ....Dr. Sean MADISON
12 President TCC Connect Campus ....Dr. Carlos MORALES
84 Assoc Vice Chanc Enrol/Acad Support ....Mr. David XIMENEZ
15 Exec Director of Human Resources ....Ms. Gloria MADDOX-POWELL
25 District Exec Dir Grants Dev/Compl ....Ms. Kim MOSS-LINNEAR
21 Assoc Vice Chancellor Finance ....Mrs. Nancy H. CHANG
20 Assoc VChanc Acad Affs/Stdnt Dev ....Vacant
111 Executive Vice Pres of Advancement ....Vacant
09 Int Exec Dir Inst Intel & Research ....Dr. Holly STOVALL
27 Exec Dir Comm/PR/Marketing ....Vacant
18 Exec Dir Real Estate/Facilities ....Mr. Okang HEMMINGS
19 Chief of Police ....Mr. Shaun WILLIAMS
20 Dist Reg & Dir Academic Supp Svcs ....Mr. John D. SPENCER
08 Director Library Services NE ....Mr. Mark DOLIVE
08 Director Library Services SO ....Ms. Laura MCKINNON
08 Director Library Services NW ....Ms. Alex POTEMKIN
08 Director Library Services SE ....Vacant
08 Director Library Services TR ....Vacant
06 Registrar South Campus ....Dr. Pedro PORTILLO
06 Registrar Northeast Campus ....Ms. Christy KLEMIUK
06 Registrar Northwest Campus ....Ms. Samantha TAYLOR
06 Registrar Southeast Campus ....Mr. Kenne EVANS
06 Registrar Trinity Campus ....Mr. Vikas RAJPUROHIT
38 Director of Counseling SO ....Vacant
38 Director of Counseling NE ....Dr. Condoa PARRENT
38 Director of Counseling NW ....Ms. Robin WASHINGTON-WHITE
38 Director of Counseling SE ....Ms. Renetta WRIGHT
38 Director of Counseling TR ....Dr. Deidra TURNER
37 District Director Financial Aid ....Ms. Samantha STALNAKER
37 Director of Financial Aid SO ....Ms. JoLynn H. SPROLE
37 Director of Financial Aid NE ....Ms. Mary BLEDSOE
37 Director of Financial Aid NW ....Ms. Trina SMITH-PATTERSON
37 Director of Financial Aid SE ....Ms. Elizabeth LANDWERMEYER
37 Director of Financial Aid TR ....Mr. William MCMULLEN
35 Dir Student Development Svcs NE ....Vacant
35 Dir Student Development Svcs SO ....Vacant
35 Dir Student Development Svcs NW ....Dr. Vesta M. MARTINEZ
35 Dir Student Development Svcs SE ....Mr. Douglas C. PEAK
35 Dir Student Development Svcs TR ....Mr. Carter BEDFORD
109 Director of Business Services ....Mrs. Kathy M. CRUSTO-WAY
96 Exec Dir of Procurement ....Mr. Michael (Mike) HERNDON
18 Exec Dir Inst Strategic Development ....Ms. Margaret K. LUTTON
07 Dist Dir of Admiss & Records ....Ms. Rebecca (Becki) GRIFFITH
28 Chief Diversity/Equity/Inclus Ofcr ....Vacant
43 Associate General Counsel ....Ms. Carol BRACKEN
100 Chief of Staff ....Vacant

Temple College (B)

2600 S First Street, Temple TX 76504-7435
County: Bell FICE Identification: 003627
Unit ID: 228608
Telephone: (254) 298-8282 Carnegie Class: Assoc/MT-VT-High Trad
FAX Number: (254) 298-8266 Calendar System: Semester
URL: www.templejc.edu
Established: 1926 Annual Undergrad Tuition & Fees (In-District): $4,512
Enrollment: 4,940 Coed
Affiliation or Control: Local IRS Status: 501(c)3
Highest Offering: Associate Degree
Accreditation: SC, ADNUR, COARC, DH, DMS, EMT, SURGT

01 President ....Dr. Christina PONCE
05 Vice Pres Academic Affairs ....Dr. Susan GUZMAN-TREVINO
10 Vice Pres Administrative Svcs/CFO ....Mr. Brandon BOZON
30 Vice Pres Development/Foundation ....Dr. Evelyn WAIWAIOLE
103 Vice Pres Workforce Development ....Ms. Dede GRIFFITH
21 AVP of Finance ....Ms. Susan ALLAMON
15 Exec Dir Human Resources ....Ms. Monica LEFNER
106 Dir Web Applications & System ....Ms. Lindsay WILLIAMS
84 Div Dir Student & Enrollment Svcs ....Mrs. Carey ROSE
08 Div Director of Learning Resources ....Ms. Carrie CRUCE
38 Director Student Advising ....Ms. Mandy HART
04 Assistant to the President & Board ....Mrs. Judith DOHNALIK
37 Director of Financial Aid ....Ms. Mary DANIEL
26 Director Marketing/Public Relations ....Ms. Ellen DAVIS
18 Dir Facilities/Physical Plant ....Mr. Jeremy ALLAMON
96 Director of Purchasing ....Mr. Brian SUPAK
32 Director Student Life ....Mrs. Ruth BRIDGES
06 Registrar ....Mrs. Toni SALAZAR
41 Athletic Director ....Mr. Craig MCMURTRY
19 Chief of Police ....Mr. Michael MARKUM
13 Dir Information Technology Svcs ....Vacant

Texarkana College (C)

2500 N Robison Road, Texarkana TX 75599
County: Bowie FICE Identification: 003628
Unit ID: 228699
Telephone: (903) 823-3456 Carnegie Class: Assoc/HVT-High Non
FAX Number: (903) 823-3451 Calendar System: Semester
URL: www.texarkanacollege.edu
Established: 1927 Annual Undergrad Tuition & Fees (In-District): $3,820
Enrollment: 3,810 Coed
Affiliation or Control: Local IRS Status: 501(c)3
Highest Offering: Associate Degree
Accreditation: SC, ADNUR, EMT

01 President ....Dr. Jason SMITH
05 Vice President of Instruction ....Dr. Donna MCDANIEL
10 Chief Finance Officer ....Mrs. Kim JONES
32 Dean of Students ....Mr. Robert JONES
13 Chief Info Technology Officer ....Mr. Bart UPCHURCH
30 Director Foundation/Development ....Mrs. Katie ANDRUS
09 Dir Inst Research & Effectiveness ....Mrs. Phyllis DEESE
18 Director Facilities Services ....Mr. Rick BOYETTE
26 Director Inst Adv/Public Relations ....Mrs. Suzy IRWIN
88 Director KTXK Radio ....Mr. Steve MITCHELL
15 Director Human Resources ....Mrs. Phyllis DEESE
103 Dean Workforce/Continuing Education ....Mr. Brandon WASHINGTON
81 Dean STEM ....Dr. Catherine HOWARD
76 Dean Health Sciences ....Mrs. Courtney SHOALMIRE
49 Dean Liberal & Performing Arts ....Mrs. Mary E. YOUNG
50 Dean Business & Social Sciences ....Dr. John Dixon BOYLES
08 Director Library/Student Support ....Dr. Tonja MACKEY
84 Enrollment Management/Registrar ....Mr. Brandon HIGGINS
07 Director of Admissions ....Mr. Lee WILLIAMS
37 Director Student Financial Aid ....Mrs. Susan JOHNSTON
04 Presidential Events Coordinator ....Mrs. Mindy PRESTON

*The Texas A & M University System Office (D)

301 Tarrow Street, 7th Floor, College Station TX 77840
County: Brazos FICE Identification: 003629
Unit ID: 228732
Telephone: (979) 458-6000 Carnegie Class: N/A
FAX Number: (979) 458-6044
URL: www.tamus.edu

01 Chancellor ....Mr. John SHARP
05 Vice Chanc for Academic Affairs ....Dr. James HALLMARK
10 Deputy Chancellor & CFO ....Mr. Billy HAMILTON
26 Vice Chanc for Marketing & Comm ....Mr. Laylan COPELIN
116 Chief Auditor ....Ms. Charlie HRNCIR
43 General Counsel ....Mr. Ray BONILLA
46 Vice Chancellor for Research ....Dr. Joe ELABD
21 Vice Chanc for Business Affairs ....Mr. Phillip RAY
13 Chief Information Officer ....Mr. Mark STONE
115 Chief Investment Ofcr/Treasurer ....Ms. Maria ROBINSON
86 Vice Chanc for Govt Relations ....Ms. Jenny JONES
88 Vice Chanc for Dis & Emerg Svc ....Chief Nim KIDD
100 Exec Assistant to the Chancellor ....Ms. Stephanie BJUNE
12 Director RELLIS Campus ....Mr. Kelly TEMPLIN

*Prairie View A & M University (E)

P.O. Box 519 Mail Stop 1337, Prairie View TX 77446-0519
County: Waller FICE Identification: 003630
Unit ID: 227526
Telephone: (936) 261-3311 Carnegie Class: DU-Higher
FAX Number: (936) 261-2115 Calendar System: Semester
URL: www.pvamu.edu
Established: 1876 Annual Undergrad Tuition & Fees (In-State): $11,099
Enrollment: 9,248 Coed
Affiliation or Control: State IRS Status: 501(c)3
Highest Offering: Doctorate
Accreditation: SC, DIETD, DIETI, MUS, NUR, NURSE, SW

02 President ....Dr. Ruth J. SIMMONS
05 Provost /Sr VP Academic Affairs ....Dr. James M. PALMER
20 Assistant Provost Academic Affairs ....Dr. Carmen CARTER
10 Sr Vice Pres Business Affairs/CFO ....Ms. Cynthia CARTER-HORN
32 AVP Student Affairs/Dean Students ....Mr. Steve RANSOM
46 VP Research/Innov/Spons Pgms ....Dr. Magesh RAJAN
41 Director of Athletics ....Mr. Donald R. REED
30 Interim Vice Pres of Development ....Ms. Andrea SANKEY
100 Chief of Staff ....Mr. Kevin HOFFMAN
84 Vice Pres Enroll Mgt/Accred Liaison ....Dr. Sarina WILLIS
21 Asst VP for Financial Accounting ....Ms. Dianne EVANS
92 Director of Honors Program ....Dr. Quincy MOORE
109 Asst VP Auxiliary Services ....Mr. Gregory BRYANT
09 AVP Institutional Research ....Mr. Dean WILLIAMSON
07 Director of Admissions ....Ms. Lenice BROWN
15 Director of Human Resources ....Ms. Cheryl GREENE
63 Director Undergrad Med Acad ....Dr. Dennis E. DANIELS
13 Chief Information Officer ....Mr. Tony MOORE
58 Dean of Graduate Studies ....Dr. Tyrone TANNER
50 Dean College of Business ....Dr. Munir QUDDUS
47 Dean Col Agriculture/Human Sciences ....Dr. Gerard D'SOUZA
66 Dean College of Nursing ....Dr. Allyssa HARRIS
49 Dean Col of Arts/Sciences ....Dr. Dorie J. GILBERT
48 Dean School of Architecture ....Dr. Ikhlas SABOUNI
88 Interim Dean Col Juvenile Justice ....Dr. Camille GIBSON
53 Dean College of Education ....Dr. Michael L. MCFRAZIER
54 Dean College of Engineering ....Dr. Pamela OBIOMON
21 Director of Treasury Services ....Ms. Equilla JACKSON
56 Administrator Coop Extension ....Dr. Carolyn J. WILLIAMS
19 AVP Public Safety/Chief of Police ....Dr. Keith JEMISON
29 Director Alumni Affairs ....Mr. Billy DAVIS
06 Registrar ....Ms. Tina MONTGOMERY
85 Exec Director Intl Programs ....Dr. Godlove FONJWENG
88 Sr Intl Student Advisor II ....Mrs. Evelyn J. MCGINTY
96 Exec Dir Proc & Disburse Svcs ....Ms. A. Marie JOHNSON
04 Executive Assistant ....Ms. Delphia ESTERS
08 Director Library Services ....Dr. Musa OLAKA
104 Executive Director Study Abroad ....Dr. Godlove FONJWENG
22 Director Affirm Action/Equal Opp ....Ms. Renee WILLIAMS
25 Director Contracts & Grants ....Dr. Theresa BAILEY
26 Exec Director Marketing & Comm ....Ms. Candace JOHNSON
37 Director Student Financial Aid ....Dr. Joy THOMAS
38 Director Student Counseling ....Dr. Bernadine DUNCAN
44 Director Annual Giving ....Ms. LaShonda WILLIAMS
39 Exec Dir Residential Engagement ....Mr. Orok OROK

*Tarleton State University (F)

1333 W Washington, Box T-0001,
Stephenville TX 76402-0001
County: Erath FICE Identification: 003631
Unit ID: 228529
Telephone: (254) 968-9000 Carnegie Class: DU-Higher
FAX Number: (254) 968-9920 Calendar System: Semester
URL: www.tarleton.edu
Established: 1899 Annual Undergrad Tuition & Fees (In-State): $8,276
Enrollment: 14,016 Coed
Affiliation or Control: State IRS Status: 501(c)3
Highest Offering: Doctorate
Accreditation: SC, ACBSP, CAATE, CACREP, DIETD, DMOLS, HT, MLS, MLTAD, MUS, NURSE, SW

02 President ....Dr. James HURLEY
100 Chief of Staff/VP University Rels ....Dr. Credence BAKER
05 Provost/Exec VPAA ....Dr. Diane STEARNS
111 Vice Pres Inst Advancement ....Mr. Tony VIDMAR
10 VP Finance/Administration ....Ms. Lori BEATY
32 Interim VP Student Affairs ....Dr. Diana ORTEGA-FEERICK
84 VP Enrollment Mgmt ....Dr. Javier GARZA
12 VP External Ops/Dean Fort Worth ....Dr. Kim MCCUISTION
46 VP Research/Innovation & Econ Dev ....Dr. Rupa IYER
20 Assoc VP Academic Administration ....Vacant
20 Assoc Provost & Dean of Faculty ....Dr. Aimee SHOUSE
36 Director of Career Services ....Ms. Alana HEFNER
18 AVP Campus Operations ....Mr. David MARTIN
35 Exec Director Univ Student Affairs ....Ms. Donna STROHMEYER
30 Asst VP Development ....Ms. Jennifer COLLEY
76 Dean Col Health Sci/Human Svcs ....Dr. Ramona PARKER
81 Dean College Science & Technology ....Dr. Michael HUGGINS
50 Dean College of Business ....Dr. Chris SHAO
47 Dean Col Agricultural/Natural Res ....Dr. Barry LAMBERT
53 Dean College of Education ....Dr. Kim RYNEARSON
49 Dean College Liberal/Fine Arts ....Dr. Eric MORROW
58 Acting Dean Col Grad/Global Studies ....Dr. Nathan HELLER
07 Director Undergraduate Admissions ....Ms. Cynthia HESS
22 Dir Disability Resources ....Mr. Martin CONTRERAS
08 Dean of University Libraries ....Dr. Katherine QUINNELL
92 Exec Dir of Honors College ....Dr. Craig CLIFFORD
37 Director Student Financial Aid ....Ms. Kathy PURVIS
13 Interim CIO ....Mr. Toby BUCKALEW
15 Director of Employee Services ....Ms. Eva LOPEZ
35 Asst VP for Student Affairs ....Dr. Lora HEVIE-MASON
26 Asst VP Marketing & Communications ....Ms. Cecilia JACOBS
41 Athletic Director ....Mr. Lonn REISMAN
23 Director Student Health Center ....Ms. Bridgette BEDNARZ
38 Director Student Counseling ....Ms. Caris THETFORD
19 University Police Chief ....Mr. Matt WELCH
124 Exec Dir of Student Engagement ....Mr. Darrell BROWN
44 Asst VP Advancement Svcs/Engagement ..Mr. Shad HANSELMAN
28 Dir Diversity/Inclusion & Intl Pgm ....Vacant
06 Interim University Registrar ....Ms. Erika GRAHAM
96 Director Procurements and Contracts ....Mr. Thad TURMAN
40 Manager Campus Bookstore ....Mr. Cliff HOY
105 Director of Web Services ....Mr. Johnny THOMPSON
04 Administrative Asst to President ....Ms. Tauna BERTSCH

29 Director Alumni Relations ... Ms. Tami CONDON
117 AVP Univ Compliance ... Mr. Kent STYRON
39 Dir Resident Life/Student Housing ... Ms. Shelly BROWN
54 Dean Mayfield Col of Engineering ... Dr. Rafael LANDAETA
108 Dir Inst Analytics/Effectiveness ... Mr. Morgan CARTER
86 Legislative Affairs Liaison ... Dr. Credence BAKER

*Texas A & M International University (A)

5201 University Boulevard, Laredo TX 78041-1900
County: Webb FICE Identification: 009651
Unit ID: 226152
Telephone: (956) 326-2001 Carnegie Class: Masters/L
FAX Number: (956) 326-2348 Calendar System: Semester
URL: www.tamiu.edu
Established: 1969 Annual Undergrad Tuition & Fees (In-State): $7,683
Enrollment: 8,525 Coed
Affiliation or Control: State IRS Status: 501(c)3
Highest Offering: Doctorate
Accreditation: SC, MPCAC, NUR, SPAA

02 President ... Dr. Pablo ARENAZ
05 Provost ... Dr. Thomas R. MITCHELL
10 Vice Pres Finance & Administration ... Mr. Juan J. CASTILLO, JR.
111 Vice Pres Institutional Advancement ... Ms. Rosanne PALACIOS
32 Interim VP for Student Success ... Mr. Juan G. GARCIA, JR.
11 AVP for Finance & Administration ... Mr. Fred JUAREZ, III
88 Dir of Compliance ... Ms. Monica PALACIOS ROBLEDO
13 Assoc VP Information Technology/CIO ... Mr. Miguel MUNOA
20 Associate Provost ... Dr. Stephen M. DUFFY
49 Dean College Arts & Sciences ... Dr. Claudia E. SAN MIGUEL
50 Dean AR Sanchez Jr Sch of Business ... Dr. Steve R. SEARS
66 Dean School of Nursing ... Dr. Marivic TORREGOSA
08 Dir Sue & Radcliffe Killam Library ... Vacant
07 Director Admissions ... Mrs. Rosie A. DICKINSON
06 Associate VP/Univ Registrar ... Mr. Juan G. GARCIA, JR.
15 Director of Human Resources ... Ms. Jan ASPELUND
26 Director Public Rels Mktg/Info Svcs ... Mr. Steve K. HARMON
37 Director Financial Aid ... Mrs. Laura M. ELIZONDO
41 Director of Athletics ... Mr. Gilbert G. ZIMMERMANN
18 Director Physical Plant ... Mr. Roberto A. GARZA
29 Assistant Director Alumni Relations ... Vacant
36 Director Career Services ... Mrs. Yelitza M. HOWARD
39 Director of Residence Life/Housing ... Mr. Manuel VELA, III
38 Dir Student Couns/Disability Svcs ... Ms. Rosabel RAMOS
96 Dir Purchasing & Support Services ... Mr. Carlos BELLA
92 Assoc Prof Director Honors Pgm ... Dr. Deborah L. BLACKWELL
21 Comptroller ... Ms. Elena M. MARTINEZ
35 Associate VP Student Success ... Mr. Juan G. GARCIA, JR.
123 Dir Grad Admissions/ Recruitment ... Mr. Guillermo F. GONZALEZ, JR.
108 Assoc VP Institutional Assessment ... Dr. Robert B. WILKINSON
97 Dean of University College ... Dr. Barbara S. HONG
53 Dean of Education ... Dr. James O'MEARA

*Texas A & M University (B)

1246 TAMU, College Station TX 77843-1246
County: Brazos FICE Identification: 003632
Unit ID: 228723
Telephone: (979) 845-2217 Carnegie Class: DU-Highest
FAX Number: (979) 845-5027 Calendar System: Semester
URL: www.tamu.edu
Established: 1876 Annual Undergrad Tuition & Fees (In-State): $12,783
Enrollment: 70,418 Coed
Affiliation or Control: State IRS Status: 501(c)3
Highest Offering: Doctorate
Accreditation: SC, CAATE, CLPSY, CONST, COPSY, DENT, DH, DIETD, DIETI, FEPAC, HSA, IPSY, LAW, LSAR, MED, NURSE, PH, PLNG, SCPSY, SPAA, VET

02 President ... Dr. M. Katherine BANKS
05 Int Provost/Exec Vice President ... Dr. Mark H. WEICHOLD
17 VP Health Science Center ... Dr. Jon E. MOGFORD
10 VP Finance/Chief Financial Officer ... Mr. John CRAWFORD
11 SVP and Chief Operating Officer ... Mr. Greg HARTMAN
26 VP Marketing/Communications ... Vacant
13 Vice President Information Tech ... Mr. Edwin PIERSON
15 VP HR & Org Effectiveness ... Dr. Jeff RISINGER
32 VP Student Affairs ... Gen. Joe E. RAMIREZ, JR.
46 Interim VP Research ... Dr. Jack G. BALDAUF
86 VP Government Relations ... Mr. Norman R. GARZA, JR.
103 Dean/VP Innovation/Econ Development ... Dr. Andrew P. MORRISS
88 VP Brand & Business Dev ... Mr. R. Shane HINCKLEY
12 VP/COO TAMU Galveston Campus ... Col. Michael E. FOSSUM
28 Interim VP/Assoc Prov Diversity ... Dr. Annie MCGOWAN
20 Interim Vice Prov Faculty Affairs ... Dr. Patrick LOUCHOUARN
84 VP Enrollment & Acad Svcs ... Mr. Joseph P. PETTIBON, II
43 Deputy General Counsel ... Mr. Brooks MOORE
47 Dean Agriculture & Life Science ... Dr. Patrick J. STOVER
48 Dean Architecture ... Dr. Jorge A. VANEGAS
50 Interim Dean Business ... Dr. R. Duane IRELAND
52 Interim Dean Dentistry ... Dr. Lynne OPPERMAN
53 Dean Education & Human Development ... Dr. Joyce M. ALEXANDER
54 Interim Dean Engineering ... Dr. John E. HURTADO
65 Dean Geosciences ... Dr. Debbie J. THOMAS
80 Dean Govt & Public Service ... Gen. Mark A. WELSH, III
61 Dean Law ... Mr. Robert B. AHDIEH
49 Interim Dean Liberal Arts ... Dr. Steven M. OBERHELMAN
63 Dean Medicine ... Dr. Amy L. WAER
66 Dean Nursing ... Dr. Nancy FAHRENWALD
67 Dean Pharmacy ... Dr. Indra K. REDDY
69 Dean Public Health ... Dr. Shawn G. GIBBS
81 Dean Science ... Dr. Valen E. JOHNSON
74 Dean Vet Med & Biomed Sci ... Dr. John R. AUGUST
08 Interim Dean/Director Libraries ... Ms. Julie MOSBO BALLESTRO
88 Dir Inst Biosciences & Tech ... Dr. Kenneth S. RAMOS
12 Dean & COO TAMU Qatar Campus ... Dr. Cesar O. MALAVE
20 Dean of Faculties/Assoc Prov ... Dr. Blanca M. LUPIANI
20 Assoc Prov Undergrad Studies ... Dr. Ann L. KENIMER
107 Assoc Prov Grad/Prof Studies ... Dr. Karen BUTLER-PURRY
07 Assoc VP Enrollment Services ... Vacant
37 Asst VP Scholarships & Fin Aid ... Ms. Delisa F. FALKS
35 Assoc VP Student Affairs ... Dr. Victoria E. DOBIYANSKI
06 Registrar ... Ms. Venesa A. HEIDICK
36 Exec Dir Career Center ... Ms. Samantha WILSON
23 Director Student Health Center ... Dr. Martha C. DANNENBAUM
38 Exec Dir Student Counseling Svcs ... Dr. Mary Ann COVEY
39 Exec Dir Residence Life/Housing ... Ms. Chareny L. RYDL
92 Assistant Provost Honors Programs ... Dr. Sumana DATTA
104 Executive Director Education Abroad ... Dr. Holly HUDSON
09 Interim Dir Data & Research Svcs ... Ms. Margot H. GOFF
102 President Texas A&M Foundation ... Mr. Tyson VOELKEL
29 Pres Assoc of Former Students ... Mr. Porter GARNER
19 Chief University Police ... Mr. J. Mike JOHNSON
41 Athletic Director ... Mr. Ross BJORK
106 Asst Prov Academic Innovation ... Dr. Jocelyn WIDMER
121 Assoc Prov Acad Affs/Stdnt Success ... Dr. Timothy P. SCOTT
18 Chf Facilities/Physical Plant Ofcr ... Ms. S. Jane SCHNEIDER
21 Asst VP Finance/Strategic Sourcing ... Mr. Dean K. ENDLER

*Texas A&M University-Central Texas (C)

1001 Leadership Place, Killeen TX 76549
County: Bell Identification: 667086
Unit ID: 483036
Telephone: (245) 519-5400 Carnegie Class: Masters/M
FAX Number: (245) 519-5482 Calendar System: Semester
URL: www.tamuct.edu
Established: 1999 Annual Undergrad Tuition & Fees (In-State): $6,483
Enrollment: 2,339 Coed
Affiliation or Control: State IRS Status: 501(c)3
Highest Offering: Master's
Accreditation: SC, ACBSP, CACREP, NURSE, SW

02 President ... Dr. Marc A. NIGLIAZZO
46 VP for Research and Economic Dev ... Dr. Russell PORTER
04 Administrative Asst to President ... Ms. Vicky FERGUSON
05 Chief Academic Officer ... Dr. Peg GRAY-VICKREY
07 Registrar/Exec Director of A&R ... Ms. Hannah MCDONALD
08 Dean of the University Library ... Ms. Bridgit MCCAFFERTY
09 Director Institutional Research ... Mr. Ryan KHAMKONGSAY
10 VP for Finance & Administration ... Mr. Todd LUTZ
13 AVP IT/CIO ... Ms. Gail WALLIN
15 Executive Director HR & Payroll ... Ms. Tina FLOREZ-NEVAREZ
22 Chief Compliance Officer ... Ms. Deserie MENSCH
111 Chief Comm & Advancement Officer ... Dr. Karen CLOS
32 AVP/Dean of Student Affairs ... Dr. Brandon GRIGGS
36 Dir Career/Professional Development ... Ms. Michelle BOLLINGER
37 Dir Student Financial Assistance ... Ms. Irene MONTALVO
50 Dean of Business Administration ... Dr. Faiza KHOJA
53 Dean of Education/Human Development ... Dr. Jeff KIRK
49 Dean of Arts & Sciences ... Dr. Allen REDMON
88 Director Military & Veteran Service ... Mr. Joshua MISSOURI
106 Dir Online Education/E-learning ... Dr. Richard SCHILKE
19 Chief of Police ... Mr. Andrew FLORES
28 Chief Diversity Officer ... Dr. Sanfrena BRITT
84 AVP for Enrollment Management ... Mr. Clifton JONES
96 Director of Purchasing ... Mr. Johnathan FUSELIER
38 Director Student Counseling ... Dr. Carmelia AMUNA
90 Director Academic Computing ... Dr. Richard SCHILKE

*Texas A & M University - Commerce (D)

PO Box 3011, Commerce TX 75429-3011
County: Hunt FICE Identification: 003565
Unit ID: 224554
Telephone: (903) 886-5000 Carnegie Class: DU-Mod
FAX Number: (903) 886-5888 Calendar System: Semester
URL: www.tamuc.edu
Established: 1889 Annual Undergrad Tuition & Fees (In-State): $9,820
Enrollment: 12,249 Coed
Affiliation or Control: State IRS Status: 501(c)3
Highest Offering: Doctorate
Accreditation: SC, ART, CACREP, MUS, #NASP, NURSE, SW

02 President & CEO ... Dr. Mark J. RUDIN
00 President Emeritus ... Dr. Ray M. KECK, III
00 President Emeritus ... Dr. Keith MCFARLAND
05 Provost & VP Academic Affairs ... Dr. Tammi VACHA-HAASE
10 VP Finance & Administration ... Ms. Tina LIVINGSTON
111 VP Div of Philanthropy/Engagement ... Mr. Devin GIROD
46 VP Research & Economic Development ... Ms. Cece GASSNER
28 VP for Inclusion ... Dr. Cephas ARCHIE
100 Chief of Staff ... Ms. Linda KING
88 Chief Ethics & Compliance Officer ... Ms. Katelyn SEVERANCE
41 Int Athletic Director ... Mr. Eric COLEMAN
26 Exec Director Marketing & Comm ... Mr. Michael JOHNSON
20 Vice Prov/Assoc VP of Stdnt Success ... Dr. Ricky DOBBS
21 AVP Finance & Admin/Comptroller ... Ms. Sarah BAKER
114 Budget Director ... Ms. Arlana MARTIN
113 Bursar & Director Student Accounts ... Mr. Charles ROBNETT
06 Registrar ... Ms. Paige BUSSELL
88 Assistant Comptroller ... Ms. Toni BURTON
08 Dean of Libraries ... Ms. Lanee DUNLAP
13 Chief Information Officer ... Mr. Jeremy GAMEZ
37 Dir Financial Aid & Scholarships ... Ms. Renee WALKER
58 Dean Graduate School ... Dr. Jennifer SCHROEDER
53 Int Dean Education & Human Svcs ... Dr. Ray GREEN
79 Dean Humanities/Social Sci & Art ... Dr. William KURACINA
54 Dean Science & Engineering ... Dr. Brent DONHAM
50 Dean Business ... Dr. Mario HAYEK
47 Dean Agric & Natural Resources ... Dr. Randy HARP
92 Dean Honors College ... Vacant
106 Dean College of Innovation & Design ... Dr. Yvonne VILLANUEVA-RUSSELL
09 Exec Dir Inst Effective & Research ... Dr. Dan SU
07 Director of Undergrad Admissions ... Vacant
88 Dir for Outreach and Post Sec Par ... Dr. Hattie POWELL
32 Int VP Stdnt Success/Dean of Stdnts ... Ms. Judy SACKFIELD
35 Assoc Dean Campus Life/Student Dev ... Vacant
29 Director of Alumni Relations ... Mr. Derryle PEACE
19 Chief of Police ... Mr. Bryan VAUGHN
56 Program Dir Extended University ... Ms. Araceli HILL
12 Director Metroplex Center ... Mr. Russell BLANCHETT
12 Director Navarro Partnership ... Ms. Virginia MONK
38 Director Counseling Center ... Dr. Nick PATRAS
39 Dir Residential Living & Learning ... Mr. Michael STARK
117 Dir of Emergency Management/Safety ... Mr. Ethan D. PREAS
23 Director Student Health Center ... Ms. Maxine MENDOZA-WELCH
85 Director International Programs ... Ms. Pri RISAL
96 Chief Procurement Ofcr & HUB Coord ... Mr. Travis BALL
105 Web Application Developer ... Mr. Rick BARR
120 LMS Coordinator ... Mr. Brett MURREY
15 Int Director of Human Resources ... Ms. Tammi THOMPSON
16 Assoc Director Human Resources ... Vacant
118 Sr Employee Benefits Rep ... Ms. Cindy TODHUNTER
18 Exec Dir Facilities Support Svcs ... Mr. Tony BRANDT
22 Int Civil Rights/Title IX Coord ... Mr. James VANBEBBER
30 Director of Philanthropy ... Vacant
44 Director Annual Programs ... Ms. Laura KRAMER-LUCAS
110 Restricted Funds & Exec Gifts Admin ... Ms. Brenda MORRIS
109 Auxiliary Services Manager ... Ms. Jennifer PERRY
84 VP Enrollment Management ... Ms. Nechell BONDS
36 Director Career Development ... Ms. Lacey HENDERSON
89 Dir New Students & Family Program ... Vacant
28 Exec Dir LATINX Outreach & Engage ... Dr. Fred FUENTES
124 Director of Student Engagement ... Ms. Amanda HORNE

*Texas A & M University - Corpus Christi (E)

6300 Ocean Drive, Corpus Christi TX 78412
County: Nueces FICE Identification: 011161
Unit ID: 224147
Telephone: (361) 825-7245 Carnegie Class: DU-Higher
FAX Number: (361) 825-5810 Calendar System: Semester
URL: www.tamucc.edu
Established: 1947 Annual Undergrad Tuition & Fees (In-State): $9,553
Enrollment: 10,820 Coed
Affiliation or Control: State IRS Status: 501(c)3
Highest Offering: Doctorate
Accreditation: SC, CAATE, CACREP, MLS, MUS, NURSE, THEA

02 President/CEO ... Dr. Kelly M. MILLER
05 Provost & VP for Acad Affairs ... Dr. Clarenda PHILLIPS
10 Exec VP for Finance/Admin ... Ms. Jaclyn MAHLMANN
111 VP Institutional Advancement ... Ms. Jaime NODARSE BARRERA
32 VP Student Engagement & Success ... Mr. Adrian RODRIGUEZ
46 VP for Research & Innovation ... Dr. Ahmed MAHDY
20 Interim Assoc Provost ... Dr. Susan MURPHY
100 Chief of Staff ... Ms. Claire SNYDER
13 Sr Assoc VP for Technology/CIO ... Mr. Edward EVANS
84 VP Enrollment Management ... Mr. Andy BENOIT
35 Assoc VP Student Engagement ... Ms. Ann DEGAISH
08 Dean of University Libraries ... Dr. Catherine RUDOWSKY
09 Exec Dir Institutional Research ... Ms. Erin MULLIGAN-NGUYEN
26 Director of Marketing ... Ms. Ashley LARRABEE
30 Asst VP Development ... Ms. Kimberly BECERRA
88 Asst VP School/Community Relations ... Dr. Margaret DECHANT
07 Exec Director of Admissions ... Mr. Oscar REYNA
37 Director of Financial Assistance ... Ms. Jeannie GAGE
31 Director Community Outreach ... Mr. Joseph MILLER
15 Director of Human Resources ... Ms. Debra CORTINAS
36 Director Career Services ... Dr. Leslie MILLS
88 Asst VP Student Support ... Dr. Lisa PEREZ
22 Dir Equal Opportunity Employee ... Mr. Sam RAMIREZ
11 Exec Dir Administrative Services ... Ms. Judy HARRAL
96 Dir Procurement & Disbursements ... Mr. Will HOBART
113 Bursar ... Ms. Christina HOLZHEUSER
58 Dean College of Grad Studies ... Dr. Karen MCCALEB
49 Dean College of Liberal Arts ... Dr. Shawnrece CAMPBELL
50 Dean College of Business ... Dr. Brian TIETJE
53 Dean College of Education ... Dr. David SCOTT
54 Interim Dean College of Sci/Engr ... Dr. Ahmed MAHDY
66 Dean College of Nursing/Health Sci ... Dr. Hassan AZIZ
04 Exec Assistant to the President ... Ms. Wendy BENDERMAN
11 Assoc VP Operations ... Mr. Scott MEARES
25 Manager Contracts ... Ms. Deborah ZENTMIRE
29 Exec Director of Alumni Relations ... Mr. Russell WAGNER
39 Manager Housing Business Operations ... Ms. Stephanie BOX
41 Athletic Director ... Mr. Jonathan PALUMBO
06 Registrar ... Ms. Missy CHAPA

*Texas A & M University - Kingsville (A)

700 University Boulevard, Kingsville TX 78363-8202
County: Kleberg FICE Identification: 003639
Unit ID: 228705
Telephone: (361) 593-2111 Carnegie Class: DU-Higher
FAX Number: (361) 593-3107 Calendar System: Semester
URL: www.tamuk.edu
Established: 1925 Annual Undergrad Tuition & Fees (In-State): $9,779
Enrollment: 6,932 Coed
Affiliation or Control: State IRS Status: 501(c)3
Highest Offering: Doctorate
Accreditation: SC, CACREP, DIETD, DIETI, MUS, NAIT, PHAR, SP, SW

02 President ... Dr. Robert VELA
43 Director of Risk & Compliance ... Dr. Shane CREEL
05 Provost & Vice President ... Dr. Lou REINISCH
10 VP Finance/Chief Financial Officer ... Mr. Jacob FLOURNOY
111 VP Institutional Advancement ... Mr. Bradley WALKER
21 Exec Dir Financial Svcs/Controller ... Ms. Joanne CASTRO
117 Exec Director Risk Management ... Dr. Shane CREEL
36 Director of Academic Success ... Ms. Christina RODRIGUEZ-GONZALEZ
109 Dir of Prop Mgmt & Auxil Services ... Mr. Crispin TREVINO
88 Director of Recreational Sports ... Vacant
84 VP Enroll Services/ Student Affair ... Dr. Rito SILVA
13 Chief Information Officer ... Vacant
119 Chief Information Security Officer ... Vacant
91 Dir Enterprise Applications ... Mr. John DOVE
35 Assistant VP Student Affairs ... Ms. Kirsten COMPARY
20 Associate VP Academic Affairs ... Dr. Jaya S. GOSWAMI
85 Dir International Student Services ... Mr. Peter LI
58 VP Research & Grad Studeis ... Vacant
22 Associate VP Student Access ... Dr. Maria MARTINEZ
47 Dean College Agriculture ... Dr. Shad NELSON
49 Dean Arts & Sciences ... Dr. Dolores GUERRERO
50 Dean Business Administration ... Dr. Natalya DELCOURE
53 Dean College of Education ... Dr. Steve BAIN
54 Dean Engineering ... Dr. Heidi A. TABOADA
121 Assoc VP for Student Success ... Dr. Shannon BAKER
26 Director Marketing & Communications ... Ms. Adriana GARZA
08 Interim Library Director ... Ms. Christine RADCLIFF
09 Institutional Research Director ... Ms. Miao ZHUANG
88 Interm Exec Director Citrus Center ... Dr. Mamoudou SETAMOU
88 Director King Ranch Institute ... Dr. Clay P. MATHIS
88 Exec Dir Wildlife Research CKWRI ... Dr. David HEWITT
06 Registrar ... Ms. Mildred SLAUGHTER
41 Exec Dir Athletics & Campus Rec ... Mr. Stephen ROACH
106 Dir Distance Learning & Instr Tech ... Mr. Rolando GARZA
110 Advancement Services Director ... Ms. Lori RUSSEK
23 Director Student Health Services ... Ms. Jo Elda CASTILLO-ALANIZ
88 Int Dir John E Conner Museum ... Ms. Kathy PAWELEK
15 Chief of People/Workplace Culture ... Mr. Henry BURGOS
18 Exec Director Physical Plant ... Mr. Andy GONZALEZ
96 Assoc VP Support Services ... Vacant
39 Exec Director Residence Life ... Mr. Tom MARTIN
88 Exec Dir Disburs/Trvl/Prop Mgmt ... Ms. Maricela CISNEROS
35 Director Student Activities ... Ms. Erin MCCLURE
19 Chief of Police ... Mr. Julian CAVAZOS
37 Director Student Financial Aid ... Mr. Raul CAVAZOS
04 Sr Exec Asst to President ... Ms. Raquel GARCIA
28 Dir of Diversity/Equity/Inclusion ... Dr. Jarett LUJAN
30 Chief Development Officer ... Ms. Ruby GONZALEZ

*Texas A & M University-San Antonio (B)

One University Way, San Antonio TX 78224
County: Bexar Identification: 666689
Unit ID: 459949
Telephone: (210) 784-1000 Carnegie Class: Masters/L
FAX Number: (210) 784-6219 Calendar System: Semester
URL: www.tamusa.edu
Established: 2009 Annual Undergrad Tuition & Fees (In-District): $8,901
Enrollment: 6,759 Coed
Affiliation or Control: State/Local IRS Status: 501(c)3
Highest Offering: Master's
Accreditation: SC

02 President ... Dr. Cynthia TENIENTE-MATSON
05 Provost/VP Academic Affairs ... Dr. Mohamed ABDELRAHMAN
10 VP Business Affairs & CFO ... Ms. Kathryn FUNK-BAXTER
111 VP for University Advancement ... Dr. Jesse PISORS
84 VP for Enrollment Management ... Dr. Brandy MCLELLAND
121 VP Student Success/Engagement ... Dr. Mari FUENTES-MARTIN
09 AVP of Institutional Effectiveness ... Ms. Jane MIMS
50 Dean College of Business ... Dr. Rohan CHRISTIE-DAVID
49 Dean College of Arts & Sciences ... Dr. Debra FEAKES
53 Interim Dean College of Education ... Dr. Suzanne MUDGE
100 Chief of Staff/Dir Pres Operation ... Ms. Jessica LOUDERMILK
29 Director Alumni Affairs ... Dr. Mary Kay COOPER
26 Dir of Marketing/Communications ... Ms. Adriana CONTRERAS
13 Chief Information Officer ... Mr. William GRIFFENBERG
07 Director of Admissions ... Ms. Melissa MORALES
37 Dir of Financial Aid & Scholarships ... Ms. Leanne JOHNSON
06 Executive Director/Registrar ... Ms. Rachel MONTEJANO
15 Chief Human Resources Officer ... Ms. Martha GONZALEZ
18 Director of Facilities ... Vacant
38 Director of Counseling ... Dr. Mary BUZZETTA
96 Dir Procurement/HUB Services ... Mr. Christopher SCOTT
41 Dir of Intercollegiate Athletics ... Mr. Darnell SMITH

*Texas A & M University - Texarkana (C)

7101 University Avenue, Texarkana TX 75503
County: Bowie FICE Identification: 031703
Unit ID: 224545
Telephone: (903) 223-3000 Carnegie Class: Masters/M
FAX Number: (903) 832-8890 Calendar System: Semester
URL: www.tamut.edu
Established: 1971 Annual Undergrad Tuition & Fees (In-State): $7,764
Enrollment: 2,171 Coed
Affiliation or Control: State IRS Status: 501(c)3
Highest Offering: Doctorate
Accreditation: SC, CACREP, NURSE, @SW

02 President ... Dr. Emily CUTRER
05 Provost/Vice Pres Academic Affairs ... Dr. Melinda ARNOLD
10 Chief Financial Officer ... Mr. Aaron HARDING
111 VP University Advancement ... Mrs. LeAnne WRIGHT
84 VP Student Engagement/Enrol/Success ... Ms. Kathy WILLIAMS
100 Chief of Staff to the President ... Ms. Vicki MELDE
13 Chief Information Officer ... Mr. Jeff HINTON
32 Assistant VP of Student Affairs ... Mr. Carl GREIG
121 Asst Vice Pres for Student Success ... Mrs. Elizabeth PATTERSON
20 Assoc Provost/SACSCOC Liaison ... Dr. Sushil SHARMA
49 Dean Col Arts & Sciences/Education ... Vacant
50 Dean Col of Bus/Engineering/Tech ... Dr. Divya CHOUDHARY
114 Director of Budgets ... Mrs. Ramona GREEN
113 Bursar ... Ms. Joni MILLICAN
37 Dir Financial Aid & Veteran Svcs ... Mr. Michael FULLER
15 Director Human Resources & EEO ... Ms. Charlotte BANKS
08 Library Director ... Vacant
19 Police Chief/Director Security ... Mr. Alex SERRANO
96 Director Purchasing and Support ... Mrs. Kristen TULLOS
07 Asst VP of Admissions/Recruiting ... Mr. Toney FAVORS
26 Director Communications ... Mr. John BUNCH
104 Director of International Studies ... Dr. Jennifer DAVIS
41 Director of Athletics ... Mr. Michael GALVAN
04 Executive Assistant to President ... Mrs. Sarah NEWMAN
06 Registrar ... Mrs. Jana BOATRIGHT
38 Director Student Counseling ... Mrs. Briana TAYLOR
29 Alumni Relations Coordinator ... Mrs. Kinley CROSS

*West Texas A & M University (D)

2501 4th Ave., Canyon TX 79016
County: Randall FICE Identification: 003665
Unit ID: 229814
Telephone: (806) 651-0000 Carnegie Class: Masters/L
FAX Number: (806) 651-2126 Calendar System: Semester
URL: www.wtamu.edu
Established: 1910 Annual Undergrad Tuition & Fees (In-State): $8,456
Enrollment: 10,036 Coed
Affiliation or Control: State IRS Status: 501(c)3
Highest Offering: Doctorate
Accreditation: SC, MUS, NURSE, SP, SW, THEA

02 President ... Dr. Walter V. WENDLER
05 Executive Vice President/Provost ... Dr. Neil W. TERRY
10 Vice Pres for Business & Finance ... Mr. Randy RIKEL
32 VP Student Enroll/Engage/Success ... Mr. Michael J. KNOX
111 VP Philanthropy & Ext Relations ... Dr. Todd W. RASBERRY
28 Chief Diversity/Inclusion Officer ... Ms. Angela ALLEN
100 Chief of Staff/Asst VP Strat Comm ... Ms. Tracee POST
06 Registrar ... Ms. Diane BRICE
07 Director of Admissions ... Mr. Jeff S. BAYLOR
08 Dir Information/Library Resources ... Ms. Shawna J. KENNEDY-WITTHAR
36 Dir Career Planning/Placement ... Ms. Kim MULLER
37 Director Student Financial Aid ... Ms. Marian K. GIESECKE
56 Director of Extended Studies ... Ms. Andrea PORTER
23 Director Medical Service ... Dr. Jim GIBBS
19 Police Chief ... Chief Shawn G. BURNS
26 AVP Marketing and Communications ... Ms. Kelly POLDEN
29 Executive Dir of Alumni Relations ... Mr. Ronnie L. HALL
38 Director Counseling Services ... Ms. Dayna SCHERTLER
41 Director of Athletics ... Mr. Michael MCBROOM
09 AVP Inst Research & Effectiveness ... Mr. Jarvis D. HAMPTON
13 VP for Information Technology/CIO ... Mr. James D. WEBB
96 Director of Purchasing ... Ms. Elaine K. CHEW
40 Manager Bookstore ... Mr. Terry S. NEPPER
15 Director of Human Resources ... Ms. Nancy HAMPTON
47 Dean Col Agri/Natural Sciences ... Dr. Kevin POND
50 Dean College of Business ... Dr. Amjad A. ABDULLAT
53 Dean Col Education/Social Sciences ... Dr. Eddie W. HENDERSON
57 Dean College Fine Arts/Humanities ... Dr. Jessica MALLARD
54 Dean College of Engineering ... Dr. Emily HUNT
46 VP for Research & Compliance ... Dr. Angela SPAULDING
66 Dean College of Nursing/Health Sci ... Dr. Dirk NELSON
104 Director Study Abroad ... Ms. Carolina GALLOWAY
122 Assoc Dir Greeks/Organiztions ... Ms. Elosia REYNA

* *Texas A & M University at Galveston* (E)

PO Box 1675, Galveston TX 77553-1675
Telephone: (409) 740-4414 FICE Identification: 010298
Accreditation: &SC

† Regional accreditation is carried under the parent institution Texas A & M University, College Station, TX.

Texas Baptist Institute and Seminary (F)

1300 Longview Drive, Henderson TX 75652
County: Rusk Identification: 667363
Telephone: (903) 657-6543 Carnegie Class: Not Classified
FAX Number: N/A Calendar System: Semester
URL: tbi.edu
Established: 1948 Annual Undergrad Tuition & Fees: N/A
Enrollment: N/A Coed
Affiliation or Control: Independent Non-Profit IRS Status: 501(c)3
Highest Offering: Doctorate
Accreditation: @BI

01 President ... Dr. Ray O. BROOKS
05 Academic Dean/CEO ... Dr. Steve BUTLER
111 Vice Pres Advancement ... Robert WALLACE
06 Registrar ... Jimmy JONES

Texas Chiropractic College (G)

5912 Spencer Highway, Pasadena TX 77505-1699
County: Harris FICE Identification: 003635
Unit ID: 228866
Telephone: (281) 487-1170 Carnegie Class: Spec-4-yr-Other Health
FAX Number: (281) 487-2009 Calendar System: Trimester
URL: www.txchiro.edu
Established: 1908 Annual Undergrad Tuition & Fees: N/A
Enrollment: 250 Coed
Affiliation or Control: Independent Non-Profit IRS Status: 501(c)3
Highest Offering: Doctorate
Accreditation: SC, CHIRO

01 President ... Dr. Stephen FOSTER
10 Controller ... Mr. David MASKELL
11 Executive Vice President ... Dr. Sandra HUGHES
84 Assoc VP of Enrollment Management ... Ms. Monique LEWIS
121 Student Success Program Coord ... Ms. Emily PYRON
100 Chief of Staff ... Dr. Kent GRAY
06 Registrar ... Ms. Sarah TROTMAN
15 Director of Human Resources ... Mrs. Sue ARNOLD
26 Graphic Designer & Communications ... Ms. Alysa CAMPOS
08 Director of Library Services ... Ms. Carol WEBB
37 Director of Financial Aid ... Mr. Arthur GOUDEAU
07 Director of Admissions ... Ms. Ericka GARDUZA
101 Exec Admin Asst/Board Liaison ... Mrs. Marian MOORE

Texas Christian University (H)

2800 S University Drive, Fort Worth TX 76129-2800
County: Tarrant FICE Identification: 003636
Unit ID: 228875
Telephone: (817) 257-7000 Carnegie Class: DU-Higher
FAX Number: N/A Calendar System: Semester
URL: www.tcu.edu
Established: 1873 Annual Undergrad Tuition & Fees: $51,660
Enrollment: 11,379 Coed
Affiliation or Control: Christian Church (Disciples Of Christ)
IRS Status: 501(c)3
Highest Offering: Doctorate
Accreditation: SC, ANEST, ART, CAATE, CACREP, CIDA, DANCE, DIETC, DIETD, JOUR, #MED, MUS, NURSE, SP, SW

01 Chancellor ... Dr. Victor J. BOSCHINI, JR.
05 Provost/Vice Chanc Academic Affairs ... Dr. Teresa A. DAHLBERG
10 Vice Chanc Finance & Administration ... Dr. William J. NUNEZ
111 Vice Chanc University Advancement ... Mr. Donald J. WHELAN, JR.
32 Vice Chancellor Student Affairs ... Dr. Kathryn CAVINS-TULL
26 Vice Chanc Mktg & Communication ... Ms. Tracy SYLER-JONES
15 Vice Chancellor Human Resources ... Ms. Yohna CHAMBERS
20 Vice Provost for Academic Affairs ... Dr. Susan M. WEEKS
41 Director Intercollegiate Athletics ... Mr. Jeremiah DONATI
115 Chief Investment Officer ... Mr. Jason SAFRAN
13 Chief Technology Officer ... Mr. Bryan LUCAS
88 Chief University Compliance Officer ... Ms. Andrea NORDMANN
28 Sr Advisor/Chief Inclusion Ofcr ... Dr. Jonathan BENJAMIN-ALVARADO
43 General Counsel ... Mr. Lee TYNER
100 Chief of Staff/Sec of the Board ... Ms. Jean PICKETT
22 Director of Institutional Equity ... Ms. Sharon GOODING
28 Dir Diversity/Inclusion Initiatives ... Ms. Aisha TORREY-SAWYER
86 Government Affairs Officer ... Dr. Lauren NIXON
60 Dean Schieffer Col Communication ... Dr. Kristie BUNTON
63 Dean School of Medicine ... Dr. Stuart FLYNN
53 Dean College of Education ... Dr. Frank HERNANDEZ
08 Dean of the Library ... Ms. Tracy HULL
81 Dean Col of Science & Engineering ... Dr. Michael KRUGER
92 Dean John V Roach Honors Col ... Dr. Ron PITCOCK
50 Dean Neeley School of Business ... Mr. Daniel W. PULLIN
57 Dean College of Fine Arts ... Ms. Amy H. TULLY
49 Dean AddRan College of Liberal Arts ... Dr. Sonja S. WATSON
66 Dean Harris Col Nurs & Health Sci ... Dr. Christopher WATTS
97 Dean School of Interdisc Stds ... Dr. Reginald WILBURN
46 Assoc Provost Research/Dean Grad ... Dr. Floyd L. WORMLEY, JR.
20 Assoc Provost Academic Plng/Budget ... Ms. Megan M. SOYER
20 Assoc Provost of Faculty Affairs ... Dr. M. Francyne HUCKABY
84 Assoc Provost of Enrollment Manage ... Mr. Mike SCOTT
07 Dean of Admission ... Mr. Heath A. EINSTEIN
07 Director of Undergraduate Admission ... Ms. Mandy CASTRO
07 Assoc Director Transfer Admission ... Ms. April YANDELL

37 Dir Scholarships & Financial Aid ..... Ms. Victoria CHEN
06 Registrar ..... Dr. Nichole FISHER
121 Assoc Vice Provost Student Success ..... Dr. Annorah MOORMAN
121 Exec Director Academic Advising ..... Dr. Angela THOMPSON
25 Director Sponsored Programs ..... Ms. LeAnn FORSBERG
51 Director Extended Education ..... Ms. Julie LOVETT
106 Dir Teaching & Learning Program ..... Dr. Joanna SCHMIDT
104 Dir Ctr Intl Studies/Study Abroad ..... Dr. Sandra CALLAGHAN
108 Director Inst Effectiveness ..... Dr. David ALLEN
09 Director Institutional Research ..... Dr. Cathan COGHLAN
35 Assoc Vice Chanc Student Affairs ..... Dr. Michael RUSSEL
35 Dean of Students ..... Dr. Karen MORGAN
88 Asst VC SA Leadership/Stdnt Involve ..... Dr. Vanessa R. BRYAN
88 Asst VC Student Affairs Admin ..... Dr. Jude KIAH
19 Asst Vice Chanc Public Safety ..... Mr. Adrian ANDREWS
93 Asst VC Multicult/Intl Impact ..... Vacant
39 Exec Dir Housing/Res & Fra/Sor Life ..... Mr. Craig ALLEN
36 Exec Dir Career Services ..... Mr. Mike CALDWELL
23 Director Health Services ..... Dr. Jane TORGERSON
85 Director International Student Svcs ..... Mr. John L. SINGLETON
38 Director Mental Health Services ..... Dr. Eric WOOD
19 Chief TCU Police ..... Mr. Robert RANGEL
42 University Chaplain ..... Rev. Todd BOLING
122 Director Fraternity & Sorority Life ..... Ms. Brooke SCOGIN
30 Assoc VC University Development ..... Mr. David NOLAN
88 Assoc VC Donor Relations ..... Ms. Julie WHITT
88 Assoc VC Strategy/Advance Admin ..... Ms. Michelle CLARK
29 Assoc Vice Chanc Alumni Relations ..... Ms. Amanda STALLINGS
110 Assoc Vice Chanc Advancement Ops ..... Mr. Travis SOYER
88 Asst VC School & College Dev ..... Mr. Adam BAGGS
44 Asst VC Loyalty Giving ..... Ms. Kristee BELL
112 Asst VC Development Major Gifts ..... Mr. Kenton WATT
102 Sr Dir Corporate/Found Relations ..... Mr. Jason BYRNE
21 Assoc Vice Chanc & Controller ..... Ms. Cheryl KENNON
18 Assoc VC Facilities & Planning ..... Mr. Todd S. WALDVOGEL
114 Sr Asst Vice Chanc for Finance ..... Ms. Veronica RIOS
116 Asst VC Internal Audit ..... Ms. Kim ADAMS
21 Asst Vice Chanc for Finance ..... Ms. Candice PAYNE
25 Director Contract Administration ..... Mr. Matthew WALLIS
96 Director of Procurement ..... Ms. Rebekah ATKINSON
113 Director Student Financial Services ..... Ms. Cori SMIT
27 Assoc Vice Chanc Communications ..... Ms. Merianne ROTH
27 Asst Vice Chanc Marketing ..... Mr. Bill HARTLEY
105 Dir Website Social Media Management ..... Mr. Corey REED
16 Assoc VC for Human Resources ..... Ms. Rachelle BLACKWELL
88 Asst VC Engage/Success/Strategy ..... Ms. Mariam MACGREGOR
118 Director of Benefits ..... Ms. Michelle WHITELEY

Texas College (A)

2404 N Grand Avenue, Tyler TX 75702-1962
County: Smith FICE Identification: 003638
Unit ID: 228884
Telephone: (903) 593-8311 Carnegie Class: Bac-Diverse
FAX Number: (903) 593-0588 Calendar System: Semester
URL: www.texascollege.edu
Established: 1894 Annual Undergrad Tuition & Fees: $10,000
Enrollment: 764 Coed
Affiliation or Control: Christian Methodist Episcopal IRS Status: 501(c)3
Highest Offering: Baccalaureate
Accreditation: SC

01 President ..... Dr. Dwight FENNELL
05 Vice President Academic Affairs ..... Dr. Jan DUNCAN
10 Vice Pres Business & Finance ..... Ms. Millicent RICKENBACKER
32 Vice Pres Student Affairs ..... Dr. Cynthia MARSHALL BIGGINS
84 Dean Enrollment Mgmt & Registrar ..... Mr. John ROBERTS
30 Development Officer ..... Vacant
42 Dean of Chapel/Campus Ministry ..... Dr. Jamie CAPERS
09 Dir Inst Research/ Effectiveness ..... Dr. Cynthia MARSHALL-BIGGINS
08 Director of Library Services ..... Mrs. Linda SIMMONS-HENRY
13 Acting Dir Information Technology ..... Mr. Yaw LABANG
15 Director Human Resources ..... Ms. Lois BOWIE
41 Athletic Director ..... Mr. Randy BUTLER
37 Director Financial Aid ..... Mrs. Shadana MINGO
18 Director Physical Plant ..... Mr. Anthony PARKER
19 Director Security/Safety ..... Mr. Derrick BROWN
26 Chief Marketing & Communications ..... Mr. Jake MARTIN
04 Exec Asst to the President ..... Mrs. Angelia FENNELL
07 Director of Admissions/Registrar ..... Mr. John ROBERTS

Texas Health and Science University (B)

4005 Menchaca Road, Austin TX 78704-6737
County: Travis FICE Identification: 031795
Unit ID: 430704
Telephone: (512) 444-8082 Carnegie Class: Spec-4-yr-Other Health
FAX Number: (512) 444-6345 Calendar System: Trimester
URL: www.thsu.edu
Established: 1990 Annual Undergrad Tuition & Fees: N/A
Enrollment: 104 Coed
Affiliation or Control: Proprietary IRS Status: Proprietary
Highest Offering: Master's; No Lower Division
Accreditation: ACICS, ACUP

01 President ..... Dr. Louis AGNESE
85 VP of International Affairs ..... Mr. Wen Huei CHEN
58 VP/MBA Director ..... Dr. Shu-Chiang LIN
05 Academic Dean/Biomed Dir Austin ..... Dr. Maoyi CAI
108 Assessment Dir ..... Ms. Martha CALLIHAM
37 Financial Aid/Intl Student Advisor ..... Mr. Antonio HOLLOWAY
08 Administrative Coordinator ..... Mrs. Iris GONG
06 Registrar/Administrator ..... Ms. Alexis SANFTNER
20 Academic Dean/Clinic Director SA ..... Dr. Roberto GUERRERO
08 Librarian SA Campus ..... Mrs. Heidi HOECKER
88 Clinic Director Austin Campus ..... Dr. Hai Tao CAO
88 Director of Herbal Department ..... Ms. Allison YU
88 Director of Acupuncture Austin ..... Dr. Sung Wook HONG
07 Director of Admissions ..... Dr. Naomi GARCIA
10 Accountant ..... Zhen SUN

† Granted candidacy at the Doctorate level by ACAOM.

Texas Lutheran University (C)

1000 W Court Street, Seguin TX 78155-5999
County: Guadalupe FICE Identification: 003641
Unit ID: 228981
Telephone: (830) 372-8000 Carnegie Class: Bac-Diverse
FAX Number: (830) 372-8001 Calendar System: Semester
URL: www.tlu.edu
Established: 1891 Annual Undergrad Tuition & Fees: $31,850
Enrollment: 1,499 Coed
Affiliation or Control: Evangelical Lutheran Church In America
IRS Status: 501(c)3
Highest Offering: Master's
Accreditation: SC, ACBSP, CAATE, MUS, NURSE

01 President ..... Dr. Debbie COTTRELL
05 VP for Academic Affairs ..... Dr. Sarah FERGUSON
10 Vice President Finance ..... Ms. Edie RICHARDSON
84 VP for Enrollment and Marketing ..... Ms. Sarah STORY
30 VP for Development/Alumni Relations ..... Ms. Renee REHFELD
32 VP/Dean of Student Life & Learning ..... Dr. Gourjoine WADE
13 VP for Administration & CIO ..... Mr. William SENTER
06 Director of Records & Registration ..... Mr. Glenn YOCKEY
08 Library Director ..... Dr. Daniel FLORES
113 Dir of Student Financial Services ..... Ms. Cathleen WRIGHT
42 Campus Pastor ..... Vacant
38 Director Counseling & Disabilities ..... Dr. Marlene MORIARITY
07 Director of Admissions ..... Ms. ALecia MCCAIN
15 Director of Human Resources ..... Ms. Toi TURNER
41 Director of Athletics ..... Mr. Bill MILLER
09 Director of Institutional Research ..... Vacant
04 Exec Assistant to the President ..... Ms. Susan RINN
102 Dir Foundation/Corporate Relations ..... Ms. Jena MCKINZIE
104 Director Study Abroad ..... Ms. Charla BAILEY
26 Director of Marketing ..... Ms. Ashlie FORD
108 Director of Academic Assessment ..... Dr. Michael CZUCHRY
18 Chief Facilities/Physical Plant ..... Mr. Kirk HERBOLD
19 University Police Chief ..... Chief Irene GARCIA
29 Director Alumni Relations ..... Ms. Taylor CARLETON
39 Director of Residence Life ..... Mr. Tim WESTMORELAND
22 Dir Affirm Action/EEO/Diversity ..... Ms. Toi TURNER
43 Dir Legal Services/General Counsel ..... Mr. James FROST
28 Chair Diversity Committee ..... Dr. Chris BOLLINGER
50 Chair Business & Econ Department ..... Dr. Fernando GARZA
53 Chair Education Department ..... Dr. Jeannette JONES
36 Director Student Placement ..... Dr. Bernadette BUCHANAN
37 Director Student Financial Aid ..... Ms. Erika MILLER
90 Director Academic Computing ..... Dr. Rodrick SHAO

Texas Southern University (D)

3100 Cleburne Street, Houston TX 77004-4584
County: Harris FICE Identification: 003642
Unit ID: 229063
Telephone: (713) 313-7011 Carnegie Class: DU-Higher
FAX Number: (713) 313-1092 Calendar System: Semester
URL: www.tsu.edu
Established: 1927 Annual Undergrad Tuition & Fees (In-State): $9,173
Enrollment: 7,015 Coed
Affiliation or Control: State IRS Status: 170(c)1
Highest Offering: Doctorate
Accreditation: SC, CAEPN, CAHIIM, COARC, DIETD, LAW, MLS, NAIT, PHAR, PLNG, SPAA, SW

01 President ..... Dr. Lesia L. CRUMPTON-YOUNG
05 Interim Provost/VP Academic Affairs ..... Dr. Lillian B. POATS
10 EVP Administration/Finance & CFO ..... Mr. Kenneth HUEWITT
111 VP Advancement/Communication ..... Ms. Melinda SPAULDING
13 VP Info Tech/Chief Information Ofcr ..... Mr. Mario BERRY
100 Chief of Staff ..... Dr. Dakota DOMAN
43 General Counsel ..... Mr. Hao LE
41 VP Intercollegiate Athletics ..... Mr. Kevin GRANGER
32 VP Student Affairs ..... Dr. Teresa MCKINNEY
09 Int Assoc Provost/Assoc VP Research ..... Dr. Adebayo O. OYEKAN
88 Dir Title III/Ofc of Sponsored Proj ..... Ms. Demetria JOHNSON-WEEKS
15 Sr Assoc VP of Human Resources ..... Ms. Yolanda EDMOND
26 Assoc VP of Communications ..... Mr. Steve SCHEFFLER
84 Assoc VP Enrollment Management ..... Mr. Wendell WILLIAMS
08 Exec Director Libraries/Museums ..... Dr. Janice L. PEYTON
50 Int Dean School of Business ..... Dr. John H. WILLIAMS
51 Int Dir Office of Cont Education ..... Dr. Melanie LAWSON
53 Dean College of Education ..... Dr. Lillian B. POATS
80 Dean School of Public Affairs ..... Dr. Theophilus HERRINGTON
61 Acting Dean School of Law ..... Dr. Gary L. BLEDSOE
67 Int Dean Col Pharmacy & Health Sci ..... Dr. Shirlette MILTON
19 Chief of Police ..... Chief Mary YOUNG
39 Director of Student Housing ..... Dr. Yvette BARKER
92 Dean Freeman Honors College .. Dr. Dianne JEMISON-POLLARD
18 Exec Dir Facilities & Maintenance ..... Mr. Bertran HARRISON
58 Dean Graduate School ..... Dr. Gregory H. MADDOX
21 Exec Dir of Business Svcs ..... Mr. Charles E. HENRY
124 Dir Acad Ret Svcs Spec Asst/Provost ..... Ms. Lori A. LABRIE
108 Exec Dir Inst Assess/Plng/Effect ..... Dr. Raijanel CROCKEM
29 Asst VP Alumni Rels/Spec Events ..... Ms. Connie L. COCHRAN
90 Senior Academic Technology Officer ..... Mr. Darnell JOSEPH
88 Associate Director of QEP Office ..... Dr. Arbolina L. JENNINGS
106 Dir Online Education/E-learning ..... Vacant
86 Director of Governmental Relations ..... Mr. Dominique CALHOUN
04 Exec Office Administrator for Pres ..... Ms. Chyenne POWELL

Texas Southmost College (E)

80 Fort Brown, Brownsville TX 78520-4993
County: Cameron FICE Identification: 003643
Unit ID: 227377
Telephone: (956) 295-3600 Carnegie Class: Assoc/HT-High Non
FAX Number: (956) 295-3384 Calendar System: Semester
URL: www.tsc.edu
Established: 1926 Annual Undergrad Tuition & Fees (In-District): $3,748
Enrollment: 8,777 Coed
Affiliation or Control: State/Local IRS Status: 501(c)3
Highest Offering: Associate Degree
Accreditation: SC, COARC, DMS, EMT, MLTAD

01 President ..... Dr. Jesus R. RODRIGUEZ
05 Vice President of Instruction ..... Dr. Joanna KILE
10 Vice Pres of Finance/Administration ..... Dr. Gisela FIGUEROA
111 Vice Pres of Inst Advancement ..... Vacant
20 Assoc VP of Instruction/Acad Svcs ..... Dr. Angelica M. FUENTES
81 Dean of STEM ..... Dr. Murad ABUSALIM
79 Dean of Humanities ..... Dr. Brian MCCORMACK
76 Dean of Health Professions ..... Dr. David PEARSE
07 Exec Dir of Admissions & Records ..... Ms. Vanessa VASQUEZ
09 Exec Director of IR & Compliance ..... Mr. Oscar O. HERNANDEZ
106 Dir Educ Technology & Online Lrng ..... Vacant
13 Vice President of Information Tech ..... Mr. Luis VILLARREAL
15 Exec Director of Human Resources . Ms. Elizabeth BALDERRAMA
25 Coord Sponsored Pgms/Grants Ctr ..... Dr. Leonor HERNANDEZ
32 Exec Director of Student Life ..... Mr. Armando PONCE
36 Coord Career & Employ Svcs ..... Mr. Rene VALDEZ
37 Director Student Financial Aid ..... Ms. Pamela JONES
96 Coordinator of Purchasing ..... Ms. Patricia SALDIVAR

Texas State Technical College Waco (F)

3801 Campus Drive, Waco TX 76705-1695
County: McLennan FICE Identification: 003634
Unit ID: 487320
Telephone: (254) 867-4891 Carnegie Class: Assoc/HVT-High Trad
FAX Number: (254) 867-3973 Calendar System: Semester
URL: www.tstc.edu
Established: 1965 Annual Undergrad Tuition & Fees (In-State): $6,169
Enrollment: 10,654 Coed
Affiliation or Control: State IRS Status: 501(c)3
Highest Offering: Associate Degree
Accreditation: SC, CAHIIM, DH, EMT, SURGT

01 Chancellor/CEO ..... Mr. Mike REESER
05 VC/Chief Academic Officer ..... Mr. Jeff KILGORE
86 SVC/Chief Govt Affairs Officer ..... Mr. Joe ARNOLD
10 VC/Chief Financial Officer ..... Mr. Jonathan HOEKSTRA
100 EVC/Chief of Staff to Chancellor ..... Mrs. Gail LAWRENCE
32 VC/Chief Student Services Officer ..... Mr. Rick HERRERA
43 VC/Chief Legal Officer ..... Mr. Ray RUSHING
88 VC/Chief Innovation Officer ..... Mr. Michael A. BETTERSWORTH
12 Provost Fort Bend County ..... Mr. Bryan BOWLING
12 Provost Harlingen ..... Ms. Cledia HERNANDEZ
12 Provost Marshall ..... Mr. Barton DAY
12 Provost West Texas ..... Mr. Andy WEAVER
12 Provost North Texas ..... Mr. Marcus BALCH
20 Interim Provost Waco ..... Mr. Jeff KILGORE
04 Exec Assistant to the Chancellor ..... Mrs. Chelsea ANFENSON
15 Associate VC Human Resources ..... Ms. Pamela MAYFIELD
18 Chief Facilities/Physical Plant Ofc ..... Mr. Ray FRIED
102 CEO TSTC Foundation ..... Ms. Beth WOOTEN
06 Registrar ..... Ms. Maria ARREDONDO
19 Police & Safety Commissioner ..... Mr. Aurelio TORRES
36 Exec Director Student Placement ..... Ms. Kacey DARNELL
37 Director Student Financial Aid ..... Ms. Jackie ADLER
96 Senior Exec Director of Purchasing ..... Ms. Melinda BOYKIN
84 Director Enrollment Management ..... Ms. Christine STUART-CARRUTHERS

*The Texas State University System (G)

601 Colorado Street, Austin TX 78701-2904
County: Travis FICE Identification: 033442
Telephone: (512) 463-1808 Carnegie Class: N/A
FAX Number: N/A
URL: www.tsus.edu

01 Chancellor ..... Brian MCCALL
05 Vice Chanc Academic & Health Affs ..... John HAYEK
43 Vice Chanc & General Counsel ..... Nelly HERRERA
10 Vice Chancellor and CFO ..... Daniel HARPER
86 Vice Chanc Government Relations ..... Sean CUNNINGHAM
26 Vice Chancellor Marketing & Comm ..... Mike WINTEMUTE
116 Chief Audit Executive ..... Carole M. FOX
11 Director of Administration ..... Laura TIBBITTS

*Lamar Institute of Technology (A)

PO Box 10043, Beaumont TX 77710-0043

County: Jefferson | FICE Identification: 036273 | Unit ID: 441760
Telephone: (409) 880-8321 | Carnegie Class: Assoc/HVT-High Trad
FAX Number: (409) 813-1844 | Calendar System: Semester
URL: www.lit.edu
Established: 1995 | Annual Undergrad Tuition & Fees (In-State): $3,602
Enrollment: 4,417 | Coed
Affiliation or Control: State | IRS Status: 501(c)3
Highest Offering: Associate Degree
Accreditation: SC, CAHIIM, COARC, DH, DMS, EMT, RAD

02 President ... Dr. Lonnie HOWARD
05 Executive Vice President/Provost ... Dr. Kerry MIX
10 Chief Business and Financial Office ... Mr. Rudolfo GONZALES
15 Director of Human Resources ... Ms. Beth KNAPE
45 Vice Pres Strategic Initiatives ... Vacant
103 AVP Strategic & Workforce Init ... Ms. Miranda PHILLIPS
32 AVP Student and Academic Success ... Dr. Angela HILL
37 Director of Financial Aid ... Ms. Linda KORNS
13 Director Information Technology ... Mr. Samuel DOCKENS
30 Exec Dir Devel/Dir LIT Foundation ... Ms. Amanda CLAYTON
26 Dir Marketing & Communication ... Mr. Chris ELLIOTT
11 Director of Administration ... Ms. Amber CLARK
21 Senior Accounting Associate ... Ms. Dawna WHITMIRE
04 Exec Assistant to the President ... Vacant

*Lamar University (B)

PO Box 10001, Beaumont TX 77710-0009

County: Jefferson | FICE Identification: 003581 | Unit ID: 226091
Telephone: (409) 880-7011 | Carnegie Class: DU-Mod
FAX Number: (409) 880-8404 | Calendar System: Semester
URL: www.lamar.edu
Established: 1923 | Annual Undergrad Tuition & Fees (In-State): $8,591
Enrollment: 16,637 | Coed
Affiliation or Control: State | IRS Status: 501(c)3
Highest Offering: Doctorate
Accreditation: SC, AAQEP, ACFEI, ART, AUD, CONST, DIETD, DIETI, MUS, NUR, SP, SW

02 President ... Dr. Jaime R. TAYLOR
05 Provost/VP Academic Affairs ... Dr. Dan BROWN
10 Chief Financial Officer ... Vacant
111 Vice Pres University Advancement ... Mr. Juan ZABALA
13 Associate Vice Pres/CIO ... Mr. Patrick STEWART
20 Associate Provost ... Vacant
15 Asst VP Human Resources/Talent Mgmt ... Mr. Anthony SANCHEZ
18 Director of Facilities Mgmt ... Mr. David MARTIN
21 Assoc Vice Pres Finance/Controller ... Ms. Jamie LARSON
58 Dean of Graduate Studies ... Dr. Jerry LIN
49 Dean College Arts & Sciences ... Dr. Lynn MAURER
50 Dean College of Business ... Dr. Dan FRENCH
53 Dean College of Educ & Human Devel ... Dr. Robert SPINA
54 Dean College of Engineering ... Dr. Brian CRAIG
57 Int Dean College of Fine Art & Comm ... Dr. Golden WRIGHT
08 Int Dean Mary and John Gray Library ... Dr. Michael SAAR
06 Registrar ... Mr. David SHORT, JR.
56 Assoc Provost of Distance Learning ... Dr. Poonam KUMAR
09 Director Institutional Research ... Vacant
23 Director Health Services ... Ms. Shawn GRAY
19 Chief University Police ... Ms. Monica RYAN
26 Assoc Dir Marketing & Communication ... Mr. Daniel MCLEMORE
29 Director Alumni Relations ... Ms. Shannon FIGUEROA
37 Exec Director Student Financial Aid ... Dr. Deidra MAYER
96 Director of Purchasing/Pymt Svcs ... Ms. Amberr MELO
07 Director of Admissions ... Vacant
04 Dir of Opers President's Office ... Ms. Amy M. TROHA
41 Athletic Director ... Mr. Jeff O'MALLEY
122 Interfraternity Council Advisor ... Mr. Canaan DANIELS

*Lamar State College Orange (C)

410 Front Street, Orange TX 77630-5802

County: Orange | FICE Identification: 023582 | Unit ID: 226107
Telephone: (409) 883-7750 | Carnegie Class: Assoc/HVT-Mix Trad/Non
FAX Number: (409) 882-3374 | Calendar System: Semester
URL: www.lsco.edu
Established: 1969 | Annual Undergrad Tuition & Fees (In-State): $3,192
Enrollment: 2,382 | Coed
Affiliation or Control: State | IRS Status: 501(c)3
Highest Offering: Associate Degree
Accreditation: SC

02 President ... Dr. Thomas A. JOHNSON
05 Executive VP/Provost ... Dr. Wendy ELMORE
10 CFO ... Mrs. Mary WICKLAND
32 Dean of Student Services ... Mr. Brian HULL
08 Director of Library Services ... Ms. Samantha SMITH
06 Registrar ... Mrs. Becky J. MCANELLEY
37 Director Student Financial Aid ... Ms. Diana KINTO
15 Human Resources Director ... Ms. Lora RIVES
18 Director of Physical Plant ... Mr. Charles MITCHELL
13 Director of Enterprise Applications ... Ms. Lisa SEDTAL
09 Coordinator Institutional Research ... Mr. Nathan CAMPOS
25 Contracts/Grants Administrator ... Mrs. Mary WICKLAND
72 Dean of Technical Studies ... Ms. Kristin WALKER
20 Dean of Academic Studies ... Dr. Suzonne CROCKETT
96 Director of Purchasing ... Ms. Alexandra QUAVE
04 Executive Assistant to President ... Ms. Stephanie JONES
19 Director Safety & Security ... Mr. Joseph HARGRAVE
26 Dir of Public Relations/Development ... Ms. Emily MELLEN

*Lamar State College-Port Arthur (D)

1500 Procter Street, Port Arthur TX 77640-6604

County: Jefferson | FICE Identification: 023485 | Unit ID: 226116
Telephone: (409) 983-4921 | Carnegie Class: Assoc/HVT-High Trad
FAX Number: (409) 984-6032 | Calendar System: Semester
URL: www.lamarpa.edu
Established: 1909 | Annual Undergrad Tuition & Fees (In-State): $4,331
Enrollment: 2,485 | Coed
Affiliation or Control: State | IRS Status: 501(c)3
Highest Offering: Associate Degree
Accreditation: SC, SURGT

02 President ... Dr. Betty REYNARD
05 Vice President Academic Affairs ... Dr. Pamela MILLSAP
10 Vice President Finance & Operations ... Ms. Mary WICKLAND
32 Dean of Student Services ... Dr. Tessie BRADFORD
04 Exec Assistant to the President ... Mrs. Judy HOFFPAUIR
08 Dean Library Services ... Ms. Helena GAWU
06 Registrar ... Ms. Robin HUMPHREY
37 Director Financial Aid ... Ms. Sharon THIBODEAUX
45 Director Inst Effectiveness ... Mr. James M. KNOWLES
18 Director of Physical Plant ... Mr. Reed RICHARD
26 Public Information Officer ... Mr. Gerry DICKERT
56 Dir External Learning Experiences ... Mr. Wayne WELLS
13 Assistant Vice President/CIO/IRM ... Mr. Samir GHORAYEB
15 Director Human Resources ... Ms. Tammy RILEY
09 Director of Institutional Research ... Mrs. Petra UZORUO
103 VP Workforce/Continuing Educ ... Dr. Ben STAFFORD
72 Dean Technical Programs ... Dr. Melissa ARMENTOR
97 Dept Chair Gen Ed & Developmental ... Dr. Michelle DAVIS
50 Dept Chair Business & Technology ... Mrs. Sheila GUILLOT
39 Director Student Housing ... Dr. Tessie BRADFORD
41 Athletic Director ... Mr. Scott STREET
96 Director of Purchasing/Contracts ... Mrs. Maria GARCIA
76 Dept Chair Allied Health ... Ms. Shirley MACNEILL
64 Dept Chair Commercial Music ... Mr. Richard VANDEWALKER
84 Director Enrollment Services ... Mr. David MORALES

*Sam Houston State University (E)

1905 University Avenue, Huntsville TX 77340

County: Walker | FICE Identification: 003606 | Unit ID: 227881
Telephone: (936) 294-1111 | Carnegie Class: DU-Higher
FAX Number: (936) 294-1465 | Calendar System: Semester
URL: www.shsu.edu
Established: 1879 | Annual Undergrad Tuition & Fees (In-State): $8,736
Enrollment: 21,912 | Coed
Affiliation or Control: State | IRS Status: Exempt
Highest Offering: Doctorate
Accreditation: SC, ART, CACREP, CAEPN, CIDA, CLPSY, DANCE, DIETD, DIETI, FEPAC, IPSY, MUS, NURSE, @OSTEO, THEA

02 President ... Dr. Alisa WHITE
05 Provost/SVP Academic Affairs ... Dr. Michael STEPHENSON
10 Interim CFO & Sr VP for Operations ... Ms. Amanda WITHERS
84 SVP Strategic Enrollment/Innovation ... Dr. Heather THIELEMANN
111 Interim VP for Univ Advancement ... Ms. Thelma MOONEY
32 Interim VP for Student Affairs ... Dr. Drew MILLER
100 Deputy to the President ... Dr. McCartney JOHNSON
41 Athletic Director ... Mr. Bobby WILLIAMS
88 Chief Strategy Officer ... MG. David GLASER
61 Dean of Criminal Justice ... Dr. Phillip LYONS
57 Dean of Arts & Media ... Dr. Ronald SHIELDS
83 Dean of Humanities/Social Sciences ... Dr. Chien-pin LI
81 Dean of Sciences & Engineering Tech ... Dr. John PASCARELLA
50 Dean of Business Administration ... Dr. Sharmistha SELF
53 Dean of Education ... Dr. Stacey EDMONSON
63 Dean of Osteopathic Medicine ... Dr. Thomas MOHR
76 Dean of Health Sciences ... Dr. Emily ROPER
58 Dean of Graduate School ... Dr. Ken HENDRICKSON
20 Vice Provost ... Dr. Anne GAILLARD
20 Assoc VP for Academic Affairs ... Ms. Somer FRANKLIN
20 Assoc Provost Research/Spons Pgm ... Dr. Chad HARGRAVE
08 Exec Director Library ... Mr. Eric OWEN
106 Assoc VP & Chief Online Educ Ofcr ... Dr. William ANGROVE
18 VP Facilities Operations/Management ... Mr. Juan NUNEZ
21 Interim Controller ... Ms. Sarah WOODS
15 Asst VP for HR & Diversity ... Ms. Rhonda BEASSIE
109 Asst VP Auxiliary Services ... Dr. Kristy VIENNE
29 Assoc VP Alumni Relations ... Mr. Charlie VIENNE
88 Museum Director ... Mr. Derrick BIRDSALL
110 Director Advancement Services ... Ms. Patricia LEWIS
06 Chief Enroll Officer/Registrar ... Mr. Jacob CHANDLER
07 Assoc VP Admissions/Recruitment ... Dr. Leah MULLIGAN
35 Assoc VP Student Affairs/Rec Sports ... Dr. Keith JENKINS
38 Exec Dir Counseling/Health Svcs ... Dr. Drew MILLER
35 Dean of Students ... Dr. Chelsea SMITH
19 Exec Dir Public Safety Services ... Mr. Kevin MORRIS
39 Exec Dir Residence Life ... Ms. Joellen TIPTON
35 Director of Student Activities ... Mr. Brandon COOPER
88 Dir of Leadership Initiatives ... Ms. Meredith CONREY
14 AVP IT Operations ... Mr. Michael DEWEY
119 Director Information Security ... Mr. Steven FREY
28 Chief Diversity Officer ... Ms. Jeanine BIAS
13 VP for Info Technology ... Mr. James BRADLEY

*Sul Ross State University (F)

PO Box C-100, Alpine TX 79832-0001

County: Brewster | FICE Identification: 003625 | Unit ID: 228501
Telephone: (432) 837-8011 | Carnegie Class: Masters/L
FAX Number: (432) 837-8334 | Calendar System: Semester
URL: www.sulross.edu
Established: 1917 | Annual Undergrad Tuition & Fees (In-State): $8,777
Enrollment: 2,345 | Coed
Affiliation or Control: State | IRS Status: 501(c)3
Highest Offering: Master's
Accreditation: SC, NURSE

02 President ... Dr. Carlos HERNANDEZ
05 Exec Vice President/Provost ... Dr. Bernardo J. CANTEÑS
10 Vice Pres Budget & Finance ... Mrs. Bonnie ALBRIGHT
84 Vice Pres Enrollment Management ... Dr. Yvonne REALIVASQUEZ
30 Asst Vice Pres Development ... Vacant
12 Dean of Academic Affairs RGC ... Ms. Patricia NICOSIA
11 Asst VP of Administration ... Vacant
09 AVP Institutional Effectiveness ... Dr. Jeanne QVARNSTROM
06 University Registrar ... Mr. Michael RENDON
08 Dean Library & Research Technology ... Ms. Betsy EVANS
32 Dean of Students ... Ms. Brandy SNYDER
92 Dir Honors Prog/Acad Ctr Excellence ... Dr. Kathy STEIN
26 Director Communications ... Mrs. Betse ESPARZA
37 Dir Financial Assistance ... Mrs. Natalie SANDOVAL
49 Dean Literature/Arts/Social Sci ... Dr. Laura PAYNE
107 Dean Education & Professional Stds ... Dr. Barbara TUCKER
47 Dean Agricult/Life & Physical Sci ... Dr. Bonnie WARNOCK
15 Director of Human Resources ... Mrs. Karlin DEVOLL
18 Asst Director of Physical Plant ... Mr. Victor ROMERO
19 Director Dept of Public Safety ... Mr. Kent DUNEGAN
21 Director of Accounting/Finance ... Ms. Corina RAMIREZ
39 Asst Director Residential Living ... Vacant
41 Athletics Director ... Ms. Amanda WORKMAN
38 Director of Counseling Center ... Dr. Mary SCHWARTZE GRISHAM
13 Chief Information Officer ... Mr. Jacob FUENTES
96 Director of Purchasing ... Vacant
88 Dir Center for Big Bend Studies ... Mr. Bryon SCHROEDER
29 Dir of Alumni Relations ... Ms. Kathy MORENO
88 Director of Upward Bound ... Mr. Rockland OWENS
88 Archivist ... Ms. Victoria CONTRERAS
88 Law Enforcement Academy Coord ... Ms. Melissa FIERRO
07 Dir Enrollment Services/Admissions ... Vacant
88 Mail Service Supervisor ... Ms. Leticia GONZALES
116 Director Office of Internal Audit ... Mr. Scott A. CUPP
36 Dir of Career Services Testing ... Ms. Amanda BARRERA
04 Exec Assistant to the President ... Mrs. Janice ESPINOZA-VALENZUELA
103 Director Workforce Development ... Ms. Elizabeth PENA
104 Director Study Abroad ... Vacant
25 Chief Contract and Grants Administr ... Dr. Eric T. FUNASAKI
28 Dean Educ & Cultural Resources ... Ms. April AULTMAN-BECKER
50 Dean of Business ... Mr. Edison MOURA

*Texas State University (G)

601 University Drive, San Marcos TX 78666-4615

County: Hays | FICE Identification: 003615 | Unit ID: 228459
Telephone: (512) 245-2111 | Carnegie Class: DU-Higher
FAX Number: (512) 245-3040 | Calendar System: Semester
URL: www.txstate.edu
Established: 1899 | Annual Undergrad Tuition & Fees (In-State): $10,855
Enrollment: 37,812 | Coed
Affiliation or Control: State | IRS Status: 170(c)1
Highest Offering: Doctorate
Accreditation: SC, CAATE, CACREP, CAHIIM, CAPRT, CIDA, COARC, CONST, DIETD, DIETI, HSA, IPSY, JOUR, MLS, MUS, NAIT, NURSE, PTA, RTT, SP, SPAA, SW

02 President ... Dr. Kelly R. DAMPHOUSSE
05 Provost/Vice Pres Academic Affairs ... Dr. Gene BOURGEOIS
11 VP University Administration ... Dr. Lisa LLOYD
32 VP Student Affairs ... Dr. Cynthia H. HERNANDEZ
10 Vice Pres Finance/Support Services ... Mr. Eric ALGOE
111 Interim VP University Advancement ... Dr. Dan PERRY
13 Vice Pres Information Technology ... Mr. Kenneth PIERCE
88 Dean College of Applied Arts ... Dr. T. Jaime CHAHIN
50 Dean McCoy Col of Business Admin ... Dr. Sanjay RAMCHANDER
57 Dean College Fine Arts & Comm ... Dr. John FLEMING
53 Dean College of Education ... Dr. Michael O'MALLEY
76 Dean College Health Professions ... Dr. Ruth B. WELBORN
79 Dean College Liberal Arts ... Dr. Mary BRENNAN
81 Dean College of Science & Engr ... Dr. Christine HAILEY
58 Dean The Graduate College ... Dr. Andrea GOLATO
97 Dean Univ Col & Dir PACE Center ... Dr. Mary Ellen CAVITT
92 Dean Honors College ... Dr. Heather GALLOWAY
20 Assoc Vice Pres Academic Affairs ... Dr. Vedaraman SRIRAMAN
15 Asst VP for Human Resources ... Ms. Carole E. CLERIE
20 Associate Provost ... Dr. Debbie M. THORNE
18 Associate VP of Facilities ... Mr. Dan COSTELLO
46 Assoc VP Research & Dir of Fed Rels ... Dr. Shreekanth A. MANDAYAM
35 Assoc VP Student Affairs ... Dr. David BYRD
108 Assoc VP for Inst Effectiveness ... Dr. Beth E. WUEST
21 Assoc VP Financial Services ... Mr. Darryl BORGONAH
84 Assoc VP Enroll Mgmt/Marketing ... Mr. Gary T. RAY
08 Associate VP University Library ... Dr. Kelly M. VISNAK

20 Associate VP for Academic Success ... Dr. Mary Ellen CAVITT
26 Asst VP for UA Communications ... Ms. Sandra PANTLIK
38 Director Counseling Center ... Dr. Lynne REEDER
07 AVP Enroll Mgmt/Dir Undergrad Admis ... Dr. Beverly WOODSON DAY
28 VP Institutional Inclusive Excell ... Dr. Mary Jane SECUBAN
110 Assoc VP University Advancement ... Dr. Dan PERRY
35 Assoc VP and Dean of Students ... Dr. Vincent MORTON
28 Asst VP IIE/Fac & Staff Initiative ... Dr. Stella SILVA
14 Assoc VP for Technology Resources ... Mr. Mark HUGHES
88 Assoc VP Technology Innovation ... Dr. Carlos SOLIS
106 Asst VP Distance & Extended Learn ... Mr. Dana WILLETT
06 University Registrar ... Ms. Martha FRAIRE-CUELLAR
91 Director Enterprise Systems ... Mr. Martin MILLS
37 Asst VP Financial Aid & Scholarship ... Dr. Christopher MURR
36 Director Career Services ... Mr. Ray ROGERS
41 Director of Athletics ... Mr. Don CORYELL
29 Asst VP & Director Alumni Affairs ... Ms. Alejandra MERHEB
27 Director Univ News Services ... Mr. Jayme L. BLASCHKE
19 Chief of Police ... Mr. Matthew CARMICHAEL
23 Asst VP/Dir Student Health Ctr ... Dr. Emilio CARRANCO
39 Exec Director Housing/Res Life ... Dr. Bill MATTERA
40 Manager University Bookstore ... Mr. John ROOT
104 Asst VP/Dir Intl Student & Scholar ... Ms. Rosario DAVIS
96 Director Purchasing ... Mr. Dan ALDEN
88 Asst VP University Marketing ... Mr. Elias L. MARTINEZ
116 Director of Audit & Analysis ... Mr. Mike MILLER
88 Director Campus Recreation ... Dr. Jen BECK
88 Director LBJ Student Center ... Mr. Jack RAHMANN
90 Assoc VP IT Assistance Center ... Mr. Benjamin ROGERS
88 Director Disability Services ... Mr. Gavin STEIGER
119 Chief Information Security Officer ... Mr. Daniel C. OWEN
88 Director Learning Spaces ... Mr. Brian SHANKS
22 Asst VP Compliance/Chief Compl Ofcr ... Mr. Bobby MASON
88 Dir Student Affairs Technology ... Mr. Kevin MCCARTY
88 Director Student Involvement ... Dr. Brenda RODRIGUEZ

*Texas Tech University System (A)

1508 Knoxville Ave, Lubbock TX 79409-2013
County: Lubbock Identification: 667242
Telephone: (806) 742-0012 Carnegie Class: N/A
FAX Number: N/A
URL: www.texastech.edu

01 Chancellor ... Dr. Tedd L. MITCHELL
10 Vice Chancellor & CFO ... Vacant
111 Vice Chancellor Inst Advancement ... Mr. Patrick KRAMER
86 Vice Chanc Government Relations ... Ms. Martha BROWN
18 Vice Chanc Facil Plng/Construction ... Mr. Billy BREEDLOVE
43 Vice Chancellor & General Counsel ... Mr. Eric D. BENTLEY
116 Vice Chancellor Audit ... Mrs. Kim TURNER

*Angelo State University (B)

2601 West Avenue N, San Angelo TX 76909-0001
County: Tom Green FICE Identification: 003541
Unit ID: 222831
Telephone: (325) 942-2555 Carnegie Class: Masters/L
FAX Number: N/A Calendar System: Semester
URL: www.angelo.edu
Established: 1928 Annual Undergrad Tuition & Fees (In-State): $7,907
Enrollment: 10,775 Coed
Affiliation or Control: State IRS Status: 501(c)3
Highest Offering: Doctorate
Accreditation: SC, ACBSP, CAATE, MUS, NURSE, PTA, SW

02 President ... Mr. Ronnie D. HAWKINS, JR.
05 Provost/Vice Pres Academic Affairs ... Dr. Donald R. TOPLIFF
111 VP for External Affairs ... Ms. Jamie MAYER
10 VP for Finance & Admin ... Ms. Angelina WRIGHT
32 VP for Student Affairs ... Dr. Ben LION
58 Dean Col of Grad Studies & Research ... Dr. David BIXLER
54 Dean of College of Sci & Engr ... Dr. Paul SWETS
50 Dean College of Business ... Dr. Andrew TIGER
53 Dean College of Education ... Dr. Scarlet CLOUSE
66 Dean College Health & Human Service ... Dr. Leslie MAYRAND
79 Dean College of Arts & Humanities ... Dr. John KLINGEMANN
06 Director of Registrar Services ... Ms. Rosalinda CASTRO
89 Dean Freshman College ... Dr. Micheal SALISBURY
108 Exec Director of Accountability ... Ms. Brandy HAWKINS
08 Exec Director of Library Services ... Mr. Chris MATZ
36 Director Career Development ... Ms. Julie J. RUTHENBECK
15 Director of Human Resources ... Mr. Kurtis R. NEAL
37 Director of Student Financial Aid ... Mr. Charles E. KERESTLY
26 Dir of Communications & Mktg ... Ms. Brittney MILLER
29 Director Development & Alumni Svcs ... Ms. Kimberly ADAMS
35 Exec Director of Student Affairs ... Dr. Bradley PETTY
18 Exec Director of Facility Services ... Mr. Cody GUINS
39 Dir of Housing & Residential Pgm ... Ms. Tracy W. BAKER
40 Manager Bookstore ... Ms. Michaela REYNOLDS
41 Athletic Director ... Mr. James REID
19 Chief of University Police ... Mr. James E. ADAMS
13 Assoc VP Information Technology/CIO ... Mr. Douglas FOX
21 Director of Business Services ... Ms. Jessica MANNING
96 Exec Director Materials Management ... Ms. Lanell NICHOLS
92 Director of Honors Program ... Dr. Shirley EOFF
04 Executive Asst to the President ... Ms. Adelina C. MORALES
104 Director of International Studies ... Ms. Meghan PENA
07 Exec Dir Admissions/Strategic Mktg ... Ms. Kerri MIKULIK
38 Director of Counseling Services ... Mr. Mark REHM
84 Director Enrollment Management ... Mr. Jeffrey SEFCIK

43 Sr Exec Asst to Pres/Gen Counsel ... Mr. Joe MUNOZ
28 Chief of Diversity & Inclusion ... Dr. Flor MADERO
30 Director of Development ... Mrs. Jennifer LOVE

† Affiliated with Texas Tech University in Lubbock, TX

*Texas Tech University (C)

2500 Broadway, Lubbock TX 79409
County: Lubbock FICE Identification: 003644
Unit ID: 229115
Telephone: (806) 742-2121 Carnegie Class: DU-Highest
FAX Number: (806) 742-2138 Calendar System: Semester
URL: www.ttu.edu
Established: 1923 Annual Undergrad Tuition & Fees (In-State): $11,600
Enrollment: 40,322 Coed
Affiliation or Control: State IRS Status: 170(c)1
Highest Offering: Doctorate
Accreditation: SC, ACPHA, ARCPA, ART, CACREP, CAEP, CIDA, CLPSY, COPSY, DANCE, DIETD, DIETI, IPSY, LAW, LSAR, MFCD, MIDWF, MUS, SPAA, SW, THEA, #VET

00 Chancellor ... Dr. Tedd L. MITCHELL
02 President ... Dr. Lawrence SCHOVANEC
101 Sec Board Regents/Ex Asst to Chanc ... Ms. Christina MARTINEZ
05 Provost and Senior Vice President ... Dr. Ron HENDRICK
10 Chief Operating Ofcr/SVP Admin/Fin ... Ms. Noel SLOAN
26 VP of Marketing/Communications ... Mr. Matthew DEWEY
111 Vice Chanc Inst Advancement ... Mr. Patrick KRAMER
86 Vice Chancellor Govt Relations ... Ms. Kristina BUTTS
43 Vice Chanc & General Counsel ... Mr. Eric D. BENTLEY
18 VC Facilities Planning Construction ... Mr. Billy BREEDLOVE
100 COS & VP for Administration ... Ms. Grace HERNANDEZ
29 EVP & CEO Texas Tech Alumni Assoc ... Mr. Curt LANGFORD
46 Vice President for Research ... Dr. Joseph HEPPERT
28 Vice Pres Institutional Diversity ... Dr. Carol A. SUMNER
84 VP Enrollment Management ... Mrs. Jamie HANSARD
21 Chief Accounting Ofcr & Controller ... Mr. Eric FISHER
82 Vice Provost International Affairs ... Dr. Elizabeth TREJOS-CASTILLO
08 Dean of Libraries ... Ms. Earnstein DUKES
60 Dean Media & Communications ... Dr. David PERLMUTTER
32 Asst Dean of Students ... Vacant
37 Exec Director Financial Aid ... Dr. Rob KNISS
13 CIO & VP for Info Technology ... Mr. Sam SEGRAN
06 Registrar ... Ms. Bobbie BROWN
07 Executive Director of Admissions ... Mr. Jason HALE
27 Dir Communications & Marketing ... Mr. Julian OLIVAS
04 Executive Asst to President ... Mrs. Mikki ROSS
88 Assoc VProvost for Outreach/Engage ... Ms. Melanie HART
23 Managing Dir Student Health Svcs ... Ms. Juli MCCAULEY
39 Sr Managing Dir Student Housing ... Ms. Tanya MASSEY
36 Director Career Center ... Mr. Jay KILLOUGH
15 Assistant VP of Human Resources ... Mrs. Jodie BILLINGSLEY
22 Asst VC/Dir of Equal Opportunity ... Ms. Dawn PAYNE
38 Director Student Counseling ... Dr. Lisa VIATOR
41 Director of Athletics ... Mr. Kirby HOCUTT
47 Dean Col Agri Science/Natural Res ... Dr. Cindy AKERS
49 Dean of Arts & Sciences ... Dr. Tosha DUPRAS
48 Dean of Architecture ... Dr. Urs Peter (Upe) FLUECKIGER
50 Dean Business Administration ... Dr. Margaret L. WILLIAMS
53 Dean of Education ... Dr. Jesse PEREZ MENDEZ
54 Acting Dean of Engineering ... Dr. Stephen BAYNE
88 Dean of Human Sciences ... Dr. Tim DODD
61 Dean School of Law ... Dr. Jack NOWLIN
58 Dean of Graduate School ... Dr. Mark SHERIDAN
92 Interim Dean Honors College ... Dr. Susan TOMLINSON
57 Dean Visual & Performing Arts ... Dr. Martin CAMACHO
19 Chief of Police ... Mr. Kyle K. BONATH
09 Managing Dir Institutional Research ... Vacant
96 Chief Procurement Officer ... Ms. Jennifer ADLING

*Texas Tech University Health Sciences Center (D)

3601 4th Street Mailstop 6258, Lubbock TX 79430-0001
County: Lubbock FICE Identification: 010674
Unit ID: 229337
Telephone: (806) 743-2900 Carnegie Class: Spec-4-yr-Eng
FAX Number: N/A Calendar System: Semester
URL: www.ttuhsc.edu
Established: 1969 Annual Undergrad Tuition & Fees (In-State): N/A
Enrollment: 5,274 Coed
Affiliation or Control: State IRS Status: 501(c)3
Highest Offering: Doctorate
Accreditation: SC, AUD, CAATE, CACREP, DMOLS, MED, MLS, NURSE, OT, PH, PHAR, PTA, SP

02 President ... Dr. Lori RICE-SPEARMAN
10 Exec VP for Finance & Operations ... Ms. Penny HARKEY
05 Provost/Chief Academic Officer ... Dr. Darrin D'AGOSTINO
26 Vice Pres External Relations ... Ms. Ashley HAMM
17 Exec Vice Pres Rural/Community Hlth ... Dr. Billy U. PHILIPS, JR.
46 Int Sr Vice President for Research ... Dr. Lance MCMAHON
13 Vice Pres Info Tech/Chief Info Ofcr ... Mr. Vince FELL
86 Sr Director Governmental Relations ... Mr. Smiley GARCIA
88 Vice President of Health Policy ... Dr. Cynthia JUMPER
28 VP Diversity/Equity & Inclusion ... Ms. Jody RANDALL
100 Executive Chief of Staff ... Mr. Coleman JOHNSON
43 Managing Attorney ... Ms. Vicki DORRIS
15 Chief People Officer ... Vacant
108 Vice Prov Effective/Accreditation ... Dr. Kari DICKSON

32 Asst Provost for Student Affairs ... Dr. Erin JUSTNYA
22 Vice Pres Inst Compliance ... Dr. Sonya CASTRO-QUIRINO
18 Vice Pres Facilities/Safety Svcs ... Dr. Harry SLIFE, JR.
63 Dean Medical Sch/EVP Clinical Affs ... Dr. Steven L. BERK
58 Dean Grad Sch Biomed Sciences ... Dr. Brandt L. SCHNEIDER
66 Dean of Nursing School ... Dr. Michael L. EVANS
76 Dean School Health Professions ... Dr. Dawndra SECHRIST
67 Dean of Pharmacy School ... Dr. Grace R. KUO
63 Reg Dean Medicine Amarillo Campus ... Dr. Richard JORDAN
63 Int Reg Dean Medicine Odessa Campus ... Dr. Timothy BENTON
66 Reg Dean Nursing Abilene ... Ms. Pearl E. MERRITT
66 Reg Dean Nursing Odessa Campus ... Dr. Sharon CANNON
76 Reg Dean Health Profession Amarillo ... Dr. Joan POTTER
76 Reg Dean Health Professions Odessa ... Dr. Deborah YORK-EDWARDS
67 Reg Dean Pharmacy Abilene ... Dr. Sara BROUSE
67 Reg Dean Pharmacy Amarillo ... Dr. Thomas THEKKUMKARA
67 Reg Dean Pharmacy Dallas ... Dr. Steven PASS
67 Reg Dean Pharmacy Lubbock ... Dr. Charles E. SEIFERT
06 Registrar ... Ms. Amanda MCSWEEN
08 Exec Director of HSC Libraries ... Vacant
21 Managing Dir Accounting Services ... Ms. Melody OLIPHINT
22 Director of Equal Employment ... Ms. Charlotte BINGHAM
25 Director of Sponsored Programs ... Ms. Erin WOODS
37 Director of Financial Aid ... Mr. Marcus WILSON
96 Managing Dir of Procurement Service ... Mr. John G. HAYNES
09 Chief Analyst Inst Research ... Mr. Kevin MCINTYRE
29 Alumni Relations Manager ... Ms. Clarissa SANCHEZ
88 Sr Director Office of Global Health ... Ms. Michelle ENSMINGER

*Texas Tech University Health Sciences Center at El Paso (E)

5001 El Paso Drive, El Paso TX 79905
County: El Paso Identification: 667243
Telephone: (915) 215-4300 Carnegie Class: Not Classified
FAX Number: N/A Calendar System: Semester
URL: www.elpaso.ttuhsc.edu
Established: 2013 Annual Undergrad Tuition & Fees (In-State): N/A
Enrollment: N/A Coed
Affiliation or Control: State IRS Status: 170(c)1
Highest Offering: Doctorate
Accreditation: SC, DENT, MED, NURSE

01 President ... Dr. Richard LANGE
05 Vice Pres for Academic Affairs ... Dr. Richard BROWER
111 Vice Pres for Inst Advancement ... Dr. Andrea TAWNEY
10 Vice Pres Finance ... Ms. Guadalupe VALENCIA-SKANES
11 Vice President for Operations ... Vacant
26 Vice Pres Outreach/Cmty Engagement ... Dr. Jose Manuel DE LA ROSA
13 Assoc VP Information Technology ... Mr. Jerry RODRIGUEZ
32 Asst VP Student Services ... Dr. Robin DANKOVICH
63 Dean School of Medicine ... Dr. Richard LANGE
66 Dean School of Nursing ... Dr. Stephanie WOODS
81 Dean Graduate School of Biomedical ... Dr. Rajkumar LAKSHMANASWAMY
52 Dean School of Dental Medicine ... Dr. Richard BLACK
04 Assistant to President ... Ms. Vanessa SOLIS
06 Registrar ... Ms. Diana ANDRADE
15 Chief Human Resources Officer ... Ms. Jennifer ERICKSON
18 Chief Facilities/Physical Plant Ofc ... Mr. Al FLORES

Texas Wesleyan University (F)

1201 Wesleyan, Fort Worth TX 76105-1536
County: Tarrant FICE Identification: 003645
Unit ID: 229160
Telephone: (817) 531-4444 Carnegie Class: DU-Mod
FAX Number: (817) 531-4425 Calendar System: Semester
URL: www.txwes.edu
Established: 1890 Annual Undergrad Tuition & Fees: $33,408
Enrollment: 2,197 Coed
Affiliation or Control: United Methodist IRS Status: 501(c)3
Highest Offering: Doctorate
Accreditation: SC, ANEST, CAATE, MFCD, MUS, NURSE

01 President ... Mr. Frederick G. SLABACH
05 Provost/Sr Vice President ... Dr. Hector QUINTANILLA
10 VP Finance & Administration ... Mrs. Donna NANCE
100 Chief of Staff and General Counsel ... Ms. Patti GEARHART TURNER
32 VP Student Affairs/Dean of Students ... Dr. Dennis HALL
111 VP University Advancement ... Ms. Jerri SCHOOLEY
26 Assoc VP Marketing/Communications ... Ms. Shannon LAMBERSON
15 AVP of Human Resources ... Dr. Angela DAMPEER
20 Assoc Provost Academic Affairs ... Dr. Steven DANIELL
20 Associate Provost ... Dr. Helena BUSSELL
41 Athletic Director ... Mr. Ricky DOTSON
53 Dean School of Education ... Dr. Carlos MARTINEZ
50 Dean of School of Business ... Dr. Sameer VAIDYA
49 Dean School of Arts & Sciences ... Dr. Ricardo RODRIGUEZ
39 Asst Dn Stdnts/Dir Residence Life ... Ms. Jill GERLOFF
06 Registrar ... Mr. Sloan WHITE
21 Controller ... Ms. Jacqueline RUTLEDGE
07 Assoc Vice Pres Enrollment ... Ms. Djuana YOUNG
42 Chaplain ... Dr. Gladys CHILDS
38 Director of Counseling ... Dr. Linda METCALF
96 Director of Purchasing ... Ms. Deborah CAVITT
36 Director Career Services/Counselor ... Dr. Gary STOUT
18 Exec Dir of Facil/Opers/Emerg Svcs ... Mr. Brian FRANKS

04 Executive Assistant to the Pres ... Mrs. Sherry SANDLES
09 Director Institutional Research ... Mr. Sean M. BRIGADIER
19 Director Campus Safety/Security ... Mr. Chris BECKRICH

Texas Woman's University (A)

304 Administration Dr, Denton TX 76204
County: Denton FICE Identification: 003646
Unit ID: 229179
Telephone: (940) 898-2000 Carnegie Class: DU-Mod
FAX Number: (940) 898-3198 Calendar System: Semester
URL: www.twu.edu
Established: 1901 Annual Undergrad Tuition & Fees (In-State): $8,255
Enrollment: 16,433 Coed
Affiliation or Control: State IRS Status: 501(c)3
Highest Offering: Doctorate
Accreditation: SC, ACBSP, CACREP, COPSY, DANCE, DH, DIETD, DIETI, HSA, LIB, MFCD, MUS, #NASP, NURSE, OT, PTA, SCPSY, SP, SW

01 Chancellor & President ... Dr. Carine FEYTEN
05 Interim Provost/Exec VP Acad Affs ... Dr. Finley GRAVES
10 VP Finance/Administration ... Mr. Jason TOMLINSON
32 VP Student Life ... Dr. Monica MENDEZ-GRANT
111 VP University Advancement ... Dr. Kimberly RUSSELL
84 Assoc VP Enrollment Management ... Dr. Javier FLORES
20 Vice Provost Faculty Success ... Dr. Kim MILOCH
88 Vice Prov Curriculum/Strat Init ... Dr. Jorge FIGUEROA
09 Vice Prov Inst Research/Improvement ... Dr. Mark S. HAMNER
15 Exec Director of Human Resources ... Ms. Amy HALL
13 Deputy CIO ... Ms. Cori TREVINO
58 Dean Graduate School ... Dr. Holly HANSEN-THOMAS
49 Dean College Arts & Sciences ... Dr. Abigail TILTON
50 Dean College of Business ... Dr. Rama YELKUR
66 Interim Dean College Nursing ... Dr. Damon COTTRELL
69 Dean College Health Sciences ... Dr. Christopher T. RAY
107 Dean College Prof Education ... Dr. Lisa HUFFMAN
46 Vice Provost Research/Innovation ... Dr. Holly HANSEN-THOMAS
121 Vice Provost Student Success ... Dr. Joshua ADAMS
08 Dean of Libraries ... Ms. Suzanne SELLERS
06 Registrar ... Ms. Jenna LEE
18 Associate VP Facilities ... Mr. Robert RAMIREZ
26 VP Marketing/Communications ... Ms. Kristina KASKEL-RUIZ
21 Associate VP Finance ... Ms. Rana ASKINS
21 Assistant VP Controller ... Ms. Melanie RAMIREZ
113 Bursar ... Mr. Glen RAY
19 Executive Dir of Public Safety ... Mr. Samuel GARRISON
41 Athletic Director ... Ms. Sandee MOTT
23 Dir Operations/Student Health Svcs ... Ms. Tanisha FREEMAN
39 Exec Director University Housing ... Ms. Jill ECKARDT
29 Exec Dir Alumni Engagement ... Ms. Jasmine CARTER
37 Exec Dir Student Financial Aid ... Ms. Lacey THOMPSON
04 Executive Asst to Chancellor/Pres ... Ms. Lorie HUSLIG
100 Chief of Staff ... Mr. Christopher JOHNSON
104 Exec Dir International Affairs ... Dr. Annie PHILLIPS MUNSON
106 Dir Teach & Learn w/Technology ... Dr. Lynda MURPHY
108 Dir Academic Assessment ... Dr. Gray SCOTT
07 Director of Admissions ... Ms. Nikki YOUNG
86 Dir Governmental/Legislative Affs ... Mr. Kevin CRUSER
43 General Counsel ... Ms. Katherine GREEN

Trinity University (B)

One Trinity Place, San Antonio TX 78212-7200
County: Bexar FICE Identification: 003647
Unit ID: 229267
Telephone: (210) 999-7011 Carnegie Class: Bac-A&S
FAX Number: (210) 999-7696 Calendar System: Semester
URL: www.trinity.edu
Established: 1869 Annual Undergrad Tuition & Fees: $46,456
Enrollment: 2,677 Coed
Affiliation or Control: Independent Non-Profit IRS Status: 501(c)3
Highest Offering: Master's
Accreditation: SC, HSA

01 President ... Dr. Danny ANDERSON
05 Vice Pres Academic Affairs ... Dr. Megan MUSTAIN
10 VP Finance and Administration ... Mr. Gary LOGAN
111 VP Alumni Relations & Development ... Mr. Michael BACON
13 VP Info Resources ... Vacant
84 VP Enrollment/Student Retention ... Mr. Eric MALOOF
32 Vice Pres Student Life ... Dr. Sheryl R. TYNES
20 Assoc VP Faculty Recruitment & Dev ... Dr. Duane COLTHARP
114 Assoc VP Budget & Research ... Dr. Jennifer HENDERSON
21 Assoc VP for Finance ... Ms. Diana HEEREN
35 AVP Student Affs/Dean of Students ... Dr. Demitrius BROWN
09 Assoc VP/Dir Institutional Research ... Ms. Kara LARKAN
109 Sr Dir Conf/Spec Pgms/Aux Svcs ... Mr. Bruce BRAVO
37 Dir Student Financial Aid ... Ms. Christina PIKLA
19 Asst VP Public Safety/Ent Risk Mgmt ... Mr. Paul CHAPA
15 Assistant VP Human Resources ... Mr. James HERTEL
06 Registrar ... Mr. Alfred RODRIGUEZ
07 Dean Enrollment Operations ... Ms. Valerie SCHWEERS
38 Sr Director Counseling/Health Svcs ... Dr. Marcy YOUNGDAHL
35 Director Student Involvement ... Ms. Jamie THOMPSON
36 Director of Career Services ... Ms. Katie RAMIREZ
13 Sr Dir Technology Operations ... Mr. David PERSALES
44 Sr Director of Annual Giving Pgms ... Ms. Kathy MCNEILL
29 Senior Director of Alumni Relations ... Mr. Ryan FINNELLY
04 Exec Assistant to the President ... Ms. Claire SMITH
18 Sr Director Facility Services ... Mr. James BAKER
42 Chaplain ... Rev. Alex SERNA-WALLENDER
96 Director of Purchasing ... Vacant
28 Director Diversity ... Ms. Jamie THOMPSON
41 Athletic Director ... Mr. Bob KING

Trinity Valley Community College (C)

100 Cardinal Drive, Athens TX 75751-2734
County: Henderson FICE Identification: 003572
Unit ID: 225308
Telephone: (903) 677-8822 Carnegie Class: Assoc/MT-VT-High Trad
FAX Number: (903) 675-6316 Calendar System: Semester
URL: www.tvcc.edu
Established: 1946 Annual Undergrad Tuition & Fees (In-District): $4,920
Enrollment: 5,600 Coed
Affiliation or Control: State/Local IRS Status: 501(c)3
Highest Offering: Baccalaureate
Accreditation: SC, ADNUR, EMT, SURGT

01 President ... Dr. Jerry KING
05 Vice President for Instruction ... Dr. Kristin SPIZZIRRI
32 Vice President Student Services ... Dr. Philip PARNELL
13 VP of Information Technology ... Mr. David GIBSON
10 Vice Pres Administrative Services ... Mr. David HOPKINS
20 Assoc VP Instruction Academic Educ ... Mrs. Erica RICHARDSON
103 Associate VP of Workforce Education ... Ms. Kelley TOWNSEND
106 AVP of Instructional Innov/Support ... Ms. Holley COLLIER
12 Assoc VP of TDCJ Programs ... Dr. Sam HURLEY
84 AVP of Enrollment Management ... Ms. Tammy DENNEY
18 Asst VP of Facilities Management ... Mr. David GRAEM
76 Provost Health Occupations ... Mr. Jason SMITH
12 Provost Kaufman County Campus ... Vacant
12 Provost Anderson County Campus ... Dr. Dreand JOHNSON
102 Executive Director of Foundation ... Ms. Emily HEGLUND
09 Dir Strategic Plng/Effect/Accred ... Mr. Spencer WAGLEY
21 Dir of Acct Services & Controller ... Ms. Stephanie GOLEM
08 Director Learning Resource Center ... Ms. Karla BRYAN
07 Dir of Admissions/Registrar ... Ms. Caroline WHITAKER
26 Director Marketing/Communications ... Vacant
28 Dir Student Engagement & Diversity ... Ms. Audrey HAWKINS
37 Dir Student Fin Aid/Veteran Svcs ... Ms. Tonya RICHARDSON-DEAN
41 Athletic Director ... Mr. Eddie KITE
19 Director of Campus Police ... Mr. Stewart NEWBY
40 Bookstore Manager ... Mrs. Beth Ann KIDD
39 Director of Housing/Judicial Ofc ... Mr. Harold JONES
51 Dir Adult/Continuing Education ... Ms. Chris HICKS
15 Director of Human Resources ... Ms. Janene DOTTS
96 Purchasing/Contracts/Ins Coord ... Ms. Lawanna SEWALT
04 Executive Asst to the President ... Ms. Norma SHERAM
25 Sr Accountant/Grants ... Ms. Delana NEWMAN
36 Director of Student Pathways ... Ms. Janet GREEN
88 Director of Dual Credit ... Ms. Mary Helen KELM
18 Dir Transportation & Logistics ... Mr. Leon HANSON
06 Registrar ... Ms. Caroline WHITAKER
29 Director Alumni Affairs ... Mrs. Darla MANSFIELD

Tyler Junior College (D)

PO Box 9020, Tyler TX 75711-9020
County: Smith FICE Identification: 003648
Unit ID: 229355
Telephone: (903) 510-2200 Carnegie Class: Bac/Assoc-Assoc Dom
FAX Number: (903) 510-2632 Calendar System: Semester
URL: www.tjc.edu
Established: 1926 Annual Undergrad Tuition & Fees (In-District): $4,762
Enrollment: 11,749 Coed
Affiliation or Control: State/Local IRS Status: 170(c)1
Highest Offering: Baccalaureate
Accreditation: SC, CAHIIM, CNEA, COARC, DA, DH, DMS, EMT, MLTAD, OTA, PTAA, RAD, SURGT

01 President/Chief Executive Officer ... Dr. Juan E. MEJIA
05 VP Acad & Stdnt Affairs/Provost ... Ms. Deana SHEPPARD
11 VP Operations/COO ... Ms. Kimberly LESSNER
10 VP Finance & Admin Affairs/CFO ... Ms. Sarah E. VAN CLEEF
111 VP Inst Advance/Exec Dir Foundation ... Mr. D. Mitch ANDREWS
88 Exec Dir Regional Cmty Development ... Mr. S. Kevin FOWLER
04 Exec Asst to President ... Ms. Debra HOLCOMB
101 Spec Asst President/Board ... Ms. Ellen MATTHEWS
13 Chief Information Officer ... Vacant
103 Assoc Vice Prov Acad & Wrkfc Affs ... Vacant
32 Assoc Vice Prov Student Affairs ... Dr. Timothy S. DRAIN
81 Dean Engineering/Math/Sciences ... Dr. J. Cliff BOUCHER
66 Dean Nursing/Health Science ... Ms. Elizabeth OLIVIA
79 Dean Humanities/Comm/Fine Arts ... Mr. Jim RICHEY
107 Dean Professional Tech Programs ... Ms. Lorretta SWAN
51 Dean Continuing Studies ... Mr. Brent WALLACE
12 Dean TJC North ... Dr. Richard NICHOLS
35 Dean of Students ... Ms. Tampa J. NANNEN
88 Exec Dir Business Services ... Ms. Carol HUTSON
21 Controller ... Mr. Hunter THROCKMORTON
108 Dir Institutional Effectiveness ... Dr. Belinda PRIHODA
22 Dir Employee Relations/Title IX ... Mr. Andrew CANTEY
15 Chief Human Resources Officer ... Dr. Rose MURILLO
18 Dir Facilities & Construction ... Mr. Mark GARTMAN
119 Director Information Security ... Ms. Kaytee HASSELL
19 Director Campus Police ... Mr. Michael SEALE
39 Director Residential Life ... Mr. Steven LOGAN
96 Director Campus Services ... Ms. Dana BALLARD
110 Dir Advancement Oper/Scholarships ... Mr. Bill WONG
41 Director Intercollegiate Athletics ... Mr. Kevin VEST
07 Director Admissions ... Mrs. Claire MIZELL
06 Director Acad Records/Registrar ... Ms. Britt SABOTA
121 Director Academic Advising/Testing ... Mr. Chris FONTAINE
37 Director Financial Aid ... Ms. Devon WIGGINS
106 Director Distance Education ... Mr. Ken CRAVER
08 Director Learning Resource Center ... Mrs. Maggie RUELLE
92 Director Honors Program ... Mr. David FUNK
35 Director Student Life ... Mrs. Lauren TYLER
29 Director Alumni Relations ... Ms. Susan FARRINGTON
26 Dir Public Affairs/Media Relations ... Mrs. Rebecca SANDERS
88 Director SBDC ... Mr. Donald W. PROUDFOOT
44 Director Annual Giving ... Vacant
112 Director Major Gifts ... Ms. Barabara GREENBAUER
118 Manager Benefits Compensation ... Mrs. Lisa BLACK
38 Counselor Learning Specialist ... Mrs. Tracey WILLIAMS
36 Specialist Career Planning ... Ms. Sherry FULLER

University of Dallas (E)

1845 E Northgate Drive, Irving TX 75062-4736
County: Dallas FICE Identification: 003651
Unit ID: 224323
Telephone: (972) 721-5000 Carnegie Class: Masters/L
FAX Number: (972) 721-5017 Calendar System: Semester
URL: www.udallas.edu
Established: 1956 Annual Undergrad Tuition & Fees: $45,160
Enrollment: 2,489 Coed
Affiliation or Control: Roman Catholic IRS Status: 501(c)3
Highest Offering: Doctorate
Accreditation: SC

01 President ... Dr. Jonathan J. SANFORD
04 Special Asst to the President ... Mr. Benjamin GIBBS
84 Assistant VP Enrollment ... Mrs. Elizabeth GRIFFIN-SMITH
10 Vice President for Finance and CFO ... Mr. Robert WATLING
05 Interim Provost ... Dr. Tammy LEONARD
111 Vice President for Advancement ... Mrs. Kristine MUNOZ-VETTER
43 VP for Board and Legal Services ... Mrs. Heather A. LACHENAUER
13 Chief Information Officer ... Mrs. Ruchi SHETH
32 Dean of Students ... Ms. Julia L. CARRANO
50 Dean College of Business ... Dr. Brett LANDRY
49 Interim Dean of Constantin College ... Dr. David A. ANDREWS
58 Dean Grad School of Liberal Arts ... Dr. Joshua S. PARENS
08 Dean of Libraries and Research ... Ms. Cherie L. HOHERTZ
06 Registrar ... Ms. Marisa DARBY
19 Police Chief ... Mr. Russell GREENE
13 Director Information Technology ... Mr. Richard HAYTER
14 Director of IT User Support Service ... Mr. Sabyasachi SANYAL
41 Director of Athletics ... Mr. Jarred SAMPLES
42 Assoc Director of Campus Ministry ... Vacant
15 Director Human Resources ... Dr. Mary FLECK
09 Dir of Institutional Effectiveness ... Dr. David MA
26 VP Marketing & Communications ... Ms. Clare VENEGAS
96 Manager of Purchasing ... Mr. Ron CARVALHO
104 Director for Rome & Summer Programs ... Mrs. Becky DAVIES
23 Physician & Dir of Health Center ... Dr. Lora RODRIGUEZ
36 Director of Career Services ... Mrs. Shannon BLATT
37 Director Financial Aid ... Mr. James HUBENER
07 Director of Undergraduate Admission ... Mr. Michael J. PROBUS
123 Director of Graduate Admissions ... Ms. Breanna COLLINS
35 Director Student Activities ... Ms. Marissa C. BROWN
39 Director Housing Operations ... Mrs. Betty PERRETTA
29 Director Alumni Relations ... Ms. Julie A. ABELL
100 Chief of Staff ... Mr. Ryan D. REEDY
22 Director Civil Rights & Title IX ... Ms. Luciana E. HAMPILOS
38 Director Counseling Center ... Mr. Johnathan M. SUMPTER
90 Director IS Apps & Security ... Mr. Blake E. PALMER
91 Director Information Systems ... Mr. Ryan M. HALLER

*University of Houston System (F)

4302 University Dr., 212 E. Cullen,
Houston TX 77204-2018
County: Harris FICE Identification: 011721
Unit ID: 229407
Telephone: (713) 743-1000 Carnegie Class: N/A
FAX Number: N/A
URL: www.uhsa.uh.edu

01 Chancellor ... Dr. Renu KHATOR
05 Sr VC for Academic Affairs/Provost ... Dr. Paula M. SHORT
10 Sr VC Administration/Finance ... Mr. Raymond BARTLETT
43 Vice Chancellor/General Counsel ... Ms. Dona H. CORNELL
32 Int Vice Chanc Student Affairs ... Dr. Dan MAXWELL
111 VC University Advancement ... Ms. Eloise D. BRICE
86 Vice Chanc Govt Relations ... Mr. Jason S. SMITH
26 Vice Chanc Marketing/Comm/Media ... Ms. Lisa K. HOLDEMAN
21 Assoc Vice Chancellor Finance ... Mr. Karin LIVINGSTON
11 Assoc VC Administration ... Dr. Emily MESSA
13 Assoc VC Information Technology/CIO ... Dr. Dennis FOUTY
100 Chief of Staff ... Mr. Michael JOHNSON
116 Director Internal Auditing ... Mr. Phillip HURD
88 Treasurer ... Ms. Roberta (Robbi) PURYEAR
15 Assoc VC Human Resources ... Mr. Gaston REINOSO
04 Sr Exec Admin Asst to the Chanc ... Ms. Carmen HERNANDEZ

*University of Houston (G)

4302 University Dr., 212 E. Cullen,
Houston TX 77204-2018
County: Harris FICE Identification: 003652
Unit ID: 225511
Telephone: (713) 743-1000 Carnegie Class: DU-Highest
FAX Number: N/A Calendar System: Semester
URL: www.uh.edu
Established: 1927 Annual Undergrad Tuition & Fees (In-State): $9,457

Enrollment: 47,090 Coed
Affiliation or Control: State IRS Status: Exempt
Highest Offering: Doctorate
Accreditation: SC, AAFCS, AAQEP, CAATE, CEA, CLPSY, CONST, COPSY, DIETD, DIETI, IPSY, LAW, #MED, MUS, NAIT, NURSE, OPT, OPTR, PHAR, SCPSY, SP, SPAA, SW

02	President	Dr. Renu KHATOR
88	Chief Energy Officer	Dr. Ramanan KRISHNAMOORTI
41	VP Intercollegiate Athletics	Mr. Chris PEZMAN
31	VP for Community Rels & Inst Access	Dr. Elwyn C. LEE
100	Chief of Staff	Mr. Mike JOHNSON
20	Vice Provost & Dean UG Stdnts	Dr. Teri E. LONGACRE
58	Vice Provost & Dean Grad School	Dr. Sarah LARSEN
21	Assoc Provost Finance & Admin	Dr. Sabrina HASSUMANI
88	Assoc Prov Educ Innov & Tech	Dr. Jeff MORGAN
88	Assoc Provost Fac Dev/Affairs	Dr. Mark CLARKE
21	Associate VC/VP Finance	Mr. Karin LIVINGSTON
05	Interim Provost	Dr. Robert H. MCPHERSON
11	Sr Assoc VC/VP Administration	Dr. Emily MESSA
35	Assoc VC/VP Student Affairs	Dr. Daniel MAXWELL
35	Assoc VP Stdnt Affs/Dean of Stdnts	Dr. Donell YOUNG
29	Assoc VP Alumni Association	Mr. Mike PEDE
13	Sr AVC/VP Information Tech/CIO	Dr. Dennis FOUTY
15	Assoc VP Human Resources	Mr. Gaston REINOSO
22	Asst VC/VP Equal Opportunity	Ms. Toni J. BENOIT
19	Asst VC/VP Public Safety/Security	Ms. Kelly BOYSEN
91	Asst VP Enterprise Sys Adm	Mr. Keith MARTIN
10	Sr Vice Pres Administration/Finance	Mr. Raymond BARTLETT
39	Asst VP Res Life/Student Housing	Mr. Don YACKLEY
63	Dean Col Medicine/VP Medical Affs	Dr. Stephen J. SPANN
48	Dean Col of Architecture/Design	Ms. Patricia Belton OLIVER
57	Dean McGovern College of the Arts	Dr. Andrew DAVIS
50	Dean Bauer Col Business Admin	Mr. Paul A. PAVLOU
49	Int Dean Col Liberal Arts/Soc Sci	Dr. Daniel P. O'CONNOR
53	Dean College of Education	Dr. Robert MCPHERSON
54	Dean Cullen College of Engineering	Dr. Joseph W. TEDESCO
92	Dean Honors College	Dr. William MONROE
88	Dean Hilton Col Htl/Restaurant Mgt	Dr. Dennis REYNOLDS
43	VP Legal Affairs & Gen Counsel	Ms. Dona H. CORNELL
61	Dean UH Law Center	Mr. Leonard M. BAYNES
81	Dean Col Natural Sci & Math	Dr. Dan WELLS
66	Dean School of Nursing	Dr. Kathryn M. TART
88	Dean College of Optometry	Dr. Michael D. TWA
85	Asst Director Global Initiatives	Ms. Corissa WANDMACHER
80	Dean Hobby School of Public Affairs	Dr. Jim GRANATO
08	Dean University Libraries	Ms. Athena JACKSON
67	Dean College of Pharmacy	Dr. Lamar PRITCHARD
70	Dean Graduate Col of Social Work	Dr. Alan DETLAFF
72	Dean College of Technology	Dr. Anthony P. AMBLER
46	VP Research/Tech Transfer	Dr. Amr ELNASHAI
101	Exec Administrator to Board	Ms. Germaine MATHISEN
27	Executive Director Media Relations	Mr. Mike S. ROSEN
37	Exec Dir Scholarships & Fin Aid	Ms. Briget JANS
07	Executive Director of Admissions	Mr. Mardell MAXWELL
25	Exec Dir Contract and Grants	Ms. Beverly RYMER
04	Sr Exec Assistant to the President	Ms. Carmen HERNANDEZ
06	University Registrar	Mr. Scott SAWYER
96	Director of Purchasing	Mr. Robert ADKINS
111	VC/VP University Advancement	Ms. Eloise D. BRICE
32	VC/VP Student Affs/Enrollment Svcs	Dr. Daniel MAXWELL
86	VP Govt & Community Relations	Mr. Jason S. SMITH
26	VC/VP for Mktg & Communications	Ms. Lisa K. HOLDEMAN

*University of Houston - Clear Lake (A)

2700 Bay Area Boulevard, Houston TX 77058
County: Harris FICE Identification: 011711
Unit ID: 225414
Telephone: (281) 283-7600 Carnegie Class: DU-Mod
FAX Number: (281) 283-2219 Calendar System: Semester
URL: www.uhcl.edu
Established: 1971 Annual Undergrad Tuition & Fees (In-State): $7,504
Enrollment: 9,053 Coed
Affiliation or Control: State IRS Status: 501(c)3
Highest Offering: Doctorate
Accreditation: SC, ABAI, CACREP, IPSY, MFCD, NUR, PSPSY, SW

02	President	Dr. Richard WALKER
05	Sr Vice Pres for Acad Affairs	Dr. Christopher MAYNARD
10	VP Administration & Finance	Mr. Mark DENNEY
04	Executive Assoc to the President	Ms. Berenice WEBSTER
20	Assoc VP Academic Affairs	Dr. Kathryn MATTHEW
111	VP University Advancement	Mr. Joseph L. STALEY
32	Vice President of Student Affairs	Vacant
21	Associate Vice Pres Finance	Ms. Sherry HAWN
121	Assoc VP Stdnt Success Initiatives	Dr. Timothy RICHARDSON
84	Int VP Strategic Enrollment Mgmt	Ms. Kara HADLEY-SHAKYA
50	Dean College Business	Dr. Edward WALLER
79	Dean College Human Sci/Humanities	Dr. Glenn SANFORD
35	Dean of Students	Mr. David A. RACHITA
28	Dir Student Diversity/Equity & Incl	Vacant
88	Exec Dir Strategic Partnerships	Dr. Natalie CLOGSTON
85	Asst VP Global Lrng/Strat/SIO	Dr. Gigi DO
45	Exec Dir Planning & Assessment	Ms. Pamela SHEFMAN
15	Interim Exec Dir Human Resources	Ms. Maureen VILLARREAL
13	Asst VP Info Technology and CIO	Dr. LeeBrian E. GASKINS
96	Exec Dir of Procurement & Payables	Ms. Debra CARPENTER
25	Exec Dir Sponsored Programs	Vacant
37	Exec Director Financial Aid	Ms. Holly NOLAN
88	Exec Dir Environment Inst Houston	Dr. George GUILLEN
51	Exec Dir Cont Educ/Dist & OC Educ	Ms. Lisa GABRIEL
26	Asst VP Marketing & Communications	Mr. Daniel RAMIREZ
29	Exec Dir University Advancement	Ms. Elbby ANTONY
36	Ex Dir Counseling/Hlth/Career Svcs	Dr. Cindy COOK
12	Dir Campus Opers/UHCL Pearland	Vacant
23	Dir Student Health Services	Ms. Regina PICKETT
07	Exec Director of Admissions	Ms. Kara HADLEY-SHAKYA
06	Registrar	Ms. Andrea CELESTINE
08	Exec Director Library	Dr. Vivienne MCCLENDON
09	Assoc Dir Institutional Research	Ms. Miriam QUMSIEH
105	Director Web & Multimedia Services	Vacant
18	Assoc VP Facilities Mgmt	Mr. David KITCHEN
19	Exec Dir Public Safety	Chief Russell L. MILLER
22	Title IX/Equal Opportunity Officer	Mr. David BRITTAIN
39	Dir Resident Life/Student Housing	Mr. Matthew PERRY
53	Dean of Education	Dr. Joan PEDRO
54	Dean of Science & Engineering	Dr. Miguel A. GONZALEZ
90	Director Academic Technologies	Ms. Sana ZEIDAN
30	Senior Development Officer	Mr. Richard J. ZALESAK
88	Director University Compliance	Dr. Yolanda NIMMER-WILLIAMS
106	Dean of Online Education/E-learning	Dr. Bianca SCHONBERG

*University of Houston - Downtown (B)

One Main Street, Houston TX 77002-1014
County: Harris FICE Identification: 003612
Unit ID: 225432
Telephone: (713) 221-8001 Carnegie Class: Masters/L
FAX Number: (713) 221-8075 Calendar System: Semester
URL: www.uhd.edu
Established: 1974 Annual Undergrad Tuition & Fees (In-State): $7,222
Enrollment: 15,239 Coed
Affiliation or Control: State IRS Status: Exempt
Highest Offering: Master's
Accreditation: SC, NURSE, SW

02	President	Dr. Loren J. BLANCHARD
100	Asst VP/Pres Affs & Constituent Rel	Dr. Liza ALONZO
22	Title IX/Equal Opportunity Officer	Ms. Lauri RUIZ
05	Senior VP & Provost	Dr. Deborah BORDELON
88	AVP Programming & Curriculum	Dr. Michelle MOOSALLY
45	AVP IE/Strategic Plng & Assessment	Vacant
08	Executive Director WI Dykes Library	Vacant
106	Exec Dir Off Campus/OL Coordinator	Mr. Louis D. EVANS, III
92	Director Honors Program	Vacant
88	Dir Teaching & Learning Excel	Dr. Gregory DEMENT
108	Exec Dir Assessment & Accred	Dr. Lea CAMPBELL
51	Dir Continuing Education	Vacant
88	Exec Dir Impact Learning	Dr. Poonam SALHOTRA
25	Exec Dir Research & Spon Pgm	Ms. Brandi SMITH-IRVING
09	Dir Institutional Research	Mrs. Carol TUCKER
50	Dean Davies College of Business	Dr. Charles E. GENGLER
117	Dir Insurance & Risk Management Ctr	Ms. Priscilla OEHLERT
79	Dean Humanities & Social Science	Dr. Wendy BURNS-ARDOLINO
88	Asst Dean Advising/Degree Comp	Ms. Reyna ROMERO
80	Dean College of Public Service	Dr. Jonathan SCHWARTZ
88	Dir Criminal Justice Center	Mr. Steven BRACKEN
88	Dir Ctr Public Svc & Com Res	Mr. Steven VILLANO
88	Dir Ctr Prof Devel Teachers	Ms. Cynae BROWN
88	Dir College Data Analytics	Mr. Richard SIMONDS
72	Dean Col Sciences & Tech	Dr. James UZMAN
88	Exec Director of Scholars Academy	Dr. Mary Jo PARKER
32	VP Student Success & Student Life	Vacant
35	Dean Student Life	Dr. Meritza TAMEZ
35	Asst Dean Student Life	Mr. Branston HARRIS
41	Director Sports & Fitness	Mr. Richard SEBASTIANI
36	Dir Career Development Center	Ms. Katherine KNAPP
124	Dir Gator Success Center	Dr. Jemma SYLVESTER-CAESAR
121	Director of Academic Support Center	Dr. Isidro GRAU
28	Dir Ctr Stdnt Diversity/Eqty/Incl	Dr. John HUDSON
38	Int Dir Counseling/Disability Svcs	Dr. Hope PAMPLIN
84	VP Enrollment Management	Dr. Daniel VILLANUEVA
07	Dir Admissions & Recruitment	Vacant
37	Director Financial Aid	Ms. LaTasha GOUDEAU
06	University Registrar	Mr. Ovidio GALVAN
88	Exec Dir Student Comm & Trans	Ms. Courtney SCHROEDER
10	VP Administration & Finance	Ms. Kimberly LAMBERT-THOMAS
13	Assoc VP Information Technology	Mr. Hossein SHAHROKHI
114	Assoc VP Business Affairs	Ms. Theresa MENELEY
18	Asst VP Facilities Management	Mr. Timothy RYCHLEC
19	Chief of Police	Mr. Casey DAVIS
90	Exec Dir Information Technology	Mr. Said FATTOUH
11	Exec Dir Admin & Finance	Ms. Stefany RECORDS
91	Director Enterprise Systems	Mr. Kong YIN
88	Dir Technology Learning Services	Mr. John LANE
14	Director Technical Services	Vacant
88	Dir User Support Services	Ms. Cheryl ROBERTSON
88	Dir IT Infrastructure & Comm Svcs	Mr. Miguel RUIZ
14	Dir PeopleSoft Bus Proc & Svc	Mr. Paul Lap LEUNG
88	Dir Auxiliary Services	Ms. Mary TORRES
113	Dir Student Business Services	Ms. Krystal LEBLANC
114	Director Budget	Mr. Preston HENG
96	Dir Univ Business Svcs/HUB Co	Ms. Lorena SANCHEZ
117	Dir Emergency Management	Ms. Cynthia VARGAS
88	Dir Environmental Health & Safety	Mr. Edward ARIAS
15	VP Employment Svcs & Operations	Ms. Ivonne MONTALBANO
118	Dir Benefits & Compensation	Ms. Erica MORALES
88	Director Payroll & Records	Ms. April FRANK
16	Dir Talent Acquisition & Mgt	Ms. Chetiqua MATTHEWS HERRON
111	VP Advancement & External Rels	Mr. Javier ZAMBRANO
26	Asst VP University Relations	Vacant
110	Exec Dir Advancement	Mr. Jacob LIPP
105	Exec Dir Marketing	Ms. Laura WAITS
27	Exec Dir Communications	Ms. Marie JACINTO
27	Director Marketing	Ms. Toye SIMMONS
88	Dir Advancement Svc & Business	Mr. Brian DRAKE

*University of Houston - Victoria (C)

3007 N Ben Wilson St., Victoria TX 77901-4450
County: Victoria FICE Identification: 013231
Unit ID: 225502
Telephone: (361) 570-4848 Carnegie Class: Masters/L
FAX Number: (361) 580-5534 Calendar System: Semester
URL: www.uhv.edu
Established: 1973 Annual Undergrad Tuition & Fees (In-State): $7,313
Enrollment: 4,922 Coed
Affiliation or Control: State IRS Status: 501(c)3
Highest Offering: Beyond Master's But Less Than Doctorate
Accreditation: SC, CACREP, NASP, NURSE

02	President	Dr. Robert K. GLENN
10	VP/CFO Administration & Finance	Dr. Beverly C. SHUFORD
05	Provost/VP Acad Affairs	Dr. Chance M. GLENN, SR.
32	Vice President Student Affairs	Dr. Jay LAMBERT
84	VP for Enrollment Management	Dr. Jose CANTU
49	Dean Col of Liberal Arts & Soc Sci	Dr. Kyoko AMANO
50	Dean College of Business	Dr. Ken COLWELL
53	Dean College of Educ & Health Prof	Dr. Rachel MARTINEZ
81	Int Dean Col of Nat & Applied Sci	Dr. Dmitri SOBOLEV
111	VP Advancement & External Relations	Dr. Amber COUNTIS
08	Director of Library	Ms. Karen LOCHER
09	Dir Inst Research/Effectiveness	Dr. Teresa SIMPSON
13	Sr Dir of Instructional Technology	Mr. Randy FAULK
22	Sr Director Equal Opportunity	Ms. Rebecca LAKE
15	Director Human Resources	Ms. Shelly FRANK
88	Dir Small Business Development Ctr	Ms. Lindsay YOUNG
06	Registrar	Ms. Denise HERNANDEZ
37	Director Financial Aid	Ms. Lashon WILLIAMS
36	Director Career Services	Ms. Amy HATMAKER
18	Director Facilities	Mr. John BURKE
21	Sr Director Finance	Ms. Erin GOODWIN
41	Director Athletics	Mr. Ashley WALYUCHOW
26	Sr Dir Marketing & Communications	Ms. Brittany MARSH
38	Counseling Center	Dr. Michael WILKINSON
35	Sr Dir Student Svcs & Judicial Affs	Dr. Michael WILKINSON
114	Director of Budget	Ms. Karen SANDERS
39	Director Residence Life & Univ Comm	Mr. Brandon W. LEE
88	Director Capital Projects	Mr. Matt ALEXANDER
04	Executive Adm Asst to President	Ms. Donna D. HOOVER
25	Dir Grants & Contracts	Ms. Angela HARTMANN
102	Sr Dir Corp/Foundation Relations	Ms. Courtney M. SIDES
29	Director Alumni/Annual Giving	Ms. Kelsey NORGARD
20	Assoc Prov Academic Affairs	Dr. Beverly TOMEK
85	Director International Programs	Ms. Ludmi HERATH
88	Asst Provost Academic Affairs	Dr. Karla DECUIR
07	Director Admissions/Recruitment	Mr. Billy LAGAL
19	Campus Security & Safety	Mr. Adam RODRIGUEZ
88	Director Student Services	Ms. Hilary KOFRON
88	Director Business Services	Mr. Tim MICHALSKI

University of the Incarnate Word (D)

4301 Broadway, San Antonio TX 78209-6397
County: Bexar FICE Identification: 003578
Unit ID: 225627
Telephone: (210) 829-6000 Carnegie Class: DU-Mod
FAX Number: (210) 829-1220 Calendar System: Semester
URL: www.uiw.edu
Established: 1881 Annual Undergrad Tuition & Fees: $32,286
Enrollment: 7,917 Coed
Affiliation or Control: Roman Catholic IRS Status: 501(c)3
Highest Offering: Doctorate
Accreditation: SC, AAQEP, ACBSP, CAATE, CIDA, DIETD, DIETI, HSA, MUS, NMT, NURSE, OPT, OPTR, OSTEO, PHAR, PTA, THEA

01	President	Dr. Thomas M. EVANS
05	Provost/Chief Academic Officer	Dr. Barbara ARANDA-NARANJO
20	Vice Provost	Dr. Glenn E. JAMES
03	Vice President Mission and Ministry	Sr. Walter MAHER
100	Chief of Staff	Ms. Cynthia S. ESCAMILLA
43	VP Legal Affairs/General Counsel	Ms. Cynthia S. ESCAMILLA
111	VP External Relations	Mr. Richard D. KIMBROUGH, III
88	Vice Pres International Affairs	Mr. Marcos FRAGOSO
10	Vice Pres Administrative Svcs/CFO	Dr. Darrell HAYDON
84	VP Strategy & Enrollment	Mr. John M. BURY
28	AVP Mission & Ministry/DEI	Dr. Arturo E. CHAVEZ
45	AVP Cap Planning/Facilities Mgmt	Mr. Philip W. LOPES, JR.
13	AVP Information Resources/CIO	Mr. Neil SCHROEDER
15	AVP for Human Resources	Ms. Annette THOMPSON
21	AVP for Finance/Comptroller	Ms. Elisa GONZALES
20	Assoc Prov Outreach/Partnerships	Dr. Osman OZTURGUT
20	Assoc Provost UG/Graduate Educ	Dr. Kevin VICHALES
17	Assoc Prov for Health Professions	Dr. Caroline GOULET
108	Assoc Provost Inst Effectiveness	Dr. David B. STEIN
121	Assoc Prov Student Success	Ms. Monica A. JIMENEZ
81	Dean Math/Science/Engineering	Dr. Carlos GARCIA
50	Dean H-E-B Sch Business & Admin	Dr. Jeannie J. SCOTT
79	Dean Humanities/Arts & Social Sci	Dr. Javier CLAVERE
66	Dean Nursing & Health Professions	Dr. Holly CASSELLS
88	Dean Media & Design	Dr. Sharon WELKEY
29	Dean of Alumni/Parent Relations	Dr. Lisa MCNARY
53	Dean Dreeben School of Education	Dr. Denise STAUDT
107	Dean School Physical Therapy	Dr. Stephen GOFFAR

67 Dean Feik School of Pharmacy ... Dr. David MAIZE
107 Dean School of Optometry ... Dr. Sandra FORTENBERRY
63 Dean School of Osteopathic Medicine ... Dr. John PHAM
08 Dean of Library Services ... Ms. Tracey MENDOZA
32 Dean of Campus Life ... Dr. Christopher A. SUMMERLIN
107 Dean Sch of Professional Studies ... Dr. Osman OZTURGUT
88 Dean Research/Graduate Supp ... Dr. Mark NIJLAND
26 Director of Comm/Marketing ... Ms. Margaret L. GARCIA
58 Director of Graduate Studies ... Dr. Trinidad MACIAS
39 Director of Residence Life ... Ms. Diane SANCHEZ
121 Director of Academic Advising ... Ms. Kedra GRANT-BRINKLEY
88 Director of Campus Ministry ... Ms. Elisabeth VILLARREAL
88 Director of Music Ministries ... Ms. Lena GOKELMAN
88 Dir Ettling Ctr for Civic Ldrs ... Dr. Ricardo GONZALEZ
41 Director of Athletics ... Mr. Richard P. DURAN
24 Director Instructional Technology ... Ms. Kathy BOTTARO
91 Director Enterprise Applications ... Mr. Jesse A. CORTINAS
14 Director IT Project Portfolio/Mgmt ... Vacant
119 Dir Infrastructure/Ops/Security ... Mr. Brian J. ANDERSON
96 Dir Procurement/Bus Support Svcs ... Vacant
18 Director Facilities/Event Mgmt ... Mr. Jose M. HERRERA
37 Director of Financial Aid ... Ms. Cristen ALICEA
07 Director of Admissions ... Ms. Jessica DELAROSA
88 Sr Director Enrollment Svcs ... Ms. Julie H. WEBER
35 Director of Campus Engagement ... Ms. Shannon S. TWUMASI
88 Director of Sports/Wellness ... Mr. Scott W. LEBLANC
88 Dir Student Advocacy/Accountability ... Vacant
09 Director of Institutional Research ... Dr. Andrew T. PAGEL
88 Sr Director Military/Veterans Aff ... Mr. Jonathan C. LOVEJOY
88 Director Ctr for Teaching/Learning ... Vacant
36 Director of Career Services ... Ms. Jessica L. WILSON
88 Director Learning Support Ctr ... Dr. Amanda J. JOHNSTON
88 Director Auxiliary Academic Svcs ... Dr. Moises J. TORRESCANO
88 Director TRIO Student Success ... Ms. Wynette H. KELLER
89 Director of First Year Engagement ... Dr. Raul ZENDEJAS
102 Dir Foundation/Corporate Relations ... Mr. Jon GILLESPIE
16 Director of Human Resources ... Ms. Shannon A. ROOT
85 Dir Intl Students/Scholar Svcs ... Mr. Jose F. MARTINEZ, JR.
112 Dir of Major Gifts/Planned Giving ... Ms. Alex A. CASTANEDA
38 Director of Counseling Svcs ... Dr. Kevin MILLIGAN
23 Director of Clinical Health ... Dr. Ronda GOTTLIEB
88 Director of International Affairs ... Dr. Javier LOZANO
88 Director Lewis Inst of the Americas ... Dr. Rafael D. HOYLE
105 Director Web & Mobile Operations ... Mr. Nicholas A. GARCIA
88 Director of Individual Giving ... Ms. Ana P. HOFF
27 Director of Presidential Comm ... Ms. Marissa A. RODRIGUEZ
88 Director of Title IX ... Ms. Alexandria SALAS, ESQ
88 Director Env Health/Safety/Risk Mgt ... Mr. Samual G. MCDANIEL
116 Dir Quality Assurance/Compliance ... Ms. Allyson M. MEDINA
23 Medical Director Health Svcs ... Dr. Shaylon D. RETTIG
114 Budget Manager ... Ms. Amy M. DEATLEY
19 University Police Chief ... Ms. Jessica A. SERBANTES
44 Annual Giving Officer ... Ms. Brittany SHARNSKY
42 Protestant Chaplain ... Rev Bp. Trevor ALEXANDER
42 University Chaplain ... Vacant
06 Registrar ... Ms. Marisol M. SCHEER
88 Associate Counsel ... Ms. Elizabeth O. PEREZ
88 Manager Vehicle Svcs/Shipping/Rcv ... Mr. Joe A. CADENA
21 Assistant Comptroller ... Ms. Kimberly S. DECKER
07 Assoc Dir Intl Admiss/Recruiting ... Ms. Amy C. DESTEFANO
04 Admin Asst Office of President ... Ms. Melissa C. MOLINA

University of Mary Hardin-Baylor (A)

900 College Street, Belton TX 76513-2578
County: Bell FICE Identification: 003588
Unit ID: 226471
Telephone: (254) 295-8642 Carnegie Class: DU-Mod
FAX Number: (254) 295-4535 Calendar System: Semester
URL: www.umhb.edu
Established: 1845 Annual Undergrad Tuition & Fees: $30,750
Enrollment: 3,876 Coed
Affiliation or Control: Southern Baptist IRS Status: 501(c)3
Highest Offering: Doctorate
Accreditation: SC, ACBSP, #ARCPA, ART, CACREP, MUS, NURSE, OT, PTA, SW

01 President/CEO ... Dr. Randy G. O'REAR
03 Sr Vice Pres Admin/COO ... Dr. Steve THEODORE
05 Provost/Sr VP Academic Affs ... Dr. John VASSAR
108 Assoc Prov for Institutional Effect ... Dr. Emily PREVOST
45 VP Campus Planning & Support ... Mr. Marvin EE
111 Vice Pres for Advancement ... Dr. Rebecca O'BANION
32 Vice Pres for Student Life ... Dr. Brandon SKAGGS
41 Vice Pres Athletics ... Mr. Mickey KERR
10 Vice Pres Business/Finance/CFO ... Mrs. Jennifer RAMM
15 Assoc Vice Pres Human Resources ... Mrs. Sherri WORLEY
13 Vice Pres Info Tech ... Mr. Greg BRANDENBURG
84 Vice Pres Enrollment Mgmt ... Dr. Gary LAMM
21 Controller ... Mrs. Charla KAHLIG
50 Dean McLane College of Business ... Dr. Ken SMITH
79 Dean of Humanities & Sciences ... Dr. Stephen BALDRIDGE
66 Interim Dean of Nursing ... Dr. Christi EMERSON
53 Dean of Education ... Dr. Joan BERRY
76 Executive Dean Health Sciences ... Dr. Colin WILBORN
88 Dean of Christian Studies ... Dr. Tim CRAWFORD
57 Dean Visual/Performing Arts ... Dr. Kathryn FOUSE
35 Dean of Students ... Dr. Michael BURNS
39 Director of Residence Life ... Dr. Kyle SMITH
04 Special Asst to President ... Mrs. Candace WILLIAMS
06 Registrar ... Mrs. Elizabeth WEBB
88 Director Strategic Engagement ... Ms. Melissa WILLIAMS
07 Director of Admissions & Recruiting ... Dr. Brent BURKS

08 Assoc Dean & Dir Learning Resources ... Mr. Alan ASHER
09 Director Institutional Research ... Mr. Trent BRIDGES
37 Director Financial Aid ... Mr. Ron BROWN
92 Director Honors Program ... Dr. David HOLCOMB
19 Director Campus Police ... Mr. Gary SARGENT
96 Purchasing Manager ... Mrs. Jennifer WEBB
29 Director Alumni Relations ... Mr. Jeff SUTTON
42 University Chaplain ... Mr. Jason PALMER
36 Director Career Services ... Mr. Don OWENS
88 Director Student Disability & Test ... Mr. Blayne ALANIZ
85 Dir International Student Services ... Mrs. Elizabeth TANAKA
110 Assoc VP for Fundraising ... Mr. Tucker GLASKE
40 Bookstore Manager ... Ms. Debbie COTTRELL
104 Director Study Abroad ... Dr. Michelle REINA
105 Dir Web Design & Development ... Mr. Joshua WURDEMANN

University of North Texas (B)

1155 Union Circle #311277, Denton TX 76203-5013
County: Denton FICE Identification: 003594
Unit ID: 227216
Telephone: (940) 565-2000 Carnegie Class: DU-Highest
FAX Number: (940) 565-7600 Calendar System: Semester
URL: www.unt.edu
Established: 1890 Annual Undergrad Tuition & Fees (In-State): $11,090
Enrollment: 40,953 Coed
Affiliation or Control: State IRS Status: 501(c)3
Highest Offering: Doctorate
Accreditation: SC, ABAI, ACPHA, ART, AUD, CACREP, CEA, CIDA, CLPSY, COPSY, FEPAC, JOUR, LIB, MUS, SP, SPAA, SW

01 President ... Dr. Neal SMATRESK
00 Chancellor ... Ms. Lesa ROE
05 Provost/VP Academic Affairs ... Dr. Michael A. MCPHERSON
10 VP Finance/Administration ... Mr. Clayton GIBSON
46 VP Research/Innovation ... Ms. Pamela PADILLA
32 Vice President Student Affairs ... Dr. Elizabeth WITH
43 Vice Chancellor/General Counsel ... Mr. Alan STUCKY
26 Int VP Brand Strategy/Communication ... Ms. Kelley REESE
30 Associate VP for Development ... Ms. Eileen P. MORAN
84 VP for Enrollment ... Mr. Shannon M. GOODMAN
13 VP for Digital Strategy/CIO ... Mr. Adam FEIN
20 Vice Provost for Academic Affairs ... Dr. Michael MCPHERSON
20 Vice Provost for Academic Resources .. Ms. Jennifer STEVENSON
20 Vice Provost Faculty Success ... Dr. Holly HUTCHINS
100 VP for Planning/Chief of Staff ... Dr. Debbie ROHWER
41 VP & Director of Athletics ... Mr. Wren BAKER
35 Asst VP and Dean of Students ... Dr. Maureen MCGUINNESS
114 Budget Director ... Vacant
121 Exec Dir Lrng Technologies ... Dr. Patrick PLUSCHT
28 VP Institutional Equity & Diversity ... Dr. Joanne WOODARD
31 Vice Prov Academic Partnerships ... Ms. Brenda KIHL
18 Assoc Vice President for Facilities ... Vacant
08 Dean of Libraries ... Ms. Diane BRUXVOORT
37 Exec Dir Fin Aid/Univ Admissions ... Ms. Zelma DELEON
49 Dean College of Liberal Arts & Sci ... Dr. Tamara BROWN
81 Dean College of Science ... Dr. Pamela PADILLA
50 Dean College Business ... Dr. Marilyn WILEY
53 Dean College of Education ... Dr. Randy BOMER
57 Dean College of CVAD ... Ms. Karen HUTZEL
69 Dean Health & Public Service ... Dr. Nicole DASH
64 Dean College of Music ... Dr. John W. RICHMOND
59 Dean Col of Merch/Hosp & Tourism ... Dr. Jana HAWLEY
77 Dean College of Information ... Dr. KINSHUK
58 Dean Toulouse Grad School ... Dr. Victor PRYBUTOK
92 Dean of TAMS/Honors College ... Dr. Glenisson DE OLIVEIRA
60 Dean Mayborn Sch of Journalism ... Dr. Andrea MILLER
54 Dean College of Engineering ... Dr. Hanchen HUANG
88 Dean New College at Frisco ... Dr. Wesley RANDALL
90 Director Acad Computing/User Svcs ... Dr. Philip C. BACZEWSKI
09 Director Institutional Research ... Dr. Mary BARTON
108 Associate Vice President DAIR ... Dr. Jason F. SIMON
88 Director of Accreditation ... Ms. Elizabeth VOGT
51 Director Lifelong Learning ... Dr. Stephanie REINKE
06 AVP Enrollment & Registrar ... Ms. Shari SCHWARTZ
15 Chief Human Capital Officer ... Ms. Sheraine GILLIAM-HOLMES
36 Exec Dir Career & Leadership ... Mr. Dan NAEGELI
19 Director/Chief of Police ... Mr. Ed REYNOLDS
39 Exec Director Housing ... Ms. Gina VANACORE
85 Vice Provost & Dean Intl Affairs ... Dr. Pia WOOD
23 Exec Dir Stdnt Health/Wellness ... Dr. Herschel VOORHEES
111 Vice President for Advancement ... Mr. Brandon BUZBEE
04 Executive Asst to President ... Ms. Louise DUNN
101 Secretary of the Institution/Board ... Dr. Rosemary R. HAGGETT
104 Director Study Abroad ... Ms. Amy SHENBERGER
88 VP Digital Strategy/Innovation ... Dr. Adam FEIN
88 Chief Compliance Officer ... Mr. Clay SIMMONS
22 AVP/Director Equal Opportunity ... Ms. Eve BELL
25 Director Pre-Awards/Contracts ... Vacant
29 Exec Director Alumni Relations ... Mr. Rob MCINTURF
38 AVP Student Counseling/Testing ... Vacant
86 Director Government Relations ... Mr. Jack MORTON

University of North Texas at Dallas (C)

7300 University Hills Blvd, Dallas TX 75241
County: Dallas Identification: 667124
Unit ID: 484905
Telephone: (972) 780-3600 Carnegie Class: Masters/L
FAX Number: (972) 780-3606 Calendar System: Semester
URL: www.untdallas.edu
Established: 2001 Annual Undergrad Tuition & Fees (In-State): $8,143
Enrollment: 4,164 Coed
Affiliation or Control: State IRS Status: 501(c)3
Highest Offering: Doctorate
Accreditation: SC, CACREP, LAW

01 President ... Robert MONG
10 Exec Vice Pres Administration & CFO ... Arthur BRADFORD
05 Provost/EVP Academic Affairs ... Dr. Betty STEWART
49 Dean of Liberal Arts & Sciences ... Dr. Orlando PEREZ
88 Dean of Human Services ... Dr. Constance LACY
04 Exec Assistant to the President ... Angie CASTILLO
06 Registrar ... Hector GOVEA
07 Director of Admissions ... Luis FRANCO
08 Chief Library Officer ... Brenda ROBERTSON
09 Exec Director Research & Dev ... Alicia BROSSETTE
106 Director Distance Learning ... Georgianna LAWS
13 Chief Information Technology Ofcr ... Kevin ROCHA
15 Chief Human Resources Officer ... Wanda BOYD
18 Chief Facilities/Physical Plant Ofc ... Wayne MCINNIS
19 Director Security/Safety ... Chris SHAW
26 Chief Public Relations Officer ... Yolanda FRANKLIN
29 Director Alumni Affairs ... Derrick MORGAN
32 Dean of Students ... Vacant
36 Director Student Placement ... Arthur LUMZY
37 Director Student Financial Aid ... Garrick HILDEBRAND
38 Director Student Counseling ... Teresa ESPINO
39 Dir Resident Life/Student Housing ... Toni MINTER
41 Athletic Director ... Jack ALLDAY
50 Dean of Business ... Dr. Karen SHUMWAY
84 Director Enrollment Management ... Stephanie HOLLEY

University of North Texas Health Science Center at Fort Worth (D)

3500 Camp Bowie Boulevard, Fort Worth TX 76107-2699
County: Tarrant FICE Identification: 009768
Unit ID: 228909
Telephone: (817) 735-2000 Carnegie Class: Spec-4-yr-Med
FAX Number: N/A Calendar System: Semester
URL: www.unthsc.edu
Established: 1966 Annual Undergrad Tuition & Fees (In-State): N/A
Enrollment: 2,329 Coed
Affiliation or Control: State IRS Status: 501(c)3
Highest Offering: Doctorate
Accreditation: SC, ARCPA, HSA, OSTEO, PH, PHAR, PTA

01 President ... Vacant
10 EVP for Finance and Operations ... Mr. Gregory R. ANDERSON
17 EVP of Health Systems ... Ms. Jessica RANGEL
05 Provost/Exec VP Academic Affairs ... Dr. Charles TAYLOR
86 Vice President Governmental Affairs ... Mr. Dan JENSEN
63 Dean Texas Col of Osteopathic Med ... Dr. Frank FILIPETTO
46 VP Research ... Dr. Brian GLADUE
58 Dean Grad Sch Biomed Sciences ... Dr. Michael MATHIS
76 Dean School of Health Professions ... Dr. J. Glenn FORISTER
69 Dean of School of Public Health ... Dr. Dennis THOMBS
37 Director Student Financial Aid ... Mr. Joseph SANCHEZ
32 Sr Vice Provost Student Affairs ... Ms. Trisha VANDUSER
19 Chief of Police ... Mr. Cliff JAYNES
111 SVP Inst Advancement/Communication ... Ms. Lacey LAPOINTE
45 VP of Culture and Experience ... Ms. Jeanie FOSTER
21 Vice President Finance & Planning ... Mr. Chuck FOX
26 AVP Marketing/Communications ... Ms. Laken RAPIER
15 Exec Director Human Resources ... Ms. Janine WATKINS
06 Dir Enrollment & Records ... Mrs. Elizabeth MEDDERS
08 Director of Lewis Library ... Mr. Daniel BURGARD
88 SVP/Chief Integrity Officer ... Mrs. Desiree RAMIREZ
100 Chief of Staff ... Mr. James MEINTJES

University of Phoenix Dallas Campus (E)

12400 Coit Road, Dallas TX 75251-2004
Telephone: (972) 385-1055 Identification: 770227
Accreditation: &HLC, ACBSP

† Branch campus of University of Phoenix, Phoenix, AZ-No longer enrolling new students

University of Phoenix Houston Campus (F)

11451 Katy Freeway, Houston TX 77079-2004
Telephone: (713) 465-9966 Identification: 770229
Accreditation: &HLC, ACBSP

† Branch campus of University of Phoenix, Phoenix, AZ-No longer enrolling new students

University of St. Augustine for Health Sciences (G)

5401 La Crosse Ave, Austin TX 78739
Telephone: (512) 394-9766 Identification: 770940
Accreditation: &WC, OT, PTA, SP

† Branch campus of University of St. Augustine for Health Sciences, San Marcos, CA.

University of St. Thomas (H)

3800 Montrose Boulevard, Houston TX 77006-4696
County: Harris FICE Identification: 003654
Unit ID: 227863
Telephone: (713) 522-7911 Carnegie Class: DU-Mod
FAX Number: (713) 525-2125 Calendar System: Semester
URL: www.stthom.edu
Established: 1947 Annual Undergrad Tuition & Fees: $31,560

Enrollment: 3,692 Coed
Affiliation or Control: Roman Catholic IRS Status: 501(c)3
Highest Offering: Doctorate
Accreditation: SC, CACREP, NURSE

01 President ... Dr. Richard LUDWICK
04 Special Assistant to the President ... Ms. Cindy VIAUD
04 Exec Assistant to the President ... Ms. Anne LAMBERT
05 Vice Pres Academic Affairs ... Dr. Chris P. EVANS
10 Vice President for Finance ... Mr. Spencer CONROY
30 Chief Development Officer ... Ms. Dawn KOENNING
32 Vice Pres Student Engagement ... Mr. Arthur ORTIZ
13 Chief Information Officer ... Mr. Reginald BRUMFIELD
84 Vice Pres Enrollment Management ... Mr. Arthur ORTIZ
26 VP Marketing/University Engagement ... Mr. Jeff OLSEN
15 Assoc VP of Human Resources ... Vacant
35 Assoc VP Student Affs/Dean Students ... Dr. Benedict NGUYEN
66 Dean School of Nursing ... Dr. Claudine DUFRENE
49 Dean Arts & Sciences ... Dr. George A. HARNE
73 Dean School of Theology ... Rev. Paul LOCKEY
50 Dean Cameron School of Business ... Dr. Mario ENZLER
53 Dean School of Education ... Dr. Ana-Lisa GONZALEZ
08 Dean of Libraries ... Mr. James PICCININNI
37 Dean of Scholarships/Financial Aid ... Ms. Lynda MCKENDREE
58 Dir Center for Thomistic Studies ... Dr. Brian CARL
82 Director Center for Intl Studies ... Dr. Richard SINDELAR
88 Director Center for Irish Studies ... Ms. Lori GALLAGHER
88 Director Center for Faith & Culture ... Fr. Binh QUACH
06 Registrar ... Mr. Nathan DUGAT
90 Director of Technical Svcs ... Ms. Wendy HODGKISS
91 Director of Application Svcs ... Ms. Alicia SMITH-GANTT
22 Director of Disability Services ... Ms. Angie MAXEY
42 Director of Campus Ministry ... Ms. Nicole LABADIE
39 Director Residence Life ... Ms. Ana Alicia LOPEZ
88 Asst Dir of Recreational Sports ... Mr. Scott LATHAM
18 Asst VP Facilities Operations ... Mr. Edgar MOCTEZUMA
21 Controller ... Mr. Keith SCHEFFLER
113 Bursar ... Mr. Richard SHUMAN
88 Director of Veteran Services ... Ms. Trisha RUIZ
27 Director of Communications ... Ms. Sandra SOLIZ
108 Dir Assessment/Inst Effectiveness ... Dr. Dominic AQUILA
19 Chief of Police ... Mr. H. E JENKINS
41 Athletic Director ... Mr. Todd SMITH
104 Director Study Abroad ... Dr. Ulyses BALDERAS
29 Director Alumni Relations ... Ms. Amy YOUNGBLOOD
88 Asst VP of Program Marketing ... Mr. Chris ZEGLIN
43 Chief Legal Counsel ... Ms. Gita BOLT

*The University of Texas System Administration (A)

210 West 7th Street, Austin TX 78701-2982
County: Travis FICE Identification: 003655
Unit ID: 229090
Telephone: (512) 499-4201 Carnegie Class: N/A
FAX Number: (512) 499-4215
URL: www.utsystem.edu

01 Chancellor ... Mr. James B. MILLIKEN
88 Sr Adv to the Chanc/Chief T&I Ofcr . Ms. Julie GOONEWARDENE
100 Chief of Staff Office of Chanc ... Mr. Art MARTINEZ
05 Exec VC Academic Affairs ... Dr. Archie L. HOLMES, JR.
17 Exec VC Health Affairs ... Dr. John M. ZERWAS
88 Sr Vice Chanc for Health Affairs ... Ms. Amy SHAW THOMAS
88 VC Health Affairs & Chief Med Ofcr ... Dr. David L. LAKEY
10 Exec Vice Chanc Business Affairs ... Mr. Jonathan C. PRUITT
43 Vice Chanc & General Counsel ... Mr. Dan SHARPHORN
86 Vice Chanc for Govt Relations ... Ms. Stacey NAPIER
26 Vice Chanc for Ext Rels/Comm & Adv ... Dr. Randa S. SAFADY
45 Assoc VC Inst Rsrch & Analysis ... Dr. David R. TROUTMAN
18 Asst VC for Capital Projects ... Mr. Stephen HARRIS
13 Assoc VC & Chief Info Officer ... Mr. David R. CRAIN
21 Assoc VC & Controller ... Ms. Veronica HINOJOSA-SEGURA
27 Director of Media Relations ... Ms. Karen E. ADLER
88 Executive Director of Real Estate ... Mr. Geoffrey RICHARDS
111 AVC for Advancement Services ... Ms. Andria BRANNON
19 Director of Police ... Mr. Michael J. HEIDINGSFIELD
04 Executive Asst to Chancellor ... Ms. Katherine IANNESSA
88 Exec Dir Systemwide Cmpl/Dpty Ofcr ... Mr. Jason KING
117 Chief Compliance & Risk Officer ... Mr. Phillip B. DENDY
119 Chief Info Security Officer ... Ms. Helen MOHRMANN

*The University of Texas at Arlington (B)

701 S Nedderman Drive, Arlington TX 76013
County: Tarrant FICE Identification: 003656
Unit ID: 228769
Telephone: (817) 272-2101 Carnegie Class: DU-Highest
FAX Number: (817) 272-5656 Calendar System: Semester
URL: www.uta.edu
Established: 1895 Annual Undergrad Tuition & Fees (In-State): $11,378
Enrollment: 48,072 Coed
Affiliation or Control: State IRS Status: 170(c)1
Highest Offering: Doctorate
Accreditation: SC, AAQEP, ART, CAATE, CEA, CIDA, LSAR, MUS, NURSE, PLNG, SPAA, SW

02 President ... Dr. Jennifer COWLEY
05 Provost & SVP Academic Affairs ... Dr. Tamara BROWN
10 VP for Business/Finance & CFO ... Mr. John DAVIDSON
32 VP Student Affairs/Dean ... Ms. Lisa NAGY
46 Vice President Research ... Dr. Kate MILLER
13 Interim Chief Information Officer ... Ms. Deepika CHALEMELA
11 Vice Pres Admin & Campus Operations ... Mr. John D. HALL
15 Chief Human Resources Officer ... Ms. Jewel WASHINGTON
84 VP for Enrollment Management ... Dr. Troy JOHNSON
111 AVP for Advancement Services ... Ms. Selma PERMENTER
45 Asst V Provost Inst Eff/Report ... Dr. Rebecca LEWIS
16 Asst Vice Pres Human Resources ... Ms. Eunice M. CURRIE
18 Int Asst VP Campus Opers/Facilities ... Mr. Don LANGE
121 Assoc V Prov Div of Stdnt Success ... Dr. Ashley PURGASON
100 VP for Planning and Chief of Staff ... Ms. Salma ADEM
58 Assoc Dean of Graduate Studies ... Mr. Raymond L. JACKSON
48 Interim Dean for CAPPA ... Dr. Maria MARTINEZ-COSIO
50 Dean College of Business ... Mr. Harry DOMBROSKI
54 Dean of Engineering ... Dr. Peter CROUCH
49 Interim Dean of Liberal Arts ... Dr. Dan CAVANAGH
66 Dean of Nursing ... Dr. Elizabeth MERWIN
81 Dean of Science ... Dr. Morteza KHALEDI
70 Dean School of Social Work ... Dr. Scott RYAN
53 Dean College of Education ... Dr. Teresa TABER DOUGHTY
92 Interim Dean Honors College ... Dr. Tim HENRY
08 Dean of Libraries ... Dr. Rebecca BICHEL
12 Exec Dir of UTA Ft Worth Center ... Vacant
37 Exec Director of Financial Aid ... Dr. Karen KRAUSE
23 Director Student Health Center ... Ms. Angela MIDDLETON
22 Director Equal Opportunity Services ... Mr. Eddie FREEMAN
41 Athletic Director ... Mr. Jon FAGG
19 Dir Environmental Health Safety ... Mr. Otu INYANG
85 Executive Director Intl Education ... Mr. Jay HORN
28 Director Multicultural Outreach ... Mr. Casey GONZALES
93 Director Multicultural Affairs ... Ms. Melanie JOHNSON
86 VP Government Relations ... Mr. Jeff JETER
43 Dir Legal Services/General Counsel ... Mr. Shelby BOSEMAN
96 Director of Purchasing ... Ms. Julia CORNWELL
29 Exec Dir for Alumni & Donor Rels ... Ms. Julie BARFIELD
04 Executive Assoc to President ... Ms. Elsa CORRAL

*University of Texas at Austin (C)

110 Inner Campus Drive, Austin TX 78705
County: Travis FICE Identification: 003658
Unit ID: 228778
Telephone: (512) 471-3434 Carnegie Class: DU-Highest
FAX Number: N/A Calendar System: Semester
URL: www.utexas.edu
Established: 1883 Annual Undergrad Tuition & Fees (In-State): $11,448
Enrollment: 50,476 Coed
Affiliation or Control: State IRS Status: 170(c)1
Highest Offering: Doctorate
Accreditation: SC, ART, AUD, CAATE, CEA, CIDA, CLPSY, COPSY, DANCE, DIETC, DIETD, IPSY, JOUR, LAW, LIB, LSAR, MED, MUS, NURSE, PCSAS, PHAR, PLNG, SCPSY, SP, SPAA, SW

02 President ... Dr. Jay C. HARTZELL
05 Int Exec Vice President & Provost ... Dr. Dan T. JAFFE
10 SVP & Chief Financial Officer ... Mr. Darrell BAZZELL
28 VP for Diversity & Cmty Engagement ... Dr. LaToya SMITH
11 Associate Vice President ... Dr. Marla MARTINEZ
46 Vice President for Research ... Dr. Alison T. PRESTON
63 Vice President for Medical Affairs ... Dr. S. Claiborne JOHNSTON
30 Vice Pres for Development ... Mr. Scott A. RABENOLD
32 VP Stdnt Affairs & Dean of Students ... Dr. Soncia REAGINS-LILLY
41 Vice President & Athletics Director ... Mr. Chris M. DEL CONTE
26 VP/Chief Marketing/Communications ... Ms. Emily REAGAN
43 Vice President Legal Affairs ... Mr. James E. DAVIS
21 Exec Dir of Finance and Admin ... Ms. Mary C. LINDHOLM
88 Deputy to the President ... Ms. Nancy BRAZZIL
04 Administrative Manager ... Ms. Christine SOBEY
88 Sr Vice Prov Resource Management ... Dr. Larry SINGELL
20 Sr Vice Prov for Faculty Affairs ... Dr. Tasha BERETVAS
85 Sr Vice Prov for Global Engagement ... Ms. Sonia FEIGENBAUM
84 Int Vice Prov for Enrollment Mgmt ... Ms. Carolyn K. CONNERAT
58 SVP for Acad Affs/Dean Grad School ... Dr. Mark SMITH
88 Chief of Staff to Exec VP/Prov ... Ms. Rosemaria MARTINELLI
16 VP Advocacy & Dispute Resolution ... Dr. Janet M. DUKERICH
25 Asst VP Res/Dir Sponsored Projects ... Ms. Renee K. GONZALES
08 Vice Provost/Director UT Libraries ... Dr. Lorraine J. HARICOMBE
20 Vice Provost Undergrad Acad Affs ... Dr. David E. PLATT
22 Vice Provost for Diversity ... Dr. Edmund T. GORDON
104 Dir of Intl Student & Scholar Svcs ... Ms. Margaret Y. LUEVANO
88 Assoc VP Strat Acad Initiatives ... Dr. Linda N. DICKENS
100 Director of Admin for President ... Mrs. Monica HORVAT
86 Deputy to Pres for Strategy & Polic ... Ms. Andrea SHERIDAN
114 Budget Office Director ... Mr. John MCGEADY
105 Web and Mobile Applications Manager ... Ms. Tracy H. BROWN
07 Asst Vice Prov for Enrollment Svcs ... Mr. Mark SIMPSON
18 Associate VP Utilities/Energy Mgmt ... Mr. Juan ONTIVEROS
15 Associate VP Human Resources ... Ms. Adrienne HOWARTH-MOORE
09 Exec Dir Inst Research & Reporting ... Dr. Shiva JAGANATHAN
37 Exec Dir Office of Financial Aid ... Ms. Diane C. TODD SPRAGUE
39 Director Housing & Food Service ... Mr. Rene RODRIGUEZ
100 Chief of Staff & Exec Sr Assoc AD ... Ms. Christine A. PLONSKY
19 Asst VP Campus Sec/Chief of Police ... Mr. David CARTER
48 Dean of School of Architecture ... Dr. Michelle ADDINGTON
50 Dean of School of Business ... Ms. Lillian MILLS
60 Dean of College of Communication ... Dr. Jay M. BERNHARDT
53 Dean of College of Education ... Dr. Charles MARTINEZ
54 Dean of School of Engineering ... Dr. Sharon L. WOOD
57 Dean of College of Fine Arts ... Dr. Douglas J. DEMPSTER
62 Dean of School of Information ... Dr. Eric T. MEYER
65 Dean of School of Geosciences ... Ms. Claudia I. MORA
61 Dean of School of Law ... Dr. Ward FARNSWORTH
49 Dean of College of Liberal Arts ... Dr. Ann STEVENS
81 Int Dean College of Natural Science . Dr. David A. VANDEN BOUT
66 Dean of School of Nursing ... Dr. Alexa M. STUIFBERGEN
67 Dean of College of Pharmacy ... Dr. Samuel POLOYAC
80 Int Dean School of Public Affairs ... Dr. David W. SPRINGER
70 Dean of School of Social Work ... Dr. Luis H. ZAYAS
97 Dean of School of Undergrad Studies ... Dr. Brent L. IVERSON
26 Director of Communications ... Mr. Joey WILLIAMS
88 Executive Director for Univ Unions ... Mr. Mulugeta FEREDE
27 Director/Editor-in-Chief ... Mr. Robert DEVENS

*The University of Texas at Dallas (D)

800 West Campbell Road, Richardson TX 75080
County: Collin FICE Identification: 009741
Unit ID: 228787
Telephone: (972) 883-2111 Carnegie Class: DU-Highest
FAX Number: (972) 883-2237 Calendar System: Semester
URL: www.utdallas.edu
Established: 1969 Annual Undergrad Tuition & Fees (In-State): $13,992
Enrollment: 28,669 Coed
Affiliation or Control: State IRS Status: 501(c)3
Highest Offering: Doctorate
Accreditation: SC, ACAE, AUD, IPSY, SP, SPAA

02 President ... Dr. Richard BENSON
100 Vice President and Chief of Staff ... Mr. Rafael O. MARTIN
05 VP Academic Affairs and Provost ... Dr. Inga MUSSELMAN
10 Vice President for Business Affairs ... Dr. Calvin D. JAMISON
32 Vice President Student Affairs ... Dr. Gene FITCH
46 VP for Research ... Dr. Joseph J. PANCRAZIO
30 Vice President for Development ... Dr. Kyle EDGINGTON
13 VP Info Technology and CIO ... Mr. Frank FEAGANS
28 Vice President of Diversity ... Dr. Yvette E. PEARSON
114 Asst VP and Chief Budget Officer ... Mr. Orkun TOROS
21 VP Finance & Controller ... Mr. Terry PANKRATZ
26 VP Public Affairs ... Ms. Amanda O. ROCKOW
45 Exec Director Strategic Planning ... Dr. Lawrence J. REDLINGER
35 Assoc VP/Dean of Students ... Dr. Amanda SMITH
58 Dean Graduate Studies ... Dr. Juan E. GONZALEZ
53 Dean Undergraduate Education ... Dr. Jessica C. MURPHY
79 Int Dean School Arts & Humanities ... Dr. Nils ROEMER
50 Dean School of Management ... Dr. Hasan PIRKUL
81 Dean Sch Natural Science/Math ... Dr. David HYNDMAN
82 Dean Sch Econ/Political Science ... Dr. Jennifer HOLMES
76 Dean Sch Behavioral/Brain Science ... Dr. Steven L. SMALL
97 Dean School General Studies ... Dr. George W. FAIR
54 Dean EJ Sch of Engr/Computer Sci ... Dr. Stephanie G. ADAMS
57 Int Dean Sch Arts/Tech/Emerg Media ... Dr. Nils ROEMER
92 Interim Dean Honors College ... Dr. Douglas C. DOW
08 Dean of Libraries ... Dr. Ellen SAFLEY
06 Registrar ... Ms. Jennifer MCDOWELL
12 Exec Director of Callier Center ... Dr. Angela SHOUP
18 Assoc VP Facilities Management ... Mr. Doug TOMLINSON
15 Assoc VP Human Resources ... Ms. Colleen DUTTON
96 Asst VP Operations (Purchasing) ... Dr. Brian BERNOUSSI
19 Chief of Police ... Mr. Larry ZACHARIAS
36 Director Career Services ... Ms. Nicolette JOHNSON
38 Assoc Dean Student Counseling ... Ms. Laura SMITH
116 Institutional Chief Audit Executive ... Ms. Toni STEPHENS
41 Director of Athletics ... Ms. Angela MARIN
78 Assoc Dir Co-operative Education ... Mr. Michael J. CHOATE
90 Assoc VP/Chief Tech Officer ... Mr. Brian DOURTY
29 Senior Director of Alumni Relations ... Ms. Jill ARREDONDO
04 Executive Associate to President ... Ms. Kimberly GOODFRIEND
105 Director Web Services ... Mr. Joe WILSON
106 Asst Provost Learning Tech ... Mr. Darren CRONE
39 Asst VP Residential Life ... Mr. Ryan WHITE
104 Director International Education ... Ms. Sara SPIEGLER
37 Director Student Financial Aid ... Ms. Sarah DORSEY
43 University Attorney ... Mr. Timothy SHAW
84 Interim Sr Director Enrollment ... Ms. Ingrid LONDON

*University of Texas at El Paso (E)

500 W University Avenue, El Paso TX 79968-8900
County: El Paso FICE Identification: 003661
Unit ID: 228796
Telephone: (915) 747-5000 Carnegie Class: DU-Highest
FAX Number: (915) 747-5111 Calendar System: Semester
URL: www.utep.edu
Established: 1914 Annual Undergrad Tuition & Fees (In-State): $9,450
Enrollment: 24,879 Coed
Affiliation or Control: State IRS Status: 501(c)3
Highest Offering: Doctorate
Accreditation: SC, CACREP, MLS, MUS, NURSE, OT, PH, PHAR, PTA, SP, SPAA, SW

02 President ... Dr. Heather WILSON
05 Provost/VP Academic Affairs ... Dr. John WIEBE
100 Vice President & Chief of Staff ... Ms. Andrea CORTINAS
10 VP Business Affairs ... Mr. Mark MCGURK
111 Vice President Inst Advancement ... Mr. Jake LOGAN
46 Vice President for Research ... Dr. Roberto OSEGUEDA
13 VP Information Resources ... Mr. Luis HERNANDEZ
32 Vice President Student Affairs ... Dr. Gary EDENS
58 Dean of Graduate School ... Dr. Stephen L. CRITES
50 Dean of Business Administration ... Dr. James E. PAYNE
53 Dean of Education ... Dr. Clifton TANABE
54 Dean of Engineering ... Dr. Kenith E. MEISSNER
49 Dean of Liberal Arts ... Dr. Anadeli BENCOMO

76 Dean of Health Sciences ... Dr. William ROBERTSON
67 Founding Dean School of Pharmacy ... Dr. Jose O. RIVERA
81 Dean of Science ... Dr. Robert KIRKEN
66 Dean of School of Nursing ... Dr. Leslie H. ROBBINS
106 Dean Extended Univ/Online Educ ... Ms. Beth L. BRUNK-CHAVEZ
18 Int Associate VP Facilities Mgmt ... Mr. Robert PARKER
08 Assoc Vice President Library ... Mr. Robert L. STAKES
26 Asst Vice Pres University Relations ... Mr. Beto LOPEZ
15 Assoc VP Human Resources ... Ms. Sandy VASQUEZ
29 Asst VP Alumni Relations ... Ms. Maribel VILLALVA
84 Asst VP Enrollment Services ... Dr. Amanda VASQUEZ
19 Chief Campus Police ... Mr. Clifton WALSH
37 Asst VP for Financial Services ... Dr. Heidi GRANGER
23 Admin Dir of Student Health Center ... Ms. Leticia PAEZ
36 Director of Career Services ... Ms. Betsy CASTRO-DUARTE
35 Associate VP/Dean of Students ... Dr. Catherine M. MCCORRY-ANDALIS
45 Assoc VP for Planning ... Dr. Roy MATHEW
39 Executive Dir of Housing Services ... Mr. Raymond GORDON
40 Manager of University Bookstore ... Mr. Nick GONZALES
41 Athletics Director ... Mr. Jim SENTER
38 Director Counseling Services ... Ms. Brian SNEED
96 Assoc VP Purchasing/General Svcs ... Dr. Diane N. DEHOYOS
27 Director Communications ... Ms. Jenn CRAWFORD
04 Exec Assistant to the President ... Ms. Patti MARTINEZ
43 Chief Legal Officer ... Ms. Priscilla CASTILLO
116 Chief Audit Executive ... Ms. Lori N. WERTZ
88 Dir/Chief Compliance & Ethics Ofcr ... Ms. Mary SOLIS
88 Title IX Coordinator ... Mr. Gabriel RAMIREZ
122 Coord Fraternity/Sorority Life ... Mr. Anthony VINCENT

*The University of Texas Rio Grande Valley (A)

1201 W University Drive, Edinburg TX 78539-2999
County: Hidalgo FICE Identification: 003599
Unit ID: 227368
Telephone: (888) 882-8201 Carnegie Class: DU-Higher
FAX Number: (956) 665-2150 Calendar System: Semester
URL: www.utrgv.edu
Established: 2015 Annual Undergrad Tuition & Fees (In-State): $8,917
Enrollment: 32,441 Coed
Affiliation or Control: State IRS Status: 501(c)3
Highest Offering: Doctorate
Accreditation: SC, ARCPA, CACREP, CAEPN, @DIET, #MED, MLS, MUS, NURSE, OT, SP, SW, THEA

02 President ... Dr. Guy BAILEY
03 Deputy President ... Dr. Janna ARNEY
05 Interim Provost ... Dr. Janna ARNEY
10 EVP for Finance and Administration ... Mr. Rick ANDERSON
46 EVP Research/Graduate Studies ... Dr. Parwinder GREWAL
111 EVP for Institutional Advancement ... Dr. Kelly NASSOUR
86 VP for Government/Cmty Relations ... Ms. Veronica GONZALES
32 Assoc Provost for Student Success ... Dr. Jonikka CHARLTON
84 Sr VP for Strategic Enrollment ... Dr. Maggie HINOJOSA
20 AVP Faculty Affairs ... Dr. Shawn SALADIN
21 Sr Assoc VP Finance & Planning ... Mr. Michael MUELLER
11 VP for Admin Support Services ... Mr. Doug ARNEY
18 Assoc VP for Facilities Planning ... Ms. Marta SALINAS-HOVAR
110 VP for Institutional Advancement ... Ms. Tracie A. ASHLOCK
88 Assoc VP for Governmental Relations ... Mr. Richard P. SANCHEZ
26 Assoc VP for University Marketing ... Mr. Patrick GONZALES
109 Assoc VP for Campus Auxiliary Svcs ... Ms. Letty BENAVIDES
31 Assoc VP for Community Engagement ... Vacant
09 AVP Strategic Analysis and Inst Res ... Ms. Susan BROWN
108 AVP Inst Accred/Pgm Dev & Analysis ... Dr. Christine SHUPALA
88 Assoc VP Acad Inst Excellence ... Dr. Laura SAENZ
53 Dean College of Educ & P-16 ... Dr. Alma RODRIGUEZ
50 Dean Business Entrepreneurship ... Dr. Lance NAIL
81 Dean College of Sciences ... Dr. Vivian INCERA
54 Dean College Engr/Comp Sci ... Dr. Ala QUBBAJ
76 Dean College of Health Professions ... Dr. Michael LEHKER
49 Dean College of Fine Arts ... Dr. Steven BLOCK
83 Dean College of Liberal Arts ... Dr. Walter DIAZ
63 Dean School of Medicine ... Dr. Michael B. HOCKER
66 Dean School of Nursing ... Dr. Sharon RADZYMINSKI
43 Chief Legal Officer ... Ms. Karen ADAMS
15 Chief Human Resources Officer ... Mr. Mike JAMES
06 University Registrar ... Ms. Sofia MONTES
22 Chief Compliance Officer ... Ms. Samantha ALLEN
13 Chief Information Officer ... Dr. Jeffrey GRAHAM
119 Chief Info Security Officer ... Dr. Kevin CROUSE
29 Exec Dir of Alumni Relations ... Mrs. Marisa CAMPIRANO
41 VP and Director of Athletics ... Mr. Chasse CONQUE
114 Dir for Budget & Ops RGSNPD ... Ms. Rosalinda SALAZAR
04 Assistant to the President ... Ms. Maria CONDE
08 Dean of Libraries ... Mr. Paul SHARPE
37 Director of Financial Aid ... Mr. Elias OZUNA
92 Dean Honors College ... Dr. Mark ANDERSEN
88 Interim Exec Dir B3 Institute ... Dr. Dania LOPEZ GARCIA
88 Chief Operating Officer SOM HA ... Ms. Sofia HERNANDEZ
116 Chief Audit Executive ... Mr. Eloy R. ALANIZ, JR.
19 Chief Police ... Mr. Adan CRUZ
28 Chief Equity & Diversity Officer ... Ms. Florence NOCAR
88 Dir Victim Advocacy & Violence ... Dr. Cynthia JONES
07 Dir of Undergraduate Admissions ... Ms. Marybel VILLASENOR
104 Director of International Programs ... Mr. Alan EARHART
30 Director of Development ... Mr. John GARZA
39 Dir Resident Life/Student Housing ... Mr. Sergio MARTINEZ
44 Director of Planned Giving ... Ms. Serena PUTEGNAT
96 Chief Procurement Officer ... Mr. Alex VALDEZ
122 Assc Dean Stdnt Involve-Frat/Sor ... Ms. Delma OLIVAREZ

*The University of Texas at San Antonio (B)

One UTSA Circle, San Antonio TX 78249-0169
County: Bexar FICE Identification: 010115
Unit ID: 229027
Telephone: (210) 458-4011 Carnegie Class: DU-Highest
FAX Number: (210) 458-4187 Calendar System: Semester
URL: www.utsa.edu
Established: 1969 Annual Undergrad Tuition & Fees (In-State): $8,566
Enrollment: 34,742 Coed
Affiliation or Control: State IRS Status: 501(c)3
Highest Offering: Doctorate
Accreditation: SC, ART, CACREP, CEA, CIDA, CONST, DIETC, MUS, NAEYC, NASP, SPAA, SW

02 President ... Dr. Taylor EIGHMY
05 Provost/Vice Pres Academic Affs ... Dr. Kimberly ANDREWS ESPY
10 SVP Business Affairs/CFO ... Ms. Veronica SALAZAR MENDEZ
46 Interim VP for Research/Econ Dev ... Ms. Jaclyn SHAW
32 SVP Student Affs/Dean of Students ... Ms. LT ROBINSON
26 VP for University Relations ... Ms. Teresa NINO
20 AVP/AV Provost Inst Initiatives ... Dr. Howard GRIMES
13 VP Information Mgmt/Technology ... Ms. Kendra KETCHUM
30 Vice Pres Development/Alumni Rels ... Mr. Karl MILLER-LUGO
28 Vice President Inclusive Excellence ... Dr. Myron ANDERSON
09 AVP Acad Compl/Inst Effectiveness ... Mr. Steve L. WILKERSON
100 Chief of Staff ... Mr. Carlos MARTINEZ
20 Sr Vice Prov/Dean Univ College ... Dr. Heather J. SHIPLEY
21 Associate VP Financial Affairs ... Ms. Sheri HARDISON
27 AVP Comm & Special Projects Officer ... Ms. Anne C. PETERS
08 Dean of Libraries ... Dr. Dean D. HENDRIX
92 Dean of Honors College ... Dr. Sean KELLY
58 Vice Prov/Dean Graduate School ... Dr. Ambika MATHUR
50 Dean College of Business ... Dr. Jonathon HALBESLEBEN
57 Dean College of Liberal & Fine Arts ... Dr. Glenn MARTINEZ
54 Dean College of Engineering ... Dr. Joann BROWNING
83 Dean College of Sciences ... Dr. David SILVA
48 Dean School of Architecture ... Prof. John MURPHY
53 Dean Col Educ/Human Development ... Dr. Mario TORRES
80 Dean College of Public Policy ... Dr. Lynne SITTIG COSSMAN
19 Chief of Police ... Ms. Stephanie SCHOENBORN
41 VP ICA and Athletics Director ... Dr. Lisa D. CAMPOS
43 Chief Legal Officer ... Mr. Jay ROSSELLO
117 Dir Inst Compliance & Risk Services ... Mr. James R. WEAVER
116 Chief Audit Executive ... Paul A. TYLER
27 AVP Communications/Marketing ... Mr. Joe IZBRAND
86 AVP Government Relations & Policy ... Mr. Albert A. CARRISALEZ
04 Assistant Office of President ... Ms. Chelsea TROTTER
07 Director of Admissions ... Ms. Beverly WOODSON DAY
88 Asst VP Strategic Initiatives ... Ms. Elvira E. LEAL
105 Associate Director of Web/Portal ... Mr. Shashi B. PINHEIRO
106 Director of Online Learning ... Ms. Marcela V. RAMIREZ
108 Assistant Vice Provost Assessment ... Dr. Kasey NEECE-FIELDER
18 Int Senior AVP for Business Affairs ... Mr. David J. RIKER
25 Dir Grants/Contracts/Financial Svcs ... Mr. Daniel ANZAK
28 Associate Provost ... Col. Lisa C. FIRMIN, RET.
37 Director of Student Financial Aid ... Ms. Diana S. MARTINEZ
38 Director Counseling Services ... Dr. Melissa HERNANDEZ
39 Director Student Housing/Residence ... Mr. Daniel L. GOCKLEY
15 Asst VP Operations/Talent Mgmt ... Ms. Rebecca ANDERSON
90 Director of Academic Computing ... Mr. John P. SOUDAH
96 Director Business Contracts ... Mr. Robert L. DICKENS
122 Mgr Stdnt Activities-Greek Life ... Ms. Rae ONABANJO

*University of Texas at Tyler (C)

3900 University Boulevard, Tyler TX 75799-6699
County: Smith FICE Identification: 011163
Unit ID: 228802
Telephone: (903) 566-7000 Carnegie Class: DU-Higher
FAX Number: (903) 566-7068 Calendar System: Semester
URL: www.uttyler.edu
Established: 1971 Annual Undergrad Tuition & Fees (In-State): $9,146
Enrollment: 9,781 Coed
Affiliation or Control: State IRS Status: 501(c)3
Highest Offering: Doctorate
Accreditation: SC, CACREP, IPSY, #MED, MUS, NAIT, NURSE, OT, PHAR, @SW

02 President ... Dr. Kirk A. CALHOUN
03 Executive Vice President ... Mr. Dwain MORRIS
05 Provost/VP Academic Affairs ... Dr. Amir MIRMIRAN
111 Vice President Univ Advancement ... Dr. Archie TUCKER
32 Vice Pres for Student Success ... Ms. Ona TOLLIVER
13 Vice President ... Dr. Sherri WHATLEY
20 Vice Provost AA/Grad Studies ... Dr. Steven IDELL
46 Assoc Provost Research/Scholarship ... Dr. Kouider MOKHTARI
10 SVP Finance/CFO ... Ms. Kris KAVASCH
15 Director of Human Resources ... Ms. Gracy BUENTELLO
86 AVP Gov & Community Relations ... Mr. Matt COPE
84 Assoc VP for Enrollment Management ... Mr. David BARRON
108 Asst Vice Pres for Assessment/IE ... Dr. Lou Ann BERMAN
49 Dean College of Arts & Sciences ... Dr. Neil GRAY
50 Dean College Business & Technology ... Dr. Krist SWIMBERGHE
53 Dean College Educ & Psych ... Dr. Wesley HICKEY
54 Dean College of Engineering ... Dr. Javier KYPUROS
66 Dean College Nursing & Health Sci ... Dr. Barbara HAAS
67 Dean College of Pharmacy ... Vacant
08 Exec Director of the Library ... Ms. Rebecca MCKAY JOHNSON
21 Director of Financial Services ... Ms. Cindy TROYER
18 VP for Operations/Strategic Init ... Dr. Andrew KROUSE
29 Exec Dir Career Success & Alumni ... Dr. Rosemary COOPER
26 Exec Dir Marketing & Communication ... Ms. Beverley GOLDEN
121 Associate Dean of Student Success ... Ms. Kim HARVEY-LIVINGSTON
39 Assoc Dean of Students ... Dr. Jennifer WATERS
06 Registrar ... Dr. Troy WHITE
09 Director Institutional Analysis ... Ms. Cindy STRAWN
19 Chief University Police ... Mr. Mike W. MEDDERS
04 Sr Executive Asst to President ... Ms. Mitzi M. HARRIS
07 Asst Director of Admissions ... Ms. Whitney RAINS
37 Director of Student Financial Aid ... Vacant
43 Chief Legal Officer ... Mr. Carl BARANOWSKI
106 Assoc Provost UG Adm & On-line Educ ... Dr. Colleen SWAIN
41 Athletic Director ... Dr. Howard PATTERSON
44 Director of Annual Giving ... Mr. Daniel ONDERKO

*The University of Texas Health Science Center at Houston (UTHealth Houston) (D)

PO Box 20036, Houston TX 77225-0036
County: Harris FICE Identification: 004951
Unit ID: 229300
Telephone: (713) 500-4472 Carnegie Class: Spec-4-yr-Eng
FAX Number: (713) 500-3026 Calendar System: Semester
URL: www.uth.edu
Established: 1972 Annual Undergrad Tuition & Fees (In-State): N/A
Enrollment: 5,608 Coed
Affiliation or Control: State IRS Status: 501(c)3
Highest Offering: Doctorate
Accreditation: SC, ANEST, CAHIIM, CAMPEP, DENT, DH, DIETI, HSA, IPSY, MED, NURSE, PERF, PH

02 President ... Dr. Giuseppe N. COLASURDO
11 Sr Exec VP & COO ... Mr. Kevin DILLON
05 Exec VP & Chief Academic Officer ... Dr. Kevin A. MORANO
32 EVP Student Affairs & Diversity ... Dr. Latanya J. LOVE
03 Senior VP & COO UT Physicians ... Mr. Andrew CASAS
63 Dean McGovern Medical School ... Dr. Richard J. ANDRASSY
69 Dean School of Public Health ... Dr. Eric BOERWINKLE
52 Dean School of Dentistry ... Dr. John A. VALENZA
58 Dean Grad Sch Biomedical Sciences ... Dr. Sharon DENT
66 Dean Cizik School of Nursing ... Dr. Diane M. SANTA MARIA
88 Dean Sch of Biomed Informatics ... Dr. Jiajie W. ZHANG
117 VP Enterprise Risk Mgmt/Compliance ... Ms. Karen K. SPILLAR
10 Sr VP Finance & Business Svcs & CFO ... Mr. Michael TRAMONTE
46 Vice Dn Rsrch/Dir Molecular Med ... Dr. John HANCOCK
30 SVP Development/Public Affairs ... Mr. Kevin J. FOYLE
15 VP/Chief Human Resources Officer ... Mr. Eric FERNETTE
43 Senior VP/Chief Legal Officer ... Mr. Melissa K. PIFKO
86 Senior VP Govt Relations ... Mr. Scott FORBES
88 VP Research & Technology ... Dr. Bruce D. BUTLER
109 VP Auxiliary Enterprises ... Mr. Charles A. FIGARI
13 VP/Chief Information Officer ... Mr. Amar YOUSIF
18 VP Facilities Planning & Engr ... Mr. Wes STEWART
90 Asst VP Academic Technology ... Dr. William A. WEEMS
116 VP & Chief Audit Officer ... Mr. Daniel SHERMAN
09 Assoc VP Institutional Research ... Ms. Deanne HERNANDEZ
06 Registrar ... Mr. Robert JENKINS
19 Assoc VP/Chief of Police ... Mr. William ADCOX
40 Executive Director HCPC/Dunn ... Dr. Jair C. SOARES
41 Director Recreation/Intramural Pgms ... Ms. Pauline M. HABETZ
85 Director International Affairs ... Ms. Rose Mary VALENCIA
39 Director University Housing ... Ms. Peree E. GRIFFIN
26 Assistant VP Public Affairs ... Ms. Meredith RAINE
37 Director Student Financial Svcs ... Ms. Heather BECKLES-BRIGHT
25 Assoc VP Sponsored Projects Admin ... Ms. Kathleen KREIDLER
91 Assoc VP Admin/Academic Tech ... Ms. Connie WOOLDRIDGE
88 Director Educational Tech Nursing ... Ms. Linda L. CRAYS
20 Senior VP/Academic & Research ... Mr. Eric J. SOLBERG
14 Assoc VP/IT Infrastructure ... Mr. Derek D. DRAWHORN
119 Assoc VP/IT Security ... Ms. Beverly Y. MOORE
88 Assoc VP/IT User Experience ... Bassel CHOUCAIR
88 Assoc VP Health Care IT ... Dr. James J. GRIFFITHS
100 Chief of Staff Office of the Pres ... Ms. Rose HOCHNER
105 Director Univ Web Svcs ... Mr. Frederick M. GREGORY
22 AVP Diversity & Equal Opportunity ... Ms. Deana K. MOYLAN

*University of Texas Health Science Center at San Antonio (E)

7703 Floyd Curl Drive, San Antonio TX 78229-3900
County: Bexar FICE Identification: 003659
Unit ID: 228644
Telephone: (210) 567-7000 Carnegie Class: Spec-4-yr-Eng
FAX Number: N/A Calendar System: Other
URL: www.uthscsa.edu
Established: 1959 Annual Undergrad Tuition & Fees (In-State): N/A
Enrollment: 3,478 Coed
Affiliation or Control: State IRS Status: 501(c)3
Highest Offering: Doctorate
Accreditation: SC, ARCPA, CAMPEP, COARC, DENT, DH, EMT, HT, IPSY, MED, MLS, NURSE, OT, PTA, RADDOS, SP

02 President ... Dr. William L. HENRICH
03 Sr Exec Vice President & COO ... Mrs. Andrea MARKS
11 EVP Facility Planning/Operations ... Mr. James D. KAZEN
10 Vice President & CFO ... Mrs. Ginny GOMEZ-LEON
05 VP Academic/Faculty/Student Affairs ... Dr. Jacqueline L. MOK
13 Vice Pres & Chief Information Ofcr ... Mr. Yeman COLLIER

46 Vice President for Research ....Dr. Andrea GIUFFRIDA
86 VP for Governmental Relations ....Mr. Gilbert LOREDO
111 VP Inst Advancement/Chief Dev Ofcr ....Ms. Anamaria REPETTI
26 VP & Chief Marketing/Comm Officer ....Ms. Heather ADKINS
15 Vice Pres of Human Resources ....Mrs. Amy TAWNEY
100 VP & Chief of Staff ....Ms. Mary G. DELAY
21 Asst Vice Pres for Business Affairs ....Mr. Gerard E. LONG
09 Asst VP Research ....Dr. Kimberly Kay SUMMERS
43 Chief Legal Officer ....Mr. Jack C. PARK
63 Dean School of Medicine ....Dr. Robert HROMAS
52 Dean School of Dentistry ....Dr. Peter M. LOOMER
58 Dean Graduate Biomed Science ....Dr. David WEISS
76 Dean School Health Professions ....Dr. David C. SHELLEDY
66 Dean School of Nursing ....Dr. Sonya HARDIN
32 Director for Student Life ....Ms. Le Keisha JOHNSON
06 Registrar ....Dr. Blanca GUERRA
08 Senior Director of Libraries ....Mr. Owen H. ELLARD
19 Chief of Police ....Mr. Michael PARKS
88 Exec Dir Acad/Fac/Stdnt Ombudspers ....Dr. Bonnie L. BLANKMEYER
37 Director Financial Aid ....Ms. Ellen NYSTROM
38 Director of Student Counseling ....Dr. Mia VEVE
96 Sr Dir Supply Chain Management ....Mr. Eric R. WALLS
07 Dir Admissions/Spec Pgm/Sch Nursing ....Mr. Henry CANTU
102 Dir Corporate/Foundation Relations ....Ms. Stephenie MCCLAIN
30 Senior Director Development ....Mr. Wes LIVESAY

*The University of Texas MD Anderson Cancer Center (A)

1515 Holcombe Boulevard, Houston TX 77030-4000
County: Harris FICE Identification: 025554
Unit ID: 416801
Telephone: (713) 792-6161 Carnegie Class: Spec-4-yr-Other Health
FAX Number: N/A Calendar System: Semester
URL: www.mdanderson.org
Established: 1941 Annual Undergrad Tuition & Fees (In-District): N/A
Enrollment: 358 Coed
Affiliation or Control: State/Local IRS Status: 501(c)3
Highest Offering: Doctorate
Accreditation: SC, CAMPEP, CGTECH, CYTO, DENT, DMOLS, HT, MLS, PAST, RAD, RADDOS, RADMAG, RTT

02 President ....Dr. Peter PISTERS
05 Chief Academic Officer ....Dr. Carin HAGBERG
10 Sr Vice President/CFO ....Mr. Omer SULTAN
17 Chief Medical Executive ....Dr. Welela TEREFFE

*The University of Texas Medical Branch (B)

301 University Boulevard, Galveston TX 77555-0129
County: Galveston FICE Identification: 004952
Unit ID: 228653
Telephone: (409) 772-1011 Carnegie Class: Spec-4-yr-Eng
FAX Number: N/A Calendar System: Semester
URL: www.utmb.edu
Established: 1891 Annual Undergrad Tuition & Fees (In-State): N/A
Enrollment: 3,458 Coed
Affiliation or Control: State IRS Status: 170(c)1
Highest Offering: Doctorate
Accreditation: SC, ARCPA, BBT, COARC, DENT, DIETI, MED, MLS, NURSE, OT, PA, PH, PTA

02 President ....Dr. Ben G. RAIMER
05 EVP/Provost/Dean Sch of Med ....Dr. Charles P. MOUTON
10 Int Chief Business/Finance Ofcr ....Mr. C. Aaron LEMAY
88 SVP & Chief Physician Executive ....Dr. Vicente RESTO
23 Chief Medical Officer ....Dr. Gulshan SHARMA
66 Sr VP & Dean of Nursing ....Dr. Deborah J. JONES
76 SVP & Dean Sch Health Professions ....Dr. David A. BROWN
58 Dean Grad School Biomed Sci ....Dr. Melinda MOORE
15 VP and Chief HR Officer ....Dr. Vivian D. KARDOW
13 VP and Chief Information Officer ....Mr. George GADDIE
21 VP Finance Academic Enterprise ....Mr. Gabe HERNANDEZ
18 VP Business Ops & Facilities ....Mr. Steven B. LEBLANC
11 VP/Chief Admin Officer AE ....Mr. Loren SKINNER
43 Sr VP General Counsel ....Ms. Carolee KING
32 Assoc Dean Student Affairs/Adm SON ....Dr. Diana PRESSLEY
25 Assoc VP Research Admin ....Ms. Claudia J. DELGADO
08 Assoc VP Library Services ....Ms. Pat CIEJKA
09 Assoc VP Inst Effectiveness ....Dr. John C. MCKEE
21 AVP Financial Capital Planning ....Mr. Matthew FURLONG
114 Assoc VP Finance CMC ....Ms. Emily MIELSCH
88 VP Finance Institution Support ....Ms. Lynn MCGINLEY
116 VP Audit Services ....Ms. Foy DESOLYN
30 VP Chief Development Officer ....Ms. Betsy B. CLARDY
88 VP & Chief Compliance Officer ....Mr. Tobin R. BOENIG
32 AVP Univ Student Svcs & Registrar ....Mr. William S. BOEH
19 VP & Chief of University Police ....Mr. Kenith ADCOX
96 VP Supply Chain Management ....Mr. Christopher TOOMES
38 Director Student Wellness Services ....Dr. Olawunmi A. AKINPELU
100 Chief of Staff ....Ms. Beth STUM
16 Assoc VP HR Ops & Employee Health ....Ms. Philesha EVANS
105 Director Digital Communications ....Mr. Eduardo VALDES
37 Director Student Financial Service ....Ms. Ann HALE
41 Field House Facilities Ops Manager ....Ms. Leslie BLACKETER
53 VP Education IE & HEC ....Dr. Janet H. SOUTHERLAND
28 Diversity & Inclusion Consultant ....Vacant
44 Sr Dir Alumni Rels & Annual Giving ....Ms. Rena LIDSTONE
86 VP Legislative Affairs ....Ms. Lauren SHEER

35 Director of Student Life ....Mr. Michael CROMIE
03 EVP Bus Dev & Chief Strategy Ofcr ....Ms. Rebecca KORENEK
17 EVP & CEO Health System ....Dr. Tim HARLIN
04 Admin Assistant to the President ....Ms. Bobbie GUYTON
07 Director of Admissions & Recruitmnt ....Dr. Pierre BANKS
26 Assoc VP Public Affairs ....Ms. Mary G. HAVARD
88 CFO HS & Chief Analytics Officer ....Mr. Dustin THOMAS
29 Director Alumni & Parent Relations ....Ms. Julie CANTINI

*University of Texas Permian Basin (C)

4901 E University Boulevard, Odessa TX 79762-0001
County: Ector FICE Identification: 009930
Unit ID: 229018
Telephone: (432) 552-2020 Carnegie Class: Masters/L
FAX Number: (432) 552-2374 Calendar System: Semester
URL: www.utpb.edu
Established: 1969 Annual Undergrad Tuition & Fees (In-State): $4,837
Enrollment: 5,530 Coed
Affiliation or Control: State IRS Status: 501(c)3
Highest Offering: Master's
Accreditation: SC, ART, CAEP, MUS, NURSE, SW

02 President ....Dr. Sandra WOODLEY
05 Provost ....Dr. Susan GANTER
32 VP Student Affairs & Leadership ....Dr. Rebecca SPURLOCK
111 Vice President of Advancement ....Mr. Wendell SNODGRASS
13 VP Information Technology/Analytics ....Mr. Bradley SHOOK
49 Interim Dean Col of Arts & Sci ....Dr. Raj DAKSHINAMURTHY
50 Dean School of Business ....Dr. Steven BEACH
53 Dean College of Education ....Dr. Larry DANIEL
66 Dean College of Nursing ....Dr. Donna BEUK
54 Dean College of Engineering ....Dr. George NNANNA
07 Director Admissions ....Ms. Lorinda TERCERO
06 Registrar ....Mr. Joe SANDERS
18 Chief Facilities/Physical Plant ....Mr. David WAYLAND
36 Director Career Services ....Ms. Megan BAEZA
29 Director of Special Projects JBS ....Ms. Kate WILLIAMSON
39 Director Student Housing ....Ms. Chermae PEEL
10 VP Business Affairs/CFO ....Mr. Cesar VALENZUELA
15 Director of Human Resources ....Mr. Ron APPLING
96 Director of Purchasing ....Ms. Elsa MONTALVO
35 Dean of Students ....Mr. Corey BENSON
04 Executive Assistant to President ....Ms. Carol GONZALEZ
41 Athletic Director ....Mr. Todd DOOLEY
08 Chief Library Officer ....Dr. Sophia KAANE
37 Director Student Financial Aid ....Mr. Scott LAPINSKI
84 Director Enrollment Management ....Ms. PJ WOOLSTON
100 Chief of Staff/Exec Dir of Comm ....Ms. Tatum HUBBARD
21 Assoc Financial/Business Officer ....Ms. Felecia BURNS
114 Chief Budget Administrator ....Ms. Griselda MEDINA
102 Director Foundation/Corporate Rels ....Ms. Marisol CHRIESMAN
104 Director Study Abroad ....Vacant
106 Director of Online Learning ....Ms. Katrieva JONES-MONROE
19 Chief of Police ....Mr. Tom HAIN
44 Annual Giving Coordinator ....Ms. Kimberly LUNA
86 Director Government Relations ....Ms. Paige COOPER
09 Director of Institutional Research ....Mr. John THOMAS
28 Director of Diversity ....Dr. LaTanya LOWERY
30 Director of Development ....Mr. Wendell SNODGRASS
121 Director Student Advising ....Ms. Veronica VIESCA

*University of Texas Southwestern Medical Center (D)

5323 Harry Hines Boulevard, Dallas TX 75390-9002
County: Dallas FICE Identification: 010019
Unit ID: 228635
Telephone: (214) 648-3111 Carnegie Class: Spec-4-yr-Eng
FAX Number: N/A Calendar System: Semester
URL: www.utsouthwestern.edu
Established: 1943 Annual Undergrad Tuition & Fees (In-State): N/A
Enrollment: 2,299 Coed
Affiliation or Control: State IRS Status: 501(c)3
Highest Offering: Doctorate
Accreditation: SC, ARCPA, CAMPEP, CLPSY, DIETC, IPSY, MED, OPE, PAST, PTA

02 President ....Dr. Daniel K. PODOLSKY
100 Chief of Staff ....Ms. Courtney ROTTMAN
05 EVP Acad Affs/Provost/Dean Med Sch ....Dr. W. P. Andrew LEE
20 Vice Provost/Sr Assoc Dean Educ ....Dr. Charles M. GINSBURG
20 Vice Provost/Sr Assoc Dean Faculty ....Dr. Dwain L. THIELE
46 Vice Provost/Dean of Basic Research ....Dr. Joan CONAWAY
17 Exec VP Health System Affairs ....Dr. John WARNER
10 Exec Vice Pres Business Affairs ....Ms. Holly CRAWFORD
111 Exec VP Institutional Advancement ....Dr. Marc A. NIVET
23 Vice President Clinical Operations ....Dr. John D. RUTHERFORD
88 VP & Chief Quality Officer ....Dr. William DANIEL
17 VP Clin Pgm & Facility Development ....Ms. Becky MCCULLEY
21 Vice President Financial Affairs ....Mr. Michael SERBER
86 Vice Pres Govt Affairs & Policy ....Ms. Angelica MARIN-HILL
15 Vice President Human Resources ....Vacant
88 VP Institutional Compliance ....Ms. Natalie A. RAMELLO
116 Vice President Internal Audit ....Ms. Valla F. WILSON
43 Vice President Legal Affairs ....Ms. Erin SINE
30 Vice President Development ....Ms. Amanda BILLINGS
102 Vice Pres Community and Corp Rels ....Mr. Ruben E. ESQUIVEL
13 Vice Pres Information Resources ....Mr. Russell POOLE
18 Vice President Facilities Mgmt ....Mr. Juan M. GUERRA, JR.
20 Vice Pres Academic Affairs/COO ....Mr. Cameron SLOCUM
88 Vice Pres/COO Medical Group ....Dr. Christopher MADDEN

58 Dean Grad School Biomedical Science ....Dr. Andrew ZINN
76 Dean School of Health Professions ....Dr. Jon WILLIAMSON
69 Interim Dean School Public Health ....Dr. Celette SKINNER
28 Assoc Dean Faculty Development ....Dr. Byron L. CRYER
28 Assoc Dean Faculty Diversity ....Dr. Quinn CAPERS, IV
88 Assoc Dean Global Health ....Dr. Fiemu E. NWARIAKU
63 Assoc Dean Grad Medical Education ....Dr. Larissa VELEZ
63 Assoc Dean Undergrad Medical Educ ....Dr. Robert REGE
32 Assoc Dean Student Affairs ....Dr. Angela MIHALIC
32 Assoc Dean Student Affairs ....Dr. Blake BARKER
93 Assoc Dean Student Diversity & Incl ....Dr. Shawna NESBITT
06 Registrar ....Mr. Adam ABERCROMBIE
07 Dir of Admissions & Recruitment ....Ms. Alanna EDWARDS
37 Director Student Financial Aid ....Ms. Melet LEAFGREEN
46 Vice Provost/Dean of Clin Research ....Dr. Eric D. PETERSON

Veritas College International Graduate School (E)

708 W. Summit Avenue, San Antonio TX 78212
County: Bexar Identification: 667395
Telephone: (210) 446-6719 Carnegie Class: Not Classified
FAX Number: N/A Calendar System: Semester
URL: www.veritascollege.org
Established: 2001 Annual Undergrad Tuition & Fees: N/A
Enrollment: N/A Coed
Affiliation or Control: Independent Non-Profit IRS Status: 501(c)3
Highest Offering: Doctorate
Accreditation: @BI

01 President ....RevDr. Bennie WOLVAARDT
05 Academic Dean ....Dr. Daniel SCOTT

Vernon College (F)

4400 College Drive, Vernon TX 76384-4092
County: Wilbarger FICE Identification: 010060
Unit ID: 229504
Telephone: (940) 552-6291 Carnegie Class: Assoc/MT-VT-High Trad
FAX Number: (940) 553-3902 Calendar System: Semester
URL: www.vernoncollege.edu
Established: 1970 Annual Undergrad Tuition & Fees (In-District): $4,520
Enrollment: 2,773 Coed
Affiliation or Control: State/Local IRS Status: 501(c)3
Highest Offering: Associate Degree
Accreditation: SC, EMT, SURGT

01 President ....Dr. Dusty R. JOHNSTON
04 Admin Secretary to the President ....Ms. Mary KING
05 Vice Pres of Instructional Services ....Dr. Elizabeth CRANDALL
10 Vice Pres Administrative Services ....Mrs. Mindi FLYNN
32 Vice President of Student Services ....Vacant
103 Dean of Instructional Services ....Ms. Shana DRURY
111 Dir Inst Advance/VC Foundation ....Ms. Michelle ALEXANDER
88 Director of Quality Enhancement ....Dr. Donnie KIRK
09 Dir of Institutional Effectiveness ....Mrs. Betsy HARKEY
37 Director Financial Aid ....Mrs. Melissa J. ELLIOTT
08 Director of Library Services ....Ms. Marion GRONA
18 Director Physical Plant ....Mr. Lyle BONNER
15 Director of Human Resources ....Mrs. Jackie POLK
39 Director of Housing ....Mr. Jesse DOMINQUEZ
35 Dean of Student Services ....Mrs. Kristin HARRIS
84 Dir of Enrollment Mgmt & Registrar ....Mrs. Amanda RAINES
66 Dir Associate Degree in Nursing ....Dr. Mary RIVARD
19 Director of Campus Police ....Mr. Kevin HOLLAND

Vet Tech Institute of Houston (G)

4669 Southwest Freeway, Suite 100, Houston TX 77027
County: Harris FICE Identification: 021448
Unit ID: 223472
Telephone: (713) 629-8940 Carnegie Class: Spec 2-yr-Health
FAX Number: (713) 629-0059 Calendar System: Semester
URL: www.vettechinstitute.edu/houston
Established: 2007 Annual Undergrad Tuition & Fees: $15,020
Enrollment: 202 Coed
Affiliation or Control: Proprietary IRS Status: Proprietary
Highest Offering: Associate Degree
Accreditation: ACCSC

01 Director/Chief Academic Officer ....Mr. Elbert HAMILTON, JR.

Victoria College (H)

2200 E Red River, Victoria TX 77901-4494
County: Victoria FICE Identification: 003662
Unit ID: 229540
Telephone: (361) 573-3291 Carnegie Class: Assoc/MT-VT-High Trad
FAX Number: (361) 572-3850 Calendar System: Semester
URL: www.victoriacollege.edu
Established: 1925 Annual Undergrad Tuition & Fees (In-District): $3,744
Enrollment: 3,274 Coed
Affiliation or Control: Local IRS Status: 501(c)3
Highest Offering: Associate Degree
Accreditation: SC, ADNUR, COARC, EMT, PTAA

01 President ....Dr. Jennifer KENT
05 Exec Vice Pres/Chief Academic Ofcr ....Ms. Cindy BUCHHOLZ
10 Vice Pres Administrative Svcs ....Mr. Keith BLUNDELL
32 Dean of Student Services ....Dr. Edrel STONEHAM
111 VP College Advance/External Affairs ....Vacant

09	Dir Inst Effect/Research/Assess	Mr. Matt WILEY
07	Registrar/Dir of Admissions	Ms. Madelyne TOLLIVER
18	Director Physical Plant	Mr. Marty DECKARD
37	Director Financial Aid	Ms. Kim OBSTA
15	Exec Director Human Resources	Ms. Terri KURTZ
26	Dir Marketing & Communications	Mr. Darin KAZMIR
38	Director Advising/Counseling	Mr. Robert CUBRIEL, III
96	Director of Purchasing	Ms. Lydia HUBER
21	Director of Finance	Ms. Tracey BERGSTROM
35	Director of Student Life	Ms. Elaine EVERETT-HENSLEY
13	Director Technology Services	Mr. Andy FARRIOR
04	Exec Admin Asst to President	Ms. Mary Ann RODRIGUEZ
102	Exec Dir Advancement/Foundation	Ms. Amy MUNDY

Wade College (A)

1950 North Stemmons Fwy, Ste 4080, Dallas TX 75207
County: Dallas — FICE Identification: 010130
Unit ID: 226879
Telephone: (214) 637-3530 — Carnegie Class: Bac-Diverse
FAX Number: (214) 637-0827 — Calendar System: Trimester
URL: www.wadecollege.edu
Established: 1962 — Annual Undergrad Tuition & Fees: $14,955
Enrollment: 180 — Coed
Affiliation or Control: Proprietary — IRS Status: Proprietary
Highest Offering: Baccalaureate
Accreditation: SC, CIDA

01	President	Dr. Harry DAVROS
05	VP of Academic/Student Affairs	Ms. Elizabeth JOHNSTON
37	VP Compliance & Financial Svcs	Ms. Lisa HOOVER
07	VP Enrollment Mgmt/Admissions	Mr. James SCHROEDER
36	Director of Career Services	Mrs. Jennifer MAGEE
08	Director Learning Resources	Ms. Rebekka GIRARD

Wayland Baptist University (B)

1900 West Seventh Street, Plainview TX 79072-6998
County: Hale — FICE Identification: 003663
Unit ID: 229780
Telephone: (806) 291-1000 — Carnegie Class: Masters/L
FAX Number: (806) 291-1975 — Calendar System: Semester
URL: www.wbu.edu
Established: 1908 — Annual Undergrad Tuition & Fees: $21,304
Enrollment: 4,062 — Coed
Affiliation or Control: Southern Baptist — IRS Status: 501(c)3
Highest Offering: Doctorate
Accreditation: SC, MUS, NUR

01	President	Dr. Bobby L. HALL
05	Vice Pres of Academic Affairs	Dr. Cindy M. MCCLENAGAN
32	Sr VP of Operations & Student Life	Dr. D. Claude LUSK
20	Vice Pres of External Campuses	Dr. David BISHOP
111	VP of Institutional Advancement	Mr. Mike HAMMACK
10	Chief Financial Officer	Mrs. Lezlie HUKILL
84	Vice President of Enrollment Mgmt	Dr. Daniel BROWN
26	Exec Dir of Marketing	Mr. Gary VAUGHN
12	Exec Dir/Campus Dean Albuquerque	Dr. Tom FISHER
12	Exec Dir/Campus Dean Wichita Falls	Dr. Jerry FAUGHT
12	Exec Dir/Campus Dean Amarillo	Dr. J. B BOREN
12	Exec Dir/Campus Dean Anchorage	Dr. Eric ASH
12	Exec Dir/Campus Dean Hawaii	Dr. Henrique REGINA
12	Exec Dir/Campus Dean Lubbock	Dr. Judy JARRATT
12	Exec Dir/Campus Dean San Antonio	Dr. Clinton LOWIN
12	Exec Dir/Camp Dn Phnx/Sierra Vista	Dr. Andrew MARQUEZ
83	Acad Dean School Behav & Soc Sci	Dr. Peter BOWEN
50	Academic Dean School of Business	Dr. Kelly WARREN
53	Academic Dean School of Education	Dr. Sarah HARTMAN
79	Acad Dean Sch of Lang & Lit	Dr. Kimberlee MENDOZA
81	Academic Dean School Math/Sciences	Dr. Adam REINHART
64	Acad Dean The Sch of Creative Arts	Dr. Ann B. STUTES
66	Academic Dean School of Nursing	Dr. Nikolaos MORAROS
73	Academic Dean Sch Christian Studies	Dr. Stephen STOOKEY
06	University Registrar	Mrs. Julie BOWEN
35	Exec Dir Student Services	Mr. Shawn THOMAS
41	Dir of Intercollegiate Athletics	Mr. Jim GIACOMAZZI
07	Director of Admissions	Mrs. Shaney BREWER
29	Director Alumni Relations	Vacant
42	Director of Spiritual Life	Mr. Donnie BROWN
30	Dir of Donor Relations/Stewardship	Mrs. Amber MCCLOUD
37	Executive Director of Financial Aid	Mrs. Christi MILLER
58	Director of Graduate Studies	Ms. Amanda STANTON
15	Exec Director of Human Resources	Mr. Rafael AGUILERA
13	Chief Information Officer	Mr. Cagan CUMMINGS
09	Dir Inst Research/Effectiveness	Dr. Gregg GREER
08	Director of Libraries	Ms. Sally QUIROZ
88	Exec Director Property Management	Mr. Trevor MORRIS
27	Director of Communications	Mr. Phillip HAMILTON
23	Director of Health Services	Mrs. Coralyn DILLARD
39	Coordinator of Student Housing	Mr. Glynn BOYDSTON
38	Dir Counseling/Career/Disability	Mrs. Brandy HEADS
40	Director of University Store	Mr. Brad HENDERSON
106	Director of WBUonline	Dr. Trish RITSCHEL-TRIFILO
88	Dir BAS/BCM & Assoc Registrar	Mrs. Caitlin BAKER
19	WBU Chief of Police	Vacant
18	Chief Facilities/Physical Plant	Mr. David MURPHREE
04	Exec Asst to President	Mrs. Cynthia TREVINO
110	Director of Advancement Services	Mrs. Amber SMITH
112	Senior Major Gift Officer	Mr. Mike MELCHER
88	Dir of Multi Tutorial Services	Dr. Brent LYNN
92	Director of Honors Program	Dr. D. Niler PYEATT
121	Director of Student Success	Dr. Rosemary PEGGRAM
88	Director of Museums	Mrs. KayLyn BEAN

Weatherford College (C)

225 College Park Drive, Weatherford TX 76086-5699
County: Parker — FICE Identification: 003664
Unit ID: 229799
Telephone: (817) 594-5471 — Carnegie Class: Assoc/MT-VT-High Trad
FAX Number: (817) 598-6210 — Calendar System: Semester
URL: www.wc.edu
Established: 1869 — Annual Undergrad Tuition & Fees (In-District): $5,130
Enrollment: 5,480 — Coed
Affiliation or Control: Local — IRS Status: 501(c)3
Highest Offering: Baccalaureate
Accreditation: SC, ADNUR, COARC, DMS, EMT, NUR, OTA, PTAA, RAD

01	President	Dr. Tod Allen FARMER
04	Exec Asst to the President	Mrs. Theresa R. HUTCHISON
10	Exec Vice Pres Finance/Admin Affs	Dr. Andra R. CANTRELL
05	VP of Instruction	Mr. Michael ENDY
111	Vice Pres Institutional Advancement	Mr. Brent BAKER
76	Dean of Health & Human Sciences	Ms. Katherine BOSWELL
20	Dean Educational/Instructional Sppt	Vacant
32	Exec Dean of Stdnt Svcs/Registrar	Mr. Adam FINLEY
103	Dean Workforce/Economic Devel	Mrs. Janetta KRUSE
26	Dir Communications/Public Relations	Mrs. Crystal WOERLY
57	Dean of Fine Arts/Education	Mr. Duane DURRETT
09	Exec Dir Inst Research	Mr. John JONES
35	Assoc Dean Student Development	Mr. Doug JEFFERSON
124	Dir Student Engage & Outreach Advis	Mr. John TURNTINE
109	Director Food Services	Ms. Erin DAVIDSON
37	Director of Financial Aid	Mrs. Nikki HARLESS
21	Controller	Mrs. Lisa SIMONS
15	Director Human Resources	Mr. Paul WILLIAMS
07	Director of Admissions	Mrs. Mika FOREMAN
13	Exec Director Info Technology	Mrs. Priscilla PARSONS
08	Director of Learning Resources Ctr	Mrs. Valorie STARR
18	Director of Facilities	Mr. Jon STARK
96	Director of Purchasing	Mrs. Jeanie HOBBS
19	Chief of Campus Police	Mr. Anthony BIGONGIARI
88	Director Upward Bound	Mr. Jeff KHALDEN
29	Director Alumni Relations	Mr. Brent BAKER
53	Director of Teacher Education	Mrs. Shannon STOKER
06	Registrar	Mr. Adam FINLEY
88	Director of Testing	Ms. Gwen CRABTREE
121	Assoc Dean Student Success	Ms. Kay LANDRUM
88	Dir Spec Populations/Pathways Spec	Mrs. Dawn KAHLDEN
39	Director Student Housing	Miss Faith STIFFLER
41	Athletic Director	Mr. Bob MCKINLEY
102	Director Foundation	Mr. Brent GOUGH
105	Director Creative/Graphic Svcs	Mrs. Katie EDWARDS
106	Director E-learning	Dr. Sarah LOCK
43	General Counsel	Mr. Dan CURLEE
25	Director Grants/Compliance & Accred	Mrs. Stephenie FIELDS
108	Director Institutional Assessment	Ms. Tracy MCKINLEY

West Coast University (D)

2323 N. Central Expressway, Richardson TX 75080
Telephone: (214) 453-4533 — Identification: 770485
Accreditation: &WC, #ARCPA

† Branch campus of West Coast University, North Hollywood, CA

Western Technical College (E)

9624 Plaza Circle, El Paso TX 79927-2105
County: El Paso — FICE Identification: 020983
Unit ID: 224679
Telephone: (915) 532-3737 — Carnegie Class: Bac/Assoc-Assoc Dom
FAX Number: (915) 532-6946 — Calendar System: Other
URL: www.westerntech.edu
Established: 1969 — Annual Undergrad Tuition & Fees: N/A
Enrollment: 1,324 — Coed
Affiliation or Control: Proprietary — IRS Status: Proprietary
Highest Offering: Associate Degree
Accreditation: ACCSC, MAC, PTAA

01	Chief Executive Officer	Mr. Brad KUYKENDALL
11	Chief Operating Officer	Ms. Mary CANO
07	Director of Admissions	Mr. Marco MARTINEZ
05	Academic Dean	Mr. Javier ZAVALA
10	Accounting Controller	Ms. Laura PLUMMER
37	Student Financial Services Director	Ms. Danielle PICCHI
36	Director Career Services	Ms. Helen GARCIA
13	Information Technology Manager	Mr. Eric PLASENCIO
18	Facilities Maintenance Director	Mr. Jose PEREZ

Western Technical College (F)

9451 Diana Drive, El Paso TX 79924-6936
Telephone: (915) 566-9621 — Identification: 666103
Accreditation: ACCSC

Western Texas College (G)

6200 College Avenue, Snyder TX 79549-6189
County: Scurry — FICE Identification: 009549
Unit ID: 229832
Telephone: (325) 573-8511 — Carnegie Class: Assoc/HT-High Non
FAX Number: (325) 573-9321 — Calendar System: Semester
URL: www.wtc.edu
Established: 1969 — Annual Undergrad Tuition & Fees (In-District): $4,200
Enrollment: 1,442 — Coed
Affiliation or Control: State/Local — IRS Status: 501(c)3
Highest Offering: Associate Degree
Accreditation: SC

01	President	Dr. Barbara R. BEEBE
04	Assistant to the President	Ms. Melanie SCHWERTNER
10	Chief Financial Officer	Ms. Patricia CLAXTON
09	Dean Inst Research & Effectiveness	Mr. Britt CANADA
05	Dean of Instructional Affairs	Ms. Stephanie DUCHENEAUX
32	VP/Dean of Student Services	Mr. Ralph RAMON
13	Dean of Technology/Info Security	Ms. Emily POWELL
103	Dean Workforce Development	Mr. Shawn FONNVILLE
41	Athletic Director	Ms. Tammy DAVIS
06	Registrar	Ms. Donna MORRIS
37	Director Financial Aid	Ms. Tevian SIDES
21	Controller	Ms. Marjann MORROW
15	Director of Human Resources	Vacant
85	Dir International Student Services	Ms. Christy DEBLIECK
96	Director of Purchasing & Compliance	Mr. Mitch CALHOUN

Wharton County Junior College (H)

911 Boling Highway, Wharton TX 77488-3298
County: Wharton — FICE Identification: 003668
Unit ID: 229841
Telephone: (979) 532-4560 — Carnegie Class: Assoc/HVT-High Trad
FAX Number: (979) 532-6526 — Calendar System: Semester
URL: www.wcjc.edu
Established: 1946 — Annual Undergrad Tuition & Fees (In-District): $3,624
Enrollment: 6,099 — Coed
Affiliation or Control: Local — IRS Status: 501(c)3
Highest Offering: Associate Degree
Accreditation: SC, CAHIIM, CNEA, CSHSE, DH, EMT, NAEYC, PTAA, RAD

01	President	Ms. Betty A. MCCROHAN
05	Vice President of Instruction	Ms. Leigh Ann COLLINS
11	Vice President Administrative Svcs	Mr. Bryce KOCIAN
84	VP of Strategy/Enrollment Mgmt	Dr. Amanda ALLEN
10	Dean of Financial & Business Svcs	Mr. Gus WESSELS
26	Dir Marketing/Comm/Advancement	Ms. Zina CARTER
06	Dean of Enrollment & Registrar	Mr. Jerry MARTINEZ
37	Director of Financial Aid	Ms. Leslie KOLOJACO
08	Director Library Info/Tech Services	Ms. Kwei HSU
18	Director of Facilities Management	Vacant
15	Dean of Human Resources	Ms. Rachel BAHNSEN
96	Director of Purchasing	Mr. Philip WUTHRICH
101	Secretary of the Institution/Board	Vacant
19	Director Security/Safety	Mr. Danny TERRONEZ
41	Athletic Director	Mr. Keith CASE

Wiley College (I)

711 Wiley Avenue, Marshall TX 75670-5199
County: Harrison — FICE Identification: 003669
Unit ID: 229887
Telephone: (903) 927-3300 — Carnegie Class: Bac-Diverse
FAX Number: (903) 938-8100 — Calendar System: Semester
URL: www.wileyc.edu
Established: 1873 — Annual Undergrad Tuition & Fees: $13,500
Enrollment: 615 — Coed
Affiliation or Control: United Methodist — IRS Status: 501(c)3
Highest Offering: Baccalaureate
Accreditation: SC, ACBSP

01	President and CEO	Dr. Herman J. FELTON, JR.
10	Sr VP for Business & Finance	Mr. George STIELL
05	VP for Academic Affairs	Dr. Howard O. GIBSON
32	Int VP Student Affairs/Enrollment	Mr. Jonas VANDERBILT
32	Int VP Student Affairs & Enrollment	Dr. Rae LUNDY
111	Sr VP Institutional Advancement	Dr. W. Anthony NEAL
11	Chief Operating Officer/VP Admin	Dr. Tashia BRADLEY
13	Chief Information Officer	Mr. Darren ASHLEY
21	Controller	Ms. Melissa BOGUE
53	Dean School of Educ & Sciences	Dr. Sophia MARSHALL-CHAPMAN
42	Dean of Chapel	Rev. Cecil DUFFIE
04	Special Asst to Pres/Dir of T3	Mrs. Cassandra M. JOHNSON
50	Dean Sch of Business & Social Sci	Dr. Stephanie COX
26	Asst VP of Mktg/Communications	Ms. Maya BROWN
08	Director of Library Services	Dr. Martha Lopez COLEMAN
06	Registrar	Mrs. Gloria MITCHELL
84	Exec Director Enrollment Mgmt	Mr. Shaquille DILLION
15	Chief Human Resource Officer	Mrs. Krystal MOODY
37	Director of Financial Aid	Mrs. Corliss COOPER
09	Exec Dir Office Institutional Rsrch	Dr. Jerelyn DUNCAN
11	Director Administrative Svcs	Mr. O. Ivan WHITE
23	Director of Health Services	Ms. Pamela BRADLEY
41	AVP of Athletics & Strategic Retent	Mr. Bruce PEIFER
96	Purchasing Manager	Mr. Johnny JOHNSON
35	Director of Student Activities	Ms. Darby SMITH
101	Secretary of the Institution/Board	Mrs. Cassandra M. JOHNSON
106	Distance/Online Educ	Vacant
19	Director of Public Safety	Mr. Howard SYLVE
39	Director of Residence Life	Mr. Howard FISHER
43	Dir Legal Services/General Counsel	Vacant
29	Executive Director of Alumni Affs	Mr. Charles CORNISH
90	Director Academic Computing	Ms. Tamisha CULBERSON
23	Associate VP Student Health	Dr. Rae LUNDY
07	Director of Admissions	Mr. Shaquille DILLION
108	Director Institutional Assessment	Dr. Jerelyn DUNCAN
18	Chf Facilities/Physical Plant Ofcr	Mr. O. I. WHITE
36	Director Student Placement	Mr. Jeremy HODGE
38	Director Student Counseling	Dr. Rae LUNDY
91	Director Administrative Computing	Ms. Tamisha CULBERSON

UTAH

Brigham Young University (A)

701 E. University Parkway, Provo UT 84602-0002
County: Utah FICE Identification: 003670
Unit ID: 230038
Telephone: (801) 422-4000 Carnegie Class: DU-Higher
FAX Number: N/A Calendar System: Semester
URL: www.byu.edu
Established: 1875 Annual Undergrad Tuition & Fees: $5,970
Enrollment: 36,461 Coed
Affiliation or Control: Latter-day Saints IRS Status: 501(c)3
Highest Offering: Doctorate
Accreditation: **NW**, ART, CAATE, CAEP, CAPRT, CLPSY, COPSY, DANCE, DIETD, DIETI, IPSY, JOUR, LAW, MFCD, MLS, MUS, NURSE, PH, SP, SPAA, SW, THEA

01 President .... Mr. Kevin J. WORTHEN
05 Academic Vice President .... Dr. C. Shane REESE
111 Advancement Vice President .... Mr. Keith VORKINK
10 VP of Finance & Administration .... Mr. Steven J. HAFEN
88 International Vice President .... Dr. Renata FORSTE
32 Student Life Vice President .... Mrs. Julie FRANKLIN
13 VP Information Tech & CIO .... Mr. Tracy W. FLINDERS
88 Belonging Vice President .... Mr. Carl HERNANDEZ, III
43 Asst to President/General Counsel .... Mr. Steven M. SANDBERG
45 Asst to Pres Planning/Assessment .... Dr. Rosemary THACKERAY
26 Asst to Pres Univ Communications .... Mrs. Carri P. JENKINS
20 Assoc Academic VP Faculty Dev .... Mr. Justin COLLINGS
20 Assoc Academic VP Faculty Rels .... Dr. Brad L. NEIGER
20 Assoc Acad VP Undergraduate Stds .... Dr. Rich OSGUTHORPE
46 Assoc Acad VP Research/Grad Stds .... Dr. Larry L. HOWELL
35 Assoc Student Life Vice Pres/Dean .... Dr. Sarah WESTERBERG
18 Asst Admin VP Physical Facilities .... Mr. Ole M. SMITH
15 Asst Admin VP Human Resource Svcs .... Mr. David TUELLER
35 Asst Admin VP/Stdnt Auxiliary Svc .... Mr. Carr KRUEGER
29 Managing Dir Alumni/Ext Rels .... Mr. Mike ROBERTS
30 Managing Dir LDS Philanthropies .... Dr. Tanise CHUNG-HOON
84 Exec Dir Enrollment Services .... Mr. Christian FAULCONER
37 Director Financial Aid/Scholarships .... Mr. Stephen E. HILL
97 Dean Undergraduate Education .... Dr. Susan RUGH
08 University Librarian .... Mr. Rick ANDERSON
58 Dean Graduate Studies .... Dr. Adam WOOLLEY
51 Dean Continuing Education .... Dr. Lee GLINES
47 Dean Life Sciences .... Dr. James P. PORTER
54 Dean Engineering & Technology .... Dr. Michael A. JENSEN
83 Dean Family Home & Social Science .... Dr. Laura PADILLA-WALKER
57 Dean Fine Arts & Communications .... Dr. Edward E. ADAMS
79 Dean Humanities .... Dr. J. Scott MILLER
61 Dean Law School .... Dr. D. Gordon SMITH
50 Dean Marriott School Management .... Dr. Brigitte MADRIAN
53 Dean McKay School of Education .... Dr. Kendray HALL-KENYON
81 Dean Physical & Math Science .... Dr. Grant JENSEN
66 Dean Nursing .... Dr. Jane H. LASSETTER
73 Dean Religious Education .... Dr. Scott ESPLIN
38 Director Counseling & Career Ctr .... Mr. Klint HOBBS
09 Dir Institutional Assess/Analysis .... Dr. Kristine MANWARING
06 University Registrar .... Mr. Barry ALLRED
07 Director Admission Services .... Ms. Lori GARDINER
96 Director of Purchasing .... Mr. W. Timothy HILL
22 Dir University Accessibility Center .... Dr. Gerilynn VORKINK
19 Managing Dir/Chief Univ Police .... Mr. James C. AUTRY
39 Director Student Housing .... Mr. Paul BARTON
41 Athletic Director .... Mr. Tom HOLMOE
88 Director BYU Broadcasting .... Mr. Jeff SIMPSON
88 University Treasurer .... Mr. David W. PAUL
14 Assistant VP Technology .... Mr. Scott H. HUNT
119 Chief Information Security Officer .... Mr. John PAYNE
43 Deputy General Counsel .... Mr. Christian A. FOX

Bottega University (B)

50 W. Broadway, Suite 300, Salt Lake City UT 84101
County: Salt Lake FICE Identification: 041292
Telephone: (801) 883-8336 Carnegie Class: Not Classified
FAX Number: (801) 855-5922 Calendar System: Trimester
URL: https://bottega.edu/
Established: 1994 Annual Undergrad Tuition & Fees: N/A
Enrollment: N/A Coed
Affiliation or Control: Proprietary IRS Status: Proprietary
Highest Offering: Master's
Accreditation: **DEAC**

01 President/Provost .... Dr. Mary Beth FINN
20 Academic Dean .... Dr. Troy ROLAND
26 Marketing Director .... Vacant
06 Registrar .... Ms. Megan BRENNAN
10 Accounting Director .... Ms. Connie TEAGUE

Broadview College (C)

1902 W 7800 S, West Jordan UT 84088-4021
County: Salt Lake FICE Identification: 011166
Unit ID: 230056
Telephone: (801) 542-7600 Carnegie Class: Spec 2-yr-Other
FAX Number: (801) 542-7601 Calendar System: Quarter
URL: www.broadview.edu
Established: 1971 Annual Undergrad Tuition & Fees: $17,712
Enrollment: 268 Coed
Affiliation or Control: Proprietary IRS Status: Proprietary
Highest Offering: Baccalaureate
Accreditation: **ACICS**

01 President .... Mr. Terry MYHRE
05 Campus Admin/Dean of Education .... Ms. Crystal DEWEERD

Eagle Gate College (D)

915 North 400 West, Layton UT 84041
Telephone: (801) 546-7500 Identification: 770812
Accreditation: **ABHES**

Eagle Gate College (E)

5588 S Green Street, Suite 150, Murray UT 84123-6965
County: Salt Lake FICE Identification: 021785
Unit ID: 230366
Telephone: (801) 333-8100 Carnegie Class: Spec-4-yr-Other Health
FAX Number: (801) 263-6520 Calendar System: Other
URL: www.eaglegatecollege.edu
Established: 1979 Annual Undergrad Tuition & Fees: $14,900
Enrollment: 271 Coed
Affiliation or Control: Proprietary IRS Status: Proprietary
Highest Offering: Master's
Accreditation: **ABHES**, NURSE

01 Campus Director .... Christine ANDERSON
06 Registrar .... Veronica GOMEZ
38 Director Student Counseling .... Niicole CROFT

Ensign College (F)

95 North 300 West, Salt Lake City UT 84101-3500
County: Salt Lake FICE Identification: 003672
Unit ID: 230418
Telephone: (801) 524-8100 Carnegie Class: Assoc/HT-High Trad
FAX Number: (801) 524-1900 Calendar System: Semester
URL: www.ensign.edu
Established: 1886 Annual Undergrad Tuition & Fees: $3,550
Enrollment: 1,829 Coed
Affiliation or Control: Latter-day Saints IRS Status: 501(c)3
Highest Offering: Associate Degree
Accreditation: **NW**, MAC

01 President .... Dr. Bruce C. KUSCH
04 Executive Admin Asst .... Ms. Kristen WILLIAMS
05 Vice Pres of Academics .... Mr. Tim SLOAN
32 Vice Pres Student Services .... Dr. Guy M. HOLLINGSWORTH
11 Vice Pres of Administration .... Mr. Mark A. RICHARDS
13 Chief Information Officer .... Mr. Paul EDEN
10 Director Financial Svcs/Controller .... Mr. Chris REITZ
106 Vice Pres Online Programs .... Mr. Alan L. YOUNG
20 Dir Curriculum/Academic Programs .... Mr. Ben MALCZYK
84 Dir Enrollment Management/Admission .... Ms. Maren LYTHGOE
15 Director of Human Resources .... Mr. David BROOKSBY
26 Manager of Public Affairs .... Mr. Kirk RAWLINS
36 Director of Career Services .... Mr. Rob BAGLEY
07 Manager of Admissions .... Ms. Rebecca AARON
08 Dir of Library/Info Resources .... Mr. Brandon BOWEN
37 Manager of Financial Aid .... Ms. Melanie CONOVER
40 Bookstore Manager .... Mr. Kent CHRISTENSEN
09 Sr Dir Institutional Effectivenes .... Mr. Jonothan NICHOLS

Fortis College (G)

3949 South 700 East, Suite 150, Salt Lake City UT 84107
Telephone: (801) 713-0915 Identification: 666762
Accreditation: **ACCSC**, ADNUR, DH

† Tuition varies by degree program.

Joyce University of Nursing and Health Sciences (H)

12257 Business Park Dr, Ste 100, Draper UT 84020
County: Salt Lake FICE Identification: 022708
Unit ID: 447263
Telephone: (801) 618-0438 Carnegie Class: Spec-4-yr-Other Health
FAX Number: (801) 816-1456 Calendar System: Semester
URL: www.ameritech.edu
Established: 1979 Annual Undergrad Tuition & Fees: $12,544
Enrollment: 1,429 Coed
Affiliation or Control: Proprietary IRS Status: Proprietary
Highest Offering: Master's
Accreditation: **NW**, ABHES, ADNUR, NURSE, OTA

01 President .... Sherry JONES
12 Campus Director .... Mike MANGELSON
10 VP of Finance .... Ashley JONES LEE
26 VP of Brand/Marketing & Strategy .... Joshua KNOTTS
15 VP Culture/People & Dir Human Res .... Ann JOHNSON
05 Associate Provost & CAO .... Dr. Ray RODRIGUEZ
32 Asst Provost Student Affairs .... Michelle RICHARDS
45 Asst Provost Inst Effectiveness .... Dr. Rebecca COLLINS
108 Asst Prov Curriculum & Assessment .... Melanie THOMPSON
07 Director of Admissions .... April FULLER
100 Chief of Staff .... Heather BAILEY
116 Chief Compliance Officer .... Colleen RUSSO
37 Sr Director of Financial Aid .... Dean RILING
32 Director of Student Services .... Wendy WINDER
20 Director Ctr Teaching & Learning .... Nicolette WATKINS
88 Director Clinical/Simulation & Lab .... Joshua RAY
88 Accreditation Liaison Officer .... Dr. Larry BANKS

Midwives College of Utah (I)

1174 E Graystone Way Suite 2,
Salt Lake City UT 84106-2671
County: Salt Lake City Identification: 666281
Unit ID: 480985
Telephone: (866) 680-2756 Carnegie Class: Spec-4-yr-Other Health
FAX Number: (866) 207-2024 Calendar System: Semester
URL: www.midwifery.edu
Established: 1980 Annual Undergrad Tuition & Fees: $7,635
Enrollment: 238 Coed
Affiliation or Control: Independent Non-Profit IRS Status: 501(c)3
Highest Offering: Master's
Accreditation: **MEAC**

01 President .... Ms. Kristi RIDD-YOUNG
05 Academic Dean .... Ms. Megan KOONTZ
06 Registrar .... Ms. Laura PARK
07 Admissions .... Ms. Allyson JUNEAU-BUTLER
13 Chief Info Technology Officer .... Mr. Alan BELLOWS
37 Financial Aid Director .... Ms. Whitney MESYEF
58 Graduate Dean .... Ms. Megan KOONTZ
26 Marketing Director .... Ms. Masha MESYEF
35 Director of Student Services .... Ms. Cheryl FURER
32 Dir Student Life/Equity & Access .... Ms. Tamara TAIT
113 Bursar .... Ms. Darliegh WEBB
30 Director of Development/Fundraising .... Ms. Masha MESYEF
15 Director of Human Resources .... Ms. Masha MESYEF

Neumont University (J)

143 South Main, Salt Lake City UT 84111
County: Salt Lake FICE Identification: 010098
Unit ID: 445692
Telephone: (801) 302-2800 Carnegie Class: Spec-4-yr-Other Tech
FAX Number: (801) 302-2811 Calendar System: Quarter
URL: www.neumont.edu
Established: 2003 Annual Undergrad Tuition & Fees: $25,440
Enrollment: 529 Coed
Affiliation or Control: Proprietary IRS Status: Proprietary
Highest Offering: Baccalaureate
Accreditation: **@NW**, ACCSC

01 President/Campus Director Utah .... Aaron REED
05 VP Academic Operations .... Tim CLARK
10 VP/Chief Financial Officer .... Andrew FULLER
32 Director of Student Affairs .... Janet HEAD-PARRISH
06 Registrar .... Alice NGUYEN
37 Director Financial Aid .... Kasie HADLEY

Nightingale College (K)

175 South Main Street, Suite 400,
Salt Lake City UT 84405
County: Salt Lake FICE Identification: 038383
Unit ID: 444787
Telephone: (801) 689-2160 Carnegie Class: Spec-4-yr-Other Health
FAX Number: (801) 689-3114 Calendar System: Semester
URL: www.nightingale.edu
Established: 2010 Annual Undergrad Tuition & Fees: N/A
Enrollment: 1,337 Coed
Affiliation or Control: Proprietary IRS Status: Proprietary
Highest Offering: Master's
Accreditation: **@NW**, ABHES, @CNEA, NURSE

01 President/CEO .... Mr. Mikhail SHNEYDER
10 EVP/Chief Financial Officer .... Mr. Thomas REAMS
26 EVP Partnerships & Business Devel .... Mr. Jonathan TANNER
06 Registrar .... Ms. Jannette ANDERSON
84 Sr Director of Enrollment .... Ms. Jeana REECE
37 Int Director Student Financial Aid .... Ms. Noemi MCCORMICK

Noorda College of Osteopathic Medicine (L)

712 East Bay Blvd, Bldg 5, Ste 300, Provo UT 84606
County: Utah Identification: 667433
Telephone: (385) 375-8724 Carnegie Class: Not Classified
FAX Number: N/A Calendar System: Other
URL: noordacom.org
Established: Annual Graduate Tuition & Fees: N/A
Enrollment: N/A Coed
Affiliation or Control: Proprietary IRS Status: Proprietary
Highest Offering: Doctorate; No Undergraduates
Accreditation: **@OSTEO**

01 Founding Dean .... Dr. John DOUGHERTY

Provo College (M)

1450 W 820 N, Provo UT 84601-1305
County: Utah FICE Identification: 023608
Unit ID: 380438
Telephone: (801) 818-8900 Carnegie Class: Spec-4-yr-Other Health
FAX Number: (801) 375-9728 Calendar System: Other
URL: www.provocollege.edu
Established: 1984 Annual Undergrad Tuition & Fees: $15,219
Enrollment: 579 Coed
Affiliation or Control: Proprietary IRS Status: Proprietary
Highest Offering: Baccalaureate

Accreditation: ABHES, NURSE, PTAA

01 Campus Director ... Ms. Kristen WHITTAKER
66 Academic Dean Nursing ... Mrs. Somerset WARNER
88 Program Director PTA ... Dr. Suzanne REESE
10 Business Office Coordinator ... Mr. Jose GUTIERREZ
37 Asst Dir of Financial Aid ... Ms. Haley GONZALES
06 Registrar ... Ms. Brieanna MADSON
32 Dir Student Services/Placement ... Ms. Christine ANDERSON

Rocky Mountain University of Health Professions (A)

122 East 1700 South, Building 3, Provo UT 84606-7379
County: Utah | FICE Identification: 041932
Unit ID: 475495
Telephone: (801) 375-5125 | Carnegie Class: Spec-4-yr-Other Health
FAX Number: (801) 375-2125 | Calendar System: Trimester
URL: www.rm.edu
Established: 1998 | Annual Graduate Tuition & Fees: N/A
Enrollment: 1,193 | Coed
Affiliation or Control: Proprietary | IRS Status: Proprietary
Highest Offering: Doctorate; No Undergraduates
Accreditation: NW, ARCPA, NURSE, PTA, SP

01 President/CEO ... Dr. Richard P. NIELSEN
05 Exec VP Academic Affairs/Provost ... Dr. Mark HORACEK
10 Exec VP Finance/CFO ... Mr. Jeff B. BATE
45 EVP Strategy & Engagement ... Dr. Sandra L. PENNINGTON
13 VP of Technology/Chief Info Officer ... Mr. David PAYNE
84 AVP Enrollment Management ... Mr. Bryce GREENBERG
20 AVP Academic Administration ... Mr. Richard PETERSON
46 Director ORSP ... Dr. Robert PETTITT
51 Director Continuing Education ... Vacant
32 AVP Student Affairs ... Ms. Lori SISK
100 VP Operations/Chief of Staff ... Dr. Cameron K. MARTIN

The Utah College of Dental Hygiene at Careers Unlimited (B)

1176 S 1480 West, Orem UT 84058-4905
County: Utah | FICE Identification: 034633
Unit ID: 448239
Telephone: (801) 426-8234 | Carnegie Class: Spec-4-yr-Other Health
FAX Number: (801) 224-5437 | Calendar System: Other
URL: www.ucdh.edu
Established: 2006 | Annual Undergrad Tuition & Fees: N/A
Enrollment: 119 | Coed
Affiliation or Control: Proprietary | IRS Status: Proprietary
Highest Offering: Baccalaureate
Accreditation: ACCSC, DH

01 College President ... Mr. Brent MOLEN
10 College VP/CFO/Director Compliance ... Ms. Krista MCCLURE
00 Director Emeritus/CEO ... Mr. Kenneth MOLEN
07 Director of Admissions ... Ms. Kaydrie TOLBERT
08 Chief Library Officer ... Ms. Lindsay LAURDSEN

*Utah System of Higher Education (C)

The Gateway, 60 S 400 W, Salt Lake City UT 84101-1284
County: Salt Lake | FICE Identification: 009339
Telephone: (801) 321-7101 | Carnegie Class: N/A
FAX Number: (801) 321-7199
URL: www.ushe.edu

01 Exec Ofcr/Int Comm of Higher Educ ... Dr. David WOOLSTENHULME
05 Assoc Comm Academic Education ... Dr. Julie HARTLEY
103 Assoc Comm Access ... Ms. Melanie HEATH
32 Chief Student Affairs Officer ... Mr. Spencer JENKINS
10 Chief Financial Officer ... Dr. Richard AMON
37 Exec Director Student Financial Aid ... Mr. David A. FEITZ
88 UESP Executive Director ... Ms. Lynne WARD

*The University of Utah (D)

201 South 1460 East, Salt Lake City UT 84112-1107
County: Salt Lake | FICE Identification: 003675
Unit ID: 230764
Telephone: (801) 581-7200 | Carnegie Class: DU-Highest
FAX Number: (801) 581-3007 | Calendar System: Semester
URL: www.utah.edu
Established: 1850 | Annual Undergrad Tuition & Fees (In-State): $8,615
Enrollment: 33,081 | Coed
Affiliation or Control: State | IRS Status: 501(c)3
Highest Offering: Doctorate
Accreditation: NW, ARCPA, AUD, CAATE, CAEP, CAMPEP, CAPRT, CARTE, CEA, CLPSY, COPSY, DANCE, DENT, DIETC, HSA, IPSY, LAW, MED, MIDWF, MLS, MPCAC, MUS, NASP, NDT, NMT, NURSE, OT, PERF, PH, PHAR, PLNG, PTA, SCPSY, SP, SPAA, SW

02 Interim President ... Dr. Michael L. GOOD
100 Chief of Staff/Secretary to Univ ... Ms. Laura SNOW
05 Sr Vice Pres Academic Affairs ... Dr. Daniel A. REED
43 General Counsel & Vice President ... Ms. Phyllis J. VETTER
32 Vice President Student Affairs ... Dr. Lori K. MCDONALD
111 Vice Pres Institutional Advancement ... Ms. Heidi D. WOODBURY
86 Vice President Government Relations ... Mr. Jason P. PERRY
22 VP Equity/Diversity & Inclusion ... Dr. Mary Ann VILLARREAL
10 CFO & VP Admin Svcs Main Campus ... Ms. Cathy ANDERSON
46 Vice President Research ... Dr. Andrew S. WEYRICH
04 Exec Asst to the President ... Ms. Brynn FRONK
04 Exec Asst to the President ... Ms. Bonnie WIESE
13 Chief Information Officer ... Dr. Stephen H. HESS
21 Chief Business Strategy Officer ... Ms. Patricia A. ROSS
85 Chief Global Officer ... Dr. Brian GIBSON
16 Chief Human Resources Officer ... Mr. Jeff C. HERRING
26 Chief Mktg & Communications Officer ... Mr. William J. WARREN
117 Interim Chief Safety Officer ... Mr. Keith SQUIRES
124 Chief Sustainability Officer ... Ms. Kerry CASE
20 Sr AVP AA & Dean Undergrad Studies ... Dr. Thomas C. HAGOOD
84 Sr Assoc VP for Enrollment Mgmt ... Mr. Steve ROBINSON
18 Chief Design & Construction Officer ... Ms. Robin BURR
88 Associate Vice President Research ... Dr. Diane E. PATAKI
20 Assoc VP Acad Affairs/Faculty ... Dr. Sarah PROJANSKY
35 AVP Student Affs/Bus/Auxil Svcs ... Dr. Jerry L. BASFORD
109 Assoc VP Admin Svc/Auxiliary Svc ... Dr. Gordon N. WILSON
48 Dean Architecture & Planning ... Dr. Keith D. MOORE
50 Dean David Eccles Sch of Business ... Dr. Taylor R. RANDALL
52 Dean School of Dentistry ... Dr. Wyatt R. HUME
53 Dean College of Education ... Dr. Nancy SONGER
54 Dean College of Engineering ... Dr. Richard B. BROWN
57 Dean Col of Fine Arts/AVP the Arts ... Dr. John W. SCHEIB
68 Dean College of Health ... Dr. David H. PERRIN
92 Dean Honors College ... Dr. Sylvia D. TORTI
79 Dean College of Humanities ... Dr. Stuart K. CULVER
61 Dean S J Quinney College of Law ... Ms. Elizabeth KRONK-WARNER
65 Dean Coll of Mines & Earth Science ... Dr. Darryl P. BUTT
63 Dean Sch Med/SVP Health Sciences ... Dr. Michael L. GOOD
66 Dean College of Nursing ... Dr. Marla DE JONG
67 Dean College of Pharmacy ... Dr. Randall T. PETERSON
81 Dean College of Science ... Dr. Peter TRAPA
88 Dean School Social/Cultural Transf ... Dr. Kathryn B. STOCKTON
83 Dean Col Social/Behav Science ... Dr. Cynthia BERG
70 Dean College of Social Work ... Dr. Martell L. TEASLEY
35 Dean of Students ... Mr. Jason RAMIREZ
06 University Registrar ... Mr. Timothy J. EBNER
17 CEO Univ Hospitals & Clinics ... Vacant
96 Director Procurement ... Mr. Glendon G. MITCHELL
94 Chair Gender Studies ... Dr. Susie S. PORTER
77 Director School of Computing ... Mr. Ross T. WHITAKER
106 AVP/Dean Online & Cont Educ ... Dr. Deborah KEYEK-FRANSSEN
88 Dir Dental Clinic/Gen Residence ... Dr. Craig PROCTOR
07 Director Admissions ... Dr. John MARFIELD
29 Int Chief Alumni Relations Officer ... Ms. Linda DUNN
112 Director Planned Giving ... Ms. Jessica NELSON
37 Exec Dir Financial Aid/Scholarships ... Dr. Anthony JONES
08 Dean MLIB/University Librarian ... Ms. Alberta D. COMER
08 Dir Eccles Health Sciences Library ... Ms. Catherine B. SOEHNER
08 Dir S J Quinney Col of Law Library ... Ms. Melissa BERNSTEIN
36 Director of Career Services ... Mr. Stan D. INMAN
38 Director Counseling Center ... Dr. Lauren WEITZMAN
39 Director Housing & Res Education ... Ms. Barbara REMSBURG
39 Director Univ Student Apartments ... Ms. Jennifer G. REED
88 Exec Dir Nat History Museum of Utah ... Dr. Jason CRYAN
19 Acting Chief of Police ... Mr. Jason HINOJOSA
40 Director Campus Bookstore ... Mr. Daniel L. ARCHER
85 Director Intl Student/Scholar Svcs ... Ms. Chelsea WELLS
25 Dir Office of Sponsored Projects ... Mr. Brent K. BROWN
31 Dir Univ Neighborhood Partners ... Ms. Jennifer A. MAYOR-GLENN
09 Director Institutional Analysis ... Dr. Michael D. MARTINEAU
41 Athletics Director ... Mr. Mark M. HARLAN
104 Exec Director Learning Abroad ... Dr. Sabine C. KLAHR
44 Interim Director Annual Giving ... Ms. Rachel ROBERTSON

*Southern Utah University (E)

351 W University Blvd, Cedar City UT 84720-2470
County: Iron | FICE Identification: 003678
Unit ID: 230603
Telephone: (435) 586-7700 | Carnegie Class: Masters/L
FAX Number: (435) 586-5475 | Calendar System: Semester
URL: www.suu.edu
Established: 1897 | Annual Undergrad Tuition & Fees (In-State): $6,770
Enrollment: 12,582 | Coed
Affiliation or Control: State | IRS Status: 501(c)3
Highest Offering: Doctorate
Accreditation: NW, ART, AAQEP, CAATE, DANCE, IPSY, MUS, NURSE, SPAA, THEA

02 President ... Ms. Mindy BENSON
05 Provost/Vice Pres Academic Affairs ... Dr. Jon ANDERSON
10 Vice Pres for Finance & Admin ... Mr. Marvin DODGE
32 Vice Pres for Student Affairs ... Mr. Jared TIPPETS
111 Vice Pres Advance/Enrollment Mgmt ... Mr. Stuart JONES
58 Assoc Provost ... Dr. James SAGE
29 Vice Pres Alumni/Community Rels ... Mr. Ron CARDON
28 Chief Diversity Officer ... Ms. Daneka SOUBERBIELLE
35 Asst Vice Pres Student Affairs ... Mr. Eric KIRBY
84 AVP Enroll Mgt Graduate/Online Pgm ... Mr. Steven MEREDITH
18 AVP of Facilities Management ... Mr. Tiger FUNK
26 Exec Dir Marketing Communication ... Ms. Nikki KOONTZ
08 Exec Director of Library ... Mr. Matt NICKERSON
114 Director of Budget and Planning ... Ms. Mary Jo ANDERSON
06 Registrar ... Vacant
15 Director Human Resources ... Mr. David T. MCGUIRE
37 Director of Financial Aid ... Mr. David HUGHES
41 Interim Athletic Director ... Mr. Todd BROWN
43 General Counsel ... Ms. Maureen REDEKER
79 Dean Col Humanities/Soc Sci ... Ms. Jean BOREEN
50 Dean School of Business ... Ms. Mary PEARSON
53 Dean College of Education ... Dr. Shawn L. CHRISTIANSEN
54 Dean College of Engineering ... Dr. Jeffrey MILLER
76 Dean College of Health Sciences ... Dr. Tony OLIVER
81 Int Dean College of Science ... Dr. Jim BRANDT
57 Dean College Performing/Visual Arts ... Mrs. Shauna MENDINI
96 Director of Purchasing ... Mr. Bradley BROWN
09 Exec Dir Inst Research/Assessment ... Mr. Christian REINER
38 Director Student Counseling ... Dr. Curtis HILL
04 Exec Assistant to the President ... Ms. Bailey BOWTHORPE
13 Chief Information Technology Office ... Mr. Matt ZUFELT
86 Exec Dir Government Rels/Dev ... Ms. Donna LAW
19 Chief of Police ... Mr. Rick BROWN
45 Chief Institutional Planning Ofcr ... Dr. Steve MEREDITH
103 Exec Director Regional Services ... Mr. Stephen LISONBEE
104 Director Study Abroad ... Dr. Kurt HARRIS
105 Director Web Services ... Ms. Jill WHITAKER
25 Chief Contract and Grants Administr ... Ms. Sylvia BRADSHAW
36 Director Career Services ... Mr. Brandon STREET
39 Dir Resident Life/Student Housing ... Mr. Christopher RALPHS

*Utah State University (F)

1400 Old Main Hill, Logan UT 84322-0001
County: Cache | FICE Identification: 003677
Unit ID: 230728
Telephone: (435) 797-1000 | Carnegie Class: DU-Highest
FAX Number: (435) 797-3880 | Calendar System: Semester
URL: www.usu.edu
Established: 1888 | Annual Undergrad Tuition & Fees (In-State): $8,764
Enrollment: 27,691 | Coed
Affiliation or Control: State | IRS Status: 501(c)3
Highest Offering: Doctorate
Accreditation: NW, AAQEP, ADNUR, ART, AUD, CACREP, CEA, CIDA, DIETC, DIETD, DIETI, IPSY, LSAR, MAAB, MFCD, MUS, NUR, PNUR, PSPSY, SCPSY, SP, SURTEC, SW, THEA

02 President ... Dr. Noelle E. COCKETT
03 Executive Vice President ... Dr. Robert WAGNER
05 Provost ... Dr. Larry H. SMITH
10 Vice President Business & Finance ... Mr. Dave COWLEY
32 Vice President Student Services ... Mr. James MORALES
43 Vice President Legal Affairs ... Ms. Mica MCKINNEY
20 VP for Academic/Instructional Svcs ... Dr. Robert WAGNER
26 VP of Marketing & Communications ... Mr. William M. PLATE
56 VP Extension & Dean Agriculture ... Dr. Kenneth L. WHITE
86 VP Government Relations ... Mr. Neil N. ABERCROMBIE
46 Vice President Research ... Dr. Lisa BERREAU
12 Interim VP Statewide Campuses ... Dr. Rich ETCHBERGER
58 Vice Provost of Graduate Stds ... Dr. Richard CUTLER
13 CIO/Assoc VP Information Technology ... Dr. Eric HAWLEY
111 VP Advancement ... Dr. Matthew WHITE
20 Assistant Vice President AIS ... Mr. John MORTENSEN
18 Associate VP for Facilities ... Mr. Ben BERRETT
47 Dean of Agriculture ... Dr. Kenneth L. WHITE
57 Dean of Arts ... Dr. Rachel NARDO
50 Dean of Business ... Mr. Douglas D. ANDERSON
53 Dean of Education ... Dr. Alan SMITH
54 Dean of Engineering ... Dr. Jagath J. KALUARACHCHI
79 Dean Humanities/Social Science ... Dr. Joseph WARD
65 Dean of Natural Resources ... Dr. Chris LUECKE
81 Interim Dean of Science ... Dr. Michelle BAKER
08 Interim Dean Libraries ... Ms. Jennifer DUNCAN
07 Director of Admissions ... Mr. Jeff SORENSEN
09 Exec Dir Analysis Assessment/Accred ... Mr. Michael TORRENS
22 Exec Director Affirmative Action ... Ms. Alison ADAMS-PERLAC
41 Athletic Director ... Mr. John HARTWELL
25 Exec Director Sponsored Programs ... Mr. Kevin PETERSON
15 Exec Director of Human Resources ... Mr. Doug BULLOCK
19 Exec Director Univ Police Dept ... Mr. Blair BARFUSS
06 Registrar ... Mr. Fran HOPKIN
36 Exec Dir Career Design Center ... Mr. Kevin SCHWEMMIN
37 Director of Financial Aid ... Ms. Christina AYRES
38 Exec Director Counseling Center ... Mr. Scott DEBERARD
40 Director of Campus Store ... Mr. Jason BROWN
92 Exec Director of Honors ... Dr. Kristine MILLER
96 Director of Purchasing ... Mr. Jeff CROSBIE
122 Asst Dir Fraternity/Sorority Life ... Mr. Ian NEMELKA

*Utah Tech University (G)

225 S University Avenue, Saint George UT 84770-3876
County: Washington | FICE Identification: 003671
Unit ID: 230171
Telephone: (435) 652-7500 | Carnegie Class: Bac-Diverse
FAX Number: (435) 656-4001 | Calendar System: Semester
URL: www.dixie.edu
Established: 1911 | Annual Undergrad Tuition & Fees (In-State): $5,662
Enrollment: 12,043 | Coed
Affiliation or Control: State | IRS Status: 501(c)3
Highest Offering: Master's
Accreditation: NW, ACBSP, ADNUR, CAATE, CAEPT, COARC, DH, EMT, MLS, MUS, NUR, PTAA, RAD, SURGT

02 President ... Dr. Richard B. WILLIAMS
05 Provost/VP Academic Affairs ... Dr. Michael LACOURSE
11 Vice Pres Administrative Services ... Mr. Paul MORRIS
32 VP Student Affairs ... Mr. Del BEATTY
111 Vice Pres Advancement ... Mr. Brad LAST
86 Asst to Pres for Govt/Comm Rels ... Mr. Henrie WALTON
79 Dean College Humanities/Social Sci ... Dr. Stephen LEE
66 Dean College Health Sciences ... Dr. Eliezer BERMUDEZ
50 Dean College of Business ... Dr. Kyle WELLS
81 Dean College Science & Technology ... Dr. Eric PEDERSEN

53 Dean College Education ... Dr. Brenda SABEY
51 Assoc Prov Cmty Global Outreach ... Dr. Nancy HAUCK
13 Chief Information Officer ... Mr. Mark WALTON
35 Asst VP/Dean of Students ... Ms. Ali THREET
15 Exec Director of Human Resources ... Mr. Travis ROSENBERG
18 Asst VP of Facilities Management ... Ms. Sherry RUESCH
08 Dean of Library/Open Learning Svcs ... Ms. Kelly PETERSON-FAIRCHILD
109 Executive Director Auxiliaries ... Mr. Seth GUBLER
37 Exec Director Financial Aid ... Mr. J. D ROBERTSON
84 Assoc Prov Enrollment Mgmt ... Ms. Darlene DILLEY
06 Registrar ... Ms. Julie STENDER
121 Director of College Advisement ... Ms. Katie ARMSTRONG
26 VP of Mktg & Communication ... Dr. Jordon SHARP
18 Director Facilities Services ... Mr. Nathan EATON
19 Interim Chief of Police ... Mr. Ron BRIDGE
41 Exec Director of Athletics ... Mr. Ken BEAZER
39 Director Housing & Residential Life ... Mr. Seth GUBLER
09 Exec Dir Institution Effectiveness ... Dr. Matt NICKODEMUS
04 Assistant to the President ... Ms. Theresa BONDAD
35 Dir Student Involvement & Ldrshp ... Mr. Luke KEROUAC
96 Director of Purchasing ... Mr. Brett WHITELAW
29 Director of Alumni Relations ... Mr. John BOWLER
36 Exec Director of Career Services ... Ms. Dottie CATLIN
105 Director of Network Services ... Mr. Allen FOX
88 Director of Payroll ... Ms. Kim SEAICH
28 Assoc VP for Campus Diversity ... Dr. Tasha TOY
43 General Counsel ... Ms. Becky BROADBENT
91 Director Administrative Computing ... Mr. James MILLER
100 Assoc VP/Chief of Staff ... Mr. Courtney WHITE
104 Director of Global Education ... Dr. Michael CARTMILL
108 Director of Assessment ... Vacant
07 Director of Admissions Operations ... Mr. Jerhett JERMAN
106 Director of UT Online ... Mr. Marc LUNDSTROM
20 Assoc Provost Acad Plng & Budget ... Dr. Pamela CANTRELL
21 Exec Dir Business Services ... Mr. Scott JENSEN
38 Director of Booth Wellness Center ... Dr. Garyn GULBRANSON
121 Sr Assoc Prov for Acad Success ... Dr. Sarah VANDERMARK

*Utah Valley University (A)

800 W University Parkway, Orem UT 84058-5999
County: Utah
FICE Identification: 004027
Unit ID: 230737
Telephone: (801) 863-8000
Carnegie Class: Masters/L
FAX Number: (801) 226-5207
Calendar System: Semester
URL: www.uvu.edu
Established: 1941
Annual Undergrad Tuition & Fees (In-State): $5,906
Enrollment: 40,936
Coed
Affiliation or Control: State
IRS Status: 501(c)3
Highest Offering: Master's
Accreditation: NW, AAQEP, ACFEI, ADNUR, #ARCPA, CEA, #COARC, DH, EMT, FEPAC, IFSAC, IPSY, MUS, NUR, SW

02 President ... Dr. Astrid TUMINEZ
05 Provost/Sr VP Academic Affairs ... Dr. Wayne VAUGHT
11 VP Administration/Strategic Rels ... Dr. Val L. PETERSON
32 VP Student Affairs ... Dr. Kyle REYES
111 VP Advancement/CEO Foundation ... Mr. Mark H. ARSTEIN
15 VP People & Culture/CHRO ... Ms. Marilyn S. MEYER
45 VP Planning/Budgets & Finance ... Ms. Linda MAKIN
13 VP Digital Transformation/CIO ... Ms. Christina BAUM
100 Chief of Staff/VP Mktg & Comm ... Ms. Kara SCHNECK
28 Chief Inclusion & Diversity Officer ... Mr. DaSheek AKWENYE
43 General Counsel ... Mr. Clark COLLINGS
10 Assoc VP Finance ... Mr. Jacob ATKIN
20 Assoc Provost Engaged Learning ... Ms. Tammy CLARK
18 Assoc VP Facilities Planning ... Mr. Frank YOUNG
20 Assoc Provost Academic Programs ... Mr. David CONNELLY
26 Assoc VP University Mktg/Comm ... Mr. Henry MOLINA
27 Assoc VP University Relations ... Mr. Steve ANDERSON
20 Deputy Provost Academic Admin ... Dr. Kathren BROWN
35 AVP Stdnt Dev/Well-Being/Dean Stdnt ... Dr. Alexis PALMER
84 Assoc VP Enrollment Management ... Ms. Michelle KEARNS
31 Assoc Provost Community Outreach ... Mr. Don CAPENER
25 Assoc VP Grants & Outreach ... Dr. William NYE
21 Controller Business Svcs ... Mr. Kedric BLACK
14 Assoc VP IT/CTO ... Dr. Troy MARTIN
119 Sr Director Product Portfolio ... Mr. Brett MCKEACHNIE
07 Director Admissions ... Mr. Chad JOHNSON
88 Assoc VP Inclusive Excellence ... Ms. Tara IVIE
54 Dean College Engineering/Technology ... Dr. Kelly FLANAGAN
57 Dean School of the Arts ... Dr. Courtney DAVIS
81 Dean College of Science ... Dr. Daniel HORNS
50 Dean School of Business ... Dr. Steven HUFF
76 Dean College Health/Public Svcs ... Dr. Cheryl HANEWICZ
53 Dean School of Education ... Dr. Vessela K. ILIEVA
79 Dean Humanities & Social Sciences ... Dr. Steven C. CLARK
37 Director Financial Aid/Scholarship ... Mr. John D. CURL
19 Dir Public Safety/Chief of Police ... Mr. Matthew D. PEDERSEN
112 Director of Gift Planning ... Ms. Cristina PIANEZZOLA
09 Director Institutional Research ... Mr. Timothy STANLEY
41 Assoc VP & Director of Athletics ... Mr. Jared M. SUMSION
24 Director Studios & Broadcast Svcs ... Mr. Will MCKINNON
40 Director Bookstore ... Ms. Louise BRIDGE
06 Registrar ... Mr. Eric HUMPHREY
28 Dir Multicultural Student Services ... Ms. Darah M. SNOW
29 Sr Director Alumni Relations ... Ms. Alexx C. TOBECK
121 Director Academic Counseling Center ... Mr. Adam BLACK
96 Sr Director of Procurement ... Mr. Ryan LINDSTROM
04 Executive Asst to President ... Ms. Annette LUND
08 Director Library ... Ms. Lesli BAKER
102 Director UVU Foundation ... Ms. Julie S. ANDERSON

36 Director Career Development ... Mr. Michael J. SNAPP
104 Chief International Officer ... Mr. Baldomero LAGO
105 Director Web Development Services ... Mr. Nathan GERBER
108 Institutional Review Board Director ... Mr. Cyrill SLEZAK
90 Director Academic IT & Analytics ... Ms. Laura BUSBY
22 Dir Affirmative Action/Equal Oppty ... Ms. Laura CARLSON
112 Assoc VP Major Gifts & Dev ... Ms. Dounia SADEGHI
44 Director Annual Giving ... Ms. Vicky HOPPER
114 Director of Budgets ... Mr. Scott WOOD
113 Bursar ... Mr. David PHILLIPS
116 Director of Internal Audit ... Mr. Peter VANDERHEIDE
118 Director of Benefits/Workforce Svcs ... Ms. Judy MARTINDALE
89 Director First Yr Experience ... Ms. Elaine LEWIS
38 Sr Director Student Health Svcs ... Mr. Bill ERB
86 Sr Director Strategic Relations ... Mr. Christian BRINTON

*Weber State University (B)

3850 Dixon Parkway, Ogden UT 84408
County: Weber
FICE Identification: 003680
Unit ID: 230782
Telephone: (801) 626-6000
Carnegie Class: Masters/L
FAX Number: (801) 626-7922
Calendar System: Semester
URL: www.weber.edu
Established: 1889
Annual Undergrad Tuition & Fees (In-State): $5,956
Enrollment: 29,596
Coed
Affiliation or Control: State
IRS Status: 501(c)3
Highest Offering: Doctorate
Accreditation: NW, AAQEP, ADNUR, ART, CAATE, CAHIIM, CIDA, COARC, DH, EMT, HSA, MLS, MLTAD, MUS, NAEYC, NUR, SW

02 President ... Dr. Brad L. MORTENSEN
05 Provost/VP Academic Affairs ... Dr. Ravi KROVI
10 Vice Pres Administrative Services ... Dr. Norm TARBOX
111 Vice Pres for Univ Advancement ... Dr. Betsy MENNELL
32 Vice Pres Student Affairs ... Dr. Brett PEROZZI
13 VP for Information Technology ... Dr. Bret ELLIS
106 Interim Dean Online/Cont Educ ... Dr. Brian STECKLEIN
28 VP for Equity/Diversity & Inclusion ... Ms. Adrienne G. ANDREWS
21 Asst VP for Financial Services ... Mr. Steven E. NABOR
15 Interim Asst VP for Human Resources ... Ms. Meagan THUNELL
88 Asst VP Regional Partnerships ... Ms. Julie SNOWBALL
18 Assoc VP for Facilities Management ... Mr. Mark HALVERSON
84 Asst Prov for Enrollment Services ... Dr. Jessica OYLER
20 Asst Prov & Dean of Undergraduates ... Dr. Brenda MARSTELLER-KOWALEWSKI
76 Dean Health Professions ... Dr. Yasmen SIMONIAN
50 Interim Dean Business/Economics . Dr. Doris GEIDE-STEVENSON
53 Dean of Education ... Dr. Kristin HADLEY
83 Dean Social/Behavioral Sciences ... Dr. Julie RICH
79 Dean of Arts & Humanities ... Dr. Deborah UMAN
81 Dean of Science ... Dr. Andrea EASTER-PILCHER
54 Dean Engr/Applied Science & Tech ... Dr. David FERRO
35 Dean of Students ... Dr. Jeffrey J. HURST
06 Registrar ... Mr. Casey D. BULLOCK
19 Director Public Safety ... Mr. Dane LEBLANC
29 Exec Director Alumni Association ... Ms. Nancy COLLINWOOD
38 Dir Counseling & Psycholog Services ... Dr. Dianna K. ABEL
36 Director of Career Services ... Dr. Winn STANGER
37 Director of Financial Aid ... Mr. Jed SPENCER
27 Director of Media Relations ... Mr. John L. KOWALEWSKI
07 Director of Admissions ... Mr. Scott TEICHERT
08 Dean of the Library ... Ms. Wendy HOLLIDAY
22 Dir Equal Opportunity/Affirm Action ... Dr. Laura THOMPSON
41 Dir of Intercollegiate Athletics ... Mr. Tim CROMPTON
40 Bookstore Director ... Mr. Tim ECK
25 Director Sponsored Projects ... Mr. James TAYLOR
85 Director Services Intl Students ... Dr. Mary A. MACHIRA
23 Director Student Health Center ... Dr. Benjamin HEATON
26 Director Public Relations ... Vacant
43 University Counsel ... Dr. G. Richard HILL
39 Int Dir Housing & Residence Life ... Ms. Angelica BETANCOURT
96 Director of Purchasing ... Ms. Nancy E. EMENGER
92 Director of Honors Program ... Dr. Dan BEDFORD
114 Dir of Financial Rep & Investments ... Mr. Wendall RICH
94 Director Women's Center ... Ms. Andrea HERNANDEZ
04 Executive Asst to the President ... Ms. Sherri COX
09 Director of Institutional Research ... Mr. Clayton ANDERSON
104 Director Study Abroad ... Ms. Rebecca SCHWARTZ
108 Dir of Institutional Effectiveness ... Dr. Gail NIKLASON
90 Director Academic Computing ... Ms. Elise WAIKART
45 Director of Strategic Initiatives ... Mr. Steven RICHARDSON
103 Director of Economic Development ... Mr. Steven NABOR
105 Director Web Services ... Mr. Peter WAITE
44 Director Annual Giving ... Ms. Nancy COLLINWOOD
86 Exec Director Government Relations ... Mr. Devin WISER
101 Secretary of the Institution/Board ... Ms. Sherri COX

*Snow College (C)

150 College Avenue, Ephraim UT 84627-1299
County: Sanpete
FICE Identification: 003679
Unit ID: 230597
Telephone: (435) 283-7000
Carnegie Class: Bac/Assoc-Assoc Dom
FAX Number: (435) 283-6879
Calendar System: Semester
URL: www.snow.edu
Established: 1888
Annual Undergrad Tuition & Fees (In-State): $3,912
Enrollment: 5,800
Coed
Affiliation or Control: State
IRS Status: 501(c)3
Highest Offering: Baccalaureate
Accreditation: NW, ACBSP, ADNUR, MUS, PNUR, THEA

02 President ... Dr. Bradley J. COOK
05 Provost ... Dr. Melanie JENKINS
10 VP Finance/Administrative Services ... Mr. Carson HOWELL
32 Vice President Student Success ... Vacant
20 Assoc Provost Academic Affairs ... Ms. Melanie JENKINS
13 Chief Info Technology Officer (CIO) ... Mr. Bill SCHUETZ
35 Director Student Life/Leadership ... Ms. Michelle BROWN
75 Dean Business & Applied Tech ... Mr. Mike MEDLEY
08 Director of Libraries ... Mr. Jon OSTLER
09 Dir Institutional Planning/Research ... Ms. Beckie HERMANSEN
15 Director Human Resources ... Mr. Randy BRABY
18 Director Campus Services Ephraim ... Ms. Leslee COOK
24 Director TTC ... Mr. Chase MITCHELL
39 Director Residential Life ... Ms. Jessica SIEGFRIED
41 Athletic Director ... Mr. Robert NIELSON
06 Registrar ... Mr. Alex SNYDER
84 AVP Enrollment Management ... Ms. Teri CLAWSON
21 Budget Director ... Ms. Sherri HANSEN
26 Marketing/Communications Director ... Mr. John STEVENS
35 Dir Student Affairs/Support Svcs ... Mr. Mike ANDERSON
37 Director Student Financial Svcs ... Mr. Jack DALENE
38 Dir Student Counseling/Wellness Ctr ... Mr. Allen RIGGS
96 Director of Purchasing ... Mr. Michael JORGENSEN
111 Director Advancement ... Ms. Janie HARRIS
27 Director of Campus Relations ... Ms. Heidi STRINGHAM
04 Sr Asst to Pres/Chief of Staff ... Ms. Marci LARSEN

*Salt Lake Community College (D)

4600 S Redwood Road, Salt Lake City UT 84123-3197
County: Salt Lake
FICE Identification: 005220
Unit ID: 230746
Telephone: (801) 957-4111
Carnegie Class: Assoc/HT-Mix Trad/Non
FAX Number: (801) 957-4444
Calendar System: Semester
URL: www.slcc.edu
Established: 1948
Annual Undergrad Tuition & Fees (In-State): $3,989
Enrollment: 27,293
Coed
Affiliation or Control: State
IRS Status: 501(c)3
Highest Offering: Associate Degree
Accreditation: NW, ACFEI, ADNUR, #COARC, DH, FUSER, OTA, PTAA, RAD, SURGT

02 President ... Dr. Deneece HUFTALIN
05 Provost for Academic Affairs ... Dr. Clifton SANDERS
10 Vice Pres Finance/Administration ... Mr. Chris MARTIN
32 VP Student Affairs/Enrollment Mgmt ... Dr. Charles LEPPER
111 Vice Pres Institutional Advancement ... Ms. Alison MCFARLANE
86 VP Govt & Community Relations ... Mr. Tim SHEEHAN
108 VP Institutional Effectiveness ... Mr. Jeffrey AIRD
28 Spec Asst to President & CDO ... Dr. Lea Lani KINIKINI
20 Assoc Provost Learning Advancement ... Dr. David HUBERT
88 Exec Dir Bus Dev Resources ... Ms. Beth COLOSIMO
103 Assoc VP Workforce & Econ Dev ... Mr. Rick BOUILLON
114 Asst VP Budget Svcs/Financial Plng ... Mr. Darren MARSHALL
21 Asst VP/Controller ... Ms. Debra GLENN
18 Assoc VP of Facilities Services ... Mr. Robert ASKERLUND
13 Chief Information/Security Officer ... Mr. Bill ZOUMADAKIS
116 Director Internal Audit ... Mr. Travis LANSING
88 Sr Dir Implementation & Planning ... Ms. Candida DARLING
19 Executive Director Public Safety ... Mr. Shane CRABTREE
41 Director Athletics ... Mr. Kevin M. DUSTIN
35 Dean of Students/Asst Vice Pres ... Dr. Kenneth STONEBROOK
84 Assoc VP Enrollment Management ... Mr. Ryan FARLEY
39 Asst VP Student Services ... Mr. Curt LARSEN
121 Asst VP Student Development ... Dr. Kathryn COQUEMONT
15 Int Asst VP of Human Resources ... Dr. Sara REED
45 Asst VP Strategy and Analysis ... Dr. Lauralea EDWARDS
20 Asst Provost Curriculum & Acad Sys ... Ms. Rachel LEWIS
09 Strategic Analysis/Accred Director ... Dr. Jessie WINITZKY-STEPHENS
30 Exec Dir Development/Foundation ... Ms. Nancy MICHALKO
26 Asst VP Inst Mktg/Communications ... Mr. Michael NAVARRE
31 Director Community Relations ... Ms. Jennifer SELTZER-STITT
43 General Counsel & Risk Management ... Mr. Chris LACOMBE
86 Director Local Govt Relations ... Mr. Scott E. BROWN
25 Director Sponsored Projects ... Ms. Nicole OMER
88 Assoc VP People & Workplace Culture ... Dr. Sara REED
60 Dean Arts/Communication/Media ... Mr. Richard SCOTT
50 Dean School of Business ... Dr. Dennis BROMLEY
72 Dean SAT/Technical Specialties ... Dr. Jennifer SAUNDERS
76 Dean School of Health Sciences ... Dr. Erica WIGHT
79 Dean Humanities/Social Sciences ... Dr. Roderic LAND
81 Dean Science/Math & Engineering ... Dr. Craig CALDWELL
07 Director of Admissions ... Ms. Kate GILDEA-BRODERICK
37 Dir Financial Aid & Scholarships ... Ms. Cristi MILLARD
36 Director of Career Services ... Ms. Ella BUTLER
121 Director Academic Advising ... Ms. Ashley SOKIA
06 Registrar & Academic Records ... Ms. MaryEtta CHASE
117 Director Risk Management ... Vacant
88 Director Special Events ... Ms. Marilee DUNN
96 Director Purchasing & AP ... Mr. Brandon THOMAS
88 Director Testing Services ... Ms. Lakiesha FEHOKO
04 Exec Asst to President & Board Sec ... Ms. Sandra LEHMAN
88 Director Concurrent Enrollment ... Mr. Brandon KOWALLIS
88 Learning Outcomes Assessment Coord ... Dr. Tom ZANE

Western Governors University (E)

4001 S 700 E, Suite 700, Salt Lake City UT 84107-2533
County: Salt Lake
FICE Identification: 033394
Unit ID: 433387
Telephone: (801) 274-3280
Carnegie Class: Masters/L
FAX Number: (801) 274-3305
Calendar System: Other
URL: www.wgu.edu
Established: 1996
Annual Undergrad Tuition & Fees: $6,670

Enrollment: 147,866   Coed
Affiliation or Control: Independent Non-Profit   IRS Status: 501(c)3
Highest Offering: Master's
Accreditation: NW, AAQEP, ACBSP, CAEP, CAHIIM, @CNEA, MAC, NURSE

01	President	Scott D. PULSIPHER
05	Provost/Chief Academic Officer	Dr. Marni B. STEIN
30	VP University Development	Dr. Sarah DEMARK
10	Vice Pres Finance/Administration	David GROW
09	Vice Pres Quality/Inst Research	Jason LEVIN
26	Vice President of Marketing	Carey HILDERBRAND
15	SVP of Human Resources	Bonnie PATTEE
37	Vice Pres of Financial Aid	Bob COLLINS
27	Vice President of Public Relations	Joan MITCHELL
86	Director Government Relations	Chris BONNELL
100	Chief of Staff	Gilbert ROJAS
13	SVP Technology/CIO	David MORALES

Westminster College (A)

1840 S 1300 E, Salt Lake City UT 84105-3697
County: Salt Lake   FICE Identification: 003681
    Unit ID: 230807
Telephone: (801) 484-7651   Carnegie Class: Masters/M
FAX Number: (801) 466-6916   Calendar System: Semester
URL: www.westminstercollege.edu
Established: 1875   Annual Undergrad Tuition & Fees: $37,960
Enrollment: 1,849   Coed
Affiliation or Control: Independent Non-Profit   IRS Status: 501(c)3
Highest Offering: Doctorate
Accreditation: NW, AAQEP, ACBSP, ANEST, CACREP, NURSE, PH

01	President	Dr. Bethami DOBKIN
05	Provost	Dr. Debbie TAHMASSEBI
10	AVP Finance & Administration	Ms. Michiko PINNINGTON
111	Vice Pres Institutional Advancement	Mr. Daniel LEWIS
84	Vice President Enrollment Mgmt	Ms. Erica JOHNSON
28	Int VP Diversity/Equity/Inclusion	Dr. Tamara STEVENSON
26	Chief Marketing Officer	Ms. Sheila YORKIN
49	Dean School of Arts & Sciences	Dr. Lance NEWMAN
66	Dean School of Nursing/Hlth Science	Dr. Sheryl STEADMAN
50	Dean School of Business	Dr. Dax JACOBSON
53	Dean School of Education	Dr. Melanie AGNEW
32	VP of Student Affairs & DOS	Dr. Glenn SMITH
29	Director Alumni Relations	Ms. Heather STRINGFELLOW
09	Director of Inst Research/Assess	Mr. David PERRY
13	VP and Chief Information Officer	Mr. Peter GRECO
43	General Counsel/Chief Risk Officer	Ms. Kathryn HOLMES
21	Director of Budget & Fin Reporting	Ms. Piper ROGERS
15	Director of Human Resources	Vacant
06	Registrar	Mr. Michael SANTAROSA
37	Director of Financial Aid	Ms. Karen HENRIQUEZ
07	Director Undergraduate Admissions	Ms. Quincey OTUAFI
18	Director Plant/Facilities	Mr. Kenton GREGORY
36	Director of Career Resource Center	Ms. Trisha JENSEN
08	Director Giovale Library	Ms. Emily SWANSON
88	Assoc. Dean of Students/Campus Life	Ms. Jessica BRAZELL-BRAYBOY
39	Director of Student Involvement	Mr. Oliver ANDERSON
88	Director of Events	Ms. Pamela SHIELDS
19	Director of Campus Safety	Ms. Bri BUCKLEY
41	Director of Athletics	Mr. Shay WYATT
42	Director of Spiritual Life	Ms. Jan SAAED
38	Director of Campus Counseling	Ms. Erin GIBSON
92	Dean of Honors College	Dr. Richard BADENHAUSEN
91	Database Administrator	Ms. Roksana REZAEI
04	Exec Asst to Pres/Dir Board Rels	Ms. Emmalee SZWEDKO
22	Title IX Coordinator/EEO Compliance	Ms. Mary ROYAL
102	Dir Foundation/Corporate Relations	Mr. Jeff DRIGGS
86	Director Government Relations	Ms. Nancy BROWN

VERMONT

Bennington College (B)

One College Drive, Bennington VT 05201-6003
County: Bennington   FICE Identification: 003682
    Unit ID: 230816
Telephone: (802) 442-5401   Carnegie Class: Bac-A&S
FAX Number: (802) 447-4269   Calendar System: Semester
URL: www.bennington.edu
Established: 1932   Annual Undergrad Tuition & Fees: $58,124
Enrollment: 799   Coed
Affiliation or Control: Independent Non-Profit   IRS Status: 501(c)3
Highest Offering: Master's
Accreditation: EH

01	President	Dr. Isabel ROCHE
05	Acting Provost	Mr. John BULLOCK
20	Acting Dean of the College	Ms. Oceana WILSON
10	SVP for Finance & Administration	Mr. Brian MURPHY
45	AVP for Institutional Initiatives	Ms. Meredith MCCOY
88	Sr VP for Strategic Partnerships	Ms. Paige BARTELS
111	VP Institutional Advancement	Vacant
84	VP for Enrollment	Mr. Tony CABASCO
28	VP for Inst Inclusion/Equity	Ms. Delia SAENZ
18	AVP for Facilities Mgmt & Planning	Mr. Andy SCHLATTER
26	Chief Communications Officer	Mr. Duncan DOBBELMANN
32	Dean of Students	Ms. Natalie BASIL
09	Dean of Research/Plng/Assessment	Mr. Zeke BERNSTEIN
08	Dean of the Library	Ms. Oceana WILSON
15	Director of Human Resources	Ms. Heather FALEY

37	Director of Financial Aid	Ms. Heather CLIFFORD
13	Director of IT	Mr. Jude HIGDON
04	Senior Exec Asst to the Pres	Ms. Shannon HOWLETT
19	Director Security/Safety	Mr. Ken COLLAMORE

Champlain College (C)

163 S Willard Street, Burlington VT 05402-0670
County: Chittenden   FICE Identification: 003684
    Unit ID: 230852
Telephone: (802) 860-2700   Carnegie Class: Masters/L
FAX Number: (802) 860-2750   Calendar System: Semester
URL: www.champlain.edu
Established: 1956   Annual Undergrad Tuition & Fees: $42,784
Enrollment: 4,137   Coed
Affiliation or Control: Independent Non-Profit   IRS Status: 501(c)3
Highest Offering: Master's
Accreditation: EH, ACBSP, ART, SW

01	President	Alejandro HERNANDEZ
100	Chief of Staff President's Office	Jennifer NICHOLLS
05	Provost and Chief Academic Officer	Monique TAYLOR
20	Associate Provost	Dr. Rosalynne WHITAKER-HECK
10	Vice President Finance and Planning	Shelley NAVARI
84	Vice President Enrollment	Robin GRONLUND
13	Vice Pres Technology & CIO	Diana MATOT
32	Vice President of Student Affairs	Danelle BERUBE
35	Assistant VP Student Affairs	Lisa MAZZARIELLO
11	Chief Operating Officer	Leslie AVERILL
21	Director Finance & Asst Treasurer	April O'DELL
111	Vice President Advancement	Sarah ANDRIANO
53	Int Dean Educ/Human Stds Div	Dr. Patricia ALDREDGE
50	Int Dean Stiller Sch of Business	Ann DEMARLE
77	Dean Information Tech/Science	Dr. Scott STEVENS
106	Interim Vice Pres Online Education	Diana MATOT
60	Interim Dean Comm & Creative Media	Amanda CRISPEL
07	Director of Admissions	Diane SOBOSKI
06	Registrar	Tara ARNESON
37	Director of Financial Aid	Gregory DAVIS
100	Director of Operations Pres Office	Liza GEDULDIG
09	Director of Institutional Research	Ellen ZEMAN
108	Director Assessment/Curriculum	Ellen ZEMAN
08	Library Director	Emily CRIST
23	Director of Student Health	Skip HARRIS
35	Dean of Students	Susan WARYCK
19	Director of Security & Safety	Bruce BOVAT
85	Senior Director Intl Education	Vacant
26	External Relations & Comm Director	Vacant
18	Director of Physical Plant	Timothy VAN WOERT
23	Medical Director	Annika HAWKINS-HILKE
88	Senior Dir Learning & Teaching	Rebecca MILLS
40	Campus Store Manager	Jeremy GREENWOOD
36	Director Career Collaborative	Dr. Tanja HINTERSTOISSER
105	Director Web Services	Brian ANDREWS
25	Chief Contracts/Grants Admin	Ted WINOKUR
44	Director Lead Giving/Donor Rels	Danielle ALTENBURG
15	Director of Human Resources	Sara QUINTANA
04	Admin Coordinator to the President	Carrie HONEMAN

Goddard College (D)

123 Pitkin Road, Plainfield VT 05667-9432
County: Washington   FICE Identification: 003686
    Unit ID: 230889
Telephone: (800) 468-4888   Carnegie Class: Masters/S
FAX Number: N/A   Calendar System: Semester
URL: www.goddard.edu
Established: 1863   Annual Undergrad Tuition & Fees: $18,210
Enrollment: 366   Coed
Affiliation or Control: Independent Non-Profit   IRS Status: 501(c)3
Highest Offering: Master's
Accreditation: EH

01	President	Dr. Dan HOCOY
05	Chief Academic Officer	Vacant
10	Chief Financial and Admin Officer	Ms. Leesa STEWART
30	Director of Development	Vacant
26	Director of Marketing	Mr. Joshua AUERBACH
13	Director of ITS	Mr. John BAKER
07	Director of Admissions	Ms. Lucy BOURGEAULT
06	Registrar	Ms. Jillehn WASHBURN
37	Director of Financial Aid	Ms. Beverly JENE
08	Director of Information Access	Ms. Eileen GATTI
18	Director of Facilities Operations	Mr. John BAKER
32	Director of Student Services	Ms. Deborah BLOOM
15	Director of Human Resources	Ms. Leesa STEWART
04	Executive Assistant to President	Ms. Lisa LARIVEE

Landmark College (E)

19 River Road South, Putney VT 05346
County: Windham   FICE Identification: 025326
    Unit ID: 247649
Telephone: (802) 387-4767   Carnegie Class: Bac/Assoc-Mixed
FAX Number: (802) 387-6868   Calendar System: Semester
URL: www.landmark.edu
Established: 1985   Annual Undergrad Tuition & Fees: $60,280
Enrollment: 559   Coed
Affiliation or Control: Independent Non-Profit   IRS Status: 501(c)3
Highest Offering: Associate Degree
Accreditation: EH

01	President	Dr. Peter A. EDEN
03	Executive Vice President	Mr. Jon A. MACCLAREN
05	VP Academic Affairs	Dr. Gail GIBSON SHEFFIELD
10	Exec VP/Chief Financial Officer	Mr. Jon MACCLAREN
111	VP Institutional Advancement	Ms. Cheryl ADOLPH
32	VP Student Affairs/Dean Campus Life	Mr. Michael LUCIANI
84	VP Enrollment Management	Mr. Kevin MAYNE
88	VP Educational Research/Innovation	Ms. Manju BANERJEE
26	VP Marketing & Communications	Mr. Mark DIPIETRO
04	Assistant to the President	Ms. Tiffany KERYLOW
13	Dir Information Technology Svcs	Ms. Tina LAFLAM
36	Director Career Connections	Ms. Jan COPLAN
18	Director of Facilities	Mr. Kyle SKROCKI
08	Director Library Services	Ms. Jennifer LANN
06	Registrar	Ms. Nichole NIETSCHE
41	Director Athletics	Ms. Kari POST
37	Director Financial Aid	Mr. Michael MERTES
38	Director of Counseling/Wellness	Ms. Jacala MILLS
23	Director of Health Services	Mr. Jeff HUYETT
15	Director Human Resources	Ms. Janie JENKINS-EVANS
21	Controller	Ms. Maureen RYAN HOFFMAN
35	Dean of Students	Ms. Kelly O'RYAN
07	Director of Admissions	Ms. Sydney RUFF
19	Director Campus Safety	Mr. Michael GIANNETTO
29	Associate Director Alumni Affairs	Ms. Tricia STANLEY
30	Sr Dir Institutional Advancement	Ms. Carol NARDINO
104	Director International Education	Ms. Peg ALDEN
106	Director Online Learning	Ms. Denise JAFFE
40	Assistant Bookstore Manager	Ms. Kimberly KEMPF

Middlebury Bread Loaf School of English (F)

75 Franklin Street, Middlebury VT 05753
Telephone: (802) 443-5418   Identification: 770119
Accreditation: &EH

† Bread Loaf School of English is a summer graduate program and the enrollment figure is for the summer term.

Middlebury College (G)

Old Chapel, Middlebury VT 05753-6200
County: Addison   FICE Identification: 003691
    Unit ID: 230959
Telephone: (802) 443-5000   Carnegie Class: Bac-A&S
FAX Number: (802) 443-2071   Calendar System: 4/1/4
URL: www.middlebury.edu
Established: 1800   Annual Undergrad Tuition & Fees: $58,316
Enrollment: 2,669   Coed
Affiliation or Control: Independent Non-Profit   IRS Status: 501(c)3
Highest Offering: Doctorate
Accreditation: EH

01	President	Dr. Laurie L. PATTON
05	Exec VP and Provost	Dr. Jeff CASON
10	Exec VP Finance & Administration	Mr. David J. PROVOST
15	VP for Human Resources	Ms. Caitlin GOSS
111	VP for Advancement	Mr. Dan COURCEY
20	VP Academic Affairs/Dean of Faculty	Dr. Sujata MOORTI
26	VP for Communications & Marketing	Mr. David J. GIBSON
32	Dean of Students	Mr. Derek DOUCET
43	General Counsel/Chief of Staff	Ms. Hannah ROSS
28	VP for Equity and Inclusion	Dr. Khuram HUSSAIN
58	VP Acad Affs/Dean of the Institute	Dr. Jeffrey DAYTON-JOHNSON
07	Dean of Admissions	Ms. Nicole CURVIN
104	Dean of International Programs	Dr. Carlos VELEZ
45	Assoc Provost for Planning	Mr. LeRoy GRAHAM
08	Dean of the Library	Mr. Michael D. ROY
37	Assoc VP Student Financial Services	Ms. Kim DOWNS-BURNS
13	VP for Information Technology/CIO	Mr. Vijay MENTA
79	VP for AA/Dean of Language Schs	Dr. Stephen SNYDER
117	VP Administration/Chief Risk Ofcr	Mr. Michael D. THOMAS
20	Dean of Curriculum	Dr. Grace SPATAFORA
09	Dean for Faculty Dev & Research	Dr. James RALPH
21	Director of Business Services	Mr. Matt CURRAN
29	Assoc VP Alumni & Parent Programs	Ms. Margaret STOREY GROVES
17	Exec Director Health & Wellness	Ms. Barbara MCCALL
23	Chief Health Ofcr/College Physician	Dr. W. Mark PELUSO
42	Dean of Spiritual/Religious Life	Mr. Mark ORTEN
41	Director of Athletics	Mr. Erin QUINN
19	Director Public Safety	Ms. Demitria KIRBY
06	Registrar	Ms. Jennifer THOMPSON
15	Director of Human Resources	Vacant
40	Assistant Bookstore Manager	Ms. Sue HEBERT
108	Dir Assessment/Inst Research	Ms. Adela LANGROCK
25	Director of Grants & Sponsored Pgm	Mr. Chuck MASON

† Tuition figure is a comprehensive fees figure.

Norwich University (H)

158 Harmon Drive, Northfield VT 05663-1000
County: Washington   FICE Identification: 003692
    Unit ID: 230995
Telephone: (802) 485-2000   Carnegie Class: Masters/L
FAX Number: (802) 485-2032   Calendar System: Semester
URL: www.norwich.edu
Established: 1819   Annual Undergrad Tuition & Fees: $42,950
Enrollment: 3,975   Coed
Affiliation or Control: Independent Non-Profit   IRS Status: 501(c)3
Highest Offering: Master's
Accreditation: EH, ACBSP, CAATE, NURSE

01 President Dr. Mark ANARUMO
05 Provost & Dean of Faculty Dr. Karen GAINES
32 SVP Student Affairs/Technology Dr. Frank VANECEK
100 Sr VP/Chief of Staff Ms. Danielle PELCZARSKI
03 Executive Vice President Mr. David J. WHALEY
30 VP of Development/Alumni Relations Ms. Elizabeth KENNEDY
88 VP Strategic Partnership Mr. Phillip SUSMANN
84 VP of Enrollment Management Mr. Greg MATTHEWS
26 VP of Communications Vacant
10 VP of Finance Mr. Martin HANIFIN
28 VP of Diversity/Equity/Inclusion Dr. Julia BERNARD
35 Commandant/VP of Student Affairs Col. William MCCOLLOUGH
107 Dean Col of Professional Schools Mr. Aron TEMKIN
83 Dean College of Liberal Arts Dr. Edward KOHN
81 Int Dean Col of Science/Mathematics Dr. Edward KOHN
80 Dean College of National Services Col. Scott CONWAY
29 Assoc VP Alumni Relations Ms. Diane SCOLARO
20 Assoc VP Academic Affairs Dr. Lea WILLIAMS
04 Exec Assistant to President Ms. Laura AMELL
35 Interim Dean of Students Mr. Greg MCGRATH
08 Interim Head Librarian Mr. Greg SAUER
41 Athletic Director Mr. Ed HOCKENBURY
18 Director Facilities/Operations Mr. Bizhan YAHYAZADEH
37 Director of Student Financial Aid Ms. Sarah HARRIS
38 Dir Student Counseling/Wellness Ms. Nicole KROTINGER
07 Director of Admissions Vacant
06 Registrar Ms. Cynthia SUTER
102 Dir Foundation/Corporate Relations Ms. Lindsay BUDNIK
103 Director Career Development Ms. Meghan OLIVER
19 Director Security/Safety Mr. Larry ROONEY
15 Director of Human Resources Mr. Dana MOSS
88 Deputy Commandant Mr. Bill PASSALACQUA

Saint Michael's College (A)

One Winooski Park, Colchester VT 05439-0001
County: Chittenden FICE Identification: 003694
Unit ID: 231059
Telephone: (802) 654-2000 Carnegie Class: Bac-A&S
FAX Number: (802) 654-2297 Calendar System: Semester
URL: www.smcvt.edu
Established: 1904 Annual Undergrad Tuition & Fees: $48,175
Enrollment: 1,724 Coed
Affiliation or Control: Roman Catholic IRS Status: 501(c)3
Highest Offering: Master's
Accreditation: EH

01 President Dr. Lorraine M. STERRITT
04 Assistant to the President Mrs. Ellen M. DEORSEY
05 VP for Academic Affairs Dr. Jeffrey TRUMBOWER
10 Vice President for Finance Mr. Robert ROBINSON
32 Vice President for Student Affairs Dr. Dawn M. ELLINWOOD
84 Vice Pres Enrollment/Marketing Ms. Kristin MCANDREW
111 Vice Pres for Inst Advancement Ms. Krystyna DAVENPORT BROWN
42 Director Edmundite Campus Ministry Rev. Brian J. CUMMINGS, SSE
07 Director of Admission Mr. Michael STEFANOWICZ
41 Director of Athletics Mr. Christopher KENNEY
26 Dir Marketing/Communications Mr. Alex BERTONI
06 Registrar Ms. Marnie OWEN
09 Director of Institutional Research Ms. Mary Jane RUSSELL
100 Chief of Staff Ms. Leandre WALDO
19 Director Security/Safety Mr. Stanley VALLES
29 Director Alumni Affairs Ms. Angela ARMOUR
37 Director Student Financial Services Ms. Diane CORBETT
102 Director Foundation/Corporate Rels Ms. Angela IRVINE
15 Director of Human Resources Ms. Kendra SMITH

School for International Training (SIT) (B)

1 Kipling Road, Brattleboro VT 05302-0676
County: Windham FICE Identification: 008860
Unit ID: 231068
Telephone: (802) 257-7751 Carnegie Class: Masters/S
FAX Number: (802) 258-3110 Calendar System: Other
URL: www.sit.edu
Established: 1964 Annual Undergrad Tuition & Fees: N/A
Enrollment: 137 Coed
Affiliation or Control: Independent Non-Profit IRS Status: 501(c)3
Highest Offering: Doctorate
Accreditation: EH

01 President Dr. Sophia HOWLETT
05 Academic Dean Ms. Aynn SETRIGHT
10 SVP Finance/CFO Mr. Kote LOMIDZE
13 Director of IT Mr. Roger BOYLE
43 General Counsel Ms. Lisa RAE
58 Dean SIT Graduate Institute Dr. Kenneth WILLIAMS
19 Dean Stdnt Safety/Health/Well-being Dr. Michael ZOLL
07 Assoc Dean of Admissions Mr. Eric WIRTH
06 Registrar Ms. Ginny NELLIS
04 Executive Asst to SIT President Ms. Adelee AUSTIN
108 Dean for Assessment & Learning Supp Dr. Kathryn INSKEEP
29 Director of Alumni Engagement Ms. Carla LINEBACK
08 Head Librarian Mr. Patrick SPURLOCK

Sterling College (C)

PO Box 72, Craftsbury Common VT 05827-0072
County: Orleans FICE Identification: 021435
Unit ID: 231095
Telephone: (802) 586-7711 Carnegie Class: Bac-Diverse
FAX Number: (802) 586-2596 Calendar System: Semester
URL: www.sterlingcollege.edu
Established: 1958 Annual Undergrad Tuition & Fees: $39,200
Enrollment: 139 Coed
Affiliation or Control: Independent Non-Profit IRS Status: 501(c)3
Highest Offering: Baccalaureate
Accreditation: EH

01 Interim President Dr. Lori COLLINS-HALL
05 Dean of Academics Dr. Laura SPENCE
07 Dean of Admission/Financial Aid Ms. Moxie MEHEGAN
111 VP for Advancement Ms. Christina GOODWIN
08 Librarian Ms. Sarah KEENER
18 Director of Facilities Mr. Kelly JONES
32 Dean of Community Ms. Favor ELLIS
06 Asst Dean of Academics & Registrar Ms. Laura Lea BERRY
26 Assoc Dean Marketing/Communications Ms. Heidi MYERS
37 Director of Financial Aid Ms. Barbara STUART

University of Vermont (D)

South Prospect Street, Burlington VT 05405-0160
County: Chittenden FICE Identification: 003696
Unit ID: 231174
Telephone: (802) 656-3131 Carnegie Class: DU-Higher
FAX Number: N/A Calendar System: Semester
URL: www.uvm.edu
Established: 1791 Annual Undergrad Tuition & Fees (In-State): $19,062
Enrollment: 13,292 Coed
Affiliation or Control: State IRS Status: 501(c)3
Highest Offering: Doctorate
Accreditation: EH, CACREP, CAEP, CLPSY, DENT, DIETC, DIETD, IPSY, MED, MLS, NURSE, PH, PTA, #RTT, SP, SPAA, SW

01 President Dr. Suresh GARIMELLA
05 Provost and Sr Vice President Dr. Patricia A. PRELOCK
10 VP for Finance & Treasurer Mr. Richard H. CATE
46 VP for Research Dr. Kirk DOMBROWSKI
30 CEO & President The UVM Foundation Dr. Monica DELISA
43 VP Legal Affairs & General Counsel Ms. Sharon REICH PAULSEN
84 VP Enrollment Management Dr. Jay JACOBS
13 Chief Information Officer Dr. Simeon ANANOU
88 Vice Provost for Faculty Affairs Dr. Jane OKECH
20 Vice Provost for Academic Affairs Dr. Jennifer DICKINSON
32 VP for Student Affairs Ms. Erica CALOIERO
28 VP for Diversity/Equity & Inclusion Dr. Amer R. AHMED
11 Chief Safety and Compliance Officer Mr. Michael SCHIRLING
15 Chief Human Resource Officer Vacant
35 Dean of Students Dr. David A. NESTOR
63 Dean College of Medicine Dr. Richard L. PAGE
66 Dean Nursing & Health Sciences Dr. Noma ANDERSON
49 Dean Arts & Sciences Dr. William A. FALLS
47 Dean Agriculture & Life Sci Dr. Leslie V. PARISE
54 Dean Engineering & Math Sciences Dr. Linda SCHADLER
53 Int Dean Education & Social Svcs Dr. Katharine SHEPHERD
50 Dean Business Administration Dr. Sanjay SHARMA
92 Dean Honors College Dr. David JENEMANN
65 Int Dean Environment/Natural Res Dr. Allan STRONG
56 Director Extension Dr. Roy BECKFORD
58 Dean Graduate College Dr. Cynthia J. FOREHAND
51 Chief Prof and Cont Educ Officer Dr. Jill IRVINE
08 Dean of University Libraries Dr. Bryn GEFFERT
06 Registrar Ms. Veronika CARTER
09 Director Institutional Research Dr. Alexander C. YIN
26 Chief Communications Officer Mr. Joel SELIGMAN
14 Assoc Chief Information Officer Vacant
25 Executive Director Research Admin Mr. Brian PRINDLE
114 University Budget Director Ms. Shari BERGQUIST
19 Chief of Police Services Mr. Timothy BILODEAU
41 Director of Athletics Mr. Jeffrey L. SCHULMAN
36 Director Career Services Ms. Sarah HEATH
23 Public Health Outreach Director Mr. John Paul GROGAN
38 Med Dir Ctr for Health & Wellbeing Dr. Michelle PAAVOLA
39 Director Residential Life Dr. Charles HOLMES-HOPE
40 Director University Bookstore Mr. Robert SANTRY
85 Int Dir Intl Education Services Ms. Emma A. SWIFT
112 VP for Principal Gifts Ms. Kathleen KELLEHER
30 VP of Development Ms. Alli LAMBERT
123 Director Graduate Admissions Vacant
07 Director Undergrad Admissions Mr. Moses MURPHY
37 Director Student Financial Services Ms. Marie D. JOHNSON
96 Director Purchasing Services Ms. Natalie L. GUILLETTE
94 Director Women's Center Ms. Melissa MURRAY
24 Access/Media Services Librarian Mr. Aaron F. NICHOLS
101 Board of Trustees Coordinator Ms. Corinne B. THOMPSON
04 Admin Assistant to the President Ms. Janis AUDET-KRANS
18 Executive Dir of Facilities Mgmt Ms. Luce HILLMAN
122 Coord for Fraternity/Sorority Llfe Mr. Aidan ANDREWS
100 Special Assistant to the President Mr. Jonathan D'AMORE

Vermont College of Fine Arts (E)

36 College Street, Montpelier VT 05602-3145
County: Washington FICE Identification: 003697
Unit ID: 455992
Telephone: (802) 828-8600 Carnegie Class: Masters/M
FAX Number: (802) 828-8649 Calendar System: Semester
URL: www.vcfa.edu
Established: 2008 Annual Graduate Tuition & Fees: N/A
Enrollment: 371 Coed
Affiliation or Control: Independent Non-Profit IRS Status: 501(c)3
Highest Offering: Master's; No Undergraduates
Accreditation: EH, ART

01 President Ms. Leslie Colis WARD
05 Academic Dean Mr. Matthew MONK
10 VP for Finance & Admin/CFO Ms. Katie GUSTAFSON
32 VP Student Services/COO Mr. David MARKOW
04 Assistant to President Ms. Kerry MACDONALD
26 Exec Dir Marketing/Communications Mr. Alastair HAYES
06 Registrar Ms. Jody MAUNSELL
08 Head Librarian Mr. Jim NOLTE
13 Director of IT Mr. Nick GINGROW
18 Dir Facilities/Operations Mr. Matthew COYNE
07 Dir Student Recruitment Ms. Ann CARDINAL
29 Director Alumni Affairs Ms. Jericho PARMS

† Carnegie Graduate Instructional Program classification is Postbac-A&S

Vermont Law School (F)

164 Chelsea Street, PO Box 96, South Royalton VT 05068-0096
County: Windsor FICE Identification: 011934
Unit ID: 231147
Telephone: (802) 831-1000 Carnegie Class: Spec-4-yr-Law
FAX Number: (802) 831-1163 Calendar System: Semester
URL: www.vermontlaw.edu
Established: 1972 Annual Graduate Tuition & Fees: N/A
Enrollment: 624 Coed
Affiliation or Control: Independent Non-Profit IRS Status: 501(c)3
Highest Offering: First Professional Degree; No Undergraduates
Accreditation: EH, LAW

01 Interim President and Dean Mr. Beth MCCORMACK
05 Vice Dean for Faculty Ms. Cynthia LEWIS
32 Vice Dean for Students Mr. Joe BRENNAN
10 Vice President for Finance Ms. Lorraine ATWOOD
07 Vice President for Enrollment Mr. John MILLER
30 Vice President for Development Ms. Brooke HERNDON
88 Director Environmental Law Ctr Ms. Jennifer RUSHLOW
35 Assoc Dean Student Affs & Diversity Ms. Shirley JEFFERSON
20 Assoc Dean for Academic Affs Vacant
106 Director of Distance Learning Ms. Sarah REITER
15 Human Resources Director Ms. Betsy ERWIN
08 Library Director Ms. Jane WOLDOW
21 Comptroller Ms. Angela CARPENTER
06 Registrar Ms. Maureen MORIARTY
37 Director of Financial Aid Ms. Mel DEFLORIO
18 Facilities Manager Mr. Jeffrey KNUDSEN
26 Director of Communications Mr. Justin CAMPFIELD
13 Technology Operations Manager Mr. Oscar TREVINO
04 Exec Asst to the President/Dean Ms. Susan FOLGER
40 Bookstore Manager Ms. Amy MCDOWELL
29 Director of Alumni Affairs Ms. Crystal BROWNELL
102 Director Foundation/Corporate Rels Mr. David THURLOW
44 Director Annual Giving Vacant
36 Director Career Services Ms. Abby ARMSTRONG

*Vermont State Colleges Office of the Chancellor (G)

PO Box 7, Montpelier VT 05601
County: Washington FICE Identification: 029162
Unit ID: 231156
Telephone: (802) 224-3000 Carnegie Class: N/A
FAX Number: (802) 224-3035
URL: www.vsc.edu

01 Chancellor Ms. Sophie ZDATNY
43 General Counsel Ms. Patty TURLEY
10 Chief Financial/Operating Officer Ms. Sharron SCOTT
05 Chief Academic/Tech Officer Dr. Yasmine ZIESLER
11 Administrative Director Ms. Jennifer PORRIER
86 Dir External/Governmental Affairs Ms. Katherine LEVASSEUR
13 Chief Information Officer Ms. Kellie CAMPBELL
13 Director of Information Technology Mr. Doug EASTMAN
15 Chief Human Resources Officer Ms. Sarah POTTER
88 Director of Payroll/Benefits Ms. Tracy SWEET
25 Grants Compliance Officer Ms. Betsy WARD

*Castleton University (H)

62 Alumni Drive, Castleton VT 05735-4454
County: Rutland FICE Identification: 003683
Unit ID: 230834
Telephone: (802) 468-5611 Carnegie Class: Masters/S
FAX Number: (802) 468-6470 Calendar System: Semester
URL: www.castleton.edu
Established: 1787 Annual Undergrad Tuition & Fees (In-State): $13,044
Enrollment: 2,211 Coed
Affiliation or Control: State IRS Status: 501(c)3
Highest Offering: Master's
Accreditation: EH, CAATE, NURSE, SW

02 President Dr. Parwinder GREWAL
04 Exec Assistant to the President Ms. Michelle GRAHAM
20 Associate Academic Dean Dr. Gillian GALLE
10 Director of Finance Ms. Laura JAKUBOWSKI
32 Dean of Students Mr. Dennis PROULX
84 Dean of Enrollment Mr. Maurice OUIMET
50 Dean College of Business Ms. Cathy KOZLIK
81 Dean College of Health & Science Dr. Francesca CATALANO
111 Assoc Dean of Advancement Mr. James LAMBERT

15	Director of Human Resources	Ms. Janet HAZELTON
06	Registrar	Ms. Heather MORRISON
37	Director Student Financial Aid	Ms. Teresa MCCORMACK
53	Director of Education	Dr. Richard REARDON
18	Director of Physical Plant	Mr. Chuck LAVOIE
36	Dir of Career Development	Ms. Renee BEAUPREWHITE
23	Wellness Center Director	Ms. Martha COULTER
13	Chief Technology Officer	Ms. Gayle MALINOWSKI

*Community College of Vermont   (A)

PO Box 489, Montpelier VT 05601

County: Washington   FICE Identification: 011167
Unit ID: 230861
Telephone: (802) 828-2800   Carnegie Class: Assoc/MT-VT-High Non
FAX Number: (802) 828-2805   Calendar System: Semester
URL: www.ccv.edu
Established: 1970   Annual Undergrad Tuition & Fees (In-State): $6,920
Enrollment: 5,102   Coed
Affiliation or Control: State   IRS Status: 501(c)3
Highest Offering: Associate Degree
Accreditation: EH

02	President	Ms. Joyce M. JUDY
11	Dean of Administration	Mr. Andrew PALLITO
05	Dean of Academic Services	Ms. Deborah STEWART
32	Dean of Student Services	Ms. Heather WEINSTEIN
20	Associate Academic Dean	Ms. Candace LEWIS
20	Associate Academic Dean	Ms. Diane HERMANN-ARTIM
35	Associate Dean of Students	Ms. Angela ALBECK
84	Dean of Enrollment & Cmty Relations	Ms. Katie MOBLEY
88	Dean of Academic Center Admin	Ms. Tapp BARNHILL
15	Director Human Resources	Mr. Robert FINNEGAN
06	Registrar	Mr. John Paul REES
07	Director of Admissions	Mr. Adam WARRINGTON
37	Director of Financial Aid	Mr. Ryan DULUDE
09	Dir Institutional Research/Planning	Ms. Laura MASSELL
26	Director of Communications	Ms. Katherine KEZEY
88	Director of Secondary Initiatives	Ms. Natalie SEARLE
36	Director of Career Training Program	Vacant
27	Dir of Marketing Operations	Ms. Danielle BRESETTE
10	Dir of Business Operations	Ms. Gisele HODGDON
30	Director of Resource Development	Ms. Aimee STEPHENSON
106	Dir of Online Teaching & Learning	Ms. Jennifer ALBERICO
13	Director of IT Infrastructure	Mr. Charles BOMBARD
90	Director of Academic Technology	Mr. Anthony HARRIS
91	Dir of Administrative Technology	Ms. Megan TUCKER
20	Associate Academic Dean	Ms. Nicole STESTON

*Northern Vermont University-Johnson   (B)

337 College Hill, Johnson VT 05656

County: Lamoille   FICE Identification: 003688
Unit ID: 230913
Telephone: (802) 635-1240   Carnegie Class: Masters/S
FAX Number: (802) 635-1230   Calendar System: Semester
URL: www.northernvermont.edu
Established: 1828   Annual Undergrad Tuition & Fees (In-State): $12,804
Enrollment: 1,999   Coed
Affiliation or Control: State   IRS Status: 501(c)3
Highest Offering: Master's
Accreditation: EH

02	President	Dr. Parwinder GREWAL
05	Provost	Dr. Nolan T. ATKINS
11	Dean of Administration	Mr. Roy M. BROCK
32	Dean of Students/Student Life	Mr. Jonathan M. DAVIS
13	Chief Info Technology Officer/CIO	Mr. Jason RYAN
35	Associate Dean of Students	Ms. Michele WHITMORE
06	Registrar	Ms. Miranda FOX
106	Assoc Dean of Distance Education	Ms. Bobbi Jo CARTER
18	Director of Physical Plant	Mr. Michael STEVENS
41	Assoc Dean Athletics/Recreation	Mr. Jamey VENTURA
38	Director of Counseling Services	Ms. Kate MCCARTHY
30	Dir Development/Alumni Relations	Ms. Lauren PHILIE
36	Director of Advising	Ms. Sara KINERSON
89	Dir First-Year Exp/Student Life	Ms. Erin ROSSETTI
19	Director of Public Safety	Mr. Michael PALAGONIA
26	Director Marketing/Communications	Ms. Sylvia PLUMB
07	Director of Admissions/Enroll Svcs	Mr. Patrick ROGERS
79	Chair Humanities	Dr. David PLAZEK
53	Chair Education	Dr. Rob SCHULZE
65	Chair Environ/Health Sciences	Dr. Elizabeth DOLCI
88	Chair Performing Arts	Mr. Isaac EDDY
57	Chair Fine Arts	Mr. Ken LESLIE
50	Chair Business Administration	Mr. William MORISON
60	Chair Writing/Literature	Dr. Sharon TWIGG
81	Chair Mathematics	Dr. Julie THEORET
83	Chair Behavioral Sciences	Dr. Susan GREEN

*Northern Vermont University-Lyndon   (C)

1001 College Road, PO Box 919,
Lyndonville VT 05851-0919

Telephone: (802) 626-6200   FICE Identification: 003689
Accreditation: &EH, EXSC

*Vermont Technical College   (D)

124 Admin Drive, PO Box 500,
Randolph Center VT 05061-0500

County: Orange   FICE Identification: 003698
Unit ID: 231165
Telephone: (802) 728-1000   Carnegie Class: Bac/Assoc-Mixed
FAX Number: (802) 728-1508   Calendar System: Semester
URL: www.vtc.edu
Established: 1866   Annual Undergrad Tuition & Fees (In-State): $16,044
Enrollment: 1,520   Coed
Affiliation or Control: State   IRS Status: 501(c)3
Highest Offering: Master's
Accreditation: EH, CNEA, COARC, DH, EMT

02	President	Ms. Patricia L. MOULTON
05	Dean of Academic Affairs	Dr. Ana GAILLAT
32	Dean of Students	Mr. Jason ENSER
11	Dean of Administration	Mr. Littleton TYLER
13	Chief Technology Officer	Ms. Kellie B. CAMPBELL
30	Assoc Dean Inst Advancement	Vacant
66	Assoc Dean of Nursing	Ms. Sarah BILLINGS-BERG
07	Asst Dean of Admissions	Ms. Jessica VAN DEREN
06	Registrar	Ms. Shelly RUSS
37	Exec Director of Student Services	Ms. Catherine MCCULLOUGH
19	Director Public Safety	Mr. Emile FREDETTE
18	Director Facilities	Mr. Theodore MANAZIR
36	Director Career Development	Ms. Karry BOOSKA
15	Director of Human Resources	Ms. Kelly-Rue RISO
26	Dir Marketing/Communications	Ms. Amanda CHAULK
08	Director of Library	Mr. James ALLEN

VIRGINIA

Advanced Technology Institute   (E)

5700 Southern Boulevard, Virginia Beach VA 23462-2409

County: City of Virginia Beach   FICE Identification: 031275
Unit ID: 231411
Telephone: (757) 490-1241   Carnegie Class: Spec 2-yr-Tech
FAX Number: (757) 499-5929   Calendar System: Semester
URL: www.auto.edu
Established: 1993   Annual Undergrad Tuition & Fees: $13,200
Enrollment: 461   Coed
Affiliation or Control: Proprietary   IRS Status: Proprietary
Highest Offering: Associate Degree
Accreditation: ACCSC

02	Vice President	Mr. Andy GLADSTEIN
05	Director of Education	Ms. Debbie WIGGINS
07	Director of Admissions	Mr. Lamont COLLINS
32	Director of Student Services	Mr. Kirk CLAYTON
37	Director Student Financial Aid	Mr. Chad MARTS
06	Registrar	Ms. Deanna MERCIER
20	Director of Training	Mr. Rob METZGER
36	Director Student Placement	Mr. Kirk CLAYTON
39	Director Student Housing	Mr. Kirk MANGHAM

American National University   (F)

1813 E Main Street, Salem VA 24153-4598

County: Roanoke   FICE Identification: 003726
Unit ID: 232797
Telephone: (540) 986-1800   Carnegie Class: Bac/Assoc-Mixed
FAX Number: (540) 444-4198   Calendar System: Quarter
URL: www.an.edu
Established: 1886   Annual Undergrad Tuition & Fees: $10,772
Enrollment: 931   Coed
Affiliation or Control: Proprietary   IRS Status: Proprietary
Highest Offering: Master's
Accreditation: DEAC, CAHIIM, MAC, NURSE

01	President	Mr. Frank E. LONGAKER
11	Sr Exec VP of Campus Operations	Mr. Joel MUSGROVE
10	Vice President of Finance	Ms. April HOWARD
05	Chief Academic Officer	Dr. Carolyn SCOTT

Appalachian College of Pharmacy   (G)

1060 Dragon Road, Oakwood VA 24631

County: Buchanan   FICE Identification: 041806
Unit ID: 449922
Telephone: (276) 498-4190   Carnegie Class: Spec-4-yr-Other Health
FAX Number: (276) 498-4193   Calendar System: Semester
URL: https://www.acp.edu/
Established: 2003   Annual Graduate Tuition & Fees: N/A
Enrollment: 180   Coed
Affiliation or Control: Independent Non-Profit   IRS Status: 501(c)3
Highest Offering: Doctorate; No Undergraduates
Accreditation: SC, PHAR

01	President	Mr. Michael G. MCGLOTHLIN
05	Dean/Chief Academic Officer	Dr. Susan L. MAYHEW
10	Chief Financial Officer	Ms. Holli HARMAN
07	Dir of Admissions/Fin Aid/Registrar	Ms. Vickie KEENE
103	Dir of Institutional Development	Vacant
32	Dir Student Services/Alumni Affairs	Mr. Jason MCGLOTHLIN
13	Dir Safety/Information Technology	Vacant
08	Library Director	Ms. Melissa SPEED

Appalachian School of Law   (H)

1169 Edgewater Drive, Grundy VA 24614-2825

County: Buchanan   FICE Identification: 035593
Unit ID: 432348
Telephone: (800) 895-7411   Carnegie Class: Spec-4-yr-Law
FAX Number: (276) 935-8261   Calendar System: Semester
URL: www.asl.edu
Established: 1995   Annual Undergrad Tuition & Fees: N/A
Enrollment: 170   Coed
Affiliation or Control: Independent Non-Profit   IRS Status: 501(c)3
Highest Offering: First Professional Degree
Accreditation: LAW

01	President and Dean	Mr. B. Keith FAULKNER
05	Chief Academic Officer	Ms. Laura WILSON
04	Executive Asst to the President	Ms. Ashley A. KELSEY
36	Director of Career Services	Ms. Lucy MCGEE
13	Director of Information Services	Mr. Brian PRESLEY
15	Director Cmty Service & Personnel	Ms. Jina M. SAULS
07	Dean of Admissions	Ms. Holly CLINE
06	Registrar	Ms. Beth STANLEY
32	Dean of Students	Mr. David WESTERN
26	Director of Communications	Mr. Mark N. KELSEY
09	Director of Institutional Research	Ms. Rebecca ENGLAND
10	Director of the Business Office	Ms. Peggy STREET
11	Chief Operating Officer	Ms. Abigail WESCOTT
08	Int Assoc Director of Library	Ms. Glenna OWENS
111	Director of Advancement	Ms. Haley ALLISON
19	Director of Campus Safety	Mr. Michael KIRKPATRICK
08	Director of the Law Library	Mr. Charlie CONDON
37	Director Student Financial Aid	Ms. Abigail WESCOTT

The Art Institute of Virginia Beach   (I)

4500 Main Street, Ste 200, Virginia Beach VA 23462

Telephone: (757) 493-6701   Identification: 770977
Accreditation: &SC, ACFEI

† Branch campus of The Art Institute of Atlanta, Atlanta, GA

Ascent College   (J)

1705 Todds Lane, Hampton VA 23666

County: Hampton City   FICE Identification: 041538
Unit ID: 458113
Telephone: (757) 826-1883   Carnegie Class: Spec-4-yr-Faith
FAX Number: (757) 826-5436   Calendar System: Semester
URL: www.ascent.edu
Established: 2004   Annual Undergrad Tuition & Fees: $8,420
Enrollment: 35   Coed
Affiliation or Control: Assemblies Of God Church   IRS Status: 501(c)3
Highest Offering: Baccalaureate
Accreditation: BI

01	President	Dr. Rob RHODEN
05	Academic Dean/Exec Vice President	Dr. Ron DEBERRY
32	Student Affairs	Vacant
06	Registrar/Dir Student Svcs	Sonji THEE
08	Librarian	Dr. Ron DEBERRY

Atlantic University   (K)

215 67th Street, Virginia Beach VA 23451-8101

County: Virginia Beach   Identification: 666653
Telephone: (757) 631-8101   Carnegie Class: Not Classified
FAX Number: (757) 631-8096   Calendar System: Trimester
URL: www.atlanticuniv.edu
Established: 1930   Annual Graduate Tuition & Fees: N/A
Enrollment: N/A   Coed
Affiliation or Control: Independent Non-Profit   IRS Status: 501(c)3
Highest Offering: Master's; No Undergraduates
Accreditation: DEAC

01	CEO	Kevin TODESCHI
05	Vice Pres Academic Affairs	James VAN AUKEN
06	Registrar	Angie BEARUP

Averett University   (L)

420 W Main Street, Danville VA 24541-3692

County: Independent City   FICE Identification: 003702
Unit ID: 231420
Telephone: (434) 791-5600   Carnegie Class: Masters/M
FAX Number: (434) 791-7181   Calendar System: Semester
URL: www.averett.edu
Established: 1859   Annual Undergrad Tuition & Fees: $36,670
Enrollment: 887   Coed
Affiliation or Control: Independent Non-Profit   IRS Status: 501(c)3
Highest Offering: Master's
Accreditation: SC, CAEP, NURSE

01	President	Dr. Tiffany M. FRANKS
05	Int Vice Pres for Academic Affairs	Ms. Ginger HENDERSON
10	Vice President Business & Finance	Mr. Don AUNGST
30	Vice Pres for Philanthropy	Ms. Melissa WOHLSTEIN
15	Director of Human Resources	Mrs. Kathie TUNE
84	Vice Pres Enrollment Management	Vacant
37	Director Student Financial Services	Mr. Carl BRADSHER
21	Controller	Ms. Sandy ISOM
08	Director of Library	Ms. Pam MCKIRDY

36 Director of Career Development ....Ms. Angie MCADAMS
06 Registrar ....Mrs. Kristi PHILLIPS
26 Dir of Marketing/Communications ....Ms. Cassie JONES
29 Director Alumni Relations ....Mr. Joel NESTER
09 Dir Institutional Research/Effect ....Ms. Dana MEHALKO
07 Assoc VP of Admissions ....Vacant
18 Chief Facilities/Physical Plant ....Mr. Bruce DEVLIN
32 VP of Student Engagement ....Dr. Venita MITCHELL
38 Director of Student Counseling ....Dr. Jennifer WAGSTAFF
04 Exec Assistant to the President ....Ms. Cyndie BASINGER
102 Dir Dev/Corporations & Foundations ....Ms. Emma SELLERS
104 Director Study Abroad ....Dr. Catherine CLARK
13 Chief Information Tech Officer ....Mr. Michael BOEHM
19 Chief of Campus Safety & Security ....Mr. Bruce DEVLIN
41 VP Operations/Athletic Director ....Ms. Meg STEVENS

Bluefield University (A)

3000 College Avenue, Bluefield VA 24605-1799
County: Tazewell FICE Identification: 003703
Unit ID: 231554
Telephone: (276) 326-3682 Carnegie Class: Masters/M
FAX Number: (276) 326-4288 Calendar System: Semester
URL: www.bluefield.edu
Established: 1922 Annual Undergrad Tuition & Fees: $27,570
Enrollment: 965 Coed
Affiliation or Control: Baptist IRS Status: 501(c)3
Highest Offering: Master's
Accreditation: **SC**, CAEPT, NURSE

01 President ....Dr. David W. OLIVE
00 Chairman of the Board ....Mr. Todd ASBURY
04 Assistant to the President ....Mrs. Jordan P. DILLON
05 Provost ....Dr. Michael SALMEIER
10 VP Finance/Administration ....Mrs. Ruth BLANKENSHIP
111 VP of Advancement/Alumni ....Mr. Josh CLINE
84 Vice President of Enrollment ....Mr. Karl HATTON
06 Registrar ....Ms. Jennifer LAMB
08 Co-Director of Library Services ....Ms. Paula BEASLEY
08 Co-Director of Library Services ....Mr. Werner LIND
110 Associate VP of Advancement ....Mr. Jacob KEY
88 Dean of Registration Services ....Dr. Paul LEMON
09 Dean Inst Effectiveness & Research ....Dr. Lewis BROGDON
37 Director of Financial Aid ....Mrs. Cary WRIGHT
42 Campus Minister ....Mr. Mason WEST
41 Athletic Director ....Mr. Corey MULLINS
40 Campus Store Manager ....Mrs. Kelley LAMBERT
18 Director of Maintenance ....Mr. Christian HERSHEY
19 Coordinator of Campus Safety ....Mr. Gary RUTH
28 Coordinator of Care & Belonging ....Mrs. Sherelle MORGAN
15 Human Resources Director ....Ms. Judy PEDNEAU
13 Chief Info Technology Officer ....Mr. Chip LAMBERT
53 Dean School of Education ....Vacant
50 Dean School of Business ....Dr. Angela CLINE
07 Director of Admissions ....Vacant
106 Exec VP of Online Education ....Dr. Patricia NEELY
26 Director Marketing/Public Relations ....Mrs. Rebecca KASEY
39 Dir Resident Life/Student Housing ....Mrs. Jessica SMITH
112 Dir Planned Giving/Major Gifts ....Mr. Vincent KEENE
14 Director of Business Intelligence ....Mr. Joshua GRUBB
14 Director of Technology Services ....Mr. Timothy ROBINETTE
88 Director of Spiritual Formation ....Dr. Henry CLARY
21 Controller ....Ms. Shirley MUTTER
21 Asst Director of Finance ....Ms. Jessy MOUNTS
88 Director of Online Admissions ....Mrs. Sherelle MORGAN
16 Human Resourses Specialist ....Mrs. Caroline DIXON
38 Director of Counseling Services ....Mrs. Emily COOK

Bon Secours Memorial College of Nursing (B)

8550 Magellan Parkway, Ste 1100, Richmond VA 23227
County: Henrico FICE Identification: 010043
Unit ID: 233356
Telephone: (804) 627-5300 Carnegie Class: Spec-4-yr-Other Health
FAX Number: (804) 627-5330 Calendar System: Semester
URL: www.bsmcon.edu
Established: 1961 Annual Undergrad Tuition & Fees: N/A
Enrollment: 456 Coed
Affiliation or Control: Independent Non-Profit IRS Status: 501(c)3
Highest Offering: Baccalaureate
Accreditation: **ABHES**, NURSE

01 Vice President ....Dr. Melanie H. GREEN
66 Dean of Nursing ....Dr. Barbara C. SORBELLO
11 Dean of Administration ....Dr. Benji DJEUKENG
32 Dean of Student Services ....Ms. Leslie WINSTON
88 Dean of Clinical Simulation Center ....Ms. Holly PUGH
10 Dean of Finance/CFO ....Ms. Amy POZZA
05 Dean of Academic Affairs ....Dr. Chris-Tenna M. PERKINS
35 Associate Dean of Student Services ....Ms. Carrie NEWCOMB
06 Registrar ....Mr. Ryan STILES
08 Librarian ....Ms. Tina METZGER
29 Director Alumni Relations ....Ms. Jennifer GOINS
121 Director of Student Success ....Ms. Lydia LISNER
37 Director Student Financial Aid ....Ms. Kelley FLORIAN

Bridgewater College (C)

402 E College Street, Bridgewater VA 22812-1599
County: Rockingham FICE Identification: 003704
Unit ID: 231581
Telephone: (540) 828-8000 Carnegie Class: Bac-A&S
FAX Number: (540) 828-5479 Calendar System: Semester
URL: www.bridgewater.edu
Established: 1880 Annual Undergrad Tuition & Fees: $37,720
Enrollment: 1,597 Coed
Affiliation or Control: Church Of The Brethren IRS Status: 501(c)3
Highest Offering: Master's
Accreditation: **SC**, CAATE, CAEP

01 President ....Dr. David W. BUSHMAN
05 Provost & Executive Vice President ....Dr. Leona SEVICK
10 Vice Pres for Finance & Treasurer ....Mr. Steve BRIGHT
111 VP for Institutional Advancement ....Dr. Maureen SILVA
26 VP Marketing & Communications ....Ms. Abbie PARKHURST
13 VP for IT & CIO ....Ms. Kristy K. RHEA
84 Vice President for Enrollment Mgmt ....Mr. Michael A. POST
40 Bookstore Manager ....Ms. Sarah LANDIS
20 Associate Dean of Academic Affairs ....Dr. Robert HAMMILL
32 VP for Student Life/Dean of Student ....Dr. Leslie FRERE
36 Associate Director Career Services ....Ms. Sherry TALBOTT
121 Director Academic Support Services ....Ms. Denise MILLER
42 Chaplain ....Rev. Robert R. MILLER
07 Director of Admissions ....Mr. Jarret L. SMITH
37 Director of Financial Aid ....Mr. Joshua NORTH
113 Director of Finance & Budget ....Ms. Penny E. REARDON
41 Director of Athletics ....Mr. Curtis L. KENDALL
38 Director of Counseling Services ....Vacant
44 Dir of Engagement & Annual Giving ....Mr. Tyler BRADLEY
09 Director of Institutional Research ....Ms. Dawn S. DALBOW
15 Director of Human Resources ....Mrs. Kimberly P. HARPER
08 Library Director ....Mr. Andrew L. PEARSON
06 Registrar ....Ms. Cynthia K. HOWDYSHELL
21 Controller ....Mr. Eric BLACK
27 Editor/Dir of Media Relations ....Ms. Jessica E. LUCK
18 Director of Facilities ....Vacant
19 Campus Police Chief ....Mr. Milton S. FRANKLIN
23 Director of Student Health Services ....Ms. Pamela GIPSON
28 Assoc Dean of Stdnts Diversity/Incl ....Dr. Gauri PITALE
109 Director of Dining Services ....Ms. Geordon DUNCAN
04 Exec Asst to President ....Ms. Courtney S. RITCHIE
39 Director Student Housing ....Mrs. Alexandra C. JOHNSON
104 Director International Education ....Mrs. Anne MARSH
30 Director of Development ....Ms. Meg RINER

Bryant & Stratton College (D)

8141 Hull Street Road, North Chesterfield VA 23235-6411
Telephone: (804) 745-2444 Identification: 666496
Accreditation: **&M**, ADNUR, MAC, PNUR

† Regional accreditation is carried under the parent institution (corporate office) in Buffalo, NY.

Bryant & Stratton College (E)

301 Centre Pointe Drive, Virginia Beach VA 23462-4417
Telephone: (757) 499-7900 FICE Identification: 010061
Accreditation: **&M**, ADNUR, MAC

† Regional accreditation is carried under the parent institution (corporate office) in Buffalo, NY.

California University of Management and Sciences Virginia (F)

12801 Fair Lakes Pkwy., Fairfax VA 22033
Telephone: (703) 663-8088 Identification: 666734
Accreditation: **ACICS**

† Branch campus of California University of Management and Sciences, Anaheim, CA.

Centra College (G)

905 Lakeside Drive, Suite A, Lynchburg VA 24501
County: Independent City FICE Identification: 021758
Unit ID: 232618
Telephone: (434) 200-3070 Carnegie Class: Spec-4-yr-Other Health
FAX Number: (434) 200-5505 Calendar System: Semester
URL: www.centracollege.edu
Established: 2011 Annual Undergrad Tuition & Fees: $12,325
Enrollment: 314 Coed
Affiliation or Control: Independent Non-Profit IRS Status: 501(c)3
Highest Offering: Baccalaureate
Accreditation: **ABHES**, CNEA

01 Dean ....Dr. Heather GABLE
66 Academic Director ADN Program ....Dr. Holly PUCKETT
66 Academic Director PN Program ....Dr. Sarah HUFFER
108 Accreditation Specialist ....Ms. Ashley HENRY
32 Director of Student Services ....Ms. Ashley FOSTER

Centura College (H)

932 Ventures Way, Chesapeake VA 23320
Telephone: (757) 549-2121 Identification: 770608
Accreditation: **ACCSC**

Centura College (I)

616 Denbigh Boulevard, Newport News VA 23608
Telephone: (757) 874-2121 Identification: 770606
Accreditation: **ACCSC**

Centura College (J)

7020 N Military Highway, Norfolk VA 23518-4202
Telephone: (757) 853-2121 Identification: 770605
Accreditation: **ACCSC**, DA

Centura College (K)

7914 Midlothian Turnpike, North Chesterfield VA 23235
County: Chesterfield FICE Identification: 031264
Unit ID: 427982
Telephone: (804) 330-0111 Carnegie Class: Not Classified
FAX Number: (804) 330-3809 Calendar System: Semester
URL: www.centuracollege.edu
Established: 1992 Annual Undergrad Tuition & Fees: $16,637
Enrollment: 160 Coed
Affiliation or Control: Proprietary IRS Status: Proprietary
Highest Offering: Associate Degree
Accreditation: **ACCSC**

01 Campus Executive Director ....Duan JOYNER
05 Director of Education ....Vacant

Centura College (L)

2697 Dean Drive, Suite 100, Virginia Beach VA 23452-7431
County: City of Virginia Beach FICE Identification: 023344
Unit ID: 232016
Telephone: (757) 340-2121 Carnegie Class: Bac/Assoc-Mixed
FAX Number: (757) 340-9704 Calendar System: Semester
URL: www.centuracollege.edu
Established: 1969 Annual Undergrad Tuition & Fees: $16,637
Enrollment: 99 Coed
Affiliation or Control: Proprietary IRS Status: Proprietary
Highest Offering: Baccalaureate
Accreditation: **ACCSC**

01 Campus Executive Director ....Dennis RYAN
05 Director of Education ....Kristy HAWKINS
06 Registrar ....Crystal PAYNE
10 Bursar ....Sarah TROUT
36 Career Services Coordinator ....Brittney FULBRIGHT
08 Librarian ....Jeffery BARBOUR
07 Director of Admissions ....Malkia LYNCH

Chamberlain University-Tyson's Corner (M)

1951 Kidwell Drive, Vienna VA 22182
Telephone: (703) 416-7300 Identification: 770497
Accreditation: **&HLC**, NURSE

† Branch campus of Chamberlain University-Addison, Addison, IL

Chester Career College (N)

751 West Hundred Road, Chester VA 23836-2516
County: Chesterfield FICE Identification: 034095
Unit ID: 437769
Telephone: (804) 751-9191 Carnegie Class: Spec 2-yr-Health
FAX Number: (804) 751-2599 Calendar System: Semester
URL: www.chestercareercollege.edu
Established: 1997 Annual Undergrad Tuition & Fees: N/A
Enrollment: 159 Coed
Affiliation or Control: Proprietary IRS Status: Proprietary
Highest Offering: Associate Degree
Accreditation: **COE**

01 School Director ....Ms. Debbie HARRIS
05 Assistant School Director ....Mr. Donte JOHNSON
06 Registrar ....Ms. Annette WHITE
08 Head Librarian ....Ms. Shanequa RAMSEY-MARTIN
36 Director Job Placement ....Mrs. Tamara KNIGHT
37 Director Student Financial Aid ....Mrs. Jennifer GLOVER

Christendom College (O)

134 Christendom Drive, Front Royal VA 22630-6534
County: Warren FICE Identification: 036653
Telephone: (540) 636-2900 Carnegie Class: Not Classified
FAX Number: (540) 636-1655 Calendar System: Semester
URL: www.christendom.edu
Established: 1977 Annual Undergrad Tuition & Fees: N/A
Enrollment: N/A Coed
Affiliation or Control: Roman Catholic IRS Status: 501(c)3
Highest Offering: Master's
Accreditation: **SC**

01 President ....Dr. Timothy T. O'DONNELL
03 Executive Vice President ....Mr. Mark ROHLENA
45 Vice President of Innovation ....Mr. Kenneth FERGUSON
05 Vice President Academic Affairs ....Dr. Gregory TOWNSEND
111 Vice President for Advancement ....Mr. Paul JALSEVAC
11 Vice President of Operations ....Mr. Michael S. FOECKLER
84 VP Enrollment & Student Success ....Mr. Thomas MCFADDEN
32 VP for Student Affairs ....Ms. Amanda GRAF
20 Academic Dean ....Dr. Kevin TRACY
10 Director of Finance ....Mr. Scott KAY
06 Registrar ....Mr. Walter A. JANARO
07 Director of Admissions ....Mr. Sam PHILLIPS
08 Director of Christendom Library ....Mr. Andrew V. ARMSTRONG

37 Financial Aid Officer ... Ms. Christine SCHMIDT
29 Dir Alumni/Donor Relations ... Mr. Vince CRISTE
13 Director of Computer Services ... Mr. Douglas S. BRIGGS
88 Registrar/Business Officer NDGS ... Miss Olivia COLVILLE
41 Athletic Director ... Mr. Patrick QUEST
04 Exec Assistant to the President ... Mrs. Brenda SEELBACH
58 Dean of the Graduate School ... Dr. Robert J. MATAVA
26 Director Marketing & Creative Svcs ... Mr. Niall O'DONNELL
44 Director Annual Giving ... Mr. Adam WILSON
39 Dir Resident Life/Student Housing ... Mrs. Pam PLASBERG

Christopher Newport University (A)

1 Avenue of the Arts, Newport News VA 23606-3072
County: Independent City FICE Identification: 003706
Unit ID: 231712
Telephone: (757) 594-7000 Carnegie Class: Masters/S
FAX Number: N/A Calendar System: Semester
URL: www.cnu.edu
Established: 1960 Annual Undergrad Tuition & Fees (In-State): $14,924
Enrollment: 4,868 Coed
Affiliation or Control: State IRS Status: 501(c)3
Highest Offering: Master's
Accreditation: SC, CAEP, MUS, SW, THEA

01 Interim President ... Mrs. Adelia P. THOMPSON
100 Interim Chief of Staff ... Dr. Robert E. COLVIN
05 Provost ... Dr. Quentin KIDD
43 University Counsel ... Ms. Maureen MATSEN
111 Vice Pres for Univ Advancement ... Mr. Keith D. ROOTS
10 Chief Financial Officer ... Mrs. Jennifer B. LATOUR
26 Int Chief Communications Officer . Mr. Bruce S. BRONSTEIN, JR.
15 Director of Human Resources ... Ms. Stephanie W. HAUTZ
07 Dean of Admission ... Mr. Robert J. LANGE
84 VP for Enroll/Student Success ... Dr. Lisa DUNCAN RAINES
32 Vice President of Student Affairs ... Dr. Kevin M. HUGHES
49 Dean College Arts & Humanities ... Dr. Jana L. ADAMITIS
83 Dean College of Social Sciences ... Dr. Tatiana P. RIZOVA
65 Dean College Nat/Behav Science ... Dr. Nicole R. GUAJARDO
50 Dean Luter School of Business ... Mr. Alan S. WITT
41 Director of Athletics ... Mr. Kyle S. MCMULLIN
21 University Comptroller ... Mrs. Diane REED
06 AVP Enrollment/University Registrar ... Mrs. Julianna M. WAIT
37 Director of Financial Aid ... Ms. Keely D. HAYNES
39 Director of Housing ... Mr. Zachary R. HOLMES
09 Director of Institutional Research ... Ms. Donna A. VARNER
13 Chief Information Officer ... Mr. Andrew B. CRAWFORD
114 Asst VP for Finance & Planning ... Ms. Ashleigh R. ANDREWS
116 Director of Internal Audit ... Ms. Faith D. BELOTE
108 Assoc Prov Assess & Accreditation ... Mr. Jason C. LYONS
96 Director Procurement Services ... Ms. Danielle Y. HENLEY
08 University Librarian ... Ms. Mary K. SELLEN
19 University Police Chief ... Mr. Daniel WOLOSZYNOWSKI
18 Director of Facilities Management ... Mr. Scott GESELE
27 Exec Dir of University Events ... Mrs. Amie G. DALE
29 Sr Director for Alumni Engagement ... Mr. Baxter VENDRICK
22 Director of Title IX and EO ... Ms. Michelle L. MOODY
38 Exec Dir Counseling/Health Services ... Dr. William V. RITCHEY
36 Director Career Planning ... Ms. Sarah M. HOBGOOD
104 Director of Study Abroad ... Ms. Amanda K. PIERCE
11 Vice Pres for Admin & Aux Services ... Ms. Christine LEDFORD
28 Chief Diversity/Equity/Inclus Ofcr ... Mr. Walter V. DICKERSON
101 Secretary of the Board ... Ms. Amie G. DALE
86 Legislative Liaison ... Mr. Thomas E. KRAMER

College of William & Mary (B)

PO Box 8795, Williamsburg VA 23187-8795
County: Independent City FICE Identification: 003705
Unit ID: 231624
Telephone: (757) 221-4000 Carnegie Class: DU-Higher
FAX Number: (757) 221-1259 Calendar System: Semester
URL: www.wm.edu
Established: 1693 Annual Undergrad Tuition & Fees (In-State): $23,628
Enrollment: 8,939 Coed
Affiliation or Control: State IRS Status: 501(c)3
Highest Offering: Doctorate
Accreditation: SC, CACREP, CAEP, CAEPN, IPSY, LAW

01 President ... Dr. Katherine A. ROWE
05 Provost/Chief Academic Officer ... Ms. Peggy AGOURIS
11 Chief Operating Officer ... Ms. Amy S. SEBRING
15 Chief Human Resources Officer ... Mr. Christopher D. LEE
32 Dean of Students ... Vacant
101 Secretary to the Board of Visitors ... Mr. Michael J. FOX
04 Executive Asst to President ... Ms. Cynthia A. BRAUER
122 Asst Dir Fraternity/Sorority Life ... Ms. Alisha CIUNCI

Columbia College (C)

8620 Westwood Center Drive, Vienna VA 22182
County: Fairfax FICE Identification: 041273
Unit ID: 455983
Telephone: (703) 206-0508 Carnegie Class: Assoc/HT-Mix Trad/Non
FAX Number: (703) 206-0488 Calendar System: Other
URL: www.ccdc.edu
Established: 1999 Annual Undergrad Tuition & Fees: N/A
Enrollment: 371 Coed
Affiliation or Control: Proprietary IRS Status: Proprietary
Highest Offering: Associate Degree
Accreditation: COE, CEA

01 President/Founder ... Dr. Richard KIM
50 Business Officer ... Vacant

Culinary Institute of Virginia (D)

2428 Almeda Avenue, Ste 106, Norfolk VA 23513-2448
Telephone: (757) 858-2433 Identification: 770960
Accreditation: &SC

Divine Mercy University (E)

45154 Underwood Ln, Sterling VA 20166
County: Loudoun FICE Identification: 038724
Unit ID: 445869
Telephone: (703) 416-1441 Carnegie Class: Spec-4-yr-Other Health
FAX Number: (703) 416-8588 Calendar System: Semester
URL: www.divinemercy.edu
Established: 1998 Annual Graduate Tuition & Fees: N/A
Enrollment: 392 Coed
Affiliation or Control: Independent Non-Profit IRS Status: 501(c)3
Highest Offering: Doctorate; No Undergraduates
Accreditation: SC, CLPSY

01 President ... Fr. Charles SIKORSKY
10 Chief Financial & Admin Ofcr ... Mr. Rigg MOHLER
05 VP Academic Affairs/Digital Lrng ... Dr. Harvey PAYNE
15 VP HR & Operations ... Mr. Antonio MAZA
84 VP Enrollment and Marketing ... Mr. Tom BROOKS
108 VP Academic & Student Support/IE ... Ms. Laura TUCKER
07 Associate VP Admissions ... Ms. Tambi SPITZ-KILHEFNER
13 IT Manager ... Vacant
08 Director of Library Services ... Mr. Jeffrey ELLIOTT
06 Registrar ... Ms. Catherine ROSASCHI
37 Director of Financial Aid ... Ms. Antoinette WORMLEY
111 Director of Inst Advancement ... Mr. Thomas CRONQUIST
121 Student Success Advisor ... Ms. Merita MCCORMACK
113 Student Accounts Administrator ... Ms. Hermela WOGAYEHU
42 Director of Campus Ministry ... Mr. Tony MACDONNELL
83 MS Counseling Program Director ... Dr. John WEST
83 MS Psychology Program Director ... Dr. Julia KLAUSLI
83 PsyD Program Director ... Dr. Lisa KLEWICKI
73 Exec Dir Spiritual Direction Cert ... Ms. Maria BRACKETT

Eastern Mennonite University (F)

1200 Park Road, Harrisonburg VA 22802-2462
County: Independent City FICE Identification: 003708
Unit ID: 232043
Telephone: (540) 432-4000 Carnegie Class: Masters/M
FAX Number: (540) 432-4444 Calendar System: Semester
URL: www.emu.edu
Established: 1917 Annual Undergrad Tuition & Fees: $39,220
Enrollment: 1,394 Coed
Affiliation or Control: Mennonite Church IRS Status: 501(c)3
Highest Offering: Doctorate
Accreditation: SC, CACREP, CAEP, NURSE, PAST, SW, THEOL

01 President ... Dr. Susan SCHULTZ-HUXMAN
05 Provost ... Dr. Fred L. KNISS
20 Associate Provost ... Vacant
111 Vice President for Advancement ... Mr. Kirk L. SHISLER
10 Vice President of Finance ... Mr. Timothy W. STUTZMAN
09 VP Institutional Strategy & CIO ... Dr. Scott BARGE
84 VP Enrollment & Strategic Growth ... Dr. Mary K. JENSEN
04 Executive Assistant to President ... Ms. Amy HARTSELL
00 Board Chairperson ... Dr. Manuel A. NUÑEZ
79 Dean Theology/Humanities/Arts ... Dr. Daniel OTT
81 Dean Science/Engr/Art/Nursing ... Dr. Tara KISHBAUGH
83 Dean Social Sciences & Professions ... Dr. David BRUBAKER
32 Dean of Students ... Ms. Shannon DYCUS
124 Assistant Provost Student Success ... Dr. Zachary YODER
06 University Registrar ... Mr. Travis TROTTER
07 Director Undergraduate Admissions ... Mr. Matthew RUTH
123 Director Graduate Recruitment ... Ms. Kirsten MCKINNEY
08 Director of Libraries ... Dr. G. Marcille H. FREDERICK
37 Director of Financial Assistance ... Ms. Michele R. HENSLEY
36 Director Career Services/Testing ... Ms. Kimberly PHILLIPS
110 Director of Advancement Services ... Ms. Laura DAILY
29 Director Alumni/Parent Engagement ... Ms. Jennifer BAUMAN
30 Director Development/Annual Giving ... Mr. Braydon HOOVER
41 Interim Athletic Director ... Ms. Carrie BERT
42 Campus Pastor ... Mr. Brian M. BURKHOLDER
18 Director of Facilities Management ... Mr. Ed LEHMAN
15 Director Human Resources ... Ms. Marilyn HARRIS
38 Director Student Counseling ... Ms. Allison COLLAZO
121 Director Academic Success Center ... Dr. Violet DUTCHER
26 Director of Communications ... Ms. Lauren JEFFERSON
28 Executive Director of Diversity ... Dr. Jacqueline FONT-GUZMÁN

Eastern Virginia Career College (G)

10304 Spotsylvania Avenue, Ste. 400,
Fredericksburg VA 22408-8605
County: Spotsylvania FICE Identification: 036543
Unit ID: 441858
Telephone: (540) 373-2200 Carnegie Class: Spec 2-yr-Health
FAX Number: (540) 373-4465 Calendar System: Other
URL: www.evcc.edu
Established: 2000 Annual Undergrad Tuition & Fees: N/A
Enrollment: 190 Coed
Affiliation or Control: Proprietary IRS Status: Proprietary
Highest Offering: Associate Degree
Accreditation: COE, @CNCE, OTA

01 Chief Executive Officer/President ... Mr. Krishna A. MADDIPATLA
03 Executive Vice President ... Ms. Jyothi PEMMASANI
05 Academic Director ... Mr. Cisco ARNOLD
07 Campus Director & Dir of Admissions ... Mr. Abdullah JOHNSON
11 Director of Operations ... Mr. Sam SHETH
37 Director of Financial Aid ... Mr. Jameson DELOATCH
36 Director of Career Services ... Ms. Cynthia ROTHELL
06 Registrar/Bursar ... Ms. Jammie ADAM
04 Admin Assistant to the President ... Vacant
10 Chief Financial/ Business Officer ... Mr. Manish KALANI

Eastern Virginia Medical School (H)

Box 1980, Norfolk VA 23501-1980
County: Independent City FICE Identification: 010338
Unit ID: 231970
Telephone: (757) 446-5600 Carnegie Class: Spec-4-yr-Eng
FAX Number: (757) 446-5135 Calendar System: Other
URL: www.evms.edu
Established: 1973 Annual Graduate Tuition & Fees: N/A
Enrollment: 1,289 Coed
Affiliation or Control: Independent Non-Profit IRS Status: 501(c)3
Highest Offering: Doctorate; No Undergraduates
Accreditation: SC, ACATE, ARCPA, CLPSY, MED, PA, PH, SURGA

88 Director for Business Management ... Ms. Tammy A. CHRISMAN
01 Interim President/Provost/Dean ... Dr. Alfred Z. ABUHAMAD
04 Sr Exec Assistant to the President ... Ms. Tracy L. MORTON
116 Director Internal Audit ... Mr. Robert B. WOOD
11 VP and Chief Operating Officer ... Mr. Brant M. COX
17 Vice Pres/Dean Sch of Health Prof ... Dr. Charles D. COMBS
88 Assoc Dean for Health Professions ... Dr. Jeffrey A. JOHNSON
10 Vice Pres Administration/Finance ... Ms. Helen HESELIUS
19 Chief of Police ... Mr. Andrew J. MITCHELL
18 Director Facilities/Physical Plant ... Mr. Doug MARTIN
28 Vice President for Diversity ... Mr. Mekbib L. GEMEDA
88 Vice Provost for Faculty Affairs ... Dr. Elza MYLONA
88 Vice Dean Clinical Affairs ... Dr. L.D BRITT
23 Interim CEO EVMS Medical Group ... Mr. Brant M. COX
05 Vice Dean Academic Affairs ... Dr. Ronald W. FLENNER
43 Vice President and General Counsel ... Ms. Stacy R. PURCELL
58 Vice Dean Grad Medical Education ... Dr. Linda R. ARCHER
09 Vice Dean for Research ... Dr. William J. WASILENKO
88 Asst Dean Hum Sub Protection/IRB ... Dr. Harry J. TILLMAN
50 Assoc Dean Business/Admin Affairs ... Mr. David E. HUBAND
84 Assoc Dean Admissions and Enroll ... Dr. Thomas D. KIMBLE
32 Assoc Dean for Student Affairs ... Dr. Allison P. KNIGHT
88 Assoc Dean Clinical Education ... Dr. Brooke HOOPER
20 Assoc Dean for Academic Affairs ... Dr. Senthil K. RAJASEKARAN
88 Assoc Dean Translational Research ... Dr. John SEMMES
88 Assoc Dean Clinical Research ... Dr. Elias SIRAJ
88 Assoc Dean Clinical Integration ... Dr. Mily KANNARKAT
08 Director of Library Services ... Ms. Kerrie S. SHAW
35 Director of Student Affairs ... Ms. Joann BAUTTI
93 Asst Dean for Diversity ... Ms. Gail C. WILLIAMS
06 Registrar ... Mr. David R. GOLAY
15 Director Human Resources ... Mr. Matthew R. SCHENK
21 Assoc VP for Financial Services ... Ms. Tammy S. CHRISMAN
37 Director Student Financial Aid ... Ms. Deborah R. BROWN
96 Director of Materials Management ... Mr. Steven LEE
13 Chief Information Officer ... Mr. Michael J. HERZOG
26 Asst VP Marketing/Communication ... Dr. Vincent A. RHODES
29 Director Alumni Relations ... Ms. Tamara N. POULSON
30 Sr Assoc VP Development and Alumni . Ms. Connie L. MCKENZIE
88 Director of the Brock Institute ... Dr. Cynthia ROMERO
51 Director for Continuing Med Educ ... Ms. Drucie A. PAPAFIL
75 Director Occupational Health ... Ms. Heather SINGLETON
25 Director Sponsored Programs ... Ms. Yolanda F. DEMORY
88 Director Rad Safety Env Health ... Mr. Courtney A. KERR
117 Director Risk Management ... Ms. Donita M. LAMARAND
118 Director Health Analytics ... Dr. Sunita DODANI
88 Director Bus Intel & Analytics ... Mr. Stephen RICHARD

† Member of Virginia Consortium for Professional Psychology.

ECPI University (I)

5555 Greenwich Road, Virginia Beach VA 23462-6554
County: Independent City FICE Identification: 010198
Unit ID: 248934
Telephone: (757) 671-7171 Carnegie Class: Masters/M
FAX Number: (757) 671-8661 Calendar System: Semester
URL: www.ecpi.edu
Established: 1966 Annual Undergrad Tuition & Fees: $16,639
Enrollment: 14,353 Coed
Affiliation or Control: Proprietary IRS Status: Proprietary
Highest Offering: Master's
Accreditation: SC, ACFEI, ADNUR, MAAB, NURSE

01 President ... Mr. Mark B. DREYFUS
05 Vice President Academic Affairs ... Vacant
32 Vice President Student Development ... Ms. Maryse LEVY

ECPI University-Newport News (J)

1001 Omni Boulevard Suite 200,
Newport News VA 23606-4388
Telephone: (757) 873-2423 FICE Identification: 022472
Accreditation: &SC, ADNUR, EMT, MAAB, NUR, PTAA, RAD

† Regional accreditation is carried under the parent institution, ECPI College of Technology, in Virginia Beach, VA.

ECPI University-Northern Virginia (A)

10021 Balls Ford Road, Ste 100, Manassas VA 20109
Telephone: (703) 330-5300 Identification: 770957
Accreditation: &SC, ADNUR, MAAB, RAD, SURTEC

ECPI University-Richmond/Innsbrook (B)

4305 Cox Road, Glen Allen VA 23060
Telephone: (804) 894-9150 Identification: 770961
Accreditation: &SC

ECPI University-Richmond/Moorefield (C)

800 Moorefield Park Drive, Richmond VA 23236
Telephone: (804) 330-5533 Identification: 770958
Accreditation: &SC, CAHIIM

ECPI University-Roanoke (D)

5234 Airport Road, Ste 200, Roanoke VA 24012
Telephone: (540) 563-8000 Identification: 770959
Accreditation: &SC, ADNUR, MAAB

Edward Via College of Osteopathic Medicine (E)

2265 Kraft Drive, Blacksburg VA 24060
County: Montgomery FICE Identification: 037093
Unit ID: 442806
Telephone: (540) 231-4000 Carnegie Class: Spec-4-yr-Med
FAX Number: (540) 231-5252 Calendar System: Semester
URL: www.vcom.edu
Established: 2002 Annual Graduate Tuition & Fees: N/A
Enrollment: 2,123 Coed
Affiliation or Control: Independent Non-Profit IRS Status: 501(c)3
Highest Offering: Doctorate; No Undergraduates
Accreditation: OSTEO

01 President ... Dr. Dixie TOOKE-RAWLINS
05 Provost ... Dr. Dixie TOOKE-RAWLINS
03 Sr Vice President ... Dr. John LUCAS
10 Vice President Finance/CFO ... Mr. Chuck SWAHA
84 Vice Pres Recruitment ... Mr. William KING
26 VP Communication/Marketing ... Ms. Cindy SHEPARD RAWLINS
11 Vice President Operations ... Mr. Bill PRICE
30 VP College Development/Alumni Rels ... Mr. Thim CORVIN
46 Vice Provost for Research ... Dr. Gunnar BROLINSON
12 Dean Carolinas Campus ... Dr. Matthew CANNON
20 Dean Virginia Campus ... Dr. Jan M. WILLCOX
12 Dean Auburn Campus ... Dr. Heath PARKER
12 Dean Louisiana Campus ... Dr. Mark SANDERS
63 Dean MABS ... Dr. Brian W. HILL
100 Sr Exec Director Administration ... Ms. Carolyn CROY
15 Director of Human Resources ... Mr. Robbie HUDSON

Emory & Henry College (F)

PO Box 947, 30461 Garnand Drive,
Emory VA 24327-0947
County: Washington FICE Identification: 003709
Unit ID: 232025
Telephone: (276) 944-4121 Carnegie Class: Masters/M
FAX Number: (276) 944-6934 Calendar System: Semester
URL: www.ehc.edu
Established: 1836 Annual Undergrad Tuition & Fees: $35,100
Enrollment: 1,230 Coed
Affiliation or Control: United Methodist IRS Status: 501(c)3
Highest Offering: Doctorate
Accreditation: SC, ARCPA, CAEP, NURSE, OT, PTA

01 President ... Dr. John W. WELLS
43 VP for Admin/General Counsel ... Mr. Mark R. GRAHAM
05 Exec VP/Provost ... Dr. Michael J. PUGLISI
76 SVP/Dean School of Health Sciences ... Dr. Louise FINCHER
10 Chief Financial Officer ... Ms. Angie EDMONDSON
28 VP Diversity/Equity/Inclusion ... Mr. John HOLLOWAY
111 VP for Advancement ... Mr. Gregory C. MCMILLAN
26 VP for Enrollment/External Affairs ... Ms. Jennifer PEARCE
09 AVP Process/Effectiveness ... Mr. Gregory G. STEINER
100 Exec Dir of Strategic Initiatives ... Mr. Ryan BOWYER
41 Director of Athletics ... Ms. Anne CRUTCHFIELD
15 Director Human Resources ... Ms. Tracy PEERY
35 Dean of Students ... Ms. Tracey L. WRIGHT
121 Dean of Student Success ... Dr. Travis PROFFITT
20 Associate Provost ... Dr. Matthew FREDERICK
29 Director of Alumni Affairs ... Ms. Monica S. HOEL
37 Director of Financial Aid ... Ms. Scarlett BLEVINS
06 Registrar ... Ms. Tammy SHEETS
36 Director of Career Center ... Mr. Lee SVETE
38 Director Student Counseling ... Mr. Todd STANLEY
08 Librarian ... Ms. Ruth CASTILLO
18 Director of Facilities ... Mr. Scott E. WILLIAMS
40 Bookstore Manager ... Mr. Terry RICHARDSON
42 Chaplain ... Rev. Sharon WRIGHT
39 Director of Housing ... Ms. Samantha LOPEZ
19 Chief of Campus Police ... Mr. Scott POORE
25 Director for Research/Grants ... Ms. Bonnie BINKLEY
104 Director Study Abroad ... Dr. Celeste GAIA
105 Web Content Manager ... Ms. Rachael WILBUR
44 Director Annual Giving ... Ms. Ronan KING
122 Asst Dir Campus Life-Greek Life ... Ms. Sam AMOS

Fairfax University of America (G)

4401 Village Drive, Fairfax VA 22030
County: Fairfax FICE Identification: 041440
Unit ID: 460376
Telephone: (703) 591-7042 Carnegie Class: Bac-Diverse
FAX Number: (703) 591-7046 Calendar System: Semester
URL: www.fxua.edu
Established: 1998 Annual Undergrad Tuition & Fees: $10,328
Enrollment: 65 Coed
Affiliation or Control: Independent Non-Profit IRS Status: 501(c)3
Highest Offering: Master's
Accreditation: ACICS

01 President ... Dr. Ahmed ALWANI
05 Executive Dean of Academic Programs ... Mr. NS HASAN
108 Accreditation/Compliance Coord ... Mr. George RADO
11 Director of Operations/Facilities ... Mr. Bayarjargal BATTULGA

Faith Bible College (H)

6330 Newtown Road, Suite 211, Norfolk VA 23502
County: Independent City Identification: 667285
Telephone: (757) 423-2095 Carnegie Class: Not Classified
FAX Number: (757) 222-1341 Calendar System: Semester
URL: www.faithbiblecollege.com
Established: 1995 Annual Undergrad Tuition & Fees: N/A
Enrollment: N/A Coed
Affiliation or Control: Independent Non-Profit IRS Status: 501(c)3
Highest Offering: Associate Degree
Accreditation: BI

05 Interim Pres/Academic Dean ... Dr. Kevin NEWMAN
26 Director Community/Church Relations ... Capt. Dale PARKER
06 Registrar ... Ms. Dawn MARTIN
10 Business Manager ... Ms. Darla BOLGER

Ferrum College (I)

PO Box 1000, 215 Ferrum Mtn Road, Ferrum VA 24151
County: Franklin FICE Identification: 003711
Unit ID: 232089
Telephone: (540) 365-2121 Carnegie Class: Bac-Diverse
FAX Number: (540) 365-4269 Calendar System: Semester
URL: www.ferrum.edu
Established: 1913 Annual Undergrad Tuition & Fees: $36,695
Enrollment: 972 Coed
Affiliation or Control: United Methodist IRS Status: 501(c)3
Highest Offering: Master's
Accreditation: SC, SW

01 President ... Dr. David L. JOHNS
05 VP for Academic Affairs ... Dr. Kevin P. REILLY
10 VP for Business and Finance ... Ms. Barb D. HATCHER
111 Vice Pres Institutional Advancement ... Mr. Wilson PAINE
84 Senior Enrollment Officer ... Mr. Eric D. GRUNDMAN
32 VP Student Dev/Campus Life ... Ms. Angie L. DAHL
42 Campus Minister ... Dr. Laura ROBINSON
101 Spec Asst to Pres/Liaison to Board ... Ms. Courtney L. BROWN
06 Registrar ... Ms. Kimberly NAJDUCH
07 Dean of Admissions ... Mr. Jason D. BYRD
09 Director of Inst Research ... Vacant
08 Director Stanley Library ... Dr. Eric RECTOR
37 Director of Financial Aid ... Ms. Heather HOLLANDSWORTH
29 Director Alumni & Family Programs ... Mrs. Tracy S. HOLLEY
26 Director of Public Relations ... Vacant
41 Director of Athletics ... Mr. John SUTYAK
18 Director of Physical Plant ... Mr. Brad BISHOP
35 Dir Student Activities ... Mr. Justin MUSE
13 Dir of Network Services ... Mr. Eugene HACKER
15 Dir of Human Resources ... Vacant
40 Bookstore Manager ... Vacant
19 Chief of Ferrum College Police Dept ... Chief J. F. OWENS
36 Dir of Career Services ... Mrs. Leslie HOLDEN
88 Director of Academic Accessibility ... Ms. Nancy S. BEACH
91 Dir Administrative Computing ... Ms. Margaret DRAKEFORD
122 Coord Fraternity/Sorority Life ... Ms. Julie AINSLEY
58 Dir School of Graduate/Online Stds ... Dr. Sandra VIA
49 Dean Sch Arts/Sciences & Business ... Dr. Jason POWELL
83 Dean Sch Health Prof/Social Science ... Dr. Angie DAHL
30 Director of Development ... Mr. Burton C. SMITH

George Mason University (J)

4400 University Drive - MSN 3A1, Fairfax VA 22030-4444
County: Fairfax FICE Identification: 003749
Unit ID: 232186
Telephone: (703) 993-1000 Carnegie Class: DU-Highest
FAX Number: N/A Calendar System: Semester
URL: www.gmu.edu
Established: 1957 Annual Undergrad Tuition & Fees (In-State): $13,014
Enrollment: 38,541 Coed
Affiliation or Control: State IRS Status: 501(c)3
Highest Offering: Doctorate
Accreditation: SC, ART, CAATE, CAEP, CAHIIM, CAPRT, CEA, CLPSY, @DIET, EXSC, HSA, IPSY, LAW, MUS, NURSE, PH, SPAA, SW

01 President ... Dr. Gregory WASHINGTON
05 Provost & Executive VP ... Dr. Mark GINSBERG
10 Int SVP of Administration/Finance ... Ms. Deb DICKENSON
100 VP Strat Initiatives/Chief of Staff ... Mr. Kenneth WALSH
28 Int VP Compliance/Diversity/Ethics ... Dr. Dietra Y. TRENT
84 Vice Pres Enrollment Management ... Mr. David BURGE
18 Vice Pres for Facilities ... Mr. Frank STRIKE
86 VP Government & Community Relations ... Mr. Paul LIBERTY
111 VP Advancement/Alumni Rels/Fndn ... Ms. Trishana BOWDEN
13 VP Information Technology/CIO ... Mr. Kevin BOREK
32 Vice President for University Life ... Ms. Rose PASCARELL
46 Int Vice President for Research ... Ms. Aurali DADE
26 VP Communications & Marketing ... Mr. Paul ALLVIN
15 VP for Human Resources/Payroll ... Mr. Lester L. ARNOLD, SR.
43 University Counsel ... Mr. Brian WALTHER
45 Assoc VP for Business Services ... Mr. Bill DRACOS
21 Vice President for Finance ... Ms. Deb DICKENSON
20 Exec Dir Academic Innovation ... Dr. Charles KREITZER
20 Assoc Prov Acad Initiatives & Svcs ... Dr. Janette MUIR
103 AVP Innovation/Economic Development ... Ms. Paula SORRELL
88 Assoc Prov for Academic Admin ... Ms. Renate H. GUILFORD
88 Assoc Prov for a Sustainable Earth ... Dr. Cody EDWARDS
35 Exec Dir Office Student Involvement ... Ms. Lauren LONG
35 Assoc Vice Pres University Life ... Ms. Pamela L. PATTERSON
06 University Registrar ... Mr. Doug MCKENNA
37 Director Student Financial Aid ... Dr. Sandra TARBOX
36 Exec Dir Univ Career Services ... Ms. Saskia CAMPBELL
08 Dean of Libraries/Univ Librarian ... Mr. John G. ZENELIS
23 Exec Dir Student Health Svcs ... Dr. Lisa PARK
29 Assoc VP Alumni Relations ... Vacant
41 Asst VP/Dir Intercol Athletics ... Mr. Brad EDWARDS
108 Assoc Prov Inst Effectiveness/Plng ... Ms. Gesele DURHAM
19 Chief of Police ... Mr. Carl ROWAN
79 Dean Col Humanities/Social Sciences ... Ms. Ann ARDIS
61 Dean School of Law ... Dr. Henry BUTLER
80 Dean Schar School of Policy & Govt ... Dr. Mark ROZELL
50 Dean School of Business ... Dr. Maury PEIPERL
53 Int Dean Col of Educ & Human Dev ... Dr. Robert BAKER
54 Dean Volgenau School of Engineering ... Dr. Kenneth BALL
66 Dean College of Health & Human Svcs ... Dr. Germaine LOUIS
81 Assoc Dean College of Science ... Mr. Ali ANDALIBI
88 Dean Sch Conflict Analysis & Resol ... Dr. Alpaslan OZERDEM
88 Dean CVPA/Exec Dir HPAC ... Dr. Rick DAVIS
38 Assoc Dean/Chief Mental Health Ofcr ... Dr. Rachel WERNICKE
09 Asst Provost Institutional Research ... Ms. Angela DETLEV
96 Chief Procurement Officer ... Mr. Cliff SHORE
04 Director of Presidential Admin ... Ms. Sharon CULLEN
101 Exec Coord to Board of Visitors ... Ms. Sarah HANBURY
21 Assoc Director Finance & Business ... Ms. Maria FIORE
25 Assoc VP Research Services ... Mr. Mike LASKOFSKI
44 Dir Annual Giving/Ofc Advancement ... Vacant
102 Dir Corporate/Foundation Relations ... Ms. Mercedes PRICE
27 Assoc Vice President for Marketing ... Mr. Eric WOODALL
106 Director Digital Learning ... Dr. Faisal MAHMUD
90 Exec Dir Learning Support Svcs ... Ms. Joy TAYLOR
07 Assoc Dean of Admissions ... Mr. Darren TROXLER
88 Director of Strategic Real Estate ... Mr. Steve GOLDIN
114 AVP Strategic Planning & Budgeting ... Ms. Rene STEWART O'NEAL
122 Assc Dir Stdnt Involve-Greek Life ... Mr. Phil MCDANIEL

Hampden-Sydney College (K)

PO Box 128, Hampden-Sydney VA 23943-0667
County: Prince Edward FICE Identification: 003713
Unit ID: 232256
Telephone: (434) 223-6000 Carnegie Class: Bac-A&S
FAX Number: N/A Calendar System: Semester
URL: www.hsc.edu
Established: 1775 Annual Undergrad Tuition & Fees: $48,110
Enrollment: 881 Male
Affiliation or Control: Presbyterian Church (U.S.A.) IRS Status: 501(c)3
Highest Offering: Baccalaureate
Accreditation: SC

01 President ... Dr. John L. STIMPERT
05 Dean of the Faculty ... Dr. Walter M. MCDERMOTT
10 VP Business Affairs & Finance ... Mr. P. Kenneth COPELAND, JR.
111 VP for College Advancement ... Ms. Heather L. KRAJEWSKI
84 VP for Enrollment ... Mr. Jeffery S. NORRIS
32 Dean of Students ... Dr. Richard M. PANTELE
121 Director for Academic Success ... Ms. Lisa A. BURNS
41 Director of Athletics ... Mr. Chad E. EISELE
08 Director of the Library & Computing ... Ms. Shaunna E. HUNTER-MCKINNEY
06 Registrar ... Ms. Dawn L. CONGLETON
37 Director of Financial Aid ... Ms. Zita M. BARREE
29 Director of Alumni Relations ... Mr. Cameron MARSHALL
18 Director of Facilities Management ... Mr. Kevin MILLER
36 Dir Career Ed/Vocational Reflection ... Ms. Stephanie N. JOYNES
15 Director of Human Resources ... Ms. Sue V. CARTER
19 Dir Public Safety/Chief of Police ... Mr. T. Mark FOWLER
09 Assoc Dean Inst Effectiveness ... Dr. Christine C. ROSS
26 Director Communications & Marketing ... Mr. Gordon W. NEAL
21 Controller ... Ms. Cheryl HILL
35 Dir of Student Affairs Operations ... Ms. Sandy P. COOKE
28 Dean of Inclusive Excellence ... Mr. John HOLLEMON
25 Grant Administrator ... Mrs. Sachiyo DINMORE
104 Dir Global Education & Study Abroad ... Dr. Daniella WIDDOWS
04 Executiv Assistant to the President ... Ms. Angela T. CLARK
38 Director of Counseling Services ... Dr. Clarence MERCKERSON
07 Dean of Admissions ... Mr. Jason FERGUSON
122 Assc Dean Stdnts/Dir Greek Life ... Col. Dwayne BOWYER

Hampton University (L)

200 William R. Harvey Way, Hampton VA 23668
County: Independent City FICE Identification: 003714
Unit ID: 232265

Telephone: (757) 727-5000 Carnegie Class: DU-Mod
FAX Number: (757) 727-5085 Calendar System: Semester
URL: www.hamptonu.edu
Established: 1868 Annual Undergrad Tuition & Fees: $29,312
Enrollment: 3,516 Coed
Affiliation or Control: Independent Non-Profit IRS Status: 501(c)3
Highest Offering: Doctorate
Accreditation: **SC**, AAB, CACREP, CAEP, IACBE, #JOUR, MUS, NURSE, PTA, SP

01 President .... LTG. Darrell K. WILLIAMS, RET.
05 Chancellor & Provost .... Dr. JoAnn W. HAYSBERT
10 Vice Pres Business Affs/Treasurer .... Mrs. Doretha J. SPELLS
11 Vice Pres for Administrative Svcs .... Dr. Barbara L. INMAN
43 Vice President/General Counsel .... Atty. Faye HARDY-LUCAS
30 Vice Pres for Development .... Mrs. Evelyn GRAHAM
13 Vice President Info Technology .... Dr. Alissa HARRISON
100 Vice President & Exec Asst to Pres .... Mrs. Joy JEFFERSON
21 Asst VP Business Affs/Comptroller .... Mrs. Denise NICHOLS
20 Asst Provost Academic Affairs .... Dr. Pollie MURPHY
26 Asst VP for Marketing .... Vacant
46 Vice President for Research .... Dr. Neelam AZAD
32 Dean of Students .... Mr. Aleczander WHITFIELD
39 Director Residential Life/Housing .... Ms. Shawneequa JAMES
07 Dean of Admissions .... Mrs. Angela BOYD
06 Registrar .... Mrs. Jorsene COOPER
36 Dir Career Counsel/Planning Ctr .... Mrs. Bessie WILLIS
38 Director Counseling Center .... Dr. Kristie NORWOOD
08 Director Harvey Library .... Mrs. Tina ROLLINS
29 Director of Alumni Affairs .... Ms. Brint MARTIN
15 Director of Human Resources .... Ms. Rikki THOMAS
37 Financial Aid Officer .... Mr. Martin MILES
27 Director of University Relations .... Mr. Matthew WHITE
09 Dir Operational Analysis & Research .... Mr. Rashad JOYNER
42 University Chaplain .... Dr. Debra L. HAGGINS
18 Director Buildings & Grounds .... Mr. Randall HARDY
87 Director of Summer Sessions .... Dr. Pollie MURPHY
19 Chief of Campus Police .... Mr. David GLOVER
86 Director Government Relations .... Mr. Wilbert L. THOMAS
96 Asst Director of Purchasing .... Ms. Debra HARDEN
40 University Bookstore Manager .... Ms. Patricia KNIGHT
53 Dean School of Liberal Arts & Educ . Dr. Linda MALONE-COLON
66 Interim Dean School of Nursing .... Dr. Arlene MONTGOMERY
50 Dean School of Business .... Dr. Ziette HAYES
54 Dean Sch of Science/Engineering .... Dr. Joyce SHIRAZI
67 Dean School of Pharmacy .... Dr. Anand IYER
58 Dean the Graduate College .... Dr. Jerald DUMAS
60 Dean Scripps Howard Sch Journ/Comm .... Ms. Julia WILSON
81 Dean School of Science .... Dr. Isi ERO-TOLLIVER
106 Dean University College .... Dr. Aresta JOHNSON
41 Athletic Director .... Mr. Eugene MARSHALL

Hollins University (A)

PO Box 9707, Roanoke VA 24020-1688
County: Roanoke FICE Identification: 003715
Unit ID: 232308
Telephone: (540) 362-6000 Carnegie Class: Bac-A&S
FAX Number: (540) 362-6642 Calendar System: 4/1/4
URL: www.hollins.edu
Established: 1842 Annual Undergrad Tuition & Fees: $40,110
Enrollment: 795 Female
Affiliation or Control: Independent Non-Profit IRS Status: 501(c)3
Highest Offering: Master's
Accreditation: **SC**, CAEPT

01 President .... Dr. Mary D. HINTON
10 Executive VP and COO .... Ms. Kerry EDMONDS
05 Provost .... Dr. Laura MCLARY
111 Vice Pres for External Relations .... Vacant
84 Vice Pres Enrollment and Marketing .... Ms. Ashley BROWNING
32 Dean of Students .... Ms. Megan CANFIELD
58 VP for Graduate Programs .... Dr. Steven E. LAYMON
04 Executive Assistant to President .... Ms. Sheyonn L. BAKER
06 Registrar .... Vacant
08 Director of the Library .... Mr. Luke VILELLE
15 Director of Human Resources .... Ms. Alicia GODZWA
26 Director of Public Relations .... Mr. Jeff HODGES
29 Director of Alumnae Relations .... Ms. Lauren WALKER
36 Director Career Dev & Life Design .... Mr. Jeffrey WHITE
37 Director Financial Aid .... Ms. Autumn NORDSTROM
41 Director of Athletics .... Mr. Chris KILCOYNE
18 Director Plant Operations/Services .... Ms. Mae RAMSEY
104 Director International Programs .... Ms. Ramona R. KIRSCH
13 Chief Info Officer .... Mr. Brad OECHSLIN
19 Director Security/Safety .... Mr. David CARLSON
09 Director of Institutional Research .... Dr. Maliha ZAMAN
28 VP for Diversity .... Dr. Nakeshia WILLIAMS

Ivy Christian College (B)

9401 Mathy Drive, Suite 380, Fairfax VA 22031
County: Fairfax Identification: 667213
Telephone: (703) 425-4143 Carnegie Class: Not Classified
FAX Number: (703) 425-4148 Calendar System: Quarter
URL: www.ivy.edu
Established: 2006 Annual Undergrad Tuition & Fees: N/A
Enrollment: N/A Coed
Affiliation or Control: Independent Non-Profit IRS Status: 501(c)3
Highest Offering: Baccalaureate
Accreditation: **TRACS**

01 President .... Dr. David Y. PAK
05 Academic Dean .... Dr. David Y. PAK
10 Chief Financial/Operating Ofcr .... Mr. John YOO
32 Director of Student Affairs .... Mr. Byung KIM
07 Director of Admissions .... Ms. Nicole ARDELEAN
06 Registrar/Finance Officer .... Mrs. Yoomin KIM
09 Librarian .... Mr. Steven KROMPF

James Madison University (C)

800 S Main Street, Harrisonburg VA 22807-0001
County: Independent City FICE Identification: 003721
Unit ID: 232423
Telephone: (540) 568-6211 Carnegie Class: DU-Higher
FAX Number: N/A Calendar System: Semester
URL: www.jmu.edu
Established: 1908 Annual Undergrad Tuition & Fees (In-State): $12,330
Enrollment: 21,594 Coed
Affiliation or Control: State IRS Status: 501(c)3
Highest Offering: Doctorate
Accreditation: **SC**, ARCPA, ART, AUD, CAATE, CACREP, CAEP, DANCE, DIETD, IPSY, MUS, NURSE, OT, PSPSY, SP, SPAA, SW, THEA

01 President .... Mr. Jonathan R. ALGER
05 Provost/Senior VP Academic Affairs .... Dr. Heather COLTMAN
10 Interim VP Admin/Finance .... Ms. Towana MOORE
32 VP Student Affairs .... Dr. Timothy M. MILLER
111 Vice Pres University Advancement .... Dr. Nick LANGRIDGE
84 VP Access and Enrollment Mgmt .... Ms. Donna L. HARPER
13 AVP Info Tech/CIO .... Ms. Robin BRYAN
81 Dean College Science/Math .... Dr. Samantha PRINS
49 Dean College Arts/Letters .... Dr. Robert AGUIRRE
76 Dean Col of Health & Behav Studies .... Dr. Sharon LOVELL
50 Dean College of Business .... Dr. Michael BUSING
57 Dean College Visual Performing Arts .... Mr. Ruben GRACIANI
53 Dean College of Education .... Dr. Mark L'ESPERANCE
72 Dean College of Int Science & Engr .... Dr. Robert KOLVOORD
58 Dean Graduate School .... Dr. Linda THOMAS
97 Vice Provost University Programs .... Vacant
08 Dean Libraries .... Dr. Bethany NOWVISKIE
43 University Counsel .... Mr. Jack KNIGHT
114 Asst Vice Pres Budget Management .... Ms. Diane L. STAMP
07 AVP Admissions Office .... Ms. Melinda WOOD
37 AVP Financial Aid & Scholarships .... Mr. Brad BARNETT
15 Director Human Resources .... Mr. Chuck FLICK
09 Director Institutional Research .... Dr. Christopher D. OREM
41 Director of Athletics .... Mr. Jeffrey T. BOURNE
26 Exec Director of Communications .... Ms. Mary-Hope VASS
06 University Registrar .... Ms. Michele M. WHITE
19 Chief of Police .... Mr. Anthony D. MATOS
31 Exec Dir Campus & Cmty Programs .... Mr. Art DEAN
29 Director Alumni Relations .... Ms. Carrie COMBS
110 Sr Dir of Advancement/Marketing .... Ms. Pam BROCK
04 Admin Assistant to the President .... Ms. Anita C. WESTFALL
102 President/CEO JMU Foundation .... Mr. Warren K. COLEMAN
104 Director Study Abroad .... Ms. Kathleen SENSABAUGH
25 Director Sponsored Programs .... Ms. Tamara T. HATCH
39 Interim Director Residence Life .... Ms. Kathleen CAMPBELL
44 Dir Advancement/Gifts & Records .... Ms. Gretchen H. ARMENTROUT
86 Director Government Relations .... Ms. Caitlyn READ
96 Director of Procurement .... Ms. Catherine B. WEAVER
100 Chief of Staff .... Dr. Mike DAVIS
28 AVP Diversity/Equity & Inclusion .... Dr. Brent LEWIS
122 Assc Dir Stdnt Life-Greek Life .... Ms. Pamela STEELE

The John Leland Center for Theological Studies (D)

1306 N Highland Street, Arlington VA 22201
County: Arlington Identification: 666340
Telephone: (703) 812-4757 Carnegie Class: Not Classified
FAX Number: (703) 812-4764 Calendar System: Other
URL: www.leland.edu
Established: 1998 Annual Graduate Tuition & Fees: N/A
Enrollment: N/A Coed
Affiliation or Control: Baptist IRS Status: 501(c)3
Highest Offering: Master's; No Undergraduates
Accreditation: **THEOL**

01 President .... RevDr. Bill H. SMITH
05 Academic Dean .... Dr. John LEE
04 Executive Assistant .... Ms. Abbie TOLBERT
08 Librarian .... Ms. Monica LEAK
06 Registrar .... Ms. Belinda BARNETT
84 Director of Enrollment .... Ms. Mindy STEWART
10 Director of Finance .... Mr. Mel HARRIS

Liberty University (E)

1971 University Boulevard, Lynchburg VA 24515
County: Independent City FICE Identification: 020530
Unit ID: 232557
Telephone: (434) 582-2000 Carnegie Class: DU-Mod
FAX Number: N/A Calendar System: Semester
URL: www.liberty.edu
Established: 1971 Annual Undergrad Tuition & Fees: $21,587
Enrollment: 93,349 Coed
Affiliation or Control: Other IRS Status: 501(c)3
Highest Offering: Doctorate
Accreditation: **SC**, AAB, ACBSP, CAATE, CACREP, CAEPN, COARC, COSMA, EXSC, FEPAC, LAW, MUS, NURSE, OSTEO, SW, THEOL

01 President .... Dr. Jerry PREVO
05 Provost .... Dr. Scott HICKS
106 Provost for Online Programs .... Mr. Shawn D. AKERS
20 Vice Provost .... Dr. Ronald E. HAWKINS
32 Sr Vice President Student Affairs .... Dr. Mark L. HINE
10 Chief Financial Officer .... Dr. Robert L. RITZ
84 Exec VP of Enrollment Mgmt & Mktg .... Mr. Ron KENNEDY
15 Exec VP Human Resources .... Mr. Steve FOSTER
42 Campus Pastor .... Mr. Jonathan FALWELL
37 VP of Student Financial Services .... Mr. Matt COOPER
26 VP of Marketing .... Ms. Kristin CONRAD
108 AVP for Institutional Effectiveness .... Mr. H. Skip KASTROLL
13 Chief Information Officer .... Mr. John GAUGER
06 University Registrar .... Mr. Jason BYRD
43 General Counsel .... Mr. David M. CORRY
08 Dean Jerry Falwell Library .... Mrs. Angela RICE
80 Dean School of Govt .... Mr. Robert HURT
18 Sr VP Campus Facilities & Transport .... Mr. Charles SPENCE
88 VP of Major Construction .... Mr. Daniel DETER
30 VP of Development .... Mr. Jim NICHOLS
41 Director of Athletics .... Mr. Ian MCCAW
49 Dean College of Arts & Sciences .... Dr. Roger D. SCHULTZ
83 Dean School of Behavioral Sciences .... Dr. Kenyon KNAPP
50 Dean School of Business .... Dr. Dave BRAT
57 Dean School of Comm & the Arts .... Dr. Scott HAYES
97 Dean CASAS .... Dr. Brian YATES
73 Interim Dean School of Divinity .... Dr. Troy TEMPLE
53 Interim Dean School of Education .... Dr. Deanna KEITH
88 VP of Campus Recreation .... Mr. Chris MISIANO
88 VP Designated Off Campus Facilities .... Mr. Scott STARNES
19 Chief of Police LUPD .... Col. Richard HINKLEY
54 Dean School of Engineering .... Dr. Mark HORSTEMEYER
97 Dean College of General Studies .... Dr. Ester WARREN
28 VP for Equity & Inclusion/CDO .... Mr. Greg DOWELL
61 Dean School of Law .... Dr. Keith FAULKNER
88 Dean School of Aeronautics .... Dr. Rick ROOF
88 Dir Center for Teaching Excellence .... Dr. Shawn BIELICKI
58 Admin Dean for Grad Education .... Dr. David CALLAND
76 Dean School of Health Sciences .... Dr. Ralph LINSTRA
63 Dean College of Osteopathic Med .... Dr. Peter BELL
64 Interim Dean School of Music .... Dr. Stephen MULLER
35 Assoc Dean of Students .... Dr. Mark HYDE
66 Dean School of Nursing .... Dr. Shanna AKERS
04 Exec Assistant to the President .... Ms. Amanda STANLEY
07 Director of UG Admissions .... Mr. Chris JONES
29 Sr Alumni Relations Officer .... Mr. Jeremy OWEN
36 Executive Director Career Services .... Mr. Richard DIDDAMS
38 Exec Director Student Counseling .... Mr. Michael KUNZINGER
96 Chief Procurement Administrator .... Mr. Americus GILL
09 Director of Institutional Research .... Ms. Sue MISJUNS

Longwood University (F)

201 High Street, Farmville VA 23909-1801
County: Prince Edward FICE Identification: 003719
Unit ID: 232566
Telephone: (434) 395-2000 Carnegie Class: Masters/M
FAX Number: (434) 395-2635 Calendar System: Semester
URL: www.longwood.edu
Established: 1839 Annual Undergrad Tuition & Fees (In-State): $13,910
Enrollment: 4,841 Coed
Affiliation or Control: State IRS Status: 501(c)3
Highest Offering: Master's
Accreditation: **SC**, CAATE, CACREP, CAEP, CAPRT, EXSC, MUS, NURSE, SP, SW, THEA

01 President .... Mr. W. Taylor REVELEY, IV
05 Provost/Vice Pres Academic Affairs .... Dr. Larissa SMITH
10 Vice Pres Administration & Finance .... Ms. Louise WALLER
32 Int Vice Pres Student Affairs .... Mr. Cameron PATTERSON
111 VP for Institutional Advancement .... Ms. Courtney HODGES
45 VP for Strategic Operations .... Ms. Victoria KINDON
13 Chief Information Officer .... Ms. Victoria KINDON
84 Assoc VP Enrollment Management .... Dr. Jennifer K. GREEN
26 AVP Marketing/Communications/Engage .... Mr. Dave HOOPER
09 Director Assessment/Inst Research .... Dr. David LEHR
06 Registrar .... Mrs. Susan HINES
08 Dean of Library .... Mr. Brent ROBERTS
28 Director Multicultural Affairs .... Mr. Jonathan E. PAGE
38 Director Student Counseling .... Dr. Maureen J. WALLS-MCKAY
121 Assoc Dir Campus Career Engagement .... Ms. Megan MILLER
37 Sr Assoc Director Financial Aid .... Ms. Sharon BIGGERS
15 Assoc VP Human Resources .... Ms. Lisa MOONEY
100 Chief of Staff/Vice President .... Mr. Justin POPE

Mary Baldwin University (G)

318 Prospect Street, Staunton VA 24401
County: Augusta FICE Identification: 003723
Unit ID: 232672
Telephone: (540) 887-7000 Carnegie Class: DU-Mod
FAX Number: (540) 886-5561 Calendar System: Other
URL: www.marybaldwin.edu
Established: 1842 Annual Undergrad Tuition & Fees: $31,110
Enrollment: 2,110 Coed
Affiliation or Control: Presbyterian Church (U.S.A.) IRS Status: 501(c)3
Highest Offering: Doctorate
Accreditation: **SC**, ANEST, ARCPA, CAEP, NURSE, OT, PTA, SW

01 President .... Dr. Pamela FOX
05 Interim Provost/Chief Academic Ofcr ... Dr. Tynisha WILLINGHAM
10 VP of Administration/CFO/Treasurer .... Mr. Sean S. SIMPLICIO

84 VP Enrollment Mgmt ... Mr. Matt MUNSEY
111 VP University Advancement ... Mr. Charles E. DAVIS, III
26 Assoc VP of Marketing ... Ms. Beth REABOLD
76 VP MDCHS/Chief Health Officer ... Dr. Deb GREUBEL
32 VP for Student Engagement ... Dr. Ernest E. JEFFRIES
28 Chief Diversity Officer ... Rev. Andrea CORNELL-SCOTT
88 Commandant VWIL/Sr Advisor to Pres ... BGen. Teresa A. DJURIC
09 Institutional Report/Research Coord ... Vacant
13 Dir of Enterprise Systems Mgmt ... Mr. Lee REID
06 Registrar ... Ms. Sheila F. TOLLEY
08 Director of Library ... Ms. Carol CREAGER
49 Dean of College of Arts & Sciences ... Dr. Martha J. WALKER
50 Dean of Col Business & Prof Stds ... Dr. Joseph R. SPRANGEL, JR.
53 Dean of College of Education ... Dr. Rachel POTTER
57 Dean of Visual & Perform Arts ... Dr. Paul MENZER
15 Director of Human Resources ... Ms. Shelly IRVINE
18 AVP of Facilities & Capital Plng ... Vacant
114 Dir of Budgets/Business Operation ... Vacant
29 Exec Director of Alumni Engagement ... Ms. Adrienne L. TEAGUE
36 Director Career to Career Center ... Ms. Nell DESMOND
37 AVP Enroll Mgmt/Dir Financial Aid ... Ms. Megan SPETH
04 Executive Presidential Assistant ... Ms. Sharon S. BOSSERMAN
41 Athletic Director ... Mr. Thomas P. BYRNES
19 Director Security/Safety ... Mr. Thomas L. BYERLY

Marymount University (A)

2807 N Glebe Road, Arlington VA 22207
County: Arlington FICE Identification: 003724
Unit ID: 232706
Telephone: (703) 522-5600 Carnegie Class: DU-Mod
FAX Number: (703) 284-1637 Calendar System: Semester
URL: www.marymount.edu
Established: 1950 Annual Undergrad Tuition & Fees: $34,540
Enrollment: 3,294 Coed
Affiliation or Control: Roman Catholic IRS Status: 501(c)3
Highest Offering: Doctorate
Accreditation: SC, ACBSP, CACREP, CAEP, CIDA, HSA, NURSE, PTA

00 Chair Board of Trustees ... Dr. Edward BERSOFF
01 President ... Dr. Irma BECERRA
125 President Emeritus ... Dr. Matthew SHANK
05 Provost & Senior VP Acad Affairs ... Dr. Hesham EL-REWINI
10 Vice Pres Finance and Operations ... Mr. Barry HARTE
26 Interim Vice Pres Marketing & Comm ... Dr. Irma BECERRA
32 VP Enroll Mgmt/Student Affairs ... Dr. William BISSET
111 Vice Pres Univ Advancement ... Mr. Dennis SLON
20 Vice Provost Academic Affairs ... Dr. Stephanie ELLIS FOSTER
09 Asst Prov Plng/Inst Effectiveness ... Dr. Richard HESS
84 Assoc VP Enrollment Management ... Mr. Evan LIPP
46 Assoc Vice Pres of Research ... Dr. Rita WONG
106 Assoc Prov Online & Grad Education ... Dr. Jason CRAIG
13 Assoc Vice Pres & CIO ... Mr. Carl WHITMAN
15 CHRO & Asst VP Human Resources ... Ms. Kendra GILLESPIE
113 Bursar/Director Stdnt Fin Affairs ... Ms. Karen WHITE
21 Asst VP Fin Affairs & Controller ... Ms. Robin WHITFIELD
23 Asst VP Student Health & Well-Being ... Dr. Laura FINKELSTEIN
39 Asst VP Res Life/Student Engag ... Mr. Richard MCNAB
109 Asst VP Campus Services ... Mr. Paul EASTON
121 Asst VP Student Success ... Dr. Michelle STEINER
88 Asst Vice Provost for Acad Affairs ... Dr. Louis FRISENDA
06 University Registrar ... Dr. Meghan ARIAS
08 University Librarian ... Ms. Alison GREGORY
50 Dean Col Bus/Innov/Leadership/Tech ... Mr. Jonathan ABERMAN
76 Dean College of Health & Education ... Dr. Kenneth HARWOOD
49 Dean College of Science/Humanities ... Dr. Marnel NILES GOINS
04 Admin Asst to President ... Ms. Allison CROSS
104 Asst VP Center Global Engagement ... Mr. Victor BETANCOURT SANTIAGO
07 Director Admissions ... Ms. Aubrey WEAVER
14 Director IT Support Services ... Mr. Oscar VENTURA-MENDOZA
16 Sr Director Human Resources ... Ms. Julie LLOYD
18 Assistant Vice President ... Ms. Onyel BHOLA
25 Dir Office of Sponsored Programs ... Ms. Janine BURGESS
30 Director Prospect Management ... Ms. Michelle RYDER
31 Director Saints Center for Service ... Vacant
36 Director Career Development ... Mr. Joe GEBBIE
37 Director Financial Aid ... Ms. Keia BROWN
38 Director Student Counseling ... Ms. Allana TAYLOR
41 Asst VP & Athletics Director ... Ms. Jill MCCABE
42 Chaplain ... Fr. Gabriel MUTERU
85 Dir International Students/Scholars ... Ms. Ashley BUS MORGAN
91 Dir Admin Information Services ... Ms. Colleen RYAN
92 Director Honors Program ... Dr. Stacy LOPRESTI-GOODMAN
96 Sr Dir Procurement & Payment Svcs ... Mr. Michael ROBINSON
114 Director Insurance & Risk Mgmt ... Ms. Pamela RYPKEMA
118 Sr HR Dir Operations Total Rewards ... Mrs. Paula POLSON
119 Director Infrastructure & Security ... Mr. David LUTES
120 Director Instructional Design ... Dr. Joseph PROVENZANO
88 Director Enrollment Support ... Ms. April COZINE
88 Director Student Access Services ... Mr. Sven JONES
88 Director Student Health Services ... Ms. Jennifer GAGNON
88 Dir Wellness Educ/Interven/Preven ... Ms. Aprile PRELLER
40 Manager Marymount Univ Bookstore ... Mr. Keith REILLY
105 Webmaster ... Mr. Jaime GAONA
29 Dir Alumni Engagement/Annual Giving ... Ms. Sarah ROSE
28 Int Dir Diversity/Equity & Inclus ... Dr. Delario LINDSEY

Norfolk State University (B)

700 Park Avenue, Norfolk VA 23504-8000
County: Independent City FICE Identification: 003765
Unit ID: 232937
Telephone: (757) 823-8600 Carnegie Class: Masters/M
FAX Number: (757) 823-2067 Calendar System: Semester
URL: www.nsu.edu
Established: 1935 Annual Undergrad Tuition & Fees (In-State): $9,622
Enrollment: 5,457 Coed
Affiliation or Control: State IRS Status: 501(c)3
Highest Offering: Doctorate
Accreditation: SC, CAEPN, CLPSY, DIETD, JOUR, KIN, MUS, NAIT, NUR, SW

01 President ... Dr. Javaune M. ADAMS-GASTON
101 Executive Advisor to Pres & BOV ... Mr. Eric W. CLAVILLE
05 Provost/Vice Pres Academic Affs ... Dr. DoVeanna FULTON
10 Vice Pres Finance and Admin ... Dr. Gerald E. HUNTER
111 Vice Pres Univ Advancement ... Mr. Clifford PORTER
32 Vice Pres Student Affairs ... Dr. Leonard E. BROWN
11 Vice Pres Operations ... Dr. Justin L. MOSES
21 AVP/University Controller ... Mrs. Karla J. AMAYA GORDON
43 University Counsel ... Ms. Pamela F. BOSTON
84 AVP Enrollment Management ... Dr. Juan M. ALEXANDER
38 Executive Dir Health & Wellness ... Dr. Vanessa C. JENKINS
06 Registrar ... Mr. Michael CARPENTER
08 Dean Library Services ... Mr. Don ESSEX
37 Director of Financial Aid ... Dr. Melissa BARNES
88 AVP Operations ... Dr. Alisha BAZEMORE
15 AVP/Chief HR Officer ... Dr. Karen H. PRUDEN
29 Dir Alumni Relations/Annual Giving ... Ms. Michelle D. HILL
49 Acting Dean College Liberal Arts ... Dr. Tommy BOGGER
50 Dean School of Business ... Mr. Glenn R. CARRINGTON
81 Dean Science/Engr/Technology ... Dr. Michael KEEVE
70 Dean of Social Work ... Dr. Isiah MARSHALL
92 Dean Honors College ... Dr. Khadijah O. MILLER
58 Dean of Graduate Studies & Research ... Dr. George E. MILLER, III
86 Advisor to Pres Govt Relations ... Mr. Eric CLAVILLE
26 AVP Communications & Marketing ... Ms. Stevalynn R. ADAMS
09 Dir Institutional Research ... Mr. Ephraim BENNETT
28 AVP for Campus Life & Diversity ... Dr. Faith M. FITZGERALD
41 Athletics Director ... Ms. Melody WEBB
18 Assoc Vice Pres Facilities Mgmt ... Mr. Anton KASHIRI
85 Dir Intl & Disability Services ... Dr. Beverly HARRIS
35 Dean of Students ... Ms. Michelle D. MARABLE
35 Assoc Vice Pres for Student Affairs ... Mrs. Bonisha PORTER
13 Chief Information Technology Office ... Ms. Sandra MONROE-DAVIS
19 Interim Chief of Police ... Mr. Brian COVINGTON
28 Exec Dir Inst Equity & EEO ... Mr. James ROBINSON
96 Director Procurement Svcs ... Ms. Ruby SPICER
100 Chief of Staff ... Ms. Tanya WHITE

† Member of Virginia Consortium for Professional Psychology.

Old Dominion University (C)

5115 Hampton Boulevard, Norfolk VA 23529-0001
County: Independent City FICE Identification: 003728
Unit ID: 232982
Telephone: (757) 683-3000 Carnegie Class: DU-Highest
FAX Number: (757) 683-4505 Calendar System: Semester
URL: www.odu.edu
Established: 1930 Annual Undergrad Tuition & Fees (In-State): $10,800
Enrollment: 24,286 Coed
Affiliation or Control: State IRS Status: 501(c)3
Highest Offering: Doctorate
Accreditation: SC, ANEST, CAATE, CACREP, CAEP, CAPRT, CLPSY, CSHSE, CYTO, DH, EXSC, LIB, MLS, MUS, NMT, NURSE, PH, PTA, SP, SPAA

01 President ... Dr. Brian O. HEMPHILL
05 Provost/VP Academic Affairs ... Dr. Austin O. AGHO
10 Vice Pres Administration & Finance ... Mr. Chad A. REED
46 Vice President for Research ... Dr. Morris W. FOSTER
15 Vice Pres for Human Resources ... Ms. September C. SANDERLIN
111 Vice Pres University Advancement ... Mr. Alonzo C. BRANDON
32 VP Student Engage/Enroll Svcs ... Dr. Donald M. STANSBERRY
100 Chief of Staff/VP Strategic Opers ... Ms. Ashley L. SCHUMAKER
88 Vice Prov Faculty Affs/Strat Init ... Dr. Katherine W. HAWKINS
20 Vice Provost Academic Affairs ... Dr. Brian K. PAYNE
20 Assoc Vice Pres Academic Affairs ... Ms. Nina R. GONSER
88 Asst VP Regional Higher Educ Ctrs ... Ms. Renee E. OLANDER
56 Assoc VP Distance Learning ... Mr. Andrew R. CASIELLO
84 Assoc Vice Pres Enrollment Mgmt ... Ms. Jane H. DANE
44 Assoc Vice Pres for Advancement ... Mr. Daniel J. GENARD
124 Assoc VP Student Engagement ... Dr. Johnny W. YOUNG
109 Dir Webb Center/Auxiliary/Bus Svcs ... Ms. Shannon M. HURT
21 Asst VP Finance/Univ Controller ... Ms. Mary C. DENEEN
13 Assoc Vice Pres University Svcs/CIO ... Mr. James R. WATERFIELD
31 Assoc VP Strategic Operations ... Ms. Karen F. MEIER
20 Asst VP Undergraduate Studies ... Ms. Judith M. BOWMAN
29 Assoc Vice Pres of Alumni Rels ... Ms. Joy L. JEFFERSON
26 AVP Strategic Comm/Marketing ... Vacant
58 Vice Prov/Dean The Graduate School ... Dr. Robert WOJTOWICZ
49 Interim Dean College Arts & Letters ... Dr. Laura DELBRUGGE
81 Dean College of Sciences ... Dr. Gail DODGE
76 Dean College of Health Sciences ... Dr. Bonnie VAN LUNEN
50 Dean Strome College of Business ... Dr. Jeff F. TANNER
53 Dean Darden College of Education ... Dr. Tammi F. DICE
54 Dean College Engineering/Tech ... Dr. Kenneth J. FRIDLEY
92 Dean Honors College ... Dr. David D. METZGER
121 Exec Dir Acad Success/Init/Support ... Ms. Marissa A. JIMENEZ
93 Exec Dir of Intercultural Relations ... Ms. Lesa C. CLARK
43 Asst Attorney General/Univ Counsel ... Mr. Allen T. WILSON
85 Senior International Officer ... Dr. Paul CURRANT
08 Dean University Libraries ... Mr. Timothy HACKMAN
06 University Registrar ... Mr. Humberto PORTELLEZ
07 Asst VP Enroll/Exec Dir Admissions ... Dr. J. Christopher FLEMING
41 Director of Athletics ... Dr. C. Wood SELIG
37 Director Student Financial Aid ... Ms. Vera E. RIDDICK
88 Director Military Affairs ... Mr. Robert E. CLARK
38 Interim Director Counseling Svcs ... Dr. Joy HIMMEL
23 Director Student Health Services ... Dr. Darylnet LYTTLE
85 Deputy Dir International Programs ... Ms. Kasie C. REYES
88 Assoc VP for Learning - SEES ... Dr. Bridget K. WEIKEL
18 Asst VP for Facilities Management ... Vacant
19 Interim Chief of Police ... Mr. Garrett L. SHELTON
28 Int Asst VP Inst Equity/Diversity ... Dr. Veleka S. GATLING
96 Director of Procurement Services ... Ms. Etta A. HENRY
94 Dir Women & Gender Equity Center ... Ms. La Wanza LETT-BREWINGTON
16 Asst VP for Human Resources ... Ms. JaRenae E. WHITEHEAD
40 University Bookstore Manager ... Ms. Rhyannon POTTER
04 Special Asst to the President ... Ms. Velvet L. GRANT
86 Assoc VP Governmental Relations ... Ms. Annie K. GIBSON
36 Director Career Development Svcs ... Vacant
88 Exec Dir Student Eng & Trad Fam Pgm ... Vacant
09 Director of Institutional Research ... Dr. Alona SMOLOVA
101 Univ Policy Mgr/Sec Bd of Visitors ... Ms. Donna W. MEEKS
103 AVP Institute Innov/Entrepreneur ... Vacant
104 Deputy Director Study Abroad ... Mr. Michael W. DEAN
108 Dir Inst Effectiveness & Assessment ... Mr. David SHIRLEY
88 Exec Dir Stdnt Engagement/Tradition ... Vacant
114 University Budget Officer ... Mr. Bruce AIRD

† Member of Virginia Consortium for Professional Psychology.

Patrick Henry College (D)

Ten Patrick Henry Circle, Purcellville VA 20132
County: Loudoun FICE Identification: 039513
Unit ID: 451927
Telephone: (540) 338-1776 Carnegie Class: Bac-A&S
FAX Number: (540) 441-8709 Calendar System: Semester
URL: www.phc.edu
Established: 2000 Annual Undergrad Tuition & Fees: $28,400
Enrollment: 340 Coed
Affiliation or Control: Non-denominational IRS Status: 501(c)3
Highest Offering: Baccalaureate
Accreditation: SC, TRACS

01 President ... Mr. Jack HAYE
125 Chancellor Emeritus ... Dr. Michael P. FARRIS
03 Executive Vice President ... Mr. Howard SCHMIDT
10 VP for Administration & Finance ... Mr. Daryl WOLKING
09 VP for Institutional Effectiveness ... Mr. Rodney J. SHOWALTER
111 Vice President for Advancement ... Mr. Tom ZIEMNICK
05 Dean of Academic Affairs ... Dr. Mark MITCHELL
32 Dean of Student Affairs ... Ms. Sandra K. CORBITT
08 Director of the Library ... Ms. Sara E. PENSGARD
07 Director of Student Recruitment ... Mr. Stephen PIERCE
26 Director of Communications ... Mr. Stephen C. ALLEN

Radford University (E)

801 East Main Street, Radford VA 24142
County: Radford City FICE Identification: 003732
Unit ID: 233277
Telephone: (540) 831-5000 Carnegie Class: DU-Mod
FAX Number: N/A Calendar System: Semester
URL: www.radford.edu
Established: 1910 Annual Undergrad Tuition & Fees (In-State): $11,416
Enrollment: 10,695 Coed
Affiliation or Control: State IRS Status: 170(c)1
Highest Offering: Doctorate
Accreditation: SC, ARCPA, ART, CAATE, CACREP, CAEP, CAPRT, CIDA, COARC, COPSY, DANCE, DIETD, EMT, MLS, MUS, NURSE, OT, OTA, PTA, SP, SURGT, SW, THEA

01 President ... Dr. Bret S. DANILOWICZ
05 Interim Provost/Senior VP Acad Affs ... Dr. Marten DENBOER
10 Interim VP Finance & Admin/CFO ... Ms. Stephanie JENNELLE
32 VP Student Affairs ... Dr. Susan TRAGESER
111 Interim VP for Adv & Univ Relations ... Ms. Penny WHITE
84 VP Enrollment Management ... Mr. Craig CORNELL
50 Dean Davis Col Business & Econ ... Dr. Joy BHADURY
53 Dean Col Education & Human Dev ... Dr. Tamara WALLACE
76 Dean Waldron Col Health/Human Svcs ... Dr. Kenneth COX
79 Dean Col Humanities/Behav Sci ... Dr. Matthew SMITH
81 Dean Artis College Sci & Tech ... Dr. Steven BACHRACH
57 Dean Col Visual & Performing Arts ... Dr. Stephanie CAULDER
58 Dean Graduate Studies/Research ... Dr. Benjamin D. CALDWELL
66 Interim Dean School of Nursing ... Dr. Wendy DOWNEY
07 Dean of Admissions ... Mr. Anthony GRAHAM
08 Interim Dean of the Library ... Dr. Laura JACOBSEN
06 Registrar ... Mr. Matthew BRUNNER
37 Director of Financial Aid ... Ms. Allison PRATT
29 Executive Dir of Alumni Relations ... Ms. Laura TURK
41 Director Intercollegiate Athletics ... Mr. Robert LINEBURG
15 Interim Asst VP for Human Resources ... Ms. Margie VEST
35 AVP Student Affs/Dean of Student ... Ms. Angela MITCHELL
19 Chief of Police ... Dr. Eric PLUMMER
09 Director of Institutional Research ... Dr. Eric LOVIK
101 Secretary to the Board of Visitors ... Ms. Karen CASTEELE
88 VP for Econ Dev & Corporate Educ ... Dr. Angela M. JOYNER
102 Dir Foundation/Corporate Relations ... Mr. Benjamin HILL
28 Director of Institutional Equity ... Dr. Andrea ZUSCHIN
44 Director Annual Giving ... Ms. Carolyn CLAYTON
86 Exec Director of Govt Relations ... Ms. Lisa GHIDOTTI
96 Exec Director of Strategic Sourcing ... Ms. Kimberly DULANEY

104 Asst Prov Ctr Global Educ & Engage .... Mr. Ismael J. BETANCOURT VELEZ
108 Dir Institutional Effectiveness .... Dr. Jessica STOWELL
11 Exec Director of Administration .... Ms. Heather MIANO
18 Asst VP for Facilities Management .... Mr. Jorge COARTNEY
25 Dir Sponsored Programs/Grants .... Mr. Thomas CRUISE
110 Assoc VP for Advancement .... Mr. Tom LILLARD
36 Dir Center for Career & Talent Dev .... Mr. Jason CLAYTON
38 Director Student Counseling Service .... Mr. Brian LUSK
39 Dir Housing & Residential Life .... Dr. Kendall PETE
122 Coord Fraternity/Sorority Life .... Mr. Kennedi JARVI
13 Assoc VP for Info Technology & CIO .... Mr. Ed OAKES

Randolph College (A)

2500 Rivermont Avenue, Lynchburg VA 24503-1555
County: Independent City FICE Identification: 003734
Unit ID: 233301
Telephone: (434) 947-8000 Carnegie Class: Bac-A&S
FAX Number: (434) 947-8139 Calendar System: Semester
URL: www.randolphcollege.edu
Established: 1891 Annual Undergrad Tuition & Fees: $25,610
Enrollment: 566 Coed
Affiliation or Control: Independent Non-Profit IRS Status: 501(c)3
Highest Offering: Master's
Accreditation: SC, CAEP

01 President .... Ms. Sue OTT ROWLANDS
05 VP Academic Affs & Dean of College .... Vacant
111 Vice Pres Institutional Advancement .... Ms. Farah MARKS
10 Vice Pres Finance & Administration .... Mr. Jonathan TYREE
32 Dean of Students .... Mr. Christopher LEMASTERS
07 Dean of Admissions .... Mr. Travis CARTER
100 Special Assistant to the President .... Mr. Steve WILLIS
20 Associate Dean of the College .... Ms. Bunny GOODJOHN
29 Director Alumnae & Alumni Relations .... Mr. Ludo LEMAITRE
09 VP for Institutional Effectiveness .... Dr. John F. KEENER
15 Director Human Resources .... Ms. Nickcole MAYNARD-ERRAMI
18 Chief Facilities/Physical Plant .... Mr. John LEARY
38 Director Student Counseling .... Ms. Jennifer BONDURANT
08 Librarian .... Ms. Lisa BROUGHMAN
06 Registrar .... Dr. John KEENER
37 Director Financial Aid .... Ms. Ashley NICKELL
36 Director of Career Development .... Ms. Maegan FALLEN
13 Director of Information Technology .... Vacant
04 Administrative Asst to President .... Ms. Cindy LYONS
19 Director Security/Safety .... Mr. Kris IRWIN
41 Athletic Director .... Mr. Thomas GALBRAITH
26 Chief Public Relations/Marketing .... Ms. Brenda EDSON

Randolph-Macon College (B)

114 College Ave, Ashland, Ashland VA 23005
County: Hanover FICE Identification: 003733
Unit ID: 233295
Telephone: (804) 752-7200 Carnegie Class: Bac-A&S
FAX Number: (804) 752-7231 Calendar System: Other
URL: www.rmc.edu
Established: 1830 Annual Undergrad Tuition & Fees: $43,940
Enrollment: 1,554 Coed
Affiliation or Control: United Methodist IRS Status: 501(c)3
Highest Offering: Master's
Accreditation: SC, #ARCPA, CAEP, NURSE

01 President .... Mr. Robert R. LINDGREN
05 Provost/VP for Academic Affairs .... Dr. Alisa J. ROSENTHAL
10 Vice Pres of Admin & Finance .... Mr. Paul DAVIES
111 Vice Pres for College Advancement .... Ms. Diane M. LOWDER
84 Vice Pres for Enroll/Admiss/Fin Aid .... Dr. David L. LESESNE
32 Vice President for Student Affairs .... Dr. Grant L. AZDELL
04 Executive Assistant to the Pres .... Mr. Tim BULLIS
07 Director of Admissions .... Ms. Erin SLATER
29 Exec Director Alumni Relations .... Ms. Rhonda TOUSSAINT
26 Assoc VP Marketing/Communications .... Ms. Beth CAMPBELL
37 Director of Financial Aid .... Mrs. Julie HICKMAN-GODOY
13 CIO and ITS Director .... Mr. Kirk BAUMBACH
06 Registrar .... Mrs. Alana DAVIS
38 Director of Counseling Services .... Dr. Beth SCHUBERT
09 Director of Institutional Research .... Dr. Katherine D. WALKER
18 Dir of Operations & Physical Plant .... Mr. John HERRON
42 Chaplain .... Rev. Kendra S. GRIMES
19 Director of Campus Safety .... Mr. Maurice J. KIELY
41 Athletic Director .... Mr. Jeffrey S. BURNS
15 Director Human Resources .... Mrs. Sharon S. JACKSON
21 Assistant VP of Finance .... Ms. Denise WATKINS
20 Associate Dean of the College .... Dr. Lauren C. BELL
36 Director of Professional Develop .... Ms. Catherine A. ROLLMAN
35 Asst Dean of Students .... Mr. James D. MCGHEE, JR.
40 Bookstore Manager .... Mrs. Barclay F. DUPRIEST
114 Director of Budget/Financial Analys .... Ms. Missy STANLEY
08 Head Librarian .... Ms. Nancy K. FALCIANI-WHITE
102 Dir Foundation/Corporate Relations .... Mr. Robert H. PATTERSON
104 Director Study Abroad .... Ms. Mayumi NAKAMURA
28 Special Asst to Pres Diversity .... Mr. Carter WALTON
39 Director Student Housing .... Ms. Sara WEINSTEIN
44 Dir Annual Giving & Alumni Rel .... Mr. Richard M. GOLEMBESKI
101 Asst Secretary of the Board .... Ms. Emily P. HARRISON

Reformed Theological Seminary (C)

8227 Old Courthouse Rd, Suite 300, Vienna VA 22182
Telephone: (703) 448-3393 Identification: 666079
Accreditation: &SC, THEOL

† Regional accreditation is carried under the parent institution in Jackson, MS.

Regent University (D)

1000 Regent University Drive,
Virginia Beach VA 23464-9800
County: Independent City FICE Identification: 030913
Unit ID: 231651
Telephone: (757) 352-4000 Carnegie Class: DU-Mod
FAX Number: (757) 352-4381 Calendar System: Semester
URL: www.regent.edu
Established: 1977 Annual Undergrad Tuition & Fees: $18,720
Enrollment: 10,483 Coed
Affiliation or Control: Independent Non-Profit IRS Status: 501(c)3
Highest Offering: Doctorate
Accreditation: SC, ACBSP, CACREP, CAEPT, CLPSY, LAW, NURSE, THEOL

01 Founder/Chancellor & CEO .... Dr. M.G. (Pat) ROBERTSON
05 Executive VP for Academic Affairs .... Dr. William L. HATHAWAY
32 Executive VP for Student Life .... Dr. Joseph UMIDI
43 Senior VP & General Counsel .... Mr. Louis A. ISAKOFF
111 Vice President for Advancement .... Mr. Chris LAMBERT
84 Exec VP for Enrollment Services .... Ms. Claire FOSTER
10 Exec VP Finance & Business Admin .... Mr. Steve BRUCE
15 VP for Human Resources & Admin .... Mrs. Martha J. SMITH
19 Vice President/Chief of Police .... Chief Chris A. MITCHELL, SR.
45 Assoc VP Strategic Initiatives .... Mr. Michael PREGITZER
07 Associate VP Enrollment Management .... Mr. Chris GRAHAM
61 Dean School of Law .... Hon. Bradley J. LINGO
49 Dean College of Arts & Sciences .... Dr. Joshua MCMULLEN
08 Dean University Library .... Dr. Esther GILLIE
50 Dean School of Business/Leadership .... Dr. Doris GOMEZ
80 Dean Robertson Sch of Government .... Hon. Michele BACHMANN
53 Dean School of Education .... Dr. Kurt KREASSIG
83 Dean Psychology & Counseling .... Dr. Anna S. ORD
73 Dean School of Divinity .... Dr. Corne BEKKER
06 Registrar .... Dr. Elizabeth BAYLESS
35 Director of Student Activities .... Ms. Jennifer GRIBBLE
37 Director of Financial Aid .... Ms. Rachael MOSER
09 Director of Institutional Research .... Dr. Amanda WYNN
18 Director of Facility Management .... Mr. Kim HEGWER
29 Dir of Alumni Rels/Annual Giving .... Ms. Andrea TATUM
42 Director of Campus Ministries .... Mr. Mark LAWRENCE
108 Director of Assessment .... Dr. Ryan MURNANE
88 Assoc Director of Military Affairs .... Mr. John CORDERO
39 Assoc VP for Student Life .... Mr. Adam WILLIAMS
96 Director of Purchasing .... Mrs. Pauline CARRAWAY
04 Assistant to the Chancellor .... Ms. Laurie Ann FINN
13 Assoc Vice Pres of Info Technology .... Mr. Jonathan HARRELL
41 Athletic Director .... Dr. Samuel BOTTA
102 Director Foundation/Corporate Rels .... Ms. Kelly FIELDER
106 Assoc Dean Online Education .... Dr. Jacqueline BRUSO
105 Director of Web Development .... Mr. John REDDY
16 Director of Human Resources .... Mrs. Patty BROWN
30 Regional Dir of Advancement .... Mrs. Melinda GIBSON
36 Assoc Director Career Services .... Mrs. Tiffany YOUNG
14 Director of IT Support .... Mr. Aaron HATFIELD

Richard Bland College (E)

11301 Johnson Road,
South Prince George VA 23805-7100
County: South Prince George FICE Identification: 003707
Unit ID: 233338
Telephone: (804) 862-6100 Carnegie Class: Spec 2-yr-Other
FAX Number: (804) 862-6207 Calendar System: Semester
URL: www.rbc.edu
Established: 1960 Annual Undergrad Tuition & Fees (In-State): $8,100
Enrollment: 2,218 Coed
Affiliation or Control: State IRS Status: 501(c)3
Highest Offering: Associate Degree
Accreditation: SC

01 President .... Dr. Debbie L. SYDOW
05 Chief Academic Officer .... Dr. Tiffany BIRDSONG
10 Chief Business Officer .... Mr. Paul EDWARDS
100 Chief of Staff .... Ms. Lashrecse D. AIRD
18 Dir Capital Assets/Chief of Opers .... Mr. Eric KONDZIELAWA
13 Chief Innovation & Strategy Officer .... Vacant
04 Executive Assistant to President .... Ms. Lisa L. POND
30 Chief Development Officer .... Dr. James T. HART
86 Director of Government Relations .... Ms. Joanne WILLIAMS
15 Director of Human Resources .... Ms. Cassandra STANDBERRY
19 Chief Campus Safety/Police .... Mr. Thomas TRAVIS
43 College Counsel .... Ms. Ramona TAYLOR
41 Director Athletics/Student Life .... Mr. Scott NEWTON
121 Director of Student Success .... Mr. Thom C. ADDINGTON
106 Director of Online Education .... Ms. Stacey SOKOL
37 Director of Financial Aid .... Ms. Lisa JOHNSON
06 Director of Records & Registration .... Vacant
07 Assoc Director of Admissions .... Mr. Kyle DOBRY
38 Dir of Counseling/Student Support .... Dr. Evanda WATTS-MARTINEZ
26 Chief Communications/Marketing Ofcr .... Mr. Jesse E. VAUGHAN
21 Controller .... Mr. Mark JACOBSON
113 Bursar .... Ms. Melissa MAHONEY
96 Procurement Manager .... Ms. Layne WARREN
119 Information Security Officer .... Ms. Deborah JAMES
14 Manager Projects & Telecom .... Mr. George JELLERSON
14 Technology Support Manager .... Mr. Bryan ROETHEL
16 HR Specialist .... Ms. Alice JABBOUR
08 Head Librarian .... Mr. Tim HURLEY
88 Director of Account & Finance .... Mr. Mark JACOBSON
88 Program Manager .... Mr. Preston BOUSMAN

Riverside College of Health Careers (F)

316 Main Street, Newport News VA 23601
County: Independent City FICE Identification: 021400
Unit ID: 233408
Telephone: (757) 240-2200 Carnegie Class: Spec 2-yr-Health
FAX Number: (757) 240-2225 Calendar System: Semester
URL: www.riverside.edu
Established: 1916 Annual Undergrad Tuition & Fees: $17,610
Enrollment: 303 Coed
Affiliation or Control: Independent Non-Profit IRS Status: 501(c)3
Highest Offering: Baccalaureate
Accreditation: ABHES, ADNUR, CVT, NUR, PNUR, PTAA, RAD, SURGT, SURTEC

01 Exec Director .... Robin M. NELHUEBEL
05 Director Academic Affairs .... Vacant
06 Registrar .... Lori ARNDER
08 Head Librarian .... Cassandra MOORE
121 Dean Student Success .... G. Michael HAMILTON
07 Senior Recruitment Coordinator .... Cynthia REDDINGTON
37 Dir Financial Aid/Student Svcs .... Saleem CHAUDHRY

Roanoke College (G)

221 College Lane, Salem VA 24153-3747
County: Independent City FICE Identification: 003736
Unit ID: 233426
Telephone: (540) 375-2500 Carnegie Class: Bac-A&S
FAX Number: (540) 375-2205 Calendar System: Semester
URL: www.roanoke.edu
Established: 1842 Annual Undergrad Tuition & Fees: $47,020
Enrollment: 1,920 Coed
Affiliation or Control: Evangelical Lutheran Church In America
IRS Status: 501(c)3
Highest Offering: Baccalaureate
Accreditation: SC, ACBSP, CAEPT

01 President .... Dr. Frank SHUSHOK
05 VP Academic/Student Affairs .... Dr. Katherine J. WOLFE
84 VP of Enroll Svcs/Dean Adm/Fin Aid .... Dr. Brenda P. POGGENDORF
10 Vice President Business Affairs .... Mr. David MOWEN
111 Vice President Advancement .... Ms. Kimberly P. BLAIR
32 Dean of Students .... Mr. Thomas A. RAMBO
26 Exec Dir/Marketing Communications .... Ms. Melanie W. TOLAN
13 Chief Information Officer .... Ms. Terri FOX
09 Dir Institutional Research .... Mr. Brandon WOLFE
20 Assoc Dean Academic Affairs .... Mrs. Sharon C. GIBBS
06 Assoc Dean Acad Affairs/Registrar .... Ms. Patricia BROKKEN
07 Director of Recruitment .... Vacant
39 Director of Residence Life/Housing .... Mr. Jimmy R. WHITED
92 Director of Honors Programs .... Dr. Chad T. MORRIS
08 Director of the Library .... Ms. Elizabeth MCCLENNEY
24 Media Technology Director .... Vacant
31 Dir of Community Programs .... Ms. Tanya RIDPATH
26 Director of Public Relations .... Ms. Teresa T. GEREAUX
29 Dir of Alumni/Family Relations .... Mr. Gregory HANLON
114 Director of Finance & Budget .... Mr. Adam NEAL
91 Database Director .... Ms. Mitzi B. STEELE
15 Director Human Resources .... Mrs. Kathy MARTIN
40 Bookstore Coordinator/Buyer .... Ms. Melissa B. RUTLEDGE
19 Director Campus Safety .... Mr. Joseph B. MILLS
23 Dir Student Health/Counseling Svcs .... Ms. Sandra W. MCGHEE
41 Athletic Director .... Mr. M. Scott ALLISON
42 Chaplain/Dean of the Chapel .... Rev. Christopher M. BOWEN
104 Director of International Education .... Ms. Sarah C. LUPTON
28 Vice Pres Cmty/Diversity/Inclusion .... Ms. Teresa JOHNSON RAMEZ
04 Executive Assistant to President .... Mrs. Whitney C. ALDRIDGE
37 Director of Financial Aid .... Mr. Thomas S. BLAIR, JR.
45 Director of Institutional Planning .... Dr. Ryan OTTO

Sentara College of Health Sciences (H)

1441 Crossways Boulevard, Ste 105,
Chesapeake VA 23320
County: Chesapeake City FICE Identification: 031065
Unit ID: 232885
Telephone: (757) 388-2900 Carnegie Class: Spec-4-yr-Other Health
FAX Number: (757) 222-7694 Calendar System: Semester
URL: www.sentara.edu
Established: 1892 Annual Undergrad Tuition & Fees: N/A
Enrollment: 341 Coed
Affiliation or Control: Independent Non-Profit IRS Status: 501(c)3
Highest Offering: Master's
Accreditation: ABHES, CVT, NURSE, SURGT, SURTEC

01 President .... Dr. Angela TAYLOR
05 Dean Academic Affairs .... Dr. Cynthia BANKS
09 Dean Inst Effectiveness/Dist Lrng .... Vacant
10 Assoc Dean Administration & Finance .... Mr. Christopher NELSON
84 Asst Dean Enrollment Management .... Mr. Joseph HOWE
06 Registrar .... Ms. Jennie POND
37 Financial Aid Advisor .... Ms. Sharon CROCKETT
07 Admissions Recruiter .... Mr. Kevin LAWRENCE

Shenandoah University (A)

1460 University Drive, Winchester VA 22601-5195
County: Independent City
FICE Identification: 003737
Unit ID: 233541
Telephone: (540) 665-4500
Carnegie Class: DU-Mod
FAX Number: N/A
Calendar System: Semester
URL: www.su.edu
Established: 1875
Annual Undergrad Tuition & Fees: $33,900
Enrollment: 4,174
Coed
Affiliation or Control: United Methodist
IRS Status: 501(c)3
Highest Offering: Doctorate
Accreditation: SC, ARCPA, CAATE, CAEP, MIDWF, NURSE, OT, PHAR, PTA

01 President ... Dr. Tracy FITZSIMMONS
05 Provost ... Dr. Cameron MCCOY
10 Vice Pres Finance/CFO ... Ms. Courtney JARRETT
32 Vice President Student Affairs ... Ms. Yolanda BARBIER GIBSON
111 Senior VP for Advancement ... Mr. Mitchell L. MOORE
84 VP for Student Success ... Dr. Yolanda BARBIER GIBSON
35 Dean of Students ... Dr. Sue O'DRISCOLL
26 Director of Media Relations ... Vacant
49 Dean of College of Arts & Sciences ... Dr. Jeffrey COKER
50 Dean of Byrd School of Business ... Dr. Astrid SHEIL
64 Dean of Shenandoah Conservatory ... Dr. Michael J. STEPNIAK
67 Dean of Dunn School of Pharmacy ... Dr. Robert DICENZO
07 Asst VP of Recruitment & Admissions ... Mr. Andy WOODALL
124 Dir of Student Engagement ... Mr. Matt LEVY
08 Director of Library Services ... Vacant
06 Registrar ... Ms. Emily HOLLINS
21 Asst VP Admin & Finance/Controller ... Ms. Courtney JARRETT
37 Student Financial Services Dir ... Dr. Karen H. BUCHER
36 Director of Career/Prof Development ... Ms. Jennifer A. SPATARO-WILSON
18 Director of Physical Plant ... Mr. Barry SCHNOOR
23 Interim Director of Wellness Center ... Mrs. Lisa DARSCH
15 Assoc Director of Human Resources ... Ms. Kim MCDONALD
41 Athletic Director ... Dr. Bridget LYONS
91 Database & System Administrator ... Mr. Seth BURKE
13 Director of Institutional Computing ... Mr. Quaiser ABSAR
66 Dean Custer School of Nursing ... Dr. Andra HANLON
88 Director Div of Athletic Training ... Dr. Rose A. SCHMIEG
76 Dir Div of Occupational Therapy ... Dr. Cathy SHANHOLTZ
76 Dir Div of Physical Therapy ... Dr. Sheri ALLEN
112 Director of Planned Gifts ... Vacant
19 Director of Public Safety ... Mr. Ricky FRYE
102 Dir of Grant Supp & Foundation Rels ... Ms. Marguerite LANDENBURGER
109 Director Auxiliary Services ... Ms. Pamela B. BURKE
88 Dir Div of Physician Asst Studies ... Dr. Anthony MILLER
20 Director Learning Services ... Ms. Holli PHILLIPS
42 Dean of Spiritual Life ... Rev Dr. Justin ALLEN
09 Director Institutional Research ... Mr. Howard BALLENTINE
40 Bookstore Manager ... Ms. Kimberly OTYENOH
96 Purchasing/Accounts Payable Manager ... Ms. Susan LANDIS
24 Coordinator Media Services ... Ms. Rebecca LAYNE
38 Director of Counseling Center ... Vacant
04 Executive Asst to President ... Ms. Kim KECKLEY
101 Exec Secretary of the BOT ... Ms. Laura CLAWSON
53 Assoc Provost School of Education ... Dr. Jill LINDSEY
104 Director International Programs . Dr. Bethany GALIPEAU-KONATE
44 Director of Annual Giving ... Ms. Aimee NUWAR
43 AVP & General Counsel ... Mr. Philip EVANS
28 Asst Dean Student Dev/ Leadership ... Ms. Margaret MCCAMPBELL LIEN
29 Executive Director Alumni Affairs ... Ms. Emily BURNER

South University (B)

2151 Old Brick Road, Glen Allen VA 23060
Telephone: (888) 422-5076
Identification: 770919
Accreditation: &SC, ACBSP, ARCPA, CACREP, NURSE, OTA, PTAA

† Branch campus of South University, Savannah, GA

South University (C)

301 Bendix Road, Suite 100, Virginia Beach VA 23452
Telephone: (877) 206-1845
Identification: 770920
Accreditation: &SC, ACBSP, CACREP, NURSE, OTA, PTAA

† Branch campus of South University, Savannah, GA

Southern Virginia University (D)

1 University Hill Drive, Buena Vista VA 24416-3097
County: Rockbridge
FICE Identification: 003738
Unit ID: 233611
Telephone: (540) 261-8400
Carnegie Class: Bac-A&S
FAX Number: (540) 266-3859
Calendar System: Semester
URL: www.svu.edu
Established: 1867
Annual Undergrad Tuition & Fees: $17,696
Enrollment: 1,140
Coed
Affiliation or Control: Independent Non-Profit
IRS Status: 501(c)3
Highest Offering: Baccalaureate
Accreditation: SC

01 President ... Dr. Reed N. WILCOX
100 Executive VP/Chief of Staff ... Mr. Brett GARCIA
05 VP of Academics/Provost ... Dr. James LAMBERT
10 Chief Financial officer ... Mr. Tyson COOPER
111 VP Institutional Advancement ... Dr. Jon WALLIN
84 VP Enrollment & Marketing ... Mr. Christopher PENDLETON
32 Dean of Students ... Mr. William BRADDY
46 VP Educational Research & Dev ... Dr. Karen M. WALKER
11 VP of Operations ... Mr. Chris PACKER
04 Administrative Asst to President ... Mrs. Kristie GIBBONS
06 University Registrar ... Ms. Whitney M. LARSEN
08 Director of Library Services ... Mrs. Stephanie K. HARDY
20 Associate Provost ... Dr. Samuel HIRT
57 Division Chair Fine & Perf Arts ... Dr. Eric HANSON
79 Division Chair Humanities ... Dr. Jan-Erik JONES
81 Div Chair Science & Mathematics ... Dr. Roger JOHNSON
83 Div Chair Social & Behavioral Sci ... Dr. Iana KONSTANTINOVA
83 Div Chair Business/Family Dev/Psych ... Dr. Jeffrey BATIS
53 Director of Teacher Education ... Ms. Kimberly KEARNEY
37 Director of Financial Aid ... Mr. Aaron CARLSON
15 Human Resources Manager ... Mr. Adam WHIPPLE
88 Title IX ... Ms. Stephanie HARDY
96 Senior Accountant ... Mr. Trenton DESPAIN
41 Athletic Director ... Ms. Deidra DRYDEN
38 Director of Student Support ... Vacant
85 Foreign Students PDSO ... Ms. Whitney M. LARSEN
19 Director Security/Safety ... Mr. Zachary ELLIOTT
109 Director of Food Services ... Mr. Joseph WHETSTONE
18 Asst Dir Facilities/Physical Plant ... Mr. Byron PORTER
101 Secretary of the Institution/Board ... Mr. Hugh REDD
13 Chief Information Technology Office ... Dr. Jeffrey SWIFT
50 Program Coordinator Business ... Dr. W. Todd BROTHERSON
07 Director of Admissions ... Ms. Madison HUGIE
09 Director of Institutional Research ... Dr. Jonathan WALLIN
39 Dir Resident Life/Student Housing ... Ms. April HARRIS

Southside College of Health Sciences (E)

430 Clairmont Court, Suite 200, Colonial Heights VA 23834
County: Independent City
FICE Identification: 012744
Unit ID: 233082
Telephone: (804) 765-5800
Carnegie Class: Spec 2-yr-Health
FAX Number: (804) 765-5944
Calendar System: Semester
URL: https://www.schs.edu/
Established: 1895
Annual Undergrad Tuition & Fees: $15,813
Enrollment: 115
Coed
Affiliation or Control: Proprietary
IRS Status: Proprietary
Highest Offering: Associate Degree
Accreditation: ABHES, ADNUR, DMS, RAD

03 Vice President ... Mrs. Cynthia SWINEFORD

Sovah School of Health Professions (F)

142 South Main Street, Danville VA 24541
County: Independent City
FICE Identification: 021116
Unit ID: 232724
Telephone: (434) 799-2271
Carnegie Class: Spec 2-yr-Health
FAX Number: (434) 799-3718
Calendar System: Semester
URL: www.danvilleregional.com
Established: 1898
Annual Undergrad Tuition & Fees: N/A
Enrollment: 13
Coed
Affiliation or Control: Proprietary
IRS Status: Proprietary
Highest Offering: Associate Degree
Accreditation: ABHES, DMS, RAD

01 Dean ... R. Alan LARSON

Standard Healthcare Services College of Nursing (G)

7704 Leesburg Pike, Suite 1000, Falls Church VA 22043
County: Fairfax
Identification: 667129
Unit ID: 483814
Telephone: (703) 891-1787
Carnegie Class: Spec 2-yr-Health
FAX Number: (703) 891-1789
Calendar System: Other
URL: www.standardcollege.edu
Established: 2004
Annual Undergrad Tuition & Fees: N/A
Enrollment: 441
Coed
Affiliation or Control: Proprietary
IRS Status: Proprietary
Highest Offering: Associate Degree
Accreditation: ABHES, @CNEA

01 Executive Director ... Dr. Isibor J. NOSEGBE
03 Deputy Executive Director ... Mrs. Heather ETTUS
06 Registrar ... Ms. Lisley M. ANCO
05 Director of Education ... Dr. Sakpa S. AMARA
32 Dean of Student Services ... Mrs. Sondra BROWN
37 Financial Aid ... Mr. Petros YOSIEF
07 Admissions ... Ms. Cara GLASER
10 Business Office ... Mrs. Brenda GARCES

Sweet Briar College (H)

134 Chapel Road, Sweet Briar VA 24595-9998
County: Amherst
FICE Identification: 003742
Unit ID: 233718
Telephone: (434) 381-6100
Carnegie Class: Bac-A&S
FAX Number: (434) 381-6173
Calendar System: Semester
URL: www.sbc.edu
Established: 1901
Annual Undergrad Tuition & Fees: $22,700
Enrollment: 362
Female
Affiliation or Control: Independent Non-Profit
IRS Status: 501(c)3
Highest Offering: Master's
Accreditation: SC

01 President ... Dr. Meredith WOO
11 VP Finance/Operations & Auxiliary ... Mr. Luther T. GRIFFITH
04 Exec Asst Office of the President ... Ms. Kim MURRAY
30 Vice Pres Alumnae Relations/Devel ... Ms. Mary Pope M. HUTSON
84 Vice Pres Enrollment Management ... Mr. Aaron BASKO
09 Dir of Institutional Effectiveness ... Ms. Kim SINHA
05 Dean of Academic Affairs ... Dr. Teresa GARRETT
13 Dir of Technology Services ... Mr. Hooshang FOROUDASTAN
41 Athletics Director ... Ms. Jodi CANFIELD
32 Dean of Student Life ... Mr. Kerry GREENSTEIN
15 Sr Human Resource Mgr ... Ms. Nickcole MAYNARD-ERRAMI
18 Director Physical Plant ... Mr. Rich MEYER
19 Director of Campus Safety ... Mr. Brian MARKER
37 Director Financial Aid ... Ms. Wanda SPRADLEY
40 Book Shop Manager ... Ms. Dottie BOONE
96 Purchasing Manager ... Ms. Karen L. THORP
88 Director of Hospitality ... Ms. Cathy MAYS
36 Director Career Services ... Ms. Barbara WATTS
26 Sr Director of Communications ... Ms. Amy OSTROTH
27 Dir of Media Rels/Content Strategy ... Ms. Dana POLESKI
06 Registrar ... Mr. Jay FLYNN
07 Director of Admissions Operations ... Ms. Melanie CAMPBELL
25 Chief Contracts/Grants Admin ... Ms. Kathleen PLACIDI
29 Director Alumnae Relations ... Ms. Claire GRIFFITH
21 Assistant VP & Controller ... Ms. Jenni SAUER

Union Presbyterian Seminary (I)

3401 Brook Road, Richmond VA 23227-4597
County: Independent City
FICE Identification: 003743
Unit ID: 233842
Telephone: (804) 355-0671
Carnegie Class: Spec-4-yr-Faith
FAX Number: (804) 355-3919
Calendar System: Semester
URL: www.upsem.edu
Established: 1812
Annual Graduate Tuition & Fees: N/A
Enrollment: 169
Coed
Affiliation or Control: Presbyterian Church (U.S.A.)
IRS Status: 501(c)3
Highest Offering: Doctorate; No Undergraduates
Accreditation: SC, THEOL

01 President ... Dr. Brian K. BLOUNT
10 Vice Pres Finance & Administration ... Ms. Jennifer D. BRITTON
111 Vice President Advancement ... Mr. Richard WONG
32 Dean of Students ... Ms. Michelle WALKER
05 Dean Union Presby Sem/Academics ... Dr. Kenneth J. MCFAYDEN
12 Dean Union Presby Sem (Charlotte) ... Dr. Richard N. BOYCE
07 Director of Admissions ... Ms. Erin BURT
06 Registrar ... Mr. J. Stanley HARGRAVES
08 Seminary Librarian ... Dr. Christopher RICHARDSON
13 Director Technology Services ... Mr. John R. WILSON
36 Director Student Services ... Ms. Susan BLANCHARD
37 Director of Financial Aid ... Ms. Michelle WALKER
15 Director of Human Resources ... Mr. Jamie COOK

University of Fairfax (J)

1813 E. Main Street, Salem VA 24153
County: Independent City
Identification: 667094
Telephone: (888) 980-9151
Carnegie Class: Not Classified
FAX Number: N/A
Calendar System: Other
URL: www.ufairfax.edu
Established: 2002
Annual Undergrad Tuition & Fees: N/A
Enrollment: N/A
Coed
Affiliation or Control: Other
IRS Status: Proprietary
Highest Offering: Doctorate
Accreditation: DEAC

01 President ... Mr. Frank LONGAKER
05 Chief Academic Officer ... Dr. Carolyn SCOTT
11 Exec Vice President Operations ... Mr. Joel MUSGROVE
26 VP Marketing & Communications ... Vacant

† Tuition is $895 per semester credit.

University of Lynchburg (K)

1501 Lakeside Drive, Lynchburg VA 24501-3199
County: Independent City
FICE Identification: 003720
Unit ID: 232609
Telephone: (434) 544-8100
Carnegie Class: DU-Mod
FAX Number: (434) 544-8539
Calendar System: Semester
URL: www.lynchburg.edu
Established: 1903
Annual Undergrad Tuition & Fees: $41,880
Enrollment: 2,692
Coed
Affiliation or Control: Christian Church (Disciples Of Christ)
IRS Status: 501(c)3
Highest Offering: Doctorate
Accreditation: SC, ACBSP, ARCPA, CAATE, CACREP, EXSC, MUS, NURSE, PTA

01 President ... Dr. Alison MORRISON-SHETLAR
05 Provost & VP for Academic Affs ... Dr. Allison JABLONSKI
10 Vice President Business & Finance ... Mr. Chris BURNLEY
111 Vice President Advancement ... Dr. J. Michael BONNETTE
84 VP Enrollment Management ... Mr. Michael JONES
32 VP & Dean of Student Development ... Mr. Eric BALDWIN
45 VP Inst Planning/Effectiveness ... Ms. Christine COLE
26 VP Communications & Marketing ... Mr. Michael JONES
50 Dean College of Business ... Dr. Nancy HUBBARD
53 Dean Col of Educ/Ldrship Stds/Couns ... Dr. Roger JONES

20 Assoc Provost ... Dr. Charles WALTON
49 Assoc Dean LC Arts & Sciences ... Dr. Oeida HATCHER
81 Assoc Dean School of Sciences ... Vacant
76 Dean College of Health Sciences ... Dr. Rusty SMITH
06 Registrar/Academic/Student Info ... Mrs. Susan KENNON
08 Director of the Library ... Mrs. Jennifer HORTON
37 Director of Financial Aid ... Ms. Elayne PELOQUIN
07 Assoc VP of Enrollment ... Mr. Aaron BASKO
25 Assoc Dir of Grants Management ... Ms. Jennifer WILLIAMS
13 Director Information and Technology ... Mrs. Jackie ALMOND
15 Human Resource Director ... Ms. Linda HALL
19 Director Security/Safety ... Vacant
28 Diversity and Inclusion Officer ... Dr. Robert CANIDA
29 Director Alumni Relations ... Ms. Heather GARNETT
39 Director Residence Life ... Ms. Kristen COOPER
41 Athletic Director ... Mr. Jon WATERS
96 Purchasing and Logistics Coord ... Mrs. Cynthia PONTON
04 Exec Assistant to the President ... Mrs. Debra WYLAND
09 Director of Institutional Research ... Dr. Aurelia KOLLASCH

University of Management & Technology (A)

1901 Fort Myer Drive, Suite 700, Arlington VA 22209-1609
County: Arlington FICE Identification: 041103
Unit ID: 437097
Telephone: (703) 516-0035 Carnegie Class: DU-Mod
FAX Number: (703) 516-0985 Calendar System: Semester
URL: www.umtweb.edu
Established: 1998 Annual Undergrad Tuition & Fees: $9,450
Enrollment: 295 Coed
Affiliation or Control: Proprietary IRS Status: Proprietary
Highest Offering: Doctorate
Accreditation: DEAC

01 President ... Dr. Yanping CHEN
05 Academic Dean ... Dr. J. Davidson FRAME

University of Mary Washington (B)

1301 College Avenue, Fredericksburg VA 22401-5300
County: Independent City FICE Identification: 003746
Unit ID: 232681
Telephone: (540) 654-1000 Carnegie Class: Bac-A&S
FAX Number: (540) 654-1073 Calendar System: Semester
URL: www.umw.edu
Established: 1908 Annual Undergrad Tuition & Fees (In-State): $13,845
Enrollment: 4,293 Coed
Affiliation or Control: State IRS Status: 501(c)3
Highest Offering: Master's
Accreditation: SC, CAEP, NURSE

01 President ... Dr. Troy PAINO
05 Provost ... Dr. Timothy O'DONNELL
100 Chief of Staff ... Dr. Jeffrey MCCLURKEN
10 VP for Admin & Finance ... Mr. Paul MESSPLAY
32 Vice President Student Affairs ... Dr. Juliette LANDPHAIR
111 Vice President for Advancement ... Ms. Katie TURCOTTE
102 CEO of UMW Foundation ... Mr. Jeffrey W. ROUNTREE
13 Chief Information Officer ... Mr. Hall CHESHIRE
88 Exec Dir Ctr Economic Development ... Mr. Brian J. BAKER
28 Assoc Provost Equity/Inclusion/CDO ... Dr. Shavonne SHORTER
15 Executive Director Human Resources ... Ms. Beth WILLIAMS
105 Director of Digital Communication ... Dr. Anand RAO
21 Director of Business Svcs ... Ms. Kathy SANDOR
20 Assoc Provost for Academic Affairs ... Vacant
84 Dean of Admissions/Assoc VP ... Ms. Melissa YAKABOUSKI
110 Assoc VP Univ Advance/Alumni Rel ... Vacant
53 Dean of College of Education ... Dr. Peter KELLY
50 Interim Dean College of Business ... Mr. Ken MACHANDE
49 Dean College of Arts & Sciences ... Dr. Keith MELLINGER
35 Dean Student Involve/Assoc VP ... Ms. Melissa JONES
37 Director of Financial Aid ... Mr. Timothy SAULNIER
09 Director of Institutional Research ... Mr. Mathew C. WILKERSON
116 Director of Internal Audit ... Vacant
39 Dean for Res Life/Asst VP ... Mr. David FLEMING
06 Registrar ... Ms. Rita DUNSTON
41 Athletic Director ... Mr. Patrick CATULLO
08 Interim University Librarian ... Ms. Carolyn PARSONS
26 Exec Dir of Univ Communications ... Ms. Amy JESSEE
88 Director of Dodd Auditorium ... Mr. Doug NOBLE
121 Assoc Provost Academic Engagement ... Vacant
19 Chief of Police ... Mr. Michael W. HALL
29 Exec Director Alumni Relations ... Mr. Mark THADEN
103 Assoc Provost Career & Workforce ... Ms. Kimberly YOUNG
38 Director of Talley Center ... Mr. Tevya ZUKOR
28 Director of Disability Resources ... Ms. Jessica MACHADO
23 University Physician/Health Center ... Ms. Nancy WANG
96 Director of Procurement Services ... Ms. Melva KISHPAUGH
09 Assoc Provost for Inst Analysis/Eff ... Dr. Debra SCHLEEF
26 Assoc VP University Relations ... Vacant
27 Asst Dir Media & Public Relations ... Ms. Lisa MARVASHTI
27 Director of University Marketing ... Mr. Malcolm HOLMES
88 Director of Design Services ... Ms. AJ NEWELL
04 Executive Office Manager ... Ms. Paula ZERO
101 Clerk of Board of Visitors ... Dr. Jeff MCCLURKEN
104 Dir Ctr for International Education ... Dr. Jose SAINZ
30 Director of Development ... Vacant
44 Director Annual Giving ... Vacant
18 Chief Facilities/Physical Plant Ofc ... Mr. Stuart SULLIVAN
25 Chief Contract/Grants Administrator ... Ms. Julie SMITH

University of North America (C)

12750 Fair Lakes Circle, Fairfax VA 22033
County: Fairfax Identification: 667241
Telephone: (571) 633-9651 Carnegie Class: Not Classified
FAX Number: (703) 890-3372 Calendar System: Semester
URL: www.uona.edu
Established: Annual Undergrad Tuition & Fees: N/A
Enrollment: N/A Coed
Affiliation or Control: Independent Non-Profit IRS Status: 501(c)3
Highest Offering: Master's
Accreditation: ACICS

00 CEO ... Claude (Marty) C. MARTIN
01 President ... Jill MARTIN
05 VP of Academic Affairs ... Peter WEST
20 VP of Educational Operations ... Jason KOO

University of the Potomac (D)

7799 Leesburg Pike, Suite 200, Falls Church VA 22043
Telephone: (202) 521-1290 Identification: 666178
Accreditation: &M

† Regional accreditation is carried under the parent institution in Washington, DC.

University of Richmond (E)

28 Westhampton Way, Richmond VA 23173-1903
County: Independent City FICE Identification: 003744
Unit ID: 233374
Telephone: (804) 289-8000 Carnegie Class: Bac-A&S
FAX Number: (804) 287-6540 Calendar System: Semester
URL: www.richmond.edu
Established: 1830 Annual Undergrad Tuition & Fees: $56,860
Enrollment: 4,056 Coordinate
Affiliation or Control: Independent Non-Profit IRS Status: 501(c)3
Highest Offering: Doctorate
Accreditation: SC, CAEPT, LAW

01 President ... Dr. Kevin HALLOCK
05 Executive VP & Provost ... Dr. Jeffrey LEGRO
10 EVP & COO Business & Finance ... Mr. David B. HALE
43 VP & General Counsel ... Ms. Shannon E. SINCLAIR
32 Vice President Student Development ... Dr. Stephen D. BISESE
111 Vice President Advancement ... Ms. Martha E. CALLAGHAN
13 VP & Chief Information Officer ... Mr. Keith W. MCINTOSH
84 Vice Pres Enrollment Management ... Dr. Stephanie DUPAUL
41 VP & Director of Athletics ... Mr. John HARDT
45 Vice President Planning & Policy ... Dr. Lori G. SCHUYLER
26 VP Communications & Marketing ... Mr. Tom ADDONIZIO
101 VP & Secretary Board of Trustees ... Dr. Ann Lloyd BREEDEN
100 Chief of Staff ... Ms. Dara GOCHESKI
22 Senior Adm Officer Equity & Comm ... Ms. Amy HOWARD
04 Assistant to President ... Ms. Meghan WALL
88 President & CIO Spider Mgmt Company ... Mr. William MCLEAN
15 Senior Assoc VP Human Resources ... Mr. Carl K. SORENSEN
18 Dir of Design/Constr/Arch ... Mr. Chuck ROGERS
30 Asst VP Development ... Mr. Jamie HUGHES
29 Asst VP Alumni & Career Services ... Ms. Denise D. SMITH
102 Int AVP Foundation/Corp/Govt Rels ... Ms. Jennifer STANCIL
42 University Chaplain ... Rev. Craig T. KOCHER
07 Interim AVP & Dean of Admission ... Ms. Marilyn E. HESSER
08 University Librarian ... Mr. Kevin BUTTERFIELD
09 Dir Institutional Effectiveness ... Ms. Melanie JENKINS
06 University Registrar ... Ms. Kristen BALL
37 AVP & Dir of Student Financial Aid ... Mr. William B. BRYAN, JR.
36 Dir Career Development Center ... Ms. Leslie W. STEVENSON
38 Director of CAPS ... Dr. Peter O. LEVINESS
96 Director Strategic Sourcing ... Vacant
28 Dean Student Equity & Inclusion . Dr. Morgan RUSSELL-STOKES
104 Director Study Abroad ... Ms. Michele D. COX
105 Director Web Services ... Mr. Bobby PAXTON
33 Dean of Richmond College ... Dr. Joseph R. BOEHMAN
34 Dean Westhampton College ... Dr. Mia R. GENONI
49 Dean School Arts & Sciences ... Dr. Jennifer J. CAVENAUGH
50 Dean School of Business ... Dr. Mickey QUIÑONES
61 Dean School of Law ... Dr. Wendy C. PERDUE
51 Dean School Continuing Studies ... Dr. Jamelle S. WILSON
88 Dean Jepson School Leader Stds ... Dr. Sandra J. PEART
104 Dean International Education ... Dr. Martha L. MERRITT
19 AVP Public Safety/Chief of Police ... Mr. David M. MCCOY
23 Director Health Center ... Dr. Latrina LEMON
40 Director University Bookstore ... Ms. Liz ST. JOHN
88 Dir of Inst Equity & Inclusion ... Dr. Glyn HUGHES
39 Dir Housing & Residence Life ... Mr. Patrick B. BENNER
91 Dir Enterprise Applications ... Mr. Lee PARKER, III
44 Director Annual Giving ... Ms. Kim LEBAR
29 Dir Alumni Relations ... Ms. Laura KRAJEWSKI
89 Dir of Student Involvement ... Mr. Andrew GURKA

University of Virginia (F)

1827 University Avenue, Charlottesville VA 22904
County: Independent City FICE Identification: 003745
Unit ID: 234076
Telephone: (434) 924-0311 Carnegie Class: DU-Highest
FAX Number: (434) 924-0938 Calendar System: Semester
URL: www.virginia.edu
Established: 1819 Annual Undergrad Tuition & Fees (In-State): $18,960
Enrollment: 25,628 Coed
Affiliation or Control: State IRS Status: 501(c)3
Highest Offering: Doctorate
Accreditation: SC, CAATE, CACREP, CAEP, CAEPT, CAMPEP, CLPSY, DENT, DIETI, IPSY, LAW, LSAR, MED, NURSE, PAST, PCSAS, PH, PLNG, PSPSY, SP

01 President ... Mr. James E. RYAN
00 Rector ... Mr. Whittington W. CLEMENT
101 Special Asst & Secretary/BOV ... Ms. Susan G. HARRIS
05 Exec Vice President & Provost ... Mr. Ian BAUCOM
03 Exec Vice Pres/Chief Operating Ofcr ... Ms. Jennifer (J.J.) WAGNER DAVIS
43 University Counsel ... Mr. Clifton ILER
116 Chief Audit Executive ... Ms. Carolyn SAINT
100 Asst VP & Chief of Staff ... Ms. Margaret S. GRUNDY
22 Assoc VP Equal Opp Pgms/Civ Rights .. Ms. Emily SPRINGSTON
17 Exec Vice Pres for Health Affairs ... Dr. K. Craig KENT
88 Chief Admin Ofcr Health Affairs ... Ms. Mary Frances SOUTHERLAND
111 Vice Pres for Advancement ... Mr. Mark LUELLEN
10 Vice President for Finance ... Ms. Melody BIANCHETTO
115 Chief Investment Officer ... Mr. Robert DURDEN
88 Exec Director The Jefferson Trust ... Mr. Brent PERCIVAL
32 VP/Chief Student Affairs Officer ... Ms. Robyn HADLEY
35 Associate VP/Dean of Students ... Ms. Julie CARUCCIO
36 Assoc VP Career & Prof Development ... Mr. Everette FORTNER
93 Dean African-American Affairs ... Dr. Maurice APPREY
23 Exec Director Student Health ... Dr. Christopher HOLSTEGE
39 Exec Dir Housing & Residence Life ... Ms. Gay PEREZ
35 Assoc VP for Student Affairs ... Ms. Susan M. DAVIS
35 Assoc VP Stdnt Affs Strat & Finance ... Ms. Elisa HOLQUIST
40 Assistant Director of UVa Bookstore ... Vacant
46 Vice Pres for Research ... Mr. Melur RAMASUBRAMANIAN
25 Sr AVP/Dir Academic Rsrch Comp ... Mr. David J. HUDSON
28 VP Diversity/Equity/Incl/Cmty Prtnr ... Mr. Kevin G. MCDONALD
41 Dir Intercollegiate Athletic Pgms ... Ms. Carla WILLIAMS
88 Director/CEO Miller Center ... William J. ANTHOLIS
15 VP/Chief Human Resources Ofcr ... Mr. John KOSKY
26 VP Communication/Chief Mktg Officer ... Mr. David W. MARTEL
12 Chancellor UVA's College at Wise ... Ms. Donna P. HENRY
11 Sr VP Operations/State Govt Rels ... Ms. Colette SHEEHY
21 Assoc VP Business Operations ... Mr. Richard A. KOVATCH
88 Architect for the University ... Ms. Alice J. RAUCHER
88 University Building Official ... Mr. Ben HAYS
18 Assoc VP & Chief Facilities Officer ... Mr. Donald E. SUNDGREN
37 Asst VP Student Financial Svcs ... Mr. Stephen A. KIMATA
96 Director Supplier Diversity ... Vacant
13 Vice Pres & Chief Information Ofcr ... Ms. Virginia H. EVANS
20 Vice Prov for Academic Affairs ... Ms. Brie GERTLER
84 Vice Provost for Enrollment ... Mr. Stephen FARMER
20 Vice Prov Academic Initiatives ... Ms. Megan BARNETT
45 Vice Provost Planning ... Mr. Adam DANIEL
108 Assoc Prov Institutional Research ... Ms. Christina MORELL
20 Vice Prov Faculty Affairs ... Ms. Manté BRANDT-PEARCE
88 Vice Prov for Administration ... Ms. Anda L. WEBB
57 Vice Prov for the Arts ... Mr. Jody K. KIELBASA
88 Vice Prov for Acad Outreach ... Mr. Louis NELSON
90 Vice Provost Academic Technology ... Mr. Ronald R. HUTCHINS
85 Vice Provost for Global Affairs ... Mr. Stephen D. MULL
06 Assoc Vice Provost and Registrar ... Ms. Laura HAWTHORNE
07 Dean of Admission ... Mr. Gregory W. ROBERTS
61 Dean School of Law ... Ms. Risa L. GOLUBOFF
49 Dean School of Arts & Sciences ... Mr. David L. HILL
63 Dean School of Medicine ... Dr. Melina R. KIBBE
66 Dean School of Nursing ... Dr. Pam CIPRIANO
54 Dean Schl Engr/Applied Science ... Ms. Jennifer L. WEST
48 Dean School of Architecture ... Ms. Malo A. HUTSON
50 Dean School of Commerce ... Ms. Nicole T. JENKINS
80 Dean Sch Leadership/Public Policy ... Mr. Ian H. SOLOMON
53 Dean School of Education ... Mr. Robert C. PIANTA
50 Dean Grad School Business Admin ... Mr. Scott C. BEARDSLEY
51 Dean Cont/Professional Studies ... Mr. Alejandro HERNANDEZ
88 Director Applied Research Inst ... Mr. Robert T. JONES
88 Director Center for Politics ... Mr. Larry J. SABATO
77 Dean School of Data Science ... Mr. Philip E. BOURNE
88 Exec Dir Biocomplexity Inst ... Mr. Christopher L. BARRETT
08 Univ Librarian/Dean of Libraries ... Mr. John M. UNSWORTH
104 Dir Intl Studies/Summer/Sp Acad Pgm ... Mr. Dudley J. DOANE
19 Associate VP Safety/Chief of Police ... Mr. Timothy LONGO
94 Dir Study in Women Gender Sexuality ... Ms. Charlotte PATTERSON
102 Director Foundation/Corporate Rels ... Ms. Katie SHEVLIN
38 Dir Counseling & Psych Services ... Dr. Nicole RUZEK
86 Exec Dir State Govt Rels/SA to Pres ... Vacant

The University of Virginia's College at Wise (G)

One College Avenue, Wise VA 24293-4412
County: Wise FICE Identification: 003747
Unit ID: 233897
Telephone: (276) 328-0100 Carnegie Class: Bac-A&S
FAX Number: (276) 376-1012 Calendar System: Semester
URL: www.uvawise.edu
Established: 1954 Annual Undergrad Tuition & Fees (In-State): $10,836
Enrollment: 1,905 Coed
Affiliation or Control: State IRS Status: 501(c)3
Highest Offering: Baccalaureate
Accreditation: SC, CAEP, MUS, NURSE

01 Chancellor ... Dr. Donna P. HENRY
05 Provost/Vice Chanc for Acad Affairs . Dr. Trisha FOLDS-BENNETT
111 VC Advancement/Alumni Engagement ... Ms. Valerie S. LAWSON
10 Vice Chanc Finance/Operations ... Mr. Joe KISER
84 Vice Chancellor Enrollment Mgmt ... Mr. Jeff BAYLOR
20 Academic Dean ... Dr. Mark CLARK

32 Vice Chancellor for Student Affairs .... Ms. Gail ZIMMERMAN
21 Comptroller .... Mrs. Kristy ROBERTSON
13 Assoc Prov for Information Svcs/CIO .... Dr. P. Scott BEVINS
06 Registrar .... Ms. Narda PORTER
15 Director of Human Resources .... Ms. Stephanie D. PERRY
29 Director of Alumni Relations .... Vacant
37 Director of Financial Aid .... Ms. Rebecca HUFFMAN
35 Asst Dir of Student Activities .... Ms. Mikaela LOGAN
36 Dir of Discovery & Planning .... Ms. Neva BRYAN
38 Personal Counselor/Health Services .... Ms. Sara SCHILL
19 Interim Campus Police Chief .... Mr. Beau BOGGS
12 Site Director UVA-Wise Programs .... Ms. Courtney L. CONNER-STRINGER
27 Director of Marketing .... Ms. Genna WELSH KASUN
24 Director of Media Services .... Ms. Rosa BOTT
40 Bookstore Manager .... Vacant
39 Director of Residence Life .... Mr. Robbie CHULICK
108 Director Institutional Assessment .... Mr. David KLOCEK
100 Chief of Staff .... Mr. Paul ROLLINS
28 AVC Diversity/Equity/Inclusion .... Ms. Tabitha SMITH

Virginia Beach Theological Seminary (A)

2221 Centerville Turnpike, Virginia Beach VA 23464-6847

County: Virginia Beach | FICE Identification: 039663 | Unit ID: 449834
Telephone: (757) 479-3706 | Carnegie Class: Spec-4-yr-Faith
FAX Number: N/A | Calendar System: Semester
URL: www.vbts.edu
Established: 1995 | Annual Graduate Tuition & Fees: N/A
Enrollment: 35 | Coed
Affiliation or Control: Baptist | IRS Status: 501(c)3
Highest Offering: Doctorate; No Undergraduates
Accreditation: TRACS

01 President .... Dr. Daniel K. DAVEY
05 Chief Academic Officer .... Dr. Eric J. LEHNER
07 Director of Admissions/Registrar .... Mr. Scott ROSEN
10 Financial Officer/Dir Operations .... Capt. Tony A. BRAZAS
08 Head Librarian .... Vacant

Virginia Bible College (B)

1006 Williamstown Dr, Dumfries VA 22026

County: Prince William | Identification: 667327
Telephone: (703) 445-9056 | Carnegie Class: Not Classified
FAX Number: (703) 445-9057 | Calendar System: Quarter
URL: vabiblecollege.edu
Established: 2011 | Annual Undergrad Tuition & Fees: N/A
Enrollment: N/A | Coed
Affiliation or Control: Independent Non-Profit | IRS Status: 501(c)3
Highest Offering: Doctorate
Accreditation: TRACS

01 Interim President .... Dr. Courtney MCBATH
05 VP of Academic & Student Affs .... Dr. Shennell JANUARY
11 VP of Administration .... Dr. Courtney MCBATH
58 Director of Graduate Studies .... Dr. James BOWERS
06 Registrar .... Vacant
08 Librarian .... Ms. Donna MCDONALD

Virginia Christian University (C)

14012-F Sullyfield Circle, Chantilly VA 20151

County: Fairfax | Identification: 667352
Telephone: (703) 629-1281 | Carnegie Class: Not Classified
FAX Number: (703) 657-0690 | Calendar System: Semester
URL: vacu.edu/
Established: 2005 | Annual Undergrad Tuition & Fees: N/A
Enrollment: N/A | Coed
Affiliation or Control: Presbyterian Church In America | IRS Status: 501(c)3
Highest Offering: Master's
Accreditation: BI

01 President .... Dr. Thomas RHEE
05 Academic Dean & Dir Graduate Pgm .... Dr. Sunik HWANG
15 Vice Pres & Dir Human Resources .... Dr. Joshua PARK
32 Dean of Students .... Dr. Hyejoo LEE
10 Director of Finance .... Ms. Enkhsetseg UDVAL
06 Director of Registration .... Ms. Sooyoung YIM
13 Director of Technology .... Mr. Junwhan KIM
07 Director of Admissions .... Ms. Hayeon KIM

Virginia Commonwealth University (D)

901 W Franklin Street, Box 842527,
Richmond VA 23284-2527

County: Independent City | FICE Identification: 003735 | Unit ID: 234030
Telephone: (804) 828-0100 | Carnegie Class: DU-Highest
FAX Number: N/A | Calendar System: Semester
URL: www.vcu.edu
Established: 1838 | Annual Undergrad Tuition & Fees (In-State): $14,710
Enrollment: 29,070 | Coed
Affiliation or Control: State | IRS Status: 501(c)3
Highest Offering: Doctorate
Accreditation: SC, ANEST, ART, CACREP, CAEP, CAEPN, CAMPEP, CEA, CIDA, CLPSY, COPSY, DANCE, DENT, DH, DIETI, DMS, EMT, FEPAC, HSA, IPSY, JOUR, MED, MLS, MUS, #NMT, NURSE, OT, PAST, PDPSY, PH, PHAR, PLNG, PTA, RAD, RTT, SPAA, SW, THEA

01 President/Pres & Chair VCU Hlth Sys .... Dr. Michael RAO
05 Provost & Sr VP Academic Affairs .... Dr. Fotis SOTIROPOULOS
17 Sr VP Health Sci/CEO VCU Hlth Sys .... Dr. Arthur KELLERMANN
10 SVP & Chief Financial Officer .... Ms. Karol GRAY
46 VP for Research & Innovation .... Dr. Srirama P. RAO
111 VP Development/Alumni Relations .... Mr. Jason DAVENPORT
86 VP External Affairs & Health Policy .... Ms. Karah L. GUNTHER
32 Vice Pres for Student Affairs .... Dr. Aaron J. HART
88 Vice Prov for Life Sciences .... Dr. Robert M. TOMBES
09 Asst VProv Inst Rsrch & Decision Su .... Ms. Monal PATEL
84 VP Strategy/Enroll Mgmt/Stdnt Succ .... Dr. Tomika LEGRANDE
13 Chief Information Officer .... Mr. Alexander L. HENSON
18 Assoc VP Facilities Management .... Mr. Richard F. SLIWOSKI
113 AVP Student Financial Svcs .... Mr. Norman F. BEDFORD
15 Asst Vice Pres for Human Resources .... Ms. Cathleen C. BURKE
08 Dean Libraries/Univ Librarian .... Ms. Irene HEROLD
43 Interim University Counsel .... Mr. Jake BELUE
41 Vice Pres & Director of Athletics .... Mr. Edward K. MCLAUGHLIN
21 Asst Vice Pres of Business Services .... Ms. Diane L. REYNOLDS
39 Exec Dir Res Life/Housing .... Mr. Gavin ROARK
06 Univ Registrar & Dir Records/Regis .... Mr. Bernard C. HAMM
37 Dir of Financial Aid & Scholarship .... Mr. Evan UDOWITCH
38 Interim AVP of Counseling Services .... Dr. Jihad N. AZIZ
36 Sr Associate Dir Career Advising .... Ms. Haley SIMS
35 Assoc Vice Prov/Dean Student Affs .... Dr. Reuban B. RODRIGUEZ
29 Assistant VP Alumni Relations .... Ms. Elizabeth BASS
88 Exec Dir Global Education Office .... Dr. Jill BLONDIN
88 Dir Ctr for Environmental Studies .... Dr. Rodney J. DYER
19 Assoc Vice Pres Public Safety .... Mr. John A. VENUTI
35 Assoc VProvost Student Affairs .... Mr. Curtis ERWIN
31 Assoc Director Svc Learning .... Ms. Katie ELLIOTT
92 Dean Honors College .... Dr. Scott BREUNINGER
67 Interim Dean of Pharmacy .... Dr. Kelechi C. OGBONNA
66 Dean of School of Nursing .... Dr. Jean GIDDENS
63 Int Dean of School of Medicine .... Dr. David CHELMOW
53 Dean School of Education .... Dr. Andrew P. DAIRE
52 Dean of Dentistry .... Dr. Lyndon F. COOPER
50 Interim Dean School of Business .... Mr. S Douglas PUGH
79 Interim Dean Humanities & Sciences .... Dr. Catherine INGRASSIA
57 Dean School of Arts .... Dr. Carmenita HIGGINBOTHAM
70 Dean School of Social Work .... Dr. Beth ANGELL
76 Dean College Health Professions .... Dr. Susan PARISH
58 Dean Graduate School .... Dr. Daniel C. BULLARD
54 Dean of School of Engineering .... Dr. Barbara D. BOYAN
96 Director Procurement Svcs .... Mr. John MCHUGH
26 Vice President University Relations .... Mr. Grant J. HESTON
104 Director Education Abroad . Ms. Stephanie DAVENPORT TIGNOR
106 Interim Exec Dir VCU Online .... Ms. Judith KORNBERG
90 Director Academic Technologies .... Ms. Colleen BISHOP
108 Dir Academic Integrity & Assessment .... Vacant
22 VP Inclusive Excellence .... Dr. Aashir NASIM
105 Deputy Dir Application Services .... Mr. James B. YUCHA
30 Sr Assoc VP for Development .... Mr. Magnus H. JOHNSSON
44 Executive Dir Strategic Initiatives .... Mr. Michael P. ANDREWS
07 Director of Admissions Operations .... Mr. Roger BUTLER

*Virginia Community College System Office (E)

300 Arboretum Place, Suite 200, Richmond VA 23236

County: Independent City | FICE Identification: 008904
Telephone: (804) 819-4901 | Carnegie Class: N/A
FAX Number: N/A
URL: www.vccs.edu

01 Chancellor .... Dr. Glenn DUBOIS
05 Sr Vice Chanc Acad/Workforce Pgms .... Dr. Sharon MORRISSEY
10 Sr Vice Chanc Admin/Finance/Tech .... Dr. Craig HERNDON
13 Chief Information Officer .... Dr. Michael RUSSELL
111 Vice Chanc Institutional Advance .... Dr. Jennifer SAGER GENTRY
15 Assoc Vice Chanc Human Resource Svc .... Ms. Malinda CARTER
18 Assoc Vice Chanc/Facility Mgmt .... Mr. Bert JONES
43 General Counsel .... Ms. Greer SAUNDERS
116 Int Director of Internal Audit .... Ms. Mary BARNETT
21 Controller .... Mr. Randall ELLIS
04 Exec Assistant to the Chancellor .... Ms. Rose Marie OWEN

*Blue Ridge Community College (F)

PO Box 80, Weyers Cave VA 24486-0080

County: Augusta | FICE Identification: 006819 | Unit ID: 231536
Telephone: (540) 234-9261 | Carnegie Class: Assoc/HT-Mix Trad/Non
FAX Number: (540) 234-8189 | Calendar System: Semester
URL: www.brcc.edu
Established: 1967 | Annual Undergrad Tuition & Fees (In-State): $5,364
Enrollment: 3,462 | Coed
Affiliation or Control: State | IRS Status: 501(c)3
Highest Offering: Associate Degree
Accreditation: SC, ADNUR

02 President .... Dr. John A. DOWNEY
05 Vice Pres Instruction/Student Svcs .... Dr. Robert YOUNG
10 VP Finance/Administration .... Ms. Anastasia SHIFLETT
15 Director of Human Resources .... Mr. Tim NICELY
30 Exec Dir Development/Foundation .... Ms. Amy L. KIGER
20 Dean of Academic Affairs .... Ms. Marlena JARBOE
20 Dean of Academic Affairs .... Dr. David URSO
51 Dean Continuing Educ/Workforce Dev .... Dr. Kevin B. RATLIFF
32 Dean Student Svcs/Acad Compliance .... Ms. Velma BRYANT
08 Head Librarian .... Ms. Dawn WALTON
26 Chief Public Relations Officer .... Ms. Bridget BAYLOR
06 Registrar/Admissions .... Ms. Lisa ADKINS

21 Director of Finance & Facilities .... Ms. Franki HAMPTON
09 Director Institutional Research .... Dr. Susan E. CROSBY
37 Financial Aid Coordinator .... Ms. Megan HARTLESS
36 Career Services/Recruitment Coord .... Ms. Carmel MURPHY-NORRIS

*Central Virginia Community College (G)

3506 Wards Road, Lynchburg VA 24502-2498

County: Independent City | FICE Identification: 004988 | Unit ID: 231697
Telephone: (434) 832-7600 | Carnegie Class: Assoc/HT-High Non
FAX Number: (434) 386-4700 | Calendar System: Semester
URL: www.centralvirginia.edu
Established: 1966 | Annual Undergrad Tuition & Fees (In-State): $4,838
Enrollment: 3,370 | Coed
Affiliation or Control: State | IRS Status: 501(c)3
Highest Offering: Associate Degree
Accreditation: SC, COARC, EMT, RAD

02 President .... Dr. John CAPPS
05 VP Student & Academic Services .... Dr. Muriel MICKLES
10 Vice President Finance & Admin Svcs .... Mr. Lewis BRYANT, III
111 Exec Dir Educational Foundation .... Vacant
13 Vice Pres of Information Technology .... Mr. David LIGHTFOOT
45 Dean Inst Effectiveness/Planning .... Dr. Kristen OGDEN
26 Dir Advancement/Public Relations .... Mr. Kenneth BUNCH
06 College Registrar .... Ms. Karen ALEXANDER
84 Dean of Enrollment Management .... Dr. Michael FARRIS
15 Human Resource Director .... Mr. Randall FRANKLIN
56 Coord Instr Tech Lib/Testing Svcs .... Mr. Ed MCGEE
08 Coordinator of Library Services .... Mr. Michael T. FEIN
75 AVP Professional & Career Studies .... Dr. Jason FERGUSON
49 AVP of Arts & Sciences .... Dr. Cynthia WALLIN
04 General Administration Coordinator .... Ms. Dianne SYKES

*Danville Community College (H)

1008 S Main Street, Danville VA 24541-4088

County: Independent City | FICE Identification: 003758 | Unit ID: 231882
Telephone: (434) 797-2222 | Carnegie Class: Assoc/MT-VT-High Non
FAX Number: (434) 797-8514 | Calendar System: Semester
URL: www.danville.edu
Established: 1967 | Annual Undergrad Tuition & Fees (In-State): $4,725
Enrollment: 2,411 | Coed
Affiliation or Control: State | IRS Status: 501(c)3
Highest Offering: Associate Degree
Accreditation: SC, NAEYC

02 President .... Dr. Jerry WALLACE
05 VP Academic Affs/Student Services .... Dr. Cornelius H. JOHNSON
10 Vice Pres Financial/Admin Services .... Mr. Wayne PETERS
30 Vice President of Development .... Mr. Shannon HAIR
103 Vice President of Workforce Service .... Vacant
09 Dir of Plng/Effectiveness/Research .... Mr. Cory POTTER
07 Coordinator of Admissions .... Ms. Cathy PULLLIAM
38 Coordinator of Counseling .... Mr. Howard GRAVES
26 Public Relations/Marketing Manager .... Ms. Faith O'NEIL
04 Exec Assistant to the President .... Ms. Connie P. WANN
08 Chief Library Officer .... Mr. Christopher FORD
15 Chief Human Resources Officer .... Vacant
37 Director Student Financial Aid .... Ms. Angela TURNER

*Eastern Shore Community College (I)

29316 Lankford Highway, Melfa VA 23410-9755

County: Accomack | FICE Identification: 003748 | Unit ID: 232052
Telephone: (757) 789-1789 | Carnegie Class: Assoc/MT-VT-High Non
FAX Number: N/A | Calendar System: Semester
URL: www.es.vccs.edu
Established: 1971 | Annual Undergrad Tuition & Fees (In-State): $4,800
Enrollment: 677 | Coed
Affiliation or Control: State | IRS Status: 501(c)3
Highest Offering: Associate Degree
Accreditation: SC

02 President .... Dr. James M. SHAEFFER
05 VP of Acad/Workforce/Student Prgms .... Dr. Patrick TOMPKINS
11 Assoc VP Administration .... Ms. Eve BELOTE
32 Coordinator of Student Services .... Mrs. Cheryll MILLS
09 Director of Institutional Research .... Ms. Judith GRIER
26 Marketing and Development Officer .... Mr. William LECATO
37 Financial Aid Coordinator .... Ms. Carole READ
15 Human Resource Officer .... Ms. Beth LUNDE
04 Admin Assistant to the President .... Ms. Raven MAXIM
19 Chief of Police .... Mr. David BRANCH
30 Director of Development .... Ms. Patricia KELLAM
06 Registrar .... Vacant
103 Business Dev & Workforce Officer .... Mr. Scott HALL
13 Chief Info Technology Officer .... Mr. Mike SMITH

*Germanna Community College (J)

2130 Germanna Highway, Locust Grove VA 22508-2102

County: Orange | FICE Identification: 008660 | Unit ID: 232195
Telephone: (540) 423-9030 | Carnegie Class: Assoc/HT-Mix Trad/Non
FAX Number: (540) 727-3207 | Calendar System: Semester
URL: www.germanna.edu
Established: 1970 | Annual Undergrad Tuition & Fees (In-State): $4,140

Enrollment: 7,679 Coed
Affiliation or Control: State IRS Status: 501(c)3
Highest Offering: Associate Degree
Accreditation: SC, ADNUR, DA, DH, EMT, PTAA

02 President .... Dr. Janet GULLICKSON
04 Exec Assistant to the President .... Ms. Lorraine PENDLETON
05 VP Academic Affairs & Workforce Dev .... Dr. Shashuna GRAY
10 VP Finance & Administrative Svcs .... Dr. John DAVIS
32 VP Student Svc/Equity Advancement .... Dr. Tiffany RAY
35 Dean of Student Services .... Dr. Frank CIRIONI
45 Director Planning/Research/Effectiv .... Mr. David DEMEDICIS
08 Head Librarian .... Ms. Tamara REMHOF
06 Registrar .... Ms. Cheri MAEA
72 Dean Professional & Technical Study .... Ms. Tina LANCE
106 Dean Distance Educ & Lrng Resources .... Dr. Yanyan YONG
66 Dean of Nursing & Health Technology .... Dr. Patti LISK
15 Associate VP of Human Resources .... Vacant
18 Director of Facilities .... Mr. Garland FENWICK
26 Director of Marketing .... Mr. William BERRY
49 Dean of Arts & Sciences .... Dr. John STROFFOLINO
19 Chief of Police .... Mr. Craig BRANCH
37 Director Student Financial Aid .... Mr. Aaron WHITACRE

*J. Sargeant Reynolds Community College (A)

PO Box 85622, Richmond VA 23285-5622
County: Henrico FICE Identification: 003759
Unit ID: 232414
Telephone: (804) 371-3000 Carnegie Class: Assoc/HVT-High Non
FAX Number: (804) 371-3650 Calendar System: Semester
URL: www.reynolds.edu
Established: 1972 Annual Undergrad Tuition & Fees (In-State): $4,998
Enrollment: 7,759 Coed
Affiliation or Control: State IRS Status: 501(c)3
Highest Offering: Associate Degree
Accreditation: SC, ACFEI, ADNUR, COARC, DA, EMT, MLTAD, OPD

02 President .... Dr. Paula P. PANDO
05 Vice President Academic Affairs .... Vacant
111 Vice President Advancement .... Mrs. Elizabeth S. LITTLEFIELD
103 VP Comm Col Workforce Alliance .... Mr. Wesley SMITH
10 VP Finance and Administration .... Ms. Amelia M. BRADSHAW
32 VP Student Affairs/Title IX Coord .... Vacant
84 VP Enroll Mgmt/Student Success .... Dr. Terricita E. SASS
45 Assoc VP Strat Plng/Inst Effective .... Dr. Timothy MERRILL
50 Dean School of Business .... Mr. David J. BARRISH
76 Dean School of Nursing/Allied Hlth .... Dr. Patricia P. LAWSON
81 Dean School of Math Sci Engineering .. Mr. Raymond A. BURTON
20 Asst VP Academic Affairs .... Dr. Lori DWYER
15 Assoc VP HR/Equal Emp Oppty Ofcr .... Ms. Corliss B. WOODSON
37 Director of Financial Aid .... Ms. Sherika CHARITY
07 Director of Admissions & Records .... Mrs. Karen M. PETTIS-WALDEN
27 Director Communications .... Mr. Joseph SHILLING
26 Director of Marketing .... Ms. Kelly A. SMITH
08 Director of Info/Library Services .... Ms. Hong WU
18 Director Facilities Mgmt/Planning .... Vacant
30 Director of Development .... Ms. Marianne S. MCGHEE
88 Director of Middle College .... Ms. Mary Jo WASHKO
06 Registrar .... Ms. Angela ROSS
19 Chief of Police .... Mr. Paul L. RONCA
04 Admin Assistant to the President .... Ms. Ann M. BUSHEY
106 Dean of Online Learning .... Dr. Danielle R. LEEK

*John Tyler Community College (B)

13101 Route 1, Chester VA 23831-5316
County: Chesterfield FICE Identification: 004004
Unit ID: 232450
Telephone: (804) 796-4000 Carnegie Class: Assoc/HT-High Non
FAX Number: (804) 796-4163 Calendar System: Semester
URL: www.jtcc.edu
Established: 1965 Annual Undergrad Tuition & Fees (In-State): $4,800
Enrollment: 9,440 Coed
Affiliation or Control: State IRS Status: 501(c)3
Highest Offering: Associate Degree
Accreditation: SC, ADNUR, EMT, FUSER

02 President .... Dr. Edward (Ted) E. RASPILLER
04 Admin Assistant to the President .... Ms. Kara ARMSTRONG
05 VP Learning & Student Success .... Dr. William FIEGE
10 VP Administration .... Ms. Susan GRINNAN
111 VP Institutional Advancement .... Ms. Rachel BIUNDO
103 VP Workforce Dev/Credential Attain .... Ms. Elizabeth CREAMER
21 Assoc VP of Financial Services .... Ms. Natolyn QUASH
32 Dean of Students .... Ms. Sandra KIRKLAND
20 Assoc VP of Learning .... Dr. Johanna WEISS
20 Assoc VP Academics .... Dr. Mikell BROWN
09 Dir Institutional Effectiveness .... Dr. Keri-Beth PETTENGILL
08 Dir of Library Services .... Ms. Suzanne SHERRY
37 Director Financial Aid .... Mr. Andrew QUINN
19 Asst Dir College Safety & Security .... Ms. Tanya BROWN
26 Public Relations Manager .... Ms. Holly WALKER
121 Assoc Dean of Advising .... Ms. Altrice SMITH
19 Dir Facilities Operations & Safety .... Mr. Chip KRAMER
06 Dir Admissions & Records/Registrar .... Mr. Leigh BAXTER

*Laurel Ridge Community College (C)

173 Skirmisher Lane, Middletown VA 22645-1745
County: Frederick FICE Identification: 008659
Unit ID: 232575
Telephone: (540) 868-7000 Carnegie Class: Assoc/MT-VT-High Non
FAX Number: (540) 868-7100 Calendar System: Semester
URL: www.lfcc.edu
Established: 1970 Annual Undergrad Tuition & Fees (In-State): $4,739
Enrollment: 6,337 Coed
Affiliation or Control: State IRS Status: 501(c)3
Highest Offering: Associate Degree
Accreditation: SC, ADNUR, CAHIIM, EMT, MLTAD, SURGT

02 President .... Dr. Kim BLOSSER
12 Provost Fauquier Campus .... Dr. Christopher COUTTS
05 VP Academic & Student Affairs .... Dr. Anne DAVIS
103 VP of Workforce & Prof Development .... Ms. Jeanian CLARK
30 AVP Development/Exec Dir Educ Fdn .... Ms. Liv HEGGOY
15 AVP Human Resources .... Ms. JoAnn ELLWOOD
09 Dir Planning/Inst Effectiveness .... Dr. John MILAM
50 Dean Business/Technology/Education .... Ms. Brenda BYARD
81 Dean Science/Eng/Math & Health .... Dr. Ia GOMEZ
83 Dean Hum/Social Sciences/Stdnt Dev .... Dr. James GILLISPIE
32 Dean of Students .... Ms. Amber FOLTZ
20 Dean Fauquier Campus .... Dr. Carolline WOOD
24 Director Learning Resources Center .... Mr. David R. GRAY
37 Director of Financial Aid .... Mr. Steven WILSON
08 Librarian .... Ms. Kerry KILPATRICK
25 Grants Manager .... Dr. Melissa DEDOMENICO-PAYNE
26 Dir Public Relations .... Ms. Brandy BOIES
21 Director Budget/Finance .... Mr. Barry ORNDORFF
84 Dean of Enrollment Svcs/Title IX .... Dr. Mia S. DEZURA
06 Registrar .... Ms. Tina Marie ANDERSON
88 Dir Marketing/Business/Ind Trng .... Mr. Guy E. CURTIS, III
20 Associate Dean of Instruction .... Ms. Heather BURTON
88 Director Small Business Dev Center .... Ms. Christine KRIZ

*Mountain Gateway Community College (D)

1000 College Drive, Clifton Forge VA 24422-1000
County: Alleghany FICE Identification: 004996
Unit ID: 231873
Telephone: (540) 863-2820 Carnegie Class: Assoc/HT-High Non
FAX Number: (540) 863-2915 Calendar System: Semester
URL: www.mgcc.edu
Established: 1962 Annual Undergrad Tuition & Fees (In-State): $4,710
Enrollment: 1,075 Coed
Affiliation or Control: State IRS Status: 501(c)3
Highest Offering: Associate Degree
Accreditation: SC, ADNUR

02 President .... Dr. John J. RAINONE
05 Vice President of Academic Affairs .... Dr. Benjamin WORTH
10 Vice Pres Financial/Admin Svcs .... Mrs. Angela GRAHAM
51 VP Continuing Educ/Workforce Svcs .... Mr. Gary S. KEENER
09 AVP of Institutional Effectiveness .... Dr. Matthew MCGRAW
32 Director of Student Services .... Ms. Suzanne OSTLING
111 Director of Inst Advancement .... Mr. Joseph HAGY
08 Director of Learning Resources .... Ms. Nova WRIGHT
13 Technical Services Manager .... Mr. Wayne RAUENZAHN
15 Director of Human Resources .... Ms. April TOLLEY
18 Buildings & Grounds Supervisor .... Mr. Steven N. RICHARDS
21 Business Manager .... Ms. Deidre WOLFE
07 Admissions Officer .... Vacant
37 Coord of Student Financial Aid .... Mrs. Coty LANFORD
04 Executive Asst to President .... Mr. Xavier STOREY
06 Registrar .... Mrs. Phyllis BARTLEY
41 Athletic Director .... Mr. Daniel CALLAHAN

*Mountain Empire Community College (E)

3441 Mountain Empire Road,
Big Stone Gap VA 24219-4634
County: Wise FICE Identification: 009629
Unit ID: 232788
Telephone: (276) 523-2400 Carnegie Class: Assoc/MT-VT-High Non
FAX Number: (276) 523-8297 Calendar System: Semester
URL: www.mecc.edu
Established: 1972 Annual Undergrad Tuition & Fees (In-State): $4,710
Enrollment: 2,253 Coed
Affiliation or Control: State IRS Status: 501(c)3
Highest Offering: Associate Degree
Accreditation: SC, ADNUR, CAHIIM, COARC

02 President .... Dr. Kristen WESTOVER
05 VP of Academic & Workforce Solution .... Dr. William BROWNSBERGER
10 Vice Pres Finance & Admin Services .... Mr. Ron VICARS
111 Vice Pres Institutional Advancement .... Dr. Amy GREEAR
32 Dean of Student Services .... Ms. Lelia BRADSHAW
07 Dean Admission/Financial Aid .... Ms. Kristy HALL
08 Director of Library Services .... Vacant
76 Dean of Health Sciences .... Ms. Kim DORTON
13 Dir Ctr Computing & Info Technology .... Mr. Ritchie DEEL
15 Director Personnel Services .... Ms. Valerie LEE
18 Chief Facilities/Physical Plant .... Mr. Preston LAYNE
49 Dean Arts & Sciences .... Dr. Derek WHISMAN
72 Dean of Industrial Tech .... Mr. Matt ROSE
26 Chief Public Relations Officer .... Ms. Amy GREEAR
19 Chief of Police .... Mr. Grayson COTHRAN
04 Exec Assistant to the President .... Ms. Peggy GIBSON

*New River Community College (F)

5251 College Drive, Dublin VA 24084
County: Pulaski FICE Identification: 005223
Unit ID: 232867
Telephone: (540) 674-3600 Carnegie Class: Assoc/MT-VT-High Non
FAX Number: (540) 674-3642 Calendar System: Semester
URL: www.nr.edu
Established: 1969 Annual Undergrad Tuition & Fees (In-State): $4,697
Enrollment: 4,137 Coed
Affiliation or Control: State IRS Status: 501(c)3
Highest Offering: Associate Degree
Accreditation: SC

02 President .... Dr. Patricia B. HUBER
05 VP for Instruction/Student Services .... Dr. Peter T. ANDERSON
10 Vice Pres for Finance & Technology ... Mr. John L. VAN HEMERT
30 VP for WD and External Relations .... Dr. Mark C. ROWH
09 Dir Inst Effectiveness/Research .... Dr. Fredrick M. STREFF
102 Executive Director of Foundation .... Ms. Angie E. COVEY
49 Dean of Arts & Sciences .... Ms. Sarah TOLBERT-HURYSZ
50 Dean of Business & Technologies .... Ms. Debra BOND
32 Dean of Student Services .... Dr. Deborah KENNEDY
15 Dir Human Resources & Business Oper .... Ms. Melissa P. ANDERSON
06 Registrar .... Mrs. Tammy SMITH
37 Financial Aid Manager .... Mrs. Shauna CROSSCUP
88 Emergency Coordination Officer .... Mr. Joseph WILLIAMS
96 Inventory and Purchasing Technician .... Ms. Monica W. CARDEN
106 Director Online Learning .... Mrs. Linda C. CLAUSSEN
08 Coordinator of Library Services .... Mrs. Sandra B. SMITH
07 Coord Admissions/Records/Stdnt Svcs .... Mrs. Tammy SMITH
18 Chief Facilities/Physical Plant .... Mr. Ronald NICHOLS
88 Coordinator of WorkKeys Center .... Mr. Ross MATNEY
88 Enrollment Coordinator .... Mrs. Lori MITCHELL
26 Public Relations Specialist .... Mrs. Jill ROSS
22 Coord Ctr for Disability Services .... Ms. Lucy J. HOWLETT
84 Enroll Mgr & Transfer Svcs Coord .... Ms. Alison WESTON
04 Administrative Asst to President .... Mrs. Kathy T. RIDPATH

*Northern Virginia Community College (G)

4001 Wakefield Chapel Road, Annandale VA 22003-3796
County: Fairfax FICE Identification: 003727
Unit ID: 232946
Telephone: (703) 323-3000 Carnegie Class: Assoc/HT-Mix Trad/Non
FAX Number: (703) 323-3767 Calendar System: Semester
URL: www.nvcc.edu
Established: 1965 Annual Undergrad Tuition & Fees (In-State): $5,610
Enrollment: 52,873 Coed
Affiliation or Control: State IRS Status: 501(c)3
Highest Offering: Associate Degree
Accreditation: SC, ADNUR, CAHIIM, COARC, DA, DH, DMS, EMT, MLTAD, NAEYC, OTA, PTAA

02 President .... Dr. Anne M. KRESS
13 VP of IET & College Computing .... Dr. Chad KNIGHTS
103 VP for Workforce & Strat Partnershp .... Mr. Steve PARTRIDGE
05 VP of Academic Affairs & CAO .... Dr. Eun-Woo CHANG
32 Vice President Student Services .... Dr. Syedur RAHMAN
84 Assoc VP Stdnt Svcs & Enroll Mgmt .... Vacant
12 Provost Alexandria Campus .... Dr. Annette HAGGRAY
12 Provost Loudoun Campus .... Dr. Julie LEIDIG
12 Provost Manassas Campus .... Dr. Molly LYNCH
102 Exec Dir NVCC Education Foundation .... Vacant
25 Director of Grants .... Dr. Syedur RAHMAN
15 AVP of Human Resources .... Ms. Charlotte M. CALOBRISI
37 Dir Stdnt Financial Aid/Support Svc .... Ms. Joan A. ZANDERS
21 Associate VP for Administration .... Mr. Cory THOMPSON
18 Director of Facilities .... Mr. Steven PATTERSON
19 Director Security/Safety .... Chief Daniel DUSSEAU
88 Office Manager .... Ms. Corinne C. HURST
09 Director of Institutional Research .... Mr. Steve PARTRIDGE

*Patrick & Henry Community College (H)

645 Patriot Avenue, Martinsville VA 24112
County: Henry FICE Identification: 003751
Unit ID: 233019
Telephone: (276) 638-8777 Carnegie Class: Assoc/HT-Mix Trad/Non
FAX Number: (276) 656-0320 Calendar System: Semester
URL: www.patrickhenry.edu
Established: 1962 Annual Undergrad Tuition & Fees (In-State): $4,720
Enrollment: 2,050 Coed
Affiliation or Control: State IRS Status: 501(c)3
Highest Offering: Associate Degree
Accreditation: SC, ADNUR, EMT, PTAA

02 President .... Dr. Greg HODGES
05 VP Academic/Student Devel Svcs .... Dr. Chris WIKSTROM
10 VP Finance & Admin Services .... Mr. John HANBURY
103 VP Workforce/Economic/Community Dev .... Mrs. Rhonda HODGES
30 Director of Development .... Mrs. Tiffani UNDERWOOD
121 Dean Academic Success/Col Transfer .... Mr. Terry YOUNG
81 Dean STEM/Health/Applied Programs .... Dr. Colin FERGUSON
66 Coordinator Nursing/Allied Health .... Ms. Amy WEBSTER
13 Dean of Technology .... Mr. David DEAL
15 Director of Human Resources .... Ms. Belinda STOCKTON
84 Dean Student Success/Enroll Svcs .... Vacant

07 Coord Admiss & Accelerated Lrng .... Ms. Meghan EGGLESTON
26 Public Relations & Mktg Mgr .... Mr. Randy FERGUSON
06 Registrar .... Ms. Jessica CARTER
37 Financial Aid/Veterans Admin .... Mrs. Cindy KELLER
08 Coord Library Services .... Ms. Marcia SEATON-MARTIN
25 Chief Contracts/Grants Admin .... Ms. Sarah B. MORRISON
41 Athletic Director .... Mr. Brian HENDERSON
09 Int Director Institutional Research .... Ms. Lisa FINLEY
18 Chief Facilities/Physical Plant .... Ms. Roberta WRIGHT
19 Director Security/Safety .... Mr. Gary DOVE
96 Director of Purchasing .... Ms. Lori CONNER
04 Administrative Asst to President .... Ms. Sue-Ann EHMANN

*Paul D. Camp Community College (A)

100 N College Drive, Franklin VA 23851-0737
County: Independent City FICE Identification: 009159
Unit ID: 233037
Telephone: (757) 569-6700 Carnegie Class: Assoc/HT-High Non
FAX Number: (757) 569-6795 Calendar System: Semester
URL: www.pdc.edu
Established: 1970 Annual Undergrad Tuition & Fees (In-State): $4,730
Enrollment: 1,237 Coed
Affiliation or Control: State IRS Status: 501(c)3
Highest Offering: Associate Degree
Accreditation: SC, ADNUR

02 President .... Dr. Corey L. MCCRAY
05 VP Academic/Student Development .... Dr. Tara ATKINS-BRADY
11 Operations Manager .... Mr. Phillip BRADSHAW
111 Dir Institutional Advancement .... Mr. Jeff ZEIGLER
32 Dean Student Services .... Dr. Trina JONES
20 Dean of Academic Programs .... Dr. Justin OLIVER
08 Coordinator of Library Services .... Ms. Cirrus GUNDLACH
103 Dir of Workforce Development .... Dr. Antoinette JOHNSON
09 Coord Inst Research/Assessment .... Ms. Damay J. BULLOCK
15 Director of Human Resources .... Ms. Michelle DANDRIDGE
37 Financial Aid Coordinator .... Dr. Teresa HARRISON
04 Assistant to the President .... Ms. Cathy CUTCHINS
06 Registrar .... Mrs. Chris RICKS
41 Athletic Director .... Dr. Justin OLIVER

*Piedmont Virginia Community College (B)

501 College Drive, Charlottesville VA 22902-7589
County: Independent City FICE Identification: 009928
Unit ID: 233116
Telephone: (434) 977-5200 Carnegie Class: Assoc/HT-High Non
FAX Number: (434) 296-8395 Calendar System: Semester
URL: www.pvcc.edu
Established: 1972 Annual Undergrad Tuition & Fees (In-State): $4,790
Enrollment: 4,864 Coed
Affiliation or Control: State IRS Status: 501(c)3
Highest Offering: Associate Degree
Accreditation: SC, ADNUR, DMS, EMT, RAD, SURGT

02 President .... Dr. Frank FRIEDMAN
05 VP Instruction/Student Svcs .... Dr. John DONNELLY
10 Vice President Finance/Admin Svcs .... Dr. Benjamin COPELAND
111 Vice Pres Advancement/Development ...... Mr. Harry STILLERMAN
79 Dean Humanities/Fine Arts/Soc Sci .... Dr. Leonda KENISTON
32 Dean of Student Svcs/Admissions .... Dr. Andrew RENSHAW
76 Dean Health & Life Sciences .... Ms. Nicole WINKLER
103 Dean Workforce Services .... Dr. Christy HAWKINS
13 Chief Information Officer .... Mr. Tom RUGGERI
09 Dir Inst Research/Planning/Effect .... Ms. Brittany RESMANN
06 Registrar .... Ms. Allyson REA
96 Business Manager .... Ms. Tracy CERSLEY
18 Facilities Manager .... Mr. Kim MCMANUS
15 Human Resources Director .... Ms. Angela NICHOLAS
26 Marketing/Media Relations Director .... Ms. Susian BROOKS
88 Outreach Manager .... Ms. Denise MCCLANAHAN
08 Director Library Services .... Ms. Crystal NEWELL
37 Director Financial Aid .... Ms. Rachel HAILEY
121 Director Advising & Transfer .... Mr. Kemper STEELE
19 Director Security/Safety .... Mr. Dwayne BOYLES
25 Mgr Grants Development & Admin .... Ms. Caitilin MOHR

*Rappahannock Community College (C)

12745 College Drive, Glenns VA 23149-0287
County: Gloucester FICE Identification: 009160
Unit ID: 233310
Telephone: (804) 333-6730 Carnegie Class: Assoc/HT-High Non
FAX Number: N/A Calendar System: Semester
URL: www.rappahannock.edu
Established: 1970 Annual Undergrad Tuition & Fees (In-State): $4,820
Enrollment: 2,629 Coed
Affiliation or Control: State IRS Status: Exempt
Highest Offering: Associate Degree
Accreditation: SC, ADNUR, EMT

02 President .... Dr. Shannon KENNEDY
10 Vice Pres Finance/Admin Services .... Ms. Tara WALKER
05 VP of Instruction .... Dr. Eric BARNA
49 Dean of Arts & Sciences .... Dr. Marty BROOKS
32 Dean Student Development .... Dr. Dave KEEL
111 VP of College Advancement .... Ms. Sarah POPE
108 Dean Research/Effectiveness/Plng .... Dr. Glenda D. HAYNIE
37 Lead Financial Aid Tech .... Mrs. Mary TOMEK
15 Director Human Resources .... Mrs. Caroline W. STELTER
18 Facilities/Physical Plant Super .... Mr. Richard LEWTER
06 Student Records/Information Coord .... Mrs. Carol BAETZ
08 Learning Resources Coordinator .... Ms. Elizabeth HADLEY
13 Chief Information Technology Ofcr .... Dr. Jeff HAYMAN

*Southside Virginia Community College (D)

109 Campus Drive, Alberta VA 23821-2930
County: Brunswick FICE Identification: 008661
Unit ID: 233639
Telephone: (434) 949-1000 Carnegie Class: Assoc/HT-High Non
FAX Number: (434) 949-7863 Calendar System: Semester
URL: www.southside.edu
Established: 1970 Annual Undergrad Tuition & Fees (In-State): $4,695
Enrollment: 3,123 Coed
Affiliation or Control: State IRS Status: 501(c)3
Highest Offering: Associate Degree
Accreditation: SC, ADNUR, EMT

02 President .... Dr. Quentin R. JOHNSON
05 VP Academics & Workforce .... Dr. Keith HARKINS
10 VP Finance & Administration .... Mrs. Shannon V. FEINMAN
84 VP Enrollment Mgmt & Stdnt Success .... Dr. Daryl MINUS
111 Director Institutional Advancement .... Mrs. Mary Jane ELKINS
09 Dir Institutional Effectiveness .... Ms. Robin DANIEL
26 Director of Communications .... Mr. Jamie JONES
13 Chief Information Officer .... Mr. Chad WOLLENBERG
15 Human Resources Manager .... Ms. Bethany W. HARRIS
66 Dean of Nursing/Health Technology .... Ms. Melissa ARTHUR
79 Dean of Humanities/Social Sciences .... Vacant
75 Dean of Career & Occup Technology .... Dr. Chad PATTON
08 College Librarian .... Ms. Marika PETERSON
37 Director of Financial Aid .... Mrs. Sally THARRINGTON
28 HR Equity and Training Consultant .... Mrs. Theresa HENDERSON
18 Buildings/Grounds Supt Christanna .... Mr. Roger WRAY
18 Buildings/Grounds Superintendent .... Mr. Eddie BENNETT
21 Business Manager .... Mrs. Toni LAMBERT
04 Exec Assistant to the President .... Ms. Angela JACKSON

*Southwest Virginia Community College (E)

Box SVCC, Richlands VA 24641-1101
County: Tazewell FICE Identification: 007260
Unit ID: 233648
Telephone: (276) 964-2555 Carnegie Class: Assoc/MT-VT-Mix Trad/Non
FAX Number: (276) 964-9307 Calendar System: Semester
URL: www.sw.edu
Established: 1967 Annual Undergrad Tuition & Fees (In-State): $4,703
Enrollment: 2,295 Coed
Affiliation or Control: State IRS Status: 501(c)3
Highest Offering: Associate Degree
Accreditation: SC, ADNUR, EMT, OTA, RAD

02 President .... Dr. Tommy F. WRIGHT
05 VP Acad & Student Services .... Dr. Robert BRANDON
10 Vice Pres Finance/Admin Svcs .... Mr. Chris LEWIS
111 VP Institutional Advancement .... Mrs. Susan L. LOWE
15 AVP Human Resources Officer .... Ms. Kimberly STEINER
13 Chief Info Technology Officer (CIO) .... Mr. Charles MUSICK
79 Dean Humanities/Soc Science .... Dr. Brian WRIGHT
81 Dean Math/Natural Sci/Health Tech .... Dr. Clint PINION
50 Dean Business/Engr & Indust Tech .... Mr. James DYE
103 Dean Workforce/Continuing Education .... Mr. Randall ROSE
32 Dean Student Success .... Mrs. Dyan E. LESTER
11 Dir Administrative Services .... Mrs. Gwendalyn STONE
09 Institutional Research Officer .... Mrs. Cathy L. SMITH-COX
102 Exec Dir Foundation/Development .... Ms. Susan LOWE
19 Campus Police Chief .... Mr. Justin MCCULLEY
21 Business Manager .... Mr. Michael BALES
18 Physical Plant Superintendent .... Mr. Tony MCGHEE
26 Dir of Strategic Communications .... Mr. John DEZEMBER
106 Director Distance Learning .... Ms. Barbie RATLIFF
25 Grants Administrator .... Ms. Phyllis ROBERTS
105 Director Web Services .... Ms. Teresa PRUETT
41 Athletic Director .... Mr. Jason VENCILL
37 Financial Aid Manager .... Mrs. Donna PRICE
08 Coordinator of Library Services .... Dr. Teresa A. YEAROUT

*Thomas Nelson Community College (F)

99 Thomas Nelson Drive, Hampton VA 23666
County: Independent City FICE Identification: 006871
Unit ID: 233754
Telephone: (757) 825-2700 Carnegie Class: Assoc/MT-VT-Mix Trad/Non
FAX Number: (757) 825-2763 Calendar System: Semester
URL: www.tncc.edu
Established: 1967 Annual Undergrad Tuition & Fees (In-State): $4,806
Enrollment: 6,256 Coed
Affiliation or Control: State IRS Status: 501(c)3
Highest Offering: Associate Degree
Accreditation: SC, ADNUR, DH, NAEYC

02 President .... Dr. Towuanna PORTER BRANNON
05 Interim VP Academic Affairs .... Dr. Lonnie J. SCHAFFER
32 Vice President for Student Affairs .... Dr. Kris RARIG
10 Vice President for Admin/Finance .... Mr. Steven R. CARPENTER
111 Vice Pres Institutional Advancement .... Ms. Cynthia CALLAWAY
15 Assistant VP Human Resources .... Vacant
121 Director of Advising .... Dr. Jeannette HOLLINS
37 Dir Financial Aid/Veteran Affairs .... Mr. Marc T. VERNON
18 Mgr Facilities/Plng/Capital Outlay .... Mr. Mark KRAMER
30 Director of Development .... Ms. Tracy ASHLEY
09 Dir Inst Research and Effectiveness .... Mr. Steven FELKER

*Tidewater Community College (G)

121 College Place, Norfolk VA 23510
County: Independent City FICE Identification: 003712
Unit ID: 233772
Telephone: (757) 822-1122 Carnegie Class: Assoc/MT-VT-Mix Trad/Non
FAX Number: (757) 822-1055 Calendar System: Semester
URL: www.tcc.edu
Established: 1968 Annual Undergrad Tuition & Fees (In-State): $5,561
Enrollment: 16,769 Coed
Affiliation or Control: State IRS Status: 501(c)3
Highest Offering: Associate Degree
Accreditation: SC, ACFEI, ADNUR, CAHIIM, COARC, DMS, EMT, FUSER, MLTAD, NAEYC, OTA, PTAA, RAD

02 President .... Dr. Marcia CONSTON
05 VP Academic Affairs & CAO .... Dr. Michelle W. WOODHOUSE
10 VP Administration & CFO .... Ms. Heather H. HARDIMAN
111 VP Institutional Advancement .... Mr. Christopher P. BRYANT
13 VP Info Systems/Inst Effectiveness .... Mr. Curtis K. AASEN
103 VP for Workforce Solutions .... Ms. Tamara S. WILLIAMS
32 VP for Student Affairs .... Dr. Karen D. CAMPBELL
12 Dean Stdnt Supp Svcs/Norfolk Dean ..... Dr. Thomas E. CHATMAN
12 Dean of Retention/Portsmouth Dean .... Ms. Dana M. HATHORN
12 Int Dean Stdnt Life & Cond/Ches Dn .... Dr. Emily HARTMAN
12 Dean Advising/VB Dean .... Dr. Kia L. HARDY
88 Special Asst to VP Academic Affairs ... Dr. Michael D. SUMMERS
15 Associate VP Human Resources/EEO .... Ms. Beth E. LUNDE
102 Chief Admin Officer Educ Foundation .... Ms. Susan M. JAMES
20 AVP for Academic Affairs .... Dr. Kellie C. SOREY
120 AVP for Distance Learning .... Mr. John MOREA
08 AVP for Libraries .... Mr. Steve E. LITHERLAND
18 AVP Facility Planning & Operations ...... Mr. Michael J. JOHNSON
88 Pathway Dean Engr/Mrtm/Skld Trds .... Mr. David EKKER
84 Dean of Enrollment Management .... Dr. Misty LYON
79 Pathway Dean Arts & Humanities .... Dr. Kerry S. RAGNO
50 Pathway Dean Business/Comp Sci/ IT .... Ms. Nancy N. PRATHER-JOHNSON
81 Pathway Dean Science & Mathematics .... Dr. Peter T. AGBAKPE
83 Pathway Dean Soc Science/Education ..... Dr. Johnna C. HARRELL
66 Discipline Dean School Nursing .... Ms. Rita T. BOUCHARD
76 Pathway Dean Health Professions .... Ms. Jennifer FERGUSON
88 Int Discipline Dean Science/Math .... Dr. Siabhon HARRIS
107 Pathway Dean Pub/Prof Svcs .... Mr. Joseph J. FAIRCHILD
88 Discipline Dean Arts/Humanities .... Ms. Marcanne ANDERSEN
88 Pathway Dean Manufacturing/Transp .... Dr. Beno RUBIN
14 Director of Programming and Systems .... Mr. Ken BALLARD
06 College Registrar .... Dr. Nicole WILSON
88 Director of Facilities .... Mr. Albert THOMPSON
19 Director of Public Safety .... Mr. Michael C. POWELL
88 Associate VP Prof Dev Solutions .... Ms. Lisa L. PETERSON
88 Exec Dir Roper Performing Arts Ctr .... Mr. Paul H. LASAKOW
96 Dir Materiel Mgmt Procurement Svcs .... Mr. Thom HUTCHINS
37 Dir Central Financial Aid .... Mr. Justin CRISTELLO
109 Director Auxiliary Services .... Ms. Tina PRICE
45 Dir of Planning & Accountability .... Dr. Kimberly M. BOVEE
25 AVP for Sponsored Programs/CTE .... Dr. Jenefer D. SNYDER
88 Dir Stdnt Resources/Empowerment Ctr .... Dr. Jeanne B. NATALI
04 Exec Asst to President .... Ms. Latesha D. JOHNSON
28 Director Diversity/Equity/Inclusion .... Dr. ClauDean KIZART
09 Assoc Dir Institutional Effective .... Mr. Anthony MACERA

*Virginia Highlands Community College (H)

PO Box 828, Abingdon VA 24212-0828
County: Washington FICE Identification: 007099
Unit ID: 233903
Telephone: (276) 739-2400 Carnegie Class: Assoc/MT-VT-Mix Trad/Non
FAX Number: (276) 739-2590 Calendar System: Semester
URL: www.vhcc.edu
Established: 1967 Annual Undergrad Tuition & Fees (In-State): $4,710
Enrollment: 2,086 Coed
Affiliation or Control: State IRS Status: 501(c)3
Highest Offering: Associate Degree
Accreditation: SC, ADNUR

02 President .... Dr. Adam HUTCHISON
05 VP Instruction & Student Services .... Dr. Stacy THOMAS
10 VP Financial & Admin Services .... Ms. Christine FIELDS
111 VP Institutional Advancement .... Ms. Laura PENNINGTON
49 Dean of Arts & Sciences Div .... Ms. Barbara MANUEL
107 Dean Professional Tech Studies Div .... Ms. Lee HUNT
09 Dir Inst Research/Effectiveness .... Mr. Robert E. MAY
66 Interim Dean of Nursing .... Dr. Elizabeth WRIGHT
103 Dean of Workforce Development .... Mr. Robert PHILLIPS
106 Dir Learning Resources/Online Lrng .... Mr. Ken FAIRBANKS
84 Dean Enrollment & Student Services .... Mr. Michael MCBRIDE
08 Coordinator of Library Services .... Ms. Sarah Beth WHITE
37 Financial Aid Coordinator .... Ms. Donna PRICE
06 Coordinator of Admissions & Records .... Ms. Paige KELLY
15 Human Resource Director .... Ms. Tiffany VANBUREN
88 Director of EXCEL .... Ms. Karen CHEERS

88 Coordinator of Dual Enrollment .... Ms. Patricia FARMER
21 Finance Manager .... Ms. Mary SNEAD
13 IT Coordinator .... Mr. Glen JOHNSON
18 Buildings & Grounds Superintendent .... Mr. Ernest L. NUNLEY
19 Campus Police Chief .... Mr. Kevin WIDENER
26 Director Marketing/Communications .... Vacant

*Virginia Western Community College (A)

3093 Colonial Avenue SW, Roanoke VA 24015-4705
County: Independent City FICE Identification: 003760
Unit ID: 233949
Telephone: (540) 857-8922 Carnegie Class: Assoc/MT-VT-Mix Trad/Non
FAX Number: (540) 857-6526 Calendar System: Semester
URL: www.virginiawestern.edu
Established: 1966 Annual Undergrad Tuition & Fees (In-State): $5,355
Enrollment: 5,738 Coed
Affiliation or Control: State IRS Status: 501(c)3
Highest Offering: Associate Degree
Accreditation: SC, ACBSP, ACFEI, ADNUR, DH, MLTAD, @PTAA, RAD, RTT

02 President .... Dr. Robert H. SANDEL
10 Vice Pres of Finance/Admin Services .... Ms. Lisa RIDPATH
05 Vice Pres Academic/Student Affs .... Dr. Elizabeth WILMER
111 Vice Pres Institutional Advancement .... Ms. Marilyn HERBERT-ASHTON
103 Vice Pres Workforce Development Svc .... Dr. Milan HAYWARD
45 AVP of Institutional Effectiveness .... Dr. Jolene HAMM
49 Dean Liberal Arts/Social Sciences .... Ms. Amy ANGUIANO
76 Dean Health Professions .... Ms. Martha SULLIVAN
81 Dean Science/Tech/Engineering/Math .... Ms. Amy WHITE
50 Dean Business/Trades/Technology .... Ms. Yvonne CAMPBELL
24 Dean Learning Resources .... Mr. Christopher PORTER
32 Dean of Student Services .... Ms. Brooke FERGUSON
09 Director Institutional Research .... Ms. Sarah CHITWOOD
18 Director of Facilities Planning .... Mr. Kevin G. WITTER
26 Director Marketing/Strategic Comm .... Vacant
06 Registrar .... Ms. Karin COLE
19 Campus Police Chief .... Mr. Craig HARRIS
37 Coord Financial Aid/Veterans Affs .... Mr. David BROD
103 Workforce Operations Supervisor .... Vacant
13 Dir Information Educ Technology .... Vacant
15 Assoc VP of Human Resources .... Vacant
21 Business Manager .... Mrs. Fredona AARON
84 Coordinator for Enrollment Services .... Ms. Tristin KITTS
08 Coordinator of the Library .... Vacant
36 Coordinator Career Services .... Ms. Shonny COOKE
25 Coord Grants Dev & Special Projects .... Ms. Marilyn J. HERBERT-ASHTON
30 Coordinator of Development .... Ms. Carole TARRANT
04 Admin Assistant to the President .... Ms. Amy BALZER

*Wytheville Community College (B)

1000 E Main Street, Wytheville VA 24382-3308
County: Wythe FICE Identification: 003761
Unit ID: 234377
Telephone: (276) 223-4700 Carnegie Class: Assoc/HT-High Non
FAX Number: (276) 223-4778 Calendar System: Semester
URL: www.wcc.vccs.edu
Established: 1963 Annual Undergrad Tuition & Fees (In-State): $4,725
Enrollment: 2,244 Coed
Affiliation or Control: State IRS Status: 501(c)3
Highest Offering: Associate Degree
Accreditation: SC, ADNUR, DH, MLTAD, PTAA

02 President .... Dr. Dean E. SPRINKLE
05 VP Academics/Inst Advancement . Dr. Rhonda K. CATRON-WOOD
10 Vice Pres Finance & Admin Services .... Vacant
103 VP Workforce Dev/Occup Programs .... Mr. Perry HUGHES
88 Dean of Transfer & Educ Partnership .... Ms. Susan EVANS
76 Interim Dean Health & Med Services .... Dr. Rita PHILLIPS
32 Dean of Student Services .... Ms. Renee THOMAS
13 Director of Technology/CIO .... Mr. Shawn MCREYNOLDS
09 Director of Inst Effectiveness .... Ms. Christine COLE
15 Director of Human Resources .... Ms. Malinda EVERSOLE
26 Public Relations & Marketing Spec .... Mr. Kenneth AKERS
08 Coordinator of Library Services .... Mr. George E. MATTIS, JR.
96 Procurement Officer .... Vacant
106 Dir Distance/Distributive Learning .... Vacant
37 Coordinator Financial Aid .... Ms. Mary Beth GALLAGHER
04 Administrative Asst to President .... Ms. Denita BURNETT
29 Development Svcs/Alumni Coordinator .... Vacant
18 Chief Facilities/Physical Plant Ofc .... Vacant
19 Director Security/Safety .... Mr. Steve BURNETTE
108 Director Institutional Assessment .... Vacant
07 Coordinator of Admissions/Records .... Ms. April MULLINS

Virginia Military Institute (C)

319 Letcher Avenue, Lexington VA 24450-0304
County: Independent City FICE Identification: 003753
Unit ID: 234085
Telephone: (540) 464-7230 Carnegie Class: Bac-A&S
FAX Number: N/A Calendar System: Semester
URL: www.vmi.edu
Established: 1839 Annual Undergrad Tuition & Fees (In-State): $19,210
Enrollment: 1,698 Coed
Affiliation or Control: State IRS Status: 501(c)3
Highest Offering: Baccalaureate
Accreditation: SC

01 Superintendent .... MG. Cedric T. WINS
05 Deputy Super/Dean of the Faculty .... BGen. Robert W. MORESCHI
10 Deputy Superintendent Finance/Admin .... Col. Dallas B. CLARK
32 Commandant of Cadets .... Col. Adrian t. BOGART, III
100 Chief of Staff .... LtCol. John M. YOUNG
04 Exec Asst to the Superintendent .... LtCol. Kevin A. RYAN
21 Treasurer .... Col. Jeffrey L. LAWHORNE
07 Interim Director of Admissions .... Col. Neil D. WHITMORE
88 Exec Director Museum Programs .... Col. Keith E. GIBSON
37 Interim Director of Financial Aid .... Mr. Pervis D. BINNS
35 Deputy Commandant .... LtCol. Jonathan T. HARTSOCK
36 Director of Career Services .... LtCol. Ammad SHEIKH
41 Director Intercollegiate Athletics .... Mr. Jim D. MILLER
26 Director Communications & Marketing ...... Col. William J. WYATT
29 Interim COO Alumni Association .... Mr. Meade B. KING
102 Exec VP VMI Foundation/Fund Raising .... Mr. Warren J. BRYAN
102 COO VMI Foundation/Keydet Club .... Mr. Meade B. KING
06 Registrar .... Col. Janet M. BATTAGLIA
15 Director Human Resources .... Vacant
18 Director Facilities Management .... Col. Thomas K. JARVIS
09 Dir Institutional Effectiveness .... Col. Lee L. RAKES
109 Director Auxiliary Services .... LtCol. Howard L. CLARK
40 Manager Bookstore .... Mr. Dalton BRILEY
42 Institute Chaplain .... Col. Robert E. PHILLIPS, SR.
17 Institute Physician .... Dr. David L. COPELAND
88 Director of Athletic Communications .... Mr. Phil R. MARCELLO
08 Director of Preston Library .... Col. Pongracz J. SENNYEY
38 Director of Cadet Counseling .... Dr. Sarah L. JONES
13 Director Information Technology .... Col. Wesley L. ROBINSON
96 Director of Procurement Services .... Col. Kathy H. TOMLIN
30 CEO Alumni Agencies .... Mr. David PRASNICKI
19 Chief VMI Police .... Chief Michael L. MARSHALL
28 Chief Diversity Officer .... LtCol. Jamica N. LOVE
44 Director Annual & Reunion Giving .... Ms. Patti COOK

† Tuition includes required room and board and quartermaster charges.

Virginia Polytechnic Institute and State University (D)

800 Drillfield Drive, Blacksburg VA 24061-0202
County: Montgomery FICE Identification: 003754
Unit ID: 233921
Telephone: (540) 231-6000 Carnegie Class: DU-Highest
FAX Number: (540) 231-9263 Calendar System: Semester
URL: www.vt.edu
Established: 1872 Annual Undergrad Tuition & Fees (In-State): $13,749
Enrollment: 37,024 Coed
Affiliation or Control: State IRS Status: 501(c)3
Highest Offering: Doctorate
Accreditation: SC, ART, CACREP, CAEP, CEA, CIDA, CLPSY, CONST, DIET, DIETD, DIETI, IPSY, LSAR, MED, MFCD, MUS, PCSAS, PH, PLNG, SPAA, THEA, VET

01 President .... Timothy D. SANDS
05 Exec Vice President & Provost .... Cyril R. CLARKE
10 EVP/Chief Business Ofcr .... Vacant
13 Vice Pres Information Tech & CIO .... Scott F. MIDKIFF
32 Int Vice President Student Affairs .... Frances KEENE
111 Vice Pres for Advancement .... Charles D. PHLEGAR
29 Assoc Vice Pres Alumni Relations .... Deborah A. DAY
28 VP Strat Affairs/Vice Prov Incl Div .... Menah PRATT-CLARKE
46 VP Research & Innovation ....Dan SUI
20 Exec Vice Provost .... G. Don TAYLOR, JR.
20 Vice Prov for Undergrad Acad Affs .... Rachel L. HOLLOWAY
58 Vice President and Dean Grad Educ .... Aimee SURPRENANT
56 VP Outreach/International Affs .... Guru GHOSH
15 Vice Pres for Human Resources .... Bryan GAREY
88 Vice Pres of Strategic Affairs .... Lisa WILKES
07 AV Prov Enrol Mgt/Dir UG Admiss .... Juan P. ESPINOZA
35 Dean of Students .... Byron A. HUGHES, JR.
43 University Counsel .... Kay K. HEIDBREDER
84 Vice Prov for Enroll & Degree Mgmt .... Luisa HAVENS
37 AVP Enroll Mgmt/Student Fin Aid .... Elizabeth ARMSTRONG
20 Vice Provost Faculty Affairs .... Ron FRICKER
88 Vice Provost Academic Resource Mgmt .... Jeff EARLEY
23 Director Schiffert Health Center .... Kanitta CHAROENSIRI
18 VP Campus Planning/Infastructure .... Christopher KIWUS
109 AVP Housing/Dining/Student Centers .... Ted FAULKNER
41 Athletic Director .... Whit BABCOCK
26 Sr Assoc Vice Pres Univ Relations .... Tracy VOSBURGH
38 Exec Dir Mental Health Initiative .... Chris FLYNN
40 Exec Dir Virginia Tech Services .... Donald J. WILLIAMS
08 Dean of University Libraries ....Tyler WALTERS
47 Dean of Agriculture/Life Sciences .... Alan GRANT
48 Int Dean Arch/Urban Studies .... Rosemary BLIESZNER
81 Dean College of Science .... Kevin PITTS
50 Interim Dean of Business .... Robin RUSSELL
54 Dean of Engineering .... Julia ROSS
79 Dean Liberal Arts & Human Sciences .... Laura BELMONTE
74 Dean of Veterinary Medicine ....Daniel GIVENS
65 Dean of Natural Resources & Environ ...... Paul M. WINISTORFER
96 Director of Procurement .... Mary HELMICK
63 Dean of VTC School of Medicine .... Lee LEARMAN
91 Assoc Vice Pres for Enterprise Sys .... Deborah M. FULTON
88 VP for Strategic Alliances .... Steven H. MCKNIGHT
12 VP/Exec Dir Innovation Campus .... Lance R. COLLINS
102 CEO Virginia Tech Foundation .... Elizabeth MCCLANAHAN
04 Special Asst to President .... Lisa WILKES
06 Assoc Vice Prov and Univ Registrar .... Rick SPARKS
101 VP for Policy and Gov/Sec to BOV .... Kim O'ROURKE
104 Director Global Education Office .... Theresa C. JOHANSSON
105 Director Web Communications .... John JACKSON
106 Exec Dir Tech-enhanced Learning .... Dale PIKE
88 Asst Provost Regional Accreditation .... Kristen BUSH
19 Chief of Police/Dir of Security .... Mac BABB
22 Assoc VP Equity and Accessibility .... Kelly OAKS
25 Director of Contracts & Agreements .... Daniel COCKRUM
86 VP Government & Community Relations .... Chris YIANILOS
76 VP for Health Sciences and Tech .... Michael J. FRIEDLANDER
88 Director of Inst Effectiveness .... Bethanny BODO
09 Assoc Vice Prov Inst Research .... R. Thulasi KUMAR
103 Director Career and Prof Dev .... Donna RATCLIFFE
90 Dir Collab Computing Solutions .... Marc T. DEBONIS

Virginia State University (E)

One Hayden Drive,
Virginia State University VA 23806-0001
County: Chesterfield FICE Identification: 003764
Unit ID: 234155
Telephone: (804) 524-5000 Carnegie Class: Masters/M
FAX Number: (804) 524-6506 Calendar System: Semester
URL: www.vsu.edu
Established: 1882 Annual Undergrad Tuition & Fees (In-State): $9,154
Enrollment: 4,020 Coed
Affiliation or Control: State IRS Status: 501(c)3
Highest Offering: Doctorate
Accreditation: SC, ACPHA, ART, CAEP, DIETD, DIETI, MUS, SW

01 President .... Dr. Makola M. ABDULLAH
10 Vice President for Finance .... Mr. Kevin DAVENPORT
05 Provost/VP for Academic Affairs .... Dr. Donald PALM
32 VP for Student Success & Engagement .... Vacant
111 VP for Institutional Advancement .... Ms. Tonya S. HALL
100 Chief of Staff .... Dr. Annie C. REDD
20 Vice Provost .... Vacant
21 Assoc Vice President for Finance .... Vacant
50 Dean Reginald F Lewis Col Business . Dr. Emmanuel OMOJOKUN
54 Dean College of Engineering & Tech .... Dr. Dawit HAILE
79 Dean Col of Humanities & Soc Sci .... Dr. Andrew KANU
47 Dean College of Agriculture .... Dr. Robert CORLEY
58 Dean Graduate Studies .... Vacant
76 Dean College of Natural Health Sci ... Dr. Lenneal J. HENDERSON
53 Dean College of Education .... Dr. Willis W. WALTER
06 Registrar .... Ms. Nedra W. JONES
09 Director Inst Planning/Assessment .... Dr. Tia A. MINNIS
37 Director of Financial Aid .... Mrs. Myra PHILLIPS
19 Chief of Police and Public Safety .... Mr. David BRAGG
18 Director of Facilities .... Mr. Gilbert HANZLIK
07 Director for Enrollment Services .... Mr. Rodney HALL
26 Director for Communication . Ms. Gwen WILLIAMS DANDRIDGE
15 HR Director .... Mrs. Tanya SIMMONS
39 Director Residence Facilities .... Mr. Derrick L. PETERSON
36 Director Career Services .... Mr. Joseph LYONS
40 Bookstore Manager .... Mr. Kevin POWELL
92 Director Honors Program .... Mr. Daniel M. ROBERTS
41 Athletic Director .... Mrs. Peggy DAVIS
42 Minister .... Rev. Jasmyn GRAHAM
29 Director of Alumni Relations .... Mr. Franklin JOHNSON
13 Deputy Chief Information Officer .... Vacant
23 Director of Student Health Services .... Dr. Cynthia S. ELLISON
25 Contract Manager .... Ms. Linda SCOTT
87 Director Summer School Session .... Dr. Vykuntapathi THOTA
96 Director of Purchasing .... Mr. Robert PHILLIPS
38 Director University Counseling .... Dr. Cynthia S. ELLISON
04 Executive Assistant to President .... Mrs. Danette JOHNSON
101 Special Asst to President & Board .... Dr. Annie REDD
43 General Counsel .... Vacant

Virginia Theological Seminary (F)

3737 Seminary Road, Alexandria VA 22304-5201
County: Independent City FICE Identification: 003731
Unit ID: 233259
Telephone: (703) 370-6600 Carnegie Class: Not Classified
FAX Number: N/A Calendar System: Semester
URL: www.vts.edu
Established: 1823 Annual Graduate Tuition & Fees: N/A
Enrollment: N/A Coed
Affiliation or Control: Protestant Episcopal IRS Status: 501(c)3
Highest Offering: Doctorate; No Undergraduates
Accreditation: THEOL

01 Dean and President .... Rev. Ian S. MARKHAM
05 VP of Academic Affairs .... Rev. Melody D. KNOWLES
111 VP of Institutional Advancement .... Mrs. Linda DIENNO
10 VP for Finance and Operations .... Ms. Jacqueline BALLOU
32 Assoc Dean of Students .... Rev. Ruthanna HOOKE
21 Director of Finance/Accounting .... Mr. Terrell WHITAKER
06 Registrar/Exec Dir Enrollment Mgmt .... Dr. Gail-Selina HEWITT-CLARKE
08 Head Librarian .... Dr. Mitzi J. BUDDE
26 Director of Communications .... Mr. Curtis PRATHER
07 Director of Admissions .... Mr. Derek GRETEN-HARRISON
04 Exec Assistant to the President .... Ms. Taryn HABBERLEY
102 Director Foundation/Corporate Rels .... Vacant
18 Chief Facilities/Physical Plnt Ofcr .... Mr. John ERBE
38 Director Student Counseling .... Mr. Derek GRETEN-HARRISON

Virginia Union University (G)

1500 N Lombardy Street, Richmond VA 23220-1784
County: Independent City FICE Identification: 003766
Unit ID: 234164
Telephone: (804) 257-5600 Carnegie Class: Bac-A&S
FAX Number: (804) 257-5818 Calendar System: Semester

URL: www.vuu.edu
Established: 1865 Annual Undergrad Tuition & Fees: $13,530
Enrollment: 1,516 Coed
Affiliation or Control: Baptist IRS Status: 501(c)3
Highest Offering: Doctorate
Accreditation: SC, ACBSP, CAEP, SW, THEOL

01 President .... Dr. Hakim J. LUCAS
11 Exec Vice President/COO .... Dr. Allia CARTER
05 Senior VP/Provost .... Dr. Terrell STRAYHORN
10 Sr VP/Chief Financial Ofcr .... Mr. Gregory LEWIS
32 VP Student Affairs .... Dr. Allia L. CARTER
111 VP Institutional Advancement .... Mr. Ralph DICKERSON
41 VP Intercollegiate Athletics .... Mr. Joseph TAYLOR
102 Sr VP Corporate & External Rels .... Mr. Maurice W. CAMPBELL
84 Int VP Enrollment Management .... Dr. Charles PRINCE
26 AVP Executive Communications .... Ms. Pam H. COX
20 Associate Provost .... Dr. Lisa T. MOON
53 Int Dean Evelyn R Syphax Sch Educ .... Dr. Alphonso LARAY SEALEY
49 Dean Arts & Sciences .... Dr. Ted L. RITTER
50 Dean Sydny Lewis Sch of Business .... Dr. Robin DAVIS
100 Chief of Staff/AVP .... Ms. Pamela COX
07 Director of Admissions .... Ms. Toyarna Y. THOMAS
103 Director Workforce Development .... Ms. Felicia COSBY
73 Dean School of Theology .... Dr. Gregory HOWARD
25 Director Sponsored Pgm/Title III .... Dr. Linda JACKSON
15 Director Human Resources .... Ms. Kendra MAYERS
06 Registrar .... Ms. Erica JACKSON
38 Director Counseling .... Dr. Shanita BROWN
29 Director of Alumni Relations .... Mr. Dominique FOWLER
08 Library Director .... Ms. Pamela B. FOREMAN
37 Director Financial Aid .... Ms. Keisha L. POPE
13 Director Bus Intel & Technology .... Ms. Doreen O. DIXON
42 University Pastor .... Rev. Angelo V. CHATMON
19 Chief University Police .... Ms. Meshia THOMAS
21 Comptroller .... Ms. Robin JEFFERSON
40 Bookstore Manager .... Ms. Terri WYATT
35 Dean of Students .... Mr. Brock MAYERS
31 Coordinator Student & Community Eng .... Vacant
18 Director Facilities Management .... Mr. Freddie ROBINSON
96 Director of Purchasing .... Ms. Beverly R. SMITH
04 Executive Asst to President .... Ms. Renee W. JOLLEY
104 Dir Ctr for International Studies .... Vacant
106 Dir Life-long Learning/Exce Ed .... Vacant
108 Director Institutional Assessment .... Dr. Lisa T. MOON
44 AVP Institutional Giving .... Vacant
101 Secretary of the Institution/Board .... Ms. Renee W. JOLLEY
105 Director Web Services .... Vacant

Virginia University of Integrative Medicine (A)

9401 Mathy Drive, Fairfax VA 22031
County: Fairfax Identification: 667208
Unit ID: 490106
Telephone: (703) 323-5690 Carnegie Class: Spec-4-yr-Other Health
FAX Number: (703) 323-5692 Calendar System: Quarter
URL: https://vuim.edu/
Established: Annual Undergrad Tuition & Fees: N/A
Enrollment: 362 Coed
Affiliation or Control: Independent Non-Profit IRS Status: 501(c)3
Highest Offering: Doctorate
Accreditation: ACUP

01 President .... Dr. Lixing LAO
05 Academic Dean .... Jeffrey MILLISON
11 COO .... John YOO
26 Chief Marketing Officer .... Byung KIM
06 Registrar .... Ji BAEK

Virginia University of Lynchburg (B)

2058 Garfield Avenue, Lynchburg VA 24501-6417
County: Independent City FICE Identification: 003762
Unit ID: 234137
Telephone: (434) 528-5276 Carnegie Class: Bac/Assoc-Mixed
FAX Number: (434) 528-4257 Calendar System: Semester
URL: www.vul.edu
Established: 1886 Annual Undergrad Tuition & Fees: $8,600
Enrollment: 244 Coed
Affiliation or Control: Independent Non-Profit IRS Status: 501(c)3
Highest Offering: Doctorate
Accreditation: TRACS

01 President .... Dr. Kathy C. FRANKLIN
05 Vice President of Academic Affairs .... Vacant
10 Vice President of Finance .... Ms. Sheila SCOTT
32 Director of Student Affairs .... Dr. Philip CAMPBELL
11 Chief Operating Officer .... Mr. Treney TWEEDY
06 Head Registrar .... Mr. Robbie ADAMS
07 Director of Admissions .... Ms. Angelique CARTER
18 Dir of Facilities/Maintenance .... Mr. Vern DEBILZAN
106 Director of Online Learning .... Ms. Katrina V. FRANKLIN
19 Director Security/Safety .... Mr. Robert CABLER, JR.
37 Director of Financial Aid .... Ms. Romena MORGAN
88 Special Assistant to the COO .... Mr. Ryan MICKLES
08 University Librarian .... Ms. Lisa KREJECKY
13 Director of IT/IE .... Vacant

Virginia Wesleyan University (C)

5817 Wesleyan Drive, Virginia Beach VA 23455
County: Independent City FICE Identification: 003767
Unit ID: 234173
Telephone: (757) 455-3200 Carnegie Class: Bac-A&S
FAX Number: (757) 461-4944 Calendar System: 4/1/4
URL: www.vwu.edu
Established: 1961 Annual Undergrad Tuition & Fees: $36,910
Enrollment: 1,347 Coed
Affiliation or Control: United Methodist IRS Status: 501(c)3
Highest Offering: Master's
Accreditation: SC, CAPRT, SW

01 President .... Dr. Scott D. MILLER
111 VP for Advance/Special Asst to Pres .... Ms. Kimberley HAMMER
11 VP for Campus Life & Oper Mgmt .... Dr. Keith E. MOORE
05 Vice President for Academic Affairs .... Dr. Sue LARKIN
10 Vice President for Finance .... Ms. Mary RYBERG
84 Vice President for Enrollment .... Ms. Heather M. CAMPBELL
101 Exec Asst to President/Board Sec .... Ms. Kelly CORDOVA
04 Admin Asst to President .... Ms. Anja SERBY-WILKENS
41 Exec Dir Intercollegiate Athletics .... Ms. Andrea HOOVER-ERBIG
21 Assoc VP for Finance .... Ms. Sylvia SCHELLY
35 Assoc VP Campus Life & Oper Mgmt .... Mr. Jason SEWARD
110 AVP Advanc/Exec Dir Alumni Rels .... Ms. Lori HARRIS
112 Asst VP for Advancement .... Mr. Sean FLYNN
20 Assoc VP for Academic Affairs .... Dr. Loren L. MARQUEZ
26 Chief Marketing Officer .... Ms. Stephanie SMAGLO
13 Chief Information Officer .... Mr. Gregory SKINNER
92 Dean Batten Honors College .... Dr. Travis MALONE
56 Dean of VWU Global Campus .... Dr. Deirdre GONSALVES-JACKSON
79 Dean Sch Arts & Humanities .... Dr. Steven EMMANUEL
81 Dean Sch Math & Natural Sciences .... Dr. Victor TOWNSEND
83 Dean Sch of Social Science .... Dr. Antje SCHWENNICKE
107 Dean of Professional Studies .... Dr. Ben DOBRIN
37 Director of Financial Aid .... Ms. Teresa L. RHYNE
96 Purchasing Manager .... Mr. Michael PETTRY
28 Chief Diversity Officer .... Dr. Felipe HUGUENO
36 Dir of Career Development .... Ms. Alice JONES
19 Director of Security .... Mr. Victor DORSEY
18 Director of Facilities Mgmt .... Mr. David PETERSON
42 Director of Student Ministries .... Ms. Marie PORTER
38 Dir of Counseling & Student Health .... Ms. April CHRISTMAN
39 Director of Residence Life .... Mr. David STUEBING
27 Content & Media Manager .... Ms. Laynee H. TIMLIN
122 Director of Student Activities .... Ms. Sarah GUZZO
40 Scribner University Store Mgr .... Ms. Kim S. BROWN
88 Director of Lifelong Learning .... Ms. Marion HIBBLER
08 Head Librarian .... Mr. Stephen LEIST
15 Dir of Human Resources .... Ms. Regina BARLETTA
06 Registrar .... Ms. Lauren NELMS
09 Director of Institutional Research .... Mr. Shane BOYD
104 Director of Global Engagement .... Ms. Amanda REINIG
119 Info Security Ofcr/Network Admin .... Ms. Marcia WILLIAMS
78 Dir Lrng Ctr/Coord Disability Svcs .... Mr. Crit MUNIZ
44 Asst Dir Annual Giving/Alumni Eng .... Mr. Nicholas MCDONALD
88 Dir of Innov Teaching/Engaged Lrng .... Dr. Denise WILKINSON
07 Director for Transfer Enrollment .... Ms. Nadine WHITE-SHOOK
88 Dir for Enrollment Batten Honors .... Ms. Brooke NOVKOVIC
102 Asst Dir Parent Rel/Crd Marlins Fdn .... Ms. Tina MILLIGAN
88 Dir of Enrollment VWU Global Campus .... Mr. Larry BELCHER
88 Director of Wesleyan Engaged .... Ms. Bethany TSIARAS

Washington and Lee University (D)

204 W Washington Street, Lexington VA 24450-2116
County: Independent City FICE Identification: 003768
Unit ID: 234207
Telephone: (540) 458-8400 Carnegie Class: Bac-A&S
FAX Number: N/A Calendar System: Other
URL: www.wlu.edu
Established: 1749 Annual Undergrad Tuition & Fees: $57,285
Enrollment: 2,183 Coed
Affiliation or Control: Independent Non-Profit IRS Status: 501(c)3
Highest Offering: Doctorate
Accreditation: SC, CAEP, JOUR, LAW

01 President .... Dr. William C. DUDLEY
26 VP Comm & Strat Init/Univ Sec .... Ms. Jessica WILLETT
05 Provost .... Dr. Lena HILL
20 Associate Provost .... Dr. Paul YOUNGMAN
88 Assoc Provost Diversity & Incl .... Dr. Kristie A. FORD
10 Vice Pres for Finance and Admin .... Mr. Steven G. MCALLISTER
111 Vice Pres University Advancement .... Mr. Thomas W. JENNINGS
32 VP Student Affs & Dean of Students .... Ms. Sidney S. EVANS
43 General Counsel .... Ms. Maria FEELEY
49 Dean of the College .... Dr. Chawne KIMBER
50 Dean of the Williams School .... Dr. Robert D. STRAUGHAN
61 Dean of the Law School .... Ms. Melanie WILSON
35 Dean of Student Life .... Mr. David M. LEONARD
35 Assoc Dean of Students .... Ms. Ronda M. BRYANT
30 Exec Dir for University Development .... Ms. Susan W. CUNNINGHAM
102 Director of Corporate/Found Rels .... Ms. Wendy W. LOVELL
41 Director of Athletics .... Ms. Janine M. HATHORN
89 Associate Dean of Students .... Mr. Jason L. RODOCKER
07 Dean of Admissions/Financial Aid .... Ms. Sally STONE RICHMOND
09 Asst Provost of Accreditation/IR .... Mr. Bryan PRICE
06 University Registrar .... Ms. Kimberly D. ROBINSON
08 University Librarian .... Dr. K.T VAUGHAN
85 Director International Education .... Dr. Mark E. RUSH
88 Sr Advisor to Univ Advancement .... Mr. Walter T. DUDLEY
15 Exec Director of Human Resources .... Ms. Jodi L. WILLIAMS
37 Director of Financial Aid .... Mr. James D. KASTER
18 Exec Dir of University Facilities .... Mr. Tom KALASKY
21 Controller .... Ms. Celia KOVAC
13 Chief Technology Officer .... Mr. David SAACKE
14 Deputy Chief Information Officer .... Ms. Kerri CHAPMAN
24 Senior Academic Technologist .... Mr. Brandon R. BUCY
29 Exec Dir of Alumni & Career Svcs .... Mr. John A. JENSEN
36 Director of Career and Prof Devel .... Ms. Molly M. STEELE
38 Director of Counseling .... Dr. Jeff RUTTER
88 Director of Dining Services .... Mr. Ryan M. MILLER
109 Exec Director of Auxiliary Services .... Mr. K. C SCHAEFER
04 Exec Assistant to the President .... Ms. Emily KING
19 Director of Public Safety .... Mr. Ethan KIPNES
28 Dean Diversity/Inclusion/Stdnt Eng .... Ms. Tamara FUTRELL
44 Senior Director Annual Giving .... Ms. Missy WITHEROW
53 Director of Teacher Education .... Dr. Haley SIGLER
122 Dir Stdnt Activities/Greek Life .... Vacant
27 Exec Dir Comm & Public Affairs .... Ms. Drewry A. SACKETT
39 Dir Resident Life/Student Housing .... Mr. Chris B. REID

Washington Theological Seminary (E)

7700 Little River Turnpike, Ste 205, Annandale VA 22003
County: Fairfax Identification: 667424
Telephone: (703) 712-7073 Carnegie Class: Not Classified
FAX Number: N/A Calendar System: Semester
URL: www.wtsva.edu
Established: 1983 Annual Undergrad Tuition & Fees: N/A
Enrollment: N/A Coed
Affiliation or Control: Non-denominational IRS Status: 501(c)3
Highest Offering: Doctorate
Accreditation: TRACS

01 President .... Ouk Sub LEE

Washington University of Science & Technology (F)

8133 Leesburg Pike, #230, Vienna VA 22182
County: Fairfax Identification: 667105
Unit ID: 483780
Telephone: (703) 941-2020 Carnegie Class: Masters/M
FAX Number: (703) 941-2025 Calendar System: Quarter
URL: www.wust.edu
Established: 2008 Annual Undergrad Tuition & Fees: $14,000
Enrollment: 254 Coed
Affiliation or Control: Proprietary IRS Status: Proprietary
Highest Offering: Master's
Accreditation: ACCSC

01 President .... Dr. Hasan KARABURK
05 VP of Distance Education .... Dr. Zafer PIRIM

Washington University of Virginia (G)

4300 Evergreen Lane, Annandale VA 22003
County: Fairfax Identification: 666234
Telephone: (703) 333-5904 Carnegie Class: Not Classified
FAX Number: (703) 333-5906 Calendar System: Semester
URL: www.wuv.edu
Established: 1982 Annual Undergrad Tuition & Fees: N/A
Enrollment: N/A Coed
Affiliation or Control: Non-denominational IRS Status: 501(c)3
Highest Offering: Doctorate
Accreditation: THEOL, TRACS, IACBE

01 President .... Dr. Peter M. CHANG
11 Exec Vice Pres Administration .... Mrs. Joyce G. PARK
84 Dean of Enrollment/Student Life .... Mr. David Y. LEE
08 Head Librarian .... Mr. Robert ROSE, JR.
50 Dean School of Business .... Mr. Won Eog KIM
06 Registrar .... Ms. Chloe AN
38 Dean Student Counseling .... Dr. Young C. YOO

WASHINGTON

Bastyr University (H)

14500 Juanita Drive NE, Kenmore WA 98028-4966
County: King FICE Identification: 022425
Unit ID: 235547
Telephone: (425) 602-3000 Carnegie Class: DU-Mod
FAX Number: (425) 823-6222 Calendar System: Quarter
URL: www.bastyr.edu
Established: 1978 Annual Undergrad Tuition & Fees: N/A
Enrollment: 904 Coed
Affiliation or Control: Independent Non-Profit IRS Status: 501(c)3
Highest Offering: Doctorate
Accreditation: NW, ACUP, DIETD, DIETI, MEAC, NATUR

01 President .... Dr. Devin BYRD
05 Senior Vice President/Provost .... Dr. Dave RULE
111 Vice Pres Advancement/Enroll Svcs .... Dr. Jeanne GALLOWAY
10 AVP Budget & Finance/CFO .... Mr. Ray OEN
32 Vice President of Student Affairs .... Ms. Susan L. WEIDER
15 Int AVP of Human Resources .... Ms. Jennifer WATSON

Bates Technical College (A)

1101 S Yakima Avenue, Tacoma WA 98405-4895
County: Pierce FICE Identification: 005306
Unit ID: 235671
Telephone: (253) 680-7000 Carnegie Class: Assoc/HVT-High Non
FAX Number: (253) 680-7101 Calendar System: Quarter
URL: www.batestech.edu
Established: 1940 Annual Undergrad Tuition & Fees (In-State): $6,628
Enrollment: 3,369 Coed
Affiliation or Control: State IRS Status: 501(c)3
Highest Offering: Associate Degree
Accreditation: NW, ACBSP, ACFEI, CNEA, DA, DT, MAC, NAEYC, OTA

01 President .... Dr. Lin ZHOU
05 Vice President of Instruction .... Mr. Johnny HU
04 Exec Asst to the President .... Ms. Karey BRYSON
32 Vice President of Student Services .... Mr. Steve ASHPOLE
15 Exec Dir of Human Resources .... Ms. Kameil BORDERS
11 Vice President Admin Services .... Mr. Nicholas LUTES
18 Exec Dir Facilities/Operations .... Ms. Dee NELONS
96 Director of General Services .... Mr. Nephtalin DRUMMER
37 Financial Aid Director .... Ms. Kimberly UPHOLD
13 Exec Dir Info Tech/CIO .... Vacant
84 Dir of Enrollment Mgt/Admission .... Vacant
19 Director Security/Safety .... Mr. Ray RICHARDSON
08 Head Librarian .... Mr. Mike WOOD
102 Director of Foundation .... Ms. LeAnn DREIER

Bellevue College (B)

3000 Landerholm Circle, SE, Bellevue WA 98007-6484
County: King FICE Identification: 003769
Unit ID: 234669
Telephone: (425) 564-1000 Carnegie Class: Bac/Assoc-Mixed
FAX Number: (425) 564-4065 Calendar System: Quarter
URL: www.bellevuecollege.edu
Established: 1965 Annual Undergrad Tuition & Fees (In-State): $3,958
Enrollment: 12,286 Coed
Affiliation or Control: State IRS Status: 501(c)3
Highest Offering: Baccalaureate
Accreditation: NW, CIDA, CNEA, #DMS, NDT, NMT, NURSE, RADDOS, RTT

01 Interim President .... Gary LOCKE
32 Int Assoc VP Student Affairs .... Christina CASTORENA
04 Exec Asst to the President .... Dr. Alicia KEATING POLSON
05 Provost .... Vacant
28 VP Diversity/Equity & Inclusion .... Dr. Consuelo GRIER
11 VP Administrative Services .... Dennis CURRAN
15 VP Human Resources .... Frances DUJON-REYNOLDS
111 VP Institutional Advancement .... Rebecca CHAWGO
13 VP Information Technology .... Rodger HARRISON
20 Assoc VP Academic Affairs .... Dr. Rob VIENS

Bellingham Technical College (C)

3028 Lindebergh Avenue, Bellingham WA 98225-1599
County: Whatcom FICE Identification: 004999
Unit ID: 234696
Telephone: (360) 752-7000 Carnegie Class: Bac/Assoc-Assoc Dom
FAX Number: (360) 676-2798 Calendar System: Quarter
URL: www.btc.edu
Established: 1957 Annual Undergrad Tuition & Fees (In-District): $3,915
Enrollment: 1,848 Coed
Affiliation or Control: State/Local IRS Status: 501(c)3
Highest Offering: Baccalaureate
Accreditation: NW, ACFEI, ADNUR, DH, SURGT

01 Interim President .... Ms. Kimberly PERRY
04 Exec Assistant to the President .... Ms. Ronda LAUGHLIN
05 Interim VP Instruction .... Dr. Heidi YPMA
32 Vice President of Student Services .... Ms. Michele WALTZ
11 VP of Administrative Services .... Ms. Chad STITELER
20 Interim Exec Dir Academic Programs .... Ms. Katie HONEYCUTT
72 Dean of Prof Technical Education .... Mr. Ray KUBISTA
66 Dean of Nursing .... Ms. Julie SAMMS
76 Interim Dean of Allied Health .... Mr. Matthew SANTOS
102 Director Foundation .... Mr. Dean FULTON
15 Int Exec Director Human Resources .... Ms. Tami WILLETT
37 Exec Dir Stdnt Financial Resources .... Ms. Chantel MCMAHAN
07 Director Registration/Enrollment .... Ms. Joan KAMMERZELL
13 Dir Computer/Info Support Svcs .... Mr. Curtis PERERA
08 Director Library Svcs & eLearning .... Ms. Dawn HAWLEY
18 Chief Facilities/Physical Plant .... Mr. David JUNGKUNTZ
26 Director Marketing/Communications .... Vacant
36 Exec Dir Student Entry & Advising .... Vacant
45 Exec Dir of Inst Planning & Advance .... Ms. RaeLyn AXLUND MCBRIDE
19 Director Security/Safety .... Mr. Foster ROBINSON
38 Student Counselor .... Ms. Nyssa HOWELL

Big Bend Community College (D)

7662 Chanute Street NE, Moses Lake WA 98837-3299
County: Grant FICE Identification: 003770
Unit ID: 234711
Telephone: (509) 793-2222 Carnegie Class: Assoc/MT-VT-Mix Trad/Non
FAX Number: (509) 762-6329 Calendar System: Quarter
URL: www.bigbend.edu
Established: 1962 Annual Undergrad Tuition & Fees (In-State): $4,484
Enrollment: 1,892 Coed
Affiliation or Control: State IRS Status: 501(c)3
Highest Offering: Baccalaureate
Accreditation: NW, ADNUR

01 President .... Dr. Sara THOMPSON TWEEDY
10 Vice Pres Administrative Services .... Ms. Linda SCHOONMAKER
05 VP Learning & Student Success .... Dr. Bryce HUMPHERYS
15 VP of Human Resources & Labor .... Mrs. Kim GARZA
103 Dean Workforce Education .... Ms. Daneen BERRY-GUERIN
32 Dean of Student Services .... Mr. Andre GUZMAN
49 Dean of Arts & Sciences .... Ms. Kathleen DUVALL
53 Dean Educ/Health/Language Skills .... Vacant
35 Director of Student Programs .... Ms. Kim JACKSON
37 Director of Financial Aid .... Ms. Casey FRY
06 Registrar .... Ms. Starr BERNHARDT
08 Director of Library Resources .... Mr. Tim FUHRMAN
41 Director of Athletics .... Vacant
102 Dir Inst Advancement/Exec Dir Found .... Mrs. LeAnne PARTON
26 Director of Communications .... Mr. Matt KILLEBREW
21 Exec Director of Business Services .... Ms. Charlene RIOS
96 Director of Purchasing .... Mr. Joe AUVIL
39 Residence Hall Coordinator .... Mr. Ammon MILLIGAN
09 Dean of Institutional Research .... Ms. Valerie PARTON
13 Director of IT .... Vacant
19 Director Security/Safety .... Vacant
04 Executive Asst to President .... Ms. Melinda DOURTE
18 Chief Facilities/Physical Plant .... Mr. John HOLTHAUS

Carrington College - Spokane (E)

10102 E Knox Avenue, Suite 200, Spokane WA 99206
Telephone: (509) 462-3722 Identification: 666385
Accreditation: &WJ, MAC, #RAD

† Regional accreditation is carried under the parent institution in Sacramento, CA.

Cascadia College (F)

18345 Campus Way, NE, Bothell WA 98011-8205
County: King FICE Identification: 034835
Unit ID: 439190
Telephone: (425) 352-8000 Carnegie Class: Bac/Assoc-Assoc Dom
FAX Number: (425) 352-8313 Calendar System: Quarter
URL: www.cascadia.edu
Established: 2000 Annual Undergrad Tuition & Fees (In-District): $4,226
Enrollment: 2,597 Coed
Affiliation or Control: State/Local IRS Status: Exempt
Highest Offering: Baccalaureate
Accreditation: NW

01 President .... Dr. Eric MURRAY
101 Exec Asst to the President .... Lily ALLEN-RICHTER
11 VP for Administrative Svcs .... Jashoda BOTHRA
15 VP for Human Resources .... Jashoda BOTHRA
05 VP for Student Learning & Success .... Dr. Kerry LEVETT
111 VP for External Rels & Planning .... Meagan WALKER
20 Dean of Student Learning-Prof Tech .... Dr. Erik TINGELSTAD
20 Dean Student Lrng-Transfer/Gen Ed .... Kristina YOUNG
32 Dean of Student Success Services .... Erin BLAKENEY
20 Dean of Student Learning-Trans Stds .... Lyn EISENHOUR
10 Interim Director of Finance .... Yan LI
13 Dir of Information Services .... Laura HEDAL
18 Dir of Facilities/Capital Projects .... Kimberlee CLARK
45 Dir Institutional Effectiveness .... Dr. Michael HORN
84 Dir Enrollment Services .... Shawn MILLER
37 Dir Student Financial Services .... Deann HOLLIDAY
121 Dir Student Adv & Support Services .... Gordon DUTRISAC
35 Dir of Student Life .... Becky RIOPEL
85 Dir of International Programs .... Yukari ZEDNICK
102 Dir of Cascadia College Foundation .... Mark COLLINS
88 Dir Organization/Professional Devel .... Samantha BROWN
28 Int Exec Dir of Equity/Inclusion .... Chari DAVENPORT
26 Manager Outreach & Marketing .... Sara GOMEZ-TAYLOR
118 Manager of Payroll .... Melissa STONER
16 Human Resources Generalist .... Elizabeth ENGLUND

Central Washington University (G)

400 E University Way, Ellensburg WA 98926-7501
County: Kittitas FICE Identification: 003771
Unit ID: 234827
Telephone: (509) 963-2111 Carnegie Class: Masters/L
FAX Number: (509) 963-3206 Calendar System: Quarter
URL: www.cwu.edu
Established: 1890 Annual Undergrad Tuition & Fees (In-State): $8,444
Enrollment: 11,174 Coed
Affiliation or Control: State IRS Status: 501(c)3
Highest Offering: Master's
Accreditation: NW, CACREP, CONST, DIETD, DIETI, EMT, IPSY, MUS

01 President .... Dr. Jim WOHLPSART
05 Provost/VP Academic & Student Life .... Dr. Michelle DENBESTE
10 VP Business & Financial Affairs .... Mr. Joel KLUCKING
100 Chief of Staff .... Vacant
20 Assoc Provost UG/Faculty Affairs .... Dr. Gail MACKIN
56 Assoc Provost Ext Learn & Outreach .... Dr. Ediz KAYKAYOGLU
32 Dean of Student Success .... Dr. Gregg HEINSELMAN
58 Dean Graduate Studies/Research .... Vacant
49 Dean College of Arts/Humanities .... Dr. Jill HERNANDEZ
50 Dean College of Business .... Mr. Jeffrey L. STINSON
53 Dean College of Educ/Prof Studies .... Dr. Sathy RAJENDRAN
83 Dean College of the Sciences .... Dr. Tim ENGLUND
08 Dean of Library Services .... Dr. Rebecca LUBAS
111 Vice Pres University Advancement .... Mr. Paul ELSTONE
28 Vice Pres of Diversity .... Dr. Delores CLEARY
13 AVP/Chief Information Officer .... Ms. Virginia TOMLINSON
15 Exec Dir Human Resources .... Ms. Staci SLEIGH-LAYMAN

Centralia College (H)

600 Centralia College Boulevard,
Centralia WA 98531-4035
County: Lewis FICE Identification: 003772
Unit ID: 234845
Telephone: (360) 736-9391 Carnegie Class: Bac/Assoc-Mixed
FAX Number: (360) 330-7108 Calendar System: Quarter
URL: www.centralia.edu
Established: 1925 Annual Undergrad Tuition & Fees (In-State): $4,652
Enrollment: 2,314 Coed
Affiliation or Control: State IRS Status: 501(c)3
Highest Offering: Baccalaureate
Accreditation: NW, CNEA

01 President .... Dr. Robert MOHRBACHER
05 Vice President Instruction .... Dr. Joyce HAMMER
32 Vice President of Students .... Mr. Robert COX
10 Vice Pres Finance/ Administration .... Ms. Leslie FOUNTAIN WILLIAMS
15 VP Human Resources/Legal Affairs .... Mr. John BOESENBERG
103 Dean Workforce Education .... Mr. Jake FAY
08 Dean of Library Services/E-Learning .... Vacant
88 Dean of Academic Transfer Programs .... Mr. Daniel TAYLOR
09 Director of Institutional Research .... Ms. Fia ELIASSON-CREEK
88 Dir WorkFirst & Worker Retraining .... Ms. Margret FRIEDLEY
84 Director of Enrollment Services .... Ms. Michelle WHEELER
37 Director of Financial Aid .... Ms. Tracy DAHL
13 Director Information Technology .... Mr. Casey SCHMIDT
41 Director of Sports Programs .... Mr. Bob PETERS
29 Director Alumni Relations .... Ms. Christine FOSSETT
96 Director of Purchasing .... Ms. Amanda WITT
26 Dir College Relations & Events .... Ms. Amanda HAINES
40 Bookstore Manager .... Ms. Tammy STRODEMIER
97 Program Coordinator .... Vacant

City University of Seattle (I)

521 Wall Street, Suite 100, Seattle WA 98121
County: King FICE Identification: 013022
Unit ID: 234915
Telephone: (206) 239-4500 Carnegie Class: DU-Mod
FAX Number: (206) 239-4802 Calendar System: Quarter
URL: www.cityu.edu
Established: 1973 Annual Undergrad Tuition & Fees: N/A
Enrollment: 2,052 Coed
Affiliation or Control: Independent Non-Profit IRS Status: 501(c)3
Highest Offering: Doctorate
Accreditation: NW, ACBSP, CACREP

01 Interim President .... Mr. Chris BRYAN
05 Provost .... Dr. Scott CARNZ
04 Exec Asst Office of the President .... Ms. Nandi MOONFLOWER
32 Vice President Student Services .... Dr. Melissa E. MECHAM
26 VP Marketing & Enrollment .... Mr. Jason ELLIOTT
10 Chief Financial Officer .... Mr. Christopher BRYAN
13 Director of Information Technology .... Mr. Kevin H. BROWN
15 Director of Human Resources .... Ms. Janet O'LEARY
20 Dean/EVP Academic Affairs .... Ms. Mary MARA
50 Dean Sch of Business & Management .... Mr. Scott CARNZ
72 Dean Sch of Technology & Computing .... Dr. Sam CHUNG
53 Dean Sch of Education & Leadership .... Dr. Vicki BUTLER
83 Dean Sch of Health & Social Science .... Dr. Pat RUSSELL
84 Director of Enrollment & Advising .... Ms. Teresa D'AMBROSIO
27 AVP Strategic Partnerships .... Ms. Kathy COX
85 Asst Provost International Educ .... Mr. Antonio ESQUEDA FLORES
08 Director Library Services .... Mr. Matthew LECHNER
37 Dir Student Financial Svcs .... Ms. Darcy KELLER
29 Alumni Relations Manager .... Mr. Alex WEBSTER
18 Facilities Manager .... Mr. Troy CRABREE
06 Registrar .... Ms. Melissa MECHAM

Clark College (J)

1933 Fort Vancouver Way, Vancouver WA 98663-3598
County: Clark FICE Identification: 003773
Unit ID: 234933
Telephone: (360) 992-2000 Carnegie Class: Bac/Assoc-Assoc Dom
FAX Number: (360) 992-2871 Calendar System: Quarter
URL: www.clark.edu
Established: 1933 Annual Undergrad Tuition & Fees (In-State): $3,957
Enrollment: 7,665 Coed
Affiliation or Control: State IRS Status: 501(c)3
Highest Offering: Baccalaureate
Accreditation: NW, ADNUR, DH, MAC

01 President .... Dr. Karin EDWARDS
05 Vice Pres of Instruction .... Mr. Paul WICKLINE
32 Vice Pres of Student Affairs .... Dr. Michele CRUSE
11 Int Executive VP of Operations .... Ms. Sabra SAND
15 Assoc Vice Pres of Human Resources .... Mr. Brad AVAKIAN
84 Dir of Enrollment/Registrar .... Ms. Mirranda SAARI
75 Dir of WF Professional Tech Ed .... Mr. Kevin THOMAS
79 Dean Engl/Comm/Hum/Basic Educ .... Mr. Jim WILKINS-LUTON
103 Dean Wkforce/Tech/Prof Educ .... Vacant
83 Dean Social Sciences/Fine Arts .... Vacant
52 Dean of Business & Health Sciences .... Ms. Brenda WALSTEAD
04 Exec Assistant to the President .... Ms. Julie TAYLOR

41 Director of Athletics .... Ms. Laura LEMASTERS
16 Associate Director Human Resources .... Ms. Thao SCHMIDT
08 Dir of Library Services .... Vacant
18 Dir of Facility Services .... Mr. Tim PETTA
26 Chief Communications Officer .... Vacant
36 Assoc Director Career Services .... Ms. Cath KEANE
37 Director of Financial Aid .... Ms. Glendi GADDIS
10 Director of Business Services .... Ms. Sabra SAND
35 Dir Stdnt Life/Multicult Stdnt Affs .... Ms. Sarah GRUHLER
121 Director of Advising Center .... Ms. Emily MEOZ
25 Director of Grant Development .... Ms. Julie ROBERTSON
28 VP Diversity/Equity/Inclusion .... Dr. Rashida WILLARD
19 Director of Security & Safety .... Mr. Michael SEE
85 International Recruitment Manager .... Ms. Csendi HOPP
40 Bookstore Manager .... Ms. Monica KNOWLES
96 Purchasing Manager .... Ms. Lisa HASART
102 Foundation CEO .... Mr. Calen OUELLETTE
105 Information Technology Specialist .... Mr. Chris CONCANNON
29 Director Alumni Relations .... Ms. Vivian MANNING
13 Interim Chief Information Officer .... Mr. Das GUPTA

Clover Park Technical College (A)

4500 Steilacoom Boulevard, SW,
Lakewood WA 98499-4004
County: Pierce FICE Identification: 005752
Unit ID: 234951
Telephone: (253) 589-5800 Carnegie Class: Bac/Assoc-Assoc Dom
FAX Number: (253) 589-5851 Calendar System: Quarter
URL: www.cptc.edu
Established: 1942 Annual Undergrad Tuition & Fees (In-State): $5,740
Enrollment: 3,591 Coed
Affiliation or Control: State IRS Status: 501(c)3
Highest Offering: Baccalaureate
Accreditation: NW, CNEA, DA, HT, MAC, MLTAD, SURGT

01 President .... Dr. Joyce LOVEDAY
04 Executive Assistant .... Cherie STEELE
05 Vice President Instruction .... Dr. Thomas BROXSON
10 Int Vice Pres Finance & Admin .... Lisa WOLCOTT
10 Int Vice Pres Finance & Admin .... Lisa BEACH
32 VP Student Success .... Scott LATIOLAIS
108 Assoc VP Inst Effectiveness .... Samantha DANA
15 Human Resources Director .... Kirk WALKER
16 Asst Dir Human Resources .... Teresa IEVERS
103 Dean of Workforce Development .... Cristeen CROUCHET
13 Dir Information Technology .... Pamela JETER
37 Director Financial Aid .... Celva BOON
18 Asst Director Facilities Services .... Chris RIDLER
18 Manager Capital Projects .... Wesley PRATER
88 Dean Pre-College Pathways .... Jenna POLLOCK
84 Dir Enrollment Services/Dean .... Cynthia MOWRY
114 Dir Budget & Finance .... Lisa WOLCOTT
121 Dean Student Success .... Dean KELLY
35 Director Student Life .... Jessica WALLACK
11 Exec Director of Operations .... Lisa BEACH
96 Purchasing & Supply Specialist .... Kimberly BILLS
26 Dir Marketing/Communication .... Jenn ADRIEN
40 Bookstore Coordinator .... Kariena MELLOR
06 Registrar .... Tracey SONGAO
88 Dean Division B .... Dr. Claire KORSCHINOWSKI
18 Dean Division C .... Michelle HILLESLAND
88 Dean Division A .... Dr. Chris CHEN MAHONEY
88 Dean Instruction .... Brandon ROGERS
28 Assoc VP Equity/Diversity/Inclusion .... Vacant
105 Web Content Manager .... Jeanna DUFOUR
28 Mgr Student Diversity Programs .... Yuko CHARTRAW
102 Exec Director Foundation .... Janet HOLM
66 Dean Nursing Programs .... Vacant

Columbia Basin College (B)

2600 N 20th Avenue, Pasco WA 99301-3397
County: Franklin FICE Identification: 003774
Unit ID: 234979
Telephone: (509) 547-0511 Carnegie Class: Bac/Assoc-Mixed
FAX Number: (509) 546-0404 Calendar System: Quarter
URL: www.columbiabasin.edu
Established: 1955 Annual Undergrad Tuition & Fees (In-State): $5,755
Enrollment: 6,745 Coed
Affiliation or Control: State IRS Status: 170(c)1
Highest Offering: Baccalaureate
Accreditation: NW, ADNUR, DH, EMT, MAC, NURSE, SURGT

01 President .... Dr. Rebekah WOODS
05 Vice President Instruction .... Dr. Michael LEE
10 Vice Pres Administrative Services .... Mr. Eduardo RODRIGUEZ
32 Vice President of Student Services .... Ms. Cheryl HOLDEN
15 VP Human Resources/Legal Affairs .... Ms. Camilla GLATT
13 Asst VP Infrastructure Services .... Mr. Brian DEXTER
26 Asst VP for Comm & External Affairs .... Ms. Elizabeth BURTNER
09 Dean for Organizational Learning .... Dr. Jason ENGLE
49 Dean Arts & Humanities .... Mr. Bill MCKAY
08 Assoc Dean Library/Instruct Svcs .... Ms. Keri LOBDELL
102 Executive Director/CEO Foundation .... Ms. Erin FISHBURN
40 Bookstore Director .... Ms. Debra BRUCE
18 Director of Plant Operations .... Mr. Kirk ENGLE
41 Athletic Director .... Mr. Scott ROGERS
26 Marketing/Communications Director .... Vacant
35 Director of Student Activities .... Ms. Alice SCHLEGEL
37 Director Student Financial Aid .... Mr. Ben BEUS
114 Director for Budget/Purchasing .... Vacant
06 Associate Registrar .... Ms. Janet GARZA
04 Executive Asst to the President .... Ms. Ronda RODGERS
84 Asst VP Enrollment Svcs & Registrar .... Ms. Kelsey MYERS
39 Director Resident Life .... Mr. Dan QUOCK
50 Int Dean Business .... Mr. Steven DANVER
83 Dean for Social Sciences/Education .... Vacant
81 Dean for Math & Sciences .... Mr. Roderick TAYLOR
76 Dean of Health Sciences .... Mr. Doug HUGHES
75 Dean for Career & Technical Educ .... Mr. Jesus MOTA
97 Dean for Transitional Studies .... Ms. Daphne LARIOS
108 Dean for Accreditation & Assessment .... Ms. Melissa MCBURNEY
124 Assoc Dean for Student Retention .... Mr. Lane SCHUMACHER
19 Director Security/Safety .... Mr. Ernesto MENDEZ

*Community Colleges of Spokane (C)

501 N Riverpoint Blvd., Spokane WA 99217
County: Spokane FICE Identification: 010784
Telephone: (509) 434-5060 Carnegie Class: N/A
FAX Number: N/A
URL: www.ccs.spokane.edu

01 Chancellor .... Dr. Christine JOHNSON
05 Provost .... Dr. Lori HUNT
10 Chief Financial Officer .... Ms. Lisa HJALTALIN
11 Chief Administration Officer .... Mr. Greg L. STEVENS
26 Public Information Officer .... Ms. Carolyn CASEY
41 Dist Director of Athletics PE/Rec .... Mr. Jim FITZGERALD
102 Executive Director CCS Foundation .... Ms. Heather BEEBE STEVENS
18 District Director of Facilities .... Mr. John GILLETTE
103 Exec Dir Ctr Wkforce/Cont Educ .... Mr. Nolan GRUVER
20 Vice Provost .... Dr. Jim MOHR
13 Chief Information Technology Ofcr .... Ms. Grace LEAF
15 Director of Human Resources .... Ms. Melody MATTHEWS
106 Director of eLearning .... Mr. Ben WHITMORE
104 Asst Dean of Global Education .... Ms. Amber MCKENZIE
116 Chief Compliance Officer .... Ms. Amy MCCOY
04 Executive Asst to the Chancellor .... Ms. Breanne RILEY
88 Executive Asst to the Provost .... Ms. Dee BLAND
19 Dist Director of Safety .... Mr. Brandon LIVINGSTON
88 Dist Director of Head Start .... Ms. Bobbi WOODRAL

*Spokane Community College (D)

1810 N. Greene Street, Spokane WA 99217-5499
County: Spokane FICE Identification: 003793
Unit ID: 236692
Telephone: (509) 533-8400 Carnegie Class: Bac/Assoc-Assoc Dom
FAX Number: N/A Calendar System: Quarter
URL: www.scc.spokane.edu
Established: 1963 Annual Undergrad Tuition & Fees (In-State): $3,727
Enrollment: 7,081 Coed
Affiliation or Control: State IRS Status: 501(c)3
Highest Offering: Baccalaureate
Accreditation: NW, ACFEI, ADNUR, CAHIIM, COARC, CVT, DA, DMS, MAC, RAD, SURGT

00 District Chancellor .... Dr. Christine JOHNSON
02 President .... Dr. Kevin BROCKBANK
05 VP of Instruction .... Ms. Jenni MARTIN
32 Vice President of Student Services .... Dr. Glen COSBY
121 Director Student Success/EDI .... Mr. Guillermo ESPINOSA
07 Director Admissions & Registration .... Ms. Chantel BLACK
35 Associate Dean Student Development .... Mr. Connan CAMPBELL
51 Dean Adult Basic Education .... Dr. Sherri FUJITA
49 Dean Arts & Sciences .... Dr. Gwendolyn JAMES
50 Dean Business/Hospitality/Info Tech .... Mr. Jeff BROWN
88 Assoc Dean Corrections Education .... Mr. Jeff WILLIAMS
56 Dean Extended Learning .... Ms. Jaclyn JACOT
76 Dean Health & Environmental Science .... Dr. J.L HENRIKSEN
66 Associate Dean of Nursing .... Dr. Cheri OSLER
75 Dean for Technical Education .... Mr. Dave COX
41 Director Athletics .... Mr. Jim FITZGERALD
09 Sr Dir Inst Effectiveness/Planning .... Dr. Roy CALIGAN
88 Assistant Dean PACE Services .... Ms. Stephanie CHILDRESS
06 Registrar .... Ms. Chantel BLACK
37 Director Financial Aid .... Ms. Tammy ZIBELL
102 District Devel Ofcr/Foundation .... Ms. Heather BEEBE-STEVENS
38 Student Counseling Department Chair .... Ms. Michelle GENDUSA
04 Executive Asst to President .... Ms. Gaylene MACRAE
104 Assoc Dean of Global Education .... Ms. Amber MCKENZIE
106 Director of E-learning .... Mr. Ben WHITMORE

*Spokane Falls Community College (E)

3410 W Whistalks Way, Spokane WA 99224-5288
County: Spokane FICE Identification: 009544
Unit ID: 236708
Telephone: (509) 533-3500 Carnegie Class: Bac/Assoc-Assoc Dom
FAX Number: (509) 533-3237 Calendar System: Quarter
URL: www.spokanefalls.edu
Established: 1967 Annual Undergrad Tuition & Fees (In-State): $3,727
Enrollment: 4,189 Coed
Affiliation or Control: State IRS Status: Exempt
Highest Offering: Baccalaureate
Accreditation: NW, OTA, PTAA

02 President .... Dr. Kimberlee MESSINA
04 Exec Asst to the President .... Ms. Megan GIBSON
05 Vice President of Learning .... Mr. Jim BRADY
32 Vice President of Student Affairs .... Mr. Patrick MCEACHERN
81 Dean Computing/Math/Science .... Dr. Sarah MARTIN
83 Dean Soc Sci/Acct/Econ/Hum Svcs .... Ms. Elodie GOODMAN
79 Dean Humanities .... Dr. Linda BEANE-BOOSE
57 Dean Visual & Performing Arts .... Dr. Bonnie GLANTZ
50 Dean Bus/Prof Stds/Workforce .... Dr. Christopher PELCHAT
121 Dean Student Support Services .... Ms. Cynthia VIGIL
84 Dir Recruit/New Stdnt Entry Center .... Ms. Leslie DAWSON
38 Counseling Department Chair .... Ms. Shawna SHELTON
37 Director of Financial Aid .... Ms. Alex BAILEY
07 Director of Admissions/Registrar .... Ms. Mindy HASENKAMP
41 Athletic Director .... Mr. James FITZGERALD
19 Director of District Security .... Mr. Ken DEMELLO
09 Dir Inst Effectiveness/Research .... Ms. Sally JACKSON
15 Chief Human Resources Officer .... Mr. Greg STEVENS
10 Chief Business Officer .... Ms. Lisa HJALTALIN
13 Chief Info Technology Officer (CIO) .... Ms. Grace LEAF
102 Exec Director CCS Foundation .... Ms. Heather BEEBE-STEVENS
85 Asst Dean for Global Education .... Ms. Amber MCKENZIE
106 District Director of e-Learning .... Mr. Ben WHITMORE
103 Chief Workforce Development Officer .... Mr. Nolan GRUVER
26 Public Information Officer .... Ms. Carolyn CASEY
18 Director of Facilities .... Mr. John GILLETTE
96 Procurement Manager .... Mr. Jim SCOTT

Cornish College of the Arts (F)

1000 Lenora Street, Seattle WA 98121-2707
County: King FICE Identification: 012315
Unit ID: 235024
Telephone: (206) 726-5151 Carnegie Class: Spec-4-yr-Arts
FAX Number: (206) 720-1011 Calendar System: Semester
URL: www.cornish.edu
Established: 1914 Annual Undergrad Tuition & Fees: $34,200
Enrollment: 482 Coed
Affiliation or Control: Independent Non-Profit IRS Status: 501(c)3
Highest Offering: Baccalaureate
Accreditation: NW

01 President .... Dr. Raymond TYMAS-JONES
05 Provost & VP Academic Affairs .... William R. SEIGH
111 VP Institutional Advancement .... Anne DERIEUX
10 VP of Finance & CFO .... Debbie TREEN
84 VP of Enrollment & Marketing .... Vacant
18 VP of Operations .... Brandon BIRD
32 Dean of Student Life .... Dr. Brittany HENDERSON
06 Dean of Academic Services/Registrar .... Adrienne M. BOLYARD
15 Director of Human Resources .... Roy BROWN, III
13 Director of Information Technology .... Jon GRAEF
100 Chief of Staff .... Rick SMITH
21 Controller .... Tina CHAMBERLAIN
08 Director of Library Services .... Bridget NOWLIN
07 Director of Admissions .... Sharron STARLING
26 Dir of Marketing & Communications .... Vacant
38 Director Student Counseling .... Lori KOSHORK
37 Director of Financial Aid .... Sara DRUMMOND
19 Manager Security & Safety .... Dean DEGRAW
30 Director of Development .... Pat BAKO
09 Director of Institutional Research .... Margaret KIRCHNER
43 General Counsel/Title IX Coord .... Tiffany DAVIS

DigiPen Institute of Technology (G)

9931 Willows Road, NE, Redmond WA 98052
County: King FICE Identification: 037243
Unit ID: 443410
Telephone: (425) 558-0299 Carnegie Class: Bac-Diverse
FAX Number: (425) 558-0378 Calendar System: Semester
URL: www.digipen.edu
Established: 1988 Annual Undergrad Tuition & Fees: $33,900
Enrollment: 1,120 Coed
Affiliation or Control: Proprietary IRS Status: Proprietary
Highest Offering: Master's
Accreditation: ACCSC

01 President .... Mr. Claude COMAIR
111 Sr VP External Affairs .... Ms. Angela KUGLER
11 COO - International .... Mr. Chris COMAIR
32 Dean of Students .... Mr. Marshall TRAVERSE
07 Director of Admissions .... Ms. Emily KIRBY

Eastern Washington University (H)

526 5th Street, Cheney WA 99004-1619
County: Spokane FICE Identification: 003775
Unit ID: 235097
Telephone: (509) 359-6200 Carnegie Class: Masters/L
FAX Number: (509) 359-6927 Calendar System: Quarter
URL: www.ewu.edu
Established: 1882 Annual Undergrad Tuition & Fees (In-State): $7,733
Enrollment: 12,349 Coed
Affiliation or Control: State IRS Status: 501(c)3
Highest Offering: Doctorate
Accreditation: NW, CAATE, CACREP, CAPRT, DH, MUS, NASP, OT, PH, PLNG, PTA, SP, SPAA, SW

01 President .... Dr. Shari MCMAHAN
05 Provost/VP for Academic Affairs .... Dr. Jonathan ANDERSON
10 Vice President for Business/Finance .... Ms. Mary VOVES
32 VP for Student Affairs .... Dr. Robert R. SAUDERS
111 Vice President of Advancement .... Ms. Barbara RICHEY
13 VP Info Technology/CIO .... Mr. Brad CHRIST
28 VP Diversity/Equity/Inclusion .... Ms. Shari J. CLARKE

20	Vice Prov Academic Admin	Dr. Brian DONAHUE
88	Int AVP Academic Planning	Ms. Heather VEEDER
41	AVP/Director of Athletics	Ms. Lynn HICKEY
21	Assoc VP Finance/Chief Fin Officer	Ms. Toni HABEGGER
18	Assoc Vice Pres for Facilities	Mr. Shawn KING
84	Assoc VP Enrollment Management	Dr. Jens LARSON
07	Assoc Dir of Admissions Operation	Mr. Boubacar BOUARÉ
15	AVP of Human Resources	Ms. Deborah DANNER
26	Asst VP Marketing/Communications	Mr. Lance KISSLER
101	Exec Assistant to the President/BOT	Ms. Chandalin BENNETT
100	Chief of Staff	Mr. Mark BALDWIN
85	Dir School of Global Learning	Dr. Gina PETRIE
37	Dir of Financial Aid & Scholarships	Ms. Kandi TEETERS
40	Director of Eagle Store	Ms. Sherri ROWE
06	Associate Registrar	Ms. Debra FOCKLER
29	AVP of Philanthropy	Ms. Laura THAYER
39	Director Housing/Residence Life	Vacant
19	Director Public Safety/Chief Police	Chief Jewell DAY
27	Director of Media Relations	Mr. David MEANY
22	Director Equal Opportunity	Mr. Ray RECTOR
79	Dean College Arts/Hum/Soc Sci	Dr. Nydia MARTINEZ
107	Dean Col Professional Pgm	Dr. Vernon LOKE
81	Dean Col Science/Technology/Math	Dr. David BOWMAN
76	Int Dean Health Sciences	Dr. Donna MANN
35	Assoc VP/Dean of Student Life	Dr. Samantha (Sam) ARMSTRONG ASH
09	Director Institutional Research	Mr. Jacob MORRISON
25	Exec Dir Grants & Research Dev	Ms. Charlene ALSPACH
86	Director Government Relations	Mr. David BURI

Edmonds College (A)

20000 68th Avenue W, Lynnwood WA 98036-5999

County: Snohomish | FICE Identification: 005001 | Unit ID: 235103

Telephone: (425) 640-1459 | Carnegie Class: Bac/Assoc-Assoc Dom

FAX Number: (425) 771-3366 | Calendar System: Quarter

URL: www.edmonds.edu

Established: 1967 | Annual Undergrad Tuition & Fees (In-State): $4,107

Enrollment: 6,545 | Coed

Affiliation or Control: State | IRS Status: 501(c)3

Highest Offering: Baccalaureate

Accreditation: NW, CONST

01	President	Dr. Amit B. SINGH
05	Vice President Instruction	Ms. Kim CHAPMAN
10	VP Finance & Operations	Mr. Jim MULIK
15	VP Human Resources/Operations	Ms. Mushka ROHANI
32	Vice President Student Services	Ms. Christina CASTORENA
84	Assoc Dean Student Enroll/Fin Aid	Ms. Christina RUSS
35	Dean Student Life/Development	Mr. Jorge DE LA TORRE
04	Exec Asst to Pres Plng/Operations	Ms. Kristen NYQUIST
124	Dean Student Success/Retention	Dr. Steve WOODARD
102	Exec Director College Foundation	Mr. Brad THOMAS
121	Director Advising	Ms. Olla IBRAHIM
25	Exec Director Grants & Research	Ms. Cat CAROTHERS
103	Dir Workforce Development/Training	Mr. Lance GROB
26	Dir Marketing/Public Information	Ms. Marisa PIERCE
13	Director Information Technology	Ms. Eva SMITH
18	Dir Facilities/Planning/Operations	Ms. Stephanie TEACHMAN
41	Athletic Director	Mr. Spencer STARK
85	Exec Dir International Student Svcs	Ms. Lisa THOMPSON
09	Institutional Researcher	Ms. Wenlan JING
28	VP Equity & Inclusion	Dr. Yvonne TERRELL-POWELL
108	Inst Effectiveness/Grants Liaison	Mr. Jim MULIK
96	Director of Finance	Ms. Heather LYONS
21	Director of Accounting	Ms. Geni TEAGUE
37	Director Financial Aid	Ms. Michelle THORSEN
38	Dir Counseling & Resource Center	Ms. Jessica BURWELL
39	Housing Dir/Housing for Students	Mr. Luke BOTZHEIM
50	Dean Business Division	Mr. Andrew WILLIAMS
29	Dir of Development/Alumni Relations	Ms. Lisa CARROLL
36	Director Entry Services	Mr. Mark DIVIRGILIO

Everett Community College (B)

2000 Tower Street, Everett WA 98201-1390

County: Snohomish | FICE Identification: 003776 | Unit ID: 235149

Telephone: (425) 388-9100 | Carnegie Class: Assoc/HT-High Non

FAX Number: (425) 388-9129 | Calendar System: Quarter

URL: www.everettcc.edu

Established: 1941 | Annual Undergrad Tuition & Fees (In-State): $3,972

Enrollment: 7,580 | Coed

Affiliation or Control: State | IRS Status: 501(c)3

Highest Offering: Associate Degree

Accreditation: NW, ADNUR, MAC

01	Interim President	Dr. Darrell L. CAIN
04	Sr Exec Asst to President	Ms. Jeri POURCHOT
04	Exec Asst to President	Ms. Rita BELVILL
05	VP of Instruction	Ms. Cathy LEAKER
32	VP of Student Services	Ms. Laurie FRANKLIN
10	Vice President of Finance	Ms. Shelby BURKE
26	Vice Pres of College Services	Vacant
28	AVP of Diversity & Equity	Dr. Phyllis ESPOSITO
88	Vice Pres of Corporate Training	Mr. John BONNER
15	Vice Pres Human Resources	Mr. Joseph WHALEN
60	Dean Communication/Social Sciences	Mr. Eugene MCAVOY
35	Int Dean of Student Development	Ms. Jennifer RHODES
81	Dean of Math & Science	Ms. Joyce BELCHER
62	Dean of Arts & Learning Resources	Ms. Lynnae DEEKEN
76	Dean Health Sciences/Public Safety	Mr. Timmothy LOVITT
53	Dean of Basic & Adult Education	Ms. Katie JENSEN
51	Director Continuing Education	Ms. Kristen MCCONAHA
84	Dean Enrollment/Student Finan Svcs	Ms. Laurie FRANKLIN
50	Dean of Business & Applied Tech	Mr. William STUFLICK
19	Dir of Campus Safety & Security	Mr. Charles MACKLIN
09	Director Institutional Research	Mr. Neal PARKER
86	Exec Dir Govt/Community Relations	Dr. John OLSON
41	Director of Athletics	Mr. Garet STUDER
40	Director of Bookstore	Ms. Rachael WATSON
22	Dir Center for Disability Services	Mr. Eric TREKELL
06	Registrar	Mr. Karl RITTER SMITH
104	Assoc Vice Pres Intl Studies	Mr. Visakan GANESON
13	Chief Information Technology Office	Mr. Tim RAGER

The Evergreen State College (C)

2700 Evergreen Parkway, NW, Olympia WA 98505-0005

County: Thurston | FICE Identification: 008155 | Unit ID: 235167

Telephone: (360) 867-6100 | Carnegie Class: Masters/M

FAX Number: N/A | Calendar System: Quarter

URL: www.evergreen.edu

Established: 1967 | Annual Undergrad Tuition & Fees (In-State): $8,325

Enrollment: 2,281 | Coed

Affiliation or Control: State | IRS Status: 501(c)3

Highest Offering: Master's

Accreditation: NW

01	President	Dr. John CARMICHAEL
05	Provost/VP for Student & Acad Life	Dr. David MCAVITY
111	Vice President College Advancement	Ms. Abby KELSO
26	AVP Marketing & Communications	Ms. Farra HAYES
28	VP Incl Excellence & Stdnt Success	Dr. Therese SALIBA
88	VP Tribal Relations/Art & Culture	Ms. Kara BRIGGS
84	Chief Enrollment Officer	Mr. John REED
15	Assoc Vice Pres for Human Resources	Ms. Laurel UZNANSKI
10	Assoc Vice Pres for Finance	Mr. Dave KOHLER
08	Dean of Library Services	Mr. Greg MULLINS
121	Dir of Academic and Career Advising	Dr. Allen THOMPSON
101	Executive Assoc/Secretary to BOT	Ms. Susan HARRIS
22	Affirm Action/Equal Opp Officer	Ms. Lorie MASTIN
13	Assoc VP Computing/Communications	Mr. Antonio ALFONSO
37	Assoc Director of Financial Aid	Mr. Colby MORELLI
06	Registrar	Ms. Lori KLATT
09	Director of Institutional Research	Vacant
11	Assoc VP for Operations	Mr. William WARD
41	Assoc Dean Wellness/Rec/Athletics	Ms. Elizabeth MCHUGH
96	Purchasing and Contracts Manager	Mr. Brant EDDY
07	Director of Admissions	Mr. Wade ARAVE
88	Director of Sustainability	Mr. Scott MORGAN
04	Admin Assistant to the President	Vacant
39	Dir Resident and Dining Services	Ms. Sharon GOODMAN
86	Director Government Relations	Mr. Nora J. SELANDER

Faith International University (D)

3504 N Pearl Street, Tacoma WA 98407-2607

County: Pierce | FICE Identification: 036894 | Unit ID: 443049

Telephone: (253) 752-2020 | Carnegie Class: Masters/S

FAX Number: (253) 759-1790 | Calendar System: Quarter

URL: www.faithiu.edu

Established: 1969 | Annual Undergrad Tuition & Fees: $11,250

Enrollment: 318 | Coed

Affiliation or Control: Interdenominational | IRS Status: 501(c)3

Highest Offering: Doctorate

Accreditation: TRACS

01	President	Dr. Michael J. ADAMS
05	Vice Pres Academic Affs/Provost	Dr. H. Wayne HOUSE
104	Executive VP/International Affairs	Dr. Kyu H. LEE
32	Executive VP/Dean of Students	Dr. John WHEELER, III
88	Admin Dean Korean Division	Miae LEE
10	Chief Financial Officer	Dr. Don BELL
07	Director of Admissions	Kim WHEELER
08	Director Library Services	Dr. Timothy HYUN
04	Exec Administrative Assistant	Kimberly ADAMS
06	Registrar	Dr. Andrew CAYANAN
108	Chief Compliance Officer	Mary VELONI
15	Chief Human Resources Officer	Alison HARDY
26	Dir Communications/Advancement	Adam BARTA
37	Director Student Financial Aid	Laura GUNNARSON
20	VP for Faculty	James TILLE

Gonzaga University (E)

502 East Boone Avenue, Spokane WA 99258-0102

County: Spokane | FICE Identification: 003778 | Unit ID: 235316

Telephone: (509) 313-4200 | Carnegie Class: DU-Mod

FAX Number: (509) 313-5718 | Calendar System: Semester

URL: www.gonzaga.edu

Established: 1887 | Annual Undergrad Tuition & Fees: $46,920

Enrollment: 7,295 | Coed

Affiliation or Control: Roman Catholic | IRS Status: 501(c)3

Highest Offering: Doctorate

Accreditation: NW, ANEST, CACREP, CEA, LAW, MUS, NASP, NURSE

01	President	Dr. Thayne M. MCCULLOH
05	Provost	Dr. Sacha E. KOPP
100	Chief of Staff	Dr. Charlita SHELTON
88	Senior Advisor to the President	Mr. John SKLUT
111	VP for University Advancement	Mr. Joe POSS
42	Acting VP for Mission Integration	Ms. Ellen MACCARONE
32	Vice Prov Student Affairs	Dr. Kent PORTERFIELD
10	Chief Financial Officer	Mr. Joe SMITH
45	Chief Strategy Officer	Mr. Chuck MURPHY
43	General Counsel	Ms. Maureen MCGUIRE
41	Director of Athletics	Mr. Chris L. STANDIFORD
28	Chief Diversity Officer	Dr. Robin KELLEY
04	Executive Asst to President	Ms. Julia BJORDAHL
101	Secretary to the Board	Ms. Maureen MCGUIRE
88	Faculty Advisor to the President	Dr. Ellen M. MACCARONE
17	Director UW-GU Health Partnership	Mr. John SKLUT
20	Assc Prov Educational Effectiveness	Dr. Ron LARGE
20	Assoc Prov Research & Initiatives	Dr. Paul BRACKE
84	Assoc Prov Enrollment Management	Ms. Julie A. MCCULLOH
06	Vice Prov Academic Affs/Registrar	Dr. Jolanta A. WEBER
93	Assoc VP for Cultural Initiatives	Dr. Raymond REYES
08	Dean of Library Services	Dr. Paul J. BRACKE
49	Dean of Arts & Sciences	Dr. Annmarie CANO
53	Dean of Education	Dr. Yoli GALLARDO
50	Dean of Business	Dr. Kenneth ANDERSON
54	Dean Engineering & Applied Sciences	Dr. Karlene HOO
61	Dean of Law	Dr. Jacob ROOKSBY
66	Dean of Nursing/Human Phys	Vacant
88	Dean of Leadership Studies	Dr. Yoli GALLARDO
12	Dean Gonzaga-In-Florence	Dr. Jason HOUSTON
106	Director of Virtual Campus	Vacant
108	Faculty Director of Assessment	Vacant
110	Asst VP Ops & Fundraising	Ms. Stephanie ROCKWELL
112	Director Planned Giving	Ms. Annette DAVIS
88	Senior Director Donor Relations	Ms. Laura GATEWOOD
27	Director of Community and PR	Ms. Mary Joan HAHN
29	Director of Engagement & Alumni	Ms. Kara HERTZ
26	AVP for Marketing/Communications	Mr. Dave SONNTAG
21	Controller	Ms. Deena PRESNELL
96	Director Purchasing	Vacant
15	VP for Human Resources	Mr. Ray KLIEWER
22	Asst Director Equity & Inclusion	Ms. Chris PURVIANCE
09	Director of Institutional Research	Dr. Maxwell KWENDA
13	Chief Information Officer	Mr. Borre ULRICHSEN
19	Director Security/Safety	Ms. Becky WILKEY
18	Director Plant Services	Mr. Ken SAMMONS
07	Director of Undergraduate Admission	Vacant
36	Asst VP Career/Prof Development	Mr. Ray ANGLE
39	Director Student Housing	Mr. Dennis COLESTOCK
37	Dean of Student Finance Services	Mr. James WHITE
35	Dean of Student Engagement	Mr. Matt LAMSMA
38	Director of Counseling Services	Dr. Fernando ORITZ
92	Director Honors Program	Dr. Linda TREDENNICK
36	Director Career Education	Mr. Jonathan BYERS
85	Dir Center for Global Engagement	Dr. Christina ISABELLI
88	Sr Publications Ed & Content Strat	Ms. Kathryn VANSKIKE
86	Liaison for External & Govt Affairs	Mr. John SKLUT
104	Director Study Abroad	Ms. Alisha LOMBARDI

Grays Harbor College (F)

1620 Edward P. Smith Drive, Aberdeen WA 98520-7500

County: Grays Harbor | FICE Identification: 003779 | Unit ID: 235334

Telephone: (360) 532-9020 | Carnegie Class: Bac/Assoc-Assoc Dom

FAX Number: (360) 538-4299 | Calendar System: Quarter

URL: www.ghc.edu

Established: 1930 | Annual Undergrad Tuition & Fees (In-District): $4,296

Enrollment: 1,553 | Coed

Affiliation or Control: State/Local | IRS Status: 501(c)3

Highest Offering: Baccalaureate

Accreditation: NW, ADNUR

01	Interim President	Dr. Ed BREWSTER
04	Senior Admin Assistant to President	Ms. Sandra ZELASKO
05	Vice President for Instruction	Ms. Nicole LACROIX
10	VP Administrative Svcs	Mr. Kwabena J. BOAKYE
32	Vice Pres for Student Services	Dr. Cal ERWIN-SVOBODA
13	Chief Exec Information Technology	Mr. Derek EDENS
20	Dean of Instruction	Ms. Evi BUELL
31	Dean Instruct/Trans Dev & Cmty Educ	Mr. Martin REIMER
35	Assoc Dean for Student Services	Vacant
08	Assoc Dn Library/Media Svcs/e-Lrng	Ms. Susan SCHREINER
07	Assoc Dean of Admissions	Vacant
15	Chief Human Resources Officer	Mr. Darin JONES
37	Director Financial Aid	Ms. Crystal BAGBY
18	Dir Campus Operations/Sfty/Security	Vacant
38	Director of Counseling	Vacant
102	Exec Dir GHC Foundation	Ms. Lisa SMITH
26	Director Public Relations	Vacant
09	Chief Inst Effect/College Relations	Ms. Kristy ANDERSON
06	Dir Enroll Svcs/Assoc Registrar	Vacant
41	Athletic Director	Mr. Tom SUTERA
106	Dir Online Education/E-Learning	Vacant

Great Northern University (G)

611 E. Indiana Avenue, Spokane WA 99207

County: Spokane | Identification: 667409

Telephone: (509) 248-7100 | Carnegie Class: Not Classified

FAX Number: N/A | Calendar System: Semester

URL: greatnorthernu.org

Established: 2018 | Annual Undergrad Tuition & Fees: N/A

Enrollment: N/A | Coed

Affiliation or Control: Independent Non-Profit | IRS Status: 501(c)3

Highest Offering: Baccalaureate

Accreditation: TRACS

01 President .... Dr. Wendy LIDDELL
05 Provost .... Dr. Jennifer MILLS

Green River College (A)

12401 SE 320th Street, Auburn WA 98092-3699
County: King FICE Identification: 003780
Unit ID: 235343
Telephone: (253) 288-3340 Carnegie Class: Bac/Assoc-Mixed
FAX Number: N/A Calendar System: Quarter
URL: www.greenriver.edu
Established: 1965 Annual Undergrad Tuition & Fees (In-State): $4,233
Enrollment: 7,493 Coed
Affiliation or Control: State IRS Status: 501(c)3
Highest Offering: Baccalaureate
Accreditation: NW, CNEA, OTA, PTAA

01 President .... Dr. Suzanne JOHNSON
05 Vice President of Instruction .... Dr. Rolita EZEONU
13 Exec Dir of Information Technology .... Camella MORGAN
10 Vice President of Business Affairs .... Shirley BEAN
15 Senior Director of Human Resources .... Mark BRUNKE
32 Vice President of Student Services . Dr. Deborah CASEY POWELL
56 VP Intl Programs/Extended Learning .... Wendy STEWART
49 Dean Fine Arts & Social Science .... Christie GILLILAND
79 Dean English/Humanities .... Jamie FITZGERALD
84 Dean of Enrollment & Completion .... David LARSEN
06 Director of Enrollment Services .... Jenny WHEELER
37 Director of Financial Aid .... Teresa BUCHMANN
111 VP of College Advancement .... George FRASIER
21 Director of Budget .... Janee SOMMERFELD
18 Capital Projects Officer .... Robert OLSON
26 Senior Director College Relations .... Philip DENMAN
12 Dean for Branch Campuses & A&P Dev .... Tsai-En CHENG
09 Dir Institutional Effectiveness .... Fia ELIASSON-CREEK
28 Dir Diversity/Equity & Inclusion .... Marwa ALMUSAWI
19 Director of Campus Safety .... Derek RONNFELDT
41 Director Athletics .... Shannon PERCELL
04 Executive Assistant to President .... Suzanne MCCUDDEN
103 Director Workforce Education .... Cathy ALSTON

Heritage University (B)

3240 Fort Road, Toppenish WA 98948-9599
County: Yakima FICE Identification: 003777
Unit ID: 235422
Telephone: (509) 865-8600 Carnegie Class: Masters/S
FAX Number: (509) 865-7976 Calendar System: Semester
URL: www.heritage.edu
Established: 1982 Annual Undergrad Tuition & Fees: $18,332
Enrollment: 999 Coed
Affiliation or Control: Independent Non-Profit IRS Status: 501(c)3
Highest Offering: Master's
Accreditation: NW, MLS, NURSE, SW

01 President .... Dr. Andrew C. SUND
05 Provost/VP Academic Affairs .... Dr. Kazuhiro SONODA
32 VP Student Affairs & Enrollment .... Dr. Melissa HILL
10 Chief Financial Officer .... Vacant
111 VP Advancement/Marketing/Comm .... Mr. David WISE
13 Director Information Technology .... Mr. Aaron KRANTZ
84 Assoc VP Enrollment Management .... Vacant
53 Chair of Education & Psychology .... Mr. Ken BERGEVIN
35 Director of Student Life/Engagement .... Mr. Isaias GUERRERO
06 Assoc Registrar .... Mr. Pablo CONTRERAS
18 Director Physical Plant/Maintenance .... Mr. Jeff BEEHLER
37 Int Director of Financial Aid .... Ms. Dianne FERNANDEZ
08 Library Dir/Reference Librarian .... Mr. Daniel LIESTMAN
07 Director of Admissions .... Mr. Gabriel PINON
26 Communications Officer .... Ms. Bonnie HUGHES
09 Inst Research Administrator .... Vacant
15 Director Human Resources .... Ms. Anita FLORES
21 Controller .... Ms. Alysia STEVENS
04 Exec Manager President's Office .... Ms. Betty J. SAMPSON
103 Director Workforce Development .... Mr. Martin VALADEZ
19 Director Security/Safety .... Mr. Joseph LAREZ

Highline College (C)

PO Box 98000, 2400 S 240th Street,
Des Moines WA 98198-9800
County: King FICE Identification: 003781
Unit ID: 235431
Telephone: (206) 878-3710 Carnegie Class: Bac/Assoc-Assoc Dom
FAX Number: (206) 870-3779 Calendar System: Quarter
URL: www.highline.edu
Established: 1961 Annual Undergrad Tuition & Fees (In-State): $4,231
Enrollment: 5,829 Coed
Affiliation or Control: State IRS Status: 501(c)3
Highest Offering: Baccalaureate
Accreditation: NW, ADNUR, COARC, MAC, NAEYC

01 President .... Dr. John MOSBY
05 VP Academic Affairs .... Dr. Emily LARDNER
11 VP Administrative Services .... Mr. Michael PHAM
32 Interim VP for Student Services .... Dr. Jamilyn PENN
111 VP for Inst Advancement .... Mr. Josh GERSTMAN
13 Executive Director of ITS and CIO .... Mr. Tim WRYE
15 Executive Dir of Human Resources .... Ms. Summer KORST
100 Executive Dir Office of the Pres .... Ms. Danielle SLOTA
103 Dean of Workforce .... Dr. Paulette LOPEZ
88 Associate Dean for BAS & Workforce .... Dr. Tanya POWERS
37 Dean for Student Support & Funding .... Mr. Ay SAECHAO
22 Assoc Dean for Access/Inclusive Ed .... Ms. Jennifer SANDLER
84 Dean for Advising & Enrollment Svcs .... Vacant
35 Associate Dean for Student Life .... Vacant
88 Associate Dean for Student Funding .... Mr. Loyal ALLEN, JR.
51 Dean for Extended Learning .... Ms. Gabrielle BACHMEIER
121 Int Assoc Dean Student Lrng/Success .... Ms. Shawna FREEMAN
88 Dean College & Career Readiness .... Mr. Justin DAMPEER
88 Dean of Academic Transfers Pathways .... Ms. Maribel JIMINEZ
09 Director of Institutional Research .... Ms. Emily COATES
19 Director Security/Safety .... Mr. David MENKE

Lake Washington Institute of Technology (D)

11605 132nd Avenue NE, Kirkland WA 98034-8506
County: King FICE Identification: 005373
Unit ID: 235699
Telephone: (425) 739-8100 Carnegie Class: Bac/Assoc-Mixed
FAX Number: (425) 739-8299 Calendar System: Quarter
URL: www.lwtech.edu
Established: 1949 Annual Undergrad Tuition & Fees (In-State): $4,510
Enrollment: 3,319 Coed
Affiliation or Control: State IRS Status: 170(c)1
Highest Offering: Baccalaureate
Accreditation: NW, ACFEI, ADNUR, DH, FUSER, MAC, OTA, PTAA

01 President .... Dr. Amy MORRISON
04 Sr Exec Asst to President and Board .... Ms. Elsa GOSSETT
32 VP Student Services .... Dr. Ruby HAYDEN
05 VP of Instruction .... Dr. Suzanne AMES
10 VP Administrative Services .... Mr. Bruce RIVELAND
53 Dean of Instruction .... Ms. Vicki CHEW
76 Dean of Instruction .... Dr. Aparna SEN
72 Dean of Instruction .... Mr. Michael RICHMOND
72 Dean of Instruction .... Mr. Mike POTTER
106 Dean of Instruction .... Ms. Sally HEILSTEDT
88 Dean High School Programs .... Mr. Tuan DANG
104 Dean of Instruction International .... Dr. David RECTOR
30 Exec Director Development .... Ms. Elisabeth SORENSEN
15 VP Human Resources .... Ms. Meena PARK
09 Director Research & Grants .... Ms. Cathy COPELAND
26 Exec Director Comm/Marketing .... Ms. Leslie SHATTUCK
13 Chief Information Officer .... Mr. Chris MCLAIN
28 Exec Director of EDI .... Mr. Robert BRITTEN
88 Assoc Dean Funeral Service Educ .... Ms. Lisa MEEHAN
66 Associate Dean Nursing Program .... Ms. Lauren CLINE
88 Director TRiO Projects .... Mr. Tien DO
08 Librarian .... Mr. Greg BEM
88 Director PTA Program .... Ms. Molly VERSCHUYL
18 Director Facilities & Operations .... Mr. Casey HUEBNER
37 Director Financial Aid .... Ms. Kimberly GEER
84 Director Enrollment Services .... Ms. Larisa AKSELRUD
103 Director Workforce Development .... Ms. Demetra BIROS
21 Director of Financial Services .... Mr. Xieng LIM
93 Director Student Programs .... Ms. Sheila WALTON
96 Manager Purchasing Service .... Mr. Isaac ROBINSON
105 Website/Digital Content Specialist .... Ms. Alisa SHTROMBERG
40 Manager Bookstore .... Mr. Russ MERKOW
19 Director Security/Safety .... Mr. Anthony BOWERS
35 Director Student Development .... Ms. Katie PEACOCK

Lower Columbia College (E)

1600 Maple Street PO Box 3010,
Longview WA 98632-0310
County: Cowlitz FICE Identification: 003782
Unit ID: 235750
Telephone: (360) 442-2311 Carnegie Class: Assoc/MT-VT-High Trad
FAX Number: (360) 442-2109 Calendar System: Quarter
URL: www.lowercolumbia.edu
Established: 1934 Annual Undergrad Tuition & Fees (In-State): $4,068
Enrollment: 2,325 Coed
Affiliation or Control: State IRS Status: 170(c)1
Highest Offering: Baccalaureate
Accreditation: NW, ADNUR, MAC

01 President .... Mr. Christopher C. BAILEY
11 Vice President Administrative Svcs .... Mr. Nolan WHEELER
05 Vice President Instruction .... Ms. Kristen FINNEL
32 Vice President Student Services .... Ms. Sue ORCHARD
15 VP Foundation/HR/Legal Affairs .... Ms. Kendra SPRAGUE
09 VP Effectiveness & Col Relations .... Ms. Wendy HALL
04 Executive Assistant to President .... Ms. Bryanna E. SMITH
66 Dean Nursing & Allied Health .... Ms. Merry BOND
20 Dean Instruction/Learning Resources .... Ms. Stefanie GILBERTI
20 Dean Instruction .... Ms. Tamra GILCHRIST
76 Executive Dean Allied Health/Nurse .... Ms. Karen JOINER
97 Dean Basic Education .... Ms. Theresa STALICK
06 Director Registration .... Mr. Magnus ALTMAYER
39 Director Stdnt Programs/Housing .... Mr. Richard ARQUETTE
19 Director Security/Safety .... Mr. Jason ARROWSMITH
104 Director International Programs .... Ms. Marie BOISVERT
88 Gallery & Programs Director .... Ms. Jennie CASTLE
88 RCA Technical Director .... Mr. Robert COCHRAN
121 Director Advising & Testing .... Mr. Byron FORD
21 Finance Director .... Ms. Desiree GAMBLE
106 Director E-learning .... Ms. Sarah GRIFFITH
18 Director Campus Services .... Mr. Richard HAMILTON
08 Library Director .... Ms. Lindsay KEEVY
88 Director Head Start .... Ms. Mindy LEASURE
40 Director Enterprise Services ... Ms. Alyssa MILANO-HIGHTOWER
88 Director DSS .... Ms. Mary Kate MORGAN
16 Director Human Resources .... Ms. Samantha ORTH
13 Director Information Technology .... Mr. Brandon RAY
88 Director TRIO Programs .... Ms. Jodi REID
88 Director Instruction Division .... Ms. Natalie RICHIE
41 Athletic Director .... Mr. Kirc J. ROLAND
88 Director Env Health/Safety .... Ms. Janel SKREEN
103 Director Workforce Programs .... Ms. Dani TRIMBLE
37 Financial Aid Director .... Vacant
88 Outreach Manager .... Ms. Nicole FABER
88 Running Start Manager .... Ms. Guadalupe RODRIGUEZ
96 Purchasing Manager .... Ms. Claudia SLABU
102 Foundation Specialist .... Mr. Jamie NELSON

Northwest College of Art & Design (NCAD) (F)

1126 Pacific Avenue, Suite 101, Tacoma WA 98402
County: Pierce FICE Identification: 026021
Unit ID: 377546
Telephone: (253) 272-1126 Carnegie Class: Spec-4-yr-Arts
FAX Number: (253) 572-9058 Calendar System: Semester
URL: www.ncad.edu
Established: 1982 Annual Undergrad Tuition & Fees: $18,100
Enrollment: 101 Coed
Affiliation or Control: Proprietary IRS Status: Proprietary
Highest Offering: Baccalaureate
Accreditation: ACCSC

01 President .... Craig FREEMAN
05 Director of Education .... Susan OGILVIE
11 Director of Operations .... Kim PERIGARD
06 Registrar .... Ashley JONES
13 IT Admin .... Skye CARLSON
07 Admissions Director .... Dan ROTHROCK
37 Financial Aid .... Julie PERIGARD
08 Head Librarian .... Dan ROTHROCK

Northwest Indian College (G)

2522 Kwina Road, Bellingham WA 98226-9217
County: Whatcom FICE Identification: 021800
Unit ID: 380377
Telephone: (360) 676-2772 Carnegie Class: Tribal
FAX Number: (360) 738-0136 Calendar System: Quarter
URL: www.nwic.edu
Established: 1973 Annual Undergrad Tuition & Fees: $6,787
Enrollment: 555 Coed
Affiliation or Control: Other IRS Status: 501(c)3
Highest Offering: Baccalaureate
Accreditation: NW

01 President .... Dr. Justin GUILLORY
10 Chief Financial Officer .... Ms. Billie KINLEY
30 Vice Pres Campus Development .... Mr. David OREIRO
25 Sponsored Programs Coordinator .... Ms. Debbie MELE MAI
04 Exec Assistant to the President .... Ms. Frances SELLARS
05 Dean of Academics .... Ms. Destiny PETROSKE
32 Dean of Students .... Ms. Victoria RETASKET
88 Pgm Coord 2-yr Programs of Study .... Mr. Rudy VENDIOLA
37 Financial Aid & Admissions Director ..... Ms. Shayna NISHIYAMA
13 IS Director .... Mr. Cameron REVARD
08 Library Director .... Ms. Valerie MCBETH
06 Registrar .... Ms. Patricia CUEVA
108 Dir of Institutional Effectiveness .... Ms. Carmen BLAND
15 Director Human Resources .... Ms. Darcilynn BOB
18 Director of Facilities Maintenance .... Mr. Jason JAMES
19 Security Manager .... Ms. Lavonne BALLEW
102 Director of NWIC Foundation .... Ms. Barbara LEWIS
78 Director of Cooperative Extension .... Vacant
88 Director Coast Salish Institute .... Ms. Sharon KINLEY
41 Athletic Director .... Mr. James MATHIAS
96 Purchasing Manager .... Mr. Charlie ROBERTS
26 Chief Public Relations/Marketing .... Ms. Natasha BRENNAN
103 Director Workforce Development .... Mr. Robert DECOTEAU
23 Director NWICCH .... Dr. William FREEMAN
88 Director Tribal Voc Rehab Institute .... Ms. Laura MAUDSLEY
88 Director Salish Sea Research Center .... Ms. Melissa PEACOCK
39 Director Resident Life Center .... Mr. Keith TOM
09 Director of Institutional Research .... Mrs. Carmen BLAND

Northwest School of Wooden Boatbuilding (H)

42 N Water Street, Port Hadlock WA 98339-8706
County: Jefferson FICE Identification: 041550
Unit ID: 458140
Telephone: (360) 385-4948 Carnegie Class: Spec 2-yr-Tech
FAX Number: (360) 385-5089 Calendar System: Other
URL: www.nwswb.edu
Established: 1981 Annual Undergrad Tuition & Fees: $16,050
Enrollment: 27 Coed
Affiliation or Control: Independent Non-Profit IRS Status: 501(c)3
Highest Offering: Associate Degree
Accreditation: ACCSC

01 Executive Director .... Ms. Betsy DAVIS
07 Admissions and Student Services .... Ms. Heidi BLEHM

Northwest University (A)

PO Box 579, Kirkland WA 98083-0579
County: King FICE Identification: 003783
Unit ID: 236133
Telephone: (425) 822-8266 Carnegie Class: Masters/M
FAX Number: (425) 889-5224 Calendar System: Semester
URL: www.northwestu.edu
Established: 1934 Annual Undergrad Tuition & Fees: $33,980
Enrollment: 1,184 Coed
Affiliation or Control: Assemblies Of God Church IRS Status: 501(c)3
Highest Offering: Doctorate
Accreditation: NW, ACBSP, COPSY, NURSE

01 President .... Dr. Joseph CASTLEBERRY
05 Provost .... Dr. Jim HEUGEL
10 Chief Financial Officer .... Mr. Ryan PORTER
111 Senior VP of Advancement .... Mr. Ken CORNELL
108 VP of Institutional Effectiveness .... Mrs. Vickie REKOW
06 Registrar .... Mrs. Sandy HENDRICKSON
07 Director of Recruitment .... Mr. Jorine JOHNSON
41 Athletic Director .... Mr. Gary MCINTOSH
08 Library Director .... Ms. Abigail DOUR
38 Director of Wellness Center .... Ms. Denise JOHNSON
15 Director of Human Resources .... Ms. Amanda BOWMAN
121 Director Academic Success/Advising .... Mrs. Traci GRANT
32 VP of Student Development .... Dr. Rick ENGSTROM
26 Senior Director of Marketing .... Mr. Steve BOSTROM
04 Sr Exec Asst to President .... Ms. Megan SCOTT
19 Director Security/Safety .... Mr. Reuben GONZALES
37 Assoc Dir of Student Financial Aid .... Mr. Roger WILSON
28 Director of Multicultural Life .... Mr. Blake SMALL
30 Sr Director of Development .... Dr. Mollie BOND
39 Associate Dean of Resident Life .... Mrs. Larissa LILLY
36 Director of Career Services .... Mr. Peter CARLSON
49 Dean College of Arts and Sciences .... Dr. Sarah DRIVDAHL
73 Dean College of Ministry .... Dr. Joshua ZIEFLE
83 Dean College of Social Sciences .... Dr. Matt NELSON
50 Dean College of Business .... Dr. Rowlanda CAWTHON
53 Dean College of Education .... Mr. Laird LEAVITT
66 Dean College of Nursing .... Dr. Erin-Joy BJORGE
106 Dean Ctr for Online Education .... Dr. George KELLEY

Olympic College (B)

1600 Chester Avenue, Bremerton WA 98337-1699
County: Kitsap FICE Identification: 003784
Unit ID: 236188
Telephone: (360) 792-6050 Carnegie Class: Bac/Assoc-Assoc Dom
FAX Number: (360) 475-7151 Calendar System: Quarter
URL: www.olympic.edu
Established: 1946 Annual Undergrad Tuition & Fees (In-State): $3,971
Enrollment: 5,357 Coed
Affiliation or Control: State IRS Status: 501(c)3
Highest Offering: Baccalaureate
Accreditation: NW, ACFEI, ADNUR, MAC, NURSE, PTAA

01 President .... Dr. Martin CAVALLUZZI
05 Vice President for Instruction .... Dr. Martin COCKROFT
11 Vice Pres Administrative Services .... Mr. Ronald ELLISON
32 Vice President for Student Services .... Dr. Brendon TAGA
22 Vice President Equity & Inclusion .... Ms. Cheryl NUÑEZ
15 Vice President of Human Resources .... Mr. Joshua MASTERS
100 Chief of Staff .... Mr. Adam MORRIS
37 Director Student Financial Services .... Ms. Heidi TOWNSEND
26 Exec Director of Communications .... Mr. Shawn DEVINE
84 Dean of Enrollment Services .... Dr. Jennifer GLASIER
18 Mgr Capital Projects .... Ms. Ariel BIRTLEY
10 Int Director of Business Services .... Ms. Angela HAMILTON
13 CIO/Exec Dir Technical Services .... Ms. Evelyn HERNANDEZ
96 Procurement Officer .... Ms. Diana LAKE
36 Director Career Center .... Ms. Teresa MCDERMOTT
09 Exec Director Inst Effectiveness .... Dr. Allison PHAYRE
28 Supervisor Multicult/Student Pgms .... Ms. Jodie COLLINS
103 Dean Workforce Development .... Ms. Amy HATFIELD
08 Dean Library/Lrng Resources/eLrng .... Ms. Erica COE
50 Dean Business & Technology .... Dr. Norma WHITACRE
81 Dean Math/Engineer/Sci/Health .... Mr. John VAUGHAN
79 Dean Humanities/Social Science .... Dr. Rebecca SEAMAN
19 Director of Campus Safety .... Mr. Stephen DAVIS
25 Director of College Grant Devel .... Ms. Sarah BROWNGOETZ
29 Exec Dir of Foundation/Alumni Assn .... Mr. Trevor ROSS
41 Director of Athletics .... Mr. Barry JANUSCH

Pacific Lutheran University (C)

12180 Park Avenue S., Tacoma WA 98447-0003
County: Pierce FICE Identification: 003785
Unit ID: 236230
Telephone: (253) 531-6900 Carnegie Class: Masters/M
FAX Number: (253) 535-8320 Calendar System: 4/1/4
URL: www.plu.edu
Established: 1890 Annual Undergrad Tuition & Fees: $46,850
Enrollment: 2,907 Coed
Affiliation or Control: Evangelical Lutheran Church In America
IRS Status: 501(c)3
Highest Offering: Doctorate
Accreditation: NW, MFCD, MUS, NURSE, SW

01 President .... Mr. Allan BELTON
101 Director of Admin & Sec to Board .... Ms. Vicky L. WINTERS
04 Asst to the President .... Ms. Julie L. MIX
05 Provost .... Dr. Joanna GREGSON
20 Assoc Provost Undergrad Programs .... Dr. Jan P. LEWIS
51 Assoc Provost for Grad & Cont Educ .... Dr. Geoffrey E. FOY
88 Dean of Inclusive Excellence .... Dr. Jennifer A. SMITH
11 Chief Operating Officer .... Ms. Teri P. PHILLIPS
111 Vice Pres for Univ Relations .... Mr. Daniel J. LEE
32 Vice Pres for Student Life .... Dr. Joanna C. ROYCE-DAVIS
84 Dean for Enrollment Management .... Mr. Michael T. FRECHETTE
121 Exec Dir Ctr for Student Success .... Ms. Kris H. PLAEHN
07 Director of Admissions .... Ms. Melody A. FERGUSON
26 Assoc VP Marketing & Comm .... Ms. Lace M. SMITH
10 Assoc VP for Finance .... Mr. Patrick D. GEHRING
42 University Pastor .... Rev. Jen L. RUDE
57 Dean School of Arts & Communication .... Dr. Cameron D. BENNETT
50 Dean School of Business .... Dr. Mark R. MULDER
53 Dean School of Educ & Kinesiology .... Dr. Karen E. MCCONNELL
66 Dean School of Nursing .... Dr. Barbara HABERMANN
79 Dean Humanities .... Dr. Kevin J. O'BRIEN
81 Dean Natural Sciences .... Dr. Ann J. AUMAN
83 Dean Social Sciences .... Dr. Michelle L. CEYNAR
35 Dean of Students .... Dr. Eva R. FREY
88 Exec Dir Wang Ctr for Global Educ .... Dr. Tamara R. WILLIAMS
41 Director of Athletics & Recreation .... Mr. Michael P. SNYDER
06 Registrar .... Ms. Kelly G. POTH
39 Assoc VP for Campus Life .... Mr. Tom A. HUELSBECK
18 Assoc VP for Facilities Management .... Mr. Ray K. ORR
19 Director of Campus Safety & Info .... Ms. Tara SIMMELINK
36 Director Career Learning & Engage .... Mr. Kevin D. ANDREW
23 Director Health Services .... Ms. Elizabeth A. HOOPER
15 Director Human Resources .... Ms. Gretchen M. HOWELL
90 Dir of Enterprise Systems & Comm .... Mr. David P. ALLEN
13 Chief Information Officer .... Ms. Ardys E. CURTIS
40 Director of Retail Services .... Mr. Josh C. GIRNUS
09 Assoc Dean Institutional Research .... Mr. Kevin A. BERG
102 Exec Director Sponsored Programs .... Ms. Erica S. LUETH
44 Director Annual Giving .... Ms. Andrea N. MICHELBACH
22 Dir Affirmative Action/EEO .... Ms. Teri P. PHILLIPS
28 Asst VP Diversity/Justice/Sustain .... Ms. Angie Z. HAMBRICK
29 Director Alumni Relations .... Ms. Jessica L. PAGEL
38 Interim Director Counseling Center .Dr. Joanna C. ROYCE-DAVIS
08 Director of the Library .... Ms. Fran R. LANE RASMUS

Pacific Northwest Christian College (D)

3021 West Clearwater Avenue, Kennewick WA 99336
County: Benton Identification: 667359
Telephone: (509) 420-4545 Carnegie Class: Not Classified
FAX Number: N/A Calendar System: Semester
URL: www.pnwcc.edu
Established: 2008 Annual Undergrad Tuition & Fees: N/A
Enrollment: N/A Coed
Affiliation or Control: Independent Non-Profit IRS Status: 501(c)3
Highest Offering: Associate Degree
Accreditation: TRACS

01 President .... Robert B. NASH
05 Dean of Academic Affairs .... Dr. Darrell PULS
06 Registrar .... Kelli TEMPLETON
07 Dir Admissions/Student Life .... Robbie FIOCCHI

Pacific Northwest University of Health Sciences (E)

111 University Parkway, Suite 202, Yakima WA 98901
County: Yakima FICE Identification: 041305
Unit ID: 455406
Telephone: (509) 452-5100 Carnegie Class: Spec-4-yr-Med
FAX Number: (509) 452-5101 Calendar System: Semester
URL: www.pnwu.edu
Established: 2005 Annual Graduate Tuition & Fees: N/A
Enrollment: 573 Coed
Affiliation or Control: Independent Non-Profit IRS Status: 501(c)3
Highest Offering: Doctorate; No Undergraduates
Accreditation: NW, OSTEO, @PTA

01 President .... Dr. Michael J. LAWLER
05 Provost .... Dr. Edward BILSKY
10 Chief Financial Officer .... Ms. Ann HITTLE
11 Chief Operations Officer .... Mr. Frank D. ALVAREZ
30 Chief Development Officer .... Ms. Michele ERICKSON
63 Dean Col of Osteopathic Medicine .... Dr. Thomas SCANDALIS
08 Head Librarian .... Ms. Anita CLEARY
13 Chief Info Technology Officer (CIO) .... Mr. Jameson WATKINS
15 Chief Human Resources Officer .... Ms. Erin MURPHY
18 Chief Facilities/Physical Plant .... Mr. Brent PERRIN
26 Chief Communications Officer .... Mr. Dean O'DRISCOLL
29 Director Alumni Relations .... Ms. Chanda ANDERSON
37 Director Student Financial Aid .... Ms. Laura PENDLETON
45 Chief Institutional Planning .... Ms. Angie GIRARD
04 Administrative Asst to President .... Ms. Vikki GORE
84 Asst Prov Enrollment Mgmt/Registrar .... Ms. LeAnn HUNTER
108 Dir Institutional Effectiveness .... Ms. Lori FULTON
32 Dean Student Affairs .... Dr. Stephen LAIRD
96 Asst Dir Procurement/Asset Mgmt .... Ms. Barbara ANDERSON
25 Chief Contract/Grants Administrator .... Ms. Anita QUINTANA
28 Director of Diversity .... Dr. Mirna RAMOS-DIAZ

Peninsula College (F)

1502 East Lauridsen Boulevard,
Port Angeles WA 98362-6698
County: Clallam FICE Identification: 003786
Unit ID: 236258
Telephone: (360) 452-9277 Carnegie Class: Bac/Assoc-Assoc Dom
FAX Number: (360) 457-8100 Calendar System: Quarter
URL: www.pencol.edu
Established: 1961 Annual Undergrad Tuition & Fees (In-District): $4,218
Enrollment: 1,727 Coed
Affiliation or Control: State/Local IRS Status: 501(c)3
Highest Offering: Baccalaureate
Accreditation: NW, CNEA, MAC

01 President .... Dr. Suzanne AMES
05 Vice President Instruction .... Dr. Steven THOMAS
10 Vice Pres Finance/Administration .... Ms. Carie EDMISTON
32 Vice President Student Services .... Mr. Jack HULS
35 Assoc Dean of Student Success .... Ms. Cathy ENGLE
41 Assoc Dean Athletics/Student Prgms .... Mr. Rick ROSS
13 Director Information Technology .... Ms. Emma JANSSEN
04 Executive Asst to the President .... Ms. Trisha HAGGERTY
26 Public Information Officer .... Ms. Kari DESSER
15 Director of Human Resources .... Ms. Krista FRANCIS
85 Dir Intl Stdnt Pgm/Stdnt Recruit .. Ms. Sophia ILIAKIS-DOHERTY
102 Interim Director College Foundation .... Ms. Getta WORKMAN
09 Director of Institutional Research .... Ms. Terye SENDERHAUF
18 Asst Director Physical Plant .... Mr. Jay Dee SMITH
40 Bookstore Manager .... Mrs. Camilla RICO

Perry Technical Institute (G)

2011 W. Washington Avenue, Yakima WA 98903
County: Yakima FICE Identification: 009387
Unit ID: 236212
Telephone: (509) 453-0374 Carnegie Class: Assoc/HVT-High Trad
FAX Number: (509) 453-0375 Calendar System: Quarter
URL: www.perrytech.edu
Established: 1939 Annual Undergrad Tuition & Fees: N/A
Enrollment: 881 Coed
Affiliation or Control: Independent Non-Profit IRS Status: 501(c)3
Highest Offering: Associate Degree
Accreditation: ACCSC

01 President .... Christine COTE
04 Executive Assistant .... Natalie RAPP
05 Dean of Education .... Nathan HULL
06 Registrar .... Jill COPE
07 Director of Admissions & Marketing .... Nicole TRAMMELL
10 VP of Finance & Administration .... Cathy STERBENZ
102 Foundation Director .... Tressa SHOCKLEY
13 Director of Information Technology .... Josh PHILLIPS
15 Director of Human Resources .... Carol HELMS
19 Director of Facilities & Safety .... Kaila LOCKBEAM
84 Asst Director of Admissions & CS .... Raul LUNA
37 Director of Financial Aid .... Jennifer SNELLINK
20 Associate Dean of Education .... Jason LAMIQUIZ
20 Associate Dean of Education .... Garet GASSELING
96 Director of Purchasing & Auxil Svcs .... Maria PULIDO

Pierce College District (H)

1601 39th Avenue SE, Puyallup WA 98374
County: Pierce FICE Identification: 005000
Unit ID: 439145
Telephone: (253) 964-6500 Carnegie Class: Not Classified
FAX Number: N/A Calendar System: Quarter
URL: www.pierce.ctc.edu
Established: 1967 Annual Undergrad Tuition & Fees (In-State): N/A
Enrollment: N/A Coed
Affiliation or Control: State IRS Status: 501(c)3
Highest Offering: Baccalaureate
Accreditation: NW, ADNUR, DH

01 District Chancellor .... Dr. Michele JOHNSON
12 President Pierce College Puyallup .... Dr. Matthew CAMPBELL
12 President Fort Steilacoom .... Dr. Julie WHITE
05 VP Learning/Student Success-PY .... Mr. Charlie PARKER
05 VP Learning/Student Success-FS .... Dr. Ilder LOPEZ
111 VP Strategic Advancement .... Mr. Mike WARK
15 VP for Human Resources .... Ms. Holly GORSKI
103 VP Workforce/Economic/Prof Devel .... Ms. Jo Ann BARIA
13 Chief Information Officer .... Mr. Andrew GLASS
84 Dean Enroll Svcs/Fin Aid/Registrar .... Ms. Anne WHITE
08 Dean Libraries & Learning Resources .... Ms. Christie FLYNN
32 Dean of Student Success .... Ms. Agnes STEWARD
26 Dir Marketing and Communications .... Mr. Brian BENEDETTI
35 Dir Student Programs-Ft Steilacoom .... Mr. Joseph ADAMS
41 Director District Athletics .... Mr. Duncan STEVENSON
35 Dir of Student Life-Puyallup .... Vacant
85 Exec Dir of International Education .... Ms. Myung PARK
19 Campus Safety Sergeant-Supervisor .... Mr. Robert ROCKEY
21 Director Fiscal Services .... Ms. Sylvia JAMES
37 District Director Financial Aid .... Ms. Trinity HUTTNER
84 Director Enrollment Services-Puy .... Vacant
09 Director Institutional Research .... Vacant
49 Dean Arts & Humanities .... Dr. Holly SMITH
88 Dean Transitional Education .... Ms. Lori GRIFFIN
76 Dean Health & Technology .... Mr. Ronald MAY
81 Dean Natural Sciences .... Mr. Eddie PERRY
83 Dean Business/Social Sciences .... Dr. Allison SIEVING

04 Exec Assistant to the President .... Ms. Christine BOITER
101 Sr Exec Assistant to Board .... Ms. Marie HARRIS
28 VP for Equity/Innovation/Engagement .... Mr. Charlie PARKER
105 Director Web Services .... Ms. Gayle RAMBEAU
18 Chief Facilities/Campus Safety Dir .... Vacant

Pima Medical Institute-Renton (A)

555 South Renton Village Place, Renton WA 98057
Telephone: (425) 228-9600 Identification: 770517
Accreditation: ABHES, COARC, OTA

† Branch campus of Pima Medical Institute-Tucson, Tucson, AZ

Pima Medical Institute-Seattle (B)

9709 3rd Avenue NE, Suite 400, Seattle WA 98115-2052
Telephone: (206) 322-6100 Identification: 666172
Accreditation: ABHES, DH, PTAA, RAD

† Branch campus of Pima Medical Institute-Tucson, Tucson, AZ

Renton Technical College (C)

3000 NE Fourth Street, Renton WA 98056-4123
County: King FICE Identification: 010434
Unit ID: 236382
Telephone: (425) 235-2352 Carnegie Class: Bac/Assoc-Assoc Dom
FAX Number: (425) 235-7832 Calendar System: Quarter
URL: www.rtc.edu
Established: 1942 Annual Undergrad Tuition & Fees (In-State): $5,671
Enrollment: 3,214 Coed
Affiliation or Control: State IRS Status: 501(c)3
Highest Offering: Baccalaureate
Accreditation: NW, ACFEI, DA, MAC, SURGT

01 President .... Dr. Yoshiko HARDEN
10 VP Finance/Administration .... Mr. Jacob JACKSON
05 Vice President Instruction .... Ms. Stephanie DELANEY
32 VP Student Services .... Ms. Jessica GILMORE ENGLISH
15 Vice President Human Resources .... Ms. Lesley HOGAN
97 Int Dean of College/Career Pathways .... Ms. Sofia MARSHAK
76 Dean Allied Health .... Mr. Christopher CARTER
66 Dean Nursing .... Ms. Yasmin ALI
103 Int Dean Workforce .... Mr. Warren TAKATA
50 Dean Bus/Educ/Hum Svcs/Gen Educ .... Ms. Sarah WAKEFIELD
102 Executive Director Foundation .... Ms. Carrie SHAW
13 Exec Director College Technology .... Mr. Jason MAYER
84 Dir Enrollment Services/Registrar .... Ms. Morenika JACOBS
111 Exec Dir Institutional Advancement .... Vacant
08 Assoc Dean of Library .... Ms. Jessica KOSHI-LUM
21 Budget/Accounting/Fin Svcs Dir .... Mr. Hui TONG
37 Director Financial Aid .... Ms. Rahel WELDU
18 Director Facilities & Grounds Svcs .... Mr. Mark DANIELS
19 Director Campus Security .... Mr. Matthew VIELBIG
88 Dean Culinary Arts/Dir Food Svcs .... Mr. Doug MEDBURY
26 Exec Dir College Relations/Mktg .... Ms. Katherine HANSEN
06 Registration Coordinator .... Ms. Ly CHANG
121 Dean Student Success .... Mr. Anthony COVINGTON
04 Executive Asst to President .... Ms. Alanna MALONE
88 Capital Projects/Space Planning Dir .... Mr. Barry BAKER
09 Director of Institutional Research .... Mr. Jichul KIM
96 Purchasing Agent .... Mr. Kawika WAIAMAU-ARIOTA

Saint Martin's University (D)

5000 Abbey Way, SE, Lacey WA 98503-7500
County: Thurston FICE Identification: 003794
Unit ID: 236452
Telephone: (360) 491-4700 Carnegie Class: Masters/S
FAX Number: (360) 459-4124 Calendar System: Semester
URL: www.stmartin.edu
Established: 1895 Annual Undergrad Tuition & Fees: $39,940
Enrollment: 1,638 Coed
Affiliation or Control: Roman Catholic IRS Status: 501(c)3
Highest Offering: Master's
Accreditation: NW, ACBSP, NURSE, SW

01 President .... Dr. Jennifer BONDS-RAACKE
00 Chancellor .... Abbot Marion NGUYEN
05 Provost/Vice Pres Academic Affairs .... Dr. Kate BOYLE
10 Vice President of Finance/CFO .... Vacant
111 Vice Pres Inst Advancement .... Vacant
26 VP of Marketing/Communications .... Ms. Genevieve CHAN
13 Associate Vice President/CIO .... Ms. Mary DONAHOO
15 Associate VP of Human Resources .... Ms. Cynthia JOHNSON
49 Dean College of Arts & Sciences .... Dr. Aaron COBY
53 Dean of Education .... Dr. Terry HICKEY
50 Dean of Business .... Dr. Chung LEE
54 Dean of Engineering .... Dr. David OLWELL
32 Dean of Students .... Ms. Melanie RICHARDSON
84 Dean Enrollment Management .... Ms. Patty LEMON
104 Associate Dean Intl Programs .... Dr. Roger DOUGLAS
21 Controller .... Ms. Burcu BRYAN
37 Director Financial Aid .... Vacant
29 Alumni Engagement Manager .... Ms. Jaima KORTLEVER
06 Assistant Registrar .... Ms. Ronda VANDERGIFF
18 Director Facilities Management .... Mr. Philip CHEEK
110 Asst Vice Pres Inst Advancement .... Ms. Katie WOJKE
36 Assoc Dean Students/Dir Career Dev .... Ms. Ann ADAMS
41 Athletic Director .... Mr. Bob GRISHAM
11 Assoc Dean Administration .... Vacant
08 Dean of Library & Learning Resource .. Ms. Stefanie GORZELSKY

42 Director Campus Ministry .... Vacant
39 Assoc Dean of Students/Dir Housing .... Mr. Justin STERN
38 Dir Office of Counseling & Wellness .... Ms. Michelle GORDON
09 Director Institutional Grants/Rsrch .... Ms. Erin HOILAND
04 Sr Exec Assistant to the President .... Ms. Brenda LUND
108 Dir of Assessment & Accreditation .... Ms. Kristine KING
19 Int Director Public Safety .... Ms. Sharon SCHNEBLY

*Seattle Colleges (E)

1500 Harvard Avenue, Seattle WA 98122-3803
County: King FICE Identification: 010106
Telephone: (206) 934-4100 Carnegie Class: N/A
FAX Number: (206) 934-3883
URL: www.seattlecolleges.edu

01 Acting Chancellor .... Dr. Rosie RIMANDO-CHAREUNSAP
05 VC Academic & Student Success .... Dr. Kurt BUTTLEMAN
13 AVP/Chief Information Officer .... Dr. Cindy RICHE
10 Int VC of Finance & Operations .... Mr. Terence HSIAO
26 Assoc VC Comms & Strat Initiatives .... Dr. Earnest PHILLIPS
111 VC of Advancement .... Ms. Kerry HOWELL
12 President South Seattle College .... Dr. Rosie RIMANDO-CHAREUNSAP
12 President North Seattle College .... Dr. Chemene CRAWFORD
12 Int Pres Seattle Central College .... Dr. Bradley LANE
15 VC of Human Resources .... Ms. Jennifer DIXON

*North Seattle College (F)

9600 College Way North, Seattle WA 98103-3599
County: King FICE Identification: 009704
Unit ID: 236072
Telephone: (206) 934-3600 Carnegie Class: Bac/Assoc-Mixed
FAX Number: (206) 934-3606 Calendar System: Quarter
URL: www.northseattle.edu
Established: 1970 Annual Undergrad Tuition & Fees (In-State): $4,123
Enrollment: 5,240 Coed
Affiliation or Control: State IRS Status: 170(c)1
Highest Offering: Baccalaureate
Accreditation: NW

02 President .... Dr. Chemene CRAWFORD
05 Vice President for Instruction .... Mr. Peter LORTZ
79 Dean Art/Humanities/Social Sciences .... Mr. Brian PALMER
81 Dean Math & Science .... Dr. Vashti BRYANT
103 Dean Workforce Instruction .... Dr. Melana YANOS
08 Interim Dean Library .... Dr. Dan TARKER
121 Executive Dean Student Success .... Ms. Alice MELLING
88 Dean Basic/Transitional Stds .... Mr. Curtis BONNEY
111 Executive Director of Advancement .... Ms. Traci RUSSELL
26 Director Marketing/Communications .... Mr. Mike SPROUSE
84 Dean Enrollment Svcs/Registrar .... Ms. Kathy RHODES
51 Director Continuing Education .... Ms. Myra KAHA
37 Director Financial Aid Services .... Ms. Brianne SANCHEZ
32 Dean of Student Support Services .... Dr. Mari ACOB-NASH
103 Director Workforce Retraining .... Ms. Jeanette MILLER
09 Exec Dir Inst Effectiveness .... Dr. Stephanie DYKES
15 Human Resources Director .... Mr. Joshua R. ERNST
18 Interim Director Facilities .... Mr. Michael SAUNDERS
38 Counselor .... Dr. Jenny MAO
13 Chief Info Technology Officer .... Dr. Cindy RICHE
19 Campus Safety and Security Director .... Mr. Patrick "Fitz" FITZPATRICK
28 Assoc Vice Chancellor EDI .... Mr. D'Andre FISHER
07 Admissions/Residency Specialist .... Mr. Fleetwood L. WILSON
04 Executive Asst to President .... Ms. Toni STANKOVIC
114 Interim Dir Budget & Business Ops .... Mr. Johnnie MOBLEY
25 Director of Grants .... Ms. Ann RICHARDSON
23 Interim Director Wellness Center .... Ms. Rose BUCHANAN

*Seattle Central College (G)

1701 Broadway, Seattle WA 98122-2400
County: King FICE Identification: 003787
Unit ID: 236513
Telephone: (206) 934-3800 Carnegie Class: Bac/Assoc-Assoc Dom
FAX Number: (206) 934-4390 Calendar System: Quarter
URL: seattlecentral.edu
Established: 1966 Annual Undergrad Tuition & Fees (In-State): $4,053
Enrollment: 5,763 Coed
Affiliation or Control: State IRS Status: 170(c)1
Highest Offering: Baccalaureate
Accreditation: NW, ACFEI, ADNUR, COARC, DA, DH, MAC, SURGT

02 Interim President .... Dr. Bradley LANE
05 Int EVP of Instruction/Fin & Plng .... Dr. Wendy ROCKHILL
32 Int Vice President Student Services .... Mr. Kao LEZHEO
103 Executive Dean Workforce Educ .... Mr. Chris SULLIVAN
37 Director of Financial Aid .... Vacant
26 Interim Director of Communications .... Mr. Adam RUSSELL
08 Dean of Library Svcs/E-learn .... Ms. Lynn KANNE
09 Exec Dir Institutional Research .... Dr. Jenni BRANSTAD
49 Dean Basic & Transitional Studies .... Dr. Saovra EAR
76 Executive Dean of Allied Health .... Vacant
81 Interim Dean of STEM .... Dr. Chelsia BERRY
83 Dean Arts/Humanities/Soc Sciences .... Dr. Jaime CARDENAS, JR.
07 Dir of International Admissions .... Mr. David ROSEBERRY
35 Dean Student Development .... Mr. Ricardo LEYVA-PUEBLA
13 IT Client Services Manager .... Ms. Maria ALES
12 Associate Dean Maritime Academy .... Mr. Dale BATEMAN
12 Int Assoc Dn Seattle Culinary Acad .... Ms. Aimee LEPAGE

19 Int Director of Safety and Security .... Mr. Sean CHESTERFIELD
18 Int Dir Facilities/Plant Operations .... Mr. Sean CHESTERFIELD
04 Executive Assistant to President .... Ms. Cassandra MCGUIRE
10 Director of Business Operations .... Vacant
15 Director Human Resources .... Mr. Scott RIXON
20 Director of Instruction Operation .... Ms. Marilyn MCCAMEY
66 Dean of Nursing .... Dr. Vicky HERTIG
106 Director of E-learning .... Mr. Kevin BOWERSOX-JOHNSON
107 Assoc Dean of Wood Technology Centr .... Mr. Robert WATT
41 Athletic Director .... Mr. Jared BLITZ
06 Dean Enrollment Services/Registrar .... Ms. Diane COLEMAN
21 Interim Associate Business Officer .... Ms. Jenny TRAN

*South Seattle College (H)

6000 16th Avenue, SW, Seattle WA 98106-1499
County: King FICE Identification: 009706
Unit ID: 236504
Telephone: (206) 934-5300 Carnegie Class: Bac/Assoc-Assoc Dom
FAX Number: (206) 934-5393 Calendar System: Quarter
URL: www.southseattle.edu
Established: 1969 Annual Undergrad Tuition & Fees (In-State): $4,214
Enrollment: 5,324 Coed
Affiliation or Control: State IRS Status: 501(c)3
Highest Offering: Baccalaureate
Accreditation: NW

02 President .... Dr. Rosie RIMANDO-CHAREUNSAP
05 Vice Pres Instruction .... Dr. Sayumi IREY
10 Vice Pres Finance/Admin Services .... Ms. Julienne DEGEYTER
32 Vice President Student Services .... Mr. Joe BARRIENTOS
45 Dean Instructional Resources .... Ms. Mary Jo WHITE
12 Exec Dean of Georgetown Campus .... Ms. Maureen SHADAIR
97 Dean Basic & Transitional Studies .... Mr. John BOWERS
20 Interim Dean of Academic Programs .... Mr. Johnny HU
35 Dean Student Life .... Mr. Daniel JOHNSON
120 Exec Dean Prof/Tech/Workforce Educ .... Ms. Veronica WADE
72 Dean Multi-Trades/Info Tech/Bus .... Vacant
84 Dean Enrollment Services .... Vacant
20 Assoc Dean Academic Programs .... Vacant
06 Assistant Registrar .... Ms. Linda MARTIN
104 Exec Dir Ctr for Intl Education .... Ms. Kathie KWILINSKI
51 Director Continuing Education .... Ms. Luisa MOTTEN
102 Director Foundation .... Vacant
103 Dir Workforce Dev/Employment Svcs .... Ms. Stephanie GUY
37 Dir Student Financial Assistance .... Ms. Corinne SOLTIS
26 Director Communications/Marketing .... Mr. Ty SWENSON
15 Director Human Resources .... Mr. Tim COLLINS
108 Exec Director Inst Effectiveness .... Mr. Greg DEMPSEY
13 Director Business Operation .... Vacant
18 Dir Facilities & Plant Operations .... Vacant
28 AVP Equity/Diversity/Inclusion .... Dr. Betsy HASEGAWA
19 Director Safety/Security .... Mr. James E. LEWIS
40 Manager Bookstore .... Vacant
04 Exec Asst to the President .... Ms. Wendy NAGASAWA

Seattle Film Institute (I)

3210 16th Avenue W., Seattle WA 98119
County: King FICE Identification: 042580
Unit ID: 488448
Telephone: (206) 568-4387 Carnegie Class: Spec-4-yr-Arts
FAX Number: (206) 299-3285 Calendar System: Quarter
URL: www.sfi.edu
Established: 1994 Annual Undergrad Tuition & Fees: $30,240
Enrollment: 96 Coed
Affiliation or Control: Proprietary IRS Status: Proprietary
Highest Offering: Master's
Accreditation: ACCSC

01 President .... David J. SHULMAN

Seattle Institute of East Asian Medicine (J)

226 South Orcas Street, Seattle WA 98108
County: King FICE Identification: 032803
Unit ID: 439914
Telephone: (206) 517-4541 Carnegie Class: Spec-4-yr-Other Health
FAX Number: (206) 299-3538 Calendar System: Trimester
URL: www.sieam.edu
Established: 1994 Annual Graduate Tuition & Fees: N/A
Enrollment: 31 Coed
Affiliation or Control: Independent Non-Profit IRS Status: 501(c)3
Highest Offering: Doctorate; No Undergraduates
Accreditation: ACUP

01 President .... Craig MITCHELL
05 Academic Dean .... Katherine TAROMINA
07 Dir Admissions/Student Services .... Iris CUTLER
08 Chief Library Officer .... Chris FLANAGAN
10 Chief Financial/Business Officer .... Peter MELINCIANU

Seattle Pacific University (K)

3307 Third Avenue W, Seattle WA 98119-1997
County: King FICE Identification: 003788
Unit ID: 236577
Telephone: (206) 281-2111 Carnegie Class: DU-Mod
FAX Number: (206) 281-2115 Calendar System: Quarter
URL: www.spu.edu
Established: 1891 Annual Undergrad Tuition & Fees: $47,244
Enrollment: 3,601 Coed

Affiliation or Control: Free Methodist IRS Status: 501(c)3
Highest Offering: Doctorate
Accreditation: NW, CACREP, CLPSY, DIETD, DIETI, MFCD, MUS, NURSE, THEOL

01 Interim President Dr. Pete C. MENJARES
05 Provost Dr. Laura C. HARTLEY
10 VP for Business & Finance Ms. Kimberly M. SAWERS
32 Vice Provost Student Formation Dr. Jeffrey C. JORDAN
111 VP for Advancement Mrs. Louise S. FURROW
84 VP for Enrollment Mgmt & Mktg Vacant
28 Vice Provost Inclusive Excellence Vacant
42 University Chaplain Rev. Lisa ISHIHARA
20 Vice Provost Academic Affairs Dr. Cynthia J. PRICE
58 Assoc Provost Grad & Prof Programs Dr. Margaret BROWN
18 Asst VP Facility Management Mr. David B. CHURCH
21 Asst VP for Financial Affairs Vacant
13 Asst VP Information Technology Mr. Micah SCHAAFSMA
37 Asst VP Student Financial Svcs Ms. Johanna DWYER
50 Dean School of Business/Govt/Econ Dr. Ross STEWART
53 Dean School of Education Dr. Nyaradzo MVUDUDU
76 Dean School of Health Sciences Dr. Tyra DEAN-OUSLEY
49 Dean College of Arts & Sciences Dr. Margaret WATKINS
59 Dean School of Psych/Fam & Cmty Dr. Katy TANGENBERG
73 Dean School of Theology Dr. Brian LUGIOYO
35 Assoc Provost for Community Life Mr. Chuck STRAWN
121 Asst Prov Exper Lrng/Stdnt Success Ms. Jenny ELSEY
08 University Librarian Mr. Michael PAULUS
38 Director Student Counseling Center . Ms. Sharon BARR-JEFFREY
07 AVP Enroll Mktg/Admissions Mr. Jobe S. KORB-NICE
07 AVP Undergraduate Admissions Ms. Ineliz SOTO-FULLER
09 Assoc Prov Inst Effectiveness Ms. Sheila STEINER
06 University Registrar Mrs. Kenda GATLIN
26 AVP Univ Communications Mrs. Alison ESTEP
27 News & Media Relations Manager Mrs. Tracy C. NORLEN
109 Asst Dir of University Services Ms. Lynn ERNSTING
19 Director of Safety & Security Mr. Mark REID
110 Director of Advancement Vacant
29 Director of Alumni/Parent Relations Ms. Amanda STUBBERT
41 Athletic Director Mr. Jackson STAVA
15 Asst VP of Human Resources Mr. Terry WINN
39 Director of Residence Life Mr. Gabe JACOBSEN
88 Director Student Programs Ms. Susie BECKER
88 Director of Multi-Ethnic Programs Vacant
104 Director of Global Engagement Ms. Caroline MAURER
04 Executive Asst to President Mrs. Ruth JACOBSEN

The Seattle School of Theology and Psychology (A)

2501 Elliot Avenue, Seattle WA 98121-1177
County: King FICE Identification: 034664
Unit ID: 441131
Telephone: (206) 876-6100 Carnegie Class: Spec-4-yr-Other Health
FAX Number: (206) 876-6195 Calendar System: Trimester
URL: www.theseattleschool.edu
Established: 2001 Annual Graduate Tuition & Fees: N/A
Enrollment: 266 Coed
Affiliation or Control: Independent Non-Profit IRS Status: 501(c)3
Highest Offering: Master's; No Undergraduates
Accreditation: NW, THEOL

01 President & Provost Dr. J. Derek MCNEIL
05 Dean for Teaching/Learning Dr. Misty Anne WINZENREID
10 Chief Financial Officer Mr. Mike ANDERSON
32 Dean/VP Students & Alumni Dev Mr. Paul STEINKE
111 VP of Advancement Dr. Jim EHRMAN
08 Dir Library Svcs/Inst Assessment Ms. Cheryl GOODWIN
06 Dir Academic Services/Registrar Ms. Kristen HOUSTON
110 Director of Advancement Mr. Andrew GREENE
13 Director Computer & Info Services Ms. Grace LA TORRA
15 Director of Human Resources Ms. Kartha HEINZ

Seattle University (B)

901 12th Avenue, Seattle WA 98122-1090
County: King FICE Identification: 003790
Unit ID: 236595
Telephone: (206) 296-6000 Carnegie Class: DU-Mod
FAX Number: N/A Calendar System: Quarter
URL: www.seattleu.edu
Established: 1891 Annual Undergrad Tuition & Fees: $48,390
Enrollment: 7,050 Coed
Affiliation or Control: Roman Catholic IRS Status: 501(c)3
Highest Offering: Doctorate
Accreditation: NW, CACREP, DMS, LAW, MFCD, MIDWF, NURSE, SPAA, SW, THEOL

01 President Mr. Eduardo M. PENALVER
05 Provost Dr. Shane MARTIN
20 Vice Provost/VP Planning Dr. Robert DULLEA
11 Executive Vice President Admin Dr. Timothy LEARY
10 VP/Chief Financial Officer Mr. Wilson GARONE
43 Vice Pres and University Counsel Ms. Mary S. PETERSEN
111 VP University Advancement Mr. Edgar GONZALEZ
32 VP Student Development Dr. Alvin STURDIVANT
88 VP Mission Integration Dr. Catherine PUNSALAN-MANLIMOS
108 Assoc Provost Inst Effectiveness Dr. Robert DUNIWAY
84 VP for Enrollment Mgmt Ms. Melore NIELSEN
26 Vice President for Univ Affairs Mr. Scott MCCLELLAN
28 VP Diversity & Inclusion Ms. Natasha MARTIN
15 Interim VP Human Resources Mr. Matthew PHILIP
31 Executive Director Cmty Engagement Mr. Kent KOTH
49 Dean of Arts & Sciences Dr. David POWERS
50 Dean of Business & Economics Dr. Joseph M. PHILLIPS
53 Dean of Education Dr. Cynthia B. DILLARD
66 Dean of Nursing Dr. Kristen SWANSON
54 Dean of Science & Engineering Dr. Amit SHUKLA
61 Dean of Law Ms. Annette C. CLARK
73 Dean of Theology & Ministry Dr. Mark MARKULY
51 Dean Schl New & Continuing Studies . Dr. Rick FEHRENBACHER
08 University Librarian Ms. Sara WATSTEIN
87 Director Summer Programs Vacant
123 Graduate Admissions Ms. Janet SHANDLEY
13 Chief Information Officer Mr. Travis NATION
124 VP Strategic Initiatives Mr. Chris VAN LIEW
18 Assoc VP Facilities Administration Mr. Robert SCHWARTZ
29 Asst VP Alumni Relations Ms. Ellen BAKER
22 Int Asst VP Inst Equity/Title IX Dr. Jill MOFFITT
112 Sr Director of Planned Giving Ms. Sarah FINNEY
44 Director of Annual Giving Ms. Margaret NEITZEL
102 Dir of Foundation & Corporate Rels .. Ms. Laura VASILOPOULOS
06 University Registrar Ms. Joyce ALLEN
07 Dean of Admissions Ms. Melore NIELSEN
09 Director of Institutional Research Dr. Irina VOLOSHIN
42 Director Campus Ministry Ms. Tammy LIDDELL
37 Asst Provost Student Financial Svcs Mr. Jordan GRANT
41 Director of Athletics Mr. Shaney FINK
19 Executive Director of Public Safety Mr. Craig BIRKLID
35 AVP/Dean of Students Dr. James WILLETTE
85 Director International Student Ctr Mr. Dale WATANABE
104 Director Education Abroad Ms. Gina LOPARDO
36 Executive Director Career Services Ms. Hilary FLANAGAN
38 Director Counseling Center Dr. Kimberly CALUZA
93 Director of Multicultural Affairs Ms. Michelle KIM-BEASLEY
39 Dir Housing & Resid Life Dr. Hilary L. LICHTERMAN
25 Director Research & Sponsored Proj Ms. Jenna ISAKSON
96 Director of Purchasing Vacant
23 Director Student Health Center Ms. Tara HICKS
100 Senior Assistant to the President Ms. Anne MORAN
105 Web Communications Manager Mr. Gaurav MANDAN
86 Manager of External Affairs Mr. Lincoln VANDER VEEN

Shoreline Community College (C)

16101 Greenwood Avenue N, Shoreline WA 98133
County: King FICE Identification: 003791
Unit ID: 236610
Telephone: (206) 546-4101 Carnegie Class: Assoc/HT-High Non
FAX Number: N/A Calendar System: Quarter
URL: www.shoreline.edu
Established: 1964 Annual Undergrad Tuition & Fees (In-State): $4,076
Enrollment: 5,382 Coed
Affiliation or Control: State IRS Status: 170(c)1
Highest Offering: Associate Degree
Accreditation: NW, ADNUR, CAHIIM, DH, MLTAD

01 President Jack KAHN
05 VP Student Lrng/Equity & Success Phillip KING
10 VP Business & Admin Services Bob WILLIAMSON
111 Assoc VP Advancement/Comm/Mktg Diana DOTTER
20 Assoc VP Acad Ops & Lrng Resources . Ann GARNSEY-HARTER
32 Assoc VP Stdnt Svcs & Intl Educ Samira PARDANANI
26 Public Information Officer Crystal BERRY
15 Exec Dir Human Resources Veronica ZURA
114 Director Budget Cliff FREDERICKSON
04 Exec Asst to the President Lori YONEMITSU
18 Director Facilities Kimberlee CLARK
19 Dir Safety & Security Gregory CRANSON
66 Dean Health Occupations & Nursing Mary BURROUGHS
84 Dir Enrollment Svcs & Fin Aid Frank FRIAS
08 Assoc Dean Library & Lrng Resources Dawn LOWE-WINCENTSEN
103 Exec Dean STEM & Workforce Guy HAMILTON
79 Exec Dean Humanities Nancy DICK
50 Exec Dean Business/Comm/Soc Sci Lucas RUCKS
41 Dir Athletics/Intram/Wellness/PE Steve ESKRIDGE
105 Assoc Director Web Strategy Adam STAFFA
106 Director eLearning Amy ROVNER
13 Dir Technology Support Svcs Gavin SMITH
21 Director Financial Services Alyshia JOSLEYN
35 Dir Stdnt Ldrshp/Residential Life Sundi MUSNICKI
88 Director Guided Pathways Brigid NULTY
88 Dean Access & Advising Chippi BELLO
121 Dean Student Support & Success Derek LEVY
88 Associate Dean Transitional Studies Jonathan MOLINARO

Skagit Valley College (D)

2405 College Way, Mount Vernon WA 98273-5899
County: Skagit FICE Identification: 003792
Unit ID: 236638
Telephone: (360) 416-7600 Carnegie Class: Bac/Assoc-Assoc Dom
FAX Number: (360) 416-7890 Calendar System: Quarter
URL: www.skagit.edu
Established: 1926 Annual Undergrad Tuition & Fees (In-State): $4,000
Enrollment: 4,227 Coed
Affiliation or Control: State IRS Status: 501(c)3
Highest Offering: Baccalaureate
Accreditation: NW, ACFEI, ADNUR, MAC

01 President Dr. Thomas KEEGAN
05 Vice President for Instruction Dr. Kenneth LAWSON
10 Vice Pres Administrative Services Mr. Ed JARAMILLO
12 Vice President of Whidbey Campus Dr. Laura CAILLOUX
15 Assoc Vice Pres of Human Resources Ms. Carolyn TUCKER
13 Dir of Information Technology Mr. Andy HEISER
103 Dean Workforce Education Mr. Darren GREENO
20 Exec Dean for Instruction Dr. Gabriel MAST
84 Assoc Dean Enrollment Services Ms. Sinead PLAGGE
36 Dir BAS Student Srvs & Wellness Ms. Sandy JORDON
32 Director of Student Life Mr. Brian MURPHY
37 Director of Financial Aid Ms. Crystal ALLISON
18 Director of Facilities & Operations Mr. Dave SCOTT
26 Chief Public Information Officer Ms. Arden AINLEY
104 Director of International Programs Ms. Christa SCHULZ
40 Bookstore Manager Ms. Kim HALL
41 Athletic Director Mr. Mitch FREEMAN
09 Director of Institutional Research Vacant

South Puget Sound Community College (E)

2011 Mottman Road, SW, Olympia WA 98512-6292
County: Thurston FICE Identification: 005372
Unit ID: 236656
Telephone: (360) 596-5200 Carnegie Class: Assoc/HT-Mix Trad/Non
FAX Number: (360) 664-0780 Calendar System: Quarter
URL: www.spscc.edu
Established: 1962 Annual Undergrad Tuition & Fees (In-State): $4,695
Enrollment: 4,665 Coed
Affiliation or Control: State IRS Status: 501(c)3
Highest Offering: Associate Degree
Accreditation: NW, ACFEI, CNEA, DA, MAC

01 President Dr. Timothy STOKES
04 Special Assistant to the President Ms. Diana TOLEDO
05 Vice President for Instruction Dr. Michelle ANDREAS
32 Vice President for Student Services Dr. David PELKEY
10 Vice Pres for Finance & Operations Dr. Tysha TOLEFREE
84 Dean of Enrollment Services Dr. Valerie ROBERTSON
18 Director of Facilities Mr. Marty MATTES
26 Exec Community Relations Officer Ms. Kelly GREEN
35 Dean Student Engagement/Retention Ms. Jennifer MANLEY
37 Dean of Student Financial Services Ms. Johanna DWYER
15 Chief Human Resources Officer Ms. Samantha DOTSON
102 Exec Director of College Foundation Ms. Tanya MOTE
28 Executive Diversity Officer Mr. Parfait BASSALE
09 Director of Institutional Research Ms. Jennifer TUIA
06 Director of Enrollment/Registrar Vacant
121 Dean of Academic Success Programs Ms. Amy KELLY
19 Director of Safety & Security Mr. Frederick CREEK
13 Executive Information Officer Mr. Rip HEMINWAY
81 Dean of Natural/Applied Sciences Mr. Bryan POWELL
72 Dean of Applied Technology Dr. Jason SELWITZ
79 Dean of Humanities/Communication Dr. Melissa MEADE
83 Dean of Social Sciences & Business Dr. Amy WARREN
96 Procurement & Supply Specialist-3 Ms. Blake MELANCON

Tacoma Community College (F)

6501 S 19th Street, Tacoma WA 98466-6100
County: Pierce FICE Identification: 003796
Unit ID: 236753
Telephone: (253) 566-5000 Carnegie Class: Bac/Assoc-Assoc Dom
FAX Number: N/A Calendar System: Quarter
URL: www.tacomacc.edu
Established: 1965 Annual Undergrad Tuition & Fees (In-State): $4,560
Enrollment: 5,823 Coed
Affiliation or Control: State IRS Status: 501(c)3
Highest Offering: Baccalaureate
Accreditation: NW, ADNUR, CAHIIM, COARC, DMS, EMT, RAD

01 President Dr. Ivan L. HARRELL, II
05 Provost/VP for Academic Affairs Ms. Marissa SCHLESINGER
11 Vice Pres Administrative Services . Ms. Patty MCCRAY-ROBERTS
32 Vice Pres Student Services Mr. Karl SMITH
111 Vice Pres for College Advancement Mr. Bill RYBERG
28 VP Equity/Diversity/Inclusion Mr. Roderick MORRISON
15 Exec Director of Human Resources Mr. Stephen SMITH
88 Dir Conduct/Compliance Ms. Dolores HAUGEN
84 Dean for Enrollment & Student Suc Mr. Patrick BROWN
124 Dean of Retention & Student Success Ms. Jennifer FOUNTAIN
10 Director Financial Services Ms. Sharon SCHRODER
18 Director Facilities/CapitalProjects Mr. Stefan MANFREDI
35 Director of Student Engagement Ms. Sonja MORGAN
37 Assoc Dir Student Financial Aid Ms. Lorena SAUCEDO
04 Executive Asst Pres Office Ms. Karyssa MATHISON
09 Director of Institutional Research Ms. Kelley SADLER
41 Athletic Director Mr. Jason PRENEVOST
13 Director Information Technology Mr. Clay KRAUSS
106 Dean Library/Learning Innovation Mr. Dale COLEMAN
19 Int Director Emergency Management Mr. Brandon KILGORE
26 Director Public Relations/Marketing Ms. Tamyra HOWSER
104 Director International Student Svcs Mr. James NEWMAN
45 Exec Director Strategic Initiatives Ms. Char GORE
07 Director of Admissions Ms. Christina NAKADA-ALM

University of Puget Sound (G)

1500 N Warner St., Tacoma WA 98416-0002
County: Pierce FICE Identification: 003797
Unit ID: 236328
Telephone: (253) 879-3100 Carnegie Class: Bac-A&S
FAX Number: (253) 879-3500 Calendar System: Semester
URL: www.pugetsound.edu
Established: 1888 Annual Undergrad Tuition & Fees: $52,775
Enrollment: 2,130 Coed

Affiliation or Control: Independent Non-Profit IRS Status: 501(c)3
Highest Offering: Doctorate
Accreditation: NW, IPSY, MUS, OT, PTA

01 President Dr. Isiaah CRAWFORD
05 Interim Provost Dr. Nick KONTOGEORGOPOULOS
10 Executive Vice President/CFO Dr. Kim KVAAL
43 VP & University Counsel/Board Sec Ms. Joanna C. CLEVELAND
100 Chief of Staff Ms. Gayle MCINTOSH
30 Vice President University Relations Mr. Victor MARTIN
84 Vice President Enrollment Dr. Matthew BOYCE
32 VP Student Affairs Ms. Sarah COMSTOCK
04 Executive Asst to President Ms. Jenna HUNTER
21 AVP Financial Planning & Analysis Ms. Janet S. HALLMAN
109 Dir Ofc Pres/Com Liaison Officer Ms. Mary Elizabeth COLLINS
28 VP Inst Equity/Diversity Dr. Lorna HERNANDEZ JARVIS
20 Associate Academic Dean Dr. Julie CHRISTOPH
58 Dean of Faculty & Grad Studies Dr. Sunil KUKREJA
20 Assoc Acad Dean Exp Lrng Vacant
53 Dean School of Education Dr. Amy RYKEN
50 Dir School of Business/Leadership Dr. Lisa JOHNSON
64 Director School of Music Dr. Tracy DOYLE
88 Dir School of Occupational Therapy Dr. Yvonne SWINTH
88 Dir School of Physical Therapy Dr. Holly ROBERTS
108 Assoc Prov IR/Plng/Stdnt Svcs Ms. Ellen PETERS
08 Director Collins Memorial Library Ms. Jane CARLIN
41 Dir of Intercollegiate Athletics Ms. Amy E. HACKETT
18 Assoc Vice Pres Facilities Services Mr. Bob KIEF
13 Interim Chief Information Officer Mr. Matthew LINK
114 Assoc VP Finance Ms. Justine JULIANI
15 AVP HR/Chief People Officer Ms. Nancy NIERAETH
29 Assoc VP Constituent Relations Ms. Allison CANNADY-SMITH
113 Assoc VP for Student Financial Svcs Ms. Maggie A. MITTUCH
42 University Chaplain Mr. Dave WRIGHT
39 Associate Dean of Students Ms. Debbie CHEE
38 Dir Counseling/Health/Wellness Svcs Dr. Kelly K. BROWN
44 Director Annual Giving Ms. Abbie LACSINA
102 Director Foundation/Corporate Rels Ms. Betty POPENUCK
26 Assoc VP Communications Vacant
06 Registrar Mr. Michael PASTORE
121 Dir Academic Advising Mr. Landon WADE
36 Director Career Services Ms. Alana HENTGES
37 Director Student Financial Aid Mr. Bryan M. GOULD
19 Director of Security Mr. Dave FERBER
90 Deputy CIO/Client Supp/Ed Tech Vacant
122 Dir Student Involvement Mr. Moe STEPHENS
104 Director International Programs Mr. Roy ROBINSON
40 Logger Store Director Ms. Kristi DOPP
105 Web Specialist Ms. Barbara WEIST
96 Procurement Manager Ms. Wendy VUI
07 Director of Admissions Mr. Robin AIJIAN

University of Washington (A)

1400 NE Campus Parkway, Seattle WA 98195-0001
County: King FICE Identification: 003798
Unit ID: 236948
Telephone: (206) 543-2100 Carnegie Class: DU-Highest
FAX Number: (206) 543-9285 Calendar System: Quarter
URL: www.washington.edu
Established: 1861 Annual Undergrad Tuition & Fees (In-State): $11,745
Enrollment: 48,149 Coed
Affiliation or Control: State IRS Status: 501(c)3
Highest Offering: Doctorate
Accreditation: NW, ARCPA, CAHIIM, CAMPEP, CLPSY, CONST, DENT, DIETC, EMT, HSA, IPSY, JOUR, LAW, LIB, LSAR, MED, MIDWF, MLS, NURSE, OPE, OT, PAST, PCSAS, PDPSY, PH, PHAR, PLNG, PTA, SCPSY, SP, SPAA, SW

01 President Dr. Ana Mari CAUCE
05 Provost/Exec Vice Pres Dr. Mark RICHARDS
12 Chancellor Bothell Campus Dr. Kristin ESTERBERG
12 Chancellor Tacoma Campus Dr. Sheila EDWARDS LANGE
28 VP Minority Affs/Vice Prov Div Dr. Rickey HALL
17 Int EVP Medical Affs/CEO UW Med Dr. Timothy DELLIT
15 Vice President Human Resources Ms. Mindy KORNBERG
13 Vice President for UW IT Mr. Andreas BOHMAN
30 Senior VP for Advancement Ms. Mary GRESCH
21 Vice President for Finance Mr. Brian MCCARTAN
26 VP of Marketing & Communications Vacant
30 Vice President for Development Ms. Tamara JOSSERAND
46 Vice Provost Research Dr. Mari OSTENDORF
51 Vice Provost UW Continuum College Dr. Rovy BRANON
45 Vice Provost Planning & Budgeting Ms. Sarah NORRIS HALL
20 Vice Prov/Dean Undergrad Acad Affs Dr. Ed TAYLOR
32 Vice President for Student Life Mr. Denzil SUITE
88 Interim VP for Academic Personnel Dr. Tanya EADIE
86 Director Federal Relations Ms. Sarah CASTRO
43 Division Chief Attorney General Mr. David M. KERWIN
06 University Registrar Ms. Helen GARRETT
29 VP Alumni & Stakeholder Engagement Mr. Paul RUCKER
17 Chief Operating Ofcr UW Medical Ctr Mr. Geoff P. AUSTIN
37 Asst VP Enroll/Exec Dir Fin Aid Ms. Kay LEWIS
09 AVP Analytics/Inst Research Ms. Erin GUTHRIE
36 Executive Director Career Center Ms. Briana RANDALL
14 CFO/UW Information Technology Mr. Bill FERRIS
18 Vice President of Facilities Mr. Lou CARIELLO
92 Director Honors Program Dr. Victoria LAWSON
41 Director Athletics Ms. Jennifer COHEN
08 Dean of Libraries Mr. Simon NEAME
96 Executive Dir Procurement Services Mr. Mark CONLEY
58 Dean Graduate School Dr. Joy WILLIAMSON-LOTT
49 Dean Arts & Sciences Dr. Dianne HARRIS
47 Dean Col of Built Environments Ms. Renee CHENG
22 EOAA Compliance Manager Mr. Brian LACOUR
50 Dean Business School Dr. Frank HODGE
54 Dean of Engineering Dr. Nancy ALLBRITTON
61 Interim Dean Law School Ms. Elizabeth PORTER
70 Dean Social Work Dr. Edwina UEHARA
52 Dean Dentistry Dr. Gary T. CHIODO
63 Interim Dean Medicine Dr. Timothy DELLIT
66 Dean Nursing Dr. Azita EMAMI
67 Dean Pharmacy Dr. Sean SULLIVAN
69 Dean School of Public Health Dr. Hilary GODWIN
53 Dean College of Education Dr. Mia TUAN
80 Dean School of Public Affairs Dr. Jodi SANDFORT
88 Dean Information School Dr. Anind DEY
88 Dean Col of Environment Ms. Maya TOLSTOY
04 Executive Asst to President Ms. Stephanie COURT
07 Director of Admissions Mr. Paul SEEGERT
104 Director Study Abroad Mr. Wolfram LATSCH
108 Director Educational Assessment Mr. Sean GEHRKE
19 Interim Chief of Police Mr. Craig WILSON
38 Director Student Counseling Dr. Natacha F. KUNE
39 Asst Vice Pres of Student Life Ms. Pam SCHREIBER
101 Secretary to the Board of Regents Mr. Tyler LANGE
102 AVP Corporate & Foundation Rels Ms. Joanna GLICKLER
44 Sr Director Annual Philanthropy Ms. Jennifer MACCORMACK
100 Chief of Staff Ms. Margaret SHEPHERD

Walla Walla Community College (B)

500 Tausick Way, Walla Walla WA 99362-9267
County: Walla Walla FICE Identification: 005006
Unit ID: 236887
Telephone: (509) 522-2500 Carnegie Class: Bac/Assoc-Assoc Dom
FAX Number: (509) 527-4480 Calendar System: Quarter
URL: www.wwcc.edu
Established: 1967 Annual Undergrad Tuition & Fees (In-State): $4,818
Enrollment: 2,940 Coed
Affiliation or Control: State IRS Status: 170(c)1
Highest Offering: Baccalaureate
Accreditation: NW, ADNUR

01 President Dr. Chad HICKOX
05 Vice President of Instruction Dr. Jess CLARK
76 Dean of Health Sciences Education Ms. Kathleen ADAMSKI
37 Financial Aid Director Ms. Maisee PERALEZ
08 Director of Library Services Ms. Jacquelyn RAY
12 Dean Clarkston Campus Dr. Chad MILTENBERGER
41 Athletic Director Mr. Jeffrey E. REINLAND
15 Vice President of Human Resources Mrs. Sharon M. HARTFORD
18 Dir Facility Svcs/Capital Projects Mr. Shane LOPER
106 Director of eLearning Ms. Lisa CHAMBERLIN
20 Dean of Transitional Studies Ms. Susan PEARSON
40 Bookstore Manager Ms. Alecia ANGELL
56 Director of Extended Learning Ms. Jodi WORDEN
26 Exec Dir Communications/Marketing Vacant
06 Registrar Ms. Erika BOCKMANN
09 Exc Dir Institutional Effectiveness Dr. Nicholas VELLUZZI
103 Dean Workforce Education Mr. Jerry ANHORN, JR.
13 Director Technology Svcs Mr. Kevin COMBS

Walla Walla University (C)

204 S College Avenue, College Place WA 99324-1198
County: Walla Walla FICE Identification: 003799
Unit ID: 236896
Telephone: (509) 527-2615 Carnegie Class: Masters/S
FAX Number: (509) 527-2397 Calendar System: Quarter
URL: www.wallawalla.edu
Established: 1892 Annual Undergrad Tuition & Fees: $29,931
Enrollment: 1,737 Coed
Affiliation or Control: Seventh-day Adventist IRS Status: 501(c)3
Highest Offering: Doctorate
Accreditation: NW, ACBSP, NURSE, SW

01 President Dr. John MCVAY
05 VP Academic Administration Dr. Pamela CRESS
10 VP Financial Administration Dr. Prakash RAMOUTAR
32 VP Student Life Dr. Doug TILSTRA
111 VP Univ Relations/Advancement Ms. Jodi WAGNER
28 Asst to President for Diversity Dr. Pedrito MAYNARD-REID
04 Executive Asst Office of President Ms. Deirdre BENWELL
20 Assoc VP Academic Administration Dr. Scott LIGMAN
21 Int AVP Financial Administration Mr. Eric JAMES
58 Assoc VP Graduate Studies Dr. Jonathan DUNCAN
84 Assoc VP of Marketing & Enrollment Mr. Trevor CONGLETON
110 Assoc VP of Alumni & Advancement Mr. Troy PATZER
35 Asst VP Stdnt Life/Dean of Students Vacant
08 Director of Libraries Ms. Carolyn GASKELL
06 Registrar Mr. Jerry ENTZE
42 Chaplain Mr. Albert HANDAL
29 Director of Parent/Alumni Relations Mrs. Claudia SANTELLANO
13 Director Information Technology Mr. Duane ANDERSON
37 Assoc Director Financial Aid Ms. Nancy CALDERA
15 Director Human Resources Ms. Erika SANDERSON
18 Director of Facility Services Mr. George BENNETT
26 Director Marketing/Public Relations Mr. Aaron NAKAMURA
07 Director of Admissions Mr. Dale MILAM
36 Director Career Development Center Vacant
38 Director Counseling/Testing Ms. Michelle NADEN
09 Director of Institutional Research Vacant
41 Interim Athletic Director Mr. Paul STARKEBAUM
19 Campus Security Director Ms. Courtney BRYANT
44 Director Gift Planning Ms. Dorita TESSIER
66 Interim Dean of School of Nursing Dr. Michaelynn PAUL
73 Dean of School of Theology Dr. Carl COSAERT
54 Int Dean of School of Engineering Dr. Delvin PETERSON
50 Dean of Business Dr. Bruce TOEWS
53 Dean of Education & Psychology Dr. Debbie MUTHERSBAUGH
70 Dean of Social Work & Sociology Dr. Deisy HAID

Washington State University (D)

PO Box 645910, Pullman WA 99164-5910
County: Whitman FICE Identification: 003800
Unit ID: 236939
Telephone: (509) 335-3564 Carnegie Class: DU-Highest
FAX Number: N/A Calendar System: Semester
URL: www.wsu.edu
Established: 1890 Annual Undergrad Tuition & Fees (In-District): $12,170
Enrollment: 31,159 Coed
Affiliation or Control: State/Local IRS Status: 501(c)3
Highest Offering: Doctorate
Accreditation: NW, CAATE, CEA, CIDA, CLPSY, CONST, COPSY, DIETC, IPSY, LSAR, MUS, NURSE, PHAR, SP, VET

01 President Dr. Kirk SCHULZ
05 Provost/Exec Vice President Dr. Elizabeth CHILTON
10 VP Finance/Administration Ms. Stacy PEARSON
111 VP Advancement/CEO WSU Foundation Mr. Mike CONNELL
106 VP Academic Outreach/Innovation Dr. David CILLAY
32 Vice Chancellor Student Affairs Dr. Ellen TAYLOR
13 VP Information Tech & CIO Mr. Sasi PILLAY
46 Vice President Research Dr. Christopher KEANE
86 VP External Affs/Government Rels Ms. Colleen KERR
26 Vice Pres Marketing/Communication Mr. Phil WEILER
20 Vice Provost for Faculty Affairs Vacant
12 Chancellor WSU Everett Dr. Paul PITRE
12 Chancellor WSU Spokane Dr. Daryll DEWALD
12 Chancellor WSU Tri-Cities Dr. Sandra HAYNES
12 Chancellor WSU Vancouver Dr. Mel NETZHAMMER
15 VP/Chief Human Resources Ofcr Ms. Theresa ELLIOT-CHESLEK
37 AVP Financial Services Ms. Joy SCOUREY
117 Chief Compliance/Risk Officer Ms. Sharyl KAMMERZELL
35 Int AVC & Dean of Students Dr. Jenna HYATT
43 Sr Assistant AG/Division Chief Mr. Nathan DEEN
58 VP for Graduate & Prof Education Dr. Tammy BARRY
47 Dean CAHNRS Dr. Wendy POWERS
50 Dean Carson College of Business Dr. Chip HUNTER
53 Dean College of Education Dr. Michael TREVISAN
54 Dean Engineering & Architecture Dr. Mary REZAK
66 Dean College of Nursing Dr. Mary KOITHAN
67 Dean College of Pharmacy Dr. Mark LEID
60 Dean College of Communication Dr. Bruce PINKLETON
49 Dean College of Arts & Sciences Dr. Todd BUTLER
74 Dean College of Veterinary Medicine Dr. Dori BORJESSON
92 Dean Honors College Dr. M. Grant NORTON
114 Assoc VP & Chief Budget Officer Vacant
18 Assoc VP Facilities Services Ms. Olivia YANG
89 Vice Prov for Academic Engagement Dr. Mary F. WACK
08 Dean Libraries Mr. Joseph STARRATT
06 University Registrar Mr. Matthew ZIMMERMAN
07 Director Admissions Mr. Andrew BREWICK
09 Exec Director Office of SPA Ms. Fran HERMANSTON
41 Director WSU Athletics Mr. Patrick CHUN
116 Director Internal Audit Ms. Heather LOPEZ
04 Administrative Asst to President Mrs. Ginger DRUFFEL
122 Dir Ctr Fraternity/Sorority Life Mr. Dan WELTER

Washington State University-Spokane (E)

412 East Spokane Falls Blvd, Spokane WA 99207-9600
Telephone: (509) 358-7500 Identification: 770948
Accreditation: &NW, EXSC, MED

Washington State University-Tri Cities (F)

2710 Crimson Way, Richland WA 99354-1671
Telephone: (509) 372-7000 Identification: 770949
Accreditation: &NW

Washington State University-Vancouver (G)

14204 NE Salmon Creek Ave, Vancouver WA 98686-9600
Telephone: (360) 549-9788 Identification: 770950
Accreditation: &NW

Wenatchee Valley College (H)

1300 Fifth Street, Wenatchee WA 98801-1799
County: Chelan FICE Identification: 003801
Unit ID: 236975
Telephone: (509) 682-6800 Carnegie Class: Bac/Assoc-Assoc Dom
FAX Number: (509) 682-6541 Calendar System: Quarter
URL: www.wvc.edu
Established: 1939 Annual Undergrad Tuition & Fees (In-State): $4,320
Enrollment: 3,090 Coed
Affiliation or Control: State IRS Status: 501(c)3
Highest Offering: Baccalaureate
Accreditation: NW, ADNUR, MAC, MLTAD, NURSE, RAD

01 President Mr. James RICHARDSON
04 Exec Assistant to President Mrs. Maria INIGUEZ
05 Vice President of Instruction Dr. Tod TREAT
11 VP of Administrative Services Mr. Brett RILEY
32 VP of Student Services & Enrollment Dr. Chio FLORES
49 Dean Lib Arts/Sciences/Basic Skills Ms. Holly BRINGHAM

103 Dean Workforce & Continuing Educ ....Ms. Riva MORGAN
66 Director of Nursing Program ....Ms. Jenny CAPELO
15 Exec Director Human Resources ....Ms. Reagan BELLAMY
18 Director of Facilities & Operations ....Mr. Rich PETERS
06 Dir of Enrollment Svcs/Registrar ....Mr. Jonathan BARNETT
08 Dir Libraries/Learning Technologies ....Ms. Jeannie HENKLE
10 Director of Fiscal Services ....Ms. Beth HAYES
26 Exec Dir of Communication Rels ....Ms. Libby SIEBENS
27 Web Marketing/Graphic Design Spec ....Ms. Sarah BAUMAN
09 Exec Director of Inst Effectiveness ....Mr. Ty JONES
19 Safety/Security & Emergency Mgr ....Ms. Maria AGNEW
28 Asst Dean Campus Life/Equity/Inclus ..Ms. Erin TOFTE-NORDVIK
102 Exec Director of WVC Foundation ....Ms. Rachel EVEY

Western Washington University (A)

516 High Street, Bellingham WA 98225-5950
County: Whatcom FICE Identification: 003802
Unit ID: 237011
Telephone: (360) 650-3000 Carnegie Class: Masters/L
FAX Number: (360) 650-3022 Calendar System: Quarter
URL: www.wwu.edu
Established: 1893 Annual Undergrad Tuition & Fees (In-State): $8,508
Enrollment: 15,197 Coed
Affiliation or Control: State IRS Status: 501(c)3
Highest Offering: Doctorate
Accreditation: NW, ART, AUD, CACREP, CAPRT, MUS, NURSE, PH, PLNG, SP

01 President ....Dr. Sabah RANDHAWA
05 Exec Vice President/Provost ....Dr. Brent CARBAJAL
03 Executive Vice President ....Dr. Brad JOHNSON
10 Vice Pres Business/Financial Affs ....Ms. Joyce LOPES
84 VP Enrollment/Student Services ....Dr. Melynda HUSKEY
26 Vice Pres for University Relations ....Ms. Donna GIBBS
111 Vice Pres University Advancement ....Ms. Kim O'NEILL
13 Vice Prov Info/Chief Info Officer ....Dr. Chuck LANHAM
58 Vice Prov Rsch/Dean Grad Sch ....Dr. David PATRICK
20 Vice Prov Undergraduate Education ....Dr. Jack HERRING
51 Vice Prov Outreach Continuing Educ ....Dr. Robert SQUIRES
35 Dean of Students ....Vacant
15 Asst VP for Human Resources ....Mr. Dennis DASHIELL
06 Registrar ....Vacant
07 Director of Admissions ....Mr. Cezar MESQUITA
36 Director Career Services Center ....Ms. Effie EISSES
37 Director Financial Aid ....Ms. Clara CAPRON
29 Executive Director Alumni Relations ....Ms. Deborah DEWEES
27 Director University Communications ....Mr. John THOMPSON
08 Dean of Libraries ....Dr. Mark GREENBERG
39 Director University Residences ....Mr. Leonard JONES
100 Chief of Staff/Secretary BOT ....Dr. Paul DUNN
09 Director of Institutional Research ....Dr. Ming ZHANG
18 Director of Facilities Management ....Mr. John A. FURMAN
19 Director of Public Safety ....Mr. Darin RASMUSSEN
41 Athletic Director ....Mr. Steven CARD
92 Director of Honors Program ....Dr. Scott LINNEMAN
96 Director of Business Services ....Mr. Pete HEILGEIST
79 Dean College of Humanities/Soc Sci ....Dr. Paqui PAREDES
72 Dean College of Science/Technology ....Dr. Brad JOHNSON
50 Dean College Business & Econ ....Dr. Scott YOUNG
65 Dean Huxley Col of the Environment . Dr. Steven HOLLENHORST
57 Dean College of Fine & Perf ....Dr. Christopher BIANCO
53 Dean Woodring College of Education ....Dr. Bruce LARSON
12 Dean Fairhaven College ....Dr. Caskey RUSSEL
04 Sr Executive Assistant to President .... Ms. Barbara A. SANDOVAL
104 Director Intl Student/Scholar Svcs ....Mr. Richard BRUCE
25 Contracts Assistant ....Ms. Andrea RODGER
38 Director Counseling Center ....Ms. Sarah GODOY
43 AAG/Chief Legal Advisor ....Ms. Kerena HIGGINS
86 Director Government Relations ....Ms. Becca KENNA-SCHENK
108 Dir Institutional Effectiveness ....Dr. John KRIEG
22 Director Diversity/Equity Office ....Dr. Jacqueline HUGHES

Whatcom Community College (B)

237 W Kellogg Road, Bellingham WA 98226-8003
County: Whatcom FICE Identification: 010364
Unit ID: 237039
Telephone: (360) 383-3000 Carnegie Class: Bac/Assoc-Assoc Dom
FAX Number: (360) 383-4000 Calendar System: Quarter
URL: www.whatcom.edu
Established: 1970 Annual Undergrad Tuition & Fees (In-State): $4,764
Enrollment: 2,719 Coed
Affiliation or Control: State IRS Status: 501(c)3
Highest Offering: Baccalaureate
Accreditation: NW, ADNUR, MAC, PTAA

01 President ....Dr. Kathi HIYANE-BROWN
05 VP for Instruction ....Mr. Barry ROBINSON
11 VP for Administrative Services ....Mr. Nate LANGSTRAAT
32 VP for Student Services ....Ms. Kerril HOLFTERY
20 Dean for Instruction ....Ms. Carla GELWICKS
08 Library Director ....Mr. Howard FULLER
10 Director for Business & Finance ....Mr. William MARTENS
06 Interim Registrar ....Mr. David KNAPP
37 Director of Financial Aid ....Mr. David KLAFFKE
85 Director of International Programs ....Mr. Kelly KESTER
40 Bookstore Manager ....Mr. Jon SPORES
18 Senior Facilities Director ....Mr. Brian KEELEY
04 Special Assistant to the President ....Ms. Rafeeka KLOKE
15 Executive Director Human Resources ....Ms. Becky RAWLINGS
09 Director for Assessment and IR ....Dr. Anne Marie KARLBERG

Whitman College (C)

345 Boyer Avenue, Walla Walla WA 99362-2083
County: Walla Walla FICE Identification: 003803
Unit ID: 237057
Telephone: (509) 527-5411 Carnegie Class: Bac-A&S
FAX Number: (509) 527-5859 Calendar System: Semester
URL: www.whitman.edu
Established: 1882 Annual Undergrad Tuition & Fees: $50,408
Enrollment: 1,360 Coed
Affiliation or Control: Independent Non-Profit IRS Status: 501(c)3
Highest Offering: Baccalaureate
Accreditation: NW

01 President ....Dr. Sarah BOLTON
05 Provost/Dean of Faculty ....Dr. Alzada TIPTON
10 Treasurer/Chief Financial Officer ....Mr. Peter W. HARVEY
30 Vice President for Development ....Mr. Steven SETCHELL
32 VP Student Affs/Dean Students ....Mr. Kazi JOSHUA
07 VP Admission & Financial Aid ....Mr. Adam MILLER
26 VP for Communications ....Ms. Gina OHNSTAD
28 VP for Diversity & Inclusion ....Dr. John JOHNSON
13 Chief Information Officer ....Mr. Dan M. TERRIO
110 Associate VP for Development ....Mr. Scott KLEINHEKSEL
20 Associate Dean Faculty Development ....Dr. Mary RASCHKO
20 Assoc Dean Academic Affairs ....Dr. Helen KIM
35 Associate Dean of Students ....Ms. Juli DUNN
18 Director of the Physical Plant ....Mr. Tony ICHSAN
08 Director of Penrose Library ....Mrs. Dalia L. CORKRUM
91 Director of Enterprise Technology ....Mr. Michael OSTERMAN
90 Dir Instructional & Learning Tech ....Mr. David SPRUNGER
41 Athletic Director ....Ms. Kim CHANDLER
38 Counseling Center Director ....Dr. Deanna ORTIZ
39 Director Residence Life & Housing ....Ms. Nancy J. TAVELLI
19 Director of Security ....Mr. Sidd SAINI
103 Dir Career/Cmty Engagement Ctr ....Mr. Noah LEAVITT
09 Director of Institutional Research ....Dr. Neal J. CHRISTOPHERSON
29 Director Alumni Relations ....Ms. Jennifer NORTHAM
15 Director Human Resources ....Ms. Telara MCCULLOUGH
104 Director of Off-Campus Studies ....Ms. Susan H. HOLME
06 Registrar ....Ms. Aimee WALKER
23 Director Health Services ....Ms. Claudia L. NESS
21 Controller ....Ms. Darlene WILSON
37 Director of Financial Aid Services ....Ms. Sandy HENRY
42 Director of Spiritual Life ....Mr. Adam M. KIRTLEY
44 Director of Annual Giving ....Ms. Cynthia COHN
36 Director for Career Development ....Ms. Kim ROLFE

Whitworth University (D)

300 W Hawthorne Road, Spokane WA 99251-0001
County: Spokane FICE Identification: 003804
Unit ID: 237066
Telephone: (509) 777-1000 Carnegie Class: Masters/M
FAX Number: (509) 777-4763 Calendar System: 4/1/4
URL: www.whitworth.edu
Established: 1890 Annual Undergrad Tuition & Fees: $46,250
Enrollment: 2,756 Coed
Affiliation or Control: Presbyterian IRS Status: 501(c)3
Highest Offering: Doctorate
Accreditation: NW, CAATE, MFCD, MPCAC, MUS, @PTA

01 President ....Dr. Scott MCQUILKIN
05 Provost & Executive Vice President ...Dr. Gregor THUSWALDNER
04 Exec Asst to President/Board ....Ms. Jaime WARFIELD
10 VP Finance & Administration ....Mr. Larry PROBUS
32 VP for Student Life/Title IX ....Ms. Rhosetta RHODES
84 VP Admissions & Financial Aid ....Mr. Greg ORWIG
111 VP Institutional Advancement ....Ms. Stacey SMITH
15 Chief Human Resources Ofcr ....Ms. Ariane OGLESBEE
21 Asst VP Finance & Administration ....Mr. Taylor HOFFARD
13 Chief Information Officer ....Mr. Kenneth BROWN
42 Dean Spiritual Life ....Dr. Forrest BUCKNER
41 Director of Athletics ....Mr. Timothy DEMANT
28 Int Chief Diversity Officer ....Ms. Roberta WILBURN
20 Associate Provost ....Dr. Stacy HILL
110 Sr AVP Institutional Advancement ....Mr. Tad WISENOR
123 Dean Cont Studies/Grad Admiss ....Dr. Brooke KIENER
108 Dir of Assessment/Accreditation ....Dr. Deanna OJENNUS
25 Dir Sponsored Program/Grants ....Vacant
88 Dir Office of Church Engagement ....Rev. Mindy SMITH
53 Dean School of Education ....Dr. Ronald JACOBSON
50 Dean School of Business ....Dr. Timothy WILKINSON
49 Dean College of Arts & Sciences ....Dr. John PELL
06 Registrar ....Mr. Jose ORTIZ
90 Dir Instructional Resources ....Mr. Kenneth PECKA
88 Assoc Dean Com Standards/Compliance ....Mr. Timothy CALDWELL
29 Dir Alumni/Parent Relations ....Mr. Dale HAMMOND
07 Director of Admissions ....Ms. Lara RAMSAY
18 Assoc VP of Facilities Services ....Mr. Christopher EICHORST
23 Director of Student Health Svcs ....Ms. Amy CUTLER
37 Director of Financial Aid ....Ms. Traci STENSLAND
39 Asst Dean Student Life ....Vacant
68 Director of Athletic Training ....Dr. Cynthia WRIGHT
26 Assoc VP Marketing & Communications ....Ms. Nancy HINES
38 Director Student Counseling Ctr ....Vacant
09 Director of Institutional Research ....Ms. Wendy OLSON
08 Dir Library/Assoc Dean Special Pgms ....Dr. Amanda CLARK
88 Interim Director MIT ....Dr. Ronald JACOBSON
19 Director Security Services ....Mr. LeRoy MCCALL
73 Dir Grad Studies in Theology ....Dr. Jeremy WYNNE
104 Dir of International Education Ctr ....Mr. Nick MCKINNEY
88 Dir US Cultural Studies ....Dr. Stacy KEOGH GEORGE
50 Dir Grad Studies Business ....Ms. Sinead VOORHEES
36 Director Career Services ....Ms. Tiffany RIDDLE

Yakima Valley College (E)

PO Box 22520, S 16th Ave & Nob Hill,
Yakima WA 98907-2520
County: Yakima FICE Identification: 003805
Unit ID: 237109
Telephone: (509) 574-4600 Carnegie Class: Bac/Assoc-Assoc Dom
FAX Number: (509) 574-6860 Calendar System: Quarter
URL: www.yvcc.edu
Established: 1928 Annual Undergrad Tuition & Fees (In-State): $4,770
Enrollment: 3,954 Coed
Affiliation or Control: State IRS Status: 170(c)1
Highest Offering: Baccalaureate
Accreditation: NW, ADNUR, DH, MAC, RAD, SURGT

01 President ....Dr. Linda KAMINSKI
05 Vice Pres Instruction/Student Svcs ....Dr. Jennifer ERNST
10 Vice Pres Administrative Services ....Dr. Teresa RICH
12 Dean Grandview Campus ....Mr. Marc COOMER
75 Dean College Career Readiness ....Mr. Marc COOMER
13 Director Tech Services ....Mr. Dilbar CHHOKAR
32 Dean Student Services ....Ms. Leslie BLACKABY
49 Dean Arts & Sciences ....Ms. Kerrie CAVANESS
103 Dean Workforce Education ....Ms. Skye FIELD
08 Library Director ....Ms. Leslie POTTER-HENDERSON
37 Director Student Financial Aid ....Mr. Oscar VERDUZCO
06 Registrar/Director of Admissions ....Ms. Lorena ALVARADO-VALDOVINOS
108 Dir Institutional Effectiveness ....Ms. Sheila DELQUADRI
26 Community Relations Coordinator ....Mr. Dustin WUNDERLICH
15 Executive Director Human Resources ....Mr. Steven SLONIKER
18 Director Facilities/Physical Plant ....Mr. Jeff MORROW
21 Director Accounting Services ....Ms. Angela ANTHONY
35 Student Life Coordinator ....Ms. Laura YOLO
04 Executive Asst to President ....Ms. Megan JENSEN
41 Athletic Director ....Mr. Ray FUNK

WEST VIRGINIA

Alderson Broaddus University (F)

101 College Hill Drive, Philippi WV 26416-4600
County: Barbour FICE Identification: 003806
Unit ID: 237118
Telephone: (800) 263-1549 Carnegie Class: Bac-Diverse
FAX Number: (304) 457-6239 Calendar System: Semester
URL: www.ab.edu
Established: 1871 Annual Undergrad Tuition & Fees: $29,220
Enrollment: 863 Coed
Affiliation or Control: American Baptist IRS Status: 501(c)3
Highest Offering: Doctorate
Accreditation: HLC, ARCPA, NUR

01 President ....Dr. James T. BARRY
05 Provost/Executive Vice President ....Dr. Andrea J. BUCKLEW
03 Executive Vice Pres Administration ....Dr. Eric M. SHOR
10 Vice Pres for Finance/CFO ....Vacant
32 Dean of Students ....Vacant
20 Associate Provost ....Dr. James M. OWSTON
111 AVP for Inst Advancement/Dir Alumni ....Mr. Joshua D. ALLEN
84 AVP for Enrollment Management . Dr. Jennifer C. HAWKINBERRY
63 Dean College of Medical Science ....Dr. Thomas F. MOORE
79 Dean Col of Humanities/Edu/Soc Sci ....Dr. Kari M. SISK
81 Dean Col Health/Science/Tech/Math ....Dr. Michael J. BOEHKE
50 Dean College of Business ....Dr. Neeley V. SATZER
106 Dean Col of Adult & Distance Edu ....Dr. Derek A. HOLBERT
06 Registrar ....Mrs. Emily J. ROSIER
08 Director of Library Services ....Mr. David E. HOXIE
41 Athletic Director ....Ms. Carrie L. BODKINS
42 Chaplain ....Pastor Jonathan L. VILLERS
21 Controller ....Mr. Chad A. MAYLE
29 Director of Alumni Relations ....Mr. Joshua D. ALLEN
44 Director of Annual Fund ....Mrs. Sandra O. FRAME
40 Director of Campus Services ....Mr. Ed P. BURDA
38 Director of Counseling Services ....Mr. Chad S. HOSTETLER
37 Director of Financial Aid ....Ms. Lora R. BRYANT
21 Director of Fiscal Operations ....Mr. Brandon C. WEAVER
18 Director of Facilities ....Mr. Lawrence J. TALLMAN
13 Director of Information Technology ....Ms. Carol WEAVER
26 Director of Mktg/Communications ....Ms. Cary L. SPONAUGLE
19 Director Security/Safety ....Mr. Michael D. KOCHKA
04 Exec Asst to Pres/Sec to the Board ....Mrs. Karla R. HIVELY
09 Director of Institutional Research ....Dr. Bob S. BUCKINGHAM
15 Director of Human Resources ....Vacant
39 Director of Housing/Residence Life ...Mr. Kevin M. MARSHBURN
30 Dir Development & Corp Relations ....Mr. Chris N. RANDOLPH
36 Director of Career Services & ACES ....Ms. Kellie J. MCMILLEN
124 Student Engagement Coordinator ....Mr. Tyler J. ZERO
88 Graphic Designer/Social Media Spec ...Mr. Joseph M. MITCHELL

American Public University System (G)

111 W Congress Street, Charles Town WV 25414-1621
County: Jefferson FICE Identification: 035393
Unit ID: 449339
Telephone: (304) 724-3700 Carnegie Class: Masters/L
FAX Number: (304) 724-3780 Calendar System: Other

URL: www.apus.edu
Established: 1991 — Annual Undergrad Tuition & Fees: $7,360
Enrollment: 50,047 — Coed
Affiliation or Control: Proprietary — IRS Status: Proprietary
Highest Offering: Doctorate
Accreditation: HLC, ACBSP, CAHIIM, IFSAC, NURSE, PH

01 President ... Dr. Wade DYKE
10 EVP/Chief Financial Officer ... Mr. Richard SUNDERLAND, JR.
05 Provost ... Dr. Vernon SMITH
20 Assoc Prov Academic & Faculty Svcs ... Dr. Michael COTTAM
11 SVP/Chief Operating Officer ... Mr. Bob GAY
21 Vice President Finance ... Ms. Claudine STUBBLEFIELD
43 VP/University Counsel ... Ms. J.J HERBERT
26 Sr VP/Chief Marketing Officer ... Ms. Beth LAGUARDIA COOPER
15 Sr VP Human Resources/Cmty Affairs ... Ms. Amy PANZARELLA
88 Sr VP Special Projects ... Mr. Peter GIBBONS
13 Exec VP/Chief Technology Officer ... Mr. Patrik DYBERG
37 VP Financial Aid & Compliance ... Mr. Keith WELLINGS
121 VP Student Support ... Mr. J.B TANNER
21 Sr VP/Controller ... Ms. Melissa FREY
32 Asst Provost Student & Alumni Affs ... Ms. Caroline SIMPSON
06 Asst Provost/Registrar ... Ms. Michelle NEWMAN
53 Dean Academic Svcs/Sch of Education ... Dr. Conrad LOTZE
124 Dean Faculty & Student Success ... Dr. Grady BATCHELOR
90 VP Academic & Instructional Tech ... Ms. Karen V. SRBA
88 Sr VP/Chief Innovation Officer ... Ms. Amy BEVILACQUA
82 Dean Security & Global Studies ... Dr. Mark T. RICCARDI
76 Dean Health Sciences ... Dr. Brian FREELAND
81 Interim Dean STEM ... Dr. Daniel WELSCH
79 Dean Arts & Humanities ... Dr. Grace GLASS
50 Dean Business ... Dr. Marie HARPER

Appalachian Bible College (A)

161 College Drive, Mount Hope WV 25880
County: Raleigh — FICE Identification: 007544
Unit ID: 237136
Telephone: (304) 877-6428 — Carnegie Class: Spec-4-yr-Faith
FAX Number: N/A — Calendar System: Semester
URL: abc.edu
Established: 1950 — Annual Undergrad Tuition & Fees: $15,536
Enrollment: 225 — Coed
Affiliation or Control: Independent Non-Profit — IRS Status: 501(c)3
Highest Offering: Master's
Accreditation: HLC, BI, CAEP

01 President ... Dr. Daniel L. ANDERSON
05 Vice President for Academics ... Mr. Tim ROWE
10 Vice President for Business ... Mr. Michael ROWE
30 Vice President for Development ... Mr. Caleb FRINK
32 Vice President for Student Services ... Mr. Kevin GULLION
42 Vice Pres for Extension Ministries ... Mr. David J. HOLLOWAY
33 Dean of Men ... Mr. Kevin GULLION
34 Dean of Women ... Mrs. Melissa GULLION
06 Registrar ... Mr. Tim ROWE
07 Director of Admissions ... Mr. Benjamin CALE
08 Librarian ... Mr. David W. DUNKERTON
37 Director of Financial Aid ... Mrs. Laura MARTIN
04 Admin Assistant to the President ... Miss Megan MULLINS
26 Director of Public Relations ... Miss Karisa A. CLARK

Bethany College (B)

31 E. Campus Drive, Bethany WV 26032-3002
County: Brooke — FICE Identification: 003808
Unit ID: 237181
Telephone: (304) 829-7000 — Carnegie Class: Bac-A&S
FAX Number: (304) 829-7700 — Calendar System: 4/1/4
URL: www.bethanywv.edu
Established: 1840 — Annual Undergrad Tuition & Fees: $30,840
Enrollment: 576 — Coed
Affiliation or Control: Christian Church (Disciples Of Christ)
IRS Status: 501(c)3
Highest Offering: Master's
Accreditation: HLC, SW

01 Interim President ... Dr. Jamie CARIDI
05 Provost/Dean of Faculty ... Dr. Anju RAMJEE
10 Vice President for Finance/CFO ... Mr. Dennis MCMASTER
111 Vice President for Advancement ... Mrs. Lori WEAVER
32 Vice President & Dean of Students ... Mr. Gerald STEBBINS
84 Vice Pres of Enrollment Management ... Ms. Dana BEARER
04 Asst to the President ... Ms. Amy VANHORN
20 Associate Provost ... Dr. Lisa REILLY
43 General Counsel ... Mr. William KIEFER
37 Director of Financial Aid ... Mrs. Laura DOTY
41 Director of Athletics & Recreation ... Mr. Brian SAMSOM
09 Dir Institutional Research/Records ... Vacant
88 Director of McCann Learning Center ... Ms. Heather TAYLOR
124 Dir Student Engag/Responsibility ... Ms. Khali BLANKENSHIP
89 Director First Year Experience ... Dr. Scott BROTHERS
104 Director of International Programs ... Dr. Harald MENZ
36 Director of Career Services ... Ms. Amy VANHORN
23 Director of the Byrd Health Center ... Ms. Amy CUPP
26 Communications Manager ... Ms. Emily LUKE
29 Director of Alumni Engagement ... Mr. Rhone THRASH
30 Director of Advancement Services ... Ms. Shirley KEMP
88 Director of Sports Communication ... Ms. Erikka SANSOM
18 Director of Physical Plant ... Mr. Jay EISENHAUER
19 Int Director of Safety & Security ... Ms. Sara DENT
15 Director of Human Resources ... Ms. Kathy BURD
39 Assistant Dean of Student Life ... Mr. Samuel GOODGE
42 Chaplain ... Vacant
08 Director of the Libraries ... Mrs. Heather MAY-RICCIUTI
06 Registrar ... Ms. Stephanie GORDON
109 Director of Dining Services ... Mr. John SHAFFER
40 Manager of the Bookstore ... Mr. Dean GEORGE
38 College Counselor ... Mrs. Terri RAWSON
07 Director of Admissions ... Ms. Laura DOTY
28 Director of Diversity ... Vacant
102 Director Foundation/Corporate Rels ... Ms. Liz SHORT
105 Director Web Services ... Mr. Edward STOUGH
25 Chief Contract and Grants Administr ... Dr. Julie WILSON
44 Director Annual Giving ... Ms. Rebecca PAULS
96 Purchase Order Processor ... Ms. Michelle BOWER

Catholic Distance University (C)

300 S. George St, Charles Town WV 25414
County: Jefferson — FICE Identification: 041242
Unit ID: 475398
Telephone: (304) 724-5000 — Carnegie Class: Spec-4-yr-Faith
FAX Number: (304) 724-5017 — Calendar System: Other
URL: www.cdu.edu
Established: 1983 — Annual Undergrad Tuition & Fees: $8,405
Enrollment: 180 — Coed
Affiliation or Control: Independent Non-Profit — IRS Status: 501(c)3
Highest Offering: Master's
Accreditation: @HLC, DEAC, THEOL

01 President ... Dr. Marianne E. MOUNT
05 Academic Dean ... Dr. Peter BROWN
88 Dean of Catechetical Programs ... Sr. Mary Margaret SCHLATHER
06 Registrar ... Mrs. Theresa SNIDER
51 Continuing Education Support ... Mrs. Kathleen WOODDELL
26 Director of Communications ... Vacant
07 Director of Admissions ... Mrs. Carol CIULLO
37 Financial Aid Officer ... Mrs. Amy SHOUSE
13 Acting Director of Technology ... Mrs. Carol DALEY
111 Director Institutional Advancement ... Mrs. Annie HAGER
04 Admin Assistant to the President ... Ms. Mary Kate WHITE
08 Librarian ... Sr. Rebecca ABEL
10 Chief Financial/Business Officer ... Mrs. Angela RUDOLPH

Davis & Elkins College (D)

100 Campus Drive, Elkins WV 26241-3996
County: Randolph — FICE Identification: 003811
Unit ID: 237358
Telephone: (304) 637-1900 — Carnegie Class: Bac-Diverse
FAX Number: (304) 637-1413 — Calendar System: Semester
URL: www.dewv.edu
Established: 1904 — Annual Undergrad Tuition & Fees: $29,960
Enrollment: 738 — Coed
Affiliation or Control: Presbyterian Church (U.S.A.) — IRS Status: 501(c)3
Highest Offering: Baccalaureate
Accreditation: HLC, ADNUR, CAEP, CNEA, IACBE, THEA

01 President ... Mr. Chris A. WOOD
03 Executive Vice President ... Dr. Rosemary M. THOMAS
05 Provost/Vice Pres Academic Affairs ... Dr. Robert J. PHILLIPS
111 Vice President for Inst Advancement ... Mr. Scott D. GODDARD
10 VP for Business & Administration ... Mr. Robert O. HARDMAN, II
15 Director Human Resources ... Ms. Jane COREY
06 Registrar ... Dr. Stephanie C. HAYNES
32 Dean of Students ... Ms. Kate GARLICK
18 Director of Physical Plant ... Mr. Ryan LABROZZI
37 Director Financial Planning ... Mr. Matthew A. SUMMERS
08 Director Booth Library ... Ms. Mary Jo DEJOICE
42 Chaplain ... Rev. Laura K. BREKKE WAGONER
41 Director of Athletics ... Mr. Patrick SNIVELY
19 Director of Public Safety ... Mr. Michael JORDON
04 Executive Asst to the President ... Ms. Beth KING
13 Chief Information Officer ... Mr. Daniel Scott TERRY
29 Dir Alumni Engagement/Support ... Ms. Wendy MORGAN
110 Sr Dir Institutional Advancement ... Ms. Cathy NOSEL
26 Communications & Marketing Coord ... Ms. Linda HOWELL SKIDMORE
07 Dir of Student Recruitment/Success ... Ms. Angie SCOTT
22 Dir Affirm Action/Equal Opportunity ... Ms. Jane COREY
38 Dir Student Counseling/Wellness ... Ms. Margaret F. FALLETTA
122 Dean of Students-Greek Life ... Ms. Kate GARLICK

Future Generations University (E)

400 Road Less Traveled, Franklin WV 26807-9201
County: Pendleton — Identification: 666714
Unit ID: 481030
Telephone: (304) 358-2000 — Carnegie Class: Spec-4-yr-Other
FAX Number: (304) 358-3008 — Calendar System: Semester
URL: www.future.edu
Established: 2003 — Annual Graduate Tuition & Fees: N/A
Enrollment: 41 — Coed
Affiliation or Control: Independent Non-Profit — IRS Status: 501(c)3
Highest Offering: Master's; No Undergraduates
Accreditation: HLC

01 President ... Dr. Daniel TAYLOR
11 Chief Operating Officer ... Stephanie HARTMAN
05 Chief Academic Officer ... Kelli FLEMING
06 Registrar ... Chris ROPER

Huntington Junior College (F)

900 Fifth Avenue, Huntington WV 25701-2004
County: Cabell — FICE Identification: 009047
Unit ID: 237437
Telephone: (304) 697-7550 — Carnegie Class: Spec 2-yr-Health
FAX Number: (304) 697-7554 — Calendar System: Quarter
URL: www.huntingtonjuniorcollege.edu
Established: 1936 — Annual Undergrad Tuition & Fees: $9,600
Enrollment: 212 — Coed
Affiliation or Control: Proprietary — IRS Status: Proprietary
Highest Offering: Associate Degree
Accreditation: HLC, MAC

01 President ... Carolyn A. SMITH
11 Director ... Lake TACKETT
05 Academic Affairs Director ... Linda J. WEST
10 Chief Fiscal Officer ... Sharon SNODDY
106 Director Online Learning ... Carol ADAMS

Martinsburg College (G)

341 Aikens Center, Martinsburg WV 25404
County: Berkeley — Identification: 667035
Unit ID: 487977
Telephone: (304) 945-0656 — Carnegie Class: Spec 2-yr-Health
FAX Number: (866) 703-6611 — Calendar System: Other
URL: www.martinsburgcollege.edu
Established: 1980 — Annual Undergrad Tuition & Fees: N/A
Enrollment: 1,691 — Coed
Affiliation or Control: Proprietary — IRS Status: Proprietary
Highest Offering: Associate Degree
Accreditation: DEAC

01 President ... Paul VIBOCH
05 Vice Pres Academic Affairs ... Rita CLAYPOLE
07 Assoc Vice Pres of Admissions ... Alyssa BUENO
10 Vice Pres of Administration ... Stella GARLICK

Mountain State College (H)

1508 Spring Street, Parkersburg WV 26101
County: Wood — FICE Identification: 005008
Unit ID: 237598
Telephone: (304) 485-5487 — Carnegie Class: Spec 2-yr-Health
FAX Number: (304) 485-3524 — Calendar System: Quarter
URL: www.msc.edu
Established: 1888 — Annual Undergrad Tuition & Fees: $8,215
Enrollment: 23 — Coed
Affiliation or Control: Proprietary — IRS Status: Proprietary
Highest Offering: Associate Degree
Accreditation: ACCSC

01 President ... Mrs. Judith SUTTON
11 Chief Operations Officer ... Mr. Kevin MERRITT
06 Registrar ... Ms. Pam RUSSELL
08 Librarian ... Mr. Roger MCCUNE
32 Dir Student Services ... Ms. Leasa DAVIS

Salem University (I)

223 W Main Street, Box 500, Salem WV 26426-0500
County: Harrison — FICE Identification: 003820
Unit ID: 237783
Telephone: (304) 326-1109 — Carnegie Class: Masters/M
FAX Number: (304) 326-1306 — Calendar System: Semester
URL: www.salemu.edu
Established: 1888 — Annual Undergrad Tuition & Fees: $16,900
Enrollment: 1,008 — Coed
Affiliation or Control: Proprietary — IRS Status: Proprietary
Highest Offering: Doctorate
Accreditation: HLC, ACBSP, CAEP, CNEA

01 CEO/President ... Mr. Danny D. FINUF
05 Provost ... Dr. Karen FERGUSON
04 Executive Asst to President ... Ms. Maria K. KENDALL
108 CITO/Accreditation Officer ... Dr. Cecil E. KIRKLAND
37 Dir Financial Aid & Compliance ... Ms. Rebecca CARR
13 Director of Information Technology ... Mr. Ibrahim GIRGIS
10 Chief Financial Officer ... Mr. Dan NELANT
21 Controller ... Ms. Virginia RICHARDS
18 Facilities Director & Business Mgr ... Mrs. Stephanie ROBERTS
06 Registrar ... Ms. Pamela GOFF
50 Dean of Business ... Dr. Marc D. GETTY
53 Dean of Educ & Inst Effectiveness ... Dr. Renee AITKEN
66 Director of Nursing Education ... Dr. Stephanie HOLADAY
08 Dean of Library Services ... Dr. Phyllis D. FREEDMAN
32 Dean of Student Affairs ... Dr. Dennis MCNABOE
19 Director of Campus Security ... Mr. Joseph E. SHAVER
41 Director of Athletics ... Mr. Alexander JOSEPH
29 Director Alumni Relations ... Ms. Carolyn BACON
39 Director Student Housing ... Mr. Mark A. NESMITH

University of Charleston (J)

2300 Maccorkle Avenue, SE, Charleston WV 25304-1099
County: Kanawha — FICE Identification: 003818
Unit ID: 237312
Telephone: (304) 357-4800 — Carnegie Class: DU-Mod
FAX Number: (304) 357-4715 — Calendar System: Semester
URL: https://www.ucwv.edu/
Established: 1888 — Annual Undergrad Tuition & Fees: $32,200

Enrollment: 2,967 Coed
Affiliation or Control: Independent Non-Profit IRS Status: 501(c)3
Highest Offering: Doctorate
Accreditation: HLC, ACBSP, ADNUR, ARCPA, CAEP, NUR, OTA, PHAR, RAD

01 President Dr. Martin S. ROTH
10 EVP of Administration & CFO Mrs. Cleta M. HARLESS
30 Vice Pres for Development Ms. Gail CARTER
05 EVP/Provost & Dean of Faculty Dr. Kim SPIEZIO
84 EVP of Enrollment Management Dr. Beth WOLFE
32 VP & Dean of Students Ms. Virginia MOORE
88 Chief Innovation Executive Mr. David RAMSBURG
06 Registrar Ms. Nicole RUPE-HAROLD
26 VP Marketing & Communications Mr. David TRAUBE
29 Director of Alumni Relations Ms. Christina CARR
21 Controller Ms. Terri UNDERHILL
13 Chief Information Officer Mr. Scott TERRY
08 Director of Library Services Mr. John ADKINS
85 Director International Student Pgms Ms. Violetta PETROSYAN
37 Director Financial Aid Ms. Christie TOMCZYK
35 Dir of Student Involvement Mr. Grant BRINSON
40 Bookstore Manager Mr. Glenn JOHNSON
18 Director of Facilities Services Mr. Gary BOYD
41 VP & Athletic Director Dr. Bren STEVENS
09 Director of Institutional Research Ms. Lisa DAWKINS
50 Dean Graduate School of Business Dr. Scott BELLAMY
51 Dean Continuing and Prof Education Dr. John BARNETTE
67 Dean School of Pharmacy Dr. Scott WESTON
49 Dean School of Arts & Sciences Dr. Tracy BRADLEY
76 Dean School of Health Sciences Dr. Mindy SMITH
15 Director Human Resources Ms. Janice GWINN
19 Director Security/Safety Mr. Eric SMITH
38 Director Student Counseling Dr. Rance BERRY
44 Director of Annual Fund Ms. Catherine ECKLEY
04 Administrative Asst to President Ms. Susan LEFEW

Valley College - Martinsburg Campus (A)

287 Aikens Center, Martinsburg WV 25404-6203
County: Berkeley FICE Identification: 026094
Unit ID: 377661
Telephone: (304) 263-0979 Carnegie Class: Bac/Assoc-Mixed
FAX Number: (304) 263-2413 Calendar System: Other
URL: www.valley.edu
Established: 1983 Annual Undergrad Tuition & Fees: N/A
Enrollment: 628 Coed
Affiliation or Control: Proprietary IRS Status: Proprietary
Highest Offering: Baccalaureate
Accreditation: ACCSC

01 Campus Director Ms. Marianela ALBERTO
05 Dir Academic Affairs-Campus Pgms Ms. Judy BAUSERMAN
106 Dir Academic Affairs-Online Pgms Ms. Shelly SMITH

*West Virginia Council for Community & Technical College Education (B)

1018 Kanawha Boulevard E, Suite 700,
Charleston WV 25301-2800
County: Kanawha Identification: 666993
Telephone: (304) 558-0265 Carnegie Class: N/A
FAX Number: (304) 558-1646
URL: www.wvctcs.edu

01 Chancellor Sarah A. TUCKER
03 Vice Chancellor Chris TREADWAY

*Blue Ridge Community and Technical College (C)

13650 Apple Harvest Drive, Martinsburg WV 25403
County: Berkeley FICE Identification: 039573
Unit ID: 446774
Telephone: (304) 260-4380 Carnegie Class: Assoc/HT-High Non
FAX Number: (304) 260-1788 Calendar System: Semester
URL: www.blueridgectc.edu
Established: 1974 Annual Undergrad Tuition & Fees (In-State): $4,128
Enrollment: 3,912 Coed
Affiliation or Control: State IRS Status: 501(c)3
Highest Offering: Associate Degree
Accreditation: HLC, ADNUR, CAHIIM, EMT, PTAA

02 President Dr. Peter G. CHECKOVICH
05 Vice President of Instruction Ms. Laura BUSEY
103 VP Engineer/Workforce Development Dr. Ann M. SHIPWAY
32 VP for Student Services Ms. Kirsten BUNCH
10 Chief Finance Officer Dr. Randall MILLER
84 VP of Enrollment Management Ms. Leslie C. SEE
11 VP of Administration Vacant
13 AVP for Technology/CIO Mr. Steven YOUNG
06 Registrar Ms. Sara SCHUMACHER
121 Director of Access & Success Ms. Brenda NEAL
37 Director of Financial Aid Ms. Anna CRAWFORD
18 Director of Facilities Mr. Larry BICKETT

*BridgeValley Community & Technical College (D)

2001 Union Carbide Drive, South Charleston WV 25303
County: Kanawha FICE Identification: 040386
Unit ID: 484932
Telephone: (304) 205-6600 Carnegie Class: Assoc/HVT-High Trad
FAX Number: N/A Calendar System: Semester
URL: www.bridgevalley.edu
Established: 2014 Annual Undergrad Tuition & Fees (In-District): $5,142
Enrollment: 1,662 Coed
Affiliation or Control: State/Local IRS Status: Exempt
Highest Offering: Associate Degree
Accreditation: HLC, ACBSP, ADNUR, COARC, DH, DMS, MLTAD

02 President Dr. Casey SACKS
05 VP of Academic Affairs Ms. Suzette BREEDEN
32 VP Student Affairs Dr. Todd JONES
103 VP Workforce Dr. Laura MCCULLOUGH
11 VP of Operations Mr. Jason STARK
10 Chief Financial Officer Ms. Cathy AQUINO
96 Chief Procurement Officer Mr. John POWELL
97 Dean of General Education Ms. Kristi ELLENBERG
20 Assoc VP Academic Affairs Vacant
84 Assoc VP of Enrollment Services Mr. Roy SIMMONS
35 Assoc VP of Student Engagement Mr. James MCDOUGLE
06 Registrar Mr. Jordan ATHA
15 Chief HR/Communications Ofcr Vacant
111 Exec Director of Inst Advancement Ms. Alicia SYNER
31 Director of Outreach Ms. Michelle WICKS
04 Exec Secretary to the President Ms. Amy MOORE
08 Director of Library Services Ms. Kaitlyn CALVERT
09 Chief Banner Officer Mr. James FAUVER
19 Chief of Police Mr. Bazra FAKHIR
88 Dean Workforce Development Ms. Heather RAINES
50 Dean Business/Legal/Human Svcs Ms. Kelly GROSE
76 Dean Allied Health/Nursing Mr. Kent WILSON
72 Dean Comp/Manufacture/Engr Tech Mr. Norm MORTENSEN
07 Director of Admissions Mr. Thomas CONNER, III
37 Director of Financial Aid Ms. Mary BLIZZARD
36 Director of Student Placement Ms. Judy WHIPKEY
38 Director of Counseling Services Ms. Carla BLANKENBUEHLER
18 Chf Facilities/Physical Plant Ofcr Mr. George BOSSIE

*Eastern West Virginia Community and Technical College (E)

316 Eastern Drive, Moorefield WV 26836-1155
County: Hardy FICE Identification: 041190
Unit ID: 438708
Telephone: (304) 434-8000 Carnegie Class: Assoc/MT-VT-Mix Trad/Non
FAX Number: (304) 434-7000 Calendar System: Semester
URL: www.easternwv.edu
Established: 1999 Annual Undergrad Tuition & Fees (In-State): $3,888
Enrollment: 374 Coed
Affiliation or Control: State IRS Status: Exempt
Highest Offering: Associate Degree
Accreditation: HLC, ADNUR

02 President Mr. Thomas STRIPLIN
10 Chief Financial Officer Ms. Trina BRANSON
05 Dean of Academic Services Mr. Curtis HAKALA
32 Dean of Student Access & Success Ms. Monica WILSON
04 President's Office Administrator Mr. Michael O'LEARY
13 Chief Information Technology Office Mr. Ronald HAMILTON
15 Human Resources Assistant III M. Jaennae SNYDER

*Mountwest Community and Technical College (F)

One Mountwest Way, Huntington WV 25701
County: Cabell FICE Identification: 040414
Unit ID: 444954
Telephone: (304) 710-3140 Carnegie Class: Assoc/HVT-Mix Trad/Non
FAX Number: (000) 000-0000 Calendar System: Semester
URL: www.mctc.edu
Established: 1975 Annual Undergrad Tuition & Fees (In-District): $4,464
Enrollment: 1,292 Coed
Affiliation or Control: State/Local IRS Status: 501(c)3
Highest Offering: Associate Degree
Accreditation: HLC, ACBSP, CAHIIM, EMT, MAC, PTAA

02 President Dr. Josh BAKER
05 Vice President of Academic Affairs Mr. Michael MCCOMAS
10 Vice President of Finance/CFO Mr. Derek ADKINS
15 VP of Student Services & HR Ms. Mesha SHAMBLIN

*New River Community and Technical College (G)

280 University Drive, Beaver WV 25813
County: Raleigh FICE Identification: 039603
Unit ID: 447582
Telephone: (304) 929-5450 Carnegie Class: Assoc/HVT-High Trad
FAX Number: (304) 929-5478 Calendar System: Semester
URL: www.newriver.edu
Established: 2003 Annual Undergrad Tuition & Fees (In-State): $4,372
Enrollment: 1,053 Coed
Affiliation or Control: State IRS Status: 501(c)3
Highest Offering: Associate Degree
Accreditation: HLC, EMT, MLTAD, @PTAA

02 President Dr. Bonny COPENHAVER
04 Exec Secretary to the President Ms. Lori A. MIDKIFF
05 Vice Pres Academic/Student Affairs Mr. Richard G. UNDERBAKKE
13 VP Information Technology Services Dr. David J. AYERSMAN
32 Dean of Student Services Mr. Pete HOEMAN
15 Director Human Resources Ms. Tina R. PANNELL
26 Director of Communications Ms. Jenni CANTERBURY
12 Campus Director/Community Outreach Vacant
12 Campus Director/Community Outreach Mr. Roger D. GRIFFITH
06 Registrar Ms. Janelle SCHOFIELD
08 Staff Librarian Mr. Robert H. COSTON
37 Director of Financial Aid Ms. Patricia HARMON
96 Director of Purchasing Ms. Anastasia CADMUS
10 Chief Financial Officer Mr. Jordan ROARK
18 Director of Physical Plant Mr. Brian SAMPSON
84 Director of Enrollment Services Ms. Tracy L. EVANS
103 Dean of Workforce/Tech Mr. Jonathan D. HARTWELL
88 Dean of Transfer/Pre-Profession Pgm Ms. Wendy PATRIQUIN

*Pierpont Community & Technical College (H)

500 Galliher Drive, Fairmont WV 26554
County: Marion FICE Identification: 040385
Unit ID: 443492
Telephone: (304) 367-4692 Carnegie Class: Assoc/HVT-High Trad
FAX Number: (304) 367-4881 Calendar System: Semester
URL: www.pierpont.edu
Established: 1974 Annual Undergrad Tuition & Fees (In-State): $4,986
Enrollment: 1,613 Coed
Affiliation or Control: State IRS Status: 501(c)3
Highest Offering: Associate Degree
Accreditation: HLC, ACFEI, CAHIIM, #COARC, @DIETT, EMT, MLTAD, NAIT, PTAA

01 Interim President Dr. Anthony HANCOCK
04 Exec Assistant to the President Ms. Amanda HAWKINBERRY
05 Provost/VP for Academic Affairs Dr. Michael P. WAIDE
10 VP for Finance and Administration Mr. Dale R. BRADLEY
111 VP Inst Advancement/Found Dir Vacant
32 Actg VP Student Svcs/Enroll Mgmt Dr. Michael WAIDE
50 Dean Sch of Bus/Aviation/Tech Dr. Kari COFFINDAFFER
76 Dean School of Health Sciences Vacant
97 Dean School Gen Educ/Business Dev Mr. David BEIGHLEY
13 Chief Information Officer Vacant
06 Registrar Mr. John DAVIS
101 Secretary of the Institution/Board Mrs. Cyndee K. SENSIBAUGH
37 Int Director Student Financial Aid Ms. Mary BLIZZARD

*Southern West Virginia Community and Technical College (I)

P. O. Box 2900, Mount Gay WV 25637-2900
County: Logan FICE Identification: 003816
Unit ID: 237817
Telephone: (304) 792-7098 Carnegie Class: Assoc/HVT-High Trad
FAX Number: (304) 792-7046 Calendar System: Semester
URL: www.southernwv.edu
Established: 1971 Annual Undergrad Tuition & Fees (In-State): $4,084
Enrollment: 1,474 Coed
Affiliation or Control: State IRS Status: 501(c)3
Highest Offering: Associate Degree
Accreditation: HLC, ADNUR, COARC, EMT, MLTAD, RAD, SURGT

02 President Dr. Pamela L. ALDERMAN
00 Board of Governors Chair Dr. Lisa J. HADDOX-HESTON
10 Chief Finance Officer Mr. Robert S. DINGESS
05 VP for Academic Affairs Dr. Tracey HUMAN
32 Chief Student Services Officer Mr. Darrell TAYLOR
103 Dir Workforce Development Mr. Jay LESTER
13 Chief Information Officer Mr. Tom COOK
111 Exec Dir Institutional Advancement Ms. Rita G. ROBERSON
07 Director of Admissions Mr. Tim OOTEN
15 Human Resources Director Ms. Debbie DINGESS
18 Dir of Facilities/Campus Operations Mr. Joe LINVILLE
04 Exec Asst to President Ms. Jennifer DOVE
09 Dir Institutional Research Mr. Charles SCOTT
12 Director Wyoming Campus Operations Mr. David LORD
12 Dir Williamson Campus Operations Mr. Doug KENNEDY
124 Dir of Advising & Retention Mr. Timothy D. OOTEN
06 Registrar Ms. Teri WELLS
37 Dir Student Financial Assistance Ms. Stella ESTEPP
08 Director of Libraries Ms. Kimberly L. MAYNARD
108 Dir Accreditation & Assessment Mr. Thomas MORRIS
22 Dir Affirmative Action/EEO Mr. Doug KENNEDY

*West Virginia Northern Community College (J)

1704 Market Street, Wheeling WV 26003-3643
County: Ohio FICE Identification: 009054
Unit ID: 238014
Telephone: (304) 233-5900 Carnegie Class: Assoc/HVT-Mix Trad/Non
FAX Number: (304) 232-4651 Calendar System: Semester
URL: www.wvncc.edu
Established: 1972 Annual Undergrad Tuition & Fees (In-State): $4,317
Enrollment: 1,253 Coed
Affiliation or Control: State IRS Status: 501(c)3
Highest Offering: Associate Degree

Accreditation: HLC, ACFEI, ADNUR, CAHIIM, EMT, MAC, RAD, SURGT

02 President .... Dr. Daniel MOSSER
05 Provost .... Dr. Jill LOVELESS
10 CFO & VP Administrative Services .... Vacant
32 Vice President Student Services .... Mrs. Janet FIKE
09 VP of Institutional Research .... Dr. Pam SHARMA
26 Director of Marketing & PR .... Mr. David BARNHARDT
18 Director of Facilities .... Ms. Trish MARKER
15 Director of Human Resources .... Mr. Robert BRAK
103 VP of Economic & Workforce Dev .... Dr. Phil KLEIN
102 Director of the Foundation .... Ms. Rana SPURLOCK
04 Executive Asst to President .... Ms. Stephanie KAPPEL

* New River Community and Technical College Greenbrier Valley Campus (A)

653 Church Street, Lewisburg WV 24901-1303
Telephone: (304) 647-6560 Identification: 770468
Accreditation: &HLC

* New River Community and Technical College Mercer County Campus (B)

1001 Mercer Street, Princeton WV 24740-8230
Telephone: (304) 425-5858 Identification: 770469
Accreditation: &HLC

* New River Community and Technical College Nicholas County Campus (C)

6101 Webster Road, Summersville WV 26651
Telephone: (304) 872-1236 Identification: 770470
Accreditation: &HLC

* Southern West Virginia Community and Technical College-Boone/Lincoln Campus (D)

3505 Daniel Boone Parkway, Suite A, Foster WV 25081-8126
Telephone: (304) 369-2952 Identification: 770471
Accreditation: &HLC

* Southern West Virginia Community and Technical College-Williamson Campus (E)

1601 Armory Drive, Williamson WV 25661
Telephone: (304) 235-6046 Identification: 770473
Accreditation: &HLC, COARC

* Southern West Virginia Community and Technical College-Wyoming/McDowell Campus (F)

128 College Drive, Saulsville WV 25876
Telephone: (304) 294-8346 Identification: 770472
Accreditation: &HLC

* West Virginia Northern Community College (G)

141 Main Street, New Martinsville WV 26155
Telephone: (304) 455-4684 Identification: 770474
Accreditation: &HLC

* West Virginia Northern Community College (H)

150 Park Avenue, Weirton WV 26062
Telephone: (304) 723-2210 Identification: 770475
Accreditation: &HLC

---

* West Virginia Higher Education Policy Commission (I)

1018 Kanawha Boulevard E, Ste 700, Charleston WV 25301-2887
County: Kanawha FICE Identification: 033440
Telephone: (304) 558-2101 Carnegie Class: N/A
FAX Number: (304) 558-5719
URL: www.wvhepc.edu

01 Chancellor .... Dr. Sarah TUCKER
88 Chancellor WV Cmty/Tech Col System .... Dr. Sarah TUCKER
46 Senior Director Science Research .... Dr. Julie SERAFIN
05 Vice Chancellor for Academic Affs .... Dr. Randall BRUMFIELD
10 Vice Chancellor for Finance .... Dr. Edward MAGEE
15 Vice Chancellor for Human Resources .... Ms. Trish HUMPHRIES
32 Senior Director of Student Services .... Ms. Elizabeth MANUEL
26 Senior Director of Communications .... Ms. Jessica TICE
43 General Counsel .... Ms. Kristin BOGGS
11 Exec Vice Chancellor Administration .... Mr. Matt TURNER
45 Senior Director Policy & Planning .... Vacant
37 Senior Director of Financial Aid .... Mr. Brian WEINGART
88 Director Administrative Services .... Ms. Cindy L. ANDERSON

* Bluefield State College (J)

219 Rock Street, Bluefield WV 24701-2198
County: Mercer FICE Identification: 003809
Unit ID: 237215
Telephone: (304) 327-4000 Carnegie Class: Bac-Diverse
FAX Number: (304) 325-7747 Calendar System: Semester
URL: www.bluefieldstate.edu
Established: 1895 Annual Undergrad Tuition & Fees (In-State): $7,680
Enrollment: 1,243 Coed
Affiliation or Control: State IRS Status: 501(c)3
Highest Offering: Baccalaureate
Accreditation: HLC, ACBSP, ADNUR, CAEP, NURSE, RAD

02 President .... Dr. Robin CAPEHART
03 Executive Vice President .... Mr. Brent BENJAMIN
05 VP of Academic Affairs/Provost .... Dr. Ted LEWIS
10 Chief Financial Officer .... Mr. J. Ronald HYPES
32 Dean of Students .... Mr. Ronald SHIDEMANTLE
27 VP of Media Relations .... Mr. Jim NELSON
06 Registrar .... Mrs. Marviene JOHNSON
08 Director Library Services .... Mr. David MCMILLAN
13 Chief Technology Officer .... Mr. John SPENCER, JR.
26 VP of Marketing .... Mr. Ansel PONDER
15 VP of Human Resources .... Ms. Jonette AUGHENBAUGH
19 Director Public Safety .... Vacant
38 Director of Counseling .... Dr. Cravor JONES
29 Director Alumni Affairs .... Ms. Deirdre GUYTON
40 Manager Bookstore .... Ms. Susan PLUMLEY
41 Athletic Director .... Mr. Derrick PRICE
50 Interim Dean School of Business .... Mrs. Karen GROGAN
54 Dean of STEM .... Vacant
53 Dean of Educ/Humanities/Social Sci .... Dr. Shelia SARGENT-MARTIN
66 Dean School Nursing/Allied Health .... Ms. Angela LAMBERT
66 ADN Program Director .... Ms. Sandra WYNN
66 BSN Program Director .... Ms. Carol COFER
88 Program Dir of Radiologic Tech .... Ms. Melissa HAYE
96 Director of Purchasing .... Mr. Paul RUTHERFORD
04 Exec Secretary to the President .... Ms. Jeanne MORICLE
100 Chief of Staff .... Mr. Keith OLSON
18 Director of Maintenance .... Mr. Charles BROWN
104 Director Study Abroad .... Dr. Sudhakar R. JAMKHANDI
108 Director Institutional Assessment .... Dr. Sarita A. RHONEMUS
84 Director Enrollment Management .... Vacant
11 Chief of Operations .... Mr. Keith OLSON

* Concord University (K)

PO Box 1000, Athens WV 24712-1000
County: Mercer FICE Identification: 003810
Unit ID: 237330
Telephone: (304) 384-3115 Carnegie Class: Masters/M
FAX Number: (304) 384-9044 Calendar System: Semester
URL: www.concord.edu
Established: 1872 Annual Undergrad Tuition & Fees (In-State): $8,385
Enrollment: 1,807 Coed
Affiliation or Control: State IRS Status: 501(c)3
Highest Offering: Master's
Accreditation: HLC, ACBSP, CAATE, CAEP, SW

02 President & CEO .... Dr. Kendra BOGGESS
05 VP & Academic Dean .... Dr. Edward HUFFSTETLER
111 VP for Advancement .... Mrs. Sarah TURNER
20 Associate Dean .... Dr. Kathy LIPTAK
32 VP Student Affairs .... Dr. Sarah BEASLEY
10 VP for Business & Finance .... Mr. John GALATIC
15 VP of Operations .... Mr. Daniel FITZPATRICK
13 Chief Info Technology Officer .... Mr. Ron HAMILTON
06 Registrar .... Ms. Sheilah SITES
08 Director of the Library .... Ms. Elizabeth CHANDLER
37 Director of Student Financial Aid .... Mrs. Tammy BROWN
29 Director Alumni & Donor Relations .... Mr. Blake FARMER
88 Director Bonner Scholars Program .... Mrs. Kathy BALL
18 Director Physical Plant .... Mr. Bill FRALEY
19 Director of Public Safety .... Chief Mark STELLA
36 Director of Career Services .... Mr. Phil LEWIS
40 Bookstore Manager .... Mrs. Sheila CONNER
41 Athletic Director .... Mr. Kevin GARRETT
21 Financial Reporting Officer .... Ms. Elizabeth J. CAHILL-MUSICK
24 Ctr for Academic Technologies .... Mr. Steve MEADOWS
25 Director of Grants and Contracts .... Vacant
12 Director of the Beckley Center .... Dr. Susan WILLIAMS
96 Contract Specialist & Business Mgr .... Ms. Andrea WEBB
121 Director of Student Success .... Dr. Sheila WOMACK
101 Exec Asst to President/BOG Liaison .... Mrs. Lora WOOLWINE
88 Program Coordinator Advancement .... Ms. Amy PITZER
110 Manager of University Advancement .... Mr. Blake FARMER
39 Asst Dean & Dir Student Housing .... Mr. Bill FRALEY
35 Asst Dean of Students .... Vacant
04 Exec Asst to Pres Events Liaison .... Mrs. Tanya BALDWIN

* Fairmont State University (L)

1201 Locust Avenue, Fairmont WV 26554-2470
County: Marion FICE Identification: 003812
Unit ID: 237367
Telephone: (304) 367-4000 Carnegie Class: Masters/S
FAX Number: (304) 367-4789 Calendar System: Semester
URL: www.fairmontstate.edu
Established: 1865 Annual Undergrad Tuition & Fees (In-State): $7,738
Enrollment: 3,848 Coed
Affiliation or Control: State IRS Status: 501(c)3
Highest Offering: Master's
Accreditation: HLC, ACBSP, ADNUR, CAEP, NURSE

02 Interim President .... Dr. Dianna PHILLIPS
05 Interim Provost/VP Academic Affairs .... Dr. Timothy OXLEY
10 Vice Pres Finance & Administration .... Ms. Christa KWIATKOWSKI
32 Vice Pres Student Success .... Mr. Kenneth FETTIG
15 VP Human/Legal Affs & Gen Counsel .... Vacant
13 VP IT & Chief Info Technology (CIO) .... Dr. Joy A. HATCH
26 VP Univ Relations & Marketing .... Vacant
108 VP Inst Effectiveness & Strat Ops .... Ms. Merri S. INCITTI
18 Asst Vice Pres for Facilities .... Vacant
06 Registrar .... Mrs. Lori SCHOONMAKER
20 Executive Director Academic Program .... Dr. Susan ROSS
49 Dean College of Liberal Arts .... Dr. Christopher KAST
72 Dean College of Science/Tech .... Dr. Steven E. ROOF
50 Dean College of Business & Aviation .... Dr. Timothy R. OXLEY
53 Dean College Educ/Hlth/Hum Perf .... Dr. Amanda METCALF
57 Dean School of Fine Arts .... Vacant
66 Dean College of Nursing .... Dr. Laura H. CLAYTON
14 Deputy CIO .... Mr. Colton GRIFFIN
91 Manager IT Strategic Operations .... Mr. George HERRICK
09 Director Institutional Research .... Mr. Jacob R. ABRAMS
124 Dir Student Retention Initiatives .... Vacant
41 Director of Athletics .... Mr. Greg BAMBERGER
19 Chief of Police & Campus Safety .... Mr. Jeffrey MCCORMICK
38 Dir of Counseling .... Vacant
37 Exec Dir Student Support Services .... Ms. Tresa WEIMER
39 Exec Dir Res/Stdnt Life .... Ms. Alicia KALKA
08 Interim Director Library Services .... Ms. Sharon MAZURE
96 Director of Procurement .... Ms. Monica J. COCHRAN
36 Exec Dir Academic & Career Success .... Dr. John DEVAULT
23 Director of Student Health Services .... Ms. Chelsie COLLINS
25 Director of Planning and Grants .... Mrs. Amantha L. COLE
90 Sr Director Banner Administration .... Dr. Senta CHMIEL
119 Chief Technology Officer .... Mr. Jon DODDS
07 Director of Admissions .... Ms. Summer BOGGESS
100 Chief of Staff .... Mrs. Serena SCULLY
104 Director Study Abroad .... Vacant
43 University General Counsel .... Vacant

* Glenville State College (M)

200 High Street, Glenville WV 26351-1292
County: Gilmer FICE Identification: 003813
Unit ID: 237385
Telephone: (304) 462-7361 Carnegie Class: Bac-Diverse
FAX Number: (304) 462-7610 Calendar System: Semester
URL: www.glenville.edu
Established: 1872 Annual Undergrad Tuition & Fees (In-State): $7,886
Enrollment: 1,583 Coed
Affiliation or Control: State IRS Status: 501(c)3
Highest Offering: Master's
Accreditation: HLC, CAEP

02 President .... Dr. Mark A. MANCHIN
05 Provost/Vice Pres Academic Affairs .... Dr. Gary MORRIS
10 Chief Financial Officer .... Mr. Bert JEDAMSKI
41 Athletic Director .... Mr. Jesse SKILES
84 VP for Enrollment & Student Affairs .... Dr. Jason YEAGER
111 Vice President for Advancement .... Mr. David E. HUTCHISON
11 VP for Administration .... Ms. Rita HELMICK
04 Executive Assistant to President .... Ms. Teresa G. STERNS
53 Dean of Education .... Dr. Jeff C. HUNTER
15 Human Resources Director .... Ms. Tegan MCENTIRE
37 Director of Financial Aid .... Ms. Stephany HARPER
18 Exective Director of Facilities .... Mr. Tom RATCLIFF
39 Director of Residence Life .... Mr. J. Trae SPRAGUE
08 Director of Library .... Mr. Jason L. GUM
21 Controller .... Ms. Caren JENKINS
96 Director of Purchasing .... Ms. Joyce E. RIDDLE
29 Dir of Alumni Affairs/Annual Giving .... Mr. Conner FERGUSON
06 Registrar .... Ms. Ann M. REED
13 Director of Information Technology .... Mr. Jason PHARES
38 Professional Counselor .... Mr. Timothy J. UNDERWOOD
19 Associate Director of Public Safety .... Mr. Ronald K. TAYLOR
20 Assoc VP for Academic Affairs .... Dr. Mari CLEMENTS
07 Director of Admissions .... Ms. Chelsea STICKELMAN

* Marshall University (N)

1 John Marshall Drive, Huntington WV 25755-0001
County: Cabell FICE Identification: 003815
Unit ID: 237525
Telephone: (304) 696-3170 Carnegie Class: DU-Higher
FAX Number: (304) 696-6565 Calendar System: Semester
URL: www.marshall.edu
Established: 1837 Annual Undergrad Tuition & Fees (In-State): $8,512
Enrollment: 11,958 Coed
Affiliation or Control: State IRS Status: Exempt
Highest Offering: Doctorate
Accreditation: HLC, ADNUR, ANEST, #ARCPA, CAATE, CACREP, CAEP, CAHIIM, CLPSY, COARC, DIETD, DIETI, DMS, FEPAC, JOUR, MED, MLS, MLTAD, MUS, NUR, PH, PHAR, PTA, SP, SW

02 President .... Dr. Brad D. SMITH
04 Admin Assistant to the President .... Ms. Cora PYLES
05 Provost/Sr VP Academic Affairs .... Dr. Avinandan MUKHERJEE
43 Gen Counsel/Chief Legal Ofcr .... Mr. Toney STROUD
10 Intrerim Chief Financial Officer .... Mr. Jason BALDWIN
100 Chief of Staff .... Ms. Virginia R. PAINTER
09 Sr VP Inst Research .... Mr. Michael J. MCGUFFEY
102 CEO MU Foundation Inc .... Dr. Ron AREA
11 Sr VP for Administration .... Ms. Brandi D. JACOBS
32 VP Student & Intercultural Affairs .... Dr. Marcie SIMMS
46 VP Research .... Mr. John MAHER
30 Vice President Development .... Mr. Lance WEST

20 Assoc VP Academic Affairs ... Dr. Karen MCCOMAS
108 Assoc VP Assessment ... Dr. Mary Beth REYNOLDS
08 Assoc VP and Dean of Libraries ... Dr. Monica BROOKS
14 Chief Technology Officer ... Mr. Allen TAYLOR
119 Chief Information Security Officer ... Mr. Jon CUTLER
07 Executive Director of Admissions ... Dr. Tammy JOHNSON
37 Dir Student Financial Aid ... Dr. Beverly BOGGS
15 Chief Talent and DEI Officer ... Mr. Bruce B. FELDER
16 Associate Human Resources Officer ... Ms. Mary CHAPMAN
06 Registrar ... Dr. Sonja G. CANTRELL
113 Bursar ... Mr. Barry BECKETT
63 Interim Dean of Medicine ... Dr. Bobby MILLER
53 Dean College of Education ... Dr. Teresa EAGLE
49 Dean College Liberal Arts ... Dr. Robert BOOKWALTER
50 Interim Dean College of Business ... Dr. Jeffrey ARCHAMBAULT
57 Interim Dean College Arts & Media ... Dr. Wendell DOBBS
67 Interim Dean School of Pharmacy ... Dr. Eric BLOUGH
66 Dean College of Health Prof ... Dr. Michael PREWITT
54 Dean Col of Engr/Comp Sci ... Dr. David DAMPIER
81 Interim College of Science ... Mr. Brian MORGAN
92 Interim Dean Honors College ... Dr. Brian HOEY
41 Director of Athletics ... Mr. Christian SPEARS
29 Executive Director Alumni Relations ... Mr. Matthew D. JAMES
39 Director Residence Services ... Ms. Mistie BIBBEE
36 Director Career Services ... Ms. Cristina C. MCDAVID
19 Director of Public Safety ... Mr. James E. TERRY
22 Director Equity Programs ... Ms. Debra HART
96 Director of Purchasing ... Ms. Angela WHITE NEGLEY
18 Director Physical Plant ... Mr. Travis BAILEY
114 Budget Director ... Ms. Katrina ESKINS
88 Sr Assoc General Counsel ... Ms. Jendonnae HOUDYSCHELL
86 Asst to Pres for External Liaison ... Mr. William BURDETTE
13 Chief Information Officer ... Ms. Jodie PENROD
26 Chief Marketing Officer ... Mr. Dave TRAUBE

*Shepherd University (A)

PO Box 5000, Shepherdstown WV 25443-5000
County: Jefferson   FICE Identification: 003822
Unit ID: 237792
Telephone: (304) 876-5000   Carnegie Class: Masters/S
FAX Number: (304) 876-3101   Calendar System: Semester
URL: www.shepherd.edu
Established: 1871   Annual Undergrad Tuition & Fees (In-State): $7,784
Enrollment: 3,159   Coed
Affiliation or Control: State   IRS Status: 501(c)3
Highest Offering: Doctorate
Accreditation: **HLC**, ART, CAEP, CAPRT, @DIETD, EXSC, IACBE, MUS, NURSE, SW

02 President ... Dr. Mary HENDRIX
05 Interim Provost ... Dr. Ben MARTZ
10 Vice President Finance ... Ms. Pam STEVENS
32 Vice President for Student Affairs ... Ms. Holly FRYE
84 Vice President for Enrollment Mgmt ... Dr. Kelly HART
43 General Counsel ... Mr. K. Alan PERDUE
11 Assoc VP Campus Services ... Mr. Jack SHAW
81 Dean College of STEM ... Dr. Robert WARBURTON
79 Dean Col Arts/Humanities/Social Sci ... Dr. Robert TUDOR
50 Dean College of Business ... Dr. Ben MARTZ
66 Dean Col of Nursing/Educ/Health ... Dr. Sharon MAILEY
58 Dean School of Grad/Prof Studies ... Dr. Richie STEVENS
26 Exec Director Univ Communications ... Ms. Dana COSTA
09 Director Institutional Research ... Ms. Sara MAENE
39 Director Residence Life ... Dr. Elizabeth SECHLER
15 Director Human Resources ... Dr. Marie DEWALT
13 Director Info Technology Services ... Mr. Joey DAGG
06 Registrar ... Ms. Tracy SEFFERS
07 Director of Admissions ... Ms. Kristen LORENZ
37 Director of Financial Aid ... Ms. Joyce CABRAL
19 Interim Univ Police Chief ... Ms. Lori MARAUGHA
53 Director Teacher Education ... Dr. Jennifer PENLAND
18 Physical Plant Manager ... Ms. Shelley SHAFFER
41 Vice President for Athletics ... Mr. Chauncey WINBUSH
96 Director of Procurement Services ... Ms. Debra LANGFORD
38 Director of Counseling ... Ms. Shanan SPENCER
29 Director of Alumni Affairs ... Ms. Katie GORDON
92 Director Honors Program ... Dr. Mark CANTRELL
30 Executive Director of Development ... Ms. Sherri JANELLE
104 Director International Affairs ... Dr. Lois JARMAN
25 Dir of Office of Sponsored Programs ... Ms. Madge MORNINGSTAR
08 Interim Co-Dean Library/CTL ... Dr. Amy DEWITT
08 Interim Co-Dean Library/CTL ... Dr. Christy WENGER
04 Executive Asst to the President ... Mrs. Sonya SHOLLEY
44 Director of Annual Giving ... Ms. Christine MEYER
102 EVP Shepherd University Foundation ... Ms. Monica LINGENFELTER
105 Dr Marketing & Digital Strategies ... Vacant
22 Dir Social Equity/Inclus/Title IX ... Ms. Annie LEWIN
28 AVP Diversity/Equity/Inclusion ... Dr. Chiquita HOWARD-BOSTIC

*West Liberty University (B)

208 University Drive, West Liberty WV 26074
County: Ohio   FICE Identification: 003823
Unit ID: 237932
Telephone: (304) 336-5000   Carnegie Class: Masters/M
FAX Number: (304) 336-8403   Calendar System: Semester
URL: www.westliberty.edu
Established: 1837   Annual Undergrad Tuition & Fees (In-State): $8,150
Enrollment: 2,481   Coed
Affiliation or Control: State   IRS Status: 501(c)3
Highest Offering: Master's
Accreditation: **HLC**, ARCPA, CAEP, DH, IACBE, MLS, MUS, NURSE, @SP, SW

02 President ... Dr. W. Franklin EVANS
05 Interim Provost ... Dr. Catherine MONTEROSO
84 Assistant VP of Enrollment Mgmt ... Ms. Katie R. COOPER
10 Executive Vice President & CFO ... Ms. Lori HUDSON
81 Dean College of Sciences ... Dr. Karen KETTLER
49 Dean College Liberal/Creative Arts .. Dr. Cecelia KONCHAR-FARR
53 Interim Dean College of Education ... Dr. Nicole ENNIS
66 Director of Nursing Programs ... Dr. Rose M. KUTLENIOS
50 Dean College of Business ... Dr. Ann SAURBIER
39 Exec Dir Housing & Student Life ... Ms. Marcella T. SNYDER
15 Chief Human Resources Officer ... Ms. Diana L. HARTO
13 Chief Information Officer ... Mr. Joseph RODELLA
09 Dir of University Effectiveness ... Vacant
41 Director of Athletics ... Mr. Lynn ULLOM
07 Exec Dir Admissions & Recruitment ... Vacant
51 Director of Cont Educ/Special Pgm ... Vacant
08 Director of Library ... Vacant
29 Director Alumni Affairs ... Ms. Amanda BENNETT
37 Director Financial Aid ... Mrs. Katie R. COOPER
111 VP of External Affairs ... Mr. Jason W. KOEGLER
109 Director of Auxiliary Services ... Vacant
38 Director of Counseling ... Mr. Christopher A. MCPHERSON
92 Director of the Honors Program ... Dr. Shannon D. HALICKI
88 Director Dental Hygiene Programs ... Ms. Stephanie MEREDITH
88 Dir Clinical Lab Science Program ... Dr. Lisa JORDAN
23 Director of Health Services ... Ms. Cheryl C. BENNINGTON
88 Dir Physician Assistant Program ... Dr. William A. CHILDERS, JR.
85 Coord International Student Rec ... Ms. Mihaela SZABO
26 Executive Director of Marketing ... Ms. Tammi SECRIST
101 Secretary of the Institution/Board ... Ms. Mary A. EDWARDS
105 Web Master ... Mr. Thomas ESTLACK
106 Dir Online Education/E-learning ... Dr. Merilee MADERA
18 Director of Physical Plant ... Mr. Joe MILLS
19 Chief of Police/Dir Public Safety ... Mr. Ronald E. FOX
96 Director of Purchasing ... Mr. Patrick KELLY
06 Registrar ... Ms. Stephanie M. NORTH
102 Executive Director Foundation ... Ms. Angela ZAMBITO-HILL
04 Admin Assistant to the President ... Ms. Mary Ann EDWARDS
25 Chief Contract & Grants Admin ... Ms. Laura MUSILLI
104 Director Study Abroad ... Dr. Felipe E. ROJAS
43 Dir Legal Services (General Counsel ... Ms. Stephanie HOOPER
28 Int Spec Asst DEI & Strategic Init ... Dr. Monique AKASSI

*West Virginia School of Osteopathic Medicine (C)

400 Lee Street North, Lewisburg WV 24901-1196
County: Greenbrier   FICE Identification: 011245
Unit ID: 237880
Telephone: (304) 645-6270   Carnegie Class: Spec-4-yr-Med
FAX Number: (304) 645-4859   Calendar System: Semester
URL: www.wvsom.edu
Established: 1972   Annual Graduate Tuition & Fees: N/A
Enrollment: 800   Coed
Affiliation or Control: State   IRS Status: 501(c)3
Highest Offering: First Professional Degree; No Undergraduates
Accreditation: **HLC**, OSTEO

01 President ... Dr. James W. NEMITZ
05 Vice Pres Academic Affairs & Dean ... Dr. Linda BOYD
10 Vice Pres Finance & Facilities ... Larry WARE
11 Vice Pres for Administration ... Dr. Edward BRIDGES
43 Vice Pres Legal/Govt Affairs ... Jeffrey SHAWVER
15 Vice Pres of Human Resources ... Leslie BICKSLER
26 Vice Pres Marketing & Communication ... Vacant
103 VP Community Engagement & Devel ... Dr. Drema MACE
58 Assoc Dean Graduate Medical Educ ... Dr. Victoria SHUMAN
20 Assoc Dean Preclinical Education ... Dr. Roy RUSS
20 Assoc Dean Research & Spons Pgms ... Dr. Jandy HANNA
108 Assoc Dean Assessment/Educ Devel ... Dr. Machelle LINSENMEYER
20 Asst Dean Osteopathic Medical Educ ... Dr. Robert FOSTER
32 Assistant Dean Student Affairs ... Dr. Rebecca MORROW
13 Chief Technology Officer ... Kimberly RANSOM
16 Director of Human Resources ... Tiffany BURNS
06 Registrar ... Jennifer SEAMS
37 Director Financial Aid ... Lisa SPENCER
30 Development Dir/WVSOM Foundation ... Vacant
29 Director of Alumni Relations ... Shannon WARREN
07 Director of Admissions ... Ronnie COLLINS
96 Director of Contracts ... Betty BAKER
08 Director of Library ... Mary ESSIG
24 Director of Media Services ... Michael FOWLER
18 Director of Physical Plant ... William ALDER
35 Director of Student Life ... Belinda EVANS
09 Coordinator Institutional Research ... Lance RIDPATH
40 Business Manager/Bookstore ... Cindi KNIGHT
21 Director of Finance ... Stella DODRILL

*West Virginia State University (D)

PO Box 1000, Institute WV 25112-1000
County: Kanawha   FICE Identification: 003826
Unit ID: 237899
Telephone: (304) 766-3000   Carnegie Class: Masters/S
FAX Number: (304) 720-2075   Calendar System: Semester
URL: www.wvstateu.edu
Established: 1891   Annual Undergrad Tuition & Fees (In-State): $8,437
Enrollment: 3,638   Coed
Affiliation or Control: State   IRS Status: 501(c)3
Highest Offering: Master's
Accreditation: **HLC**, ACBSP, CAEP, SW

02 President ... Mr. Ericke S. CAGE
10 VP for Business and Finance ... Ms. Christina DALTON
05 Int Provost/VP for Academic Affairs ... Dr. J. Paige CARNEY
84 VP Enroll Mgmt/Student Affairs ... Vacant
111 VP for University Advancement ... Ms. Patricia J. SCHUMANN
20 Assoc Prov/AVP Academic Affairs ... Vacant
100 Interim VP/Chief of Staff ... Mr. Ericke S. CAGE
46 VP for Research & Public Service ... Dr. Jose TOLEDO
79 Dean Col of Arts & Humanities ... Dr. Robert WALLACE
81 Dean Col of Natural Sci/Math ... Dr. Naveed ZAMAN
107 Dean Col of Prof Studies ... Dr. J. Paige CARNEY
50 Dean Col of Business/Social Science ... Vacant
26 Assistant VP of Comm & Marketing ... Mr. Jack BAILEY
13 Director of Information Technology ... Mr. Alan SKIDMORE
18 Int Director Physical Facilities ... Mr. Dayton WILSON
06 Director Records & Registration ... Vacant
19 Director of Public Safety ... Vacant
15 Asst VP Human Resource ... Vacant
08 Director of Drain-Jordan Library ... Dr. Willette STINSON
37 Int Dir Student Financial Asst ... Ms. Gwen BAUSLEY
29 Director of Alumni Relations ... Ms. Belinda FULLER
36 Dir of Career Services & Coop Educ ... Vacant
07 Director of Admissions ... Vacant
89 Coordinator of New Student Programs ... Vacant
96 Director of Purchasing ... Vacant
106 Dir of Center for Online Learning ... Dr. Thomas KIDDIE
41 Athletic Director ... Vacant
39 Dir of Housing and Residence Life ... Mr. Derrien WILLIAMS
04 Exec Assistant to the President ... Ms. Crystal WALKER
32 AVP Student Affairs/Student Life ... Mr. Joe ODEN, JR.
86 Director Government Relations ... Vacant

*West Virginia University (E)

1500 University Avenue, PO Box 6201, Morgantown WV 26506
County: Monongalia   FICE Identification: 003827
Unit ID: 238032
Telephone: (304) 293-0111   Carnegie Class: DU-Highest
FAX Number: (304) 293-5883   Calendar System: Semester
URL: www.wvu.edu
Established: 1867   Annual Undergrad Tuition & Fees (In-State): $8,976
Enrollment: 26,269   Coed
Affiliation or Control: State   IRS Status: 501(c)3
Highest Offering: Doctorate
Accreditation: **HLC**, ABAI, ANEST, #ARCPA, ART, AUD, CAATE, CACREP, CAEP, CAHIIM, CEA, CLPSY, COPSY, DENT, DH, DIETD, DIETI, DMS, EXSC, FEPAC, HT, IPSY, JOUR, LAW, LSAR, MED, MLS, MUS, NMT, NURSE, OT, PA, PAST, PH, PHAR, PTA, RAD, RADMAG, RTT, SP, SPAA, SW, THEA

02 President/Chief Exec Officer ... Mr. E. Gordon GEE
05 Provost & VP Acad Affairs ... Ms. Maryanne REED
10 VP & CFO ... Ms. Paula CONGELIO
26 Vice Pres for University Relations ... Ms. Sharon L. MARTIN
17 Chancellor/Exec Dean Health Science ... Dr. Clay B. MARSH
46 Vice President for Research ... Mr. Fred L. KING
102 Pres/CEO WVU Foundation ... Ms. Cindi ROTH
15 VP for Talent & Culture ... Mr. Cris DEBORD
20 Vice Provost Academic Affairs ... Dr. Paul KREIDER
20 Assoc Provost Academic Personnel ... Dr. Tracy MORRIS
88 Director Research & Rural Health ... Ms. Sandra Y. POPE
100 Senior Advisor to President ... Mr. John J. COLE
88 Exec Officer for Policy Development ... Dr. Jennifer L. FISHER
45 VP Strategic Initiatives ... Mr. Rob ALSOP
28 VP Diversity Equity & Inclusion ... Ms. Meshea L. POORE
29 VP Alumni Rels/CEO Alumni Assn ... Mr. Kevin BERRY
21 Assoc Vice Pres for Finance ... Ms. Anjali HALABE
56 Int Dean & Director Extension Svcs ... Dr. Jorge ATILES
13 Assoc Provost IT/CIO ... Mr. Brice KNOTTS
18 Sr Assoc VP Facilities & Svcs ... Mr. Jamie F. KOSIK
35 Assoc Vice Pres Student Affairs ... Mr. Michael A. ELLINGTON
76 Asst VP Hlth Sci & Tech Academy ... Ms. Ann L. CHESTER
84 Assoc VP Enroll Mgmt Svcs ... Mr. George ZIMMERMAN
88 Assoc VP Strategic Initiatives ... Ms. Elizabeth P. REYNOLDS
88 Int Director Corporate Relations ... Mr. Jack THOMPSON
25 Asst VP Office of Research Admin ... Mr. Alan B. MARTIN
09 Director of Institutional Research ... Ms. Donielle R. MAUST
39 Director Res Life/Dean of Students ... Ms. Trish CENDANA
41 Dir & Assoc VP Intercoll Athletics ... Mr. Shane LYONS
37 Asst VP Financial Aid ... Ms. Sandra K. OERLY-BENNETT
06 University Registrar ... Mr. Josh IMES
08 Dean of Library Services ... Ms. Karen DIAZ
19 Chief of Police/Univ Police Dept ... Capt. W. P. CHEDESTER
109 Sr Assoc VP Auxiliary Services ... Mr. Edward T. SVEHLIK
85 VP Global Strategies ... Dr. Amber BRUGNOLI
69 Assoc VP & Dean Public Health ... Dr. Jeffrey COBEN
50 Dean & VP Business & Economics ... Dr. Josh HALL
49 Dean of Arts & Sciences ... Dr. Gregory DUNAWAY
57 Dean College of Creative Arts ... Dr. Keith JACKSON
61 Dean of Law ... Dr. Amelia RINEHART
63 Executive Dean & VP of Medicine ... Dr. Clay B. MARSH
52 Dean of Dentistry ... Dr. Stephen PACHUTA
54 Dean of Engr/Mineral Resources ... Dr. Pedro MAGO
47 Dean of Davis Agric & Forestry ... Dr. Darrell DONAHUE
67 Dean of Pharmacy ... Dr. William P. PETROS
60 Dean of College of Media ... Dr. Diana MARTINELLI
66 Dean of Nursing ... Dr. Tara HULSEY
92 Dean of Honors College ... Mr. Kenneth P. BLEMINGS
106 Dean Online Programs ... Vacant
88 Dean Col of Applied Human Sciences ... Dr. Autumn CYPRES
36 Director Career Services ... Mr. David L. DURHAM

20 Assoc Provost Intl Acad Affairs ..... Dr. David STEWART
20 Campus Provost-WVUIT ..... Dr. Joan NEFF
58 Assoc Provost Grad Acad Affairs ..... Dr. Richard THOMAS
35 Assoc VP & Dean of Students ..... Mr. G. Corey FARRIS
105 Director Web Services ..... Ms. Cathy ORNDORFF
88 Asst VP Entrepreneurship & Innov ..... Ms. Carrie WHITE
116 Director Internal Audit ..... Mr. Bryan D. SHAVER
122 Dir Ctr Fraternal Values/Ldrshp ..... Dr. Matthew RICHARDSON
04 Admin Assistant to the President ..... Ms. Bonnie ANDERSON

*West Virginia University at Parkersburg (A)

300 Campus Drive, Parkersburg WV 26104-8647
County: Wood FICE Identification: 003828
Unit ID: 237686
Telephone: (304) 424-8000 Carnegie Class: Bac/Assoc-Mixed
FAX Number: (304) 424-8315 Calendar System: Semester
URL: www.wvup.edu
Established: 1961 Annual Undergrad Tuition & Fees (In-State): $3,890
Enrollment: 2,624 Coed
Affiliation or Control: State IRS Status: 501(c)3
Highest Offering: Baccalaureate
Accreditation: HLC, ACBSP, ADNUR, CAEP, NUR, SURGT

02 President ..... Dr. Christopher GILMER
18 VP Facilities/Internal Affairs ..... Mr. Brady WHIPKEY
05 Provost/Vice PresAcademic Affairs ..... Dr. Chad CRUMBAKER
10 Vice Pres Finance/Administration ..... Ms. Alice HARRIS
84 Exec VP Enrollment Management ..... Dr. Steven SMITH
111 Exec VP Institutional Advancement ..... Dr. Torie JACKSON
13 Chief Information Officer ..... Mr. Doug ANTHONY
103 Exec Dir Workforce/Economic Develop ..... Ms. Michele WILSON
22 Exec Dir Equity/Inclus/Compliance ..... Mrs. Debbie RICHARDS
20 Dean for Academic Affairs ..... Dr. Cynthia GISSY
32 Exec Dir Student Support Services ..... Mr. Kurt KLETTNER
110 Exec Dir Institutional Advancement ..... Ms. Senta GOUDY
15 Director Human Resources ..... Mr. Scott POE
09 Dean Institutional Research ..... Mr. Jeremy STARKEY
06 Registrar/Dir Center Student Svcs ..... Mrs. Leslie SIMS
37 Director of Financial Aid ..... Mrs. Heather SKIDMORE
21 Exec Dir of CPO ..... Ms. Jeannine RATLIFFE
08 Director of Library ..... Mr. Stephen HUPP
29 Exec Dir Alumni Relations ..... Ms. Nancy BREMAR
50 Chair Business/Economics/Math Div ..... Mr. Jeff HOLLAND
53 Chair Education ..... Dr. David LANCASTER
81 Chair STEM Division ..... Dr. Jared GUMP

West Virginia Junior College (B)

5514 Big Tyler Road Suite 200, Cross Lanes WV 25313
County: Kanawha FICE Identification: 010573
Unit ID: 237987
Telephone: (304) 769-0011 Carnegie Class: Assoc/HVT-High Trad
FAX Number: (304) 769-0013 Calendar System: Quarter
URL: www.wvjc.edu
Established: 1892 Annual Undergrad Tuition & Fees: $14,335
Enrollment: 218 Coed
Affiliation or Control: Proprietary IRS Status: Proprietary
Highest Offering: Associate Degree
Accreditation: ABHES

01 Campus President ..... Ms. Michelle MILES
05 Academic Dean ..... Ms. Katie HARVEY
06 Registrar ..... Ms. Jennifer BIRD
37 Director Student Financial Aid ..... Ms. Christina HAYSLETT

West Virginia Junior College (C)

148 Willey Street, Morgantown WV 26505-5596
County: Monongalia FICE Identification: 005007
Unit ID: 237996
Telephone: (304) 296-8282 Carnegie Class: Assoc/HVT-Mix Trad/Non
FAX Number: (304) 581-6990 Calendar System: Quarter
URL: www.wvjc.edu
Established: 1922 Annual Undergrad Tuition & Fees: $13,950
Enrollment: 622 Coed
Affiliation or Control: Proprietary IRS Status: Proprietary
Highest Offering: Associate Degree
Accreditation: ABHES, ADNUR

01 President ..... Ms. Samantha ESPOSITO
05 Academic Dean ..... Ms. Rachael SALVUCCI
37 Financial Aid Director ..... Ms. Patricia CALLEN

West Virginia Junior College-Bridgeport (D)

176 Thompson Drive, Bridgeport WV 26330
Telephone: (304) 842-4007 Identification: 770823
Accreditation: ABHES

West Virginia Wesleyan College (E)

59 College Avenue, Buckhannon WV 26201-2699
County: Upshur FICE Identification: 003830
Unit ID: 237969
Telephone: (304) 473-8000 Carnegie Class: Bac-Diverse
FAX Number: N/A Calendar System: Semester
URL: www.wvwc.edu
Established: 1890 Annual Undergrad Tuition & Fees: $32,252
Enrollment: 1,066 Coed
Affiliation or Control: United Methodist IRS Status: 501(c)3
Highest Offering: Doctorate
Accreditation: HLC, CAATE, CAEP, MUS, NURSE

01 President ..... Dr. Joel THIERSTEIN
05 Dean of Faculty/Chief Academic Ofcr ..... Dr. James MOORE
84 VP Enrollment Mgmt & Admissions ..... Mr. John WALTZ
111 VP Advancement ..... Mr. Robert SKINNER
10 Chief Financial Officer ..... Dr. Scott MCKINNEY
42 Dean of the Chapel ..... Rev. Lauren WEAVER
102 Director Foundation/Govt Relations ..... Ms. Nicki BENTLEY-COLTHART
11 Director of Administrative Services ..... Mr. Robert KIMBLE
37 Director Financial Aid ..... Ms. Susan GEORGE
29 Assoc VP Adv & Alumni Relations ..... Mr. William ARMISTEAD
08 Director of Library Services ..... Mr. Brett MILLER
36 Director Academic & Career Services ..... Ms. Tammy FREDERICK
39 Director Campus Life & Housing ..... Ms. Alisa LIVELY
09 Director of Institutional Research ..... Ms. Tammy CRITES
15 Director of Human Resources ..... Ms. Vickie CROWDER
18 Director of the Physical Plant ..... Mr. Vaughn HARTLEY
30 Director Advancement Operations ..... Ms. Rose Ellen LOUDIN
88 Director of Learning Center ..... Dr. Shawn KUBA
06 Registrar ..... Ms. Tammy FREDERICK
41 Director of Athletics ..... Mr. Randall TENNEY
10 Controller ..... Mr. Randall CRITES
40 Retail Store Manager ..... Ms. Jennifer FLETCHER
92 Director Honors Program ..... Ms. Jordana LAFANTASIE
93 Director Multicultural Programs ..... Mr. Robert QUARLES
112 Planned Giving Coordinator ..... Rev. David PETERS
38 Director of Counseling Services ..... Ms. Lori THOMPSON
31 Asst Dir of Community Engagement ..... Ms. Jessica VINCENT
13 Director of Computing Services ..... Mr. Neil ROTH
04 Administrative Asst to President ..... Ms. Deborah K. MULLENS
19 Director of Security ..... Mr. David PARKS
43 Dir Legal Services/General Counsel ..... Mr. David W. MCCAULEY
101 Secretary of the Institution/Board ..... Ms. Deborah K. MULLENS
104 Director Study Abroad ..... Dr. Tamara BAILEY

Wheeling University (F)

316 Washington Avenue, Wheeling WV 26003-6295
County: Ohio FICE Identification: 003831
Unit ID: 238078
Telephone: (304) 243-2000 Carnegie Class: Masters/M
FAX Number: (304) 243-2243 Calendar System: Semester
URL: www.wheeling.edu
Established: 1954 Annual Undergrad Tuition & Fees: $29,290
Enrollment: 857 Coed
Affiliation or Control: Roman Catholic IRS Status: 501(c)3
Highest Offering: Doctorate
Accreditation: #HLC, ACBSP, CAATE, NURSE, PTA

01 President ..... Ms. Ginny FAVEDE
05 Int VP for Academic Affairs ..... Ms. Jackie MCGLADE
32 VP for Student Services ..... Mr. Andrew LEWIS
84 Vice Pres of Enrollment Management ..... Mr. Justin SCHWARZ
13 Acting Dir Information Technology ..... Mr. Ron MAGERS
37 Interim Director Financial Aid ..... Ms. Dawn LANGDON
06 Acting Registrar ..... Mr. John L'ECUYER
08 Librarian ..... Vacant
42 Director of Campus Ministry ..... Dr. I. Hadi SASMITA, SJ
41 Athletic Director ..... Mr. Patrick SNIVELY
18 Director of Facilities ..... Mr. Michael CONNER
04 Executive Asst to President ..... Ms. Melissa ROSE
106 Dir Online Education/E-learning ..... Mr. D. Jason FRITZMAN
19 Director Public Safety ..... Mr. Larry PALMER
29 Director Alumni Relations ..... Vacant
38 Director of Counseling Center ..... Ms. Tina TORDELLA

WISCONSIN

Alverno College (G)

3400 S 43rd Street, Box 343922,
Milwaukee WI 53234-3922
County: Milwaukee FICE Identification: 003832
Unit ID: 238193
Telephone: (414) 382-6000 Carnegie Class: Masters/L
FAX Number: (414) 382-6066 Calendar System: Semester
URL: www.alverno.edu
Established: 1887 Annual Undergrad Tuition & Fees: $30,658
Enrollment: 1,876 Female
Affiliation or Control: Independent Non-Profit IRS Status: 501(c)3
Highest Offering: Doctorate
Accreditation: HLC, MUS, NURSE, SW

01 Interim President ..... Dr. Joseph FOY
100 Vice Pres and Chief of Staff ..... Ms. Jill DESMOND
10 Vice Pres Finance/Administration ..... Ms. Dawn PETERSON
111 Vice President for Advancement ..... Ms. Christa SHIELDS
84 VP for Enrollment & Student Success ..... Ms. Kate LUNDEEN
32 VP for Student Devel & Success ..... Dr. Heidi ANDERSON-ISAACSON
07 Director of Admissions ..... Ms. Janet STIKEL
20 Assoc Vice Pres ..... Sr. Marlene NEISES
06 Registrar ..... Ms. Lori SZARZYNSKI
08 Director Library ..... Mr. Larry DUERR
36 Executive Director Career Studio ..... Vacant
13 Chief Information Officer ..... Mr. John JERIES
37 Director of Financial Aid ..... Ms. Naomi COE
110 Executive Director of Advancement ..... Ms. Kim MUENCH
29 Alumni Engagement Manager ..... Vacant
121 Director Academic Advising ..... Ms. Kate TISCH
15 Director Human Resources ..... Ms. MJ GILFILLAN
41 Director of Athletics ..... Ms. Katari KEY
42 Campus Minister ..... Vacant
96 Purchasing Coordinator ..... Ms. Anne MCCARRON
66 Dean School of Nursing ..... Dr. Laurie KUNKEL-JORDAN
107 Dean of Professional/Grad Studies ..... Dr. Jodi EASTBERG
49 Dean School of Arts & Sciences ..... Dr. Kevin CASEY
51 Dean School of Adult Learning ..... Ms. Meghan WALSH
04 Exec Assistant to the President ..... Ms. Morgan DICOSOLA
18 Director Plant Operations ..... Mr. John MARKS
19 Director Security/Safety ..... Mr. Jason PILARSKI

Bellin College, Inc. (H)

3201 Eaton Road, Green Bay WI 54311
County: Brown FICE Identification: 006639
Unit ID: 238324
Telephone: (920) 433-6699 Carnegie Class: Spec-4-yr-Other Health
FAX Number: (920) 433-1923 Calendar System: Semester
URL: www.bellincollege.edu
Established: 1909 Annual Undergrad Tuition & Fees: $21,685
Enrollment: 626 Coed
Affiliation or Control: Independent Non-Profit IRS Status: 501(c)3
Highest Offering: Doctorate
Accreditation: HLC, DMS, NURSE, @PTA, RAD

01 President & CEO of the College ..... Dr. Connie J. BOERST
10 VP of Business & Finance ..... Mrs. Ginger B. KRUMMEN SCHRAVEN
66 Dean of Nursing ..... Dr. Mary K. ROLLOFF
76 Dean of Allied Health Sciences ..... Dr. Mark A. BAKE
32 Dean of Student Services ..... Dr. Mark A. BAKE
07 VP of Admissions and Marketing ..... Mr. Matt G. RENTMEESTER
13 Director of Technology ..... Mr. Travis A. SMITH
06 Registrar ..... Mr. Russell J. LEARY
37 Director Financial Aid ..... Mrs. Lena C. GOODMAN
04 Executive Assistant to President ..... Mrs. Jamie L. ARBEITER
08 Head Librarian ..... Ms. Cindy M. REINL
111 VP of Advancement ..... Mr. Thomas J. SHEFCHIK

Beloit College (I)

700 College Street, Beloit WI 53511-5595
County: Rock FICE Identification: 003835
Unit ID: 238333
Telephone: (608) 363-2000 Carnegie Class: Bac-A&S
FAX Number: (608) 363-2717 Calendar System: Semester
URL: www.beloit.edu
Established: 1846 Annual Undergrad Tuition & Fees: $53,348
Enrollment: 978 Coed
Affiliation or Control: Independent Non-Profit IRS Status: 501(c)3
Highest Offering: Baccalaureate
Accreditation: HLC

01 President ..... Dr. Scott BIERMAN
05 Provost ..... Dr. Eric BOYNTON
100 Chief of Staff ..... Ms. Erica I. DANIELS
45 VP Budget & Planning ..... Ms. Stacie SCOTT
111 VP Development & Alumni Relations ..... Ms. Amy WILSON
15 VP Human Resources and Operations ..... Ms. Lori RHEAD
84 VP Enrollment ..... Ms. Leslie DAVIDSON
32 Dean Equity/Cmty/Student Success ..... Mr. Cecil YOUNGBLOOD
13 Chief Information Officer ..... Mr. Ted WILDER
26 Chief Comm & Integ Mktg Officer ..... Ms. Elizabeth CONLISK
108 Dir Strategic Research & Assessment ..... Ms. Ellie ANDERYRNE
09 Dir Inst Research/Assmt/Planning ..... Vacant
06 Registrar ..... Dr. Yaffa GROSSMAN
07 Director of Admissions ..... Ms. Martha STOLZE
18 Director of Facilities ..... Mr. Robert OEHLER
39 Director Resident Life/Conferences ..... Mr. Ryan SCHAMP
36 Director of Career Development ..... Ms. Jessica FOX-WILSON
37 Director of Financial Aid ..... Ms. Betsy HENKEL
41 Athletic Director ..... Mr. Dave DEGEORGE

Cardinal Stritch University (J)

6801 N Yates Road, Milwaukee WI 53217-3985
County: Milwaukee FICE Identification: 003837
Unit ID: 238430
Telephone: (414) 410-4000 Carnegie Class: DU-Mod
FAX Number: (414) 410-4239 Calendar System: Semester
URL: www.stritch.edu
Established: 1937 Annual Undergrad Tuition & Fees: $33,770
Enrollment: 1,646 Coed
Affiliation or Control: Roman Catholic IRS Status: 501(c)3
Highest Offering: Doctorate
Accreditation: HLC, ACBSP, NUR, NURSE

01 President ..... Dr. Daniel J. SCHOLZ
04 Exec Assistant to the President ..... Ms. Yanelis RODRIGUEZ
05 Vice Pres Academic Affairs ..... Dr. Daniel J. SCHOLZ
84 VP Enrollment Management ..... Ms. Tracy A. FISCHER
32 Vice Pres Student Affairs ..... Ms. Donney MORONEY
21 Interim Chief Financial Officer ..... Mrs. Mel L. AUSTIN
42 Director University Ministry ..... Mr. Gino GRIVETTI
41 Director of Athletics ..... Mr. Danny KUKLINSKI
13 Director Infrastructure Support ..... Mr. Steven W. TRACY
66 Dean College of Nursing/HealthSci ..... Dr. Vince SALYERS
76 Assoc Dean Col Nursing/Health Sci ..... Dr. Crystal-Rae WALTON
53 Dean Col of Educ/Literacy/Leaders ..... Dr. Janice JONES
49 Dean College of Arts and Sciences ..... Dr. Carl D. MUELLER

35 Dean of Students ... Ms. Donney MORONEY
15 Director of Human Resources/Payroll ... Ms. Jackie L. KLENZ
06 University Registrar ... Ms. Christine GLYNN
37 Dir of Financial Aid ... Mr. Mark W. QUISTORF
36 Asst Dir Internships/Career Engage ... Mr. Tom E. KIPP
38 Dir for Counseling/Mental Wellness ... Ms. Mary Beth WISNIEWSKI
104 Director International Education ... Ms. Sarah R. SWEENEY
108 Dir of Institutional Effectiveness ... Mr. William L. MARCOU
91 Director of Enterprise Systems ... Ms. Susan L. INGLES
08 Director of University Library ... Ms. Dyan E. BARBEAU
26 Sr Dir University Communications ... Ms. Kathleen M. HOHL
18 Director of Facilities ... Mr. Donald PAJEWSKI
88 Director Mission Integration ... Dr. Barbara SPIES

Carroll University (A)

100 N East Avenue, Waukesha WI 53186-5593
County: Waukesha FICE Identification: 003838
Unit ID: 238458
Telephone: (262) 547-1211 Carnegie Class: Masters/L
FAX Number: (262) 524-7646 Calendar System: Semester
URL: www.carrollu.edu
Established: 1846 Annual Undergrad Tuition & Fees: $34,010
Enrollment: 3,451 Coed
Affiliation or Control: Presbyterian Church (U.S.A.) IRS Status: 501(c)3
Highest Offering: Doctorate
Accreditation: HLC, ARCPA, CAATE, @CNEA, MUS, NURSE, OT, PTA

01 President ... Dr. Cindy GNADINGER
05 Provost/Vice Pres Academic Affairs ... Dr. Mark BLEGEN
10 Vice Pres Finance/Administration ... Ms. Dana STUART
84 Vice President for Enrollment ... Mr. Teege METTILLE
111 Vice President for Advancement ... Ms. Victoria DOWLING
32 Vice President Student Affairs ... Dr. Theresa BARRY
26 Vice Pres Marketing & Communication ... Ms. Tiffany WYNN
13 Chief Technology Officer ... Vacant
06 Registrar ... Ms. Ann HANDFORD
21 Assoc VP Finance & Administration ... Ms. Deidre ERWIN
37 Assoc VP Enroll/Dir Fin Aid ... Ms. Dawn M. SCOTT
15 Director of Human Resources ... Ms. Kelly PEARSE
08 Library Director ... Mr. Joe HARDENBROOK
41 Athletic Director ... Mr. Mike SCHULIST
107 Dir of Non-Trad Adult/Prof Studies ... Ms. Lynn NOVAK
28 Assoc Dean Multicult Affairs . Ms. Vanessa PEREZ-TOPCZEWSKI
29 Sr Director Alumni Engagement ... Ms. Dolores M. BROWN
109 Sr Director Auxiliary & Gen Svcs ... Vacant
07 Director of Trad & Intl Admissions ... Ms. Annie J. ASCHENBRENNER
18 Facilities Director ... Mr. Tom HEFFERNAN
38 Director Student Counseling ... Ms. Angie R. BRANNAN
04 Exec Assistant to the President ... Ms. Gina M. EHLER
123 Director Graduate Admissions ... Ms. Cindy HOLAHAN
121 Director of Student Success ... Mr. Jeff MCNAMARA
19 Director Security/Safety ... Mr. Mike BAGIN
22 Director of Compliance ... Ms. Suzanne LIDTKE
43 Director of Legal Services ... Ms. Cat JORGENS
50 Dean School of Business ... Dr. Hamid AKBARI
49 Dean College of Arts & Sciences ... Dr. Kareem MOHAMMAD
76 Dean Health Sciences ... Dr. Thomas PAHNKE
09 Director of Institutional Research ... Mr. Joshua MITCHELL
25 Sr Director of Sponsored Projects ... Vacant
122 Dir Ofc Fraternity/Sorority Life ... Ms. Alexandra SMITH

Carthage College (B)

2001 Alford Park Drive, Kenosha WI 53140-1994
County: Kenosha FICE Identification: 003839
Unit ID: 238476
Telephone: (262) 551-8500 Carnegie Class: Masters/S
FAX Number: (262) 551-6208 Calendar System: 4/1/4
URL: www.carthage.edu
Established: 1847 Annual Undergrad Tuition & Fees: $31,500
Enrollment: 2,763 Coed
Affiliation or Control: Evangelical Lutheran Church In America
IRS Status: 501(c)3
Highest Offering: Master's
Accreditation: HLC, CAATE, MUS, NURSE, SW

01 President/Chief Executive Officer ... Dr. John R. SWALLOW
04 Special Assistant to the President ... Ms. Dana KROLL
05 Provost/Chief Operating Officer ... Dr. David TIMMERMAN
10 AVP Finance & Administration/CFO ... Mr. Vince CEJA
111 VP for Institutional Advancement ... Dr. Thomas KLINE
26 Assoc VP Marketing/Communications ... Ms. Elizabeth YOUNG
84 VP for Enrollment ... Mr. Nick MULVEY
32 VP Student Affairs/Dean of Students ... Dr. Kimberlie GOLDSBERRY
108 VP Institutional Effectiveness ... Dr. Abigail HANNA
41 Interim Athletic Director ... Mr. Nathan STEWART
42 Campus Pastor ... Ms. Kara BAYLOR
06 Registrar ... Mr. Brandon PORTER
104 Director Study Abroad ... Dr. Erik KULKE
15 Director of Human Resources ... Ms. Marianne MARSHALL
19 Director of Public Safety ... Vacant
37 Director of Financial Aid ... Mr. Jeff TEAGUE
122 Asst Dir Involvement-Greek Life ... Mr. Lance THOMSON

College of Menominee Nation (C)

PO Box 1179, Keshena WI 54135-1179
County: Menominee FICE Identification: 031251
Unit ID: 413617
Telephone: (800) 567-2344 Carnegie Class: Tribal
FAX Number: (715) 799-1336 Calendar System: Semester
URL: www.menominee.edu
Established: 1992 Annual Undergrad Tuition & Fees: $6,200
Enrollment: 173 Coed
Affiliation or Control: Tribal Control IRS Status: 501(c)3
Highest Offering: Baccalaureate
Accreditation: HLC

01 Interim President ... Mr. Christopher M. CALDWELL
05 Chief Academic Officer ... Ms. Geraldine SANAPAW
10 Interim Chief Financial Officer ... Mr. George OTRADOVEC
51 Dean of Continuing Education ... Mr. Brian KOWALKOWSKI
124 Director of Retention ... Mr. Norman SHAWANOKASIC
100 Chief of Staff ... Ms. Melinda COOK
09 Director Institutional Research ... Ms. Geraldine SANAPAW
13 IT Director ... Mr. Edward BOWKER
15 Human Resources Generalist ... Ms. Sarah LYONS
06 Registrar/Bursar ... Ms. Geraldine SANAPAW
37 Financial Aid Mgr ... Mr. Austin RETZLAFF
07 Admissions/Enrollment Manager ... Mr. Luis ORTIZ
78 Director of Vocational Rehab ... Ms. Myrna WARRINGTON
08 Director of Library Services ... Ms. Maria ESCALANTE
96 Director of Purchasing ... Ms. Darla ASENBRENER

College of Menominee Nation (D)

2733 S Ridge Road, Green Bay WI 54304
Telephone: (715) 799-5600 Identification: 770424
Accreditation: &HLC

Concordia University Wisconsin (E)

12800 N Lake Shore Drive, Mequon WI 53097-2402
County: Ozaukee FICE Identification: 003842
Unit ID: 238616
Telephone: (262) 243-5700 Carnegie Class: DU-Mod
FAX Number: (262) 243-4351 Calendar System: 4/1/4
URL: www.cuw.edu
Established: 1881 Annual Undergrad Tuition & Fees: $31,182
Enrollment: 5,492 Coed
Affiliation or Control: Lutheran Church - Missouri Synod
IRS Status: 501(c)3
Highest Offering: Doctorate
Accreditation: HLC, #ARCPA, CAATE, DMS, IACBE, MAC, NURSE, OT, PHAR, PTA, @SP, SW

01 Interim President ... Dr. William R. CARIO
11 Executive VP & Chief Oper Ofcr ... Mr. Allen J. PROCHNOW
05 Interim Provost/Chief Accred Ofcr ... Dr. Leah M. DVORAK
10 CFO/Senior VP of Finance ... Rev Dr. Roy PETERSON
111 Interim VP of Advancement ... Mr. Dean D. RENNICKE
13 VP of Information Technology ... Mr. Thomas G. PHILLIP
32 VP of Student Life ... Dr. Steven P. TAYLOR
84 Vice Provost of Student Enrollment ... Dr. Michael D. UDEN
121 Asst VP Academics/Student Success ... Dr. Elizabeth A. POLZIN
07 Asst Vice President Admissions ... Mr. Robert J. NOWAK
26 Asst VP Strategic Communications ... Ms. Lisa LILJEGREN
85 Asst VP International Affairs ... Vacant
42 Campus Pastor ... Rev. Steven N. SMITH
42 Campus Pastor ... Rev. Randall S. DUNCAN
88 Chair Faculty Senate ... Mr. Jordan P. BECK
49 Dean School Arts/Sciences ... Dr. Steven R. MONTREAL
50 Dean School of Business ... Dr. Matthew W. HURTIENNE
53 Dean School of Education ... Dr. James A. PINGEL
76 Dean School of Health Professions ... Dr. Linda M. SAMUEL
66 Dean School of Nursing ... Dr. Diane AMES
67 Dean School of Pharmacy ... Dr. Erik JORVIG
35 Dean of Students ... Dr. Steven W. GERNER
06 Registrar ... Mr. Erik W. HALLING
29 Director of Alumni Relations ... Mr. Gregory P. WITTO
41 Director of Athletics ... Dr. Rob M. BARNHILL
19 Director Campus Safety ... Mr. Michael STOLTE
38 Director of Counseling ... Mr. David T. ENTERS
36 Director of Career Engagement ... Mr. Tyler R. LANDERS
37 Director of Financial Aid ... Mr. Kevin P. SHERIDAN
15 Asst VP Human Resources ... Ms. Kimberly R. MASENTHIN
09 Exec Director Inst Effectiveness ... Dr. Tamara R. FERRY
24 Director Instructional Technology ... Mr. Sean B. YOUNG
08 Director of Library Services ... Mr. Christian R. HIMSEL
39 Director of Residence Life ... Ms. Beckie KRUSE
51 Exec Director Cont & Dist Educ ... Ms. Sarah A. PECOR
18 Superintendent Buildings & Grounds ... Mr. Stephen V. HIBBARD
40 Bookstore Manager ... Ms. Kia LOR

Edgewood College (F)

1000 Edgewood College Drive, Madison WI 53711-1997
County: Dane FICE Identification: 003848
Unit ID: 238661
Telephone: (608) 663-4861 Carnegie Class: DU-Mod
FAX Number: (608) 663-3291 Calendar System: Semester
URL: www.edgewood.edu
Established: 1927 Annual Undergrad Tuition & Fees: $31,700
Enrollment: 2,007 Coed
Affiliation or Control: Roman Catholic IRS Status: 501(c)3
Highest Offering: Doctorate
Accreditation: HLC, ACBSP, NURSE

01 President ... Dr. Andrew P. MANION
05 VP Academic Affairs/Academic Dean ... Dr. William MANGAN
15 VP Admin/Chief HR Officer ... Ms. Arhelia DALLA COSTA BEHM
84 VP Enrollment Mgmt ... Mr. Paul EGGERS
10 VP Financial Affairs/CFO ... Ms. Amanda BERG
111 VP Institutional Advancement ... Ms. Katie VESPERMAN
28 VP Mission/Values & Inclusion ... Dr. Milton JAVIER BRAVO
32 VP Student Dev/Dean of Students ... Mr. Matthew SULLIVAN
100 Chief of Staff/Chief Comm Officer ... Mr. Edward TAYLOR
04 Admin Assistant to President ... Ms. Julie IBINGER
37 AVP Enrollment Mgmt/Financial Aid ... Ms. Kari GRIBBLE
110 Assoc VP Institutional Advancement ... Mr. Mike SWEITZER-BECKMAN
07 Assoc VP New Student Enrollment ... Ms. Tess FERZOCO
49 Dean Liberal Arts/Educ/Sciences ... Dr. William MANGAN
66 Dean Nursing/Bus/Health Sciences ... Dr. Margaret NOREUIL
50 Assoc Dean Bus/Comms/Innovation ... Dr. Victoria PALMISANO
53 Assoc Dean Education ... Dr. Julie LUECKE
44 Director Advancement Services ... Ms. Erin BORIS
29 Director Alumni Relations ... Ms. Abby BJERKE
41 Director Athletics ... Mr. Al BRISACK
42 Director Campus Ministry ... Ms. Laurin DODGE
36 Director Career Development ... Ms. Sheila KRONBERG
78 Director Curriculum/Instruction ... Dr. Tom HOLUB
18 Director Facility Operations ... Ms. Susan VANDERSANDEN
23 Director Health Services ... Ms. Suzanne WALLACE
13 Director Information Technology ... Mr. Patrick GUMIENY
30 Director Leadership Giving ... Ms. Jen STEWART
08 Director Library ... Dr. Nathan DOWD
58 Director Master's of Art Therapy ... Dr. Jill MCNUTT
106 Director Online Learning ... Ms. Rebecca ZAMBRANO
38 Director Personal Counseling Svcs .. Dr. Megan COBB-SHEEHAN
19 Director Security/Risk Management ... Mr. Jack LESKOVAR
39 Director Student Life ... Ms. Claire MAND
104 Director Study Abroad/Intl Students ... Dr. Sara LIANG
07 Director Undergraduate Admissions ... Mr. Ryan O'DELL
21 Controller ... Ms. Jane WILHELM
06 Registrar ... Mr. David JOHNSON

George Williams College of Aurora University (G)

PO Box 210, Williams Bay WI 53191-0210
Telephone: (262) 245-5564 Identification: 770066
Accreditation: &HLC

† Branch campus of Aurora University, Aurora, IL

Herzing University (H)

5218 E Terrace Drive, Madison WI 53718-8340
County: Dane FICE Identification: 009621
Unit ID: 240392
Telephone: (608) 249-6611 Carnegie Class: Masters/L
FAX Number: (608) 249-8593 Calendar System: Semester
URL: www.herzing.edu
Established: 1965 Annual Undergrad Tuition & Fees: $14,200
Enrollment: 2,392 Coed
Affiliation or Control: Independent Non-Profit IRS Status: 501(c)3
Highest Offering: Master's
Accreditation: HLC, IACBE, NURSE

00 President ... Ms. Renee HERZING
01 Regional President Madison Campus ... Dr. Jeff HILL
10 CFO & Vice President of Finance ... Mr. Robert HERZOG
05 Academic Dean ... Dr. Steve MCEVOY
37 Educational Funding Manager ... Mr. Clayton GROTH
32 Dir of Student Services/Registrar ... Ms. Amy HERFEL
07 Director of Admissions ... Ms. Danielle OEST
36 Career Development Coach ... Ms. Chris SZOLYGA

Herzing University Brookfield Campus (I)

15895 W Bluemound Rd, Brookfield WI 53005
Telephone: (262) 649-1710 Identification: 770429
Accreditation: &HLC, NURSE, PTAA

Herzing University Kenosha Campus (J)

5800 7th Avenue, Kenosha WI 53140
Telephone: (262) 671-0675 Identification: 770430
Accreditation: &HLC, NURSE

Herzing University Online (K)

W140N8917 Lilly Road, Menomonee Falls WI 53051
Telephone: (866) 508-0748 Identification: 770431
Accreditation: &HLC, CAHIIM

Lac Courte Oreilles Ojibwe College (L)

13466 W Trepania Road, Hayward WI 54843-2181
County: Sawyer FICE Identification: 025322
Unit ID: 260372
Telephone: (715) 634-4790 Carnegie Class: Tribal
FAX Number: (715) 634-5049 Calendar System: Semester
URL: www.lco.edu
Established: 1982 Annual Undergrad Tuition & Fees: $4,590
Enrollment: 278 Coed
Affiliation or Control: Tribal Control IRS Status: 501(c)3
Highest Offering: Master's
Accreditation: HLC

01 President ... Dr. Russell SWAGGER
10 Chief Financial Officer ... Ms. Lydia DENASHA
05 Provost ... Ms. Lisa MUNIVE

32 Dean of Students & Cmty Engagement ....Ms. Amber MARLOW
11 Chief Operating Officer ....Mr. Mark MONTANO
35 Dean of Continuous Improvement ....Dr. Odawa WHITE
111 Dir Inst Advancement/ Development ....Ms. Jessica WAGNER-SCHULTZ
37 Director of Financial Aid ....Ms. Kimberly PAULSON
13 Information Technology Systems Admn ....Mr. Tristan STEVENS
15 Director of Human Resources ....Ms. Tamara THIMM
07 Recruitment/Admissions ....Ms. Jaclynn SULLEY
08 Chief Library Officer ....Ms. Caryl PFAFF
100 Chief of Staff ....Ms. Karen BREIT
41 Athletic Director ....Mr. Tristan STEVENS
06 Dean of Records/Registrar ....Ms. Stephanie ST. GERMAINE

Lakeland University (A)

W3718 South Dr, Plymouth WI 53073
County: Sheboygan FICE Identification: 003854
Unit ID: 238980
Telephone: (920) 565-1000 Carnegie Class: Masters/L
FAX Number: (920) 565-1060 Calendar System: Semester
URL: www.lakeland.edu
Established: 1862 Annual Undergrad Tuition & Fees: $30,777
Enrollment: 2,753 Coed
Affiliation or Control: United Church Of Christ IRS Status: 501(c)3
Highest Offering: Master's
Accreditation: HLC, NURSE

01 President ....Dr. Beth M. BORGEN
04 Assistant to the President ....Mr. Stuart J. SCHMIDT
125 Former President/President Emeritus ....Dr. David R. BLACK
101 Liaison to the Board of Trustees ....Mr. Stuart J. SCHMIDT
00 Board Chairperson ....Mr. Jeffrey SPENCE
05 Vice President of Academic Affairs ....Dr. Joshua P. KUTNEY
12 Vice President Lakeland U Japan ....Dr. Brian T. FRINK
10 Vice President Finance & Operation ....Ms. Amy M. WIRTZ
32 Vice President Campus Life ....Mr. David R. SIMON
15 Vice President Human Resources ....Dr. James JONES
41 Director of Athletics ....Dr. April A. ARVAN
108 Chief Innovation Officer ....Dr. Michael P. DUNLAP
84 Vice President Enrollment Mgmt ....Mr. Sam G. POULLETTE
20 Dean Academic Support Services ....Dr. Margaret L. ALBRINCK
55 Dean William R. Kellett School .... Dr. Rachel J. WARE-CARLTON
79 Dean Humanities & Fine Arts ....Rev. Karl A. KUHN
50 Dean Schilcutt School ....Dr. Paul PICKHARDT
26 Director of External Relations ....Mr. David D. GALLIANETTI
27 Director of Marketing ....Mr. Michael P. LACKOVIC
111 Assoc Vice President Advancement ....Mr. Tylor S. LOEST
78 Assoc Vice President Co-Op/Career .Ms. Jessica N. LAMBRECHT
21 Controller ....Ms. Kathy NEITZEL
37 Sr Dir of Financial Aid & Ed Fund ....Ms. Patty L. TAYLOR
09 Director Institutional Research ....Dr. Paul M. WHITE
06 Registrar ....Ms. Amanda J. HRUSKA
39 Director Residence Life ....Mr. Mark T. EDMOND
38 Director Health & Counseling ....Ms. Alex LIOSATOS
42 Chaplain/Ethicist in Residence ....Rev. Julie A. MAVITY-MADDALENA
08 Director Library Services ....Ms. Ann PENKE
29 Director Alumni Rels/Annual Giving ....Ms. Andrea M. SCHMITZ
102 Dir Corporation & Foundation Rels ....Vacant
114 Financial Analyst ....Mr. Chris J. GROTEGUT
113 Bursar ....Ms. Jalesa C. FREESE
19 Director Campus Security ....Mr. Christopher J. RINGEL
13 Director Technology Services ....Mr. Charles M. GRUBISIC
106 Director Online Learning ....Ms. Florence E. SIEBERT
120 Director Instructional Design ....Mr. Andrew R. DAMP
123 Sr Director Graduate Recruitment ....Ms. Jane A. BOUCHE
04 Sr Advisor International Affairs ....Dr. Stephen SIM

Lawrence University (B)

711 E. Boldt Way, Appleton WI 54911
County: Outagamie FICE Identification: 003856
Unit ID: 239017
Telephone: (920) 832-7000 Carnegie Class: Bac-A&S
FAX Number: (920) 832-6978 Calendar System: Other
URL: www.lawrence.edu
Established: 1847 Annual Undergrad Tuition & Fees: $50,958
Enrollment: 1,430 Coed
Affiliation or Control: Independent Non-Profit IRS Status: 501(c)3
Highest Offering: Baccalaureate
Accreditation: HLC, MUS

01 President ....Ms. Laurie CARTER
04 Executive Asst to the President ....Ms. Alice BOECKERS
05 Provost and Dean of the Faculty ....Ms. Catherine KODAT
10 VP Finance & Administration ....Ms. Mary Alma NOONAN
30 VP Development/Alumni Rels ....Mr. Calvin D. HUSMANN
32 VP for Student Life ....Mr. Christopher D. CARD
29 VP Alumni/Constituency Engagement ....Mr. Mark D. BRESEMAN
28 VP for Diversity & Inclusion ....Vacant
26 Assoc Vice Pres Communications ....Ms. Megan J. SCOTT
44 Campaign Dir/Principal Gifts Ofcr ....Mr. Lucas A. BROWN
110 Assoc Vice Pres Development ....Ms. Stacy J. MARA
21 Controller ....Ms. Amy PRICE
64 Dean Conservatory of Music ....Mr. Brian G. PERTL
36 Dean of Career Services ....Mr. Mike K. O'CONNOR
121 Dean of Academic Success ....Ms. Monita M. GRAY
20 Associate Dean of the Faculty ....Dr. Peter A. BLITSTEIN
28 Asst Dean Students Multicul Affs ....Ms. Brittany M. BELL
09 Director of Research Administration ....Ms. Kristin L. MCKINLEY
84 Vice Pres Enrollment/ Communications ....Mr. Kenneth L. ANSELMENT

37 Director of Financial Aid ....Mr. Ryan L. GEBLER
06 Registrar ....Ms. Angi LONG
08 Librarian ....Mr. Peter J. GILBERT
41 Athletic Director ....Ms. Kim TATRO
13 Director Information Tech Svcs ....Mr. Steven M. ARMSTRONG
15 Assoc Director of Human Resources ....Ms. Tina L. HARRIG
38 Assoc Dean Stdnts Health/Wellness ....Mr. Rich L. JAZDZEWSKI

Maranatha Baptist University (C)

745 West Main Street, Watertown WI 53094-7600
County: Jefferson FICE Identification: 023172
Unit ID: 239071
Telephone: (920) 261-9300 Carnegie Class: Masters/S
FAX Number: (920) 261-9109 Calendar System: Semester
URL: www.mbu.edu
Established: 1968 Annual Undergrad Tuition & Fees: $17,650
Enrollment: 916 Coed
Affiliation or Control: Independent Non-Profit IRS Status: 501(c)3
Highest Offering: Doctorate
Accreditation: HLC, NURSE

00 Chief Executive Officer ....Dr. Matthew DAVIS
01 President ....Dr. Martin MARRIOTT
05 Vice President for Academic Affairs ....Dr. William LICHT
111 Vice President for Inst Advancement ....Vacant
10 Vice President for Business Affairs ....Mr. Donald DONOVAN
32 Dean of Students ....Dr. Andrew GOODWILL
06 Registrar ....Mr. Lance SAXON
07 Director of Admissions ....Mr. Peter WRIGHT
30 Director of Development ....Vacant
09 Director of Institutional Research ....Mr. Jonathan COLEMAN
15 Director Personnel Services ....Mr. Eric HASSENPLUG
26 Chief Public Relations Officer ....Mr. Jonathan SHEELEY
41 Athletic Director ....Mr. Robert THOMPSON
08 Librarian ....Miss Jennifer DUNLOP
35 Director Student Affairs ....Mr. Luke DEWALD
29 Director Alumni Relations ....Mr. Peter WRIGHT
37 Director Student Financial Aid ....Mr. Matthew UPLINGER
13 Chief Info Technology Officer ....Mr. Scott RILEY
19 Director Security/Safety ....Mr. Robert FULLER
106 Dir Online Education/E-learning ....Mrs. Dana DAVIS
18 Chief Facilities/Physical Plant ....Mr. Jared CHESLEY
50 Dean School of Business ....Dr. Tracy FOSTER
53 Dean School of Education ....Dr. Thomas GRAHAM, JR.

Marian University (D)

45 S National Avenue, Fond Du Lac WI 54935-4699
County: Fond Du Lac FICE Identification: 003861
Unit ID: 239080
Telephone: (920) 923-7600 Carnegie Class: Masters/M
FAX Number: (920) 923-7154 Calendar System: Semester
URL: www.marianuniversity.edu
Established: 1936 Annual Undergrad Tuition & Fees: $28,560
Enrollment: 1,593 Coed
Affiliation or Control: Roman Catholic IRS Status: 501(c)3
Highest Offering: Doctorate
Accreditation: HLC, NURSE, RAD, SW

01 President ....Dr. Michelle E. MAJEWSKI
05 VP Academic Affairs ....Dr. Ken R. MULLIKEN
10 VP Finance & Administration ....Dr. Daisy H. HALVORSON
32 VP Student Life/Diversity ....Mr. Jason BARTELT
111 Interim SVP Advancement/Alumni Rels ....Ms. Kathleen CANDEE
26 Senior VP for University Relations ....Dr. George E. KOONCE, JR.
101 Secretary of the Corporation ....Ms. Carey C. GARDIN
04 Executive Assistant to President ....Ms. Sharon P. FISCHER
21 Controller ....Mr. Michael R. MOOS
107 Dean College of the Professions ....Vacant
49 Dean College Arts/Sciences/Letters ....Vacant
18 Operations Manager/Facilities ....Mr. Todd BUSS
90 Assoc VP Academic Administration ....Ms. Lynda K. SCHULTZ
35 Assistant Dean of Students ....Ms. Pamela C. WARREN
37 Director of Financial Aid ....Ms. Wendy A. HILVO
42 Director of Campus Ministry ....Sr. Edie A. CREWS, CSA
27 Asst VP Marketing & Communication ....Ms. Lisa L. KIDD
84 Asst VP & Dean of Enrollment ....Ms. Shannon S. LALUZERNE
15 Interim Director of Human Resources ....Ms. Amanda J. BAKER
41 Interim Director of Athletics ....Mr. Tony D. DRAVES
23 Director of Health Services ....Ms. Jodi S. SCHRAUTH
36 Director of Career Services ....Ms. Teri A. DURKIN
40 Director of Spirit Store ....Mr. Charles W. RUFFING
38 Director of Counseling ....Ms. Robyn A. WILLIAMS
92 Director Honors Program ....Dr. Michael T. GARVEY
39 Director of Residence Life ....Ms. Severa KRUEGER
104 Director of Study Abroad ....Dr. Matthew P. SZROMBA
19 Lead Security Supervisor ....Mr. Christopher M. GURECKI
121 Dean of Student Success ....Ms. Jennifer K. FARVOUR
89 Director of First Year Studies ....Ms. Juliet V. LOCKWOOD
06 Interim Registrar ....Ms. Bianca Y. BIRSCHBACH

Marquette University (E)

PO Box 1881, Milwaukee WI 53201-1881
County: Milwaukee FICE Identification: 003863
Unit ID: 239105
Telephone: (414) 288-7700 Carnegie Class: DU-Higher
FAX Number: (414) 288-3300 Calendar System: Semester
URL: www.marquette.edu
Established: 1881 Annual Undergrad Tuition & Fees: $45,666
Enrollment: 11,550 Coed
Affiliation or Control: Roman Catholic IRS Status: 501(c)3
Highest Offering: Doctorate
Accreditation: HLC, ANEST, ARCPA, CAATE, CACREP, CLPSY, COPSY, DENT, EXSC, LAW, MIDWF, MLS, NURSE, PTA, SP, THEA

01 President ....Dr. Michael R. LOVELL
05 Provost/EVP Academic Affairs ....Dr. Kimo AH YUN
10 Sr Vice President/COO ....Mr. Joel POGODZINSKI
15 Vice President Human Resources ....Ms. Claudia PAETSCH
32 Vice President Student Affairs ....Dr. Xavier A. COLE
09 Vice Pres Research and Innovation ....Dr. Jeanne M. HOSSENLOPP
42 Vice Pres Mission & Ministry ....Rev. James VOISS, S.J.
20 Senior Vice Prov Faculty Affairs ....Dr. Gary MEYER
26 VP Univ Relations/Gen Counsel ....Mr. Paul JONES
41 Vice Pres and Director of Athletics ....Mr. Bill SCHOLL
111 Vice Pres University Advancement ....Mr. Tim MCMAHON
28 Vice Pres Inclusive Excellence ....Dr. Christine NAVIA
21 Vice President Finance ....Mr. Ian GONZALEZ
20 VProv Acad Affairs/Student Success ....Dr. John J. SU
84 Vice Pres Enrollment Management ....Dr. John BAWOROWSKY
06 University Registrar ....Mr. Seth ZLOTOCHA
07 Dean of Undergrad Admissions ....Mr. Brian TROYER
60 Dean of Communication ....Dr. Sarah FELDNER
76 Dean of Health Sciences ....Dr. William CULLINAN
61 Dean of the Law School ....Mr. Joseph D. KEARNEY
52 Dean of Dentistry ....Dr. William K. LOBB
49 Dean Arts & Sciences/Education ....Dr. Heidi BOSTIC
54 Opus Dean of Engineering ....Dr. Kristina ROPELLA
50 Acting Dean of Business Admin ....Mr. Tim HANLEY
08 Dean of Libraries ....Dr. Tara BAILLARGEON
101 Sr Advisor to Pres/Corp Secretary ....Mr. Steven W. FRIEDER
66 Acting Dean of Nursing ....Dr. Jill GUTTORMSON
58 VProv Grad/Prof Stds/Dn of Grad Sch ....Dr. Douglas WOODS
13 Chief Information Officer ....Ms. Laurie PANELLA
114 Asst Provost Budget & Div Ops ....Ms. Sallly DOYLE
35 Dean of Students ....Dr. Stephanie QUADE
30 Senior Philanthropic Advisor ....Mr. Timothy RIPPINGER
102 Asst VP Corp & Foundation Relations ....Ms. Jaclyn NESS
21 Director Finance ....Ms. Tari BLAZEI
45 VP Planning/Facilities Mgmt ....Ms. Lora STRIGENS
86 Assoc VP Public Affairs ....Ms. Rana ALTENBURG
25 Exec Dir Research & Sponsored Prog ....Ms. Katherine DURBEN
23 Exec Dir University Medical Clinic ....Mrs. Keli WOLLMER
88 Chief of Staff for Office of SVP ....Ms. Jean DOLE
88 Asst Provost/Chief of Staff ....Ms. Cindy PETRITES
36 Dir Career Services Center ....Ms. Courtney HANSON
38 Director Counseling Center ....Ms. Brenda LENZ
18 Asst Dir Facilities Services ....Mr. Christopher BARTOLONE
37 Assoc VProv Fin Aid/Enrollment Svcs ....Ms. Susan M. TEERINK
29 Sr Engagement Director ....Mr. Daniel DEWEERDT
19 Chief of Police ....Ms. Edith HUDSON
96 Director of Purchasing ....Ms. Jenny ALEXANDER
04 Executive Asst to President ....Mrs. Stacy ROMANT
39 Director Residence Life ....Ms. Mary JANZ
44 Director Annual Giving ....Mrs. Angela BARTOSIK
108 Assessment Director ....Dr. Nick CURTIS

Medical College of Wisconsin (F)

PO Box 26509, Milwaukee WI 53226-0509
County: Milwaukee FICE Identification: 024535
Unit ID: 239169
Telephone: (414) 955-8296 Carnegie Class: Spec-4-yr-Eng
FAX Number: (414) 955-6560 Calendar System: Other
URL: www.mcw.edu
Established: 1893 Annual Graduate Tuition & Fees: N/A
Enrollment: 1,506 Coed
Affiliation or Control: Independent Non-Profit IRS Status: 501(c)3
Highest Offering: Doctorate; No Undergraduates
Accreditation: HLC, AA, CAMPEP, IPSY, MED, PDPSY, PH, PHAR

01 President & CEO ....Dr. John R. RAYMOND, SR.
05 Provost/Exec VP/Dean ....Dr. Joseph E. KERSCHNER
04 Executive Asst to President ....Vacant
88 Sr VP Strategic Acad Partnerships ....Dr. Cheryl A. MAURANA
10 Exec VP/COO Finance ....Mr. Christopher P. KOPS
81 Dean Grad Sch Biomedical Science ....Dr. Ravi P. MISRA
30 Vice Pres of Development ....Mr. Mitchell BECKMAN
15 VP & Chief People Officer ....Ms. Adrienne MITCHELL
86 VP Government & Community Relations ....Ms. Kathryn A. KUHN
117 VP Corporate Compliance/Risk Mgmt ....Mr. Carlos BROWN
26 SVP Univ Engagement/Strategic Plan ....Ms. Mara LORD
13 VP Information Services/CIO ....Mr. David C. HOTCHKISS
27 Assoc VP Communications ....Ms. Mary REINKE
20 Sr Assoc Dean Med Education ....Dr. Jose FRANCO
20 Associate Provost Faculty Affairs ....Dr. Christina RUNGE
110 Asst VP Engagement ....Mr. James PECK
28 VP Inclusion & Diversity ....Dr. C. Greer JORDAN
22 Assoc Dean Student Div & Inclusion ....Dr. Malika SIKER
58 Sr Assoc Dean Graduate Med Educ ....Dr. Kenneth B. SIMONS
88 Assoc Dean Neuroscience Rsrch Ctr ....Dr. Cecilia J. HILLARD
20 Associate Dean Curriculum ....Dr. Martin MUNTZ
114 Assoc Director Budget ....Ms. Lisa SCHEELE
14 Director Application Development ....Ms. Rebecca L. MORRISON
08 Director Medical Libraries ....Ms. Ellen N. SAYED
07 Dir Recruitment/Admissions ....Ms. Alexis MEYER
06 Registrar ....Vacant
18 VP Facilities & Operations ....Mr. Jeffrey BORNEMANN
37 Director Student Financial Services ....Ms. Kristin J. STUHR-MOOTZ
25 Director Grants & Contracts ....Ms. April HAVERTY
29 Exec Director Alumni Relations ....Ms. Angela NELSON
96 Dir Purchasing & Payables ....Ms. Joan AGUADO WARE
40 Manager of Bookstore ....Ms. Cathy GRANFIELD
19 Director Public Safety ....Mr. David C. FELLER

43 Sr VP General Counsel ... Mr. John NEWSOME
21 Chief Financial Officer ... Ms. Shelisa DALTON
32 Chief Student Affairs/Life Officer ... Dr. Jennifer KUSCH
67 Dean School of Pharmacy ... Dr. George MACKINNON
88 Managed Care Contract Mgr ... Mr. Jeffrey WOJNOWSKI
46 Assoc Provost for Research ... Dr. Ann NATTINGER
88 Assoc VP Financial Plng & Analysis ... Mr. Kevin EIDE
101 Liaison to Board of Trustees ... Ms. Kristin NIEMIEC
44 Director Annual Giving ... Ms. Elsa KNYSAK
09 Director of Institutional Research ... Dr. Maureen E. PYLMAN
100 Chief of Staff ... Ms. Jenny BULTMAN

Midwest College of Oriental Medicine (A)

6232 Bankers Road, Racine WI 53403-9747
County: Racine   FICE Identification: 030612
Unit ID: 383020
Telephone: (800) 593-2320   Carnegie Class: Spec-4-yr-Other Health
FAX Number: (262) 554-7475   Calendar System: Quarter
URL: www.acupuncture.edu
Established: 1979   Annual Undergrad Tuition & Fees: N/A
Enrollment: 62   Coed
Affiliation or Control: Proprietary   IRS Status: Proprietary
Highest Offering: Master's; No Lower Division
Accreditation: **ACUP**

01 President ... Dr. William J. DUNBAR
05 Director of Academics ... Dr. Robert CHELNICK
12 Evanston Campus Director ... Dr. Kristine L. LA POINT
37 Director of Financial Aid ... Mr. Douglas R. PITTMAN
07 Admissions Coord/Transfer Credit ... Ms. Stephanie PITTMAN
06 Records Officer/Registrar ... Ms. Amy L. BENISH
08 Librarian ... Mr. John BALLARINI
32 Dean of Students ... Ms. Olga GAJDOSIK
09 Research Director ... Vacant
108 Clinic Tracking/Inst Evaluation ... Ms. Deirdre M. DUNBAR
91 Information Systems ... Mr. William H. LEHMAN
26 Marketing/Student Affairs ... Mr. Chris A. KRAJNIAK
88 Office Manager ... Vacant

Milwaukee Career College (B)

3077 North Maryfair Road, Suite 300,
Milwaukee WI 53222
County: Milwaukee   FICE Identification: 041174
Unit ID: 449861
Telephone: (800) 754-1009   Carnegie Class: Assoc/HVT-Mix Trad/Non
FAX Number: (414) 727-9557   Calendar System: Other
URL: www.mkecc.edu
Established: 2002   Annual Undergrad Tuition & Fees: N/A
Enrollment: 231   Coed
Affiliation or Control: Proprietary   IRS Status: Proprietary
Highest Offering: Associate Degree
Accreditation: **ABHES**, SURTEC

01 President ... Jack TAKAHASHI

Milwaukee Institute of Art & Design (C)

273 E Erie Street, Milwaukee WI 53202-6003
County: Milwaukee   FICE Identification: 020771
Unit ID: 239309
Telephone: (414) 847-3200   Carnegie Class: Spec-4-yr-Arts
FAX Number: (414) 291-8077   Calendar System: Semester
URL: www.miad.edu
Established: 1974   Annual Undergrad Tuition & Fees: $39,560
Enrollment: 925   Coed
Affiliation or Control: Independent Non-Profit   IRS Status: 501(c)3
Highest Offering: Baccalaureate
Accreditation: **HLC**, ART

01 President ... Mr. Jeff MORIN
04 Executive Assistant to President ... Ms. Mary EGGERT
05 VP of Academic Affairs ... Mr. Steven HANSEN
10 VP for Financial Affairs ... Ms. Brenda JONES
111 VP for Institutional Advancement ... Ms. Tracy MILKOWSKI
84 VP for Enrollment Management ... Mr. Mark FETHERSTON
06 Registrar ... Ms. Jean WEIMER
32 Dean of Students ... Ms. Lindy STEIN
35 Assoc Dean of Students ... Ms. Jennifer CRANDALL
39 Director of Residential Living ... Ms. Marianne DI ULIO
37 Executive Director of Financial Aid ... Ms. Kristina ALVAREZ
07 Director of Admissions ... Ms. Molly NOYES
88 Asst Dir of Transfer Admissions ... Mr. Matthew SOTHAN
09 Institutional Research Analyst ... Mr. Bryan VOSS
08 Director of Library Services ... Ms. Nancy SIKER
36 Exec Dir of Advising & Career Svcs ... Mr. Duane P. SEIDENSTICKER
121 Director of Advising ... Ms. Monica LLOYD
51 Dir Pre-College & Continuing Educ ... Mr. Corbett TOOMSEN
19 Director Security/Safety ... Mr. Keith A. KOTOWICZ
15 Director of Human Resources ... Mr. Dustin HOOT
18 Director of Facilities & Logistics ... Ms. Marie COUTURE
18 Director of Building & Grounds ... Mr. Michael A. GOETZ
13 Director of Technology ... Mr. Matt OGDEN
20 Dir of Academic Adminstration ... Ms. Jennifer KRANTZ
20 Dir of Academic Affairs ... Ms. Marie LARSON
88 Director of Emerging Technology ... Mr. Ben DEMBROSKI
88 Exec Director of Innovation Center ... Mr. Drew MAXWELL
21 Director of Accounting ... Ms. Kelly BERES
26 Director of Marketing ... Ms. Stacey STEINBERG
28 Director of Equity & Inclusion ... Mr. Richard ANDERSON-MARTINEZ
29 Dir Alumni Relations/Annual Giving ... Mr. Kyle HERNANDEZ
25 Grants Manager ... Ms. Maren KNUTSEN
44 Devel Database & Donor Svcs Mgr ... Ms. Anne KIRSCHMANN

Milwaukee School of Engineering (D)

1025 N Broadway, Milwaukee WI 53202-3109
County: Milwaukee   FICE Identification: 003868
Unit ID: 239318
Telephone: (414) 277-7300   Carnegie Class: Masters/M
FAX Number: (414) 277-7454   Calendar System: Quarter
URL: www.msoe.edu
Established: 1903   Annual Undergrad Tuition & Fees: $43,575
Enrollment: 2,673   Coed
Affiliation or Control: Independent Non-Profit   IRS Status: 501(c)3
Highest Offering: Master's
Accreditation: **HLC**, NURSE, PERF

01 President ... Dr. John WALZ
05 Executive Vice President Academics ... Dr. Eric BAUMGARTNER
10 Vice President of Finance and CFO ... Ms. Dawn THIBEDEAU
111 VP of University Advancement ... Mr. Jeff SNOW
18 VP of Campus Infrastructure ... Dr. Steve WILLIAMS
32 VP of Student Services/Enroll Mgmt ... Dr. Timothy VALLEY
88 Dean of Applied Research ... Mr. Sheku KAMARA
48 Chair Architectural Engr Dept ... Dr. Christopher RAEBEL
54 Chair Electrical Engr/CPU Sci Dept ... Dr. Sheila ROSS
79 Chair Humanities Department ... Dr. Alicia DOMACK
81 Chair Physics/Chemistry/Mathematics ... Dr. Matey KALTCHEV
66 Chair Nursing Department ... Dr. Carol SABEL
06 Registrar ... Ms. Mary F. NIELSEN
13 Senior Director of IT ... Mr. Rick THOMAS
26 VP Marketing & Community Engagement ... Mr. Sebastian THACHENKARY
27 Sr Dir Comm/Media Relations ... Ms. JoEllen BURDUE
15 Director of Human Resources ... Ms. Rebecca PLOECKELMAN
30 Senior Director of Development ... Mr. Greg CASEY
41 Director Athletics ... Mr. Brian MILLER
08 Director of Library & Info Services ... Mr. Gary S. SHIMEK
29 Director Alumni Affairs ... Ms. Cathy VAREBROOK
07 Dean of Admissions ... Mr. Paul BORENS
36 Director of Career Services ... Ms. Julie WAY
40 Bookstore Manager ... Mr. David P. ABRAHAMSON
04 Executive Admin to the President ... Ms. Kellyann M. REUTER
20 Assoc VP Academic Success ... Dr. Jill MEYER
19 Director of Public Safety ... Mr. Billy FYFE
37 Director of Financial Aid ... Ms. Stephanie MEALY
38 Director Counseling Services ... Ms. Colleen CHRISTANSEN
39 Director Residence Life ... Ms. Elizabeth ALBRECHT
44 Director Annual Giving ... Ms. Jessica TEDAMRONGWANISH

Mount Mary University (E)

2900 N Menomonee River Parkway,
Milwaukee WI 53222-4597
County: Milwaukee   FICE Identification: 003869
Unit ID: 239390
Telephone: (414) 930-3000   Carnegie Class: Masters/L
FAX Number: (414) 930-3712   Calendar System: Semester
URL: www.mtmary.edu
Established: 1913   Annual Undergrad Tuition & Fees: $32,790
Enrollment: 1,200   Female
Affiliation or Control: Roman Catholic   IRS Status: 501(c)3
Highest Offering: Doctorate
Accreditation: **HLC**, CACREP, CIDA, DIET, DIETC, DIETI, NURSE, OT, SW

01 President ... Dr. Isabelle CHERNEY
10 VP Finance & Admin Services ... Mr. Robert O'KEEFE
05 VP Academic Affairs ... Dr. Karen FRIEDLEN
84 Vice Pres Enrollment Services ... Mr. David WEGENER
30 Vice Pres Development ... Ms. Pamela OWENS
88 Vice President Mission/Identity ... Vacant
32 Vice Pres Student Affairs ... Ms. Keri ALIOTO
28 VP Diversity/Equity/Inclusion ... Vacant
50 Dean School Business/Arts & Design ... Mr. Robert SCHWARTZ
81 Dean School Nat & Health Sci/Educ ... Dr. Cheryl BAILEY
79 Dean Sch Hum/Social Sci/Interdisc ... Dr. Wendy WEAVER
121 Dean Student Success ... Ms. Beth FELCH
58 Dean of Graduate Education ... Vacant
21 Sr Dir of Business Ofc/Controller ... Ms. Nicole BIDDLE
06 Registrar ... Ms. Rachel FISCHER
110 Senior Development Officer ... Ms. Lisa BREITSPRECKER
26 Dir of Communications ... Ms. Kathy VAN ZEELAND
29 Director of Alumnae Relations ... Vacant
123 Director of Graduate Admission ... Mr. Kirk HELLER DE MESSER
07 Director of Undergraduate Admission ... Ms. Kathryn SCHUMACHER
09 Director of Inst Research ... Ms. Leah ADAMS-CURTIS
08 Director of Library ... Mr. Daniel VINSON
13 Senior Director of IT ... Vacant
37 Director Financial Aid ... Ms. Angela SARNI
39 Dir Student Engagement/Resid Living ... Ms. Hannah CRONIN
36 Dir of Advising/Career Development ... Vacant
104 Director of International Studies ... Ms. Nan METZGER
15 Senior Director of Human Resources ... Ms. Tonya VLASIK
41 Athletic Director ... Ms. Natalie BALLETO
42 Director of Campus Ministry ... Ms. Theresa UTSCHIG
18 Director of Buildings & Grounds ... Ms. Tara BEAUCHINE
19 Director of Public Safety ... Mr. Dan BRAUER
40 Mgr Barnes & Noble Bookstore ... Mr. Timothy STERNKE
04 Executive Assistant to President ... Ms. Kim NEWMAN
102 Exec Dir Corp Rels/Foundation/WLI ... Ms. Alexandra HOSLET

Nashotah House (F)

2777 Mission Road, Nashotah WI 53058-9793
County: Waukesha   FICE Identification: 003874
Unit ID: 239424
Telephone: (262) 646-6500   Carnegie Class: Spec-4-yr-Faith
FAX Number: (262) 646-6504   Calendar System: Semester
URL: www.nashotah.edu
Established: 1842   Annual Graduate Tuition & Fees: N/A
Enrollment: 106   Coed
Affiliation or Control: Protestant Episcopal   IRS Status: 501(c)3
Highest Offering: Doctorate; No Undergraduates
Accreditation: **THEOL**

01 President/Dean ... Dr. Garwood P. ANDERSON
11 Senior Director of Operations ... Rev. Jason TERHUNE
05 Provost ... Dr. Garwood P. ANDERSON
111 Exec VP Institutional Advancement ... Mr. Labin L. DUKE
13 Director Information Systems ... Mr. Matt BILLS
30 Senior Development Officer ... Mr. Jim WATKINS
09 Asst Dean Institutional Research ... Rev. Esther KRAMER
32 Senior Director of Students ... Rev. Jason TERHUNE
101 Secretary of the Board of Trustees ... Rev. R. Brien KOEHLER
06 Registrar ... Ms. Carolee PUCHTER
07 Director of Admissions ... Ms. Kristen OLVER
08 Dir Francis Donaldson Library ... Dr. David G. SHERWOOD
26 Director Marketing/Communications ... Ms. Lisa SWAN
42 Director of Church Relations ... Ms. Carolyn BARTKUS
18 Director B&G/Maintenance ... Mr. Ricco MEDINA

Northland College (G)

1411 Ellis Avenue, Ashland WI 54806-3999
County: Ashland   FICE Identification: 003875
Unit ID: 239512
Telephone: (715) 682-1699   Carnegie Class: Bac-Diverse
FAX Number: (715) 682-1308   Calendar System: Other
URL: www.northland.edu
Established: 1892   Annual Undergrad Tuition & Fees: $38,596
Enrollment: 570   Coed
Affiliation or Control: United Church Of Christ   IRS Status: 501(c)3
Highest Offering: Baccalaureate
Accreditation: **HLC**

01 President ... Dr. Karl SOLIBAKKE
100 Chief of Staff ... Ms. Dawn RIVARD
11 Chief Operating Officer ... Vacant
20 Dean of Academic Affairs ... Dr. Alan BREW
32 Dean of Students ... Dr. Joseph COOPER
07 Director of Admissions ... Mr. Alex PATTERSON
111 Director of Advancement ... Vacant
26 Sr Director Marketing/Comm ... Ms. Angela HOFFMAN-COOPER
29 Director of Alumni Relations ... Ms. Jackie MOORE
41 Director Intercollegiate Athletics ... Mr. Seamus GREGORY
13 Exec Director Information Svcs Tech ... Mr. Todd PYDO
15 Exec Director Human Resources ... Ms. Sherri VENERO
08 Library Director ... Ms. Julia WAGGONER
39 Director of Residential Life ... Ms. DeeDee DUSEK
25 Director of Grants/Sponsored Awards ... Ms. Lisa WILLIAMSON
37 Director of Financial Aid ... Ms. Kelly DUNN
38 Campus Counselor ... Vacant
23 Health Services Manager ... Ms. Jennifer NEWAGO
21 Chief Business Officer ... Ms. Sherri VENERO
28 Diversity and Inclusion Coordinator ... Vacant
06 Registrar ... Ms. Michelle BITZER
18 Director of Operations ... Mr. Paul WEBB
19 Campus Safety Director ... Mr. Dawayne LAMPSON
04 Admin Assistant to the President ... Ms. Molly B. LARSON

Ottawa University Brookfield, WI (H)

245 South Executive Drive, Ste 340, Brookfield WI 53005
Telephone: (262) 879-0200   Identification: 666084
Accreditation: **&HLC**

† Regional accreditation is carried under the parent institution in Ottawa, KS.

Rasmussen University - Green Bay (I)

904 South Taylor Street, Building 1, Green Bay WI 54303
Telephone: (920) 593-8400   Identification: 667063
Accreditation: **&HLC**, ADNUR, MAAB

† Regional accreditation is carried under the parent institution in Saint Cloud, MN. The tuition figure is an average, actual tuition may vary.

Ripon College (J)

300 West Seward Street, PO Box 248,
Ripon WI 54971-0248
County: Fond du Lac   FICE Identification: 003884
Unit ID: 239628
Telephone: (920) 748-8115   Carnegie Class: Bac-A&S
FAX Number: (920) 748-7243   Calendar System: Semester
URL: www.ripon.edu
Established: 1851   Annual Undergrad Tuition & Fees: $47,123
Enrollment: 816   Coed
Affiliation or Control: Independent Non-Profit   IRS Status: 501(c)3

Highest Offering: Baccalaureate
Accreditation: HLC

01 President Zachariah P. MESSITTE
05 Vice Pres/Dean of Faculty John E. SISKO
111 VP for Advancement Shawn F. KARSTEN
10 Vice President for Finance Andrea N. YOUNG
32 Vice President/Dean of Students Christophor M. OGLE
84 Vice President for Enrollment Jennifer L. MACHACEK
06 Assoc Dean of Faculty/Registrar Michele A. WITTLER
36 Dir of Career/Prof Development Mary HATLEN
21 Associate VP for Finance Lori A. SCHULZE
08 Access Services Librarian Karlyn M. SCHUMACHER
35 Dir Student Activities/Orientation Sara VANSTEENBERGEN
121 Director Student Support Svcs Daniel J. KRHIN
39 Director of Residence Life Mark B. NICKLAUS
27 Dir of Creative & Social Media Richard T. DAMM
13 Sr Dir of Information Technology Brian DISTERHAFT
18 Director Physical Plant Brian SKAMRA
41 Director of Athletics Ryan KANE
29 Dir Constituent Engagement Amy L. GERRETSEN
15 Director of Human Resource Paula STETTBACHER
38 Director of Counseling Services Cynthia S. VIERTEL
37 Director Financial Aid Linda KINZIGER
28 Dir of Multicultural Affairs Maria MENDOZA-BAUTISTA
44 Director Annual Giving Kelly A. NIELSEN
90 Director Academic Computing Andrew P. DESCH
91 Director Administrative Computing Gary S. RODMAN
100 Chief of Staff Kara K. JANKOWSKI

Sacred Heart Seminary and School of Theology (A)

7335 S Highway 100, P.O. Box 429,
Hales Corners WI 53130-0429
County: Milwaukee FICE Identification: 020780
Unit ID: 239637
Telephone: (414) 425-8300 Carnegie Class: Spec-4-yr-Faith
FAX Number: (414) 529-6999 Calendar System: Semester
URL: www.shsst.edu
Established: 1933 Annual Graduate Tuition & Fees: N/A
Enrollment: 98 Coed
Affiliation or Control: Roman Catholic IRS Status: 501(c)3
Highest Offering: Master's; No Undergraduates
Accreditation: HLC, THEOL

01 President-Rector V. Rev. Raúl L. GOMEZ-RUIZ, SDS
10 VP Finance & Administration Mr. Tyler GALSTAD
05 VP Intellectual Formation/CAO Dr. Paul MONSON
42 Vice Rector Rev. Zbigniew MORAWIEC, SCJ
111 VP for Institutional Advancement Ms. Monica MISEY
88 VP Intercultural Prep for Ministry Vacant
26 VP Marketing & Communications Vacant
08 Director Library & Acad Supp Svcs Ms. Jennifer BARTHOLOMEW
88 Director Liturgy and Music/Organist Dr. Benjamin STONE
88 Interim Director Lux Center Mr. Jon SWEENEY
07 Director of Admissions Ms. Lynn KAESTNER
18 Director Plant Operations Mr. Michael J. ERATO
88 Director Hispanic Min Prep Program Rev. José GONZÁLEZ
88 Faculty Council Chair Dr. Steven SHIPPEE
06 Registrar/Academic Planning Officer Ms. Laura SOKOLOSKY
15 Finance Manager/HR Officer Ms. Shari WIEMER
13 Information Systems Coordinator Vacant
88 Design Project Manager Ms. Ruth MARKWORTH
04 Manager President-Rector Office Ms. Brittany HAGER MCNEELY
108 Accreditation Spec & Title IX Coord Vacant
32 VP Student Services/Spec Projects Dr. Julie A. O'CONNOR
108 Dir Accreditation & Assessment Dr. Robert GOTCHER
88 VP Formation Programs Rev. John MACK

Saint Norbert College (B)

100 Grant Street, De Pere WI 54115-2099
County: Brown FICE Identification: 003892
Unit ID: 239716
Telephone: (920) 403-3181 Carnegie Class: Bac-A&S
FAX Number: (920) 403-4008 Calendar System: Semester
URL: www.snc.edu
Established: 1898 Annual Undergrad Tuition & Fees: $40,885
Enrollment: 1,939 Coed
Affiliation or Control: Roman Catholic IRS Status: 501(c)3
Highest Offering: Master's
Accreditation: HLC

01 Interim President Mr. Thomas KUNKEL
05 Interim VP Academic Affairs Sr. Andrea LEE
10 Vice President Business & Finance Ms. Autumn ANFANG
111 Vice Pres Institutional Advancement Mr. Jon ENSLIN
32 Vice Pres Student Affairs Mr. Joe WEBB
84 Vice Pres Enrollment Mgmt/Comm Mr. Edward LAMM
13 Vice Pres Info Tech & CIO Mr. Marc BELANGER
110 Assoc Vice Pres Inst Advancement Ms. Lia KAMPMAN
09 Dir Institutional Effectiveness Ms. Carolyn UHL
20 Dean Faculty Affairs & Development Dr. Lisa VANWORMER
36 Director Career Services Ms. Mary Ellen OLSON
38 Dir Counseling/Career Programs Mr. Bruce ROBERTSON
07 Exec Director of Admissions Mr. Mark SELIN
29 Director Alumni & Parent Relations Mr. William FALK
21 Director of Finance Ms. Elizabeth MILLER
37 Director of Financial Aid Ms. Jessica RAFELD
26 Dir Communications/Marketing Ms. Nina ROUSE
08 Director of Library Ms. Alaina MORALES
15 Asst Vice Pres Human Resources Ms. Heather BUTTERFIELD
41 Director Physical Educ/Athletics Mr. Cam FULLER
06 Registrar Ms. Lauren GAECKE
104 Assoc Academic Dir Global Affairs Mr. Dan STOLL
28 Dir Multicultural Student Services Ms. Bridgit MARTIN
18 Director Facilities/Physical Plant Mr. Chris DAHLKE
40 Manager Bookstore Operations Mr. Ryan SILER
04 Executive Asst to President Ms. Jamie MCGUIRE
102 Dir Foundation/Corporate Relations Ms. Amy KUNDINGER
100 Chief of Staff Ms. Julie MASSEY
19 Director Security/Safety Mr. Eric DUNNING
39 Director Student Housing Mr. Michael PECKHAM
44 Director Annual Giving Ms. Monica MCCLURE
50 Dean of Business Mr. Dan HEISER

*University of Wisconsin System (C)

1220 Linden Dr, 1720 Van Hise Hall,
Madison WI 53706-1559
County: Dane FICE Identification: 003894
Unit ID: 240435
Telephone: (608) 262-2321 Carnegie Class: N/A
FAX Number: (608) 262-3985
URL: www.wisconsin.edu

01 President Jay O. ROTHMAN
100 Chief of Staff Dean STEINBERG
05 VP Academic/Student Affairs Anny MORROBEL-SOSA
11 Int VP Administration James LANGDON
10 VP Finance Sean NELSON
30 Int VP University Relations Jeff BUHRANDT
15 Assoc VP HR & CHRO Dan CHANEN
117 Assoc VP Administrative Services Ruth ANDERSON
116 Assoc VP Cap Planning & Budget Alexandria ROE
119 Assoc VP Info Security Kathy MAYER
120 Assoc VP Learning/Info Tech Steven HOPPER
88 Int Exec Dir Shared Services Stacey ROLSTON
121 Associate VP Student Success Christine NAVIA
20 AVP Acad Pgms/Faculty Advancement Carleen VANDE ZANDE
56 Sr AVP & Exec Dir Extended Campus Aaron BROWER
09 Assoc VP Policy and Research Ben PASSMORE
21 Sr Assoc VP Financial Admin Julie GORDON
114 Asst VP Budget/Planning Renee STEPHENSON
88 Director Trust Funds Douglas HOERR
88 Exec Dir Business & Entrepreneur Mark LANGE
26 Exec Dir Public & Community Affairs Jack JABLONSKI
27 Dir of Strategic Communications Heather LAROI
86 AVP Government Relations Jeff BUHRANDT
43 General Counsel Quinn WILLIAMS
28 System Sr EDI Officer Warren ANDERSON
101 ED & Corp Sec to Board of Regents Jessica LATHROP
04 Sr Exec Assistant to the President Nicole SMENT

*University of Wisconsin-Madison (D)

500 Lincoln Drive, Madison WI 53706-1380
County: Dane FICE Identification: 003895
Unit ID: 240444
Telephone: (608) 262-1234 Carnegie Class: DU-Highest
FAX Number: (608) 262-0123 Calendar System: Semester
URL: www.wisc.edu
Established: 1848 Annual Undergrad Tuition & Fees (In-State): $10,742
Enrollment: 44,640 Coed
Affiliation or Control: State IRS Status: 501(c)3
Highest Offering: Doctorate
Accreditation: HLC, ARCPA, ART, AUD, CAATE, CACREP, CAMPEP, CIDA, CLPSY, COPSY, DANCE, DIET, DIETD, DMS, IPSY, LAW, LIB, LSAR, MED, MUS, NURSE, PCSAS, PH, PHAR, PLNG, PTA, SCPSY, SP, SW, VET

02 Chancellor Dr. Jennifer MNOOKIN
05 Provost Academic Affairs Dr. Karl SCHOLZ
46 Vice Chanc Research/Graduate Educ Dr. Steven ACKERMAN
11 Vice Chancellor Administration Mr. Robert CRAMER
100 Chancellor's Int Chief of Staff Ms. Jennifer NOYES
26 Vice Chanc University Relations Mr. Charles HOSLET
32 Vice Chanc Student Affairs Dr. Lori REESOR
84 Vice Provost Enrollment Management Mr. Derek KINDLE
13 CIO/Vice Prov Info Technology Ms. Lois BROOKS
18 Assoc VC Facilities Plng/Mgmt Mr. Robert CRAMER
28 Vice Provost Diversity/Climate Dr. LaVar CHARLESTON
20 Vice Provost Faculty/Staff Pgms Dr. Beth MEYERAND
20 Vice Provost Teaching/Learning Dr. John ZUMBRUNNEN
10 Assoc Vice Chanc Finance/Admin Mr. David MURPHY
21 Asst Vice Chanc Business Svcs Mr. David HONMA
35 Chief of Staff/Student Affairs Mr. Argyle WADE
58 Dean Graduate School Dr. William J. KARPUS
49 Dean College Letters & Science Dr. Eric WILCOTS
63 Dean Medicine and Public Health Dr. Robert N. GOLDEN
53 Dean School of Education Dr. Diana HESS
50 Dean School of Business Dr. Vallabh SAMBAMURTHY
67 Dean School of Pharmacy Dr. Steven M. SWANSON
54 Dean of College of Engineering Dr. Ian ROBERTSON
47 Dean of Agricultural/Life Sciences Dr. Kathryn VANDENBOSCH
66 Dean of School of Nursing Dr. Linda SCOTT
59 Dean of Human Ecology Dr. Soyeon SHIM
74 Dean of Veterinary Medicine Dr. Mark D. MARKEL
61 Dean of the Law School Dr. Daniel TOKAJI
82 Dean International Studies Dr. Guido PODESTÁ
43 Director of Admin Legal Services Ms. Nancy LYNCH
88 Dean Nelson Inst Environmental Stds Dr. Paul ROBBINS
41 Director Intercollegiate Athletics Mr. Christopher MCINTOSH
88 Int Director of Physical Plant Mr. James BOGAN
88 Director of the Arboretum Dr. Karen OBERHAUSER
88 Director State Lab of Hygiene Dr. James SCHAUER
88 Director of Wisconsin Union Mr. Mark C. GUTHIER
07 Director of Admissions Mr. Andre PHILLIPS
08 Director of Libraries Ms. Lisa CARTER
27 Director University Communications Mr. John LUCAS
102 President UW Foundation Dr. Michael M. KNETTER
37 Director Student Financial Aid Ms. Helen FAITH
38 Director Mental Health Services Dr. Sarah NOLAN
15 Int Chief Human Resources Mr. Patrick SHEEHAN
39 Director of University Housing Dr. Jeffrey NOVAK
51 Dean Continuing Studies Dr. Jeffrey RUSSELL
19 Chief of University Police Ms. Kristen ROMAN
88 Director of Archives Ms. Katie NASH
23 Director University Health Svcs Dr. Jake BAGGOTT
88 Director of Space Management Mr. Brent LLOYD
17 CEO Hospital & Clinics Dr. Alan KAPLAN
109 Dir Auxiliary Operations Analysis Ms. Donna HALLERAN
06 Registrar Mr. Scott OWCZAREK
88 Secretary of the Faculty Ms. Heather DANIELS
88 Secretary of Academic Staff Mr. Jake SMITH
88 Director of Recreational Sports Mr. Aaron HOBSON
85 Dir International Student Svcs Ms. Samantha MCCABE
22 Dir Office of Equity & Diversity Mr. Luis A. PINERO
96 Director of Purchasing Ms. Lori VOSS
09 Int Dir Inst Rsrch/Acd Plng/Anlysis Ms. Allison LATARTE
88 Sr Special Asst to Provost Dr. Eden INOWAY-RONNIE
86 Sr Special Asst to Chanc Fed Rels Mr. Michael LENN

*University of Wisconsin-Eau Claire (E)

105 Garfield Avenue, PO Box 4004,
Eau Claire WI 54702-4004
County: Eau Claire FICE Identification: 003917
Unit ID: 240268
Telephone: (715) 836-2637 Carnegie Class: Masters/M
FAX Number: N/A Calendar System: Semester
URL: www.uwec.edu
Established: 1916 Annual Undergrad Tuition & Fees (In-State): $8,870
Enrollment: 11,017 Coed
Affiliation or Control: State IRS Status: 501(c)3
Highest Offering: Doctorate
Accreditation: HLC, CAATE, JOUR, MUS, NURSE, SP, SW

02 Chancellor Dr. James C. SCHMIDT
05 Prov/Vice Chanc Academic Affairs Dr. Patricia A. KLEINE
100 Chief of Staff Ms. Mary Jane BRUKARDT
84 Vice Chanc Enrollment Management Mr. Billy FELZ
10 Vice Chanc Finance/Administration Ms. Grace CRICKETTE
28 VC Div/Equity/Inclusion/Stdnt Affs Dr. Olga DIAZ
46 Asst VC Research/Sponsored Pgm Dr. Erica BENSON
111 Asst Chanc Foundation/Advancement Ms. Kimera K. WAY
20 Assoc Vice Chanc Academic Affairs Dr. Mary HOFFMAN
20 Assoc Vice Chanc Academic Affairs Dr. Louisa RICE
26 Executive Director Mktg & Planning Ms. Mary Jane BRUKARDT
26 Chief Communications Officer Ms. Paula GILBECK
22 Director of Affirmative Action Ms. Teresa E. O'HALLORAN
102 Exec Dir of Foundation Ms. Kimera K. WAY
32 Interim Dean of Students Mr. Gregory HEINSELMAN
08 Director of Libraries Dr. Jill S. MARKGRAF
18 Director of Facilities Mr. Troy TERHARK
14 Dir Learning & Technology Services Mr. Kent GERBERICH
15 Interim Director of Human Resources Ms. Tracy DRIER
37 Director of Financial Aid Ms. Nicole S. ANDREWS
38 Director of Counseling Dr. Riley C. MCGRATH
06 Registrar Ms. Kimberly B. O'KELLY
36 Assoc Director Career Services Ms. Staci L. HEIDTKE
23 Director of Student Health Services Dr. Kim FRODL
39 Director of Housing & Res Life Mr. J. Quincy CHAPMAN
41 Director of Athletics Mr. Daniel J. SCHUMACHER
85 Interim Lead Intl Education Ms. Colleen C. MARCHWICK
92 Director of Honors Program Dr. Heather FIELDING
27 Director of Integrated Marketing Ms. Rebecca J. DIENGER
09 Institutional Planner Mr. Casey ROZOWSKI
108 Director of Assessment Dr. Mary F. HOFFMAN
49 Dean Col of Arts & Sciences Dr. Aleks STERNFELD-DUNN
66 Dean Col of Nursing/Health Sciences Dr. Sonja MEIERS
53 Dean Col Education/Human Sciences Dr. Carmen K. MANNING
50 Dean College of Business Dr. Brewer DORAN
04 Exec Asst to Chancellor Ms. Kelly OLSON

*University of Wisconsin-Green Bay (F)

2420 Nicolet Drive, Green Bay WI 54311-7001
County: Brown FICE Identification: 003899
Unit ID: 240277
Telephone: (920) 465-2000 Carnegie Class: Masters/M
FAX Number: (920) 465-2032 Calendar System: Semester
URL: www.uwgb.edu
Established: 1965 Annual Undergrad Tuition & Fees (In-State): $7,873
Enrollment: 8,954 Coed
Affiliation or Control: State IRS Status: 501(c)3
Highest Offering: Doctorate
Accreditation: HLC, ART, CAATE, CAHIIM, @DIET, DIETD, DIETI, MUS, NURSE, SW

02 Chancellor Dr. Michael ALEXANDER
05 Provost/Vice Chanc Acad Affs Dr. Kathleen BURNS
12 CEO UW Manitowoc Mr. Jamie SCHRAMM
12 CEO UW Marinette Vacant
12 CEO UW Sheboygan Mr. Jamie SCHRAMM

10	SVC Inst Strategy/Chf Business Ofcr	Ms. Sheryl VAN GRUENSVEN
111	Vice Chanc University Advancement	Mr. Tony WERNER
41	Athletic Director	Mr. Josh MOON
32	Vice Chanc for Student Affairs	Dr. Corey KING
20	Assoc Provost for Acad Affairs	Dr. Courtney SHERMAN
53	Dean Health/Education/Social Well	Dr. Susan GALLAGHER-LEPAK
50	Dean Cofrin School of Business	Dr. Mathew DORNBUSH
49	Dean of Arts/Humanities	Dr. Chuck RYBAK
81	Dean of Science/Engr & Tech	Dr. John KATERS
07	Exec Director of Admissions	Ms. Rachele BAKIC
15	Asst VC Policy & Compliance	Mr. Christopher PAQUET
35	Asst Vice Chanc for Student Affairs	Ms. Gail SIMS-AUBERT
35	Dean of Students	Mr. Mark OLKOWSKI
18	Dir Facilities Management/Planning	Mr. Joe HARVEY
19	Director of Public Safety	Chief Tony DECKER
21	Controller	Ms. SuAnn DETAMPEL
84	Asst Vice Chanc Enrollment Services	Ms. Jennifer JONES
46	Director of Institute for Research	Mr. Bojan LJUBENKO
37	Director Financial Aid	Mr. Rich BORUSZEWSKI
39	Director of Residence Life	Ms. Gail SIMS-AUBERT
24	Director Media Svcs/Telecomm	Vacant
23	Director Health Services	Ms. Amy HENNIGES
100	Chief of Staff	Mrs. Susan GRANT ROBINSON
26	Director University Communications	Ms. Janet BONKOWSKI
36	Director Career Services	Ms. Linda G. PEACOCK-LANDRUM
29	Director Alumni Relations	Mr. Brian RAMMER
35	Director Student Life	Ms. Katherine LESPERANCE
06	Registrar	Mr. Daniel VANDE YACHT
04	Administrative Asst to President	Vacant
104	Director Study Abroad	Mr. Brent BLAHNIK
28	Diversity Director	Ms. Mai LO LEE
30	Director of Development	Mr. Jacob DEPAS
13	Asst Vice Chancellor for IT	Ms. Wendy WOODWARD
102	Director Foundation	Mr. Anthony WERNER
51	Asst Vice Chanc Continuing Educ	Ms. Jess LAMBRECHT
54	Dean of Engineering	Dr. John KATERS
86	Director Government Relations	Mrs. Janet BONKOWSKI
96	Assistant Director of Procurment	Vacant

*University of Wisconsin-La Crosse (A)

1725 State Street, La Crosse WI 54601-3788

County: La Crosse — FICE Identification: 003919 — Unit ID: 240329

Telephone: (608) 785-8000 — Carnegie Class: Masters/L

FAX Number: (608) 785-8492 — Calendar System: Semester

URL: www.uwlax.edu

Established: 1909 — Annual Undergrad Tuition & Fees (In-State): $9,160

Enrollment: 10,531 — Coed

Affiliation or Control: State — IRS Status: 501(c)3

Highest Offering: Doctorate

Accreditation: HLC, ANEST, ARCPA, CAATE, CAPRT, MUS, #NASP, NMT, OT, PH, PTA, RADDOS, RTT

02	Chancellor	Dr. Joe GOW
05	Vice Chanc/Provost Acad Affairs	Dr. Betsy MORGAN
111	Vice Chancellor Advancement	Mr. Greg REICHERT
10	Vice Chancellor Admin & Finance	Dr. Bob HETZEL
50	Dean of Business Administration	Dr. Taggert BROOKS
53	Dean School of Education	Dr. Marcie WYCOFF-HORN
79	Dean of Liberal Studies	Dr. Karl KUNKEL
81	Dean Science/Health	Dr. Ju KIM
32	Vice Chancellor Student Affairs	Dr. Vitaliano FIGUEROA
13	Chief Information Officer	Mr. David KIM
58	Dean of Graduate & Extended Lrng	Dr. Meredith THOMSEN
08	Director of Library	Mr. John JAX
85	Dir International Education & Engag	Ms. Karolyn BALD
07	Director ES/Admissions	Mr. Corey SJOQUIST
37	Director ES/Financial Aid	Ms. Louise L. JANKE
36	Director of Career Services	Ms. Becky VIANDEN
41	Athletic Director	Ms. Kim BLUM
26	Director News and Marketing	Mr. Brad R. QUARBERG
29	Director Alumni Relations	Ms. Janie M. MORGAN
23	Student Health Center Admin	Mr. Ben CRENSHAW
09	Director Institutional Research	Ms. Graciela ENGEN
28	Vice Chancellor Diversity/Inclusion	Ms. Dina ZAVALA
22	Director Affirmative Action	Ms. Antoiwana WILLIAMS
106	Dir CATL	Ms. Kristin KOEPKE
39	Director Residence Life	Ms. Jenni BRUNDAGE
06	Registrar	Ms. Leanne VIGUE
15	Chief Human Resources Officer	Mr. John ACARDO

*University of Wisconsin-Milwaukee (B)

PO Box 413, Milwaukee WI 53201-0413

County: Milwaukee — FICE Identification: 003896 — Unit ID: 240453

Telephone: (414) 229-1122 — Carnegie Class: DU-Highest

FAX Number: (414) 229-6329 — Calendar System: Semester

URL: www.uwm.edu

Established: 1885 — Annual Undergrad Tuition & Fees (In-State): $9,254

Enrollment: 24,565 — Coed

Affiliation or Control: State — IRS Status: 501(c)3

Highest Offering: Doctorate

Accreditation: HLC, ART, ATECH, CAATE, CEA, CLPSY, COPSY, DANCE, DMS, HSA, LIB, MLS, MPCAC, MUS, NASP, NURSE, OT, PH, PLNG, PTA, RAD, SCPSY, SP, SW

02	Chancellor	Dr. Mark A. MONE
05	Interim Provost	Dr. Scott GRONERT
10	Vice Chanc Finance & Admin Affs	Ms. Robin L. VAN HARPEN
30	VC Development & Alumni Relations	Ms. Joan NESBITT
32	VC Student Affairs	Ms. Kelly HAAG
46	Vice Provost of Research	Dr. Mark T. HARRIS
28	VC Diversity/Equity and Inclusion	Dr. Chia VANG
20	Assoc Vice Chanc Academic Affairs	Dr. Devarajan VENUGOPALAN
20	Assoc Vice Chanc Academic Affairs	Dr. Phyllis KING
84	Associate VC for Enrollment Mgmt	Ms. Kay EILERS
13	Assoc Vice Chanc/CIO	Dr. Robert J. BECK
18	Assoc VC Facilities Planning/Mgmt	Ms. Melissa SPADANUDA
102	President UWM Foundation	Mr. David H. GILBERT
76	Int Dean College Health Sciences	Dr. Mark HARRIS
48	Interim Dean Arch & Urban Planning	Dr. Mo ZELL
50	Dean School of Business	Dr. Kaushal CHARI
53	Acting Dean School of Education	Dr. Tina FREIBURGER
54	Dean College Engr & Applied Science	Dr. Brett PETERS
57	Interim Dean Peck School of Arts	Mr. Kevin HARTMAN
65	Int Dean Sch of Freshwater Science	Dr. Rebecca KLAPER
69	Acting Dean School Public Health	Dr. Amy HARLEY
58	Dean Graduate School	Mr. Mark HARRIS
49	Acting Dean College Letters/Science	Dr. Nigel ROTHFELS
62	Interim Dean School Info Studies	Dr. Tina FREIBURGER
66	Dean of College of Nursing	Dr. Kim LITWACK
70	Dean School Social Welfare	Dr. Tina FREIBURGER
51	Provost's Deputy for Continuing Ed	Dr. Nancy NELSON
32	Dean of Students	Mr. Adam JUSSEL
22	Dir Equity/Diversity Services	Mr. Jamie CIMPL-WIEMER
08	Associate Vice Provost of Libraries	Dr. Michael DOYLEN
43	Dir Legal Affairs	Ms. Joely B. URDAN
06	Registrar	Ms. Kristin HILDEBRANDT
15	Assoc Vice Chanc Human Resources	Ms. Makda FESSAHAYE
19	Chief of University Police	Mr. David SALAZAR
25	Dir Office Sponsored Research	Ms. Kate MOLLEN
23	Dir Health Center	Dr. Aamir SIDDIQI
108	Dir Assess/Institutional Research	Dr. Jonathan HANES
37	Director Financial Aid	Mr. Timothy OPGENORTH
41	Athletic Director	Ms. Amanda BRAUN
36	Exec Dir Student Experience/Talent	Ms. Laurie MARKS
27	Sr Dir Integrated Mktg & Comm	Ms. Michelle JOHNSON
21	Assoc Vice Chanc Business & Finance	Mr. Drew KNAB
29	Director Alumni/Advancement & Ops	Ms. Amy TATE
96	Director of Procurement	Vacant
114	Dir Budget & Planning	Ms. Cindy KLUGE
105	Dir Web & Mobile Services	Mr. Mark JACOBSON
106	Executive Director UWM Online	Ms. Laura PEDRICK
112	Dir of Gift Planning & Agreements	Ms. Gretchen MILLER
97	Dean College of General Studies	Dr. Simon BRONNER
04	Admin Assistant to the Chancellor	Ms. Christine ADAMS-MATT
07	Executive Director of Admissions	Mr. Marc YOUNG
09	Director of Institutional Research	Dr. Jonathan HANES
100	Chief of Staff	Ms. Suzanne WESLOW
104	Director Study Abroad	Ms. Sharon GOSZ
39	Director University Housing	Ms. Arcetta KNAUTZ
44	Director Annual Giving	Mr. Thomas BJORNSTAD

*University of Wisconsin Oshkosh (C)

800 Algoma Boulevard, Oshkosh WI 54901

County: Winnebago — FICE Identification: 003920 — Unit ID: 240365

Telephone: (920) 424-1234 — Carnegie Class: DU-Mod

FAX Number: (920) 424-7317 — Calendar System: Semester

URL: www.uwosh.edu

Established: 1871 — Annual Undergrad Tuition & Fees (In-State): $7,717

Enrollment: 15,314 — Coed

Affiliation or Control: State — IRS Status: 501(c)3

Highest Offering: Doctorate

Accreditation: HLC, ANEST, CAATE, CACREP, IFSAC, JOUR, MUS, NURSE, SW

02	Chancellor	Dr. Andrew J. LEAVITT
03	Vice Chancellor	Dr. John KOKER
05	Provost & VC Academic Affairs	Ms. Carmen FAYMONVILLE
20	Asst Vice Chanc Acad Support	Dr. Sylvia CAREY-BUTLER
121	AVC Curric Affs/Stdnt Acad Achvmt	Dr. Charles HILL
32	Vice Chancellor Student Affairs	Vacant
10	Vice Chanc Finance/Administration	Dr. James FLETCHER
21	Associate Vice Chanc Admin Svcs	Vacant
06	Registrar	Ms. Lisa M. DANIELSON
22	Affirmative Action Officer	Vacant
09	Director of Institutional Research	Mr. Michael W. WATSON
38	Director of Counseling Center	Dr. Sandy COX
13	CIO Director Info Technology	Mr. Mark CLEMENTS
50	Dean Business	Dr. Barbara L. RAU
66	Dean Nursing	Dr. Judith WESTPHAL
53	Dean Education & Human Svcs	Dr. Linda HALING
49	Interim Dean Letters & Sciences	Dr. Colleen MCDERMOTT
102	Pres Univ of Wisc Oshkosh Foundatn	Vacant
29	Director of Alumni Association	Ms. Christine M. GANTNER
37	Director of Financial Aid	Mr. Kim DONAT
26	Int Exec Dir Marketing/Comms	Ms. Peggy BREISTER
35	Dean of Students	Dr. Art MUNIN
58	Director Graduate Studies	Mr. Gregory WYPISZYNSKI
07	Director of Admissions	Mr. Paul GEDLINSKE
15	AVC Human Resources/Int Dir EO/AA	Ms. Shawna KUETHER
18	Facilities/Physical Plant Director	Mr. Brian KRUEGER
36	Director of Career Services	Ms. Jaime PAGE-STADLER
92	Director University Honors Program	Dr. Laurence CARLIN
08	Interim Director Library	Ms. Sarah NEISES
04	Administrative Asst to President	Ms. Suzette THIBADEAU
104	Director Study Abroad	Ms. Jennifer GRAFF
41	Athletic Director	Mr. Darryl SIMS
90	Director Academic Computing	Ms. Laura KNAAPEN
122	Program Advisor Frat/Sorority Life	Ms. Angela ZEMKE

*University of Wisconsin-Parkside (D)

900 Wood Road, Box 2000, Kenosha WI 53141-2000

County: Kenosha — FICE Identification: 005015 — Unit ID: 240374

Telephone: (262) 595-2345 — Carnegie Class: Masters/M

FAX Number: (262) 595-2202 — Calendar System: Semester

URL: www.uwp.edu

Established: 1968 — Annual Undergrad Tuition & Fees (In-State): $7,444

Enrollment: 4,452 — Coed

Affiliation or Control: State — IRS Status: 501(c)3

Highest Offering: Master's

Accreditation: HLC, CAHIIM, MLS

02	Chancellor	Deborah L. FORD
05	Provost/Vice Chancellor	Robert DUCOFFE
111	Asst Chanc Univ Rels/Advancement	Willie JUDE, II
20	Vice Provost Academic Affairs	Gary WOOD
32	Vice Provost Student Affs & Enroll	Tammy MCGUCKIN
10	Vice Pres Finance/Administration	Scott MENKE
28	University Diversity & Inclusion	Tyler LENZ-FISHER
35	Dean of Students	Steve WALLNER
50	Dean Col of Bus Econ & Comput	Dirk BALDWIN
49	Dean College of Arts & Humanities	Lesley WALKER
81	Dean College of Nat & Hlth Sciences	Emmanual OTU
83	Dean Social Sci & Prof Studies	Peggy JAMES
51	Dir Continuing Educ & Cmty Engage	Debra KARP
08	Director of the Library	Anna STADICK
13	Chief Information Officer	Jordania LEON-JORDAN
35	Asst Dean of Students	Damian EVANS
21	Dir Business Services/Controller	Ann IVERSON
15	Asst Vice Chanc Human Resources	Sheronda GLASS
19	Dir Campus Police/Public Safety	James HELLER
37	Director Financial Aid	Kristina KLEMENS
44	Annual Fund/Stewardship Coordinator	Linnea BOOHER
06	Registrar	Rhonda KIMMEL
36	Dir of Advising/Career Center	Neil BAUMGARTNER
18	Director Facilities Management	John BRUCH
94	Director of Women's Studies	Linda CRAFTON
38	Dir Health/Counseling/Disability	Renee KIRBY
40	Manager Bookstore	Kim FLANNERY
07	Interim Director of Admissions	Richard BARTH
04	Administrative Asst to Chancellor	Karen GRABHER
104	Admin Program Manager Intl Educ	Elaine PHILIPPA
39	Asst Director Residence Life	Jenna SWARTZ
41	Athletic Director	Andrew GAVIN
105	Director Web Services	Kimberly SEKAS
26	Chief Public Relations/Marketing	Vacant

*University of Wisconsin-Platteville (E)

1 University Plaza, Platteville WI 53818-3099

County: Grant — FICE Identification: 003921 — Unit ID: 240462

Telephone: (608) 342-1491 — Carnegie Class: Masters/L

FAX Number: (608) 342-1232 — Calendar System: Semester

URL: www.uwplatt.edu

Established: 1866 — Annual Undergrad Tuition & Fees (In-State): $7,873

Enrollment: 7,547 — Coed

Affiliation or Control: State — IRS Status: 501(c)3

Highest Offering: Master's

Accreditation: HLC, MUS, NAIT

02	Chancellor	Mr. Dennis J. SHIELDS
05	Provost/Vice Chanc Acad Affairs	Dr. Tammy EVETOVICH
111	Vice Chanc University Relations	Ms. Rose M. SMYRSKI
10	Vice Chanc Admin Services	Ms. Paige SMITH
30	Asst Vice Chanc Dev/Alum Engagement	Mr. Josh BOOTS
06	Registrar	Mr. David S. KIECKHAFER
84	Vice Chanc Enroll/Student Support	Ms. Angela M. UDELHOFEN
37	Asst Director of Financial Aid	Mr. Brian BIRD
38	Director Student Counseling	Ms. Deirdre L. DALSING
26	Chief Communications Officer	Mr. Paul J. ERICKSON
41	Director Intercollegiate Athletics	Dr. Kristina M. NAVARRO
39	Director of Residence Life	Mrs. Linda A. MULROY-BOWDEN
15	Director Human Resources/AA/EED	Ms. Sarah VOSBERG
19	Director Security/Safety	Chief Joseph M. HALLMAN
08	Head Librarian	Mr. Todd ROLL
18	Engineer/Facilities Management	Mrs. Katrina M. HECIMOVIC
18	Facilities/Building Maintenance	Mr. John D. NIEHAUS
36	Director of Career Center	Mr. Trapper MITCHELL
51	Director Continuing Education	Ms. Kerie WEDIGE
20	Int Assoc VC for Academic Affairs	Dr. Melissa E. GORMLEY
54	Int Dean Col of Engr/Math/Science	Dr. Philip J. PARKER
49	Int Dean Col of Lib Arts/Educ	Dr. Kory G. WEIN
47	Dean Business Life Sci/Agric	Dr. Wayne C. WEBER
100	Chief Staff/Asst Chanc Div/Inclus	Ms. Angela M. MILLER
13	Chief Information Officer	Mr. Tony HAYES
21	Comptroller	Ms. Cathy J. RIEDL-FARREY
35	Dean of Students	Ms. Kate DEMERSE
07	Director Admissions	Ms. Heidi TUESCHER-GILLE
23	Admin Director Student Health Svcs	Ms. Rachel HERMAN
121	Director Student Support Services	Ms. Laura A. FRANKLIN
104	Director International Programs	Ms. Kari M. HILL
124	Director Retention/Acad Support	Ms. Karen MCLEER
20	Asst Prov Grad Pgms/Assess/Dist	Dr. Carolyn KELLER
25	Director Research & Sponsored Pgm	Mr. William C. HOYER

*University of Wisconsin-River Falls (A)

410 S Third Street, River Falls WI 54022-5013
County: Pierce FICE Identification: 003923
Unit ID: 240471
Telephone: (715) 425-3201 Carnegie Class: Masters/M
FAX Number: (715) 425-4487 Calendar System: Semester
URL: www.uwrf.edu
Established: 1874 Annual Undergrad Tuition & Fees (In-State): $8,063
Enrollment: 5,855 Coed
Affiliation or Control: State IRS Status: 501(c)3
Highest Offering: Doctorate
Accreditation: HLC, CACREP, MACTE, MUS, NASP, SP, SW

02 Chancellor … Dr. Maria GALLO
05 Vice Chancellor & Provost … Dr. David TRAVIS
10 Vice Chanc Finance/Administration … Mr. David RUHLAND
111 Asst Chancellor Advancement … Mr. Richard FOY
20 Associate Provost … Dr. Wesley CHAPIN
32 Asst Chancellor for Student Success … Dr. Jamie ZAMJAHN
21 Controller … Ms. Jody NICHOLS
47 Dean Agricult/Food/Environ Sci … Dr. Dale GALLENBERG
53 Interim Dean Educ & Prof Studies … Dr. Dawn HUKAI
49 Dean of Arts & Sciences … Dr. Dean YOHNK
50 Interim Dean Business & Economics … Dr. Dawn HUKAI
13 Chief Information Officer … Mr. Joseph KMIECH
15 Human Resources Director … Ms. Michelle BEST
18 Exec Dir Facilities Management … Mr. Alan SYMICEK
22 Director Integrity & Compliance … Ms. Jennifer LARIMORE
06 Registrar … Mrs. Kelly BROWNING
07 Executive Director of Admissions … Mrs. Sarah NELSON
46 Director Grants & Research … Ms. Molly VAN WAGNER
08 Director of Library … Ms. Maureen OLLE-LAJOIE
41 Athletic Director … Mrs. Crystal LANNING
37 Director Financial Assistance … Mr. Robert BODE
19 Director of Protective Services … Mr. Karl FLEURY
96 Director of Purchasing Services … Ms. Brandee DRINKEN
121 Dir Student Success Center … Mr. Ian STROUD
29 Director Alumni Relations … Mr. Pedro RENTA
92 Director Honors Program … Dr. Kathleen HUNZER
38 Director Stdnt Health & Counseling … Ms. Debra JANIS
51 Director Continuing Education … Mr. Randy ZIMMERMANN
92 McNair Scholars Director … Dr. Sierra HOWRY
26 Director Communications & Marketing … Ms. Dina FASSINO
39 Director of Residence Life … Ms. Karla THOENNES
40 Manager Bookstore … Ms. Julie EKLUND
04 Executive Assistant to Chancellor … Ms. Jenna LINDSETH
100 Chief of Staff … Ms. Beth SCHOMMER
28 Dir Diversity/Equity & Inclusion … Mr. Derek BRADLEY
35 Dean of Students … Dr. Katie JACKSON

*University of Wisconsin-Stevens Point (B)

2100 Main Street, Stevens Point WI 54481-3871
County: Portage FICE Identification: 003924
Unit ID: 240480
Telephone: (715) 346-0123 Carnegie Class: Masters/M
FAX Number: (715) 346-4841 Calendar System: Semester
URL: https://www.uwsp.edu/Pages/default.aspx
Established: 1894 Annual Undergrad Tuition & Fees (In-State): $8,300
Enrollment: 8,302 Coed
Affiliation or Control: State IRS Status: 501(c)3
Highest Offering: Doctorate
Accreditation: HLC, ART, AUD, CAATE, CAHIIM, CIDA, DANCE, DIETD, MLS, MUS, NURSE, SP, SW, THEA

02 Chancellor … Dr. Thomas GIBSON
05 Provost & Vice Chancellor … Dr. La Vonne CORNELL-SWANSON
10 Chief Financial Officer … Ms. Pratima GANDHI
32 Vice Chancellor Student Affairs … Dr. Al THOMPSON
20 AVC for Tech/Learning/Acad Pgms … Dr. Todd HUSPENI
100 Chief of Staff … Dr. Robert MANZKE
15 AVC Person/Bdgt/Grants/Summer Pgms … Dr. Katie JORE
51 Exec Dir UWSP Continuing Education … Vacant
21 Controller … Ms. Christina RICKERT
07 Director Admissions … Mr. Justin WILLIS
37 Director of Financial Aid … Ms. Mandy SLOWINSKI
19 Director Safety & Loss Control … Vacant
111 Vice Chanc Univ Advancement … Vacant
29 Director of Alumni Affairs … Ms. Laura GEHRMAN ROTTIER
26 Dir Univ Relations/Communications … Ms. Lana POOLE
38 Director Counseling Center … Dr. Stacey GERKEN
13 Dir of Information Technology … Mr. Peter ZUGE
22 Director Equity/Affirmative Action … Dr. Eric ROESLER
08 Director University Library … Ms. Mindy KING
06 Interim Registrar … Ms. Anne ECKENROD
18 Chief Facilities/Physical Plant … Mr. Paul HASLER
36 Associate Director Career Services … Ms. Sue KISSINGER
96 Purchasing Manager … Ms. Heidi WALLNER
57 Dean Col Fine Arts/Commun … Dr. Valerie CISLER
49 Dean Col of Letters & Sciences … Dr. Joshua HAGEN
65 Dean Col of Natural Resources … Dr. Brian SLOSS
107 Dean Col of Professional Studies … Dr. Marty LOY
35 Director Student Affairs … Dr. Al THOMPSON
04 Administrative Asst to President … Ms. Sara BRANDL-REEVES
104 Director Study Abroad … Mr. Brad VANDENELZEN
41 Athletic Director … Mr. Brad DUCKWORTH
50 Dean of Business … Dr. Kevin NEUMAN
86 Director Government Relations … Dr. Robert MANZKE
39 Director Student Housing … Mr. Brian FAUST

09 Director of Institutional Research … Dr. Katie JORE
84 Director Enrollment Management … Ms. Lana POOLE

*University of Wisconsin-Stout (C)

712 South Broadway, Menomonie WI 54751-0790
County: Dunn FICE Identification: 003915
Unit ID: 240417
Telephone: (715) 232-1122 Carnegie Class: Masters/L
FAX Number: N/A Calendar System: 4/1/4
URL: www.uwstout.edu
Established: 1891 Annual Undergrad Tuition & Fees (In-State): $9,488
Enrollment: 7,970 Coed
Affiliation or Control: State IRS Status: 501(c)3
Highest Offering: Doctorate
Accreditation: HLC, ACBSP, ACPHA, ART, CEA, CIDA, CONST, DIETD, DIETI, MFCD, @PTA

02 Chancellor … Dr. Katherine P. FRANK
05 Provost & Vice Chancellor … Dr. Glendali RODRIGUEZ
100 Head of Staff … Ms. Kristi KRIMPELBEIN
20 Associate Vice Chancellor … Ms. Tamara BRANTMEIER
10 Vice Chanc Business/Fin/Admin … Mr. Eric GUENARD
111 Vice Chanc Univ Advance/Alumni Rel … Mr. Willie JOHNSON
84 VChanc Enrollment/Strat Initiative … Ms. Laura KING
45 Asst Chanc Plng/Assess/Rsrch/Qlty … Dr. Meridith WENTZ
53 Dean CAHS … Dr. Maria ALM
81 Interim Dean CSTEMM … Dr. Gindy NEIDERMYER
32 Dean of Students … Ms. Sandi SCOTT
15 Senior Human Resources Officer … Mr. Terry MCCANN
26 Senior Marketing Officer … Mr. Michael HUGGINS
06 Registrar … Mr. Josh LIND
28 Asst Chanc Diversity/Equity/Incl … Ms. Quin BROOKS
36 Director Career Services … Mr. Bryan BARTS
08 Interim Library Director … Ms. Kate KRAMSCHUSTER
37 Director Financial Aid … Mr. Joe KAUFFMAN
13 Asst Chanc for Learning & IT/CIO … Ms. Suzanne TRAXLER
38 Director Counseling Center … Dr. Chasidy FAITH
23 Director Student Health Services … Vacant
44 Development Program Specialist … Ms. Jennifer RUDIGER
85 Director International Educ … Mr. Scott PIERSON
18 Director Facilities Management … Mr. Justin UTPADEL
96 Director Purchasing … Mr. Carley SCRIVENER
39 Interim Dir University Housing … Mr. Adam LUDWIG
41 Athletic Director … Mr. Duey NAATZ
117 Pgm Mgr/Dir of Safety & Risk Mgmt … Mr. Jim UHLIR
19 Chief of Police/Director of Parking … Mr. Jason SPETZ
106 Assoc Director Stout Online … Dr. Amy GULLIXSON
07 Director of Admissions … Ms. Joan EBNET
35 Assoc Dean of Students … Ms. Jacqueline BONNEVILLE
114 Budget Director … Mr. Curtis WIELAND
122 Civic Engagement/Greek Life Coord … Ms. Jessica KIELCHESKI

*University of Wisconsin-Superior (D)

Belknap and Catlin, PO Box 2000,
Superior WI 54880-4500
County: Douglas FICE Identification: 003925
Unit ID: 240426
Telephone: (715) 394-8101 Carnegie Class: Masters/M
FAX Number: (715) 394-8454 Calendar System: Semester
URL: www.uwsuper.edu
Established: 1893 Annual Undergrad Tuition & Fees (In-State): $8,140
Enrollment: 2,560 Coed
Affiliation or Control: State IRS Status: 501(c)3
Highest Offering: Beyond Master's But Less Than Doctorate
Accreditation: HLC, MUS, SW

02 Chancellor … Dr. Renee WACHTER
05 Provost/Vice Chanc Academic Affairs … Dr. Maria CUZZO
111 Vice Chanc University Advancement … Ms. Jeanne E. THOMPSON
10 Vice Chanc Administration/Finance … Mr. Jeff KAHLER
26 Senior Communications Officer … Ms. Jordan MILAN
41 Athletic Director … Mr. Nick BURSIK
32 Assoc Vice Chanc of Student Affairs … Mr. Harry ANDERSON
15 Senior Human Resource Officer … Mr. Cory KEMPF
28 Interim Dir of Equity/Div/Inclusion … Ms. Salisa HOCHSTETLER
06 Registrar … Ms. Janie CAMPBELL
84 Senior Enrollment Officer … Mr. Jeremy NERE
21 Controller … Mr. Robert B. WAKSDAHL
37 Interim Director Financial Aid … Ms. Chelsie PARRISH
51 Director Continuing Education … Ms. Kathryn GUIMOND
08 Director CLIC & Library … Dr. Jamie WHITE-FARNHAM
40 Director Bookstore … Mr. Vaughn N. RUSSOM
29 Director of Alumni Relations … Ms. Heather THOMPSON
121 Asst Dir Academic Advising … Ms. Kristen JASPERSON
18 Director Facilities Management … Mr. Dustin JOHNSON
04 Executive Assistant to Chancellor … Ms. Debbie SEGUIN
88 Int Exec Admin Officer to Provost … Ms. Michelle STARRY
09 Dir Inst Research & Spons Pgms … Ms. Emily NEUMANN
19 Chief of Police … Mr. Joseph EICKMAN
39 Director Residence Life … Mr. Ryan KREUSER
13 Senior Technology Officer … Mr. David WAGNER
20 Dean of Academic Affairs … Dr. Nick DANZ
07 Director International Admissions … Mr. Mark MACLEAN
38 Director Counseling Services … Mr. Randy BARKER

*University of Wisconsin-Whitewater (E)

800 W Main Street, Whitewater WI 53190-1790
County: Walworth FICE Identification: 003926
Unit ID: 240189
Telephone: (262) 472-1918 Carnegie Class: Masters/L
FAX Number: (262) 472-1518 Calendar System: Semester
URL: www.uww.edu
Established: 1868 Annual Undergrad Tuition & Fees (In-State): $7,735
Enrollment: 11,989 Coed
Affiliation or Control: State IRS Status: 501(c)3
Highest Offering: Doctorate
Accreditation: HLC, ART, CACREP, IPSY, MUS, NASP, SP, SW

02 Interim Chancellor … Dr. John CHENOWETH
05 Prov/Vice Chanc Academic Affs … Dr. John CHENOWETH
32 Vice Chancellor Student Affairs … Dr. Artanya WESLEY
111 Interim Vice Chanc Univ Relations … Ms. Katharine KUZNACIC
11 Int Vice Chanc Administrative Affs … Mr. Jeff ARNOLD
100 Chief of Staff/Exec Asst to Chanc … Mrs. Kari HEIDENREICH
20 Assoc VC Academic Affairs … Ms. Kristin PLESSEL
13 Asst Vice Chanc Information Tech … Dr. Elena POKOT
84 Assoc Vice Chanc Enroll/Retention … Mr. Matt ASCHENBRENER
09 Chief of Inst Research/Planning … Ms. Lynsey SCHWABROW
37 Director of Financial Aid … Mr. William TRIPPETT
26 AVC University Relations … Ms. Katharine KUZNACIC
36 Dir of Career & Leadership Dev … Mr. Ron BUCHHOLZ
15 Chief Human Resources Officer … Ms. Janelle CROWLEY
85 Dir Center for Global Education … Ms. Candace A. CHENOWETH
102 CFO Foundation … Ms. Debbie PETRASEK
18 Director Facility Planning/Mgmt … Ms. Tami MCCULLOUGH
28 AVC Diversity/Equity/Inclusion … Dr. Kenny YARBROUGH
92 Director of Honors Program … Dr. Elizabeth KIM
57 Dean Arts/Communication … Dr. Eileen M. HAYES
50 Dean of Business & Economics … Vacant
53 Int Dean Education/Prof Studies … Dr. Robin FOX
49 Dean Letters & Sciences … Dr. Franklin GOZA
58 Dean Grad Stds/Continuing Educ … Dr. Seth MEISEL
41 Athletic Director … Mr. Ryan CALLAHAN
122 Greek Community/Svcs Coord … Mr. Tyler HENDERSON

*University of Wisconsin-Platteville Baraboo Sauk County (F)

1006 Connie Road, Baraboo WI 53913
Telephone: (608) 355-5200 Identification: 770450
Accreditation: &HLC

*University of Wisconsin-Eau Claire - Barron County (G)

1800 College Drive, Rice Lake WI 54868
Telephone: (715) 788-6244 Identification: 770457
Accreditation: &HLC

*University of Wisconsin-Stevens Point at Marshfield (H)

2000 West 5th Street, Marshfield WI 54449
Telephone: (715) 389-6530 Identification: 770455
Accreditation: &HLC

*University of Wisconsin-Platteville Richland (I)

1200 Highway 14 West, Richland Center WI 53581-1316
Telephone: (608) 647-6186 Identification: 770458
Accreditation: &HLC

*University of Wisconsin-Stevens Point at Wausau (J)

518 South 7th Avenue, Wausau WI 54401
Telephone: (715) 261-6100 Identification: 770461
Accreditation: &HLC

*University of Wisconsin-Whitewater at Rock County (K)

2909 Kellogg Avenue, Janesville WI 53546
Telephone: (608) 758-6565 Identification: 770452
Accreditation: &HLC

Viterbo University (L)

900 Viterbo Court, La Crosse WI 54601-8802
County: La Crosse FICE Identification: 003911
Unit ID: 240107
Telephone: (608) 796-3000 Carnegie Class: Masters/L
FAX Number: (608) 796-3050 Calendar System: Semester
URL: www.viterbo.edu
Established: 1890 Annual Undergrad Tuition & Fees: $29,350
Enrollment: 2,516 Coed
Affiliation or Control: Roman Catholic IRS Status: 501(c)3
Highest Offering: Doctorate
Accreditation: HLC, ACBSP, CACREP, DIETC, DIETI, MUS, NURSE, SW

01 President … Dr. Rick TRIETLEY
05 Vice Pres Academics … Dr. Sara COOK
32 EVP Student Success … Vacant
28 VP Diversity/Equity & Inclusion … Dr. Marlene DE LA CRUZ-GUZMAN
84 VP Enrollment Management … Dr. Michelle KRONFELD
10 VP Administration/Finance … Dr. Lillian WANJAGI
111 VP Advancement … Mr. Jim SALMO
21 Assistant Vice President Finance … Ms. Kristen SANBORN

42 University Chaplain ....Fr. Conrad A. TARGONSKI
66 Chief Nursing Officer ....Vacant
54 Dean Engr/Letters/Sciences ....Vacant
09 Asst VP Institutional Effectiveness ....Dr. Timothy SCHORR
57 Conservatory Director ....Vacant
50 Dean Business/Ldrship/Ethics/Educ ....Dr. Tonya WAGNER
58 Dean Graduate/Prof/Adult Education ....Vacant
88 Director of Ethics in Leadership ....Dr. Richard L. KYTE
06 Registrar ....Ms. Kori SALASKI
08 Director of Library ....Ms. Kim OLSON-KOPP
13 Director Instruct/Info Technology ....Ms. Sarah BEARBOWER
41 Athletic Director ....Mr. Barry J. FRIED
37 Director of Financial Aid ....Ms. Terry W. NORMAN
26 Director of Marketing ....Mr. Roger HARTWELL
29 Director Alumni Relations ....Ms. Kathleen A. DUERWACHTER
36 Director Career Planning/Placement ....Ms. Beth D. DOLDER-ZIEKE
15 Asst Director of Human Resources ....Ms. Kayla BERG
108 Dir Assessment/Inst Research ....Ms. Naomi R. STENNES-SPIDAHL
18 Director Physical Plant ....Mr. Eugene M. MCCURDY
38 Dir Counseling/Student Development ....Mr. Justin MCKNIGHT
39 Interim Director of Residence Life ....Ms. Joann STACEY
53 Director Grad Studies in Education ....Vacant
19 Director Campus Safety ....Mr. Brian BARTELT
07 Asst Director of Admissions ....Vacant
04 Executive Asst to President ....Ms. Sheila SEVERSON

Wisconsin Lutheran College (A)

8800 W Bluemound Road, Milwaukee WI 53226-4699

County: Milwaukee FICE Identification: 021366
Unit ID: 240338
Telephone: (414) 443-8800 Carnegie Class: Bac-Diverse
FAX Number: (414) 443-8514 Calendar System: Semester
URL: www.wlc.edu
Established: 1973 Annual Undergrad Tuition & Fees: $31,754
Enrollment: 1,166 Coed
Affiliation or Control: Independent Non-Profit IRS Status: 501(c)3
Highest Offering: Master's
Accreditation: HLC, EXSC, NURSE

01 President ....Dr. Daniel W. JOHNSON
05 Provost & VP of Academic Affairs ....Dr. John D. KOLANDER
11 Vice President Operations ....Mr. Ryan OERTEL
32 VP of Student Life ....Mr. Jon BOCHE
10 Vice Pres Finance ....Mrs. Diane HOEHNKE
26 Exec Dir Marketing & Communication ....Vacant
30 Vice Pres Development ....Mr. Richard MANNISTO
15 Exec Director of Human Resources ....Mr. Jon FLANAGAN
07 Vice President of Enrollment ....Mr. Lucas FAUST
06 Registrar ....Mr. Brett VALERIO
08 Director of Library Services ....Vacant
37 Director Student Financial Aid ....Mrs. Linda L. LOEFFEL
42 Campus Pastor ....Rev. Greg LYON
53 Director Teacher Education ....Prof. James HOLMAN
39 Director Residential Life/Housing ....Mr. Adam VOLBRECHT
41 Athletic Director ....Mr. Edward NOON
88 Director of Arts Programming ....Mrs. Loni BOYDL
13 Director of Information Technology ....Mr. John MEYER
29 Director of Alumni Relations ....Mrs. Lisa LEFFEL
88 Research Analyst ....Mr. Robert JUNE
24 Media Services Coordinator ....Mr. Tim SNYDER
04 Exec Assistant to the President ....Mrs. Barb MATTEK
09 Director of Institutional Research ....Mr. Rob HAHN
19 Director Security/Safety ....Mr. Dan SMITH
49 Dean College of Arts & Sciences ....Dr. Jarrod ERBE
107 Dean College Professional Studies ....Mr. David BRIGHTSMAN
76 Dean College of Health Sciences ....Dr. Robert BALZA, JR.

Wisconsin School of Professional Psychology (B)

9120 W Hampton Avenue #212,
Milwaukee WI 53225-4960

County: Milwaukee FICE Identification: 022713
Unit ID: 240213
Telephone: (414) 464-9777 Carnegie Class: Spec-4-yr-Other Health
FAX Number: (414) 358-5590 Calendar System: Semester
URL: www.wspp.edu
Established: 1979 Annual Graduate Tuition & Fees: N/A
Enrollment: 80 Coed
Affiliation or Control: Independent Non-Profit IRS Status: 501(c)3
Highest Offering: Doctorate; No Undergraduates
Accreditation: HLC, CLPSY

01 President ....Dr. Kathleen M. RUSCH
05 Dean ....Dr. Kristin A. JUERGENS
04 Assistant to the President ....Ms. Veronica V. EGERSON
17 Director Clinical Training ....Dr. Jamal R. CUNNINGHAM
08 Head Librarian ....Ms. Rebecca DOUGHERTY
37 Director Student Financial Aid ....Mr. Erik MOZOLIK

*Wisconsin Technical College System (C)

PO Box 7874, Madison WI 53707-7874

County: Dane Identification: 666185
Telephone: (608) 266-1207 Carnegie Class: N/A
FAX Number: N/A
URL: www.wtcsystem.edu

01 President ....Dr. Morna K. FOY
03 Executive Vice President ....Mr. James ZYLSTRA
05 Provost/Vice President ....Dr. Colleen MCCABE
04 Executive Staff Assistant ....Ms. Julie DRAKE

*Blackhawk Technical College (D)

PO Box 5009, Janesville WI 53547-5009

County: Rock FICE Identification: 005390
Unit ID: 238397
Telephone: (608) 758-6900 Carnegie Class: Assoc/HVT-Mix Trad/Non
FAX Number: (608) 757-7740 Calendar System: Semester
URL: www.blackhawk.edu
Established: 1912 Annual Undergrad Tuition & Fees (In-District): $4,505
Enrollment: 2,232 Coed
Affiliation or Control: State/Local IRS Status: 501(c)3
Highest Offering: Associate Degree
Accreditation: HLC, ACFEI, ADNUR, CSHSE, DA, DMS, MAC, MLTAD, PTAA, RAD, SURGT

02 President ....Dr. Tracy P. PIERNER
05 Vice President Academic Affairs ....Dr. Karen R. SCHMITT
10 Vice Pres Finance & College Opers ....Ms. Renea L. RANGUETTE
15 Exec Director/Chief HR Officer ....Ms. Kathleen BROSKE
09 Exec Dir Institutional Research ....Dr. Jon TYSSE
32 Exec Dir Student Services ....Mr. Anthony LANDOWSKI
04 Asst to President/District Board ....Ms. Julie M. BARREAU
13 Director IT Services ....Mr. Mitch MILLER
26 Exec Dir Marketing & Communications ....Ms. Elizabeth P. PAULSEN
97 Dean General Education ....Dr. Helen PROEBER
88 Learning Support Manager ....Mr. Darian SNOW
76 Dean Health Sciences/Public Safety ....Ms. Moira LAFAYETTE
19 Manager of Campus Safety & Security ....Mr. Brad K. SMITH
88 EMS Fire Service & Paramedic Coord ....Mr. Robert BALSAMO
72 Dean Advanced Mfg/Transport/Tech ....Mr. Greg PHILLIPS
50 Dean Business ....Dr. Helen PROEBER
21 Controller ....Mr. Gerri DOWNING
25 Grants Administration ....Ms. Amy E. ANDERSON
37 Financial Aid Manager ....Mr. Craig SCHULTZ
06 Registrar ....Ms. Michelle KELLEY
18 Facilities Director ....Mr. Steve KORMANAK
96 Accounting & Procurement Manager ....Ms. Kristine BYL
08 Dir Teaching & Learning Resources ....Ms. Lynn NEITZEL
102 Dir Foundation & Advancement ....Ms. Lisa HURDA
103 Director Workforce & Community Dev ....Mr. Mark BOROWICZ
88 Program Admin Law Enforcement ....Mr. Troy R. EGGERS

*Chippewa Valley Technical College (E)

620 W Clairemont Avenue, Eau Claire WI 54701-6162

County: Eau Claire FICE Identification: 005304
Unit ID: 240116
Telephone: (715) 833-6200 Carnegie Class: Assoc/HVT-High Non
FAX Number: (715) 833-6470 Calendar System: Semester
URL: www.cvtc.edu
Established: 1912 Annual Undergrad Tuition & Fees (In-District): $4,505
Enrollment: 7,367 Coed
Affiliation or Control: Local IRS Status: 501(c)3
Highest Offering: Associate Degree
Accreditation: HLC, ACBSP, ACFEI, ADNUR, CAHIIM, COARC, DH, DMS, EMT, MAC, MLTAD, NAEYC, PTAA, RAD, SURGT

02 President ....Dr. Sunem BEATON-GARCIA
05 Provost/VP of Academic Affairs ....Dr. Lynette LIVINGSTON
32 Vice President Student Services ....Vacant
10 Vice President Finance & Facilities ....Kirk L. MOIST
13 Vice President IT/CIO ....Tom J. LANGE
15 VP of Talent & Culture ....Tam BURGAU
26 VP of Strategic Comm & Cmty Engage ....Joni GEROUX
111 VP of Institutional Advancement ....Karen KOHLER
50 Exec Dean Bus/Arts/Science & Acad ....Vacant
88 Assoc Dean Emergency Services/RF ....Eric ANDERSON
75 Dean of Appr/Eng/Mfg/IT ....Jeff SULLIVAN
47 Dean Ag/Energy/Transport/Emer Serv ....Adam WEHLING
66 Dean of Nursing ....Gina PETRIE
20 Dean Academic/Development Services ....Holly HASSEMER
20 Director of Curriculum & Prof Devel ....Rachelle PHAKITTHONG
108 Dir of College Effectiveness ....Shana SCHMIDT
18 Director of Facilities ....Rod BAGLEY
21 Director of Finance & Budgeting ....Sara J. NICK
84 Director of Enrollment Services ....Jennifer ANDEREGG
88 Dir Advisement/Title IX Coordinator ....Natalyn M. MARLAIRE
119 Network & Infrastructure Manager ....Nate RUNGE
12 Bus Dev/Menomonie Campus Manager ....Daniel LYTLE
12 Bus Dev/Chip Falls Campus Manager ....Angela ECKMAN
88 Recruitment & Bus Dev Manager ....Kendra WEBER
06 Registrar ....Jessica SCHWARTZ
37 Director Financial Aid ....Kim YODER
105 Marketing & Digital Exp Manager ....Sara PERTZ
88 Director K-12 Initiatives ....Kristel TAVARE
19 Public Safety Manager ....Mark PROVOST
35 Director of Student Central ....Forrest BUCK
35 Director of Student Life ....Alisa S. SCHLEY
96 Purchasing Coordinator ....Jody SCHNEIDER
28 Diversity Manager ....Mitch BARONI
88 Assistant Registrar ....Kristin CREVISTON
107 Director of Professional Dev ....Claire RODER
04 Executive Asst to President & Board ....Lauren SULLIVAN

*Fox Valley Technical College (F)

1825 N Bluemound Drive, Appleton WI 54914-1643

County: Outagamie FICE Identification: 009744
Unit ID: 238722
Telephone: (920) 735-5600 Carnegie Class: Assoc/HVT-High Non
FAX Number: (920) 735-2582 Calendar System: Semester
URL: www.fvtc.edu
Established: 1967 Annual Undergrad Tuition & Fees (In-District): $4,677
Enrollment: 11,711 Coed
Affiliation or Control: State/Local IRS Status: 501(c)3
Highest Offering: Associate Degree
Accreditation: HLC, ACFEI, ADNUR, CAHIIM, DA, DH, EMT, MAC, MLTAD, NDT, OTA, PNUR

02 President/CEO ....Dr. Chris MATHENY
05 VP Learning/CAO ....Dr. Jennifer LANTER
32 VP Student Success ....Mrs. Elizabeth BURNS
15 Int VP Human Resources/CHRO ....Ms. Susan KAUFMAN
10 VP Financial Svcs & Facilities/CFO ....Ms. Amy VAN STRATEN
13 VP Information Tech/CIO ....Mr. Troy KOHL
28 VP Diversity/Equity/Inclusion ....Mr. Rayon BROWN
97 Dean General Studies ....Dr. Jennifer LANTER
47 Dean Mfg/Construction & Agric ....Mr. Steve STRAUB
102 Exec Dir FVTC Foundation/Cmty Rels ....Ms. Rebecca BOULANGER
12 Associate VP Regional Campuses ....Ms. Deb HEATH
37 Director Student Financial Svcs ....Ms. Stacy DORAN
06 Registrar ....Ms. Shannon GERKE-CORRIGAN
26 Director College Marketing ....Ms. Barb DREGER
118 Director Compensation & Benefits ....Ms. Heather ZWEIGER
88 Director Venture Center ....Ms. Amy PIETSCH
108 AVP College Effectiveness & Accred ....Dr. Kim OLSON

*Gateway Technical College (G)

3520 30th Avenue, Kenosha WI 53144-1690

County: Kenosha FICE Identification: 005389
Unit ID: 238759
Telephone: (262) 564-2200 Carnegie Class: Assoc/HVT-Mix Trad/Non
FAX Number: (262) 564-2201 Calendar System: Semester
URL: www.gtc.edu
Established: 1911 Annual Undergrad Tuition & Fees (In-District): $4,621
Enrollment: 7,839 Coed
Affiliation or Control: State/Local IRS Status: 501(c)3
Highest Offering: Associate Degree
Accreditation: HLC, ACBSP, ADNUR, CAHIIM, CSHSE, DA, EMT, MAC, PTAA, SURGT

*Lakeshore Technical College (H)

1290 North Avenue, Cleveland WI 53015-1414

County: Manitowoc FICE Identification: 009194
Unit ID: 239008
Telephone: (920) 693-1000 Carnegie Class: Assoc/HVT-High Non
FAX Number: (920) 693-8078 Calendar System: Semester
URL: www.gotoltc.edu
Established: 1912 Annual Undergrad Tuition & Fees (In-District): $4,417
Enrollment: 2,420 Coed
Affiliation or Control: State/Local IRS Status: 501(c)3
Highest Offering: Associate Degree
Accreditation: HLC, ACFEI, ADNUR, CAHIIM, EMT, MAAB, PNUR, RAD

02 President ....Dr. Paul CARLSEN
04 Executive Assistant ....Ms. Heidi SOODSMA
05 Vice President of Instruction ....Mr. James LEMEROND
32 Vice President of Student Success ....Ms. Polly ABTS
11 Vice President of Administration ....Ms. Brenda RIESTERER
45 Vice Pres of Strategy/Outreach ....Ms. Tanya WASMER
111 Vice President of Advancement ....Ms. Kristin LIPHART

*Madison Area Technical College (I)

1701 Wright Street, Madison WI 53704-2599

County: Dane FICE Identification: 004007
Unit ID: 238263
Telephone: (608) 246-6100 Carnegie Class: Assoc/HVT-Mix Trad/Non
FAX Number: (608) 246-6880 Calendar System: Semester
URL: www.madisoncollege.edu
Established: 1912 Annual Undergrad Tuition & Fees (In-District): $4,530
Enrollment: 13,057 Coed
Affiliation or Control: State/Local IRS Status: 501(c)3
Highest Offering: Associate Degree
Accreditation: HLC, ACFEI, ADNUR, COARC, CSHSE, DH, EMT, MAC, MLTAD, OPTT, OTA, RAD, SURGT

02 President ....Dr. Jack E. DANIELS, III
04 Exec Asst to the President ....Ms. Kristin ROLLING
05 Provost/EVP Academic Affairs ....Dr. Turina BAKKEN
45 VP Academic Strategy & Planning ....Dr. Shawna M. CARTER
26 Chief Marketing Officer ....Ms. Kristin UTTECH
32 EVP Student Affairs ....Dr. Timothy L. CASPER
10 EVP Finance/Administration ....Dr. Mark THOMAS
84 VP Strategic Enrollment Management ....Mr. Ali R. ZARRINNAM
15 VP Human Resources ....Ms. Rosemary BUSCHHAUS
11 VP Administration ....Ms. Sylvia RAMIREZ
13 Chief Information Officer ....Dr. Shawn BELLING
103 Dean Workforce Education ....Ms. Schauna RASMUSSEN
88 Dean Academic Advancement ....Dr. Leslie PETTY
20 Vice Provost ....Dr. Denise REIMER
49 Dean Arts/Hum & Soc Sciences ....Mr. Brian SHORT

50 Dean Business & Applied Arts ....Dr. Ramon ORTIZ
76 Exec Dean Health Sciences/Nursing .... Dr. Marsha TWEEDY
88 VP Industry & Regional Affairs .... Mr. Bryan M. WOODHOUSE
54 Dean Engr/Science & Math .... Dr. Kevin MIRUS
35 Dean of Students ....Dr. Geraldo G. VILACRUZ
35 Director Student Life ....Ms. Renee M. ALFANO
06 Registrar ....Mr. Bill W. DOUGHERTY
08 Director Library Services ....Ms. Julie C. GORES
41 Athletic Director .... Mr. Jason VERHELST
22 Dir Disability Res and Testing ....Mr. Scott RITTER
21 CFO/Controller ....Ms. Laurie M. GRIGG
102 Chief Exec Officer Foundation ....Ms. Tammy THAYER
12 VP Goodman South Campus ....Ms. Valentina AHEDO
37 Dean Student Access & Success ....Dr. Keyimani ALFORD
28 VP Equity/Diversity/Cmty Relations .... Dr. Damira GRADY
19 Director Public Safety ....Mr. John FLANNERY

*Mid-State Technical College (A)

500 32nd Street N, Wisconsin Rapids WI 54494-5599
County: Wood FICE Identification: 005380
Unit ID: 239220
Telephone: (715) 422-5300 Carnegie Class: Assoc/HVT-High Non
FAX Number: (715) 422-5345 Calendar System: Semester
URL: www.mstc.edu
Established: 1967 Annual Undergrad Tuition & Fees (In-District): $4,451
Enrollment: 2,648 Coed
Affiliation or Control: State/Local IRS Status: 501(c)3
Highest Offering: Associate Degree
Accreditation: HLC, ADNUR, CAHIIM, COARC, EMT, MAC, SURGT

02 President ....Dr. Shelly MONDEIK
05 Vice President Academics ....Dr. Deb STENCIL
32 Vice Pres Student Svcs/Enroll Mgmt ....Dr. Mandy LANG
10 Vice President Finance/Facilities ....Mr. Greg BRUCKBAUER
15 Vice President HR & Org Dev .... Dr. Karen BRZEZINSKI
103 Vice President Workforce & Pub Rels ....Dr. Bobbi DAMROW
97 Dean Gen Educ & Learning Resource .... Ms. Amber STANCHER
50 Dean Business & Technology .... Dr. Missy SKURZEWSKI-SERVANT
65 Dean Trans/Agric/Nat Res & Constr .... Mr. Ryan KAWSKI
76 Dean Health/Protective & Human Svcs ....Dr. Colleen KANE
12 Dean Stevens Point Campus ....Mr. Ben NUSZ
12 Dean Marshfield Campus .... Dr. Alex LENDVED
35 Dean Student Support .... Ms. Christina LORGE-GROVER
26 Director Marketing & Communication ..Mr. John Eric HOFFMANN
102 Director Foundation and Alumni ....Ms. Jill STECKBAUER
18 Director Facilities/Procurement ....Mr. Craig WAGNER
06 Registrar .... Ms. Jennifer CONWELL
04 Executive Administrative Assistant ....Ms. Angela SUSA
37 Manager Financial Aid .... Ms. Shelly WEICHELT

*Milwaukee Area Technical College (B)

700 W State Street, Milwaukee WI 53233-1443
County: Milwaukee FICE Identification: 003866
Unit ID: 239248
Telephone: (414) 297-6600 Carnegie Class: Assoc/HVT-High Trad
FAX Number: (414) 297-7990 Calendar System: Semester
URL: www.matc.edu
Established: 1912 Annual Undergrad Tuition & Fees (In-District): $4,730
Enrollment: 12,618 Coed
Affiliation or Control: Local IRS Status: 501(c)3
Highest Offering: Associate Degree
Accreditation: HLC, ACFEI, ADNUR, AT, CAHIIM, COARC, CVT, DH, DIETT, EMT, FUSER, MAC, MLTAD, NAEYC, OTA, PNUR, PTAA, RAD, SURGT

02 President ....Dr. Vicki J. MARTIN
05 VP Learning .... Dr. Mohammad DAKWAR
06 Registrar ....Dr. Sarah ADAMS
10 Vice President of Finance .... Mr. Jeffrey HOLLOW
43 Interim General Counsel .... Ms. Kristen DECATO
13 Chief Information Officer ....Mr. David ROWE
23 Dean Healthcare Pathway ....Dr. Eric GASS
12 Campus Exec Dir West Allis Campus ...Dr. Richard BUSALACCHI
24 VP/General Manager Milwaukee PBS .... Mr. Bohdan ZACHARY
35 VP of Retention & Completion ....Dr. Jeff JANZ
08 Dean of Student Experience ....Mr. Equan BURROWS
37 Director Financial Aid .... Ms. Christine ZOLLICOFFER
90 Director Technical Services ....Mr. Michael GAVIN
21 Controller ....Ms. Eva KUETHER
19 Lieutenant Public Safety ....Lt. Karina TAYLOR
07 Director Admissions .... Dr. Nicole TANNER
09 Director of Institutional Research ....Dr. Yan WANG
84 Manager Recruitment .... Ms. Sophia WILLIAMS
29 Vice Pres Coll Advancement/Ext Comm ....Ms. Laura BRAY
108 VP Institutional Effectiveness ....Dr. Christine MANION
26 Coord Design Center/Mktg & Comm .... Ms. Kathryn KAESERMANN
96 Procurement Manager ....Ms. Laura MOORE
41 Coordinator Athletics ....Mr. Randy CASEY
28 Chf Diversity/Equity/Inclusion Ofcr .... Ms. Eva MARTINEZ-POWLESS
121 Exec Vice President Student Success .... Dr. Naydeen GONZALEZ-DE JESUS
15 Vice Pres Human Resource Services ....Ms. Elle BONDS

*Moraine Park Technical College (C)

235 N National Avenue, Fond Du Lac WI 54936-1940
County: Fond Du Lac FICE Identification: 009256
Unit ID: 239372
Telephone: (920) 922-8611 Carnegie Class: Assoc/HVT-Mix Trad/Non
FAX Number: (920) 929-2471 Calendar System: Semester
URL: www.morainepark.edu
Established: 1967 Annual Undergrad Tuition & Fees (In-District): $4,505
Enrollment: 2,654 Coed
Affiliation or Control: State/Local IRS Status: 501(c)3
Highest Offering: Associate Degree
Accreditation: HLC, ADNUR, CAHIIM, COARC, EMT, MAC, MLTAD, RAD, SURGT

02 President ....Bonnie BAERWALD
05 Vice President Academic Affairs .... James R. EDEN
10 VP Finance and Administration ....Carrie KASUBASKI
32 Vice President Student Services ....James BARRETT
13 Chief Information Officer .... Jerry RICHARDS
20 Dean of Applied Technology & Trades .... Fred RICE
23 Dean of Health & Human Services .... Barb JASCR
97 Dean of General Education .... Lane HOLTE
103 Dean Economic & Workforce Devel .... JoAnn HALL
12 Dean of the West Bend Campus ....Peter J. RETTLER
35 Dean of Students .... Scott LIEBURN
111 Director of College Advancement ....Dana BOURLAND
26 Dir Marketing/Communications ....Mandy POTTS
09 Director of Inst Effectiveness .... Laura WAURIO
21 Director of Finance .... Tara WENDT
08 Library Services Coordinator .... Hans BAIERL
18 Facilities Operation Manager ....Benjamin HILL
96 Purchasing Manager .... Timothy KEENAN
19 Security Manager ....John FAEH
04 Admin Assistant to the President ....Jaclyn JELINEK

*Nicolet Area Technical College (D)

5364 College Drive, PO Box 518,
Rhinelander WI 54501-0518
County: Oneida FICE Identification: 005384
Unit ID: 239442
Telephone: (715) 365-4493 Carnegie Class: Assoc/HVT-Mix Trad/Non
FAX Number: (715) 365-4445 Calendar System: Trimester
URL: www.nicoletcollege.edu
Established: 1967 Annual Undergrad Tuition & Fees (In-State): $4,505
Enrollment: 1,236 Coed
Affiliation or Control: State IRS Status: 501(c)3
Highest Offering: Associate Degree
Accreditation: HLC, ADNUR, MAC

02 President ....Ms. Kate FERREL
05 Executive VP Acad & Student Affs ....Vacant
10 VP for Finance/Administration ....Mr. John VAN DE LOO
15 Director of Human Resources ....Vacant
13 CIO .... Mr. Greg MILJEVICH
66 Dean of Health Occupations .... Ms. Candy DAILEY
103 Exec Dir Economic/Community Dev .... Ms. Sandy BISHOP
49 Dean of Univ Transfer/Liberal Arts ......Ms. Laura WIND-NORTON
88 Dean of Trade/Industry/Apprentice ....Mr. Jeff LABS
19 Assoc Dean/Dir Pub Safety/Security .... Mr. Jason GOELDNER
18 Director of Facilities ....Mr. Pete VANNEY
37 Financial Aid Manager .... Mr. Patrick BURNS
102 Foundation Executive Director ....Ms. Heather SCHALLOCK
108 Dir Inst Effectiveness/Staff Dev .... Ms. Kelly HAVERKAMPF
45 Dir Instructional Effectiveness ......Ms. Penny MERTZ KUCKKAHN
06 Registrar ....Mr. Joseph HAFERMAN
04 Exec Asst to President/Board ....Ms. Anne E. WIEDMAIER
08 Manager of Library Services ....Ms. Nora CRAVEN
28 Diversity and Tribal Outreach Coord ....Ms. Susan CRAZY THUNDER

*Northcentral Technical College (E)

1000 W Campus Drive, Wausau WI 54401-1880
County: Marathon FICE Identification: 005387
Unit ID: 239460
Telephone: (715) 675-3331 Carnegie Class: Assoc/HVT-High Non
FAX Number: (715) 675-9776 Calendar System: Semester
URL: www.ntc.edu
Established: 1912 Annual Undergrad Tuition & Fees (In-District): $3,673
Enrollment: 5,939 Coed
Affiliation or Control: Local IRS Status: 501(c)3
Highest Offering: Associate Degree
Accreditation: HLC, #ACBSP, ADNUR, DH, EMT, MAC, MLTAD, RAD, SURGT

01 President .... Dr. Jeannie M. WORDEN
05 VP for Learning ....Dr. Darren ACKLEY
32 VP Student Services ....Dr. Sarah DILLON
10 VP of Finance & General Counsel .... Ms. Roxanne LUTGEN
102 Dir Resource Dev/Exec Dir Found .... Dr. Vicki JEPPESEN
13 AVP Info Tech/Chf Information Ofcr .... Dr. Chet A. STREBE
15 VP of HR & Risk Management ....Ms. Cher VINK
18 AVP of Facilities Management ....Mr. Rob ELLIOTT
86 VP of Community & Govt Relations ....Mrs. Katrina FELCH
107 Exec Dean of Academic Excellence .... Dr. Emily STUCKENBRUCK
50 Dean Business and Virtual College ....Dr. Brandy BREUCKMAN
76 Dean of Health Sciences .... Ms. Marlene ROBERTS
22 Employment Coord/Affirm Action Ofcr ....Ms. Cindy THELEN
84 Senior Dir Enrollment Strategy ....Mr. Nick BLANCHETTE
19 Director of Security .... Mr. Jordan SCHULT
06 Registrar ....Mrs. Wendi LUDWIG
121 Dean of Student Success ....Dr. Shannon LIVINGSTON
103 Dean Workforce Training/Prof Devel .... Dr. Brad GAST
04 Executive Asst to President .... Mrs. Nicole KOPP
37 Director Student Financial Aid .... Mr. Jeff CICHON
47 Dean Agricultural Sciences .... Dr. Greg CISEWSKI
97 Dean of General Studies .... Dr. Brooke SCHINDLER
54 Dean Engineering/Adv Manufacturing .... Mr. Iain CAMERON

44 Director Annual Giving .... Ms. Sheila ROSSMILLER
106 Dean of Academic Technology .... Mr. Jon DEGROOT
07 Director of Enrollment .... Mr. Nick LAMPONE

*Northeast Wisconsin Technical College (F)

PO Box 19042, 2740 W Mason Street,
Green Bay WI 54307-9042
County: Brown FICE Identification: 005301
Unit ID: 239488
Telephone: (920) 498-5444 Carnegie Class: Assoc/HVT-Mix Trad/Non
FAX Number: (920) 498-6260 Calendar System: Semester
URL: www.nwtc.edu
Established: 1913 Annual Undergrad Tuition & Fees (In-District): $4,659
Enrollment: 10,763 Coed
Affiliation or Control: State/Local IRS Status: 501(c)3
Highest Offering: Associate Degree
Accreditation: HLC, ACBSP, ADNUR, CAHIIM, COARC, DA, DH, DMS, EMT, MAC, MLTAD, PNUR, PTAA, RAD, SURGT

02 President ....Dr. H. Jeffrey RAFN
05 Vice President of Learning .... Dr. Kathryn ROGALSKI
32 Vice President of Student Services ....Dr. Colleen SIMPSON
111 Vice Pres of College Advancement ....Ms. Meridith K. JAEGER
15 Vice President of Human Resources ....Vacant
13 Chief Information Officer ....Mr. Daniel MINCHEFF
10 VP Business & Finance ....Dr. Robert MATHEWS
12 Dean Regional Learning ....Ms. Jan SCOVILLE
50 Dean College of Business ....Mr. Michael VANDER HEIDEN
76 Dean Health Science ....Mr. Scott ANDERSON
72 Dean Trades & Engr Technologies ....Dr. Amy KOX
97 Dean General Education .... Ms. Michaeline SCHMIT
19 Dean Public Safety .... Ms. Cynthia ESTRUP
20 Dean Learning Solutions ....Ms. Jennifer STOLPA FLATT
103 Dean Corp Training/Economic Dev ....Vacant
121 Dean of Student Success ....Vacant
07 Dean Enrollment Services/Registrar .... Mr. Mark FRANKS
37 Financial Aid Director ....Ms. Stephanie FEUCHT
102 Foundation Director .... Ms. Crystal HARRISON
40 Director Bookstore .... Mr. Patrick SORELLE
26 Public Relations/Comm Specialist .... Ms. Tara CRIBB
18 Director of Facilities ....Mr. Chet LAMERS
08 Manager Library Services ....Ms. Kim LAPLANTE
104 Mgr Student Involvement/Intl Pgm ....Ms. Megan POPKEY
04 Administrative Asst to President ....Ms. Janel KARBAN
09 Institutional Researcher .... Mr. Jeff GREBINOSKI
105 Director Web Services ....Ms. Erica PLAZA
28 Director of Diversity ....Vacant
19 Director Security/Safety .... Mr. Philip SCHAEFER
96 Dir of Procurement & Distribution ....Ms. Jennifer CANAVERA

*Northwood Technical College (G)

1900 College Drive, Rice Lake WI 54868
County: Barron FICE Identification: 011824
Unit ID: 240198
Telephone: (715) 234-7082 Carnegie Class: Assoc/HVT-High Non
FAX Number: (715) 234-1241 Calendar System: Semester
URL: www.northwoodtech.edu
Established: 1968 Annual Undergrad Tuition & Fees (In-State): $4,917
Enrollment: 2,818 Coed
Affiliation or Control: State IRS Status: Exempt
Highest Offering: Associate Degree
Accreditation: HLC, ADNUR, CAHIIM, DA, OTA

02 President ....Dr. John WILL
10 VP Admin Svcs/CFO/RL Campus Admin .... Mr. Steven DECKER
05 Vice President Academic Affairs ....Dr. Aliesha R. CROWE
32 VP Student Affs/Ashland Campus Adm .... Dr. Steve BITZER
103 Dean Workforce/Cmty Development .... Ms. Bambi PATTERMAN
09 VP Inst Effective/Richmond Camp Adm ....Ms. Susan YOHNK LOCKWOOD
13 Sr Director Technology Services ....Mr. Bill HODGE
37 Director Financial Aid ....Mr. Terry KLEIN
06 Registrar .... Mr. Shane EVENSON
84 Director of Enrollment Services .... Ms. Laura SULLIVAN
26 AVP Mktg/Comms/Superior Campus Adm .... Ms. Jena VOGTMAN
15 Director Human Resources ....Ms. Amanda GOHDE

*Southwest Wisconsin Technical College (H)

1800 Bronson Boulevard, Fennimore WI 53809-9778
County: Grant FICE Identification: 007669
Unit ID: 239910
Telephone: (608) 822-3262 Carnegie Class: Assoc/HVT-High Non
FAX Number: (608) 822-6019 Calendar System: Semester
URL: www.swtc.edu
Established: 1967 Annual Undergrad Tuition & Fees (In-District): $4,500
Enrollment: 2,581 Coed
Affiliation or Control: State/Local IRS Status: Exempt
Highest Offering: Associate Degree
Accreditation: HLC, ADNUR, CAHIIM, MAC, MEAC, MLTAD, PTAA

02 President ....Dr. Jason S. WOOD
10 VP for Administrative Services ....Mr. Caleb WHITE
05 Chief Academic Officer ....Dr. Kathleen E. GARRITY
47 Dean of Industry/Trades/Agriculture .... Dr. Derek DACHELET
32 Chief Student Services Officer ....Ms. Holly CLENDENEN
15 Chief Human Resources Officer .... Ms. Krista WEBER

108	Manager of College Effectiveness	Ms. Mandy HENKEL
102	Director of Foundation	Ms. Kim SCHMELZ
13	Director of IT Services	Mr. Heath AHNEN
101	Executive Services Director	Ms. Karen M. CAMPBELL
18	Director of Facilities	Mr. Dan IMHOFF
37	Financial Aid Manager	Ms. Corabeth HALVORSON
19	Director of Public Safety	Ms. Kris WUBBEN
20	Innovative/Alternative Learning Dir	Ms. Kim MAIER
21	Controller	Ms. Kelly KELLY
88	Director of Pre-College Programs	Ms. Julie PLUEMER
06	Registrar	Ms. Danielle SEIPPEL
109	Dining Services Manager	Mr. Rex SMITH
76	Dean of Health Occupations/Service	Ms. Cynde LARSEN

*Waukesha County Technical College (A)

800 Main Street, Pewaukee WI 53072-4696
County: Waukesha — FICE Identification: 005294
Unit ID: 240125
Telephone: (262) 691-5566 — Carnegie Class: Assoc/HVT-High Non
FAX Number: (262) 691-5593 — Calendar System: Semester
URL: www.wctc.edu
Established: 1923 — Annual Undergrad Tuition & Fees (In-District): $4,588
Enrollment: 6,952 — Coed
Affiliation or Control: State/Local — IRS Status: 501(c)3
Highest Offering: Associate Degree
Accreditation: HLC, ACFEI, ADNUR, CAHIIM, DH, EMT, MAC, NAEYC, SURGT

02	President	Dr. Richard G. BARNHOUSE
05	Provost	Dr. Ann KRAUSE-HANSON
20	VP Learning	Dr. Bradley PIAZZA
32	VP Student Services	Ms. Angela FRAZIER
10	VP Finance	Dr. Jane KITTEL
15	VP Human Resource Svcs	Mr. David BROWN
13	Chief Information Officer	Mr. Rodney NOBLES
102	Dir Foundation/Corporate Relations	Ms. Ellen PHILLIPS
50	Dean Business Occupations	Mr. Jon KOCH
38	Dean Support/Couns/Advs & Access	Dr. Christopher DAOOD
75	Dean Industrial Occupations	Mr. Michael SHIELS
88	Dean Service Occupations	Dr. Greg WEST
97	Dean Acad Foundation & General Stds	Ms. Bethany LEONARD
76	Dean Health Occupations	Ms. Michele NELSON
26	Director PR/Marketing & Outreach	Mr. Andrew PALEN
18	Director Facilities Services	Mr. Jeffrey LEVERENZ
06	Registrar	Ms. Rachel BURLING
36	Mgr Career Development Services	Ms. Debra WEBER
51	Dir Corporate Training Ctr	Mr. James DRAEGER
28	Chief Officer Diversity	Ms. Sherry SIMMONS
07	Mgr Admissions/Testing Svcs	Ms. Kathleen KAZDA
88	Director Academic Excellence	Dr. Randall COOROUGH
09	Director of Institutional Research	Dr. Viktor BRENNER
37	Manager Financial Aid	Mr. Justin KEHRING
35	Coordinator Student Life	Mr. Jonathan N. PEDRAZA
08	Director of Library Services	Ms. Amy MANION
19	Environ Health & Safety Supervisor	Mr. Bruce NEUMANN
27	Specialist Public Relations	Ms. Michelle NELSON
96	Purchasing Specialist	Ms. Victoria NASH
04	Admin Assistant to the President	Ms. Kristan GOCHENAUER

*Western Technical College (B)

400 N Seventh Street, La Crosse WI 54601-3368
County: La Crosse — FICE Identification: 003840
Unit ID: 240170
Telephone: (608) 785-9200 — Carnegie Class: Assoc/HVT-High Trad
FAX Number: (608) 785-9205 — Calendar System: Trimester
URL: www.westerntc.edu
Established: 1912 — Annual Undergrad Tuition & Fees (In-District): $4,500
Enrollment: 4,240 — Coed
Affiliation or Control: State/Local — IRS Status: 501(c)3
Highest Offering: Associate Degree
Accreditation: HLC, ADNUR, CAHIIM, COARC, DA, EMT, MAC, MLTAD, OTA, PTAA, RAD, SURGT

02	President	Dr. Roger STANFORD
10	Vice President Finance/Operations	Mr. Wade HACKBARTH
32	VP Student Service & Engagement	Ms. Amy THORNTON
102	Executive Director Foundation	Mr. Michael SWENSON
37	Financial Aid Manager	Ms. Jerolyn R. GRANDALL
21	Controller	Ms. Christina HEIT
103	Director of Business/Industry Svcs	Ms. Angie MARTIN
07	Director of Enrollment Services	Ms. Debra HETHER
36	Director Advising & Career Service	Ms. Barb KELSEY
38	Director of Counseling & Case Mgmt	Ms. Ann BRANDAU-HYNEK
06	Registrar/Stdnt Info System Coord	Ms. Sandy PETERSON
35	Dean of Students	Ms. Shelley MCNEELY
72	Dean Integrated Technology	Mr. Josh GAMER
76	Dean Health & Public Safety	Mr. Kevin DEAN
97	Dean General Education	Mr. John GILLETTE
50	Dean Business Education	Mr. Gary BROWN
13	Director Information Technology	Ms. Joan PIERCE
26	Director Marketing & Communications	Ms. Julie LEMON
29	Manager Alumni Relations	Ms. Stephanie KNUTSON
40	Manager Campus Shop	Mr. David R. WIGNES
15	Director Human Resources	Mr. John HEATH
09	Exec Dir Planning & Org Excellence	Ms. Tracy DRYDEN

*Chippewa Valley Technical College-Gateway (C)

2320 Alpine Road, Eau Claire WI 54703
Telephone: (715) 874-4600 — Identification: 770420

*Chippewa Valley Technical College River Falls Campus (D)

500 South Wasson Lane, River Falls WI 54722
Telephone: (715) 425-3301 — Identification: 770423
Accreditation: &HLC

*Chippewa Valley Technical College-West (E)

4000 Campus Road, Eau Claire WI 54703
Telephone: (715) 852-1394 — Identification: 770421
Accreditation: &HLC

*Madison Area Technical College Commercial Avenue Education Center (F)

2125 Commercial Avenue, Madison WI 53704
Telephone: (608) 246-6100 — Identification: 770436
Accreditation: &HLC

*Madison Area Technical College Downtown Education Center (G)

1701 Wright Street, Madison WI 53704
Telephone: (608) 246-6100 — Identification: 770437
Accreditation: &HLC

*Madison Area Technical College Fort Atkinson (H)

827 Banker Road, Fort Atkinson WI 53538
Telephone: (920) 568-7200 — Identification: 770435
Accreditation: &HLC

*Madison Area Technical College Portage (I)

330 West Collins Street, Portage WI 53901
Telephone: (608) 745-3100 — Identification: 770438
Accreditation: &HLC

*Madison Area Technical College Reedsburg (J)

300 Alexander Avenue, Reedsburg WI 53959
Telephone: (608) 524-7800 — Identification: 770439
Accreditation: &HLC

*Madison Area Technical College Watertown (K)

1300 West Main Street, Watertown WI 53098
Telephone: (920) 206-8000 — Identification: 770440
Accreditation: &HLC

*Moraine Park Technical College (L)

700 Gould Street, Beaver Dam WI 53916
Telephone: (920) 887-1428 — Identification: 770446
Accreditation: &HLC

*Moraine Park Technical College (M)

2151 North Main Street, West Bend WI 53090
Telephone: (262) 335-5713 — Identification: 770447
Accreditation: &HLC

*Northeast Wisconsin Technical College-Marinette Campus (N)

1601 University Drive, Marinette WI 54143
Telephone: (715) 735-9361 — Identification: 770448
Accreditation: &HLC

*Northeast Wisconsin Technical College-Sturgeon Bay Campus (O)

229 N 14th Avenue, Sturgeon Bay WI 54235
Telephone: (920) 746-4900 — Identification: 770449
Accreditation: &HLC

*Northwood Technical College-Ashland Campus (P)

2100 Beaser Avenue, Ashland WI 54806
Telephone: (715) 682-8040 — Identification: 770463
Accreditation: &HLC

*Northwood Technical College-New Richmond Campus (Q)

1019 S Knowles Avenue, New Richmond WI 54017
Telephone: (715) 246-6561 — Identification: 770464
Accreditation: &HLC, MAC

*Northwood Technical College-Superior Campus (R)

600 North 21st Street, Superior WI 54880
Telephone: (715) 394-6677 — Identification: 770466

Accreditation: &HLC, MAC

Wright Graduate University for the Realization of Human Potential (S)

N7698 County Highway H, Elkhorn WI 53121
County: Walworth — Identification: 667224
Unit ID: 486460
Telephone: (262) 742-4444 — Carnegie Class: Spec-4-yr-Other
FAX Number: (262) 721-0752 — Calendar System: Quarter
URL: www.wrightgrad.edu
Established: 2006 — Annual Graduate Tuition & Fees: N/A
Enrollment: 30 — Coed
Affiliation or Control: Independent Non-Profit — IRS Status: 501(c)3
Highest Offering: Doctorate; No Undergraduates
Accreditation: DEAC, IACBE

00	Chief Executive Officer	Dr. Bob WRIGHT
01	Chancellor/CFO	Dr. Michael ZWELL
05	Chief Academic Officer	Dr. Judith WRIGHT
11	Campus Director	Ms. Kate HOLMQUEST

WYOMING

Casper College (T)

125 College Drive, Casper WY 82601-2458
County: Natrona — FICE Identification: 003928
Unit ID: 240505
Telephone: (307) 268-2110 — Carnegie Class: Assoc/MT-VT-Mix Trad/Non
FAX Number: (307) 268-2682 — Calendar System: Semester
URL: www.caspercollege.edu
Established: 1945 — Annual Undergrad Tuition & Fees (In-District): $3,882
Enrollment: 3,551 — Coed
Affiliation or Control: Local — IRS Status: 501(c)3
Highest Offering: Associate Degree
Accreditation: HLC, ACBSP, ADNUR, ART, COARC, DANCE, EMT, MLTAD, MUS, NAEYC, OTA, RAD, THEA

01	President	Dr. Darren D. DIVINE
05	Vice President Academic Affairs	Dr. Brandon KOSINE
32	Vice President Student Services	Ms. Kim BYRD
10	Vice Pres Administrative Services	Ms. Lynnde COLLING
15	Director Human Resources	Ms. Rhonda FRANZEN
07	Director Admissions/Student Success	Ms. Leanne LOYA
26	Director of Public Relations	Mr. Chris LORENZEN
18	Director Physical Plant	Mr. Eric RULOFSON
38	Director Student Counseling	Ms. Erin FORD
08	Director of the Library	Ms. Katrina BROWN
13	Director Information Technology	Mr. Kent BROOKS
121	Director of Student Success Service	Ms. Leanne LOYA
39	Director of Housing	Mr. Corey PEACOCK
41	Athletic Director	Mr. Paul MARBEL
19	Director Campus Security	Mr. John BECKER
102	Exec Director Foundation	Ms. Denise BRESSLER
09	Institutional Researcher	Mr. Michael DEAL
37	Director of Student Financial Aid	Mrs. Shannon ESKAM
21	Dir Financial Services/Controller	Ms. Robyn LANDEN
96	Purchasing Coordinator	Mr. Shane PULLIAM
06	Registrar	Ms. Linda NICHOLS
29	Director Alumni Relations	Vacant
04	Executive Asst to President	Ms. Tina SILVA
108	Director Institutional Assessment	Dr. Michael BROOKS
25	Grant Coordinator	Ms. Katie MCMILLAN

Central Wyoming College (U)

2660 Peck Avenue, Riverton WY 82501-1520
County: Fremont — FICE Identification: 007289
Unit ID: 240514
Telephone: (307) 855-2000 — Carnegie Class: Assoc/MT-VT-Mix Trad/Non
FAX Number: (307) 855-2095 — Calendar System: Semester
URL: www.cwc.edu
Established: 1966 — Annual Undergrad Tuition & Fees (In-District): $4,500
Enrollment: 1,755 — Coed
Affiliation or Control: Local — IRS Status: 501(c)3
Highest Offering: Associate Degree
Accreditation: HLC, ADNUR

01	President	Dr. Brad TYNDALL
04	Exec Asst to the President/Board	Ms. Linda BENDER
05	Vice Pres Academic Affairs	Dr. Katherine WELLS
10	Vice Pres Admin Svcs/CFO	Mr. Willie NOSEEP
32	Vice Pres Student Affairs	Dr. Cory DALY
13	Chief Information Officer	Mr. John WOOD
18	Chief Facilities/Physical Plant	Mr. Wayne ROBINSON
08	Director of Library	Ms. Staci GREEN
26	Exec Director of Marketing/Pub Rels	Ms. Jennifer MARSHALL
15	Dir for Human Resources	Mr. Scott MILLER
21	Finance Officer	Ms. Lindy PASKETT
19	Director of Campus Safety/Security	Mr. Chuck CARR
103	Dean Business/Technical & Workforce	Ms. Lynne MCAULIFFE
35	Dean of Students	Mr. Steve BARLOW
06	Registrar	Ms. Connie NYBERG
49	Dean for Arts & Sciences	Dr. Mark NORDEEN
102	Exec Director CWC Foundation	Ms. Beth MONTEIRO
09	Director of Institutional Research	Vacant

Eastern Wyoming College (A)

3200 W C Street, Torrington WY 82240-1699
County: Goshen FICE Identification: 003929
Unit ID: 240596
Telephone: (307) 532-8200 Carnegie Class: Assoc/HVT-High Non
FAX Number: (307) 532-8229 Calendar System: Semester
URL: ewc.wy.edu/
Established: 1948 Annual Undergrad Tuition & Fees (In-District): $4,110
Enrollment: 1,430 Coed
Affiliation or Control: State/Local IRS Status: 501(c)3
Highest Offering: Associate Degree
Accreditation: HLC

01 President .... Dr. Jeffry HAWES
04 Exec Asst to President/Board .... Ms. Sally WATSON
05 VP for Academic Services .... Mr. Roger HUMPHREY
10 VP for Admin Services .... Mr. Kwin WILKES
32 VP for Student Services .... Ms. Tami AFDAHL
12 VP for Douglas Campus .... Dr. Margaret FARLEY
30 Dir of Institutional Development .... Mr. John HANSEN
08 Director of Library Services .... Mrs. Casey DEBUS
41 Director of College Athletics .... Mr. Tom ANDERSEN
26 Director of College Relations .... Mr. Brad STAMAN
18 Director of Physical Plant .... Mr. Keith JARVIS
39 Director of Residence Life .... Mr. Jim RORABAUGH
37 Director of Financial Aid .... Ms. Becky MCALLISTER
15 Director Human Resources .... Mr. Patrick KORELL
21 Business Office Director .... Ms. Karen PARRIOTT
06 Registrar .... Ms. Sue SCHMIDT
13 Chief Information Tech Officer .... Mr. Tyler VASKO

Eastern Wyoming College-Douglas Campus (B)

800 South Wind River Drive, Douglas WY 82633
Telephone: (307) 624-7000 Identification: 770476
Accreditation: &HLC, ADNUR

Gillette College (C)

300 West Sinclair, Gillette WY 82718
Telephone: (307) 681-6000 Identification: 770478
Accreditation: &HLC

Laramie County Community College (D)

1400 E College Drive, Cheyenne WY 82007-3299
County: Laramie FICE Identification: 009259
Unit ID: 240620
Telephone: (307) 778-5222 Carnegie Class: Assoc/HVT-Mix Trad/Non
FAX Number: (307) 778-1399 Calendar System: Semester
URL: www.lccc.wy.edu
Established: 1968 Annual Undergrad Tuition & Fees (In-District): $4,432
Enrollment: 3,838 Coed
Affiliation or Control: State/Local IRS Status: 501(c)3
Highest Offering: Baccalaureate
Accreditation: HLC, ADNUR, CAHIIM, DH, DMS, EMT, PTAA, RAD, SURGT

01 President .... Dr. Joe SCHAFFER
05 Vice Pres Academic Affairs .... Dr. Kari BROWN-HERBST
10 Vice Pres of Administration/Finance .... Mr. Rick JOHNSON
32 Vice President of Student Services .... Dr. Melissa STUTZ
13 Chief Technology Officer .... Mr. Chad MARLEY
15 Executive Director Human Resources .... Ms. Tammy MAAS
111 Assoc VP Institutional Advancement .... Ms. Lisa TRIMBLE
12 Int Assoc VP Albany County Campus .... Dr. Clark HARRIS
45 Assc VP Institutional Effectiveness .... Dr. Kim BENDER
08 Assoc Dean Library/Learning Commons .... Vacant
37 Director of Financial Aid .... Ms. Brandi PAYNE CERVERA
18 Director of Physical Plant .... Mr. Bill ZINK
21 Comptroller .... Ms. Nola ROCHA
29 Dir Alumni Affairs/Event Plans .... Vacant
09 Director of Institutional Research .... Dr. Mark PERKINS
07 Dir of Admissions and Welcome Ctr .... Ms. Sarah HANNES
06 Registrar .... Ms. Stacy MAESTAS
49 Int Dean Sch of Arts & Humanities .... Dr. Jonathan CARRIER
50 Dean School of BATS .... Dr. Jill KOSLOSKY
76 Dean Sch of Health Sci & Wellness .... Ms. Starla MASON
81 Dean School Math & Science .... Mr. Bryan WILSON
103 Dean Sch of Outreach/Workforce Dev .... Ms. Maryellen TAST
19 Risk Manager Director Campus Safety .... Mr. Jesse BLAIR
41 Int Exec Dir Athletics & Exercise .... Dr. Cynthia HENNING
04 Executive Asst to President .... Ms. Vicki BOREING
26 Manager Strategic Communications .... Mr. Troy RUMPF
39 Director Residential Living .... Ms. Diana WILSON

Laramie County Community College Albany County Campus (E)

1125 Boulder Drive, Laramie WY 82070
Telephone: (307) 721-5138 Identification: 770477
Accreditation: &HLC

Northern Wyoming Community College District (F)

1 Whitney Way, Sheridan WY 82801-1500
County: Sheridan FICE Identification: 003930
Unit ID: 240666
Telephone: (307) 675-0505 Carnegie Class: Assoc/MT-VT-High Non
FAX Number: (307) 675-0684 Calendar System: Semester
URL: www.sheridan.edu
Established: 1948 Annual Undergrad Tuition & Fees (In-District): $4,290
Enrollment: 3,741 Coed
Affiliation or Control: Local IRS Status: 501(c)3
Highest Offering: Associate Degree
Accreditation: HLC, ADNUR, DH

01 President .... Dr. Walter TRIBLEY
05 VP Academic Affairs .... Dr. Estella CASTILLO-GARRISON
10 VP Administration/CFO .... Mr. Craig ACHORD
12 VP Gillette College/CEO .... Ms. Janell OBERLANDER
32 VP Student Affairs .... Ms. Jenn CROUSE
75 Dean Career/Technical Education .... Mr. Jed JENSEN
15 AVP for Human Resources .... Ms. Jennifer MCARTHUR
26 VP Strategic Comm/Public Info Ofcr .... Ms. Wendy M. SMITH
37 Director Financial Aid Services .... Ms. Heidi BALSTER
13 AVP for Info Tech Svcs/CIO .... Mr. Brady R. FACKRELL
09 AVP for Institutional Research .... Mr. Jason BROWNING
21 Director of Finance/Controller .... Ms. Gina KIDNEIGH
07 Exec Director of Admissions Svcs .... Mr. Joe B. MUELLER
39 Director Housing/Residential Educ .... Ms. Larissa B. BONNET
88 Director Veteran Services-Sheridan .... Mr. Tyler JENSEN
88 Director Veteran Services-Gillette .... Mr. Loren GROVES
18 AVP Facilities Management .... Mr. Kent A. ANDERSEN
18 Director Gillette Facilities .... Mr. Mark N. ANDERSEN
08 Librarian .... Ms. Katrina M. BROWN
19 Police Chief .... Mr. Jason VELA
41 Athletic Director .... Vacant
100 Executive Office Manager .... Ms. Jana CLEMENTS
20 Assoc Academic Officer-Sheridan .... Ms. Martha DAVEY
20 Assoc Academic Officer-Gillette .... Dr. Matt EWERS
29 Alumni Relations .... Ms. Bobbi MITZEL
102 Exec Dir Sheridan Foundation .... Ms. Jenn CROUSE
102 Exec Dir Gillette Foundation .... Ms. Heidi GROSS
38 Dir Student Svc/Counselor Gillette .... Ms. Susan SERGE
38 Coord Counseling ADA Svcs-Sheridan .... Ms. Amy BROWNING
84 Director Enrollment Management .... Mr. Micah OLSEN

Northwest College (G)

231 W 6th St, Powell WY 82435
County: Park FICE Identification: 003931
Unit ID: 240657
Telephone: (307) 754-6000 Carnegie Class: Assoc/MT-VT-Mix Trad/Non
FAX Number: (307) 754-6245 Calendar System: Semester
URL: www.nwc.edu
Established: 1946 Annual Undergrad Tuition & Fees (In-District): $4,330
Enrollment: 1,438 Coed
Affiliation or Control: State/Local IRS Status: 501(c)3
Highest Offering: Baccalaureate
Accreditation: HLC, ADNUR, ART, MUS

01 President .... Ms. Lisa WATSON
05 Vice Pres Academic Affairs .... Dr. Gerald GIRAUD
11 Vice Pres Admin Services/Finance .... Ms. Lisa WATSON
102 Executive Director NWC Foundation .... Ms. Shelby WETZEL
08 Library Director .... Ms. Nancy MILLER
10 Finance Director .... Mr. Brad BOWEN
15 Human Resources Director .... Ms. Jill ANDERSON
13 Computing Services Director .... Mr. Casey DEARCORN
18 Interim Facilities Director .... Mr. Dennis QUILLEN
84 Enrollment Services Director .... Mr. West HERNANDEZ
37 Financial Aid/Scholarships Director .... Mr. Shaman QUINN
39 Interim Residence Life Director .... Mr. Lee BLACKMORE
04 Exec Secretary to President & Board .... Ms. Keli BORDERS
07 Admissions Coordinator .... Ms. Kendle JEFFS
09 Institutional Research Manager .... Ms. Lisa SMITH
26 Communications & Marketing Director .... Ms. Carey MILLER
19 Campus Security Coordinator .... Mr. Lee BLACKMORE
41 Athletic Director .... Mr. Brian ERICKSON

University of Wyoming (H)

1000 E University Avenue, Dept 3434, Laramie WY 82071-3434
County: Albany FICE Identification: 003932
Unit ID: 240727
Telephone: (307) 766-1121 Carnegie Class: DU-Higher
FAX Number: (307) 766-2271 Calendar System: Semester
URL: www.uwyo.edu
Established: 1886 Annual Undergrad Tuition & Fees (In-State): $5,791
Enrollment: 11,829 Coed
Affiliation or Control: State IRS Status: 501(c)3
Highest Offering: Doctorate
Accreditation: HLC, CACREP, CAEPN, CLPSY, CONST, DIETD, LAW, MLS, MUS, NURSE, PHAR, SP, SW

01 President .... Mr. Edward SEIDEL
05 Provost/VP Academic Affairs .... Dr. Kevin CARMAN
10 SVP Finance & Administration .... Dr. Neil THEOBALD
31 Interim Vice Pres Community Affairs .... Mr. Chris BOSWELL
46 Vice Pres Research & Economic Dev . Dr. Edmund SYNAKOWSKI
32 Vice President Student Affairs .... Ms. Kim CHESTNUT
13 Vice President Information Tech .... Mr. Robert R. AYLWARD
111 Vice Pres Institutional Advancement .... Mr. W. Ben BLALOCK, III
43 Vice President & General Counsel .... Ms. Tara EVANS
20 Vice Provost Academic Personnel .... Dr. Tami BENHAM-DEAL
20 AVP Undergrad Academic Affairs .... Dr. Steven BARRETT
84 Associate VP Enrollment Management .... Mr. Kyle MOORE
21 AVP Budget and Inst Planning .... Mr. David JEWELL
35 AVP/Dean of Students/Dir Fin Aid .... Dr. Nycole COURTNEY
110 Assoc VP Institutional Advancement .... Mr. John D. STARK
26 Assoc VP Communication/Marketing .... Mr. Chad BALDWIN
41 Director Intercollegiate Athletics .... Mr. Tom BURMAN
47 Dean of Agriculture/Natural Res .... Dr. Barbara RASCO
49 Dean of Arts & Sciences .... Dr. Danny DOLE
50 Dean of Business .... Dr. David SPROTT
53 Int Dean of Education .... Dr. Leslie RUSH
54 Interim Dean of Engineering .... Dr. Cameron WRIGHT
76 Dean of Health Sciences .... Dr. David JONES
61 Dean of Law .... Dr. Klint ALEXANDER
12 Assoc Dean/Director UW at Casper .... Dr. Jeff EDGENS
08 Dean of Libraries .... Dr. Ivan GAETZ
65 Dean Sch Environ/Nat Resources .... Dr. John KOPROWSKI
07 Director of Admissions .... Ms. Shelley DODD
36 Director Advising/Career Services .... Ms. Evelyn J. CHYTKA
29 Exec Director Alumni Affairs .... Mr. Keener FRY
88 Director American Heritage Center .... Ms. Bridgit BURKE
88 Exec Dir School of Energy Resources .... Ms. Holly KRUTKA
88 Director Art Museum .... Ms. Marianne WARDLE
88 Director Campus Recreation .... Mr. Patrick MORAN
15 Int Assoc VP Human Resources .... Ms. Deborah MARUTZKY
18 Assoc Vice President UW Operations .... Mr. John R. DAVIS
92 Dean Honors College .... Mr. Peter PAROLIN
86 Director of Govt Relations .... Ms. Meredith ASAY
39 Exec Dir Res Life/Dining/Stdnt Un .... Mr. Eric WEBB
37 Int Director Student Financial Aid .... Ms. Carrie GOSE
06 Registrar .... Ms. Kwanna KING
23 Director Student Health Clinic .... Dr. Richelle KEINATH
19 Chief University Police Dept .... Mr. Mike SAMP
38 Director Counseling Center .... Dr. Toi GEIL

Western Wyoming Community College (I)

2500 College Drive, Rock Springs WY 82901
County: Sweetwater FICE Identification: 003933
Unit ID: 240693
Telephone: (307) 382-1600 Carnegie Class: Assoc/HVT-High Non
FAX Number: (307) 382-1636 Calendar System: Semester
URL: www.westernwyoming.edu
Established: 1959 Annual Undergrad Tuition & Fees (In-District): $3,456
Enrollment: 2,776 Coed
Affiliation or Control: State/Local IRS Status: 501(c)3
Highest Offering: Baccalaureate
Accreditation: HLC, ADNUR

01 President .... Dr. Kim K. DALE
05 VP for Student Learning .... Dr. Clifford WITTSTRUCK, III
11 VP for Administrative Services .... Mr. Burt REYNOLDS
15 Assoc VP of Human Resources .... Ms. Joy ADAMS
10 Assoc VP of Finance .... Ms. Debbie BAKER
84 Dean of Enrollment Management .... Mr. Eric FRY
06 Registrar .... Mr. Stuart MOORE
37 Director of Financial Aid .... Mr. James HEU
08 Director of Library Services .... Mr. Christopher MURRY
18 Director of Facilities .... Mr. Chris DEVER
32 Dean of Students .... Mr. Dustin CONOVER
40 Bookstore Manager .... Ms. Natalie LANE
41 Athletic Director .... Dr. Lu SWEET
92 Director of Honors Program .... Vacant
09 Assoc VP of Inst Effectiveness .... Mr. Mark REMBACZ
26 Coord of Marketing/Public Info .... Ms. Kimberly REMBACZ
30 Dir Community College Relations .... Mr. David TATE
22 Dir Student Counseling/Disability .... Ms. Amy GALLEY
96 Director of Purchasing .... Ms. Tammy REGISTER
04 Executive Asst to President .... Ms. Kandy FRINK
19 Protective Services Supervisor .... Mr. Mark PADILLA
13 Director of Information Technology .... Mr. Derek ROBINSON
20 Dean of Academics .... Vacant
103 Dean of Outreach & Workforce Devel .... Ms. Amy MURPHY

Wyoming Catholic College (J)

306 Main Street, Lander WY 82520
County: Fremont Identification: 667227
Telephone: (307) 332-2930 Carnegie Class: Not Classified
FAX Number: (307) 332-2918 Calendar System: Semester
URL: www.wyomingcatholic.edu
Established: 2005 Annual Undergrad Tuition & Fees: N/A
Enrollment: N/A Coed
Affiliation or Control: Roman Catholic IRS Status: 501(c)3
Highest Offering: Baccalaureate
Accreditation: HLC

01 President .... Dr. Glen ARBERY
03 Executive Vice President .... Mr. Richard ROLLINO
05 Interim Academic Dean .... Mr. Kyle WASHUT
111 Vice President Advancement .... Mr. Joseph SUSANKA
32 Vice President Student Affairs .... Mr. Jonathan TONKOWICH
06 Registrar .... Ms. Jennifer WESTMAN
35 Director of Student Life .... Dr. Lucas PREBLE
07 Director of Admissions .... Miss Madeleine TRULL
37 Director Student Financial Aid .... Mrs. Christina BOLIN

WyoTech (K)

1889 Venture Drive, Laramie WY 82070
County: Albany FICE Identification: 009157
Unit ID: 240718
Telephone: (307) 742-3776 Carnegie Class: Spec 2-yr-Tech
FAX Number: (307) 755-2484 Calendar System: Other
URL: www.wyotech.edu
Established: 1966 Annual Undergrad Tuition & Fees: N/A
Enrollment: 585 Coed

Affiliation or Control: Proprietary IRS Status: Proprietary
Highest Offering: Associate Degree
Accreditation: ACCSC

01 President .... Mr. Jim MATHIS
11 Vice President of Operation .... Mr. Kyle MORRIS
05 Vice President of Training .... Mr. Shawn NUNLEY
84 VP of Enrollment Services .... Ms. Alyson MOYER
07 Vice President of Admissions .... Mr. Steve MEYER
06 Registrar .... Ms. Jennifer BALDWIN
36 Director of Career Services .... Mr. Greg TAYLOR
32 Director of Student Life .... Mr. Gabe LUCERO
18 Director of Facilities .... Mr. David KUHN

US SERVICE SCHOOLS

Air Force Institute of Technology (A)

2950 Hobson Way, Wright-Patterson AFB OH 45433-7765
County: Greene FICE Identification: 003009
Unit ID: 200697
Telephone: (937) 255-6565 Carnegie Class: DU-Higher
FAX Number: (937) 656-7600 Calendar System: Quarter
URL: www.afit.edu
Established: 1919 Annual Graduate Tuition & Fees: N/A
Enrollment: 1,129 Coed
Affiliation or Control: Federal IRS Status: Exempt
Highest Offering: Doctorate; No Undergraduates
Accreditation: HLC

01 Director and Chancellor .... Dr. Walter F. JONES
05 Chief Academic Officer and Provost .... Dr. Heidi R. RIES
54 Dean Graduate School of Engr & Mgt .... Dr. Adedeji B. BADIRU
46 Dean for Research .... Dr. Darryl K. AHNER
10 Chief Financial Officer .... Ms. Danielle THOMAS
09 Director Institutional Research .... Dr. Andrea BAKKER
06 Director Admissions/Registrar .... Ms. Kathleen K. BURDEN
32 Dean of Students .... Lt Col. Christopher M. RONDEAU
20 Associate Dean for Academic Affairs .... Dr. Paul J. WOLF
13 Interim Dir Comm & Information .... Mr. Joseph E. LAMB
08 Director D'Azzo Research Library .... Dr. Ellis BETECK
15 Director Personnel Services .... Ms. Sonja B. MARSH
18 Chief Facilities/Physical Plant .... Mr. Dennis K. SHUTTLEWORTH
29 Manager Alumni Affairs .... Ms. Kathleen E. SCOTT
85 Director of Intl Student Affairs .... Mr. Michael J. PAPROCKI
106 Dir Online Education/E-learning .... Mr. John A. REISNER
111 Manager Institutional Advancement .... Ms. Katie E. SCOTT

Air University (B)

55 LeMay Plaza South, Maxwell AFB AL 36112-6335
County: Montgomery FICE Identification: 001001
Telephone: (334) 953-5613 Carnegie Class: Masters/L
FAX Number: (334) 953-2749 Calendar System: Other
URL: www.airuniversity.af.mil
Established: 1946 Annual Undergrad Tuition & Fees: N/A
Enrollment: N/A Coed
Affiliation or Control: Federal IRS Status: Exempt
Highest Offering: Doctorate
Accreditation: SC

01 Commander and President .... LtGen. Andrea D. TULLOS
03 Vice Commander .... MajGen. William G. HOLT, II
05 Chief Academic Officer .... Dr. Mark J. CONVERSINO
32 Vice Chancellor Student Affairs .... Vacant
06 Registrar .... Dr. Mehmed ALI

† Parent institution of Community College of the Air Force, School of Advanced Air and Space Studies, and the Air Force Institute of Technology

Community College of the Air Force (C)

100 South Turner Blvd,
Maxwell AFB, Gunter Annex AL 36114-3011
Telephone: (334) 649-5000 FICE Identification: 012308
Accreditation: &SC

† Regional accreditation is carried under the parent institution, Air University, Maxwell AFB, AL.

Defense Language Institute (D)

1759 Lewis Road, Monterey CA 93944
County: Monterey FICE Identification: 001195
Unit ID: 428222
Telephone: (831) 242-5291 Carnegie Class: Spec 2-yr-Other
FAX Number: (831) 242-6495 Calendar System: Other
URL: www.dliflc.edu
Established: 1941 Annual Undergrad Tuition & Fees: N/A
Enrollment: N/A Coed
Affiliation or Control: Federal IRS Status: Exempt
Highest Offering: Associate Degree
Accreditation: WJ

01 Commandant .... Col. James KIEVIT
03 Assistant Commandant .... Col. Jennifer SARACENO
05 Provost .... Dr. Robert SAVUKINAS
20 Associate Provost .... Dr. Hiam KANBAR
100 Chief of Staff .... Mr. Steven COLLINS
32 Dean of Students .... Lt Col. Jorge AVILA

† Associate Arts in Foreign Language authorized by US Congress in December 2001 and approved by ACCJC/WASC in June 2002.

59th Dental Training Squadron (E)

Bldg 3352, JBSA, Lackland AFB TX 78236
Telephone: (210) 292-8850 Identification: 770122
Accreditation: &M

† Branch campus of Uniformed Services University of the Health Sciences, Bethesda, MD

Joint Forces Staff College (F)

7800 Hampton Boulevard, Norfolk VA 23511-1702
Telephone: (757) 443-6124 Identification: 770121
Accreditation: &M

† Branch campus of National Defense University, Washington, DC

The Judge Advocate General's Legal Center & School (G)

600 Massie Road, Charlottesville VA 22903-1781
County: Albermarle Identification: 666974
Telephone: (434) 971-3300 Carnegie Class: Not Classified
FAX Number: (434) 971-3338 Calendar System: Quarter
URL: https://tjaglcs.army.mil/
Established: 1951 Annual Graduate Tuition & Fees: N/A
Enrollment: N/A Coed
Affiliation or Control: Federal IRS Status: Exempt
Highest Offering: Master's; No Undergraduates
Accreditation: LAW

01 Commander/Commandant .... BGEN. Alison C. MARTIN
05 Dean .... COL. Tonya L. BLACKWELL
20 Associate Dean of Academics .... Mr. Maurice A. LESCAULT, JR.
32 Associate Dean of Students .... LTC. Melvin WILLIAMS

Marine Corps University (H)

2076 South Street, Quantico VA 22134-5068
County: Prince William Identification: 666745
Telephone: (703) 784-2105 Carnegie Class: Not Classified
FAX Number: (703) 784-1271 Calendar System: Semester
URL: www.usmcu.edu
Established: 1989 Annual Graduate Tuition & Fees: N/A
Enrollment: N/A Coed
Affiliation or Control: Federal IRS Status: Exempt
Highest Offering: Master's; No Undergraduates
Accreditation: SC

01 President .... BGen. Maura M. HENNIGAN
05 Vice President for Academic Affairs .... Dr. Rebecca J. JOHNSON
11 VP for Operations & Planning .... Mr. Jay HATTON
10 VP Business Affairs .... Mr. Keil GENTRY
100 Chief of Staff .... Col. Paul M. MELCHIOR

National Defense University (I)

Fort Lesley J. McNair, Washington DC 20319-5066
FICE Identification: 031893
Unit ID: 423494
Telephone: (202) 685-3924 Carnegie Class: Spec-4-yr-Other
FAX Number: (202) 685-3920 Calendar System: Semester
URL: www.ndu.edu
Established: 1976 Annual Graduate Tuition & Fees: N/A
Enrollment: N/A Coed
Affiliation or Control: Federal IRS Status: Exempt
Highest Offering: Master's; No Undergraduates
Accreditation: M

01 President .... LGen. Michael T. PLEHN
03 Senior Vice President .... Amb. John F. HOOVER
05 Interim Provost of AA .... Dr. Cynthia A. WATSON
11 Chief Operating Officer .... Mrs. Kathryn L. KOLBE
43 General Counsel .... Ms. Mollie MURPHY
46 Sr Dir Research/Strategic Support .... Dr. Laura J. JUNOR
88 Chancellor CISA .... Amb. Greta C. HOLTZ
88 Commandant ES .... BGen. Joy L. CURRIERA
88 Commandant NWC .... BGen. Jeffrey H. HURLBERT
88 Chancellor CIC .... Dr. Cassandra C. LEWIS
88 Commandant JFSC .... BGen. Voris W. MCBURNETTE
107 Deputy Director CAPSTONE .... Mr. Gerard M. MAUER, JR.
32 Director of OIRPA .... Dr. B.J MILLER
06 University Registrar .... Mr. Larry JOHNSON
42 Chaplain .... COL. Ken WILLIAMS
26 Director of Strategic Communication .... Mr. Mark PHILLIPS
10 Chief Financial Officer .... Mrs. Barbara J. GILCHRIST
105 Web/Social Media Manager .... Ms. Jennifer RUSSELL
23 Director Health Fitness .... Mr. Tony SPINOSA
15 Director Human Resources .... Mr. John N. FREEMAN
08 Director Libraries .... Mr. Mohan RAMASWAMY
85 Dir International Student Mgmt Ofc .... Mr. Harrington T. MATTHEW
18 Chief Facilities/Physical Plant .... LTC. Crystal L. PROVENCHER
19 Director Security .... Mr. Kutchak D. NICHOLAS
102 President/CEO NDU Foundation .... Mr. James SCHMELING

National Intelligence University (J)

Roberdeau Hall ICC-B, Washington DC 20511
Identification: 666393
Telephone: (301) 243-2094 Carnegie Class: Not Classified
FAX Number: (301) 227-7067 Calendar System: Quarter
URL: www.ni-u.edu
Established: 1962 Annual Undergrad Tuition & Fees: N/A
Enrollment: N/A Coed
Affiliation or Control: Federal IRS Status: Exempt
Highest Offering: Master's
Accreditation: M

01 President .... Dr. J. Scott CAMERON
03 Exec VP .... Ms. Patricia LARSEN
20 Associate Provost Acad & Faculty .... Dr. Anna WAGGENER
32 Associate Provost Student Affairs .... Dr. Duane C. YOUNG
09 VP Research .... Mr. Manolis PRINIOTAKIS
46 Associate VP for Research .... Mr. Andrew BORENE
08 Director Library Services .... Ms. Elizabeth E. VENTURA
108 Dir Institutional Effectiveness .... Dr. Jeffrey CHEN
10 VP Finance & Infrastructure .... Mr. Stephen J. KERDA
19 Security Officer .... Mr. John SAWYER
06 Registrar .... Ms. Heather BISSON
58 Dean College Strategic Intel .... Dr. Amy KARDELL
12 Director NSA Campus .... Ms. Bobbi LALLEY
12 Dir Exec Reserve Monthly Pgm .... Dr. Christopher BAILEY
12 Director European Academic Ctr .... Dr. Erik JENS
12 Director Southern Academic Ctr .... Mr. Christopher MARSHALL
12 Director Quantico Academic Ctr .... Ms. Janet NELSON
58 Dean School of Science & Tech Intel .... Dr. Thomas PIKE
26 Acting VP Engagement .... Mr. Kyle WALDEN
05 Acting Provost .... Dr. Susan PERLMAN
29 Director Alumni Affairs .... Mr. Thomas VAN WAGNER
04 Admin Assistant to the President .... Ms. Bessie JOHNSON
84 Assoc Provost Acad Integrity & Svcs .... Dr. David SHIN
07 Director of Admissions .... Ms. Melanie D'ANGELO
11 Chief of Operations/Administration .... COL. Jennifer MCAFEE

Naval Postgraduate School (K)

1 University Circle, Room M10, Monterey CA 93943-5100
County: Monterey FICE Identification: 001310
Unit ID: 119678
Telephone: (831) 656-2441 Carnegie Class: Masters/L
FAX Number: (831) 656-2921 Calendar System: Quarter
URL: www.nps.edu
Established: 1909 Annual Undergrad Tuition & Fees: N/A
Enrollment: 2,866 Coed
Affiliation or Control: Federal IRS Status: Exempt
Highest Offering: Doctorate
Accreditation: WC, SPAA

01 President .... VAdm. Ann Elisabeth RONDEAU, RET.
05 Provost/Academic Dean .... Dr. Scott GARTNER
100 Chief of Staff .... CAPT. Philip E. OLD
20 Vice Provost for Academic Affairs .... Dr. Joseph HOOPER
46 Vice Provost for Research .... Dr. Kevin SMITH
32 Dean of Students .... CAPT. Brandon BRYAN
11 Chief Operations Officer .... Vacant
10 Comptroller .... Ms. Laura COLE
13 Director Information Technology .... Mr. Scott BISCHOFF
08 University Librarian .... Mr. Thomas ROSKO
06 Registrar .... Ms. Jessica BAWDON
15 Director Human Resources .... Ms. Jennifer AMORIN
56 Director of CED3 .... Mr. Dennis LESTER
07 Director of Admissions .... Ms. Sue DOOLEY
88 Director of Programs .... CDR. Sabina PAMARAN
04 Admin Assistant to the President .... Mr. Michael WEATHERFORD

Naval War College (L)

686 Cushing Road, Newport RI 02841-1207
County: Newport FICE Identification: 003413
Telephone: (401) 841-3089 Carnegie Class: Not Classified
FAX Number: (401) 841-1297 Calendar System: Trimester
URL: www.usnwc.edu
Established: 1884 Annual Graduate Tuition & Fees: N/A
Enrollment: N/A Coed
Affiliation or Control: Federal IRS Status: Exempt
Highest Offering: Master's; No Undergraduates
Accreditation: EH

01 President .... RADM. Shoshana CHATFIELD
04 Exec Assistant to the President .... LCDR. Jorge VARGAS
05 Interim Provost .... Dr. Jay HICKEY
20 Deputy Provost .... Mr. Richard R. MENARD
20 Associate Provost .... Dr. Tom GIBBONS
100 Vice Pres/Chief of Staff .... CAPT. Joseph C. GIRARD
20 Dean of Academic Affairs .... Dr. Phil HAUN
88 Int Dean Center for Warfare Studies .... Dr. Peter A. DUTTON
32 Dean of Students .... CAPT. Cindy DIETERLY
08 Director H.E. Eccles Library .... Dr. Allen C. BENSON
106 Dean College of Distance Education .... Prof. Leonard Walter WILDEMANN
06 Registrar .... CAPT. Cindy DIETERLY
46 Chairman Strategy & Policy .... Prof. David STONE
88 Chairman National Security Affairs .... Prof. Derek REVERON
88 Chairman Joint Military Operations .... CAPT. Edmund HERNANDEZ
10 Chief Business Officer .... Mr. Robert SAMPSON
108 Dir Institutional Effectiveness .... Dr. Edward GILLEN
15 Director Military Personnel Svcs .... Vacant
15 Civilian Human Resources Officer .... Ms. Charlene HANSON
18 Chief Facilities/Physical Plant .... Mr. Shawn BOGDAN
26 Chief Public Relations Officer .... CDR. Gary ROSS
13 Chief Information Officer .... Mr. Joseph PANGBORN
19 Director of Security .... Mr. James HULL
29 Director Alumni Affairs .... Prof. Julia GAGE
104 Dean International Programs .... Prof. Thomas MANGOLD
88 Director of Events .... Ms. Karen SELLERS
88 Int Dn Maritime Operational Warfare .... Mr. Sean P. HENSELER
88 Dean Leadership and Ethics .... Prof. Peg KLEIN

School of Advanced Air and Space Studies (A)

125 Chennault Circle, Maxwell AFB AL 36112-6424
Telephone: (334) 953-5155 Identification: 666746
Accreditation: &SC

† Regional accreditation is carried under the parent institution, Air University, Maxwell AFB, AL.

Uniformed Services University of the Health Sciences (B)

4301 Jones Bridge Road, Bethesda MD 20814-4799
County: Montgomery FICE Identification: 021610
Unit ID: 164137
Telephone: (301) 295-3013 Carnegie Class: Spec-4-yr-Eng
FAX Number: (301) 295-3431 Calendar System: Quarter
URL: www.usuhs.edu
Established: 1972 Annual Undergrad Tuition & Fees: N/A
Enrollment: N/A Coed
Affiliation or Control: Federal IRS Status: Exempt
Highest Offering: Doctorate
Accreditation: M, ANEST, CLPSY, DENT, HSA, MED, NURSE, PH

01 University President .... Dr. Jonathan WOODSON
05 SVP University Programs South .... Vacant
05 SVP Academic Operations .... Dr. William ROBERTS
10 Vice Pres Finance & Admin .... Mr. Walter TINLING
26 Vice Pres External Affairs .... Dr. Jeffrey LONGACRE
46 Vice President for Research .... Dr. Mark KORTEPETER
04 Special Assistant to the President .... Ms. Lorraine BREEN
21 AVP Resource Management .... Vacant
100 Chief of Staff .... Mr. Robert J. THOMPSON
63 Dean School of Medicine .... Dr. Eric ELSTER
66 Dean Graduate School of Nursing .... Dr. Carol ROMANO
76 Dean School Allied Health Sci .... Dr. Lula PELAYO
52 Dean Postgraduate Dental School .... COL. Drew FALLIS
52 Executive Dean Postgrad Dental .... Vacant
58 Assoc Dean Graduate Education .... Dr. Saibal DEY
07 Assoc Dean Admiss & Recruiting SOM .... CDR. Robert LIOTTA
88 Assoc Dean Graduate Medical Educ .... CAPT. Jerri CURTIS
32 Assoc Dean Student Affairs .... COL. Pamela WILLIAMS
20 Assoc Dean for Curriculum .... Dr. Arnyce POCK
88 Sr Assoc Dean for Faculty .... Dr. Jessica SERVEY
88 Assoc Dean for Medical Education .... COL. Catherine WITKOP
88 Assistant Dean Academic Support .... Vacant
88 Associate Dean Clinical Services .... COL. Ashley MARANICH
20 Sr Assoc Dean Academic Affairs .... Dr. Brian REAMY
13 Chief Information Officer .... Mr. Timothy RAPP
43 Acting General Counsel .... Mr. Samuel J. SMITH
46 Director AFRRI .... COL. Mohammed NAEEM
15 Director Civilian Human Res .... Mr. Darryl BROWN
08 Director University Librarian .... Ms. Alison ROLLINS
18 Director of Facilities .... Ms. Florence RICHARDSON
96 Director of Contracting .... Mr. Stephen DAVIS
29 Director Alumni Relations .... Ms. Sharon HOLLAND
19 Director Security/Safety .... Mr. Christopher MOTTLER
06 AVP Records/Registrar .... Dr. Wendy LISHEN
108 Director Institutional Assessment .... Mr. Stephen HENSKE

United States Air Force Academy (C)

2304 Cadet Drive,, USAF Academy CO 80840-5002
County: El Paso FICE Identification: 001369
Unit ID: 128328
Telephone: (800) 443-9266 Carnegie Class: Bac-Diverse
FAX Number: N/A Calendar System: Semester
URL: www.usafa.af.mil
Established: 1954 Annual Undergrad Tuition & Fees: N/A
Enrollment: 4,307 Coed
Affiliation or Control: Federal IRS Status: Exempt
Highest Offering: Baccalaureate
Accreditation: HLC, DENT

01 Superintendent .... LtGen. Richard M. CLARK
05 Chief Acad Officer/Dean of Faculty .... BGen. Linell A. LETENDRE
101 Vice Superintendent .... Col. Benjamin R. JONSSON
100 Chief of Staff/Vice COM Cadets .... Ms. Gail B. COLVIN
09 Director of Institutional Research .... Col. Douglas W. WARNOCK, JR.
10 Chief Financial Officer .... Lt Col. Casey WYMAN
37 Director Student Financial Aid .... Lt Col. Casey WYMAN
103 Dir Workforce/Career Development .... Dr. Steven K. JONES
104 Director Study Abroad .... Maj. Braden B. REYNOLDS
11 Command Chief .... CMSgt. Randall D. KWIATKOWSKI
13 Chief Technology Officer (CTO) .... Mr. Michael M. ANDREWS
15 Director Personnel Services .... Mr. Dale A. HOGUE
18 Chief Facilities/Physical Plant .... Mr. Carlos R. CRUZ-GONZALEZ
19 Director Security/Safety .... Lt Col. Reuben J. LITTON
22 Dir Affirmative Action/EO .... Mr. Larry C. JONES
26 Chief Public Affairs .... Lt Col. Brian L. MAGUIRE
28 Director of Diversity .... Mr. Joseph D. LOONEY
29 Director Alumni Relations .... Ms. Nicole J. COX
30 Chief Development/Advancement .... Dr. Harold A. TAYLOR
32 Commandant of Cadets .... BGen. Paul D. MOGA
36 Director Student Placement .... Ms. Laura A. ANGELES
39 Director Student Housing .... Ms. Jennifer M. JONES
41 Exec Director of Athletic Programs .... Ms. Jennifer A. BLOCK
41 Athletic Director .... Mr. Nathan A. PINE
43 Dir Legal Services/General Counsel .... Col. Michael W. SAFKO
45 Chief Institutional Planning .... Col. Patrick E. GRUBER
50 Head Dept of Management .... Col. Troy R. HARTING
54 Pgm Head Environmental Engineering .... Dr. Thomas J. PHELAN
08 Head Librarian .... Mrs. Diana G. KLARE
84 Director Enrollment Management .... Col. Arthur W. PRIMAS, JR.
90 Director Academic Computing .... Mr. Eugene K. KAUPPILA
91 Director Administrative Computing .... Ms. Paula J. BURMEISTER
96 Director of Purchasing .... Mr. James A. ANDERSON
06 Registrar .... Dr. Harold A. TAYLOR
07 Director of Admissions .... Col. Arthur PRIMAS, JR.
105 Marketing Chief .... Vacant
108 Director Institutional Assessment .... Mr. Dixon D. DYKMAN
44 Director Annual Giving .... Mrs. Carla J. HUNSTAD
86 Director Government Relations .... Mr. James R. CUTCHIN
102 Dir Foundation/Corporate Rels .... Mr. Michael PETERSON
25 Chief Contract Grants Administrator .... Mr. James A. ANDERSON
27 Chief Information Officer .... Col. Angela K. HERRON
27 Director Strategic Communications .... Lt Col. Brian L. MAGUIRE

United States Army Command and General Staff College (D)

100 Stimson Avenue, Fort Leavenworth KS 66027-1352
County: Leavenworth FICE Identification: 001947
Unit ID: 156055
Telephone: (913) 684-3097 Carnegie Class: Spec-4-yr-Other
FAX Number: (913) 684-2906 Calendar System: Trimester
URL: https://usacac.army.mil/organizations/cace/cgsc
Established: 1881 Annual Graduate Tuition & Fees: N/A
Enrollment: N/A Coed
Affiliation or Control: Federal IRS Status: Exempt
Highest Offering: Master's; No Undergraduates
Accreditation: HLC

01 Commandant .... LTG. Theodore D. MARTIN
100 Deputy Commandant .... BG. Don H. HILL
05 Dean of Academics .... Dr. Jack D. KEM
20 Assoc Dean of Academics .... Vacant
58 Director Graduate Degree Programs .... Dr. Robert BAUMANN
08 Director of Library .... Mrs. Beata MOORE
32 Director CGSS School .... Col. Scott A. GREEN
06 Registrar .... Dr. Thomas E. CREVISTON

United States Army War College (E)

122 Forbes Avenue, Carlisle PA 17013-5050
County: Cumberland Identification: 666235
Telephone: (717) 245-4711 Carnegie Class: Not Classified
FAX Number: (717) 245-4721 Calendar System: Other
URL: www.carlisle.army.mil
Established: 1901 Annual Graduate Tuition & Fees: N/A
Enrollment: N/A Coed
Affiliation or Control: Federal IRS Status: Exempt
Highest Offering: Master's; No Undergraduates
Accreditation: M

01 Commandant .... MG. David C. HILL
05 Provost .... Dr. Jim G. BRECKENRIDGE
100 Chief of Staff .... Col. Lance D. OSKEY

United States Coast Guard Academy (F)

31 Mohegan Avenue, New London CT 06320
County: New London FICE Identification: 001415
Unit ID: 130624
Telephone: (860) 444-8444 Carnegie Class: Bac-Diverse
FAX Number: (860) 444-8288 Calendar System: Semester
URL: https://www.uscga.edu/
Established: 1876 Annual Undergrad Tuition & Fees: N/A
Enrollment: 1,056 Coed
Affiliation or Control: Federal IRS Status: Exempt
Highest Offering: Baccalaureate
Accreditation: EH

01 Superintendent .... RADM. William G. KELLY
03 Assistant Superintendent .... CAPT. Michael A. TURDO
45 Planning Officer .... CDR. Nolan J. CUEVAS
05 Provost .... Dr. Amy K. DONOHUE
20 Associate Provost Academic Admin .... CAPT. Russell E. BOWMAN
20 Associate Provost Academic Affairs .... Dr. Eric J. PAGE
07 Assoc Director of Admissions .... LCDR. Tony BORRUSO
32 Commandant of Cadets .... CAPT. Arthus L. RAY
06 Registrar .... Mr. Miguel O. GONZALEZ
08 Librarian .... Ms. Lucia MAZIAR
10 Comptroller .... CDR. Micheal FRIEND
26 External Affairs .... CDR. Krystn E. PECORA
09 Institutional Research .... Dr. Leonard M. GIAMBRA
13 Head of Information Services .... CDR. Grant C. WYMAN
16 Personnel Management Specialist .... Ms. Julie A. KELLY
15 Chief Personnel/Administration .... CAPT. William SMITH
18 Chief Facilities Engineer .... CDR. Michael N. COST
22 Civil Rights Officer .... Mr. Roy P. ZIEGENGEIST
23 Clinic Director .... LCDR. Scott BLANCETT
38 Chief Cadet Counselor .... Dr. Daria PAPALIA
40 Bookstore Manager .... Ms. Heidii H. CRESTURO
41 Director of Athletics .... Dr. Dan C. ROSE
42 Command Chaplain .... CDR. Jamie J. STALL-RYAN, CHC
43 Staff Legal Officer .... CDR. Aaron J. CASAVANT
85 International Cadet Advisor .... Dr. Kassim M. TARHINI
28 Director Inclusion and Diversity .... Dr. Aram DEKOVEN

United States Merchant Marine Academy (G)

300 Steamboat Road, Kings Point NY 11024-1634
County: Nassau FICE Identification: 002892
Unit ID: 197027
Telephone: (516) 773-5000 Carnegie Class: Bac-Diverse
FAX Number: (516) 773-5582 Calendar System: Trimester
URL: www.usmma.edu
Established: 1943 Annual Undergrad Tuition & Fees: $1,095
Enrollment: 1,045 Coed
Affiliation or Control: Federal IRS Status: Exempt
Highest Offering: Master's
Accreditation: M

01 Superintendent .... RADM. Jack BUONO
03 Deputy Superintendent .... RDML. Susan L. DUNLAP
05 Academic Dean & Provost .... Dr. John R. BALLARD
32 Commandant of Midshipmen .... Vacant
20 Assistant Academic Dean .... Ms. Dianne TAHA
18 Asst Supt for Facilities .... CAPT. Theodore DOGONNIUCK
26 Director Office of External Affairs .... Mr. George RHYNEDANCE
07 Director of Admissions .... CDR. Michael BEDRYK
06 Registrar .... Ms. Lisa JERRY
13 Director Computer/Information Mgmt .... Vacant
15 Director Human Resources .... Vacant
10 Chief Financial Officer .... Mr. David SOCOLOF
29 Director Alumni Relations .... Mr. Jim TOBIN
36 Dir of Prof Develop/Career Services .... CAPT. Gene ALBERT
37 Director Student Financial Aid .... Mr. Joseph BECKER
96 Director of Purchasing .... Mr. Max DIAH
09 Director of Institutional Research .... Ms. Lori TOWNSEND
41 Athletic Director .... Ms. Maureen WHITE
108 Director Institutional Assessment .... Ms. Lori TOWNSEND
43 Dir Legal Services/General Counsel .... Ms. Ilene KREITZER
11 Chief of Administration .... Mr. John DEMERS
19 Director Security/Safety .... Mr. Jeffrey THOMAS
22 Director Affirmative Action/EEO .... Mr. Marvin WILLIAMS
04 Admin Assistant to the President .... Ms. Cynthia FLYNN
08 Chief Library Officer .... Ms. Donna SELVAGGIO

United States Military Academy (H)

646 Swift Rd., West Point NY 10996-5000
County: Orange FICE Identification: 002893
Unit ID: 197036
Telephone: (845) 938-4041 Carnegie Class: Bac-A&S
FAX Number: (845) 938-3021 Calendar System: Semester
URL: www.westpoint.edu
Established: 1802 Annual Undergrad Tuition & Fees: N/A
Enrollment: 4,536 Coed
Affiliation or Control: Federal IRS Status: Exempt
Highest Offering: Baccalaureate
Accreditation: M

01 Superintendent/President .... LTG. Darryl A. WILLIAMS
32 Commandant of Cadets .... BG. Mark QUANDER
05 Dean of Academic Board .... BG. Shane REEVES
41 Director Intercollegiate Athletics .... Mr. Mike BUDDIE
100 Chief of Staff .... COL. Mark WEATHERS
88 Garrison Commander .... COL. Evangeline ROSEL
07 Director of Admissions .... COL. Deborah MCDONALD
20 Vice Dean Academic Affairs .... Dr. Susan CARTER
06 Associate Dean for Registrar .... Dr. Jim DALTON
46 Associate Dean for Research .... Dr. Ken WICKISER
88 Dir Center for Teaching Excellence .... Dr. Mark EVANS
121 Dir Ctr for Enhanced Performance .... COL. Darcy SCHNACK
08 USMA Library .... Mr. Christopher BARTH
38 Dir Center for Personal Development .... LTC. Michell GRIFFITH
88 Director of Cadet Activities .... COL. Tom HANSBARGER
13 Chief Information Officer .... COL. Edward TEAGUE
15 Chief Strength Management .... COL. Jennifer HICKS-MCGOWAN
26 Public Affairs Officer .... LTC. Beth SMITH
10 Director of Resource Management .... Ms. Melissa CARDONA
108 Dir Institutional Effectiveness .... Dr. Gerald KOBYLSKI
09 Director Institutional Research .... LTC. Brian NOVOSELICH
18 Director of Public Works .... Mr. William KILLOUGH
28 Chief Diversity Officer .... Vacant

United States Naval Academy (I)

121 Blake Road, Annapolis MD 21402
County: Anne Arundel FICE Identification: 030430
Unit ID: 164155
Telephone: (410) 293-1000 Carnegie Class: Bac-A&S
FAX Number: (410) 293-3734 Calendar System: Semester
URL: www.usna.edu
Established: 1845 Annual Undergrad Tuition & Fees: N/A
Enrollment: 4,594 Coed
Affiliation or Control: Federal IRS Status: Exempt
Highest Offering: Baccalaureate
Accreditation: M

01 Superintendent .... VADM. Sean S. BUCK
100 Chief of Staff/Dep Superintendent .... CAPT. James BATES
32 Commandant of Midshipmen .... Col. James P. MCDONOUGH
05 Academic Dean & Provost .... Dr. Andrew T. PHILLIPS
41 Athletic Director .... Mr. Chet GLADCHUK
07 Dean of Admissions .... Mr. Bruce J. LATTA
10 CFO/Deputy for Finance .... Mr. Joseph RUBINO
13 Chief Information Officer .... Mr. Louis J. GIANNOTTI

20 Vice Provost ... Dr. Daniel W. O'SULLIVAN
20 Assoc Provost for Academic Affairs ... Dr. Samarra FIREBAUGH
21 Assoc Provost Finance/Mil Affairs ... Mr. Peter A. NARDI
108 Assoc Provost for Planning & Assess ... Katherine CERMAK
54 Dean School of Engineering & Weps ... CAPT. Robert WOLF
81 Dean School of Math & Science ... CAPT. Benjamin SHUPP
79 Dean School of Hum/Social Sciences ... Col. Michael STYSKAL
35 Deputy Commandant of Midshipmen ... CAPT. David FORMAN
107 Deputy Commandant Professional Dev ... CAPT. Bo JOHNS
88 Dir Leadership Educ/Development ... CAPT. Jason RIMMER
121 Dean Student Academic Development ... Ms. Pamela SCHMITT
08 Assoc Dean Information Svcs/Library ... Mr. Larry CLEMENS
06 Registrar ... Dr. Christopher A. DAVIS
26 Public Affairs Officer ... CDR. Alana GARAS
29 Alumni Assoc Director of Engagement .. Mr. Craig WASHINGTON
21 Comptroller ... Mr. Todd W. HAUGE
09 Director Institutional Research ... Mr. Robert J. BRENNAN
18 Deputy Facilities & Construction ... Ms. Sara PHILLIPS
42 Command Chaplain ... CAPT. Richard BONNETTE
15 Director Human Resources ... Mr. William COFFIN
28 Chief Diversity Officer ... CAPT. Herbert E. LACY
43 Staff Judge Advocate ... CAPT. Andrew HOUSE
86 Director Government Relations ... Mr. Mike BRADY
104 Director International Programs ... Mr. Tim DISHER
04 Admin Assistant to the President ... Maj. Alexandra FITZGERALD

AMERICAN SAMOA

American Samoa Community College (A)

PO Box 2609, Pago Pago AS 96799-2609
County: American Samoa FICE Identification: 010010
Unit ID: 240736
Telephone: (684) 699-2722 Carnegie Class: Bac/Assoc-Assoc Dom
FAX Number: (684) 699-6259 Calendar System: Semester
URL: www.amsamoa.edu
Established: 1970 Annual Undergrad Tuition & Fees (In-State): $3,950
Enrollment: 1,081 Coed
Affiliation or Control: State IRS Status: 501(c)3
Highest Offering: Baccalaureate
Accreditation: WJ

01 President ... Dr. Rosevonne M. PATO
32 VP Cmty/Academic/Student Affairs ... Dr. Letupu MOANANU
11 VP Admin/Finance & Accred Liaison ... Mr. Sonny LEOMITI
05 Dean of Academic Affairs ... Dr. Siamaua ROPETI
88 Dir of Samoan Studies Institute .Mrs. Okenaisa FAUOLO-MANILA
108 Executive Director of IE ... Mr. Tauvela FALE
88 Director of Land Grant/ACNR ... Mr. Ropeti ARETA
88 Director of UCEDD ... Ms. Tafaimamao TUPUOLA
51 Director of Adult Education-LEL ... Vacant
53 Teacher Educ Program Director ... Ms. Shirley DE LA ROSA
66 Nursing Program Director ... Ms. Lele V. AH MU
72 Trade and Tech Program Director ... Mr. Frederick R. SUISALA
32 Dean of Student Services ... Dr. Emilia LE'I
38 Program Director of Counseling ... Ms. Annie PANAMA
06 Registrar/Records Officer ... Mrs. Sifagatogo TUITASI
08 Program Director of Library Svcs ... Mrs. Faailoa AFALAVA
37 Financial Aid Officer ... Ms. Shanell TAUILIILI
07 Admission Officer ... Mrs. Elizabeth LEUMA
10 Financial Officer ... Ms. Elsie LESA
13 Chief Information Officer ... Mrs. Grace TULAFONO-ASI
18 Physical Facilities Maint Officer ... Mr. Lokeni LOKENI
15 Human Resources Officer ... Mrs. Sereima ASIFOA
96 Procurement Officer ... Mrs. Jessie SU'ESU'E
40 Bookstore Officer ... Mrs. Alofia AFALAVA
04 Executive Secretary ... Mrs. Alofagia PANAPA
101 Board Secretary ... Mrs. Tiare TUPUA
19 Security Officer ... Mr. Toetu SAILI

FEDERATED STATES OF MICRONESIA

College of Micronesia-FSM (B)

PO Box 159 Kolonia, Pohnpei FM 96941-0159
FICE Identification: 010343
Unit ID: 243638
Telephone: (691) 320-2480 Carnegie Class: Bac/Assoc-Assoc Dom
FAX Number: (691) 320-2479 Calendar System: Semester
URL: www.comfsm.fm
Established: 1963 Annual Undergrad Tuition & Fees (In-State): $4,750
Enrollment: 1,861 Coed
Affiliation or Control: State IRS Status: 501(c)3
Highest Offering: Associate Degree
Accreditation: WJ

01 Interim President/CEO ... Mrs. Karen SIMION
05 Vice Pres for Instructional Affairs ... Mrs. Karen SIMION
84 Vice Pres Enroll Mgmt/Student Svcs ... Mr. Joey ODUCADO
11 Vice President Admin Services ... Mr. Joseph HABUCHMAI
12 Dean Chuuk Campus ... Mr. Kind KANTO
12 Dean Kosrae Campus ... Mr. Nena MIKE
12 Dean Yap Campus/VP Instruct Affs ... Ms. Lourdes ROBOMAN
10 Comptroller ... Mrs. Roselle TOGONON
15 Director Human Resources ... Ms. Rencelly NELSON
20 Dean of Academic Programs ... Mrs. Maria DISON
08 Director Learning Resource Center ... Mrs. Jennifer HELIEISAR
75 Dir Career & Technical Education ... Mr. Grilly JACK
18 Director Physical Plant/Maintenance ... Mr. Francisco MENDIOLA
06 Registrar ... Mr. Doman DAOAS
21 Business Officer Manager ... Ms. Ritchie VALENCIA
37 Acting Director of Financial Aid ... Ms. Arinda SWINGLY
38 Lead Counselor ... Ms. Penselyn SAM
13 Director Information Technology ... Mr. Shaun SULIOL
19 Supervisor Security/Safety ... Mr. Terry MARCUS

GUAM

Guam Community College (C)

P.O. Box 23069, Barrigada GU 96921-3069
County: Guam FICE Identification: 015361
Unit ID: 240745
Telephone: (671) 735-5531 Carnegie Class: Assoc/MT-VT-High Trad
FAX Number: (671) 734-5238 Calendar System: Semester
URL: www.guamcc.edu
Established: 1977 Annual Undergrad Tuition & Fees (In-District): $3,414
Enrollment: 1,716 Coed
Affiliation or Control: State/Local IRS Status: 501(c)3
Highest Offering: Associate Degree
Accreditation: WJ, ACFEI

01 President ... Dr. Mary Y. OKADA
05 Vice President Academic Affairs ... Dr. Virginia C. TUDELA
32 Dean Technology & Student Services ... Dr. Michael L. CHAN
10 Controller ... Mr. Edwin E. LIMTUATCO
88 Dean Trade & Prof Svcs ... Ms. Pilar WILLIAMS
51 Asst Dir Cont Educ & Workforce Dev . Ms. Denise M. MENDIOLA
45 Asst Dir Planning & Development ... Dr. Julie U. ULLOA HEATH
26 Asst Dir Communications & Promo ... Mr. John DELA ROSA
04 Private Secretary ... Ms. Esther A. MUNA
101 Admin Secretary II BOT-Pres Ofc ... Ms. Bertha M. GUERRERO
07 Coordinator Admissions/Registration ... Ms. Ava M. GARCIA
09 Asst Director AIER ... Ms. Marlena O. PANGELINAN
15 Chief Human Resources Ofcr ... Ms. Apolline SAN NICOLAS
35 Assoc Dean Tech & Student Svcs ... Mr. Gerald A. CRUZ
18 Facilities Engineer Administrator ... Vacant
08 Librarian ... Ms. Christine B. MATSON
20 Admin Ofcr VP's Ofc-Academic Affs .... Ms. Jadeline A. MULLIKIN
55 Pgm Spc Adult Basic Educ ... Ms. Yolonda T. TOPASNA
88 Pgm Spc TRIO Programs ... Vacant
88 Pgm Spc Ctr Student Involvement ... Ms. Tara Rose PASCUA
23 LPN Health Services Center ... Ms. Eva Marie L. MUI
37 Coordinator Student Financial Aid ... Ms. Charmaine F. BELZER
88 Inventory Mgmt Officer ... Mr. Isaac K. WILLIAMS
29 Pgm Specialist Alum & Fundraising ... Ms. Bonnie Mae M. DATUIN
96 Supply Management Administrator .Ms. Joleen M. EVANGELISTA
13 Chief Info Tech Officer MIS ... Mr. Adrian ATALIG
19 Environ Health & Safety Ofcr ... Mr. Huan F. HOSEI
40 Bookstore Manager ... Mr. Roland MANGLONA
88 Pgm Spc Night Administrator ... Mr. Arjay A. REYES
39 Pgm Spc Accommodative Svcs ... Mr. John F. PAYNE
88 Sustainability/Project Coordinator ... Mr. Francisco E. PALACIOS

Pacific Islands University (D)

172 Kinney's Road, Mangilao GU 96913
County: Guam FICE Identification: 034383
Unit ID: 439862
Telephone: (671) 734-1812 Carnegie Class: Bac-A&S
FAX Number: (671) 734-1813 Calendar System: Semester
URL: www.piu.edu
Established: 1976 Annual Undergrad Tuition & Fees: $6,110
Enrollment: 273 Coed
Affiliation or Control: Independent Non-Profit IRS Status: 501(c)3
Highest Offering: Master's
Accreditation: TRACS

01 President ... Dr. Mihamm KIM-RAUCHHOLZ
10 Chief Financial Officer ... Ms. Edlyn DALISAY
05 Vice President Academic Affairs ... Ms. Joanna GREEN
49 Liberal Studies Chair ... Ms. Pamela JENKINS
73 Biblical Studies Chair ... Mr. Iotaka CHORAM
32 Vice President Student Development ... Mr. Delight SUDA
21 Director of Operations ... Ms. Celia ATOIGUE
04 Admin Assistant to the President ... Mr. Kevin GRAHAM
08 Library Director ... Mr. Paul DRAKE
15 Human Resource Director ... Mr. Joshua COMBS
84 Enrollment Mgmt Dir/Registrar ... Mr. Joshua COMBS
37 Financial Aid Officer ... Mr. Delight SUDA

University of Guam (E)

UOG Station, Mangilao GU 96923-1800
County: Guam FICE Identification: 003935
Unit ID: 240754
Telephone: (671) 735-2990 Carnegie Class: Masters/M
FAX Number: (671) 734-2296 Calendar System: Semester
URL: www.uog.edu
Established: 1952 Annual Undergrad Tuition & Fees (In-State): $5,846
Enrollment: 3,449 Coed
Affiliation or Control: State IRS Status: 501(c)3
Highest Offering: Master's
Accreditation: WC, AAQEP, IACBE, NUR, SPAA, SW

01 President ... Dr. Thomas W. KRISE
05 Senior VP & Provost ... Dr. Anita B. ENRIQUEZ
10 Vice Pres Administration & Finance ... Mr. Randall V. WIEGAND
46 Director Research & Sponsored Pgm ... Dr. Rachael T. LEON GUERRERO
43 University General Counsel ... Mr. Anthony R. CAMACHO
13 Chief Information Officer ... Mr. Vincent DELA CRUZ
22 Acting Director EEO & Title IX/ADA . Ms. Elaine FACULO-GOGUE
100 Int Chief of Staff & Board Liaison ... Mr. David S. OKADA
26 Chief Mktg & Comm Officer ... Mr. Jonas D. MACAPINLAC
45 Acting Chief Planning Officer ... Mr. James R. HOLLYER
29 Director Alumni Affairs ... Mr. Norman ANALISTA
102 Exec Director Endowment Foundation ... Ms. Katrina PEREZ
108 Vice Provost Inst Effectiveness ... Ms. Deborah D. LEON GUERRERO
20 Vice Provost Academic Excellence .Dr. Sharleen SANTOS-BAMBA
49 Dean Col of Lib Arts & Social Sci ... Dr. James D. SELLMANN
47 Dean Col of Natural & Applied Sci ... Dr. Lee S. YUDIN
50 Dean Sch Business & Pub Admin ... Dr. Annette T. SANTOS
53 Dean School of Education ... Dr. Alicia AGUON
76 Dean School of Health ... Dr. Margaret HATTORI-UCHIMA
54 Interim Dean School of Engineering ... Dr. Lee YUDIN
84 Dean Enroll Mgmt & Student Svcs .... Dr. Lawrence F. CAMACHO
06 Interim Associate Dean/Registrar ... Ms. Arline E. LEON GUERRERO
37 Financial Aid Director ... Mr. Mark A. DUARTE
32 Student Life Officer ... Vacant
88 Interim Director Guam CEDDERS ... Ms. June DE LEON
08 Dean University Libraries ... Dr. Monique STORIE
88 Dir Micronesia Area Res Center ... Dr. Carlos MADRID
88 Interim Director Marine Laboratory ... Dr. Laurie RAYMUNDO
88 Dir Water Env Rsrch Inst Wstrn Pac ... Dr. John JENSON
88 Dir Ctr for Island Sustainability ... Dr. Austin SHELTON
104 Dir Global Learning & Engagement ... Mr. Carlos TAITANO
15 Actg Chief Human Resources Officer ... Mr. Joseph B. GUMATAOTAO
18 Int Chief Plant/Facility Officer ... Mr. David S. OKADA
41 Field House/Athletics Director ... Mr. Doug PALMER
19 Safety Administrator ... Mr. Alfred GARRIDO
40 Interim Bookstore & Auxiliary Svcs ... Mr. Jonas MACAPINLAC
21 Comptroller ... Ms. Abigail MARTIN
39 Director of Residence Halls ... Mr. Mark MENDIOLA
30 Director of Development ... Mr. Norman S. ANALISTA

MARSHALL ISLANDS

College of the Marshall Islands (F)

PO Box 1258, Majuro MH 96960-1258
County: Marshalls FICE Identification: 030224
Unit ID: 376695
Telephone: (692) 625-3394 Carnegie Class: Bac/Assoc-Assoc Dom
FAX Number: (692) 625-7203 Calendar System: Semester
URL: www.cmi.edu
Established: 1989 Annual Undergrad Tuition & Fees (In-State): $4,900
Enrollment: 1,162 Coed
Affiliation or Control: State IRS Status: 501(c)3
Highest Offering: Associate Degree
Accreditation: WJ

01 President ... Dr. Irene J. TAAFAKI
05 Vice Pres Academic/Student Affairs ... Dr. Elizabeth SWITAJ
10 Vice Pres Business & Admin Affairs ... Mr. Stevenson KOTTON
88 Vice President for Land Grant ... Mr. Stanley LORENNIJ
20 Dean of Academic Affairs ... Ms. Vasemaca SAVU
32 Dean of Student Success ... Vacant
06 Registrar ... Ms. Monica GORDON
07 Director of Admissions & Records ... Ms. Jomi CAPELLE
08 Director of Library ... Ms. Verenaisi BAVADRA
15 Human Resources Director ... Ms. Agnes KOTOISUVA
18 Director Physical Plant ... Mr. Linus KEBOS
13 Director Information & Technology ... Mr. Bonifacio SANCHEZ
88 Director Nuclear Institute ... Ms. Mary L. SILK
37 Financial Aid Director ... Ms. Sali ANDRIKE
49 Chair Liberal Arts ... Ms. Oyinada OGUNMOKUN
03 Executive Vice President ... Mr. William REIHER
50 Chair Business & IT ... Ms. Meitaka KENDALL-LEKKA
66 Chair Nursing ... Ms. Florence L. PETER
19 Director Security/Safety ... Mr. David DEBRUM
38 Director of Counseling ... Ms. Demiana NAUSI KUMORU
09 Dir Inst Research/Assessment ... Ms. Cheryl T. VILA
04 Admin Assistant to the President ... Ms. Takbar ISHIGURO
101 Executive Officer ... Ms. Kelly Luce SEBASTIAN
105 Director Web Services ... Mr. John A. VILLAFANIA

NORTHERN MARIANAS

Northern Marianas College (G)

PO Box 501250, Saipan MP 96950-1250
FICE Identification: 030330
Unit ID: 240790
Telephone: (670) 234-5498 Carnegie Class: Bac/Assoc-Mixed
FAX Number: (670) 234-1270 Calendar System: Semester
URL: www.marianas.edu
Established: 1976 Annual Undergrad Tuition & Fees (In-District): $4,038
Enrollment: 1,255 Coed
Affiliation or Control: State/Local IRS Status: Exempt
Highest Offering: Baccalaureate
Accreditation: WC

01 President ... Dr. Galvin DELEON GUERRERO
05 Dean of Academic Programs/Services ... Dr. Randy YATES

10 Chief Financial Officer .... Mr. David ATTAO
04 Executive Secretary to President .... Ms. Becky SABLAN
20 Dean Learning & Student Success .... Ms. Charlotte CEPEDA
13 Dir Information Technology .... Mr. Adrian ATALIG
09 Dir Institutional Effectiveness .... Dr. Wesley WILSON
18 Director of Facilities .... Mr. Vincent MERFALEN
53 Director School of Education .... Mr. Roland MERAR
51 Director of Adult Basic Education .... Ms. Lorraine C. MAUI
37 Director of Financial Aid .... Ms. Daisy MANGLONA-PROPST
96 Procurement Manager .... Ms. Anita C. CAMACHO
106 Director of Distance Learning .... Mr. William HUNTER
06 Registrar .... Ms. Marji TAROPE
101 Executive Secretary to the Board .... Ms. Helen B. CAMACHO
84 Director Enrollment Services .... Mr. Manny CASTRO

PALAU

Palau Community College (A)

PO Box 9, Koror PW 96940-0009
County: Koror | FICE Identification: 011009 | Unit ID: 243647
Telephone: (680) 488-2470 | Carnegie Class: Assoc/HT-High Trad
FAX Number: (680) 488-2447 | Calendar System: Semester
URL: www.palau.edu
Established: 1969 | Annual Undergrad Tuition & Fees: $3,610
Enrollment: 553 | Coed
Affiliation or Control: Federal | IRS Status: Exempt
Highest Offering: Associate Degree
Accreditation: WJ

01 President .... Dr. Patrick U. TELLEI
05 Vice President Education & Training .... Vacant
11 Vice Pres Administration & Finance .... Mr. Jay OLEGERIIL
46 Vice Pres Cooperative Rsrch/Exten . Dr. Christopher U. KITALONG
04 Exec Assistant to the President .... Mr. Todd NGIRAMENGIOR
32 Dean of Students/Dir Student Life .... Ms. Hilda N. REKLAI
20 Dean of Academic Affairs .... Ms. Deikola OLIKONG
51 Dean of Continuing Education .... Mr. Jefferson THOMAS
30 Director of Development .... Mr. Tchuzie TADAO
37 Director of Financial Aid .... Ms. Isumechraard K. NGIRAIRIKL
07 Director of Admissions and Records .... Ms. Lesley B. ADACHI
15 Director of Human Resources .... Ms. Marie A. ANDERSON
18 Director of Physical Plant .... Mr. Clement KAZUMA
13 Director of Computer Systems .... Mr. Bruce RIMIRCH
10 Director of Finance .... Ms. Uroi N. SALII
08 Interim Director Library Services .... Ms. Pioria ASITO

PUERTO RICO

American University of Puerto Rico (B)

Box 2037, Bayamon PR 00960-2037
County: Bayamon | FICE Identification: 011941 | Unit ID: 241100
Telephone: (787) 620-2040 | Carnegie Class: Bac-Diverse
FAX Number: (787) 785-7377 | Calendar System: Other
URL: www.aupr.edu
Established: 1963 | Annual Undergrad Tuition & Fees: $6,555
Enrollment: 294 | Coed
Affiliation or Control: Independent Non-Profit | IRS Status: 501(c)3
Highest Offering: Master's
Accreditation: M

01 President .... Mr. Juan C. NAZARIO TORRES
03 Executive Vice President .... Mr. Jaime GONZALEZ
05 Vice President Acad/Student Affairs .... Dr. Jose RAMIREZ-FIGUEROA
32 Dean Student Affairs .... Prof. Claribel RODRIGUEZ-VARGAS
07 Admissions Officer .... Ms. Keren LLANOS
08 Learning Resources Center Director .... Vacant
37 Coordinator Financial Aid .... Mrs. Nelly DUARTE
21 Director Accounting .... Mr. Anderson MONTERO-RIVERA
38 Director Guidance Counseling .... Mrs. Luz S. HERNANDEZ
24 Director Educational Media .... Ms. Carol SANTIAGO
41 Athletic Director .... Mr. Manfredo VEGA
15 Director Human Resources .... Mr. Jorge ESCALERA MUÑOZ
12 Director Manati Campus .... Prof. Milagros RIVERA-OTERO
09 Dir Research/Institutional Planning .... Vacant
18 Chief Facilities/Physical Plant .... Mr. Efrain LUGO
36 Director of Student Placement .... Vacant
96 Coordinator of Purchasing .... Mr. Felix REYES-RIVERA
92 Director of Honors Program .... Prof. Claribel RODRIGUEZ
30 Chief Development .... Mr. Jaime GONZALEZ
20 Associate Academic Officer .... Prof. Zahira GARCIA
13 Director Computer Center .... Vacant
53 Dept Chair School of Education .... Dr. Jose RAMIREZ
50 Dept Chair Business Admin/Sec Sci .... Vacant
49 Department Chair Arts & Sciences .... Vacant
100 Chief of Staff .... Ms. Rosabel VAZQUEZ
102 Dir Foundation/Corporate Relations .... Vacant
105 Director Web Services .... Vacant
19 Director Security/Safety .... Ms. Rosabel VAZQUEZ
45 Chief Institutional Planning ... Prof. Bolivar RAMIREZ-CARLO, III
04 Administrative Asst to President .... Mrs. Carmen ARROYO

Atenas College (C)

Paseo de las Atenas #101, Manati PR 00674
FICE Identification: 035443 | Unit ID: 440651
Telephone: (787) 884-3838 | Carnegie Class: Spec-4-yr-Other Health
FAX Number: (787) 854-4530 | Calendar System: Semester
URL: www.atenascollege.edu
Established: 1996 | Annual Undergrad Tuition & Fees: $7,370
Enrollment: 558 | Coed
Affiliation or Control: Independent Non-Profit | IRS Status: 501(c)3
Highest Offering: Baccalaureate
Accreditation: M, ADNUR, NURSE

01 President .... Dra. Maria L. HERNANDEZ NUNEZ
05 VP Academic Affairs .... Prof. Widalys GONZALEZ
32 VP of Student Affairs .... Dr. José M. DONATE
45 VP Inst Planning & Development .... Mrs. Ingrid Y. COLON
10 VP Finance & Administrative Affairs ..... Mrs. Astrid Y. MELENDEZ
20 Associate VP of Academic Affairs .... Dra. Cenia K. ROMANO
21 Assoc VP of Finance & Admin Affs .... Mrs. Zulay SOTO
37 Financial Aid Administrator .... Mr. Manuel RAMIREZ

Atlantic University College (D)

PO Box 3918, Guaynabo PR 00970
County: Guaynabo | FICE Identification: 025054 | Unit ID: 241216
Telephone: (787) 720-1022 | Carnegie Class: Masters/S
FAX Number: (787) 720-1092 | Calendar System: Quarter
URL: www.atlanticu.edu
Established: 1983 | Annual Undergrad Tuition & Fees: $7,500
Enrollment: 1,584 | Coed
Affiliation or Control: Independent Non-Profit | IRS Status: 501(c)3
Highest Offering: Master's
Accreditation: ACCSC

01 President .... Dr. Jaime SANTIAGO
05 Academic Dean .... Prof. Maria VILLALONGA
10 Asst Dean of Administration .... Ms. Viviana SANTIAGO
06 Registrar .... Ms. Edna I. GUTIERREZ
38 Dir Student Counseling/Placement .... Prof. Maria C. LOPEZ-CEPERO RAMOS
37 Director Financial Aid .... Mrs. Janice RIVERA
08 Head Librarian .... Mrs. Awilda MORAN
07 Director of Admissions .... Mr. Joel MONTERO
21 Director Business Office .... Mrs. María del C MONTESINO
15 Officer of Human Resources .... Ms. Viviana SANTIAGO

Caribbean University (E)

Box 493, Bayamon PR 00960-0493
County: Bayamon | FICE Identification: 012525 | Unit ID: 241377
Telephone: (787) 780-0070 | Carnegie Class: Masters/S
FAX Number: N/A | Calendar System: Semester
URL: www.caribbean.edu
Established: 1969 | Annual Undergrad Tuition & Fees: $5,496
Enrollment: 987 | Coed
Affiliation or Control: Independent Non-Profit | IRS Status: 501(c)3
Highest Offering: Doctorate
Accreditation: M

01 President/CEO .... Dr. Ana E. CUCURELLA-ADORNO
03 Executive Director .... Mr. Victor T. ADORNO
45 VP of Planning and Development .... Mrs. Lillian MATOS
11 VP Administration Affairs .... Mr. Hector GRACIA
32 Dean of Student Affairs .... Mr. Alex CLAUDIO
15 Int Director Human Resources .... Dr. Rebecca QUINTANA
37 Coordinator Student Financial Aid .... Mrs. Lorell NUÑEZ
06 Registrar .... Ms. Rosalie MORALES
08 Librarian/Director Audio-Visual .... Mrs. Cynthia MIRANDA
12 Director of Carolina Campus .... Dr. Reinaldo DEL VALLE
12 Director of Ponce Campus .... Dr. Rafael NEGRON
12 Director Vega Baja Campus .... Prof. Rafael MARRERO
26 Director of Marketing/Admissions .... Prof. Gricelie TORRES
58 Academic Dean Graduate Programs .... Dr. Zoraida ALONSO
49 Director Department of Liberal Arts .... Prof. Arelis NEVAREZ
50 Coordinator Dept Business Admin .... Prof. Carmen RODRIGUEZ
76 Director Dept Allied Sciences .... Dr. Ricardo MELGAREJO
54 Director Department Engineering/IT .... Dr. Hermes CALDERON
66 Coordinator Department of Nursing .... Prof. Noemi SANTOS
53 Dir Dept Education/Liberal Arts .... Prof. Arelis NEVAREZ
18 Chief Facilities/Physical Plant .... Mr. Ibrahim MESTRES
38 Director Counseling Center (CIOSE) .... Lic. Maria PEREZ
41 Athletic Director .... Mr. Xavier PIZARRO
22 Director of Compliance/Student Svcs .... Mrs. Elena GARCIA
12 Director of Bayamon Campus .... Prof. Alex CLAUDIO
04 Admin Assistant to the President .... Ms. Judith ROMAN
10 Chief Financial/Business Officer .... Mr. Edwin C. LOZADA
19 Director Security/Safety .... Ms. Ana SANCHEZ

Carlos Albizu University (F)

Box 9023711, San Juan PR 00902-3711
County: San Juan | FICE Identification: 010724 | Unit ID: 241331
Telephone: (787) 725-6500 | Carnegie Class: Spec-4-yr-Other Health
FAX Number: (787) 721-7187 | Calendar System: Semester
URL: www.albizu.edu
Established: 1966 | Annual Undergrad Tuition & Fees: $7,434
Enrollment: 2,344 | Coed
Affiliation or Control: Independent Non-Profit | IRS Status: 501(c)3
Highest Offering: Doctorate
Accreditation: M, CLPSY, IPSY, SP

01 President .... Dr. Jose PONS MADERA
00 Chair Board of Trustees ..... Mrs. Maria FELICIANO DE LA CRUZ
03 Chancellor .... Dr. Julio SANTANA MARINO
05 Provost/Dean of Academic Affairs .... Dr. José A. PEREZ - SANTIAGO
10 Chief Financial Officer .... Ms. Angel ORTIZ GARCIA
32 Dean of Student Services .... Ms. Carmen RIVERA
84 Dean of Enrollment Management .... Ms. Rosa BELVIS LOPEZ
07 Interim Director of Admissions .... Mrs. Kareline SANTIAGO TORRES
21 Director of Finance .... Mr. Hector PENA
09 Dir of Planning/Inst Research .. Mr. Yoel A. VELAZQUEZ-OLIVER
46 Director Research/Training Program .... Dr. Lymaries PADILLA
51 Director Continuing Education .... Ms. Luaida OYOLA
37 Director Financial Aid .... Mrs. Doris QUERO-MENDEZ
08 Director Library .... Ms. Yolanda ROSARIO-ROSARIO
06 Registrar .... Ms. Maria de Lourdes RIVERA-NIEVES
88 Dir Industrial/Org Psych Program .... Dr. Ramón RODRÍGUEZ MONTALBAN
13 Director Information Systems .... Mr. Juan RIVERA RIVERA
88 Administrator Community Svcs Clinic .... Mr. Epifanio RIVERA
88 Director Community Services Clinic .... Dr. Vanessa RIVERA
88 Dir PhD Clinical Psychology Program .... Mr. Marcos REYES
15 Human Resources Director .... Ms. Carmen M. ACEVEDO RIOS
30 Director Development .... Vacant
97 Director Bachelor's Program .... Dr. Arlene VELEZ
38 President Student Counseling .... Mr. Jose A. GARCIA
11 Director Administration .... Mr. Epifanio RIVERA
108 Dir Assessment and Accreditation .... Mr. Rafael MELENDEZ
58 Director of Graduate Education .... Dr. Luaida OYOLA
04 Admin Assistant to the President .... Ms. Vanessa RAMOS
100 Chief of Staff .... Dr. Angel ORTIZ

CEM College (G)

Calle Degetau #25, Bayamon PR 00961
Telephone: (787) 780-8900 | Identification: 770590
Accreditation: ACCSC

CEM College (H)

Calle Dr. Vidal #8 y #53, Humacao PR 00791
Telephone: (787) 852-5505 | Identification: 770589
Accreditation: ACCSC

CEM College (I)

Ext San Agustin,Calle 13 #1206, San Juan PR 00926
County: San Juan | FICE Identification: 021891 | Unit ID: 241517
Telephone: (787) 765-4210 | Carnegie Class: Spec-4-yr-Other Health
FAX Number: (787) 765-4277 | Calendar System: Semester
URL: www.cemcollege.edu
Established: 1980 | Annual Undergrad Tuition & Fees: $8,616
Enrollment: 277 | Coed
Affiliation or Control: Independent Non-Profit | IRS Status: 501(c)3
Highest Offering: Baccalaureate
Accreditation: ACCSC

02 President .... Mr. Juan C. PAGANO SOTO
11 Campus Director .... Mr. Hector M. DAVILA RIVERA

Center for Advanced Studies On Puerto Rico and the Caribbean (J)

PO Box 902-3970, Old San Juan PR 00902-3970
County: San Juan | FICE Identification: 021660 | Unit ID: 241793
Telephone: (787) 723-4481 | Carnegie Class: Masters/S
FAX Number: (787) 723-1023 | Calendar System: Semester
URL: www.ceaprc.edu
Established: 1976 | Annual Graduate Tuition & Fees: N/A
Enrollment: 507 | Coed
Affiliation or Control: Independent Non-Profit | IRS Status: 501(c)3
Highest Offering: Doctorate; No Undergraduates
Accreditation: M

01 Chancellor .... Dr. Olga A. BENITEZ
05 Dean of Academic Affairs .... Dr. Maritza TORRES
06 Registrar .... Mr. Raul R. HERNANDEZ
08 Head Librarian .... Mr. Enrique L. PIMENTEL
11 Administration Director .... Ms. Marie L. RIVERA
32 Students Affairs Dean .... Mr. Raul R. HERNANDEZ
37 Financial Aid Director .... Mr. Jose F. PEREZ-RODRIGUEZ
07 Admissions Officer .... Ms. Maria TORRES
38 Director Student Counseling .... Mrs. Carmen B. ORTIZ
04 Chancellor's Assistant .... Ms. Clarissa SANTIAGO-TORO

Colegio de Cinematografia, Artes y Television (K)

51 Calle Dr. Santiago Veve, Bayamon PR 00961
County: Bayamon | FICE Identification: 031576 | Unit ID: 430935
Telephone: (787) 779-2500 | Carnegie Class: Assoc/MT-VT-High Trad
FAX Number: (787) 995-2525 | Calendar System: Semester
URL: www.ccatpuertorico.com
Established: 1993 | Annual Undergrad Tuition & Fees: $6,660
Enrollment: 619 | Coed
Affiliation or Control: Proprietary | IRS Status: Proprietary
Highest Offering: Associate Degree

Accreditation: ACCSC

01 President .... Ms. Carola GARCIA
05 Director of Academics .... Mr. Harry VAZQUEZ
32 Dean of Student Affairs .... Ms. Diana CASTILLO

Colegio Universitario de San Juan (A)

180 Jose R. Oliver Avenue, San Juan PR 00918
County: San Juan FICE Identification: 010567
Unit ID: 241720
Telephone: (787) 480-2400 Carnegie Class: Bac-Diverse
FAX Number: (787) 250-7395 Calendar System: Semester
URL: www.cunisanjuan.edu
Established: 1972 Annual Undergrad Tuition & Fees (In-District): $2,340
Enrollment: 840 Coed
Affiliation or Control: Local IRS Status: 501(c)3
Highest Offering: Baccalaureate
Accreditation: M, ADNUR, NURSE

01 Interim Chancellor .... Ms. Deborah A. DRAHUS-CAPO
45 Dir Planning/Inst Research/Ext Revs .... Dr. Karla COLON
05 Interim Dean Academic Affairs .... Prof. Mercy FALERO
32 Interim Dean Student Affairs .... Mr. Omar RIVERA-MELENDEZ
11 Interim Dean Administrative Affairs .... Dr. Haydee ZAYAS-HERNANDEZ
51 Dir Continuing Educ/Extension Pgm .... Mrs. Deborah RIVERA
37 Manager Student Financial Aid .... Mrs. Kennia I. SANTOS-PEREZ
08 Head Librarian .... Mrs. Sheila VERA-MORALES
06 Registrar .... Mrs. Michel ORTIZ
38 Counselor .... Mrs. Mara MALAVE-LASSO
36 Placement Officer .... Prof. Waleska Y. ROSA-NUNEZ
13 Administrator Info Systems/ Telecomm .... Mr. Zacarias POUERIET-DE LA CRUZ
72 Dir Science & Technology Dept .... Prof. Marcus DROZ-RAMOS
76 Dir Health Related Science Dept .... Prof. Elizabeth ROSARIO-RODRIGUEZ
50 Dir Business Administration Dept .... Prof. Nilda E. RODRIGUEZ-MOLINA
97 Manager General Education Dept .... Prof. Carmen J. RODRIGUEZ-VINCENTY
88 Dir Behavioral Related Profess Dept .... Prof. Maria T. PEREZ-CASANOVA
04 Chancellor Assistant .... Prof. Annelis RIVERA
15 Chief Human Resources Officer .... Ms. Isabel LOZADA-CRUZ

Columbia Central University (B)

PO Box 9120, Caguas PR 00726-9120
County: Caguas FICE Identification: 008902
Unit ID: 241304
Telephone: (787) 704-1020 Carnegie Class: Spec-4-yr-Other Health
FAX Number: N/A Calendar System: Semester
URL: www.columbiacentral.edu
Established: 1966 Annual Undergrad Tuition & Fees: $7,180
Enrollment: 798 Coed
Affiliation or Control: Proprietary IRS Status: Proprietary
Highest Offering: Master's
Accreditation: M

01 President & CEO .... Mr. Jose CORDOVA
05 VP Academic Affairs .... Mrs. Betsy VIDAL
20 Assoc VP of Curricular Innovation .... Ms. Maria CRUZ
45 VP of Planning/Assessment & Accred .... Mrs. Lina VEGA
10 VP Finance and Administration .... Mrs. Magda CANCEL
32 VP Student Affairs .... Dr. Raul MEDINA
26 VP Marketing and Admissions .... Mrs. Josie ARROYO
07 Institutional Admissions Director .... Ms. Zaida LOZADA
12 Chancellor of Caguas Campus .... Mrs. Wilda VELEZ
12 Chancellor of Yauco Branch .... Mr. Juan ORENGO
12 Chancellor of Bayam=n Branch .... Mr. Fernando GONZALEZ
12 Chancellor of Carolina Branch .... Mr. Rafael GUZMAN
06 Registrar - Caguas Branch .... Mrs. Sheila DAVILA
06 Registrar - Carolina Branch .... Ms. Enid LOPEZ
06 Registrar - Bayamon Branch .... Ms. Jeannette TORRES
06 Registrar - Yauco Branch .... Mr. Luis ALMODOVAR
38 Student Counselor Caguas Branch .... Mrs. Iris SANTIAGO
38 Student Counselor - Carolina Branch .... Mr. David BAEZ
38 Student Counselor Bayamon Branch .... Ms. Zuleika COTTO
124 Retention Officer Caguas .... Mrs. Sandra SANTIAGO
124 Retention Officer Bayamon .... Ms. Vanessa OJEDA
36 Student Placement Officer - Caguas .... Ms. Wanda DEL VALLE
36 Student Placement Officer Carolina .... Ms. Boamari MENDEZ
36 Student Placement Officer Bayamon .... Ms. Keimily MELENDEZ
36 Student Placement Officer Yauco .... Mr. Salvador IRIZARRY
113 Treasury Officer Caguas .... Ms. Ineabelle CINTRON
113 Treasury Officer Caguas .... Mrs. Ana MERCED
113 Treasury Officer Carolina .... Ms. Karelie SUAZO
113 Treasury Officer Bayamon .... Ms. Wanda ESTREMERA
113 Treasury Officer Yauco .... Ms. Yolanda NIEVES
15 Director Human Resources .... Mrs. Norelis RODRIGUEZ
18 Facilities & Purchases Director .... Mrs. Aracelis MOLINA
13 IT Director .... Mr. Efrain GUADALUPE
37 Financial Aid Institutional Dir .... Mrs. Gloria MIRABAL

Conservatory of Music of Puerto Rico (C)

951 Ponce de Leon Ave. Miramar, Santurce PR 00907
County: San Juan FICE Identification: 010819
Unit ID: 241766
Telephone: (787) 751-0160 Carnegie Class: Spec-4-yr-Arts
FAX Number: (787) 766-1216 Calendar System: Semester
URL: www.cmpr.edu
Established: 1959 Annual Undergrad Tuition & Fees (In-State): $3,370
Enrollment: 370 Coed
Affiliation or Control: State IRS Status: 501(c)3
Highest Offering: Master's
Accreditation: M, MUS

01 Chancellor .... Dr. Manuel CALZADA
05 Dean of Academic/Student Affairs .... Mrs. Helen GONZALEZ
20 Assoc Dean of Academic/Student Affs .... Mr. Ernesto V. RAMOS
10 Dean of Finance/Administration .... Ms. Gloryber LABOY
37 Director Financial Aid .... Mr. Luis R. DIAZ
88 Director of Preparatory School .... Mr. Orlando MALDONADO
07 Admission Coordinator .... Mrs. Ana Marta ARRAIZA
08 Librarian .... Mrs. Maria del Carmen MALDONADO
15 Human Resources Director .... Ms. Johanna BERMUDEZ
38 Counselor .... Mrs. Indira L. BHAJAN
06 Registrar .... Mrs. Waleska MARTINEZ RIVERA
09 Director of Institutional Research .... Mrs. Eutimia SANTIAGO
18 Chief Facilities/Physical Plant .... Mr. Jose MATOS
13 Information Systems Coordinator .... Mr. Edwin FUMERO

Dewey University (D)

PO Box 19538, San Juan PR 00910-1538
County: San Juan FICE Identification: 031121
Unit ID: 431309
Telephone: (787) 710-8999 Carnegie Class: Not Classified
FAX Number: (787) 751-4660 Calendar System: Trimester
URL: www.dewey.edu
Established: 1992 Annual Undergrad Tuition & Fees: N/A
Enrollment: N/A Coed
Affiliation or Control: Independent Non-Profit IRS Status: 501(c)3
Highest Offering: Master's
Accreditation: ABHES

01 President/CEO .... Mr. Carlos A. QUINONES
03 Executive Vice President .... Ms. Yelitza FELICIANO
15 Chief Human Resources Officer .... Ms. Glenis VELEZ
07 Director of Admissions .... Ms. Yesenia MACHUCA
105 Director Web Services .... Ms. Yosanalis TORRES
106 Director Online Education .... Ms. Miriam DELGADO
37 Director Student Financial Aid .... Ms. Mayra VILANOVA
10 Chief Financial/Business Officer .... Ms. Yesenia CARRION

Dewey University-Carolina (E)

Carr. #3, Km. 11, Lote 7, Carolina PR 00987
Telephone: (787) 769-1515 Identification: 770776
Accreditation: ABHES

Dewey University-Juana Diaz (F)

Rd 149, KM 55.9 Lomas Industrial PK, Juana Diaz PR 00795
Telephone: (787) 260-1023 Identification: 770774
Accreditation: ABHES

Dewey University-Manati (G)

Rd 604,Km 49.1 Tierra Nueva Salient, Manati PR 00674
Telephone: (789) 854-3800 Identification: 770807
Accreditation: ABHES

EDP University of Puerto Rico (H)

PO Box 192303, San Juan PR 00919-2303
County: San Juan FICE Identification: 021651
Unit ID: 243832
Telephone: (787) 765-3560 Carnegie Class: Bac/Assoc-Mixed
FAX Number: (787) 777-0025 Calendar System: Semester
URL: www.edpuniversity.edu
Established: 1968 Annual Undergrad Tuition & Fees: $6,200
Enrollment: 1,349 Coed
Affiliation or Control: Independent Non-Profit IRS Status: 501(c)3
Highest Offering: Master's
Accreditation: M, ADNUR, NUR

01 President .... Mrs. Gladys T. NIEVES
05 Exec Vice President/Provost .... Dr. Marilyn PASTRANA
20 Dean of Academic Affairs .... Prof. María RIVERA
10 Vice President of Finance .... Mr. Luis RIVERA
111 AVP for Strategic Advancement .... Prof. Mayra RIVERA
108 AVP Institutional Compliance .... Dr. Alberto LOPEZ
13 AVP Administration and Technology .... Eng. Luis FUSTER
85 AVP Educational Innovation .... Prof. Sandra ARROYO
21 AVP for Financial Affairs .... Mrs. Marie Luz PASTRANA
09 AVP Assessment & Research .... Prof. Nydia RIVERA
14 Technology Affairs Dean .... Dr. Ramon MALLOL
06 Registrar .... Mrs. Marien DE JESÚS
08 Librarian .... Mrs. Igrí ENRIQUEZ
32 Dean of Student Affairs .... Prof. Alba FERRER
37 Director of Financial Aid .... Mr. Yaitzaenid GONZALEZ
07 Director of Admissions .... Mrs. Dendy VILA
15 Director Human Resources .... Mr. Héctor VAZQUEZ
36 Director Student Placement .... Ms. Tamara MORALES

EDP University of Puerto Rico (I)

PO Box 1674, 49 Betances Street, San Sebastian PR 00685-1674
Telephone: (787) 896-2252 Identification: 666488
Accreditation: &M

† Regional accreditation is carried under the parent institution in San Juan, PR.

Escuela de Artes Plasticas de Puerto Rico (J)

PO Box 9021112, San Juan PR 00902-1112
County: San Juan FICE Identification: 025694
Unit ID: 241951
Telephone: (787) 725-8120 Carnegie Class: Spec-4-yr-Arts
FAX Number: N/A Calendar System: Semester
URL: www.eap.edu
Established: 1966 Annual Undergrad Tuition & Fees (In-State): $3,942
Enrollment: 405 Coed
Affiliation or Control: State IRS Status: 501(c)3
Highest Offering: Baccalaureate
Accreditation: M, ART

01 Chancellor .... Dra. Ileana MUNOZ LANDRON
100 Chief of Staff .... Ms. Zolen BARRETO
05 Dean Academic Affairs .... Prof. Mayda IRIZARRY MERCADO
32 Dean Student Affairs .... Dra. Lilliam MARTINEZ ROLON
11 Dean of Administration .... Vacant
06 Registrar .... Ms. Ileana MALDONADO
07 Officer of Admissions .... Vacant
13 Chief Information Technology .... Ms. Limaris SOTO AQUINO
37 Director Student Financial Aid .. Mr. Victor M. MELENDEZ ORTIZ
45 Director of Planning & Budget .... Mr. Carlos E. RIVERA
09 Institutional Research .... Dr. Shirley A. TAVARES
10 Chief Financial Officer .... Mr. Omar FALU MENDEZ
18 Coord Facilities/Physical Plant .... Mr. Edwin ALICEA
56 Coordinator Extension Program .... Prof. Veronica SOSA
38 Counselor Student Life/Counseling .. Ms. Lisneisy NIEVES PEREZ
88 Coordinator Cultural Activities ... Mr. Adrian O. RIVERA NEGRON
105 Director Web Services .... Mr. Celso E. PORTELA IRIGOYEN
08 Library Director .... Ms. Estrella VAZQUEZ
20 Asst Dean Acad/Student Affairs .... Vacant
15 Director Human Resources .... Vacant
57 Director Art Education .... Dra. Grisselle SOTO VELEZ
97 Director General Studies .... Dr. Maria VAZQUEZ
88 Director Fashion Design .... Prof. Ana COLORADO
88 Director Industrial Design .... Prof. Vladimir GARCIA
88 Director Graphic Design .... Dr. Mauricio CONEJO
88 Director Painting .... Prof. Linda SANCHEZ PINTOR
88 Director Sculpture .... Prof. Linda SANCHEZ PINTOR
88 Director Printmaking .... Prof. Haydee LANDING
88 Director Image and Movements .... Vacant

Evangelical Seminary of Puerto Rico (K)

Ponce De Leon Avenue 776, San Juan PR 00925-9907
County: San Juan FICE Identification: 006823
Unit ID: 243498
Telephone: (787) 763-6700 Carnegie Class: Spec-4-yr-Faith
FAX Number: N/A Calendar System: Semester
URL: www.se-pr.edu
Established: 1919 Annual Undergrad Tuition & Fees: N/A
Enrollment: 155 Coed
Affiliation or Control: Interdenominational IRS Status: 501(c)3
Highest Offering: Doctorate
Accreditation: M, THEOL

01 President .... Dr. Juan R. MEJIAS-ORTIZ
05 Dean Academic & Student Affairs .... Dr. Agustina LUVIS-NÚÑEZ
10 Financial Director .... Mr. Raul F. SANTIAGO-RIVERA
18 Director of General Services .... Ms. Myrna E. PEREZ-LOPEZ
06 Registrar .... Mrs. Keina TRONCOSO-FERNANDEZ
08 Head Librarian .... Mrs. Milka VIGO-VERESTÍN
37 Student Financial Aid Officer .... Ms. Damaris MERCADO-LÓPEZ
04 Administrative Asst to President .. Mrs. Ruth E. CRUZ-GONZÁLEZ
88 Technician of Information Systems .... Mr. Héctor R. GONZÁLEZ-SANTANA
108 Director Institutional Assessment .... Dr. Juan R. MEJIAS-ORTIZ
16 Human Resources Officer .... Mrs. Janet SANTIAGO-LÓPEZ
51 Coordinator of Continuing Education .... Mrs. Keina TRONCOSO-FERNÁNDEZ

Huertas College (L)

PO Box 8429, Caguas PR 00726-8429
County: Caguas FICE Identification: 022608
Unit ID: 242112
Telephone: (787) 746-1400 Carnegie Class: Spec-4-yr-Other Health
FAX Number: (787) 743-0203 Calendar System: Semester
URL: www.huertas.edu
Established: 1945 Annual Undergrad Tuition & Fees: $7,165
Enrollment: 488 Coed
Affiliation or Control: Proprietary IRS Status: Proprietary
Highest Offering: Baccalaureate
Accreditation: M, CAHIIM, OTA

01 President .... Dr. Isaac ESQUILIN-CASTRO
05 Vice Pres Academic/Student Affairs .... Norma SANTIAGO
32 Dean of Student Success .... Yolanda ROSARIO
06 Registrar .... Krishna MARQUEZ
08 Head Librarian .... Vionis ACEVEDO
38 Director Student Counseling .... Mayra FLORES
07 Director of Admissions .... Karla SANCHEZ
36 Director Student Placement .... Ingrid SANCHEZ
37 Director Financial Aid .... Wanda ORTIZ

Humacao Community College (A)

PO Box 9139, Humacao PR 00792-9139
County: Humacao FICE Identification: 023406
Unit ID: 242121
Telephone: (787) 852-1430 Carnegie Class: Bac/Assoc-Mixed
FAX Number: (787) 850-1577 Calendar System: Trimester
URL: www.hccpr.edu
Established: 1978 Annual Undergrad Tuition & Fees: $5,742
Enrollment: 301 Coed
Affiliation or Control: Independent Non-Profit IRS Status: 501(c)3
Highest Offering: Baccalaureate
Accreditation: ACCSC

01 President ... Lic. Jorge E. MOJICA
03 Executive Vice President ... Prof. Aida E. RODRIGUEZ
81 STEM Project Director ... Mr. Jaime RIVERA
37 Director Student Financial Aid ... Mrs. Milagros CRUZ
36 Student Placement Officer ... Mrs. Coralis LOPEZ
07 Director Admissions ... Vacant
06 Registrar ... Mr. Israel LOPEZ
08 Head Librarian ... Mrs. Lourdes ELIZA
10 Treasury Officer (Finance) ... Mrs. Joelis CAPRILES
38 Student Counselor ... Mrs. Maria UREÑA
11 Chief College Administrator ... Mrs. Marianne BERRIOS
04 Admin Asst to Pres/Dir Personnel ... Vacant

ICPR Junior College (B)

558 Munoz Rivera Avenue, Hato Rey PR 00919-0304
County: San Juan FICE Identification: 011940
Unit ID: 243841
Telephone: (787) 753-6000 Carnegie Class: Assoc/HVT-High Trad
FAX Number: (787) 622-3416 Calendar System: Semester
URL: www.icprjc.edu
Established: 1946 Annual Undergrad Tuition & Fees: $7,010
Enrollment: 431 Coed
Affiliation or Control: Proprietary IRS Status: Proprietary
Highest Offering: Associate Degree
Accreditation: M

01 President/Chief Executive Officer ... Dr. Olga RIVERA
12 Hato Rey Campus Director ... Mrs. Awilda FONTANEZ
05 Academic Affairs Dean ... Mrs. Elsa RODRIGUEZ
07 Dir Admissions/Marketing Hato Rey ... Mrs. Laysa FUENTES
07 Dir Admissions/Marketing Mayaguez . Mrs. Lorraine CONTRERAS
07 Dir Admissions/Marketing Arecibo ... Mr. Carlos CONCEPCIÓN
07 Dir Admissions/Marketing Manati ... Mrs. Mariela CRUZ
10 Chief Financial Officer ... Mrs. Arelis DIAZ
37 Financial Aid Director ... Ms. Palmira ARROYO
12 Mayaguez Campus Director ... Dr. Sylvia RAMIREZ
12 Arecibo Campus Director ... Mrs. Magdalena VEGA
12 Manati Campus Director ... Mr. Henberto RODRIGUEZ
06 Registrar Mayaguez ... Mrs. Olga NEGRON
06 Registrar Arecibo ... Mrs. Yaritza SANTIAGO
06 Registrar Manati ... Mrs. Vanessa TRINIDAD
26 Enrollment & Advertising Manager ... Mrs. Vimarie ASENCIO
13 Chief Information Officer ... Mr. Nelson MEJIAS
08 Learning Res Librarian Hato Rey ... Mr. Angel FIGUEROA
08 Lrng Resources Librarian Mayaguez ... Vacant
08 Lrng Resources Librarian Arecibo ... Mrs. Irma JIMENEZ
08 Learning Resources Librarian ... Mr. Martin ROSADO
38 Professional Counselor Mayaguez .. Mrs. Maraynette CARABALLO
38 Professional Counselor Arecibo ... Mrs. Delva PEREZ
38 Professional Counselor Manati ... Mrs. Josephin BORRERO
38 Professional Counselor Hato Rey ... Vacant
15 Human Resources Director ... Mrs. Daisy CASTRO
43 Institutional Compliance Director ... Mrs. Lizzette VARGAS
56 Bayamon Extension Assoc Director ... Mrs. Awilda FONTÁNEZ
20 Academic Coordinator Mayaguez ... Mrs. Erudina ROSAS
20 Academic Coordinator Arecibo ... Mrs. Edith RAMOS
20 Academic Coordinator Manati ... Mrs. Maribel TORRES
20 Academic Coordinator Hato Rey ... Mrs. Catalina FELICIANO

ICPR Junior College-Arecibo Campus (C)

20 Ave San Patricio, Arecibo PR 00614
Telephone: (787) 878-6000 Identification: 770166
Accreditation: &M

ICPR Junior College-Manati Branch Campus (D)

PO Box 49, Manati PR 00674-0049
Telephone: (787) 884-6000 Identification: 770168
Accreditation: &M

ICPR Junior College-Mayaguez Campus (E)

PO Box 1108, Mayaguez PR 00681-9913
Telephone: (787) 832-6000 Identification: 770167
Accreditation: &M

Instituto de Banca y Comercio (F)

709 Ferrocarril Street, Ponce PR 00717
Telephone: (787) 840-6119 Identification: 770773
Accreditation: &M, ACFEI

Instituto de Banca y Comercio (G)

61 Ponce de Leon Ave, San Juan PR 00917
Telephone: (787) 754-7120 Identification: 667107
Accreditation: &M, ACFEI

*Inter American University of Puerto Rico Central Office (H)

PO Box 363255, San Juan PR 00936-3255
County: San Juan FICE Identification: 008242
Unit ID: 242671
Telephone: (787) 766-1912 Carnegie Class: N/A
FAX Number: (787) 751-3375
URL: www.inter.edu

01 Acting President ... Dr. Rafael RAMÍREZ
05 VP Academic & Student Affairs ... Mrs. Jacqueline ALVAREZ
10 VP Financial Affairs/Services ... Mrs. Olga LUNA
42 Vice President Religious Affairs ... Rev. Norberto DOMINGUEZ
20 Associate VP Academic Affairs ... Vacant
21 Assoc VP Financial Affairs/Services ... Vacant
32 Associate Vice Pres Student Affairs ... Dr. Patricia ALVAREZ
21 Assoc VP Accounting/Finance ... Mr. Orlando GONZALEZ
100 Exec Dir to Pres/Chief of Staff ... Vacant
26 Exec Dir Public Rels/Communications ... Mrs. Zaima NEGRON
84 Dir Inst Promo/Student Recruitment ... Mr. Antonio PANTOJA
09 Exec Director Inst Research ... Dr. Isaac SANTIAGO
13 Exec Dir Information/Telecom ... Mrs. Jossie SALGUERO
43 Exec Director Legal Services ... Mrs. Lorraine JUARBE
43 Exec Director Federal Legal Svcs ... Mr. Vladimir ROMAN
15 Exec Director Human Resources ... Mrs. Maggie COLON
30 Exec Director Devel/Alumni Affairs . Dr. Nelida RIVERA-CLAUDIO

*Inter American University of Puerto Rico Aguadilla Campus (I)

Box 20000, Aguadilla PR 00605-9001
County: Aguadilla FICE Identification: 003939
Unit ID: 242626
Telephone: (787) 891-0925 Carnegie Class: Masters/S
FAX Number: (787) 882-3020 Calendar System: Other
URL: aguadilla.inter.edu
Established: 1957 Annual Undergrad Tuition & Fees: $5,974
Enrollment: 3,517 Coed
Affiliation or Control: Independent Non-Profit IRS Status: 501(c)3
Highest Offering: Master's
Accreditation: M, ADNUR, CAEPT, NUR, SW

02 Chancellor ... Dr. Elie AGESILAS
05 Dean of Academic Affairs ... Dr. Evelyn CASTILLO
20 Associate Dean of Academic Affairs ... Dr. Zenaida SANJURJO
10 Dean of Administrative Affairs ... Mr. Israel AYALA
21 Asst Dean Administrative Affairs ... Mr. Irvin CANALES
32 Dean of Student Affairs ... Mrs. Nararly CLAUDIO
35 Asst Dean Student Affairs ... Mrs. Nayda SOTO
84 Enrollment Manager ... Prof. Myriam MARCIAL
30 Development and Alumni Director ... Mrs. Dolores SEPULVEDA
08 Library Director ... Mrs. Lizzie COLÓN
13 Director Information and Technology ... Mr. Asdrubal JIMENEZ
07 Admissions Director ... Mrs. Doris PEREZ
06 Registrar ... Mrs. Maria PEREZ
37 Financial Aid Director ... Mrs. Gloria CORTÉS
113 Bursar ... Mr. Hancy MUNIZ
15 Human Resources Director ... Mr. Jose R. AREIZAGA
96 Purchasing Officer ... Mrs. Lissette REILLO
121 Student Support Services Director ... Mrs. Ivonne ACEVEDO
81 Sciences and Technology Director ... Prof. Alfredo RIVERA
53 Education & Hum Studies Director ... Prof. Michelle RIVERA
50 Economic & Adm Sciences Director ... Prof. Raul MENDOZA
83 Social Sciences & Behavior Director ... Prof. Janice LORENZO
42 Chaplain ... Mr. Jaime B. GALVAN
88 Director of Upward Bound Program ... Ms. Mayra ROZADA
92 Honor Program Educational Director ... Mrs. Yamilette PROSPER
18 Building Maintenance Director ... Mr. Jose CABAN
38 Counseling Office Director ... Ms. Dary ACEVEDO
41 Sports Director ... Ms. Yolanda PAGAN
19 Univ Security Guard Supervisor ... Mr. Efrain RAMOS
120 Distance Education Director ... Prof. Bernabe SOTO
88 Director Upward Bound Math/Sciences ... Mrs. Geidy ACEVEDO
76 Health Sciences Director ... Dr. Lourdes OLAVARRIA
58 Graduate Studies Director ... Dr. Aris ROMAN

*Inter American University of Puerto Rico Arecibo Campus (J)

PO Box 4050, Arecibo PR 00614-4050
County: Arecibo FICE Identification: 005026
Unit ID: 242635
Telephone: (787) 878-5475 Carnegie Class: Masters/M
FAX Number: (787) 880-1624 Calendar System: Semester
URL: www.arecibo.inter.edu
Established: 1957 Annual Undergrad Tuition & Fees: $5,986
Enrollment: 3,359 Coed
Affiliation or Control: Independent Non-Profit IRS Status: 501(c)3
Highest Offering: Doctorate
Accreditation: M, ANEST, CAEP, NUR, SW

02 Chancellor ... Dr. Rafael RAMIREZ-RIVERA
05 Dean of Academic Affairs ... Dr. Karen WOOLCOCK
11 Dean of Administrative Affairs ... Dr. Grisel CASTELLANOS
32 Dean of Student Affairs ... Mrs. Ilvis AGUIRRE
20 Assoc Dean of Academic Affairs ... Dr. Wanda I. BALSEIRO
08 Educational Resources Center Dir ... Mrs. Sara ABREU
113 Bursar ... Mr. Victor MALDONADO
37 Student Financial Aid Director ... Mr. Angel MENDEZ
06 Registrar ... Mrs. Carmen RODRIGUEZ
07 Director of Admissions ... Mrs. Brenda ROMÁN
04 Executive Assistant to Chancellor ... Mrs. Enid ARBELO
56 Distance Learning Director ... Prof. Ebigaly OLIVER
45 Planning Director ... Mrs. Enid ARBELO
42 Religious Life Director ... Mr. Amilcar SOTO
15 Personnel Director ... Mrs. Ada VELEZ
41 Athletic Department ... Ms. Ileana MORALES
50 Dir Econ/Admin Sciences Dept ... Dr. Alexander ROSADO
51 Continuing Education Director ... Dr. Inia ROSADO
53 Director of Education Department ... Dr. Auris MARTINEZ
66 Director of Nursing Department ... Dr. Frances CORTES
79 Dir of Humanities Department ... Dr. Angel TRINIDAD
81 Director of Sciences & Tech Dept ... Dr. Lizbeth ROMERO
83 Director of Social Sciences Dept ... Dr. Lourdes CARRION
30 Development Director ... Vacant
38 Director Student Counseling ... Ms. Abigail TORRES
13 Director of Computing Center ... Mr. Jose SEGARRA
58 Director Graduate Program in Educ ... Dra. Ramonita DIAZ
18 Chief Facilities/Physical Plant ... Vacant
84 Director Enrollment Management ... Mrs. Carmen MONTALVO
88 Dir Graduate Program Anesthesia ... Prof. Ivan MOLINA
96 Purchasing Officer ... Mrs. Iris GONZALEZ
92 Coordinator Honor Program ... Ms. Vilmaris VAZQUEZ
108 Director Institutional Assessment ... Dr. Pedro RIVERA
26 Director of Marketing ... Mr. Juan RODRIGUEZ

*Inter American University of Puerto Rico Barranquitas Campus (K)

PO Box 517, Barranquitas PR 00794-0517
County: Barranquitas FICE Identification: 005027
Unit ID: 242644
Telephone: (787) 857-3600 Carnegie Class: Bac-Diverse
FAX Number: (787) 857-2244 Calendar System: Semester
URL: www.br.inter.edu
Established: 1957 Annual Undergrad Tuition & Fees: $5,974
Enrollment: 1,303 Coed
Affiliation or Control: Independent Non-Profit IRS Status: 501(c)3
Highest Offering: Doctorate
Accreditation: M, NURSE

02 Chancellor ... Dr. Juan A. NEGRON-BERRIOS
05 Dean Academic Affairs ... Dra. Filomena CINTRON-SERRANO
11 Dean Administrative Affairs ... Mr. José E. ORTIZ-ZAYAS
32 Dean Student Affairs/Athletic Dir ... Mrs. Diomary MELÉNDEZ-PAGÁN
15 Director Human Resources ... Mr. Jonathan ORTIZ-MORALES
113 Bursar Director ... Mr. Cristian J. RIOS-COLON
06 Registrar ... Mrs. Sandra M. MORALES-RODRIGUEZ
07 Director Admissions/Financial Aid ... Mrs. Ana I. COLON-ALONSO
81 Dir Natural Sciences/Technology .. Mrs. Yesenia RIVERA-RIVERA
76 Dir Health Department ... Dra. Damaris COLON-RIVERA
38 Director Upward Bound Program ... Mrs. Saraliz GONZALEZ-MELENDEZ
51 Director Continuing Education ... Mrs. Irisvel ORTIZ-FONTANEZ
88 Evaluation and Monitoring Officer ... Mrs. Carmen C. ROSADO-BERRIOS
29 Coord Alumni Relations ... Mrs. Aixa SERRANO-FEBO
88 CAI-TC Director ... Mrs. Eleane ROSADO-LOPEZ
42 Chaplain ... Mr. Arnaldo L. CINTRON-MIRANDA

*Inter American University of Puerto Rico Bayamon Campus (L)

500 Dr. John Will Harris Road, Bayamon PR 00957-6257
County: Bayamon FICE Identification: 005028
Unit ID: 242705
Telephone: (787) 279-1912 Carnegie Class: Bac-Diverse
FAX Number: (787) 279-2205 Calendar System: Semester
URL: bayamon.inter.edu
Established: 1912 Annual Undergrad Tuition & Fees: $6,012
Enrollment: 4,123 Coed
Affiliation or Control: Independent Non-Profit IRS Status: 501(c)3
Highest Offering: Master's
Accreditation: M, AAB, ACBSP, NURSE, OPTR

02 Acting Chancellor ... Dr. Carlos J. OLIVARES
04 Assistant to Chancellor ... Dr. Rafael R. CANALES
30 Chief Development ... Mr. Jaime COLON
05 Chief Academic Officer ... Dr. Anthony RIVERA
20 Associate Academic Officer ... Dra. Nydia I. FELICIANO
20 Associate Academic Officer ... Dr. Rafael SALGADO
08 Head Librarian ... Mrs. Sandra ROSA
85 Director of International Relations ... Mrs. Maritza ZAMBRANA
88 Interim Dean School of Aeronautics ... Dr. Jonathan VELAZQUEZ
54 Dean School of Engineering ... Dr. Javier QUINTANA
54 Director Electrical Engr Dept ... Prof. Ruben FLORES
54 Director Industrial Engr Dept ... Prof. Catherine AGUILAR
54 Director Mechanical Engr Dept ... Dr. Otoniel DIAZ
81 Director Mathematics/Sciences ... Dra. Rosamil REY
50 Dir Business Administration Dept ... Prof. Edward VICENTE
60 Director Communications Dept ... Prof. Yanira HERNANDEZ
77 Director Computer Sciences Dept ... Prof. Jose A. RODRIGUEZ
76 Director of Health Science ... Prof. Jose M. CRUZ
79 Director Humanities/Language Dept ... Dra. Gisela CARRERAS
75 Director Tech Institute ... Mrs. Liza FREYTES
32 Chief Students Life Officer ... Prof. David LOPEZ
38 Director Student Counseling ... Vacant
41 Athletic Director ... Mr. Reynaldo ROLON
10 Chief Financial/Business Officer ... Mr. Serafin RIVERA

96 Purchasing Officer .... Mrs. Gladys ARROYO
18 Chief Facilities/Physical Plant .... Eng. Jose A. FUENTES
15 Human Resources Director .... Mrs. Wilma FIGUEROA
84 Director Enrollment Services .... Miss Ivette NIEVES
35 Director of Students Services .... Mrs. Aurelis BAEZ
06 Registrar .... Mrs. Suhail BRUNET
13 Director Information Technology .... Mr. Edwin RIVERA
42 Director of Chaplaincy Office .... Rvda. Carmen I. PEREZ
106 Dir Online Education/E-learning .... Dra. Vanesa SANTIAGO
39 Housing Administrator .... Mr. Angel MARTINEZ
108 Coordinator of Institutional Assess .... Dr. Eduardo PEREZ
113 Director Bursar Office .... Sr. Eduardo BERRIOS
26 Chief Pub Rels/Marketing/Comm Ofcr .... Vacant

*Inter American University of Puerto Rico Fajardo Campus (A)

Call Box 70003, Fajardo PR 00738-7003
County: Fajardo | FICE Identification: 022828
Unit ID: 242680
Telephone: (787) 863-2390 | Carnegie Class: Bac-Diverse
FAX Number: (787) 860-3470 | Calendar System: Semester
URL: fajardo.inter.edu
Established: 1960 | Annual Undergrad Tuition & Fees: $6,012
Enrollment: 1,609 | Coed
Affiliation or Control: Independent Non-Profit | IRS Status: 501(c)3
Highest Offering: Master's
Accreditation: M, CAEP, SW

02 Chancellor .... Dr. Paula SAGARDIA OLIVERA
05 Dean Academic Affairs .... Dr. Marielis E. RIVERA RUIZ
11 Dean Administrative Affairs .. Mrs. Monica GONZALEZ PACHECO
32 Dean for Student Affairs .... Mrs. Francheska E. DE JESUS CEBALLOS
06 Registrar .... Mrs. Arlene PARRILLA
07 Director of Admissions .... Mrs. Ada CARABALLO
37 Director Student Financial Aid .... Mrs. Marilyn MARTINEZ
08 Librarian .... Ms. Angie COLON
15 Director of Personnel Office .... Mr. Angel J. RUIZ
09 Planning Director .... Ms. Hilda L. ORTIZ
41 Athletic Director .... Vacant
18 Director Physical Plant .... Mr. Eliezer GARCIA
42 Chaplain/Director Campus Ministry .... Vacant
50 Chairperson Business Department .... Prof. Wilfredo DEL VALLE
53 Chairperson Educ & Social Sci Dept .... Dr. Porfirio MONTES
79 Chairperson Humanities Dept .... Dr. Yolanda LOPEZ-MEDERO
81 Chairperson Math/Science Dept .... Dr. Millie GONZALEZ
84 Director Enrollment Management .... Mrs. Glenda DIAZ

*Inter American University of Puerto Rico Guayama Campus (B)

Call Box 10004, Guayama PR 00785
County: Guayama | FICE Identification: 022827
Unit ID: 242699
Telephone: (787) 864-2222 | Carnegie Class: Bac-Diverse
FAX Number: (787) 866-5006 | Calendar System: Semester
URL: www.guayama.inter.edu
Established: 1958 | Annual Undergrad Tuition & Fees: $5,974
Enrollment: 1,687 | Coed
Affiliation or Control: Independent Non-Profit | IRS Status: 501(c)3
Highest Offering: Master's
Accreditation: M, NURSE

02 Acting President .... Dr. Rafael RAMIREZ
00 Chancellor .... Dr. Angela DE JESUS-ALICEA
06 Registrar .... Mr. Oscar SANTIAGO
08 Librarian .... Mrs. Edny SANTIAGO
113 Bursar .... Ms. Teresa MANAUTOU
05 Dean of Academic Affairs .... Mrs. Elia COLON
11 Dean of Administration .... Mr. Jose ROMERO
32 Dean of Students .... Vacant
07 Director Admissions .... Mrs. Laura FERRER
37 Director Financial Aid .... Mrs. Neidalis DAVIS
29 Director Alumni Relations .... Dr. Jose ROMERO
51 Director Continuing Education .... Mrs. Leida VELAZQUEZ
15 Human Resources Officer .... Mrs. Maria MARES
42 Chaplain Director .... Rvdo. Ismael VAZQUEZ
84 Director Enrollment Management .... Dr. Eileen RIVERA
96 Director of Purchasing .... Mr. Rinaldo ROBLES
31 Dir of Community & New Student Rels .... Mrs. Luz ORTIZ
23 Director Health Services .... Mrs. Arcilia RIVERA
66 Director Nursing Program .... Dr. Marisol VELAZQUEZ
55 Dir Adult Higher Education Program .... Vacant
50 Dir Dept Business Admin/Econ Sci .... Prof. Juan L. TORRES
53 Dir Dept Education/Soc Sci/Hum Std .... Prof. Angel R. ORTIZ
81 Dir Dept Natural & Applied Science .... Dr. Maria G. RIVERA
09 Director of Institutional Research .... Dr. Isaac SANTIAGO

*Inter American University of Puerto Rico / Metropolitan Campus (C)

PO Box 191293, San Juan PR 00919-1293
County: San Juan | FICE Identification: 003940
Unit ID: 242653
Telephone: (787) 250-1912 | Carnegie Class: Masters/L
FAX Number: (787) 250-0742 | Calendar System: Semester
URL: www.metro.inter.edu
Established: 1962 | Annual Undergrad Tuition & Fees: $8,655
Enrollment: 6,826 | Coed
Affiliation or Control: Independent Non-Profit | IRS Status: 501(c)3
Highest Offering: Doctorate
Accreditation: M, ADNUR, CAEP, MLS, NUR, @SP, SW

02 Chancellor .... Prof. Marilina L. WAYLAND
00 Chief Executive Officer .... Dr. Rafael RAMIREZ
05 Dean of Studies .... Prof. Migdalia TEXIDOR
32 Dean of Students .... Dr. Carmen OQUENDO
83 Director School of Psychology .... Dr. Jaime SANTIAGO
79 Dean Faculty of Humanities .... Dr. Oscar CRUZ
66 Director of Nursing .... Dr. Maria J. COLÓN
72 Director of Medical Technology .... Dr. Ida A. MEJIAS
81 Dean Faculty of Science & Tech .... Dr. Yogani GOVENDER
06 Registrar .... Ms. Lisette RIVERA
84 Enrollment Manager .... Mr. Luis E. RUIZ
20 Associate Dean of Studies .... Ms. Liliam GAYA
08 Dir of Ctr for Access Info/Library ....Ms. Maria de Lourdes RESTO
15 Human Resources Officer .... Mrs. Darlin TORRES
37 Director of Financial Aid .... Ms. Lillian CONCEPCION
18 Dir Conservation & General Services .... Vacant
38 Dir Stdnt Placement/Guidance/Couns .... Ms. Beatriz RIVERA
70 Director School of Social Work .... Dr. Alex CASIANO
53 Director School of Education .... Dr. Margarita MARICHAL
85 Coord International Rels Office .... Dr. Ramon AYALA
83 Dean of Education & Behavioral Scie .... Vacant
73 Dir School of Theology .... Dr. Angel VELEZ
88 Dir School of Criminal Justice .... Prof. Luis SOTO
13 Director Informatic/Telecomm Center .... Mr. Eduardo ORTIZ
36 Director Student Placement .... Vacant
07 Dir of Recruit & Admission Office .... Mr. Reinaldo ROBLES
30 Development & Fund Raising .... Vacant
96 Purchasing Officer .... Mrs. Patricia GONZALEZ
92 Coordinator of Honors Program .... Prof. Mariusz JACKO
113 Bursar .... Ms. Carmen RIVERA
106 Dir Online Education/E-learning .... Mr. Jairo PULIDO
19 Director Security/Safety .... Mr. George RIVERA
41 Athletic Director .... Mr. Jesus CORA
04 Admin Assistant to the President .... Ms. Isabel CAMACHO
09 Director of Institutional Research .... Dr. Isaac SANTIAGO
10 Chief Financial/Business Officer .... Ms. Olga LUNA
101 Secretary of the Institution/Board .... Dr. Jose-Luis COLON
108 Director Institutional Assessment .... Prof. Rose VINCENTY
22 Director Affirm Action/Equal Opp .... Mr. Jaime CASASNOVAS
25 Chief Contract and Grants Administr .... Mr. Amaury BOSCIO
26 Chief Public Relations Officer .... Ms. Zyma NEGRON
29 Director Alumni Affairs .... Dra. Nelida RIVERA
43 Director Legal Services .... Lic. Loraine JUARBE
45 Chief Institutional Planning Office .... Ms. Yoisa GONZALEZ
50 Dean of Business .... Lic. Fredrick VEGA

*Inter American University of Puerto Rico Ponce Campus (D)

104 Turpo Industrial Park Road, #1,
Mercedita PR 00715-1602
County: Ponce | FICE Identification: 005029
Unit ID: 242662
Telephone: (787) 284-1912 | Carnegie Class: Bac-Diverse
FAX Number: (787) 841-0103 | Calendar System: Semester
URL: ponce.inter.edu
Established: 1962 | Annual Undergrad Tuition & Fees: $5,986
Enrollment: 3,910 | Coed
Affiliation or Control: Independent Non-Profit | IRS Status: 501(c)3
Highest Offering: Doctorate
Accreditation: M, NURSE, #PTAA

02 Chancellor .... Dr. Vilma E. COLON
05 Dean of Academic Affairs .... Dr. Victor A. FELIBERTY
32 Dean of Students .... Mrs. Miriam MARTINEZ
11 Dean Administrative Affairs .... Mr. Julio MUNOZ
100 Chief Executive Assistant .... Mrs. Hilda V. STELLA
13 Director Information Technology .... Mr. Antonio RAMOS
42 Chaplain .... Rev. Lucy ROSARIO
26 Dir Marketing & Student Promotion .... Mrs. Ginady RIVERA
06 Registrar .... Mrs. Maria del C PEREZ
106 Director Online Education Division .... Dr. Hector L. FELICIANO
08 Director Education Resource Center .... Mrs. Karina TORRES
15 Human Resource Director .... Mrs. Yinaira SANTIAGO
37 Director Student Financial Aid .... Ms. Karen CAQUIAS
07 Director of Admissions .... Mr. Franco L. DIAZ
113 Bursar .... Mr. Brian HERNANDEZ
50 Director Business & Administration .... Dr. Eunice CORDERO
79 Act Dir Humanistics/Pedagogical Std .... Dr. Orlando GONZALEZ
81 Director Sciences and Technology .... Dr. Yvette RIVERA
83 Dir Social/Behavioral Science .... Ms. Lidis L. JUSINO
66 Director Health Science .... Mrs. Raquel GONZALEZ
58 Director of Graduate Programs .... Dr. Lisbel CORREA
38 Dir Univ Integration Services Ofc .... Mr. Hector MARTINEZ
51 Adult Education Director .... Mrs. Marilyn OLIVERAS
41 Athletic Director .... Mr. Raul HERNANDEZ
19 Supervisor of University Guard .... Mr. Reinaldo ROSADO
36 Director Student Placement .... Mr. Hector MARTINEZ

*Inter American University of Puerto Rico San German Campus (E)

PO Box 5100, San German PR 00683-9801
County: San German | FICE Identification: 003938
Unit ID: 242617
Telephone: (787) 264-1912 | Carnegie Class: Masters/S
FAX Number: (787) 264-4448 | Calendar System: Semester
URL: www.intersg.edu
Established: 1912 | Annual Undergrad Tuition & Fees: $6,012
Enrollment: 3,710 | Coed
Affiliation or Control: Independent Non-Profit | IRS Status: 501(c)3
Highest Offering: Doctorate
Accreditation: M, IACBE, MLS, NURSE, RAD

02 Chancellor .... Prof. Agnes MOJICA
05 Acting Dean of Academic Affairs .... Prof. Vilma MARTINEZ
11 Dean of Administration .... Mrs. Frances CARABALLO
32 Dean of Students .... Mr. Raúl MEDINA
20 Associate Dean of Academic Affairs .... Prof. Vilma MARTÍNEZ
109 Auxiliary Dean of Administration .... Mrs. Marisol GONZÁLEZ
35 Associate Dean of Students .... Mrs. Idalmy RAMOS
15 Director of Human Resources .... Mrs. Evelyn TORRES
18 Acting Director Physical Plant .... Mr. José BERRÍOS
37 Director Financial Aid .... Mrs. Brunilda FERRER
06 Acting Registrar .... Mrs. Rosa VELEZ
07 Director of Admissions .... Mrs. Mildred CAMACHO
08 Director of Library .... Mrs. Mayra RODRÍGUEZ
38 Director Student Counseling .... Mrs. Daisy PEREZ
09 Dir Planning/Assessment/Development .... Dr. Caroline AYALA
19 Director of Security .... Mr. Francisco BARBOSA
13 Director of Computer Center .... Mr. Rogelio TORO-ZAPATA
41 Athletic Director .... Prof. Francisco ACEVEDO
39 Director of Men Student Housing .... Mrs. Erlinda VEGA
39 Director of Women Student Housing .... Mrs. Erlinda VEGA
42 Dir Chaplaincy/Spiritual Well-being .... Rev. Pablo CARABALLO
04 Special Assistant of the Chancellor .... Mrs. Tary GARCÍA
04 Special Assistant of the Chancellor ..Mrs. Janine HADERTHAUER
51 Acting Director Continuing Educ .... Prof. Vilma MARTÍNEZ
58 Director Graduate Programs .... Dr. Carlos IRIZARRY
109 Manager of Food Services .... Mr. Orlando MOLINA
17 Health Services Officer .... Mrs. Neisha TORRES
30 Chief Development Officer .... Mrs. Tary GARCÍA
96 Director of Purchasing .... Mr. Israel CRUZ
113 Director Bursar's Office .... Mr. Carlos SEGARRA
53 Director of Education .... Dr. Nancy COLÓN
83 Dir Social Sciences & Liberal Arts .... Dr. Kenneth DILORENZO
50 Director of Entrepreneurial & Mgmt .... Dr. Ailin PADILLA
88 Director of Biology & Environmental .... Prof. Iris SEDA
72 Director of Technical Studies .... Prof. Mildred ORTIZ
64 Director o Fine Arts/Music .... Dr. Gary MORALES
76 Director of Health Sciences .... Dr. Héctor MERCADO
92 Director of Honor Program .... Mrs. Sulmarie MORALES
26 Acting Coord External Resources .... Dr. Ramón FERNÁNDEZ
106 Dir Online Education/E-learning .... Prof. Luis ZORNOSA
57 Director of Fine Arts/Arts .... Dr. María GARCIA

*Inter American University of Puerto Rico School of Law (F)

PO Box 70351, San Juan PR 00936-8351
County: San Juan | Identification: 666813
Unit ID: 242723
Telephone: (787) 751-1912 | Carnegie Class: Spec-4-yr-Law
FAX Number: (787) 751-2975 | Calendar System: Semester
URL: www.derecho.inter.edu
Established: 1961 | Annual Graduate Tuition & Fees: N/A
Enrollment: 712 | Coed
Affiliation or Control: Independent Non-Profit | IRS Status: 501(c)3
Highest Offering: First Professional Degree; No Undergraduates
Accreditation: M, LAW

02 President .... Mr. Manuel J. FERNOS
61 Dean .... Dr. Julio E. FONTANET-MALDONADO
05 Dean for Academic Affairs .... Dr. Yanira REYES-GIL
32 Dean of Students .... Dr. Iris M. CAMACHO-MELENDEZ
11 Dean of Administration ...Mr. Juan C. HERNÁNDEZ-FERNÁNDEZ
06 Registrar .... Mr. Jose A. LOPEZ-RODRÍGUEZ
08 Head Librarian .... Mr. Hector R. SANCHEZ-FERNANDEZ
88 Director of Legal Aid Clinic .. Mr. Rafael E. RODRÍGUEZ-RIVERA
37 Director of Financial Aid .... Mr. Ricardo CRESPO NEVAREZ
07 Director of Admissions .... Mrs. Angela TORRES
18 Chief Facilities/Physical Plant .... Mr. Jose A. RIVERA
113 Director of Bursar Office .... Mrs. Ileana PIÑERO
88 Exec Asst Planning/Eval/ Development .... Mrs. Edith C. PABON-RODRIGUEZ
121 Dir of Academic Support Program .. Mrs. Patricia OTÓN-OLIVIERI
88 Master Program Coordinator .. Mr. Cesar A. ALVARADO-TORRES
04 Executive Asst to President .... Mr. Dominique GILORMINI
13 Chief Info Technology Officer .Mr. Omar A. PEDRAZA-GUEVARA
15 Acting Director Personnel Services .Mrs. Sonia I. NUÑEZ-LISBOA
19 Director Security/Safety .... Mrs. Erika SANCHEZ
30 Dir Development/Alumni Rels .... Mrs. Sheila GOMEZ
36 Assoc Dean Stdnts/ Plcmt/Empl Ofc .... Mrs. Lin COLLAZO
51 Assoc Dean Acad Affs/Grad Pgm/ CLE .... Mr. Cesar ALVARADO-TORRES
38 Counselor/Title IX Coord .... Ms. Yarelis PEREZ-RODRIGUEZ

*Inter American University of Puerto Rico School of Optometry (G)

500 John Will Harris Road, Bayamon PR 00957-6257
County: Bayamon | Identification: 666601
Unit ID: 404222
Telephone: (787) 765-1915 | Carnegie Class: Spec-4-yr-Other Health
FAX Number: (787) 767-3920 | Calendar System: Semester
URL: www.optonet.inter.edu
Established: 1981 | Annual Graduate Tuition & Fees: N/A
Enrollment: 214 | Coed
Affiliation or Control: Independent Non-Profit | IRS Status: 501(c)3
Highest Offering: First Professional Degree; No Undergraduates
Accreditation: M, OPT

02 Dean .... Dr. Andres PAGAN

05 Dean for Academic Affairs ......Dr. Angel F. ROMERO
11 Dean of Administration ......Mr. Francisco RIVERA
32 Dean of Student Affairs ......Dr. Iris R. CABELLO
42 Director Religious Life ......Rev. Julio R. VARGAS
30 Executive Assistant of the Dean ......Ms. Gloriana SALGADO
17 Dean of Clinical Affairs ......Dr. Damaris PAGAN
08 Library Director ......Ms. Wilma MARRERO
15 Director Human Resources ......Mrs. Janice A. MARTINEZ
37 Financial Aid Officer ......Mrs. Raquel ROJAS
04 Executive Assistant of the Dean ......Mrs. Jannette ARROYO
06 Registrar ......Mrs. Luz OCASIO
07 Director of Admissions ......Mrs. Sirimarie MARTINEZ

Mech-Tech College (A)

PO Box 6118, Caguas PR 00726

County: Caguas FICE Identification: 030255
Unit ID: 414461
Telephone: (787) 744-1060 Carnegie Class: Assoc/HVT-High Trad
FAX Number: (787) 744-1035 Calendar System: Quarter
URL: www.mechtech.edu
Established: 1984 Annual Undergrad Tuition & Fees: $9,618
Enrollment: 1,947 Coed
Affiliation or Control: Proprietary IRS Status: Proprietary
Highest Offering: Associate Degree
Accreditation: CNCE

01 President ......Mr. Edwin J. COLON COSME

National University College (B)

PMB452, PO Box 144035, Arecibo PR 00614-4035
Telephone: (787) 879-5044 Identification: 666489
Accreditation: &M

National University College (C)

P.O. Box 2036, Bayamon PR 00960

County: Puerto Rico FICE Identification: 022606
Unit ID: 242972
Telephone: (787) 780-5134 Carnegie Class: Masters/L
FAX Number: (787) 786-9093 Calendar System: Trimester
URL: www.nuc.edu
Established: 1982 Annual Undergrad Tuition & Fees: $6,675
Enrollment: 25,999 Coed
Affiliation or Control: Proprietary IRS Status: Proprietary
Highest Offering: Doctorate
Accreditation: M, ADNUR, CAEP, NUR, #PTAA

00 President ......Mr. Michael BANNETT
01 Campus Chancellor ......Mr. Wigdalys NEGRON-COLON
05 Dean Academic Affairs ......Dr. Waleska MUNIZ-MUNOZ
32 Director Student Affairs ......Vacant
113 Bursar ......Mr. Juan ORTIZ-BELTRAN
37 Director Financial Aid ......Ms. Zorymar GONZALEZ-ZAMBRANA
06 Registrar ......Ms. Glorimar RODRIGUEZ-ANDUJAR

National University College (D)

190 Ave Gautier Benftez, Caguas PR 00725
Telephone: (787) 653-4733 Identification: 770928
Accreditation: &M

† Branch campus of National University College, Bayamon, PR.

National University College Ponce Campus (E)

PO Box 801243, Coto Laurel PR 00780-1243
Telephone: (787) 840-4474 Identification: 770169
Accreditation: &M

National University College Rio Grande Campus (F)

PO Box 3064, Rio Grande PR 00745
Telephone: (787) 809-5100 Identification: 770170
Accreditation: &M

Ponce Health Sciences University (G)

PO Box 7004, Ponce PR 00732-7004

County: Ponce FICE Identification: 024824
Unit ID: 243081
Telephone: (787) 840-2575 Carnegie Class: Spec-4-yr-Med
FAX Number: (787) 840-9756 Calendar System: Semester
URL: www.psm.edu
Established: 1977 Annual Undergrad Tuition & Fees: N/A
Enrollment: 699 Coed
Affiliation or Control: Independent Non-Profit IRS Status: 501(c)3
Highest Offering: Doctorate
Accreditation: M, CLPSY, IPSY, MED, NURSE, PH

01 President/CEO ......Dr. David LENIHAN
05 Provost/VP Academic Affairs ......Dr. Jose TORRES-RUIZ
32 Vice Pres Student Affairs ......Dr. Elisandra RODRIGUEZ
15 Vice President of Human Resources ......Mrs. Susan G. HEMMER
45 VP of Strategic Planning ......Mr. Israel A. RUIZ
10 Chief Financial Officer ......Mr. Carlos ROJAS
04 Admin Assistant to the President ......Ms. Quetsy M. ROBLES
08 Chief Library Officer ......Mrs. Carmen MALAVET
06 Registrar ......Mrs. Ivette OLIVERAS
37 Director of Financila Aid ......Mr. Adam L. COLVIN
07 Director of Admissions ......Mrs. Emsley VAZQUEZ
106 Director of Educ Tech & Online Lrng ......Mr. Carlos SELLAS
13 Information Technology Officer ......Ms. Damaris TORRES
19 Director Security/Safety ......Mrs. Miriam PEREZ
38 Student Counseling ......Mr. Jose A. SOTO-FRANCESCHINI
96 Director of Purchasing ......Mr. Jose GONZALEZ

The Pontifical Catholic University of Puerto Rico (H)

2250 Blvd. Luis A. Ferre, Suite 564,
Ponce PR 00717-9997

County: Ponce FICE Identification: 003936
Unit ID: 241410
Telephone: (787) 841-2000 Carnegie Class: DU-Mod
FAX Number: (787) 651-2034 Calendar System: Semester
URL: www.pucpr.edu
Established: 1948 Annual Undergrad Tuition & Fees: $5,510
Enrollment: 6,614 Coed
Affiliation or Control: Roman Catholic IRS Status: 501(c)3
Highest Offering: Doctorate
Accreditation: M, CACREP, CAEP, @DIETC, LAW, MLS, NUR, @SP, SW

00 Chancellor ......M.Rev. Ruben A. GONZALEZ MEDINA, CMF
01 President ......Dr. Jorge I. VELEZ AROCHO
04 Executive Assistant to President ......Lic. Liza RIESTRA
05 Vice President Academic Affairs ......Dr. Leandro COLON ALICEA
10 Vice President of Finance ......Lic. Jose A. FRONTERA AGENJO
32 Vice President for Student Affs ......Prof. Myriam D. LOPEZ
20 Assoc Vice Pres Academic Affairs ......Prof. Maria MUNIZ GARCIA
35 Assoc Vice Pres Student Affairs ......Prof. Wanda SOTO MALDONADO
09 Vice Pres Inst Rsrch/Dev/Planning ......Dr. Felix CORTES
12 Rector Arecibo Branch ......Dr. Edwin HERNANDEZ
12 Rector Mayaguez Branch ......Dr. Olga HERNÁNDEZ
06 Registrar ......Dr. Juan A. RODRIGUEZ LABOY
07 Director of Admissions ......Prof. Carmen Z. TORRES
08 Director of the Library ......Prof. Magda VARGAS
37 Director of Student Aid ......Mrs. Maria NOLASCO
36 Director of Placement Services ......Mr. Enrique ARROYO
13 Director Computer Center ......Mr. Moises CABRERA
24 Director Educational Technology ......Dr. Edgar RODRIGUEZ
79 Dean of Arts & Humanities ...Rev. Juan Luis NEGRON DELGADO
81 Dean of Sciences ......Dra. Alma L. SANTIAGO
61 Dean of the School of Law ......Lic. Fernando MORENO ORAMA
50 Dean Business Administration ......Dr. David ZAYAS
53 Dean of Education ......Prof. Ana I. BAEZ
58 Dean Col of Behav Sci/Cmty Affs ......Dra. Ilia ROSARIO-NIEVES
48 Dean School of Architecture ......Mr. Luis V. BADILLO-LOZANO
51 Coord Continuing Education Inst ......Mrs. Karen G. MORALES
27 Communications ......Mrs. Jalibeth RODRIGUEZ
29 Alumni Relations Officer ......Mrs. Maria S. MASCARO
15 Director Human Resources ......Mr. Wilfredo CORNIER
40 Director Bookstore ......Mrs. Ashley VELEZ
41 Interim Athletic Director ......Mr. Marcos GUIGLIOTTI ACEVEDO
42 Chaplain ......Rev. Luis OTIZ ALVAREZ
109 Director Auxiliary Enterprises ......Lic. Waddy MERCADO
26 Director Public Relations ......Vacant
38 Director Student Counseling ......Dr. Arvin BAEZ
18 Physical Plant/Safety & Security ......Mr. Julio PALMER
113 Treasurer Bursar's Office ......Mr. Juan E. ROMAN
96 Director of Purchasing ......Sra. Hilda TORRES COLON
88 Director of Biotechnology ......Hna. Nancy ARROYO
88 Accreditation Liaison Officer ......Dra. Maritza RIVERA MORET
30 Infrastructure Director ......Ing. Armando RODRIGUEZ
84 Coord Institutional Recruitment ......Sr. Rene MARRERO
89 Director of Freshmen ......Dra. Elizabeth MARTINEZ
106 Dir Online Education/E-learning ......Dra. Ivette TORRES
19 Director Security/Safety ......Mr. Julio PALMER
43 Dir Legal Services/General Counsel ......Lic. Carolyn COSTAS
86 Director Government Relations ......Vacant
100 Chief of Staff ......Lic. Liza RIESTRA
108 Director Institutional Assessment ......Prof. Mishelle RIVERA
39 Director Student Housing .Hna. Gloria N. CARABALLO TURRELL
102 Dir Foundation/Corporate Relations ......Sra. Gladys M. DIAZ
104 Director Study Abroad ......Sr. Joel VELEZ
105 Webmaster II ......Mr. Francisco SUAREZ
88 Director of Compliance ......Lic. Waddy MERCADO

Pontifical Catholic University of Puerto Rico-Arecibo Campus (I)

Box 144045, Arecibo PR 00614-4045
Telephone: (787) 881-1212 Identification: 666603
Accreditation: &M

† Regional accreditation is carried under the parent institution in Ponce, PR.

Pontifical Catholic University of Puerto Rico-Mayaguez Campus (J)

Box 1326, Mayaguez PR 00681-1326
Telephone: (787) 834-5151 Identification: 666605
Accreditation: &M

† Branch campus of The Pontifical Catholic University of Puerto Rico, Ponce, PR.

Puerto Rico School of Nurse Anesthetists (K)

656 Ponce de Leon Avenue, Floor 1, Hato Rey PR 00918

County: San Juan Identification: 667341
Telephone: (787) 998-8997 Carnegie Class: Not Classified
FAX Number: (787) 998-8998 Calendar System: Semester
URL: www.eeapr.org
Established: Annual Undergrad Tuition & Fees: N/A
Enrollment: N/A Coed
Affiliation or Control: Proprietary IRS Status: Proprietary
Highest Offering: Doctorate
Accreditation: M

01 President ......Mr. Carlos J. BORRERO-RIOS
05 Dean of Academic Affs & Accred ......Dr. Noraida DOMINGUEZ-FLORES
10 Chief Financial Officer ......Denisse RIVERA-MELENDEZ
37 Director Student Financial Aid ......Jelitza CINTRON ANDINO
07 Director of Admissions/Registrar ......Diana TORRUELLA
66 Dean of Nursing ......Joseline LOPEZ-LEBRON
88 Director Master Science in Nursing ......Dr. Karen MORA-HERAS
08 Chief Library Officer ......Dr. Noraida DOMINGUEZ-FLORES
113 Bursar Officer ......Ariana BAEZ-ZABALA

San Juan Bautista School of Medicine (L)

PO Box 4968, Carretera 172, Caguas PR 00726-4968

County: San Juan FICE Identification: 031773
Unit ID: 430670
Telephone: (787) 743-3038 Carnegie Class: Spec-4-yr-Med
FAX Number: (787) 746-3093 Calendar System: Semester
URL: www.sanjuanbautista.edu
Established: 1978 Annual Undergrad Tuition & Fees: $9,192
Enrollment: 344 Coed
Affiliation or Control: Proprietary IRS Status: Proprietary
Highest Offering: First Professional Degree
Accreditation: M, #ARCPA, MED, NURSE

01 President/Dean ......Dr. Yocasta BRUGAL-MENA
11 Dean of Administration/HR ......Mr. Carlos F. ABREU
05 Chief Academic Officer ......Dr. Irving MALDONADO-RIVERA
06 Registrar ......Mrs. Nildalee MELENDEZ
08 Head Librarian ......Mr. Carlos ALTAMIRANO
10 Chief Business Officer ......Mr. Juan C. CASTRO
32 Chief Student Affairs/Student Life ......Dr. Yolanda MIRANDA
37 Director Student Financial Aid ......Miss Beatriz DE LEON
07 Director of Admissions ......Ms. Jaymi SANCHEZ
13 Chief Info Technology Officer (CIO) ......Mr. Jorge TORRES
38 Director Student Counseling ......Ms. Ilsa CENTENO

Seminario Teologico de Puerto Rico (M)

458 Jose Canals #301, San Juan PR 00918
Telephone: (787) 274-1142 Identification: 770142
Accreditation: &M

† Branch campus of Nyack College, Nyack, NY

Universal Technology College of Puerto Rico (N)

111 Comercio Street, Aguadilla PR 00603

County: Aguadilla FICE Identification: 030297
Unit ID: 376385
Telephone: (787) 882-2065 Carnegie Class: Spec-4-yr-Other Health
FAX Number: (787) 891-2370 Calendar System: Semester
URL: www.unitecpr.edu
Established: 1987 Annual Undergrad Tuition & Fees: N/A
Enrollment: 108 Coed
Affiliation or Control: Independent Non-Profit IRS Status: 501(c)3
Highest Offering: Baccalaureate
Accreditation: ABHES

01 Chief Executive Officer ......Mrs. Keila LOPEZ
06 Registrar ......Ms. Maria ALVAREZ
08 Director of Library ......Ms. Airlyn VAZQUEZ
10 Accountant ......Ms. Nancy MORALES
12 Director of Branch Campus ......Ms. Nelida CARDONA
13 Director Computer Center ......Mr. Zain CORDERO
15 Director Human Resources ......Vacant
18 Chief Facilities/Physical Plant ......Mr. Danily NIEVES
07 Placement & Admissions Director ......Mrs. Evelyn TORRES
37 Director Student Financial Aid ......Mr. Samuel HERNANDEZ
38 Director Student Counsel ......Mrs. Dalia SANTIAGO
96 Purchasing Officer ......Mrs. Dolores MITJANS
23 Healthcare Services ......Mr. Silverio JIMENEZ
76 Health Related Sciences Department ......Ms. Esther SANTIAGO

Universidad Adventista de las Antillas (O)

Box 118, Mayaguez PR 00681-0118

County: Mayaguez FICE Identification: 005019
Unit ID: 241191
Telephone: (787) 834-9595 Carnegie Class: Masters/S
FAX Number: (787) 834-9597 Calendar System: Semester
URL: www.uaa.edu
Established: 1961 Annual Undergrad Tuition & Fees: $7,250
Enrollment: 1,056 Coed

Affiliation or Control: Seventh-day Adventist IRS Status: 501(c)3
Highest Offering: Master's
Accreditation: M, #COARC, NURSE

01 President .... Dr. Myrna COLON
05 Vice President Academic Affairs .... Prof. Yolanda PEREZ
10 Vice President Financial Affairs .... Mr. Luis F. ACOBE
32 Vice President for Students Affairs .... Dr. Sigfredo MORALES
20 Associate VP Academic Affairs .... Mrs. Mayra SOTO
21 Associate Financial Vice President .... Mrs. Madeline CRUZ
113 Director Student Finance Office .... Mrs. Gisselle RIVERA
66 Dean of the School of Nursing .... Dr. Amarilys IRIZARRY
66 Director School of Nursing .... Mr. Hector GONZALEZ
53 Dean of the School of Education .... Dr. Ileanex PEREZ
50 Director of Business Administration .... Prof. Yanitza OLIVENCIA
81 Director Mathematics/Sciences/ Comp .... Mrs. Alicia MORADILLOS-DELGADO
73 Dir Theology/Music Department .... Prof. Erick MENDIETA
06 Registrar .... Mrs. Ana D. TORRES
07 Director of Admissions .... Mrs. Yolanda FERRER
37 Director of Student Financial Aid .... Mrs. Awilda MATOS
26 Dir Public Relations & Promotion .... Miss Lorell VARELA
108 Dir of Institutional Effectiveness .... Dr. Digna WILLIAMS
13 Director ITS .... Mr. Heber VAZQUEZ
08 Librarian .... Mrs. Aixa VEGA
38 Counselor .... Mrs. Ivelisse PEREZ
88 Environmental Services Director .... Mr. Legna VARELA
18 Chief Facilities/Physical Plant .... Mr. Abel RODRIGUEZ
33 Dean of Men .... Mr. Hector MONTILLA
04 Admin Assistant to the President .... Ms. Ruth B. RIVERA OCASIO
15 Chief Human Resources Officer .... Ms. Frances A. IZQUIERDO

*Universidad Ana G. Mendez (A)

Apartado 21345, Rio Piedras PR 00928-1341
County: San Juan FICE Identification: 029078
Unit ID: 242060
Telephone: (787) 751-0178 Carnegie Class: N/A
FAX Number: (787) 766-1706
URL: www.uagm.edu

01 President .... Mr. Jose F. MENDEZ
05 Vice President for Academic Affairs .... Dr. José E. MALDONADO
10 Vice Pres Financial Affairs .... Mr. Carmelo TORRES
32 Vice Chancellor Student Affairs .... Dr. Gisela NEGRÓN
11 Executive & Operations Vice Pres .... Mr. Ricardo RODRIGUEZ
15 Vice President Human Resources .... Dr. Victoria DE JESUS
88 Acting Vice Pres International Affs .... Dr. Rafael NADAL
13 Chief Information Officer .... Vacant
26 Associate Vice Pres for Public Rels .... Ms. Maria MARTINEZ
04 Exec Assistant to President .... Ms. Lydia I. MASSARI

*Universidad Ana G. Mendez Carolina Campus (B)

Carr #190 Ave. Principal Sabana, Carolina PR 00983-2010
County: San Juan FICE Identification: 003941
Unit ID: 243346
Telephone: (787) 257-7373 Carnegie Class: Masters/L
FAX Number: (787) 776-1220 Calendar System: Semester
URL: https://carolina.uagm.edu/
Established: 1949 Annual Undergrad Tuition & Fees: $5,820
Enrollment: 7,892 Coed
Affiliation or Control: Independent Non-Profit IRS Status: 501(c)3
Highest Offering: Master's
Accreditation: M, ACBSP, ACFEI, ACPHA, ADNUR, CAEP, NUR, SW

00 President .... Mr. José F. MENDEZ
02 Chancellor .... Dr. Félix R. HUERTAS GONZÁLEZ
05 Vice Chancellor Academic Affairs .... Dr. Evelyza CRESPO
32 Vice Chancellor Student Affairs .... Dr. María G. VEAZ
84 Assoc VC Enrollment Management .... Mrs. Magda E. OSTOLAZA
15 Vice Pres Human Resources .... Dr. Victoria DE JESÚS
88 Dean Intl Sch Hosp/Culinary Arts .... Mrs. Terestella GONZÁLEZ
107 Dean Professional Studies .... Mrs. Mildred Y. RIVERA
06 Registrar .... Mrs. Elisa QUILES
08 Director of Library .... Mrs. Elsa MARIANI
26 Director Public Relations .... Mrs. Ivonne D. ARROYO
83 Dean of Social and Human Sciences .... Dr. Evelyza CRESPO
50 Dean of Business Administration .... Dr. José E. BERRÍOS
72 Dean of Science and Technology .... Dr. Marielis E. RIVERA
76 Dean of Health Science .... Dr. Vanessa ORTIZ
19 Director Security/Safety .... Mr. José E. MACHUCA

*Universidad Ana G. Mendez Cupey Campus (C)

PO Box 21150, San Juan PR 00928-1150
County: San Juan FICE Identification: 025875
Unit ID: 241739
Telephone: (787) 766-1717 Carnegie Class: Masters/L
FAX Number: (787) 759-7663 Calendar System: Semester
URL: https://cupey.uagm.edu/
Established: 1980 Annual Undergrad Tuition & Fees: $5,820
Enrollment: 8,893 Coed
Affiliation or Control: Independent Non-Profit IRS Status: 501(c)3
Highest Offering: Doctorate
Accreditation: M, ACBSP, ADNUR, CAEPT, NUR, SW

00 UAGM President .... Mr. Jose F. MENDEZ
02 Vice Chancellor/CEO .... Dr. Lorna MARTINEZ
05 Dean of Academic Affairs .... Dr. Jose E. BERRIOS
10 Vice President of Financial Affairs .... Mr. Carmelo TORRES
108 Director Institutional Assessment .... Prof. Sarai TORRES
30 Interim Director Inst Development .... Dr. Maria I. DE GUZMAN
32 Dean of Student Affairs .... Dr. Rafael J. RODRIGUEZ
85 Executive Director Intl Affairs .... Dr. Zaida VEGA
26 Assoc Director External Resources .... Vacant
88 Director of Accreditation/Licensing .... Dr. Giselle TAPIA
11 Dean of Institutional Effectiveness .... Mrs. Brenda L. ORTIZ
15 Director of Human Resources .... Mrs. Aymee VEGA
13 Director Telecomm and Informatics .... Mr. Rafael I. GARCIA
114 Director of Analysis & Budget .... Mrs. Aixa ALDARONDO
45 Director of Planning .... Dr. Mariela COLLAZO
124 Director of Retention .... Mrs. Margie CRUZ
49 Dean of Liberal Arts .... Dr. Evelyza CRESPO
50 Dean of Business/Tourism & Entrep .... Dr. Juan C. SOSA
53 Academic Program Director Education .... Dr. Héctor M. MORALES
76 Director of Health Sciences Dept .... Dr. Aleyda SIACA
81 Director Science/Technology & Envir .... Mrs. Fabiola TRIGO
75 Dean Professional/Technical Studies .... Dr. Mildred Y. RIVERA
107 Director of Professional Studies .... Mrs. Melissa GUILLIANI
97 Director General Education .... Dr. Jorge L. TORRES
08 Head Librarian .... Mrs. Balbina J. ROJAS
18 Manager Operations & Facilities .... Mr. Reynaldo NIEVES
66 Director of Nursing Department .... Dr. Tayra J. PEREZ
06 Assoc Registrar .... Mrs. Laura E. RIVERA
12 Additional Location Dir Bayamon .... Dr. Luis A. MARRERO
12 Additional Location Dir Aguadilla .... Mr. Luis A. RUIZ
07 Director Recruitment and Admissions .... Mrs. Iris R. CRUZ
07 Director Recruitment and Admissions .... Mr. Erick A. BONILLA
41 Director Sports/Wellness and Act .... Mr. Edgar I. DIAZ
19 Director of Security .... Mr. Julio A. MANGUAL
36 Assoc Director Student Placement .... Mr. Braulio GONZALEZ
37 Assoc Dir Student Financial Aid .... Mrs. Navia ORTIZ
38 Director of Student Wellness .... Mrs. Arelis VILLANUEVA

*Universidad Ana G. Mendez Gurabo Campus (D)

Estacion Universidad, Box 3030, Gurabo PR 00778-3030
County: Gurabo FICE Identification: 011719
Unit ID: 243601
Telephone: (787) 743-7979 Carnegie Class: DU-Mod
FAX Number: (787) 744-5394 Calendar System: Semester
URL: https://gurabo.uagm.edu/
Established: 1972 Annual Undergrad Tuition & Fees: $5,820
Enrollment: 13,553 Coed
Affiliation or Control: Independent Non-Profit IRS Status: 501(c)3
Highest Offering: Doctorate
Accreditation: M, CAEP, COPSY, DIETC, IPSY, JOUR, LSAR, MLS, NATUR, NURSE, SW

02 Chancellor .... Dr. David MENDEZ
11 Actg Vice Chancellor Admin Affairs .... Ms. Mari G. GONZALEZ
05 Vice Chancellor .... Dra. Nydia BOU
32 Vice Chancellor of Student Affairs .... Dra. Brunilda APONTE
08 Vice Chancellor Information Res .... Dr. Sarai LASTRA
92 Internship & Honors Program Coord .... Ms. Wanda I. GONZÁLEZ
88 Asst Vice Chanc Eval & Development .... Ms. Lizbeth RIVERA
21 Director of Admin Affairs .... Mrs. Belinda ROSA
53 Dean Education .... Dra. Elaine GUADALUPEZ
50 Dean Business and Entrepreneurship .... Dr. Juan Carlos SOSA
54 Dean Engineering .... Dr. Rolando GARCIA
81 Dean Natural Science & Technology .... Dr. Teresa LIPSETT
83 Dean Social Sciences/ Communications .... Dra. Maria del C. SANTOS
48 Dean Architecture/Design .... Ms. Aurorisa MATEO
76 Acting Dean Health Sciences .... Dra. Nydia BOU
72 Dean Technical Studies .... Ms. Maria E. FLORES
107 Dean Professional Stds & Cont Educ .... Ms. Mildred Y. RIVERA
58 Associate Dean of Graduate Studies .... Dr. Sharon CANTRELL
06 Registrar .... Mrs. Zoraida ORTIZ
97 Dean of Liberal Arts & Gen Studies .... Mr. Felix R. HUERTAS
26 Director of Marketing .... Vacant
37 Director Office of Financial Aid .... Mrs. Carmen J. RIVERA
26 Director Public Relations .... Ms. Iris SERRANO
18 Chief Facilities/Physical Plant .... Ms. Mayra RODRIGUEZ
29 Coordinator Alumni Relations .... Mr. Wilfredo HILLS
30 Chief Development Officer .... Mr. Rene S. RONDA
96 Director of Purchasing .... Ms. Norma C. DONEZ
07 Director of Admissions .... Mrs. Diriee Y. RODRIGUEZ
45 Aux Vice President of Planning .... Ms. Mari G. GONZALEZ
15 Aux Vice President Human Resources .... Mrs. Iris BERRIOS
36 Assoc Vice Chanc Student Placement .... Ms. Carmen PULLIZA
84 Asst Vice Chanc Enrollment Mgmt .... Ms. Maria V. FIGUEROA
114 Aux Vice President of Budget .... Ms. Camille LAMBOY
38 Assoc Vice Chanc Student Counseling .... Ms. Samaris COLLAZO
106 Dir Online Education/E-learning .... Mr. Israel RODRIGUEZ
108 Asst Vice Chanc Assessment .... Mr. Ernesto ESPINOZA
41 Athletic Director .... Mr. Felix A. CARRASQUILLO

Universidad Central de Bayamon (E)

PO Box 1725, Bayamon PR 00960-1725
County: Bayamon FICE Identification: 005022
Unit ID: 241225
Telephone: (787) 786-3030 Carnegie Class: Masters/S
FAX Number: (787) 740-2200 Calendar System: Semester
URL: www.ucb.edu.pr
Established: 1961 Annual Undergrad Tuition & Fees: $5,462
Enrollment: 1,146 Coed
Affiliation or Control: Roman Catholic IRS Status: 501(c)3
Highest Offering: Master's
Accreditation: M, NURSE, SW, THEOL

01 President .... Br. Oscar MORALES CRUZ, OP
100 President Assistant .... Mr. Angel VALENTIN
05 Academic Dean .... Dr. Maritza DEL VALLE
10 Dean Admin/Finance .... Vacant
32 Dean of Students .... Mrs. Niza ZAYAS
49 Dir Col Liberal Arts/Humanities/ Ed .... Dr. Luz E. ROBLES BERMÚDEZ
50 Dir Business Development & Tech .... Dr. Nidia COLON
15 Director of Human Resources .... Dr. Julitza ARROYO
07 Director of Admissions .... Mrs. Wanda APONTE
37 Director Student Financial Aid .... Mrs. Elaine NUÑEZ
38 Dir Guidance/Counseling Center Int .... Mr. Cesar LOPEZ
35 Coord Center Learning Stre (CFAEE) .... Mrs. Myrna PEREZ
13 Director of Information System .... Mr. Marcos CRUZ RIVERA
18 Director Physical Facilities .... Mrs. Enid RIVERA
96 Purchase Officer .... Mrs. Jessica OJEDA
09 Institutional Research Officer .... Mrs. Luz M. PALACIOS
20 Associate Academic Dean .... Vacant
81 Dir College Sciences/Health Prof .... Dr. Pedro ROBLES
04 Administrative Asst to President .... Vacant
106 Dir Online Education/E-learning .... Mr. Jorge L. DIAZ
108 Director Institutional Assessment .... Mrs. Vivian A. PADILLA
41 Athletic Director .... Mr. Juan A. FIGUEROA
08 Chief Library Officer .... Ms. Yanit DELGADO
06 Registrar .... Dr. Kendra ORTIZ

Universidad Central Del Caribe (F)

PO Box 60327, Bayamon PR 00960-6032
County: Bayamon FICE Identification: 021633
Unit ID: 243568
Telephone: (787) 798-3001 Carnegie Class: Spec-4-yr-Med
FAX Number: (787) 798-6836 Calendar System: Semester
URL: www.uccaribe.edu
Established: 1976 Annual Undergrad Tuition & Fees: $8,387
Enrollment: 547 Coed
Affiliation or Control: Independent Non-Profit IRS Status: 501(c)3
Highest Offering: Doctorate
Accreditation: M, CHIRO, MED

01 President .... Dr. Waleska CRESPO-RIVERA
10 VP of Finances and Operations .... Mr. Ariel DAVILA
05 Dean for Academic Affairs .... Dr. Nereida DIAZ-RODRIGUEZ
20 Asst Dean of Curriculum Development .... Dr. Alvaro PEREZ
76 Dean Health Sciences & Tech .... Dr. Luz N. RAMOS-VARGAS
88 Interim Director Med Imaging Tech .... Prof. Elaine RUIZ
11 Dean Administrative Affairs .... Ms. Emilia SOTO
32 Dean Student Affairs .... Dr. Omar PEREZ
35 Asst Dean Student Affairs .... Dr. Jose L. OLIVER
63 Dean of Medicine .... Dr. Jose A. CAPRILES
88 Associate Dean of Medicine .... Mrs. Zilka RIOS
06 Registrar .... Ms. Nilda MONTANEZ-LOPEZ
07 Director of Admissions .... Ms. Irma L. CORDERO
37 Director Student Financial Aid .... Mr. Edwin SANCHEZ
21 Director of Finances .... Mrs. Iris J. FONT
08 Librarian .... Ms. Mildred RIVERA
51 Director of Continuing Medical Educ .... Dr. Frances GARCIA
38 Counselor .... Mrs. Lileana BRUNO
46 Assoc Dean Research & Grad Studies .... Vacant
20 Assoc Dean Clinical & Fac Affairs .... Dr. Harry MERCADO
30 Dean of Inst Devel & Strategic Plng .... Ms. Mildred RIVERA-MARRERO
13 Chief Information Technology Office .... Dr. Legier ROJAS

Universidad Pentecostal Mizpa (G)

Bo Caimito Rd 199 km 0.3, Rio Piedras PR 00928
County: San Juan FICE Identification: 031983
Unit ID: 441690
Telephone: (787) 720-4476 Carnegie Class: Spec-4-yr-Faith
FAX Number: N/A Calendar System: Semester
URL: www.mizpa.edu
Established: 1937 Annual Undergrad Tuition & Fees: $4,220
Enrollment: 165 Coed
Affiliation or Control: Pentecostal Church of God IRS Status: 501(c)3
Highest Offering: Master's
Accreditation: BI

01 President .... Mrs. Naury Y. SANCHEZ CINTRON
05 Dean of Academic Affairs .... Mrs. Joan JIMENEZ MARRERO
10 Dean Administration/Finance .... Mrs. Maureen DE LEON MULLERT
32 Dean of Student Affairs .... Mr. Jorge A. BURGOS CARRION
42 Chaplain/Director Campus Ministry .... Mr. Harry MUNOZ COLON
35 Associate Student/Affairs Life .... Mrs. Daulan NIEVES GARCIA
06 Registrar .... Mr. Leonardo MELENDEZ LEON
08 Librarian .... Mrs. Melanie RODRIGUEZ MARTINEZ
37 Student Financial Aid Officer .... Mrs. Myriam JUARBE REY
26 Chief Public Relations Officer .... Mr. Rafael LABOY FUSTER
113 Bursar .... Mr. Geserie CRUZADO ROSADO
04 Administrative Asst to President .... Miss Jaydee A. GUZMAN QUILES

Universidad Politecnica de Puerto Rico (H)

Ponce de Leon 377, Box 192017,
San Juan PR 00919-2017
County: San Juan FICE Identification: 021000
Unit ID: 243577
Telephone: (787) 622-8000 Carnegie Class: Masters/M
FAX Number: (787) 754-8268 Calendar System: Trimester
URL: www.pupr.edu

Established: 1966 Annual Undergrad Tuition & Fees: $8,640
Enrollment: 4,367 Coed
Affiliation or Control: Independent Non-Profit IRS Status: 501(c)3
Highest Offering: Doctorate
Accreditation: M, #LSAR

01 President .... Eng. Ernesto VAZQUEZ-MARTINEZ
03 Executive Vice President .... Vacant
84 Vice Pres Enrollment Management .... Mr. Carlos PEREZ
05 Chief Academic Officer .... Dr. Miguel A. RIESTRA
06 Registrar .... Mrs. Mayra I. LOPEZ
07 Director Admissions .... Mrs. Teresa CARDONA
08 Head Librarian .... Mrs. Digna DELGADO
37 Director Financial Aid .... Mr. Sergio VILLOLDO
15 Director Personnel Services .... Ms. Ana CASTELLANO
18 Chief Facilities/Physical Plant .... Mr. Herminio ROMERO
29 Alumni Relations .... Ms. Glenda M. COLON-RAMOS
32 Director Student Affairs .... Mr. Carlos PEREZ
36 Director Student Placement .... Mrs. Angie ESCALANTE
38 Director Student Counseling .... Ms. Sheila VAZQUEZ
96 Director of Purchasing .... Ms. Alba LLOMPART
19 Director Security/Safety .... Mr. Miguel ALBARRAN
41 Athletic Director .... Mr. Roberto MEDINA-ORTIZ
50 Dean of Business .... Dr. Enrique MUNOZ-GIL
49 Dean of Arts and Science/Education .... Dr. Horacio GARCIA
54 Dean of Engineering .... Dr. Carlos J. GONZALEZ
106 Dir Online Education/E-learning .... Dr. Cuauhtemoc GODOY
108 Director Institutional Assessment .... Dr. Miguel A. RIESTRA-FERNANDEZ
91 Director Administrative Computing .... Mr. Pedro PEREZ-DORTA
09 Director of Institutional Research .... Dr. Miguel A. RIESTRA
101 Secretary of the Institution/Board .... Arch. Ricardo LEFRANC-MORALES
13 Chief Information Tech Officer .... Mr. Pedro PEREZ
39 Dir Resident Life/Student Housing .... Mr. William KORBER

Universidad Teologica Del Caribe (A)

PO Box 901, Saint Just PR 00978-0901
County: Trujillo Alto FICE Identification: 023355
Unit ID: 241614
Telephone: (787) 761-0640 Carnegie Class: Spec-4-yr-Faith
FAX Number: (787) 748-9220 Calendar System: Semester
URL: www.utcpr.edu
Established: 1956 Annual Undergrad Tuition & Fees: $6,366
Enrollment: 433 Coed
Affiliation or Control: Church Of God IRS Status: 501(c)3
Highest Offering: Master's
Accreditation: BI

01 President .... Francisco ORTIZ
05 Academic Dean .... Carmen AYALA
06 Registrar .... Awilda MORALES
10 Administration Dean .... Frankie NEGRON
32 Students Dean .... Wilfredo ADORNO
37 Financial Aid Director .... Claudia RODRIGUEZ
08 Librarian .... Graciela TORRES
45 Planning & Development Officer .... Ana CEPERO
106 Online Program Coordinator .... Renaldo FIGUEROA
58 Graduate School Coordinator .... Samuel CARABALLO
12 North-Central (Dorado) Campus Coord .... Richard D'COSTA
04 Administrative Asst to the Pres .... Waleska VEGA
07 Admissions Officer .... Avianny PAULINO

*University of Puerto Rico-Central Administration (B)

Flamboy n st 1187 Jardin Bot nico S,
San Juan PR 00926-1117
County: San Juan FICE Identification: 003942
Unit ID: 243160
Telephone: (787) 250-0000 Carnegie Class: N/A
FAX Number: (787) 759-6917
URL: www.upr.edu

01 President .... Dr. Jorge HADDOCK-ACEVEDO
03 Executive Director .... Lcda. Soniemi RODRIGUEZ DAVILA
05 Executive Vice President .... Dr. Ubaldo M. CORDOVA-FIGUEROA
108 Vice Pres for Acred & Assessment .... Dr. Jennifer ALICEA-CASTILLO
32 Vice Pres - Student Affairs .... Dr. Jose PERDOMO
46 Vice Pres for Research & Technology .... Mrs. Carmen BACHIER
88 Director of Institutional Planning .... Dr. Félix LOPEZ-ROMÁN
88 Director of Intellectual Property .... Eng. Yahveh COMAS-TORRES
88 Director Compliance/Integrity .... Mr. Carlos RODRIGUEZ-RIVERA
88 Dir Innovation/Entreprenurship .... Dr. Jose L. AYALA
12 Chancellor UPR-Rio Piedras Campus .... Dr. Luis A. FERRAO-DELGADO
12 Chanc UPR-Mayaguez Campus .... Dr. Agustin RULLAN TORO
12 Acting Chanc UPR-Medical Sci Campus .... Dr. Wanda MALDONADO
12 Chancellor UPR-Cayey Campus .... Dr. Glorivee ROSARIO-PEREZ
12 Chancellor UPR-Humacao Campus .... Dr. Aida RODRIGUEZ-ROIG
12 Chancellor UPR-Bayamon Campus .... Dr. Miguel VELEZ-RUBIO
12 Chancellor UPR-Ponce Campus .... Dr. Tessie CRUZ-RIVERA
12 Acting Chanc UPR-Carolina Campus .... Dr. Jose I. MEZA PEREIRA
12 Chancellor UPR-Utuado Campus .... Dr. Luis TAPIA-MALDONADO
12 Chancellor UPR-Aguadilla Campus .... Dr. Sonia RIVERA GONZÁLEZ
12 Chancellor UPR-Arecibo Campus .... Dr. Carlos A. ANDÚJAR-ROJAS
30 Dir Devel & Alumni Affairs Office .... Mrs. Margarita MENDEZ ESCUDERO
10 Director Finance Office .... Mr. Antonio TEJERA-ROCAFORT
15 Acting Dir Human Resources Office .... Mr. Nelson RIVERA-VILLANUEVA
11 Director Administrative Service .... Mrs. Myriam MARTINEZ FIGUEROA
13 Dir Information Systems Ofc .... Mr. Jose PABÓN PAGÁN
37 Director Student Financial Aid .... Vacant
43 Acting Director Legal Affairs Ofc .... Lcda. Soniemi RODRÍGUEZ-DÁVILA
88 Acting Dir Botanical Garden .... Mr. Carlos R. DIAZ-PÉREZ
26 Acting Dir Press & Communications .... Ms. Joan M. HERNÁNDEZ-MARRERO
101 Exec Sec University Board .... Dr. Ana E. FALCON EMANUELLI
114 Acting Director Budget Office .... Dr. Osvaldo GUZMÁN LÓPEZ
18 Actg Dir Phys Dev/Infrastrcture Ofc .... Arch. Jennifer LUGO CARDONA
04 Admin Assistant to the President .... Mrs. Adaliz PEREZ COLÓN
07 Director of Admissions .... Mrs. Ivonne CALDERÓN GARCÍA
102 Director Foundation/Corporate Rels .... Arch. Wilma L. SANTIAGO GABRIELINI
105 Director Web Services .... Mr. José MUÑOZ ALVAREZ
106 Dean of Online Education/E-learning .... Lcda. Lisa M. NIEVES OSLÁN
19 Director Security/Safety .... Mrs. Lillyvette CARRAU MARTY
45 Chief Institutional Planning Office .... Mrs. Rosa TORRES-MOLINA
88 Director of Academic Planning .... Dr. Eunice PEREZ-MEDINA
96 Director of Purchasing .... Mr. Nelson QUIÑONES SANTIAGO
09 Director of Institutional Research .... Mrs. Rosa H. TORRES-MOLINA

*University of Puerto Rico-Aguadilla (C)

PO Box 6150, Aguadilla PR 00604-6150
County: Aguadilla FICE Identification: 012123
Unit ID: 243106
Telephone: (787) 890-2681 Carnegie Class: Bac-Diverse
FAX Number: (787) 891-3455 Calendar System: Semester
URL: www.uprag.edu
Established: 1972 Annual Undergrad Tuition & Fees (In-State): $4,768
Enrollment: 2,444 Coed
Affiliation or Control: State IRS Status: 501(c)3
Highest Offering: Baccalaureate
Accreditation: M, ACBSP, #CAEP

02 Chancellor .... Dr. Sonia RIVERA-GONZALEZ
05 Dean Academic Affairs .... Dr. Walleska DE JESUS BONILLA
11 Dean Administrative Affairs .... Mrs. Veronica LOPEZ-PADUA
32 Dean Student Affairs .... Dr. Sharon RIVERA-RUIZ
06 Registrar .... Mrs. Wanda FELICIANO-MÉNDEZ
07 Admissions Officer .... Mrs. Melba SERRANO
08 Head Librarian .... Prof. Elsa MATOS
13 Director of Computer Center .... Mr. Carlos JIMENEZ
15 Director of Personnel .... Mrs. Luz A. HERNANDEZ
19 Director of Security/Safety .... Mr. Edwin VAZQUEZ MEDINA
37 Director Student Financial Aid .... Mrs. Marta A. SOTO
51 Director Continuing Education .... Sr. Birilo SANTIAGO-VELÁZQUEZ
38 Director Student Counseling .... Dr. Gilberto HERRERA
45 Dir Planning/Inst Research Office .... Mr. Gerardo JAVARIZ
18 Chief Facilities/Physical Plant . Mrs. Marjorie MORALES-MATIAS
29 Director Alumni Relations .... Mrs. Jeannette AQUINO
92 Purchasing Supervisor .... Mrs. Widylia MEDINA

*University of Puerto Rico at Arecibo (D)

Call Box 4010, Arecibo PR 00614-4010
County: Arecibo FICE Identification: 007228
Unit ID: 243115
Telephone: (787) 815-0000 Carnegie Class: Bac-Diverse
FAX Number: (787) 880-2245 Calendar System: Semester
URL: www.upra.edu
Established: 1967 Annual Undergrad Tuition & Fees (In-State): $4,178
Enrollment: 3,414 Coed
Affiliation or Control: State IRS Status: 501(c)3
Highest Offering: Baccalaureate
Accreditation: M, ACBSP, ADNUR, CAEP, JOUR, NUR

02 Chancellor .... Dr. Carlos A. ADNÚJUAR ROJAS
05 Dean for Academic Affairs .... Dr. Weyna QUINONES
11 Dean of Administrative Affairs .... Dr. Inocencio RODRÍGUEZ
32 Dean of Student Affairs .... Dr. Yeidi ALTIERI
10 Director of Finances .... Vacant
09 Dir Planning/Institutional Research .... Dr. Geissa TORRES
06 Interim Registrar .... Mrs. Igmarie SOTO
07 Director of Admissions .... Mrs. Magaly MENDEZ
08 Head Librarian .... Prof. Víctor MALDONADO
15 Director Human Resources .... Vacant
38 Director Student Counseling .... Prof. Celia MEDINA
04 Assistant to the Chancellor .... Dr. José SOTO
37 Director Student Financial Aid .... Ms. Daliana FRESSE
41 Athletic Director .... Mr. Alexieyi RIVERA
13 Computing & Information Management .... Prof. Luis COLON
20 Assoc Dean of Academic Affairs .... Dra. Elizabeth CORTÉS
92 Director Honors Program .... Dra. Vanessa MORA

*University of Puerto Rico at Bayamon (E)

Carr. 174, Industrial Minillas 170,
Bayamon PR 00959-1919
County: Bayamon FICE Identification: 010975
Unit ID: 243133
Telephone: (787) 993-0000 Carnegie Class: Bac-Diverse
FAX Number: (787) 993-8900 Calendar System: Semester
URL: www.uprb.edu
Established: 1971 Annual Undergrad Tuition & Fees (In-State): $4,198
Enrollment: 3,592 Coed
Affiliation or Control: State IRS Status: 501(c)3
Highest Offering: Baccalaureate
Accreditation: M, ACBSP, CAEP

02 Chancellor .... Dr. Miguel VELEZ-RUBIO
05 Dean Academic Affairs .... Dr. Jorge ROVIRA-ALVAREZ
32 Dean Student Affairs .... Dr. Lenis TORRES-BERRIOS
06 Registrar .... Ms. Elizabeth ORTIZ-VARGAS
07 Director Admissions .... Ms. Minerva HERNÁNDEZ-BERNIER
08 Director Learning Resources .... Dr. Myrna L. TORRES-PEREZ
11 Dean Administrative Affairs .... Prof. Jose I. HERNANDEZ-SUAREZ
15 Director Human Resources . Ms. Carina FIGUEROA-RODRÍGUEZ
35 Director Student Activities .... Mr. Manuel COLON-AYALA
37 Director Student Financial Aid .... Mr. Marcos DE JESÚS
38 Director Student Counseling .. Dr. Irma J. SANTIAGO-SANTIAGO
81 Director Biology .... Dr. Darinel ORTIZ-PADILLAT
50 Director Business Administration .... Dr. Peggy Y. SANTIAGO-LOPEZ
09 Director Planning & Inst Research .... Mr. Javier ZAVALA-QUIÑONES
53 Director Education .... Dr. Maria A. GONZALEZ
54 Director Engineering .... Prof. Luis PAGAN
68 Director Physical Education .... Dr. Mario VEGA-GEBOYEAUX
79 Director Humanities .... Dr. Luis PABÓN-BATLLE
83 Director Social Sciences .... Dr. Elizabeth CRESPO-KEBLER
77 Director Computer Science .... Dr. Omar DIAZ-RIVERA
75 Director Secretarial Sciences .... Dr. Peggy SANTIAGO-LÓPEZ
72 Director Electronics .... Prof. Elias BEAUCHAMP-RODRIGUEZ
23 Director Health Services .... Dr. Kimberly RIVERA-SANTIAGO
96 Director Purchasing .... Ms. Allison M. BRACHE-MELLO
88 Director Special Services .... Ms. Shelciy COLLAZO-CASTRO
81 Director Physics .... Dr. Javier AVALOS-SÁNCHEZ
88 Director English .... Prof. Carmen SKERRETT-LLANOS
88 Director Spanish .... Dr. Amarilis TORRES-FUENTES
81 Director Mathematics .... Prof. Angel MORERA-GONZÁLEZ
88 Director Chemistry .... Dr. Marisol CORDERO-RIVERA
18 Coord Facilities/Physical Plant .... Mr. Luis MUNOZ-ALVARADO
114 Director Budget .... Mr. Javier L. ZAVALA-QUINONES
10 Director Finance .... Ms. Mayra NAVARRO-FIGUEROA
13 Director Information Systems . Ms. Barbara LANDRAU-ESPINOSA
105 Director Web Services .... Mr. Orlando ORENGO-ORTEGA
19 Director Security/Safety .... Mr. Nestor RODRÍGUEZ
41 Athletic Director .... Mr. Gerardo BATISTA-SANTIAGO
43 Dir Legal Services/General Counsel .... Mr. Angel MARRERO-HERNÁNDEZ

*University of Puerto Rico-Carolina (F)

PO Box 4800, Carolina PR 00984-4800
County: San Juan FICE Identification: 030160
Unit ID: 243142
Telephone: (787) 257-0000 Carnegie Class: Bac-Diverse
FAX Number: (787) 750-7940 Calendar System: Quarter
URL: www.uprc.edu
Established: 1974 Annual Undergrad Tuition & Fees (In-State): $6,252
Enrollment: 2,580 Coed
Affiliation or Control: State IRS Status: 501(c)3
Highest Offering: Baccalaureate
Accreditation: M, ACBSP, ACPHA

02 Chancellor .... Dr. Jose I. MEZA
05 Int Dean of Academic Affairs .... Dr. Rafael MENDEZ
11 Int Dean Administrative Affairs .... Mr. Gregory BERMUDEZ
32 Int Dean Student Affairs .... Ms. Myrna SANCHEZ
06 Registrar .... Mrs. Ana Y. RIVERA
15 Human Resources Director .... Mrs. Sheila D. SABAT
09 Director of Planning/Inst Research .... Dra. Cristina MARTINEZ
08 Director Learning Resources Center .... Prof. Stanley PORTELA
51 Director Continuing Education .... Prof. Miguel PERÉZ
07 Admissions Director .... Mrs. Celia MENDEZ
13 Director Information Systems .... Mr. Juan CRUZ
37 Financial Aid Director .... Mr. Rafael RUIZ
22 Affirmative Action Officer .... Vacant
48 Director Graphic Arts/Advertising .... Prof. Orlando TORRES
50 Director Banking/Finance/Insurance .... Dr. George OTERO
81 Director Natural Sciences .... Dra. Karilys GONZALEZ
88 Director Secretarial Sciences .... Prof. Josefina RODRIGUEZ
83 Director Social Sciences .... Dr. Kathia WALKERS
68 Director Physical Education .... Prof. Walbert MARCANO
88 Director Auto Tech/Mech Engineering .... Dr. Jose MEZA
79 Director Humanities .... Dr. Bianca APONTE
88 Director Spanish .... Dra. Zulma PENCHI
88 Director English .... Prof. Wanda RODRIGUEZ
88 Dean Hotel Administration School .... Prof. Miguel E. PEREZ
23 Director Health Care .... Dr. Zaida DIAZ
18 Supt Operations & Maintenance .... Mr. Herman MUNIZ
41 Athletic Director .... Mr. Arcadio OCASIO
10 Director of Finance .... Mr. Victor GONZALEZ

*University of Puerto Rico at Cayey (A)

PO BOX 372230, Cayey PR 00737-2230

County: Cayey FICE Identification: 007206
Unit ID: 243151
Telephone: (787) 738-2161 Carnegie Class: Bac-A&S
FAX Number: N/A Calendar System: Semester
URL: www.cayey.upr.edu
Established: 1967 Annual Undergrad Tuition & Fees (In-State): $4,208
Enrollment: 2,984 Coed
Affiliation or Control: State IRS Status: 501(c)3
Highest Offering: Baccalaureate
Accreditation: M, ACBSP, CAEP

02 Chancellor .... Dr. Glorivee ROSARIO PEREZ
05 Acting Dean of Academic Affairs .... Dr. Jose ALONSO
11 Actg Dean of Administration Affairs .... Prof. Isamel QUILES
32 Acting Dean of Student Affairs .... Mr. Jesus MARTINEZ
20 Actg Assoc Dean of Academic Affairs .... Dr. Dalia GONZALEZ
08 Director Library .... Prof. Angel RIOS
06 Registrar .... Mrs. Daisy RAMOS
15 Director Human Resources .... Mrs. Enerida RODRIGUEZ
56 Head Extension Division .... Dr. Aurora GONZALEZ
37 Director Student Financial Aid .... Mrs. Pedro AYALA
38 Director Student Counseling .... Dr. Lino HERNANDEZ
13 Director Computer Center .... Mrs. Minerva DIAZ
45 Director Planning .... Mr. Gabriel APONTE
07 Director Admissions .... Mrs. Elsandra RIVERA
18 Director Facilities/Physical Plant .... Mr. Luis ARROYO
23 Director Health Services .... Dr. Idellisse BALBES
19 Director Security/Safety .... Mr. Luis LOPEZ
92 Director Honor Program .... Vacant
41 Director Athletic Program .... Mr. Ismael RAMOS
43 Director Legal Services .... Ms. Sheila DIAZ
88 Student Ombudsman .... Prof. Efrain COLON
53 Education .... Vacant
79 Humanities .... Vacant
83 Social Sciences .... Vacant
106 Distance Education .... Dr. Margie ALVAREZ
88 Hispanic Studies .... Vacant
88 English .... Dr. Nelly VAZQUEZ
81 Chemistry .... Dr. Wilfredo RESTO
65 Natural Science .... Dr. Maria DE JESUS
88 Biology .... Dr. Edwin VAZQUEZ
94 Women's Studies .... Dr. Lizandra TORRES
88 Occupational Health and Safety .... Mr. Gabriel APONTE
10 Chief Business Officer .... Ms. Glorimar ORTIZ
114 Director Budgeting .... Mrs. Maria SANTIAGO
81 Mathematics/Physics .... Dr. Maytee CRUZ
50 Business Administration .... Dr. Xiomara SANTIAGO
88 RISE Program .... Dr. Juan SANTANA
88 Interdisciplinary Research Inst .... Ms. Vionex MARTI
88 Museum .... Mr. Jonathan BERRIOS
100 Chief of Staff .... Prof. Gladys RAMOS
101 Secretary of the Institution/Board .... Ms. Katherine VAZQUEZ
26 Chief PR/Mktg/Communications Ofcr .... Mr. Angel HOYOS
104 Director Study Abroad .... Ms. Elsandra RIVERA
105 Director Web Services .... Ms. Minerva DIAZ
28 Director of Cultural Activities .... Mr. Eleric RIVERA
108 Dir Institutional Assessment/Rsrch .... Dr. Margie ALVAREZ
22 Dir Affirm Action/Equal Opportunity .... Mrs. Kiara DE JESUS

*University of Puerto Rico-Humacao (B)

Call Box 860, Humacao PR 00792

County: Humacao FICE Identification: 003943
Unit ID: 243179
Telephone: (787) 850-0000 Carnegie Class: Bac-Diverse
FAX Number: (787) 852-4638 Calendar System: Semester
URL: www.uprh.edu
Established: 1962 Annual Undergrad Tuition & Fees (In-State): $4,208
Enrollment: 3,106 Coed
Affiliation or Control: State IRS Status: 501(c)3
Highest Offering: Baccalaureate
Accreditation: M, ACBSP, JOUR, NUR, #PTAA, SW

02 Chancellor .... Dr. Aida I. RODRIGUEZ ROIG
05 Dean of Academic Affairs .... Dr. Hector L. AYALA
11 Dean Administrative Affairs .... Mrs. Mariolga ROTGER
04 Assistant to the Chancellor .... Dr. Iris L. GARCIA
32 Dean of Student Affairs .... Dr. Ivelisse BLASINI
20 Associate Dean Academic Affairs .... Dr. Deborah E. NIEVES
45 Director Planning Office .... Prof. Ivette IRIZARRY
06 Registrar .... Mrs. Carmen B. RODRIGUEZ
07 Director of Admissions .... Mrs. Carmen RIVERA
08 Director of the Library .... Prof. Evelyn RODRIGUEZ
13 Director System Info Ofc .... Mr. Hiram ORTIZ
15 Director Human Resources .... Mrs. Elsa SANTOS
10 Director of Finance .... Mrs. Ines SANCHEZ
37 Director Financial Aid .... Mr. Jose R. JIMENEZ
38 Director Counseling Office .... Dr. Magaly RODRIGUEZ
51 Dir Continuing Education/Extension .... Dr. Lilliam MORALES
23 Director Health Services .... Dr. Gini CRUZ
18 Chief Facilities/Physical Plant .... Mrs. Sandra CARRADERO
19 Director Security/Transit .... Mrs. Lilliam TAPIA
41 Athletic Activities Director .... Mrs. Clarisa Z. ROSADO
114 Director of Budget Office .... Mrs. Adiary LAVIENA
108 Office of Institutional Assessment .... Dr. Mildred CUADRADO
101 Sec of Academic Senate/Adm Board .... Prof. Amelia MALDONADO
26 Press Relations .... Ms. Ingrid VAZQUEZ
50 Director Business Administration .... Prof. Aida KALIL
88 Director of Biology Dept .... Dr. Esther Z. VEGA
88 Director of Chemistry Dept .... Dr. Tania MALAVE
60 Director of Communication Dept .... Dr. Hector PINERO
53 Director of Education Dept .... Dr. Ramon D. GARCIA BARRIOS
88 Director of English Dept .... Dr. Nilsa L. LUGO
79 Director of Humanities Dept .... Prof. Luis P. SANCHEZ LONGO
81 Director of Mathematics Dept .... Prof. Barbara I. SANTIAGO
66 Director of Nursing Dept .... Dr. Alba I. PEREZ
88 Director Occup Therapy Dept .... Prof. Madeline ORTIZ
88 Dir Office System Admin Dept .... Prof. Ivelisse REYES
76 Director Physical Therapy Dept .... Prof. Eneida SILVA
88 Director Physics & Elect Dept .... Dr. Rogerio FURLAN
83 Director Social Science Dept .... Dr. Luis R. RODRIGUEZ
70 Director of Social Work Dept .... Prof. Vanessa SANCHEZ
88 Director of Spanish Dept .... Dr. Jeandelize GONZALEZ
88 Graphics Art Supervisor .... Mr. Carlos LAZU
22 Dir Affirmative Action/EEO .... Mrs. Mariolga ROTGER
46 Dir Subsidized Research & Programs .... Dr. Daniel RODRIGUEZ HOWELL
88 Director Day Care Center .... Mrs. Maggaly POMALAZA
88 Student Support Service Director .... Prof. Olga L. BERRIOS
88 Upward Bound Director .... Mrs. Myriam CINTRON
88 Director of ExTgesis Journal .... Dr. Carlos R. GOMEZ
21 Director of Accounting Office .... Mrs. Wanda FLORES

*University of Puerto Rico-Mayaguez Campus (C)

Call Box 9000, Mayaguez PR 00681-9000

County: Mayaguez FICE Identification: 003944
Unit ID: 243197
Telephone: (787) 832-4040 Carnegie Class: Masters/M
FAX Number: (787) 834-3031 Calendar System: Semester
URL: www.uprm.edu
Established: 1911 Annual Undergrad Tuition & Fees (In-State): $4,168
Enrollment: 12,825 Coed
Affiliation or Control: State IRS Status: 501(c)3
Highest Offering: Doctorate
Accreditation: M, ACBSP, CAEP, NUR

02 Chancellor .... Dr. Agustin RULLAN TORO
05 Dean of Academic Affairs .... Dr. Betsy MORALES
11 Dean of Administration .... Dr. Omar I. MOLINA BAS
32 Dean of Students .... Dr. Jonathan MUNOZ BARRETO
49 Dean of Arts & Sciences .... Dr. Fernando GILBES SANTAELLA
54 Dean of Engineering .... Dr. Bienvenido VELEZ RIVERA
47 Dean Agricultural Sciences .... Dr. Raul E. MACCHIAVELLI
50 Dean Business Administration .... Dr. Maria AMADOR DUMOIS

*University of Puerto Rico-Medical Sciences Campus (D)

PO Box 365067, San Juan PR 00936-5067

County: San Juan FICE Identification: 024600
Unit ID: 243203
Telephone: (787) 758-2525 Carnegie Class: Spec-4-yr-Med
FAX Number: (787) 758-2556 Calendar System: Other
URL: www.rcm.upr.edu
Established: 1950 Annual Undergrad Tuition & Fees (In-State): N/A
Enrollment: 2,218 Coed
Affiliation or Control: State IRS Status: 501(c)3
Highest Offering: Doctorate
Accreditation: M, ANEST, AUD, CAHIIM, CYTO, DA, DENT, @DIET, DIETI, HSA, MED, MLS, NMT, NURSE, OT, PH, PHAR, PTA, #RAD, SP

02 Chancellor .... Dr. Segundo RODRIGUEZ
05 Interim Dean Academic Affairs .... Dr. Debora H. SILVA-DIAZ
32 Dean Students Affairs .... Dr. Maria HERNANDEZ
11 Interim Dean of Administration .... Mr. Carlos A. ORTIZ REYES
63 Dean School of Medicine .... Dr. Agustin RODRIGUEZ
52 Dean School of Dental Medicine .... Dr. Jose MATOS
69 Dean Grad School Public Health .... Dr. Dharma VAZQUEZ
67 Dean School of Pharmacy .... Dr. Wanda MALDONADO
76 Dean School of Health Professions .... Dr. Barbara SEGARRA
66 Dean School of Nursing .... Dr. Suane SANCHEZ
100 Chief of Staff .... Dr. Ramon F. GONZALEZ
20 Associate Academic Officer .... Dr. Jose CAPRILES
13 CIT Acting Director .... Mr. Angel D. COLON
43 Director Legal Services .... Ms. Cristina PARES
26 Chief Information Officer .... Ms. Vivian VAZQUEZ
06 Registrar .... Mr. Abelardo MARTINEZ
08 Library Director .... Dr. Carmen M. SANTOS
09 Director Inst & Academic Research .... Dr. Wanda BARRETO
24 Director Educational Media .... Vacant
35 Assoc Dean Student Affairs .... Dr. Blanca AMOROS
07 Director of Admissions .... Mrs. Maribel ORTIZ
38 Director of Student Counseling .... Prof. Blanca AMOROS
37 Director of Student Financial Aid .... Mrs. Yolanda RIVERA
10 Chief Financial Officer .... Vacant
15 Director Personnel Services .... Mr. Manuel CARDONA
18 Chief Facilities/Physical Plant .... Mr. Julio A. COLLAZO
96 Director of Purchasing .... Mr. Miguel BOBE
19 Director Security Office .... Mr. William FIGUEROA
108 Director Institutional Assessment .... Dr. Jose CAPRILES
25 Chief Contracts/Grants Admin .... Ms. Lysette BARRERAS

*University of Puerto Rico at Ponce (E)

PO Box 7186, Ponce PR 00732-7186

County: Ponce FICE Identification: 009652
Unit ID: 243212
Telephone: (787) 844-8181 Carnegie Class: Bac-Diverse
FAX Number: N/A Calendar System: Semester
URL: www.uprp.edu
Established: 1970 Annual Undergrad Tuition & Fees (In-State): $4,198
Enrollment: 2,382 Coed
Affiliation or Control: State IRS Status: 501(c)3
Highest Offering: Baccalaureate
Accreditation: M, ACBSP, CAEP, #PTAA

02 Chancellor .... Dr. Tessie H. CRUZ RIVERA
04 Assistant to the Chancellor .... Prof. Carmen A. BRACERO
05 Interim Dean Academic Affairs .... Dr. Ineabelle MONTES
11 Dean Administrative Affairs .... Mr. Isaac COLON
32 Dean Student Affairs .... Prof. Carlos H. PAGAN
20 Associate Academic Dean .... Dr. Joahana RAMOS
45 Dir Inst Research/Planning Officer .... Dr. Diana LOPEZ
08 Director Library .... Prof. Jose OLIVERAS
06 Registrar .... Mrs. Marya Z. SANTIAGO
38 Director Student Counseling .... Dr. Marisel RAMIREZ
07 Director of Admissions .... Mrs. Emily MATOS
37 Director of Financial Aid .... Mrs. Vanessa VELEZ
15 Director of Personnel Services .... Dr. Ericka RODRIGUEZ
13 Director of Computer Center .... Mrs. Damarys HERNANDEZ
18 Chief Facilities/Physical Plant .... Mr. Alberto GARCIA
40 Director Bookstore .... Vacant
41 Athletic Director .... Mr. Anibal MONTES
23 Director Health Services .... Dr. Yiselle LOPEZ
29 Director Alumni Relations .... Mrs. Joanne E. VALLS
30 Chief Development .... Vacant
19 Director of Security/Traffic .... Mr. William BERMEJO
88 Coordinator Security/Safety .... Mrs. Celia GONZALEZ
22 Coordinator Affirmative Action .... Dr. Yesenia QUINONES
10 Chief Financial/Business Officer .... Mrs. Romarie MESA
43 Director Legal Services .... Mr. Gaddiel MORALES
90 Director Academic Computing .... Mr. Edward GRACIA
96 Director of Purchasing .... Mrs. Rubis M. SANTIAGO

*University of Puerto Rico-Rio Piedras Campus (F)

10 Ave Universidad, Ste 1001, San Juan PR 00925-2530

County: San Juan FICE Identification: 007108
Unit ID: 243221
Telephone: (787) 763-7099 Carnegie Class: DU-Higher
FAX Number: (787) 764-8799 Calendar System: Semester
URL: www.uprrp.edu
Established: 1903 Annual Undergrad Tuition & Fees (In-State): $4,198
Enrollment: 13,892 Coed
Affiliation or Control: State IRS Status: 501(c)3
Highest Offering: Doctorate
Accreditation: M, ACBSP, CACREP, CAEP, CLPSY, DIETD, JOUR, LAW, LIB, PLNG, SPAA, SW

02 Chancellor .... Dra. Angelica VARELA LLAVONA
05 Dean Academic Affairs .... Dra. Nivia FERNÁNDEZ HERNANDEZ
11 Dean of Administration .... Mrs. Anaisa LOPEZ
32 Dean of Students .... Dr. Gloria DIAZ URBINA
20 Associate Dean Academic Affairs .... Dr. Nellie TORRADO PEREZ
50 Dean Business Administration .... Dr. Rafael MARRERO DIAS
48 Dean of Architecture .... Arq. Mayra JIMÉNEZ MONTANO
81 Dean of Natural Sciences .... Dr. Néstor CARBALLEIRA
83 Dean of Social Sciences .... Dr. Milagros MENDEZ CASTILLO
61 Dean of Law .... Dr. Vivian NEPTUNE RIVERA
97 Dean of General Studies .... Dr. Carlos SANCHEZ ZAMBRANA
79 Dean of Humanities .... Dr. Agnes BOSCH IRIZARRY
58 Dean Graduate Studies/ Research .... Dr. Carlos I. GONZÁLEZ VARGAS
53 Dean of Education .... Dr. Grace CARRO
35 Asst Dean Student Affairs .... Dr. Marilu PEREZ HERNÁNDEZ
38 Director of Student Counseling .... Dr. María JIMÉNEZ CHAFEY
30 Dean Aux Devel & Alumni Relations .... Mrs. Sandra SANCHEZ GONZÁLEZ
06 Registrar .... Mrs. Zulyn RODRIGUEZ REYES
08 Director of Library System .... Dr. Nancy ABREU BAEZ
15 Director of Human Resources .... Ms. Nydza IRIZARRY ALGARÍN
07 Director of Admissions .... Dr. Jessica A. MORALES TORRES
13 Director of Computer Center .... Mr. Ruben RODRÍGUEZ OCASIO
62 Director Grad Sch Library/Info Sci .... Dr. Nancy ABREU BAEZ
60 Dean School of Communication .... Dr. Jorge SANTIAGO PINTOR
58 Dir Graduate Sch of Planning .... Dr. Norma PEÑA RIVERA
51 Dir Continuing Educ/Extension .... Dr. Somar RAMOS
09 Director of Institutional Research .... Dr. Isabel MONTANEZ
18 Chief Planning/Physical Devel Ofc .... Mr. Ramón BAYÓN TORRES
26 Chief Public Relations Officer .... Mr. Mario ALEGRE
37 Director of Student Financial Aid .... Mr. Anibal ALVALLE
96 Director of Purchasing .... Mr. Edgardo DIAZ LABRADOR
19 Director Security/Safety .... Mr. Victor ROSARIO DELGADO
10 Chief Financial/Business Officer .... Mr. Roberto SEGARRA
102 Director Foundation/Corporate Rels .... Dr. Carmen RUIZ DE FIISCHLER
105 Director Web Services .... Mrs. Wilmarie SANTIAGO LOPEZ
22 Director Affirm Action/Equal Opp .... Mr. Gabriel I. GONZALEZ
28 Director of Diversity .... Mrs. Orializ OCASIO
29 Director Alumni Affairs .... Arq. Luis IRIZARRY RAMÍREZ
39 Dir Resident Life/Student Housing .... Arq. Darwin J. MARRERO CARRER
41 Athletic Director .... Mr. Ramon HERNANDEZ CRUZ
43 Director Legal Services .... Mrs. Miriam TOLEDO DAVID

*University of Puerto Rico at Utuado (G)

PO Box 2500, Utuado PR 00641-2500

County: Utuado FICE Identification: 029384
Unit ID: 243188
Telephone: (787) 894-2828 Carnegie Class: Bac/Assoc-Mixed

FAX Number: (787) 894-1081   Calendar System: Semester
URL: www.uprutuado.edu
Established: 1979   Annual Undergrad Tuition & Fees (In-State): $4,168
Enrollment: 554   Coed
Affiliation or Control: State   IRS Status: 501(c)3
Highest Offering: Baccalaureate
Accreditation: **M**, ACBSP

02	Chancellor/Rector	Dr. Luis A. TAPIA MALDONADO
05	Academic Dean	Dr. Ana M. ARCE
10	Dean of Administration	Mrs. Zoila GONZALEZ
32	Chief Student Life Officer	Dr. Jessica ROMERO
08	Library Director	Prof. Catalina SOTO
09	Director Institutional Research	Vacant
06	Registrar	Vacant
07	Director of Admission	Mrs. Maria V. ROBLES
15	Director Human Resources	Mrs. Zoila GONZALEZ
38	Director Student Counseling	Dr. Victor M. HERNANDEZ
37	Director Student Financial Aid	Mrs. Daliana FRESSE
13	Director Information Systems	Mr. Juan MARTINEZ
19	Director Security/Safety	Vacant
41	Director of Athletics	Vacant
47	Director of Agriculture	Prof. Luis E. DIAZ
50	Dir Office Systems/Business Admin	Dr. Frank RIVAS
96	Director of Purchasing	Ms. Luz E. MARTINEZ
51	Director Continuing Education	Mrs. Livette REYES
65	Director Natural Sciences	Prof. Luis E. DIAZ
79	Director Humanities/Spanish/English	Vacant

University of the Sacred Heart   (A)

PO Box 12383, San Juan PR 00914-8505
County: San Juan   FICE Identification: 003937
    Unit ID: 243443
Telephone: (787) 728-1515   Carnegie Class: Masters/M
FAX Number: (787) 728-1692   Calendar System: Semester
URL: www.sagrado.edu
Established: 1935   Annual Undergrad Tuition & Fees: $6,000
Enrollment: 4,501   Coed
Affiliation or Control: Roman Catholic   IRS Status: 501(c)3
Highest Offering: Master's
Accreditation: **M**, NURSE, SW

01	President	Gilberto J. MARXUACH-TORROS
04	Admin Assistant to the President	Gloriana YDRACH
05	Provost	Anuchka RAMOS RUIZ
06	Registrar	Marcelo RIVERA GONZALEZ
07	Director of Admissions	Katherine CASTILLO
10	Chief Financial Officer & CIO	Miguel A. MERCADO
15	VP/Chief Human Resources Officer	Camelia FERNANDEZ
32	Interim VP Student Affairs	Madeline ORTIZ
37	Director Student Financial Aid	Johanel RIOS
39	Dir Resident Life/Student Housing	Mayra HERNANDEZ
41	Athletic Director	Rafael COLON
43	Director Legal Services	Camelia FERNANDEZ
50	Dean of Business	Dennis ROMAN ROA

VIRGIN ISLANDS

University of the Virgin Islands   (B)

#2 John Brewers Bay, Saint Thomas VI 00802-9990
    FICE Identification: 003946
    Unit ID: 243665
Telephone: (340) 776-9200   Carnegie Class: Masters/S
FAX Number: (340) 693-1005   Calendar System: Semester
URL: www.uvi.edu
Established: 1962   Annual Undergrad Tuition & Fees (In-State): $5,235
Enrollment: 1,838   Coed
Affiliation or Control: State   IRS Status: 501(c)3
Highest Offering: Doctorate
Accreditation: **M**, ACBSP, NUR, @SW

01	President	Dr. David HALL
88	VP Business Development/Innovation	Dr. Haldane DAVIES
04	Director of Presidential Operations	Ms. Una DYER
101	Board Liaison	Ms. Gail T. STEELE
05	Provost/VP of Academic Affairs	Dr. Camille A. MCKAYLE
46	Interim Vice Provost/ECC/RPS	Vacant
53	Dean School of Education	Dr. Karen H. BROWN
81	Int Dean College of Science/Math	Dr. Sandra ROMANO
50	Dean School of Business	Dr. Kendra L. HARRIS
49	Dean Col Liberal Arts/Social Sci	Dr. Kimarie ENGERMAN
66	Dean School of Nursing	Ms. Beverley A. LANSIQUOT
104	Assoc Provost Grad/Global Acad Affs	Dr. James S. MADDIRALA
84	VP Access/Enroll Services	Vacant
07	Coordinator Enrollment Services	Ms. Charmaine I. SMITH
06	Registrar	Ms. Monifa J. POTTER
37	Director of Financial Aid	Ms. Cheryl A. ROBERTS
32	Dean of Students-STT Campus	Ms. Verna J. RIVERS
36	Director Counseling/Career Services	Ms. Patricia TOWAL
111	VP Institutional Advancement	Mr. Mitchell NEAVES
44	Director of Annual Giving	Vacant
30	Capital Campaign Manager	Mr. Jose Raul CARRILLO
10	VP Administration & Finance	Ms. Shirley L. LAKE-KING
21	Acting Controller	Ms. Stacey CHADOS
15	Director of HR/Org Development	Mr. Charles Ronald MEEK
19	Chief Campus Police/Security	Mr. Theodore E. GLASFORD
18	Director of Physical Plant	Mr. Charles MARTIN
13	VP Info Services/Inst Assessment	Ms. Sharlene J. HARRIS
08	Library Manager	Mrs. Celia P. PRINCE-RICHARD

32	Dean of Students-STC Campus	Ms. Hedda T. FINCH-SIMPSON
09	Director of Institutional Research	Ms. Laurie BLAKE

University of the Virgin Islands-St. Croix   (C)

RR1, Box 10,000, Kingshill VI 00850-9781
Telephone: (340) 778-1620   Identification: 770173
Accreditation: **&M**

Index of Key Administrators

ABREU, Katie .... 410-334-2904 205 A
kabreu@worwic.edu
ABREU, Sara .... 787-878-5475 506 J
sabreu@arecibo.inter.edu
ABREU BAEZ, Nancy .... 787-764-0000 511 F
nancy.abreu1@upr.edu
ABREU-HERNANDEZ,
Viviana .... 508-854-4380 215 D
vabreu@qcc.mass.edu
ABREU-HORNBOSTEL,
Esmilda .... 718-862-8000 304 K
eabreuhornbostel01@manhattan.edu
ABROMAITIS, James ..... 203-773-8578.. 85 C
jabromaitis@albertus.edu
ABSAR, Quaiser .... 540-665-4937 470 A
qabsar@su.edu
ABSHIRE, Aimee .... 337-482-5519 192 F
aimee.abshire@louisiana.edu
ABSHIRE, Elaine .... 979-209-7547 430 I
eabshire@blinn.edu
ABSHIRE, Martha Ann .. 225-490-1685 186 H
martha.abshire@franu.edu
ABSTON, Kara .... 501-279-4332.. 19 G
kabston@harding.edu
ABTS, Polly .... 920-693-1221 497 H
polly.abts@gotoltc.edu
ABUHAMAD, Alfred, Z .. 757-446-5800 465 H
abuhamaz@evms.edu
ABUSALIM, Murad .... 956-295-3568 448 E
murad.abusalim@tsc.edu
ABUSHABAN, Sahar ...... 619-644-7575.. 44 F
sahar.abushaban@gcccd.edu
ABUTIN, Albert .... 714-992-7076.. 54 D
aabutin@fullcoll.edu
ACARDO, John .... 608-785-8697 495 A
jacardo@uwlax.edu
ACCARDI, Christen .... 585-785-1231 299 E
christen.accardi@flcc.edu
ACCARDI, Jon .... 315-279-5690 303 D
jaccardi@keuka.edu
ACCIARDO, Linda, A ..... 401-874-2116 404 E
lindaa@uri.edu
ACEBO, JR., Andre .... 201-200-2039 278 F
aacebo@njcu.edu
ACEVEDO, Beatriz .... 212-924-5900 321 C
bursar@swedishinstitute.edu
ACEVEDO, Dary .... 787-891-0925 506 I
dacevedo@aguadilla.inter.edu
ACEVEDO, Francisco ..... 787-892-5700 507 E
facevedo@intersg.edu
ACEVEDO, Geidy .... 787-891-0925 506 I
geacevedo@aguadilla.inter.edu
ACEVEDO, Ivonne .... 787-891-0925 506 I
iacevedo@aguadilla.inter.edu
ACEVEDO, Mauricio ...... 818-702-1421.. 56 H
mauricio.acevedo@pepperdine.edu
ACEVEDO, Tony .... 512-428-1319 441 N
tonya@stedwards.edu
ACEVEDO, Vionis .... 787-746-1400 505 L
vacevedo@huertas.edu
ACEVEDO RIOS,
Carmen, M .... 787-725-6500 504 F
cacevedo@albizu.edu
ACEVES, Salvador, D .... 303-458-4144.. 83 B
saceves@regis.edu
ACEY, Stacy .... 770-228-7372 125 F
stacy.acey@sctech.edu
ACHAN, Jennifer .... 661-395-4482.. 47 B
jennifer.achan@bakersfieldcollege.edu
ACHARYA, Mukul .... 908-737-3358 277 F
macharya@kean.edu
ACHARYA, Suresh .... 269-749-7666 229 G
sacharya@olivetcollege.edu
ACHARYA, Sushil .... 412-397-6227 396 E
acharya@rmu.edu
ACHENBACH, USMS,
Gerard .... 231-995-1203 228 F
gachenbach@nmc.edu
ACHESON, Carol .... 503-253-3443 374 E
cacheson@ocom.edu
ACHEY, Becky .... 610-921-7663 377 F
bachey@albright.edu
ACHIPA, Joshua .... 405-491-6351 369 G
jachipa@snu.edu
ACHIVARE-HILL,
Rachael .... 918-595-7941 370 B
rachael.achivarehill@tulsacc.edu
ACHORD, Craig .... 307-675-0505 500 F
ACHS, Carol .... 480-461-7742.. 13 F
carol.achs@mesacc.edu
ACIERNO, Lou .... 212-752-1530 303 G
lou.acierno@limcollege.edu
ACKER, Janet .... 207-326-2220 195 G
janet.acker@mma.edu
ACKER, Lorraine .... 585-395-2772 317 B
ldacker@brockport.edu
ACKER, Scott .... 806-371-5160 428 F
s0311868@actx.edu
ACKER, Shelia .... 248-341-2121 228 H
smacker@oaklandcc.edu
ACKERLEY, Roseanne .... 513-487-3234 300 H
rackerley@huc.edu
ACKERLY, David, D .... 510-642-7171.. 68 N
dackerly@berkeley.edu
ACKERMAN, Ari .... 305-944-0035 114 B
ACKERMAN, Denise ...... 845-758-7526 290 G
ackerman@bard.edu
ACKERMAN, Hannah ..... 518-327-6021 310 G
hackerman@paulsmiths.edu
ACKERMAN, Kathy .... 828-395-1522 335 B
kackerman@isothermal.edu
ACKERMAN, Steven ...... 973-328-5550 276 A
sackerman@ccm.edu
ACKERMAN, Steven ...... 608-262-1044 494 D
saackerm@wisc.edu
ACKERMAN, Tom .... 618-664-6620 138 D
tom.ackerman@greenville.edu
ACKERMAN, Tom .... 352-271-2905 107 G
thomas.ackerman@sfcollege.edu
ACKERMAN-BEHR, Glen 906-932-4231 224 A
glena@gogebic.edu
ACKLEH, Azmy .... 337-482-6986 192 F
azmy.ackleh@louisiana.edu
ACKLEY, Darren .... 715-675-3331 498 E
ackley@ntc.edu
ACKLEY, Denise .... 815-965-8616 147 I
ACKLEY, Jared .... 601-318-6102 249 B
jackley@wmcarey.edu
ACKMAN, Elizabeth, R .. 315-684-6043 320 E
ackmaner@morrisville.edu
ACKMAN, Robin .... 217-786-2762 142 F
robin.ackman@llcc.edu
ACOB-NASH, Mari .... 206-934-3643 482 F
maria.acob-nash@seattlecolleges.edu
ACOBE, Luis, F .... 787-834-9595 508 O
lacobe@uaa.edu
ACOLASTE, Ras .... 703-878-2800.. 93 H
ACOSTA, Anna Lisa .... 775-445-4262 271 A
annalisa.acosta@wnc.edu
ACOSTA, Araceli .... 210-924-4338 430 D
araceli.acosta@bua.edu
ACOSTA, Claudia .... 619-482-6359.. 65 K
cacosta@swccd.edu
ACOSTA, Daniel .... 650-949-7514.. 42 J
acostadaniel@fhda.edu
ACOSTA, Erica .... 570-408-7856 402 B
erica.acosta@wilkes.edu
ACOSTA, Esmeralda, M . 623-845-3012.. 13 E
esmeralda.acosta@gccaz.edu
ACOSTA, Kathy .... 214-860-1464 434 A
kacosta@dcccd.edu
ACOSTA, Kirsten .... 760-245-4271.. 74 D
kirsten.acosta@vvc.edu
ACOSTA, Sara .... 708-524-6288 137 A
sacosta@dom.edu
ACQUAAH, George .... 301-860-3610 203 D
gacquaah@bowiestae.edu
ACQUAH, Ken .... 718-518-4369 293 F
kacquah@hostos.cuny.edu
ACREE, Cheryl .... 229-333-2126 127 F
cheryl.acree@wiregrass.edu
ACUFF, Keith .... 660-596-7301 259 D
kacuff@sfccmo.edu
ACUNA, Angela .... 408-498-5133.. 73 A
aacuna@cogswell.edu
ACUNTO, Rob, L .... 864-833-8242 410 E
rlacunto@presby.edu
ADACHI, Lesley, B .... 680-488-2471 504 A
lesleyadachi@palau.edu
ADADE, Anthony .... 508-929-8714 213 D
aadade@worcester.edu
ADADEVOH, Vidal .... 205-929-1603.... 6 B
vadadevoh@miles.edu
ADAIR, Adam .... 870-512-7801.. 18 C
adam_adair@asun.edu
ADAIR, Charles .... 934-420-2198 320 C
charles.adair@farmingdale.edu
ADAIR, Hollie .... 541-956-7442 375 G
hadair@roguecc.edu
ADAIR, Kathy .... 906-248-3354 221 I
kadair@bmcc.edu
ADAIR, Matt .... 580-327-8418 367 A
wmadair@nwosu.edu
ADAIR, Matthew .... 952-829-2459 233 H
matt.adair@bethfel.org
ADAIR, Suzanne, C .... 814-863-0471 391 F
sca917@psu.edu
ADAM, Jammie .... 540-373-2200 465 G
jadam@evcc.edu
ADAM, Terri .... 207-974-4691 195 A
tadam@emcc.edu
ADAM, Wendy .... 413-597-2353 220 A
ga1@williams.edu
ADAMCHAK, Andrea ..... 765-658-4440 154 G
andreaadamchak@depauw.edu
ADAMCZYK, Julie, L ..... 989-837-4436 228 G
adamczyk@northwood.edu
ADAMCZYK, Stephanie . 412-392-4205 395 H
sadamczyk@pointpark.edu
ADAME, Belinda .... 847-628-2468 141 A
belinda.adame@judsonu.edu
ADAMIEC, Larissa .... 630-829-6000 133 B
ADAMITIS, Jana, L .... 757-594-7057 465 A
jadam@cnu.edu
ADAMO, Clare .... 860-632-3009.. 88 B
cadamo@holyapostles.edu
ADAMO, Paul, J .... 607-436-2535 316 C
paul.adamo@oneonta.edu
ADAMS, Adam .... 712-722-6006 165 E
adam.adams@dordt.edu
ADAMS, Alex .... 559-489-2225.. 67 A
alex.adams@fresnocitycollege.edu
ADAMS, Alexandra .... 816-501-2400 249 H
alexandra.adams@avila.edu
ADAMS, Amanda .... 864-592-4276 411 E
adams@sccsc.edu
ADAMS, Amy .... 740-389-4636 355 F
adamsa@mtc.edu
ADAMS, Ann .... 312-491-2869 146 C
a-adams@northwestern.edu
ADAMS, Ann .... 360-486-8842 482 D
aadams@stmartin.edu
ADAMS, Ann Clay .... 404-687-4524 117 D
adamsa@ctsnet.edu
ADAMS, Barbara, L .... 803-536-8980 410 H
badams@scsu.edu
ADAMS, Betsy .... 336-758-5000 344 A
ADAMS, Billy, W .... 903-693-2028 440 E
badams@panola.edu
ADAMS, Brad .... 865-251-1800 422 G
badams@south.edu
ADAMS, Brenda .... 501-450-1226.. 19 I
adams@hendrix.edu
ADAMS, Brett, C .... 443-352-4250 202 C
bcadams@stevenson.edu
ADAMS, Brian .... 225-771-2520 190 K
brian_adams@subr.edu
ADAMS, Bruce .... 504-286-5432 191 A
badams@suno.edu
ADAMS, Carey .... 812-866-7005 155 D
adamsc@hanover.edu
ADAMS, Carol .... 678-717-2233 126 G
carol.adams@ung.edu
ADAMS, Carol .... 304-697-7550 486 F
ADAMS, Caroline .... 805-893-3285.. 70 E
caroline.adams@ucsb.edu
ADAMS, Caroline .... 601-426-6346 248 C
cadams@southeasternbaptist.edu
ADAMS, Charles, H .... 813-974-3087 111 B
chadams@honors.usf.edu
ADAMS, Chris .... 503-251-5767 377 A
chadams@uws.edu
ADAMS, Colby, T .... 817-921-8714 444 D
cadams@swbts.edu
ADAMS, Dave .... 218-299-4000 234 K
ADAMS, David .... 620-331-4100 174 E
dadams@indycc.edu
ADAMS, David, J .... 513-556-5511 361 I
davidj.adams@uc.edu
ADAMS, Dean .... 270-384-8036 183 D
adamsd@lindsey.edu
ADAMS, Denise .... 530-895-2329.. 27 F
adamsde@butte.edu
ADAMS, Doug .... 217-443-8832 136 E
d.adams@dacc.edu
ADAMS, Ed .... 870-633-4480.. 19 E
eadams@eacc.edu
ADAMS, Edward .... 646-312-1190 292 F
edward.adams@baruch.cuny.edu
ADAMS, Edward, E .... 801-422-8611 458 A
ed_adams@byu.edu
ADAMS, Elizabeth .... 661-952-5015.. 30 C
ADAMS, Emily .... 541-962-3130 372 H
eadams5@eou.edu
ADAMS, Grace .... 716-926-8928 301 C
gadams@hilbert.edu
ADAMS, Grantley .... 860-738-6333.. 87 A
gadams@nwcc.edu
ADAMS, Guy .... 408-727-1060.. 46 A
ADAMS, James .... 850-474-2080 111 E
jadams1@uwf.edu
ADAMS, James, E .... 325-942-2071 450 B
james.adams@angelo.edu
ADAMS, Jamie .... 620-229-6104 177 D
jamie.adams@sckans.edu
ADAMS, Jamie .... 716-829-8000 298 C
adamsj@dyc.edu
ADAMS, Jamie .... 609-984-1105 283 D
jadams@tesu.edu
ADAMS, Janieth .... 601-979-0928 245 G
janieth.f.wilson_adams@jsums.edu
ADAMS, Jann .... 404-639-0999 122 H
jann.adams@morehouse.edu
ADAMS, Jason .... 303-762-6936.. 80 G
jason.adams@denverseminary.edu
ADAMS, Jeff .... 479-788-7221.. 22 A
jeff.adams@uafs.edu
ADAMS, Jeffrey .... 406-243-4330 263 D
jeffrey.adams@umontana.edu
ADAMS, Jeffrey, M .... 336-841-4581 329 E
jeadams@highpoint.edu
ADAMS, Jennie .... 714-564-6433.. 58 F
adams_jennie@sac.edu
ADAMS, Jennifer .... 925-473-7302.. 40 I
jadams@losmedanos.edu
ADAMS, Jennifer .... 334-347-2623.... 2 A
jadams@escc.edu
ADAMS, Jennifer .... 334-844-7326.... 4 E
jennifer.adams@auburn.edu
ADAMS, Jennifer .... 315-792-7810 320 F
jennifer.adams@sunypoly.edu
ADAMS, Jennifer .... 614-236-6170 348 I
jadams@capital.edu
ADAMS, Joetta .... 870-743-3000.. 20 F
jadams@northark.edu
ADAMS, John, E .... 828-262-6432 340 G
adamsje2@appstate.edu
ADAMS, Johnnie .... 310-434-4302.. 63 B
adams_johnnie@smc.edu
ADAMS, Joseph .... 253-964-6598 481 H
jadams@pierce.ctc.edu
ADAMS, Josh .... 707-524-1731.. 63 C
jadams2@santarosa.edu
ADAMS, Joshua .... 707-524-1731.. 63 C
jadams2@santarosa.edu
ADAMS, Joshua .... 940-898-4108 451 A
jadams15@twu.edu
ADAMS, Joy .... 307-382-1832 500 I
jadams@westernwyoming.edu
ADAMS, Julie .... 423-746-5251 425 C
jadams@tnwesleyan.edu
ADAMS, Julius, G .... 716-645-1971 315 F
jgadams2@buffalo.edu
ADAMS, Karen .... 956-296-1416 455 A
karen.adams@utrgv.edu
ADAMS, Karen, H .... 812-856-5596 156 B
kadams@iu.edu
ADAMS, Kari .... 620-276-9638 173 H
kari.adams@gcccks.edu
ADAMS, Kate .... 518-244-4594 312 D
adamsk2@sage.edu
ADAMS, Kathryn, F .... 717-337-6660 384 C
kadams@gettysburg.edu
ADAMS, Kelly, L .... 315-792-3047 323 G
kadams@utica.edu
ADAMS, Kenneth .... 718-482-5050 294 D
presidentadams@lagcc.cuny.edu
ADAMS, Kent .... 620-450-2140 176 I
kenta@prattcc.edu
ADAMS, Kim .... 817-257-4506 447 H
kim.adams@tcu.edu
ADAMS, Kimberly .... 325-942-2122 450 B
kimberly.adams@angelo.edu
ADAMS, Kimberly .... 253-752-2020 479 D
kimadams@faithiu.edu
ADAMS, Kylie .... 913-758-6219 177 I
kylie.adams@stmary.edu
ADAMS, Landon .... 417-667-8181 251 E
ladams@cottey.edu
ADAMS, Larry .... 606-368-6030 178 D
larryadams@alc.edu
ADAMS, Lita .... 413-748-3641 218 E
ladams@springfield.edu
ADAMS, Lynne, I .... 301-546-0500 201 D
adamsil@pgcc.edu
ADAMS, Michael .... 910-893-1686 327 C
adams@campbell.edu
ADAMS, Michael, J .... 888-777-7675 479 D
mjadams@faithiu.edu
ADAMS, Michelle .... 773-291-6211 135 B
madams@ccc.edu

AGGARWAL, Reena .... 202-687-3784.. 92 D
aggarwal@georgetown.edu

AGHA, Farooq .... 919-516-4129 339 G
fmagha@st-aug.edu

AGHAEI, Oxana .... 559-243-7511.. 66 G
oxana.aghaei@scccd.edu

AGHO, Austin, O ...... 757-683-3079 468 C
aagho@odu.edu

AGID, Shana .... 212-229-8950 307 E
agids@newschool.edu

AGIDIUS, Erin .... 208-885-4285 132 C
erina@uidaho.edu

AGINNIES, Dessalines .. 501-374-6305.. 21 B

AGJMURATI, Nick ...... 212-592-2002 314 I
nagjmurati@sva.edu

AGLAN, Heshmat .... 334-727-8355.... 7 D
aglan@tuskegee.edu

AGLER, Brian .... 937-327-6458 364 C
aglerb1@wittenberg.edu

AGLIETTI, Annette .... 954-322-1612.. 99 E

AGNE, Anissa .... 904-620-2698 111 A
anissa.agne@unf.edu

AGNER, Christy .... 828-227-3553 343 D
cagner@wcu.edu

AGNESE, Louis .... 512-444-8082 448 B
agnese@thsu.edu

AGNEW, Andrea .... 251-662-5363.... 1 E
aagnew@bishop.edu

AGNEW, Ina .... 918-293-4761 368 B
ina.agnew@okstate.edu

AGNEW, Maria .... 509-682-6659 484 H
magnew@wvc.edu

AGNEW, Melanie .... 801-832-2474 461 A
magnew@westminstercollege.edu

AGO, Emmanuel .... 718-862-7996 304 K
emmanuel.ago@manhattan.edu

AGOLLI, Aba .... 718-368-6725 294 C
aba.agolli@kbcc.cuny.edu

AGOONS, Akwai .... 678-466-4000 117 A
akwaiagoons@clayton.edu

AGOSTINI, Stephen .... 919-962-3795 342 B
steve.agostini@unc.edu

AGOSTO, Liz .... 413-542-2337 205 D
lagosto@amherst.edu

AGOURIS, Peggy .... 757-221-1693 465 B

AGOVINO, Vikki .... 970-247-7100.. 80 H
vmagovino@fortlewis.edu

AGRAS, James, R .... 412-359-1000 399 D
jagras@triangle-tech.edu

AGRAS, Rudy .... 512-359-1000 399 D
ragras@triangle-tech.edu

AGRAWAL, C. Mauli .... 816-235-1101 260 D
chancellor@umkc.edu

AGRELA, Ramona .... 949-824-5962.. 69 C
ragrela@uci.edu

AGRESTI, Aric .... 650-508-3652.. 54 G
aagresti@ndnu.edu

AGRON, David .... 626-617-0527 250 J
dagron@accreditation101.com

AGUADO WARE, Joan . 414-955-8227 492 F
jaguado@mcw.edu

AGUAYO, Mary .... 909-448-4970.. 71 C
maguayo@laverne.edu

AGUERO-TROTTER,
Dianne .... 973-761-9500 282 K
dianne.aguero-trotter@shu.edu

AGUIAR, Ara .... 818-719-6408.. 49 H

AGUILAR, Brittany .... 949-794-9090.. 66 C
baguilar@stanbridge.edu

AGUILAR, Carmen .... 401-865-2816 403 G
caguilar@providence.edu

AGUILAR, Catherine ..... 787-279-1912 506 L
caguilar@bayamon.inter.edu

AGUILAR, Elmer .... 559-925-3127.. 75 A
elmeraguilar@whccd.edu

AGUILAR, Gary .... 916-484-8354.. 50 J
aguilag@arc.losrios.edu

AGUILAR, Hugo, H .... 562-804-1239.. 45 C
hugoa@healthcarecareercollege.edu

AGUILAR, Jose, A .... 951-827-3878.. 70 B
jose.aguilar@ucr.edu

AGUILAR, Nathaly .... 408-864-8705.. 42 K
aguilarnathaly@fhda.edu

AGUILAR, Priscilla .... 210-486-3964 428 B
plopez136@alamo.edu

AGUILAR, Richard .... 559-934-2333.. 74 L
richardaguilariii@whccd.edu

AGUILAR-VILLARREAL,
Elizabeth .... 210-486-3711 428 B
eaguilar-villarr@alamo.edu

AGUILERA, Rafael .... 806-291-3451 457 B
aguilerar@wbu.edu

AGUILERA-GOERNER,
Carmen .... 915-831-7784 435 B
cagui205@epcc.edu

AGUILERA LAWRENSON,
Lisa .... 209-954-5018.. 61 H
lisa.lawrenson@deltacollege.edu

AGUINALDO, Nicole .. 408-741-2164.. 75 C
nicole.aguinaldo@missioncollege.edu

AGUIRRE, Ilvis .... 787-878-5475 506 J
iaguirre@arecibo.inter.edu

AGUIRRE, Juan Carlos . 956-872-6782 443 B
jcaguirre@southtexascollege.edu

AGUIRRE, Katherine ..... 631-451-4022 320 G
aguirrk@sunysuffolk.edu

AGUIRRE, Katherine ..... 631-451-4022 321 A
aguirrk@sunysuffolk.edu

AGUIRRE, Robert .... 540-568-7044 467 C
aguirrrd@jmu.edu

AGUIRRE, Tomas, A ...... 607-746-4440 320 A
aguirrta@delhi.edu

AGUIRRE, Vanessa .... 909-621-8026.. 37 E

AGUON, Alicia .... 671-735-2444 503 E
aliciaaguon@triton.uog.edu

AH MU, Lele, V .... 684-699-2722 503 A
leleahmu@ymail.com

AH YUN, Kimo .... 414-288-8033 492 E
james.ahyun@marquette.edu

AHA, Christian .... 856-225-6140 281 A
christian.aha@camden.rutgers.edu

AHAD, Badia, S .... 773-915-7478 142 G
bahad@luc.edu

AHDIEH, Robert, B .... 817-212-3838 446 B
dean@law.tamu.edu

AHEARN, Colleen .... 815-836-5475 142 C
cahearn@lewisu.edu

AHEARN, Mary Colleen 815-836-5471 142 C
cahearn@lewisu.edu

AHEDO, Valentina .... 608-246-6461 497 I
vahedo@madisoncollege.edu

AHERN, Catherine .... 585-785-1273 299 E
catherine.ahern@flcc.edu

AHERN, Joseph, F .... 845-758-7178 290 G
ahern@bard.edu

AHERN, Kathleen .... 718-390-3100 324 B

AHERN, Kathleen .... 203-285-2092.. 86 D
kahern@gatewayct.edu

AHERN, Martin .... 617-984-1635 217 G
mahern@quincycollege.edu

AHERN, Rob .... 614-236-7115 348 I
rahern@capital.edu

AHERON, Michelle .... 910-898-9610 336 A
aheronm@montgomery.edu

AHI, Sibel .... 610-568-1473 378 C
sibel.ahi@alvernia.edu

AHLBERG, Tim .... 630-617-3309 137 E
ahlbergt@elmhurst.edu

AHLEMANN, Tina .... 843-574-6142 411 I
tina.ahlemann@tridenttech.edu

AHLERSMEYER, Jordan . 847-735-6232 141 F
jahlersmeyer@lakeforest.edu

AHLFELDT,
Stephanie, L .... 218-299-3001 234 K
ahlfeldt@cord.edu

AHLQUIST, Judy .... 916-660-7602.. 64 B
jahlquist@sierracollege.edu

AHLQUIST, Lauren .... 717-477-1123 394 D
lrahliquist@ship.edu

AHLSCHWEDE, Karri . 402-465-2375 267 J
studenthealth@nebrwesleyan.edu

AHLUWALIA, Sanjam .. 928-523-8709.. 14 J
sanjam.ahluwalia@nau.edu

AHMAD, Catherine .... 609-497-7804 279 D

AHMAD, Rafeeque .... 718-793-2330 309 A

AHMAD, Shahzad .... 320-308-4287 240 C
shah@stcloudstate.edu

AHMAD-POST, Aisha .. 303-871-6200.. 84 C
aisha.ahmad-post@du.edu

AHMADI, Goodarz .... 315-268-6544 295 E
gahmadi@clarkson.edu

AHMED, Adil .... 510-466-7200.. 56 I

AHMED, Amel .... 413-545-4135 211 D
aahmed@umass.edu

AHMED, Amer, R .... 802-656-8426 462 D
amer.ahmed@uvm.edu

AHMED, Furquan .... 313-943-4000 232 B
fahmed1@wcccd.edu

AHMED, Furquan .... 313-496-2674 232 B
fahmed1@wccd.edu

AHMED, Haseeb .... 810-762-7969 225 F
hahmed@kettering.edu

AHMED, Juzar .... 812-465-7160 162 B
juzar@usi.edu

AHMED, Michael .... 904-632-3153 101 A
michael.ahmed@fscj.edu

AHMED, Monir .... 707-664-2310.. 34 C

AHMED, Sadia .... 505-747-5016 287 C
sadia.ahmed@nnmc.edu

AHMED, Shahid .... 215-392-2938 395 B

AHMED, Shariq .... 562-985-8115.. 32 A
shariq.ahmed@csulb.edu

AHMEDNA, Mohamed ... 336-285-4794 341 C
ahmedna@ncat.edu

AHMIDOUCH, Abdellah 336-334-7567 341 C
abdellah@ncat.edu

AHN, Anne .... 714-533-1495.. 64 G
anneahn@southbaylo.edu

AHN, David .... 718-270-5118 294 E
dahn@mec.cuny.edu

AHN, Diane .... 916-577-2200.. 76 C
dahn@jessup.edu

AHN, Hongjun .... 714-533-3946.. 34 D
finance@calums.edu

AHN, Hongjun .... 714-533-3946.. 34 D
registrar@calums.edu

AHN, Mary .... 508-856-3837 212 A
mary.ahn@umassmed.edu

AHNEN, Heath .... 608-822-2327 498 H
hahnen@swtc.edu

AHNER, Darryl, K .... 937-255-3636 501 A
darryl.ahner@afit.edu

AHOLA, Scott .... 605-642-6359 415 F
scott.ahola@bhsu.edu

AHORRIO, Beatriz .... 212-694-1000 291 F
bahorrio@boricuacollege.edu

AHRENS, Rebecca .... 417-873-7523 252 A
bahrens@drury.edu

AHRENS, Shanna .... 559-934-2160.. 74 K
shannaahrens@whccd.edu

AHUJA, Sima Saran .... 845-575-3000 305 C

AHUJA, Sunil .... 740-351-3472 360 E
sahuja@shawnee.edu

AIELLO, Frank .... 517-371-5140 232 K
aiellof@cooley.edu

AIELLO, Karen, M .... 973-655-4212 278 C
aiellok@montclair.edu

AIELLO, Megan .... 864-587-4008 411 F
aiellom@smcsc.edu

AIGOTTI, Claire .... 317-940-9900 153 H
caigotti@butler.edu

AIJIAN, Robin .... 253-879-3986 483 G
rbaijian@pugetsound.edu

AIKEN, Donn .... 518-464-8765 299 B
daiken@excelsior.edu

AIKEN, Irene .... 910-521-6271 343 A
irene.aiken@uncp.edu

AIKEN, Jane .... 336-758-5000 344 A

AIKEN, Ryan .... 413-775-1309 214 C
aikenr@gcc.mass.edu

AIKENS, Jane .... 641-472-1260 168 A
jaikens@miu.edu

AIKENS, Laura, M .... 616-331-6000 224 D
laura.aikens@gvsu.edu

AIKONS, Latisha .... 773-371-5470 134 C
laikons@ctu.edu

AILSTER, Felicia .... 770-962-7580 121 B
failster@gwinnetttech.edu

AILSTER, Felicia .... 404-297-9522 119 G

AILSTOCK, M. Stephen . 410-777-2230 197 C
smailstock@aacc.edu

AIME, Marty .... 225-214-1953 186 H
morton.aime@franu.edu

AIMONE, Chris .... 406-447-4445 262 E
caimone@carroll.edu

AINA, Wendy .... 678-916-2674 115 G
waina@johnmarshall.edu

AINBINDER, Meredith .. 617-824-8908 208 G
meredith_ainbinder@emerson.edu

AINBINDER,
Meredith, L .... 781-736-4205 207 D
mainbinder@brandeis.edu

AINLEY, Arden .... 360-416-7716 483 D
arden.ainley@skagit.edu

AINSLEIGH, Susan .... 413-565-1000 205 I
sainsleigh@baypath.edu

AINSLEY, Julie .... 540-365-2121 466 I

AINSLEY, Sharon .... 908-852-1400 275 H
sharon.ainsley@centenaryuniversity.edu

AINSLIE, Andrew .... 585-275-3316 323 E
andrew.ainslie@simon.rochester.edu

AINSWORTH, Emma, L . 662-685-4771 244 D
eainsworth@bmc.edu

AINSWORTH, Troy .... 928-428-8225.. 12 H
troy.ainsworth@eac.edu

AIONA, Barbara .... 712-749-2637 164 A
aionab@bvu.edu

AIRD, Bruce .... 757-683-3127 468 C
baird@odu.edu

AIRD, Jeffrey .... 801-957-4090 460 D
jeffrey.aird@slcc.edu

AIRD, Lashrecse, D .... 804-862-6100 469 E
laird@rbc.edu

AIREY, Jennifer, L .... 918-631-2000 371 C
jennifer-airey@utulsa.edu

AIRO, Robert .... 479-788-7188.. 22 A
robert.airo@uafs.edu

AIROZO, Paul .... 508-830-5051 213 A
pairozo@maritime.edu

AITKEN, Derek .... 510-885-3877.. 31 C
derek.aitken@csueastbay.edu

AITKEN, Meghan .... 973-290-4427 282 G
maitken@steu.edu

AITKEN, Renee .... 304-326-1109 486 I
renee.aitken@salemu.edu

AITSON-ROESSLER,
Mechelle .... 405-733-7308 369 D
maitson-roessler@rose.edu

AIVARS, Paul .... 269-294-4276 223 J
paivars@glenoaks.edu

AJAYI, Gloria .... 312-225-1700 139 B
gajayi@ico.edu

AJE, John .... 609-984-1130 283 D
jaje@tesu.edu

AJIBADE, Victoria .... 718-270-3058 316 E
victora.ajibade@downstate.edu

AJIBOYE, Oluwasayo .... 903-303-7853 441 E

AKAKPO, Koffi, C .... 859-246-6501 181 B
koffi.akakpo@kctcs.edu

AKASSI, Monique .... 304-336-8289 489 B
monique.akassi@westliberty.edu

AKAU, Sherri .... 808-932-7407 129 A
akau714@hawaii.edu

AKBARI, Hamid .... 262-547-1211 491 A
hakbari@carrollu.edu

AKCHIN, Lisa, G .... 410-455-2889 202 G
akchin@umbc.edu

AKENS, Cathy .... 336-334-5099 342 D
caakens@uncg.edu

AKERS, Adam .... 316-284-5261 171 I
akersa@bethelks.edu

AKERS, Brandy .... 800-686-1883 222 B
bakers@cleary.edu

AKERS, Cindy .... 806-742-2808 450 C
cindy.akers@ttu.edu

AKERS, Daniel .... 951-552-8579.. 27 J
dakers@calbaptist.edu

AKERS, Kathleen .... 931-472-3453 424 A
kathleen.akers@nscc.edu

AKERS, Kenneth .... 276-223-4118 475 B
kakers@wcc.vccs.edu

AKERS, Larry .... 850-973-9477 104 K
akersl@nfc.edu

AKERS, Mary Anne .... 909-869-2704.. 30 B

AKERS, Mary Anne .... 443-885-3225 200 F
maryanne.akers@morgan.edu

AKERS, Matthew, P .... 330-972-4933 361 G
akers1@uakron.edu

AKERS, Shanna .... 434-592-3618 467 E
sakers@liberty.edu

AKERS, Shawn, D .... 434-592-5451 467 E
sdakers@liberty.edu

AKERS, Tina .... 209-954-5039.. 61 H
tina.akers@deltacollege.edu

AKEY, Lynn .... 507-389-2419 238 L
lynn.akey@mnsu.edu

AKHTAR, Shama .... 410-337-6062 198 G
shama.akhtar@goucher.edu

AKHTAR, Sumaira .... 510-356-4760.. 77 E

AKIN, Christopher, L ..... 813-974-0898 111 B
cakin@usf.edu

AKIN, Daniel, L .... 919-761-2222 340 B
dakin@sebts.edu

AKIN, Jacob, J .... 507-933-7510 235 E
jakin@gustavus.edu

AKIN, Johnathan .... 615-966-6150 420 B
johnathan.akin@lipscomb.edu

AKIN, Paul .... 502-897-4043 184 D
pakin@sbts.edu

AKIN, Renea .... 270-534-3388 182 G
renea.akin@kctcs.edu

AKINCI, Fevzi .... 412-396-5303 382 E
akincif@duq.edu

AKINJIDE, Kofi .... 831-477-3548.. 27 E

AKINLEYE, Johnson, O . 919-530-6104 341 D
johnson.akinleye@nccu.edu

AKINOLA, Ayodele .... 775-673-7617 270 I
aakinola@tmcc.edu

ALEXANDER, Alicia 386-506-3650 98 A alicia.alexander@daytonastate.edu
ALEXANDER, Amber 217-773-4441 141 H aalexander@lakelandcollege.edu
ALEXANDER, Andrea 408-223-6796 62 F andrea.alexander@evc.edu
ALEXANDER, Beth, A 317-940-6378 153 H balexand@butler.edu
ALEXANDER, Bishop 256-765-4201 8 E jmalexander@una.edu
ALEXANDER, Bryant, K 310-338-7430 51 C bryantkeithalexander@lmu.edu
ALEXANDER, Candi 559-453-3448 43 D candi.alexander@fresno.edu
ALEXANDER, Carol 701-349-5776 346 G carolalexander@trinitybiblecollege.edu
ALEXANDER, Charlene, M 765-285-5558 153 E calexander@bsu.edu
ALEXANDER, Chaz 907-563-7575 9 E chaz.alexander@alaskacareercollege.edu
ALEXANDER, Chris, D 717-358-3912 383 G christine.alexander@fandm.edu
ALEXANDER, Dannie 269-488-4298 225 C dalexander@kvcc.edu
ALEXANDER, Debra 989-328-1276 227 G debraj@montcalm.edu
ALEXANDER, Desire 912-871-1801 123 F dalexander@ogeecheetech.edu
ALEXANDER, Donalyn 325-670-1198 439 A donalyn.alexander@phssn.edu
ALEXANDER, Donalyn 325-670-1198 436 B donalyn.alexander@hsutx.edu
ALEXANDER, Gary 617-731-3500 210 D
ALEXANDER, Gary 617-850-1294 210 D galexander@hchc.edu
ALEXANDER, Gary 617-850-1322 210 D galexander@hchc.edu
ALEXANDER, Ginny 904-646-2205 101 A ginny.alexander@fscj.edu
ALEXANDER, Herman 504-526-4745 190 C hermana@nationsu.edu
ALEXANDER, Jeffery 805-546-3138 41 A jeffery_alexander@cuesta.edu
ALEXANDER, Jeffrey 775-673-7090 270 I jalexander@tmcc.edu
ALEXANDER, Jennifer 352-588-8298 107 B jennifer.alexander@saintleo.edu
ALEXANDER, Jenny 414-288-7362 492 E jenny.alexander@marquette.edu
ALEXANDER, Jessica 734-487-6570 223 F jalexande1@emich.edu
ALEXANDER, Joyce, M 979-862-6649 446 B joycemalexander@tamu.edu
ALEXANDER, Juan, M 757-823-8396 468 B jmalexander@nsu.edu
ALEXANDER, Karen 434-832-7623 472 G alexanderk2@centralvirginia.edu
ALEXANDER, Katie 734-432-5837 226 G ksalexander@madonna.edu
ALEXANDER, Katy 317-738-8090 155 A kalexander@franklincollege.edu
ALEXANDER, Keith 928-428-8279 12 H keith.alexander@eac.edu
ALEXANDER, Kerri 504-520-7359 193 C kalexa12@xula.edu
ALEXANDER, Kevin 970-943-0120 85 B
ALEXANDER, Kevin, L 714-449-7450 51 D kalexander@ketchum.edu
ALEXANDER, Kimberly 845-758-7516 290 G kalexand@bard.edu
ALEXANDER, Klint 307-766-6416 500 H klint.alexander@uwyo.edu
ALEXANDER, Laurence, B 870-575-8535 22 F alexanderl@uapb.edu
ALEXANDER, Linda 913-782-3529 175 H lalexand@mnu.edu
ALEXANDER, Lisa 315-464-4700 316 F alexandl@upstate.edu
ALEXANDER, Lorraine 229-430-6624 114 G lalexander@albanytech.edu
ALEXANDER, Lynn, M 731-881-7490 426 E lalexand@utm.edu
ALEXANDER, Mark 610-519-7005 401 B alexander@law.villanova.edu
ALEXANDER, Mary 605-995-2656 414 A mary.alexander@dwu.edu
ALEXANDER, Matt 361-570-4823 452 C alexanderm@uhv.edu
ALEXANDER, Michael 805-678-5580 74 A malexander@vcccd.edu
ALEXANDER, Michael 920-465-2207 494 F alexandm@uwgb.edu
ALEXANDER, Michael, B 617-243-2221 210 G malexander@lasell.edu
ALEXANDER, Michelle 940-552-6291 456 F malexander@vernoncollege.edu
ALEXANDER, Missy 203-837-8400 86 A alexanderm@wcsu.edu
ALEXANDER, Nathan 501-374-6305 21 B nathan.alexander@shortercollege.edu
ALEXANDER, Paige, E 404-420-5100 118 D paige.eve.alexander@emory.edu
ALEXANDER, Paul 508-362-2131 214 B palexander@capecod.edu
ALEXANDER, Paul 701-349-5444 346 G paulalexander@trinitybiblecollege.edu
ALEXANDER, Paul, H 714-879-3901 45 J palexander@hiu.edu
ALEXANDER, Pearl 404-894-0300 119 D pearl.alexander@ohr.gatech.edu
ALEXANDER, Rebecca 770-962-7580 121 B ralexander@gwinnetttech.edu
ALEXANDER, Ricky 785-227-3380 171 H alexanderrd@bethanylb.edu
ALEXANDER, Ross, C 256-765-5950 8 E ralexander3@una.edu
ALEXANDER, Sanquita 334-291-4996 1 H sanquita.alexander@cv.edu
ALEXANDER, Scott 207-786-6000 193 D salexan2@bates.edu
ALEXANDER, Seth 617-253-4900 215 G
ALEXANDER, State, W 704-216-6067 330 D salexan@livingstone.edu
ALEXANDER, Stephanie 740-245-7366 363 A alexandr@rio.edu
ALEXANDER, Taylor 606-326-2432 180 I
ALEXANDER, Thomas 978-542-6000 213 B thomas.alexander@salemstate.edu
ALEXANDER, Tim 205-665-6155 8 D talexand@montevallo.edu
ALEXANDER, Trevor 210-829-3130 452 D alexande@uiwtx.edu
ALEXANDER, Tyson 325-674-2878 427 G tma08a@acu.edu
ALEXANDER, Whitney 605-331-6793 416 C whitney.alexander@usiouxfalls.edu
ALEXANDER-HERRIOTT, Vicki 641-472-1161 168 A dof@miu.edu
ALEXANDER-HUNT, Shirley 617-521-2000 218 C
ALEXANDER-WALLACE, Linda 718-518-4432 293 F lalexander@hostos.cuny.edu
ALEXIS, Christina 404-527-7767 121 I calexis@itc.edu
ALEXIS STEPHENS, Grace 312-922-1884 143 D chancellor@maccormac.edu
ALEXO, JR., Kenneth 973-596-8293 278 G kenneth.alexo@njit.edu
ALEXO, Michael 302-831-2129 91 A malexo@udel.edu
ALEY, Danielle 828-395-1633 335 B daley@isothermal.edu
ALFANO, Anthony 610-519-7730 401 B anthony.alfano@villanova.edu
ALFANO, Michael 203-365-7621 88 H alfanom3@sacredheart.edu
ALFANO, Renee, M 608-243-4539 497 I ralfano@madisoncollege.edu
ALFANO, Tara 914-594-2726 308 J tara_alfano@nymc.edu
ALFARO, Carolina 209-667-3982 33 D calfaro@csustan.edu
ALFARO, Christina 619-594-1354 33 E calfaro@sdsu.edu
ALFARO, Richard 408-855-5145 75 C richard.alfaro@missioncollege.edu
ALFERNESS, Rod 805-893-3141 70 E alferness@engineering.ucsb.edu
ALFIE, Dario 305-642-4104 106 D
ALFIE, Rebeca 305-642-4104 106 D
ALFONSO, Antonio 360-867-6238 479 C alfonsoa@evergreen.edu
ALFONSO, Daniel 954-262-8835 104 M djalfonso@nova.edu
ALFONSO, Gena 719-549-2687 79 G gena.alfonso@csupueblo.edu
ALFORD, Andrew 601-276-3704 248 D aalford@smcc.edu
ALFORD, Brian 212-678-8195 321 H ba2361@tc.columbia.edu
ALFORD, Cynthia 336-838-6111 338 H clalford287@wilkescc.edu
ALFORD, Elise 208-426-1417 130 F elisealford@boisestate.edu
ALFORD, Keith 315-443-4110 321 D kalford@syr.edu
ALFORD, Keith, A 716-645-1267 315 F sw-dean@buffalo.edu
ALFORD, Keyimani 608-246-6320 497 I klalford@madisoncollege.edu
ALFORD, Michael 850-644-1079 110 B ad@athletics.fsu.edu
ALFORD, Rodney 256-890-4733 1 F rodney.alford@calhoun.edu
ALFORD, Sara 972-899-8414 439 I salford@nctc.edu
ALFORD, Stephanie 410-337-6431 198 G stephanie.alford@goucher.edu
ALFORQUE, Patrick 312-341-2277 148 A palforque@roosevelt.edu
ALFRED, Reina 718-270-2611 316 E reina.alfred@downstate.edu
ALFRED, Tangelia 323-241-5333 49 I alfredtm@lasc.edu
ALFULTIS, Michael, A 718-409-7271 320 D
ALGARIN, Richard, J 845-569-3598 307 B richard.algarin@msmc.edu
ALGATE, Jill 800-280-0307 153 B jill.algate@ace.edu
ALGER, Jalissa 864-941-8364 410 D alger.j@ptc.edu
ALGER, Jonathan, R 540-568-6868 467 C president@jmu.edu
ALGIER, Anne-Marie 585-275-4085 323 E anne-marie.algier@rochester.edu
ALGOE, Eric 512-245-2244 449 G e_a231@txstate.edu
ALI, Adel 320-308-3110 240 C alali@stcloudstate.edu
ALI, Amjad 412-397-6461 396 E alia@rmu.edu
ALI, Asim 334-844-8728 4 E aliasim@auburn.edu
ALI, Cheryl 609-497-7757 279 D cheryl.ali@ptsem.edu
ALI, Ibrahim 310-900-1600 39 H
ALI, Jamal 256-372-8344 1 A jamal.ali@aamu.edu
ALI, Jamal 256-372-5230 1 A jamal.ali@aamu.edu
ALI, Khaliff 386-267-0565 97 R director@daytonacollege.edu
ALI, Mahmood 641-472-1126 168 A housing@miu.edu
ALI, Mansoor 401-225-2321 200 B mali01@mica.edu
ALI, Mehmed 334-953-4827 501 B
ALI, Mohammad 937-376-6191 349 H mali@centralstate.edu
ALI, Neena 571-553-3601 92 C neena20147@gwu.edu
ALI, Omar 336-334-5538 342 D ohali@uncg.edu
ALI, Radman 803-934-3284 409 H rali@morris.edu
ALI, Yasmin 718-951-5000 293 A yali@brooklyn.cuny.edu
ALI, Yasmin 425-235-5728 482 C yali@rtc.edu
ALIBERTI, Fred 518-629-7210 302 A f.aliberti@hvcc.edu
ALICANDRO, Jean 860-832-1664 85 F alicandro@ccsu.edu
ALICEA, Cristen 210-805-1238 452 D gimenez@uiwtx.edu
ALICEA, Edwin 787-725-8120 505 J ealicea@eap.edu
ALICEA, Robert 410-225-2398 200 B ralicea@mica.edu
ALICEA, Victor, G 212-694-1000 291 F valicea@boricuacollege.edu
ALICEA-CASTILLO, Jennifer 787-250-0000 510 B jennifer.alicea@upr.edu
ALICEA-MALDONADO, Rafael 585-345-6820 300 D ralicea-maldonado@genesee.edu
ALICES, Krystal 252-399-6543 326 H kralices@barton.edu
ALIMBOYOGUEN, Maribel 847-376-7053 146 E malimboyoguen@oakton.edu
ALIMO, Craig 707-256-7000 53 E
ALINDER, Jasmine 831-459-2696 71 A humanities@ucsc.edu
ALIOTO, Keri 414-930-3525 493 E aliotok@mtmary.edu
ALIOTTA, Jackie 717-871-4636 394 B
ALIPOE, Dovi 601-877-6543 244 B alipoe@alcorn.edu
ALIVISATOS, Paul 773-702-8001 151 B
ALIX, Jeff 419-289-5093 347 H jalix@ashland.edu
ALJOE, Jaria 203-576-4183 89 A jaljoe@bridgeport.edu
ALKIRE, Amy 612-330-1188 233 G alkirea@augsburg.edu
ALL, Jessica 803-812-7398 412 E allj@mailbox.sc.edu
ALLAHBACHAYO, Salima 626-852-6439 37 B sallahbachayo@citruscollege.edu
ALLAIN, Ashlynn, R 508-929-8000 213 D aallain3@worcester.edu
ALLAIN, Kimberly 909-869-5152 30 B kgallain@cpp.edu
ALLAIRE, Aaron 209-667-3016 33 D aallaire@csustan.edu
ALLAIRE, André 212-229-5662 307 E allairea@newschool.edu
ALLAMON, Jeremy 254-298-8692 445 B jeremy.allamon@templejc.edu
ALLAMON, Susan 254-298-8452 445 B susan.allamon@templejc.edu
ALLAN, Kevin 845-451-1460 297 E kevin.allan@culinary.edu
ALLAN, Lee 215-641-6300 390 A lallan@mc3.edu
ALLAR, Holly 909-537-3680 33 B holly.allar@csusb.edu
ALLARD, Dei 662-325-3555 247 A da1112@msstate.edu
ALLARD, Ingrid, M 518-262-5919 289 C allardi@amc.edu
ALLARD, Lee 716-566-7879 297 F lallard@daemen.edu
ALLARD, Lee 719-587-7631 77 F lallard@adams.edu
ALLARD, Monique 213-740-2421 73 C msallard@usc.edu
ALLBRITTEN, Jeffery 239-489-9211 100 G president@fsw.edu
ALLBRITTON, Nancy 206-543-1829 484 A nlallbr@uw.edu
ALLCOCK, Melissa 270-534-3090 182 G melissa.allcock@kctcs.edu
ALLCORN, Terry, A 417-268-6003 250 A tallcorn@gobbc.edu
ALLCORN, Terry, L 606-474-3258 180 G tallcorn@kcu.edu
ALLDAY, Jack 972-780-3600 453 C jack.allday@untdallas.edu
ALLDREDGE, Brian 415-514-0421 70 D brian.alldredge@ucsf.edu
ALLDREDGE, Kari 865-974-1350 426 C kalldre1@utk.edu
ALLEE, Amanda 719-255-3838 84 A aallee@uccs.edu
ALLEE, Kelly 217-234-5215 141 H kallee@lakelandcollege.edu
ALLEE, Rodney 317-632-5553 158 V rallee@lincolntech.edu
ALLEGRETTO, Stephen, A 203-582-7962 88 F stephen.allegretto@quinnipiac.edu
ALLEMAN, Michael 337-550-1308 189 B malleman@lsue.edu
ALLEMAN-BEYERS, Natalie 913-468-8500 174 F nalleman@jccc.edu
ALLEN, Alex 812-237-2584 155 H alex.allen@indstate.edu
ALLEN, Amanda 979-532-6468 457 H allena@wcjc.edu
ALLEN, Amy 559-278-6034 31 D aallen@mail.fresnostate.edu
ALLEN, Andre 309-671-2779 143 I aallen@methdistcol.edu
ALLEN, Andrew 619-260-4816 72 H andrewt@sandiego.edu
ALLEN, Angela 806-651-8482 447 D aallen@wtamu.edu

ALLMOND, Tim .... 229-468-2241 127 F timothy.allmond@wiregrass.edu
ALLRED, Barry .... 801-422-8386 458 A barry_allred@byu.edu
ALLRED, Ben .... 913-722-0272 174 G
ALLRED, John .... 605-642-6599 415 F john.allred@bhsu.edu
ALLSUP, Laura .... 251-380-3865.... 6 H lallsup@shc.edu
ALLTOP, Jeremy .... 859-572-5207 184 B alltopj1@nku.edu
ALLUP, Dahly .... 910-221-2224 330 G dallup@manna.edu
ALLVIN, Paul .... 703-993-1000 466 J
ALLWOOD, Steven .... 470-639-0231 122 H steven.allwood@morehouse.edu
ALM, Deborah .... 413-748-3216 218 E dalm@springfield.edu
ALM, Maria .... 715-232-2687 496 C almm@uwstout.edu
ALMAN, Shelly .... 704-922-6406 334 E alman.shelly@gaston.edu
ALMANDREZ, Mary Grace .... 401-874-7077 404 E mgalmandrez@uri.edu
ALMANZA, Manny .... 903-983-8623 437 G malmanza@kilgore.edu
ALMANZAR, Karoline .... 909-469-5318.. 75 G kalmanzar@westernu.edu
ALMAROAD, Megan .... 423-279-7630 424 B mlalmaroad@northeaststate.edu
ALMASI-BUSH, Ann .... 843-805-5507 407 D
ALMEDA, Delilah .... 305-237-2951 104 E dalmeda1@mdc.edu
ALMEIDA, Mark .... 510-885-4376.. 31 C mark.almeida@csueastbay.edu
ALMEIDA, Paul, A .... 202-687-3883.. 92 D almeidap@georgetown.edu
ALMLI, Jennifer .... 406-377-9410 262 G jalmli@dawson.edu
ALMOAYYED, Jasmine .... 319-398-5525 167 H jasmine.almoayyed@kirkwood.edu
ALMODOVAR, Luis .... 787-856-0845 505 B lalmodovar@columbiacentral.edu
ALMON, Robert, C .... 212-346-1200 310 F ralmon@pace.edu
ALMOND, Jackie .... 434-544-8457 470 K almond.j@lynchburg.edu
ALMOND, James, S .... 765-494-9706 159 G jsalmond@purdue.edu
ALMONTE, Loreto .... 305-821-3333 100 C lalmonte@fnu.edu
ALMORADIE, Joel .... 718-522-9073 290 B jalmoradie@asa.edu
ALMQUIST, Brian .... 843-574-6011 411 I brian.almquist@tridenttech.edu
ALMQUIST, Cathy .... 843-574-6057 411 I cathy.almquist@tridenttech.edu
ALMQUIST, Jennifer .... 970-351-1890.. 84 D
ALMUSAWI, Marwa .... 253-833-9111 480 A malmusawi@greenriver.edu
ALMY, Marilynn .... 912-525-5000 124 G malmy@scad.edu
ALNAJJAR, Hisham .... 860-768-4846.. 89 E alnajjar@hartford.edu
ALNUTT, Mark, M .... 716-645-6811 315 F ub-athleticdirector@buffalo.edu
ALO, Richard .... 850-412-5978 109 E richard.alo@famu.edu
ALOISIO, Simone .... 707-826-5086.. 30 A simone.aloisio@humboldt.edu
ALONSO, Carlos, J .... 212-854-6935 296 H ca2201@columbia.edu
ALONSO, Jose .... 787-738-2161 511 A jose.alonso@upr.edu
ALONSO, Zoraida .... 787-780-0070 504 E zalonso@caribbean.edu
ALONZO, Joseph .... 714-628-5040.. 58 G alonzo_joseph@sccollege.edu
ALONZO, Liza .... 713-221-8682 452 B alonzol@uhd.edu
ALONZO, Mia .... 909-607-9192.. 37 E mia.alonzo@claremont.edu
ALOYO, JR., Victor .... 609-688-1941 279 D victor.aloyo@ptsem.edu
ALP, Nesli .... 812-237-3166 155 H nesli.alp@indstate.edu
ALP, Nesli .... 570-320-2400 392 S nesli.alp@pct.edu
ALPAY, Pamir .... 860-486-6917.. 89 B pamir.alpay@uconn.edu
ALPERN, Robert, J .... 203-785-4672.. 90 B robert.alpern@yale.edu
ALPI, Kristine .... 503-494-0455 374 F alpi@ohsu.edu
ALPIN, Jolie .... 760-366-5210.. 40 K jalpin@cmccd.edu
ALREFAE, Omar .... 660-831-4000 256 B
ALSHEIMER, Michael .... 315-792-7210 320 F michael.alsheimer@sunypoly.edu
ALSING, Melissa .... 724-830-1850 397 F malsing@setonhill.edu
ALSOBROOKS, Scott .... 662-476-5060 245 C salsobrooks@eastms.edu
ALSOP, Rob .... 304-293-5841 489 E rob.alsop@mail.wvu.edu
ALSOP, Robert .... 641-585-8130 170 E alsopb@waldorf.edu
ALSPACH, Charlene .... 509-359-2479 478 H calspach@ewu.edu
ALSTER, Samuel .... 732-765-9126 284 E ygocb@yeshivanet.com
ALSTER, Shimon .... 732-765-9126 284 E ygocb@yeshivanet.com
ALSTON, Alvin, S .... 803-934-6613 409 H aalston@morris.edu
ALSTON, Cathy .... 253-833-9111 480 A calston@greenriver.edu
ALSTON, Dawn .... 404-270-5077 126 A dalston@spelman.edu
ALSTON, Ellen .... 501-450-1263.. 19 I alston@hendrix.edu
ALSTON, Kay .... 270-789-5360 179 G klalston@campbellsville.edu
ALSTON, Kenyon .... 205-366-8980.... 7 A kalston@stillman.edu
ALSTON, Micah, N .... 714-879-3901.. 45 J mnalston@hiu.edu
ALSTON, Shana .... 303-871-2246.. 84 C shana.alston@du.edu
ALSTON, Sharon .... 202-885-6053.. 91 D salston@american.edu
ALSTON, Susan .... 860-512-2903.. 86 F salston@manchestercc.edu
ALSTON, Vickie .... 479-979-1303.. 24 A valston@ozarks.edu
ALSTON FORBES, Lakesha .... 252-328-6804 340 H alstonl@ecu.edu
ALSUP, Margaret .... 870-307-7474.. 20 D margaret.alsup@lyon.edu
ALT, Susan .... 406-994-3344 263 G salt@montana.edu
ALT, Tamara .... 319-398-4509 167 H tamara.alt@kirkwood.edu
ALTAMIRANO, Carlos .... 787-743-3038 508 L caltamirano@sanjuanbautista.edu
ALTAMIRANO, Rodolfo, R .... 215-573-6332 399 J rudiea@pobox.upenn.edu
ALTARRIBA, Jeanette .... 518-442-5004 315 D jaltarriba@albany.edu
ALTAYLI, Benek .... 719-255-3257.. 84 A zaltayli@uccs.edu
ALTEGOER, Diana, B .... 215-898-8493 399 J altegoer@upenn.edu
ALTEMOSE, Jane .... 610-758-4637 388 C jca209@lehigh.edu
ALTENBURG, Danielle .... 802-865-8473 461 C daltenburg@champlain.edu
ALTENBURG, Rana .... 414-288-7430 492 E rana.altenburg@marquette.edu
ALTERIO, Christopher .... 315-279-5483 303 D calterio1@keuka.edu
ALTHAUS, Lindsay .... 336-217-7221 329 B lindsay.althaus@greensboro.edu
ALTIC, Scott .... 402-557-7355 265 A saltic@bellevue.edu
ALTIER, Jeffrey, P .... 386-822-8100 111 F jaltier@stetson.edu
ALTIER, Matthew .... 504-568-3712 189 C matthewaltier@lsuhsc.edu
ALTIERE, Ralph .... 303-724-2887.. 84 B ralph.altiere@ucdenver.edu
ALTIERI, Anthony .... 561-237-7275 103 W aaltieri@lynn.edu
ALTIERI, Yeidi .... 787-815-0000 510 D yeidi.altieri@upr.edu
ALTIZER, Sonia .... 706-542-9251 126 F saltizer@uga.edu
ALTMAN, Carolyn .... 912-486-1149 120 A caltman@georgiasouthern.edu
ALTMAN, Don .... 480-219-6008 249 C daltman@atsu.edu
ALTMAN, J.J .... 912-871-1648 123 F jaltman@ogeecheetech.edu
ALTMAN, Joanne, D .... 336-841-9613 329 E jaltman0@highpoint.edu
ALTMAN, Kip .... 864-488-4012 409 C caltman@limestone.edu
ALTMAN, Miranda .... 410-778-7261 204 E maltman2@washcoll.edu
ALTMAN, Stacey .... 252-328-2973 340 H altmans@ecu.edu
ALTMAN-COSGROVE, Megan .... 716-286-8314 309 F mcosgrove@niagara.edu
ALTMANN, Barbara, K .... 717-358-3971 383 G president@fandm.edu
ALTMAYER, Magnus .... 360-442-2372 480 E maltmayer@lowercolumbia.edu
ALTOBELLO, Maria, R .... 617-322-3505 210 F maria_altobello@laboure.edu
ALTONGY-MAGEE, Kristy .... 508-373-5726 216 B kristy.altongy-magee@mcphs.edu
ALTOUNIAN, David .... 401-341-2163 404 D david.altounian@salve.edu
ALTSHULER, Gina .... 215-335-0800 388 E galtshuler@lincolntech.edu
ALTUSKY, Shlomo Avidgor .... 718-868-2300 290 J
ALTVATER, Fran .... 860-768-4055.. 89 E altvater@hartford.edu
ALTWINE, Chad .... 605-668-1502 414 F chad.altwine@mountmarty.edu
ALVA, Sylvia, A .... 562-951-4710.. 29 J salva@calstate.edu
ALVALLE, Anibal .... 787-764-0000 511 F anibal.alvalle@upr.edu
ALVARADO, Christian .... 949-582-4340.. 65 C calvarado@saddleback.edu
ALVARADO, George .... 559-443-8627.. 67 A george.alvarado@fresnocitycollege.edu
ALVARADO, Jose Luis .... 212-636-6470 300 A alvarado@fordham.edu
ALVARADO, Miguel .... 617-422-7423 217 B malvarado@nesl.edu
ALVARADO, Nelly .... 310-900-1600.. 39 H nalvarado@compton.edu
ALVARADO, Norman .... 718-779-1430 310 I nalvarado@plazacollege.edu
ALVARADO-TORRES, Cesar .... 787-751-1912 507 F calvarado@juris.inter.edu
ALVARADO-TORRES, Cesar, A .... 787-751-1912 507 F calvarado@juris.inter.edu
ALVARADO-VALDOVINOS, Lorena .... 509-574-4702 485 E lalvarado-valdovinos@yvcc.edu
ALVAREZ, Alex .... 323-466-6663.. 44 A
ALVAREZ, Alvin .... 415-338-6480.. 34 A aalvarez@sfsu.edu
ALVAREZ, Amanda .... 213-207-6884.. 67 I amandaalvarez@toa.edu
ALVAREZ, Ana .... 305-284-3584 112 K aalvarez@miami.edu
ALVAREZ, Arlene .... 909-558-4567.. 48 J sm8026@bncollege.com
ALVAREZ, Brian .... 516-364-0808 308 C balvarez@nycollege.edu
ALVAREZ, Celso .... 718-429-6600 323 I celso.alvarez@vaughn.edu
ALVAREZ, Cristina .... 909-537-5669.. 33 B cristina.alvarez@csusb.edu
ALVAREZ, Eduardo .... 352-371-2833.. 98 D academicdean@dragonrises.edu
ALVAREZ, Emiyaril .... 717-871-5100 394 B emiyaril.alvarez@millersville.edu
ALVAREZ, Frank, D .... 509-452-5100 481 E falvarez@pnwu.edu
ALVAREZ, Ivonne .... 619-388-2689.. 61 A ialvarez@sdccd.edu
ALVAREZ, Jacqueline .... 787-763-5845 506 H jalvarez@inter.edu
ALVAREZ, Jim .... 574-535-7557 155 B alvarez@goshen.edu
ALVAREZ, Jon .... 617-253-1727 215 G
ALVAREZ, Kristina .... 414-847-3271 493 C kristinaalvarez@miad.edu
ALVAREZ, Linda .... 507-389-2986 238 L linda.alvarez@mnsu.edu
ALVAREZ, Lourdes .... 210-431-4187 440 D lalvarez@ollusa.edu
ALVAREZ, Lucy .... 408-846-4964.. 43 H lalvarez@gavilan.edu
ALVAREZ, Margie .... 787-738-2161 511 A margie.alvarez@upr.edu
ALVAREZ, Maria .... 787-882-2065 508 N malvarez@unitecpr.edu
ALVAREZ, Maria, L .... 305-899-3085.. 96 A malvarez@barry.edu
ALVAREZ, Patricia .... 787-766-1912 506 H palvarez@inter.edu
ALVAREZ, Rebecca .... 408-741-2072.. 75 C rebecca.alvarez@westvalley.edu
ALVAREZ, Rebecca .... 408-741-2072.. 75 B rebecca.alvarez@wvm.edu
ALVAREZ, René .... 408-288-3115.. 62 G rene.alvarez@sjcc.edu
ALVAREZ, Rory .... 503-399-2594 372 A rory.alvarez@chemeketa.edu
ALVAREZ, Ruby .... 407-582-1548 113 C ralvarez15@valenciacollege.edu
ALVAREZ, Timothy .... 719-384-6871.. 82 C timothy.alvarez@otero.edu
ALVAREZ-ORTIZ, Genette .... 516-572-7664 307 C genette.ortiz@ncc.edu
ALVAREZ-ROBINSON, Sonia .... 404-385-3306 119 D sonia@consulting.gatech.edu
ALVARO, Eusebio .... 520-360-3599.. 37 F eusebio.alvaro@cgu.edu
ALVERSON, Amelia, J .... 212-851-7929 296 H amelia.alverson@columbia.edu
ALVES, Catherine .... 212-393-6329 294 B calves@jjay.cuny.edu
ALVES, Daniel .... 203-672-6654.. 85 C dalves@albertus.edu
ALVES, Eddie .... 541-881-5590 376 E ealves@tvcc.cc
ALVES, Melisa .... 508-929-8965 213 D malves2@worcester.edu
ALVIN, Glenda .... 615-963-5000 425 A
ALVIS, Robert .... 812-357-6543 160 G ralvis@saintmeinrad.edu
ALVITI, Eileen .... 617-747-2375 206 D hroperations@berklee.edu
ALVOET, Patricia, E .... 210-297-9630 430 A
ALWANI, Ahmed .... 703-591-7042 466 G aalwani@fxua.edu
ALWAY, Tom .... 231-843-5967 232 I talway@westshore.edu
ALYAN, Nafez .... 906-635-2831 226 C nalyan@lssu.edu
AMACK, April .... 970-542-3187.. 81 M april.amack@morgancc.edu
AMADI, Emmanual .... 662-254-3363 247 C amadi@mvsu.edu
AMADOR, Lui .... 562-860-2451.. 35 O lamador@cerritos.edu
AMADOR, Steve .... 209-588-5142.. 76 J amadors@yosemite.edu
AMADOR, Tristen .... 303-458-4174.. 83 B tamador@regis.edu
AMADOR DUMOIS, Maria .... 787-833-8918 511 C decano.adem@upr.edu
AMALFITANO, Andrea .... 517-355-9616 227 C amalfit1@msu.edu
AMAN, Edward .... 864-231-2000 405 F eaman@andersonuniversity.edu
AMAN, Rick .... 208-535-5366 130 I rick.aman@cei.edu
AMANO, Kyoko .... 361-570-4200 452 C amanok@uhv.edu
AMAR, Angela .... 702-895-3360 270 J angela.amar@unlv.edu
AMAR, Salomon .... 914-594-4900 308 J
AMAR, Salomon .... 914-594-3036 322 B salomon_amar@nymc.edu
AMAR, Salomon .... 914-594-3036 322 C salomon_amar@nymc.edu
AMAR, Vikram .... 217-333-0931 151 F amar@illinois.edu
AMARA, Sakpa, S .... 703-891-1787 470 G samara@standardcollege.edu
AMARI, Jonathan .... 781-768-7019 217 H
AMARO, Marco .... 773-878-8756 148 F
AMAROK, Barbara .... 907-443-8402.. 10 B bjamarok@alaska.edu
AMARONE, Ben .... 203-787-8635.. 85 C bamarone@albertus.edu
AMASON, Allen .... 912-478-2622 120 A aamason@georgiasouthern.edu
AMATO, Christina .... 937-512-3703 360 F christina.amato@sinclair.edu
AMATO, John .... 515-271-2849 165 F john.amato@drake.edu

ANDERSON, Carla .... 310-506-4149.. 56 H
carla.anderson@pepperdine.edu
ANDERSON, Cary, M .... 610-660-1045 397 A
cander01@sju.edu
ANDERSON, Casey .... 610-957-6037 398 B
canders4@swarthmore.edu
ANDERSON, Cathy .... 315-445-4300 303 F
anderscr@lemoyne.edu
ANDERSON, Cathy .... 801-581-6940 459 D
cathy.anderson@utah.edu
ANDERSON, Chanda ...... 509-452-5100 481 E
cmanderson@pnwu.edu
ANDERSON, Charlise .... 615-963-5000 425 A
ANDERSON, Cheryl .... 503-517-1206 377 B
clanderson@warnerpacific.edu
ANDERSON, Chris .... 507-537-6272 240 G
chris.anderson@smsu.edu
ANDERSON, Chris .... 704-527-9909 209 G
canderson3@gordonconwell.edu
ANDERSON, Chris .... 704-527-9909 209 G
canderson3@gcts.edu
ANDERSON, Christine ... 801-333-8100 458 E
ANDERSON, Christine ... 801-818-8900 458 M
christine.anderson@provocollege.edu
ANDERSON, Cindy, L ... 304-558-4016 488 I
cindy.anderson@wvhepc.edu
ANDERSON, Clayton ..... 801-626-6465 460 B
canderson@weber.edu
ANDERSON, Cliff .... 763-433-1100 236 H
clifford.anderson@anokaramsey.edu
ANDERSON, Clifford ..... 763-433-1100 237 A
clifford.anderson@anokaramsey.edu
ANDERSON, Corey .... 701-845-7216 345 E
corey.anderson@vcsu.edu
ANDERSON, Corey .... 541-684-7354 371 H
canderson@bushnell.edu
ANDERSON, Cynthia ..... 708-974-5347 144 G
anderson@morainevalley.edu
ANDERSON, Cynthia ..... 605-642-6341 415 F
cynthia.anderson@bhsu.edu
ANDERSON, Daisy .... 717-796-1800 389 F
anderson@messiah.edu
ANDERSON, Dan .... 336-278-2000 328 H
andersd@elon.edu
ANDERSON, Daniel, G .. 541-278-5743 371 G
daanderson@bluecc.edu
ANDERSON, Daniel, L .. 304-877-6428 486 A
president@abc.edu
ANDERSON, Danielle .... 989-328-1217 227 G
daniellea@montcalm.edu
ANDERSON, Danny .... 210-999-8401 451 B
tupresident@trinity.edu
ANDERSON, Daphne ..... 312-949-7000 139 B
danderson@ico.edu
ANDERSON, Darrel .... 913-971-3294 175 H
dwanderson@mnu.edu
ANDERSON, Daryl .... 718-779-1430 310 I
danderson1@mail.plazacollege.edu
ANDERSON, Dave .... 877-476-8674 435 G
ANDERSON, David .... 903-586-2518 437 D
ANDERSON, David .... 616-234-3638 224 C
danderso@grcc.edu
ANDERSON, David .... 423-775-6596 421 I
ANDERSON, David, R ... 507-786-3000 242 I
anderson@stolaf.edu
ANDERSON, DaVida ...... 410-386-8217 197 G
danderson3@carrollcc.edu
ANDERSON, Deanna ..... 601-266-5020 248 H
deedee.anderson@usm.edu
ANDERSON, Deb .... 508-541-1940 208 E
danderson@dean.edu
ANDERSON, Delia, C .... 617-732-2910 216 B
delia.anderson@mcphs.edu
ANDERSON, Dennis ...... 731-286-3292 423 E
danderson@dscc.edu
ANDERSON, Diane, K ... 269-387-2152 232 J
diane.anderson@wmich.edu
ANDERSON, Diann .... 256-372-8094.... 1 A
diann.anderson@aamu.edu
ANDERSON, Donald ...... 785-242-5200 176 F
donald.anderson@ottawa.edu
ANDERSON, Donna .... 406-243-2212 263 D
donna.anderson@umontana.edu
ANDERSON, Dorothy .... 505-277-5824 288 C
unmvphr@unm.edu
ANDERSON, Dorothy .... 405-325-0311 370 J
ANDERSON, Doug .... 208-769-3300 132 A
ANDERSON,
Douglas, D .... 435-797-2376 459 F
douglas.anderson@usu.edu
ANDERSON, Duane .... 509-527-2205 484 C
duane.anderson@wallawalla.edu

ANDERSON, Elizabeth ... 706-295-6846 119 F
eanderson@gntc.edu
ANDERSON, Elizabeth ... 609-586-4800 277 H
andersoe@mccc.edu
ANDERSON, Emily .... 575-439-3806 286 H
emilyt@nmsu.edu
ANDERSON, Eric .... 712-707-7132 169 A
eric.anderson@nwciowa.edu
ANDERSON, Eric .... 715-855-7512 497 E
eanderson72@cvtc.edu
ANDERSON, Eric, R ...... 614-236-6606 348 I
eanderson@capital.edu
ANDERSON, Erin .... 575-492-2676 286 E
eanderson@nmjc.edu
ANDERSON, Eugene ..... 315-443-9601 321 D
genea@syr.edu
ANDERSON, Francis ..... 314-367-8700 260 A
francis.anderson@uhsp.edu
ANDERSON,
Garwood, P .... 262-646-6500 493 F
ganderson@nashotah.edu
ANDERSON,
Garwood, P .... 262-646-6523 493 F
ganderson@nashotah.edu
ANDERSON, Gary .... 601-977-6177 248 E
ganderson@tougaloo.edu
ANDERSON, Gary, C ..... 612-624-3908 242 K
ander018@umn.edu
ANDERSON, Glenn .... 318-342-1600 193 A
ganderson@ulm.edu
ANDERSON, Grace .... 208-792-2465 131 F
glanderson@lcsc.edu
ANDERSON, Gregory .... 951-222-8804.. 59 D
ANDERSON, Gregory .... 601-979-2144 245 G
gregory.l.anderson@jsums.edu
ANDERSON, Gregory, R 817-735-7600 453 D
gregory.anderson@unthsc.edu
ANDERSON, Harry .... 715-394-8241 496 D
handerso@uwsuper.edu
ANDERSON, Heidi, M .... 410-651-6101 203 B
hmanderson@umes.edu
ANDERSON, Holly .... 541-885-1389 374 G
holly.anderson@oit.edu
ANDERSON, JR.,
Horace, E .... 914-422-4407 310 F
ANDERSON, Ian .... 207-699-5033 194 G
ianderson@meca.edu
ANDERSON, Izzy .... 713-718-8570 436 E
izzy.anderson@hccs.edu
ANDERSON, Jacqui .... 620-343-4600 173 D
janderson@fhtc.edu
ANDERSON, James .... 508-999-8042 211 F
jim.anderson@umassd.edu
ANDERSON, James, A .. 719-333-2074 502 C
james.anderson@afacademy.af.edu
ANDERSON, James, A .. 800-443-9266 502 C
james.anderson@afacademy.af.edu
ANDERSON, James, D .. 217-333-7404 151 F
janders@illinois.edu
ANDERSON, James, T .. 973-655-7022 278 C
andersonja@montclair.edu
ANDERSON, Jamie .... 863-667-5000 108 I
ANDERSON, Jannette .... 801-689-2160 458 K
janderson@nightingale.edu
ANDERSON, Jay .... 614-685-9015 358 E
anderson.4180@osu.edu
ANDERSON, Jeanette .... 626-571-8811.. 73 D
jeanettea@uwest.edu
ANDERSON, Jeff .... 808-245-8384 129 H
jeffa@hawaii.edu
ANDERSON, Jeffrey ...... 607-778-5021 317 A
andersonj6@sunybroome.edu
ANDERSON, Jeffrey, J .. 847-574-5210 141 G
janderson@lfgsm.edu
ANDERSON, Jennifer .... 785-539-3571 175 F
janderson@mccks.edu
ANDERSON, Jennifer .... 203-254-4000.. 87 G
janderson@fairfield.edu
ANDERSON, Jennifer .... 614-287-5581 351 B
jander02@cscc.edu
ANDERSON, Jennifer .... 503-594-6222 372 B
jennifer.anderson@clackamas.edu
ANDERSON, Jeremy ...... 218-751-8670 241 Q
jeremyanderson@oakhills.edu
ANDERSON, Jerry .... 515-271-3985 165 F
jerry.anderson@drake.edu
ANDERSON, Jill .... 480-988-8884.. 13 B
jill.anderson@cgc.edu
ANDERSON, Jill .... 307-754-6401 500 G
jill.anderson@nwc.edu
ANDERSON, Jill .... 717-393-0654 387 F
ANDERSON, Jill, C .... 610-625-7910 390 D
andersonj@moravian.edu

ANDERSON, Jody .... 706-778-8500 124 B
jandersonl@piedmont.edu
ANDERSON, John .... 601-925-7100 246 D
jpanders@mc.edu
ANDERSON, John .... 612-330-1616 233 G
andersj1@augsburg.edu
ANDERSON, John, M ... 202-806-4830.. 92 E
john_m_anderson@howard.edu
ANDERSON, Jon .... 435-586-7700 459 E
jonanderson@suu.edu
ANDERSON, Jon (Jay) .. 979-209-7296 430 I
jay.anderson@blinn.edu
ANDERSON, Jonathan ... 509-359-6246 478 H
janderson@ewu.edu
ANDERSON, Joshua ...... 602-429-4432.. 15 D
janderson@ps.edu
ANDERSON, JP .... 585-594-6832 310 A
anderson_jp@roberts.edu
ANDERSON, Julie .... 507-222-4321 234 C
janderso@carleton.edu
ANDERSON, Julie .... 507-457-5122 241 A
julie.anderson@winona.edu
ANDERSON, Julie .... 309-556-3780 140 E
janders3@iwu.edu
ANDERSON, Julie, S ..... 801-863-5378 460 A
julie.anderson@uvu.edu
ANDERSON, Justin .... 603-646-3661 272 F
justin.anderson@dartmouth.edu
ANDERSON, Kali .... 260-452-2251 154 F
kali.anderson@ctsfw.edu
ANDERSON, Katherine .. 617-747-2274 206 D
financialaid@berklee.edu
ANDERSON, Kathy .... 501-370-5306.. 21 A
kanderson@philander.edu
ANDERSON, Kay .... 478-445-6286 119 A
kay.anderson@gcsu.edu
ANDERSON, Kelly .... 417-268-6002 250 A
kanderson@gobbc.edu
ANDERSON, Kelsi .... 402-481-8602 265 B
kelsi.anderson@bryanhealthcollege.edu
ANDERSON, Kenneth .... 202-806-2550.. 92 E
kenneth.anderson@howard.edu
ANDERSON, Kenneth .... 509-313-3404 479 E
anderson@gonzaga.edu
ANDERSON, Kent .... 701-483-2214 345 A
kent.w.anderson@dickinsonstate.edu
ANDERSON, Kevin .... 251-380-3006..... 6 H
jkanderson@shc.edu
ANDERSON, Kevin .... 617-747-2359 206 D
physicalplant@berklee.edu
ANDERSON, Kevin .... 239-432-6706 100 G
kevin.anderson@fsw.edu
ANDERSON, Kevin, L .... 563-589-0211 170 G
kanderson@wartburgseminary.edu
ANDERSON, Kim .... 800-561-2606 388 F
kanderson@lincoln.edu
ANDERSON, Kimberly ... 602-285-7466.. 13 H
kimberly.anderson@phoenixcollege.edu
ANDERSON, Kirk, D ...... 309-794-7203 132 H
kirkanderson@augustana.edu
ANDERSON, Kristina ..... 334-222-6591..... 2 I
kgriffin@lbwcc.edu
ANDERSON, Kristine ..... 231-777-0447 228 C
kristine.anderson@muskegoncc.edu
ANDERSON, Kristy .... 360-538-4151 479 F
kristy.anderson@ghc.edu
ANDERSON,
LaTonya, R .... 405-466-2231 366 B
ANDERSON, OFM,
Lawrence .... 518-783-2331 314 K
landerson@siena.edu
ANDERSON, Layne .... 218-477-2447 239 A
layne.anderson@mnstate.edu
ANDERSON, Layton ...... 870-541-7858.. 20 B
ANDERSON, Leif, B .... 612-330-1497 233 G
andersol@augsburg.edu
ANDERSON, Leslie .... 870-733-6732.. 18 A
landerson@asumidsouth.edu
ANDERSON, Leslie .... 408-498-5100.. 73 A
landerson@cogswell.edu
ANDERSON, Linda .... 256-726-7095..... 6 C
landerson@oakwood.edu
ANDERSON, Lisa .... 718-270-5000 294 E
lisa@mec.cuny.edu
ANDERSON, Liz .... 479-619-4176.. 20 G
eanderson14@nwacc.edu
ANDERSON, Lois .... 301-387-3042 198 F
lois.anderson@garrettcollege.edu
ANDERSON, Lori .... 828-227-7271 343 D
landerson@wcu.edu
ANDERSON, Luke .... 404-727-6123 118 D
luke@emory.edu

ANDERSON, Maria .... 708-656-8000 145 B
maria.anderson@morton.edu
ANDERSON, Maria .... 973-655-5225 278 C
andersonmar@montclair.edu
ANDERSON, Marianne .. 410-386-8000 197 G
manderson@carrollcc.edu
ANDERSON, Marie .... 909-469-5485.. 75 G
manderson@westernu.edu
ANDERSON, Marie, A .... 680-488-2470 504 A
mariea@palau.edu
ANDERSON, Mark .... 908-709-7010 283 E
mark.anderson2@ucc.edu
ANDERSON, Mark, D .... 937-775-3570 364 D
mark.anderson@wright.edu
ANDERSON, Marlene .... 701-224-5578 345 F
marlene.anderson@bismarckstate.edu
ANDERSON, Mary .... 850-474-2384 111 E
manderson1@uwf.edu
ANDERSON, Mary Jo .... 435-865-8491 459 E
andersonm@suu.edu
ANDERSON,
Mary Kaye, G .... 615-898-2670 421 C
marykaye.anderson@mtsu.edu
ANDERSON, Matt, J ...... 651-286-7525 243 E
mjanderson@unwsp.edu
ANDERSON, Melinda, F 318-619-2916 189 A
manderson@lsua.edu
ANDERSON,
Melinda, R .... 252-335-3187 341 A
mranderson@ecsu.edu
ANDERSON, Melissa ..... 620-331-4100 174 E
manderson@indycc.edu
ANDERSON, Melissa ..... 785-833-4512 175 C
melissa.anderson@kwu.edu
ANDERSON, Melissa ..... 330-263-2082 350 H
melanderson@wooster.edu
ANDERSON, Melissa, L 336-841-9220 329 E
manderson@highpoint.edu
ANDERSON, Melissa, P 540-674-3635 473 F
manderson@nr.edu
ANDERSON, Michael .... 318-345-9261 188 A
michaelanderson19@ladelta.edu
ANDERSON,
Michelle, J .... 718-951-5671 293 A
bcpresident@brooklyn.cuny.edu
ANDERSON,
Michelle, O .... 214-777-6433 440 I
ANDERSON, Mike .... 503-255-0332 374 A
mikeanderson@multnomah.edu
ANDERSON, Mike .... 435-283-7393 460 C
mike.anderson@snow.edu
ANDERSON, Mike .... 206-876-6107 483 A
manderson@theseattleschool.edu
ANDERSON, Myron .... 210-458-4011 455 B
myron.anderson@utsa.edu
ANDERSON,
N. Douglas .... 740-376-4536 355 E
doug.anderson@marietta.edu
ANDERSON, Nathan ...... 701-858-3064 345 C
nathan.c.anderson@minotstateu.edu
ANDERSON, Nathan ...... 520-795-0787.. 10 J
ANDERSON, Neal .... 303-963-3463.. 78 D
nanderson@ccu.edu
ANDERSON, Neil .... 423-648-2673 422 D
nanderson@richmont.edu
ANDERSON, Nick .... 651-290-6358 241 N
nick.anderson@mitchellhamline.edu
ANDERSON, Nickoel ..... 218-733-5990 238 A
nickoel.anderson@lsc.edu
ANDERSON, Nina .... 732-571-7551 278 B
nanderso@monmouth.edu
ANDERSON, Noma .... 901-490-2989 462 D
noma.anderson@uvm.edu
ANDERSON, Oliver .... 801-832-2242 461 A
oanderson@westminstercollege.edu
ANDERSON, Paula .... 641-784-5148 166 B
pkanders@graceland.edu
ANDERSON, Pauline ...... 850-729-6485 104 L
ander113@nwfsc.edu
ANDERSON, Per, M ...... 218-299-3932 234 K
anderson@cord.edu
ANDERSON, Peter .... 216-987-3538 351 D
peter.anderson@tri-c.edu
ANDERSON, Peter, T ..... 540-674-3631 473 F
ptanderson@nr.edu
ANDERSON, Randy .... 513-618-1925 350 B
randerson@ccms.edu
ANDERSON, Rayelle ..... 208-769-5978 132 A
rayelle_anderson@nic.edu
ANDERSON, Raymond .. 480-965-9911.. 11 A
ray.anderson@asu.edu
ANDERSON, Rebecca .... 210-458-4132 455 B
rebecca.anderson@utsa.edu

ANGELIS, Peter .... 310-825-4941 .. 69 D
pangelis@ha.ucla.edu

ANGELL, Alecia .... 509-527-3683 484 B
alecia.angell@wwcc.edu

ANGELL, Beth .... 804-827-1030 472 D
keangell@vcu.edu

ANGELL,
Kathryn (Beth) .... 734-764-5347 231 A
bangell@umich.edu

ANGELL, Tracey .... 401-874-2326 404 E
tracey@uri.edu

ANGELO, Caroline .... 404-225-4545 115 F
cangelo@atlantatech.edu

ANGELO, Jack, D .... 330-471-8251 355 D
jangelo@malone.edu

ANGELO, Lisa .... 215-968-8048 379 B
lisa.angelo@bucks.edu

ANGELONI, Lisa .... 609-771-3080 275 J
angeloni@tcnj.edu

ANGELOS, Peter .... 218-879-0839 237 F
peter.angelos@fdltcc.edu

ANGELOVA, Milena ...... 831-770-6854 .. 44 J
mangelova@hartnell.edu

ANGEMI, Karen .... 909-621-8384 .. 44 K
kangemi@hmc.edu

ANGEMI, Karen .... 909-621-8384 .. 44 K
karen_angemi@hmc.edu

ANGENY, Karen .... 610-861-5460 391 B
kangeny@northampton.edu

ANGER, Paul .... 928-428-8334 .. 12 H
paul.anger@eac.edu

ANGIOLETTI, Lindsey .... 516-572-9634 307 C
lindsey.angioletti@ncc.edu

ANGION, Stanford ...... 334-872-2533 .... 6 F
stanfordangion@gmail.com

ANGLE, Jay Scott .... 352-392-1971 110 E
jangle@ufl.edu

ANGLE, Ray .... 509-313-4100 479 E
angle@gonzaga.edu

ANGLE, Steven, R .... 423-425-4141 426 D
steven-angle@utc.edu

ANGLESIO, Marco ...... 610-861-4585 391 B
manglesio@northampton.edu

ANGLIM, Sean .... 315-568-3092 309 H
sanglim@northeastcollege.edu

ANGLIN, Pamela, D ..... 903-785-7661 440 F
panglin@parisjc.edu

ANGLIN, Roland .... 216-687-2174 350 G
r.anglin@csuohio.edu

ANGLIN, Roland .... 216-687-5269 350 G
r.anglin@csuohio.edu

ANGLIN, Thad .... 254-442-5111 431 J
thad.anglin@cisco.edu

ANGLIONGTO,
Maryanne .... 636-481-3318 253 G
manglion@jeffco.edu

ANGOLA HARPER,
Tameka .... 334-727-8421 .... 7 D
tharper@tuskegee.edu

ANGRIST, Michele, P .... 518-388-6234 323 B
angristm@union.edu

ANGROVE, William ...... 936-294-2774 449 E
wla002@shsu.edu

ANGRY, Rose .... 719-502-4106 .. 82 D
rose.angry1@pikespeak.edu

ANGSMAN, Rhonda ...... 317-921-4479 158 B
rangsman@ivytech.edu

ANGST, JR., Arthur, H .. 516-876-3094 318 A
angsta@oldwestbury.edu

ANGUIANO, Amy .... 540-857-7254 475 A
aanguiano@virginiawestern.edu

ANGUIANO, Maria ...... 855-278-5080 .. 11 A
maria.anguiano.1@asu.edu

ANGULO, Angelina ..... 305-821-3333 100 C
aangulo@fnu.edu

ANGULO, Michael ...... 609-626-6072 283 A
michael.angulo@stockton.edu

ANHORN, JR., Jerry .... 509-527-4299 484 B
jerry.anhorn@wwcc.edu

ANICETTI, Rachel ...... 925-473-7446 .. 40 I
ranicetti@losmedanos.edu

ANISFELD, Sharon, C .. 617-559-8773 210 C
sanisfeld@hebrewcollege.edu

ANISKOVICH, William ... 203-773-8550 .. 85 C
waaniskovich@albertus.edu

ANKE, Sharla, M .... 724-287-8711 379 C
sharla.anke@bc3.edu

ANKENY, Carrie .... 630-829-6028 133 B
croberts@ben.edu

ANKER, Laura, M .... 516-876-3460 318 A
ankerl@oldwestbury.edu

ANKERBERG, Erik ...... 708-209-3278 136 G
erik.ankerberg@cuchicago.edu

ANKERSON, Katherine .. 402-472-3751 269 A
ankerson@unl.edu

ANKROM, Jeff .... 336-272-7102 329 B
jeff.ankrom@greensboro.edu

ANN, Elina .... 215-392-2938 395 B
eann@pitc.edu

ANNABLE, Ross .... 716-614-6407 309 E
rannable@niagaracc.suny.edu

ANNAN, Vidal .... 908-737-4866 277 F
vannan@kean.edu

ANNARELLI, James, J .. 727-864-8243 .. 98 G
annarejj@eckerd.edu

ANNAVARJULA, Madan 401-232-6227 403 B
mannavar@bryant.edu

ANNEAR, Patricia, T .... 724-287-8711 379 C
patricia.annear@bc3.edu

ANNINO, Lou .... 203-932-7153 .. 89 F
lannino@newhaven.edu

ANNIS, Stephen .... 423-318-2736 424 G
stephen.annis@ws.edu

ANNUNZIATA,
Margaret, H .... 828-395-1300 335 B
mannunziata@isothermal.edu

ANSARI, Sami .... 978-542-7015 213 B
sami.ansari@salemstate.edu

ANSBOURY, Pamela .... 210-485-0307 427 H
pansboury@alamo.edu

ANSBRO, Dawn .... 845-341-4337 310 D
dawn.ansbro@sunyorange.edu

ANSCHUTZ, Mendi ..... 785-738-9090 176 C
manschutz@ncktc.edu

ANSEL, Ryan .... 313-664-1425 222 C
ransel@collegeforcreativestudies.edu

ANSELMENT,
Kenneth, L .... 920-832-6992 492 B
ken.anselment@lawrence.edu

ANSEVIN-ALLEN, Scott . 603-899-4151 272 G
ansevis@franklinpierce.edu

ANSLEY, Kelly .... 706-880-8311 121 K
kansley@lagrange.edu

ANSTOETTER, Don ..... 314-792-6120 253 J
anstoetter@kenrick.edu

ANT, Susan .... 952-358-8906 239 C
susan.ant@normandale.edu

ANTARIKSA, Kara ...... 661-362-2269 .. 51 E
kantariksa@masters.edu

ANTECOL, Heather ..... 909-607-8067 .. 37 G
heather.antecol@claremontmckenna.edu

ANTELMAN, Kristin ..... 805-893-3256 .. 70 E
kantelman@ucsb.edu

ANTER, David .... 805-378-1415 .. 73 I
danter@vcccd.edu

ANTHOINE, Sandra ..... 401-341-2102 404 D
sandra.anthoine@salve.edu

ANTHOLIS, William, J .. 434-924-6061 471 F
wja8yh@virginia.edu

ANTHONY, Angela ..... 509-574-4651 485 E
aanthony@yvcc.edu

ANTHONY, Cynthia, T .. 205-929-6300 .... 2 H
canthony@lawsonstate.edu

ANTHONY, David .... 315-464-8047 316 F
anthonyd@upstate.edu

ANTHONY, Doug .... 304-424-8280 490 A
doug.anthony@wvup.edu

ANTHONY, Eric .... 951-571-6282 .. 59 B
eric.anthony@mvc.edu

ANTHONY, Jason, S ... 401-456-8234 404 A
janthony@ric.edu

ANTHONY, Kathy .... 610-526-6045 385 F
kanthony@harcum.edu

ANTHONY, Kelly .... 219-464-6700 162 C
kelly.anthony@valpo.edu

ANTHONY, Linda .... 866-492-5336 243 G
linda.anthony@laureate.net

ANTHONY, Marra .... 301-546-4180 201 D
marratj@pgcc.edu

ANTHONY, Michael, D . 708-709-3501 147 A
manthony@prairiestate.edu

ANTHONY, Ryan .... 704-290-5870 337 F
ranthony@spcc.edu

ANTHONY, Takeia ...... 502-597-6008 183 A
takeia.anthony@kysu.edu

ANTHWAL, Sunny ...... 845-398-4061 314 D
sunny@stac.edu

ANTIGUA, Brian .... 786-391-1167 .. 95 G
ANTIGUA, Diony .... 786-391-1167 .. 95 G
ANTIGUA, Jose .... 786-391-1167 .. 95 G

ANTKOWIAK, Bruce .... 724-805-2940 397 C
bruce.antkowiak@stvincent.edu

ANTKOWIAK, Bruce .... 724-805-2940 397 D
bruce.antkowiak@stvincent.edu

ANTLE, Austin .... 518-458-5435 296 E
antlea@strose.edu

ANTLE, Jay .... 913-469-8500 174 F
jantle@jccc.edu

ANTMAN, Karen, H .... 617-358-9600 207 C
kha4@bu.edu

ANTOINE, Kevin .... 215-968-8093 379 B
kevin.antoine@bucks.edu

ANTOINE, Linda .... 225-771-4580 190 J
linda_antoine@subr.edu

ANTOINE, Linda, B ..... 225-771-4587 190 K
linda_antoine@subr.edu

ANTOINE, Tanesha ..... 281-478-2742 442 C
tanesha.antoine@sjcd.edu

ANTOINE, Tanesha ..... 281-922-3453 442 E
tanesha.antoine@sjcd.edu

ANTON, Vanessa .... 918-444-3701 366 G
anton@nsuok.edu

ANTONAKAKIS, Helen .. 856-227-7200 275 F
hantonakakis@camdencc.edu

ANTONE, Blaine .... 520-383-0075 .. 16 D
bantone@tocc.edu

ANTONELLI, Fred .... 585-582-8201 298 E
fredantonelli@elim.edu

ANTONELLO, Michael .. 561-237-7960 103 W
mantonello@lynn.edu

ANTONIKOWSKI,
Angela .... 518-262-5848 289 C
antonia@amc.edu

ANTONIO, Edward ...... 218-299-3894 234 K
eantonio@cord.edu

ANTONISHEN, Ashley .. 231-348-6600 228 D
aantonishen@ncmich.edu

ANTONOVICS, Kate .... 858-246-5340 .. 70 C
seventhprovost@ucsd.edu

ANTONOWICZ, Joseph . 908-737-3150 277 F
jantonow@kean.edu

ANTONUCCI, Carl ...... 860-832-2099 .. 85 F
antonucci@ccsu.edu

ANTONUCCI-DURGAN,
Dana .... 631-451-4539 321 A
antonud@sunysuffolk.edu

ANTONY, Elbby .... 281-283-2016 452 A
antonye@uhcl.edu

ANTROBUS, Barbara ... 859-858-2285 178 G
Barbara

ANTROP-GONZÁLEZ,
René .... 845-257-2800 316 B
antropgr@newpaltz.edu

ANTRUM, Curtis .... 203-857-7090 .. 87 B
cantrum@norwalk.edu

ANTUNES, Nancy .... 781-891-2686 206 C
nantunes@bentley.edu

ANTURKAR, Anjali, N .. 734-764-5132 231 A
anturkar@umich.edu

ANUMBA, Chimay ...... 352-392-4836 110 E
anumba@ufl.edu

ANUNDSON, Brock ..... 907-474-7780 .. 10 B
bsanundson@alaska.edu

ANVINSON, Kimberly ... 701-231-7761 345 D
kimberley.anvinson@ndsu.edu

ANYANWU,
Fitzpatrick, U .... 337-421-6905 188 H
fitzpatrick.anyanwu@sowela.edu

ANZAK, Daniel .... 210-458-5905 455 B
daniel.anzak@utsa.edu

ANZALDUA, Ricardo .... 212-237-8316 294 B
ranzaldua@jjay.cuny.edu

ANZALONE, Alessandro 772-462-5604 102 E
aanzalone@irsc.edu

ANZALONE, Nancy ..... 619-297-9700 .. 68 A
janzalone@mdc.edu

ANZALOTTA, Jaime .... 305-237-3336 104 E
janzalot@mdc.edu

ANZINGER, John .... 240-629-7858 198 E
janzinger@frederick.edu

ANZUONI, Rebecca ..... 617-373-7780 217 D
AOUN, Joseph, E ...... 617-373-2101 217 D

AOYAMA, Yuko .... 508-793-7403 207 F
yaoyama@clarku.edu

APANEL, Stephen, J .... 570-577-1195 379 A
stephen.apanel@bucknell.edu

APANOVICH, Val .... 570-674-6749 389 H
vapanovich@misericordia.edu

APARICIO, Sally .... 520-515-8757 .. 11 O
aparicios@cochise.edu

APAW, David .... 410-225-2464 200 B
dapaw@mica.edu

APEL, Scott .... 562-985-1658 .. 32 A
scott.apel@csulb.edu

APFELBAUM, Randy .... 646-592-4227 325 R
randy.apfelbaum@yu.edu

APFELTHALER, Gerhard 805-493-3352 .. 29 E
apfeltha@callutheran.edu

APGAR, Travis .... 518-276-6266 311 J
apgart@rpi.edu

APICELLA, Paul .... 215-895-1403 382 D
pwa29@drexel.edu

APICERNO, Amy .... 727-864-8058 .. 98 G
apiceral@eckerd.edu

APIGIAN, Charles ...... 615-460-6278 417 B
charlie.apigian@belmont.edu

APIGO, Mary-Jo .... 310-287-4110 .. 50 C
apigomj@wlac.edu

APODACA, John .... 505-428-1630 287 H
john.apodaca1@sfcc.edu

APODACA, Phillip, C .. 719-389-6613 .. 78 E
papodaca@coloradocollege.edu

APOLLO, Richard, M ... 516-463-5405 301 E
richard.apollo@hofstra.edu

APOLLONIO, Heather .. 914-674-7394 305 H
hapollonio@mercy.edu

APONTE, Bianca .... 787-257-0000 510 F
bianca.aponte1@upr.edu

APONTE, Brunilda ...... 787-743-7979 509 F
baponte@suagm.edu

APONTE, Gabriel .... 787-738-2161 511 A
gabriel.aponte5@upr.edu

APONTE, Gabriel .... 787-738-2161 511 A
gabriel.aponte2@upr.edu

APONTE, Giancarlo ..... 305-821-3333 100 C
gaponte@fnu.edu

APONTE, Madelene ..... 845-574-4492 312 C
maponte@sunyrockland.edu

APONTE, Wanda .... 787-786-3030 509 F
waponte@ucb.edu.pr

APOSTOLAKIS, Vy ..... 504-568-6518 189 C
vpham@lsuhsc.edu

APOSTOLAKOS,
Michael, J .... 585-275-4786 323 E
michael_apostolakos@urmc.rochester.edu

APPAVOO, Suresh ..... 909-706-7045 .. 75 G
sappavoo@westernu.edu

APPEANING,
V. Alexander .... 225-771-2705 190 J
appeaning@sus.edu

APPEANING,
Vladimir, A .... 225-771-2705 190 K
appeaning@sus.edu

APPEL, Anize .... 610-625-7701 390 D
appela@moravian.edu

APPEL, Elizabeth, H .... 410-777-7383 197 C
ehappel@aacc.edu

APPEL, Heidi .... 419-530-6031 363 B
heidi.appel@utoledo.edu

APPEL, Kellie .... 678-547-6397 122 C
appel_k@mercer.edu

APPEL, Michelle .... 301-405-0475 202 E
mappel@umd.edu

APPEL, Shari, A .... 330-471-8116 355 D
sappel@malone.edu

APPEL, Steve .... 575-492-2147 288 I
sappel@usw.edu

APPELGET, Kristin ...... 609-258-3018 279 E
appelget@princeton.edu

APPELT, Uschi .... 812-866-7221 155 D
appelt@hanover.edu

APPIAH-PADI,
Stephen, K .... 570-577-3796 379 A
s.appiahpadi@bucknell.edu

APPIARIUS, Don .... 505-747-2255 287 C
don.appiarius@nnmc.edu

APPLE, Monique .... 605-455-6055 414 H
mapple@olc.edu

APPLE, Ryan .... 517-321-0242 224 E
rapple@glcc.edu

APPLEBAUM, Melanie . 314-505-7117 251 D
applebaumm@csl.edu

APPLEBY, Alice .... 803-822-3588 409 E
applebya@midlandstech.edu

APPLEBY, Karen .... 208-282-2171 131 E
karenappleby@isu.edu

APPLEBY, Leigh .... 860-723-0617 .. 85 E
APPLEBY, Scott .... 574-631-6972 161 G
rappleby@nd.edu

APPLEGARTH, Crystal .. 660-263-3900 250 G
crystalapplegarth@cccb.edu

APPLEMAN, Boomer ... 505-566-3318 287 E
applemanb@sanjuancollege.edu

APPLETON, Abigail ..... 352-588-6720 107 B
abigail.appleton@saintleo.edu

APPLETON, Amber ..... 503-253-3443 374 E
amber.appleton@ocom.edu

APPLETON, Kevin ...... 847-543-2631 135 B
kappleton1@clcillinois.edu

APPLETON, LeoNard ... 773-291-6313 135 B

ARMSTRONG, Katie .... 435-652-7975 459 G
katie.armstrong@utahtech.edu
ARMSTRONG, Keith ...... 719-590-6758.. 80 B
karmstrong@coloradotech.edu
ARMSTRONG, Kelli .... 401-341-2337 404 D
kelli.armstrong@salve.edu
ARMSTRONG, Kevin ...... 402-375-7510 267 I
kearmst1@wsc.edu
ARMSTRONG, Kim .... 501-332-0231.. 18 D
karmstrong@asutr.edu
ARMSTRONG, Kim .... 309-694-5599 138 I
kim.armstrong@icc.edu
ARMSTRONG,
La Kiesha .... 615-460-6619 417 B
lakiesha.armstrong@belmont.edu
ARMSTRONG, LaTonya . 773-291-6613 135 B
tarmstrong11@ccc.edu
ARMSTRONG, Lori .... 618-634-3313 149 C
loria@shawneecc.edu
ARMSTRONG, Lori, B ... 410-704-3570 204 B
larmstrong@towson.edu
ARMSTRONG, Myeshia . 510-885-3803.. 31 C
myeshia.armstrong@csueastbay.edu
ARMSTRONG, Neal, R ... 520-621-6044.. 16 H
nra@arizona.edu
ARMSTRONG, Patricia ... 773-602-5000 135 A
ARMSTRONG,
Patricia, J .... 615-353-3758 424 A
patricia.armstrong@nscc.edu
ARMSTRONG, Rhonda .. 423-869-6436 420 A
rhonda.armstrong@lmunet.edu
ARMSTRONG,
Steven, M .... 920-832-6769 492 B
steven.m.armstrong@lawrence.edu
ARMSTRONG, Susan ..... 937-393-3431 360 G
slarmstrong1@sscc.edu
ARMSTRONG, Tamara ... 916-568-3021.. 50 I
armstrt@losrios.edu
ARMSTRONG, Tamara ... 310-568-6219.. 51 C
tamara.armstrong@lmu.edu
ARMSTRONG, Wesley ... 828-262-2190 340 G
armstrongwr@appstate.edu
ARMSTRONG ASH,
Samantha (Sam) .... 509-359-7852 478 H
sarmstrong@ewu.edu
ARMSTRONG-SMITH,
Gina .... 925-631-4123.. 59 I
gga2@stmarys-ca.edu
ARNABOLDI,
D. Clinton .... 718-793-2330 309 A
ARNADE, Peter .... 808-956-6460 129 B
parnade@hawaii.edu
ARNDER, Lori .... 757-240-2200 469 F
lori.arnder@rivhs.com
ARNDT, Chase .... 423-652-4341 419 F
chasevarndt@king.edu
ARNDT, Daniel .... 914-633-2520 302 C
darndt@iona.edu
ARNDT, Justin .... 406-994-4647 263 G
justin.arndt@montana.edu
ARNDT, Serenna .... 217-234-5253 141 H
ARNDT, Theresa .... 717-245-1750 382 B
arndtt@dickinson.edu
ARNDT, Wayne .... 732-987-2237 277 B
warndt@georgian.edu
ARNER, Joe .... 352-588-7426 107 B
joseph.arner@saintleo.edu
ARNER, Katelynn .... 910-410-1761 336 G
kdarner@richmondcc.edu
ARNER, Robert .... 610-292-9852 396 C
robert.arner@reseminary.edu
ARNER, Timothy .... 641-269-4529 166 D
arnertim@grinnell.edu
ARNESON, Dean .... 912-201-6123 125 D
darneson@southuniversity.edu
ARNESON, Eric .... 470-578-6000 121 J
ARNESON, Stephen .... 707-664-2848.. 34 C
ARNESON, Tara .... 802-865-5702 461 C
tarneson@champlain.edu
ARNET, Lisa .... 716-286-8689 309 F
larnet@niagara.edu
ARNETT, Carrie .... 510-879-9270.. 60 C
carnett@samuelmerritt.edu
ARNETT, David, J .... 978-478-3400 217 E
darnett@northpoint.edu
ARNETT, Katy, E .... 240-895-4451 201 F
kearnett@smcm.edu
ARNETT, LaTondra .... 901-678-2234 426 A
larnett@memphis.edu
ARNETT, Nathan .... 618-985-3741 140 G
nathanarnett@jalc.edu
ARNETTE, Drew .... 502-413-8801 184 F
darnette@sullivan.edu
ARNETTE ERZ, Bradley . 305-821-3333 100 C
berz@fnu.edu
ARNEY, Doug .... 956-882-7145 455 A
doug.arney@utrgv.edu
ARNEY, Janna .... 956-882-8833 455 A
janna.arney@utrgv.edu
ARNEY, Karl .... 215-455-2300 378 F
ARNHOLT, JoAnn .... 848-932-7692 281 B
arnholt@echo.rutgers.edu
ARNITZ, Deborah .... 602-429-4927.. 15 D
darnitz@ps.edu
ARNN, Larry .... 517-607-2301 224 G
larnn@hillsdale.edu
ARNO, Marlene .... 716-851-1431 299 A
arno@ecc.edu
ARNOLD, Alicia .... 402-481-8752 265 B
alicia.arnold@bryanhealthcollege.edu
ARNOLD, Amelia .... 317-977-7778 258 H
amelia.arnold@slu.edu
ARNOLD, Amesha .... 706-396-8132 123 I
aarnold@paine.edu
ARNOLD, Angela .... 952-358-9045 239 C
angela.arnold@normandale.edu
ARNOLD, Audrey .... 505-277-2511 288 C
aaronld5@unm.edu
ARNOLD, Brent .... 609-652-4501 283 A
brent.arnold@stockton.edu
ARNOLD, Brian .... 575-492-2104 288 I
barnold@usw.edu
ARNOLD, Brian .... 704-406-4732 328 I
barnold@gardner-webb.edu
ARNOLD, Brian .... 602-850-8000.. 15 D
ARNOLD, Carl .... 903-233-4310 438 C
carlarnold@letu.edu
ARNOLD, Cisco .... 540-373-2200 465 G
carnold@evcc.edu
ARNOLD, Eli .... 404-364-8885 123 G
earnold@oglethorpe.edu
ARNOLD, Jeff .... 270-852-3300 183 B
jeff.arnold@kwc.edu
ARNOLD, Jeff .... 262-472-1918 496 E
ARNOLD, Joe .... 254-867-4891 448 F
joe.arnold@tstc.edu
ARNOLD, Jon .... 714-895-8183.. 38 E
jarnold@gwc.cccd.edu
ARNOLD, Jon .... 931-540-2538 423 D
jarnold15@columbiastate.edu
ARNOLD, Joseph, E ...... 202-885-8649.. 94 D
jearnold@wesleyseminary.edu
ARNOLD, Joshua .... 714-879-3901.. 45 J
jarnold@hiu.edu
ARNOLD, Josi .... 308-367-5200 269 D
jarnold7@unl.edu
ARNOLD, Julie .... 419-448-2953 353 D
jarnold3@heidelberg.edu
ARNOLD, Kathy, R .... 651-962-6510 243 F
arno2932@stthomas.edu
ARNOLD, Kenneth, L .... 707-256-7777.. 53 E
karnold@napavalley.edu
ARNOLD, SR.,
Lester, L .... 703-993-2602 466 J
llarnold@gmu.edu
ARNOLD, Melinda .... 903-223-3004 447 C
marnold@tamut.edu
ARNOLD, Paloma .... 805-965-0581.. 62 M
ARNOLD, Richard .... 617-243-2217 210 G
rarnold@lasell.edu
ARNOLD, Rodney .... 870-743-3000.. 20 F
rarnold@northark.edu
ARNOLD, Shirley, E ...... 828-641-0762 327 A
arnoldse@brevard.edu
ARNOLD, Shonta .... 501-370-5271.. 21 A
sarnold@philander.edu
ARNOLD, Sue .... 281-998-6003 447 G
sarnold@txchiro.edu
ARNOLD, Susan .... 610-647-4400 385 K
sarnold@immaculata.edu
ARNOLD, Tai .... 518-587-2100 320 B
tai.arnold@esc.edu
ARNOLD, Timothy .... 716-338-1125 302 G
timothyarnold@mail.sunyjcc.edu
ARNOLD, III, W. Ellis .. 501-450-1351.. 19 I
arnold@hendrix.edu
ARNOLD, William .... 517-371-5140 232 K
arnoldw@cooley.edu
ARNOULD, Karen, A ...... 810-762-3344 231 C
karnould@umich.edu
ARNQUIST, Lynn .... 320-762-4464 236 G
lynn.arnquist@alextech.edu
ARNST, Scott .... 810-762-3123 231 C
sarnst@umich.edu
ARNUSH, Michael, F ..... 518-580-5462 315 A
marnush@skidmore.edu
AROCHA, Karen .... 305-443-9170 106 M
karocha@sabercollege.edu
AROCHO, Ashley .... 212-650-6460 293 B
aarocho@ccny.cuny.edu
AROMANDO, Drew, C .. 609-896-5367 280 D
aromando@rider.edu
ARONIN, Heidi, J .... 718-270-1025 316 E
heidi.aronin@downstate.edu
ARONSON, Ann .... 612-624-1755 242 K
aronson@umn.edu
ARONSON, Krista, M .... 207-786-6280 193 D
karonson@bates.edu
ARONSON, Seth .... 609-984-3430 283 D
saronson@tesu.edu
ARONSON, Stacey .... 320-589-6250 243 C
aronsosp@morris.umn.edu
ARONSTEIN, A-J .... 212-854-7758 290 H
aaronste@barnard.edu
ARORA, Deepa .... 478-934-6588 122 D
deepa.arora@mga.edu
ARORA SINGH, Alka ..... 623-845-3968.. 13 E
alka.arora.singh@gccaz.edu
AROSKAR, Rajarshi ...... 518-454-2122 296 E
aroskarr@strose.edu
ARQUETTE, Richard ...... 360-442-2443 480 E
rarquette@lowercolumbia.edu
ARQUETTE, Toby .... 563-333-6294 169 D
arquettetoby@sau.edu
ARRAIZA, Ana Marta .... 787-751-0160 505 C
aarraiza@cmpr.pr.gov
ARRASTIA, Anna .... 502-897-4121 184 D
aarrastia@sbts.edu
ARREAZOLA, David .... 956-764-5950 438 A
darreazola@laredo.edu
ARREDONDO, Jill .... 972-883-5380 454 D
jill.arredondo@utdallas.edu
ARREDONDO, Maria ..... 965-364-4322 448 F
paula.arredondo@tstc.edu
ARREDONDO, Michael .. 214-860-8639 434 B
marredondo@dcccd.edu
ARREDONDO SAMSON,
Marisol .... 714-628-7339.. 36 D
arredond@chapman.edu
ARRIAZA, Cecilia .... 714-992-7087.. 54 D
carriaza@fullcoll.edu
ARRIETA, Cynthia .... 626-914-8597.. 37 B
carrieta@citruscollege.edu
ARRIETA, Jesus .... 520-452-2665.. 11 O
arrietaj@cochise.edu
ARRINGTON, Jeffrey ...... 334-386-7105.... 5 D
jarrington@faulkner.edu
ARRINGTON, Justin ...... 229-333-5351 127 C
juarrington@valdosta.edu
ARRINGTON,
Manuel, A .... 301-546-0635 201 D
arringma@pgcc.edu
ARRINGTON, Pam .... 330-966-5460 360 I
parrington@starkstate.edu
ARRINGTON,
Stephanie, K .... 765-285-8304 153 E
skarrington@bsu.edu
ARRINGTON, Tom .... 281-459-7613 442 D
tom.arrington@sjcd.edu
ARRIOLA, JR., Ben .... 915-778-4001 444 A
ARRIOLA, Stephanie ...... 903-983-8228 437 G
sarriola@kilgore.edu
ARRIOLA, Susan .... 559-442-8237.. 67 A
susan.arriola@fresnocitycollege.edu
ARROWOOD, Roarke ..... 828-835-4305 338 C
rarrowood@tricountycc.edu
ARROWSMITH, Jason ... 360-442-2270 480 E
jarrowsmith@lowercolumbia.edu
ARROYO, Carmen .... 787-620-2040 504 B
carroyo@aupr.edu
ARROYO, Daniel .... 916-306-1628.. 67 E
darroyo@sum.edu
ARROYO, Enrique .... 787-841-2000 508 H
earroyo@pucpr.edu
ARROYO, Erica .... 305-284-1724 112 K
earroyo@miami.edu
ARROYO, George .... 740-500-0684 358 A
garroyo@ohiochristian.edu
ARROYO, Gladys .... 787-279-1912 506 L
garroyo@bayamon.inter.edu
ARROYO, Ivonne, D ...... 787-257-7323 509 B
ARROYO, Jannette .... 787-765-1915 507 G
jarroyo@opto.inter.edu
ARROYO, Josie .... 787-704-1020 505 B
jarroyo@columbiacentral.edu
ARROYO, Julitza .... 787-786-3030 509 E
jarroyo@ucb.edu.pr
ARROYO, Luis .... 787-738-2161 511 A
luis.arroyo20@upr.edu
ARROYO, Nancy .... 787-841-2000 508 H
nancy_arroyo@pucpr.edu
ARROYO, Palmira .... 787-753-6335 506 B
parroyo@icprjc.edu
ARROYO, Patti .... 800-462-7845.. 79 F
ARROYO, Rina .... 386-822-7773 111 F
rarroyo@stetson.edu
ARROYO, Sandra .... 787-765-3560 505 H
sandraarroyo@edpuniversity.edu
ARRUDA, Yvonne, D ..... 401-865-2480 403 G
yarruda@providence.edu
ARRUTI, Duane .... 505-277-8125 288 C
darruti@unm.edu
ARSENAULT, Randi .... 207-859-4000 194 B
ARSHANAPALLI, Bala .... 219-980-6919 157 A
barshana@iu.edu
ARSTEIN, Mark, H .... 801-863-5189 460 A
mark.arstein@uvu.edu
ARTALE, Maureen, P ..... 607-436-3216 316 C
maureen.artale@oneonta.edu
ARTAMENKO, Dan .... 620-417-1550 177 C
dan.artamenko@sccc.edu
ARTAZ, Nancy .... 316-295-5514 173 G
artaz@friends.edu
ARTEAGA, Elizabeth ...... 714-628-5051.. 58 G
arteaga_elizabeth@sccollege.edu
ARTEAGA, Monica .... 305-821-3333 100 C
marteaga@fnu.edu
ARTEAGA, Sandy .... 850-729-5259 104 L
arteagas@nwfsc.edu
ARTER, Neil .... 405-425-5906 367 C
neil.arter@oc.edu
ARTERBURN, Matt .... 785-670-1561 178 A
matt.arterburn@washburn.edu
ARTHUR, Candis .... 859-985-3192 179 E
arthurc@berea.edu
ARTHUR, Chandra .... 216-987-4659 351 D
chandra.arthur@tri-c.edu
ARTHUR, Christon .... 269-471-3404 220 H
christon@andrews.edu
ARTHUR, David .... 617-746-1990 210 E
david.arthur@hult.edu
ARTHUR, Mark .... 405-789-7661 369 H
mark.arthur@swcu.edu
ARTHUR, Melissa .... 434-736-2027 474 D
melissa.arthur@southside.edu
ARTHUR, Scott .... 303-724-8469.. 84 B
scott.arthur@cuanschutz.edu
ARTHUR, Virginia .... 651-793-1900 238 B
ginny.arthur@metrostate.edu
ARTIGUES, Jay .... 985-549-2395 192 E
jay.artigues@selu.edu
ARTIM, Chris .... 219-473-4314 154 A
cartim@ccsj.edu
ARTIS, Christine .... 718-933-6700 306 J
cartis@monroecollege.edu
ARTIS, Lori .... 618-468-3000 142 B
lartis@lc.edu
ARTIS, Roslyn, C .... 803-705-4681 405 G
roslyn.artis@benedict.edu
ARTZ, Liz .... 937-327-7820 364 C
artze@wittenberg.edu
ARTZE VEGA, Isis .... 407-582-3055 113 C
iartzevega@valenciacollege.edu
ARUCK, Janette .... 585-785-1298 299 E
janette.aruck@flcc.edu
ARUSH, Ilan .... 661-824-2977.. 53 H
ARVAN, April, A .... 920-565-1000 492 A
arvanaa@lakeland.edu
ARVAY, Anna .... 570-504-9695 384 A
aarvay@som.geisinger.edu
ARVIDSON, Susie .... 620-223-2700 173 F
susiea@fortscott.edu
ARVIZU, Dan .... 575-646-2035 286 G
chancellor.arvizu@nmsu.edu
ARVIZU, Primavera .... 559-791-2218.. 47 D
prarvizu@portervillecollege.edu
ARWINE, Troy .... 850-478-8496 105 F
tarwine@pcci.edu
ARWOOD, Katie .... 989-328-1291 227 G
katiea@montcalm.edu
ARWOOD, Robin .... 719-549-3327.. 82 I
robin.arwood@pueblocc.edu
ARZOUMANIAN, Arineh 213-763-7000.. 50 A
ARZROUNI-CHAHINIAN,
Chaghig .... 510-925-4282.. 25 P
carzroun@aua.am
ASAAD, Diana .... 415-561-6555.. 58 B
ASAD, Ray .... 626-584-5460.. 43 E
rayasad@fuller.edu
ASAGBA, Tempress .... 214-333-5340 433 D
tempress@dbu.edu

Index of Key Administrators | ASAMOAH – ATKINS 527

ASAMOAH, Yaw ... 724-357-2280 393 G
yaw.asamoah@iup.edu
ASAMSAMA-ACUNA, Gabriella ... 805-289-6044 74 B
gasamsamaacuna@vcccd.edu
ASANTE, Javonda ... 973-313-6211 282 K
javonda.asante@shu.edu
ASARO, Linda ... 212-817-7490 293 D
intstu@gc.cuny.edu
ASAWA, Archibald, E ... 949-480-4006 64 E
asawa@soka.edu
ASAY, Meredith ... 307-766-2238 500 H
masay@uwyo.edu
ASBURY, Adrienne ... 570-955-1494 387 A
asburya@lackawanna.edu
ASBURY, Amber ... 719-384-6834 82 C
amber.asbury@otero.edu
ASBURY, Arthur ... 617-670-5438 209 D
aasbury@fisher.edu
ASBURY, Phil ... 847-491-8557 146 C
phil.asbury@northwestern.edu
ASBURY, Sean ... 614-287-2525 351 B
sasbury@cscc.edu
ASBURY, Todd ... 276-326-3682 464 A
ASCENCIO, Jorge ... 714-895-8107 38 E
jascencio@gwc.cccd.edu
ASCENCIO, Mario ... 626-396-2231 26 G
mario.ascencio@artcenter.edu
ASCH, Emily ... 651-690-6650 242 F
ejasch@stkate.edu
ASCHEMAN, SVD, Thomas ... 563-876-3353 165 D
tascheman@dwci.edu
ASCHENBRENER, Matt ... 262-472-1570 496 E
aschenbm@uww.edu
ASCHENBRENNER, Annie, J ... 262-524-7224 491 A
aaschenb@carrollu.edu
ASCHER, Marie ... 914-594-4208 308 J
marie_ascher@nymc.edu
ASCHER, Tom ... 815-939-5011 146 F
tascher@olivet.edu
ASCHMANN, Leah ... 713-348-0000 441 K
ASCIONE, Lou ... 619-388-7873 61 B
lascione@sdccd.edu
ASDEL, Bryan ... 760-252-2411 26 L
basdel@barstow.edu
ASENBRENER, Darla ... 800-567-2344 491 C
dasenbrener@menominee.edu
ASENCIO, Vimarie ... 787-753-6000 506 B
vasencio@icprjc.edu
ASENCIO-PINTO, Aida ... 708-209-3492 136 D
aida.asencio-pinto@cuchicago.edu
ASETTA, Eric ... 617-824-3075 208 G
eric_asetta@emerson.edu
ASFAW, Abel ... 651-450-3685 237 H
aasfaw@inverhills.edu
ASGARALLI, Abigail ... 212-280-1396 323 C
aasgaralli@uts.columbia.edu
ASGARIAN, Gabrielle ... 530-435-5451 60 A
registrar@spots.edu
ASGEIRSDOTTIR, Aslaug ... 207-786-6066 193 D
aasgeirs@bates.edu
ASH, Beth ... 740-474-8896 358 A
bash@ohiochristian.edu
ASH, Carol ... 505-224-4138 285 B
cash2@cnm.edu
ASH, Eric ... 907-375-4515 457 B
ash@wbu.edu
ASH, Karen ... 541-917-4999 373 F
ASH, Kenya, D ... 513-529-7157 356 A
ashkd@miamioh.edu
ASH, Michael ... 402-559-3389 269 B
michael.ash@unmc.edu
ASH, Michael ... 319-208-5050 169 I
mash@scciowa.edu
ASH, Steven ... 352-854-2322 97 L
ashs@cf.edu
ASHAOLU, John ... 412-392-3911 395 H
jashaolu@pointpark.edu
ASHBURN, Maureen ... 617-735-9838 209 A
ashburnm@emmanuel.edu
ASHBURN-NARDO, Leslie ... 215-895-2000 382 D
la574@drexel.edu
ASHBY, Lisa ... 402-643-7419 265 I
lisa.ashby@cune.edu
ASHBY, Mae ... 407-708-2170 108 B
ashbym@seminolestate.edu
ASHBY, Mindy ... 618-634-3200 149 C
mindya@shawneecc.edu
ASHBY, Pamela ... 207-834-7516 196 G
pam.ashby@maine.edu
ASHBY, Patti ... 405-912-9017 368 H
pashby@ru.edu
ASHBY, Todd ... 843-863-7984 406 C
tashby@csuniv.edu
ASHCRAFT, Brent, G ... 208-496-3405 130 G
ashcraftb@byui.edu
ASHCRAFT, Katie ... 317-788-3533 161 F
ashcraftke@uindy.edu
ASHCRAFT, Matthew ... 480-731-8121 13 A
matthew.ashcraft@domail.maricopa.edu
ASHDOWN, Jonathan ... 518-629-7149 302 A
j.ashdown@hvcc.edu
ASHE, Susan ... 818-333-3558 53 J
deanstudentsla@nyfa.edu
ASHER, Adam ... 815-928-5554 146 F
adam@989group.com
ASHER, Alan ... 254-295-4636 453 A
aasher@umhb.edu
ASHER, Joy ... 859-238-5284 179 H
joy.asher@centre.edu
ASHER, Nancy ... 660-785-4143 259 J
nasher@truman.edu
ASHER, Steve ... 314-421-0949 259 G
ASHER, Trevor ... 218-751-8670 241 Q
trevorasher@oakhills.edu
ASHERIAN, Armen ... 702-651-7481 270 F
armen.asherian@csn.edu
ASHERIAN, Vartouhi ... 702-651-5860 270 F
vartouhi.asherian@csn.edu
ASHFORD, Prentice ... 615-966-5210 420 B
prentice.ashford@lipscomb.edu
ASHFORD, Rebecca ... 423-697-4455 423 B
rebecca.ashford@chattanoogastate.edu
ASHFORD, Scott ... 541-737-1211 374 H
scott.ashford@oregonstate.edu
ASHFORTH-ASHWORTH, Nikita ... 662-243-2641 245 C
nashworth@eastms.edu
ASHISH, Joshi ... 901-678-4514 426 A
ajoshi7@memphis.edu
ASHLEY, Annalee ... 912-478-5331 120 A
aashley@georgiasouthern.edu
ASHLEY, Annalee ... 912-478-5953 120 A
aashley@georgiasouthern.edu
ASHLEY, Darren ... 903-923-2406 457 I
dashley@wileyc.edu
ASHLEY, Donna ... 646-717-9706 300 C
ashley@gts.edu
ASHLEY, Evelyn ... 413-545-2684 211 D
eashley@umass.edu
ASHLEY, Flynn ... 859-344-3530 184 G
ashleyf@thomasmore.edu
ASHLEY, Kurt ... 630-617-3262 137 E
kurt.ashley@elmhurst.edu
ASHLEY, Lance ... 704-669-4092 333 C
ashleyl@clevelandcc.edu
ASHLEY, Mark ... 909-621-8090 44 K
mark_ashley@hmc.edu
ASHLEY, Mea ... 662-329-7416 247 B
meashley@muw.edu
ASHLEY, Peter ... 812-866-7014 155 D
ashley@hanover.edu
ASHLEY, Richard ... 704-272-5463 337 F
rashley@spcc.edu
ASHLEY, Talia ... 404-835-6118 422 D
tashley@richmont.edu
ASHLEY, Tim, M ... 315-267-2222 318 D
ashleytm@potsdam.edu
ASHLEY, II, Timothy ... 315-386-7777 319 E
ashleytm@canton.edu
ASHLEY, Tracy ... 757-258-6674 474 F
ashleyt@tncc.edu
ASHLINE, Melesa ... 520-515-3638 11 O
ashlinem@cochise.edu
ASHLOCK, Tracie, A ... 956-665-6431 455 A
tracie.ashlock@utrgv.edu
ASHMON, Scott ... 949-214-3735 40 E
scott.ashmon@cui.edu
ASHMYAN, Ilya ... 201-360-4693 277 D
iashmyan@hccc.edu
ASHPOLE, Steve ... 253-680-7005 477 A
sashpole@batestech.edu
ASHRAF, Mitu ... 910-521-6464 343 A
mohammed.ashraf@uncp.edu
ASHRAF, Sadie ... 510-723-6716 35 Q
sashraf@chabotcollege.edu
ASHTON, Andrew ... 845-437-5787 323 H
anashton@vassar.edu
ASHTON, Catherine ... 641-269-3450 166 D
ashtonca@grinnell.edu
ASHTON, Nadine ... 313-664-1495 222 C
nashton@collegeforcreativestudies.edu
ASHWORTH, Ken ... 202-806-6100 92 E
ASHWORTH, Marieca ... 501-205-8826 19 B
mashworth@cbc.edu
ASHWORTH, Pope ... 406-243-5661 263 D
pope.ashworth@umontana.edu
ASIAMAH-ANDRADE, Akua ... 856-225-6322 281 A
andradea@camden.rutgers.edu
ASIFOA, Sereima ... 684-699-2722 503 A
s.asifoa@amsamoa.edu
ASIP, Cailin ... 336-249-4688 333 G
cailin_asip@davidsondavie.edu
ASITO, Pioria ... 680-488-2471 504 A
pasito1149@gmail.com
ASKA, Aaron ... 201-200-3035 278 F
aaska@njcu.edu
ASKAR, Majd ... 951-571-6341 59 B
majd.askar@mvc.edu
ASKERLUND, Robert ... 801-957-4101 460 D
robert.askerlund@slcc.edu
ASKEW, George, R ... 864-656-3140 406 F
gaskew@clemson.edu
ASKEW, J. Alicia ... 864-833-8215 410 E
jaaskew@presby.edu
ASKEW, Jipaum ... 618-634-3423 149 C
jipauma@shawneecc.edu
ASKEW, Joseph ... 731-989-6651 418 H
jaskew@fhu.edu
ASKEW, Susan, S ... 931-598-1710 422 F
saskew@sewanee.edu
ASKEW, Tara ... 706-649-1901 117 F
taskew@columbustech.edu
ASKEW-ELLIOTT, Shalunda ... 901-435-1477 419 I
shalunda_askew-elliott@loc.edu
ASKEY, Angela ... 520-494-5485 11 M
angela.askey@centralaz.edu
ASKILDSON, Lance ... 808-735-4825 128 C
lance.askildson@chaminade.edu
ASKINS, Eric ... 510-642-6000 68 N
ASKINS, Rana ... 940-898-3505 451 A
raskins@twu.edu
ASLAM, Ersal ... 973-596-5303 278 G
ersal.aslam@njit.edu
ASLAM, Naveela ... 706-379-3111 128 A
ASLANIAN, Artour ... 310-287-4361 50 C
aslania@wlac.edu
ASLANYAN, Agasi ... 213-387-4242 48 B
ASMUS, Jeremy ... 518-327-6463 310 G
jasmus@paulsmiths.edu
ASMUTH, Shawn ... 904-620-2730 111 A
shawn.asmuth@unf.edu
ASOODEH, Mike, M ... 985-549-2314 192 E
asoodeh@selu.edu
ASP, Martin ... 617-746-1990 210 E
martin.asp@hult.edu
ASPEGREN, Eric ... 402-465-7734 267 J
easpegre@nebrwesleyan.edu
ASPELUND, Jan ... 956-326-2361 446 A
jan.aspelund@tamiu.edu
ASPER, Kris ... 713-718-6858 436 E
kris.asper@hccs.edu
ASPERGER, Joseph ... 810-762-9749 225 F
jasperge@kettering.edu
ASPINWALL, Neil ... 337-421-6965 188 H
neil.aspinwall@sowela.edu
ASPRION, Chris ... 985-549-2118 192 E
christopher.asprion@selu.edu
ASSAD, Arjang, A ... 412-648-1556 400 A
aassad@pitt.edu
ASSANIS, Dennis ... 302-831-2111 91 A
president@udel.edu
ASSER, Neala ... 561-683-1400 94 F
nasser@anho.edu
ASSERSON, Elizabeth ... 406-994-4531 263 G
basserson@montana.edu
ASSMANN, James ... 718-262-2218 295 D
jassmann@york.cuny.edu
ASSUDANI, Rashmi ... 513-745-1082 364 F
assudanir@xavier.edu
ASTARITA, Susan ... 973-720-2201 283 I
astaritas@wpunj.edu
ASTI, Tony ... 602-286-8000 13 D
anthony.asti@gatewaycc.edu
ASTOLFI, Amy ... 978-232-2286 209 B
aastolfi@endicott.edu
ASTON, Mary Kay ... 570-941-5984 400 C
marykay.aston@scranton.edu
ASTORGA, Heather, N ... 610-499-4139 401 I
hnastorga@widener.edu
ASTORGA, Juan Carlos ... 818-710-2248 49 H
astorgjc@piercecollege.edu
ASTORINA, Nicolina ... 718-390-3100 324 B
ASTUTO, James ... 603-342-3022 272 E
jastuto@ccsnh.edu
ASUKILE, Imani, D ... 727-816-3192 105 E
asukili@phsc.edu
ATALIG, Adrian ... 670-234-5498 503 G
adrian.atalig@marianas.edu
ATALIG, Adrian ... 671-734-0540 503 C
adrian.atalig@guamcc.edu
ATALLAH, Ibrahim ... 313-845-9749 224 F
iatallah@hfcc.edu
ATALLAH, Zahi ... 618-544-8657 139 E
atallahz@iecc.edu
ATALLAH, Zahi ... 618-544-8657 139 E
atallaz@iecc.edu
ATAPATTY, Nalin ... 805-482-2755 59 G
natapatty@stjohnsem.edu
ATCHINSON, KC ... 816-235-6705 260 D
atchinson@umkc.edu
ATCHISON, Eric ... 501-660-1000 17 G
eatchison@asusystem.edu
ATCHLEY, Connie ... 541-885-1720 374 G
connie.atchley@oit.edu
ATCHLEY, Paul ... 813-974-4051 111 B
patchley@usf.edu
ATCHLEY, Ruth Ann ... 813-974-7175 111 B
ratchley@usf.edu
ATCHLEY, Tony ... 251-981-3771 5 B
tony.atchley@columbiasouthern.edu
ATEN, Kevin ... 970-564-6222 82 I
kevin.aten@pueblocc.edu
ATEN, Shawn ... 800-658-4308 266 J
atens@mpcc.edu
ATENCIO, Elaine ... 619-260-4520 72 H
atencio@sandiego.edu
ATENCIO, Yvette ... 719-846-5538 83 I
yvette.atencio@trinidadstate.edu
ATES, Kerry, A ... 410-516-8068 199 E
kates1@jhu.edu
ATEWOLOGUN, Adenuga ... 507-433-0607 240 A
adenuga.atewologun@riverland.edu
ATHA, Jordan ... 304-205-6704 487 D
jordan.atha@bridgevalley.edu
ATHERTON, Beth ... 512-313-4101 432 N
beth.atherton@concordia.edu
ATHERTON, Joe ... 707-467-3067 51 F
jatherton@mendocino.edu
ATHIS, Joslin "Joe" ... 305-626-0207 100 B
joslin.athis@fmuniv.edu
ATHMAN, Meredith, L ... 320-308-2102 240 C
mlathman@stcloudstate.edu
ATIEH, Lute ... 816-279-7000 249 D
lute@abtu.edu
ATIEH, Ramsey ... 816-279-7000 249 D
ramsey@abtu.edu
ATIEH, Ramsey ... 567-200-6829 353 A
ramsey.atieh@globaltech.edu
ATIENZA, Johanna ... 626-529-8007 55 E
ATILES, Jorge ... 304-293-6967 489 E
jorge.atiles@mail.wvu.edu
ATKERSON, Emily ... 918-495-7032 368 F
eatkerson@oru.edu
ATKIN, Jacob ... 801-863-8576 460 A
jacob.atkin@uvu.edu
ATKINS, Angie, S ... 662-329-7126 247 B
asatkins@muw.edu
ATKINS, Caroline ... 606-783-2097 183 H
c.atkins@moreheadstate.edu
ATKINS, Colette ... 319-398-5431 167 H
colette.atkins@kirkwood.edu
ATKINS, Colette ... 718-518-4407 293 F
catkins@hostos.cuny.edu
ATKINS, Courtney, B ... 910-898-9602 336 A
atkinsc@montgomery.edu
ATKINS, Darian ... 318-345-9265 188 A
datkins@ladelta.edu
ATKINS, David ... 423-585-6934 424 G
david.atkins@ws.edu
ATKINS, David, P ... 423-439-4337 418 D
atkinsdp@etsu.edu
ATKINS, Deb ... 763-424-0993 239 D
datkins@nhcc.edu
ATKINS, Elizabeth ... 856-225-2521 281 A
atkins1@camden.rutgers.edu
ATKINS, Elizabeth, A ... 856-225-2521 281 A
atkins1@camden.rutgers.edu
ATKINS, Laura ... 216-397-1886 353 O
latkins@jcu.edu
ATKINS, Michael ... 301-860-4362 203 D
matkins@bowiestate.edu
ATKINS, Michele ... 731-661-5465 425 F
matkins@uu.edu

ATKINS, Nolan, T 802-626-6406 463 B nolan.atkins@northernvermont.edu
ATKINS, Paula 318-797-5116 189 E paula.atkins@lsus.edu
ATKINS, Regina 812-237-2510 155 H regina.atkins@indstate.edu
ATKINS, Rodney 903-730-4890 437 E ratkins@jarvis.edu
ATKINS, Vicky 401-232-6026 403 B vatkins@bryant.edu
ATKINS, Victoria 610-399-2097 393 D vatkins@cheyney.edu
ATKINS, Warren 504-671-5416 187 I watkin@dcc.edu
ATKINS-BRADY, Tara 757-569-6713 474 A tatkins-brady@pdc.edu
ATKINSON, Blaire 405-385-5100 367 G batkinson@osugiving.com
ATKINSON, Charles 606-218-5194 185 F charlesatkinson@upike.edu
ATKINSON, Denese 606-886-3863 181 A denese.atkinson@kctcs.edu
ATKINSON, Eva, G 270-686-4282 179 F eva.atkinson@brescia.edu
ATKINSON, Judith 856-415-2115 280 F jatkinson@rcsj.edu
ATKINSON, Juli 918-495-7650 368 F juatkinson@oru.edu
ATKINSON, Kacey 561-683-1400 94 F katkinson@anho.edu
ATKINSON, Maryanne 617-228-2027 214 A matkinso@bhcc.edu
ATKINSON, Rebekah 817-257-8309 447 H r.j.atkinson@tcu.edu
ATKINSON, Rose 406-768-6317 262 I ratkinson@fpcc.edu
ATKINSON, Sander 601-484-8707 246 B satkinso@meridiancc.edu
ATKINSON, Sheri 530-752-8787 69 A slatkinson@ucdavis.edu
ATKINSON, Simon 785-864-7298 177 G satkinson@ku.edu
ATKINSON, Susan 870-245-5581 20 H atkinsons@obu.edu
ATKINSON, Timothy 931-221-7011 416 H atkinsont@apsu.edu
ATKINSON-WILLOUGHBY, Brenda 202-687-5677 92 D ba3@georgetown.edu
ATLAN, Stephanie 213-613-2200 65 D stephanie_atlan@sciarc.edu
ATOIGUE, Celia 671-734-1812 503 D catoigue@piu.edu
ATON, Rob 541-888-1623 376 B rob.aton@socc.edu
ATTALLA, Mohamed 646-664-2605 292 E mohamed.attalla@cuny.edu
ATTAO, David 670-237-6887 503 G david.attao@marianas.edu
ATTEBERY, Phillip 903-586-2501 430 C phillip.attebery@bmats.edu
ATTEMA, Staci 605-331-6814 416 C staci.attema@usiouxfalls.edu
ATTI, Stephanie 716-829-8158 298 C attis@dyc.edu
ATTIPOE, Sherika 256-306-2560 1 F sherika.attipoe@calhoun.edu
ATTORD, DeNeen 813-663-0100 93 H
ATWATER, Caryn 336-272-7102 329 B caryn.atwater@greensboro.edu
ATWATER, Harry, A 626-395-4100 29 B haa@its.caltech.edu
ATWATER, Ken 813-253-7050 102 A katwater@hccfl.edu
ATWELL, Patrick 573-288-6424 251 I patwell@culver.edu
ATWOOD, Andrew 615-297-7545 416 G atwooda@aquinascollege.edu
ATWOOD, Lorraine 802-831-1204 462 F latwood@vermontlaw.edu
ATWOOD, Peter 617-585-0200 206 E peter.atwood@the-bac.edu
ATWOOD, Steve 573-840-9708 259 I satwood@trcc.edu
ATWOOD, Thomas 419-530-2833 363 B thomas.atwood@utoledo.edu
ATZERT, Andy 516-877-3424 288 L aatzert@adelphi.edu
AU, Gerard 909-537-5100 33 B gau@csusb.edu
AU, Peggy 510-628-8038 48 G peggyau@lincolnuca.edu
AU, Valerie 508-999-8826 211 F valerie.au@umassd.edu
AU-MULLANEY, Rebecca 212-659-3601 303 E rau@tkc.edu
AU-YEUNG, Michael 909-537-3132 33 B michael.au-yeung@csusb.edu
AUBE, Maureen 207-755-5235 194 J maube@cmcc.edu
AUBERT, Griselda 575-624-7149 285 F griselda.aubert@roswell.enmu.edu
AUBERT, OSB, Jerome 985-867-2294 190 I brjerome@sjasc.edu
AUBERT, Ronald 401-863-9858 403 A ronald_aubert@brown.edu
AUBREY, Karen 704-406-4239 328 I kaubrey@gardner-webb.edu
AUBRY, Ann 309-556-3874 140 E aaubry@iwu.edu
AUBRY, Dawn, M 248-370-3228 229 F dmaubry@oakland.edu
AUBURGER, Colleen 301-445-1936 202 D cauburger@usmd.edu
AUCHINCLOSS, Robin 718-960-8226 293 E robin.auchincloss@lehman.cuny.edu
AUCOIN, Brent 765-448-1986 154 I
AUCOIN, Martin, C 704-461-6258 326 I martinaucoin@bac.edu
AUD, Peggy, R 240-895-3060 201 F praud@smcm.edu
AUDANT, Babette 718-518-4241 293 F baudant@hostos.cuny.edu
AUDAS, JP 405-224-3140 371 B jpaudas@usao.edu
AUDET, Shirley 860-465-5337 85 G audets@easternct.edu
AUDET, Suzanne 508-999-8076 211 F saudet@umassd.edu
AUDET-KRANS, Janis 802-656-7878 462 D janis.audet-krans@uvm.edu
AUDETTE, Bert 207-974-4682 195 A baudette@emcc.edu
AUDETTE, Jordan 316-295-5658 173 G jordan_audette@friends.edu
AUDUSSEAU, Loic 310-660-3593 41 J laudusseau@elcamino.edu
AUDYATIS, Todd 508-531-2608 212 B taudyatis@bridgew.edu
AUER, Matthew, R 706-542-2059 126 F matthew.auer@uga.edu
AUER, Susanne 605-455-6097 414 H sauer@olc.edu
AUER, Susanne 605-455-6049 414 H sauer@olc.edu
AUERBACH, Joshua 802-322-1619 461 D joshua.auerbach@goddard.edu
AUERNHEIMER, Brent 559-278-4373 31 D brent_auernheimer@csufresno.edu
AUGENSTEIN, Amee 317-813-2320 157 G aaugenstein@ibcindianapolis.edu
AUGENSTEIN, Heather 928-428-8333 12 H heather.augenstein@eac.edu
AUGENSTEIN, Mike 740-386-4138 355 F augensteinm@mtc.edu
AUGESTINE-COLLINS, Sandy 518-244-2274 312 D augsts@sage.edu
AUGHENBAUGH, Barbara 410-837-5719 204 C baughenbaugh@ubalt.edu
AUGHENBAUGH, Jonette 304-327-4049 488 J jaughenbaugh@bluefieldstate.edu
AUGHENBAUGH, Lisa 410-386-8494 197 G laughenbaugh@carrollcc.edu
AUGHINBAUGH, David 864-592-4482 411 E aughinbaughd@sccsc.edu
AUGOSTINI, Christopher 404-712-6018 118 D christopher.l.augostini@emory.edu
AUGSBURGER, Lee 215-887-5511 401 G leeaugsburger@wts.edu
AUGUST, Avery 607-253-4045 297 D aa749@cornell.edu
AUGUST, James 805-437-2099 30 D jim.august@csuci.edu
AUGUST, John, R 979-845-5053 446 B j-august@tamu.edu
AUGUST, Michele 620-241-0723 172 H michele.august@centralchristian.edu
AUGUSTINE, Gina 740-264-5591 352 B gaugustine@egcc.edu
AUGUSTINE, Jacqueline 760-245-4271 74 D jacqueline.augustine@vvc.edu
AUGUSTINE, Lailani 570-674-6248 389 H laugustine@misericordia.edu
AUGUSTINE, TJ 312-413-1454 151 D aaugustn@uic.edu
AUGUSTINE-PLAISANCE, Lu-Ann 718-409-7302 320 D laugustine@sunymaritime.edu
AUGUSTUS, Edward 508-541-1658 208 E chancellor@dean.edu
AUKAI-PAIA, Lori 808-735-4785 128 C lori.aukai-paia@chaminade.edu
AULICINO, Christy, L 727-816-3443 105 E aulicic@phsc.edu
AULISIO, George 570-941-4008 400 C george.aulisio@scranton.edu
AULL, JR., Zeke 251-460-6609 9 A zaull@southalabama.edu
AULT, Jill 530-242-7689 64 A jault@shastacollege.edu
AULT, Jill 530-242-7500 64 A
AULT, Kathy 308-635-6350 269 E aultk@wncc.edu
AULTMAN-BECKER, April 432-837-8121 449 F axa15ee@sulross.edu
AUM, SeokJoo 213-487-0110 41 I president@dula.edu
AUMAN, Ann, J 253-535-8485 481 C aumanaj@plu.edu
AUMAN, Timothy, L 336-758-5210 344 A aumantl@wfu.edu
AUNAI, Samasoni 559-934-2222 74 L samaunai@whccd.edu
AUNE, Dave 763-433-1306 236 H david.aune@anokaramsey.edu
AUNE, Krystyna 808-956-7541 129 B krystyna@hawaii.edu
AUNE, Mark 724-938-4535 394 C aune@calu.edu
AUNE, Richard, S 507-933-7676 235 E raune@gustavus.edu
AUNE, Tami 507-933-6113 235 E taune@gustavus.edu
AUNGST, Don 434-791-5651 463 L daungst@averett.edu
AUPPERLE, Jared 302-831-8156 91 A jaup@udel.edu
AUPPERLE, Jeff 765-998-4553 161 A jeffry_aupperle@taylor.edu
AURICCHIO, Laura 212-636-6300 300 A lauricchio@fordham.edu
AURIGEMMA, Maureen 845-758-6822 290 G
AURINGER, Melissa 303-458-3510 83 B mauringer@regis.edu
AURITI, Brian 239-410-4147 326 J bauriti@bennett.edu
AURO, Fadi 314-792-6119 253 J auro@kenrick.edu
AURORA, Teri 770-533-6918 121 L taurora@laniertech.edu
AUSBAND, Avrohom 718-601-3523 325 Q
AUSBORN, Dawn 910-630-7610 331 B dausborn@methodist.edu
AUSBURY, Brad 417-862-9533 252 H bausbury@globaluniversity.edu
AUSBURY, D. Bradley 417-862-9533 252 H bausbury@globaluniversity.edu
AUSDEMORE, Jayma 402-826-8670 266 A jayma.ausdemore@doane.edu
AUSEL, Jill 412-365-1244 380 F jausel@chatham.edu
AUSMAN, David, J 412-397-5424 396 E ausman@rmu.edu
AUSTER, Julie 646-592-4335 325 R julie.auster@yu.edu
AUSTIN, Adelee 802-258-3359 462 B adelee.austin@worldlearning.org
AUSTIN, Alton 352-854-2322 97 L austina@cf.edu
AUSTIN, Amber 502-863-7008 180 E amber_austin@georgetowncollege.edu
AUSTIN, Ann, E 517-353-5300 227 C aaustin@msu.edu
AUSTIN, Ann, E 517-355-1734 227 C aaustin@msu.edu
AUSTIN, Anne 870-612-2058 23 B anne.austin@uaccb.edu
AUSTIN, April 404-270-5153 126 A aprila@spelman.edu
AUSTIN, Bob 318-473-6571 189 A raustin@lsua.edu
AUSTIN, Bob, C 806-371-5024 428 F rcaustin@actx.edu
AUSTIN, Christine 479-880-4282 18 E caustin@atu.edu
AUSTIN, Christopher 225-578-2841 188 K ccaustin@lsu.edu
AUSTIN, Dale, F 616-395-7950 224 H austin@hope.edu
AUSTIN, Deborah 717-261-4381 402 D daustin@wilson.edu
AUSTIN, Geoff, P 206-598-8318 484 A graustin@uw.edu
AUSTIN, Jonathan 502-897-4121 184 D jaustin@sbts.edu
AUSTIN, Kathryn 516-572-7759 307 C kathryn.austin@ncc.edu
AUSTIN, Kristin 610-436-1725 394 F kaustin@wcupa.edu
AUSTIN, Laurie 718-960-8706 293 E laurie.austin@lehman.cuny.edu
AUSTIN, Marc 706-721-0211 115 I
AUSTIN, Marcia, M 727-816-3264 105 E austinm@phsc.edu
AUSTIN, Mel, L 414-410-4002 490 J mlaustin@stritch.edu
AUSTIN, Michael 812-488-1178 161 E ma352@evansville.edu
AUSTIN, Rashonda 402-554-5958 269 C raustin@unomaha.edu
AUSTIN, Renee 615-230-3587 424 F renee.austin@volstate.edu
AUSTIN, Renee 931-393-1640 423 G raustin1@mscc.edu
AUSTIN, Sheila 334-244-3425 4 F saustin1@aum.edu
AUSTIN, Susan 212-229-8950 307 E austins@newschool.edu
AUSTIN, Suzanne 843-953-4983 407 D austinse@cofc.edu
AUSTIN, Taylor, J 405-325-3916 370 J tjaustin@ou.edu
AUSTIN, Tiffany 201-559-3620 277 A austint@felician.edu
AUSTIN, Tracey, M 603-526-3886 271 H taustin@colby-sawyer.edu
AUSTIN, William 908-689-7618 283 H will@warren.edu
AUSTIN-KETCH, Tammy 315-464-3900 316 F austinkt@upstate.edu
AUTERO, Esa 954-545-4500 108 C academics@sfbc.edu
AUTHIER, Adam 734-462-4400 230 B aauthier@schoolcraft.edu
AUTIO, Wesley 413-545-2963 211 D autio@umass.edu
AUTREY, Krista, M 724-847-6636 384 B kmautrey@geneva.edu
AUTRY, Dean 270-686-4464 182 C dean.autry@kctcs.edu
AUTRY, James, C 801-422-3928 458 A autry@byu.edu
AUVENSHINE, Donnie 325-649-8002 437 A dauvenshine@hputx.edu
AUVIL, Joe 509-793-2016 477 D joea@bigbend.edu
AUXENTIOS, Bishop 530-467-3544 60 A rector@spots.edu
AVAKIAN, Brad 360-992-2986 477 J bavakian@clark.edu
AVAKIAN, Satenik 510-925-4282 25 P savakian@aua.am
AVALONE, Valarie, L 585-292-3021 306 K vavalone@monroecc.edu
AVALOS, Jesse 617-236-8827 209 D javalos@fisher.edu
AVALOS, Juan 949-582-4566 65 C javalos@saddleback.edu
AVALOS, Marlena 773-252-6464 146 D marlena.avalos@oakpoint.edu
AVALOS, Natalie 818-767-0888 76 D natalie.avalos@woodbury.edu
AVALOS, Natalie 818-252-5107 76 D natalie.avalos@woodbury.edu
AVALOS, Robert 323-343-3060 32 B ravalo10@calstatela.edu
AVALOS, Yesenia Noreeka 219-989-2872 160 A yavalos@pnw.edu
AVALOS-SÁNCHEZ, Javier 787-993-8863 510 E javier.avalos@upr.edu
AVALTRONI, Michael 201-692-7094 276 I mavaltro@fdu.edu
AVANT, Robin 203-332-5984 86 E ravant@housatonic.edu

AVANT, Tamara .... 252-399-6497 326 H tavant@barton.edu
AVANT, Toni, D .... 662-915-7174 248 F tavant@olemiss.edu
AVEDESIAN, Starr .... 714-628-4862.. 58 G avedesian_starr@sccollege.edu
AVEGALIO, Daniel .... 660-596-7393 259 D davegalio@sfccmo.edu
AVELINO, Melanie .... 336-633-0256 336 F mlavelino@randolph.edu
AVENDANO, John .... 904-632-5032 101 A john.avendano@fscj.edu
AVENIA, Bradford .... 303-273-3548.. 79 A bavenia@mines.edu
AVENT, Jenna .... 336-272-7102 329 B jenna.avent@greensboro.edu
AVENT, Randy, K .... 863-583-9050 110 A
AVERBECK, Daniel, H ... 513-519-9671.. 96 B daverbeck@appliedassessmentsinc.com
AVERETT, Mike .... 812-488-2050 161 E ma479@evansville.edu
AVERILL, Gary .... 916-306-1628.. 67 E gaverill@sum.edu
AVERILL, Leslie .... 802-865-5715 461 C laverill@champlain.edu
AVERITT, Brad .... 931-221-6373 416 H averittb@apsu.edu
AVERY, Alycia .... 603-626-9490 273 E a.avery@snhu.edu
AVERY, Cynthia .... 619-260-4588.. 72 H cynthiaavery@sandiego.edu
AVERY, Diane .... 661-362-3640.. 38 H diane.avery@canyons.edu
AVERY, Hannah .... 606-693-5000 182 H havery@kmbc.edu
AVERY, James .... 731-661-5326 425 F javery@uu.edu
AVERY, Jared .... 214-887-5201 434 G javery@dts.edu
AVERY, Kathy .... 918-293-4988 368 B kathy.avery@okstate.edu
AVERY, Lisa .... 541-917-4200 373 F averyl@linnbenton.edu
AVERY, Martin .... 315-386-7222 319 E averym@canton.edu
AVERY, Michelle, D ...... 719-884-5000.. 82 A mdavery@nbc.edu
AVERY, Rebecca .... 610-896-1230 385 H ravery@haverford.edu
AVERY, Sherri, M .... 781-736-3706 207 D savery@brandeis.edu
AVERY, Thomas .... 419-517-8893 355 C tavery@lourdes.edu
AVERYT, Kati .... 541-956-7346 375 G kaveryt@roguecc.edu
AVETISYAN, Lucy .... 310-206-6771.. 69 D lucyavetisyan@ucla.edu
AVILA, Alyssa .... 657-278-2998.. 31 E alavila@fullerton.edu
AVILA, Brandi .... 951-571-6159.. 59 B brandi.avila@mvc.edu
AVILA, Esmerelda .... 954-378-2400.. 93 H
AVILA, Holly .... 405-422-6283 368 I holly.avila@redlandscc.edu
AVILA, Jason .... 562-938-4313.. 48 K javila@lbcc.edu
AVILA, Jennifer .... 626-571-8811.. 73 D jennifera@uwest.edu
AVILA, Jorge .... 831-242-5291 501 D
AVILA, Kelly .... 209-384-6000.. 52 B kelly.avila@mccd.edu
AVILA, Mitch .... 805-437-8400.. 30 D
AVILA, Pedro .... 707-524-1647.. 63 C pavila@santarosa.edu
AVILA, Pedro .... 408-848-4712.. 43 H pedroavila@gavilan.edu
AVILA, Susan .... 510-594-3661.. 28 D savila@cca.edu
AVILES, Gladys, M .... 248-204-4123 226 E gaviles@ltu.edu
AVILES, Jose .... 225-578-1175 188 K javiles1@lsu.edu
AVILES, Jose .... 225-578-2111 188 J
AVIOLA, Joseph, P .... 302-295-1165.. 91 C joseph.p.aviola@wilmu.edu
AVIS ROGERS, Julie ...... 617-824-8036 208 G julie_avisrogers@emerson.edu
AVISSAR, Roni .... 305-421-4000 112 K avissar@miami.edu
AW, Fanta .... 202-885-3357.. 91 D fanta@american.edu
AWADALLAH, Baha .... 773-602-5068 135 A bawadallah@ccc.edu
AWAN, Seher .... 408-855-5122.. 75 C
AWE, Jacqueline .... 912-358-3114 124 H awej@savannahstate.edu
AWES-FREEMAN, Jennifer .... 651-255-6140 242 J jawes-freeman@unitedseminary.edu
AWONIYI, Beatrice .... 352-395-5513 107 G bea.awoniyi@sfcollege.edu
AWOPETU, Lawrence ..... 870-575-8649.. 22 F awopetul@uapb.edu
AWUAH, Agatha .... 315-498-2500 310 C awuaha@sunyocc.edu
AWUAH, Emmanuel ...... 320-308-5030 240 D emmanuel.awuah@sctcc.edu
AWWAD, Elise .... 630-515-3105 136 G eawwad@devry.edu
AXLUND MCBRIDE, RaeLyn .... 360-752-8344 477 C raelyn.axlund.mcbride@btc.edu
AXON, Diane .... 910-221-2224 330 G daxon@manna.edu
AXTELL, Denise .... 530-242-7771.. 64 A daxtell@shastacollege.edu
AXVIG, Samantha .... 218-299-4562 234 K axvig@cord.edu
AYABE, John .... 530-226-4152.. 64 C jayabe@simpsonu.edu
AYAD, Nada .... 212-353-4302 297 C nada.ayad@cooper.edu
AYALA, Aurora .... 619-482-6320.. 65 K aayala@swccd.edu
AYALA, Carmen .... 787-761-0640 510 A decanaacademica@utcpr.edu
AYALA, Caroline .... 787-264-1912 507 E caroline_ayala@intersg.edu
AYALA, Hector, L .... 787-850-9303 511 B hector.ayala5@upr.edu
AYALA, Ingrid .... 305-377-8817.. 95 K ingrid.ayala@atlantisuniversity.edu
AYALA, Israel .... 787-891-0925 506 I iayala@aguadilla.inter.edu
AYALA, Javier .... 619-644-7158.. 44 H javier.ayala@gcccd.edu
AYALA, Jose, L .... 787-250-0000 510 B jose.ayala5@upr.edu
AYALA, Mary .... 575-562-2421 285 E mary.ayala@enmu.edu
AYALA, Oliva .... 818-364-7795.. 49 G sancheo@lamission.edu
AYALA, Pedro .... 787-738-2161 511 A pedro.ayala1@upr.edu
AYALA, Ramon .... 787-250-1912 507 C rayala@intermetro.edu
AYALA, Sharon .... 619-849-2988.. 57 J sharonayala@pointloma.edu
AYALA, Shawn .... 617-588-1352 206 B sayala@bfit.edu
AYALA-JIMENEZ, Monica .... 210-486-3338 428 B mayala5@alamo.edu
AYAR, Christina .... 586-445-7302 226 F ayarc84@macomb.edu
AYARS, Daniel .... 937-328-6040 350 D ayarsd@clarkstate.edu
AYARS, Matthew, I .... 601-366-8880 249 A miayars@wbs.edu
AYCOCK, Allan .... 706-542-1546 126 F aaycock@uga.edu
AYCOCK, Allan .... 706-542-9902 126 F aaycock@uga.edu
AYCOCK, Greg .... 951-739-7802.. 59 C greg.aycock@norcocollege.edu
AYCOCK, Jim .... 662-246-6331 246 E jaycock@msdelta.edu
AYCOCK, Larry .... 909-389-3663.. 60 E laycock@sbccd.cc.ca.us
AYER, Dorothy, R .... 805-437-8517.. 30 D dorothy.ayer@csuci.edu
AYERS, Benjamin, C ..... 706-542-8100 126 F busdean@uga.edu
AYERS, James, P .... 716-880-2179 305 F james.p.ayers@medaille.edu
AYERS, Julia .... 470-578-6033 121 J jayers30@kennesaw.edu
AYERS, Kenya .... 817-515-6200 445 A kenya.ayers@tccd.edu
AYERS, Lee .... 541-552-6505 376 A ayersl@sou.edu
AYERS, Mary .... 662-562-3438 247 E
AYERS, Megan .... 252-328-6105 340 H ayersm@ecu.edu
AYERS, Michael .... 718-758-8127 293 A mrayers@brooklyn.cuny.edu
AYERS, Peggy .... 479-964-0532.. 18 E payers@atu.edu
AYERS, Sheli .... 209-954-5139.. 61 H sayers@deltacollege.edu
AYERS, Susan .... 978-232-2066 209 B sayers@endicott.edu
AYERS, Tom .... 810-762-9787 225 F tayers@kettering.edu
AYERSMAN, David, J ..... 304-256-0281 487 G dayersman@newriver.edu
AYEVA, Maawiya .... 323-731-2383.. 55 G
AYKROID, David .... 847-543-2259 135 G daykroid@clcillinois.edu
AYLESBURY, Charles, T 626-568-8850.. 49 B tom@lacm.edu
AYLETT, Ashley .... 870-584-1125.. 22 G aaylett@cccua.edu
AYLWARD, Denise .... 570-422-3203 393 F daylward@esu.edu
AYLWARD, Paige .... 785-309-3100 177 B paige.johnson@salinatech.edu
AYLWARD, Robert, R .... 307-766-4860 500 H raylward@uwyo.edu
AYMER, Margaret .... 512-404-4821 429 K maymer@austinseminary.edu
AYNES, Danny .... 541-917-4999 373 F aynesd@linnbenton.edu
AYON, Carlos .... 714-992-7042.. 54 D cayon@fullcoll.edu
AYON, Carlos .... 714-992-7033.. 54 D cayon@fullcoll.edu
AYON, Maria .... 928-505-3300.. 14 H mayon@mohave.edu
AYOUCH, Karen .... 315-866-0300 301 B ayouchka@herkimer.edu
AYRAVAINEN, Eija .... 212-772-4878 294 A eija.ayravainen@hunter.cuny.edu
AYRES, Amy .... 405-208-7910 367 E aayres@okcu.edu
AYRES, Bill .... 330-675-8823 354 A rayres1@kent.edu
AYRES, Christina .... 435-797-1455 459 F christina.ayres@usu.edu
AYRES, Christina, M ..... 573-202-6959 252 D christina.ayres@eastcentral.edu
AYRES, Dana .... 214-768-2841 443 G dwayres@smu.edu
AYRES, Deb .... 636-949-4405 254 B dayres@lindenwood.edu
AYRES, Jessica .... 650-433-3824.. 55 K jayres@paloaltou.edu
AZAD, Neelam .... 757-637-2539 466 L neelam.azad@hamptonu.edu
AZAMA, Anthony, J ...... 314-935-5000 261 B anthony.j.azama@wustl.edu
AZAR, Eve .... 908-835-2335 283 H azar@warren.edu
AZDELL, Grant, L .... 804-752-7266 469 B gazdell@rmc.edu
AZEVEDO, Filipe .... 918-495-6813 368 F fazevedo@oru.edu
AZEVEDO, Steve .... 480-461-7974.. 13 F steve.azevedo@mesacc.edu
AZIZ, Hassan .... 361-825-2649 446 E hassan.aziz@tamucc.edu
AZIZ, Jihad, N .... 804-828-6200 472 D jnaziz@vcu.edu
AZIZ, Majdouline .... 864-424-8046 412 H azizma@mailbox.sc.edu
AZIZI, Kate .... 843-792-4281 409 D azizi@musc.edu
AZKOUL, Emilie .... 616-222-1447 222 F emilie.azkoul@cornerstone.edu
AZURE, Lane .... 605-698-3966 415 C lazure@swcollege.edu
AZURE, Lisa .... 701-255-3285 346 I lazure@uttc.edu
AZURE, Tracy .... 701-477-7809 346 H tazure@tm.edu
AZZAM-GOMEZ, Shady . 631-451-4920 320 G azzamgs@sunysuffolk.edu
AZZARA, Thomas .... 934-420-2599 320 C azzaratf@farmingdale.edu
AZZARELLO, Tony .... 419-227-3141 362 F amazzare@unoh.edu
AZZI, Amanda, R .... 607-871-2325 289 E ruscitto@alfred.edu
AZZU, Heather .... 336-734-7273 334 D hazzu@forsythtech.edu
A'SEE, Carlito, D .... 803-536-7485 410 H cdasee@scsu.edu

B

BAACH, Laurence, A ..... 212-217-3400 299 C laurence_baach@fitnyc.edu
BAACK, Cathryn .... 614-781-1085 352 F cbaack@felbrycollege.edu
BAADE, Lamanda .... 815-802-8837 141 B lbaade@kcc.edu
BAAR, Tricia .... 501-337-5000.. 18 D tbaar@asutr.edu
BAAR, Tricia .... 501-332-0238.. 18 D tbaar@asutr.edu
BAARMAND, Fanak .... 321-674-8885 100 A fbaarman@fit.edu
BAART, Aaron .... 712-722-6079 165 E aaron.baart@dordt.edu
BAARTMAN, Randy .... 712-324-5061 168 H rbaartman@nwicc.edu
BAAS, Beth .... 712-722-6990 165 E beth.baas@dordt.edu
BAAS, John .... 712-722-6020 165 E john.baas@dordt.edu
BAAS, Mark .... 507-431-2202 240 A mark.baas@riverland.edu
BAATZ, Stephanie .... 605-256-5675 415 G stephanie.baatz@dsu.edu
BABAKER, Jessica .... 352-335-2332.. 94 E
BABALIS, Eva .... 718-779-1430 310 I ebabalis@plazacollege.edu
BABANI, Henry .... 305-442-9223 104 G hbabani@mru.edu
BABASOLOUKIAN, Alin . 212-217-4000 299 C alin_babasoloukian@fitnyc.edu
BABB, Billy .... 636-229-7900 261 A bbabb@upci.org
BABB, Brian .... 386-506-4457.. 98 A brian.babb@daytonastate.edu
BABB, Brian, T .... 386-506-4457.. 98 A brian.babb@daytonastate.edu
BABB, Charmaine .... 302-857-7009.. 90 D cbabb@desu.edu
BABB, Mac .... 540-231-5123 475 D wmb1@vt.edu
BABB, Michael .... 614-287-2473 351 B mbabb6@cscc.edu
BABB, Stephanie .... 559-324-6463.. 66 H stephanie.babb@cloviscollege.edu
BABB, Tina, M .... 806-371-5420 428 F tmbabb@actx.edu
BABBITT, Terry .... 505-277-2626 288 C tbabbitt@unm.edu
BABCOCK, Daphne, H ... 972-378-8835 432 I dbabcock@collin.edu
BABCOCK, Ed .... 309-694-5337 138 I ebabcock@icc.edu
BABCOCK, Jamie, T ...... 607-871-2460 289 E babcock@alfred.edu
BABCOCK, Rob .... 402-461-7344 266 C rbabcock@hastings.edu
BABCOCK, Whit .... 540-231-3977 475 D hokiead@vt.edu
BABCOCK-DEPEW, Elizabeth .... 219-989-2367 160 A ebabcock@pnw.edu
BABENCHUK, Iaroslava . 631-451-4409 320 G babenci@sunysuffolk.edu
BABER, III, Jimmie .... 734-677-5359 232 A jbaberiii@wccnet.edu
BABER, Kathleen .... 336-334-3147 342 D kababer@uncg.edu
BABER, Thomas .... 919-573-5350 340 A tbaber@shepherds.edu
BABETZ, Jeff .... 843-863-7921 406 C jbabetz@csuniv.edu
BABETZ, Jeffrey .... 843-863-7921 406 C jbabetz@csuniv.edu
BABIC, Djuradj .... 323-260-8120.. 49 D babicd@elac.edu
BABIN, Lisa .... 318-675-8769 189 D lisa.babin@lsuhs.edu
BABINGTON, Lynn .... 808-735-4741 128 C president@chaminade.edu
BABOWICZ, Debra, P ... 315-684-6078 320 E babowidp@morrisville.edu
BABUSZCZAK, Keith ..... 919-866-5817 338 E kbabuszczak@waketech.edu
BACA, Amy .... 575-538-6169 288 J amy.baca@wnmu.edu
BACA, Brad .... 970-943-2186.. 85 B bbaca@western.edu
BACA, Clair .... 909-667-4481.. 38 A cbaca@claremontlincoln.edu
BACA, Diana .... 505-428-1267 287 H diana.baca@sfcc.edu

BACA, Janice 505-747-2115 287 C janice.baca@nnmc.edu
BACA, Jim 806-345-5561 428 F j0512060@actx.edu
BACA, Josepha 805-378-4133 73 I jbaca@vcccd.edu
BACA, Julie 970-943-2061 85 B jfeier@western.edu
BACA, Lori 505-747-2186 287 C lbaca@nnmc.edu
BACA, Max 505-454-3272 286 C mbaca@nmhu.edu
BACA, Sylvia 505-426-2048 286 C sbaca@nmhu.edu
BACARISSE, Charles 281-649-3428 436 D cbacarisse@hbu.edu
BACCAM, Stephanie 712-722-6014 165 E stephanie.baccam@dordt.edu
BACCAR, Cindy 503-725-5533 375 D baccarc@pdx.edu
BACCARY, Annie 303-541-1321 83 L annie.baccary@cu.edu
BACCHETTA, Aldo 816-802-3334 253 H abacchetta@kcai.edu
BACH, Alex 913-234-0610 172 I alex.bach@cleveland.edu
BACH, Jacqueline 225-578-6867 188 K jbach@lsu.edu
BACH, Julie 708-524-6366 137 A jbach@dom.edu
BACH, Ken 717-477-1201 394 D ktbach@ship.edu
BACH, Larry, C 612-343-4703 241 O lcbach@northcentral.edu
BACH MCELWAIN, Emily 719-549-2067 79 G emiy.mcelwain@csupueblo.edu
BACHAND, Donald, J 989-964-4041 229 L dbachand@svsu.edu
BACHAS, Leonidas, G 305-284-4117 112 K bachas@miami.edu
BACHHER, Jagdeep, S 510-987-0260 68 M jagdeep.baccher@ucop.edu
BACHIER, Carmen 787-250-0000 510 B carmen.bachier1@upr.edu
BACHLE, Lori 402-552-6127 265 G bachle@clarksoncollege.edu
BACHMAN, Katie 760-384-6150 47 C katie.bachman@cerrocoso.edu
BACHMAN, Sara 215-898-5511 399 J sbachman@upenn.edu
BACHMANN, Kirk 303-494-7988 77 I
BACHMANN, Michele 757-352-4302 469 D mbachmann@regent.edu
BACHMEIER, Gabrielle 206-878-3710 480 C gbachmeier@highline.edu
BACHMEIER, Jim 231-591-2164 223 H jimbachmeier@ferris.edu
BACHMEIER, Mark 828-262-6483 340 G bachmeiermd@appstate.edu
BACHRACH, Gavriel 847-982-2500 138 G bachrach@htc.edu
BACHRACH, Steven 540-831-5958 468 E sbachrach@radford.edu
BACHRI, Abdel 870-235-4290 21 E agbachri@saumag.edu
BACHTEL, Tara 903-923-2119 435 A tbachtel@etbu.edu
BACIGALUPI, Michael 606-218-5510 185 F mbacigalupi@upike.edu
BACIK, Valerie 814-871-5571 383 H bacik001@gannon.edu
BACK, Roxanne 863-680-4982 100 F rback@flsouthern.edu
BACK, Tony 606-487-3302 181 E tony.back@kctcs.edu
BACKER, Joni 402-375-7200 267 I jobacke1@wsc.edu
BACKES, Karen 320-308-5087 240 D karen.backes@sctcc.edu
BACKES, Karen 320-363-5933 234 I kbackes@csbsju.edu
BACKHAUS, Kristin 845-257-2930 316 B backhauk@newpaltz.edu
BACKLIN, William 785-833-4511 175 C bill.backlin@kwu.edu
BACKMAN, Andrea 202-419-0400 93 H
BACKMAN, Kelli 402-467-9052 266 A kelli.backman@doane.edu
BACKOFEN, Susan 229-226-1621 126 B sbackofen@thomasu.edu
BACKUS, Karlyn 585-345-6850 300 D kmbackus@genesee.edu
BACKUS, Robert, H 607-746-4677 320 A backusrh@delhi.edu
BACON, Amy 417-447-2660 257 B bacona@otc.edu
BACON, Bo 409-933-8401 432 H tbacon@com.edu
BACON, Carolyn 304-326-1242 486 I carolyn.bacon@salemu.edu
BACON, Gus 406-395-4875 264 I gbacon@stonechild.edu
BACON, Jen 610-436-0045 394 F jbacon@wcupa.edu
BACON, John 252-493-7229 336 E jbacon@email.pittcc.edu
BACON, Karen 646-592-4150 325 R kbacon@yu.edu
BACON, Kristen 315-279-5000 303 D kbacon@keuka.edu
BACON, Lyne 503-517-1212 377 B lbacon@warnerpacific.edu
BACON, Michael 210-999-7320 451 B mbacon@trinity.edu
BACON, Pamela 320-363-5401 234 I pbacon@csbsju.edu
BACON, Pamela 320-363-5167 242 G pbacon@csbsju.edu
BACON, Robbie 717-815-6818 402 G rbacon2@ycp.edu
BACON, Scott 904-256-7543 102 G sbacon@ju.edu
BACON, Scott, A 317-381-6028 162 E sbacon@vinu.edu
BACOTE, Jenia 478-471-3627 122 D jenia.bacote@mga.edu
BACOTE-CHARLES, Terri, K 301-546-0409 201 D bacotetk@pgcc.edu
BACOW, Lawrence, S 617-495-1502 210 B president@harvard.edu
BACZEWSKI, Philip, C 940-565-3886 453 B baczewski@unt.edu
BADAKHSH, Diane 912-478-5555 120 A dbadakhsh@georgiasouthern.edu
BADAL, Amy, A 570-577-1601 379 A amy.badal@bucknell.edu
BADAL, Joel 832-252-4615 431 M joel.badal@cbshouston.edu
BADALOV, Michael 847-275-9896 66 F mjb@dvcg.co
BADALYAN, Anna 323-953-4000 49 E badalya@lacitycollege.edu
BADAR, Bryan 330-490-7417 363 E bbadar@walsh.edu
BADASZEWSKI, Philip 716-878-3000 317 C badaszpd@buffalostate.edu
BADE, Robert, E 727-816-3413 105 E badeb@phsc.edu
BADEAU, Melissa 607-871-2698 289 E badeau@alfred.edu
BADEAUX, Margo 985-448-4518 192 C margo.badeaux@nicholls.edu
BADEN, Cory 407-646-2264 106 L cbaden@rollins.edu
BADENES, José 310-338-7684 51 C jose.badenes@lmu.edu
BADENHAUSEN, Richard 801-832-2460 461 A rbadenhausen@westminstercollege.edu
BADER, Greg 740-587-0810 351 K
BADER, Irv 718-820-4877 322 C irv.bader@touro.edu
BADER, Irv 718-820-4877 322 B irv.bader@touro.edu
BADER, Jerad 740-474-8896 358 A jbader@ohiochristian.edu
BADER, Melissa 951-372-7062 59 C melissa.bader@norcocollege.edu
BADER-SAYE, Scott 512-472-4133 442 H scott.bader-saye@ssw.edu
BADIA, Janet 260-481-6895 159 H badiaj@pfw.edu
BADILLO, Adriana 657-287-8280 31 E abadillo@fullerton.edu
BADILLO, Maria Antonieta 919-831-6755 435 B mbadill4@epcc.edu
BADILLO-LOZANO, Luis, V 787-841-2000 508 H luis_badillo@pucpr.edu
BADIRU, Adedeji, B 937-255-3025 501 A adedeji.badiru@afit.edu
BADMAN, Jodie 574-239-8404 155 E jbadman@hcc-nd.edu
BADOVINAC, Amanda 406-496-4828 264 C abadovinac@mtech.edu
BADOVINAC, Michele 209-468-9141 67 H mbadovinac@sjcoe.net
BADOWSKA, Eva 718-817-4400 300 A badowska@fordham.edu
BADOWSKI, Ryan 415-442-7833 44 B rbadowski@ggu.edu
BADZEK, Laurie, A 814-863-9734 391 F lzb340@psu.edu
BAE, Brian 215-368-5000 389 G bbae@missio.edu
BAEFSKY, Laurie 406-243-4987 263 D laurie.baefsky@umontana.edu
BAEK, Ji 703-323-5690 476 A registrar@vuim.edu
BAEK, Ju Young 213-385-2322 76 E
BAEK, Kyunghee 310-739-0132 41 C
BAEK, Seongyul 714-525-0088 44 C
BAER, Candace 401-454-6426 404 B cbaer@risd.edu
BAER, Christopher 240-500-2341 199 A wcbaer@hagerstowncc.edu
BAER, Dana 724-852-3295 401 E dbaer@waynesburg.edu
BAER, James 607-735-1840 298 G jbaer@elmira.edu
BAER, Lori 816-802-3448 253 H lbaer@kcai.edu
BAER, Miriam 718-780-7517 291 G miriam.baer@brooklaw.edu
BAERWALD, Bonnie 920-929-2127 498 C bbaerwald@morainepark.edu
BAETZ, Carol 804-333-6741 474 C cbaetz@rappahannock.edu
BAEZ, Ana, I 787-841-2000 508 H abaez@pucpr.edu
BAEZ, Arvin 787-841-2000 508 H arvin_baez@pucpr.edu
BAEZ, Aurelis 787-279-1912 506 L abaez@bayamon.inter.edu
BAEZ, David 787-701-5100 505 B dbaez@columbiacentral.edu
BAEZ, Jeanette, G 909-869-4088 30 B jgbaez@cpp.edu
BAEZ, Juan 310-233-4427 49 F baezrj@lahc.edu
BAEZ, Juan 212-650-7555 293 B juan@ccny.cuny.edu
BAEZ, Lorenley 212-229-5459 307 E baezl@newschool.edu
BAEZ, Thomas 864-294-3031 408 I thomas.baez@furman.edu
BAEZ MILAN, Tony 724-653-2183 382 C tbaez@dec.edu
BAEZ-ZABALA, Ariana 787-998-8997 508 K abaez@eeapr.org
BAEZA, Marco 714-438-4707 38 C mbaeza2@cccd.edu
BAEZA, Megan 432-552-2893 456 C baeza_me@utpb.edu
BAEZA-ORTEGO, Gilda 575-538-6358 288 J ortegog@wnmu.edu
BAFFA, Joe 714-556-3610 73 G joe.baffa@vanguard.edu
BAGANHA, Margarida 508-531-2877 212 B m1baganha@bridgew.edu
BAGASRA, Nisreen 617-627-6333 219 A nisreen.bagasra@tufts.edu
BAGATELIA, Eleonora, G 248-522-3491 228 H egbagate@oaklandcc.edu
BAGBY, Crystal 360-538-4082 479 F crystal.bagby@ghc.edu
BAGBY, Don 254-710-8400 430 F don_bagby@baylor.edu
BAGBY, Sara 606-693-5000 182 H srichardson@kmbc.edu
BAGBY, Tammy, A 610-399-2534 393 D tbagby@cheyney.edu
BAGDAZIAN, Robert, A 805-421-5927 67 J rbagdazian@thomasaquinas.edu
BAGG, Eva 760-252-2411 26 L ebagg@barstow.edu
BAGG, Mary Beth 317-788-3262 161 F bagg@uindy.edu
BAGGETT, Ryan 859-622-8261 180 B ryan.baggett@eku.edu
BAGGOTT, Jake 608-262-1885 494 D jake.baggott@wisc.edu
BAGGS, Adam 817-257-6814 447 H a.baggs@tcu.edu
BAGGS, David 843-863-7513 406 C dbaggs@csuniv.edu
BAGILEO, Nick, J 202-526-3799 93 E nbagileo@johnpaulii.edu
BAGIN, Mike 262-547-1211 491 A mbagin@carrollu.edu
BAGLEY, Elizabeth 404-471-6339 114 E ebagley@agnesscott.edu
BAGLEY, Judy 864-294-2320 408 I judy.bagley@furman.edu
BAGLEY, Michael 530-741-5564 77 D mbagley@yccd.edu
BAGLEY, Michelle, M 971-722-4497 375 C michelle.bagley@pcc.edu
BAGLEY, Rob 801-524-1952 458 F robbagley@ldsbc.edu
BAGLEY, Rod 715-833-6480 497 E rbagley1@cvtc.edu
BAGLEY, Shawn 330-823-2280 362 E bagleysp@mountunion.edu
BAGLIVO, Mary 212-346-1200 310 F
BAGNALL, James 928-428-8414 12 H jim.bagnall@eac.edu
BAGNELL, Brendan 916-306-1628 67 E bbagnell@sum.edu
BAGNELL, William 252-328-6858 340 H bagnellw@ecu.edu
BAGNOLI, Joseph, P 641-269-3600 166 D bagnolij@grinnell.edu
BAGSTAD, Kristi 563-588-6314 164 C kristi.bagstad@clarke.edu
BAGTAS-CARMONA, Emy 415-457-8811 39 B ebagtascarmona@marin.edu
BAGWELL, Christopher 228-896-2500 246 F christopher.bagwell@mgccc.edu
BAGWELL, Dana 814-871-7238 383 H bagwell002@gannon.edu
BAGWELL, Jack 252-335-0821 333 E
BAH, Ibrahim 919-546-8565 339 I ibrahim.bah@shawu.edu
BAHAM, Anthony 337-521-9049 188 G anthony.baham@solacc.edu
BAHAM, Liz 510-501-5075 58 H lbaham@reach.edu
BAHAM, Tracey 662-325-6941 247 A tbaham@oire.msstate.edu
BAHAMONDE, Rafael, E 317-274-2344 157 B rbahamon@iupui.edu
BAHAN, Rebecca 314-977-2500 258 H rebecca.bahan@slu.edu
BAHARANYI, Ntam 334-727-8659 7 D nbaharanyi@tuskegee.edu
BAHE, Rebecca 701-231-6255 345 D rebecca.bahe@ndsu.edu
BAHLS, Steven, C 309-794-7208 132 H stevenbahls@augustana.edu
BAHNSEN, Rachel 979-532-4560 457 H
BAHR, Brett 218-755-2599 237 B brett.bahr@bemidjistate.edu
BAHR, Jon 517-750-1200 230 F jonathan.bahr@arbor.edu
BAHREMAND, Manijeh 610-399-2260 393 D mbahremand@cheyney.edu
BAI, Kang 815-836-5640 142 C kbai@lewisu.edu
BAI, Lynn 516-739-1545 308 E admissions@nyctcm.edu
BAI, Monica, S 928-523-6514 14 J monica.bai@nau.edu
BAI, Shuming 337-475-5514 192 B sbai@mcneese.edu
BAI, Tracy 626-571-5110 48 I tracybai@les.edu
BAI, Yifeng 973-748-9000 275 C yifeng_bai@bloomfield.edu
BAIA, Larissa 603-366-5215 271 K lbaia@ccsnh.edu
BAIA, Larissa 813-253-7755 102 A lbaia@hccfl.edu
BAIARDI, Janet 313-993-1208 230 H baiardjm@udmercy.edu
BAICKER, Katherine 773-702-0711 151 B kbaicker@uchicago.edu
BAIDA, Ana 470-578-6555 121 J abaida@kennesaw.edu
BAIDOO, Christopher, E 619-239-0391 34 H cbaidoo@cwsl.edu
BAIER, Henry, D 734-764-3402 231 A hbaier@umich.edu
BAIER, Valerie, A 570-326-3761 392 S vbaier@pct.edu

BAIERL, Hans 920-924-3112 498 C hbaierl@morainepark.edu

BAILARD, Rhiannon 415-851-8858 69 B bailardrhiannon@uchastings.edu

BAILER, Joseph 910-678-8585 334 C bailerj@faytechcc.edu

BAILEY, Albert 937-502-3750 363 G a_bailey@wilberforce.edu

BAILEY, Alex 509-533-3402 478 E alexandra.bailey@sfcc.spokane.edu

BAILEY, Alison 309-438-2947 140 C baileya@ilstu.edu

BAILEY, Amanda 617-358-6887 207 C baileya1@bu.edu

BAILEY, Andrew 563-387-1507 167 J bailan01@luther.edu

BAILEY, Angela, W 252-335-3513 341 A awbailey@ecsu.edu

BAILEY, Anthony 213-740-2852 73 C arbailey@usc.edu

BAILEY, Aprille 828-652-0629 335 H

BAILEY, Barbara 773-252-5311 146 D barbara.bailey@oakpoint.edu

BAILEY, Brad 228-497-7627 246 F brad.bailey@mgccc.edu

BAILEY, Brian 312-567-6937 139 H bbailey4@iit.edu

BAILEY, Cassy 785-594-8431 171 C cassy.bailey@bakeru.edu

BAILEY, Cassy 785-594-8484 171 C cassy.bailey@bakeru.edu

BAILEY, Chad 423-354-5370 424 B cmbailey@northeaststate.edu

BAILEY, Charla 830-372-8098 448 C cbailey@tlu.edu

BAILEY, Cheryl 414-930-3111 493 E baileyc@mtmary.edu

BAILEY, Christine 315-268-6578 295 E cbailey@clarkson.edu

BAILEY, Christopher 815-825-9592 141 D cbailey4@kish.edu

BAILEY, Christopher 301-243-2271 501 J christopher.bailey@dodiis.mil

BAILEY, Christopher 570-372-4149 398 A baileycj@susqu.edu

BAILEY, Christopher 401-254-3124 404 C cjbailey@rwu.edu

BAILEY, Christopher, C 360-442-2101 480 E cbailey@lowercolumbia.edu

BAILEY, Clint 252-328-2606 340 H baileyrc@ecu.edu

BAILEY, David, C 574-631-1097 161 G bailey.77@nd.edu

BAILEY, Denise 909-274-4425 52 K dbailey@mtsac.edu

BAILEY, Denise 903-233-3100 438 C denisebailey@letu.edu

BAILEY, JR., Dexter, F 626-395-6307 29 B dbailey@caltech.edu

BAILEY, Dixon 325-668-9657 441 D dbailey@rangercollege.edu

BAILEY, Ed 231-995-1215 228 F ebailey@nmc.edu

BAILEY, Guy 956-665-9102 455 A president@utrgv.edu

BAILEY, Heather 801-618-0438 458 H hbailey@ameritech.edu

BAILEY, Helen 423-869-6434 420 A helen.bailey@lmunet.edu

BAILEY, Jack 304-766-4109 489 D jbaile19@wvstateu.edu

BAILEY, Jack, S 585-275-2121 323 E

BAILEY, Jalynda 918-293-5266 368 B jalynda@okstate.edu

BAILEY, Jeff 870-972-3077 17 I jbailey@astate.edu

BAILEY, Jessika 580-559-5252 365 J jbailey@ecok.edu

BAILEY, Jodi 704-637-4292 327 H jsbailey21@catawba.edu

BAILEY, Jodi 201-200-3507 278 F jbailey2@njcu.edu

BAILEY, Joseph, A 585-345-6900 300 D jabailey@genesee.edu

BAILEY, Julie 404-687-4593 117 D baileyj@ctsnet.edu

BAILEY, Keith 402-872-2257 267 H kbailey@peru.edu

BAILEY, Kelly 724-738-4223 394 E kelly.bailey@sru.edu

BAILEY, Kevin 704-687-0350 342 C baileyk@uncc.edu

BAILEY, Kevin, S 573-882-1639 260 C baileyks@missouri.edu

BAILEY, Kimberly 252-398-6526 328 A ksbailey@chowan.edu

BAILEY, Laura 423-439-1000 418 D

BAILEY, Lisa 909-652-6532 36 B lisa.bailey@chaffey.edu

BAILEY, Mara 515-961-1684 169 G mara.bailey@simpson.edu

BAILEY, Mary Kaye 702-651-7437 270 F marykaye.bailey@csn.edu

BAILEY, Michael 352-588-8464 107 B michael.bailey@saintleo.edu

BAILEY, Michael, A 202-687-6021 92 D baileyma@georgetown.edu

BAILEY, Michael, A 919-530-6298 341 D mabailey@nccu.edu

BAILEY, Mike 620-417-1044 177 C mike.bailey@sccc.edu

BAILEY, Mitchell, A 650-574-6510 62 H baileym@smccd.edu

BAILEY, Monique 606-337-3196 180 A

BAILEY, Patrick 818-677-4452 32 E patrick.bailey@csun.edu

BAILEY, Paul 256-352-8359 4 A paul.bailey@wallacestate.edu

BAILEY, Phillip 501-450-3262 23 K phillipb@uca.edu

BAILEY, JR., Richard, J 541-552-6111 376 A presidentsoffice@sou.edu

BAILEY, Rita 470-578-2364 121 J rbaile62@kennesaw.edu

BAILEY, Robyn 847-635-1428 146 E rbailey@oakton.edu

BAILEY, Shaun 559-934-2254 74 L shaunbailey@whccd.edu

BAILEY, Sybil, F 401-825-2311 403 D sfbailey@ccri.edu

BAILEY, Tamara 304-473-8424 490 E bailey_t@wvwc.edu

BAILEY, Tammy 252-789-0253 335 F tammy.bailey@martincc.edu

BAILEY, Theresa 936-261-1570 445 E tlbailey@pvamu.edu

BAILEY, Thomas, R 212-678-3131 321 H tb3@tc.columbia.edu

BAILEY, Tonya 517-483-1116 226 D bailet20@lcc.edu

BAILEY, Travis 304-696-3032 488 N bailey53@marshall.edu

BAILEY, Trish 312-369-7342 136 C pbailey@colum.edu

BAILEY-CHEN, Robin 323-856-7764 25 M rbaileychen@afi.com

BAILEY FISCHER, Valerie 413-597-2483 220 A vb7@williams.edu

BAILEY-JONES, Jenny 662-472-9174 245 E jbailey@holmescc.edu

BAILEY MURPHY, Krista 215-248-7142 380 G murphyk@chc.edu

BAILIFF, Lara 512-313-4705 432 N lara.bailiff@concordia.edu

BAILLARGEON, Betty 860-215-9207 87 D bbaillargeon@threerivers.edu

BAILLARGEON, Tara 414-288-5213 492 E tara.baillargeon@marquette.edu

BAILO, Carole Anne 480-212-1704 15 R caroleanne@sessions.edu

BAILY, Jessica 914-674-7611 305 H jbaily@mercy.edu

BAIN, Abbey 318-427-4468 189 A abbey@lsua.edu

BAIN, Ann 501-916-3204 22 C abbain@ualr.edu

BAIN, Joe 785-628-4233 173 E jbbain@fhsu.edu

BAIN, Steve 361-593-2802 447 A steve.bain@tamuk.edu

BAIN-SELBO, Eric 765-455-9280 156 E ebainsel@iu.edu

BAIN-SELBO, Eric 573-651-2154 258 J ebainselbo@semo.edu

BAINE, Brad 870-248-4000 18 H brad.baine@blackrivertech.edu

BAINS, Divinder 530-741-6700 77 B

BAINTER, Bradley 309-298-1808 152 I bl-bainter@wiu.edu

BAIR, Ava 719-336-1574 81 J ava.bair@lamarcc.edu

BAIR, Matthew, S 260-422-5561 156 A msbair@indianatech.edu

BAIR, Ryan 309-677-2697 133 H rbair@fsmail.bradley.edu

BAIRD, Andrea 901-726-1977 427 E abaird@mooretech.edu

BAIRD, Anthony, M 315-792-3310 323 G ambaird@utica.edu

BAIRD, Bridget, R 423-439-8222 418 D bairdb@etsu.edu

BAIRD, David 860-685-2119 90 A dbaird@wesleyan.edu

BAIRD, Denise 651-690-6720 242 F dmbaird417@stkate.edu

BAIRD, Jeffrey 352-323-1977 96 B jbaird@beaconcollege.edu

BAIRD, Nicole 301-846-2646 198 E nbaird@frederick.edu

BAIRD, Rebecca 973-720-2713 283 I bairdr3@wpunj.edu

BAIRD, Sara Lynn 256-765-4288 8 E sbaird@una.edu

BAIRD, Susan 662-243-2682 245 C sbaird@eastms.edu

BAIRD, Thomas, A 734-647-6030 231 A baird@umich.edu

BAIRD, Timothy, R 724-847-6490 384 B trbaird@geneva.edu

BAIRD-JAMES, Allison 310-794-8686 69 D abaird-james@finance.ucla.edu

BAIRD-JAMES, Allison 310-825-3444 69 D abaird-james@finance.ucla.edu

BAIRSTOW-ALLEN, Deirdre 212-229-5150 307 E bairstod@newschool.edu

BAISEY, Michael 301-624-2892 198 E mbaisey@frederick.edu

BAJEUX-BESNAINOU, Isabelle 412-268-5596 380 B tepperdean@andrew.cmu.edu

BAJOR, William 570-422-3588 393 F wbajor@esu.edu

BAJRAMI, Diana 510-748-2301 57 A dbajrami@peralta.edu

BAJWA, Sreekala 406-994-5154 263 G sreekala.bajwa@montana.edu

BAKAMITSOS, Yiorgos 386-822-7432 111 F bakamitsos@stetson.edu

BAKANE, Samir 973-655-7773 278 C bakanes@montclair.edu

BAKAR, Senem 202-885-3352 91 D bakar@american.edu

BAKARI, R. Sentwali 516-877-3151 288 L sbakari@adelphi.edu

BAKE, Mark, A 920-433-6626 490 H mark.bake@bellincollege.edu

BAKEMEIER, Emily, P 203-432-9492 90 B emily.bakemeier@yale.edu

BAKER, Adria 713-348-6095 441 K abaker@rice.edu

BAKER, Aja 701-255-3285 346 I abaker@uttc.edu

BAKER, Alvin 606-326-2422 180 I alvin.baker@kctcs.edu

BAKER, Amanda, J 920-923-8082 492 D ajbaker31@marianuniversity.edu

BAKER, Amy 573-288-6493 251 I abaker@culver.edu

BAKER, S.T.D., Andrew, R 301-447-5295 201 A baker@msmary.edu

BAKER, Angela 717-264-2630 402 D angela.baker@wilson.edu

BAKER, Barry 425-235-5839 482 C bbaker@rtc.edu

BAKER, Betty 304-793-6873 489 C bbaker@osteo.wvsom.edu

BAKER, Bonnie 928-523-0090 14 J bonnie.baker@nau.edu

BAKER, Brad 610-459-0905 390 G bakerb@neumann.edu

BAKER, Brent 765-641-4138 153 D babaker@anderson.edu

BAKER, Brent 817-598-6275 457 C bbaker@wc.edu

BAKER, Brian 812-749-1212 159 E bbaker@oak.edu

BAKER, Brian 336-278-7453 328 H bbaker7@elon.edu

BAKER, Brian, J 540-654-1302 471 B bbaker@umw.edu

BAKER, Bryan 740-454-2501 364 H bbaker@zanestate.edu

BAKER, Byron 501-205-8939 19 B bbaker@cbc.edu

BAKER, Caitlin 806-291-3575 457 B bakerc@wbu.edu

BAKER, Carey 870-235-4042 21 E clbaker@saumag.edu

BAKER, Caroline 410-455-8171 202 G cbaker@umbc.edu

BAKER, Casey 412-536-1022 386 H casey.baker@laroche.edu

BAKER, Cindy 863-669-2898 106 A cbaker@polk.edu

BAKER, Colleen 530-251-8854 47 I cbaker@lassencollege.edu

BAKER, Credence 254-968-9464 445 F cbaker@tarleton.edu

BAKER, Dan 217-424-3757 144 D drbaker@millikin.edu

BAKER, David, A 541-737-3871 374 H david.baker@oregonstate.edu

BAKER, Debbie 307-382-1611 500 I dbaker@westernwyoming.edu

BAKER, Deborah 413-565-1000 205 I dbaker@baypath.edu

BAKER, Debra 662-246-6301 246 E dbaker@msdelta.edu

BAKER, Derrick 217-351-2524 146 G dbaker@parkland.edu

BAKER, Diane 269-927-6287 226 B baker@lakemichigancollege.edu

BAKER, Dylan 301-405-5632 202 E dbaker@umd.edu

BAKER, Elissa 518-629-8196 302 A e.baker@hvcc.edu

BAKER, Elizabeth 252-222-6216 332 G bakere@carteret.edu

BAKER, Elizabeth, A 312-942-2702 148 C elizabeth_baker@rush.edu

BAKER, Ellen 206-296-5570 483 B ellenwb@seattleu.edu

BAKER, Emily 909-748-8047 72 E emily_baker@redlands.edu

BAKER, Emma 843-377-2410 406 B ebaker@charlestonlaw.edu

BAKER, Frankie 513-569-1453 350 C frankie.baker@cincinnatistate.edu

BAKER, Gail, F 619-260-4553 72 H provost@sandiego.edu

BAKER, Gary 941-752-5431 109 C bakerg@scf.edu

BAKER, Gisella 319-296-4465 166 E gisella.baker@hawkeyecollege.edu

BAKER, Hilary 818-677-7750 32 E hilary.baker@csun.edu

BAKER, Hunter 731-661-5312 425 F hbaker@uu.edu

BAKER, James 210-999-8076 451 B jbaker5@trinity.edu

BAKER, Jean 214-860-8885 434 B jeanbaker@dcccd.edu

BAKER, Jeff 859-371-9393 179 C jbaker@beckfield.edu

BAKER, Jeffrey, A 704-687-8457 342 C jbaker88@uncc.edu

BAKER, Jennifer 410-516-7490 199 E jbaker94@jhu.edu

BAKER, Jerry 229-391-4782 114 D jbaker@abac.edu

BAKER, Jimmy 513-562-8762 347 G jbaker@artacademy.edu

BAKER, Jimmy, H 334-293-4524 1 C jimmy.baker@accs.edu

BAKER, John 802-490-5159 461 D john.baker@goddard.edu

BAKER, John, T 508-856-5538 212 A john.baker@umassmed.edu

BAKER, Josh 304-710-3355 487 F bakerj@mctc.edu

BAKER, Joshua, C 623-572-3426 144 C jbaker@midwestern.edu

BAKER, Karen 570-702-8908 386 D kbaker@johnson.edu

BAKER, Kathryn, R 865-354-3000 424 D bakerkr@roanestate.edu

BAKER, Kecia 972-524-3341 444 E kecia.baker@swcc.edu

BAKER, Keith 602-489-5300 10 G keith.baker@arizonachristian.edu

BAKER, Ken 412-918-3086 125 D kbaker@southuniversity.edu

BAKER, Kevin 662-227-2222 245 E kbaker@holmescc.edu

BAKER, Leigh 386-822-8900 111 F labaker@stetson.edu

BAKER, Lesli .... 801-863-8286 460 A
lbaker@uvu.edu
BAKER, Libba .... 205-652-3878.... 9 B
lbaker@uwa.edu
BAKER, Linda .... 610-799-1584 388 B
lbaker4@lccc.edu
BAKER, Lindsay .... 607-735-1774 298 G
lbaker@elmira.edu
BAKER, Lisa .... 252-246-1310 339 A
lbaker@wilsoncc.edu
BAKER, Lori .... 507-537-6251 240 G
lori.baker@smsu.edu
BAKER, Luanne .... 205-247-8147.... 7 A
lbaker@stillman.edu
BAKER, Matt .... 660-562-1219 256 G
mcbaker@nwmissouri.edu
BAKER, Matt, D .... 215-951-6803 398 G
bakerm@philau.edu
BAKER, Melinda .... 859-246-6819 181 B
melinda.baker@kctcs.edu
BAKER, Michael .... 765-641-4237 153 D
mtbaker@anderson.edu
BAKER, Michael .... 814-886-6368 390 E
mbaker@mtaloy.edu
BAKER, Michael, F .... 508-856-3040 212 A
michael.baker@umassmed.edu
BAKER, Michael, L .... 423-478-7702 421 J
mbaker@ptseminary.edu
BAKER, Michelle .... 435-797-7131 459 F
michelle.baker@usu.edu
BAKER, Mickey .... 334-556-2485.... 2 C
mbaker@wallace.edu
BAKER, Mike .... 859-442-4188 181 D
mike.baker@kctcs.edu
BAKER, Nancy .... 704-636-6882 329 F
nbaker@hoodseminary.edu
BAKER, Natalie .... 404-880-6879 116 I
nbaker@cau.edu
BAKER, Nelson .... 404-894-8920 119 D
nelson.baker@pe.gatech.edu
BAKER, Nick .... 989-275-5000 225 H
nick.baker@kirtland.edu
BAKER, Nikki, M .... 336-334-4227 342 D
nmwilson@uncg.edu
BAKER, Ric .... 203-931-2905.. 89 F
rbaker@newhaven.edu
BAKER, Richard .... 812-249-9188 197 F
rebaker@captechu.edu
BAKER, Richard .... 601-643-8302 244 G
richard.baker@colin.edu
BAKER, Richard .... 713-348-4350 441 K
BAKER, Rick .... 828-689-1215 330 H
rbaker@mhu.edu
BAKER, Robert .... 703-993-2004 466 J
rbaker2@gmu.edu
BAKER, Robert, T .... 336-758-5224 344 A
bakerrt@wfu.edu
BAKER, Robin, E .... 503-554-2101 372 I
rbaker@georgefox.edu
BAKER, Ross .... 618-664-7115 138 D
ross.baker@greenville.edu
BAKER, Russell, D .... 317-921-4313 158 A
rbaker80@ivytech.edu
BAKER, Ruth, E .... 410-334-2825 205 A
rbaker@worwic.edu
BAKER, Sarah .... 910-672-1918 341 B
sdbaker@uncfsu.edu
BAKER, Sarah .... 903-886-5045 446 D
sarah.baker@tamuc.edu
BAKER, Scott .... 828-339-4249 337 H
scottb@southwesterncc.edu
BAKER, Seth .... 312-850-7038 135 E
sbaker71@ccc.edu
BAKER, Shannon .... 361-593-3290 447 A
shannon.baker@tamuk.edu
BAKER, Sharon .... 423-478-7898 421 J
sbaker@ptseminary.edu
BAKER, Shawn .... 314-340-5095 253 E
bakers@hssu.edu
BAKER, Sherry .... 731-286-3242 423 E
baker@dscc.edu
BAKER, Sheyonn, L ...... 540-362-6287 467 A
bakersl@hollins.edu
BAKER, Stephen, N .... 401-874-2109 404 E
snbaker@uri.edu
BAKER, Steve .... 619-644-7155.. 44 H
steve.baker@gcccd.edu
BAKER, Steve .... 805-565-7156.. 75 I
stbaker@westmont.edu
BAKER, Steven .... 301-387-3791 198 F
steven.baker@garrettcollege.edu
BAKER, Thomas, N .... 315-267-2900 318 D
bakertn@potsdam.edu
BAKER, Todd .... 208-467-8011 132 B
toddbaker@nnu.edu
BAKER, Tracy, W .... 325-942-2035 450 B
tracy.baker@angelo.edu
BAKER, Uchenna .... 973-443-8935 276 I
uchennabaker@fdu.edu
BAKER, Wanda .... 314-838-8858 261 A
assessment@ugst.edu
BAKER, Wayne .... 432-335-6574 440 C
wbaker@odessa.edu
BAKER, Wren .... 940-565-2789 453 B
wren.baker@unt.edu
BAKER, Yvonne .... 513-569-4942 350 C
yvonne.baker@cincinnatistate.edu
BAKER, Zeb .... 513-529-3398 356 A
zeb.baker@miamioh.edu
BAKER-DEMARAY,
Twyla .... 701-627-4738 346 D
tbaker@nhsc.edu
BAKER-FLOWERS,
Kimberly .... 510-885-2809.. 31 C
kimberly.bakerflowers@csueastbay.edu
BAKER-WATSON, Stevie 765-658-6075 154 G
steviebaker-watson@depauw.edu
BAKEWELL-SACHS,
Susan .... 503-494-7445 374 F
sondeansoffice@ohsu.edu
BAKHIT, Kathy .... 661-362-5042.. 38 H
kathy.bakhit@canyons.edu
BAKHIT, Norman .... 574-372-5100 155 C
bakhitn@grace.edu
BAKHTIARI, Nick .... 605-995-7227 414 E
nick.bakhtiari@mitchelltech.edu
BAKIC, Rachele .... 920-465-2111 494 F
bakicr@uwgb.edu
BAKKAM, Nathan .... 312-369-7292 136 C
nbakkum@colum.edu
BAKKE, Lisa .... 702-651-4211 270 F
lisa.bakke@csn.edu
BAKKE, Sarah .... 845-437-7751 323 H
BAKKEN, Jim .... 205-934-3887.... 8 A
jimb@uab.edu
BAKKEN, John .... 919-866-5611 338 E
jrbakken@waketech.edu
BAKKEN, Phillip .... 402-472-7554 268 I
pbakken@nebraska.edu
BAKKEN, Turina .... 608-246-6516 497 I
bakken@madisoncollege.edu
BAKKEN, Virgil .... 218-755-3370 237 B
virgil.bakken@bemidjistate.edu
BAKKER, Andrea .... 937-255-3636 501 A
andrea.bakker@afit.edu
BAKKER, Theresa .... 907-474-6218.. 10 B
uaf-alumni@alaska.edu
BAKO, Pat .... 206-726-5052 478 F
pbako@cornish.edu
BAKOYEMA, Bryn .... 334-229-4100.... 4 B
bbakoyema@alasu.edu
BAKSH-JARRETT, Gail ... 718-482-5116 294 D
gailbj@lagcc.cuny.edu
BAKSHI, Mona .... 512-505-3002 437 B
officeofthepresident@htu.edu
BAKSI, Christine .... 717-245-1916 382 B
baksic@dickinson.edu
BAKST, M, S .... 248-968-3360 233 C
BAKST, Y .... 248-968-3360 233 C
BAKTHAKUMAR, Davi ... 954-545-4500 108 C
dbakthakumar@sfbc.edu
BAKULA, Timothy, L ..... 319-273-2722 163 G
tim.bakula@uni.edu
BALA, Devi .... 713-718-8430 436 E
devi.bala@hccs.edu
BALA, Kavita .... 607-255-1383 297 D
kavitabala@cornell.edu
BALABAN, Mark .... 845-431-8044 298 B
mark.balaban@sunydutchess.edu
BALAJADIA, Blake .... 408-288-3160.. 62 G
blake.balajadia@sjcc.edu
BALAKOFF, Gary .... 610-647-4400 385 K
gbalakoff@immaculata.edu
BALAKRISHNAN,
Jaydeep .... 916-278-6578.. 33 A
cob@csus.edu
BALAKRISHNAN, Raju .. 313-593-5248 231 B
rajub@umich.edu
BALAKRISHNAN,
Venkataramanan .... 216-368-3227 349 B
cse-dean@case.edu
BALANA MOLTER,
Sarah .... 317-955-6319 159 A
sbalanamolter@marian.edu
BALARIN, Alfredo .... 518-629-7348 302 A
a.balarin@hvcc.edu
BALASUBRAMANIAN,
Ramprasad .... 508-999-8827 211 F
r.bala@umassd.edu
BALASUBRAMANIAN,
Sunder .... 573-681-5138 254 A
balasubramanians@lincolnu.edu
BALASZ, Anne .... 419-530-2087 363 B
anne.balasz@utoledo.edu
BALATBAT, Joseph .... 212-924-5900 321 C
jbalatbat@swedishinstitute.edu
BALAZSI, Jessica .... 252-618-6502 334 B
balazsij@edgecombe.edu
BALBACH, Donna .... 812-357-6525 160 G
dbalbach@saintmeinrad.edu
BALBES, Idellisse .... 787-738-2161 511 A
idelisse.balbes@upr.edu
BALCAZAR, Genaro .... 708-524-6562 137 A
gbalcazar@dom.edu
BALCER, Jesse .... 215-248-7046 380 G
balcerj@chc.edu
BALCH, Craig .... 817-760-5504 436 C
cbalch@hillcollege.edu
BALCH, Maggie .... 413-572-5300 213 C
BALCH, Marcus .... 972-617-4128 448 F
marcus.balch@tstc.edu
BALCH, Robert .... 575-835-5143 286 D
robert.balch@nmt.edu
BALCH-LINDSAY,
Suzanne .... 575-562-2314 285 E
suzanne.balch@enmu.edu
BALCHAK, Sharon .... 216-373-5295 357 F
sbalchak@ndc.edu
BALCOM, David, A .... 410-651-6199 203 B
dabalcom@umes.edu
BALD, Karolyn .... 608-785-8017 495 A
kbald@uwlax.edu
BALDA, Jose .... 201-200-3381 278 F
jbalda@njcu.edu
BALDASSARO, Sarah .... 202-885-1000.. 91 D
sarahgb@american.edu
BALDAUF, Jack, G .... 979-845-8585 446 B
jbaldauf@tamu.edu
BALDERAS, Ulyses .... 713-525-3533 453 H
balderj@stthom.edu
BALDERRAMA,
Elizabeth .... 956-295-3600 448 E
BALDIN, Antoinette .... 419-995-8406 360 B
baldin.a@rhodesstate.edu
BALDINI, Fred .... 510-879-0784.. 60 C
fbaldini@samuelmerritt.edu
BALDISSERI, Richard .... 503-281-4181 372 F
BALDONEDO, Claudia .. 718-482-5236 294 D
claudiab@lagcc.cuny.edu
BALDRIDGE, Amber ...... 706-880-8238 121 K
abjohnson@lagrange.edu
BALDRIDGE, Stephen .... 254-295-4732 453 A
sbaldridge@umhb.edu
BALDUCCI, Laureen ...... 408-864-8945.. 42 K
balduccilaureen@deanza.edu
BALDWIN, Ally .... 617-236-8878 209 D
abaldwin@fisher.edu
BALDWIN, Anne, E .... 585-245-5547 317 E
baldwina@geneseo.edu
BALDWIN, Beth .... 208-496-1706 130 G
baldwinb@byui.edu
BALDWIN, Calene .... 502-272-8234 179 D
cbaldwin@bellarmine.edu
BALDWIN, Candice .... 301-624-2867 198 E
cbaldwin@fredreick.edu
BALDWIN, Chad .... 307-766-2929 500 H
cbaldwin@uwyo.edu
BALDWIN, Christine, A . 714-850-4800.. 83 H
baldwin@taftu.edu
BALDWIN, Christine, A . 714-850-4800.. 67 G
baldwin@taftu.edu
BALDWIN, Darin .... 334-745-6437.... 3 G
dbaldwin@suscc.edu
BALDWIN, Deborah, J .. 501-320-5780.. 22 C
djbaldwin@ualr.edu
BALDWIN, Diane .... 617-353-4377 207 C
dbaldwin@bu.edu
BALDWIN, Dirk .... 262-595-2379 495 D
baldwin@uwp.edu
BALDWIN, Eric .... 434-544-8226 470 K
baldwin_e@lynchburg.edu
BALDWIN, Erin .... 515-294-7971 163 E
baldwine@iastate.edu
BALDWIN, Jason .... 304-696-6603 488 N
baldwinja@marshall.edu
BALDWIN, Jeff .... 863-292-3743 106 A
jbaldwin@polk.edu
BALDWIN, Jennifer .... 307-742-3776 500 K
jbaldwin@wyotech.edu
BALDWIN, Julie .... 406-243-5778 263 D
julie.baldwin@umontana.edu
BALDWIN, Kate .... 207-602-4828 194 F
kbaldwin@landingschool.edu
BALDWIN, Latosha .... 202-274-6604.. 94 B
latosha.baldwin@udc.edu
BALDWIN, Laura .... 215-572-2909 378 E
baldwinl@arcadia.edu
BALDWIN, Mark .... 509-359-6312 478 H
mbaldwin@ewu.edu
BALDWIN, Naomi .... 716-673-3456 316 A
naomi.baldwin@fredonia.edu
BALDWIN, R. Chad .... 636-584-6609 252 D
robert.baldwin@eastcentral.edu
BALDWIN, Sarah, T ...... 859-858-3511 178 H
sarah.baldwin@asbury.edu
BALDWIN, Stan .... 601-925-3321 246 D
sbaldwin@mc.edu
BALDWIN, Tanya .... 304-384-5223 488 K
tlbaldwin@concord.edu
BALDWIN, Terri .... 740-588-1210 364 H
tbaldwin2@zanestate.edu
BALDWIN, Undra .... 850-644-6031 110 B
ubaldwin@fsu.edu
BALDWIN-DIMEO,
Caren, L .... 603-526-3714 271 H
cbaldwin-dimeo@colby-sawyer.edu
BALENTINE, Jerry .... 516-686-3999 308 H
jerry.balentine@nyit.edu
BALENTINE, Kim .... 417-626-1234 257 A
BALES, Jennifer .... 913-621-8733 173 B
jennifer@donnelly.edu
BALES, Michael .... 276-964-7323 474 E
michael.bales@sw.edu
BALES, William, J .... 615-898-5014 421 C
joe.bales@mtsu.edu
BALES-SHERROD, Lesli . 865-694-6638 424 C
lbalessherrod@pstcc.edu
BALESTRA, Elisa .... 914-813-9242 314 H
ebalestra@sarahlawrence.edu
BALESTRERI, Teresa, A . 314-516-5002 260 E
tkb@umsl.edu
BALFOUR, Stephen, P .. 706-357-0049 126 F
stephen.balfour@uga.edu
BALI, Sunjay .... 412-809-5180 395 F
bali.sunjay@ptcollege.edu
BALIGH, Mohamed .... 518-255-5473 318 F
saeedmg@cobleskill.edu
BALINSKI, Joseph .... 231-348-6600 228 D
jbalinski@ncmich.edu
BALINSKI, Joseph .... 231-439-6347 228 D
jbalinski@ncmich.edu
BALINT, Elizabeth .... 530-541-4660.. 47 H
balint@ltcc.edu
BALINT, William, S .... 724-357-7854 393 G
wsbalint@iup.edu
BALKAN, Grace .... 517-607-2301 224 G
gbalkan@hillsdale.edu
BALKIN, David .... 716-842-2770 299 A
BALKIN, Timothy, P ..... 716-888-2480 291 M
balkin4@canisius.edu
BALKISSOON, Tony ...... 212-237-8000 294 B
BALKON, Victoria .... 718-990-1512 313 B
colev@stjohns.edu
BALL, Charnee .... 863-680-4449 100 F
cball@flsouthern.edu
BALL, Christine .... 706-771-4150 115 H
cball@augustatech.edu
BALL, Diane .... 352-588-8417 107 B
diane.ball@saintleo.edu
BALL, Don .... 330-494-6170 360 I
dball@starkstate.edu
BALL, Donald .... 330-494-6170 360 I
dball@starkstate.edu
BALL, Doug .... 620-235-4107 176 H
dbball@pittstate.edu
BALL, Gregory, F .... 301-405-4175 202 E
gball@umd.edu
BALL, Gregory, F .... 301-405-4175 202 F
gball@umd.edu
BALL, James, D .... 410-386-8188 197 G
jball@carrollcc.edu
BALL, Jamie .... 618-650-2333 149 H
jball@siue.edu
BALL, Jason .... 561-297-3440 109 F
jball@fau.edu
BALL, Jennifer .... 785-670-1648 178 A
jennifer.ball@washburn.edu
BALL, Jennifer .... 315-268-4208 295 E
jball@clarkson.edu
BALL, John .... 504-568-4500 189 C
jball@lsuhsc.edu

BANNENBERG, David, S ..... 602-243-8062.. 14 C david.bannenberg@southmountaincc.edu
BANNER, Josephina ..... 215-646-7300 384 G banner.j@gmercyu.edu
BANNETT, Michael ..... 787-780-5134 508 C
BANNIN, Bernard ..... 419-289-5291 347 H bbannin2@ashland.edu
BANNING, Susan ..... 901-321-3248 417 G sbanning@cbu.edu
BANNISTER, Darlene ..... 830-792-7356 442 G registrar@schreiner.edu
BANNISTER, Dustin ..... 919-299-4817 340 E dbannister@umo.edu
BANNISTER, Justin ..... 575-646-5981 286 G jbannist@nmsu.edu
BANNISTER, Kathleen ... 770-426-2787 122 A kstavovy@life.edu
BANNISTER, Mark ..... 208-426-1000 130 F markbannister724@boisestate.edu
BANNON, Logan, D ..... 412-578-6258 380 A lgbannon@carlow.edu
BANNON, Stephen ..... 401-232-6001 403 B sbannon@bryant.edu
BANSAVICH, John ..... 415-422-5529.. 72 I bansavich@usfca.edu
BANSCHBACH, Valerie .. 503-943-7760 376 H banschba@up.edu
BANTILLO, Karl ..... 443-352-5018 202 C jbantillo@stevenson.edu
BANTON, Cris ..... 503-554-2167 372 I cbanton@georgefox.edu
BANUELOS, Francisco .. 559-730-3942.. 39 C franciscob@cos.edu
BANUELOS, Javier ..... 562-860-2451.. 35 O jbanuelos@cerritos.edu
BANUSH, David ..... 504-865-5131 191 D dbanush@tulane.edu
BANYACSKI, Mark ..... 609-586-4800 277 H banyacsm@mccc.edu
BAOUA, Kesha ..... 501-450-3824.. 19 I baoua@hendrix.edu
BAPTISTE, April ..... 315-228-7203 296 C abaptiste@colgate.edu
BAPTISTE, Brian ..... 215-951-1425 386 I
BAPTISTE, JoRae ..... 808-245-8323 129 H jorae@hawaii.edu
BAPTISTE-SEXTON, Candice ..... 212-650-7905 293 B csexton@ccny.cuny.edu
BAR, Rosann ..... 732-255-0400 279 A rbar@ocean.edu
BARABE, Becky ..... 559-443-8514.. 67 A becky.barabe@fresnocitycollege.edu
BARABINO, Gilda, A ..... 781-292-2301 209 E
BARAGONA, Michelle ... 662-720-7375 247 D mabaragona@nemcc.edu
BARAHONA, Cynthia .... 949-794-9090.. 66 C cbarahona@stanbridge.edu
BARAKAT, Nabeel, M .... 310-233-4351.. 49 F barakanm@lahc.edu
BARALDI, Michael ..... 919-209-2051 335 D m_baraldi@johnstoncc.edu
BARAM, Elan ..... 646-565-6036 322 B elan.bar-am@touro.edu
BARAN, Kelley ..... 508-531-2492 212 B kelley.baran@bridgew.edu
BARAN, Victoria ..... 716-488-3021 302 F victoriabaran@jbc.edu
BARANOVIC, Mike ..... 970-204-8255.. 80 I mike.baranovic@frontrange.edu
BARANOWSKI, Carl ..... 903-566-6475 455 C cbaranowski@uttyler.edu
BARATO, Ruben ..... 508-588-9100 214 F
BARATO, Ruben ..... 914-606-6777 324 F ruben.barato@sunywcc.edu
BARATTA, Peter ..... 609-626-6080 283 A peter.baratta@stockton.edu
BARBA, Jesse, D ..... 413-542-5485 205 D jbarba@amherst.edu
BARBARI, Tim ..... 303-273-3000.. 79 A tbarbari@mines.edu
BARBARICK, Cliff ..... 325-674-3767 427 G cab11c@acu.edu
BARBATIS, Peter ..... 561-868-3142 105 C barbatip@palmbeachstate.edu
BARBAULD, Ryan, J ..... 812-888-4313 162 E ryan.barbauld@vinu.edu
BARBE, Tammy, D ..... 678-547-6741 122 C barbe_td@mercer.edu
BARBEAU, Dyan, E ..... 414-410-4118 490 J debarbeau@stritch.edu
BARBEE, Brent ..... 910-410-1809 336 G btbarbee@richmondcc.edu
BARBEE, Danielle ..... 856-225-2965 281 A danielle.barbee@camden.rutgers.edu
BARBEE, Holly ..... 252-493-7206 336 E hbarbee@email.pittcc.edu
BARBEE, Julianna ..... 505-747-2206 287 C jbarbee@nnmc.edu
BARBEE, Kelsey ..... 719-384-6824.. 82 C kelsey.barbee@otero.edu
BARBEITO, Patricia ..... 401-709-6575 404 B pbarbeit@risd.edu
BARBER, Adrianne ..... 208-459-5268 131 A abarber@collegeofidaho.edu
BARBER, Angela ..... 785-227-3380 171 H barberao@bethanylb.edu
BARBER, Billy ..... 252-789-0303 335 F billy.barber@martincc.edu
BARBER, Carolyn ..... 816-235-6151 260 D barberce@umkc.edu
BARBER, Charles ..... 202-994-6503.. 92 C cbarber@gwu.edu
BARBER, Christina ..... 518-454-2142 296 E barberc@strose.edu
BARBER, Cindy ..... 870-307-7527.. 20 D cindy.barber@lyon.edu
BARBER, DiAnna ..... 919-739-7021 338 F wcc-bookstore@waynecc.edu
BARBER, Eric ..... 402-460-5722 266 E ebarber@marylanning.org
BARBER, Gary ..... 740-374-8716 363 F gbarber@wscc.edu
BARBER, Isaac, C ..... 260-359-4328 155 G ibarber@huntington.edu
BARBER, Jacques ..... 516-877-4800 288 L jbarber@adelphi.edu
BARBER, Jeff ..... 843-863-7080 406 C jbarber@csuniv.edu
BARBER, Jennifer ..... 916-278-3634.. 33 A jbarbar@csus.edu
BARBER, Kim ..... 252-792-1521 335 F
BARBER, Kimberly ..... 850-644-6127 110 B kabarber@admin.fsu.edu
BARBER, Lori ..... 208-535-5419 130 I lori.barber@cei.edu
BARBER, Luanne ..... 870-612-2119.. 23 B luanne.barber@uaccb.edu
BARBER, Melinda ..... 352-435-6351 103 U barberm@lssc.edu
BARBER, Richard ..... 724-503-1001 401 D rbarber@washjeff.edu
BARBER, Robbi ..... 502-863-7047 180 E robbi_barber@georgetowncollege.edu
BARBER, Sarah ..... 315-229-5083 313 F sbarber@stlawu.edu
BARBER, Tracy ..... 719-255-7507.. 84 A tbarber@uccs.edu
BARBER, Trent, J ..... 860-512-3283.. 86 F tbarber@manchestercc.edu
BARBER, Wendi ..... 937-395-8520 354 J wendi.barber@ketteringhealth.org
BARBERA, Anthony ..... 516-876-3135 318 A barberaa@oldwestbury.edu
BARBERA, Bridget ..... 718-960-8559 293 E bridget.barbera@lehman.cuny.edu
BARBERIAN, Wazkein ... 818-988-2300.. 53 F
BARBERICH, Kim ..... 609-896-5000 280 D kbarberich@rider.edu
BARBIER GIBSON, Yolanda ..... 540-665-4500 470 A
BARBIER GIBSON, Yolanda ..... 540-665-4783 470 A ygibson@su.edu
BARBONE, Tony ..... 626-585-3203.. 56 D tbarbone@pasadena.edu
BARBOSA, Francisco ..... 787-264-1912 507 E fbarbosa@intersg.edu
BARBOSA, Miguel ..... 570-422-3545 393 F mbarbosa@esu.edu
BARBOUR, A. Sandy .... 814-865-1086 391 F asb25@psu.edu
BARBOUR, Anthony ..... 704-272-5393 337 F abarbour@spcc.edu
BARBOUR, Channell ..... 859-985-3251 179 E barbourc@berea.edu
BARBOUR, Cheryl ..... 303-546-3565.. 81 N cheryl@naropa.edu
BARBOUR, Darrell ..... 641-585-8138 170 E darrell.barbour@waldorf.edu
BARBOUR, Denise ..... 770-412-5740 125 F denise.barbour@sctech.edu
BARBOUR, Jeffery ..... 757-340-2121 464 L librariancvab@centura.edu
BARBOUR, Monica ..... 313-993-1951 230 H barboumm@udmercy.edu
BARBOUR, Suzanne, W 919-962-7791 342 B sbarbour@unc.edu
BARCLAY, Beth ..... 563-884-5586 169 C beth.barclay@palmer.edu
BARCLAY, Kent ..... 978-232-2282 209 B kbarclay@endicott.edu
BARCLAY, Raymond ..... 989-463-7143 220 F barclayrd@alma.edu
BARCLAY, Ryan ..... 813-988-5131.. 99 M barclayr@floridacollege.edu
BARCLAY, Tosha ..... 713-718-6140 436 E tosha.barclay@hccs.edu
BARCO, Jessica ..... 657-278-5256.. 31 E jbarco@fullerton.edu
BARCO, Nicole, S ..... 989-774-3902 221 M sparl1nl@cmich.edu
BARCUS, Krista ..... 660-562-1128 256 G kbarcus@nwmissouri.edu
BARD, JR., Branville .... 410-516-3486 199 E branville.bard@jhu.edu
BARD, Melissa, L ..... 302-831-2171.. 91 A bardm@udel.edu
BARD, Sharon, K ..... 704-463-3428 339 C sharon.bard@pfeiffer.edu
BARD, Stephanie ..... 218-755-2263 237 B stephanie.bard@bemidjistate.edu
BARDEGUEZ, Lemuel .... 405-682-7814 367 D lbardeguez@occc.edu
BARDEN, John ..... 203-432-3262.. 90 B john.barden@yale.edu
BARDEN, JR ..... 512-404-4805 429 K jrbarden@austinseminary.edu
BARDNEY, Eileen ..... 845-569-3254 307 B eileen.bardney@msmc.edu
BARE, Benita ..... 423-636-5096 425 E bbare@tusculum.edu
BAREFIELD, Kevin ..... 662-685-4771 244 D kbarefield@bmc.edu
BAREFOOT, Jon ..... 317-921-4882 158 A jon.barefoot@ivytech.edu
BAREFOOT, Russell ..... 908-526-1200 280 C russell.barefoot@raritanval.edu
BARELA, Lara ..... 505-467-6816 288 A larabarela@swc.edu
BARELA-EUBANK, Corey ..... 575-234-9404 287 I ceubank@senmc.edu
BARELMAN, Jason ..... 402-375-7327 267 I jabarel1@wsc.edu
BAREN, Jill ..... 215-596-8800 400 B
BARFIELD, Carnelia ..... 318-274-6375 191 G barfieldc@gram.edu
BARFIELD, Julie ..... 817-272-2584 454 B barfield@uta.edu
BARFIELD, Kem ..... 860-215-9210.. 87 D kbarfield1@threerivers.edu
BARFIELD, Randall, K ... 708-209-3304 136 D randall.barfield@cuchicago.edu
BARFOOT, D. Scott ..... 214-887-5151 434 G sbarfoot@dts.edu
BARFUSS, Blair ..... 435-797-1000 459 F
BARGA, Brian ..... 619-201-8951.. 65 F brian.barga@socalsem.edu
BARGAS, DeLynn ..... 575-562-2175 285 E delynn.bargas@enmu.edu
BARGAS, Theresa ..... 512-859-7239 429 H tbargas@escoffier.edu
BARGE, Scott ..... 540-432-4304 465 F scott.barge@emu.edu
BARGE-MILES, Linda .... 850-599-3225 109 E linda.bargemiles@famu.edu
BARGER, Debbie, M ..... 515-263-6012 166 C dbarger@grandview.edu
BARGER, Eric, C ..... 503-943-7507 376 H barger@up.edu
BARGER, Judith ..... 678-916-2653 115 G jbarger@johnmarshall.edu
BARGER, Melanie ..... 573-592-6050 261 F melanie.barger@westminster-mo.edu
BARGER, Mollie ..... 601-928-6264 246 F mollie.barger@mgccc.edu
BARGER, Peter, S ..... 630-637-5362 145 E psbarger@noctrl.edu
BARGERHUFF, Eric ..... 727-376-6911 112 F eric.bargerhuff@trinitycollege.edu
BARGHOTHI, Jane ..... 828-262-2090 340 G janebar@appstate.edu
BARGO, Sarah ..... 417-447-7813 257 B bargos@otc.edu
BARGOOT, Carolyn ..... 617-373-2000 217 D
BARHAM, James ..... 731-286-3371 423 E jbarham@dscc.edu
BARHAM, Michael ..... 510-204-0738.. 37 A mbarham@cdsp.edu
BARHAM, Stephanie ..... 423-279-7633 424 B srbarham@northeaststate.edu
BARHAM, Treva ..... 903-233-3470 438 C trevabarham@letu.edu
BARHORST, Michael, D 937-512-3612 360 F michael.barhorst@sinclair.edu
BARIA, Jo Ann ..... 253-964-6640 481 H jbaria@pierce.ctc.edu
BARIL, Kathleen, T ..... 419-772-2180 358 D k-baril@onu.edu
BARILE, Becca ..... 315-781-3827 301 D barile@hws.edu
BARILOVITS, Karlyn ..... 866-492-5336 243 G karlyn.barilovits@mail.waldenu.edu
BARIOLA, Kristi ..... 662-246-6376 246 E kbariola@msdelta.edu
BARISH, Robert ..... 312-413-0340 151 D rbarish@uic.edu
BARKAN, Chester ..... 516-572-7131 307 C chester.barkan@ncc.edu
BARKE, Brady, L ..... 573-651-2227 258 J bbarke@semo.edu
BARKER, Aaron ..... 320-308-3030 240 D abarker@sctcc.edu
BARKER, Anita, S ..... 530-898-6470.. 31 A abarker@csuchico.edu
BARKER, Blake ..... 214-648-2168 456 D blake.barker@utsouthwestern.edu
BARKER, Brian ..... 970-945-8691.. 78 H
BARKER, Bruce ..... 828-227-3100 343 D bbarker@wcu.edu
BARKER, Christopher .... 203-392-6025.. 85 H barkerc7@southernct.edu
BARKER, Curtis ..... 336-841-9372 329 E cbarker@highpoint.edu
BARKER, Eddie ..... 606-337-3196 180 A
BARKER, Ellie ..... 919-508-2041 344 D erbarker@peace.edu
BARKER, Greg ..... 815-753-1000 145 H
BARKER, Jennifer ..... 970-675-3233.. 78 P jennifer.barker@cncc.edu
BARKER, John, D ..... 864-294-2106 408 I john.barker@furman.edu
BARKER, John, F ..... 716-286-8220 309 F jfb@niagara.edu
BARKER, Marco ..... 402-472-3751 269 A marco.barker@unl.edu
BARKER, Michael ..... 919-962-4314 342 B michael_barker@unc.edu
BARKER, Neva ..... 909-621-8306.. 63 E neva.barker@scrippscollege.edu
BARKER, Randy ..... 715-394-8394 496 D rbarker@uwsuper.edu
BARKER, Ryan ..... 315-470-5710 291 E ryanbarker@crouse.org
BARKER, Sandy ..... 336-812-7234 125 D sbarker@southuniversity.edu
BARKER, Tess ..... 765-455-9360 156 E tessbark@iu.edu
BARKER, Yvette ..... 713-313-7201 448 D yvette.barker@tsu.edu
BARKHAMER, Kim ..... 215-596-8800 400 B
BARKIS, Kimberly ..... 310-506-6110.. 56 H kimberly.barkis@pepperdine.edu
BARKLEY, Beatrice, L ... 215-368-5000 389 G bbarkley@missio.edu
BARKLEY, Bill ..... 866-492-5336 243 G william.barkley@mail.waldenu.edu
BARKLEY, Brian ..... 770-836-6830 127 E brian.barkley@westgatech.edu
BARKLEY, Lisa, C ..... 252-536-6399 334 G lbarkley150@halifaxcc.edu
BARKLEY-GIFFIN, Adrienne ..... 618-985-3741 140 G adriennebarkley@jalc.edu
BARKLIND, Amanda ..... 651-450-3887 237 H abarklind@inverhills.edu
BARKO, Valerie ..... 808-245-8336 129 H vabarko@hawaii.edu
BARKOFF, Larry ..... 734-677-5413 232 A lbarkoff@wccnet.edu
BARKOWITZ, Daniel, T . 407-582-1458 113 C dbarkowitz@valenciacollege.edu
BARKSDALE, Debra, J ... 336-334-5177 342 D djbarksdale@uncg.edu
BARKSDALE, Elizabeth .. 706-295-6592 119 F ebarksdale@gntc.edu
BARKSDALE, Glasetta ... 312-850-7288 135 E gbarksdale@ccc.edu

BARRAGAN, Domingo .. 520-494-5461.. 11 M
domingo.barragan@centralaz.edu
BARRAGAN, Joseph ...... 254-526-1427 431 E
joseph.barragan@ctcd.edu
BARRAZA, Ana Lilia ..... 562-907-4912.. 76 A
abarraza@whittier.edu
BARRE, Todd .... 256-824-6350.... 8 B
todd.barre@uah.edu
BARREAU, Julie, M ...... 608-757-7772 497 D
jbarreau@blackhawk.edu
BARREDO, Ronald .... 615-963-5924 425 A
rbarredo@tnstate.edu
BARREE, Zita, M .... 434-223-6265 466 K
zbarree@hsc.edu
BARRENECHE, Gabriel .. 706-236-2297 116 A
gbarreneche@berry.edu
BARRENTINE, Jim .... 719-502-2148.. 82 D
jim.barrentine@pikespeak.edu
BARRENTINE, Roger ..... 636-481-3106 253 G
rbarrent@jeffco.edu
BARRERA, Amanda .... 432-837-8178 449 F
amanda.barrera@sulross.edu
BARRERA, Kirsten .... 877-559-3621.. 28 J
BARRERA, Rosa, M .... 316-284-5241 171 I
rbarrera@bethelks.edu
BARRERA, Taurin .... 415-503-6311.. 61 E
tbarrera@sfcm.edu
BARRERAS, Lysette .... 787-758-2525 511 D
lysette.barreras@upr.edu
BARRESE, Anthony .... 201-216-8768 282 L
abarrese@stevens.edu
BARRESI, JR., Joseph .. 401-598-1000 403 E
joseph.barresi@jwu.edu
BARRET, Karrie .... 775-327-2382 270 G
karrie.barrett@gbcnv.edu
BARRETO, Betsy .... 240-895-4410 201 F
cbbarreto@gmail.com
BARRETO, Wanda .... 787-758-2480 511 D
wanda.barreto@upr.edu
BARRETO, Xavier .... 718-270-6131 294 E
xbarreto@mec.cuny.edu
BARRETO, Zolen .... 787-725-8120 505 J
zbarreto@eap.edu
BARRETT, Ashley .... 619-596-2766.. 26 I
abarrett@ata.edu
BARRETT, Brenda .... 620-276-0481 173 H
brenda.barrett@gcccks.edu
BARRETT, Brielle .... 785-670-1927 178 A
brielle.barrett@washburn.edu
BARRETT,
Christopher, L .... 434-924-0311 471 F
clb5xe@virginia.edu
BARRETT, Dustin .... 912-650-6250 125 D
dbarrett@southuniversity.edu
BARRETT, Dwight .... 909-558-4578.. 48 J
dbarrett@llu.edu
BARRETT, Edith .... 412-365-2970 380 F
e.barrett@chatham.edu
BARRETT, Gary .... 910-323-5614 327 E
gbarrett@ccbs.edu
BARRETT, James .... 920-924-6431 498 C
jbarrett8@morainepark.edu
BARRETT, James, F ...... 330-325-6274 357 D
jbarrett@neomed.edu
BARRETT, Jeannie .... 309-438-8999 140 C
jebarr@ilstu.edu
BARRETT, Joan .... 417-447-6914 257 B
barrettj@otc.edu
BARRETT, Laura .... 845-257-3520 316 B
barrettl@newpaltz.edu
BARRETT, Lawrence ...... 386-752-1822.. 99 P
lawrence.barrett@fgc.edu
BARRETT, Leah .... 402-844-7055 268 A
lbarrett@northeast.edu
BARRETT, Linda .... 401-874-2509 404 E
lindab@uri.edu
BARRETT, Mary, C .... 607-735-1790 298 G
mbarrett@elmira.edu
BARRETT, Michael .... 616-432-3412 229 H
michael.barrett@prts.edu
BARRETT, Michele .... 812-237-7829 155 H
michele.barrett@indstate.edu
BARRETT, Pam, J .... 770-534-6176 116 C
pbarrett@brenau.edu
BARRETT, Pamela .... 505-438-8884 287 J
pamela@acupuncturecollege.edu
BARRETT, Richard .... 319-363-1323 168 D
rbarrett@mtmercy.edu
BARRETT, Sarah .... 518-244-2441 312 D
barres2@sage.edu
BARRETT, Scott .... 310-243-3787.. 31 B
sbarrett@csudh.edu
BARRETT, Steve .... 651-793-1278 238 B
steve.barrett@metrostate.eduetrostate.edu
BARRETT, Steve .... 507-389-2015 238 L
steve.barrett@mnsu.edu
BARRETT, Steven .... 307-766-4286 500 H
BARRETT, Tracy .... 704-922-6309 334 E
barrett.tracy@gaston.edu
BARRETT, Zunilka .... 617-287-7050 211 C
zbarrett@umassp.edu
BARRETTA, Jacqueline .. 503-370-6004 377 E
jbarretta@willamette.edu
BARRETTE, Catherine .... 313-577-1615 232 H
c.barrette@wayne.edu
BARRETTO, Kelly .... 919-807-7100 331 I
BARRICELLI, Franca ...... 978-665-3627 212 C
fbarrice@fitchburgstate.edu
BARRICK, Bradley .... 405-733-7961 369 D
bbarrick@rose.edu
BARRIENTOS, Joe .... 206-934-6788 482 H
joe.barrientos@seattlecolleges.edu
BARRIER, Jeremy .... 256-766-6610.... 5 F
jbarrier@hcu.edu
BARRINEAU, Annette ...... 904-381-3724 101 A
annette.barrineau@fscj.edu
BARRINGER, Bryan .... 901-321-4409 417 G
bbarring@cbu.edu
BARRINGER, Judy .... 212-659-7215 303 E
jbarringer@tkc.edu
BARRINGER, Susan, J .. 336-430-8880 329 B
susan.barringer@greensboro.edu
BARRINGER, Tony .... 239-590-7849 109 G
tbarring@fgcu.edu
BARRINGHAUS, Jill .... 660-248-6977 250 H
jbarring@centralmethodist.edu
BARRINGTON, Beverly .. 850-599-8316 109 E
beverly.barrington@famu.edu
BARRIO, Brian .... 410-455-2207 202 G
bbarrio@umbc.edu
BARRIO-SOTILLO,
Ramona .... 818-240-1000.. 43 J
rbarrio@glendale.edu
BARRIOS, Bella .... 563-588-7206 167 I
marbella.barrios@loras.edu
BARRIOS, Kristin .... 626-568-8850.. 49 B
kristin@lacm.edu
BARRIOS, Sharon, A ..... 530-898-4473.. 31 A
sbarrios@csuchico.edu
BARRIS, Brad .... 706-236-2272 116 A
bbarris@berry.edu
BARRISH, David, J .... 804-523-5934 473 A
dbarrish@reynolds.edu
BARRON, Caulyne .... 602-648-5750.. 12 G
cbarron@dunlap-stone.edu
BARRON, David .... 903-566-7051 455 C
dbarron@uttyler.edu
BARRON, Dori .... 828-448-3170 338 G
dbarron@wpcc.edu
BARRON, Jose .... 575-624-8263 286 F
barron@nmmi.edu
BARRON, Kim, M .... 716-878-5550 317 C
barronkm@buffalostate.edu
BARRON, Lee .... 314-275-3510 147 B
lee.barron@principia.edu
BARRON, Nicole .... 312-341-2114 148 A
nbarron03@roosevelt.edu
BARRON, Sebastian ...... 903-434-8260 440 A
sbarron@ntcc.edu
BARRON, Travis .... 229-500-4004 114 F
travis.barron@asurams.edu
BARROS, Ben .... 419-530-7877 363 B
ben.barros@utoledo.edu
BARROSO, Laura .... 805-652-5500.. 73 H
BARROTT, James .... 423-697-3211 423 B
jim.barrott@chattanoogastate.edu
BARROW, Carla .... 229-225-5077 125 G
cbarrow@southernregional.edu
BARROW, Danny .... 225-578-1175 188 K
dbarrow1@lsu.edu
BARROW, Deborah, L ... 940-397-4212 439 F
debbie.barrow@msutexas.edu
BARROW, Laurie .... 717-901-5143 385 G
lbarrow@harrisburgu.edu
BARROW, Terry .... 620-792-9318 171 F
barrowt@bartonccc.edu
BARROWS, James .... 520-515-5339.. 11 O
barrowsj@cochise.edu
BARROWS, Jamie .... 251-981-3771.... 5 B
james.barrows@columbiasouthern.edu
BARROWS, Karen, A ..... 585-475-2396 312 A
karen.barrows@rit.edu
BARROWS, Karen, A ..... 585-475-2396 312 A
kab7050@rit.edu
BARROWS, Kimberly ..... 406-353-2607 262 B
kbarrows@ancollege.edu
BARROWS, Robert .... 617-228-2241 214 A
rbarrows@bhcc.mass.edu
BARRY, Ben .... 212-229-5600 307 E
barryb@newschool.edu
BARRY, Bernard .... 913-621-8765 173 B
bbarry@donnelly.edu
BARRY, Carol .... 225-578-1480 188 K
carolbarry@lsu.edu
BARRY, Catherine .... 603-578-8900 272 B
cbarry@ccsnh.edu
BARRY, Chris .... 217-786-2410 142 F
chris.barry@llcc.edu
BARRY, Christy .... 229-931-2053 120 B
christy.barry@gsw.edu
BARRY, Colleen .... 607-255-2000 297 D
cbarry@cornell.edu
BARRY, Danyell .... 478-827-3232 118 E
barnesd@fvsu.edu
BARRY, Ernie .... 214-768-2004 443 G
ebarry@smu.edu
BARRY, Heather .... 718-940-5796 313 C
BARRY, Heather .... 631-687-5109 313 C
hbarry@sjcny.edu
BARRY, James, T .... 304-457-6317 485 F
barryjt@ab.edu
BARRY, Jeannette .... 402-375-7466 267 I
jebarry1@wsc.edu
BARRY, Jessica .... 937-294-0592 356 D
jessica.barry@themodern.edu
BARRY, Kevin, A .... 213-477-2875.. 52 J
kbarry@msmu.edu
BARRY, Kevin, G .... 302-295-1170.. 91 C
kevin.g.barry@wilmu.edu
BARRY, Lisa .... 508-856-6507 212 A
lisa.barry@umassmed.edu
BARRY, Liz, M .... 734-764-6270 231 A
lizbarry@umich.edu
BARRY, Maria .... 202-885-2121.. 91 D
mariab@american.edu
BARRY, Marie .... 443-394-9818 202 C
mbarry@stevenson.edu
BARRY, Michael, F .... 713-646-1819 443 C
mbarry@stcl.edu
BARRY, Richard .... 610-526-6532 378 J
rbarry@brynmawr.edu
BARRY, Tammy .... 509-335-6424 484 D
tammy.barry@wsu.edu
BARRY, Taylor .... 828-898-3368 330 A
barryt@lmc.edu
BARRY, Theresa .... 262-524-7334 491 A
tbarry@carrollu.edu
BARSAM, Steven, N ...... 636-529-0000 258 B
snbarsam@slchc.edu
BARSOM, Michelle .... 770-836-4712 127 E
michelle.barsom@westgatech.edu
BARTA, Adam .... 888-777-7675 479 D
abarta@faithiu.edu
BARTA, Gary .... 319-335-9435 163 F
gary-barta@uiowa.edu
BARTA, Lou .... 217-641-4215 140 H
lbarta@jwcc.edu
BARTEE, Robert .... 402-559-4203 269 B
bbartee@unmc.edu
BARTEK, Jennifer, J ...... 724-738-2339 394 E
jennifer.bartek@sru.edu
BARTEL, Charles, R ...... 412-396-1090 382 E
bartelc@duq.edu
BARTEL, OSB, Martin ... 724-805-2146 397 D
martin.bartel@stvincent.edu
BARTELL, LaNeil, R .... 605-336-6588 415 B
lbartell@kairos.edu
BARTELL, William .... 605-331-6703 416 C
bill.bartell@usiouxfalls.edu
BARTELS, Paige .... 802-440-4300 461 B
pbartels@bennington.edu
BARTELS, Rob .... 417-865-2815 252 F
bartels4@evangel.edu
BARTELS, Roy .... 830-792-7213 442 G
rbartels@schreiner.edu
BARTELS, Suzanne, M .. 336-316-2046 329 C
bartelssm@guilford.edu
BARTELSON, Jon .... 401-456-8200 404 A
jbartelson@ric.edu
BARTELT, Brian .... 608-796-3912 496 L
bebartelt@viterbo.edu
BARTELT, Jason .... 920-923-8090 492 D
jbartelt@marianuniversity.edu
BARTFIELD, Joel .... 518-262-7302 289 C
bartfij@amc.edu
BARTH, Christopher ...... 845-938-3833 502 H
christopher.barth@westpoint.edu
BARTH, Doug .... 785-594-4526 171 C
doug.barth@bakeru.edu
BARTH, Richard .... 262-595-2495 495 D
barthr@uwp.edu
BARTH, Richard .... 864-656-5463 406 F
rbarth@clemson.edu
BARTH, Rick .... 256-233-8176.... 4 D
rick.barth@athens.edu
BARTH, Sean .... 407-708-4570 108 B
barths@seminolestate.edu
BARTHA, Jaimee .... 847-628-2514 141 A
jbartha@judsonu.edu
BARTHEL, Jamie .... 763-422-6082 236 H
jbarthel@anokatech.edu
BARTHELMAS, Rick .... 518-244-2200 312 D
barthf@sage.edu
BARTHOLOMAE, Dan .... 269-387-3061 232 J
daniel.bartholomae@wmich.edu
BARTHOLOMEW, Diane 660-831-4146 256 B
bartholomewd@moval.edu
BARTHOLOMEW, Diane 913-234-0665 172 I
diane.bartholomew@cleveland.edu
BARTHOLOMEW,
Jennifer .... 414-425-8300 494 A
jbartholomew@shsst.edu
BARTHOLOMEW, Leslie 610-282-1100 382 A
leslie.bartholomew@desales.edu
BARTHOLOMEW-FEIS,
Dixee .... 712-749-1803 164 A
bartholomew@bvu.edu
BARTINDALE, Becky ..... 650-949-6107.. 42 J
bartindalebecky@fhda.edu
BARTINE, Hunt .... 610-526-6012 385 F
hbartine@harcum.edu
BARTKOWSKI, Frances . 973-353-5444 281 C
franb@newark.rutgers.edu
BARTKOWSKI, Reggie ... 850-478-8496 105 F
rbartkowski@pcci.edu
BARTKUS, Carolyn .... 262-422-1686 493 F
cbartkus@nashotah.edu
BARTL, Noelle .... 575-562-2412 285 E
noelle.bartl@enmu.edu
BARTLE, John, R .... 402-554-3989 269 C
jbartle@unomaha.edu
BARTLETT, Abby .... 913-360-7400 171 G
abartlett@benedictine.edu
BARTLETT, Andy .... 218-755-2746 237 B
andy.bartlett@bemidjistate.edu
BARTLETT, Anne .... 973-290-4418 282 G
abartlett@steu.edu
BARTLETT, Anne .... 979-230-3202 431 A
anne.bartlett@brazosport.edu
BARTLETT, Annemarie ... 401-341-2117 404 D
annemarie.bartlett@salve.edu
BARTLETT, Jay .... 478-960-7969 127 D
jbartlett@wesleyancollege.edu
BARTLETT, Julia .... 651-846-1314 240 E
julia.bartlett@saintpaul.edu
BARTLETT, Lynlea .... 620-441-5289 172 M
lynlea.bartlett@cowley.edu
BARTLETT, Raymond ..... 832-842-5550 451 F
rbartlett@uh.edu
BARTLETT, Raymond ..... 832-842-5530 451 G
rbartlett@uh.edu
BARTLETT, Stacey .... 530-242-7730.. 64 A
sbartlett@shastacollege.edu
BARTLETT, Stacy .... 706-385-1100 124 C
stacy.bartlett@point.edu
BARTLEY, Mary, E .... 515-961-1511 169 G
mimi.bartley@simpson.edu
BARTLEY, Phyllis .... 540-863-2823 473 D
pbartley@mgcc.edu
BARTLING, Jonathan ..... 615-248-1258 425 D
jdbartling@trevecca.edu
BARTLING, Kelly, H ...... 308-865-8455 268 J
bartlingkh@unk.edu
BARTLOW, Jon, A .... 620-235-4761 176 H
jbartlow@pittstate.edu
BARTMESS, Lana .... 641-782-1456 170 B
bartmess@swcciowa.edu
BARTO, Christopher, E . 212-752-1530 303 G
cbarto@limcollege.edu
BARTO, Daniel .... 727-341-3051 107 C
barto.daniel@spcollege.edu
BARTOLD, Milissa .... 312-949-7440 139 B
mbartold@ico.edu
BARTOLINI, Brian, J ..... 401-865-1554 403 G
bbartoli@providence.edu
BARTOLOMEI, Chris, J . 716-645-2227 315 F
cbartolo@buffalo.edu
BARTOLOMEO, Jamin ... 240-567-1993 200 E
jamin.bartolomeo@montgomerycollege.edu

BARTOLOMEO, Joseph . 413-545-2554 211 D jbartolo@uww.umass.edu
BARTOLONE, Christopher 414-288-6103 492 E christopher.bartolone@marquette.edu
BARTON, Allison 615-220-7826 423 G abarton@mscc.edu
BARTON, Amanda 501-977-2028.. 23 D barton@uaccm.edu
BARTON, Andrea, M 503-943-8715 376 H barton@up.edu
BARTON, April 412-396-6280 382 E ambarton@duq.edu
BARTON, II, Barkley 706-542-2112 126 F barkely.barton@uga.edu
BARTON, Charles (Lennie) 919-760-8375 331 A bartonl@meredith.edu
BARTON, Jennifer, K 520-626-0314.. 16 H barton@arizona.edu
BARTON, Ken 870-780-1262.. 17 F kbarton@smail.anc.edu
BARTON, Mary 940-565-2085 453 B mary.barton@unt.edu
BARTON, Michael 256-782-5277.... 6 A msbarton@jsu.edu
BARTON, Michelle 760-744-1150.. 56 B mbarton@palomar.edu
BARTON, Oscar 443-885-3621 200 F oscar.barton@morgan.edu
BARTON, Patricia 510-136-1220.. 45 H barton@hnu.edu
BARTON, Paul 801-422-2738 458 A paul_barton@byu.edu
BARTON, Sara 310-506-4275.. 56 H sara.barton@pepperdine.edu
BARTOSIK, Angela 414-288-8436 492 E angela.bartosik@marquette.edu
BARTOVICS, Laura 718-482-5073 294 D lbartovics@lagcc.cuny.edu
BARTOW, Patricia 619-216-6795.. 65 K pbartow@swccd.edu
BARTRUG, Reba 740-374-8716 363 F rbartrug@wscc.edu
BARTS, Bryan 715-232-1469 496 C bartsb@uwstout.edu
BARTSCH, Melissa 859-622-1303 180 B melissa.bartsch@eku.edu
BARTUNEK, Tami 913-288-7166 174 H tbartunek@kckcc.edu
BARTUSIK, LisaMarie ... 850-484-2007 105 G lbartusik@pensacolastate.edu
BARUA, Susamma 657-278-3362.. 31 E sbarua@fullerton.edu
BARUSEFSKI, Ronald 412-312-8383 379 D housefather@bcs.edu
BARWICK, Ruth 202-319-5100.. 91 G barwick@cua.edu
BARZACCHINI, Mike 847-925-6510 138 E mbarzacc@harpercollege.edu
BAS QUINTERO, Sascha 305-629-2929 107 F sbas@sanignaciouniversity.edu
BASALA, Nissim 732-370-1560 274 H
BASCH, Hersch 718-438-1002 306 A
BASCOM, Shawn 208-282-5304 131 E bascshaw@isu.edu
BASCOMB, Cheryl, A 603-646-2258 272 F cheryl.a.bascomb@dartmouth.edu
BASDEN ARNOLD, Lorin 610-683-4000 394 A
BASEL, Barbara 609-586-4800 277 H baselb@mccc.edu
BASER, Ric 210-486-4908 427 H rbaser@alamo.edu
BASFORD, Jerry, L 801-581-3435 459 D jbasford@sa.utah.edu
BASGEN, Brian 617-824-8186 208 G brian_basgen@emerson.edu
BASGIER, Christopher ... 334-844-7475.... 4 E crb0085@auburn.edu
BASHAM, Lori 706-756-4589 127 E lori.basham@westgatech.edu
BASHARA, Teri 318-678-6000 187 E tbashara@bpcc.edu
BASHAW, Ed 620-341-5274 173 C ebashaw@emporia.edu
BASHET, Abuzafar, M ... 972-860-7158 433 I azbashet@dcccd.edu
BASHIR, Rashid 217-333-2150 151 F rbashir@illinois.edu
BASHKIHARATEE, Kisha 951-493-6753.. 77 A kbashkiharatee@yacollege.edu
BASICH, Tammy 219-464-5115 162 C tammy.basich@valpo.edu
BASIL, Meredith 657-278-2648.. 31 E mbasil@fullerton.edu
BASIL, Natalie 802-440-4390 461 B
BASILE, Carole, G 480-965-4064.. 11 A carole.basile@asu.edu
BASILIO, Shelle 315-781-3880 301 D basilio@hws.edu
BASINGER, Cyndie 434-791-5671 463 L cbasinger@averett.edu
BASINGER, David 585-594-6550 311 L basingerd@roberts.edu
BASINGER, Jim 814-332-3355 378 A jbasinger@allegheny.edu
BASINGER, Randall, G .. 717-796-5375 389 F rbasinge@messiah.edu
BASKEL, Elise 719-598-0200.. 80 B ebaskel@coloradotech.edu
BASKERVILLE, Elizabeth 323-563-5929.. 36 E ebaskerville@cdrewu.edu
BASKERVILLE, Rebecca . 402-472-5393 269 A rlbaskerville@unl.edu
BASKETTE, Shawna 562-860-2451.. 35 O sbaskette@cerritos.edu
BASKI, Alison 909-869-3600.. 30 B aabaski@cpp.edu
BASKI, Alison, A 909-869-3600.. 30 B aabaski@cpp.edu
BASKIN, Brent 706-233-7281 125 A bbaskin@shorter.edu
BASKIN, Dennis 269-965-3931 225 D baskind@kellogg.edu
BASKO, Aaron 434-544-8300 470 K basko_a@lynchburg.edu
BASKO, Aaron 434-381-6142 470 H abasko@sbc.edu
BASLER, Danielle 573-518-2307 255 G dbasler@mineralarea.edu
BASLER, Joella 618-634-3274 149 C joellab@shawneecc.edu
BASLER, Julie 303-369-5151.. 82 H julie.basler@plattcolorado.edu
BASS, Angela 816-415-5902 261 G bassa@william.jewell.edu
BASS, Barbara 202-994-2987.. 92 C bbass@gwu.edu
BASS, Brandie 318-487-7339 187 B brandie.bass@lcuniversity.edu
BASS, Brenda, L 319-273-2221 163 G brenda.bass@uni.edu
BASS, Candace 405-425-5931 367 C candace.bass@oc.edu
BASS, Charles 619-260-4819.. 72 H charlesb@sandiego.edu
BASS, Donna 334-222-6591.... 2 I dbass@lbwcc.edu
BASS, Elizabeth 804-828-8192 472 D eebass@vcu.edu
BASS, Gordon 904-357-8891 101 A gbass@fscj.edu
BASS, Jimmy 910-962-4292 343 B bassj@uncw.edu
BASS, Kengie, R 919-516-4160 339 G krbass@st-aug.edu
BASS, Leonard, C 407-582-2745 113 C lbass11@valenciacollege.edu
BASS, Mary, T 252-618-6560 334 B bassm@edgecombe.edu
BASS, Michelle 205-391-5810.... 3 E mbass@sheltonstate.edu
BASS, Randall 202-687-6400.. 92 D bassr@georgetown.edu
BASS, Royce, D 386-312-4204 107 A roycebass@sjrstate.edu
BASS KEER, Wendy 818-712-2619.. 49 H basskew@piercecollege.edu
BASSALE, Parfait 360-596-5356 483 E pbassale@spscc.edu
BASSARD, Kathy 901-843-3795 422 C bassardk@rhodes.edu
BASSEN, Amy 402-323-3406 268 D abassen@southeast.edu
BASSETT, Carolyn, S 413-577-1057 211 D cbassett@umass.edu
BASSETT, Ellen 404-894-3380 119 D ellen.bassett@design.gatech.edu
BASSETT, Heidi, M 972-860-7255 433 I hbassett@dcccd.edu
BASSETT, John 309-649-6303 150 D john.bassett@src.edu
BASSETT, Susan 607-274-3209 302 E sbassett@ithaca.edu
BASSETTI, Mimi 215-572-2941 378 E bassetti@arcadia.edu
BASSI-COOK, Teresa 724-838-4295 397 F tbassicook@setonhill.edu
BASSIE, Carol 973-408-3838 276 B cbassie@drew.edu
BASSINGER, Donnie 828-726-2214 332 E dbassinger@cccti.edu
BASSO, Sharon 909-621-8485.. 37 G sharon.basso@cmc.edu
BAST, Andy 616-392-8555 233 B andy@westernsem.edu
BASTA, Tania 270-745-7003 186 A tania.basta@wku.edu
BASTECKI-PEREZ, Victoria 215-641-6482 390 A vbasteck@mc3.edu
BASTIAN, Joni 618-537-6555 143 G jjbastian@mckendree.edu
BASTIAN, Kayla 605-773-3455 415 D kayla.bastian@sdbor.edu
BASTIN, Judy 316-322-3235 172 B jbastin@butlercc.edu
BASTON, Michael, A 216-987-4000 351 D
BASTONE, Linda 914-251-6000 318 E
BASU, Andra 570-945-8252 386 F andra.basu@keystone.edu
BASUALDO, Maria 607-778-5030 317 A basualdomi@sunybroome.edu
BASURTO, Brandi 402-481-8760 265 B brandi.basurto@bryanhealthcollege.edu
BATALAMA, Stella 561-297-3426 109 F sbatalama@fau.edu
BATCH, Mary 603-535-3278 274 B
BATCHELDER, Joseph ... 518-255-5620 318 F batchejb@cobleskill.edu
BATCHELLER, Tamara 313-993-1246 230 H batchets@udmercy.edu
BATCHELOR, Chelle 503-838-8886 377 C batchelorc@wou.edu
BATCHELOR, Grady 304-724-3700 485 G gbatchelor@apus.edu
BATCHELOR, Jennifer 603-665-7481 273 E j.batchelor@snhu.edu
BATCHELOR, Laura 609-343-5632 274 E lbatchel@atlantic.edu
BATCHELOR, Susan 618-545-3033 141 C sbatchelor@kaskaskia.edu
BATCHER, Shelly 770-426-2653 122 A sbatcher@life.edu
BATE, Jeff, B 801-375-5125 459 A jeff.bate@rm.edu
BATE, Jennifer 201-327-8877 276 F jbate@eastwick.edu
BATE, Joel, C 208-732-6836 131 B jbate@csi.edu
BATEK, Petra 317-274-2548 157 B pbatek@iupui.edu
BATEMAN, Dale 206-934-2905 482 G dale.bateman@seattlecolleges.edu
BATEMAN, Douglas, R .. 318-678-6000 187 E rbateman@bpcc.edu
BATEMAN, Heather 800-686-1883 222 B hbateman@cleary.edu
BATEMAN, Jamie 863-784-7181 108 D jamie.bateman@southflorida.edu
BATEMAN, Joyce 417-447-6966 257 B batemanj@otc.edu
BATEMAN, Justin 432-335-6460 440 C jbateman@odessa.edu
BATEMAN, Mathew 814-866-8148 387 C mbateman@lecom.edu
BATEMAN, Sharon 931-303-1697 423 G sbateman@mscc.edu
BATENHORST, Jamie 402-461-7300 266 C jamie.batenhorst@hastings.edu
BATES, Alicia 225-768-1797 186 H alicia.bates@franu.edu
BATES, Alisa 503-847-2627 377 A abates@uws.edu
BATES, Anthony 708-235-7431 138 C abates99@govst.edu
BATES, Brent 660-596-7223 259 D bbates@sfccmo.edu
BATES, Brian 408-924-6518.. 34 B brian.bates@sjsu.edu
BATES, Carese 410-778-5822 204 E cbates2@washcoll.edu
BATES, Cortny 940-397-4000 439 F cortny.bates@msutexas.edu
BATES, Dakota 417-255-7960 256 A dakotabates@missouristate.edu
BATES, Damien 928-317-5892.. 11 B damien.bates@azwestern.edu
BATES, Doug 931-372-3408 425 B dbates@tntech.edu
BATES, Holly 770-533-7007 121 L hbates@laniertech.edu
BATES, James 410-293-1568 502 I jbates@usna.edu
BATES, Julie 501-660-1002.. 17 G jbates@asusystem.edu
BATES, Larry 865-694-6404 424 C lbates@pstcc.edu
BATES, Leslie 937-769-1345 347 F lbates@antioch.edu
BATES, Lynette 909-558-4561.. 48 J lbates@llu.edu
BATES, Lynette 719-846-5559.. 83 I lynette.bates@trinidadstate.edu
BATES, Mary Lou, W 518-580-5588 315 A mbates@skidmore.edu
BATES, Michael 573-876-7172 259 F mbates@stephens.edu
BATES, Michael 847-925-6290 138 E mbates@harpercollege.edu
BATES, Michael, M 585-292-2821 306 K mbates@monroecc.edu
BATES, Michele 575-624-8096 286 F bates@nmmi.edu
BATES, Starnell 803-822-3235 409 E batess@midlandstech.edu
BATES, Tierney 919-843-7100 342 B tjbates@email.unc.edu
BATES, Trevor, M 937-481-2200 363 H trevor.bates@wilmington.edu
BATES, Wendy 831-646-4226.. 52 H wbates@mpc.edu
BATES-REESE, Fannie .... 205-391-2214.... 3 E freese@sheltonstate.edu
BATESON, Carrie 918-595-7868 370 B carrie.bateson@tulsacc.edu
BATH, Michael, J 906-227-2151 228 E mbath@nmu.edu
BATHERSFIELD, Olivia .. 240-965-3628 197 F ombathersfield@captechu.edu
BATHOLOMEW, Lindsay 864-488-4557 409 C lbartholomew@limestone.edu
BATIC, Marjorie 317-955-6150 159 A mbatic@marian.edu
BATIE, Larry 205-929-1446.... 6 B lbatie@miles.edu
BATIS, Jeffrey 540-261-8400 470 D jeff.batis@svu.edu
BATISTA, Freddie 239-992-4624.. 96 E
BATISTA, Hector 646-664-9106 292 E hector.batista@cuny.edu
BATISTA, Jorge 347-964-8600 291 F jbatista@boricuacollege.edu
BATISTA, Michelle 530-541-4660.. 47 H batista@ltcc.edu
BATISTA-SANTIAGO, Gerardo 787-993-8950 510 E gerardo.batista@upr.edu
BATSON, Marie 251-442-2370.... 8 C mbatson@umobile.edu
BATSON, Rebecca 302-857-7887.. 90 D rbatson@desu.edu
BATSON, Robert 937-775-2869 364 D robert.batson@wright.edu
BATSON, Trice 269-488-4119 225 C tbatson@kvcc.edu
BATT, Joe 918-343-7624 369 A jbatt@rsu.edu
BATT, Mark 724-589-2157 398 F mbatt@thiel.edu
BATT, Marylou 617-349-8564 210 H mbatt@lesley.edu
BATT, Megan 419-267-1366 357 E mbatt@northweststate.edu
BATTAGLIA, Janet, M ... 540-464-7213 475 C battagliajm@vmi.edu
BATTAGLIA, John, A 417-268-1000 249 G battagliaj@evangel.edu
BATTAGLINO, JR., John 617-353-4126 207 C jbattag@bu.edu
BATTEE-FREEMAN, Katherine 217-206-8503 151 E kathyy@uis.edu
BATTELL, Victoria, L 518-861-2571 305 B vbattell@mariacollege.edu
BATTEN, Debbie 252-618-6503 334 B battend@edgecombe.edu

BATTEN, Kelsey .... 317-917-5732 158 A
kbatten1@ivytech.edu
BATTEN, Melissa .... 843-349-5228 409 A
melissa.batten@hgtc.edu
BATTEN-MICKENS,
Meloyde, R .... 301-546-0763 201 D
mbatte101373@pgcc.edu
BATTINELLI, David .... 516-463-7384 301 E
david.battinelli@hofstra.edu
BATTINKOFF, Robert ... 989-686-9145 223 E
robertbattinkoff@delta.edu
BATTISTA, Doug .... 858-646-3100.. 62 L
BATTISTA, Joe, N .... 407-582-6622 113 C
jbattista@valenciacollege.edu
BATTISTA, Marc .... 847-635-1423 146 E
mbattista@oakton.edu
BATTISTA, Vince .... 312-567-8625 139 H
vbattista@iit.edu
BATTLE, Chris .... 323-343-3000... 32 B
cbattle3@calstatela.edu
BATTLE, Emily .... 312-369-7480 136 C
ebattle@colum.edu
BATTLE, III, George ...... 919-445-1248 342 B
gbattle@ad.unc.edu
BATTLE, Kara .... 919-536-7200 334 A
battlek@durhamtech.edu
BATTLE, Kiana .... 708-974-5372 144 G
battlek@morainevalley.edu
BATTLE, Leslee, S .... 336-750-2263 343 E
shepardl@wssu.edu
BATTLE, Lydée .... 301-891-4128 204 D
lbattle@wau.edu
BATTLE-BROWN,
LaToya .... 973-353-1374 281 C
lbbrown@rutgers.edu
BATTLES, Denise, A ...... 585-245-5501 317 E
battles@geneseo.edu
BATTLES, Jason, J .... 479-575-3836.. 21 H
jasonjb@uark.edu
BATTLES, Linnea .... 251-380-2240... 6 H
lbattles@shc.edu
BATTOE, Whitney, E ...... 305-628-6590 107 D
wbattoe@stu.edu
BATTRAW, Danny .... 928-428-8605.. 12 H
danny.battraw@eac.edu
BATTS, JR., Battinto ...... 602-496-5555... 11 A
battinto.batts@asu.edu
BATTS, Martha .... 214-818-1317 433 A
mbatts@criswell.edu
BATTULGA, Bayarjargal . 703-591-7042 466 G
bayarjargal@fxua.edu
BATTURS, Beth Anne .... 410-777-7352 197 C
babatturs@aacc.edu
BATTY, Philip .... 616-331-8650 224 D
battyp@gvsu.edu
BATTY-HERBERT,
Kimberly .... 928-226-4362.. 12 B
kimberly.batty-herbert@coconino.edu
BATTYE, Karen .... 334-844-2544... 4 E
klb0002@auburn.edu
BAU, Krista .... 605-626-3007 415 H
krista.bau@northern.edu
BAUCOM, Devin .... 704-991-0190 338 A
dbaucom0142@stanly.edu
BAUCOM, Eva .... 704-233-8633 344 E
e.baucom@wingate.edu
BAUCOM, Ian .... 434-924-3728 471 F
ibb4n@virginia.edu
BAUCUM, Natasha ...... 601-928-6281 246 F
natasha.baucum@mgccc.edu
BAUDOUIN, Ashley ...... 864-294-2000 408 I
BAUDOUX, Brandy ...... 352-245-4119 112 D
brandy.barnett@taylorcollege.edu
BAUDRY YOUNG,
Rebecca .... 513-529-3438 356 A
baudryrm@miamioh.edu
BAUER, Amanda .... 661-763-7853... 67 F
abauer@taftcollege.edu
BAUER, Amie .... 785-227-3380 171 H
baueral@bethanylb.edu
BAUER, Angela, C ...... 336-841-9501 329 E
abauer@highpoint.edu
BAUER, Blanca .... 337-482-6306 192 F
blanca.bauer@louisiana.edu
BAUER, C. Jon .... 636-584-6501 252 D
jon.bauer@eastcentral.edu
BAUER, Christine ...... 208-426-5903 130 F
christinebauer@boisestate.edu
BAUER, Cortney, A ...... 402-280-3533 265 J
cortneybauer@creighton.edu
BAUER, Dan .... 724-738-2773 394 E
dan.bauer@sru.edu
BAUER, Daniel .... 314-367-8700 260 A
daniel.bauer@uhsp.edu

BAUER, David .... 859-858-3581 178 G
BAUER, Denise .... 845-451-1345 297 I
denise.bauer@culinary.edu
BAUER, Dennis .... 479-308-2282... 17 E
dennis.bauer@acheedu.org
BAUER, James .... 863-680-4186 100 F
jbauer@flsouthern.edu
BAUER, Jason, K ...... 515-263-2887 166 C
jbauer@grandview.edu
BAUER, Jeffrey .... 740-351-3208 360 E
jbauer@shawnee.edu
BAUER, Jeffrey, C ...... 513-732-5209 362 B
jeff.bauer@uc.edu
BAUER, Jeremy ...... 203-596-8359.. 88 C
jebauer@post.edu
BAUER, Joanna .... 909-667-4411.. 38 A
BAUER, Joy .... 918-540-6720 366 F
joyb@neo.edu
BAUER, Kara .... 619-594-0489.. 33 E
kbauer@sdsu.edu
BAUER, Kathryn .... 575-835-5260 286 D
kathryn.bauer@nmt.edu
BAUER, Kelli .... 620-252-7180 172 K
bauer.kelli@coffeyville.edu
BAUER, Marc .... 308-865-8332 268 J
bauermd@unk.edu
BAUER, Mark, D ...... 507-354-8221 236 D
bauermd@mlc-wels.edu
BAUER, Mary .... 718-405-3233 296 D
mary.bauer@mountsaintvincent.edu
BAUER, Matt .... 919-739-7030 338 F
mjbauer@waynecc.edu
BAUER, Sarah .... 657-278-2929.. 31 E
sarahbauer@fullerton.edu
BAUER, Stacy .... 605-229-8405 414 I
stacy.bauer@presentation.edu
BAUER, Stacy .... 605-626-2521 415 H
stacy.bauer@northern.edu
BAUER, Susan .... 646-592-4090 325 R
susan.bauer@yu.edu
BAUER, Tawana .... 662-243-1923 245 C
tbauer@eastms.edu
BAUER, Tom .... 650-358-6782.. 62 H
bauert@smccd.edu
BAUER, Warren, K ...... 515-574-1120 166 G
bauer@iowacentral.edu
BAUGH, Anita, G ...... 320-308-5936 240 D
abaugh@sctcc.edu
BAUGH, Frank .... 601-318-6772 249 B
frank.baugh@wmcarey.edu
BAUGH, Robbie .... 940-668-3338 439 I
rbaugh@nctc.edu
BAUGH, Suzi .... 850-201-6083 112 B
suzi.baugh@tcc.fl.edu
BAUGHMAN, Leslie ...... 305-428-5700 104 F
BAUGHMAN, Linda, M . 651-962-6053 243 F
lmbaughman@stthomas.edu
BAUGHMAN, Matthew . 618-453-2341 149 G
baughman@siu.edu
BAUGHMAN, Philip ...... 515-271-1340 165 C
philip.baughman@dmu.edu
BAUGHMAN, Sara ...... 828-669-8012 331 H
sara.baughman@montreat.edu
BAUGHMAN, Terry ...... 314-838-8858 261 A
lifepastoraz@gmail.com
BAUGHN, Jeffrey ...... 615-966-7650 420 B
jeff.baughn@lipscomb.edu
BAUGOUS, Amanda ...... 309-794-7340 132 H
amandabaugous@augustana.edu
BAUGUESS, Seth ...... 937-912-0622 364 D
seth.bauguess@wright.edu
BAUM, Benjamin ...... 410-626-2522 201 E
benjamin.baum@sjc.edu
BAUM, Christina ...... 801-863-8405 460 A
christina.baum@uvu.edu
BAUM, Cynthia .... 609-984-1100 283 D
provost@tesu.edu
BAUM, Dan, B .... 410-777-2011 197 C
dbbaum@aacc.edu
BAUM, Lucy .... 404-378-8821 117 D
BAUM, Richard .... 212-998-2345 309 D
BAUMAN, Jennifer ...... 540-432-4294 465 F
baumanj@emu.edu
BAUMAN, Joel .... 412-396-5002 382 E
baumanj@duq.edu
BAUMAN, Michael ...... 312-935-4242 140 F
mbauman@icsw.edu
BAUMAN, Sandra ...... 406-447-6928 263 F
sandra.bauman@helenacollege.edu
BAUMAN, Sarah ...... 509-682-6473 484 H
sbauman@wvc.edu

BAUMAN POWER,
Angie .... 319-895-4818 164 E
abaumanpower@cornellcollege.edu
BAUMANN, Diana .... 785-623-6150 176 C
dbaumann@ncktc.edu
BAUMANN, Erick ...... 708-524-5054 137 A
ebauman@dom.edu
BAUMANN, Joseph ...... 480-506-0039 173 A
jbaumann@dc3.edu
BAUMANN, Robert ...... 913-684-2741 502 D
robert.baumann@leavenworth.army.mil
BAUMANN, Todd ...... 308-432-6245 267 G
tbaumann@csc.edu
BAUMBACH, Kirk ...... 804-752-7263 469 B
kirkbaumbach@rmc.edu
BAUMBERGER, Jessica . 217-206-8384 151 E
jbaum02s@uis.edu
BAUMEISTER, Barbara .. 405-736-0208 369 D
bbaumeister@rose.edu
BAUMER, Brian ...... 718-990-3292 313 B
baumerb@stjohns.edu
BAUMET, Robert ...... 315-279-5328 303 D
rbaumet@keuka.edu
BAUMGARD, Heath ...... 651-423-8298 237 E
heath.baumgard@dctc.edu
BAUMGARDNER,
Brice, D .... 573-629-3280 253 D
bbaumgardner@hlg.edu
BAUMGARDNER,
Deidra .... 317-738-8189 155 A
dbaumgardner@franklincollege.edu
BAUMGARDNER, Doug . 574-372-5100 155 C
doug.baumgardner@grace.edu
BAUMGART, Reilly ...... 618-262-8641 139 G
baumgartr@iecc.edu
BAUMGARTNER, Aileen . 914-241-3500 305 D
abaumgartner@mmm.edu
BAUMGARTNER,
Danielle .... 815-921-4849 147 H
d.baumgartner@rockvalleycollege.edu
BAUMGARTNER, Eric ... 414-277-7190 493 D
BAUMGARTNER, Erin ... 503-838-8348 377 C
baumgare@wou.edu
BAUMGARTNER,
Gretchen .... 530-283-0202.. 42 E
gbaumgartner@frc.edu
BAUMGARTNER, Holly .. 800-541-6682 104M
BAUMGARTNER, Neil ... 262-595-2151 495 D
baumgarn@uwp.edu
BAUMGARTNER, Renee . 408-554-5344.. 63 A
rbaumgartner@scu.edu
BAUMHOVER, Lynne ...... 563-589-0300 170 G
lbaumhover@wartburgseminary.edu
BAUMUNK, Jeffrey ...... 310-660-3593.. 41 J
jbaumunk@elcamino.edu
BAUN, Dan .... 507-537-6978 240 G
dan.baun@smsu.edu
BAUN, Jeff .... 610-436-2705 394 F
jbaun@wcupa.edu
BAUR, Cheryl .... 570-740-0368 388 G
cbaur@luzerne.edu
BAURAIN, Thomas ...... 816-311-0110 250 E
thomas.baurain@calvary.edu
BAUSANO, Darren ...... 906-487-7396 223 I
jason.sullivan@finlandia.edu
BAUSCH, Suzanne ...... 330-972-4688 361 G
sbausch@uakron.edu
BAUSERMAN, Judy ...... 304-263-0979 487 A
BAUSINGER, Patricia, E 570-321-4049 388 H
baus@lycoming.edu
BAUSLEY, Gwen ...... 304-766-4366 489 D
gbausley@wvstateu.edu
BAUSS, Celia, N ...... 864-592-4754 411 E
baussc@sccsc.edu
BAUTE, Aaron .... 765-446-1154 158 A
abaute@ivytech.edu
BAUTE, Brian .... 704-229-2070 339 D
bauteb@queens.edu
BAUTISTA, Adrian ...... 518-580-5352 315 A
BAUTISTA, Annabelle .... 859-344-3572 184 G
bautista@thomasmore.edu
BAUTISTA, Maria ...... 808-734-9519 129 E
mariab@hawaii.edu
BAUTISTA MOLLER,
Lydia .... 954-607-4344 112 I
BAUTTI, Joann .... 757-446-5244 465 H
bauttij@evms.edu
BAVA, Brian .... 208-459-5271 131 A
bava@collegeofidaho.edu
BAVADRA, Verenaisi ...... 692-625-3394 503 F
BAVER, Debra .... 610-921-7256 377 F
dbaver@albright.edu

BAVISI, Lata .... 505-922-2889 285 G
lata@eccu.edu
BAVISI, Sanjay .... 505-922-2889 285 G
BAWA, Opinder .... 415-422-2787.. 72 I
osbawa@usfca.edu
BAWCOM, Amy .... 512-223-7619 429 E
amy.bawcom@austincc.edu
BAWCUM, Audrey ...... 334-699-2266... 1 B
ambawcum@acom.edu
BAWDON, Jessica ...... 831-656-1062 501 K
jessica.bawdon@nps.edu
BAWOROWSKY, John .. 414-288-4976 492 E
john.baworowsky@marquette.edu
BAX, Conny .... 231-843-5710 232 I
cbax@westshore.edu
BAXTER, Agnes .... 919-546-8212 339 I
abaxter@shawu.edu
BAXTER, Aimee, F ...... 318-257-2641 192 A
abaxter@latech.edu
BAXTER, Herman ...... 214-887-5267 434 G
hbaxter@dts.edu
BAXTER, Hilary .... 617-327-6777 219 E
hilary_baxter@williamjames.edu
BAXTER, Jamie .... 513-745-2800 364 F
baxterj1@xavier.edu
BAXTER, John .... 504-526-4745 190 C
BAXTER, Kathleen ...... 951-372-8080.. 45 G
hisuniv@yahoo.com
BAXTER, Keith .... 580-745-2250 369 F
kbaxter@se.edu
BAXTER, Leigh .... 804-706-5214 473 B
lbaxter@jtcc.edu
BAXTER, Melissa ...... 315-568-3271 309 H
mbaxter@northeastcollege.edu
BAXTER, Randl .... 866-617-6446 190 C
BAXTER, Susanna ...... 706-880-8230 121 K
sbaxter@lagrange.edu
BAYÓN TORRES,
Ramón .... 787-764-0000 511 F
ramon.bayon@upr.edu
BAY, Kelly .... 309-467-6431 137 G
kbay@eureka.edu
BAY, Willow, C .... 213-740-6180.. 73 C
wbay@usc.edu
BAYARDELLE, Eddy ...... 718-289-5185 292 H
eddy.bayardelle@bcc.cuny.edu
BAYER, Amy .... 305-395-1121.. 98 B
amy@dolphins.org
BAYER, Kristy .... 816-501-4854 257 K
kristy.bayer@rockhurst.edu
BAYER, Michelle ...... 605-688-5585 416 A
michelle.bayer@sdstate.edu
BAYLES, Kenneth ...... 402-559-4945 269 B
kbayles@unmc.edu
BAYLESS, Elizabeth ...... 757-352-5152 469 F
ebayless@regent.edu
BAYLESS, Laura .... 978-665-3215 212 C
lbayless@fitchburgstate.edu
BAYLISS-CARR, Sandy . 252-638-4755 333 F
bayliss-carrs@cravencc.edu
BAYLOR, Bridget ...... 540-453-2358 472 F
baylorb@brcc.edu
BAYLOR, Jeff .... 276-328-0322 471 G
fyc6tr@uvawise.edu
BAYLOR, Jeff, S .... 806-651-2020 447 D
jbaylor@wtamu.edu
BAYLOR, Kara .... 262-551-5812 491 B
kbaylor@carthage.edu
BAYNE, Deann .... 402-481-8718 265 B
deann.bayne@bryanhealthcollege.edu
BAYNE, Stephen ...... 806-742-3533 450 C
stephen.bayne@ttu.edu
BAYNES, Leonard, M .. 713-743-2478 451 G
lbaynes@uh.edu
BAYOUMI, Magdy, A .... 337-482-6147 192 F
mab@louisiana.edu
BAYS, Lindsay .... 620-341-5221 173 C
lbays@emporia.edu
BAYSDEN, Jennifer, M .. 252-328-9194 340 H
baysdenj@ecu.edu
BAYTO, Tammy .... 478-274-7852 123 E
tbayto@oftc.edu
BAYUS, Jenelle .... 330-569-5287 353 F
bayusj1@hiram.edu
BAZAN, Yamilet ...... 951-785-2100.. 47 F
ybazan@lasierra.edu
BAZANT, Robert, S ...... 724-222-5330 391 E
rbazant@penncommercial.edu
BAZARSKY, Debbie ...... 717-396-7833 392 Q
dbazarsky@pcad.edu
BAZEMORE, Alisha ...... 757-823-2406 468 B
albazemore@nsu.edu

Index of Key Administrators BAZEMORE – BEAZLEY 539

BAZEMORE, Hannah ..... 910-893-1326 327 C
bazemoreh@campbell.edu
BAZEMORE, Michael ..... 406-657-2369 263 H
michael.bazemore@msubillings.edu
BAZEMORE,
Qiana Anngel .... 336-744-0900 327 D
qiana.bazemore@carolina.edu
BAZIL, Ted .... 914-961-8313 314 E
ted@svots.edu
BAZILE, Samantha .... 845-398-4102 314 D
sbazile@stac.edu
BAZIN, Angela .... 860-465-0147.. 85 G
bazina@easternct.edu
BAZZEL, Matthew .... 706-419-1126 117 G
matthew.bazzel@covenant.edu
BAZZEL, Mitchell .... 256-233-8161.... 4 D
mitchell.bazzel@athens.edu
BAZZELL, Darrell .... 512-471-1422 454 C
bazzell@austin.utexas.edu
BC, Hikmat .... 813-253-7236 102 A
hbc@hccfl.edu
BEA, David .... 520-206-4519.. 15 E
dbea@pima.edu
BEACH, Adam, R .... 765-285-1300 153 E
arbeach@bsu.edu
BEACH, David .... 913-288-7163 174 H
dbeach@kckcc.edu
BEACH, Justin .... 406-377-9410 262 G
jbeach@dawson.edu
BEACH, Lisa .... 253-589-5603 478 A
lisa.beach@cptc.edu
BEACH, Michael .... 913-288-7645 174 H
mbeach@kckcc.edu
BEACH, Nancy, S .... 540-365-4529 466 I
nbeach@ferrum.edu
BEACH, Natalie .... 503-399-5105 372 A
natalie.beach@chemeketa.edu
BEACH, Scott, R .... 412-624-4141 400 A
scottb@pitt.edu
BEACH, Steven .... 432-552-2170 456 C
beach_s@utpb.edu
BEACH, Vincent .... 641-585-8133 170 E
vince.beach@waldorf.edu
BEACH, Wendy .... 906-635-2213 226 C
wbeach1@lssu.edu
BEACHAM, David, M .... 864-597-4206 413 E
beachamdm@wofford.edu
BEACHAM, Ralph .... 620-724-0390 173 F
ralphb@fortscott.edu
BEACHE, Vidda, P .... 240-500-2357 199 A
vpbeache@hagerstowncc.edu
BEACHLER, Kelly .... 941-309-4022 106 J
kbeachle@ringling.edu
BEACHNAU, Andy .... 616-331-3585 224 D
beachnaa@gvsu.edu
BEACHY, Jeff .... 408-554-5360.. 63 A
jdbeachy@scu.edu
BEADLES, Cindy .... 309-457-2114 144 E
cbeadles@monmouthcollege.edu
BEAGHAN, John .... 828-669-8012 331 H
john.beaghan@montreat.edu
BEAGLE, Donald .... 704-461-6740 326 I
donaldbeagle@bac.edu
BEAGLE, Mike .... 541-552-6127 376 A
beaglem@sou.edu
BEAKMAN, Andrew, W . 315-792-3111 323 G
awbeakma@utica.edu
BEAL, Jean .... 413-572-8574 213 C
jbeal@westfield.ma.edu
BEAL, Jennifer .... 940-668-3315 439 I
jbeal@nctc.edu
BEAL, Kyle .... 765-677-2497 157 F
kyle.beal@indwes.edu
BEAL, Maureen .... 412-624-6832 400 A
mbeal@cfo.pitt.edu
BEAL, Stephen .... 510-594-3630.. 28 D
sbeal@cca.edu
BEALE, Connie, L .... 973-761-9401 282 K
concetta.beale@shu.edu
BEALE, Tyson .... 843-383-8000 407 C
tbeale@coker.edu
BEALE, Tyson, J .... 301-546-0412 201 D
bealetj@pgcc.edu
BEALES, Sharon .... 610-861-5451 391 B
sbeales@northampton.edu
BEALKA, JT .... 651-450-3386 237 H
jbealka@inverhills.edu
BEALL, David .... 773-508-2391 142 G
dbeall@luc.edu
BEALS, Brandi .... 602-383-8228.. 16 G
bbeals@uat.edu
BEALS, Linda .... 937-327-6324 364 C
lbeals@wittenberg.edu
BEALS, Michael, J .... 714-556-3610.. 73 G
officeofthepresident@vanguard.edu
BEAM, Brian .... 309-438-8404 140 C
babeam@ilstu.edu
BEAM, Faithe .... 910-893-1540 327 C
beam@campbell.edu
BEAM, John .... 510-464-3474.. 57 B
jbeam@peralta.edu
BEAM, Julie .... 574-807-7020 153 G
julie.beam@bethelunivesity.edu
BEAM, Tony .... 864-977-2008 410 A
tony.beam@ngu.edu
BEAMER, Denise .... 252-428-7327 336 B
dmbeamer917@nashcc.edu
BEAN, Al .... 207-780-5588 196 J
albean@maine.edu
BEAN, Andrew, J .... 312-942-3589 148 C
andrew_j_bean@rush.edu
BEAN, Gary .... 315-792-7222 320 F
gary.bean@sunypoly.edu
BEAN, Joanna .... 719-255-3180.. 84 A
jbean2@uccs.edu
BEAN, KayLyn .... 806-291-3662 457 B
jdmuseum@wbu.edu
BEAN, Kellie .... 740-245-7014 363 A
kbean@rio.edu
BEAN, Leslie .... 423-461-8712 421 E
labean@milligan.edu
BEAN, Linda .... 479-964-3217.. 18 E
lbean@atu.edu
BEAN, Miho .... 603-206-8101 272 A
msbean@ccsnh.edu
BEAN, Shirley .... 253-833-9111 480 A
sbean@greenriver.edu
BEAN, Stacey .... 937-778-7844 352 D
sbean@edisonohio.edu
BEAN, Steve .... 218-293-6850 238 D
steven.bean@minnesotanorth.edu
BEAN, Tracy .... 610-799-1121 388 B
tbean@lccc.edu
BEANE, Michael .... 563-441-4016 165 J
mbeane@eicc.edu
BEANE-BOOSE, Linda ... 509-533-3567 478 E
linda.beane-boose@sfcc.spokane.edu
BEANS, Jessica .... 937-395-8601 354 J
jessica.beans@kc.edu
BEANS, Trip .... 717-871-4636 394 B
trip.beans@millersville.edu
BEAR, Thomas .... 812-877-8691 160 C
bear@rose-hulman.edu
BEARBOWER, Sarah ...... 608-796-3860 496 L
sbearbower@viterbo.edu
BEARCE, Karen .... 610-861-5434 391 B
kbearce@northampton.edu
BEARD, Alison .... 828-726-2311 332 E
abeard@cccti.edu
BEARD, Audrey, W .... 919-530-5327 341 D
awbeard@nccu.edu
BEARD, Brian, C .... 302-356-6989.. 91 C
bcbeard@wilmu.edu
BEARD, Clete .... 205-652-3543.... 9 B
cbeard@uwa.edu
BEARD, Elizabeth .... 318-427-4460 189 A
ebeard@lsua.edu
BEARD, Jonathan .... 419-448-3018 361 C
beardjw@tiffin.edu
BEARD, Jordan .... 229-391-5050 114 D
jbeard2@abac.edu
BEARD, Julia .... 208-426-1459 130 F
juliabeard@boisestate.edu
BEARD, Katie .... 205-652-3852.... 9 B
kbeard@uwa.edu
BEARD, Kyanna .... 501-812-2230.. 23 E
kbeard@uaptc.edu
BEARD, Richard, L .... 717-867-6363 388 A
rbeard@lvc.edu
BEARD, Tanika, L .... 803-535-5471 406 E
tbeard@claflin.edu
BEARD, Timothy, L .... 727-816-3400 105 E
beardt@phsc.edu
BEARD, Virginia .... 616-395-7544 224 H
beard@hope.edu
BEARDEN, David .... 541-737-5774 374 H
beardend@ohsu.edu
BEARDEN, Karen .... 386-481-2054.. 96 D
beardenk@cookman.edu
BEARDEN, Katherine ..... 318-869-5039 186 C
kbearden@centenary.edu
BEARDEN, Shae .... 501-420-1203.. 17 D
shae.bearden@arkansasbaptist.edu
BEARDMORE, Kevin ...... 270-686-4504 182 C
kevin.beardmore@kctcs.edu
BEARDMORE,
Melissa, A .... 410-777-2532 197 C
mabeardmore@aacc.edu
BEARDSALL,
Christopher .... 210-486-7018 428 C
cbeardsall@alamo.edu
BEARDSLEE, Gene .... 402-872-2270 267 H
gbeardslee@peru.edu
BEARDSLEY, Jason .... 310-434-8054.. 63 B
beardsley_jason@smc.edu
BEARDSLEY, Kathleen ... 215-572-2838 378 E
beardsley@arcadia.edu
BEARDSLEY, Scott, C .... 434-924-7481 471 F
scb4v@virginia.edu
BEARER, Dana .... 716-673-3251 316 A
dana.bearer@fredonia.edu
BEARER, Dana .... 304-829-7591 486 B
dbearer@bethanywv.edu
BEARMAN, Alan .... 785-670-1855 178 A
alan.bearman@washburn.edu
BEARROWS, Thomas, R 312-996-7762 151 C
bearrows@uillinois.edu
BEARROWS, Thomas, R 312-996-7762 151 D
bearrows@uillinois.edu
BEARSS, Carrie .... 810-989-5501 230 A
cbearss@sc4.edu
BEARUP, Angie .... 757-631-8101 463 K
BEASIMER, Linda, M .... 845-431-8979 298 B
beasimer@sunydutchess.edu
BEASLAND, Matthew ..... 708-596-2000 149 D
mbeasland@ssc.edu
BEASLEY, Alicia .... 601-635-2111 245 B
abeasley@eccc.edu
BEASLEY, Debbie .... 870-574-4481.. 21 F
dbeasley@sautech.edu
BEASLEY, Gerald, R ...... 607-255-3393 297 D
libadmin@cornell.edu
BEASLEY, Jerri .... 706-754-7704 123 C
jbeasley@northgatech.edu
BEASLEY, Joan .... 386-822-7251 111 F
jlbeasle@stetson.edu
BEASLEY, Laura .... 507-433-0676 240 A
laura.beasley@riverland.edu
BEASLEY, Paula .... 276-326-4269 464 A
pbeasley@bluefield.edu
BEASLEY, Sarah .... 304-384-6035 488 K
sbeasley@concord.edu
BEASLEY, Shelly .... 870-236-6901.. 19 D
sebeasley@crc.edu
BEASLEY, Stephanie ...... 901-678-5021 426 A
sbeasly1@memphis.edu
BEASLEY, Vanessa .... 615-322-4948 427 B
vanessa.beasley@vanderbilt.edu
BEASSIE, Rhonda .... 936-294-2425 449 E
rvbeassie@shsu.edu
BEATA, Anthony .... 316-942-4291 176 B
beataa@newmanu.edu
BEATIE, Jennifer .... 918-595-7668 370 B
jennifer.beatie@tulsacc.edu
BEATON, Kim .... 530-283-0202.. 42 E
kbeaton@frc.edu
BEATON-GARCIA,
Sunem .... 954-201-7350.. 96 F
BEATON-GARCIA,
Sunem .... 715-833-6221 497 E
sbeatongarcia@cvtc.edu
BEATSON, Bonnie .... 808-235-7374 130 C
beatson@hawaii.edu
BEATTIE, Eric, L .... 508-831-6231 220 C
elbeattie@wpi.edu
BEATTIE, Matthew .... 734-432-5386 226 G
mbeattie@madonna.edu
BEATTIE, Terry .... 610-436-3317 394 F
tbeattie@wcupa.edu
BEATTY, Amy .... 863-667-5523 108 I
arbeatty@seu.edu
BEATTY, Anthany .... 859-257-8200 185 D
anthany.beatty@uky.edu
BEATTY, Bernadette .... 575-624-8001 286 F
noriega@nmmi.edu
BEATTY, Del .... 435-652-7514 459 G
del.beatty@utahtech.edu
BEATTY, Jane .... 301-846-2657 198 E
jbeatty@frederick.edu
BEATTY, Kelli .... 740-284-5222 352 I
kbeatty@franciscan.edu
BEATTY, Kimberly .... 816-604-1011 254 E
kimberly.beatty@mcckc.edu
BEATTY, Luke .... 217-245-3020 139 A
luke.beatty@ic.edu
BEATTY, Luke .... 563-333-6241 169 D
beattyluke@sau.edu
BEATTY, Michael .... 415-338-1124.. 34 A
mbeatty@sfsu.edu
BEATTY, Tracy .... 269-965-3931 225 D
beattyt@kellogg.edu
BEATY, Andrew .... 309-846-3544 144 F
andrew.beaty@moody.edu
BEATY, Kimberly, L ...... 716-888-2301 291 M
beatyk@canisius.edu
BEATY, Lori .... 254-968-9877 445 F
lbeaty@tarleton.edu
BEAUCHAMP, Cheryl, L 518-629-8177 302 A
c.beauchamp@hvcc.edu
BEAUCHAMP, Lance ..... 904-588-2104 102 G
lbeauch@ju.edu
BEAUCHAMP, Robbin ... 617-989-4112 219 D
beauchampr1@wit.edu
BEAUCHAMP, Stepheny 303-273-3000.. 79 A
sbeauchamp@mines.edu
BEAUCHAMP-RODRIGUEZ,
Elias .... 787-993-8878 510 E
elias.beauchamp@upr.edu
BEAUCHINE, Tara .... 414-930-3534 493 E
beauchit@mtmary.edu
BEAUCOURT, Kim .... 405-945-8650 368 C
kim.beaucourt@okstate.edu
BEAUDIN, Giselda .... 407-646-2466 106 L
gbeaudin@rollins.edu
BEAUDIN, Paul, M .... 631-451-4089 320 G
beaudip@sunysuffolk.edu
BEAUDOIN, Kraig .... 212-431-2143 308 I
kraig.beaudoin@nyls.edu
BEAUDRY, George .... 334-670-3215.... 7 C
gbeaudry@troy.edu
BEAUGENE, Rosa .... 281-649-3801 436 D
rbeaugene@hbu.edu
BEAUJON, Francis .... 530-251-8879.. 47 I
fbeaujon@lassencollege.edu
BEAULIEU, Elizabeth ..... 860-701-5028.. 88 C
beaulieu_e@mitchell.edu
BEAULIEU, Ellen .... 207-602-2334 197 A
ebeaulieu@une.edu
BEAULIEU, Gary, R .... 317-940-9624 153 H
gbeaulie@butler.edu
BEAULIEU, Sharen .... 864-294-2217 408 I
sharen.beaulieu@furman.edu
BEAUMAN, Jesse .... 704-687-1242 342 C
jbeauman@uncc.edu
BEAUMONT, Ben .... 501-686-2531.. 21 G
bbeaumont@uasys.edu
BEAUMONT, David .... 313-496-2795 232 B
dbeaumont@wcccd.edu
BEAUMONT,
Samuel (Lee) .... 210-690-9000 436 A
sbeaumont@hallmarkuniversity.edu
BEAUPRE, David, R ...... 610-660-1320 397 A
dbeaupre@sju.edu
BEAUPRE, Walt .... 410-287-1469 198 A
wbeaupre@cecil.edu
BEAUPREWHITE, Renee 802-468-1339 462 H
renee.beauprewhite@castleton.edu
BEAUREGARD, Amy ...... 419-866-0261 361 A
abeauregard@stautzenberger.com
BEAUREGARD, Jenna .... 518-564-4604 318 C
case8736@plattsburgh.edu
BEAUREGARD, Jill .... 320-589-6036 243 C
beaureja@morris.umn.edu
BEAUREGARD, Nicole ... 401-232-6161 403 B
nbeaureg@bryant.edu
BEAUREGARD, Stephen 508-565-1375 218 F
sbeauregard@stonehill.edu
BEAUVAIS, Laura .... 401-874-1000 404 E
BEAVER, Jeff, S .... 864-388-8208 409 B
jbeaver@lander.edu
BEAVER, Nancy .... 770-533-7001 121 L
nbeaver@laniertech.edu
BEAVER, Noele, M .... 641-422-4004 168 E
noele.beaver@niacc.edu
BEAVER, Robert .... 651-779-5744 237 D
robert.beaver@century.edu
BEAVER, Stephanie .... 870-508-6180.. 18 B
sbeaver@asumh.edu
BEAVERS, Gayonne .... 940-397-3298 439 F
gayonne.beavers@msutexas.edu
BEAVERS, Jeff .... 517-884-1301 227 C
jbeavers@msu.edu
BEAVERS, Judy .... 517-321-0242 224 E
jbeavers@glcc.edu
BEAVERS, Kristin .... 714-289-2020.. 36 D
kbeavers@chapman.edu
BEAVERS, Philip, E .... 517-321-0242 224 E
pbeavers@glcc.edu
BEAZER, Ken .... 435-652-7526 459 G
ken.beazer@utahtech.edu
BEAZLEY, Michael .... 906-632-6841 226 C
mbeazley@lssu.edu

BEBBER, Glenda, H ...... 704-233-8742 344 E
gbebber@wingate.edu
BEBER, Melissa .... 531-622-2236 266 G
mlbeber@mccneb.edu
BEBOUT, Angel .... 615-966-1788 420 B
angel.bebout@lipscomb.edu
BECCA, Meirielly .... 404-627-2681 116 B
meirielly.becca@beulah.edu
BECENTI, Tonilee .... 505-387-7411 286 B
tbecenti@navajotech.edu
BECERRA, Cynthia .... 209-478-0800.. 45 L
cbecerra@humphreys.edu
BECERRA, Gilberto .... 210-486-3930 428 B
gbecerra8@alamo.edu
BECERRA, Irma .... 703-284-1598 468 A
ibecerra@marymount.edu
BECERRA, Kimberly .... 361-825-2639 446 E
kimberly.becerra@tamucc.edu
BECHARD, Deanna .... 603-665-2595 273 E
d.bechard@snhu.edu
BECHARD, Matthew ...... 785-243-1435 172 J
mbechard@cloud.edu
BECHEN, Gene, F .... 563-333-6380 169 D
becheneugenef@sau.edu
BECHEN, Linda .... 319-363-1323 168 D
lbechen@mtmercy.edu
BECHER, Amy .... 412-365-1139 380 F
abecher@chatham.edu
BECHER, Dave .... 305-284-4020 112 K
davebecher@miami.edu
BECHER, Gregory, J ...... 805-525-4417.. 67 J
gbecher@thomasaquinas.edu
BECHERER, Jeffery .... 212-431-2345 308 I
jeff.becherer@nyls.edu
BECHTEL, Brian .... 816-604-1059 254 E
brian.bechtel@mcckc.edu
BECK, Amanda .... 601-925-3253 246 D
abeck@mc.edu
BECK, Bruce .... 617-731-3500 210 D
BECK, Carina .... 406-994-7627 263 G
cbeck@montana.edu
BECK, Cherie .... 517-371-5140 232 K
beckc@cooley.edu
BECK, Chris .... 661-362-2766.. 51 E
cbeck@masters.edu
BECK, Connie .... 901-321-3529 417 G
cbeck1@cbu.edu
BECK, Donald .... 336-249-8186 333 G
donald_beck@davidsondavie.edu
BECK, Erika, D .... 818-677-2121.. 32 E
BECK, Gretchen .... 814-332-2754 378 A
gbeck@allegheny.edu
BECK, Jacob .... 214-887-5067 434 G
jbeck@dts.edu
BECK, Jeffery .... 765-361-6346 162 G
beckj@wabash.edu
BECK, Jen .... 512-245-2940 449 G
jb32@txstate.edu
BECK, Jennifer, M .... 512-448-8516 441 N
jbeck@stedwards.edu
BECK, Jordan, P .... 262-243-5700 491 E
jordan.beck@cuw.edu
BECK, Judy .... 803-641-3269 412 B
judyb@usca.edu
BECK, Leesa .... 805-893-4165.. 70 E
leesa.beck@sa.ucsb.edu
BECK, Martin .... 949-480-4024.. 64 E
mbeck@soka.edu
BECK, Maryann, M .... 334-833-4431.... 5 H
registrar@hawks.huntingdon.edu
BECK, Michael, J .... 310-825-2411.. 69 D
michaelbeck@ucla.edu
BECK, Mike .... 479-394-7622.. 23 F
mbeck@uarichmountain.edu
BECK, Raphe .... 541-346-6317 376 G
apheb@uoregon.edu
BECK, Richard .... 918-343-7797 369 A
rbeck@rsu.edu
BECK, Robert, J .... 414-229-3713 495 B
rjbeck@uwm.edu
BECK, Ronda .... 517-371-5140 232 K
beckr@cooley.edu
BECK, Stacie .... 480-423-6520.. 14 B
stacie.beck@scottsdalecc.edu
BECK, Tamara .... 336-838-6496 338 H
tlbeck371@wilkescc.edu
BECK, Victor .... 870-508-6133.. 18 B
vbeck@asumh.edu
BECK, Wanda .... 336-903-3141 338 H
whbeck366@wilkescc.edu
BECK, Zach .... 937-512-4603 360 F
zachary.beck@sinclair.edu

BECKA, Nathan .... 510-594-3787.. 28 D
n.becka@cca.edu
BECKA, Roberta .... 310-973-3134.. 41 J
rbecka@elcamino.edu
BECKEL, Constance .... 724-838-4219 397 F
beckel@setonhill.edu
BECKEMEYER, Wendy ... 319-895-4173 164 E
wbeckemeyer@cornellcollege.edu
BECKENDORF, Kristina . 979-830-4122 430 I
kbeckendorf@blinn.edu
BECKENSTEIN MBUVI,
Amanda .... 215-576-0800 396 B
BECKER, Alex .... 870-460-1022.. 22 E
beckera@uamont.edu
BECKER, Alexis .... 605-995-2617 414 A
alexis.becker@dwu.edu
BECKER, Amy .... 612-874-3799 236 E
amy_naughton@mcad.edu
BECKER, Ashley .... 618-235-2700 150 B
ashley.becker@swic.edu
BECKER, Betsie .... 617-266-1400 206 D
ile@berklee.edu
BECKER, Brian .... 619-849-2679.. 57 J
bbecker@pointloma.edu
BECKER, Brian .... 512-492-3017 429 B
bbecker@aoma.edu
BECKER, Carol .... 212-854-9847 296 H
cbecker@columbia.edu
BECKER, Christopher .... 626-300-5444.. 57 F
cbecker@plattcollege.edu
BECKER, Dennis, M ...... 303-871-3897.. 84 C
dbecker@du.edu
BECKER, Jim .... 812-855-4884 156 B
jambecke@iu.edu
BECKER, John .... 307-268-2672 499 T
j.becker@caspercollege.edu
BECKER, Jonathan .... 845-758-7378 290 G
jbecker@bard.edu
BECKER, Jonathan .... 903-586-2518 437 D
jbecker@jacksonville-college.edu
BECKER, Joseph .... 516-773-5000 502 G
beckerj@usmma.edu
BECKER, Kate .... 505-272-2111 288 C
katebecker@salud.unm.edu
BECKER, Kelly .... 847-635-1973 146 E
kbecker@oakton.edu
BECKER, Keri .... 616-331-8800 224 D
beckeker@gvsu.edu
BECKER, Laura .... 805-922-6966.. 24 L
laura.becker@hancockcollege.edu
BECKER, Laurel .... 970-943-7004.. 85 B
lbecker@western.edu
BECKER, Maureen .... 718-262-2000 295 D
mbecker@york.cuny.edu
BECKER, Maureen .... 718-262-5310 295 D
mbecker@york.cuny.edu
BECKER, Sara, M .... 856-225-6409 281 A
sara.becker@rutgers.edu
BECKER, Sheila, R .... 844-642-2338 168 F
beckers@nicc.edu
BECKER, Susie .... 206-281-2553 482 K
sbecker@spu.edu
BECKER, Tawney .... 719-587-8305.. 77 F
tbecker@adams.edu
BECKER, Theresa .... 760-921-5444.. 56 A
theresa.becker@paloverde.edu
BECKER-LUTZ, Jill .... 303-797-5882.. 77 H
jill.becker-lutz@arapahoe.edu
BECKETT, Barry .... 304-696-2207 488 N
beckett@marshall.edu
BECKETT, Karen, J .... 305-284-5749 112 K
kbeckett@miami.edu
BECKFORD, Dillon .... 803-535-5301 406 E
dbeckford@claflin.edu
BECKFORD, Roy .... 802-656-3131 462 D
fitzroy.beckford@uvm.edu
BECKHAM, Vanessa .... 863-680-6285 100 F
vbeckham@flsouthern.edu
BECKHORN, Nisha .... 916-484-8376.. 50 J
beckhon@arc.losrios.edu
BECKHORN, Roy .... 916-568-3190.. 50 I
beckhor@losrios.edu
BECKLER, Larry .... 843-525-8282 411 G
lbeckler@tcl.edu
BECKLES-BRIGHT,
Heather .... 713-500-3871 455 D
heather.m.beckles@uth.tmc.edu
BECKLEY, Clark .... 913-234-0609 172 I
clark.beckley@cleveland.edu
BECKLEY, Jodie .... 734-462-4400 230 B
jbeckley@schoolcraft.edu
BECKMAN, Amy .... 620-242-0400 175 G
beckmana@mcpherson.edu

BECKMAN, John, H .... 212-998-6848 309 D
john.beckman@nyu.edu
BECKMAN, Mitchell ...... 414-955-4871 492 F
mrbeckman@mcw.edu
BECKMAN, Seth .... 765-285-5495 153 E
svbeckman@bsu.edu
BECKNELL, James .... 606-546-1233 185 B
james.becknell@unionky.edu
BECKNER, Andrew .... 864-231-2000 405 F
abeckner@andersonuniversity.edu
BECKNER, Michael .... 985-549-2318 192 E
michael.beckner@selu.edu
BECKNER, Scott .... 319-335-5026 163 F
scott-beckner@uiowa.edu
BECKRICH, Chris .... 817-531-4251 450 F
cabeckrich@txwes.edu
BECKS, Crystal .... 661-654-3012.. 30 C
cbecks@csub.edu
BECKSTROM, Brian .... 219-464-6514 162 C
brian.beckstrom@valpo.edu
BECKSTROM, Ron .... 218-755-2743 237 B
ronald.beckstrom@bemidjistate.edu
BECKWITH, Jill .... 508-531-2757 212 B
jbeckwith@bridgew.edu
BECKWITH, Melissa ...... 317-940-9900 153 H
mbeckwit@butler.edu
BECKWITH, Rachel .... 413-559-5765 210 A
rbeckwith@hampshire.edu
BECKWITH-MCMANUS,
Ellie, F .... 419-772-2073 358 D
e-mcmanus.1@onu.edu
BECTON, Bret .... 601-266-4659 248 H
bret.becton@usm.edu
BEDA, Cheri .... 308-398-7437 265 C
cheribeda@cccneb.edu
BEDARD, Brooke .... 413-265-2314 208 B
bedardb@elms.edu
BEDDARD, Wesley .... 252-789-0222 335 F
wb07479@martincc.edu
BEDELL, Duane .... 906-248-3354 221 I
BEDELL, Honey .... 563-336-3302 165 G
hbedell@eicc.edu
BEDELL, Michael, D ...... 773-442-6150 145 G
m-bedell@neiu.edu
BEDELL, Todd .... 603-271-6484 272 C
tbedell@ccsnh.edu
BEDETTE, Kathryn .... 470-578-6000 121 J
BEDFORD, Allen .... 218-755-2015 237 B
allen.bedford@bemidjistate.edu
BEDFORD, April .... 718-951-5214 293 A
abedford@brooklyn.cuny.edu
BEDFORD, Carter .... 817-515-1193 445 A
carter.bedford@tccd.edu
BEDFORD, Dan .... 801-626-8091 460 B
dbedford@weber.edu
BEDFORD, David .... 864-578-8770 410 G
dbedford@sherman.edu
BEDFORD, Grant .... 209-946-2537.. 71 E
gbedford@pacific.edu
BEDFORD, Michelle .... 770-412-4005 125 F
michelle.bedford@sctech.edu
BEDFORD, Norm .... 702-774-8000 270 J
norm.bedford@unlv.edu
BEDFORD, Norman, F .. 804-828-3618 472 D
bedfordn@vcu.edu
BEDI, Param, S .... 570-577-1557 379 A
param.bedi@bucknell.edu
BEDIENT, Sonya .... 971-722-7686 375 C
sonya.bedient@pcc.edu
BEDILLION, Char .... 336-316-2410 329 C
cbedillion@guilford.edu
BEDINGFIELD, Eric .... 864-250-8700 408 J
eric.bedingfield@gvltec.edu
BEDNARZ, Bridgette ..... 254-968-9271 445 F
bednarz@tarleton.edu
BEDNARZ, Jeffrey .... 413-205-3208 205 C
jeffrey.bednarz@aic.edu
BEDNEY, Donald, A ...... 269-471-3122 220 H
dbedney@andrews.edu
BEDNEY, Elynda, A ...... 269-471-6040 220 H
bedney@andrews.edu
BEDOLLA, Juan .... 559-638-0300.. 67 C
juan.bedolla@reedleycollege.edu
BEDOYA, Eduardo .... 231-777-0332 228 C
eduardo.bedoya@muskegoncc.edu
BEDRYK, Michael .... 516-726-5644 502 G
bedrykm@usmma.edu
BEDTKE, James .... 507-457-1458 242 H
jbedtke@smumn.edu
BEDWELL, Deborah, A .. 812-888-7777 162 E
dbedwell@vinu.edu
BEEBE, Barbara, R .... 325-574-6501 457 G
bbeebe@wtc.edu

BEEBE, Craig .... 970-943-2314.. 85 B
cbeebe@western.edu
BEEBE, Gayle, D .... 805-565-6024.. 75 I
president@westmont.edu
BEEBE, Jennifer .... 716-338-1404 302 G
jenniferbeebe@mail.sunyjcc.edu
BEEBE, Norman .... 413-775-1333 214 C
beebe@gcc.mass.edu
BEEBE STEVENS,
Heather .... 509-434-5123 478 C
h.beebe-stevens@ccs.spokane.edu
BEEBE-STEVENS,
Heather .... 509-434-5125 478 E
heather.beebe-stevens@ccs.spokane.
edu
BEEBE-STEVENS,
Heather .... 509-434-5123 478 D
heather.beebe-stevens@ccs.spokane.
edu
BEEBY, James .... 603-358-2112 274 A
james.beeby@keene.edu
BEECH, Amanda .... 661-255-1050.. 28 I
abeech@calarts.edu
BEECHER, Brian .... 616-234-3869 224 C
brianbeecher@grcc.edu
BEECHER, Shan, L .... 515-574-1985 166 G
beecher@iowacentral.edu
BEEHLER, Jeff .... 509-865-0446 480 B
beehler_j@heritage.edu
BEEK, Ashtyn .... 641-844-5715 167 E
ashtyn.beek@iavalley.edu
BEEKE, Joel, R .... 616-432-3403 229 H
joel.beeke@prts.edu
BEEKE, Jonathon .... 616-432-3408 229 H
jonathon.beeke@prts.edu
BEEKEY, Mark .... 203-371-7783.. 88 H
beekeym@sacredheart.edu
BEELEN, Joan .... 616-957-6027 221 K
jrb44@calvinseminary.edu
BEELER, Jeremy .... 908-835-2301 283 H
jbeeler@warren.edu
BEELER, Sydney .... 724-925-4050 401 H
beelers@westmoreland.edu
BEEMAN, Greg .... 646-378-6100 289 F
greg.beeman@nyack.edu
BEEMAN, Meredith .... 252-249-1851 336 C
mbeeman@pamlicocc.edu
BEEMER, Matthew .... 904-596-2473 112 E
mbeemer@tbc.edu
BEEN, Nicole .... 918-781-7321 365 B
beenn@bacone.edu
BEERMANN, Tawnya ..... 712-274-6400 170 H
tawnya.beermann@witcc.edu
BEERS, Amy .... 716-673-4925 316 A
amy.beers@fredonia.edu
BEERS, Peter .... 717-560-8200 387 D
pbeers@lbc.edu
BEERS, Stephen, T .... 479-524-7252.. 20 C
sbeers@jbu.edu
BEESLEY, Wendy .... 845-688-1980 322 K
beesleyw@sunyulster.edu
BEESON, Duane, L .... 712-707-7116 169 A
beeson@nwciowa.edu
BEEZLEY, Erin .... 970-247-7429.. 80 H
ebeezley@fortlewis.edu
BEGANY, James .... 502-852-5555 185 E
jim.begany@louisville.edu
BEGAY, Janice .... 785-749-8419 174 A
janice.begay@bie.edu
BEGAY, Karen, F .... 520-621-0964.. 16 H
kfbegay@arizona.edu
BEGAY, Melissa .... 575-835-5120 286 D
melissa.begay@nmt.edu
BEGAYE, Nolan, S .... 928-724-6857.. 12 F
nsbegaye@dinecollege.edu
BEGG, Melissa .... 212-851-2289 296 H
mdb3@columbia.edu
BEGGS, Beth .... 828-898-2417 330 A
beggsb@lmc.edu
BEGGS, Gail .... 251-405-7021.... 1 E
gbeggs@bishop.edu
BEGGS, Gail .... 251-580-2154.... 1 I
gail.beggs@coastalalabama.edu
BEGIN, Gene, P .... 508-286-3223 219 F
begin_gene@wheatoncollege.edu
BEGIN, Russell .... 207-453-5123 195 B
rbegin@kvcc.me.edu
BEGLAU, Gregg .... 815-802-8304 141 B
gbeglau@kcc.edu
BEGLEY, John, B .... 270-384-8505 183 D
begleyj@lindsey.edu
BEGLEY, Kimberly .... 610-606-4666 380 C
kimberly.begley@cedarcrest.edu

BELLING, Karen ... 630-752-5021 152 K
karen.belling@wheaton.edu
BELLING, Shawn ... 608-243-4180 497 I
sbelling@madisoncollege.edu
BELLINGER, Andrew ... 315-792-7141 320 F
abellinger@sunypoly.edu
BELLINGER, Patricia ... 617-495-6495 210 B
patricia_bellinger@harvard.edu
BELLINGS, Andy ... 563-588-6420 164 C
andy.bellings@clarke.edu
BELLINI, Michel ... 217-265-5297 151 F
bellini@illinois.edu
BELLINO, Maria ... 480-517-8220.. 14 A
maria.bellino@riosalado.edu
BELLIVEAU, Brian ... 303-753-6046.. 83 C
bbelliveau@rmcad.edu
BELLMORE, Aimee ... 912-525-5000 124 G
abellmor@scad.edu
BELLO, Chippi ... 206-546-4101 483 C
cbello@shoreline.edu
BELLO, Deborah, A ... 240-895-4289 201 F
dabello@smcm.edu
BELLO, Diane ... 631-632-6179 316 D
diane.bello@stonybrook.edu
BELLO-DECASTRO,
Leigh ... 973-877-3483 276 G
bellodecastro@essex.edu
BELLOT, Dario ... 610-526-6614 385 F
dbellot@harcum.edu
BELLOW, Kathleen, D ... 504-520-7691 193 C
ibcs@xula.edu
BELLOWS, Alan ... 801-649-5230 458 I
technicalsupport@midwifery.edu
BELLOWS, Charlene ... 508-793-2514 208 A
cbellows@holycross.edu
BELLOWS, Laurie ... 402-472-3755 269 A
lbellows1@unl.edu
BELLUCCI, Anthony, D .. 973-378-2655 282 K
anthony.bellucci@shu.edu
BELLUCCI, Keith ... 617-732-2145 216 B
keith.bellucci@mcphs.edu
BELLUM, Jon ... 704-403-3077 327 B
jon.bellum@cabarruscollege.edu
BELLUM, Kim ... 605-886-6777 414 F
kimberly.bellum@mountmarty.edu
BELMAN, David ... 925-473-7423.. 40 I
dbelman@losmedanos.edu
BELMAR, Ricardo ... 305-607-6123 104 M
belmar@nova.edu
BELMONT, Amanda ... 701-349-5416 346 G
amandabelmont@trinitybiblecollege.edu
BELMONT, Heather ... 772-462-7215 102 E
hbelmont@irsc.edu
BELMONTE, Laura ... 540-231-6779 475 D
belmonte@vt.edu
BELOBRAJDIC, Scott ... 618-650-2298 149 H
sbelobr@siue.edu
BELOTE, Eve ... 757-789-1767 472 I
ebelote@es.vccs.edu
BELOTE, Faith, D ... 757-594-7618 465 A
faith.belote@cnu.edu
BELOW, Debbie ... 573-986-6888 258 J
dbelow@semo.edu
BELSER, Andrew ... 402-472-9339 269 A
abelser2@unl.edu
BELSER, Nakia ... 205-929-1569.... 6 B
BELSKY, Marianne ... 202-651-5031.. 92 B
marianne.belsky@gallaudet.edu
BELT, Jennifer ... 479-788-7007.. 22 A
jennifer.belt@uafs.edu
BELTER, Joe ... 541-888-7800 376 B
joseph.belter@socc.edu
BELTON, Ada, A ... 803-705-4327 405 G
ada.belton@benedict.edu
BELTON, Allan ... 253-535-7101 481 C
allan.belton@plu.edu
BELTON, Ray ... 225-771-4680 190 K
ray_belton@sus.edu
BELTON, Ray, L ... 225-771-4680 190 J
ray_belton@sus.edu
BELTON, Tammie ... 216-791-5000 350 F
tamatha.belton@cim.edu
BELTRAN, Adrian ... 559-730-3885.. 39 C
adrianb@cos.edu
BELTRAN, Dulce ... 305-348-7347 109 H
dulce.beltran@fiu.edu
BELTRAN, Jacque ... 870-566-7330 152 F
jbeltran@usml.edu
BELTRAN, Jake ... 847-970-4961 152 F
jbeltran@usml.edu
BELTRAN, Philip ... 408-554-4161.. 63 A
pjbeltran@scu.edu
BELTRAN, Renz ... 808-954-4934 128 D
rbeltran@hmi.edu
BELUE, Jake ... 804-828-6610 472 D
jabelue@vcu.edu
BELVILL, Rita ... 425-388-9202 479 B
rbelvill@everettcc.edu
BELVINS, Walter ... 510-723-6648.. 35 Q
wbelvins@clpccd.org
BELVIS LOPEZ, Rosa ... 787-725-6500 504 F
rbelvis@albizu.edu
BELZER, Charmaine, F .. 671-735-5544 503 C
financialaid@guamcc.edu
BEM, Greg ... 425-739-8100 480 D
greg.bem@lwtech.edu
BEMBRY, Deborah ... 229-500-2141 114 F
deborah.bembry@asurams.edu
BEMBRY, John ... 850-644-9452 110 B
jbembry@fsu.edu
BEMIS, Scot, R ... 314-935-1112 261 B
bemis@wustl.edu
BENABESS, Najiba ... 717-361-3590 383 B
benabessn@etown.edu
BENANDER, Mark ... 413-565-1000 205 I
mbenander@baypath.edu
BENAVIDES, Dominique 510-748-5264.. 57 A
dbenavides@peralta.edu
BENAVIDES, Elma, F ... 512-863-1441 444 F
benavide@southwestern.edu
BENAVIDES, Letty ... 956-665-2255 455 A
letty.benavides@utrgv.edu
BENAVIDES-DOMINGUEZ,
Patricia ... 361-698-2250 434 H
studentaffairs@delmar.edu
BENBOW, Camilla, P ... 615-322-8407 427 B
camilla.benbow@vanderbilt.edu
BENBROOK, Tabitha ... 918-335-6854 368 E
tbenbrook@okwu.edu
BENCOMO, Anadeli ... 915-747-7018 454 E
abencomo5@utep.edu
BENDABOUT, Cynthia ... 918-444-3413 366 G
bendabou@nsuok.edu
BENDAPUDI, Neeli ... 814-865-4700 391 F
BENDARSH, Joe ... 646-592-4615 325 R
joe.bednarsh@yu.edu
BENDELE, Jennifer ... 419-227-3141 362 F
jennifer@unoh.edu
BENDER, Christina ... 267-341-3017 385 I
cbender@holyfamily.edu
BENDER, Jennie, M ... 606-474-3226 180 G
jbender@kcu.edu
BENDER, Jim ... 651-635-2378 233 J
j-bender@bethel.edu
BENDER, Karla ... 713-718-8247 436 E
karla.bender@hccs.edu
BENDER, Kim ... 307-778-4337 500 D
kbender@lccc.wy.edu
BENDER, Linda ... 307-855-2102 499 U
lbender@cwc.edu
BENDER, Loren, J ... 407-582-3408 113 C
lbender2@valenciacollege.edu
BENDER, Marian ... 814-472-3931 396 I
mbender@francis.edu
BENDER, Rick ... 432-685-4529 439 E
rbender@midland.edu
BENDER, Starr, S ... 407-303-5765.. 95 A
starr.bender@ahu.edu
BENDER, IV,
Thomas, B ... 504-866-7426 190 E
library@nds.edu
BENDER, Virginia ... 201-761-6024 282 H
vbender@saintpeters.edu
BENDER, Yaakov ... 718-868-2300 290 J
BENDER SHETLER, Jan . 574-535-7108 155 B
jans@goshen.edu
BENDERMAN, Wendy ... 361-825-2621 446 E
wendy.benderman@tamucc.edu
BENDERS, Alison ... 408-554-4064.. 63 A
ambenders@scu.edu
BENDEZU PALOMINO,
Cyndi ... 661-362-3278.. 38 H
cyndi.palomino@canyons.edu
BENDICK, Emily ... 405-208-5000 367 E
ebendick@okcu.edu
BENDL, Colleen ... 740-593-1630 358 L
bendl@ohio.edu
BENEDETTI, Brian ... 253-864-3235 481 H
bbenedetti@pierce.ctc.edu
BENEDICT, Barbara ... 719-549-3039.. 82 I
barbara.benedict@pueblocc.edu
BENEDICT, David ... 860-486-2725.. 89 B
david.benedict@uconn.edu
BENEDICT, JR.,
Gregory ... 908-709-7520 283 E
gregory.benedict@ucc.edu
BENEDICT, Jody, C ... 585-385-8322 313 A
jbenedict@sjfc.edu
BENEDICT, Sherri, J ... 315-655-7245 292 B
sjbenedict@cazenovia.edu
BENEDICT-JONES,
Michelle ... 607-255-5056 297 D
mbenedict-jones@cornell.edu
BENEDIK, Marijean ... 330-569-5132 353 F
benedikm@hiram.edu
BENEFIEL, Lori ... 541-383-7572 371 I
lbenefiel@cocc.edu
BENEFIEL, Patricia ... 619-574-6909.. 55 D
pbenefiel@pacificcollege.edu
BENEFIEL, Ron ... 619-849-2613.. 57 J
ronbenefiel@pointloma.edu
BENEKE, Thomas, J ... 515-574-1050 166 G
beneke@iowacentral.edu
BENET, Micol, A ... 415-485-9502.. 39 B
mabenet@marin.edu
BENET, Suzeanne ... 616-331-2400 224 D
benets@gvsu.edu
BENEVENTO, Erin ... 410-386-4821 200 D
ebenevento@mcdaniel.edu
BENFANTI, William, J ... 716-878-5557 317 C
benfanwj@buffalostate.edu
BENFER, Pamela, A ... 570-577-1561 379 A
pam.benfer@bucknell.edu
BENFORD, Jeffrey ... 925-473-7425.. 40 I
jbenford@losmedanos.edu
BENGE, Robert ... 423-236-2855 422 H
rcbenge@southern.edu
BENGEL, Kristi ... 513-244-4624 356 F
kristi.bengel@msj.edu
BENGFORT, Joseph ... 415-476-1000.. 70 D
joe.bengfort@ucsf.edu
BENHAM, Maenette ... 808-689-2770 129 C
mbenham@hawaii.edu
BENHAM, Rebekah ... 503-375-7093 372 G
rbenham@corban.edu
BENHAM-DEAL, Tami ... 307-766-4286 500 H
benham@uwyo.edu
BENINGHOVE, Linda ... 201-216-5412 282 L
linda.beninghove@stevens.edu
BENISH, Amy, L ... 262-554-2010 493 A
albenish@aol.com
BENITEZ, Hubert, M ... 413-205-3202 205 C
BENITEZ, Leyda, L ... 610-519-3976 401 B
leyda.benitez@villanova.edu
BENITEZ, JR., Michael . 303-615-2063.. 81 L
mbenite4@msudenver.edu
BENITEZ, Olga, A ... 787-723-4481 504 J
olga.benitez@ceaprc.edu
BENITIZ, Yvette ... 575-527-7552 287 A
ybenitiz@nmsu.edu
BENJAMIN, Brent ... 304-327-4014 488 J
bbenjamin@bluefieldstate.edu
BENJAMIN, Eric ... 240-567-5267 200 E
BENJAMIN, Eric, M ... 240-567-5048 200 E
eric.benjamin@montgomerycollege.edu
BENJAMIN, Jeffrey ... 706-542-7369 126 F
jeffrey.benjamin@uga.edu
BENJAMIN, Jodi ... 402-941-6102 267 B
benjamin@midlandu.edu
BENJAMIN, Kathi ... 508-289-2705 220 B
kbenjamin@whoi.edu
BENJAMIN, Kyle ... 865-471-3447 417 E
kbenjamin@cn.edu
BENJAMIN, Robert ... 617-745-3595 208 F
robert.j.benjamin@enc.edu
BENJAMIN, Valerie, C .. 585-385-7247 313 A
vbenjamin@sjfc.edu
BENJAMIN-ALVARADO,
Jonathan ... 817-257-5566 447 H
j.ba@tcu.edu
BENKE, Jack ... 573-642-3361 261 F
BENKE, Jack ... 573-592-6231 261 F
jack.benke@westminster-mo.edu
BENKERT, Stuart ... 719-549-2090.. 79 G
stuart.benkert@csupueblo.edu
BENKESER, Kristina ... 724-738-2052 394 E
kristina.benkeser@sru.edu
BENKO, Hope ... 512-472-4133 442 H
hope.benko@ssw.edu
BENKO, Jared ... 912-478-5047 120 A
jbenko@georgiasouthern.edu
BENKO, Richard, A ... 724-287-8711 379 C
richard.benko@bc3.edu
BENLOLO, Henri ... 352-854-2322.. 97 L
benloloh@cf.edu
BENMAMOUN, Abbas ... 919-684-4997 328 D
elabbas.benmamoun@duke.edu
BENN MARSHALL,
Karen ... 256-726-8044.... 6 C
kmarshall@oakwood.edu
BENNANI, Wissem ... 650-306-3100.. 62 I
BENNEIAN, Teresa ... 717-290-8748 387 F
tbenneian@lancasterseminary.edu
BENNER, Brent, W ... 813-257-3002 113 B
bbenner@ut.edu
BENNER, Patrick ... 707-965-6242.. 55 H
pbenner@puc.edu
BENNER, Patrick, B ... 804-289-8930 471 E
pbenner@richmond.edu
BENNER, Paul ... 610-282-1100 382 A
paul.benner@desales.edu
BENNER, Shawn ... 208-426-1839 130 F
sbenner@boisestate.edu
BENNER, Tracy ... 614-823-1580 359 G
tbenner@otterbein.edu
BENNER-IIAMES, Annie 937-481-2200 363 H
annie.benner-iiames@wilmington.edu
BENNETT, Amanda ... 423-697-4400 423 B
BENNETT, Amanda ... 304-336-8844 489 B
amanda.bennett@westliberty.edu
BENNETT, Amy ... 317-955-6768 159 A
abennett@marian.edu
BENNETT, Angela ... 865-251-1800 422 G
abennett@south.edu
BENNETT, Anthony, T ... 910-672-1314 341 B
abennett@uncfsu.edu
BENNETT, Breely ... 816-802-3420 253 H
bbennett@kcai.edu
BENNETT, Brian ... 615-248-7782 425 D
bmbennett2@trevecca.edu
BENNETT, Cameron, D . 253-535-7150 481 C
bennetcd@plu.edu
BENNETT, Candida ... 719-255-3868.. 84 A
candida.bennett@uccs.edu
BENNETT, Carol ... 330-941-3001 364 G
clbennett04@ysu.edu
BENNETT, Carolyn ... 516-876-3203 318 A
bennettc@oldwestbury.edu
BENNETT, Chandalin ... 509-359-6362 478 H
cmbennett@ewu.edu
BENNETT, Curtis ... 562-985-5559.. 32 A
curtis.bennett@csulb.edu
BENNETT, Daniel ... 828-669-8012 331 H
dbennett@montreat.edu
BENNETT, David, A ... 606-474-3256 180 G
dbennett@kcu.edu
BENNETT, David, P ... 202-806-6100.. 92 E
david.bennett@howard.edu
BENNETT, Dorine ... 605-256-5137 415 G
dorine.bennett@dsu.edu
BENNETT, Douglas ... 714-432-5126.. 38 F
dbennett@occ.cccd.edu
BENNETT, Eddie ... 434-736-2055 474 D
eddie.bennett@southside.edu
BENNETT, Elaine ... 724-805-2602 397 C
elaine.bennett@stvincent.edu
BENNETT, Elbert ... 870-575-8504.. 22 F
bennette@uapb.edu
BENNETT, Elizabeth, C .. 949-824-7982.. 69 C
bennette@uci.edu
BENNETT, Elizabeth, P .. 717-396-7833 392 Q
ebennet@pcad.edu
BENNETT, Ephraim ... 757-823-8214 468 B
ejbennett@nsu.edu
BENNETT, Erika ... 314-505-7286 251 D
bennette@csl.edu
BENNETT, Gary ... 919-668-3420 328 D
gary.bennett@duke.edu
BENNETT, Gene ... 870-780-1201.. 17 F
gbennett@smail.anc.edu
BENNETT, George ... 509-527-2092 484 C
george.bennett@wallawalla.edu
BENNETT, Heather ... 309-796-5301 133 D
bennetth@bhc.edu
BENNETT, Holly, L ... 561-868-3279 105 C
bennetth@palmbeachstate.edu
BENNETT, Jabbar, R ... 517-353-3924 227 C
jrb1619@msu.edu
BENNETT, Janice, G ... 563-588-8000 165 K
jbennett@emmaus.edu
BENNETT, Jeffrey, L ... 570-321-4031 388 H
bennett@lycoming.edu
BENNETT, Jen ... 918-631-2276 371 C
jsb8472@utulsa.edu
BENNETT, Jim ... 913-288-7259 174 H
jbennett@kckcc.edu
BENNETT, JoAnn ... 937-327-6185 364 C
jbennett@wittenberg.edu
BENNETT, Kari ... 518-783-2368 314 K
kbennett@siena.edu

BERGER, Aron 845-426-3276 324 I ydm@thejnet.com
BERGER, Donna, S 845-575-3000 305 C donna.berger@marist.edu
BERGER, Doris 212-217-3400 299 C doris_berger@fitnyc.edu
BERGER, Jane 567-661-7459 359 H jane_berger2@owens.edu
BERGER, Jessica 760-750-4400 33 C jberger@csusm.edu
BERGER, John 303-273-3000 79 A jberger@mines.edu
BERGER, Joseph 617-287-5600 211 E
BERGER, Kellie 517-265-5161 220 D kberger@adrian.edu
BERGER, Kelly 315-470-6740 319 A kmberger@esf.edu
BERGER, Mark 404-364-8303 123 G mberger@oglethorpe.edu
BERGER, Martin 312-899-5100 149 B
BERGER, Michael 602-639-7500 12 L
BERGER, Scott 320-762-4475 236 G scottb@alextech.edu
BERGER, Sheri 310-900-1600 39 H sberger@compton.edu
BERGER, Travis 484-254-2107 378 C travis.berger@alvernia.edu
BERGER, Yaakov 845-393-4308 325 C admin@kessertorah.org
BERGER-SWEENEY, Joanne 860-297-2086 88 I president@trincoll.edu
BERGERON, Bette, S 315-267-2108 318 D bergerbs@potsdam.edu
BERGERON, Billie Jo 405-682-1611 367 D billiejo.bergeron@occc.edu
BERGERON, Ian 413-662-5592 212 F ian.bergeron@mcla.edu
BERGERON, Iva 561-868-3162 105 C bergeroi@palmbeachstate.edu
BERGERON, Iva 214-860-8735 434 B ibergeron@dcccd.edu
BERGERON, Katherine 860-439-2666 87 F katherine.bergeron@conncoll.edu
BERGERON, Mindy 510-841-9230 76 F financialaid@wi.edu
BERGERSON, Amy, A 513-529-6721 356 A bergera9@miamioh.edu
BERGESON, Patricia 312-369-7478 136 C pbergeson@colum.edu
BERGESON, Rachel 631-632-6740 316 D rachel.bergeson@stonybrook.edu
BERGESON, Rachel, D 218-299-4728 234 K bergeson@cord.edu
BERGETZ, Carl 312-942-6886 148 C carl_bergetz@rush.edu
BERGEVIN, Ken 509-865-0746 480 B bergevin_k@heritage.edu
BERGGREN, Kent, E 208-535-5373 130 I kent.berggren@cei.edu
BERGGREN, Stacey 208-467-8011 132 B slberggren@nnu.edu
BERGH, Anna 952-829-2408 233 H anna.bergh@bethanygu.edu
BERGH, David 315-655-7126 292 B dgbergh@cazenovia.edu
BERGHOFF, Peter 312-225-6288 152 G
BERGIN, Bonita, M 707-545-3647 27 A bonnie@berginu.edu
BERGLER, Michael 949-214-3187 40 E michael.bergler@cui.edu
BERGLUND, Lars 916-703-9120 69 A lberglund@ucdavis.edu
BERGMAN, Charles 505-984-6066 287 F charles.bergman@sjc.edu
BERGMAN, Helen 903-463-8698 435 H bergmanh@grayson.edu
BERGMAN, Joe 309-694-5367 138 I joe.bergman@icc.edu
BERGMAN, Matthew 217-228-5432 147 C bergmma@quincy.edu
BERGMAN, Rebecca, M 507-933-7538 235 E president@gustavus.edu
BERGMANN, Donald, J 570-941-7400 400 C donald.bergmann@scranton.edu
BERGMANN, Leah 785-738-9062 176 C lbergmann@ncktc.edu
BERGMANN, Michelle 541-440-4620 376 F michelle.bergmann@umpqua.edu
BERGMANN, Tom 847-947-5516 145 C tbergmann@nl.edu
BERGQUIST, Shari 802-656-3427 462 D shari.bergquist@uvm.edu
BERGREN, Rebecca, A 717-337-6866 384 C rbergren@gettysburg.edu
BERGRUD, Erik 816-584-6412 257 E erik.bergrud@park.edu
BERGS, Thomas 651-846-1322 240 E thomas.bergs@saintpaul.edu
BERGSMA, Brad 785-890-3641 176 E brad.bergsma@nwktc.edu
BERGSTROM, Amy 218-723-6067 234 J abergstrom@css.edu
BERGSTROM, Mary 217-228-5432 147 C m.bergstrom11@quincy.edu
BERGSTROM, Tracey 361-582-2565 456 H tracey.bergstrom@victoriacollege.edu
BERHIE, Girmay 601-979-6386 245 G girmay.berhie@jsums.edu
BERHORST, Todd 323-860-1199 53 D toddb@mi.edu
BERICH, Anthony 609-652-1776 283 A anthony.berich@stockton.edu
BERIGAN, Jennifer 513-936-1734 362 A jennifer.berigan@uc.edu
BERK, Anne-Marie 217-619-9884 144 D aberk@millikin.edu
BERK, Steven, L 806-743-3000 450 D steven.berk@ttuhsc.edu
BERKE, Deborah 203-436-8057 90 B deborah.berke@yale.edu
BERKELEY, Amy 401-254-3302 404 C aberkeley@rwu.edu
BERKEY, Jessica 864-294-2267 408 I jessica.berkey@furman.edu
BERKEY, Jonathan 704-894-2529 328 C joberkey@davidson.edu
BERKHEIMER, Eric, J 410-677-6553 204 A ejberkheimer@salisbury.edu
BERKHEIMER, Karen 410-334-2915 205 A kberkheimer@worwic.edu
BERKINSHAW, Stewart, M 405-325-1271 370 J sberkinshaw@ou.edu
BERKLAS, Jennifer, L 909-607-7976 63 E jberklas@scrippscollege.edu
BERKLE, Paul 941-752-5000 109 C
BERKLEY, Shelley 702-777-1776 68 B shelley.berkley@tun.touro.edu
BERKNER, Donna 817-202-6214 444 B dberkner@swau.edu
BERKNER, Paul, D 207-859-4460 194 B paul.berkner@colby.edu
BERKOWITZ, Bobbie 212-305-3582 296 H bb2509@columbia.edu
BERKSHIRE, Sarah 270-706-8836 181 C sarah.berkshire@kctcs.edu
BERKUN, Mike 718-409-4841 320 D
BERLEY, Susan, A 828-448-6125 338 G sberley@wpcc.edu
BERLIN, Beth 518-320-1100 315 C beth.berlin@suny.edu
BERLIN, Linda 231-995-1533 228 F lberlin@nmc.edu
BERLO, Joshua 303-871-3399 84 C josh.berlo@du.edu
BERMAN, Ari 212-960-5300 325 R president@yu.edu
BERMAN, Bruce 714-895-8315 38 E bberman@gwc.cccd.edu
BERMAN, Daniel 215-204-2044 398 D daniel.berman@temple.edu
BERMAN, Joel 954-262-2130 104 M jb@nsu.nova.edu
BERMAN, Larry, S 404-413-5570 120 C larryberman@gsu.edu
BERMAN, Lou Ann 903-566-7052 455 C lberman@uttyler.edu
BERMAN, Marc 619-961-4271 68 A mberman@tjsl.edu
BERMAN, Mark 518-782-6957 314 K mberman@siena.edu
BERMAN, Paula 617-277-3915 207 B bermanp@bgsp.edu
BERMEA, Gilbert, S 830-758-4111 443 I gbermea@swtjc.edu
BERMEJO, William 787-844-8181 511 E william.bermejo@upr.edu
BERMEL, John 507-222-4427 234 C jbermel@carleton.edu
BERMEL, Rhea 903-463-8628 435 H bermelr@grayson.edu
BERMUDEZ, Eliezer 453-879-4817 459 G eliezer.bermudez@utahtech.edu
BERMUDEZ, Gregory 787-257-0000 510 F
BERMUDEZ, Johanna 787-751-0160 505 C jbermudez@cmpr.pr.gov
BERNA, Laurie 603-578-8900 272 B
BERNABE, Arnaldo 718-518-6888 293 F abernabe@hostos.cuny.edu
BERNAL, Eduardo (Eddie) 626-571-8811 73 D eddieb@uwest.edu
BERNAL, Jesse, M 616-331-3296 224 D bernalje@gvsu.edu
BERNAL, Omar 708-237-5050 146 B obernal@nc.edu
BERNAL-OLSON, Patricia 937-229-4211 362 C pbernalolson1@udayton.edu
BERNARD, Barbara 781-239-2629 214 E bbernard@massbay.edu
BERNARD, Bryce 503-375-7034 372 G bbernard@corban.edu
BERNARD, Chris 405-695-5533 366 A cbernard@familyoffaith.edu
BERNARD, Gregory 203-392-6501 85 H bernardg2@southernct.edu
BERNARD, Julia 802-485-3162 461 H jbernar3@norwich.edu
BERNARD, Kacey 610-341-1459 383 A kbernard@eastern.edu
BERNARD, Ken 803-778-6668 406 A bernardkd@cctech.edu
BERNARD, Kyle 518-580-5820 315 A kbernar1@skidmore.edu
BERNARD, Marci 207-221-4419 197 A mbernard4@une.edu
BERNARD, Marcus 502-597-5758 183 A marcus.bernard@kysu.edu
BERNARD, Michelle 706-379-3111 128 A mmbernard@yhc.edu
BERNARD, Pamela 919-684-3955 328 D pam.bernard@duke.edu
BERNARD, Renee 814-472-2766 396 I rbernard@francis.edu
BERNARD-AMOS, Marion 484-365-7224 388 F mba@lincoln.edu
BERNARDINI, Paola 305-223-4561 106 N pbernardini@sjvcs.edu
BERNARDIS, Tim 406-638-3113 262 J tim@lbhc.edu
BERNARDO, Antonio 310-825-4321 69 D a.bernardo@anderson.ucla.edu
BERNARDO, Lisa, M 209-667-3094 33 D lbernardo@csustan.edu
BERNARDO-SOUSA, Marie 401-598-1754 403 E marie.bernardo-sousa@jwu.edu
BERNATOW, Andy 605-668-1523 414 F abernatow@mountmarty.edu
BERNATZ, Richard 563-387-2000 167 J bernatzr@luther.edu
BERNAUER, Edmund 808-521-2288 128 G dean@orientalmedicine.edu
BERNAUER, Jeanne 808-521-2288 128 G
BERNDT, Michael 651-450-3641 237 H michael.berndt@minnstate.edu
BERNDT, Michael, D 651-423-8000 237 E michael.berndt@minnstate.edu
BERNE, Jennifer, I 248-341-2051 228 H jiberne@oaklandcc.edu
BERNER, JR., Howard, E 314-275-3514 147 B howard.berner@principia.edu
BERNER, Jason 510-215-4131 40 G jberner@contracosta.edu
BERNER, Nancy, J 931-598-1172 422 F nberner@sewanee.edu
BERNHARD, Bo 702-895-3201 270 J
BERNHARD, Robert, J 574-631-3902 161 G bernhard.9@nd.edu
BERNHARD, William 217-333-6677 151 F bernhard@illinois.edu
BERNHARDSON, Bonnie 218-879-0828 237 F bonnie@fdltcc.edu
BERNHARDSON, Mark 218-879-0703 237 F mbernhar@fdltcc.edu
BERNHARDT, Jay, M 512-471-8100 454 C moody.dean@austin.utexas.edu
BERNHARDT, Starr 509-793-2065 477 D starrb@bigbend.edu
BERNHARDT, Thomas 804-763-6300 93 H
BERNHEIM, Michelle 562-902-3343 65 H michellebernheim@scuhs.edu
BERNIER, Brandon 970-491-1833 79 E brandon.bernier@colostate.edu
BERNIER, Carrie 203-857-7270 87 B cbernier@norwalk.edu
BERNIER, Jose 386-822-7045 111 F jbernier@stetson.edu
BERNOI, Verna, A 443-518-4773 199 D vbernoi@howardcc.edu
BERNOT, C. Tina 270-809-3250 184 A cbernot@murraystate.edu
BERNOT, Elizabeth 518-564-2080 318 C
BERNOTAS, Scott, C 412-624-9510 400 A bernotas@pitt.edu
BERNOTSKY, R. Lorraine 610-436-6977 394 F lbernotsky@wcupa.edu
BERNOUSSI, Brian 972-883-2676 454 D brian_bernoussi10@utdallas.edu
BERNSTEIN, Alan, M 229-333-5860 127 C abernste@valdosta.edu
BERNSTEIN, Andy 203-582-7882 88 F andy.bernstein@qu.edu
BERNSTEIN, David 845-406-4308 325 C
BERNSTEIN, Melissa 801-581-3386 459 D melissa.bernstein@law.utah.edu
BERNSTEIN, Pamela 603-880-8308 273 F pbernstein@thomasmorecollege.edu
BERNSTEIN, Robin 402-557-7300 265 A robin.bernstein@bellevue.edu
BERNSTEIN, Zeke 802-440-4594 461 B zbernstein@bennington.edu
BEROWSKI, Alfred 315-866-0300 301 B berowskfj@herkimer.edu
BERQUE, David 765-658-4359 154 G vpaa@depauw.edu
BERREAU, Lisa 435-797-3509 459 F lisa.berreau@usu.edu
BERRETH, Dwight 208-467-8011 132 B dberreth@nnu.edu
BERRETT, Ben 435-797-1957 459 F ben.berrett@usu.edu
BERRIDGE, Bob 773-256-0783 143 C bberridg@lstc.edu
BERRIEN, Joel 712-749-2379 164 A berrienj@bvu.edu
BERRIEN, Tara 443-885-3559 200 F tara.berrien@morgan.edu
BERRIOS, Anthony 305-821-3333 100 C aberrios@fnu.edu
BERRIOS, Eduardo 787-603-1515 506 L eberrios@bayamon.inter.edu
BERRIOS, Eric 814-864-6666 384 E ericb@glit.edu
BERRIOS, Iris 787-743-7979 509 D ac_irberrios@suagm.edu
BERRIOS, Jennifer, D 617-627-5540 219 A jennifer.berrios@tufts.edu
BERRIOS, Jonathan 787-738-2161 511 A jonathan.berrios@upr.edu
BERRIOS, Jose, E 787-766-1717 509 C jberrios34@uagm.edu
BERRIOS, Marianne 787-852-1430 506 A mberrios@hccpr.edu
BERRIOS, Olga, L 787-850-9340 511 B olga.berrios@upr.edu
BERRIOS, William 212-592-2043 314 I wberrios@sva.edu
BERRY, Abby 315-655-7292 292 B alberry@cazenovia.edu
BERRY, Alex 217-786-4912 142 F alex.berry@llcc.edu
BERRY, Alex 217-424-6217 144 D aberry@millikin.edu
BERRY, Anna 413-775-1868 214 C
BERRY, Anthony, T 860-297-2177 88 I anthony.berry@trincoll.edu
BERRY, Benny 423-652-4333 419 F blberry@king.edu
BERRY, Brian 870-777-5722 23 C brian.berry@uaht.edu
BERRY, Cammie, S 803-536-8961 410 H cberry@scsu.edu
BERRY, Chad 859-985-3730 179 E berryc@berea.edu
BERRY, Chelsia 206-934-4077 482 G chelsia.berry@seattlecolleges.edu
BERRY, Clay 870-508-6124 18 B cberry@asumh.edu
BERRY, Crystal 206-546-4101 483 C crystal.berry@shoreline.edu
BERRY, Doug 602-787-7668 13 G doug.berry@paradisevalley.edu
BERRY, Elizabeth, D 607-746-4573 320 A berryee@delhi.edu

BERRY, Emily ... 513-529-9625 356 A emily.berry@miamioh.edu
BERRY, Gwennette, C ... 319-273-2820 163 G gwenne.berry@uni.edu
BERRY, Joan ... 254-295-4010 453 A joan.berry@umhb.edu
BERRY, Joan, E ... 610-566-1776 402 C jberry@williamson.edu
BERRY, John ... 740-364-9510 349 D berry.19@cotc.edu
BERRY, John, K ... 865-981-8145 420 C john.berry@maryvillecollege.edu
BERRY, Keith ... 813-253-7714 102 A kberry@hccfl.edu
BERRY, Kevin ... 304-293-4731 489 E kbberry@mail.wvu.edu
BERRY, Larry ... 423-614-8086 419 H lberry@leeuniversity.edu
BERRY, Laura Lea ... 802-586-7711 462 C lberry@sterlingcollege.edu
BERRY, Linda, C ... 708-209-3209 136 D linda.berry@cuchicago.edu
BERRY, Mariane ... 541-956-7028 375 G mberry@roguecc.edu
BERRY, Mario ... 501-370-5336.. 21 A mberry@philander.edu
BERRY, Mario ... 713-313-7011 448 D
BERRY, Marla, J ... 808-956-8838 129 B mberry@hawaii.edu
BERRY, Michael ... 724-222-5330 391 E
BERRY, Rance ... 304-357-4862 486 J ranceberry@ucwv.edu
BERRY, Ronald, L ... 318-342-1010 193 A rberry@ulm.edu
BERRY, Steve ... 530-541-4660.. 47 H sberry@ltcc.edu
BERRY, Steve ... 919-365-7711 340 C sberry@sfwbc.edu
BERRY, Steven ... 410-386-8145 197 G sberry@carrollcc.edu
BERRY, Theodorea ... 407-823-2373 110 D theodorea.berry@ucf.edu
BERRY, Tina ... 520-494-5972.. 11 M tina.berry@centralaz.edu
BERRY, Trey ... 870-235-4001.. 21 E tcberry@saumag.edu
BERRY, William ... 386-481-2060.. 96 D berryw@cookman.edu
BERRY, William ... 540-423-9069 472 J wberry@germanna.edu
BERRY-GUERIN, Daneen ... 509-793-2053 477 D daneenb@bigbend.edu
BERRY-HUNG, Rima ... 313-593-5190 231 B rberry@umich.edu
BERRYHILL, Kelly, M ... 989-774-2849 221 M berry1km@cmich.edu
BERRYMAN, Cynthia ... 708-237-5050 146 B cberryman@nc.edu
BERRYMAN, Jennifer ... 508-856-2900 212 A jennifer.berryman@umassmed.edu
BERRYMAN, Todd ... 501-450-1322.. 19 I berryman@hendrix.edu
BERRÍOS, José ... 787-264-1912 507 E jfberrio@intersg.edu
BERRÍOS, José, E ... 787-257-7373 509 B jberrios34@uagm.edu
BERSANE, Angie ... 575-624-7168 285 F angie.bersane@roswell.enmu.edu
BERSCHBACK, Emily ... 313-883-8500 229 J berschback.emily@shms.edu
BERSHAD, Carolyn ... 607-753-4728 317 D carolyn.bershad@cortland.edu
BERSOFF, Edward ... 703-522-5600 468 A
BERT, Carrie ... 540-432-4331 465 F carrie.bert@emu.edu
BERT, Melissa ... 320-589-6113 243 C mbert@morris.umn.edu
BERTACCO, Valeria ... 734-763-0395 231 A vale@umich.edu
BERTAUX, Audrey ... 513-300-3117 347 G audrey.bertaux@artacademy.edu
BERTE, Hope ... 718-982-2400 293 C hope.berte@csi.cuny.edu
BERTHEL, Michael ... 516-299-3328 304 C michael.berthel@liu.edu
BERTHELOTE, Antony ... 406-275-4080 264 H antony_berthelote@skc.edu
BERTHELSEN, Michael .. 612-624-3557 242 K berth004@umn.edu
BERTHIAUME, Joe ... 209-946-2331.. 71 E jberthiaume@pacific.edu
BERTHIAUME, Scott ... 972-708-7338 434 F dean-academic@diu.edu
BERTHOLF, David ... 906-487-7222 223 I david.bertholf@finlandia.edu
BERTIE, Brett ... 620-331-4100 174 E bbertie@indycc.edu
BERTLING, Crystal ... 954-545-4500 108 C cbertling@sfbc.edu
BERTOLINE, Gary, R ... 765-494-4600 159 G
BERTOLINI, David ... 701-231-9588 345 D david.bertolini@ndsu.edu
BERTOLINO, Joe ... 203-392-5250.. 85 H president@southernct.edu
BERTONAZZI, Laura ... 781-768-7060 217 H laura.bertonazzi@regiscollege.edu
BERTONE, Alicia, L ... 614-292-9490 358 E bertone.1@osu.edu
BERTONE, Christopher .. 215-571-4085 382 D ctb332@drexel.edu
BERTONE, David, J ... 914-694-1122 291 A djb@berkeleycollege.edu
BERTONE, David, J ... 914-694-1122 274 J djb@berkeleycollege.edu
BERTONI, Alex ... 802-654-2536 462 A abertoni@smcvt.edu
BERTOT, John ... 301-405-4252 202 E jbertot@umd.edu
BERTOTTO, Dwayne ... 952-806-3958 241 R dwayne.bertotto@rasmussen.edu
BERTRAM, Alissa ... 401-341-2287 404 D alissa.bertram@salve.edu
BERTRAM, Brian ... 517-264-7676 230 C bbertram@sienaheights.edu
BERTRAM, Mary ... 847-970-4801 152 F mbertram@usml.edu
BERTRAN, Colette ... 515-576-7201 166 G
BERTRAND, Cindy ... 619-239-0391.. 34 H cbertrand@cwsl.edu
BERTRAND, Colleen ... 315-279-5000 303 D cbertrand@keuka.edu
BERTSCH, Lynda ... 701-858-3360 345 C lynda.bertsch@minotstateu.edu
BERTSCH, Tauna ... 254-968-9921 445 F bertsch@tarleton.edu
BERTSCHE, Allen ... 719-227-8280.. 78 E abertsche@coloradocollege.edu
BERTUCCI, Roy ... 337-421-6565 188 H
BERUBE, Beth ... 906-217-4036 221 J beth.berube@baycollege.edu
BERUBE, Brian ... 978-665-3025 212 C bberube3@fitchburgstate.edu
BERUBE, Danelle ... 802-865-5460 461 C dberube@champlain.edu
BERUMEN, Daniel ... 714-992-7000.. 54 D dberumen@fullcoll.edu
BERUMEN, Yvonne ... 909-621-8129.. 57 E yvonne_berumen@pitzer.edu
BERWICK, Robert ... 904-256-7092 102 G rberwic@ju.edu
BESANA, GianMario ... 312-362-5554 136 F gbesana@depaul.edu
BESEAU, Steven, P ... 614-885-5585 359 K sbeseau@pcj.edu
BESELER THOMPSON, Joel ... 701-231-8286 345 D joel.d.thompson@ndsu.edu
BESHARA, Alexa ... 732-255-0400 279 A abeshara@ocean.edu
BESHEARS, Brenda ... 217-228-5520 133 G beshearsb@brcn.edu
BESIKOF, Rudy ... 510-464-3236.. 57 B rbesikof@peralta.edu
BESLER, Shane ... 563-589-3115 170 C
BESMER, Matthew ... 559-243-7103.. 66 G matthew.besmer@scccd.edu
BESNETTE HAUSER, Carrie ... 970-945-8691.. 78 H
BESONG, Jeffrey, D ... 412-392-3819 395 H jbesong@pointpark.edu
BESONG, Marsha ... 856-225-6108 281 A marsha.besong@rutgers.edu
BESPALOV, Oleg ... 805-553-4176.. 73 I obespalov@vcccd.edu
BESS MYERS, Donna ... 314-977-9378 258 H donnabess.myers@slu.edu
BESSETTE, Bill ... 301-934-4753 198 C wrbessette@csmd.edu
BESSETTE, James ... 912-279-5704 117 C jbessette@ccga.edu
BESSETTE, Mark ... 518-381-1353 319 G bessetma@sunysccc.edu
BESSETTE, Nancy, A ... 401-456-8033 404 A nbessette@ric.edu
BESSLER, Joseph, A ... 918-270-6448 368 G joe.bessler@ptstulsa.edu
BESSLER, Timothy (Tim) ... 210-431-3331 442 A tbessler@stmarytx.edu
BEST, JR., A. Reginald . 313-317-1700 224 F arbest1@hfcc.edu
BEST, Kathy ... 919-635-2788 340 E kbest@umo.edu
BEST, Lisa ... 712-749-2415 164 A bestl@bvu.edu
BEST, Matthew ... 716-270-5262 299 A bestm@ecc.edu
BEST, Michelle ... 715-425-3073 496 A michelle.best@uwrf.edu
BEST, Roger ... 660-543-4112 259 K president@ucmo.edu
BEST, Ruth ... 212-463-0400 322 C ruth.best@touro.edu
BEST, Sara ... 701-349-5793 346 G sarabest@trinitybiblecollege.edu
BESTAVROS, Azer ... 617-353-9726 207 C best@bu.edu
BESTE, Jeff ... 937-766-3645 349 C bestej@cedarville.edu
BESWICK, Patrick, T ... 724-738-4855 394 E patrick.beswick@sru.edu
BETANCOURT, Angelica 801-626-6033 460 B abetancourt@weber.edu
BETANCOURT, Gigi ... 619-574-5816.. 43 B jbetancourt@fst.edu
BETANCOURT, Tammy, L ... 217-443-8778 136 E t.betancourt@dacc.edu
BETANCOURT-RUIZ, Yeisha ... 773-481-8183 135 D ybetancourt-ruiz@ccc.edu
BETANCOURT SANTIAGO, Victor ... 703-284-1677 468 A victor.betancourt@marymount.edu
BETANCOURT VELEZ, Ismael, J ... 540-831-6200 468 E ibetancourtvelez@radford.edu
BETARIE, Breanna ... 570-422-3045 393 F bbetarie@esu.edu
BETCHER, Tom ... 937-766-7681 349 C tbetcher@cedarville.edu
BETECK, Ellis ... 937-255-3636 501 A ellis.beteck@afit.edu
BETHANY, Lea Ann ... 601-968-8724 244 C lbethany@belhaven.edu
BETHARDS, Troy ... 417-328-1757 258 K tbethards@sbuniv.edu
BETHE, Rhonda ... 785-833-4503 175 C rhonda.bethe@kwu.edu
BETHEL, Genna ... 903-813-3001 429 I gbethel@austincollege.edu
BETHKE, Jeffrey ... 312-567-3000 139 H
BETHUNE, Andrew, J ... 989-964-4071 229 L ajbethune@svsu.edu
BETIT, Brian ... 352-787-0981.. 96 B bbetit@beaconcollege.edu
BETLER, Yamayra ... 251-460-6133.... 9 A ybetler@southalabama.edu
BETSCHART, Joseph, V . 503-845-3335 373 G joseph.betschart@mtangel.edu
BETSINGER, Alicia ... 512-326-7002 441 N abetsing@stedwards.edu
BETSWORTH, Sharon ... 405-208-5602 367 E sbetsworth@okcu.edu
BETSWORTH, Sharon ... 913-253-5018 177 A sharon.betsworth@spst.edu
BETTELYOUN, Kim ... 605-455-6093 414 H kbettelyoun@olc.edu
BETTENCOURT, Patrick .. 209-575-6221.. 76 K bettencourtp@mjc.edu
BETTENDORF, Anthony . 507-933-7529 235 E abettend@gustavus.edu
BETTERSON, April ... 559-934-2323.. 74 L aprilbetterson@whccd.edu
BETTERSWORTH, Michael, A ... 512-647-8790 448 F michael.bettersworth@tstc.edu
BETTINGER, Michael ... 215-461-1105 390 A mbettinger@mc3.edu
BETTIS, Donna ... 423-697-2551 423 B
BETTS, Bill ... 765-285-1264 153 E wrbetts@bsu.edu
BETTS, David ... 831-646-4000.. 52 H
BETTS, Keith ... 203-837-8600.. 86 A bettsk@wcsu.edu
BETTS, Steve ... 405-789-6400 369 G sbetts@snu.edu
BETZ, Bridgette, K ... 573-341-4282 260 F berry@mst.edu
BETZ, Cheri ... 517-264-7100 230 C cbetz@sienaheights.edu
BETZ, Kimberly ... 609-258-3000 279 E kbetz@princeton.edu
BETZ, Leslie ... 309-556-3161 140 E registrar@iwu.edu
BETZ, Michael ... 866-492-5336 243 G
BETZ, Phil ... 765-983-1600 154 H betzph@earlham.edu
BETZ, Stacey ... 610-799-1737 388 B sbetz1@lccc.edu
BEUK, Donna ... 432-552-2579 456 C beuk_d@utpb.edu
BEURSKENS, Benny ... 620-331-0815 174 E bbeurskens@indycc.edu
BEURY, Carey ... 812-465-7175 162 B clbeury@usi.edu
BEUS, Ben ... 509-542-4811 478 B bbeus@columbiabasin.edu
BEUS, Yifen ... 808-675-4300 128 B yifen.beus@byuh.edu
BEUSCHER, Barbara ... 814-871-7464 383 H beuscher001@gannon.edu
BEUTEL, Kate ... 419-517-8880 355 C kbeutel@lourdes.edu
BEVAN, Olivia ... 740-245-7370 363 A obevan@rio.edu
BEVER, Edward ... 516-876-3998 318 A bevere@oldwestbury.edu
BEVERAGE, JR., Morris, W ... 440-525-7118 354 L mbeverage@lakelandcc.edu
BEVERIDGE, Kim ... 800-869-7223 124 G kbeverid@scad.edu
BEVERIDGE, Thomas ... 805-565-6017.. 75 I tbeverid@westmont.edu
BEVERLY, Beth ... 270-707-3869 181 G ebeverly0003@kctcs.edu
BEVERLY, Jacqueline ... 251-981-3771.... 5 B jacqueline.beverly@columbiasouthern.edu
BEVERLY, Jason ... 601-928-6267 246 F jason.beverly@mgccc.edu
BEVERLY, Kiah ... 775-673-7300 271 A kiah.beverly@dri.edu
BEVERLY, Michael ... 402-399-2313 265 H mbeverly@csm.edu
BEVERLY, Pearlie ... 254-710-4466 430 F pearl_beverly@baylor.edu
BEVERLY, Sharon ... 860-768-4145.. 89 E sbeverly@hartford.edu
BEVILACQUA, Amy ... 304-724-3700 485 G abevilacqua@apus.edu
BEVILACQUA, Linda ... 305-899-3010.. 96 A lbevilacqua@barry.edu
BEVILL, Yolanda ... 970-491-2359.. 79 E yolanda.bevill@colostate.edu
BEVILLE, Glenn ... 504-526-4745 190 C glennb@nationsu.edu
BEVILLE, Jill ... 336-334-4013 342 D jmbevill@uncg.edu
BEVINS, P. Scott ... 276-328-0144 471 G pb8q@uvawise.edu
BEVIS, Kara ... 618-985-3741 140 G karabevis@jalc.edu
BEVIVINO, DJ ... 315-255-1743 292 A dbevin@cayuga-cc.edu
BEY, Adrienne, M ... 302-295-1140.. 91 C adrienne.m.bey@wilmu.edu
BEYAH, Raheem ... 404-894-2531 119 D rbeyah@coe.gatech.edu
BEYDA-LORIE, Sandra .. 773-442-5528 145 G s-beyda@neiu.edu
BEYDLER, Julie ... 970-542-3129.. 81 M julie.beydler@morgancc.edu
BEYELER, Jodi ... 574-535-7572 155 B jodihb@goshen.edu
BEYER, Charlotte ... 224-570-7900 148 B charlotte.beyer@rosalindfranklin.edu
BEYER, Christian ... 814-824-2915 389 E cbeyer@mercyhurst.edu
BEYER, Christopher ... 309-794-2686 132 H christopherbeyer@augustana.edu
BEYL, Caula ... 865-974-7303 426 C cbeyl@utk.edu
BEYMER, Lisa ... 812-855-0271 156 C libeymer@iu.edu
BEYROUTY, Craig ... 301-405-2072 202 E beyrouty@umd.edu
BEZEK, Cory ... 716-673-3251 316 A cory.bezek@fredonia.edu

BEZEL, Jill .... 212-431-2100 308 I
jbezel@nyls.edu
BEZET, Jared .... 561-912-1211.. 99 C
jbezet@evergladesuniversity.edu
BHADA, Farokh .... 401-232-6005 403 B
fbhada@bryant.edu
BHADURY, Joy .... 540-831-5300 468 E
jbhadury@radford.edu
BHAJAN, Indira, L .... 787-751-0160 505 C
ibhajan@cmpr.pr.gov
BHALLA, Raman, S .... 585-475-2555 312 A
rsbetc@rit.edu
BHARADWAJ,
Prashanth .... 724-357-7889 393 G
pnb@iup.edu
BHARGAVA, Suman ...... 833-637-0866.. 46 J
sumanb@itu.edu
BHASIN, Rohit .... 978-681-0800 216 A
ro@mslaw.edu
BHAT, Manju .... 336-750-2214 343 E
bhatj@wssu.edu
BHATI, Divya .... 843-953-9443 407 D
bhatid@cofc.edu
BHATIA, Amit .... 503-375-7125 372 G
abhatia@corban.edu
BHATT, Juhi .... 201-692-2187 276 I
juhi_bhatt26@fdu.edu
BHATTACHARYA,
Kaushik .... 626-395-6365.. 29 B
vpr@caltech.edu
BHATTACHARYA,
Manish .... 844-283-2246.. 93 C
BHATTACHARYA,
Somnath .... 217-206-6600 151 E
sbhat23@uis.edu
BHATTACHARYYA,
Abhijit .... 870-972-3565.. 17 I
abhattacharyya@astate.edu
BHATTI, Ilyas .... 617-989-4590 219 D
bhattii@wit.edu
BHAUMIK, Nila .... 646-313-8000 295 C
nila.bhaumik@guttman.cuny.edu
BHOLA, Onyel .... 703-284-1491 468 A
onyel.bhola@marymount.edu
BIAGAS, Lisa .... 215-972-2038 392 P
lbiagas@pafa.edu
BIALEK, Kelly, A .... 330-972-6153 361 G
kaf58@uakron.edu
BIALK, Kathy .... 859-257-6547 185 D
kathy.bialk@uky.edu
BIALKOWSKI, Richard .. 518-255-5317 318 F
bialkort@cobleskill.edu
BIALOWAS, John .... 912-201-8049 125 D
jbialowas@southuniversity.edu
BIANCARDI, Joseph, M 651-631-5178 243 E
jmbiancardi@unwsp.edu
BIANCHETTO, Melody ... 434-982-2347 471 F
msb2p@virginia.edu
BIANCHI, Amy, M .... 617-333-2236 208 D
abianchi@curry.edu
BIANCHI, Ashley .... 413-597-4181 220 A
abb5@williams.edu
BIANCHI, Gina, L .... 217-424-6330 144 D
gbianchi@millikin.edu
BIANCHI, Timothy .... 717-299-7793 398 E
bianchi@stevenscollege.edu
BIANCO, Annamarie ...... 202-687-0100.. 92 D
amb504@georgetown.edu
BIANCO, Christopher .... 360-650-4076 485 A
christopher.bianco@wwu.edu
BIANCO, Gena .... 401-254-5602 404 C
gbianco@rwu.edu
BIANCO, Michelle .... 906-353-8400 225 G
mbianco@kbocc.edu
BIANCO, Theresa .... 906-353-8400 225 G
hr@kbocc.edu
BIANCO MAJERI, Kim .. 202-651-5005.. 92 B
kim.bianco.majeri@gallaudet.edu
BIANGONE, Marianne ... 916-646-2779.. 60 C
mbiangone@samuelmerritt.edu
BIAS, Jeanine .... 936-294-3026 449 E
jrb023@shsu.edu
BIAS, Joseph .... 803-738-7604 409 E
biasj@midlandstech.edu
BIBB-SANDERS,
Angelia .... 323-860-0789.. 50 E
BIBBEE, Mistie .... 304-696-3152 488 N
bibbeem@marshall.edu
BIBBENS, Matt .... 909-621-8111.. 37 G
matthew.bibbens@cmc.edu
BIBBO, Chris, J .... 727-816-3261 105 E
bibboc@phsc.edu
BIBEAU, Guy .... 508-849-3333 205 E
gbibeau@annamaria.edu

BIBLE, Brice, J .... 716-645-7979 315 F
bible@buffalo.edu
BIBLER, Nicole .... 913-758-6123 177 I
nicole.bibler@stmary.edu
BIBO, JR., Tim .... 410-704-4685 204 B
tbibo@towson.edu
BICE, Matthew .... 785-594-6451 171 C
matthew.bice@bakeru.edu
BICE, Patricia .... 914-251-6360 318 E
patricia.bice@purchase.edu
BICHEL, Rebecca .... 817-272-1413 454 B
rbichel@uta.edu
BICHELMEYER, Barbara . 785-864-4904 177 G
bichelmeyer@ku.edu
BICICCHI, Rachel .... 217-424-3692 144 D
rbicicchi@millikin.edu
BICKART, Thomas .... 605-394-4800 414 G
BICKERTON, Molly .... 912-871-1600 123 F
mbickerton@ogeecheetech.edu
BICKETT, Brian .... 847-970-4861 152 F
bbickett@usml.edu
BICKETT, Larry .... 304-260-4380 487 C
lbickett@blueridgectc.edu
BICKFORD, Deborah, J . 937-229-5360 362 C
dbickford1@udayton.edu
BICKING, Michael .... 610-341-1720 383 A
michael.bicking@eastern.edu
BICKLEY, Craig .... 724-357-4874 393 G
cbickley@iup.edu
BICKNELL, Brian .... 603-206-8002 272 A
bbicknell@ccsnh.edu
BICKNELL, Patricia .... 215-951-1430 386 I
bicknell@lasalle.edu
BICKNELL, Teresa .... 865-531-4108 420 A
teresa.bicknell@lmunet.edu
BICKSLER, Leslie .... 304-647-6279 489 C
lbicksler@osteo.wvsom.edu
BIDDINGER, Mark .... 618-664-6610 138 D
mark.biddinger@greenville.edu
BIDDINGS-MURO,
Regina .... 805-493-3828.. 29 E
rbiddingsmuro@callutheran.edu
BIDDLE, Elizabeth, A .... 570-326-3761 392 S
ebiddle@pct.edu
BIDDLE, Nicole .... 414-930-3663 493 E
biddlen@mtmary.edu
BIDLE, Kelly .... 609-895-5418 280 D
kbidle@rider.edu
BIDWELL, Joe .... 423-439-5671 418 D
bidwell@etsu.edu
BIDWELL, Mary .... 860-253-3118.. 86 B
mbidwell@asnuntuck.edu
BIEBER, Ann, D .... 610-799-1581 388 B
abieber@lccc.edu
BIEBER, Harold .... 678-916-2690 115 G
hbieber@johnmarshall.edu
BIEBER, Joshua .... 785-227-3380 171 H
bieberjb@bethanylb.edu
BIEBUYCK, Bill .... 563-588-6405 164 C
bill.biebuyck@clarke.edu
BIECHLER, Laura .... 508-531-1341 212 B
lbiechler@bridgew.edu
BIEDERMANN, Heather . 507-389-7223 240 F
heather.biedermann@southcentral.edu
BIEDERMANN, Scott ..... 209-946-2011.. 71 E
BIEDERMANN, Scott ..... 209-946-2166.. 71 E
sbiedermann@pacific.edu
BIEGEL, Peter .... 561-868-3532 105 C
biegelp@palmbeachstate.edu
BIEGER, Mark .... 225-578-7244 188 K
mbieger@lsu.edu
BIEHL, Peter .... 831-459-3336.. 71 A
pbiehl@ucsc.edu
BIEHN, Christopher, M 585-385-5251 313 A
mbiehn@sjfc.edu
BIEK, David .... 478-757-2544 122 D
david.biek@mga.edu
BIEL, Kirsten .... 317-917-5988 158 A
kbiel@ivytech.edu
BIEL, Michael, J .... 219-989-2510 160 A
bielm@pnw.edu
BIELAT SOLTOW, Keely 585-245-5566 317 E
ksoltow@geneseo.edu
BIELAWSKI, Bill .... 312-329-8047 144 F
bill.bielawski@moody.edu
BIELBY, Steve .... 864-977-0249 410 A
steve.bielby@ngu.edu
BIELFELDT, Dennis .... 605-692-9337 414 B
president@ilt.edu
BIELICKI, Shawn .... 434-582-3035 467 E
smbielicki@liberty.edu
BIELITZ, Colleen, Q ...... 203-392-5459.. 85 H
bielitzc1@southernct.edu

BIELSER, Silvia .... 510-780-4500.. 48 D
sbielser@lifewest.edu
BIENVENUE, Scott .... 603-578-8900 272 B
sbienvenue@ccsnh.edu
BIENZ, Richard, A .... 260-399-7700 162 A
rbienz@sf.edu
BIER, Debbie .... 412-521-6200 396 F
debbie.bier@rosedaletech.org
BIERBAUM, Joseph .... 203-287-3031.. 88 D
BIERGANS, Matthew ..... 909-621-8205.. 57 K
matthew.biergans@pomona.edu
BIERIG, Samuel .... 816-414-3731 255 F
sbierig@mbts.edu
BIERLE, Brad .... 763-544-9501 235 D
BIERLE, Sarah .... 763-544-9501 235 D
sarah.bierle@flbc.edu
BIERMAN, Cindy .... 909-607-3305.. 37 F
cindy.bierman@cgu.edu
BIERMAN, Derek .... 402-826-8333 266 A
derek.bierman@doane.edu
BIERMAN, Matt .... 309-556-3021 140 E
mbierman@iwu.edu
BIERMAN, Matthew, J .. 217-581-2921 137 C
BIERMAN, Scott .... 608-363-2201 490 I
biermans@beloit.edu
BIERMANN, Mark, L ..... 217-854-3231 133 F
BIERMANN, Matt .... 989-275-5000 225 H
matt.biermann@kirtland.edu
BIERNBAUM, John .... 309-298-3320 152 I
j-biernbaum@wiu.edu
BIERSCHBACH, Richard 313-577-3933 232 H
rbierschbach@wayne.edu
BIESCHKE, Kathleen ...... 814-863-7494 391 F
kxb11@psu.edu
BIESCHKE, Walt .... 615-322-7311 427 B
BIESECKER, James .... 717-337-6700 384 C
jbieseck@gettysburg.edu
BIESTY, Cathy .... 518-243-4471 290 K
biestyc@ellismedicine.org
BIESZKE, Jay .... 630-752-7091 152 K
jay.bieszke@wheaton.edu
BIETELCHIES, Wade ...... 517-265-5161 220 D
wbietelchies@adrian.edu
BIG SPRING, Anita .... 406-275-4974 264 H
anita_bigspring@skc.edu
BIGALK, Roberta .... 970-542-3113.. 81 M
roberta.bigalk@morgancc.edu
BIGAM, Evan .... 607-778-5676 317 A
bigame@sunybroome.edu
BIGARD, Heather .... 352-365-3525 103 U
bigardh@lssc.edu
BIGBEE, Leah, M .... 205-853-1200.... 2 G
leah.bigbee@jeffersonstate.edu
BIGELOW, Bethany .... 503-375-7172 372 G
bbigelow@corban.edu
BIGELOW, Shannon ...... 317-632-5553 158 V
sbigelow@lincolntech.edu
BIGGANE, Michael, J ... 716-851-1416 299 A
biggane@ecc.edu
BIGGER, Kimberly .... 870-248-4000.. 18 H
kim.bigger@blackrivertech.edu
BIGGERS, Sharon .... 434-395-2209 467 F
drinkardsf@longwood.edu
BIGGERSTAFF,
D. Patrick .... 704-233-8247 344 E
dpbigg@wingate.edu
BIGGERSTAFF,
Elizabeth .... 704-233-8368 344 E
erogers@wingate.edu
BIGGS, Aaron, A .... 405-325-4861 370 J
abiggs@ou.edu
BIGGS, Clay .... 573-629-3211 253 D
cbiggs@hlg.edu
BIGGS, Jessie, N .... 260-422-5561 156 A
jnbiggs@indianatech.edu
BIGGS, Michelle .... 985-549-2150 192 E
michelle.biggs@selu.edu
BIGGS, Patsy .... 501-420-1201.. 17 D
patsy.biggs@arkansasbaptist.edu
BIGGS, Shirley, A .... 803-535-5268 406 E
sbiggs@claflin.edu
BIGGS, Theresa .... 207-834-7665 196 G
theresa.biggs@maine.edu
BIGGS, Vicki .... 314-505-7266 251 D
biggsv@csl.edu
BIGGS GARBUIO, Judi . 202-319-5619.. 91 G
judibg@cua.edu
BIGHAM, Bill .... 937-775-2350 364 D
bill.bigham@wright.edu
BIGHAM-STEPHENS,
Dana .... 850-729-6469 104 L
stephed@nwfsc.edu

BIGNOLI, Callan .... 781-292-2386 209 E
cbignoli@olin.edu
BIGONGIARI, Anthony .. 817-599-6320 457 C
abigongiari@wc.edu
BIGWOOD, Christine .... 401-232-6348 403 B
cbigwood@bryant.edu
BILACH, Bernadett .... 480-994-9244.. 16 C
bernadettb@swiha.edu
BILAL, Waheedah .... 573-681-5505 254 A
bilald@lincolnu.edu
BILBRUCK, Tom .... 661-362-3235.. 38 H
tom.bilbruck@canyons.edu
BILBY, Lesley, S .... 859-238-5217 179 H
lesley.bilby@centre.edu
BILDERBACK, Rebecca .. 620-901-6351 171 A
bilderback@allencc.edu
BILEN-GREEN, Canan .... 701-231-7040 345 D
canan.bilen.green@ndsu.edu
BILES, Brad .... 816-584-6888 257 E
brad.biles@park.edu
BILGER, Audrey .... 503-777-7500 375 F
abilger@reed.edu
BILGER, Bonnie .... 760-366-5285.. 40 K
bbilger@cmccd.edu
BILKER, Mitch .... 215-248-7084 380 G
bilkerm@chc.edu
BILL, Rhonda .... 281-484-1900 442 E
BILLEAUDEAU, Kim, A .. 337-262-5300 192 F
kimberlyb@louisiana.edu
BILLECI, Celesta .... 805-893-3437.. 70 E
celesta.billeci@sa.ucsb.edu
BILLECI-GARD, Phil ...... 510-436-1049.. 45 H
billecigard@hnu.edu
BILLEN, Isabelle .... 405-733-7580 369 D
ibillen@rose.edu
BILLET, Bill .... 805-969-3626.. 55 I
bbillet@pacifica.edu
BILLETT, Carrie .... 606-589-3152 182 F
cbillett0002@kctcs.edu
BILLETTA, Michael .... 610-718-1844 390 A
mbilletta@mc3.edu
BILLEY, Terry .... 580-928-5533 369 I
terry.billey@swosu.edu
BILLHARTZ, Scott, L ..... 618-537-6869 143 G
slbillhartz@mckendree.edu
BILLIE, Marie .... 650-574-6161.. 62 J
BILLINGS, Amanda .... 214-648-2344 456 D
amanda.billings@utsouthwestern.edu
BILLINGS, Eve .... 602-557-1731.. 16 L
eve.krahe@phoenix.edu
BILLINGS, James .... 866-776-0331.. 54 E
jbillings@ncu.edu
BILLINGS, Lora .... 973-655-5108 278 C
billingsl@montclair.edu
BILLINGS, Maria .... 201-216-9901 276 C
maria.billings@eicollege.edu
BILLINGS, Mindi .... 866-294-3974 154 E
BILLINGS, Molly .... 402-280-4722 265 J
mollybillings@creighton.edu
BILLINGS, Patricia .... 413-552-2248 214 D
pbillings@hcc.edu
BILLINGS, Stephanie, L 828-262-2366 340 G
billingssl@appstate.edu
BILLINGS-BERG, Sarah . 802-728-1586 463 D
sberg@vtc.edu
BILLINGSLEY, Jennifer .. 217-540-3588 141 H
jbillingsley@lakelandcollege.edu
BILLINGSLEY, Jodie .... 806-742-2020 450 C
jodie.billingsley@ttu.edu
BILLINGSLEY, Joel .... 251-460-6697.... 9 A
lewis@southalabama.edu
BILLINGSLEY, Linda ...... 318-487-7630 187 B
linda.billingsley@lcuniversity.edu
BILLINGSLEY, Mark .... 901-321-3278 417 G
mark.billingsley@cbu.edu
BILLINGSLEY, Sarah ..... 916-278-7737.. 33 A
sarah.billingsley@csus.edu
BILLINGSLEY, Scott ...... 910-521-6224 343 A
scott.billingsley@uncp.edu
BILLINGTON, Dave .... 517-607-2451 224 G
dbillington@hillsdale.edu
BILLITIER, Rick .... 585-594-7777 311 L
billitier_rick@roberts.edu
BILLMAN, Carol .... 724-838-4204 397 F
billman@setonhill.edu
BILLMAN, Tyler .... 618-252-5400 149 E
tyler.billman@sic.edu
BILLS, Andy .... 336-841-4538 329 E
abills@highpoint.edu
BILLS, Kimberly .... 253-589-5846 478 A
kimberly.bills@cptc.edu
BILLS, Matt .... 262-646-6513 493 F
mbills@nashotah.edu

BILLS, Matthew .... 563-387-1189 167 J
bills@luther.edu
BILLS, Melissa .... 563-387-1042 167 J
billma02@luther.edu
BILLS-WINDT, Caryn, A 312-413-8145 151 D
cabw@uic.edu
BILLUPS, Kim .... 215-368-5000 389 G
kbillups@missio.edu
BILLUPS, Kyle .... 408-848-4901.. 43 H
kbillups@gavilan.edu
BILLY, Amanda .... 904-256-7161 102 G
abilly1@ju.edu
BILLY, Cameron .... 406-395-4875 264 I
cbilly@stonechild.edu
BILODEAU, Leta .... 207-859-1201 196 A
bilodeaul@thomas.edu
BILODEAU, Timothy ...... 802-316-0078 462 D
timothy.bilodeau@uvm.edu
BILOKONSKY, George ... 740-374-8716 363 F
gbilokonsky@wscc.edu
BILOTTA, Bobbie, J ...... 716-880-2265 305 F
bbilotta@medaille.edu
BILSKY, Edward .... 509-452-5100 481 E
ebilsky@pnwu.edu
BILYEU, Bethany .... 217-206-7122 151 E
bilyeu.bethany@uis.edu
BIMER, Tammy, C .... 734-763-9954 231 A
tammyc@umich.edu
BIMONTE, Maria 561-237-7173 103W
mbimonte@lynn.edu
BINDER, Maureen .... 407-823-2771 110 D
maureen.binder@ucf.edu
BING, Andrea .... 415-565-4733.. 69 B
wellesan@uchastings.edu
BING, Sarah .... 870-743-3000.. 20 F
sbing@northark.edu
BINGAMON, Cindy .... 660-263-3900 250 G
cindybingamon@cccb.edu
BINGEMAN, Jeff .... 717-396-7833 392 Q
jbingeman@pcad.edu
BINGHAM, Brent .... 515-650-3198 163 C
brentbingham@theartofeducation.edu
BINGHAM, Charlotte ..... 806-742-3627 450 D
charlotte.bingham@ttu.edu
BINGHAM, Erin .... 252-638-7328 333 F
binghame@cravencc.edu
BINGHAM, Jeffrey .... 817-921-8613 444 D
jbingham@swbts.edu
BINGHAM, Vicki, L .... 662-846-4268 245 A
vbingham@deltastate.edu
BINK, Cynthia .... 718-260-5030 294 F
cbink@citytech.cuny.edu
BINKERD, James .... 707-638-5935.. 68 B
james.binkerd@tu.edu
BINKLEY, Bonnie .... 276-944-6921 466 F
bbinkley@ehc.edu
BINLEY, Jane, W .... 412-578-8880 380 A
jwbinley@carlow.edu
BINNEY, Craig .... 508-565-1107 218 F
cbinney@stonehill.edu
BINNEY, Diane, M .... 626-395-6651.. 29 B
dbinney@caltech.edu
BINNICKER, Paul .... 816-423-4710 166 B
binnicke@graceland.edu
BINNS, Pervis, D .... 540-464-7164 475 C
binnspd@vmi.edu
BINSFELD, Doug .... 563-425-5284 170 D
binsfeldd08@uiu.edu
BINSTOCK, Jonathan ..... 585-276-8902 323 E
jbinstock@mag.rochester.edu
BIONDO, Drew .... 631-451-4776 320 G
biondodr@sunysuffolk.edu
BIRCH, Andrea, C .... 770-718-5325 116 C
abirch@brenau.edu
BIRCH, Brian .... 607-431-4101 300 G
birchb@hartiwck.edu
BIRCH, Jenna .... 610-436-2813 394 F
jbirch@wcupa.edu
BIRCH, Laura, A .... 217-420-6661 144 D
lbirch@millikin.edu
BIRCH, Sara .... 269-294-4287 223 J
sbirch@glenoaks.edu
BIRCHARD, Michael ...... 651-290-6416 241 N
michael.birchard@mitchellhamline.edu
BIRCHWOOD, Rachel .... 845-452-9600 297 E
rachel.birchwood@culinary.edu
BIRCK, Ken .... 513-231-2223 348 A
kwbirck@athenaeum.edu
BIRCKBICHLER,
Carrie, J .... 724-738-2150 394 E
carrie.birckbichler@sru.edu
BIRD, Barb .... 765-998-4571 161 A
brbird@taylor.edu
BIRD, Brandon .... 206-315-5024 478 F
bbird@cornish.edu
BIRD, Brian .... 608-342-7584 495 E
birdbr@uwplatt.edu
BIRD, Christopher .... 740-264-5591 352 B
cbird@egcc.edu
BIRD, David .... 785-242-5200 176 F
david.bird@ottawa.edu
BIRD, Jamie .... 909-370-4800.. 29 H
BIRD, Jennifer .... 304-769-0011 490 B
jbird@wvjc.edu
BIRD, Jessica .... 316-942-4291 176 B
birdj@newmanu.edu
BIRD, Karla .... 406-338-5441 262 D
BIRD, Su Ann .... 229-931-2110 125 C
sbird@southgatech.edu
BIRD, Veronica, A .... 610-917-1422 400 D
rabird@valleyforge.edu
BIRDSALL, Derrick .... 936-294-3931 449 E
dcb031@shsu.edu
BIRDSELL, David .... 908-737-3457 277 F
BIRDSELL, Rebecca .... 217-245-3035 139 A
becky.birdsell@ic.edu
BIRDSONG, Jeff .... 918-540-6348 366 F
jbirdsong@neo.edu
BIRDSONG, Tiffany .... 804-862-6100 469 E
BIRDWELL, Cindy, A ..... 517-264-7194 230 C
cbirdwell@sienaheights.edu
BIRDWELL, Kim .... 940-521-0720 439 I
kbirdwell@nctc.edu
BIRENBAUM, Hylah ...... 828-627-4544 335 A
hebirenbaum@haywood.edu
BIRGE, James .... 413-662-5201 212 F
james.birge@mcla.edu
BIRGE, Susan, N .... 203-254-4000.. 87 G
sbirge@fairfield.edu
BIRKAM, Sally .... 231-773-9131 228 C
BIRKEL, Michelle .... 402-323-3411 268 D
mbirkel@southeast.edu
BIRKLAND, Amy .... 320-222-5977 239 H
amy.birkland@ridgewater.edu
BIRKLID, Craig .... 206-296-5999 483 B
cbirklid@seattleu.edu
BIRMAN, Julio .... 410-334-2966 205 A
jbirman@worwic.edu
BIRNBAUM, Jeremiah ... 415-824-7000.. 61 F
BIRNEY, Vanessa .... 740-264-5591 352 B
vbirney@egcc.edu
BIRNIE, Christine, R ...... 585-385-7202 313 A
cbirnie@sjfc.edu
BIRON, Louise .... 518-255-5623 318 F
bironl@cobleskill.edu
BIROS, Demetra .... 425-739-8315 480 D
demetra.biros@lwtech.edu
BIRSCHBACH,
Bianca, Y .... 920-923-7619 492 D
bybirschbach76@marianuniversity.edu
BIRTLEY, Ariel .... 360-475-7814 481 B
abirtley@olympic.edu
BIRX, Donald, L .... 603-535-2210 274 B
dlbirx@plymouth.edu
BISANTZ, Ann, M .... 716-645-8989 315 F
bisantz@buffalo.edu
BISBEE, Karin .... 717-796-5220 389 F
kbisbee@messiah.edu
BISBEE, Nina .... 610-526-7935 378 J
nbisbee@brynmawr.edu
BISBEE, Yolanda .... 208-885-2468 132 C
yobiz@uidaho.edu
BISCARI, Janine .... 516-323-3000 306 I
BISCEGLIE, Kara .... 504-280-6990 189 F
kmbisceg@uno.edu
BISCHOFF, Richard, W . 216-368-5445 349 B
richard.bischoff@case.edu
BISCHOFF, Scott .... 831-656-1998 501 K
scott.bischoff@nps.edu
BISCOE, Belinda, P .... 405-325-0473 370 J
bpbiscoe@ou.edu
BISESE, Stephen, D ...... 804-289-8615 471 E
sbisese@richmond.edu
BISH, Courtney, D .... 315-386-7120 319 E
bish@canton.edu
BISH, Dennis .... 724-589-2186 398 F
dbish@thiel.edu
BISH, Gregory .... 585-567-9524 301 G
greg.bish@houghton.edu
BISH, Kevin .... 859-858-2272 178 G
BISH, Nathan .... 724-357-3809 393 G
nathan.bish@iup.edu
BISHKO, David .... 907-474-7700.. 10 B
dbishko@alaska.edu
BISHKO, David .... 907-450-8200.... 9 I
dbishko@alaska.edu
BISHKO, David .... 907-796-6100.. 10 C
ua-hr@alaska.edu
BISHOP, Ben .... 208-376-7731 130 E
bbishop@boisebible.edu
BISHOP, Brad .... 540-365-4250 466 I
bradbishop@ferrum.edu
BISHOP, Brandan .... 616-222-1954 222 F
brandan.bishop@cornerstone.edu
BISHOP, Carl .... 704-290-5281 337 F
cbishop@spcc.edu
BISHOP, Catherine .... 612-330-1117 233 G
bishopc@augsburg.edu
BISHOP, Chanel .... 773-907-4724 134 N
cbishop13@ccc.edu
BISHOP, Colleen .... 804-828-9914 472 D
cbishop4@vcu.edu
BISHOP, David .... 806-291-3417 457 B
bishopd@wbu.edu
BISHOP, Eric .... 510-659-6200.. 54 J
ebishop@ohlone.edu
BISHOP, Janet .... 909-621-8026.. 37 E
janet.bishop@claremont.edu
BISHOP, Janet .... 909-621-8924.. 37 F
janetbishop@claremont.edu
BISHOP, Jeff .... 770-720-5966 124 E
wjb@reinhardt.edu
BISHOP, Jesse .... 706-368-7776 119 C
jebishop@highlands.edu
BISHOP, Joseph .... 616-554-5687 222 H
joseph.bishop@davenport.edu
BISHOP, Joshua .... 315-781-3900 301 D
bishop@hws.edu
BISHOP, Kara .... 570-941-7400 400 C
kara.bishop@scranton.edu
BISHOP, Kaylee .... 405-789-7661 369 H
kaylee.bishop@swcu.edu
BISHOP, Kim .... 641-782-1413 170 B
kbishop@swcciowa.edu
BISHOP, Kristy .... 724-925-4212 401 H
bishopkr@westmoreland.edu
BISHOP, Laura .... 561-803-2012 105 B
laura_bishop@pba.edu
BISHOP, Melanie .... 314-392-2323 255 H
melanie.bishop@mobap.edu
BISHOP, Michelle .... 870-612-2070.. 23 B
michelle.bishop@uaccb.edu
BISHOP, Nancy .... 803-778-6638 406 A
bishopnw@cctech.edu
BISHOP, Penny .... 207-581-1865 196 D
BISHOP, Rebekah .... 931-221-1277 416 H
bishopr@apsu.edu
BISHOP, Richard .... 209-476-7840.. 67 D
rbishop@clc.edu
BISHOP, Robert, H .... 813-974-3864 111 B
robertbishop@usf.edu
BISHOP, Sandy .... 715-365-4564 498 D
sbishop@nicoletcollege.edu
BISHOP, Sasha .... 843-470-8396 411 G
sbishop@tcl.edu
BISHOP, Steve .... 601-276-3701 248 D
bishop@smcc.edu
BISHOP, Valerie .... 601-484-8642 246 B
vbishop@meridiancc.edu
BISHOP, William .... 916-278-7469.. 33 A
william.bishop@csus.edu
BISHOP -SAMUELS,
Kellei .... 334-724-4777.... 7 D
ksamuels@tuskegee.edu
BISHOP BENTLEY,
Ember .... 478-471-2723 122 D
ember.bentley@mga.edu
BISIGNANO, Chris .... 914-251-6530 318 E
chris.bisignanoi@purchase.edu
BISKUPIAK, Walter, H .. 406-447-5521 262 E
bbiskupi@carroll.edu
BISPING, Timothy .... 936-468-3101 444 H
bispingto@sfasu.edu
BISSELL, Monika .... 207-795-2846 194 H
bisselmo@mchp.edu
BISSELL, Sally .... 419-783-2366 351 J
sbissell@defiance.edu
BISSEN, Randi .... 712-325-3428 167 G
rbissen@iwcc.edu
BISSET, Matthew, S ...... 727-864-8482.. 98 G
bissetms@eckerd.edu
BISSET, William .... 703-284-1646 468 A
william.bisset@marymount.edu
BISSINGER, Mary .... 805-482-2755.. 59 G
mbissinger@stjohnsem.edu
BISSON, Heather .... 301-243-2093 501 J
heather.heartley@dodiis.mil
BISSONETTE, David .... 218-855-8178 237 C
david.bissonette@clcmn.edu
BISSONETTE, Matt .... 507-280-3152 240 B
matt.bissonette@rctc.edu
BISSONNETTE, Ali .... 530-541-4660.. 47 H
bissonnette@ltcc.edu
BISSONNETTE, Mignon . 954-262-7239 104M
mbissonnet@nova.edu
BISSOONDIAL, Laxmi ... 508-929-8543 213 D
lbissoondial@worcester.edu
BISWAS, Harun .... 678-466-4240 117 A
harunbiswas@clayton.edu
BISWAS, Pratim .... 305-284-5986 112 K
pbiswas@miami.edu
BITNER, Scott .... 410-706-3822 202 F
sbitner@umaryland.edu
BITNER, Teddy .... 816-322-0110 250 E
teddy.bitner@calvary.edu
BITSÓI, LeManuel .... 781-736-4411 207 D
lbitsoi@brandeis.edu
BITTEL, Jill .... 412-809-5250 395 F
bittel.jill@ptcollege.edu
BITTER, Michael .... 808-932-7095 129 A
bitter@hawaii.edu
BITTERBAUM, Erik, J .... 607-753-2201 317 D
erik.bitterbaum@cortland.edu
BITTERMAN, Kevin .... 336-770-1442 343 C
bittermank@uncsa.edu
BITTINGER, Dale .... 410-455-2278 202 G
bittinger@umbc.edu
BITTINGER, Sara Beth .. 301-687-3130 203 F
sbittinger@frostburg.edu
BITTLE, Tyler .... 501-882-8936.. 17 H
tdbittle@asub.edu
BITTNER, Lauren .... 605-626-2550 415 H
lauren.bittner@northern.edu
BITTON, Yoram .... 513-824-2261 300 H
ybitton@huc.edu
BITTORF, David, C .... 240-500-2266 199 A
dcbittorf@hagerstowncc.edu
BITTRICH, Meredith ...... 508-289-3379 220 B
meredith.bittrich@whoi.edu
BITZER, Michelle .... 715-682-1484 493 G
mbitzer@northland.edu
BITZER, Steve .... 715-685-3034 498 G
steve.bitzer@northwoodtech.edu
BIUNDO, Rachel .... 804-594-1479 473 B
rbiundo@jtcc.edu
BIVINS, B. Peyton .... 806-371-5324 428 F
bpbivins@actx.edu
BIVINS, Chip .... 205-348-5260.... 7 F
cbivins@uasystem.edu
BIVINS, Christy .... 706-754-7772 123 C
cbivins@northgatech.edu
BIVINS, Dallas .... 480-941-1993.. 43 G
dallasbivins@gs.edu
BIXBY, David, E .... 626-815-5334.. 26 K
dbixby@apu.edu
BIXBY, Gary .... 610-436-3200 394 F
gbixby@wcupa.edu
BIXEL, Patricia .... 207-941-7104 194 D
bixelp@husson.edu
BIXLER, David .... 325-942-2169 450 B
david.bixler@angelo.edu
BIXLER, Kirk, J .... 317-738-8803 155 A
kbixler@franklincollege.edu
BIXLER, Luke .... 909-388-6900.. 60 D
BIXLER, Sharon, G .... 859-858-3511 178 H
sharon.bixler@asbury.edu
BIZOT, Kenny .... 601-925-3819 246 D
kbizot@mc.edu
BIZOUKAS, Tim .... 630-466-7900 152 H
tbizoukas@waubonsee.edu
BIZZARRO, Deana .... 518-458-5373 296 E
bizzarrd@strose.edu
BJELLA, Traci, A .... 407-582-1016 113 C
tbjella@valenciacollege.edu
BJELLAND, David .... 320-762-4407 236 G
davidb@alextech.edu
BJERKE, Abby .... 608-663-2309 491 F
abjerke@edgewood.edu
BJERKLIE, J. R .... 607-431-4997 300 G
bjerkliej@hartwick.edu
BJERKLIE, Joseph .... 607-431-4997 300 G
bjerkliej@hartwick.edu
BJERKLIE-BARRY, Jane . 603-641-7371 273 C
jberkliebarry@anselm.edu
BJOKNE, Daniel, H .... 515-964-0601 166 A
bjokned@faith.edu
BJORDAHL, Julia .... 509-313-6102 479 E
bjordahl@gonzaga.edu
BJORGAN, Heather .... 309-796-5340 133 D
bjorganh@bhc.edu
BJORGE, Erin-Joy .... 425-889-5760 481 A
erin-joy.bjorge@northwestu.edu

© COPYRIGHT HIGHER EDUCATION PUBLICATIONS, INC. 2022

BJORK, Johanna .... 208-792-2395 131 F
jcbjork@lcsc.edu
BJORK, Ross .... 979-845-5129 446 B
feedback@athletics.tamu.edu
BJORN, Thorr, D .... 401-874-5245 404 E
tbjorn@uri.edu
BJORNSTAD,
Christopher, S .... 770-394-8300 114 J
BJORNSTAD,
Halcyon, D .... 319-352-8409 170 F
halcyon.bjornstad@wartburg.edu
BJORNSTAD, Thomas ... 414-229-3298 495 B
bjornsta@uwm.edu
BJUNE, Stephanie ...... 979-458-6000 445 D
sbjune@tamus.edu
BLAAKMAN, Michelle ... 585-594-6837 311 L
blaakman_michelle@roberts.edu
BLACHE, Corinne .... 225-771-4680 190 J
corinne_blache@sus.edu
BLACHE, Corinne .... 225-771-4680 190 K
corinne_blache@sus.edu
BLACHFORD, Charles ... 215-368-5000 389 G
cblachford@missio.edu
BLACK, Adam .... 801-863-6378 460 A
blackad@uvu.edu
BLACK, Adrian .... 410-617-2000 199 G
abblack@loyola.edu
BLACK, Angela .... 479-968-0417.. 18 E
ablack9@atu.edu
BLACK, Ann .... 505-428-1811 287 H
ann.black@sfcc.edu
BLACK, April .... 405-789-7661 369 H
april.black@swcu.edu
BLACK, Bernadette .... 619-644-7100.. 44 H
bernadette.black@gcccd.edu
BLACK, Carrie .... 813-988-5131.. 99 M
blackc@floridacollege.edu
BLACK, Chantel .... 509-533-7067 478 D
chantel.black@scc.spokane.edu
BLACK, Connie .... 208-562-3252 131 C
connieblack@cwi.edu
BLACK, David, R .... 920-565-1101 492 A
blackdr@lakeland.edu
BLACK, Diane .... 251-442-2209.... 8 C
dblack@umobile.edu
BLACK, Downey .... 318-345-9297 188 A
harryblack@ladelta.edu
BLACK, Ellen .... 843-349-5211 409 A
ellen.black@hgtc.edu
BLACK, Eric .... 540-828-5487 464 C
eblack@bridgewater.edu
BLACK, Erynn .... 803-508-7337 405 C
blacke@atc.edu
BLACK, G.L .... 615-322-7311 427 B
BLACK, Gary .... 440-826-2900 348 C
gblack@bw.edu
BLACK, Heather .... 712-749-2656 164 A
blackh@bvu.edu
BLACK, Janet, M .... 303-963-3357.. 78 D
jblack@ccu.edu
BLACK, Jason .... 205-726-3673.... 6 E
jjblack@samford.edu
BLACK, Jeremy .... 864-424-8081 412 H
jdblack@mailbox.sc.edu
BLACK, Jessica .... 205-726-2487.... 6 E
jblack@samford.edu
BLACK, Joann .... 936-468-2201 444 H
blackjoann@sfasu.edu
BLACK, John .... 248-689-8282 231 E
jblack@walshcollege.edu
BLACK, John Paul .... 252-527-6223 335 E
jpblack73@lenoircc.edu
BLACK, Joshua .... 864-941-8542 410 D
black.j@ptc.edu
BLACK, Joshua .... 423-614-8370 419 H
jblack@leeuniversity.edu
BLACK, Katherine, A ..... 860-768-4505.. 89 E
kablack@hartford.edu
BLACK, Kedric .... 801-863-8536 460 A
kedric.black@uvu.edu
BLACK, Kevin .... 717-531-4803 391 F
kpb4@psu.edu
BLACK, Kim .... 970-351-1102.. 84 D
kim.black@unco.edu
BLACK, Laura .... 505-566-3837 287 G
blackl@sanjuancollege.edu
BLACK, Lendley, C .... 218-726-7106 243 A
chan@d.umn.edu
BLACK, Linda .... 207-288-5015 194 C
BLACK, Lisa .... 903-510-2417 451 D
lisa.black@tjc.edu
BLACK, Lynda, K .... 336-838-6148 338 H
lkblack932@wilkescc.edu
BLACK, Mary .... 217-424-6220 144 D
mblack@millikin.edu
BLACK, Matthew .... 606-337-3196 180 A
BLACK, Michael, M .... 229-333-7838 127 C
mmblack@valdosta.edu
BLACK, Richard .... 915-215-4320 450 E
richard.black@ttuhsc.edu
BLACK, Rochelle, A ...... 248-370-3658 229 F
black@oakland.edu
BLACK, Sara .... 864-977-2094 410 A
sara.black@ngu.edu
BLACK, Shaun, C .... 315-445-4569 303 F
blacksc@lemoyne.edu
BLACK, Sul .... 803-934-3419 409 H
sulblack@morris.edu
BLACK, Susan .... 903-983-8236 437 G
sblack@kilgore.edu
BLACK, Tanja .... 864-424-8080 412 H
trblack@mailbox.sc.edu
BLACK HUDGINS, Carri 386-506-3000.. 98 A
BLACK-PATEL, Jennifer . 706-419-1136 117 G
jennifer.blackpatel@covenant.edu
BLACKABY, Leslie .... 509-574-6806 485 E
lblackaby@yvcc.edu
BLACKBURN, Amanda .. 404-835-6114 422 D
ablackburn@richmont.edu
BLACKBURN, Amber ..... 336-838-6419 338 H
alblackburn893@wilkescc.edu
BLACKBURN, Brenda .... 828-694-1773 332 C
bc_blackburn@blueridge.edu
BLACKBURN, Brian .... 919-658-7889 340 E
bblackburn@umo.edu
BLACKBURN, Fred .... 619-201-8780.. 60 G
fred.blackburn@sdcc.edu
BLACKBURN, J. Blair .... 903-923-2222 435 A
bblackburn@etbu.edu
BLACKBURN, James ..... 404-413-2000 120 C
BLACKBURN, Jan .... 706-437-6811 115 H
jan.blackburn@augustatech.edu
BLACKBURN,
Jessamine .... 217-786-3441 142 F
jessie.blackburn@llcc.edu
BLACKBURN, JR .... 614-292-2424 358 E
blackburn.23@osu.edu
BLACKBURN, Kellye ...... 318-274-3350 191 G
blackburnk@gram.edu
BLACKBURN, Kristi .... 323-241-5218.. 49 I
blackbkv@lasc.edu
BLACKBURN, Lisa .... 606-218-5296 185 F
lisablackburn@upike.edu
BLACKBURN, Mark .... 605-274-4124 413 G
mark.blackburn@augie.edu
BLACKBURN, Sean .... 605-626-3007 415 H
sean.blackburn@northern.edu
BLACKBURN-SMITH,
Jefferson .... 614-823-1031 359 G
jblackburnsmith@otterbein.edu
BLACKETER, Leslie .... 409-772-1304 456 B
lmblacke@utmb.edu
BLACKFORD, Ben .... 660-562-1282 256 G
blkfrd@nwmissouri.edu
BLACKFORD, Devin, K .. 260-422-5561 156 A
dkblackford@indianatech.edu
BLACKHURST, Anne ...... 218-477-2243 239 A
anne.blackhurst@mnstate.edu
BLACKIE, Crisanne .... 207-581-1359 196 D
cblackie@maine.edu
BLACKINGTON,
Christopher .... 603-427-7600 271 J
BLACKLANCE, Charles .. 218-855-8119 237 C
charles.blacklance@clcmn.edu
BLACKLAW, Stuart .... 412-237-8182 381 C
sblacklaw@ccac.edu
BLACKMAN, Bret .... 402-554-2227 269 C
bblackman@unomaha.edu
BLACKMAN, Bret, R ...... 402-554-2227 268 I
bblackman@nebraska.edu
BLACKMAN, Cheryl, H ... 301-860-3257 203 D
cblackman@bowiestate.edu
BLACKMER, Jennifer ..... 765-285-2783 153 E
jsblackmer@bsu.edu
BLACKMON, Bruce .... 704-687-7010 342 C
ablackm8@uncc.edu
BLACKMON, Jamie .... 256-352-8461.... 4 A
jamie.blackmon@wallacestate.edu
BLACKMON, Luke .... 843-863-8004 406 C
lblackmon@csuniv.edu
BLACKMON, Paul .... 334-420-4461.... 3 H
pblackmon@trenholmstate.edu
BLACKMON, Terry, W ... 731-426-7601 419 G
tblackmon@lanecollege.edu
BLACKMORE, Lee .... 307-754-6067 500 G
lee.blackmore@nwc.edu
BLACKSHER DIABATE,
Dafina .... 484-365-7785 388 F
ddiabate@lincoln.edu
BLACKSMITH, Lourdes .. 847-214-7274 137 D
lblacksmith@elgin.edu
BLACKSON, Ginny .... 503-883-2517 373 E
gblackson@linfield.edu
BLACKSTON, Darren ..... 302-857-6143.. 90 D
dblackston@desu.edu
BLACKSTON, Misty .... 912-650-6233 125 D
mblackston@southuniversity.edu
BLACKSTONE, Barbara .. 207-768-9415 196 I
barbara.blackstone@maine.edu
BLACKWELDER,
Mark, A .... 731-989-6624 418 H
mblackwelder@fhu.edu
BLACKWELDER, Megan . 847-467-1730 146 C
megan.blackwelder@northwestern.edu
BLACKWELL, Amy .... 864-294-3496 408 I
amy.blackwell@furman.edu
BLACKWELL, Barbara .... 314-275-3521 147 B
barbara.blackwell@principia.edu
BLACKWELL,
Deborah, L .... 956-326-2628 446 A
dblackwell@tamiu.edu
BLACKWELL, Jody .... 405-912-9463 368 H
jblackwell@ru.edu
BLACKWELL, Joe .... 405-789-7661 369 H
joe.blackwell@swcu.edu
BLACKWELL, Joshua ..... 763-488-0236 239 D
joshua.blackwell@nhcc.edu
BLACKWELL, Karen ...... 336-256-0396 342 D
kmblackw@uncg.edu
BLACKWELL, Mark .... 860-768-4103.. 89 E
blackwell@hartford.edu
BLACKWELL, Rachelle ... 817-257-5920 447 H
r.blackwell@tcu.edu
BLACKWELL, Tiffiny ...... 864-646-1492 411 H
tblackw7@tctc.edu
BLACKWELL, Tonya, L .. 434-971-3303 501 G
tanya.l.blackwell4.mil@army.mil
BLACKWOOD, David ..... 575-392-6561 288 I
BLACKWOOD, Edwin ..... 412-731-6000 396 D
eblackwood@rpts.edu
BLACKWOOD, James .... 706-880-8050 121 K
jblackwood@lagrange.edu
BLACKWOOD, Jothany .. 615-366-1505 423 A
BLAD, Cory .... 718-862-7345 304 K
cory.blad@manhattan.edu
BLADE, Michael .... 541-463-5566 373 C
bladem@lanecc.edu
BLAETTNER, Wendy ...... 830-792-7212 442 G
careerdevelopment@schreiner.edu
BLAGUSZEWSKI,
Edward, F .... 413-545-0444 211 D
edblag@admin.umass.edu
BLAHNIK, Brent .... 920-465-2190 494 F
blahnikb@uwgb.edu
BLAHNIK, Hannah, K .... 651-628-3332 243 E
hkblahnik@unwsp.edu
BLAHNIK, Jeffrey, J ...... 405-325-2151 370 J
jblahnik@ou.edu
BLAICH, Charles, F .... 765-361-6311 162 G
blaichc@wabash.edu
BLAIN, Judy .... 931-221-7691 416 H
blainj@apsu.edu
BLAIR, Alan .... 413-572-5582 213 C
alan@westfield.ma.edu
BLAIR, Audrey, D .... 563-333-6364 169 D
blairaudreyd@sau.edu
BLAIR, Austin .... 309-624-8980 148 G
BLAIR, Brian .... 202-885-2842.. 91 D
bblair@american.edu
BLAIR, Brian .... 267-502-2407 378 I
brian.blair@brynathyn.edu
BLAIR, Bryan .... 419-530-4987 363 B
bryan.blair@utoledo.edu
BLAIR, Caroline .... 616-234-4164 224 C
carolineblair@grcc.edu
BLAIR, Chastity .... 901-321-3552 417 G
cblair3@cbu.edu
BLAIR, Cinnamon .... 505-277-1806 288 C
cblair@unm.edu
BLAIR, Daniel .... 978-556-3820 215 C
dblair@necc.mass.edu
BLAIR, Darren .... 815-939-5265 146 F
dblair1@olivet.edu
BLAIR, Douglas .... 574-239-8380 155 E
dblair@hcc-nd.edu
BLAIR, Elaine .... 219-473-4218 154 A
eblair@ccsj.edu
BLAIR, Eric .... 816-415-5217 261 G
blaire@william.jewell.edu
BLAIR, Jeff .... 614-251-4735 358 B
blairj@ohiodominican.edu
BLAIR, Jesse .... 307-778-1340 500 D
jblair@lccc.wy.edu
BLAIR, Jim .... 925-969-2025.. 40 H
jblair@dvc.edu
BLAIR, John Paul .... 270-745-6520 186 A
jp.blair@wku.edu
BLAIR, Julie .... 713-646-1793 443 C
jblair@stcl.edu
BLAIR, Kathryn .... 207-453-5000 195 B
kblair@kvcc.me.edu
BLAIR, Kimberly, P .... 540-375-2592 469 G
kblair@roanoke.edu
BLAIR, Kristine .... 412-396-6388 382 E
blairk2@duq.edu
BLAIR, Lisa .... 785-890-3641 176 E
lisa.blair@nwktc.edu
BLAIR, Matthew .... 605-225-1634 414 I
matthew.blair@presentation.edu
BLAIR, Neil, B .... 913-253-5090 177 A
neil.blair@spst.edu
BLAIR, Patti .... 805-652-5502.. 73 H
pblair@vcccd.edu
BLAIR, Paul, G .... 574-372-5100 155 C
blairp@grace.edu
BLAIR, Robbie, M .... 806-716-2336 443 A
rblair@southplainscollege.edu
BLAIR, Sara, B .... 734-764-9290 231 A
sbblair@umich.edu
BLAIR, Selena, S .... 864-488-4394 409 C
ssblair@limestone.edu
BLAIR, Shelly .... 714-241-6251.. 38 D
sblair12@coastline.edu
BLAIR, Thomas, A .... 770-216-2960 121 F
tab@ict.edu
BLAIR, JR., Thomas, S 540-375-2235 469 G
blair@roanoke.edu
BLAIR, Wray .... 419-289-5118 347 H
wblair@ashland.edu
BLAIR, Zulema .... 718-270-6127 294 E
zblair@mec.cuny.edu
BLAISDELL, John .... 845-575-3000 305 C
john.blaisdell@marist.edu
BLAISDELL, Stephanie .. 845-257-3260 316 B
blaisdes@newpaltz.edu
BLAKE, Charles, E .... 901-322-0120 416 E
BLAKE, Christopher ...... 478-471-2712 122 D
christopher.blake@mga.edu
BLAKE, Christopher, T .. 631-451-4283 321 A
blakec@sunysuffolk.edu
BLAKE, Corey .... 251-626-3303.... 7 E
cblake@ussa.edu
BLAKE, Dave .... 619-239-0391.. 34 H
dblake@cwsl.edu
BLAKE, David .... 912-525-5000 124 G
dblake@scad.edu
BLAKE, Debbie, G .... 410-651-8382 203 B
dgblake@umes.edu
BLAKE, Karen .... 203-575-8269.. 86 H
kblake@nv.edu
BLAKE, Keiana .... 713-718-5059 436 E
keiana.blake@hccs.edu
BLAKE, Laurie .... 340-776-9200 512 B
lblake@uvi.edu
BLAKE, Lawrence .... 651-962-6561 243 F
blak0035@stthomas.edu
BLAKE, M. Brian .... 404-413-1300 120 C
president@gsu.edu
BLAKE, Melody, A .... 478-757-5229 127 D
mblake@wesleyancollege.edu
BLAKE, Monique .... 954-201-6455.. 96 F
mblake@broward.edu
BLAKE, Nicquet .... 415-514-2440.. 70 D
nicquet.blake@ucsf.edu
BLAKE, Reginald .... 718-260-5560 294 F
rblake@citytech.cuny.edu
BLAKE, Scott .... 906-487-7242 223 I
scott.blake@finlandia.edu
BLAKE, Susan .... 828-327-7000 332 H
skillian@cvcc.edu
BLAKELY, Christopher .. 239-590-7900 109 G
cblakely@fgcu.edu
BLAKELY, Colette .... 541-969-3088 373 G
colette.blakely@mtangel.edu
BLAKELY, Craig, H .... 502-852-3297 185 E
crag.blakely@louisville.edu
BLAKELY, Dedria, A ...... 573-334-6825 258 I
dblakely@sehcollege.edu
BLAKEMORE, Arthur ..... 480-965-9032.. 11 A
arthur.blakemore@asu.edu
BLAKEMORE, Jerry, D .. 336-334-3067 342 D
j_blakem@uncg.edu

Index of Key Administrators BLAKEMORE – BLOCKETT 549

BLAKEMORE, Molly ...... 707-476-4254.. 58 I
molly-blakemore@redwoods.edu
BLAKEMORE, Patricia ... 401-739-5000 403 F
pblakemore@neit.edu
BLAKENEY, Erin .... 425-352-8534 477 F
eblakeney@cascadia.edu
BLAKENEY, Nicolas .... 210-486-3777 428 B
nblakeney@alamo.edu
BLAKES, Cara .... 205-226-4727.... 5 A
clblakes@bsc.edu
BLAKESLEE, Amber .... 707-826-5702.. 30 A
amber.blakeslee@humboldt.edu
BLAKEY, Linda .... 734-973-3606 232 A
lblakey@wccnet.edu
BLAKLEY, Jacquelyn ..... 864-646-1305 411 H
jblakle1@tctc.edu
BLAKLEY, Linda .... 312-362-7734 136 F
lblakley@depaul.edu
BLALARK, Frank .... 919-684-2813 328 D
registrar@duke.edu
BLALOCK, John .... 864-488-4615 409 C
jblalock@limestone.edu
BLALOCK, III, W. Ben .. 307-766-3948 500 H
bblalock@uwyo.edu
BLANC, Doug .... 607-729-1581 297 G
dblanc@davisny.edu
BLANCETT, Scott .... 860-444-8352 502 F
BLANCHARD, Gina, A ... 740-392-6868 356 G
gina.blanchard@mvnu.edu
BLANCHARD, Gordon ... 847-578-3232 148 B
gordon.blanchard@rosalindfranklin.edu
BLANCHARD, Jack .... 301-405-8438 202 E
jblancha@umd.edu
BLANCHARD, Jeffrey ..... 201-559-6170 277 A
blanchardj@felician.edu
BLANCHARD, Jon, A ..... 207-768-2795 195 C
jblanch@nmcc.edu
BLANCHARD, Joyce ...... 207-621-3403 196 E
joyceb@maine.edu
BLANCHARD,
Kristen, A .... 302-622-8000.. 90 C
kblanchard@dcad.edu
BLANCHARD, Kym .... 815-921-4015 147 H
k.blanchard@rockvalleycollege.edu
BLANCHARD, Lloyd ...... 860-486-3455.. 89 B
lloyd.blanchard@uconn.edu
BLANCHARD, Lloyd ...... 860-486-0930.. 89 B
lloyd.blanchard@uconn.edu
BLANCHARD, Lloyd ...... 860-486-4240.. 89 B
lloyd.blanchard@uconn.edu
BLANCHARD, Loren, J .. 713-221-8001 452 B
BLANCHARD, Susan ..... 804-278-4204 470 I
sblanchard@upsem.edu
BLANCHARD, Troy .... 225-578-8273 188 K
troy@lsu.edu
BLANCHET, Robert, C ... 315-684-6046 320 E
blanchrc@morrisville.edu
BLANCHETT, Russell ..... 972-882-7520 446 D
russell.blanchett@tamuc.edu
BLANCHETT, Wanda ...... 848-932-7496 281 B
wanda.blanchett@gse.rutgers.edu
BLANCHETTE, Dawn ...... 401-598-1857 403 E
dawn.blanchette@jwu.edu
BLANCHETTE, Jennifer .. 815-802-8816 141 B
jblanchette@kcc.edu
BLANCHETTE, Nick .... 715-675-3331 498 E
blanchet@ntc.edu
BLANCHIER, Andree ...... 530-242-7511.. 64 A
ablanchier@shastacollege.edu
BLANCK, Mark .... 913-758-6326 177 I
mark.blanck@stmary.edu
BLANCO, Cynthia .... 956-872-2112 443 B
cblanco9@southtexascollege.edu
BLANCO, Eva .... 408-554-5251.. 63 A
eblanco@scu.edu
BLAND,
Bartholomew, F .... 718-960-8731 293 E
bartholomew.bland@lehman.cuny.edu
BLAND, Carmen .... 360-676-2772 480 G
cbland@nwic.edu
BLAND, Dee .... 509-434-5060 478 C
dee.bland@ccs.spokane.edu
BLAND, Jacob .... 501-332-0235.. 18 D
jbland@asutr.edu
BLAND, James .... 937-393-3431 360 G
jbland@sscc.edu
BLAND, Janet, L .... 740-376-4741 355 E
janet.bland@marietta.edu
BLAND, Marissa .... 816-415-5938 261 G
blandm@william.jewell.edu
BLAND, Mary .... 330-569-5080 353 F
blandme@hiram.edu
BLAND, Sharon .... 240-567-3080 200 E
sharon.bland@montgomerycollege.edu
BLAND, Tamara .... 708-524-6386 137 A
tbland@dom.edu
BLAND, Terry .... 662-862-8282 245 F
tgbland@iccms.edu
BLANDFORD, David, K . 989-463-7147 220 F
blandford@alma.edu
BLANDFORD,
Jonathan, W .... 502-272-7404 179 D
jblandford@bellarmine.edu
BLANDIZZI, Maria, Q ... 209-946-2011.. 71 E
BLANDON, Darwin .... 423-648-2678 422 D
dblandon@richmont.edu
BLANK, Dave, L .... 336-278-6705 328 H
dblank@elon.edu
BLANK, Lisa .... 928-226-7625.. 12 B
lisa.blank@coconino.edu
BLANK, Michelle .... 260-665-4179 161 C
blankm@trine.edu
BLANK, Natalia .... 716-829-8124 298 C
blankn@dyc.edu
BLANKE, Raymond .... 405-733-7306 369 D
rblanke@rose.edu
BLANKENBAKER,
Zarina .... 817-515-7750 445 A
zarina.blankenbaker@tccd.edu
BLANKENBUEHLER,
Carla .... 304-205-6706 487 D
carla.blankenbuehler@bridgevalley.edu
BLANKENHEIM, Kim ..... 319-368-6464 168 D
kblankenheim@mtmercy.edu
BLANKENSHIP,
Bryan, P .... 859-858-2228 178 G
BLANKENSHIP, Daniel .. 785-628-4234 173 E
djblankenship@fhsu.edu
BLANKENSHIP, Karen ... 281-476-1850 442 C
karen.blankenship@sjcd.edu
BLANKENSHIP, Kevin ... 615-230-3428 424 F
kevin.blankenship@volstate.edu
BLANKENSHIP, Khali ... 304-829-7064 486 B
kblankenship@bethanywv.edu
BLANKENSHIP,
Mark, V .... 859-280-1250 183 C
mblankenship@lextheo.edu
BLANKENSHIP, Michael 585-567-9554 301 G
michael.blankenship@houghton.edu
BLANKENSHIP, Michael 910-592-8081 337 D
mblankenship@sampsoncc.edu
BLANKENSHIP,
Michelle .... 212-343-1234 306 C
mblankenship@mcny.edu
BLANKENSHIP, Mike .... 601-605-3315 245 E
mblankenship@holmescc.edu
BLANKENSHIP, Paul, D 407-582-5415 113 C
pblankenship1@valenciacollege.edu
BLANKENSHIP, Randy .. 419-755-4767 357 B
rblankenship@ncstatecollege.edu
BLANKENSHIP, Rosalie . 765-658-4211 154 G
rosalieblankenship@depauw.edu
BLANKENSHIP, Ruth ..... 276-326-4556 464 A
rblankenship@bluefield.edu
BLANKENSHIP, Vince ... 903-923-2002 435 A
vblankenship@etbu.edu
BLANKMEYER,
Bonnie, L .... 210-567-2691 455 E
blankmeyer@uthscsa.edu
BLANSON, Archie .... 281-765-7999 438 E
archie.blanson@lonestar.edu
BLANTON, Angela .... 412-268-6011 380 B
ablanton@andrew.cmu.edu
BLANTON, Emily .... 870-230-5000.. 19 H
BLANTON, James .... 205-929-6317.... 2 H
jblanton@lawsonstate.edu
BLANTON, Jay, D .... 859-257-6605 185 D
jay.blanton@uky.edu
BLANTON, Julie .... 620-665-3510 174 D
BLANTON, Kristin .... 704-669-4004 333 C
blantonk@clevelandcc.edu
BLANTON, Michael .... 213-740-4577.. 73 C
michael.blanton@usc.edu
BLANTON, Michelle ...... 740-474-8896 358 A
mblanton@ohiochristian.edu
BLANTON, Ryan .... 580-349-1550 367 F
rblanton@opsu.edu
BLANTON, Sharon .... 609-771-3353 275 J
blantons@tcnj.edu
BLASCHKE, Jayme, L .... 512-245-2180 449 G
jb71@txstate.edu
BLASDEL, Amy .... 618-537-6330 143 G
bookstores@mckendree.edu
BLASE, Kristen .... 603-428-2226 272 I
kblase@nec.edu
BLASER, Martin, J .... 848-445-9834 281 B
blaser@cabm.rutgers.edu
BLASHAK, Ted .... 800-995-3159 262 A
BLASINI, Ivelisse .... 787-850-9328 511 B
ivelisse.blasini@upr.edu
BLASZCZAK, SJ,
Gerry, R .... 203-254-4000.. 87 G
gblaszczak@fairfield.edu
BLATCHFORD, Alicia ..... 305-284-5155 112 K
awb49@miami.edu
BLATT, Evelynne .... 610-625-7854 390 D
blatte@moravian.edu
BLATT, Keath .... 212-678-8000 303 A
keblatt@jtsa.edu
BLATT, Shannon .... 972-721-4135 451 E
sblatt1@udallas.edu
BLATTNER, Allan .... 919-962-5401 342 B
allan_blattner@unc.edu
BLATTNER, Carolyn .... 919-508-2048 344 D
cmblattner@peace.edu
BLATTNER, Nancy .... 314-889-1419 252 G
nblattner@fontbonne.edu
BLAU, Mendel .... 718-774-3430 292 D
BLAUFUSS, Mary .... 314-918-2537 252 E
mblaufuss@eden.edu
BLAYLOCK, Andrew .... 217-786-4533 142 F
andrew.blaylock@llcc.edu
BLAYLOCK, Arlene .... 240-567-7308 200 E
arlene.blaylock@montgomerycollege.
edu
BLAYLOCK, Jennifer ...... 501-812-2864.. 23 E
jblaylock@uaptc.edu
BLAYLOCK, Reginald, S 909-869-3805.. 30 B
rsblaylock@cpp.edu
BLAZEI, Tari .... 414-288-5163 492 E
theresa.blazei@marquette.edu
BLAZEK, Brent .... 816-501-4375 257 K
brent.blazek@rockhurst.edu
BLAZER, Joshua .... 415-955-2100.. 25 A
BLAZER, Lisa .... 314-496-7080 261 D
lisablazer@webster.edu
BLAZEY, Jerry .... 815-753-1883 145 H
gblazey@niu.edu
BLAZIS, Enoch .... 507-786-3002 242 I
blazis@stolaf.edu
BLEA, Kimberly .... 505-454-3566 286 C
kjvaldez@nmhu.edu
BLEAM, Holly .... 570-321-4041 388 H
bleam@lycoming.edu
BLECHMAN, Mindy .... 215-635-7300 384 D
mblechman@gratz.edu
BLECHSCHMIDT,
Allison .... 610-625-7912 390 D
blechschmidta@moravian.edu
BLEDSOE, Chad, A .... 910-898-9601 336 A
bledsoec@montgomery.edu
BLEDSOE, Christopher .. 212-998-2040 309 D
christopher.bledsoe@nyu.edu
BLEDSOE, D'Awana .... 601-977-7919 248 E
dlbledsoe@tougaloo.edu
BLEDSOE, Gary, L .... 713-313-1071 448 D
gary.bledsoe@tmslaw.tsu.edu
BLEDSOE, Jennifer .... 423-472-7141 423 C
jbledsoe01@clevelandstatecc.edu
BLEDSOE, Mary .... 817-515-6792 445 A
mary.bledsoe@tccd.edu
BLEDSOE, W. Craig .... 615-966-1789 420 B
craig.bledsoe@lipscomb.edu
BLEE, Kathleen, M .... 412-624-6094 400 A
kblee@pitt.edu
BLEEKER, Josh .... 303-357-5817.. 80 G
josh.bleeker@denverseminary.edu
BLEGEN, Mark .... 262-524-7364 491 A
mglegen@carrollu.edu
BLEHAR, Timothy .... 315-470-6611 319 A
tmblehar@esf.edu
BLEHM, Heidi .... 360-385-4948 480 H
heidi.blehm@nwswb.edu
BLEIBDREY, Jarod .... 361-354-2339 431 L
jbleibdrey@coastalbend.edu
BLEIFIELD, Elaina .... 651-450-3618 237 H
elaina.bleifield@inverhills.edu
BLEMINGS, Kenneth, P . 304-293-2100 489 E
ken.blemings@mail.wvu.edu
BLENIS, Brian .... 484-664-3631 390 F
brianblenis@muhlenberg.edu
BLESSO, Thomas .... 480-947-6644.. 15 B
thomas.blesso@pennfoster.edu
BLEVINS, Beth .... 417-690-2438 250 K
eblevins@cofo.edu
BLEVINS, Bob .... 601-318-6155 249 B
bblevins@wmcarey.edu
BLEVINS, Brooke .... 208-885-7921 132 C
bblevins@uidaho.edu
BLEVINS, Donna .... 907-563-7575.... 9 E
donna.blevins@alaskacareercollege.edu
BLEVINS, Elisabeth .... 336-838-6145 338 H
ekblevins580@wilkescc.edu
BLEVINS, Elizabeth .... 740-351-3112 360 E
eblevins@shawnee.edu
BLEVINS, Justin .... 859-257-4784 185 D
j.blevins@uky.edu
BLEVINS, Karen .... 606-326-2063 180 I
karen.blevins@kctcs.edu
BLEVINS, Keisha .... 313-593-5252 231 B
kgipson@umich.edu
BLEVINS, N. Leann .... 615-547-1357 418 C
lblevins@cumberland.edu
BLEVINS,
Phillip Andrew .... 479-575-7330.. 21 H
blevins@uark.edu
BLEVINS, Rick .... 785-442-6111 174 C
rblevins@highlandcc.edu
BLEVINS, Ryan .... 219-464-5411 162 C
ryan.blevins@valpo.edu
BLEVINS, Scarlett .... 276-944-6229 466 F
scblevins@ehc.edu
BLEW, Chad .... 405-744-6604 367 G
chad.blew@okstate.edu
BLEWETT, Patrick, A ..... 530-226-4144.. 64 C
pblewett@simpsonu.edu
BLEWETT, Paul, F .... 805-421-5924.. 67 J
pblewett@thomasaquinas.edu
BLIER, Helen .... 412-924-1346 395 G
hblier@pts.edu
BLIESZNER, Rosemary .. 540-231-6416 475 D
rmb@vt.edu
BLIFFEN, John .... 901-375-4400 421 A
johnbliffen@midsouthchristian.edu
BLIGH, Michelle .... 909-621-8647.. 37 F
michelle.bligh@cgu.edu
BLIGHT, Meaghan, K .... 478-757-5212 127 D
mblight@wesleyancollege.edu
BLINE, David .... 440-943-7600 360 D
dbline@dioceseofcleveland.org
BLINKA, Sonja .... 409-933-8474 432 H
sblinka@com.edu
BLISS, Gretchen .... 719-255-8227.. 84 A
gbliss@uccs.edu
BLISS, Jeremy .... 217-786-4646 142 F
jeremy.bliss@llcc.edu
BLISS, Kathy .... 312-341-3801 148 A
kbliss@roosevelt.edu
BLISS, Nishanga .... 510-666-8248.. 24 G
clinicdirector@aimc.edu
BLITSTEIN, Peter, A ...... 920-832-6528 492 B
peter.a.blitstein@lawrence.edu
BLITZ, Jared .... 206-934-4152 482 G
jared.blitz@seattlecolleges.edu
BLITZ, Y .... 248-968-3360 233 C
BLIWISE, Nancy .... 404-727-7452 118 D
nancy.bliwise@emory.edu
BLIXT-DIAZ, Carrie .... 708-974-5349 144 G
blixtdiasc@morainevalley.edu
BLIZINSKI, Bob .... 626-585-7502.. 56 D
rblizinski@pasadena.edu
BLIZZARD, Angie .... 919-739-6801 338 F
asblizzard@waynecc.edu
BLIZZARD, Mary .... 304-205-6750 487 D
mary.blizzard@bridgevalley.edu
BLIZZARD, Mary .... 304-367-4692 487 H
BLOCHER, Larry .... 334-670-3869.... 7 C
lblocher@troy.edu
BLOCK, Clifford, A .... 989-964-4285 229 L
cablock@svsu.edu
BLOCK, Gene, D .... 310-825-2151.. 69 D
chancellor@conet.ucla.edu
BLOCK, Jayme, E .... 410-543-6156 204 A
jeblock@salisbury.edu
BLOCK, Jennifer, A .... 719-333-4008 502 C
jennifer.block@afacademy.af.edu
BLOCK, Joel .... 212-686-9244 289 G
BLOCK, Kailey .... 970-339-6433.. 77 G
kailey.block@aims.edu
BLOCK, Kelly, J .... 217-244-0102 151 C
kjb@uillinois.edu
BLOCK, Steven .... 956-665-2175 455 A
steven.block@utrgv.edu
BLOCK, William, A .... 423-439-6317 418 D
block@etsu.edu
BLOCKER, Bill .... 832-252-4624 431 M
bill.blocker@cbshouston.edu
BLOCKER, Robert, L ..... 203-432-4160.. 90 B
robert.blocker@yale.edu
BLOCKETT, Charles .... 501-708-0600.. 93 H

BLOCKSIDGE, Katie .... 740-364-9513 349 D
blocksidge.3@osu.edu
BLODGETT, Barbara ...... 412-924-1383 395 G
bblodgett@pts.edu
BLODGETT, Bruce, M .... 315-294-8544 292 A
blodgett@cayuga-cc.edu
BLODGETT, Hannah ...... 916-568-3021.. 50 I
BLODORN, Lori .... 661-654-3206.. 30 C
lblodorn@csub.edu
BLOEBAUM, Christina ... 330-672-2892 354 A
cbloebau@kent.edu
BLOEMKER,
Geraldine, A .... 610-499-4107 401 I
gabloemker@widener.edu
BLOHM, Christopher ..... 985-545-1500 188 B
BLOHM, David .... 410-617-5635 199 G
dblohm@loyola.edu
BLOHM, John .... 337-482-0911 192 F
jib@louisiana.edu
BLOHM, Melvin .... 248-218-2119 229 I
mblohm@rochesteru.edu
BLOHM-THOMPSON,
Amanda .... 270-831-9849 181 F
amanda.blohm@kctcs.edu
BLOM, Alyssa .... 616-988-3624 226 A
ablom@kuyper.edu
BLOMBERG,
Thomas, G .... 850-644-7380 110 B
tblomber@fsu.edu
BLOME, Christian .... 812-481-5918 162 E
cblome@vinu.edu
BLOME, Shelley .... 701-671-2191 346 B
shelley.blome@ndscs.edu
BLOMGREN, Laura .... 610-892-1536 393 B
lblomgren@pit.edu
BLONDE, Mitchell .... 419-448-3584 361 C
blondemp@tiffin.edu
BLONDEL, Elizabeth ...... 312-662-4003 132 D
eblondel@adler.edu
BLONDIN, Jill .... 804-828-8471 472 D
jblondin@vcu.edu
BLONDIN, Jo, A .... 937-328-6001 350 D
blondinj@clarkstate.edu
BLONDIN, Monica, M .. 508-767-7157 205 F
mm.blondin@assumption.edu
BLONIGEN, Bruce .... 541-346-3902 376 G
bruceb@uoregon.edu
BLOOD, Melanie .... 585-245-5952 317 E
blood@geneseo.edu
BLOOM, Deborah .... 802-322-1624 461 D
deborah.bloom@goddard.edu
BLOOM, John, S .... 214-887-5591 434 G
jbloom@dts.edu
BLOOM, Melanie .... 402-554-4989 269 C
melaniebloom@unomaha.edu
BLOOM, Vicki .... 574-520-4448 157 C
vdbloom@iusb.edu
BLOOM, Yvonne .... 314-539-5150 258 C
ybloom1@stlcc.edu
BLOOMBERG, Laura ...... 612-625-0608 242 K
bloom004@umn.edu
BLOOMBERG, Laura, J . 216-687-3583 350 G
laura.bloomberg@csuohio.edu
BLOOMBERG, Steven .... 870-543-5907.. 21 D
sbloomberg@seark.edu
BLOOMER, Dennis, L ... 864-488-4561 409 C
dbloomer@limestone.edu
BLOOMER, Richard, J ... 901-678-4316 426 A
rbloomer@memphis.edu
BLOOMER, Sherm .... 541-737-0123 374 H
BLOOMFIELD, Stewart .. 212-938-5540 319 B
sbloomfield@sunyopt.edu
BLOSHINSKI, John .... 570-422-3631 393 F
jbloshinski@esu.edu
BLOSS, Kim, K .... 870-235-4057.. 21 E
kkbloss@saumag.edu
BLOSSER, Joseph, D .... 336-841-9337 329 E
jblosser@highpoint.edu
BLOSSER, Kim .... 540-868-7101 473 C
kblosser@lfcc.edu
BLOSSER, Rob .... 810-762-9940 225 F
rblosser@kettering.edu
BLOSSOM, Marcus .... 402-280-1435 265 J
marcusblossom@creighton.edu
BLOUCH, Christine .... 309-677-2395 133 H
blouch@fsmail.bradley.edu
BLOUGH, Alisaa .... 805-437-8916.. 30 D
alissa.blough@csuci.edu
BLOUGH, Eric .... 304-696-7302 488 N
blough@marshall.edu
BLOUNT, Amanda .... 863-680-6221 100 F
ablount@flsouthern.edu
BLOUNT, Brian, K .... 804-278-4200 470 I
bblount@upsem.edu
BLOUNT, Lori .... 610-558-5630 390 G
blountl@neumann.edu
BLOUNT, Nicole .... 513-556-3233 361 I
nicole.blount@uc.edu
BLOUNT, Pamela .... 850-412-5072 109 E
pamela.blount@famu.edu
BLOUNT-FENNEY, Alice 201-200-3094 278 F
ablountfenny@njcu.edu
BLOWERS, Amanda .... 315-781-3309 301 D
blowers@hws.edu
BLOWERS, Kelsy .... 218-683-8543 239 E
kelsy.blowers@northlandcollege.edu
BLOYE, Alex .... 231-995-2929 228 F
abloye@nmc.edu
BLUE, Bob .... 318-869-5127 186 C
vpfa@centenary.edu
BLUE, Crystal .... 870-612-2044.. 23 B
crystal.blue@uaccb.edu
BLUE, Janeal .... 805-922-6966.. 24 L
janeal.blue@hancockcollege.edu
BLUE, Jean .... 910-695-3739 337 E
bluej@sandhills.edu
BLUE, Joe .... 270-824-1828 182 A
joe.blue@kctcs.edu
BLUE, Katina .... 910-521-6000 343 A
BLUE, Paula, B .... 585-340-9648 296 B
pblue@crcds.edu
BLUE, Shella .... 847-578-8807 148 B
shella.blue@rosalindfranklin.edu
BLUEBAUGH, Wade ...... 301-687-3175 203 F
ewadebluebaugh@frostburg.edu
BLUEHORSE, Byron ...... 907-474-5439.. 10 B
bdbluehorse@alaska.edu
BLUHM, Jamie, L .... 716-645-7777 315 F
jlbluhm@buffalo.edu
BLUM, Aron .... 718-522-6646 325 E
BLUM, Christian .... 716-884-9120 291 I
cmblum@bryantstratton.edu
BLUM, Dominika .... 605-626-7802 415 H
dominika.blum@northern.edu
BLUM, Eric .... 909-554-3814.. 54 H
BLUM, Janet .... 978-837-5000 216 D
blumj@merrimack.edu
BLUM, Janice .... 317-274-1020 157 B
jblum@iupui.edu
BLUM, Janice, S .... 317-278-1715 157 B
jblum@iupui.edu
BLUM, Jonathan .... 712-274-5408 168 C
blumj@morningside.edu
BLUM, Kim .... 608-785-8616 495 A
kblum@uwlax.edu
BLUM, Thomas .... 914-395-2203 314 H
tblum@sarahlawrence.edu
BLUM, Thomas, L .... 914-395-2203 314 H
tblum@sarahlawrence.edu
BLUM, Victoria .... 312-322-1700 150 C
BLUM MALLEY,
Suzanne .... 910-630-7005 331 B
smalley@methodist.edu
BLUMBERG, Elizabeth ... 781-239-2762 214 E
eblumberg@massbay.edu
BLUMBERG, James, J ... 309-556-3066 140 E
jblumber@iwu.edu
BLUME, Travis .... 906-217-4116 221 J
travis.blume@baycollege.edu
BLUMENAUER, Michael 517-264-7163 230 C
mblumen1@sienaheights.edu
BLUMENSTEIN, Robert .. 610-282-1100 382 A
robert.blumenstein@desales.edu
BLUMENTHAL, Chava ... 212-678-8072 303 A
chblumenthal@jtsa.edu
BLUMENTHAL, Eric .... 971-722-4200 375 C
eric.blumenthal2@pcc.edu
BLUMENTRITT, Timothy 470-578-2075 121 J
tblument@kennesaw.edu
BLUML, Joel .... 785-670-2100 178 A
joe.bluml@washburn.edu
BLUMMER, Brian .... 219-864-2400 159 D
BLUNDELL, Keith .... 361-582-2535 456 H
keith.blundell@victoriacollege.edu
BLUNK, Shelly, R .... 515-574-1901 166 G
blunk@iowacentral.edu
BLUNT, Shelly, B .... 812-465-1617 162 B
sblunt@usi.edu
BLUTH, Ellen .... 563-336-3331 165 G
ebluth@eicc.edu
BLUTREICH, Peter .... 912-478-5406 120 A
pblutreich@georgiasouthern.edu
BLYTHE, Gretchen .... 816-604-2631 254 H
gretchen.blythe@mcckc.edu
BLYTHE, Janett .... 270-534-3079 182 G
janett.blythe@kctcs.edu
BLYTHE, Jeff .... 912-478-1193 120 A
jblythe@georgiasouthern.edu
BLYTHE, Keith .... 336-734-7212 334 D
kblythe@forsythtech.edu
BOADA, Maria, F .... 845-431-8966 298 B
maria.boada@sunydutchess.edu
BOAK, Bradley .... 919-761-2404 340 B
bboak@sebts.edu
BOAKYE, Augustine, A . 973-877-4462 276 G
aboakye@essex.edu
BOAKYE, Kwabena, J .... 360-538-4221 479 F
kwabena.boakye@ghc.edu
BOAKYE-BOATEN, Agya 828-350-4564 342 A
aboaten@unca.edu
BOARD, Afarah .... 909-554-3814.. 54 H
BOARDER, Matthew ...... 610-796-8243 378 C
matthew.boarder@alvernia.edu
BOARDMAN, David .... 215-204-4822 398 D
david.boardman@temple.edu
BOARDMAN, Jennifer ... 570-504-9638 384 A
jboardman@som.geisinger.edu
BOAST, Gary .... 814-262-6483 393 A
gboast@pennhighlands.edu
BOATENG, Henry .... 716-829-8349 298 C
boatengh@dyc.edu
BOATRIGHT, Bryan .... 330-823-6596 362 E
boatribr@mountunion.edu
BOATRIGHT, Christine .. 386-752-1822.. 99 P
christine.boatright@fgc.edu
BOATRIGHT, Jana .... 903-223-3047 447 C
jboatright@tamut.edu
BOATRIGHT, Jill .... 504-865-3864 190 A
boatrigh@loyno.edu
BOATWRIGHT, Betty, R . 803-536-8556 410 H
bboatwright@scsu.edu
BOATWRIGHT, Kim .... 803-738-7601 409 E
boatwrightk@midlandstech.edu
BOATWRIGHT, Shane ... 903-785-7661 440 F
sboatwright@parisjc.edu
BOB, Darcilynn .... 360-676-2772 480 G
dbob@nwic.edu
BOBADILLA, Leobardo .. 305-237-2598 104 E
lbobadi1@mdc.edu
BOBART, David .... 410-837-4331 204 C
dbobart@ubalt.edu
BOBBIN, Michael .... 904-256-7055 102 G
mbobbin@ju.edu
BOBBIN, Steffi .... 617-559-8640 210 C
sbobbin@hebrewcollege.edu
BOBBIT, Lindy .... 410-337-6000 198 G
lindy.bobbit@goucher.edu
BOBBITT, Donald, R ..... 501-686-2505.. 21 G
dbobbitt@uasys.edu
BOBBOUINE, Art .... 570-342-8000 383 F
abobbouine@fortisinstitute.edu
BOBE, Miguel .... 787-758-2525 511 D
miguel.bobe2@upr.edu
BOBEA, Jenny .... 201-360-4381 277 D
jbobea@hccc.edu
BOBICK, Aaron, F .... 314-935-6350 261 B
afb@wustl.edu
BOBINCHOCK, Edward .. 412-536-1209 386 H
edward.bobinchock@laroche.edu
BOBINSKI, Mary Anne .. 404-712-8815 118 D
mary.anne.bobinski@emory.edu
BOBLEY, Laurie .... 212-463-0400 322 C
laurie.bobley@touro.edu
BOBO, David .... 205-853-1200.... 2 G
dbobo@jeffersonstate.edu
BOBO, Kristen .... 205-391-2211..... 3 E
kbobo@sheltonstate.edu
BOBOC, Marius .... 216-687-4700 350 G
m.boboc@csuohio.edu
BOCANEGRA, Melanie .. 818-677-2969.. 32 E
elizabeth.t.adams@csun.edu
BOCCACINO, Samantha 585-785-1459 299 E
samantha.boccacino@flcc.edu
BOCCALANDRO, Maria . 972-860-2973 433 H
mboccalandro@dcccd.edu
BOCCHICCHIO, Rebecca 916-660-7502.. 64 B
rbocchicchio@sierracollege.edu
BOCHE, Jon .... 414-443-8825 497 A
jonathan.boche@wlc.edu
BOCK, Darrell, L .... 214-887-5251 434 G
dbock@dts.edu
BOCK, Jim .... 610-328-8529 398 B
jbock1@swarthmore.edu
BOCK, Wendy .... 309-796-5180 133 D
bockw@bhc.edu
BOCKMANN, Erika .... 509-527-4282 484 B
erika.bockmann@wwcc.edu
BOCKORNY, Kristi .... 605-626-3001 415 H
kristi.bockorny@northern.edu
BOCKSTEIN, Mindy .... 212-393-6340 294 B
mbockstein@jjay.cuny.edu
BOCZER, Amy .... 203-254-4000.. 87 G
aboczer@fairfield.edu
BODAH, Matthew, H ..... 401-874-2497 404 E
mbodah@uri.edu
BODDIE-FORBES,
Rasheda .... 662-325-2033 247 A
rboddie-forbes@saffairs.msstate.edu
BODDIE-LA VAN,
Jeanine, Y .... 229-333-5709 127 C
jyboddielavan@valdosta.edu
BODE, Lori .... 314-434-4044 251 F
lori.bode@covenantseminary.edu
BODE, Robert .... 715-425-3141 496 A
robert.bode@uwrf.edu
BODEEN, Rob .... 657-278-2339.. 31 E
rbodeen@fullerton.edu
BODEN, Alison .... 609-258-6244 279 E
aboden@princeton.edu
BODEN, Stacia .... 316-978-6792 178 B
stacia.boden@wichita.edu
BODEN-ALBALA,
Bernadette .... 949-824-5735.. 69 C
bbodenal@uci.edu
BODENHAUSEN,
Bradley .... 417-836-3292 255 J
bradbodenhausen@missouristate.edu
BODENSCHATZ,
Matthew .... 814-262-6456 393 A
mbodenschatz@pennhighlands.edu
BODENSTEINER, Jill, R . 610-660-1707 397 A
jbodenst@sju.edu
BODENSTEINER, Joann . 585-475-3947 312 A
BODIE, Matthew .... 727-791-2415 107 C
bodie.matthew@spcollege.edu
BODIFORD, Glenn .... 216-881-1700 358 K
gbodiford@ohiotech.edu
BODIFORD, John .... 229-500-2926 114 F
john.bodiford@asurams.edu
BODIN, Joy .... 952-995-1300 237 G
BODKINS, Carrie, L ...... 304-457-6347 485 F
bodkinscl@ab.edu
BODMER, Brad .... 518-782-6907 314 K
bbodmer@siena.edu
BODNAR, Jennifer .... 504-520-7503 193 C
jbodnar@xula.edu
BODNAR, Molly .... 719-389-6351.. 78 E
mbodnar@coloradocollege.edu
BODNAR, Seth .... 406-243-2311 263 D
thepresident@umontana.edu
BODO, Bethanny .... 540-231-6003 475 D
bbodo@vt.edu
BODONI, June .... 978-867-4217 209 F
june.bodoni@gordon.edu
BODOR, Jim .... 619-201-8725.. 60 G
jim.bodor@sdcc.edu
BODOR, Jim .... 619-201-8700.. 60 G
jim.bodor@sdcc.edu
BODREY, Kari .... 229-931-2700 125 C
kbodrey@southgatech.edu
BODUR, Niyazi .... 607-777-3621 315 E
nbodur@binghamton.edu
BODVARSSON, Orn .... 503-370-6868 377 E
obodvarsson@willamette.edu
BOE, Chris .... 704-463-1360 339 C
christopher.boe@pfeiffer.edu
BOE, Cindy .... 320-589-6065 243 C
cindyboe@morris.umn.edu
BOE, Jennifer .... 816-802-3436 253 H
jboe@kcai.edu
BOE, Ken .... 504-568-6130 189 C
kboe@lsuhsc.edu
BOE, Michelle .... 712-279-5428 163 H
michelle.boe@briarcliff.edu
BOE, Natasha .... 507-537-6448 240 G
natasha.boe@smsu.edu
BOECK, Mark .... 515-294-8959 163 E
mboeck@foundation.iastate.edu
BOECKENSTEDT, Jon .... 541-737-0123 374 H
BOECKERS, Alice .... 920-832-6525 492 B
alice.o.boeckers@lawrence.edu
BOECKMAN, Linda, A ... 717-262-2616 402 D
linda.boeckman@wilson.edu
BOEDEKER, Katrina, P .. 260-399-7700 162 A
kboedeker@sf.edu
BOEDER, John, C .... 507-354-8221 236 D
boederjc@mlc-wels.edu
BOEDING, Laurie .... 843-574-6172 411 I
laurie.boeding@tridenttech.edu
BOEGEL, Thomas .... 415-239-3322.. 37 C
tboegel@ccsf.edu

BOEH, William, S .... 409-772-9803 456 B
wsboeh@utmb.edu
BOEHKE, Michael, J ..... 304-457-6300 485 F
boehkemj@ab.edu
BOEHLEIN, Sandi .... 314-918-2691 252 E
sboehlein@eden.edu
BOEHM, Beth .... 502-852-5110 185 E
beth.boehm@louisville.edu
BOEHM, Michael .... 402-472-2871 269 A
mboehm3@unl.edu
BOEHM, Michael .... 434-791-7273 463 L
mboehm@averett.edu
BOEHM, Michael, J .. 402-472-2871 268 I
mboehm3@unl.edu
BOEHM, Pamela .... 254-659-7501 436 C
pboehm@hillcollege.edu
BOEHMAN, Joseph, R .. 804-289-8061 471 E
jboehman@richmond.edu
BOEHME, Laura .... 541-383-7219 371 I
lboehme@cocc.edu
BOEHMER, Ann .... 636-584-6679 252 D
ann.boehmer@eastcentral.edu
BOEHMER, Brian ...... 740-364-9535 349 D
boehmer.23@osu.edu
BOEHMER, Jennifer ...... 541-917-4214 373 F
boehmj@linnbenton.edu
BOEHMER, Jennifer ..... 503-517-1064 377 B
jboehmer@warnerpacific.edu
BOEHMER, Nick ...... 660-831-4228 256 B
boehmern@moval.edu
BOEHMLER, Brook, S ... 641-422-4212 168 E
boehmbro@niacc.edu
BOEHNE, Cheryl .... 618-545-3486 141 C
cboehne@kaskaskia.edu
BOEKE, Joseph .... 208-426-2328 130 F
josephboeke@boisestate.edu
BOEKELHEIDE, Alex ... 626-585-7422.. 56 D
aboekelheide@pasadena.edu
BOELCKE, Renee, E ... 269-337-7248 225 B
renee.boelcke@kzoo.edu
BOELE, Erin .... 599-278-2345.. 31 D
eboele@csufresno.edu
BOELHAUF, Kate .... 314-529-9531 254 D
cboelhauf@maryville.edu
BOELSCHE, Shelbilynn .. 704-406-4244 328 I
sboelsche@gardner-webb.edu
BOELTER, Pearl .... 657-278-4345.. 31 E
pboelter@fullerton.edu
BOENIG, Catrina .... 337-475-5145 192 B
cboenig@mcneese.edu
BOENIG, Tobin, R .... 409-747-8702 456 B
trboenig@utmb.edu
BOENINGER, Candace .. 740-593-4120 358 L
boeningc@ohio.edu
BOER, Wiebe, K .... 616-526-6100 221 L
president@calvin.edu
BOERGER, Dan .... 972-708-7340 434 F
daniel_boerger@diu.edu
BOERIO, Regina .... 740-284-5361 352 I
rboerio@franciscan.edu
BOERNER, Bill .... 315-781-3922 301 D
boerner@hws.edu
BOERNGEN, Alan .... 618-545-3301 141 C
aboerngen@kaskaskia.edu
BOERSIG, Pam .... 337-421-6954 188 H
pam.boersig@sowela.edu
BOERSMA, Ken .... 616-988-1000 222 D
ken.b@compass.edu
BOERSMA, Paul, H ...... 616-395-7145 224 H
boersma@hope.edu
BOERST, Connie, J ...... 920-433-6622 490 H
connie.boerst@bellincollege.edu
BOERWINKLE, Eric ..... 713-500-9050 455 D
eric.boerwinkle@uth.tmc.edu
BOES, Shelley .... 231-843-5806 232 I
rboes@westshore.edu
BOESCH, Ron .... 563-884-5567 169 C
ron.boesch@palmer.edu
BOESEL, Terry .... 714-997-6818.. 36 D
boesel@chapman.edu
BOESENBERG, John ... 360-623-8474 477 H
john.boesenberg@centralia.edu
BOEVE, Jim .... 402-461-7468 266 C
jboeve@hastings.edu
BOEVE, Traci .... 402-461-7789 266 C
tboeve@hastings.edu
BOEVE, Wallace .... 515-271-1400 165 C
BOFFI, William .... 508-767-7262 205 F
wl.boffi@assumption.edu
BOFILL, Krista .... 386-822-7000 111 F
BOGAN, James .... 608-262-5689 494 D
james.bogan@wisc.edu

BOGARD, Michele, K .... 402-280-2775 265 J
bogard@creighton.edu
BOGARD, William .... 317-921-4718 158 A
wfbogard@ivytech.edu
BOGART, III, Adrian, t .. 540-464-7313 475 C
bogartat@vmi.edu
BOGART, William, T ..... 803-786-3178 407 E
tbogart@columbiasc.edu
BOGDALEK, Steven, J .. 248-204-3925 226 E
sbogdalek@ltu.edu
BOGDAN, John .... 704-687-8454 342 C
jbogdan1@uncc.edu
BOGDAN, Shawn .... 401-841-6103 501 L
shawn.bogdan@usnwc.edu
BOGEN, David .... 617-747-2150 206 D
academicaffairs@berklee.edu
BOGEN, Janice, M ...... 215-503-4335 398 G
janice.bogen@jefferson.edu
BOGER, Marybeth .... 973-596-3470 278 G
marybeth.boger@njit.edu
BOGER-HAWKINS,
Caitlin .... 860-738-6441.. 86 B
cboger-hawkins@nwcc.commnet.edu
BOGER-HAWKINS,
Caitlin .... 860-738-6441.. 87 A
cboger-hawkins@nwcc.edu
BOGERT, Brian .... 570-408-4015 402 B
brian.bogert@wilkes.edu
BOGGER, Tommy .... 757-823-2430 468 B
tlbogger@nsu.edu
BOGGESS, Kendra ..... 304-384-5224 488 K
president@concord.edu
BOGGESS, Summer .... 304-367-4000 488 L
summer.boggess@fairmontstate.edu
BOGGS, Beau .... 276-328-0190 471 G
sbb5w@uvawise.edu
BOGGS, Beverly .... 304-696-3162 488 N
boggsb@marshall.edu
BOGGS, Brad .... 662-862-8271 245 F
bdboggs@iccms.edu
BOGGS, Gretchen, M .. 410-250-1088 203 B
contedoc@ezy.net
BOGGS, Jamie .... 602-639-7500.. 12 L
BOGGS, Kristin .... 304-558-0695 488 I
kristin.boggs@wvhepc.edu
BOGGS, Paul, R .... 903-233-3981 438 C
paulboggs@letu.edu
BOGGS, Rainie .... 859-251-4722 180 C
rainie.boggs@frontier.edu
BOGGS, Steven, E ..... 858-534-6882.. 70 C
dean-ps@ucsd.edu
BOGHOSSIAN, Fikru ..... 443-885-3160 200 F
fikru.boghossian@morgan.edu
BOGIER, Stacy .... 314-454-7770 253 A
stacy.bogier@barnesjewishcollege.edu
BOGLE, Barry, J .... 915-831-7116 435 B
bbogle@epcc.edu
BOGLE, Jason, K ...... 570-326-3671 392 S
jkb20@pct.edu
BOGLE, Yvonne .... 413-782-1594 219 E
yvonne.bogle@wne.edu
BOGLE JUBINVILLE,
Kimberly .... 603-665-3348 273 E
k.boglejubinville@snhu.edu
BOGOSIAN, Deborah ... 212-229-5600 307 E
deborah.bogosian@newschool.edu
BOGUE, Melissa .... 903-927-3213 457 I
msbogue@wileyc.edu
BOGUES, Diane, A ...... 712-290-8709 387 F
dbogues@lancasterseminary.edu
BOGUSH, Tom .... 570-955-1509 387 A
bogusht@lackawanna.edu
BOHACZ, Candy ...... 269-294-4232 223 J
cbohacz@glenoaks.edu
BOHALL, Rob .... 503-554-2416 372 I
rbohall@georgefox.edu
BOHAM, Kenneth, A .... 919-934-3051 335 D
BOHAM, Nihtawneemiw 406-275-4884 264 H
tawnee_boham@skc.edu
BOHAM, Sandra ...... 406-275-4974 264 H
sandra_boham@skc.edu
BOHANNON, Larry .... 323-343-3700.. 32 B
lbohannon@calstatela.edu
BOHANNON, Sherri ..... 318-797-5063 189 E
sherri.bohannon@lsus.edu
BOHASKA, Chris .... 410-225-2490 200 B
cbohaska@mica.edu
BOHL, Coreen .... 315-268-6633 295 E
cbohl@clarkson.edu
BOHL, Kyle .... 616-538-2330 224 B
kbohl@gracechristian.edu
BOHLANDER, Brad ...... 919-515-7373 341 E
bcbohlan@ncsu.edu

BOHLANDER, Elena, M . 260-982-5968 158 W
embohlander@manchester.edu
BOHLEKE, Chuck ...... 208-535-5400 130 I
chuck.bohleke@cei.edu
BOHLENDER, Kristi ...... 970-491-6533.. 79 E
kristi.bohlender@colostate.edu
BOHM, Tiffany .... 913-288-7126 174 H
tbohm@kckcc.edu
BOHMAN, Andreas ...... 206-616-1172 484 A
abohman@uw.edu
BOHMAN, Robert ...... 229-226-1621 126 B
rbohman@thomasu.edu
BOHN, Donna .... 913-288-7634 174 H
dbohn@kckcc.edu
BOHN, Hannah .... 419-251-8993 355 G
hannah.bohn@mercycollege.edu
BOHN, Mike .... 213-740-4154.. 73 C
mbohn@usc.edu
BOHNENBLUST, Delyna 620-421-6700 175 D
delynab@labette.edu
BOHNERT, David ...... 402-375-7394 267 I
dabohne1@wsc.edu
BOHNSACK, Derek ...... 660-831-4000 256 B
BOHNY, David .... 973-618-3440 275 E
dbohny@caldwell.edu
BOHORQUEZ, Tanya .... 559-325-3600.. 28 F
tbohorquez@chsu.edu
BOHRER, Karen ...... 781-283-2127 219 E
kbohrer@wellesley.edu
BOHRER, Robert ...... 330-569-5125 353 F
bohrerr@hiram.edu
BOICE, Daniel .... 870-460-1080.. 22 E
boice@uamont.edu
BOICE, Paul .... 708-239-4837 150 H
paul.boice@trnty.edu
BOICE-PARDEE, Heath . 585-475-2268 312 A
hbpvsa@rit.edu
BOIES, Brandy .... 540-868-7161 473 C
bboies@lfcc.edu
BOIKE, Allan .... 216-707-8004 354 A
aboike1@kent.edu
BOIRE, Abby .... 802-735-2646 289 A
abby.boire@acphs.edu
BOISCLAIR, Terrah ..... 334-291-4981.... 1 H
terrah.boisclair@cv.edu
BOISE, Craig, M ...... 315-443-9580 321 D
cmboise@law.syr.edu
BOISE, Dustin .... 352-638-9726.. 96 B
dboise@beaconcollege.edu
BOISELLE, Philip .... 203-582-5301.. 88 F
philip.boiselle@quinnipiac.edu
BOISER, Romel .... 863-680-3908 100 F
rboiser@flsouthern.edu
BOISSELLE, Vincent ...... 508-767-7272 205 F
vg.boisselle@assumptiuon.edu
BOISVERT, Marie ...... 360-442-2313 480 E
mboisvert@lowercolumbia.edu
BOITER, Christine ...... 253-840-8417 481 H
cboiter@pierce.ctc.edu
BOIVERT, David .... 941-487-5000 110 C
dboivert@ncf.edu
BOIVIN, Janet .... 808-544-1187 128 E
jboivin@hpu.edu
BOIVIN-MCGHEE, Mary 510-436-1249.. 45 H
boivin-mcghee@hnu.edu
BOJORQUEZ, Cathy .... 805-289-6354.. 74 B
cbojorquez@vcccd.edu
BOKIL, Vrushali ...... 541-737-4811 374 H
BOKTOR, Monir ...... 949-794-9090.. 66 C
mboktor@stanbridge.edu
BOLAND, Chris .... 570-504-7000 384 A
cboland@som.geisinger.edu
BOLAND, Jennifer .... 209-954-5151.. 61 H
BOLAND, Kristine ..... 419-783-2469 351 J
kboland@defiance.edu
BOLAND, Mary Kate ..... 610-647-4400 385 K
mboland@immaculata.edu
BOLAND, Wendy ...... 202-885-1976.. 91 D
boland@american.edu
BOLAS, Michelle .... 919-225-2607 342 B
michelle.bolas@unc.edu
BOLDEN, Edward ...... 216-368-1500 349 B
edward.bolden@case.edu
BOLDEN, Michael ...... 601-979-2522 245 K
michael.j.bolden@jsums.edu
BOLDENOW, Jill ...... 952-358-8218 239 C
jill.boldenow@normandale.edu
BOLDING, Regina ...... 864-644-5532 411 D
rbolding@swu.edu
BOLDIZAR, Jeff .. 814-472-3200 396 I
jboldizar@francis.edu
BOLDMAN, Rachael ...... 815-479-7572 143 F
rboldman@mchenry.edu

BOLDON, Diana ...... 330-672-3930 354 A
dboldon@kent.edu
BOLDT, Deborah ...... 505-428-1704 287 H
deborah.boldt@sfcc.edu
BOLDUC, Casey ...... 843-863-7196 406 C
cbolduc@csuniv.edu
BOLDUC, Michael, C .... 561-237-7180 103 W
mbolduc@lynn.edu
BOLEN, Deb, L ...... 717-245-1798 382 B
bolend@dickinson.edu
BOLEN, Kari .... 626-585-7786.. 56 D
kbolen@pasadena.edu
BOLEN, Tracey .... 218-726-7520 243 A
tbolen@d.umn.edu
BOLENDER, James .... 619-260-6824.. 72 H
bolender@sandiego.edu
BOLENDER, Sean, R .... 740-368-3945 359 F
srbolender@owu.edu
BOLES, Janie, A .... 334-844-6176.... 4 E
bolesja@auburn.edu
BOLES, Michael .... 207-602-4813 194 F
mboles@landingschool.edu
BOLGER, Darla ...... 757-423-2095 466 H
BOLGER, Eric ...... 417-690-2278 250 K
bolger@cofo.edu
BOLIEK, Davis, I ...... 919-962-2211 342 B
david.boliek@unc.edu
BOLIN, Christina .... 307-332-2930 500 J
cbolin@wyomingcatholic.edu
BOLIN, Joseph ...... 951-343-4714.. 27 J
jbolin@calbaptist.edu
BOLIN, Mark .... 256-352-8102.... 4 A
mark.bolin@wallacestate.edu
BOLIN, Mary, C ...... 859-257-8701 185 D
marychandler.bolin@uky.edu
BOLIN, Ray .... 513-487-1248 361 E
ray.bolin@myunion.edu
BOLINDER, Megan ..... 479-936-5145.. 20 G
mbolinder@nwacc.edu
BOLINE, Krista .... 678-331-4399 122 A
krista.boline@life.edu
BOLING, Todd .... 817-257-7830 447 H
t.boling@tcu.edu
BOLINSKI, Linda .... 210-341-1366 440 B
lbolinski@ost.edu
BOLLANA, Daniel, C .... 315-792-3191 323 G
dcbollan@utica.edu
BOLLER, Greg .... 901-678-3633 426 A
gboller@memphis.edu
BOLLERO, German ...... 217-333-0460 151 F
gbollero@illinois.edu
BOLLERUD, Julie ...... 760-795-6610.. 52 G
jbollerud@miracosta.edu
BOLLHEIMER, Meredith 814-824-3363 389 E
mbollheimer@mercyhurst.edu
BOLLHORST, Robin .... 217-875-7200 147 G
rbollhor@richland.edu
BOLLIER, John, H ...... 203-432-6754.. 90 B
john.bollier@yale.edu
BOLLING, Phyllis .... 973-596-3420 278 G
phyllis.bolling@njit.edu
BOLLING, Vicky .... 770-689-5017 114 J
vbolling@aii.edu
BOLLINGER, Bruce ..... 701-231-6177 345 D
bruce.bollinger@ndsu.edu
BOLLINGER, Chris ...... 830-372-8019 448 C
cbollinger@tlu.edu
BOLLINGER, Emily ...... 970-248-1536.. 78 F
ejbollinger@coloradomesa.edu
BOLLINGER, Karen ...... 903-463-8790 435 H
bollingerk@grayson.edu
BOLLINGER, Lee, C ..... 212-854-9970 296 H
bollinger@columbia.edu
BOLLINGER, Michelle .. 254-519-5748 446 C
michellebollinger@tamuct.edu
BOLLMAN, Dan, J ...... 517-355-3366 227 C
dbollman@ipf.msu.edu
BOLLMAN-DALANSKY,
Terri, L .... 814-641-3424 386 E
bollmat@juniata.edu
BOLMAN, Ann .... 605-718-2401 416 D
ann.bolman@wdt.edu
BOLMAN, Dave .... 602-383-8228.. 16 G
dbolman@uat.edu
BOLOGA, James .... 717-757-1100 402 J
BOLOGNA, Brynn ...... 816-584-6714 257 E
brynn.bologna@park.edu
BOLOGNONE,
John (Buddy) .... 213-624-1200.. 42 F
bbolognone@fidm.edu
BOLSER, Chad ...... 765-966-2656 158 A
cmbolser@ivytech.edu

BOLSTER, Jeff ... 619-849-2480 57 J jeffbolster@pointloma.edu
BOLT, Barb ... 814-868-9900 383 C barbb@erieit.edu
BOLT, Brian ... 616-526-7526 221 L brb8@calvin.edu
BOLT, Gita ... 713-522-7911 453 H boltg@stthom.edu
BOLT, Joy ... 678-717-3466 126 G joy.bolt@ung.edu
BOLT, Mary, W ... 410-287-1025 198 A mbolt@cecil.edu
BOLT, Susan ... 614-823-1354 359 G bolt1@otterbein.edu
BOLT-MICHEWICZ, Jilliane ... 570-321-4144 388 H michewicz@lycoming.edu
BOLTON, Adrienne ... 985-448-4091 192 C adrienne.bolton@nicholls.edu
BOLTON, Brooke ... 513-618-1927 350 B bbolton@ccms.edu
BOLTON, David ... 417-328-1538 258 K dbolton@sbuniv.edu
BOLTON, James ... 484-664-3400 390 F jimbolton@muhlenberg.edu
BOLTON, Julia ... 706-233-7233 125 A jbolton@shorter.edu
BOLTON, Lance ... 719-502-2200 82 D lance.bolton@pikespeak.edu
BOLTON, Meghann ... 512-313-4115 432 N meghann.bolton@concordia.edu
BOLTON, Robert, D ... 517-750-1200 230 F rbolton@arbor.edu
BOLTON, Sarah ... 330-263-2139 350 H sbolton@wooster.edu
BOLTON, Sarah ... 509-527-5132 485 C sbolton@whitman.edu
BOLTON, Shantay, N ... 314-935-1070 261 B sbolton@wustl.edu
BOLTON, Tonya ... 870-759-4130 24 B tbolton@williamsbu.edu
BOLUCH WOOD, Elizabeth ... 610-328-8317 398 B lwood1@swarthmore.edu
BOLYARD, Adrienne, M 206-726-5021 478 F abolyard@cornish.edu
BOLYARD, Gregory ... 412-809-5349 395 F bolyard.gregory@ptcollege.edu
BOMAN, Jeff ... 918-540-6226 366 F jboman@neo.edu
BOMAN, Victoria ... 205-247-8164 7 A vboman@stillman.edu
BOMAR, Jimmy ... 731-352-4034 417 C bomarj@bethelu.edu
BOMBACK, Larry ... 215-717-3171 381 I larry.bomback@curtis.edu
BOMBARD, Charles ... 802-654-0505 463 A clb10040@ccv.vsc.edu
BOMELEY, Bruce ... 203-332-5034 86 E bbomely@housatonic.edu
BOMER, Randy ... 940-565-2231 453 B randy.bomer@unt.edu
BOMMER, Sharon ... 937-328-6038 350 D bommers@clarkstate.edu
BOMOTTI, Gerry ... 951-827-7310 70 B gerry.bomotti@ucr.edu
BONACOSSA, Pietro ... 305-389-7256 96 A pbonacossa@barry.edu
BONADIE, Heidi ... 909-599-5433 48 E hbonadie@lifepacific.edu
BONADUCE DE NIGRIS, Francesca ... 713-646-1811 443 C fbonaducedenigris@stcl.edu
BONAGURA, Thom ... 712-749-2271 164 A bonagura@bvu.edu
BONAHUE, Edward ... 631-451-4112 320 G bonahue@sunysuffolk.edu
BONAMASSA, Alexis ... 910-893-1200 327 C abonamassa@campbell.edu
BONAMICI, Andrew ... 973-408-3322 276 B abonamici@drew.edu
BONANNO, Joseph, A ... 812-855-4440 156 C jbonanno@indiana.edu
BONAPARTE, Donna ... 781-239-6434 205 G dbonaparte@babson.edu
BONAPARTE, Rachel, N 301-546-0767 201 D bonaparn@pgcc.edu
BONATH, Kyle, K ... 806-742-3931 450 C kyle.k.bonath@ttu.edu
BONATO, Frederick ... 201-761-6020 282 H fbonato@saintpeters.edu
BONAVIA, Jan ... 708-709-7844 147 A jbonavia@prairiestate.edu
BONCHI, Joseph ... 973-596-3002 278 G joseph.bonchi@njit.edu
BOND, Alicia ... 570-408-6024 402 B alicia.bond@wilkes.edu
BOND, Bradley ... 815-753-9403 145 H bbond@niu.edu
BOND, Christopher ... 207-509-7179 196 B cbond@unity.edu
BOND, Dawn ... 413-545-2100 211 D dbond@umass.edu
BOND, Deanna ... 614-236-6011 348 I
BOND, Debra ... 540-674-3607 473 F dbond@nr.edu
BOND, Enoch, D ... 252-335-3224 341 A edbond@ecsu.edu
BOND, Erin ... 212-431-2199 308 I erin.bond@nyls.edu
BOND, Helen ... 202-806-0870 92 E hbond@howard.edu
BOND, James ... 219-473-4299 154 A jbond@ccsj.edu
BOND, Lynette ... 413-662-5106 212 F lynette.bond@mcla.edu
BOND, Meredith ... 216-687-9364 350 G m.bond40@csuohio.edu
BOND, Merry ... 360-442-2851 480 E mbond@lowercolumbia.edu
BOND, Michelle ... 334-386-7275 5 D mbond@faulkner.edu
BOND, Millie ... 610-526-7805 378 J mbond@brynmawr.edu
BOND, Mollie ... 425-889-6178 481 A mollie.bond@northwestu.edu
BOND, Scott ... 916-348-4689 42 B sbond@epic.edu
BOND, Terrance ... 309-268-8238 138 F terrance.bond@heartland.edu
BOND, Travis ... 800-995-3159 262 A
BONDAD, Theresa ... 435-652-7502 459 G theresa.bondad@utahtech.edu
BONDEROFF, Mary, H ... 607-746-4000 320 A bondermh@delhi.edu
BONDI, Nathanael ... 303-273-3537 79 A nbondi@mines.edu
BONDOC, Salvador ... 412-365-1199 380 F s.bondoc@chatham.edu
BONDS, Elle ... 414-297-6422 498 B bonds12@matc.edu
BONDS, Janna ... 256-840-4184 3 F janna.bonds@snead.edu
BONDS, Jess ... 209-478-0800 45 L jbonds@humphreys.edu
BONDS, Nechell ... 903-886-5101 446 D nechell.bonds@tamuc.edu
BONDS, Nell ... 870-743-3000 20 F nbonds@northark.edu
BONDS, Rodney ... 803-793-5170 408 A bondsr@denmarktech.edu
BONDS-RAACKE, Jennifer ... 360-438-4307 482 D president@stmartin.edu
BONDURANT, Jennifer ... 434-947-4113 469 A jbondurant@randolphcollege.edu
BONDURANT, Joy ... 214-333-5104 433 D joyb@dbu.edu
BONDY, Angelica, L ... 412-578-6123 380 A albondy@carlow.edu
BONDY, Jeff ... 406-994-2661 263 G jbondy@montana.edu
BONDY, Kaylyn ... 701-224-5638 345 F kaylyn.bondy@bismarckstate.edu
BONE, Jennifer ... 618-235-2700 150 B jennifer.bone@swic.edu
BONE, Rodney ... 256-228-6001 3 B bonejr@nacc.edu
BONEBRIGHT, Terri ... 501-450-1273 19 I bonebright@hendrix.edu
BONERI, Jacqueline ... 954-776-4476 103 B jboneri@keiseruniversity.edu
BONES, Whit ... 816-802-3532 253 H wbones@kcai.edu
BONEWALD, Karen, I ... 603-526-3748 271 H kbonewald@colby-sawyer.edu
BONFANTI, Phil ... 601-928-8402 246 F phil.bonfanti@mgccc.edu
BONFIL, Terry ... 626-968-1328 47 J
BONGARTZ, Michael ... 816-235-1515 260 D bongartzm@umkc.edu
BONGIOVANNI, Lynne ... 718-405-3753 296 D lynne.bongiovanni@mountsaintvincent.edu
BONIADI, Ani ... 818-252-5224 76 D ani.boniadi@woodbury.edu
BONIECKI, Kurt, A ... 501-450-3126 23 K kurtb@uca.edu
BONIFAS, Angela ... 309-298-2010 152 I aj-bonifas@wiu.edu
BONIFER, Duane ... 309-457-2321 144 E dbonifer@monmouthcollege.edu
BONIFIELD, Susan ... 404-727-9252 118 D susan.bonifield@emory.edu
BONIFORTI, Chris, G ... 561-237-7163 103 W cboniforti@lynn.edu
BONILLA, Angelita ... 973-353-1037 281 C bonillan@newark.rutgers.edu
BONILLA, David ... 406-771-4425 264 B dbonilla@gfcmsu.edu
BONILLA, Erick, A ... 787-766-1717 509 C erbonilla@uagm.edu
BONILLA, Kathleen ... 559-489-2221 67 A kathy.bonilla@fresnocitycollege.edu
BONILLA, Mary Kay ... 406-771-5123 264 B mbonilla@gfcmsu.edu
BONILLA, Matthew, F ... 212-463-0400 322 B matthew.bonilla3@touro.edu
BONILLA, Matthew, F ... 212-463-0400 322 C matthew.bonilla@touro.edu
BONILLA, Ray ... 979-458-6128 445 D rbonilla@tamus.edu
BONIN, Keith ... 336-758-5000 344 A
BONITATIBUS, Alexandra ... 518-587-2100 320 B
BONK, Sharon, B ... 617-588-1356 206 B sbonk@bfit.edu
BONKOWSKI, Janet ... 920-465-2067 494 F bonkowsj@uwgb.edu
BONKOWSKI, Janet ... 920-465-2527 494 F bonkowsj@uwgb.edu
BONLARRON, Rachael, E ... 561-868-3140 105 C bonlarr@palmbeachstate.edu
BONN, Cynthia, L ... 401-874-7100 404 E cynthia_bonn@uri.edu
BONNEAU, Lisa ... 605-658-3853 415 E lisa.bonneau@usd.edu
BONNEE, Peter ... 504-286-5258 191 A pbonnee@suno.edu
BONNEKESSEN, Barbara, E ... 217-581-2922 137 C bbonnekessen@eiu.edu
BONNELL, Chris ... 801-274-3280 460 E chris.bonnell@wgu.edu
BONNELL, Dawn, A ... 215-898-7236 399 J vpr@pobox.upenn.edu
BONNER, Carol ... 937-512-4463 360 F carol.bonner@sinclair.edu
BONNER, Connie, C ... 260-359-4006 155 G cbonner@huntington.edu
BONNER, Davita ... 386-481-2143 96 D bonnerd@cookman.edu
BONNER, Jo ... 251-460-6111 9 A
BONNER, John ... 425-276-9520 479 B jbonner@everettcc.edu
BONNER, Kenyon, R ... 412-648-1006 400 A krb114@pitt.edu
BONNER, Lisa ... 212-229-5600 307 E bonner@newschool.edu
BONNER, Lyle ... 940-552-6291 456 F lbonner@vernoncollege.edu
BONNER, Mason ... 205-366-8814 7 A mbonner@stillman.edu
BONNER, Tiffany ... 909-537-5211 33 B tiffany.bonner@csusb.edu
BONNER, Tommy ... 507-222-4199 234 C tbonner@carleton.edu
BONNET, Larissa, B ... 307-675-0511 500 F lbonnet@sheridan.edu
BONNETTE, Clarence ... 803-793-5264 408 A bonnettec@denmarktech.edu
BONNETTE, J. Michael ... 434-544-8907 470 K bonnette@lynchburg.edu
BONNETTE, Richard ... 410-293-1104 502 I bonnette@usna.edu
BONNEVILLE, Jacqueline ... 715-232-1181 496 C bonnevillej@uwstout.edu
BONNEVILLE, Janice ... 309-438-5507 140 C jbonnev@ilstu.edu
BONNEY, Curtis ... 206-934-4551 482 F curtis.bonney@seattlecolleges.edu
BONNEY, Emily ... 657-278-2715 31 E ebonney@fullerton.edu
BONNEY, Keith ... 863-298-6843 106 A kbonney@polk.edu
BONNIN, Linda ... 901-843-3852 422 C bonninl@rhodes.edu
BONONES, Patrick ... 404-471-6396 114 E pbonones@agnesscott.edu
BONSER, Matthew ... 719-389-6345 78 E mbonser@coloradocollege.edu
BONTATIBUS, Donna ... 860-343-5745 86 G smathis@mxcc.edu
BONTE, Kathleen, M ... 614-823-1289 359 G kbonte@otterbein.edu
BONTRAGER, Bonita ... 406-683-7520 263 E bonita.bontrager@umwestern.edu
BONTRAGER, Karen ... 419-358-3629 348 E bontragerk@bluffton.edu
BONUCHI, Molly ... 308-635-6112 269 E bonuchim@wncc.edu
BONVENUTO, Christopher ... 310-434-4508 63 B bonvenuto_chris@smc.edu
BOODY, Kathleen ... 732-987-2490 277 B kboody@georgian.edu
BOODY, Kathleen ... 732-987-2229 277 B kboody@georgian.edu
BOOG, Melissa, M ... 410-543-6330 204 A mmboog@salisbury.edu
BOOHER, Linnea ... 262-595-2404 495 D booher@uwp.edu
BOOHER, Mark ... 805-922-6966 24 L mbooher@pcpa.org
BOOKAS, Olga ... 860-685-2122 90 A obookas@wesleyan.edu
BOOKER, Alicia ... 216-987-3048 351 D alicia.booker@tri-c.edu
BOOKER, Ansley, A ... 478-301-2856 122 C booker_aa@mercer.edu
BOOKER, James, W ... 301-860-4035 203 D jbooker@bowiestate.edu
BOOKER, Kevin ... 470-639-0355 122 H kevin.booker@morehouse.edu
BOOKER, Kevin ... 470-639-0309 122 H kevin.booker@morehouse.edu
BOOKER, Latoya ... 616-554-5819 222 H latoya.booker@davenport.edu
BOOKER, Lonnie ... 785-833-4360 175 C lonnie.booker@kwu.edu
BOOKER, Marc ... 205-934-9847 8 A mbooker@uab.edu
BOOKER, Mary ... 302-831-2126 91 A mbooker@udel.edu
BOOKER, Michael ... 636-481-3312 253 G mbooker@jeffco.edu
BOOKER, Ndala ... 407-303-6413 95 A ndala.booker@ahu.edu
BOOKER, Pamela ... 478-757-2647 122 D pamela.booker@mga.edu
BOOKER, Steve ... 407-646-2395 106 L sbooker@rollins.edu
BOOKER, Suzy ... 865-981-8203 420 C suzy.booker@maryvillecollege.edu
BOOKHART, Nancy ... 706-396-7597 123 I nbookhart@paine.edu
BOOKOUT, James ... 334-670-3617 7 C jbookout@troy.edu
BOOKOUT, Jeff ... 870-358-8614 18 C jeff_bookout@asun.edu
BOOKS, Sandra ... 530-891-6900 27 H
BOOKWALA, Jamila ... 610-330-5070 387 B bookwalj@lafayette.edu
BOOKWALTER, Robert ... 304-696-2350 488 N bookwalt@marshall.edu
BOOM, Philip ... 563-588-8000 165 K pboom@emmaus.edu
BOOMER, Brian ... 559-934-2152 74 K brianboomer@whccd.edu
BOOMGAARDEN, Donald, R ... 718-940-5902 313 C dboomgaarden@sjcny.edu
BOOMS, Carole ... 734-462-4400 230 B cbooms@schoolcraft.edu
BOON, Celva ... 253-589-5822 478 A celva.boon@cptc.edu
BOON, Rachel, L ... 515-281-3332 163 D rachel.boon@iowaregents.edu
BOON, Stephanie, C ... 610-566-1776 402 C sboon@williamson.edu
BOONE, Addie ... 601-276-3720 248 D aboone@smcc.edu
BOONE, Becky ... 843-349-5274 409 A becky.boone@hgtc.edu
BOONE, Beth ... 352-392-1311 110 E bboone@ufl.edu
BOONE, Brenda ... 770-426-2808 122 A brenda.boone@life.edu
BOONE, Dan ... 615-248-1251 425 D dboone@trevecca.edu

BOONE, Debbie .... 205-853-1200.... 2 G
dboone@jeffersonstate.edu
BOONE, Dottie .... 434-381-6106 470 H
dboone@sbc.edu
BOONE, Jessica .... 316-295-5900 173 G
jessica_boone@friends.edu
BOONE, Kim .... 219-464-5002 162 C
kim.boone@valpo.edu
BOONE, Kyle .... 616-331-2120 224 D
booneky@gvsu.edu
BOONE, Megan .... 606-783-2233 183 H
m.boone@moreheadstate.edu
BOONE, Nichole, N .... 972-378-8573 432 I
nboone@collin.edu
BOONE, Nicole .... 252-538-4326 334 G
nboone@halifaxcc.edu
BOONE, Rebecca .... 318-357-5621 192 D
booner@nsula.edu
BOONE, Scott .... 678-916-2638 115 G
sboone@johnmarshall.edu
BOONE, Steve, E ...... 501-686-7348.. 22 D
seboone@uams.edu
BOONE, Zak .... 541-383-7212 371 I
zboone@cocc.edu
BOONSTRA, Brenda .... 706-778-8500 124 B
bboonstra@piedmont.edu
BOONTHAVONGKHAM,
Bonnie .... 559-325-5205.. 66 H
bonnie.boonthavongkham@
cloviscollege.edu
BOOR, Kathryn, J .... 607-255-5864 297 D
dean_gradschool@cornell.edu
BOOROM, Richard .... 303-867-1155.. 83 H
boorom@taft.edu
BOOS, David .... 605-995-3065 414 E
david.boos@mitchelltech.edu
BOOS, Jean .... 843-355-4167 413 C
boosj@wiltech.edu
BOOS, Matt .... 440-684-6021 363 C
mboos@ursuline.edu
BOOSKA, Karry .... 802-728-1320 463 D
kbooska@vtc.edu
BOOSKOS, George ...... 609-343-5116 274 E
gbooskos@atlantic.edu
BOOTE, Marlys .... 319-335-2043 163 F
marlys-boote@uiowa.edu
BOOTH, Daria .... 530-898-4054.. 31 A
dbooth3@csuchico.edu
BOOTH, Derrick .... 916-484-8411.. 50 J
boothd@arc.losrios.edu
BOOTH, Diana .... 847-574-5152 141 G
dbooth@lfgsm.edu
BOOTH, H. Austin .... 212-998-1212 309 D
BOOTH, Jane, E .... 212-854-0286 296 H
jeb@gc.columbia.edu
BOOTH, Jennifer .... 803-754-4100 407 F
BOOTH, Laura .... 706-993-1115 119 E
lbooth@gmc.edu
BOOTH, Mary .... 918-540-6998 366 F
mary.booth@neo.edu
BOOTH, Melinda .... 989-463-7111 220 F
boothml@alma.edu
BOOTH, Ronald .... 706-721-3393 115 I
ronbooth@augusta.edu
BOOTH, Scott .... 315-568-3052 309 H
sbooth@northeastcollege.edu
BOOTH, Scott .... 336-734-7317 334 D
dbooth@forsythtech.edu
BOOTH, Susan, A .... 573-629-3002 253 D
sbooth@hlg.edu
BOOTH-CARO, Erin ..... 562-985-4151.. 32 A
erin.booth-caro@csulb.edu
BOOTHE, Shane 832-252-4646 431M
shane.boothe@cbshouston.edu
BOOTON, Katie .... 402-280-5833 265 J
kbooton@creighton.edu
BOOTON, Steven .... 402-472-2625 269 A
sbooton2@unl.edu
BOOTS, Josh .... 608-342-3961 495 E
bootsj@uwplatt.edu
BOOTS, Lori .... 620-331-4100 174 E
lboots@indycc.edu
BOOTY, Connie .... 479-979-1242.. 24 A
cbooty@ozarks.edu
BOOZ, Jennifer .... 907-786-1800.. 10 A
BOOZANG, Kathleen .... 973-642-8501 282 K
kathleen.boozang@shu.edu
BOOZE, David .... 714-484-7432.. 54 C
dbooze@cypresscollege.edu
BOPKO, Patricia .... 909-652-6152.. 36 B
patricia.bopko@chaffey.edu
BOPP, Jayne .... 808-455-0597 130 A
pbopp@hawaii.edu

BOQUET, OSB,
Gregory, M .... 985-867-2232 190 I
rector@sjasc.edu
BORAH, Jeffrey .... 934-420-2661 320 C
borahj@farmingdale.edu
BORCH, Claire .... 607-274-1926 302 E
cborch@ithaca.edu
BORCHERDING, Alan .... 314-505-7763 251 D
borcherdinga@csl.edu
BORCHERDING,
Matthew .... 218-736-1506 238 K
matthew.borcherding@minnesota.edu
BORCHERS, Mitch .... 816-604-1345 254 E
mitch.borchers@mcckc.edu
BORCHERS, Tim .... 402-872-2222 267 H
tborchers@peru.edu
BORCHERT, Anne, M ... 216-368-0242 349 B
amb14@case.edu
BORCHERT, Lisa .... 570-674-6265 389 H
lborchert@misericordia.edu
BORDEAUX, Debra ...... 605-856-5880 415 A
debra.bordeaux@sintegleska.edu
BORDEAUX, Lionel ...... 605-856-5880 415 A
lionel.bordeaux@sintegleska.edu
BORDELON, Ann .... 479-575-5828.. 21 H
bordelon@uark.edu
BORDELON, Deborah ... 713-221-8003 452 B
bordelond@uhd.edu
BORDEN, M. Paige .... 407-823-4765 110 D
paige.borden@ucf.edu
BORDEN, Rae .... 504-520-7539 193 C
rborden@xula.edu
BORDEN, Susan .... 410-626-2506 201 E
susan.borden@sjc.edu
BORDERS, Kameil .... 253-680-7000 477 A
BORDERS, Keli .... 307-754-6409 500 G
keli.borders@nwc.edu
BORDEYNE, Philippe ... 202-526-3799.. 93 E
BORDNICK, Patrick ...... 504-862-3482 191 D
bordnick@tulane.edu
BORDONARO, Vilma .... 914-594-4900 308 J
vilma_bordonaro@nymc.edu
BORDT, Elisabet .... 859-846-5310 183 G
ebordt@midway.edu
BOREEN, Jean .... 435-586-7898 459 E
jeanboreen@suu.edu
BOREING, Vicki .... 307-778-1102 500 D
vboreing@lccc.wy.edu
BOREK, Kevin .... 703-993-8728 466 J
kborek@gmu.edu
BORELLI, Alysa .... 707-864-7000.. 64 F
alysa.borelli@solano.edu
BORELLI, Gina .... 949-359-0045.. 29 C
BORELLI, Tricia, S ...... 563-588-7085 167 I
tricia.borelli@loras.edu
BOREN, J. B .... 806-352-5207 457 B
borenjb@wbu.edu
BOREN, Laura, D .... 229-931-2339 120 B
laura.boren@gsw.edu
BORENE, Andrew .... 301-243-2261 501 J
andrew.borene@odni.gov
BORENS, Paul .... 414-277-7593 493 D
borens@msoe.edu
BORES, Gerald .... 503-552-2007 374 B
gbores@nunm.edu
BORFITZ, Joanne .... 315-228-7120 296 C
jborfitz@colgate.edu
BORGEN, Beth, M .... 920-565-1101 492 A
borgenbm@lakeland.edu
BORGER, Jennika .... 610-861-1583 390 D
borgerj@moravian.edu
BORGES, Dan .... 408-741-2674.. 75 B
dan.borges@wvm.edu
BORGES, Dan .... 408-741-2674.. 75 C
dan.borges@wvm.edu
BORGES, Donald .... 209-575-6198.. 76 K
borgesd@mjc.edu
BORGES, Ed .... 281-649-3299 436 D
eborges@hbu.edu
BORGES-JOHNSON,
Catherine .... 301-736-3631 200 A
BORGES-O'DELL,
Cynthia .... 209-667-6635.. 33 D
cborgesodell@csustan.edu
BORGESI, Susan .... 614-891-3200 357 A
BORGIA, Daniel, J ...... 508-213-2335 217 C
daniel.borgia@nichols.edu
BORGMAN,
Cathleen, M .... 203-254-4081.. 87 G
cborgman@fairfield.edu
BORGMANN-INGWERSEN,
Marian .... 402-465-2415 267 J
mborgman@nebrwesleyan.edu

BORGMEYER, Anita ...... 314-977-2500 258 H
anita.borgmeyer@slu.edu
BORGONAH, Darryl ..... 512-245-2550 449 G
djb129@txstate.edu
BORGSTEDTE, Ashley ... 432-685-4734 439 E
aborgstedte@midland.edu
BORGSTROM,
Henrik, C .... 716-286-8342 309 F
hcb@niagara.edu
BORGSTROM, Shelly .... 918-343-7668 369 A
sborgstrom@rsu.edu
BORIA, Selina, M .... 508-854-4368 215 D
sboria@qcc.mass.edu
BORILL, Brandon .... 337-550-1233 189 B
bborill@lsue.edu
BORIS, Barbara, A ...... 610-409-3605 400 E
bboris@ursinus.edu
BORIS, Erin .... 608-663-2377 491 F
eboris@edgewood.edu
BORIS, Lenore, L .... 315-448-5040 313 D
lenore.boris@sjhcon.edu
BORIS, LuAnn .... 330-490-7186 363 E
lboris@walsh.edu
BORISYUK, Dima .... 978-867-4103 209 F
dima.borisyuk@gordon.edu
BORJESSON, Dori .... 509-335-9515 484 D
dori.borjesson@wsu.edu
BORJORQUEZ, Lina ..... 213-738-6719.. 66 A
finaid@swlaw.edu
BORK, Rocky .... 985-545-1500 188 B
BORKOWSKI, Alina ..... 402-354-7230 267 E
alina.borkowski@methodistcollege.edu
BORKOWSKI,
Donald, V .... 207-725-3947 194 A
dborkows@bowdoin.edu
BORLAND, Jeanine ...... 909-469-3457.. 75 G
jmann@westernu.edu
BORMANN, Gregory ..... 661-722-6300.. 26 E
gbormann@avc.edu
BORMANN, Holly .... 918-647-1200 365 D
hbbormann@carlalbert.edu
BORN, John .... 773-244-5771 145 F
jborn@northpark.edu
BORN, Lauren, E .... 610-917-1465 400 D
leborn@valleyforge.edu
BORN, Matthew .... 610-436-2231 394 F
mborn@wcupa.edu
BORNE, Jade .... 410-462-7416 197 E
jborne@bccc.edu
BORNEMANN, Jeffrey ... 414-955-8793 492 F
jbornemann@mcw.edu
BORNER, John .... 518-562-4121 295 F
john.borner@clinton.edu
BORNHOLDT, Claudia ... 843-349-2746 407 B
bornholdt@coastal.edu
BORNHORST, Mary ...... 937-778-7837 352 D
mbornhorst@edisonohio.edu
BORNSTEIN, Eva .... 718-960-8490 293 E
eva.bornstein@lehman.cuny.edu
BORNSTEIN, Ilisabeth .. 401-232-6000 403 B
ibornstein@bryant.edu
BORNSTEIN, Leah, L .... 970-339-6210.. 77 G
leah.bornstein@aims.edu
BOROWICK, Matthew ... 973-378-9801 282 K
matthew.borowick@shu.edu
BOROWICZ, Laurie ...... 815-825-9333 141 D
lborowicz@kish.edu
BOROWICZ, Mark .... 608-757-7723 497 D
mborowicz@blackhawk.edu
BOROZAN, Susan .... 941-309-5455 106 J
sborozan@ringling.edu
BORQUERO, Jason ...... 562-860-2451.. 35 O
jborquero@cerritos.edu
BORR, Mike .... 701-231-9535 345 D
mike.borr@ndsu.edu
BORRACCINI, Martha .... 610-647-4400 385 K
mborraccini@immaculata.edu
BORREGARD, Andrea .... 270-686-4521 182 C
andrea.borregard@kctcs.edu
BORREGO, Tom .... 316-323-6729 172 B
tborrego@butlercc.edu
BORRELL, Anthony ...... 813-757-2111 102 A
aborrell2@hccfl.edu
BORREN, Tammy, S .... 931-540-2534 423 D
tborren@columbiastate.edu
BORRERO, Jennifer, S .. 718-982-2335 293 C
jennifer.borrero@csi.cuny.edu
BORRERO, Josephin .... 787-884-6000 506 B
jborrero@icprjc.edu
BORRERO-RIOS,
Carlos, J .... 787-998-8997 508 K
cborrero@eeapr.org
BORRETT, Stuart .... 919-962-7430 343 B
borretts@uncw.edu

BORROR, Brenn .... 503-255-0332 374 A
brennborror@multnomah.edu
BORROR, Kelly .... 503-517-1839 377 D
kborror@westernseminary.edu
BORRUSO, Tony .... 860-444-8444 502 F
BORS, Lisa .... 585-340-9647 296 B
lbors@crcds.edu
BORSKI, Brian .... 972-860-4116 433 G
bborski@dcccd.edu
BORST, Andy .... 217-300-3957 151 F
ajb168@illinois.edu
BORSZ, Michael .... 315-498-2097 310 C
m.a.borsz@sunyocc.edu
BORTH, Adam .... 620-223-2700 173 F
adamb@fortscott.edu
BORTNER, Arlis .... 209-381-6570.. 52 B
arlis.bortner@mccd.edu
BORTON, Jeff .... 734-462-4400 230 B
jborton@schoolcraft.edu
BORTON, Shawn .... 719-384-6892.. 82 C
shawn.borton@otero.edu
BORTUNK, Ayelet .... 305-653-8770 114 C
abortunk@lecfl.com
BORUCKI, Jennifer, C ... 818-947-2433.. 50 B
fongjc@lavc.edu
BORUFF-JONES, Polly .. 248-370-2459 229 F
boruffjones@oakland.edu
BORUM, John .... 214-333-5973 433 D
johnb@dbu.edu
BORUSZEWSKI, Rich .... 920-465-2075 494 E
boruszer@uwgb.edu
BORUSZEWSKI,
Richard .... 810-762-0533 228 E
richard.boruszewski@mcc.edu
BORYCZKA, Jocelyn ..... 203-254-4000.. 87 G
jboryczka@fairfield.edu
BORZELLINO, Joseph ... 805-756-5192.. 29 K
jborzell@calpoly.edu
BOS, Angela .... 208-426-1368 130 F
schoolofpublicservice@boisestate.edu
BOS, James .... 712-722-6030 165 E
jim.bos@dordt.edu
BOS, Timothy .... 559-325-3600.. 28 E
tbos@chsu.edu
BOSACK-KOSEK,
Carol, A .... 570-408-4063 402 B
carol.bosack@wilkes.edu
BOSCH IRIZARRY,
Agnes .... 787-767-4300 511 F
agnes.bosch@upr.edu
BOSCHINI, Debbie ...... 661-654-2154.. 30 A
dboschini@csub.edu
BOSCHINI, JR.,
Victor, J .... 817-257-7783 447 H
v.boschini@tcu.edu
BOSCIO, Amaury .... 787-766-1912 507 C
aboscio@inter.edu
BOSCO, SJ, Mark ...... 202-687-1395.. 92 D
mb2263@georgetown.edu
BOSE, Mohua .... 518-782-6737 314 K
mbose@siena.edu
BOSE, Shantanu .... 630-829-0281 136 G
sbose@devry.edu
BOSE, Stacey .... 215-702-4276 379 E
dbose@cairn.edu
BOSELL, Sue .... 218-726-7101 243 A
vcfo@d.umn.edu
BOSEMAN, Shelby ...... 817-272-2142 454 E
sboseman@uta.edu
BOSEN, Patricia .... 518-580-5550 315 A
pbosen@skidmore.edu
BOSHART, David .... 574-295-3726 153 C
dboshart@ambs.edu
BOSHKOFF, Katharine .. 617-746-1990 210 E
katharine.boshkoff@hult.edu
BOSIO, Amy .... 610-647-4400 385 K
abosio@immaculata.edu
BOSKET, David .... 570-585-9218 381 A
dbosket@clarkssummitu.edu
BOSLET, Diane .... 518-736-3622 300 B
diane.boslet@fmcc.suny.edu
BOSLEY, Amy, N .... 407-582-8255 113 C
abosley@valenciacollege.edu
BOSLEY, Barry .... 717-358-4663 383 G
barry.bosley@fandm.edu
BOSLEY, Mike .... 407-582-7007 113 C
mbosley@valenciacollege.edu
BOSLEY-BOYCE,
Annette .... 203-773-6685.. 85 C
abosleyboyce@albertus.edu
BOSS, Alyssa .... 401-874-1000 404 E
BOSS, Diane .... 479-936-5172.. 20 G
dboss@nwacc.edu

BOSS, Shannon 215-780-1318 397 E sboss@salus.edu
BOSSALLER, Andy 314-792-6100 253 J andybossaller@kenrick.edu
BOSSANGE, Patricia 508-626-4996 212 D pbossange@framingham.edu
BOSSARD, Jennifer 402-826-8275 266 A jennifer.bossard@doane.edu
BOSSERMAN, Sharon, S 540-887-7026 467 G sbosserman@marybaldwin.edu
BOSSERT, Elizabeth (Becky) 909-558-4517 48 J bbossert@llu.edu
BOSSIE, George 304-205-6615 487 D george.bossie@bridgevalley.edu
BOST, Rachel, R 662-915-7448 248 F rbost@olemiss.edu
BOSTANIC, George 909-599-5433 48 E gbostanic@lifepacific.edu
BOSTIAN, Susan 605-626-2520 415 H susan.bostian@northern.edu
BOSTIC, Blake 704-991-0183 338 A sbostic2222@stanly.edu
BOSTIC, Heidi 414-288-3224 492 E heidi.bostic@marquette.edu
BOSTIC, Melodie 314-505-7626 251 D bosticm@csl.edu
BOSTIC, Peter 310-233-4288 49 F bosticpf@lahc.edu
BOSTICK, William 504-520-5243 193 C wbostick@xula.edu
BOSTON, Denise 866-492-5336 243 G denise.boston@mail.waldenu.edu
BOSTON, Genyne 850-599-3276 109 E genyne.boston@famu.edu
BOSTON, Joanna 212-343-1234 306 C jboston@mcny.edu
BOSTON, Kay 318-678-6000 187 E kboston@bpcc.edu
BOSTON, Ken 308-635-6736 269 E bostonk1@wncc.edu
BOSTON, Melissa 914-798-2734 305 A melissa.boston@mville.edu
BOSTON, Pamela, F 757-823-2293 468 B pfboston@nsu.edu
BOSTON, Pasiley 256-761-8520 7 B pboston@talladega.edu
BOSTON, Troy 641-673-1170 170 I troy.boston@wmpenn.edu
BOSTROM, Steve 425-889-5321 481 A steve.bostrom@northwestu.edu
BOSTWICK, Keri 918-335-6291 368 E kbostwick@okwu.edu
BOSWELL, Angela 870-230-5320 19 H boswela@hsu.edu
BOSWELL, Chris 307-766-6934 500 H chris.boswell@uwyo.edu
BOSWELL, Erin 314-529-9333 254 D eboswell@maryville.edu
BOSWELL, Katherine 817-598-6216 457 C kboswell@wc.edu
BOSWELL, Kirstin 336-278-7729 328 H kboswell4@elon.edu
BOSWELL, Samantha 478-471-2430 122 D samantha.boswell@mga.edu
BOSWELL, Talisa 662-252-8000 248 B tboswell@rustcollege.edu
BOSWORTH, Theresa 541-278-5957 371 G tbosworth@bluecc.edu
BOTANA, II, Joseph, D 870-307-7589 20 D joseph.botana@lyon.edu
BOTCHAN, Michael, R 510-642-5716 68 N mbotchan@berkeley.edu
BOTERO, Cecilia 662-915-5858 248 F cbotero@olemiss.edu
BOTERO, Nancy, R 954-201-7414 96 F
BOTHE, Dan 619-849-2290 57 J danbothe@pointloma.edu
BOTHNER, Peter, G 585-389-2196 307 D pbothne4@naz.edu
BOTHOF, Ken 859-572-6639 184 B bothofk1@nku.edu
BOTHRA, Jashoda 425-352-8000 477 F
BOTMAN, Selma 212-960-5217 325 R selma.botman@yu.edu
BOTSOLIS, Nicholas 617-850-1231 210 D nbotsolis@hchc.edu
BOTSTEIN, Leon 845-758-7423 290 G president@bard.edu
BOTT, Greg 610-799-1585 388 B
BOTT, Rebecca 605-688-5268 416 A rebecca.bott@sdstate.edu
BOTT, Rosa 276-328-0312 471 G grb5u@uvawise.edu
BOTTA, Michael 412-392-3833 395 H mfbotta@pointpark.edu
BOTTA, Samuel 757-352-4491 469 D sambott@regent.edu
BOTTARO, Kathy 210-805-2591 452 D bottaro@uiwtx.edu
BOTTELBERGHE, John 303-360-4718 80 C john.bottelberghe@ccaurora.edu
BOTTEM, Lisa 218-683-8544 239 E lisa.bottem@northlandcollege.edu
BOTTI, Romayne 848-932-1991 281 B romayne.botti@rutgers.edu
BOTTINELLI, Stasi 303-751-8700 78 A bottinelli@belrea.edu
BOTTRILL, Michael, S 212-924-5900 321 C
BOTZHEIM, Luke 425-640-1946 479 A luke.botzheim@edcc.edu
BOTZMAN, Thomas, J 330-823-6050 362 E botzmatj@mountunion.edu
BOU, Nydia 787-743-7979 509 D ut_nbou@suagm.edu
BOUARÉ, Boubacar 509-359-6449 478 H bbouare@ewu.edu
BOUCHARD, Norma 714-997-6826 36 D nbouchard@chapman.edu
BOUCHARD, Rita, T 757-822-2308 474 G rbouchard@tcc.edu
BOUCHE, Jane, A 920-565-1000 492 A boucheja@lakeland.edu
BOUCHER, Gery 252-638-7283 333 F boucherg@cravencc.edu
BOUCHER, Helen 617-628-5000 219 A helen.boucher@tufts.edu
BOUCHER, J. Cliff 903-510-2546 451 D cliff.boucher@tjc.edu
BOUCHER, Jeanne 207-985-7976 194 F jeanne@landingschool.edu
BOUCHER, John 907-450-8389 9 I jbouche1@alaska.edu
BOUCHER, Robert 207-755-5100 194 J rboucher@cmcc.edu
BOUCHER, Susan 315-792-3013 323 G salberi@utica.edu
BOUCHER-JARVIS, Allison 973-720-2123 283 I boucherjarvisa@wpunj.edu
BOUCHER MORRIS, Kelly 212-228-1888 311 I
BOUCHEY, BettyJo 312-261-3505 145 C bbouchey@nl.edu
BOUCKAERT, Rebecca 402-354-7034 267 E rebecca.bouckaert@methodistcollege.edu
BOUDO, Lori 978-542-7404 213 B lori.boudo@salemstate.edu
BOUDREAU, Charles 630-466-7900 152 H cboudreau@waubonsee.edu
BOUDREAU, John 860-906-5071 86 C jboudreau@capitalcc.edu
BOUDREAU, Mark 413-775-1311 214 C boudreaum@gcc.mass.edu
BOUDREAU, Vincent, G 212-650-7285 293 B vboudreau@ccny.cuny.edu
BOUDREAUX, Carol 225-752-4233 187 A cboudreaux@iticollege.edu
BOUDREAUX, Gregory 330-494-6170 360 I gboudreaux@starkstate.edu
BOUFAS, Maureen 315-866-0300 301 B boufasmn@herkimer.edu
BOUGHEY, Robin 502-245-6177 183 F
BOUGHIDA, Karim 631-632-1067 316 D belkacemkarim.boughida@stonybrook.edu
BOUGHIDA, Karim, B 401-874-4602 404 E boughida@uri.edu
BOUGHMAN, Joann 301-445-1992 202 D jboughman@usmd.edu
BOUILLON, Rick 801-957-5158 460 D rick.bouillon@slcc.edu
BOUKHMAN, Anna 718-522-9073 290 B aboukhman@asa.edu
BOULANGER, Brie 316-295-5525 173 G brie_boulanger@friends.edu
BOULANGER, Rebecca 920-735-2407 497 F boulanger@fvtc.edu
BOULDEN, Billy 515-294-4111 163 E
BOULDIN, Randy 615-966-5711 420 B randy.bouldin@lipscomb.edu
BOULDING, William 919-660-7822 328 D bb1@duke.edu
BOULERSOX, Kate 573-875-8700 251 A
BOULES, Raouf 860-231-5803 89 G rboules@usj.edu
BOULOS, Alan, S 518-262-6008 289 C boulosa@amc.edu
BOULTER, Brandon 415-257-1334 41 H
BOULTON, April 301-696-3811 199 C boulton@hood.edu
BOULTON, Kenneth 605-626-2497 415 H kenneth.boulton@northern.edu
BOULUKOS, Tracy 561-297-3531 109 F tbouluko@fau.edu
BOULWARE, Jan 386-481-2298 96 D boulwarej@cookman.edu
BOUNDS, Roger 928-523-4331 14 J roger.bounds@nau.edu
BOUQUOT, Gregory 860-486-3903 89 B gregory.bouquot@uconn.edu
BOURA, Ahmad 530-898-5830 31 A aboura@csuchico.edu
BOURDON, Marsha 603-271-6484 272 C
BOURDON, Marsha 603-366-5206 271 K mbourdon@ccsnh.edu
BOURG, Chris 617-253-5297 215 G
BOURGEAULT, Lucy 802-322-1676 461 D lucy.bourgeault@goddard.edu
BOURGEOIS, Angi 662-325-2202 247 A abourgeois@caad.msstate.edu
BOURGEOIS, Donna 504-865-3523 190 A dhbourg@loyno.edu
BOURGEOIS, Gene 512-245-2205 449 G eb04@txstate.edu
BOURGEOIS, Thomas 662-325-3611 247 A thomasb@saffairs.msstate.edu
BOURGET, Jose 269-471-3211 220 H bourget@andrews.edu
BOURHIS NOLAN, Ellen 845-569-3116 307 B ellen.nolan@msmc.edu
BOURLAND, Dana 920-924-3225 498 C dbourland1@morainepark.edu
BOURLAND HUIZENGA, Annette 563-589-3858 170 C ahuizenga@dbq.edu
BOURLIER, Julie 310-660-3383 41 J jbourlier@elcamino.edu
BOURN, Brenda 423-461-8414 421 E bsbourn@milligan.edu
BOURNE, Anthony 419-448-2316 353 D tbourne1@heidelberg.edu
BOURNE, Brandy 828-251-6639 342 A bbourne@unca.edu
BOURNE, Don, E 208-535-5360 130 I don.bourne@cei.edu
BOURNE, Jeffrey, T 540-568-6164 467 C bournejt@jmu.edu
BOURNE, Philip, E 434-924-6867 471 F peb6a@virginia.edu
BOURQUE, Alicia 504-865-3835 190 A aabourqu@loyno.edu
BOURQUE, Daniel, F 617-552-6067 207 A daniel.bourque@bc.edu
BOURQUE, Kathleen 413-565-1000 205 I kbourque@baypath.edu
BOURQUE, Michael, J 617-552-0343 207 A michael.bourque.2@bc.edu
BOURQUE, Nancy 773-878-2998 148 F
BOURQUE, Nicole 603-342-3030 272 E nbourque@ccsnh.edu
BOUSCHER, Jordan 724-847-6556 384 B jdbousch@geneva.edu
BOUSLAUGH, Megan 949-854-8002 40 E
BOUSMAN, Preston 804-862-6100 469 E pbousman@rbc.edu
BOUSSON, Eduardo 402-465-2222 267 J ebousson@nebrwesleyan.edu
BOUTE, Bradley 480-393-1396 16 C bradb@swiha.edu
BOUTELLE, Ken 866-776-0331 54 E kboutelle@ncu.edu
BOUTIN, Karyn 508-588-9100 214 F kboutin@massasoit.mass.edu
BOUTIN, Kelly 401-232-6855 403 B kboutin1@bryant.edu
BOUVIN, David 850-718-2380 97 E bouvind@chipola.edu
BOUWHUIS, Ryan 928-776-2195 17 B ryan.bouwhuis@yc.edu
BOUYEA, Aaron, M 585-292-2833 306 K abouyea@monroecc.edu
BOUZAS, Maria 973-761-9081 282 K maria.bouzas@shu.edu
BOUZIGARD, Cambria 985-448-4101 192 C cambria.bouzigard@nicholls.edu
BOVA, Keith 716-829-7551 298 C bovak@dyc.edu
BOVAT, Bruce 802-860-2755 461 C bovat@champlain.edu
BOVEE, Kimberly, M 757-822-1913 474 G kbovee@tcc.edu
BOVIA, Wendy 860-738-6325 87 A wbovia@nwcc.edu
BOVIA, Wendy 860-773-1420 87 E wbovia@commnet.edu
BOVINGDON, Ali 406-449-9166 263 C abovingdon@montana.edu
BOWAB, Lynn 978-681-0800 216 A bowab@mslaw.edu
BOWAN, Carmen 626-316-5312 63 D cbowan@saybrook.edu
BOWAR, Alicia 712-722-6022 165 E alicia.bowar@dordt.edu
BOWDEN, Michael 410-951-6280 203 E mbowden@coppin.edu
BOWDEN, Nathan, E 805-437-3719 30 D nathan.bowden@csuci.edu
BOWDEN, Ron 903-434-8157 440 A rbowden@ntcc.edu
BOWDEN, Steve 207-699-5010 194 G sbowden@meca.edu
BOWDEN, Trishana 703-993-8756 466 J tbowden2@gmu.edu
BOWDEN, Vicky 626-815-2034 26 K vbowden@apu.edu
BOWDEN, Zach 937-766-7901 349 C zbowden@cedarville.edu
BOWDEN-EVANS, Andrea 205-391-2452 3 E abowden@sheltonstate.edu
BOWDITCH, Nathaniel 603-535-3500 274 B
BOWDRE, Paul 812-749-1431 159 E pbowdre@oak.edu
BOWE, Terry 812-535-5284 160 E terry.bowe@smwc.edu
BOWEN, Alyncia 614-947-6226 352 J alyncia.bowen@franklin.edu
BOWEN, Bonnie 616-331-2400 224 D bowenb@gvsu.edu
BOWEN, Brad 864-508-0107 411 D bbowen@swu.edu
BOWEN, Brad 307-754-6404 500 G brad.bowen@nwc.edu
BOWEN, Brandon 801-524-8181 458 F bowenbrandon@ensign.edu
BOWEN, Carmen 626-316-5312 63 D cbowen@saybrook.edu
BOWEN, Christopher, M 540-375-2300 469 G bowen@roanoke.edu
BOWEN, Eve 254-659-7500 436 C
BOWEN, Heath 845-398-4380 314 D hbowen@stac.edu
BOWEN, Jennifer 330-263-2008 350 H jbowen@wooster.edu
BOWEN, Julie 806-291-3470 457 B bowenj@wbu.edu
BOWEN, Kenneth 910-272-3375 337 A kbowen@robeson.edu
BOWEN, Kim, T 517-750-1200 230 F kbowen@arbor.edu
BOWEN, Lance 410-777-2873 197 C ldbowen1@aacc.edu
BOWEN, Laura 704-669-4106 333 C bowen@clevelandcc.edu
BOWEN, Lauren 814-641-3121 386 E bowenl@juniata.edu
BOWEN, Marie 617-287-5150 211 E marie.bowen@umb.edu
BOWEN, Mark 478-445-4467 119 A mark.bowen@gcsu.edu
BOWEN, Nicole 605-256-5121 415 G nicole.bowen@dsu.edu
BOWEN, Patricia, A 606-693-5000 182 H pbowen@kmbc.edu
BOWEN, Peter 806-291-1171 457 B pbowen@wbu.edu
BOWEN, Rachel 610-526-6157 385 F rbowen@harcum.edu
BOWEN, Randyll 716-878-3694 317 C bowenrp@buffalostate.edu
BOWEN, Robert 603-271-6484 272 C
BOWEN, Robin, E 479-968-0228 18 E rbowen@atu.edu
BOWEN, Roxanne 423-585-6806 424 G roxanne.bowen@ws.edu
BOWEN, Sam 320-222-5206 239 H sam.bowen@ridgewater.edu

BOYETT, Chris ... 270-707-3711 181 G
chris.boyett@kctcs.edu
BOYETT, Patricia ... 504-865-3082 190 A
pbboyett@loyno.edu
BOYETTE, Alan, J ... 336-334-5494 342 D
jaboyett@uncg.edu
BOYETTE, Rick ... 903-823-3274 445 C
ricky.boyette@texarkanacollege.edu
BOYKIN, Celyn ... 504-280-6225 189 F
ccboykin@uno.edu
BOYKIN, Coretta ... 251-578-1313 ... 3 D
cboykin@rstc.edu
BOYKIN, Gregory ... 252-985-5117 339 B
gboykin@ncwc.edu
BOYKIN, Justin ... 251-981-3771 ... 5 B
justin.boykin@columbiasouthern.edu
BOYKIN, Melinda ... 254-867-3761 448 F
melinda.boykin@tstc.edu
BOYKIN, Regena ... 601-635-2111 245 B
rboykin@eccc.edu
BOYKIN, Sutonia ... 724-480-3423 381 G
sutonia.boykin@ccbc.edu
BOYKIN, Ted ... 570-585-9327 381 A
tboykin@clarkssummitu.edu
BOYKIN, Tiffany ... 410-777-1239 197 C
tfboykin@aacc.edu
BOYKIN, Tiffany, F ... 410-777-1239 197 C
tfboykin@aacc.edu
BOYLAN, Erin ... 607-753-2516 317 D
erin.boylan@cortland.edu
BOYLAN, Joyce ... 562-977-6041 .. 43 C
joyce.boylan@fremont.edu
BOYLAN, Stanley ... 646-565-6412 322 C
stanley.boylan@touro.edu
BOYLAN, Stanley, L ... 646-565-6412 322 B
stanley.boylan@touro.edu
BOYLE, Alicia ... 740-284-5453 352 I
aboyle@franciscan.edu
BOYLE, Allison, J ... 410-576-7644 201 F
aboyle@oag.state.md.us
BOYLE, Ann ... 480-219-6107 249 C
aboyle@atsu.edu
BOYLE, Ann, L ... 610-799-1736 388 B
aboyle@lccc.edu
BOYLE, Antonio ... 302-857-6351 .. 90 D
aboyle@desu.edu
BOYLE, Brian ... 251-442-2287 ... 8 C
bboyle@umobile.edu
BOYLE, Carol Ann ... 516-877-3775 288 L
boyle@adelphi.edu
BOYLE, Chandler ... 336-278-7423 328 H
kboyle8@elon.edu
BOYLE, Jeffery ... 864-592-4823 411 E
boylej@sccsc.edu
BOYLE, Kate ... 360-438-4310 482 D
kboyle@stmartin.edu
BOYLE, Kevin ... 973-618-3372 275 E
kboyle@caldwell.edu
BOYLE, Kevin ... 570-408-6302 402 B
kevin.boyle2@wilkes.edu
BOYLE, Paula ... 646-795-4510 322 C
paula.pashkoff@touro.edu
BOYLE, Robert, J ... 904-620-4663 111 A
rboyle@unf.edu
BOYLE, Roger ... 202-464-6464 462 B
roger.boyle@worldlearning.org
BOYLE, Sharon, I ... 215-926-2200 398 D
sharon.boyle@temple.edu
BOYLE, Tracy ... 267-341-3616 385 I
tboyle2@holyfamily.edu
BOYLE JONES, Becky ... 218-477-4000 239 A
BOYLES, Bruce ... 704-406-3275 328 I
bboyles@gardner-webb.edu
BOYLES, Dwayne ... 434-961-5488 474 B
dboyles@pvcc.edu
BOYLES, Erin, I ... 412-578-8774 380 A
eiboyles@carlow.edu
BOYLES, Joel ... 662-562-3451 247 E
jsboyles@northwestms.edu
BOYLES, John Dixon ... 903-823-3192 445 C
johndixon.boyles@texarkanacollege.edu
BOYLES, Patrice ... 773-821-2453 134 J
pboyles@csu.edu
BOYLES, Shery ... 919-760-8581 331 A
boyless@meredith.edu
BOYNTON, Andrew, C .. 617-552-4107 207 A
andy.boynton@bc.edu
BOYNTON,
Christopher, E ... 207-581-1484 196 D
christopher.boynton@maine.edu
BOYNTON, Diane ... 831-646-4097 .. 52 H
dboynton@mpc.edu
BOYNTON, Eric ... 608-363-2667 490 I
boyntone@beloit.edu
BOYSEN, Kelly ... 713-743-2841 451 G
krboysen@uh.edu
BOYSUN, Virginia ... 406-377-9404 262 G
vboysun@dawson.edu
BOZARTH, Diane ... 573-288-6473 251 I
dbozarth@culver.edu
BOZARTH, Sandra ... 661-654-3042 .. 30 C
sbozarth2@csub.edu
BOZIAN, Charles ... 718-262-5165 295 D
cbozian@york.cuny.edu
BOZINSKI, Glenn ... 570-674-6434 389 H
gbozinski@misericordia.edu
BOZON, Brandon ... 254-298-8606 445 B
bozonb819@templejc.edu
BOZYLINSKY, Garry ... 860-465-5537 .. 85 G
bozylinskyg@easternct.edu
BOZYM, Rebecca ... 412-536-1158 386 H
rebecca.bozym@laroche.edu
BOZZA, Brian ... 239-590-1250 109 G
bbozza@fgcu.edu
BRAATZ, Brady, J ... 913-971-3452 175 H
bbraatz@mnu.edu
BRABHAM, Sherry, F ... 212-217-4020 299 C
sherry_brabham@fitnyc.edu
BRABO, Andria ... 970-339-6518 .. 77 G
andria.brabo@aims.edu
BRABY, Randy ... 435-283-7058 460 C
randy.braby@snow.edu
BRACCIANO, Susan ... 816-271-4214 256 C
braccian@missouriwestern.edu
BRACCO, Anthony ... 212-237-8613 294 B
abracco@jjay.cuny.edu
BRACERO, Carmen, A ... 787-844-8181 511 E
carmen.bracero@upr.edu
BRACEROS, Amy ... 909-537-3224 .. 33 B
abracero@csusb.edu
BRACEY,
Christopher, A ... 202-994-6510 .. 92 C
cbracey@gwu.edu
BRACEY,
Christopher, A ... 202-994-6510 .. 92 C
cabracey@gwu.edu
BRACEY, David ... 714-772-3330 .. 26 B
BRACEY, Matthew ... 615-675-5329 427 D
mbracey@welch.edu
BRACH, Philip ... 704-461-5073 326 I
philipbrach@bac.edu
BRACHE-MELLO,
Allison, M ... 787-993-8886 510 E
allison.brache@upr.edu
BRACKE, Paul ... 509-313-6533 479 E
bracke@gonzaga.edu
BRACKE, Paul, J ... 509-313-6533 479 E
bracke@gonzaga.edu
BRACKEN, Carol ... 817-515-5137 445 A
carol.bracken@tccd.edu
BRACKEN, Damien, S ... 617-747-2221 206 D
admissions@berklee.edu
BRACKEN, Diane ... 850-484-1175 105 G
dbracken@pensacolastate.edu
BRACKEN, Gary ... 239-938-7700 102 C
BRACKEN, Lisa ... 803-778-6652 406 A
brackenlm@cctech.edu
BRACKEN, Steven ... 713-226-5276 452 B
brackens@uhd.edu
BRACKETT, Geoffrey, L . 845-575-3000 305 C
geoffrey.brackett@marist.edu
BRACKETT, Maria ... 703-416-1441 465 E
mbrackett@divinemercy.edu
BRACKETT, Robert ... 708-563-1577 139 H
rbrackett@iit.edu
BRACKETT, Stacey ... 828-328-7309 330 B
stacey.brackett@lr.edu
BRACKETT, Suzanne ... 252-985-5102 339 B
sbrackett@ncwc.edu
BRACKIN, Anita ... 901-333-4018 424 E
abrackin@southwest.tn.edu
BRACKIN, Chad ... 225-578-4736 188 J
cmb@lsu.edu
BRACKIN, Stewart ... 731-989-6911 418 H
sbrackin@fhu.edu
BRACKMANN, Sarah ... 512-863-1987 444 F
brackmas@southwestern.edu
BRACY, Judy ... 504-520-7317 193 C
jbracy@xula.edu
BRACY, Marion ... 504-520-7507 193 C
mbracy@xula.edu
BRADACH, Carmen ... 218-749-7743 238 D
c.bradach@minnesotanorth.edu
BRADBERRY, Martha ... 336-217-7221 329 B
BRADBERRY, Richard ... 443-885-3488 200 F
richard.bradberry@morgan.edu
BRADBURN, Chelsea ... 810-762-9770 225 F
cbradburn@kettering.edu
BRADBURY, Amy ... 850-201-8519 112 B
amy.bradbury@tcc.fl.edu
BRADBURY, Nikki ... 205-665-6044 ... 8 D
bradburynp@montevallo.edu
BRADDOCK, Glenn ... 518-782-6567 314 K
gbraddock@siena.edu
BRADDOCK, Heather, C 423-652-4742 419 F
hcbraddock@king.edu
BRADDOCK, Reb ... 850-644-0453 110 B
rbraddock@admin.fsu.edu
BRADDY, Linda ... 972-860-4806 433 G
BRADDY, William ... 540-261-8450 470 D
bill.braddy@svu.edu
BRADEN, Kale ... 916-484-8408 .. 50 J
bradenk@arc.losrios.edu
BRADEN, Kimberly, M .. 724-589-2167 398 F
kbraden@thiel.edu
BRADFIELD, Brett ... 605-331-6712 416 C
brett.bradfield@usiouxfalls.edu
BRADFIELD, Carol ... 407-303-9585 .. 95 A
carol.bradfield@ahu.edu
BRADFIELD, Jennifer, S 440-775-8400 357 G
jennifer.bradfield@oberlin.edu
BRADFIELD, Tanisha ... 714-432-5509 .. 38 F
tbradfield@occ.cccd.edu
BRADFORD, Adam ... 208-282-2490 131 E
adambradford@isu.edu
BRADFORD, Arthur ... 972-780-3600 453 C
arthur.bradford@untdallas.edu
BRADFORD, Ashlee ... 325-793-4984 439 A
bradford.ashlee@mcm.edu
BRADFORD, Brian ... 323-466-6663 .. 44 A
BRADFORD, Carmen ... 501-370-5214 .. 21 A
cebradford@philander.edu
BRADFORD, Carol, R ... 614-685-4411 358 E
bradford.885@osu.edu
BRADFORD, SR., Corey 708-235-7421 138 C
cbradford2@govst.edu
BRADFORD, Darryl ... 616-432-3418 229 H
darryl.bradfor@prts.edu
BRADFORD, George ... 909-607-8709 .. 37 I
george_bradford@kgi.edu
BRADFORD, John ... 303-273-3000 .. 79 A
jbradford@mines.edu
BRADFORD, Kelema, K . 718-289-5100 292 H
kelema.bradford@bcc.cuny.edu
BRADFORD, Kevin ... 606-878-4718 182 D
kevin.bradford@kctcs.edu
BRADFORD, Lawrence .. 323-241-5280 .. 49 I
bradfoll@lasc.edu
BRADFORD, Michael ... 860-486-4037 .. 89 B
michael.bradford@uconn.edu
BRADFORD, Paul ... 805-565-6033 .. 75 I
pbradford@westmont.edu
BRADFORD, Rebecca ... 843-355-4121 413 C
bradfordr@wiltech.edu
BRADFORD, Tessie ... 409-984-6156 449 D
bradfordts@lamarpa.edu
BRADFORD, Todd ... 706-236-2231 116 A
tbradford@berry.edu
BRADFORD DIAZ,
Morgan ... 641-784-5108 166 B
mjbradfo@graceland.edu
BRADLEY, Alana ... 740-474-8896 358 A
abradley@ohiochristian.edu
BRADLEY, Angela ... 228-497-7630 246 F
angela.bradley@mgccc.edu
BRADLEY, Anna, S ... 310-825-3935 .. 69 D
aspainbradley@equity.ucla.edu
BRADLEY, Bonita ... 912-358-3159 124 H
bradleyb@savannahstate.edu
BRADLEY, Brandon ... 660-263-3900 250 G
brandonbradley@cccb.edu
BRADLEY, Carla ... 404-894-2575 119 D
carla.bradley@studentlife.gatech.edu
BRADLEY, Cedric ... 228-896-2519 246 F
cedric.bradley@mgccc.edu
BRADLEY, Christian ... 918-293-5440 368 B
christian.bradley@okstate.edu
BRADLEY, Dale, R ... 304-367-4692 487 H
dale.bradley@pierpont.edu
BRADLEY, Dana ... 202-994-8500 .. 92 C
dana_bradley@gwu.edu
BRADLEY, Dana ... 443-543-5628 202 G
bradleyd@umbc.edu
BRADLEY, Derek ... 715-425-3300 496 A
derek.bradley@uwrf.edu
BRADLEY, Desirae' ... 903-923-2321 435 A
desiraeb@etbu.edu
BRADLEY, Earlhagi ... 315-229-5311 313 F
ebradley@stlawu.edu
BRADLEY, Elizabeth ... 845-437-7200 323 H
elbradley@vassar.edu
BRADLEY, Gerry ... 502-852-5295 185 E
tgerald.bradley@louisville.edu
BRADLEY, Gerry ... 502-852-5295 185 E
tgerard.bradley@louisville.edu
BRADLEY, Heather ... 229-732-5928 114 I
heatherbradley@andrewcollege.edu
BRADLEY, James ... 936-294-1900 449 E
jim@shsu.edu
BRADLEY, Jennifer ... 319-398-5537 167 H
jennifer.bradley@kirkwood.edu
BRADLEY, Jennifer ... 808-734-9890 129 E
jbradley@hawaii.edu
BRADLEY, Jon-Pierre ... 630-617-6458 137 E
jon-pierre.bradley@elmhurst.edu
BRADLEY, Joseph ... 410-617-2865 199 G
jbradley@loyola.edu
BRADLEY, Julie, M ... 972-758-3821 432 I
jbradley@collin.edu
BRADLEY, Karen ... 951-552-8913 .. 27 J
kbradley@calbaptist.edu
BRADLEY, Katy ... 405-789-6400 369 G
kbradley@snu.edu
BRADLEY, Katy ... 405-491-6336 369 G
kbradley@snu.edu
BRADLEY, Kim, S ... 704-687-5700 342 C
kim.bradley@uncc.edu
BRADLEY, Kirk ... 850-484-1764 105 G
kbradley@pensacolastate.edu
BRADLEY, LaKisha ... 831-646-4261 .. 52 H
lbradley@mpc.edu
BRADLEY, Marcy, K ... 607-871-2350 289 E
bradlemk@alfred.edu
BRADLEY, Mark ... 360-882-2200 .. 43 G
markbradley@gs.edu
BRADLEY, Mary Jane ... 870-972-3057 .. 17 I
mbradley@astate.edu
BRADLEY, Monica ... 817-257-7513 431 B
monica.bradley@tcu.edu
BRADLEY, Nedra ... 601-484-8674 246 B
nbradley@meridiancc.edu
BRADLEY, Pamela ... 903-927-3260 457 I
pbradley@wileyc.edu
BRADLEY, Patricia ... 410-704-0203 204 B
pbradley@towson.edu
BRADLEY, Rebecca ... 559-453-2021 .. 43 D
rebecca.bradley@fresno.edu
BRADLEY, Renee ... 419-995-8200 360 B
bradley.l@rhodesstate.edu
BRADLEY, Roger ... 386-267-0565 .. 97 R
BRADLEY, Ryan ... 205-348-8327 ... 7 G
ryan.bradley@ua.edu
BRADLEY, Ryan ... 503-552-1862 374 B
rbradley@nunm.edu
BRADLEY, Sha ... 909-621-8277 .. 63 E
sbradley@scrippscollege.edu
BRADLEY, Shane ... 864-379-8766 408 F
bradley@erskine.edu
BRADLEY, Shannon ... 575-527-7524 287 A
shanbrad@nmsu.edu
BRADLEY, Stephen, L ... 864-242-5100 405 H
BRADLEY, Susie ... 352-245-4119 112 D
susie.bradley@taylorcollege.edu
BRADLEY, Tashia ... 937-708-5648 363 G
tbradley@wilberforce.edu
BRADLEY, Tashia ... 903-927-3329 457 I
tbradley@wileyc.edu
BRADLEY, Tina ... 870-508-6130 .. 18 B
tbradley@asumh.edu
BRADLEY, Tracey ... 865-539-7158 424 C
tcbradley@pstcc.edu
BRADLEY, Tracy ... 304-357-4813 486 J
tracybradley@ucwv.edu
BRADLEY, Trish ... 610-902-8131 379 E
pl722@cabrini.edu
BRADLEY, Tyler ... 540-828-5745 464 C
tbradley2@bridgewater.edu
BRADLEY, Vinson ... 251-580-2103 ... 1 I
vinson.bradley@coastalalabama.edu
BRADLEY-ARMSTRONG,
Akirah ... 831-459-4287 .. 71 A
vcsas@ucsc.edu
BRADLEY BRENNAN,
Dolores ... 404-681-3643 126 A
BRADLEY-HASTY,
Barbara ... 252-536-3386 334 G
bhasty399@halifaxcc.edu
BRADSHAW, Amanda ... 910-592-8081 337 D
jbradshaw@sampsoncc.edu

BRASEL, Steve .... 312-329-4194 144 F
steve.brasel@moody.edu
BRASFIELD, Logan .... 870-633-4480.. 19 E
lbrasfield@eacc.edu
BRASFIELD, Molly, A .... 601-984-1010 248 G
mbrasfield@umc.edu
BRASHEAR, Allison .... 716-829-3955 315 F
vphs@buffalo.edu
BRASHEAR, Jenna .... 270-852-3291 183 B
jbrashear@kwc.edu
BRASHEAR, Pam .... 714-895-8234.. 38 E
pbrashear@gwc.cccd.edu
BRASHEARS, Randolph .. 978-934-2384 211 G
randolph_brashears@uml.edu
BRASHIER, Jason .... 731-989-6009 418 H
jbrashier@fhu.edu
BRASIER, Terry .... 828-398-7146 331 K
terrygbrasier@abtech.edu
BRASKAMP, Corey .... 605-256-5227 415 G
corey.braskamp@dsu.edu
BRASSEUR, Gary, V ...... 989-964-4259 229 L
gvb@svsu.edu
BRASSEUR, Susan, M .... 989-964-6016 229 L
brasseur@svsu.edu
BRASSIL, Kristoffer, W .. 617-358-7000 207 C
kbrassil@bu.edu
BRASURE, III, Ralph ..... 860-515-3873.. 85 D
BRASWELL, Debbi .... 601-968-5920 244 C
dbraswell@belhaven.edu
BRASWELL, Don .... 318-257-2120 192 A
braswell@latech.edu
BRASWELL, Jody .... 417-690-3376 250 K
braswell@cofo.edu
BRASWELL, Kevin .... 931-372-6092 425 B
kbraswell@tntech.edu
BRASWELL, Macy .... 870-235-4078.. 21 E
macybraswell@saumag.edu
BRASWELL, Macy .... 870-235-4991.. 21 E
macybraswell@saumag.edu
BRASWELL, Mavour .... 432-264-5025 436 H
mbraswell@howardcollege.edu
BRAT, Dave .... 434-582-7367 467 E
dabrat@liberty.edu
BRATANOV, Michael ...... 216-791-5000 350 F
michael.bratanov@cim.edu
BRATCHER, James .... 636-922-8238 258 A
BRATHWAITE, Ormond . 216-987-5008 351 D
ormond.brathwaite@tri-c.edu
BRATHWAITE, Renea, C 612-343-4166 241 O
rcbrathw@northcentral.edu
BRATSCH, John .... 559-730-3830.. 39 C
johnbr@cos.edu
BRATSCH-PRINCE,
Dawn .... 515-294-6410 163 E
deprince@iastate.edu
BRATTEN, Amy .... 863-667-5238 108 I
anbratten@seu.edu
BRATTIN, Emily .... 913-288-7601 174 H
ebrattin@kckcc.edu
BRATTON, John .... 501-332-0276.. 18 D
jbratton@asutr.edu
BRATTON, Kevin .... 248-942-3214 228 H
kmbratto@oaklandcc.edu
BRATTON, Marissa .... 808-544-0249 128 E
mbratton@hpu.edu
BRATTON, Tara .... 501-337-5000.. 18 D
tbratton@asutr.edu
BRATULIN, Paul .... 909-384-8978.. 60 F
pbratulin@sbccd.cc.ca.us
BRAUCKMULLER, Lois .. 352-854-2322.. 97 L
brauckml@cf.edu
BRAUD, Terry .... 985-448-4017 192 C
terry.braud@nicholls.edu
BRAUER, Cynthia, A ..... 757-221-1693 465 B
cabra1@wm.edu
BRAUER, Dan .... 414-930-3121 493 E
brauerd@mtmary.edu
BRAUER, Douglas .... 904-632-5151 101 A
douglas.brauer@fscj.edu
BRAULT, Kelly, N .... 248-370-4921 229 F
brault@oakland.edu
BRAUN, Amanda .... 414-229-6599 495 B
abraun25@uwm.edu
BRAUN, Bernie .... 225-578-1295 188 K
bbraun@lsu.edu
BRAUN, Dennis .... 850-729-6493 104 L
braund@nwfsc.edu
BRAUN, Eric .... 740-351-3542 360 E
ebraun@shawnee.edu
BRAUN, Frank .... 440-826-3566 348 C
fbraun@bw.edu
BRAUN, Gregory .... 815-280-2263 140 I
gbraun@jjc.edu
BRAUN, Gretchen .... 864-294-3137 408 I
gretchen.braun@furman.edu
BRAUN, Keith, V .... 727-816-3336 105 E
braunk@phsc.edu
BRAUN, Lynn .... 419-783-2548 351 J
lbraun@defiance.edu
BRAUN, Mark, J .... 515-281-6426 163 D
mark.braun@iowaregents.edu
BRAUN, Mary, C .... 319-273-6144 163 G
mary.braun@uni.edu
BRAUN, Ronald .... 620-947-3121 177 F
ronb@tabor.edu
BRAUN, Sara .... 903-923-2136 435 A
sbraun@etbu.edu
BRAUN, Shannon .... 909-607-8170.. 37 I
sbraun@kgi.edu
BRAUNGARD, John ...... 518-629-4507 302 A
j.braungard@hvcc.edu
BRAUNGARD, John ...... 518-276-6000 311 J
BRAUSCH, Anthony, R .. 513-231-2223 348 A
abrausch@athenaeum.edu
BRAVEK, Karen .... 605-688-4451 416 A
karen.bravek@sdstate.edu
BRAVER, Joel .... 845-782-1380 326 C
BRAVMAN, John, C .... 570-577-1511 379 A
john.bravman@bucknell.edu
BRAVO, Amy .... 212-261-1538 308 H
abravo@nyit.edu
BRAVO, Bruce .... 210-999-7601 451 B
bbravo@trinity.edu
BRAVO, Deyse .... 423-236-2789 422 H
dbravo@southern.edu
BRAVO, Karen, E .... 317-274-2581 157 B
kbravo@iupui.edu
BRAWLEY, Susan .... 336-917-5455 339 H
susan.brawley@salem.edu
BRAXTON, Asella .... 404-270-5078 126 A
aybraxton@spelman.edu
BRAXTON, Joanne, E .... 631-451-4160 320 G
braxtoj@sunysuffolk.edu
BRAXTON, Pamela .... 610-519-4032 401 B
pamela.braxton@villanova.edu
BRAY, Brian .... 207-859-4730 194 B
brain.bray@colby.edu
BRAY, Brittney .... 909-793-2121.. 72 E
BRAY, Corey .... 405-208-5301 367 E
cbray@okcu.edu
BRAY, Crystal .... 405-382-9287 369 E
c.bray@sscok.edu
BRAY, John .... 765-677-1771 157 F
john.bray@indwes.edu
BRAY, Kevin .... 803-822-3586 409 E
brayk@midlandstech.edu
BRAY, Kristen .... 315-279-5000 303 D
kbray@keuka.edu
BRAY, Laura .... 414-297-6048 498 B
braylm@matc.edu
BRAY, Lee .... 252-493-7264 336 E
lbray@email.pittcc.edu
BRAY, Paul .... 515-964-0601 166 A
brayp@faith.edu
BRAY, Rich .... 979-209-7285 430 I
richard.bray@blinn.edu
BRAY, Sean .... 410-617-2838 199 G
sbray@loyola.edu
BRAY, Stefanie .... 319-895-4243 164 E
sbray@cornellcollege.edu
BRAY MCNATT,
Rosemary .... 510-430-3335.. 66 F
rbraymcnatt@sksm.edu
BRAYBOY, Bryan .... 480-965-5327.. 11 A
bryan.brayboy@asu.edu
BRAZAS, Tony, A .... 757-479-3706 472 A
tbrazas@vbts.edu
BRAZELL, Frank .... 910-221-2224 330 G
fbrazell@manna.edu
BRAZELL-BRAYBOY,
Jessica .... 801-832-2235 461 A
jbrazell-brayboy@westminstercollege.edu
BRAZELTON, Kent .... 713-646-1889 443 C
kbrazelton@stcl.edu
BRAZIEL, Ellen .... 503-883-2492 373 E
BRAZIER, Elise .... 512-313-3000 432 N
elise.brazier@concordia.edu
BRAZIL-CRUZ, Lisceth .. 530-661-5700.. 77 C
BRAZILL, Derrick .... 718-262-2780 295 D
dbrazill@york.cuny.edu
BRAZZIL, Nancy .... 512-471-1232 454 C
nancy@po.utexas.edu
BREAM, Insiya .... 301-985-7000 203 C
insiya.bream@umgc.edu
BREAU, Walter, C .... 413-265-2222 208 B
breauw@elms.edu
BREAUX, Aminta .... 301-860-3555 203 D
president@bowiestate.edu
BREAUX, Danielle .... 985-448-7041 192 C
danielle.breaux@nicholls.edu
BREAUX, Megan .... 337-482-1394 192 F
mbreaux@louisiana.edu
BREAUX, Paula .... 337-482-6981 192 F
paula.breaux@louisiana.edu
BREAVLT, Donna .... 201-200-2101 278 F
dbreavlt@njcu.edu
BREAZEAL, Cynthia .... 617-253-1000 215 G
BREAZILE, Chad .... 816-279-7000 249 D
chad@abtu.edu
BRECHER, Sharon .... 305-534-7050 112 C
sbrecher@talmudicu.edu
BRECHTEL, Scott .... 704-687-7329 342 C
sjbrecht@uncc.edu
BRECKENRIDGE, James 650-433-3826.. 55 K
jbreckenridge@paloaltou.edu
BRECKENRIDGE,
Jim, G .... 717-245-4711 502 E
james.g.breckenridge.civ@mail.mil
BRECKHEIMER, Debra ... 310-660-5182.. 41 J
dbreckhe@elcamino.edu
BRECKINRIDGE, Robert 610-861-1478 390 D
breckinridger@moravian.edu
BRECKNER, Laura, S .... 517-750-1200 230 F
lowen@arbor.edu
BRECZINSKI, Christian . 218-755-3883 237 B
christian.breczinski@bemidjistate.edu
BREDEMAN, Blaine .... 573-681-5187 254 A
bredemanb@lincolnu.edu
BREDESON, Janna .... 770-426-2700 122 A
janna.bredeson@life.edu
BREED, Terre .... 409-212-5724 430 B
BREEDEN, Ann Lloyd .... 804-289-8732 471 E
abreeden@richmond.edu
BREEDEN, Suzette .... 304-205-6614 487 D
BREEDLOVE, Billy .... 806-742-2011 450 A
BREEDLOVE, Billy .... 806-742-2116 450 C
billy.breedlove@ttu.edu
BREEDLOVE, Paul .... 541-880-2239 373 B
breedlove@klamathcc.edu
BREEMS, Jennifer .... 712-722-6043 165 E
jenni.breems@dordt.edu
BREEN, David .... 413-542-2254 205 D
dbreen@amherst.edu
BREEN, Dennis .... 740-284-5201 352 I
dbreen@franciscan.edu
BREEN, Lorraine .... 301-295-3007 502 B
lorraine.breen@usuhs.edu
BREER, Mary .... 217-234-5401 141 H
mbreer@lakelandcollege.edu
BREERWOOD, Adam, J . 601-403-1201 247 F
abreerwood@prcc.edu
BREES, Chris .... 641-844-5679 167 E
chris.brees@iavalley.edu
BREESE, Eric .... 312-567-3153 139 H
ebreese@iit.edu
BREESE, Jeffrey, R .... 330-823-2690 362 E
breesejr@mountunion.edu
BREGE, Nicholas .... 989-358-7202 220 G
bregen@alpenacc.edu
BREGOVI, Tiffany .... 215-641-6300 390 A
tbregovi@mc3.edu
BREHENY, Marie .... 413-775-1397 214 C
brehenym@gcc.mass.edu
BREHLER, Elizabeth ...... 336-506-4138 331 J
elizabeth.brehler@alamancecc.edu
BREINER, Ozzie .... 610-758-3500 388 C
lb05@lehigh.edu
BREISTER, Peggy .... 920-424-1133 495 C
BREIT, Karen .... 715-634-4790 491 L
kbreit@lco.edu
BREITBACH, William ..... 530-242-7555.. 64 A
wbreitbach@shastacollege.edu
BREITBARTH,
Jonathan, S .... 651-641-8796 235 A
breitbarth@csp.edu
BREITENBACH, Edward . 231-777-0526 228 C
edward.breitenbach@muskegoncc.edu
BREITFELD, Adrian .... 310-476-9777.. 25 N
adrian.breitfeld@aju.edu
BREITFELD, Erika .... 517-371-5140 232 K
breitfee@cooley.edu
BREITHART, Jodi .... 269-337-7228 225 B
jodi.breithart@kzoo.edu
BREITHAUPT, Jeff .... 917-493-4702 304 L
jbreithaupt@msmnyc.edu
BREITHAUPT, Scott .... 706-238-5897 116 A
sbreithaupt@berry.edu
BREITIGAN, Katie .... 585-567-9227 301 G
katie.breitigan@houghton.edu
BREITLER, Alex .... 209-954-5151.. 61 H
alex.breitler@deltacollege.edu
BREITLING, Nathan .... 626-966-4576.. 56 F
nate@agu.edu
BREITMEYER, Chris ...... 503-338-2425 372 C
cbreitmeyer@clatsopcc.edu
BREITSPRECKER, Lisa ... 414-930-3131 493 E
breitspl@mtmary.edu
BREJA, Lisa .... 641-844-5576 167 C
lisa.breja@iavalley.edu
BREJC, Jessica .... 303-546-5291.. 81 N
jbrejc@naropa.edu
BREKKE, Paul .... 701-858-3485 345 C
paul.brekke@minostateu.edu
BREKKE WAGONER,
Laura, K .... 304-637-1267 486 D
brekkel@dewv.edu
BRELAND, Barbara .... 585-340-9631 296 B
bbreland@crcds.edu
BRELAND, Byron, D .... 408-274-6700.. 62 E
byron.breland@sjeccd.edu
BRELAND, Jennifer, R ... 205-934-3555..... 8 A
jbreland@uab.edu
BRELAND, Moddie .... 914-674-7325 305 H
mbreland@mercy.edu
BREMAR, Nancy .... 304-424-8000 490 A
nancy.bremar@wvup.edu
BREMER, Cheryl .... 574-372-5100 155 C
bremercl@grace.edu
BREMER, Cris, M .... 559-489-2220.. 67 A
crism.bremer@fresnocitycollege.edu
BREMER-MILLER,
Heather .... 319-296-4283 166 E
heather.bremermiller@hawkeyecollege.edu
BREMNER, Ellen .... 860-439-2413.. 87 F
ebremner@conncoll.edu
BREMS, Nora .... 317-738-8864 155 A
nbrems@franklincollege.edu
BRENBERG, Brian .... 212-659-7200 303 E
bbrenberg@tkc.edu
BRENDT, Lucette .... 254-526-1205 431 E
lucette.brendt@ctcd.edu
BRENEMAN, Curt .... 518-276-6305 311 J
brenec@rpi.edu
BRENEMAN, Jeff .... 269-387-2071 232 J
jeff.breneman@wmich.edu
BRENEMAN, Matt .... 714-449-7480.. 51 D
mbrenema@ketchum.edu
BRENES, Omar .... 913-288-7386 174 H
obrenes@kckcc.edu
BRENN, James, E .... 803-535-5326 406 E
jbrenn@claflin.edu
BRENNAN, Anna .... 610-989-1200 400 F
BRENNAN, Anne .... 847-376-7046 146 E
abrennan@oakton.edu
BRENNAN, Catherine .... 973-596-3124 278 G
catherine.brennan@njit.edu
BRENNAN,
Christopher, P .... 727-864-8122.. 98 G
brennacp@eckerd.edu
BRENNAN, David .... 410-857-2284 200 D
dbrennan@mcdaniel.edu
BRENNAN, Joe .... 802-831-1244 462 F
jbrennan@vermontlaw.edu
BRENNAN, Jonathan ..... 518-629-7311 302 A
j.brennan@hvcc.edu
BRENNAN, Joseph, A ... 973-655-3054 278 C
brennanjos@montclair.edu
BRENNAN, Joyce .... 508-678-2811 213 F
joyce.brennan@bristolcc.edu
BRENNAN, Kate .... 856-225-6577 281 A
katecb@camden.rutgers.edu
BRENNAN, Kelly .... 843-953-1642 406 D
kbrenna1@citadel.edu
BRENNAN, Kristin .... 207-725-3000 194 A
BRENNAN, Kwi .... 201-200-3489 278 F
kbrennan@njcu.edu
BRENNAN, Kyle .... 309-438-5626 140 C
ksbren1@ilstu.edu
BRENNAN, Lipa .... 718-438-2727 326 D
rlb@novominsk.com
BRENNAN, Mary .... 512-245-2317 449 G
mb18@txstate.edu
BRENNAN, Megan .... 801-883-8336 458 B
BRENNAN, Michael .... 813-253-7124 102 A
mbrennan@hccfl.edu
BRENNAN, Monica .... 207-453-5129 195 B
mbrennan@kvcc.me.edu
BRENNAN, Natasha .... 360-676-2772 480 G
nmbrennan@nwic.edu

Index of Key Administrators BRENNAN – BRIGHAM 559

BRENNAN, Robert, J ..... 301-447-7432 201 A
brennan@msmary.edu
BRENNAN, Robert, J ..... 410-293-1482 502 I
rbrennan@usna.edu
BRENNAN, Terence .... 303-753-6046.. 83 C
tbrennan@rmcad.edu
BRENNAN, Terrence, P . 972-881-5734 432 I
tbrennan@collin.edu
BRENNAN, Victoria .... 805-482-2755.. 59 G
vbrennan@stjohnsem.edu
BRENNAN, William, J ... 207-326-2221 195 G
bill.brennan@mma.edu
BRENNAN-SOKOLOWSKI,
Kelley .... 848-445-2620 281 B
brennank@registrar.rutgers.edu
BRENNAN-TONETTA,
Margaret .... 848-932-3776 281 C
mbrennan@rutgers.edu
BRENNEMAN, Brockton 951-552-8865.. 27 J
bbrenneman@calbaptist.edu
BRENNEMAN, Darnell ... 740-857-1311 360 C
dbrenneman@rosedale.edu
BRENNEMAN, David ..... 812-855-0608 156 C
davabren@indiana.edu
BRENNEMAN, James, E 510-841-1905.. 27 B
jbrenneman@bst.edu
BRENNEMAN, Todd ...... 334-386-7662.... 5 D
tbrenneman@faulkner.edu
BRENNEMANN, Chris ... 217-228-5432 147 C
c.brennemann14@quincy.edu
BRENNER, Beth .... 530-754-2023.. 69 A
blbrenner@ucdavis.edu
BRENNER, Christina ..... 610-436-3511 394 F
cbrenner@wcupa.edu
BRENNER, Jim .... 562-947-8755.. 65 H
jimbrenner@scuhs.edu
BRENNER, Jordan .... 216-881-1700 358 K
jbrenner@ohiotech.edu
BRENNER, Matthew ...... 610-359-5070 381 J
mbrenner@dccc.edu
BRENNER, Viktor .... 262-691-5577 499 A
vbrenner@wctc.edu
BRENNER JOHNSON,
Hannah .... 619-239-0391.. 34 H
hbrenner@cwsl.edu
BRENNER-SCOTTI,
Laura .... 609-984-1141 283 D
lbrennerscotti@tesu.edu
BRENNIE, Matthew .... 845-688-6068 322 K
brenniem@sunyulster.edu
BRENT, Daniel .... 617-327-6777 219 G
dan_brent@williamjames.edu
BRENT, OP, James .... 202-495-3853.. 93 D
jbrent@dhs.edu
BRENTLINGER, Ann, M . 605-394-1604 415 I
ann.brentlinger@sdsmt.edu
BRESE, James .... 808-356-5272 128 E
jbrese@hpu.edu
BRESEE, Mikel .... 313-664-1546 222 C
mbresee@collegeforcreativestudies.edu
BRESEMAN, Mark, D .... 920-832-6519 492 B
mark.d.breseman@lawrence.edu
BRESETTE, Danielle .... 802-828-2800 463 A
dmd05080@ccv.vsc.edu
BRESLIN, James .... 502-272-7403 179 D
jbreslin@bellarmine.edu
BRESLIN, Kate .... 267-341-3352 385 I
kbreslin@holyfamily.edu
BRESLIN, Kyleen .... 406-994-2042 263 G
kyleen.breslin@montana.edu
BRESLIN, Matt .... 207-859-1111 196 A
breslinm@thomas.edu
BRESNAHAN, Barb .... 973-408-3348 276 B
bbresnahan@drew.edu
BRESNAHAN, Mary .... 508-767-7198 205 F
mbresnah@assumption.edu
BRESNAHAN, Nicole ..... 202-885-2822.. 91 D
nlbres@american.edu
BRESSETTE, Andrew ...... 706-290-2166 116 A
abressette@berry.edu
BRESSLER, Coleen .... 402-844-7006 268 A
coleen@northeast.edu
BRESSLER, Denise .... 307-268-2256 499 T
bressler@caspercollege.edu
BRESSLER, Rebecca, B . 662-915-7735 248 F
rbbressl@olemiss.edu
BRESSOUD, Suzanne .... 740-618-6173 349 D
bressoud.2@cotc.edu
BRETCH, Allyson .... 678-839-4107 127 A
abretch@westga.edu
BRETON, Susan .... 212-217-4260 299 C
susan_breton@fitnyc.edu
BRETSCHER, David .... 217-786-2238 142 F
david.bretscher@llcc.edu
BRETT, Jennifer .... 203-576-4122.. 89 A
acup@bridgeport.edu
BRETT, Maryellen .... 508-588-9100 214 F
BRETTSCHNEIDER,
Susan .... 763-576-4134 237 A
sbrettschneider@anokatech.edu
BRETZ, James .... 215-641-6643 390 A
jbretz@mc3.edu
BRETZ, Laurel .... 217-782-1086 142 F
laurel.bretz@llcc.edu
BREUCKMAN, Brandy ... 715-675-3331 498 E
breuckman@ntc.edu
BREUER, Catherine .... 952-806-3966 241 R
cappy.breuer@rasmussen.edu
BREUNINGER, Matthew 740-284-5363 352 I
mbreuninger@franciscan.edu
BREUNINGER, Rebecca . 215-968-8114 379 B
rebecca.breuninger@bucks.edu
BREUNINGER, Scott ...... 804-828-1803 472 D
breuningersc@vcu.edu
BREVIK, Eric .... 618-453-2469 149 G
eric.brevik@siu.edu
BREW, Alan .... 715-682-1329 493 G
abrew@northland.edu
BREWER, Brent .... 269-782-1276 230 D
bbrewer01@swmich.edu
BREWER, Carol .... 320-308-6158 240 D
carol.brewer@sctcc.edu
BREWER, Cecelia .... 913-288-7533 174 H
cbrewer@kckcc.edu
BREWER, Chris .... 615-494-8803 421 C
chris.brewer@mtsu.edu
BREWER, David, J .... 770-831-8882 121 E
BREWER, Debbie .... 614-825-6255 347 C
dbrewer@aiam.edu
BREWER, Deborah .... 813-988-5131.. 99 M
brewerd@floridacollege.edu
BREWER, Deborah .... 716-614-5911 309 E
dbrewer@niagaracc.suny.edu
BREWER, George .... 706-272-4456 118 A
gbrewer@daltonstate.edu
BREWER, Helen .... 409-933-8619 432 H
hbrewer1@com.edu
BREWER, Janet .... 501-760-4221.. 20 E
janet.brewer@np.edu
BREWER, Jerry, T .... 803-777-5783 412 A
jerry-brewer@sc.edu
BREWER, Joan .... 620-341-5367 173 C
jbrewer@emporia.edu
BREWER, John .... 301-687-4895 203 F
jbrewer@frostburg.edu
BREWER, Marcus .... 405-585-4102 367 B
marcus.brewer@okbu.edu
BREWER, Margaret .... 207-755-5285 194 J
mbrewer@cmcc.edu
BREWER, Margaret .... 719-549-2368.. 79 G
meg.brewer@csupueblo.edu
BREWER, Nancy, A .... 631-451-4064 320 G
brewern@sunysuffolk.edu
BREWER, Regina, L ...... 336-628-4554 336 F
rlbrewer@randolph.edu
BREWER, Rick .... 318-487-7401 187 B
rick.brewer@lcuniversity.edu
BREWER, Robb .... 817-722-1670 437 H
robb.brewer@tku.edu
BREWER, Robert, W ...... 336-272-7102 329 B
rbrewer@greensboro.edu
BREWER, Shaney .... 806-291-3500 457 B
brewers@wbu.edu
BREWER, Tiffany .... 708-709-3653 147 A
tbrewer@prairiestate.edu
BREWER, Tim .... 704-878-3205 335 I
tbrewer@mitchellcc.edu
BREWER, Timothy .... 310-825-9570.. 69 D
tbrewer@conet.ucla.edu
BREWICK, Andrew .... 509-335-3280 484 D
andrew.brewick@wsu.edu
BREWINGTON,
Donald, E .... 512-505-3054 437 B
debrewington@htu.edu
BREWINGTON, Mark ..... 910-630-7149 331 B
sbrewington@methodist.edu
BREWS, Peter, J .... 803-777-3176 412 A
peter.brews@moore.sc.edu
BREWSTER, Derrick .... 334-229-4241.... 4 B
dbrewster@alasu.edu
BREWSTER, Ed .... 360-538-4000 479 F
ed.brewster@ghc.edu
BREWSTER, Jay .... 310-506-4261.. 56 H
jay.brewster@pepperdine.edu
BREWSTER, Larissa .... 617-451-0010 217 B
BREWSTER, LaRita .... 662-252-8000 248 B
lbrewster@rustcollege.edu
BREY, Amanda .... 805-893-2529.. 70 E
amanda.brey@ucsb.edu
BREY, Nick .... 607-778-5379 317 A
breynh@sunybroome.edu
BREYER, Julia .... 760-773-2507.. 39 A
jbreyer@collegeofthedesert.edu
BREZIL, Chris .... 212-229-5300 307 E
brezilc@newschool.edu
BREZINA, Jenniffer .... 615-230-3557 424 F
jennifer.brezina@volstate.edu
BREZINSKI, Donald ...... 603-645-3109 273 E
d.brezinski@snhu.edu
BRHEL, Jan .... 607-844-8222 321 I
jmb068@tompkinscortland.edu
BRIAN, Robert, M .... 912-583-3107 116 D
rbrian@bpc.edu
BRIAND, Simone .... 913-234-0810 172 I
simone.briand@cleveland.edu
BRIAR, Jason .... 620-278-4218 177 E
jason.briar@sterling.edu
BRIAR, John .... 559-325-3600.. 28 F
jbriar@chsu.edu
BRICCA, Gregory .... 410-386-8229 197 G
gbricca@carrollcc.edu
BRICE, Diane .... 806-651-4902 447 D
dbrice@wtamu.edu
BRICE, Eloise, D .... 713-743-8872 451 F
edbrice@uh.edu
BRICE, Eloise, D .... 713-743-8165 451 G
edbrice@uh.edu
BRICELAND, Cynthia ..... 724-503-1001 401 D
cbriceland@washjeff.edu
BRICENO, Jaime .... 773-380-6780 133 C
BRICKER, Adrienne .... 614-292-9330 358 E
bricker.164@osu.edu
BRICKER, Erin .... 707-527-4679.. 63 C
ebricker@santarosa.edu
BRICKER, Lizette .... 650-574-6590.. 62 J
brickerl@smccd.edu
BRICKER, Rich .... 931-424-2049 426 F
rbricke1@utsouthern.edu
BRICKHOUSE,
Katelyn, M .... 716-878-3023 317 C
brickkm@buffalostate.edu
BRICKHOUSE,
Nancy, W .... 254-710-3601 430 F
nancy_brickhouse@baylor.edu
BRICKLE, Colleen .... 952-358-8158 239 C
colleen.brickle@normandale.edu
BRICKLEY, Ashley, M ... 573-882-4696 260 C
brickleya@missouri.edu
BRIDENSTINE, Amy ...... 620-417-1111 177 C
amy.bridenstine@sccc.edu
BRIDGE, Louise .... 801-863-8689 460 A
bridgelo@uvu.edu
BRIDGE, Morgan .... 970-248-1169.. 78 F
mbridge@coloradomesa.edu
BRIDGE, Ron .... 435-236-4002 459 G
ron.bridge@utahtech.edu
BRIDGEFORTH, Valerie . 601-318-6188 249 B
vbridgeforth@wmcarey.edu
BRIDGEMAN, Doris ...... 601-977-7836 248 E
dbridgeman@tougaloo.edu
BRIDGEMAN, Lindsay ... 800-955-2527.. 22 B
lbridgeman@grantham.edu
BRIDGEMAN, Lindsey ... 800-955-2527.. 22 B
lbridgeman@grantham.edu
BRIDGEMAN, Stella .... 865-329-3101 424 C
jcbridgeman@pstcc.edu
BRIDGEMAN, Valerie .... 740-362-3482 355 H
jbridgeman@mtso.edu
BRIDGES, Antoinette ..... 815-753-6727 145 H
abridges3@niu.edu
BRIDGES, Carl .... 217-443-8771 136 E
c.bridges@dacc.edu
BRIDGES, Chris .... 800-323-5692 347 G
chris.bridges@artacademy.edu
BRIDGES, Clarence, F ... 312-413-5946 151 D
cbridges@uic.edu
BRIDGES, Cynthia .... 361-698-1218 434 H
cbridges@delmar.edu
BRIDGES, Darryl .... 843-661-1201 408 H
dbridges@fmarion.edu
BRIDGES, David .... 404-894-7700 119 D
david.bridges@innovate.gatech.edu
BRIDGES, Edward .... 304-647-6439 489 C
ebridges@osteo.wvsom.edu
BRIDGES, Felicia, L ...... 510-981-2852.. 56 J
fbridges@peralta.edu
BRIDGES, Harold, A ...... 310-338-2700.. 51 C
drew.bridges@lmu.edu
BRIDGES, J. Thomas .... 704-847-5600 340 D
jbridges@ses.edu
BRIDGES, Katie .... 202-462-2101.. 93 A
kbridges@iwp.edu
BRIDGES, Kermit, S ...... 972-825-4652 444 C
president@sagu.edu
BRIDGES, LaDonna .... 508-626-4906 212 D
lbridges@framingham.edu
BRIDGES, Martin .... 910-410-1818 336 G
mwbridges@richmondcc.edu
BRIDGES, Michael, W ... 412-396-1813 382 E
bridgesm@duq.edu
BRIDGES, Robert .... 470-578-3622 121 J
rbridge7@kennesaw.edu
BRIDGES, Robert .... 912-583-3218 116 D
rbridges@bpc.edu
BRIDGES, Ruth .... 254-298-8309 445 B
ruth.bridges@templejc.edu
BRIDGES, Sharekka .... 843-921-6965 410 B
sbridges@netc.edu
BRIDGES, Steven, J ...... 812-464-1849 162 B
sjbridge@usi.edu
BRIDGES, Trent .... 254-295-8645 453 A
tbridges@umhb.edu
BRIDGES, Vernon, D ..... 818-947-2541.. 50 B
bridgevd@lavc.edu
BRIDGES, Vincent .... 405-682-7534 367 D
vincent.e.bridges@occc.edu
BRIDGES-KEE, Lorinnsa 202-274-5449.. 94 B
BRIDGESMITH, Lance ... 310-506-4700.. 56 H
lance.bridgesmith@pepperdine.edu
BRIDGMON, Phillip ...... 660-543-4116 259 K
bridgmon@ucmo.edu
BRIDWELL, Joy .... 406-395-4875 264 I
jbridwell@stonechild.edu
BRIELL, Scott .... 410-532-5105 201 C
sbriell@ndm.edu
BRIEN, Jane .... 845-758-4294 290 G
brien@bard.edu
BRIESKE, Sonya .... 480-732-7308.. 13 B
sonya.brieske@cgc.edu
BRIGADIER, Sean, M .... 817-531-7511 450 F
brigadier@txwes.edu
BRIGATI, Arthur, J .... 205-929-1448.... 6 B
ajb@miles.edu
BRIGG, Ronald .... 470-578-6000 121 J
BRIGGER, Clark .... 303-492-6301.. 83 M
clark.brigger@colorado.edu
BRIGGS, Alissa .... 508-793-7534 207 F
abriggs@clarku.edu
BRIGGS, Brittany .... 937-328-6543 350 D
briggsb@clarkstate.edu
BRIGGS, Catherine, R ... 856-222-9311 280 E
cbriggs@rcbc.edu
BRIGGS, Chad .... 847-628-2018 141 A
chad.briggs@judsonu.edu
BRIGGS, Darcy .... 605-394-2219 415 I
darcy.briggs@sdsmt.edu
BRIGGS, Douglas, S ..... 540-636-2900 464 O
dougb@christendom.edu
BRIGGS, Jeff .... 785-628-4200 173 E
jbriggs@fhsu.edu
BRIGGS, Jeffrey, C .... 513-244-4803 356 F
jeffrey.briggs@msj.edu
BRIGGS, SR., Jerryl ...... 662-254-3088 247 C
jerryl.briggs@mvsu.edu
BRIGGS, Julie, A .... 585-245-5616 317 E
briggsja@geneseo.edu
BRIGGS, Justine .... 585-395-5118 317 B
jabriggs@brockport.edu
BRIGGS, Kara .... 360-867-5344 479 C
BRIGGS, Kristin .... 336-249-8186 333 G
kristin_briggs@davidsondavie.edu
BRIGGS, Phillip .... 805-289-6036.. 74 B
pbriggs@vcccd.edu
BRIGGS, Stephen, R ..... 706-236-2281 116 A
sbriggs@berry.edu
BRIGGS, Susan .... 406-683-7303 263 E
susan.briggs@umwestern.edu
BRIGGS, Tammie .... 334-876-9236.... 2 D
tammie.briggs@wccs.edu
BRIGGS, Thyra .... 909-607-4408.. 44 K
thyra_briggs@hmc.edu
BRIGGS, Traci .... 254-526-1331 431 E
traci.briggs@ctcd.edu
BRIGGS, Wayne .... 214-333-5111 433 D
wayne@dbu.edu
BRIGGS, William .... 406-477-6215 262 F
wbriggs@cdkc.edu
BRIGGS-PICKETT,
Jodi, M .... 508-929-5000 213 D
BRIGHAM, Doug .... 208-459-5268 131 A
dbrigham@collegeofidaho.edu
BRIGHAM, Reginald ...... 573-466-4087 252 D
reginald.brigham@eastcentral.edu

BRIGHENTI, Kenneth .... 614-885-5585 359 K kbrighenti@pcj.edu
BRIGHT, Brett .... 402-323-3400 268 D
BRIGHT, Brett .... 620-665-3579 174 D brightb@hutchcc.edu
BRIGHT, David .... 863-667-5310 108 I drbright@seu.edu
BRIGHT, Harold .... 480-219-6036 249 C hbright@atsu.edu
BRIGHT, Harry .... 641-472-1178 168 A hbright@miu.edu
BRIGHT, Josh .... 805-893-8000.. 70 E
BRIGHT, Kristina .... 573-642-3361 261 F
BRIGHT, Sarah .... 636-481-3218 253 G sbright@jeffco.edu
BRIGHT, Steve .... 937-512-2524 360 F steve.bright@sinclair.edu
BRIGHT, Steve .... 540-828-8113 464 C sbright2@bridgewater.edu
BRIGHTON, Robyn, M .. 407-582-3895 113 C rbrighton1@valenciacollege.edu
BRIGHTSMAN, David .... 414-443-8739 497 A david.brightsman@wlc.edu
BRIGMAN, Kate .... 949-824-9351.. 69 C kate.brigman@uci.edu
BRIGNONI, Linda, M .... 818-677-2085.. 32 E linda.brignoni@csun.edu
BRIKER, Olga .... 610-795-6079 385 H obriker@haverford.edu
BRILEY, Dalton .... 540-464-7637 475 C brileydc@vmi.edu
BRILL, Ann, M .... 785-864-4755 177 G abrill@ku.edu
BRILL, Seth .... 601-925-7844 246 D sbrill@mc.edu
BRILLEY, Amy .... 217-362-6488 144 D abrilley@millikin.edu
BRILLHART, David .... 740-366-9319 349 D brillhart.5@cotc.edu
BRIM, Catherlyn .... 865-573-4517 419 E cbrim@johnsonu.edu
BRIMBERRY, Ryan .... 812-877-8621 160 C brimberr@rose-hulman.edu
BRIMHALL, Carrie .... 218-736-1503 238 K carrie.brimhall@minnesota.edu
BRIMHALL, Joseph .... 503-251-5712 377 A jebrimhall@uws.edu
BRIMLEY, Pamela .... 501-420-1219.. 17 D pamela.brimley@arkansasbaptist.edu
BRIMMER, Suzette .... 713-718-6158 436 E suzette.brimmer@hccs.edu
BRIMMER, Zachary .... 518-783-2302 314 K zbrimmer@siena.edu
BRIMMERMAN, Roger .. 620-242-0435 175 G
BRINDLE, Denise .... 978-665-3454 212 C dbrindl1@fitchburgstate.edu
BRINDLEY, Peter .... 423-266-4574 422 D
BRINDLEY, Roger, N .... 814-863-4030 391 F rnb5238@psu.edu
BRINER, Clare .... 708-974-5376 144 G brinerc@morainevalley.edu
BRINER, Sean .... 760-750-4404.. 33 C sbriner@csusm.edu
BRINEY, Colleen .... 479-575-5459.. 21 H cbriney@uark.edu
BRINGER, Michael .... 573-288-6528 251 I mbringer@culver.edu
BRINGHAM, Holly .... 509-682-6705 484 H hbringham@wvc.edu
BRINGLEY, Courtney .... 518-327-6059 310 G cbringley@paulsmiths.edu
BRINING, Patricia .... 215-968-8091 379 B patricia.brining@bucks.edu
BRINK, Ben .... 314-246-7150 261 D benjaminbrink87@webster.edu
BRINK, Laura .... 617-521-2127 218 C laura.brink@simmons.edu
BRINK, Stephanie .... 573-823-8594 250 H sbrink@centralmethodist.edu
BRINK-DRESCHER, Judith .... 516-323-3925 306 I jdrescher@molloy.edu
BRINKER, JR., Thomas, M .... 215-572-4039 378 E brinkert@arcadia.edu
BRINKLEY, Bill .... 660-543-4123 259 K brinkley@ucmo.edu
BRINKLEY, David .... 270-745-6140 186 A david.brinkley@wku.edu
BRINKLEY, Derek .... 312-369-7493 136 C dbrinkley@colum.edu
BRINKLEY, Frank .... 336-770-3349 343 C brinkleyt@uncsa.edu
BRINKLEY, Martin .... 919-962-4417 342 B martin92@unc.edu
BRINKLEY-KENNEDY, Rhonda .... 513-861-6400 361 E
BRINKMAN, Kevin .... 513-618-1926 350 B kbrinkman@ccms.edu
BRINKMAN, Matt .... 423-614-8395 419 H mmbrinkman@leeuniversity.edu
BRINKMANN, Robert .... 815-753-1061 145 H rbrinkmann@niu.edu
BRINSON, Bruce .... 214-379-5573 440 H bbrinson@pqc.edu
BRINSON, Donna .... 770-533-6921 121 L dbrinson@laniertech.edu
BRINSON, Grant .... 304-357-4741 486 J grantbrinson@ucwv.edu
BRINSON, Lawrence .... 704-406-2361 328 I
BRINSON, Leigh, T .... 309-341-7130 141 E ltbrinson@knox.edu
BRINSON, Reginald .... 404-756-8458 123 A rwbrinson@msm.edu
BRINSON, Sarah .... 229-500-2173 114 F sarah.brinson@asurams.edu
BRINSON, Willie, L .... 919-735-5151 338 F wlbrinson@waynecc.edu
BRINTON, Christian .... 801-863-8000 460 A christian.brinton@uvu.edu
BRIONES, Evonne .... 816-472-4852 253 H ebriones@kcai.edu
BRISACK, Al .... 608-663-3289 491 F abrisack@edgewood.edu
BRISBON, T. Muriel .... 610-896-1250 385 H tbrisbon@haverford.edu
BRISCO, JaMeece .... 918-495-7701 368 F jabrisco@oru.edu
BRISCOE, Chad, C .... 574-372-5100 155 C chad.briscoe@grace.edu
BRISCOE, Connie .... 407-646-2194 106 L cbriscoe@rollins.edu
BRISCOE-ALBA, Susana 845-569-3414 307 B susana.alba@msmc.edu
BRISENO, Jason .... 512-223-7550 429 J jbrisen2@austincc.edu
BRISKEY, Barbara .... 845-758-6822 290 G
BRISKEY, Marvin .... 614-947-6002 352 J marv.briskey@franklin.edu
BRISLIN, Shawn, P .... 607-746-4670 320 A brislisp@delhi.edu
BRISSON, Michelle .... 973-408-3454 276 B mbrisson@drew.edu
BRISTER, Amelia .... 318-345-9143 188 A ameliabrister@ladelta.edu
BRISTLE, Shawn .... 928-757-0860.. 14 H sbristle@mohave.edu
BRISTOL, Amanda .... 423-461-8490 421 E abristol@milligan.edu
BRISTOL, Caterina .... 334-229-4297.... 4 B cbristol@alasu.edu
BRISTOR, Patricia .... 724-852-3315 401 E pbristor@waynesburg.edu
BRISTOW, Aimee .... 573-592-5365 261 F aimee.bristow@westminster-mo.edu
BRISTOW, Cliff .... 405-912-9037 368 H cbristow@ru.edu
BRITE, Chris .... 660-944-2863 251 B cbrite@conception.edu
BRITIGAN, Bradley, E .... 402-599-8878 269 B bradley.britigan@unmc.edu
BRITO, Alfredo .... 860-906-5048.. 86 C abrito@ccc.commnet.edu
BRITO, Jaclyn .... 909-687-1454.. 43 G
BRITT, Allysceaeioun .... 615-327-6457 420 D abritt@mmc.edu
BRITT, Amber, N .... 601-643-8301 244 G nikki.britt@colin.edu
BRITT, Denise .... 404-752-1500 123 A dbritt@msm.edu
BRITT, Eddie .... 601-643-8628 244 G eddie.britt@colin.edu
BRITT, Frank .... 480-947-6644.. 15 B frank.britt@pennfoster.edu
BRITT, Jeanette .... 814-824-2247 389 E jbritt@mercyhurst.edu
BRITT, Josh .... 843-921-6997 410 B jbritt@netc.edu
BRITT, Kenith .... 317-955-6209 159 A kbritt@marian.edu
BRITT, Kimberly .... 602-285-7607.. 13 H kimberly.britt@phoenixcollege.edu
BRITT, L.D .... 757-446-8996 465 H brittld@evms.edu
BRITT, Sanfrena .... 254-519-5447 446 C sanfrena.britt@tamuct.edu
BRITT, Shane .... 785-738-9075 176 C sbritt@ncktc.edu
BRITT, Sharda, D .... 252-862-1307 336 H sdbritt0117@roanokechowan.edu
BRITT, Tammy, T .... 704-233-8111 344 E tbritt@wingate.edu
BRITTAIN, David .... 281-283-2305 452 A brittaind@uhcl.edu
BRITTAIN, Kate .... 732-445-3783 281 B k.brittain@admissions.rutgers.edu
BRITTAIN, Kate .... 212-678-3000 321 H kwb2121@tc.columbia.edu
BRITTAIN, Linda, D .... 717-264-3787 402 D lbrittain@wilson.edu
BRITTAN, Steven, J .... 949-376-6000.. 47 G
BRITTEN, Robert .... 425-739-8100 480 D robert.britten@lwtech.edu
BRITTEN, Scott .... 734-973-5981 232 A csbritten@wccnet.edu
BRITTICH, Glen .... 630-617-3368 137 E glen.brittich@elmhurst.edu
BRITTINGHAM, Diane .... 719-587-7011.. 77 F dbrittingham@adams.edu
BRITTO, Vanessa .... 401-863-5970 403 A vanessa_britto@brown.edu
BRITTON, Bill .... 805-756-2190.. 29 K bibritto@calpoly.edu
BRITTON, Dana, J .... 800-233-4220 389 F dbritton@messiah.edu
BRITTON, Danielle .... 607-778-5203 317 A brittondf@sunybroome.edu
BRITTON, Elizabeth .... 620-450-2194 176 I elizabethb@prattcc.edu
BRITTON, JB .... 616-526-6695 221 L jbritton@calvin.edu
BRITTON, Jennifer, D .. 804-355-0671 470 I
BRITTON, Karen .... 781-239-3101 214 E kbritton@massbay.edu
BRITTON, Keith, E .... 803-938-3882 412 G kbritton@uscsumter.edu
BRITTON, Lesley .... 617-745-3897 208 F lesley.britton@enc.edu
BRITTON, Mark .... 419-289-5057 347 H mbritto3@ashland.edu
BRITTON-SPEARS, Ona . 918-463-2931 365 I ona.britton-spears@connorsstate.edu
BRIX, Timothy .... 636-922-8211 258 A tbrix@stchas.edu
BRIZUELA, Barbara .... 617-627-4230 219 A barbara.brizuela@tufts.edu
BRIZUELA, Erika .... 310-289-5123.. 68 E erika.brizuela@wcui.edu
BRNCICH, Lisa .... 815-479-7589 143 F lbrncich@mchenry.edu
BROADBENT, Becky .... 435-879-4242 459 G becky.broadbent@utahtech.edu
BROADDUS, Mary, E .... 502-597-6958 183 A maryellen.broaddus@kysu.edu
BROADDUS, Matthew .... 865-573-4517 419 E mbroaddus@johnsonu.edu
BROADHURST, Gary .... 315-792-5573 306 G gbroadhurst@mvcc.edu
BROADIE, II, Paul .... 352-395-5164 107 G paul.broadie@sfcollege.edu
BROADWATER, III, Colby, M .... 843-577-5245 405 E
BROADWATER, Jen .... 303-914-6254.. 82 L jen.broadwater@rrcc.edu
BROADWATER, Kimberly .... 662-254-3484 247 C kbroadwater@mvsu.edu
BROADWATER, Melanie, R .... 724-589-2754 398 F mbroadwater@thiel.edu
BROADWAY, Emily .... 803-778-6655 406 A broadwayec@cctech.edu
BROADWAY, Shane .... 501-660-1001.. 17 G sbroadway@asusystem.edu
BROADWELL, Phyllis .... 912-279-5816 117 C pbroadwell@ccga.edu
BROBERG, Loretta .... 402-878-2380 266 D loretta.broberg@littlepriest.edu
BROBERG, Sarah .... 828-251-6967 342 A sbroberg@unca.edu
BROBERG, Vic .... 610-292-9852 396 C vic.broberg@reseminary.edu
BROCCHINI, Jenna .... 602-383-8228.. 16 G jbrocchini@uat.edu
BROCIOUS, Heather .... 973-720-2705 283 I brocioush@wpunj.edu
BROCK, Casson .... 501-332-0410.. 18 D cbrock@asutr.edu
BROCK, James .... 805-893-4151.. 70 E
BROCK, Jeffrey .... 203-432-2550.. 90 B
BROCK, Jessica .... 479-356-2188.. 18 E jbrock15@atu.edu
BROCK, Lisa .... 256-840-4185.... 3 F lisa.brock@snead.edu
BROCK, Marcius .... 507-389-1180 238 L marcius.brock@mnsu.edu
BROCK, Marty, A .... 662-329-7152 247 B mabrock@muw.edu
BROCK, Michael, G .... 610-989-1246 400 F mbrock@vfmac.edu
BROCK, Michele .... 559-737-5441.. 39 C michelebr@cos.edu
BROCK, Michelle .... 704-290-5357 337 F mbrock@spcc.edu
BROCK, Pam .... 540-568-3191 467 C brockps@jmu.edu
BROCK, Roy, M .... 802-635-1240 463 B
BROCKBANK, Kevin .... 509-533-7042 478 D kevin.brockbank@scc.spokane.edu
BROCKEL, Amber .... 605-229-8427 414 I amber.brockel@presentation.edu
BROCKELBANK, Steve ... 231-591-2861 223 H stevebrockelbank@ferris.edu
BROCKETT, Lori .... 760-750-4405.. 33 C brockett@csusm.edu
BROCKGREITENS, Kathy .... 636-922-8229 258 A kbrockgreitens@stchas.edu
BROCKHOFF, Jennifer ... 502-585-9911 184 E jbrockhoff@spalding.edu
BROCKIE, Clarena .... 406-353-2607 262 B cbrockie@ancollege.edu
BROCKIE, John .... 562-985-4101.. 32 A john.brockie@csulb.edu
BROCKIE, Kim .... 406-353-2607 262 B kbrockie@ancollege.edu
BROCKIE, Michele .... 406-353-2607 262 B mbrockie@ancollege.edu
BROCKMAN, Beverly .... 812-488-2954 161 E bb318@evansville.edu
BROCKMAN, Diane .... 660-596-7205 259 D dbrockman@sfccmo.edu
BROCKMAN, Mark .... 513-745-4842 364 F brockmanm1@xavier.edu
BROCKMAN, Tom .... 614-251-4453 358 B brockmat2@ohiodominican.edu
BROCKMAN, Tracy .... 614-985-2324 359 K tbrockman@pcj.edu
BROCKSMITH, Susan .... 812-888-4588 162 E
BROCKWELL, Matthew, D .... 405-325-5161 370 J matt.brockwell@ou.edu
BROD, David .... 540-857-6675 475 A dbrod@virginiawestern.edu
BRODA, Joanna .... 212-346-1652 310 F jbroda@pace.edu
BRODA, Mary .... 517-750-1200 230 F mary.broda@arbor.edu
BRODE, Andrea .... 352-787-0114.. 96 B abrode@beaconcollege.edu
BRODERICK, Daniela .... 815-479-7873 143 F dbroderick@mchenry.edu
BRODERICK, Jo .... 978-921-4242 216 F jo.broderick@montserrat.edu
BRODERICK, Kimberley 413-755-4490 215 F kebroderick@stcc.edu
BRODERICK, Mac .... 603-513-1327 273 I mac.broderick@granite.edu
BRODERICK, Mac, J .... 603-535-2215 274 B mac.broderick@plymouth.edu
BRODERICK, Michael .... 860-515-3885.. 85 D mbroderick@charteroak.edu
BRODERSEN, Lisa .... 319-226-2034 163 A lisa.brodersen@allencollege.edu
BRODIGAN, Rebecca, H .... 207-859-4692 194 B becky.brodigan@colby.edu
BRODL, Mark .... 309-556-3101 140 E provost@iwu.edu
BRODMERKEL, Darcy .... 570-674-6466 389 H dbrodmerkel@misericordia.edu
BRODSKY, Aryeh .... 732-765-9126 284 E ygocb@yeshivanet.com
BRODSKY, Mikhail .... 510-208-2803.. 48 G president@lincolnuca.edu
BRODSKY, Stephen .... 212-346-1274 310 F sbrodksy@pace.edu
BRODY, Charmain .... 610-398-5300 388 D cbrody@lincolntech.edu
BRODY, Matthew .... 919-962-4651 340 F msbrody@northcarolina.edu

BROWN, Angelyne .... 803-327-7402 407 A
abrown@clintoncollege.edu
BROWN, Anita .... 937-319-6164 347 E
abrown@antiochcollege.edu
BROWN, Ann .... 919-516-5083 339 G
abrown@st-aug.edu
BROWN, Anne .... 704-687-5770 342 C
abrow316@uncc.edu
BROWN, Anthony .... 718-951-5000 293 A
anthony.brown@brooklyn.cuny.edu
BROWN, Anthony .... 866-217-9823 187 D
BROWN, Art .... 515-964-6394 164 F
acbrown9@dmacc.edu
BROWN, Arthur .... 507-372-3495 239 B
arthur.brown@mnwest.edu
BROWN, Ashley .... 845-687-5000 322 K
brownas@sunyulster.edu
BROWN, Barbara .... 229-430-3504 114 G
bbrown@albanytech.edu
BROWN, Barry .... 406-243-6800 263 D
barry.brown@umontana.edu
BROWN, Beth .... 305-284-1570 112 K
bgbrown@miami.edu
BROWN, Beverly .... 718-262-2238 295 D
bbrown@york.cuny.edu
BROWN, Beverly .... 704-978-5479 335 I
bbrown2@mitchellcc.edu
BROWN, Beverly, D ...... 239-590-1051 109 G
bdbrown@fgcu.edu
BROWN, Bill .... 919-760-2367 331 A
brownw@meredith.edu
BROWN, Bob .... 707-476-4239.. 58 I
bob-brown@redwoods.edu
BROWN, Bobbie .... 806-742-3661 450 C
bobbie.brown@ttu.edu
BROWN, Bonita .... 859-572-5172 184 B
brownb33@nku.edu
BROWN, Bradley .... 435-586-7871 459 E
brown@suu.edu
BROWN, Brent, K .... 801-581-3003 459 D
brent.brown@osp.utah.edu
BROWN, Brian .... 315-364-3207 324 E
bbrown@wells.edu
BROWN, JR., Buck, F .. 864-379-8805 408 F
brown@erskine.edu
BROWN, Calvin .... 404-880-6042 116 I
cbrown@cau.edu
BROWN, Calvin .... 205-348-5966.... 7 G
cbrown@alumni.ua.edu
BROWN, Camille .... 781-280-3200 214 G
BROWN, Candice .... 678-359-5010 120 D
candiceb@gordonstate.edu
BROWN, Carl .... 614-947-6080 352 J
carl.brown@franklin.edu
BROWN, Carlos .... 414-955-8826 492 F
carlosbrown@mcw.edu
BROWN, Carmen .... 662-246-6275 246 E
cbrown@msdelta.edu
BROWN, Carmen .... 803-812-7318 412 E
cdbrown@mailbox.sc.edu
BROWN, Carolanne ...... 561-803-2050 105 B
carolanne_brown@pba.edu
BROWN, Carolus .... 408-498-5100.. 73 A
cbrown@cogswell.edu
BROWN, Carolyn .... 229-500-2821 114 F
carolyn.brown@asurams.edu
BROWN, Catherine .... 716-614-5950 309 E
cbrown@niagaracc.suny.edu
BROWN, Cathy .... 620-241-0723 172 H
cathy.brown@centralchristian.edu
BROWN, Cedric .... 618-468-6205 142 B
cedbrown@lc.edu
BROWN, Chad .... 918-647-1375 365 D
cbrown@carlalbert.edu
BROWN, Chad, M .... 740-588-1201 364 H
cbrown@zanestate.edu
BROWN, Charles .... 304-327-4196 488 J
cbrown@bluefieldstate.edu
BROWN, Chasley .... 256-228-6001.... 3 B
brownchasley@nacc.edu
BROWN, Chelsea .... 301-934-2251 198 C
crclute@csmd.edu
BROWN, Chris .... 205-934-1294.... 8 A
csbrown@uab.edu
BROWN, Chris .... 845-257-3231 316 B
browncl@newpaltz.edu
BROWN, Chris .... 507-389-1713 238 L
christopher.brown@mnsu.edu
BROWN, Christi .... 985-545-1500 188 B
BROWN, Christine .... 773-995-2386 134 J
cbrown@csu.edu
BROWN, Christopher .... 785-864-4904 177 G
jcbrown2@ku.edu
BROWN, Christopher .... 949-376-6000.. 47 G
cbrown@lcad.edu
BROWN,
Christopher, P .... 803-934-3235 409 H
cbrown@morris.edu
BROWN, Cindy .... 417-455-5540 251 H
cindybrown@crowder.edu
BROWN, Claude, E .... 601-977-6181 248 E
cebrown@tougaloo.edu
BROWN, Coleen .... 573-875-8700 251 A
BROWN, Constandina ... 617-731-3500 210 D
cbrown@hchc.edu
BROWN, Courtney, L .... 540-365-4201 466 I
cbrown@ferrum.edu
BROWN, Craig .... 208-562-3412 131 C
craigbrown@cwi.edu
BROWN, Curressia .... 662-254-3600 247 C
cbrown@mvsu.edu
BROWN, Cynae .... 713-223-7943 452 B
browncy@uhd.edu
BROWN, Dale .... 413-552-2420 214 D
dbrown@hcc.edu
BROWN, Damon .... 989-463-7151 220 F
browndm@alma.edu
BROWN, Dan .... 409-880-7785 449 B
dbrown109@lamar.edu
BROWN, Dana, A .... 601-877-4713 244 B
dagbrown@alcorn.edu
BROWN, Daniel .... 806-291-3416 457 B
dbrown@wbu.edu
BROWN, Danielle .... 570-372-4757 398 A
browndd@susqu.edu
BROWN, Darrell .... 254-968-9497 445 F
dwbrown@tarleton.edu
BROWN, Darryl .... 301-295-3412 502 B
darryl.brown@usuhs.edu
BROWN, David .... 412-624-4141 400 A
dbb37@pitt.edu
BROWN, David .... 910-668-3331 439 I
dbrown@nctc.edu
BROWN, David .... 262-691-5346 499 A
dbrown@wctc.edu
BROWN, David .... 270-745-4449 186 A
david.brown@wku.edu
BROWN, David .... 256-233-8187.... 4 D
david.brown@athens.edu
BROWN, David, A .... 409-772-3001 456 B
davibrow@utmb.edu
BROWN, Davin .... 916-558-2142.. 51 B
brownd@scc.losrios.edu
BROWN, Deborah .... 202-319-6915.. 91 G
browndl@cua.edu
BROWN, Deborah, R .... 757-446-5828 465 H
browndr@evms.edu
BROWN, Demetrius ...... 601-974-1225 246 C
browndl@millsaps.edu
BROWN, Demitrius .... 210-999-8844 451 B
dbrown7@trinity.edu
BROWN, Denelle .... 570-577-2071 379 A
denelle.brown@bucknell.edu
BROWN, Derek .... 620-862-5252 171 E
BROWN, Derek .... 303-404-5492.. 80 I
derek.brown@frontrange.edu
BROWN, Derrick .... 903-593-8311 448 A
dbrown@texascollege.edu
BROWN, Diane, M .... 484-365-7400 388 F
dbrown@lincoln.edu
BROWN, Dina .... 603-897-8232 273 B
dbrown@rivier.edu
BROWN, Dolores, M .... 262-524-7133 491 A
docampo@carrollu.edu
BROWN, Donna .... 951-372-8080.. 45 G
hisuniv_accreditation@yahoo.com
BROWN, Donna .... 479-248-7236.. 19 F
dbrown@ecollege.edu
BROWN, Donna .... 701-477-7862 346 H
dbrown@tm.edu
BROWN, Donnie .... 806-291-1168 457 B
brownd@wbu.edu
BROWN, Douglas .... 508-588-9100 214 F
dbrown43@massasoit.mass.edu
BROWN, Douglas, E ..... 515-964-0601 166 A
brownd@faith.edu
BROWN, Ed .... 406-657-2044 263 H
edward.brown2@msubillings.edu
BROWN, Edna, D .... 513-585-1853 350 A
edna.brown@thechristcollege.edu
BROWN, Edward .... 303-615-0060.. 81 L
ebrow100@msudenver.edu
BROWN, Elizabeth .... 504-862-8335 191 D
beth@tulane.edu
BROWN, Emily .... 910-592-8081 337 D
ebrown@sampsoncc.edu
BROWN, Emmett .... 616-988-1000 222 D
emmett.b@compass.edu
BROWN, Eric .... 207-778-7276 196 F
brown.eric@maine.edu
BROWN, Eric .... 530-221-4275.. 63 G
ebrown@shasta.edu
BROWN, Erik .... 650-203-4865.. 24 J
BROWN, Erik .... 218-726-8891 243 A
etbrown@d.umn.edu
BROWN, Erika .... 404-752-1723 123 A
etbrown@msm.edu
BROWN, Erin .... 405-789-7661 369 H
erin.brown@swcu.edu
BROWN, Erinn .... 308-345-8112 266 J
browne@mpcc.edu
BROWN, Fran .... 248-476-1122 227 B
fbrown@msp.edu
BROWN, Gary .... 608-785-9167 499 B
browng@westerntc.edu
BROWN, Gary, L .... 252-335-3277 341 A
glbrown@ecsu.edu
BROWN, Gary, M .... 919-497-3213 330 E
gmbrown@louisburg.edu
BROWN, Geeta, A .... 714-712-7900.. 46 F
BROWN, George, H ...... 828-227-7028 343 D
ghbrown@wcu.edu
BROWN, Gina, S .... 202-806-6100.. 92 E
gina.brown@howard.edu
BROWN, Glenn .... 973-684-5402 279 B
gbrown@pccc.edu
BROWN, Gloria, M .... 252-335-3268 341 A
gmbrown@ecsu.edu
BROWN, H. David .... 816-271-4327 256 C
browndav@missouriwestern.edu
BROWN, Harold .... 415-452-5163.. 37 C
hbrown@ccsf.edu
BROWN, Haywood .... 813-974-4373 111 B
haywood@usf.edu
BROWN, Heather .... 916-686-7400.. 29 G
BROWN, Heather .... 423-472-7141 423 C
hbrown@clevelandstatecc.edu
BROWN, Hubert .... 352-392-0466 110 E
hub.brown@ufl.edu
BROWN, Ivey .... 336-750-2108 343 E
browniv@wssu.edu
BROWN, J. Steven .... 202-319-4738.. 91 G
brownj@cua.edu
BROWN, J.J .... 828-262-2060 340 G
brownjj1@appstate.edu
BROWN, Jackie .... 803-705-4971 405 G
jackie.brown@benedict.edu
BROWN, James .... 615-230-3787 424 F
james.brown@volstate.edu
BROWN, James .... 570-389-4410 393 E
jbrown@bloomu.edu
BROWN, III, James, E .. 661-824-2977.. 53 H
jbrown@ntps.edu
BROWN, James, M .... 570-340-6044 389 B
jmbrown@marywood.edu
BROWN, Jared .... 417-455-5566 251 H
jaredbrown@crowder.edu
BROWN, Jasmin, K ...... 910-630-7035 331 B
jabrown@methodist.edu
BROWN, Jason .... 435-797-3322 459 F
jason.brown@usu.edu
BROWN, Jeff .... 215-489-2208 381 K
jeffrey.brown@delval.edu
BROWN, Jeff .... 570-320-2400 392 S
jbrown@pct.edu
BROWN, Jeff .... 509-533-7373 478 D
jeff.brown@scc.spokane.edu
BROWN, Jeffery .... 202-885-3165.. 91 D
jtbrown@american.edu
BROWN, Jeffrey .... 217-333-2747 151 F
brownjr@illinois.edu
BROWN, Jefrey .... 309-298-1544 152 I
j-brown2@wiu.edu
BROWN, Jennifer .... 785-738-9085 176 C
jbrown@ncktc.edu
BROWN, Jennifer .... 860-465-0781.. 85 G
brownje@easternct.edu
BROWN, Jennifer .... 808-235-7370 130 C
jb26@hawaii.edu
BROWN, Jennifer, G ..... 203-582-8200.. 88 F
jennifer.brown@quinnipiac.edu
BROWN, Jennifer, L ..... 909-869-4182.. 30 B
jlbrown1@cpp.edu
BROWN, Jeremy .... 951-639-5404.. 53 A
jebrown@msjc.edu
BROWN, Jeremy .... 530-741-6700.. 77 D
jbrown2@yccd.edu
BROWN, Jeremy .... 530-741-6766.. 77 D
jbrown2@yccd.edu
BROWN, Jeremy .... 970-248-1962.. 78 F
jbrown@coloradomesa.edu
BROWN, Jerri .... 928-350-2113.. 15 O
jbrown@prescott.edu
BROWN, Jerri .... 928-350-2100.. 15 O
BROWN, Jessica .... 706-821-8235 123 I
jbrown@paine.edu
BROWN, Jessyca .... 254-659-7504 436 C
jbrown@hillcollege.edu
BROWN, Jill .... 660-562-1642 256 G
jillb@nwmissouri.edu
BROWN, John .... 404-270-5227 126 A
jbrow109@spelman.edu
BROWN, John .... 614-236-6771 348 I
jbrown18@capital.edu
BROWN, John, V .... 919-684-0539 328 D
jbrown@duke.edu
BROWN, Jonathan .... 336-249-8186 333 G
jonathan_brown@davidsondavie.edu
BROWN, Jordan .... 706-886-6831 126 C
jbrown@tfc.edu
BROWN, Joseph .... 910-246-4957 337 E
brownjo@sandhills.edu
BROWN, Joseph .... 903-923-2270 435 A
jbrown@etbu.edu
BROWN, Joyce, F .... 212-217-4000 299 C
joyce_brown@fitnyc.edu
BROWN, Julia .... 662-472-9011 245 E
jubrown@holmescc.edu
BROWN, Julie .... 718-625-2200 291 G
julie.brown@brooklaw.edu
BROWN, Justin .... 740-392-6868 356 G
justin.brown@mvnu.edu
BROWN, Justin, C .... 402-472-3484 269 A
justin.brown@unl.edu
BROWN, Kali .... 253-492-2061 338 D
brownk@vgcc.edu
BROWN, Kanika .... 405-208-5501 367 E
kbrown2@okcu.edu
BROWN, Karen .... 815-599-3402 138 H
karen.brown@highland.edu
BROWN, Karen .... 502-597-6434 183 A
karend.brown@kysu.edu
BROWN, Karen, A .... 607-436-2524 316 C
karen.brown@oneonta.edu
BROWN, Karen, H .... 340-693-1324 512 B
karen.brown@uvi.edu
BROWN, Karen, J .... 603-899-4280 272 G
brownkj@franklinpierce.edu
BROWN, Kathleen, M .... 574-284-4557 160 F
kbrown@saintmarys.edu
BROWN, Kathren .... 801-863-8517 460 A
kbrown@uvu.edu
BROWN, Kathryn .... 318-876-2401 187 F
BROWN, Katie .... 303-333-4224.. 11 C
registrar@aspen.edu
BROWN, Katie .... 843-377-2432 406 B
kbrown@charlestonlaw.edu
BROWN, Katina .... 910-410-1817 336 G
kwbrown@richmondcc.edu
BROWN, Katrina .... 307-268-2036 499 T
katrina.brown@caspercollege.edu
BROWN, Katrina, M ...... 307-675-0221 500 F
kbrown@sheridan.edu
BROWN, Keia .... 703-284-1530 468 A
kabrown@marymount.edu
BROWN, Keith .... 443-674-1915 198 A
kbrown@cecil.edu
BROWN, Keith .... 440-366-7692 355 B
BROWN, Keith, A .... 205-853-1200.... 2 G
kbrown@jeffersonstate.edu
BROWN, Kelli, R .... 828-227-7100 343 D
kbrown@wcu.edu
BROWN, Kelly .... 443-482-6575 201 E
kelly.brown@sjc.edu
BROWN, Kelly, K .... 253-879-3778 483 G
kkbrown@pugetsound.edu
BROWN, Ken .... 620-278-4217 177 E
kbrown@sterling.edu
BROWN, Kendra .... 580-774-3785 369 I
kendra.brown@swosu.edu
BROWN, Kendrick, T ..... 404-639-0999 122 H
kendrick.brown@morehouse.edu
BROWN, Kenneth .... 318-675-3395 189 D
kenny.brown@lsuhs.edu
BROWN, Kenneth .... 509-777-4486 485 D
kbrown@whitworth.edu
BROWN, Kevin .... 517-750-1200 230 F
kbrown@arbor.edu
BROWN, Kevin .... 812-866-7061 155 D
brownk@hanover.edu
BROWN, Kevin .... 843-349-5398 409 A
kevin.brown@hgtc.edu

BROWN, Tammy .... 304-384-5358 488 K
tbrown@concord.edu
BROWN, Tanya .... 804-594-1414 473 B
tbrown01@jtcc.edu
BROWN, Tavonda .... 870-743-3000.. 20 F
tbrown@northark.edu
BROWN, Teresa .... 404-297-9522 119 G
BROWN, Teresa .... 507-285-7217 240 B
teresa.brown@rctc.edu
BROWN, Teressa .... 479-401-6021.. 17 E
teressa.brown@acheedu.org
BROWN, Terrance .... 270-745-2344 186 A
terrance.brown@wku.edu
BROWN, Terrence .... 901-751-8453 420 G
tbrown@mabts.edu
BROWN, Terri .... 478-289-2062 118 B
thbrown@ega.edu
BROWN, Theodore .... 256-726-7070.... 6 C
tbrown@oakwood.edu
BROWN, Thomas, W .... 507-933-7005 235 E
brownie@gustavus.edu
BROWN, Tim .... 843-574-6211 411 I
tim.brown@tridenttech.edu
BROWN, Timi .... 909-652-6322.. 36 B
timi.brown@chaffey.edu
BROWN, Timothy .... 704-847-5600 340 D
tbrown@ses.edu
BROWN, Todd .... 435-586-7700 459 E
BROWN, Toni .... 919-536-7200 334 A
brownt@durhamtech.edu
BROWN, Tracy, H .... 512-475-9411 454 C
tbrown@tacc.utexas.edu
BROWN, Travis .... 419-372-6067 348 F
brownst@bgsu.edu
BROWN, Trevor, L .... 614-292-4533 358 E
brown.2296@osu.edu
BROWN, Troy .... 310-342-5256.. 73 E
BROWN, Tucker .... 931-221-7725 416 H
brownt@apsu.edu
BROWN, Veronica .... 334-876-9335.... 2 D
veronica.brown@wccs.edu
BROWN, Victor .... 718-960-8222 293 E
victor.brown@lehman.cuny.edu
BROWN, Vintress .... 864-503-5553 413 A
vbrown@uscupstate.edu
BROWN, Wanda .... 336-750-2446 343 E
brownwa@wssu.edu
BROWN, Wilfred, E .... 805-893-4155.. 70 E
willie.brown@auxiliary.ucsb.edu
BROWN, William .... 301-696-3402 199 C
brownw@hood.edu
BROWN, William .... 719-549-3144.. 82 I
william.brown@pueblocc.edu
BROWN, William, T ...... 203-285-2000.. 86 D
BROWN, Zakiya .... 573-681-5502 254 A
brownz@lincolnu.edu
BROWN-ALDRIDGE,
Linda .... 708-596-2000 149 D
lbrown@ssc.edu
BROWN-CORNELIUS,
Denise .... 502-272-8270 179 D
dbrowncornelius@bellarmine.edu
BROWN CORNELIUS,
Lisa .... 216-397-4408 353 O
lmbrown@jcu.edu
BROWN-ELIZE, Rashitta 661-722-6300.. 26 E
rbrownelize@avc.edu
BROWN GORDAN,
Loria .... 601-979-2107 245 G
loria.c.brown@jsums.edu
BROWN-HARRIS,
Brandi .... 618-537-6813 143 G
BROWN-HAYWOOD,
Felicia .... 717-867-6210 388 A
bhaywood@lvc.edu
BROWN-HERBST, Kari .. 307-778-1103 500 D
kherbst@lccc.wy.edu
BROWN-JOHNSON,
Leah .... 973-748-9000 275 C
leah_brown@bloomfield.edu
BROWN-LAVEIST,
Cynthia .... 443-885-4720 200 F
cynthia.brownlaveist@morgan.edu
BROWN LEONARD,
Jeannie .... 785-532-3370 175 A
brownleonard@ksu.edu
BROWN MARSDEN,
Margaret .... 940-397-4253 439 F
margaret.brownmarsden@msutexas.edu
BROWN-NAGIN,
Tomiko .... 617-495-8602 210 B
tbrownnagin@radcliffe.harvard.edu
BROWN WYATT, Donna 660-626-2790 249 C
dbrown@atsu.edu
BROWN YOUNG,
Danita .... 217-300-1300 151 F
dbyoung@illinois.edu
BROWNAWELL,
Carolyn .... 303-556-2400.. 84 B
carolyn.brownawell@ucdenver.edu
BROWNE, Brian .... 718-990-2762 313 B
browneb@stjohns.edu
BROWNE, Doug .... 620-417-1201 177 C
doug.browne@sccc.edu
BROWNE, Jacob .... 727-864-8846.. 98 G
brownejh@eckerd.edu
BROWNE, Jason .... 504-278-6421 188 E
jbrowne@nunez.edu
BROWNE, Joan .... 386-481-2469.. 96 D
brownej@cookman.edu
BROWNE, Joan, M .... 202-806-7513.. 92 E
jmbrowne@howard.edu
BROWNE, Kathleen .... 740-587-6654 351 K
brownek@denison.edu
BROWNE, Kevin .... 312-413-3471 151 D
kbrowne@uic.edu
BROWNE, Lorraine .... 860-509-9501.. 88 A
lbrowne@hartfordinternational.edu
BROWNE, Nadine .... 718-368-5109 294 C
nadine.browne@kbcc.cuny.edu
BROWNE, Patrick .... 503-256-3180 377 A
pbrowne@uws.edu
BROWNE, Robert .... 603-641-7287 273 C
rbrowne@anselm.edu
BROWNE, Teri .... 803-777-6258 412 A
brownetm@mailbox.sc.edu
BROWNE-BOATSWAIN,
Venoreen .... 763-422-6094 236 H
venoreen.browne-boatswain@anokaramsey.edu
BROWNE-BOATSWAIN,
Venoreen .... 763-422-6094 237 A
venoreen.browne-boatswain@anokaramsey.edu
BROWNELL, Crystal ...... 802-831-1339 462 F
cbrownell@vermontlaw.edu
BROWNELL, Jayne, E ... 513-529-4631 356 A
browneje@miamioh.edu
BROWNELL, Jennifer ..... 336-506-4237 331 J
jennifer.brownell@alamancecc.edu
BROWNGOETZ, Sarah ... 360-475-7129 481 B
sbrowngoetz@olympic.edu
BROWNIE, Ronald .... 605-626-2568 415 H
ronald.brownie@northern.edu
BROWNING, Allison ...... 740-474-8896 358 A
abrowning@ohiochristian.edu
BROWNING, Amy .... 307-675-0122 500 F
abrowning@sheridan.edu
BROWNING, Angela ...... 772-462-4703 102 E
abrownin@irsc.edu
BROWNING, Ashley ...... 540-362-6210 467 A
abrowning@hollins.edu
BROWNING, David .... 336-917-5472 339 H
david.browning@salem.edu
BROWNING, Eric .... 740-392-6868 356 G
eric.browning@mvnu.edu
BROWNING, Janelle ..... 617-747-2358 206 D
jbrowning@berklee.edu
BROWNING, Jason .... 307-675-0210 500 F
jbrowning@sheridan.edu
BROWNING, Jay .... 215-641-6543 390 A
jbrowning@mc3.edu
BROWNING, Joann .... 210-458-7379 455 B
joann.browning@utsa.edu
BROWNING, Kelly .... 715-425-3342 496 A
kelly.browning@uwrf.edu
BROWNING, Lynn .... 225-768-1724 186 H
lynn.browning@franu.edu
BROWNING, Mark .... 541-278-5950 371 G
mbrowning@bluecc.edu
BROWNING, Peter .... 417-873-7231 252 A
pbrowning@drury.edu
BROWNING, Reggie ...... 864-488-4522 409 C
rbrowning@limestone.edu
BROWNING, Shea .... 828-227-7116 343 D
srbrowning@wcu.edu
BROWNING, Steve .... 870-235-4102.. 21 E
dsbrowning@saumag.edu
BROWNING, Tyler .... 618-544-8657 139 E
browningt@iecc.edu
BROWNLEE, David, W .. 610-558-5628 390 G
dbrownle@neumann.edu
BROWNLEE, Jamie .... 619-849-6785.. 57 J
jamiebrownlee@pointloma.edu
BROWNLEE,
Mordecai, I .... 303-360-4775.. 80 C
mordecai.brownlee@ccaurora.edu
BROWNLEE, Reb .... 814-262-3842 393 A
rbrownlee@pennhighlands.edu
BROWNLEE, Robert .... 707-527-4964.. 63 C
rbrownlee@santarosa.edu
BROWNLEE DELL, Erin . 610-328-8321 398 B
edell1@swarthmore.edu
BROWNLOW, Antonio ... 662-254-3411 247 C
abrownlow@mvsu.edu
BROWNSBERGER,
William .... 276-523-2400 473 E
bbrownsberger@mecc.edu
BROWNSTEIN, Sheri ..... 623-572-3824 144 C
sbrown1@midwestern.edu
BROXSON, Thomas .... 253-589-5510 478 A
thomas.broxson@cptc.edu
BROYLES, Ken .... 423-461-8734 421 E
kbroyles@milligan.edu
BROYLES, Kevin .... 334-699-2266.... 1 B
krbroyles@acom.edu
BROYLES, Steven .... 626-300-5444.. 57 F
sbroyles@plattcollege.edu
BROYLES, Wendy .... 334-983-6556.... 7 C
whuckabee@troy.edu
BROZ, Roger .... 612-659-6805 238 C
roger.broz@minneapolis.edu
BROZOVICH, Jennifer ... 785-227-3380 171 H
brozovichjm@bethanylb.edu
BRUBACHER, Don .... 517-607-3130 224 G
dbrubacher@hillsdale.edu
BRUBAKER, David .... 585-567-9484 301 G
david.brubaker@houghton.edu
BRUBAKER, David .... 540-432-4423 465 F
dean-ssp@emu.edu
BRUBAKER, Karl .... 620-327-8216 174 B
karl.brubaker@hesston.edu
BRUBAKER, Sam, R ...... 208-496-9817 130 G
brubakers@byui.edu
BRUBAKER, Sara .... 620-242-0413 175 G
brubakes@mcpherson.edu
BRUBAKER-COLE,
Susie .... 650-723-2300.. 66 D
susiebc@stanford.edu
BRUCE, Aaron .... 626-396-2200.. 26 G
aaron.bruce@artcenter.edu
BRUCE, Alex, M .... 931-598-1187 422 F
ambruce@sewanee.edu
BRUCE, Allison .... 915-831-2164 435 B
abruce@epcc.edu
BRUCE, Ben .... 706-292-3900 125 A
bbruce@shorter.edu
BRUCE, Bernadette .... 954-262-8856 104 M
bb968@nova.edu
BRUCE, Dagmara .... 864-503-5000 413 A
BRUCE, David .... 617-521-2000 218 C
BRUCE, Debra .... 509-542-4604 478 B
dbruce@columbiabasin.edu
BRUCE, Dustin .... 502-897-4555 184 D
dbruce@sbts.edu
BRUCE, Gonzalo .... 208-426-2272 130 F
gonzalobruce@boisestate.edu
BRUCE, Heidi .... 443-885-4850 200 F
heidi.bruce@morgan.edu
BRUCE, Jeanne .... 740-474-8896 358 A
jbruce@ohiochristian.edu
BRUCE, Jennifer .... 503-375-7032 372 G
jbruce@corban.edu
BRUCE, Joe .... 904-826-8708.. 99 D
jbruce@flagler.edu
BRUCE, Josh .... 954-771-0376 103 S
jbruce@knoxseminary.edu
BRUCE, Kimberly .... 318-345-9147 188 A
kbruce@ladelta.edu
BRUCE, Lori, M .... 931-372-3224 425 B
lbruce@tntech.edu
BRUCE, Philip .... 518-276-6234 311 J
brucep@rpi.edu
BRUCE, R. Todd .... 216-397-1600 353 O
rbruce@jcu.edu
BRUCE, Richard .... 360-650-6517 485 A
richard.bruce@wwu.edu
BRUCE, Robert .... 713-348-2599 441 K
rgbruce@rice.edu
BRUCE, Steve .... 574-520-4457 157 C
stbruce@iusb.edu
BRUCE, Steve .... 757-352-4429 469 D
stepbru@regent.edu
BRUCE, Susan .... 704-233-8015 344 E
s.bruce@wingate.edu
BRUCE, William, P .... 615-327-3927 419 D
pbruce@guptoncollege.edu
BRUCE-SMITH, Soo Lee 208-792-2378 131 F
slbruce@lcsc.edu
BRUCELAS, Joy .... 510-215-3841.. 40 G
jbrucelas@contracosta.edu
BRUCH, Anna .... 815-224-0320 140 D
anna_bruch@ivcc.edu
BRUCH, Courtney .... 505-747-2244 287 C
courtney.bruch@nnmc.edu
BRUCH, John .... 262-595-2228 495 D
bruch@uwp.edu
BRUCKBAUER, Greg ..... 715-422-5327 498 A
greg.bruckbauer@mstc.edu
BRUCKENTHAL, Patricia 631-444-1041 316 D
patricia.bruckenthal@stonybrookmedicine.edu
BRUCKI, Mark, J .... 248-204-2310 226 E
mbrucki@ltu.edu
BRUCKSTEIN, Irving ..... 401-341-2400 404 D
irving.bruckstein@salve.edu
BRUDER, Edward, C ..... 717-815-1314 402 G
ebruder@ycp.edu
BRUDER, Remylin .... 248-218-2281 229 I
rbruder@rochesteru.edu
BRUDNICKI, James .... 856-222-9311 280 E
jbrudnic@rcbc.edu
BRUDNOCK, Ben .... 724-938-4725 394 C
brudnock@calu.edu
BRUDNOK, Celine .... 724-805-2720 397 D
celine.brudnok@stvincent.edu
BRUDNOK, Celine, R .... 724-805-2720 397 C
celine.brudnok@email.stvincent.edu
BRUECK, Joshua .... 217-641-4320 140 H
jbrueck@jwcc.edu
BRUEHL, Allen, A .... 508-767-7311 205 F
abruehl@assumption.edu
BRUEHL, Amanda .... 732-247-5241 278 E
BRUFFEY, L. Mark .... 763-417-8250 234 D
mbruffey@centralseminary.edu
BRUGAL-MENA,
Yocasta .... 787-743-3038 508 L
ybrugal@sanjuanbautista.edu
BRUGGEMAN, Michael . 313-664-1440 222 C
mikeb@collegeforcreativestudies.edu
BRUGH, Suzanne .... 814-262-6463 393 A
sbrugh@pennhighlands.edu
BRUGNOLI, Amber .... 304-293-9298 489 E
amber.brugnoli@mail.wvu.edu
BRUHN, Gregory .... 718-990-1951 313 B
bruhng@stjohns.edu
BRUINGTON, Toni .... 620-331-4100 174 E
bbruington@indycc.edu
BRUINSMA, Paul .... 618-842-3711 139 D
bruinsmap@iecc.edu
BRUKARDT, Mary Jane ... 715-836-2320 494 E
brukarmj@uwec.edu
BRUKLEY, Reuben .... 313-317-6573 224 F
rjbrukley@hfcc.edu
BRUMBACH, Mary .... 214-378-1549 433 F
mbrumbach@dcccd.edu
BRUMBAUGH, Douglas 330-972-6824 361 G
dbrumbaugh@uakron.edu
BRUMBAUGH, Pete, S .. 913-971-3275 175 H
pjbrumbaugh@mnu.edu
BRUMBERG, Joshua ...... 212-817-7242 293 D
jbrumberg@gc.cuny.edu
BRUMFIELD, Adele .... 734-763-5837 231 A
vpadele@umich.edu
BRUMFIELD, Amy .... 208-535-5361 130 I
amy.brumfield@cei.edu
BRUMFIELD, Randall ..... 304-558-0261 488 I
randall.brumfield@wvhepc.edu
BRUMFIELD, Reginald .. 713-522-7911 453 H
reginald.brumfield@stthom.edu
BRUMFIELD, Sean .... 770-229-3269 125 F
sean.brumfield@sctech.edu
BRUMITT, Jane .... 312-629-6184 149 B
jbrumitt@saic.edu
BRUMLEY, Jessica .... 305-284-5314 112 K
jbrumley@miami.edu
BRUMLEY, Larry, D ...... 478-301-5700 122 C
brumley_ld@mercer.edu
BRUMMEL, Joe .... 641-628-7648 164 B
brummelj@central.edu
BRUMMER, James, M ... 651-962-6595 243 F
jbrummer@stthomas.edu
BRUMMOND, Kristin, A 330-972-7869 361 G
brummon@uakron.edu
BRUMMUND, Barry .... 520-621-9723.. 16 H
brummund@arizona.edu
BRUNACINI, Kelly .... 585-271-3657 312 E
kelly.brunacini@stbernards.edu.edu
BRUNDAGE, Alice .... 215-395-8962 395 B
abrundage@pitc.edu

BRUNDAGE, Christina .. 570-348-6247 389 B
brundage.c@marywood.edu
BRUNDAGE, Isaac .... 530-898-6131.. 31 A
ibrundage@csuchico.edu
BRUNDAGE, Jenni .... 608-785-8075 495 A
jbrundage@uwlax.edu
BRUNDAGE, Kelley, L .... 785-532-6254 175 A
kbrundage@ksu.edu
BRUNDAGE, Ken .... 814-871-7551 383 H
brundage001@gannon.edu
BRUNDAGE, Tracy .... 229-391-5050 114 D
BRUNDIGE, Patricia ...... 518-243-4473 290 K
BRUNE, Carolyn .... 847-574-5154 141 G
cbrune@lfgsm.edu
BRUNEAU, Patrice .... 803-323-2266 413 D
bruneaup@winthrop.edu
BRUNEEL, Greta .... 805-565-6101.. 75 I
gbruneel@westmont.edu
BRUNELLE, Christopher 909-652-6591.. 36 B
christopher.brunelle@chaffey.edu
BRUNELLE, Maria .... 413-552-2431 214 D
mbrunelle@hcc.edu
BRUNELLI, Leslie .... 303-871-3750.. 84 C
leslie.brunelli@du.edu
BRUNEN, Meredith .... 678-839-6447 127 A
mbrunen@westga.edu
BRUNER, Brett .... 816-271-4200 256 C
BRUNER, Darl, L .... 208-467-8843 132 B
dlbruner@nnu.edu
BRUNER, Deborah, W ... 404-727-6123 118 D
deborah.w.bruner@emory.edu
BRUNER, Greg, S .... 815-939-5249 146 F
gbruner@olivet.edu
BRUNER, Joe, W .... 859-858-3511 178 H
joe.bruner@asbury.edu
BRUNER, Jon .... 325-674-2757 427 G
jon.bruner@acu.edu
BRUNER, Judith .... 858-246-1800.. 70 C
jbruner@ucsd.edu
BRUNER, Monique .... 405-733-7524 369 D
mbruner@rose.edu
BRUNER, Ted .... 828-689-1242 330 H
tbruner@mhu.edu
BRUNER-TRACEY, Anne-Marie .... 318-869-5059 186 C
abrunertracey@centenary.edu
BRUNET, Kathleen .... 973-328-5052 276 A
kbrunet@ccm.edu
BRUNET, Suhail .... 787-279-1912 506 L
sbrunet@bayamon.inter.edu
BRUNETTA, Stephanie ... 607-431-4000 300 G
brunettas@hartwick.edu
BRUNETTO, Kathryn ...... 201-879-9294 274 I
kplessing@bergen.edu
BRUNGARDT, Cherie .... 970-521-6787.. 82 B
cherie.brungardt@njc.edu
BRUNGARDT, Heather ... 970-521-6623.. 82 B
heather.brungardt@njc.edu
BRUNGARDT, Heather ... 970-521-6690.. 82 B
heather.brungardt@njc.edu
BRUNI, Summer .... 650-508-3503.. 54 G
sbruni@ndnu.edu
BRUNICARDI, F. Charles .... 718-270-1000 316 E
BRUNING, Kathryn .... 617-333-2120 208 D
kathryn.bruning@curry.edu
BRUNING, Zachary .... 213-738-6721.. 66 A
zbruning@swlaw.edu
BRUNK-CHAVEZ, Beth, L .... 915-747-6318 454 E
blbrunk@utep.edu
BRUNKE, Mark .... 253-833-9111 480 A
mbrunke@greenriver.edu
BRUNKOW, Alan .... 402-761-8259 268 D
abrunkow@southeast.edu
BRUNN, Troy .... 316-978-5585 178 B
troy.brunn@wichita.edu
BRUNNER, Brian .... 636-949-4903 254 B
bbrunner@lindenwood.edu
BRUNNER, Diane .... 419-473-2700 351 I
dbrunner@daviscollege.edu
BRUNNER, Jon, L .... 239-590-7950 109 G
jbrunner@fgcu.edu
BRUNNER, Karen, L ...... 865-882-4606 424 D
brunnerkl@roanestate.edu
BRUNNER, Lisa .... 218-935-0417 244 A
lisa.brunner@wetcc.edu
BRUNNER, Ludwig .... 716-375-7666 312 F
lbrunner@sbu.edu
BRUNNER, Marc .... 931-221-7887 416 H
brunnerm@apsu.edu
BRUNNER, Marta .... 518-580-5506 315 A
mbrunner@skidmore.edu
BRUNNER, Matthew ...... 540-851-5271 468 E
msbrunner@radford.edu
BRUNNER, Sharon .... 410-386-8142 197 G
sbrunner@carrollcc.edu
BRUNNER, Tim .... 419-473-2700 351 I
tbrunner@daviscollege.edu
BRUNO, Andrea .... 818-252-5102.. 76 D
andrea.bruno@woodbury.edu
BRUNO, Ann .... 518-828-4181 296 G
ann.bruno@sunycgcc.edu
BRUNO, Bonnie .... 336-278-6603 328 H
bbruno2@elon.edu
BRUNO, Christopher ..... 470-578-5483 121 J
cbruno3@kennesaw.edu
BRUNO, Dave .... 615-966-7133 420 B
dave.bruno@lipscomb.edu
BRUNO, Gene .... 865-524-8079 419 A
gene.bruno@huhs.edu
BRUNO, Lileana .... 787-798-3001 509 F
lileana.bruno@uccaribe.edu
BRUNO, Michael .... 808-956-8447 129 B
mbruno2@hawaii.edu
BRUNO, Michael .... 914-367-8251 313 E
fr.michael.bruno@archny.org
BRUNO, SC, Teresa ...... 973-957-0188 274 D
academicdean@acs350.org
BRUNOLD, Timothy ...... 213-740-6753.. 73 C
admdean@usc.edu
BRUNS, David .... 419-995-8177 360 B
bruns.d@rhodesstate.edu
BRUNS, Lisa .... 934-420-2245 320 C
lisa.bruns@farmingdale.edu
BRUNS, Michelle .... 605-867-5856 414 H
mbruns@olc.edu
BRUNSON, JR., Larry ... 909-384-8949.. 60 F
lbrunson@sbccd.cc.ca.us
BRUNSTING, Diane .... 708-293-4918 150 H
diane.brunsting@trnty.edu
BRUNTMYER, Eric, I ..... 325-670-1850 436 B
eric.bruntmyer@hsutx.edu
BRUSATI, Gerianne .... 845-341-4020 310 D
gerianne.brusati@sunyorange.edu
BRUSCATO, Brandon ..... 318-342-5314 193 A
bruscato@ulm.edu
BRUSO, Jacqueline .... 757-352-4259 469 D
jacqbru@regent.edu
BRUSTKERN, Kari .... 406-447-5422 262 E
kbrustkern@carroll.edu
BRUSUELAS-JAMES, Rebecca .... 714-456-5456.. 69 C
rbrusuel@uci.edu
BRUTON, Muniece .... 323-241-5338.. 49 I
brutonmr@lasc.edu
BRUTSMAN, Lauren .... 732-224-2392 275 D
lbrutsman@brookdalecc.edu
BRUUN, Matthew .... 978-665-4694 212 C
mbruun@fitchburgstate.edu
BRUXVOORT, Deb .... 641-628-7675 164 B
bruxvoortd@central.edu
BRUXVOORT, Diane ...... 940-565-3025 453 B
diane.bruxvoort@unt.edu
BRY, Jay .... 978-665-3131 212 C
jbry@fitchburgstate.edu
BRYAN, Angela .... 850-474-2894 111 E
abryan@uwf.edu
BRYAN, Ben, J .... 864-597-4556 413 E
bryanbj@wofford.edu
BRYAN, Brandon .... 831-656-3690 501 K
brandon.bryan@nps.edu
BRYAN, Burcu .... 360-688-2450 482 D
bbryan@stmartin.edu
BRYAN, Chris .... 206-239-4500 477 I
BRYAN, Christine .... 978-934-3936 211 G
christine_bryan@uml.edu
BRYAN, Christopher ..... 206-239-4500 477 I
BRYAN, Dave .... 718-951-5352 293 A
dbryan@brooklyn.cuny.edu
BRYAN, Karla .... 903-675-6229 451 C
kbryan@tvcc.edu
BRYAN, Neva .... 276-328-0126 471 G
njd8r@uvawise.edu
BRYAN, Paul .... 215-893-5252 381 I
paul.bryan@curtis.edu
BRYAN, Robert (Bob) ... 216-987-4684 351 D
bob.bryan@tri-c.edu
BRYAN, Robin .... 540-568-7063 467 C
bryanra@jmu.edu
BRYAN, Stephen .... 217-333-0050 151 F
spbryan@illinois.edu
BRYAN, Susan .... 417-865-2815 252 F
bryans@evangel.edu
BRYAN, Terry .... 832-252-4676 431 M
terry.bryan@cbshouston.edu
BRYAN, Timothy, A ...... 330-471-8539 355 D
tbryan@malone.edu
BRYAN, Vanessa, R ...... 817-257-7855 447 H
v.r.bryan@tcu.edu
BRYAN, Warren, J .... 540-464-7287 475 C
bbryan@vmiaa.org
BRYAN, JR., William, B .... 804-289-8438 471 E
wbryan@richmond.edu
BRYAN-SMITH, Malinda .... 913-469-8500 174 F
mbryan@jccc.edu
BRYAN WILLIAMS, Pamela .... 314-529-9614 254 D
pbryanwilliams@maryville.edu
BRYANT, Alex, L .... 417-268-1000 249 G
bryanta@evangel.edu
BRYANT, Alfred .... 910-893-1632 327 C
abryant@campbell.edu
BRYANT, Allison .... 202-806-1605.. 92 E
allison.bryant@howard.edu
BRYANT, Amanda .... 252-222-6225 332 G
bryanta@carteret.edu
BRYANT, Amie .... 970-247-7212.. 80 H
arbryant@fortlewis.edu
BRYANT, Amy .... 765-983-1302 154 H
bryanam@earlham.edu
BRYANT, Angie .... 615-460-6407 417 B
angie.bryant@belmont.edu
BRYANT, Brigette .... 215-572-2900 378 E
bryantb@arcadia.edu
BRYANT, Bryan .... 303-914-6346.. 82 L
bryan.bryant@rrcc.edu
BRYANT, Chad .... 423-585-2677 424 G
chad.bryant@ws.edu
BRYANT, Chip .... 865-974-9557 426 C
bryant00@utk.edu
BRYANT, Christopher, P .... 757-822-1076 474 G
cbryant@tcc.edu
BRYANT, Clarence, V .... 301-546-0656 201 D
bryantcv@pgcc.edu
BRYANT, Cody .... 931-372-3292 425 B
cdbryant@tntech.edu
BRYANT, Courtney .... 501-852-0804.. 23 K
cbryant13@uca.edu
BRYANT, Courtney .... 509-527-2613 484 C
courtney.bryant@wallawalla.edu
BRYANT, Cynthia, D ..... 225-771-3631 190 K
cynthia_bryant@subr.edu
BRYANT, David .... 423-279-3680 424 B
dlbryant@northeaststate.edu
BRYANT, Don .... 910-521-6648 343 A
don.bryant@uncp.edu
BRYANT, Elisa .... 417-625-3039 255 I
bryant-e@mssu.edu
BRYANT, Essie, L .... 662-254-3440 247 C
elbryant@mvsu.edu
BRYANT, Felicia .... 856-227-7200 275 F
fbryant@camdencc.edu
BRYANT, Gerard .... 646-781-5625 294 B
gwbryant@jjay.cuny.edu
BRYANT, Gregory .... 936-261-1702 445 E
gebryant@pvamu.edu
BRYANT, Jack .... 405-422-1260 368 I
jack.bryant@redlandscc.edu
BRYANT, III, James, S . 803-535-1330 410 C
bryantj@octech.edu
BRYANT, Jody .... 864-231-2000 405 F
jbryant@andersonuniversity.edu
BRYANT, John .... 309-556-3449 140 E
jbryant@iwu.edu
BRYANT, John .... 630-844-5683 133 A
jbryant@aurora.edu
BRYANT, Kelly .... 704-314-4920 329 F
kbryant@hoodseminary.edu
BRYANT, LaSonya .... 214-388-5466 434 E
lbryant@dallasinstitute.edu
BRYANT, III, Lewis .... 434-832-7615 472 G
bryantl@centralvirginia.edu
BRYANT, Lindsey .... 432-335-6400 440 C
BRYANT, Lora, R .... 304-457-6354 485 F
bryantlr@ab.edu
BRYANT, Luke .... 214-887-3904 434 G
lbryant@dts.edu
BRYANT, Marcean .... 510-522-7221.. 57 A
mbryant@peralta.edu
BRYANT, Martha .... 337-482-6391 192 F
martha.bryant@louisiana.edu
BRYANT, Melanie .... 805-267-1690.. 48 A
BRYANT, Michael .... 843-863-7518 406 C
mbryant@csuniv.edu
BRYANT, Missy .... 610-409-3590 400 E
mbryant@ursinus.edu
BRYANT, Natalie .... 903-983-8620 437 G
nbryant@kilgore.edu
BRYANT, Nate .... 978-542-6134 213 B
nate.bryant@salemstate.edu
BRYANT, Paul .... 606-248-2001 182 F
paul.bryant@kctcs.edu
BRYANT, Rachel .... 415-575-6257.. 29 A
rbryant@ciis.edu
BRYANT, Richard, T ...... 714-997-6849.. 36 D
rbryant@chapman.edu
BRYANT, Rick .... 352-294-0963 110 E
rjbryant@ufl.edu
BRYANT, Robbie .... 417-328-1550 258 K
rbryant@sbuniv.edu
BRYANT, Ronda, M .... 540-458-4111 476 D
rbryant2@wlu.edu
BRYANT, Rosalynn .... 314-362-9253 253 A
rosalynn.bryant@barnesjewishcollege.edu
BRYANT, Scott .... 903-923-2069 435 A
sbryant@etbu.edu
BRYANT, Shannon .... 817-515-2515 445 A
shannon.bryant@tccd.edu
BRYANT, Sheila, M .... 931-221-7178 416 H
bryantsm@apsu.edu
BRYANT, Stephan .... 712-325-3310 167 G
sbryant@iwcc.edu
BRYANT, Vashti .... 206-934-3747 482 F
vashti.bryant@seattlecolleges.edu
BRYANT, Velma .... 540-453-2582 472 F
bryantv@brcc.edu
BRYANT, Vickie .... 817-461-8741 429 C
vbryant@abu.edu
BRYANT, Wayne .... 318-274-6118 191 G
bryantw@gram.edu
BRYANT, Wayne, H .... 318-670-9230 191 B
wbryant@ssla.edu
BRYANT-FRIEDRICH, Amanda .... 313-577-1324 232 H
ag3496@wayne.edu
BRYANT HOWE, Marcio .... 501-812-2342.. 23 E
mbryanthowe@uaptc.edu
BRYANT-SHANKS, Cheryl .... 336-334-4822 334 F
cmbryantshanks@gtcc.edu
BRYANT-THIGPEN, Patrice .... 863-298-6847 106 A
pthigpen@polk.edu
BRYARS, Beth .... 251-580-2227.... 1 I
beth.bryars@coastalalabama.edu
BRYCH, Jarda .... 415-581-8902.. 69 B
brychj@uchastings.edu
BRYDE, Beverly .... 610-902-8331 379 E
beverly.reilly.bryde@cabrini.edu
BRYDEN, David, L .... 336-841-9101 329 E
dbryden@highpoint.edu
BRYDON, Lucinda, C ... 607-746-4603 320 A
brydonlm@delhi.edu
BRYENTON, John .... 270-686-4615 182 C
john.bryenton@kctcs.edu
BRYER, Eason .... 316-978-7921 178 B
eason.bryer@wichita.edu
BRYMER, Allison .... 205-726-2762.... 6 E
abrymer@samford.edu
BRYS-WILSON, Jessica . 252-985-5186 339 B
jbrys-wilson@ncwc.edu
BRYSON, Cynthia .... 916-361-1660.. 35 D
BRYSON, Karey .... 253-680-7119 477 A
kbryson@batestech.edu
BRYSON, Matthew, S .... 601-923-1600 248 A
mbryant@rts.edu
BRYSON, Terri .... 931-393-1688 423 G
tbryson@mscc.edu
BRYSON, Tonya, K .... 864-597-4014 413 E
brysontk@wofford.edu
BRZEZINSKI, Karen .... 715-422-5325 498 A
karen.brzezinski@mstc.edu
BRZINSKI, Joanne .... 404-727-6054 118 D
poljb@emory.edu
BRZORAD, John .... 828-328-7606 330 B
john.brzorad@lr.edu
BRZOZOWSKI, Eileen .... 321-433-5493.. 98 F
brzozowskie@easternflorida.edu
BRZYCKI, Shelly .... 847-578-8355 148 B
shelly.brzycki@rosalindfranklin.edu
BSULLAK, Nik .... 207-699-5060 194 G
nbsullak@meca.edu
BUBB, Paul .... 309-298-1190 152 I
pa-bubb@wiu.edu
BUBB, Terry .... 615-230-3398 424 F
terry.bubb@volstate.edu
BUBBLE, Tara .... 315-228-6581 296 C
tbubble@colgate.edu

BUBLITZ, Greg ... 818-343-2890.. 39 F
BUBNOVA, Elena ... 775-673-8240 270 I
ebubnova@tmcc.edu
BUCARO, S. Ted ... 937-229-4122 362 C
sbucaro1@udayton.edu
BUCCINO, Mike ... 410-455-2766 202 G
mbuccino@umbc.edu
BUCELLO, Glenn, R ... 716-878-4128 317 C
bucellgr@buffalostate.edu
BUCHA, Edward ... 724-738-9000 394 E
edward.bucha@sru.edu
BUCHANAN, Amanda ... 828-694-1806 332 C
a.buchanan@blueridge.edu
BUCHANAN, Amanda ... 828-766-1224 335 G
albuchanan@mayland.edu
BUCHANAN, Barbara ... 336-322-2106 336 D
barbara.buchanan@piedmontcc.edu
BUCHANAN, Bernadette 830-372-6412 448 C
bbuchanan@tlu.edu
BUCHANAN, Connie ... 830-703-1555 443 I
cwbuchanan@swtjc.edu
BUCHANAN, Cristallea .. 805-493-3058.. 29 E
cristallea@callutheran.edu
BUCHANAN, Dorothy ... 909-607-1232.. 37 G
dorothy.buchanan@cmc.edu
BUCHANAN, Emily, B ... 336-694-8042 336 D
emily.buchanan@piedmontcc.edu
BUCHANAN, Evelyn ... 510-885-4602.. 31 C
evelyn.buchanan@csueastbay.edu
BUCHANAN, James ... 570-585-9235 381 A
BUCHANAN, Jenna ... 863-638-7209 113 D
jenna.buchanan@warner.edu
BUCHANAN, Julie ... 575-492-2597 286 E
jbuchanan@nmjc.edu
BUCHANAN, Kelly ... 619-201-8702.. 60 G
kelly.buchanan@sdcc.edu
BUCHANAN, Kent ... 719-587-7622.. 77 F
kbuchanan@adams.edu
BUCHANAN, Kyrel ... 256-765-4937.... 8 E
kbuchanan1@una.edu
BUCHANAN, Lauren, A . 724-346-2073 379 C
lauren.buchanan@bc3.edu
BUCHANAN, Linda, R ... 229-732-5926 114 I
lindabuchanan@andrewcollege.edu
BUCHANAN, Mercedes . 205-226-4979.... 5 A
mdbucha1@bsc.edu
BUCHANAN, Pamela ... 828-227-7640 343 D
pmbuchanan@wcu.edu
BUCHANAN, Rose ... 206-934-4591 482 F
rose.buchanan@seattlecolleges.edu
BUCHANAN, Shasta ... 512-223-7053 429 J
shasta.buchanan@austincc.edu
BUCHANAN, Tony ... 910-843-5304 330 F
tony@buchanan.net
BUCHANAN, Trey ... 512-313-5002 432 N
trey.buchanan@concordia.edu
BUCHANAN MILLER,
Pamela ... 251-442-2360.... 8 C
pbuchanan@umobile.edu
BUCHBAUER, Victoria ... 717-477-1484 394 D
vmbuchbauer@ship.edu
BUCHE, Nathan ... 620-665-3569 174 D
buchen@hutchcc.edu
BUCHELE, Ann ... 541-917-4211 373 F
buchela@linnbenton.edu
BUCHEN, Lucas ... 309-649-6230 150 D
lucas.buchen@src.edu
BUCHER, Denise ... 303-404-5481.. 80 I
denise.bucher@frontrange.edu
BUCHER, Fred ... 706-778-8500 124 B
BUCHER, Jacob ... 708-524-6694 137 A
jbucher@dom.edu
BUCHER, Jennifer ... 570-372-4136 398 A
bucherjennifer@susqu.edu
BUCHER, Karen, H ... 540-665-4621 470 A
kbucher@su.edu
BUCHER, Lisa ... 860-832-2556.. 85 F
bucherl@ccsu.edu
BUCHER, Mary ... 864-503-5197 413 A
mbucher@uscupstate.edu
BUCHHEIT, Cynthia ... 256-306-2675.... 1 F
cynthia.buchheit@calhoun.edu
BUCHHEIT, Rudolph ... 859-257-1687 185 D
rudolph.buchheit@uky.edu
BUCHHOLZ, Cindy ... 361-582-2587 456 H
cindy.buchholz@victoriacollege.edu
BUCHHOLZ, Erica ... 701-845-7235 345 E
erica.buchholz@vcsu.edu
BUCHHOLZ, Meagan ... 314-434-4044 251 F
meagan.buchholz@covenantseminary.edu
BUCHHOLZ, Richard ... 405-422-6204 368 I
richard.buchholz@redlandscc.edu
BUCHHOLZ, Ron ... 262-472-1498 496 E
buchholr@uww.edu
BUCHKO, Lindsay ... 202-448-7037.. 92 B
lindsay.buchko@gallaudet.edu
BUCHLEITER, Melanie ... 505-428-5954 285 H
melanie.buchleiter@iaia.edu
BUCHMAN, Ashley ... 870-512-7812.. 18 C
ashley_buchman@asun.edu
BUCHMANN, Teresa ... 253-833-9111 480 A
tbuchmann@greenriver.edu
BUCHOLTZ, Ehren ... 314-367-8700 260 A
ehren.bucholtz@uhsp.edu
BUCHTERKIRCHEN,
Rebekah ... 503-517-1910 377 D
rbuchterkirchen@westernseminary.edu
BUCHWALD, Adam ... 503-768-7227 373 D
buchwald@lclark.edu
BUCHWALD, Carrie ... 847-574-5164 141 G
cbuchwald@lfgsm.edu
BUCHWALD, Staci ... 541-552-6998 376 A
buchwalds@sou.edu
BUCHWALDER,
Mary, P ... 937-229-3131 362 C
mbuchwalder1@udayton.edu
BUCIOR, Autumn ... 973-275-2259 282 K
autumn.bucior@shu.edu
BUCK, Angela ... 207-760-1128 195 C
nabuck@nmcc.edu
BUCK, Charles ... 208-292-1737 132 C
buck@uidaho.edu
BUCK, Eric ... 603-456-2656 273 A
ebuck@magdalen.edu
BUCK, Forrest ... 715-833-6232 497 E
fbuck@cvtc.edu
BUCK, Heather ... 570-702-8906 386 D
hbuck@johnson.edu
BUCK, Jason ... 603-428-2241 272 I
jbuck@nec.edu
BUCK, John ... 314-968-6980 261 D
buckjh@webster.edu
BUCK, Joseph, E ... 610-758-4711 388 C
job316@lehigh.edu
BUCK, Katherine ... 973-290-4203 282 G
kbuck@steu.edu
BUCK, Kevan ... 405-208-5498 367 E
kbuck@okcu.edu
BUCK, Laurie ... 217-206-6724 151 E
lbuck01s@uis.edu
BUCK, Leah ... 207-768-2768 195 C
lbuck@nmcc.edu
BUCK, Luther, S ... 301-736-3631 200 A
BUCK, Sean, S ... 410-293-1500 502 I
sbuck@usna.edu
BUCKALEW, Toby ... 254-968-9963 445 F
buckalew@tarleton.edu
BUCKEL, Maria ... 314-889-4533 252 G
mbuckel@fontbonne.edu
BUCKELS, Carol ... 386-738-6686 111 F
cbuckels@stetson.edu
BUCKENMEYER, Janet ... 812-237-2919 155 H
janet.buckenmeyer@indstate.edu
BUCKHAULTS, Tex ... 806-874-3571 431 K
tex.buckhaults@clarendoncollege.edu
BUCKHAULTS,
Tresea, L ... 318-342-5247 193 A
buckhaults@ulm.edu
BUCKINGHAM, Bob, S . 304-457-6588 485 F
buckinghamrs@ab.edu
BUCKINGHAM,
David, E ... 404-378-8821 117 D
BUCKINGHAM, Richard 617-573-8605 218 G
rbuckingham@suffolk.edu
BUCKINGHAM, Stacy ... 618-985-2828 140 G
stacybuckingham@jalc.edu
BUCKLER, C. Adam ... 317-896-9324 161 D
abuckler@ubca.org
BUCKLER, Christina ... 845-434-5750 321 B
BUCKLES, Beverly, J ... 909-558-4528.. 48 J
bbuckles@llu.edu
BUCKLES, Cassie ... 386-752-1822.. 99 P
cassandra.buckles@fgc.edu
BUCKLES, Dale ... 270-706-8431 181 C
dale.buckles@kctcs.edu
BUCKLES, Jennifer ... 423-425-4677 426 D
jennifer-buckles@utc.edu
BUCKLES, Michael ... 337-475-5192 192 B
mbuckles@mcneese.edu
BUCKLESS, Frank ... 919-515-5560 341 E
buckless@ncsu.edu
BUCKLEW, Andrea, J ... 304-457-6438 485 F
bucklewaj@ab.edu
BUCKLEY, Alison ... 845-687-5050 322 K
BUCKLEY, Anne, L ... 858-534-7572.. 70 C
albuckley@ucsd.edu
BUCKLEY, Bri ... 801-832-2529 461 A
bbuckley@westminstercollege.edu
BUCKLEY, Candice ... 404-297-9522 119 G
buckleyc@gptc.edu
BUCKLEY, Cathy ... 719-389-6707.. 78 E
cbuckley@coloradocollege.edu
BUCKLEY, Cynthia, S ... 405-466-3204 366 B
cynthia.buckley@langston.edu
BUCKLEY, Dawn ... 228-897-3835 246 F
dawn.buckley@mgccc.edu
BUCKLEY, Emily ... 913-621-8731 173 B
ebuckley@donnelly.edu
BUCKLEY, Erin ... 610-519-8881 401 B
erin.buckley@villanova.edu
BUCKLEY, Gabrielle, M . 773-508-8435 142 G
gbuckley1@luc.edu
BUCKLEY, Gerard ... 315-781-3701 301 D
buckley@hws.edu
BUCKLEY, Gerard, J ... 585-475-6317 312 A
gjbcfo@ntid.rit.edu
BUCKLEY, Jennifer ... 630-844-6155 133 A
jbuckley@aurora.edu
BUCKLEY, Jerry, L ... 559-638-0300.. 67 C
jerry.buckley@reedleycollege.edu
BUCKLEY, John, M ... 302-857-1200.. 90 H
john.buckley@dtcc.edu
BUCKLEY, John, W ... 718-817-4000 300 A
jbuckley@fordham.edu
BUCKLEY, Keith ... 503-352-2180 375 B
buckleyk@pacificu.edu
BUCKLEY, Kelley ... 615-871-2260.. 93 H
BUCKLEY, Linda, J ... 978-556-3224 215 C
lbuckley@necc.mass.edu
BUCKLEY, Neil ... 781-239-3193 214 E
nbuckley@massbay.edu
BUCKLEY, Nicholas ... 580-559-5602 365 J
nicpbuc@ecok.edu
BUCKLEY, Noah ... 541-737-4411 374 H
osuadmit@oregonstate.edu
BUCKLEY, Patricia ... 518-458-5444 296 E
buckleyp@strose.edu
BUCKLEY, Sally ... 508-286-3857 219 F
buckley_sally@wheatoncollege.edu
BUCKLEY, Tera ... 701-777-4941 344 H
tera.buckley@und.edu
BUCKLEY, Toni ... 413-236-3075 213 E
tbuckley@berkshirecc.edu
BUCKLEY-BURNELL,
Addye ... 617-358-5732 207 C
addyebb@bu.edu
BUCKLIN, Carolyn ... 515-643-6744 168 B
cbucklin@mercydesmoines.org
BUCKMAN, Anna ... 270-384-8033 183 D
buckmana@lindsey.edu
BUCKMAN, Julie ... 605-698-3966 415 C
jbuckman@swcollege.edu
BUCKMAN, Michael, R . 724-458-3355 384 F
mrbuckman@gcc.edu
BUCKNER, Edmund ... 601-877-6137 244 B
ebuckner@alcorn.edu
BUCKNER, Forrest ... 509-777-4506 485 D
fbuckner@whitworth.edu
BUCKNER, Hope ... 615-460-6645 417 B
hope.buckner@belmont.edu
BUCKNER, Jeremy ... 865-471-3219 417 E
jbuckner@cn.edu
BUCKNER, Melody ... 520-626-9484.. 16 H
mbuckner@arizona.edu
BUCKNER, Nichole ... 828-689-1103 330 H
nbuckner@mhu.edu
BUCKNER, R. Ty ... 336-316-2248 329 C
rbuckner@guilford.edu
BUCKNER, S. Jamila ... 415-442-7079.. 44 B
BUCKNER, Terry ... 859-246-6397 181 B
terry.buckner@kctcs.edu
BUCKNER-BROWN,
Joyce ... 601-877-6528 244 B
jbucknerbrown@alcorn.edu
BUCKNER INNISS,
Lolita ... 303-492-8047.. 83 M
lawdean@colorado.edu
BUCKOVICH, John ... 912-525-5000 124 G
jbuckovi@scad.edu
BUCKRIDGE, Brett ... 610-902-8781 379 E
beb99@cabrini.edu
BUCKSON, Ryan ... 803-750-2500.. 93 H
BUCKTHORPE, Ryan, R . 813-253-6010 102 A
rbuckthorpe@hccfl.edu
BUCKWALTER, John ... 208-426-4062 130 F
johnbuckwalter@boisestate.edu
BUCKWALTER, Kristine . 828-669-8012 331 H
kristine.buckwalter@montreat.edu
BUCY, Brandon, R ... 540-458-8651 476 D
bucyb@wlu.edu
BUCZKOWSKI,
Stephanie ... 716-286-8720 309 F
sbuczkowski@niagara.edu
BUDA, Pawel ... 507-433-0620 240 A
pawel.buda@riverland.edu
BUDDE, Bruce ... 309-694-5477 138 I
bbudde@icc.edu
BUDDE, Jill ... 641-683-5111 166 F
jill.budde@indianhills.edu
BUDDE, Mitzi, J ... 703-370-6600 475 F
BUDDEN, LaNae, R ... 803-786-3856 407 E
lrbriggs@columbiasc.edu
BUDDIE, Mike ... 845-938-3701 502 H
allison.wright@westpoint.edu
BUDDIN, Laura ... 919-739-6867 338 F
lrbuddin@waynecc.edu
BUDELL, Andrew ... 615-343-3896 427 B
andrew.m.budell@vanderbilt.edu
BUDESKI, Brittany ... 406-791-5207 264 J
brittany.budeski@uprovidence.edu
BUDGE, Aaron ... 507-389-5998 238 L
aaron.budge@mnsu.edu
BUDIG, Michelle ... 413-545-5972 211 D
budig@soc.umass.edu
BUDINE, Julie ... 217-228-5432 147 C
hendrju@quincy.edu
BUDNIK, Lindsay ... 802-485-2824 461 H
lbudnik@norwich.edu
BUDNY, Jill ... 724-925-4185 401 H
budnyj@westmoreland.edu
BUDNY, Steve ... 724-925-4085 401 H
budnys@westmoreland.edu
BUDWAY, Joshua ... 480-947-6644.. 15 B
BUDWORTH, Tim ... 602-243-8050.. 14 C
tim.budworth@southmountaincc.edu
BUDZIAK, Chase ... 815-825-1708 141 D
cbudziak@kish.edu
BUDZICK, Danielle ... 440-366-7278 355 B
BUDZILOWICZ, Mary ... 610-902-8352 379 E
mary.m.budzilowicz@cabrini.edu
BUECHELE, Angela, K ... 937-229-2941 362 C
abuechele1@udayton.edu
BUECHELE, Thomas ... 312-899-7420 149 B
tbuechele@saic.edu
BUEHLER, Charlie ... 612-351-0631 235 I
cbuehler@ipr.edu
BUEHLER, Julie ... 585-245-5601 317 E
buehler@geneseo.edu
BUEHLER, Lesley ... 510-659-6082.. 54 J
lbuehler@ohlone.edu
BUEHRER, Danielle ... 470-578-4426 121 J
dbuehrer@kennesaw.edu
BUEHRER, Danielle, S .. 478-301-2070 122 C
buehrer_ds@mercer.edu
BUEL, Kevin, A ... 646-378-6143 289 F
kevin.buel@nyack.edu
BUELL, Evi ... 360-538-4013 479 F
evi.buell@ghc.edu
BUENO, Alyssa ... 304-263-6262 486 G
BUENO, Leo ... 310-338-2775.. 51 C
leo.bueno@lmu.edu
BUENTELLO, Gracy ... 903-566-7480 455 C
gbuentello@uttyler.edu
BUETTNER, John ... 443-352-4494 202 C
jbuettner@stevenson.edu
BUETTNER, Rita ... 410-617-2146 199 G
rfbuettner@loyola.edu
BUFANO, Suzanne ... 843-953-6799 406 D
suzanne.bufano@citadel.edu
BUFF, Sam ... 704-825-6260 334 E
buff.sam@gaston.edu
BUFFINGTON, Brooke ... 336-278-6009 328 H
bbuffington@elon.edu
BUFFINGTON, Chelsea . 925-631-4595.. 59 I
cpb6@stmarys-ca.edu
BUFFINGTON, James ... 714-437-9697.. 38 B
BUFFONE, Nancy ... 413-577-1101 211 D
buffone@admin.umass.edu
BUFFUM, Don ... 662-325-2861 247 A
dbuffum@procurement.msstate.edu
BUFORD, Ron ... 541-888-7229 376 B
ronald.buford@socc.edu
BUGADO, Lai Sha ... 808-932-7365 129 A
sdelo@hawaii.edu
BUGAIGHIS, Elizabeth .. 610-332-6272 391 B
ebugaighis@northampton.edu
BUGAIGHIS, Yasmin ... 610-861-1480 390 D
bugaighisy@moravian.edu

BUGAJSKI, Kenneth, A . 260-399-7700 162 A
kbugajski@sf.edu
BUGAJSKI, OFS,
Trish, J .... 260-399-7700 162 A
tbugajski@sf.edu
BUGGS, Richard .... 415-575-6116.. 29 A
rbuggs@ciis.edu
BUGLIONE, Suzanne ..... 508-678-2811 213 F
suzanne.buglione@bristolcc.edu
BUGOS, Michelle .... 251-580-2100.... 1 I
michelle.bugos@coastalalabama.edu
BUHAGIAR, Jon .... 412-809-5216 395 F
buhagiar.jon@ptcollege.edu
BUHL, Patrick .... 952-358-8595 239 C
patrick.buhl@normandale.edu
BUHLER, Doug, D .... 517-355-0123 227 C
buhler@msu.edu
BUHR, Brian .... 612-625-7173 242 K
bbuhr@umn.edu
BUHR, Connie .... 319-296-4281 166 E
connie.buhr@hawkeyecollege.edu
BUHR, Heather .... 812-866-7097 155 D
buhr@hanover.edu
BUHRANDT, Jeff .... 608-262-2321 494 C
BUHRANDT, Jeff .... 608-262-1312 494 C
jbuhrandt@uwsa.edu
BUHRMASTER, John ..... 305-899-3336.. 96 A
jbuhrmaster@barry.edu
BUHROW, William, C ... 503-554-2340 372 I
bbuhrow@georgefox.edu
BUI, Brooke .... 949-451-5336.. 65 B
bbui21@ivc.edu
BUI, Derek .... 714-241-6594.. 38 D
vbui34@coastline.edu
BUI, Thomas .... 310-434-4554.. 63 B
bui_thomas@smc.edu
BUIE, Melissa, K .... 601-857-3927 245 D
melissa.buie@hindscc.edu
BUISKER, Tracy .... 605-882-5284 414 D
tracy.buisker@lakeareatech.edu
BUISMAN, Kevin .... 507-389-6111 238 L
kevin.buisman@mnsu.edu
BUJAK, Jeanette, K ...... 704-233-8149 344 E
jbujak@wingate.edu
BUJAK, Valerie .... 816-331-5700 257 F
BUJAKI, Jim .... 989-774-1771 221 M
bujak1jf@cmich.edu
BUKOWSKI, Mark .... 863-784-7104 108 D
mark.bukowski@southflorida.edu
BUKOWSKI, Tamzin ...... 320-762-4415 236 G
tamzinb@alextech.edu
BULAN, Anita .... 718-951-5000 293 A
BULCOCK, John .... 507-389-1111 238 L
BULEY, Paula Marie ..... 603-897-8202 273 B
pbuley@rivier.edu
BULGER, Stephanie .... 541-463-5200 373 C
bulgers@lanecc.edu
BULITTA, Sue .... 309-694-5522 138 I
sue.bulitta@icc.edu
BULKLEY, Katrina .... 973-655-2063 278 C
bulkleyk@montclair.edu
BULL, Amy .... 614-508-7277 353 M
BULL, Bernard .... 402-643-3651 265 I
BULL, Joe .... 937-481-2263 363 H
joe.bull@wilminton.edu
BULL, Kam .... 530-895-1352.. 27 F
bullka@butte.edu
BULL, Karen .... 336-315-7044 342 D
kzbull@uncg.edu
BULL, Prince .... 704-406-4402 328 I
pbull@gardner-webb.edu
BULL CHIEF, Emerson .. 406-638-3131 262 J
bullchiefe@lbhc.edu
BULLARD, Anthony .... 662-685-4771 244 D
abullard@bmc.edu
BULLARD, Bobby .... 512-448-8569 441 N
bobbyb@stedwards.edu
BULLARD, Cora .... 910-521-6219 343 A
cora.bullard@uncp.edu
BULLARD, Daniel, C ..... 804-828-2233 472 D
bullarddc@vcu.edu
BULLARD, Eric .... 310-825-5551.. 69 D
ebullard@unex.ucla.edu
BULLARD, Jayne .... 417-269-3473 251 G
jayne.bullard@coxcollege.edu
BULLARD, Roland .... 504-816-4916 186 F
rbullard@dillard.edu
BULLARD, Scott, W ...... 704-463-3030 339 C
scott.bullard@pfeiffer.edu
BULLINGER, Cheryl .... 605-394-4800 414 G
BULLINGHAM, Bree .... 212-517-0532 305 D
bbullingham@mmm.edu
BULLINGTON, Jeffrey .... 719-587-7820.. 77 F
jsbullington@adams.edu
BULLINS, Chris .... 419-372-2343 348 F
chrishb@bgsu.edu
BULLINS, David .... 704-978-5446 335 I
dbullins@mitchellcc.edu
BULLIS, Tim .... 804-752-7315 469 B
timbullis@rmc.edu
BULLOCK, Ann .... 336-278-5900 328 H
abullock9@elon.edu
BULLOCK, Brian .... 610-519-4070 401 B
brian.bullock@villanova.edu
BULLOCK, Casey, D ...... 801-626-6750 460 B
caseybullock@weber.edu
BULLOCK, Charles .... 949-753-4774.. 71 D
BULLOCK, Damay, J ..... 757-569-6704 474 A
dbullock@pdc.edu
BULLOCK, Doug .... 435-797-1812 459 F
doug.bullock@usu.edu
BULLOCK, James .... 949-824-6022.. 69 C
bullock@uci.edu
BULLOCK, James, R ..... 336-978-0688 344 E
j.bullock@wingate.edu
BULLOCK, Jeffrey, F ..... 563-589-3224 170 C
jbullock@dbq.edu
BULLOCK, John .... 802-440-4406 461 B
jbullock@bennington.edu
BULLOCK, Josh .... 217-234-5222 141 H
jbullock@lakelandcollege.edu
BULLOCK, Kelly .... 602-386-4104.. 10 G
kelly.bullock@arizonachristian.edu
BULLOCK, Quintin, B .... 412-237-4413 381 C
brichardson@ccac.edu
BULLUCK, Bruce .... 256-551-5210.... 2 E
bruce.bulluck@drakestate.edu
BULLUCK, Travis .... 828-227-7733 343 D
tlbulluck@email.wcu.edu
BULLWINKEL,
Michelle, L .... 727-816-3212 105 E
bullwim@phsc.edu
BULMER, Sandra .... 203-392-6993.. 85 H
bulmers1@southernct.edu
BULTMAN, Jenny .... 414-955-8193 492 F
jbultman@mcw.edu
BULZONI, Donna, R ...... 570-422-3117 393 F
dbulzoni@esu.edu
BUMGARNER, Jennifer . 252-514-6715 333 F
bumgarnerj@cravencc.edu
BUMILLER, Taylor .... 636-327-4645 255 E
taylorbumiller@gmail.com
BUMIN, Kirill, M .... 508-565-1877 218 F
kbumin@stonehill.edu
BUMPERS, Claude .... 251-665-4139.... 1 E
cbumpers@bishop.edu
BUMPERS, Eddie .... 417-328-1500 258 K
eddiebumpers@crosswaybc.org
BUMPOUS, Debbi .... 605-626-2283 415 H
debbi.bumpous@northern.edu
BUMPS, Heather .... 309-341-7000 141 E
hsbumps@knox.edu
BUNCE, Heather .... 517-321-0242 224 E
hbunce@glcc.edu
BUNCE, Larry .... 419-289-5032 347 H
lbunce@ashland.edu
BUNCH, Ella .... 252-335-0821 333 E
ella_bunch44@albemarle.edu
BUNCH, John .... 903-334-6628 447 C
john.bunch@tamut.edu
BUNCH, Kenneth .... 434-832-6691 472 G
bunchk@centralvirginia.edu
BUNCH, Kirsten .... 828-694-1804 332 C
kirstenb@blueridge.edu
BUNCH, Kirsten .... 304-260-4380 487 C
BUNCH, Martha, M .... 336-272-7102 329 B
bunchm@greensboro.edu
BUNCH, Tara .... 315-445-4155 303 F
campoltm@lemoyne.edu
BUNCH, Tom .... 817-202-6207 444 B
buncht@swau.edu
BUNCH, Wes .... 828-327-7000 332 H
wbunch@cvcc.edu
BUNDERS, Lisa .... 610-606-4666 380 C
lisa.bunders@cedarcrest.edu
BUNDICK, Chris .... 504-398-2125 191 E
cbundick@uhcno.edu
BUNDICK, Tim .... 325-793-4780 439 A
bundick.tim@mcm.edu
BUNDY, Alfred .... 973-877-3156 276 G
abundy@essex.edu
BUNDY, Barbara .... 213-624-1200.. 42 F
bbundy@fidm.edu
BUNDY, Bill .... 806-720-7126 438 F
bill.bundy@lcu.edu
BUNDY, Brad, M .... 513-529-4029 356 A
bundybm@miamioh.edu
BUNDY, James, A .... 203-432-1505.. 90 B
james.bundy@yale.edu
BUNDY, III, O. Richard 814-863-4826 391 F
orb100@psu.edu
BUNGAY, Sophia .... 505-438-8884 287 J
admissions@acupuncturecollege.edu
BUNGER, Ron .... 404-835-6120 422 D
rbunger@richmont.edu
BUNING, Tom .... 808-739-8578 128 C
thomas.buning@chaminade.edu
BUNIS, David .... 508-831-4993 220 C
dabunis@wpi.edu
BUNJER, Alice .... 515-964-0601 166 A
bunjera@faith.edu
BUNJER, Jeff .... 515-964-0601 166 A
bunjerj@faith.edu
BUNKER, Aaron .... 918-335-6875 368 E
abunker@okwu.edu
BUNKER, Michael .... 303-871-2334.. 84 C
michael.bunker@du.edu
BUNKOWSKI, Elise .... 775-674-7544 270 I
ebunkowski@tmcc.edu
BUNN, Colleen .... 607-431-4504 300 G
bunnc@hartwick.edu
BUNN JONES, Yvette .... 443-840-5426 198 D
yjones@ccbcmd.edu
BUNNELL, Bob .... 856-351-2239 282 I
bbunell@salemcc.edu
BUNNELL, Stephen, P .. 208-496-3000 130 G
bunnells@byui.edu
BUNNELL-RHYNE,
Melinda .... 301-369-2543 197 F
mabunnell-rhyne@captechu.edu
BUNNING, Matt .... 859-441-4500 181 D
matt.bunning@kctcs.edu
BUNT, Stephanie .... 714-556-3610.. 73 G
stephanie.bunt@vanguard.edu
BUNTEN, Tricia .... 218-726-6995 243 A
tbunten@d.umn.edu
BUNTING, Amy .... 334-699-2266.... 1 B
aebunting@southeasthealth.org
BUNTING, Gene .... 336-841-9583 329 E
gbunting@highpoint.edu
BUNTING, Taryn .... 618-395-7777 139 F
buntingt@iecc.edu
BUNTON, Kristie .... 817-257-6550 447 H
k.bunton@tcu.edu
BUNTON, Thomas .... 501-916-3010.. 22 C
tebunton@ualr.edu
BUNTON, Tim, M .... 217-443-8780 136 E
t.bunton@dacc.edu
BUONICONTI, Bridget ... 781-768-7895 217 H
bridget.buoniconti@regiscollege.edu
BUONO, Jack .... 516-773-5000 502 G
BUONO, Lisa .... 805-493-3663.. 29 E
llbuono@callutheran.edu
BUONOPANE, Gerald .... 973-761-9121 282 K
gerard.buonopane@shu.edu
BUOY, Kristen .... 678-664-0529 127 E
kristen.buoy@westgatech.edu
BURA, Dona .... 515-964-6443 164 F
dmbura@dmacc.edu
BURBACK, Michael .... 202-884-9812.. 94 A
burbackm@trinitydc.edu
BURBANTE, Gilberto ..... 985-448-4208 192 C
gilberto.burbante@nicholls.edu
BURBEY, Denise .... 607-962-9000 319 F
BURBINE, Jeff .... 207-307-3900 193 E
jburbine@beal.edu
BURCH, Ann Lee .... 480-219-6061 249 C
aburch@atsu.edu
BURCH, Beth .... 503-568-9941 374 E
bburch@ocom.edu
BURCH, Brian, W .... 864-242-5100 405 H
BURCH, Chuck, S .... 704-406-4342 328 I
cburch@gardner-webb.edu
BURCH, Daphne .... 912-478-5054 120 A
dburch@georgiasouthern.edu
BURCH, Melissa .... 706-771-4823 115 H
melissa.burch@augustatech.edu
BURCHAM, Andy .... 806-720-7408 438 F
andy.burcham@lcu.edu
BURCHAM, Joshua .... 336-734-7714 334 D
jburcham@forsythtech.edu
BURCHARD, Eric .... 740-593-1804 358 L
burchard@ohio.edu
BURCHARD, Robert .... 573-875-8700 251 A
BURCHETT, Amy .... 432-264-5063 436 H
aburchett@howardcollege.edu
BURCHETT, Bonnie, L ... 423-439-4446 418 D
bonnie@etsu.edu
BURCHETT, Jennifer ...... 760-252-2411.. 26 L
BURCHETT, Lance .... 470-578-6033 121 J
BURCHETT, Rachelle ..... 606-788-2863 181 A
rachelle.burchett@kctcs.edu
BURCHFIELD, Doug ...... 828-564-5128 335 A
ddburchfield@haywood.edu
BURCHINAL, Mitzi, W .. 336-334-4036 342 D
mjwilder@uncg.edu
BURCIAGA, Alfredo .... 719-846-5458.. 83 I
alfredo.burciaga@trinidadstate.edu
BURCIAGA, Alfredo .... 719-846-5545.. 83 I
alfredo.burciaga@trinidadstate.edu
BURCIAGA, Armando .... 303-914-6761.. 82 L
armando.burciaga@rrcc.edu
BURCIAGA, Jeremy .... 915-778-4001 444 A
BURCKARDT, Jennifer ... 860-486-2337.. 89 B
BURCKEL, Daryl, V .... 337-475-5556 192 B
dburckel@mcneese.edu
BURCKHALTER, Regina . 406-604-4300 262 C
r.burckhalter@apollos.edu
BURD, Gail, D .... 520-621-1856.. 16 H
gburd@arizona.edu
BURD, Kathy .... 304-829-7131 486 B
kburd@bethanywv.edu
BURD, Randy .... 516-299-2917 304 C
randy.burd@liu.edu
BURDA, Ed, P .... 304-457-6238 485 F
burdaep@ab.edu
BURDA, Jeffrey .... 860-768-4482.. 89 E
burda@hartford.edu
BURDEN, Chris .... 619-260-4655.. 72 H
cburden@sandiego.edu
BURDEN, John .... 502-585-9911 184 E
jburden@spalding.edu
BURDEN, Kathleen, K .... 937-255-3636 501 A
kathleen.burden@afit.edu
BURDEN, Matthew .... 630-637-5433 145 E
mburden@noctrl.edu
BURDEN, Susan .... 660-263-4100 256 D
susanburden@macc.edu
BURDETTE, Darcy .... 319-208-5050 169 I
dburdette@scciowa.edu
BURDETTE, Vinson .... 706-754-7711 123 C
vinson.burdette@northgatech.edu
BURDETTE, Vinson .... 803-508-7244 405 C
burdettv@atc.edu
BURDETTE, William .... 304-696-6523 488 N
burdette@marshall.edu
BURDICK, Alexis .... 805-765-9307.. 39 E
alexisburdick@collegesoflaw.edu
BURDICK, Anne .... 626-396-2200.. 26 G
provost@artcenter.edu
BURDICK, David .... 607-962-9328 319 F
dburdic4@corning-cc.edu
BURDICK, Gary .... 269-471-3501 220 H
gburdick@andrews.edu
BURDICK, Jonathan .... 607-255-2000 297 D
jrb538@cornell.edu
BURDICK, Kirsten, N .... 205-934-4319.... 8 A
knburdick@uab.edu
BURDICK, Phillip .... 520-206-4850.. 15 E
pburdick@pima.edu
BURDICK, Scott .... 401-874-2383 404 E
sburdick@uri.edu
BURDINE, Mike .... 208-459-5663 131 A
mburdine@collegeofidaho.edu
BURDSALL, Mark, D ..... 412-624-8038 400 A
pauab5@pitt.edu
BURDUE, JoEllen .... 414-277-7117 493 D
burdue@msoe.edu
BURFITT, William .... 619-849-2540.. 57 J
williamburfitt@pointloma.edu
BURFORD, Amy .... 309-341-5497 134 A
aburford@sandburg.edu
BURFORD, Chris .... 541-962-4101 372 H
cburford@eou.edu
BURFORD, Kristina .... 501-450-1362.. 19 I
burford@hendrix.edu
BURFORD, Kyla .... 618-252-5400 149 E
kyla.burford@sic.edu
BURFORD, Nancy .... 816-501-3618 249 H
BURG, Karen, J .... 706-542-4582 126 F
kburg@uga.edu
BURGAD, Allen .... 701-845-7184 345 E
allen.a.burgad@vcsu.edu
BURGARD, Bambi .... 816-802-3455 253 H
bburgard@kcai.edu
BURGARD, Daniel .... 817-735-2589 453 D
daniel.burgard@unthsc.edu
BURGAU, Tam .... 715-858-1377 497 E
tburgau@cvtc.edu
BURGAY, Stephen, P .... 617-353-1168 207 C
burgay@bu.edu

BURGE, David .... 703-993-5487 466 J
dburge@gmu.edu
BURGE, Jennifer, G ...... 309-677-4939 133 H
jgruening@bradley.edu
BURGE, Timothy .... 402-826-2161 266 A
timothy.burge@doane.edu
BURGENER, Ricki .... 562-985-7502.. 32 A
ricki.burgener@csulb.edu
BURGER, Alissa .... 583-288-6350 251 I
aburger@culver.edu
BURGER, Arnold .... 615-329-8516 418 E
aburger@fisk.edu
BURGER, Betsy .... 517-483-1200 226 D
BURGER, Cindy, L .... 717-796-1800 389 F
cburger@messiah.edu
BURGER, Crystal .... 870-733-6831.. 18 A
ccburger@asumidsouth.edu
BURGER, Tony .... 734-936-1320 231 A
tburger@umich.edu
BURGER, Wes .... 662-325-7552 247 A
w.burger@msstate.edu
BURGESS, Adam .... 850-474-2244 111 E
aburgess1@uwf.edu
BURGESS, Amanda .... 612-330-1791 233 G
burgessa@augsburg.edu
BURGESS, Brandi .... 610-291-9389 390 G
burgessb@neumann.edu
BURGESS, Brandy .... 303-273-3282.. 79 A
burgess@mines.edu
BURGESS, Brenda, K ..... 580-774-3000 369 I
brenda.burgess@swosu.edu
BURGESS, Craig .... 706-507-8800 117 E
burgess_craig@columbusstate.edu
BURGESS, Esther .... 803-981-7075 413 F
eburgess@yorktech.edu
BURGESS, Jamie .... 315-386-7390 319 E
burgessj@canton.edu
BURGESS, Janine .... 703-908-7644 468 A
janine.burgess@marymount.edu
BURGESS, Leandra, H ... 803-705-4604 405 G
leandra.burgess@benedict.edu
BURGESS, Lillie, A .... 803-253-5000 405 G
BURGESS, Linda .... 913-288-7450 174 H
lburgess@kckcc.edu
BURGESS, Marcus, H ... 803-535-5238 406 E
mburgess@claflin.edu
BURGESS, Norma .... 615-966-5062 420 B
norma.burgess@lipscomb.edu
BURGESS, Rick .... 607-255-2000 297 D
ffb7@cornell.edu
BURGESS, Robert .... 870-512-8617.. 18 C
robert_burgess@asun.edu
BURGESS, Ronald, L ..... 334-844-4650.... 4 E
rlb0029@auburn.edu
BURGESS, Shane, C ..... 520-621-7621.. 16 H
sburgess@cals.arizona.edu
BURGESS, Valerie .... 603-880-8308 273 F
vburgess@thomasmorecollege.edu
BURGGRAFF, Lucy .... 919-573-5350 340 A
lburggraff@shepherds.edu
BURGIN, Jeffery .... 256-761-6274.... 7 B
jburgin@talladega.edu
BURGIN, Vicki .... 251-442-2238.... 8 C
vburgin@umobile.edu
BURGMAYER, Sharon ..... 610-526-5106 378 J
sburmay@brynmawr.edu
BURGNER, Ryan .... 308-635-6798 269 E
burgnerr@wncc.edu
BURGOS, Henry .... 361-593-2258 447 A
henry.burgos@tamuk.edu
BURGOS, Kathy .... 562-860-2451.. 35 O
kburgos@cerritos.edu
BURGOS, Victoria .... 336-721-2627 339 H
victoria.burgos@salem.edu
BURGOS, Victoria .... 701-483-2014 345 A
victoria.burgos@sodexo.com
BURGOS CARRION,
Jorge, A .... 787-720-4476 509 G
decanatoestudiantes@mizpa.edu
BURGRAFF, Tom .... 970-943-2237.. 85 B
tburgraff@western.edu
BURGREEN, Sheena ...... 256-765-4328.... 8 E
sldickerson@una.edu
BURGUNDER-JOHNSON,
Dominique .... 574-535-7568 155 B
dominiquebj@goshen.edu
BURHANNA, Kenneth .... 330-672-1660 354 A
kburhann@kent.edu
BURI, David .... 509-359-6200 478 H
dburi@ewu.edu
BURILLO-HOPKINS,
Madeline .... 713-718-7748 436 E
madeline.burillo@hccs.edu

BURINGTON, Stacie ...... 563-425-5899 170 D
buringtons63@uiu.edu
BURK, Ann, M .... 308-432-6311 267 G
aburk@csc.edu
BURKE, Alison .... 610-921-6711 377 F
aburke@albright.edu
BURKE, Andrew .... 575-646-2431 286 G
aburke@nmsu.edu
BURKE, Belinda .... 828-771-2000 344 B
bburke@warren-wilson.edu
BURKE, Brenda .... 330-672-6000 354 A
bburke21@kent.edu
BURKE, Brian, W .... 413-545-2204 211 D
bwburke@umass.edu
BURKE, Bridgit .... 307-766-3753 500 H
BURKE, Brigid .... 973-443-8520 276 I
brigid_burke@fdu.edu
BURKE, Cathleen, C ..... 804-828-6549 472 D
ccburke@vcu.edu
BURKE, Christina .... 301-687-4467 203 F
cnburke@frostburg.edu
BURKE, Christy .... 740-376-4708 355 E
christy.burke@marietta.edu
BURKE, Colleen .... 215-572-2785 378 E
burkec@arcadia.edu
BURKE, Courtney .... 518-262-9590 289 C
burkec4@amc.edu
BURKE, Derek, A .... 252-398-6369 328 A
burked@chowan.edu
BURKE, Elizabeth .... 626-571-8811.. 73 D
elizabethb@uwest.edu
BURKE, Gary .... 301-369-2544 197 F
gaburke@captechu.edu
BURKE, Greg .... 318-357-5251 192 D
burkeg@nsula.edu
BURKE, Greg .... 812-749-1288 159 E
gburke@oak.edu
BURKE, Indy .... 203-432-5109.. 90 B
indy.burke@yale.edu
BURKE, James .... 216-397-4484 353 O
burke@jcu.edu
BURKE, Jeanmarie .... 315-568-3869 309 H
jburke@northeastcollege.edu
BURKE, Jim .... 601-974-1036 246 C
BURKE, John .... 845-848-4079 298 A
john.burke@dc.edu
BURKE, John .... 361-570-4550 452 C
burkej@uhv.edu
BURKE, John, D .... 617-552-3387 207 A
john.burke.7@bc.edu
BURKE, Jon .... 816-604-6620 254 G
jon.burke@mcckc.edu
BURKE, Jonathan, L ..... 816-604-6620 254 F
jon.burke@mcckc.edu
BURKE, Jonica .... 740-351-3863 360 E
jburke@shawnee.edu
BURKE, Joy .... 814-371-2090 399 B
jburke@triangle-tech.edu
BURKE, Judith, M .... 978-656-3116 214 G
BURKE, Kathleen .... 213-763-7000.. 50 A
BURKE, Katie .... 860-231-5364.. 89 G
kathrynburke@usj.edu
BURKE, Keri .... 503-883-2269 373 E
kburke@linfield.edu
BURKE, SJ, Kevin, F .... 303-458-4087.. 83 B
kburke@regis.edu
BURKE, Lucy .... 315-859-4999 300 F
lburke@hamilton.edu
BURKE, Marcilynn .... 541-346-3836 376 G
maburke@uoregon.edu
BURKE, Mary, E .... 215-707-3023 398 D
maryburke@temple.edu
BURKE, Matthew .... 978-665-3313 212 C
mburke4@fitchburgstate.edu
BURKE, Pamela, B .... 540-665-4925 470 A
pburke2@su.edu
BURKE, Patty .... 513-487-1287 361 E
patty.burke@myunion.edu
BURKE, Paula .... 660-831-4105 256 B
burkep@moval.edu
BURKE, Robyn .... 907-852-1838.... 9 H
robyn.burke@ilisagvik.edu
BURKE, Sandra .... 662-252-8000 248 B
sburke@rustcollege.edu
BURKE, Sara, K .... 330-471-8288 355 D
sburke@malone.edu
BURKE, Scott, M .... 404-413-2088 120 C
sburke@gsu.edu
BURKE, Sean .... 563-387-2110 167 J
burke.sean@luther.edu
BURKE, Seth .... 540-665-6257 470 A
sburke@su.edu

BURKE, Shelby .... 425-388-9254 479 B
saburke@everettcc.edu
BURKE, Thomas .... 410-864-3602 202 A
tburke@stmarys.edu
BURKE, Vic .... 229-225-3978 125 G
vburke@southernregional.edu
BURKE, William .... 570-702-8907 386 D
wburke@johnson.edu
BURKERT, Amy, L .... 412-268-5865 380 B
ak11@andrew.cmu.edu
BURKES, Kate .... 479-619-4299.. 20 G
kburkes@nwacc.edu
BURKET, Jamie .... 904-256-7542 102 G
jburket@ju.edu
BURKETT, Brad .... 731-881-7641 426 E
bburkett@utm.edu
BURKETT, Kaia .... 510-587-7890.. 57 C
kburkett@peralta.edu
BURKHALTER, Sheila .... 803-323-2251 413 D
burkhalters@winthrop.edu
BURKHARDT, Bonnie .... 973-275-4673 282 K
bonnie.burkhardt@shu.edu
BURKHARDT, Janet .... 303-871-4757.. 84 C
janet.burkhardt@du.edu
BURKHARDT, Paul .... 928-350-4100.. 15 O
pburkhardt@prescott.edu
BURKHARDT, Paul .... 269-749-7625 229 G
pburkhardt@olivetcollege.edu
BURKHARDT, Ronald ..... 856-351-2608 282 I
rburkhardt@salemcc.edu
BURKHART, Allison ...... 303-963-3437.. 78 D
aburkhart@ccu.edu
BURKHART, Cindy .... 910-938-6145 333 D
burkhartc@coastalcarolina.edu
BURKHART, John .... 419-358-3320 348 E
burkhartj@bluffton.edu
BURKHART, Manda .... 520-417-4115.. 11 O
burkhartm@cochise.edu
BURKHOLDER,
Brian, M .... 540-432-4132 465 F
brian.burkholder@emu.edu
BURKHOLDER, Mary, E 419-783-2360 351 J
mburkholder@defiance.edu
BURKHOLDER,
Robert, C .... 215-503-6249 398 G
robert.burkholder@jefferson.edu
BURKINK, Tim, J .... 308-865-1547 268 J
burkinktj@unk.edu
BURKITT, David .... 419-517-8968 355 C
dburkitt@lourdes.edu
BURKITT, David .... 309-672-5513 143 I
dburkitt@methodistcol.edu
BURKLO, Daniel .... 419-267-1342 357 E
dburklo@northweststate.edu
BURKMAN, Roger .... 502-585-9911 184 E
rburkman@spalding.edu
BURKS, A. Wesley .... 919-966-4161 342 B
wesley.burks@unc.edu
BURKS, Brent .... 254-295-4514 453 A
bburks@umhb.edu
BURKS, Bryan .... 501-279-4312.. 19 G
bburks@harding.edu
BURKS, Cherryl .... 770-229-3409 125 F
cherryl.burks@sctech.edu
BURKS, Eric .... 785-738-9057 176 C
eburks@ncktc.edu
BURKS, Gwenevera, E .. 559-453-2010.. 43 D
gwen.burks@fresno.edu
BURKS, Scott, A .... 502-852-4661 185 E
scott.burks@louisville.edu
BURKULE, Adit .... 507-222-5635 234 C
adit@carleton.edu
BURKY, Heather .... 717-391-6935 398 E
burky@stevenscollege.edu
BURLEIGH-JONES,
Bronte .... 202-885-3283.. 91 D
jonesbro@american.edu
BURLESON, Brooke .... 828-766-1269 335 G
bburleson@mayland.edu
BURLESON, Burt .... 254-710-3517 430 F
burt_burleson@baylor.edu
BURLESON, Rachel .... 603-899-4080 272 G
burlesonr@franklinpierce.edu
BURLESON, Susan, D .... 336-224-4840 333 G
susan_burleson@davidsondavie.edu
BURLEW, Jon .... 606-451-6748 182 D
jon.burlew@kctcs.edu
BURLEW, Lynette .... 318-473-6401 189 A
lburlew@lsua.edu
BURLEY, Diana .... 202-885-1000.. 91 D
dburley@american.edu
BURLEY, Hansel, E .... 505-277-6525 288 C
hburley@unm.edu

BURLING, Rachel .... 262-691-5266 499 A
rburling@wctc.edu
BURLINGAME, Kathy .... 502-410-6200 180 D
kburlingame@galencollege.edu
BURLINGAME, Suzette .. 330-829-8175 362 E
burlinsu@mountunion.edu
BURMA, William, H ...... 515-263-2975 166 C
bburma@grandview.edu
BURMAN, Tom .... 307-766-2292 500 H
tburman@uwyo.edu
BURMEISTER, Justin .... 718-429-6600 323 I
justin.burmeister@vaughn.edu
BURMEISTER, Paula, J . 719-333-3450 502 C
paula.burmeister.ctr@afacademy.af.edu
BURMENKO, Neil .... 510-464-3520.. 57 B
nburmenko@peralta.edu
BURMESTER, Aimee ...... 605-626-2550 415 H
aimee.burmester@northern.edu
BURNELL, Hope .... 207-786-8388 193 D
hburnell@bates.edu
BURNER, Emily .... 540-665-3489 470 A
eburner@su.edu
BURNET-JONES, Sylvie . 303-492-7631.. 83 M
sylvie.burnet-jones@colorado.edu
BURNETT, Allie .... 805-756-2925.. 29 K
alburnet@calpoly.edu
BURNETT, Amber .... 909-599-5433.. 48 E
aburnett@lifepacific.edu
BURNETT, Belinda .... 520-417-4028.. 11 O
burnettb@cochise.edu
BURNETT, Ben .... 601-318-6495 249 B
pres@wmcarey.edu
BURNETT, Bradley, T .... 405-325-9899 370 J
bburnett@ou.edu
BURNETT, Brian .... 205-934-4011.... 8 A
brianburnett@uab.edu
BURNETT, Catherine, G 713-646-1831 443 C
cburnett@stcl.edu
BURNETT, Denita .... 276-223-4769 475 B
dburnett@wcc.vccs.edu
BURNETT, Edward, T .... 508-286-8214 219 F
burnett_edward@wheatoncollege.edu
BURNETT, Farah .... 718-270-2488 316 E
farah.burnett@downstate.edu
BURNETT, Grace .... 208-882-1566 131 H
registrar@nsa.edu
BURNETT, Jake .... 740-826-8042 356 H
jburnett@muskingum.edu
BURNETT, John .... 724-938-5425 394 C
burnett@calu.edu
BURNETT, Kimberly ...... 205-226-4906.... 5 A
kmburnet@bsc.edu
BURNETT, Lenora .... 863-292-3765 106 A
lburnett@polk.edu
BURNETT, Lindsay .... 870-972-2586.. 17 I
lburnett@astate.edu
BURNETT, Lonnie .... 251-442-2201.... 8 C
lburnett@umobile.edu
BURNETT, Mary .... 717-477-1279 394 D
meburnett@ship.edu
BURNETT, Myra .... 404-270-5027 126 A
mburnett@spelman.edu
BURNETT, Sean .... 818-702-1400.. 56 H
sean.burnett@pepperdine.edu
BURNETT, Sharron, T ... 904-470-8012.. 98 I
s.burnett@ewc.edu
BURNETT, Shirley .... 601-979-2127 245 G
shirley.f.burnett@jsums.edu
BURNETT-HACKBARTH,
Kimberly .... 563-876-3353 165 D
kburnetthackbarth@dwci.edu
BURNETTE, Brittany ..... 832-252-0737 431 M
brittany.burnette@cbshouston.edu
BURNETTE, Daarel .... 502-597-6000 183 A
daarel.burnette@kysu.edu
BURNETTE, Heather ...... 704-991-0215 338 A
hburnette9430@stanly.edu
BURNETTE, Monica .... 973-761-9147 282 K
monica.burnette@shu.edu
BURNETTE, Rick .... 850-644-1532 110 B
rburnette@admin.fsu.edu
BURNETTE, Steve .... 276-223-4705 475 B
sburnette@wcc.vccs.edu
BURNEY, David .... 479-524-7427.. 20 C
dburney@jbu.edu
BURNEY, Linda .... 910-879-5519 332 B
lburney@bladencc.edu
BURNEY, Michelle .... 662-227-2304 245 E
mburney@holmescc.edu
BURNEY, Rolanda, C .... 413-545-2211 211 D
rburney@umass.edu
BURNFIELD, Robert ...... 954-731-8880.. 97 O

BUSH, Justin ... 352-588-8361 107 B justin.bush@saintleo.edu
BUSH, Keith ... 218-751-8670 241 Q it@oakhills.edu
BUSH, Kelsey, R ... 240-895-4259 201 F krbush@smcm.edu
BUSH, Kristen ... 540-231-1796 475 D khbush@vt.edu
BUSH, Lisa, F ... 828-398-7202 331 K lbush@abtech.edu
BUSH, Maureen ... 410-617-5817 199 G mwfaux@loyola.edu
BUSH, Mike ... 505-526-4745 190 C mikeb@dmisys.com
BUSH, Polly ... 585-340-9633 296 B pbush@crcds.edu
BUSHA, Michael ... 269-337-4400 233 A
BUSHAW, Lisa ... 734-462-4400 230 B lbushaw@schoolcraft.edu
BUSHELL, Shawna ... 312-850-7313 135 E sbushell@ccc.edu
BUSHEY, Ann, M ... 804-371-3000 473 A abushey@reynolds.edu
BUSHKIN, Alan ... 954-492-5353.. 97 G abushkin@citycollege.edu
BUSHMAN, David, W ... 540-828-5605 464 C dbushman@bridgewater.edu
BUSHONG, Sara ... 419-372-2856 348 F sbushon@bgsu.edu
BUSHUNOW, Alexei ... 530-467-3544.. 60 A apb@spots.edu
BUSHWAY, Deborah ... 952-885-5410 241 P dbushway@nwhealth.edu
BUSING, Michael ... 540-568-3254 467 C busingme@jmu.edu
BUSKIRK, Joseph ... 443-412-2377 199 B jbuskirk@harford.edu
BUSKIRK, Susan ... 410-706-4937 202 F sbuskirk@umaryland.edu
BUSS, James ... 859-572-5946 184 B bussj1@nku.edu
BUSS, Rob ... 309-694-5494 138 I rob.buss@icc.edu
BUSS, Todd ... 920-923-8762 492 D tcbuss45@marianuniversity.edu
BUSSELL, Helena ... 817-531-4405 450 F hbussell@txwes.edu
BUSSELL, Jeff ... 714-619-6615.. 73 G jeff.bussell@vanguard.edu
BUSSELL, Paige ... 903-468-3209 446 D paige.bussell@tamuc.edu
BUSSELL, Rachelle ... 909-558-4544.. 48 J rbussell@llu.edu
BUSSELL, Tom ... 504-526-4745 190 C
BUSSEY, Brenda ... 508-929-8455 213 D bbussey@worcester.edu
BUSSEY, Tosha ... 404-225-4596 115 F tbussey@atlantatech.edu
BUSSI, Mary ... 415-422-5555.. 72 I mebussi@usfca.edu
BUSSIKI, Marcelo ... 979-209-7460 430 I mbussiki@blinn.edu
BUSTAMANTE, Alexander ... 510-987-9090.. 68 M alexander.bustamante@ucop.edu
BUSTAMANTE, JR., Tom ... 909-218-3253.. 25 J tbustamantejr@americancareercollege.edu
BUSTARD, James ... 217-351-2211 146 G jbustard@parkland.edu
BUSTER, Larissa ... 402-399-2674 265 H lbuster@csm.edu
BUSTER, Marcella ... 406-657-1043 264 G marcella.buster@rocky.edu
BUSTINZA, Reggie ... 815-753-8821 145 H rbustinza@niu.edu
BUSTOS, Adam ... 505-454-3053 286 C adambustos@nmhu.edu
BUSTOS, Leon ... 505-454-3366 286 C leonbustos@nmhu.edu
BUSTOS-WORKS, Carmen ... 707-826-3722.. 30 A carmen.works@humboldt.edu
BUTCHER, Claudette ... 918-293-5256 368 B claudette.butcher@okstate.edu
BUTCHER, Greg ... 724-589-2031 398 F gbutcher@thiel.edu
BUTCHER, Matt ... 928-757-0861.. 14 H mbutcher@mohave.edu
BUTCHER, Michael ... 912-279-5815 117 C mbutcher@ccga.edu
BUTCHER, Michelle, C .. 859-858-3511 178 H michelle.butcher@asbury.edu
BUTCHKO, Thomas ... 570-208-5928 386 G thomasbutchko@kings.edu
BUTDORFF, Carla ... 419-747-5401 357 B 196mgr@fheg.follett.com
BUTERA, Peter ... 716-286-8060 309 F pbutera@niagara.edu
BUTERA, Rae-Anne ... 617-521-2000 218 C
BUTERA, Robert ... 404-894-2935 119 D rbutera@gatech.edu
BUTERA, Vince ... 847-578-8374 148 B vince.butera@rosalindfranklin.edu
BUTEYN, Derek ... 712-722-6076 165 E derek.buteyn@dordt.edu
BUTKOVICH, Michelle ... 248-204-2111 226 E mbutkovic@ltu.edu
BUTLER, Amy ... 202-885-1000.. 91 D aebutler@american.edu
BUTLER, Andra ... 606-546-1224 185 B abutler@unionky.edu
BUTLER, Andrew ... 508-831-6634 220 C abutler@wpi.edu
BUTLER, Andrew, J ... 205-934-5149.... 8 A andrewbutler@uab.edu
BUTLER, Barry ... 386-226-6000.. 98 J butlerb@erau.edu
BUTLER, Blake ... 501-760-4176.. 20 E blake.butler@np.edu
BUTLER, Brady ... 412-536-1300 386 H brady.butler@laroche.edu
BUTLER, Brian, S ... 205-348-4786.... 7 G bsbutler@ua.edu
BUTLER, Bruce, D ... 713-500-3369 455 D bruce.d.butler@uth.tmc.edu
BUTLER, Bryant ... 601-968-5930 244 C bbutler@belhaven.edu
BUTLER, Carmen ... 704-406-3980 328 I cbutler@gardner-webb.edu
BUTLER, Chorissa ... 928-350-2104.. 15 O
BUTLER, David, L ... 615-898-2182 421 C david.butler@mtsu.edu
BUTLER, Debra ... 662-252-8000 248 B dbutler@rustcollege.edu
BUTLER, Duan ... 540-374-4300.. 93 H
BUTLER, Ella ... 801-957-4592 460 D ella.butler@slcc.edu
BUTLER, Fay ... 718-482-5281 294 D fbutler@lagcc.cuny.edu
BUTLER, Heidi ... 251-380-4000.... 6 H
BUTLER, Henry ... 703-993-8644 466 J hnbutler@gmu.edu
BUTLER, Isaac ... 314-367-8700 260 A isaac.butler@uhsp.edu
BUTLER, John, L ... 773-442-4219 145 G j-butler1@neiu.edu
BUTLER, S.J., John, T .. 617-552-6855 207 A john.butler@bc.edu
BUTLER, Kevin ... 702-992-2351 270 H kevin.butler@nsc.edu
BUTLER, Kim, I ... 515-263-2841 166 C maintenance@grandview.edu
BUTLER, Kristi ... 740-386-4110 355 F butlerk@mtc.edu
BUTLER, JR., Lee, H ... 918-610-6466 368 G lee.butler@ptstulsa.edu
BUTLER, LeRoy ... 815-836-5923 142 C butlerle@lewisu.edu
BUTLER, Linc ... 919-843-6298 342 B linc_butler@unc.edu
BUTLER, Lisa, J ... 478-301-2951 122 C butler_lj@mercer.edu
BUTLER, Malcolm, B ... 704-687-8997 342 C malcom.butler@uncc.edu
BUTLER, Malinda ... 601-877-6141 244 B mbutler@alcorn.edu
BUTLER, Mark ... 864-231-2000 405 F mbutler@andersonuniversity.edu
BUTLER, Michael ... 909-469-5534.. 75 G mbutler@westernu.edu
BUTLER, Randy ... 903-593-8311 448 A rbutler@texascollege.edu
BUTLER, Rebecca ... 614-287-2180 351 B rbutler17@cscc.edu
BUTLER, Renee ... 470-578-5414 121 J rbutle35@kennesaw.edu
BUTLER, Rhett ... 334-833-4474.... 5 H chaplain@hawks.huntingdon.edu
BUTLER, Robert ... 617-824-8953 208 G robert_butler@emerson.edu
BUTLER, Roger ... 804-828-0100 472 D butlerr3@vcu.edu
BUTLER, Sandy ... 404-261-1441 123 G
BUTLER, Sara ... 760-776-7365.. 39 A sbutler@collegeofthedesert.edu
BUTLER, Shai ... 413-755-4197 215 F slbutler@stcc.edu
BUTLER, Stephen, M ... 412-383-3547 400 A smb285@pitt.edu
BUTLER, Steve ... 903-657-6543 447 F
BUTLER, Tamaka ... 313-577-6606 232 H tamaka.butler@wayne.edu
BUTLER, Todd ... 509-335-3854 484 D butlert@wsu.edu
BUTLER, Vicki ... 206-239-4500 477 I
BUTLER, Walter ... 731-352-4000 417 C butlerw@bethelu.edu
BUTLER-JOHNSON, Serena ... 202-274-5670.. 94 B sbutlerjohnson@udc.edu
BUTLER-PURRY, Karen . 979-845-3631 446 B ogaps@tamu.edu
BUTRUM, Herb ... 713-798-4951 430 E
BUTT, Darryl, P ... 801-581-8767 459 D darryl.butt@utah.edu
BUTT, Ryan ... 815-836-5267 142 C rbutt@lewisu.edu
BUTT, Steven ... 269-276-3253 232 J steven.butt@wmich.edu
BUTTAFARRO, JR., Thomas ... 716-375-2155 312 F tbuttafa@sbu.edu
BUTTARS, Ryan, J ... 208-496-2710 130 G buttarsr@byui.edu
BUTTERFIELD, Heather .. 920-403-3210 494 B
BUTTERFIELD, Kevin ... 804-289-8456 471 E kbutterf@richmond.edu
BUTTERFIELD, Robyn ... 781-239-2605 214 E rbutterfield@massbay.edu
BUTTERFIELD, Sherri-Ann, P ... 973-353-5541 281 C sbutter@newark.rutgers.edu
BUTTERFIELD, Valerie ... 616-234-4105 224 C registrars@grcc.edu
BUTTIMER, Richard, J .. 904-620-5280 111 A richard.buttimer@unf.edu
BUTTLEMAN, Kurt ... 206-934-4111 482 E kurt.buttleman@seattlecolleges.edu
BUTTON, Emiley ... 270-384-7442 183 D buttone@lindsey.edu
BUTTON, Mark ... 402-472-6262 269 A mbutton2@unl.edu
BUTTRICK, Hilary ... 317-940-8748 153 H
BUTTRY, Tonya ... 573-334-6825 258 I tbuttry@sehcollege.edu
BUTTS, Cory ... 719-549-3064.. 82 I cory.butts@pueblocc.edu
BUTTS, Dawn ... 803-508-7332 405 C buttsd@atc.edu
BUTTS, Emily, J ... 507-786-3503 242 I butts2@stolaf.edu
BUTTS, Gary ... 212-241-8276 302 B gary.butts@mssm.edu
BUTTS, Jeffrey ... 212-237-8486 294 B jbutts@jjay.cuny.edu
BUTTS, John ... 252-618-6598 334 B buttsj@edgecombe.edu
BUTTS, Joseph ... 432-685-4569 439 E jbutts@midland.edu
BUTTS, Kristina ... 806-834-2850 450 C kristina.butts@ttu.edu
BUTTS, Tracy ... 530-898-5146.. 31 A tbutts@csuchico.edu
BUTTS-FREEMAN, Jolene ... 470-453-0428 116 I jbuttsfreeman@cau.edu
BUTTY, David, C ... 313-496-2526 232 B dbutty1@wcccd.edu
BUTTZ, William ... 724-357-4844 393 G wbuttz@iup.edu
BUTWELL, Justin ... 845-575-3000 305 C justin.butwell@marist.edu
BUTWIN, Bridget, K ... 812-237-4141 155 H bridget.butwin@indstate.edu
BUTZ, Michael ... 216-421-7417 350 E mcbutz@cia.edu
BUTZER, Hans, E ... 405-325-3505 370 J butzer@ou.edu
BUVINGER, Nancy ... 562-860-2451.. 35 O nbuvinger@cerritos.edu
BUXBAUM, Hannah ... 812-855-4350 156 B hbuxbaum@iu.edu
BUXBAUM, Hannah ... 812-855-4350 156 C hbuxbaum@iu.edu
BUXTON, Jasmine ... 302-857-7987.. 90 D jbuxton@desu.edu
BUXTON, John, B ... 919-536-7200 334 A president@durhamtech.edu
BUXTON, Kimberly ... 401-598-4471 403 E kimberly.buxton@jwu.edu
BUYSSE, James ... 909-388-6900.. 60 D
BUYSSE, Rustin ... 507-537-6876 240 G rustin.buysse.2@smsu.edu
BUZAK, Anne ... 916-323-0853.. 26 H abuzak@asher.edu
BUZAY, Aaron ... 401-254-3198 404 C abuzay@rwu.edu
BUZBEE, Brandon ... 940-565-2000 453 B
BUZHARDT, Landee ... 803-321-5106 409 I landee.buzhardt@newberry.edu
BUZZANCA, Cristine ... 239-280-2511.. 95 M cristine.buzzanca@avemaria.edu
BUZZARD, Janet ... 918-444-2900 366 G buzzardj@nsuok.edu
BUZZETTA, Mary ... 210-784-1336 447 B mary.buzzetta@tamusa.edu
BYAM, Latrice ... 202-806-2705.. 92 E latrice.byam@howard.edu
BYARD, Brenda ... 540-868-7208 473 C bbyard@lfcc.edu
BYAS, Renee ... 401-277-4955 404 B rbyas@risd.edu
BYBEE, Paivi ... 816-501-4832 257 K paivi.bybee@rockhurst.edu
BYBEE, Tamika ... 443-518-1000 199 D
BYCURA, Samantha ... 412-809-5144 395 F bycura.samantha@ptcollege.edu
BYCZEK, Sara ... 313-593-5430 231 B sbyczek@umich.edu
BYE, Ryan ... 219-454-5150 162 C ryan.bye@valpo.edu
BYER, Larry ... 805-969-3626.. 55 I lbyer@pacifica.edu
BYER, Shanda ... 217-786-2290 142 F shanda.byer@llcc.edu
BYERLEY, Julie ... 570-504-7290 384 A jbyerley1@som.geisinger.edu
BYERLY, Alison, R ... 507-222-4000 234 C
BYERLY, Michele ... 562-903-4701.. 27 E michele.byerly@biola.edu
BYERLY, Thomas, L ... 540-887-7000 467 G tbyerly@marybaldwin.edu
BYERS, Ashley ... 618-537-6532 143 G aabyers@mckendree.edu
BYERS, Asia ... 615-868-6503 421 B
BYERS, Eric, C ... 240-500-2501 199 A ecbyers@hagerstowncc.edu
BYERS, Fred ... 970-675-3407.. 78 P fred.byers@cncc.edu
BYERS, Jonathan ... 509-313-4667 479 E byers@gonzaga.edu
BYERS, Merrie ... 970-675-3204.. 78 P merrie.byers@cncc.edu
BYERS, Michelle, C ... 319-273-2422 163 G michelle.byers@uni.edu
BYERS, Mike ... 828-227-7321 343 D mtbyers@wcu.edu
BYERS, Randy ... 214-333-5691 433 D randy@dbu.edu
BYERS, Rhonda ... 573-341-4241 260 F byersrf@mst.edu
BYERS, Tiffany ... 501-279-4856.. 19 G tbyers@harding.edu
BYFIELD, Natalie ... 718-990-1976 313 B byfieldn@stjohns.edu
BYHAM, Joseph ... 215-503-3997 398 G joseph.byham@jefferson.edu
BYINGTON, Carrie ... 510-987-0700.. 68 M
BYINGTON, Scott ... 919-718-7425 333 A sbyington@cccc.edu
BYL, Kristine ... 608-757-6328 497 D kbyl@blackhawk.edu
BYLAND, KK ... 800-280-0307 153 B kk.byland@ace.edu
BYLAND, Tammy ... 785-532-6318 175 A tbyland@ksu.edu
BYLSMA, Thomas, W ... 616-395-7781 224 H bylsma@hope.edu
BYNOG, Jennie ... 318-797-5058 189 E jennie.bynog@lsus.edu
BYNUM, Chris ... 616-949-5300 222 F chris.bynum@cornerstone.edu
BYNUM, Jo Ellen ... 443-334-2880 205 A jbynum@worwic.edu
BYNUM, Leroy ... 503-725-3340 375 D lbynumjr@pdx.edu
BYNUM, Torrance ... 415-550-4348.. 37 C tbynum@ccsf.edu
BYRD, Ajani ... 650-949-7777.. 43 A
BYRD, Alexander ... 713-348-4026 441 K axb@rice.edu

CAIRY, Timothy, J ... 610-499-1193 401 I
tjcairy@widener.edu
CAISON, Anthony ... 919-866-6101 338 E
amcaison@waketech.edu
CAISON, Santrell ... 919-866-5428 338 E
smcaison@waketech.edu
CAJTHAML, Alanna ... 626-969-3434.. 26 K
CAKE, John ... 301-891-4008 204 D
jcake@wau.edu
CAL, John ... 305-348-4001 109 H
john.cal@fiu.edu
CAL, Mark ... 575-439-3622 286 H
mcal@nmsu.edu
CALABA, George ... 610-799-1114 388 B
gcalaba@lccc.edu
CALABRESE, Lisa ... 203-575-8151.. 86 H
lcalabrese@nv.edu
CALABRESE, Nancy ... 410-626-2553 201 E
nancy.calabrese@sjc.edu
CALABRESE, Shelly ... 518-244-2442 312 D
calabs@sage.edu
CALABRO, Gina ... 910-893-1652 327 C
CALAHAN, John ... 936-468-1025 444 H
calahanje@sfasu.edu
CALAIS, Debra ... 337-482-6199 192 F
dcalais@louisiana.edu
CALAIS, Erica ... 225-342-6950 191 F
erica.calais@ulsystem.edu
CALAIS, Kyle ... 337-482-6367 192 F
kyle.calais@louisiana.edu
CALAMETTI, Jeffrey, D .. 251-442-2242.... 8 C
jcalametti@umobile.edu
CALAMIA, James ... 732-255-0400 279 A
jcalamia@ocean.edu
CALANDRA, Viviana ... 407-303-7894.. 95 A
viviana.calandra@ahu.edu
CALARESE, Mary ... 508-831-5423 220 C
mcalarese@wpi.edu
CALARESO, Joe ... 305-595-9500.. 94 G
admissions@amcollege.edu
CALDARELLO, Beth ... 660-359-3948 256 F
bcaldarello@mail.ncmissouri.edu
CALDBECK, Kellie ... 406-275-4744 264 H
kellie_caldbeck@skc.edu
CALDERÓN GARCÍA,
Ivonne ... 787-250-0000 510 B
ivonne.calderon@upr.edu
CALDERA, Nancy ... 509-527-2315 484 C
nancy.caldera@wallawalla.edu
CALDERHEAD, Kyle, D .. 330-471-8631 355 D
kcalderhead@malone.edu
CALDERO FIGUEROA,
Ana, J ... 407-582-1431 113 C
acalderofigueroa@valenciacollege.edu
CALDERON, Alfredo, B .. 215-455-1300 378 F
acalderon@aspirapa.org
CALDERON, Amalia ... 661-395-4066.. 47 B
amalia.calderon@bakersfieldcollege.edu
CALDERON, Ann Marie . 615-230-3401 424 F
annmarie.calderon@volstate.edu
CALDERON, Christina ... 760-252-2411.. 26 L
ccalderon@barstow.edu
CALDERON, Colleen ... 408-274-7900.. 62 F
colleen.calderon@evc.edu
CALDERON, Hermes ... 787-780-0070 504 E
hcalderon@caribbean.edu
CALDERON, Janet ... 407-303-6108.. 95 A
janet.calderon@ahu.edu
CALDERON, Nancy, T ... 408-554-4400.. 63 A
ntcalderon@scu.edu
CALDERON, Paula ... 985-549-2217 192 E
paula.calderon@selu.edu
CALDERON, Rosa ... 310-338-8839.. 51 C
rosa.calderon@lmu.edu
CALDERONE, Jackie ... 508-541-1530 208 E
0558mgr@fheg.follett.com
CALDERONE, Jennifer ... 812-488-2021 161 E
jj130@evansville.edu
CALDERWOOD, Jon ... 810-406-4825 228 B
jon.calderwood@mcc.edu
CALDWELL, Adonna ... 901-572-2592 417 A
adonna.caldwell@baptistu.edu
CALDWELL, Agnes ... 419-783-2402 351 J
acaldwell@defiance.edu
CALDWELL, Anthony ... 803-705-4348 405 G
anthony.caldwell@benedict.edu
CALDWELL, Benjamin ... 903-233-3200 438 C
benjamincaldwell@letu.edu
CALDWELL,
Benjamin, D ... 540-831-5723 468 E
bcaldwell13@radford.edu
CALDWELL, Brinda, W .. 828-398-7134 331 K
bcaldwell@abtech.edu
CALDWELL, Bryan ... 305-899-3250.. 96 A
bcaldwell@barry.edu
CALDWELL, Cate ... 605-642-6371 415 F
cate.caldwell@bhsu.edu
CALDWELL,
Christopher, M ... 800-567-2344 491 C
CALDWELL, Craig ... 801-957-5180 460 D
craig.caldwell@slcc.edu
CALDWELL, Dallas ... 405-974-2631 370 H
dcaldwell@uco.edu
CALDWELL, Daniel ... 601-318-6101 249 B
dcaldwell@wmcarey.edu
CALDWELL, David ... 323-259-2500.. 54 I
caldwelld@oxy.edu
CALDWELL, Donna ... 706-864-1410 126 G
donna.caldwell@ung.edu
CALDWELL, Gail ... 256-726-7024.... 6 C
gcaldwell@oakwood.edu
CALDWELL, Helen ... 704-378-1014 329 H
hcaldwell@jcsu.edu
CALDWELL, Hollie ... 651-641-8278 235 A
hcaldwell@csp.edu
CALDWELL, James ... 970-675-3236.. 78 P
james.caldwell@cncc.edu
CALDWELL, James ... 215-780-1306 397 E
jcaldwell@salus.edu
CALDWELL, Jim ... 215-780-1313 397 E
jcaldwell@salus.edu
CALDWELL, Jodi, K ... 912-478-5541 120 A
jodic@georgiasouthern.edu
CALDWELL, Katrina ... 410-516-7564 199 E
kcaldwell@jhu.edu
CALDWELL, Kisha ... 423-697-3250 423 B
kisha.caldwell@chattanoogastate.edu
CALDWELL, Larry, W ... 605-336-6588 415 B
lcaldwell@kairos.edu
CALDWELL, Mike ... 817-257-7523 447 H
m.a.caldwell@tcu.edu
CALDWELL, Nina ... 314-529-9485 254 D
ncaldwell@maryville.edu
CALDWELL, Patrice ... 575-562-2315 285 E
patrice.caldwell@enmu.edu
CALDWELL, Richard ... 708-974-5202 144 G
caldwellr8@morainevalley.edu
CALDWELL, Samuel ... 518-956-8112 315 D
sjcaldwell@albany.edu
CALDWELL, Sheila ... 217-545-8080 149 F
sheila.caldwell@siu.edu
CALDWELL, Stephanie ... 973-408-3061 276 B
scaldwell@drew.edu
CALDWELL, OSB,
Teresio ... 503-845-3169 373 G
teresio.caldwell@mtangel.edu
CALDWELL, Timothy ... 509-777-3749 485 D
tcaldwell@whitworth.edu
CALDWELL, Troy ... 740-695-9500 348 D
tcaldwell@belmontcollege.edu
CALDWELL, IV,
William, B ... 478-387-4775 119 E
wcaldwell@gmc.edu
CALDWELL, Yolanda ... 518-485-3133 296 E
caldwely@strose.edu
CALDWELL-KAN, Sara ... 907-786-4070.. 10 A
CALE, Benjamin ... 304-877-6428 486 A
admissions@abc.edu
CALEB, Peter ... 917-493-4507 304 L
library@msmnyc.edu
CALEFFI-PRICHARD,
Vivi ... 503-365-4723 372 A
vivi.caleffi.prichard@chemeketa.edu
CALFIN, Matthew ... 805-378-1448.. 73 I
mcalfin@vcccd.edu
CALHOUN, Angela ... 319-399-8699 164 D
acalhoun@coe.edu
CALHOUN, Austin ... 651-846-1361 240 E
austin.calhoun@saintpaul.edu
CALHOUN, Cheryl ... 303-797-5702.. 77 H
cheryl.calhoun@arapahoe.edu
CALHOUN, David ... 863-583-9050 110 A
CALHOUN, Dominique .. 713-313-7640 448 D
dominique.calhoun@tsu.edu
CALHOUN, Grace ... 401-863-2972 403 A
grace_calhoun@brown.edu
CALHOUN, Kirk, A ... 903-566-7325 455 C
mitziharris@uttyler.edu
CALHOUN, Larry ... 912-538-3101 125 E
lcalhoun@southeasterntech.edu
CALHOUN, Linda ... 270-686-4473 182 C
linda.calhoun@kctcs.edu
CALHOUN, Lozanne ... 870-850-4826.. 21 D
lcalhoun@seark.edu
CALHOUN, Matthew ... 601-276-3718 248 D
mattc@smcc.edu
CALHOUN, Mitch ... 325-574-7612 457 G
mcalhoun@wtc.edu
CALHOUN, Paula, M ... 330-471-8236 355 D
pcalhoun@malone.edu
CALHOUN, Ralph ... 901-435-1276 419 I
ralph_calhoun@loc.edu
CALHOUN, Ric ... 678-359-5018 120 D
ricc@gordonstate.edu
CALHOUN, Rica ... 850-412-5479 109 E
rica.calhoun@famu.edu
CALHOUN, Rochelle ... 609-258-3056 279 E
rochelle.calhoun@princeton.edu
CALHOUN, Roy ... 229-430-1729 114 G
rcalhoun@albanytech.edu
CALHOUN, Shawn ... 415-422-6167.. 72 I
calhouns@usfca.edu
CALHOUN, JR.,
Thomas ... 662-254-3636 247 C
thomas.calhoun@mvsu.edu
CALHOUN-BROWN,
Allison ... 404-413-2067 120 C
acalhounbrown@gsu.edu
CALHOUN-BROWN,
Allison ... 404-413-2579 120 C
acalhounbrown@gsu.edu
CALICA, Corinna ... 415-485-9132.. 39 B
cdyliacco@marin.edu
CALIGAN, Roy ... 509-533-8861 478 D
roy.caligan@scc.spokane.edu
CALIHAN, Heather ... 910-938-6241 333 D
calihanh@coastalcarolina.edu
CALILAN,
James (Kimo) ... 707-864-7264.. 64 F
james.calilan@solano.edu
CALISE, Lisa ... 617-287-7050 211 C
lcalise@umassp.edu
CALISE, Thomasina, L .. 203-857-7003.. 87 B
tcalise@norwalk.edu
CALISSI, Barbara ... 212-678-8009 303 A
bacalissi@jtsa.edu
CALKA, Anna ... 973-313-6314 282 K
anna.calka@shu.edu
CALKINS, Kevin ... 863-583-9050 110 A
CALKINS, Sheila ... 617-573-8027 218 G
scalkins@suffolk.edu
CALLAGHAN, Carolyn ... 828-227-3068 343 D
ccallaghan@wcu.edu
CALLAGHAN, Connor ... 415-503-6235.. 61 E
ccallaghan@sfcm.edu
CALLAGHAN, James ... 478-445-4789 119 A
james.callaghan@gcsu.edu
CALLAGHAN, Karen, A .. 305-899-3401.. 96 A
kcallaghan@barry.edu
CALLAGHAN, Martha, E 804-287-1256 471 E
mcallagh@richmond.edu
CALLAGHAN, MaryEllen 914-633-2512 302 C
mcallaghan@iona.edu
CALLAGHAN, Sandra ... 817-257-6483 447 H
s.callaghan@tcu.edu
CALLAHAN, Audra ... 508-999-8620 211 F
audra.callahan@umassd.edu
CALLAHAN, Brigid ... 847-947-5409 145 C
bcallahan2@nl.edu
CALLAHAN, Caitlin ... 617-449-7038 219 B
caitlin.callahan@urbancollege.edu
CALLAHAN, Candice ... 718-779-1499 310 I
cmc2@plazacollege.edu
CALLAHAN, Caroline ... 718-779-1499 310 I
cmc@plazacollege.edu
CALLAHAN, III,
Charles, E ... 718-779-1499 310 I
cec3@plazacollege.edu
CALLAHAN, IV,
Charles, E ... 718-779-1499 310 I
cec4@plazacollege.edu
CALLAHAN, Christena ... 321-674-8927 100 A
ccallahan@fit.edu
CALLAHAN,
Christopher ... 209-946-2011.. 71 E
CALLAHAN, Clara, A ... 215-955-6983 398 G
clara.callahan@jefferson.edu
CALLAHAN, Daniel ... 540-863-2828 473 D
dcallahan@mgcc.edu
CALLAHAN, Emile (EJ) . 661-654-2497.. 30 C
ecallahan@csub.edu
CALLAHAN, JR.,
Jack, F ... 203-432-1185.. 90 B
jack.callahan@yale.edu
CALLAHAN, Janet ... 906-487-2005 227 D
callahan@mtu.edu
CALLAHAN, Margaret ... 215-517-2654 378 E
callahanm@arcadia.edu
CALLAHAN,
Margaret, F ... 708-216-9222 142 G
mcallahan3@luc.edu
CALLAHAN, Mark ... 402-461-5177 266 E
CALLAHAN, Meghan ... 607-274-3306 302 E
mcallahan1@ithaca.edu
CALLAHAN, Michael ... 805-289-6344.. 74 B
mcallahan@vcccd.edu
CALLAHAN, Ryan ... 262-472-4661 496 E
callahanrm19@uww.edu
CALLAHAN, Scott ... 843-349-7105 409 A
scott.callahan@hgtc.edu
CALLAHAN, Sean ... 678-872-8542 119 C
scallaha@highlands.edu
CALLAHAN, Tristin ... 256-840-4219.... 3 F
tristin.callahan@snead.edu
CALLAN, Pam ... 325-481-8300 436 H
pcallan@howardcollege.edu
CALLAND, Dana ... 606-759-7141 182 B
dana.calland@kctcs.edu
CALLAND, David ... 434-592-7336 467 E
dcalland@liberty.edu
CALLAND, David ... 423-775-7200 417 D
dcalland2423@bryan.edu
CALLANDRILLO, Traci ... 202-885-1000.. 91 D
callandr@american.edu
CALLAWAY, Cynthia ... 757-825-2725 474 F
callawayc@tncc.edu
CALLEN, Patricia ... 304-296-8282 490 C
pcallen@wvjc.edu
CALLEY, Addison ... 850-478-8496 105 F
acalley@pcci.edu
CALLICO, Jason ... 504-398-2143 191 E
jcallico@uhcno.edu
CALLICOTT, Robin ... 803-641-3342 412 B
robinc@usca.edu
CALLIER, Theodore ... 504-816-4018 186 F
tcallier@dillard.edu
CALLIES, Kathryn ... 605-256-5143 415 G
kathy.callies@dsu.edu
CALLIHAM, Jimmy ... 830-591-7333 443 I
jwcalliham@swtjc.edu
CALLIHAM, Martha ... 512-444-8082 448 B
mcalliham@thsu.edu
CALLINAN, Dennis ... 845-574-4481 312 C
dcallina@sunyrockland.edu
CALLIS, Jennifer ... 785-309-3120 177 B
jennifer.callis@salinatech.edu
CALLISTER, Melanie ... 507-285-7461 240 B
melanie.callister@rctc.edu
CALLISTO, Anthony ... 315-443-2225 321 D
acallist@syr.edu
CALLOW-WRIGHT,
Katie ... 773-795-3361 151 B
ccallow@uchicago.edu
CALLOWAY, Brad ... 336-841-9841 329 E
scallowa@highpoint.edu
CALLOWAY, Terence ... 850-599-3256 109 E
terence.calloway@famu.edu
CALOBRISI,
Charlotte, M ... 703-323-3110 473 G
ccalobrisi@nvcc.edu
CALOCA, Luis ... 208-562-3396 131 C
luiscaloca@cwi.edu
CALOIERO, Erica ... 802-656-3858 462 D
erica.caloiero@uvm.edu
CALOVINE, Iris ... 203-932-7297.. 89 F
icalovine@newhaven.edu
CALPIN, Fran ... 570-945-8170 386 F
fran.calpin@keystone.edu
CALTABIANO, Ronald ... 312-362-7256 136 F
rcalt@depaul.edu
CALTER, Mimi ... 314-935-5415 261 B
mimi@wustl.edu
CALUS-MCLAIN, Martha 503-352-2764 375 B
martha@pacificu.edu
CALUZA, Kimberly ... 206-296-6090 483 B
caluzak@seattleu.edu
CALVARUSO, Joe ... 517-629-0210 220 E
CALVELLI, Louis ... 718-862-7977 304 K
lcalvelli01@manhattan.edu
CALVERT, Chandra ... 605-718-2419 416 D
chandra.calvert@wdt.edu
CALVERT, Christopher ... 513-569-1586 350 C
christopher.calvert@cincinnatistate.edu
CALVERT, Kaitlyn ... 304-205-6697 487 D
kaitlyn.calvert@bridgevalley.edu
CALVERT, Linda ... 423-323-0222 424 B
lwcalvert@northeaststate.edu
CALVERT, Mike ... 620-672-2700 176 I
michaelc@prattcc.edu
CALVIN, Anitra ... 504-520-7365 193 C
acalvin3@xula.edu

CAMPBELL, Ralph .... 623-935-8051.. 13 C
ralph.campbell@estrellamountain.edu
CAMPBELL, Randy .... 607-778-5196 317 A
campbellrj@sunybroome.edu
CAMPBELL, Rebecca ..... 575-646-3203 286 G
rjpc@nmsu.edu
CAMPBELL, Richard ...... 336-334-4314 342 D
rtcampbell@uncg.edu
CAMPBELL, Rina .... 619-201-8753.. 60 G
rina.campbell@sdcc.edu
CAMPBELL, Robin .... 336-721-2600 339 H
robin.campbell@salem.edu
CAMPBELL, Samerah ..... 559-243-7122.. 66 G
samerah.campbell@scccd.edu
CAMPBELL, Sara .... 423-614-8525 419 H
scampbell@leeuniversity.edu
CAMPBELL, Saskia .... 703-993-3738 466 J
scampb22@gmu.edu
CAMPBELL, Scott .... 773-834-3390 151 B
scottcampbell@uchicago.edu
CAMPBELL, Scott, L ...... 740-392-6868 356 G
scott.campbell@mvnu.edu
CAMPBELL, Shannon ..... 228-865-4531 248 H
shannon.campbell@usm.edu
CAMPBELL, Shawnrece . 361-825-2659 446 E
shawnrece.campbell@tamucc.edu
CAMPBELL,
Shoshanna, M .... 718-780-7501 291 G
shoshanna.campbell@brooklaw.edu
CAMPBELL, Stacy .... 352-245-4119 112 D
CAMPBELL, Staphea ...... 404-225-4422 115 F
scampbell@atlantatech.edu
CAMPBELL, Stephanie ... 904-470-8114.. 98 I
s.campbell@ewc.edu
CAMPBELL, Steven .... 601-928-6224 246 F
steven.campbell@mgccc.edu
CAMPBELL, Susan .... 623-845-3876.. 13 E
susan.j.campbell@gccaz.edu
CAMPBELL, Suzanne ...... 620-417-1403 177 C
suzanne.campbell@sccc.edu
CAMPBELL, Tami .... 660-359-3948 256 F
tcampbell@mail.ncmissouri.edu
CAMPBELL, Terrance ...... 630-752-5490 152 K
terrance.campbell@wheaton.edu
CAMPBELL, Terri .... 303-458-4231.. 83 B
tcampbell007@regis.edu
CAMPBELL, Terri .... 402-399-2419 265 H
tcampbell@csm.edu
CAMPBELL, Timothy, G .. 859-858-3511 178 H
tim.campbell@asbury.edu
CAMPBELL, Tom .... 615-966-7164 420 B
tom.campbell@lipscomb.edu
CAMPBELL, Toma .... 406-353-2607 262 B
tcampbell@ancollege.edu
CAMPBELL, Yvonne ...... 540-857-6829 475 A
ycampbell@virginiawestern.edu
CAMPBELL-BROWN,
Andrea .... 423-614-8600 419 H
acampbell@leeuniversity.edu
CAMPBELL-FOSTER,
Jason .... 617-353-4126 207 C
dos@bu.edu
CAMPBELL-GOLDEN,
Carolyn .... 724-503-1001 401 D
ccampbellgolden@washjeff.edu
CAMPBELL JACKSON,
Candace .... 315-443-3494 321 D
candace1@syr.edu
CAMPEAU, Tony .... 406-994-5541 263 G
tcampeau@montana.edu
CAMPELLO, Luca .... 661-824-2977.. 53 H
CAMPER, Shannon .... 845-451-1352 297 E
shannon.camper@culinary.edu
CAMPER, Starr .... 704-669-4066 333 C
camper@clevelandcc.edu
CAMPFIELD, Justin .... 802-831-1228 462 F
jcampfield@vermontlaw.edu
CAMPION, Alyssa .... 218-736-1502 238 K
alyssa.campion@minnesota.edu
CAMPION, Setareh .... 701-252-3467 346 J
setareh.campion@uj.edu
CAMPIRANO, Marisa .... 956-665-3137 455 A
marisa.campirano01@utrgv.edu
CAMPLESE, Cole .... 617-373-2752 217 D
CAMPO, Carlos .... 419-289-5050 347 H
ccampo@ashland.edu
CAMPO, Jeffrey .... 973-655-7081 278 C
campoj@montclair.edu
CAMPO, Juan, E .... 805-893-3945.. 70 E
jcampo@religion.ucsb.edu
CAMPOS, Alysa .... 281-487-1170 447 G
acampos@txchiro.edu
CAMPOS, Brian .... 805-482-2755.. 59 G
registrar-sjs@stjohnsem.edu
CAMPOS, Cesar .... 312-939-0111 137 B
cesar@eastwest.edu
CAMPOS, Darcie, R .... 708-534-5000 138 C
dcampos@govst.edu
CAMPOS, Diana .... 575-234-9227 287 I
dcampos@senmc.edu
CAMPOS, Javier .... 559-453-4600.. 43 D
javier.campos@fresno.edu
CAMPOS, Jesus .... 956-872-8330 443 B
jhcampos@southtexascollege.edu
CAMPOS, Juan .... 213-738-6800.. 66 A
juancampos@swlaw.edu
CAMPOS, Lisa, D .... 210-458-8149 455 B
lisa.campos@utsa.edu
CAMPOS, Luis .... 575-646-2101 286 G
campos1@nmsu.edu
CAMPOS, Nathan .... 409-882-3305 449 C
nathan.campos@lsco.edu
CAMPOS, Nicolette .... 910-521-6695 343 A
nicolette.campos@uncp.edu
CAMPOS, Nicolette, S ... 910-521-6000 343 A
CAMPOS, Susan .... 708-456-0300 151 A
susancampos@triton.edu
CAMPOS FACCHINATO,
Ana .... 562-947-8755.. 65 H
anafacchinato@scuhs.edu
CAMPS, Manel .... 831-459-2411.. 71 A
mcamps@ucsc.edu
CAMUTI, Alice .... 931-372-6006 425 B
acamuti@tntech.edu
CANAAN, Shirley .... 203-371-7946.. 88 H
canaans@sacredheart.edu
CANACARIS, Diana .... 865-981-8198 420 C
diana.canacaris@maryvillecollege.edu
CANADA, Allison, M ...... 410-334-2918 205 A
acanada@worwic.edu
CANADA, Britt .... 325-574-7671 457 G
bcanada@wtc.edu
CANADA, Jeff, H .... 410-543-6056 204 A
jhcanada@salisbury.edu
CANADA, Mark .... 765-455-9227 156 E
canadam@iuk.edu
CANAL, Marcie .... 213-738-6800.. 66 A
administrativeservices@swlaw.edu
CANALE, Brad .... 906-227-2610 228 E
bcanale@nmu.edu
CANALE, Mary .... 315-312-5558 318 B
mary.canale@oswego.edu
CANALES, Irvin .... 787-891-0925 506 I
icanales@aguadilla.inter.edu
CANALES, Jason .... 413-662-5413 212 F
jason.canales@mcla.edu
CANALES, Leticia .... 805-289-6064.. 74 B
lcanales@vcccd.edu
CANALES, Rafael, R ...... 787-279-1912 506 L
rrcanales@bayamon.inter.edu
CANAN, Michelle .... 918-293-5494 368 B
michelle.canan@okstate.edu
CANARY, Sharnie .... 845-569-3548 307 B
sharnie.canary@msmc.edu
CANAS, Carlos .... 305-626-3698 100 B
carlos.canas@fmuniv.edu
CANAVAN, Brian .... 617-258-6409 215 G
CANAVAN, Linda, T .... 781-292-2341 209 E
linda.canavan@olin.edu
CANAVERA, Jennifer ..... 920-498-5406 498 F
jennifer.canavera@nwtc.edu
CANCEL, Magda .... 787-704-1020 505 B
mcancel@columbiacentral.edu
CANDA, Angela .... 216-397-1531 353 O
acanda@jcu.edu
CANDANEDO, Jose .... 602-286-8371.. 13 D
jose.candanedo@gatewaycc.edu
CANDEE, Kathleen .... 920-923-8727 492 D
kcandee@marianuniversity.edu
CANDELARIA,
J. Randel .... 336-734-7311 334 D
jcandelaria@forsythtech.edu
CANDELARIA, Lorenzo .. 615-322-7311 427 B
CANDLER, George, B .... 212-327-7801 312 B
candler@rockefeller.edu
CANDLISH, Karen .... 317-955-6190 159 A
kcandlish@marian.edu
CANEDO, Francis .... 480-461-7343.. 13 F
francis.canedo@mesacc.edu
CANEIRO-LIVINGSTON,
Graciela .... 402-465-2110 267 J
gcaneiro@nebrwesleyan.edu
CANEPA, Janet, A .... 203-254-4280.. 87 G
jcanepa@fairfield.edu
CANER, Emir .... 706-865-2134 126 D
ecaner@truett.edu
CANFIELD, Barbara .... 607-962-9231 319 F
bcanfie2@corning-cc.edu
CANFIELD, Clarke .... 207-741-5575 195 D
ccanfield@smccme.edu
CANFIELD, Jodi .... 434-381-6100 470 H
jcanfield@sbc.edu
CANFIELD, Kathleen ...... 847-925-6437 138 E
kcanfiel@harpercollege.edu
CANFIELD, Kipton .... 309-341-5325 134 A
kcanfield@sandburg.edu
CANFIELD, Megan .... 540-362-6018 467 A
canfieldm@hollins.edu
CANFIELD, Susan .... 641-628-7642 164 B
canfields@central.edu
CANGELLARIS,
Andreas, C .... 217-333-6677 151 F
provost@illinois.edu
CANGEMI, Livia .... 212-772-4475 294 A
livia.cangemi@hunter.cuny.edu
CANGIANO, George .... 781-891-2380 206 C
gcangiano@bentley.edu
CANHAM, Drew .... 254-299-8645 438 G
dcanham@mclennan.edu
CANIA, Sal .... 315-267-2174 318 D
caniasj@potsdam.edu
CANIDA, Robert .... 434-544-8540 470 K
canida_rl@lynchburg.edu
CANIGLIA, Alan, S .... 717-358-3934 383 G
alan.caniglia@fandm.edu
CANINE, Chris .... 402-486-2502 268 G
chris.canine@ucollege.edu
CANINE, Kim .... 402-486-2507 268 G
kim.canine@ucollege.edu
CANINO, Terri .... 501-450-3184.. 23 K
tcanino@uca.edu
CANIPE, Steve .... 866-492-5336 243 G
stephen.canipe@mail.waldenu.edu
CANIZALES, Rafael .... 937-395-8837 354 J
rafael.canizales@kc.edu
CANNADA, JR.,
Robert, C .... 601-923-1600 248 A
rcannada@rts.edu
CANNADAY SAULNY,
Helen .... 202-994-6710.. 92 C
saulnyh@gwu.edu
CANNADY, Sharell .... 704-378-3572 329 H
scannady@jcsu.edu
CANNADY-SMITH,
Allison .... 253-879-3450 483 G
acannadysmith@pugetsound.edu
CANNAN, Erin .... 845-758-7454 290 G
cannan@bard.edu
CANNIFF, James, F .... 617-228-2435 214 A
jfcanniff@bhcc.mass.edu
CANNING, John, B .... 401-232-6020 403 B
jcanning@bryant.edu
CANNING, Kathleen .... 713-348-4810 441 K
CANNINGS, Pierre .... 214-887-5000 434 G
pcannings@dts.edu
CANNISTRACI, Patti .... 518-268-5131 314 G
patricia.cannistraci@sphp.com
CANNON, Amy .... 270-901-1012 182 E
amy.cannon@kctcs.edu
CANNON, Barbie .... 318-797-5116 189 E
barbie.cannon@lsus.edu
CANNON, Brenda .... 931-393-1548 423 G
bcannon@mscc.edu
CANNON, Chris .... 251-460-6161.... 9 A
ccannon@southalabama.edu
CANNON, D. Glen .... 770-962-7580 121 B
gcannon@gwinnetttech.edu
CANNON, Gordon .... 601-266-5116 248 H
gordon.cannon@usm.edu
CANNON, Gregory .... 973-720-6268 283 I
cannong@wpunj.edu
CANNON, Jason .... 256-840-4150.... 3 F
jason.cannon@snead.edu
CANNON, Julie .... 386-752-1822.. 99 P
julie.cannon@fgc.edu
CANNON, Kathleen .... 503-847-2557 377 A
kcannon@uws.edu
CANNON, Matthew .... 864-327-9800 466 E
mcannon@vcom.vt.edu
CANNON, Rebecca .... 225-768-0810 186 H
rebecca.cannon@franu.edu
CANNON, Sharon .... 432-703-5270 450 D
sharon.cannon@ttuhsc.edu
CANNON, Thomas .... 646-592-4327 325 R
thomas.cannon@yu.edu
CANNON, Uzzie .... 828-641-0436 327 A
ucannon@brevard.edu
CANNON SMITH, Betsy 413-542-2031 205 D
ecsmith@amherst.edu
CANO, Annmarie .... 509-313-3883 479 E
cano@gonzaga.edu
CANO, Leticia, R .... 559-278-7459.. 31 D
lreyna@csufresno.edu
CANO, Mary .... 915-566-9621 457 E
mcano@westerntech.edu
CANO, Mary .... 901-333-4462 424 E
mcano1@southwest.tn.edu
CANO, Omar .... 719-846-5497.. 83 I
omar.cano@trinidadstate.edu
CANO-MORALES,
Anna, M .... 401-456-8810 404 A
acanomorales@ric.edu
CANON, Susan .... 507-786-3647 242 I
canon@stolaf.edu
CANOY, Eugenio .... 408-274-7900.. 62 F
eugenio.canoy@evc.edu
CANOY, Robert, W .... 704-406-4395 328 I
rcanoy@gardner-webb.edu
CANSLER, Charles .... 843-953-6982 406 D
ccansler@citadel.edu
CANT, Greg .... 570-408-4000 402 B
greg.cant@wilkes.edu
CANTELMO, Douglas ..... 973-761-9152 282 K
douglas.cantelmo@shu.edu
CANTER, Bridget .... 270-534-3088 182 G
bridget.canter@kctcs.edu
CANTER, Bridget .... 270-534-3155 182 G
bridget.canter@kctcs.edu
CANTERBURY, Jay .... 419-434-4076 362 D
canterbury@findlay.edu
CANTERBURY, Jenni ...... 304-929-6727 487 G
jcanterbury@newriver.edu
CANTERINO, Patricia ...... 610-647-4400 385 K
pcanterino@immaculata.edu
CANTEY, Andrew .... 903-510-2186 451 D
acan2@tjc.edu
CANTEÑS, Bernardo, J .. 432-837-8866 449 F
bernie.cantens@sulross.edu
CANTILLO, Abel .... 516-572-9786 307 C
abel.cantillo@ncc.edu
CANTINI, Julie .... 409-772-2351 456 B
jucantin@utmb.edu
CANTLEY, Adam, D .... 302-831-8939.. 91 A
adamcan@udel.edu
CANTONIS, George, M .. 617-731-3500 210 D
CANTOR, Franklyn .... 215-717-6023 399 I
fcantor@uarts.edu
CANTOR, Nancy, E .... 973-353-5541 281 C
nancy.cantor@rutgers.edu
CANTOR, Ronald, G .... 315-294-9070 292 A
rcantor@cayuga-cc.edu
CANTRELL, Andra, R ...... 817-598-6260 457 C
acantrell@wc.edu
CANTRELL, Betsy .... 678-717-3941 126 G
betsy.cantrell@ung.edu
CANTRELL, Dwayne .... 661-654-2160.. 30 C
dcantrell2@csub.edu
CANTRELL, Hampton ...... 626-395-4187.. 29 B
cantrell@caltech.edu
CANTRELL, Hampton ...... 925-631-8097.. 59 I
hnc2@stmarys-ca.edu
CANTRELL, Jill .... 770-533-6903 121 L
cantrell@laniertech.edu
CANTRELL, Mark .... 304-876-5528 489 A
mcantrel@shepherd.edu
CANTRELL, Pamela .... 435-879-4260 459 G
pam.cantrell@utahtech.edu
CANTRELL, Paul .... 361-354-2520 431 L
pcantrell@coastalbend.edu
CANTRELL, Shannon ...... 479-619-3103.. 20 G
scantrell3@nwacc.edu
CANTRELL, Sharon .... 501-907-6670.. 23 E
scantrell@uaptc.edu
CANTRELL, Sharon .... 787-743-7979 509 D
scantrel@suagm.edu
CANTRELL, Sirena .... 601-266-6028 248 H
sirena.cantrell@usm.edu
CANTRELL, Sonja, G ...... 304-696-2258 488 N
cantrel1@marshall.edu
CANTRELL, Tiffany .... 334-386-7450.... 5 D
tcantrell@faulkner.edu
CANTRELL, Will .... 906-487-2326 227 D
cantrell@mtu.edu
CANTU, Brenda .... 830-591-7252 443 I
bmcantu@swtjc.edu
CANTU, Dean .... 479-788-7840.. 22 A
dean.cantu@uafs.edu
CANTU, Gaston .... 210-486-3941 428 B
gcantu@alamo.edu
CANTU, Henry .... 210-567-5807 455 E
cantuh@uthsca.edu

CANTU, Jose .... 361-570-4149 452 C cantujl1@uhv.edu
CANTU, Laura, B .... 818-364-7635.. 49 G cantulb@lamission.edu
CANTU DELGADO, Illiana .... 651-523-2100 235 F icantudelgado01@hamline.edu
CANTUTI-CASTELVETRI, Ippolita, A .... 617-627-6696 219 A ippolita.cantuti_castelvetri@tufts.edu
CANTWELL, Bethan .... 517-355-9273 227 C cantwelb@msu.edu
CANTWELL, Elizabeth, R .... 520-626-0631.. 16 H ecantwell@arizona.edu
CANTWELL, Jaclyn .... 217-424-3503 144 D jcantwell@millikin.edu
CANTWELL, Kevin .... 478-471-0229 122 D kevin.cantwell@mga.edu
CANTWELL, Matilda .... 413-585-2753 218 D mcantwel@smith.edu
CANTY, Joan .... 712-749-2626 164 A cantyj@bvu.edu
CANUP, Karen .... 864-578-8770 410 G kcanup@sherman.edu
CAO, Hai Tao .... 512-444-8082 448 B tcao@thsu.edu
CAO, Jian .... 847-467-1032 146 C jcao@northwestern.edu
CAO, Nina .... 773-907-4473 134 N ncao@ccc.edu
CAPÓ, Rafael .... 305-474-6981 107 D rcapo@stu.edu
CAPACCIO, Mike .... 843-953-4806 406 D mcapaccio@citadel.edu
CAPACI, Eric .... 501-623-2272.. 19 C
CAPACI, Josiah .... 501-623-2272.. 19 C
CAPADONA, Kimberly, A .... 973-761-9190 282 K kimberly.capadona@shu.edu
CAPALDI, Shannon .... 909-448-4901.. 71 C scapaldi@laverne.edu
CAPE, Coleen .... 620-792-1136 171 F capec@bartonccc.edu
CAPEBIANCO, Joseph ... 954-492-5353.. 97 G
CAPECI, James .... 417-625-9806 255 I capeci-j@mssu.edu
CAPEHART, Robin .... 304-327-4030 488 J officeofthepresident@bluefieldstate.edu
CAPELL, Carey, M .... 843-953-6847 406 D carey.capell@citadel.edu
CAPELLA, Carrie .... 315-268-6445 295 E ccapella@clarkson.edu
CAPELLA, Michael .... 504-864-7946 190 A mcapella@loyno.edu
CAPELLE, Jomi .... 692-625-3291 503 F jcapelle@cmi.edu
CAPELLE, Mitchell .... 603-526-3610 271 H mitch.capelle@colby-sawyer.edu
CAPELO, Jenny .... 509-682-6662 484 H jcapelo@wvc.edu
CAPENER, Don .... 801-863-6768 460 A donc@uvu.edu
CAPERS, Jamie .... 903-593-8311 448 A jcapers@texascollege.edu
CAPERS, Meggin .... 610-341-5902 383 A mcapers@eastern.edu
CAPERS, IV, Quinn .... 214-648-0390 456 D quinn.capers@utsouthwestern.edu
CAPERS, Willette .... 605-274-4313 413 G willette.capers@augie.edu
CAPEZUTI, Elizabeth .... 212-481-7689 294 A ec773@hunter.cuny.edu
CAPEZZA, Kristen .... 516-877-3021 288 L kcapezza@adelphi.edu
CAPILOUTO, Eli, I .... 859-257-1703 185 D pres@uky.edu
CAPISCIOLTO, Ken .... 616-988-3676 226 A kcapisciolto@kuyper.edu
CAPLES, Gwen .... 601-979-2282 245 G gwendolyn.caples@jsums.edu
CAPLOW, Stacy .... 718-780-7944 291 G stacy.caplow@brooklaw.edu
CAPO, Laura .... 714-556-3610.. 73 G laura.capo@vanguard.edu
CAPO, Leslie, L .... 504-568-4806 189 C lcapo@lsuhsc.edu
CAPO, Rachael .... 518-276-8327 311 J kruser@rpi.edu
CAPOCCIA-WHITE, Rozanne .... 714-432-5072.. 38 F
CAPON, Sandy .... 515-964-0601 166 A capons@faith.edu
CAPONE, Lisa .... 337-482-0927 192 F lisa.capone@louisiana.edu
CAPONE, Lisa .... 314-516-4278 260 E lcapone@umsl.edu
CAPONI, Kimberly .... 630-466-7900 152 H kcaponi@waubonsee.edu
CAPORALE, Matthew ..... 203-932-7451.. 89 F mcaporale@newhaven.edu
CAPORUSCIO, Josie .... 718-636-3649 311 A jcaporus@pratt.edu
CAPP, James .... 561-297-3061 109 F jcapp1@fau.edu
CAPP, Maureen .... 561-868-3333 105 C cappm@palmbeachstate.edu
CAPPARELLI, Tim .... 312-949-7000 139 B tcapparelli@ico.edu
CAPPELLO, Manny .... 408-741-2513.. 75 B manny.cappello@wvm.edu
CAPPELLO, Phillip .... 516-572-7300 307 C phillip.cappello@ncc.edu
CAPPS, Jenn .... 707-826-3722.. 30 A jenn.capps@humboldt.edu
CAPPS, John .... 434-832-7601 472 G cappsj@centralvirginia.edu
CAPPS, Steve .... 936-633-5281 429 A scapps@angelina.edu
CAPPS, Tammy .... 618-634-3280 149 C tammyc@shawneecc.edu
CAPRARIO, Janet .... 619-849-2958.. 57 J janetcaprario@pointloma.edu
CAPRILES, Joelis .... 787-852-1430 506 A jcapriles@hccpr.edu
CAPRILES, Jose .... 787-758-2525 511 D jose.capriles@upr.edu
CAPRILES, Jose, A .... 787-798-3001 509 F jose.capriles@uccaribe.edu
CAPRIO, Mark, J .... 401-865-1996 403 G mcaprio1@providence.edu
CAPRIOGLIO, Helen .... 719-549-2207.. 79 G helen.caprioglio@csupueblo.edu
CAPRON, Clara .... 360-650-3470 485 A clara.capron@wwu.edu
CAPSOURAS, Barbara .... 973-328-5059 276 A bcapsour@ccm.edu
CAPUANO, Christopher . 201-692-7100 276 I capuano@fdu.edu
CAPUANO, Jamie .... 845-687-5051 322 K capuanoj@sunyulster.edu
CAPUNAY, Martin .... 718-429-6600 323 I martin.capunay@vaughn.edu
CAPUNO, Jayson .... 818-575-6800.. 68 C jayson.capuno@tuw.edu
CAPUTO, Brian .... 630-942-2800 135 F caputob@cod.edu
CAPUTO, Michael .... 845-575-3000 305 C michael.caputo@marist.edu
CAQUIAS, Karen .... 787-284-1912 507 D kcaquias@ponce.inter.edu
CARA, Robert .... 704-688-4222 248 A rcara@rts.edu
CARABALLO, Ada .... 787-863-2390 507 A ada.caraballo@fajardo.inter.edu
CARABALLO, Frances .... 787-892-2315 507 E frances_caraballo@intersg.edu
CARABALLO, Maraynette .... 787-832-6000 506 B mcaraballo@icprjc.edu
CARABALLO, Pablo .... 787-264-1912 507 E pablo_caraballo_rodriguez@intersg.edu
CARABALLO, Samuel .... 787-761-0640 510 A escuelagraduada@utcpr.edu
CARABALLO TURRELL, Gloria, N .... 787-841-2000 508 H gloria_caraballo@pucpr.edu
CARABANNA, Viviana ... 305-899-3949.. 96 A vcarabanna@barry.edu
CARACCI, Corinna .... 845-257-4444 316 B caraccic@newpaltz.edu
CARACO, Candace .... 410-837-5243 204 C ccaraco@ubalt.edu
CARAHER, Stephen .... 315-781-3776 301 D caraher@hws.edu
CARAS, Zoe .... 928-350-2100.. 15 O
CARAWAY, Tom .... 907-852-1852.... 9 H tom.caraway@ilisagvik.edu
CARBAJAL, Brent .... 360-650-3480 485 A provost@wwu.edu
CARBALLEIRA, Néstor ... 787-765-9695 511 F nestor.carballeira1@upr.edu
CARBALLO, Lauren .... 516-671-8355 324 C lcarballo@webb.edu
CARBALLO, Manuel .... 440-775-8411 357 G manuel.carballo@oberlin.edu
CARBONARO, Dennis ... 610-785-6525 396 H dcarbonaro@scs.edu
CARBONARO, Gene .... 562-938-4624.. 48 K gcarbonaro@lbcc.edu
CARBONE, Cindy, L .... 248-246-2512 228 H clcarbon@oaklandcc.edu
CARBONE, Shaylah .... 860-343-5757.. 86 G scarbone@commnet.edu
CARBONELL, John .... 731-661-5081 425 F jcarbone@uu.edu
CARBONI, Cuauhtemoc 619-660-4505.. 44 G cuauhtemoc.carboni@gcccd.edu
CARBONI, Cuauhtemoc 760-355-6323.. 45 N temo.carboni@imperial.edu
CARBONI, Michelle, L .. 815-224-0417 140 D michelle_carboni@ivcc.edu
CARCANA, Yolanda, S .. 252-335-3318 341 A yscarcana@ecsu.edu
CARCIA, Erin .... 781-239-5946 205 G ecarcia@babson.edu
CARCILLO, Anthony, J .. 302-356-3475.. 91 C anthony.j.carcillo@wilmu.edu
CARCOPA, Joshua .... 239-513-1122 102 C jcarcopa@hodges.edu
CARD, Christopher, D ... 920-832-6596 492 B christopher.card@lawrence.edu
CARD, Steven .... 360-650-3489 485 A steven.card@wwu.edu
CARDAMONE, Rich .... 717-780-2528 385 A rmcardam@hacc.edu
CARDAMONE, Samuel .. 585-245-5567 317 E cardamone@geneseo.edu
CARDEN, Gloria .... 864-250-8114 408 J studentrecords@gvltec.edu
CARDEN, Monica, W .... 540-674-3600 473 F mcarden@nr.edu
CARDENAS, Anthony ..... 386-752-1822.. 99 P anthony.cardenas@fgc.edu
CARDENAS, Daniel .... 510-780-4500.. 48 D dcardenas@lifewest.edu
CARDENAS, Eric, D .... 813-253-6232 113 B ecardenas@ut.edu
CARDENAS, JR., Jaime . 206-934-4348 482 G jaime.cardenas@seattlecolleges.edu
CARDENAS, Jenni .... 520-494-5420.. 11 M jenni.cardenas@centralaz.edu
CARDENAS, Kerstin .... 507-222-4068 234 C kcardena@carleton.edu
CARDENAS, Maria .... 970-542-3169.. 81 M maria.cardenas@morgancc.edu
CARDENAS, Miguel, A .. 619-934-0797.. 61 C
CARDENAS, JR., Miguel, A .... 619-934-0797.. 61 C
CARDENAS, Roosbelinda .... 413-549-4600 210 A rccsi@hampshire.edu
CARDENAS, Sonia .... 860-297-4193.. 88 I sonia.cardenas@trincoll.edu
CARDENAS, Veronica .... 956-722-0521 438 A
CARDENAS-ADAME, Patricia .... 623-935-8812.. 13 C patricia.cardenas-adame@estrellamountain.edu
CARDILLO, Charlie .... 323-259-2937.. 54 I ccardillo@oxy.edu
CARDILLO, Rosaleen ..... 845-437-5843 323 H roecardillo@vassar.edu
CARDIN, Chad .... 706-295-6552 119 F ccardin@gntc.edu
CARDIN, Matt .... 870-743-3000.. 20 F matt.cardin@northark.edu
CARDIN, Matthew .... 914-633-2741 302 C mcardin@iona.edu
CARDINAL, Ann .... 802-828-8600 462 E
CARDINAL, Jason .... 952-358-9462 239 C jason.cardinal@normandale.edu
CARDINAL, Mark .... 218-733-2032 238 A mark.cardinal@lsc.edu
CARDINAS, Emily .... 213-738-6817.. 66 A ecardinas@swlaw.edu
CARDINE, Darla, S .... 630-466-7900 152 H dcardine@waubonsee.edu
CARDON, Ron .... 435-586-7763 459 E cardonr@suu.edu
CARDONA, Joe .... 856-256-4236 280 H cardona@rowan.edu
CARDONA, Manuel .... 787-758-2525 511 D manuel.cardona1@upr.edu
CARDONA, Margarita .... 410-837-6191 204 C mcardona@ubalt.edu
CARDONA, Melissa .... 845-938-6947 502 H melissa.cardona@westpoint.edu
CARDONA, Michelle, D 909-869-2154.. 30 B mdcardona@cpp.edu
CARDONA, Nelida .... 787-262-5786 508 N ncardona@unitecpr.edu
CARDONA, Pablo .... 305-266-7678 104 A
CARDONA, Teresa .... 787-622-8000 509 H tcardona@pupr.edu
CARDONE, Stephen .... 609-497-7706 279 D housing@ptsem.edu
CARDONICK, Mariann ... 215-717-6187 399 I mcardonick@uarts.edu
CARDOSO, Elizabeth ..... 888-360-1588.. 93 H
CARDOZA, Emy .... 212-854-2096 290 H ecardoza@barnard.edu
CARDOZA, II, Frederick 574-372-5100 155 C freddy.cardoza@grace.edu
CARDOZA, Lisa .... 916-278-7043.. 33 A lisa.cardoza@csus.edu
CARDWELL, Becky .... 916-361-1660.. 35 D bcardwell@carrington.edu
CARDWELL, Catherine ... 775-784-6500 270 K ccardwell@unr.edu
CAREAGA, Andrew, P ... 573-341-4183 260 F acareaga@mst.edu
CARELLA, Emily .... 704-463-3047 339 C emily.carella@pfeiffer.edu
CARELLA, Terry .... 517-371-5140 232 K carellat@cooley.edu
CAREW, Patrick .... 925-631-4572.. 59 I pcarew@stmarys-ca.edu
CAREW, Tara .... 410-777-2204 197 C tcarew@aacc.edu
CAREY, Alexa .... 616-632-2882 221 A ajc004@aquinas.edu
CAREY, Amy .... 734-763-0395 231 A amycarey@umich.edu
CAREY, Culeen .... 216-373-5335 357 F ccarey@ndc.edu
CAREY, Elaine .... 248-370-4535 229 F ecarey@oakland.edu
CAREY, Elaine .... 219-989-2366 160 A careye@pnw.edu
CAREY, Joe .... 317-896-9324 161 D jcarey@ubca.org
CAREY, Karen .... 907-796-6272.. 10 C ktcarey@alaska.edu
CAREY, Kevin .... 309-556-3111 140 E kcarey@iwu.edu
CAREY, Lynley .... 740-245-7183 363 A lcarey@rio.edu
CAREY, Russell .... 401-863-9650 403 A russell_carey@brown.edu
CAREY, Seamus .... 914-633-2203 302 C president@iona.edu
CAREY, Sherri .... 706-245-7226 118 C sherricarey@ec.edu
CAREY, Tom .... 217-443-8856 136 E t.carey@dacc.edu
CAREY, Val .... 303-282-3427.. 83 E val.carey@archden.org
CAREY, Vanessa .... 423-614-8500 419 H vcarey@leeuniversity.edu
CAREY, William .... 845-451-1300 297 E william.carey@culinary.edu
CAREY-BUTLER, Sylvia .. 401-863-2216 403 A sylvia_carey-butler@brown.edu
CAREY-BUTLER, Sylvia .. 920-424-0348 495 C careybus@uwosh.edu
CARFAGNA, Angelo .... 201-692-7025 276 I angelo@fdu.edu
CARGILE, Mechelle .... 501-205-8813.. 19 B mcargile@cbc.edu
CARHART, Kaitlyn .... 315-279-5212 303 D kcarhart@keuka.edu
CARIDI, Jamie .... 304-829-7111 486 B jcaridi@bethanywv.edu
CARIE, Laura .... 812-888-5116 162 E laura.carie@vinu.edu
CARIELLO, Lou .... 206-685-1428 484 A cariello@uw.edu
CARILLO, Ryan .... 401-874-9463 404 E ryancarrillo@uri.edu
CARIO, William, R .... 262-243-5700 491 E william.cario@cuw.edu
CARISTA, Jessica .... 315-268-3873 295 E jcarista@clarkson.edu
CARISTO, David .... 215-885-2360 389 A dcaristo@manor.edu
CARITO, Paige .... 860-932-4098.. 87 C pcarito@qvcc.edu
CARL, Ashley .... 813-253-7158 102 A acarl@hccfl.edu

CARL, Bailey 870-574-4558 21 F bcarl@sautech.edu
CARL, Brian 713-522-7911 453 H carlbt@stthom.edu
CARL, Courtney 319-385-6386 167 F courtney.carl@iw.edu
CARL, Diane 570-321-4101 388 H carl@lycoming.edu
CARL, Heidi, A 765-494-4600 159 G
CARL, Jessica 203-332-5105 86 E jcarl@housatonic.edu
CARL, Rebecca 812-855-9634 156 B rebcarl@iu.edu
CARL, Rebecca 812-855-9634 156 C rebcarl@iu.edu
CARL, Steven, B 508-767-7267 205 F sb.carl@assumption.edu
CARLAND, J. Paul 407-708-2363 108 B carlandp@seminolestate.edu
CARLAND, Tammy Rae 510-594-3649 28 D tcarland@cca.edu
CARLBLOM, Shelia 765-677-2191 157 F sheila.carlblom@indwes.edu
CARLE, Sarah 213-321-4248 71 A sacarle@ucsc.edu
CARLES, Gilberto 574-631-0946 161 G gcarlesb@nd.edu
CARLESSO, Dennis 313-993-3360 230 H carlesdm@udmercy.edu
CARLETON, Dia, M 607-436-2518 316 C dia.carleton@oneonta.edu
CARLETON, Taylor 830-372-8026 448 C tcarleton@tlu.edu
CARLETON, Tori 707-664-2880 34 C
CARLEY, Christelle 318-487-7051 187 B christelle.carley@lcuniversity.edu
CARLEY, Michael 559-791-2275 47 D mcarley@portervillecollege.edu
CARLILE, Kimberly, L 806-371-5017 428 F k0153833@actx.edu
CARLIN, Donna 409-944-1387 435 F dcarlin@gc.edu
CARLIN, Jane 253-879-3118 483 G jcarlin@pugetsound.edu
CARLIN, Laurence 920-424-7364 495 C carlin@uwosh.edu
CARLIN, Michael 704-687-8485 342 C mike.carlin@uncc.edu
CARLINEO, Renee, M 716-878-5561 317 C carlinrm@buffalostate.edu
CARLISLE, David, M 323-563-4987 36 E davidcarlisle@cdrewu.edu
CARLISLE, Elizabeth 812-749-1241 159 E lcarlisle@oak.edu
CARLISLE, Nahomi 617-228-3311 214 A nahomi.carlisle@bhcc.edu
CARLISLE, Sandi 320-629-5140 239 G sandi.carlisle@pine.edu
CARLISLE, Shayla, D 260-422-5561 156 A sdcarlisle@indianatech.edu
CARLISLE, Susan 931-424-4063 426 F scarlis2@utsouthern.edu
CARLOCK, Myra 731-352-4090 417 C carlockm@bethelu.edu
CARLON, Elizabeth 602-872-7753 14 C elizabeth.carlon@southmountaincc.edu
CARLOS, Amaya 915-831-2640 435 B camaya3@epcc.edu
CARLOS, Raymond 909-384-8253 60 F rcarlos@sbccd.cc.ca.us
CARLOW, Regina 410-704-3288 204 B rcarlow@towson.edu
CARLSEN, Paul 920-693-1123 497 H paul.carlsen@gotoltc.edu
CARLSON, Aaron 540-261-8503 470 D aaron.carlson@svu.edu
CARLSON, Anna 218-755-2737 237 B anna.carlson@bemidjistate.edu
CARLSON, Ashley 406-683-7115 263 E ashley.carlson@umwestern.edu
CARLSON, Beth, L 724-847-6666 384 B bcarlson@geneva.edu
CARLSON, Bob 630-682-6002 139 H carlson@iit.edu
CARLSON, Britt 978-867-4221 209 F britt.carlson@gordon.edu
CARLSON, Brooke 212-217-4300 299 C brooke_carlson@fitnyc.edu
CARLSON, Bryan 951-827-4592 70 B bryan.carlson@ucr.edu
CARLSON, Buff 215-248-6392 399 H bcarlson@uls.edu
CARLSON, Casey 530-893-7544 27 F carlsonca@butte.edu
CARLSON, Catherina 781-891-2989 206 C ccarlson@bentley.edu
CARLSON, Catherine 513-732-5233 362 B carlsoc2@ucmail.uc.edu
CARLSON, Cathy 507-222-4075 234 C ccarlson@carleton.edu
CARLSON, Christopher 978-867-4073 209 F chris.carlson@gordon.edu
CARLSON, Craig 203-857-3344 87 B ccarlson@norwalk.edu
CARLSON, David 540-362-6675 467 A dcarlson@hollins.edu
CARLSON, Deb 402-354-7257 267 E deb.carlson@methodistcollege.edu
CARLSON, Dennis 817-984-0550 93 H
CARLSON, Dillon 507-847-7978 239 B dillon.carlson@mnwest.edu
CARLSON, Douglas 415-476-4527 70 D doug.carlson@ucsf.edu
CARLSON, Jennifer 517-264-3124 220 D jennycarlson@adrian.edu
CARLSON, Jessica 406-586-3585 263 A jmcarlson@montanabiblecollege.edu
CARLSON, Jim 985-545-1500 188 B
CARLSON, Jim 225-743-8500 188 F jcarlson@rpcc.edu
CARLSON, Julie 402-844-7142 268 A juliec@northeast.edu
CARLSON, Karen 413-565-6850 205 I kcarlson@baypath.edu
CARLSON, Kathleen 574-284-4543 160 F kcarlson@saintmarys.edu
CARLSON, Kathleen 773-298-3305 148 I carlson@sxu.edu
CARLSON, Kevin, R 563-333-6070 169 D carlsonkevinr@sau.edu
CARLSON, Kirk 507-933-6362 235 E kcarlson@gustavus.edu
CARLSON, Laina 651-423-8000 237 E laina.carlson@dctc.edu
CARLSON, Laina 651-450-3654 237 H lcarlso@inverhills.edu
CARLSON, Laura 302-831-2101 91 A lcarlson@udel.edu
CARLSON, Laura 801-863-5704 460 A lcarlson@uvu.edu
CARLSON, Lisa 605-394-5261 415 I lisa.carlson@sdsmt.edu
CARLSON, Mary 704-669-6000 333 C carlsone141@clevelandcc.edu
CARLSON, Molly 240-629-7905 198 E mcarlson@frederick.edu
CARLSON, Nicholas 309-457-2391 144 E ncarlson@monmouthcollege.edu
CARLSON, Nicki 218-683-8546 239 E nicki.carlson@northlandcollege.edu
CARLSON, Nicole 763-493-0597 239 D ncarlson@nhcc.edu
CARLSON, Paul 815-802-8652 141 B pcarlson@kcc.edu
CARLSON, Peggy 402-486-2600 268 G peggy.carlson@ucollege.edu
CARLSON, Peter 425-889-5208 481 A peter.carlson@northwestu.edu
CARLSON, Renee 712-324-5061 168 H rcarlson@nwicc.edu
CARLSON, Robert 785-227-3380 171 H carlsonr@bethanylb.edu
CARLSON, Ruth 906-217-4032 221 J ruth.carlson@baycollege.edu
CARLSON, Skye 253-272-1126 480 F scarlson@ncad.edu
CARLSON, Steve 906-217-4080 221 J steve.carlson@baycollege.edu
CARLSON, Steve 937-298-3399 354 J steve.carlson@ketteringhealth.org
CARLSON, Steven 269-782-1305 230 D scarlson01@swmich.edu
CARLSON, Susan 510-987-0728 68 M susan.carlson@ucop.edu
CARLSON ANDERSON, Kerri 612-238-4556 242 H kscarlso@smumn.edu
CARLSON-KENLEY, Wendi 605-256-5149 415 G wendi.carlson-kenley@dsu.edu
CARLTON, Christopher 717-477-1481 394 D cocarlton@ship.edu
CARLTON, Edith 731-286-3300 423 E carlton@dscc.edu
CARLTON, Theresa 312-553-5922 134 M tcarlton@ccc.edu
CARLTON, William 912-279-5892 117 C wcarlton@ccga.edu
CARMAN, James 989-463-7111 220 F
CARMAN, Jeff 541-962-3293 372 H jcarman@eou.edu
CARMAN, Kevin 307-766-4286 500 H provost@uwyo.edu
CARMAN, Kristi 678-839-5306 127 A kcarman@westga.edu
CARMAN, Robert 562-938-4238 48 K rcarman@lbcc.edu
CARMEL, Julie 508-929-8754 213 D jcarmel@worcester.edu
CARMEN, Kim 318-675-5207 189 D kimberly.carmen@lsuhs.edu
CARMER, Laura 978-468-7111 209 G lcarmer@gcts.edu
CARMICHAEL, Aaron 970-351-1890 84 D aaron.carmichael@unco.edu
CARMICHAEL, Brenda 620-343-4600 173 D bcarmichael@fhtc.edu
CARMICHAEL, Demetrius, L 309-677-3155 133 H dcarmichael@fsmail.bradley.edu
CARMICHAEL, Jason 678-839-6533 127 A jcarmichael@westga.edu
CARMICHAEL, John 360-867-6100 479 C carmichj@evergreen.edu
CARMICHAEL, Lisandra 912-478-5116 120 A lcarmichael@georgiasouthern.edu
CARMICHAEL, Matthew 512-245-8336 449 G fhx6@txstate.edu
CARMICHAEL, Paul 860-343-5787 86 G pcarmichael@mxcc.edu
CARMICHAEL, Tracy 562-938-5082 48 K tcarmichael@lbcc.edu
CARMIGNANI, Courtney 925-631-4577 59 I ccarmign@stmarys-ca.edu
CARMITCHEL, Michelle 913-758-4359 177 I michelle.carmitchel@stmary.edu
CARMODY, Kevin 616-331-9530 224 D carmodke@gvsu.edu
CARMONA, Josefina 575-527-7639 287 A jocarmon@nmsu.edu
CARNAHAN, Brian 479-394-7622 23 F
CARNAHAN, Diane 209-468-9155 67 H dcarnahan@sjcoe.net
CARNAROLI, Craig 215-898-6693 399 J carnarol@upenn.edu
CARNAVAS, Ria 718-390-3131 324 B ria.carnavas@wagner.edu
CARNE, Kim 906-217-4027 221 J carnek@baycollege.edu
CARNELL, James 972-825-4700 444 C jcarnell@sagu.edu
CARNES, Gregory, A 256-765-4245 8 E gacarnes@una.edu
CARNES, Martin 706-865-2134 126 D mcarnes@truett.edu
CARNEVALE, David 714-532-6049 36 D carneva@chapman.edu
CARNEY, Chuck 812-855-1892 156 B ccarney@indiana.edu
CARNEY, Ginger 208-885-6195 132 C gingercarney@uidaho.edu
CARNEY, J. Paige 304-766-3194 489 D pcarney@wvstateu.edu
CARNEY, Jennifer 585-785-1388 299 E jennifer.carney@flcc.edu
CARNEY, Lindsey 229-391-5066 114 D lroberts@abac.edu
CARNEY, Marty 864-250-8166 408 J marty.carney@gvltec.edu
CARNEY, Michelle 785-864-8975 177 G mmcarney@ku.edu
CARNEY, RSM, Sheila, A 412-578-6424 380 A sacarney@carlow.edu
CARNEY, Susie 620-278-4228 177 E susie.carney@sterling.edu
CARNEY, Timothy 202-319-5619 91 G carneyt@cua.edu
CARNEY-DEBORD, Nan 740-587-6428 351 K carneydebord@denison.edu
CARNEY-HALL, Karla 309-556-3111 140 E dstudent@iwu.edu
CARNIE, Andrew, H 520-621-7815 16 H carnie@arizona.edu
CARNLEY, Lisa 334-222-6591 2 I lcarnley@lbwcc.edu
CARNS, Doug 724-805-2673 397 D doug.carns@stvincent.edu
CARNS, Mary Lee 843-525-5692 411 G mcarns@tcl.edu
CARNZ, Scott 206-239-4500 477 I
CARNZ, Scott 206-239-4500 477 I provost@cityu.edu
CARO, Mary Ellen 215-670-9201 391 D president@peirce.edu
CAROLAN, Brian, V 203-365-4657 88 H carolanb2@sacredheart.edu
CAROLIN, Robert 760-750-4089 33 C rcarolin@csusm.edu
CAROLIN, Robert 701-777-4202 344 H robert.carolin@und.edu
CAROLLO, Sandy 212-616-7200 301 A scarollo@helenefuld.edu
CARON, Elizabeth 620-241-0723 172 H elizabeth.caron@centralchristian.edu
CARON, John 518-464-8500 299 B
CARON, John, V 413-565-1000 205 I
CARON, Justine 978-762-4000 215 B jcaron@northshore.edu
CARON, Lenn 410-455-3260 202 G carlen@umbc.edu
CARON, Lesley 530-898-6116 31 A
CARON, Paul 310-506-4621 56 H paul.caron@pepperdine.edu
CAROTHERS, Amy 775-784-6620 270 K acarothers@unr.edu
CAROTHERS, Cat 425-640-1112 479 A cat.carothers@edcc.edu
CAROTHERS, Robert 401-752-2640 403 C
CAROZZA, Christopher 516-686-1080 308 H ccarozza@nyit.edu
CARPEN, Katie 716-338-1210 302 G katiecarpen@mail.sunyjcc.edu
CARPENTER, Amanda 805-437-3565 30 D amanda.carpenter@csuci.edu
CARPENTER, Angela 802-831-1209 462 F acarpenter@vermontlaw.edu
CARPENTER, Ariel 314-935-7679 261 B arielc@wustl.edu
CARPENTER, B. Stephen 814-865-2591 391 F bsc5@psu.edu
CARPENTER, Barbara 225-771-2016 190 J barbara_carpenter@subr.edu
CARPENTER, Barbara, W 225-771-2613 190 K barbara_carpenter@subr.edu
CARPENTER, Beth 615-230-3560 424 F beth.carpenter@volstate.edu
CARPENTER, Betsy 413-585-2052 218 D ewcarpen@smith.edu
CARPENTER, Carol 616-977-5520 222 F carol.carpenter@cornerstone.edu
CARPENTER, Carol 505-984-6102 201 E carol.carpenter@sjc.edu
CARPENTER, Catherine 213-738-6875 66 A ccarpenter@swlaw.edu
CARPENTER, Charles 817-921-5883 444 D ccarpenter@swbts.edu
CARPENTER, David 913-722-0272 174 G david.carpenter@kansaschristian.edu
CARPENTER, Deanna 620-901-6338 171 A carpenter@allencc.edu
CARPENTER, Deb 765-998-5200 161 A dbcarpenter@taylor.edu
CARPENTER, Debra 281-283-2150 452 A carpenter@uhcl.edu
CARPENTER, Hedy, L 818-677-2138 32 E hcarpenter@csun.edu
CARPENTER, Jane 785-670-1526 178 A jane.carpenter@washburn.edu
CARPENTER, Jenna 910-814-4018 327 C carpenter@campbell.edu
CARPENTER, Jennifer 407-303-5727 95 A jennifer.carpenter@ahu.edu
CARPENTER, Jessica 607-735-1812 298 G jcarpenter@elmira.edu
CARPENTER, Karen 843-383-8130 407 C kcarpenter@coker.edu
CARPENTER, Kathryn, H 312-996-8974 151 D khc@uic.edu
CARPENTER, Kristy 208-732-6209 131 B kcarpenter@csi.edu
CARPENTER, Larry 423-614-8440 419 H lcarpenter@leeuniversity.edu
CARPENTER, Marla 336-770-3337 343 C carpem@uncsa.edu

CARSTENS, Lisa 503-352-3065 375 B carstens@pacificu.edu
CARSTENSEN, Lundie 619-201-8705 60 G lundie.carstensen@sdcc.edu
CARSWELL, Justin 417-690-3446 250 K carswell@cofo.edu
CARSWELL, Pamela 386-752-1822 99 P pamela.carswell@fgc.edu
CARSWELL, Will 843-661-1678 408 H will.carswell@fmarion.edu
CARTER, Abby 229-227-3177 125 G acarter@southernregional.edu
CARTER, Allia 804-257-5719 475 G alcarter@vuu.edu
CARTER, Allia, L 804-924-5507 475 G alcarter@vuu.edu
CARTER, Amanda 860-701-5061 88 C carter_a@mitchell.edu
CARTER, Amber 859-442-1712 181 D amber.carter@kctcs.edu
CARTER, Angela, M 336-334-4822 334 F amcarter@gtcc.edu
CARTER, Angelique 434-528-5276 476 B
CARTER, Ashley 770-534-6164 116 C acarter@brenau.edu
CARTER, Ben 317-916-7825 158 B bcarter145@ivytech.edu
CARTER, Bessie 405-945-3211 368 C bessie.carter@okstate.edu
CARTER, Beth 910-630-7425 331 B bcarter@methodist.edu
CARTER, Bobbi Jo 802-635-1381 463 B bobbijo.carter@northernvermont.edu
CARTER, Brenda, C 469-365-1988 432 I bcarter@collin.edu
CARTER, Brett 336-334-5514 342 D bacarte2@uncg.edu
CARTER, Carla 501-370-5210 21 A ccarter@philander.edu
CARTER, Carmen 936-261-3502 445 E crcarter@pvamu.edu
CARTER, Caroline 919-516-4000 339 G
CARTER, Charlie 515-964-0601 166 A carterc@faith.edu
CARTER, Chris 864-587-4003 411 F carterc@smcsc.edu
CARTER, Christina 918-631-3530 371 C christina-carter@utulsa.edu
CARTER, Christopher 425-235-2352 482 C ccarter@rtc.edu
CARTER, Christopher 517-264-7606 230 C ccarter9@sienaheights.edu
CARTER, Christopher, C 610-758-5802 388 C ccc317@lehigh.edu
CARTER, Christy 316-295-8701 173 G christy_carter@friends.edu
CARTER, Cindy 641-585-8130 170 E carterc@waldorf.edu
CARTER, Cindy 906-217-4107 221 J carterc@baycollege.edu
CARTER, Clark 843-863-8008 406 C ccarter@csuniv.edu
CARTER, Clay 252-940-6357 332 A clay.carter@beaufortccc.edu
CARTER, SR., Dameon, R 410-951-3906 203 E damecarter@coppin.edu
CARTER, Daniel 651-641-8866 235 A dcarter@csp.edu
CARTER, Danita 314-918-2625 252 E dcarter@eden.edu
CARTER, Darryl 716-878-6522 317 C carterdc@buffalostate.edu
CARTER, David 800-785-0585 39 F
CARTER, David 909-607-7692 37 I david_carter@kgi.edu
CARTER, David 512-232-6400 454 C david.carter@austin.utexas.edu
CARTER, Dawn 910-962-2659 343 B carterdb@uncw.edu
CARTER, Dedric, A 314-935-3591 261 B dedric@wustl.edu
CARTER, Deena 909-687-1465 43 G deenacarter@gs.edu
CARTER, Derek 410-951-3748 203 E dcarter@coppin.edu
CARTER, Derrell 573-876-7111 259 F decarter@stephens.edu
CARTER, Diana 404-727-4264 118 D diana.carter@emory.edu
CARTER, Dione 310-434-4858 63 B carter_dione@smc.edu
CARTER, Don 928-523-1605 14 J don.carter@nau.edu
CARTER, Edythe, L 806-335-4228 428 F elcarter@actx.edu
CARTER, Erin 352-854-5835 97 L cartere@cf.edu
CARTER, Evonne 252-335-0821 333 E evonne_carter@albemarle.edu
CARTER, FeRita 951-222-8837 59 D ferita.carter@rcc.edu
CARTER, Gail 304-357-4849 486 J gailcarter@ucwv.edu
CARTER, Glenn 302-831-3358 91 A gcarter@udel.edu
CARTER, Helene, T 706-821-8323 123 I hcarter@paine.edu
CARTER, Holly 812-488-1040 161 E hc110@evansville.edu
CARTER, Hope 601-974-1000 246 C carterhm@millsaps.edu
CARTER, Hugh 334-222-6591 2 I hcarter@lbwcc.edu
CARTER, Jade 405-682-1611 367 D jade.j.carter@occc.edu
CARTER, Jaime 912-260-4367 125 B jaime.carter@sgsc.edu
CARTER, Jamail 323-241-5328 49 I carterjd2@lasc.edu
CARTER, Janet 912-427-5817 117 B jcarter@coastalpines.edu
CARTER, Jasmine 940-898-3869 451 A jcarter21@twu.edu
CARTER, Jason 216-987-4883 351 D jason.carter@tri-c.edu
CARTER, Jeffrey 252-335-0821 333 E jeffrey_carter@albemarle.edu
CARTER, Jeffrey, J 919-866-5148 338 E jjcarter@waketech.edu
CARTER, Jeffrey, W 800-287-8822 153 F president@bethanyseminary.edu
CARTER, Jennifer 318-257-4730 192 A jcarter@latech.edu
CARTER, Jennings 618-545-3169 141 C jcarter@kaskaskia.edu
CARTER, Jeremiah 808-735-4774 128 C jeremiah.carter@chaminade.edu
CARTER, Jeremy 317-274-4170 157 B carterjg@iupui.edu
CARTER, Jeremy 501-370-5330 21 A jcarter@philander.edu
CARTER, Jessica 276-656-0312 473 H jcarter@patrickhenry.edu
CARTER, Jimmy 919-573-5350 340 A jcarter@shepherds.edu
CARTER, John, B 413-542-2771 205 D jbcarter@amherst.edu
CARTER, June 864-503-5881 413 A junecar@uscupstate.edu
CARTER, Karen 318-487-7519 187 B karen.carter@lcuniversity.edu
CARTER, Kathleen 706-778-8500 124 B kcarter@piedmont.edu
CARTER, Keith 662-915-6684 248 F jkcarter@olemiss.edu
CARTER, Kenneth 770-784-8439 118 D kcart01@emory.edu
CARTER, Kevin 501-450-5382 23 K kacarter@uca.edu
CARTER, Kim, C 859-257-8310 185 D kccarter.1@uky.edu
CARTER, Larance 404-880-8074 116 I lcarter@cau.edu
CARTER, Laurie 920-832-6525 492 B laurie.carter@lawrence.edu
CARTER, Laurie, J 570-372-4288 398 A carterl@susqu.edu
CARTER, Lawrence, E 470-639-0323 122 H lawrence.carter@morehouse.edu
CARTER, Linda 816-604-3081 255 A linda.carter@mcckc.edu
CARTER, Lindsey 859-622-3541 180 B lindsey.carter@eku.edu
CARTER, Linnie, S 717-780-2321 385 A lscarter@hacc.edu
CARTER, Lisa 608-262-1234 494 D lisa.carter@wisc.edu
CARTER, Lucinda 617-747-2316 206 D ootp@berklee.edu
CARTER, Luther, F 843-661-1210 408 H lcarter@fmarion.edu
CARTER, Malika 315-470-6866 319 A mcarte06@esf.edu
CARTER, Malinda 804-819-4685 472 E mcarter@vccs.edu
CARTER, Mariel 906-217-4076 221 J mariel.carter@baycollege.edu
CARTER, Matt 505-277-3003 288 C mdcarter@unm.edu
CARTER, Melodie 919-546-8320 339 I melodie.carter@shawu.edu
CARTER, Melondia, R 205-726-2278 6 E mcarte10@samford.edu
CARTER, Michael 937-512-3883 360 F michael.carter@sinclair.edu
CARTER, Michele 254-526-1331 431 E michele.carter@ctcd.edu
CARTER, Michelle 225-578-3202 188 K michellec@lsu.edu
CARTER, Mike (Robert) 918-495-6150 368 F mcarter@oru.edu
CARTER, Miranda 406-656-9950 263 B mcarter@yellowstonechristian.edu
CARTER, Morgan 254-968-1967 445 F mcarter@tarleton.edu
CARTER, Pamela 301-985-7000 203 C pamela.carter@umgc.edu
CARTER, Parris 937-502-3649 363 G pcarter@wilberforce.edu
CARTER, Paul 863-667-5000 108 I prcarter@seu.edu
CARTER, Peggy 731-352-4096 417 C carterp@bethelu.edu
CARTER, Phyllis 925-229-6944 40 F
CARTER, Pinkey 803-536-7053 410 H pcarter@scsu.edu
CARTER, Quamina 909-621-8965 37 F quamina.carter@cgu.edu
CARTER, Regina, W 501-916-5310 22 C rswade@ualr.edu
CARTER, Richard 251-460-6283 9 A rcarter@southalabama.edu
CARTER, Rock 562-907-4972 76 A rcarter@whittier.edu
CARTER, Ronald, L 909-558-7616 48 J rcarter@llu.edu
CARTER, Ronald, L 909-558-4528 48 J rcarter@llu.edu
CARTER, Saundra 202-274-5531 94 B scarter@udc.edu
CARTER, Scott, N 423-439-4343 418 D cartersn@etsu.edu
CARTER, Seth, M 785-460-5400 172 L seth.carter@colbycc.edu
CARTER, Shanel 602-243-8200 14 C shanel.carter@southmountaincc.edu
CARTER, Shawna, M 608-246-6249 497 I smcarter@madisoncollege.edu
CARTER, Sheila 312-369-7187 136 C scarter@colum.edu
CARTER, Shermanetta 404-458-6085 123 B
CARTER, Sherryl 562-860-2451 35 O scarter@cerritos.edu
CARTER, Shree 714-556-3610 73 G vutrustees@vanguard.edu
CARTER, Shree 714-556-3610 73 G scarter@vanguard.edu
CARTER, Shree 714-556-3610 73 G vaschoolcertifyingofficial@vanguard.edu
CARTER, Steven, J 215-887-5511 401 G scarter@wts.edu
CARTER, Sue 831-459-3275 71 A sacarter@ucsc.edu
CARTER, Sue, V 434-223-6220 466 K svcarter@hsc.edu
CARTER, Susan 845-938-4041 502 H susan.carter@westpoint.edu
CARTER, Tasha 251-343-8200 6 D
CARTER, Ted, E 402-472-8636 268 I president@nebraska.edu
CARTER, Thomas, E 315-470-6691 319 A tecarter@esf.edu
CARTER, Tina, P 919-866-5419 338 E tcarter@waketech.edu
CARTER, Todd 316-322-3201 172 B tcarter@butlercc.edu
CARTER, Tomeika 909-652-6536 36 B tomeika.carter@chaffey.edu
CARTER, Toure 510-780-4500 48 D
CARTER, Tracie 334-420-4426 3 H tcarter@trenholmstate.edu
CARTER, Travis 434-947-8000 469 A
CARTER, Veronika 802-656-0589 462 D vlcarter@uvm.edu
CARTER, Zina 979-532-6417 457 H zinac@wcjc.edu
CARTER-CONWAY, Joan 443-885-3950 200 F joan.carterconway@morgan.edu
CARTER-FISHER, Andrea 910-879-5512 332 B acarterfisher@bladencc.edu
CARTER-FRANCIQUE, Akilah 803-253-5000 405 G akilah.francique@benedict.edu
CARTER-HARBOUR, Courtney 972-860-7335 433 I courtneycarter@dcccd.edu
CARTER-HORN, Cynthia 936-261-2153 445 E cacarterhorn@pvamu.edu
CARTER OWENS, David 918-540-6250 366 F david.carter.owens@neo.edu
CARTER-STEVENS, Marilyn 718-862-7958 304 K marilyn.carter@manhattan.edu
CARTER-TELLISON, Katrina 561-237-7412 103 W kcartertellison@lynn.edu
CARTIER, Cheryl 203-582-8431 88 F cheryl.cartier@quinnipiac.edu
CARTIER, Jennifer 207-509-7282 196 B jcartier@unity.edu
CARTIER, Jolie, L 619-239-0391 34 H jcartier@cwsl.edu
CARTIER, Missy, M 559-323-2100 61 G mcartier@sjcl.edu
CARTLEDGE, Ernest 240-567-7991 200 E ernest.cartledge@montgomerycollege.edu
CARTMILL, Christopher 716-375-7888 312 F
CARTMILL, Michael 435-652-7899 459 G michael.cartmill@utahtech.edu
CARTNAL, Ryan 805-546-3933 41 A rcartnal@cuesta.edu
CARTNEY, Michael, D 605-882-5284 414 D cartneym@lakeareatech.edu
CARTOLANO, Joseph 718-631-6231 295 B jcartolano@qcc.cuny.edu
CARTRIGHT, Jonathan 573-882-2011 260 B cartrightj@umsystem.edu
CARTWRIGHT, Alexander, N 407-823-1823 110 D alexander.cartwright@ucf.edu
CARTWRIGHT, Bill 415-422-5417 72 I jcartwri@usfca.edu
CARTWRIGHT, David, R 401-598-4826 403 E david.cartwright@jwu.edu
CARTWRIGHT, Marla 931-540-2618 423 D mcartwright1@columbiastate.edu
CARTWRIGHT, Michael, G 317-788-3233 161 F mcartwright@uindy.edu
CARTWRIGHT, Roengsak 760-366-3791 40 K
CARTWRIGHT-COLLINS, Carissa 317-921-4717 158 B ccartwright2@ivytech.edu
CARTY, Cheryl 478-471-5235 122 D cheryl.carty@mga.edu
CARTY, Karenann 718-933-6700 306 J kcarty@monroecollege.edu
CARTY, Raymond, W 573-629-3094 253 D rcarty@hlg.edu
CARUCCIO, Julie 434-924-4836 471 F jwi2p@virginia.edu
CARULLO, Susan, H 843-792-5802 409 D carullos@musc.edu
CARUOLO, Michael 401-341-2334 404 D michael.caruolo@salve.edu
CARUSO, Anne-Marie 617-989-4174 219 D carusoa@wit.edu
CARUSO, Katharine, H 281-618-1148 438 E katharine.h.caruso@lonestar.edu
CARUSO, Matthew 908-737-5263 277 F mcaruso@kean.edu
CARUSO, Michele, E 985-448-4081 192 C michele.caruso@nicholls.edu
CARUSO, Nicole 770-216-2960 121 F nicole@ict.edu
CARUTHERS, Janet 573-875-7372 251 A jaocaruthers@ccis.edu
CARVAJAL, Lorelei 623-845-3729 13 E lorelei.carvajal@gccaz.edu
CARVAJAL, Richard 229-333-5952 127 C rcarvajal@valdosta.edu
CARVAJALINO, Calos 305-821-3333 100 C ccarvajalino@fnu.edu
CARVALHO, Andrea 831-476-9424 42 I scadmin@fivebranches.edu

CASTELINO, Paul .... 740-593-1616 358 L
castelin@ohio.edu
CASTELLANO, Ana .... 787-622-8000 509 H
acastellano@pupr.edu
CASTELLANO, Cecilia .... 419-372-7803 348 F
ccast@bgsu.edu
CASTELLANO,
Melissa, C .... 562-903-4883.. 27 E
melissa.c.castellano@biola.edu
CASTELLANO, Paul .... 561-912-1211.. 99 C
paul.castellano@evergladesuniversity.edu
CASTELLANO, Stephen .. 215-871-6977 395 A
stephenca1@pcom.edu
CASTELLANOS, Grisel .... 787-878-5475 506 J
gcastellanos@arecibo.inter.edu
CASTELLANOS, Joshua .. 562-938-4343.. 48 K
jcastellanos@lbcc.edu
CASTELLANOS, Victoria . 570-941-6305 400 C
victoria.castellanos@scranton.edu
CASTELLO, Sergio .... 704-233-8147 344 E
s.castello@wingate.edu
CASTELLOE, Stephen ..... 336-334-4822 334 F
srcastelloe@gtcc.edu
CASTER, Ryan .... 716-926-8820 301 C
rcaster@hilbert.edu
CASTER, Tia .... 281-649-3289 436 D
tcaster@hbu.edu
CASTERTON, Deanna ..... 563-387-1038 167 J
castde01@luther.edu
CASTETE, Ralynn, F .... 337-475-5140 192 B
rcastete@mcneese.edu
CASTEÑEDA, Mari .... 413-545-2483 211 D
mari@comm.umass.edu
CASTIGLIA, Ashley .... 973-684-6868 279 B
acastiglia@pccc.edu
CASTIGLIONE,
Joseph, R .... 405-325-8208 370 J
jcastiglione@ou.edu
CASTIGLIONE, Thomas . 212-650-8150 293 B
tcastiglione@ccny.cuny.edu
CASTILAW, Timothy ...... 660-543-4113 259 K
castilaw@ucmo.edu
CASTILLA, Rafael .... 201-327-8877 276 F
rcastilla@eastwick.edu
CASTILLA, Sandra .... 518-262-4019 289 C
castils@amc.edu
CASTILLE, Carrie .... 865-974-7342 426 C
ccastil4@utk.edu
CASTILLE, Laura .... 575-646-3635 286 G
castille@nmsu.edu
CASTILLO, Angie .... 972-780-3600 453 C
angie.castillo@untdallas.edu
CASTILLO, Carlos .... 305-348-2103 109 H
carlos.castillo8@fiu.edu
CASTILLO, Dale .... 785-309-3108 177 B
dale.castillo@salinatech.edu
CASTILLO, David .... 831-479-6213.. 27 G
dacastil@cabrillo.edu
CASTILLO, David .... 559-934-2166.. 74 K
davidcastillo2@whccd.edu
CASTILLO, Diana .... 254-526-1348 431 E
diana.castillo@ctcd.edu
CASTILLO, Diana .... 787-779-2500 504 K
CASTILLO, Elisa .... 978-542-6410 213 B
elisa.castillo@salemstate.edu
CASTILLO, Evelyn .... 787-891-0925 506 I
ecastillo@aguadilla.inter.edu
CASTILLO, Henry .... 718-862-7249 304 K
bookstore@manhattan.edu
CASTILLO, Jaime .... 585-245-5716 317 E
jcastillo@geneseo.edu
CASTILLO, Jay .... 510-436-1648.. 45 H
jcastillo@hnu.edu
CASTILLO, JR., Juan, J . 956-326-2380 446 A
jjcastillo@tamiu.edu
CASTILLO, Katherine ..... 787-728-1515 512 A
katherine.castillo@sagrado.edu
CASTILLO, Kelly .... 516-686-7902 308 H
kcasti08@nyit.edu
CASTILLO, Maggie .... 623-935-8839.. 13 C
maggie.castillo@estrellamountain.edu
CASTILLO, Mario, K .... 832-813-6655 438 E
mario.k.castillo@lonestar.edu
CASTILLO, Mayra .... 410-287-1043 198 A
mcastillo@cecil.edu
CASTILLO, Nicole .... 209-946-2496.. 71 E
ncastillo@pacific.edu
CASTILLO, Pio .... 818-364-7866.. 49 G
castilpg@lamission.edu
CASTILLO, Priscilla .... 915-747-5850 454 E
castillop@utep.edu
CASTILLO, Ramon .... 323-343-2810.. 32 B
rcastill@calstatela.edu
CASTILLO, Roy .... 661-362-3418.. 38 H
roy.castillo@canyons.edu
CASTILLO, Ruth .... 276-944-6754 466 F
rcastillo@ehc.edu
CASTILLO, Salvador ...... 541-737-8083 374 H
salvador.castillo@oregonstate.edu
CASTILLO, Toni .... 405-733-7498 369 D
tcastillo@rose.edu
CASTILLO-ALANIZ,
Jo Elda .... 361-593-2382 447 A
jcastillo-alaniz@tamuk.edu
CASTILLO CLARK,
Evette .... 503-768-7110 373 D
vpsl@lclark.edu
CASTILLO-FRICK, Iliana . 305-237-0294 104 E
ifrick@mdc.edu
CASTILLO-GARRISON,
Estella .... 307-675-0819 500 F
egarrison@sheridan.edu
CASTILLO-JOHNSON,
Grace .... 323-343-3342.. 32 B
gcasti70@calstatela.edu
CASTILLON, Carrie .... 209-478-0800.. 45 L
carrie.castillon@humphreys.edu
CASTLE, Ashley .... 919-301-6500.. 93 H
CASTLE, Carey .... 606-451-6602 182 D
carey.castle@kctcs.edu
CASTLE, Cathy .... 620-947-3121 177 F
CASTLE, Clinton .... 218-683-8600 239 E
clinton.castle@northlandcollege.edu
CASTLE, Constance .... 870-575-8963.. 22 F
castlec@uapb.edu
CASTLE, Gretchen .... 765-983-1689 154 H
castlgr@earlham.edu
CASTLE, Jennie .... 360-442-2510 480 E
jcastle@lowercolumbia.edu
CASTLE, Lyle .... 208-282-7880 131 E
castlyle@isu.edu
CASTLE, Tom .... 319-363-1323 168 D
tcastle@mtmercy.edu
CASTLEBERRY, Joseph .. 425-889-4202 481 A
joseph.castleberry@northwestu.edu
CASTLEBERRY, Joshua .. 803-778-6601 406 A
castleberryjs@cctech.edu
CASTLEBERRY, Mike ..... 512-404-4811 429 K
mcastleberry@austinseminary.edu
CASTLEBERRY, Phillip ... 585-475-7721 312 A
pdcdar@rit.edu
CASTLEBERRY, Rita .... 405-703-8247 366 C
rita.castleberry@macu.edu
CASTLEBURY, Lisa .... 812-357-6515 160 G
lcastlebury@saintmeinrad.edu
CASTLES, Steve .... 661-253-3071.. 28 I
scastles@calarts.edu
CASTO, Lisa .... 305-428-5700 104 F
CASTON, Everett, E .... 662-846-4000 245 A
ecaston@deltastate.edu
CASTONGUAY, Sharon .... 860-685-3377.. 90 A
scastonguay@wesleyan.edu
CASTORENA, Christina .. 425-564-1000 477 B
christina.castorena@bellevuecollege.edu
CASTORENA, Christina .. 425-640-1668 479 A
christina.castorena@edcc.edu
CASTRIOTTA, Sue .... 603-358-2112 274 A
scastrio@keene.edu
CASTRO, Adam .... 914-674-7548 305 H
acastro@mercy.edu
CASTRO, Cynthia .... 208-885-6307 132 C
cynthiacastro@uidaho.edu
CASTRO, Daisy .... 787-753-6335 506 B
dcastro@icprjc.edu
CASTRO, Evelyn .... 718-804-8805 294 E
ecastro@mec.cuny.edu
CASTRO, Francia, L .... 212-694-1000 291 F
fcastro@boricuacollege.edu
CASTRO, Joanne .... 361-593-3085 447 A
joanne.castro@tamuk.edu
CASTRO, Juan, C .... 787-743-3038 508 L
jcastro@sanjuanbautista.edu
CASTRO, Kaye .... 239-687-5343.. 95 L
kcastro@avemarialaw.edu
CASTRO, Mandy .... 817-257-7490 447 H
m.castro@tcu.edu
CASTRO, Manny .... 670-237-6772 503 G
manny.castro@marianas.edu
CASTRO, Maria, V .... 562-860-2451.. 35 O
mvcastro@cerritos.edu
CASTRO, Melba .... 714-628-4886.. 58 G
castro_melba@sccollege.edu
CASTRO, Monaco .... 561-237-7035 103 W
mocastro@lynn.edu
CASTRO, Rosalinda .... 325-942-2043 450 B
rosalinda.castro@angelo.edu
CASTRO, Roz .... 630-953-3681 134 E
rcastro@chamberlain.edu
CASTRO, Sarah .... 202-624-1426 484 A
smcastro@uw.edu
CASTRO, Shirley .... 406-604-4300 262 C
s.castro@apollos.edu
CASTRO-DUARTE, Betsy 915-747-5640 454 E
bcastro@utep.edu
CASTRO-QUIRINO,
Sonya .... 806-743-3949 450 D
sonya.castro@ttuhsc.edu
CASTRUITA, Javier .... 408-741-2042.. 75 B
javier.castruita@wvm.edu
CASUCCIO, Anthony ...... 716-896-0700 324 A
acasuccio@villa.edu
CATALANO, Francesca .. 802-468-1214 462 H
francesca.catalano@castleton.edu
CATALANO, Philip .... 315-279-5252 303 D
pcatalano@keuka.edu
CATALANO, Steven .... 718-489-5309 312 H
scatalano@sfc.edu
CATALDI, Amy, E .... 405-208-5446 367 E
acataldi@okcu.edu
CATALDI, Jennifer .... 317-738-8256 155 A
jcataldi@franklincollege.edu
CATALDO, Adrienne .... 803-938-3906 412 G
cataldo@uscsumter.edu
CATALLOZZI, Lori, A ..... 617-228-2048 214 A
lacatallozzi@bhcc.mass.edu
CATANESE, Matthew ...... 313-664-7496 222 C
mcatanese@collegeforcreativestudies.edu
CATANIA, Nancy, M ...... 610-566-1776 402 C
ncatania@williamson.edu
CATARUZOLO,
Aleksandra .... 212-220-8011 292 G
acataruzolo@bmcc.cuny.edu
CATCHING,
Christopher, C .... 609-652-4225 283 A
christopher.catching@stockton.edu
CATCHINGS, Robert ...... 202-806-6700.. 92 E
rcatchings@howard.edu
CATE, Fred, H .... 812-856-2096 156 B
fcate@iu.edu
CATE, Fred, H .... 812-856-2096 156 C
vpr@iu.edu
CATE, Patrick .... 603-366-5281 271 K
pcate@ccsnh.edu
CATE, Richard, H .... 802-656-0219 462 D
richard.cate@uvm.edu
CATER, Ben .... 619-849-2932.. 57 J
bcater@pointoma.edu
CATERINICCHIO,
Madeline .... 732-906-2519 278 A
mcaterinicchio@middlesexcc.edu
CATES, Carl .... 870-972-3973.. 17 I
ccates@astate.edu
CATES, Chris .... 423-585-2618 424 G
chris.cates@ws.edu
CATES, Jared .... 417-255-7233 256 A
jaredcated@missouristate.edu
CATES, Jo .... 312-369-8781 136 C
jcates@colum.edu
CATES, Sarah .... 615-460-5588 417 B
sarah.cates@belmont.edu
CATHCART, Chris .... 704-330-6647 333 B
chris.cathcart@cpcc.edu
CATHELINE, Jim .... 724-964-8811 391 A
jcatheline@ncstrades.edu
CATHER, Darci .... 618-634-3260 149 C
darcic@shawneecc.edu
CATHEY, Edie .... 405-382-9717 369 E
CATHEY, Imogene .... 724-552-4499 397 F
icathey@setonhill.edu
CATHEY, Joyce .... 972-524-3341 444 E
jcath@swcc.edu
CATHEY, Patrice, A .... 716-878-4055 317 C
catheypc@mail.buffalostate.edu
CATHEY, Ron .... 318-257-4336 192 A
rcathey@latech.edu
CATHEY, Vernesha .... 972-524-3341 444 E
swccactivties@mail.com
CATINO, Yvonne .... 570-422-3580 393 F
ycatino@esu.edu
CATLAN, Laura .... 212-472-1500 309 B
proffice@nysid.edu
CATLETT, Darlene .... 570-585-9203 381 A
dcatlett@clarkssummitu.edu
CATLETT, Deborrah, L ... 859-246-6810 181 B
deborrah.catlett@kctcs.edu
CATLETT, Jennifer .... 865-471-3530 417 E
jcatlett@cn.edu
CATLETT, Nick .... 217-443-8864 136 E
n.catlett@dacc.edu
CATLIN, Carter .... 615-963-5319 425 A
ccatlin@tnstate.edu
CATLIN, Cutrina .... 816-584-6582 257 E
cutrina.catlin@park.edu
CATLIN, Dottie .... 435-652-7737 459 G
dottie.catlin@utahtech.edu
CATLIN, Michele, E .... 812-221-1714 162 D
michelecatlin@vbc.edu
CATO, Amie .... 903-785-7661 440 F
acato@parisjc.edu
CATO, Jim .... 937-766-7610 349 C
catoj@cedarville.edu
CATO, Michael .... 207-725-3050 194 A
mcato@bowdoin.edu
CATON, Brock, E .... 207-778-7033 196 F
brock.caton@maine.edu
CATON, Claire .... 713-646-1799 443 C
ccaton@stcl.edu
CATON, Lisa .... 979-627-0286 430 I
lisa.caton@blinn.edu
CATON, Rebecca, A ...... 630-515-6190 144 C
rcaton@midwestern.edu
CATON, Rhonda .... 479-788-7073.. 22 A
rhonda.caton@uafs.edu
CATON, Sheron .... 325-794-4530 431 J
sheron.caton@cisco.edu
CATONE, Christopher, J 610-921-7581 377 F
ccatone@albright.edu
CATOTA, Claudia .... 661-654-2137.. 30 C
ccatota@csub.edu
CATRON, Kathleen .... 907-474-7721.. 10 B
kacatron@alaska.edu
CATRON, Susan, D .... 530-754-9158.. 69 A
sdcatron@ucdavis.edu
CATRON-WOOD,
Rhonda, K .... 276-223-4772 475 B
rcatronwood@wcc.vccs.edu
CATT, Helen .... 229-430-3506 114 G
hcatt@albanytech.edu
CATTANI, Jessica .... 213-624-1200.. 42 F
jcattani@fidm.edu
CATTERSON, Anna .... 309-268-8297 138 F
anna.catterson@heartland.edu
CATTOLICA, Carollee ..... 707-256-7161.. 53 E
ccattolica@napavalley.edu
CATTON, Heather .... 936-468-5597 444 H
hcatton@sfasu.edu
CATTOOR, Chad, A .... 314-505-7304 251 D
cattoorc@csl.edu
CATULLO, LeeAnna .... 863-680-4108 100 F
lcatullo@flsouthern.edu
CATULLO, Patrick .... 540-654-2489 471 B
pcatullo@umw.edu
CAUBLE, Christie .... 828-641-0450 327 A
caublecl@brevard.edu
CAUCE, Ana Mari .... 206-543-5010 484 A
pres@uw.edu
CAUDILL, Alicia, D .... 843-953-5522 407 D
caudillad@cofc.edu
CAUDILL, Brenda .... 859-622-6327 180 B
brenda.caudill2@eku.edu
CAUDILL, Sarah .... 859-985-3037 179 E
caudillsar@berea.edu
CAUDILL, Stephen .... 859-622-4997 180 B
steve.caudill@eku.edu
CAUDLE, Grainger .... 828-689-1127 330 H
gcaudle@mhu.edu
CAUDLE, Mary Anne ..... 252-789-0280 335 F
maryanne.caudle@martincc.edu
CAUDLE, Patricia, M ..... 909-748-8171.. 72 E
pat_caudle@redlands.edu
CAULDER, Stephanie ..... 540-831-5265 468 E
scaulder@radford.edu
CAULEY, Cleon .... 302-857-7827.. 90 D
ccauley@desu.edu
CAULEY, Phil .... 828-227-7317 343 D
cauley@wcu.edu
CAULFIELD, Julene .... 914-323-7285 305 A
julene.caulfield@mville.edu
CAULFIELD, Kim .... 267-341-3481 385 I
kcaulfield@holyfamily.edu
CAUSBY, Cory .... 828-227-3142 343 D
causby@wcu.edu
CAUSEY, Bruce .... 256-306-2569.... 1 F
bruce.causey@calhoun.edu
CAUSEY, Joy .... 229-500-3023 114 F
joy.causey@asurams.edu
CAUSEY, Katherine .... 901-435-1259 419 I
katherine_causey@loc.edu
CAUSLAND, Luann .... 678-407-5231 119 B
lcausland@ggc.edu
CAUTHEN, Leigha .... 256-782-5278.... 6 A
lcauthen@jsu.edu

CHAFFEE, Brandy .... 218-281-8434 243 B
brandy@umn.edu
CHAFFEE, Cynthia .... 312-567-3084 139 H
cchaffee@iit.edu
CHAFFEE, Julie, A .... 508-929-5000 213 D
CHAFFEE, Reta .... 603-513-1350 273 I
reta.chaffee@granite.edu
CHAFFIN, Doug .... 580-327-8645 367 A
dechaffin@nwosu.edu
CHAFFIN, Jason .... 828-726-2200 332 E
CHAFFIN, Jason .... 910-362-7275 332 F
jchaffin@cfcc.edu
CHAGOYA, Felix .... 530-541-4660.. 47 H
chagoya@ltcc.edu
CHAHAL, Monica .... 559-325-5214.. 66 H
monica.chahal@cloviscollege.edu
CHAHAL, Sonia .... 415-565-4788.. 69 B
chahalsonia@uchastings.edu
CHAHIN, T. Jaime .... 512-245-3333 449 G
tc03@txstate.edu
CHAHINO, Michael .... 847-214-7161 137 D
mchahino@elgin.edu
CHAI, Lin .... 407-888-8689.. 99 N
lchai@fcim.edu
CHAIDEZ, Beatriz, S ..... 408-223-6704.. 62 E
beatriz.chaidez@sjeccd.edu
CHAIMOV, John .... 319-399-8594 164 D
jchaimov@coe.edu
CHAISSON, Rebecca ..... 504-286-5469 191 A
rchaisson@suno.edu
CHAJES, Michael, J ...... 302-831-6756.. 91 A
chajes@udel.edu
CHAKA, Wendi .... 508-999-8711 211 F
wchaka@umassd.edu
CHAKRABARTI, Parth .... 508-856-5610 212 A
parth@umassmed.edu
CHAKRABORTY, David .. 781-283-2474 219 C
dchakraborty@wellesley.edu
CHALEMELA, Deepika ... 817-272-5602 454 B
deepika@uta.edu
CHALENBURG, Mike ..... 501-279-4041.. 19 G
chalenburg@harding.edu
CHALEUNPHONH,
Seuth .... 812-941-2319 157 D
schaleun@ius.edu
CHALFONTE, Barb .... 413-545-0941 211 I
bchalfonte@umass.edu
CHALK, Gregg .... 508-541-1668 208 E
gchalk@dean.edu
CHALMERS, John .... 617-451-0010 217 B
CHALMERS, Scott .... 773-256-0685 143 C
schalmer@lstc.edu
CHALOUX, Matthew, P .. 561-237-7699 103W
mchaloux@lynn.edu
CHAMARS, Chris .... 518-562-4103 295 F
chris.chamars@clinton.edu
CHAMARTHI, Raju .... 844-872-8680.. 72 J
CHAMBALA, Bryan ...... 607-844-8222 321 I
chambab@tompkinscortland.edu
CHAMBERLAIN, Anna ... 808-235-7471 130 C
arc8@hawaii.edu
CHAMBERLAIN, Brad .... 563-387-1627 167 J
brad.chamberlain@luther.edu
CHAMBERLAIN,
Daphne .... 601-977-7804 248 E
dchamberlain@tougaloo.edu
CHAMBERLAIN, Jared ... 623-572-3695 144 C
jchamb@midwestern.edu
CHAMBERLAIN,
Jonathan .... 704-216-3765 337 C
jonathan.chamberlain@rccc.edu
CHAMBERLAIN, Kendra . 619-201-8700.. 60 G
kendra.chamberlain@sdcc.edu
CHAMBERLAIN,
LaShanda .... 228-897-3886 246 F
lashanda.chamberlain@mgccc.edu
CHAMBERLAIN,
MaryEllen .... 518-891-2915 309 G
mchamberlain@nccc.edu
CHAMBERLAIN,
Michelle .... 909-607-8555.. 37 G
michelle.chamberlain@
claremontmckenna.edu
CHAMBERLAIN,
Michelle .... 909-621-8111.. 37 G
michelle.chamberlain@
claremontmckenna.edu
CHAMBERLAIN, Tina ..... 206-726-5197 478 F
tchamberlain@cornish.edu
CHAMBERLIN,
Christopher .... 212-353-4099 297 C
c.m.chamberlin@gmail.com
CHAMBERLIN, Lisa ...... 509-527-5145 484 B
lisa.chamberlin@wwcc.edu

CHAMBERLIN, Mona ..... 918-631-2656 371 C
mona-chamberlin@utulsa.edu
CHAMBERS, Amy .... 309-341-7200 141 E
adchambers@knox.edu
CHAMBERS, Andy .... 314-392-2201 255 H
andy.chambers@mobap.edu
CHAMBERS, Ashlee ...... 301-891-4177 204 D
achamber@wau.edu
CHAMBERS, Bryan ...... 817-722-1651 437 H
bryan.chambers@tku.edu
CHAMBERS, Cynthia .... 562-988-2278.. 26 A
clchambers@auhs.edu
CHAMBERS, Danielle .... 618-235-2700 150 B
danielle.chambers@swic.edu
CHAMBERS, Danielle .... 323-343-3200.. 32 B
dchambe8@calstatela.edu
CHAMBERS, Eric .... 573-651-2249 258 J
echambers@semo.edu
CHAMBERS,
Franklin, D .... 607-436-2513 316 C
franklin.chambers@oneonta.edu
CHAMBERS, Jamila, J ... 323-259-2500.. 54 I
CHAMBERS, Jason ...... 828-835-4297 338 C
jchambers@tricountycc.edu
CHAMBERS, Jeffrey ..... 903-434-8106 440 A
jchambers@ntcc.edu
CHAMBERS, Jessica ..... 937-778-8600 352 J
CHAMBERS, John 561-237-7973 103W
jchambers@lynn.edu
CHAMBERS, Karen ...... 574-284-4594 160 F
kchambers@saintmarys.edu
CHAMBERS, Kathleen ... 413-796-2080 219 E
kathleen.chambers@wne.edu
CHAMBERS, Kemba ..... 334-420-4216... 3 H
kchambers@trenholmstate.edu
CHAMBERS, Lee .... 740-392-6868 356 G
lee.chambers@mvnu.edu
CHAMBERS, Melody ..... 660-626-2164 249 C
melodychambers@atsu.edu
CHAMBERS, Robert ..... 617-879-7117 212 E
rchambers@massart.edu
CHAMBERS, Sarah ...... 203-285-2132.. 86 D
sarahchambers@gatewayct.edu
CHAMBERS, Shanna .... 828-398-7178 331 K
shannarchambers@abtech.edu
CHAMBERS, Yohna ...... 817-257-7790 447 H
y.chambers@tcu.edu
CHAMBERS-KLATT,
Elizabeth .... 309-556-3849 140 E
echamber@iwu.edu
CHAMBLAS, Dimitri ...... 661-253-7898.. 28 I
dchamblas@calarts.edu
CHAMBLEE, Marquita ... 313-577-2200 232 H
mtchamblee@wayne.edu
CHAMBLESS, Greta ..... 334-244-3750... 4 F
gchamble@aum.edu
CHAMBLIN, Dana .... 816-235-5807 260 D
chamblind@umkcfoundation.org
CHAMBLISS, Chandra ... 334-727-8503... 7 D
cchambliss@tuskegee.edu
CHAMBLISS, Keith ...... 870-460-1335.. 22 E
chamblissk@uamont.edu
CHAMBLISS, Kevin ...... 254-710-3763 430 F
kevin_chambliss@baylor.edu
CHAMBLISS, Myron ..... 803-738-7173 409 E
chamblissm@midlandstech.edu
CHAMP, Karli .... 716-338-1046 302 G
karlichamp@mail.sunyjcc.edu
CHAMPA, Kristin .... 317-931-2310 154 D
kchampa@cts.edu
CHAMPAGNE, Gerald .... 734-462-4400 230 B
gchampag@schoolcraft.edu
CHAMPAGNE, Keith, M . 773-508-3890 142 G
kchampagne@luc.edu
CHAMPAGNE, Michael .. 225-752-4233 187 A
mchampagne@iticollege.edu
CHAMPION, Belinda ..... 931-393-1765 423 G
bchampion@mscc.edu
CHAMPION, Grace ...... 828-898-8828 330 A
championg@lmc.edu
CHAMPION, Laura ...... 616-526-6187 221 L
ldc4@calvin.edu
CHAMPION, Marion ..... 760-346-8041.. 39 A
mchampion@collegeofthedesert.edu
CHAMPION, Vincent .... 717-245-1013 382 B
championv@dickinson.edu
CHAMPNESS, Robert .... 516-572-9971 307 C
robert.champness@ncc.edu
CHAMPOLI, John, F ..... 717-361-3736 383 B
champolij@etown.edu
CHAMPS, Melissa ...... 773-481-8453 135 D
mchamps@ccc.edu

CHAMRA, Louay, M ..... 248-370-2217 229 F
chamra@oakland.edu
CHAMSAZ, Amir .... 410-706-3802 202 F
achamsaz@umaryland.edu
CHAN, Andy .... 336-758-4662 344 A
achan@wfu.edu
CHAN, Ann .... 630-844-3866 133 A
achan@aurora.edu
CHAN, Bill .... 614-947-6054 352 J
bill.chan@franklin.edu
CHAN, Caleb, K .... 517-750-1200 230 F
cchan@arbor.edu
CHAN, Claudia .... 718-482-5005 294 D
cichan@lagcc.cuny.edu
CHAN, David, C .... 626-395-2670.. 29 B
dchan@caltech.edu
CHAN, Emily .... 719-389-6679.. 78 E
echan@coloradocollege.edu
CHAN, Eva .... 718-270-6487 294 E
echan@mec.cuny.edu
CHAN, Genevieve .... 360-438-4332 482 D
gchan@stmartin.edu
CHAN, Hokeung, C ..... 626-917-9482.. 36 H
cliffc@cesna.edu
CHAN, Juliet .... 510-430-3335.. 66 F
registrar@sksm.edu
CHAN, Kara .... 412-521-6200 396 F
kara.chan@rosedaletech.org
CHAN, Michael, L ...... 671-735-5573 503 C
michael.chan@guamcc.edu
CHAN, Paul, H .... 303-871-4646.. 84 C
phchan@du.edu
CHAN, Regina .... 212-517-0501 305 D
rchan@mmm.edu
CHAN, Stephen .... 617-373-2000 217 D
CHAN, Yau-Gene ...... 833-637-0866.. 46 J
ygchan@itu.edu
CHANCE, Chelsey ...... 318-797-5364 189 E
chelsea.chance@lsus.edu
CHANCE, Dayne .... 908-709-7089 283 E
chance@ucc.edu
CHANCE, Katie .... 256-551-5214... 2 E
katie.chance@drakestate.edu
CHANCE, Kenneth, B ... 216-368-3266 349 B
kenneth.b.chance@case.edu
CHANCE, Mary .... 903-693-1142 440 E
mchance@panola.edu
CHANCE MERCURIUS,
Karen .... 585-275-1710 323 E
karen.mercurius@rochester.edu
CHANCELLOR, Ashley .. 314-838-8858 261 A
achancellor@ugst.edu
CHANCELLOR, Beth ..... 573-882-2434 260 B
chancellorb@umsystem.edu
CHANCELLOR, Beth, C . 573-882-2434 260 C
chancellorb@missouri.edu
CHANCELLOR, John .... 979-830-4590 430 I
john.chancellor@blinn.edu
CHANCEY, Debra .... 251-442-2332... 8 C
dchancey@umobile.edu
CHANCEY, Todd .... 903-586-2518 437 D
CHANDI, Balbir .... 661-362-5416.. 38 H
balbir.chandi@canyons.edu
CHANDLER, Alison ...... 773-298-3017 148 I
chandler@sxu.edu
CHANDLER, Brandon ... 856-225-6471 281 A
brandonc@scarletmail.rutgers.edu
CHANDLER, Cullen ...... 570-321-4173 388 H
chandler@lycoming.edu
CHANDLER, Debbie ..... 318-675-5341 189 D
debbie.chandler@lsuhs.edu
CHANDLER, Elizabeth ... 304-384-5366 488 K
echandler@concord.edu
CHANDLER, Erica .... 901-572-2452 417 A
erica.chandler@baptistu.edu
CHANDLER, G. Thomas 803-777-5032 412 A
tchandler@sc.edu
CHANDLER, Jacob ...... 936-294-1034 449 E
jacob.chandler@shsu.edu
CHANDLER, Joe .... 205-226-4667... 5 A
jchandle@bsc.edu
CHANDLER, Kevin ...... 586-445-7244 226 F
chandlerk85@macomb.edu
CHANDLER, Kim .... 509-527-5288 485 C
chandlkc@whitman.edu
CHANDLER, Kimberly ... 502-863-7057 180 E
kimberly_chandler@georgetowncollege.
edu
CHANDLER, Kirk .... 336-334-4822 334 F
kdchandler@gtcc.edu
CHANDLER, Kristin ..... 318-342-5327 193 A
morris@ulm.edu

CHANDLER, Marissa .... 931-221-6851 416 H
chandlerm@apsu.edu
CHANDLER, Mary .... 315-445-4300 303 F
richermm@lemoyne.edu
CHANDLER, Meghan .... 562-368-3001.. 65 H
meghanchandler@scuhs.edu
CHANDLER, Morgan .... 205-853-1200.... 2 G
morgan.chandler@jeffersonstate.edu
CHANDLER, Navarro .... 541-956-7030 375 G
tchandler@roguecc.edu
CHANDLER, Norma ...... 602-787-7073.. 13 G
norma.chandler@paradisevalley.edu
CHANDLER, Prentice .... 931-221-7511 416 H
chandlerp@apsu.edu
CHANDLER, Rebecca ... 310-338-2723.. 51 C
rchandler@lmu.edu
CHANDLER, Roger ...... 303-963-3341.. 78 D
rchandler@ccu.edu
CHANDLER, Scott .... 208-467-8550 132 B
scottchandler@nnu.edu
CHANDLER, Sean .... 406-353-2607 262 B
schandler@ancollege.edu
CHANDLER, Shannon ... 205-391-2360.... 3 E
schandler@sheltonstate.edu
CHANDLER, Shelly ...... 352-638-9710.. 96 B
schandler@beaconcollege.edu
CHANDLER, Susan ...... 607-962-9329 319 F
schandl2@corning-cc.edu
CHANDLER, Vernita ..... 256-469-7333..... 5 I
reg@hbc1.edu
CHANDLER, Vicki .... 415-649-7658.. 52 F
CHANDO, Kristen ...... 610-499-4142 401 I
kmchando@widener.edu
CHANDO, Michael ...... 856-415-2282 280 I
mchando@rcsj.edu
CHANDRAKASAN,
Anantha .... 617-258-0818 215 G
CHANDRASEKAR,
Edwin .... 847-635-1876 146 E
echandra@oakton.edu
CHANEN, Dan .... 608-890-0291 494 C
dchanen@uwsa.edu
CHANEY, Christi .... 605-882-5284 414 D
christi.chaney@lakeareatech.edu
CHANEY, Colleen .... 859-622-1000 180 B
colleen.chaney@eku.edu
CHANEY, Jayn .... 641-269-3200 166 D
chaneyj@grinnell.edu
CHANEY, Jeff .... 859-281-3690 185 A
jchaney@transy.edu
CHANEY, Katie .... 765-973-8484 156 D
kabaldwi@iue.edu
CHANEY, Kelly .... 712-274-5540 168 C
chaneyk@morningside.edu
CHANEY, Kevin .... 740-392-6868 356 G
kevin.chaney@mvnu.edu
CHANEY, Matthew, C .. 937-775-2501 364 D
matthew.chaney@wright.edu
CHANEY, Susan .... 505-438-8884 287 J
susan@acupuncturecollege.edu
CHANFRAU, Gersende .. 401-456-8392 404 A
gchanfrau@ric.edu
CHANG, Chaw-ye ...... 610-436-3043 394 F
cchang@wcupa.edu
CHANG, Christopher ... 845-687-5096 322 K
changc@sunyulster.edu
CHANG, Dean .... 301-314-8121 202 E
deanc@umd.edu
CHANG, Diane, T ...... 510-464-3294.. 57 B
dtchang@peralta.edu
CHANG, Eun-Woo ...... 703-323-3087 473 G
echang@nvcc.edu
CHANG, Frank .... 213-740-4623.. 73 C
fjc@usc.edu
CHANG, Garret .... 808-518-4791 128 H
garretchang@pacrim.edu
CHANG, George .... 908-737-3600 277 F
gchang@kean.edu
CHANG, Jimmy .... 727-341-4305 107 C
chang.jimmy@spcollege.edu
CHANG, Jin .... 626-395-2908.. 29 B
jin.chang@caltech.edu
CHANG, Joann .... 928-317-6000.. 11 B
joann.chang@azwestern.edu
CHANG, Ling Ling ...... 516-739-1545 308 E
library@nyctcm.edu
CHANG, Ly .... 425-235-2352 482 C
lchang@rtc.edu
CHANG, Malina, A ..... 626-395-3309.. 29 B
machang@caltech.edu
CHANG, Mari .... 808-934-2526 129 F
changm@hawaii.edu

CHAVEZ, Melanie .... 831-582-5404.. 32 D
mchavez@csumb.edu

CHAVEZ, Michael ...... 661-654-3183... 30 C
mchavez14@csub.edu

CHAVEZ, Patricia ...... 201-684-7622 280 B
pchavez@ramapo.edu

CHAVEZ, Robert ...... 215-576-0800 396 B
rchavez@rrc.edu

CHAVEZ, Robert ...... 615-460-6670 417 B
robert.chavez@belmont.edu

CHAVEZ, Steven ...... 575-538-6403 288 J
steve.chavez@wnmu.edu

CHAVEZ, Susan ...... 505-425-7511 286 C
srchavez@nmhu.edu

CHAVEZ, Todd ...... 813-974-1642 111 B
tchavez@usf.edu

CHAVEZ, Vanessa .... 785-442-6016 174 C
vchavez@highlandcc.edu

CHAVEZ-SILVA, Monica 641-269-3900 166 D
chavezsm@grinnell.edu

CHAVIRA, Melissa .... 575-646-4571 286 G
chavira@nmsu.edu

CHAVIRA, Rejoice ...... 909-389-3456.. 60 C
rchavira@craftonhills.edu

CHAVIS, Gordon .... 407-823-3004 110 D
gordon.chavis@ucf.edu

CHAVIS, Keesha ...... 610-499-1301 401 I
kchavis@widener.edu

CHAVIS, Kimberly .... 847-925-6507 138 E
kchavis@harpercollege.edu

CHAVOUS, Tabbye, M ... 734-764-3982 231 A
tchavous@umich.edu

CHAWANA, John ...... 816-604-1160 254 E
john.chawana@mcckc.edu

CHAWGO, Rebecca ..... 425-564-3061 477 B
rebecca.chawgo@bellevuecollege.edu

CHAYA, Patricia ...... 585-343-0055 300 D
pechaya@genesee.edu

CHAYKIN, Rachelle ...... 610-892-1528 393 B
rchaykin@pit.edu

CHAZHUR, Bess .... 914-594-2730 308 J
bchazhur@nymc.edu

CHEAGLE, Dorothy, S ... 803-934-3227 409 H
dcheagle@morris.edu

CHEAK, Laura .... 501-686-2901.. 21 G
lcheak@uasys.edu

CHEAL, Sheryl ...... 617-732-2880 216 B
sheryl.cheal@mcphs.edu

CHEARO, David ...... 508-793-7443 207 F
dchearo@clarku.edu

CHEASTY, Michelle .... 816-279-7000 249 D

CHEASTY, Michelle ...... 567-200-6829 353 A
michellecheasty@globaltech.edu

CHEATEM, Michelle ...... 410-617-5171 199 G
mlcheatem@loyola.edu

CHEATHAM,
Amberdawn .... 410-777-2653 197 C
acheatham@aacc.edu

CHEATHAM,
Christopher .... 269-387-2357 232 J
chris.cheatham@wmich.edu

CHEATHAM, Judy, B .... 931-363-9823 426 F
jbcheat@utsouthern.edu

CHEATHAM, Laura .... 773-907-4365 134 N
lcheatham2@ccu.edu

CHECKOVICH, Peter, G . 304-260-4380 487 C
pcheckov@blueridgectc.edu

CHEDESTER, W, P ...... 304-293-3136 489 E

CHEE, Debbie .... 253-879-2640 483 G
dchee@pugetsound.edu

CHEEK, Annesa .... 301-846-2440 198 E
acheek@frederick.edu

CHEEK, Barb ...... 614-885-5585 359 K
bcheek@pcj.edu

CHEEK, Crystal ...... 580-745-2470 369 F
ccheek@se.edu

CHEEK, Debbie ...... 843-661-8302 408 G
debbie.cheek@fdtc.edu

CHEEK, Philip ...... 360-688-2361 482 D
philip.cheek@stmartin.edu

CHEEK, Zulema ...... 908-709-7093 283 E
cheek@ucc.edu

CHEEKS, James ...... 714-712-7900.. 46 F

CHEEKS, Jeremi ...... 919-530-7298 341 D
jcheeks3@nccu.edu

CHEERS, Karen ...... 276-739-2561 474 H
kcheers@vhcc.edu

CHEEVER, Fumi ...... 218-477-2959 239 A
fumi.cheever@mnstate.edu

CHEEVER, Rex ...... 620-665-3382 174 D
cheeverr@hutchcc.edu

CHEIN, Zalman ...... 718-774-5050 321 G

CHELBERG, Gene .... 415-405-3728.. 34 A
chelberg@sfsu.edu

CHELL, Travis, L ...... 423-652-6368 419 F
tlchell@king.edu

CHELLADURAI,
Benjamin .... 832-252-4616 431 M
benjamin.chelladurai@cbshouston.edu

CHELMOW, David ...... 804-828-9788 472 D
peter.buckley@vcuhealth.org

CHELNICK, Robert ...... 773-975-1295 493 A
krisbob1@cs.com

CHELSEN, Paul, O ...... 630-752-5026 152 K
paul.chelsen@wheaton.edu

CHELSTROM, Gina ...... 323-265-3746.. 49 D
chelstg@elac.edu

CHEMBARS, Joanie .... 706-864-1838 126 G
joanie.chembars@ung.edu

CHEMERINSKY, Erwin .. 510-642-6483.. 68 N
echemerinsky@law.berkeley.edu

CHEMISHANOVA,
Marieta .... 973-596-3602 278 G
marieta.p.chemishanova@njit.edu

CHEN, Allan ...... 661-255-1050.. 28 I
achen@calarts.edu

CHEN, Bill ...... 626-571-8811.. 73 D
billchen@uwest.edu

CHEN, Chau-Kuang ...... 615-327-6848 420 D
ckchen@mmc.edu

CHEN, Chunju ...... 978-542-2046 213 B
chunju.chen@salemstate.edu

CHEN, I ...... 650-508-3587.. 54 C
ichen@ndnu.edu

CHEN, Jane ...... 212-472-1500 309 B
info@nysid.edu

CHEN, Jeffrey ...... 301-243-2212 501 J
jeffrey.chen2@dodiis.mil

CHEN, Julie ...... 978-934-2204 211 G
chancellor@uml.edu

CHEN, Karen ...... 405-744-4366 367 G
karen.chen@okstate.edu

CHEN, Kevin ...... 408-433-2280.. 36 I

CHEN, Leslie ...... 949-502-6252.. 74 E

CHEN, Letty ...... 626-448-0023.. 46 K

CHEN, Liana ...... 408-345-2633.. 42 I
accountant@fivebranches.edu

CHEN, Liana ...... 408-260-0208.. 42 H
accountant@fivebranches.edu

CHEN, Lisa ...... 401-874-4638 404 E
lchen@uri.edu

CHEN, Luke ...... 626-289-7719.. 24 K
lchen@amu.edu

CHEN, Meghan ...... 909-274-5140.. 52 K
mchen@mtsac.edu

CHEN, Meng ...... 660-543-4218 259 K
mchen@ucmo.edu

CHEN, Oliver ...... 573-341-4011 260 F
chenhs@mst.edu

CHEN, Oliver ...... 215-871-6486 395 A
hsinliangch@pcom.edu

CHEN, Shaw ...... 401-874-4339 404 E
schen@uri.edu

CHEN, Stephen ...... 415-338-7348.. 34 A
stephenchen@sfsu.edu

CHEN, Victoria ...... 817-257-5169 447 H
v.chen@tcu.edu

CHEN, Vivian ...... 503-821-1266 374 G
vivian.chen@oit.edu

CHEN, Wen Huei ...... 512-444-8082 448 B
wchen@thsu.edu

CHEN, Xiangming ...... 860-297-5170.. 88 I
xiangming.chen@trincoll.edu

CHEN, Yanping ...... 703-516-0035 471 A
yanping.chen@umtweb.edu

CHEN, Yemeng ...... 516-739-1545 308 E
president@nyctcm.edu

CHEN, Ze (Wade) ...... 812-888-4156 162 E
zchen@vinu.edu

CHEN-LAU, Sandra .... 323-856-7680.. 25 M
schenlau@afi.com

CHEN MAHONEY,
Chris .... 253-589-6004 478 A
chris.mahoney@cptc.edu

CHEN-MENICHINI,
Desiree .... 630-617-3033 137 E
chend@elmhurst.edu

CHENAIL, Ronald, J ...... 954-262-5796 104 M
ron@nova.edu

CHENARD, Susan ...... 203-285-2000.. 86 D

CHENEY, Austin, C .... 217-581-3526 137 C
acheney@eiu.edu

CHENEY, John ...... 413-542-2331 205 D
jtcheney@amherst.edu

CHENEY, Victor ...... 904-819-6213.. 99 D
vcheney@flagler.edu

CHENG, Debbie ...... 408-260-0208.. 42 H
daomassociate@fivebranches.edu

CHENG, Emily ...... 405-945-3385 368 C
emily.cheng@okstate.edu

CHENG, Judy ...... 714-895-8382.. 38 E
jcheng@gwc.cccd.edu

CHENG, Michael ...... 305-919-4506 109 H
michael.cheng@fiu.edu

CHENG, Renee ...... 206-616-2442 484 A
rycheng@uw.edu

CHENG, Terrence ...... 860-723-0011.. 85 E

CHENG, Tsai-En ...... 253-833-9111 480 A
tcheng@greenriver.edu

CHENG, Weili ...... 203-432-1940.. 90 B
weili.cheng@yale.edu

CHENG-LEVINE, Jia-Yi .. 661-362-5806.. 38 H
jia-yi.cheng-levine@canyons.edu

CHENIER, Jessie ...... 413-265-2288 208 B
chenierj@elms.edu

CHENKIN, David ...... 212-353-4122 297 C

CHENOWETH,
Candace, A .... 262-472-1592 496 E
chenowec@uww.edu

CHENOWETH, Gregg, A 815-939-5221 146 F
gachenoweth@olivet.edu

CHENOWETH, John ...... 262-472-1672 496 E
chenowej@uww.edu

CHEOKAS, Gaynor ...... 229-931-2090 120 B
gaynor.cheokas@gsw.edu

CHEPLICK, Katelyn ...... 315-279-5726 303 D
kcheplick@keuk.edu

CHERAGHI, S. Hossein . 413-782-1272 219 E
cheraghi@wne.edu

CHERAMIE, Robin ...... 470-578-6425 121 J
rcheram1@kennesaw.edu

CHERENEGAR, Jessica . 605-331-6671 416 C
jessica.cherenegar@usiouxfalls.edu

CHERETTA, Robson ...... 718-405-3200 296 D
cheretta.robson@mountsaintvincent.edu

CHEREWICK, Daniel, P . 248-232-4622 228 H
dpcherew@oaklandcc.edu

CHERKAOUI,
Mohammed .... 516-299-2501 304 C
mohammed.cherkaoui@liu.edu

CHERLAND, Ryan, M .... 949-824-4521.. 69 C
ryan.cherland@uci.edu

CHERNER, Barbara ...... 602-285-7777.. 13 H

CHERNEY, Isabelle ...... 414-930-3639 493 E
cherneyi@mtmary.edu

CHERNOBILSKY, Ellina . 973-618-3951 275 E
echernobilsky@caldwell.edu

CHERRIN, Bruce, E ...... 505-277-1740 288 C
cherrin@unm.edu

CHERRY, Evonne ...... 254-267-7042 441 D
echerry@rangercollege.edu

CHERRY, Jazmine ...... 318-274-6206 191 G
cherryj@gram.edu

CHERRY, Jennifer ...... 252-789-0316 335 F
jennifer.cherry@martincc.edu

CHERRY, Jermaine ...... 336-334-7500 341 C
jcherry@jcsu.edu

CHERRY, Jermaine ...... 704-330-1110 329 H

CHERRY, Jessica ...... 617-984-1734 217 G
jcherry@quincycollege.edu

CHERRY, Kristina ...... 601-984-4104 248 G
kacherry@umc.edu

CHERRY, Luke ...... 661-362-2603.. 51 E
lcherry@masters.edu

CHERRY, Mark ...... 321-433-7031.. 98 F
cherrym@easternflorida.edu

CHERRY, Paul ...... 501-205-8805.. 19 B
pcherry@cbc.edu

CHERRY, Shirley ...... 870-575-8461.. 22 F
cherrys@uapb.edu

CHERRY, Stephanie ...... 319-296-2320 166 F
stephanie.cherry@hawkeyecollege.edu

CHERRY, Tonya ...... 321-433-7094.. 98 F
cherryt@easternflorida.edu

CHERRY-VOGT,
Kimberly .... 618-235-2700 150 B
kimberly.cherryvogt@swic.edu

CHERUBINI, Angela ...... 914-395-2567 314 H
acherubini@sarahlawrence.edu

CHERUVELIL, Kendra, S 517-353-6486 227 C
ksc@msu.edu

CHERWIEN, Jeremiah .... 870-307-7078.. 20 D
jeremiah.cherwien@lyon.edu

CHESHIRE, Diana ...... 843-953-5163 406 D
diana.cheshire@citadel.edu

CHESHIRE, Grace .... 828-835-4207 338 C
gcheshire@tricountycc.edu

CHESHIRE, Hall ...... 540-654-1379 471 B
hcheshir@umw.edu

CHESLEY, Amy ...... 402-437-2711 268 C
achesley@southeast.edu

CHESLEY, Colin ...... 386-506-3720.. 98 A
colin.chesley@daytonastate.edu

CHESLEY, Jared ...... 920-390-2820 492 C
jared.chesley@mbu.edu

CHESLEY, Laurie ...... 541-383-7201 371 I
lchesley@cocc.edu

CHESNEY, Linda, H ...... 718-262-5119 295 D
chesney@york.cuny.edu

CHESNEY, Robert ...... 973-655-6804 278 C
chesneyr@montclair.edu

CHESNEY, Thom, D ...... 563-588-6385 164 C
thom.chesney@clarke.edu

CHESNUT, Meghann ...... 606-546-1758 185 B
mchesnut@unionky.edu

CHESNUT, Renae ...... 515-271-1814 165 F
renae.chesnut@drake.edu

CHESNUT, Robert, W .... 217-581-8453 137 C
rwchesnut@eiu.edu

CHESNUTWOOD,
Shawn .... 301-846-2688 198 E
schesnutwood@frederick.edu

CHESTER, Ann, L ...... 304-293-1026 489 E
achester@hsc.wvu.edu

CHESTER, Brandi ...... 870-248-4000.. 18 H
brandic@blackrivertech.edu

CHESTER, Bruce ...... 510-780-4500.. 48 D
bchester@lifewest.edu

CHESTER, Cathie ...... 914-251-5976 318 E
cathie.chester@purchase.edu

CHESTER, Detrenyona ... 904-470-8244.. 98 I
d.chester@ewc.edu

CHESTER, Heather ...... 239-489-9354 100 G
hchester1@fsw.edu

CHESTER, Kate ...... 971-722-8233 375 C
kate.chester@pcc.edu

CHESTER, Shellond ...... 504-520-5470 193 C
schester@xula.edu

CHESTER, Steven ...... 860-343-5864.. 86 G
schester@mxcc.edu

CHESTER, Timothy, M ... 706-542-3145 126 F
tchester@uga.edu

CHESTERFIELD, Sean .. 206-934-5437 482 G
sean.chesterfield@seattlecolleges.edu

CHESTERFIELD, Sean .. 206-934-6968 482 G
sean.chesterfield@seattlecolleges.edu

CHESTNUT, Kim ...... 307-766-5123 500 H
studentaffairs@uwyo.edu

CHESTNUT, Lisa ...... 303-797-5746.. 77 H
lisa.chestnut@arapahoe.edu

CHEU, Susan ...... 650-949-6202.. 42 J
cheususan@fhda.edu

CHEUNG, Alvin ...... 916-686-8883.. 29 G

CHEUNG, Chu ...... 212-752-1530 303 G
chu.cheung@limcollege.edu

CHEUNG, Floyd ...... 413-585-2241 218 D
fcheung@smith.edu

CHEUNG, Wilson ...... 833-637-0866.. 46 J
wcheung@itu.edu

CHEVALIER, David ...... 478-289-2370 118 C
dchevalier@ega.edu

CHEVALIER, Jason ...... 909-652-6901.. 36 K
jason.chevalier@chaffey.edu

CHEVALIER, JR.,
Joseph .... 404-756-5773 123 A
jchevalier@msm.edu

CHEVALIER, Lizette ...... 504-280-4384 189 F
lizette.chevalier@uno.edu

CHEVERTON, Holly ...... 518-783-2323 314 K
hcheverton@siena.edu

CHEVES, Brad, E ...... 214-768-2667 443 G
bcheves@smu.edu

CHEW, Elaine, K ...... 806-651-2110 447 D
echew@wtamu.edu

CHEW, Kenneth ...... 812-237-3939 155 H
kenneth.chew@indstate.edu

CHEW, Vicki ...... 425-739-8311 480 D
vicki.chew@lwtech.edu

CHEYNE, Larry ...... 503-316-3279 372 A
larry.cheyne@chemeketa.edu

CHEZUM, Kelly, O ...... 315-268-4483 295 E
kchezum@clarkson.edu

CHHOKAR, Dilbar ...... 507-574-4710 485 C
dchhokar@yvcc.edu

CHI, Robert ...... 949-502-6252.. 74 E

CHIA, Israel ...... 973-313-6128 282 K
israel.chia@shu.edu

CLARK, Jeanian ... 540-868-7122 473 C jclark@lfcc.edu
CLARK, Jennifer ... 805-378-1412 73 I jclark@vcccd.edu
CLARK, Jennifer ... 724-589-2858 398 F jclark@thiel.edu
CLARK, Jennifer, R ... 773-508-7450 142 G jclark7@luc.edu
CLARK, Jess ... 509-527-4289 484 B jess.clark@wwcc.edu
CLARK, Jessica ... 410-543-6020 204 A jkclark@salisbury.edu
CLARK, Jessica ... 309-677-3185 133 H jclark@bradley.edu
CLARK, Jill ... 712-325-3285 167 G jclark@iwcc.edu
CLARK, Jimmy ... 479-979-1484 24 A jclark@ozarks.edu
CLARK, John ... 919-497-3250 330 E jclark@louisburg.edu
CLARK, John, S ... 865-694-6601 424 C jclark@pstcc.edu
CLARK, Joy ... 334-244-3539 4 F jclark@aum.edu
CLARK, Joye ... 313-577-2161 232 H joye.clark@wayne.edu
CLARK, Kara ... 724-503-1001 401 D kclark@washjeff.edu
CLARK, Karen ... 765-973-8242 156 D krclark@iue.edu
CLARK, Karen ... 937-529-2201 361 F kclark@united.edu
CLARK, Karen ... 254-299-8689 438 G kclark@mclennan.edu
CLARK, Karen, M ... 708-344-4700 142 E kclark@lincolntech.edu
CLARK, Karen, R ... 765-973-8242 157 D krclark@indiana.edu
CLARK, Karisa, A ... 304-877-6428 486 A publicrelations@abc.edu
CLARK, Kathleen ... 305-809-3188 97 M kathleen.clark2@cfk.edu
CLARK, Kelly ... 918-595-7000 370 B kelly.clark@tulsacc.edu
CLARK, Kimberlee ... 425-352-8204 477 F kclark@cascadia.edu
CLARK, Kimberlee ... 206-546-4101 483 C kclark@shoreline.edu
CLARK, Kristin ... 559-934-2131 74 K kristinclark@whccd.edu
CLARK, Kyle ... 850-644-4444 110 B kyle@fsu.edu
CLARK, L. Nathan, N ... 775-241-4445 269 G nclark@ccnn4u.com
CLARK, Lanette ... 406-758-6328 262 I lclark@fpcc.edu
CLARK, Laura ... 870-777-5722 23 C laura.clark@uaht.edu
CLARK, Laura, B ... 615-898-5405 421 C laura.clark@mtsu.edu
CLARK, Laurie ... 979-830-4336 430 I laurie.clark@blinn.edu
CLARK, Lawrence, S ... 318-797-5234 189 E larry.clark@lsus.edu
CLARK, Leann ... 573-840-9682 259 I leannclark@trcc.edu
CLARK, Lesa, C ... 757-683-4406 468 C lclark@odu.edu
CLARK, Letitia ... 949-582-4920 65 A lclark31@socccd.edu
CLARK, Linda ... 662-332-8750 246 E liclark@msdelta.edu
CLARK, Lindsay ... 217-732-3168 142 D
CLARK, Luann ... 252-399-6309 326 H lwclark@barton.edu
CLARK, Madelyn ... 517-607-2714 224 G mclark2@hillsdale.edu
CLARK, Mandi ... 541-885-1087 374 G mandi.clark@oit.edu
CLARK, Marcy, R ... 413-545-3359 211 D mroeclark@umass.edu
CLARK, Mark ... 515-964-6213 164 F maclark@dmacc.edu
CLARK, Mark ... 276-376-4576 471 G mwc4n@uvawise.edu
CLARK, Marla ... 269-927-8762 226 B mclark@lakemichigancollege.edu
CLARK, Marta ... 718-482-5080 294 D maclark@lagcc.cuny.edu
CLARK, Mary ... 863-297-1009 106 A mclark@polk.edu
CLARK, Mary ... 501-977-2011 23 D clark@uaccm.edu
CLARK, Mary ... 303-871-2966 84 C mary.clark@du.edu
CLARK, Matt ... 217-853-6130 144 D mfclark@millikin.edu
CLARK, Matt ... 910-892-3189 329 D mclark@heritagebiblecollege.edu
CLARK, OSB, Matthew ... 985-867-2245 190 I mrclark@sjasc.edu
CLARK, Melinda ... 813-226-4858 107 B melinda.clark@saintleo.edu
CLARK, Michael ... 570-321-4249 388 H clark@lycoming.edu
CLARK, Michelle ... 954-262-1384 104 M miclark@nova.edu
CLARK, Michelle ... 817-257-5262 447 H m.clark@tcu.edu
CLARK, Michelle, R ... 626-395-6832 29 B michelle.clark@caltech.edu
CLARK, Nelson ... 256-782-8557 6 A nclark@jsu.edu
CLARK, Nora ... 301-846-2565 198 E nclark@frederick.edu
CLARK, Pam ... 989-686-9225 223 E pamelaclark@delta.edu
CLARK, Patricia ... 910-272-3505 337 A pclark@robeson.edu
CLARK, Patrick, E ... 513-556-2628 361 I patrick.clark@uc.edu
CLARK, Rachel, E ... 319-352-8655 170 F rachel.clark@wartburg.edu
CLARK, Richard ... 404-894-4154 119 D rick.clark@admission.gatech.edu
CLARK, Richard ... 702-895-1469 270 J richard.clark@unlv.edu
CLARK, Richard ... 865-573-4517 419 E rclark@johnsonu.edu
CLARK, Richard, M ... 800-443-9266 502 C richard.clark@afacademy.af.edu
CLARK, Robert, A ... 207-941-7138 194 D clarkr@husson.edu
CLARK, Robert, E ... 757-683-3018 468 C reclark@odu.edu
CLARK, Rodney ... 701-777-3391 344 H rodney.e.clark@und.edu
CLARK, Ryan ... 971-722-7800 375 C ryan.clark13@pcc.edu
CLARK, Sara ... 419-530-4039 363 B sara.clark2@utoledo.edu
CLARK, Sarah ... 215-951-1732 386 I clarks@lasalle.edu
CLARK, Sarah, E ... 863-667-5463 108 I seclark@seu.edu
CLARK, Scott, D ... 716-888-8357 291 M clarks@canisius.edu
CLARK, Sharon ... 607-844-8222 321 I
CLARK, Sherri ... 606-248-2224 182 F sherril.clark@kctcs.edu
CLARK, Stephanie ... 850-474-2492 111 E sclark2@uwf.edu
CLARK, Steve ... 541-737-4875 374 H steve.clark@oregonstate.edu
CLARK, Steven, C ... 801-863-8082 460 A steven.clark@uvu.edu
CLARK, Susan ... 517-629-0798 220 E sclark@albion.edu
CLARK, Tammie, L ... 252-451-8372 336 B tlckark215@nashcc.edu
CLARK, Tammy ... 801-863-4626 460 A clarktj@uvu.edu
CLARK, Terry ... 618-453-7960 149 G tclark@business.siu.edu
CLARK, Tim ... 801-302-2800 458 J tim.clark@neumont.edu
CLARK, Todd ... 870-972-2947 17 I tclark@astate.edu
CLARK, Todd ... 909-469-5473 75 G tclark@westernu.edu
CLARK, Traci ... 318-345-9185 188 A traciclark@ladelta.edu
CLARK, Tracie ... 704-330-6022 333 B tracie.clark@cpcc.edu
CLARK, Treka ... 870-236-6901 19 D tclark@crc.edu
CLARK, Treva ... 717-867-6106 388 A tclark@lvc.edu
CLARK, Tricia ... 316-394-5227 171 I tclark@bethelks.edu
CLARK, Victoria ... 618-664-7101 138 D victoria.clark@greenville.edu
CLARK, Whitney ... 212-659-7200 303 E whitney_clark@tkc.edu
CLARK, Wil ... 618-453-6239 149 G wil.clark@siu.edu
CLARK, Wil ... 618-536-2384 149 G wil.clark@siu.edu
CLARK, William ... 856-351-2602 282 I clark@salemcc.edu
CLARK, William (Bill) ... 740-376-4601 355 E wbc001@marietta.edu
CLARK, Yvette ... 603-645-9623 273 E y.clark@snhu.edu
CLARK, Yvette ... 615-898-5570 421 C yvette.clark@mtsu.edu
CLARK, Zak ... 907-786-1215 10 A
CLARK-FAGGS, Diane ... 202-408-2400 93 H
CLARK-GOFF, Kylah ... 325-649-8148 437 A kclarkgoff@hputx.edu
CLARKBERG, Marin, E ... 607-255-9101 297 D mec30@cornell.edu
CLARKE, Anthony ... 336-334-4822 334 F
CLARKE, Arlene, V ... 404-527-5264 121 I avclarke@itc.edu
CLARKE, Beth ... 601-974-1062 246 C
CLARKE, Calaundra ... 225-771-2552 191 C cclarke@sulc.edu
CLARKE, Cara ... 606-759-7141 182 B cara.clarke@kctcs.edu
CLARKE, Courtney ... 216-987-5504 351 D courtney.clarke@tri-c.edu
CLARKE, Cyril, R ... 540-231-6122 475 D provost@vt.edu
CLARKE, Debbi ... 919-445-0956 342 B clarked@email.unc.edu
CLARKE, Deborah ... 480-965-7405 11 A deborah.clarke@asu.edu
CLARKE, Ed ... 610-758-5154 388 C ehc222@lehigh.edu
CLARKE, Ginger ... 606-759-7141 182 B ginger.clarke@kctcs.edu
CLARKE, Helen ... 507-222-4183 234 C hclarke@carleton.edu
CLARKE, Judith, B ... 631-632-6270 316 D judith.b.clarke@stonybrook.edu
CLARKE, Karen ... 808-518-4791 128 H karenclarke@pacrim.edu
CLARKE, Kristen ... 815-226-2840 147 J kclarke@rockford.edu
CLARKE, Malaine ... 212-621-4101 294 B maclarke@jjay.cuny.edu
CLARKE, Mark ... 713-743-9854 451 G mclarke@uh.edu
CLARKE, Mayra ... 978-542-6134 213 B mclarke@salemstate.edu
CLARKE, Megan ... 906-248-8435 221 I mclarke@bmcc.edu
CLARKE, Rachel, M ... 218-299-4816 234 K rclarke@cord.edu
CLARKE, Rachelle ... 480-517-8544 14 A rachelle.clarke@riosalado.edu
CLARKE, Raymond ... 912-358-4338 124 H clarker@savannahstate.edu
CLARKE, Shari, J ... 509-359-4742 478 H sclarke5@ewu.edu
CLARKE-ANDERSON, Shannon ... 718-270-5143 294 E shannon@mec.cuny.edu
CLARKE-GLOVER, Jazzmine ... 718-390-3280 324 B j.clarke-glover@wagner.edu
CLARKSON, Gerry ... 325-649-8153 437 A gclarkson@hputx.edu
CLARO, Aida ... 305-899-3674 96 A aclaro@barry.edu
CLARY, Bruce ... 620-242-0506 175 G claryb@mcpherson.edu
CLARY, Dean ... 309-649-6316 150 D dean.clary@src.edu
CLARY, Gail ... 229-931-2318 125 C gclary@southgatech.edu
CLARY, Henry ... 276-326-4471 464 A hclary@bluefield.edu
CLARY, Shalena ... 607-962-9428 319 F sclary@corning-cc.edu
CLARY, Stephanie ... 270-686-9550 179 F stephanie.clary@brescia.edu
CLASBY, Caroline ... 314-889-4509 252 G cclasby@fontbonne.edu
CLASEMANN-RYAN, Corey ... 317-917-5707 158 A cclasemann@ivytech.edu
CLAUDIO, Alex ... 787-780-0070 504 E aclaudio@caribbean.edu
CLAUDIO, Nararly ... 787-891-0925 506 I nclaudio@aguadilla.inter.edu
CLAUSEN, Beth ... 651-793-1618 238 B beth.clausen@metrostate.edu
CLAUSEN, Janice ... 661-654-3360 30 C jclausen@csub.edu
CLAUSS, Daniel ... 949-582-4547 65 C dclauss@saddleback.edu
CLAUSS, Karl, W ... 315-228-7489 296 C kclauss@colgate.edu
CLAUSS, Sandy ... 210-366-2701 441 C clauss@questcollege.edu
CLAUSSEN, Linda, C ... 540-674-3614 473 F lclaussen@nr.edu
CLAUSSEN, Nicole ... 605-256-5744 415 G nicole.claussen@dsu.edu
CLAVELL, Edward ... 602-489-5300 10 G edward.clavell@arizonachristian.edu
CLAVELLE, Martha ... 619-644-7000 44 H martha.clavelle@gcccd.edu
CLAVER, Jennifer ... 336-744-0900 327 D cla@outfitters4.com
CLAVERE, Javier ... 210-829-3877 452 D clavere@uiwtx.edu
CLAVERIE, Mark ... 518-587-2100 320 B mark.claverie@esc.edu
CLAVIER, Cheri ... 423-439-7483 418 D clavier@etsu.edu
CLAVIER, Sophie ... 415-338-7160 34 A sclavier@sfsu.edu
CLAVILLE, Eric ... 757-823-8670 468 B ewclaville@nsu.edu
CLAVILLE, Eric, W ... 757-823-8683 468 B ewclaville@nsu.edu
CLAW, Chandra ... 520-383-8401 16 D
CLAWSON, Laura ... 540-665-4505 470 A lclawson@su.edu
CLAWSON, Teri ... 435-283-7154 460 C teri.clawson@snow.edu
CLAXTON, Brenda ... 432-264-5160 436 H bclaxton@howardcollege.edu
CLAXTON, Patricia ... 325-574-7607 457 G pclaxton@wtc.edu
CLAXTON, Stephanie, L ... 315-267-2154 318 D claxtosc@potsdam.edu
CLAY, Aileen ... 603-206-8175 272 A aclay@ccsnh.edu
CLAY, Angel ... 301-548-5500 93 H
CLAY, Antoinette, M ... 732-255-0400 279 A aclay@ocean.edu
CLAY, Claire ... 419-358-3456 348 E clayc@bluffton.edu
CLAY, Daniel ... 319-335-5380 163 F daniel-clay@uiowa.edu
CLAY, Doreen ... 818-710-2510 49 H claydj@piercecollege.edu
CLAY, Elonda ... 740-362-3435 355 H eclay@mtso.edu
CLAY, George, W ... 864-656-0723 406 F gclay@clemson.edu
CLAY, John, L ... 256-469-7333 5 I president@hbc1.edu
CLAY, Karen ... 662-329-7104 247 B kgclay@muw.edu
CLAY, Kristi ... 870-245-5417 20 H clayk@obu.edu
CLAY, Lauren ... 601-484-8618 246 B lclay1@meridiancc.edu
CLAY, Martyn ... 813-757-2110 102 A mclay6@hccfl.edu
CLAY, Melanie, N ... 678-839-0627 127 A melaniec@westga.edu
CLAY, Mercedes ... 419-783-2362 351 J mclay@defiance.edu
CLAY, Patricia ... 201-360-4351 277 D pclay@hccc.edu
CLAY, Philip, N ... 508-831-5507 220 C pclay@wpi.edu
CLAY, Phillip, H ... 502-597-6041 183 A phillip.clay@kysu.edu
CLAY, Quinton ... 314-889-1478 252 G qclay@fontbonne.edu
CLAY, Robert ... 563-387-1001 167 J clay@luther.edu
CLAY, Stacey ... 417-625-9521 255 I clay-s@mssu.edu
CLAYBAUGH, Tracy, L ... 603-535-2550 274 B tlclaybaugh@plymouth.edu
CLAYBON, John ... 405-682-1611 367 D jclaybon@occc.edu
CLAYBORN, Kathy ... 501-450-3134 23 K kathyc@uca.edu
CLAYBOURNE, Hilary ... 256-824-6422 8 B hilary.claybourne@uah.edu
CLAYBROOK, Jennifer ... 662-329-7962 247 B jlclaybrook@muw.edu

CLOUSTON, Heather, O . 336-633-0286 336 F
hoclouston@randolph.edu
CLOUTIER, Adam 269-269-4250 223 J
acloutier@glenoaks.edu
CLOUTIER, Adam 440-525-7079 354 L
acloutier1@lakelandcc.edu
CLOUTIER, Julie, H 860-297-2403.. 88 I
julie.cloutier@trincoll.edu
CLOUTIER, Michael 978-665-3590 212 C
mclouti4@fitchburgstate.edu
CLOUTIER, Michelle 401-232-6722 403 B
mcloutier@bryant.edu
CLOUTIER MIHAL,
Christine 201-599-6074 277 A
mihalc@felician.edu
CLOUTIER MIHAL,
Christine 201-559-6000 277 A
CLOVER, Susan 508-588-9100 214 F
sclover@massasoit.mass.edu
CLOVIS, Stephen 503-845-3570 373 G
stephen.clovis@mtangel.edu
CLOW, William 309-298-1552 152 I
wt-clow@wiu.edu
CLOWER, Matthew 334-808-6313.... 7 C
mclower@troy.edu
CLOWERS, Laurie, C 919-866-5929 338 E
lcclowers@waketech.edu
CLOWERS, Linda 562-860-2451.. 35 O
lclowers@cerritos.edu
CLOWNEY-JOHNSON,
Shannon 501-370-5276.. 21 A
sclowney@philander.edu
CLOYD, Angela 859-858-3581 178 G
CLOYD, Benjamin 662-246-6256 246 E
bcloyd@msdelta.edu
CLOYD, Sherri, L 417-836-8500 255 J
sherricloyd@missouristate.edu
CLOYD, Timothy 417-873-7201 252 A
jtcloyd16@drury.edu
CLUETT, Jennifer, A 508-831-5286 220 C
jcluett@wpi.edu
CLUM, Gerald 678-331-4366 122 A
gerard.clum@life.edu
CLUM, Lauren 510-780-4500.. 48 D
lclum@lifewest.edu
CLUM, Randy 845-758-7468 290 G
clum@bard.edu
CLUNE, Jay 985-448-4003 192 C
jay.clune@nicholls.edu
CLUNE, Michael 415-476-0944.. 70 D
michael.clune@ucsf.edu
CLUNIE, Chris 704-894-2337 328 C
chclunie@davidson.edu
CLUNIS, Tamara, T 806-371-5226 428 F
ttclunis@actx.edu
CLUSSERATH, Michael .. 770-426-4479 122 A
michael.clusserath@life.edu
CLUTE, Claire 610-902-8201 379 E
cc736@cabrini.edu
CLUTE, David 913-234-0642 172 I
david.clute@cleveland.edu
CLUTTER, Archie 402-472-7084 269 A
aclutter2@unl.edu
CLYBURN, Sonya 443-885-3034 200 F
sonya.clyburn@morgan.edu
CLYDE, Jamie, C 530-898-6411.. 31 A
jcamaren@csuchico.edu
CLYDE, Katherine 252-493-7262 336 E
kclyde@email.pittcc.edu
CLYDE, JR., William 516-572-0607 307 C
william.clyde@ncc.edu
CLYDESDALE, Timothy .. 609-771-1855 275 J
clydesda@tcnj.edu
CLYMER, Timothy 440-646-8301 363 C
tim.clymer@ursuline.edu
CLYNE, Dylan 203-596-4500.. 88 E
COACH, Michelle 860-253-3002.. 86 B
mcoach@asnuntuck.edu
COACHMAN, Kenneth ... 205-929-1457.... 6 B
kcoachman@miles.edu
COACHMAN, Lorie 407-708-2380 108 B
coachmanl@seminolestate.edu
COAD, Alex 985-493-3304 192 C
alex.coad@nicholls.edu
COADY, Barbara 610-785-6201 396 H
bcoady@scs.edu
COAKLEY, Katrina 312-341-3542 148 A
kcoakley01@roosevelt.edu
COAKLEY, Sarah 678-872-8015 119 C
stesar@highlands.edu
COALLEY, Justin 706-865-2134 126 D
jcoalley@truett.edu

COARTNEY, Jorge 540-831-7803 468 E
jcoartne@radford.edu
COATES, Emily 206-878-3710 480 C
ecoates@highline.edu
COATES, Jeff 407-882-2326 110 D
jeff.coates@ucf.edu
COATNEY, Julie 402-872-2365 267 H
jcoatney@peru.edu
COATS, Bruce 419-434-4250 364 B
bcoats@winebrenner.edu
COATS, Karen 601-266-4369 248 H
karen.coats@usm.edu
COATS, Lindsay 603-428-2358 272 I
lcoats@nec.edu
COATS, Meagan 870-850-3124.. 21 D
mcoats@seark.edu
COAXUM, Julian 704-894-2915 328 C
jucoaxum@davidson.edu
COBANE, Craig 270-745-2085 186 A
craig.cobane@wku.edu
COBB, Anika, V 803-376-5717 405 D
acobb@allenuniversity.edu
COBB, Brian 937-481-2243 363 H
brian.cobb@wilmington.edu
COBB, Charles 270-706-8566 181 C
charles.cobb@kctcs.edu
COBB, Charles, G 404-413-4000 120 C
ccobb13@gsu.edu
COBB, Charlie 865-354-3000 424 D
cobbcc@roanestate.edu
COBB, Christopher 323-343-3942.. 32 B
ccobb3@calstatela.edu
COBB, David 615-329-8848 418 E
dcobb@fisk.edu
COBB, Donna 405-974-5298 370 H
dcobb@uco.edu
COBB, James 931-372-3524 425 B
jimcobb@tntech.edu
COBB, JR., James 410-888-9048 200 C
COBB, Jeffrey 231-995-1338 228 F
jcobb@nmc.edu
COBB, Katharine 646-660-6660 292 F
katharine.cobb@baruch.cuny.edu
COBB, Keith 310-900-1600.. 39 H
kcobb@compton.edu
COBB, Mary 318-675-6065 189 D
mcobb@lsuhsc.edu
COBB, Michael 910-362-7347 332 F
mcobb203@mail.cfcc.edu
COBB, Nickie 502-213-5333 181 H
nicole.cobb@kctcs.edu
COBB, P. Denise 618-650-3779 149 H
pcobb@siue.edu
COBB, Raisha 336-750-2092 343 E
cobbr@wssu.edu
COBB, Rebecca 626-585-7385.. 56 D
rcobb1@pasadena.edu
COBB, Ron, K 770-484-1204 122 B
rob.cobb@lutherrice.edu
COBB, Ryan 910-410-1759 336 G
racobb@richmondcc.edu
COBB, Tim 503-370-6280 377 E
tcobb@willamette.edu
COBB, Tommi 870-584-1158.. 22 G
tcobb@cccua.edu
COBB, Travis 334-699-2266..... 1 B
tcobb@acom.edu
COBB, Velma, L 212-463-0400 322 C
velma.cobb@touro.edu
COBB-SHEEHAN,
Megan 608-663-4861 491 F
mcobbsheehan@edgewood.edu
COBEN, Jeffrey 304-293-2362 489 E
jcoben@hsc.wvu.edu
COBIAN, Oscar 805-678-5847.. 74 A
ocobian@vcccd.edu
COBINE, Stewart, T 812-855-7657 156 B
scobine@iu.edu
COBLE, Chris 501-760-4177.. 20 E
chris.coble@np.edu
COBLE, Keith 662-325-3006 247 A
keith.cobl@msstate.edu
COBLE, Kristopher 614-947-6728 352 J
kristopher.coble@franklin.edu
COBOS, Luzmar 832-252-4670 431 M
luzmar.cobos@cbshouston.edu
COBURN, Amy 505-277-9289 288 C
acoburn@unm.edu
COBURN, Danielle 205-853-1200.... 2 G
dcoburn@jeffersonstate.edu
COBURN, Walter 575-492-2721 286 E
wcoburn@nmjc.edu

COBY, Aaron 360-438-4564 482 D
acoby@stmartin.edu
COCA, Anthony 505-424-2327 285 H
acoca@iaia.edu
COCANOUGHER,
Carolyn 713-798-9091 430 E
cocanoug@bcm.edu
COCCIOLO, Anthony 718-636-3702 311 A
acocciol@pratt.edu
COCCO, Melissa 917-493-4584 304 L
mcocco@msmnyc.edu
COCCO DE FILIPPIS,
Daisy 718-518-4300 293 F
president@hostos.cuny.edu
COCHIS, Toni 919-497-3240 330 E
tcochis@louisburg.edu
COCHRAN, Bob 503-594-6790 372 B
bobc@clackamas.edu
COCHRAN, Carolyn 214-329-4447 429 L
carolyn.cochran@bgu.edu
COCHRAN, Connie, L ... 713-313-7606 448 D
cochrancl@tsu.edu
COCHRAN, Doug 865-471-3559 417 E
dcochran@cn.edu
COCHRAN, Eli 415-703-9500.. 28 D
ecochran@cca.edu
COCHRAN, Glenn 508-626-4636 212 D
gcochran@framingham.edu
COCHRAN, Jason, A 256-765-5241.... 8 E
jacochran@una.edu
COCHRAN, Jeanne 619-849-2513.. 57 J
jeannecochran@pointloma.edu
COCHRAN, Karen 407-882-2861 110 D
karen.cochran@ucf.edu
COCHRAN, Keirsh, A 260-359-4035 155 G
kcochran@huntington.edu
COCHRAN, Matt 918-444-3926 366 G
cochranm@nsuok.edu
COCHRAN, Michelle 203-773-8535.. 85 C
mcochran@albertus.edu
COCHRAN, Monica, J ... 304-367-4711 488 L
monica.cochran@fairmontstate.edu
COCHRAN, Nathan 504-520-7329 193 C
ncochran@xula.edu
COCHRAN, Ralph 614-236-6181 348 I
rcochran@capital.edu
COCHRAN, Raylene 850-478-8496 105 F
rcochran@pcci.edu
COCHRAN, Robert 360-442-2277 480 E
rcochran@lowercolumbia.edu
COCHRAN, Tamara 480-517-8000.. 14 A
COCHRAN, W. Scott 864-587-4236 411 F
COCHRANE, Ashley 859-985-3605 179 E
cochranea@berea.edu
COCHRANE, John, T 319-352-8470 170 F
john.cochrane@wartburg.edu
COCHRANE, Ken, S 937-529-2201 361 F
kscochrane@united.edu
COCHRANE, Paul 207-228-8598 196 J
paul.cochrane@maine.edu
COCKERELL, K.T 210-341-1366 440 B
ktcockerell@ost.edu
COCKERHAM, Richard ... 318-678-6000 187 E
rcockerham@bpcc.edu
COCKETT, Noelle, E 435-797-7172 459 F
noelle.cockett@usu.edu
COCKFIELD, Barbara 518-244-4720 312 D
b.cockfield@sage.edu
COCKRELL, Grant 205-391-2384.... 3 E
gcockrell@sheltonstate.edu
COCKRELL, Jordan 251-380-3470.... 6 H
COCKRELL, Phillip, A 216-687-2048 350 G
p.cockrell@csuohio.edu
COCKRELL, Todd 281-649-3417 436 D
tcockrell@hbu.edu
COCKROFT, Martin 360-792-6050 481 B
COCKRUM, Colton 901-678-2156 426 A
ccockrum@memphis.edu
COCKRUM, Daniel 540-231-8897 475 D
dcockrum@vt.edu
COCKRUM, Larry, L 606-539-4201 185 C
presoff@ucumberlands.edu
COCLANIS-LODING,
Chris 815-479-8713 143 F
ccoclanis-loding@mchenry.edu
COCO, Karen 318-670-9324 191 B
kcoco@susla.edu
COCOZZA, Christopher . 610-282-1100 382 A
christopher.cocozza@desales.edu
COCOZZOLI, Gary, R 248-204-3006 226 E
gcocozzol@ltu.edu
CODDINGTON, Andrew . 315-228-6921 296 C
acoddington@colgate.edu

CODDINGTON, Leslie ... 501-450-3237.. 23 K
lcoddington@uca.edu
CODERKO, Charles 217-206-7375 151 E
ccode2@uis.edu
CODJOE, Henry 706-272-4406 118 A
hcodjoe@daltonstate.edu
CODNER, Jackie 580-745-2810 369 F
jcodner@se.edu
CODNER, Kolton 724-480-3460 381 G
kolton.codner@ccbc.edu
CODNER, Renee 619-688-0800.. 40 D
CODY, Liz 507-222-4013 234 C
lcody@carleton.edu
CODY, Mary Ellen 203-285-2296.. 86 D
mcody@gatewayct.edu
COE, Erica 360-475-7263 481 B
ecoe@olympic.edu
COE, Lea 229-931-2381 125 C
lcoe@southgatech.edu
COE, Naomi 414-382-6040 490 G
naomi.coe@alverno.edu
COE REGAN,
Jo Ann, R 202-319-5454.. 91 G
cua-ncsss@cua.edu
COEHOORN, Joel 402-363-5603 269 F
jcoehoorn@york.edu
COELHO, Marty 707-476-4358.. 58 I
marty-coelho@redwoods.edu
COES, Alvie 864-941-8417 410 D
coes.a@ptc.edu
COFER, Caitlyn 912-344-3248 120 A
ccofer@georgiasouthern.edu
COFER, Carol 304-327-4144 488 J
ccofer@bluefieldstate.edu
COFER, Shayne 773-442-5919 145 G
r-shaynecofer@neiu.edu
COFFARO, Joananne 732-906-7707 278 A
jcoffaro@middlesexcc.edu
COFFEE, Carol, L 260-399-7700 162 A
ccoffee@sf.edu
COFFEY, Amanda, A 717-796-1800 389 F
acoffey@messiah.edu
COFFEY, Brittany 812-258-9510 154 B
bcoffey@cariscollege.edu
COFFEY, Charle 931-393-1816 423 G
ccoffey@mscc.edu
COFFEY, Elijah 270-789-5005 179 G
evcoffey@campbellsville.edu
COFFEY, Paul 312-899-5176 149 B
pcoffey@saic.edu
COFFEY, Peter 312-362-7144 136 F
pcoffey2@depaul.edu
COFFEY, Rachel 423-614-8430 419 H
rcoffey@leeuniversity.edu
COFFEY, Randon 417-667-8181 251 E
rcoffey@cottey.edu
COFFEY, Ron, L 260-359-4029 155 G
rcoffey@huntington.edu
COFFIN, Gordie 402-465-2544 267 J
gcoffin@nebrwesleyan.edu
COFFIN, Lee, A 603-646-2604 272 F
lee.a.coffin@dartmouth.edu
COFFIN, William 410-293-2809 502 I
coffin@usna.edu
COFFINDAFFER, Kari 304-367-4638 487 H
kari.coffindaffer@pierpont.edu
COFFMAN, Benjamin, S 989-774-3581 221 M
coffm1bs@cmich.edu
COFFMAN, Curt 812-888-4373 162 E
ccoffman@vinu.edu
COFFMAN, David, W 803-947-2052 409 I
david.coffman@newberry.edu
COFFMAN, Michael 972-758-3805 432 I
mcoffman@collin.edu
COFFMAN, Michelle 405-912-9058 368 H
mcoffman@ru.edu
COFFMAN, Renee 702-968-2020 271 D
rcoffman@roseman.edu
COFIELD, Bridgette, N .. 412-578-8897 380 A
bncofield@carlow.edu
COFONE, Albin 631-451-4335 321 A
cofonea@sunysuffolk.edu
COGBURN, Jeff 423-425-2345 426 D
jeff-cogburn@utc.edu
COGBURN, Troy 914-694-2200 305 A
COGER, Robin, N 252-328-5419 340 H
rncoger@ecu.edu
COGGESHALL, Ken 513-761-2020 350 B
COGGIN, Rod 662-720-7306 247 D
rbcoggin@nemcc.edu
COGGINS, Patrick 940-397-4239 439 F
patrick.coggins@msutexas.edu

COLEMAN, Jonathan, B 501-916-3035 22 C jbcoleman@ualr.edu
COLEMAN, LaMar 860-465-0072 85 G colemanla@easternct.edu
COLEMAN, LaShonda 310-506-4436 56 H lashonda.coleman@pepperdine.edu
COLEMAN, Laura 906-217-4244 221 J colemanl@baycollege.edu
COLEMAN, La'Tia 952-918-1966 233 H latia.coleman@bethanygu.edu
COLEMAN, Lisa 212-998-1212 309 D
COLEMAN, Lynn, C 443-518-4749 199 D lcoleman@howardcc.edu
COLEMAN, Mark 270-384-8040 183 D colemanm@lindsey.edu
COLEMAN, Martha Lopez 903-972-3275 457 I mlcoleman@wileyc.edu
COLEMAN, Mary 646-313-8000 295 C mary.coleman@guttman.cuny.edu
COLEMAN, Melinda, L 843-953-8180 407 D colemanm@cofc.edu
COLEMAN, Michael 828-565-4220 335 A mwcoleman@haywood.edu
COLEMAN, Michael 919-866-6226 338 E mccoleman@waketech.edu
COLEMAN, Michelle 410-888-9048 200 C mcoleman@muih.edu
COLEMAN, Mychal 616-331-2215 224 D colemamy@gvsu.edu
COLEMAN, Nana, E 832-826-6230 430 E necolema@bcm.edu
COLEMAN, Nancy 617-495-2930 210 B dce_dean@fas.harvard.edu
COLEMAN, Rachel, C 620-417-1125 177 C rachel.coleman@sccc.edu
COLEMAN, Robert 518-694-7357 289 A robert.coleman@acphs.edu
COLEMAN, Robert 210-436-3605 442 A rcoleman3@stmarytx.edu
COLEMAN, Sandy 508-286-3504 219 F coleman_sandra@wheatoncollege.edu
COLEMAN, Scott 859-246-6422 181 B scott.coleman@kctcs.edu
COLEMAN, Sean 406-657-1092 264 G colemans@rocky.edu
COLEMAN, Sean 412-365-1164 380 F scoleman1@chatham.edu
COLEMAN, Stephanie 252-328-6975 340 H colemans@ecu.edu
COLEMAN, Stephany 512-505-3039 437 B slcoleman@htu.edu
COLEMAN, JR., Sterling, J 937-328-6023 350 D colemans@clarkstate.edu
COLEMAN, Steve, B 864-941-8603 410 D coleman.s@ptc.edu
COLEMAN, Tammy 870-584-1149 22 G tcoleman@cccua.edu
COLEMAN, Tekayiha 352-638-9745 96 B tcoleman@beaconcollege.edu
COLEMAN, Teresa 912-538-3103 125 E tcoleman@southeasterntech.edu
COLEMAN, Tia 704-878-3345 335 I tcoleman@mitchellcc.edu
COLEMAN, Todd 319-363-8213 168 D
COLEMAN, Tonya, R 678-359-5435 120 D tonya_c@gordonstate.edu
COLEMAN, Tracy 251-460-6574 9 A tcoleman@southalabama.edu
COLEMAN, Valorie 417-690-2212 250 K vcoleman@cofo.edu
COLEMAN, Vicki 336-285-4185 341 C vcoleman@ncat.edu
COLEMAN, Warren, K 540-568-3187 467 C colemawk@jmu.edu
COLEMAN, Wendy 334-229-4232 4 B wcoleman@alasu.edu
COLEMAN, Wes 848-932-2916 281 C samcolem@finance.rutgers.edu
COLEMAN, Woodie 405-682-1611 367 D rcoleman@occc.edu
COLEMAN-CARTER, Margaree 973-655-7548 278 C carterm@montclair.edu
COLEMAN-DUNN, Olivia 502-863-8007 180 E olivia_coleman@georgetowncollege.edu
COLEMAN-FERRELL, Tunjarnika 561-868-3474 105 C ferrelln@palmbeachstate.edu
COLEMAN-FOSTER, Barbara 407-708-2373 108 B colemanb@seminolestate.edu
COLEMAN-MARTINS, Shelly 316-978-3456 178 B shelly.coleman-martins@wichita.edu
COLEMER, Dena 763-424-0853 239 D dcolemer@nhcc.edu
COLES, Natalie 937-708-4023 363 G ncoles@wilberforce.edu
COLESTOCK, Dennis 509-313-4103 479 E colestock@gonzaga.edu
COLESTOCK, Kian 949-824-4059 69 C kcolestock@uci.edu
COLETTI, Jocelyn, J 617-422-7228 217 B jcoletti@nesl.edu
COLEY, Camille 415-422-5368 72 I ccoley@usfca.edu
COLEY, Derrick 301-860-4076 203 D dcoley@bowiestate.edu
COLEY, Jason 518-861-2598 305 B jcoley@mariacollege.edu
COLEY, JR., Norman 308-635-6123 269 E coleyn@wncc.edu
COLEY, Phylicia 518-454-5295 296 E coleyp@strose.edu
COLEY, Soraya, M 909-869-2290 30 B president@cpp.edu
COLGAN, Ann 610-436-3505 394 F acolgan@wcupa.edu
COLGAN, OSB, Tobias 812-357-6304 160 G tcolgan@saintmeinrad.edu
COLGATE, Beverly 805-893-2218 70 E beverly.colgate@ucsb.edu
COLGROVE, Marianne, M 503-777-7792 375 F mcolgrov@reed.edu
COLIN, Cherie 650-574-6161 62 J
COLIN, Cherie 650-738-4346 62 K colinc@smccd.edu
COLIN, Jennifer 616-222-3000 226 A jcolin@kuyper.edu
COLIP, Mark, K 312-949-7700 139 B mcolip@ico.edu
COLITON, John 240-567-5031 200 E john.coliton@montgomerycollege.edu
COLL, James, P 601-266-4491 248 H james.coll@usm.edu
COLL, Jose 503-725-4712 375 D coll@pdx.edu
COLL, Ryan 717-262-2612 402 D ryan.coll@wilson.edu
COLL, Stephen, W 212-854-6056 296 H steve.coll@columbia.edu
COLLAMORE, Ken 802-440-4420 461 B kcollamore@bennington.edu
COLLARD, Jordan 903-983-8198 437 G jcollard1@kilgore.edu
COLLAROS, Phelosha 505-984-6109 287 F pcollaros@sjc.edu
COLLAROS, Phelosha 505-984-6000 287 F phelosha.collaros@sjc.edu
COLLAZO, Allison 540-432-4314 465 F allison.collazo@emu.edu
COLLAZO, Julio, A 787-758-2525 511 D julio.collazo@upr.edu
COLLAZO, Lin 787-751-1912 507 F lcollazo@juris.inter.edu
COLLAZO, Luis 973-278-5400 291 A luis-collazo@berkeleycollege.edu
COLLAZO, Luis 973-278-5400 274 J luis_collazo@berkeleycollege.edu
COLLAZO, Mariela 787-766-1717 509 C mcollazo@uagm.edu
COLLAZO, Samaris 787-743-7979 509 D s_collazo@suagm.edu
COLLAZO-CASTRO, Shelciy 787-993-8876 510 E shelciy.collazo@upr.edu
COLLER, Barry, S 212-327-7490 312 B collerb@rockefeller.edu
COLLET, Jason 575-538-6444 288 J jason.collet@wnmu.edu
COLLETTA, Louis 504-568-3126 189 C lcolletta@lsuhsc.edu
COLLETTE, Sherwin 240-567-9033 200 E sherwin.collette@montgomerycollege.edu
COLLEY, Debra 716-286-8317 309 F dcolley@niagara.edu
COLLEY, Jennifer 254-968-9769 445 F jcolley@tarleton.edu
COLLEY, Karen 312-413-2548 151 D karenc@uic.edu
COLLEY, Scott 318-473-6490 189 A scolley@lsua.edu
COLLIE, Richard 256-233-8100 4 D richard.collie@athens.edu
COLLIER, Annina 918-595-7050 370 B annina.collier@tulsacc.edu
COLLIER, Barry, S 317-940-8421 153 H bcollier@butler.edu
COLLIER, Brenda 585-582-8220 298 E brendacollier@elim.edu
COLLIER, Bridget 773-702-5671 151 B bcollier@uchicago.edu
COLLIER, Eartha, W 405-466-3210 366 B eartha.collier@langston.edu
COLLIER, Gail 405-491-6333 369 G gcollier@snu.edu
COLLIER, Hemie 319-895-5950 164 E hcollier@cornellcollege.edu
COLLIER, Holley 903-677-8822 451 C holley.collier@tvcc.edu
COLLIER, Isaiah 785-670-1723 178 A isaiah.collier@washburn.edu
COLLIER, Jackie 859-985-3110 179 E collierj@berea.edu
COLLIER, Jay 402-375-7325 267 I jacolli1@wsc.edu
COLLIER, Kristen, L 937-327-7523 364 C kcollier@wittenberg.edu
COLLIER, Li 707-524-1797 63 C lcollier@santarosa.edu
COLLIER, Rhonda 334-725-2307 7 D rcollier@tuskegee.edu
COLLIER, Sam 859-442-1146 181 D sam.collier@kctcs.edu
COLLIER, Yeman 210-567-7052 455 E colliery@uthscsa.edu
COLLIER-WALKER, Crystal 717-264-4141 402 D
COLLIGAN, Amanda 617-984-1727 217 G acolligan@quincycollege.edu
COLLIGNON, Kaitlyn 916-558-2442 51 B colligk@scc.losrios.edu
COLLING, Lynnde 307-268-2247 499 T lcolling@caspercollege.edu
COLLINGS, Clark 801-863-8898 460 A ccollings@uvu.edu
COLLINGS, Justin 801-422-0684 458 A justin_collings@byu.edu
COLLINGSWORTH, Rob 214-818-1319 433 A rcollingsworth@criswell.edu
COLLINGWOOD, Marlin 603-535-2475 274 B mcollingwood@plymouth.edu
COLLINS, Aaron 251-981-3771 5 B aaron.collins@columbiasouthern.edu
COLLINS, Alvin 713-718-8363 436 E alvin.collins@hccs.edu
COLLINS, Aristide, J 202-994-6500 92 C aristide@gwu.edu
COLLINS, Arthur 978-630-9188 215 A acollins@mwcc.mass.edu
COLLINS, Ashley 703-729-8800 93 H
COLLINS, Berkeley 202-885-6074 94 D bcollins@wesleyseminary.edu
COLLINS, Bob 801-274-3280 460 E robert.collins@wgu.edu
COLLINS, Breanna 972-721-5304 451 E bcollins@udallas.edu
COLLINS, Bryan 256-830-2626 5 D bcollins@faulkner.edu
COLLINS, Candy 301-423-3600 93 H
COLLINS, Carl 256-331-8010 3 C carl.collins@nwscc.edu
COLLINS, Carla 863-667-5012 108 I cdcollins@seu.edu
COLLINS, Carrie 215-871-6154 395 A carrieco@pcom.edu
COLLINS, Charlie 912-871-1632 123 F cpcollins@ogeecheetech.edu
COLLINS, Chelsea 229-928-4116 120 B chelsea.collins@gsw.edu
COLLINS, Chelsie 304-367-4214 488 L chelsea.collins@fairmontstate.edu
COLLINS, Christopher, J 651-962-5200 243 F christopher.collins@stthomas.edu
COLLINS, Craig 859-323-0301 185 D craig.collins@email.uky.edu
COLLINS, Dakota 765-983-1344 154 H collida@earlham.edu
COLLINS, Dana 580-349-1574 367 F dcollins@opsu.edu
COLLINS, Darron 207-801-5601 194 C dcollins@coa.edu
COLLINS, Dave 937-512-5182 360 F dave.collins@sinclair.edu
COLLINS, Dawn, M 773-508-3802 142 G dcollins4@luc.edu
COLLINS, Dean, C 706-385-1094 124 C dean.collins@point.edu
COLLINS, Deanne 770-533-6924 121 L dcollins@laniertech.edu
COLLINS, Deborah 309-647-7030 141 H dcollins@lakelandcollege.edu
COLLINS, Debra 860-773-1350 87 E dcollins@tunxis.edu
COLLINS, Denise 812-237-3087 155 H denise.collins@indstate.edu
COLLINS, Derrick, K 773-995-3505 134 J dkcollins@csu.edu
COLLINS, Donald 318-473-6427 189 A dcollins@lsua.edu
COLLINS, Elizabeth 303-860-5600 83 L elizabeth.collins@cu.edu
COLLINS, Ellen 617-323-6662 219 G ellen_collins@williamjes.edu
COLLINS, Emmanuel 502-852-6281 185 E emmanuel.collins@louisville.edu
COLLINS, Erin Michelle 909-621-8147 57 K erin.collins@pomona.edu
COLLINS, Ernest 215-635-7300 384 D ecollins@gratz.edu
COLLINS, Gary 478-301-2970 122 C collins_g@mercer.edu
COLLINS, Gregory 530-251-8889 47 I gcollins@lassencollege.edu
COLLINS, Holly 651-523-2800 235 F
COLLINS, Jacqueline, M 410-651-6407 203 B jmcollins@umes.edu
COLLINS, James, E 563-588-7103 167 I jim.collins@loras.edu
COLLINS, Jamie 910-272-3500 337 A jcollins@robeson.edu
COLLINS, Janna 651-635-8003 233 J j-collins@bethel.edu
COLLINS, Jennifer 504-816-4263 186 F jcollins@dillard.edu
COLLINS, Jennifer 850-599-8347 109 E jennifer.bowers@famu.edu
COLLINS, Jennifer 901-843-3730 422 C president@rhodes.edu
COLLINS, Jim 319-385-6280 167 F jim.collins@iw.edu
COLLINS, Jodie 360-475-7682 481 B jcollins@olympic.edu
COLLINS, John 315-228-7714 296 C jhcollins@colgate.edu
COLLINS, John, D 727-816-3310 105 E collinj@phsc.edu
COLLINS, Joseph 763-424-0964 239 D jcollins@nhcc.edu
COLLINS, Kamari 410-827-5858 198 B kcollins@chesapeake.edu
COLLINS, Ken 440-366-7738 355 B
COLLINS, Kimberley 585-292-2105 306 K kcollins@monroecc.edu
COLLINS, Kris 208-426-2484 130 F kcollin@boisestate.edu
COLLINS, Kristy 310-506-4116 56 H kristy.collins@pepperdine.edu
COLLINS, Kyle 515-965-7304 164 F kcollins16@dmacc.edu
COLLINS, Kyle 314-977-5353 258 H kyle.collins@health.slu.edu
COLLINS, Kyle, T 844-642-2338 168 F collinsky@nicc.edu
COLLINS, Lamont 757-490-1241 463 E lcollins@degree.auto.edu
COLLINS, Lance, R 571-384-4839 475 D lrcollins@vt.edu
COLLINS, Latrina 225-771-4312 190 K latrina_collinis@subr.edu
COLLINS, Leigh Ann 979-532-6520 457 H lacollins@wcjc.edu
COLLINS, Loleta 937-778-8600 352 D
COLLINS, Mark 425-352-8260 477 F mcollins@cascadia.edu
COLLINS, Mark, G 407-582-2375 113 C mcollins68@valenciacollege.edu
COLLINS, Mary 660-562-1599 256 G maryc@nwmissouri.edu
COLLINS, Mary, K 315-445-4791 303 F collinsm@lemoyne.edu
COLLINS, Mary Elizabeth 253-879-3237 483 G lcollins@pugetsound.edu
COLLINS, Matthew 989-463-7111 220 F collinsms@alma.edu

CONGER, Heather .... 609-894-9311 280 E
hconger@rcbc.edu
CONGLETON, Dawn, L .. 434-223-6203 466 K
dcongleton@hsc.edu
CONGLETON, Jonell .... 973-877-3068 276 G
jcongleton@essex.edu
CONGLETON, Trevor ..... 509-527-2256 484 C
trevor.congleton@wallawalla.edu
CONGLETON, Yasemin .. 859-246-6487 181 B
yasemin.congleton@kctcs.edu
CONI, Ilir .... 610-527-0200 396 G
ilir.coni@rosemont.edu
CONINE, Chris .... 423-614-8102 419 H
cconine@leeuniversity.edu
CONINE, Darren .... 978-837-5154 216 D
conined@merrimack.edu
CONKLIN, Christina ...... 716-488-3023 302 F
chrissyconklin@jbc.edu
CONKLIN, Claudia .... 601-925-3943 246 D
cconklin@mc.edu
CONKLIN, David .... 716-488-3026 302 F
davidconklin@jbc.edu
CONKLIN, Kathleen .... 517-371-5140 232 K
conklink@cooley.edu
CONKLIN, Lara, L .... 217-443-8798 136 E
l.conklin@dacc.edu
CONKLIN, Peggy .... 606-589-3336 182 F
peggy.conklin@kctcs.edu
CONKLIN, Peter .... 603-513-1384 273 I
peter.conklin@granite.edu
CONKLIN, Robin .... 845-574-4484 312 C
rconklin@sunyrockland.edu
CONKLIN, Shane, R ...... 413-545-1581 211 D
sconklin@admin.umass.edu
CONKLIN, Shannon ...... 609-771-2161 275 J
conklins@tcnj.edu
CONKLIN BUESCHEL,
Andrea .... 848-932-7454 281 A
andrea.bueschel@rutgers.edu
CONKLIN BUESCHEL,
Andrea .... 848-932-7454 281 B
andrea.bueschel@rutgers.edu
CONKLIN BUESCHEL,
Andrea .... 848-932-7454 281 C
andrea.bueschel@rutgers.edu
CONLEY, Amanda, K ..... 606-759-7141 182 B
amanda.conley@kctcs.edu
CONLEY, Carlotta .... 847-543-2345 135 G
chd340@clcillinois.edu
CONLEY, Cynthia .... 651-690-6525 242 F
caconley@stkate.edu
CONLEY, Dennis .... 618-395-7777 139 F
conleyd@iecc.edu
CONLEY, Fatimah, R ..... 302-831-7361.. 91 A
fconley@udel.edu
CONLEY, Jen .... 860-768-4665.. 89 E
jconley@hartford.edu
CONLEY, Jerome .... 513-529-2800 356 A
conleyj@miamioh.edu
CONLEY, Kelli .... 256-840-4101.... 3 F
kelli.conley@snead.edu
CONLEY, Laura, H .... 330-972-5793 361 G
lhc1@uakron.edu
CONLEY, Mark .... 206-543-4211 484 A
mconley@uw.edu
CONLEY, Tony .... 870-759-4166.. 24 B
tconley@williamsbu.edu
CONLIN, Katryn .... 651-385-6364 238 J
kconlin@southeastmn.edu
CONLIN, Pam .... 419-372-7678 348 F
pconlin@bgsu.edu
CONLISK, Elizabeth .... 608-363-2625 490 I
conliske@beloit.edu
CONLON, Cindy .... 256-765-4274.... 8 E
chconlon@una.edu
CONLON, Cindy, H .... 256-765-4293.... 8 E
chconlon@una.edu
CONLON, Jim .... 609-896-5188 280 D
jconlon@rider.edu
CONLON, Maureen .... 732-255-0400 279 A
mconlon@ocean.edu
CONN, Brian .... 423-614-8621 419 H
bconn@leeuniversity.edu
CONN, Cameron, A ...... 901-572-2538 417 A
cameron.conn@baptistu.edu
CONN, Jeana Rae .... 918-343-7707 369 A
jconn@rsu.edu
CONN, Megan .... 603-206-8005 272 A
mconn@ccsnh.edu
CONN, Michael .... 618-395-7777 139 F
connm@iecc.edu
CONN, Nerissa .... 215-455-2300 378 F
CONN, Robert .... 618-262-8641 139 G
connr@iecc.edu
CONN, Steve .... 903-233-4431 438 C
steveconn@letu.edu
CONNAGHAN, Stephen . 202-319-5055.. 91 G
connaghan@cua.edu
CONNEELY, James .... 706-864-1818 126 G
james.conneely@ung.edu
CONNELL, Dan, J .... 606-783-2612 183 H
d.connell@moreheadstate.edu
CONNELL, Gregory .... 321-674-8095 100 A
gconnell@fit.edu
CONNELL, Jack .... 617-745-3703 208 F
jack.connell@enc.edu
CONNELL, Joseph .... 201-684-7462 280 B
jconnell@ramapo.edu
CONNELL, Matthew .... 212-634-2231 322 B
matthew.connell2@touro.edu
CONNELL, Mike .... 509-335-5865 484 D
connell@wsu.edu
CONNELL, Steven .... 215-972-2027 392 P
sconnell@pafa.edu
CONNELLY, Christian .... 914-888-5226 305 H
cconnelly@mercy.edu
CONNELLY, David .... 801-863-8642 460 A
dconnelly@uvu.edu
CONNELLY, Judy .... 815-280-2265 140 I
jconnell@jjc.edu
CONNELLY, Katherine ... 212-875-4515 290 F
kconnelly@bankstreet.edu
CONNELLY, Krysti, H .... 618-537-6861 143 G
khconnelly@mckendree.edu
CONNELLY, Maureen, T 888-576-3348.. 46 M
CONNELLY, Pamela, W . 412-396-6000 382 E
CONNELLY, Robert .... 215-489-2346 381 K
robert.connelly@delval.edu
CONNELLY, Scott .... 815-772-7218 145 A
CONNELLY, Susan .... 602-275-7133.. 15 P
susan.connelly@rsi.edu
CONNELLY GOIDAS,
Traci .... 215-641-6529 390 A
tconnellygoidas@mc3.edu
CONNELY, Colby .... 641-784-5141 166 B
connely@graceland.edu
CONNER, Arabie .... 785-242-5200 176 F
arabie.conner@ottawa.edu
CONNER, Barbara .... 207-741-5571 195 D
bconner@smccme.edu
CONNER, Cassandra ...... 228-702-1829 249 B
cconner@wmcarey.edu
CONNER, Dyonne .... 601-979-2021 245 G
0364mgr@follett.com
CONNER, Jamelle .... 727-341-3344 107 C
conner.jamelle@spcollege.edu
CONNER, Kristin .... 707-864-7000.. 64 F
kristin.conner@solano.edu
CONNER, Lori .... 276-656-0286 473 H
lconner@patrickhenry.edu
CONNER, Marc, C .... 518-580-5700 315 A
mconner@skidmore.edu
CONNER, Michael .... 304-243-2317 490 F
mconner@wheeling.edu
CONNER, Sheila .... 304-384-5385 488 K
conners@concord.edu
CONNER, Steven .... 850-644-2145 110 B
sconner@fsu.edu
CONNER, III, Thomas .... 304-205-6738 487 D
thomas.conner@bridgevalley.edu
CONNER, Tracy .... 815-802-8405 141 B
tconner@kcc.edu
CONNER-STRINGER,
Courtney, L .... 276-619-4317 471 G
cstringer@uvawise.edu
CONNERAT, Carolyn, K . 512-475-9223 454 C
connerat@austin.utexas.edu
CONNETT, David .... 909-469-5423.. 75 G
dconnett@westernu.edu
CONNIRY, Charles .... 503-517-1860 377 D
cconniry@westernseminary.edu
CONNOLLY, Ann Marie . 313-883-8500 229 J
connolly.annmarie@shms.edu
CONNOLLY, Barbara ..... 845-569-3202 307 B
barbara.connolly@msmc.edu
CONNOLLY, Derry .... 858-653-6740.. 46 L
dconnolly@jpcatholic.com
CONNOLLY, James .... 203-332-5090.. 86 E
jconnolly@hcc.commnet.edu
CONNOLLY, Jerry .... 239-489-9203 100 G
jconnolly1@fsw.edu
CONNOLLY, Jim .... 617-305-5123 218 G
jconnolly2@suffolk.edu
CONNOLLY, Jon, H .... 973-300-2120 283 B
jconnolly@sussex.edu
CONNOLLY, Justin .... 256-766-6610.... 5 F
jconnolly@hcu.edu
CONNOLLY, Laura .... 970-351-2707.. 84 D
laura.connolly@unco.edu
CONNOLLY, Lidy .... 858-653-6740.. 46 L
lconnolly@jpcatholic.com
CONNOLLY, Mary .... 314-977-7121 258 H
mary.connolly@slu.edu
CONNOLLY, Melissa, A 516-463-4160 301 E
melissa.a.connolly@hofstra.edu
CONNOLLY, Michael ...... 320-363-2737 242 G
mconnolly@csbsju.edu
CONNOLLY, Michael ...... 320-363-3512 242 G
mconnolly@csbsju.edu
CONNOLLY, Robert .... 404-894-2500 119 D
robert.connolly@police.gatech.edu
CONNOLLY, Sandra .... 910-893-1241 327 C
sconnolly@campbell.edu
CONNOLLY, Shawn, M . 973-655-5427 278 C
connollys@montclair.edu
CONNOLLY, Tara .... 515-964-6447 164 F
tkconnolly@dmacc.edu
CONNOR, Andrea .... 847-735-5200 141 F
conner@lakeforest.edu
CONNOR, Anissa .... 203-672-6661.. 85 C
aconner@albertus.edu
CONNOR, Cammie .... 314-340-5089 253 E
connorc@hssu.edu
CONNOR, James .... 510-592-9688.. 61 D
jim.connor@npu.edu
CONNOR, Kate .... 773-907-4452 134 N
kconnor@ccc.edu
CONNOR, Kevin .... 501-623-2272.. 19 C
CONNOR, Liz .... 386-822-7736 111 F
econnor@stetson.edu
CONNOR, Rianne .... 707-476-4187.. 58 I
rianne-connor@redwoods.edu
CONNOR, Terry, D .... 859-344-3308 184 G
connort@thomasmore.edu
CONNORS,
Anne-Marie, E .... 216-523-7221 350 G
a.e.connors@csuohio.edu
CONNORS, Brian .... 516-323-3504 306 I
bconnors@molloy.edu
CONNORS, Cheryl, C .... 401-739-5000 403 F
cconnors@neit.edu
CONNORS, Christopher 609-652-4836 283 A
chris.connors@stockton.edu
CONNORS, Joan .... 863-297-1039 106 A
jconnors@polk.edu
CONNORS, John .... 215-596-8973 400 B
j.connors@usciences.edu
CONNORS, Natalie .... 219-989-2600 160 A
natalie.connors@pnw.edu
CONNORS, Robert .... 216-397-1946 353 O
rconnors@jcu.edu
CONNOT, Matthew .... 209-588-5383.. 76 J
connotm@yosemite.edu
CONOLEY, Jane, C .... 562-985-4121.. 32 A
csulb-president@csulb.edu
CONOVER, David .... 419-267-1462 357 E
dconover@northweststate.edu
CONOVER, Dustin .... 307-382-1644 500 I
dconover@westernwyoming.edu
CONOVER, Melanie .... 801-524-1927 458 F
conoverm@ldsbc.edu
CONOVER, Phillip .... 217-228-5432 147 C
conoverp@quincy.edu
CONQUE, Chasse .... 956-665-5301 455 A
chasse.conque@utrgv.edu
CONQUEST, Jonathon ... 810-762-9932 225 F
jconques@kettering.edu
CONRAD, Ann .... 216-987-2464 351 D
ann.conrad@tri-c.edu
CONRAD, Ben .... 913-469-8500 174 F
bconrad5@jccc.edu
CONRAD, Craig .... 309-298-2442 152 I
ca-conrad1@wiu.edu
CONRAD, Cynthia, M ... 314-516-4148 260 E
cconrad@umsl.edu
CONRAD, Deb .... 775-445-4236 271 A
deb.conrad@wnc.edu
CONRAD, Jacqueline .... 518-580-5733 315 A
jconrad@skimore.edu
CONRAD, James, A ...... 509-535-4051 144 F
jim.conrad@moody.edu
CONRAD, Jon .... 717-290-8713 387 F
CONRAD, Jon, B .... 610-861-1527 390 D
conradj@moravian.edu
CONRAD, Karen .... 518-438-2586 305 B
kconrad@mariacollege.edu
CONRAD, Kari, M .... 570-577-1217 379 A
kari.conrad@bucknell.edu
CONRAD, Kelley .... 231-777-0321 228 C
kelley.conrad@muskegoncc.edu
CONRAD, Kristin .... 434-592-4941 467 E
klconrad@liberty.edu
CONRAD, Lara .... 614-251-4718 358 B
conradl@ohiodominican.edu
CONRAD, Rhonda .... 641-683-5115 166 F
rhonda.conrad@indianhills.edu
CONRAD, Sonya .... 484-664-3126 390 F
sonyaconrad@muhlenberg.edu
CONRAD SKOGLUND,
Marcie .... 612-767-7097 233 E
marcie.skoglund@alfedadler.edu
CONRAD WEISMAN,
Sarah .... 315-312-3557 318 B
sarah.weisman@oswego.edu
CONRADSEN, Susan ..... 706-236-5494 116 A
sconradsen@berry.edu
CONREY, Meredith .... 936-294-3602 449 E
meredithconrey@shsu.edu
CONROY, Kristen .... 617-732-1714 209 A
conroyk@emmanuel.edu
CONROY, Kristie .... 516-323-4836 306 I
kconroy@molloy.edu
CONROY, Sarah .... 510-849-8200.. 55 F
CONROY, Spencer .... 713-525-6960 453 H
conroysc@stthom.edu
CONSELYEA, Mark, E .... 614-293-2562 358 E
conselyea.1@osu.edu
CONSIDINE-FONTES,
Lisa, M .... 401-825-2444 403 D
lfontes@ccri.edu
CONSOLVO, Justin .... 843-953-5600 406 D
consolvoj1@citadel.edu
CONSTABLE, Amanda .... 610-519-6456 401 B
amanda.constable@villanova.edu
CONSTABLE, Peter .... 217-333-2760 151 F
constabl@illinois.edu
CONSTANT, Jason .... 318-342-1028 193 A
bconstant@ulm.edu
CONSTANT, Kristin, P ... 515-294-3337 163 E
constant@iastate.edu
CONSTANTINE, OSB,
Cyprian, G .... 724-805-2332 397 D
cyprian.constantine@stvincent.edu
CONSTANTINE, Liane .... 314-516-6983 260 E
constantinel@umsl.edu
CONSTANTINE, Thomas 518-388-6358 323 B
constant@union.edu
CONSTANTINO, John .... 808-245-8245 129 H
johncons@hawaii.edu
CONSTANTINO, Patricia 617-745-3724 208 F
patricia.constantino@enc.edu
CONSTANTINO, Rocco .. 805-965-0581.. 62 M
rfconstantino@sbcc.edu
CONSTANTINOU,
Constantia .... 215-898-7091 399 J
cc1@upenn.edu
CONSTON, Marcia .... 757-822-1122 474 G
CONTARDI, Heather ...... 570-342-8000 383 F
hcontardi@fortisinstitute.edu
CONTARINO, Sue .... 847-925-6200 138 E
scontari@harpercollege.edu
CONTE, Andrew .... 412-392-8055 395 H
aconte@pointpark.edu
CONTE, Angela .... 562-985-5146.. 32 A
angela.conte@csulb.edu
CONTENTO, Anthony ..... 315-684-6367 320 E
contental@morrisville.edu
CONTESSA, Teresa .... 607-778-5407 317 A
contessatl99@sunybroome.edu
CONTINETTI, Robert, E . 858-534-3131.. 70 C
savcaa@ucsd.edu
CONTOMANOLIS,
Laurel .... 585-275-3166 323 E
laurel.contomanolis@rochester.edu
CONTRERAS, Adriana ..... 210-784-1115 447 B
acontreras@tamusa.edu
CONTRERAS,
Eduardo, R .... 503-943-8266 376 H
contrera@up.edu
CONTRERAS,
Frances, E .... 949-824-4732.. 69 C
frances.contreras@uci.edu
CONTRERAS, Gilbert .... 714-992-7074.. 54 D
gcontreras@fullcoll.edu
CONTRERAS, Lorraine ... 787-753-6000 506 B
lcontreras@icprjc.edu
CONTRERAS, Martin ..... 254-968-9650 445 F
mcontreras1@tarleton.edu
CONTRERAS, Pablo .... 509-865-8606 480 B
contreras_p@heritage.edu
CONTRERAS, Rita .... 303-458-4347.. 83 B
rcontreras001@regis.edu
CONTRERAS, Rosalie .... 212-799-5000 303 B

COOPER, Ian .... 410-287-1625 198 A
mcooper@cecil.edu
COOPER, James .... 619-239-0391.. 34 H
jcooper@cwsl.edu
COOPER, Jamie .... 803-327-8000 413 F
jcooper@yorktech.edu
COOPER, Jeffrey .... 215-898-1388 399 J
jeffcoop@upenn.edu
COOPER, Jennifer .... 423-697-2437 423 B
COOPER, Jeremy .... 303-466-1714.. 83 G
jeremy.cooper@spartan.edu
COOPER, Jessica .... 606-783-5159 183 H
j.cooper@moreheadstate.edu
COOPER, Jessica .... 210-486-2217 428 C
jshaw36@alamo.edu
COOPER, Jim .... 610-902-8275 379 E
jc7027@cabrini.edu
COOPER, Jonathan, A ... 410-543-6202 204 A
jacooper@salisbury.edu
COOPER, Jorsene .... 757-727-5323 466 L
jorsene.cooper@hamptonu.edu
COOPER, Joseph .... 715-682-1230 493 G
jcooper@northland.edu
COOPER, Joy .... 212-472-1500 309 B
giving@nysid.edu
COOPER, Karen .... 603-897-8508 273 B
kcooper@rivier.edu
COOPER, Karen, S .... 650-723-0198.. 66 D
karen.cooper@stanford.edu
COOPER, Katie, R .... 304-336-8131 489 B
katie.cooper@westliberty.edu
COOPER, Kenneth .... 925-424-1013.. 36 A
kcooper@laspositascollege.edu
COOPER, Kevin .... 501-375-9845.. 21 A
kcooper@philander.edu
COOPER, Kevin .... 772-462-7546 102 E
kcooper@irsc.edu
COOPER, Kevin .... 734-384-4128 227 F
kcooper@monroeccc.edu
COOPER, Kristen .... 434-544-8112 470 K
cooper.k@lynchburg.edu
COOPER, Kyle .... 432-264-5044 436 H
kcooper@howardcollege.edu
COOPER, Layton .... 605-626-2544 415 H
layton.cooper@northern.edu
COOPER, Lesley .... 815-802-8370 141 B
lcooper@kcc.edu
COOPER, Linda .... 260-665-4124 161 C
cooperl@trine.edu
COOPER, Lisa, A .... 229-931-2921 120 B
lisa.cooper@gsw.edu
COOPER, Lyndon, F ...... 804-828-7235 472 D
cooperlf@vcu.edu
COOPER, Mark .... 614-251-4576 358 B
cooperm2@ohiodominican.edu
COOPER, Mary Kay .... 210-784-1121 447 B
mary.cooper@tamusa.edu
COOPER, Mary-Beth, A . 413-748-3241 218 E
mbcooper@springfield.edu
COOPER, Matt .... 434-592-6376 467 E
mcooper9@liberty.edu
COOPER, Matthew .... 609-292-6317 283 D
mcooper@tesu.edu
COOPER, Matthew .... 907-450-8080.... 9 I
mcooper10@alaska.edu
COOPER, Micah .... 937-766-7905 349 C
micahcooper@cedarville.edu
COOPER, Michelle .... 678-916-2675 115 G
mcooper@johnmarshall.edu
COOPER, Mila .... 937-767-0123 347 E
mcooper@antiochcollege.edu
COOPER, Natalie, F .... 270-824-8599 182 A
natalie.cooper@kctcs.edu
COOPER, Paige .... 512-568-1422 456 C
cooper_p@utpb.edu
COOPER, Pam .... 479-498-6028.. 18 E
pcooper@atu.edu
COOPER, Paul .... 631-451-4445 320 G
cooperp@sunysuffolk.edu
COOPER, Peter .... 423-236-2165 422 H
cooperp@southern.edu
COOPER, Rick .... 251-981-3771.... 5 B
rick.cooper@columbiasouthern.edu
COOPER, Rosemary ...... 903-565-5535 455 C
rcooper@uttyler.edu
COOPER, Ruth .... 512-313-3000 432 N
ruth.cooper@concordia.edu
COOPER, Shelly .... 504-282-4455 190 D
COOPER, Stephanie ...... 973-300-2161 283 B
scooper@sussex.edu
COOPER, Susan .... 270-706-8564 181 C
scooper0151@kctcs.edu
COOPER, Tana .... 620-792-9241 171 F
coopert@bartonccc.edu
COOPER, Tara, L .... 606-546-1241 185 B
tcooper@unionky.edu
COOPER, Tiffany .... 202-274-6085.. 94 B
tecooper@udc.edu
COOPER, Tomekia .... 229-430-3605 114 G
tcooper@albanytech.edu
COOPER, Tyson .... 540-261-8463 470 D
tyson.cooper@svu.edu
COOPER, Yolanda .... 216-368-3508 349 B
ylc6@case.edu
COOPER-JOHNSON,
Chrystal .... 910-672-1073 341 B
ccooper3@uncfsu.edu
COOPER WHITEHEAD,
Shawna .... 617-552-4796 207 A
shawna.cooper.whitehead@bc.edu
COOPER WILKINS, Lisa 415-239-3382.. 37 C
lcooperwilkins@ccsf.edu
COOPERRIDER-FRYMAN,
Theigha .... 541-881-5792 376 E
tcooperrider-fryman@tvcc.cc
COOROUGH, Randall .... 262-691-5168 499 A
rcoorough@wctc.edu
COOTER, Raelynn .... 215-503-6595 398 G
raelynn.cooter@jefferson.edu
COOTS, Frank .... 315-859-4144 300 F
fcoots@hamilton.edu
COOTS, Kevin .... 610-372-4721 396 A
kcoots@racc.edu
COP, Kenneth, B .... 732-932-7211 281 B
kcop@aps.rutgers.edu
COPAN, Walter .... 303-273-3000.. 79 A
wcopan@mines.edu
COPE, Aaron .... 616-538-2330 224 B
acope@gracechristian.edu
COPE, Jill .... 509-453-0374 481 G
jill.cope@perrytech.edu
COPE, Joe .... 585-245-5531 317 E
cope@geneseo.edu
COPE, Joey .... 325-674-2000 427 G
copej@acu.edu
COPE, Marla .... 913-234-0687 172 I
marla.cope@cleveland.edu
COPE, Matt .... 903-566-7325 455 C
mcope@uttyler.edu
COPE, Michael .... 310-506-4270.. 56 H
mike.cope@pepperdine.edu
COPE, Tara .... 518-782-6987 314 K
tcope@siena.edu
COPELAND, Ashley .... 678-664-0525 127 E
ashley.copeland@westgatech.edu
COPELAND, Benjamin ... 434-961-5207 474 B
bcopeland@pvcc.edu
COPELAND, Cathy .... 425-739-8156 480 D
cathy.copeland@lwtech.edu
COPELAND, D. Gayle .... 559-453-2031.. 43 D
gayle.copeland@fresno.edu
COPELAND, David, L .... 540-464-7218 475 C
copelanddl@vmi.edu
COPELAND, Ebony, R ... 202-806-7540.. 92 E
ebony.copeland@howard.edu
COPELAND, Jackie .... 919-962-2315 342 B
jackie_copeland@unc.edu
COPELAND, Kristopher . 918-595-7224 370 B
kristopher.copeland@tulsacc.edu
COPELAND, Leigh .... 843-525-8231 411 G
lcopeland@tcl.edu
COPELAND, Lena .... 321-433-5631.. 98 F
copelandl@easternflorida.edu
COPELAND, Marcus .... 870-574-4778.. 21 F
mcopelan@sautech.edu
COPELAND, Maura .... 912-478-7481 120 A
mconley@georgiasouthern.edu
COPELAND, Michele ..... 612-659-6248 238 C
michele.copeland@minneapolis.edu
COPELAND, JR.,
P. Kenneth .... 434-223-6216 466 K
kcopeland@hsc.edu
COPELAND, Richard ...... 918-444-2536 366 G
copelanr@nsuok.edu
COPELAND-MORGAN,
Youlonda .... 310-825-2665.. 69 D
ycopeland-morgan@saonet.ucla.edu
COPELIN, Laylan .... 979-458-6425 445 D
lcopelin@tamus.edu
COPENHAVER, Bonny ... 304-929-5472 487 G
bcopenhaver@newriver.edu
COPENHAVER, Diane, L 717-871-4950 394 B
diane.copenhaver@millersville.edu
COPENHAVER, Kristin .. 810-984-3881 230 A
COPENHAVER, Michael . 619-644-7000.. 44 H
michael.coppenhaver@gcccd.edu
COPLAN, Jan .... 802-387-7175 461 E
jancoplan@landmark.edu
COPLAND, Katherine ..... 917-493-4030 304 L
kcopland@msmnyc.edu
COPLEN, Amy .... 503-352-7252 375 B
amy.coplen@pacificu.edu
COPLEY, Gordon .... 562-985-5566.. 32 A
gordon.copley@csulb.edu
COPLEY-SPIVEY, Aaron . 773-256-0771 143 C
aaron.copley@lstc.edu
COPLIN, Kimberly, A .... 740-587-6243 351 K
coplin@denison.edu
COPLIN, Louis .... 518-629-7307 302 A
l.coplin@hvcc.edu
COPONITI, Laura, I ...... 405-224-3140 371 B
lcoponiti@usao.edu
COPONITI, Mick, D .... 405-224-3140 371 B
mcoponiti@usao.edu
COPONITI, Mike .... 405-224-3140 371 B
mcoponiti@usao.edu
COPP, Crista .... 310-338-1745.. 51 C
crista.copp@lmu.edu
COPPAGE, Chaste .... 405-466-3217 366 B
chaste.coppage@langston.edu
COPPEDGE, Robin .... 580-387-7000 366 E
rcoppedge@mscok.edu
COPPER, Christine .... 419-755-4753 357 B
ccopper@ncstatecollege.edu
COPPER GLENZ, Becky . 978-665-3564 212 C
bcopperg@fitchburgstate.edu
COPPERSMITH, Clifford 410-827-5802 198 B
ccoppersmith@chesapeake.edu
COPPERSMITH, Terri ..... 212-353-4136 297 C
terri.coppersmith@cooper.edu
COPPERWHEAT,
Melissa .... 315-792-5499 306 G
mcopperwheat@mvcc.edu
COPPINGER, Katherine . 914-674-7238 305 H
kcoppinger@mercy.edu
COPPLA, Colleen .... 973-655-4214 278 C
copplac@montclair.edu
COPPLE, Chad .... 618-437-5321 147 F
copplec@rlc.edu
COPPLE, James (Dean) . 865-694-6536 424 C
jdcopple@pstcc.edu
COPPLE, Ryan .... 760-921-5548.. 56 A
ryan.copple@paloverde.edu
COPPLE, Therese .... 712-279-5433 163 H
therese.copple@briarcliff.edu
COPPOLA, David .... 203-365-4809.. 88 H
coppolad@sacredheart.edu
COPPOLA, John .... 410-617-2345 199 G
jccoppola@loyola.edu
COPPOLA, Sandra .... 973-278-5400 274 J
sec@berkeleycollege.edu
COPPOLA, Sandra, E .... 973-278-5400 291 A
sec@berkeleycollege.edu
COPPOLA, Stephen, A .. 704-687-5965 342 C
scoppola@uncc.edu
COPPOLA, William .... 817-515-3001 445 A
william.coppola@tccd.edu
COPPOLA-WALLACE,
Rita .... 413-597-3493 220 A
rc2@williams.edu
COPPRUE, Lisa .... 972-860-8147 433 H
lcopprue@dcccd.edu
COQUEMONT, Kathryn .. 801-957-4186 460 D
kathryn.coquemont@slcc.edu
COQUEREL, Phoebe ...... 803-327-8000 413 F
CORA, Jesus .... 787-250-1912 507 C
jacora@metro.inter.edu
CORACE-LANGBEEN,
Annaliese .... 734-432-5245 226 G
acoracelangbeen@madonna.edu
CORAGGIO, Jackie .... 212-752-1530 303 G
jackie.coraggio@limcollege.edu
CORAZZINI, Joseph ...... 508-793-7614 207 F
jcorazzini@clarku.edu
CORBELL, Alicia .... 505-566-4034 287 G
corbella@sanjuancollege.edu
CORBELL, Kristen .... 336-334-4822 334 F
kacorbell@gtcc.edu
CORBETT, Ann .... 207-621-3145 196 E
annie@maine.edu
CORBETT, Diane .... 802-654-2000 462 A
dcorbett@smcvt.edu
CORBETT, Faith .... 718-260-5564 294 F
fcorbett@citytech.cuny.edu
CORBETT, Heather .... 207-753-6930 193 D
hcorbett@bates.edu
CORBETT, Lisa .... 607-431-4162 300 G
corbettl@hartwick.edu
CORBETT, Martin .... 315-781-3656 301 D
corbett@hws.edu
CORBETT, Patricia .... 603-428-2775 272 I
pcorbett@nec.edu
CORBETT, Reide .... 252-475-5428 340 H
corbettd@ecu.edu
CORBIE, Giselle .... 919-843-8271 342 B
gcorbie@med.unc.edu
CORBIN, David .... 866-323-0233.. 58 D
CORBIN, Donna .... 781-280-3200 214 G
CORBIN, Edith .... 856-222-9311 280 E
ecorbin@rcbc.edu
CORBIN, Kirsten .... 916-484-8363.. 50 J
corbink@arc.losrios.edu
CORBIN, Lisa .... 864-644-5035 411 D
lcorbin@swu.edu
CORBIN, Mark .... 610-399-2178 393 D
mcorbin@cheyney.edu
CORBIN, Russ .... 315-498-2831 310 C
corbinr@sunyocc.edu
CORBIN, Sue .... 216-373-5429 357 F
scorbin@ndc.edu
CORBITT, Sandra, K ...... 540-338-1776 468 D
slife@phc.edu
CORBITT, Timothy .... 315-229-5392 313 F
tcorbitt@stlawu.edu
CORBITT, Zach .... 864-596-9215 407 G
zach.corbitt@converse.edu
CORBY, John, T .... 330-972-7345 361 G
jcorby@uakron.edu
CORCHADO, Regina ...... 570-208-5900 386 G
reginacorchado@kings.edu
CORCORAN, D.J .... 978-934-3328 211 G
dj_corcoran@uml.edu
CORCORAN, Jerry, M .... 815-224-0404 140 D
jerry_corcoran@ivcc.edu
CORCORAN, Kate .... 610-902-8571 379 E
clc722@cabrini.edu
CORCORAN, Kristen ...... 814-472-3386 396 I
kcorcoran@francis.edu
CORCORAN, Kristen ...... 570-740-0429 388 G
CORCORAN, Paul .... 507-389-2267 238 L
paul.corcoran@mnsu.edu
CORCORAN, William ..... 570-208-5846 386 G
wmcorcor@kings.edu
CORDA HADJAOUI,
Jamie .... 217-238-8286 141 H
jcorda12886@lakelandcollege.edu
CORDAHL, Susan .... 701-788-4767 345 B
susan.cordahl@mayvillestate.edu
CORDANO,
Roberta (Bobbi) .... 202-651-5005.. 92 B
roberta.cordano@gallaudet.edu
CORDEIRO, Aaron .... 541-485-1780 374 C
aaroncordeiro@newhope.edu
CORDEIRO, Uilani .... 541-485-1780 374 C
uilanicordeiro@newhope.edu
CORDEIRO, Wayne .... 541-485-1780 374 C
waynecordeiro@newhope.edu
CORDELL, Heather .... 562-944-0351.. 27 E
heather.cordell@biola.edu
CORDELL, Michelle .... 479-619-4361.. 20 G
mcordell@nwacc.edu
CORDELL, Stacey .... 318-342-1982 193 A
ulm@campuscornerinc.com
CORDER, Brad .... 214-818-1340 433 A
bcorder@criswell.edu
CORDER, Matt .... 903-463-8638 435 H
corderm@grayson.edu
CORDERO, April .... 619-849-2328.. 57 J
acordero@pointloma.edu
CORDERO, Edwin .... 864-578-8770 410 G
ecordero@sherman.edu
CORDERO, Eunice .... 787-284-1912 507 D
ecordero@ponce.inter.edu
CORDERO, Irma, L .... 787-740-1611 509 F
irma.cordero@uccaribe.edu
CORDERO, Javier .... 575-646-3553 286 G
javierco@nmsu.edu
CORDERO, John .... 757-352-4752 469 D
jacordero@regent.edu
CORDERO, Zain .... 787-882-2065 508 N
zcordero@unitecpr.edu
CORDERO-RIVERA,
Marisol .... 787-993-8874 510 E
marisol.cordero@upr.edu
CORDERY, Simon .... 706-864-1819 126 G
simon.cordery@ung.edu
CORDISCO, Shelli .... 607-778-5222 317 A
cordiscosl@sunybroome.edu
CORDLE, Emma .... 706-236-2267 116 A
ecordle@berry.edu
CORDOBA-VELÁSQUEZ,
Natalia .... 619-388-6723.. 60 H
ncordoba@sdccd.edu

CORDOVA, Andrea .... 719-255-3056.. 84 A
andrea.cordova@uccs.edu
CORDOVA, Anthony ...... 661-395-4787.. 47 B
anthony.cordova@bakersfieldcollege.edu
CORDOVA, Ferando ...... 318-342-1537 193 A
fcordova@ulm.edu
CORDOVA, Francie .... 505-277-5251 288 C
fcordova3@unm.edu
CORDOVA, Gary .... 808-735-4772 128 C
gary.cordova@chaminade.edu
CORDOVA, Jose .... 787-704-1020 505 B
jcordova@columbiacentral.edu
CORDOVA, Kelly .... 757-455-3366 476 C
kcordova@vwu.edu
CORDOVA, Lonita .... 209-954-5632.. 61 H
lonita.cordova@deltacollege.edu
CORDOVA, Matthew ...... 505-454-2559 285 I
mcordova@luna.edu
CORDOVA, Mitch .... 239-590-1522 109 G
mcordova@fgcu.edu
CORDOVA, Ryan .... 505-747-2288 287 C
rcordova@nnmc.edu
CORDOVA-CHAVARRY,
Edna .... 310-287-4429.. 50 C
chavarer@wlac.edu
CORDOVA-FIGUEROA,
Ubaldo, M .... 787-765-5955 510 B
ubaldom.cordova@upr.edu
CORDOVA-KIBIGER,
Michelle, J 260-470-2746 158W
mjcordova-kibiger@manchester.edu
CORDOVA QUERO,
Hugo .... 510-430-3335.. 66 F
hquero@sksm.edu
CORDRAY, Mary .... 843-208-8139 412 C
marymac@uscb.edu
CORDREY, Terri .... 605-882-5284 414 D
terri.cordrey@lakeareatech.edu
CORDULACK, Tricia ...... 217-875-7211 147 G
tcordulack@richland.edu
CORE, Kate .... 903-813-2050 429 I
kshelley@austincollege.edu
COREIL, Paul .... 318-473-6444 189 A
chancellor@lsua.edu
CORELLA, Yvanna .... 303-914-6905.. 82 L
yvanna.corella@rrcc.edu
COREY, Barry, H .... 562-903-4701.. 27 E
president@biola.edu
COREY, George, A .... 413-577-5211 211 D
gcorey@uhs.umass.edu
COREY, Jane .... 304-637-1344 486 D
coreym@dewv.edu
COREY, Laura .... 217-245-3010 139 A
lcorey@ic.edu
COREY, Leslie .... 662-325-2228 247 A
lcorey@hrm.msstate.edu
COREY, Shannon .... 404-413-1800 120 C
scorey@gsu.edu
COREY, Steven .... 312-369-7844 136 C
scorey@colum.edu
COREY, Steven, M .... 269-749-7642 229 G
presidentsoffice@olivetcollege.edu
CORGAN, Sean .... 215-951-1011 386 I
CORIA, Elizabeth .... 805-546-3116.. 41 A
elizabeth_coria@cuesta.edu
CORIA-NAVIA, Anneris .. 269-471-3249 220 H
anneris@andrews.edu
CORINO, Mark, A .... 973-618-3412 275 E
mcorino@caldwell.edu
CORK, Mark .... 208-467-8773 132 B
mcork@nnu.edu
CORKILL, Jim, R .... 805-893-5882.. 70 E
jim.corkill@bfs.ucsb.edu
CORKISH, Michele .... 208-467-8373 132 B
mcorkish@nnu.edu
CORKRAN, Ken .... 508-541-1700 208 E
kcorkran@dean.edu
CORKRUM, Dalia, L ...... 509-527-5193 485 C
corkrum@whitman.edu
CORKUM, David .... 617-552-4500 207 A
david.corkum@bc.edu
CORLE, Trish .... 814-262-3841 393 A
tcorle@pennhighlands.edu
CORLEW, Amy .... 931-221-6131 416 H
corlewa@apsu.edu
CORLEY, Chris .... 507-389-5953 238 L
christopher.corley@mnsu.edu
CORLEY, David .... 530-257-6181.. 47 I
dcorley@lassencollege.edu
CORLEY, Jazalyn .... 701-854-8073 346 F
jazalyn.corley@sittingbull.edu
CORLEY, Michelle .... 937-376-6276 349 H
mcorley@centralstate.edu
CORLEY, Robert .... 804-524-5999 475 E
rcorley@vsu.edu
CORLEY, Scott .... 615-460-5547 417 B
scott.corley@belmont.edu
CORLEY, Stacey .... 941-359-7674 106 J
scorley@ringling.edu
CORLEY, Thomas .... 785-242-5200 176 F
thomas.corley@ottawa.edu
CORLISS, Bruce .... 401-874-6222 404 E
bcorliss@uri.edu
CORLISS, Cindy .... 603-622-9941 272 A
0970mgr@follett.com
CORMACK, Ellen .... 706-864-1993 126 G
ellen.cormack@ung.edu
CORMACK, Jody .... 562-985-4128.. 32 A
jody.cormack@csulb.edu
CORMICAN, Beverly ...... 864-242-5100 405 H
CORMIER, Barbara .... 978-665-4342 212 C
bcormier8@fitchburgstate.edu
CORMIER, Craig, C .... 207-768-3425 196 I
craig.cormier@maine.edu
CORMIER, Garth .... 207-941-7626 194 D
cormierg@husson.edu
CORMIER, Linda .... 213-621-2200.. 38 G
CORN, Melanie .... 614-222-3220 351 A
mcorn@ccad.edu
CORNACCHIA,
Eugene, J .... 201-761-6010 282 H
ecornacchia@saintpeters.edu
CORNACCHIA, Lindsay .. 212-639-2496 304 H
cornaccl@mskcc.org
CORNACCHIO, Jennifer . 716-896-0700 324 A
jcornacchio@villa.edu
CORNEJO, Silvia .... 619-216-6755.. 65 K
scornejo@swccd.edu
CORNELISON, Steve .... 731-424-3520 423 F
scornelison@jscc.edu
CORNELIUS, Adrian, R .. 301-314-8249 202 E
adrianc@umd.edu
CORNELIUS, Allisa .... 432-335-6797 440 C
acornelius@odessa.edu
CORNELIUS, Amanda .... 928-523-8960.. 14 J
amanda.cornelius@nau.edu
CORNELIUS, Andrew ..... 208-467-8011 132 B
acornelius@nnu.edu
CORNELIUS, Barbara ..... 903-813-2536 429 I
bcornelius@austincollege.edu
CORNELIUS, Caleb .... 954-201-7350.. 96 F
CORNELIUS, Carrie .... 785-832-6659 174 A
ccornelius@haskell.edu
CORNELIUS, Jerod, L ... 651-631-5320 243 E
jlcornelius@unwsp.edu
CORNELIUS, Katherine .. 615-460-6856 417 B
katherine.cornelius@belmont.edu
CORNELIUS, Melvin ...... 773-298-3540 148 I
cornelius@sxu.edu
CORNELIUS, Owen .... 314-773-0083 250 C
ocornelius@brookes.edu
CORNELIUS, Susan .... 859-622-6216 180 B
susan.cornelius@eku.edu
CORNELIUS, Tim .... 479-619-3117.. 20 G
tcornelius@nwacc.edu
CORNELL, Cecilia .... 217-206-7230 151 E
ccorn1@uis.edu
CORNELL, Craig .... 540-831-6044 468 E
cwcornell@radford.edu
CORNELL, Dona, H .... 713-743-0949 451 G
dhcornell@uh.edu
CORNELL, Dona, H .... 832-842-0949 451 F
dhcornell@uh.edu
CORNELL, Karyn .... 707-654-1000.. 32 C
CORNELL, Ken .... 425-889-7800 481 A
ken.cornell@northwestu.edu
CORNELL, Lisa .... 706-880-8240 121 K
lcornell@lagrange.edu
CORNELL, Paul .... 845-368-7212 314 F
CORNELL, Robert .... 617-745-3705 208 F
robert.cornell@enc.edu
CORNELL, Starr .... 810-762-9759 225 F
scornell@kettering.edu
CORNELL, Tracey .... 207-216-4320 195 F
CORNELL-SCOTT,
Andrea .... 540-887-7380 467 G
ascott@marybaldwin.edu
CORNELL-SWANSON,
La Vonne .... 715-346-4686 496 B
lcornell@uwsp.edu
CORNELLI, Francesca .... 847-491-2840 146 C
francesca.cornelli@kellogg.northwestern.edu
CORNELY,
Pierre Richard .... 229-333-5699 127 C
pcornely@valdosta.edu
CORNER, Kimberly .... 402-465-7783 267 J
kcorner@nebrwesleyan.edu
CORNER, William, T ..... 616-526-6451 221 L
wtc2@calvin.edu
CORNETT, Doug .... 859-622-7286 180 B
doug.cornett@eku.edu
CORNETT, Jessalynn ..... 502-863-8302 179 B
jessalynn.cornett@bsk.edu
CORNETT, Scott .... 606-368-6120 178 D
scottcornett@alc.edu
CORNETT, Vicki .... 785-227-3380 171 H
cornettv@bethanylb.edu
CORNETTI, Bobbi Jo .... 724-287-8711 379 C
bobbi.cornetti@bc3.edu
CORNETTO, Kevin .... 215-702-4339 379 F
ccornetto@cairn.edu
CORNIE, Brandy .... 251-626-3303.... 7 E
bcornie@ussa.edu
CORNIER, Wilfredo .... 787-841-2000 508 H
wcornier@pucpr.edu
CORNILLE, Keith .... 309-268-8106 138 F
keith.cornille@heartland.edu
CORNISH, Charles .... 903-927-3253 457 I
chcornish@wileyc.edu
CORNISH, Denise .... 909-469-5672.. 75 G
dcornish@westernu.edu
CORNISH, La Jerne, T .. 607-274-3111 302 E
president@ithaca.edu
CORNMAN, Candy .... 573-876-7299 259 F
ccornman@stephens.edu
CORNMAN, Thomas ...... 503-375-7000 372 G
president@corban.edu
CORNOG, Jackie .... 617-588-1364 206 B
jcornog@bfit.edu
CORNWELL, Grant, H .... 407-646-2120 106 L
president@rollins.edu
CORNWELL, John, M .... 713-348-3227 441 K
cornwell@rice.edu
CORNWELL, Julia .... 817-272-2194 454 B
cornwell@uta.edu
CORONA, Guadalupe .... 619-482-6544.. 65 K
gcorona@swccd.edu
CORONA, Jamie, L .... 248-232-4513 228 H
jlcorona@oaklandcc.edu
CORONA, Robert .... 315-464-4238 316 F
coronar@upstate.edu
CORONA, Stacie .... 530-898-5103.. 31 A
scorona@csuchico.edu
CORONADO, Ian .... 541-463-5824 373 C
coronadoi@lanecc.edu
CORONADO, John .... 312-413-1401 151 D
jcoronad@uic.edu
CORONEL, Angel .... 305-821-3333 100 C
acoronel@fnu.edu
CORONEL, Roberto .... 714-744-7959.. 36 D
coronel@chapman.edu
CORP, Cory .... 803-786-3886 407 E
bookstore@columbiasc.edu
CORP, Stephanie .... 518-587-2100 320 B
stephanie.corp@esc.edu
CORPENING, Brian .... 831-582-3366.. 32 D
bcorpening@csumb.edu
CORR, Daniel, P .... 928-344-7501.. 11 B
daniel.corr@azwestern.edu
CORR, Marianne .... 574-631-6411 161 G
mcorr1@nd.edu
CORR, Michael .... 610-861-1365 390 D
corrm@moravian.edu
CORRADETTI, Arthur ..... 718-631-6350 295 B
acorradetti@qcc.cuny.edu
CORRADO, Colleen .... 610-436-2552 394 F
ccorrado@wcupa.edu
CORRADO, Kim .... 412-536-1152 386 H
kimberly.corrado@laroche.edu
CORRAL, Elsa .... 817-272-2101 454 B
corral@uta.edu
CORRAL, Nohel .... 562-938-4156.. 48 K
ncorral@lbcc.edu
CORREA, Alma .... 760-366-5279.. 40 K
acorrea@cmccd.edu
CORREA, Frank .... 714-966-8500.. 74 C
fcorrea@ves.edu
CORREA, Lisbel .... 787-284-1912 507 D
lmcorrea@ponce.inter.edu
CORREA, Magaly .... 860-773-1433.. 87 E
mcorrea@tunxis.edu
CORREA, Omar .... 651-962-5000 243 F
CORREALES, Robert ...... 702-895-2406 270 J
robert.correales@unlv.edu
CORRELL, Jen .... 717-728-2362 380 D
jencorrell@centralpenn.edu
CORRELL, Mary .... 610-409-3698 400 E
mcorrell@ursinus.edu
CORRELL, Scott .... 701-777-2711 344 H
scott.correll@und.edu
CORRELL-HUGHES,
Larry .... 386-822-7730 111 F
lcorrell-hughes@stetson.edu
CORRIGAN, Boo .... 919-515-2109 341 E
ecorrig@ncsu.edu
CORRIGAN, Constance . 215-497-8717 379 B
constance.corrigan@bucks.edu
CORRIGAN, JR.,
Robert, F .... 713-798-6392 430 E
corrigan@bcm.edu
CORRINGAN, Terrance .. 713-718-7278 436 E
terrance.corrigan@hccs.edu
CORRINGTON, Jesse .... 909-469-5417.. 75 G
jcorrington@westernu.edu
CORRINNE-HARVEY,
Janet, K .... 724-925-4091 401 H
corrinnej@westmoreland.edu
CORRY, David, M .... 434-592-4008 467 E
dcorry@liberty.edu
CORRY, Janie .... 864-488-4473 409 C
jcorry@limestone.edu
CORRY, Shauna .... 208-885-9301 132 C
scorry@uidaho.edu
CORSARO, Louis .... 412-392-6190 395 H
lcorsaro@pointpark.edu
CORSELLO, Christine .... 704-403-4336 327 B
christine.corsello@atriumhealth.org
CORSI, Richard .... 503-725-8393 375 D
rcorsi@pdx.edu
CORSINI, Kevin .... 619-201-8701.. 60 G
dr.kevin.corsini@sdcc.edu
CORSO, Michael .... 973-720-2202 283 I
corsom1@wpunj.edu
CORSO, Phaedra .... 470-578-6354 121 J
pcorso@kennesaw.edu
CORSON, Charles .... 229-209-5239 114 I
charlescorson@andrewcollege.edu
CORSON, Christina .... 517-264-3999 220 D
ccorson@adrian.edu
CORTÉS, Elizabeth .... 787-815-0000 510 D
elizabeth.cortes@upr.edu
CORTÉS, Gloria .... 787-891-0925 506 I
gcortes@aguadilla.inter.edu
CORTELL, Sabrina .... 619-594-0336.. 33 E
scortell@sdsu.edu
CORTES, Dario, A .... 305-442-9223 104 G
CORTES, Felix .... 787-841-2000 508 H
fcortes@pucpr.edu
CORTES, Frances .... 787-878-5475 506 J
fcortes@arecibo.inter.edu
CORTES, Gabriel .... 210-924-4338 430 D
gabriel.cortes@bua.edu
CORTES, Jorge .... 706-446-5732 115 I
jcortes1@augusta.edu
CORTES, Stephanie .... 352-854-2322.. 97 L
cortess@cf.edu
CORTES, Tammy, A .... 832-813-6820 438 E
tammy.a.cortes@lonestar.edu
CORTESIO, Cynthia .... 865-354-3000 424 D
cortesiocl@roanestate.edu
CORTEZ, Alicia .... 408-864-5338.. 42 K
cortezalicia@deanza.edu
CORTEZ, Carrie .... 985-448-7936 187 J
carrie.cortez@fletcher.edu
CORTEZ, Christina .... 210-486-2894 428 C
ccortez109@alamo.edu
CORTEZ, Dorinna .... 808-934-2510 129 F
dorinna@hawaii.edu
CORTEZ, Lori, A .... 815-835-6260 149 A
lori.a.cortez@svcc.edu
CORTEZ, Sandra .... 956-794-4982 438 A
sandra.cortez@laredo.edu
CORTEZ-DIAZ, Marisol . 954-201-7350.. 96 F
CORTINA, Mary .... 516-877-3259 288 L
cortina@adelphi.edu
CORTINAS, Andrea .... 915-747-5555 454 E
acortinas@utep.edu
CORTINAS, Debra .... 361-825-5743 446 E
debra.cortinas@tamucc.edu
CORTINAS, Jesse, A ..... 210-829-3830 452 D
jacortin@uiwtx.edu
CORTNER, Laquetta .... 614-837-4088 363 D
cortnerl@valorcollege.edu
CORUJO, Shaneen .... 803-705-4673 405 G
shaneen.corujo@benedict.edu
CORUM, Amanda .... 719-549-3163.. 82 I
amanda.corum@pueblocc.edu
CORVIN, Thim .... 540-231-7189 466 E
tcorvin@vcom.vt.edu
CORVINO, John .... 505-224-4639 285 B
jcorvino@cnm.edu

CORVINO, John ... 313-577-3030 232 H ae9123@wayne.edu
CORWIN, Jay ... 972-549-6320 432 I jcorwin@collin.edu
CORWIN, Katherine ... 631-687-5149 313 C kcorwin@sjcny.edu
CORWIN, Rhonda ... 620-665-3500 174 D corwinr@hutchcc.edu
CORYELL, Don ... 512-245-2114 449 G dc33@txstate.edu
COSAERT, Carl ... 509-527-2194 484 C carl.cosaert@wallawalla.edu
COSBY, Felicia ... 804-257-5616 475 G fdcosby@vuu.edu
COSBY, Glen ... 509-533-7015 478 D glen.cosby@scc.spokane.edu
COSBY, Kevin, W ... 502-776-1443 184 C kcosby@simmonscollegeky.edu
COSBY, Nadine ... 914-633-2354 302 C ncosby@iona.edu
COSBY, Sheliah ... 423-869-6353 420 A sheliah.cosby@lmunet.edu
COSCIA, Danielle ... 914-395-2365 314 H dcoscia@sarahlawrence.edu
COSCIA, Paul ... 336-917-5577 339 H paul.coscia@salem.edu
COSENTINO, Guy, T ... 315-255-1743 292 A gcosentino@cayuga-cc.edu
COSENTINO, Lauren ... 310-506-4898.. 56 H lauren.cosentino@pepperdine.edu
COSENTINO, Richard, E 864-388-8300 409 B cosentino@lander.edu
COSGROVE, Ellen ... 518-262-5919 289 C cosgroe@amc.edu
COSGROVE, Theresa ... 707-654-1000.. 32 C
COSIMO, Julie ... 815-836-5332 142 C gcosimo@lewisu.edu
COSKRAN, John ... 612-330-1000 233 G coskranj@augsburg.edu
COSMA, Allan ... 734-699-7008 232 B acosma1@wcccd.edu
COSNER BERZIN, Stephanie ... 617-521-2000 218 C
COSPER, Emily ... 504-671-6323 187 I ecospe@dcc.edu
COSS, Laura ... 724-852-7629 401 E lcoss@waynesburg.edu
COSS, Reydecel ... 575-562-2108 285 E reydecel.coss@enmu.edu
COSSAR, Nigel ... 215-898-9073 399 J ncossar@upenn.edu
COSSE, Ted ... 626-584-5501.. 43 E ted_cosse@fuller.edu
COSSEY, Jeannie ... 870-972-2030.. 17 I jcossey@astate.edu
COSSICH, Marc ... 850-474-2022 111 E mcossich@uwf.edu
COST, Michael, N ... 860-701-6727 502 F michael.n.cost@uscg.mil
COST, Timothy, P ... 904-256-7016 102 G tcost@ju.edu
COSTA, Dana ... 304-876-5465 489 A dcosta@shepherd.edu
COSTA, Daniel ... 831-459-2464.. 71 A costa@ucsc.edu
COSTA, Darin ... 310-233-4450.. 49 F costadv@lahc.edu
COSTA, Erik ... 860-701-5787.. 88 C costa_e@mitchell.edu
COSTA, Karen ... 716-829-7640 298 C costak@dyc.edu
COSTA, Kris ... 559-925-3218.. 75 A kriscosta@whccd.edu
COSTA, Linda, J ... 848-932-7711 281 B smeds@gradadm.rutgers.edu
COSTA, Vic ... 410-778-5080 204 E vcosta2@washcoll.edu
COSTANTINIDIS, Teresa 505-277-7520 288 C tcostant@unm.edu
COSTANTINO, Tracie ... 661-255-1050.. 28 I provost@calarts.edu
COSTANZA, Laina, T ... 334-387-3878.... 4 C lainacostanza@amridgeuniversity.edu
COSTANZO, Brian ... 570-961-7841 387 A costanzob@lackawanna.edu
COSTAS, Carolyn ... 787-841-2000 508 H ccostas@pucpr.edu
COSTAS, Pamela, G ... 312-915-6194 142 G pcostas@luc.edu
COSTELLO, Bernard, J ... 412-648-1938 400 A bjc1@pitt.edu
COSTELLO, Dan ... 512-245-9244 449 G cpo32@txstate.edu
COSTELLO, Dennis ... 586-445-7318 226 F costellod@macomb.edu
COSTELLO, Gregory, W . 507-344-7305 233 I gregory.costello@blc.edu
COSTELLO, Jamie ... 617-879-7703 212 E jcostello@massart.edu
COSTELLO, Kevin ... 617-327-6777 219 G kevin_costello@williamjames.edu
COSTELLO, Leon ... 406-994-4226 263 G lcostello@msubobcats.com
COSTELLO, Melanie ... 815-753-2111 145 H melcostello@niu.edu
COSTELLO, Richard, J ... 219-989-2539 160 A rick@pnw.edu
COSTELLO, sean ... 215-785-0111 392 O
COSTIGAN, Harry ... 610-359-5288 381 J hcostigan@dccc.edu
COSTIGAN, Rosemary ... 401-825-2142 403 D rcostigan@ccri.edu
COSTIN, Dondi, E ... 843-863-7502 406 C dcostin@csuniv.edu
COSTLEY, Lucien ... 830-895-7116 442 G vpaf@schreiner.edu
COSTNER, Beth ... 803-323-2151 413 D costnerb@winthrop.edu
COSTNER, Kelly ... 866-492-5336 243 G kelley.costner@mail.waldenu.edu
COSTOLA, Sergio ... 512-863-1373 444 F costolas@southwestern.edu
COSTON, Andrew ... 507-933-7575 235 E acoston@gustavus.edu
COSTON, Linda ... 229-430-2751 114 G lcoston@albanytech.edu
COSTON, Robert, H ... 304-647-6575 487 G rcoston@newriver.edu
COSTON, Sophia ... 216-659-7200 303 E sophia_coston@tkc.edu
COT, Alea ... 504-280-7484 189 F amcot@uno.edu
COTA, Clarissa ... 702-651-2728 270 F clarissa.cota@csn.edu
COTA, Marco ... 909-384-8630.. 60 F mcota@sbccd.cc.ca.us
COTE, Christine ... 509-453-0374 481 G christine.cote@perrytech.edu
COTE, Christy ... 907-745-3201.... 9 C ccote@akbible.edu
COTE, Erik ... 617-989-4590 219 D cotee1@wit.edu
COTE, Lori, A ... 401-865-1961 403 G lcote4@providence.edu
COTE, Matthew ... 907-745-3201.... 9 C mcote@akbible.edu
COTE, Melissa ... 603-752-1060 272 E mcote@ccsnh.edu
COTE, Robin ... 617-287-5777 211 E robin.cote@umb.edu
COTE-BONANNO, Joanne, F ... 973-655-6234 278 C bonannoj@montclair.edu
COTHAM, Brian ... 559-278-2111.. 31 D bcotham@csufresno.edu
COTHRAN, Ginger ... 580-387-7112 366 E gcothran@mscok.edu
COTHRAN, Grayson ... 276-523-7473 473 E gcothran@mecc.edu
COTHRAN, Rick ... 864-646-1701 411 H rcothran@tctc.edu
COTNOIR, Paul ... 508-798-4394 207 F pcotnoir@clarku.edu
COTO, Jennifer ... 714-628-4775.. 58 G coto_jennifer@sccollege.edu
COTSONES, Rena ... 815-753-9503 145 H rcotsones@niu.edu
COTSONIS, Joachim ... 617-850-1243 210 D jcotsonis@hchc.edu
COTTAM, Michael ... 304-724-3700 485 G mcottam@apus.edu
COTTER, Bob ... 513-487-1144 361 E bob.cotter@myunion.edu
COTTER, George ... 813-974-3340 111 B gcotter@usf.edu
COTTER, Jennifer, M ... 989-774-7155 221 M reihl1jm@cmich.edu
COTTER, Michael ... 914-594-3675 308 J michael_cotter@nymc.edu
COTTET, Sarah ... 914-594-4574 308 J sarah_cottet@nymc.edu
COTTI, Nadia ... 661-259-7800.. 38 H nadia.cotti@canyons.edu
COTTINGHAM, Ryan, T . 517-750-1200 230 F ryanc@arbor.edu
COTTO, JR., Jay ... 563-677-6633 169 B jcotto@orion.edu
COTTO, Zuleika ... 787-665-7910 505 B zucotto@columbiacentral.edu
COTTON, Art ... 405-974-3575 370 H acotton4@uco.edu
COTTON, Charles ... 269-387-1000 232 J charles.e.cotton@wmich.edu
COTTON, George ... 870-575-8911.. 22 F cottong@uapb.edu
COTTON, Gina ... 662-476-5063 245 C gcotton@eastms.edu
COTTON, Gregory ... 319-895-4454 164 E gcotton@cornellcollege.edu
COTTON, Leonard ... 662-329-7409 247 B sm8076@bncollege.com
COTTON, Nyla ... 310-434-4495.. 63 B cotton_nyla@smc.edu
COTTON, Renee ... 601-857-3364 245 D renee.cotton@hindscc.edu
COTTON, Sabrina ... 256-726-7408.... 6 C cotton@oakwood.edu
COTTON, Todd ... 205-726-4144.... 6 E tcotton@samford.edu
COTTON KELLY, Montique ... 860-486-2240.. 89 B mcottonkelly@foundation.uconn.edu
COTTONE, John ... 607-753-2701 317 D john.cottone@cortland.edu
COTTONER, Brittany ... 812-258-9510 154 B bcottoner@cariscollege.edu
COTTONHAM, Patricia ... 337-482-6266 192 F patcottonham@louisiana.edu
COTTRELL, Bryan ... 254-442-5173 431 J bryan.cottrell@cisco.edu
COTTRELL, Damon ... 940-898-2401 451 A dcottrell@twu.edu
COTTRELL, Danny ... 501-337-5000.. 18 D dcottrell@asutr.edu
COTTRELL, Debbie ... 830-372-8001 448 C president@tlu.edu
COTTRELL, Debbie ... 254-295-5059 453 A dcottrell@umhb.edu
COTTRELL, Jeffrey ... 325-670-1484 436 B jcottrell@hsutx.edu
COTTRELL, Liesl ... 773-252-5114 146 D liesl.cottrell@oakpoint.edu
COTTRELL, Terrance, L .. 815-740-5041 152 E tcottrell@stfrancis.edu
COTTRILL, Liesl ... 708-209-3053 136 D liesl.cottrill@cuchicago.edu
COUCH, Charlie ... 970-351-2231.. 84 D charlie.couch@unco.edu
COUCH, Cheryl ... 402-363-5696 269 F ccouch@york.edu
COUCH, Laurie, L ... 606-783-2434 183 H l.couch@moreheadstate.edu
COUCH, Lisa ... 760-384-6230.. 47 C lcouch@cerrocoso.edu
COUGHENOUR, Russ ... 931-372-6153 425 B rcoughenour@tntech.edu
COUGHLIN, Cass ... 620-341-5264 173 C ccoughli@emporia.edu
COUGHLIN, Chris ... 623-845-3205.. 13 E chris.coughlin@gccaz.edu
COUGHLIN, III, Jay, J .. 443-518-4032 199 D jcoughlin@howardcc.edu
COUGHLIN, JR., Kevin . 305-348-2320 109 H kevin.coughlinjr@fiu.edu
COUGHLIN, Mary Ann .. 413-748-3959 218 E mcoughlin@springfield.edu
COUGHLIN, Robert, D .. 860-685-2543.. 90 A rdcoughlin@wesleyan.edu
COUILLARD, Michael ... 719-502-3352.. 82 D mike.couillard@pikespeak.edu
COULE, Phillip, L ... 706-721-1083 115 I pcoule@augusta.edu
COULING, Mike ... 972-660-5701 438 D mcouling@lincolntech.com
COULLIETTE, Holly ... 904-808-7441 107 A hollycoulliette@sjrstate.edu
COULOMBE, Jennifer, B ... 336-734-7957 334 D jcoulombe@forsythtech.edu
COULON, Richard ... 949-824-4533.. 69 C rcoulon@uci.edu
COULOUTE, Clifford ... 718-997-5100 295 A clifford.couloute@qc.cuny.edu
COULSON, Joseph ... 877-248-6724.. 12 M jcoulson@hmu.edu
COULSTON, Susan ... 269-782-1396 230 D scoulston@swmich.edu
COULSTON BAUMANN, Liz ... 574-284-4569 160 F ecoulston@saintmarys.edu
COULTER, Ann ... 641-782-1340 170 B coulter@swcciowa.edu
COULTER, Cindy ... 828-327-7000 332 H ccoulter@cvcc.edu
COULTER, Denise ... 609-343-5007 274 E dcoulter@atlantic.edu
COULTER, Laurie ... 903-813-2900 429 I lcoulter@austincollege.edu
COULTER, Lisa ... 610-683-4072 394 A coulter@kutztown.edu
COULTER, Martha ... 802-468-1314 462 H martha.coulter@castleton.edu
COULTER, Seana ... 443-885-3110 200 F seana.coulter@morgan.edu
COUNCIL, Juanette ... 910-672-1208 341 B jcouncil@uncfsu.edu
COUNCIL, Mark ... 910-362-7009 332 F mcouncil@cfcc.edu
COUNCIL, Timothy ... 909-607-7811.. 37 F admissions@cgu.edu
COUNLEY, Meagan ... 402-472-3417 269 A mcounley2@unl.edu
COUNTEE, Jerome ... 559-243-7262.. 66 G jerome.countee@scccd.edu
COUNTIS, Amber ... 361-570-4829 452 C
COUNTS, LaNeta ... 404-471-6483 114 E lcounts@agnesscott.edu
COUNTS, Richard ... 501-977-2000.. 23 D
COUNTZ, Karen ... 803-780-1181 413 B kcountz@voorhees.edu
COUP, Brett ... 908-526-1200 280 C brett.coup@raritanval.edu
COUPE, Maria ... 845-398-4038 314 D mcoupe@stac.edu
COURCEY, Dan ... 802-443-5000 461 G dcourcey@middlebury.edu
COUREY, Scott ... 616-394-4287 222 F scott.courey@cornerstone.edu
COUREY, Susan ... 212-463-0400 322 C susan.courey@touro.edu
COURNOYER, Gerald ... 918-683-4581 365 B cournoyerg@bacone.edu
COURNOYER, Jennifer .. 603-542-7744 272 D jcournoyer@ccsnh.edu
COURSEY, Greg ... 706-437-6808 115 H gcoursey@augustatech.edu
COURSEY, Laura ... 903-923-2326 435 A lcoursey@etbu.edu
COURT, Christine ... 330-363-6347 348 B registrar@aultmancollege.edu
COURT, Cynthia ... 706-236-2261 116 A ccourt@berry.edu
COURT, Stephanie ... 206-543-5010 484 A shcourt@uw.edu
COURTEAU, Lindsay, M 724-847-6577 384 B lmcourte@geneva.edu
COURTEMANCHE, Brian 978-927-2278 209 B bcourtem@endicott.edu
COURTEY, Susan ... 818-240-1000.. 43 J susan@glendale.edu
COURTNEY, Dan ... 765-641-4004 153 D dacourtney@anderson.edu
COURTNEY, Daniel ... 765-641-4114 153 D dacourtney@anderson.edu
COURTNEY, Nycole ... 307-766-3920 500 H nf@uwyo.edu
COURTNEY, Sharon, P .. 504-988-3390 191 D sharonc@tulane.edu
COURVILLE, Barb ... 309-796-5000 133 D
COUSE, Leslie ... 603-862-0638 273 H leslie.couse@unh.edu
COUSINS, Amirah ... 718-289-5155 292 H amirah.cousins@bcc.cuny.edu
COUSINS, James, P ... 270-852-3117 183 B james.cousins@kwc.edu
COUSINS, Shelley ... 973-972-6715 281 C cousinsh@oit.rutgers.edu
COUTANT, Richard ... 860-738-6317.. 87 A rcoutant@nwcc.edu
COUTS, LeeAnn ... 740-392-6868 356 G leeann.couts@mvnu.edu
COUTS, Suzann ... 864-388-8335 409 B scouts@lander.edu
COUTTS, Christopher ... 540-351-1513 473 C ccoutts@lfcc.edu
COUTURE, Brandy ... 406-275-4977 264 H brandy_couture@skc.edu
COUTURE, Marie ... 414-847-3334 493 C mariecouture@miad.edu

CRAFT, Edwin .... 662-846-4760 245 A
ecraft@deltastate.edu
CRAFT, Jonathan .... 256-216-3310.... 4 D
jonathan.craft@athens.edu
CRAFT, Shonda, M .... 320-308-4894 240 C
smcraft@stcloudstate.edu
CRAFT, Tina .... 740-474-8896 358 A
tcraft@ohiochristian.edu
CRAFT, William, J .... 218-299-3000 234 K
president@cord.edu
CRAFTON, Linda .... 262-595-2341 495 D
crafton@uwp.edu
CRAFTON, Teresa .... 478-274-7833 123 E
tcrafton@oftc.edu
CRAFTS, Deborah .... 617-879-7805 212 E
dcrafts@massart.edu
CRAFTS, Deborah .... 978-556-3691 215 C
dcrafts@necc.mass.edu
CRAGAR, Beth .... 931-598-1312 422 F
bcragar@sewanee.edu
CRAGER, Cindy .... 609-626-3658 283 A
cindy.crager@stockton.edu
CRAGG, Michael .... 315-781-3740 301 D
cragg@hws.edu
CRAGG, Michael .... 718-990-6223 313 B
craggm@stjohns.edu
CRAGLE, Rachael, C .... 865-539-7219 424 C
rccragle@pstcc.edu
CRAHEN, Sherri .... 216-397-4423 353 O
scrahen@jcu.edu
CRAIDER, Holly .... 216-987-2006 351 D
holly.craider@tri-c.edu
CRAIG, Adrienne, M .... 336-334-5513 342 D
amcraig2@uncg.edu
CRAIG, Barbara .... 269-927-8147 226 B
craig@lakemichigancollege.edu
CRAIG, Brian .... 409-880-8804 449 B
brian.craig@lamar.edu
CRAIG, Calvin .... 704-922-6357 334 E
craig.calvin@gaston.edu
CRAIG, Camilla .... 301-423-3600.. 93 H
CRAIG, Carissa .... 925-473-7491.. 40 I
ccraig@losmedanos.edu
CRAIG, Christopher, J .. 417-836-5215 255 J
chriscraig@missouristate.edu
CRAIG, Cornell .... 516-463-5102 301 E
cornell.craig@hofstra.edu
CRAIG, Dennis .... 607-436-2500 316 C
dennis.craig@oneonta.edu
CRAIG, Erin .... 616-632-2853 221 A
ebc001@aquinas.edu
CRAIG, Jaimie .... 662-476-5728 245 C
jcraig@eastms.edu
CRAIG, James .... 520-206-6916.. 15 E
jcraig7@pima.edu
CRAIG, Jason .... 703-284-5988 468 A
jason.craig@marymount.edu
CRAIG, Jim .... 208-885-6125 132 C
jimcraig@uidaho.edu
CRAIG, John .... 610-436-3133 394 F
jcraig@wcupa.edu
CRAIG, Johnny .... 219-473-4301 154 A
jcraig@ccsj.edu
CRAIG, Johnny .... 407-708-2166 108 B
craigj@seminolestate.edu
CRAIG, Kimberly .... 651-641-8718 235 A
craig@csp.edu
CRAIG, Kris .... 952-358-8150 239 C
kris.craig@normandale.edu
CRAIG, Marci .... 330-821-5320 362 E
CRAIG, Marva .... 212-220-8131 292 G
mcraig@bmcc.cuny.edu
CRAIG, Michael .... 816-501-4065 257 K
michael.craig@rockhurst.edu
CRAIG, Myrana .... 478-757-4024 127 D
mcraig@wesleyancollege.edu
CRAIG, Sandy .... 618-262-8641 139 G
craigs@iecc.edu
CRAIG, Scot .... 334-291-4954.... 1 H
scot.craig@cv.edu
CRAIG, William, G .... 732-571-3427 278 B
craig@monmouth.edu
CRAIG-MARIUS, Renee . 408-848-4760.. 43 H
rcraigmarius@gavilan.edu
CRAIGG, Dorende .... 336-315-7800.. 93 H
CRAIGMILES, Janet .... 863-638-7524 113 D
janet.craigmiles@warner.edu
CRAIK, Rebecca, L .... 215-572-2143 378 E
craikr@arcadia.edu
CRAIN, David, R .... 469-284-7366 454 A
dcrain@utsystem.edu
CRAIN, John, L .... 985-549-2280 192 E
jcrain@selu.edu
CRAIN, Lena .... 570-577-1617 379 A
lkc007@bucknell.edu
CRAIN, Rick .... 678-717-3623 126 G
rick.crain@ung.edu
CRAIN, Stacey .... 407-265-8383.. 96 H
CRAKES, Aileen .... 619-388-2896.. 61 A
acrakes@sdccd.edu
CRAM-RAHLF, Shelly .... 563-288-6011 165 I
scramrahlf@eicc.edu
CRAMER, Alicia .... 713-646-1808 443 C
acramer@stcl.edu
CRAMER, Devin .... 303-492-9048.. 83 M
deanofstudents@colorado.edu
CRAMER, Gregory, D .... 630-889-6467 145 D
gcramer@nuhs.edu
CRAMER, Joel .... 317-738-8197 155 A
jcramer@franklincollege.edu
CRAMER, John .... 860-439-5226.. 87 F
jcramer@conncoll.edu
CRAMER, Kenneth .... 603-456-2656 273 A
kcramer@magdalen.edu
CRAMER, Laura .... 603-456-2656 273 A
lcramer@magdalen.edu
CRAMER, Renee .... 515-271-3751 165 F
renee.cramer@drake.edu
CRAMER, Robert .... 608-262-3488 494 D
rgcramer@wisc.edu
CRAMER, Tricia, A .... 517-750-1200 230 F
tr700519@arbor.edu
CRAMER, Walter .... 203-837-8547.. 86 A
cramerw@wcsu.edu
CRAMPTON,
Anne-Marie .... 719-336-1520.. 81 J
anne-marie.crampton@lamarcc.edu
CRAMPTON, Donald .... 508-362-2131 214 B
CRAMPTON, Scott .... 719-336-1681.. 81 J
scott.crampton@lamarcc.edu
CRAMPTON, Troy, D .... 515-574-1114 166 G
crampton@iowacentral.edu
CRAMSEY, Rachel .... 217-228-5520 133 G
cramseyr@brcn.edu
CRANDALL, Donald, W . 479-524-7150.. 20 C
dcrandal@jbu.edu
CRANDALL, Elizabeth .... 940-552-6291 456 F
lisa.crandall@vernoncollege.edu
CRANDALL, James .... 530-242-7989.. 64 A
jcrandall@shastacollege.edu
CRANDALL, Jennifer .... 414-847-3344 493 C
jennifercrandall@miad.edu
CRANDALL, Jill .... 607-871-2164 289 E
crandallj@alfred.edu
CRANDALL, Krystal .... 515-574-1034 166 G
crandall_k@iowacentral.edu
CRANDALL, Laura .... 315-470-4865 319 A
ldcranda@esf.edu
CRANDALL, Mariella .... 916-660-7340.. 64 B
mcrandall4@sierracollege.edu
CRANE, David .... 508-531-6145 212 B
dcrane@bridgew.edu
CRANE, Ellen, E .... 989-964-4109 229 L
ecrane@svsu.edu
CRANE, Jeff .... 707-826-4491.. 30 A
jeffrey.crane@humboldt.edu
CRANE, Jeff .... 270-384-8150 183 D
cranej@lindsey.edu
CRANE, Katie .... 717-245-1389 382 B
craink@dickinson.edu
CRANE, Lindsay .... 585-395-5616 317 B
lcrane@brockport.edu
CRANE, Paul .... 810-762-9887 225 F
pcrane@kettering.edu
CRANE, Rob, M .... 913-288-7283 174 H
rcrane@kckcc.edu
CRANE, Ron .... 972-825-4818 444 C
rcrane@sagu.edu
CRANE, Susan, L .... 989-964-4350 229 L
scrane@svsu.edu
CRANFORD, Bill .... 601-925-3283 246 D
cranford@mc.edu
CRANFORD, Elizabeth ... 864-231-2000 405 F
ecranford@andersonuniversity.edu
CRANFORD, Shannon ... 580-628-6229 366 J
shannon.cranford@noc.edu
CRANFORD, Timothy .... 510-879-9223.. 60 C
tcranford@samuelmerritt.edu
CRANHAM, John, B .... 919-508-2336 344 D
jbcranham@peace.edu
CRANK, Ned .... 859-257-4691 185 D
ncranksh@uky.edu
CRANMORE, Jill, A .... 217-443-8756 136 E
j.cranmore@dacc.edu
CRANNELL, Annalisa .... 717-358-4283 383 G
annalisa.crannell@fandm.edu
CRANSON, Gregory .... 206-546-4503 483 C
gcranson@shoreline.edu
CRANSTON, Carolyn .... 412-924-1375 395 G
ccranston@pts.edu
CRAPPELL, Courtney .... 816-235-2900 260 D
conservatory@umkc.edu
CRAPSER, Bryce .... 860-465-5778.. 85 G
crapserb@easternct.edu
CRARY, Shara .... 408-270-6448.. 62 F
shara.crary@evc.edu
CRAST, Justin .... 760-795-2121.. 52 G
jcrast@miracosta.edu
CRASTRO-BOLIN, Irene . 914-594-4470 308 J
icrastro@nymc.edu
CRATER, Lucas .... 217-545-9362 149 F
lcrater@siumed.edu
CRATER, Matt .... 805-378-1457.. 73 I
mcrater@vcccd.edu
CRATTY, Frederic, W .... 203-837-8665.. 86 A
crattyf@wcsu.edu
CRAUN, Elizabeth .... 413-549-4600 210 A
ecpp@hampshire.edu
CRAVATH, Maureen .... 570-945-8117 386 F
maureen.cravath@keystone.edu
CRAVEN, Bryan, C .... 850-718-2375.. 97 E
cravenb@chipola.edu
CRAVEN, Christa .... 330-263-2576 350 H
ccraven@wooster.edu
CRAVEN, Deborah .... 303-678-3868.. 80 I
deborah.craven@frontrange.edu
CRAVEN, Heather .... 973-328-5281 276 A
hcraven@ccm.edu
CRAVEN, Katherine .... 781-239-5955 205 G
kcraven@babson.edu
CRAVEN, Kendra .... 402-354-7848 267 E
kendra.craven@methodistcollege.edu
CRAVEN, Leo .... 805-267-1690.. 48 A
CRAVEN, Nora .... 715-365-4576 498 D
ncraven@nicoletcollege.edu
CRAVEN, Randy .... 423-236-2076 422 H
rlcraven@southern.edu
CRAVENS, Alyssa .... 918-343-7612 369 A
acravens@rsu.edu
CRAVENS, Keith .... 770-859-9779 121 A
CRAVENS, Michael .... 419-824-3620 355 C
mcravens@sistersosf.org
CRAVENS, Peyton .... 620-441-5290 172 M
peyton.cravens@cowley.edu
CRAVER, Ken .... 903-510-2591 451 D
kcra@tjc.edu
CRAVER, Robert .... 303-369-5151.. 82 H
robert.craver@plattcolorado.edu
CRAVER, Travis .... 325-670-1856 436 B
travis.craver@hsutx.edu
CRAVER, III, William .... 229-668-3172 395 A
williamcr@pcom.edu
CRAWFORD, Abby .... 863-638-7248 113 D
abby.crawford@warner.edu
CRAWFORD, Adrian .... 318-678-6000 187 E
acrawford@bpcc.edu
CRAWFORD, Andrew .... 216-987-2053 351 D
andrew.crawford@tri-c.edu
CRAWFORD, Andrew, B 757-594-7663 465 A
andrew.crawford@cnu.edu
CRAWFORD, Anna .... 304-260-4380 487 C
acrawfor@blueridgectc.edu
CRAWFORD, Arminda ... 614-985-2241 359 K
acrawford@pcj.edu
CRAWFORD, Audrey .... 205-665-6030.... 8 D
acrawford@montevallo.edu
CRAWFORD, Bill .... 619-201-8700.. 60 G
bill.crawford@sdcc.edu
CRAWFORD, Brittany .... 334-683-2382.... 3 A
bcrawford@marionmilitary.edu
CRAWFORD, Bruce .... 205-929-6312.... 2 H
bcrawford@lawsonstate.edu
CRAWFORD, Bryan .... 719-562-7001.. 82 I
bryan.crawford@pueblocc.edu
CRAWFORD, Cali .... 734-462-4400 230 B
ccrawfor@schoolcraft.edu
CRAWFORD, RET.,
Cardon .... 843-953-5092 406 D
crawfordc1@citadel.edu
CRAWFORD, Cardon, B 843-953-6966 406 D
cardon.crawford@citadel.edu
CRAWFORD, Chemene .. 206-934-3601 482 F
chemene.crawford@seattlecolleges.edu
CRAWFORD, Chemene .. 206-934-3601 482 E
chemene.crawford@seattlecolleges.edu
CRAWFORD, Chris .... 903-923-2225 435 A
chrisc@etbu.edu
CRAWFORD, Chyna, N . 252-335-3113 341 A
cncrawford@ecsu.edu
CRAWFORD, Clinton .... 718-270-5140 294 E
crawford@mec.cuny.edu
CRAWFORD, Colin .... 415-442-7000.. 44 B
CRAWFORD, Crystal .... 864-597-4199 413 E
crawfordcr@wofford.edu
CRAWFORD, David .... 303-404-5000.. 80 I
david.crawford@frontrange.edu
CRAWFORD, David .... 773-947-6301 143 E
dcrawford@mccormick.edu
CRAWFORD, David, S ... 202-526-3799.. 93 E
dcrawford@johnpaulii.edu
CRAWFORD, Debbie .... 970-945-8691.. 78 H
CRAWFORD, Deborah .... 865-974-3053 426 C
dcrawf19@utk.edu
CRAWFORD, Dickie .... 318-257-2445 192 A
crawford@latech.edu
CRAWFORD, Ethan .... 319-296-4204 166 E
ethan.crawford@hawkeyecollege.edu
CRAWFORD, Gina .... 405-208-5900 367 E
gcrawford@okcu.edu
CRAWFORD,
Gregory, P .... 513-529-2345 356 A
president@miamioh.edu
CRAWFORD, Holly .... 214-648-3572 456 D
holly.crawford@utsouthwestern.edu
CRAWFORD, Ilene .... 319-895-4210 164 E
icrawford@cornellcollege.edu
CRAWFORD, Isiaah .... 253-879-3201 483 G
president@pugetsound.edu
CRAWFORD, James .... 336-517-1818 326 J
jcrawford@bennett.edu
CRAWFORD, III,
James, W .... 201-355-1426 277 A
president@felician.edu
CRAWFORD, Jenn .... 915-747-7526 454 E
jwcrawford@utep.edu
CRAWFORD, John .... 979-845-1321 446 B
crawford@tamu.edu
CRAWFORD, John, D .... 229-333-5939 127 C
jdcrawford@valdosta.edu
CRAWFORD, Jonas .... 805-678-5870.. 74 A
jcrawford@vcccd.edu
CRAWFORD, Karen .... 603-358-2487 274 A
kcrawford@keene.edu
CRAWFORD, Kenneth .... 803-793-5100 408 A
crawfordk@denmarktech.edu
CRAWFORD, Kevin .... 803-641-3495 412 B
kevincr@usca.edu
CRAWFORD, Kevin, L ... 240-500-2412 199 A
klcrawford@hagerstowncc.edu
CRAWFORD, Lauri .... 817-807-5463 216 H
crawfordl@neco.edu
CRAWFORD, Martha, J . 203-371-7999.. 88 H
crawfordm4@sacredheart.edu
CRAWFORD, Matthew ... 740-351-3132 360 E
mcrawford@shawnee.edu
CRAWFORD, Michelle ... 805-756-2324.. 29 K
mcrawf02@calpoly.edu
CRAWFORD, Peg .... 617-732-2132 216 B
peg.crawford@mcphs.edu
CRAWFORD, Ray Scott . 318-678-6000 187 E
rcrawford@bpcc.edu
CRAWFORD, Sabrina .... 727-341-3118 107 C
crawford.sabrina@spcollege.edu
CRAWFORD, Scott .... 309-341-7662 141 E
rscrawford@knox.edu
CRAWFORD, Steve .... 614-823-3200 359 G
crawford2@otterbein.edu
CRAWFORD, Teresa .... 863-784-7061 108 D
teresa.crawford@southflorida.edu
CRAWFORD, Teri .... 281-998-6151 442 B
teri.crawford@sjcd.edu
CRAWFORD,
Thomas, P .... 412-624-5822 400 A
tom.crawford@ia.pitt.edu
CRAWFORD, Tim .... 254-295-4180 453 A
tcrawford@umhb.edu
CRAWFORD, Trish .... 423-354-2552 424 B
tscrawford@northeaststate.edu
CRAWFORD, Wendy .... 870-733-6711.. 18 A
wcrawford@asumidsouth.edu
CRAWFORD GROSS,
Tania .... 859-246-6522 181 B
tania.crawford@kctcs.edu
CRAWFORD-PARKER,
Sarah .... 785-864-4225 177 G
scrawpar@ku.edu
CRAWFORD-SPINELLI,
John, R .... 330-672-2760 354 A
jcrawfo1@kent.edu
CRAWFORD-WHITE,
Demarus .... 937-376-6574 349 H
dcrawford-white@centralstate.edu

CROMBE, Katie .... 989-463-7245 220 F
crombekm@alma.edu
CROMER, Elyse .... 765-641-4039 153 D
emcromer@anderson.edu
CROMER, Julie .... 740-593-1711 358 L
jcromer@ohio.edu
CROMIE, Michael .... 409-772-3958 456 B
mcromie@utmb.edu
CROMPTON, Tim .... 801-626-8078 460 B
tcrompton@weber.edu
CROMWELL, Susan .... 617-373-2101 217 D
CRONAN, David .... 815-836-5270 142 C
CRONAN, David .... 630-617-3020 137 E
david.cronan@elmhurst.edu
CRONAUER, OSB,
Patrick, T .... 724-805-2324 397 D
patrick.cronauer@stvincent.edu
CRONE, Darren .... 972-883-4826 454 D
darren.crone@utdallas.edu
CRONE, Kimberly .... 860-231-5360.. 89 G
kcrone@usj.edu
CRONE, Paula .... 909-469-5563.. 75 G
pcrone@westernu.edu
CRONIN, Corey .... 978-542-7517 213 B
corey.cronin@salemstate.edu
CRONIN, Debra .... 773-256-0700 143 C
debra.cronin@lstc.edu
CRONIN, Elizabeth .... 585-389-2461 307 D
ecronin5@naz.edu
CRONIN, Hannah .... 414-930-3324 493 E
croninh@mtmary.edu
CRONIN, Laura .... 212-229-5662 307 E
croninl@newschool.edu
CRONIN, Mark, W .... 603-641-7250 273 C
mwcronin@anselm.edu
CRONIN, Marta .... 541-506-6103 372 E
mcronin@cgcc.edu
CRONIN, Shawn .... 978-762-4000 215 B
scronin@northshore.edu
CRONIN, Trish .... 508-793-7305 207 F
tcronin@clarku.edu
CRONK, Brian, C .... 716-878-6326 317 C
cronkbc@buffalostate.edu
CRONK, Keith .... 501-279-5700.. 19 G
kcronk@harding.edu
CRONK, Shantel .... 406-265-3594 264 A
shantel.cronk@msun.edu
CRONLEY, Maria .... 931-221-7676 416 H
cronleym@apsu.edu
CRONMILLER, Janelle ...... 610-647-4400 385 K
jcronmiller@immaculata.edu
CRONQUIST, Thomas .... 703-416-1441 465 E
tcronquist@divinemercy.edu
CRONQVIST, Henrik ...... 714-997-6819.. 36 D
hcronqvist@chapman.edu
CROOK, Amy .... 615-460-8796 417 B
amy.crook@belmont.edu
CROOK, Chris .... 785-864-9331 177 G
ccrook@ku.edu
CROOK, Evonne .... 423-236-2830 422 H
ercrook@southern.edu
CROOK, Patricia .... 615-963-5280 425 A
pcrook@tnstate.edu
CROOK, Rebecca .... 321-674-8099 100 A
bcrook@fit.edu
CROOKENDALE,
Humphrey .... 212-343-1234 306 C
hcrookendale@mcny.edu
CROOKER, Benjamin ...... 718-817-3048 300 A
crooker@fordham.edu
CROOKS, John .... 740-264-5591 352 B
jcrooks@egcc.edu
CROOM, H. Edward ...... 919-658-7745 340 E
hcroom@umo.edu
CROPPER, USMS,
Thomas, A .... 707-654-1011.. 32 C
tacropper@csum.edu
CROSBIE, Jeff .... 435-797-1042 459 F
jeff.crosbie@usu.edu
CROSBY, Anita, L .... 334-387-3877.... 4 C
anitacrosby@amridgeuniversity.edu
CROSBY, Cheryl .... 352-854-2322.. 97 L
crosbyc@cf.edu
CROSBY, Devin .... 561-237-7213 103 W
dcrosby@lynn.edu
CROSBY, Devin .... 530-749-3804.. 77 B
dcrosby@yccd.edu
CROSBY, Gary, B .... 973-290-4475 282 G
gcrobsy@steu.edu
CROSBY, Jason .... 859-238-5473 179 H
jason.crosby@centre.edu
CROSBY, Jean, K .... 765-285-7057 153 E
jkcrosby@bsu.edu
CROSBY, Karen .... 225-771-4845 190 K
karen_crosby@subr.edu
CROSBY, Kim .... 870-307-7275.. 20 D
kim.crosby@lyon.edu
CROSBY, Lynne .... 931-221-6240 416 H
crosbyl@apsu.edu
CROSBY, Mark .... 207-859-5500 194 B
mark.crosby@colby.edu
CROSBY, Michael .... 207-985-7976 194 F
CROSBY, Stephanie .... 805-922-6966.. 24 L
stephanie.crosby@hancockcollege.edu
CROSBY, Susan, E .... 540-453-2363 472 F
crosbys@brcc.edu
CROSBY LEHMANN,
Carl .... 507-786-3894 242 I
lehmann@stolaf.edu
CROSBY-WEEKS, Cherie 215-885-2360 389 A
ccrosby@manor.edu
CROSE, Brian .... 407-708-2396 108 B
croseb@seminolestate.edu
CROSE, Sarah .... 563-387-1477 167 J
sarah.crose@luther.edu
CROSLIN, Joey .... 405-208-5075 367 E
jcroslin@okcu.edu
CROSON, Rachel .... 612-626-1616 242 K
CROSS, Allison .... 703-284-1598 468 A
allison.cross@marymount.edu
CROSS, Berri, V .... 336-334-4822 334 F
bvcross@gtcc.edu
CROSS, Cara, R .... 417-865-2815 249 G
crossca@evangel.edu
CROSS, Charles, E .... 415-422-6522.. 72 I
cross@usfca.edu
CROSS, Cheryl .... 870-512-7827.. 18 C
cheryl_cross@asun.edu
CROSS, Chip .... 828-652-6021 335 H
CROSS, Connie .... 417-865-2815 252 F
crossc@evangel.edu
CROSS, David .... 713-718-8636 436 E
david.cross@hccs.edu
CROSS, Jeffrey .... 248-476-1122 227 B
jcross@msp.edu
CROSS, Jesse .... 336-334-4822 334 F
jlcross@gtcc.edu
CROSS, Jon .... 937-708-5254 363 G
jcross@wilberforce.edu
CROSS, Kinley .... 903-223-3057 447 C
kcross@tamut.edu
CROSS, Laura .... 605-256-5023 415 G
laura.cross@dsu.edu
CROSS, Mary, M .... 615-353-3301 424 A
mary.cross@nscc.edu
CROSS, Nigel .... 310-544-6424.. 60 B
nigel.cross@usw.salvationarmy.org
CROSS, Penny .... 828-652-6021 335 H
pennyc@mcdowelltech.edu
CROSS, Reece .... 626-365-1934.. 67 I
reecec@toa.edu
CROSS, Solomon .... 972-860-8120 433 H
scross@dcccd.edu
CROSS, Stacy .... 310-544-6442.. 60 B
stacy.cross@usw.salvationarmy.org
CROSS, Terry .... 423-614-8140 419 H
tcross@leeuniversity.edu
CROSSCUP, Shauna ...... 540-674-3615 473 F
scrosscup@nr.edu
CROSSLAND, Martin ...... 913-971-3514 175 H
mcrossland@mnu.edu
CROSSLAND, Shannon .. 806-457-4200 435 D
CROSSLIN, Cara .... 205-391-3905.... 3 E
ccrosslin@sheltonstate.edu
CROSSMAN,
Raymond, E .... 312-662-4001 132 D
rec@adler.edu
CROSWELL, Kat, A .... 510-841-1905.. 27 B
CROSWELL, Lauren, C .. 714-850-4800.. 67 G
croswell@taftu.edu
CROTEAU, Cate .... 630-829-6522 133 B
ccroteau@ben.edu
CROTEAU, David .... 803-754-4100 407 F
CROTEAU, Melissa .... 978-630-9211 215 A
mcroteau@mwcc.mass.edu
CROTHERS, Bill, S .... 864-644-5011 411 D
president@swu.edu
CROTHERS, Tammy .... 309-467-6309 137 G
tcrothers@eureka.edu
CROTTE, Kirsten .... 614-823-1525 359 G
kcrotte@otterbein.edu
CROTTY, Kaitlin .... 918-343-7715 369 A
kcrotty@rsu.edu
CROUCH, Alicia .... 859-256-3100 180 H
alicia.crouch@kctcs.edu
CROUCH, Dani .... 541-956-7199 375 G
dcrouch@roguecc.edu
CROUCH, Leon .... 541-552-6885 376 A
crouchl@sou.edu
CROUCH, Michael, A .... 205-726-2820.... 6 E
mcrouch@samford.edu
CROUCH, Mike .... 620-343-4600 173 D
mcrouch@fhtc.edu
CROUCH, Peter .... 817-272-2571 454 B
peter.crouch@uta.edu
CROUCH, Robert .... 415-575-6100.. 29 A
rcrouch@ciis.edu
CROUCH, Suzanne .... 903-813-2059 429 I
scrouch@austincollege.edu
CROUCH, Tony .... 620-229-6368 177 D
tony.crouch@sckans.edu
CROUCHET, Cristeen ...... 253-589-5895 478 A
cristeen.crouchet@cptc.edu
CROUGHAN, May .... 530-752-4964.. 69 A
provost@ucdavis.edu
CROUNSE, Cheryl .... 978-542-7591 213 B
cheryl.crounse@salemstate.edu
CROUSE, Abigail .... 651-962-5000 243 F
CROUSE, Jenn .... 307-675-0701 500 F
jcrouse@sheridan.edu
CROUSE, Justin .... 319-352-8719 170 F
justin.crouse@wartburg.edu
CROUSE, Kevin .... 956-665-7823 455 A
kevin.crouse@utrgv.edu
CROUSE, Steve .... 864-977-7022 410 A
steve.crouse@ngu.edu
CROUSO, Lena .... 405-789-6400 369 G
lcrouso@snu.edu
CROUSO, Lena .... 405-491-6304 369 G
lcrouso@snu.edu
CROUT, David .... 765-658-4090 154 G
davidcrout@depauw.edu
CROUTHER, Deveta ...... 501-370-5333.. 21 A
nurse@philander.edu
CROW, Amy .... 937-778-8600 352 D
CROW, Angela .... 479-968-0271.. 18 E
acrow@atu.edu
CROW, Brook .... 314-838-8858 261 A
bcrow@ugst.edu
CROW, Cecily .... 706-236-2293 116 A
ccrow@berry.edu
CROW, Jeff .... 870-245-4258.. 20 H
crowj@obu.edu
CROW, Michael, M .... 480-965-8972.. 11 A
michael.crow@asu.edu
CROW, Scott .... 916-484-8647.. 50 J
crows@arc.losrios.edu
CROWDER, Darren .... 417-328-1797 258 K
dcrowder@sbuniv.edu
CROWDER, Jim .... 732-224-1987 275 D
jcrowder@brookdalecc.edu
CROWDER, Michael, W 513-529-3734 356 A
crowdemw@miamioh.edu
CROWDER, Sabrina ...... 334-229-4156.... 4 B
scrowder@alasu.edu
CROWDER,
Stephanie, B .... 773-896-2400 134 K
sbcrowder@ctschicago.edu
CROWDER, Vickie .... 304-473-8032 490 E
crowder_v@wvwc.edu
CROWE, Aliesha, R .... 715-788-7208 498 G
aliesha.crowe@northwoodtech.edu
CROWE, Beth .... 618-524-3471 149 C
bethc@shawneecc.edu
CROWE, Ellen .... 816-604-3108 255 A
ellen.crowe@mcckc.edu
CROWE, Ken .... 706-864-1499 126 G
ken.crowe@ung.edu
CROWE, Lindsey .... 270-852-3118 183 B
lcrowe@kwc.edu
CROWE, Michael .... 270-745-5429 186 A
michael.crowe@wku.edu
CROWE, Peggy .... 270-745-3159 186 A
peggy.crowe@wku.edu
CROWE, Sarah .... 770-533-7009 121 L
scrowe@laniertech.edu
CROWE, Shad, M .... 315-792-3472 323 G
smcrowe@utica.edu
CROWE, JR., Terry, M .. 865-694-6619 424 C
tmcrowe1@pstcc.edu
CROWE, Thomas .... 847-543-2473 135 G
tcrowe@clcillinois.edu
CROWELL, Anthony .... 212-431-2840 308 I
anthony.crowell@nyls.edu
CROWELL, Heidi .... 603-897-8630 273 B
hcrowell@rivier.edu
CROWELL, Scott .... 507-537-6844 240 G
scott.crowell@smsu.edu
CROWETIPTON, Vaughn 864-294-2138 408 I
vaughn.crowetipton@furman.edu
CROWFOOT, Dara .... 312-996-8586 151 D
CROWL, Ronald .... 330-829-2756 362 E
crowlrl@mountunion.edu
CROWLEY, Cara, J .... 806-345-5518 428 F
cjcrowley@actx.edu
CROWLEY, Janelle .... 708-235-6807 138 C
jcrowley3@govst.edu
CROWLEY, Janelle .... 262-472-1918 496 E
CROWLEY, Jason .... 567-661-7032 359 H
jason_crowley2@owens.edu
CROWLEY, Karlyn, A ..... 740-368-3101 359 F
kacrowley@owu.edu
CROWLEY, Kimberly, A . 806-354-6087 428 F
kacrowley@actx.edu
CROWLEY, Merritt .... 508-286-3464 219 F
crowley_merritt@wheatoncollege.edu
CROWLEY, Michael .... 508-213-2428 217 C
michael.crowley@nichols.edu
CROWLEY, Michael .... 408-554-4300.. 63 A
mcrowley@scu.edu
CROWLEY, Tanya .... 978-665-3441 212 C
tcrowle7@fitchburgstate.edu
CROWLEY, Tim .... 660-543-8059 259 K
crowley@ucmo.edu
CROWLEY, Timothy, D .. 207-768-2811 195 C
tcrowley@nmcc.edu
CROWN, Deborah, F ..... 407-646-2405 106 L
dcrown@rollins.edu
CROWSON, Natalie .... 978-626-7111 209 G
ncrowson@gcts.edu
CROWTHER, Lori .... 620-792-9216 171 F
crowtherl@bartonccc.edu
CROWTHER, Steven ...... 910-221-2224 330 G
scrowther@manna.edu
CROY, Carolyn .... 540-231-6059 466 E
ccroy@vcom.vt.edu
CROYLE, Kristin .... 315-312-2285 318 B
kristin.croyle@oswego.edu
CROYLE, Randi .... 208-885-5522 132 C
rcroyle@uidaho.edu
CROZIER, Nate .... 305-284-5766 112 K
nac132@miami.edu
CRUCE, Carrie .... 254-298-8425 445 B
carrie.cruce@templejc.edu
CRUCIANI, Mark .... 570-941-4274 400 C
mark.cruciani@scranton.edu
CRUCITTI, Thomas .... 203-837-9090.. 86 A
crucittit@wcsu.edu
CRUDDAS, Shanti .... 408-847-4060.. 52 I
CRUESS, Alison .... 904-620-2583 111 A
acruess@unf.edu
CRUICKSHANK, Cam ...... 704-403-1521 327 B
cameron.cruickshank@atriumhealth.org
CRUICKSHANK, Laura ... 860-486-1656.. 89 B
laura.cruickshank@uconn.edu
CRUISE, Thomas .... 540-831-5479 468 E
tcruise@radford.edu
CRULL, Matthew .... 815-825-2086 141 D
mcrull@kish.edu
CRUM, Denise .... 765-983-1203 154 H
crumde@earlham.edu
CRUM, Kelly .... 517-796-8470 225 A
crumkellya@jccmi.edu
CRUM, Lyndsey .... 970-351-2551.. 84 D
lyndsey.crum@unco.edu
CRUMBAKER, Chad ...... 304-424-8242 490 A
chad.crumbaker@wvup.edu
CRUMBLEY, Dean .... 229-931-2074 120 B
dean.crumbley@gsw.edu
CRUME, Gene .... 847-628-2002 141 A
gene.crume@judsonu.edu
CRUMEDY, Ron, C .... 409-944-1237 435 F
rcrumedy@gc.edu
CRUMIT-HANCOCK,
Lisa .... 419-783-2332 351 J
lcrumithancock@defiance.edu
CRUMLEY, Christopher . 281-476-1801 442 C
christopher.crumley@sjcd.edu
CRUMLEY, Kristie .... 410-386-8408 197 G
kcrumley@carrollcc.edu
CRUMLEY, Terri .... 319-273-2311 163 G
theresa.crumley@uni.edu
CRUMP, Amanda .... 315-386-7019 319 E
crumpa@canton.edu
CRUMP, D'adra .... 718-940-5869 313 C
dcrump@sjcny.edu
CRUMP-DICKENS,
Tanya .... 386-481-2514.. 96 D
dickenst@cookman.edu

CUMMINGS, Andrea, M 904-470-8220.. 98 I a.cummings@ewc.edu
CUMMINGS, Andrew ..... 503-845-3505 373 G andrew.cummings@mtangel.edu
CUMMINGS, Bobby, L .. 302-857-6060.. 90 D bcummings@desu.edu
CUMMINGS, Brian .... 313-577-1574 232 H ac6308@wayne.edu
CUMMINGS, SSE, Brian, J .... 802-654-2386 462 A bcummings@smcvt.edu
CUMMINGS, Brittany ..... 405-491-6365 369 G bcummings@snu.edu
CUMMINGS, Cagan .... 806-291-3542 457 B cummingsc@wbu.edu
CUMMINGS, Carmen ..... 850-599-3707 109 E carmen.cummings@famu.edu
CUMMINGS, Cassidy .... 910-843-5304 330 F office@lumbeeriver.edu
CUMMINGS, Chris .... 937-778-8600 352 D
CUMMINGS, Christopher .... 508-588-9100 214 F cwcummings@massasoit.mass.edu
CUMMINGS, Corlis .... 678-466-5505 117 A corliscummings@clayton.edu
CUMMINGS, Dana .... 317-738-8235 155 A dcummings@franklincollege.edu
CUMMINGS, Edie .... 318-869-5191 186 C ecummings@centenary.edu
CUMMINGS, Eric .... 615-547-1323 418 C ecummings@cumberland.edu
CUMMINGS, Evangeline 352-294-7158 110 E ecummings@ufl.edu
CUMMINGS, Glenn, T ... 207-780-4480 196 J glennc@maine.edu
CUMMINGS, Jan .... 850-718-2201.. 97 E cummingsj@chipola.edu
CUMMINGS, John .... 518-782-6932 314 K jcummings@siena.edu
CUMMINGS, Katherine .. 570-740-0420 388 G
CUMMINGS, Keith .... 405-491-6396 369 G kcummings@snu.edu
CUMMINGS, Kevin, R ... 914-594-4536 308 J kevin_cummings@nymc.edu
CUMMINGS, Liz .... 910-775-4155 343 A liz.cummings@uncp.edu
CUMMINGS, JR., McDuffie .... 910-521-6690 343 A mcduffie.cummings@uncp.edu
CUMMINGS, Robin, G .. 910-521-4471 343 A chancellor@uncp.edu
CUMMINGS, Simone ..... 314-968-5951 261 D simonecummings84@webster.edu
CUMMINGS, Terri .... 217-443-8786 136 E t.cummings@dacc.edu
CUMMINGS, Torreya ..... 415-551-9227.. 28 D tcummings@cca.edu
CUMMINGS, Wanda ...... 314-362-6590 253 A wanda.cummings@barnesjewishcollege.edu
CUMMINGS-DANSON, Gail, L .... 518-580-5370 315 A gcumming@skidmore.edu
CUMMINGS-DANSON, Gail, L .... 518-580-5730 315 A gcumming@skidmore.edu
CUMMINS, Bev .... 402-437-2554 268 D bcummins@southeast.edu
CUMMINS, Carla .... 406-874-6214 262 K cumminsc@milescc.edu
CUMMINS, Kendra .... 918-540-6201 366 F kendra.cummins@neo.edu
CUMMINS, Michelle ...... 812-888-4573 162 E mcummins@vinu.edu
CUMMINS, Stephen, B .. 530-898-5917.. 31 A sbcummins@csuchico.edu
CUMMO, Salvatrice .... 626-585-7693.. 56 D scummo@pasadena.edu
CUMPSTSON, Jennifer ... 630-942-3570 135 F cumpstonj@cod.edu
CUNDIFF, Dianna .... 812-488-1083 161 E dc114@evansville.edu
CUNEO, Allison .... 443-334-2063 202 C acuneo@stevenson.edu
CUNEO, Sean, P .... 814-824-2118 389 E scuneo@mercyhurst.edu
CUNION, Jessica .... 330-823-6051 362 E cunionjs@mountunion.edu
CUNION, William .... 216-987-2341 351 D william.cunion@tri-c.edu
CUNNIFF, Megan .... 508-830-5059 213 A mcunniff@maritime.edu

CUNNINGHAM, Anne, S .... 765-658-4200 154 G annecunningham@depauw.edu
CUNNINGHAM, Beverly 765-361-6221 162 G cunningb@wabash.edu
CUNNINGHAM, Brent ... 256-782-8773.... 6 A brentc@jsu.edu
CUNNINGHAM, Chad ... 563-588-8000 165 K ccunningham@emmaus.edu
CUNNINGHAM, Dana ..... 785-628-4424 173 E dacunningham@fhsu.edu
CUNNINGHAM, Dayna .. 617-628-5000 219 A dayna.cunningham@tufts.edu
CUNNINGHAM, Denise, S .... 516-463-6473 301 E denise.cunningham@hofstra.edu
CUNNINGHAM, Eric ...... 573-875-7649 251 A ercunningham@ccis.edu
CUNNINGHAM, Gary .... 651-201-1818 236 F gary.cunningham@minnstate.edu
CUNNINGHAM, Huie, J 601-979-1111 245 G huie.t.cunningham@jsums.edu
CUNNINGHAM, Jamal, R .... 414-464-9777 497 B cunningham.jamal@wspp.edu
CUNNINGHAM, James .. 315-279-5228 303 D jcunning@keuka.edu
CUNNINGHAM, Janet ... 954-771-0376 103 S jcunningham@knoxseminary.edu
CUNNINGHAM, Jen ...... 815-226-4010 147 J jcunningham@rockford.edu
CUNNINGHAM, Jennifer, L .... 610-758-5799 388 C jlc516@lehigh.edu
CUNNINGHAM, Jill .... 209-381-6470.. 52 B jill.cunningham@mccd.edu
CUNNINGHAM, Jim ...... 660-596-7208 259 D jcunningham@sfccmo.edu
CUNNINGHAM, John, A .... 513-556-0626 361 I bearcat.ad@uc.edu
CUNNINGHAM, Joi, M . 248-370-2190 229 F cunning3@oakland.edu
CUNNINGHAM, Karla, K .... 317-940-9570 153 H kcunning@butler.edu
CUNNINGHAM, Kathy ... 610-372-4721 396 A kcunningham@racc.edu
CUNNINGHAM, Kay ..... 901-321-3430 417 G kay.cunningham@cbu.edu
CUNNINGHAM, Kelly, E 607-255-5201 297 D president@cornell.edu
CUNNINGHAM, Kevin, A .... 563-884-5898 169 C kevin.cunningham@palmer.edu
CUNNINGHAM, Kim ..... 951-343-4227.. 27 J kcunningham@calbaptist.edu
CUNNINGHAM, Kima ... 937-376-6566 349 H kcunningham@centralstate.edu
CUNNINGHAM, Larry .... 843-377-2145 406 B lcunningham@charlestonlaw.edu
CUNNINGHAM, Lawrence (Bubba), R .. 919-962-8200 342 B bubba.cunningham@unc.edu
CUNNINGHAM, Linda ... 402-559-7394 269 B lcunningham@unmc.edu
CUNNINGHAM, Mark ... 404-756-4654 115 E mcunningham@atlm.edu
CUNNINGHAM, Matt ..... 773-298-3109 148 I mcunningham@sxu.edu
CUNNINGHAM, Michael .... 504-865-5261 191 D mcunnin1@tulane.edu
CUNNINGHAM, Michael .... 201-684-7666 280 B mcunning@ramapo.edu
CUNNINGHAM, II, Michael, J .... 401-333-7121 403 D mjcunningham2@ccri.edu
CUNNINGHAM, Michael, R .... 858-642-8101.. 53 I mcunningham@nu.edu
CUNNINGHAM, Nicole .. 508-793-2265 208 A ncunning@holycross.edu
CUNNINGHAM, Pat ...... 615-460-6617 417 B pat.cunningham@belmont.edu
CUNNINGHAM, Patricia, A .... 205-940-7800.... 5 E pcunningham@fortisinstitute.edu
CUNNINGHAM, Phillip . 205-366-8979.... 7 A pcunninghan@stillman.edu
CUNNINGHAM, Rebecca, M .... 734-764-1185 231 A stroh@umich.edu

CUNNINGHAM, Richardo .... 563-589-3115 170 C
CUNNINGHAM, Sandy .. 985-867-2234 190 I cunninghams@sjasc.edu
CUNNINGHAM, Sarah ... 314-977-2226 258 H sarah.cunningham@slu.edu
CUNNINGHAM, Sarah ... 401-454-6100 404 B scunning@risd.edu
CUNNINGHAM, Sean .... 512-463-4930 448 G sean.cunningham@tsus.edu
CUNNINGHAM, Stephen .... 607-753-5565 317 D stephen.cunningham@cortland.edu
CUNNINGHAM, Susan, W .... 540-458-8489 476 D scunningham@wlu.edu
CUNNINGHAM, Tamara 201-200-3454 278 F tcunningham@njcu.edu
CUNNINGHAM, Tamara 951-487-3116.. 53 A tcunningham@msjc.edu
CUNNINGHAM, Todd, D .... 724-357-7872 393 G todd.cunningham@iup.edu
CUNNINGHAM, William 636-584-6651 252 D william.cunningham@eastcentral.edu
CUNNINGHAM, William 215-248-7120 380 G cunninghamw@chc.edu
CUNNINGS, Chris .... 217-424-6244 144 D ccunnings@millikin.edu
CUP, Jo Beth .... 312-662-4101 132 D jcup@adler.edu
CUPICH, Blase .... 847-566-6401 152 F
CUPICH, Krista .... 402-280-1823 265 J kristacupich@creighton.edu
CUPP, Amy .... 304-829-7567 486 B acupp@bethanywv.edu
CUPP, Craig .... 870-236-6901.. 19 D ccupp@crc.edu
CUPP, Jason .... 312-506-4634.. 39 F jason.cupp@columbiacollege.edu
CUPP, Julie .... 773-298-5167 148 I cupp@sxu.edu
CUPP, Scott, A .... 432-837-8303 449 F scott.cupp@sulross.edu
CUPPETT, Cathy .... 843-383-8121 407 C ccuppett@coker.edu
CUPPLES, Tamara .... 212-217-4069 299 C tamara_cupples@fitnyc.edu
CURBO, Billy, D .... 254-659-7701 436 C bdcurbo@hillcollege.edu
CURCHACK, Barb .... 651-450-3739 237 H bcurchack@inverhills.edu
CURCI, Roberto .... 708-524-6321 137 A rcurci@dom.edu
CURCIO, Ellen .... 610-409-3600 400 E ecurcio@ursinus.edu
CURD, Michael .... 877-248-6724.. 12 M mcurd@hmu.edu
CURFMAN, Mike .... 218-683-8630 239 E mike.curfman@northlandcollege.edu
CURIEL, Erika .... 714-997-6736.. 36 D curiel@chapman.edu
CURKO, Sandy .... 914-633-2201 302 C scurko@iona.edu
CURL, Bridget .... 309-438-2236 140 C kbcurl@ilstu.edu
CURL, Bruce .... 707-826-3626.. 30 A bruce.curl@humboldt.edu
CURL, John, D .... 801-863-6746 460 A jcurl@uvu.edu
CURLE, Thomas .... 919-508-2366 344 D tocurle@peace.edu
CURLEE, Dan .... 817-598-6227 457 C dcurlee@wc.edu
CURLEY, Amy .... 928-757-0801.. 14 H acurley@mohave.edu
CURLEY, Chad .... 740-245-7278 363 A ccurley@rio.edu
CURLEY, Greg, M .... 814-641-3521 386 E curleyg@juniata.edu
CURLEY, Jami .... 419-824-3708 355 C jcurley@lourdes.edu
CURLEY, Lauren .... 781-239-2572 214 E lcurley@massbay.edu
CURLEY, Scott .... 815-224-0301 140 D scott_curley@ivcc.edu
CURNUTT, Deana .... 575-624-8040 286 F curnutt@nmmi.edu
CURPHEY, Richena .... 805-525-4417.. 67 J rcurphey@thomasaquinas.edu
CURRAN, Dennis .... 425-564-2446 477 B dennis.curran@bellevuecollege.edu
CURRAN, Jack .... 718-862-7934 304 K jack.curran@manhattan.edu

CURRAN, James .... 914-594-3723 308 J jcurran6@nymc.edu
CURRAN, Jennifer, M ... 860-685-3338.. 90 A jcurran@wesleyan.edu
CURRAN, Joel, G .... 574-631-6798 161 G jcurran9@nd.edu
CURRAN, John, A .... 785-864-3975 177 G jacurran@ku.edu
CURRAN, Kathy .... 541-776-9942 375 A kathy.c@pacificbible.edu
CURRAN, Lizzy, E .... 402-280-2221 265 J lizzycurran@creighton.edu
CURRAN, Matt .... 802-443-5835 461 G matthewc@middlebury.edu
CURRAN, Sheri, L .... 309-794-8058 132 H shericurran@augustana.edu
CURRAN, Terrence .... 904-620-5063 111 A terrence.curran@unf.edu
CURRAN-HEADLEY, Marie .... 518-255-5127 318 F curranmc@cobleskill.edu
CURRANT, Paul .... 757-683-3956 468 C pcurrant@odu.edu
CURREN, Kerry .... 207-236-8581 195 H kcurren@mainemedia.edu
CURRENT, Lori, M .... 800-287-8822 153 F currelo@bethanyseminary.edu
CURRERI, Michelle .... 401-874-4462 404 E mcurreri@uri.edu
CURRIE, Catherine .... 401-232-6369 403 B ccurrie@bryant.edu
CURRIE, David .... 978-468-7111 209 G dcurrie@gcts.edu
CURRIE, Eunice, M .... 817-272-5554 454 B currie@uta.edu
CURRIE, Jennifer .... 508-531-2338 212 B j1currie@bridgew.edu
CURRIE, John .... 215-887-5511 401 G jcurrie@wts.edu
CURRIE, John, D .... 336-758-5000 344 A
CURRIE, Kathy .... 734-677-5143 232 A kcurrie@wccnet.edu
CURRIE, Wayne .... 603-222-4282 273 C wcurrie@anselm.edu
CURRIER, Christine .... 785-248-2562 176 F christine.currier@ottawa.edu
CURRIER, Nicole, A ...... 301-546-0560 201 D curriena@pgcc.edu
CURRIERA, Joy, L .... 202-685-4278 501 I joy.l.curriera.mil@ndu.edu
CURRIN, Bruce, A .... 402-472-3105 269 A bcurrin1@unl.edu
CURRINGTON, Adrienne .... 530-226-4788.. 64 C acurrington@simpsonu.edu
CURRIVAN, Megan, D ... 617-322-3568 210 F megan_currivan@laboure.edu
CURRY, Adora .... 501-812-2771.. 23 E acurry@uaptc.edu
CURRY, Angela .... 502-852-5777 185 E angela.curry@louisville.edu
CURRY, Ashley .... 312-755-2250 137 F acurry@erikson.edu
CURRY, Carolyn, S .... 240-895-4282 201 F cscurry@smcm.edu
CURRY, Christa .... 513-244-4614 356 F christa.curry@msj.edu
CURRY, Gina .... 916-278-7461.. 33 A curryg@skymail.csus.edu
CURRY, James .... 402-844-7063 268 A jamesc@northeast.edu
CURRY, James .... 718-997-5545 295 A james.curry@qc.cuny.edu
CURRY, Jason, R .... 615-329-8697 418 E jcurry@fisk.edu
CURRY, Kathleen .... 413-265-2412 208 B curryk@elms.edu
CURRY, Keith .... 310-900-1600.. 39 H kcurry@compton.edu
CURRY, Kristin .... 212-343-1234 306 C kcurry@mcny.edu
CURRY, Leann .... 940-397-4138 439 F leann.curry@msutexas.edu
CURRY, Marilyn .... 662-252-8000 248 B mcurry@rustcollege.edu
CURRY, R. Esther .... 954-492-5353.. 97 G ecurry@citycollege.edu
CURRY, Reva .... 989-686-9298 223 E revacurry@delta.edu
CURRY, Robert .... 646-660-6000 292 F robert.curry@baruch.cuny.edu
CURRY, Robert .... 706-542-7066 126 F bob.currey@uga.edu

DAICHENDT, Jim .... 619-849-2412.. 57 J
jimdaichendt@pointloma.edu
DAIG, Bart .... 989-729-3350 221 B
bdaig01@baker.edu
DAIGLE, Anna .... 504-865-3158 190 A
apdaigle@loyno.edu
DAIGLER, David .... 207-629-4017 194 I
ddaigler@mccs.me.edu
DAIGNAULT, Lorraine ... 401-232-6000 403 B
ldaignault@bryant.edu
DAILEY, Bracken, J .... 951-827-3427.. 70 B
bracken.dailey@ucr.edu
DAILEY, Brian .... 910-962-3711 343 B
daileyb@uncw.edu
DAILEY, Candy .... 715-365-4539 498 D
csdailey@nicoletcollege.edu
DAILEY, John .... 919-684-6571 328 D
john.dailey@duke.edu
DAILEY, Michael .... 502-597-6238 183 A
michael.dailey@kysu.edu
DAILEY, Shawn .... 740-427-5151 354 I
daileys@kenyon.edu
DAILEY, Stash .... 614-885-5585 359 K
sdailey@pcj.edu
DAILEY-WEAVER,
Amanda, M .... 812-941-2482 157 D
ammdaile@ius.edu
DAILY, Daniel, R .... 605-658-3369 415 E
dan.daily@usd.edu
DAILY, David .... 479-979-1456.. 24 A
ddaily@ozarks.edu
DAILY, Joseph .... 719-365-1160.. 83 K
joseph.daily@uchealth.org
DAILY, Laura .... 540-432-4597 465 F
laura.daily@emu.edu
DAILY, Laurie .... 605-274-5211 413 G
laurie.daily@augie.edu
DAILY, Nathan, B .... 256-766-6610.... 5 F
ndaily@hcu.edu
DAIN, Claudette, E .... 626-914-8886.. 37 B
cdain@citruscollege.edu
DAIR, Desmond .... 415-422-2772.. 72 I
ddair@usfca.edu
DAIRE, Andrew, P .... 804-827-2670 472 D
apdaire@vcu.edu
DAIS, Olga .... 646-312-3320 292 F
olga.dais@baruch.cuny.edu
DAISEY, Mary Beth .... 856-225-6044 281 A
daisey@camden.rutgers.edu
DAISY, Jennifer .... 620-432-2808 176 A
jdaisy@neosho.edu
DAISY, Joseph .... 808-245-8210 129 H
jdaisy@hawaii.edu
DAITCH, Jonathan .... 909-469-8522.. 75 G
jdaitch@westernu.edu
DAJUSTE, Billy (Malik) . 386-481-2606.. 96 D
dajusteb@cookman.edu
DAKE, Michael .... 520-626-5394.. 16 H
mddake@arizona.edu
DAKSHINAMURTHY,
Raj .... 432-552-2220 456 C
dakshinamurthy_r@utpb.edu
DAKWAR, Mohammad .. 414-297-8087 498 B
dakwarmm@matc.edu
DALABA, Stacia .... 315-279-5000 303 D
sdalaba@keuka.edu
DALAGER, Jon .... 651-201-1800 236 F
DALBOW, Dawn, S .... 540-828-5310 464 C
ddalbow@bridgewater.edu
DALE, Amie, G .... 757-594-7672 465 A
amie.dale@cnu.edu
DALE, Andrew .... 662-562-3319 247 E
adale@northwestms.edu
DALE, Cheryl .... 601-318-6199 249 B
cheryl.dale@wmcarey.edu
DALE, David .... 516-463-6611 301 E
david.dale@hofstra.edu
DALE, Deb .... 585-275-6030 323 E
debora.dale@rochester.edu
DALE, Elizabeth .... 215-503-5138 398 G
elizabeth.dale@jefferson.edu
DALE, Jeffrey .... 770-720-5522 124 E
jdale@reinhardt.edu
DALE, Jenn .... 303-360-4730.. 80 C
jennifer.dale@ccaurora.edu
DALE, Kim, K .... 307-382-1602 500 I
kdale@westernwyoming.edu
DALE, Kory, J .... 479-524-7116.. 20 C
kdale@jbu.edu
DALE, Marc .... 630-466-7900 152 H
mdale@waubonsee.edu
DALE-CARTER, April .... 909-384-8922.. 60 F
acarter@sbccd.cc.ca.us
DALEKE, David .... 812-855-6902 156 C
daleked@indiana.edu
DALENBERG, David .... 765-361-6288 162 G
dalenbed@wabash.edu
DALENE, Jack .... 435-283-7130 460 C
jack.dalene@snow.edu
DALES, Sandra .... 910-246-4133 337 E
daless@sandhills.edu
DALEY, Ben .... 619-929-9748.. 45 F
bdaley@hightechhigh.org
DALEY, Carol .... 540-338-2700 486 C
cdaley@cdu.edu
DALEY, Elizabeth, M ..... 213-740-2804.. 73 C
edaley@cinema.usc.edu
DALEY, George, Q .... 617-432-1501 210 B
george_daley@hms.harvard.edu
DALEY, Karen .... 203-365-4508.. 88 H
daleyk3@sacredheart.edu
DALEY, Karen .... 616-698-7111 222 H
kdaley@davenport.edu
DALEY, Kathy, A .... 843-349-6407 407 B
kdaley@coastal.edu
DALEY, Lauren .... 773-907-4725 134 N
ldaley@ccc.edu
DALEY, Maggie .... 617-746-1990 210 E
maggie.daley@hult.edu
DALGLISH, Lucy, A .... 301-405-8806 202 E
dalglish@umd.edu
DALISAY, Edlyn .... 671-734-1812 503 D
edalisay@piu.edu
DALLA COSTA BEHM,
Arhelia .... 608-663-2387 491 F
adallacostabehm@edgewood.edu
DALLAS, Deedra .... 928-774-3890.. 12 N
DALLAS, Marty .... 602-557-1453.. 16 L
martha.dallas@phoenix.edu
DALLIS-COMENTALE,
Diane .... 812-855-4848 156 C
DALLIS-COMENTALE,
Diane, M .... 812-855-5679 156 B
ddallis@indiana.edu
DALLMANN, Denise ...... 503-251-2800 377 A
ddallmann@uws.edu
DALLY, Brenda .... 580-581-2230 365 C
brendad@cameron.edu
DALMAGE, Sharon .... 818-710-2523.. 49 H
dalmagsc@piercecollege.edu
DALOLA, Lorie, A .... 252-399-6300 326 H
ldalola@barton.edu
DALPE, J. Kyle .... 775-445-4431 271 A
kyle.dalpe@wnc.edu
DALPIAZ, Antonia .... 303-369-5151.. 82 H
antonia.dalpiaz@plattcolorado.edu
DALRYMPLE, Jenason ... 303-385-1070 352 A
jenason.dalrymple@eastohio.edu
DALRYMPLE, Jim .... 417-626-1234 257 A
dalrymple.jim@occ.edu
DALSING, Deirdre, L ..... 608-342-1865 495 E
dalsingd@uwplatt.edu
DALSKE, James .... 707-654-1070.. 32 C
jdalske@csum.edu
DALSKE, James .... 760-355-6457.. 45 N
james.dalske@imperial.edu
DALTON, Brenda .... 972-860-4677 433 G
bdalton@dcccd.edu
DALTON, Brett .... 254-710-3554 430 F
brett_dalton@baylor.edu
DALTON, Brian .... 901-321-3605 417 G
bdalton@cbu.edu
DALTON, Christina .... 304-766-3061 489 D
christina.dalton@wvstateu.edu
DALTON, Cody .... 828-327-7000 332 H
cdalton880@cvcc.edu
DALTON, Dana, L .... 336-272-7102 329 B
dana.dalton@greensboro.edu
DALTON, Diane .... 317-813-2300 157 G
DALTON, Jaime .... 620-235-4241 176 H
jdalton@pittstate.edu
DALTON, James .... 205-348-4892.... 7 G
jim.dalton@ua.edu
DALTON, Jim .... 845-768-3991 502 H
jim.dalton@westpoint.edu
DALTON, John .... 765-973-8450 156 D
jodalton@iue.edu
DALTON, Judith .... 215-572-4088 378 E
daltonj@arcadia.edu
DALTON, Matthew .... 413-545-4475 211 D
matthew.dalton@umass.edu
DALTON, Shelisa .... 414-955-8740 492 F
sdalton@mcw.edu
DALTON, Valerie .... 404-215-2666 122 H
valerie.dalton@morehouse.edu
DALTRY, Rachel .... 610-436-2301 394 F
rdaltry@wcupa.edu
DALY, Adrian .... 213-621-2200.. 38 G
DALY, Arthur .... 740-266-5591 352 B
adaly@egcc.edu
DALY, Cory .... 307-855-2186 499 U
cdaly@cwc.edu
DALY, Erin .... 952-358-8834 239 C
erin.daly@normandale.edu
DALY, Jacqueline .... 908-835-2309 283 H
jdaly@warren.edu
DALY, Jillian .... 209-575-6159.. 76 K
dalyj@mjc.edu
DALY, Jon, C .... 315-655-7225 292 B
jcdaly@cazenovia.edu
DALY, Jonathan, P .... 805-421-5901.. 67 J
jdaly@thomasaquinas.edu
DALY, Kelly .... 714-432-0202.. 38 F
kdaly@occ.cccd.edu
DALY, Kenneth, D .... 845-398-4000 314 D
DALY, Mark .... 620-341-6522 173 C
mdaly@emporia.edu
DALY, Maura .... 312-893-7110 137 F
mdaly@erikson.edu
DALY, Melissa .... 856-227-7200 275 F
mdaly@camdencc.edu
DALY, Rebecca .... 906-487-7253 223 I
rebecca.daly@finlandia.edu
DALY-EIMER, Anne .... 856-227-7200 275 F
adalyeimer@camdencc.edu
DALZIEL, Murray .... 410-837-4955 204 C
mdalziel@ubalt.edu
DAMAR, Andrea .... 718-409-7200 320 D
DAMARJIAN, Steve ...... 312-850-7140 135 E
sdamarjian@ccc.edu
DAMAS, Tammi, L .... 202-806-4859.. 92 E
tammi.damas@howard.edu
DAMATO, Haylee .... 910-788-6343 337 G
haylee.damato@sccnc.edu
DAMES, Christopher ..... 314-516-6473 260 E
cdames@umsl.edu
DAMES, Jeanine .... 203-432-8040.. 90 B
jeanine.dames@yale.edu
DAMES, K. Matthew ...... 574-631-7790 161 G
kmdames@nd.edu
DAMIANI, Joel, J .... 716-851-1405 299 A
damiani@ecc.edu
DAMIANI, Susan, M ..... 718-990-7562 313 B
damianis@stjohns.edu
DAMIANO, Ann .... 315-223-2568 323 G
aedamiano@utica.edu
DAMIANO, Fred .... 315-781-3955 301 D
damiano@hws.edu
DAMIANO, Maureen ..... 610-409-3607 400 E
mdamiano@ursinus.edu
DAMICO, Debra, L .... 718-862-7213 304 K
debra.damico@manhattan.edu
DAMM, Christine .... 217-228-5432 147 C
dammch@quincy.edu
DAMM, Richard, T .... 920-748-8322 493 J
dammr@ripon.edu
DAMMERS, Rick .... 856-256-4551 280 H
dammers@rowan.edu
DAMMON, Dave .... 815-825-9538 141 D
ddammon@kish.edu
DAMODARAN, Purush .. 815-753-5660 145 H
pdamodaran@niu.edu
DAMON, Jud .... 904-819-6252.. 99 D
jdamon@flagler.edu
DAMP, Andrew, R .... 920-565-1000 492 A
dampar@lakeland.edu
DAMPEER, Angela .... 817-531-4403 450 F
adampeer@txwes.edu
DAMPEER, Justin .... 206-592-3301 480 C
jdampeer@highline.edu
DAMPHOUSSE, Kelly, R 512-245-2121 449 G
president@txstate.edu
DAMPIER, David .... 304-696-3066 488 N
dampierd@marshall.edu
DAMPIER, Paula .... 770-297-5896 116 C
pland@brenau.edu
DAMRAUER, Robert .... 303-315-2131.. 84 B
robert.damrauer@ucdenver.edu
DAMRON, Barbara .... 505-277-2498 288 C
bdamron@salud.unm.edu
DAMRON, Donald, M ... 606-474-3151 180 G
dmdamron@kcu.edu
DAMRON, Karla .... 214-860-2473 434 A
kdamron@dcccd.edu
DAMRON, Nancy .... 913-971-3393 175 H
nldamron@mnu.edu
DAMROW, Bobbi .... 715-422-5421 498 A
bobbi.damrow@mstc.edu
DAMS, Scott .... 610-861-1601 390 D
damss@moravian.edu
DAMSCHRODER,
Matthew .... 814-641-3151 386 E
damschm@juniata.edu
DAN, Chong .... 704-216-6035 330 D
cdan@livingstone.edu
DANA, Robert, Q .... 207-581-1405 196 D
rdana@maine.edu
DANA, Samantha .... 253-589-4520 478 A
samantha.dana@cptc.edu
DANCE, Andrea .... 252-335-0821 333 E
andrea_dance@albemarle.edu
DANCER, Erin .... 770-426-2974 122 A
erin.dancer@life.edu
DANCHO, Michelle .... 336-757-3710 334 D
mdancho@forsythtech.edu
DANCY, Gerlinde .... 963-638-2941 113 E
dancygl@webber.edu
DANCY, Regina, M .... 704-636-6454 329 F
rdancy@hoodseminary.edu
DANDOURAS, Spiros .... 516-686-1034 308 H
sdandour@nyit.edu
DANDRIDGE, Michelle .. 757-569-6791 474 A
mdandridge@pdc.edu
DANE, Jane, H .... 757-683-6702 468 C
jhdane@odu.edu
DANE, Stephanie .... 314-889-1467 252 G
sdane@fontbonne.edu
DANELL, Allison .... 252-328-6249 340 H
danella@ecu.edu
DANELL, James, N .... 507-354-8221 236 D
danelljc@mlc-wels.edu
DANES, Mark .... 515-271-1661 165 C
mark.danes@dmu.edu
DANFORD, Richard, K .. 740-376-4736 355 E
richard.danford@marietta.edu
DANFORTH, Brian .... 352-846-1849 110 E
bdanforth@uff.ufl.edu
DANFORTH, Dave .... 218-281-8490 243 B
danfo002@umn.edu
DANFORTH, Elizabeth ... 406-994-3836 263 G
danforth@montana.edu
DANG, Hung, D .... 805-437-8918.. 30 D
hung.dang@csuci.edu
DANG, Jessica .... 510-763-7787.. 24 F
DANG, Tuan .... 425-739-8818 480 D
tuan.dang@lwtech.edu
DANG-WILLIAMS, Thao 314-246-8757 261 D
thaodangwilliams@webster.edu
DANGELANTONIO,
Sarah .... 603-899-4278 272 G
dangelantonios@franklinpierce.edu
DANGER-JAMES, Renee 828-771-4066 344 B
DANGERFIELD, Deneen . 410-777-2830 197 C
drdangerfield@aacc.edu
DANHEISER,
Priscilla, R .... 678-547-6028 122 C
danheiser_p@mercer.edu
DANICA, Kathleen .... 518-244-4552 312 D
bouchk2@sage.edu
DANIEL, Adam .... 434-924-4052 471 F
ard2a@virginia.edu
DANIEL, Andrea, D .... 706-355-5111 115 C
adaniel@athenstech.edu
DANIEL, Bina .... 302-857-7403.. 90 D
bdaniel@desu.edu
DANIEL, Chett .... 417-455-5740 251 H
chettdaniel@crowder.edu
DANIEL, Chris .... 770-229-3327 125 F
chris.daniel@sctech.edu
DANIEL, Chris .... 813-974-2972 111 B
cldaniel@usf.edu
DANIEL, Eileen .... 585-395-5505 317 B
edaniel@brockport.edu
DANIEL, Ethel .... 617-217-9887 206 A
edaniel@baystate.edu
DANIEL, Julie .... 478-757-3803 127 D
jdaniel@wesleyancollege.edu
DANIEL, Juliet .... 828-225-3993 328 B
admissions@daoisttraditions.edu
DANIEL, Ken .... 541-278-5775 371 G
kdaniel@bluecc.edu
DANIEL, Kenya .... 404-225-4454 115 F
kdaniel@atlantatech.edu
DANIEL, Kevin, S .... 719-587-7741.. 77 F
ksdaniel@adams.edu
DANIEL, Larry .... 432-552-2120 456 C
daniel_l@utpb.edu
DANIEL, Mary .... 254-298-8362 445 B
mary.daniel@templejc.edu
DANIEL, Meredith .... 864-941-8442 410 D
meredith.d@ptc.edu

DAVENPORT, Bethany ... 319-363-1323 168 D
bdavenport@mtmercy.edu
DAVENPORT, Catherine, M .... 717-245-1231 382 B
davenpor@dickinson.edu
DAVENPORT, Chari .... 425-352-8000 477 F
cdavenport@cascadia.edu
DAVENPORT, Floyd ...... 573-651-2217 258 J
fdavenport@semo.edu
DAVENPORT, Jason ...... 804-828-0880 472 D
jedavenport@vcu.edu
DAVENPORT, John .... 309-438-2230 140 C
jmdaven@ilstu.edu
DAVENPORT, Kevin .... 256-306-2574.... 1 F
kevin.davenport@calhoun.edu
DAVENPORT, Kevin .... 804-524-5995 475 E
pdjackson@vsu.edu
DAVENPORT, LeChelle .. 901-722-3223 422 I
lhunt-davenport@sco.edu
DAVENPORT, Mike .... 270-824-8661 182 A
mike.davenport@kctcs.edu
DAVENPORT, Mona ...... 217-581-6690 137 C
mydavenport@eiu.edu
DAVENPORT, Robert ..... 313-577-4302 232 H
hd5623@wayne.edu
DAVENPORT, Robert ..... 405-585-5301 367 B
robert.davenport@okbu.edu
DAVENPORT, Robin ...... 973-618-3905 275 E
rdavenport@caldwell.edu
DAVENPORT, Sara .... 315-294-8597 292 A
davenport@cayuga-cc.edu
DAVENPORT, Susan, C . 609-652-4521 283 A
susan.davenport@stockton.edu
DAVENPORT, Zebulun ... 610-436-3301 394 F
zdavenport@wcupa.edu
DAVENPORT BROWN, Krystyna .... 802-654-2470 462 A
kdavenportbr@smcvt.edu
DAVENPORT TIGNOR, Stephanie .... 804-827-7882 472 D
davenportse@vcu.edu
DAVENPORTE, Cynthia .. 678-916-2604 115 G
cdavenporte@johnmarshall.edu
DAVES, Renate .... 714-241-6146.. 38 D
rakins1@coastline.edu
DAVEY, Daniel, K .... 757-479-3706 472 A
dkdavey@vbts.edu
DAVEY, Martha .... 307-675-0822 500 F
mdavey@sheridan.edu
DAVEY, Patrick .... 202-319-6907.. 91 G
daveyp@cua.edu
DAVEY, Stephen .... 919-573-5350 340 A
DAVID, Craig, A .... 573-882-9570 260 C
davidcr@missouri.edu
DAVID, Erin .... 312-369-7589 136 C
egenide@colum.edu
DAVID, Jerad .... 985-448-4303 192 C
jerad.david@nicholls.edu
DAVID, Kentiner .... 530-898-6451.. 31 A
kdavid@csuchico.edu
DAVID, Kim .... 478-553-2054 123 D
kdavid@oftc.edu
DAVID, Kimberly, C ...... 713-798-1543 430 E
kcotner@bcm.edu
DAVID, Kyle .... 774-455-7100 211 C
kdavid@umassp.edu
DAVID, Marc .... 843-661-8101 408 G
marc.david@fdtc.edu
DAVID, Marcella .... 312-369-7495 136 C
mdavid@colum.edu
DAVID, Matthew .... 934-249-3048 320 C
bksfarmingdale@bncollege.com
DAVID, Prabu .... 517-355-3410 227 C
pdavid@msu.edu
DAVID, Samantha, L ..... 610-917-1402 400 D
sldavid@valleyforge.edu
DAVID, Taylor .... 866-217-9823 187 D
DAVIDOWITZ, Menachem .... 585-473-2810 321 E
tiunyfax@gmail.com
DAVIDS, Cheryl .... 828-339-7018 337 H
c_davids@southwesterncc.edu
DAVIDSEN, Susanna ..... 866-492-5336 243 G
susanna.davidsen@mail.waldenu.edu
DAVIDSON, Anthony, R 718-817-4602 300 A
ardavidson@fordham.edu
DAVIDSON, Camille ...... 618-453-8761 149 G
camille.davidson@siu.edu
DAVIDSON, Charity ...... 248-218-2011 229 I
DAVIDSON, Cheryl .... 812-877-8686 160 C
clapp@rose-hulman.edu
DAVIDSON, Diana .... 870-777-5722.. 23 C
diana.davidson@uaht.edu
DAVIDSON, Erin .... 817-598-6285 457 C
edavidson@wc.edu
DAVIDSON, James, A ... 410-827-5846 198 B
jdavidson@chesapeake.edu
DAVIDSON, Jamie .... 702-895-3627 270 J
jamie.davidson@unlv.edu
DAVIDSON, Janet .... 724-925-4215 401 H
davidsonj@westmoreland.edu
DAVIDSON, Janine, A ... 303-615-0060.. 81 L
davidson@msudenver.edu
DAVIDSON, Jennifer ..... 708-456-3033 151 A
jenniferdavidson@triton.edu
DAVIDSON, Jennifer ..... 510-649-2441.. 44 E
DAVIDSON, John .... 817-272-5420 454 B
john.davidson@uta.edu
DAVIDSON, Jonathan ... 251-580-2222.... 1 I
jonathan.davidson@coastalalabama.edu
DAVIDSON, Jonathan ... 828-771-3029 344 B
jdavidson@warren-wilson.edu
DAVIDSON, Katrena, J .. 330-941-1712 364 G
katrena.davidson@ysu.edu
DAVIDSON, Laura .... 919-760-8531 331 A
davidsonl@meredith.edu
DAVIDSON, Laura-Lee .. 202-274-6260.. 94 B
lauralee.davidson@udc.edu
DAVIDSON, Leslie .... 608-363-2380 490 I
davidsonl@beloit.edu
DAVIDSON, Maryanne .. 475-210-6392.. 88 H
davidsonm6@sacredheart.edu
DAVIDSON, Meaghan ... 410-532-5195 201 C
mdavidson@ndm.edu
DAVIDSON, Megan .... 912-358-4002 124 H
davidsonm@savannahstate.edu
DAVIDSON, Michael ..... 617-552-3358 207 A
michael.davidson.3@bc.edu
DAVIDSON, Michael, E . 404-413-3154 120 C
mdavidson@gsu.edu
DAVIDSON, Mitch .... 260-481-6196 159 H
davidsom@pfw.edu
DAVIDSON, Nick .... 616-632-2475 221 A
nwd001@aquinas.edu
DAVIDSON, Quincy .... 607-274-3115 302 E
mdavidson1@ithaca.edu
DAVIDSON, Richard ...... 248-689-8282 231 E
rdavidson@walshcollege.edu
DAVIDSON, Roger .... 916-485-6028.. 50 J
davidsr@arc.losrios.edu
DAVIDSON, Sharon ...... 718-262-2155 295 D
sdavid@york.cuny.edu
DAVIDSON, Steed .... 773-947-6341 143 E
sdavidson@mccormick.edu
DAVIDSON, Stephanie .. 405-692-3241 366 C
stephanie.davidson@macu.edu
DAVIDSON, Stuart .... 336-272-7102 329 B
davidsons@greensboro.edu
DAVIDSON, Suellen ...... 870-368-2059.. 20 I
sdavidson@ozarka.edu
DAVIDSON, Sydnie .... 405-585-5801 367 B
sydnie.davidson@okbu.edu
DAVIDSON, Tracy .... 406-657-1015 264 G
tracy.davidson@rocky.edu
DAVIDSON, Tyler .... 205-349-4240.... 7 A
tdavidson@stillman.edu
DAVIDSON, Veronica .... 937-294-0592 356 D
veronica.davidson@themodern.edu
DAVIDSON-BOYD, Leslie .... 909-537-3252.. 33 B
lboyd@csusb.edu
DAVIE, Fred .... 212-280-1408 323 C
fdavie@uts.columbia.edu
DAVIE, Karen .... 646-378-6121 289 F
karen.davie@nyack.edu
DAVIE, Keith, A .... 646-564-6760 289 F
keith.davie@nyack.edu
DAVIES, Becky .... 972-721-5206 451 E
bdavies@udallas.edu
DAVIES, Cindy .... 828-448-6048 338 G
cdavies@wpcc.edu
DAVIES, David .... 585-567-9315 301 G
david.davies@houghton.edu
DAVIES, Elizabeth .... 617-587-5787 216 H
daviese@neco.edu
DAVIES, Elizabeth .... 815-740-3819 152 E
edavies@stfrancis.edu
DAVIES, II, Elizabeth .... 773-995-2438 134 J
edavie21@csu.edu
DAVIES, H. Dele, O ...... 402-559-5131 269 B
dele.davies@unmc.edu
DAVIES, Haldane .... 340-693-1004 512 B
hdavies@uvi.edu
DAVIES, Kim .... 706-737-1738 115 I
kdavies1@augusta.edu
DAVIES, Lincoln, L ...... 614-292-0574 358 E
davies.473@osu.edu
DAVIES, Lorelle .... 719-502-2447.. 82 D
lorelle.davies@pikespeak.edu
DAVIES, Lorelle .... 541-506-6000 372 E
idavies@cgcc.edu
DAVIES, Mark .... 607-436-2541 316 C
mark.davies@oneonta.edu
DAVIES, Patty .... 303-914-6298.. 82 L
patty.davies@rrcc.edu
DAVIES, Paul .... 804-752-7399 469 B
pauldavies@rmc.edu
DAVIES, Robert, O .... 989-774-3131 221 M
president@cmich.edu
DAVIES, Susan, B .... 706-721-0211 115 I
sdavies@augusta.edu
DAVIES, William, E .... 301-447-5234 201 A
davies@msmary.edu
DAVILA, Alberto .... 573-651-2112 258 J
adavila@semo.edu
DAVILA, Ariel .... 787-798-3001 509 F
ariel.davila@uccaribe.edu
DAVILA, David .... 361-698-1561 434 H
ddavila23@delmar.edu
DAVILA, Heydi .... 305-266-7678 104 A
h.davila@miuniversity.edu
DAVILA, Sheila .... 787-743-4041 505 B
sdavila@columbiacentral.edu
DAVILA RIVERA, Hector, M .... 787-765-4210 504 I
DAVINGMAN, Stephanie .... 217-351-2210 146 G
sdavingman@parkland.edu
DAVIS, Abby .... 479-356-2033.. 18 E
adavis@atu.edu
DAVIS, Abigail, H .... 706-886-6831 126 C
abdavis@tfc.edu
DAVIS, AJ .... 423-425-5860 426 D
aj-davis@utc.edu
DAVIS, Alan, B .... 205-853-1200.... 2 G
adavis@jeffersonstate.edu
DAVIS, Alana .... 804-752-7227 469 B
adavis@rmc.edu
DAVIS, Alfred .... 918-465-1894 365 K
adavis3@eosc.edu
DAVIS, Andrew .... 334-347-2623.... 2 A
adavis@escc.edu
DAVIS, Andrew .... 816-584-6411 257 E
andrew.davis@park.edu
DAVIS, Andrew .... 541-383-7592 371 I
apdavis@cocc.edu
DAVIS, Andrew .... 713-743-3009 451 G
adavis5@uh.edu
DAVIS, Angela .... 229-430-1710 114 G
adavis@albanytech.edu
DAVIS, Angela .... 919-536-7244 334 A
davisa@durhamtech.edu
DAVIS, Angelic .... 909-274-5512.. 52 K
adavis@mtsac.edu
DAVIS, Angiah .... 678-359-5076 120 D
adavis1@gordonstate.edu
DAVIS, Anita .... 860-297-4251.. 88 I
anita.davis@trincoll.edu
DAVIS, Anne .... 540-868-7000 473 C
DAVIS, Annette .... 509-313-6142 479 E
davis@gonzaga.edu
DAVIS, Anthony .... 718-262-5228 295 D
adavis13@york.cuny.edu
DAVIS, Anthony, J .... 704-216-6098 330 D
adavis@livingstone.edu
DAVIS, Audrey .... 301-546-0124 201 D
davisac@pgcc.edu
DAVIS, Betsy .... 360-385-4948 480 H
betsy@nwswb.edu
DAVIS, Billy .... 936-261-1550 445 E
bcdavis@pvamu.edu
DAVIS, Blake .... 214-768-3738 443 G
bbdavis@smu.edu
DAVIS, Brad .... 707-522-2824.. 63 C
bdavis@santarosa.edu
DAVIS, Brad .... 405-789-7661 369 H
brad.davis@swcu.edu
DAVIS, Bradley .... 814-824-2559 389 E
bdavis2@mercyhurst.edu
DAVIS, Bradley, J .... 408-741-2421.. 75 B
bradley.davis@wvm.edu
DAVIS, Brealle .... 423-461-8335 421 E
bkdavis@milligan.edu
DAVIS, Brenda .... 423-775-6596 421 I
bdavis@ogs.edu
DAVIS, Brent .... 559-730-3912.. 39 C
brentd@cos.edu
DAVIS, Brian .... 870-236-6901.. 19 D
bdavis@crc.edu
DAVIS, Britt .... 910-893-1215 327 C
davisb@campbell.edu
DAVIS, Brittany .... 662-846-4675 245 A
bdavis@deltastate.edu
DAVIS, Brittany .... 334-833-4428.... 5 H
finaid@hawks.huntingdon.edu
DAVIS, Bryan .... 951-343-4721.. 27 J
bdavis@calbaptist.edu
DAVIS, Bryan, P .... 229-928-1361 120 B
bryan.davis@gsw.edu
DAVIS, Bryson .... 270-745-2051 186 A
bryson.davis@wku.edu
DAVIS, Carenado .... 919-532-5759 338 E
cdavis19@waketech.edu
DAVIS, Carissa .... 708-656-8000 145 B
carissa.davis@morton.edu
DAVIS, Carolyn .... 601-877-6246 244 B
cadavis@alcorn.edu
DAVIS, Casey .... 713-221-5811 452 B
davisca@uhd.edu
DAVIS, Catherine, C ..... 609-497-7882 279 D
student.relations@ptsem.edu
DAVIS, Chad .... 701-477-7847 346 H
cdavis@tm.edu
DAVIS, Charity .... 330-325-6365 357 D
cdavis6@neomed.edu
DAVIS, III, Charles, E .. 540-887-7240 467 G
cedavis@marybaldwin.edu
DAVIS, Charles, N .... 706-542-1704 126 F
cndavis@uga.edu
DAVIS, Chris .... 706-385-1041 124 C
chris.davis@point.edu
DAVIS, Chris .... 910-672-1683 341 B
cdavis18@uncfsu.edu
DAVIS, Christina .... 617-585-1313 217 A
christina.davis@necmusic.edu
DAVIS, Christine .... 314-539-5000 258 C
DAVIS, Christine .... 479-619-3156.. 20 G
cdavis22@nwacc.edu
DAVIS, Christopher .... 765-674-6901 157 F
christopher.davis3@indwes.edu
DAVIS, Christopher, A .. 410-293-6381 502 I
cdavis@usna.edu
DAVIS, Cindy .... 785-442-6054 174 C
cdavis@highlandcc.edu
DAVIS, Claire .... 818-677-6105.. 32 E
claire.davis@csun.edu
DAVIS, Cliff .... 417-447-2652 257 B
davisc@otc.edu
DAVIS, Cody .... 501-977-2087.. 23 D
davis@uaccm.edu
DAVIS, Colin .... 309-649-6395 150 D
colin.davis@src.edu
DAVIS, Connie .... 985-549-2094 192 E
cdavis@selu.edu
DAVIS, Cory .... 402-280-2796 265 J
sm8335@bncollege.com
DAVIS, Courtney .... 256-372-8653.... 1 A
courtney.davis@aamu.edu
DAVIS, Courtney .... 801-863-8118 460 A
davisco@uvu.edu
DAVIS, Craig .... 781-768-7000 217 H
DAVIS, D. Scott .... 478-301-2110 122 C
davis_ds@mercer.edu
DAVIS, Damita, A .... 585-395-2772 317 B
ddavis@brockport.edu
DAVIS, Dana .... 863-667-5020 108 I
dcdavis@seu.edu
DAVIS, Dana .... 920-206-2323 492 C
dana.davis@mbu.edu
DAVIS, Daniel .... 212-854-6939 290 H
ddavis@barnard.edu
DAVIS, Danny, R .... 252-398-6250 328 A
drdavis@chowan.edu
DAVIS, Darin .... 405-789-7661 369 H
darin.davis@swcu.edu
DAVIS, Daryl, J .... 407-582-1255 113 C
djdavis@valenciacollege.edu
DAVIS, Deidra .... 207-326-2138 195 G
deidra.davis@mma.edu
DAVIS, Derek .... 646-664-9210 292 E
derek.davis@cuny.edu
DAVIS, Derek .... 816-268-5400 256 E
dldavis@nts.edu
DAVIS, Diana .... 513-244-4301 356 F
diana.davis@msj.edu
DAVIS, Diane .... 319-385-6215 167 F
diane.davis@iw.edu
DAVIS, Dirk .... 951-343-3905.. 27 J
ddavis@calbaptist.edu

DAVIS, Rick .... 703-993-8624 466 J
rdavi4@gmu.edu

DAVIS, Rick, C .... 402-280-1785 265 J
richarddavis@creighton.edu

DAVIS, JR., Robert, W . 570-941-7500 400 C
robert.davis@scranton.edu

DAVIS, Roberta .... 803-705-4411 405 G
roberta.davis@benedict.edu

DAVIS, Robin .... 804-257-5710 475 G
revrod1983@aol.com

DAVIS, Rodney, L .. 573-999-2145 174 G
revrod1983@aol.com

DAVIS, Rodrigo ..... 727-712-5720 107 C
davis.rod@spcollege.edu

DAVIS, Roger, W .. 724-480-3400 381 G
roger.davis@ccbc.edu

DAVIS, Rosario ...... 512-245-9222 449 G
rd31@txstate.edu

DAVIS, Sandra, S .... 803-535-1218 410 C
davisss@octech.edu

DAVIS, Sara .... 251-580-2100 ... 1 I
sara.davis@coastalalabama.edu

DAVIS, Scott .... 575-562-2425 285 E
scott.davis@enmu.edu

DAVIS, Shanda ...... 320-308-5538 240 D
shanda.davis@sctcc.edu

DAVIS, Shannon ..... 931-540-2705 423 D
shannon.davis@columbiastate.edu

DAVIS, Sharon .... 254-526-1346 431 E
sharon.davis@ctcd.edu

DAVIS, Sharon ...... 803-765-6029 405 D
sdavis@allenuniversity.edu

DAVIS, Sheila, J .... 706-542-9167 126 F
sjames@uga.edu

DAVIS, Shelby ..... 520-494-5492.. 11M
shelby.davis@centralaz.edu

DAVIS, Sheri .... 401-874-5654 404 E
sdavis@uri.edu

DAVIS, Sherri .... 205-929-6357.... 2 H
sdavis@lawsonstate.edu

DAVIS, Sherri .... 828-398-7900 331 K
sherrijdavis@abtech.edu

DAVIS, Sherry .... 812-221-1714 162 D
sherrydavis@vbc.edu

DAVIS, Sherry .... 254-659-7818 436 C
sdavis@hillcollege.edu

DAVIS, Stephanie .. 615-547-1387 418 C
sdavis@cumberland.edu

DAVIS, Stephen ...... 360-475-7805 481 D
sdavis2@olympic.edu

DAVIS, Stephen .... 301-295-3062 502 B
stephen.davis@usuhs.edu

DAVIS, Steve, J .... 208-496-3305 130 G
daviss@byui.edu

DAVIS, Steven .... 707-638-5270.. 68 B
steven.davis@tu.edu

DAVIS, Stewart ... 256-549-8603.... 2 B
sdavis@gadsdenstate.edu

DAVIS, Stuart .... 760-862-1333.. 39 A
stdavis@collegeofthedesert.edu

DAVIS, Sue .... 225-768-1802 186 H
sue.davis@franu.edu

DAVIS, Susan, M .... 434-924-4639 471 F
smd5r@virginia.edu

DAVIS, Suzanne ... 618-664-7000 138 D
suzanne.davis@greenville.edu

DAVIS, Suzanne, E ...... 315-268-6493 295 E
sdavis@clarkson.edu

DAVIS, Taisheika ..... 225-771-2790 190 K
taisheika_davis@subr.edu

DAVIS, Taishieka ..... 225-771-4530 190 J
taishieka_davis@subr.edu

DAVIS, Tamara ...... 317-274-8362 156 C
tamsdavi@iu.edu

DAVIS, Tamara, S ...... 317-274-8362 157 B
tamsdavi@iu.edu

DAVIS, Tammy ...... 325-574-7695 457 G
tdavis@wtc.edu

DAVIS, Tania .... 251-626-3303.... 7 E
tdavis@ussa.edu

DAVIS, Teresa .... 336-433-5570 341 C
tmdavis4@ncat.edu

DAVIS, Terry Daily .... 314-340-3688 253 E
davist@hssu.edu

DAVIS, Thom .... 661-654-2287.. 30 C
tdavis31@csub.edu

DAVIS, Thomas .... 520-206-4769.. 15 E
tdavis53@ppima.edu

DAVIS, Tiffany .... 206-726-5099 478 F
tdavis@cornish.edu

DAVIS, Tom .... 334-670-3981.... 7 C
tomdavis@troy.edu

DAVIS, Tonisha .... 870-575-8052.. 22 F
davistn@uapb.edu

DAVIS, Traci .... 309-796-5408 133 D
davist@bhc.edu

DAVIS, Tracy .... 951-763-0500.. 55 A
davist10@springfield.edu

DAVIS, Troy .... 714-484-7271.. 54 C
tdavis@cypresscollege.edu

DAVIS, Troy .... 413-748-3108 218 E
tdavis10@springfield.edu

DAVIS, Ty .... 770-457-2021 120 G
davist@iecc.edu

DAVIS, Wain .... 618-393-2982 139 C
davist@iecc.edu

DAVIS, Warren ..... 972-860-2944 433 H
wldavis@dcccd.edu

DAVIS, Warren ..... 972-860-2994 434 B
jarreddavis@dcccd.edu

DAVIS, Wartyna ..... 973-720-2731 283 I
davisw@wpunj.edu

DAVIS, Wayne .... 214-333-5163 433 D
wayned@dbu.edu

DAVIS, Weldon .... 865-573-4517 419 E
wdavis@johnsonu.edu

DAVIS, Wendy ...... 501-812-2273.. 23 E
wdavis@uaptc.edu

DAVIS, Wendy ...... 520-515-3623.. 11 O
davisd@cochise.edu

DAVIS, Wendy ...... 330-363-6347 348 B
wendy.davis@aultmancollege.edu

DAVIS, Wesley ...... 701-477-7853 346 H
wdavis1@tm.edu

DAVIS, Wesley ...... 828-669-8012 331 H
wesley.davis@montreat.edu

DAVIS, Whitney ...... 478-757-5170 127 D
wdavis@wesleyancollege.edu

DAVIS, William .... 708-534-4105 138 C
wdavis3@govst.edu

DAVIS, William .... 830-792-7415 442 G
deanoffaculty@schreiner.edu

DAVIS, William .... 610-359-6500 381 J
wdavis@dccc.edu

DAVIS, Zabe .... 662-562-3314 247 E
DAVIS-BAXTER, Angela . 704-636-6023 329 F
adavisbaxter@hoodseminary.edu

DAVIS-EYENE, Mishawn 857-701-1230 215 H
mdeyene@rcc.mass.edu

DAVIS-FREEMAN,
Juana .... 803-934-3464 409 H
jdavis@morris.edu

DAVIS-HAYNES, Angela 770-689-4779 114 J
ahaynes@aii.edu

DAVIS-JOHNSON, Max . 208-426-3033 130 F
maxdavis-johnson@boisestate.edu

DAVIS JONES, Chrissy . 800-222-4222 385 A
DAVIS-KAHL, Stephanie 309-556-3350 140 E
sdaviska@iwu.edu

DAVIS-KEPHART, Renee 334-386-7230.... 5 D
rkephart@faulkner.edu

DAVIS-LOWE, Eda ..... 407-582-3057 113 C
edavislowe@valenciacollege.edu

DAVIS-MAHONEY,
Robyn .... 212-678-3976 321 H
rd3034@tc.columbia.edu

DAVIS-SAMUELS,
Ivanetta .... 615-327-6141 420 D
isamuel@mmc.edu

DAVIS-SHINE, Zupenda . 609-626-6088 283 A
zupenda.davis-shine@stockton.edu

DAVIS-STREET, Jeanean 508-531-6151 212 B
jeanean.davisstreet@bridgew.edu

DAVISON, Frieda, M .. 864-503-5610 413 A
fdavison@uscupstate.edu

DAVISON, James .. 252-335-0821 333 E
james_davison99@albemarle.edu

DAVISON, Kimberly, A . 972-985-3781 432 I
kdavison@collin.edu

DAVISON, Natalie ..... 208-459-5188 131 A
ndavison@collegeofidaho.edu

DAVITT, Jeffrey .... 904-819-6489.. 99 D
jdavitt@flagler.edu

DAVITT, Kristin .... 412-647-6504 400 A
davitt@pitt.edu

DAVITZ, Pamela, K ..... 314-505-7010 251 D
davitzp@csl.edu

DAVOLA, Michela ...... 978-921-4242 216 F
michela.davola@montserrat.edu

DAVOUD, Mohammad . 912-478-7412 120 A
mdavoud@georgiasouthern.edu

DAVRAY, Niranjan ...... 315-228-7995 296 C
ndavray@colgate.edu

DAVROS, Harry .... 214-637-3530 457 A
hdavros@wadecollege.edu

DAW, Michael .... 415-442-6682.. 44 B
mdaw@ggu.edu

DAWE, Chris .... 660-562-1348 256 G
cdawe@nwmissouri.edu

DAWE, Richard, L .... 870-368-2006... 20 I
rdawe@ozarka.edu

DAWES, Daniel ...... 404-752-1833 123 A
ddawes@msm.edu

DAWES, Doug .... 702-968-5568 271 D
ddawes@roseman.edu

DAWES, Elliott ...... 646-312-4542 292 F
elliott.dawes@baruch.cuny.edu

DAWES, Trevor, A ...... 302-831-2231.. 91 A
lib-vplm@udel.edu

DAWIDOWICZ,
Christina .... 406-791-5366 264 J
christina.dawidowicz@uprovidence.edu

DAWKINS, Lisa ...... 304-357-4374 486 J
lisadawkins@ucwv.edu

DAWKINS, Norman .. 212-431-2142 308 I
norman.dawkins@nyls.edu

DAWKINS, Sandra, C ... 662-252-8000 248 E
sdawkins@rustcollege.edu

DAWN, Brett .... 417-667-8181 251 E
bdawn@cottey.edu

DAWN, Russell ...... 708-771-8300 136 D
president@cuchicago.edu

DAWSEY, Brian ...... 912-358-4154 124 H
dawseyb@savannahstate.edu

DAWSON, Brandon ...... 860-231-5430.. 89 G
bdawson@usj.edu

DAWSON, Bridgette ...... 740-699-3804 348 D
bdawson@belmontcollege.edu

DAWSON, Caroline .. 209-386-6730.. 52 B
DAWSON, Dani ...... 619-239-0391.. 34 H
ddawson@cwsl.edu

DAWSON, Greg ...... 615-248-1507 425 D
gdawson@trevecca.edu

DAWSON, Keith ...... 574-520-4480 157 C
khdawson@iusb.edu

DAWSON, Kevin ..... 202-806-6100.. 92 E
DAWSON, Leslie ..... 509-533-3527 478 E
leslie.dawson@sfcc.spokane.edu

DAWSON, Marcus .. 517-629-0224 220 E
mdawson@albion.edu

DAWSON, Marsha .. 607-274-3141 302 E
mdawson@ithaca.edu

DAWSON, Patrick .... 410-455-2356 202 G
pdawson@umbc.edu

DAWSON, Rachel ...... 660-596-7478 259 D
rdawson1@sfccmo.edu

DAWSON, Randall ...... 210-486-2534 428 C
rdawson@alamo.edu

DAWSON, Renita ...... 919-739-6980 338 F
rddawson@waynecc.edu

DAWSON, JR.,
Thomas, E .... 410-951-3792 203 E
thdawson@coppin.edu

DAWSON, Travis, M .. 716-888-2793 291M
dawsont@canisius.edu

DAWSON, Trey ...... 918-540-6113 366 F
jhdawso@neo.edu

DAWSON-SCULLY, Ken . 800-541-6682 104M
DAWTON, Dennis ..... 215-965-4073 390 C
academic@moore.edu

DAXENBICHLER, Amy . 309-694-5573 138 I
amy.daxenbichler@icc.edu

DAY, Alexandra, H ...... 609-258-8771 279 E
ahday@princeton.edu

DAY, Barbara .... 828-726-2471 332 E
bday@cccti.edu

DAY, Barton ...... 953-923-3201 448 F
bart.day@tstc.edu

DAY, Ben .... 508-626-4640 212 D
bday@framingham.edu

DAY, Blake .... 605-626-2550 415 H
blake.day@northern.edu

DAY, Charles ...... 518-262-3777 289 C
dayc1@amc.edu

DAY, Christopher .... 405-208-5210 367 E
cday@okcu.edu

DAY, Dani .... 505-454-2500 285 I
DAY, David .... 412-536-1070 386 H
david.day@laroche.edu

DAY, Deborah, A ...... 540-231-6285 475 D
alumni@vt.edu

DAY, Ian .... 734-432-5343 226 G
iday@madonna.edu

DAY, Jackson ...... 585-582-1230 298 E
jacksonday@elim.edu

DAY, Jeffrey .... 561-912-2166.. 99 C
jeday@evergladesuniversity.edu

DAY, Jewell .... 509-359-6924 478 H
jday@ewu.edu

DAY, John, R ...... 404-413-2564 120 C
jday@gsu.edu

DAY, John Mark .... 765-658-4199 154 G
johnmarkday@depauw.edu

DAY, Lawrence ...... 315-792-3099 323 G
lday@utica.edu

DAY, Levi .... 541-881-5875 376 E
lday@tvcc.cc

DAY, Mark .... 949-376-6000.. 47 G
mday@lcad.edu

DAY, Mellani, J .... 303-963-3434.. 78 D
mday@ccu.edu

DAY, Michael .... 812-941-2244 157 D
micaday@ius.edu

DAY, Michael .... 760-744-1150.. 56 B
mday1@palomar.edu

DAY, Michelle ...... 406-768-6351 262 I
mday@fpcc.edu

DAY, Mitzi .... 231-591-3800 223 H
mitziday@ferris.edu

DAY, Patricia ...... 518-828-4181 296 C
day@sunycgcc.edu

DAY, Patrick, K ...... 408-924-5900.. 34 B
DAY, Richard ..... 216-397-1904 353 O
rday@jcu.edu

DAY, Stuart .... 913-897-4903 177 G
day@ku.edu

DAY, Terri .... 615-230-3350 424 F
terri.day@volstate.edu

DAY-HAIRSTON, Beth .. 478-825-6856 118 E
beth.dayhairston@fvsu.edu

DAYAL, Ravinder ...... 916-361-5100.. 35 C
DAYHOFF, Brenda, K .. 301-447-5207 201 A
b.k.dayhoff@msmary.edu

DAYHOFF, Sharon, S ... 717-337-6276 384 C
sdayhoff@gettysburg.edu

DAYNES, Gary ...... 336-721-2617 339 H
gary.daynes@salem.edu

DAYTNER, Katrina ...... 309-298-1690 152 I
km-daytner@wiu.edu

DAYTON, Nancy .... 765-998-5204 161 A
nndayton@taylor.edu

DAYTON-JOHNSON,
Jeffrey .... 831-647-4647 461 G
jdaytonjohnson@middlebury.edu

DAYZIE, Merle ...... 928-724-6950.. 12 F
mtdayzie@dinecollege.edu

DE, Suvranu ...... 850-644-2525 110 B
sde@eng.famu.fsu.edu

DE ARAUJO, Pedro ...... 719-389-6687.. 78 E
pedro@coloradocollege.edu

DE ARMOND, Maureen 515-271-3133 165 F
maureen.dearmond@drake.edu

DE BAEZ SNYDER,
Tracey .... 724-830-1125 397 F
snyderdebaez@setonhill.edu

DE BERLY, Geraldine .... 413-755-4434 215 F
gndeberly@stcc.edu

DE BOER, David, S ...... 773-508-2530 142 G
ddeboer@luc.edu

DE BONO, Chad ...... 719-336-1517.. 81 J
chad.debono@lamarcc.edu

DE BOTTON, Leonard . 973-278-5400 291 A
len@berkeleycollege.edu

DE BOTTON, Leonard . 973-278-5400 274 J
len@berkeleycollege.edu

DE CAMPOS, Mateus . 978-468-7111 209 G
mdecampos@gordonconwell.edu

DE COOKE, Peggy, A . 315-386-7202 319 E
decookep@canton.edu

DE DIOS, Paul .... 714-484-7335.. 54 C
pdedios@cypresscollege.edu

DE FREITAS, Lisa, M .. 864-597-4203 413 E
defreitaslh@wofford.edu

DE FRIES, Carol ...... 215-496-6122 381 H
cdefries@ccp.edu

DE GELDERE,
La Donna, K .... 701-231-8522 345 D
ladonna.degeldere@ndsu.edu

DE GRAFFENREID,
Ellen .... 641-269-4605 166 D
graffeel@grinnell.edu

DE GROAT, II,
Arthur, S .... 785-532-0369 175 A
degroata@ksu.edu

DE GUZMAN, Maria, I .. 787-766-1717 509 C
ac_mguzman@uagm.edu

DE GUZMAN, Pedro .. 561-586-0121 101 P
DE HAAS PHILLIPS,
Sylvia .... 413-565-1000 205 I
sdphillips@baypath.edu

DE HARO, Oscar ...... 707-256-7160.. 53 E
odeharo@napavalley.edu

DE JESUS, Kiara ...... 787-738-2161 511 A
kiara.dejesus1@upr.edu

DEBOEF, Ryan ... 417-836-8500 255 J
ryandeboef@missouristate.edu
DEBOER, Eileen ... 318-487-7222 187 B
eileen.deboer@lcuniversity.edu
DEBOER, Keith ... 616-222-1247 222 F
keith.deboer@cornerstone.edu
DEBOER, Michael ... 334-386-7547 ... 5 D
mdeboer@faulkner.edu
DEBOLT, Ken ... 315-781-3146 301 D
debolt@hws.edu
DEBOLT, Patricia ... 918-631-2308 371 C
patricia-zumwalt@utulsa.edu
DEBOLT, Peg ... 260-359-4068 155 G
pdebolt@huntington.edu
DEBONA, OSB, Guerric 812-357-6549 160 G
gdebona@saintmeinrad.edu
DEBONI, Toni ... 805-437-8962 .. 30 D
toni.deboni@csuci.edu
DEBONIS, Marc, T ... 540-231-2728 475 D
marcd@vt.edu
DEBONO, Vincent ... 636-227-2100 254 C
DEBORD, Cris ... 304-293-2545 489 E
cris.debord@mail.wvu.edu
DEBORD, Kristy, L ... 770-720-9146 124 E
kristy.debord@reinhardt.edu
DEBORD, Toni Lynn ... 412-563-6673 125 D
tdebord@southuniversity.edu
DEBOSE, Diedre ... 716-926-8816 301 C
ddebose@hilbert.edu
DEBRAGGIO,
Michael, J ... 315-859-4654 300 F
mdebragg@hamilton.edu
DEBRUM, David ... 692-625-6416 503 F
ddebrum@cmi.edu
DEBURE, Olivier ... 727-864-8366 .. 98 G
debureoc@eckerd.edu
DEBURRO, Jennifer ... 207-602-2132 197 A
jdeburro@une.edu
DEBUS, Casey ... 307-532-8311 500 A
cdebus@ewc.wy.edu
DEC, Matthew ... 937-319-6082 347 E
mdec@antiochcollege.edu
DEC, Ted ... 631-687-5155 313 C
tdec@sjcny.edu
DECAIRE, Maryann ... 847-578-8810 148 B
maryann.decaire@rosalindfranklin.edu
DECAMP, Suzanne ... 406-756-3801 262 H
sdecamp@fvcc.edu
DECAPUA-RINCK,
Nicole ... 201-761-6023 282 H
ndecapuarinck@saintpeters.edu
DECARIE, Linette, A ... 617-353-7118 207 C
decarie@bu.edu
DECARLI, Jamila ... 619-388-3513 .. 60 I
jdecarli@sdccd.edu
DECARO, Peter ... 718-862-7379 304 K
pdecaro01@manhattan.edu
DECAROLIS, Crystal ... 845-905-4632 297 E
crystal.decarolis@culinary.edu
DECAROLIS, Donna, M . 215-895-1795 382 D
donna.marie.decarolis@drexel.edu
DECARVALHO,
Meghan, M ... 401-341-2348 404 D
meghan.decarvalho@salve.edu
DECATO, Kristen ... 414-297-6719 498 B
decatok@matc.edu
DECATUR, Jane ... 508-626-4585 212 D
jdecatur@framingham.edu
DECATUR, Sean ... 740-427-5111 354 I
decatur@kenyon.edu
DECAY, Jarlene ... 972-860-8071 433 H
jdecay@dcccd.edu
DECELLE, Michael, P ... 603-641-4107 273 H
mike.decelle@unh.edu
DECENT, Bridgette ... 901-678-5502 426 A
bdecent@memphis.edu
DECESARE, Renee ... 617-552-4400 207 A
renee.decesare@bc.edu
DECEW, Dave ... 603-428-2292 272 I
ddecew@nec.edu
DECHAMBEAU,
Aimee, L ... 330-972-7488 361 G
aimee@uakron.edu
DECHANT, Margaret ... 361-825-2863 446 E
margaret.dechant@tamucc.edu
DECHARINTE, Janeen ... 815-836-5263 142 C
decharja@lewisu.edu
DECHIARO, Thomas ... 215-895-1434 382 D
tdechiaro@drexel.edu
DECHTER, Gadi ... 609-258-4611 279 E
DECKARD, Marty ... 361-582-2469 456 H
marty.deckard@victoriacollege.edu
DECKER, Craig ... 719-255-4338 .. 84 A
cdecker@uccs.edu
DECKER, David, R ... 614-947-6017 352 J
david.decker@franklin.edu
DECKER, Douglas ... 724-983-0700 387 I
ddecker@laurel.edu
DECKER, Evan ... 510-215-3977 .. 40 G
edecker@contracosta.edu
DECKER, Jarron, P ... 518-276-6216 311 J
deckej3@rpi.edu
DECKER, Jedda ... 419-772-2403 358 D
j-decker@onu.edu
DECKER, John ... 989-964-4612 229 L
jdecker1@svsu.edu
DECKER, Kimberly, S ... 210-829-2782 452 D
kdecker@uiwtx.edu
DECKER, Marlene ... 563-876-3353 165 D
mdecker@dwci.edu
DECKER, SVD, Mike ... 563-876-3353 165 D
midecker@dwci.edu
DECKER, Nancy ... 724-983-0700 387 I
ndecker@laurel.edu
DECKER, Nancy, M ... 724-439-4900 387 H
ndecker@laurel.edu
DECKER, Randy ... 903-589-7143 437 D
rdecker@jacksonville-college.edu
DECKER, Stacy ... 513-244-4619 356 F
stacy.decker@msj.edu
DECKER, Steven ... 715-788-7113 498 G
steve.decker@northwoodtech.edu
DECKER, Susan ... 785-594-8454 171 C
susan.decker@bakeru.edu
DECKER, Timothy ... 845-298-0755 298 B
tdecker@sunydutchess.edu
DECKER, Tony ... 920-465-2300 494 F
deckera@uwgb.edu
DECKER, William, C ... 501-916-3328 .. 22 C
wcdecker@ualr.edu
DECKER, William, C ... 501-916-3302 .. 22 C
wcdecker@ualr.edu
DECKERT, Amanda ... 315-386-7688 319 E
wood121@canton.edu
DECKERT, Glenn ... 978-867-4736 209 F
glenn.deckert@gordon.edu
DECKINGA, Mike ... 219-864-2400 159 D
mdeckinga@midamerica.edu
DECLASS, SVD, Sonny .. 563-876-3353 165 D
edeclass@dwci.edu
DECLEENE, Rob ... 574-520-4872 157 C
DECOCINIS, Anthony ... 717-815-6579 402 G
adecocinis@ycp.edu
DECONNO, David ... 518-580-5718 315 A
ddeconno@skidmore.edu
DECOSTA, Leah ... 617-552-4700 207 A
leah.decosta@bc.edu
DECOSTANZA, John ... 708-524-6685 137 A
jdecostanza@dom.edu
DECOSTER, Daisy ... 201-761-6465 282 H
ddecoster@saintpeters.edu
DECOTEAU, Brian ... 701-221-1604 346 I
bdecoteau@uttc.edu
DECOTEAU, Jolene ... 701-255-3285 346 I
jolene.decoteau@uttc.edu
DECOTEAU, Katina ... 701-255-3285 346 I
kdecoteau@uttc.edu
DECOTEAU, Robert ... 360-392-4293 480 G
rdecoteau@nwic.edu
DECOURCY, Michael ... 502-597-5550 183 A
michael.decourcy@kysu.edu
DECOURSEY, Paul, A ... 515-574-1055 166 G
decoursey@iowacentral.edu
DECRISTO, James ... 336-734-2862 343 C
decristoj@uncsa.edu
DECRISTO, Jim ... 336-734-2862 343 C
decristoj@uncsa.edu
DECRISTOFARO,
Richard ... 617-984-1776 217 G
rdecristofaro@quincycollege.edu
DECROSTRA, Joseph ... 412-396-5180 382 E
decrostra@duq.edu
DECUIR, Bobbie ... 337-482-1000 192 F
bobbie@louisiana.edu
DECUIR, Karla ... 281-396-3792 452 C
decuirk@uhv.edu
DECUIR, JR.,
Winston, G ... 225-578-2111 188 J
DECUIR, JR.,
Winston, G ... 225-578-2111 188 K
wdecuirjr@lsu.edu
DEDDO, Gary ... 980-495-3978 329 A
DEDEAUX, Ebby ... 601-925-3310 246 D
ededeaux@mc.edu
DEDEAUX, Raynoid ... 601-877-6500 244 B
rdedeaux@alcorn.edu
DEDMON, Nicola ... 714-992-7035 .. 54 D
ndedmon@fullcoll.edu
DEDOMENICO-PAYNE,
Melissa ... 540-868-7000 473 C
DEDOMINICI, Peter ... 703-329-9100 .. 93 H
DEDONATO, Joy ... 516-572-0670 307 C
joy.dedonato@ncc.edu
DEDWYLDER, Jason ... 601-477-4075 246 A
jason.dedwylder@jcjc.edu
DEDWYLDER, Kari ... 601-477-4040 246 A
kari.dedwylder@jcjc.edu
DEE, Edward ... 718-779-1499 310 I
edee@plazacollege.edu
DEE, Edward ... 718-862-7597 304 K
edee02@manhattan.edu
DEE, Kay, C ... 812-877-8502 160 C
dee@rose-hulman.edu
DEE, Shawn, G ... 336-334-4822 334 F
sgdee@gtcc.edu
DEE, Tina ... 231-777-0660 228 C
tina.dee@muskegoncc.edu
DEEB, Bassam, M ... 716-827-2423 322 J
deebb@trocaire.edu
DEEB, Tiffni ... 612-659-6600 238 C
tiffni.deeb@minneapolis.edu
DEEDS, Brad ... 530-541-4660 .. 47 H
deeds@ltcc.edu
DEEG, Richard ... 215-204-7443 398 D
DEEGAN, Michele ... 484-664-3130 390 F
deanofacademiclife@muhlenberg.edu
DEEKEN, Lynnae ... 425-388-9502 479 B
ldeeken@everettcc.edu
DEEL, Ritchie ... 276-523-2400 473 E
rdeel@mecc.edu
DEEL, Susan, M ... 989-463-7176 220 F
deel@alma.edu
DEEM, Marie ... 412-536-1128 386 H
marie.deem@laroche.edu
DEEMER, Cindy ... 231-995-1058 228 F
cdeemer@nmc.edu
DEEN, Christopher ... 907-564-8282 ... 9 F
cdeen@alaskapacific.edu
DEEN, Michael ... 903-813-2306 429 I
mdeen@austincollege.edu
DEEN, Nathan ... 509-335-2636 484 D
nathan_deen@wsu.edu
DEER, Susan ... 845-574-4280 312 C
sdeer@sunyrockland.edu
DEES, Margaret ... 904-256-7020 102 G
mdees@ju.edu
DEES, Meg, K ... 704-637-4394 327 H
mkdees12@catawba.edu
DEES-BURNETT,
Keichanda ... 816-235-5628 260 D
deesk@umkc.edu
DEESE, Phyllis ... 903-823-3355 445 C
phyllis.deese@texarkanacollege.edu
DEESS, Eugene, P ... 973-596-3110 278 G
eugene.p.deess@njit.edu
DEETER, Anne ... 708-524-6846 137 A
adeeter@dom.edu
DEETER, Daniel, P ... 864-597-4232 413 E
deeterdp@wofford.edu
DEETZ, Kristi, R ... 812-888-5333 162 E
kdeetz@vinu.edu
DEEULIS, Chris ... 810-762-3000 231 C
cdeeulis@umich.edu
DEEVERS, Shari ... 269-965-3931 225 D
deevers@kellogg.edu
DEFALCO, Cindy ... 609-343-4900 274 E
DEFALCO, Julie ... 860-832-2551 .. 85 F
julie.defalco@ccsu.edu
DEFATTA, Jerry ... 601-266-5013 248 H
jerry.defatta@usm.edu
DEFAZIO, Harmony, R .. 520-626-9211 .. 16 H
defazioh@arizona.edu
DEFEDE, Kathryn ... 559-925-3145 .. 75 A
kathryndefede@whccd.edu
DEFEIS, Evelyn ... 973-684-5900 279 B
edefeis@pccc.edu
DEFELICE, Jonathan, P . 603-641-7010 273 C
jdefelice@anselm.edu
DEFELICE, Stacey ... 516-876-3009 318 A
defelices@oldwestbury.edu
DEFEO, William ... 252-335-0821 333 E
william_defeo@albemarle.edu
DEFFENBACHER, Mark .. 559-453-2239 .. 43 D
mark.deffenbacher@fresno.edu
DEFILIPPIS, Brian, J ... 410-704-2358 204 B
bdefilippis@towson.edu
DEFILIPPIS, Nunzio ... 818-333-3558 .. 53 J
nunzio.defilippis@nyfa.edu
DEFILY, James ... 708-524-6979 137 A
jdefily@dom.edu
DEFLORIO, Mel ... 802-831-1037 462 F
mdeflorio@vermontlaw.edu
DEFOOR, Keith ... 706-379-3111 128 A
kdefoor@yhc.edu
DEFORD, Victoria ... 763-424-0955 239 D
vdeford@nhcc.edu
DEFORE, Jody ... 678-359-5990 120 D
jody@gordonstate.edu
DEFORE, Matt ... 205-726-4021 ... 6 E
mdefore@samford.edu
DEFOREST, Kristin, A ... 607-746-4590 320 A
deforeka@delhi.edu
DEFOREST, Lori ... 616-259-1112 223 H
lorideforest@ferris.edu
DEFORREST, Matthew ... 704-378-1238 329 H
mdeforrest@jcsu.edu
DEFRAIN, Steven, R ... 610-917-1430 400 D
srdefrain@valleyforge.edu
DEFRANCO, Jeff ... 530-541-4660 .. 47 H
defranco@ltcc.edu
DEFREECE, Michele, T .. 607-746-4652 320 A
defreemt@delhi.edu
DEFRONZO, Jennifer ... 508-626-4923 212 D
jdefronzo@framingham.edu
DEFUSCO-SULLIVAN,
Andrea ... 978-762-4000 215 B
adefusco@northshore.edu
DEGAIN, Sabrina ... 336-506-4161 331 J
sabrina.degain@alamancecc.edu
DEGAISH, Ann ... 361-825-2481 446 E
ann.degaish@tamucc.edu
DEGARMO, David, L ... 417-862-9533 252 H
ddegarmo@globaluniversity.edu
DEGEARE, Chris ... 636-481-3467 253 G
cdegear1@jeffco.edu
DEGENHARDT, Brian ... 660-626-2304 249 C
bdegenhardt@atsu.edu
DEGENHARDT, Nancy ... 412-578-6423 380 A
nadegenhardt@carlow.edu
DEGEORGE, Dave ... 608-363-2039 490 I
degeorge@beloit.edu
DEGERMAN, Roger ... 336-316-2123 329 C
degermanre@guilford.edu
DEGEUS, Brianna ... 602-787-6500 .. 13 G
brianna.degeus@paradisevalley.edu
DEGEYTER, Julienne ... 530-754-2293 .. 69 A
jdegeyter@ucdavis.edu
DEGEYTER, Julienne ... 206-934-5300 482 H
DEGIOIA,
John (Jack), J ... 202-687-4134 .. 92 D
president@georgetown.edu
DEGIOVANNI, Kim ... 301-387-3040 198 F
kim.degiovanni@garrettcollege.edu
DEGITZ, Russ, J ... 260-359-4002 155 G
rdegitz@huntington.edu
DEGN, Jason ... 479-619-4337 .. 20 G
jdegn@nwacc.edu
DEGNER, Katie ... 352-424-1719 107 B
katie.degner@saintleo.edu
DEGRAW, Dean ... 206-726-5120 478 F
ddegraw@cornish.edu
DEGRAW, Mary ... 815-836-5815 142 C
degrawma@lewisu.edu
DEGRAY, Chris ... 413-236-3015 213 E
cdegray@berkshirecc.edu
DEGRAY, Terrance ... 408-270-6401 .. 62 E
terrance.degray@sjeccd.edu
DEGREGORIS,
Bernadette ... 617-731-3500 210 D
bdegregoris@hchc.edu
DEGREVE, Lou Ann ... 630-829-6197 133 B
DEGROAT, Kevin ... 718-405-3400 296 D
kevin.degroat@mountsaintvincent.edu
DEGROFT, Michael ... 717-391-3506 398 E
degroft@stevenscollege.edu
DEGROOT, Jon ... 715-675-3331 498 E
degroot@ntc.edu
DEGRUY, Theresa ... 504-941-8500 187 I
tdegru@dcc.edu
DEGUGLIELMO,
Michael ... 978-934-4807 211 G
michael_deguglielmo@uml.edu
DEGUIRE, Adam ... 480-965-0969 .. 11 A
adam.deguire@asu.edu
DEGYARFAS, Bridgette .. 213-738-6831 .. 66 A
bdegyarfas@swlaw.edu
DEHAAN, Brandon ... 616-331-3255 224 D
dehaanb@gvsu.edu
DEHAAN, Brian ... 866-323-0233 .. 58 D
DEHAAN, Laura ... 616-526-7114 221 L
ldehaan@calvin.edu

DELLACONTRADA, John .... 716-645-6969 315 F dellacon@buffalo.edu
DELLAPIETRA, Lynn ...... 215-968-8272 379 B lynn.dellapietra@bucks.edu
DELLAPORTA, Pamela ... 718-933-6700 306 J pdellaporta@monroecollege.edu
DELLAROCAS, Chrysanthos (Chris) ... 617-358-0831 207 C dell@bu.edu
DELLASALA, Kristen ...... 845-569-3439 307 B kristen.dellasala@msmc.edu
DELLATORRE, Bonnie ... 714-449-7495.. 51 D bdellatorre@ketchum.edu
DELLE, James .... 717-871-7462 394 B james.delle@millersville.edu
DELLE, James, A .... 717-871-7462 394 B james.delle@millersville.edu
DELLERT, Mary, E .... 217-786-2200 142 F mary.dellert@llcc.edu
DELLEY, Debra .... 512-505-3096 437 B ddelley@htu.edu
DELLI GATTI, Barbara ... 510-780-4500.. 48 D bdelligatti@lifewest.edu
DELLICARPINI, Casey ... 914-633-2122 302 C cdellicarpini@iona.edu
DELLICARPINI, Dominic, F .... 717-815-1303 402 G dcarpini@ycp.edu
DELLINGER, Dewey ...... 704-922-6207 334 E dellinger.dewey@gaston.edu
DELLINGER, Jade .... 239-489-9313 100 G jdellinger@fsw.edu
DELLINGER, Tim .... 731-425-2610 423 F tdellinger1@jscc.edu
DELLIT, Timothy .... 206-543-3106 484 A thdellit@uw.edu
DELLO BUONO, Ricardo .... 718-862-7527 304 K ricardo.dellobuono@manhattan.edu
DELLWO, Sarah .... 406-447-6908 263 F sarah.dellwo@helenacollege.edu
DELL'AQUILO, Bobbie .. 516-686-7851 308 H rdellaqu@nyit.edu
DELL'OMO, Gregory ..... 609-896-5001 280 D gdellomo@rider.edu
DELMARK, Cary .... 281-649-3703 436 D cdelmark@hbu.edu
DELMOLINO, Nick .... 413-236-3070 213 E ndelmolino@berkshirecc.edu
DELMONT, Angie .... 815-825-9686 141 D adelmont@kish.edu
DELO, Carl .... 718-409-7412 320 D cdelo@sunymaritime.edu
DELOACH, C. Gregory .. 678-547-6620 122 C deloach_cg@mercer.edu
DELOATCH, Jameson .... 540-373-2200 465 G jdeloatch@evcc.edu
DELONG, Allen .... 207-786-8305 193 D adelong@bates.edu
DELONG, Brian, C .... 610-799-1179 388 B bdelong2@lccc.edu
DELONG, Cliff .... 605-455-6079 414 H cdelong@olc.edu
DELONG, Lori .... 251-442-2302.... 8 C ldelong@umobile.edu
DELONG, Rhonda .... 313-317-6800 224 F rdelong@hfcc.edu
DELONG, Stephannie .... 620-229-6241 177 D stephannie.delong@sckans.edu
DELONGORIA, Maria .... 718-270-4850 294 E mdelongoria@mec.cuny.edu
DELONGPRE JOHNSTON, Dedee, I .... 336-758-3256 344 A
DELONIS, Alex .... 765-361-6375 162 G delonisa@wabash.edu
DELOREN, Dianne .... 505-467-6807 288 A diannedeloren@swc.edu
DELORENZO, Michael ... 217-333-1300 151 F michaeld@illinois.edu
DELORENZO, Robin .... 518-861-2513 305 B robind@mariacollege.edu
DELORIE, Jim .... 207-859-1183 196 A jim.delorie@thomas.edu
DELORME, Teresa .... 701-477-7862 346 H tdelorme@tm.edu
DELORT, Greg .... 785-539-3571 175 F gdelort@mccks.edu
DELOS REYES DAVIS, Mark .... 831-459-2654.. 71 A mdrdavis@ucsc.edu
DELP, Mark Damien ..... 510-356-4760.. 77 E
DELPLANQUE, Jean-Pierre .... 530-754-8380.. 69 A delplanque@ucdavis.edu
DELPRETE, Angela .... 440-375-7230 354 K adelprete@lec.edu
DELPRIORE, Michael ... 717-464-7050 387 E
DELQUADRI, Sheila ...... 509-574-4655 485 E sdelquadri@yvcc.edu
DELUCA, Anthony, L ..... 516-876-3177 318 A delucaa@oldwestbury.edu
DELUCA, Cynthia, A ...... 813-974-3077 111 B deluca@usf.edu
DELUCA, Eileen .... 239-985-3498 100 G eileen.deluca@fsw.edu
DELUCA, Mick .... 310-206-1753.. 69 D mdeluca@recreation.ucla.edu
DELUCA, Rocko .... 530-752-1011.. 69 A
DELUCA, Thomas .... 541-737-4279 374 H
DELUCA, Vincent, J ...... 212-817-7500 293 D vdeluca@gc.cuny.edu
DELUCA FERNÁNDEZ, Sonia .... 303-492-5822.. 83 M sdf@colorado.edu
DELUCCHI, Jennifer ...... 916-568-3039.. 50 I deluccj@losrios.edu
DELUCIA, Andrea .... 619-574-5809.. 43 B adelucia@fst.edu
DELUCIA, Melissa .... 203-773-8538.. 85 C mdelucia@albertus.edu
DELUNG, Jim .... 303-340-7520.. 80 C jim.delung@ccaurora.edu
DELVA, Jorge .... 617-353-3760 207 C jdelva@bu.edu
DELVECCHIO, Edie .... 201-200-3159 278 F edelvecchio@njcu.edu
DELVISCIO, Gregory ...... 607-777-2175 315 E gregdelv@binghamton.edu
DEMA, Anne, C .... 816-415-5912 261 G demaa@william.jewell.edu
DEMAEGD, Gwen .... 574-239-8349 155 E gdemaegd@hcc-nd.edu
DEMAGGIO, Steve .... 530-895-2327.. 27 F demaggiost@butte.edu
DEMAGISTRIS, Jared ..... 518-736-3622 300 B jdmagis@fmcc.edu
DEMAN, Shane .... 314-792-6132 253 J shanedeman@kenrick.edu
DEMANT, Timothy .... 509-777-3600 485 D tdemant@whitworth.edu
DEMARAIS, Melanie ...... 508-767-7332 205 F demarais@assumption.edu
DEMARCO, Anthony ...... 610-607-6294 396 A ademarco@racc.edu
DEMARCO, Deborah ...... 508-856-2903 212 A deborah.demarco@umassmed.edu
DEMARCO, Joanne .... 914-888-5215 305 H jdemarco1@mercy.edu
DEMARCO, Patricia .... 508-286-3458 219 F demarco_patricia@wheatoncollege.edu
DEMARCO, Rosanna ..... 617-287-7500 211 E rosanna.demarco@umb.edu
DEMARCO, Thomas ...... 610-519-4550 401 B tom.demarco@villanova.edu
DEMARCO FUENTES, Wendy .... 212-817-7187 293 D wdemarco@gc.cuny.edu
DEMARESKI, Roger .... 610-519-4530 401 B roger.demareski@villanova.edu
DEMARESKI, Roger .... 610-330-5133 387 B demaresr@lafayette.edu
DEMARK, Sarah .... 801-274-3280 460 E sarah.demark@wgu.edu
DEMARLE, Ann .... 802-860-2725 461 C ademarle@champlain.edu
DEMARS, Kerry .... 708-802-6154 138 A kdemars@foxcollege.edu
DEMART-KRAUS, Gina .. 440-646-8334 363 C gdemart@ursuline.edu
DEMARTE, Daniel, T ..... 716-338-1060 302 G danieldemarte@mail.sunyjcc.edu
DEMARTINO, Amanda ... 609-771-2231 275 J demartia@tcnj.edu
DEMAS, Christopher ..... 423-354-2588 424 B cddemas@northeaststate.edu
DEMAYO PUGNO, Courtney .... 419-448-2510 353 D cdemayo@heidelberg.edu
DEMBROSKI, Ben .... 414-847-3285 493 C bendembroski@miad.edu
DEMBSKEY, Evan .... 269-294-4315 223 J edembskey@glenoaks.edu
DEMCIE, Christine .... 716-829-7874 298 C demciec@dyc.edu
DEMEDEIROS, Joe .... 512-233-1443 441 N joed@stedwards.edu
DEMEDICIS, David .... 540-834-1026 472 J ddemedicis@germanna.edu
DEMEL, Tammy .... 470-578-6383 121 J tdemel@kennesaw.edu
DEMELIA, Andrew .... 401-232-6082 403 B ademelia@bryant.edu
DEMELLO, Ken .... 509-533-3407 478 E kenneth.demello@ccs.spokane.edu
DEMELO, Amy .... 417-269-3667 251 G amy.demelo@coxcollege.edu
DEMENT, Gregory .... 713-221-8280 452 B dementg@uhd.edu
DEMENT, Jennifer .... 503-491-7385 373 H jennifer.dement@mhcc.edu
DEMENT, Laura .... 303-373-2008.. 83 D ldement@rvu.edu
DEMENT, Paul .... 732-263-5679 278 B pdement@monmouth.edu
DEMENT, Randal .... 806-720-7508 438 F randal.dement@lcu.edu
DEMERCHANT, Melissa . 207-768-9462 196 I melissa.demerchant@maine.edu
DEMERITT, Dan .... 207-581-1865 196 D
DEMERRITT, Stan .... 806-716-2360 443 A sdemerritt@southplainscollege.edu
DEMERS, Amanda .... 410-287-1005 198 A mdemers@cecil.edu
DEMERS, Ben .... 323-241-5401.. 49 I demersbk@lasc.edu
DEMERS, Danielle .... 508-531-2744 212 B d1demers@bridgew.edu
DEMERS, David .... 207-621-3417 196 C david.demers@maine.edu
DEMERS, John .... 516-773-5000 502 G demersj@usmma.edu
DEMERS, Lisa .... 336-316-2178 329 C ldemers@guilford.edu
DEMERS, Patti .... 712-749-2167 164 A demersp@bvu.edu
DEMERS, Susan, S .... 727-791-2501 107 C demers.susan@spcollege.edu
DEMERSE, Kate .... 608-342-1854 495 E demersek@uwplatt.edu
DEMERSSEMAN, Anne .. 308-432-6224 267 G ademersseman@csc.edu
DEMERY, Rodney .... 318-274-3831 191 G demeryr@gram.edu
DEMETRIOU, Sophia ..... 212-925-6625 293 B sdemetriou@ccny.cuny.edu
DEMETRULIAS, Diana ... 617-731-3500 210 D
DEMEZZO, Robert, C .... 203-392-5886.. 85 H demezzor1@southernct.edu
DEMICHAEL, Mark .... 765-677-2317 157 F mark.demichael@indwes.edu
DEMING, Brett .... 970-247-7491.. 80 H deming_b@fortlewis.edu
DEMING, Faith .... 845-434-5750 321 B
DEMIR, Kristin .... 517-884-6142 227 C
DEMIRBAG, Jocelyn Romero .... 808-984-3471 130 B jocelyn.romerodemirbag@uhfoundation.org
DEMISHKEVICH, Maya .. 410-386-8157 197 G mdemishkevich@carrollcc.edu
DEMISSIE, Kitaw .... 718-270-1056 316 E kitaw.demissie@downstate.edu
DEMISSIE, Yoseph .... 313-496-2959 232 B ykidane1@wcccd.edu
DEMKO, Amy .... 513-244-4408 356 F amy.demko@msj.edu
DEMLEITNER, Nora, V .. 410-626-2510 201 E nora.demleitner@sjc.edu
DEMMERLE, Jennifer ..... 216-987-4709 351 D jennifer.demmerle@tri-c.edu
DEMMERS, Dan .... 559-638-0300.. 67 C dan.demmers@reedleycollege.edu
DEMMINGS, Elizabeth ... 765-658-4221 154 G betsydemmings@depauw.edu
DEMMONS, Daniel, C ... 401-865-1755 403 G ddemmons@providence.edu
DEMOND, Ramon, S .... 260-399-7700 162 A rdemond@sf.edu
DEMONTINEY, Jessie .... 406-395-4875 264 I
DEMORST, Wendi .... 310-434-4271.. 63 B demorst_wendi@smc.edu
DEMORY, Yolanda, F .... 757-446-8498 465 H demoryyf@evms.edu
DEMPSEY, Greg .... 206-934-5201 482 H greg.dempsey@seattlecolleges.edu
DEMPSEY, John, R .... 910-695-3700 337 E dempseyj@sandhills.edu
DEMPSEY, Matthew .... 972-273-3501 434 C mdempsey@dcccd.edu
DEMPSEY, Ron .... 812-749-1213 159 E rdempsey@oak.edu
DEMPSEY, Van, O .... 910-962-3354 343 B dempseyv@uncw.edu
DEMPSEY-SWOPES, Danielle .... 785-670-1906 178 A danielle.dempsey-swopes@washburn.edu
DEMPSTER, Douglas, J . 512-471-9601 454 C ddempster@austin.utexas.edu
DEMPSTER, Joan .... 310-506-6997.. 56 H joan.dempster@pepperdine.edu
DEMPSTER, John .... 215-885-2360 389 A jdempster@manor.edu
DEMSETZ, Laura .... 650-574-6581.. 62 J demsetz@smccd.edu
DEMUTH, Paul .... 651-450-3536 237 H pdemuth@inverhills.edu
DEMUTH, Paul .... 651-423-8370 237 E paul.demuth@dctc.edu
DEN DULK, Kevin .... 616-526-6234 221 L krd33@calvin.edu
DENARD, Letitia, J .... 404-270-5143 126 A ldenard@spelman.edu
DENARDIS, Leslie .... 860-632-3010.. 88 B
DENARDIS, Nick .... 313-577-4540 232 H ndenardis@wayne.edu
DENARDO, Hope .... 612-874-3700 236 E hdenardo@mcad.edu
DENARO, Jessica .... 914-606-8571 324 F jessica.denaro@sunywcc.edu
DENASHA, Lydia .... 715-634-4790 491 L ldenasha@lco.edu
DENBESTE, Michelle ..... 509-963-1400 477 G michelle.denbeste@cwu.edu
DENBOER, Marten .... 540-831-5404 468 E mdenboer@radford.edu
DENBY-BRINSON, Ramona .... 919-962-2211 342 B rdenby-brinson@unc.edu
DENCH, Emma .... 617-496-1464 210 B dench@fas.harvard.edu
DENDY, Phillip, B .... 512-499-4652 454 A pdendy@utsystem.edu
DENEAU, Kathleen .... 517-884-1136 227 C deneauk@msu.edu
DENEEN, Mary, C .... 757-683-3211 468 C mdeneen@odu.edu
DENENMARK, Lisa .... 415-575-6282.. 29 A ldenenmark@ciis.edu
DENEUI, Dan .... 541-552-6913 376 A deneuid@sou.edu
DENG, Qi .... 909-895-7138.. 45 K kiki@huca.edu
DENG, Yi .... 215-895-6824 382 D yd362@drexel.edu
DENG, Zhengtao .... 256-372-5560.... 1 A zhengtao.deng@aamu.edu
DENGEL, Daniel .... 215-204-7276 398 D daniel.dengel@temple.edu
DENHAM, Cynthia .... 256-840-4133.... 3 F cynthia.denham@snead.edu
DENHAM, Mark .... 313-993-3250 230 H denhamma@udmercy.edu
DENICOLA, Maura .... 201-355-1433 277 A denicolaa@felician.edu
DENIO, John .... 401-232-6046 403 B jdenio@bryant.edu
DENISTON, Paul .... 719-255-4665.. 84 A pdenisto@uccs.edu
DENK, Laurie .... 785-227-3380 171 H denkll@bethanylb.edu
DENLEA, Gregory, R ..... 864-644-5050 411 D gdenlea@swu.edu
DENLINGER, Keith .... 574-372-5100 155 C denlinka@grace.edu
DENMAN, Barbara .... 301-546-0185 201 D denmanbx@pgcc.edu
DENMAN, Brian, S .... 254-710-2663 430 F brian_denman@baylor.edu
DENMAN, Philip .... 253-833-9111 480 A pdenman@greenriver.edu
DENMARK, Stephanie ... 850-484-1605 105 G sdenmark@pensacolastate.edu
DENNARD, Rhonesia ..... 813-253-7006 102 A rdennard@hccfl.edu
DENNARD, Shajuana .... 256-761-8849.... 7 B sdennard@talladega.edu
DENNEHY, Kathryn .... 317-738-8083 155 A kdennehy@franklincollege.edu
DENNEY, Jon .... 650-723-2300.. 66 D

Index of Key Administrators DENNEY – DESPAIN 615

DENNEY, Jon .... 314-773-0083 250 C jdenney@brookes.edu
DENNEY, Karen .... 828-627-4546 335 A kdenney@haywood.edu
DENNEY, Mark .... 281-283-2100 452 A denney@uhcl.edu
DENNEY, Steve .... 419-289-4142 347 H
DENNEY, Tammy .... 903-675-6306 451 C tdenney@tvcc.edu
DENNIE, Deidra .... 859-233-8300 185 A ddennie@transy.edu
DENNIN, Michael .... 949-824-7761.. 69 C mdennin@uci.edu
DENNING, Jacob .... 303-292-0015.. 80 F jdenning@denvercollegeofnursing.edu
DENNING, CSC, John, F .... 508-565-1301 218 F jdenning@stonehill.edu
DENNING, Rusty .... 864-941-8417 410 D denning.r@ptc.edu
DENNING, Timothy .... 404-413-3517 120 C tdenning@gsu.edu
DENNIS, Alecia .... 614-251-4500 358 B
DENNIS, Anne .... 515-643-6640 168 B adennis@mercydesmoines.org
DENNIS, Edward, J .... 212-986-4343 274 J edward-dennis@berkeleycollege.edu
DENNIS, Edward, J .... 212-986-4343 291 A edward-dennis@berkeleycollege.edu
DENNIS, Fay .... 831-476-9424.. 42 I scextension@fivebranches.edu
DENNIS, James .... 615-329-8696 418 E jdennis@fisk.edu
DENNIS, Jason .... 419-448-5136 361 C dennisja@tiffin.edu
DENNIS, Jennifer .... 580-581-2339 365 C jdennis@cameron.edu
DENNIS, Kale .... 720-890-8922.. 81 H registrar@itea.edu
DENNIS, Larinee .... 405-585-4253 367 B larinee.dennis@okbu.edu
DENNIS, Larry .... 850-644-5804 110 B larry.dennis@cci.fsu.edu
DENNIS, Michelle .... 312-662-4000 132 D
DENNIS, Pam .... 704-406-4298 328 I pdennis@gardner-webb.edu
DENNIS, Paul .... 909-384-8286.. 60 F pdennis@sbccd.cc.ca.us
DENNIS, Peggy .... 419-372-8495 348 F fayed@bgsu.edu
DENNIS, Sarah .... 281-649-3350 436 D sdennis@hbu.edu
DENNIS, Terry .... 863-680-4148 100 F vdennis@flsouthern.edu
DENNIS, Vicki .... 318-678-6000 187 E vdennis@bpcc.edu
DENNIS, Yolanda .... 508-588-9100 214 F ydennis@massasoit.mass.edu
DENNISON, Anne .... 207-699-5054 194 G adennison@meca.edu
DENNISON, Jaimi .... 740-392-6868 356 G jaimi.dennison@mvnu.edu
DENNISON, Lori, R .... 315-859-4412 300 F ldenniso@hamilton.edu
DENNISON, Marla, K .... 651-631-5395 243 E mkdennison@unwsp.edu
DENNISON, Mary .... 507-285-7233 240 B mary.dennison@rctc.edu
DENNISON, Tracy .... 626-395-4068.. 29 B tkd@hss.caltech.edu
DENNISON, Wayne .... 812-877-8858 160 C dennison@rose-hulman.edu
DENNISTON, James .... 937-775-2821 364 D james.denniston@wright.edu
DENNO, Linda .... 520-626-2422.. 16 H ldenno@arizona.edu
DENNY, Lou Ann .... 480-965-7302.. 11 A ldenny@asu.edu
DENON, Gregory .... 978-934-2418 211 G gregory_denon@uml.edu
DENSE, Angela .... 417-865-2815 249 G densea@evangel.edu
DENSE, Angela .... 417-865-2815 252 F densea@evangel.edu
DENSMORE, Carrie .... 919-934-3051 335 D
DENSMORE, Timothy ..... 607-844-8222 321 I tad@tompkinscortland.edu
DENSON, Jeff .... 510-845-5373.. 29 D jeff@cjc.edu
DENSON, John .... 205-665-6237.... 8 D jdenson1@montevallo.edu
DENSON, Kiwana .... 361-698-2411 434 H kdenson1@delmar.edu
DENSON, Michael .... 415-476-5455.. 70 D mike.denson@ucsf.edu
DENSON, Rob .... 515-964-6638 164 F rjdenson@dmacc.edu
DENT, David, D .... 202-994-6706.. 92 C ddent@gwu.edu
DENT, Deborah .... 601-979-4299 245 G deborah.f.dent@jsums.edu
DENT, Sara .... 304-829-7744 486 B sdent@bethanywv.edu
DENT, Sharon .... 713-500-9850 455 D sharon.dent@uth.tmc.edu
DENT, Valerie .... 518-320-1100 315 C valerie.dent@suny.edu
DENTINO, Daniel .... 740-283-6346 352 I ddentino@franciscan.edu
DENTLER, James .... 330-337-6403 347 B registrar@awc.edu
DENTON, Aaron .... 252-985-5276 339 B adenton@ncwc.edu
DENTON, Amy .... 800-686-1883 222 B adenton@cleary.edu
DENTON, Andrew .... 952-446-4112 235 B dentona@crown.edu
DENTON, Andrew, C ..... 612-343-4745 241 O acdenton@northcentral.edu
DENTON, Carol .... 704-922-6484 334 E denton.carol@gaston.edu
DENTON, Christine .... 808-739-8597 128 C christine.denton@chaminade.edu
DENTON, Justin .... 815-224-0450 140 D justin_denton@ivcc.edu
DENTON, Melissa .... 913-234-0750 172 I melissa.denton@cleveland.edu
DENTON, SaVana .... 580-477-7712 371 D
DENU, Kim .... 805-565-6007.. 75 I kdenu@westmont.edu
DENVER, Genae .... 785-539-3571 175 F gdenver@mccks.edu
DENYS, Mark .... 215-204-7500 398 D mark.denys@temple.edu
DENYSSCHEN, Carol, A 716-878-4698 317 C denyssca@buffalostate.edu
DEOGHARE, Harsha ...... 909-469-5437.. 75 G hdeoghare@westernu.edu
DEOLALIKAR, Anil .... 951-827-2310.. 70 B anil.deolalikar@ucr.edu
DEOLIVEIRA, Shushawna .... 718-270-4744 316 E shushawna.deoliveira@downstate.edu
DEORSEY, Ellen, M .... 802-654-2212 462 A edeorsey@smcvt.edu
DEOSTHALE, Duleep ..... 716-285-1212 309 F ddeosthale@niagara.edu
DEPACE, Paul .... 401-874-2725 404 E pauldepace@uri.edu
DEPAOLA, John .... 518-262-6008 289 C depaolj@amc.edu
DEPAOLA, Natacha .... 312-567-3009 139 H depaola@iit.edu
DEPAS, Jacob .... 920-465-2000 494 F depasj@uwgb.edu
DEPASS, Donald .... 607-431-4112 300 G depassd@hartwick.edu
DEPAULL, Mark .... 607-753-2111 317 D mark.depaull@cortland.edu
DEPEDER, Suzanne .... 312-362-8648 136 F sdepeder@depaul.edu
DEPEW, Chris .... 845-434-5750 321 B cdepew@sunysullivan.edu
DEPEW, Monette .... 620-450-2211 176 I monetted@prattcc.edu
DEPINET, Andrea .... 419-372-8844 348 F adepine@bgsu.edu
DEPINTO, Michael .... 908-526-1200 280 C michael.depinto@raritanval.edu
DEPOUTOT, Al .... 727-376-6911 112 F adepoutot@trinitycollege.edu
DEPOY, Bryan .... 440-375-7028 354 K bdepoy@lec.edu
DEPPONG, Greg, J .... 517-355-5020 227 C deppong@msu.edu
DEPRETTO-BEHAN, Melissa .... 215-895-6154 382 D med87@drexel.edu
DEPRINZIO, OSA, Kevin .... 610-519-5431 401 B kevin.deprinzio@villanova.edu
DEPRON, Dianna .... 225-771-5050 190 K dianna_gilbert@subr.edu
DEPSEE, Kelly .... 973-278-5400 274 J kme@berkeleycollege.edu
DEPSEE, Kelly .... 973-278-5400 291 A kme@berkeleycollege.edu
DEPTA, Linda .... 269-488-4821 225 C ldepta@kvcc.edu
DEPTULA, Bill .... 603-428-2296 272 I wdeptula@nec.edu
DEPUTY, Meghan .... 386-312-4169 107 A meghandeputy@sjrstate.edu
DEPUY, Amy .... 419-434-5832 362 D adepuy@findlay.edu
DEPUY, Gail .... 502-852-0115 185 E depuy@louisville.edu
DER, Brenda .... 410-837-4813 204 C bder@ubalt.edu
DERAMUS, Danny .... 501-279-4339.. 19 G dderamus@harding.edu
DERBY, Amy .... 712-279-5396 163 H amy.derby@briarcliff.edu
DERBY, Andre .... 954-532-9614 102 D
DERBY, Breon .... 605-642-6590 415 F breon.derby@bhsu.edu
DERBY, Dustin, C .... 563-884-5682 169 C dustin.derby@palmer.edu
DERBY-TALBOT, Ryan .... 760-572-2000.. 41 D dean@deepsprings.edu
DERBYSHIRE, Lynne ..... 401-874-4732 404 E derbyshire@uri.edu
DERCOLE, Steve .... 212-237-8000 294 B
DERDA, Bob .... 412-392-6157 395 H rderda@pointpark.edu
DERDEN, Deborah .... 417-873-6939 252 A dderden@drury.edu
DERDEN, Wade .... 501-760-4203.. 20 E wade.derden@np.edu
DERDERIAN, Todd .... 508-767-7392 205 F tderderi@assumption.edu
DERDIARIAN, Armine ... 805-678-5029.. 74 A aderdiarian@vcccd.edu
DERDIK, Ari .... 347-619-9074 326 B
DEREE, Jeanne .... 508-626-4523 212 D jderee1@framingham.edu
DERFUS, Stephanie .... 912-443-5828 124 I sderfus@savannahtech.edu
DERIA, Jamilla .... 413-545-3517 211 D jderia@umass.edu
DERICO, Sherika .... 205-929-6437.... 2 H sderico@lawsonstate.edu
DERIEUX, Anne .... 206-726-5171 478 F aderieux@cornish.edu
DERIGGI, Nancy .... 914-923-2699 310 F
DERING, Allison .... 337-421-6955 188 H allison.dering@sowela.edu
DERK, Malcolm .... 570-372-4571 398 A derk@susqu.edu
DERMER, Shannon .... 708-534-8396 138 C sdermer@govst.edu
DERMISHYAN, Sima ..... 916-877-7977.. 59 E sima@sui.edu
DERMODY, Sean, B ...... 518-564-3606 318 C dermodsb@plattsburgh.edu
DEROCHE, Jessica .... 940-498-6282 439 I jderoche@nctc.edu
DEROCHE, Jessica .... 972-899-8402 439 I jderoche@nctc.edu
DEROCHER, Cynthia ..... 989-358-7394 220 G derocherc@alpenacc.edu
DEROCHI, Jack .... 803-323-2275 413 D derochij@winthrop.edu
DEROSA, John .... 203-837-9806.. 86 A derosaj@wcsu.edu
DEROSA, Michael .... 510-879-9280.. 60 C mderosa@samuelmerritt.edu
DEROSE, Michelle .... 616-632-2826 221 A derosmic@aquinas.edu
DEROSE, Paul .... 602-285-7517.. 13 H paul.derose@phoenixcollege.edu
DEROSSE, Anthony .... 919-573-5350 340 A aderosse@shepherds.edu
DEROUIN, Erika .... 719-587-7901.. 77 F ederouin@adams.edu
DERR, Colleen .... 765-677-3467 157 F colleen.derr@indwes.edu
DERRICK, Ann .... 512-381-7252 429 H aderrick@escoffier.edu
DERRICK, Damon .... 936-468-4305 444 H derrickdc@sfasu.edu
DERRICK, Diahann .... 541-881-5827 376 E dderrick@tvcc.cc
DERRICK, Joey .... 803-777-3205 412 A jcderric@mailbox.sc.edu
DERRICO, Cindy .... 805-437-3340.. 30 D cindy.derrico@csuci.edu
DERRITT, Shawn .... 913-288-7437 174 H sderritt@kckcc.edu
DERRIVAN, Kevin .... 617-217-9000 206 A
DERRY, John .... 972-241-3371 433 E
DERSTINE, Andria .... 440-775-8665 357 G andria.derstine@oberlin.edu
DERUBBO, Jeff .... 724-938-4415 394 C derubbo@calu.edu
DERUITER, Mark .... 269-749-7133 229 G mderuiter@olivetcollege.edu
DERWOSTYP, William ... 832-813-6281 438 E william.derwostyp@lonestar.edu
DESAI, Rebekah .... 512-637-1924 441 N rebekahn@stedwards.edu
DESALVO, Dianne, S ..... 989-774-4308 221 M desal1ds@cmich.edu
DESALVO, Stephen .... 718-429-6600 323 I stephen.desalvo@vaughn.edu
DESANCTIS, Greg .... 908-526-1200 280 C greg.desanctis@raritanval.edu
DESANCTIS, Marielena .. 303-352-6990.. 80 D marielena.desanctis@ccd.edu
DESANDRE, Carolynn ... 706-867-2778 126 G carolynn.desandre@ung.edu
DESANTIS, Charles, E ... 202-687-1787.. 92 D ced33@georgetown.edu
DESANTIS, Melanie .... 617-989-4590 219 D desantism@wit.edu
DESANTIS, Melissa .... 303-724-1748.. 84 B melissa.desantis@ucdenver.edu
DESANTIS, Susan .... 239-489-9234 100 G susan.desantis@fsw.edu
DESANTIS, Victor .... 717-871-7001 394 B victor.desantis@millersville.edu
DESANTIS, Victor, S ..... 717-871-5742 394 B victor.desantis@millersville.edu
DESAUTELS-POLIQUIN, Lisa .... 207-859-1243 196 A desautelsl@thomas.edu
DESCH, Andrew, P .... 920-748-8849 493 J descha@ripon.edu
DESCHENES, Marilyn, E 401-865-2074 403 G mdeschen@providence.edu
DESHAW, Carla, M .... 315-655-7147 292 B cmdeshaw@cazenovia.edu
DESHIELDS, Richard ..... 406-874-6226 262 K deshieldsr@milescc.edu
DESHLER, Kirsten .... 805-893-4588.. 70 E kirsten.deshler@ia.ucsb.edu
DESHONG, Jelanie .... 718-270-1490 316 E jelanie.deshong@downstate.edu
DESHPANDE, Satish ..... 269-387-5067 232 J satish.deshpande@wmich.edu
DESIMIO, Angelica .... 816-802-3461 253 H adesimio@kcai.edu
DESIMIO, Terese .... 575-527-7675 287 A tdesimio@nmsu.edu
DESIMONE, Barbara ...... 716-614-5904 309 E desimone@niagaracc.suny.edu
DESIMONE, Thomas ...... 732-255-0400 279 A tdesimone@ocean.edu
DESIR, JR., Serge .... 530-898-4177.. 31 A sdesirjr@csuchico.edu
DESJARDINS, Karla .... 860-932-4000.. 87 C kdesjardins@qvcc.edu
DESJARDINS, Linda ...... 413-775-1105 214 C desjardins@gcc.mass.edu
DESJEANS, Karen .... 413-552-2168 214 D kdesjeans@hcc.edu
DESMARAIS, Mark .... 603-342-3009 272 E mdesmarais@ccsnh.edu
DESMARAIS, Rachel, M 252-492-2061 338 D desmarais@vgcc.edu
DESMARTEAU, Doug ..... 620-901-6245 171 A desmarteau@allencc.edu
DESMOND, Bill .... 309-796-5437 133 D desmondw@bhc.edu
DESMOND, Daneisha ..... 336-744-0900 327 D frontoffice@carolina.edu
DESMOND, Jennifer ...... 207-581-1865 196 D
DESMOND, Jill .... 414-382-6067 490 G jill.desmond@alverno.edu
DESMOND, Nell .... 540-887-7225 467 G hdesmond@marybaldwin.edu
DESNOES, Davina, A ..... 607-255-9332 297 D davinadesnoes@cornell.edu
DESOLYN, Foy .... 409-747-3277 456 B defoy@utmb.edu
DESORMEAUX, Amy ..... 337-482-6293 192 F amyd@louisiana.edu
DESOUZA, Priscila .... 650-543-3786.. 52 A priscila.desouza@menlo.edu
DESPAIN, Robbyn, W ... 229-333-5980 127 C rdespain@valdosta.edu
DESPAIN, Trenton .... 540-261-8453 470 D trenton.despain@svu.edu

DESPATHY, Carol .... 603-206-8136 272 A
cdespathy@ccsnh.edu
DESPLAS, Edward .... 505-566-3253 287 G
desplase@sanjuancollege.edu
DESRAVINES, Melissa ... 212-280-1531 323 C
finaid@utsnyc.edu
DESROCHES, Reginald .. 713-348-4500 441 K
president@rice.edu
DESROSIERS, Candace .. 281-649-3049 436 D
cdesrosiers@hbu.edu
DESRUISSEAUX, Lisa .... 617-984-1619 217 G
ldesruisseaux@quincycollege.edu
DESSER, Kari .... 360-417-6291 481 F
kdesser@pencol.edu
DESTEFANO, Amy, C .... 210-805-5707 452 D
adestefa@uiwtx.edu
DESTEFANO,
Joanne, M .... 607-255-4242 297 D
jmd11@cornell.edu
DESTEIGUER, John .... 405-425-5100 367 C
john.desteiguer@oc.edu
DESTER, Lisa .... 518-743-2232 319 D
desterl@sunyacc.edu
DESVIGNE, LaVora .... 718-482-5114 294 D
ldesvigne@lagcc.cuny.edu
DESWERT, David .... 413-585-2200 218 D
ddeswert@smith.edu
DETAMPEL, SuAnn .... 920-465-2302 494 F
detampes@uwgb.edu
DETAR, Eric .... 315-279-5378 303 D
edetar@keuka.edu
DETEMPLE, Jon Jay ...... 610-526-6119 385 F
jdetemple@harcum.edu
DETER, Daniel .... 434-592-4172 467 E
ddeter@liberty.edu
DETERMANN, Nic .... 641-585-8164 170 E
nic.determann@waldorf.edu
DETIEGE, Jacques, J .... 504-283-8822 186 F
jdetiege@dillard.edu
DETLAFF, Alan .... 713-743-7819 451 G
ajdettlaff@uh.edu
DETLEFSEN, Karen .... 215-898-7225 399 J
karen.detlefsen@provost.upenn.edu
DETLEV, Angela .... 703-993-8969 466 J
adetlev@gmu.edu
DETRICK, Jeffrey .... 979-230-3383 431 A
DETRIE, Pam .... 901-843-3835 422 C
detriep@rhodes.edu
DETTELIS, Mary .... 716-896-0700 324 A
mdettelis@villa.edu
DETTLOFF, Kathy, L ...... 410-455-2939 202 G
dettloff@umbc.edu
DETTMER, Sharon, A .... 315-655-7258 292 B
sdettmer@cazenovia.edu
DETTY, Aaron .... 619-388-3706.. 60 I
adetty@sdccd.edu
DETUCCIO, James .... 352-588-8920 107 B
james.detuccio@saintleo.edu
DETWEILER, Craig .... 602-639-7500.. 12 L
DETWILER, David .... 970-248-1303.. 78 F
detwiler@coloradomesa.edu
DETWILER, Tim .... 616-988-3790 226 A
tdetwiler@kuyper.edu
DEUCHARS, Julie .... 503-399-5000 372 A
julie.deuchars@chemeketa.edu
DEUTER, Clayton .... 605-995-7132 414 E
clayton.deuter@mitchelltech.edu
DEUTSCH, Daniela .... 619-684-8790.. 53 K
ddeutsch@newschoolarch.edu
DEUTSCH, Gail, S .... 714-449-7459.. 51 D
gdeutsch@ketchum.edu
DEUTSCH, Josef .... 347-558-8422 321 F
jdeutsch11219@gmail.com
DEUTSCH, Nicole .... 410-462-7443 197 E
ndeutsch@bccc.edu
DEUTSCH, Yeruchem .... 718-963-9770 323 D
ed@utsb.org
DEUTSCHMAN, Robert .. 636-481-3386 253 G
rdeutsch2@jeffco.edu
DEVAN, Rhonda .... 828-669-8012 331 H
rhondadevan@montreat.edu
DEVANE, Lisa .... 910-879-5516 332 B
ldevane@bladencc.edu
DEVANEY, Chevy .... 315-781-3700 301 D
devaney@hws.edu
DEVASAGAYAM, Raj ..... 732-263-5550 278 B
raj@monmouth.edu
DEVAUGHN, Michael ..... 503-943-7155 376 H
devaughn@up.edu
DEVAUGHN, Misty .... 662-720-7200 247 D
mwdevaughn@nemcc.edu
DEVAULT, John .... 304-367-4644 488 L
jdevault3@fairmontstate.edu

DEVEAU, Shawn .... 617-287-5800 211 E
shawn.deveau@umb.edu
DEVENNEY, Michael ...... 215-503-3509 398 G
michael.devenney@jefferson.edu
DEVENS, Robert .... 512-232-7615 454 C
rdevens@utpress.utexas.edu
DEVER, Chris .... 307-382-1696 500 I
cdever@westernwyoming.edu
DEVER, David .... 310-434-4384.. 63 B
dever_david@smc.edu
DEVER, Lydia .... 770-426-2709 122 A
ldever@life.edu
DEVER, Rhea .... 906-227-2330 228 E
rdever@nmu.edu
DEVEREAUX, Kent .... 410-337-6040 198 G
president@goucher.edu
DEVEREAUX, Rebecca ... 305-626-3666 100 B
rebecca.devereaux@fmuniv.edu
DEVEREUX, Mandy .... 503-370-6924 377 E
mdevereux@willamette.edu
DEVERICKS,
Lynne Marie .... 856-222-9311 280 E
ldevericks@rcbc.edu
DEVERO, Susan .... 479-308-2289.. 17 E
susan.devero@acheedu.org
DEVERS, Monica, C ...... 612-330-1000 233 G
devers@augsburg.edu
DEVERY, Dennis .... 609-777-5693 283 D
ddevery@tesu.edu
DEVERY, Fletcher .... 251-380-4000.... 6 H
fdevery@shc.edu
DEVIER, David .... 269-294-4221 223 J
ddevier@glenoaks.edu
DEVILBISS, Mark .... 203-582-8721.. 88 F
mark.devilbiss@quinnipiac.edu
DEVINE, Carol .... 859-252-0361 183 C
DEVINE, Flora .... 912-358-4000 124 H
devinef@savannahstate.edu
DEVINE, Shawn .... 360-475-7106 481 B
sdevine@olympic.edu
DEVINNE, Christine ...... 440-646-8101 363 C
cdevinne@ursuline.edu
DEVINO, Terrence .... 617-732-1608 209 A
devinot@emmanuel.edu
DEVITO, Don .... 952-806-3910 241 R
DEVITO, Rose, M .... 617-984-1620 217 G
rdevito@quincycollege.edu
DEVITO, Theresa .... 413-565-1000 205 I
tdevito@baypath.edu
DEVITT, Amanda .... 860-231-5322.. 89 G
adevitt@usj.edu
DEVITT, Deondra .... 219-464-6370 162 C
deondra.devitt@valpo.edu
DEVIVO, Sharon, B .... 718-429-6600 323 I
sharon.devivo@vaughn.edu
DEVKOTA, Tripti .... 704-403-1639 327 B
tripti.devkota@atriumhealth.org
DEVLESCHOWARD,
Brian .... 269-783-2706 230 D
bdevleschoward@swmich.edu
DEVLIN, Bruce .... 434-791-5600 463 L
bdevlin@wffservices.com
DEVLIN, Bruce .... 434-791-5780 463 L
bdevlin@wffservices.com
DEVLIN, Catherine .... 413-775-1147 214 C
devlinc@gcc.mass.edu
DEVLIN, George, A .... 803-705-4417 405 G
george.devlin@benedict.edu
DEVLIN, Kathy .... 704-378-6776 329 H
kdevlin@jcsu.edu
DEVLIN, Kimberly .... 607-436-3024 316 C
kimberly.devlin@oneonta.edu
DEVLIN, Maura .... 413-565-1000 205 I
mdevlin@baypath.edu
DEVLIN, Sarah .... 704-216-3706 337 C
sarah.devlin@rccc.edu
DEVLIN, Thomas, C .... 510-642-3461.. 68 N
tcd@berkeley.edu
DEVOE, Kelsey, R .... 508-793-2276 208 A
krdevoe@holycross.edu
DEVOE OLBRYCH,
Dawne .... 518-243-4471 290 K
DEVOGE, Savala .... 218-281-8507 243 B
devog007@crk.umn.edu
DEVOLL, Karlin .... 432-837-8652 449 F
kdevoll@sulross.edu
DEVOND, Lesa .... 937-376-6163 349 H
ldevond@centralstate.edu
DEVONISH, Cheryl .... 203-857-7024.. 87 B
cdevonish@norwalk.edu
DEVONISH, Natalie .... 609-343-5083 274 E
ndevonis@atlantic.edu

DEVORA-JONES, Kayla .. 361-354-2532 431 L
kdjones@coastalbend.edu
DEVORE, Debra .... 740-392-6868 356 G
debra.devore@mvnu.edu
DEVORE, Lauren .... 713-646-1828 443 C
ldevore@stcl.edu
DEVRIES, Kristen .... 269-387-8785 232 J
kristen.devries@wmich.edu
DEVRIES, Susann .... 270-745-6422 186 A
susann.devries@wku.edu
DEW, JR.,
James Kenneth .... 504-282-4455 190 D
jdew@nobts.edu
DEW, Wendi, M .... 407-582-3841 113 C
wdew@valenciacollege.edu
DEWAAL, Rachel .... 615-514-2787 421 H
rdewaal@nossi.edu
DEWALD, Daryll .... 509-358-7521 484 D
daryll.dewald@wsu.edu
DEWALD, Luke .... 920-206-2339 492 C
luke.dewald@mbu.edu
DEWALD, Marylou .... 785-248-2550 176 F
marylou.dewald@ottawa.edu
DEWALT, Daniel .... 310-506-7427.. 56 H
danny.dewalt@pepperdine.edu
DEWALT, Marie .... 304-876-5299 489 A
mdewalt@shepherd.edu
DEWALT, Sheryl .... 207-307-3900 193 E
sdewalt@beal.edu
DEWAN, Craig .... 315-792-3393 323 G
cpdewan@utica.edu
DEWAN, Julie .... 315-731-5716 306 G
jdewan@mvcc.edu
DEWAN, Mantosh .... 315-464-4513 316 F
dewanm@upstate.edu
DEWAN, Rajiv .... 315-443-2736 321 D
rdewan@syr.edu
DEWAR, Cynthia .... 415-239-3292.. 37 C
cdewar@ccsf.edu
DEWBERRY, Angela, B . 704-894-2227 328 C
andewberry@davidson.edu
DEWBERRY, Thomas ..... 541-683-5141 373 A
cdewberry@gutenberg.edu
DEWBRE, Dane .... 806-716-2211 443 A
ddewbre@southplainscollege.edu
DEWBRE, Jeri Ann .... 806-894-9611 443 A
jdewbre@southplainscollege.edu
DEWEASE, Brandon .... 601-481-1340 246 B
bdewease@meridiancc.edu
DEWEERD, Crystal .... 801-542-7600 458 C
DEWEERDT, Daniel .... 414-288-4740 492 E
daniel.deweerdt@marquette.edu
DEWEERTH, Jennifer ..... 315-731-5818 306 G
jdeweerth@mvcc.edu
DEWEERTH, Stephen, P 610-758-5308 388 C
spd416@lehigh.edu
DEWEES, Bridget, P ...... 803-535-5793 406 E
bdewees@claflin.edu
DEWEES, Deborah .... 360-560-3353 485 A
deborah.dewees@wwu.edu
DEWEESE, Theodore ...... 410-955-7068 199 E
deweese@jhmi.edu
DEWELL, Roger .... 325-649-8825 437 A
rdewell@hputx.edu
DEWESE, Jerima .... 914-251-6000 318 E
DEWESE, Jerima .... 718-997-5565 295 A
jerima.dewese@qc.cuny.edu
DEWEY, Amy .... 575-234-9222 287 I
adewey@senmc.edu
DEWEY, Marvin, L .... 724-847-6880 384 B
marvin.dewey@geneva.edu
DEWEY, Matthew .... 806-742-2136 450 C
mdewey@ttu.edu
DEWEY, Michael .... 936-294-1325 449 E
mld072@shsu.edu
DEWEY, Robin .... 410-386-4699 200 D
rdewey@mcdaniel.edu
DEWEY, Tom .... 706-419-1105 117 G
tom.dewey@covenant.edu
DEWINTER, Naomi .... 563-288-6003 165 I
ndewinter@eicc.edu
DEWITT, Amy .... 304-876-5480 489 A
adewitt@shepherd.edu
DEWITT, David, C .... 812-941-2569 157 D
davdewit@ius.edu
DEWITT, Deborah .... 828-694-1862 332 C
deborah_dewitt@blueridge.edu
DEWITT, Jeffrey .... 785-864-0938 177 G
jeff.dewitt@ku.edu
DEWITT, Katelyn .... 417-268-1059 249 G
dewittk@evangel.edu
DEWITT, Kelly .... 479-308-2207.. 17 E
kelly.dewitt@acheedu.org

DEWITT, Lillian, M .... 617-258-8475 215 G
DEWITT, Linda .... 918-610-0027 365 H
ldewitt@communitycarecollege.edu
DEWITT, Siobhan, K ..... 412-578-6651 380 A
skdewitt@carlow.edu
DEWITT, William .... 828-641-0116 327 A
dewittwm@brevard.edu
DEWOLFE, Melissa .... 812-357-6610 160 G
mdewolfe@saintmeinrad.edu
DEWYRE, Lynne .... 330-569-5281 353 F
dewyrel@hiram.edu
DEXHEIMER, David .... 573-629-3124 253 D
david.dexheimer@hlg.edu
DEXTER, Brian .... 509-542-4727 478 B
bdexter@columbiabasin.edu
DEXTER, Kimberly .... 508-626-4951 212 D
kdexter@framingham.edu
DEY, Anind .... 206-685-9937 484 A
anind@uw.edu
DEY, Anita .... 989-964-4236 229 L
adey@svsu.edu
DEY, Farouk .... 410-516-0874 199 E
fdey@jhu.edu
DEY, Farouk .... 650-723-1983.. 66 D
fdey@stanford.edu
DEY, Saibal .... 301-295-3449 502 B
saibal.dey@usuhs.edu
DEYAMPERT, Fredi .... 906-487-7301 223 I
fredi.deyampert@finlandia.edu
DEYO, Sarah .... 225-214-6975 186 H
sarah.deyo@franu.edu
DEYOUNG, Michael ...... 702-968-2006 271 D
mdeyoung@roseman.edu
DEYOUNG, Renee .... 231-348-6618 228 D
rdeyoung@ncmich.edu
DEYTON, Patricia, H ..... 617-521-3876 218 C
patricia.deyton@simmons.edu
DEZARN, Andrew .... 859-251-4569 180 C
andrew.dezarn@frontier.edu
DEZEMBER, John .... 276-964-7332 474 E
john.dezember@sw.edu
DEZURA, Mia, S .... 540-868-7087 473 C
mleggettdezura@lfcc.edu
DHALIWAL, Amol .... 727-614-7292 107 C
dhaliwal.amol@spcollege.edu
DHALIWAL, Jasbir .... 901-678-1592 426 A
jdhaliwl@memphis.edu
DHANKHER, Veena .... 413-552-2543 214 D
vdhankher@hcc.edu
DHARMARAJ,
Premkumar .... 626-448-0023.. 46 K
DHAWAN, Atam, P .... 973-596-3220 278 G
atam.p.dhawan@njit.edu
DHAWAN, Reetika .... 928-344-7650.. 11 B
reetika.dhawan@azwestern.edu
DHILLON, Harpal .... 510-254-3756.. 48 G
hdhillon@lincolnuca.edu
DHILLON, Mona .... 415-869-2900 210 E
mona.dhillon@hult.edu
DHILLON, Upinder, S ... 607-777-2314 315 E
dhillon@binghamton.edu
DHILLON, Vineeta .... 707-654-1283.. 32 C
vdhillon@csum.edu
DHINGRA, Pawan, H ..... 413-542-2334 205 D
pdhingra@amherst.edu
DHRUV, Krista .... 717-337-6960 384 C
kdhruv@gettysburg.edu
DHUPELIA, Aarti .... 312-261-3484 145 C
adhupelia@nl.edu
DI BENEDETTO,
Eileen, M .... 212-854-7732 290 H
edibened@barnard.edu
DI DIO, Stephen .... 718-631-6044 295 B
sdidio@qcc.cuny.edu
DI LELLO, Joseph .... 914-367-8237 313 E
joseph.dilello@archny.org
DI LEO, Russell .... 215-898-6425 399 J
rdileo@upenn.edu
DI LIBERTO, James, G . 631-691-8733 302 D
dilibertoj@idti.edu
DI LIBERTO, John, G ... 631-691-8733 302 D
johng@idti.edu
DI NARDI, Jason .... 914-594-4668 308 J
jason_dinardi@nymc.edu
DI PIERO, Robert .... 209-954-5000.. 61 H
rdipiero@deltacollege.edu
DI SANTO, Dusty .... 303-762-6982.. 80 G
dusty.disanto@denverseminary.edu
DI ULIO, Marianne .... 414-847-3246 493 C
mariannediulio@miad.edu
DIAB, Dorey .... 419-755-4811 357 B
ddiab@ncstatecollege.edu

DIEHM, Perry .... 405-789-6400 369 G
pdiehm@snu.edu
DIEKMAN, Larry .... 269-294-4312 223 J
ldiekman@glenoaks.edu
DIEKMANN, Beth .... 507-285-7259 240 B
beth.diekmann@rctc.edu
DIEL-HUNT, Sarah .... 309-268-8593 138 F
sarah.dielhunt@heartland.edu
DIELE, Brian .... 631-655-1600 322 C
brian.diele@touro.edu
DIELS, Janie .... 989-463-7176 220 F
diels@alma.edu
DIEMER, Maria .... 815-394-5112 147 J
mdiemer@rockford.edu
DIENES, Tye, A .... 518-388-6000 323 B
DIENG, Samba .... 225-578-8242 188 K
sdieng1@lsu.edu
DIENGER, Rebecca, J .... 715-836-4423 494 E
diengerj@uwec.edu
DIENNO, Linda .... 703-370-6600 475 F
DIEP, Kyle .... 847-735-5035 141 F
diep@lakeforest.edu
DIERINGER, Deanna, L . 907-474-6629.. 10 B
dldieringer@alaska.edu
DIERMEIER, Daniel .... 615-322-7311 427 B
DIERS, Jennifer .... 641-628-5443 164 B
diersj@central.edu
DIERS, Jody .... 970-248-1366.. 78 F
jmdiers@coloradomesa.edu
DIETER, Mary .... 765-658-4286 154 G
marydieter@depauw.edu
DIETERICH, Scott .... 718-409-7204 320 D
sdieterich@sunymaritime.edu
DIETERLY, Cathy .... 954-492-5353.. 97 G
cdieterly@citycollege.edu
DIETERLY, Cindy .... 401-841-6594 501 L
cindy.dieterly@usnwc.edu
DIETRICH, Kim, E .... 260-399-7700 162 A
kdietrich@sf.edu
DIETRICH, Nathan .... 916-278-3725.. 33 A
nathan.dietrich@csus.edu
DIETRICH, Robb .... 570-321-4401 388 H
dietrich@lycoming.edu
DIETRICH, Sandra, L .... 919-866-5674 338 E
sldietrich@waketech.edu
DIETZ, Elizabeth .... 606-693-5000 182 H
edietz@kmbc.edu
DIETZ, Fred .... 940-397-4533 439 F
fred.dietz@msutexas.edu
DIETZ, Jonathan .... 620-792-9271 171 F
dietzj@bartonccc.edu
DIETZ, Kelley .... 919-508-2220 344 D
kelley.dietz@peace.edu
DIETZ, Maya .... 618-374-5162 147 B
maya.dietz@principia.edu
DIETZ, Timothy, D .... 240-567-7998 200 E
tim.dietz@montgomerycollege.edu
DIETZ, Timothy, N .... 530-226-4103.. 64 C
tdietz@simpsonu.edu
DIETZE, Jane .... 401-867-3986 403 A
jane_dietze@brown.edu
DIETZEL, Lea .... 231-348-6667 228 D
ldietzel@ncmich.edu
DIETZOLD, Heather .... 850-729-6922 104 L
dietzolh@nwfsc.edu
DIEUDONNE, Jose .... 484-664-3464 390 F
josedieudonne@muhlenberg.edu
DIEUJUSTE, Slandie ...... 413-748-3131 218 E
sdieujuste@springfield.edu
DIEUJUSTE, Slandie ...... 508-588-9100 214 F
sdieujus1@massasoit.mass.edu
DIEZ, Mickey .... 936-468-3401 444 H
DIEZ ROUX, Ana, V ...... 215-571-4013 382 D
ana.v.diezroux@drexel.edu
DIFFEN, Marta .... 830-792-7201 442 G
mdiffen@schreiner.edu
DIFFENDERFER, Jason .. 914-633-2373 302 C
jdiffenderfer@iona.edu
DIFFEY, Stephanie .... 662-472-9101 245 E
scdiffey@holmescc.edu
DIFFEY, Steve .... 662-472-9068 245 E
sdiffey@holmescc.edu
DIFINI, Marcelo .... 858-653-3000.. 29 F
mdifini@calmu.edu
DIFINO, Heather .... 315-268-6477 295 E
hdifino@clarkson.edu
DIFONZO, Kari .... 781-283-2360 219 C
cmacgreg@wellesley.edu
DIFRANCO, Heidi .... 803-641-3397 412 B
heidid@usca.edu
DIGGORY, Parker .... 518-580-8340 315 A
kdiggory@skidmore.edu
DIGGS, Amanda .... 334-670-5782.... 7 C
amdiggs@troy.edu
DIGGS, Christina .... 212-217-3900 299 C
christina_diggs@fitnyc.edu
DIGGS, Jeannie (Carol) 507-433-0571 240 A
jeannie.diggs@riverland.edu
DIGGS, Tina .... 740-203-8012 351 B
tdiggs4@cscc.edu
DIGIOACCHINO,
Dominic .... 973-803-5000 279 C
ddigioacchino@pillar.edu
DIGIRONIMO, Joseph ... 215-468-8800 386 C
director@culinaryarts.edu
DIGIRONIMO, Nicole .... 215-468-8800 386 C
DIGMAN, Jo-Ann .... 314-539-5358 258 C
jdigman1@stlcc.edu
DIGMANN, Ashley .... 605-995-2891 414 A
ashley.digmann@dwu.edu
DIGORIO, Jeremy .... 386-822-7022 111 F
jdigorio@stetson.edu
DIGRAZIA, Lauren .... 919-962-8289 342 B
lauren.digrazia@unc.edu
DIGREGORIO, Antonia .. 516-876-3156 318 A
digregorioa@oldwestbury.edu
DILAURO, Nanette .... 212-854-2154 290 H
ndilauro@barnard.edu
DILBECK, Cindy .... 805-546-3118.. 41 A
cynthia_dilbeck@cuesta.edu
DILBECK, David .... 479-394-7622.. 23 F
ddilbeck@uarichmountain.edu
DILBECK, Edie .... 573-840-9698 259 I
edilbeck@trcc.edu
DILBECK, LeAnn .... 479-394-7622.. 23 F
ldilbeck@uarichmountain.edu
DILENO, Susan .... 213-477-2535.. 52 J
sdileno@msmu.edu
DILES, David .... 906-635-2625 226 C
ddiles@lssu.edu
DILGER, Patrick .... 203-392-6586.. 85 H
dilgerp1@southernct.edu
DILL, Chris .... 601-605-3363 245 E
cdill@holmescc.edu
DILL, Deborah .... 325-649-8610 437 A
ddill@hputx.edu
DILL, Elizabeth .... 860-768-4268.. 89 E
dill@hartford.edu
DILL, Jeremy .... 207-741-5821 195 D
jdill@smccme.edu
DILL, Ken .... 864-644-5431 411 D
kdill@swu.edu
DILL, Marian .... 423-614-8304 419 H
mdill@leeuniversity.edu
DILLA, Bethany .... 541-684-7282 371 H
bdilla@bushnell.edu
DILLARD, Anthony .... 740-474-8896 358 A
adillard@ohiochristian.edu
DILLARD, Coralyn .... 806-291-3763 457 B
dillardc@wbu.edu
DILLARD, Cynthia, B .... 206-296-5758 483 B
cdillard@seattleu.edu
DILLARD, Helene .... 530-752-1605.. 69 A
hrdillard@ucdavis.edu
DILLARD, Paulette .... 919-719-3860 339 I
pdillard@shawu.edu
DILLARD, V. Harrison ... 610-861-1409 390 D
dillardv@moravian.edu
DILLBECK, Michael .... 641-472-1187 168 A
sdillbeck@miu.edu
DILLBECK, Susan .... 641-472-1187 168 A
sdillbeck@miu.edu
DILLE, Wayne .... 641-628-5336 164 B
dille@central.edu
DILLENGER, Jennifer ..... 864-587-4295 411 F
dillengerj@smcsc.edu
DILLER, Lisa .... 423-236-2417 422 H
ldiller@southern.edu
DILLER, Matthew .... 212-636-6875 300 A
diller@fordham.edu
DILLEY, Darlene .... 435-652-7704 459 G
darlene.dilley@utahtech.edu
DILLIHAY, Elliot .... 843-746-5100.. 93 H
DILLION, Shaquille .... 903-927-3214 457 I
sdillion@wileyc.edu
DILLMAN, Ray .... 405-703-8226 366 C
ray.dillman@macu.edu
DILLMAN, Stephanie, C 610-861-1566 390 D
dillmans@moravian.edu
DILLON, Anastacia .... 503-768-7095 373 D
adillon@lclark.edu
DILLON, Diana .... 605-856-8182 415 A
diana.dillon@sintegleska.edu
DILLON, Ellen .... 308-635-6787 269 E
dillone@wncc.edu
DILLON, Jennifer .... 216-397-1976 353 O
jdillon@jcu.edu
DILLON, John .... 603-641-7349 273 C
jdillon@anselm.edu
DILLON, John .... 610-683-4002 394 A
dillon@kutztown.edu
DILLON, Jordan, P .... 276-326-4201 464 A
jdillon@bluefield.edu
DILLON, Karen .... 641-269-3000 166 D
dillonka@grinnell.edu
DILLON, Katherine, E .... 914-594-4527 308 J
katherine_dillion@nymc.edu
DILLON, Kendall .... 515-263-6129 166 C
kdillon@grandview.edu
DILLON, Kevin .... 713-500-3535 455 D
kevin.dillon@uth.tmc.edu
DILLON, Mark .... 978-867-4900 209 F
mark.dillon@gordon.edu
DILLON, Mary Ellen ...... 704-922-6475 334 E
dillon.maryellen@gaston.edu
DILLON, Michele, M ...... 603-862-2062 273 H
michele.dillon@unh.edu
DILLON, Nate .... 661-722-6300.. 26 E
ndillon@avc.edu
DILLON, Patricia .... 215-951-1430 386 I
dillonp@lasalle.edu
DILLON, Patrick .... 508-830-5103 213 A
pdillon@maritime.edu
DILLON, Sarah .... 715-675-3331 498 E
dillon@ntc.edu
DILLOW, Al .... 217-245-3168 139 A
al.dillow@ic.edu
DILLS-ALLEN,
Michael, C .... 530-898-5142.. 31 A
mcdills-allen@csuchico.edu
DILLSWORTH, Gary .... 716-926-8920 301 C
gdillsworth@hilbert.edu
DILONE, Odile .... 860-906-5141.. 86 C
odilone@ccc.commnet.edu
DILORENZO, Judith ...... 518-629-7204 302 A
j.dilorenzo@hvcc.edu
DILORENZO, Kenneth ... 787-264-1912 507 E
kenneth_dilorenzo@intersg.edu
DILORENZO, Molly .... 617-735-9876 209 A
dilorenzom@emmanuel.edu
DILORENZO, Vicki .... 518-694-7331 289 A
vicki.dilorenzo@acphs.edu
DILS, Keith .... 724-738-2292 394 E
keith.dils@sru.edu
DILUCA, Susan .... 502-895-3411 183 E
sdiluca@lpts.edu
DILUSTRO, John .... 252-398-6220 328 A
dilusj@chowan.edu
DILWORTH, Paulette, P 205-934-0541.... 8 A
ppddei@uab.edu
DIMAGGIO, Jacqueline . 864-250-8179 408 J
jacqui.dimaggio@gvltec.edu
DIMANNA, Nicholas .... 303-410-2416.. 83 G
nicholas.dimanna@spartan.edu
DIMARCO, Erin .... 302-356-6924.. 91 C
erin.j.dimarco@wilmu.edu
DIMARCO, Scott .... 570-662-4689 393 E
sdimarco@mansfield.edu
DIMARIA, David .... 410-455-2624 202 G
dimaria@umbc.edu
DIMARINO, Nicholas .... 610-558-5626 390 G
dimarinn@neumann.edu
DIMARIO, Joseph, X .... 847-578-8494 148 B
joseph.dimario@rosalindfranklin.edu
DIMARZIO, Denise .... 508-678-2811 213 F
denise.dimarzio@bristolcc.edu
DIMARZO, Dean .... 845-569-3219 307 B
dean.dimarzo@msmc.edu
DIMATTIA, Andrea .... 570-504-9634 384 A
adimattia@som.geisinger.edu
DIMATTIO, David .... 563-588-6432 164 C
david.dimattio@clarke.edu
DIMATTIO,
Mary Jane, K .... 570-941-7400 400 C
maryjane.dimattio@scranton.edu
DIMAURO, Alfredo .... 860-253-3031.. 86 B
adimauro@asnuntuck.edu
DIMAURO, Giorgio .... 212-854-7430 290 H
gdimauro@barnard.edu
DIMAURO, Michael .... 315-781-3691 301 D
dimauro@hws.edu
DIMEMMO, Kristine ...... 951-222-8265.. 59 D
kristine.dimemmo@rcc.edu
DIMET, Emily .... 989-328-1245 227 G
emily.dimet@montcalm.edu
DIMIDIK, George .... 937-481-2543 363 H
george_dimidik@wilmington.edu
DIMING, Mianta' .... 219-980-6620 157 A
mdiming@iun.edu
DIMINO, Laura, R .... 717-728-2419 380 D
lauradimino@centralpenn.edu
DIMINO, Solweig .... 973-300-2215 283 B
sdimino@sussex.edu
DIMITCH, Jessica .... 701-662-1546 346 A
jessica.l.dimitch@lrsc.edu
DIMITRI, Nick .... 510-215-3848.. 40 G
ndimitri@contracosta.edu
DIMITRIOU, Kathy .... 313-845-9650 224 F
kdimitriou@hfcc.edu
DIMITROV, Danielle, E . 718-982-2335 293 C
danielle.dimitrov@csi.cuny.edu
DIMITROVA, Diana .... 604-274-3306 302 E
ddimitrova@ithaca.edu
DIMOFF, Danielle .... 419-372-2356 348 F
ddimoff@bgsu.edu
DIMOLITSAS, Spiros ..... 202-687-3730.. 92 D
seniorvp@georgetown.edu
DIMOND, David .... 914-632-5400 306 J
ddimond@monroecollege.edu
DIMOPLON, Vera .... 617-873-0614 207 E
vera.dimoplon@cambridgecollege.edu
DIMURA, Maria .... 704-461-6717 326 I
mariadimura@bac.edu
DIN, Kristine .... 508-565-1411 218 F
kdin@stonehill.edu
DINALLO, JR.,
Benjamin .... 201-559-3507 277 A
dinallob@felician.edu
DINAN, Abigail .... 315-279-5289 303 D
adinan@keuka.edu
DINAN, Richard .... 856-225-2910 281 A
richard.dinan@rutgers.edu
DINAN, Susan .... 516-877-3803 288 L
sdinan@adelphi.edu
DINDY, Bill .... 706-854-4718 121 C
bdindy@helms.edu
DINE, Andrea, B .... 781-736-3620 207 D
dine@brandeis.edu
DINEEN-THACKERAY,
Lorrie .... 707-654-1086.. 32 C
ldineen-thackeray@csum.edu
DINEGAR, Leonard .... 303-860-5600.. 83 L
leonard.dinegar@cu.edu
DINEHART, Laura .... 305-348-3790 109 H
laura.dinehart@fiu.edu
DINELLA, Amy .... 352-245-4119 112 D
amy.dinella@taylorcollege.edu
DINEROS, Jedrek .... 717-358-3860 383 G
jdineros@fandm.edu
DING, Xiaoting .... 626-289-7719.. 24 K
registrar@amu.edu
DINGER, Julie .... 580-349-1402 367 F
julie.dinger@opsu.edu
DINGES, Danielle .... 406-874-6182 262 K
dingesd@milescc.edu
DINGESS, Debbie .... 304-792-7098 487 I
DINGESS, Robert, S ...... 304-792-7098 487 I
DINGLE, Terry .... 843-661-8321 408 G
terry.dingle@fdtc.edu
DINGMANN, Melissa .... 218-477-2085 239 A
melissa.dingmann@mnstate.edu
DINGUS-EASON,
Jeannine .... 401-456-8110 404 A
jdinguseason@ric.edu
DINH, Chris .... 616-957-8619 221 K
crd081@calvinseminary.edu
DINH, Katie .... 941-281-6784 387 C
kdinh@lecom.edu
DINKENS, Sedaric .... 903-730-4890 437 E
sdinkens@jarvis.edu
DINKINS, Elizabeth .... 502-272-7958 179 D
edinkins@bellarmine.edu
DINMORE, Sachiyo .... 434-223-6392 466 K
sdinmore@hsc.edu
DINNAN, Matthew, A .... 203-254-4000.. 87 G
madinnan@fairfield.edu
DINNO, Christopher ..... 707-664-2870.. 34 C
christopher.dinno@sonoma.edu
DINOTO, Sandra .... 518-262-5034 289 C
dinotos@amc.edu
DINOVO, Carolyn .... 614-985-2211 359 K
cdinovo@pcj.edu
DINSMAN, Joshua .... 631-656-3137 299 G
joshua.dinsman@ftc.edu
DINSMORE, Eric .... 717-815-1226 402 G
edinsmore@ycp.edu
DINUCCI, Jo Ellen .... 208-426-1200 130 F
jedinucc@boisestate.edu
DIONNE, Kathryn .... 239-280-2565.. 95 M
kathryn.dionne@avemaria.edu
DIONNE, Trisha .... 603-271-6484 272 C
tdionne@ccsnh.edu

Index of Key Administrators DIORIO – DOBRANSKY 619

DIORIO, Annette .... 610-330-5082 387 B diorioa@lafayette.edu
DIOUF, OSB, Francois .. 724-805-2500 397 C francois.diouf@stvincent.edu
DIPALMA, Jordan .... 701-231-8011 345 D
DIPAOLA, Robert .... 859-257-2911 185 D provost@uky.edu
DIPAOLO, John .... 415-565-4804.. 69 B dipaolojohn@uchastings.edu.edu
DIPAOLO, Lawrence ...... 610-558-5507 390 G dipaolol@neumann.edu
DIPASQUALE, Ray .... 508-588-9100 214 F
DIPIERO, Thomas .... 214-768-3212 443 G tdipiero@smu.edu
DIPIETRO, Mark .... 802-387-1632 461 E markdipietro@landmark.edu
DIPIETRO, Rachael .... 203-857-7162.. 87 B rdipietro@norwalk.edu
DIPLOCK, Peter .... 860-486-2915.. 89 B peter.diplock@uconn.edu
DIPPEL, Holger .... 508-999-9181 211 F hdippel@umassd.edu
DIPRETA, Lauren, R .... 516-463-6180 301 E lauren.dipreta@hofstra.edu
DIRAIMONDO, John ..... 815-226-4006 147 J jdiraimondo@rockford.edu
DIRICO, Rocco .... 617-627-3583 219 A rocco.dirico@tufts.edu
DIRIENZO, Denise .... 716-829-8000 298 C dirienzd@dyc.edu
DIRINGER, Haley .... 269-749-7570 229 G hdiringer@olivetcollege.edu
DIRISIO, Mary .... 910-678-7351 334 C dirisiom@faytechcc.edu
DIRK, Brian .... 440-375-7220 354 K bdirk@lec.edu
DIRKS, Kathleen, M ...... 815-835-6386 149 A kathleen.m.dirks@svcc.edu
DIRKS, Kurt, T .... 314-935-4074 261 B dirks@wustl.edu
DIRKSCHNEIDER, Carla 402-552-6295 265 G dirkschneider@clarksoncollege.edu
DIRKSEN, Andrew .... 507-452-4430 242 H adirksen@smumn.edu
DIRKSEN, Dawn .... 866-323-0233.. 58 D admin@providencecc.edu
DIRKSEN, Debra .... 575-538-6427 288 J debra.dirksen@wnmu.edu
DIRMANN, Rachel .... 504-864-7768 190 A rdirmann@loyno.edu
DIROFF, Raquel .... 313-664-7650 222 C rdiroff@collegeforcreativestudies.edu
DISABATINO, Gail .... 516-876-3000 318 A
DISALVO, Anthony .... 510-659-6220.. 54 J tdisalvo@ohlone.edu
DISALVO, Stephen .... 314-529-9521 254 D sdisalvo@maryville.edu
DISALVO, Steven .... 978-232-2000 209 B sdisalvo@endicott.edu
DISANO, Maria .... 401-874-7078 404 E mdisano@uri.edu
DISANTI, Francis, J ...... 610-660-1506 397 A disanti@sju.edu
DISANTO, Amy, S .... 630-620-2101 146 A adisanto@seminary.edu
DISBROW, Lynn .... 470-578-3550 121 J ldisbrow@kennesaw.edu
DISBROW, Nancy .... 910-755-7391 332 D
DISCALA, Anthony .... 480-517-8411.. 14 A anthony.discala@riosalado.edu
DISCENZA, Tobias .... 239-489-9329 100 G tobias.discenza@fsw.edu
DISCH, Keri, A .... 314-935-5959 261 B keri.disch@wustl.edu
DISCHINGER, Rainier .... 928-344-7726.. 11 B rainier.dischinger@azwestern.edu
DISHER, Tim .... 410-293-2981 502 I disher@usna.edu
DISHMAM, Julie .... 765-983-1523 154 H dishmju@earlham.edu
DISHMAN, Laurie .... 615-547-1278 418 C ldishman@cumberland.edu
DISHMAN, Marcie .... 919-718-7491 333 A mdishman@cccc.edu
DISHMAN, Megan .... 212-659-3604 303 E mdishman@tkc.edu
DISHMAN, Mike .... 470-578-7588 121 J mdishma2@kennesaw.edu
DISHMAN, Mike .... 678-839-6570 127 A
DISHMAN, Molly .... 858-566-1200.. 41 E mdishman@disd.edu
DISIENA, Michael .... 518-464-8500 299 B
DISKIN, Becca, L .... 417-659-5422 255 I diskin-b@mssu.edu
DISMUKES, David .... 225-578-4400 188 K dismukes@lsu.edu
DISMUKES, Mary Claire .... 615-460-6490 417 B maryclaire.dismukes@belmont.edu
DISNEW, Carolyn .... 212-752-1530 303 G carolyn.disnew@limcollege.edu
DISNEY, Deica .... 731-286-3321 423 E disney@dscc.edu
DISON, Maria .... 691-320-2480 503 B mdison@comfsm.fm
DISPAGNA, Diane .... 845-848-4118 298 A diane.dispagna@dc.edu
DISQUE, Carol .... 336-506-4138 331 J carol.disque@alamancecc.edu
DISRUDE, Jim .... 815-479-7746 143 F jdisrude@mchenry.edu
DISS, Brian .... 574-631-5646 161 G bdiss@nd.edu
DISTASI, Vincent, F ...... 724-458-2116 384 F vfdistasi@gcc.edu
DISTEFANO, JR., Augustine .... 215-596-8800 400 B
DISTEFANO, Phillip, P .. 303-492-8908.. 83 M phil.distefano@colorado.edu
DISTEFANO, Tammy ..... 716-829-7639 298 C distefan@dyc.edu
DISTERHAFT, Brian .... 920-748-8381 493 J disterhaftb@ripon.edu
DITCHFIELD, Dora .... 205-726-2980.... 6 E dditchfi@samford.edu
DITLEFSEN, Ed .... 208-732-6847 131 B editlefsen@csi.edu
DITMAN, Mark .... 713-348-5441 441 K mditman@rice.edu
DITMYER, Marcia .... 989-964-4508 229 L mditmyer@svsu.edu
DITOMMSO, Anthony .... 412-237-4413 381 C adtommaso@ccac.edu
DITONNO, Joey .... 406-477-6215 262 F
DITORO, Tim .... 936-633-5204 429 A tditoro@angelina.edu
DITTEMORE, Nancy .... 951-785-2300.. 47 F ndittemo@lasierra.edu
DITTMAN, Jeff, L .... 605-256-5229 415 G jeff.dittman@dsu.edu
DITTMAR, Amy .... 713-348-4026 441 K adittmar@rice.edu
DITTMER, Christine .... 858-646-3100.. 62 L
DITTO, John .... 979-230-3157 431 A john.ditto@brazosport.edu
DITTO, Liz .... 419-434-4510 362 D dittoe@findlay.edu
DITULLIO, Daniel, F ..... 508-767-7321 205 F df.ditullio@assumption.edu
DITUSA, John, F .... 317-274-0625 157 B jfditusa@iu.edu
DIVALERIO, Thomas, J . 856-225-6050 281 A tdivaler@camden.rutgers.edu
DIVEL, Kristin .... 402-471-2505 267 F kdivel@nscs.edu
DIVELY, Mary Jo .... 412-268-9519 380 B mjdively@andrew.cmu.edu
DIVEN-BROWN, Laura .. 662-915-5788 248 F ldivenbr@olemiss.edu
DIVENTI, Monique .... 815-394-4376 147 J mdiventi@rockford.edu
DIVER, Bryan .... 217-424-6253 144 D bdiver@millikin.edu
DIVINCENZO, Mark .... 617-452-2082 215 G
DIVINE, Darren, D .... 307-268-2548 499 T darrendivine@caspercollege.edu
DIVINEY, Shelley .... 979-230-3422 431 A shelley.diviney@brazosport.edu
DIVINITY, Veleicia .... 312-341-2213 148 A vdivinity@roosevelt.edu
DIVINO, Claudio, F .... 252-334-2049 331 C claudio.divino@macuniversity.edu
DIVIRGILIO, Mark .... 425-640-1582 479 A mark.divirgilio@edcc.edu
DIVITO, Robert .... 518-454-5204 296 E divitor@strose.edu
DIVITO, Timothy .... 856-225-6565 281 A tdivito@camden.rutgers.edu
DIWARA, Patrica .... 719-502-2037.. 82 D patricia.diawar@pikespeak.edu
DIX, Jennifer .... 413-662-5272 212 F j.dix@mcla.edu
DIX, Therol, J .... 610-819-2070 390 A tdix@mc3.edu
DIXEY, Mary .... 413-552-2261 214 D mdixey@hcc.edu
DIXIE, Wendy, D .... 502-597-7000 183 A wendy.dixie@kysu.edu
DIXON, Annya .... 909-537-3753.. 33 B annya.dixon@csusb.edu
DIXON, Ashlee .... 870-230-5000.. 19 H dixona@hsu.edu
DIXON, Brad .... 660-248-6267 250 H bdixon@centralmethodist.edu
DIXON, Caroline .... 276-326-4594 464 A cdixon@bluefield.edu
DIXON, Cassie .... 704-403-1798 327 B cassie.dixon@atriumhealth.org
DIXON, Catherine .... 410-626-2548 201 E cathy.dixon@sjc.edu
DIXON, Cheryl .... 918-631-2525 371 C cheryl-dixon@utulsa.edu
DIXON, Colleen .... 334-876-9373.... 2 D colleen.dixon@wccs.edu
DIXON, Collette .... 314-516-5396 260 E mclemorec@umsl.edu
DIXON, David .... 216-649-8700 354 A ddixon@kent.edu
DIXON, Dawn, S .... 919-464-2373 335 D dsdixon@johnstoncc.edu
DIXON, Deanna .... 413-585-2523 218 D ddixon@smith.edu
DIXON, Doreen, O .... 804-257-5630 475 G ddixon@vuu.edu
DIXON, Jacqueline .... 727-553-3369 111 B jdixon@usf.edu
DIXON, Jennifer .... 928-681-5656.. 14 H jdixon@mohave.edu
DIXON, Jennifer .... 206-934-4101 482 E jennifer.dixon@seattlecolleges.edu
DIXON, Jeremy .... 205-726-2732.... 6 E jgdixon@samford.edu
DIXON, John .... 859-622-5094 180 B john.dixon@eku.edu
DIXON, John .... 843-661-1335 408 H jdixon@fmarion.edu
DIXON, Joyce, A .... 662-254-3308 247 C jadixon@mvsu.edu
DIXON, Karrie, G .... 252-335-3228 341 A chancellor@ecsu.edu
DIXON, Laquala, C .... 601-979-2329 245 G laquala.m.coleman@jsums.edu
DIXON, Leon .... 507-457-1617 242 H ldixon@smumn.edu
DIXON, Lloyd .... 501-420-1200.. 17 D
DIXON, Lynn .... 512-223-1222 429 J cdixon@austincc.edu
DIXON, Margaret .... 662-621-4670 244 E mdixon@coahomacc.edu
DIXON, Melanie .... 916-484-8212.. 50 J dixonm2@arc.losrios.edu
DIXON, Michael .... 432-685-4503 439 E mdixon@midland.edu
DIXON, Michael, D .... 812-465-7015 162 B mdixon@usi.edu
DIXON, Mikkel .... 561-912-1211.. 99 C midixon@evergladesuniversity.edu
DIXON, P. Grady .... 785-628-4790 173 E pgdixon@fhsu.edu
DIXON, Patrick .... 919-466-4400.. 93 H
DIXON, Patrick .... 757-493-6000.. 93 H
DIXON, Ramona .... 610-399-2442 393 D rdixon@cheyney.edu
DIXON, Robert .... 312-413-1878 151 D robd@uic.edu
DIXON, Robert .... 405-744-6512 367 G robert.dixon@okstate.edu
DIXON, Shawn .... 918-781-7317 365 B dixons@bacone.edu
DIXON, Siri .... 503-281-4181 372 F
DIXON, Sonja .... 806-796-8800 438 F sonja.dixon@lcu.edu
DIXON, Steve .... 918-540-6275 366 F steve.dixon10@neo.edu
DIXON, Terrance .... 404-954-6520 122 H terrance.dixon@morehouse.edu
DIXON, Terrance .... 919-592-4292 339 I terrance.dixon@shawu.edu
DIXON, Tiffany .... 312-850-7013 135 E tdixon10@ccc.edu
DIXON, Traci .... 575-624-7413 285 F traci.dixon@roswell.enmu.edu
DIXON, William .... 585-292-3031 306 K wdixon5@monroecc.edu
DIXON HALL, Maria ..... 214-768-3393 443 G madixon@smu.edu
DIXON-PETERS, Earic ... 562-908-3489.. 58 M edixon-peters@riohondo.edu
DIXON-REEVES, Regina 619-260-7455.. 72 H cid@sandiego.edu
DIXON-SAXON, Savitri . 866-492-5336 243 G savitri.dixon-saxon@mail.waldenu.edu
DIXON SAXON, Savitri . 952-806-3910 241 R
DIZIK, Elizabeth .... 248-645-3273 222 G edizik@cranbrook.edu
DIZON, Richard .... 650-325-5621.. 59 J richard.dizon@stpsu.edu
DJEDI, Anthony .... 650-574-6161.. 62 J
DJERLEK, Jeffrey .... 850-474-3027 111 E jdjerlek@uwf.edu
DJEUKENG, Benji .... 804-627-5300 464 B benjamin_djeukeng@bshsi.org
DJUKIC, Stevan .... 918-876-2529 368 E sdjukic@okwu.edu
DJUNAIDI, Harry .... 931-540-2523 423 D hdjunaidi@columbiastate.edu
DJURIC, Teresa, A .... 540-887-7243 467 G tdjuric@marybaldwin.edu
DLUGOS, James, S .... 207-893-7711 195 I jdlugos@sjcme.edu
DLUGOS, Joseph .... 605-394-2416 415 I joseph.dlugos@sdsmt.edu
DLUGOS, OSA, Raymond .... 978-837-5130 216 D dlugosr@merrimack.edu
DLUGOSZ, Joy .... 610-225-5660 383 A jdlugosz@eastern.edu
DO, Dao .... 714-484-7316.. 54 C ddo@cypresscollege.edu
DO, Gigi .... 281-283-2750 452 A dogigi@uhcl.edu
DO, Tien .... 425-739-8353 480 D tien.do@lwtech.edu
DOAK, Bryan, E .... 928-344-7617.. 11 B bryan.doak@azwestern.edu
DOAK, Joshua, M .... 417-659-4460 255 I doak-j@mssu.edu
DOAN, Kathi .... 231-843-5933 232 I kdoan1@westshor.edu
DOAN, Kathleen .... 207-741-5805 195 D kdoan@smccme.edu
DOAN, Linh .... 714-903-2762.. 68 I
DOAN, Ryan .... 213-262-3939.. 46 H
DOANE, Dudley, J .... 434-982-3013 471 F djd4j@virginia.edu
DOANE, Tonya .... 336-517-2185 326 J tdoane@bennett.edu
DOBBELMANN, Duncan 802-440-4400 461 B duncand@bennington.edu
DOBBERT, Thomas .... 775-673-7800 270 I tdobbert@tmcc.edu
DOBBINS, Courtney ...... 864-587-4271 411 F dobbinsc@smcsc.edu
DOBBINS, Daniel, C ..... 618-537-6936 143 G dcdobbins@mckendree.edu
DOBBINS, Kenneth .... 336-506-4126 331 J kenneth.dobbins@alamancecc.edu
DOBBINS, Tabbetha ...... 856-256-4467 280 H dobbins@rowan.edu
DOBBS, Brian .... 208-732-6266 131 B bdobbs@csi.edu
DOBBS, Chris .... 406-994-6543 263 G chris.dobbs@montana.edu
DOBBS, Gwen .... 479-636-4245.. 20 G gdobbs@nwacc.edu
DOBBS, Melissa .... 903-983-8203 437 G mdobbs@kilgore.edu
DOBBS, Ricky .... 903-468-8707 446 D ricky.dobbs@tamuc.edu
DOBBS, Trent .... 405-425-5913 367 C trent.dobbs@oc.edu
DOBBS, Wendell .... 304-696-2964 488 N dobbs@marshall.edu
DOBELL, Daniel .... 845-574-4156 312 C ddobell@sunyrockland.edu
DOBI, Hanko, H .... 203-932-7191.. 89 F hdobi@newhaven.edu
DOBIE, Elizabeth, A ...... 607-871-2137 289 E dobie@alfred.edu
DOBISH, Rodney, W ..... 412-396-4781 382 E dobish@duq.edu
DOBIYANSKI, Victoria, E .... 979-845-4728 446 B vdobiyanski@tamu.edu
DOBKIN, Bethami .... 801-832-2550 461 A bdobkin@westminstercollege.edu
DOBKINS, Debra .... 770-534-6299 116 C
DOBRANSKY, Mary .... 402-557-7160 265 A mary.dobransky@bellevue.edu

DOBRIN, Ben .... 757-455-3412 476 C
bdobrin@vwu.edu
DOBRINSKY,
Herbert, C .... 212-960-0850 325 R
dobrinsk@yu.edu
DOBROWSKI, Pauline 508-565-1363 218 F
pdobrowski@stonehill.edu
DOBRY, Kyle .... 804-862-6100 469 E
DOBSON, Alyssa 724-738-2220 394 E
alyssa.dobson@sru.edu
DOBYNS, Keith ..... 951-222-8001 .. 59 A
keith.dobyns@rccd.edu
DOCETT, AJ .... 678-916-2665 115 G
ajdoucett@johnmarshall.edu
DOCHERTY, Karen 480-517-8432 .. 14 A
karen.docherty@riosalado.edu
DOCKENDORF, Amy, L 605-256-5130 415 G
amy.dockendorf@dsu.edu
DOCKENS, Samuel 409-880-8195 449 A
sjdockens@lit.edu
DOCKERY, David, S ...... 817-921-8600 444 D
provost@swbts.edu
DOCKERY, Julie .... 630-829-2172 133 B
jdockery@ben.edu
DOCKERY, Rachael, M 417-836-8507 255 J
rmdockery@missouristate.edu
DOCKERY, Sheila 910-788-6250 337 G
sheila.dockery@sccnc.edu
DOCKERY, Tim .... 239-280-1695 .. 95 M
timothy.dockery@avemaria.edu
DOCKING, Jeffrey, R 517-265-5161 220 D
jdocking@adrian.edu
DOCKINS, Tiffany 601-979-3950 245 G
tiffany.h.dockins@jsums.edu
DOCKTER, Jason 217-786-4947 142 F
jason.dockter@llcc.edu
DOCTOR, John ...... 650-738-4166 .. 62 K
doctorj@smccd.edu
DOCTOR, OFM, John 217-228-5432 147 C
docotjo@quincy.edu
DOCTOR, OFM, John 218-228-5432 147 C
doctojo@quincy.edu
DODANI, Sunita 757-446-7944 465 H
dodanis@evms.edu
DODD, Kendra, Q 651-631-5330 243 E
kqdodd@unwsp.edu
DODD, Olivia ...... 256-228-6001 .. 3 B
doddo@nacc.edu
DODD, Paul .... 530-754-7806 .. 69 A
pdodd@ucdavis.edu
DODD, Shelley ...... 307-766-4273 500 H
shelley@uwyo.edu
DODD, Susan .... 408-848-4895 .. 43 H
sdodd@gavilan.edu
DODD, Tim .... 806-742-3031 450 C
tim.dodd@ttu.edu
DODDROE, Josh 480-857-5521 .. 13 B
josh.doddroe@cgc.edu
DODDS, David, L 701-777-5529 344 H
david.dodds@und.edu
DODDS, Jon ..... 304-367-4275 488 L
jon.dodds@fairmontstate.edu
DODGE, Carolina 301-387-3050 198 F
carolina.dodge@garrettcollege.edu
DODGE, Gail .... 757-683-3432 468 C
gdodge@odu.edu
DODGE, Georgina 301-405-2838 202 E
gdodge1@umd.edu
DODGE, Kevin .... 301-387-3328 198 F
kevin.dodge@garrettcollege.edu
DODGE, Lauren 217-854-5509 133 F
lauren.dodge@blackburn.edu
DODGE, Laurin 608-663-3233 491 F
ldodge@edgewood.edu
DODGE, Marvin ..... 435-586-7721 459 E
marvindodge@suu.edu
DODGE, Michelle 503-847-2560 377 A
mdodge@uws.edu
DODGE, Norma Jean 620-417-1171 177 C
normajean.dodge@sccc.edu
DODGE, Randall 858-695-8587 155 F
rdodge@horizonuniversity.edu
DODGE, Rhonda, M 727-816-3401 105 E
dodger@phsc.edu
DODOSH, Gabrielle 316-942-4291 176 B
dodoshg@newmanu.edu
DODRILL, Stella 304-647-6310 489 C
sdodrill@osteo.wvsom.edu
DODSON, Andrea 575-492-2107 288 I
adodson@usw.edu
DODSON, Jennifer 269-294-4255 223 J
jdodson@glenoaks.edu

DODSON, Jerry 254-442-5152 431 J
jerry.dodson@cisco.edu
DODSON, Preston 910-893-1310 327 C
dodsonp@campbell.edu
DODSON, Renee 620-278-2173 177 E
DODSON, Shelley 765-973-8332 156 D
midodson@iue.edu
DODSON, Wendy, B 910-246-2868 337 E
dodsonw@sandhills.edu
DODSON-REED,
Candace .... 410-455-2065 202 G
cdodreed@umbc.edu
DOEBLE, Gina ...... 239-489-9029 100 G
gdoeble@fsw.edu
DOEHNE, Ben ...... 612-351-0631 235 I
bdoehne@ipr.edu
DOELL, Margaret 719-587-8383 .. 77 F
mjdoell@adams.edu
DOEPKER, Joel 636-584-6527 252 D
joel.doepker@eastcentral.edu
DOERGE, Rebecca, W 412-268-5124 380 B
rwdoerge@andrew.cmu.edu
DOERING, Douglas 207-699-5082 194 G
doug@meca.edu
DOERING, Laura, J 515-294-0760 163 E
ljdoeri@iastate.edu
DOERMANN, Thomas 319-363-1323 168 D
tdoermann@mtmercy.edu
DOERR, Cara ...... 618-634-3247 149 C
carad@shawneecc.edu
DOGBEVIA, Moses 402-461-7466 266 C
mdogbevia@hastings.edu
DOGGETT, Jeffrey 978-837-5207 216 D
doggettj@merrimack.edu
DOGONNIUCK,
Theodore .... 516-773-5000 502 G
dogonniuckt@usmma.edu
DOHENY, Sarah 423-323-0233 424 B
scdoheny@northeaststate.edu
DOHERTY, Brian 337-482-6396 192 F
brian.doherty@louisiana.edu
DOHERTY, Elizabeth 401-863-7845 403 A
elizabeth_doherty@brown.edu
DOHERTY, Jennifer 818-836-5038 142 C
dohert@lewisu.edu
DOHERTY, Kathleen, T 717-780-2496 385 A
ktdohert@hacc.edu
DOHERTY, Kenneth 313-577-3756 232 H
ken-doherty@wayne.edu
DOHERTY, Kevin ..... 620-421-6700 175 D
kevind@labette.edu
DOHERTY, Kristal 864-250-8417 408 J
kristal.doherty@gvltec.edu
DOHERTY, Laura 914-637-2710 302 C
ldoherty@iona.edu
DOHERTY, Leanna, J 620-421-6700 175 D
leannan@labette.edu
DOHERTY, Mark 650-325-5621 .. 59 J
mark.doherty@stpsu.edu
DOHERTY, Sharon 651-690-6783 242 F
sldoherty@stkate.edu
DOHERTY, Tiffany 603-513-1328 273 I
tiffany.doherty@granite.edu
DOHNALIK, Judith 254-298-8600 445 B
j.dohnalik@templejc.edu
DOI, Keiko ...... 626-396-2439 .. 26 G
keiko.doi@artcenter.edu
DOIGUCHI, Farah 808-235-7430 130 C
farah@hawaii.edu
DOIRON, Gail, M 978-665-3101 212 C
gdoiron@fitchburgstate.edu
DOLAK, Lisa, A 315-443-1860 321 D
ladolak@syr.edu
DOLAN, Cathy 212-616-7278 301 A
DOLAN, Christy 502-863-8022 180 E
christy_dolan@georgetowncollege.edu
DOLAN, Daniel 212-237-8900 294 B
ddolan@jjay.cuny.edu
DOLAN, Elizabeth 610-758-1888 388 C
bdk3@lehigh.edu
DOLAN, Gayle 617-277-3915 207 B
dolang@bgsp.edu
DOLAN, Jill, S 609-258-3040 279 E
jsdolan@princeton.edu
DOLAN, Kevin 617-732-2144 216 B
kevin.dolan@mcphs.edu
DOLAN, Matthew 202-319-5142 .. 91 G
dolan@cua.edu
DOLAN, Sarah 617-984-1666 217 G
sdolan@quincycolleg.edu
DOLAN, Scott 518-464-8500 299 B
DOLAN, Scott 614-234-1076 356 E
sdolan@mccn.edu

DOLAN, Stacey, L 312-788-1147 152 G
sdolan@vandercook.edu
DOLAN, Tim .... 808-956-3711 129 B
timdolan@hawaii.edu
DOLAN, Timothy 808-376-7801 128 I
info@uhfoundation.org
DOLAN, Tina, M 781-283-3501 219 C
cdolan@wellesley.edu
DOLAN-WILSON,
Allison .... 978-556-3624 215 C
adolanwilson@necc.mass.edu
DOLBERRY, Carol 229-732-5962 114 I
caroldolberry@andrewcollege.edu
DOLBOW, David 702-567-1920 270 D
DOLCI, Elizabeth 802-635-1482 463 B
elizabeth.dolci@northernvermont.edu
DOLD, Julie ...... 315-257-2350 318 D
doldjm@potsdam.edu
DOLDER-ZIEKE,
Beth, D .... 608-796-3828 496 L
bdzieke@viterbo.edu
DOLE, Danny ...... 307-766-1121 500 H
DOLE, Jean .... 414-288-0285 492 E
jean.dole@marquette.edu
DOLE, John, M 919-515-2191 341 E
DOLE, Robin, L 610-499-4352 401 I
rldole@widener.edu
DOLEN, Tom ...... 408-864-8764 .. 42 K
dolentom@deanza.edu
DOLEZAL, Marlo 316-677-1690 178 C
mdolezal@wsutech.edu
DOLEZAL, Vernon 316-295-5679 173 G
vernon_dolezal@friends.edu
DOLHEIMER, Mary, E 717-815-1584 402 C
mdolheim@ycp.edu
DOLINAR, Jon ...... 216-987-4354 351 D
jon.dolinar@tri-c.edu
DOLIVE, Mark 817-515-2113 445 A
mark.dolive@tccd.edu
DOLL, Bill .... 828-395-1676 335 B
wdoll@isothermal.edu
DOLL, Christopher 740-366-9383 349 D
doll.4@cotc.edu
DOLL, Christopher 563-589-3215 170 C
cdoll@dbq.edu
DOLL, DeAnn .... 863-583-9050 110 A
DOLL, DeAnne 641-673-2118 170 I
dollde@wmpenn.edu
DOLLA, Marie ..... 718-779-1499 310 I
mdolla@plazacollege.edu
DOLLAR, Andrew 256-216-5364 .... 4 D
andrew.dollar@athens.edu
DOLLOFF, Brad 417-690-2325 250 K
bdolloff@cofo.edu
DOLLYHITE, Ronald 336-838-6149 338 H
radollyhite367@wilkescc.edu
DOLPH, Annette 708-709-3502 147 A
adolph@prairiestate.edu
DOLPHIN, Jen 712-274-5110 168 C
dolphinj@morningside.edu
DOLS, Kenn .... 218-855-8132 237 C
kenneth.dols@clcmn.edu
DOLSON, Scott 812-855-4848 156 C
DOLSON, Scott, M 812-855-0866 156 B
sdolson@iu.edu
DOLTER, Kathryn 319-398-5630 167 H
kathryn.dolter@kirkwood.edu
DOMACK, Alicia 414-277-7351 493 D
domack@msoe.edu
DOMAN, Dakota 713-313-7011 448 D
DOMAN-FLYGARE,
Sarah .... 763-424-0755 239 D
sdoman-flygare@nhcc.edu
DOMANN, Britney 816-604-1317 254 E
britney.domann@mcckc.edu
DOMAS, Matthew 662-562-3494 247 C
DOMBROSKI, Harry 817-272-2882 454 B
harry.dombroski@uta.edu
DOMBROWSKI, Kirk 802-656-2918 462 D
kirk.dombrowski@uvm.edu
DOMENE, Douglas, S 714-879-3901 .. 45 J
dsdomene@hiu.edu
DOMENICI, Bob 650-574-6161 .. 62 J
DOMES, Chris, E 610-558-5501 390 C
cdomes@neumann.edu
DOMIANO, Sam 985-549-2282 192 E
sdomiano@selu.edu
DOMINGO,
Courtney, N 808-956-6486 128 I
cmnd@hawaii.edu
DOMINGO, Junior 626-914-8656 .. 37 B
jdomingo@citruscollege.edu

DOMINGUEZ, Aaron 202-319-5244 .. 91 G
provost@cua.edu
DOMINGUEZ, Carmen 818-947-2625 .. 50 B
domingmc@lavc.edu
DOMINGUEZ, Israel 949-582-4777 .. 65 C
idominguez@saddleback.edu
DOMINGUEZ, Joe 323-953-4000 .. 49 E
domingjn@lacitycollege.edu
DOMINGUEZ, Mary 805-922-6966 .. 24 L
mary.dominguez@hancockcollege.edu
DOMINGUEZ, Norberto 787-296-0453 506 H
dominguez@inter.edu
DOMINGUEZ, Victoria 626-914-8794 .. 37 B
vdominguez@citruscollege.edu
DOMINGUEZ-FLORES,
Noraida .... 787-998-8997 508 K
ndominguez@eeapr.org
DOMINICIS, Erick 305-237-6583 104 E
edominic@mdc.edu
DOMINICK, Jay 609-258-5601 279 E
jdominick@princeton.edu
DOMINICK, Tara 541-881-5928 376 E
tdominick@tvcc.cc
DOMINIQUE, Ezechiel 203-857-7154 .. 87 B
edominique@norwalk.edu
DOMINQUEZ, Jesse 940-552-6291 456 F
jdominguez@vernoncollege.edu
DOMINY, Carol 478-218-3700 116 F
cjones@centralgatech.edu
DOMINY, Robert 478-757-3579 116 F
rdominy@centralgatech.edu
DOMKE-DAMONTE,
Darla, J .... 843-349-2129 407 B
ddamonte@coastal.edu
DOMMER, David 919-658-7854 340 E
ddommer@umo.edu
DOMNWACHUKWU,
Chinaka .... 909-537-5600 .. 33 B
chinaka.domnwachukwu@csusb.edu
DOMZALSKI, Jim 570-740-0342 388 G
jdomzalski@luzerne.edu
DON, John ..... 864-231-2100 405 F
jdon@andersonuniversity.edu
DONA, David 541-383-7209 371 I
ddona@cocc.edu
DONAE, Deserie 707-826-3011 .. 30 A
deserie.donae@humboldt.edu
DONAGER, Sedef 617-989-4590 219 D
donagers@wit.edu
DONAGHUE,
Jennifer, H .... 202-994-4477 .. 92 C
iso@gwu.edu
DONAGHY, Maureen 856-225-6131 281 A
maureen.donaghy@rutgers.edu
DONAHOO, Mary 360-438-8772 482 D
mdonahoo@stmartin.edu
DONAHUE, Bob 614-947-6010 352 J
robert.donahue@franklin.edu
DONAHUE, Brian 509-359-6345 478 H
bdonahue@ewu.edu
DONAHUE, Colin 818-677-2333.. 32 E
colin.donahue@csun.edu
DONAHUE, Darrell 304-293-2395 489 E
darrell.donahue@mail.wvu.edu
DONAHUE, Gerard 610-902-8546 379 E
gd7006@cabrini.edu
DONAHUE, James, P 423-652-6002 419 E
jpd@king.edu
DONAHUE, Lorraine 814-262-3822 393 A
ldonahue@pennhighlands.edu
DONAHUE, Maura, S 740-368-3350 359 F
msdonahue@owu.edu
DONAHUE, Nancy 865-694-6541 424 C
ndonahue@pstcc.edu
DONAHUE, Pat 812-855-5234 156 B
donahued@iu.edu
DONAHUE, Sean 772-462-7751 102 C
sdonahue@irsc.edu
DONAHUE, Susan 212-346-1200 310 F
DONAIRE-CIRSOVIUS,
Maria .... 904-632-3346 101 A
maria.donaire.cirsovius@fscj.edu
DONALD, Rebecca 570-321-4082 388 H
donald@lycoming.edu
DONALD, Todd 662-887-2876 246 E
tdonald@msdelta.edu
DONALDSON, Colleen 404-364-8319 123 G
cdonaldson@oglethorpe.edu
DONALDSON, Devin 620-432-0402 176 A
ddonaldson@neosho.edu
DONALDSON, Jody 319-398-7186 167 H
jody.donald@kirkwood.edu
DONALDSON, Paul 985-545-1500 188 B

DOTSON, Barry .... 912-538-3141 125 E
bdotson@southeasterntech.edu
DOTSON, Brandon .... 423-323-0205 424 B
brdotson@northeaststate.edu
DOTSON, Carolyn .... 731-352-4020 417 C
dotsonc@bethelu.edu
DOTSON, Donald .... 334-229-6995.... 4 B
ddotson@alasu.edu
DOTSON, Kaitlin .... 912-443-5874 124 I
kdotson@savannahtech.edu
DOTSON, Kit .... 423-461-8708 421 E
kdotson@milligan.edu
DOTSON, Mark .... 706-379-3111 128 A
mcdotson@yhc.edu
DOTSON, Ricky .... 817-531-4874 450 F
rdotson@txwes.edu
DOTSON, Samantha .... 360-596-5361 483 E
ssoto@spscc.edu
DOTSON, Tawny, M ...... 530-741-6707.. 77 D
tdotson@yccd.edu
DOTSON, Tom .... 614-222-3280 351 A
tdotson@ccad.edu
DOTSON COX, Renee ... 575-758-8914 286 A
DOTTER, Anne .... 913-469-8500 174 F
adotter@jccc.edu
DOTTER, Diana .... 206-546-4101 483 C
ddotter@shoreline.edu
DOTTS, Janene .... 903-675-6215 451 C
janene.dotts@tvcc.edu
DOTY, Angela .... 541-684-7289 371 H
adoty@bushnell.edu
DOTY, Brett .... 901-321-4321 417 G
bdoty@cbu.edu
DOTY, Craig .... 913-667-5700 172 G
cdoty@cbts.edu
DOTY, Jessica .... 701-777-0500 344 H
jessica.doty@und.edu
DOTY, Kate .... 317-955-6475 159 A
kdoty@marian.edu
DOTY, Laura .... 916-660-7655.. 64 B
ldoty@sierracollege.edu
DOTY, Laura .... 304-829-7142 486 B
ldoty@bethanywv.edu
DOTY, Laura .... 304-829-7601 486 B
ldoty@bethanywv.edu
DOTY, Steve .... 212-799-5000 303 B
DOUCET, Derek .... 802-443-3103 461 G
ddoucet@middlebury.edu
DOUCET, Gayle .... 318-678-6000 187 E
gdoucet@bpcc.edu
DOUCET, John .... 985-448-4385 192 C
john.doucet@nicholls.edu
DOUCET, Shelly .... 816-235-5123 260 D
doucets@umkcfoundation.org
DOUCETT, Sandra, L ..... 413-585-2686 218 D
sdoucett@smith.edu
DOUCETTE, Dennis .... 858-566-1200... 41 E
dennis@disd.edu
DOUCETTE, Margot .... 858-566-1200... 41 E
margot@disd.edu
DOUCETTE, Mary .... 775-327-2120 270 G
mary.doucette@gbcnv.edu
DOUCETTPERRY, Maria . 775-784-1547 270 K
mdoucettperry@unr.edu
DOUD, Megan, F .... 734-647-6000 231 A
mdoud@umich.edu
DOUET, Lelanya .... 337-482-1278 192 F
ldouet@louisiana.edu
DOUGAL, Ian .... 617-746-1990 210 E
ian.dougal@hult.edu
DOUGALL, Jennifer, L .. 330-325-6484 357 D
jdougall@neomed.edu
DOUGHERTY, Bill, W .... 608-246-6223 497 I
wdougherty@madisoncollege.edu
DOUGHERTY, Brian, C . 812-244-4009 160 C
brian.dougherty@rhventures.org
DOUGHERTY,
Christopher .... 215-248-7130 380 G
doughertyc@chc.edu
DOUGHERTY, Clint, C .. 760-355-6207.. 45 N
clint.dougherty@imperial.edu
DOUGHERTY, Dennis .... 610-647-4400 385 K
ddougherty1@immaculata.edu
DOUGHERTY,
Dennis, A .... 626-395-3646.. 29 B
dadougherty@caltech.edu
DOUGHERTY, Gabe .... 503-838-9396 377 C
doughertyg@wou.edu
DOUGHERTY, John .... 385-375-8724 458 L
DOUGHERTY, Kaila .... 623-572-3415 144 C
kosmot@midwestern.edu
DOUGHERTY, Kathleen . 603-899-4178 272 G
doughertyk@franklinpierce.edu

DOUGHERTY, OSF,
Kathy .... 610-558-5511 390 G
dougherk@neumann.edu
DOUGHERTY, Kevin ...... 541-737-8748 374 H
deanofstudents@oregonstate.edu
DOUGHERTY, Lisa .... 201-360-4111 277 D
ldougherty@hccc.edu
DOUGHERTY, Mark .... 864-646-1871 411 H
mdougher@tctc.edu
DOUGHERTY,
Michele, R .... 215-955-6656 398 G
michele.dougherty@jefferson.edu
DOUGHERTY, Rebecca .. 414-464-9777 497 B
dougherty.rebecca@wspp.edu
DOUGHERTY, Robert .... 740-283-6223 352 I
rdougherty@franciscan.edu
DOUGHERTY, Sharon ... 215-248-7036 380 G
doughertys@chc.edu
DOUGHERTY,
Susan-Ellis .... 301-314-1713 202 E
sdougher@umd.edu
DOUGHERTY, Tracy, D . 806-371-5106 428 F
tsdougherty@actx.edu
DOUGHERTY, Troy, J ... 208-496-9220 130 G
doughertyt@byui.edu
DOUGHERTY, Veronica . 410-287-1947 198 A
vdougherty@cecil.edu
DOUGHERTY DURHAM,
Danielle .... 208-459-5004 131 A
ddurham@collegeofidaho.edu
DOUGHTIE, Michael ...... 973-877-3301 276 G
mdoughti@essex.edu
DOUGHTY, Catherine .... 717-464-7050 387 E
DOUGHTY, JR., Clyde .. 301-860-3559 203 D
cdoughty@bowiestate.edu
DOUGHTY, Del .... 812-464-1735 162 B
ddoughty1@usi.edu
DOUGHTY, Ellen .... 207-581-5840 196 C
edoughty@maine.edu
DOUGHTY, Harry .... 504-286-5312 191 A
hdoughty@suno.edu
DOUGLAS, Alicia, R ...... 816-501-4306 257 K
alicia.douglas@rockhurst.edu
DOUGLAS, Amy, K .... 334-844-3604.... 4 E
douglak@auburn.edu
DOUGLAS, Bernadine .... 305-891-8182.. 96 A
bdouglas@barry.edu
DOUGLAS, Blake .... 702-895-2399 270 J
blake.douglas@unlv.edu
DOUGLAS, Brianna .... 843-383-8175 407 C
bbuncedouglas@coker.edu
DOUGLAS, C.D .... 402-375-7213 267 I
cddougl1@wsc.edu
DOUGLAS, Dana .... 504-286-5000 191 A
ddouglas@suno.edu
DOUGLAS, Darcy .... 713-646-1803 443 C
ddouglas@stcl.edu
DOUGLAS, Denise .... 440-365-5222 355 B
DOUGLAS, Derek .... 773-702-3627 151 B
drbdouglas@uchicago.edu
DOUGLAS, Duane .... 618-474-7120 149 H
rodougl@siue.edu
DOUGLAS, Georgio .... 318-274-2611 191 G
douglasge@gram.edu
DOUGLAS, Hallie .... 203-773-6678.. 85 C
hdouglas@albertus.edu
DOUGLAS, Jamie .... 765-361-5592 162 G
douglasj@wabash.edu
DOUGLAS, Jerome, N ... 610-917-1403 400 D
jndouglas@valleyforge.edu
DOUGLAS, Joan .... 281-495-0078 436 G
DOUGLAS, Kristen .... 706-227-5375 115 C
kdouglas@athenstech.edu
DOUGLAS, Kristin .... 309-794-3443 132 H
kristindouglas@augustana.edu
DOUGLAS, Laura, L ...... 508-678-2811 213 F
laura.douglas@bristolcc.edu
DOUGLAS, Lee .... 562-938-4209.. 48 K
ldouglas@lbcc.edu
DOUGLAS, Mary .... 870-508-6101.. 18 B
mdouglas@asumh.edu
DOUGLAS, Michelle ...... 850-644-7950 110 B
mbdouglas@fsu.edu
DOUGLAS, Natacha .... 636-227-2100 254 C
DOUGLAS, Roger .... 360-438-4375 482 D
ddouglas@stmartin.edu
DOUGLAS, Tiffanie .... 972-860-4256 433 I
tdouglas@dcccd.edu
DOUGLAS-BROWN,
Laura, E .... 404-727-9507 118 D
l.douglasbrown@emory.edu
DOUGLASS, David .... 208-459-5259 131 A
ddouglass@collegeofidaho.edu

DOUGLASS, James .... 507-433-0611 240 A
james.douglass@riverland.edu
DOUGLASS, Laura .... 978-998-7750 209 B
ldouglas@endicott.edu
DOUGLIS, Evan .... 518-276-6460 311 J
douglis@rpi.edu
DOUGNAC, Carlos .... 352-273-4000 110 E
cdougnac@ufl.edu
DOUILLARD, Paul .... 508-767-7550 205 F
pr.douillard@assumption.edu
DOULIS, Peter .... 215-871-6900 395 A
peterd@pcom.edu
DOUMA, Debbie .... 850-484-1705 105 G
ddouma@pensacolastate.edu
DOUMA, Jason .... 605-331-6750 416 C
jason.douma@usiouxfalls.edu
DOUMA, Ross .... 712-722-6234 165 E
ross.douma@dordt.edu
DOUR, Abigail .... 425-889-5201 481 A
abigail.dour@northwestu.edu
DOURLEIN, Peter .... 520-621-9414.. 16 H
dourlein@arizona.edu
DOURTE, Melinda .... 509-793-2001 477 D
melindad@bigbend.edu
DOURTY, Brian .... 972-883-6600 454 D
brian.dourty@utdallas.edu
DOUSSETT, Courtney ..... 760-776-7339.. 39 A
cdoussett@collegeofthedesert.edu
DOUTHIT, James .... 828-262-3020 340 G
douthitjr1@appstate.edu
DOUTHIT, Tricia .... 303-273-3383.. 79 A
tdouthit@mines.edu
DOVAL, Christy .... 806-457-4200 435 D
DOVE, Bill .... 719-389-6389.. 78 E
wdove@coloradocollege.edu
DOVE, Gary .... 276-656-5494 473 H
gdove@patrickhenry.edu
DOVE, Jennifer .... 304-792-7098 487 I
DOVE, John .... 361-593-2704 447 A
john.dove@tamuk.edu
DOVE, John .... 843-349-5296 409 A
john.dove@hgtc.edu
DOVE, Shirley .... 254-442-5134 431 J
shirley.dove@cisco.edu
DOVE, Tangila .... 210-486-5000 427 I
DOVER, Lydia .... 618-634-3200 149 C
lydiad@shawneecc.edu
DOVI, Anthony .... 201-684-7305 280 B
adovi@ramapo.edu
DOVIAK, Jason .... 607-587-4630 319 C
doviakjm@alfredstate.edu
DOW, Douglas, C .... 972-883-4295 454 D
dougdow@utdallas.edu
DOW, Marilyn .... 313-993-1090 230 H
dowmk@udmercy.edu
DOW, Steven, R .... 402-465-2255 267 J
sdow@nebrwesleyan.edu
DOWD, Bonnie Ann ...... 619-388-6975.. 60 H
bdowd@sdccd.edu
DOWD, Carolyn, R .... 817-554-5950 439 C
cdowd@messengercollege.edu
DOWD, Denny .... 214-333-5102 433 D
denny@dbu.edu
DOWD, Jay .... 843-953-1411 406 D
jdowd1@citadel.edu
DOWD, Nathan .... 608-663-2837 491 F
ndowd@edgewood.edu
DOWD, Sarah .... 843-574-6624 411 I
sarah.dowd@tridenttech.edu
DOWD, Sean, R .... 973-596-3041 278 G
sean.r.dowd@njit.edu
DOWD-HIGGINS,
Caroline .... 812-327-4884 158 A
cdowdhiggins@ivytech.edu
DOWDALL, Alexandria .. 810-762-0293 228 B
alexandria.dowdall@mcc.edu
DOWDELL-WHITE,
Ambe .... 712-325-3371 167 G
adowdellwhite@iwcc.edu
DOWDLE, Deedie, K ..... 765-285-2304 153 E
deedie.dowdle@bsu.edu
DOWDY, Chris .... 214-376-1000 440 H
cdowdy@pqc.edu
DOWE, Pearl .... 770-784-4761 118 D
pearl.dowe@emory.edu
DOWE, Peter .... 585-395-2531 317 B
pdowe@brockport.edu
DOWELL, JR., Adrain ... 402-554-2305 269 C
adriandowell@unomaha.edu
DOWELL, Adrian, E ...... 402-280-4483 265 J
adriandowell@creighton.edu
DOWELL, Aileen .... 912-478-3326 120 A
adowell@georgiasouthern.edu

DOWELL, David .... 606-337-3196 180 A
DOWELL, Greg .... 434-592-3888 467 E
dgdowell@liberty.edu
DOWELL, Luke .... 620-417-1012 177 C
luke.dowell@sccc.edu
DOWEN, Chris .... 303-315-2550.. 84 B
chris.dowen@ucdenver.edu
DOWER, Julia .... 603-542-7744 272 D
jdower@ccsnh.edu
DOWER, Kellori .... 714-564-5600.. 58 F
dower_kellori@sac.edu
DOWER, Kellori .... 714-484-7142.. 54 C
kdower@cypresscollege.edu
DOWLAND, Pam .... 812-357-6515 160 G
pdowland@saintmeinrad.edu
DOWLESS, Donald, V .... 706-233-7201 125 A
chimes@shorter.edu
DOWLING, Audra .... 765-455-9204 156 E
aedowlin@iu.edu
DOWLING, Beth .... 603-428-2239 272 I
edowling@nec.edu
DOWLING, Diana .... 928-776-2391.. 17 B
diana.dowling@yc.edu
DOWLING, Joseph, B ... 714-895-7711.. 38 E
jdowling@gwc.cccd.edu
DOWLING, Victoria .... 262-524-7132 491 A
vdowling@carrollu.edu
DOWN, Cody .... 808-543-8024 128 E
cdown@hpu.edu
DOWN, Ron .... 402-643-7133 265 I
ronald.down@cune.edu
DOWNER, James .... 814-472-3286 396 I
jdowner@francis.edu
DOWNES, Christine, M . 914-633-7704 302 C
cdownes@iona.edu
DOWNES, John .... 770-426-2646 122 A
jdownes@life.edu
DOWNES, Kathy .... 316-978-3586 178 B
kathy.downes@wichita.edu
DOWNES, Kelly .... 618-437-5321 147 F
downes@rlc.edu
DOWNES, Kelly .... 617-266-1400 206 D
equity@berklee.edu
DOWNEY, Christina ...... 765-455-9385 156 E
downeyca@iuk.edu
DOWNEY, John, A .... 540-453-2200 472 F
downeyj@brcc.edu
DOWNEY, John, P .... 610-499-1265 401 I
jpdowney@widener.edu
DOWNEY, Liesl, V .... 773-442-4248 145 G
l-downey@neiu.edu
DOWNEY, Mechell .... 405-382-9260 369 E
m.downey@sscok.edu
DOWNEY, Nancy .... 207-859-4503 194 B
nancy.downey@colby.edu
DOWNEY, Nora .... 610-785-6582 396 H
ndowney@scs.edu
DOWNEY, Wendy .... 540-831-7700 468 E
wrdowney@radford.edu
DOWNING, SJ, Andrew 201-761-6014 282 H
rdowning@saintpeters.edu
DOWNING, Arthur .... 646-312-1026 292 F
arthur.downing@baruch.cuny.edu
DOWNING, Arthur .... 646-312-1020 292 F
arthur.downing@baruch.cuny.edu
DOWNING, Beverly, L .. 512-505-3127 437 B
bldowning@htu.edu
DOWNING, Chris .... 309-268-8587 138 F
chris.downing@heartland.edu
DOWNING, Cynthia ...... 336-334-7755 341 C
downingc@ncat.edu
DOWNING, Gerri .... 608-757-7759 497 D
gdowning1@blackhawk.edu
DOWNING, John .... 910-362-7846 332 F
jfdowning296@mail.cfcc.edu
DOWNING, Julie .... 541-383-7238 371 I
jdowning@cocc.edu
DOWNING, Kimberly ...... 513-556-5028 361 I
kimberly.downing@uc.edu
DOWNING, Michael ...... 508-336-8700 403 E
michael.downing@jwu.edu
DOWNING, Nancy .... 513-745-3502 364 F
downingn@xavier.edu
DOWNING, Scott .... 620-278-2173 177 E
scott.downing@sterling.edu
DOWNING, Shelby .... 904-596-2452 112 E
sdowning@tbc.edu
DOWNING, Stacey .... 860-231-5373.. 89 G
sdowning@usj.edu
DOWNING, Stacy, L ..... 308-736-2454.. 90 D
sdowning@desu.edu
DOWNING, Steve .... 317-955-6351 159 A
sdowning@marian.edu

Index of Key Administrators DOWNING – DRODDY 623

DOWNING, Valerie 610-606-4609 380 C vdowning@cedarcrest.edu
DOWNS, Amy 717-815-1781 402 G adowns@ycp.edu
DOWNS, Craig 312-899-5100 149 B
DOWNS, Gilbert 805-678-5813 74 A gdowns@vcccd.edu
DOWNS, Jesse, G 225-578-7180 188 K jdowns@lsu.edu
DOWNS, Matthew 251-442-2588 8 C mdowns@umobile.edu
DOWNS, Nate 580-774-3700 369 I nate.downs@swosu.edu
DOWNS, Timothy 707-826-3011 30 A timothy.downs@humboldt.edu
DOWNS, Timothy 607-274-3118 302 E tdowns@ithaca.edu
DOWNS, William, M 704-406-4236 328 I presidentdowns@gardner-webb.edu
DOWNS-BURNS, Kim 802-443-5208 461 G kdowns@middlebury.edu
DOWNWIND, Chrissy 218-755-2141 237 B chrissy.downwind@bemidjistate.edu
DOWTY, Dean 310-233-4216 49 F dowtydl@lahc.edu
DOXEY, Tia, M 919-530-7269 341 D tdoxey@nccu.edu
DOYEL, Sheri 815-479-7563 143 F sdoyel@mchenry.edu
DOYLE, Amanda 337-482-6730 192 F amandad@louisiana.edu
DOYLE, Anne 617-663-7054 210 G adoyle@lasell.edu
DOYLE, Barbara 805-765-9300 39 E
DOYLE, Brianna 207-755-5358 194 J bdoyle@cmcc.edu
DOYLE, Catherine 585-389-2123 307 D cdoyle0@naz.edu
DOYLE, Cathleen, H 410-777-2902 197 C chdoyle@aacc.edu
DOYLE, Christy 208-769-3481 132 A cadoyle@nic.edu
DOYLE, Damian 410-455-3872 202 G damian.doyle@umbc.edu
DOYLE, Dorothy (Darcy) 610-647-4400 385 K ddoyle1@immaculata.edu
DOYLE, Eileen 914-633-2483 302 C edoyle@iona.edu
DOYLE, Francis, J 617-495-5829 210 B dean@seas.harvard.edu
DOYLE, Griffin 706-542-8096 126 F gdoyle@uga.edu
DOYLE, James 845-398-4395 314 D jdoyle@stac.edu
DOYLE, Jamie 877-559-3621 28 J info@ciat.edu
DOYLE, Jeanette 508-373-5733 216 B jeanette.doyle@mcphs.edu
DOYLE, Johnna 719-549-2130 79 G johnna.doyle@colostate.edu
DOYLE, Leslie 641-472-1241 168 A ldoyle@miu.edu
DOYLE, Oliver, J 406-791-5300 264 J president@uprovidence.edu
DOYLE, SHCJ, Peg 610-527-0200 396 G margaret.doyle@rosemont.edu
DOYLE, Peter 973-748-9000 275 C peter_doyle@bloomfield.edu
DOYLE, Rock, D 716-878-6711 317 C doylerd@buffalostate.edu
DOYLE, Sallly 414-288-5153 492 E sally.doyle@marquette.edu
DOYLE, Sheila 607-777-3844 315 E sdoyle@binghamton.edu
DOYLE, Teresa 530-895-2568 27 F doylete@butte.edu
DOYLE, Timothy 901-321-3548 417 G tdoyle1@cbu.edu
DOYLE, Tracy 253-879-3700 483 G tadoyle@pugetsound.edu
DOYLE-TADDUNI, MaryElizabeth 610-282-1100 382 A maryelizabeth.tadduni@desales.edu
DOYLEN, Michael 414-251-9061 495 B doylenm@uwm.edu
DOZIER, John 617-253-1000 215 G
DOZIER, Luann, D 504-865-5794 191 D ldozier@tulane.edu
DOZIER, Monique 951-827-1012 70 B
DOZIER, Monique 470-639-0545 122 H monique.dozier@morehouse.edu
DOZIER, Rodney 620-276-9536 173 H rodney.dozier@gcccks.edu
DRABIK, Mary, A 954-545-4500 108 C mdrabik@sfbc.edu
DRABIK, Thomas 954-637-2268 108 C financialaid@sfbc.edu
DRACHMAN, Annette, R 843-792-4063 409 D drachmar@musc.edu
DRACOS, Bill 703-993-8199 466 J wdracos@gmu.edu
DRAEGER, James 262-695-7833 499 A jdraeger5@wctc.edu
DRAEGER CATTADORIS, Ellen 507-786-3451 242 I cattad1@stolaf.edu
DRAGAN, Kimberly 860-738-6418 87 A kdragan@nwcc.edu
DRAGANIC, Darko 701-255-3285 346 I ddraganic@uttc.edu
DRAGNA, Janine 559-325-3600 28 F jdragna@chsu.edu
DRAGON, Emily 207-602-2451 197 A edragon@une.edu
DRAGOUN, Mary Beth 805-581-1233 42 C mdragoun@eternitybiblecollege.com
DRAGSETH, Debora 701-483-2330 345 A deb.dragseth@dickinsonstate.edu
DRAGUSHANSKAYA, Ludmilla 718-522-9073 290 B mdragush@asa.edu
DRAHUS-CAPO, Deborah, A 787-480-2370 505 A ddrahus@sanjuan.pr
DRAIN, Deborah 315-781-3312 301 D drain@hws.edu
DRAIN, Jerome 713-718-5261 436 E jerome.drain@hccs.edu
DRAIN, Timothy, S 903-510-2320 451 D tim.drain@tjc.edu
DRAKE, Bo 423-697-2606 423 B bo.drake@chattanoogastate.edu
DRAKE, Brent 702-895-3011 270 J brent.drake@unlv.edu
DRAKE, Brian 713-221-8045 452 B drakeb@uhd.edu
DRAKE, Brittney 714-816-0366 68 G brittney.drake@trident.edu
DRAKE, David 706-865-2134 126 D ddrake@truett.edu
DRAKE, Edna 601-977-7876 248 E edrake@tougaloo.edu
DRAKE, Howard 863-669-2321 106 A hdrake@polk.edu
DRAKE, Jennifer 616-331-2495 224 D clas-dean@gvsu.edu
DRAKE, Jill 678-839-6445 127 A jdrake@westga.edu
DRAKE, Julie 608-267-9066 497 C julie.drake@wtcsystem.edu
DRAKE, Kay, L 859-238-5467 179 H kay.drake@centre.edu
DRAKE, Kourtney 816-279-7000 249 D registrar@abtu.edu
DRAKE, Lawrence 386-481-2001 96 D drakel@cookman.edu
DRAKE, Michael, V 510-987-0700 68 M president@ucop.edu
DRAKE, Natricia 910-521-6000 343 A
DRAKE, Paul 671-734-1812 503 D pdrake@piu.edu
DRAKE, Peter 212-842-5970 308 A pdrake@nyaa.edu
DRAKE, Roger, D 660-248-6221 250 H rdrake@centralmethodist.edu
DRAKE, Tyler 480-212-1704 15 R tyler@sessions.edu
DRAKE, Web 864-977-7137 410 A web.drake@ngu.edu
DRAKEFORD, Margaret 540-365-4365 466 I mdrakeford@ferrum.edu
DRALE, Christina, S 501-916-3200 22 C csdrale@ualr.edu
DRAMIS, Jenni 513-745-3639 364 F dramisj@xavier.edu
DRANKA, Scott 413-748-3110 218 E sdranka@springfield.edu
DRAPEAU, Guy 860-297-4210 88 I guy.drapeau@trincoll.edu
DRAPER, Diana, M 203-254-4125 87 G ddraper@fairfield.edu
DRAPER, Jason 724-830-1014 397 F jdraper@setonhill.edu
DRAPER, Marla 303-273-3297 79 A mdraper@mines.edu
DRAPER, Matthew 315-268-6763 295 E mdraper@clarkson.edu
DRAPER, Nancy, J 405-912-9024 368 H ndraper@ru.edu
DRASGOW, Fritz 217-333-1480 151 F fdrasgow@illinois.edu
DRASIN, Joseph 301-314-1019 202 E jdrasin@umd.edu
DRATCH, Joseph 845-848-7600 298 A joseph.dratch@dc.edu
DRAUD, Matt 325-793-3806 439 A draud.matt@mcm.edu
DRAVES, Patricia, H 641-784-5111 166 B pat.draves@graceland.edu
DRAVES, Tony, D 920-923-8140 492 D tddraves32@marianuniversity.edu
DRAWHORN, Derek, D 713-486-2083 455 D derek.d.drawhorn@uth.tmc.edu
DRAYER, Judy 602-274-1885 15 C jdrayer@pihma.edu
DRAYFAHL, Perry, M 610-499-1291 401 I pmdrayfahl@widener.edu
DRAYTON, Rebecca 610-398-5300 388 D rdrayton@lincolntech.edu
DRAYTON, William 240-965-2501 197 F wmdrayton@captechu.edu
DRAZEN, Brock 510-436-2545 57 C bdrazen@peralta.edu
DRAZKOWSKI, Amy 507-453-1479 238 J amy.drazkowski@southeastmn.edu
DREES, Betty, M 816-926-4400 253 C
DREES, John 502-852-6739 185 E john.drees@louisville.edu
DREESZEN, Joseph 617-747-2012 206 D alumniaffairs@berklee.edu
DREESZEN, Megan 402-354-7026 267 E megan.dreeszen@methodistcollege.edu
DREGER, Barb 920-735-4776 497 F dreger@fvtc.edu
DREGIER, Denise, M 443-412-2428 199 B ddregier@harford.edu
DREHER, Karolina 610-796-8218 378 C karolina.dreher@alvernia.edu
DREIER, Alexander 203-432-4949 90 B alexander.dreier@yale.edu
DREIER, LeAnn 253-680-7000 477 A
DREILING, Lori 620-235-4187 176 H ldreiling@pittstate.edu
DREIMILLER, Gretchen 352-638-9754 96 B gdreimiller@beaconcollege.edu
DREITCER, Andrew 909-447-2521 37 H adreitcer@drew.edu
DREIZLER, Robin 310-660-5487 41 J rdreizle@elcamino.edu
DRELL, Persis 650-724-4074 66 D provost@stanford.edu
DRENKOW, Daniel, D 605-274-5251 413 G dan.drenkow@augie.edu
DRENNEN, III, James, K 412-396-6377 382 E drennen@duq.edu
DRENNEN, Rebecca, J 212-986-4343 291 A rjd@berkeleycollege.edu
DRENNEN, Rebecca, J 973-278-5400 274 J rjd@berkeleycollege.edu
DRENOVSKY, Rebecca 216-397-4451 353 O rdrenovsky@jcu.edu
DRESCHER, Debra 518-631-9847 295 E ddresche@clarkson.edu
DRESCHER, Greg 916-416-6476 297 E greg.drescher@culinary.edu
DRESCHER, Marc 310-434-4547 63 B drescher_marc@smc.edu
DRESDNER, Lisa 203-575-8116 86 H ldresdner@nv.edu
DRESSEN, Barbara, J 507-344-7317 233 I barb.dressen@blc.edu
DRESSER-RECKTENWALD, Wendy 607-587-4025 319 C dressews@alfredstate.edu
DRETZKA, Susan 323-856-7852 25 M sdretzka@afi.com
DREW, Daniel, J 716-888-2569 291 M drewd@canisius.edu
DREW, John 617-287-6047 211 E john.drew@umb.edu
DREW, Michael 252-985-5263 339 B mdrew@ncwc.edu
DREW, Ned 973-353-1187 281 C ndrew@newark.rutgers.edu
DREW, Nichole 503-554-2182 372 I ndrew@georgefox.edu
DREWELOW, Lonna 319-363-1323 168 D ldrewelow@mtmercy.edu
DREWENSKI, Shirley 708-596-2000 149 D sdrewenski@ssc.edu
DREWES, James 419-267-1439 357 E jdrewes@northweststate.edu
DREWS, Dani 585-245-5343 317 E ddrews@geneseo.edu
DREXEL, Penny, M 814-332-4311 378 A pdrexel@allegheny.edu
DREXLER, Brad 610-861-5475 391 B bdrexler@northampton.edu
DREXLER, Jim 706-419-1408 117 G jim.drexler@covenant.edu
DREXLER, Julie 229-333-2100 127 F julie.drexler@wiregrass.edu
DREXLER, Matthew 302-831-3348 91 A mdrexler@udel.edu
DREYER, Allen, R 570-585-9317 381 A adreyer@clarkssummitu.edu
DREYFUS, Kristen 252-328-9492 340 H springerk@ecu.edu
DREYFUS, Mark, B 757-671-7171 465 I president@ecpi.edu
DREYFUSS, Shannon 303-963-3411 78 D sdreyfuss@ccu.edu
DRIBBEN, Anthony 772-462-7520 102 E adribben@irsc.edu
DRIEDGER, Derek 605-995-2635 414 A derek.driedger@dwu.edu
DRIER, Tracy 715-836-5182 494 E driert@uwec.edu
DRIES, Kelly 909-748-8030 72 E kelly_dries@redlands.edu
DRIESSEN, Daniel 701-662-1508 346 A daniel.driessen@lrsc.edu
DRIESSEN, Mary 480-461-7489 13 F mary.driessen@mesacc.edu
DRIGGS, Jeff 801-832-2737 461 A jdriggs@westminstercollege.edu
DRIMMER, Alan 800-686-1883 222 B
DRINAN, Helen 610-902-8201 379 E pres@cabrini.edu
DRINDAK, Desiree 518-587-2100 320 B desiree.drindak@esc.edu
DRINKEN, Brandee 715-425-4597 496 A brandee.drinken@uwrf.edu
DRISCOLL, Alisa 714-289-2098 36 D driscoll@chapman.edu
DRISCOLL, Daniel 630-889-6609 145 D ddriscoll@nuhs.edu
DRISCOLL, Laura 218-935-0417 244 A laura.driscoll@wetcc.edu
DRISCOLL, Lori 850-769-1551 101 O ldriscoll@gulfcoast.edu
DRISCOLL, Mary 803-641-3448 412 B maryc@usca.edu
DRISCOLL, Mary Erina 781-768-7000 217 H
DRISCOLL, Michael, A 724-357-2200 393 G michael.driscoll@iup.edu
DRISCOLL, Micheline 718-368-5436 294 C mdriscoll@kbcc.cuny.edu
DRISCOLL, Michelle 816-501-3608 249 H michelle.driscoll@avila.edu
DRISCOLL, Nite 770-242-7716 115 D
DRISCOLL, Shellie 909-599-5433 48 E sdriscoll@lifepacific.edu
DRISH, Michael 413-545-0222 211 D mdrish@umass.edu
DRISKELL, Chad 601-266-6525 248 H chad.driskell@usm.edu
DRISKELL, Lindsay 502-213-2141 181 H lindsay.driskell@kctcs.edu
DRISKILL, Karen 405-425-5205 367 C karen.driskill@oc.edu
DRISKILL, Kristen 585-594-6106 311 L driskill_kristen@roberts.edu
DRISKILL, Sarah 325-793-3808 439 A driskill.sarah@mcm.edu
DRIVDAHL, Sarah 425-889-7826 481 A sarah.drivdahl@northwestu.edu
DRIVER, Berry 502-897-4807 184 D bdriver@sbts.edu
DRIVER, Dale 678-839-6587 127 A ddriver@westga.edu
DRIVER, Louise 406-683-7511 263 E louise.driver@umwestern.edu
DRODDY, Jason, J 225-578-5745 188 K jdroddy@lsu.edu

DROEGEMUELLER, Heidi 651-641-3528 236 A hdroegemueller001@luthersem.edu
DRONGOWSKI, OP, Stanley 616-632-8900 221 A sad004@aquinas.edu
DROOG, Sue 712-722-6017 165 E sue.droog@dordt.edu
DROPKIN, Keith 617-559-8783 210 C kdropkin@hebrewcollege.edu
DROSS, Megan 904-361-6213 101 A megan.dross@fscj.edu
DROST, Jack 256-824-7407 8 B jack.drost@uah.edu
DROUILLARD, Shelly 419-530-7800 363 B shelly.drouillard@utoledo.edu
DROWNE, Kate 573-341-4687 260 F kdrowne@mst.edu
DROZ-RAMOS, Marcus 787-480-2442 505 A mdroz@sanjuan.pr
DRUCKENMILLER, Patrick 907-474-6939 10 B psdruckenmiller@alaska.edu
DRUCKER, David 508-541-1508 208 E ddrucker@dean.edu
DRUCKER, Monique 203-582-8723 88 F monique.drucker@quinnipiac.edu
DRUEKE, Tim 803-323-4862 413 D drueket@winthrop.edu
DRUFFEL, Ginger 509-335-4200 484 D gkdruffel@wsu.edu
DRUIN, Allison 718-687-5543 311 A adruin@pratt.edu
DRUM, Tim 864-587-4282 411 F drumt@smcsc.edu
DRUMM, Jennifer 303-384-2604 79 A jdrumm@mines.edu
DRUMM, Kevin 607-778-5100 317 A drummke@sunybroome.edu
DRUMM, Meaghan, M 585-475-5520 312 A mmdsfa@rit.edu
DRUMMER, Carlee 518-828-4181 296 G carlee.drummer@sunycgcc.edu
DRUMMER, Ebony 216-987-4069 351 D ebony.drummer@tri-c.edu
DRUMMER, Nephtalin 253-680-7150 477 A ndrummer@batestech.edu
DRUMMOND, Carl 260-481-6116 159 H drummond@pfw.edu
DRUMMOND, Cynthia 281-401-5327 438 E cynthia.drummond@lonestar.edu
DRUMMOND, Gordon 480-212-1704 15 R gordon@sessions.edu
DRUMMOND, Hugh 508-849-3345 205 E hdrummond@annamaria.edu
DRUMMOND, Marcy 323-953-4000 49 E drummomj@lacitycollege.edu
DRUMMOND, Michael 954-597-9279 112 J mdrummond@uftl.edu
DRUMMOND, Nancy 503-517-1135 377 B ndrummond@warnerpacific.edu
DRUMMOND, Sara 206-726-5035 478 F sdrummond@cornish.edu
DRURY, Cooper, C 573-884-3971 260 C drury@missouri.edu
DRURY, David 760-355-6215 45 N david.drury@imperial.edu
DRURY, Leesa 218-751-8670 241 Q leesadrury@oakhills.edu
DRURY, Scott 864-644-5013 411 D sdrury@swu.edu
DRURY, Shana 940-552-6291 456 F sdrury@vernoncollege.edu
DRYDEN, Deidra 540-261-8501 470 D deidra.dryden@svu.edu
DRYDEN, JR., Gary 502-213-2646 181 H gary.dryden@kctcs.edu
DRYDEN, Jonathan, N 440-366-4052 355 B
DRYDEN, Tracy 608-789-6179 499 B drydent@westerntc.edu
DRYE, Theresa 856-256-4139 280 H drye@rowan.edu
DRYER, Christy 410-287-1013 198 A cdryer@cecil.edu
DRYER, Michael 215-951-2677 398 G michael.dryer@jefferson.edu
DRYER, Peter 602-489-5300 10 G peter.dryer@arizonachristian.edu
DRYSDALE, Robin 415-565-4852 69 B drysdale@uchastings.edu
DU, Wendy 619-298-1829 65 J wdu@ssu.edu
DU MONT, Malia 845-758-7800 290 G mdumont@bard.edu
DU VIVIER, Derick 503-494-5657 374 F derik@ohsu.edu
DUA, Sumeet 318-257-2871 192 A dua@latech.edu
DUARTE, Ivette 305-348-2423 109 H fduartei@fiu.edu
DUARTE, Kelly 207-221-4772 197 A kduarte@une.edu
DUARTE, Khioverny 732-743-3800 93 H
DUARTE, Maria 575-492-2141 288 I mduarte@usw.edu
DUARTE, Mark, A 671-735-2266 503 E mduarte@triton.uog.edu
DUARTE, Mirna 559-443-8680 67 A mirna.duarte@fresnocitycollege.edu
DUARTE, Nelly 787-620-2040 504 B duarten@aupr.edu
DUBAK, Izabela 630-889-6576 145 D idubak@nuhs.edu
DUBAL, Deepa 859-233-8515 185 A ddubal@transy.edu
DUBBE, Della 406-447-6943 263 F della.dubbe@helenacollege.edu
DUBE, Benoit 215-898-6081 399 J bedube@upenn.edu
DUBE, Vicki 401-874-5275 404 E vdube@uri.edu
DUBENION, Brian 484-365-7705 388 F ddubenion@lincoln.edu
DUBIEL, Mandy 517-629-0600 220 E adubiel@albion.edu
DUBINETT, Steven 310-825-5687 69 D sdubinett@mednet.ucla.edu
DUBINSKY, Julie 816-415-5085 261 G dubinskyj@william.jewell.edu
DUBINSKY, Zalman 973-267-8005 279 G zalmandubinsky@gmail.com
DUBITSKY, Pamela 301-624-2754 198 E pdubitsky@frederick.edu
DUBLON, Felice 312-629-6800 149 B fdublon@saic.edu
DUBMAN, Jillian 978-232-2013 209 B jdubman@endicott.edu
DUBOFF, Brian 505-428-1343 287 H brian.duboff@sfcc.edu
DUBOFF, Katie 610-527-0200 396 G kathleen.duboff@rosemont.edu
DUBOIS, Beth, A 260-359-4080 155 G bdubois@huntington.edu
DUBOIS, Darcy 401-456-8240 404 A ddubois1@ric.edu
DUBOIS, Deb 515-650-3198 163 C debdubois@theartofeducation.edu
DUBOIS, Glenn 804-819-4903 472 E gdubois@vccs.edu
DUBOIS, Gregory, E 561-297-3000 109 F duboisg@fau.edu
DUBOSE, Alexis, W 843-355-4165 413 C dubosea@wiltech.edu
DUBOSE, Cheryl 843-355-4162 413 C dubosec@wiltech.edu
DUBOSE, Derek 303-871-3597 84 C derek.dubose@du.edu
DUBOSE, JR., James 252-335-3400 341 A
DUBOSE, Laticia 334-347-2623 2 A ldubose@escc.edu
DUBOSE, Nicole 205-391-5860 3 E ndubose@sheltonstate.edu
DUBRAY, Robert, R 412-365-2716 380 F rdubray@chatham.edu
DUBRON, Denise 718-522-9073 290 B ddubron@asa.edu
DUBROY, Tashni-Ann 202-806-2258 92 E tashni.dubroy@howard.edu
DUBUC, Lisa 716-614-6798 309 E dubuc@niagaracc.suny.edu
DUBUIS, Dina 734-432-5309 226 G ddubuis@madonna.edu
DUBUQUE, Betsy 508-531-2100 212 B edubuque@bridgew.edu
DUBUQUE, Melissa 573-288-6343 251 I mdubuque@culver.edu
DUCA, Jacqueline 706-737-1632 115 I jduca@augusta.edu
DUCHARME, Gaylene 406-338-5441 262 D gatk@bfcc.edu
DUCHARME, Lisa 413-572-8370 213 C lducharme@westfield.ma.edu
DUCHENEAUX, Stephanie 325-574-6502 457 G sducheneaux@wtc.edu
DUCHETTE, Katharine 207-741-5726 195 D kduchette@smccme.edu
DUCHSCHERER, Eric, D 315-267-2350 318 D duchsced@potsdam.edu
DUCIOAME, Lynn 940-397-4676 439 F lynn.ducioame@msutexas.edu
DUCK, Joseph, T 617-628-5000 219 A joseph.duck@tufts.edu
DUCKETT, Danny 423-746-5318 425 C dduckett@tnwesleyan.edu
DUCKETT, Skye 404-894-2499 119 D skye.duckett@hr.gatech.edu
DUCKHAM, James 765-285-1832 153 E jaduckham@bsu.edu
DUCKWORTH, Anthony 229-500-2847 114 F anthony.duckworth@asurams.edu
DUCKWORTH, Brad 715-346-2694 496 B brad.duckworth@uwsp.edu
DUCKWORTH, Melinda 301-784-5000 197 B
DUCKWORTH, Robert, C 214-887-5089 434 G rduckworth@dts.edu
DUCLOS, Victoria 401-341-2345 404 D duclosv@salve.edu
DUCOFFE, Robert 262-595-2261 495 D ducoffe@uwp.edu
DUCOTE, Melissa 318-342-5141 193 A ducote@ulm.edu
DUCSAY, Teresa 412-809-5275 395 F barbour.teresa@ptcollege.edu
DUDA, David 215-489-2356 381 K david.duda@delval.edu
DUDA, Heather 330-829-6127 362 E dudahe@mountunion.edu
DUDA, Teri 973-278-5400 274 J td@berkeleycollege.edu
DUDAS, Bertalan 814-866-8142 387 C bdudas@lecom.edu
DUDAS, Jon 520-626-6350 16 H jondudas@arizona.edu
DUDGEON, Ashley 859-846-4421 183 G adudgeon@midway.edu
DUDGEON, David 305-899-3727 96 A ddudgeon@barry.edu
DUDGEON, Hollis 502-863-8056 180 E hollis_dudgeon@georgetowncollege.edu
DUDGEON, Mark 614-287-2508 351 B mdudgeon@cscc.edu
DUDICH, Jason 317-788-3301 161 F dudichj@uindy.edu
DUDLEY, Brad, D 310-506-4184 56 H brad.dudley@pepperdine.edu
DUDLEY, Christopher, H 336-841-9127 329 E cdudley@highpoint.edu
DUDLEY, Jacklyn 270-809-3774 184 A jdudley@murraystate.edu
DUDLEY, Jason 239-985-8368 100 G jason.dudley@fsw.edu
DUDLEY, John 605-658-3830 415 E john.dudley@usd.edu
DUDLEY, Kaitlin 404-297-9522 119 G
DUDLEY, Kristine 603-206-8161 272 A kdudley@ccsnh.edu
DUDLEY, Manuel 336-334-4822 334 F mcdudley@gtcc.edu
DUDLEY, Roland, Q 417-268-6108 250 A rdudley@gobbc.edu
DUDLEY, Sharese 219-980-6791 157 A shaadudl@iun.edu
DUDLEY, Tina 618-634-3200 149 C tinad@shawneecc.edu
DUDLEY, Waller, T 540-458-8470 476 D wdudley@wlu.edu
DUDLEY, William, C 540-458-8700 476 D president@wlu.edu
DUDONIS, Shirlin 510-666-8248 24 G accounting@aimc.edu
DUDONIS, Shirlin 510-666-8248 24 G registrar@aimc.edu
DUDT, Susan 770-426-2700 122 A sdudt@life.edu
DUDUIT, Angie 740-351-3322 360 E aduduit@shawnee.edu
DUDUIT, James 864-231-2000 405 F jduduit@andersonuniversity.edu
DUDZIK, Kim 619-660-4453 44 G kim.dudzik@gcccd.edu
DUECK, Jeffrey 646-378-6100 289 F jeffrey.dueck@nyack.edu
DUELL, Charles 303-914-6517 82 L charles.duell@rrcc.edu
DUELLMAN, Scott 314-977-8283 258 H scott.duellman@slu.edu
DUENAS, Francisca 530-898-6345 31 A fiduenas@csuchico.edu
DUENAS, Hector 305-273-4499 96 I hector@cbt.edu
DUENAS, Miguel 323-265-8835 49 D duenasma@elac.edu
DUENAS, Tina 530-242-7622 64 A tduenas@shastacollege.edu
DUENKEL, Priscilla 865-981-5302 424 C pduenkel@pstcc.edu
DUERK, Jeffrey 305-284-6318 112 K jeffrey.duerk@miami.edu
DUERR, Larry 414-382-6173 490 G larry.duerr@alverno.edu
DUERR, William 864-250-7000 93 H
DUERWACHTER, Kathleen, A 608-796-3072 496 L kaduerwachter@viterbo.edu
DUESING, Jason, G 816-414-3740 255 F jduesing@mbts.edu
DUET, Jodi 985-448-7946 187 J jodi.duet@fletcher.edu
DUETSCH, Craig 773-995-2042 134 J cduetsch@csu.edu
DUETT, Belinda, G 334-833-4519 5 H bduett@hawks.huntingdon.edu
DUEWEKE, Jerome 317-940-8000 153 H
DUEÑAS, Felicia 805-289-6562 74 B fduenas@vcccd.edu
DUEÑEZ, Nydia 213-738-6871 66 A deanofstudents@swlaw.edu
DUFAU, Nancy 410-704-5822 204 B ndufau@towson.edu
DUFAULT-HUNTER, David, R 818-677-3700 32 E ddh@csun.edu
DUFF, Evan 252-985-5136 339 B eduff@ncwc.edu
DUFFEL, Cary Beth 901-751-8453 420 G
DUFFIE, Cecil 903-923-2455 457 I cduffie@wileyc.edu
DUFFIE, James 561-868-3077 105 C duffiej@palmbeachstate.edu
DUFFIELD, Stacy 701-231-7012 345 D stacy.duffield@ndsu.edu
DUFFINS, Varo, L 610-328-8360 398 B vduffin1@swarthmore.edu
DUFFY, Arwen, S 413-545-4200 211 D arwen.duffy@umass.edu
DUFFY, Brian 215-972-2030 392 P bduffy@pafa.edu
DUFFY, Camisha 270-809-3155 184 A cduffy@murraystate.edu
DUFFY, Chris 813-974-0658 111 B cduffy@usf.edu
DUFFY, Chrissie 334-222-6591 2 I cduffy@lbwcc.edu
DUFFY, Deborah 215-717-6387 399 I deduffy@uarts.edu
DUFFY, Dolly 574-631-2788 161 G eduffy@nd.edu
DUFFY, Elizabeth 240-629-7886 198 E eduffy@frederick.edu
DUFFY, James, P 717-337-6240 384 C jpduffy@gettysburg.edu
DUFFY, Julia, A 203-254-4000 87 G jduffy@fairfield.edu
DUFFY, Kelly 315-470-5922 291 E kellyduffy@crouse.org
DUFFY, Kevin 609-586-4800 277 H duffyk@mccc.edu
DUFFY, Kristine 518-743-2237 319 D duffyk@sunyacc.edu
DUFFY, Matthew 218-726-8829 243 A duffy@d.umn.edu
DUFFY, Michael 517-265-5161 220 D mduffy@adrian.edu
DUFFY, Rachelle, M 517-265-5161 220 D rduffy@adrian.edu
DUFFY, Raymond 610-519-4237 401 B raymond.duffy@villanova.edu
DUFFY, Sean 518-244-4536 312 D duffys2@sage.edu
DUFFY, Stephen, M 956-326-2543 446 A sduffy@tamiu.edu
DUFFY, Susan 617-989-4590 219 D duffys7@wit.edu
DUFFY, Susan 781-239-6425 205 G sduffy@babson.edu
DUFFY, Thomas 845-431-8305 298 B thomas.duffy1@sunydutchess.edu
DUFFY, II, William, R 563-425-5221 170 D duffyw@uiu.edu

DUNLAP, Doug ... 620-901-6261 171 A
ddunlap@allencc.edu
DUNLAP, John ... 617-287-7050 211 C
jdunlap@umassp.edu
DUNLAP, Lanee ... 903-886-5738 446 D
lanee.dunlap@tamuc.edu
DUNLAP, Michael, P ... 920-565-1000 492 A
dunlapmp@lakeland.edu
DUNLAP, Ruth ... 662-562-3202 247 E
rdunlap@northwestms.edu
DUNLAP, Scott ... 973-720-3232 283 I
dunlaps@wpunj.edu
DUNLAP, Stacey ... 870-512-7811.. 18 C
stacey_dunlap@asun.edu
DUNLAP, Susan, L ... 516-726-5816 502 G
dunlaps@usmma.edu
DUNLAY, Robert, W ... 402-280-2600 265 J
robertdunlay@creighton.edu
DUNLEAVY, James, F ... 610-861-5463 391 B
jdunleavy@northampton.edu
DUNLOP, Jennifer ... 920-206-2375 492 C
jennifer.dunlop@mbu.edu
DUNLOP, Kath ... 413-597-4286 220 A
kdk2@williams.edu
DUNMIRE, Brad ... 419-755-4765 357 B
bdunmire@ncstatecollege.edu
DUNN, Alaina ... 650-417-2055.. 55 K
adunn@paloaltou.edu
DUNN, Amy ... 202-379-7808.. 93 H
DUNN, Andrew ... 714-438-4611.. 38 C
wdunniii@cccd.edu
DUNN, Ashley ... 818-778-5518.. 50 B
dunnae@lavc.edu
DUNN, Barbara ... 870-543-5957.. 21 D
bdunn@seark.edu
DUNN, Barry, H ... 605-688-4111 416 A
barry.dunn@sdstate.edu
DUNN, Becky ... 816-271-4200 256 C
DUNN, Brad ... 512-863-1944 444 F
dunnb@southwestern.edu
DUNN, Charissa ... 918-335-6822 368 E
cdunn@okwu.edu
DUNN, Chris ... 816-271-4200 256 C
DUNN, Christopher ... 617-482-3103 211 D
cdunn@admin.umass.edu
DUNN, Corey ... 404-471-6176 114 E
cdunn@agnesscott.edu
DUNN, Daniel ... 312-329-4451 144 F
daniel.dunn@moody.edu
DUNN, Darren ... 970-351-2362.. 84 D
darren.dunn@unco.edu
DUNN, Deborah ... 734-432-5313 226 G
ddunn@madonna.edu
DUNN, Derrek, B ... 410-651-6348 203 B
ddunn@umes.edu
DUNN, Doug ... 606-693-5000 182 H
ddunn@kmbc.edu
DUNN, Elizabeth ... 607-436-2520 316 C
elizabeth.dunn@oneonta.edu
DUNN, Elizabeth ... 607-436-3458 316 C
elizabeth.dunn@oneonta.edu
DUNN, Florence ... 559-325-3600.. 28 F
fdunn@chsu.edu
DUNN, Gary ... 831-459-2628.. 71 A
gmdunn@ucsc.edu
DUNN, Jaime ... 410-626-2500 201 E
jaime.dunn@sjc.edu
DUNN, James ... 559-325-3600.. 28 F
jdunn@chsu.edu
DUNN, James, J ... 336-758-4240 344 A
jdunn@vergercapital.com
DUNN, Jena ... 361-991-9403 444 G
DUNN, Jim ... 918-335-6234 368 E
jdunn@okwu.edu
DUNN, Jimmy ... 559-325-3600.. 28 F
jdunn@chsu.edu
DUNN, John, B ... 617-552-3350 207 A
jack.dunn@bc.edu
DUNN, Juli ... 509-522-4403 485 C
dunnjl@whitman.edu
DUNN, Keith ... 601-974-1010 246 C
keith.dunn@millsaps.edu
DUNN, Kelly ... 715-682-1351 493 G
kdunn@northland.edu
DUNN, Kevin ... 617-627-2816 219 A
kevin.dunn@tufts.edu
DUNN, Kevin ... 859-246-6716 181 B
kevin.dunn@kctcs.edu
DUNN, Linda ... 801-581-6996 459 D
linda.dunn@alumni.utah.edu
DUNN, Lisa ... 602-274-1885.. 15 C
ldunn@pihma.edu
DUNN, Louise ... 940-565-4307 453 B
louise.dunn@unt.edu
DUNN, Marilee ... 801-957-4490 460 D
marilee.dunn@slcc.edu
DUNN, Michael, K ... 240-895-4105 201 F
mkdunn@smcm.edu
DUNN, Patricia, A ... 815-599-3408 138 H
pat.dunn@highland.edu
DUNN, Paul ... 860-701-7739.. 88 C
dunn_p@mitchell.edu
DUNN, Paul ... 360-650-3472 485 A
paul.dunn@wwu.edu
DUNN, Rose Ellen ... 609-497-7818 279 D
rose.ellen.dunn@ptsem.edu
DUNN, Shari ... 704-687-5723 342 C
shari.dunn@uncc.edu
DUNN, Sharon ... 318-813-2941 189 D
sharon.dunn@lsuhs.edu
DUNN, Stanley ... 518-276-8433 311 J
dunns6@rpi.edu
DUNN, Susan, C ... 407-582-6871 113 C
sdunn18@valenciacollege.edu
DUNN, Timothy ... 415-503-6281.. 61 E
tdunn@sfcm.edu
DUNN, Timothy ... 212-659-3604 303 E
tdunn@tkc.edu
DUNN, Todd ... 910-678-8236 334 C
dunnt@faytechcc.edu
DUNN, Tom ... 516-299-2537 304 D
tom.dunn@liu.edu
DUNN, Tracy ... 859-233-8148 185 A
tdunn@transy.edu
DUNN, Tracy ... 803-705-4694 405 G
tracy.dunn@benedict.edu
DUNN, W. Brent ... 417-836-6666 255 J
brentdunn@missouristate.edu
DUNN, Will ... 386-506-4486.. 98 A
will.dunne@daytonastate.edu
DUNN CARLTON,
Heather ... 209-667-6635.. 33 D
hdunncarlton@csustan.edu
DUNN CARPENTER,
Christina ... 913-758-6267 177 I
christina.dunn_carpenter@stmary.edu
DUNN-RAMSAY, Sheri ... 910-410-1907 336 G
srdunn-ramsay@richmondcc.edu
DUNNAGAN, Tim ... 208-426-3917 130 F
timdunnagan@boisestate.edu
DUNNE, Jennifer ... 617-333-2271 208 D
jdunne1213@curry.edu
DUNNE, Nicole ... 831-646-3007.. 52 H
ndunne@mpc.edu
DUNNE, Timothy ... 207-741-5506 195 D
tdunne@smccme.edu
DUNNE-CASCIO,
Colleen ... 541-962-3476 372 H
ccascio@eou.edu
DUNNING, Carol ... 312-553-2500 134 L
cdunning6@ccc.edu
DUNNING, Eric ... 920-403-1346 494 B
eric.dunning@snc.edu
DUNNING, Jim ... 805-756-5551.. 29 K
jdunning@calpoly.edu
DUNNING, Katherine ... 615-879-2022 419 C
DUNNING, Kathy ... 251-442-2281.... 8 C
kdunning@umobile.edu
DUNNING, Scott ... 317-274-4860 157 B
DUNNING, Scott ... 765-973-8435 156 D
sdunning@iu.edu
DUNNING, Sue ... 863-638-2937 113 E
dunnings@webber.edu
DUNNINGTON, Renee ... 614-236-6701 348 I
rdunning@capital.edu
DUNNIVANT, Stephen ... 954-201-7350.. 96 F
DUNNUCK, John ... 954-201-7405.. 96 F
jdunnuck@broward.edu
DUNPHY, Michael ... 330-490-7123 363 E
mdunphy@walsh.edu
DUNSCOMBE, William ... 908-709-7570 283 E
dunscombe@ucc.edu
DUNSEATH, Jennifer ... 401-254-3275 404 C
jdunseath@rwu.edu
DUNSMORE, Tara ... 410-857-2798 200 D
tdunsmore@mcdaniel.edu
DUNSTAN, Dani ... 208-282-3343 131 E
dunsdani@isu.edu
DUNSTON, Julie ... 618-453-3430 149 G
dunston@siu.edu
DUNSTON, Karen ... 503-352-2713 375 B
dunstonk@pacificu.edu
DUNSTON, Rita ... 540-654-1265 471 B
rdunston@umw.edu
DUNSWORTH,
Richard, L ... 479-979-1242.. 24 A
rdunsworth@ozarks.edu
DUNTLEY, Mark ... 503-768-7082 373 D
hmhiman@lclark.edu
DUNTON, Renee ... 207-307-3900 193 E
rdunton@beal.edu
DUONG, Kimberly ... 559-324-6423.. 66 H
kimberly.duong@cloviscollege.edu
DUONG, Tom ... 714-903-2762.. 68 I
DUPAUL, Stephanie ... 804-287-6442 471 E
sdupaul@richmond.edu
DUPAY, Abbie ... 812-941-2115 157 D
aedupay@ius.edu
DUPEE, II, Dan, J ... 315-786-2230 302 I
ddupee@sunyjefferson.edu
DUPLANTIS, Josh ... 251-990-0445.... 1 I
joshua.duplantis@coastalalabama.edu
DUPLER, Terry ... 719-587-7208.. 77 F
dtdupler@adams.edu
DUPLESSIS, Raymond ... 504-671-6480 187 I
rduple@dcc.edu
DUPLESSIS, Tamika ... 504-671-5050 187 I
tduple@dcc.edu
DUPONT, Collise ... 337-521-8912 188 G
collise.dupont@solacc.edu
DUPONT, Jeffrey ... 970-247-7153.. 80 H
dupont_j@fortlewis.edu
DUPONT, Joseph ... 617-552-3430 207 A
joseph.dupont@bc.edu
DUPONT, Michael ... 817-515-3015 445 A
michael.dupont@tccd.edu
DUPONT, Randall ... 318-427-4489 189 A
rdupont@lsua.edu
DUPONT, Richard ... 203-332-5991.. 86 E
rdupont@hcc.commnet.edu
DUPRA, JoAnn ... 870-543-5993.. 21 D
jdupra@seark.edu
DUPRAS, Tosha ... 806-742-3831 450 C
tosha.dupras@ttu.edu
DUPRE, Tara ... 985-549-2001 192 E
tara.dupre@selu.edu
DUPRE, Terry, G ... 985-448-4031 192 C
terry.dupre@nicholls.edu
DUPREE, Jason, M ... 580-774-7081 369 I
jason.dupree@swosu.edu
DUPREE, Leslie, M ... 309-794-7626 132 H
lesliedupree@augustana.edu
DUPREE, Paul ... 704-216-7114 337 C
paul.dupree@rccc.edu
DUPREE, Paul, J ... 859-858-3511 178 H
pdupree@asbury.edu
DUPRIEST, Barclay, F ... 804-752-7371 469 B
bdupries@rmc.edu
DUPUIS, Chris ... 860-768-7866.. 89 E
cdupuis@hartford.edu
DUPUIS, Mishelle ... 910-938-6251 333 D
dupuism@coastalcarolina.edu
DURAJ, Jonathan ... 937-327-7817 364 C
jduraj@wittenberg.edu
DURALL, Changamire ... 504-520-7490 193 C
cdurall1@xula.edu
DURAN, Alexandra ... 408-274-6700.. 62 E
DURAN, Armando ... 626-585-7148.. 56 D
axduran@pasadena.edu
DURAN, Cristina ... 505-454-3456 286 C
duranc@nmhu.edu
DURAN, Jennie Marie ... 518-320-1851 315 C
DURAN, Michael, S ... 505-984-6000 287 F
msduran@sjc.edu
DURAN, Richard, P ... 210-829-6968 452 D
rduran@uiwtx.edu
DURAN, Rosie ... 575-624-7093 285 F
rosie.duran@roswell.enmu.edu
DURAN, Veronica ... 520-494-5481.. 11 M
veronica.duran@centralaz.edu
DURAN-CERDA,
Dolores ... 520-206-4999.. 15 E
dcerda@pima.edu
DURAND,
Alain-Philippe ... 520-621-9294.. 16 H
adurand@arizona.edu
DURAND, Gene ... 707-527-4011.. 63 C
DURANT, Ben ... 201-200-2597 278 F
bdurant@njcu.edu
DURANT, Brian, M ... 315-255-1743 292 A
bdurant@cayuga-cc.edu
DURANT, Leroy, A ... 803-535-5341 406 E
ldurant@claflin.edu
DURANT, Natalie ... 860-768-5565.. 89 E
ndurant@hartford.edu
DURANT, Richard ... 909-794-1084.. 39 G
DURANT DANCEL,
Samantha ... 415-703-9577.. 28 D
sdurant@cca.edu
DURANT-JONES, Lisa ... 585-389-2775 307 D
ldurant4@naz.edu
DURANTE, Kate ... 860-297-2072.. 88 I
kate.durante@trincoll.edu
DURAZO, Marco, A ... 805-482-2755.. 59 G
rector@stjohnsem.edu
DURBAK, Andres ... 773-907-4708 134 N
adurbak@ccc.edu
DURBEN, Katherine ... 414-288-5470 492 E
katherine.durben@marquette.edu
DURBIN, Bryce ... 706-236-2282 116 A
bdurbin@berry.edu
DURBIN, Daniel ... 502-852-5555 185 E
daniel.durbin.1@louisville.edu
DURBIN, Kelly ... 505-428-1814 287 H
kelly.durbin@sfcc.edu
DURBIN, Rachel ... 503-494-7800 374 F
finaid@ohsu.edu
DURDELLA, Caroline ... 562-908-3412.. 58 M
cdurdella@riohondo.edu
DURDEN, Lori, S ... 912-871-1638 123 F
ldurden@ogeecheetech.edu
DURDEN, Robert ... 434-218-4540 471 F
uvimco@uvimco.org
DURDEN, Tracey ... 734-432-5673 226 G
tdurden@madonna.edu
DUREN, Brad ... 580-349-1498 367 F
duren@opsu.edu
DUREN, Brad ... 918-595-7066 370 B
brad.duren@tulsacc.edu
DURFEE, Jeffrey, A ... 904-620-2820 111 A
jdurfee@unf.edu
DURGIN, Tricia ... 208-885-6469 132 C
triciadurgin@uidaho.edu
DURGLO, Dan ... 406-275-4972 264 H
dan_durglo@skc.edu
DURHAM, Claiborn ... 501-420-1211.. 17 D
claiborn.durham@arkansasbaptist.edu
DURHAM, Danielle ... 660-831-4177 256 B
DURHAM, David, L ... 304-293-8220 489 E
david.durham@mail.wvu.edu
DURHAM, Ed ... 410-287-1010 198 A
edurham@cecil.edu
DURHAM, Gesele ... 703-993-5883 466 J
gedurham@gmu.edu
DURHAM, Greg ... 402-280-2987 265 J
gregdurham@creighton.edu
DURHAM, John, R ... 610-519-7164 401 B
john.durham@villanova.edu
DURHAM, Kimberly ... 954-262-8730 104 M
durham@nova.edu
DURHAM, Leslie ... 208-426-1414 130 F
ldurham@boisestate.edu
DURHAM, Monica ... 419-755-4896 357 B
mdurham@ncstatecollege.edu
DURHAM, Morgan ... 870-886-6741.. 24 B
DURHAM, Robert ... 501-812-2318.. 23 E
rdurham@uaptc.edu
DURHAM, Tammara ... 785-864-4060 177 G
tdurham@ku.edu
DURHAM, Tammie ... 734-763-4119 231 A
tldurham@umich.edu
DURHAM, Teresa ... 269-965-3931 225 D
durhamt@kellogg.edu
DURHAM, Terry ... 615-220-7885 423 G
tdurham@mscc.edu
DURHAM, Tracey ... 239-513-1122 102 C
DURHAM, William, H ... 704-233-8811 344 E
durham@wingate.edu
DURIAN-GAMBELL,
Angella ... 641-673-1076 170 I
gambella@wmpenn.edu
DURIAN-GAMBELL,
Angella, M ... 641-673-1076 170 I
gambella@wmpenn.edu
DURICK, Brian ... 949-480-4018.. 64 E
bdurick@soka.edu
DURIE, Dale ... 651-638-6400 233 J
d-durie@bethel.edu
DURKEE, David ... 616-632-2944 221 A
ddd003@aquinas.edu
DURKIN, Karen ... 856-415-2284 280 F
kdurkin@rcsj.edu
DURKIN, Rebecca ... 847-578-8351 148 B
rebecca.durkin@rosalindfranklin.edu
DURKIN, Teri, A ... 920-923-7161 492 D
tadurkin33@marianuniversity.edu
DURLER, Jamie ... 620-276-0473 173 H
jamie.durler@gcccks.edu

D'ELIA, Christopher ...... 225-578-8574 188 K
cdelia@lsu.edu
D'EMILIO, Deanne, H ... 215-641-5548 384 G
demilio.d@gmercyu.edu
D'IORIO, Cinzia .... 201-612-7488 274 I
cdiorio@bergen.edu
D'ITALIA, Alexandra ..... 213-738-5729.. 66 A
aditalia@swlaw.edu
D'LENA, Brandye .... 520-206-2610.. 15 E
bdlena@pima.edu
D'MONTE, Loreto .... 909-448-4983.. 71 C
ldmonte@laverne.edu
D'OLIVO, Amy .... 908-852-1400 275 H
dolivoa@centenaryuniversity.edu
D'OYLEY, Alicia, A .... 617-228-3267 214 A
alicia.doyley@bhcc.edu
D'SA, Vinessa .... 314-838-8858 261 A
vdsa@ugst.edu
D'SOUZA, Gerard .... 936-261-2212 445 E
gedsouza@pvamu.edu
D'ZMURA, Anne .... 562-985-7886.. 32 A
anne.dzmura@csulb.edu

E

EACKER, Anne .... 888-576-3348.. 46 M
EACONA, Travis .... 770-381-7200 120 F
EADE, Chuck .... 218-477-2131 239 A
chuck.eade@mnstate.edu
EADES, Annemarie .... 678-839-6100 127 A
aeades@westga.edu
EADES, Timothy .... 405-491-6600 369 G
teades@snu.edu
EADIE, Danielle .... 716-839-8337 297 F
dseadie@daemen.edu
EADIE, Tanya .... 206-221-1405 484 A
teadie@uw.edu
EADLINE, Madalyn .... 610-758-3000 388 C
EADS, Amy .... 423-869-6751 420 A
amy.eads@lmunet.edu
EADS, Jessica, L .... 516-463-6318 301 E
jessica.l.eads@hofstra.edu
EADS, Sonja .... 606-759-7141 182 B
sonja.eads@kctcs.edu
EADY, Daniel, P .... 214-768-3999 443 G
deady@smu.edu
EADY, Niya .... 404-225-4452 115 F
neady@atlantatech.edu
EAFFORD, Felisa .... 216-987-5229 351 D
felisa.eafford@tri-c.edu
EAGAN, Johanna .... 303-384-2589.. 79 A
jeagan@mines.edu
EAGAN, John .... 617-333-2974 208 D
jeagan1008@curry.edu
EAGAN, Paige .... 269-488-4468 225 C
peagan@kvcc.edu
EAGEN, Michael, J .... 413-545-2554 211 D
meagen@provost.umass.edu
EAGER, Trenton .... 251-405-7034.... 1 E
teager@bishop.edu
EAGLE, Teresa .... 304-746-8924 488 N
thardman@marshall.edu
EAGLEMAN, Frances .... 406-638-3111 262 J
eaglemanf@lbhc.edu
EAHEART, Maggie .... 773-298-3301 148 I
eaheart@sxu.edu
EAKER, David .... 602-319-7697.. 15 P
david.eaker@rsi.edu
EAKER, Jodie .... 815-772-7218 145 A
jeaker@morrisontech.edu
EAKIN, Amber .... 757-382-9900.. 93 H
EAKINS, Lewis .... 208-282-2515 131 E
eakilewi@isu.edu
EAMES, Michael .... 216-687-3604 350 G
EANES, Berenecea, J .... 718-262-2350 295 D
bjeanes@york.cuny.edu
EANOCHS, LaDonna ...... 601-877-6123 244 B
lweanochs@alcorn.edu
EAPEN, Jacob .... 215-751-8029 381 H
jeapen@ccp.edu
EAPEN, Johnson .... 717-358-3971 383 G
EAR, Saovra .... 206-934-6964 482 G
saovra.ear@seattlecolleges.edu
EARHART, Alan .... 956-665-3572 455 A
alan.earhart@utrgv.edu
EARICK, Mary .... 505-454-3146 286 C
maryearick@nmhu.edu
EARL, Brittany .... 417-328-1500 258 K
bearl@sbuniv.edu
EARL, Bryan .... 313-593-5070 231 B
earlb@umich.edu
EARL, Danielle .... 914-961-8313 314 E
dearl@svots.edu
EARL, Todd .... 417-328-1843 258 K
tearl@sbuniv.edu
EARL, Twyler .... 405-789-6400 369 G
tearl@snu.edu
EARL-REPLOGLE,
Melanie .... 417-873-7444 252 A
mearl@drury.edu
EARLE, David .... 620-278-2173 177 E
EARLE, Heather, A .... 603-646-9442 272 F
heather.a.earle@dartmouth.edu
EARLE, Jonathan, H ...... 225-578-2735 188 K
jearle@lsu.edu
EARLE, Steven, R .... 562-903-4740.. 27 E
steve.earle@biola.edu
EARLEY, Jeff .... 540-231-6905 475 D
jearley@vt.edu
EARLEY, Rita .... 828-766-1290 335 G
rearley@mayland.edu
EARLY, Johnnie .... 850-599-3301 109 E
johnnie.early@famu.edu
EARLY, Lisa .... 410-951-3666 203 E
learly@coppin.edu
EARLY, Loretta .... 410-822-5400 198 B
learly@chesapeake.edu
EARLY, Patrick .... 785-670-1711 178 A
patrick.early@washburn.edu
EARNEST, Bruce .... 251-442-2325.... 8 C
bearnest@umobile.edu
EARNEST, Greta .... 212-217-4370 299 C
greta_earnest@fitnyc.edu
EARNEST, Mike .... 907-474-7500.. 10 B
wmearnest@alaska.edu
EARNEST, Sarah .... 978-232-2042 209 B
searnest@endicott.edu
EARP, Christy .... 336-838-6117 338 H
cbearp774@wilkescc.edu
EARP, Samantha .... 413-585-2618 218 D
searp@smith.edu
EASLEY, Dawn .... 763-576-4268 237 A
dawn.easley@anokatech.edu
EASLEY, II, Jacob .... 212-463-0400 322 B
jacob.easley@touro.edu
EASLEY, II, Jacob .... 212-463-0400 322 C
jacob.easley@touro.edu
EASLEY, Mike .... 704-233-8299 344 E
m.easley@wingate.edu
EASOM, Lauren .... 478-445-5384 119 A
lauren.easom@gcsu.edu
EASON, Rod .... 641-472-1204 168 A
reason@miu.edu
EAST, Jen .... 610-527-0200 396 G
jennifer.east@rosemont.edu
EASTBERG, Jodi .... 414-382-6231 490 G
jodi.eastberg@alverno.edu
EASTER, Tammy .... 312-329-4000 144 F
EASTER-PILCHER,
Andrea .... 801-626-6159 460 B
aeasterpilcher@weber.edu
EASTERBROOK,
Jonathan .... 860-768-5096.. 89 E
easterbro@hartford.edu
EASTERLING, Mayson ..... 864-231-2000 405 F
measterling@andersonuniversity.edu
EASTERLING, Vonda ...... 919-582-4293 339 I
vonda.easterling@shawu.edu
EASTERLING,
W. Samuel .... 515-294-9988 163 E
wse@iastate.edu
EASTERWOOD, Allyson . 601-266-5005 248 H
allyson.easterwood@usm.edu
EASTHAM, Sabine .... 270-384-8236 183 D
easthams@lindsey.edu
EASTHAM, Yvette .... 270-707-3731 181 G
yvette.eastham@kctcs.edu
EASTHOPE, Jennifer ...... 219-464-5982 162 C
jennifer.easthope@valpo.edu
EASTIN, Elizabeth .... 602-383-8228.. 16 G
eeastin@uat.edu
EASTIN, Graig, R .... 518-276-6247 311 J
eastig@rpi.edu
EASTIN, Todd, B .... 602-243-8245.. 14 C
todd.eastin@southmountaincc.edu
EASTLICK, Beth .... 919-681-0405 328 D
beth.eastlick@duke.edu
EASTMAN, Deborah .... 860-439-2030.. 87 F
daeas@conncoll.edu
EASTMAN, Diana .... 605-394-2497 415 I
diana.eastman@sdsmt.edu
EASTMAN, Doug .... 802-224-3009 462 G
doug.eastman@vsc.edu
EASTMAN, Karen .... 423-697-4791 423 B
karen.eastman@chattanoogastate.edu
EASTMAN, Katharine, G 617-333-2935 208 D
garrett.eastman@curry.edu
EASTMAN, Ken .... 405-744-5064 367 G
ken.eastman@okstate.edu
EASTMAN, Lori .... 518-580-5640 315 A
leastman@skidmore.edu
EASTMAN, Michele, A .. 301-405-5025 202 E
meastman@umd.edu
EASTMAN, Mindy, R ...... 641-422-4363 168 E
eastmmin@niacc.edu
EASTMAN, Nancy .... 816-802-3466 253 H
neastman@kcai.edu
EASTMAN, Rayshawn ..... 513-244-4467 356 F
rayshawn.eastman@msj.edu
EASTON, Celia, A .... 585-245-5541 317 E
easton@geneseo.edu
EASTON, Nancy .... 773-442-4650 145 G
n-easton@neiu.edu
EASTON, Patricia .... 909-607-3318.. 37 F
patricia.easton@cgu.edu
EASTON, Paul .... 703-526-6804 468 A
paul.easton@marymount.edu
EASTON, Rebecca .... 806-371-5982 428 F
rreaston@actx.edu
EASTON, Stephen, D ..... 701-483-2326 345 A
steve.easton@dickinsonstate.edu
EASTON, Tanya .... 570-674-6368 389 H
teaston@misericordia.edu
EASTON-BROOKS,
Donald .... 775-682-7853 270 K
deastonbrooks@unr.edu
EASTRIDGE, Julie .... 641-844-5571 167 C
julie.eastridge@iavalley.edu
EASTRIDGE, Julie .... 641-844-5571 167 E
julie.eastridge@iavalley.edu
EASTRIDGE, June .... 702-992-2863 270 H
june.eastridge@nsc.edu
EASTWICK, Thomas .... 973-661-0600 276 E
teastwick@eastwick.edu
EASTWICK, Thomas .... 201-327-8877 276 F
teastwick@eastwick.edu
EASTWICK, Thomas, M . 201-488-9400 276 D
tomeastwick@aol.com
EASTWOOD, Matt .... 405-682-1611 367 D
matthew.a.eastwood@occc.edu
EATMAN, Lynne .... 318-670-6000 191 B
EATMON, Joe .... 205-391-2936.... 3 E
jeatmon@sheltonstate.edu
EATON, Adrienne .... 848-932-9503 281 B
eaton@smlr.rutgers.edu
EATON, Amy .... 503-943-8551 376 H
eaton@up.edu
EATON, Andrew .... 856-222-9311 280 E
aeaton@rcbc.edu
EATON, Brett .... 336-758-5237 344 A
eatonbd@wfu.edu
EATON, Charlee .... 603-899-4097 272 G
eatonc@franklinpierce.edu
EATON, Emily .... 309-467-6826 137 G
eeaton@eureka.edu
EATON, Nathan .... 435-652-7553 459 G
nathan.eaton@utahtech.edu
EATON, Patrick, D .... 662-720-7165 247 D
pdeaton@nemcc.edu
EATON, Robert .... 401-456-8776 404 A
reaton@ric.edu
EATON, Rosalyn .... 507-786-3615 242 I
reaton@stolaf.edu
EATON, Stephanie .... 314-516-5765 260 E
stephanie@umsl.edu
EATON, Tim .... 812-888-4450 162 E
teaton@vinu.edu
EATON, Timothy, W ...... 405-912-9456 368 H
teaton@ru.edu
EATON-SMITH, Janet .... 419-517-8987 355 C
jeaton-smith@lourdes.edu
EAVENSON, Dave .... 910-630-7182 331 B
deavenson@methodist.edu
EAVES, Jerry .... 502-776-1443 184 C
jeaves@simmonscollegeky.edu
EAVES, Robert .... 803-934-3229 409 H
reaves@morris.edu
EAVES, Stephen .... 615-460-8118 417 B
stephen.eaves@belmont.edu
EAVES-MCLENNAN,
Kristi .... 919-760-8455 331 A
eavesk@meredith.edu
EBARB, Lisa .... 318-675-6505 189 D
lisa.ebarb@lsuhs.edu
EBBING, Jeff .... 319-208-5060 169 I
jebbing@scciowa.edu
EBBOTT, Mary .... 508-793-2335 208 A
mebbott@holycross.edu
EBEL, Jeffrey .... 618-235-2700 150 B
jeffrey.ebel@swic.edu
EBEL, Malia, M .... 603-526-3375 271 H
malia.ebel@colby-sawyer.edu
EBER, Hayley .... 212-353-4220 297 C
hayley.eber@cooper.edu
EBERHARDT, David .... 205-226-4731.... 5 A
deberhar@bsc.edu
EBERHARDT, Lauren ...... 949-794-9090.. 66 C
leberhardt@stanbridge.edu
EBERHARDT, Russell ..... 605-698-3966 415 C
reberhardt@swcollege.edu
EBERHART, Becky, J ...... 847-866-3938 138 B
becky.eberhart@garrett.edu
EBERHART, John .... 269-782-1207 230 D
jeberhart@swmich.edu
EBERL, Jason .... 314-977-2500 258 H
jason.eberl@slu.edu
EBERLE, Jeanette .... 863-638-2978 113 E
eberleja@webber.edu
EBERLE, John .... 615-248-1234 425 D
jeberle@trevecca.edu
EBERLY, Jamie .... 402-872-2436 267 H
jeberly@peru.edu
EBERSOLE, Erin .... 301-934-7621 198 C
erebersole@scmd.edu
EBERSOLE, Susan .... 718-960-8000 293 E
susan.ebersole@lehman.cuny.edu
EBERT, Chris .... 559-791-2370.. 47 D
chris.ebert@portervillecollege.edu
EBERT, Kellie .... 405-744-2122 367 G
kellie.ebert@okstate.edu
EBERT, Stacy .... 281-756-5601 428 E
sebert@alvincollege.edu
EBERT, Tina, L .... 417-268-6006 250 A
tebert@gobbc.edu
EBERT-HOLBERG, Olga . 865-539-7283 424 C
odeberthiberg@pstcc.edu
EBERTS, Keirsten .... 260-665-4675 161 C
ebertsk@trine.edu
EBERTZ, Susan J, S ..... 563-589-0265 170 G
library@wartburgseminary.edu
EBNER, Laura .... 773-244-5726 145 F
lmebner@northpark.edu
EBNER, Timothy, J .... 801-581-5808 459 D
tim.ebner@utah.edu
EBNET, Joan .... 715-232-2276 496 C
ebnetj@uwstout.edu
EBRAHIMPOUR, Maling 401-874-4244 404 E
mebrahimpour@uri.edu
EBRON, Kienesha .... 252-618-6675 334 B
ebronk@edgecombe.edu
EBY, Larry .... 302-225-6289.. 90 I
ebylw@gbc.edu
ECABERT, Gayle .... 859-371-9393 179 C
gecabert@beckfield.edu
ECCLES, Tom .... 845-758-7598 290 G
ccs@bard.edu
ECHAMBADI, Raj .... 312-567-3106 139 H
ECHEVARRI, Richard ..... 215-780-1410 397 E
rech@salus.edu
ECHEVARRIA, Charlotte . 607-735-1707 298 G
cechevarria@elmira.edu
ECHEVARRIA, Joseph .... 305-243-5677 112 K
j.echevarria@miami.edu
ECHEVARRIA, Martha .... 973-618-3000 275 E
mechevarria@caldwell.edu
ECHOLS, Deanna .... 912-201-8000 125 D
dechols@southuniversity.edu
ECHOLS, Marti .... 305-760-7500 103 V
ECHOLS, Steven, F .... 912-583-2241 116 D
sechols@bpc.edu
ECK, Douglas .... 312-369-7221 136 C
deck@colum.edu
ECK, James, C .... 770-531-3129 116 C
jeck@brenau.edu
ECK, Kristi .... 315-312-2212 318 B
kristi.eck@oswego.edu
ECK, Stephen .... 405-425-5106 367 C
stephen.eck@oc.edu
ECK, Stephen, M .... 973-596-3306 278 G
steven.eck@njit.edu
ECK, Tammy .... 405-744-4188 367 G
tammy.eck@okstate.edu
ECK, Tim .... 801-626-6352 460 B
teck@weber.edu
ECKARDT, Jill .... 940-898-3676 451 A
jeckardt@twu.edu
ECKART, Natasha .... 814-332-2701 378 A
neckart@allegheny.edu
ECKENROD, Anne .... 715-346-3612 496 B
ECKER, Brian .... 717-262-2017 402 D
brian.ecker@wilson.edu
ECKERDT, Zack .... 406-447-5509 262 E
zeckerdt@carroll.edu

EDWARDS, Natasha ...... 718-489-2035 312 H
nedwards2@sfc.edu
EDWARDS, Nigel .... 850-599-3183 109 E
nigel.edwards@famu.edu
EDWARDS, Paul .... 804-861-6100 469 E
pedwards@rbc.edu
EDWARDS, JR.,
Quinton, T .... 662-915-3785 248 F
qtedward@olemiss.edu
EDWARDS, Romney ... 314-340-3340 253 E
edwardro@hssu.edu
EDWARDS, Rosie .... 334-514-5063.... 2 F
rosie.edwards@istc.edu
EDWARDS, Sadie .... 217-443-8760 136 E
s.edwards@dacc.edu
EDWARDS, Sarah .... 270-706-8447 181 C
sarah.edwards@kctcs.edu
EDWARDS, Scarlet ... 919-866-5457 338 D
stedwards@waketech.edu
EDWARDS, Sharon ... 931-393-1663 423 G
sedwards@mscc.edu
EDWARDS, Shawn ... 843-953-6989 406 D
shawn.edwards@citadel.edu
EDWARDS, Sheryl ... 870-235-5090.. 21 E
saedwards@saumag.edu
EDWARDS, Stephen ... 719-884-5000.. 82 A
sfedwards@nbc.edu
EDWARDS, Steve .... 912-583-3218 116 D
sedwards@bpc.edu
EDWARDS, Susan ... 617-254-2610 218 A
susan.edwards@sjs.edu
EDWARDS, Susan, L ... 937-775-2312 364 D
susan.edwards@wright.edu
EDWARDS, TerCraig, D 410-651-8420 203 B
tdedwards@umes.edu
EDWARDS, Thomas ...... 207-859-1362 196 A
edwardst@thomas.edu
EDWARDS, Tim .... 205-652-3457.... 9 B
tedwards@uwa.edu
EDWARDS, Timothy ... 208-882-1566 131 H
timedwards@nsa.edu
EDWARDS, Tina, L 260-982-5001 158W
tledwards@manchester.edu
EDWARDS, Tracy ...... 405-945-3376 368 C
tracy.edwards@okstate.edu
EDWARDS, Verneda ...... 785-594-6451 171 C
verneda.edwards@bakeru.edu
EDWARDS, Wanda ... 910-275-6364 335 C
wedwards@jamessprunt.edu
EDWARDS, Wayne .... 516-876-3207 318 A
edwardsw@oldwestbury.edu
EDWARDS LANGE,
Sheila .... 253-692-5646 484 A
sredward@uw.edu
EDWARDS-NEFF,
Denise .... 626-815-6000.. 26 K
EDWIN, Shirin .... 651-793-1727 238 B
shirin.edwin@metrostate.edu
EDYTHE, Abdullah, E ... 904-620-5408 111 A
e.abdullah@unf.edu
EE, Marvin .... 254-295-8620 453 A
mee@umhb.edu
EFFROS, Michelle ...... 626-395-6249.. 29 B
effros@caltech.edu
EFTHIMIOU, Chris ...... 718-289-5169 292 H
chris.efthimiou@bcc.cuny.edu
EFTHYMIOU,
Lampeto (Betty) ... 718-631-6611 295 B
lefthymiou@qcc.cuny.edu
EFURD, Melissa ...... 479-308-2284.. 17 E
melissa.efurd@arcomedu.org
EGAN, Brian .... 973-684-5999 279 B
began@pccc.edu
EGAN, Carolyn ...... 850-644-4440 110 B
cegan@fsu.edu
EGAN, Danielle ...... 860-439-2030.. 87 F
regan1@conncoll.edu
EGAN, Jodi ...... 575-654-0963 434 F
humanresources@diu.edu
EGAN, Jonathon ...... 562-947-8755.. 65 H
jonathonegan@scuhs.edu
EGAN, Kristen ...... 847-628-2017 141 A
kristen.egan@judsonu.edu
EGAN, Maryan .... 239-590-1130 109 G
megan@fgcu.edu
EGAN, Michael ...... 309-794-8965 132 H
mikeegan@augustana.edu
EGAN, Michelle ...... 574-284-4601 160 F
mlegan@saintmarys.edu
EGAN, Russi ...... 530-541-4660.. 47 H
egan@ltcc.edu
EGAN, Thomas ...... 215-572-2900 378 E
egant@arcadia.edu

EGBE, Daniel .... 501-370-5268.. 21 A
degbe@philander.edu
EGBE, Emmanuel .... 718-270-5170 294 E
egbe@mec.cuny.edu
EGBERT, Edwin, C ...... 605-342-0317 414 C
eegbert@jwc.edu
EGBERT, Jean ...... 651-385-6349 238 J
jegbert@southeastmn.edu
EGBERT, Jeb ...... 949-783-4800.. 74 I
jegbert@westcoastuniversity.edu
EGBERT, Jeb ...... 818-299-5500.. 74 I
jegbert@westcoastuniversity.edu
EGENESS, Cynthia ...... 651-690-6864 242 F
cnegeness@stkate.edu
EGERSON, Veronica, V . 414-464-9777 497 B
egerson.veronica@wspp.edu
EGERSTEDT, Magnus, B 949-824-6002.. 69 C
magnus@uci.edu
EGGEBRECHT, Erin ...... 815-967-7302 147 I
eeggebrecht@rockfordcareercollege.
edu
EGGENSPERGER,
Martin .... 870-248-4000.. 18 H
martin.eggensperger@blackrivertech.
edu
EGGER, Thomas, J ...... 314-505-7011 251 E
eggert@csl.edu
EGGERS, Paul ...... 608-663-3431 491 F
peggers@edgewood.edu
EGGERS, Ron ...... 252-399-6417 326 H
reggers@barton.edu
EGGERS, Troy ...... 212-854-5939 296 H
te99@columbia.edu
EGGERS, Troy, R ...... 608-757-6963 497 D
tegger1@blackhawk.edu
EGGERS-BUTTES,
Jessica, H ...... 260-399-7700 162 A
jbuttes@sf.edu
EGGERT, Katherine ... 303-735-5345.. 83M
katherine.eggert@colorado.edu
EGGERT, Mary ...... 414-847-3211 493 C
maryeggert@miad.edu
EGGIMAN, Jessica ... 864-596-9055 407 G
jessica.eggiman@converse.edu
EGGIMANN, Becky ... 630-752-5646 152 K
becky.eggimann@wheaton.edu
EGGLESTON, Joseph ... 562-947-8755.. 65 H
josepheggleston@scuhs.edu
EGGLESTON,
Kathryn, K .... 972-238-6364 434 D
keggleston@dcccd.edu
EGGLESTON, Kevin ... 724-938-1626 394 C
eggleston@calu.edu
EGGLESTON, Meghan . 276-656-0285 473 H
megeggleston@patrickhenry.edu
EGGLESTON, Tami ... 618-537-6926 143 G
teggleston@mckendree.edu
EGGLESTON, Tami ... 618-537-4481 143 G
teggleston@mckendree.edu
EGLE, Don ...... 903-233-3290 438 C
donegle@letu.edu
EGUARAS, Agnes ...... 818-240-1000.. 43 J
aeguaras@glendale.edu
EHLER, Gina, M ...... 262-524-7247 491 A
gehler@carrollu.edu
EHLERS, Chris ...... 918-781-7233 365 B
ehlersc@bacone.edu
EHLERS, Kathleen ...... 617-670-4501 209 D
kehlers@fisher.edu
EHLERT, Alycia ...... 386-506-3769.. 98 A
alycia.ehlert@daytonastate.edu
EHLING, Andrew ...... 620-242-0582 175 G
ehlinga@mcpherson.edu
EHLING, Andrew ...... 505-454-3351 286 C
aehling@nmhu.edu
EHLING, William ...... 252-328-6387 340 H
ehlingw16@ecu.edu
EHMAN, Amanda ...... 740-245-7443 363 A
amandae@rio.edu
EHMANN, Sue-Ann ... 276-656-0206 473 H
sehmann@patrickhenry.edu
EHMEN, Stacy, L ...... 217-443-8746 136 E
s.ehmen@dacc.edu
EHMIG, Ashley ...... 503-244-0726 371 E
ehmig@ashley
EHMKE, Pamela ...... 620-432-0400 176 A
pehmke@neosho.edu
EHNOT, Jillian ...... 406-791-5307 264 J
jillian.ehnot@uprovidence.edu
EHRESMAN, Terry ...... 620-278-4264 177 E
tehresman@sterling.edu
EHRHARDT, Kristal ... 269-387-4478 232 J
kristal.ehrhardt@wmich.edu
EHRHART, Christopher . 218-281-6510 243 B
EHRLICH, Anne ...... 717-337-6921 384 C
aehrlich@gettysburg.edu

EHRLICH, Brian ...... 321-674-8832 100 A
behrlich@fit.edu
EHRLICH, Robert ...... 660-626-2297 249 C
rehrlich@atsu.edu
EHRMAN, Jim ...... 206-876-6100 483 A
ehrman@theseattleschool.edu
EHRMAN, Sheryl ...... 408-924-3800.. 34 B
sheryl.ehrman@sjsu.edu
EHST, Suzanne ...... 574-535-7839 155 B
sehst@goshen.edu
EICHELROTH, Kathleen . 508-929-8098 213 D
keichelroth@worcester.edu
EICHENBERGER, Julie ... 620-223-2700 173 F
juliee@fortscott.edu
EICHENSTEIN, Joseph . 732-985-6533 279 F
EICHER, Michael ...... 614-292-9858 358 E
eicher@osu.edu
EICHHORN, Emily ...... 256-824-6203.... 8 B
emily.eichhorn@uah.edu
EICHHORN, Gregory ... 203-932-7492.. 89 F
geichhorn@newhaven.edu
EICHHORN, Kristen, C 315-312-3152 318 B
kristen.eichhorn@oswego.edu
EICHHORST, Amy ...... 301-405-2102 202 E
aeich@umd.edu
EICHINGER, Stephen ... 212-517-0400 305 D
EICHLER, Richard ...... 212-854-2878 296 H
re1@columbia.edu
EICHNER, John ...... 716-614-6431 309 E
jeichner@niagaracc.suny.edu
EICHOLTZ, Kristin ...... 610-282-1100 382 A
kristin.eicholtz@desales.edu
EICHORST, Christopher . 509-777-4780 485 D
ceichorst@whitworth.edu
EICKE, Dustin ...... 308-635-6026 269 E
eicked@wncc.edu
EICKEN, Hajo ...... 907-474-7331.. 10 B
heicken@alaska.edu
EICKHOFF, Chad, A ... 928-523-8558.. 14 J
chad.eickhoff@nau.edu
EICKHOLT, Marcia ...... 419-227-3141 362 F
marcia@unoh.edu
EICKHORST, Lindsay ... 309-268-8031 138 F
lindsay.eickhorst@heartland.edu
EICKMAN, Joseph ...... 715-394-8155 496 D
jeickman@uwsuper.edu
EID, Haitham ...... 504-286-5010 191 A
heid@suno.edu
EIDE, Kevin ...... 414-955-4888 492 F
keide@mcw.edu
EIDELMAN, Lipa ...... 732-370-1560 274 H
EIDGAHY, Saeid ...... 714-564-6606.. 58 F
eidgahy_saeid@sac.edu
EIDSON, Kevin ...... 615-966-7190 420 B
kevin.eidson@lipscomb.edu
EIDSON, Kristi ...... 270-686-4216 179 F
kristi.eidson@brescia.edu
EIDSON, Natasha ...... 580-349-1356 367 F
natasha.eidson@opsu.edu
EIDSON, Paul ...... 406-799-1515 262 C
dreidson@apollos.edu
EIDSON, Scott ...... 406-604-4320 262 C
drscott@apollos.edu
EIFERT, Robert ...... 217-824-4004 141 H
reifert@lakelandcollege.edu
EIGENBROT, Steven, C . 410-704-3936 204 B
seigenbrot@towson.edu
EIGHMY, Sunny ...... 641-628-5272 164 B
eighmys@central.edu
EIGHMY, Taylor ...... 210-458-4101 455 B
president.eighmy@utsa.edu
EIKE, Claire ...... 312-629-9379 149 B
ceike@saic.edu
EIKENBERRY, Michael . 317-940-8940 153 H
meikenbe@butler.edu
EILER, Claire ...... 610-917-1461 400 D
cmeiler@valleyforge.edu
EILERS, Karen ...... 828-669-8012 331 H
karen.eilers@montreat.edu
EILERS, Kay ...... 414-229-7194 495 B
kceilers@uwm.edu
EILOLA, William, T ...... 419-772-2261 358 E
w-eilola@onu.edu
EIMERS, Mardy, T ...... 573-882-4077 260 C
eimersm@missouri.edu
EINOLF, Karl, W ...... 260-422-5561 156 A
kweinolf@indianatech.edu
EINSPAHR, Kent ...... 402-643-7315 265 I
kent.einspahr@cune.edu
EINSTEIN, Heath, A ...... 817-257-7490 447 H
h.einstein@tcu.edu
EIS, Linda ...... 417-625-3797 255 I
eis-l@mssu.edu

EISELE, Chad, E ...... 434-223-6151 466 K
ceisele@hsc.edu
EISEMAN, Margaret ... 412-396-6061 382 F
eiseman@duq.edu
EISEN, Jeffrey, M ...... 919-658-7759 340 E
jeisen@umo.edu
EISEN, Karen ...... 718-780-0343 291 G
karen.eisen@brooklaw.edu
EISEN SANCHEZ,
Amber .... 507-389-7354 240 F
amber.eisensanchez@southcentral.edu
EISENBACH, Regina ...... 760-750-4329.. 33 C
regina@csusm.edu
EISENBEISER, Colleen . 410-777-1249 197 C
ckeisenbeiser@aacc.edu
EISENBERG, Ann ...... 734-487-0341 223 F
aeisenbe@emich.edu
EISENBERG, Eric ...... 813-974-2804 111 B
eisenberg@usf.edu
EISENBERG, Joshua ...... 617-745-3719 208 F
joshua.eisenberg@enc.edu
EISENBERG, Judith ...... 718-289-5132 292 H
judith.eisenberg@bcc.cuny.edu
EISENBERGER, Israel ... 845-362-3053 290 I
EISENBERT, Eric ...... 813-974-2011 111 B
EISENHART, Pamela ... 717-337-6010 384 C
peisenha@gettysburg.edu
EISENHAUER, James ...... 218-879-0743 237 F
james.eisenhauer@fdltcc.edu
EISENHAUER, Jay ...... 304-829-7465 486 B
jeisenhauer@bethanywv.edu
EISENHAUER, Joseph .. 313-993-1204 230 H
eisenhjg@udmercy.edu
EISENHAUER, Ryan, L ... 575-624-8291 286 F
eisenhauer@nmmi.edu
EISENHAUER, Thomas .. 816-415-5990 261 G
eisenhauer@william.jewell.edu
EISENHOUR, Lyn ...... 425-352-8548 477 F
leisenhour@cascadia.edu
EISENMAN, Ann ...... 563-244-7040 165 H
aeisenman@eicc.edu
EISENMENGER, Paul ...... 847-317-7083 150 J
pweisenmenger@tiu.edu
EISENMENGER,
Paul, W .... 309-341-7212 141 E
pweisenmenger@knox.edu
EISENSTEIN, Laya ...... 718-268-4700 311 H
EISENTRAGER, Pete ... 816-235-2665 260 D
eisentragerp@umkc.edu
EISGRUBER,
Cristopher, L .... 609-258-3026 279 E
eisgrube@princeton.edu
EISLER, David, L ...... 231-591-2500 223 H
davideisler@ferris.edu
EISLER, John ...... 978-630-9477 215 A
jeisler@mwcc.mass.edu
EISMEIER, Michael .... 301-445-2783 202 D
meismeier@usmd.edu
EISNER, Alan ...... 508-793-7368 207 F
aeisner@clarku.edu
EISNER, SND, Janet ...... 617-735-9825 209 A
president@emmanuel.edu
EISSES, Effie ...... 360-650-7610 485 E
eissese@wwu.edu
EITEL, Norine ...... 660-626-2391 249 C
neitel@atsu.edu
EITLE, Tami ...... 317-274-8448 157 B
teitle@iupui.edu
EITZEN, Amy ...... 570-389-4005 393 E
aeitzen@bloomu.edu
EJIGIRI, Damien ...... 225-771-3103 190 K
dejigiri@yahoo.com
EJIMA, Tricia, R ...... 808-956-4304 129 B
ejimat@hawaii.edu
EKANGER, Holger ...... 716-338-1332 302 G
holgerekanger@mail.sunyjcc.edu
EKARIUS, John ...... 215-503-5017 398 G
john.ekarius@jefferson.edu
EKE, Kenoye ...... 903-730-4890 437 E
keke@jarvis.edu
EKKER, David ...... 757-822-7197 474 E
dekker@tcc.edu
EKLUND, Julie ...... 715-425-3962 496 A
0375mgr@follett.com
EKMEKTIOGLU, Lerna . 617-253-9621 215 G
EKNESS, Ray ...... 406-243-4154 263 D
ray.ekness@umontana.edu
EKOUE TOTOU, Patrick . 415-883-2211.. 39 B
pekouetotou@marin.edu
EKSTROM, Rodney ...... 603-535-2217 274 B
raekstrom@plymouth.edu
EL-AMIN, Aisha .... 312-413-3450 151 D
aelami2@uic.edu

ELLIS, Erin .... 254-710-2371 430 F
e_ellis@baylor.edu
ELLIS, Favor .... 802-586-7711 462 C
fellis@sterlingcollege.edu
ELLIS, Gwen .... 423-461-8492 421 E
ghellis@milligan.edu
ELLIS, Jan .... 614-287-2640 351 B
jellis@cscc.edu
ELLIS, Jason .... 325-674-2305 427 G
jwe95i@acu.edu
ELLIS, Jay, J .... 318-274-6344 191 G
ellisj@gram.edu
ELLIS, Jerry .... 918-647-1365 365 D
jwellis@carlalbert.edu
ELLIS, Joan .... 504-571-1290 187 I
jellis@dcc.edu
ELLIS, Jon .... 860-515-3881.. 85 D
jeellis@charteroak.edu
ELLIS, Karen .... 870-762-3158.. 17 F
kellis@smail.anc.edu
ELLIS, Kathy .... 863-680-4106 100 F
kellis@flsouthern.edu
ELLIS, Kristie .... 505-566-3408 287 G
ellisk@sanjuancollege.edu
ELLIS, Larry .... 607-729-1581 297 G
lellis@davisny.edu
ELLIS, Larry .... 570-585-9210 381 A
lellis@clarkssummitu.edu
ELLIS, Lee .... 618-374-5180 147 B
lee.ellis@principia.edu
ELLIS, Mark .... 308-865-8767 268 J
ellismr@unk.edu
ELLIS, Missie .... 731-989-6029 418 H
mellis@fhu.edu
ELLIS, Monica .... 508-831-5000 220 C
ELLIS, Pamela .... 828-395-1456 335 B
pellis@isothermal.edu
ELLIS, Pelema .... 603-862-1234 273 H
pelema.ellis@unh.edu
ELLIS, R. Darin .... 313-577-2024 232 H
rdellis@wayne.edu
ELLIS, Randall .... 804-819-4922 472 E
rellis@vccs.edu
ELLIS, Reggie .... 310-434-3780.. 63 B
ellis_reggie@smc.edu
ELLIS, Reuben .... 818-394-3316.. 76 D
reuben.ellis@woodbury.edu
ELLIS, Rod .... 714-772-3330.. 26 B
ELLIS, Rodney, A .... 318-670-9312 191 B
rellis@susla.edu
ELLIS, Ronald, L .... 951-343-4210.. 27 J
jarmentrout@calbaptist.edu
ELLIS, Rudolph, K .... 318-274-7723 191 G
ellisr@gram.edu
ELLIS, Sabrina .... 212-998-1205 309 D
sabrina.ellis@nyu.edu
ELLIS, Samuel .... 207-216-4434 195 F
sellis@yccc.edu
ELLIS, Shannon .... 775-784-6196 270 K
elliss@unr.edu
ELLIS, Sharmina .... 302-292-6100.. 93 H
ELLIS, Susan .... 580-774-6039 369 I
susan.ellis@swosu.edu
ELLIS, Tom, M .... 423-425-4687 426 D
tom-ellis@utc.edu
ELLIS, Trevor .... 918-495-6492 368 F
tellis@oru.edu
ELLIS, Wade .... 626-914-8897.. 37 B
wellis@citruscollege.edu
ELLIS, William .... 828-766-1227 335 G
wellis@mayland.edu
ELLIS, William, C .... 918-495-7308 368 F
wellis@oru.edu
ELLIS FOSTER,
Stephanie .... 703-284-6478 468 A
sfoster@marymount.edu
ELLIS-FOULTZ,
Kathleen .... 302-622-8000.. 90 C
kellis-foultz@dcad.edu
ELLIS-HILL, Ralonda ..... 216-987-5544 351 D
ralonda.ellis-hill@tri-c.edu
ELLISON, Brian .... 510-925-4282.. 25 P
ELLISON, Cynthia, S ..... 804-524-5654 475 E
cellison@vsu.edu
ELLISON, Cynthia, S ..... 804-524-5845 475 E
cellison@vsu.edu
ELLISON, Diane .... 585-475-7284 312 A
dmeges@rit.edu
ELLISON, Jared .... 732-743-3800.. 93 H
ELLISON, Maderia .... 928-532-6743.. 14 L
maderia.ellison@npc.edu
ELLISON, Marjorie .... 573-288-6541 251 I
mellison@culver.edu
ELLISON, Mark .... 828-339-4229 337 H
m_ellison@southwesterncc.edu
ELLISON, Ron .... 209-946-7372.. 71 E
rellison1@pacific.edu
ELLISON, Ronald .... 360-792-6050 481 B
ELLISOR, Kimberly, M .. 843-661-1190 408 H
kellisor@fmarion.edu
ELLRICH, Lisa .... 207-778-7054 196 F
ellrich@maine.edu
ELLSPERMANN, Sue, J . 317-921-4980 158 A
sellspermann@ivytech.edu
ELLSWORTH, Laura .... 301-546-0620 201 D
ellswolr@pgcc.edu
ELLSWORTH, Laura, R .. 301-546-0553 201 D
ellswolr@pgcc.edu
ELLSWORTH, Tim .... 731-661-5215 425 F
tellsworth@uu.edu
ELLWOOD, JoAnn .... 540-868-7000 473 C
ELM, Dana .... 203-596-2153.. 86 H
delm@nv.edu
ELMAN, Beth .... 712-362-7947 166 H
belman@iowalakes.edu
ELMBORG, James .... 205-348-2719.... 7 G
jkelmborg@ua.edu
ELMENDORF, Douglas .. 617-495-1122 210 B
doug_elmendorf@hks.harvard.edu
ELMORE, Amanda .... 864-646-1401 411 H
amandal.elmore@tctc.edu
ELMORE, Amelia .... 910-592-8081 337 D
aelmore@sampsoncc.edu
ELMORE, Amy .... 270-534-3118 182 G
amy.elmore@kctcs.edu
ELMORE, Bryan .... 334-844-3664.... 4 E
elmorbj@auburn.edu
ELMORE, Chris .... 336-272-7102 329 B
chris.elmore@greensboro.edu
ELMORE, Dana .... 601-925-3371 246 D
elmore@mc.edu
ELMORE, George .... 803-780-1211 413 B
gelmore@voorhees.edu
ELMORE, Kenneth .... 508-541-1658 208 E
president@dean.edu
ELMORE, Kevin .... 219-980-6841 157 A
kdelmore@iun.edu
ELMORE, Mary .... 704-403-3218 327 B
mary.elmore@atriumhealth.org
ELMORE, R. Duane .... 814-863-0273 391 F
rde9@psu.edu
ELMORE, Robert .... 513-875-3344 349 K
robert.elmore@chatfield.edu
ELMORE, Trent .... 910-893-1635 327 C
telmore@campbell.edu
ELMORE, Wendy .... 409-882-3077 449 C
wendy.elmore@lsco.edu
ELNASHAI, Amr .... 713-743-5797 451 G
elnashai@uh.edu
ELNICK, William .... 215-572-2172 378 E
elnickb@arcadia.edu
ELNICKI, Patrice .... 716-614-5933 309 E
pelnicki@niagaracc.suny.edu
ELOFIR, Stacy .... 410-704-4414 204 B
selofir@towson.edu
ELOI, Kaylarge .... 770-232-2717 124 D
kay.eloi@runiv.edu
ELOWSKY, Joel .... 314-505-7106 251 D
elowskyj@csl.edu
ELQUIZABAL,
Christopher .... 562-860-2451.. 35 O
celquizabal@cerritos.edu
ELROD, David .... 706-272-4473 118 A
delrod@daltonstate.edu
ELROD, David .... 615-966-5887 420 B
david.elrod@lipscomb.edu
ELROD, Eileen, R .... 408-554-4136.. 63 A
eelrod@scu.edu
ELROD, Susan .... 574-520-4220 157 C
slelrod@iusb.edu
ELS, Jason .... 606-546-1231 185 B
jels@unionky.edu
ELSBERRY, Meagan 561-237-7233 103W
melsberry@lynn.edu
ELSE, George .... 610-989-1200 400 F
gelse@vfmac.edu
ELSEN, Jake .... 615-244-5848 422 E
ELSENBAUMER, Ronald 260-481-6103 159 H
chancellor@pfw.edu
ELSENER, Daniel, J .... 317-955-6100 159 A
delsener@marian.edu
ELSEY, Jenny .... 206-281-2340 482 K
elseyj@spu.edu
ELSHAYEB, Tarek, A ..... 704-687-7859 342 C
telshaye@uncc.edu
ELSISHANS, Nicholas .... 415-703-9500.. 28 D
ELSMORE, Kathleen ...... 610-989-1330 400 F
kelsmore@vfmac.edu
ELSTER, Eric .... 301-295-3017 502 B
eric.elster@usuhs.edu
ELSTON, Ken, D .... 336-841-2848 329 E
kelston@highpoint.edu
ELSTON, Timothy, G ..... 803-321-5110 409 I
timothy.elston@newberry.edu
ELSTONE, Paul .... 509-963-2111 477 G
paul.elstone@cwu.edu
ELSTONE, Paul .... 541-346-2166 376 G
pelstone@uoregon.edu
ELSWICK, Clark .... 575-562-4490 285 E
clark.elswick@enmu.edu
ELTON, Nathan .... 302-831-8574.. 91 A
nelton@udel.edu
ELTON, Terri .... 651-523-1822 236 A
telton@luthersem.edu
ELTRINGHAM, TJ .... 570-955-1487 387 A
eltringhamj@lackawanna.edu
ELUFIEDE, Babafemi ..... 229-500-2255 114 F
babafemi.elufiede@asurams.edu
ELUSKIE, Robert .... 616-538-2330 224 B
beluskie@gracechristian.edu
ELVARD, Lesly .... 410-888-9048 200 C
lelvard@muih.edu
ELVERSON, Katie .... 412-536-1079 386 H
katie.elverson@laroche.edu
ELVOVE, Naomi .... 415-257-1380.. 41 H
naomi.elvove@dominican.edu
ELWELL, David .... 617-253-3795 215 G
ELWELL, Marcene .... 308-635-7431 269 E
elwellm1@wncc.edu
ELWOOD, Steve .... 765-998-4907 161 A
stelwood@taylor.edu
ELY, Susan .... 559-325-3600.. 28 F
sely@chsu.edu
ELY, Tim .... 610-526-1862 385 F
tely@harucm.edu
ELY, Tim .... 610-526-1862 385 F
tely@harcum.edu
ELZINGA, Gregory, J .... 616-526-6097 221 L
gje3@calvin.edu
EMAMI, Azita .... 206-221-2472 484 A
emamia@uw.edu
EMANUS, Melissa .... 718-260-5173 294 F
memanus@citytech.cuny.edu
EMBACHER, Barbara ..... 507-433-0659 240 A
barb.embacher@riverland.edu
EMBERTON,
Sherilyn, R .... 260-359-4050 155 G
semberton@huntington.edu
EMBLER, Marc .... 843-863-7000 406 C
membler@csuniv.edu
EMBREE, Catherine .... 212-678-3991 321 H
cme11@tc.columbia.edu
EMBRY, Jason .... 303-444-0202.. 81 N
EMBRY, Kelli .... 501-760-4222.. 20 E
EMBRY, Robin .... 803-323-2229 413 D
embryr@winthrop.edu
EMDY, Jim .... 831-476-9424.. 42 I
librarian@fivebranches.edu
EMEHISER, Theresa ...... 623-245-4600.. 16 F
temehiser@uti.edu
EMEKA, Amon .... 518-580-8111 315 A
aemeka@skidmore.edu
EMENGER, Nancy, E ..... 801-626-6017 460 B
nemenger@weber.edu
EMERICK, Brian, J .... 740-368-3177 359 F
bjemeric@owu.edu
EMERICK, Laura .... 740-389-4636 355 F
emerickl@mtc.edu
EMERICK, Mary .... 781-280-3624 214 G
emerickm@middlesex.mass.edu
EMERICK, Sandra, M .... 330-325-6759 357 D
semerick@neomed.edu
EMERSON, Adam .... 413-236-2132 213 E
aemerson@berkshirecc.edu
EMERSON, Brian .... 716-896-0700 324 A
bemerson@villa.edu
EMERSON, Christi .... 254-295-5014 453 A
christi.emerson@umhb.edu
EMERSON, Colleen .... 401-341-2908 404 D
emersonc@salve.edu
EMERSON, Dana .... 714-241-6184.. 38 D
demerson3@coastline.edu
EMERSON, Eleanor .... 512-326-7013 441 N
eemerson@stedwards.edu
EMERSON, Jessica .... 315-786-2416 302 I
jemerson@sunyjefferson.edu
EMERSON, Matthew ...... 405-585-4426 367 B
matthew.emerson@okbu.edu
EMERSON, Mitchell, R .. 623-572-3501 144 C
memers@midwestern.edu
EMERSON, Peter .... 985-549-3894 192 E
peter.emerson@selu.edu
EMERSON, Steve .... 951-343-4415.. 27 J
semerson@calbaptist.edu
EMERSON, Steve .... 208-467-8528 132 B
sdemerson@nnu.edu
EMERSON, Yolanda .... 562-908-3457.. 58M
yemerson@riohondo.edu
EMERT, John .... 765-285-1024 153 E
jemert@bsu.edu
EMERY, Donna .... 512-472-4133 442 H
donna.emery@ssw.edu
EMERY, Lisa .... 903-813-2423 429 I
lemery@austincollege.edu
EMERY, Matthew .... 870-236-6901.. 19 D
memery@crc.edu
EMERY, Melissa .... 269-927-6114 226 B
memery@lakemichigancollege.edu
EMILIO, Linda .... 909-469-8421.. 75 G
lemilio@westernu.edu
EMIRU, Tadael .... 916-691-7913.. 50 K
emirut@crc.losrios.edu
EMISON, Barry .... 662-407-1409 245 F
blemison@iccms.edu
EMM, Willliam .... 315-786-2401 302 I
wemm@sunyjefferson.edu
EMMA, Janine .... 732-255-0400 279 A
jemma@ocean.edu
EMMANUEL, Steven ...... 757-455-3405 476 C
semmanuel@vwu.edu
EMMER, Karen .... 520-515-5417.. 11 O
emmerk@cochise.edu
EMMERT, Gary .... 901-678-4831 426 A
gemmert@memphis.edu
EMMICK, Joe .... 847-866-3923 138 B
joe.emmick@garrett.edu
EMMIL, Bruce .... 701-224-5758 345 F
bruce.emmil@bismarckstate.edu
EMMONS, Carol-Ann ..... 312-567-3827 139 H
emmons@iit.edu
EMMONS, Lee .... 270-534-3084 182 G
lee.emmons@kctcs.edu
EMO, Ann .... 315-279-5465 303 D
aemo@keuka.edu
EMONS, Margaret .... 402-399-2467 265 H
memons@csm.edu
EMORY, Cynthia, M ...... 717-264-2192 402 D
cynthia.emory@wilson.edu
EMORY, Julie, W .... 252-398-6252 328 A
emoryj@chowan.edu
EMORY, Rose .... 800-323-5692 347 G
rose.emory@artacademy.edu
EMORY, Sid .... 803-793-5147 408 A
emorys@denmarktech.edu
EMPET, Audriana, L ...... 570-326-3761 392 S
alm56@pct.edu
EMR, Linda .... 201-879-7206 274 I
lemr@bergen.edu
EMRICH, Dawn .... 310-506-4700.. 56 H
dawn.emrich@pepperdine.edu
EMRICH, Whitney .... 601-974-1000 246 C
whitney.emrich@millsaps.edu
EMRICH, Whitney .... 601-974-1105 246 C
whitney.emrich@millsaps.edu
EMSELLEM, Dawn .... 401-341-2336 404 D
dawn.emsellem@salve.edu
EMSICKE, Dan .... 513-244-4955 356 F
dan.emsicke@msj.edu
ENAMAIT, John .... 704-991-0220 338 A
jenamait1211@stanly.edu
ENAYAT, Sharmeen .... 619-574-5800.. 43 B
senayat@fst.edu
ENCARNACION, Zaneta . 619-482-6301.. 65 K
ENCINA, Rosalinda .... 210-486-4609 428 A
rencina@alamo.edu
ENCISO, Martha .... 657-278-8655.. 31 E
maenciso@fullerton.edu
ENDEAN, Kristopher ..... 480-245-7993.. 12 O
kristopher.endean@ibcs.edu
ENDERS, Naulayne, R ... 606-474-3276 180 G
nenders@kcu.edu
ENDICOTT, Alicia .... 660-359-3948 256 F
aendicott@mail.ncmissouri.edu
ENDICOTT, Daniel, D .... 904-620-2019 111 A
dendicot@unf.edu
ENDICOTT, David .... 218-894-5172 237 C
david.endicott@clcmn.edu
ENDICOTT, Jon .... 559-453-3484.. 43 D
jon.endicott@fresno.edu
ENDLER, Dean, K .... 979-845-0099 446 B
d-endler@tamu.edu

ERDLE, Jennie .... 585-785-1263 299 E
jennie.erdle@flcc.edu
ERDMAN, Brian, J .... 773-508-7592 142 G
berdman@luc.edu
ERDMANN, Alex .... 407-582-1389 113 C
aerdmann@valenciacollege.edu
ERDMANN, Joel .... 251-460-7121.... 9 A
jerdmann@southalabama.edu
ERDMANN, Paul .... 620-441-5264 172 M
paul.erdmann@cowley.edu
ERDMANN, Stephanie ... 406-771-4305 264 B
stephanie.erdmann@gfcmsu.edu
EREMITA, Nicholas .... 301-985-7000 203 C
ERFAN, Shahir .... 718-482-5501 294 D
serfan@lagcc.cuny.edu
ERFFMEYER, Kenneth .... 626-584-5200.. 43 E
kerffmeyer@thefullerfoundation.org
ERFOURTH, Stavroula ... 989-729-3431 221 G
serfou01@baker.edu
ERGIN, Laure .... 302-831-7364.. 91 A
lbergin@udel.edu
ERHARDT, Niclas .... 219-464-5035 162 C
niclas.erhardt@valpo.edu
ERHEMJAMTS,
Otgontsetseg .... 415-422-5555.. 72 I
oerhemjamts@usfca.edu
ERICKSEN, Janet, S ...... 320-589-6020 243 C
ericksja@morris.umn.edu
ERICKSON, Angela .... 573-518-2323 255 G
aerickson@mineralarea.edu
ERICKSON, Angela .... 507-933-7595 235 E
aerick13@gustavus.edu
ERICKSON, Brian .... 307-754-6210 500 G
brian.erickson@nwc.edu
ERICKSON, Chris .... 952-829-1919 233 H
chris.erickson@bethfel.org
ERICKSON, Christine .... 209-667-3177.. 33 D
cerickson2@csustan.edu
ERICKSON, Deb .... 619-849-2323.. 57 J
deberickson@pointloma.edu
ERICKSON, Ethan, E ..... 785-532-6242 175 A
eerickson@ksu.edu
ERICKSON, Ethan, E ..... 785-532-6226 175 A
eerickson@ksu.edu
ERICKSON, Gary .... 314-838-8858 261 A
gerickson@ugst.edu
ERICKSON, Jeff .... 775-445-4223 271 A
jeffrey.erickson@wnc.edu
ERICKSON, Jennifer ...... 320-308-5940 240 D
jennifer.erickson@sctcc.edu
ERICKSON, Jennifer ...... 915-215-4145 450 E
jennifer.erickson@ttuhsc.edu
ERICKSON, Jessica .... 707-256-7205.. 53 E
jerickson@napavalley.edu
ERICKSON, John .... 402-557-7291 265 A
ERICKSON, Jon .... 320-762-4405 236 G
jon.erickson@alextech.edu
ERICKSON, Karen .... 701-224-5424 345 F
karen.erickson@bismarckstate.edu
ERICKSON, Kevin .... 402-486-2504 268 G
kevin.erickson@ucollege.edu
ERICKSON, Kim .... 909-652-6021.. 36 B
kim.erickson@chaffey.edu
ERICKSON, Lori .... 423-439-4457 418 D
ericksol@etsu.edu
ERICKSON, Marc .... 706-419-1645 117 G
marc.erickson@covenant.edu
ERICKSON, Mark .... 845-451-1295 297 E
mark.erickson@culinary.edu
ERICKSON, Michael .... 619-660-4000.. 44 G
ERICKSON, Michele .... 509-452-5100 481 E
merickson@pnwu.edu
ERICKSON, Michelle ..... 617-735-9825 209 A
erickson@emmanuel.edu
ERICKSON, Paul, J .... 608-342-1194 495 E
ericksop@uwplatt.edu
ERICKSON, Steve .... 218-846-3721 238 K
steve.erickson@minnesota.edu
ERICKSON-PESETSKI,
Stacy, L .... 260-982-5391 158 W
slerickson-pesetski@manchester.edu
ERICKSTAD, Jade .... 701-662-1553 346 A
jade.erickstad@lrsc.edu
ERICSON, III, Ed .... 479-238-8669.. 20 C
eericson@jbu.edu
ERICSON, Kendra .... 712-279-3149 169 E
kendra.ericson@stlukescollege.edu
ERIKSEN, Jennifer .... 704-337-2217 339 D
eriksenj@queens.edu
ERILUS, Nedzer, C .... 401-865-1151 403 G
nerilus@providence.edu
ERIQUEZZO, Michael .... 413-737-7000 205 C
ERJAVEC, Patricia .... 719-549-3213.. 82 I
patty.erjavec@pueblocc.edu
ERLACHER, Ryan .... 678-466-4672 117 A
ryanerlacher@clayton.edu
ERLANGER, Esrael .... 718-645-0536 306 F
ERMATINGER, James .... 217-206-6512 151 E
jerma2@uis.edu
ERMER, Scott .... 319-398-4944 167 H
scott.ermer@kirkwood.edu
ERMER, Scott .... 716-851-1977 299 A
ermer@ecc.edu
ERMIS, Lisa .... 830-591-2935 443 I
ldermis@swtjc.edu
ERMOLI, Victor .... 912-525-5000 124 G
vermoli@scad.edu
ERNE, Richard .... 208-459-5179 131 A
rerne@collegeofidaho.edu
ERNEST, Matthew, S ..... 914-968-6200 313 E
mernest@archny.org
ERNEST, Ralynn .... 614-825-6255 347 C
rernest@aiam.edu
ERNEVAD, David .... 503-768-7979 373 D
davidernevad@lclark.edu
ERNEY, Thomas .... 614-287-2532 351 B
terney@cscc.edu
ERNST, Carrie .... 859-622-7973 180 B
carrie.ernst@eku.edu
ERNST, Chris .... 502-456-6506 184 F
cernst@sullivan.edu
ERNST, Donna .... 502-852-6538 185 E
donna.ernst@louisville.edu
ERNST, Jennifer .... 509-574-4641 485 E
jernst@yvcc.edu
ERNST, John .... 859-344-3524 184 G
ernstj@thomasmore.edu
ERNST, Joshua, R .... 206-934-4710 482 F
josh.ernst@seattlecolleges.edu
ERNST, Nathan .... 630-515-6342 144 C
nernst@midwestern.edu
ERNST, Robert, D .... 734-647-8160 231 A
robernst@umich.edu
ERNST-LEONARD,
Amber .... 305-809-3531.. 97 M
amber.ernstleonard@cfk.edu
ERNSTBERGER, Jon ...... 706-880-8155 121 K
jernstberger@lagrange.edu
ERNSTER, Michael .... 563-884-5667 169 C
mike.ernster@palmer.edu
ERNSTING, Brian .... 603-888-1311 273 B
bernsting@rivier.edu
ERNSTING, Lynn .... 206-281-2778 482 K
russel@spu.edu
ERNY, Michael .... 850-729-6051 104 L
ernym@nwfsc.edu
ERO-TOLLIVER, Isi .... 757-727-5239 466 L
isi.erotolliver@hamptonu.edu
ERPELDING, Augustine . 623-845-4526.. 13 E
augustine.erpelding@gccaz.edu
ERPENBACH, Steve .... 605-697-7475 416 A
steve.erpenbach@sdstatefoundation.org
ERPESTAD, Hanna .... 218-733-7667 238 A
hanna.erpestad@lsc.edu
ERRICO, James .... 845-398-4000 314 D
ERRTHUM, Amy .... 563-588-6683 164 C
amy.errthum@clarke.edu
ERSIG, Nathan .... 563-387-1510 167 J
nersig@luther.edu
ERSKINE, Tina .... 207-454-1002 195 E
terskine@wccc.me.edu
ERSTE, SR., Mark, A ..... 740-284-5234 352 I
merste@franciscan.edu
ERTEL, Mia .... 978-646-7111 209 G
mertel@gcts.edu
ERTEL, Rebecca .... 937-376-6495 349 H
rertel@centralstate.edu
ERTEL, Stefanie .... 910-221-2224 330 G
sertel@manna.edu
ERTEL, Steve .... 615-343-8506 427 B
steve.ertel@vanderbilt.edu
ERUZIONE, Vincent .... 617-333-2202 208 D
veruzion@curry.edu
ERVIN, Archie .... 404-385-3686 119 D
archie.ervin@vpid.gatech.edu
ERVIN, Carrie .... 765-983-1758 154 H
ervinca@earlham.edu
ERVIN, Elonda .... 812-237-8513 155 H
elonda.ervin@indstate.edu
ERVIN, Jennifer .... 404-880-8051 116 I
jervin@cau.edu
ERVIN, Korrie .... 910-898-9603 336 A
ervink@montgomery.edu
ERVIN, Leisa .... 662-325-7353 247 A
lbryant@audit.msstate.edu
ERVIN, Martha .... 864-644-5011 411 D
mervin@swu.edu
ERVIN, Timothy, R .... 217-786-9605 142 F
tim.ervin@llcc.edu
ERWIN, Betsy .... 802-831-1225 462 F
berwin@vermontlaw.edu
ERWIN, Curtis .... 804-828-7666 472 D
cgerwin@vcu.edu
ERWIN, Deidre .... 262-524-7201 491 A
derwin@carrollu.edu
ERWIN, Gary .... 313-993-1254 230 H
erwingj@udmercy.edu
ERWIN, John .... 508-856-8200 212 A
john.erwin@umassmed.edu
ERWIN, John, O .... 616-985-2230 359 K
jerwin@pcj.edu
ERWIN, Leslie .... 419-448-2000 353 D
ERWIN, Lisa .... 218-726-8501 243 A
laerwin@d.umn.edu
ERWIN, Paul .... 205-975-8970.... 8 A
perwin@uab.edu
ERWIN, R. Guy .... 717-338-3000 399 H
president@uls.edu
ERWIN, Ryan .... 903-923-2226 435 A
rerwin@etbu.edu
ERWIN, Steve .... 620-235-4231 176 H
serwin@pittstate.edu
ERWIN, Steve .... 661-362-5917.. 38 H
steve.erwin@canyons.edu
ERWIN-SVOBODA, Cal .. 360-538-4067 479 F
cal.erwin-svoboda@ghc.edu
ESAU, Joshua .... 602-489-5300.. 10 G
joshua.esau@arizonachristian.edu
ESAU, Sheri .... 620-327-8147 174 B
sheri.esau@hesston.edu
ESCAGY, Marsha .... 718-270-6984 294 E
mescagy@mec.cuny.edu
ESCAJEDA, Jackie .... 408-855-5038.. 75 C
jacqueline.escajeda@missioncollege.edu
ESCALANTE, Angie .... 787-765-5974 509 H
aescalante@pupr.edu
ESCALANTE, Eddie .... 626-571-8811.. 73 D
eddiee@uwest.edu
ESCALANTE, John .... 773-442-4110 145 G
j-escalante3@neiu.edu
ESCALANTE, Maria .... 800-567-2344 491 C
mescalante@menominee.edu
ESCALERA, Liya .... 617-287-5862 211 E
liya.escalera@umb.edu
ESCALERA MUÑOZ,
Jorge .... 787-620-2040 504 B
jescalera@aupr.edu
ESCALLIER, Lori, A .... 718-270-7632 316 E
lori.escallier@downstate.edu
ESCAMILLA, Cynthia, S . 210-829-3136 452 D
cyescami@uiwtx.edu
ESCAMILLA, Mark .... 361-698-1203 434 H
mescamilla@delmar.edu
ESCAMILLA, Phil .... 916-577-2200.. 76 C
pescamilla@jessup.edu
ESCH, Marj .... 989-275-5000 225 H
marj.esch@kirtland.edu
ESCH, Richard, T .... 814-362-5140 400 A
esch@pitt.edu
ESCH, Rod .... 970-351-1890.. 84 D
rodney.esch@unco.edu
ESCHBACH, Jeanne .... 607-962-9335 319 F
eschbach@corning-cc.edu
ESCHENBACHER, Elaine 612-330-1492 233 G
eschenba@augsburg.edu
ESCHENBAUM, Matt ...... 303-871-4256.. 84 C
matt.eschenbaum@du.edu
ESCHENBERG, Ardis ...... 808-235-7402 130 C
ardise@hawaii.edu
ESCHENBRENNER,
Nancy .... 860-773-1304.. 87 E
neschenbrenner@tunxis.edu
ESCHER, Nancy .... 401-341-2157 404 D
nancy.escher@salve.edu
ESCLAVON, Annette .... 972-241-3371 433 E
ESCOBAR, Fabio .... 716-270-6688 299 A
escobar@ecc.edu
ESCOBAR, Jorge, L .... 408-270-6452.. 62 E
jorge.escobar@sjeccd.edu
ESCOBAR, Luis .... 650-738-4124.. 62 K
escobarluis@smccd.edu
ESCOBEDO, Beatriz .... 619-934-0797.. 61 C
ESCOBEDO, Maria .... 805-591-6220.. 41 A
maria_escobedo@cuesta.edu
ESCOFFERY, Ciaran .... 212-799-5000 303 B
ESCOLAS, Roger .... 614-222-3264 351 A
rescolas@ccad.edu
ESGUERRA, Genevieve .. 619-388-3924.. 60 I
gesguerr@sdccd.edu
ESHLEMAN, Kristen .... 860-297-2525.. 88 I
kristen.eshleman@trincoll.edu
ESHLEMAN, Kristen ...... 704-894-2583 328 C
kreshleman@davidson.edu
ESHLEMAN, Robert .... 406-656-9950 263 B
reshleman@yellowstonechristian.edu
ESKAM, Shannon .... 307-268-2596 499 T
seskam@caspercollege.edu
ESKANDARI, Sepehr ..... 406-657-2367 263 H
sepehr.eskandari@msubillings.edu
ESKANDARIAN, Ali .... 443-334-2160 202 C
aeskandarian@stevenson.edu
ESKER, Brian .... 312-899-5177 149 B
besker@saic.edu
ESKEW, Natalie .... 872-972-2042.. 17 I
neskew@astate.edu
ESKINS, Katrina .... 304-696-7096 488 N
eskinsk@marshall.edu
ESKOW, Robin .... 619-260-2928.. 72 H
reskow@sandiego.edu
ESKRIDGE, Steve .... 206-546-4553 483 C
seskridge@shoreline.edu
ESLAND, Melanie .... 248-689-8282 231 E
mesland@walshcollege.edu
ESLINGER, Elise .... 507-222-5597 234 C
eeslinger@carleton.edu
ESLINGER, Nichole .... 281-756-3500 428 E
neslinger@alvincollege.edu
ESMAEILI, Ali .... 956-872-7270 443 B
esmaeili@southtexascollege.edu
ESMIEU, Paola .... 214-379-5444 440 H
pesmieu@pqc.edu
ESPARZA, Betse .... 432-837-8451 449 F
betse.esparza@sulross.edu
ESPARZA, Victor .... 580-349-1324 367 F
coachvic@opsu.edu
ESPERDY, Gabrielle ...... 973-596-3072 278 G
gabrielle.esperdy@njit.edu
ESPERIAS, Kelly .... 909-607-9651.. 37 I
kelly_esperias@kgi.edu
ESPESET, Rick .... 260-982-5390 158 W
rbespeset@manchester.edu
ESPESETH, Jeremy .... 860-932-4079.. 87 C
jespeseth@qvcc.edu
ESPICH, Whitney, T ...... 617-253-8231 215 G
ESPINA, Maritza .... 563-333-6266 169 D
espinamaritza@sau.edu
ESPINAL, Jeanette .... 727-736-3812 108 A
jeanette.espinal@schiller.edu
ESPINO, Teresa .... 972-338-1783 453 C
teresa.espino@untdallas.edu
ESPINOSA, Dora .... 847-578-8524 148 B
dora.espinosa@rosalindfranklin.edu
ESPINOSA, Guillermo ... 509-533-7033 478 D
guillermo.espinosa@scc.spokane.edu
ESPINOSA, Juan Carlos 305-348-4100 109 H
juancarlos.espinosa@fiu.edu
ESPINOSA, Martin .... 615-687-6960 416 F
mespinosa@abcnash.edu
ESPINOSA, Rafael .... 209-667-3137.. 33 D
respinosa@csustan.edu
ESPINOSA, Rene .... 210-341-1366 440 B
respinosa@ost.edu
ESPINOSA, Zoila .... 305-642-4104 106 D
ESPINOSA-PIEB,
Christina, G .... 408-864-8940.. 42 K
espinosapiebchristina@deanza.edu
ESPINOZA, Anthony .... 936-468-5822 444 H
anthony.espinoza@sfasu.edu
ESPINOZA, Benjamin .... 585-594-6803 310 A
espinoza_benjamin@roberts.edu
ESPINOZA, Elizabeth ..... 760-355-6551.. 45 N
elizabeth.espinoza@imperial.edu
ESPINOZA, Ernesto .... 787-743-7979 509 D
eespinoza@suagm.edu
ESPINOZA, Juan, P ...... 540-231-3554 475 D
juespino@vt.edu
ESPINOZA, Judy .... 316-978-3540 178 B
judy.espinoza@wichita.edu
ESPINOZA, Julissa .... 909-448-4745.. 71 C
jespinoza@laverne.edu
ESPINOZA, Michael .... 541-506-6000 372 E
mespinoza@cgcc.edu
ESPINOZA, Roberta .... 310-338-4405.. 51 C
roberta.espinoza@lmu.edu
ESPINOZA, Suzanne ...... 510-885-3646.. 31 C
suzanne.espinoza@csueastbay.edu
ESPINOZA, Tony .... 209-954-5176.. 61 H
tony.espinoza@deltacollege.edu

ESPINOZA, Yolanda 480-423-6163 14 B yolanda.espinoza@scottsdalecc.edu
ESPINOZA-MOLINA, Humberto 210-431-5570 440 D hespinoza-mol@ollusa.edu
ESPINOZA-PARRA, Oscar 760-674-7792 39 A oespinoza-parra@collegeofthedesert.edu
ESPINOZA-VALENZUELA, Janice 432-837-8000 449 F janice.espinoza-valenzuela@sulross.edu
ESPIRITU, David 619-216-6759 65 K despiritu@swccd.edu
ESPIRITU, Kira, A 619-260-4598 72 H kespiritu@sandiego.edu
ESPLIN, Daniel 928-774-3890 12 N desplin@indianbible.org
ESPLIN, Scott 801-422-2424 458 A scott_esplin@byu.edu
ESPOSITO, Antoinette 212-472-1500 309 B finaid@nysid.edu
ESPOSITO, Christopher 215-780-1307 397 E cesposito@salus.edu
ESPOSITO, Donna 617-627-5740 219 A donna.esposito@tufts.edu
ESPOSITO, James 212-678-8095 303 A jaesposito@jtsa.edu
ESPOSITO, Joseph, P 213-738-5743 66 A jesposito@swlaw.edu
ESPOSITO, Juliana 508-854-4276 215 D jesposito@qcc.mass.edu
ESPOSITO, Mark 309-796-5427 133 D espositom@bhc.edu
ESPOSITO, Nicole 860-512-3000 86 F
ESPOSITO, Phyllis 425-388-9979 479 B pesposito@everettcc.edu
ESPOSITO, Phyllis 503-517-4762 375 F espositop@reed.edu
ESPOSITO, Richard 843-863-8044 406 C resposito@csuniv.edu
ESPOSITO, Richard, C 412-396-6607 382 E esposito@duq.edu
ESPOSITO, Samantha 304-296-8282 490 C sesposito@wvjc.edu
ESPOSITO, Scott 203-254-4000 87 G sesposito@fairfield.edu
ESPOSITO-NOY, Celia 707-864-7112 64 F celia.esposito-noy@solano.edu
ESPY, Tracy 860-701-5000 88 C
ESQUEDA, Melissa, G 512-448-8400 441 N mellissaesqueda@stedwards.edu
ESQUEDA FLORES, Antonio 206-239-4500 477 I
ESQUILIN-CASTRO, Isaac 787-746-1400 505 L
ESQUIVEL, Carlos 212-875-4615 290 F cesquivel@bankstreet.edu
ESQUIVEL, Daniel 806-379-2702 428 F dmesquivel@actx.edu
ESQUIVEL, Ruben, E 214-648-0448 456 D ruben.esquivel@utsouthwestern.edu
ESQUIVEL, Shelley 865-354-3000 424 D esquivelsl@roanestate.edu
ESSENBURG, Curt 616-988-3654 226 A cessenburg@kuyper.edu
ESSER, Kurt 407-708-2092 108 B esserk@seminolestate.edu
ESSES, Levi, K 301-447-6122 201 A l.k.esses@msmary.edu
ESSEX, Don 757-823-8481 468 B dlessex@nsu.edu
ESSEX, T.A 972-773-8300 93 H
ESSHAKI, Teresa 248-689-8282 231 E tesshaki@walshcollege.edu
ESSIG, Linda 646-660-6500 292 F provost.office@baruch.cuny.edu
ESSIG, Mary 304-647-6213 489 C messig@osteo.wvsom.edu
ESSL, Michael (Mike) 212-353-4203 297 C essl@cooper.edu
ESTABROOK, Madeleine, A 617-373-2772 217 D
ESTAPHAN, Charles 508-793-3014 208 A cestapha@holycross.edu
ESTEBAN, A. Gabriel 312-362-8890 136 F president@depaul.edu
ESTEBAN, Grace 415-239-3556 37 C mesteban@ccsf.edu
ESTELLA, Marlon 909-599-5433 48 E mestella@lifepacific.edu
ESTELLE, Holly 970-247-7364 80 H hkestell@fortlewis.edu
ESTEN, Phil, J 651-962-5901 243 F phil.esten@stthomas.edu
ESTENSON, Chad 701-662-1521 346 A chad.estenson@lrsc.edu
ESTEP, Alison 206-378-5056 482 K estep@spu.edu
ESTEPP, Stella 304-896-7060 487 I stella.estepp@southernwv.edu
ESTER, Joyce, C 952-358-8150 239 C joyce.ester@normandale.edu
ESTERBERG, Kristin 425-352-5220 484 A uwbchlr@uw.edu
ESTERBERG, Kristin, G 315-267-2100 318 D president@potsdam.edu
ESTERS, Chris 336-278-7482 328 H cesters@elon.edu
ESTERS, Delphia 936-261-2111 445 E dmesters@pvamu.edu
ESTERS, Llatetra 410-837-5429 204 C lesters@ubalt.edu
ESTERS, Lorenzo 317-917-5935 158 B lorenzo.esters@ivytech.edu
ESTERS, Randy, E 318-345-9262 188 A randyesters@ladelta.edu
ESTES, Amy 404-835-6124 422 D aestes@richmont.edu
ESTES, Brandee 260-982-5288 158W bjestes@manchester.edu
ESTES, Eric 401-863-1800 403 A eric_estes@brown.edu
ESTES, Hollie 610-398-5300 388 D hestes@lincolntech.edu
ESTES, Joel David 609-497-7805 279 D admissions@ptsem.edu
ESTES, Jonathan 731-989-6901 418 H jestes@fhu.edu
ESTES, Kelly 865-573-4517 419 E kestes@johnsonu.edu
ESTES, Kerry 239-280-2519 95 M kerry.estes@avemaria.edu
ESTES, Lane 205-226-4640 5 A lestes@bsc.edu
ESTES, Makenna 405-425-5961 367 C makenna.estes@oc.edu
ESTES, Scott 928-317-6000 11 B scott.estes@azwestern.edu
ESTES, Wendy 678-717-3845 126 G wendy.estes@ung.edu
ESTES, William 423-614-8175 419 H bestes@leeuniversity.edu
ESTEVES, Gabriela 305-237-3008 104 E gesteve1@mdc.edu
ESTEVEZ, Jean 617-353-9286 207 C estevezj@bu.edu
ESTEY, Alicia 208-426-1417 130 F aliciaestey@boisestate.edu
ESTEY, Amanda 641-648-4611 167 D amanda.estey@iavalley.edu
ESTEY, Amanda 405-382-9210 369 E a.estey@sscok.edu
ESTILL, April 601-266-4829 248 H april.estill@usm.edu
ESTILL, Donna 256-306-2756 1 F donna.estill@calhoun.edu
ESTILL, Gabe 773-481-8182 135 D jestill@ccc.edu
ESTLACK, Scarlet 806-874-3571 431 K scarlet.estlack@clarendoncollege.edu
ESTLACK, Thomas 304-336-8275 489 B thomas.estlack@westliberty.edu
ESTLOW, Stephanie 714-708-0722 83 H student_support@taftu.edu
ESTLUND, Karen 970-491-1101 79 E karen.estlund@colostate.edu
ESTOCK, Steven 575-562-2632 285 E steven.estock@enmu.edu
ESTRADA, Adriana 310-660-3593 41 J aestrada@elcamino.edu
ESTRADA, Brenda 714-564-6212 58 F estrada_brenda@sac.edu
ESTRADA, Ella Mae 212-431-2888 308 I ellamae.estrada@nyls.edu
ESTRADA, George 530-242-7929 64 A gestrada@shastacollege.edu
ESTRADA, Jeri 970-521-6730 82 B jeri.estrada@njc.edu
ESTRADA, Jose 239-489-9358 100 G jose.estrada@fsw.edu
ESTRADA, Judith 831-459-0111 71 A judi@ucsc.edu
ESTRADA, Maria 323-267-3715 49 D estradmc@elac.edu
ESTRADA, Nicolas 406-791-5261 264 J nicolas.estrada@uprovidence.edu
ESTRADA, Rebecca 505-428-1604 287 H rebecca.estrada@sfcc.edu
ESTRADA, Robert 925-473-7540 40 I restrada@losmedanos.edu
ESTRADA-HAMBY, Lisa 940-397-4076 439 F lisa.hamby@msutexas.edu
ESTRADA-HOWELL, Claudia 619-388-7392 61 B cestrada@sdccd.edu
ESTRELLA, Jeremy 971-722-7228 375 C jeremy.estrella@pcc.edu
ESTREMERA, Wanda 787-665-7910 505 B westremera@columbiacentral.edu
ESTRIN, David 718-522-9073 290 B david@asa.edu
ESTRUP, Cynthia 920-498-5505 498 F cynthia.estrup@nwtc.edu
ESTWICK, Daphne 845-848-4121 298 A daphne.estwick@dc.edu
ESZTERHAS, Gabriel 910-521-6000 343 A
ETCHBERGER, Rich 435-797-4106 459 F rich.etchberger@usu.edu
ETCHISON, Matt 317-921-5739 158 A metchison@ivytech.edu
ETE, Sonia 310-360-8888 27 D
ETE, Thierry 310-360-8888 27 D
ETEZADY, Cameron 215-204-6542 398 D cameron.etezady@temple.edu
ETHERIDGE, Joey 859-341-5800 184 G
ETHERIDGE, Lori 270-852-3284 183 B letheridge@kwc.edu
ETHERTON, Scott 503-370-6707 377 E swetherton@willamette.edu
ETHIER, Lori 402-941-6481 267 B ethier@midlandu.edu
ETHINGTON, Robert 707-527-4573 63 C rethington@santarosa.edu
ETHRIDGE, Jennifer 815-740-2286 152 E jethridge@stfrancis.edu
ETHRIDGE, Lewis 615-327-6800 420 D lethridge@mmc.edu
ETHRIDGE, Rebecca 912-538-3107 125 E rethridge@southeasterntech.edu
ETIENNE, Guy 754-312-2898 103 R registrar@keycollege.edu
ETIENNE, John 904-276-6859 107 A johnetienne@sjrstate.edu
ETIENNE-CUMMINGS, Ralph 410-516-8770 199 E retienne@jhu.edu
ETINGE, Elias, E 706-396-7609 123 I eetinge@paine.edu
ETSCHMAIER, Gale 850-644-5211 110 B getschmaier@fsu.edu
ETTENSOHN, Clare 973-290-4240 282 G cettensohn@steu.edu
ETTENSOHN, Mark 916-686-7400 29 G
ETTINGER, Sherri 617-521-2451 218 C sherri.ettinger@simmons.edu
ETTLICH, Sherry 541-552-6576 376 A ettlich@sou.edu
ETTNER, Susan 310-206-2281 69 D settner@grad.ucla.edu
ETTRICH, Rudi, H 305-760-7500 103 V
ETTUS, Heather 703-891-1787 470 G hettus@standardcollege.edu
ETUGE, OFM CAP, Akolla 610-358-4202 390 G etugea@neumann.edu
ETZEL, Brent 630-752-5955 152 K brent.etzel@wheaton.edu
EUBANK, Charlotte 573-840-9105 259 I ceubank@trcc.edu
EUBANK, Lee 618-374-5096 147 B lee.eubank@principia.edu
EUBANKS, Colin 205-853-1200 2 G ceubanks@jeffersonstate.edu
EUBANKS, David 864-294-2025 408 I david.eubanks@furman.edu
EUBANKS, Gail 912-443-3022 124 I geubanks@savannahtech.edu
EUBANKS, Greta 205-366-8817 7 A greubanks@stillman.edu
EUBANKS, Jon 903-785-7661 440 F jeubanks@parisjc.edu
EUBANKS, Karla 912-427-5899 117 B keubanks@coastalpines.edu
EUBANKS, Michelle 256-765-4225 8 E meubanks@una.edu
EUBANKS, Nekita 704-216-3778 337 C nekita.eubanks@rccc.edu
EUBANKS, Philip 865-573-4517 419 E peubanks@johnsonu.edu
EUDY, Cristine 704-403-4571 327 B cristine.eudy@atriumhealth.org
EUEN, Mandy, L 513-529-8776 356 A euenal@miamioh.edu
EULE, Anne 603-578-8900 272 B aeule@ccsnh.edu
EUN OH, Jea 310-739-0132 41 C
EURE, Darius, D 252-335-8530 341 A ddeure@ecsu.edu
EURY, Brian 610-902-8734 379 E brian.eury@cabrini.edu
EUSER, Andrea 740-376-4477 355 E eusermia@marietta.edu
EVAN, Joseph 570-208-5895 386 G josephevan@kings.edu
EVANCOE, Ryan 812-888-8888 162 E
EVANGELIST, Andrea 352-395-5413 107 G andrea.evangelist@sfcollege.edu
EVANGELISTA, Joleen, M 671-735-5540 503 C materialsmanagement@guamcc.edu
EVANGELISTA, Jordan 717-867-6324 388 A evangeli@lvc.edu
EVANGELISTA, Nancy, J 740-826-8123 356 H nancye@muskingum.edu
EVANS, Adam 909-448-4498 71 C aevans@laverne.edu
EVANS, Alice, C 309-655-3450 148 G alice.c.evans@osfhealthcare.org
EVANS, Ana 478-387-0580 122 D ana.evans@mga.edu
EVANS, Angela 269-782-1323 230 D aevans14@swmich.edu
EVANS, April 765-455-9226 156 E aplevans@iu.edu
EVANS, Atlas 617-726-5164 216 E aevans3@mghihp.edu
EVANS, Belinda 304-647-6401 489 C bevans@osteo.wvsom.edu
EVANS, Betsy 432-837-8312 449 F bxe16ie@sulross.edu
EVANS, Beverly, A 717-815-1228 402 G behinger@ycp.edu
EVANS, Bill 402-481-3967 265 B bill.evans@bryanhealthcollege.edu
EVANS, Brenda 978-934-5021 211 G brenda_evans@uml.edu
EVANS, Brian 502-863-8223 180 E brian_evans@georgetowncollege.edu
EVANS, Brian 423-697-2417 423 B brian.evans@chattanoogastate.edu
EVANS, Charlotte 402-554-2772 269 B charlotte.evans@unmc.edu
EVANS, Charlotte 402-554-2772 269 C cevans@unomaha.edu
EVANS, Chas 601-635-2111 245 B cevans@eccc.edu
EVANS, Chris, P 713-831-7863 453 H evanscp@stthom.edu
EVANS, Damian 262-595-2540 495 D damian.evans@uwp.edu
EVANS, Damon 301-314-0013 202 E devans16@umd.edu
EVANS, Dana 601-718-5900 93 H
EVANS, David 209-667-3153 33 D devans@csustan.edu
EVANS, David 972-273-3561 434 C devans@dcccd.edu
EVANS, Dianne 936-261-1905 445 E dtevan@pvamu.edu
EVANS, Donna 937-319-0211 347 E devans@antiochcollege.edu
EVANS, Edward 361-825-2693 446 E ed.evans@tamucc.edu
EVANS, Edward 718-489-2008 312 H eevans3@sfc.edu
EVANS, Eric 440-375-7056 354 K erevans@lec.edu
EVANS, Eric 602-384-2555 11 H eric.evans@bryanuniversity.edu
EVANS, Eric 606-546-1653 185 B eevans@unionky.edu
EVANS, Eric, D 781-981-7000 215 G
EVANS, Erik 570-389-4047 393 E eevans@bloomu.edu
EVANS, Ernest, C 317-738-8091 155 A eevans@franklincollege.edu
EVANS, Frederick 803-536-7180 410 H fevans@scsu.edu

EVANS, Garry, W .... 214-491-6271 432 I
gevans@collin.edu
EVANS, Gary .... 607-753-2302 317 D
gary.evans@cortland.edu
EVANS, George .... 618-545-3010 141 C
gevans@kaskaskia.edu
EVANS, JR., Gilbert, L .. 386-312-4126 107 A
gilbertevans@sjrstate.edu
EVANS, Greg .... 541-463-5340 373 C
evansg@lanecc.edu
EVANS, Ivan .... 858-534-2247.. 70 C
ercprovost@ucsd.edu
EVANS, J. David .... 470-578-6194 121 J
devans@kennesaw.edu
EVANS, James .... 407-277-0311.. 99 C
jaevans@evergladesuniversity.edu
EVANS, Jami .... 606-451-6726 182 D
jami.evans@kctcs.edu
EVANS, Janet, D .... 412-392-3824 395 H
jevans@pointpark.edu
EVANS, Jason .... 401-508-1880 403 E
jason.evans@jwu.edu
EVANS, Jennifer, M ...... 717-867-6271 388 A
jevans@lvc.edu
EVANS, Jill .... 208-496-9812 130 G
evansj@byui.edu
EVANS, Jocelyn .... 850-474-2158 111 E
jevans@uwf.edu
EVANS, John .... 901-678-2209 426 A
jevans@memphis.edu
EVANS, Johnny .... 912-279-5960 117 C
jevans@ccga.edu
EVANS, June .... 301-546-8235 201 D
evansjl1@pgcc.edu
EVANS, Kamira .... 610-892-1504 393 B
kevans@pit.edu
EVANS, Kathleen .... 315-312-2823 318 B
kathleen.evans@oswego.edu
EVANS, Katie .... 281-649-3000 436 D
kevans@hbu.edu
EVANS, Katina .... 619-201-8700.. 60 G
katina.evans@sdcc.edu
EVANS, Keigan .... 229-500-3062 114 F
keigan.evans@asurams.edu
EVANS, Keniese .... 319-399-8843 164 D
kevans@coe.edu
EVANS, Kenne .... 817-515-3055 445 A
kenneth.evans1@tccd.edu
EVANS, Kenneth, R ...... 405-208-5032 367 E
kevans@okcu.edu
EVANS, Kris .... 413-585-2840 218 D
kevans@smith.edu
EVANS, Krista, D .... 610-683-4000 394 A
kevans@kutztown.edu
EVANS, Laura .... 909-448-4180.. 71 C
levans2@laverne.edu
EVANS, Layna .... 214-333-5275 433 D
layna@dbu.edu
EVANS, Liz .... 412-392-5945 395 H
eevans@pointpark.edu
EVANS, III, Louis, D .. 713-221-2766 452 B
evansl@uhd.edu
EVANS, Marcheta, P ... 973-748-9000 275 C
marcheta_evans@bloomfield.edu
EVANS, Mario .... 843-574-6053 411 I
mario.evans@tridenttech.edu
EVANS, Mark .... 845-938-5502 502 H
mark.evans@westpoint.edu
EVANS, Melissa .... 315-386-7123 319 E
evansm@canton.edu
EVANS, Michael .... 402-872-2239 267 H
mevans@peru.edu
EVANS, Michael, L .... 806-743-2738 450 D
michael.evans@ttuhsc.edu
EVANS, Mike .... 503-399-2391 372 A
mike.evans@chemeketa.edu
EVANS, Murry .... 510-849-8200.. 55 F
EVANS, Nancy .... 484-365-5167 388 F
nevans@lincoln.edu
EVANS, Nate .... 704-406-4254 328 I
njevans@gardner-webb.edu
EVANS, Nicole .... 907-852-1768.. 9 H
nicole.evans@ilisagvik.edu
EVANS, Nita .... 909-667-4411.. 38 A
EVANS, Patricia .... 310-265-6143.. 60 B
patricia.evans@usw.salvationarmy.org
EVANS, Pervis .... 432-335-6412 440 C
pevans@odessa.edu
EVANS, Philesha .... 409-772-8695 456 B
paevans@utmb.edu
EVANS, Philip .... 540-665-4515 470 A
pevans@su.edu
EVANS, Rick .... 818-677-6285.. 32 E
rick.evans@csun.edu

EVANS, Robbie .... 760-252-2411.. 26 L
revans@barstow.edu
EVANS, Runan .... 859-246-6305 181 B
runan.evans@kctcs.edu
EVANS, Ruth .... 215-572-2187 378 E
evansr@arcadia.edu
EVANS, Sammara .... 864-503-7352 413 A
sammarae@uscupstate.edu
EVANS, Sara .... 610-359-5302 381 J
sevans28@dccc.edu
EVANS, Sharmyne .... 678-622-0390 122 H
sharmyne.evans@morehouse.edu
EVANS, Sidney .... 443-885-3144 200 F
sidney.evans@morgan.edu
EVANS, Sidney, S .... 540-458-8754 476 D
sevans@wlu.edu
EVANS, Susan .... 276-223-4740 475 B
sevans@wcc.vccs.edu
EVANS, Suzanne, M ...... 386-312-4041 107 A
suzanneevans@sjrstate.edu
EVANS, Tara .... 307-766-4019 500 H
tevans15@uwyo.edu
EVANS, Tasha .... 337-482-1325 192 F
tasha.evans@louisiana.edu
EVANS, Taylor .... 803-323-2133 413 D
evanst@winthrop.edu
EVANS, Terry .... 502-863-8038 180 L
terry_evans@georgetowncollege.edu
EVANS, Terry, R .... 904-620-2624 111 A
terry.evans@unf.edu
EVANS, Thomas, M ...... 210-829-3900 452 D
tevans@uiwtx.edu
EVANS, Tiffany .... 785-462-3984 172 L
EVANS, Todd .... 865-539-7164 424 C
jtevans@pstcc.edu
EVANS, Toner .... 205-726-2484.... 6 E
jevans1@samford.edu
EVANS, Tonya .... 620-421-6700 175 D
tevans@labette.edu
EVANS, Tracy, L .... 304-929-5480 487 G
tevans@newriver.edu
EVANS, Virginia, H ...... 434-982-2249 471 F
veb5u@virginia.edu
EVANS, W. Franklin .. 304-336-8000 489 B
president@westliberty.edu
EVANS, William, B .... 617-552-4445 207 A
william.evans@bc.edu
EVANS-DINNEEN,
Laurie .... 907-564-8880.... 9 F
levansdinneen@alaskapacific.edu
EVANS GOODCHILD,
Joy .... 231-995-1084 228 F
jevans@nmc.edu
EVANS JONES, Cheryl . 706-821-8230 123 I
cevansjones@paine.edu
EVANS-PLANTS, Penny . 706-232-5374 116 A
peplants@berry.edu
EVANS TAYLOR,
Genevieve .... 818-677-2121.. 32 E
genevieve.evanstaylor@csun.edu
EVANS WILSON, Kelly .. 937-313-3832 352 J
kelly.evans-wilson@franklin.edu
EVANSON, Mary .... 515-294-3959 163 B
mevanson@foundation.iastate.edu
EVE, Debra .... 406-353-2607 262 B
deve@ancollege.edu
EVEILLARD, Angela, M .6 813-259-6589 102 A
aeveillard@hccfl.edu
EVELAND, David .... 865-573-4517 419 E
develand@johnsonu.edu
EVELAND, Jessica, A ... 614-292-1132 358 E
eveland.9@osu.edu
EVELAND, Peter .... 909-954-3502.. 34 E
EVELYN, Tom .... 864-294-2151 408 I
tom.evelyn@furman.edu
EVENER, Julie .... 800-241-1027.. 72 F
jevener@usa.edu
EVENSON, Amanda ... 479-380-2266.. 17 E
amande.evenson@arcomedu.org
EVENSON, Brad .... 620-278-4221 177 E
bevenson@sterling.edu
EVENSON, Shane ...... 715-645-7037 498 G
shane.evenson@northwoodtech.edu
EVENSON, Tresse ...... 605-274-5520 413 G
tresse.evenson@augie.edu
EVENSVOLD, Marty ... 620-251-7700 172 K
evensvold.marty@coffeyville.edu
EVERETT, Darcy .... 843-953-0749 407 D
everettdc@cofc.edu
EVERETT, Dennis ...... 850-718-2216.. 97 E
everettd@chipola.edu
EVERETT, Dennis, T .... 850-718-2216.. 97 E
everettd@chipola.edu

EVERETT, Donna .... 601-635-2111 245 B
deverett@eccc.edu
EVERETT, Frankie .... 541-956-7104 375 G
feverett@roguecc.edu
EVERETT, Jim .... 208-459-5268 131 A
jeverett@collegeofidaho.edu
EVERETT, John .... 512-404-4871 429 K
jeverett@austinseminary.edu
EVERETT, John, C ...... 704-636-6545 329 F
jeverett@hoodseminary.edu
EVERETT, Julia .... 256-228-6001.... 3 B
everettj@nacc.edu
EVERETT, Kaitlin .... 732-255-0400 279 A
keverett@ocean.edu
EVERETT, Kelly .... 229-931-2351 125 C
keverett@southgatech.edu
EVERETT, Leonard ...... 352-854-2322.. 97 L
everettl@cf.edu
EVERETT, Marcia, K ...... 330-471-8335 355 D
meverett@malone.edu
EVERETT, Margaret ...... 401-254-3726 404 C
meverett@rwu.edu
EVERETT, Mark .... 561-697-9200 125 D
maeverett@southuniversity.edu
EVERETT, Patricia ...... 734-432-5388 226 G
peverett@madonna.edu
EVERETT, Sophia ...... 205-391-2326.... 3 E
severett@sheltonstate.edu
EVERETT, Steve .... 212-817-7200 293 D
provost@gc.cuny.edu
EVERETT, Thomas ...... 912-537-8875 116 D
teverett@mccn.edu
EVERETT, Todd .... 614-234-5177 356 E
teverett@mccn.edu
EVERETT-HAYNES,
La Monica .... 619-594-0232.. 33 E
leveretthaynes@sdsu.edu
EVERETT-HENSLEY,
Elaine .... 361-572-6440 456 H
elaine.hensley@victoriacollege.edu
EVERHART, Bruce ...... 312-329-2040 144 F
bruce.everhart@moody.edu
EVERHART, Clinton, D .. 501-686-5113.. 22 D
cdeverhart@uams.edu
EVERHART, Derrick ...... 828-771-2081 344 B
deverhart@warren-wilson.edu
EVERHART, Kim .... 937-775-5414 364 D
kim.everhart@wright.edu
EVERHEART, Jazmine .. 863-680-3004 100 F
jeverheart@flsouthern.edu
EVERITT, David .... 508-793-7297 207 F
deveritt@clarku.edu
EVERS, Cynthia .... 202-806-6100.. 92 E
cynthia.evers@howard.edu
EVERS-MANLY, Shirley . 601-304-4302 244 B
severs-manly@alcorn.edu
EVERSLEY BRADWELL,
Nicole .... 607-274-3124 302 E
neversley@ithaca.edu
EVERSOLE, Danielle ...... 863-667-5000 108 I
dmeversole@seu.edu
EVERSOLE, Malinda ...... 276-223-4869 475 B
meversole@wcc.vccs.edu
EVERSON, Melvin ...... 770-962-7580 121 B
meverson@gwinnettech.edu
EVERTS, Sheri .... 828-262-2040 340 G
evertssn@appstate.edu
EVERY, Janice, S .... 620-421-6700 175 D
janicee@labette.edu
EVETOVICH, Tammy .... 608-342-1261 495 E
evetovicht@uwplatt.edu
EVEY, Rachel .... 509-682-6415 484 H
revey@wvc.edu
EWALD, Jennifer .... 203-254-4000.. 87 G
jewald@fairfield.edu
EWALD, Stanley .... 503-251-5717 377 A
sewald@uws.edu
EWANOW, Scott .... 585-245-5651 317 E
ewanow@geneseo.edu
EWART, Dan .... 208-885-2127 132 C
dewart@uidaho.edu
EWELL, Clint .... 928-776-2166.. 17 B
clint.ewell@yc.edu
EWELL, Robbi .... 619-388-3870.. 60 I
rewell@sdccd.edu
EWEN, Amy .... 617-573-8034 218 G
amy.ewen@suffolk.edu
EWEN, Amy .... 401-598-4370 403 E
amy.ewen@jwu.edu
EWEN, Bernadette ...... 812-877-8697 160 C
ewen@rose-hulman.edu
EWEN, Kurt .... 713-718-8176 436 E
kurt.ewen@hccs.edu
EWERS, Matt .... 307-681-6022 500 F
mewers@sheridan.edu

EWIN, Tammy .... 330-972-5766 361 G
tewin@uakron.edu
EWING, April .... 706-821-8307 123 I
aewing@paine.edu
EWING, April .... 706-396-8118 123 I
aewing@paine.edu
EWING, Chris .... 303-492-7059.. 83 M
chris.ewing@colorado.edu
EWING, Deborah .... 979-230-3632 431 A
deborah.ewing@brazosport.edu
EWING, Greg .... 812-535-1191 160 E
greg.ewing@smwc.edu
EWING, Jennifer .... 619-201-8967.. 65 F
jennifer.ewing@socalsem.edu
EWING, Matthew .... 208-426-4231 130 F
mnewing@boisestate.edu
EWING, Mel .... 406-683-7382 263 E
mel.ewing@umwestern.edu
EWING, Melvin .... 406-447-6932 263 E
mel.ewing@helenacollege.edu
EWING, Michele, Y ...... 410-337-6000 198 G
michele.ewing@goucher.edu
EWING, Mike, J .... 320-363-5605 234 I
mjewing@csbsju.edu
EWING, Nadia .... 574-284-4560 160 F
newing@saintmarys.edu
EWING, II, Rick, M ...... 419-289-5893 347 H
pewing@ashland.edu
EWING, Rob .... 510-845-5373.. 29 C
rob@cjc.edu
EWING, Sarah .... 814-871-7618 383 F
ewing003@gannon.edu
EWING, Sunnie .... 901-722-3231 422 I
sewing@sco.edu
EWING, Terry .... 918-610-8303 368 G
terry.ewing@ptstulsa.edu
EWING-MORGAN,
Dawn .... 718-960-8111 293 E
dawn.ewing-morgan@lehman.cuny.edu
EXANTUS, Yveline .... 617-405-5912 217 G
yexantus@quincycollege.edu
EXELER, Brandy .... 859-371-9393 179 C
bexeler@beckfield.edu
EXLER, Michael, J .... 215-895-6488 382 D
mexler@drexel.edu
EXLEY, Robert, J .... 281-756-3598 428 E
rexley@alvincollege.edu
EXLINE, Teresa, D .... 812-237-7783 155 H
teresa.exline@indstate.edu
EXNER, Allen .... 301-369-2470 197 F
ahexner@captechu.edu
EXSTEEN, Shaun .... 561-237-7839 103 W
exsteen@lynn.edu
EXSTROM, Bruce .... 402-323-3389 268 D
bexstrom@southeast.edu
EYE, John .... 601-266-4241 248 H
john.eye@usm.edu
EYERLY, Mark .... 610-330-5120 387 B
eyerlym@lafayette.edu
EYERMAN, Sandra ...... 518-629-7737 302 A
s.eyerman@hvcc.edu
EYLE, Chris .... 972-758-3891 432 I
ceyle@collin.edu
EYLER, Stephanie ...... 918-631-2539 371 C
stephanie-eyler@utulsa.edu
EYLERS, Hinrich .... 602-557-7428.. 16 L
hinrich.eylers@phoenix.edu
EYMANN, Stephanie ..... 815-599-3439 138 H
stephanie.eymann@highland.edu
EYNON, Craig, S .... 330-325-6663 357 D
ceynon@neomed.edu
EYNON, Matthew .... 717-358-4144 383 G
matthew.eynon@fandm.edu
EYNOUF, Erica .... 413-755-4064 215 F
eweynouf@stcc.edu
EYRING, Henry, J .... 208-496-1111 130 G
eyringh@byui.edu
EYSTER, Kevin .... 734-432-5307 226 G
keyster@madonna.edu
EZELL, Monica .... 251-460-6111.... 9 A
monicae@southalabama.edu
EZEOKE, Benedict ...... 507-457-5331 241 A
bezeoke@winona.edu
EZEONU, Rolita .... 253-833-9111 480 A
rezeonu@greenriver.edu
EZZEDDINE, Ahmad .. 313-577-4450 232 H
a.m.ezzeddine@wayne.edu
EZZELL, Russell .... 325-649-8040 437 A
rezzell@hputx.edu
EZZI, Ricardo .... 724-805-2251 397 D
ezzi.ricardo@stvincent.edu

FARABEE, Lars, C .... 336-841-9604 329 E
lfarabee@highpoint.edu
FARAD, Timothy .... 303-329-6355.. 79 C
FARADAY, Christine ...... 516-572-7401 307 C
christine.faraday@ncc.edu
FARAGALLA, Sameh ..... 973-661-0600 276 E
sfaragalla@eastwick.edu
FARAH ABDIGANNI,
Abdulahi .... 507-372-3423 239 B
abdullahi.farahabdigaani@mnwest.edu
FARAHANI, Eric .... 631-656-2144 299 G
eric.farahani@ftc.edu
FARAHANI, Gohar .... 301-846-2451 198 E
gfarahani@frederick.edu
FARANDA, Nicholas ...... 914-261-9758 307 E
farandan@newschool.edu
FARB, Erin .... 303-404-5537.. 80 I
erin.farb@frontrange.edu
FARBANIEC, David .... 845-257-3196 316 B
farbanid@newpaltz.edu
FARCHMIN, Eileen .... 863-638-1431 113 E
FARFAN, Erika, M .... 740-427-5571 354 I
farfane@kenyon.edu
FARGASON, Renee .... 850-245-0466 109 D
renee.fargason@flbog.edu
FARHA, Darron, C .... 219-464-6702 162 C
darron.farha@valpo.edu
FARIA, Mary .... 512-233-9466 429 B
mfaria@aoma.edu
FARIAS, Teddy .... 281-998-6150 442 D
teddy.farias@sjcd.edu
FARIAS-EISNER, Robin .. 909-469-5200.. 75 G
FARIDIAN, Fred .... 650-685-6616.. 44 I
ffaridian@gurnick.edu
FARINA, Amanda .... 910-275-6126 335 C
afarina@jamessprunt.edu
FARINA, Jonathan .... 973-761-9388 282 K
jonathan.farina@shu.edu
FARINA, Matthew, R ..... 212-592-2126 314 I
mfarina@sva.edu
FARINELLI, Robert .... 814-262-6474 393 A
rfarinelli@pennhighlands.edu
FARKAS, Esther .... 718-252-0847 325 P
FARKAS, John .... 814-886-6331 390 E
jfarkas@mtaloy.edu
FARLAND, Lisa .... 310-338-7896.. 51 C
lisa.farland@lmu.edu
FARLAY, Grace, R .... 800-686-1883 222 B
FARLESS, John, A .... 812-228-5157 162 B
jafarless@usi.edu
FARLEY, Barbara, A ...... 217-245-3001 139 A
barbara.farley@ic.edu
FARLEY, Catherine .... 805-922-6966.. 24 L
catherine.farley@hancockcollege.edu
FARLEY, Christy .... 602-872-2555.. 14 J
christy.farley@nau.edu
FARLEY, Jerry, B .... 785-670-1022 178 A
jerry.farley@washburn.edu
FARLEY, Kathleen .... 401-341-2206 404 D
kathleen.farley2@salve.edu
FARLEY, Margaret .... 307-624-7010 500 A
mfarley@ewc.wy.edu
FARLEY, Patrick .... 301-891-4551 204 D
pfarley@wau.edu
FARLEY, Rebecca .... 661-395-4610.. 47 B
rebecca.farley@bakersfieldcollege.edu
FARLEY, Ryan .... 801-957-4681 460 D
ryan.farley@slcc.edu
FARLEY, Tiombe .... 518-381-1279 319 G
farleyts@sunysccc.edu
FARLEY, Troy .... 616-331-3311 224 D
farleytr@gvsu.edu
FARLOW, Carolyn .... 515-965-7067 164 F
cdfarlow@dmacc.edu
FARLOW, Rita .... 727-302-6526 107 C
farlow.rita@spcollege.edu
FARMER, Blake .... 304-384-6065 488 K
bfarmer@concord.edu
FARMER, Blake .... 304-384-6056 488 K
bfarmer@concord.edu
FARMER, Bradley .... 614-287-2787 351 B
bfarmer@cscc.edu
FARMER, Brandon .... 916-577-2200.. 76 C
bfarmer@jessup.edu
FARMER, Carter .... 717-290-8701 387 F
cfarmer@lancasterseminary.edu
FARMER, David .... 910-695-3914 337 E
farmerdj@sandhills.edu
FARMER, Elizabeth, M .. 412-624-6304 400 A
efarmer@pitt.edu
FARMER, James .... 740-351-3264 360 E
jfarmer@shawnee.edu
FARMER, Joyce .... 610-282-1100 382 A
joyce.farmer@desales.edu
FARMER, Kaymon .... 903-434-8265 440 A
kfarmer@ntcc.edu
FARMER, Kris .... 785-243-1435 172 J
krisfarmer@cloud.edu
FARMER, Lindsey .... 910-695-3907 337 E
farmerl@sandhills.edu
FARMER, Patricia .... 276-739-2480 474 H
pfarmer@vhcc.edu
FARMER, Patricia J, B .. 315-229-5265 313 F
pfarmer@stlawu.edu
FARMER, Patrick .... 618-664-7079 138 D
patrick.farmer@greenville.edu
FARMER, Stephen .... 434-924-3728 471 F
smf4t@virignia.edu
FARMER, Tod Allen ...... 817-594-6271 457 C
tafarmer@wc.edu
FARMER, Yolanda .... 815-280-6691 140 I
yfarmer@jjc.edu
FARMER, Yvonne .... 314-889-1419 252 G
yfarmer@fontbonne.edu
FARMER-DIXON,
Cherae .... 615-327-6207 420 D
cdixon@mmc.edu
FARMER-KAISER, Mary . 337-482-6965 192 F
kaiser@louisiana.edu
FARMER-NEAL,
Rochonda .... 254-710-3684 430 F
rochonda_farmer-neal@baylor.edu
FARMER NOONAN,
Erin .... 617-735-9991 209 A
farmer@emmanuel.edu
FARMIGA, Adriana .... 212-353-4200 297 C
adriana.farmiga@cooper.edu
FARNAM, Boyd, A .... 248-370-3110 229 F
farnam@oakland.edu
FARNAN, Christiane ...... 518-783-2353 314 K
farnan@siena.edu
FARNAN, JR.,
Joseph, J .... 302-356-6817.. 91 C
ashley.r.mundy@wilmu.edu
FARNEY, Kirk .... 630-752-5016 152 K
kirk.farney@wheaton.edu
FARNSWORTH, Tracy .... 208-795-4266 131 D
FARNSWORTH, Vicki ..... 423-425-4393 426 D
vicki-farnsworth@utc.edu
FARNSWORTH, Vicki ..... 423-425-1755 426 D
vicki-farnsworth@utc.edu
FARNSWORTH, Ward .... 512-232-1120 454 C
wf@law.utexas.edu
FARQUAHARSON,
Robert .... 617-373-2000 217 D
FARQUHAR,
Sherry Leigh .... 334-833-4562.... 5 H
internships@hawks.huntingdon.edu
FARQUHARSON,
Donald .... 816-523-9140 261 E
don.f@wellspring.edu
FARQUHARSON, Hope .. 951-487-6752.. 53 A
hfarquharson@msjc.edu
FARR, Matthew .... 856-222-9311 280 E
mfarr@rcbc.edu
FARR, Paul .... 229-931-2482 125 C
pfarr@southgatech.edu
FARR, Sharon .... 573-288-6633 251 I
sfarr@culver.edu
FARRAH, Anne .... 800-818-6136.. 55 K
afarrah@palaoltou.edu
FARRAR, Griffen .... 712-325-3487 167 G
gfarrar@iwcc.edu
FARRE, Matias .... 760-750-8111.. 33 C
mfarre@csusm.edu
FARRELL, Allison .... 315-445-4275 303 F
cudaal@lemoyne.edu
FARRELL, Chris .... 814-631-9633 393 A
cfarrell@pennhighlands.edu
FARRELL, Diane .... 706-864-1951 126 G
diane.farrell@ung.edu
FARRELL, Dina .... 971-722-2851 375 C
dina.farrell@pcc.edu
FARRELL, Dolly .... 239-590-7638 109 G
dofarrell@fgcu.edu
FARRELL, Donna .... 423-354-2407 424 B
dsfarrell@northeaststate.edu
FARRELL, Erin, P .... 317-788-2127 161 F
farrelle@uindy.edu
FARRELL, Gregory .... 212-220-1379 292 G
gfarrell@bmcc.cuny.edu
FARRELL, Jill .... 305-899-3649.. 96 A
jfarrell@barry.edu
FARRELL, Jillian .... 864-578-8770 410 G
jfarrell@sherman.edu
FARRELL, Kathleen .... 914-251-6090 318 E
kathleen.farrell@purchase.edu
FARRELL, Kathleen, A ... 402-472-9500 268 I
kfarrell2@unl.edu
FARRELL, Kathy .... 402-472-9500 269 A
kfarrell2@unl.edu
FARRELL, Kevin .... 570-961-4725 389 B
kfarrell@marywood.edu
FARRELL, Lauren, M ..... 724-925-4079 401 H
farrelll@westmoreland.edu
FARRELL, Lisa, M .... 636-584-6558 252 D
lisa.farrell@eastcentral.edu
FARRELL, Maggie .... 702-895-2286 270 J
maggie.farrell@unlv.edu
FARRELL, Natasha .... 315-445-4460 303 F
farrelnt@lemoyne.edu
FARRELL, Patricia .... 918-781-7394 365 B
farrellp@bacone.edu
FARRELL, Robert, B .... 570-941-6213 400 C
robert.farrell@scranton.edu
FARRELL, Shawn .... 909-537-3015.. 33 B
shawn.farrell@csusb.edu
FARRELL, Thomas .... 585-275-1837 323 E
farrellt@rochester.edu
FARRELL, Tony .... 858-513-9240.. 16 I
courtney.farrell@ashford.edu
FARRELL, Tony .... 858-513-9240.. 16 I
tony.farrell@ashford.edu
FARREN, Chelsea .... 215-248-7011 380 G
farrenc@chc.edu
FARRIER, Jasmine .... 502-852-6924 185 E
j.farrier@louisville.edu
FARRINGTON, Keisha ... 214-860-2032 434 A
kfarrington@dcccd.edu
FARRINGTON, Susan .... 903-510-2371 451 D
susan.farrington@tjc.edu
FARRIOR, Andy .... 361-582-2547 456 H
andy.farrior@victoriacollege.edu
FARRIS, Deborah .... 970-351-1273.. 84 D
deborah.farris@unco.edu
FARRIS, G. Corey .... 304-293-5811 489 E
corey.farris@mail.wvu.edu
FARRIS, Kent .... 662-728-7751 247 D
FARRIS, Kimberly .... 312-225-6288 152 G
FARRIS, Kristie .... 423-697-3143 423 B
kristie.farris@chattanoogastate.edu
FARRIS, Michael .... 434-832-7891 472 G
farrism@centralvirginia.edu
FARRIS, Michael, P ...... 540-338-1776 468 D
chancellor@phc.edu
FARRIS, Rachel .... 251-981-3771.... 5 B
rachel.farris@columbiasouthern.edu
FARRIS, Rachel .... 301-687-4878 203 F
rfarris@frostburg.edu
FARRIS, Rachel .... 612-330-1476 233 G
farrisr@augsburg.edu
FARRIS, Thomas, N ...... 848-445-1640 281 B
tfarris@rutgers.edu
FARROW, Joseph .... 530-752-3113.. 69 A
jafarrow@ucdavis.edu
FARRY, Gavin .... 847-578-3252 148 B
gavin.farry@rosalindfranklin.edu
FARSAD, Sarah .... 518-388-6013 323 B
FARTHING, Scott .... 949-582-4907.. 65 C
sfarthing@saddleback.edu
FARVARDIN, Nariman ... 201-216-5213 282 L
president@stevens.edu
FARVOUR, Jennifer, K .. 920-923-8725 492 D
jkfarvour37@marianuniversity.edu
FARWELL, Chris .... 918-631-5613 371 C
chris-farwell@utulsa.edu
FARWELL, Kamrhan ...... 573-882-4523 260 B
FARWELL, Kamrhan, M . 573-882-4523 260 C
farwellk@missouri.edu
FARWELL, Keenan .... 207-778-7009 196 F
keenan.farwell@maine.edu
FARWELL, Susan .... 217-732-3168 142 D
FARYNIAK, Karen, N ..... 717-245-1323 382 B
faryniak@dickinson.edu
FASANELLA, Karen .... 973-748-9000 275 C
karen_fasanella@bloomfield.edu
FASANO, Ralph .... 978-665-3354 212 C
rfasano@fitchburgstate.edu
FASSERO, Matt .... 913-360-7420 171 G
mfassero@benedictine.edu
FASSETT, Lori .... 989-386-6692 227 E
lfassett1@midmich.edu
FASSINO, Dina .... 715-425-4306 496 A
dina.fassino@uwrf.edu
FASSLER, Suli .... 914-893-4036 288 K
sfassler@ajr.edu
FAST, Doreen .... 620-229-6223 177 D
doreen.fast@sckans.edu
FAST, Katie .... 541-737-4514 374 H
FASTNOW, Chris .... 406-994-2870 263 G
cfastnow@montana.edu
FATHALLAH, Fadi .... 530-754-9707.. 69 A
fathallah@ucdavis.edu
FATHERLY, Sarah .... 704-337-2568 339 D
fatherlys@queens.edu
FATIMA, Nasrin .... 607-777-2365 315 E
nfatima@binghamton.edu
FATOOL, Kirk .... 765-448-1986 154 I
FATTOUH, Said .... 713-221-8059 452 B
fattouhs@uhd.edu
FAUCETT, Trinity .... 919-718-7291 333 A
tfaucett@cccc.edu
FAUCHET, Philippe, M .. 615-322-0720 427 B
philippe.m.fauchet@vanderbilt.edu
FAUCI, Darcy .... 607-777-2131 315 E
dfauci@binghamton.edu
FAUDREE, Donna .... 574-807-7752 153 G
donna.faudree@betheluniversity.edu
FAUGHANAN, Timothy . 607-777-2275 315 E
tfaughn@binghamton.edu
FAUGHT, Jerry .... 580-481-5243 457 B
jerry.faught@wbu.edu
FAUGHT, Norma .... 575-392-5018 286 E
nfaught@nmjc.edu
FAUL, Michelle .... 916-278-3625.. 33 A
michelle.faul@csus.edu
FAULCONER, Christian . 801-422-4690 458 A
christian_faulconer@byu.edu
FAULK, Colene .... 910-788-6269 337 G
colene.faulk@sccnc.edu
FAULK, Jeremy .... 573-681-5431 254 A
faulkj@lincolnu.edu
FAULK, Randy .... 361-570-4397 452 C
faulkr@uhv.edu
FAULKNER, B. Keith ..... 276-244-1283 463 H
bkfaulkner@asl.edu
FAULKNER,
Jacqueline, A .... 901-333-5722 424 E
jfaulkner@southwest.tn.edu
FAULKNER, Jessica ...... 501-205-8800.. 19 B
jfaulkner@cbc.edu
FAULKNER, Karen, R .... 812-888-5640 162 E
kfaulkner@vinu.edu
FAULKNER, Keith .... 434-592-5351 467 E
bkfaulkner@liberty.edu
FAULKNER, Kenya, M ... 404-727-2237 118 D
kenya.mann.faulkner@emory.edu
FAULKNER, Michael ..... 336-386-3436 338 B
faulknerm@surry.edu
FAULKNER, Renee .... 507-222-4896 234 C
rfaulkner@carleton.edu
FAULKNER, Ryan .... 208-535-5417 130 I
ryan.faulkner@cei.edu
FAULKNER, Ted .... 540-231-5618 475 D
thfaulkn@vt.edu
FAULKNER, William ...... 718-631-6244 295 B
FAULSTICK, Donald, R .. 413-542-8266 205 D
drfaulstick@amherst.edu
FAULSTICK, Lindsay ...... 812-866-7079 155 D
faulstick@hanover.edu
FAUNCE, Rhonda .... 607-735-1732 298 G
rfaunce@elmira.edu
FAUOLO-MANILA,
Okenaisa .... 684-699-2722 503 A
o.fauolo@amsamoa.edu
FAUROT, Sara .... 609-652-4469 283 A
sara.faurot@stockton.edu
FAUST, Anthony .... 402-844-7717 268 A
anthonyf@northeast.edu
FAUST, Brian .... 715-346-3511 496 B
brian.faust@uwsp.edu
FAUST, Brian, A .... 502-852-2898 185 E
brian.faust@louisville.edu
FAUST, Joanne .... 860-343-5890.. 86 G
jfaust@mxcc.edu
FAUST, Kimberly, A ...... 803-323-2225 413 D
faustk@winthrop.edu
FAUST, Lucas .... 414-443-8720 497 A
lucas.faust@wlc.edu
FAUST, Mary Catherine 770-426-2771 122 A
cfaust@life.edu
FAUSTINO, James .... 808-675-3739 128 B
james.faustino@byuh.edu
FAUSZ, Kevin .... 210-431-4066 440 D
kpfausz@ollusa.edu
FAUTAS, Jason .... 330-490-7437 363 E
jfautas@walsh.edu
FAUVER, James .... 304-734-6614 487 D
james.fauver@bridgevalley.edu
FAVARA, JR., Leonard .. 620-241-0723 172 H
lenny.favara@centralchristian.edu

Index of Key Administrators FAVARA – FELTY 639

FAVARA, Tina .... 603-427-7600 271 J
FAVAZZA, Erin .... 301-985-7077 203 C
erin.favazza@umuc.edu
FAVAZZA, Joseph, A .... 603-641-7010 273 C
jfavazza@anselm.edu
FAVEDE, Ginny .... 304-243-2233 490 F
president@wheeling.edu
FAVERTY, Patrick .... 916-520-7472.. 71 E
pfaverty@pacific.edu
FAVORIT, Mike, D .... 407-582-1336 113 C
mfavorit@valenciacollege.edu
FAVORS, Toney .... 903-223-3061 447 C
toney.favors@tamut.edu
FAVOUR OKORO,
Ifeoma .... 405-789-7661 369 H
FAVRE, David .... 919-866-5258 338 E
dlfavre@waketech.edu
FAW, Kim, E .... 336-838-6293 338 H
kefaw728@wilkescc.edu
FAWBUSH, Donna .... 605-256-5084 415 G
donna.fawbush@dsu.edu
FAWBUSH, Douglas ...... 570-740-0305 388 G
FAWBUSH, Greg .... 615-675-5255 427 D
gfawbush@welch.edu
FAWCETT, Andrew .... 631-451-4879 320 G
fawceta@sunysuffolk.edu
FAWCETT, III,
Frederick, J .... 207-602-4804 194 F
sf@landingschool.edu
FAWCETT, Jeffrey, K ...... 574-372-5100 155 C
fawcettj@grace.edu
FAWCETT, Tonya, L .... 574-372-5100 155 C
fawcettl@grace.edu
FAWKS, Melinda, D ...... 717-477-1121 394 D
mdfawk@ship.edu
FAY, Dana .... 630-515-7166 144 C
dfayxx@midwestern.edu
FAY, Derek, R .... 208-496-7310 130 G
fayd@byui.edu
FAY, Jake .... 360-623-8400 477 H
jake.fay@centralia.edu
FAY, Laurie .... 518-783-2307 314 K
fay@siena.edu
FAY, Michael .... 630-515-6382 144 C
mfayxx@midwestern.edu
FAY, Sue .... 847-543-2218 135 G
sfay@clcillinois.edu
FAY-REILLY, Tara .... 718-862-7939 304 K
tfayreilly01@manhattan.edu
FAYEK, Moaty .... 408-864-8896.. 42 K
fayekmoaty@deanza.edu
FAYETTE, Theodore .... 973-673-3900 275 A
fayette0101@gmail.com
FAYMONVILLE, Carmen 920-424-0890 495 C
faymonvc@uwosh.edu
FAZ, Isaac .... 214-378-1793 433 F
isaac.faz@dcccd.edu
FAZEKAS, Jennifer .... 203-932-7274.. 89 F
jfazekas@newhaven.edu
FAZIO, James, I .... 619-201-8978.. 65 F
james.fazio@socalsem.edu
FAZIO, Jamie .... 585-389-2308 307 D
jfazio1@naz.edu
FAZIO, Jennifer .... 732-255-0400 279 A
jfazio@ocean.edu
FAZIO, Kari .... 610-526-5641 378 J
kfazio@brynmawr.edu
FAZZINI, Beth, M .... 412-578-8780 380 A
emfazzini@carlow.edu
FEAGANS, Frank .... 972-883-6900 454 D
frank.feagans@utdallas.edu
FEAGLE, Wayne .... 503-491-6422 373 H
wayne.feagle@mhcc.edu
FEAGLEY, Jordan .... 412-731-6000 396 D
jfeagley@rpts.edu
FEAKES, Debra .... 210-784-2403 447 B
dfeakes@tamusa.edu
FEAR, Kevin, G .... 724-653-2222 382 C
kfear@dec.edu
FEARN, Odell .... 865-882-4679 424 D
fearnao@roanestate.edu
FEARN, Odell .... 865-354-3000 424 D
fearnao@roanestate.edu
FEARRINGTON, Valerie . 336-506-4133 331 J
vfearrington969@alamancecc.edu
FEASEL, Edward, M ...... 949-480-4133.. 64 E
feasel@soka.edu
FEATHER, Nancy .... 412-809-5266 395 F
feather.nancy@ptcollege.edu
FEATHERLING, Adam .... 740-366-9301 349 D
featherling.2@osu.edu
FEATHERSTON, Guy ...... 972-775-7250 439 G
guy.featherston@navarrocollege.edu
FEATHERSTONE, Jamal . 919-546-8369 339 I
jamal.featherstone@shawu.edu
FEAVER, John, H .... 405-224-3140 371 B
jfeaver@usao.edu
FEBBO, Jenny .... 216-987-4854 351 D
jenny.febbo@tri-c.edu
FEBO-GOMEZ, Yamillet . 732-906-2602 278 A
yfebo-gomez@middlesexcc.edu
FEBUS, Vivian .... 718-262-2350 295 D
vfebus@york.cuny.edu
FECHO, Susan .... 252-399-6480 326 H
sfecho@barton.edu
FECHTER, Sharon .... 240-567-7563 200 E
sharon.fechter@montgomerycollege.edu
FEDDER, Carolyn .... 934-420-2239 320 C
fedderc@farmingdale.edu
FEDE, Marie, A .... 516-572-7310 307 C
marie.fede@ncc.edu
FEDER, Mary, M .... 631-451-4256 320 G
federm@sunysuffolk.edu
FEDERER, Gina .... 972-273-3006 434 C
gfederer@dcccd.edu
FEDERMAN, Robin .... 213-884-4133.. 24 D
rfederman@ajrca.edu
FEDIN, Andrey .... 408-498-5151.. 73 A
afedin@cogswell.edu
FEDOR, Michael .... 717-728-2333 380 D
michaelfedor@centralpenn.edu
FEDORCHAK, Lynn .... 607-778-5319 317 A
fedorchaklm@sunybroome.edu
FEDOREK, Jeffrey .... 724-653-2204 382 C
jfedorek@dec.edu
FEDORKO, Kathleen, C . 215-968-8220 379 B
kathleen.fedorko@bucks.edu
FEDRICK, Marion .... 229-500-2000 114 F
marion.fedrick@asurams.edu
FEDRIZZI-WILLIAMS,
Linda .... 717-728-2219 380 D
lindafedrizzi@centralpenn.edu
FEELER, William .... 432-685-4626 439 E
bfeeler@midland.edu
FEELEY, Brian .... 336-278-7446 328 H
bfeeley@elon.edu
FEELEY, Maria .... 540-458-8940 476 D
mfeeley@wlu.edu
FEELY, SND, Katherine . 216-397-1966 353 O
kfeely@jcu.edu
FEENEY, Gregory .... 859-246-6329 181 B
greg.feeney@kctcs.edu
FEERER, Pam .... 620-252-7135 172 K
feerer.pam@coffeyville.edu
FEEST, Amy .... 860-773-1631.. 87 E
afeest@tunxis.edu
FEEZELL, Travis .... 704-461-6214 326 I
travisfezzell@bac.edu
FEGAN, Kevin, G .... 903-875-7306 439 G
kevin.fegan@navarrocollege.edu
FEGAN, Maryanne .... 908-852-1400 275 H
maryanne.fegan@centenaryuniversity.edu
FEGLEY, Jill .... 650-325-5621.. 59 J
jill.fegley@stpsu.edu
FEGLEY, Laura .... 510-883-2068.. 41 G
lfegley@dspt.edu
FEHER, Katie .... 567-661-7532 359 H
katie_feher2@owens.edu
FEHLING, Patricia .... 518-580-5742 315 A
pfehling@skidmore.edu
FEHN, Heather .... 609-771-2101 275 J
hfehn@tcnj.edu
FEHOKO, Lakiesha .... 801-957-4278 460 D
lakiesha.fehoko@slcc.edu
FEHR, Eric .... 740-474-8896 358 A
efehr@ohiochristian.edu
FEHR, Joy, A .... 951-785-2020.. 47 F
president@lasierra.edu
FEHRENBACHER,
Dwayne .... 618-634-3335 149 C
dwaynef@shawneecc.edu
FEHRENBACHER, Rick ... 206-220-8269 483 B
fehrenbacher@seattleu.edu
FEICHTER, Kathryn .... 330-966-5452 360 I
kfeichter@starkstate.edu
FEICK, Andrew .... 610-328-8276 398 B
afeick1@swarthmore.edu
FEIERMAN, Michael ...... 212-678-3438 321 H
mf192@tc.columbia.edu
FEIFER, Amy .... 610-896-1181 385 H
afeifer@haverford.edu
FEIG, Daniel .... 864-503-5140 413 A
dfeig@uscupstate.edu
FEIGENBAUM, Sonia ..... 512-232-4438 454 C
sfeigenbaum@austin.utexas.edu
FEIGERT, James, M ...... 949-582-4342.. 65 C
jfeigert@saddleback.edu
FEIGERT, Kendra, M ..... 717-867-6126 388 A
feigert@lvc.edu
FEILMEIER, Paul .... 402-844-7060 268 A
pfeilme1@northeast.edu
FEIN, Adam .... 940-565-2000 453 B
FEIN, Adam .... 940-565-2624 453 B
adam.fein@unt.edu
FEIN, Gene .... 718-817-3900 300 A
fein@fordham.edu
FEIN, Jason .... 207-786-6341 193 D
jfein@bates.edu
FEIN, Michael, R .... 401-598-1736 403 E
michael.fein@jwu.edu
FEIN, Michael, T .... 434-832-7751 472 G
feinm@centralvirginia.edu
FEINBERG, Diane .... 405-974-2658 370 H
dfeinberg@uco.edu
FEINBERG, Elisha .... 718-268-4700 311 H
FEINBERG, Kari .... 212-228-1888 311 I
FEINFELD, Amy, S .... 212-678-8007 303 A
registrar@jtsa.edu
FEINGOLD, Ruth, P ...... 503-370-6285 377 E
feingold@willamette.edu
FEINMAN, Shannon, V . 434-949-1005 474 D
shannon.feinman@southside.edu
FEINSTEIN, Andrew .... 970-351-2121.. 84 D
andy.feinstein@unco.edu
FEIS, Alicia, E .... 623-572-3901 144 C
afeis@midwestern.edu
FEIST, Donna, L .... 610-758-3156 388 C
dlf210@lehigh.edu
FEIST, K. Cameron .... 315-859-4413 300 F
cfeist@hamilton.edu
FEIST-PRICE, Sonja .... 810-762-3177 231 C
sfprice@umich.edu
FEISTHAMEL, Kevin, P .. 330-569-5952 353 F
feisthamelkp@hiram.edu
FEISTRITZER, Emily .... 844-283-2246.. 93 C
FEISTRITZER, Richard ... 844-283-2246.. 93 C
FEIT, Christopher, R ..... 563-588-7109 167 I
christopher.feit@loras.edu
FEITZ, David, A .... 801-321-7211 459 C
dfeitz@ushe.edu
FEKE, Donald, L .... 216-368-4389 349 B
dlf4@case.edu
FEKETE, Erin .... 317-788-8030 161 F
feketee@uindy.edu
FELCH, Beth .... 414-930-3640 493 E
felchb@mtmary.edu
FELCH, Katrina .... 715-675-3331 498 E
felch@ntc.edu
FELD, Rachel, M .... 507-354-8221 236 D
feldrm@mlc-wels.edu
FELDER, Andrea .... 202-885-6000.. 91 D
FELDER, Brandon .... 864-388-8398 409 B
bfelder@lander.edu
FELDER, Bruce, B .... 304-696-3983 488 N
felder1@marshall.edu
FELDER, Luther .... 706-821-8295 123 I
lfelder@paine.edu
FELDER, Theresa .... 443-412-2475 199 B
tfelder@harford.edu
FELDHAUS, Heather ...... 570-389-3870 393 E
hfeldhau@bloomu.edu
FELDHAUS, Jeffrey, J .... 402-280-3994 265 J
jeffreyfeldhaus@creighton.edu
FELDHAUS, Rachel .... 815-599-3455 138 H
rachel.feldhaus@highland.edu
FELDHUES, Nicole .... 412-396-6644 382 E
feldhuesn@duq.edu
FELDHUS, Karima .... 949-582-6160.. 65 C
kfeldhus@saddleback.edu
FELDMAN, Aharon .... 410-484-7200 201 B
raf@nirc.edu
FELDMAN, Cecile .... 848-445-4633 281 B
l.c.feldman@rutgers.edu
FELDMAN, Chandra ...... 785-738-9080 176 C
cfeldman@ncktc.edu
FELDMAN, Dan .... 781-736-8405 207 D
feldman@brandeis.edu
FELDMAN, Ilana .... 202-994-7728.. 92 C
ifeldman@gwu.edu
FELDMAN, Jason .... 907-796-6100.. 10 C
FELDMAN, Nell .... 240-567-3120 200 E
nell.feldman@montgomerycollege.edu
FELDMAN, Rachelle ...... 919-445-8325 342 B
rachelle_feldman@unc.edu
FELDNER, Sarah .... 414-288-3491 492 E
sarah.feldner@marquette.edu
FELDSTEIN, Andrew ...... 785-628-4788 173 E
apfeldstein@fhsu.edu
FELDSTEIN, Jay, S .... 215-871-6800 395 A
jfeldstein@pcom.edu
FELDT, Alison, J .... 507-786-3193 242 I
feldt@stolaf.edu
FELDT, Tina .... 318-869-5424 186 C
tfeldt@centenary.edu
FELEKE, Yoseph .... 941-355-9080.. 98 E
FELIBERTY, Victor, A ..... 787-284-1912 507 D
vfeliber@ponce.inter.edu
FELICE, Michael .... 717-477-1123 394 D
mjfelice@ship.edu
FELICIANO, Catalina ..... 787-753-6000 506 B
cfeliciano@icprjc.edu
FELICIANO, Hector, L ... 787-284-1912 507 D
hlfelic@ponce.inter.edu
FELICIANO, Jose .... 607-753-4711 317 D
jose.feliciano@cortland.edu
FELICIANO, Nydia, I ..... 787-279-1912 506 L
nfeliciano@bayamon.inter.edu
FELICIANO, Patsy .... 813-974-3827 111 B
pfelicia@admin.usf.edu
FELICIANO, Yelitza .... 787-710-8999 505 D
yelitza.feliciano@dewey.edu
FELICIANO DE LA CRUZ,
Maria .... 787-725-6500 504 F
mfeliciano@albizu.edu
FELICIANO-MÉNDEZ,
Wanda .... 787-890-2681 510 C
wanda.feliciano1@upr.edu
FELIO, John .... 518-694-7319 289 A
john.felio@acphs.edu
FELIX, Dionne .... 423-236-2912 422 H
felixd@southern.edu
FELIX, Vivienne .... 724-503-1001 401 D
vfelix@washjeff.edu
FELKER, Sharon, M .... 303-963-3369.. 78 D
sfelker@ccu.edu
FELKER, Steven .... 757-825-2716 474 F
felkers@tncc.edu
FELKS, Stephanie .... 803-533-3957 410 H
sfelks@scsu.edu
FELL, Julie .... 319-335-0224 163 F
julie-fell@uiowa.edu
FELL, Katherine, R .... 419-434-4510 362 D
fell@findlay.edu
FELL, Vince .... 806-743-7013 450 D
vince.fell@ttuhsc.edu
FELLER, Cory .... 218-683-8633 239 E
cory.feller@northlandcollege.edu
FELLER, David .... 352-294-7439 110 E
dbf@ufl.edu
FELLER, David, C .... 414-955-8424 492 F
dfeller@mcw.edu
FELLER, Scott, E .... 765-361-6221 162 G
fellers@wabash.edu
FELLINGER, Jennifer ..... 616-395-7860 224 H
fellinger@hope.edu
FELSER, Francis, J .... 716-250-7500 291 H
fjfelser@bryantstratton.edu
FELSKE, Eileen .... 973-618-3419 275 E
efelske@caldwell.edu
FELT, Bryan .... 973-761-9492 282 K
bryan.felt@shu.edu
FELTHOUSEN, Robert .... 541-956-7147 375 G
rfelthousen@roguecc.edu
FELTNER, Michael, E .... 310-506-4280.. 56 H
michael.feltner@pepperdine.edu
FELTON, Dean .... 310-287-4349.. 50 C
feltond@wlac.edu
FELTON, JR.,
Herman, J .... 903-927-3201 457 I
seventeen@wileyc.edu
FELTON, III, James .... 609-771-2423 275 J
feltonj@tcnj.edu
FELTON, John .... 336-272-7102 329 B
john.felton@greensboro.edu
FELTON, Rob .... 503-554-2129 372 I
rfelton@georgefox.edu
FELTON, Shawn .... 607-255-5241 297 D
admissions@cornell.edu
FELTON, Shawn .... 239-590-7511 109 G
sfelton@fgcu.edu
FELTON, Terence .... 630-466-7900 152 H
tfelton@waubonsee.edu
FELTS, Cynthia .... 812-488-1046 161 E
cf128@evansville.edu
FELTS, Jessica .... 706-583-2893 115 C
jfelts@athenstech.edu
FELTS, Joanna .... 559-251-4215.. 28 B
jfelts@calchristiancollege.edu
FELTS, Ronald .... 661-726-1911.. 68 L
ron.felts@uav.edu
FELTY, Darren .... 843-958-5813 411 I
darren.felty@tridenttech.edu

FELTY, James 717-867-6698 388 A
felty@lvc.edu
FELVER, Richard 413-236-2151 213 E
rfelver@berkshirecc.edu
FELZ, Billy 715-836-2715 494 E
felzwl@uwec.edu
FEMINELLA,
Catherine, A 610-499-4392 401 I
cafeminella@widener.edu
FEMINO, Donny 978-232-5201 209 B
dfemino@endicott.edu
FEML, Nicole, A 315-267-2128 318 D
conantna@potsdam.edu
FENCSIK, Alissa 510-204-0727 37 A
afencsik@cdsp.edu
FENDER, Samantha 828-689-1126 330 H
sfender@mhu.edu
FENDERS, Nancy 207-941-7153 194 D
fendersn@husson.edu
FENDRICH, Chris 719-549-2054 79 G
chris.fendrich@csupueblo.edu
FENERCI, Sercan 617-936-1998 214 A
sfenerci@bhcc.edu
FENG, Alice 858-784-8469 63 F
FENG, Jin 641-269-4464 166 D
fengjin@grinnell.edu
FENG, Xiaodong 916-686-7400 29 G
FENG, Xiaodong 916-686-8066 29 G
FENLASON, Julie 320-762-4531 236 G
julief@alextech.edu
FENLASON, Laurie 413-585-2170 218 D
lfenlaso@smith.edu
FENLON, Matt 617-287-5000 211 E
matt.fenlon@umb.edu
FENNEBERG, Leanna 609-896-5313 280 D
lfenneberg@rider.edu
FENNELL, Angelia 903-593-8311 448 A
afennell@texascollege.edu
FENNELL, Barbara 432-686-4250 439 E
bfennell@midland.edu
FENNELL, Catherine 610-896-1221 385 H
cfennell@haverford.edu
FENNELL, Dwight 903-593-8311 448 A
dfennell@texascollege.edu
FENNELL, Katie 740-376-4369 355 E
katie.cretin@marietta.edu
FENNELL, Sabrina 716-839-8228 297 F
sfennell@daemen.edu
FENNEMA, Timothy, G 616-526-7112 221 L
tf27@calvin.edu
FENNER, Felicia 706-821-8320 123 I
ffenner@paine.edu
FENNERN, Nikki 847-628-2521 141 A
nikki.fennern@judsonu.edu
FENNESSY, Sara 352-854-2322 97 L
fennesss@cf.edu
FENNING, Julie 218-793-2463 239 E
julie.fenning@northlandcollege.edu
FENOGLIO, Sharon 314-516-6788 260 E
fenoglios@umsl.edu
FENSKE, Susanne 724-938-4000 394 C
FENSTERMACHER,
Deanne 610-282-1100 382 A
deanne.fenstermacher@desales.edu
FENSTERMACHER, Erin 610-606-4612 380 C
erin.fenstermacher@cedarcrest.edu
FENTON, Jane 952-358-8143 239 C
jane.fenton@normandale.edu
FENTON, Kimberly 716-286-8566 309 F
kfenton@niagara.edu
FENTON, Michael 219-464-6757 162 C
michael.fenton@valpo.edu
FENTRESS, Brittany 209-667-3395 33 D
bfentress@csustan.edu
FENTRESS, Craig, M 240-500-2352 199 A
cmfentress@hagerstowncc.edu
FENVES, Gregory, L 404-727-6013 118 D
president@emory.edu
FENWICK, Brad 620-665-3417 174 D
fenwickb@hutchcc.edu
FENWICK, Garland 540-423-9046 472 J
gfenwick@germanna.edu
FERALDI, Corey 803-641-3280 412 B
coreyf@usca.edu
FERALDI, Patricia, A 716-673-3553 316 A
patricia.feraldi@fredonia.edu
FERBER, Dave 253-879-3313 483 G
dferber@pugetsound.edu
FERBER, David 402-399-2319 265 H
dferber@csm.edu
FERBER, Moshe 718-601-3523 325 Q
mosheferber@ytariverdale.org
FERBER, Paul 636-481-3420 253 G
pferber@jeffco.edu
FERBRACHE, Jeanne 402-559-3937 269 B
jferbrache@unmc.edu
FERDARKO, Mark 770-792-6100 122 A
mark.ferdarco@life.edu
FERDINAND, Jason 256-726-7277 6 C
jferdinand@oakwood.edu
FERDON, Joel 704-991-0261 338 A
jferdon0525@stanly.edu
FEREBEE, Cheryl 678-916-2615 115 G
cferebee@johnmarshall.edu
FEREDAY, Alicia 207-221-4373 197 A
afereday@une.edu
FEREDE, Mulugeta 512-475-6600 454 C
mferede@utexas.edu
FEREIRA, James 864-231-2000 405 F
jfereira@andersonuniversity.edu
FERENCE, Jonathan, D 570-408-4271 402 B
jonathan.ference@wilkes.edu
FERENCHAK, Greg 903-785-7661 440 F
gferenchak@parisjc.edu
FERES, Brandon 303-340-7563 80 C
brandon.feres@ccaurora.edu
FERGEL, Mike 701-349-5421 346 G
mfergel@trinitybiblecollege.edu
FERGERSON, Scott 816-584-6352 257 E
scott.fergerson@park.edu
FERGUS, Roy 516-299-2278 304 C
roy.fergus@liu.edu
FERGUSON, Annette 281-425-6887 438 B
aferguson@lee.edu
FERGUSON, Brooke 540-857-6348 475 A
bferguson@virginiawestern.edu
FERGUSON, Charity, F 270-384-8100 183 D
fergusonc@lindsey.edu
FERGUSON, Chris 209-946-2011 71 E
FERGUSON, Colin 276-656-0349 473 H
cferguson@patrickhenry.edu
FERGUSON, Conner 304-462-6116 488 M
conner.ferguson@glenville.edu
FERGUSON, Darla 321-433-7080 98 F
fergusond@easternflorida.edu
FERGUSON, David 765-285-8971 153 E
dferguson@bsu.edu
FERGUSON, Douglas, J 610-359-7399 381 J
dferguson4@dccc.edu
FERGUSON, Glenda 478-757-5241 127 D
gferguson@wesleyancollege.edu
FERGUSON, Jason 434-832-7797 472 G
fergusonj@centralvirginia.edu
FERGUSON, Jason 434-223-6327 466 K
jferguson@hsc.edu
FERGUSON, Jason 601-928-6230 246 F
jason.ferguson@mgccc.edu
FERGUSON, Jennifer 757-822-7330 474 G
jferguson@tcc.edu
FERGUSON, Joseph, C 915-831-7730 435 B
jfergu11@epcc.edu
FERGUSON, Julie 570-941-4330 400 C
julie.ferguson@scranton.edu
FERGUSON, Karen 304-326-1465 486 I
karen.ferguson@salemu.edu
FERGUSON, Keith 256-233-8215 4 D
keith.ferguson@athens.edu
FERGUSON, Kenneth 540-636-2900 464 O
ken.ferguson@christendom.edu
FERGUSON, Kim 914-395-2371 314 H
kferguson@sarahlawrence.edu
FERGUSON, Kris 620-331-4100 174 E
FERGUSON, Larry 606-326-2042 180 I
larry.ferguson@kctcs.edu
FERGUSON, Lee 903-923-2048 435 A
lferguson@etbu.edu
FERGUSON, Lisa 270-789-5109 179 G
lgferguson@campbellsville.edu
FERGUSON, Lisa, M 740-284-5894 352 I
lferguson@franciscan.edu
FERGUSON, Mark 202-319-5188 91 G
cua-architecture@cua.edu
FERGUSON, Mark 973-290-4238 282 G
mferguson@steu.edu
FERGUSON, Megan, R 605-342-0317 414 C
library@jwc.edu
FERGUSON, Melissa 937-294-0592 356 D
melissa.ferguson@themodern.edu
FERGUSON, Melody, A 253-535-7077 481 C
fergusma@plu.edu
FERGUSON, Nancy 706-542-6147 126 F
nferg@uga.edu
FERGUSON, Nicole 719-549-2210 79 G
nicole.ferguson@csupueblo.edu
FERGUSON, Noreen 248-204-3106 226 E
nferguson@ltu.edu
FERGUSON, Pamela 973-720-2615 283 I
fergusonp4@wpunj.edu
FERGUSON, Paul, W 626-812-3075 26 K
president@apu.edu
FERGUSON, Randi 856-225-6760 281 A
randi.ferguson@camden.rutgers.edu
FERGUSON, Randy 276-656-0229 473 H
rferguson@patrickhenry.edu
FERGUSON, Sam 325-793-4631 439 A
ferguson.sam@mcm.edu
FERGUSON, Sara 423-266-4574 422 D
FERGUSON, Sarah 972-860-4854 433 G
sferguson@dcccd.edu
FERGUSON, Sarah 830-372-8002 448 C
sferguson@tlu.edu
FERGUSON, Shiantal 412-809-5362 395 F
ferguson.shiantal@ptcollege.edu
FERGUSON, Stephanie 575-492-2643 286 E
sferguson@nmjc.edu
FERGUSON, Timothy 859-572-7770 184 B
fergusont2@nku.edu
FERGUSON, Vicki 925-969-2005 40 H
vferguson@dvc.edu
FERGUSON, Vicky 254-519-5720 446 C
vferguson@tamuct.edu
FERGUSON STEGER,
Emily 406-243-6268 263 D
emily.steger@umontana.edu
FERLAND, Chris 478-445-3350 119 A
chris.ferland@gcsu.edu
FERLAND, William, R 401-825-1210 403 D
wferland@ccri.edu
FERLAZZO, Mike 570-577-2000 379 A
mike.ferlazzo@bucknell.edu
FERLEGER, Naomi, A 845-575-3000 305 C
naomi.ferleger@marist.edu
FERMAN, Pamela 716-375-2351 312 F
pferman@sbu.edu
FERME, Valerio 513-556-2588 361 I
provost@uc.edu
FERNÁNDEZ, Camelia 787-728-1515 512 A
cameliac.fernandez@sagrado.edu
FERNÁNDEZ, Ramón 787-264-1912 507 E
ramon_fernandez@sangerman.inter.edu
FERNÁNDEZ HERNANDEZ,
Nivia 787-751-0500 511 F
nivia.fernandez@upr.edu
FERNÁNDEZ-KETCHAM,
Evelyn 718-518-6667 293 F
efernandez-ketcham@hostos.cuny.edu
FERN, Abigail 620-235-4122 176 H
afern@pittstate.edu
FERN, M. Scott 405-682-1611 367 D
michael.s.fern@occc.edu
FERNALD, Julian, L 831-459-4341 71 A
jfernald@ucsc.edu
FERNANDER, Kevin, A 561-868-3143 105 C
fernandk@palmbeachstate.edu
FERNANDES, Brian 845-848-7807 298 A
brian.fernandes@dc.edu
FERNANDES, Jamie 404-894-7162 119 D
jamie.fernandes@business.gatech.edu
FERNANDES, Jane 937-767-1286 347 E
FERNANDES, Kim 816-604-1418 254 E
kim.fernandes@mcckc.edu
FERNANDES, Sidney 813-974-7927 111 B
sfernand@health.usf.edu
FERNANDEZ, Angela 937-512-2917 360 F
angela.fernandez@sinclair.edu
FERNANDEZ, Axel 541-506-6000 372 E
FERNANDEZ,
Damian, J 727-864-8211 98 G
president@eckerd.edu
FERNANDEZ, Dianne 509-865-8500 480 B
fernandez_d@heritage.edu
FERNANDEZ, Edel 507-389-7200 240 F
edel.fernandez@southcentral.edu
FERNANDEZ, Edith 702-992-2358 270 H
edith.fernandez@nsc.edu
FERNANDEZ, Eva 914-674-7138 305 H
efernandez@mercy.edu
FERNANDEZ, Frank 614-236-6504 348 I
ffernand@capital.edu
FERNANDEZ, Henry, B 954-486-7728 112 J
uftlchancellor@uftl.edu
FERNANDEZ, Hilary 212-353-4100 297 C
FERNANDEZ, Jazmine 954-776-4476 103 B
jazminef@keiseruniversity.edu
FERNANDEZ, Jorge 973-748-9000 275 C
jorge_fernandez@bloomfield.edu
FERNANDEZ, Jose 973-684-6107 279 B
jfernandez@pccc.edu
FERNANDEZ, Julie 843-863-7914 406 C
jfernandez@csuniv.edu
FERNANDEZ, Marco 915-831-6498 435 B
mferna56@epcc.edu
FERNANDEZ, Marco, A 915-831-6498 435 B
mferna56@epcc.edu
FERNANDEZ, Marla 660-785-4130 259 J
mfernandez@truman.edu
FERNANDEZ, Mike 615-966-5186 420 B
mike.fernandez@lipscomb.edu
FERNANDEZ,
Rodolfo, J 305-284-4085 112 K
rudyfernandez@miami.edu
FERNANDEZ, Serafin 707-524-1704 63 C
sfernandez2@santarosa.edu
FERNANDEZ, Terry 202-885-2554 91 D
tfernan@american.edu
FERNANDEZ, Vivian 848-932-7821 281 B
FERNANDEZ, Yaniris 413-559-5781 210 A
ymfpr@hampshire.edu
FERNANDO, Gihan 202-885-1829 91 D
gihan@american.edu
FERNANDO, Lionel 910-362-7890 332 F
lsfernando826@mail.cfcc.edu
FERNANDO, Mayanthi 831-459-4512 71 A
mfernan3@ucsc.edu
FERNANDO, Rukshan 626-969-3434 26 K
FERNETTE, Eric 713-500-3110 455 D
eric.fernette@uth.tmc.edu
FERNHALL, Bo 312-996-6695 151 D
fernhall@uic.edu
FERNIANY, Will 205-975-5362 8 A
ferniany@uab.edu
FERNOS, Manuel, J 787-766-1912 507 F
mfernos@inter.edu
FERNS, Nathalie 603-206-8132 272 A
nferns@ccsnh.edu
FERNSTRUM, Ross 712-707-7416 169 A
rfenstr@nwciowa.edu
FERO, Laura 651-690-6358 242 F
ljfero284@stkate.edu
FEROE, Louise, H 914-323-5240 305 A
louise.feroe@mville.edu
FERRAND, Jill 615-353-3305 424 A
jill.ferrand@nscc.edu
FERRANTE, John 516-918-2787 324 C
jferrante@webb.edu
FERRANTE, Regina 860-512-3632 86 F
rferrante@manchestercc.edu
FERRAO-DELGADO,
Luis, A 787-763-3930 510 B
luis.ferrao@upr.edu
FERRARA, Brandi 315-781-3517 301 D
bferrara@hws.edu
FERRARA, Hania 201-692-2381 276 I
ferrara@fdu.edu
FERRARA, Maria 201-447-7236 274 I
mferrara@bergen.edu
FERRARA, Michael 603-862-1178 273 H
mike.ferrara@unh.edu
FERRARA, Victoria 914-674-3094 305 H
vferrara@mercy.edu
FERRARE, Dino 805-898-4018 42 G
dferrare@fielding.edu
FERRARI, Cynthia 724-830-4639 397 F
ferrari@setonhill.edu
FERRARI, Laura 617-573-8157 218 G
lferrari@suffolk.edu
FERRARI, Loretta 212-229-5860 307 E
ferraril@newschool.edu
FERRARI, Susan 641-269-4983 166 D
ferraris@grinnell.edu
FERRARO, Johnathan 419-434-4749 362 D
ferraro@findlay.edu
FERRARO, Michael 212-217-4018 299 C
michael_ferraro@fitnyc.edu
FERRATO, Christy 505-566-3299 287 G
ferratoc@sanjuancollege.edu
FERRAUILO-DAVIS,
Mary-Jo 518-736-3622 300 B
mary-jo.ferrauilo-davis@fmcc.suny.edu
FERRE, Loren 785-670-1794 178 A
loren.ferre@washburn.edu
FERREIRA, David 860-515-3727 85 D
dferreira@charteroak.edu
FERREIRA, David 860-738-6319 87 A
dferreira@nwcc.edu
FERREIRA, Kenneth 603-899-4186 272 G
ferreirak@franklinpierce.edu
FERREIRA, Lisa 619-961-4202 68 A
lisaf@tjsl.edu

FIGUEROA, William ...... 787-758-2525 511 D william.figueroa2@upr.edu
FIGUEROA, Wilma .... 787-279-1912 506 L wfigueroa@bayamon.inter.edu
FIGUEROA-RAY, Kelly ... 651-523-2750 235 F kfigueroaray01@hamline.edu
FIGUEROA-RODRÍGUEZ, Carina .... 787-993-8897 510 E carina.figueroa@upr.edu
FIJAL, Amanda .... 773-702-7659 151 B afijal@uchicago.edu
FIKE, David, J .... 415-442-7059.. 44 B dfike@ggu.edu
FIKE, Janet .... 304-214-8837 487 J jfike@wvncc.edu
FIKE, Nancy .... 810-762-9925 225 F nfike@kettering.edu
FIKE-CURRY, Esther ..... 407-831-9816.. 97 F efike@citycollege.edu
FILA, Jennifer .... 607-436-2491 316 C jennifer.fila@oneonta.edu
FILAK, Andrew .... 513-558-7333 361 I andrew.filak@uc.edu
FILARDI, Salvatore .... 203-582-8800.. 88 F salvatore.filardi@quinnipiac.edu
FILARDO, Amy .... 443-840-5215 198 D afilardo@ccbcmd.edu
FILE, Carter .... 620-665-3505 174 D filec@hutchcc.edu
FILEMYR, Ann .... 505-467-6823 288 A annfilemyr@swc.edu
FILES, Sylvia .... 310-233-4011.. 49 F filesss@lahc.edu
FILIATREAU, Amy .... 561-237-7000 103 W afiliatreau@lynn.edu
FILION, Diane .... 816-235-1107 260 D filiond@umkc.edu
FILIPCHUK, Danielle ..... 567-661-7970 359 H danielle_filipchuk@owens.edu
FILIPETTO, Frank .... 817-735-2221 453 D frank.filipetto@unthsc.edu
FILIPPONE, Anne .... 610-902-8407 379 E anne.filippone@cabrini.edu
FILKO, Jeffrey, D .... 407-582-1709 113 C jfilko@valenciacollege.edu
FILLER, Daniel, M .... 215-571-4705 382 D daniel.m.filler@drexel.edu
FILLING-BROWN, Michelle .... 610-902-8502 379 E mlf57@cabrini.edu
FILLPOT, Jim .... 909-652-7676.. 36 B jim.fillpot@chaffey.edu
FILOSA, Bruce .... 718-951-5366 293 A bfilosa@brooklyn.cuny.edu
FILS, Guerda .... 212-938-5883 319 B gfils@sunyopt.edu
FILS AIME, Andel, P ..... 407-582-1388 113 C afilsaime4@valenciacollege.edu
FILSON, Cori .... 518-580-5355 315 A cfilson@skidmore.edu
FILSON, David .... 215-887-5511 401 G dfilson@wts.edu
FINALY, Roy .... 818-575-6800.. 68 C yoram.neumann@tuw.edu
FINALY, Roy .... 818-575-6800.. 68 C roy.finaly@tuw.edu
FINCANNON, Angie, L .. 260-422-5561 156 A alfincannon@indianatech.edu
FINCH, Amanda .... 607-436-2513 316 C amanda.finch@oneonta.edu
FINCH, Christopher ...... 201-559-6084 277 A finchc@felician.edu
FINCH, Jim .... 626-396-2456.. 26 G jim.finch@artcenter.edu
FINCH, Joanna .... 314-246-7114 261 D joannafinch84@webster.edu
FINCH, Judy .... 503-768-7328 373 D finchj@lclark.edu
FINCH, Kathryn .... 912-688-6922 123 F kfinch@ogeecheetech.edu
FINCH, Kim .... 985-545-1500 188 B
FINCH, Manicia .... 314-340-3383 253 E finchm@hssu.edu
FINCH, Manicia, J .... 803-536-8622 410 H mfinch@scsu.edu
FINCH, Marissa .... 315-792-4575 323 G mmfinch@utica.edu
FINCH, Tony .... 662-720-7304 247 D tfinch@nemcc.edu
FINCH, Tracy .... 870-972-2031.. 17 I tfinch@astate.edu
FINCH-SIMPSON, Hedda, T .... 340-692-4228 512 B hfinch@uvi.edu
FINCHAM, Brian, S .... 515-964-0601 166 A finchamb@faith.edu
FINCHER, David, B .... 660-263-3900 250 G president@cccb.edu
FINCHER, Justin .... 631-632-6265 316 D justin@stonybrook.edu
FINCHER, Ken .... 541-885-1118 374 G ken.fincher@oit.edu
FINCHER, Louise .... 276-944-6342 466 F lfincher@ehc.edu
FINCHER, Wade .... 501-882-8866.. 17 H wade@asub.edu
FINCK, Brandy .... 207-621-3037 196 E brandy.finck@maine.edu
FINCK, Victoria .... 903-586-2518 437 D
FINDLEN, Sean, T .... 207-786-6328 193 D sfindlen@bates.edu
FINDLEY, Lauren .... 256-782-5265.... 6 A lsthomas@jsu.edu
FINDLEY, Mike, T .... 402-280-5746 265 J mikefindley@creighton.edu
FINE, David .... 303-605-5234.. 81 L dfine2@msudenver.edu
FINE, Elizabeth .... 310-453-8300.. 41 K efine@emperors.edu
FINE, Kimberly .... 910-788-6305 337 G kimberly.fine@sccnc.edu
FINEGAN, SC, Carol, M 718-405-3349 296 D carol.finegan@mountsaintvincent.edu
FINEGOLD, David .... 412-365-1160 380 F finegold@chatham.edu
FINELLI, Chris .... 910-962-3787 343 B finellic@uncw.edu
FINGER, Mary .... 724-838-4211 397 F mfinger@setonhill.edu
FINGER, Richard .... 718-960-7825 293 E richard.finger@lehman.cuny.edu
FINGEROTE, Paul .... 510-845-5373.. 29 D
FINHOLT, Thomas, A .... 734-763-1282 231 A finholt@umich.edu
FINK, Brenda .... 626-914-8830.. 37 B bfink@citruscollege.edu
FINK, Ed .... 657-278-2945.. 31 E efink@fullerton.edu
FINK, Ernest .... 718-409-5265 320 D efink@sunymaritime.edu
FINK, Gayle, M .... 301-860-3403 203 D gfink@bowiestate.edu
FINK, Michael .... 909-652-6453.. 36 B michael.fink@chaffey.edu
FINK, Pete .... 815-235-6121 138 H pete.fink@highland.edu
FINK, Shaney .... 206-296-5915 483 B finks@seattleu.edu
FINKE, John .... 317-955-6202 159 A jfinke@marian.edu
FINKEL, Barry .... 323-469-3300.. 25 G
FINKEL, Max .... 215-884-8942 402 E registrar@woninstitute.edu
FINKELSTEIN, Ellen .... 646-592-4491 325 R ellen.finkelstein@yu.edu
FINKELSTEIN, Eric, M ... 718-990-2417 313 B finkelse@stjohns.edu
FINKELSTEIN, Jerry .... 212-229-1671 307 E finkelsj@newschool.edu
FINKELSTEIN, Laura ...... 703-526-6861 468 A laura.finkelstein@marymount.edu
FINKEN, Mark .... 303-369-5151.. 82 H mark.finken@plattcolorado.edu
FINLAY, Amy .... 313-593-5151 231 B akaraban@umich.edu
FINLAY, Stephen .... 580-387-7303 366 E sfinlay@mscok.edu
FINLAYSON, Al .... 218-733-7600 238 A alan.finlayson@lsc.edu
FINLAYSON, Alexander (Sandy) ...... 215-572-3823 401 G sfinlayson@wts.edu
FINLAYSON, Jeanne ...... 508-565-1337 218 F jfinlayson@stonehill.edu
FINLAYSON, Matthew .... 860-701-3540.. 88 C finlayson_m@mitchell.edu
FINLEY, Adam .... 817-598-8831 457 C afinley@wc.edu
FINLEY, Allison .... 850-973-1613 104 K finleya@nfc.edu
FINLEY, Brad .... 309-694-8557 138 I bfinley@icc.edu
FINLEY, Bryan .... 212-659-7200 303 E bfinley@tkc.edu
FINLEY, David .... 229-931-2068 125 C dfinley@southgatech.edu
FINLEY, David, R .... 231-348-6601 228 D dfinley@ncmich.edu
FINLEY, Gerald .... 662-846-4740 245 A gfinley@deltastate.edu
FINLEY, Janene, R .... 563-333-6177 169 D finleyjanener@sau.edu
FINLEY, Jerry .... 806-716-2340 443 A jfinley@southplainscollege.edu
FINLEY, Lisa .... 276-656-0230 473 H lfinley@patrickhenry.edu
FINLEY, Rebecca .... 215-503-9000 398 G rebecca.finley@jefferson.edu
FINLEY, Terence .... 314-340-5770 253 E finleyt@hssu.edu
FINN, Alan .... 765-285-1033 153 E atfinn@bsu.edu
FINN, Alicia, A .... 603-641-7600 273 C afinn@anselm.edu
FINN, Anna .... 831-459-3276.. 71 A annaf@ucsc.edu
FINN, Erin .... 215-503-1040 398 G erin.finn@jefferson.edu
FINN, Erin, M .... 215-503-1040 398 G erin.finn@jefferson.edu
FINN, Janice .... 267-620-4112 378 E finn@arcadia.edu
FINN, Kevin .... 248-204-4100 226 E kfinn@ltu.edu
FINN, Laurie Ann .... 757-352-4036 469 D lfinn@regent.edu
FINN, Mary, A .... 517-355-2192 227 C mfinn@msu.edu
FINN, Mary Beth .... 801-883-8336 458 B
FINN, Nancy .... 617-585-0200 206 E nancy.finn@the-bac.edu
FINN, Nathan .... 864-977-7011 410 A nathan.finn@ngu.edu
FINN, Troy .... 603-862-1234 273 H troy.finn@unh.edu
FINN, William .... 708-974-5727 144 G finn@morainevalley.edu
FINNEGAN, John .... 612-625-1179 242 K finne001@umn.edu
FINNEGAN, Lorna .... 708-216-5448 142 G lfinnegan2@luc.edu
FINNEGAN, Paul, J .... 617-495-1000 210 B
FINNEGAN, Robert .... 802-828-2800 463 A rjf12090@ccv.vsc.edu
FINNEL, Kristen .... 360-442-2501 480 E kfinnel@lowercolumbia.edu
FINNELL, JoRene .... 831-646-4272.. 52 H jfinnell@mpc.edu
FINNELLY, Ryan .... 210-999-8490 451 B rfinnell@trinity.edu
FINNEMORE, Cathi .... 207-236-8581 195 H cfinnemore@mainemedia.edu
FINNEN, Mary .... 646-660-6549 292 F mary.finnen@baruch.cuny.edu
FINNERAN, Christina, M .... 207-725-3897 194 A cfinnera@bowdoin.edu
FINNERN, Julie .... 651-638-6400 233 J j-finnern@bethel.edu
FINNERTY, Bob .... 585-475-4733 312 A refuns@rit.edu
FINNERTY, James, M .... 716-878-4324 317 C finnerjm@buffalostate.edu
FINNEY, Andy .... 208-769-3266 132 A andy_finney@nic.edu
FINNEY, George .... 214-768-3950 443 G gfinney@smu.edu
FINNEY, Jennifer .... 979-230-3395 431 A jennifer.finney@brazosport.edu
FINNEY, Lesley, M .... 717-361-1445 383 B finneylm@etown.edu
FINNEY, Malcolm .... 562-985-5212.. 32 A malcolm.finney@csulb.edu
FINNEY, Sarah .... 206-296-6962 483 B sfinney@seattleu.edu
FINNEY, Terry .... 870-972-2398.. 17 I tfinney@astate.edu
FINNIN, Meredith .... 212-752-1530 303 G meredith.finnin@limcollege.edu
FINO, Danielle .... 508-289-3624 220 B dfino@whoi.edu
FINO, Mike .... 760-757-2121.. 52 G mfino@miracosta.edu
FINO, Mireli, W .... 617-474-3250 212 A mireli.fino@umassmed.edu
FINTON, Tabby .... 612-343-4743 241 O tjfinton@northcentral.edu
FINUF, Danny, D .... 304-326-1522 486 I dan.finuf@salemu.edu
FIOCCHI, Robbie .... 509-420-4545 481 D robbie@gather4him.net
FIOCHETTA, Joe .... 215-489-2927 381 K joe.fiochetta@delval.edu
FIORE, Douglas, J .... 515-643-6600 168 B dfiore@mercydesmoines.org
FIORE, Elizabeth .... 914-323-5171 305 A elizabeth.fiore@mville.edu
FIORE, Francesca .... 516-686-7403 308 H ffiore@nyit.edu
FIORE, Linda .... 215-248-7307 399 H lfiore@uls.edu
FIORE, Maria .... 703-993-4739 466 J mfiore1@gmu.edu
FIORE, Susan .... 718-289-5913 292 H susan.fiore@bcc.cuny.edu
FIORE CONTE, Johann .. 607-777-2221 315 E jmfconte@binghamton.edu
FIORELLA, Cynthia .... 270-686-4445 182 C cindy.fiorella@kctcs.edu
FIORELLO, Laury .... 479-968-0300.. 18 E lfiorello@atu.edu
FIORENTINO, Chris .... 610-436-6973 394 F cfiorentino@wcupa.edu
FIORENZA, Jennifer ...... 863-298-6845 106 A jfiorenza@polk.edu
FIORENZA, Keren .... 515-271-3918 165 F keren.fiorenza@drake.edu
FIPPS, Corey, C .... 606-474-3137 180 G ccfipps@kcu.edu
FIRE, David .... 785-749-8443 174 A david.fire@bie.edu
FIREBAUGH, Samarra .... 410-293-1586 502 I firebaug@usna.edu
FIREMAN, Gary .... 617-305-6368 218 G gfireman@suffolk.edu
FIRESTONE, Lauren, A .. 717-544-9051 383 G lauren.firestone@fandm.edu
FIRMIN, RET., Lisa, C .. 210-458-6097 455 B lisa.firmin@utsa.edu
FIROZA, Karin .... 617-353-2000 207 C
FIRSDON, Jodi .... 419-434-6914 362 D firsdon@findlay.edu
FIRTH, Ann, M .... 574-631-9164 161 G firth.2@nd.edu
FISCELLA, Elizabeth .... 413-662-5591 212 F elizabeth.fiscella@mcla.edu
FISCHER, Ashley .... 580-327-8601 367 A affischer@nwosu.edu
FISCHER, Barry .... 212-217-3560 299 C barry_fischer@fitnyc.edu
FISCHER, Beth .... 336-334-3876 342 D beth.fischer@uncg.edu
FISCHER, Bruce .... 618-545-3173 141 C bfischer@kaskaskia.edu
FISCHER, III, Charles .... 412-924-1362 395 G cfischer@pts.edu
FISCHER, Daniel .... 254-526-1116 431 E daniel.fischer@ctcd.edu
FISCHER, Gabriella .... 865-251-1800 422 G gfischer@south.edu
FISCHER, OSU, Helena . 270-686-4248 179 F helena.fischer@brescia.edu
FISCHER, Holly .... 563-884-5257 169 C holly.fischer@palmer.edu
FISCHER, Katie .... 651-641-8278 235 A laviolette@csp.edu
FISCHER, Lisa, C .... 716-888-2995 291 M fischer7@canisius.edu
FISCHER, Luke .... 319-895-4133 164 E lfischer@cornellcollege.edu
FISCHER, Mark, T .... 585-275-3340 323 E mfische8@ur.rochester.edu
FISCHER, Marsha .... 573-884-3222 260 B fischermb@umsystem.edu
FISCHER, Marsha, B ..... 573-882-2148 260 C fischermb@missouri.edu
FISCHER, Megan .... 605-367-4624 416 B megan.fischer@southeasttech.edu
FISCHER, Melissa .... 614-825-6255 347 C mfischer@aiam.edu
FISCHER, Michael .... 207-646-9282 195 F mfischer@yccc.edu
FISCHER, Paige .... 580-327-8533 367 A plfischer@nwosu.edu
FISCHER, Rachel .... 619-482-6369.. 65 K rfischer@swccd.edu
FISCHER, Rachel .... 619-482-6315.. 65 K rfischer@swccd.edu
FISCHER, Rachel .... 414-930-3195 493 E fischerr@mtmary.edu
FISCHER, Robert .... 270-745-2297 186 A robert.fischer@wku.edu

FISCHER, Samuel 718-302-7500 326 A
FISCHER, Sharon, P 920-923-7617 492 D spfischer85@marianuniversity.edu
FISCHER, Stacy 973-408-3047 276 B sfischer@drew.edu
FISCHER, Suzie 712-279-5405 163 H suzie.fischer@briarcliff.edu
FISCHER, Tammi 620-227-9262 173 A tfischer@dc3.edu
FISCHER, Tracy, A 414-410-4266 490 J tafischer@stritch.edu
FISCHER, William, M 937-229-3682 362 C wfischer1@udayton.edu
FISCHER-FREE, Todd 815-226-3385 147 J tfree@rockford.edu
FISCHER-SMITH, Jeffrey 510-849-8200 55 F
FISCUS, Tricia 406-447-6926 263 F tricia.fiscus@helenacollege.edu
FISER, Harvey 601-974-1000 246 C
FISH, Jacqueline 843-863-7504 406 C jfish@csuniv.edu
FISHBACH, Alisa 909-607-2593 57 K alisa.fishbach@pomona.edu
FISHBACK, Lauren 559-730-3921 39 C laurenfi@cos.edu
FISHBANE, Simcha 646-565-6000 322 B simcha.fishbane@touro.edu
FISHBANE, Simcha 646-565-6000 322 C simcha.fishbane@touro.edu
FISHBURN, Erin 509-542-4436 478 B efishburn@columbiabasin.edu
FISHBURN, Jill 785-227-3380 171 H fishburnjd@bethanylb.edu
FISHER, Amy 479-524-7128 20 C afisher@jbu.edu
FISHER, Andrew 603-271-6484 272 C
FISHER, Anne, E 941-487-4254 110 C fisher@ncf.edu
FISHER, Anthony 912-525-5000 124 G afisher@scad.edu
FISHER, Barrett 651-638-6083 233 J fisbar@bethel.edu
FISHER, Barry 620-450-2179 176 I barryf@prattcc.edu
FISHER, Beth 901-722-3285 422 I bfisher@sco.edu
FISHER, Bill 571-483-8002 93 F
FISHER, Brock 201-447-7100 274 I bfisher1@bergen.edu
FISHER, Bryan 479-968-0674 18 E pfisher1@atu.edu
FISHER, Carol 405-609-6622 365 F
FISHER, Courtney 870-762-3105 17 F cfisher@smail.anc.edu
FISHER, Craig 325-674-4985 427 G cdf11a@acu.edu
FISHER, Dalene 918-335-6217 368 E dfisher@okwu.edu
FISHER, David 918-540-6233 366 F dfisher@neo.edu
FISHER, David, A 864-242-5100 405 H
FISHER, Dawn 940-397-4787 439 F dawn.fisher@msutexas.edu
FISHER, D'Andre 206-934-3655 482 F dandre.fisher@seattlecolleges.edu
FISHER, Ed 202-885-2167 91 D edfisher@american.edu
FISHER, Edward 714-872-5692 51 D efisher@ketchum.edu
FISHER, Ellen 505-277-6128 288 C vpr@unm.edu
FISHER, Ellen 212-472-1500 309 B academicaffairs@nysid.edu
FISHER, Emily 501-812-2366 23 E efisher@uaptc.edu
FISHER, Emily 404-727-6719 118 D emily.fisher@emory.edu
FISHER, Emily 405-733-7300 369 D efisher@rose.edu
FISHER, Eric 806-742-2985 450 C eric.fisher@ttu.edu
FISHER, Howard 903-927-0183 457 I hlfisher@wileyc.edu
FISHER, Jami 479-964-0543 18 E jfisher26@atu.edu
FISHER, Jane 516-877-3220 288 L fisher2@adelphi.edu
FISHER, Jay 931-598-1142 422 F jafisher@sewanee.edu
FISHER, Jen 317-921-4885 158 A jfisher147@ivytech.edu
FISHER, Jennifer, L 304-293-8531 489 E jennifer.fisher@mail.wvu.edu
FISHER, Jeremy, M 402-280-3819 265 J jfisher@creighton.edu
FISHER, Johanna 661-489-5026 47 D johanna.fisher@kccd.edu
FISHER, Joseph, B 210-690-9000 436 A jfisher@hallmarkuniversity.edu
FISHER, Joseph, E 901-322-0120 416 E
FISHER, Joy 208-885-4000 132 C joyfish@uidaho.edu
FISHER, Judith 269-471-3470 220 H jfisher@andrews.edu
FISHER, Julie 410-857-2218 200 D jfisher@mcdaniel.edu
FISHER, Katie 828-328-7247 330 B katie.fisher@lr.edu
FISHER, Kristie 641-844-5720 167 C kristie.fisher@iavalley.edu
FISHER, Kristie 641-752-4643 167 E
FISHER, Kyle 270-534-3086 182 G kyle.fisher@kctcs.edu
FISHER, Kyle 954-262-2119 104 M kfisher@nova.edu
FISHER, L. Dean 208-732-6220 131 B deanfisher@csi.edu
FISHER, Lee 216-687-2300 350 G l.fisher@law.csuohio.edu
FISHER, Lisa 405-945-9185 368 C lisa.fisher@okstate.edu
FISHER, Marc 510-642-3507 68 N
FISHER, Maurissa 503-330-5012 373 G maurissa.fisher@mtangel.edu
FISHER, Michael 440-525-7788 354 L mfisher@lakelandcc.edu
FISHER, Michael 707-826-3646 30 A mdf15@humboldt.edu
FISHER, Michael 541-383-7755 371 I mfisher@cocc.edu
FISHER, Michael 858-785-1458 299 E michael.fisher@flcc.edu
FISHER, Nevan 585-389-2370 307 D nfisher2@naz.edu
FISHER, Nichole 817-257-7237 447 H nichole.fisher@tcu.edu
FISHER, Patsy 781-736-4107 207 D fpfisher@brandeis.edu
FISHER, Patti, J 574-807-7625 153 G patti.fisher@betheluniversity.edu
FISHER, Rebecca 877-248-6724 12 M rfisher@hmu.edu
FISHER, Robert 859-344-4066 184 G fisherr@thomasmore.edu
FISHER, Robert 507-457-6658 242 H rfisher@smumn.edu
FISHER, Russell 859-846-5400 183 G fisher-russell@aramark.com
FISHER, Ryan 901-678-2350 426 A rfisher3@memphis.edu
FISHER, Susan 814-262-3833 393 A sfisher@pennhighlands.edu
FISHER, Tabor 315-445-4256 303 F fisherct@lemoyne.edu
FISHER, Tammy 661-824-2977 53 H tfisher@ntps.edu
FISHER, Thomas 574-520-4207 157 C fishert@iu.edu
FISHER, Tom 505-323-9282 457 B twfisher@wbu.edu
FISHER, Venus 505-922-2889 285 G
FISHER, Witney 864-592-4620 411 E fisherw@sccsc.edu
FISHER, Yasmin 518-783-2335 314 K yfisher@siena.edu
FISHER-BAMMER, Doreen 717-221-1309 385 A dmfisher@hacc.edu
FISHER-EGGE, Anita 507-222-5478 234 C afisheregge@carleton.edu
FISHER GARDIAL, Sarah 615-460-6175 417 B sarah.gardial@belmont.edu
FISHMAN, Ann 904-620-2514 111 A ann.fishman@unf.edu
FISHMAN, David 845-406-4308 325 C
FISHMAN, Moshe 718-972-3772 297 B
FISHMAN, Yisroel 718-645-0536 306 F
FISHNER, Carrie, J 607-746-4635 320 A fishnecj@delhi.edu
FISK, Cheryl 651-638-6043 233 J caf74526@bethel.edu
FISK, Cheryl 952-446-4172 235 B fiskc@crown.edu
FISK, Deanna 815-280-2701 140 I dfisk@jjc.edu
FISK, Gerald 716-673-3101 316 A gerald.fisk@fredonia.edu
FISK, Janessa 724-266-3838 399 F janessa.fisk@tsm.edu
FISK, Justin 724-266-3838 399 F justin.fisk@tsm.edu
FISK, Mitch 952-446-4142 235 B fiskm@crown.edu
FISKE, Joshua, A 315-268-6718 295 E jfiske@clarkson.edu
FISS, Beverly, J 618-235-2700 150 B beverly.fiss@swic.edu
FISTER, K. Renee 270-809-2491 184 A kfister@murraystate.edu
FISTER-TUCKER, Mary 606-783-2053 183 H m.fister@moreheadstate.edu
FITCH, Brent 303-753-6046 83 C bfitch@rmcad.edu
FITCH, CD 620-862-5252 171 E cd.fitch@barclaycollege.edu
FITCH, Gene 972-883-6236 454 D gene.fitch@utdallas.edu
FITCH, James 814-332-2381 378 A jfitch@allegheny.edu
FITCH, Marilyn 919-573-5350 340 A mfitch@shepherds.edu
FITCH, Megan 610-896-2958 385 H mfitch@haverford.edu
FITCH, Michelle 712-279-3503 169 E michelle.fitch@stlukescollege.edu
FITCH, Poppy 858-513-9240 16 I poppy.fitch@ashford.edu
FITE, Clare 936-468-2401 444 H fitec@sfasu.edu
FITE-MORGAN, Amber 256-765-4487 8 E afitemorgan@una.edu
FITHIAN, David, B 508-793-7320 207 F presidentsoffice@clarku.edu
FITSIMMONS, Gary, N 423-775-7196 417 D gary.fitsimmons@bryan.edu
FITTA, Kevin, J 401-456-9885 404 A kfitta@ric.edu
FITTA, Kevin, J 401-456-8000 404 A
FITTERLING, Lori 816-654-7262 253 I lfitterling@kcumb.edu
FITTS, Alex 907-474-7980 10 B affitts@alaska.edu
FITTS, Michael, A 504-865-5201 191 D maf@tulane.edu
FITZ, Franzetta 850-599-3460 109 E franzetta.fitz@famu.edu
FITZ, SM, James, F 937-229-2899 362 C jfitz1@udayton.edu
FITZER, Robert 718-817-0667 300 A rfitzer@fordham.edu
FITZGERALD, Alexandra 410-293-1503 502 I afitzger@usna.edu
FITZGERALD, Barrie, D 229-333-7836 127 C bdfitzgerald@valdosta.edu
FITZGERALD, Brian 603-456-2656 273 A bfitzgerald@magdalen.edu
FITZGERALD, Diedre 406-874-6188 262 K fitzgeraldd@milescc.edu
FITZGERALD, Ed 618-252-5400 149 E eddie.fitzgerald@sic.edu
FITZGERALD, Eileen 978-921-4242 216 F catherine.robertson@montserrat.edu
FITZGERALD, Erin 860-723-0013 85 E fitzgeralde@ct.edu
FITZGERALD, Erin 401-341-3108 404 D erin.fitzgerald@salve.edu
FITZGERALD, Faith, M 757-785-3866 468 B fmfitzgerald@nsu.edu
FITZGERALD, Francis 860-509-9520 88 A ffitzgerald@hartfordinternational.edu
FITZGERALD, Glynis 610-796-8340 378 C glynis.fitzgerald@alvernia.edu
FITZGERALD, Gregory 410-532-5109 201 C gfitzgerald@ndm.edu
FITZGERALD, Ione 312-461-0600 132 F ifitzgerald@aaart.edu
FITZGERALD, James 509-533-3631 478 E james.fitzgerald@ccs.spokane.edu
FITZGERALD, Jamie 253-833-9111 480 A jfitzgerald@greenriver.edu
FITZGERALD, Jim 509-533-3631 478 C james.fitzgerald@ccs.spokane.edu
FITZGERALD, Jim 509-533-7000 478 D james.fitzgerald@ccs.spokane.edu
FITZGERALD, Joanne 585-389-2070 307 D jfitzge0@naz.edu
FITZGERALD, Joseph 314-529-9476 254 D jfitzgerald@maryville.edu
FITZGERALD, SJ, Kevin 402-280-1849 265 J kevinfitzgerald@creighton.edu
FITZGERALD, Margaret 701-231-7131 345 D margaret.fitzgerald@ndsu.edu
FITZGERALD, Mark 208-426-4127 130 F markfitzgerald@boisestate.edu
FITZGERALD, Marty 773-371-5400 134 C mfitzgerald@ctu.edu
FITZGERALD, Paul 814-868-9900 383 C paulf@erieit.edu
FITZGERALD, SJ, Paul, J 415-422-6762 72 I pjfitzgerald@usfca.edu
FITZGERALD, Paula 440-646-8327 363 C paula.fitzgerald@ursuline.edu
FITZGERALD, Robert 401-863-2500 403 A robert_fitzgerald@brown.edu
FITZGERALD, Ryan 806-716-2341 443 A rfitzgerald@southplainscollege.edu
FITZGERALD, Sherry 973-300-2127 283 B sfitzgerald@sussex.edu
FITZGERALD, Teresa, L 786-331-1000 104 H tfitzgerald@maufl.edu
FITZGERALD, JR., Walter, L 208-282-2175 131 E fitzwalt@isu.edu
FITZGERALD-BOCARSLY, Patricia 973-972-5233 281 B bocarsly@njms.rutgers.edu
FITZGIBBON, Cecelia 215-965-4000 390 C cfitzgibbon@moore.edu
FITZGIBBON, James 510-231-5000 46 N james.x.fitzgibbon@kp.org
FITZGIBBONS, SJ, John, P 303-458-4190 83 B president@regis.edu
FITZHENRY, Leigh 541-888-7222 376 B lfitzhenry@socc.edu
FITZHUGH, Clayton 215-503-1418 398 G clayton.fitzhugh@jefferson.edu
FITZMAURICE, Patricia 212-752-1530 303 G patricia.fitzmaurice@limcollege.edu
FITZPATRICK, Catherine 973-353-1882 281 C catherine.fitzpatrick@rutgers.edu
FITZPATRICK, Daniel 304-384-5276 488 K dfitzpatrick@concord.edu
FITZPATRICK, Holly 413-775-1813 214 C fitzpatrickh@gcc.mass.edu
FITZPATRICK, James, D 203-254-4000 87 G jfitzpatrick@fairfield.edu
FITZPATRICK, Jane 606-783-2053 183 H j.fitzpatrick@moreheadstate.edu
FITZPATRICK, Jane, V 606-783-2053 183 H j.fitzpatrick@moreheadstate.edu
FITZPATRICK, Kenneth 209-476-7840 67 D kfitzpatrick@clc.edu
FITZPATRICK, Laura 432-264-5039 436 H lfitzpatrick@howardcollege.edu
FITZPATRICK, Nivla 310-506-4210 56 H nivla.fitzpatrick@pepperdine.edu
FITZPATRICK, Patrick "Fitz" 206-934-3646 482 F patrick.fitzpatrick@seattlecolleges.edu
FITZPATRICK, Ralph 502-852-6026 185 E ralph.fitzpatrick@louisville.edu
FITZPATRICK, Sharon 405-945-3292 368 C sharon.fitzpatrick@okstate.edu
FITZPATRICK, Tamara 209-476-7840 67 D tfitzpatrick@clc.edu
FITZPATRICK, Timothy, J 352-273-1325 110 E timf@ufl.edu
FITZPATRICK, Tod 702-895-5120 270 J tod.fitzpatrick@unlv.edu
FITZPATRICK, Tracy 914-251-6105 318 E tracy.fitzpatrick@purchase.edu
FITZSIMMONS, Debra, L 724-357-2202 393 G dfitzsim@iup.edu
FITZSIMMONS, Joanne 518-445-2324 289 B jfitz@albanylaw.edu
FITZSIMMONS, Katie 701-328-4109 344 G katie.fitzsimmons@ndus.edu
FITZSIMMONS, Linda 207-454-1033 195 E lfitzsimmons@wccc.me.edu
FITZSIMMONS, Stephanie 732-224-2369 275 D sfitzsimmons@brookdalecc.edu
FITZSIMMONS, Tracy 540-665-4505 470 A tfitzsim@su.edu
FITZSIMONS, Orla 914-674-7574 305 H ofitzsimons@mercy.edu
FIVECOAT, Frederick 610-892-1519 393 B ffivecoat@pit.edu

FJELDOS, Calista .... 712-279-5416 163 H
calista.fjeldos@briarcliff.edu
FLAA, Carol .... 701-224-5519 345 F
carol.flaa@bismarckstate.edu
FLACK, Adrienne .... 717-391-3595 398 E
flack@stevenscollege.edu
FLACK, Anna .... 631-451-4008 320 G
flacka@sunysuffolk.edu
FLACK, Tamala .... 315-228-7014 296 C
tflack@colgate.edu
FLADELAND, Diane .... 701-355-8140 347 A
dflade@umary.edu
FLADRY, Robert .... 303-753-6046.. 83 C
rfladry@rmcad.edu
FLAGEL, Jennifer .... 781-891-2740 206 C
jflagel@bentley.edu
FLAGG, Chuck, S .... 248-232-4811 228 H
csflagg@oaklandcc.edu
FLAGSTAD, Paul .... 952-446-4152 235 B
flagstadp@crown.edu
FLAHERTY, Anne, G .... 217-581-3221 137 C
agflaherty@eiu.edu
FLAHERTY, John .... 212-817-7761 293 D
jflaherty@gc.cuny.edu
FLAHERTY, Kathryn .... 843-857-4227 407 C
kflaherty@coker.edu
FLAHERTY, Mary .... 585-594-6533 311 L
flahertym@roberts.edu
FLAHERTY, Pamela, B .... 781-280-3631 214 G
flahertyp@middlesex.mass.edu
FLAIG, Thomas .... 303-724-8155.. 84 B
thomas.flaig@ucdenver.edu
FLAKUS, Zack .... 605-626-3005 415 H
zack.flakus@northern.edu
FLAMER, Keith .... 707-476-4170.. 58 I
keith-flamer@redwoods.edu
FLAMINIO, Becca .... 630-844-5475 133 A
bflaminio@aurora.edu
FLAMM, Andrew, R .... 574-372-5100 155 C
drew.flamm@grace.edu
FLAMM, Drew .... 574-372-5100 155 C
drew.flamm@grace.edu
FLANAGAN, Chris .... 206-517-4541 482 J
cflanagan@sieam.edu
FLANAGAN, Gareth .... 617-451-0010 217 B
FLANAGAN, Hilary .... 206-220-6088 483 B
hflanagan@seattleu.edu
FLANAGAN, James .... 212-247-3434 304 J
jflanagan@mandl.edu
FLANAGAN, James, P .... 603-641-6025 273 C
jflanagan@anselm.edu
FLANAGAN, John .... 510-642-3414.. 68 N
jgflanagan@berkeley.edu
FLANAGAN, Jon .... 414-443-8826 497 A
jon.flanagan@wlc.edu
FLANAGAN, Joseph .... 716-375-2375 312 F
jflan@sbu.edu
FLANAGAN, Karla .... 979-209-7445 430 I
karla.flanagan@blinn.edu
FLANAGAN, Kelly .... 801-863-4848 460 A
kelly.flanagan@uvu.edu
FLANAGAN, Liesl .... 314-529-9360 254 D
lflanagan@maryville.edu
FLANAGAN, Lori .... 314-516-5661 260 E
flanagamlo@umsl.edu
FLANAGAN, Mary Jane . 989-774-7393 221 M
flana1mj@cmich.edu
FLANAGAN, Melissa .... 770-962-7580 121 B
mflanagan@gwinnetttech.edu
FLANARY, Trevor .... 800-607-6377.. 60 C
tflanary@samuelmerritt.edu
FLANDERS, Lorene .... 251-460-7021.... 9 A
lflanders@southalabama.edu
FLANIGAN, Alyce .... 256-352-8295.... 4 A
alyce.malcolm@wallacestate.edu
FLANIGAN, Michael, G . 718-270-6955 294 E
mflanigan1@mec.cuny.edu
FLANIGAN, Rod .... 701-671-2221 346 B
rod.flanigan@ndscs.edu
FLANIGAN, Virginia .... 973-877-3056 276 G
vflaniga@essex.edu
FLANIK, Greg, G .... 440-826-2700 348 C
gflanik@bw.edu
FLANNAGAN, Larnell .... 773-995-3764 134 J
lflannag@csu.edu
FLANNERY, Brenda .... 507-389-9423 238 L
brenda.flannery@mnsu.edu
FLANNERY, John .... 608-246-6052 497 I
jflannery1@madisoncollege.edu
FLANNERY, Kathleen .... 620-235-4769 176 H
kflannery@pittstate.edu
FLANNERY, Kim .... 262-595-2301 495 D
bookstore@uwp.edu
FLANNERY, Patrick .... 517-607-2239 224 G
pflannery@hillsdale.edu
FLASH, Lacretia .... 617-266-1400 206 D
lflash@berklee.edu
FLATLEY, Kate .... 314-889-1447 252 G
kflatley@fontbonne.edu
FLATT, Jennifer .... 912-201-8000 125 D
jflatt@southuniversity.edu
FLATTERY, Tim .... 313-664-7696 222 C
tflattery@collegeforcreativestudies.edu
FLATZ, Connor .... 914-968-6200 313 E
cflatz@corriganlibrary.org
FLAUGHER, Amanda .... 989-317-4760 229 K
aflaugher@sagchip.edu
FLAX-HYMAN,
Cheryl, L .... 850-872-3800 101 O
cflax-hyman@gulfcoast.edu
FLAYTON, Brad .... 605-331-6575 416 C
brad.flayton@usiouxfalls.edu
FLEAGLE, Steven, R .... 319-384-0595 163 F
steve-fleagle@uiowa.edu
FLECK, Alicia .... 860-632-3012.. 88 B
afleck@holyapostles.edu
FLECK, Mary .... 972-721-4054 451 E
mfleck@udallas.edu
FLECK, Theresa .... 636-227-2100 254 C
FLEEGER, Christina, M . 724-287-8711 379 C
tina.fleeger@bc3.edu
FLEEGER, Christina, M . 724-287-8711 379 C
christine.fleeger@bc3.edu
FLEENER, Katie .... 559-453-7121.. 43 D
katie.fleener@fresno.edu
FLEENOR, James .... 478-757-5140 127 D
jfleenor@wesleyancollege.edu
FLEENOR, Rick .... 606-539-4154 185 C
rick.fleenor@ucumberlands.edu
FLEETWOOD, Nick .... 619-596-2766.. 26 I
nfleetwood@ata.edu
FLEISCHER, Amy .... 805-756-2132.. 29 K
afleisch@calpoly.edu
FLEISCHER ROWLAND,
Theresa .... 925-485-5244.. 35 P
trowland@clpccd.org
FLEISCHMAN, Linda .... 704-337-2543 339 D
fleischmanl@queens.edu
FLEISCHMAN, Robert .... 231-591-3797 223 H
robertfleischman@ferris.edu
FLEISCHMANN, Anne .... 916-660-8000.. 64 B
afleischmann@sierracollege.edu
FLEISCHMANN,
Kenneth .... 314-367-8700 260 A
kenneth.fleischmann@uhsp.edu
FLEISHMAN, Michael .... 301-860-4331 203 D
mfleishman@bowiestate.edu
FLEITAS, Dionisio .... 214-333-5481 433 D
dionisio@dbu.edu
FLEMING, A.L .... 229-500-3286 114 F
al.fleming@asurams.edu
FLEMING, Allyson .... 615-327-6235 420 D
afleming@mmc.edu
FLEMING, Amanda .... 910-962-3122 343 B
flemingac@uncw.edu
FLEMING, Andrea .... 419-251-2182 355 G
andrea.fleming@mercycollege.edu
FLEMING, Angela .... 607-735-1893 298 G
afleming@elmira.edu
FLEMING, April .... 239-489-9319 100 G
april.fleming@fsw.edu
FLEMING, Candace, C .. 973-655-4040 278 C
flemingc@montclair.edu
FLEMING, David .... 269-782-1201 230 D
dfleming@swmich.edu
FLEMING, David .... 540-654-1058 471 B
dflemin3@umw.edu
FLEMING, Drew .... 269-965-3931 225 D
flemingd@kellogg.edu
FLEMING, Elizabeth .... 413-565-1000 205 I
lfleming@baypath.edu
FLEMING, Ian .... 678-872-8007 119 C
ifleming@highlands.edu
FLEMING,
J. Christopher .... 757-683-3603 468 C
jcflemin@odu.edu
FLEMING, Jennifer .... 479-498-6020.. 18 E
jfleming@atu.edu
FLEMING, John .... 512-245-2308 449 G
jf18@txstate.edu
FLEMING, OP,
John Mary .... 615-256-5486 416 G
education@op-tn.org
FLEMING, Julie .... 704-406-4491 328 I
jcfleming@gardner-webb.edu
FLEMING, Justin .... 507-786-3615 242 I
flemingj@stolaf.edu
FLEMING, Katherine .... 212-998-3660 309 D
katherine.fleming@nyu.edu
FLEMING, Kelli .... 304-358-2000 486 E
kelli.fleming@future.edu
FLEMING, Kevin .... 951-739-7880.. 59 C
kevin.fleming@norcocollege.edu
FLEMING, Kirsten .... 970-351-1890.. 84 D
FLEMING, Lora .... 619-849-2298.. 57 J
lfleming@pointloma.edu
FLEMING, Lyesha, J .... 570-422-3896 393 F
lfleming@esu.edu
FLEMING, Mark .... 973-655-5225 278 C
flemingm@montclair.edu
FLEMING, Patrick .... 919-807-7100 331 I
FLEMING, Philip .... 714-484-7394.. 54 C
pfleming@cypresscollege.edu
FLEMING, Rachel .... 410-626-2558 201 E
rachel.fleming@sjc.edu
FLEMING, Rita .... 870-230-5820.. 19 H
fleminr@hsu.edu
FLEMING, Sindy .... 507-222-5439 234 C
sfleming@carleton.edu
FLEMING, Tawny .... 707-826-4273.. 30 A
tb36@humboldt.edu
FLEMING, Tracey .... 773-777-7900 135 D
tfleming22@ccc.edu
FLEMING, Tricia .... 610-526-6001 385 F
tfleming@harcum.edu
FLEMING, Wanda .... 601-877-6188 244 B
wcfleming@alcorn.edu
FLEMING-RANDLE,
Marche .... 316-978-5932 178 B
marche.fleming-randle@wichita.edu
FLEMMING, Damon .... 805-756-1302.. 29 K
dmf@calpoly.edu
FLEMMING, Rachel .... 978-232-2714 209 B
rflemming@endicott.edu
FLENIKEN, Tracey .... 940-668-4207 439 I
tfleniken@nctc.edu
FLENNER, Ronald, W .... 757-446-5829 465 H
flennerw@evms.edu
FLESCHNER, Julius .... 706-368-7732 119 C
jfleschn@highlands.edu
FLESHLER, David .... 216-368-2399 349 B
david.fleshler@case.edu
FLESNER, Brian .... 402-826-8228 266 A
brian.flesner@doane.edu
FLETCHER, Antonio .... 478-825-6304 118 E
antonio.fletcher@fvsu.edu
FLETCHER, Bill .... 502-852-4740 185 E
bill.fletcher@louisville.edu
FLETCHER, Brandi .... 931-372-3317 425 B
bhill@tntech.edu
FLETCHER, Carol .... 575-562-2611 285 E
carol.fletcher@enmu.edu
FLETCHER, Charles, H .. 808-956-6182 129 B
c.fletcher@hawaii.edu
FLETCHER, Evie .... 662-252-8000 248 B
efletcher@rustcollege.edu
FLETCHER, Francis .... 916-608-6500.. 51 A
FLETCHER, James .... 920-424-3030 495 C
fletcher@uwosh.edu
FLETCHER, Jennifer .... 304-473-8017 490 E
fletcher.j@wvwc.edu
FLETCHER, Kiely .... 312-996-5563 151 D
kfletch@uic.edu
FLETCHER, Kristina .... 845-451-1405 297 E
kristina.fletcher@culinary.edu
FLETCHER, Lauronda .... 610-399-2224 393 D
lfletcher@cheyney.edu
FLETCHER, Linda .... 256-469-7333.... 5 I
students@hbc1.edu
FLETCHER, Linda .... 252-492-2061 338 D
fletcherl@vgcc.edu
FLETCHER, Martha .... 615-675-5264 427 D
mfletcher@welch.edu
FLETCHER, Randy .... 321-433-7380.. 98 F
fletcherr@easternflorida.edu
FLETCHER, Rob .... 773-291-6143 135 B
FLETCHER, Scott .... 503-768-6001 373 D
graddean@lclark.edu
FLETCHER, T-Ray .... 812-749-1576 159 E
tfletcher@oak.edu
FLEURY, Karl .... 715-425-3133 496 A
karl.fleury@uwrf.edu
FLEURY, Sam .... 573-875-8700 251 A
FLEWELLEN, Vincent .... 314-246-8250 261 D
vincentflewellen@webster.edu
FLEWELLING, Travis .... 252-246-1210 339 A
tflewelling@wilsoncc.edu
FLICK, Chuck .... 540-568-3825 467 C
flickco@jmu.edu
FLICK, Ethan .... 810-984-3881 230 A
FLICK, Matt .... 937-294-0592 356 D
matt.flick@themodern.edu
FLICK, Zeke .... 641-683-5282 166 F
zeke.flick@indianhills.edu
FLICKEMA, Aubree .... 847-628-1572 141 A
aubree.flickema@judsonu.edu
FLICKER, John .... 928-350-4100.. 15 O
john.flicker@prescott.edu
FLICKINGER, Annette .... 317-921-4341 158 A
alamb37@ivytech.edu
FLICKINGER, Catherine . 516-686-7792 308 H
catherine.flickinger@nyit.edu
FLIDER, Robert .... 217-300-5348 151 F
rfflider@illinois.edu
FLIGER, Jerry .... 409-933-8229 432 H
jfliger@com.edu
FLINDERS, Tracy, W .... 801-422-3142 458 A
tracy_flinders@byu.edu
FLING, Corey .... 619-849-2583.. 57 J
coreyfling@pointloma.edu
FLINK, Janet .... 860-231-5272.. 89 G
jflink@usj.edu
FLINK, Sara .... 413-265-2447 208 B
flinks@elms.edu
FLINN, Cara .... 479-979-1467.. 24 A
cflinn@ozarks.edu
FLINN, Eileen .... 724-805-2897 397 D
eileen.flinn@stvincent.edu
FLINN, Gordon .... 916-577-2200.. 76 C
gflinn@jessup.edu
FLINT, Juanita .... 972-860-4694 433 G
juanitazf@dcccd.edu
FLINT, Mary Ann .... 601-643-8414 244 G
maryann.flint@colin.edu
FLINT, Michelle .... 508-793-4378 207 F
mflint@clarku.edu
FLINT, Randy .... 714-546-7600.. 38 D
FLINT, Tora .... 310-577-3000.. 76 H
registrar@yosan.edu
FLINT, Wendy .... 503-554-2332 372 I
wflint@georgefox.edu
FLINT-HAMILTON,
Kimberly .... 315-229-5011 313 F
kflint@stlawu.edu
FLINTOFT, Rebecca .... 303-273-3050.. 79 A
rflintof@mines.edu
FLIPSE, Vanessa .... 785-628-4494 173 E
vmflipse@fhsu.edu
FLISS, Diana .... 507-223-1317 239 B
diana.fliss@mnwest.edu
FLOCK, Gretchen .... 724-805-2209 397 C
gretchen.flock@email.stvincent.edu
FLOCK, Zach .... 724-805-2660 397 D
zachary.flock@stvincent.edu
FLOCK, Zachary .... 724-805-2660 397 C
zachary.flock@stvincent.edu
FLOCKEN, Lise .... 760-757-2121.. 52 G
lflocken@miracosta.edu
FLOM, Sheldon .... 541-917-4999 373 F
floms@linnbenton.edu
FLOOD, Eileen, M .... 718-990-5741 313 B
floode@stjohns.edu
FLOOD, Kathy .... 619-574-5805.. 43 B
kflood@fst.edu
FLOOD, Michael .... 404-752-1500 123 A
mflood@msm.edu
FLOOD, Thomas .... 718-489-5443 312 H
thomasflood@sfc.edu
FLOOD, Tim .... 760-757-2121.. 52 G
tflood@miracosta.edu
FLOOD, Tom .... 336-278-6549 328 H
tflood@elon.edu
FLOOD-WEINER,
Christie .... 614-253-3502 358 B
weinerc@ohiodominican.edu
FLORA, Heidi, S .... 620-421-6700 175 D
heidif@labette.edu
FLORA, Kristin, C .... 317-738-8784 155 A
kflora@franklincollege.edu
FLORA, William, F .... 423-439-6872 418 D
floraw@etsu.edu
FLORATOS, Mary .... 516-572-7222 307 C
mary.floratos@ncc.edu
FLOREA, Carleen .... 716-896-0700 324 A
cflorea@villa.edu
FLORENCE, Brad .... 563-876-3353 165 D
bflorence@dwci.edu
FLORENDO, Heather .... 808-844-2310 129 G
heather.florendo@hawaii.edu
FLORENTINE, Dennis .... 908-835-2326 283 H
dflorentine@warren.edu
FLORES, Al .... 915-215-4491 450 E

FOLLETT, Naomi .... 530-541-4660.. 47 H
follett@ltcc.edu
FOLLIARD, Peter ...... 605-274-5233 413 G
peter.folliard@augie.edu
FOLLICK, David .... 516-572-7346 307 C
david.follick@ncc.edu
FOLLICK, Edwin ...... 714-533-1495.. 64 C
edfollick@southbaylo.edu
FOLLONI, Laura ...... 508-531-1343 212 B
lfolloni@bridgew.edu
FOLLOWELL, Coleen .... 562-985-4121.. 32 A
coleen.followell@csulb.edu
FOLLOWELL, Wendell .... 859-256-3100 180 H
wendell.followell@kctcs.edu
FOLSE, Dick .... 309-556-3058 140 E
dfolse@iwu.edu
FOLSE, Vickie .... 309-556-3052 140 E
vfolse@iwu.edu
FOLSE, Vickie .... 309-556-3051 140 E
nursing@iwu.edu
FOLSOM, Jing .... 650-738-4221.. 62 K
folsomj@smccd.edu
FOLSOM, Michele .... 716-888-8367 291 M
folsom@canisius.edu
FOLT, Carol, L ...... 213-740-2311.. 73 C
president@usc.edu
FOLTZ, Amber .... 540-869-0799 473 C
afoltz@lfcc.edu
FOLTZ, Kathy .... 805-893-4774.. 70 E
foltz@lifesci.ucsb.edu
FOMENKO, Juliana .... 215-972-2003 392 P
jfomenko@pafa.edu
FON, Lael .... 415-575-6100.. 29 A
lfon@ciis.edu
FONDILLER, Jennifer .. 212-854-2817 290 H
jfondill@barnard.edu
FONFA, Raven .... 845-451-1323 297 E
raven.fonfa@cuilnary.edu
FONG, Chun, M ...... 626-917-9482.. 36 K
chunmingfong@cesna.edu
FONG, Lindy .... 323-780-6738.. 49 D
fonglw@elac.edu
FONG, Steve .... 503-552-1584 374 B
sfong@nunm.edu
FONG, Valerie .... 650-949-7135.. 43 A
fongvalerie@fhda.edu
FONG, Wyman .... 925-485-5261.. 35 Q
wfong@clpccd.org
FONG, Wyman .... 952-485-5261.. 35 P
wfong@clpccd.org
FONJWENG, Godlove .... 936-261-2119 445 E
gtfonjweng@pvamu.edu
FONJWENG, Godlove .... 936-261-2119 445 E
gtfongweng@pvamu.edu
FONNVILLE, Shawn ...... 325-574-7645 457 G
sfonville@wtc.edu
FONOIMOANA, David .... 808-675-3565 128 B
david.fonoimoana@byuh.edu
FONSECA, Anthony .... 413-265-2280 208 A
fonsecaa@elms.edu
FONTÁNEZ, Awilda .... 787-523-6000 506 B
afontanez@icprjc.edu
FONT, Iris, J .... 787-740-4282 509 F
iris.font@uccaribe.edu
FONT-GUZMÁN,
Jacqueline .... 540-432-4398 465 F
jackie.font@emu.edu
FONTAINE, Andrea .... 208-562-3000 131 C
andreafontaine@cwi.edu
FONTAINE, Chris ...... 903-510-2496 451 D
chris.fontaine@tjc.edu
FONTAINE, David .... 315-792-3050 323 G
dsfontaine@utica.edu
FONTAINE, Deborah .... 904-633-8163 101 A
deborah.fontaine@fscj.edu
FONTAINE, Linda ...... 512-492-3014 429 B
lfontaine@aoma.edu
FONTAINE, Paul, V .... 401-865-1575 403 G
fontaine@providence.edu
FONTAINE, Sheryl .... 657-278-2651.. 31 E
sfontaine@fullerton.edu
FONTANA, Janine ...... 641-628-5229 164 B
fontanaj@central.edu
FONTANA, Jeanette ...... 209-575-6498.. 76 K
fontanaj@mjc.edu
FONTANET-MALDONADO,
Julio, E .... 787-751-1912 507 F
jfontana@juris.inter.edu
FONTANEZ, Awilda .... 787-753-6000 506 B
afontanez@icprjc.edu
FONTENETTE, Edward .... 870-575-8410.. 22 F
fontenette@uapb.edu
FONTENOT, Karen ...... 985-549-2101 192 E
kfontenot@selu.edu

FONTENOT, Lana .... 337-521-9026 188 G
lana.fontenot@solacc.edu
FONTENOT, Olufunke .... 478-825-6330 118 E
olufunke.fontenot@fvsu.edu
FONTENOT, Patrick .... 210-486-4431 428 A
pfontenot@alamo.edu
FONTENOT, Roxane .... 337-475-5090 192 B
rfontenot@mcneese.edu
FONTES, Elizabeth .... 845-848-7826 298 A
elizabeth.fontes@dc.edu
FONTES, Marianne .... 831-755-6700.. 44 J
mfontes@hartnell.edu
FONTOURA, Ana, M .... 201-692-2653 276 I
ana_maria_fontoura66@fdu.edu
FONTS, Raul, A ...... 401-865-2754 403 G
rfonts@providence.edu
FOOS, Jacque .... 419-559-2370 361 B
jafoos@terra.edu
FOOSE, David ...... 913-234-0650 172 I
david.foose@cleveland.edu
FOOTE, Amy .... 661-362-3574.. 38 H
amy.foote@canyons.edu
FOOTE, Bruce ...... 815-740-3403 152 E
bfoote@stfrancis.edu
FOOTE, Chandra .... 716-286-8549 309 F
cjf@niagara.edu
FOOTE, Jeffrey, C .... 518-255-5830 318 F
footejc@cobleskill.edu
FOOTE, Monica, W .... 718-939-5100 304 B
mfoote@libi.edu
FOOTE, Nicola .... 412-624-6880 400 A
nfoote@pitt.edu
FORBEAR, Lori ...... 815-836-5498 142 C
lforbear@lewisu.edu
FORBES, Claudia .... 303-352-3035.. 80 D
claudia.forbes@ccd.edu
FORBES, DeChelle .... 410-951-3390 203 E
dforbes@coppin.edu
FORBES, Digna ...... 615-327-6204 420 D
dforbes@mmc.edu
FORBES, J. Thomas .... 812-855-5700 156 B
forbesjt@iu.edu
FORBES, John .... 805-378-1403.. 73 I
jforbes@vcccd.edu
FORBES, Lindi ...... 620-421-6700 175 D
lindif@labette.edu
FORBES, Lisa, R ...... 402-486-2897 268 G
lisa.r.forbes@ucollege.edu
FORBES, Scott .... 713-500-3289 455 D
scott.forbes@uth.tmc.edu
FORBES, Tonya ...... 269-965-3931 225 D
forbest@kellogg.edu
FORBES, Valery ...... 561-297-3301 109 F
veforbes@fau.edu
FORBES, Valery, E .... 612-624-2244 242 K
veforbes@umn.edu
FORBES BERTHOUND,
Diane .... 410-706-7727 202 F
dforbes@umaryland.edu
FORBUS, Amy .... 501-450-1426.. 19 I
forbus@hendrix.edu
FORCE, Daniel ...... 402-486-2534 268 G
daniel.force@ucollege.edu
FORCE, Maria ...... 973-408-3515 276 B
mforce@drew.edu
FORCE, Rex .... 208-282-3848 131 E
forcrex@isu.edu
FORCH, Aron .... 847-317-6400 150 J
agforch@tiu.edu
FORD, Allison ...... 985-448-4002 192 C
allison.ford@nicholls.edu
FORD, Amy .... 580-559-5725 365 J
aford@ecok.edu
FORD, Andrea ...... 202-274-2303.. 94 C
andrea.ford@potomac.edu
FORD, Ashlie ...... 830-372-8064 448 C
aford@tlu.edu
FORD, Beth .... 216-373-5351 357 F
bford@ndc.edu
FORD, Bryant ...... 401-863-3476 403 A
bryant_ford@brown.edu
FORD, Byron .... 360-442-2354 480 E
bford@lowercolumbia.edu
FORD, Cathy ...... 567-661-7398 359 H
catherine_ford@owens.edu
FORD, Charlotte .... 205-665-6110.... 8 D
cford6@montevallo.edu
FORD, Chris ...... 270-686-4291 179 F
chris.ford@brescia.edu
FORD, Christopher .... 434-797-8598 472 H
christopher.ford@danville.edu
FORD, Claudia, J .... 315-267-2184 318 D
fordcj@potsdam.edu

FORD, Daryl .... 401-254-3148 404 C
dford@rwu.edu
FORD, David .... 925-631-4818.. 59 I
dford@stmarys-ca.edu
FORD, David, M ...... 989-774-1870 221 M
se@cmich.edu
FORD, Deborah, L .... 262-595-2211 495 D
deborah.ford@uwp.edu
FORD, Debra ...... 402-280-2551 265 J
debraford@creighton.edu
FORD, Elgin .... 718-262-2135 295 D
eford1@york.cuny.edu
FORD, Erin .... 307-268-2621 499 T
erin.ford@caspercollege.edu
FORD, Glenn .... 503-847-2570 377 A
gford@uws.edu
FORD, Gregory ...... 504-286-5381 191 A
gford@uws.edu
FORD, Henri .... 305-243-5677 112 K
hford@med.miami.edu
FORD, James .... 805-893-2706.. 70 E
j.ford@summer.ucsb.edu
FORD, Jeff .... 417-690-3290 250 K
jford@cofo.edu
FORD, Jermaine, M .... 843-661-8000 408 G
jermaine.ford@fdtc.edu
FORD, Jesse .... 617-670-4536 209 D
jford02@fisher.edu
FORD, Josh .... 575-492-2183 288 I
jford@usw.edu
FORD, Keith .... 661-395-4299.. 47 B
keith.ford@bakersfieldcollege.edu
FORD, Kimberly .... 843-863-7050 406 C
kcford@csuniv.edu
FORD, Kimberly .... 330-337-6403 347 B
ie@awc.edu
FORD, Kristie, A .... 540-458-8418 476 D
kford@wlu.edu
FORD, Madeline .... 718-518-4211 293 F
mford@hostos.cuny.edu
FORD, Mark, C .... 913-971-3614 175 H
mford@mnu.edu
FORD, Mary Beth .... 412-396-2061 382 E
fordmb@duq.edu
FORD, Melody ...... 318-274-6238 191 G
form@gram.edu
FORD, Michael ...... 312-341-2322 148 A
mford@roosevelt.edu
FORD, Miriam ...... 914-674-7860 305 H
mford@mercy.edu
FORD, Nadine ...... 919-536-7200 334 A
fordn@durhamtech.edu
FORD, Pari .... 785-227-3380 171 H
fordpl@bethanylb.edu
FORD, Regenia ...... 865-471-3212 417 E
rford@cn.edu
FORD, Ricky, G .... 662-720-7730 247 D
rgford@nemcc.edu
FORD, Rochelle, L ...... 504-816-4640 186 F
rford@dillard.edu
FORD, Shamika ...... 215-885-2360 389 A
sford@manor.edu
FORD, Sharhonda, L .... 305-626-3103 100 B
sharhonda.ford@fmuniv.edu
FORD, Sherry ...... 970-943-7052.. 85 B
sford@western.edu
FORD, Sue .... 518-264-4334 289 C
fords@amc.edu
FORD, Tami ...... 619-594-4723.. 33 E
tford2@sdsu.edu
FORD, Terrance ...... 972-224-5481 443 E
tford@washjeff.edu
FORD, Theresa ...... 724-503-1001 401 D
tford@washjeff.edu
FORD, Tracey ...... 336-770-3283 343 C
fordt@uncsa.edu
FORD, Tracey, D .... 419-783-2354 351 J
tford@defiance.edu
FORD, Tracy ...... 601-968-8840 244 C
tford@belhaven.edu
FORD FISHER,
Margaret .... 713-718-8011 436 E
margaret.fordfisher@hccs.edu
FORD-KEE, Dianthia .... 662-254-3550 247 C
dfkee@mvsu.edu
FORD-THOMAS,
Manisha .... 314-977-5510 258 H
manisha.fordthomas@slu.edu
FORD TURBOW, Eboni .707-826-3361.. 30 A
eboni.turnbow@humboldt.edu
FORDE, Althea ...... 718-960-8066 293 E
althea.forde@lehman.cuny.edu
FORDE, Christopher .... 618-544-8657 139 E
fordec@iecc.edu

FORDE, Dermot, M ...... 419-372-9475 348 F
dforde@bgsu.edu
FORDE, Dorothy ...... 256-726-7287.... 6 C
deforde@oakwood.edu
FORDE, Kevin .... 701-858-3042 345 C
kevin.forde@minotstateu.edu
FORDE, Nokoia ...... 484-365-7275 388 F
nforde@lincoln.edu
FORDE, Timothy ...... 708-534-7053 138 C
tforde@govst.edu
FORDHAM, Traci .... 971-722-4667 375 C
traci.fordham@pcc.edu
FORDHAM, Traci .... 971-722-5841 375 C
traci.fordham@pcc.edu
FORDHAM, Tracy .... 941-377-4880 104 D
tfordham@meridian.edu
FORDIS, JR.,
C. Michael .... 713-798-8256 430 E
fordis@bcm.edu
FORDYCE, Amanda .... 440-375-7015 354 K
afordyce@lec.edu
FORE, Marilyn, J .... 843-349-5201 409 A
marilyn.fore@hgtc.edu
FORE, Shonna ...... 417-328-1689 258 K
sfore@sbuniv.edu
FORE, Sue .... 252-249-1851 336 C
sfore@pamlicocc.edu
FOREHAND, Cynthia, J .802-656-8060 462 E
cynthia.forehand@uvm.edu
FOREMAN, Adam .... 601-484-8615 246 B
tforeman@meridiancc.edu
FOREMAN, Artie .... 601-635-2111 245 B
aforeman@eccc.edu
FOREMAN, David .... 610-328-8625 398 D
dforema1@swarthmore.edu
FOREMAN, Hank, T .... 828-262-2040 340 G
foremanht@appstate.edu
FOREMAN, Margo .... 508-793-7351 207 F
mforeman@clarku.edu
FOREMAN, Margo .... 515-294-0143 163 E
mrforma@iastate.edu
FOREMAN, Michelle .... 717-477-1475 394 E
mtforeman@ship.edu
FOREMAN, Mika .... 817-598-6354 457 C
mforeman@wc.edu
FOREMAN, Pamela, B .... 804-257-5821 475 G
pforeman@vuu.edu
FOREMAN, Todd ...... 518-956-8120 315 D
todd.foreman@albany.edu
FORESE, Joseph ...... 770-426-2741 122 A
joseph.forese@life.edu
FOREST, Colleen ...... 805-437-8537.. 30 E
colleen.forest@csuci.edu
FOREST, Mark ...... 609-771-2247 275 J
forestm@tcnj.edu
FORESTER, David .... 252-536-7213 334 G
dforester@halifaxcc.edu
FORESTER, David, L .... 252-536-7213 334 G
dforester483@halifaxcc.edu
FORESTER, Erin ...... 706-778-8500 124 B
rforeste@aum.edu
FORESTER, Robin .... 334-244-3676.... 4 F
rforeste@aum.edu
FORESTER, Sherri, L .... 270-901-1115 182 E
sherri.forester@kctcs.edu
FORGER, James, B .... 517-355-4583 227 C
forger@msu.edu
FORGETTE, Adrienne .... 505-566-3217 287 F
forgettea@sanjuancollege.edu
FORGEY, Glendon .... 806-457-4200 435 D
gforgey@fpctx.edu
FORGUES, Chalea .... 657-278-7758.. 31 E
ceforgues@fullerton.edu
FORGUES, David .... 657-278-8351.. 31 E
dforgues@fullerton.edu
FORISTER, J. Glenn .... 817-735-2762 453 D
glenn.forister@unthsc.edu
FORKNER, Peter .... 781-891-2274 206 C
pforkner@bentley.edu
FORLINES, Jon ...... 615-675-5299 427 D
jforlines@welch.edu
FORLINES, Susan .... 615-675-5259 427 D
susan@welch.edu
FORMAN, David .... 410-293-7006 502 I
dforman@usna.edu
FORMAN, Robert, J .... 718-990-7552 313 B
formanj@stjohns.edu
FORMAN, Robin .... 504-865-5261 191 D
rforman@tulane.edu
FORMAN,
Scheherazade, W .... 301-546-0884 201 D
formansw@pgcc.edu
FORMOSO,
Eusebio (Seb) .... 646-664-2365 292 E
seb.formoso@cuny.edu

FOWL, Steve .... 410-617-2327 199 G
sfowl@loyola.edu
FOWLER, Andrea .... 615-248-1798 425 D
afowler@trevecca.edu
FOWLER, Bill .... 870-864-7146.. 21 C
bfowler@southark.edu
FOWLER, Carla .... 828-328-1741 330 B
carlton.fowler@mcckc.edu
FOWLER, Carlton ...... 816-604-4101 255 B
carlton.fowler@mcckc.edu
FOWLER, Charles ...... 865-471-3200 417 E
cfowler@cn.edu
FOWLER, Charlotte ..... 760-471-1316.. 72 G
chris.fowler@csulb.edu
FOWLER, Chris .... 562-985-4121.. 32 A
chris.fowler@csulb.edu
FOWLER, Craig .... 828-227-7282 343 D
cfowler@wcu.edu
FOWLER, David .... 334-386-7415.... 5 D
dfowler@faulkner.edu
FOWLER, Dominique .... 804-257-5219 475 G
dmfowler@vuu.edu
FOWLER, Gregory .... 301-985-7000 203 C
FOWLER, James, R ...... 401-341-2908 404 C
jim.fowler@salve.edu
FOWLER, Jason .... 850-201-7773 112 B
jason.fowler@tcc.fl.edu
FOWLER, Jason .... 919-761-2252 340 B
jfowler@sebts.edu
FOWLER, Judy .... 214-818-1301 433 A
jfowler@criswell.edu
FOWLER, Justin .... 503-552-1517 374 B
jfowler@nunm.edu
FOWLER, Kelly .... 909-274-5414.. 52 K
kfowler@mtsac.edu
FOWLER, Kristy .... 949-214-3064.. 40 E
kristy.fowler@cui.edu
FOWLER, Leigh .... 706-779-8110 123 C
leigh.fowler@northgatech.edu
FOWLER, Liesl, A ...... 309-794-7211 132 H
lieslfowler@augustana.edu
FOWLER, Lisa .... 303-914-6302.. 82 L
lisa.fowler@rrcc.edu
FOWLER, Logan .... 208-792-2200 131 F
ljfowler@lcsc.edu
FOWLER, Matt .... 618-262-8641 139 G
fowlerm@iecc.edu
FOWLER, Michael .... 304-793-6869 489 C
mfowler@osteo.wvsom.edu
FOWLER, Mike .... 502-451-0815 184 F
mfowler@sullivan.edu
FOWLER, Paul .... 337-550-1433 189 B
pfowler@lsue.edu
FOWLER, Paul .... 404-727-0512 118 D
pgfowle@emory.edu
FOWLER, Peter .... 617-573-8000 218 G
peter.fowler@suffolk.edu
FOWLER, Peter, A ...... 518-388-6176 323 B
FOWLER, Rhonda .... 734-487-2587 223 F
rfowler@emich.edu
FOWLER, Robert .... 315-866-0300 301 B
fowlerrc@herkimer.edu
FOWLER, S. Kevin .... 903-510-2307 451 D
kfow@tjc.edu
FOWLER, Sandra .... 530-661-5700.. 77 C
FOWLER, Shaun .... 585-582-1230 298 E
shaunfowler@elim.edu
FOWLER, Sky .... 618-252-5400 149 E
sky.fowler@sic.edu
FOWLER, T. Mark .... 434-223-6164 466 K
mfowler@hsc.edu
FOWLER, Tammy .... 901-572-2774 417 A
tammy.fowler@baptistu.edu
FOWLER, Walter, B ...... 412-365-1105 380 F
wfowler@chatham.edu
FOWLER, Wes .... 319-398-7797 167 H
wes.fowler@kirkwood.edu
FOWLES, Gareth 561-237-7601 103W
gfowles@lynn.edu
FOWLES, Michelle, R .... 818-947-2437.. 50 B
fowlesmr@lavc.edu
FOWLKES, April .... 215-242-7704 380 G
fowlkesa@chc.edu
FOWLKES, Bruce, M ..... 309-467-6423 137 G
bfowlkes@eureka.edu
FOWLKES, Carl .... 410-455-3377 202 G
cfowlkes@umbc.edu
FOWLKES, Rodney .... 937-769-1356 347 F
rfowlkes@antioch.edu
FOX, Allen .... 435-652-7938 459 G
allen.fox@utahtech.edu
FOX, Amanda .... 205-665-6040.. 8 D
foxat@montevallo.edu
FOX, Amanda .... 516-572-7436 307 C
amanda.fox@ncc.edu

FOX, Amber .... 218-935-0417 244 A
amber.fox@wetcc.edu
FOX, Amelia .... 334-514-4018.... 2 F
amelia.fox@istc.edu
FOX, Andrea .... 606-337-3196 180 A
FOX, Andrew .... 314-529-9584 254 D
afox@maryville.edu
FOX, Ashley .... 270-789-5216 179 G
amfarmer@campbellsville.edu
FOX, Bridget, E ...... 724-847-6674 384 B
befox@geneva.edu
FOX, Carole, M ...... 512-463-9471 448 G
carole.fox@tsus.edu
FOX, Charles .... 318-626-1565 189 D
charles.fox@lsuhs.edu
FOX, Charles .... 313-883-8563 229 J
fox.charles@shms.edu
FOX, Christian, A ...... 801-422-8417 458 A
cfox@byu.edu
FOX, Chuck .... 817-735-5030 453 D
chuck.fox@unthsc.edu
FOX, Dan .... 303-273-3000.. 79 A
dfox@mines.edu
FOX, David .... 570-561-1818 397 B
fr.david.fox@stots.edu
FOX, Debbie .... 225-768-1727 186 H
deborah.fox@franu.edu
FOX, Debbie .... 502-272-7777 179 D
dfox@bellarmine.edu
FOX, Deborah .... 785-442-6010 174 C
dfox@highlandcc.edu
FOX, Djuan .... 727-341-3334 107 C
fox.djuan@spcollege.edu
FOX, Donnie, S ...... 606-337-1530 180 A
president@ccbbc.edu
FOX, Douglas .... 325-942-2333 450 B
doug.fox@angelo.edu
FOX, Gary .... 601-936-5553 245 D
gmfox@hindscc.edu
FOX, Glen .... 978-630-9267 215 A
gfox1@mwcc.mass.edu
FOX, Janelle .... 843-863-8052 406 C
jmfox@csuniv.edu
FOX, Jeanne, E ...... 574-807-7243 153 C
jeanne.fox@betheluniversity.edu
FOX, Jennifer .... 252-222-6081 332 G
foxj@carteret.edu
FOX, Jeromy .... 309-467-6394 137 G
jfox@eureka.edu
FOX, John .... 410-455-2591 202 C
johnfox@umbc.edu
FOX, Kelly .... 713-348-4193 441 K
kelly.fox@rice.edu
FOX, Kimberley .... 215-965-4035 390 C
kifox@moore.edu
FOX, Laurie .... 585-245-5577 317 E
fox@geneseo.edu
FOX, Levi .... 417-328-2072 258 K
lfox@sbuniv.edu
FOX, Lori .... 646-313-8000 295 C
lori.fox@cuny.edu
FOX, Mark .... 704-669-4175 333 C
foxm@clevelandcc.edu
FOX, Mary David ...... 864-503-5040 413 A
mdfox@uscupstate.edu
FOX, Matthew .... 413-782-1410 219 E
mfox@wne.edu
FOX, Melanie .... 828-251-6700 342 A
mrfox@unca.edu
FOX, Melissa .... 607-753-2305 317 D
melissa.fox@cortland.edu
FOX, Michael .... 716-851-1639 299 A
ascfoxm@ecc.edu
FOX, Michael, J ...... 207-941-7000 194 D
foxm@husson.edu
FOX, Michael, J ...... 757-221-1693 465 B
mjfox1@wm.edu
FOX, Michelle .... 406-604-4300 262 C
mfox@apollos.edu
FOX, Miranda .... 802-635-1257 463 B
FOX, Noah .... 419-824-3873 355 C
nfox@lourdes.edu
FOX, Pamela .... 540-887-7026 467 G
pfox@marybaldwin.edu
FOX, Paul .... 254-710-2900 430 F
paul.fox@baylor.edu
FOX, Pete .... 989-686-9565 223 E
petefox@delta.edu
FOX, Ray .... 208-535-5378 130 I
ray.fox@cei.edu
FOX, Robert .... 502-852-6745 185 E
bob.fox@louisville.edu

FOX, Robin .... 262-472-5821 496 E
foxr@uww.edu
FOX, Ronald, E ...... 304-336-8021 489 B
ronald.fox@westliberty.edu
FOX, Sabrina .... 308-432-7024 267 G
sfox@csc.edu
FOX, Sandra .... 541-885-1107 374 G
sandra.fox@oit.edu
FOX, Teresa .... 330-490-7503 363 E
tfox@walsh.edu
FOX, Terri .... 540-375-2403 469 G
austin@roanoke.edu
FOX, Tim .... 954-771-0376 103 S
tfox@knoxseminary.edu
FOX, Toyin .... 618-985-2828 140 G
toyinfox@jalc.edu
FOX, Tricia .... 309-672-5957 143 I
tfox@methodistcol.edu
FOX-WILSON, Jessica .. 608-363-2647 490 I
foxjs@beloit.edu
FOXMAN, Philip, R ...... 814-332-5383 378 A
pfoxman@allegheny.edu
FOXMAN, Ruth .... 860-231-5221.. 89 G
rfoxman@usj.edu
FOXWORTH, Derrick .... 971-722-4980 375 C
derrick.foxworth@pcc.edu
FOXX, LaMisa, M .... 919-530-7361 341 D
lmccoy@nccu.edu
FOXX-DAWODU,
Paulette, R .... 301-546-0995 201 D
foxxdapr@pgcc.edu
FOY, Allsion .... 864-294-3464 408 I
allison.foy@furman.edu
FOY, Geoffrey, E ...... 253-535-7126 481 C
foy@plu.edu
FOY, Joseph .... 414-382-6044 490 G
joseph.foy@alverno.edu
FOY, Morna, K ...... 608-267-9066 497 C
president@wtcsystem.edu
FOY, Richard .... 715-425-3505 496 A
richard.foy@uwrf.edu
FOY, William .... 903-785-7661 440 F
bfoy@parisjc.edu
FOY-BURROUGHS,
Wanda .... 704-378-1023 329 H
wfburroughs@jcsu.edu
FOYE, Shanen .... 949-675-4451.. 46 G
shanen@idi.edu
FOYLE, Kevin, J ...... 713-500-4472 455 H
kevin.j.foyle@uth.tmc.edu
FRAASE, Justin .... 605-626-3007 415 H
justin.fraase@northern.edu
FRABONI, David ...... 260-665-4310 161 C
FRACE, Lisa .... 517-355-5016 227 C
lfrace@msu.edu
FRACKER, Julie .... 248-645-3300 222 G
jfracker@cranbrook.edu
FRACTION, Lynette, M .. 651-290-6310 241 N
lynette.fraction@mitchellhamline.edu
FRADEN, Rena .... 209-946-2023.. 71 E
rfraden@pacific.edu
FRADEN, Sarah .... 904-538-1000.. 93 H
FRAGALE, Stephen ...... 518-381-1378 319 G
fragalsa@sunysccc.edu
FRAGOSO, Marcos ...... 210-805-3014 452 B
fragoso@uiwtx.edu
FRAGUADA, Saul .... 718-289-5876 292 H
saul.fraguada@bcc.cuny.edu
FRAHM, Karyn .... 661-726-1911.. 68 L
karyn.frahm@uav.edu
FRAIMAN, Keren .... 312-322-1728 150 C
FRAINIER, Janine, L .... 317-940-9228 153 H
jfrainie@butler.edu
FRAIRE, John .... 831-582-4363.. 32 D
jfraire@csumb.edu
FRAIRE-CUELLAR,
Martha .... 512-245-2367 449 G
mf29@txstate.edu
FRAKES, Jamie .... 870-762-3126.. 17 F
jfrakes@smail.anc.edu
FRAKES, Robert .... 661-654-3986.. 30 A
rfrakes1@csub.edu
FRALEY, Bill .... 304-384-5377 488 K
bfraley@concord.edu
FRALEY, Bill .... 304-384-6334 488 K
bfraley@concord.edu
FRALEY, James .... 217-420-6765 144 D
jfraley@millikin.edu
FRALEY, Meghann ...... 740-245-7267 363 A
mfraley@rio.edu
FRALEY, Taryn .... 806-457-4200 435 D
tfraley@fpctx.edu

FRALEY, Todd .... 252-737-5083 340 H
fraleyt@ecu.edu
FRALIC, Bradley .... 713-348-4927 441 K
bradley.w.fralic@rice.edu
FRALIX, Brandon .... 973-748-9000 275 C
brandon_fralix@bloomfield.edu
FRAMBACH, Nathan ...... 563-589-0207 170 G
nframbach@wartburgseminary.edu
FRAME, Adrienne, O .... 407-823-6960 110 D
adrienne.frame@ucf.edu
FRAME, Brenda .... 507-280-2814 240 B
brenda.frame@rctc.edu
FRAME, Charles .... 952-358-9211 239 C
charles.frame@normandale.edu
FRAME, J. Davidson ..... 703-516-0035 471 A
davidson.frame@umtweb.edu
FRAME, Michael .... 315-792-7400 320 F
mframe@sunypoly.edu
FRAME, Rachel .... 610-799-1034 388 B
rframe@lccc.edu
FRAME, Rose .... 620-450-2169 176 I
rosef@prattcc.edu
FRAME, Sandra, O ...... 304-457-6324 485 F
frameso@ab.edu
FRAMPTON, Danica, D .. 512-448-8418 441 N
danicad@stedwards.edu
FRAMPTON, Travis ...... 830-792-7371 442 G
provost@schreiner.edu
FRANCE, Lucy .... 406-243-4742 263 D
lucy.france@umontana.edu
FRANCE, Melissa, H .... 918-631-2516 371 C
melissa-france@utulsa.edu
FRANCEL, James .... 208-562-2032 131 C
jamesfrancel@cwi.edu
FRANCESCHELLI, James 570-504-9679 384 A
jfranceschelli@som.geisinger.edu
FRANCESCHINI,
Geralynn .... 202-885-2121.. 91 D
geralynn@american.edu
FRANCHAK, Jen .... 513-529-3831 356 A
jen.franchak@miamioh.edu
FRANCIES, Karen .... 281-649-3450 436 B
kfrancies@hbu.edu
FRANCIOSI, Adrienne .... 617-243-2214 210 G
afranciosi@lasell.edu
FRANCIS, Aisha .... 617-588-1342 206 B
afrancis@bfit.edu
FRANCIS, Anthony .... 618-537-4481 143 G
FRANCIS, Charlie .... 402-472-3886 269 A
cfrancis3@unl.edu
FRANCIS, JR.,
D. Morgan .... 336-838-6102 338 H
dmfrancis058@wilkescc.edu
FRANCIS, Diana .... 219-473-4211 154 A
dfrancis@ccsj.edu
FRANCIS, Eddie .... 504-816-4024 186 F
efrancis@dillard.edu
FRANCIS, Garrett .... 620-252-7046 172 K
FRANCIS, Jane, C ...... 213-738-6710.. 66 A
jfrancis@swlaw.edu
FRANCIS, Jeff .... 972-825-4731 444 C
jfrancis@sagu.edu
FRANCIS, Jeffrey .... 918-631-2084 371 C
jeffrey-francis@utulsa.edu
FRANCIS, Jennifer .... 919-613-6814 328 D
jfrancis@duke.edu
FRANCIS, John-Mark .... 270-745-7024 186 A
john-mark.francis@wku.edu
FRANCIS, Kathy .... 240-629-7804 198 C
kfrancis@frederick.edu
FRANCIS, Krista .... 360-417-6212 481 F
kfrancis@pencol.edu
FRANCIS, Leon, J ...... 610-558-5584 390 G
francisl@neumann.edu
FRANCIS, Mark, J ...... 847-467-5456 146 C
mark.francis@northwestern.edu
FRANCIS, Mary .... 605-256-5205 415 G
mary.francis@dsu.edu
FRANCIS, Melanie .... 916-306-1628.. 67 E
mfrancis@sum.edu
FRANCIS, Melissa, A .... 252-940-6236 332 A
melissa.francis@beaufortccc.edu
FRANCIS, Morgan .... 336-838-6102 338 H
dmfrancis058@wilkescc.edu
FRANCIS, Rebecca .... 270-852-3222 183 B
rfrancis@kwc.edu
FRANCIS, Sean .... 410-617-5922 199 G
sefrancis@loyola.edu
FRANCIS, Wilbur .... 661-259-7800.. 38 D
wilbur.francis@canyons.edu
FRANCIS GARLAND,
Kay .... 651-403-4035 240 E
kay.francisgarland@saintpaul.edu

FREDERICK, Tammy ...... 303-473-8046 490 E
frederick_t@wvwc.edu

FREDERICK, Tammy ...... 304-473-8440 490 E
frederick_t@wvwc.edu

FREDERICK, Teresa ...... 417-836-4383 255 J
teresafrederick@missouristate.edu

FREDERICK, Todd ...... 805-546-3118.. 41 A
tfrederi@cuesta.edu

FREDERICK, Wayne ...... 202-806-2500.. 92 E
wfrederick@howard.edu

FREDERICKS, Jason ...... 908-526-1200 280 C
jason.fredericks@raritanval.edu

FREDERICKS, Kimberly . 518-292-1782 312 D
fredek1@sage.edu

FREDERICKS, Rachel ..... 931-598-3208 422 F
rlfreder@sewanee.edu

FREDERICKSON, Cliff .. 206-546-6955 483 C
cfrederickson@shoreline.edu

FREDERICKSON, Derek . 954-771-0376 103 S
admissions@knoxseminary.edu

FREDERICKSON, Joel .. 651-638-6317 233 J
frejoe@bethel.edu

FREDERIKSEN, Jens ...... 615-329-8762 418 E
jfrederiksen@fisk.edu

FREDETTE, Brenda ...... 724-938-4169 394 C
fredette@calu.edu

FREDETTE, Emile ...... 802-728-1292 463 D
efrederltt@vtc.edu

FREDETTE, Melissa ...... 617-746-1990 210 E
melissa.fredette@hult.edu

FREDIN, Alyssa ...... 906-487-2622 227 J
alwood@mtu.edu

FREDOTOVIC, Ivana ..... 305-237-7450 104 E
ifredoto@mdc.edu

FREDRICH, Rachel, R .... 507-354-8221 236 C
fredrirr@mlc-wels.edu

FREDRICK, Kay ...... 605-626-2518 415 H
kay.fredrick@northern.edu

FREDRICK, Travis ...... 803-780-1360 413 B
tfredrick@voorhees.edu

FREDRICKSON, Angela . 402-375-7220 267 I
anfredr1@wsc.edu

FREDRICKSON, Kurt ..... 626-584-5654.. 43 E
kurtf@fuller.edu

FREDRICKSON, Lang .... 323-856-7600.. 25 M
lfredrickson@afi.com

FREDRICKSON-LAOUINI,
Kendra ...... 909-447-2592.. 37 H
kfredrickson-laouini@cst.edu

FREE, Carolyn, G ...... 803-536-8402 410 H
cfree@scsu.edu

FREE, Espie ...... 714-879-3901.. 45 J
efree@hiu.edu

FREE, Rhona, C ...... 860-231-5221.. 89 G
rfree@usj.edu

FREE, Travella ...... 336-278-6259 328 H

FREEBOURN, Randal ..... 904-256-8000 102 G
rfreebo@ju.edu

FREEBURG, Beth ...... 605-658-3850 415 E
beth.freeburg@usd.edu

FREED, Curt ...... 970-542-3105.. 81 M
curt.freed@morgancc.edu

FREED, Doug ...... 309-298-1965 152 I
da-freed@wiu.edu

FREED, Rebekah ...... 402-643-7405 265 I
rebekah.freed@cune.edu

FREED, Sarah ...... 610-436-3411 394 F
sfreed@wcupa.edu

FREED, Ty ...... 812-888-5308 162 E
tfreed@vinu.edu

FREEDLAND,
Gregory, E ...... 717-871-5874 394 B
gregory.freedland@millersville.edu

FREEDMAN, Daniel ...... 845-257-3728 316 B
freedmad@newpaltz.edu

FREEDMAN, Eric ...... 312-369-8222 136 C
efreedman@colum.edu

FREEDMAN, Michael ...... 301-985-7200 203 C
michael.freedman@umuc.edu

FREEDMAN, Michael, J 716-286-8584 309 F
mfreedman@niagara.edu

FREEDMAN, Phyllis, D . 304-326-1390 486 I
pfreedman@salemu.edu

FREEDMAN, Wendy, A . 845-437-5700 323 H
wefreedman@vassar.edu

FREELAND, Brian ...... 304-724-3700 485 G
bfreeland@apus.edu

FREELAND, Melissa ...... 843-792-4364 409 D
freelan@musc.edu

FREELANDER, Geoffrey . 405-491-6396 369 G
gfree@snu.edu

FREELS, Cindy ...... 573-288-6511 251 I
cfreels@culver.edu

FREEMAN, Abby ...... 402-472-9531 269 A
abby.freeman@unl.edu

FREEMAN, Abby ...... 313-496-2997 232 B
afreema2@wcccd.edu

FREEMAN, Adam ...... 813-974-9047 111 B
adamfreeman@usf.edu

FREEMAN, Andrew ...... 585-292-2189 306 K
afreeman@monroecc.edu

FREEMAN, Angela ...... 404-752-1657 123 A
afreeman@msm.edu

FREEMAN, Carla ...... 404-727-6059 118 D
cfree01@emory.edu

FREEMAN, Catharine ...... 319-296-4041 166 E
catharine.freeman@hawkeyecollege.edu

FREEMAN, Craig ...... 253-272-1126 480 F
cfreeman@ncad.edu

FREEMAN, Deborah ...... 209-946-7362.. 71 E
dfreeman@pacific.edu

FREEMAN, Eddie ...... 817-272-2106 454 B
efreeman@uta.edu

FREEMAN, Eric ...... 910-272-3600 337 A
efreeman@robeson.edu

FREEMAN, Gary ...... 402-461-7752 266 C
gfreeman@hastings.edu

FREEMAN, Ginger, C ...... 615-898-2922 421 C
ginger.freeman@mtsu.edu

FREEMAN, Heather ...... 731-425-2602 423 F
hfreeman@jscc.edu

FREEMAN, Heather ...... 225-771-7827 190 J
heather_freeman@sus.edu

FREEMAN, Heather ...... 225-771-4955 190 K
heather_freeman@subr.edu

FREEMAN, Jacqueline ... 517-371-5140 232 K
freemanj@cooley.edu

FREEMAN, Jason ...... 252-789-0304 335 F
jason.freeman@martincc.edu

FREEMAN, Jeremy ...... 315-229-5286 313 F
jfreeman@stlawu.edu

FREEMAN, Jerrid ...... 918-444-2010 366 G
freema22@nsuok.edu

FREEMAN, Jim ...... 417-690-3248 250 K
jfreeman@cofo.edu

FREEMAN, John, H ...... 202-685-3921 501 I
john.n.freeman.civ@ndu.edu

FREEMAN, Jordan ...... 662-915-7211 248 F
kfreeman@sunyjefferson.edu

FREEMAN, Karen ...... 315-786-2404 302 I
kfreeman@sunyjefferson.edu

FREEMAN, Kevin ...... 405-974-2446 370 H
kfreeman7@uco.edu

FREEMAN, Linda ...... 916-900-2850.. 26 H
lfreeman@asher.edu

FREEMAN, Lisa ...... 202-885-1000.. 91 D
lisaf@american.edu

FREEMAN, Lisa ...... 413-572-5204 213 C
lfreeman@asher.edu

FREEMAN, Lisa, C ...... 815-753-9500 145 H
lfreeman1@niu.edu

FREEMAN, Michael ...... 413-572-5300 213 C
FREEMAN, Mike ...... 712-274-5464 168 C
freemanm@morningside.edu

FREEMAN, Mitch ...... 360-416-7771 483 D
mitch.freeman@skagit.edu

FREEMAN, Sharon ...... 662-254-3811 247 C
sharonf@mvsu.edu

FREEMAN, Shawna ...... 206-878-3710 480 C
sfreeman@highline.edu

FREEMAN, Sheila, D ...... 662-685-4771 244 D
sfreeman@bmc.edu

FREEMAN, Sherryta ...... 610-330-5530 387 B
freemasy@lafayette.edu

FREEMAN, Stacy ...... 912-538-3129 125 E
sfreeman@southeasterntech.edu

FREEMAN, Susan ...... 863-680-3952 100 F
sfreeman@flsouthern.edu

FREEMAN, Susan, L ...... 312-942-9511 148 C
susan_l_freeman@rush.edu

FREEMAN, Tamara ...... 706-542-2222 126 F
tjf35176@uga.edu

FREEMAN, Tanisha ...... 940-898-3845 451 A
tfreeman1@twu.edu

FREEMAN, William ...... 360-676-2772 480 G
wfreeman@nwic.edu

FREEMAN, Yancy ...... 423-425-4303 426 D
yancy-freeman@utc.edu

FREEMAN-PATTON,
Dena ...... 310-243-3877.. 31 B
dfreemanpatton@csudh.edu

FREEMAN-PATTON,
Dena ...... 443-885-3344 200 F
dena.freemanpatton@morgan.edu

FREEMYER, Sara ...... 816-271-4287 256 C
sfreemyer1@missouriwestern.edu

FREER, Doug ...... 909-537-5130.. 33 B
dfreer@csusb.edu

FREER, Michael ...... 651-290-6322 241 N
michael.freer@mitchellhamline.edu

FREESE, Jalesa, C ...... 920-565-1000 492 A
freesej@lakeland.edu

FREESE, John ...... 951-343-4323.. 27 J
jfreese@calbaptist.edu

FREET, Dan ...... 314-516-5157 260 E
freetd@umsl.edu

FREEZE, Kimberly ...... 541-956-7117 375 G
kfreeze@roguecc.edu

FREI, Jennifer ...... 541-463-5306 373 C
freij@lanecc.edu

FREIBERG, Brittany ...... 815-921-4502 147 H
b.freiberg@rockvalleycollege.edu

FREIBERGER, Amy, M . 918-631-3727 371 C
amy-freiberger@utulsa.edu

FREIBURGER, Chevy .. 641-628-7637 164 B
freiburgerc@central.edu

FREIBURGER, Lisa ...... 616-234-4025 224 C
lfreiburger@grcc.edu

FREIBURGER, Tina ...... 414-229-6134 495 B
freiburg@uwm.edu

FREID, Laura ...... 207-699-5011 194 G
lfreid@meca.edu

FREIJE, Margaret ...... 508-793-2541 208 A
mfreije@holycross.edu

FREILER, Dan ...... 717-396-7833 392 Q
dfreiler@pcad.edu

FREIRE, Bethany ...... 952-996-1303 233 H
bethany.freire@bethfel.org

FREIRE, Kenneth ...... 952-996-1316 233 H
kenneth.freire@bethfel.org

FREITAG, Nancy ...... 312-413-2411 151 D
nfreitag@uic.edu

FREIWALD, Susan ...... 415-422-6304.. 72 I
freiwald@usfca.edu

FREKING, Lise ...... 651-423-8000 237 E
lfreking@inverhills.edu

FREKING, Lise ...... 651-450-3551 237 H
lfreking@inverhills.edu

FRELICH, Daryl ...... 202-250-2282.. 92 B
daryl.frelich@gallaudet.edu

FRENCH, Alexandra, S . 808-956-5495 129 B
afrench@hawaii.edu

FRENCH, Angie ...... 870-248-4000.. 18 H
angie.french@blackrivertech.edu

FRENCH, Brian ...... 406-243-2565 263 D
brian.french@umontana.edu

FRENCH, Christopher .... 860-297-5204.. 88 I
christopher.french@trincoll.edu

FRENCH, Cortney ...... 603-513-1345 273 I
cortney.french@granite.edu

FRENCH, Dan ...... 409-880-8603 449 B
dfrench2@lamar.edu

FRENCH, Dan ...... 419-251-1967 355 C
dan.french@mercycollege.edu

FRENCH, Daniel, J ...... 315-443-9732 321 D
djfrench@syr.edu

FRENCH, Daphne ...... 912-260-4233 125 B
daphne.french@sgsc.edu

FRENCH, JR.,
George, T ...... 404-880-8500 116 I
caupresident@cau.edu

FRENCH, Heather ...... 314-889-1410 252 G
hfrench@fontbonne.edu

FRENCH, Jeffrey ...... 210-486-2105 428 C
jfrench21@alamo.edu

FRENCH, Joy ...... 303-724-2516.. 84 B
joy.french@ucdenver.edu

FRENCH, Kelly ...... 859-344-3619 184 G
frenchk@thomasmore.edu

FRENCH, CSSP,
Raymond ...... 412-396-5286 382 E
french@duq.edu

FRENCH-HART, Holly .... 318-678-6000 187 E
hfrench@bpcc.edu

FRENCH-HOLLOWAY,
Michelle ...... 310-954-4056.. 52 J
mfrench@msmu.edu

FRENDO, Cristina ...... 313-593-5156 231 B
vatalaro@umich.edu

FRENK, Julio ...... 305-284-5155 112 K
jfrenk@miami.edu

FRENZA, Linda ...... 909-469-5356.. 75 G
lfrenza@westernu.edu

FRERE, Leslie ...... 540-828-5380 464 C
lfrere@bridgewater.edu

FRERICHS, Chris ...... 515-961-1711 169 G
chris.frerichs@simpson.edu

FRESCAS, Christina, C . 915-831-6735 435 B
ccasta16@epcc.edu

FRESHOUR, Brett ...... 724-552-4372 397 E
bfreshour@setonhill.edu

FRESHOUR, Missy ...... 928-523-3611.. 14 J
missy.freshour@nau.edu

FRESHWATER,
Laurie, A ...... 252-222-6281 332 G
freshwaterl@carteret.edu

FRESQUEZ, Julie ...... 951-343-4302.. 27 J
jfresquez@calbaptist.edu

FRESSE, Daliana ...... 787-894-2828 511 G
daliana.fresse@upr.edu

FRESSE, Daliana ...... 787-815-0000 510 D
daliana.fresse@upr.edu

FRETT, Sean ...... 212-431-2100 308 I
sfrett@nyls.edu

FREUDENHEIM, Lisa ..... 617-451-0010 217 B
clfreund@ucsd.edu

FREUND, Caroline ...... 858-534-1946.. 70 C
clfreund@ucsd.edu

FREUND, Debra ...... 860-512-3107.. 86 F
dfreund@manchestercc.edu

FREUND, Scott, A ...... 401-739-5000 403 F
sfreund@neit.edu

FREVILLE, Ben ...... 708-524-6557 137 A
freville@dom.edu

FREW, Jeremy ...... 517-796-8409 225 A
frewjeremy@jccmi.edu

FREW, R. Scott ...... 603-646-6401 272 F
r.scott.frew@dartmouth.edu

FREW, Stuart ...... 706-355-5052 115 C
sfrew@athenstech.edu

FREWALDT, Megan ...... 605-626-3007 415 H
megan.frewaldt@northern.edu

FREY, Carolyn, A ...... 859-238-5275 179 H
carrie.frey@centre.edu

FREY, Eva, R ...... 253-535-7159 481 C
eva.frey@plu.edu

FREY, James ...... 229-931-2039 125 C
jfrey@southgatech.edu

FREY, Jason ...... 773-896-2400 134 K
FREY, Jason ...... 773-896-2400 134 K
jason.frey@ctschicago.edu

FREY, Len, T ...... 870-972-3303.. 17 I
lfrey@astate.edu

FREY, Mandy ...... 605-367-4236 416 B
mandy.frey@southeasttech.edu

FREY, Melissa ...... 304-724-3700 485 G
mfrey@apus.edu

FREY, Melissa ...... 503-589-7652 372 A
melissa.frey@chemeketa.edu

FREY, Michelle ...... 660-263-4100 256 E
michellefrey@macc.edu

FREY, Sarah ...... 209-228-4400.. 70 A
FREY, Steven ...... 936-294-2739 449 E
saf001@shsu.edu

FREY, Susan, M ...... 570-348-6267 389 B
sfrey@marywood.edu

FREY, Tim ...... 402-826-8648 266 A
timothy.frey@doane.edu

FREYBERG, Ian ...... 256-549-8266.... 2 B
ifreyberg@gadsdenstate.edu

FREYTES, Liza ...... 787-279-1912 506 L
lfreytes@bayamon.inter.edu

FRIANT, Jakim ...... 910-362-7212 332 G
jfriant@cfcc.edu

FRIAR, Shirley ...... 334-724-4667.... 7 D
sfriar@tuskegee.edu

FRIAR, Tobyn, L ...... 773-508-7704 142 G
tfriar@luc.edu

FRIAS, Frank ...... 206-546-4613 483 C
ffrias@shoreline.edu

FRICK, Jeffrey ...... 724-503-1001 401 D
jfrick@washjeff,.edu

FRICK, Kelly ...... 302-831-2226.. 91 A
kfrick@udel.edu

FRICK, Lillian ...... 989-386-6605 227 E
lfrick@midmich.edu

FRICK, Richard, A ...... 201-692-2001 276 I
rfrick@fdu.edu

FRICK, Wanda ...... 910-898-9637 336 A
frickw@montgomery.edu

FRICK-RUPPER,
Jennifer ...... 828-641-0298 327 A
jefrick@brevard.edu

FRICKE, Erik ...... 805-965-0581.. 62 M
fricke@sbcc.edu

FRICKER, Ron ...... 540-231-7754 475 D
rf@vt.edu

FRIDAY, Vivienne ...... 860-913-2355.. 87 H
vfriday@goodwin.edu

FRIDAY, Yolanda ...... 909-652-6840.. 36 B
yolanda.friday@chaffey.edu

FRIDAY-STROUD,
Shawnta ...... 850-599-3491 109 E
shawnta.friday@famu.edu

Index of Key Administrators FRIDAY-STROUD – FUENTEALBA 651

FRIDAY-STROUD, Shawnta ..... 850-599-3565 109 E shawnta.friday@famu.edu
FRIDDLE, Adrienne ..... 336-249-8186 333 G adrienne_friddle@davidsondavie.edu
FRIDGE, Rob ..... 417-873-7526 252 A rfridge001@drury.edu
FRIDLEY, Kenneth, J ..... 757-683-3765 468 C kfridley@odu.edu
FRIDRIKSSON, Julius ... 803-777-5931 412 A fridriks@mailbox.sc.edu
FRIEBIS, Michael ..... 607-962-9203 319 F mfriebis@corning-cc.edu
FRIED, Barry, J ..... 608-796-3811 496 L bjfried@viterbo.edu
FRIED, Hindie ..... 516-239-9002 314 J hfried@shoryoshuv.org
FRIED, Linda, P ..... 212-305-9300 296 H lpfried@columbia.edu
FRIED, Marc ..... 785-670-1712 178 A marc.fried@washburn.edu
FRIED, Ray ..... 325-235-7320 448 F ray.fried@tstc.edu
FRIED, Sandy ..... 701-224-2423 345 F sandra.fried@bismarckstate.edu
FRIED-WALKENFELD, Faye ..... 212-742-8770 322 C faye.fried-walkenfeld@touro.edu
FRIEDEL, Kristin, M ..... 315-859-4637 300 F kfriedel@hamilton.edu
FRIEDEMAN, Elijah ..... 601-366-8880 249 A efriedeman@wbs.edu
FRIEDER, Steven, W ..... 414-288-7752 492 E steven.frieder@marquette.edu
FRIEDHOFF, AJ ..... 314-889-1429 252 G afriedhoff@fontbonne.edu
FRIEDLANDER, Michael, J ..... 540-231-2013 475 D friedlan@vt.edu
FRIEDLEN, Karen ..... 414-930-3349 493 E friedlek@mtmary.edu
FRIEDLEY, Margret ..... 360-623-8410 477 H margret.friedley@centralia.edu
FRIEDLI, Deidre ..... 208-459-5025 131 A dfriedli@collegeofidaho.edu
FRIEDLINE, Patrick ..... 312-329-4414 144 F patrick.friedline@moody.edu
FRIEDMAN, Adam ..... 718-687-5546 311 A afriedm3@pratt.edu
FRIEDMAN, David ..... 410-484-7200 201 B dfreidman@nirc.edu
FRIEDMAN, Elea ..... 213-884-4133.. 24 D registrar@ajrca.edu
FRIEDMAN, Elizabeth .... 718-518-4314 293 F efriedman@hostos.cuny.edu
FRIEDMAN, Eric, M ..... 201-447-7237 274 I efriedman@bergen.edu
FRIEDMAN, Erik ..... 312-369-7790 136 C efriedman@colum.edu
FRIEDMAN, Frank ..... 434-977-1620 474 B ffriedman@pvcc.edu
FRIEDMAN, Jay, R ..... 530-898-4890.. 31 A jfriedman1@csuchico.edu
FRIEDMAN, Jill ..... 508-793-7681 207 F jifriedman@clarku.edu
FRIEDMAN, Joshua ..... 305-284-4111 112 K jmfriedman@miami.edu
FRIEDMAN, Melissa ..... 212-280-6001 303 A mefriedman@jtsa.edu
FRIEDMAN, Rachel ..... 562-988-2278.. 26 A rfriedman@auhs.edu
FRIEDMAN, Robert ..... 646-592-6255 325 R robert.freidman@yu.edu
FRIEDMAN, Ronald ..... 260-481-5750 159 H friedmar@pfw.edu
FRIEDMAN, Sandra, V .. 516-572-7326 307 C sandra.friedman@ncc.edu
FRIEDMAN, Scott ..... 708-974-5359 144 G friedmans5@morainevalley.edu
FRIEDMAN, Scott ..... 310-825-8607.. 69 D friedman@idre.ucla.edu
FRIEDMAN, Yaakov ..... 847-982-2500 138 G yfriedman@htc.edu
FRIEDMANN, Jonathan . 213-884-4133.. 24 D jfriedmann@ajrca.edu
FRIEDRICH, Brian ..... 651-641-8211 235 A
FRIEDRICH, David ..... 617-253-2811 215 G
FRIEDRICHSEN, Steven, W ..... 909-706-3911.. 75 G sfriedrichsen@westernu.edu
FRIEDT, Barbara ..... 440-525-7510 354 L bfriedt@lakelandcc.edu
FRIEL, Lydia ..... 215-780-1251 397 E lfriel@salus.edu
FRIEL, Wm. Jake ..... 724-287-8711 379 C jake.friel@bc3.edu
FRIEND, Damian ..... 303-273-3154.. 79 A dfriend@mines.edu
FRIEND, Dane ..... 713-798-1544 430 E dfriend@bcm.edu
FRIEND, Dave ..... 531-622-2647 266 G djfriend@mccneb.edu
FRIEND, Jennifer ..... 816-501-4076 257 K jennifer.friend@rockhurst.edu
FRIEND, John ..... 251-460-7051.... 9 A jfriend@southalabama.edu
FRIEND, Micheal ..... 860-444-8444 502 F micheal.friend@uscg.mil
FRIEND, Ricky ..... 205-348-1370.... 7 G rdfriend@bama.ua.edu
FRIER, Jessica ..... 952-777-3134 241 P jfrier@nwhealth.edu
FRIERSON, Georita ..... 973-761-9022 282 K georita.frierson@shu.edu
FRIERSON, Kenneth ..... 312-935-4232 140 F kfrierson@icsw.edu
FRIES, Ben ..... 269-294-4271 223 J bfries@glenoaks.edu
FRIES, Jane ..... 970-542-3106.. 81 M jane.fries@morgancc.edu
FRIES, Ruth, A ..... 651-628-3241 243 E rafries@unwsp.edu
FRIESEN, Brandon ..... 805-893-8125.. 70 E brandon.friesen@ucsb.edu
FRIESEN, Joshua ..... 864-250-8994 408 J joshua.friesen@gvltec.edu
FRIESEN, Kay ..... 531-622-2878 266 G kfriesen@mccneb.edu
FRIESON, Dawn ..... 419-372-2865 348 F dfreison@bgsu.edu
FRIESSEN, Lisa ..... 580-774-3149 369 I lisa.friessen@swosu.edu
FRIGGE, Maria ..... 334-670-3736.... 7 C lfrigge@troy.edu
FRINK, Brian, T ..... 920-565-1000 492 A frinkbt@lakeland.edu
FRINK, Caleb ..... 304-877-6428 486 A developmentvp@abc.edu
FRINK, Dorothy ..... 219-980-6994 157 A defrink@iun.edu
FRINK, Kandy ..... 307-382-1602 500 I kfrink@westernwyoming.edu
FRISBEE, Robert ..... 620-235-4365 176 H rfrisbee@pittstate.edu
FRISBEE, Stephen ..... 315-792-5399 306 G sfrisbee@mvcc.edu
FRISBIE, Kathy ..... 970-542-3240.. 81 M kathy.frisbie@morgancc.edu
FRISBY, Anthony ..... 215-503-4990 398 G anthony.frisby@jefferson.edu
FRISBY, Anthony ..... 215-503-8848 398 G anthony.frisby@jefferson.edu
FRISBY, Kylie ..... 405-325-3163 370 J kylie.frisby@ou.edu
FRISCH, Kevin ..... 315-279-5889 303 D kfrisch@keuka.edu
FRISCH, Kim ..... 303-458-4909.. 83 B kfrisch@regis.edu
FRISENDA, Louis ..... 703-247-8341 468 A louis.frisenda@marymount.edu
FRISINA, Warren ..... 516-463-4783 301 E warren.frisina@hofstra.edu
FRISK, Madeline ..... 503-725-3000 375 D
FRISKICS, Scott ..... 406-353-2607 262 B friskics@hotmail.com
FRISONE, Al ..... 510-409-7939.. 60 C afrisone@samuelmerritt.edu
FRISQUE, Megan ..... 512-863-1584 444 F frisquem@southwestern.edu
FRIST, Matthew, J ..... 412-396-6063 382 E frist@duq.edu
FRITCH, John, E ..... 319-273-2725 163 G john.fritch@uni.edu
FRITCH, Todd ..... 941-752-5000 109 C
FRITH, Karen ..... 256-824-6669.... 8 B karen.frith@uah.edu
FRITSCH, Denise ..... 859-442-1113 181 D denise.fritsch@kctcs.edu
FRITSCHI, Ramona ..... 717-697-6027 389 F rfritschi@messiah.edu
FRITZ, Cheryl ..... 314-246-7055 261 D cherylfritz49@webster.edu
FRITZ, John ..... 410-455-6596 202 G fritz@umbc.edu
FRITZ, Simon ..... 216-368-2595 349 B srf@case.edu
FRITZ, Ted, P ..... 412-624-0072 400 A tfritz@pitt.edu
FRITZ, Thomas, R ..... 814-472-3006 396 I tfritz@francis.edu
FRITZ, Tim ..... 805-969-3626.. 55 I tfritz@pacifica.edu
FRITZE, Kellie ..... 907-474-6265.. 10 B kfritze@alaska.edu
FRITZEN, Scott, A ..... 405-325-4387 370 J sfritzen@ou.edu
FRITZMAN, D. Jason ..... 304-243-2043 490 F jfritzman@wheeling.edu
FRIZZA-POMPA, Julio ... 619-265-0107.. 57 I jfrizza@platt.edu
FRIZZELL, Douglas ..... 412-396-3234 382 E frizzelld@duq.edu
FRIZZELL, Monica ..... 479-979-1215.. 24 A mfrizzell@ozarks.edu
FRKAL, Robin ..... 508-213-2254 217 C robin.frkal@nichols.edu
FROCKT, Daniel ..... 502-272-8263 179 D dfrockt@bellarmine.edu
FRODL, Kim ..... 715-836-5360 494 E frodlka@uwec.edu
FROEDGE, Claudia ..... 270-384-8519 183 D froedgec@lindsey.edu
FROHARDT, Russell ..... 210-486-4136 428 A rfrohardt@alamo.edu
FROHOCK, Richard ..... 405-744-6799 367 G richard.frohock@okstate.edu
FROHOFF, Katherine ..... 816-501-4151 257 K katherine.frohoff@rockhurst.edu
FROMBGEN, Elizabeth .. 620-229-6223 177 D elizabeth.frombgen@sckans.edu
FROMMELT, Steve ..... 309-796-5933 133 D frommelts@bhc.edu
FRONHEISER, Joey ..... 405-947-4421 368 C
FRONK, Brynn ..... 801-581-5701 459 D brynn.fronk@utah.edu
FRONTERA, Daniel ..... 716-851-1832 299 A vafrontera@ecc.edu
FRONTERA AGENJO, Jose, A ..... 787-841-2000 508 H jose_frontera@pucpr.edu
FRONTERHOUSE, Misti . 719-336-1511.. 81 J misti.fronterhouse@lamarcc.edu
FRONTIERA, Charlene ... 650-574-6312.. 62 J frontierac@smccd.edu
FROONJIAN, John ..... 609-626-3626 283 A john.froonjian@stockton.edu
FROSCH, Jeff ..... 512-313-4105 432 N jeff.frosch@concordia.edu
FROSLID JONES, Karen, L ..... 202-885-6155.. 91 D kfroslid@american.edu
FROSS, Sharon ..... 301-985-7000 203 C sharon.fross@umgc.edu
FROST, Amy ..... 319-296-4214 166 E amy.frost@hawkeyecollege.edu
FROST, Dana, L ..... 864-644-5004 411 D dfrost@swu.edu
FROST, David ..... 843-349-2227 407 B dfrost@coastal.edu
FROST, Donny ..... 479-979-1000.. 24 A dfrost@ozarks.edu
FROST, Dustin ..... 850-201-8484 112 B dustin.frost@tcc.fl.edu
FROST, James ..... 830-303-0404 448 C frost@frostlawoffice.com
FROST, John ..... 402-399-2350 265 H jfrost@csm.edu
FROST, Kimberly ..... 619-482-6309.. 65 K kfrost@swccd.edu
FROST, Leanne ..... 406-771-4372 264 B leanne.frost@gfcmsu.edu
FROST, Linda ..... 423-425-5922 426 D linda-frost@utc.edu
FROST, Mark ..... 518-783-4100 314 K mfrost@siena.edu
FROST, Mary ..... 563-884-5664 169 C mary.frost@palmer.edu
FROST, Misty ..... 770-729-8400 115 A
FROST, Pamela ..... 614-825-6255 347 C pfrost@aiam.edu
FROST, Richard, A ..... 616-395-7800 224 H frost@hope.edu
FROST, Stacy ..... 507-537-6483 240 G stacy.frost@smsu.edu
FROSTBAUM, Stephanie, D ..... 404-712-2155 118 D stephanie.frostbaum@emory.edu
FROUDE, Bill ..... 859-572-5112 184 B froudew1@nku.edu
FRUCHTHANDLER, Abraham, H ..... 718-377-0777 311 B
FRUGE, Alfred ..... 337-475-5183 192 B ffruge@mcneese.edu
FRUGE, Cheryl ..... 337-521-6670 188 G cheryl.fruge@solacc.edu
FRUGE, Courtney ..... 337-550-1201 189 B crfruge@lsue.edu
FRUGE, Jason ..... 973-300-2256 283 B jfruge@sussex.edu
FRUITTICHER, Lee ..... 478-445-5650 119 A lee.fruitticher@gcsu.edu
FRULAND, Bonnie ..... 719-549-2332.. 79 G bonnie.fruland@csupueblo.edu
FRUM, Jennifer, L ..... 706-542-6126 126 F jfrum@uga.edu
FRY, Alyssa ..... 614-234-4760 356 E afry@mchs.com
FRY, Angela ..... 870-574-4523.. 21 F afry@sautech.edu
FRY, Blake ..... 816-604-1412 254 E blake.fry@mcckc.edu
FRY, Casey ..... 509-793-2031 477 D caseyf@bigbend.edu
FRY, Donna ..... 810-237-6503 231 C donnafry@umich.edu
FRY, Eric ..... 307-382-1790 500 I efry@westernwyoming.edu
FRY, John, A ..... 215-895-2100 382 D jaf@drexel.edu
FRY, Justyn ..... 937-376-6386 349 H jfry@centralstate.edu
FRY, Keener ..... 307-766-4166 500 H keener.fry@uwyo.edu
FRY-BOWERS, Eileen .... 415-422-2959.. 72 I efrybowers@usfca.edu
FRYAR, Ben ..... 208-496-1896 130 G fryarb@byui.edu
FRYAR, David ..... 252-985-5222 339 B dfryar@ncwc.edu
FRYDA, Megan, M ..... 308-865-8934 268 J frydamm@unk.edu
FRYE, Brandon ..... 936-468-2701 444 H brandon.frye@sfasu.edu
FRYE, Holly ..... 304-876-5402 489 A hfrye@shepherd.edu
FRYE, Jeffrey ..... 419-434-4501 362 D frye@findlay.edu
FRYE, Karen ..... 910-898-9620 336 A fryek@montgomery.edu
FRYE, Kevin ..... 937-708-5628 363 G kfrye@wilberforce.edu
FRYE, Lela ..... 352-395-5420 107 G lela.frye@sfcollege.edu
FRYE, Ricky ..... 540-545-7338 470 A rfrye2@su.edu
FRYKBERG, Jay ..... 310-342-5200.. 73 E
FRYLING, Andrea ..... 616-988-3639 226 A afryling@kuyper.edu
FRYLING, Michelle, S ... 724-357-2302 393 G mfryling@iup.edu
FRYLING, Mitch ..... 323-343-4303.. 32 B mfrylin2@calstatela.edu
FRYNS, Jennifer ..... 352-854-2322.. 97 L frynsj@cf.edu
FU, Di ..... 954-763-9840.. 95 J fudi@atom.edu
FU, Siqi ..... 856-225-2349 281 A sfu@camden.rutgers.edu
FU, Xuanning ..... 559-278-2636.. 31 D xfu@csufresno.edu
FU, Xudong ..... 516-739-1545 308 E xudfu@nyctcm.edu
FUCHKO, III, John, M .. 706-507-8800 117 E
FUCHS, Caroline ..... 718-990-5050 313 B fuchsc@stjohns.edu
FUCHS, Kris ..... 815-921-4013 147 H k.fuchs@rockvalleycollege.edu
FUCHS, Lisa ..... 402-354-7065 267 E lisa.fuchs@methodistcollege.edu
FUCHS, Tina, M ..... 503-838-8220 377 C fuchst@wou.edu
FUCHS, W. Kent ..... 352-392-1311 110 E president@ufl.edu
FUCHSER, Kathy ..... 402-562-1211 265 C kathyfuchser@cccneb.edu
FUDALA, Amanda ..... 303-871-2394.. 84 C amanda.fudala@du.edu
FUDALLY, Steve ..... 218-733-7600 238 A steve.fudally@lsc.edu
FUENTEALBA, Carmen .. 516-299-3342 304 D carmen.fuentealba@liu.edu

FUENTES, Alan .... 718-933-1604 292 H
alan.fuentes@bcc.cuny.edu
FUENTES, Angel .... 510-464-3224.. 57 B
afuentes@peralta.edu
FUENTES, Angeles .... 831-582-4136.. 32 D
afuentes@csumb.edu
FUENTES, Angelica, M .. 956-295-3383 448 E
angelica.fuentes@tsc.edu
FUENTES, Fred .... 903-886-5067 446 D
fred.fuentes@tamuc.edu
FUENTES, Jacob .... 432-837-8885 449 F
jacob.fuentes@sulross.edu
FUENTES, Jonathan .... 432-553-6493 440 C
jfuentes@odessa.edu
FUENTES, Jose, A .... 787-279-1912 506 L
jfuentes@bayamon.inter.edu
FUENTES, Laysa .... 787-753-6000 506 B
lfuentes@icprjc.edu
FUENTES, Montserrat .... 512-448-8411 441 N
mfuentes@stedwards.edu
FUENTES, Rachael .... 605-698-3966 415 C
rfuentes@swcollege.edu
FUENTES, Renee .... 805-437-3608.. 30 D
renee.fuentes@csuci.edu
FUENTES, Ricky .... 575-769-4076 285 C
ricky.fuentes@clovis.edu
FUENTES, Sandra .... 559-638-0300.. 67 C
sandra.fuentes@reedleycollege.edu
FUENTES, Vilma .... 352-395-5030 107 G
vilma.fuentes@sfcollege.edu
FUENTES-MARTIN, Mari 210-784-1527 447 B
mfuentes@tamusa.edu
FUENTEZ, Tammy .... 620-421-6700 175 D
tammyf@labette.edu
FUENZALIDA, Bracey .... 212-659-7200 303 E
bfuenzalida@tkc.edu
FUERST, Barbara .... 636-922-8363 258 A
bfuerst@stchas.edu
FUERST, Nathan .... 860-486-1463.. 89 B
nathan.fuerst@uconn.edu
FUEST, Cana .... 585-582-8218 298 E
canafuest@elim.edu
FUGATE, Amy .... 989-275-5000 225 H
amy.fugate@kirtland.edu
FUGATE, Edna .... 606-218-5625 185 F
ednafugate@upike.edu
FUGATE, Megan .... 620-421-6700 175 D
mfugate@labette.edu
FUGATE, Stu .... 606-487-3196 181 E
stu.fugate@kctcs.edu
FUGATE, Wesley, R .... 717-262-2000 402 D
FUGATE-CATE, Kassie ... 620-223-2700 173 F
kassief@fortscott.edu
FUGATT, John .... 559-278-2083.. 31 D
johnfugatt@csufresno.edu
FUGAZZOTTO, Sam .... 702-895-0892 270 J
sam.fugazzotto@unlv.edu
FUGETT, David .... 941-487-4877 110 C
dfugett@ncf.edu
FUGIEL, Lisa .... 413-755-4786 215 F
lfugiel@stcc.edu
FUHRMAN, Dane .... 573-876-7210 259 F
dfuhrman@stephens.edu
FUHRMAN, Hillary .... 330-941-2453 364 G
hlfuhrman@ysu.edu
FUHRMAN, Tim .... 509-793-2351 477 D
timf@bigbend.edu
FUHRMANN, Donald, J 814-824-2104 389 E
dfuhrmann@mercyhurst.edu
FUITH, Leanne .... 651-290-7526 241 N
leanne.fuith@mitchellhamline.edu
FUJA, Thomas .... 574-631-8052 161 G
tfuja@nd.edu
FUJA, Thomas, E .... 574-631-5534 161 G
tfuja@nd.edu
FUJII, Stephanie .... 303-797-5701.. 77 H
stephanie.fujii@arapahoe.edu
FUJIMOTO, Kell .... 408-924-5910.. 34 B
kell.fujimoto@sjsu.edu
FUJIMURA, Takahiro ..... 808-983-4120 128 F
htic@tokai.edu
FUJITA, Sherri .... 509-279-6241 478 D
sherri.fujita@scc.spokane.edu
FUJIYOSHI, Lois, M ..... 808-932-7664 129 A
lfujiyos@hawaii.edu
FULBRIGHT, Brittney ..... 757-340-2121 464 L
careercvab@centura.edu
FULBRIGHT, Kyle .... 423-746-5327 425 C
kfulbright@tnwesleyan.edu
FULBRIGHT, Marshall ... 619-644-7104.. 44 H
marshall.fulbright@gcccd.edu
FULCHER, Kerry .... 619-849-2651.. 57 J
kerryfulcher@pointloma.edu
FULCOMER, Eric, W ...... 815-226-4010 147 J
efulcomer@rockford.edu
FULFORD, Leroy .... 740-377-2520 361 D
leroy.fulford@tsbc.edu
FULFORD, Tim .... 843-574-6116 411 I
tim.fulford@tridenttech.edu
FULIGNI, Paul .... 515-294-2631 163 E
pfuligni@iastate.edu
FULK, Scott .... 219-980-6792 157 A
sfulk@iun.edu
FULK, Sheryl, E .... 812-877-8514 160 C
fulk1@rose-hulman.edu
FULKERSON, Cathy .... 775-445-4405 271 A
cathy.fulkerson@wnc.edu
FULKERSON,
Christopher, D .... 336-278-5003 328 H
fulkers@elon.edu
FULKERSON, Steven ...... 501-686-2925.. 21 G
sfulkerson@uasys.edu
FULKS, Mark, A .... 423-439-8550 418 D
fulks@etsu.edu
FULKS, Steve .... 252-399-6570 326 H
sfulks@barton.edu
FULLANA, Yaremis, P .... 407-582-3037 113 C
yfullana@valenciacollege.edu
FULLBRIGHT, Kalyn ...... 405-585-5000 367 B
kalyn.fullbright@okbu.edu
FULLEM, Wendy .... 973-300-2120 283 B
wfullem@sussex.edu
FULLER, Andrew .... 801-302-2800 458 J
andrew.fuller@neumont.edu
FULLER, April .... 801-618-0438 458 H
afuller@ameritech.edu
FULLER, Belinda .... 304-766-3387 489 D
bfuller@wvstateu.edu
FULLER, Brad .... 269-956-3931 225 D
fullerb@kellogg.edu
FULLER, Brad .... 870-460-1050.. 22 E
fullerb@uamont.edu
FULLER, Cam .... 920-403-3030 494 B
cam.fuller@snc.edu
FULLER, Candy .... 361-354-2251 431 L
fuller_c@coastalbend.edu
FULLER, Chris .... 615-547-1336 418 C
cfuller@cumberland.edu
FULLER, Christopher ..... 207-893-7705 195 I
cfuller@sjcme.edu
FULLER, David .... 478-471-5365 122 D
david.fuller@mga.edu
FULLER, Dayna .... 251-981-3771.... 5 B
dayna.fuller@columbiasouthern.edu
FULLER, JR., Henry, M 843-953-5185 406 D
hank.fuller@citadel.edu
FULLER, Howard .... 360-383-3295 485 B
hfuller@whatcom.edu
FULLER, Karen .... 716-338-1034 302 G
karenfuller@mail.sunyjcc.edu
FULLER, Kyle .... 740-753-7009 353 G
fullerk@hocking.edu
FULLER, Leanna .... 412-924-1459 395 G
lfuller@pts.edu
FULLER, Mark .... 740-753-7129 353 G
fullerm@hocking.edu
FULLER, Mark .... 508-999-8004 211 F
chancellor@umassd.edu
FULLER, Marshall, R ..... 919-536-7200 334 A
fullerm@durhamtech.edu
FULLER, Melanie .... 919-508-2311 344 D
mjfuller@peace.edu
FULLER, Michael .... 903-223-3060 447 C
michael.fuller@tamut.edu
FULLER, Michael .... 541-684-7248 371 H
mfuller@bushnell.edu
FULLER, Mickey .... 405-945-8645 368 C
mickey.fuller@okstate.edu
FULLER, Peggy .... 318-678-6000 187 E
pfuller@bpcc.edu
FULLER, Robert .... 920-206-2332 492 C
robert.fuller@mbu.edu
FULLER, Rose .... 239-590-1356 109 G
rfuller@fgcu.edu
FULLER, Sherry .... 903-510-3346 451 D
sherry.fuller@tjc.edu
FULLER, Stephanie .... 336-272-7102 329 B
stephanie.fuller@greensboro.edu
FULLER, Sunny .... 417-328-1512 258 K
sfuller@sbuniv.edu
FULLER, Swanita .... 336-322-2281 336 D
swanita.fuller@piedmontcc.edu
FULLER-WILLIAMS,
Vonetta .... 972-438-6932 440 G
FULLERTON, Adam .... 712-274-5247 168 C
fullertona@morningside.edu
FULLERTON, John .... 208-795-4266 131 D
FULLMAN, Leah .... 334-386-7395.... 5 D
lfullman@faulkner.edu
FULLMER, Matt .... 610-358-4568 390 G
fullmerm@neumann.edu
FULLMER, Ryan .... 310-342-5200.. 73 E
FULLUM-CAMPBELL,
Marissa .... 916-712-3945.. 71 A
mfc@ucsc.edu
FULLWOOD, Carla .... 336-278-5017 328 H
cfullwood@elon.edu
FULMER, David .... 478-387-4890 119 E
dfulmer@gmc.edu
FULMER, Gregory, L ..... 610-921-2381 377 F
FULMER, Hal .... 334-670-3112.... 7 C
hfulmer@troy.edu
FULMER, Ingrid .... 848-445-4519 281 B
ifulmer@smlr.rutgers.edu
FULMER, Janet .... 316-284-5248 171 I
jfulmer@bethelks.edu
FULMER, Judy .... 334-670-3102.... 7 C
jfulmer@troy.edu
FULMER, Sarah .... 575-769-4085 285 C
sarah.fulmer@clovis.edu
FULOP, Ann .... 309-467-6440 137 G
afulop@eureka.edu
FULOP, Ann .... 309-467-6301 137 G
afulop@eureka.edu
FULTINEER, Scheri .... 401-454-6100 404 B
sfultine@risd.edu
FULTON, Dean .... 360-752-8378 477 C
dfulton@btc.edu
FULTON, Deborah, M ... 540-231-0735 475 D
dfulton@vt.edu
FULTON, DoVeanna ...... 757-823-8408 468 B
provost@nsu.edu
FULTON, Jodie .... 541-956-7200 375 G
jfulton@roguecc.edu
FULTON, Lori .... 509-452-5100 481 E
lfulton@pnwu.edu
FULTON, Neil .... 605-658-3508 415 E
neil.fulton@usd.edu
FULTON, Tara Lynn ...... 603-862-1506 273 H
taralynn.fulton@unh.edu
FULTON, Tom .... 412-924-1434 395 G
tfulton@pts.edu
FULTZ, Angela .... 606-759-7141 182 B
angela.fultz@kctcs.edu
FULTZ, Bob .... 502-863-8029 180 E
bob_fultz@georgetowncollege.edu
FULTZ, Larenda .... 731-286-3234 423 E
fultz@dscc.edu
FULTZ, Rob .... 423-614-8420 419 H
rfultz@leeuniversity.edu
FULWOOD, III, Sam ..... 202-885-1000.. 91 D
sfulwood@american.edu
FUMERO, Edwin .... 787-751-0160 505 C
efumero@cmpr.pr.gov
FUNARO, Janette .... 925-969-2347.. 40 H
jfunaro@dvc.edu
FUNASAKI, Eric, T .... 432-837-8109 449 F
etf14xz@sulross.edu
FUNCHES, Amanda .... 478-757-2500 122 D
amanda.funches@mga.edu
FUNDERBURG,
Stephanie .... 617-873-0238 207 E
stephanie.funderburg@
cambridgecollege.edu
FUNDERBURK, Annette . 334-290-3265.... 2 F
annette.funderburk@istc.edu
FUNDERBURK, Dana ..... 660-626-2391 249 C
FUNG, Eileen .... 415-422-6083.. 72 I
fung@usfca.edu
FUNK, Andrea .... 805-765-9300.. 39 E
FUNK, Chad .... 916-484-8452.. 50 J
funkc@arc.losrios.edu
FUNK, David .... 903-510-3078 451 D
dfun@tjc.edu
FUNK, Julie .... 520-626-8550.. 16 H
juliefunk@arizona.edu
FUNK, Ray .... 509-574-4722 485 E
rfunk@yvcc.edu
FUNK, Tiger .... 435-586-7888 459 E
funk@suu.edu
FUNK-BAXTER, Kathryn 210-784-2000 447 B
kbaxter@tamusa.edu
FUNKE, Rebecca .... 515-964-6328 164 F
rsfunke@dmacc.edu
FUNSTON, Terry Lyn .... 815-825-9338 141 D
tfunston@kish.edu
FUQUA, Amy .... 605-642-6221 415 F
amy.fuqua@bhsu.edu
FUQUA, Chad .... 417-268-6022 250 A
cfuqua@gobbc.edu
FUQUA, Julie .... 850-718-2478.. 97 E
fuquaj@chipola.edu
FURDA, Jenifer .... 719-255-3185.. 84 A
jfurda@uccs.edu
FURE-SLOCUM, Carolyn 507-222-4003 234 C
cfureslo@carleton.edu
FURER, Cheryl .... 866-680-2756 458 I
studentservices@midwifery.edu
FURGE, Laura .... 484-664-3134 390 F
laurafurge@muhlenberg.edu
FURLAN, Rogerio .... 787-850-9006 511 B
rogerio.furlan@upr.edu
FURLONG, Deborah .... 315-312-2345 318 B
deborah.furlong@oswego.edu
FURLONG, Matthew ...... 409-772-5113 456 B
mfurlong@utmb.edu
FURLONG, Patty .... 914-633-2548 302 C
mfurlong@iona.edu
FURLONG, Scott, R .... 315-312-2290 318 B
scott.furlong@oswego.edu
FURLONG, Sumita .... 914-633-2485 302 C
sfurlong@iona.edu
FURLONG, Victoria, L .... 315-312-2222 318 B
victoria.furlong@oswego.edu
FURLONG, William .... 603-641-7121 273 C
wfurlong@anselm.edu
FURMAN, Ellen .... 413-205-3503 205 C
ellen.furman@aic.edu
FURMAN, John, A .... 360-650-3497 485 A
john.furman@wwu.edu
FURNO, Mike .... 303-871-2361.. 84 C
mike.furno@du.edu
FURQUIM, Fernando ..... 612-659-6000 238 C
fernando.furquim@minneapolis.edu
FURR, Angela .... 601-643-8332 244 G
angela.furr@colin.edu
FURR, Brandi .... 903-463-8650 435 H
furrb@grayson.edu
FURR, Jennifer .... 402-643-7341 265 I
alumni@cune.edu
FURR, Laci .... 620-417-1151 177 C
laci.furr@sccc.edu
FURR, Myra .... 704-991-0202 338 A
mfurr7711@stanly.edu
FURR, Tim .... 320-308-5177 240 D
tim.furr@sctcc.edu
FURROW, Louise, S ..... 206-281-2998 482 K
lfurrow@spu.edu
FURST, Mary .... 828-898-8743 330 A
furstm@lmc.edu
FURST-BOWE, Julie ...... 479-968-0319.. 18 E
jfurstbowe@atu.edu
FURUTA, Lisa .... 808-739-4746 128 C
lisa.furuta@chaminade.edu
FURUTO, Brian .... 808-734-9572 129 E
bfuruto@hawaii.edu
FURUTO, Sandra, K ...... 808-956-7487 128 I
yano@hawaii.edu
FUSARO, Graziela .... 516-299-4192 304 D
graziela.fusaro@liu.edu
FUSCO, Joseph .... 610-902-8245 379 E
jf693@cabrini.edu
FUSCO, Valerie .... 315-792-7111 320 F
valerie.fusco@sunypoly.edu
FUSELIER, Johnathan .... 254-519-5477 446 C
j.fuselier@tamuct.edu
FUSELIER, Teresa .... 918-631-3551 371 C
teresa-fuselier@utulsa.edu
FUSER, Mindi .... 918-631-2582 371 C
mjf3917@utulsa.edu
FUSTER, Bradley .... 315-279-5202 303 D
bfuster@keuka.edu
FUSTER, Luis .... 787-765-3560 505 H
lfuster@edpuniversity.edu
FUTHEY, Tracy .... 919-684-8111 328 D
futhey@duke.edu
FUTRELL, Tamara .... 540-458-8766 476 D
tfutrell@wlu.edu
FUTTERER, Julie .... 815-740-3826 152 E
jfutterer@stfrancis.edu
FYDENKEVEZ,
Mary Ellen .... 413-775-1469 214 C
fydenkevez@gcc.mass.edu
FYDENKEVEZ,
Mary Ellen .... 413-775-1000 214 C
FYE, Marty .... 402-826-8261 266 A
marty.fye@doane.edu
FYE, Marty .... 402-826-8215 266 A
marty.fye@doane.edu
FYFE, Billy .... 414-277-2339 493 D

FYFFE, Cecily, B 740-885-5620 363 F
cfyffe@wscc.edu
FYNAARDT, Tamara 712-707-7115 169 A
fynaardt@nwciowa.edu
FYNES, Daniel 330-569-6107 353 F
fynesda@hiram.edu

G

GAAL, John 215-276-6070 397 E
jgaal@salus.edu
GAALSWYK, Terry 507-372-3491 239 B
terry.gaalswyk@mnwest.edu
GABA, Barbara 609-343-4901 274 E
president@atlantic.edu
GABBARD, Clinton, E 815-455-8725 143 F
cgabbard@mchenry.edu
GABBARD, Kurt, A 609-497-7705 279 D
kurt.gabbard@ptsem.edu
GABBERT, Jeri Pat 219-981-4242 157 A
jgabbert@iun.edu
GABEHART, Luci 432-264-5074 436 H
lgabehart@howardcollege.edu
GABEL, Ann-Marie 949-582-4664 65 A
agabel@socccd.edu
GABEL, Barb 419-448-2183 353 D
bgabel@heidelberg.edu
GABEL, Joan, T 612-626-1616 242 K
upres@umn.edu
GABER, Sharon, L 704-687-5723 342 C
sharon.gaber@uncc.edu
GABERT, Susan, S 603-641-7231 273 C
sgabert@anselm.edu
GABLE, Carol 315-859-4313 300 F
cgable@hamilton.edu
GABLE, Heather 434-200-3070 464 G
GABLE, Jill 312-942-5681 148 C
jill_gable@rush.edu
GABLE, Justin 559-453-2215 43 D
justin.gable@fresno.edu
GABLE, Marsha 619-644-7110 44 H
marsha.gable@gcccd.edu
GABOR, Octavian 309-671-2970 143 I
ogabor@methodistcol.edu
GABOURY, Mario 203-932-7253 89 F
mgaboury@newhaven.edu
GABRIEL, Lisa 281-212-1788 452 A
gabriel@uhcl.edu
GABRIEL, Mary 970-339-6248 77 G
mary.gabriel@aims.edu
GABRIEL, Peter 913-288-7484 174 H
pgabriel@kckcc.edu
GABRIEL, Robert 510-659-6269 54 J
rgabriel@ohlone.edu
GABRIEL, Robert 510-742-3101 54 J
rgabriel@ohlone.edu
GABRIEL, Sherine, E 312-942-7100 148 C
sherine_l-gabriel@rush.edu
GABRIELE, Erin 610-902-8304 379 E
eg574@cabrini.edu
GABRIELSON, Rudy 207-780-4235 196 C
william.gabrielson@maine.edu
GABY FISHER, Robin 973-353-3739 281 C
rofisher@newark.rutgers.edu
GACHETTE, Yves, M 716-878-4521 317 C
gachetym@buffalostate.edu
GACHIGO, David 718-390-4345 313 B
gachigod@stjohns.edu
GACKLE, Joel 605-274-5238 413 G
joel.gackle@augie.edu
GADBERRY, Brad 678-341-6615 121 L
bgadberry@laniertech.edu
GADD, Holly 423-236-2961 422 H
hgadd@southern.edu
GADDIE, George 409-266-1600 456 B
ggaddie@utmb.edu
GADDIS, Glendi 360-992-2260 477 J
ggaddis@clark.edu
GADDIS, Todd 706-769-1472 115 B
GADDY, James 973-300-2306 283 B
jgaddy@sussex.edu
GADE-JONES, Tish 402-465-2114 267 J
tgadejon@nebrwesleyan.edu
GADES, Andrew 208-459-5172 131 A
agades@collegeofidaho.edu
GADSBY, Peter 845-758-7457 290 G
gadsby@bard.edu
GADSON, Alecia, S 302-857-6030 90 D
agadson@desu.edu
GADSON, Mark 610-409-3582 400 E
mgadson@ursinus.edu
GADSON, Nadia 225-771-2613 190 K
nadia_gadson@subr.edu

GADSON, Tyrone 413-841-0394 399 H
tgadson@uls.edu
GADZINSKI, James, G 906-227-2971 228 E
jgadzins@nmu.edu
GAECKE, Lauren 920-403-3981 494 B
lauren.gaecke@snc.edu
GAERTE, Phyllis 585-567-9620 301 G
phyllis.gaerte@houghton.edu
GAERTNER, Michelle 615-248-1463 425 D
mgaertner@trevecca.edu
GAETA, Alexa 404-471-6054 114 E
agaeta@agnesscott.edu
GAETA, Maria 805-482-2755 59 G
mgaeta@stjohnsem.edu
GAETJE, Lisa 714-484-7188 54 C
lgaetje@cypresscollege.edu
GAETZ, Ivan 307-766-3279 500 H
igaetz@uwyo.edu
GAFFEY, Pat 480-947-6644 15 B
GAFFIN, John 859-572-6611 184 B
gaffinj@nku.edu
GAFFNEY, Elizabeth 516-299-2273 304 C
elizabeth.gaffney@liu.edu
GAFFNEY, Eva 508-531-1337 212 B
egaffney@bridgew.edu
GAFFNEY, Michelle 330-823-2496 362 E
gaffnemi@mountunion.edu
GAFFNEY, Tiffany, D 401-865-2191 403 G
tgaffne1@providence.edu
GAFFORD, Brian 931-393-1576 423 G
bgafford@mscc.edu
GAGAN, Adam 212-799-5000 303 B
GAGE, Adrian 508-929-8563 213 D
agage@worcester.edu
GAGE, Brent 319-335-3839 163 F
brent-gage@uiowa.edu
GAGE, Chris 615-460-6785 417 B
chris.gage@belmont.edu
GAGE, Doug 517-355-0306 227 C
gage@msu.edu
GAGE, Jeannie 361-825-2332 446 E
jeannie.gage@tamucc.edu
GAGE, Julia 401-841-6535 501 L
julia.gage@usnwc.edu
GAGE, Michael 719-549-3011 82 I
michael.gage@pueblocc.edu
GAGER, Sarah 203-575-8086 86 H
sgager@nv.edu
GAGLIANO, Patricia 772-462-7565 102 E
pgaglian@irsc.edu
GAGLIANO, Tiffany, N 845-569-3650 307 B
tiffany.gagliano@msmc.edu
GAGLIARDI, Elaine 406-243-5094 263 D
elaine.gagliardi@umontana.edu
GAGLIARDI, Stephen 440-525-7241 354 L
sgagliardi@lakelandcc.edu
GAGNE, Bob 314-977-2506 258 H
bob.gagne@slu.edu
GAGNE, Cathy, A 401-865-2540 403 G
caragao@providence.edu
GAGNE-HAWES, Anna 907-474-5142 10 B
algagnehawes@alaska.edu
GAGNE PENDLETON,
Lori 860-515-3858 85 D
lpendleton@charteroak.edu
GAGNON, Jennifer 703-284-1610 468 A
jennifer.gagnon@marymount.edu
GAGNON, Joel 925-424-1420 36 A
jgagnon@laspositascollege.edu
GAGNON, Patrick 315-229-5906 313 F
pgagnon@stlawu.edu
GAGNON, Pauline 678-839-5450 127 A
pgagnon@westga.edu
GAGNON, Rick 978-927-0585 209 B
rgagnon@endicott.edu
GAGNOW, Robin, W 440-826-8153 348 C
rgagnow@bw.edu
GAHAGANS, Steve 479-575-6626 21 H
steveg@uark.edu
GAHBAUER, Martin 630-617-3625 137 E
martin.gahbauer@elmhurst.edu
GAIA, Celeste 276-944-6917 466 F
cgaia@ehc.edu
GAIK, Molly 773-298-3293 148 I
gaik@sxu.edu
GAIKO, Sylvia 724-357-2555 393 G
sylvia.gaiko@iup.edu
GAIL, Keli, A 413-597-4233 220 A
kg8@williams.edu
GAILEY, Andrew 706-865-2134 126 D
agailey@truett.edu
GAILEY, Kim 970-943-3140 85 B
kgailey@western.edu

GAILLARD, Anne 936-294-1006 449 E
bio_arg@shsu.edu
GAILLAT, Ana 802-728-1533 463 D
agaillat@vtc.edu
GAIMARO, Amy 516-323-4415 306 I
agaimaro@molloy.edu
GAINER, Amy, T 972-548-6650 432 I
againer@collin.edu
GAINER, Jeanmarie 773-298-3316 148 I
gainer@sxu.edu
GAINER, Nancy 610-436-4164 394 F
ngainer@wcupa.edu
GAINES, Angela 225-771-2552 191 C
againes@sulc.edu
GAINES, Angie 573-897-5000 259 E
GAINES, Chad 660-248-6228 250 H
cgaines@centralmethodist.edu
GAINES, Cliff 254-501-3101 431 E
cgaines@ctcd.edu
GAINES, Freda 478-471-4394 121 C
GAINES, Gina 914-606-7612 324 F
gina.gaines@sunywcc.edu
GAINES, Glynnis 254-299-8306 438 G
ggaines@mclennan.edu
GAINES, Jill 502-585-9911 184 E
jgaines01@spalding.edu
GAINES, Karen 802-485-2025 461 H
kgaines@norwich.edu
GAINES, Kellie 415-503-6214 61 E
kgaines@sfcm.edu
GAINES, Kim 256-306-2592 1 F
kim.gaines@calhoun.edu
GAINES, Larry 856-225-6095 281 A
gaines@camden.rutgers.edu
GAINES, LaTysha 973-278-5400 274 J
latysha-gaines@berkeleycollege.edu
GAINES, Sarah 512-505-3037 437 B
srgaines@htu.edu
GAINES, Steven, D 805-893-7363 70 E
gaines@ucsb.edu
GAINES, Willie 877-476-8674 435 G
GAINOR, Birma 864-656-2451 406 F
bgainor@clemson.edu
GAISSERT, John 706-355-5039 115 C
jgaissert@athenstech.edu
GAITAN, Deborah 210-486-4454 428 A
dgaitan@alamo.edu
GAITAN, Susie 361-354-2714 431 L
mgaitan@coastalbend.edu
GAITERS-JORDAN,
Jacquelyn 719-502-2000 82 D
GAITERS-JORDAN,
Jacquelyn 719-502-3078 82 D
jacquelyn.gaitersjordan@pikespeak.edu
GAITHER, Kenn 336-278-5776 328 H
tgaither@elon.edu
GAITHER, Kim 573-288-6340 251 I
kgaither@culver.edu
GAITHER, Sonya 678-466-4334 117 A
sonyagaither@clayton.edu
GAITO, Madalyn 828-652-0630 335 H
madalyng@mcdowelltech.edu
GAITOR, Sherissa 256-761-8843 7 B
skgaitor@talladega.edu
GAJDOSIK, Olga 262-554-2010 493 A
olgag6542@yahoo.com
GAJEWSKI, Linda 219-473-4217 154 A
GAJEWSKI, Linda 219-473-4217 154 A
lgajewski@ccsj.edu
GAJRIA, Meenakshi 845-398-4154 314 D
mgajria@stac.edu
GALAN, Brady 646-313-8000 295 C
brady.galan@guttman.cuny.edu
GALANO, Hector 714-879-3901 45 J
hgalano@hiu.edu
GALANSKI, Kay, A 724-946-7218 401 F
galanska@westminster.edu
GALANSKY, Galia 212-772-4511 294 A
galia.galansky@hunter.cuny.edu
GALATIC, John 304-384-5190 488 K
jgalatic@concord.edu
GALBAVY, Colton 406-395-4875 264 I
cgalbavy@stonechild.edu
GALBAVY, Tiffany 406-395-4875 264 I
tgalbavy@stonechild.edu
GALBIERZ, Todd 636-922-8359 258 A
tgalbierz@stchas.edu
GALBRAITH, Drew 860-297-2057 88 I
drew.galbraith@trincoll.edu
GALBRAITH, Gretchen 315-267-2231 318 D
galbragr@potsdam.edu
GALBRAITH, II, Jay, R 407-582-3420 113 C
jgalbraith1@valenciacollege.edu

GALBRAITH, Jennifer 909-274-4600 52 K
jgalbraith@mtsac.edu
GALBRAITH, Joan 973-805-8099 276 B
jgalbrai@drew.edu
GALBRAITH, Joseph, P 864-656-4233 406 F
joegalb@clemson.edu
GALBRAITH, Thomas 434-947-8537 469 A
tgalbraith@randolphcollege.edu
GALBREATH, Dodd 615-966-1771 420 B
dodd.galbreath@lipscomb.edu
GALBREATH, Susan, C 615-966-5952 420 B
susan.galbreath@lipscomb.edu
GALCHINSKY, Michael 404-413-2578 120 C
mgalchinsky@gsu.edu
GALDIERI, Viriginia 201-684-7506 280 B
vgaldier@ramapo.edu
GALE, Jason 615-297-7545 416 G
galej@aquinascollege.edu
GALE, Jennifer, D 610-917-1488 400 D
jdgale@valleyforge.edu
GALE, Jesse 610-526-6526 378 J
jgale@brynmawr.edu
GALE, Mary 952-885-5437 241 P
mgale@nwhealth.edu
GALE, Nicole, L 410-651-6458 203 B
nlgale@umes.edu
GALEA, Sandro 617-358-1840 207 C
sgalea@bu.edu
GALEANO, Angela 410-951-3931 203 E
agaleano@coppin.edu
GALEWSKI, Matt 781-891-2000 206 C
GALFORD, Shaun 615-879-2022 419 C
GALGON, Aquila 209-946-2421 71 E
agalgon@pacific.edu
GALIANI, Colette 415-257-1392 41 H
colette.galiani@dominican.edu
GALICIA, Delia 805-482-2755 59 G
dgalicia@stjohnsem.edu
GALICK, Rob 847-925-6380 138 E
rgalick@harpercollege.edu
GALICKI, Stan 601-974-1405 246 C
galics@millsaps.edu
GALIME, Steve 518-956-8030 315 D
sgalime@albany.edu
GALINDO, Diana 760-776-7358 39 A
digalindo@collegeofthedesert.edu
GALINSKI, Bonnie 978-542-2532 213 B
bonnie.galinski@salemstate.edu
GALIPEAU, Jennifer 401-598-1813 403 E
jennifer.galipeau@jwu.edu
GALIPEAU-KONATE,
Bethany 540-542-6285 470 A
bgalipea@su.edu
GALITZ, Todd 718-951-5099 293 A
todd.galitz@brooklyn.cuny.edu
GALL, Connie 405-692-3258 366 C
connie.gall@macu.edu
GALL, Cory 309-341-5273 134 A
cgall@sandburg.edu
GALL, Rob 707-765-1836 52 C
GALLAGHER, Aimee 619-644-7572 44 F
aimee.gallagher@gcccd.edu
GALLAGHER, Amber 949-582-4860 65 C
agallagher4@saddleback.edu
GALLAGHER, Amie 908-526-1200 280 C
amie.gallagher@raritanval.edu
GALLAGHER, Bonnie 845-431-8631 298 B
bonnie.gallagher@sunydutchess.edu
GALLAGHER, Connie 610-558-5501 390 G
gallaghc@neumann.edu
GALLAGHER, Daniel 518-485-3390 296 E
gallaghd@strose.edu
GALLAGHER, Ed 256-766-6610 5 F
egallagher@hcu.edu
GALLAGHER, Elizabeth 925-631-4223 59 I
egallagh@stmarys-ca.edu
GALLAGHER, Ellen 570-408-3893 402 B
ellen.gallagher@wilkes.edu
GALLAGHER, Heather 973-300-2110 283 B
hgallagher@sussex.edu
GALLAGHER, Jennifer 410-810-7765 204 E
jrunyon2@washcoll.edu
GALLAGHER, Joanna 215-646-7300 384 G
gallagher.j@gmercyu.edu
GALLAGHER, John 573-341-4286 260 F
gallagherjo@mst.edu
GALLAGHER, Karen 607-753-4717 317 D
karen.gallagher@cortland.edu
GALLAGHER, Kathleen 215-503-6959 398 G
kathleen.gallagher@jefferson.edu
GALLAGHER, Leslie, D 281-425-6301 438 B
lgallagher@lee.edu

GALLAGHER, Lori .... 713-525-3592 453 H irishstudies@stthom.edu
GALLAGHER, Mary .... 323-953-4000.. 49 E gallagmp@lacitycollege.edu
GALLAGHER, Mary Beth .... 276-223-4765 475 B mgallagher@wcc.vccs.edu
GALLAGHER, Maureen .. 914-395-2385 314 H mgallagh@sarahlawrence.edu
GALLAGHER, Miles, P .. 717-871-7210 394 B miles.gallagher@millersville.edu
GALLAGHER, Patrick ..... 412-624-4200 400 A pdg@pitt.edu
GALLAGHER, Patrick ..... 646-592-4008 325 R patrick.gallagher@yu.edu
GALLAGHER, Patrick ..... 908-709-7045 283 E gallagher@ucc.edu
GALLAGHER, Samantha 970-247-7435.. 80 H smgallagher@fortlewis.edu
GALLAGHER, Steve .... 650-723-2300.. 66 D
GALLAGHER, Steve .... 336-631-1217 343 C gallaghers@uncsa.edu
GALLAGHER, Susan ...... 410-777-2124 197 C sgallagher5@aacc.edu
GALLAGHER, Susan ...... 503-312-5425 373 G susan.gallagher@mtangel.edu
GALLAGHER, Terri .... 724-480-3427 381 G terri.gallagher@ccbc.edu
GALLAGHER, Thomas .... 406-243-7852 263 D tom.gallagher@umontana.edu
GALLAGHER, Todd .... 916-686-7300.. 29 G
GALLAGHER-LEPAK, Susan .... 920-465-2034 494 F galaghs@uwgb.edu
GALLAHER, Connie .... 614-251-4690 358 B connie.gallaher@ohiodominican.edu
GALLAHER, James .... 412-624-7000 400 A james.gallaher@pitt.edu
GALLAHER, Kent .... 806-720-7402 438 F kent.gallaher@lcu.edu
GALLANT, Darren .... 207-786-6216 193 D dgallant@bates.edu
GALLANT, Mary .... 518-402-0281 315 D mgallant@albany.edu
GALLANT, Suzanna .... 207-755-5396 194 J sgallant@cmcc.edu
GALLARDO, Ignacio ...... 805-893-4412.. 70 E ignacio.gallardo@ucsb.edu
GALLARDO, Katherine ... 949-824-7676.. 69 C klgallar@uci.edu
GALLARDO, Mark .... 573-341-4981 260 F gallardom@mst.edu
GALLARDO, Ruben, C .. 915-831-6306 435 B rgalla16@epcc.edu
GALLARDO, Yoli .... 509-313-6115 479 E gallardoy@gonzaga.edu
GALLE, Gillian .... 802-468-1344 462 H gillian.galle@castleton.edu
GALLEGOS, Jeremy .... 316-295-5871 173 G jeremy_gallegos@friends.edu
GALLEGOS, Joel, A .... 704-687-7755 342 C jagalleg@uncc.edu
GALLEGOS, Jose Alfred 323-242-5511.. 49 I gallegja@lasc.edu
GALLEGOS, Renee, D .... 562-463-7271.. 58 M rdgallegos@riohondo.edu
GALLENBERG, Dale .... 715-425-3841 496 A dale.gallenberg@uwrf.edu
GALLERY, Tracy .... 800-955-2527.. 22 B tgallery@grantham.edu
GALLEY, Amy .... 307-382-1645 500 I agalley@westernwyoming.edu
GALLIANETTI, David, D . 920-565-1000 492 A gallianettidd@lakeland.edu
GALLICHIO, Kathy .... 973-300-2100 283 B kgallichio@sussex.edu
GALLIE, Alain .... 770-559-0580 123 H
GALLIGAN, Chad .... 623-935-8075.. 13 C chad.galligan@estrellamountain.edu
GALLIGAN, Kathleen ..... 503-206-3217 377 A kgalligan@uws.edu
GALLIGAN, Laura .... 401-598-2163 403 E laura.galligan@jwu.edu
GALLIHER, Shelbey .... 310-338-7854.. 51 C shelbey.galliher@lmu.edu
GALLIHUGH, Joel .... 313-993-1235 230 H gallihja@udmercy.edu
GALLIMORE, Alec, D .... 734-647-7008 231 A rasta@umich.edu
GALLIMORE, Jennie ...... 419-372-7581 348 F jgallim@bgsu.edu
GALLIMORE, Mark, K ... 716-888-8353 291 M gallimom@canisius.edu
GALLIMORE, Sarah .... 717-815-6470 402 G sgallimo@ycp.edu
GALLINA, Nancy .... 212-463-0400 322 C nancy.gallina@touro.edu
GALLINI, Brian .... 503-370-6402 377 E bgallini@willamette.edu
GALLION, Melanie .... 843-525-8224 411 G mgallion@tcl.edu
GALLIPEAU, Jean, B ..... 315-443-3765 321 D jbgallip@syr.edu
GALLIVAN, Mary .... 505-224-4000 285 B mgallivan@cnm.edu
GALLMAN, Kathleen ...... 252-638-7233 333 F gallmank@cravencc.edu
GALLO, James .... 215-646-7300 384 G gallo.j@gmercyu.edu
GALLO, James, D .... 646-664-3013 292 E james.gallo@cuny.edu
GALLO, John, D .... 724-847-6796 384 B jdgallo@geneva.edu
GALLO, Kathleen .... 516-463-4074 301 E kathleen.gallo@hofstra.edu
GALLO, Kelly .... 562-902-3316.. 65 H kellygallo@scuhs.edu
GALLO, Kristen .... 215-204-7981 398 D kgallo@temple.edu
GALLO, Maria .... 715-425-3201 496 A maria.gallo@uwrf.edu
GALLO, Nancy .... 973-300-2181 283 B ngallo@sussex.edu
GALLO-MURPHY, Meredith .... 773-907-4650 134 N mgallo-murphy@ccc.edu
GALLON-STUBBS, Valencia .... 386-481-2035.. 96 D stubbsv@cookman.edu
GALLONIO, Anthony ..... 401-454-6636 404 B agalloni@risd.edu
GALLOT, JR., Richard ... 318-274-3811 191 G prez@gram.edu
GALLOWAY, Carolina .... 806-651-5309 447 D cgalloway@wtamu.edu
GALLOWAY, David .... 808-675-3368 128 B david.galloway@byuh.edu
GALLOWAY, David .... 651-603-6263 235 A galloway@csp.edu
GALLOWAY, Heather ..... 512-245-2266 449 G hg02@txstate.edu
GALLOWAY, Jeanne ...... 425-602-3007 476 H jgalloway@bastyr.edu
GALLOWAY, Jeannie ..... 606-368-6113 178 D jeanniegalloway@alc.edu
GALLOWAY, Merrill .... 606-589-3079 182 F merrill.galloway@kctcs.edu
GALLOWAY, Pamela ..... 919-760-8360 331 A davisp@meredith.edu
GALLOWAY, Peter .... 610-436-1015 394 F pgalloway@wcupa.edu
GALLOWAY, Robert .... 713-646-2927 443 C rgalloway@stcl.edu
GALLOWAY, Robin .... 319-296-4292 166 E robin.galloway@hawkeyecollege.edu
GALLOWAY, Sean .... 717-358-4210 383 G sean.galloway@fandm.edu
GALLOWAY, Sheila .... 910-755-7312 332 D galloways@brunswickcc.edu
GALLOWAY, Stephen ..... 714-997-6765.. 36 D sgalloway@chapman.edu
GALLOWGLAS, Robin .... 916-484-8401.. 50 J gallowr@arc.losrios.edu
GALLUCCI, Kathleen ...... 585-275-2121 323 E
GALLUZZO, Benjamin ... 315-268-2387 295 E bgalluzz@clarkson.edu
GALOPE, Richard .... 909-382-4034.. 60 D rgalope@sbccd.cc.ca.us
GALOYAN, Nazy .... 408-864-8292.. 42 K galoyannazy@deanza.edu
GALSTAD, Tyler .... 414-425-8300 494 A tgalstad@shsst.edu
GALT, Cindy .... 561-433-2330 108 H
GALTNEY, Alfred .... 601-877-6124 244 B agaltney@alcorn.edu
GALUKYAN, Armine ...... 626-585-7201.. 56 D agalukyan@pasadena.edu
GALVAN, Adriana .... 310-206-3961.. 69 D agalvan@college.ucla.edu
GALVAN, Betty .... 210-528-7183 440 D bagalvan@ollusa.edu
GALVAN, Dennis, C ...... 541-346-5851 376 G dgalvan@uoregon.edu
GALVAN, Jaime, B .... 787-891-0925 506 I jgalvan@aguadilla.inter.edu
GALVAN, Juan, M .... 956-872-5051 443 B jmiguel@southtexascollege.edu
GALVAN, Michael .... 903-223-3013 447 C michael.galvan@tamut.edu
GALVAN, Ovidio .... 713-221-8967 452 B galvano@uhd.edu
GALVAN, Racheal .... 785-309-3147 177 B racheal.galvan@salinatech.edu
GALVAN, Sonia .... 443-412-2545 199 B sgalvan@harford.edu
GALVANONI, Mark .... 630-889-6661 145 D mgalvanoni@nuhs.edu
GALVEZ, Jocelin .... 870-584-1163.. 22 G
GALVIN, Carroll .... 410-532-5314 201 C cgalvin@ndm.edu
GALVIN, Elizabeth .... 401-341-2904 404 D elizabeth.galvin@salve.edu
GALVIN, Garrett .... 619-574-5801.. 43 B ggalvin@fst.edu
GALVIN, Jeanne .... 718-631-6220 295 B jgalvin@qcc.cuny.edu
GALVIN, Michael .... 973-655-7761 278 C galvinm@montclair.edu
GALVIN, Sophia .... 954-201-7350.. 96 F
GALVINHILL, Paul .... 508-793-3363 208 A pgalvin@holycross.edu
GALYEAN, Paul .... 903-589-7135 437 D pgalyean@jacksonville-college.edu
GALZERANO, Jacqueline .... 813-253-6219 113 B jgalzerano@ut.edu
GAMA, Kristal .... 909-607-7821.. 37 F kristal.gama@cgu.edu
GAMARRA, Rachel .... 765-998-2751 161 A rachel_gamarra@taylor.edu
GAMBA, Melissa .... 267-502-6038 378 I
GAMBA, Raymond .... 530-541-4660.. 47 H gamba@ltcc.edu
GAMBILL, Jon .... 816-501-2436 249 H jon.gambill@avila.edu
GAMBILL, Todd .... 864-388-8182 409 B tgambill@lander.edu
GAMBINO, Ellen, M ...... 845-431-8954 298 B egambino@sunydutchess.edu
GAMBLE, Desiree .... 360-442-2202 480 E dgamble@lowercolumbia.edu
GAMBLE, Gregory .... 856-225-6388 281 A gambleg@camden.rutgers.edu
GAMBLE, Jason .... 717-867-6060 388 A jgamble@lvc.edu
GAMBLE, Jim .... 616-538-2330 224 B jgamble@gracechristian.edu
GAMBLE, Kristina .... 859-985-3795 179 E gamblek@berea.edu
GAMBLE, Richard .... 423-775-6596 421 I rgamble@ogs.edu
GAMBLE, Rob .... 408-855-5255.. 75 C rob.gamble@missioncollege.edu
GAMBLES, Freddie, A ... 256-372-5230.... 1 A freddie.gambles@aamu.edu
GAMBOA, Jorge .... 714-992-7048.. 54 D jgamboa@fullcoll.edu
GAMBOA, Noel .... 718-262-2372 295 D ngamboa@york.cuny.edu
GAMBOA, Patricia .... 479-575-6247.. 21 H pgamboa@uark.edu
GAMBRELL-BOONE, Letizia .... 401-341-2205 404 D letizia.gboone@salve.edu
GAMBRO, John, S .... 815-740-3829 152 E jgambro@stfrancis.edu
GAMER, Josh .... 608-785-9088 499 B gamerj@westerntc.edu
GAMES, Susie .... 252-638-7451 333 F gamess@cravencc.edu
GAMET, Nate .... 660-359-3948 256 F ngamet@mail.ncmissouri.edu
GAMEZ, Jeremy .... 903-886-5969 446 D jeremy.gamez@tamuc.edu
GAMEZ, Robert .... 785-532-6420 175 A audi@ksu.edu
GAMMEL-SMITH, Hollie 936-468-7249 444 H hsmith@sfasu.edu
GAMMELL, William .... 860-723-0054.. 85 E gammellw@ct.edu
GAMMILL, Brandon ...... 417-873-7410 252 A bgammill@drury.edu
GAMMILL, Josh .... 662-407-1569 245 F jegammill@iccms.edu
GAMMON, Kristeen, R .. 407-582-2909 113 C kchristian6@valenciacollege.edu
GAMMON, Marcia, L .... 480-245-7946.. 12 O marcia.gammon@ibcs.edu
GAMMON, Steve .... 406-496-4127 264 C sgammon@mtech.edu
GAMMON, JR., Willey .. 404-756-4000 115 E
GAMMONS, Andy .... 765-998-5565 161 A andy_gammons@taylor.edu
GAMMONS, Debra, J .... 843-377-2429 406 B dgammons@charlestonlaw.edu
GANAC, Lynn .... 657-278-8474.. 31 E lganac@fullerton.edu
GANCHUK, Thomas ...... 256-761-6590.... 7 B thomas.ganchuk@thompsonfacilities.com
GANDHI, Pratima .... 715-346-2641 496 B pgandhi@uwsp.edu
GANDIA, Antonio .... 239-992-4624.. 96 E
GANDIA, Antonio .... 954-753-6869.. 99 B
GANDRE, James .... 917-493-4438 304 L jgandre@msmnyc.edu
GANDU, Bobby .... 316-978-5675 178 B bobby.gandu@wichita.edu
GANESON, Visakan .... 425-388-9378 479 B vganeson@everettcc.edu
GANG, Marty .... 208-792-2888 131 F mpgang@lcsc.edu
GANGER, Trisha .... 224-293-5858.. 10 F tganger@aiuniv.edu
GANGI, Maria .... 914-831-0350 296 F mgangi@cw.edu
GANGL, Brad .... 701-228-2277 345 G brad.gangl@dakotacollege.edu
GANIC, Emir .... 718-758-8125 293 A eganic@brooklyn.cuny.edu
GANIM, Russell .... 319-335-3500 163 F russell-ganim@uiowa.edu
GANLEY, DeLacy .... 909-621-8075.. 37 F delacy.ganley@cgu.edu
GANLEY, Kristin .... 908-737-3323 277 F kganley@kean.edu
GANN, Alexander .... 516-367-6890 296 A ganna@cshl.edu
GANN, Brian .... 919-866-5701 338 E bwgann@waketech.edu
GANN, Scott .... 870-543-5900.. 21 D sgann@seark.edu
GANNAWAY, Anne, M .. 563-333-6382 169 D gannawayannem@sau.edu
GANNON, Angela .... 808-984-3576 130 B yarnall@hawaii.edu
GANNON, David .... 401-232-6336 403 B dgannon@bryant.edu
GANNON, Debbie, K ..... 515-263-6020 166 C dgannon@grandview.edu
GANNON, John .... 631-451-4000 321 A
GANNON, Marcy .... 301-934-7560 198 C mdgannon@csmd.edu
GANSCHOW, Darby .... 605-658-3632 415 E darby.ganschow@usd.edu
GANT, Jeffrey, D .... 845-257-7869 316 B
GANT, Jon, P .... 919-530-7438 341 D jpgant@nccu.edu
GANTER, Susan .... 432-552-2020 456 C ganter_s@utpb.edu
GANTHER, Breanna .... 610-740-3725 380 C bookstore@cedarcrest.edu
GANTHER, Felicia, L ..... 215-968-8221 379 B felicia.ganther@bucks.edu
GANTI, Sridevi .... 844-872-8680.. 72 J
GANTNER, Christine, M 920-424-0625 495 C gantner@uwosh.edu
GANTT, Bernard .... 718-289-5887 292 H bernard.gantt@bcc.cuny.edu
GANTT, Calvin .... 607-777-2791 315 E cgantt@binghamton.edu
GANTT, Calvin, J .... 585-292-2122 306 K cgant@monroecc.edu
GANTZ, Katherine, L ..... 240-895-4922 201 F klgantz@smcm.edu
GANTZ, Walter .... 812-855-1621 156 C gantz@indiana.edu
GANUES, Jeff .... 567-661-7334 359 H jeffrey_ganues@owens.edu
GANZ, Gerald, J .... 501-916-3202.. 22 C gjganz@ualr.edu
GANZ BLYTHE, Sarah ... 401-454-6686 404 B sganz@risd.edu
GANZAR, John .... 303-751-8700.. 78 A ganzar@belrea.edu
GANZEL, Toni .... 502-852-5192 185 E toni.ganzel@louisville.edu
GANZEL, Toni .... 502-852-1499 185 E toni.ganzel@louisville.edu
GAO, Jing .... 215-646-7300 384 G gao.j@gmercyu.edu

GARDNER, Brian .... 978-468-7111 209 G
bgardner3@gcts.edu
GARDNER, Brian .... 610-861-4137 391 B
bgardner@northampton.edu
GARDNER, Chris .... 913-288-7613 174 H
cgardner@kckcc.edu
GARDNER, Chris .... 910-410-1731 336 G
csgardner@richmondcc.edu
GARDNER, Chris, L .... 864-597-4236 413 E
gardnercl@wofford.edu
GARDNER, Christina ..... 619-849-2246.. 57 J
christinagardner@pointloma.edu
GARDNER,
Christopher, L .... 864-597-4000 413 E
gardnercl@wooford.edu
GARDNER, Daniel .... 718-862-7301 304 K
dgardner01@manhattan.edu
GARDNER, Denise .... 865-974-4373 426 C
d.gardner@utk.edu
GARDNER, Donna .... 816-415-7622 261 G
gardnerd@william.jewell.edu
GARDNER, Eileen .... 251-442-2234.... 8 C
egardner@umobile.edu
GARDNER, Gretchen ...... 412-809-5302 395 F
gardner.gretchen@ptcollege.edu
GARDNER, Iva, L .... 803-516-4616 410 H
igardner@scsu.edu
GARDNER, Jackie .... 909-537-5000.. 33 B
GARDNER, James .... 617-745-3716 208 F
james.gardner@enc.edu
GARDNER, Jared .... 541-888-7316 376 B
jgardner@socc.edu
GARDNER, Kasey .... 530-661-5700.. 77 C
GARDNER, Kathleen ...... 989-774-3111 221 M
gardn2k@cmich.edu
GARDNER, Kevin .... 502-852-6356 185 E
kevin.gardner@louisville.edu
GARDNER, Kevin, D ...... 330-494-6170 360 I
kdgardner@starkstate.edu
GARDNER, Laurie, A ..... 207-778-7272 196 F
lgardner@maine.edu
GARDNER, Lisa .... 208-426-1698 130 F
lisagardner@boisestate.edu
GARDNER, Lizz .... 312-850-7889 135 E
egardner17@ccc.edu
GARDNER, Marie .... 785-242-2067 176 A
mgardner@neosho.edu
GARDNER, Marilyn .... 617-322-3566 210 F
marilyn_gardner@laboure.edu
GARDNER, Mary Jo ...... 651-450-3835 237 H
mgardner@inverhills.edu
GARDNER, Melissa .... 330-823-6092 362 E
gardnemf@mountunion.edu
GARDNER, Mike .... 484-460-6067 390 F
mikegardner@muhlenberg.edu
GARDNER, Nathan .... 518-262-5251 289 C
gradnen@amc.edu
GARDNER, Phil .... 864-977-7014 410 A
phil.gardner@ngu.edu
GARDNER, Rebecca ...... 502-776-1443 184 C
rsmith@simmonscollegeky.edu
GARDNER, Richard .... 212-924-5900 321 C
rgardner@swedishinstitute.edu
GARDNER, Ron .... 559-297-4500.. 46 C
rgardner@iot.edu
GARDNER, Sarah .... 415-485-3239.. 41 H
sarah.gardner@dominican.edu
GARDNER, Scott .... 208-496-4012 130 G
gardners@byui.edu
GARDNER,
Stephanie, F .... 501-686-5689.. 22 D
sfgardner@uams.edu
GARDNER, Susan .... 541-737-0123 374 H
susan.gardner@oregonstate.edu
GARDNER, Tyshawn ..... 205-366-8838.... 7 A
tgardner@stillman.edu
GARDNER, William .... 301-546-0652 201 D
gardnewx@pgcc.edu
GARDNER SMITH,
Catie, K .... 651-696-6315 236 C
GARDUZA, Ericka .... 281-487-1170 447 G
egarduza@txchiro.edu
GARDUÑO, Anna .... 505-454-2501 285 I
agarduno@luna.edu
GARDUÑO-CRESPIN,
Inca .... 505-454-2500 285 I
GARDZINA, Matt .... 614-222-4014 351 A
mgardzina@ccad.edu
GAREIS, Martha .... 970-521-6662.. 82 B
martha.gareis@njc.edu
GARELICK, Rhonda .... 212-229-8916 307 E
garelicr@newschool.edu
GAREY, Bryan .... 540-231-7457 475 D
bgarey@vt.edu
GAREY, Kelly .... 503-552-1603 374 B
kgarey@nunm.edu
GARFIELD, Dana .... 401-598-5235 403 E
dana.garfield@jwu.edu
GARFIN, Steven .... 858-534-1783.. 70 C
sgarfin@ucsd.edu
GARG, Amita .... 562-804-1239.. 45 C
amitag@healthcarecareercollege.edu
GARGIULO, Colette .... 201-489-5836 277 E
GARGIULO, Donald .... 213-252-5100.. 24 C
dgargiulo@alu.edu
GARGIULO, Leslie .... 213-252-5100.. 24 C
lgargiulo@alu.edu
GARIBAY JENKS, Dina . 575-624-7112 285 F
dina.jenks@roswell.enmu.edu
GARIEPY, Maria .... 508-929-8784 213 D
mgariepy1@worcester.edu
GARIFO, Sarah .... 301-891-4222 204 D
sgarifo@wau.edu
GARIMELLA, Suresh ..... 802-656-7878 462 D
suresh.garimella@uvm.edu
GARIMELLA, Umadevi ... 610-359-5282 381 J
ugarimella@dccc.edu
GARLAND,
Christopher, D .... 302-857-6909.. 90 D
cgarland@desu.edu
GARLAND, Colleen .... 740-427-5154 354 I
garland1@kenyon.edu
GARLAND, Elizabeth ..... 503-370-6209 377 E
ecarson@willamette.edu
GARLAND, Philip .... 619-260-4724.. 72 H
pgarland@sandiego.edu
GARLAND, Rebecca, R . 815-740-3648 152 E
rgarland@stfrancis.edu
GARLAND, Sheila .... 402-354-7063 267 E
sheila.garland@methodistcollege.edu
GARLAND, Tom .... 813-988-5131.. 99 M
garlandt@floridacollege.edu
GARLICK, Bill .... 517-483-1780 226 D
garliw@lcc.edu
GARLICK, Kate .... 304-637-1900 486 D
GARLICK, Rebecca .... 979-743-5222 430 I
bgarlick@blinn.edu
GARLICK, Stella .... 304-263-6262 486 G
GARLING, Brittany .... 712-749-2065 164 A
garling@bvu.edu
GARLING, Jessica .... 712-749-2500 164 A
garlingj@bvu.edu
GARLINGTON, Gina, D . 404-627-2681 116 B
gina.garlington@beulah.edu
GARLITZ, John .... 541-962-3114 372 H
jgarlitz@eou.edu
GARMAN, Deanna .... 423-585-6897 424 G
deanna.garman@ws.edu
GARMER, Nancy .... 321-674-7542 100 A
ngarmer@fit.edu
GARN, Gregg, A .... 405-325-7576 370 J
garn@ou.edu
GARN, Jonathan .... 989-686-9160 223 E
jonathangarn@delta.edu
GARNAR, Martin, L ...... 413-542-2373 205 D
library@amherst.edu
GARNER, Alison .... 617-585-1100 217 A
GARNER, Amber .... 662-720-7256 247 D
acgarner@nemcc.edu
GARNER, Amy .... 937-327-7457 364 C
daltona@wittenberg.edu
GARNER, Brian .... 615-329-8690 418 E
bgarner@fisk.edu
GARNER, Clayton .... 719-255-3924.. 84 A
cgarner@uccs.edu
GARNER, David, B .... 215-572-3811 401 G
dgarner@wts.edu
GARNER, Graham .... 936-468-2166 444 H
graham.garner@sfasu.edu
GARNER, Gregg .... 615-879-2022 419 C
GARNER, Jeffrey .... 239-590-1083 109 G
jgarner@fgcu.edu
GARNER, John .... 334-670-3712.... 7 C
jcgarner@troy.edu
GARNER, Jon .... 205-348-7880.... 7 F
jgarner@uasystem.edu
GARNER, III, Joseph .... 573-629-3049 253 D
joseph.garner@hlg.edu
GARNER, Josh .... 770-720-5928 124 E
josh.garner@reinhardt.edu
GARNER, Latonya .... 662-254-3421 247 C
lcgarner@mvsu.edu
GARNER, LaTrina .... 773-252-6464 146 D
GARNER, Lyn .... 281-998-6150 442 D
lyn.garner@sjcd.edu
GARNER, Mesha .... 618-650-3839 149 H
megarne@siue.edu
GARNER, Michael .... 859-846-5839 183 G
michael.garner@midway.edu
GARNER, Porter .... 979-845-7514 446 B
porter-garner@tamu.edu
GARNER, Regina .... 214-860-8561 434 B
garnerre@dcccd.edu
GARNER, Roger .... 256-765-6341.... 8 E
wgarner@una.edu
GARNER, Sam .... 402-363-5620 269 F
sgarner@york.edu
GARNER, Tashania .... 912-279-5806 117 C
tgarner@ccga.edu
GARNER, Tim .... 256-782-8220.... 6 A
tgarner@jsu.edu
GARNER-FERRIS,
Chelsea .... 941-309-4098 106 J
cferris@ringling.edu
GARNETT, Heather .... 434-544-8431 470 K
garnett_h@lynchburg.edu
GARNSEY-HARTER, Ann 206-546-5879 483 C
agarnsey@shoreline.edu
GAROFALO, Giovanni ... 412-365-1292 380 F
g.garofalo@chatham.edu
GARONE, Wilson .... 206-296-6148 483 B
wgarone@seattleu.edu
GARR, Bethany .... 864-596-9595 407 G
healthservices@converse.edu
GARRANT, Ines .... 617-358-0513 207 C
igarrant@bu.edu
GARRELL, Robin, L .... 212-817-7100 293 D
president@gc.cuny.edu
GARREN, Cynthia .... 863-784-7177 108 D
cynthia.garren@southflorida.edu
GARRETSON, Angela, R 973-596-3108 278 G
angela.r.garretson@njit.edu
GARRETT, Allen .... 619-201-8700.. 60 G
algarrett@sdcc.edu
GARRETT, Bonnie, J ..... 410-777-2503 197 C
bjgarrett@aacc.edu
GARRETT, Brian .... 212-616-7200 301 A
GARRETT, Candace .... 256-761-6590.... 7 B
cgarrett@talladega.edu
GARRETT, Craig .... 504-282-4455 190 D
cgarrett@nobts.edu
GARRETT, Daniel .... 605-225-1634 414 I
GARRETT, Don .... 325-674-2213 427 G
dlg09a@acu.edu
GARRETT, Geoff .... 213-740-6422.. 73 C
dean@marshall.usc.edu
GARRETT, Gina .... 870-307-7557.. 20 D
gina.garrett@lyon.edu
GARRETT, Glenda .... 214-860-8591 434 B
ghall@dcccd.edu
GARRETT, Helen .... 206-685-2553 484 A
helenbg@uw.edu
GARRETT, James .... 502-597-5951 183 A
james.garrett@kysu.edu
GARRETT, JR.,
James, H .... 412-268-3260 380 B
garrett@andrew.cmu.edu
GARRETT, Jason .... 731-661-5367 425 F
jgarrett@uu.edu
GARRETT, Katrina .... 601-484-8724 246 B
kgarret2@meridiancc.edu
GARRETT, Kevin .... 304-384-5340 488 K
garrettad@concord.edu
GARRETT, Kristi .... 205-860-7845.... 7 A
kgarrett@stillman.edu
GARRETT, Kristina .... 507-786-3419 242 I
garrettk@stolaf.edu
GARRETT, Krystal .... 217-351-2533 146 G
kgarrett@parkland.edu
GARRETT, LaCharlotte ... 504-284-5435 191 A
lgarrett@suno.edu
GARRETT, Leonard .... 214-860-3697 434 B
lgarrett@dcccd.edu
GARRETT, Mandy .... 785-890-3641 176 E
mandy.garrett@nwktc.edu
GARRETT, Mark .... 270-901-1065 182 E
mark.garrett@kctcs.edu
GARRETT, Mechelle ...... 503-375-8189 372 G
mgarrett@corban.edu
GARRETT, Natasha .... 412-536-1296 386 H
natasha.garrett@laroche.edu
GARRETT, Nicole, L ...... 919-658-7896 340 E
ngarrett@umo.edu
GARRETT, Rachele .... 936-468-2504 444 H
nixonhr@sfasu.edu
GARRETT, Rachele .... 936-468-2403 444 H
nixonhr@sfasu.edu
GARRETT, Rick .... 765-641-4156 153 D
ragarrett@anderson.edu
GARRETT, Robert, J ...... 208-496-1124 130 G
garrettr@byui.edu
GARRETT, Robin .... 254-526-1733 431 E
robin.garrett@ctcd.edu
GARRETT, Scott .... 216-687-5119 350 G
s.garrett1@csuohio.edu
GARRETT, Shana .... 866-492-5336 243 G
shana.garrett@mail.waldenu.edu
GARRETT, Teresa .... 434-381-6205 470 H
tgarrett@sbc.edu
GARRETT, Tiffani .... 702-968-2033 271 D
tgarrett@roseman.edu
GARRETT, Todd, L .... 913-971-3278 175 H
tgarrett@mnu.edu
GARRETT FINSTER,
Susan .... 619-239-0391.. 34 H
sgf@cwsl.edu
GARRETT-KOJU, Stacey 615-238-6350 418 E
skoju@bonelaw.com
GARRICK, Connie, S ..... 281-290-2923 438 E
connie.s.garrick@lonestar.edu
GARRICK, Sean, C .... 217-244-3674 151 F
sgarrick@illinois.edu
GARRICK DUHANEY,
Laurel .... 845-257-3561 316 B
duhaneyl@newpaltz.edu
GARRIDO, Alfred .... 671-735-2372 503 E
garridoa3216@triton.uog.edu
GARRIDO, Lillian .... 407-303-7747.. 95 A
lillian.garrido@ahu.edu
GARRIGO, Jose, I .... 406-791-5300 264 J
jose.garrigo@uprovidence.edu
GARRINGER, Jim .... 765-998-4912 161 A
jmgarringer@taylor.edu
GARRIOCH, Shay .... 845-451-4365 297 E
shay.garrioch@culinary.edu
GARRIS, Daffie, H .... 336-633-0290 336 F
dhgarris@randolph.edu
GARRIS, Eric .... 843-661-1136 408 H
egarris@fmarion.edu
GARRIS, Rick .... 303-963-3290.. 78 D
rgarris@ccu.edu
GARRISION, Phil .... 512-454-1188 429 B
pgarrison@aoma.edu
GARRISON, Anne .... 508-856-2285 212 A
anne.garrison@umassmed.edu
GARRISON, Anthony ..... 925-631-4235.. 59 I
anthony@stmarys-ca.edu
GARRISON, Christie ...... 417-873-7200 252 A
cgarrsion@drury.edu
GARRISON, Cindy .... 931-526-3660 418 F
cynthia.stephenson@fortisinstitute.edu
GARRISON, Deborah ..... 716-829-8447 298 C
garrisod@dyc.edu
GARRISON, Diane .... 609-626-3842 283 A
diane.garrison@stockton.edu
GARRISON, James .... 913-971-3626 175 H
jgarriso@mnu.edu
GARRISON, Jennifer ...... 812-464-1862 162 B
jlgarrison@usi.edu
GARRISON, Joseph, L .. 989-774-5251 221 M
garri2jl@cmich.edu
GARRISON, Julie, A ...... 269-387-5202 232 J
julie.garrison@wmich.edu
GARRISON, Kristen .... 940-397-6305 439 F
kristen.garrison@msutexas.edu
GARRISON, Makenna .... 918-463-2931 365 I
makenna.garrsion@connorsstate.edu
GARRISON, Mark .... 443-885-3185 200 F
mark.garrison@morgan.edu
GARRISON, Melissa .... 610-330-5005 387 B
garrisom@lafayette.edu
GARRISON, Renetta .... 530-752-1011.. 69 A
GARRISON, Ryan .... 828-652-6021 335 H
GARRISON, Samuel .... 213-740-5371.. 73 C
sam.garrison@usc.edu
GARRISON, Samuel .... 940-898-2911 451 A
sgarrison1@twu.edu
GARRISON, Shane .... 270-789-5541 179 G
msgarrison@campbellsville.edu
GARRISON, Steve .... 940-397-4978 439 F
steve.garrison@msutexas.edu
GARRISON, Tom .... 208-792-2247 131 F
tgarrison@lcsc.edu
GARRITY, Christopher .. 413-737-7000 205 C
christopher.garrity@aic.edu
GARRITY, Geraldine ...... 928-724-6814.. 12 F
ggarrity@dinecollege.edu
GARRITY, Kathleen, E ... 608-822-2471 498 H
kgarrity@swtc.edu

GARRITY, Michael ... 708-456-0300 151 A michaelgarrity@triton.edu
GARRITY, Mitch ... 505-277-2626 288 C mgarrity@unm.edu
GARROW, Steve ... 816-268-5400 256 E sgarrow@nts.edu
GARRY, Kirby ... 831-582-3015 .. 32 D kgarry@csumb.edu
GARSTECKI, Marcus ... 605-229-8492 414 I marcus.garstecki@presentation.edu
GARTEN, Aimee ... 909-607-2370 .. 37 F aimee.garten@cgu.edu
GARTENMAYER, Charles ... 913-360-7583 171 G cgartenmayer@benedictine.edu
GARTIN, Stanton ... 785-309-3160 177 B stanton.gartin@salinatech.edu
GARTLAND, Myles ... 816-501-4563 257 K myles.gartland@rockhurst.edu
GARTMAN, Mark ... 903-510-2254 451 D mark.gartman@tjc.edu
GARTNER, Scott ... 831-656-2371 501 K scott.gartner@nps.edu
GARTRELL, Carla ... 623-572-6364 144 C cgartr@midwestern.edu
GARVER, Beth ... 617-585-0200 206 E blg@the-bac.edu
GARVER, Joseph ... 954-532-9614 102 D
GARVER, Robert, A ... 419-866-0261 361 A ragarver@stautzenberger.com
GARVEY, Judy ... 714-241-6230 .. 38 D jgarvey@coastline.edu
GARVEY, Kevin ... 973-720-2861 283 I garveyk@wpunj.edu
GARVEY, Michael, T ... 920-923-8790 492 D mtgarvey04@marianuniversity.edu
GARVIN, Kalindi ... 319-363-8213 168 D kgarvin@mtmercy.edu
GARVIN, Lisa ... 214-768-4507 443 G garvinl@smu.edu
GARVIN, Lynda ... 318-487-5443 187 G lyndagarvin@cltcc.edu
GARVIN, Maureen ... 912-525-5000 124 G mgarvin@scad.edu
GARVIN, Natara ... 615-329-8635 418 E ngarvin@fisk.edu
GARVIN, William ... 417-873-7482 252 A wgarvin@drury.edu
GARVIN AQUILINO, Rose ... 240-567-4249 200 E rosegarvinaquilino@montgomerycollege.edu
GARVIN-LEIGHTON, Timothy ... 706-778-8500 124 B tleighton@piedmont.edu
GARWOOD, Erika ... 619-260-4524 .. 72 H egarwood@sandiego.edu
GARY, Alex ... 828-227-7338 343 D agary@wcu.edu
GARY, Cynthia ... 405-682-1611 367 D cgary@occc.edu
GARY, Jay ... 918-495-6713 368 F jgary@oru.edu
GARY, Jay ... 662-246-6302 246 E jgary@msdelta.edu
GARY, Joe ... 270-707-3790 181 G joe.gary@kctcs.edu
GARY, Teresa ... 614-891-3200 357 A
GARY, William ... 216-987-3110 351 D william.gary@tri-c.edu
GARZA, Adriana ... 361-593-4979 447 A adriana.garza@tamuk.edu
GARZA, Daniel ... 408-288-3163 .. 62 G daniel.garza@sjcc.edu
GARZA, Fernando ... 830-372-6056 448 C fgarza@tlu.edu
GARZA, Hector ... 303-404-5117 .. 80 I hector.garza@frontrange.edu
GARZA, Janet ... 509-547-0511 478 B jgarza@columbiabasin.edu
GARZA, Javier ... 254-968-0787 445 F garza@tarleton.edu
GARZA, John ... 956-665-3298 455 A john.garza@utrgv.edu
GARZA, Kim ... 509-793-2010 477 D kimg@bigbend.edu
GARZA, Monique ... 559-638-0300 .. 67 C monique.garza@reedleycollege.edu
GARZA, JR., Norman, R ... 979-845-2217 446 B ngarza@tamu.edu
GARZA, PJ ... 916-577-2200 .. 76 C pgarza@jessup.edu
GARZA, Rebecca, J ... 214-860-2618 434 A rgarza@dcccd.edu
GARZA, Robert ... 210-486-3960 427 H
GARZA, Robert ... 210-486-3000 428 B
GARZA, Roberto, A ... 956-326-2325 446 A roberto.garza1@tamiu.edu
GARZA, Rolando ... 361-593-5501 447 A rolando.garza@tamuk.edu
GARZA, Tambera ... 218-855-8123 237 C tambera.garza@clcmn.edu
GARZA, Vicente ... 361-354-2749 431 L vgarza@coastalbend.edu
GARZA, JR., Victor ... 408-270-6434 .. 62 F victor.garza@evc.edu
GARZA-RODERICK, Jessie ... 209-833-7900 .. 61 H jgarza-roderick@deltacollege.edu
GARZANELLI, Melissa ... 660-785-7480 259 J melissag@truman.edu
GARZANELLI, Mike ... 660-785-4153 259 J michaelg@truman.edu
GARZARELLI, Todd ... 724-357-4295 393 G tgarzare@iup.edu
GASAWAY, Debbie ... 870-460-1622 .. 22 E gasaway@uamont.edu
GASCHE, Currie ... 847-574-5158 141 G cgasche@lfgsm.edu
GASEVIC, Sarah ... 701-788-4647 345 B sarah.gasevic@mayvillestate.edu
GASH, Brandon ... 417-873-7257 252 A bgash@drury.edu
GASH, James, A ... 310-506-4451 .. 56 H jim.gash@pepperdine.edu
GASH, Justin ... 317-738-8213 155 A jgash@franklincollege.edu
GASHAW, Abigail ... 309-677-3083 133 H algashaw@fsmail.bradley.edu
GASHI, Agron ... 845-848-4058 298 A agron.gashi@dc.edu
GASKELL, Carolyn ... 509-527-2107 484 C carolyn.gaskell@wallawalla.edu
GASKELL, Millicent ... 610-519-6371 401 B millicent.gaskell@villanova.edu
GASKIN, Cathy, M ... 503-370-6492 377 E cmccann@willamette.edu
GASKIN, Elizabeth ... 772-462-7225 102 E egaskin@irsc.edu
GASKINS, LeeBrian, E ... 281-283-2905 452 A gaskins@uhcl.edu
GASOSKE, Betsy ... 314-434-4044 251 F registrar@covenantseminary.edu
GASPAR, Leigh ... 617-824-3877 208 G leigh_gaspar@emerson.edu
GASPAR, Nicholas ... 810-762-3200 231 C ngaspar@umich.edu
GASPARD, Harold ... 504-671-6247 187 I hgaspa@dcc.edu
GASPARICH, Gail ... 717-871-7555 394 B gail.gasparich@millersville.edu
GASPARRO, Paul, F ... 740-699-3037 348 D pgasparro@belmontcollege.edu
GASPER, Kim ... 916-900-2850 .. 26 H kgasper@asher.edu
GASPER JARVIS, Donna ... 207-221-4237 197 A dgasper@une.edu
GASQUE, Tarlough ... 240-567-7588 200 E tarlough.gasque@montgomerycollege.edu
GASS, Beth ... 423-305-7783 417 F beth.gass@chattanoogacollege.edu
GASS, Eric ... 414-297-6263 498 B gasse@matc.edu
GASSELING, Garet ... 509-453-0374 481 G garet.gasseling@perrytech.edu
GASSER, George ... 573-651-2930 258 J gmgasser@semo.edu
GASSER, Ray, F ... 517-884-4996 227 C gasserra@msu.edu
GASSERT, Alden ... 315-781-3616 301 D gassert@hws.edu
GASSIOT, Ken ... 912-478-3326 120 A kgassiot@georgiasouthern.edu
GASSMAN, Chad ... 641-585-8183 170 E chad.gassman@waldorf.edu
GASSNER, Cece ... 903-246-1194 446 D cece.gassner@tamuc.edu
GAST, Brad ... 715-675-3331 498 E gast@ntc.edu
GASTINEAU, Zane ... 501-279-4464 .. 19 G zgastineau@harding.edu
GASTON, Amy ... 717-396-7833 392 Q agaston@pcad.edu
GASTON, David ... 785-864-3624 177 G adgaston@ku.edu
GASTON, David ... 800-280-0307 153 B david.gaston@ace.edu
GASTON, Lori ... 704-894-2208 328 C logaston@davidson.edu
GASTON, Patricia ... 518-629-7292 302 A p.gaston@hvcc.edu
GASTON, Rachel ... 870-574-4423 .. 21 F rgaston@sautech.edu
GASWICK, Kari ... 308-432-6202 267 G kgaswick@csc.edu
GATCH, Delana ... 912-478-7354 120 A dgatch@georgiasouthern.edu
GATCH, Maura ... 406-265-3536 264 A maura.gatch@msun.edu
GATELY, Kevin ... 978-837-5385 216 D gatelykm@merrimack.edu
GATES, Charles, B ... 415-338-2765 .. 34 A charlesbg@sfsu.edu
GATES, Dinecia ... 314-838-8858 261 A dgates@ugst.edu
GATES, Gladys ... 989-317-4760 229 K ggates@sagchip.edu
GATES, Jane ... 860-723-0058 .. 85 E gatesj@ct.edu
GATES, Jeffrey ... 315-792-3006 323 G jtgates@utica.edu
GATES, John ... 765-494-4600 159 G
GATES, Margaret, A ... 607-777-2000 315 E
GATES, Michelle ... 480-517-8000 .. 14 A
GATES, Reginald ... 817-515-5001 445 A reginald.gates@tccd.edu
GATES, Sean ... 310-577-3000 .. 76 H sgates@yosan.edu
GATES, Sharon ... 312-942-3670 148 C sharon_gates@rush.edu
GATES, Victor ... 254-526-1168 431 E victor.gates@ctcd.edu
GATES, Yvonne ... 303-444-0202 .. 81 N
GATES BLACK, L. Joy ... 610-359-5100 381 J jgatesblack@dccc.edu
GATEWOOD, Algie, C ... 336-506-4150 331 J algie.gatewood@alamancecc.edu
GATEWOOD, Jace, C ... 678-916-2601 115 G jgatewood@johnmarshall.edu
GATEWOOD, Laura ... 509-313-6381 479 E gatewood@gonzaga.edu
GATHERS, Khaleel, M ... 716-878-6625 317 C gathersm@buffalostate.edu
GATHJE, Peter ... 901-334-5830 420 E pgathje@memphisseminary.edu
GATINS, Deborah ... 845-575-3000 305 C deborah.gatins@marist.edu
GATKE, Brandon ... 503-352-1510 375 B bgatke@pacificu.edu
GATLIFF, Hope ... 713-348-4500 441 K hg4@rice.edu
GATLIN, Brandon ... 406-657-2147 263 H brandon.gatlin@msubillings.edu
GATLIN, Greg ... 617-573-8428 218 G ggatlin@suffolk.edu
GATLIN, Kenda ... 206-281-2569 482 K kgatlin@spu.edu
GATLIN, Patricia ... 585-385-8241 313 A pgatlin@sjfc.edu
GATLING, Veleka, S ... 757-683-3141 468 C vgatling@odu.edu
GATRELL, Jay, D ... 217-581-2121 137 C jgatrell@eiu.edu
GATRJYAN, Berj ... 510-925-4282 .. 25 P
GATTAS, Jeff ... 858-534-2230 .. 70 C jgattas@ucsd.edu
GATTEAU, Richard ... 631-632-6700 316 D richard.gatteau@stonybrook.edu
GATTI, Eileen ... 802-322-1603 461 D eileen.gatti@goddard.edu
GATTIS, Gerald ... 251-460-6133 .... 9 A ggattis@southalabama.edu
GATTIS, Tom ... 614-222-3237 351 A tgattis@ccad.edu
GATTONI, Susanna ... 405-325-4124 370 J sgattoni@ou.edu
GATTOZZI, Nicholas ... 330-672-3000 354 A ngattozz@kent.edu
GATTUSO, Vince ... 312-563-7527 148 C vince_gattuso@rush.edu
GATZKE, Meredith ... 201-447-7100 274 I
GAU, Karalynn ... 617-879-7065 212 E kgau@massart.edu
GAUBATZ, Dale ... 303-273-3225 .. 79 A dgaubatz@mines.edu
GAUBATZ, Noreen ... 803-323-3707 413 D gaubatzn@winthrop.edu
GAUDELIUS, Yvonne ... 814-863-1864 391 F ymg100@psu.edu
GAUDELLI, William ... 610-758-3221 388 C wig318@lehigh.edu
GAUDETTE, Helen ... 212-217-5380 299 C helen_gaudette@fitnyc.edu
GAUDINO-GOERING, Elizabeth, A ... 516-572-7775 307 C elizabeth.gaudino-goering@ncc.edu
GAUDREAU, Alison, K ... 248-364-6117 229 F agaudreau@oakland.edu
GAUGER, John ... 434-582-8946 467 E jmgauger@liberty.edu
GAUGHAN, Cheryl ... 619-849-2499 .. 57 J cherylgaughan@pointloma.edu
GAUGHF, Natalie, W ... 601-845-6436 248 G nwgaughf1@umc.edu
GAUL, Julie, M ... 412-578-6042 380 A jmgaul@carlow.edu
GAUL, Yvonne ... 718-482-5559 294 D
GAULDEN, Susan ... 201-684-7500 280 B sgaulden@ramapo.edu
GAUNCE, Lori ... 606-759-7141 182 B lori.gaunce@kctcs.edu
GAUNDER, Alisa ... 512-863-1418 444 F gaundera@southwestern.edu
GAUNTT, Kamille ... 706-865-2134 126 D kgauntt@truett.edu
GAURMER, Terry ... 303-458-1629 .. 83 B tgaurmer@regis.edu
GAURON, Patricia, M ... 978-556-3000 215 C pgauron@necc.mass.edu
GAUSE, Genell ... 843-661-8351 408 G genell.gause@fdtc.edu
GAUSTAD, Gabrielle, G ... 607-871-2953 289 E gaustad@alfred.edu
GAUTAM, Mridul ... 775-327-2363 270 K mgautam@unr.edu
GAUTHIER, Theresa ... 585-785-1304 299 E theresa.gauthier@flcc.edu
GAUTIER, Angela ... 575-835-6619 286 D angela.gautier@nmt.edu
GAUVAIN, Ignatius ... 570-561-1818 397 B ignatius.gauvain@stots.edu
GAUVIN, Keith ... 843-953-6964 406 D kgauvin@citadel.edu
GAUVIN, Olivia ... 207-307-3900 193 E registrar@beal.edu
GAVARRA-OH, Mary Anne ... 818-710-2234 .. 49 H gavarrm@piercecollege.edu
GAVENTA, Sarah ... 512-404-4885 429 K sgaventa@austinseminary.edu
GAVER, Bob ... 402-363-5721 269 F bagaver@york.edu
GAVIGAN, Lisa ... 508-286-3799 219 F gavigan_lisa@wheatoncollege.edu
GAVIN, Andrew ... 262-595-2485 495 D gavin@uwp.edu
GAVIN, Carrie ... 850-599-3076 109 E carrie.gavin@famu.edu
GAVIN, Diane ... 210-486-2431 428 C dgavin7@alamo.edu
GAVIN, Joseph ... 713-718-6015 436 E joseph.gavin@hccs.edu
GAVIN, Michael ... 414-297-6760 498 B gavinmj@matc.edu
GAVIN, Michael ... 973-655-5105 278 C
GAVIN, Michael, H ... 989-686-9000 223 E michaelgavin@delta.edu
GAVIN, Mike ... 828-395-1295 335 B mgavin@isothermal.edu
GAVIN, Paul ... 319-363-1323 168 D pgavin@mtmercy.edu
GAVIN, Paula ... 386-752-1822 .. 99 P paula.gavin@fgc.edu
GAVINI, Srinivas, R ... 225-771-2277 190 K reddy_gavini@subr.edu
GAVLICK, Christopher ... 718-636-3579 311 A cgavlick@pratt.edu
GAVLIK, Deborah ... 937-512-3060 360 F deborah.gavlik@sinclair.edu
GAW, Kevin ... 401-232-6090 403 B kgaw@bryant.edu
GAWEL, Matthew ... 207-893-6609 195 I mgawel@sjcme.edu
GAWELEK, Mary Ann ... 419-824-3809 355 C mgawelek@lourdes.edu
GAWENDA, Matt ... 312-922-1884 143 D mgawenda@maccormac.edu
GAWLICK, Craig ... 650-949-7777 .. 43 A

GAWLIK, Terry ... 208-885-0216 132 C tlg@uidaho.edu
GAWRONSKI, JR., Michael ... 845-341-4284 310 D michael.gawronski@sunyorange.edu
GAWTHROP, Larry ... 810-762-0235 228 B larry.gawthrop@mcc.edu
GAWU, Helena ... 409-984-6216 449 D arthurh@lamarpa.edu
GAXIOLA-ROWLES, Thomas ... 559-443-8612.. 67 A thom.gaxiola@fresnocitycollege.edu
GAY, Aaron ... 859-246-6565 181 B aaron.gay@kctcs.edu
GAY, Bob ... 304-724-3700 485 G rgay@apus.edu
GAY, Chris ... 706-771-4145 115 H cgay@augustatech.edu
GAY, Claudine ... 617-495-1566 210 B fasdean@fas.harvard.edu
GAY, Cliff ... 478-289-2025 118 B cgay@ega.edu
GAY, John ... 410-386-8434 197 G jgay@carrollcc.edu
GAY, Michelle ... 704-403-1758 327 B michelle.gay@atriumhealth.org
GAYA, Liliam ... 787-250-1912 507 C lgaya@intermetro.edu
GAYER, Richard, H ... 213-262-3939.. 46 H
GAYLE, Helene ... 404-270-5001 126 A helenegayle@spelman.edu
GAYLER, Sarah ... 270-686-6416 179 F sarah.gayler@brescia.edu
GAYLOR, IV, Charles ... 919-739-7161 338 F cpgaylor@waynecc.edu
GAYMON, Joffery ... 334-844-6428.... 4 E jag0124@auburn.edu
GAYNOR, Dona, E ... 321-674-7394 100 A dgaynor@fit.edu
GAYNOR, Julie ... 940-397-4353 439 F julie.gaynor@msutexas.edu
GAYNOR, Lynnette ... 919-365-7711 340 C lgaynor@sfwbc.edu
GAYNOR, Michael, M ... 610-519-4000 401 B michael.gaynor@villanova.edu
GAYNOR, Timothy ... 919-365-7711 340 C tgaynor@sfwbc.edu
GAYTAN, Alejandra ... 909-607-4404.. 37 F alejandra.gaytan@cgu.edu
GAYTAN, Andrea ... 916-375-5513.. 51 B gaytana@scc.losrios.edu
GAYTAN, Andrea ... 916-375-5505.. 51 B gaytana@scc.losrios.edu
GAYTAN, Franco, X ... 773-244-5740 145 F fgaytan@northpark.edu
GAYTAN, Maribel ... 530-741-6700.. 77 B
GAYTON, Linda ... 973-684-6104 279 B lgayton@pccc.edu
GAZAL, Andre ... 406-586-3585 263 A andre.gazal@montanabiblecollege.edu
GAZAL, Mary ... 724-805-2627 397 C mary.gazal@stvincent.edu
GAZAL, Mary ... 724-805-2555 397 D mary.gazal@stvincent.edu
GAZZALE, Bob ... 323-856-7600.. 25 M bgazzale@afi.com
GAZZARA HESS, Margaret ... 508-588-9100 214 F mhess2@massasoit.mass.edu
GAZZILLO, Sara ... 201-684-7610 280 B sgazzill@ramapo.edu
GEAGHAN, Tom ... 216-687-4745 350 G t.geaghan@csuohio.edu
GEAR, Lisa, L ... 213-738-6834.. 66 A admissions@swlaw.edu
GEARAN, Dan ... 603-428-2372 272 I dgearan@nec.edu
GEARAN, Mark, D ... 315-781-3309 301 D gearan@hws.edu
GEARHART, Gregory, L ... 717-691-6007 389 F gearhart@messiah.edu
GEARHART, Victoria ... 301-687-4714 203 F vmgearhart@frostburg.edu
GEARHART, Zach ... 316-978-5859 178 B zachary.gearhart@wichita.edu
GEARHART TURNER, Patti ... 817-531-5820 450 F pturner@txwes.edu
GEARING-KALILL, Allison ... 413-565-1000 205 I agkalill@baypath.edu
GEARY, Cale ... 724-838-4282 397 F cgeary@setonhill.edu
GEARY, Colette ... 718-862-7200 304 K cgeary01@manhattan.edu
GEARY, Jason ... 848-932-9360 281 B jgeary@mgsa.rutgers.edu
GEARY, MaryLee ... 303-678-3642.. 80 I marylee.geary@frontrange.edu
GEARY, Parrish ... 916-484-8172.. 50 J gearyp@arc.losrios.edu
GEASEY, David, W ... 607-436-3314 316 C david.geasey@oneonta.edu
GEBBIE, Joe ... 703-284-5960 468 A jgebbie@marymount.edu
GEBEKE, Mike ... 309-438-8851 140 C mdgebek@ilstu.edu
GEBHARDT, Matthias ... 951-763-0500.. 55 A
GEBHARDT, Maureen ... 978-927-0585 209 B mgebhard@endicott.edu
GEBHARDT, Michael, B 215-204-8635 398 D michael.gebhardt@temple.edu
GEBHARDT, Robert ... 503-517-1813 377 D bgebhardt@westernseminary.edu
GEBKE, Jill ... 314-367-8700 260 A jill.gebke@uhsp.edu
GEBLER, Ryan, L ... 920-832-6584 492 B ryan.l.gebler@lawrence.edu
GEBO, John ... 607-844-8222 321 I geboj@tompkinscortland.edu
GEBREMICHAEL, Miliite 651-793-1876 238 B miliite.gebremichael@metrostate.edu
GEBRU, Amanuel ... 805-553-4065.. 73 I agebru@vcccd.edu
GEDDINGS, Scarlet ... 803-535-1243 410 C geddingss@octech.edu
GEDLINSKE, Paul ... 920-424-0404 495 C gedlinsk@uwosh.edu
GEDNALSKE, Julie ... 605-331-6683 416 C julie.gednalske@usiouxfalls.edu
GEDRO, Julie ... 585-224-3222 320 B julie.gedro@esc.edu
GEDULDIG, Liza ... 802-651-5938 461 C lgeduldig@champlain.edu
GEE, E. Gordon ... 304-293-5531 489 E gordon.gee@mail.wvu.edu
GEE, Henry ... 562-692-0921.. 58 M hgee@riohondo.edu
GEE, Robert ... 909-794-1084.. 39 G
GEE, Terry ... 619-594-2853.. 33 E tgee@sdsu.edu
GEEHAN, Margaret ... 518-629-7151 302 A m.geehan@hvcc.edu
GEEL, Donna ... 207-454-1013 195 E dgeel@wccc.me.edu
GEER, Caroline ... 423-775-6596 421 I carolinegeer@gmail.com
GEER, Cynthia ... 513-745-3119 364 F geer@xavier.edu
GEER, John, G ... 615-936-6366 427 B john.geer@vanderbilt.edu
GEER, Kimberly ... 425-739-8119 480 D kimberly.geer@lwtech.edu
GEETER, Andy ... 229-732-5934 114 I andygeeter@andrewcollege.edu
GEETER, Candy ... 248-341-2138 228 H crgeeter@oaklandcc.edu
GEETTER, Erika ... 617-353-2326 207 C egeetter@bu.edu
GEFELL, Michele, D ... 315-786-2271 302 I mgefell@sunyjefferson.edu
GEFFERT, Bryn ... 802-656-2020 462 D bryn.geffert@uvm.edu
GEFROH, Heidi ... 605-367-4625 416 B heidi.gefroh@southeasttech.edu
GEGENHEIMER BALDASSARO, Sarah ... 202-994-5152.. 92 C sarahgb@gwu.edu
GEHBAUER, Daryl ... 636-481-3120 253 G dgehbaue@jeffco.edu
GEHLERT, Sarah ... 213-740-2311.. 73 C
GEHLHAUSEN, Keith ... 812-488-2943 161 E kg77@evansville.edu
GEHRICH, Michael, D ... 317-381-6016 162 E mgehrich@vinu.edu
GEHRING, Dennis ... 319-363-1323 168 D dgehring@mtmercy.edu
GEHRING, Patrick, D ... 253-535-7119 481 C gehrinpd@plu.edu
GEHRINGER, Steve ... 610-409-3598 400 E sgehringer@ursinus.edu
GEHRKE, Sean ... 206-543-9956 484 A sjgehrke@uw.edu
GEHRKE, Shelly ... 620-341-5421 173 C rgehrke@emporia.edu
GEHRMAN ROTTIER, Laura ... 715-346-3903 496 B laura.gehrman.rottier@uwsp.edu
GEIBEL, Randy ... 631-656-2157 299 G
GEIDE-STEVENSON, Doris ... 801-626-6063 460 B dgsteven@weber.edu
GEIER, Cathy ... 202-884-9545.. 94 A geierc@trinitydc.edu
GEIER, Doug ... 415-369-5275.. 44 B dgeier@ggu.edu
GEIGER, Debra ... 912-443-5783 124 I dgeiger@savannahtech.edu
GEIGER, Douglas ... 773-838-7984 135 C dgeiger3@ccc.edu
GEIGER, Hope ... 918-631-2715 371 C hope-geiger@utulsa.edu
GEIGER, Joseph ... 215-222-4200 401 C jgeiger@walnuthillcollege.edu
GEIGER, Karen ... 610-527-0200 396 G karen.geiger@rosemont.edu
GEIGER, Martha ... 513-936-1691 362 A martha.geiger@uc.edu
GEIKEN, Jason ... 479-968-0400.. 18 E jgeiken@atu.edu
GEIL, Carol ... 641-844-5747 167 E carol.geil@iavalley.edu
GEIL, Toi ... 307-766-2187 500 H
GEIS, Jodi ... 828-327-7000 332 H jgeis@manufacturingsolutionscenter.org
GEIS, Quint ... 402-826-8501 266 A quinton.geis@doane.edu
GEISEN, Kathleen ... 701-483-2137 345 A kathleen.geisen@dickinsonstate.edu
GEISER, Laura ... 314-977-2543 258 H laura.geiser@slu.edu
GEISER-GETZ, Glenn ... 585-245-5531 317 E geisergetz@geneseo.edu
GEISLER, Allison ... 218-293-6850 238 D allison.geisler@minnesotanorth.edu
GEISMAN, Cami ... 225-342-6950 191 F cami.geisman@ulsystem.edu
GEISSINGER, Peter ... 541-962-3638 372 H pgeissinger@eou.edu
GEISSLER, Nancy ... 217-228-5432 147 C geissna@quincy.edu
GEIST, Alan ... 937-766-7768 349 C geista@cedarville.edu
GEIST, Amanda ... 630-466-7900 152 H ageist@waubonsee.edu
GELAYE, Enku ... 404-727-5693 118 D enku.gelaye@emory.edu
GELB, Edward ... 919-573-5350 340 A assessment@shepherds.edu
GELBACK-DIAZ, Christy 317-921-4746 158 A cgelback@ivytech.edu
GELDZAHLER, Daniel ... 718-633-4715 311 G collegeoy@gmail.com
GELENTER, Sue ... 410-626-2504 201 E sue.gelenter@sjc.edu
GELERNTER, Mark ... 303-315-1020.. 84 B mark.gelernter@ucdenver.edu
GELFUSO, Andrew ... 401-232-6406 403 B agelfuso@bryant.edu
GELINA, Denise ... 573-875-8700 251 A
GELL, Barry ... 518-255-5440 318 F gellbf@cobleskill.edu
GELLER, Jack, M ... 813-253-6262 113 B jgeller@ut.edu
GELLER, Laurie ... 701-858-3310 345 C laurie.geller@minotstateu.edu
GELLER, Mary, A ... 320-363-5601 234 I mgeller@csbsju.edu
GELLER, Steve ... 952-358-8954 239 C steve.geller@normandale.edu
GELLES, Karen ... 934-420-2420 320 C gelleska@farmingdale.edu
GELLMAN, Sarah, M ... 724-946-7340 401 F gellmasm@westminster.edu
GELO, Erica ... 218-879-0746 237 F erica@fdltcc.edu
GELSTON, Nicole ... 860-486-5796.. 89 B nicole.gelston@uconn.edu
GELUZ, Ramon ... 562-804-1239.. 45 C ramong@healthcarecareercollege.edu
GELWICKS, Carla ... 360-383-3222 485 B cgelwick@whatcom.edu
GELY, Gilda ... 616-554-5183 222 H gilda.gely@davenport.edu
GEMEDA, Mekbib, L ... 757-446-7151 465 H gemedam@evms.edu
GEMME, Terese ... 203-392-5499.. 85 H gemmet1@southernct.edu
GEMMEL, Jeanine ... 845-451-1302 297 E jeanine.gemmel@culinary.edu
GEMMELL, Ann ... 651-290-6434 241 N ann.gemmell@mitchellhamline.edu
GEMMER, Pete ... 513-936-1632 362 A peter.gemmer@uc.edu
GEMPERLEIN, Monica, P ... 919-334-1520 338 E mpgemperlein@waketech.edu
GENANDT, James ... 785-320-4500 175 E jamesgenandt@manhattantech.edu
GENARD, Daniel, J ... 757-683-5747 468 C dgenard@odu.edu
GENARDO, Patricia ... 630-889-6597 145 D pgenardo@nuhs.edu
GENCO, Caroline ... 617-628-5000 219 A
GENDRON, Dennis ... 716-926-8922 301 C dgendron@hilbert.edu
GENDRON, Dennis ... 615-327-6894 420 D dgendron@mmc.edu
GENDUSA, Michelle ... 509-533-8196 478 D michelle.gendusa@scc.spokane.edu
GENECIN, Paul ... 203-432-0076.. 90 B paul.genecin@yale.edu
GENELIUS, Sandy ... 413-542-5785 205 D sgenelius@amherst.edu
GENERALS, Donald ... 215-751-8000 381 H ggenerals@ccp.edu
GENES, Marna ... 408-924-1550.. 34 B marna.genes@sjsu.edu
GENESE, Carol ... 914-632-5400 306 J cgenese@monroecollege.edu
GENESER, Michael ... 319-399-8663 164 D mgeneser@coe.edu
GENETTI, Carol ... 805-893-2013.. 70 E cgenetti@graddiv.ucsb.edu
GENFI, Henrieta ... 973-618-3589 275 E hgenfi@caldwell.edu
GENGLER, Charles, E ... 713-221-8017 452 B
GENIG, Dennis ... 734-462-4400 230 B dgenig@schoolcraft.edu
GENIN, Larisa ... 316-978-3200 178 B larisa.genin@wichita.edu
GENKINGER, Mark ... 701-231-8788 345 D mark.genkinger@ndsu.edu
GENNA, Angela ... 602-285-7357.. 13 H angela.genna@phoenixcollege.edu
GENNARO, Gwen ... 719-255-3153.. 84 A ggennaro@uccs.edu
GENNETTE, Heather ... 785-243-1435 172 J hgennette@cloud.edu
GENO, Amanda ... 413-565-1150 205 I ageno@baypath.edu
GENONI, Mia, R ... 804-289-8468 471 E mgenoni@richmond.edu
GENOVESE, Erin ... 309-677-3160 133 H egenovese@bradley.edu
GENT, Barbara ... 606-248-0142 182 F barbara.gent@kctcs.edu
GENTEMAN, Kurt ... 706-769-1472 115 B
GENTHON, Paulette ... 402-556-4456 268 H paulettegenthon@ucha.edu
GENTILE, Julie ... 330-941-3700 364 G jgentile@ysu.edu
GENTILE, Kim ... 330-972-6345 361 G gentile@uakron.edu
GENTILE, Kimberly ... 610-499-4498 401 I kmgentile@widener.edu
GENTILE, Maria ... 563-588-7639 167 I maria.gentile@loras.edu
GENTILE, Maria ... 415-257-1307.. 41 H maria.gentile@dominican.edu
GENTILE, Marla ... 828-898-3841 330 A gentilem@lmc.edu
GENTIUS, Paula ... 919-515-2191 341 E paula_gentius@ncsu.edu
GENTLEWARRIOR, Sabrina ... 508-531-1429 212 B sabrina.gentlewarrior@bridgew.edu
GENTNER, Becky ... 810-984-3881 230 A
GENTRY, Amanda ... 256-840-4210.... 3 F amanda.gentry@snead.edu
GENTRY, Eric, C ... 859-572-5129 184 B egentry@nku.edu
GENTRY, Holly ... 303-914-6341.. 82 L holly.wren@rrcc.edu
GENTRY, Jeff ... 575-562-2733 285 E jeff.gentry@enmu.edu
GENTRY, Jeffrey ... 270-809-3420 184 A jgentry@murraystate.edu

GHEE, Hailey .... 404-962-3002 127 B
hailey.ghee@usg.edu
GHERBI, Naima .... 860-439-2411.. 87 F
nghe@conncoll.edu
GHIDIU, Katherine, E ... 585-292-2320 306 K
kghidiu@monroecc.edu
GHIDOTTI, Lisa .... 540-831-5000 468 E
lghidotti@radford.edu
GHILONI, Adam .... 864-646-1583 411 H
aghiloni@tctc.edu
GHINASSI, Frank .... 848-932-3818 281 B
ghinassi@ubhc.rutgers.edu
GHOLSON, Robert, D ..... 601-266-4466 248 H
robert.gholson@usm.edu
GHOLSON, Shari .... 270-534-3412 182 G
shari.gholson@kctcs.edu
GHOLSON, Shari .... 270-534-3372 182 G
shari.gholson@kctcs.edu
GHOLSTON, Kim .... 215-895-2582 382 D
kjg88@drexel.edu
GHORAYEB, Samir .... 409-984-6484 449 D
samir.ghorayeb@lamarpa.edu
GHORI, Zaid .... 650-738-7088.. 62 K
ghoriz@smccd.edu
GHORMOZ, Jacquelyn .. 570-504-9073 384 A
jghormoz@som.geisinger.edu
GHORPADE, Anuja .... 518-694-7337 289 A
anuja.ghorpade@acphs.edu
GHOSAL, Bobby .... 601-928-6207 246 F
bobby.ghosal@mgccc.edu
GHOSH, Avijit .... 217-333-3077 151 C
ghosha@uillinois.edu
GHOSH, Avijit .... 217-265-0263 151 C
ghosha@uillinois.edu
GHOSH, Guru .... 540-231-3205 475 D
gghosh@vt.edu
GHOSH, Jayati .... 989-964-4064 229 L
jghosh@svsu.edu
GHOSH, Melanie Mala . 617-627-2000 219 A
mala.ghosh@tufts.edu
GHOSH, Sibdas .... 412-578-6072 380 A
sghosh@carlow.edu
GHOSH, Soumitra .... 312-362-8610 136 F
GHOUS, Mostafa .... 831-386-7100.. 44 J
mghous@hartnell.edu
GHOUSSAINI, Nizar ...... 402-280-2700 265 J
GHRAYEB, Omar .... 815-753-0494 145 H
oghrayeb@niu.edu
GIACOBBE, Jeff .... 973-655-5373 278 C
giacobbej@montclair.edu
GIACOMAZZI, James ..... 925-424-1281.. 36 A
jgiacomazzi@laspositascollege.edu
GIACOMAZZI, Jim .... 806-291-3801 457 B
giacomazzij@wbu.edu
GIACOMELLI, Jodi .... 814-871-7741 383 H
organ002@gannon.edu
GIACOMINI, Kathy .... 415-476-8010.. 70 D
kathy.giacomini@ucsf.edu
GIACOMINI, Michael .... 661-336-5124.. 47 A
michael.giacomini@bakersfieldcollege.edu
GIACOMINI, Mike .... 661-395-4203.. 47 B
mike.giacomini@bakersfieldcollege.edu
GIAGO, Don .... 605-455-6000 414 H
dgiago@olc.edu
GIAMBRA, Leonard, M . 860-701-6679 502 F
leonard.m.giambra@uscg.mil
GIAMPAOLI, Michael .... 702-463-2122 271 G
GIAMPAOLI, Michael .... 702-463-2122 271 G
mgiampaoli@wongu.org
GIAMPIETRO, Michael .. 413-565-1000 205 I
mgiampietro@baypath.edu
GIANCATARINO, Kate ... 610-519-6285 401 B
kate.giancatarino@villanova.edu
GIANCOLA, Grace .... 518-244-2008 312 D
giancg@sage.edu
GIANNELLIS, Emmanuel, P .... 607-255-7200 297 D
epg2@cornell.edu
GIANNESCHI, Matt .... 970-945-8691.. 78 H
mgianneschi@coloradomtn.edu
GIANNET, Stanley, M ... 727-816-3490 105 E
giannes@phsc.edu
GIANNETTINO, Val .... 319-208-5065 169 I
vgiannettino@scciowa.edu
GIANNETTO, Michael .... 802-387-4767 461 E
GIANNINI, Gaetan .... 610-796-8305 378 C
gaetan.giannini@alvernia.edu
GIANNINI, Renee .... 209-664-6652.. 33 D
rgiannini@csustan.edu
GIANNOBILE, William, V .... 617-495-1000 210 B
william_giannobile@hsdm.harvard.edu
GIANNOTTI, Louis, J .... 410-293-1400 502 I
giannott@usna.edu
GIANOLI, Mary Beth ..... 317-955-6697 159 A
sgianoli@marian.edu
GIANOTTI, Timothy, J ... 773-281-4700 132 G
GIARDULLO, Kelly .... 781-891-2014 206 C
kgiardullo@bentley.edu
GIATAS, Domna .... 207-621-3495 196 E
domna.giatas@maine.edu
GIBAJA, Marcia .... 904-256-7077 102 G
mgibaja@ju.edu
GIBB, Deborah .... 212-229-5667 307 E
gibbd@newschool.edu
GIBB, Randy .... 602-639-7500.. 12 L
GIBBINGS, Emily .... 413-579-3040 213 C
egibbings@westfield.ma.edu
GIBBON, Lori, A .... 316-942-4291 176 B
gibbonl@newmanu.edu
GIBBONS, Arthur .... 845-758-7442 290 G
gibbons@bard.edu
GIBBONS, Beth .... 202-499-6776.. 92 B
beth.gibbons@gallaudet.edu
GIBBONS, Dennis .... 315-792-5361 306 G
dgibbons@mvcc.edu
GIBBONS, Jeremy .... 910-362-7054 332 F
jgibbons@cfcc.edu
GIBBONS, Kristie .... 540-261-4100 470 D
kristie.gibbons@svu.edu
GIBBONS, Megan .... 781-768-7843 217 H
megan.gibbons@regiscollege.edu
GIBBONS, Meghan .... 240-567-7185 200 E
meghan.gibbons@montgomerycollege.edu
GIBBONS, Peter .... 304-724-3700 485 G
pgibbons@apus.edu
GIBBONS, Susan .... 203-432-1810.. 90 B
susan.gibbons@yale.edu
GIBBONS, Thomas, F .... 312-503-3011 146 C
tgibbons@northwestern.edu
GIBBONS, Tom .... 401-841-4008 501 L
gibbonst@usnwc.edu
GIBBONS, William .... 315-267-2000 318 D
GIBBS, Benjamin .... 972-721-5203 451 E
bgibbs@udallas.edu
GIBBS, Cassidy .... 334-347-2623.... 2 A
cgibbs@escc.edu
GIBBS, Chymeka .... 229-293-2100 127 F
chymeka.gibbs@wiregrass.edu
GIBBS, Danny .... 615-366-3921 423 A
danny.gibbs@tbr.edu
GIBBS, Donna .... 360-650-3482 485 A
donna.gibbs@wwu.edu
GIBBS, J. D .... 252-527-6223 335 E
jdgibbs27@lenoircc.edu
GIBBS, Jamie .... 252-249-1851 336 C
jgibbs@pamlicocc.edu
GIBBS, Jeffery .... 407-971-5172 108 B
gibbsj@seminolestate.edu
GIBBS, Jeffery .... 407-404-6060 108 B
gibbsj@seminolestate.edu
GIBBS, Jeremiah .... 317-788-2058 161 F
gibbsj@uindy.edu
GIBBS, Jim .... 806-651-3287 447 D
jgibbs@wtamu.edu
GIBBS, Lincoln .... 231-591-2273 223 H
lincolngibbs@ferris.edu
GIBBS, Martin .... 208-792-2325 131 F
mlgibbs@lcsc.edu
GIBBS, Renisha .... 850-644-8082 110 B
rgibbs@admin.fsu.edu
GIBBS, Robert .... 520-452-2684.. 11 O
gibbsr@cochise.edu
GIBBS, Robert, C .... 512-428-1060 441 N
rgibbs@stedwards.edu
GIBBS, Ryan .... 806-716-2207 443 A
rgibbs@southplainscollege.edu
GIBBS, Sarah .... 919-209-2086 335 D
sfgibbs@johnstoncc.edu
GIBBS, Sharon, C .... 540-375-2204 469 G
sgibbs@roanoke.edu
GIBBS, Shawn, G .... 979-436-9322 446 B
sgibbs@tamu.edu
GIBBS, SherRhonda ...... 970-351-1890.. 84 D
sherrhonda.gibbs@unco.edu
GIBBS, Tanya, R .... 203-285-2061.. 86 D
tgibbs@gatewayct.edu
GIBBS, Thomas, C .... 314-434-4044 251 F
tom.gibbs@covenantseminary.edu
GIBBS DRAYTON, Marilyn .... 803-535-5309 406 E
mgibbs@claflin.edu
GIBERTI, Bruno .... 805-756-2246.. 29 K
bgiberti@calpoly.edu
GIBISCH, Elizabeth .... 256-824-6926.... 8 B
elizabeth.gibisch@uah.edu
GIBLER, Rhonda, K .... 573-882-2094 260 C
giblerr@missouri.edu
GIBLIN, Harvey, M .... 512-691-1717 429 F
hgiblin@aii.edu
GIBLIN, Patrick .... 314-246-7174 261 D
patrickgiblin61@webster.edu
GIBLIN, Tara .... 714-432-5093.. 38 F
tgiblin@occ.cccd.edu
GIBNEY, Regan .... 412-578-6654 380 A
rpgibney@carlow.edu
GIBOUT, Holly .... 847-970-4929 152 F
hgibout@usml.edu
GIBRALTER, Jonathan ... 315-364-3265 324 E
president@wells.edu
GIBSON, Alivia .... 352-854-2322.. 97 L
gibsona@cf.edu
GIBSON, Amy, B .... 630-515-7198 144 C
agibso@midwestern.edu
GIBSON, Andrea .... 386-506-3337.. 98 A
andrea.gibson@daytonastate.edu
GIBSON, Annie, K .... 757-683-3156 468 C
akmorris@odu.edu
GIBSON, Ashley, M .... 918-270-6405 368 G
ashley.gibson@ptstulsa.edu
GIBSON, Bernard .... 805-289-6121.. 74 B
agibson@vcccd.edu
GIBSON, Brenda .... 503-375-7110 372 G
bgibson@corban.edu
GIBSON, Brian .... 504-278-6420 188 E
bgibson@nunez.edu
GIBSON, Brian .... 801-581-8305 459 D
brian.gibson@utah.edu
GIBSON, Camille .... 936-261-5205 445 E
cbgibson@pvamu.edu
GIBSON, Cedrick .... 904-779-4045 101 A
cedrick.gibson@fscj.edu
GIBSON, Chris .... 650-574-6161.. 62 J
GIBSON, Christoper, P . 518-783-2302 314 K
cgibson@siena.edu
GIBSON, Christopher .... 650-738-4343.. 62 K
gibsonc@smccd.edu
GIBSON, Clayton .... 940-565-2055 453 B
clayton.gibson@unt.edu
GIBSON, Crystal, L .... 240-895-4295 201 F
clgibson@smcm.edu
GIBSON, Dan .... 214-333-5931 433 D
danielg@dbu.edu
GIBSON, Danielle .... 402-844-7115 268 A
dgibson@northeast.edu
GIBSON, David .... 903-675-6393 451 C
david.gibson@tvcc.edu
GIBSON, David, J .... 802-443-5834 461 G
djgibson@middlebury.edu
GIBSON, Denise .... 505-454-2500 285 I
GIBSON, Donald .... 718-862-7440 304 K
dgibson01@manhattan.edu
GIBSON, Donna, S .... 212-639-2109 304 H
gibsond@mskcc.org
GIBSON, Dwight .... 847-317-7005 150 J
dgibson@tiu.edu
GIBSON, Edie, B .... 731-881-7508 426 E
edgibson@utm.edu
GIBSON, Erin .... 801-832-2237 461 A
egibson@westminstercollege.edu
GIBSON, Gloria, J .... 773-442-5400 145 G
gjgibson@neiu.edu
GIBSON, Godfrey .... 760-750-4020.. 33 C
ggibson@csusm.edu
GIBSON, Howard, O ...... 903-923-1620 457 I
hgibson@wileyc.edu
GIBSON, Ian .... 949-824-7948.. 69 C
ihgibson@uci.edu
GIBSON, J. Murray .... 850-410-6161 109 E
jmgibson@eng.famu.fsu.edu
GIBSON, Jane .... 901-375-4400 421 A
janegibson@midsouthchristian.edu
GIBSON, Janell .... 251-981-3771.... 5 B
janell.gibson@columbiasouthern.edu
GIBSON, Jeanine .... 203-332-5000.. 86 E
jgibson@hcc.commnet.edu
GIBSON, Jeanne .... 719-549-2704.. 79 G
jeanne.gibson@csupueblo.edu
GIBSON, Jeff .... 319-895-4357 164 E
jgibson@cornellcollege.edu
GIBSON, Jeff .... 417-625-9727 255 I
gibson-j@mssu.edu
GIBSON, Jeffrey .... 580-559-5204 365 J
jgibson@ecok.edu
GIBSON, Jeremy .... 978-837-5306 216 D
gibsonj@merrimack.edu
GIBSON, Jonathan .... 503-517-1806 377 D
jgibson@westernseminary.edu
GIBSON, Joseph .... 843-574-6311 411 I
joe.gibson@tridenttech.edu
GIBSON, Keith, E .... 540-464-7334 475 C
gibsonke@vmi.edu
GIBSON, Kelly .... 913-971-3392 175 H
krgibson@mnu.edu
GIBSON, Kody .... 602-850-8000.. 15 D
GIBSON, Lloyd .... 914-674-7159 305 H
lgibson@mercy.edu
GIBSON, Lynn .... 662-685-4771 244 D
lgibson@bmc.edu
GIBSON, Mandi .... 713-646-1702 443 C
mgibson@stcl.edu
GIBSON, Marc .... 318-675-4928 189 D
marc.gibson@lsuhs.edu
GIBSON, Maribeth .... 601-366-8880 249 A
mgibson@wbs.edu
GIBSON, Matthew .... 816-926-4400 253 C
GIBSON, Megan .... 509-533-3535 478 E
megan.gibson@sfcc.spokane.edu
GIBSON, Melinda .... 757-352-4222 469 D
mgibson@regent.edu
GIBSON, Michael .... 256-840-4124.... 3 F
michael.gibson@snead.edu
GIBSON, Nathan .... 719-255-3075.. 84 A
ngibson@uccs.edu
GIBSON, Nola, R .... 601-974-1132 246 C
gibsonk@millsaps.edu
GIBSON, Pamela .... 910-486-3930 334 C
gibsonp@faytechcc.edu
GIBSON, Peggy .... 276-523-2400 473 E
pgibson@mecc.edu
GIBSON, Rick .... 734-764-6270 231 A
gibsonrl@umich.edu
GIBSON, Rob .... 620-341-6694 173 C
rgibson1@emporia.edu
GIBSON, Robert .... 541-552-7672 376 A
GIBSON, Ryan .... 606-368-6130 178 D
ryangibson@alc.edu
GIBSON, Ryan, W .... 217-581-1904 137 C
rwgibson@eiu.edu
GIBSON, Sally .... 816-271-4369 256 C
sgibson14@missouriwestern.edu
GIBSON, Shanan .... 386-226-7283.. 98 J
shanan.gibson@erau.edu
GIBSON, Stacey .... 208-282-3964 131 E
gibssta2@isu.edu
GIBSON, Susan .... 404-880-8757 116 I
sgibson@cau.edu
GIBSON, Tammy .... 706-379-3111 128 A
tgibson@yhc.edu
GIBSON, Tera .... 325-670-1077 436 B
tera.gibson@hsutx.edu
GIBSON, Thomas .... 715-346-2123 496 B
GIBSON, Tim .... 212-659-7207 303 E
tgibson@tkc.edu
GIBSON, Tim .... 405-692-3287 366 C
tim.gibson@macu.edu
GIBSON, Todd, D .... 724-458-2147 384 F
tdgibson@gcc.edu
GIBSON, Tonia, R .... 270-824-1739 182 A
tonia.gibson@kctcs.edu
GIBSON-GAYLE, Gale .... 718-489-5240 312 H
ggibson-gayle@sfc.edu
GIBSON SHEFFIELD, Gail .... 802-387-6797 461 E
gailsheffield@landmark.edu
GIBSON-SHREVE, Lada . 330-494-6170 360 I
lshreve@starkstate.edu
GIDDENS, Elizabeth ...... 619-260-4823.. 72 H
egiddens@sandiego.edu
GIDDENS, Jean .... 804-828-5174 472 D
jgiddens@vcu.edu
GIDDINGS, Matthew ..... 701-224-5789 345 F
matthew.giddings@bismarckstate.edu
GIDEON, Amy, C .... 615-868-6503 421 B
amy@mtsa.edu
GIDEON, Ryan .... 320-363-5225 234 I
rgideon001@csbsju.edu
GIDJUNIS, Rebecca ...... 610-341-1576 383 A
rgidjuni@eastern.edu
GIE, Lori .... 504-520-5730 193 C
lgie@xula.edu
GIELOW, Bob .... 617-559-8610 210 C
bgielow@hebrewcollege.edu
GIENGER, Crystal .... 985-448-7909 187 J
crystal.gienger@fletcher.edu
GIER, David .... 734-764-0584 231 A
dgier@umich.edu
GIER, Matt .... 208-459-5846 131 A
mgier@collegeofidaho.edu

GILLILAND, Eric ...... 702-992-2322 270 H
eric.gilliland@nsc.edu
GILLIN, Douglas, P ...... 828-262-7781 340 G
gillindp@appstate.edu
GILLING RAYNOR,
Beatrice .... 718-951-5778 293 A
braynor@brooklyn.cuny.edu
GILLINS, Dawn .... 914-606-6844 324 F
dawn.gillins@sunywcc.edu
GILLIS, Diane .... 617-984-1700 217 G
GILLIS, Lynette ...... 512-313-5301 432 N
lynette.gillis@concordia.edu
GILLISPIE, James ...... 540-868-7042 473 C
jgillispie@lfcc.edu
GILLISS, Catherine ...... 415-476-1805.. 70 D
catherine.gilliss@ucsf.edu
GILLMAN, Howard, A .... 949-824-5111.. 69 C
chancellor@uci.edu
GILLMAN, Sally ...... 605-688-6094 416 A
sally.gillman@sdstate.edu
GILLS, Twyla ...... 832-252-0716 431 M
twyla.gills@cbshouston.edu
GILLUM, Deborah ...... 574-807-7015 153 G
deborah.gillum@betheluniversity.edu
GILLUM-CLEMONS,
Nikki .... 610-902-8206 379 E
ng7009@cabrini.edu
GILLUS, Raynaldo ...... 662-254-3636 247 C
raynaldo.gillus@mvsu.edu
GILMAN, Daniel ...... 412-396-6000 382 E
GILMAN, Isaac ...... 503-352-1401 375 B
gilmani@pacificu.edu
GILMAN, James, T ...... 203-932-7015.. 89 F
jgilman@newhaven.edu
GILMAN, Jim ...... 941-351-4742 106 J
jgilman1@ringling.edu
GILMAN, Wendy ...... 518-255-5520 318 F
gilmanwc@cobleskill.edu
GILMARTIN, Kevin, M .. 626-395-6100.. 29 B
kmg@hss.caltech.edu
GILMER, Christopher .. 304-424-8200 490 H
president@wvup.edu
GILMER, Ray ...... 240-567-7970 200 E
ray.gilmer@montgomerycollege.edu
GILMORE, Blaine ...... 859-572-6449 184 B
gilmoreb@nku.edu
GILMORE, Bradley ...... 706-802-5479 119 C
bgilmore@highlands.edu
GILMORE, Brent ...... 562-938-4311.. 48 K
bgilmore@lbcc.edu
GILMORE, Calvin, L ...... 336-272-7102 329 E
gilmorec@greensboro.edu
GILMORE, Darwin ...... 850-718-2270.. 97 E
gilmored@chipola.edu
GILMORE, David ...... 617-989-4328 219 D
gilmored@wit.edu
GILMORE, Derrick, C .... 205-349-4240.. 7 A
dgilmore@stillman.edu
GILMORE, Donna ...... 239-590-7582 109 G
dgilmore@fgcu.edu
GILMORE, Eric, J ...... 402-280-2100 265 J
ericgilmore@creighton.edu
GILMORE, John, W ...... 609-497-7700 279 D
john.gilmore@ptsem.edu
GILMORE, Katrina ...... 661-654-3330.. 30 C
kgilmore2@csub.edu
GILMORE, Lindsey ...... 502-272-7275 179 D
lgilmore@bellarmine.edu
GILMORE, Paul ...... 848-932-0990 281 B
paul.gilmore@rutgers.edu
GILMORE, Paul ...... 516-299-2900 304 D
paul.gilmore@liu.edu
GILMORE, Thomas ...... 712-325-3288 167 G
tgilmore@iwcc.edu
GILMORE, Usha ...... 312-567-3000 139 H
GILMORE, Wayne ...... 617-353-8289 207 C
waygil@bu.edu
GILMORE-CLEVELAND,
Sherie .... 925-631-4552.. 59 I
sbg2@stmarys-ca.edu
GILMORE ENGLISH,
Jessica .... 425-235-2463 482 C
jgilmoreenglishl@rtc.edu
GILMOUR, Davie, J .... 570-320-8010 391 F
djg120@psu.edu
GILORMINI, Dominique 787-766-1912 507 F
dgilormini@inter.edu
GILPERT, Jessica ...... 610-647-4400 385 K
jgilpert@immaculata.edu
GILPIN, Sandy ...... 505-566-3022 287 G
gilpins@sanjuancollege.edu
GILREATH, Scott ...... 765-677-6515 157 F
scott.gilreath@indwes.edu

GILROY, Janice ...... 914-606-6610 324 F
janice.gilroy@sunywcc.edu
GILROY, Maryellen ...... 518-783-2328 314 K
mgilroy@siena.edu
GILSON, Jannie ...... 508-588-9100 214 F
jgilson1@massasoit.mass.edu
GILSON, Jannie ...... 909-621-8471.. 57 E
jannie_gilson@pitzer.edu
GILSTRAP, Bryon ...... 312-369-7940 136 C
bgilstrap@colum.edu
GILSTRAP, Donald ...... 205-348-7561.... 7 G
dlgilstrap@ua.edu
GILSTRAP, Matthew .... 864-388-8000 409 B
mgilstrap@lander.edu
GILTNER, Greg ...... 405-425-5501 367 C
greg.giltner@oc.edu
GILTNER, Scott ...... 573-288-6382 251 I
sgiltner@culver.edu
GINDER, Greg ...... 317-955-6018 159 A
ginder@marian.edu
GINDICESSI, Beth ...... 415-503-6285.. 61 E
egindicessi@sfcm.edu
GINEVAN, Douglas, W .. 207-786-6093 193 D
dginevan@bates.edu
GINGERELLA, David .... 508-999-8051 211 F
dgingerella@umassd.edu
GINGERICH, Jeff ...... 716-375-2222 312 F
jgingerich@sbu.edu
GINGERICH, Tamara ..... 219-464-6196 162 C
tamara.gingerich@valpo.edu
GINGLES, Haley, N ...... 336-750-3152 343 E
gingleshn@wssu.edu
GINGRAS, Jim ...... 312-369-7736 136 C
jgingras@colum.edu
GINGROW, Nick ...... 802-828-8600 462 E
GINN, Bryan ...... 678-225-7500 395 A
bginn@pcom.edu
GINN, Julie ...... 781-239-2734 214 E
jginn@massbay.edu
GINN, Mark ...... 828-262-2070 340 G
ginnmc@appstate.edu
GINN, Phill ...... 704-847-5600 340 D
pginn@ses.edu
GINNETTI, Jennifer ...... 215-646-7300 384 G
ginnetti.j@gmercyu.edu
GINSBERG, Amy ...... 973-720-2594 283 I
ginsberga3@wpunj.edu
GINSBERG, Mark ...... 703-993-5399 466 J
mginsber@gmu.edu
GINSBERG, Richard ...... 718-289-5770 292 H
richard.ginsberg@bcc.cuny.edu
GINSBERG, Rick ...... 785-864-4297 177 G
ginsberg@ku.edu
GINSBURG, Charles, M 214-648-8597 456 D
charles.ginsburg@utsouthwestern.edu
GINTER, Judy ...... 859-985-3767 179 E
ginterj@berea.edu
GINTER, Matthew ...... 419-434-5624 362 D
ginterm@findlay.edu
GINTNER, Robin ...... 541-867-8516 374 D
robin.gintner@oregoncoast.edu
GINTY, Kevin ...... 773-508-2204 142 G
kginty@luc.edu
GIOIOSO, JR.,
Domenic .... 603-526-3698 271 H
domenic.gioioso@colby-sawyer.edu
GIORDANO,
Christopher .... 810-762-3434 231 C
giordanc@umich.edu
GIORDANO, Matthew ... 716-896-0700 324 A
giordano@villa.edu
GIORDANO,
Nicholas, J .... 334-844-5737.... 4 E
njg0003@auburn.edu
GIORDANO, Rose ...... 916-558-2279.. 51 B
giordar@scc.losrios.edu
GIORDANO, Steve ...... 615-547-1225 418 C
sgiordano@cumberland.edu
GIORDANO, Victoria ...... 863-680-5080 100 F
vgiordano@flsouthern.edu
GIOVAGNOLI, Michelle . 570-208-5847 386 G
michellegiovagnoli@kings.edu
GIOVANETTI, Tracy ...... 870-733-6874.. 18 A
tmclaughlin@asumidsouth.edu
GIOVANNELLI, Tony ...... 724-964-8811 391 A
tgiovannelli@ncstrades.edu
GIPE, Jason ...... 919-658-7637 340 E
jgipe@umo.edu
GIPKO, Jesse ...... 740-699-9500 348 D
jgipko@belmontcollege.edu
GIPSON, Amy ...... 386-822-7220 111 F
agipson@stetson.edu
GIPSON, Cory ...... 903-730-4890 437 E
cgipson@jarvis.edu

GIPSON, Dee ...... 239-304-7977.. 95 M
dee.gipson@avemaria.edu
GIPSON, Maurice ...... 573-882-3394 260 B
mdgipson@missouri.edu
GIPSON, Maurice, D .... 573-882-3394 260 C
mdgipson@missouri.edu
GIPSON, Pamela ...... 540-515-3749 464 C
pgipson@bridgewater.edu
GIPSON, Patrick ...... 773-602-5524 135 A
pgipson2@ccc.edu
GIPSON, Tim ...... 760-872-2000.. 41 D
tgipson@deepsprings.edu
GIPSON, William ...... 215-898-0809 399 J
wgipson@exchange.upenn.edu
GIPSON-RAYFORD, Rita 662-252-8000 248 B
rrayford@rustcollege.edu
GIRALDO, Luis ...... 805-965-0581.. 62 M
lggiraldo@sbcc.edu
GIRALDO, Maribel ...... 914-594-4696 308 J
mgiraldo2@nymc.edu
GIRANDOLA, Joe ...... 513-562-8750 347 G
president@artacademy.edu
GIRARD, Angie ...... 509-452-5100 481 E
agirard@pnwu.edu
GIRARD, David ...... 719-384-6818.. 82 C
david.girard@otero.edu
GIRARD, Don ...... 310-434-4287.. 63 B
girard_donald@smc.edu
GIRARD, Gary ...... 531-622-2541 266 G
gagirard@mccneb.edu
GIRARD, Joseph, C ...... 401-841-2245 501 L
joseph.girard@usnwc.edu
GIRARD, Preble ...... 337-475-5243 192 B
preble@mcneese.edu
GIRARD, Rebekka ...... 214-637-3530 457 A
GIRARD, Samantha ...... 619-216-6762.. 65 K
sgirard@swccd.edu
GIRARD-MALLEY,
Jenny .... 510-436-1081.. 45 H
girard-malley@hnu.edu
GIRARDEAU, Cathy ...... 912-650-5672 125 D
cgirardeau@southuniversity.edu
GIRARDIN, Lindsay ...... 909-607-5934.. 37 F
lindsay.lease@cgu.edu
GIRARDOT, Steven ...... 404-894-5551 119 D
steven.girardot@gatech.edu
GIRAUD, Gerald ...... 307-754-6235 500 G
gerald.giraud@nwc.edu
GIRGENTE, Irene ...... 501-332-0208.. 18 D
igirgente@asutr.edu
GIRGIS, Bassem ...... 949-376-6000.. 47 G
bgirgis@lcad.edu
GIRGIS, Ibrahim ...... 304-326-1259 486 I
ibrahim.girgis@salemu.edu
GIRNUS, Josh, C ...... 253-535-7476 481 C
girnusjc@plu.edu
GIRO, Sasha ...... 305-629-2929 107 F
sgiro@sanignaciouniversity.edu
GIROD, Devin ...... 903-468-8198 446 D
devin.girod@tamuc.edu
GIROD, Douglas, A ...... 785-864-3131 177 G
dgirod@ku.edu
GIROD, Mark ...... 503-838-8471 377 C
girodm@wou.edu
GIROIR, Elizabeth ...... 337-482-5930 192 F
elizabeth.giroir@louisiana.edu
GIROUX, Jenifer ...... 401-456-8990 404 A
jgiroux@ric.edu
GIRTON, Carrie ...... 740-245-7382 363 A
cgirton@rio.edu
GIRTON, Kaitlin ...... 718-390-3100 324 B
GISH, Jennifer ...... 518-337-5694 296 E
gishj@strose.edu
GISH, Joanne ...... 805-565-6066.. 75 I
jgish@westmont.edu
GISS, Gary ...... 315-279-2969 303 D
ggiss@keuka.edu
GISSELER, Adam ...... 815-825-2086 141 D
agisseler@kish.edu
GISSENDANNER,
Cindy, L .... 410-704-5456 204 B
cgissendanner@towson.edu
GISSY, Cynthia ...... 304-424-8259 490 A
cindy.gissy@wvup.edu
GIST, Vicki ...... 406-265-3706 264 A
gist@msun.edu
GITAU, Peter ...... 530-895-2511.. 27 F
GITLIN, Laura, N ...... 267-359-5957 382 D
laura.gitlin@drexel.edu
GITTELL, Ross ...... 401-232-6008 403 B
rgitt@bryant.edu
GITTENS, Brian, E ...... 501-603-1159.. 22 D
bgittens@uams.edu

GITTENS, Carol Ann ..... 925-631-4012.. 59 I
cgittens@stmarys-ca.edu
GITTINGS, Karen ...... 843-661-1688 408 H
kgittings@fmarion.edu
GIUFFI, Krista ...... 312-942-2569 148 C
krista_m_giuffi@rush.edu
GIUFFRIDA, Andrea ...... 210-567-4219 455 E
giuffrida@uthscsa.edu
GIUFRE, Matt ...... 845-257-3910 316 B
giufrem@newpaltz.edu
GIUNTA, Bridget ...... 570-408-4134 402 B
bridget.giunta@wilkes.edu
GIUSTI, Linda ...... 916-577-2200.. 76 C
lgiusti@jessup.edu
GIUSTI, Rebecca ...... 909-706-3519.. 75 G
rgiusti@westernu.edu
GIVAN, Lisa, D ...... 260-422-5561 156 A
ldgivan@indianatech.edu
GIVAN, Natalie ...... 212-757-1190 289 H
ngivan@aami.edu
GIVENS, Christen ...... 850-201-8466 112 B
christen.givens@tcc.fl.edu
GIVENS, Daniel ...... 540-231-7910 475 D
dangivens@vt.edu
GIVENS, Earl ...... 704-637-4212 327 H
ebgivens15@catawba.edu
GIVENS, Gregg ...... 816-584-6429 257 F
gregg.givens@park.edu
GIVENS, Hali ...... 251-442-2212.... 8 C
hgivens@umobile.edu
GIVENS, Natisha ...... 704-290-5828 337 F
ngivens@spcc.edu
GIVENS, Rita ...... 870-574-4495.. 21 F
rgivens@sautech.edu
GIVINS, Ashlee ...... 508-853-2300 215 B
agivins@qcc.mass.edu
GIVOGLU, Wendy, L ..... 407-582-2822 113 C
wgivoglu@valenciacollege.edu
GJERDE, Michelle ...... 719-549-2512.. 79 G
michelle.gjerde@csupueblo.edu
GJERDE, Ryan ...... 563-387-1288 167 J
gjerdery@luther.edu
GLACKIN, Barbara ...... 573-986-6011 258 J
bglackin@semo.edu
GLADCHUK, Chet ...... 410-293-2429 502 I
gladchuk@usna.edu
GLADDEN, James, M .... 317-278-3635 157 B
jamglad@iupui.edu
GLADDEN, Josh ...... 662-915-2780 248 B
jgladden@olemiss.edu
GLADDEN, Samuel ...... 504-280-1278 189 F
sgladden@uno.edu
GLADE, Fiona ...... 240-567-1845 200 E
fiona.glade@montgomerycollege.edu
GLADNEY, Don ...... 561-868-4116 105 C
gladneyd@palmbeachstate.edu
GLADNEY, Sandra, K ..... 541-346-0696 376 G
skgladney@uoregon.edu
GLADSTEIN, Andy ...... 757-490-1241 463 E
agladstein@auto.edu
GLADUE, Angel ...... 701-477-7825 346 H
agladue@tm.edu
GLADUE, Brian ...... 817-735-5083 453 E
brian.gladue@unthsc.edu
GLADWIN, Mark, T ...... 410-706-7410 202 F
mgladwin@som.umaryland.edu
GLADWIN, Sonja ...... 410-777-2927 197 C
srgladwin@aacc.edu
GLADYS, Niki ...... 775-445-3239 271 A
niki.gladys@wnc.edu
GLANCY, Susan, K ...... 212-854-9977 296 H
skg56@columbia.edu
GLANDER, Mindy ...... 706-754-7790 123 C
mglander@northgatech.edu
GLANDON,
Constance, J .... 641-422-4332 168 E
glandcon@niacc.edu
GLANTZ, Bonnie ...... 509-533-3339 478 E
bonnie.glantz@sfcc.spokane.edu
GLANZ, Melissa, A ...... 330-494-6170 360 I
mglanz@starkstate.edu
GLANZER, Chris ...... 620-947-3121 177 F
chrisg@tabor.edu
GLAPA-GROSSKLAG,
James .... 661-362-3632.. 38 H
james.glapa-grossklag@canyons.edu
GLASCO, Gerald ...... 810-762-3480 231 C
gglasco@umich.edu
GLASCO, Lisa ...... 870-972-3449.. 17 I
lglasco@astate.edu
GLASENER, Jacquelyn .. 559-278-2586.. 31 D
jacquig@csufresno.edu
GLASER, Brian ...... 309-796-5238 133 D
glaserb@bhc.edu

Index of Key Administrators GLASER – GODFREY 663

GLASER, Cara .... 703-891-1787 470 G
admissions@standardcollege.edu
GLASER, David .... 936-294-1010 449 E
dpg016@shsu.edu
GLASER, James .... 617-627-4230 219 A
james.glaser@tufts.edu
GLASER, Katelyn .... 440-826-8016 348 C
kglaser@bw.edu
GLASER, Kyle .... 412-365-2734 380 F
k.glaser@chatham.edu
GLASER, Stacey .... 907-442-3400.. 10 B
slglaser@alaska.edu
GLASER, Stephanie .... 704-894-2114 328 C
stglaser@davidson.edu
GLASFORD,
Theodore, E .... 340-693-1535 512 B
tglasfo@uvi.edu
GLASGAL, Rana .... 617-373-8565 217 D
GLASGOW,
Mary Ellen, S .... 412-396-6554 382 E
glasgowm@duq.edu
GLASGOW, Michael ...... 860-486-3619.. 89 B
michael.glasgow@uconn.edu
GLASGOW, Sara .... 231-348-6604 228 D
sglasgow@ncmich.edu
GLASGOW, Terri .... 269-749-7623 229 G
tglasgow@olivetcollege.edu
GLASGOW, Wayne, C ... 478-301-5599 122 C
glasgow_wc@mercer.edu
GLASIER, Jennifer .... 360-475-7128 481 B
GLASKE, Tucker .... 254-295-4281 453 A
tglaske@umhb.edu
GLASMACHER, Thomas . 517-908-7710 227 C
glasmacher@frib.msu.edu
GLASPER, Janice .... 702-651-5698 270 F
janice.glasper@csn.edu
GLASS, Amber .... 580-349-1376 367 F
amber.glass@opsu.edu
GLASS, AmyBeth .... 609-652-4849 283 A
amybeth.glass@stockton.edu
GLASS, Andrew .... 253-964-6534 481 H
aglass@pierce.ctc.edu
GLASS, Art .... 845-569-3210 307 B
arthur.glass@msmc.edu
GLASS, Brent .... 651-201-1673 236 F
brent.glass@minnstate.edu
GLASS, Carrie .... 504-520-7522 193 C
cglass1@xula.edu
GLASS, Cheryl, A .... 651-631-5344 243 E
caglass@unwsp.edu
GLASS, Chris .... 202-462-2101.. 93 A
cglass@iwp.edu
GLASS, Cynthia, M .... 212-217-3650 299 C
cynthia_glass@fitnyc.edu
GLASS, Grace .... 304-724-3700 485 G
gglass@apus.edu
GLASS, Jamie .... 205-929-3407.... 2 H
jglass@lawsonstate.edu
GLASS, Jeff .... 919-660-5386 328 D
jeff.glass@duke.edu
GLASS, Jim .... 229-225-5068 125 G
jglass@southernregional.edu
GLASS, Marc .... 207-780-4141 196 J
marc.glass@maine.edu
GLASS, JR., Robert .... 706-776-0111 124 B
bglass@piedmont.edu
GLASS, Sheronda .... 262-595-2230 495 D
glasss@uwp.edu
GLASS, Stacy .... 630-960-3934 144 C
sglass@midwestern.edu
GLASS, Stewart .... 914-606-8501 324 F
stewart.glass@sunywcc.edu
GLASS, Tameka .... 770-426-2705 122 A
tameka.glass@life.edu
GLASS, Wendy, G .... 207-786-6096 193 D
wglass@bates.edu
GLASS PEREZ, Kristen .. 847-491-7256 146 C
kristen.glassperez@northwestern.edu
GLASS-SHOWLER,
Rachel .... 918-335-6212 368 E
rglassshowler@okwu.edu
GLASSBURN, Suzanne .. 617-452-2081 215 G
GLASSCOCK, Darrell, R . 210-434-6711 440 D
drglasscock@ollusa.edu
GLASSCOE, Toni .... 517-483-9909 226 D
glassct@lcc.edu
GLASSER, Karen .... 406-756-3841 262 H
kglasser@fvcc.edu
GLASSER, Paul .... 646-565-6030 322 C
paul.glasser@touro.edu
GLASSER, Paul .... 646-565-6030 322 B
paul.glasser@touro.edu
GLASSFORD, Darwin ..... 616-222-3000 226 A
dglassford@kuyper.edu
GLASSFORD, Samantha 732-255-0400 279 A
sglassford@ocean.edu
GLASSMAN, Beth .... 610-328-8397 398 B
bglassm1@swarthmore.edu
GLASSMAN, David, M .. 217-581-2011 137 C
dglassman@eiu.edu
GLASSMAN, Jody .... 305-348-7596 109 H
jody.glassman@fiu.edu
GLASSMAN, Paul .... 646-592-4106 325 R
paul.glassman@yu.edu
GLATMAN, Elena .... 617-521-2000 218 C
GLATT, Camilla .... 509-542-5548 478 B
GLATTER, Bryan .... 337-521-8994 188 G
bryan.glatter@solacc.edu
GLAUS, Beth .... 573-651-5923 258 J
baglaus@semo.edu
GLAVIN, Keith .... 508-289-2229 220 B
kglavin@whoi.edu
GLAZE, Doug .... 314-529-9606 254 D
dglaze@maryville.edu
GLAZER, David .... 973-278-5400 274 J
dvg@berkeleycollege.edu
GLAZER, David .... 973-278-5400 291 A
dvg@berkeleycollege.edu
GLAZER, Meir .... 718-268-4700 311 H
GLAZER, Randy .... 323-259-2500.. 54 I
GLAZEWSKI, Eleanor .... 732-842-1900 275 D
GLEAN, Randy .... 309-298-1920 152 I
r-glean@wiu.edu
GLEASON, Allyson .... 610-359-5341 381 J
agleason@dccc.edu
GLEASON, Ann, C .... 919-760-8521 331 A
gleasona@meredith.edu
GLEASON, Brenda .... 314-367-8700 260 A
brenda.gleason@uhsp.edu
GLEASON, David .... 410-455-2709 202 G
gleason@umbc.edu
GLEASON, Grace .... 212-659-7200 303 E
ggleason@tkc.edu
GLEASON, James .... 503-375-7585 372 G
board@corban.edu
GLEASON-ZEEFF, Paula 616-732-1203 222 H
paula.gleason-zeeff@davenport.edu
GLEBER, Richard .... 601-403-1352 247 F
GLECKLER, Bryan .... 217-786-2253 142 F
bryan.gleckler@llcc.edu
GLEESON-KREIG,
JoAnn .... 518-564-2195 318 C
gleesojm@plattsburgh.edu
GLEIM, Jeffrey .... 618-453-2408 149 G
jeffg@alumni.siu.edu
GLEITMAN, Claire .... 607-274-3102 302 E
gleitman@ithaca.edu
GLEIXNER, Stacy .... 408-741-2150.. 75 D
stacy.gleixner@westvalley.edu
GLEJZER, Richard .... 413-662-5242 212 F
richard.glejzer@mcla.edu
GLEN, Nicole .... 508-531-2483 212 B
nglen@bridgew.edu
GLENDENNING,
Danielle .... 845-451-1314 297 E
danielle.glendenning@culinary.edu
GLENMAYE, Linnea .... 316-978-5054 178 B
linnea.glenmaye@wichita.edu
GLENN, Brooke .... 402-465-7518 267 J
bglenn@nebrwesleyan.edu
GLENN, SR.,
Chance, M .... 361-570-4321 452 C
glennc1@uhv.edu
GLENN, Crystal .... 828-327-7000 332 H
cglenn@cvcc.edu
GLENN, Darrell .... 212-217-4075 299 C
darrell_glenn@fitnyc.edu
GLENN, Deborah .... 610-526-1399 378 D
deborah.glenn@theamericancollege.edu
GLENN, Debra .... 801-957-4084 460 D
debra.glenn@slcc.edu
GLENN, Elise .... 724-357-3402 393 G
eglenn@iup.edu
GLENN, Jenna .... 630-889-6620 145 D
jglenn@nuhs.edu
GLENN, Jonathan, A ..... 501-450-3126.. 23 K
jona@uca.edu
GLENN, Kimberlin .... 602-787-7102.. 13 G
kimberlin.glenn@paradisevalley.edu
GLENN, Lane, A .... 978-556-3855 215 C
lglenn@necc.mass.edu
GLENN, Mark .... 319-656-2447 169 F
mark.glenn@shilohuniversity.edu
GLENN, Micah, A .... 314-505-7224 251 D
glennm@csl.edu
GLENN, Nancy .... 208-426-2933 130 F
nancyglenn@boisestate.edu
GLENN, Peggy .... 918-444-4207 366 G
glennsum@nsuok.edu
GLENN, Robert, K .... 361-570-4332 452 C
glennrk@uhv.edu
GLENN, Tammy, S .... 800-287-8822 153 F
glennta@bethanyseminary.edu
GLENN-JONES, Patrice .. 904-766-6044.... 4 B
pajones@alasu.edu
GLENNON, Jennifer ...... 410-857-2403 200 D
jglennon@mcdaniel.edu
GLESNER FINES,
Barbara .... 816-235-1007 260 D
glesnerb@umkc.edu
GLEW, Karen .... 207-453-5820 195 B
kglew@kvcc.me.edu
GLICK, Carol .... 313-593-6751 231 B
cglick@umich.edu
GLICK, Nicole .... 562-938-4695.. 48 K
nglick@lbcc.edu
GLICKLER, Joanna .... 206-221-3095 484 A
glickler@uw.edu
GLIDDEN, Stacey, T ...... 978-468-7111 209 G
sglidden@gcts.edu
GLIEM, Allegra .... 856-482-4200.. 93 H
GLIEM, Allegra .... 609-835-6000.. 93 H
GLIEM, Valerie .... 727-864-8408.. 98 G
gliemvm@eckerd.edu
GLIKAS, Emily .... 575-769-4109 285 C
emily.glikas@clovis.edu
GLINES, Carol, A .... 563-333-6328 169 D
glinescarola@sau.edu
GLINES, Carol, A .... 563-333-6329 169 D
glinescarola@sau.edu
GLINES, Lee .... 801-422-4147 458 A
lee.glines@byu.edu
GLINES, Neil .... 707-864-7000.. 64 F
neil.glines@solano.edu
GLISCH, John .... 321-433-7017.. 98 F
glischj@easternflorida.edu
GLODEN CARLSON,
Sarah .... 402-559-8932 269 B
sarah.glodencarlson@unmc.edu
GLOMSRUD, Ryan .... 760-480-8474.. 75 H
academicdean@wscal.edu
GLOOR, Kathryn .... 740-376-4620 355 E
kathryn.gloor@marietta.edu
GLORIA, Doriane, K .... 646-664-3308 292 E
doriane.gloria@cuny.edu
GLORIA, Jackie .... 858-566-1200.. 41 E
jgloria@disd.edu
GLOSE, Karen .... 610-861-4589 391 B
kglose@northampton.edu
GLOSTER, Clay .... 336-285-2366 341 C
cgloster@ncat.edu
GLOVASKI, Matthew, T . 914-633-2311 302 C
mglovaski@iona.edu
GLOVER, B.J .... 405-585-5701 367 B
beverly.glover@okbu.edu
GLOVER, Brandi .... 660-263-4100 256 D
brandiglover@macc.edu
GLOVER, David .... 757-727-5259 466 L
david.glover@hamptonu.edu
GLOVER, Gail .... 607-431-4041 300 G
gloverg@hartwick.edu
GLOVER, Gail .... 845-431-8405 298 B
gail.glover@sunydutchess.edu
GLOVER, Glenda .... 615-963-7401 425 A
president@tnstate.edu
GLOVER, Ja'Net .... 352-273-2316 110 E
jglover@ufsa.ufl.edu
GLOVER, Jeannette .... 309-649-6603 150 D
jeannette.glover@src.edu
GLOVER, Jennifer .... 804-425-5797 464 N
jglover@ccc-va.com
GLOVER, John .... 701-231-6800 345 D
john.glover@ndsualumni.com
GLOVER, Joseph .... 352-392-2404 110 E
jglover@aa.ufl.edu
GLOVER, Joseph, M ..... 812-941-2661 157 D
joglover@ius.edu
GLOVER, Kerri .... 828-398-7900 331 K
kerriaglover@abtech.edu
GLOVER, Kisalan .... 773-907-4493 134 N
kglover31@ccc.edu
GLOVER, Laura .... 906-227-2244 228 E
lglover@nmu.edu
GLOVER, Leonardo .... 870-575-8291.. 22 F
gloverlp@uapb.edu
GLOVER, Oveta .... 803-376-5732 405 D
oglover@allenuniversity.edu
GLOWIENKA, Jennifer ... 406-447-4461 262 E
jglowienka@carroll.edu
GLYER-CULVER, Betty ... 916-568-3068.. 50 I
glyercb@losrios.edu
GLYMPH, Minnie .... 404-727-6055 118 D
minnie.glymph@emory.edu
GLYNN, Amy, C .... 413-545-8500 211 D
aglynn@admin.umass.edu
GLYNN, Christine .... 414-410-4083 490 J
clglynn@stritch.edu
GLYNN, Luke .... 508-856-4653 212 A
luke.glynn@umassmed.edu
GMEINER, Rebecca .... 678-466-4145 117 A
rebeccagmeiner@clayton.edu
GMITTER, Elizabeth .... 312-850-4595 135 E
egmitter@ccc.edu
GNADINGER, Cindy ...... 262-524-7246 491 A
cgnadinger@carrollu.edu
GNAN, Peter, D .... 708-209-3192 136 D
peter.gnan@cuchicago.edu
GNARRA, James .... 941-782-5957 387 C
jgnarra@lecom.edu
GOATELY, Virginia .... 518-442-5080 315 D
vgoatley@albany.edu
GOBEN, Jason .... 606-693-5000 182 H
jgoben@kmbc.edu
GOBER, Jaclyn .... 215-572-5511 401 G
jgober@wts.edu
GOBER, Steve .... 859-858-3581 178 G
GOBER, T. Kale .... 602-639-7500.. 12 L
GOBERIS, Lisa .... 303-273-3230.. 79 A
lgoberis@mines.edu
GOBERISH, John, S ...... 724-480-3450 381 G
john.goberish@ccbc.edu
GOBIEL, Eric .... 508-767-7086 205 F
ep.gobiel@assumption.edu
GOBLIRSCH, James ...... 507-457-5045 241 A
jgoblirsch@winona.edu
GOCHENAUER, Kristan . 262-691-5211 499 A
kgochenauer@wctc.edu
GOCHENAUR,
Heather, K .... 260-982-5873 158 W
hkgochenaur@manchester.edu
GOCHESKI, Dara .... 804-289-8088 471 E
dgochesk@richmond.edu
GOCHIS, Cheryl .... 254-710-2000 430 F
cheryl_gochis@baylor.edu
GOCHIS, Suzanne .... 816-604-1033 254 E
suzanne.gochis@mcckc.edu
GOCIAL, Tammy .... 314-529-6893 254 D
tgocial@maryville.edu
GOCKLEY, Daniel, L ...... 214-458-6200 455 B
daniel.gockley@utsa.edu
GODARD, Michael .... 573-651-2063 258 J
mgodard@semo.edu
GODBEE, Sara .... 443-334-2688 202 C
sgodbee@stevenson.edu
GODDARD, Amy .... 405-224-3140 371 B
agoddard@usao.edu
GODDARD, Courtney .... 660-543-4157 259 K
cgoddard@ucmo.edu
GODDARD, Deanna ...... 507-457-2493 241 A
dgoddard@winona.edu
GODDARD, Jerry .... 661-946-2274.. 74 G
GODDARD, Jill, P .... 508-565-1070 218 F
jgoddard@stonehill.edu
GODDARD, Kelly .... 484-581-1272 383 A
kelly.goddard@eastern.edu
GODDARD, Lisa .... 916-306-1628.. 67 E
lgoddard@sum.edu
GODDARD, Nick .... 303-352-3053.. 80 D
nick.goddard@ccd.edu
GODDARD, Scott, D ...... 304-637-1352 486 D
goddards@dewv.edu
GODDARD MCGUIRK,
Lisa .... 814-871-7664 383 H
mcguirk001@gannon.edu
GODDEN, Barb .... 712-325-3320 167 G
bgodden@iwcc.edu
GODDEN, Barbara .... 641-782-1452 170 B
godden@swcciowa.edu
GODDEN, Marv .... 641-782-1317 170 B
mgodden@swcciowa.edu
GODDING, Jesse .... 972-825-4811 444 C
jgodding@sagu.edu
GODDU, Jessica .... 203-932-7000.. 89 F
GODEK, Jim .... 949-376-6000.. 47 G
jgodek@lcad.edu
GODES, Iris .... 508-541-1547 208 E
igodes@dean.edu
GODFREY, Rodney .... 662-241-7636 247 B
ragodfrey@muw.edu

GODFREY, SJ,
Timothy, S .... 415-422-6272.. 72 I
tgodfrey@usfca.edu
GODFREY-DAWSON,
Angela, R .... 252-335-0821 333 E
adawson@albemarle.edu
GODINA, Rafael .... 773-838-7516 135 C
rgodina1@ccc.edu
GODINET, Michelle .... 785-670-1509 178 A
michelle.godinet@washburn.edu
GODINEZ, Bobby .... 323-780-6722.. 49 D
godinerj@elac.edu
GODLESKI, Kasha .... 315-445-4772 303 F
godleska@lemoyne.edu
GODLESKI, Mark, G ...... 315-445-4520 303 F
godlesmg@lemoyne.edu
GODLEY, Amanda, J ..... 412-624-2137 400 A
agodley@pitt.edu
GODMAN, Christi .... 859-442-1684 181 D
christi.godman@kctcs.edu
GODNEY, Elmer .... 979-209-7575 430 I
elmer.godney@blinn.edu
GODO, James .... 630-637-5809 145 E
jwgodo@noctrl.edu
GODOY, Cuauhtemoc ... 787-622-8000 509 H
cgodoy@pupr.edu
GODOY, Sarah .... 360-650-3164 485 A
sarah.godoy@wwu.edu
GODSEY, R. Kirby .... 478-501-1501 122 C
godsey_rk@gmail.com
GODULA, Amanda .... 724-552-1369 397 F
agodula@setonhill.edu
GODWIN, Donald, A ..... 505-272-0907 288 C
dgodwin@salud.unm.edu
GODWIN, Hilary .... 206-543-1144 484 A
hgodwin@uw.edu
GODWIN, King .... 207-834-7500 196 G
king.godwin@maine.edu
GODWIN, Lewis .... 301-846-2674 198 E
lgodwin@frederick.edu
GODWIN, Norman .... 334-844-5774.... 4 E
godwinh@auburn.edu
GODWIN, Wendell .... 580-559-5212 365 J
wgodwin@ecok.edu
GODZWA, Alicia .... 540-362-6660 467 A
agodzwa@hollins.edu
GOEBEL, Dan .... 585-395-5537 317 B
dgoebel@brockport.edu
GOEBELBECKER, Eric .... 407-303-9798.. 95 A
eric.goebelbecker@ahu.edu
GOEBELER, Stefanie ...... 803-695-3687 409 E
goebelers@midlandstech.edu
GOEDEREIS, Eric .... 314-246-7513 261 D
ericgoedereis18@webster.edu
GOEHRING, Crystal ...... 740-397-6868 356 G
crystal.goehring@mvnu.edu
GOEL, Meeta .... 661-722-6300.. 26 E
mgoel@avc.edu
GOELDNER, Jason .... 715-365-4534 498 D
jgoeldner@nicoletcollege.edu
GOELLNER, Erik .... 401-598-1251 403 E
erik.goellner@jwu.edu
GOEMAN, Peter .... 919-573-5350 340 A
pgoeman@shepherds.edu
GOEN, Brandon .... 806-720-7313 438 F
brandon.goen@lcu.edu
GOEN, Jennifer .... 239-590-1020 109 G
jgoen@fgcu.edu
GOEPPINGER,
Kathleen, H .... 630-515-7300 144 C
drgoeppinger@midwestern.edu
GOES, Paulo .... 504-865-5407 191 D
pgoes@tulane.edu
GOETCHIUS,
Stephen, H .... 860-215-9002.. 87 D
sgoetchius@threerivers.edu
GOETSCH, John .... 661-946-2274.. 74 G
GOETSCH, Steven .... 603-641-7500 273 C
sgoetsch@anselm.edu
GOETZ, Beth .... 765-285-5625 153 E
bgoetz@bsu.edu
GOETZ, Michael, A .... 414-847-3305 493 C
mikegoetz@miad.edu
GOETZ, Michele .... 619-594-1862.. 33 E
mgoetz@sdsu.edu
GOETZ, Whitney .... 423-439-1000 418 D
GOFF, David .... 303-724-7304.. 84 B
david.goff@ucdenver.edu
GOFF, Jason .... 949-794-9090.. 66 C
jgoff@stanbridge.edu
GOFF, Jay .... 202-994-6710.. 92 C
jwgoff@gwu.edu
GOFF, Karen .... 440-775-8462 357 G
kgoff@oberlin.edu

GOFF, Kim .... 916-558-2054.. 51 B
goffk@scc.losrios.edu
GOFF, Margot, H .... 979-845-7293 446 B
margot_goff@tamu.edu
GOFF, Pamela .... 304-326-1304 486 I
pgoff@salemu.edu
GOFF, Sue .... 503-594-3110 372 B
sue.goff@clackamas.edu
GOFF, Travis .... 785-864-3143 177 G
kuathletics@ku.edu
GOFF-CREWS, Kimberly 203-432-6602.. 90 B
kimberly.goff-crews@yale.edu
GOFFAR, Stephen .... 210-283-6477 452 D
goffar@uiwtx.edu
GOFFE, Lorraine .... 847-491-8400 146 C
lorraine.goffe@northwestern.edu
GOFFE, Lorraine .... 814-863-6188 391 F
lag5792@psu.edu
GOFFE-MCNISH, Jackie . 845-431-8445 298 B
mcnish@sunydutchess.edu
GOFFNEY,
Jacqueline, A .... 832-813-6814 438 E
jacqueline.a.goffney@lonestar.edu
GOFORTH, Blake .... 618-634-3337 149 C
blakeg@shawneecc.edu
GOFORTH, Cheri, D ...... 501-686-5850.. 22 D
goforthcherid@uams.edu
GOFORTH, Glen .... 936-633-3209 429 A
ggoforth@angelina.edu
GOFORTH, Jonathan ..... 919-761-2413 340 B
admissions@sebts.edu
GOGA, Nedzad .... 718-636-3599 311 A
ngoga@pratt.edu
GOGAL, Mark .... 910-521-6000 343 A
GOGERTY, Andrew .... 515-964-0601 166 A
gogertya@faith.edu
GOGOLA, Eva .... 313-593-5495 231 B
egronows@umich.edu
GOGU, Longin .... 281-290-3772 438 E
longin.gogu@lonestar.edu
GOH, Michael .... 612-624-0594 242 K
mgoh@umn.edu
GOHDE, Amanda .... 715-645-7042 498 G
amanda.gohde@northwoodtech.edu
GOHEEN, Peter .... 207-551-5765 195 C
pgoheen@nmcc.edu
GOHL, Pam .... 605-331-6652 416 C
pam.gohl@usiouxfalls.edu
GOHMANN, Jennifer ...... 502-585-9911 184 E
jgohmann@spalding.edu
GOIN, JR., Randy .... 717-720-4010 393 C
rgoin@passhe.edu
GOINES, Pamela .... 513-792-8625 362 A
pamela.goines@uc.edu
GOINGS, Andrea .... 419-995-8302 360 B
goings.a@rhodesstate.edu
GOINS, Jennifer .... 804-627-5300 464 B
jennifer_goins@bshsi.org
GOINS, Jessica, D .... 864-488-4590 409 C
jgoins@limestone.edu
GOINS, Jody .... 423-869-6725 420 A
jody.goins@lmunet.edu
GOINS, LaKeya .... 205-366-8150.... 7 A
lgoins@stillman.edu
GOINS, Scot .... 678-916-2652 115 G
sgoins@johnmarshall.edu
GOINS, Scott, E .... 337-475-5456 192 B
sgoins@mcneese.edu
GOKCEK, Gigi .... 415-482-2427.. 41 H
gigi.gokcek@dominican.edu
GOKE-PARIOLA,
Abiodun .... 630-637-5356 145 E
agokepariola@noctrl.edu
GOKELMAN, Lena .... 210-832-3207 452 D
mgokelma@uiwtx.edu
GOLA, Kate .... 413-585-2200 218 D
kgola@smith.edu
GOLABEK, Sue .... 843-208-8144 412 C
sgolabek@uscb.edu
GOLAN, Linda .... 754-312-2898 103 R
GOLAND, Lois .... 518-782-6673 314 K
lgoland@siena.edu
GOLAR, Norman .... 205-349-4240.... 7 A
ngolar@stillman.edu
GOLATO, Andrea .... 512-245-2581 449 G
a_g554@txstate.edu
GOLAY, David, R .... 757-446-5890 465 H
golaydr@evms.edu
GOLBA, Gina .... 816-802-3397 253 H
ggolba@kcai.edu
GOLD, Chris .... 310-660-3735.. 41 J
cgold@elcamino.edu

GOLD, E .... 212-964-2830 306 B
egold@mtj.edu
GOLD, Ellen .... 734-487-1107 223 F
egold@emich.edu
GOLD, Harriet, B .... 270-384-8018 183 D
goldh@lindsey.edu
GOLD, Jeffery, P .... 402-559-4201 269 B
jeffrey.gold@unmc.edu
GOLD, Jeffrey .... 402-472-7117 268 I
jeffrey.gold@nebraska.edu
GOLD, Jered .... 626-396-2251.. 26 G
jered.gold@artcenter.edu
GOLD, Kimberly .... 919-807-7100 331 I
GOLDAMMER, Diana ..... 605-995-2997 414 A
diana.goldammer@dwu.edu
GOLDBERG, Amy .... 212-674-5300 300 H
GOLDBERG, Amy, J ...... 215-707-8773 398 D
amy.goldberg@temple.edu
GOLDBERG, David .... 517-265-5161 220 D
dgoldberg@adrian.edu
GOLDBERG, Dovid .... 440-943-5300 360 A
dgoldberg@telsheyeshiva.edu
GOLDBERG, Elaine .... 646-565-6136 322 B
elaine.goldberg@touro.edu
GOLDBERG, Elaine .... 646-565-6136 322 C
elaine.goldberg@touro.edu
GOLDBERG, Jesse .... 716-614-6741 309 E
jgoldberg@niagaracc.suny.edu
GOLDBERG, Maureen ... 805-965-0581.. 62 M
mmgoldberg@pipeline.sbcc.edu
GOLDBERG, Robert .... 610-328-8316 398 B
rgoldbe2@swarthmore.edu
GOLDBERG, Steven .... 706-446-4482 115 I
stgoldberg@augusta.edu
GOLDBERG, Yisroel ...... 973-267-9404 279 G
financialaid@rca.edu
GOLDBERGBELLE,
Jonathan .... 217-206-8319 151 E
jgold1@uis.edu
GOLDBERGER, David .... 845-783-9901 323 F
GOLDBERGER, Jo .... 212-229-5192 307 E
jogo@newschool.edu
GOLDBLUM, Tom .... 610-989-1329 400 F
tgoldblum@vfmac.edu
GOLDEN, Andrew, K ..... 609-258-4136 279 E
agolden@princeton.edu
GOLDEN, Beverley .... 903-566-7303 455 C
bgolden@uttyler.edu
GOLDEN, Cheryl .... 316-942-4291 176 B
goldenc@newmanu.edu
GOLDEN, Cynthia .... 412-624-3335 400 A
goldenc@pitt.edu
GOLDEN, Denise .... 814-871-7663 383 H
golden007@gannon.edu
GOLDEN, Kathie, S .... 662-254-3800 247 C
ksgolden@mvsu.edu
GOLDEN, Leslie, B .... 407-582-3466 113 C
lgolden@valenciacollege.edu
GOLDEN, Matthew .... 973-596-5286 278 G
matthew.golden@njit.edu
GOLDEN, Paul .... 570-586-2400 381 A
pgolden@clarkssummitu.edu
GOLDEN, Rebecca .... 386-752-1822.. 99 P
rebecca.golden@fgc.edu
GOLDEN, Robert, N ...... 608-263-4910 494 D
rngolden@wisc.edu
GOLDEN, Teresa .... 580-745-2286 369 F
tgolden@se.edu
GOLDEN-BATTLE, Julia . 617-732-2058 216 B
julia.golden-battle@mcphs.edu
GOLDEN-BOTTI, Julie ... 561-297-4204 109 F
goldenj@fau.edu
GOLDENBERG, Isabel ... 202-741-2656.. 92 C
iag@gwu.edu
GOLDENBERG, Jay .... 646-216-2862 308 F
jgoldenberg@nycda.edu
GOLDENBERG, Mary ..... 847-491-2005 146 C
m-goldenberg@northwestern.edu
GOLDEY, Ellen, S .... 859-238-5226 179 H
ellen.goldey@centre.edu
GOLDFEIZ, Emanuel ..... 410-653-0433 201 B
dorm@nirc.edu
GOLDGEIER, Eileen .... 401-863-9900 403 A
eileen_goldgeier@brown.edu
GOLDHABER,
Yochanan .... 718-232-7800 325 D
GOLDIN, Michael .... 269-965-3931 225 D
goldinm@kellogg.edu
GOLDIN, Steve .... 703-993-8294 466 J
sgoldin2@gmu.edu
GOLDING, Geissler .... 850-474-2555 111 E
ggolding@uwf.edu

GOLDING, Tena .... 985-549-2316 192 E
provost@selu.edu
GOLDMAN, Cassandra .. 618-262-8641 139 C
goldmanc@iecc.edu
GOLDMAN, Dana .... 213-740-0350.. 73 C
GOLDMAN, Lee .... 212-305-2752 296 H
lg2379@columbia.edu
GOLDMAN, Lynn, R ...... 202-994-1000.. 92 C
goldmanl@gwu.edu
GOLDMAN, Marc .... 717-337-6616 384 C
mgoldman@gettysburg.edu
GOLDMAN, Patricia ...... 914-813-9201 314 H
pgoldman@sarahlawrence.edu
GOLDMON, Moses .... 870-460-1053.. 22 E
goldmon@uamont.edu
GOLDNER, Lauren .... 213-884-4133.. 24 D
lgoldner@arjca.edu
GOLDNER, Lauren .... 213-884-4133.. 24 D
lgoldner@ajrca.edu
GOLDSBERRY,
Kimberlie .... 262-551-5800 491 B
kgoldsberry@carthage.edu
GOLDSBY, Michael .... 765-285-9002 153 E
mgoldsby@bsu.edu
GOLDSCHMIDT, Robert . 646-565-6421 322 B
robert.goldschmidt@touro.edu
GOLDSCHMIDT, Robert . 646-565-6421 322 C
robert.goldschmidt@touro.edu
GOLDSCHMIDTS,
Walter .... 516-367-6890 296 A
GOLDSMITH, Andrea, J 609-258-3000 279 E
ajgoldsmith@princeton.edu
GOLDSMITH, Carole ..... 559-243-7100.. 66 G
GOLDSMITH, Christine . 605-718-2403 416 D
christine.goldsmith@wdt.edu
GOLDSMITH, Diane .... 401-874-4218 404 E
dgoldsmith@uri.edu
GOLDSMITH, Glenn, A .. 574-269-5344 155 C
goldsmga@grace.edu
GOLDSMITH, Meredith .. 610-409-3404 400 E
mgoldsmith@ursinus.edu
GOLDSTEIN, Aaron .... 314-434-4044 251 F
aaron.goldstein@covenantseminary.edu
GOLDSTEIN, Adam .... 336-758-5226 344 A
GOLDSTEIN, Alexis .... 847-982-2500 138 G
GOLDSTEIN, Benjamin .. 707-527-4880.. 63 C
bgoldstein@santarosa.edu
GOLDSTEIN, Bill .... 641-472-1183 168 A
bgoldstein@miu.edu
GOLDSTEIN, Brian .... 760-591-3012.. 72 F
cao@usa.edu
GOLDSTEIN, Jeffrey, E .. 610-330-5001 387 B
goldstej@lafayette.edu
GOLDSTEIN, Jeremy ..... 401-225-2419 200 B
jgoldstein@mica.edu
GOLDSTEIN, Joel .... 304-760-1700.. 93 H
GOLDSTEIN, Lindsey .... 310-825-6322.. 69 D
lgoldstein@saonet.ucla.edu
GOLDSTEIN, Robert, S .. 502-852-6169 185 E
rsgold03@louisville.edu
GOLDSTEIN, Serge, J ... 609-258-6059 279 E
serge@princeton.edu
GOLDSTEIN, Sharon ..... 973-684-6919 279 B
sgoldstein@pccc.edu
GOLDSTEIN, Steve .... 949-824-5926.. 69 C
vcha@health.uci.edu
GOLDSTEIN, Stuart .... 973-720-2978 283 I
goldsteins@wpunj.edu
GOLDSTON, David .... 202-789-1828 215 G
GOLDSTONE, Matthew .. 914-893-4035 288 K
mgoldstone@ajr.edu
GOLDWARE, Rebeccah . 951-222-8111.. 59 A
rebeccah.goldware@rccd.edu
GOLDWATER,
Joanne, A .... 240-895-4270 201 F
jagoldwater@smcm.edu
GOLDYS, Michelle .... 386-506-3331.. 98 A
michelle.goldys@daytonastate.edu
GOLEM, Stephanie .... 903-670-2688 451 C
stephanie.golem@tvcc.edu
GOLEMAN, Michael .... 606-451-6864 182 D
michael.goleman@kctcs.edu
GOLEMBESKI,
Richard, M .... 804-752-3288 469 B
richardgolembesi@rmc.edu
GOLEMME, Donna .... 781-292-2300 209 E
GOLETTI, Cristina .... 970-351-2515.. 84 D
cristina.goletti@unco.edu
GOLETZ, Gregory .... 610-606-4666 380 C
gregory.goletz@cedarcrest.edu
GOLEY, Julie .... 706-737-1604 115 I
jgoley@augusta.edu

GONZALEZ, Jennifer ..... 201-216-9901 276 C jennifer.gonzalez@eicollege.edu
GONZALEZ, Jeremy ...... 312-553-5641 134 M jgonzalez@ccc.edu
GONZALEZ, Jesse .... 714-480-7401.. 58 E gonzalez_jesse@rsccd.edu
GONZALEZ, Jorge, G .... 269-337-7220 225 B jorge.gonzalez@kzoo.edu
GONZALEZ, Jose .... 787-840-2575 508 G jogonzalez@psm.edu
GONZALEZ, Joselyn ...... 214-860-2447 434 A joselyngonzalez@dcccd.edu
GONZALEZ, Juan, E ...... 972-883-2234 454 D jgonzal@utdallas.edu
GONZALEZ, Julio .... 951-571-6409.. 59 B julio.gonzalez@mvc.edu
GONZALEZ, Karilys .... 787-257-0000 510 F karilys.gonzalez@upr.edu
GONZALEZ, Leonore ...... 212-220-8044 292 G lgonzalez@bmcc.cuny.edu
GONZALEZ, Leslie .... 563-674-6633 169 B lgonzalez@orion.edu
GONZALEZ, Lizbeth ...... 603-578-8900 272 B lgonzalez@ccsnh.edu
GONZALEZ, Luis .... 661-259-7800.. 38 H luis.gonzalez@canyons.edu
GONZALEZ, Luis .... 805-678-5949.. 74 A lgonzalez@vcccd.edu
GONZALEZ, Luz .... 559-278-3003.. 31 D luz_gonzalez@csufresno.edu
GONZALEZ, Mari, G ...... 787-743-7979 509 D mggonzalez@suagm.edu
GONZALEZ, Maria .... 951-372-7137.. 59 C maria.gonzalez@norcocollege.edu
GONZALEZ, Maria, A .... 787-993-8872 510 E maria.gonzalez34@upr.edu
GONZALEZ, Maria De La Luz .... 559-925-3244.. 75 A mariadelaluzgonzalez@whccd.edu
GONZALEZ, Marlib .... 915-831-2290 435 B mgonz618@epcc.edu
GONZALEZ, Martha .... 210-784-2059 447 B martha.gonzalez@tamusa.edu
GONZALEZ, Matthew ...... 860-632-3068.. 88 B megonzalez@holyapostles.edu
GONZALEZ, Matthew .... 860-632-3010.. 88 B mgonzalez@holyapostles.edu
GONZALEZ, Melissa ..... 281-312-1644 438 E melissa.gonzalez@lonestar.edu
GONZALEZ, Miguel, A .. 281-283-3705 452 A gonzalezmig@uhcl.edu
GONZALEZ, Miguel, O .. 860-444-8444 502 F miguel.o.gonzalez@uscga.edu
GONZALEZ, Millie .... 787-863-2390 507 A millie.gonzalez@fajardo.inter.edu
GONZALEZ, Millie .... 508-626-4651 212 D vgonzalez@framingham.edu
GONZALEZ, Natalie .... 214-379-5438 440 H ngonzalez@pqc.edu
GONZALEZ, Nichole, J . 717-361-1179 383 B gonazleznichole@etown.edu
GONZALEZ, Orlando ...... 787-766-1912 506 H ogonzale@inter.edu
GONZALEZ, Orlando ..... 787-284-1912 507 D ochevere@ponce.inter.edu
GONZALEZ, Paco .... 316-942-4291 176 B gonzalezp@newmanu.edu
GONZALEZ, Patricia ...... 787-250-1912 507 C pgonzalez@metro.inter.edu
GONZALEZ, Paulette, B 718-990-6521 313 B gonzalep@stjohns.edu
GONZALEZ, Ramon, F .. 787-758-2525 511 D ramon.gonzalez5@upr.edu
GONZALEZ, Raquel .... 787-284-1912 507 D rgonzalez@ponce.inter.edu
GONZALEZ, Raul .... 305-899-3000.. 96 A rgonzalez@barry.edu
GONZALEZ, Reinishia .... 252-618-6636 334 B gonzalezr@edgecombe.edu
GONZALEZ, Reyes .... 773-878-7502 148 F rgonzalez@staugustine.edu
GONZALEZ, Ricardo ..... 210-283-6423 452 D rigonza4@uiwtx.edu
GONZALEZ, Richard ...... 239-992-4624.. 96 E
GONZALEZ, Rick .... 424-207-3727.. 55 B rgonzalez@otis.edu
GONZALEZ, Rick .... 714-997-6763.. 36 D rigonzalez@chapman.edu
GONZALEZ, Ricky .... 763-433-1137 236 H ricardo.gonzalez@anokaramsey.edu
GONZALEZ, Robert, A ... 505-277-2903 288 C ragonzalez@unm.edu
GONZALEZ, Roberto ..... 310-287-4314.. 50 C gonzalro@wlac.edu
GONZALEZ, Roberto, O 310-287-4248.. 50 C gonzalro@wlac.edu
GONZALEZ, Rocelia, T .. 904-620-2870 111 A rrgonz@unf.edu
GONZALEZ, Roenice ..... 914-367-8208 313 E roenice.gonzalez@archny.org
GONZALEZ, Ruby .... 361-593-4338 447 A ruby.gonzalez@tamuk.edu
GONZALEZ, Ruth .... 860-738-6315.. 87 A rgonzalez@nwcc.edu
GONZALEZ, Samantha .. 860-512-2663.. 86 F sgonzalez@manchestercc.edu
GONZALEZ, Sergio .... 401-863-5402 403 A sergio_gonzalez@brown.edu
GONZALEZ, Sonia .... 760-776-7441.. 39 A sgonzalez@collegeofthedesert.edu
GONZALEZ, Sonia .... 562-860-2451.. 35 O smgonzalez@cerritos.edu
GONZALEZ, Sophia .... 210-486-2247 428 C fklein@alamo.edu
GONZALEZ, Stacy .... 518-244-4557 312 D gonzas@sage.edu
GONZALEZ, Susana ...... 281-998-6129 442 B susana.gonzalez@sjcd.edu
GONZALEZ, Tania .... 209-228-4400.. 70 A
GONZALEZ, Tanya .... 785-532-4797 175 A tgonzale@ksu.edu
GONZALEZ, Ted .... 254-526-1668 431 E ted.gonzalez@ctcd.edu
GONZALEZ, Tina .... 212-799-5000 303 B
GONZALEZ, Victor .... 956-872-2336 443 B vgonzalez99@southtexascollege.edu
GONZALEZ, Victor .... 787-257-0000 510 F
GONZALEZ, Widalys ...... 787-884-3838 504 C wgonzalez@atenascollege.edu
GONZALEZ, Wilson .... 610-861-1554 390 D gonzalezw02@moravian.edu
GONZALEZ, Yaitzaenid .. 787-765-3560 505 H ygonzalez@edpuniversity.edu
GONZALEZ, Yoisa .... 787-766-1912 507 C ygonzalez@inter.edu
GONZALEZ, Zoila .... 787-894-2828 511 G zoila.gonzalez@upr.edu
GONZALEZ-DE JESUS, Naydeen .... 414-297-6436 498 B gonzan43@matc.edu
GONZALEZ-LEVY, Sandra .... 305-348-7235 109 H sandra.gonzalez-levy@fiu.edu
GONZALEZ MEDINA, CMF, Ruben, A .... 787-848-5265 508 H ruben_gonzalez@pucpr.edu
GONZALEZ-MELENDEZ, Saraliz .... 787-857-3600 506 K sgonzalez@br.inter.edu
GONZALEZ PACHECO, Monica .... 787-863-2390 507 A monica.gonzalez@fajardo.inter.edu
GONZALEZ-ZAMBRANA, Zorymar .... 787-780-5134 508 C
GOO, Brian .... 408-855-5204.. 75 C brian.goo@missioncollege.edu
GOO, Brian .... 510-723-7564.. 35 Q bgoo@chabotcollege.edu
GOO, Shannon .... 617-217-9000 206 A
GOOCH, Cheryl .... 518-381-1382 319 G goochcrg@sunysccc.edu
GOOCH, Jackie .... 256-233-8211.... 4 D jackie.gooch@athens.edu
GOOCH, Josh .... 620-665-3594 174 D goochj@hutchcc.edu
GOOCH, Zanetta .... 615-963-7401 425 A zgooch@tnstate.edu
GOOCH-GRAYSON, Cynthia .... 531-622-2649 266 G ckgoochgrayson@mccneb.edu
GOOD, Amy .... 641-752-4643 167 E amy.good@iavalley.edu
GOOD, Andrew .... 818-364-7800.. 49 G gooda@lamission.edu
GOOD, Darrin, S .... 402-465-2217 267 J president@nebrwesleyan.edu
GOOD, Gayle, A .... 402-363-5621 269 F gagood@york.edu
GOOD, Glenn .... 352-392-3261 110 E ggood@coe.ufl.edu
GOOD, Heather .... 313-664-7440 222 C hgood@collegeforcreativestudies.edu
GOOD, Jason .... 941-359-7690 106 J jgood@ringling.edu
GOOD, Jeff .... 309-672-5538 143 I jgood@methodistcol.edu
GOOD, Lisa .... 717-396-7833 392 Q lgood@pcad.edu
GOOD, Michael, L .... 801-581-5701 459 D president@utah.edu
GOOD, Michael, L .... 801-581-7480 459 D michael.good@hsc.utah.edu
GOOD, RT .... 561-237-7458 103 W rgood@lynn.edu
GOOD KAUFMANN, Cynthia .... 574-535-7351 155 B cynthiagk@goshen.edu
GOOD LUCK, Aldean ..... 406-638-3118 262 J goodluckav@lbhc.edu
GOODALE, Brian .... 518-587-2100 320 B brian.goodale@esc.edu
GOODALE, Nathan .... 315-859-4615 300 F ngoodale@hamilton.edu
GOODALE, Timothy, A .. 252-335-3767 341 A tagoodale@ecsu.edu
GOODBERLET, Amy ...... 314-744-7699 255 H amy.goodberlet@mobap.edu
GOODBURN, Amy .... 402-472-3751 269 A agoodburn1@unl.edu
GOODE, David .... 662-692-1508 247 D dtgoode@nemcc.edu
GOODE, Greg, J .... 812-237-7778 155 H greg.goode@indstate.edu
GOODE, Jacqueline ...... 610-399-2038 393 D jgoode@cheyney.edu
GOODE, Jess .... 312-567-3970 139 H jgoode1@iit.edu
GOODE, Jodi .... 325-646-8075 437 A jgoode@hputx.edu
GOODE, Kevin .... 814-866-8406 387 C kgoode@lecom.edu
GOODE, Mike .... 704-894-2143 328 C migoode@davidson.edu
GOODE, Nikki .... 256-824-4739.... 8 B nikki.goode@uah.edu
GOODE, Tyler .... 828-339-4394 337 H t_goode@southwesterncc.edu
GOODELL, Adam .... 201-879-7033 274 I agoodell@bergen.edu
GOODELL, Adam .... 201-879-3673 274 I agoodell@bergen.edu
GOODEN, Amoaba .... 330-672-2442 354 A agooden@kent.edu
GOODEN, Benny, L .... 479-308-2294.. 17 E benny.gooden@acheedu.org
GOODEN, Lancelot, A ... 407-299-5000 113 C lgooden5@valenciacollege.edu
GOODENOW, Andrew ... 816-235-1107 260 D goodenowa@umkc.edu
GOODFELLOW, Geoffrey .... 312-949-7016 139 B ggoodfel@ico.edu
GOODFELLOW, Tim ...... 503-554-2585 372 I tgoodfellow@georgefox.edu
GOODFRIEND, Kimberly .... 972-883-2201 454 D kimberly.goodfriend@utdallas.edu
GOODGAME, Henry ...... 470-639-0400 122 H henry.goodgame@morehouse.edu
GOODGE, Samuel .... 304-829-7905 486 B sgoodge@bethanywv.edu
GOODHEART, Marc .... 617-496-9480 210 B marc_goodheart@harvard.edu
GOODHIND, Deborah ... 413-545-5542 211 D deb.goodhind@umass.edu
GOODHUE LYNCH, Mary .... 508-588-9100 214 F mgoodhuel@massasoit.mass.edu
GOODING, Betsy .... 903-434-8137 440 A bgooding@ntcc.edu
GOODING, JR., Dale, E 330-972-5908 361 G dale2@uakron.edu
GOODING, Michelle ..... 305-899-3058.. 96 A migooding@barry.edu
GOODING, Sharon .... 817-257-4748 447 H s.gooding@tcu.edu
GOODJOHN, Bunny ...... 434-947-8126 469 A bgoodjohn@randolphcollege.edu
GOODKIND, Hilary .... 650-574-6196.. 62 J goodkindh@smccd.edu
GOODLAND, Jennifer .... 719-336-1541.. 81 J jennifer.goodland@lamarcc.edu
GOODLING, Barry, G .... 717-796-5064 389 F bgoodlin@messiah.edu
GOODMAN, Adam .... 205-853-1200.... 2 G akgoodman@jeffersonstate.edu
GOODMAN, Ann .... 575-646-1722 286 G anng@nmsu.edu
GOODMAN, Brent .... 619-849-2371.. 57 J brentgoodman@pointloma.edu
GOODMAN, Carl .... 301-860-3460 203 D cgoodman@bowiestate.edu
GOODMAN, David, M ... 617-552-3900 207 A david.goodman@bc.edu
GOODMAN, Dawn .... 617-564-9390 219 G dawn_goodman@williamjames.edu
GOODMAN, Dennis, S .. 573-341-4284 260 F dgoodman@mst.edu
GOODMAN, Elodie .... 509-533-3694 478 E elodie.goodman@sfcc.spokane.edu
GOODMAN, Grayson .... 407-303-1631.. 95 A grayson.goodman@ahu.edu
GOODMAN, Gwen .... 518-327-6242 310 G ggoodman@paulsmiths.edu
GOODMAN, Hunter, P .. 937-229-4915 362 C hgoodman1@udayton.edu
GOODMAN, Jacque .... 641-844-5640 167 C jacque.goodman@iavalley.edu
GOODMAN, James .... 808-455-0668 130 A goodmanj@hawaii.edu
GOODMAN, Jeremy .... 781-292-2373 209 E jeremy.goodman@olin.edu
GOODMAN, Lena, C ..... 920-433-6638 490 H lena.goodman@bellincollege.edu
GOODMAN, Marc, P ..... 310-506-4607.. 56 H marc.goodman@pepperdine.edu
GOODMAN, Mark .... 646-565-6000 322 C mark.goodman6@touro.edu
GOODMAN, Mark .... 646-565-6000 322 B mark.goodman6@touro.edu
GOODMAN, Matthew .... 207-741-5507 195 D mgoodman@smccme.edu
GOODMAN, Michael ..... 504-865-5725 191 D mgoodman@tulane.edu
GOODMAN, Patricia ...... 574-535-7700 155 B pgoodman@goshen.edu
GOODMAN, Richard, H 503-494-5078 374 F goodmanr@ohsu.edu
GOODMAN, Shannon, M .... 940-565-4510 453 B shannon.goodman@unt.edu
GOODMAN, Sharon .... 360-867-6333 479 C goodmans@evergreen.edu
GOODMAN, Walt .... 318-487-7000 187 B walt.goodman@lcuniversity.edu
GOODMAN, Willie, F .... 404-527-5735 121 I wgoodman@itc.edu
GOODMON, Cindy .... 661-654-2346.. 30 C cgoodmon@csub.edu
GOODMUNDSON, Doug .... 952-829-4181 233 H doug.goodmundson@bethfel.org
GOODNER, Asha, L ...... 330-569-5419 353 F goodneral@hiram.edu
GOODNER, Jason .... 501-882-4475.. 17 H jsgoodner@asub.edu
GOODNIGHT, Lisa .... 219-989-2323 160 A ljgoodni@pnw.edu
GOODRICH, Mark .... 707-654-1563.. 32 C mgoodrich@csum.edu
GOODRICH, Oliver .... 607-255-6003 297 D og68@cornell.edu
GOODRICH, Shannon ... 208-769-3303 132 A sgoodrich@nic.edu
GOODRIDGE, Ellengold 256-726-7093.... 6 C egoodridge@oakwood.edu
GOODROW, Darrin .... 315-229-1818 313 F dgoodrow@stlawu.edu
GOODSON, Alyn .... 252-335-2972 341 A agoodson@ecsu.edu
GOODSON, Bart .... 919-962-1000 340 F
GOODSON, Drew .... 919-718-7445 333 A dgoodson@cccc.edu
GOODSON, Indigo .... 212-752-1530 303 G indigo.goodson@limcollege.edu
GOODSON, Leigh .... 918-595-7868 370 B leigh.goodson@tulsacc.edu
GOODSON, Linda .... 334-699-2266.... 1 B lgoodson@acom.edu
GOODSON, Paul .... 252-249-1851 336 C pgoodson@pamlicocc.edu
GOODSPEED, Emily ...... 518-743-2200 319 D goodspeede@sunyacc.edu
GOODSTEIN, Eban .... 845-758-7067 290 G ebangood@bard.edu
GOODWILL, Andrew ..... 920-206-2332 492 C andrew.goodwill@mbu.edu
GOODWIN, Amy .... 719-587-7912.. 77 F 1559mgr@follett.com
GOODWIN, Andrea .... 301-314-8428 202 E agoodwin@umd.edu
GOODWIN, Ann, E .... 859-238-5760 179 H ann.goodwin@centre.edu

GOSSEN, Larry 308-367-5200 269 D larry.gossen@unl.edu

GOSSEN, Timothy 507-457-1597 242 H tgossen@smumn.edu

GOSSETT, Betty 716-673-3321 316 A betty.gossett@fredonia.edu

GOSSETT, Elsa 425-739-8200 480 D elsa.gossett@lwtech.edu

GOSSETT, John 828-398-7112 331 K johndgossett@abtech.edu

GOSSMAN, Diane 563-387-1408 167 J gossmand@luther.edu

GOSWAMI, Jaya, S 361-593-2170 447 A jaya.goswami@tamuk.edu

GOSZ, Mike 312-567-3198 139 H gosz@iit.edu

GOSZ, Sharon 414-229-5346 495 B schetney@uwm.edu

GOTANDA, John 808-544-0203 128 E president@hpu.edu

GOTAY, Yaritza 931-393-1690 423 G

GOTCHER, Ashley 405-691-3800 366 C ashley.gotcher@macu.edu

GOTCHER, Mike 931-372-3366 425 B mgotcher@tntech.edu

GOTCHER, Robert 414-425-8300 494 A rgotcher@shsst.edu

GOTHAM, Cece, R 716-888-2758 291 M gothamc@canisius.edu

GOTHAM, Kerry 585-395-2068 317 B kgotham@brockport.edu

GOTHARD, Mathew, J 303-963-3223 78 D mgothard@ccu.edu

GOTJEN, Lynne 207-795-7166 194 H gotjenly@mchp.edu

GOTO, Joy 559-278-2448 31 D jgoto@csufresno.edu

GOTSCH, Sarah, A 574-631-3903 161 G sgotsch@nd.edu

GOTSCHALL, Matthew 308-398-7300 265 C mgotschall@cccneb.edu

GOTSMAN, Craig 973-596-5488 278 G craig.gotsman@njit.edu

GOTT, Jared 731-989-6649 418 H jgott@fhu.edu

GOTTARDY, John 716-645-2450 315 F johngott@buffalo.edu

GOTTLIEB, Jane 212-799-5000 303 B

GOTTLIEB, Mel 213-884-4133 24 D mgottlieb@ajrca.edu

GOTTLIEB, Neal 732-431-1600 283 C taofnj@gmail.com

GOTTLIEB, Ronda 210-829-6017 452 D rgottlie@uiwtx.edu

GOTTSCHALK, Katherine 765-983-1267 154 H gottska@earlham.edu

GOTTSCHALK, Mark 806-894-9611 443 A mgottschalk@southplainscollege.edu

GOTTSHALL, Lori 954-771-0376 103 S lgottshall@knoxseminary.edu

GOTTULA, Todd 308-865-8454 268 J gottulatm@unk.edu

GOTZMAN, Ron 763-417-8250 234 D rgotzman@centralseminary.edu

GOUDEAU, Arthur 281-487-1170 447 G agoudeau@txchiro.edu

GOUDEAU, LaTasha 713-221-8162 452 B goudeaul@uhd.edu

GOUDY, Senta 304-424-8000 490 A senta.goudy@wvup.edu

GOUGER, Tammy 585-395-2126 317 B tgouger@brockport.edu

GOUGH, Allison 808-544-1109 128 E agough@hpu.edu

GOUGH, Annette 732-571-3402 278 B gough@monmouth.edu

GOUGH, Brent 817-598-6275 457 C

GOUGH, Darby 816-501-3660 249 H darby.gough@avila.edu

GOUGH, Jenna 909-607-3731 57 E jenna_gough@pitzer.edu

GOUGH, Pam 251-981-3771 5 B pam.gough@columbiasouthern.edu

GOUGH, Richard, J 843-525-8247 411 G rgough@tcl.edu

GOUGHNOUR, Karla 417-328-1823 258 K kgoughnour@sbuniv.edu

GOULD, Amanda 413-565-1000 205 I agould@baypath.edu

GOULD, Bryan, M 253-879-3355 483 G bmgould@pugetsound.edu

GOULD, Deborah, M 413-545-2554 211 D dmgould@admin.umass.edu

GOULD, Greg 406-275-4991 264 H greg_gould@skc.edu

GOULD, Janet 336-316-2135 329 C jgould@guilford.edu

GOULD, Jenkin 413-755-4061 215 F jgould@stcc.edu

GOULD, Jon, B 949-824-5466 69 C jon.gould@uci.edu

GOULD, Kenneth 718-951-3136 293 A kgould@brooklyn.cuny.edu

GOULD, Kimberly 215-893-5252 381 I

GOULD, Kyle 765-998-4635 161 A kygould@taylor.edu

GOULD, Nicholas 202-779-9399 92 B nicholas.gould@gallaudet.edu

GOULD, Rachel 607-274-3306 302 E rgould@ithaca.edu

GOULD, Robert 612-330-1582 233 G gouldr@augsburg.edu

GOULD, Shari 814-860-5151 387 C sgould@lecom.edu

GOULD, Thomas 252-493-7406 336 E tgould@email.pittcc.edu

GOULD, Trent 601-266-5253 248 H trent.gould@usm.edu

GOULET, Bonnie 203-576-8752 86 H bgoulet@nv.edu

GOULET, Caroline 210-283-6924 452 D goulet@uiwtx.edu

GOURD, Samantha 701-766-4415 344 F

GOURDINE, Raji 334-876-9292 2 D ragi.gourdine@wccs.edu

GOURJI, Konstantin 650-685-6616 44 I kgourji@gurnick.edu

GOURLEY, Bridget, L 765-658-4359 154 G bgourley@depauw.edu

GOURNEAU, Haven 406-768-6300 262 I hgourneau@fpcc.edu

GOURNEAU, Kim 218-755-3948 237 B kim.gourneau@bemidjistate.edu

GOURNEAU, Kim 218-755-3948 239 F kim.gourneau@bemidjistate.edu

GOURNIAK, Allison 419-289-5622 347 H agournia@ashland.edu

GOUSE, Richard, I 401-739-5000 403 F rgouse@neit.edu

GOUVEIA, Jan 808-956-6405 129 B jgouveia@hawaii.edu

GOUVEIA, Jan, N 808-956-6405 128 I jgouveia@hawaii.edu

GOVAN, Jennifer 212-678-3022 321 H govan@tc.columbia.edu

GOVE, Scott 918-595-7523 370 B scott.gove@tulsacc.edu

GOVEA, Hector 972-780-3600 453 C hector.govea@untdallas.edu

GOVEA, Rene 815-479-7619 143 F rgovea@mchenry.edu

GOVEA, Sam 972-860-4216 433 G sgovea@dcccd.edu

GOVENDER, Yogani 787-250-1912 507 C ygovender@metro.inter.edu

GOVER, Bruce 606-679-8501 182 D bruce.gover@kctcs.edu

GOVER, Kristie 904-256-7070 102 G kgover1@ju.edu

GOVINDARAJU, Venugopal 716-645-3321 315 F vpr@buffalo.edu

GOVINDARAJULU, Chitti 765-455-9275 156 E cgovinda@iu.edu

GOVINDASWAMY, Parvadha 636-584-6627 252 D parvadha.govindaswamy@eastcentral.edu

GOVITZ, Leanne 989-686-9490 223 E leannegovitz@delta.edu

GOW, Joe 608-785-8004 495 A jgow@uwlax.edu

GOWAN, Mary, A 706-864-1800 126 G mary.gowan@ung.edu

GOWANS, Faye 803-822-3251 409 E gowansf@midlandstech.edu

GOWDY, Stephen 616-538-2330 224 B sgowdy@gracechristian.edu

GOWEN, Claire 610-341-5849 383 A claire.gowen@eastern.edu

GOWEN, Karla 312-553-2500 134 L kgowen@ccc.edu

GOWER, Ana Maria 510-628-8034 48 G agower@lincolnuca.edu

GOWER, Molly 574-284-4886 160 F mgower@saintmarys.edu

GOWER, Paula 405-585-5410 367 B paula.gower@okbu.edu

GOWER, Rena 618-544-8657 139 E gowerr@iecc.edu

GOWER, Ryan 618-393-2982 139 C gowerry@iecc.edu

GOWER, Scott 570-945-8231 386 F scott.gower@keystone.edu

GOWING, James 913-288-7240 174 H jgowing@kckcc.edu

GOWING, Wendi 303-762-6887 80 G wendi.gowing@denverseminary.edu

GOYETTE, Carey 518-562-4111 295 F cary.goyette@clinton.edu

GOYETTE, John 805-421-5916 67 J jgoyette@thomasaquinas.edu

GOYETTE, Sylvain 815-836-5974 142 C goyettsy@lewisu.edu

GOYUNYAN, Gevorg 510-925-4282 25 P gevorg@aua.am

GOZA, Franklin 262-472-1712 496 E gozaf@uww.edu

GOZIK, Nick 617-552-3827 207 A nick.gozik@bc.edu

GOZIK, Nick 336-278-6700 328 H ngozik@elon.edu

GOZUM, Allan 937-769-1304 347 F agozum@antioch.edu

GRAB, Kelly 708-608-4019 144 G grabk2@morainevalley.edu

GRABER, Brent 574-296-6221 153 C it@ambs.edu

GRABER, David 402-375-7257 267 I dagrabe1@wsc.edu

GRABER, Linda 866-931-4300 257 J linda.graber@rockbridge.edu

GRABHER, Karen 262-595-2211 495 D grabher@uwp.edu

GRABLE, Bettye 850-599-3379 109 E bettye.grable@famu.edu

GRABLE, Pamela 719-549-3026 82 I pamela.grable@pueblocc.edu

GRABOWSKI, Jeremiah 716-829-8392 298 C grabowsj@dyc.edu

GRABOWSKI, John, F 410-777-2231 197 C jfgrabowski@aacc.edu

GRABOWSKI, Mark 417-328-1556 258 K mgrabowski@sbuniv.edu

GRABOWSKI, Rodney, M 716-645-2925 315 F rodneyg@buffalo.edu

GRABSKI, Joanna 480-727-1568 11 A joanna.grabski@asu.edu

GRACE, Anna 503-253-3443 374 E anna.grace@ocom.edu

GRACE, Audrey 781-768-7000 217 H

GRACE, Chris 641-472-1104 168 A stuact@miu.edu

GRACE, Colton 864-592-4619 411 E gracec@sccsc.edu

GRACE, Glenda, G 646-664-9108 292 E glenda.grace@cuny.edu

GRACE, Janet 620-441-5564 172 M janet.grace@cowley.edu

GRACE, Joe 270-707-3771 181 G joe.grace@kctcs.edu

GRACE, Kittie 402-463-2402 266 C kgrace@hastings.edu

GRACE, Lynn 734-973-3518 232 A lgmartin@wccnet.edu

GRACE, Michelle, M 847-543-2274 135 G mgrace@clcillinois.edu

GRACE, Nabil, F 248-204-2500 226 E ngrace@ltu.edu

GRACE, Sherie 256-228-6001 3 B graces@nacc.edu

GRACE, Susan 513-487-1217 361 E susan.grace@myunion.edu

GRACHAN, Bart 845-574-4294 312 C bart.grachan@sunyrockland.edu

GRACIA, Edward 787-844-8181 511 E edward.gracia@upr.edu

GRACIA, Hector 787-780-0070 504 E graciah@caribbean.edu

GRACIANI, Ruben 540-568-4850 467 C graciarg@jmu.edu

GRACIAS, Vicente, H 732-235-6300 281 B graciavh@rbhs.rutgers.edu

GRACOMBE, Sarah 508-565-1724 218 F sgracombe@stonehill.edu

GRACYALNY, David 410-225-2220 200 B dgracyal@mica.edu

GRADDY, Elizabeth 213-740-6715 73 C graddy@usc.edu

GRADDY, Kathryn 781-736-8616 207 D kgraddy@brandeis.edu

GRADOWSKI, Charles 484-365-8049 388 F cgradowski@lincoln.edu

GRADY, Amber, N 870-759-4188 24 B agrady@williamsbu.edu

GRADY, Catherine 937-229-1000 362 C

GRADY, Damira 608-246-6025 497 I dgrady3@madisoncollege.edu

GRADY, Darryl 910-592-8081 337 D dgrady@sampsoncc.edu

GRADY, Francis 314-516-5404 260 E fgrady@umsl.edu

GRADY, Helene 443-997-3359 199 E hgrady1@jhu.edu

GRADY, Jessica 781-283-2088 219 C jg101@wellesley.edu

GRADY, Jonathan 909-869-3850 30 B jgrady@cpp.edu

GRADY, Meghan 610-606-4666 380 C meghan.grady@cedarcrest.edu

GRADY, Sandra, K 518-861-2579 305 B sgrady@mariacollege.edu

GRADY, Sara 508-929-8130 213 D sara.grady@worcester.edu

GRADY, Sarah 718-409-7262 320 D sgrady@sunymaritime.edu

GRADY, Susan 817-202-6755 444 B sgrady@swau.edu

GRAEF, Jon 206-726-5028 478 F jgraef@cornish.edu

GRAEM, David 903-675-6364 451 C dgraem@tvcc.edu

GRAESER, Kristin 717-736-4103 385 A kgraeser@hacc.edu

GRAESSLE, Tammy 814-472-3222 396 I tgraessle@francis.edu

GRAF, Amanda 540-636-2900 464 O agraf@christendom.edu

GRAF, Bob 651-696-6280 236 C rgraf@macalester.edu

GRAF, Mel 401-598-4949 403 E mary.graf@jwu.edu

GRAFF, Brenda 217-641-4530 140 H bgraff@jwcc.edu

GRAFF, Eric, S 614-885-5585 359 K egraff@pcj.edu

GRAFF, Jennifer 920-424-0775 495 C graff@uwosh.edu

GRAFF, Leslie 901-321-3271 417 G leslie.graff@cbu.edu

GRAFF, Michael 440-525-7060 354 L

GRAFF, Robin 914-606-7756 324 F robin.graff@sunywcc.edu

GRAFFAGNINO, Jason 706-865-2134 126 D jgraffagnino@truett.edu

GRAFFEO, Mary Ann 719-389-6142 78 E mgraffeo@coloradocollege.edu

GRAFFIUS, Jeffrey 740-374-8716 363 F jgraffius@wscc.edu

GRAFIUS, Brandon 313-831-5200 223 G bgrafius@etseminary.edu

GRAFTON, Anthony 870-307-7315 20 D anthony.grafton@lyon.edu

GRAFTON, Donald 541-485-1780 374 C donaldgrafton@newhope.edu

GRAFTON, Floria 541-485-1780 374 C floriagrafton@newhope.edu

GRAFTON, Karla 860-509-9564 88 A dgrafton@hartfordinternational.edu

GRAFTON, Phillip 937-766-7834 349 C graftonp@cedarville.edu

GRAFTON, Robert 318-257-2111 192 A rgrafton@latec.edu

GRAFTON, Steve, C 734-763-9730 231 A sgrafton@umich.edu

GRAGG, Derrick 847-491-8880 146 C derrick.gragg@northwestern.edu

GRAGG, Matt 909-748-8108 72 E matt_gragg@redlands.edu

GRAGG, Philip, T 619-239-0391 34 H pgragg@cwsl.edu

GRAHAM, Amy 315-470-7858 291 E amygraham@crouse.org

GRAHAM, Angela 540-863-2806 473 D agraham@mgcc.edu

GRAHAM, Annette 845-451-1610 297 E annette.graham@culinary.edu

Index of Key Administrators **GRAHAM – GRANT ROBINSON 669**

GRAHAM, Anthony .... 540-831-5508 468 E argraham1@radford.edu
GRAHAM, Anthony .... 336-750-2206 343 E grahama@wssu.edu
GRAHAM, April .... 661-362-3248.. 38 H april.graham@canyons.edu
GRAHAM, Bobby .... 318-345-9301 188 A robertgraham4@ladelta.edu
GRAHAM, Carlos .... 573-681-5912 254 A grahamc@lincolnu.edu
GRAHAM, Chad .... 601-484-8698 246 B cgraham@meridiancc.edu
GRAHAM, Chris .... 757-352-4231 469 D chrigr1@regent.edu
GRAHAM, Christopher .. 214-818-1390 433 A cgraham@criswell.edu
GRAHAM, Christy .... 423-869-6314 420 A christina.graham@lmunet.edu
GRAHAM, Chuck .... 352-335-2332.. 94 E
GRAHAM, Chuck .... 412-237-3184 381 C cgraham@ccac.edu
GRAHAM, Daria .... 909-537-5185.. 33 B daria.graham@csusb.edu
GRAHAM, Daria .... 909-537-7172.. 33 B daria.graham@csusb.edu
GRAHAM, David .... 704-894-2052 328 C dagraham@davidson.edu
GRAHAM, Dean .... 207-581-1714 196 D dean.graham@maine.edu
GRAHAM, Dennis .... 616-949-5300 222 F dennis.graham@cornerstone.edu
GRAHAM, Earl .... 203-332-5290.. 86 E egraham@housatonic.edu
GRAHAM, Elizabeth ...... 909-607-2269.. 57 K elizabeth.graham@pomona.edu
GRAHAM, Emily, J .... 843-661-1145 408 H emily.graham3@fmarion.edu
GRAHAM, Erika .... 254-968-0547 445 F egraham@tarleton.edu
GRAHAM, Eva .... 661-255-1050.. 28 I egraham@calarts.edu
GRAHAM, Evelyn .... 757-728-5357 466 L evelyn.graham@hamptonu.edu
GRAHAM, Helen .... 713-718-8566 436 E helen.graham@hccs.edu
GRAHAM, James, F ...... 660-543-4279 259 K graham@ucmo.edu
GRAHAM, Jamil .... 973-877-3064 276 G
GRAHAM, Jasmyn .... 804-524-5214 475 E jgraham@vsu.edu
GRAHAM, Jeff .... 301-687-4311 203 F jlgraham@frostburg.edu
GRAHAM, Jeffrey .... 956-665-2683 455 A jeff.graham@utrgv.edu
GRAHAM, Jennifer .... 478-445-5004 119 A
GRAHAM, Joan .... 585-475-6079 312 A
GRAHAM, Joan, E .... 585-475-6079 312 A jegirp@rit.edu
GRAHAM, Jocelyn .... 910-775-4471 343 A jocelyn.hunt@uncp.edu
GRAHAM, John-Bauer .. 256-782-5255..... 6 A jgraham@jsu.edu
GRAHAM, Jonathan ...... 800-287-8822 153 F grahajo@bethanyseminary.edu
GRAHAM, Jonathan ...... 615-220-7839 423 G jgraham@mscc.edu
GRAHAM, Kathleen .... 570-577-3607 379 A kathy.graham@bucknell.edu
GRAHAM, Keith .... 901-375-4400 421 A keithgraham@midsouthchristian.edu
GRAHAM, Keith .... 570-740-0302 388 G kgraham@luzerne.edu
GRAHAM, Kelli .... 315-655-7227 292 B kgraham@cazenovia.edu
GRAHAM, Kerwin .... 336-750-2078 343 E grahamkw@wssu.edu
GRAHAM, Kevin .... 671-734-1812 503 D kgraham@piu.edu
GRAHAM, Larry .... 479-979-1425.. 24 A lgraham@ozarks.edu
GRAHAM, Latonya .... 334-833-4302..... 5 H hccounseling@hawks.huntingdon.edu
GRAHAM, LeRoy .... 802-443-5669 461 G leroyg@middlebury.edu
GRAHAM, JR., Lewis, P .... 803-934-3274 409 H lgraham@morris.edu
GRAHAM, JR., Lewis, P .... 803-934-3404 409 H lgraham@morris.edu
GRAHAM, Lindsey .... 978-556-3621 215 C lgraham@necc.mass.edu
GRAHAM, Mark, R .... 276-944-6104 466 F mgraham@ehc.edu
GRAHAM, Mary, S .... 601-928-6280 246 F mary.graham@mgccc.edu
GRAHAM, Megan .... 909-554-3814.. 54 H
GRAHAM, Michael .... 847-947-5333 145 C michael.graham@nl.edu
GRAHAM, Michelle .... 802-728-1252 462 H michelle.graham@vtc.edu
GRAHAM, Patrick .... 870-574-4701.. 21 F pgraham@sautech.edu
GRAHAM, Rachael .... 413-559-5724 210 A rgraham@hampshire.edu
GRAHAM, Robbie .... 907-786-1190.... 9 I rlgraham3@alaska.edu
GRAHAM, Robert .... 773-602-5265 135 A rgraham24@ccc.edu
GRAHAM, Ronald .... 518-562-4200 295 F ronald.graham@clinton.edu
GRAHAM, Samuel .... 301-405-3868 202 E samuelg@umd.edu
GRAHAM, Scott .... 617-353-1344 207 C scgraham@bu.edu
GRAHAM, Sharon, D .... 913-897-8767 177 G sgraham@ku.edu
GRAHAM, Shelci .... 212-217-3600 299 C shelci_graham@fitnyc.edu
GRAHAM, Stephanie, M .... 847-467-6270 146 C smg@northwestern.edu
GRAHAM, Stephen .... 202-806-2273.. 92 E stephen.graham@howard.edu
GRAHAM, Stephen .... 650-723-2750.. 66 D
GRAHAM, Steve .... 252-492-2061 338 D grahams@vgcc.edu
GRAHAM, Terri .... 772-462-2505 102 E tgraham@irsc.edu
GRAHAM, Terri, A .... 407-582-6801 113 C tgraham34@valenciacollege.edu
GRAHAM, Thomas .... 740-264-5591 352 B tegraham@egcc.edu
GRAHAM, JR., Thomas 920-206-2345 492 C thomas.grahamjr@mbu.edu
GRAHAM, Toby .... 706-542-0621 126 F tgraham@uga.edu
GRAHAM, Tymon .... 904-470-8360.. 98 I t.graham@ewc.edu
GRAHAM, Van .... 903-233-3900 438 C vangraham@letu.edu
GRAHAM, Zebedee .... 828-448-6196 338 G zgraham@wpcc.edu
GRAIN, Vanessa, M ...... 575-835-5600 286 D vanessa.grain@nmt.edu
GRAJEWSKI, Tracy, L ... 814-641-3194 386 E grajewt@juniata.edu
GRAMELSPACHER, Dave .... 812-357-8429 160 G dgramelspacher@saintmeinrad.edu
GRAMENZ, Gary .... 559-453-5574.. 43 D gary.gramenz@fresno.edu
GRAMLICH, Annalisa .... 816-501-4714 257 K annalia.gramlich@rockhurst.edu
GRAMLING, Gary .... 325-649-8404 437 A ggramling@hputx.edu
GRAMLING, Kelly .... 513-875-3344 349 K kelly.gramling@chatfield.edu
GRAMLING, P.J .... 325-649-8406 437 A pgramling@hputx.edu
GRAMLING, Patrick .... 800-241-1027.. 72 F pgramling@usa.edu
GRAMLING, Shelly .... 765-998-5202 161 A shgramling@taylor.edu
GRAMLING, Tim .... 951-552-8324.. 27 J tgramling@calbaptist.edu
GRAMMER, Jody .... 918-293-4890 368 B jody.grammer@okstate.edu
GRAMOPADHYE, Anand .... 864-656-3202 406 F agramop@clemson.edu
GRAN, Tracey .... 651-690-6043 242 F tlgran@stkate.edu
GRANADOS, Alexander . 816-322-0110 250 E alexander.granados@calvary.edu
GRANADOS, Pattie .... 760-252-2411.. 26 L pgranados@barstow.edu
GRANART, Heather, L .... 630-844-5448 133 A hgranart@aurora.edu
GRANAT, Bonnie .... 718-613-8534 316 E bonnie.granat@downstate.edu
GRANATA, Brian .... 215-572-2194 378 E granatab@arcadia.edu
GRANATO, Jim .... 713-743-8887 451 G jgranato@uh.edu
GRANATOWSKI, Doris .. 480-212-1704.. 15 R doris@sessions.edu
GRANBERG, Ellen .... 585-475-6399 312 A emgpro@rit.edu
GRAND PRÉ, Paul .... 508-588-9100 214 F pgrandpre@massasoit.mass.edu
GRAND PRE, Donna .... 617-573-8460 218 G dgrandpre@suffolk.edu
GRANDA, Cecilia .... 914-323-5357 305 A cecilia.granda@mville.edu
GRANDALL, Jerolyn, R . 608-785-9576 499 B grandallj@westerntc.edu
GRANDCHAMP, Michael, N .... 401-341-2142 404 D grandchm@salve.edu
GRANDINETTI, Margie .. 610-282-1100 382 A margie.grandinetti@desales.edu
GRANDINETTI, Mary Aurora .... 502-272-7954 179 D mgrandinetti@bellarmine.edu
GRANDJEAN, Miley .... 575-674-2366 284 P mgrandjean@burrell.edu
GRANDJEAN, Peter, W . 662-915-7900 248 F pwg@olemiss.edu
GRANDSTAFF, Kelly ...... 850-478-8496 105 F kgrandstaff@pcci.edu
GRANDY, Carla .... 650-574-6161.. 62 J
GRANDY, Jody .... 252-335-3275 341 A jograndy@ecsu.edu
GRANEC, Rodney .... 205-652-3592..... 9 B rgranec@uwa.edu
GRANEY, Carol .... 215-717-6393 399 I cgraney@uarts.edu
GRANEY, Daniel .... 401-874-2098 404 E dgraney@uri.edu
GRANFIELD, Cathy .... 414-955-8566 492 F mcw@matthewsstores.com
GRANFIELD, Robert ...... 716-645-3594 315 F rgranfie@buffalo.edu
GRANGER, Cherice .... 518-564-2010 318 C grangecg@plattsburgh.edu
GRANGER, Gary .... 503-777-7379 375 F grangerg@reed.edu
GRANGER, Heidi .... 915-747-7390 454 E hgranger@utep.edu
GRANGER, Jill .... 828-227-7383 343 D jngranger@wcu.edu
GRANGER, Joey .... 601-984-1199 248 G jgranger@umc.edu
GRANGER, Kevin .... 713-313-4378 448 D kevin.granger@tsu.edu
GRANGER, Sarah .... 574-284-4584 160 F sgranger@saintmarys.edu
GRANGER, Vern .... 860-486-1478.. 89 B vern.granger@uconn.edu
GRANILLO, Lillian .... 718-522-9073 290 B lgranillo@asa.edu
GRANLE, Ken .... 312-341-3500 148 A
GRANNAS, Amanda ...... 610-519-5858 401 B amanda.grannas@villanova.edu
GRANNUM-MOSLEY, Andrea, K .... 610-799-1083 388 B agrannummosley@lccc.edu
GRANOT, Elad .... 419-289-5932 347 H egranot@ashland.edu
GRANOT, Elad .... 216-397-1886 353 O egranot@jcu.edu
GRANT, Alan .... 540-231-4152 475 D algrant@vt.edu
GRANT, Allen, C .... 315-267-2515 318 D grant@potsdam.edu
GRANT, Amy .... 310-660-3350.. 41 J agrant@elcamino.edu
GRANT, Angela .... 617-824-8655 208 G angela_grant@emerson.edu
GRANT, Benjamin .... 716-829-8336 298 C grantb@dyc.edu
GRANT, Bob .... 937-775-2771 364 D bob.grant@wright.edu
GRANT, Brad .... 912-525-5000 124 G bgrant@scad.edu
GRANT, Brian, T .... 315-268-6463 295 E bgrant@clarkson.edu
GRANT, Caitlin .... 207-646-9282 195 F ycgrant@yccc.edu
GRANT, Caleb .... 518-255-5526 318 F grantcr@cobleskill.edu
GRANT, Caleb .... 518-255-5525 318 F grantcr@cobleskill.edu
GRANT, Christine .... 603-342-3005 272 E cgrant@ccsnh.edu
GRANT, Christine .... 860-768-4220.. 89 E cgrant@hartford.edu
GRANT, Christy .... 615-248-1447 425 D cgrant@trevecca.edu
GRANT, Claudia .... 352-395-5496 107 G claudia.grant@sfcollege.edu
GRANT, Connie .... 518-736-3622 300 B cgrant@fmcc.edu
GRANT, Dave .... 562-944-0351.. 27 E dave.grant@biola.edu
GRANT, Deena .... 860-509-9536.. 88 A dgrant@hartfordinternational.edu
GRANT, Erica .... 251-981-3771.... 5 B erica.grant@columbiasouthern.edu
GRANT, G. Anthony ...... 303-615-0539.. 81 L ggrant5@msudenver.edu
GRANT, G. Anthony ...... 617-253-4498 215 G
GRANT, Gary .... 321-674-6160 100 A ggrant@fit.edu
GRANT, Jacqueline .... 570-208-5899 386 G jacquelinegrant@kings.edu
GRANT, Jamie .... 864-596-9010 407 G jamie.grant@converse.edu
GRANT, Janis .... 718-270-4900 294 E
GRANT, Jeff .... 229-245-3852 127 C jgrant@valdosta.edu
GRANT, Jesse .... 216-421-7427 350 E jlgrant@cia.edu
GRANT, Jordan .... 206-296-5852 483 B jgrant1@seattleu.edu
GRANT, Karen .... 508-854-4382 215 D kgrant@qcc.mass.edu
GRANT, Kevin .... 805-756-7487.. 29 K kgrant04@calpoly.edu
GRANT, Kizuwanda .... 214-379-5500 440 H kgrant@pqc.edu
GRANT, Laura .... 636-922-8391 258 A lgrant@stchas.edu
GRANT, Linda .... 334-637-3151.... 1 I linda.grant@coastalalabama.edu
GRANT, Madeline .... 714-564-6750.. 58 F grant_madeline@sac.edu
GRANT, Mary, K .... 617-879-7100 212 E mkgrant@massart.edu
GRANT, Meagan .... 978-921-4242 216 F meagan.grant@montserrat.edu
GRANT, Michael .... 484-809-7770.. 93 H
GRANT, Michael .... 302-292-6100.. 93 H
GRANT, Michele .... 215-335-0800 388 E mgrant@lincolntech.edu
GRANT, Nathan .... 207-778-7864 196 F nathan.grant@maine.edu
GRANT, Nina .... 319-296-4218 166 E nina.grant@hawkeyecollege.edu
GRANT, Nina .... 803-323-2141 413 D grantn@winthrop.edu
GRANT, Nina .... 843-863-8020 406 C ngrant@csuniv.edu
GRANT, Pamela .... 216-987-5020 351 D pamela.grant@tri-c.edu
GRANT, Ralph .... 973-803-5000 279 C rgrant@pillar.edu
GRANT, Renee .... 315-781-3319 301 D grant@hws.edu
GRANT, Robert .... 563-333-6419 169 D grantrobert@sau.edu
GRANT, Sharone, V ...... 410-651-6597 203 B svgrant@umes.edu
GRANT, Shauna .... 907-786-1517.. 10 A smgrant@alaska.edu
GRANT, Shaunette .... 301-860-3402 203 D sgrant@bowiestate.edu
GRANT, Shaunette .... 305-899-4888.. 96 A sgrant@barry.edu
GRANT, Shearese, G ..... 334-420-4216.... 3 H sgrant@trenholmstate.edu
GRANT, Tim .... 843-863-7000 406 C tgrant@csuniv.edu
GRANT, Timothy .... 609-771-2167 275 J tgrant@tcnj.edu
GRANT, Traci .... 425-889-7823 481 A traci.grant@northwestu.edu
GRANT, Tyler .... 574-807-7124 153 G tyler.grant@betheluniversity.edu
GRANT, Tyler, C .... 574-807-7124 153 G tyler.grant@betheluniversity.edu
GRANT, Velvet, L .... 757-683-3159 468 C vlgrant2@odu.edu
GRANT-BRINKLEY, Kedra .... 210-805-5814 452 D kegrant@uiwtx.edu
GRANT ROBINSON, Susan .... 920-465-2067 494 F grantros@uwgb.edu

© COPYRIGHT HIGHER EDUCATION PUBLICATIONS, INC. 2022

GRANTHAM, Kimberly .. 901-678-2930 426 A kimberly.grantham@memphis.edu
GRANTHAM, Lisa, P ..... 512-448-8774 441 N lisag@stedwards.edu
GRANTNER, Elizabeth ... 312-949-7079 139 B egrantner@ico.edu
GRANZOW, Daniel .... 636-922-8508 258 A dgranzow@stchas.edu
GRAPENTHIEN, Robert .. 847-925-6245 138 E rgrapent@harpercollege.edu
GRASELL, James, F ...... 610-660-1299 397 A jgrasell@sju.edu
GRASSADONIA, Jane .... 570-577-3786 379 A jmg064@bucknell.edu
GRASSEL, OSB, Martin . 503-845-3326 373 G martin.grassel@mtangel.edu
GRASSMAN, Sandy .... 216-373-5283 357 F sgrassman@ndc.edu
GRASSO, Dominico .... 313-593-5500 231 B grasso@umich.edu
GRASSO, Eliot .... 541-683-5141 373 A
GRASSO, Joseph, E ...... 315-445-4174 303 F grassoje@lemoyne.edu
GRASSO, Richard .... 718-489-3450 312 H richardgrasso@sfc.edu
GRATSON, Emily .... 616-949-5300 222 F emily.gratson@cornerstone.edu
GRATZ, Bruce, A .... 507-344-7367 233 I bruce.gratz@blc.edu
GRAU, Isidro .... 713-221-8494 452 B graui@uhd.edu
GRAU, Leeann .... 740-389-4636 355 F graul@mtc.edu
GRAU, Melissa .... 269-927-6172 226 B grau@lakemichigancollege.edu
GRAU, Monica, C .... 607-436-2255 316 C monica.grau@oneonta.edu
GRAUBERGER, Renee ... 602-383-8228.. 16 G rgrauberger@uat.edu
GRAUMAN, Greg .... 808-543-8061 128 E ggrauman@hpu.edu
GRAUSE, Candice .... 850-201-6219 112 B candice.grause@tcc.fl.edu
GRAVATT, Tomi .... 217-234-5253 141 H tgravatt@lakelandcollege.edu
GRAVEL, Matthew .... 413-755-4623 215 F mgravel@stcc.edu
GRAVEL, Tammy .... 508-373-5682 216 B tammy.gravel@mcphs.edu
GRAVELINE, Michele, A 508-767-7386 205 F mgraveli@assumption.edu
GRAVELLE, Andrea .... 410-386-8419 197 G agravelle@carrollcc.edu
GRAVERATTE, Jacqueline .... 989-317-4760 229 K jgraveratte@sagchip.edu
GRAVES, Barry .... 205-853-1200.... 2 G barry.graves@jeffersonstate.edu
GRAVES, Becky .... 256-352-8159.... 4 A becky.graves@wallacestate.edu
GRAVES, Bennie .... 979-830-4701 430 I bennie.graves@blinn.edu
GRAVES, Carla .... 985-867-2232 190 I humanresources@sjasc.edu
GRAVES, Carla .... 904-470-8237.. 98 I carla.graves@ewc.edu
GRAVES, Devin .... 620-441-5595 172 M devin.graves@cowley.edu
GRAVES, Elizabeth, E .... 859-238-5200 179 H elizabeth.graves@centre.edu
GRAVES, Finley .... 940-898-3500 451 A fgraves@twu.edu
GRAVES, Frank .... 254-299-8126 438 G fgraves@mclennan.edu
GRAVES, Howard .... 434-797-8460 472 H howard.graves@danville.edu
GRAVES, Howard, E ...... 516-463-6429 301 E howard.e.graves@hofstra.edu
GRAVES, Jeana .... 740-377-2520 361 D jeana.graves@tsbc.edu
GRAVES, Julie .... 901-435-1526 419 I julie_graves@loc.edu
GRAVES, Kathleen .... 563-884-5102 169 C kathleen.graves@palmer.edu
GRAVES, Kimberly .... 330-490-7296 363 E kgraves@walsh.edu
GRAVES, Lisa, E .... 269-337-4400 233 A
GRAVES, Loreatha, D .... 336-285-2702 341 C loretha@ncat.edu
GRAVES, Lucheia .... 336-517-1501 326 J lgraves@bennett.edu
GRAVES, Mallis .... 859-442-1608 181 D mallis.graves@kctcs.edu
GRAVES, Marquita, J .... 336-750-3331 343 E gravesmj@wssu.edu
GRAVES, Randy, K .... 269-471-3854 220 H gravesr@andrews.edu
GRAVES, Robbie .... 606-759-7141 182 B robbie.graves@kctcs.edu
GRAVES, Robbie .... 731-661-5008 425 F rgraves@uu.edu
GRAVES, Sara .... 256-824-6064.... 8 B sara.graves@uah.edu
GRAVES, Treva .... 507-847-7945 239 B treva.graves@mnwest.edu
GRAVES, William .... 316-942-4291 176 B gravesw@newmanu.edu
GRAVES, William, R ...... 515-294-2682 163 E graves@iastate.edu
GRAVES, William, T ...... 318-342-1961 193 A graves@ulm.edu
GRAVES-BAYAZITOGLU, Rebecca .... 609-258-3000 279 E
GRAVETT, Erika .... 760-750-4437.. 33 C egravett@csusm.edu
GRAVETT, Sharon, L ...... 229-333-5950 127 C sgravett@valdosta.edu
GRAVIETTE, Kimberly, K .... 402-461-7387 266 C kgraviette@hastings.edu
GRAVINA, Kevin .... 303-273-3351.. 79 A kgravina@mines.edu
GRAVLEY-STACK, Kara .. 218-477-4000 239 A kara.gravleystack@mnstate.edu
GRAWROCK, Matt .... 315-684-6072 320 E grawromd@morrisville.edu
GRAY, Amy .... 630-844-5467 133 A agray@aurora.edu
GRAY, Amy .... 815-280-2246 140 I amgray@jjc.edu
GRAY, Brandy .... 315-792-3228 323 G bgray@utica.edu
GRAY, Charlotte .... 417-967-5466 259 H
GRAY, Charlotte .... 417-777-5062 250 B cgray@texascountytech.edu
GRAY, Chris .... 913-469-8500 174 F chrisgray@jccc.edu
GRAY, Christine .... 303-722-5724.. 81 K cgray@lincolntech.edu
GRAY, Courtney .... 903-730-4890 437 E cgray@jarvis.edu
GRAY, Cynthia, B .... 386-481-2000.. 96 D
GRAY, David, R .... 540-868-7154 473 C dgray@lfcc.edu
GRAY, Gregory, S .... 334-727-8011.... 7 D gsgray@tuskegee.edu
GRAY, Hannah .... 972-279-6511 428 G hgray@amberton.edu
GRAY, Holly .... 662-862-8381 245 F ehgray@iccms.edu
GRAY, Isabel .... 856-227-7200 275 F igray@camdencc.edu
GRAY, James .... 205-247-8001.... 7 A jgray@stillman.edu
GRAY, Jeff .... 870-733-6731.. 18 A wjgray@asumidsouth.edu
GRAY, Jeff .... 478-387-4781 119 E jgray@gmc.edu
GRAY, Jeffrey, L .... 718-817-4750 300 A gray@fordham.edu
GRAY, Jennifer .... 405-425-1936 367 C jennifer.gray@oc.edu
GRAY, Jim .... 413-585-2426 218 D jwgray@smith.edu
GRAY, John, C .... 302-295-1139.. 91 C john.c.gray@wilmu.edu
GRAY, Julianna, R .... 607-871-2256 289 E gray@alfred.edu
GRAY, Karol .... 804-828-1200 472 D kgray8@vcu.edu
GRAY, Kathleen .... 718-489-5340 312 H kgray4@sfc.edu
GRAY, Kelly, A .... 419-755-4823 357 B kgray@ncstatecollege.edu
GRAY, Kent .... 281-487-1170 447 G kgray@txchiro.edu
GRAY, Kilen .... 502-895-3411 183 E kgray@lpts.edu
GRAY, Kristen .... 616-395-7945 224 H gray@hope.edu
GRAY, Kristina .... 309-341-5456 134 A kgray@sandburg.edu
GRAY, Lee .... 704-687-5737 342 C legray@uncc.edu
GRAY, Lisa, G .... 410-546-6390 204 A lggray@salisbury.edu
GRAY, Lloyd .... 601-974-1000 246 C lloyd.gray@millsaps.edu
GRAY, Lydia, E .... 718-862-7231 304 K lydia.gray@manhattan.edu
GRAY, Marisa .... 443-885-4714 200 F marisa.gray@morgan.edu
GRAY, Megan .... 607-431-4170 300 G graym@hartwick.edu
GRAY, Michelle .... 541-956-7084 375 G mgray@roguecc.edu
GRAY, Mike .... 606-546-4151 185 B mgray@unionky.edu
GRAY, Monita, M .... 920-832-6697 492 B monita.m.gray@lawrence.edu
GRAY, Neil .... 903-566-7368 455 C ngray@uttyler.edu
GRAY, Nicholas .... 765-361-6188 162 G grayn@wabash.edu
GRAY, Peter, W .... 931-598-1274 422 F pwgray@sewanee.edu
GRAY, Ronald .... 718-862-7352 304 K
GRAY, Ronald .... 828-448-6068 338 G rgray@wpcc.edu
GRAY, Ronald, A .... 201-559-3541 277 A grayr@felician.edu
GRAY, Sarah .... 309-649-6265 150 D sarah.gray@src.edu
GRAY, Scott .... 402-844-7036 268 A sgray7@northeast.edu
GRAY, Sean .... 319-385-6271 167 F sean.gray@iw.edu
GRAY, Seth .... 904-596-2451 112 E
GRAY, Shashuna .... 540-891-3032 472 J sgray@germanna.edu
GRAY, Shaun .... 207-741-5580 195 D sgray@smccme.edu
GRAY, Shawn .... 409-880-8466 449 B shawn.gray@lamar.edu
GRAY, Simon .... 716-285-1212 309 F sgray@niagara.edu
GRAY, Teresa .... 575-624-8213 286 F tgray@nmmi.edu
GRAY, Tiffaney .... 662-252-8000 248 B tgray@rustcollege.edu
GRAY, Tiffiney .... 662-252-8000 248 B tgray@rustcollege.edu
GRAY, Tim .... 303-937-4420.. 77 J tim.gray@augustineinstitute.org
GRAY, Timothy .... 704-216-6284 330 D tgray@livingstone.edu
GRAY, Toni, B .... 806-371-2912 428 F tbgray@actx.edu
GRAY, Tracy .... 858-695-8587 155 F tgray@horizonuniversity.edu
GRAY, Tuesday, A .... 225-216-8403 187 D grayt@mybrcc.edu
GRAY, Tyler .... 256-215-4284.... 1 G tgray@cacc.edu
GRAY, Van .... 901-751-8453 420 G
GRAY, Vance .... 773-291-6100 135 B
GRAY, William .... 417-777-5062 250 B bgray@texascountytech.edu
GRAY, William .... 517-607-2736 224 G wgray@hillsdale.edu
GRAY-DEVINE, Sherry ... 580-387-7212 366 E sgray@mscok.edu
GRAY-VICKREY, Peg ..... 254-519-5447 446 C gray-vickrey@tamuct.edu
GRAYBEAL, David .... 252-399-6599 326 H jdgraybeal@barton.edu
GRAYBEAL, Susan .... 423-354-2529 424 B segraybeal@northeaststate.edu
GRAYBILL, Jody, D .... 570-577-3351 379 A jody.graybill@bucknell.edu
GRAYBILL, Jolie .... 701-231-8887 345 D jolie.graybill@ndsu.edu
GRAYBILL, Mark, S .... 610-499-1008 401 I msgraybill@widener.edu
GRAYLEE, Laleh .... 657-278-2304.. 31 E lgraylee@fullerton.edu
GRAYS, Shantay .... 713-718-5115 436 E shantay.grays@hccs.edu
GRAYSON, Denise, R .... 605-256-5152 415 G denise.grayson@dsu.edu
GRAYSON, Micki .... 951-571-6382.. 59 B micki.clowney@mvc.edu
GRAZIANO, Carl .... 570-961-7899 387 A grazianoc@lackawanna.edu
GRAZIANO, Lisa .... 716-851-1499 299 A grazianol@ecc.edu
GRAZIOSO, Amanda ...... 603-535-2260 274 B ajgrazioso@plymouth.edu
GRAZULIS, Michele ...... 617-373-2000 217 D
GRAZZINI-OLSON, Nancy .... 952-851-0066 233 D
GREAGOFF, Amy .... 337-550-1416 189 B agreagof@lsue.edu
GREANEY, Brendan .... 419-995-8416 360 B greaney.b@rhodesstate.edu
GREANEY, Bryan .... 917-493-4448 304 L bgreaney@msmnyc.edu
GREANEY, KC .... 707-778-4188.. 63 C kgreaney@santarosa.edu
GREATHOUSE, Jo .... 979-230-3234 431 A jo.greathouse@brazosport.edu
GREAVES, Brandee .... 352-588-8200 107 B
GREAVES, Matthew, C .. 202-687-3488.. 92 D mcg3@georgetown.edu
GREB, Cynthia, W .... 240-895-4203 201 F cwgreb@smcm.edu
GREBIN, Kevin .... 605-331-6772 416 C kevin.grebin@usiouxfalls.edu
GREBINOSKI, Jeff .... 920-498-7193 498 F jeffrey.grebinoski@nwtc.edu
GRECO, Anne .... 215-751-8217 381 H agreco@ccp.edu
GRECO, Frank, M .... 412-365-1680 380 F greco@chatham.edu
GRECO, Gary .... 310-660-3593.. 41 J ggreco@elcamino.edu
GRECO, Gil .... 541-683-5141 373 A ggreco@gutenberg.edu
GRECO, Juneann .... 570-340-6004 389 B greco@marywood.edu
GRECO, Maria .... 865-573-4517 419 E mgreco@johnsonu.edu
GRECO, Michelle .... 504-671-6006 187 I mgreco@dcc.edu
GRECO, Michelle .... 504-671-5091 187 I mgreco@dcc.edu
GRECO, Peter .... 801-832-2005 461 A pgreco@westminstercollege.edu
GRECO, Richard .... 413-781-7822 215 F rdgreco@stcc.edu
GRECOL, Joseph .... 216-373-5407 357 F jgrecol@ndc.edu
GREDEN, Leigh .... 734-487-2211 223 F lgreden@emich.edu
GREEAR, Amy .... 276-523-7480 473 E agreear@mecc.edu
GREELEY, Darryl .... 480-423-6522.. 14 B darryl.greeley@scottsdalecc.edu
GREEN, Adam, S .... 423-439-4211 418 D greenas@etsu.edu
GREEN, Andre .... 850-599-3400 109 E andre.green@famu.edu
GREEN, Andrew .... 443-997-1288 199 E andrew.green@jhu.edu
GREEN, Ashley .... 817-722-1656 437 H ashley.green@tku.edu
GREEN, Becky .... 806-457-4200 435 D bgreen@fpctx.edu
GREEN, Bernice .... 334-727-8011.... 7 D
GREEN, Bevley .... 251-460-6796.... 9 A bwgreen@southalabama.edu
GREEN, Brenda .... 479-725-4669.. 20 G bgreen@nwacc.edu
GREEN, C. Scott .... 208-885-6365 132 C president@uidaho.edu
GREEN, Carmen, R .... 212-650-5277 293 B carmeng@med.cuny.edu
GREEN, Carol, C .... 517-750-1200 230 F ca368436@arbor.edu
GREEN, Carrie .... 405-692-3176 366 C carrie.green@macu.edu
GREEN, Charlotte .... 601-318-6495 249 B cgreen@wmcarey.edu
GREEN, Cheryl .... 212-229-5600 307 E greenck@newschool.edu
GREEN, Cheryl, F .... 708-534-4130 138 C cgreen@govst.edu
GREEN, Chris .... 805-546-3902.. 41 A cgreen@cuesta.edu
GREEN, Chris .... 859-985-3727 179 E greenchr@berea.edu
GREEN, Cindy .... 334-222-6591.... 2 I cgreen@lbwcc.edu
GREEN, Cindy .... 314-539-5227 258 C cgreen2@stlcc.edu
GREEN, Clarence .... 660-562-1110 256 G cgreen@nwmissouri.edu
GREEN, Danielle, M ...... 217-581-5313 137 C dmgreen@eiu.edu
GREEN, David, M .... 818-947-2679.. 50 B greendm@lavc.edu

GREEN, Deborah .... 816-415-7572 261 G
greend@william.jewell.edu
GREEN, Don .... 412-392-3990 395 H
dgreen@pointpark.edu
GREEN, Donna .... 562-985-5468.. 32 A
donna.green@csulb.edu
GREEN, Donna .... 562-985-5471.. 32 A
donna.green@csulb.edu
GREEN, Dwayne .... 256-372-8672.... 1 A
dwayne.green@aamu.edu
GREEN, Elaine .... 215-248-7063 380 G
greene@chc.edu
GREEN, Ellen .... 662-846-4100 245 A
esgreen@deltastate.edu
GREEN, Evan .... 248-218-2114 229 I
egreen@rochesteru.edu
GREEN, E'Lisa .... 904-256-8000 102 G
GREEN, Finley .... 423-652-4865 419 F
flgreen@king.edu
GREEN, Garrett .... 706-721-0211 115 I
gagreen@augusta.edu
GREEN, Gedalya, A ...... 732-367-1060 275 B
ggreen@bmg.edu
GREEN, Geoff .... 805-965-0581.. 62 M
green@sbccfoundation.org
GREEN, Gina, L .... 212-870-1233 309 C
ggreen@nyts.edu
GREEN, Gordon .... 909-580-9661.. 34 E
GREEN, James .... 314-340-3502 253 E
greenja@hssu.edu
GREEN, Janet .... 903-677-8822 451 C
janet.green@tvcc.edu
GREEN, Jasmine .... 773-907-4445 134 N
jgreen14@ccc.edu
GREEN, Jeffrey .... 281-649-3197 436 D
jgreen@hbu.edu
GREEN, Jennifer .... 909-621-8000.. 44 K
jgreen@hmc.edu
GREEN, Jennifer .... 860-932-4140.. 87 C
jgreen@qvcc.edu
GREEN, Jennifer, K ...... 434-395-2944 467 F
greenjk@longwood.edu
GREEN, Jeremy .... 410-386-8335 197 G
jgreen@carrollcc.edu
GREEN, Jessica .... 660-831-4000 256 B
GREEN, Joanna .... 671-734-1812 503 D
jgreen@piu.edu
GREEN, John .... 661-362-3684.. 38 H
john.green@canyons.edu
GREEN, John .... 252-222-6273 332 G
greenj@carteret.edu
GREEN, Jonathan .... 570-372-4018 398 A
supres@susqu.edu
GREEN, Judith .... 201-684-7523 280 B
jgreen2@ramapo.edu
GREEN, Katherine .... 239-590-1067 109 G
kcgreen@fgcu.edu
GREEN, Katherine .... 940-898-3250 451 A
kgreen33@twu.edu
GREEN, Kathleen .... 412-924-1420 395 G
kgreen@pts.edu
GREEN, Kathy .... 303-556-2400.. 84 B
GREEN, Kelli .... 888-378-9988 415 G
kelli.green@dsu.edu
GREEN, Kelly .... 360-596-5214 483 E
kgreen@spscc.edu
GREEN, Laura .... 856-351-2616 282 I
lgreen@salemcc.edu
GREEN, Leif .... 951-493-6753.. 77 A
lgreen@youngamericans.org
GREEN, Lindsay .... 518-783-6822 314 K
lgreen@siena.edu
GREEN, Lisa .... 315-792-3736 323 G
lcgreen@utica.edu
GREEN, Mark .... 267-341-3308 385 I
mgreen2@holyfamily.edu
GREEN, Marra .... 585-292-2102 306 K
mgreen90@monroecc.edu
GREEN, Mary .... 269-965-3931 225 D
greenm@kellogg.edu
GREEN, Matthew .... 518-828-4181 296 G
matthew.green@sunycgcc.edu
GREEN, Matthew .... 805-546-3924.. 41 A
mgreen@cuesta.edu
GREEN, Maureen .... 252-789-0297 335 F
maureen.green@martincc.edu
GREEN, Melanie, H .... 804-627-5300 464 B
melanie_green@bshsi.org
GREEN, Meredith .... 864-294-2163 408 I
meredith.green@furman.edu
GREEN, Michael .... 205-391-2257.... 3 E
mgreen@sheltonstate.edu
GREEN, Michael .... 508-856-5330 212 A
michael.green@umassmed.edu
GREEN, Mike .... 541-737-2447 374 H
GREEN, Monica .... 951-372-7016.. 59 C
monica.green@norcocollege.edu
GREEN, Monica .... 951-372-7016.. 59 A
monica.green@norcocollege.edu
GREEN, Monica .... 770-229-3328 125 F
monica.green@sctech.edu
GREEN, Murrell .... 408-741-2136.. 75 D
murrell.green@westvalley.edu
GREEN, Myrtes, D .... 205-929-6305.... 2 H
mdgreen@lawsonstate.edu
GREEN, Nancy .... 704-403-3599 327 B
nancy.green@atriumhealth.org
GREEN, Nathan .... 615-343-7626 427 B
nathan.green@vanderbilt.edu
GREEN, Nicole .... 310-825-0768.. 69 D
ngreen@caps.ucla.edu
GREEN, O. Jerome .... 501-374-6305.. 21 B
jerome.green@shortercollege.edu
GREEN, Paul .... 785-833-4387 175 C
green@kwu.edu
GREEN, Ragan .... 478-275-7865 123 E
rgreen@oftc.edu
GREEN, Ramona .... 903-223-3058 447 C
ramona.green@tamut.edu
GREEN, Ray .... 903-886-5181 446 D
raymond.green@tamuc.edu
GREEN, Rebecca .... 760-355-6499.. 45 N
becky.green@imperial.edu
GREEN, Rob .... 765-448-1986 154 I
GREEN, Ronnie, D .... 402-472-2116 269 A
rgreen@unl.edu
GREEN, Ruvain .... 845-352-5852 324 I
GREEN, Ryan .... 859-622-6932 180 B
ryan.green@eku.edu
GREEN, Samantha .... 973-720-2107 283 I
greens19@wpunj.edu
GREEN, Sandra .... 225-342-6950 191 F
sandra.green@ulsystem.edu
GREEN, Sandy, B .... 864-488-8348 409 C
sgreen@limestone.edu
GREEN, Scott, A .... 913-684-4298 502 D
GREEN, Sherri .... 503-253-3443 374 E
sherri.green@ocom.edu
GREEN, Sholom .... 845-352-5852 324 I
GREEN, Staci .... 307-855-2232 499 U
sgreen@cwc.edu
GREEN, Stacy .... 207-974-4679 195 A
sgreen@emcc.edu
GREEN, Stephen .... 734-462-4400 230 B
sjgreen@schoolcraft.edu
GREEN, Susan .... 802-635-1308 463 B
susan.green@northernvermont.edu
GREEN, Teresa .... 806-716-2205 443 A
tgreen@southplainscollege.edu
GREEN, Tica, D .... 336-272-7102 329 B
tica.green@greensboro.edu
GREEN, Tiffany .... 256-551-7265.... 2 E
tiffany.green@drakestate.edu
GREEN, Timothy, M ...... 615-248-1378 425 D
tgreen@trevecca.edu
GREEN, Tom .... 216-421-7491 350 E
tgreen@cia.edu
GREEN, Tony .... 585-276-3262 323 E
tony.green@rochester.edu
GREEN, Tracy, A .... 440-366-7557 355 B
GREEN, Travis .... 386-752-1822.. 99 P
travis.green@fgc.edu
GREEN, Wayne .... 601-968-5940 244 C
GREEN, William .... 423-614-8240 419 H
wgreen@leeuniversity.edu.edu
GREEN, William .... 336-734-7520 334 D
bgreen@forsythtech.edu
GREEN, Zachariah .... 602-489-5300.. 10 G
zachariah.green@arizonachristian.edu
GREEN-HAMANN,
Matthew .... 207-992-4951 194 D
green-hamannm@husson.edu
GREENBAUER,
Barbara .... 903-533-5468 451 D
barbara.greenbauer@tjc.edu
GREENBERG, Aaron ...... 561-237-7915 103 W
agreenberg@lynn.edu
GREENBERG, Bryce ...... 801-375-5125 459 A
bryce.greenberg@rm.edu
GREENBERG, Cindy ...... 657-278-3245.. 31 E
cgreenberg@fullerton.edu
GREENBERG, David ...... 212-854-4446 296 H
david.greenberg@columbia.edu
GREENBERG, Elizabeth . 207-236-8581 195 H
egreenberg@mainemedia.edu
GREENBERG, Mark .... 360-650-3051 485 A
mark.greenberg@wwu.edu
GREENBERG, Moshe ..... 845-426-3110 325 M
GREENBERGER, Alan .... 215-895-6364 382 D
ajg42@drexel.edu
GREENE, Aimee .... 225-490-1652 186 H
aimee.howard@franu.edu
GREENE, Andrew .... 206-876-6100 483 A
agreene@theseattleschool.edu
GREENE, Andrew, S ...... 717-867-6200 388 A
greene@lvc.edu
GREENE, Barbara .... 251-675-5990.... 8 C
bgreene@umobile.edu
GREENE, Brendan .... 504-816-4546 186 F
bgreene@dillard.edu
GREENE, C. Allen .... 334-844-9891.... 4 E
cag0083@auburn.edu
GREENE, Carlnita, P ..... 617-228-2312 214 A
carlnita.greene@bhcc.edu
GREENE, Cary .... 910-695-3781 337 E
greenec@sandhills.edu
GREENE, Cheryl .... 936-261-1748 445 E
ckgreene@pvamu.edu
GREENE, Christina .... 910-362-7551 332 F
csgreene85@mail.cfcc.edu
GREENE, Clark, M .... 401-456-8440 404 A
cgreene@ric.edu
GREENE, Dale .... 706-542-4741 126 F
wdgreene@uga.edu
GREENE, David .... 575-838-5880 286 D
david.greene@nmt.edu
GREENE, David, A .... 207-859-4604 194 B
david.greene@colby.edu
GREENE, Dawn .... 847-317-7138 150 J
GREENE, Debra .... 443-518-4101 199 D
dgreene@howardcc.edu
GREENE, Diane .... 617-253-6700 215 G
GREENE, Doug .... 641-782-1324 170 B
greene@swcciowa.edu
GREENE, Eric .... 606-337-1457 180 A
eric.greene@ccbbc.edu
GREENE, Eric .... 269-965-3931 225 D
greenee@kellogg.edu
GREENE, Eric, J .... 606-337-1457 180 A
eric.greene@ccbbc.edu
GREENE, Gayle .... 919-866-5143 338 E
dggreene@waketech.edu
GREENE, Gloria .... 256-824-2657.... 8 B
gloria.greene@uah.edu
GREENE, Holly .... 229-333-2100 127 F
holly.greene@wiregrass.edu
GREENE, Jason .... 256-824-6277.... 8 B
jason.greene@uah.edu
GREENE, Jeffrey .... 207-602-2274 197 A
jgreene2@une.edu
GREENE, Jessica, A ...... 617-552-3111 207 A
jessica.greene.2@bc.edu
GREENE, Joseph, J .... 401-598-1038 403 E
joseph.greene@jwu.edu
GREENE, Julie .... 860-512-3372.. 86 F
jgreene@manchestercc.edu
GREENE, Kaliah .... 631-451-4213 320 G
greenek@sunysuffolk.edu
GREENE, Kami, S .... 724-847-6557 384 B
ksgreene@geneva.edu
GREENE, Kelly .... 337-521-9032 188 G
kelly.greene@solacc.edu
GREENE, Kenneth .... 718-368-5069 294 C
kenneth.greene@kbcc.cuny.edu
GREENE, Kim .... 816-604-3036 255 A
kim.greene@mcckc.edu
GREENE, Linda, S .... 517-432-6993 227 C
dean.greene@law.msu.edu
GREENE, Lori .... 317-940-6086 153 H
lgreene@butler.edu
GREENE, Marcia .... 707-638-5870.. 68 B
GREENE, Matthew .... 605-718-4038 416 D
matthew.greene@wdt.edu
GREENE, Michael .... 480-732-7146.. 13 B
mike.greene@cgc.edu
GREENE, Michelle .... 256-824-5203.... 8 B
michelle.greene@uah.edu
GREENE, Mike .... 870-248-4000.. 18 H
mikeg@blackrivertech.edu
GREENE, Ondrea .... 641-784-5447 166 B
ondrea2@graceland.edu
GREENE, Patricia .... 843-521-4117 412 C
pagreene@uscb.edu
GREENE, Robert .... 832-519-2902 438 E
robert.greene@lonestar.edu
GREENE, Robyn .... 401-341-2337 404 D
robyn.greene@salve.edu
GREENE, Russell .... 972-721-5395 451 E
rgreene@udallas.edu
GREENE, Sheila, M .... 312-942-5762 148 C
sheila_m_greene@rush.edu
GREENE, Shelley, W ..... 336-633-0174 336 F
swgreene@randolph.edu
GREENE, Thomas .... 718-636-3784 311 A
tgreene@pratt.edu
GREENE, Timothy, D ..... 315-655-7377 292 B
tdgreene@cazenovia.edu
GREENE, Tracy .... 605-688-5248 416 A
tracy.greene@sdstate.edu
GREENE, Travis .... 218-755-2075 237 B
travis.greene@bemidjistate.edu
GREENE-RAINEY, Velva . 484-365-7335 388 F
vgrainey@lincoln.edu
GREENER, Daniel .... 631-691-8733 302 D
finaid@idti.edu
GREENFELD, Solomon .. 718-782-7070 323 D
sgreenfeld@utsny.edu
GREENFIELD, Adam ...... 404-727-6123 118 D
ahgree4@emory.edu
GREENFIELD, Brenda, T 315-470-6683 319 A
bgreenfield@esf.edu
GREENFIELD, OSFS,
James, J .... 610-282-1100 382 A
james.greenfield@desales.edu
GREENFIELD, Jon .... 646-592-4414 325 R
greenfield@yu.edu
GREENFIELD, Karli .... 706-865-2134 126 D
kgreenfield@truett.edu
GREENFIELD, Meg .... 504-278-6424 188 E
mgreenfield@nunez.edu
GREENFIELD, Nicolas .... 706-865-2134 126 D
ngreenfield@truett.edu
GREENFIELD, Steve .... 240-567-2583 200 E
steve.greenfield@montgomerycollege.edu
GREENGART, Eli .... 410-484-7200 201 B
egreengart@nirc.edu
GREENHALL, Kim .... 714-744-7045.. 36 D
kgreenha@chapman.edu
GREENHAW, Eric .... 479-524-7285.. 20 C
egreenhaw@jbu.edu
GREENHOW, Andrew .... 412-924-1367 395 G
agreenhow@pts.edu
GREENING, Kris .... 870-743-3000.. 20 F
kgreening@northark.edu
GREENLEAF, Maxine, R 601-877-3900 244 B
mgreenleaf@alcorn.edu
GREENLEAF, Sara .... 315-781-3007 301 D
greenleaf@hws.edu
GREENLEE, Carmen, M . 207-725-3286 194 A
cgreenle@bowdoin.edu
GREENLEE, Geol .... 865-354-3000 424 D
greenlee@roanestate.edu
GREENLEE, Mitchelle .... 619-574-5806.. 43 B
mgreenlee@fst.edu
GREENLEE, Pam, S .... 815-939-5211 146 F
pgreenle@olivet.edu
GREENLEE, Zach .... 314-744-7639 255 H
greenleez@mobap.edu
GREENMAN, David .... 716-880-2000 305 F
GREENO, Darren .... 360-416-7729 483 D
darren.greeno@skagit.edu
GREENO, Jimmie .... 215-972-2303 392 P
jgreeno@pafa.edu
GREENO, John, G .... 412-396-5103 382 E
greenoj@duq.edu
GREENO, Stephanie ...... 845-434-5750 321 B
sgreeno@sunysullivan.edu
GREENSLADE, Ernestine 978-556-3862 215 C
egreenslade@necc.mass.edu
GREENSLADE-SMITH,
Toni .... 614-292-8266 358 E
greenslade-smith.1@osu.edu
GREENSTEIN, Benjamin 401-254-3337 404 C
bgreenstein@rwu.edu
GREENSTEIN, Daniel ..... 717-720-4010 393 C
chancellor@passhe.edu
GREENSTEIN, Kerry .... 434-381-6221 470 H
kgreenstein@sbc.edu
GREENTHAL, Joe .... 864-388-8305 409 B
jgreenthal@lander.edu
GREENTHAL, Joseph, T 607-587-3938 319 C
greentjt@alfredstate.edu
GREENTREE, John .... 208-467-8523 132 B
jgreentree@nnu.edu
GREENUP, Troy .... 562-907-4287.. 76 A
greenup@whittier.edu
GREENWALD, J. Patrick 716-888-8216 291 M
greenwal@canisius.edu
GREENWALD, Kellye ..... 301-696-3714 199 C
greenwald@hood.edu

GREENWALD, Phil .... 405-692-3176 366 C
president@macu.edu

GREENWALD, Richard ... 203-254-4000.. 87 G
rgreenwald@fairfield.edu

GREENWALT, Riane, B .. 618-650-2852 149 H
rgreenw@siue.edu

GREENWAY, Adam, W .. 817-921-8710 444 D
presoffice@swbts.edu

GREENWAY, Janet .... 605-995-7194 414 E
janet.greenway@mitchelltech.edu

GREENWAY, Jill .... 605-995-3023 414 E
jill.greenway@mitchelltech.edu

GREENWAY, Lidell .... 229-468-2240 127 F
lidell.greenway@wiregrass.edu

GREENWAY, Pamela ...... 864-596-9050 407 G
pamela.greenway@converse.edu

GREENWELL, Brian .... 330-490-7282 363 E
bgreenwell@walsh.edu

GREENWELL, Natalie, G 972-985-3768 432 I
ngreenwell@collin.edu

GREENWOD, Steve .... 209-932-2815.. 71 E
sgreenwood@pacific.edu

GREENWOOD, Diane .... 610-409-3316 400 E
dgreenwood@ursinus.edu

GREENWOOD, Grant ..... 325-793-4785 439 A
greenwood.grant@mcm.edu

GREENWOOD, Jeremy .. 802-860-2754 461 C
jgreenwood@champlain.edu

GREENWOOD, Marisol . 469-454-3400.. 93 H

GREENWOOD, Paul ...... 813-257-3095 113 B
pgreenwood@ut.edu

GREENWOOD-BLACKSHEAR,
Sheila .... 410-706-2281 202 F
sheila.blackshear@umaryland.edu

GREER, Bobby .... 843-377-4901 406 B
bgreer@charlestonlaw.edu

GREER, Bradley .... 864-424-8039 412 H
greerm@mailbox.sc.edu

GREER, Carrie .... 636-481-3220 253 G
cgreer4@jeffco.edu

GREER, Charles .... 951-827-3093.. 70 B
charles.greer@ucr.edu

GREER, Christine, G ..... 906-227-1700 228 E
cgreer@nmu.edu

GREER, Gregg .... 806-291-3406 457 B
greerg@wbu.edu

GREER, Jay .... 616-988-1000 222 D
jay.g@compass.edu

GREER, Jennifer .... 859-257-2000 185 D
jgr357@uky.edu

GREER, Jeremy .... 870-245-5526.. 20 H
greerj@obu.edu

GREER, Karla, J .... 972-860-7173 433 I
kgreer@dcccd.edu

GREER, Marisa .... 606-546-1730 185 B
mgreer@unionky.edu

GREER, Melodie .... 267-502-2407 378 I
melodie.greer@brynathyn.edu

GREER, Nyssa .... 712-329-4743 167 G
ngreer@iwcc.edu

GREER, Qubieinique ..... 573-681-5456 254 A
greerq@lincolnu.edu

GREER, Rebecca .... 914-361-6220 307 A
rgreer@montefiore.org

GREER, Sheree .... 606-474-3186 180 G
sgreer@kcu.edu

GREER, Sherman, D ..... 901-333-4101 424 E
sdgreer@southwest.tn.edu

GREER, T. Richard .... 585-594-6160 311 L
greerr@roberts.edu

GREER, Todd .... 251-442-2218.... 8 C
tgreer@umobile.edu

GREER, Tristin .... 724-805-2176 397 D
tristin.greer@stvincent.edu

GREER, William .... 734-763-3571 231 A
wggreer@umich.edu

GREER, William, B .... 423-461-8710 421 E
bgreer@milligan.edu

GREGERSEN, Denise ..... 707-545-3647.. 27 A
denise@berginu.edu

GREGERSON, Robert, G 724-836-9911 400 A
rgregers@pitt.edu

GREGERSON,
Sandra, G .... 832-813-6835 438 E
sandra.g.gregerson@lonestar.edu

GREGG, Carla .... 712-274-5463 168 C
gregg@morningside.edu

GREGG, Carole .... 605-856-8213 415 A
carole.gregg@sintegleska.edu

GREGG, Claire .... 864-596-9213 407 G
claire.gregg@converse.edu

GREGG, Cody .... 361-698-1931 434 H
cgregg2@delmar.edu

GREGG, Judy .... 740-392-6868 356 G
judy.gregg@mvnu.edu

GREGG, Marisa .... 508-793-2720 208 A

GREGG, Matt .... 503-517-1370 377 B
mgregg@warnerpacific.edu

GREGG, Phyllis .... 312-362-8850 136 F
pgregg@depaul.edu

GREGG, Rachel .... 619-594-2078.. 33 E
rgregg@sdsu.edu

GREGG, Robert, S .... 609-652-4542 283 A
robert.gregg@stockton.edu

GREGG, Stacy .... 803-536-8743 410 H
sgregg7@scsu.edu

GREGG, Tara .... 402-465-2488 267 J
tgregg@nebrwesleyan.edu

GREGO, Katherine .... 706-721-0211 115 I
kgrego@augusta.edu

GREGOIRE, David, P ..... 518-564-3613 318 C
david.gregoire@plattsburgh.edu

GREGOIRE, JR.,
Paul, E .... 504-282-4455 190 D
pgregoire@nobts.edu

GREGOIRE, Tom .... 614-292-9426 358 E
gregoire.5@osu.edu

GREGOR, Jeffrey .... 630-870-7900 152 H
jgregor@waubonsee.edu

GREGORIO, Anthony ..... 504-280-6068 189 F
agregor1@uno.edu

GREGORSKI, Ryan .... 231-843-5985 232 I
rgregorski@westshore.edu

GREGORY, Alison .... 703-284-1673 468 A
alison.gregory@marymount.edu

GREGORY, Anne 260-982-5285 158W
aggregory@manchester.edu

GREGORY, Anne .... 219-989-2086 160 A
gregor43@pnw.edu

GREGORY,
Archimandrite .... 530-467-3544.. 60 A
frg@spots.edu

GREGORY, Brent .... 601-276-2000 248 D

GREGORY, Brent .... 601-635-6200 245 B
bgregory@eccc.edu

GREGORY, Carolyn .... 216-368-5276 349 B
carolyn.gregory@case.edu

GREGORY, Charles .... 630-829-6004 133 B
cgregory@ben.edu

GREGORY, Charlie .... 308-635-6740 269 E
gregor43@wncc.edu

GREGORY, Christopher . 508-626-4510 212 D
cgregory@framingham.edu

GREGORY, Dan .... 320-308-4909 240 C
ddgregory@stcloudstate.edu

GREGORY, Dan .... 512-313-3000 432 N
daniel.gregory@concordia.edu

GREGORY, Danyelle ...... 231-591-2617 223 H
danyellegregory@ferris.edu

GREGORY, David .... 615-460-6400 417 B
david.gregory@belmont.edu

GREGORY, David .... 615-460-6538 417 B
david.gregory@belmont.edu

GREGORY, David, L .... 606-783-5100 183 H
d.gregory@moreheadstate.edu

GREGORY, Denise .... 205-726-2725.... 6 E
djgregor@samford.edu

GREGORY, Derek .... 570-961-7839 387 A
gregoryd@lackawanna.edu

GREGORY, Dianne .... 651-846-1538 240 E
dianne.gregory@saintpaul.edu

GREGORY, Elizabeth ..... 660-263-4100 256 D
elizabethgregory@macc.edu

GREGORY, Ellen, D .... 859-846-6046 183 G
egregory@midway.edu

GREGORY,
Frederick, M .... 713-500-3296 455 D
frederick.m.gregory@uth.tmc.edu

GREGORY, James, W ... 386-226-6060.. 98 J
jim.gregory@erau.edu

GREGORY, Jenny .... 706-865-2134 126 D
jgregory@truett.edu

GREGORY, Katherine .... 617-552-2867 207 A
katherine.gregory@bc.edu

GREGORY, Kenton .... 801-832-2530 461 A
kgregory@westminstercollege.edu

GREGORY, Kimberly ...... 252-335-0821 333 E
kimberly_gregory73@albemarle.edu

GREGORY, Matthew ...... 617-322-3506 210 F
matthew_gregory@laboure.edu

GREGORY, Melissa .... 240-567-5036 200 E
melissa.gregory@montgomerycollege.edu

GREGORY, Melissa .... 419-530-5507 363 B
melissa.gregory@utoledo.edu

GREGORY, Miraglia ...... 707-654-4528.. 53 E
mgregory@napavalley.edu

GREGORY, Patrick .... 334-386-7259..... 5 D
pgregory@faulkner.edu

GREGORY, Rhonda .... 615-230-3675 424 F
rhonda.gregory@volstate.edu

GREGORY, Sadie .... 410-951-1295 203 E
srgregory@coppin.edu

GREGORY, Seamus .... 715-682-1395 493 G
sgregory@northland.edu

GREGORY, Tony .... 864-424-8000 412 H
gregorga@mailbox.sc.edu

GREGORYK, Kerry .... 701-845-7480 345 E
kerry.gregoryk@vcsu.edu

GREGSON, Joanna .... 253-535-7126 481 C
gregson@plu.edu

GREIDER, Lauren .... 317-274-5924 157 B
lgreider@iupui.edu

GREIG, Carl .... 903-223-3062 447 C
carl.greig@tamut.edu

GREIMAN, Judith .... 631-632-6302 316 D
judith.greiman@stonybrook.edu

GREIMAN, Judith .... 631-632-6538 316 D
judith.greiman@stonybrook.edu

GREINER, Stephanie ..... 515-271-1386 165 C
stephanie.greiner@dmu.edu

GREISDORF, Steven ...... 978-646-4052 209 G
sgreisdorf@gcts.edu

GREISDORF, Steven ...... 978-921-4242 216 F
steven.greisdorf@montserrat.edu

GREITZ MILLER,
Roxanne .... 714-628-2628.. 36 D
rgmiller@chapman.edu

GRELINGER, Adam .... 316-942-4291 176 B
grelingera@newmanu.edu

GREMMELS, Gillian .... 515-271-4776 165 F
gillian.gremmels@drake.edu

GRENDER, Teresa .... 606-368-6044 178 D
teresagrender@alc.edu

GRENIER, Christine .... 630-617-3071 137 E
cgrenier@elmhurst.edu

GRENZ, Jonathan .... 561-803-2295 105 B
jon_grenz@pba.edu

GRESCH, Mary .... 206-543-8222 484 A
mgresch@uw.edu

GRESH, Bethany .... 216-421-7957 350 E
bggresh@cia.edu

GRESHAM, Joanne .... 209-476-7840.. 67 D
jgresham@clc.edu

GRESHAM, Kathryn .... 828-641-0324 327 A
greshakb@brevard.edu

GRESHAM, Pamela, M .. 302-857-6261.. 90 D
pgresham@desu.edu

GRESS, Andrew .... 515-643-6637 168 B
agress@mercydesmoines.org

GRESS, Vicky .... 217-333-4885 151 F
gress@illinois.edu

GRESS, Vicky .... 217-333-4493 151 F
gress@illinois.edu

GRETCH, Jim .... 406-791-5320 264 J
james.gretch@uprovidence.edu

GRETEN-HARRISON,
Derek .... 703-370-6600 475 F

GRETEN-HARRISON,
Derek .... 703-370-6600 475 F
dgreten-harrison@vts.edu

GREUBEL, Deb .... 540-887-7370 467 G
dgreubel@marybaldwin.edu

GREUFE, Sandra .... 641-648-4611 167 D
sandra.greufe@iavalley.edu

GREVE, Jennifer .... 402-844-7062 268 A
jenniferg@northeast.edu

GREVE, Scott .... 740-284-5891 352 I
sgreve@franciscan.edu

GREVING, John .... 402-465-2486 267 J
jgreving@nebrwesleyan.edu

GREW-GILLEN, Cheryl .. 701-777-4200 344 H
cheryl.grewgillen@und.edu

GREWAL, Daman .... 650-574-6550.. 62 H
grewald@smccd.edu

GREWAL, Parwinder ...... 802-635-1240 463 B

GREWAL, Parwinder ...... 802-728-1252 462 H
parwinder.grewal@vermontstate.vsc.edu

GREWAL, Parwinder ...... 956-665-3883 455 A
parwinder.grewal@utrgv.edu

GREWE, Mike .... 612-330-1499 233 G
grewe@augsburg.edu

GREY, Gregory, D .... 410-334-2933 205 A
ggrey@worwic.edu

GREY, Marge .... 209-946-2311.. 71 E
mgrey@pacific.edu

GREY, Mary .... 413-796-2267 219 E
mgrey@wne.edu

GREY, Pam .... 408-864-8209.. 42 K
greypam@deanza.edu

GREY, Shenequa .... 225-771-2552 191 C
sgrey@sulc.edu

GREY, Valerie .... 518-320-1100 315 C
valerie.grey@suny.edu

GREY GILBERT,
Jeannette .... 406-994-4284 263 G
jeannette.greygilbert@montana.edu

GREYDANUS, John .... 541-737-9099 374 H
john.greydanus@oregonstate.edu

GRGICAK, Catherine ..... 856-225-6142 281 A
cmg369@camden.rutgers.edu

GRIBB, Molly .... 309-677-2721 133 H
mgribb@bradley.edu

GRIBBEN, Les .... 212-817-7414 293 D
lgribben@gc.cuny.edu

GRIBBIN, David .... 478-289-2047 118 B
dgribbin@ega.edu

GRIBBLE, Jennifer .... 757-352-4924 469 D
jgribble@regent.edu

GRIBBLE, Kari .... 608-663-2305 491 F
kgribble@edgewood.edu

GRIBBLE, Scott .... 308-632-6933 268 F
sgribble@summitcc.edu

GRIBBLE, Shannon, L .... 301-687-7588 203 F
slgribble@frostburg.edu

GRIBBONS, Barry, C ..... 818-947-2321.. 50 B
gribbobc@lavc.edu

GRIBLIN, Diana .... 316-942-4291 176 B
griblind@newmanu.edu

GRICAR, Jeff .... 713-718-7431 436 E
jeff.gricar@hccs.edu

GRICE, Ronnie, D .... 785-532-1131 175 A
raker@ksu.edu

GRICE, Sharon .... 319-895-4162 164 E
sgrice@cornellcollege.edu

GRIECCI, Christina .... 800-877-4723 207 E
christina.griecci@cambridgecollege.edu

GRIECO, Debra .... 630-515-7600 144 C

GRIEFF, Jamie .... 203-576-4961.. 89 A

GRIEGO, Esperanza .... 505-467-6593 288 A
esperanzagriego@swc.edu

GRIEGO, Orlando .... 575-624-8020 286 F
ogriego@nmmi.edu

GRIER, Consuelo .... 425-564-2232 477 B
consuelo.grier@bellevuecollege.edu

GRIER, Ed .... 408-554-4523.. 63 A
egrier@scu.edu

GRIER, Judith .... 757-789-1753 472 I
jgrier@es.vccs.edu

GRIES, Kathie .... 269-782-1425 230 D
kgries@swmich.edu

GRIESHEIMER, Tina .... 303-797-5901.. 77 H
tina.griesheimer@arapahoe.edu

GRIEVE, Kimberly .... 605-658-3555 415 E
kimberly.grieve@usd.edu

GRIEVE, Robyn .... 408-260-0208.. 42 H
daom@fivebranches.edu

GRIEWISCH, Carl .... 828-898-8862 330 A
griewischc@lmc.edu

GRIFFEL, Michael, M ...... 541-346-2667 376 G
mgriffel@uoregon.edu

GRIFFEN, Emily .... 413-542-2265 205 D
egriffen@amherst.edu

GRIFFENBERG, William 210-784-4357 447 B
william.griffenberg@tamusa.edu

GRIFFIN, Aishia .... 336-517-2229 326 J
agriffin@bennett.edu

GRIFFIN, Amy .... 317-917-5956 158 B
agriffin76@ivytech.edu

GRIFFIN, Bruce .... 925-485-5247.. 35 P
bgriffin@clpccd.org

GRIFFIN, Bryan, L 989-774-7112 221M
alumni@cmich.edu

GRIFFIN, Clifton, P .... 410-548-3894 204 A
cpgriffin@salisbury.edu

GRIFFIN, Colton .... 304-333-3688 488 L
colton.griffin@fairmontstate.edu

GRIFFIN, Courtney .... 909-635-0250 207 E
courtney.griffin@cambridgecollege.edu

GRIFFIN, Dan .... 731-661-5120 425 F
dgriffin@uu.edu

GRIFFIN, David .... 617-824-8495 208 G
david_griffin@emerson.edu

GRIFFIN, David .... 903-923-2340 435 A
dgriffin@etbu.edu

GRIFFIN, Derika .... 256-395-2211.... 3 G

GRIFFIN, Donitha .... 334-876-9302.... 2 D
donitha.griffin@wccs.edu

GRIFFIN, Elaine .... 615-966-5818 420 B
elaine.griffin@lipscomb.edu

GRIFFIN, Erica .... 618-252-5400 149 E
erica.griffin@sic.edu

GROGG, Ben .... 785-539-3571 175 F
bgrogg@mccks.edu
GROGG, Sam .... 516-877-3810 288 L
sgrogg@adelphi.edu
GROGG, Sam .... 336-517-8620 326 J
sgrogg@bennett.edu
GROH, Sara .... 315-228-6134 296 C
sgroh@colgate.edu
GROLEAU, Richard, A ... 815-835-6331 149 A
richard.a.groleau@svcc.edu
GROLEAU, Ron, W .... 815-224-0482 140 D
ron_groleau@ivcc.edu
GROMAKOV, Max .... 800-686-1883 222 B
GROMATZKY, Steven .... 913-360-7511 171 G
sgromatzky@benedictine.edu
GROMIS, Jeffrey .... 610-341-1775 383 A
jgromis@eastern.edu
GRONA, Marion .... 940-552-6291 456 F
mgrona@vernoncollege.edu
GROND, Greta .... 712-707-7248 169 A
ggrond@nwciowa.edu
GRONDA, Hellene .... 503-223-8188 375 E
hellene.gronda@processwork.edu
GRONDIN, Megan .... 817-722-1741 437 H
megan.grondin@tku.edu
GRONERT, Scott .... 414-229-5895 495 B
sgronert@uwm.edu
GRONEWALD, Kate .... 903-233-3291 438 C
kategronewald@letu.edu
GRONLUND, Robin .... 802-651-5911 461 C
rgronlund@champlain.edu
GRONNIGER, Eileen, C . 785-442-6010 174 C
egronniger@highlandcc.edu
GRONO, Anthony .... 718-817-4943 300 A
grono@fordham.edu
GRONSKY, Jennifer .... 215-503-8189 398 G
jennifer.gronsky@jefferson.edu
GRONSKY, Jennifer, M . 215-503-8189 398 G
jennifer.gronsky@jefferson.edu
GROOBY, Stuart .... 302-857-6000.. 90 D
sgrooby@desu.edu
GROOM, Julie .... 617-243-2176 210 G
jgroom@lasell.edu
GROOM, Ruth .... 513-529-9210 356 A
groomra@miamioh.edu
GROOMS, Catherine ..... 661-362-5151.. 38 H
catherine.grooms@canyons.edu
GROOMS, Daniel, L .... 515-294-9860 163 E
dgrooms@iastate.edu
GROOMS, Kenya .... 312-922-1884 143 D
kgrooms@maccormac.edu
GROPP, Jonathan .... 864-231-2000 405 F
jgropp@andersonuniversity.edu
GROPPER, Daniel .... 561-297-3635 109 F
dgropper@fau.edu
GROPPI, Kelly .... 530-938-5555.. 39 D
GROS, Kathy, R .... 504-865-3237 190 A
kgros@loyno.edu
GROSBY, Karen .... 954-262-5885 104 M
grosby@nsu.nova.edu
GROSCH, Darren .... 323-953-4000.. 49 E
groschda@lacitycollege.edu
GROSE, Kelly .... 304-734-6636 487 D
kelly.grose@bridgevalley.edu
GROSPITCH, Eric .... 785-670-2100 178 A
eric.grospitch@washburn.edu
GROSS, Amanda, R .... 716-839-8210 297 F
agross@daemen.edu
GROSS, Bryan, J .... 413-782-1233 219 E
bryan.gross@wne.edu
GROSS, Calvin .... 859-985-3274 179 E
grossj@berea.edu
GROSS, Candace .... 870-512-7716.. 18 C
candace_gross@asun.edu
GROSS, Carla, E .... 717-796-1800 389 F
cgross@messiah.edu
GROSS, Charles .... 406-447-5480 262 E
cgross@carroll.edu
GROSS, Daryl, J .... 323-343-3080.. 32 B
dgross4@calstatela.edu
GROSS, Dawn .... 508-999-8665 211 F
dgross1@umassd.edu
GROSS, Dolores .... 915-831-6484 435 B
dgross2@epcc.edu
GROSS, Erik, E .... 603-862-1584 273 H
erik.gross@unh.edu
GROSS, Germaine .... 641-269-9700 166 D
grossger@grinnell.edu
GROSS, Heidi .... 307-681-6400 500 F
hgross@sheridan.edu
GROSS, Henry .... 706-649-1883 117 F
hgross@columbustech.edu
GROSS, Laura .... 518-255-5531 318 F
grossll@cobleskill.edu
GROSS, Lois .... 516-739-1545 308 E
studentservices@nyctcm.edu
GROSS, Michael .... 732-987-2373 277 B
mgross@georgian.edu
GROSS, Michael, L .... 610-921-7672 377 F
mgross@albright.edu
GROSS, Monika .... 301-860-4091 203 D
mgross@bowiestate.edu
GROSS, Scott .... 606-487-3528 181 E
scott.gross@kctcs.edu
GROSS, Steven .... 973-698-4944.. 16 L
steven.gross@phoenix.edu
GROSS, Susan .... 201-216-8142 282 L
susan.gross@stevens.edu
GROSSI, OSB, Anthony 724-537-4554 397 C
anthony.grossi@email.stvincent.edu
GROSSI, Donna .... 412-365-1231 380 F
d.grossi@chatham.edu
GROSSKOPF, John .... 850-973-1601 104 K
grosskopfj@nfc.edu
GROSSMAN, David .... 714-992-7046.. 54 D
dgrossman@fullcoll.edu
GROSSMAN, LuAnn ...... 605-331-6738 416 C
luann.grossman@usiouxfalls.edu
GROSSMAN, Michal .... 732-414-2834 284 K
ytcbks@gmail.com
GROSSMAN, Pam .... 215-898-7014 399 J
grossman@gse.upenn.edu
GROSSMAN, Seth .... 202-885-2121.. 91 D
sethg@american.edu
GROSSMAN, Yaffa .... 608-363-2219 490 I
grossman@beloit.edu
GROSSMAN BLOOM,
Stacie .... 212-998-1212 309 D
GROSVENOR, Ari .... 978-921-4242 216 F
ari.grosvenor@montserrat.edu
GROSVENOR, Christy .... 303-762-6902.. 80 G
christy.grosvenor@denverseminary.edu
GROTE, Justin .... 740-588-1361 364 H
jgrote@zanestate.edu
GROTEGUT, Chris, J ..... 920-565-1000 492 A
grotegutcj@lakeland.edu
GROTH, Clayton .... 608-249-6611 491 H
cgroth@herzing.edu
GROTH, Dennis .... 812-856-1079 156 B
iuldean@indiana.edu
GROTTON, Chris .... 207-941-7785 194 D
grottonc@husson.edu
GROTZINGER, John, P . 626-395-6005.. 29 B
grotz@gps.caltech.edu
GROUNDS, Cynthia .... 785-749-8418 174 A
cynthia.grounds@bie.edu
GROUP, Lynda .... 616-632-8900 221 A
GROURKE, Stephen, J .. 610-526-1389 378 D
stephen.grourke@theamericancollege.edu
GROVE, Allison, A .... 570-326-3761 392 S
aab14@pct.edu
GROVE, Jessica .... 314-539-5000 258 C
GROVE, Laurie .... 717-396-7188 398 E
grove@stevenscollege.edu
GROVE, Luke, J .... 515-574-1062 166 G
grove@iowacentral.edu
GROVE, Melinda, F .... 330-972-8574 361 G
mgrove@uakron.edu
GROVE, Shannon, D ..... 814-886-6391 390 E
sgrove@mtaloy.edu
GROVEMAN, Susan .... 661-763-7942.. 67 F
sgroveman@taftcollege.edu
GROVENSTEIN,
Elizabeth .... 919-807-7070 331 I
GROVER, Arthur, G .... 610-660-1111 397 A
agrover@sju.edu
GROVER, Carol .... 315-781-3339 301 D
groverc@hws.edu
GROVER, Dustin .... 918-540-6202 366 F
dugrover@neo.edu
GROVER-BISKER, Edna . 573-341-4292 260 F
egroverb@mst.edu
GROVES, Allen .... 315-443-1870 321 D
GROVES, Devany .... 904-620-2506 111 A
dgroves@unf.edu
GROVES, Katharina .... 719-389-6974.. 78 E
kgroves@coloradocollege.edu
GROVES, Kathy .... 800-995-3159 262 A
GROVES, Loren .... 307-681-6460 500 F
lgroves@sheridan.edu
GROVES, Robert, M ...... 202-687-6400.. 92 D
provost@georgetown.edu
GROVES, Shelley .... 405-789-7661 369 H
shelley.groves@swcu.edu
GROVES, William .... 937-769-1345 347 F
bgroves@antioch.edu
GROVES-SCOTT,
Victoria .... 501-450-3175.. 23 K
vickigs@uca.edu
GROW, David .... 801-274-3280 460 E
dgrow@wgu.edu
GROW, Tamera, J .... 660-562-1146 256 G
tammi@nwmissouri.edu
GROYSMAN, Natasga .... 954-492-5353.. 97 G
ngroysman@citycollege.edu
GROZA, Adam .... 909-687-1450.. 43 G
adamgroza@gs.edu
GRREEN-ROGERS,
Martine Kei .... 336-770-3243 343 C
GRUBAUGH, Jessica ..... 740-392-6868 356 G
jessica.grubaugh@mvnu.edu
GRUBB, Autumn .... 863-680-5118 100 F
agrubb@flsouthern.edu
GRUBB, Derek .... 303-914-6516.. 82 L
derek.grubb@rrcc.edu
GRUBB, John .... 423-354-5144 424 B
jmgrubb@northeaststate.edu
GRUBB, Joshua .... 276-326-4211 464 A
jgrubb@bluefield.edu
GRUBB, Kevin .... 610-519-4060 401 B
kevin.c.grubb@villanova.edu
GRUBB, Lillie .... 620-223-2700 173 F
lillieg@fortscott.edu
GRUBBS, Norris, C .... 504-282-4455 190 D
provostadmin@nobts.edu
GRUBBS, Roe .... 601-925-3844 246 D
rgrubbs@mc.edu
GRUBE, AJ .... 828-227-3028 343 D
agrube@wcu.edu
GRUBER,
Christopher, J .... 704-894-2710 328 C
chgruber@davidson.edu
GRUBER, Jay .... 202-687-7014.. 92 D
jg1502@georgetown.edu
GRUBER, Jennifer .... 530-898-5415.. 31 A
jlgruber@csuchico.edu
GRUBER, Patrick, E .... 719-333-2251 502 C
patrick.gruber@afacademy.af.edu
GRUBISIC, Charles, M .. 920-565-1000 492 A
grubisiccm@lakeland.edu
GRUCZELAK, Jennifer ... 415-575-6100.. 29 A
jgruczelak@ciis.edu
GRUDZINSKI, Shanelle . 402-844-7215 268 A
shanelle@northeast.edu
GRUENIG, Gwendolyn .. 907-450-8190.... 9 I
gdgruenig@alaska.edu
GRUENWALD, John ...... 610-399-2051 393 D
jgruenwald@cheyney.edu
GRUETT, Jon .... 636-584-6575 252 D
jon.gruett@eastcentral.edu
GRUHLER, Sarah .... 360-992-2406 477 J
sgruhler@clark.edu
GRUICHICH, Dawn .... 480-732-7050.. 13 B
dawn.gruichich@cgc.edu
GRUITS, Christopher, A 215-898-5828 399 J
GRUMMONS, Beth .... 315-568-3103 309 H
bgrummons@northeastcollege.edu
GRUNBLATT, Akiva .... 718-268-4700 311 H
GRUNDEN, Ken .... 614-837-4088 363 D
grundenk@valorcollege.edu
GRUNDER, Mark .... 989-358-7376 220 G
grunderm@alpenacc.edu
GRUNDIG, John .... 863-680-6212 100 F
jgrundig@flsouthern.edu
GRUNDMAN, Eric, D ..... 540-365-4551 466 I
egrundman@ferrum.edu
GRUNDY, Christopher .. 314-918-2584 252 E
cgrundy@eden.edu
GRUNDY, Christy .... 419-289-5306 347 H
cgrundy@ashland.edu
GRUNDY, Dallas, A ...... 330-972-8877 361 G
dgrundy@uakron.edu
GRUNDY, Margaret, S .. 434-982-6409 471 F
mg8r@virginia.edu
GRUNEIRO, Nieves .... 973-328-5400 276 A
ngruneiro@ccm.edu
GRUNEIRO-ROADCAP,
Nieves .... 570-422-3494 393 F
ngruneiror@esu.edu
GRUNENWALD,
Matthew .... 406-791-5223 264 J
matthew.grunenwald@uprovidence.edu
GRUNKEMEYER, Heidi .. 402-280-1272 265 J
heidigrunkemeyer@creighton.edu
GRUNKLEE, David .... 319-296-4042 166 E
david.grunklee@hawkeyecollege.edu
GRUNOW, Tamie, L .... 513-556-1015 361 I
grunowtl@ucmail.uc.edu
GRUNWALD, Gerald ...... 215-503-8982 398 G
gerald.grunwald@jefferson.edu
GRUPP, Laurie .... 203-254-4000.. 87 G
lgrupp@fairfield.edu
GRUS, Shannon .... 573-897-5000 259 E
GRUSE, Douglas .... 518-244-4593 312 D
grused@sage.edu
GRUSKA, Julie .... 320-363-3395 242 G
jgruska@csbsju.edu
GRUSKA, Julie, E .... 320-363-3395 234 I
jgruska@csbsju.edu
GRUSKOS, Cynthia .... 732-224-2204 275 D
cgruskos@brookdalecc.edu
GRUTZIK, Cynthia .... 415-338-2686.. 34 A
cgrutzik@sfsu.edu
GRUVER, Nolan .... 509-533-8481 478 C
nolan.gruver@ccs.spokane.edu
GRUVER, Nolan .... 509-434-8481 478 E
nolan.gruver@ccs.spokane.edu
GRUVER, Randi .... 515-574-1148 166 G
gruver@iowacentral.edu
GRUYS, Melissa .... 260-481-6461 159 H
gruysm@pfw.edu
GRYCENKOV, Tina .... 848-932-7305 281 B
grycenko@irap.rutgers.edu
GRYNSPAN, Dévora ...... 312-503-2903 146 C
devora@northwestern.edu
GRYSKEVICZ, Rose .... 570-208-5900 386 G
rosegryskevicz@kings.edu
GRZAN, Dawn .... 516-686-7737 308 H
dgrzan@nyit.edu
GRZENDA, Jana, T .... 641-422-4269 168 E
jana.grzenda@niacc.edu
GRZESIAK, Michael .... 440-775-8273 357 G
mgrzesia@oberlin.edu
GRZYBOWSKI, Mark, J . 815-224-0393 140 D
mark_grzybowski@ivcc.edu
GSTALDER, Steven .... 203-773-0129.. 85 C
sgstalder@albertus.edu
GUADA, Hannah .... 740-753-7067 353 G
guadah@hocking.edu
GUADAGNINO, Frank ... 814-867-4088 391 F
ftg2@psu.edu
GUADALUPE, Efrain ...... 787-704-1020 505 B
eguadalupe@columbiacentral.edu
GUADALUPE, Sarah ...... 248-370-3266 229 F
saguadal@oakland.edu
GUADALUPEZ, Elaine .... 787-743-7979 509 D
eguadalupe@suagm.edu
GUADARRAMA, Janet .... 210-436-3725 442 A
jguadarrama2@stmarytx.edu
GUAJARDO, Aaron .... 972-825-4706 444 C
aguajardo@sagu.edu
GUAJARDO, Nicole, R .. 757-594-8214 465 A
nguajard@cnu.edu
GUALTIERI, Kelly .... 207-326-2215 195 G
kelly.gualtieri@mma.edu
GUAN, Sharon .... 773-325-7726 136 F
xguan@depaul.edu
GUANTE, Alfred .... 203-285-2000.. 86 D
GUANZON, Kimberly .... 831-582-3632.. 32 D
kguanzon@csumb.edu
GUARD, Louis .... 315-781-3309 301 D
guard@hws.edu
GUARDINO, Lauren ...... 610-989-1240 400 F
lguardino@vfmac.edu
GUARDINO, JR., Ron ... 919-497-3327 330 E
rguardino@louisburg.edu
GUARIN-KLEIN, Natalia 718-951-5696 293 A
nataliag@brooklyn.cuny.edu
GUARINO, Joy, A .... 716-878-5331 317 C
guarinja@buffalostate.edu
GUARINO, Mindy .... 708-344-4700 142 E
mguarino@lincolntech.edu
GUARJARDO, George ... 979-830-4743 430 I
george.guarjardo@blinn.edu
GUASTELLA, Rosaria ..... 504-398-2240 191 E
rguastella@uhcno.edu
GUAY, Tanya .... 207-699-5071 194 G
tguay@meca.edu
GUAY, Veronica .... 978-630-9533 215 A
vguay@mwcc.mass.edu
GUBAN, Philip .... 440-943-7600 360 D
pguban@dioceseofcleveland.org
GUBAN, Philip .... 440-943-7676 360 D
pguban@dioceseofcleveland.org
GUBKIN, Liora .... 760-750-4200.. 33 C
lgubkin@csusm.edu
GUBLER, Seth .... 435-652-7571 459 G
seth.gubler@utahtech.edu
GUBLER, Seth .... 435-652-7570 459 G
seth.gubler@utahtech.edu

HAHN, Derek .... 507-433-0569 240 A
derek.hahn@riverland.edu
HAHN, Karen .... 352-588-8522 107 B
karen.hahn@saintleo.edu
HAHN, Kathryn .... 612-330-1013 233 G
hahn@augsburg.edu
HAHN, Keith .... 269-387-1900 232 J
keith.hahn@wmich.edu
HAHN, Kelli .... 269-927-6701 226 B
khahn@lakemichigancollege.edu
HAHN, Lenell .... 573-986-6012 258 J
lhahn@semo.edu
HAHN, Lisa .... 516-572-7169 307 C
lisa.hahn@ncc.edu
HAHN, Marc, B .... 816-654-7102 253 I
mhahn@kcumb.edu
HAHN, Marcela .... 212-875-4400 290 F
mhahn@bankstreet.edu
HAHN, Mary Joan .... 509-313-6095 479 E
hahn@gonzaga.edu
HAHN, Rob .... 414-443-8944 497 A
rob.hahn@wlc.edu
HAHN, Sarah .... 530-752-8990.. 69 A
shahn@shcs.ucdavis.edu
HAHN, Tony .... 812-888-5101 162 E
thahn@vinu.edu
HAHN, Troy .... 718-997-3009 295 A
troy.hahn@qc.cuny.edu
HAHN SCHNIPPER,
Jenny .... 636-922-8244 258 A
jschnipper@stchas.edu
HAHUES, Sven .... 239-590-1337 109 G
shahues@fgcu.edu
HAID, Deisy .... 509-527-2389 484 C
deisy.haid@wallawalla.edu
HAIDLE, Shirley .... 541-881-5842 376 E
shaidle@tvcc.cc
HAIDLE, Sue, E .... 740-368-3104 359 F
sehaidle@owu.edu
HAIGHT, Aaron .... 616-331-3585 224 D
haighta@gvsu.edu
HAIGLER, Steve .... 831-646-4040.. 52 H
shaigler@mpc.edu
HAILE, Amy .... 207-221-4228 197 A
ahaile@une.edu
HAILE, Bob, A .... 309-649-6331 150 D
bob.haile@src.edu
HAILE, Dawit .... 804-524-1141 475 E
dhaile@vsu.edu
HAILE, Gregory Adam ... 954-201-7401.. 96 F
HAILEY, Christine .... 512-245-2119 449 G
ceh138@txstate.edu
HAILEY, Maryann .... 903-875-7305 439 G
maryann.hailey@navarrocollege.edu
HAILEY, Mechele .... 620-227-9377 173 A
mhailey@dc3.edu
HAILEY, Rachel .... 434-961-6547 474 B
rhailey@pvcc.edu
HAILEY PENN, Carla ..... 973-353-5541 281 C
carla.hpenn@rutgers.edu
HAIMINDRA, Mario ...... 203-857-7000.. 87 B
mhaimindra@ncc.commnet.edu
HAIMOVICH, Inbal .... 646-546-5000 322 B
inbal.haimovich@touro.edu
HAIN, Brooke .... 410-857-2546 200 D
bhain@mcdaniel.edu
HAIN, Cathy .... 585-475-2627 312 A
cathy.hain@rit.edu
HAIN, Peggy, S .... 402-465-2137 267 J
phain@nebrwesleyan.edu
HAIN, Tom .... 432-552-2780 456 C
hain_t@utpb.edu
HAINES, Amanda .... 360-623-8428 477 H
amanda.haines@centralia.edu
HAINES, Asher .... 704-687-8693 342 C
ahaines3@uncc.edu
HAINES, Chuck .... 805-893-8541.. 70 E
chuck.haines@ucsb.edu
HAINES, Darla, V 260-982-5949 158W
dvhaines@manchester.edu
HAINES, Gary .... 719-884-5000.. 82 A
gwhaines@nbc.edu
HAINES, Lynne .... 912-650-5673 125 D
lhaines@southuniversity.edu
HAINES, Rhonda .... 315-792-7100 320 F
rhaines@sunypoly.edu
HAINES, Terry .... 913-266-8601 176 F
terry.haines@ottawa.edu
HAINES-FRANK,
Bridget .... 215-619-7453 390 A
bhainesfrank@mc3.edu
HAINGRAY, Donald ...... 585-567-9287 301 G
donald.haingray@houghton.edu

HAINLINE, Benjamin ..... 580-628-6250 366 J
ben.hainline@noc.edu
HAIR, Neil, F .... 585-475-6322 312 A
nfhbbu@rit.edu
HAIR, Shannon .... 434-797-8495 472 H
shannon.hair@danville.edu
HAIRE, Helen, M .... 319-273-2712 163 G
helen.haire@uni.edu
HAIRE, Jacqueline .... 254-526-1903 431 E
jacqueline.haire@ctcd.edu
HAIRR, Blair .... 910-592-8081 337 D
ahairr@sampsoncc.edu
HAIRSTON, Creasie .... 312-996-3219 151 D
cfh@uic.edu
HAIRSTON, Gertrude, J . 410-651-6404 203 B
gjhairston@umes.edu
HAISCH, Craig .... 503-883-2675 373 E
chaisch@linfield.edu
HAISMA, Dale .... 616-632-3037 221 A
haismdal@aquinas.edu
HAIZLIP, Kim .... 402-354-7000 267 E
kimberly.haizlip@methodistcollege.edu
HAJ-HARIRI, Hossein ... 803-777-7356 412 A
hhh@mailbox.sc.edu
HAJDER, Michelle .... 866-492-5336 243 G
michelle.hajder@mail.waldenu.edu
HAJELA, Prabhat .... 518-276-6487 311 J
hajelap@rpi.edu
HAJIR, Farshid .... 413-545-6330 211 D
hajir@provost.umass.edu
HAJIR, Tracy, F .... 410-543-6012 204 A
tfhajir@salisbury.edu
HAJJAR, Souraya .... 915-831-4143 435 B
shajjar@epcc.edu
HAKALA, Curtis .... 304-434-8000 487 E
curtis.hakala@easternwv.edu
HAKE, Eric .... 704-637-4293 327 H
erhake@catawba.edu
HAKIM, George .... 810-762-3223 231 C
geohak@umich.edu
HAKIM, Iman, A .... 520-626-7083.. 16 H
ihakim@arizona.edu
HAKKAKIAN, Eliyahu .... 410-484-7200 201 B
dorm@nirc.edu
HAKKILA, Jon .... 256-824-6339.... 8 B
jon.hakkila@uah.edu
HALABE, Anjali .... 304-293-8768 489 E
anjali.halabe@mail.wvu.edu
HALADA, Robert .... 402-471-2505 267 F
rhalada@nscs.edu
HALARIS, Dimitris .... 914-633-2649 302 C
dhalaris@iona.edu
HALAS, Wally .... 203-254-4000.. 87 G
whalas@fairfield.edu
HALASZ, Tom .... 252-328-6050 340 H
halaszt18@ecu.edu
HALBERSTADT, Joseph . 718-438-1002 306 A
yhalberstadt@yeshivanet.com
HALBERSTAM, Lisa .... 646-565-6326 322 B
lisa.halberstam@touro.edu
HALBERSTAM, Lisa .... 646-565-6326 322 C
lisa.halberstam@touro.edu
HALBERT, Debora .... 808-956-6897 128 I
halbert@hawaii.edu
HALBESLEBEN,
Jonathon .... 205-348-6330.... 7 G
jrhalbesleben@ua.edu
HALBESLEBEN,
Jonathon .... 210-458-4011 455 B
jonathon.halbesleben@utsa.edu
HALBROOK, Anna .... 501-208-5310.. 23 D
halbrook@uaccm.edu
HALCOMB, Jonda .... 361-698-1219 434 H
jhalcomb@delmar.edu
HALCUMB, Cambrea ...... 573-840-9658 259 I
chalcumb@trcc.edu
HALDEMAN, Andrea ...... 717-867-6136 388 A
haldeman@lvc.edu
HALDEMAN, Bill .... 612-626-5148 242 K
HALE, Ann .... 409-772-9796 456 B
aehale@utmb.edu
HALE, Barry .... 903-923-2021 435 A
bhale@etbu.edu
HALE, Cassandra .... 417-455-5675 251 H
cassandrahale@crowder.edu
HALE, Charles, R .... 805-893-8354.. 70 E
ssdean@ltsc.ucsb.edu
HALE, Dale .... 901-321-3264 417 G
dale.hale@cbu.edu
HALE, Dana .... 601-643-8658 244 G
dana.hale@colin.edu
HALE, David, B .... 804-289-8150 471 E
dhale2@richmond.edu

HALE, Don .... 404-413-3025 120 C
dhale@gsu.edu
HALE, Jason .... 806-742-1480 450 C
jason.hale@ttu.edu
HALE, Jean, M .... 724-946-7368 401 F
halejm@westminster.edu
HALE, Jeff, A .... 504-520-5797 193 C
jhale@xula.edu
HALE, Jeremy .... 503-375-7000 372 G
president@corban.edu
HALE, Jerold .... 423-425-4633 426 D
jerold-hale@utc.edu
HALE, Jessica .... 618-468-5110 142 B
jeehale@lc.edu
HALE, Jimmie .... 864-488-4519 409 C
jhale@limestone.edu
HALE, Kandi .... 207-941-7138 194 D
halek@husson.edu
HALE, Katie .... 718-399-4551 311 A
khale@pratt.edu
HALE, Kayla .... 918-631-2745 371 C
kayla-hale@utulsa.edu
HALE, Kimberly .... 217-228-5432 147 C
haleki@quincy.edu
HALE, LaToya .... 443-394-3377.. 93 H
HALE, Mallie .... 256-824-6501.... 8 B
mallie.hale@uah.edu
HALE, Mario .... 760-921-5409.. 56 A
mario.hale@paloverde.edu
HALE, Mark .... 214-333-5503 433 D
markh@dbu.edu
HALE, Melina .... 773-702-2102 151 B
mhale@uchicago.edu
HALE, Mike .... 503-552-1555 374 B
HALE, Nori .... 785-242-5200 176 F
nori.hale@ottawa.edu
HALE, Philip, D .... 773-508-7452 142 G
phale@luc.edu
HALE, Ryan .... 941-408-1405 109 C
haler@scf.edu
HALE, Shawn .... 803-780-1129 413 B
shale@voorhees.edu
HALE, Ted .... 860-906-5053.. 86 C
thale@capitalcc.edu
HALE, Tracy .... 507-457-2319 241 A
thale@winona.edu
HALE, Tricia, A .... 229-333-5940 127 C
tahale@valdosta.edu
HALEAMAU-KAM,
Raynette (Kalei) .... 808-969-8804 129 F
haleamau@hawaii.edu
HALES, Brent .... 814-865-4028 391 F
bdh5347@psu.edu
HALES, Erin .... 714-463-7554.. 51 D
ehales@ketchum.edu
HALES, Jessica .... 410-334-2808 205 A
jhales@worwic.edu
HALEY, Christopher ...... 207-326-2232 195 G
christopher.haley@mma.edu
HALEY, Donna .... 678-839-6438 127 A
dhaley@westga.edu
HALEY, John .... 315-445-4520 303 F
haleyjr@lemoyne.edu
HALEY, John, R .... 315-445-4689 303 F
haleyjr@lemoyne.edu
HALEY, Meghan .... 610-527-0200 396 G
meghan.haley@rosemont.edu
HALEY, Melissa .... 847-578-8756 148 B
melissa.haley@rosalindfranklin.edu
HALEY, Tara .... 904-633-8285 101 A
tara.haley@fscj.edu
HALEY, Taylor .... 606-337-3196 180 A
HALEY, Ted .... 508-767-7215 205 F
thaley@assumption.edu
HALEY-THOMSON, Lisa 518-454-5239 296 E
thomsonl@strose.edu
HALIBURTON, Willie ..... 503-725-4406 375 D
willie@pdx.edu
HALICKI, Shannon, D ... 304-336-8075 489 B
shalicki@westliberty.edu
HALIEMUN, Cynthia ...... 217-228-5432 147 C
haliecy@quincy.edu
HALIKIAS, Philip .... 617-731-3500 210 D
compliance@hchc.edu
HALIMI, Shpresa .... 503-352-2864 375 B
shalimi@pacificu.edu
HALING, Linda .... 920-424-3322 495 C
HALKITIS, Perry, N .... 732-235-9700 281 B
perry.halkitis@rutgers.edu
HALL, Allyson .... 860-465-5283.. 85 G
hallall@easternct.edu
HALL, Amber, L .... 501-450-3663.. 23 K
amberh@uca.edu

HALL, Amy .... 225-214-6979 186 H
amy.hall@franu.edu
HALL, Amy .... 940-898-3544 451 A
ahall@twu.edu
HALL, Anders, W .... 615-322-2451 427 B
anders.hall@vanderbilt.edu
HALL, Andrew .... 404-523-8520 126 A
ahall@follett.com
HALL, Andy .... 423-585-6801 424 G
robert.hall@ws.edu
HALL, Andy .... 423-585-6801 424 G
andy.hall@ws.edu
HALL, Benjamin .... 740-362-3448 355 H
bhall@mtso.edu
HALL, Bobby, L .... 806-291-3401 457 B
hallb@wbu.edu
HALL, Brian .... 207-768-2707 195 C
nbhall@nmcc.edu
HALL, Brian .... 312-850-7899 135 E
bhall44@ccc.edu
HALL, Carol .... 860-515-3889.. 85 D
chall@charteroak.edu
HALL, Carol .... 860-515-3880.. 85 D
chall@charteroak.edu
HALL, Cecily .... 212-686-9244 289 G
HALL, Charles .... 410-209-6020 197 E
chall@bccc.edu
HALL, Chaundra .... 501-686-2921.. 21 G
chall@uasys.edu
HALL, Cheryl .... 985-549-5312 192 E
chall@selu.edu
HALL, Chris .... 410-827-5859 198 B
chall@chesapeake.edu
HALL, Chris .... 618-537-6833 143 G
chall@mckendree.edu
HALL, Christina .... 973-618-3670 275 E
chall@caldwell.edu
HALL, Christopher .... 803-934-3216 409 H
chall@morris.edu
HALL, Clarence, E .... 252-862-1224 336 H
cehall@roanokechowan.edu
HALL, Cynthia .... 530-283-0202.. 42 E
chall@frc.edu
HALL, Dan .... 319-895-4242 164 E
dhall@cornellcollege.edu
HALL, Dan, J .... 412-578-6591 380 A
djhall@carlow.edu
HALL, Danielle .... 517-371-5140 232 K
halld@cooley.edu
HALL, David .... 501-279-4407.. 19 G
dhall@harding.edu
HALL, David .... 340-693-1000 512 B
dhall@uvi.edu
HALL, David, A .... 417-836-8444 255 J
dhall@missouristate.edu
HALL, Davyd .... 317-917-3951 159 B
dhall@martin.edu
HALL, Dennis .... 817-531-6504 450 F
dhall@txwes.edu
HALL, Derek .... 906-227-2716 228 E
halld@nmu.edu
HALL, Dessie .... 404-225-4588 115 F
dhall@atlantatech.edu
HALL, Donald .... 585-273-5000 323 E
donald.hall@rochester.edu
HALL, Donald, E .... 607-777-2141 315 E
dehall@binghamton.edu
HALL, Gene .... 503-517-1119 377 B
ghall@warnerpacific.edu
HALL, Gwen .... 610-526-1441 378 D
gwendolyn.hall@theamericancollege.
edu
HALL, Gwenn .... 318-345-9126 188 A
ghall@ladelta.edu
HALL, Haley .... 520-795-0787.. 10 J
HALL, Heather .... 251-445-9400.... 9 A
heatherhall@southalabama.edu
HALL, Hollie, M .... 607-587-4200 319 C
hallhm@alfredstate.edu
HALL, Jack, C .... 386-312-4293 107 A
jackhall@sjrstate.edu
HALL, Jackie .... 606-487-3180 181 E
jackie.hall@kctcs.edu
HALL, James .... 934-420-2479 320 C
jim.hall@farmingdale.edu
HALL, James .... 585-475-2295 312 A
jchcms@rit.edu
HALL, James, R .... 864-597-4351 413 E
halljr@wofford.edu
HALL, Jami .... 706-272-4428 118 A
jhall@daltonstate.edu
HALL, Jean .... 914-323-5412 305 A
jean.hall@mville.edu

HALVORSON, Corabeth . 608-822-2316 498 H chalverson@swtc.edu
HALVORSON, Daisy ...... 605-229-8453 414 I daisy.halvorson@presentation.edu
HALVORSON, Daisy, H . 920-923-8576 492 D dhhalvorson88@marianuniversity.edu
HALVORSON, Eric .... 714-836-7500 150 J ehhalvorson@tiu.edu
HALVORSON, J. Derek .. 706-419-1117 117 G derek.halvorson@covenant.edu
HALVORSON, Kurt .... 218-935-0417 244 A kurt.halvorson@wetcc.edu
HALVORSON, Lloyd ...... 701-662-1681 346 A lloyd.halvorson@lrsc.edu
HAM, Brandy .... 432-335-6651 440 C bham@odessa.edu
HAM, Dwight .... 661-362-2733.. 51 E dham@masters.edu
HAM, Gary .... 978-762-4000 215 B gham@northshore.edu
HAM, Jeoung, H .... 636-327-4645 255 E reg@midwest.edu
HAM, Michelle .... 912-279-5744 117 C mham@ccga.edu
HAM, Michelle .... 912-260-4320 125 B michelle.ham@sgsc.edu
HAM, Nicole .... 252-940-6204 332 A nicole.ham@beaufortccc.edu
HAM, Paige .... 919-739-6740 338 F peham@waynecc.edu
HAMACHER, Lori .... 719-389-6710.. 78 E lhamacher@coloradocollege.edu
HAMAD, James .... 630-844-4910 133 A jhamad@aurora.edu
HAMADA, Larisa .... 562-985-8256.. 32 A larisa.hamada@csulb.edu
HAMADEH, Yousef, A .... 423-425-5703 426 D yousef-hamadeh@utc.edu
HAMAKAWA, Curt .... 413-782-3111 219 E curt.hamakawa@wne.edu
HAMANN, Dick .... 407-708-2258 108 B hamannd@seminolestate.edu
HAMANN, Melanie .... 573-840-9665 259 I mhamann@trcc.edu
HAMBERGER, Elizabeth . 934-420-5362 320 C studyabroad@farmingdale.edu
HAMBEY, Anthony .... 205-226-4850.... 5 A ahambey@bsc.edu
HAMBLIN, Carolyn .... 928-758-3926.. 14 H chamblin@mohave.edu
HAMBLIN, John .... 503-491-7384 373 H john.hamblin@mhcc.edu
HAMBRICK, Angie, Z .... 253-535-8108 481 C hambriaz@plu.edu
HAMBRIGHT, Beverly .... 850-718-2223.. 97 E hambrightb@chipola.edu
HAMBY, Jamie .... 423-472-7141 423 C jhamby@clevelandstatecc.edu
HAMEL, Dale, M .... 508-626-4580 212 D dhamel@framingham.edu
HAMEL, John .... 508-849-3306 205 E jhamel@annamaria.edu
HAMEL, Kayte .... 815-825-9447 141 D khamel@kish.edu
HAMEL, Lowell .... 269-473-2222 220 H
HAMEL, Nicholas .... 207-755-5284 194 J nhamel@cmcc.edu
HAMELINE, Walter .... 718-390-3488 324 B whamelin@wagner.edu
HAMEN, Laurie .... 320-363-5505 234 I csbpres@csbsju.edu
HAMERLA, R. Rich .... 405-325-9286 370 J rhamerla@ou.edu
HAMERSKY, Steve .... 316-942-4291 176 B hamerskys@newmanu.edu
HAMES, Anne .... 731-352-4066 417 C hamesa@bethelu.edu
HAMES, Joe .... 731-352-4000 417 C hamesj@bethelu.edu
HAMET, Shelby .... 480-750-4470.. 15 Q shamet@tsoa.edu
HAMID, Faisal .... 510-356-4760.. 77 E
HAMID, Hadi .... 803-571-4022 408 A hamidh@denmarktech.edu
HAMILL, Chad, S .... 928-523-3849.. 14 J chad.hamill@nau.edu
HAMILL, Nancy, G .... 510-987-9720.. 70 E nancy.hamill@ucop.edu
HAMILL, Tara .... 732-247-5241 278 E thamill@nbts.edu
HAMILL, Timothy .... 267-341-3514 385 I thamill@holyfamily.edu
HAMILTON, Aaron .... 772-546-5534 102 B
HAMILTON, Adam .... 415-565-4767.. 69 B hamiltoa@uchastings.edu
HAMILTON, Alice .... 785-442-6025 174 C ahamilton@highlandcc.edu
HAMILTON, Alicia .... 972-825-4612 444 C ahamilton@sagu.edu
HAMILTON, Amber .... 806-371-5303 428 F ahbrookshire@actx.edu
HAMILTON, Andrew ...... 641-269-3800 166 D hamiltoa@grinnell.edu
HAMILTON, Andrew ...... 212-998-2345 309 D andrew.hamilton@nyu.edu
HAMILTON, Andrew ...... 336-334-5000 342 D a_hamilt@uncg.edu
HAMILTON, Angela .... 360-475-7504 481 B ahamilton2@olympic.edu
HAMILTON, Angela, M . 724-480-3440 381 G angela.hamilton@ccbc.edu
HAMILTON, Ann .... 661-362-3310.. 38 H ann.hamilton@canyons.edu
HAMILTON, Ann .... 213-763-7000.. 50 A
HAMILTON, Ann .... 323-953-4000.. 49 E hamiltae@lacitycollege.edu
HAMILTON, Anna .... 270-706-8649 181 C ahamilton0062@kctcs.edu
HAMILTON, Barbara ...... 870-837-4003.. 21 F bhamilto@sautech.edu
HAMILTON, Billie Jo .... 813-974-3039 111 B bjhamilton@usf.edu
HAMILTON, Billy .... 979-458-6421 445 D bhamilton@tamus.edu
HAMILTON, Cara .... 864-646-1797 411 H chamilt5@tctc.edu
HAMILTON, Christine ... 913-758-6242 177 I christine.hamilton@stmary.edu
HAMILTON, Cliff .... 843-953-6802 407 D hamiltoncm@cofc.edu
HAMILTON, Crystal ...... 270-852-3130 183 B clhamilton@kwc.edu
HAMILTON, Daniel, W .. 702-895-1876 270 J daniel.hamilton@unlv.edu
HAMILTON, David, L .... 413-542-2167 205 D dhamilton@amherst.edu
HAMILTON, DaVina ...... 904-256-7067 102 G dhamilt3@ju.edu
HAMILTON, Debbie .... 713-718-5041 436 E debbie.hamilton@hccs.edu
HAMILTON, Dorthy .... 786-391-1167.. 95 G
HAMILTON, JR., Elbert . 713-629-1500 456 G
HAMILTON, Eldrie .... 318-274-6321 191 G hamiltoneb@gram.edu
HAMILTON, Eric .... 843-574-6272 411 I eric.hamilton@tridenttech.edu
HAMILTON, Erin .... 502-895-3411 183 E ehamilton@lpts.edu
HAMILTON, Ethan .... 619-849-2621.. 57 J ethanhamilton@pointloma.edu
HAMILTON, G. Michael 757-240-2206 469 F michael.hamilton@rivhs.com
HAMILTON, Glenn .... 708-524-6795 137 A hamilton@dom.edu
HAMILTON, Glenn, R .... 859-858-3511 178 H glenn.hamilton@asbury.edu
HAMILTON, Guy .... 206-533-6638 483 C ghamilton@shoreline.edu
HAMILTON, Heather ..... 303-273-3951.. 79 A hhamilton@mines.edu
HAMILTON, Jared .... 508-213-2045 217 C jared.hamilton@nichols.edu
HAMILTON, Jeff .... 740-351-3393 360 E jhamilton@shawnee.edu
HAMILTON, Jeffrey, S ... 254-710-2657 430 F jeffrey_hamilton@baylor.edu
HAMILTON, Jody .... 919-546-8416 339 I jhamilton@shawu.edu
HAMILTON, Karen .... 310-578-1080 347 F khamilton1@antioch.edu
HAMILTON, Kate .... 517-264-7143 230 C khamilton@sienaheights.edu
HAMILTON, Katie .... 603-206-8152 272 A khamilton@ccsnh.edu
HAMILTON, Keith, J ...... 907-822-3201.... 9 D keith@akcc.org
HAMILTON, Kelly .... 949-794-9090.. 66 C khamilton@stanbridge.edu
HAMILTON, Kevin .... 217-332-5833 151 F kham@illinois.edu
HAMILTON, Laura .... 501-202-7937.. 18 G laura.hamilton@baptist-health.org
HAMILTON, Leah .... 214-245-3199 139 A leah.hamilton@ic.edu
HAMILTON, JR., Leroy . 502-597-6417 183 A leroy.hamilton@kysu.edu
HAMILTON, LoriRae ...... 719-846-5524.. 83 I lorirae.hamilton@trinidadstate.edu
HAMILTON, Louis, I ..... 973-642-7664 278 G louis.i.hamilton@njit.edu
HAMILTON, Marty .... 423-236-2806 422 H mlhamil@southern.edu
HAMILTON, Michelle .... 618-985-3741 140 G michellehamilton@jalc.edu
HAMILTON, Nakeysha ... 216-373-5316 357 F nhamilton@ndc.edu
HAMILTON, Nardos ...... 516-572-7759 307 C nardos.hamilton@ncc.edu
HAMILTON, Nicky .... 931-598-1796 422 F nhamilto@sewanee.edu
HAMILTON, Penny .... 585-785-1201 299 E penny.hamilton@flcc.edu
HAMILTON, Phillip .... 806-291-3588 457 B hamiltonp@wbu.edu
HAMILTON, Richard ...... 360-442-2263 480 E rhamilton@lowercolumbia.edu
HAMILTON, Ron .... 734-218-0045 488 K rhamilton@concord.edu
HAMILTON, Ronald .... 304-434-8000 487 E ron.hamilton@easternwv.edu
HAMILTON, Ryan .... 419-267-1273 357 E rhamilton@northweststate.edu
HAMILTON, Shadel .... 813-221-6302 107 B shadel.hamilton@saintleo.edu
HAMILTON, Shelley ...... 760-921-5483.. 56 A shamilton@paloverde.edu
HAMILTON, Sondra ...... 931-221-7667 416 H hamiltons@apsu.edu
HAMILTON, Ted .... 605-856-8259 415 A ted.hamilton@sintegleska.edu
HAMILTON, Thomas, H 813-988-5131.. 99 M hamiltont@floridacollege.edu
HAMILTON, William ...... 352-588-6610 107 B william.hamilton02@saintleo.edu
HAMILTON-DRAGER, Catrina .... 717-254-8935 382 B hamiltoc@dickinson.edu
HAMILTON-HONEY, Emily .... 315-386-7071 319 E hamiltone@canton.edu
HAMILTON SLANE, Sandra .... 530-242-7799.. 64 A sslane@shastacollege.edu
HAMLETT, Rebecca .... 816-415-7620 261 G hamlettr@william.jewell.edu
HAMLETT, Tiffany .... 816-995-2844 257 I tiffany.hamlett@researchcollege.edu
HAMLETT, Willie .... 626-815-3890.. 26 K whamlett@apu.edu
HAMLIN, Annemarie ..... 541-383-7523 371 I ahamlin@cocc.edu
HAMLIN, Annemarie ..... 541-383-7205 371 I ahamlin@cocc.edu
HAMLIN, April .... 541-956-7255 375 G ahamlin@roguecc.edu
HAMLIN, John .... 337-550-1301 189 B jhamlin@lsue.edu
HAMLIN, Marcus .... 312-369-7605 136 C mhamlin@colum.edu
HAMLIN, Toby .... 518-608-8218 299 B thamlin@excelsior.edu
HAMLUK, Brian, F .... 716-645-2982 315 F bfhamluk@buffalo.edu
HAMM, Ashley .... 806-743-1445 450 D ashley.hamm@ttuhsc.edu
HAMM, Bernard, C .... 804-828-1233 472 D bchamm2@vcu.edu
HAMM, Darryl .... 562-951-4500.. 31 D dhamm@calstate.edu
HAMM, Jennifer .... 828-327-7000 332 H jhamm@cvcc.edu
HAMM, Jolene .... 540-857-7311 475 A jhamm@virginiawestern.edu
HAMM, Joy .... 706-379-3111 128 A kjhamm@yhc.edu
HAMM, Lee, L .... 504-988-5462 191 D lhamm@tulane.edu
HAMM, Michelle .... 404-471-5443 114 E mhamm@agnesscott.edu
HAMM, Reggie .... 678-359-5103 120 D reggieh@gordonstate.edu
HAMM, Rod .... 620-947-3121 177 F rodneyhamm@tabor.edu
HAMMACK, Brian .... 641-683-4270 166 F brian.hammack@indianhills.edu
HAMMACK, Mike .... 806-291-3428 457 B hammackm@wbu.edu
HAMMACK, Mike .... 325-670-1278 436 B mhammack@hsutx.edu
HAMMAN, Emily .... 937-775-3843 364 D emily.hamman@wright.edu
HAMMAN, John .... 240-567-9006 200 E john.hamman@montgomerycollege.edu
HAMMAR, Matt .... 503-554-2162 372 I mhammar@georgefox.edu
HAMMAT, Jennifer, R ... 812-464-1862 162 B jhammat@usi.edu
HAMMEKE, Curtis .... 785-628-4050 173 E chammeke@fhsu.edu
HAMMEL, Rachel .... 330-490-7452 363 E rhammel@walsh.edu
HAMMEN, Matthew .... 563-387-2174 167 J hammma03@luther.edu
HAMMER, Adam .... 320-762-4901 236 G adam.hammer@alextech.edu
HAMMER, Bradley, C .... 419-434-6922 362 D hammer@findlay.edu
HAMMER, Debbie .... 610-989-1200 400 F dhammer@vfmac.edu
HAMMER, Elizabeth ...... 504-520-5141 193 C eyhammer@xula.edu
HAMMER, Jaime, S ...... 334-844-5176.... 4 E jsh0073@auburn.edu
HAMMER, Joyce .... 360-623-8486 477 H joyce.hammer@centralia.edu
HAMMER, Kathryn .... 716-839-8364 297 F khammer@daemen.edu
HAMMER, Katie .... 617-715-5940 215 G
HAMMER, Kimberley ..... 757-455-3205 476 C khammer@vwu.edu
HAMMER, Larry .... 828-227-7216 343 D hammer@wcu.edu
HAMMERMAN, Adam, D .... 914-594-4570 308 J adam_hammerman@nymc.edu
HAMMERSLEY, Lisa .... 916-278-4655.. 33 A hammersley@csus.edu
HAMMES, Meg .... 563-387-1375 167 J hammma01@luther.edu
HAMMETT, Amy, S .... 216-368-4318 349 B registrar@case.edu
HAMMETT, Maria, A ...... 478-301-2226 122 C hammett_ma@mercer.edu
HAMMETT, Matthew, K . 864-597-4000 413 E hammettmk@wofford.edu
HAMMETT, Steve .... 216-421-7000 350 E shammett@cia.edu
HAMMILL, Graham, L ... 716-645-6003 315 F ghammill@buffalo.edu
HAMMILL, Robert .... 540-828-5719 464 C rhammill@bridgewater.edu
HAMMING, Jeanne .... 318-869-5240 186 C jhamming@centenary.edu
HAMMITT, Stephanie ..... 218-879-0804 237 F shammitt@fdltcc.edu
HAMMOCK, Susan .... 478-240-5162 123 D shammock@oftc.edu
HAMMOND, Beth .... 706-754-7789 123 C beth.hammond@northgatech.edu
HAMMOND, Bradley ...... 918-343-7852 369 A bhammond@rsu.edu
HAMMOND, Brady .... 508-853-2300 215 D bhammond@qcc.mass.edu
HAMMOND, Caroline .... 870-864-7102.. 21 C chammond@southark.edu
HAMMOND, Charles ..... 646-378-6131 289 F charles.hammond@nyack.edu
HAMMOND, Charles, A 302-225-6352.. 90 I hammond@gbc.edu
HAMMOND, Christine ... 816-995-2856 257 I christine.hammond@researchcollege.edu
HAMMOND, Dale .... 509-777-3730 485 D dhammond@whitworth.edu
HAMMOND, Denise ...... 870-584-1118.. 22 G dhammond@cccua.edu
HAMMOND, Erin .... 314-256-8808 249 F hammond@ai.edu
HAMMOND, Jaime .... 203-575-8199.. 86 H jhammond@nv.edu
HAMMOND, Jeff .... 601-264-4629 248 H jeff.hammond@usm.edu
HAMMOND, Joanna ...... 903-923-2051 435 A jhammond@etbu.edu
HAMMOND, Karen, S ... 240-500-2241 199 A kshammond@hagerstowncc.edu
HAMMOND, Klavdiya .... 973-655-7087 278 C hammondkl@montclair.edu
HAMMOND, Mark .... 910-893-1211 327 C hammond@campbell.edu
HAMMOND, Paul .... 848-932-8404 281 B paul.hammond@rutgers.edu

HAMMOND, Troy, D ..... 630-637-5454 145 E
tdhammond@noctrl.edu
HAMMOND, Vanessa .... 423-614-8511 419 H
vhammond@leeuniversity.edu
HAMMOND NASS,
Holly .... 207-602-2306 197 A
hnass@une.edu
HAMMONDS, Curtis ..... 660-596-7110 259 D
chammonds@sfccmo.edu
HAMMONDS, Diane, M 610-526-1409 378 D
diane.hammonds@theamericancollege.edu
HAMMONDS, Jennifer .. 270-745-5030 186 A
jennifer.hammonds@wku.edu
HAMMONDS, Luke ...... 601-477-4058 246 A
luke.hammonds@jcjc.edu
HAMMONS, Stacy .... 765-677-3061 157 F
stacy.hammons@indwes.edu
HAMMONTREE, Tonya .. 501-205-8809.. 19 B
thammontree@cbc.edu
HAMMRICH, Penny .... 215-895-5929 382 D
plh33@drexel.edu
HAMMS, Gavin .... 318-274-7701 191 G
hammsg@gram.edu
HAMNER, Elise .... 541-888-7211 376 B
elise.hamner@socc.edu
HAMNER, Mark, S .... 940-898-3013 451 A
mhamner@twu.edu
HAMOND, Michael .... 978-867-4800 209 F
president@gordon.edu
HAMPEL-KOZAR, Vesna 612-624-4390 242 K
hampe004@umn.edu
HAMPILOS, Luciana, E . 972-721-5056 451 E
lhampilos@udallas.edu
HAMPSHIRE, Audrey, N 260-982-5036 158 W
anhampshire@manchester.edu
HAMPTON, Austin .... 785-212-0855 171 H
hamptonaj@bethanylb.edu
HAMPTON, Diane .... 870-733-6880.. 18 A
dhampton@asumidsouth.edu
HAMPTON, Franki .... 540-453-2285 472 F
hamptonf@brcc.edu
HAMPTON, Iyisha .... 334-244-3674.... 4 F
ihampton@aum.edu
HAMPTON, Jarvis, D .... 806-651-3451 447 D
jhampton@wtamu.edu
HAMPTON, Joyce .... 413-265-2423 208 B
hamptonj@elms.edu
HAMPTON, Julie .... 309-649-6201 150 D
julie.hampton@src.edu
HAMPTON, Logan, C .... 731-426-7595 419 G
lhampton@lanecollege.edu
HAMPTON, Marie .... 925-485-5233.. 35 Q
mhampton@clpccd.org
HAMPTON, Michael ...... 503-883-2442 373 E
mhampton@linfield.edu
HAMPTON, Nancy .... 504-520-5083 193 C
nhampton@xula.edu
HAMPTON, Nancy .... 806-651-2116 447 D
nhampton@wtamu.edu
HAMPTON, Robert .... 863-784-7411 108 D
robert.hampton@southflorida.edu
HAMPTON, Tabatha ...... 870-762-3121.. 17 F
thampton@smail.anc.edu
HAMPTON, Todd .... 925-969-2018.. 40 H
thampton@dvc.edu
HAMPTON, Victoria .... 203-582-7446.. 88 F
victoria.hampton@quinnipiac.edu
HAMPTON, William .... 903-730-4890 437 E
whampton@jarvis.edu
HAMRIC, Janice .... 281-646-1109 430 H
janice.hamric@thebibleseminary.edu
HAMRICK, Elizabeth ...... 704-290-5251 337 F
ehamrick@spcc.edu
HAMRICK, Robin, G ..... 704-406-3996 328 I
rhamrick@gardner-webb.edu
HAMS, Susan, D .... 480-732-7075.. 13 B
sue.hams@cgc.edu
HAMSTRA, Brent .... 423-236-2203 422 H
bhamstra@southern.edu
HAMSTRA, Pete .... 866-323-0233.. 58 D
HAMTAK, Chelsie .... 775-445-3288 271 A
chelsie.hamtak@wnc.edu
HAN, David, S .... 423-478-7524 421 J
dhan@ptseminary.edu
HAN, Jenjen .... 407-888-8689.. 99 N
HAN, Jin .... 212-870-1211 309 C
jhan@nyts.edu
HAN, Ki Won .... 714-527-0691.. 42 D
HAN, Luoheng .... 205-348-4890.... 7 G
luoheng.han@ua.edu
HAN, Peter .... 303-273-3000.. 79 A
phan@mines.edu
HAN, Priscilla .... 423-478-7723 421 J
phan@ptseminary.edu
HAN, Woo Jin .... 714-533-1495.. 64 G
whan@southbaylo.edu
HAN, Yuan-Yuan .... 407-888-8689.. 99 N
y2han@fcim.edu
HANADA, Karen .... 808-984-3527 130 B
tkhanada@hawaii.edu
HANADA,
Tomone Karen .... 808-984-3527 130 B
tkhanada@hawaii.edu
HANAFIAH, Michelle ..... 805-546-3279.. 41 A
michelle_hanafiah@cuesta.edu
HANAK, Casey .... 912-279-4561 117 C
chanak@ccga.edu
HANAK, Lesley .... 912-525-5000 124 G
lhanak@scad.edu
HANAN, Sandi .... 541-885-1000 374 G
HANBURY, II,
George, L .... 954-262-7575 104 M
hanbury@nsu.nova.edu
HANBURY, John .... 276-656-0205 473 H
jhanbury@patrickhenry.edu
HANBURY, Sarah .... 703-993-1000 466 J
HANCOCK, Amy .... 912-260-4461 125 B
amy.hancock@sgsc.edu
HANCOCK, Anthony ...... 304-367-4933 487 H
HANCOCK, Ashley .... 580-774-7051 369 I
ashley.hancock@swosu.edu
HANCOCK, Bert .... 803-778-6679 406 A
hancockhi@cctech.edu
HANCOCK, Darryl .... 478-827-3857 118 E
darryl.hancock@fvsu.edu
HANCOCK, Daryl, R ...... 618-537-6870 143 G
drhancock@mckendree.edu
HANCOCK, Heather ...... 918-595-7842 370 B
heather.hancock@tulsacc.edu
HANCOCK, John .... 713-500-7356 455 D
john.f.hancock@uth.tmc.edu
HANCOCK, Kristina .... 661-362-3400.. 38 H
kristina.hancock@canyons.edu
HANCOCK, Mara .... 510-594-5080.. 28 D
mhancock@cca.edu
HANCOCK, Marcia .... 410-864-4000 202 A
HANCOCK, Merodie, A . 609-984-1105 283 D
president@tesu.edu
HANCOCK, Nathan .... 630-617-3080 137 E
nathan.hancock@elmhurst.edu
HANCOCK, Nick .... 408-260-0208.. 42 H
nwhancock@fivebranches.edu
HANCOCK, Sean, C ...... 760-384-6100.. 47 C
HANCOCK, Shannon ...... 913-253-5084 177 A
shannon.hancock@spst.edu
HANCOCK, Tara, A .... 508-929-5000 213 D
HANCOCK, Wanda .... 229-225-5089 125 G
whancock@southernregional.edu
HAND, David .... 601-968-8703 244 C
dhand@belhaven.edu
HAND, Erica .... 814-371-2090 399 B
ehand@triangle-tech.edu
HAND, Greg .... 316-978-3600 178 B
gregory.hand@wichita.edu
HAND, Jason .... 215-751-8806 381 H
jhand@ccp.edu
HAND, Jeffrey .... 856-256-5186 280 H
handj@rowan.edu
HAND, Julie .... 517-990-1382 225 A
handjulier@jccmi.edu
HAND, Kelli .... 704-637-4416 327 H
kmhand@catawba.edu
HAND, Mary .... 518-743-2248 319 D
handm@sunyacc.edu
HAND, Natalie .... 484-664-3804 390 F
nataliehand@muhlenberg.edu
HAND, Theresa .... 518-244-2301 312 D
handt@sage.edu
HANDAL, Albert .... 509-527-2343 484 C
albert.handal@wallawalla.edu
HANDCOX, Jenelle .... 910-521-6255 343 A
jenelle.handcox@uncp.edu
HANDEL, Greg .... 318-357-4330 192 D
handelg@nsula.edu
HANDFIELD, Sandy ...... 321-433-5502.. 98 F
handfields@easternflorida.edu
HANDFORD, Ann .... 262-524-7211 491 A
ahandfor@carrollu.edu
HANDLER, Jeffrey .... 516-876-3000 318 A
HANDLEY, Jim .... 815-921-4754 147 H
j.handley@rockvalleycollege.edu
HANDLEY, Kristen .... 907-796-6100.. 10 C
HANDOJO, Jeanne .... 626-584-5366.. 43 E
jeanne@fuller.edu
HANDS, Ashanti .... 619-388-2678.. 61 A
ahands@sdccd.edu
HANDS, Colette .... 847-635-7675 146 E
chands@oakton.edu
HANDS, Ronnie .... 619-216-6617.. 65 K
rhands@swccd.edu
HANDWERK, Phil .... 336-758-5244 344 A
handwepg@wfu.edu
HANDWORK, David ...... 870-972-2066.. 17 I
dhandwork@astate.edu
HANDY, Cromwell .... 334-229-4309.... 4 B
chandy@alasu.edu
HANDY, Cynthia, H ...... 404-752-1654 123 A
cynthia@msm.edu
HANDY, Eric .... 916-484-8011.. 50 J
handye@arc.losrios.edu
HANDY, Gary .... 785-594-6451 171 C
gary.handy@bakeru.edu
HANDY, Patricia .... 225-771-4680 190 K
patricia_handy@sus.edu
HANDY, Ty, J .... 502-213-2121 181 H
ty.handy@kctcs.edu
HANDYSIDES, Robert .... 909-558-4683.. 48 J
rhandysides@llu.edu
HANDZLIK, Diane, M ... 716-896-0700 324 A
dianeh@villa.edu
HANEFIELD, Robert .... 580-581-2417 365 C
rhanefield@cameron.edu
HANEL, Lois .... 785-738-9060 176 C
lhanel@ncktc.edu
HANELINE, Kendra .... 704-669-4094 333 C
hanelinek274@clevelandcc.edu
HANER, Eric .... 231-591-3802 223 H
erichaner@ferris.edu
HANES, Austin .... 251-981-3771.... 5 B
austin.hanes@columbiasouthern.edu
HANES, Carol .... 903-875-7594 439 G
carol.hanes@navarrocollege.edu
HANES, Jonathan .... 414-251-6678 495 B
jmhanes@uwm.edu
HANES, Jonathan .... 414-251-6778 495 B
jmhanes@uwm.edu
HANES, Mackenzie .... 859-846-5385 183 G
mhanes@midway.edu
HANES, Madlyn, L .... 814-863-0327 391 F
mqh3@psu.edu
HANES, Rick .... 937-778-8600 352 D
rhanes@edisonohio.edu
HANES-GOODLANDER,
Lisa .... 651-846-1383 240 E
lisa.hanes@saintpaul.edu
HANES-RAMOS,
Melanie .... 843-208-8023 412 C
hanesml@uscb.edu
HANETA, Irene .... 408-848-4754.. 43 H
ihaneta@gavilan.edu
HANEWICZ, Cheryl .... 801-863-6539 460 A
hanewich@uvu.edu
HANEY, Alecia .... 313-664-7461 222 C
ahaney@collegeforcreativestudies.edu
HANEY, Asia .... 512-505-3023 437 B
aehaney@htu.edu
HANEY, Cindy, M .... 610-799-1122 388 B
chaney1@lccc.edu
HANEY, David .... 931-526-3660 418 F
david.haney@fortisinstitute.edu
HANEY, David, P .... 330-569-5120 353 F
haneydp@hiram.edu
HANEY, Frank .... 913-234-0788 172 I
frank.haney@cleveland.edu
HANEY, Genelle .... 770-426-2725 122 A
genelle.haney@life.edu
HANEY, Liz .... 765-285-5085 153 E
elizabeth.haney@bsu.edu
HANEY, Michele .... 303-914-6215.. 82 L
michele.haney@rrcc.edu
HANEY, Pamela .... 708-974-5204 144 G
haney@morainevalley.edu
HANEY, Randy .... 606-788-2817 181 A
randy.haney@kctcs.edu
HANEY, Regina .... 806-457-4200 435 D
rhaney@fpctx.edu
HANEY, Shannon .... 870-612-2017.. 23 B
shannon.haney@uaccb.edu
HANEY, Teresa .... 417-836-5517 255 J
teresahaney@missouristate.edu
HANEY KEITH, Latonia . 208-459-5009 131 A
lhaneykeith@collegeofidaho.edu
HANG, Ducha .... 401-456-8884 404 A
dhang@ric.edu
HANG, MayKao, Y .... 651-962-4727 243 F
maykao.hang@stthomas.edu
HANGEN, Susan .... 201-684-7407 280 B
shangen@ramapo.edu
HANICAK, Mary Ann .... 216-397-1886 353 O
HANIFIN, Martin .... 802-485-2040 461 H
mhanifin@norwich.edu
HANINCIK, Amanda ...... 610-330-5338 387 B
hanincia@lafayette.edu
HANKERSON, Brian ...... 954-486-7728 112 J
bhankersoncfo@uftl.edu
HANKERSON, Kimberly . 850-599-3491 109 E
kimberly.hankerson@famu.edu
HANKERSON, Reggie .... 662-621-4231 244 E
rhankerson@coahomacc.edu
HANKES, Doug .... 334-844-5123.... 4 E
hankedm@auburn.edu
HANKIN, Brette .... 785-462-3984 172 L
HANKIN, Jennifer .... 518-454-2852 296 E
hankinj@strose.edu
HANKINS, Ashley .... 501-882-8809.. 17 H
anhankins@asub.edu
HANKINS, Ashley .... 870-236-6901.. 19 D
ahankins@crc.edu
HANKINS, Bruce .... 870-612-2121.. 23 B
bruce.hankins@uaccb.edu
HANKINS, Doris .... 510-466-7374.. 57 C
dhankins@peralta.edu
HANKINS, Jeff .... 501-660-1004.. 17 G
jhankins@asusystem.edu
HANKINS, Kim .... 815-455-8778 143 F
khankins@mchenry.edu
HANKINS, Orlando, E ... 919-516-4860 339 G
oehankins@st-aug.edu
HANKINS, Paul .... 479-788-7431.. 22 A
paul.hankins@uafs.edu
HANKINSON, Carol, A .. 252-862-1239 336 H
cahankinson@roanokechowan.edu
HANKINSON, Holbrook 765-658-4538 154 G
holbrookhankinson@depauw.edu
HANKS, Justin .... 513-233-2223 348 A
jhanks@athenaeum.edu
HANKS, Mary .... 205-652-3668.... 9 B
mhanks@uwa.edu
HANKS, Timothy .... 337-482-6449 192 F
timothy.hanks@louisiana.edu
HANLEY, Darla, S .... 617-747-2664 206 D
dhanley@berklee.edu
HANLEY, James .... 215-204-5578 398 D
jhanley@bncollege.com
HANLEY, Peggy .... 318-274-6546 191 G
peggy@gram.edu
HANLEY, Rodney, S ...... 906-635-2202 226 C
president@lssu.edu
HANLEY, Tim .... 414-288-7141 492 E
timothy.hanley@marquette.edu
HANLEY-MAXWELL,
Cheryl .... 217-333-6677 151 F
cherylhm@illinois.edu
HANLON, Andra .... 540-665-4500 470 A
HANLON, Chris .... 610-921-2381 377 F
HANLON, Christopher .. 410-532-5369 201 C
chanlon@ndm.edu
HANLON, Erin .... 617-322-3531 210 F
erin_hanlon@laboure.edu
HANLON, Gregory .... 540-375-2074 469 G
hanlon@roanoke.edu
HANLON, Philip, J .... 603-646-2223 272 F
philip.j.hanlon@dartmouth.edu
HANN, Charlesa .... 704-233-6035 344 E
c.hann@wingate.edu
HANN, Nancy .... 614-234-1135 356 E
nhann@mccn.edu
HANNA, Aaron .... 210-431-3335 442 A
ahanna1@stmarytx.edu
HANNA, Abigail .... 262-551-8500 491 B
ahanna@carthage.edu
HANNA, Bashar, W .... 570-389-4526 393 E
bhanna@bloomu.edu
HANNA, Bryce .... 970-943-2126.. 85 B
bhanna@western.edu
HANNA, Chris .... 616-432-3407 229 H
chris.hanna@prts.edu
HANNA, Diane, R .... 607-746-4430 320 A
hannadr@delhi.edu
HANNA, Dorothy .... 785-833-4468 175 C
dahanna@kwu.edu
HANNA, Heather .... 406-657-2131 263 H
heather.hanna@msubillings.edu
HANNA, Jandy .... 304-647-6366 489 C
jhanna@osteo.wvsom.edu
HANNA, Jenette .... 620-441-5214 172 M
jenette.hanna@cowley.edu
HANNA, Kim .... 931-372-3203 425 B
khanna@tntech.edu
HANNA, Mae .... 513-732-5332 362 B
mae.hanna@uc.edu

HANNA, Mark 708-239-4705 150 H
mark.hanna@trnty.edu
HANNA, Rame 719-255-4762 84 A
edi@uccs.edu
HANNA, Rame 508-831-5000 220 C
HANNA, Randy 850-770-2102 110 B
rhanna@fsu.edu
HANNAFORD, Bo, S 580-327-8400 367 A
bshannaford@nwosu.edu
HANNAFORD, Erin, E 717-867-6071 388 A
hannafor@lvc.edu
HANNAFORD, Tara 580-327-8540 367 A
tlhannaford@nwosu.edu
HANNAH, Felisa 559-791-2316 47 D
felisa.hannah@portervillecollege.edu
HANNAH, Katie 269-783-2185 230 D
khannah@swmich.edu
HANNAH, Marcus 334-876-9360 2 D
marcus.hannah@wccs.edu
HANNAH, Russ 870-972-3303 17 I
rhannah@astate.edu
HANNAH-JEFFERSON, Floressa 601-979-2127 245 G
floressa.j.hannah-jefferson@jsums.edu
HANNAN, Amanda 618-634-3277 149 C
amandah@shawneecc.edu
HANNAN, Christopher 319-291-2705 166 E
christopher.hannan@hawkeyecollege.edu
HANNAN, James 315-445-4125 303 F
hannanjp@lemoyne.edu
HANNAR, Christine 636-949-4625 254 B
channar@lindenwood.edu
HANNERS, Rodney 323-442-9775 73 C
rod.hanners@med.usc.edu
HANNES, Sarah 307-778-1178 500 D
shannes@lccc.wy.edu
HANNI, Rachel 440-375-7000 354 K
HANNIGAN, Robyn, E 610-409-3587 400 E
president@ursinus.edu
HANNIGAN, Scott 501-279-4407 19 G
shannigan@harding.edu
HANNING, Chris 610-430-4178 394 F
channing@wcupa.edu
HANNMANN, Richard 518-608-8198 299 B
rhannmann@excelsior.edu
HANNON, James 330-672-0566 354 A
jhannon5@kent.edu
HANNON, Jim, M 563-333-6359 169 D
hannonjamesm@ambrose.sau.edu
HANNON, Ken 210-341-1366 440 B
khannon@ost.edu
HANNON, Kristin 330-490-7226 363 E
khannon@walsh.edu
HANNON, Kristina 909-388-6900 60 D
HANNON, Lauretta 706-295-6273 119 F
lhannon@gntc.edu
HANNON, Lauretta 404-756-4666 115 E
lhannon@atlm.edu
HANNUM, Joshua 520-795-0787 10 J
president@asaom.edu
HANNUM, Natalie 925-473-7401 40 I
nhannum@losmedanos.edu
HANOFEE, Rosemarie 845-434-5750 321 B
rhanofee@sunysullivan.edu
HANOLD, John, W 814-863-0768 391 F
jhh6@psu.edu
HANRAHAN, Chelsea 603-428-2291 272 I
chanrahan@nec.edu
HANRAHAN, Mark 740-283-6860 352 I
mhanrahan@franciscan.edu
HANRAHAN, Neil, S 212-998-4581 309 D
nsh2@nyu.edu
HANRAHAN, Susan, N 870-972-3112 17 I
hanrahan@astate.edu
HANRAHAN, Thomas, M 717-867-6030 388 A
hanrahan@lvc.edu
HANRAHAN, Timothy 816-584-2102 257 E
thanrahan@park.edu
HANS, Peter 919-962-1000 340 F
HANSARD, Anna, M 248-341-2121 228 H
amhansar@oaklandcc.edu
HANSARD, Betsy 903-983-8105 437 G
bhansard@kilgore.edu
HANSARD, Jamie 806-742-1482 450 C
jamie.hansard@ttu.edu
HANSBARGER, Tom 845-938-2715 502 H
tom.hansbarger@westpoint.edu
HANSBURG, David 303-273-3300 79 A
hansburg@mines.edu
HANSCOM, Marcus 401-254-3345 404 C
mhanscom@rwu.edu
HANSELMAN, Jennifer 978-665-4187 212 C
jhanselm@fitchburgstate.edu
HANSELMAN, Jennifer 413-572-8702 213 C
jhanselman@westfield.ma.edu
HANSELMAN, Shad 254-968-1756 445 F
shanselman@tarleton.edu
HANSEN, Andy 605-229-8378 414 I
andrew.hansen@presentation.edu
HANSEN, Anne, W 518-564-2090 318 C
hansenaw@plattsburgh.edu
HANSEN, Blaine, J 828-898-8838 330 A
hansenb@lmc.edu
HANSEN, Chris 423-236-2802 422 H
chansen@southern.edu
HANSEN, Christian 207-453-5128 195 B
chansen@kvcc.me.edu
HANSEN, Christopher 978-867-4500 209 F
chris.hansen@gordon.edu
HANSEN, Cynthia 641-269-3099 166 D
hansency@grinnell.edu
HANSEN, Dan 605-688-4237 416 A
dan.hansen@sdstate.edu
HANSEN, Dan 405-491-6309 369 G
dhansen@snu.edu
HANSEN, David 843-574-6021 411 I
david.hansen@tridenttech.edu
HANSEN, David 605-367-7568 415 D
dave.hansen@sdbor.edu
HANSEN, Dean 662-915-1945 248 F
dlhansen@olemiss.edu
HANSEN, Eric 325-481-8300 436 H
ehansen@howardcollege.edu
HANSEN, Gregg 978-468-7111 209 G
ghansen@gcts.edu
HANSEN, Jill 815-825-9517 141 D
jhansen1@kish.edu
HANSEN, John 515-576-7201 166 G
hansen_j@iowacentral.edu
HANSEN, John 307-532-8304 500 A
jhansen@ewc.wy.edu
HANSEN, Jory 605-995-2151 414 A
jory.hansen@dwu.edu
HANSEN, Katherine 425-235-2356 482 C
khansen@rtc.edu
HANSEN, Kathy 320-363-5307 234 I
kghansen@csbsju.edu
HANSEN, Kenneth 402-559-5301 269 B
hansenkl@unmc.edu
HANSEN, Kent, A 909-558-2644 48 J
khansen@claysonlaw.com
HANSEN, Kevin 319-398-5625 167 H
kevin.hansen@kirkwood.edu
HANSEN, Kristine 651-793-1300 238 B
kristine.hansen@metrostate.edu
HANSEN, Lynn 407-823-2362 110 D
lynn.hansen@ucf.edu
HANSEN, Mandy 719-255-7528 84 A
mhansen2@uccs.edu
HANSEN, Marie 207-973-1081 194 D
hansenm@my.husson.edu
HANSEN, Martina 301-985-7000 203 C
studentaffairs@umgc.edu
HANSEN, Micah 605-367-5550 416 B
micah.hansen@southeasttech.edu
HANSEN, Michele, J 317-278-2618 157 B
mjhansen@iupui.edu
HANSEN, Milton 706-864-1941 126 G
milton.hansen@ung.edu
HANSEN, Noah 619-594-4808 33 E
nhansen@sdsu.edu
HANSEN, Peter 210-436-3324 442 A
phansen@stmarytx.edu
HANSEN, Rachel 217-641-4514 140 H
rhansen@jwcc.edu
HANSEN, Robyn 402-552-6119 265 G
hansenrobyn@clarksoncollege.edu
HANSEN, Sarah 319-335-3557 163 F
sarah-hansen@uiowa.edu
HANSEN, Sherri 435-283-7251 460 C
sherri.hansen@snow.edu
HANSEN, Steven 414-847-3205 493 C
stevenhansen@miad.edu
HANSEN, Susan 978-869-1122 439 B
HANSEN, Terry 432-264-5600 436 H
thansen@howardcollege.edu
HANSEN, Zeynep 208-426-3314 130 F
zeynephansen@boisestate.edu
HANSEN-KIEFFER, Kristin, M 717-796-5234 389 F
khansen@messiah.edu
HANSEN-THOMAS, Holly 940-898-3415 451 A
hhansenthomas@twu.edu
HANSEN-THOMAS, Holly 940-898-2749 451 A
hhansenthomas@twu.edu
HANSLEY, Emily 704-748-5259 334 E
hansley.emily@gaston.edu
HANSON, Andrew 208-792-2218 131 F
ahanson@lcsc.edu
HANSON, Andrew 702-895-2267 270 J
andrew.hanson@unlv.edu
HANSON, Anita 218-879-0805 237 F
anita.hanson@fdltcc.edu
HANSON, Charlene 401-841-6541 501 L
charlene.hanson@usnwc.edu
HANSON, Cheryl 208-282-2533 131 E
hanscher@isu.edu
HANSON, Christina, R 717-796-1800 389 F
chanson@messiah.edu
HANSON, Courtney 414-288-3577 492 E
courtney.hanson@marquette.edu
HANSON, Cyndi 402-241-6405 268 A
cyndih@northeast.edu
HANSON, Denise 319-226-2012 163 A
denise.hanson@allencollege.edu
HANSON, Eric 540-261-8400 470 D
eric.hanson@svu.edu
HANSON, Gary, A 310-506-4405 56 H
gary.hanson@pepperdine.edu
HANSON, Janet, K 507-786-3018 242 I
jhanson@stolaf.edu
HANSON, Jim 507-389-7387 240 F
jim.hanson@southcentral.edu
HANSON, Julie 970-945-8691 78 H
HANSON, Karen 701-662-1539 346 A
karen.e.hanson@lrsc.edu
HANSON, Ken 817-202-6519 444 B
ken.hanson@swau.edu
HANSON, Kent 763-433-1179 236 H
kent.hanson@anokaramsey.edu
HANSON, Kent 763-576-4700 237 A
kent.hanson@anokatech.edu
HANSON, Kristen 386-506-4506 98 A
kristen.hanson@daytonastate.edu
HANSON, Leon 903-675-6349 451 C
lhanson@tvcc.edu
HANSON, Lisa 309-341-5212 134 A
lhanson@sandburg.edu
HANSON, Margaret 513-556-5858 361 I
margaret.hanson@uc.edu
HANSON, Michelle 605-331-6714 416 C
michelle.hanson@usiouxfalls.edu
HANSON, Patti, L 641-422-4170 168 E
hansopat@niacc.edu
HANSON, Peter 513-875-3344 349 K
peter.hanson@chatfield.edu
HANSON, Rhoda 503-842-8222 376 D
rhodahanson@tillamookbaycc.edu
HANSON, Sara 860-343-5883 86 G
shanson@mxcc.edu
HANSON, Steven, D 517-355-2352 227 C
hansons@msu.edu
HANSON, Susanah 724-266-3838 399 F
shanson@tsm.edu
HANSON, Terry 903-988-7495 437 G
thanson@kilgore.edu
HANSON, Tonya 952-358-8213 239 C
tonya.hanson@normandale.edu
HANSTEN, LaDeane 209-588-5087 76 J
hanstenl@yosemite.edu
HANTL, Bill 216-881-1700 358 K
bhantl@ohiotech.edu
HANTON, Donna, C 803-533-3647 410 H
djordan2@scsu.edu
HANTON, Tracy 215-496-6175 381 H
thanton@ccp.edu
HANUSCIN, R. Douglas 419-755-4871 357 B
dhanusci@ncstatecollege.edu
HANYCZ, Colleen, M 513-745-3502 364 F
president@xavier.edu
HANZLIK, Gilbert 804-524-3698 475 E
ghanzik@vsu.edu
HAO, Lan 626-914-8521 37 B
lhao@citruscollege.edu
HAPNER, Leslie 850-873-3511 101 O
lhapner@gulfcoast.edu
HAPPE, Doyle 713-529-2778 431 D
happe@paralegal.edu
HAPPEL, Harriet 661-362-3653 38 H
harriet.happel@canyons.edu
HAPSMITH, Linda, M 907-474-1849 10 B
lhapsmith@alaska.edu
HAQUE, MD 909-448-4791 71 C
mhaque@laverne.edu
HARA, Lou 785-749-8440 174 A
lhara@haskell.edu
HARA, Michael 651-690-6845 242 F
mehara140@stkate.edu
HARARI-RAFUL, Joseph 347-394-1036 291 B
rjraful@ateret.net
HARAWAY, Malcolm 512-505-3009 437 B
mxharaway@htu.edu
HARAYDA, Daniel 978-681-0800 216 A
HARB, Sam 337-521-9041 188 G
sam.harb@solacc.edu
HARBACH, Heather 319-273-2332 163 G
heather.harbach@uni.edu
HARBAUGH, Ian 251-461-1390 9 A
iharbaugh@southalabama.edu
HARBAUGH, Melinda, B 229-333-5952 127 C
mharbaugh@valdosta.edu
HARBAUGH, Merisa 717-477-1211 394 D
mlharbaugh@ship.edu
HARBER, Zachery 870-612-2081 23 B
zach.harber@uaccb.edu
HARBIDGE LITTLE, Michelle 904-819-6288 99 D
mharbidge@flagler.edu
HARBIN, Averl 716-286-8405 309 F
aharbin@niagara.edu
HARBIN, Glenn 256-551-7299 2 E
glenn.harbin@drakestate.edu
HARBIN, Suzanne 256-352-8144 4 A
suzanne.harbin@wallacestate.edu
HARBISON, Amanda 205-391-5878 3 E
aharbison@sheltonstate.edu
HARBOLD, Lisa 270-707-3728 181 G
lisa.harbold@kctcs.edu
HARBOR, John 317-208-5311 159 F
HARBOURT, Ellen, K 740-427-5121 354 I
harbourte@kenyon.edu
HARCOURT, Charles, F 315-655-7107 292 B
cfharcourt@cazenovia.edu
HARCOURT, Tracy, J 315-267-2667 318 D
harcoutj@potsdam.edu
HARCUM, Michael 215-619-7312 390 A
mharcum@mc3.edu
HARDAWAY, Gail 864-455-7992 412 F
admissions@greenvillemed.sc.edu
HARDCASTLE, Beth 734-487-1047 223 F
bhardcas@emich.edu
HARDCASTLE, Bob 610-359-5182 381 J
bhardcastle@dccc.edu
HARDEE, Catherine 619-239-0391 34 H
chardee@cwsl.edu
HARDEE, Sheri 706-864-1800 126 G
sheri.hardee@ung.edu
HARDEE, Teresa 504-286-5000 191 A
HARDEMAN, Sara 706-865-2134 126 D
shardeman@truett.edu
HARDEMON, Rhonda 312-850-7894 135 E
rhardemon@ccc.edu
HARDEN, Daniel 916-348-4689 42 B
dharden@epic.edu
HARDEN, Daphne 229-732-5923 114 I
daphneharden@andrewcollege.edu
HARDEN, Debra 757-727-5477 466 L
debra.harden@hamptonu.edu
HARDEN, Erica 478-553-2068 123 D
eharden@oftc.edu
HARDEN, Erica, I 478-553-2068 123 E
eharden@oftc.edu
HARDEN, Justin 231-591-2678 223 H
justinharden@ferris.edu
HARDEN, Kelly 731-661-5946 425 F
kharden@uu.edu
HARDEN, Ronald, W 916-348-4689 42 B
rharden@epic.edu
HARDEN, Yoshiko 425-235-2235 482 C
yharden@rtc.edu
HARDENBERGH, Catherine 906-227-1083 228 E
caharden@nmu.edu
HARDENBROOK, Joe 262-650-4887 491 A
jhardenb@carrollu.edu
HARDER, Kenette 816-414-3730 255 F
kharder@mbts.edu
HARDER, Maria 402-465-2117 267 J
mharder@nebrwesleyan.edu
HARDER, Natalie 843-383-8010 407 C
nharder@coker.edu
HARDER, Robert 503-554-2788 372 I
bharder@georgefox.edu
HARDESKI, Grace, L 215-955-6618 398 G
grace.hardeski@jefferson.edu

HARP, Elizabeth, R 815-282-7900 148 E bethharp@sacn.edu
HARP, Jeff 405-974-2800 370 H jharp@uco.edu
HARP, John, W 319-895-4234 164 E jharp@cornellcollege.edu
HARP, Randy 903-886-5351 446 D randy.harp@tamuc.edu
HARP-STEPHENS, Becky 859-246-6498 181 B becky.harp@kctcs.edu
HARPE, Cicely 706-771-4156 115 H charpe@augustatech.edu
HARPE, John Michael 803-356-5906 405 D jmharpe@allenuniversity.edu
HARPER, Alexie 571-483-8002 93 F
HARPER, Brian 516-686-4018 308 H bharper@nyit.edu
HARPER, Charles 615-460-6403 417 B charles.harper@belmont.edu
HARPER, Christine 859-257-3458 185 D christine.harper@uky.edu
HARPER, Daniel 212-472-1500 309 B academicaffairs@nysid.edu
HARPER, Daniel 512-463-6449 448 G daniel.harper@tsus.edu
HARPER, Daniel, S 901-321-3577 417 G dharper3@cbu.edu
HARPER, David 410-827-5806 198 B dharper@chesapeake.edu
HARPER, David 412-396-5589 382 E harperd1@duq.edu
HARPER, Donna, L 540-568-3705 467 C harperdl@jmu.edu
HARPER, Doreen, C 205-934-5360 8 A dcharper@uab.edu
HARPER, Erick 702-895-4729 270 J
HARPER, Heather 615-230-3519 424 F heather.harper@volstate.edu
HARPER, Holly 620-441-5240 172 M holly.harper@cowley.edu
HARPER, Jennifer 619-482-6551 65 K jharper@swccd.edu
HARPER, Jimmy 912-260-4314 125 B jimmy.harper@sgsc.edu
HARPER, Joann 706-245-7226 118 C jharper@ec.edu
HARPER, John 507-389-7433 240 F john.harper@southcentral.edu
HARPER, Jonathan 603-897-8529 273 B jharper@rivier.edu
HARPER, Josh 503-255-0332 374 A jharper@multnomah.edu
HARPER, Karla 937-376-6444 349 H kharper@centralstate.edu
HARPER, Kelly 513-569-1647 350 C kelly.harper@cincinnatistate.edu
HARPER, Kimberly, P 540-828-5393 464 C kharper@bridgewater.edu
HARPER, Kristin 205-226-4720 5 A kharper@bsc.edu
HARPER, Larisa 740-588-1216 364 H lharper@zanestate.edu
HARPER, Lauren 409-933-8690 432 H lharper1@come.edu
HARPER, Lisa, D 859-858-3511 178 H lisa.harper@asbury.edu
HARPER, Marie 304-724-3700 485 G mharper@apus.edu
HARPER, Marjoree 318-678-6000 187 E mharper@bpcc.edu
HARPER, Pam 270-706-8434 181 C pamela.harper@kctcs.edu
HARPER, Randy 870-574-4590 21 F rharper@sautech.edu
HARPER, Rita 251-460-6111 9 A rharper@southalabama.edu
HARPER, Ross 620-421-6700 175 D rossharper@labette.edu
HARPER, Sandra 325-793-3800 439 A harper.sandra@mcm.edu
HARPER, Stephany 304-462-6171 488 M stephany.harper@glenville.edu
HARPER, Stephen 952-995-1617 237 G stephen.harper@hennepintech.edu
HARPER, Teresa, B 502-213-2121 181 H teresa.harper@kctcs.edu
HARPER, Terral 501-337-5000 18 D tharper@asutr.edu
HARPER, Vernon 661-654-2154 30 C vharper@csub.edu
HARPER-LANE, Destiny 210-486-2157 428 C dharper24@alamo.edu
HARPHAM, Jennifer, E 330-972-5860 361 G jharpham@uakron.edu
HARPINE, Annette 910-938-6789 333 D harpinea@coastalcarolina.edu
HARPOLE, Jessica 662-329-7129 247 B jjharpole@muw.edu
HARPOLE, Theresa 662-476-5274 245 C tharpole@eastms.edu
HARPOOL, David 866-776-0331 54 E president@ncu.edu
HARPOOL, David 866-776-0331 54 E dharpool@ncu.edu
HARPOOL, Drew 615-494-8812 421 C drew.harpool@mtsu.edu
HARPS, Trynette Lottie 231-777-0559 228 C trynette.lottie-harps@muskegoncc.edu
HARPST, Steve 845-341-4230 310 D steve.harpst@sunyorange.edu
HARR, Jon 423-652-4773 419 F jharr@king.edu
HARR, Shannon, L 606-783-2330 183 H s.harr@moreheadstate.edu
HARRA, Alice 503-517-7421 375 F harraa@reed.edu
HARRAL, Judy 361-825-2495 446 E judy.harral@tamucc.edu
HARRAL, Kevin 650-949-7223 43 A harralkevin@foothill.edu
HARRELL, Alfred 225-771-3911 190 K alfred@sutrueblue.org
HARRELL, Alfred, E 225-771-3911 190 K alfred_harrell@sus.edu
HARRELL, III, Alfred, E 225-771-3911 190 J alfred_harrell@sus.edu
HARRELL, Angela 260-399-7700 162 A aharrell@sf.edu
HARRELL, Brandan 706-204-2209 119 C bharrell@highlands.edu
HARRELL, Brenda 904-470-8081 98 I b.harrell@ewc.edu
HARRELL, Bryant, L 860-727-6756 87 H bharrell@goodwin.edu
HARRELL, Evelyn 504-286-5234 191 A eharrell@suno.edu
HARRELL, II, Ivan, L 253-566-5100 483 F iharrell@tacomacc.edu
HARRELL, Jessica 336-506-4113 331 J jessica.harrell@alamancecc.edu
HARRELL, Jessica 828-694-1882 332 C j.harrell@blueridge.edu
HARRELL, Johnna, C 757-822-2381 474 G jcharrell@tcc.edu
HARRELL, Jonathan 757-352-4453 469 D jonahar@regent.edu
HARRELL, Joseph, H 513-558-4635 361 I joseph.harrell@uc.edu
HARRELL, Katie 605-668-1491 414 F katie.harrell@mountmarty.edu
HARRELL, Kim 252-862-1288 336 H kharrell@roanokechowan.edu
HARRELL, Kimberley 623-935-8033 13 C kimberley.harrell@estrellamountain.edu
HARRELL, Lee 941-359-7532 106 J lharrell@ringling.edu
HARRELL, Lisa 229-430-3396 114 G lharrell@albanytech.edu
HARRELL, Maeleesa 580-387-7220 366 E mharrell@mscok.edu
HARRELL, Pamela, J 919-209-2048 335 D pjharrell@johnstoncc.edu
HARRELL, Shereada 850-599-3700 109 E shereada.harrell@famu.edu
HARRELL, Zach 212-229-5150 307 E harrellz@newschool.edu
HARRELSON, Chris 505-566-3284 287 G harrelsonc@sanjuancollege.edu
HARRI, Robert 563-387-2103 167 J harrro01@luther.edu
HARRIER, Briana, K 515-964-0601 166 A harrierb@faith.edu
HARRIES, Peter, J 919-515-1989 341 E pjharrie@ncsu.edu
HARRIG, Tina, L 920-832-6541 492 B tina.l.harrig@lawrence.edu
HARRILL, Thad 828-395-1624 335 B tharrill@isothermal.edu
HARRIMAN, Melinda 805-565-6045 75 I mharriman@westmont.edu
HARRIMAN, Tayler 510-594-3633 28 D tayler.harriman@cca.edu
HARRING, Christopher 410-225-2255 200 B charring@mica.edu
HARRING, Kathleen 484-664-3125 390 F president@muhlenberg.edu
HARRINGTON, Billie 864-578-8770 410 G bharrington@sherman.edu
HARRINGTON, Constance 240-965-2494 197 F cpharrington@captechu.edu
HARRINGTON, Donna 505-467-6831 288 A donnaharrington@swc.edu
HARRINGTON, Heather 901-321-3260 417 G hharring@cbu.edu
HARRINGTON, Jaclyn 315-866-0300 301 B harringjp@herkimer.edu
HARRINGTON, Jamee 541-956-7017 375 G jharrington@roguecc.edu
HARRINGTON, Jermaine 215-368-5000 389 G jharrington@missio.edu
HARRINGTON, Kahlil 323-953-4000 49 E harrinkg@lacitycollege.edu
HARRINGTON, Kate 413-542-2000 205 D
HARRINGTON, Kimberly 704-216-6151 330 D kharrington@livingstone.edu
HARRINGTON, Krista 843-574-6077 411 I krista.harrington@tridenttech.edu
HARRINGTON, Lynn 708-974-5704 144 G harrington@morainevalley.edu
HARRINGTON, Marcie 617-333-2947 208 D marcie.harrington@curry.edu
HARRINGTON, Mark, R 716-888-2937 291 M harring4@canisius.edu
HARRINGTON, Melinda 620-276-9514 173 H melinda.harrington@gcccks.edu
HARRINGTON, Melissa 302-857-6656 90 D mharrington@desu.edu
HARRINGTON, Michael 718-429-6600 323 I michael.harrington@vaughn.edu
HARRINGTON, Michael, J 415-422-2790 72 I harrington@usfca.edu
HARRINGTON, Rob 605-331-6645 416 C rob.harrington@usiouxfalls.edu
HARRINGTON, Ryan 573-518-2236 255 G rkharrin@mineralarea.edu
HARRINGTON, Sherre, L 706-236-2285 116 A sharrington@berry.edu
HARRINGTON, Stacey 314-977-7124 258 H stacey.harrington@slu.edu
HARRINGTON-HOPE, Sharon 617-243-2145 210 G sharrington-hope@lasell.edu
HARRIOTT, Danielle 815-965-8616 147 I dharriott@rockfordcareercollege.edu
HARRIOTT, Wendy 732-263-5905 278 B wharriot@monmouth.edu
HARRIS, Alex 208-769-3300 132 A
HARRIS, Alexis 251-981-3771 5 B alexis.harris@columbiasouthern.edu
HARRIS, Alice 304-424-8224 490 A alice.harris@wvup.edu
HARRIS, Allatia 281-459-7140 442 B allatia.harris@sjcd.edu
HARRIS, Allyssa 713-797-7000 445 E alharris@pvamu.edu
HARRIS, Alvin 501-370-5284 21 A aharris@philander.edu
HARRIS, Andrew 415-338-1471 34 A a1harris@sfsu.edu
HARRIS, Angie 415-565-4645 69 B harrisangie@uchastings.edu
HARRIS, Angie 717-245-1556 382 B harrisa@dickinson.edu
HARRIS, Anna-Lize 201-216-5208 282 L anna-lize.harris@stevens.edu
HARRIS, Anne 641-269-3000 166 D president@grinnell.edu
HARRIS, Anthony 802-828-2800 463 A ajh03150@ccv.vsc.edu
HARRIS, April 540-261-8400 470 D april.harris@svu.edu
HARRIS, Ari 989-774-3197 221 M ucomm@cmich.edu
HARRIS, Becky 214-638-0484 437 F bharris@kdstudio.com
HARRIS, Bennie, L 404-752-1955 123 A bharris@msm.edu
HARRIS, Bennie, L 803-503-5200 413 A bennieh@uscupstate.edu
HARRIS, Beryl 410-951-6280 203 E bharris@coppin.edu
HARRIS, Beth 203-287-3023 88 D paierartlibrary@snet.net
HARRIS, Bethany, W 434-949-1007 474 D bethany.harris@southside.edu
HARRIS, Beverly 757-823-2409 468 B bbharris@nsu.edu
HARRIS, Bill 972-708-7340 434 F bill_harris@diu.edu
HARRIS, Branston 713-221-8056 452 B harrisb@uhd.edu
HARRIS, Caleb 208-882-1566 131 H charris15@nsa.edu
HARRIS, Carol, B 605-342-0317 414 C charris@jwc.edu
HARRIS, Caroline 252-536-7265 334 G charris@halifaxcc.edu
HARRIS, Chelsia 615-966-6650 420 B chelsia.harris@lipscomb.edu
HARRIS, Chelsy 719-502-3034 82 D chelsy.harris@pikespeak.edu
HARRIS, Chonnea 661-726-1911 68 L chonnea.harris@uav.edu
HARRIS, Chris 949-214-3169 40 E chris.harris@cui.edu
HARRIS, Chris 606-218-5537 185 F chrisharris@upike.edu
HARRIS, Christina 530-422-7923 74 F charris@weimar.edu
HARRIS, Christine 320-762-4435 236 G christine.harris@alextech.edu
HARRIS, Clark 307-772-4245 500 D charris@lccc.wy.edu
HARRIS, Clark 580-628-6201 366 J president@noc.edu
HARRIS, Clayton 216-987-4425 351 D clayton.harris@tri-c.edu
HARRIS, Craig 540-857-7797 475 A charris@virginiawestern.edu
HARRIS, Crystal 816-271-5827 256 C crharris@missouriwestern.edu
HARRIS, Danielle 828-627-4507 335 A ldharris@haywood.edu
HARRIS, David 718-268-4700 311 H
HARRIS, David 843-574-6615 411 I david.harris@tridenttech.edu
HARRIS, David, P 909-558-7600 48 J dpharris@llu.edu
HARRIS, David, R 518-388-6101 323 B harrisd@union.edu
HARRIS, David, W 319-273-2470 163 G david.harris@uni.edu
HARRIS, Dawn 225-771-2680 190 K dawn_harris@subr.edu
HARRIS, Debbie 804-751-9191 464 N dharris@ccc-va.com
HARRIS, Delores, R 919-530-6681 341 D dharr226@nccu.edu
HARRIS, Denise, M 716-878-5811 317 C harrisdm@buffalostate.edu
HARRIS, Derrell 912-287-5855 117 B dharris@coastalpines.edu
HARRIS, Dianne 206-543-5340 484 A dsh1@uw.edu
HARRIS, Dina 574-520-4131 157 C dlharris@iusb.edu
HARRIS, Doris, M 301-546-0129 201 D harrisdm@pgcc.edu
HARRIS, Eboneigh 940-397-4567 439 F eboneigh.harris@msutexas.edu
HARRIS, Erica 606-539-4250 185 C erica.harris@ucumberlands.edu
HARRIS, Eugenia 903-813-2371 429 I eharris@austincollege.edu
HARRIS, SR., Forrest, E 615-256-1463 416 F officeofthepresident@abcnash.edu
HARRIS, Frank 520-795-0787 10 J admissions@asaom.edu
HARRIS, G. Duncan 860-906-5100 86 C gharris@capitalcc.edu
HARRIS, G. Duncan 860-906-5100 86 C gharris@ccc.commnet.edu
HARRIS, Gail 423-746-5208 425 C gharris@tnwesleyan.edu
HARRIS, Gary, L 202-806-2550 92 E gharris@howard.edu
HARRIS, Gheretta 231-591-3947 223 H gherettaharris@ferris.edu
HARRIS, Hayley 607-274-3011 302 E hharris@ithaca.edu
HARRIS, J. Loyd 850-747-3211 101 O lharris@gulfcoast.edu
HARRIS, Jacob 512-233-1447 441 N jharri15@stedwards.edu

HART, Chris 410-837-5739 204 C chart@ubalt.edu
HART, Christi 503-491-6961 373 H christi.hart@mhcc.edu
HART, Daniel 856-225-6741 281 A daniel.hart@rutgers.edu
HART, Deanna 562-860-2451 35 O dhart@cerritos.edu
HART, Debra 304-696-2597 488 N hart70@marshall.edu
HART, Edward 843-953-6532 407 D harte@cofc.edu
HART, Erick 585-395-2579 317 B ehart@brockport.edu
HART, Erin 336-285-2470 341 C ehhart@ncat.edu
HART, Erin 814-871-5603 383 H hart022@gannon.edu
HART, Eyvonne 912-486-7784 123 F ehart@ogeecheetech.edu
HART, George, K 401-825-2233 403 D ghart3@ccri.edu
HART, Geraldine 516-463-6605 301 E geraldine.hart@hofstra.edu
HART, James, R 904-264-2172 106 K president@iws.edu
HART, James, T 804-862-6100 469 E jhart@rbc.edu
HART, Jan 918-549-2800 365 G
HART, Jeni, L 573-884-1402 260 C hartjl@missouri.edu
HART, Jennifer 717-871-7001 394 B jennifer.hart@millersville.edu
HART, Jimmy 205-348-3485 7 G jimmy.hart@ua.edu
HART, Jimmy, W 615-898-5131 421 C jimmy.hart@mtsu.edu
HART, Joan 314-256-8800 249 F
HART, John 937-766-3400 349 C johnhart@cedarville.edu
HART, Jon 605-995-2152 414 A jon.hart1@dwu.edu
HART, Joy 502-852-6976 185 E jlhart01@louisville.edu
HART, Julie 315-498-2214 310 C hartj@sunyocc.edu
HART, Kelly 304-876-5016 489 A khart08@shepherd.edu
HART, Kristy 916-608-6993 51 A hartk@flc.losrios.edu
HART, La Toya 601-979-7030 245 G latoya.m.hart@jsums.edu
HART, Mandy 254-298-8634 445 B mandy.hart@templejc.edu
HART, Melanie 212-229-5400 307 E melanie.hart@newschool.edu
HART, Melanie 806-742-2392 450 C melanie.hart@ttu.edu
HART, Melissa 605-642-6549 415 F melissa.hart@bhsu.edu
HART, Michael 207-741-5500 195 D mhart@smccme.edu
HART, Mischon 765-641-4083 153 D mnhart@anderson.edu
HART, Patrick 718-658-0006 308 B
HART, Richard, H 909-558-4540 48 J rhart@llu.edu
HART, Richard, L 214-768-4301 443 G rlhart@smu.edu
HART, Samatha 570-577-1554 379 A samatha.hart@bucknell.edu
HART, Sarah 813-253-6239 113 B sarahhart@ut.edu
HART, Susan 615-343-6604 427 B susan.hart@vanderbilt.edu
HART, Tara 308-432-6078 267 G thart@csc.edu
HART, Thomas 412-396-6002 382 E hartt1@duq.edu
HART, Tim 316-978-6192 178 B tim.hart@wichita.edu
HART, Wade 607-735-1770 298 G whart@elmira.edu
HART RUTHENBECK, Robin 740-427-5136 354 I hartruthenbeck1@kenyon.edu
HARTE, Barry 703-284-3847 468 A barry.harte@marymount.edu
HARTE, Tim 610-526-5000 378 J
HARTE WEYANT, Meghan 828-251-6474 342 A mhweyant@unca.edu
HARTENBURG, Dale 706-721-3356 115 I dhartenburg@augusta.edu
HARTENBURG, Gary 281-649-3630 436 D ghartenburg@hbu.edu
HARTER, Jeff 415-476-3001 70 D jeff.harter@ucsf.edu
HARTER, Jill 314-367-8700 260 A jill.harter@uhsp.edu
HARTER, Kris 937-298-3399 354 J kris.harter@kc.edu
HARTER, Michelle 912-583-3245 116 D mharter@bpc.edu
HARTFORD, Sharon, M 509-527-4323 484 B sharon.hartford@wwcc.edu
HARTFORD, Stephanie 618-985-2828 140 G stephaniehartford@jalc.edu
HARTGE, Gary 352-395-5835 107 G gary.hartge@sfcollege.edu
HARTGRAVE, Matt 208-732-6333 131 B mlhartgrave@csi.edu
HARTHORN, Karen, M 651-962-6353 243 F kmharthorn@stthomas.edu
HARTIG, Elizabeth 734-384-4202 227 F
HARTIGAN, Gretchen 617-358-6361 207 C hartigan@bu.edu
HARTIGAN, Sheenah 732-255-0400 279 A shartigan@ocean.edu
HARTING, Troy, R 719-333-4130 502 C troy.harting@afacademy.af.edu
HARTING, William 317-955-6015 159 A bharting@marian.edu
HARTL, Renae 563-387-1244 167 J hartre01@luther.edu
HARTLAUB, Elizabeth 859-441-4500 181 D elizabeth.hartlaub@kctcs.edu
HARTLESS, Megan 540-453-2209 472 F hartlessm@brcc.edu
HARTLEY, Bill 817-257-8227 447 H w.hartley@tcu.edu
HARTLEY, Gary 916-558-2408 51 B hartleg@scc.losrios.edu
HARTLEY, Greg, L 916-348-4689 42 B ghartley@epic.edu
HARTLEY, James 870-762-1020 17 F jehartley@smail.anc.edu
HARTLEY, Julie 801-321-7101 459 C jhartley@ushe.edu
HARTLEY, Katherine 909-537-5000 33 B katherine.hartley@csusb.edu
HARTLEY, Keri 334-386-7179 5 D khartley@faulkner.edu
HARTLEY, Laura 316-942-4291 176 B hartleyl@newmanu.edu
HARTLEY, Laura, C 206-281-2125 482 K lhartley@spu.edu
HARTLEY, Leslie 205-387-0511 1 D leslie.hartley@bscc.edu
HARTLEY, Patricia 970-351-1890 84 D
HARTLEY, Roger 410-837-5359 204 C rhartley@ubalt.edu
HARTLEY, Timothy 330-337-6403 347 B thartley@awc.edu
HARTLEY, Tracey 610-989-1200 400 F
HARTLEY, Vaughn 304-473-8367 490 E hartley.v@wvwc.edu
HARTLEY-HUTTON, Kelley 260-481-6643 159 H hartleyk@pfw.edu
HARTLINE, Michael 850-644-4747 110 B mhartline@fsu.edu
HARTLINE, Michael 850-644-4405 110 B mhartline@cob.fsu.edu
HARTMAN, Brandi, P 864-488-4617 409 C bhartman@limestone.edu
HARTMAN, C. Max 650-306-3132 62 I hartmanmax@smccd.edu
HARTMAN, Carolyn, S 910-962-4103 343 B hartmanc@uncw.edu
HARTMAN, Chris, T 215-885-2360 389 A chartman@manor.edu
HARTMAN, Christine 717-796-1800 389 F chartman@messiah.edu
HARTMAN, Dean, A 706-880-8246 121 K dhartman@lagrange.edu
HARTMAN, Emily 757-822-5201 474 G ehartman@tcc.edu
HARTMAN, Fritz 574-535-7423 155 B fritzdh@goshen.edu
HARTMAN, Greg 979-458-8679 446 B ghartman@tamu.edu
HARTMAN, James 609-896-5016 280 D jhartman@rider.edu
HARTMAN, Jennifer 316-322-3101 172 B jhartman7@butlercc.edu
HARTMAN, Joseph 978-934-2168 211 G joseph_hartman@uml.edu
HARTMAN, Joseph 972-825-4774 444 C jhartman@sagu.edu
HARTMAN, Katie 740-593-2600 358 L hartmank@ohio.edu
HARTMAN, Kerry 701-627-4738 346 D khartm@nhsc.edu
HARTMAN, Kevin 414-229-4594 495 B hartman@uwm.edu
HARTMAN, Kimberly 727-712-5876 107 C hartman.kimberly@spcollege.edu
HARTMAN, Laurie 315-792-7400 320 F laurie.hartman@sunypoly.edu
HARTMAN, Lianne 215-641-6595 390 A lhartman@mc3.edu
HARTMAN, Lynne 718-517-7753 314 B lhartman@edaff.com
HARTMAN, Paulla 641-844-5767 167 E paulla.hartman@iavalley.edu
HARTMAN, Rob 803-754-4100 407 F
HARTMAN, Robin 714-879-3901 45 J rhartman@hiu.edu
HARTMAN, Sarah 806-291-1045 457 B harmans@wbu.edu
HARTMAN, Sherry 410-287-1025 198 A shartman@cecil.edu
HARTMAN, Stephanie 304-358-2000 486 E stephanie@future.edu
HARTMAN, Thomas 336-506-4201 331 J thomas.hartman@alamancecc.edu
HARTMANN, Angela 361-570-4374 452 C hartmanna@uhv.edu
HARTMANN, Lori, L 859-238-5371 179 H lori.hartmann@centre.edu
HARTMANN, Steve 631-451-4000 321 A hartmas@sunysuffolk.edu
HARTNESS, Darrin, L 336-249-8186 333 G darrin_hartness@davidsondavie.edu
HARTNETT, Mary 716-839-8451 297 F mhartnet@daemen.edu
HARTNETT, Ryan 716-896-0700 324 A hartnettr@villa.edu
HARTO, Diana, L 304-336-8139 489 B diana.harto@westliberty.edu
HARTOG, III, John 712-324-5061 168 H jhartog@nwicc.edu
HARTOG, Paul, A 515-964-0601 166 A hartogp@faith.edu
HARTON, Mary Kay 847-925-6221 138 E mharton@harpercollege.edu
HARTRANFT, Joshua 717-871-5889 394 B josh.hartranft@millersville.edu
HARTS, Melissa, L 727-816-3466 105 E hartsm@phsc.edu
HARTSELL, Amy 540-432-4100 465 F springer@emu.edu
HARTSELL, Angela 239-489-9427 100 G ahartsell1@fsw.edu
HARTSELL, Dawn 843-792-3088 409 D hartsell@musc.edu
HARTSHORN, Kevin 610-861-1374 390 D hartshornk@moravian.edu
HARTSHORN, Tricia 620-242-0441 175 G hartshot@mcpherson.edu
HARTSOCK, Jonathan, T 540-464-7709 475 C hartsockjt@vmi.edu
HARTSOCK, Michael 217-424-6265 144 D mhartsock@millikin.edu
HARTSON, Michelle 931-431-9700 421 G mhartson@nci.edu
HARTSON, Michelle 931-431-9700 421 G financialaid@nci.edu
HARTUNG, Benjamin 716-673-4725 316 A benjamin.hartung@fredonia.edu
HARTWELL, John 435-797-2060 459 F john.hartwell@usu.edu
HARTWELL, Jonathan, D 304-929-1045 487 G jhartwell@newriver.edu
HARTWELL, Richard, H 610-361-2336 390 G hartwelr@neumann.edu
HARTWELL, Roger 608-796-3040 496 L rwhartwell@viterbo.edu
HARTWELL, Stephanie 313-577-2519 232 H gr2312@wayne.edu
HARTWIG, Elizabeth 336-273-4431 326 J elizabeth.hartwig@bennett.edu
HARTWIG, Ryan 303-963-3426 78 D rhartwig@ccu.edu
HARTY, Kristin 412-365-2769 380 F kharty@chatham.edu
HARTY, Molly 610-902-8131 379 E mh10962@cabrini.edu
HARTZ, James 270-686-4630 182 C jim.hartz@kctcs.edu
HARTZ, Rachel 570-348-6211 389 B rhartz@marywood.edu
HARTZELL, Jay, C 512-471-1232 454 C president@utexas.edu
HARTZELL, Rick 563-425-5293 170 D hartzellr53@uiu.edu
HARTZLER, Murray, G 843-661-1237 408 H mhartzler@fmarion.edu
HARTZLER, Tracy 505-224-4415 285 B thartzler@cnm.edu
HARTZOG, Bryan 706-754-7807 123 C bryan.hartzog@northgatech.edu
HARTZOG, Randy 504-278-6363 188 E rhartzog@nunez.edu
HARTZSCH, Hannah 413-737-7000 205 C
HARVEN, Gabriel 925-969-2082 40 H gharven@dvc.edu
HARVEY, Andrew 301-387-3025 198 F andrew.harvey@garrettcollege.edu
HARVEY, Ashley 850-718-2487 97 E harveya@chipola.edu
HARVEY, Bart 219-464-5987 162 C bart.harvey@valpo.edu
HARVEY, Binti 909-621-8152 63 E bharvey@scrippscollege.edu
HARVEY, Cameron 901-381-3939 427 C cameron@visible.edu
HARVEY, Christopher 727-398-8407 107 C harvey.chris@spcollege.edu
HARVEY, Diana 510-642-6448 68 N diana.harvey@berkeley.edu
HARVEY, Diana 510-987-0700 68 M
HARVEY, Donna, J 812-941-2026 157 D djharvey@ius.edu
HARVEY, Erik 518-891-2915 309 G eharvey@nccc.edu
HARVEY, George 919-761-2203 340 B harvey@sebts.edu
HARVEY, Janice 870-248-4000 18 H janice.harvey@blackrivertech.edu
HARVEY, Jay 800-227-2013 248 A jharvey@rts.edu
HARVEY, Jennifer 515-271-3751 165 F jennifer.harvey@drake.edu
HARVEY, Joe 920-465-2373 494 F harveyj@uwgb.edu
HARVEY, Katie 304-769-0011 490 B kharvey@wvjc.edu
HARVEY, Kim 585-389-2023 307 D kharvey8@naz.edu
HARVEY, Laurie 516-686-7711 308 H lharve05@nyit.edu
HARVEY, Marcus 816-604-4121 255 B marcus.harvey@mcckc.edu
HARVEY, Marilyn 951-639-5436 53 A mharvey@msjc.edu
HARVEY, Michael 410-778-7202 204 E mharvey2@washcoll.edu
HARVEY, Michael 864-592-4991 411 E harveym@sccsc.edu
HARVEY, Peter, W 509-527-5145 485 C harvey@whitman.edu
HARVEY, Roberta 856-256-5140 280 H harvey@rowan.edu
HARVEY, Ryan, D 740-826-8051 356 H harvey@muskingum.edu
HARVEY, Sally 480-858-9100 16 B s.harvey@scnm.edu
HARVEY, Sandra 318-678-6000 187 E sharvey@bpcc.edu
HARVEY, Sandra 704-468-2155 327 F sandra.harvey@carolinascollege.edu
HARVEY, Sandra 704-403-3202 327 B sandra.harvey@atriumhealth.org
HARVEY, Scott 864-646-1556 411 H sharvey@tctc.edu
HARVEY, Shannon, S 814-865-2044 391 F sxs205@psu.edu
HARVEY, Sonja, K 217-786-4913 142 F sonja.harvey@llcc.edu
HARVEY, Stephen 212-731-3419 302 B stephen.harvey@mssm.edu
HARVEY, Stewart, A 207-581-2668 196 D stewarth@maine.edu
HARVEY-LIVINGSTON, Kim 903-566-7197 455 C klivingston@uttyler.edu

HEBERT, Bill .... 916-278-7550.. 33 A
bhebert@csus.edu
HEBERT, Carolyn .... 860-515-3880.. 85 D
chebert@charteroak.edu
HEBERT, Gurdeep .... 559-325-5378...66 H
gurdeep.hebert@cloviscollege.edu
HEBERT, Jaimie .... 337-482-6454 192 F
jaimie.hebert@louisiana.edu
HEBERT, Joseph .... 281-998-6150 442 E
joseph.hebert@sjcd.edu
HEBERT, Karen .... 803-934-3196 409 H
khebert@morris.edu
HEBERT, Katie .... 508-626-4575 212 D
khebert@framingham.edu
HEBERT, Kimberly .... 510-883-2073.. 41 G
khebert@dspt.edu
HEBERT, Lisa .... 903-463-8651 435 H
hebertl@grayson.edu
HEBERT, Martial, H .... 412-268-5704 380 B
hebert@cs.cmu.edu
HEBERT, Richard .... 203-576-4804.. 89 A
rhebert@bridgeport.edu
HEBERT, Ronnie .... 256-824-5599.... 8 B
ronnie.hebert@uah.edu
HEBERT, Sarah .... 603-542-7744 272 D
shebert@ccsnh.edu
HEBERT, Scott .... 337-482-2001 192 F
scott.hebert@louisiana.edu
HEBERT, Sue .... 802-443-2673 461 G
hebert@middlebury.edu
HEBERT, Trace .... 615-966-5325 420 B
trace.hebert@lipscomb.edu
HEBERT-MACCARO,
Karen .... 781-239-4355 205 G
maccaro@babson.edu
HEBRA, Jada .... 603-665-7173 273 E
j.hebra@snhu.edu
HEBREARD, Dana .... 616-632-8900 221 A
HECHT, Amy .... 850-644-5590 110 B
ahecht@fsu.edu
HECHT, Bill .... 901-321-3396 417 G
whecht@cbu.edu
HECHT, Boruch .... 973-267-9404 279 G
boruch.hecht@gmail.com
HECHT, Jason .... 828-398-7900 331 K
HECHT, Pinchas .... 718-645-0536 306 F
phecht@thejnet.com
HECHTER, Alissa 954-262-7300 104M
HECIMOVIC, Katrina, M 608-342-1155 495 E
hecimovick@uwplatt.edu
HECK, Annie .... 541-737-0790 374 H
annie.heck@oregonstate.edu
HECK, Ashlee .... 580-559-5625 365 J
aheck@ecok.edu
HECK, Julia .... 734-487-0074 223 F
emu_ombuds@emich.edu
HECKAMAN, Daniel, A .. 218-477-2300 239 A
daniel.heckaman@mnstate.edu
HECKAMAN, Judith, M . 717-560-8278 387 D
jheckaman@lbc.edu
HECKENDORN, Sally ...... 717-245-1518 382 B
heckendo@dickinson.edu
HECKENLAIBLE, Anna ... 605-331-6651 416 C
anna.heckenlaible@usiouxfalls.edu
HECKENLAIBLE, John ... 623-845-3809.. 13 E
john.heckenlaible@gccaz.edu
HECKLER, Casey .... 812-866-7000 155 D
HECKLER, Pamela .... 410-706-5631 202 F
pheckler@umaryland.edu
HECKLINGER, Jill .... 410-617-2627 199 G
jphecklinger@loyola.edu
HECKMAN, Mary Ellen .. 610-372-4721 396 A
mheckman@racc.edu
HECKMANN, John .... 815-753-2900 145 H
jheckmann@niu.edu
HECTOR, Gerald .... 407-823-2387 110 D
gerald.hector@ucf.edu
HECTOR, Leticia .... 909-384-8535.. 60 F
lhector@sbccd.cc.ca.us
HEDAL, Laura .... 425-352-8186 477 F
lhedal@cascadia.edu
HEDAYAT, Nasser .... 407-582-3326 113 C
nhedayat@valenciacollege.edu
HEDBERG, Rick .... 701-858-4483 345 C
rick.hedberg@minotstateu.edu
HEDDEN, Gregory .... 419-559-2302 361 B
ghedden01@terra.edu
HEDDLESTON,
Patrick, D .... 330-823-6599 362 E
heddlepd@mountunion.edu
HEDEEN, Deborah .... 207-834-7504 196 G
deborah.hedeen@maine.edu

HEDEGARD, Heidi .... 603-862-0967 273 G
heidi.hedegard@usnh.edu
HEDGE, Becca .... 816-501-4287 257 K
becca.hedge@rockhurst.edu
HEDGE, Dennis .... 605-688-4173 416 A
dennis.hedge@sdstate.edu
HEDGEPATH, Donna ..... 270-789-5231 179 G
drhedgepath@campbellsville.edu
HEDGES, Jennifer .... 217-234-5241 141 H
jhedges@lakelandcollege.edu
HEDGES, Jerris, R .... 808-692-0899 129 B
jerris@hawaii.edu
HEDGES, Joseph .... 661-654-2515.. 30 C
jhedges@csub.edu
HEDGES, Tammy .... 901-678-2843 426 A
thedges@memphis.edu
HEDIN, Norma .... 214-333-5599 433 D
norma@dbu.edu
HEDINGER, Andrew .... 503-517-1807 377 D
ahedinger@westernseminary.edu
HEDLUN, Erin .... 417-865-2815 252 F
hedlune@evangel.edu
HEDLUN, Erin .... 417-865-2815 249 G
hedlune@evangel.edu
HEDLUN, Randy, J .... 417-862-9533 252 H
rhedlun@globaluniversity.edu
HEDLUND, Evan .... 503-375-7126 372 G
ehedlund@corban.edu
HEDLUND, Traci .... 816-960-2008 250 J
billing@cityvision.edu
HEDMAN, Miranda .... 228-497-7639 246 F
miranda.hedman@mgccc.edu
HEDMAN, Shawn .... 507-537-6292 240 G
shawn.hedman@smsu.edu
HEDRICK, Noemi .... 952-829-1479 233 H
noemi.hedrick@bethfel.org
HEDRICK, Van .... 940-668-7347 439 I
vhedrick@nctc.edu
HEDSTROM, Lori .... 843-953-7777 406 D
lhedstro@citadel.edu
HEDTKE, Abram .... 612-728-5206 242 H
ahedtke@smumn.edu
HEEKE, Dave .... 520-621-4622.. 16 H
dheeke@arizona.edu
HEERDINK, Joe .... 270-831-9615 181 F
joe.heerdink@kctcs.edu
HEERDINK, Joe .... 270-831-9615 182 A
joe.heerdink@kctcs.edu
HEEREMA, Lynne .... 616-988-1000 222 D
lynne.h@compass.edu
HEEREN, Diana .... 210-999-7163 451 B
dheeren@trinity.edu
HEEREN, Matthew .... 660-626-2522 249 C
mheeren@atsu.edu
HEERMAN, Heather, L .. 508-565-1301 218 F
hheerman@stonehill.edu
HEERMANN, Keith .... 417-862-9533 252 H
kheermann@globaluniversity.edu
HEERSINK, Heather .... 719-587-7759.. 77 F
heather_heersink@adams.edu
HEERSINK, Jordan .... 303-963-3388.. 78 D
joheersink@ccu.edu
HEETER, Brenda .... 859-218-0416 185 D
brenda.heeter@uky.edu
HEETLAND, David, L ..... 847-866-3970 138 B
david.heetland@garrett.edu
HEFFERN, Tim .... 562-938-4346.. 48 K
theffern@lbcc.edu
HEFFERNAN, Emily .... 941-487-4225 110 C
eheffernan@ncf.edu
HEFFERNAN, Tom .... 262-524-7343 491 A
theffernan@carrollu.edu
HEFFNER, Brian .... 231-995-1014 228 F
bheffner@nmc.edu
HEFLIN, Sherry .... 717-815-1257 402 G
sheflin@ycp.edu
HEFNER, Alana .... 254-968-9078 445 F
hefner@tarleton.edu
HEFNER, April .... 615-460-6000 417 B
april.hefner@belmont.edu
HEFNER, Beth .... 770-533-6607 121 L
bhefner@laniertech.edu
HEFNER, Kelli .... 662-720-7411 247 D
kehefner@nemcc.edu
HEFNER, Todd .... 417-667-8181 251 E
thefner@cottey.edu
HEFTKA, Chris .... 815-479-7661 143 F
cheftka@mchenry.edu
HEFTON, Ryan .... 214-333-5424 433 D
ryanh@dbu.edu
HEGAB, Hisham .... 318-257-4647 192 A
hhegab@latech.edu

HEGAMIN, Tonya .... 718-270-4846 294 E
thegamin@mec.cuny.edu
HEGARTY, Joseph .... 207-509-7292 196 B
jhegarty@unity.edu
HEGARTY, Mary .... 714-564-6904.. 58 F
hegarty_mary@sac.edu
HEGARTY, Michelle .... 952-885-5465 241 P
mhegarty@nwhealth.edu
HEGEDUS, Stephen .... 203-392-5900.. 85 H
schoolofeducation@southernct.edu
HEGEMAN, Jay .... 301-687-4738 203 F
jhegeman@frostburg.edu
HEGER, Laura .... 570-389-4179 393 E
lheger@bloomu.edu
HEGGEMEYER, Terri ...... 402-844-7263 268 A
terrih@northeast.edu
HEGGOY, Liv .... 540-868-4091 473 C
lheggoy@lfcc.edu
HEGLUND, Emily .... 903-670-2664 451 C
emily.heglund@tvcc.edu
HEGLUND, Miranda ...... 906-932-4231 224 A
mirandah@gogebic.edu
HEGWER, Kim .... 757-352-4005 469 D
khegwer@regent.edu
HEGWOOD, Johnetta .... 310-342-5290.. 73 E
HEHL, Jim .... 239-590-1313 109 G
jhehl@fgcu.edu
HEIDA, Debbie .... 706-236-2227 116 A
dheida@berry.edu
HEIDBREDER, Kay, K .... 540-231-6293 475 D
heidbred@vt.edu
HEIDE, Erin .... 701-845-7113 345 E
erin.heide@vcsu.edu
HEIDELBERG, Roy .... 225-578-1397 188 K
royh@lsu.edu
HEIDEMAN, Carl, E ...... 616-395-7670 224 H
heideman@hope.edu
HEIDEMANN, Kathryn ... 216-421-7410 350 E
kjheidemann@cia.edu
HEIDEMANN, Molly ...... 513-529-8600 356 A
mheidemann@miamioh.edu
HEIDENDAL, Egon .... 660-562-1254 256 G
egon@nwmissouri.edu
HEIDENFELDER, Jason . 630-829-1389 133 B
jheidenfelder@ben.edu
HEIDENREICH, Kari .... 262-472-1921 496 E
heidenreka12@uww.edu
HEIDENREICH, Lisa .... 651-290-7678 241 N
lisa.heidenreich@mitchellhamline.edu
HEIDER, Don .... 408-554-7898.. 63 A
dheider@scu.edu
HEIDERICH, Gail .... 504-526-4745 190 C
gailh@nationsu.edu
HEIDICK, Venesa, A ...... 979-845-1059 446 B
vheidick@tamu.edu
HEIDINGSFIELD,
Michael, J .... 512-499-4688 454 A
mheidingsfield@utsystem.edu
HEIDKE, Stephen .... 314-392-2372 255 H
heidkesj@mobap.edu
HEIDLE, Wayne .... 714-463-7589.. 51 D
wheidle@ketchum.edu
HEIDRICH, Mark .... 208-459-5199 131 A
mheidrich@collegeofidaho.edu
HEIDRICK, Judy .... 785-738-9058 176 C
jheidrick@ncktc.edu
HEIDT, Matthew .... 716-926-8792 301 C
mheidt@hilbert.edu
HEIDTKE, Staci, L .... 715-836-5358 494 E
heidtksl@uwec.edu
HEIFNER, Bryan .... 432-335-6512 440 C
bheifner@odessa.edu
HEIGHT, Linda, L .... 248-204-2159 226 E
lheight@ltu.edu
HEIGLE, Chris .... 870-838-2945.. 17 F
cheigle@smail.anc.edu
HEIKKILA, Christina ...... 910-362-7313 332 F
cheikkila@cfcc.edu
HEIKKINEN, Melinda .... 314-977-2500 258 H
melinda.heikkinen@slu.edu
HEIL, Elissa .... 717-262-2018 402 D
elissa.heil@wilson.edu
HEIL, Mandy .... 928-317-6000.. 11 B
mandy.heil@azwestern.edu
HEIL, Scott .... 951-827-3296.. 70 B
scott.heil@ucr.edu
HEILAND, Donna .... 718-636-3744 311 A
dheiland@pratt.edu
HEILBRON, Shawn, R ... 631-632-7205 316 D
shawn.heilbron@stonybrook.edu
HEILGEIST, Pete .... 360-650-3127 485 A
pete.heilgeist@wwu.edu

HEILMAN, Carl, R .... 620-792-9301 171 F
heilmanc@bartonccc.edu
HEILSKOV, Heidi .... 515-964-6264 164 F
haheilskov@dmacc.edu
HEILSTEDT, Sally .... 425-739-8233 480 D
sally.heilstedt@lwtech.edu
HEIM, Bret .... 251-380-3871.... 6 H
HEIM, Dianna .... 717-264-2064 402 D
dianna.heim@wilson.edu
HEIM, Edward .... 610-796-2838 378 C
edward.heim@alvernia.edu
HEIM, Peggy, M .... 610-799-1532 388 B
pheim@lccc.edu
HEIM, Reanna .... 712-325-3207 167 G
rheim@iwcc.edu
HEIMANN, Anne .... 402-552-3100 265 G
heimannanne@clarksoncollege.edu
HEIMBAUGH, Sharon ... 773-442-5805 145 G
s-heimbaugh@neiu.edu
HEIMBURGER, David, F 314-977-3139 258 H
david.heimburger@slu.edu
HEIMLICH, Dana .... 212-986-4343 291 A
dana-heimlich@berkeleycollege.edu
HEIMLICH, Dana .... 973-278-5400 274 J
dana-heimlich@berkeleycollege.edu
HEIMMERMANN,
Daniel .... 803-641-3276 412 B
daniel.heimmermann@usca.edu
HEIMOVITZ, Issac .... 718-438-1002 306 A
HEIN, Anna .... 386-481-2894.. 96 D
heina@cookman.edu
HEIN, Beth .... 651-779-3438 237 D
beth.hein@century.edu
HEIN, Steven, M .... 912-478-0831 120 A
shein@georgiasouthern.edu
HEINBAUGH, JoElle ...... 717-757-1100 402 J
HEINDEL, Patricia .... 973-290-4102 282 G
pheindel@steu.edu
HEINDL, Michael, J ...... 662-562-3227 247 E
mheindl@northwestms.edu
HEINE, Caroline .... 502-585-9911 184 E
cheine@spalding.edu
HEINE, Kelly .... 620-341-5473 173 C
kheine1@emporia.edu
HEINEMAN, Linda .... 978-656-3228 214 G
heinemanl@middlesex.mass.edu
HEINEMAN, Pete .... 402-557-7146 265 A
pete.heineman@bellevue.edu
HEINEMAN, William ..... 978-762-4000 215 B
wheinema@northshore.edu
HEINEMANN, Yosef ...... 732-367-1060 275 B
HEINEN, James .... 847-970-4809 152 F
jheinen@usml.edu
HEINERICHS, Scott .... 610-436-2733 394 F
sheinerichs@wcupa.edu
HEINEY, James .... 915-831-6441 435 B
jheiney@epcc.edu
HEINHORST, Sabine ..... 601-266-4533 248 H
sabine.heinhorst@usm.edu
HEINITZ, Adam .... 605-574-5529 413 G
adam.heinitz@augie.edu
HEINLE, Nicole .... 701-252-3467 346 J
nicole.heinle@uj.edu
HEINONEN, Pamela ...... 928-523-9342.. 14 J
pamela.heinonen@nau.edu
HEINRICH, Peggy .... 847-214-7635 137 D
pheinrich@elgin.edu
HEINRICH, Robert .... 609-652-6039 283 A
robert.heinrich@stockton.edu
HEINRICHER, Art .... 508-831-5000 220 C
HEINS, Marshall, B .... 713-718-8464 436 E
marshall.heins@hccs.edu
HEINSELMAN, Gregg .... 509-963-1515 477 G
gregory.heinselman@cwu.edu
HEINSELMAN, Gregory . 715-836-2637 494 E
HEINTZ, Jill .... 315-792-5584 306 G
jheintz@mvcc.edu
HEINTZ, Katharine .... 408-551-3332.. 63 A
kheintz@scu.edu
HEINTZ, Paul .... 937-778-8600 352 D
HEINTZ, Ryan .... 561-912-1211.. 99 C
rheintz@evergladesuniversity.edu
HEINTZ, Tim .... 303-292-0015.. 80 F
theintz@denvercollegeofnursing.edu
HEINY, Dani .... 507-433-0517 240 A
dani.heiny@riverland.edu
HEINZ, Amy .... 612-238-4549 242 H
aheinz@smumn.edu
HEINZ, Cheryl .... 630-829-6581 133 B
cheinz@ben.edu
HEINZ, Kartha .... 206-876-6100 483 A
kheinz@theseattleschool.edu

HEINZE, Edward .... 502-897-4700 184 D
eheinze@sbts.edu
HEINZE, Steven .... 419-358-3236 348 E
heinzes@bluffton.edu
HEINZEKEHR, Justin ..... 574-535-7110 155 B
justinbh@goshen.edu
HEINZEKEHR, Justin ..... 574-535-7000 155 B
justinbh@goshen.edu
HEINZELMAN, Wendi .... 585-275-3958 323 E
wendi.heinzelman@rochester.edu
HEINZERLING, Kelly ..... 734-384-4275 227 F
kheinzerling@monroeccc.edu
HEIRD, Josh .... 502-852-3858 185 E
josh.heird@louisville.edu
HEISER, Andy .... 360-416-7745 483 D
andy.heiser@skagit.edu
HEISER, Dan .... 920-403-3447 494 B
dan.heiser@snc.edu
HEISER, Donna .... 239-687-5402.. 95 L
dheiser@avemarialaw.edu
HEISER, Eric .... 740-755-7275 349 D
heiser.68@mail.cotc.edu
HEISEY, Jennifer .... 513-556-4344 361 I
heiseyj@ucmail.uc.edu
HEISS, Beth, L .... 517-265-5161 220 D
bheiss@adrian.edu
HEIST, Daniel, P .... 814-865-1359 391 F
dph3@psu.edu
HEISTAD, Deirdre, A ..... 319-273-2633 163 G
d.heistad@uni.edu
HEIT, Christina .... 608-785-9139 499 B
heitc@westerntc.edu
HEITHAUS, Michael ...... 305-348-2866 109 H
michael.heithaus@fiu.edu
HEITKAMP, Andrew .... 701-858-4002 345 C
andy.heitkamp@minotstateu.edu
HEITKAMP, Mike .... 641-585-8695 170 E
mike.heitkamp@waldorf.edu
HEITMAN, Tom .... 251-981-3771.... 5 B
tom.heitman@columbiasouthern.edu
HEITZENRATER, Kim, D 931-598-1948 422 F
kheitzen@sewanee.edu
HEIZ, Andrew .... 845-341-4251 310 D
andrew.heiz@sunyorange.edu
HEJL, Cindy .... 303-964-5758.. 83 B
chejl@regis.edu
HEJL, Talitha .... 970-675-3217.. 78 P
talitha.hejl@cncc.edu
HELBIG, Suzanne, C ..... 949-824-7366.. 69 C
shelbig@uci.edu
HELBIG, Tuesdi .... 270-745-3250 186 A
tuesdi.helbig@wku.edu
HELBLE, Joseph, J .... 610-758-3156 388 C
jjh282@lehigh.edu
HELBLING, Brenda .... 208-885-9191 132 C
brendah@uidaho.edu
HELD, II, John .... 573-341-6533 260 F
heldjohn@mst.edu
HELD, Joshua .... 847-317-4188 150 J
jrheld@tiu.edu
HELDEROP, Sue .... 248-364-6135 229 F
helderop@oakland.edu
HELDT, Amy .... 812-749-1303 159 E
aheldt@oak.edu
HELEAN, Cathy .... 941-487-4150 110 C
chelean@ncf.edu
HELENS, Joyce .... 775-327-2108 270 G
joyce.helens@gbcnv.edu
HELFRICH, Sarah .... 740-593-4400 358 L
helfrich@ohio.edu
HELGESEN, Pete .... 913-360-7476 171 G
phelgesen@benedictine.edu
HELGESON, Grant .... 808-455-0645 130 A
helgeson@hawaii.edu
HELGESON, Stu .... 610-989-1276 400 F
shelgeson@vfmac.edu
HELIEISAR, Jennifer ...... 691-320-2480 503 B
jenniferh@comfsm.fm
HELITZER, Deborah, L .. 602-496-0789.. 11 A
deborah.helitzer@asu.edu
HELLA, Lori, L .... 989-774-2010 221 M
hella1ll@cmich.edu
HELLDOBLER, Richard .. 973-720-2222 283 I
helldoblerr@wpunj.edu
HELLEMAN, Kathryn ...... 419-434-4256 364 B
khelleman@winebrenner.edu
HELLEN, Sharla .... 870-743-3000.. 20 F
sharla.hellen@northark.edu
HELLER, Amanda .... 503-244-0726 371 E
admissions@achs.edu
HELLER, Dana .... 734-487-4344 223 F
dheller@emich.edu
HELLER, Jacob .... 516-628-5076 318 A
hellerj@oldwestbury.edu
HELLER, James .... 262-595-2455 495 D
james.heller@uwp.edu
HELLER, Jennifer .... 816-584-6755 257 E
jennifer.heller@park.edu
HELLER, Jennifer .... 828-328-7154 330 B
jennifer.heller@lr.edu
HELLER, Joshua, W ...... 585-785-1335 299 E
joshua.heller@flcc.edu
HELLER, Lauren .... 706-290-2688 116 A
lheller@berry.edu
HELLER, Laurent .... 410-516-2373 199 E
lheller8@jhu.edu
HELLER, Mary .... 610-989-1345 400 F
mheller@vfmac.edu
HELLER, Michael .... 814-824-2390 389 E
mheller@mercyhurst.edu
HELLER, Nathan .... 254-968-9420 445 F
heller@tarleton.edu
HELLER, Tracy .... 858-635-4535.. 25 A
theller@alliant.edu
HELLER, Tracy .... 858-635-4772.. 25 B
theller@alliant.edu
HELLER DE MESSER,
Kirk .... 414-930-3221 493 E
hellerk@mtmary.edu
HELLERUD, Nancy .... 314-246-7440 261 D
nancyhellerud@webster.edu
HELLING, Nathan, M .... 605-336-6588 415 B
nhelling@kairos.edu
HELLMAN, Caroline ...... 718-260-5400 294 F
chellman@citytech.cuny.edu
HELLMAN, Joel .... 202-687-0100.. 92 D
jhellman@georgetown.edu
HELLMAN, Shari .... 419-434-4570 362 D
shellman@findlay.edu
HELLMICH, David, M .... 815-835-6303 149 A
david.m.hellmich@svcc.edu
HELLUMS, Paula .... 337-421-6965 188 H
paula.hellums@sowela.edu
HELLWIG, Beth .... 701-777-3000 344 H
HELLYER, Brenda .... 281-998-6100 442 B
brenda.hellyer@sjcd.edu
HELM, Brian, C .... 717-361-1568 383 B
helmb@etown.edu
HELM, Deborah .... 619-388-3450.. 60 I
dhelm@sdccd.edu
HELM, Heather .... 970-351-1890.. 84 D
heather.helm@unco.edu
HELM, Jonathan, C .... 412-624-7600 400 A
jch127@pitt.edu
HELM, Scott .... 641-782-1481 170 B
helm@swcciowa.edu
HELM-STEVENS,
Roxanne .... 626-969-3434.. 26 K
HELMBOLT, Shawn .... 605-688-4008 416 A
shawn.helmbolt@sdstate.edu
HELMBRECHT, Alex .... 308-432-6212 267 G
ahelmbrecht@csc.edu
HELMER, Robert, C ...... 440-826-2424 348 C
rhelmer@bw.edu
HELMER, Shannon .... 610-799-1857 388 B
shelmer@lccc.edu
HELMICK, Mary .... 540-231-6221 475 D
mhelmick@vt.edu
HELMICK, Rita .... 304-462-6178 488 M
rita.helmick@glenville.edu
HELMICK, Tom .... 724-852-3210 401 E
thelmick@waynesburg.edu
HELMINCK, Aloysius ..... 808-956-6451 129 B
helminck@hawaii.edu
HELMKE, Jonathan .... 936-468-1537 444 H
helmkej@sfasu.edu
HELMS, Barbara .... 440-646-8126 363 C
barbara.helms@ursuline.edu
HELMS, Bryan .... 334-293-4522.... 1 C
bryan.helms@accs.edu
HELMS, Carol .... 509-453-0374 481 G
carol.helms@perrytech.edu
HELMS, Chris .... 828-766-1291 335 G
chelms@mayland.edu
HELMS, Clint .... 706-233-7265 125 A
chelms@shorter.edu
HELMS, Jaclyn .... 646-313-8000 295 C
jaclyn.helms@guttman.cuny.edu
HELMS, Lance .... 912-538-3207 125 E
lhelms@southeasterntech.edu
HELMS, Marilyn .... 706-272-2600 118 A
mhelms@daltonstate.edu
HELMS, Mark .... 704-330-6127 333 B
mark.helms@cpcc.edu
HELMS, Michael .... 334-347-2623.... 2 A
mhelms@escc.edu
HELMS, Paula .... 334-347-2623.... 2 A
phelms@escc.edu
HELMS, Sherrie .... 478-289-2360 118 B
shelms@ega.edu
HELMS, Steve .... 334-222-6591.... 2 I
shelms@lbwcc.edu
HELMSING, Debra, F ..... 260-665-4240 161 C
helmsingd@trine.edu
HELMSTETTER, Ashley .. 419-448-2231 353 D
ahelmste@heidelberg.edu
HELMUS, Aimee .... 910-362-7012 332 F
ahelmus@cfcc.edu
HELSEL, Jeannie .... 513-558-9964 362 B
helselje@foundation.uc.edu
HELSPER, Lauren .... 661-259-7800.. 38 H
laura.helsper@canyons.edu
HELTON, Kasey .... 404-894-1822 119 D
kasey.helton@gatech.edu
HELTON, Todd .... 580-774-3227 369 I
todd.helton@swosu.edu
HELVERING, Christal ..... 765-641-4205 153 D
crhelvering@anderson.edu
HELWIG, Anna .... 708-596-2000 149 D
ahelwig@ssc.edu
HELYER, Kella .... 503-838-8475 377 C
helyerk@wou.edu
HELZLSOUER, William .. 610-436-3109 394 F
whelzlsouer@wcupa.edu
HEMANN, Patty .... 507-433-0816 240 A
patty.hemann@riverland.edu
HEMANS, Peter .... 828-694-1723 332 C
peterh@blueridge.edu
HEMBREE, Jennifer .... 707-654-1780.. 32 C
jhembree@csum.edu
HEMBREE, Kelly .... 828-835-4291 338 C
khembree@tricountycc.edu
HEMENWAY, Courtney .. 269-782-2179 230 D
chemenway@swmich.edu
HEMENWAY, Robin .... 612-238-4542 242 H
rhemenwa@smumn.edu
HEMINGWAY, Jennie ..... 217-245-3006 139 A
jennie.hemingway@ic.edu
HEMINGWAY, Liana ...... 727-864-8316.. 98 G
heminglo@eckerd.edu
HEMINWAY, Rip .... 360-596-5353 483 E
rheminway@spscc.edu
HEMKER, Judy .... 618-545-3105 141 C
jhemker@kaskaskia.edu
HEMKIN, Sheryl .... 740-427-5093 354 I
hemkins@kenyon.edu
HEMLICK, Lisa, M .... 610-341-5830 383 A
lhemlick@eastern.edu
HEMMER, David .... 906-487-2156 227 D
djhemmer@mtu.edu
HEMMER, Katie .... 212-842-5962 308 A
khemmer@nyaa.edu
HEMMER, Laura .... 314-505-7203 251 D
hemmerl@csl.edu
HEMMER, Susan, G ...... 787-840-2575 508 G
shemmer@psm.edu
HEMMERT, Stewart .... 513-562-6282 347 G
stuart.hemmert@artacademy.edu
HEMMESCH, Michael ..... 320-363-2595 242 G
mhemmesch@csbsju.edu
HEMMESCH, Michael ..... 320-363-2595 234 I
mhemmesch@csbsju.edu
HEMMIG, Bill .... 215-504-8611 379 B
bill.hemmig@bucks.edu
HEMMILA, Deanna .... 906-227-2637 228 E
dhemmila@nmu.edu
HEMMINGS, Okang .... 817-515-6742 445 A
okang.hemmings@tccd.edu
HEMMINGSEN, Jens ..... 614-236-6105 348 I
jhemming@capital.edu
HEMPEN, Laurie .... 319-208-5063 169 I
lhempen@scciowa.edu
HEMPHILL, Brian, O ..... 757-683-3159 468 C
bhemphill@odu.edu
HEMPHILL, Bryon .... 208-467-8673 132 B
bdhemphill@nnu.edu
HEMPSEY, John Paul .... 928-524-7418.. 14 L
paul.hempsey@npc.edu
HEMPSEY, Paul .... 928-524-7418.. 14 L
paul.hempsey@npc.edu
HEMPSTEAD,
Barbara, L .... 212-746-1818 297 D
blhempst@med.cornell.edu
HEMPTON, David, N ..... 617-495-4513 210 B
dhempton@hds.harvard.edu
HEMRIC, Cheryl .... 910-272-3241 337 A
chemric@robeson.edu
HEMRICK, Robert, D ..... 731-425-2636 423 F
dhemrick@jscc.edu
HEMWAY, Joseph .... 718-399-4293 311 A
jhemway@pratt.edu
HENAHAN, David .... 518-587-2100 320 B
david.henahan@esc.edu
HENAO, Felipe .... 516-686-1224 308 H
fhenao@nyit.edu
HENARD, Kevin .... 817-760-5831 436 C
khenard@hillcollege.edu
HENCHY, Dolores .... 201-355-1133 277 A
henchyd@felician.edu
HENCK, Anita .... 626-815-5348.. 26 K
ahenck@apu.edu
HENDEA, Corina .... 508-849-3444 205 E
chendea@annamaria.edu
HENDERSHOT, Debra .... 256-306-2581.... 1 F
debi.hendershot@calhoun.edu
HENDERSHOT,
Stephanie, N .... 412-262-6251 396 E
hendershot@rmu.edu
HENDERSON, Alexis ..... 708-239-4808 150 H
alexis.henderson@trnty.edu
HENDERSON, Allan .... 816-322-0110 250 E
allan.henderson@calvary.edu
HENDERSON, Amy .... 410-287-1910 198 A
ahenderson@cecil.edu
HENDERSON, Andre ..... 412-237-2224 381 C
ahenderson@ccac.edu
HENDERSON, April .... 650-949-7777.. 43 A
HENDERSON, Ashley .... 610-409-3718 400 E
ahenderson@ursinus.edu
HENDERSON, Brad .... 660-596-7250 259 D
rhenderson9@sfccmo.edu
HENDERSON, Brad .... 806-291-3616 457 B
brad.henderson@wbu.edu
HENDERSON, Brian ...... 479-979-1304.. 24 A
bhenderson@ozarks.edu
HENDERSON, Brian ...... 276-656-0313 473 H
bhenderson@patrickhenry.edu
HENDERSON, Brittany ... 206-726-5174 478 F
bhenderson@cornish.edu
HENDERSON, Brittney ... 678-664-0515 127 E
brittney.henderson@westgatech.edu
HENDERSON, Carol, E .. 404-727-3127 118 D
carol.e.henderson@emory.edu
HENDERSON, Carolyn .. 256-551-3226.... 2 E
carolyn.henderson@drakestate.edu
HENDERSON,
Chiquita, A .... 727-816-3205 105 E
henderc@phsc.edu
HENDERSON, Christina 515-271-1501 165 C
christina.henderson@dmu.edu
HENDERSON, Christine 773-371-5450 134 C
chenderson@ctu.edu
HENDERSON,
Clifford, L .... 205-348-6405.... 7 G
mrwilcox@eng.ua.edu
HENDERSON, Darren .... 219-473-4346 154 A
dhenderson@ccsj.edu
HENDERSON, Eddie, W 806-651-2600 447 D
ehenderson@wtamu.edu
HENDERSON, George ... 704-330-4806 333 B
george.henderson@cpcc.edu
HENDERSON, Ginger .... 434-791-5630 463 L
vhenderson@averett.edu
HENDERSON, Glendell .. 316-322-3232 172 B
ghenderson@butlercc.edu
HENDERSON, Howard ... 580-349-1380 367 F
howardh@opsu.edu
HENDERSON, James, B 225-342-6950 191 F
jim.henderson@ulsystem.edu
HENDERSON, Jennifer .. 210-999-7561 451 B
jhender4@trinity.edu
HENDERSON, John .... 951-827-1012.. 70 B
HENDERSON, Keli .... 724-938-5985 394 C
henderson_k@calu.edu
HENDERSON, Ken .... 617-373-4798 217 D
HENDERSON, Kristin, R 205-853-1200.... 2 G
khenderson@jeffersonstate.edu
HENDERSON, Kyle, W .. 740-427-5729 354 I
hendersonk@kenyon.edu
HENDERSON, Lacey ...... 903-886-5108 446 D
lacey.henderson@tamuc.edu
HENDERSON, Laretta .... 217-581-2524 137 C
lhenderson2@eiu.edu
HENDERSON,
Lenneal, J .... 804-524-1162 475 E
lhenderson@vsu.edu
HENDERSON, Lisa .... 440-826-2767 348 C
lhenders@bw.edu
HENDERSON, Mantra .... 662-254-3495 247 C
mlhenderson@mvsu.edu

© COPYRIGHT HIGHER EDUCATION PUBLICATIONS, INC. 2022

HENDERSON, Mark .... 818-833-3333.. 49 G hendersml@elac.edu
HENDERSON, Mark .... 818-947-2600.. 50 B henderme@piercecollege.edu
HENDERSON, Mark .... 412-624-4141 400 A hendersm@pitt.edu
HENDERSON, Michelle . 760-252-2411.. 26 L mhenderson@barstow.edu
HENDERSON, Nancy 319-296-4448 166 E nancy.henderson@hawkeyecollege.edu
HENDERSON, Paul .... 207-602-2302 197 A phenderson@une.edu
HENDERSON, Peter .... 410-455-3263 202 G phenders@umbc.edu
HENDERSON, Sarah ...... 309-457-2190 144 E shenderson@monmouthcollege.edu
HENDERSON, Sean .... 559-442-8295.. 67 A sean.henderson@fresnocitycollege.edu
HENDERSON, Silvester . 510-466-5379.. 57 A shenderson@peralta.edu
HENDERSON, Stacie ...... 334-727-8643.... 7 D shenderson@tuskegee.edu
HENDERSON, Susan ..... 843-383-8264 407 C shenderson@coker.edu
HENDERSON, Taja-Nia . 973-353-5834 281 C tajania@law.rutgers.edu
HENDERSON, Tammy ... 850-484-1766 105 G thenderson@pensacolastate.edu
HENDERSON, Theresa .. 434-949-1089 474 D theresa.henderson@southside.edu
HENDERSON, Tracy ...... 870-886-6741.. 24 B
HENDERSON, Trenton ... 217-228-5432 147 C t.henderson39@quincy.edu
HENDERSON, Trevonda 225-248-1015 186 G
HENDERSON, Triss .... 217-353-2101 146 G thenderson@parkland.edu
HENDERSON, Tyler .... 262-472-1918 496 E
HENDERSON, Virginia .. 601-968-8778 244 C vhenderson@belhaven.edu
HENDERSON-BROWN, Tessa .... 415-239-3530.. 37 C thenders@ccsf.edu
HENDERSON-GASSER, Ellen .... 217-357-3129 134 A ehenderson@sandburg.edu
HENDRICK, Ron .... 806-742-2184 450 C ron.hendrick@ttu.edu
HENDRICK, Sarah .... 661-654-3370.. 30 C shendrick@csub.edu
HENDRICK, Sarah .... 860-932-4096.. 87 C shendrick@qvcc.edu
HENDRICKS, Andrew ..... 317-738-8121 155 A ahendricks@franklincollege.edu
HENDRICKS, Bill .... 214-887-5252 434 G bhendricks@dts.edu
HENDRICKS, Cher .... 970-248-1273.. 78 F chendricks@coloradomesa.edu
HENDRICKS, Constance 334-727-8282.... 7 D chendricks@tuskegee.edu
HENDRICKS, Dawn .... 570-321-4022 388 H henddawn@lycoming.edu
HENDRICKS, Dennis ..... 510-204-0754.. 37 A dhendricks@cdsp.edu
HENDRICKS, Jeff .... 270-852-8977 182 C jhendricks0008@kctcs.edu
HENDRICKS, Jeff .... 336-278-5587 328 H jhendrick4@elon.edu
HENDRICKS, Julie .... 805-893-4581.. 70 E julie.hendricks@dcs.ucsb.edu
HENDRICKS, Lori .... 508-999-8188 211 F lhendricks@umassd.edu
HENDRICKS, Lynn Nicole .... 203-582-8753.. 88 F lynn.hendricks@quinnipiac.edu
HENDRICKS, Mark .... 916-278-1999.. 33 A mark.hendricks@csus.edu
HENDRICKS, Michelle, M .... 570-577-2404 379 A michelle.jones@bucknell.edu
HENDRICKS, Richard ..... 703-233-7469 125 A rhendricks@shorter.edu
HENDRICKS, Richard, J 708-974-5203 144 G hendricksr4@morainevalley.edu
HENDRICKS, Susan ...... 765-455-9288 156 E shendric@iu.edu
HENDRICKS, Taylor Ann .... 641-422-4001 168 E
HENDRICKS, Tom, M .... 248-232-4312 228 H tmhendri@oaklandcc.edu
HENDRICKS, W. Michael .... 813-253-6211 113 B whendricks@ut.edu
HENDRICKSEN, David ... 502-456-6504 184 F dhendricksen@sullivan.edu
HENDRICKSON, Anthony, R .... 402-280-2852 265 J anthonyhendrickson@creighton.edu
HENDRICKSON, Brittney .... 417-447-8656 258 K bhendrickson@sbuniv.edu
HENDRICKSON, Dan ..... 859-622-1000 180 B dan.hendrickson@eku.edu
HENDRICKSON, SJ, Daniel, S .... 402-280-2770 265 J president@creighton.edu
HENDRICKSON, Jennifer .... 678-407-5818 119 B jhendrickson@ggc.edu
HENDRICKSON, Kathy .. 763-424-0881 239 D kathy.hendrickson@nhcc.edu
HENDRICKSON, Ken ..... 936-294-2359 449 E his_keh@shsu.edu
HENDRICKSON, Kristine .... 401-341-2148 404 D hendrick@salve.edu
HENDRICKSON, Loretta 607-962-9228 319 F hendrickson@corning-cc.edu
HENDRICKSON, Nathan 541-880-2273 373 B hendrickson@klamathcc.edu
HENDRICKSON, Philip .. 402-643-7358 265 I philip.hendrickson@cune.edu
HENDRICKSON, Ryan, C .... 217-581-2220 137 C rchendrickson@eiu.edu
HENDRICKSON, Sandy . 425-889-5232 481 A sandy.hendrickson@northwestu.edu
HENDRICKSON, Scott ... 906-487-7307 223 I
HENDRICKSON, Taisha . 617-745-3773 208 F taisha.hendrickson@enc.edu
HENDRICKSON, Vicki, A .... 918-631-2526 371 C vicki-hendrickson@utulsa.edu
HENDRIKSMA, Jane, E . 616-526-6117 221 L jhendrik@calvin.edu
HENDRIX, Andrew .... 803-641-3490 412 B andrewh@usca.edu
HENDRIX, Dean, D .... 210-458-4889 455 B dean.hendrix@utsa.edu
HENDRIX, Grace .... 208-882-1566 131 H ghendrix@nsa.edu
HENDRIX, Jill .... 704-922-6521 334 E hendrix.jill@gaston.edu
HENDRIX, Joan .... 228-267-8643 246 F joan.hendrix@mgccc.edu
HENDRIX, Kristi .... 706-886-6831 126 C khendrix@tfc.edu
HENDRIX, Mary .... 304-876-5107 489 A mhendrix@shepherd.edu
HENDRIX, Mary Helen .. 803-822-3077 409 E hendrixca@midlandstech.edu
HENDRIX, Sherri .... 517-750-1200 230 F shendrix@arbor.edu
HENDRIX, Tommy .... 828-669-8012 331 H tommy.hendrix@montreat.edu
HENDRYX, Julie, A .... 260-422-5561 156 A jahendryx@indianatech.edu
HENEGAR, Kellie .... 618-545-3025 141 C khenegar@kaskaskia.edu
HENEISE, Rachael .... 417-777-5062 250 B rhammon@texascountytech.edu
HENESSEE, Valerie .... 319-385-6290 167 F valerie.henessee@iw.edu
HENFER, Marsha .... 773-442-5412 145 G m-henfer@neiu.edu
HENG, Preston .... 713-221-8606 452 B hengp@uhd.edu
HENG-MOSS, Tiffany ..... 402-472-2797 269 A thengmoss2@unl.edu
HENGGELER, Christina . 678-946-1105 119 C chenggel@highlands.edu
HENGST, Timothy .... 805-493-3555.. 29 E thengst@callutheran.edu
HENICK, Steven, T .... 410-777-2429 197 C sthenick@aacc.edu
HENKE, Brian .... 816-802-3493 253 H bhenke@kcai.edu
HENKE, Corrine .... 208-426-4045 130 F chenke@boisestate.edu
HENKE, Hilary .... 309-779-7700 150 I
HENKEL, Betsy .... 608-363-2662 490 I henkelb@beloit.edu
HENKEL, Mandy .... 608-822-2475 498 H mhenkel@swtc.edu
HENKEL, Taylor .... 650-543-3885.. 52 A taylor.henkel@menlo.edu
HENKELMAN, Amy .... 415-257-1304.. 41 H amy.henkelman@dominican.edu
HENKING, Susan, E ...... 315-364-3311 324 E shenking@wells.edu
HENKLE, Jeannie .... 509-682-6718 484 H jhenkle@wvc.edu
HENLEY, Amy .... 701-777-2135 344 H amy.henley@und.edu
HENLEY, Antonio .... 704-330-1320 329 H ahenley@jcsu.edu
HENLEY, Brian .... 916-278-7766.. 33 A brian.henley@csus.edu
HENLEY, Danielle, Y ..... 757-594-7635 465 A danielle.henley@cnu.edu
HENLEY, Keldon .... 870-245-5405.. 20 H henleyk@obu.edu
HENLEY, Kyle .... 213-740-7000.. 73 C khenley@adm.usc.edu
HENLEY, Marilynn, D ... 602-614-2337.. 10 E
HENLEY, Marsia .... 215-751-8902 381 H mhenley@ccp.edu
HENLEY, Wade .... 301-860-3744 203 D whenley@bowiestate.edu
HENNEBERG, Sylvia ...... 606-783-2650 183 H s.henneberg@moreheadstate.edu
HENNEHA, Jack .... 405-744-7013 367 G jack.henneha@okstate.edu
HENNES, Jake .... 651-641-3502 236 A jhennes001@luthersem.edu
HENNESSEY, Brendan ... 575-562-2424 285 E brendan.hennessey@enmu.edu
HENNESSEY, David .... 617-243-2478 210 G dhennessey@lasell.edu
HENNESSEY-GREENE, Megan .... 508-910-6958 211 F mhennesseygreene@umassd.edu
HENNESSY, Bill .... 701-349-5779 346 G bhennessy@trinitybiblecollege.edu
HENNESSY, Catherine ... 516-463-6820 301 E catherine.hennessy@hofstra.edu
HENNESSY, John, L ...... 650-723-2300.. 66 D
HENNESSY, Kelly .... 609-771-3455 275 J hennessk@tcnj.edu
HENNESSY, Lynne, M ... 203-773-8529.. 85 C lhennessy@albertus.edu
HENNICK-KAMINSKI, Heidi .... 919-962-1205 342 B h2kamins@email.unc.edu
HENNIGAN, Ed .... 570-740-0399 388 G ehennigan@luzerne.edu
HENNIGAN, Maura, M .. 703-784-2105 501 H
HENNIGES, Amy .... 920-465-2380 494 F hennigea@uwgb.edu
HENNING, Amy .... 215-572-2900 378 E henninga@arcadia.edu
HENNING, Anna .... 563-588-8000 165 K ahenning@emmaus.edu
HENNING, Arnold .... 217-206-6600 151 E ahenn6@uis.edu
HENNING, Cynthia .... 307-778-1185 500 D chenning@lccc.wy.edu
HENNING, Kana .... 773-508-3489 142 G kwibben@luc.edu
HENNING, Kent, L .... 515-263-2802 166 C khenning@grandview.edu
HENNING, Mimi .... 251-981-3771.... 5 B mimi.henning@columbiasouthern.edu
HENNING, Patricia .... 505-277-6128 288 C henning@unm.edu
HENNING, Stefanie .... 617-747-2246 206 D careercenter@berklee.edu
HENNING, Stephanie ..... 407-646-2258 106 L shenning@rollins.edu
HENNING, Tiffany .... 503-768-7325 373 D thenning@lclark.edu
HENNING, Toni .... 734-432-5672 226 G thenning@madonna.edu
HENNINGER, Ed .... 541-962-3672 372 H eahenninger@eou.edu
HENNINGSEN, James, D .... 352-873-5835.. 97 L jim.henningsen@cf.edu
HENRICH, William, L .... 210-567-2050 455 E henrich@uthscsa.edu
HENRICKSON, Melanie, L .... 410-777-2237 197 C mlscherer@aacc.edu
HENRIE, Stephen, E ...... 313-577-5929 232 H fj9065@wayne.edu
HENRIKSEN, J.L .... 509-533-7295 478 D jl.henriksen@scc.spokane.edu
HENRIKSEN, Melanie .... 503-552-1702 374 B president@nunm.edu
HENRIKSEN, Smokey .... 406-338-5441 262 D smokeyh@bfcc.edu
HENRIQUES, Richard .... 402-486-2121 268 G richard.henriqes@ucollege.edu
HENRIQUES, Shilo .... 508-588-9100 214 F shenrique@massasoit.mass.edu
HENRIQUEZ, Karen .... 801-832-2502 461 A khenriquez@westminstercollege.edu
HENRY, Amber .... 314-392-2224 255 H amber.henry@mobap.edu
HENRY, Amir .... 336-750-8033 343 E henryaa@wssu.edu
HENRY, Amy .... 404-894-7475 119 D amy.henry@oie.gatech.edu
HENRY, Ashley .... 434-200-7029 464 G ashley.henry@centracollege.edu
HENRY, Barb .... 404-364-8443 123 G bhenry@oglethorpe.edu
HENRY, Barbara, L .... 419-372-4825 348 F bhenry@bgsu.edu
HENRY, Beverly .... 815-753-9283 145 H bwhenry@niu.edu
HENRY, Brian .... 847-543-2264 135 G bhenry1@clcillinois.edu
HENRY, Carolyn, J .... 573-882-3768 260 C henryc@missouri.edu
HENRY, Charles, E .... 713-313-4343 448 D henryce@tsu.edu
HENRY, Christy, S .... 478-757-5219 127 D chenry@wesleyancollege.edu
HENRY, Cynthia .... 850-599-3225 109 E cynthia.henry@famu.edu
HENRY, Deena, H .... 919-209-2017 335 D dhhenry@johnstoncc.edu
HENRY, Donna, P .... 276-328-0122 471 G dph3p@uvawise.edu
HENRY, Donna, P .... 276-328-0122 471 F dph3p@virginia.edu
HENRY, Douglas, V ...... 254-710-4860 430 F douglas_henry@baylor.edu
HENRY, Ed .... 717-338-3000 399 H
HENRY, Etta, A .... 757-683-5889 468 C ehenry@odu.edu
HENRY, Frank, M .... 405-325-6151 370 J fhenry@ou.edu
HENRY, Gary .... 303-735-6624.. 83 M gary.henry@colorado.edu
HENRY, Gary .... 302-831-2394.. 91 A gthenry@udel.edu
HENRY, Geneva .... 202-994-6455.. 92 C genevahenry@gwu.edu
HENRY, Heather .... 518-629-8143 302 A h.henry@hvcc.edu
HENRY, Jamie .... 618-544-8657 139 E henryj@iecc.edu
HENRY, Jennifer .... 314-529-9552 254 D jhenry@maryville.edu
HENRY, Jerlynn .... 505-387-7362 286 B jhenry@navajotech.edu
HENRY, Jerry, W .... 361-698-2178 434 H jhenry12@delmar.edu
HENRY, Jonathan .... 207-621-3304 196 E jonathan.henry@maine.edu
HENRY, Kim .... 712-325-3276 167 G khenry@iwcc.edu
HENRY, Laurie, A .... 410-543-6335 204 A lahenry@salisbury.edu
HENRY, Linda .... 913-360-7500 171 G lhenry@benedictine.edu
HENRY, Marci .... 970-521-6617.. 82 B marci.henry@njc.edu
HENRY, Melody .... 903-434-8148 440 A mhenry@ntcc.edu
HENRY, Mitch .... 334-386-7103.... 5 D mhenry@faulkner.edu
HENRY, Nick .... 404-756-4442 115 E
HENRY, Nick .... 706-272-4435 118 A nhenry@daltonstate.edu
HENRY, Ronald .... 850-599-3560 109 E ronald.henry@famu.edu
HENRY, Sandra .... 334-983-6556.... 7 C shenry@troy.edu
HENRY, Sandy .... 509-527-5986 485 C henrys@whitman.edu
HENRY, Scott .... 859-257-5781 185 D scott.henry@uky.edu
HENRY, Tamara .... 212-870-1205 309 C thenry@nyts.edu
HENRY, Tim .... 817-272-7215 454 B dr.henry@uta.edu
HENRY, Yvette .... 973-877-3084 276 G yhenry@essex.edu
HENRY POWELL, Jonita 704-379-6800.. 93 H

HERNANDEZ, Linda ...... 903-730-4890 437 E
lhernandez@jarvis.edu
HERNANDEZ, Lino .... 787-738-2161 511 A
lino.hernandez@upr.edu
HERNANDEZ, Lisa .... 951-343-4767.. 27 J
lihernandez@calbaptist.edu
HERNANDEZ, Lisa, H ... 412-397-5968 396 E
hernandezl@rmu.edu
HERNANDEZ, Loana ..... 361-664-2981 431 L
lhernandez@coastalbend.edu
HERNANDEZ, Lola .... 806-894-9611 443 A
lhernandez@southplainscollege.edu
HERNANDEZ, Luis .... 915-747-5308 454 E
lehernan@utep.edu
HERNANDEZ, Luz, A ..... 787-890-2681 510 C
luz.hernandez6@upr.edu
HERNANDEZ, Luz, S ..... 787-620-2040 504 B
lhernandez@aupr.edu
HERNANDEZ,
Madelline .... 818-364-7618.. 49 G
hernanm@lamission.edu
HERNANDEZ, Maria ...... 787-758-2525 511 D
maria.hernandez15@upr.edu
HERNANDEZ, Marisa .... 989-837-4337 228 G
toschkof@northwood.edu
HERNANDEZ,
Mary Lou .... 520-494-5200.. 11M
marylou.hernandez@centralaz.edu
HERNANDEZ, Mayra ..... 787-728-1515 512 A
mayra.hernandez@sagrado.edu
HERNANDEZ, Melissa ... 210-458-4140 455 B
melissa.hernandez@utsa.edu
HERNANDEZ, Mina .... 760-795-2121.. 52 G
mihernandez@miracosta.edu
HERNANDEZ, Myrna ..... 330-263-2011 350 H
myhernandez@wooster.edu
HERNANDEZ, Oscar, O . 956-295-3451 448 E
oscar.hernandez@tsc.edu
HERNANDEZ, JR.,
Pablo .... 956-872-2182 443 B
phernan@southtexascollege.edu
HERNANDEZ, JR.,
Pablo .... 956-872-8372 443 B
phernan@southtexascollege.edu
HERNANDEZ, Page .... 281-649-3487 436 D
phernandez@hbu.edu
HERNANDEZ, Rachelle .. 410-516-5028 199 E
rachellehernandez@jhu.edu
HERNANDEZ, Ramon .... 860-832-1619.. 85 F
hernandez@ccsu.edu
HERNANDEZ, Raul .... 787-284-1912 507 D
rhernand@ponce.inter.edu
HERNANDEZ, Raul, R ... 787-723-4481 504 J
raul.hernandez@ceaprc.edu
HERNANDEZ, Rebecca .. 503-554-2147 372 I
rhernandez@georgefox.edu
HERNANDEZ, Richard ... 760-252-2411.. 26 L
rhernandez@barstow.edu
HERNANDEZ, Rita .... 361-698-1277 434 H
rhernandez18@delmar.edu
HERNANDEZ, Roberto ... 713-692-0077 433 B
rhernandez@ciaml.com
HERNANDEZ, Rosa .... 305-821-3333 100 C
rhernandez@fnu.edu
HERNANDEZ, Samuel .... 787-882-2065 508 N
shernandez@unitecpr.edu
HERNANDEZ, Sofia .... 956-296-1445 455 A
sofia.hernandez@utrgv.edu
HERNANDEZ, Sorangel . 818-947-2324.. 50 B
hernansp@lavc.edu
HERNANDEZ, Sylvia ..... 718-997-3460 295 A
sylvia.hernandez@qc.cuny.edu
HERNANDEZ,
Thomas, J .... 585-395-2510 317 B
thernand@brockport.edu
HERNANDEZ, Todd .... 419-267-1310 357 E
thernandez@northweststate.edu
HERNANDEZ, Victor, M 787-894-2828 511 G
victor.hernandez23@upr.edu
HERNANDEZ, Wanda .... 646-565-6000 322 B
wanda.hernandez@touro.edu
HERNANDEZ, Wanda .... 646-565-6000 322 C
wanda.hernandez@touro.edu
HERNANDEZ, West .... 307-754-6103 500 G
west.hernandez@nwc.edu
HERNANDEZ, Yanira ..... 787-279-1912 506 L
yhernandez@bayamon.inter.edu
HERNANDEZ-AGOSTO,
Emmanuel .... 727-712-5407 107 C
hernandez.emmanuel@spcollege.edu
HERNANDEZ CRUZ,
Ramon .... 787-764-0000 511 F
ramon.hernandez19@upr.edu

HERNANDEZ FRIEDMAN,
Yvonne .... 843-349-2303 407 B
yfriedman@coastal.edu
HERNANDEZ HUNTER,
Anna .... 503-838-8000 377 C
HERNANDEZ JARVIS,
Lorna .... 253-879-3207 483 G
lhernandezjarvis@pugetsound.edu
HERNANDEZ MEJIA,
Jesus, O .... 507-933-7687 235 E
jhernan2@gustavus.edu
HERNANDEZ NUNEZ,
Maria, L .... 787-884-3838 504 C
mlhernandez@atenascollege.edu
HERNANDEZ PRIMMER,
Marianly .... 954-776-4476 103 B
HERNANDEZ-STEVENSON,
Britney .... 270-824-8671 182 A
britney.hernandezstevenson@kctcs.edu
HERNANDEZ-SUAREZ,
Jose, I .... 787-993-8881 510 E
jose.hernandez54@upr.edu
HERNDON, Brooke .... 802-831-1078 462 F
bherndon@vermontlaw.edu
HERNDON, Craig .... 804-819-4782 472 E
cherndon@vccs.edu
HERNDON, Doug .... 916-484-8101... 50 J
herndod@arc.losrios.edu
HERNDON,
Kimmetha, D .... 205-726-2198.... 6 E
kherndon@samford.edu
HERNDON, OSB, Linda 913-360-7553 171 G
lherndon@benedictine.edu
HERNDON, Linda, M .... 229-226-1621 126 B
lherndon@thomasu.edu
HERNDON,
Michael (Mike) .... 817-515-1502 445 A
michael.herndon@tccd.edu
HERNDON, Nicole .... 501-760-4300.. 20 E
nicole.herndon@np.edu
HERNDON, Renee .... 205-929-3419.... 2 H
rherndon@lawsonstate.edu
HERNDON, Steven, T ... 937-229-3317 362 C
sherndon1@udayton.edu
HERNE, Jaclyn .... 716-839-8245 297 F
jherne@daemen.edu
HERNESS, Scott .... 973-655-4368 278 C
hernesss@montclair.edu
HERNON, Joseph .... 315-228-4087 296 C
jhernon@colgate.edu
HERNQUIST, Angela ..... 800-462-7845.. 79 F
HEROD, Kevin .... 256-761-8757.... 7 B
krherod@talladega.edu
HEROLD, Dale .... 352-638-9778.. 96 B
dherold@beaconcollege.edu
HEROLD, Irene .... 804-828-0100 472 D
heroldi@vcu.edu
HERON, Keith .... 212-217-4210 299 C
keith_heron@fitnyc.edu
HERONIMUS, Katie .... 507-372-3455 239 B
katie.heronimus@mnwest.edu
HEROY, Darci .... 503-370-6195 377 E
dheroy@willamette.edu
HERR, Beth, J .... 402-280-5769 265 J
bherr@creighton.edu
HERR, Don .... 850-201-6168 112 B
don.herr@tcc.fl.edu
HERR, Duane .... 410-777-2346 197 C
dpherr@aacc.edu
HERR, Robert .... 518-327-6031 310 G
rherr@paulsmiths.edu
HERRELL, Kate .... 636-627-2555 254 B
kherrell@lindenwood.edu
HERREN, Johnna .... 618-985-3741 140 G
johnnaherren@jalc.edu
HERREN, Melissa .... 405-945-3297 368 C
melissa.herren@okstate.edu
HERRERA, Antoinette .... 408-274-7900... 62 F
antoinette.herrera@evc.edu
HERRERA, Cynthia .... 805-652-5944.. 73 H
cynthia_herrera@vcccd.edu
HERRERA, Gilberto .... 787-890-2681 510 C
gilberto.herrera@upr.edu
HERRERA, Gregory .... 212-229-5323 307 E
herrerag@newschool.edu
HERRERA, Holly .... 312-369-6499 136 C
hherrera@colum.edu
HERRERA, Jorge, D ...... 512-404-4829 429 K
jherrera@austinseminary.edu
HERRERA, José .... 319-273-2517 163 G
jose.herrera@uni.edu
HERRERA, Jose, M .... 210-832-3299 452 D
herreraj@uiwtx.edu

HERRERA, Nelly .... 512-463-1808 448 G
netty.herrera@tsus.edu
HERRERA, Rick .... 956-364-5002 448 F
rick.herrera@tstc.edu
HERRERA LINDSTROM,
Cynthia, E .... 312-996-3719 151 D
cynthiar@uic.edu
HERRERO, Veronica ...... 312-553-2500 134 L
vherrero@ccc.edu
HERRICK, Alice .... 207-326-2445 195 G
alice.herrick@mma.edu
HERRICK, George .... 304-367-4883 488 L
george.herrick@fairmontstate.edu
HERRICK, James, S ...... 619-594-0213... 33 E
herrick1@sdsu.edu
HERRICK, Jessica .... 989-328-1228 227 G
jessicah@montcalm.edu
HERRICK, Jim .... 619-594-8236... 33 E
herrick1@sdsu.edu
HERRIDGE, Curt .... 214-768-4197 443 G
herridge@smu.edu
HERRIDGE, Mary .... 254-710-3435 430 F
mary_herridge@baylor.edu
HERRIG, Becky .... 563-588-6321 164 C
becky.herrig@clarke.edu
HERRIN, Andraea .... 803-376-5758 405 D
aherrin@allenuniversity.edu
HERRIN, Brice .... 229-732-5980 114 I
briceherrin@andrewcollege.edu
HERRIN, Bridget .... 619-388-2509.. 61 A
bherrin@sdccd.edu
HERRIN, Carl .... 508-929-8263 213 D
cherrin@worcester.edu
HERRIN, Timothy, D ..... 704-233-8150 344 E
herrin@wingate.edu
HERRIN, William .... 209-946-2650.. 71 E
wherrin@pacific.edu
HERRING, Andrew .... 303-273-3000.. 79 A
aherring@mines.edu
HERRING, Angela .... 252-246-1363 339 A
aherring@wilsoncc.edu
HERRING, April .... 410-386-8444 197 G
aherring@carrollcc.edu
HERRING, Charles .... 410-704-2505 204 B
cherring@towson.edu
HERRING, Jack .... 360-650-4900 485 A
jack.herring@wwu.edu
HERRING, Jeff, C .... 801-585-0928 459 D
jeff.herring@utah.edu
HERRING, Natalie .... 217-206-8660 151 E
nherr4@uis.edu
HERRING, Nathan .... 765-677-2257 157 F
nathan.herring@indwes.edu
HERRING, Paula .... 229-333-2109 127 F
paula.herring@wiregrass.edu
HERRING, Robin .... 717-262-2017 402 D
rherring@wilson.edu
HERRING, Ryan .... 208-562-3227 131 C
ryanherring@cwi.edu
HERRING, Susan .... 215-968-8364 379 B
susan.herring@bucks.edu
HERRINGER,
Gretchen, B .... 413-585-2550 218 D
gherringer@smith.edu
HERRINGTON, Ashley ...... 928-344-7501.. 11 B
ashley.herrington@azwestern.edu
HERRINGTON, James ...... 816-654-7910 253 I
jherrington@kcumb.edu
HERRINGTON, Jere .... 662-562-3214 247 E
recruiting@northwestms.edu
HERRINGTON, Kristine .. 904-620-1672 111 A
k.herrington@unf.edu
HERRINGTON, Marla .... 318-342-5320 193 A
lindsey@ulm.edu
HERRINGTON,
Theophilus .... 713-313-7827 448 D
theo.herrington@tsu.edu
HERRMAN, Kathy .... 785-628-4251 173 E
kaherrman@fhsu.edu
HERRMANN, Anthony ...... 914-323-5406 305 A
anthony.herrmann@mville.edu
HERRMANN, Bryan .... 320-589-6113 243 C
herrmanb@morris.umn.edu
HERRMANN, John, L ...... 740-284-5215 352 I
jherrmann@franciscan.edu
HERRMANN, Mark .... 907-474-7116.. 10 B
mlherrmann@alaska.edu
HERRMANN, Matthew ...... 910-938-6236 333 D
herrmannm@coastalcarolina.edu
HERRMANN, Tracy .... 513-745-5689 362 A
tracy.herrmann@ec.edu
HERROD, Lindsay .... 724-925-4059 401 H
herrodl@westmoreland.edu

HERRON, Alex .... 512-313-3000 432 N
alexandra.herron@concordia.edu
HERRON, Angela, K ...... 719-333-8856 502 C
angela.herron@afacademy.af.edu
HERRON, Crystal .... 314-286-0236 257 H
cherron@ranken.edu
HERRON, Jeffrey .... 732-906-2515 278 A
jherron@middlesexcc.edu
HERRON, John .... 804-752-7244 469 B
johnherron@rmc.edu
HERRON, Kimberly .... 903-785-7661 440 F
kimberlyherron@parisjc.edu
HERRON, Margaret .... 785-248-2360 176 F
margaret.herron@ottawa.edu
HERRON, Martin, T .... 515-964-0601 166 A
herronm@faith.edu
HERRON, Matthew .... 410-777-2707 197 C
mtherron@aacc.edu
HERRON, Robert .... 251-626-3303.... 7 E
rherron@ussa.edu
HERSCH, Lisa .... 301-687-7085 203 F
ldhersch@frostburg.edu
HERSCH, Tonya .... 415-457-8811.. 39 B
thersch@marin.edu
HERSCHEDE, Kathryn, J 610-499-4101 401 I
kjherschede@widener.edu
HERSETH SANDLIN,
Stephanie .... 605-274-4111 413 G
stephanie.hersethsandlin@augie.edu
HERSHBERGER, Bernie . 207-725-3069 194 A
bhershbe@bowdoin.edu
HERSHBERGER, Del .... 620-327-8602 174 B
del.hershberger@hesston.edu
HERSHBERGER,
Michael .... 512-448-8538 441 N
jhershbe@stedwards.edu
HERSHENSON, Jay .... 718-997-5648 295 A
jay.hershenson@qc.cuny.edu
HERSHEY, Christian ...... 276-245-0507 464 A
chershey@bluefield.edu
HERSHEY, J. David .... 717-396-7833 392 Q
dhershey@pcad.edu
HERSHEY, Jean .... 717-947-6150 392 R
jlhershe@pacollege.edu
HERSHKOWITZ, Meyer . 845-207-0330 290 C
HERSHOCK, Martin .... 313-593-5490 231 B
mhershoc@umich.edu
HERSI, Afra .... 410-617-2546 199 G
ahersi@loyola.edu
HERSKER, Alan, L .... 315-267-3445 318 D
herskeal@potsdam.edu
HERSKOWITZ, Isaac .... 212-463-0400 322 C
issac.herskowitz@touro.edu
HERSKOWITZ, Issac .... 212-463-0400 322 C
issac.herskowitz@touro.edu
HERSKOWITZ,
Mordechai .... 732-367-1060 275 B
HERSON, Mendy .... 973-267-9404 279 G
ymmherson@rca.edu
HERSON, Moshe .... 973-267-9404 279 G
rabbiherson@rca.edu
HERT, Darlene .... 406-657-2320 263 H
dhert@msubillings.edu
HERTEL, Elisabeth .... 701-854-8000 346 F
elisabeth.hertel@sittingbull.edu
HERTEL, James .... 210-999-7551 451 B
jhertel@trinity.edu
HERTEL, Jeffrey .... 616-395-7770 224 H
hertelj@hope.edu
HERTEL, Tina, L .... 484-664-3550 390 F
tinahertel@muhlenberg.edu
HERTH, Cam .... 269-927-6284 226 B
cherth@lakemichigancollege.edu
HERTIG, Vicky .... 206-934-6962 482 G
vicky.hertig@seattlecolleges.edu
HERTS, Rolando .... 662-846-4311 245 A
rherts@deltastate.edu
HERTZ, Adam .... 410-386-4043 200 D
ahertz@mcdaniel.edu
HERTZ, David .... 440-775-6671 357 G
david.hertz@oberlin.edu
HERTZ, Elisa .... 646-313-8000 295 C
elisa.hertz@guttman.cuny.edu
HERTZ, Kara .... 509-313-5981 479 E
hertzk@gonzaga.edu
HERTZOG, Matthew .... 773-235-5549 146 D
matthew.hertzog@oakpoint.edu
HERVEY, Brian, T .... 949-824-8941.. 69 C
bhervey@uci.edu
HERWICK, Shawna .... 402-323-3637 268 D
sherwick@southeast.edu
HERZING, Renee .... 608-249-6611 491 H
rherzing@herzing.edu

HICKS, Danielle .... 913-234-0735 172 I
danielle.hicks@cleveland.edu
HICKS, Derrick .... 973-748-9000 275 C
derrick_hicks@bloomfield.edu
HICKS, Diana .... 916-484-8654.. 50 J
hicksd@arc.losrios.edu
HICKS, Elena, D .... 214-768-4115 443 G
ehicks@smu.edu
HICKS, Heather .... 325-794-4401 431 J
heather.hicks@cisco.edu
HICKS, J. David .... 423-652-4782 419 F
jdhicks@king.edu
HICKS, Janet, K .... 570-586-2400 381 A
jhicks@clarkssummitu.edu
HICKS, Jennifer .... 706-295-6371 119 C
jhicks@highlands.edu
HICKS, Jim .... 423-425-4246 426 D
jim-hicks@utc.edu
HICKS, Joel .... 318-677-3100 192 D
hicksj@nsula.edu
HICKS, Juanita .... 404-962-3265 127 B
juanita.hicks@usg.edu
HICKS, Julie .... 252-492-2061 338 D
hicksj@vgcc.edu
HICKS, Kasey .... 717-728-2272 380 D
kaseyhicks@centralpenn.edu
HICKS, Mallory .... 706-754-7724 123 C
mhicks@northgatech.edu
HICKS, Mandy .... 812-258-9510 154 B
mhicks@cariscollege.edu
HICKS, Maryanne .... 925-473-7766.. 40 I
mhicks@losmedanos.edu
HICKS, Megan .... 319-895-4828 164 E
mhicks@cornellcollege.edu
HICKS, Renee, G .... 985-493-2556 192 C
renee.hicks@nicholls.edu
HICKS, Rick .... 714-895-8270.. 38 E
rhick@gwc.cccd.edu
HICKS, Rosemary .... 662-252-8000 248 B
rhicks@rustcollege.edu
HICKS, Samantha .... 843-349-2348 407 B
shicks@coastal.edu
HICKS, Scott .... 434-592-4808 467 E
smhicks@liberty.edu
HICKS, Shawn .... 619-644-7163.. 44 H
shawn.hicks@gcccd.edu
HICKS, Stephanie .... 334-833-4571.... 5 H
stephanie.hicks@hawks.huntingdon.edu
HICKS, Tara .... 206-296-6300 483 B
hickst@seattleu.edu
HICKS, Timothy, J .... 315-859-4790 300 F
thicks@hamilton.edu
HICKS, Travis .... 209-381-6047.. 52 B
HICKS-MCGOWAN,
Jennifer .... 945-938-6104 502 H
jennifer.hicksmcgowan@westpoint.edu
HICSWA, Stefani .... 406-657-2300 263 H
stefani.hicswa@msubillings.edu
HIDALGO, Troy .... 337-475-5748 192 B
shidalgo@mcneese.edu
HIDLEBAUGH, Laura ..... 319-234-5748 166 E
laura.hidlebaugh@hawkeyecollege.edu
HIEBERT, Sandra .... 620-327-8231 174 B
sandra.hiebert@hesston.edu
HIEDEMAN, Ann .... 218-477-2066 239 A
ann.hiedeman@mnstate.edu
HIEL, Edwin .... 619-388-3036.. 60 I
ehiel@sdccd.edu
HIEMENZ, Karen, A ...... 320-308-5017 240 D
khiemenz@sctcc.edu
HIEN, Denise .... 848-445-0749 281 B
denise.hien@smithers.rutgers.edu
HIESTAND, Nathaniel .... 320-308-5009 240 D
nhiestand@sctcc.edu
HIETAPELTO, Amy .... 218-726-7281 243 A
vcaa@d.umn.edu
HIETSCH, Stephen .... 315-229-5896 313 F
shietsch@stlawu.edu
HIETT, Lee Ann .... 713-266-6594 435 C
HIGA, Pat .... 949-582-4585.. 65 C
phiga@saddleback.edu
HIGA-KING, Jennifer ..... 808-845-9110 129 G
higaking@hawaii.edu
HIGASHI, Lori .... 541-485-1780 374 C
lorihigashi@enewhope.edu
HIGASHIDA, Carol .... 805-553-4771.. 73 I
chigashida@vcccd.edu
HIGBEE, Isabelle .... 601-974-1220 246 C
higbeie@millsaps.edu
HIGDON, Abert .... 573-629-3007 253 D
ahigdon@hlg.edu
HIGDON, Beth .... 641-784-5064 166 B
mhigdon@graceland.edu
HIGDON, Charles .... 251-578-1313.... 3 D
chigdon@rstc.edu
HIGDON, Hal, L .... 417-447-2602 257 B
higdonh@otc.edu
HIGDON, Jude .... 802-440-4485 461 B
judehigdon@bennington.edu
HIGDON, Leon .... 334-244-3028.... 4 F
lhigdon@aum.edu
HIGGINBOTHAM,
Amanda .... 610-921-7636 377 F
ahigginbotham@albright.edu
HIGGINBOTHAM,
Carmenita .... 804-828-2787 472 D
artsdean@vcu.edu
HIGGINBOTHAM,
Debra .... 940-397-4120 439 F
debra.higginbotham@msutexas.edu
HIGGINBOTHAM, Karen 212-472-1500 309 B
deanofstudents@nysid.edu
HIGGINBOTHAM, Ray ... 931-393-1737 423 G
rhigginbotham@mscc.edu
HIGGINS, Brandon .... 903-823-3024 445 C
brandon.higgins@texarkanacollege.edu
HIGGINS, Carla .... 419-783-2571 351 J
chiggins@defiance.edu
HIGGINS, Dalton .... 918-335-6865 368 E
dhiggins@okwu.edu
HIGGINS, Dawn .... 603-271-6484 272 C
dhiggins@ccsnh.edu
HIGGINS, Elizabeth .... 207-780-4632 196 J
bhiggins@maine.edu
HIGGINS, Holly .... 207-699-5047 194 G
hhiggins@meca.edu
HIGGINS, Holly .... 800-650-4772.. 48 H
hhiggins@issaonline.edu
HIGGINS, Jenee .... 432-264-5154 436 H
jhiggins@howardcollege.edu
HIGGINS, Joe .... 617-715-2616 215 G
HIGGINS, Kacey .... 325-670-1368 436 B
kacey.higgins@hsutx.edu
HIGGINS, Kerena .... 360-650-2040 485 A
kerena.higgins@wwu.edu
HIGGINS, Mark .... 570-941-4049 400 C
mark.higgins@scranton.edu
HIGGINS, Rhonda .... 440-934-3101 357 I
HIGGINS, Ronnell, A ..... 203-432-9455.. 90 B
ronnell.higgins@yale.edu
HIGGINS, Rosemary ..... 239-590-7021 109 G
rhiggins@fgcu.edu
HIGGINS, Sandra .... 718-260-5700 294 F
shiggins@citytech.cuny.edu
HIGGINS, Terri .... 641-782-1431 170 B
thiggins@swcciowa.edu
HIGGINS, Wendy .... 707-654-1194.. 32 C
whiggins@csum.edu
HIGGINS, Will .... 918-647-1373 365 D
whiggins@carlalbert.edu
HIGGINSON, Jason .... 252-744-2201 340 H
higginsonj@ecu.edu
HIGGS, Fred .... 713-348-5923 441 K
higgs@rice.edu
HIGGS, Jessica .... 309-677-2700 133 H
jhiggs@bradley.edu
HIGGS, John .... 724-480-3558 381 G
john.higgs@ccbc.edu
HIGGS, Michael .... 903-813-2342 429 I
mhiggs@austincollege.edu
HIGGS, Michelle .... 520-452-2633.. 11 O
higgsm@cochise.edu
HIGH, Andrew .... 310-289-5123.. 68 E
andrew.high@wcui.edu
HIGH, Elizabeth .... 910-788-6367 337 G
elizabeth.high@sccnc.edu
HIGH, Jennifer .... 252-399-6397 326 H
jmhigh@barton.edu
HIGH, Lucrecia, A .... 252-451-8387 336 B
lahigh756@nashcc.edu
HIGH, Troy .... 610-790-2849 378 C
troy.high@alvernia.edu
HIGHAM, Pamela, S ..... 814-332-3576 378 A
phigham@allegheny.edu
HIGHERS, Cami .... 918-444-4200 366 G
highersc@nsuok.edu
HIGHFILL, Katie .... 417-447-4820 257 B
highfilk@otc.edu
HIGHFILL, Melanie .... 559-638-0300.. 67 C
melanie.highfill@reedleycollege.edu
HIGHLAND, Jean Anne . 217-234-5329 141 H
jhighland@lakelandcollege.edu
HIGHLANDER, Paula ..... 406-657-2278 263 H
paula.highlander@msubillings.edu
HIGHLEY, Melinda, C .... 606-783-2033 183 H
m.highley@moreheadstate.edu
HIGHSMITH, Rotanetta .. 718-793-2330 309 A
HIGHSMITH, Stephen .... 610-902-1070 379 E
smh395@cabrini.edu
HIGHSMITH, Vanessa ... 818-702-1387.. 56 H
vanessa.highsmith@pepperdine.edu
HIGHTOWER, Jodie ...... 870-612-2016.. 23 B
jodie.hightower@uaccb.edu
HIGHTOWER-MITCHELL,
Damara .... 803-780-1234 413 B
dhmitchell@voorhees.edu
HIGHUM, Mark .... 906-217-4083 221 J
mark.highum@baycollege.edu
HIGINBOTHAM,
Lynn, E .... 212-998-4444 309 D
lynn.higinbotham@nyu.edu
HIGLEY, William, J .... 570-586-2400 381 A
whigley@clarkssummitu.edu
HIJEK, Barbara .... 754-312-2898 103 R
HIJLEH, Mark .... 828-669-8012 331 H
mark.hijleh@montreat.edu
HILBELINK, Amy .... 865-251-1800 422 G
ahilbelink@south.edu
HILBERT, Jim .... 651-290-6423 241 N
jim.hilbert@mitchellhamline.edu
HILBERT, Stephen .... 216-987-3501 351 D
stephen.hilbert@tri-c.edu
HILBURN, Nancy .... 843-574-6564 411 I
nancy.hilburn@tridenttech.edu
HILDEBRAND, Garrick ... 972-780-3600 453 C
garrick.hildebrand@untdallas.edu
HILDEBRAND, Stephen . 740-284-5313 352 I
shildebrand@franciscan.edu
HILDEBRANDT, Kristin .. 414-229-6031 495 B
hildebra@uwm.edu
HILDERBRAND, Carey .. 801-274-3280 460 E
carey.hilderbrand@wgu.edu
HILDRETH, Brandon ...... 818-947-2929.. 50 B
hildrebm@lavc.edu
HILDRETH, SR.,
James E.K .... 615-327-6904 420 D
jhildreth@mmc.edu
HILES, Jason .... 602-639-7500.. 12 L
HILGEDICK, Brianne ..... 660-248-6210 250 H
bhilgedi@centralmethodist.edu
HILGERSOM, Karin .... 775-673-7025 270 I
khilgersom@tmcc.edu
HILKE, David .... 805-493-3960.. 29 E
dhilke@callutheran.edu
HILL, Adriane .... 212-870-1212 309 C
ahill@nyts.edu
HILL, Amanda .... 215-545-6400 391 D
amhill@peirce.edu
HILL, Amber .... 928-524-7381.. 14 L
amber.hill@npc.edu
HILL, Andrew .... 906-227-2531 228 E
anhill@nmu.edu
HILL, Angela .... 409-880-8188 449 A
ajhill@lit.edu
HILL, Araceli .... 214-954-3610 446 D
araceli.hill@tamuc.edu
HILL, Ben .... 319-384-3400 163 F
benjamin-hill-1@uiowa.edu
HILL, Benjamin .... 540-831-2311 468 E
bhill59@radford.edu
HILL, Benjamin .... 920-929-2136 498 C
bhill@morainepark.edu
HILL, Bernard .... 706-585-0028 124 C
bernard.hill@point.edu
HILL, Beth .... 520-515-3613.. 11 O
hillb@cochise.edu
HILL, Beverly .... 479-619-2679.. 20 G
bhill3@nwacc.edu
HILL, Brad .... 252-618-6640 334 B
hillb@edgecombe.edu
HILL, Brandon .... 765-677-2200 157 F
brandon.hill@indwes.edu
HILL, Brandon .... 580-559-5208 365 J
bhill@ecok.edu
HILL, Brian, W .... 540-231-5107 466 E
bhill@vcom.vt.edu
HILL, Calvin, R .... 413-748-3552 218 E
chill@springfield.edu
HILL, Carol .... 580-349-1566 367 F
carol.hill@opsu.edu
HILL, Cassandra .... 815-753-0380 145 H
chill14@niu.edu
HILL, Charles .... 920-424-3190 495 C
hill@uwosh.edu
HILL, Cheryl .... 434-223-6219 466 K
chill@hsc.edu
HILL, Christina .... 704-669-4545 333 C
bellch@clevelandcc.edu
HILL, Christopher, D .... 404-413-2572 120 C
chill@gsu.edu
HILL, Christopher, J ..... 412-392-4707 395 H
chill@pointpark.edu
HILL, Craig, C .... 214-768-2534 443 G
craighill@smu.edu
HILL, Crystal .... 252-985-5202 339 B
chill@ncwc.edu
HILL, Curtis .... 435-865-8621 459 E
hillc@suu.edu
HILL, David .... 973-290-4345 282 G
dhill@steu.edu
HILL, David, C .... 717-245-4400 502 E
david.c.hill10.mil@mail.mil
HILL, David, L .... 434-982-4728 471 F
dh2t@virginia.edu
HILL, Deana .... 570-484-2014 393 E
dhill@lockhaven.edu
HILL, Diane .... 973-353-1634 281 C
dianeh@newark.rutgers.edu
HILL, Dometrius .... 281-425-6849 438 B
dhill@lee.edu
HILL, Don, H .... 913-684-5401 502 D
HILL, Doree .... 252-222-6282 332 G
hilld@carteret.edu
HILL, Doris .... 651-793-1852 238 B
doris.hill@metrostate.edu
HILL, Edward .... 314-340-3352 253 E
hille@hssu.edu
HILL, Eileen .... 831-479-6458.. 27 G
eihill@cabrillo.edu
HILL, Emily .... 319-335-1684 163 F
emily-hill@uiowa.edu
HILL, Erin .... 916-577-2200.. 76 C
ehill@jessup.edu
HILL, G. Richard .... 801-626-7313 460 B
grhill@weber.edu
HILL, Gary .... 573-681-5496 254 A
hillg@lincolnu.edu
HILL, Heather .... 704-330-6730 333 B
heather.hill@cpcc.edu
HILL, Holly, L .... 904-826-8636.. 99 D
hhill@flagler.edu
HILL, Jack .... 870-633-4480.. 19 E
jhill@eacc.edu
HILL, Jacqueline .... 305-623-4281 100 B
jacqueline.hill@fmuniv.edu
HILL, Jamie .... 309-796-5284 133 D
hillj@bhc.edu
HILL, Janeen .... 714-628-7223.. 36 D
jhill@chapman.edu
HILL, Janeen, M .... 714-628-7223.. 36 D
jhill@chapman.edu
HILL, Jeff .... 608-249-6611 491 H
HILL, Jerell .... 626-529-8500.. 55 E
HILL, Jody .... 901-334-5809 420 E
jhill@memphisseminary.edu
HILL, John .... 310-243-2056.. 31 B
johill@csudh.edu
HILL, Jolia .... 734-487-2421 223 F
jhill105@emich.edu
HILL, Jonathan, H .... 212-346-1810 310 F
HILL, Joyce .... 575-439-3879 286 H
joyhill@nmsu.edu
HILL, Kameshia .... 601-979-1325 245 G
kameshia.m.hill@jsums.edu
HILL, Karen .... 310-665-6910.. 55 B
khill@otis.edu
HILL, Kari, M .... 608-342-1555 495 E
hillkar@uwplatt.edu
HILL, Katherine .... 303-352-6938.. 80 D
katy.hill@ccd.edu
HILL, Katrina .... 937-298-3399 354 J
katrina.hill@kc.edu
HILL, Kelli .... 309-268-8121 138 F
kelli.hill@heartland.edu
HILL, Ken .... 207-801-5630 194 C
khill@coa.edu
HILL, Kevin .... 423-636-7300 425 E
khill@tusculum.edu
HILL, Kimberly .... 252-527-6223 335 E
krhill01@lenoircc.edu
HILL, Laura, A .... 559-325-5200.. 66 H
laura.hill@cloviscollege.edu
HILL, Leah .... 252-985-5293 339 B
lhill@ncwc.edu
HILL, Leia .... 601-484-8786 246 B
lhill@meridiancc.edu
HILL, Lena .... 540-458-8418 476 D
lmhill@wlu.edu
HILL, Leroy .... 619-201-8959.. 65 F
leroy.hill@socalsem.edu

HILL, Lisa .... 410-337-6000 198 G
lisa.hill@goucher.edu
HILL, Lisa .... 252-940-6417 332 A
lisa.hill@beaufortccc.edu
HILL, Malcolm .... 207-786-6066 193 D
mhill@bates.edu
HILL, Mark .... 651-641-8223 235 A
hill@csp.edu
HILL, Mark, J .... 315-470-6670 319 A
mjhill@esf.edu
HILL, Mary, M .... 989-774-3331 221 M
hill1mm@cmich.edu
HILL, Mathew, B ...... 651-631-5362 243 E
mbhill@unwsp.edu
HILL, Melinda .... 910-898-9634 336 A
hillm@montgomery.edu
HILL, Melissa .... 509-865-0411 480 B
hill_m@heritage.edu
HILL, Michael .... 610-328-8067 398 B
mhill1@swarthmore.edu
HILL, Michael, E ...... 919-530-5214 341 D
mhill73@nccu.edu
HILL, Michelle, D .... 757-823-8135 468 B
mdhill@nsu.edu
HILL, Mike .... 704-687-1054 342 C
athleticdirector@uncc.edu
HILL, Miriam .... 651-638-6415 233 J
m-hill@bethel.edu
HILL, Nicholas .... 803-535-5689 406 E
nhill@claflin.edu
HILL, Nicole .... 717-477-1371 394 D
nrhill@ship.edu
HILL, Nicole, R .... 717-477-1373 394 D
nrhill@ship.edu
HILL, Penny .... 518-629-7294 302 A
p.hill@hvcc.edu
HILL, Peter .... 774-392-1646 220 B
phill@whoi.edu
HILL, Redgina .... 574-284-4834 160 F
rhill@saintmarys.edu
HILL, Reggie, B ...... 314-516-6471 260 E
reggiehill@umsl.edu
HILL, Reinhold, R ...... 812-348-7226 157 B
reihill@iupuc.edu
HILL, Robert, A .... 617-353-3560 207 C
rahill@bu.edu
HILL, Rory .... 216-397-3015 353 O
rhill@jcu.edu
HILL, Salena .... 406-243-5776 263 D
salena1.hill@umontana.edu
HILL, Samantha ...... 850-484-4680 105 G
smhill@pensacolastate.edu
HILL, Sandra, B ...... 973-720-2565 283 I
hills21@wpunj.edu
HILL, Sarah .... 217-234-5440 141 H
shill@lakelandcollege.edu
HILL, Sean .... 618-468-6000 142 B
shill@lc.edu
HILL, Shane .... 806-894-9611 443 A
shill@southplainscollege.edu
HILL, Shannon .... 805-546-3279.. 41 A
shannon_hill@cuesta.edu
HILL, Sharon .... 770-229-3454 125 F
sharon.hill@sctech.edu
HILL, Sherri .... 203-837-8774.. 86 A
hills@wcsu.edu
HILL, Soni .... 513-569-4215 350 C
soni.hill@cincinnatistate.edu
HILL, Stacy .... 509-777-4657 485 D
shill@whitworth.edu
HILL, Stephanie ...... 937-376-6591 349 H
shill2@centralstate.edu
HILL, Stephanie ...... 817-515-5210 445 A
stephanie.hill@tccd.edu
HILL, Stephen, E ...... 801-422-8153 458 A
steve_hill@byu.edu
HILL, Sydney .... 870-460-1453.. 22 E
hillsg@uamont.edu
HILL, Tami .... 541-463-3655 373 C
hilltk@lanecc.edu
HILL, Tim .... 541-440-4707 376 F
tim.hill@umpqua.edu
HILL, Tina .... 717-262-2012 402 D
tina.hill@wilson.edu
HILL, Toni, E .... 301-546-0688 201 D
hill@pgcc.edu
HILL, Tonya, L .... 217-443-8772 136 E
t.hill@dacc.edu
HILL, Travis, R .... 315-859-4023 300 F
thill@hamilton.edu
HILL, Trey .... 918-293-4895 368 B
trey.hill@okstate.edu

HILL, W. Timothy ..... 801-422-7011 458 A
7714@byu.edu
HILL, Walter, A .... 334-727-8157.... 7 D
hillwa@tuskegee.edu
HILL, William .... 713-646-1764 443 C
whill@synermarkprop.com
HILL, II, William, L ...... 215-965-4022 390 C
whill@moore.edu
HILL, Willy .... 205-652-3471.... 9 B
whill@uwa.edu
HILL, Wynn, N .... 208-496-9200 130 G
hillw@byui.edu
HILL, Yasmine .... 334-699-2266.... 1 B
yhill@acom.edu
HILL, Z. JoAnna ...... 303-292-0015.. 80 F
zhill@denvercollegeofnursing.edu
HILL-CHEATOM, Petrina 716-851-1120 299 A
cheatom@ecc.edu
HILL-CLARKE, Kandi ...... 901-678-5495 426 A
kyhill@memphis.edu
HILL-FARON, Jennifer ...... 850-484-4443 105 G
jhillfaron@pensacolastate.edu
HILL-HANNA, Shantey 718-940-5759 313 C
shill4@sjcny.edu
HILL-HANNA, Shantey . 631-687-1445 313 C
shill4@sjcny.edu
HILL-STANFORD, Holly . 417-328-1725 258 K
hhill@sbuniv.edu
HILLA, Jose .... 707-664-2880.. 34 C
HILLARD, Cecilia, J ...... 414-955-8493 492 C
chillard@mcw.edu
HILLEBRAND, Kayli ...... 714-556-3610.. 73 G
kayli.hillebrand@vanguard.edu
HILLENBRAND, Hilary . 812-488-2163 161 E
hm38@evansville.edu
HILLER, Renee .... 906-487-2800 227 D
rlhiller@mtu.edu
HILLER, Renee .... 320-308-3203 240 C
renee.hiller@stcloudstate.edu
HILLER-FREUND,
Darby, L .... 937-327-7930 364 C
hillerd@wittenberg.edu
HILLERMAN, Donnie ...... 660-359-3948 256 F
dhillerman@mail.ncmissouri.edu
HILLERY, Barbara ...... 516-876-3257 318 A
hilleryb@oldwestbury.edu
HILLESLAND, Michelle . 253-589-5586 478 A
michelle.hillesland@cptc.edu
HILLGROVE, Jennifer . 303-751-8700.. 78 A
hillgrove@belrea.edu
HILLIARD, Aaron ...... 269-488-4409 225 C
ahilliard@kvcc.edu
HILLIARD, Eva .... 510-879-9200.. 60 C
ehilliard@samuelmerritt.edu
HILLIARD, Zach .... 724-357-7942 393 G
zhilliar@iup.edu
HILLIKER, Robert ...... 856-256-4988 280 H
hilliker@rowan.edu
HILLIKER, Tommy ...... 866-931-4300 257 J
tommy.hilliker@rockbridge.edu
HILLIS, Ed .... 512-863-1066 444 F
hillise@southwestern.edu
HILLIS, Greg .... 575-439-3624 286 H
ghillis@nmsu.edu
HILLIS, Michael .... 805-493-3422.. 29 E
mhillis@callutheran.edu
HILLMAN, George ...... 214-887-5261 434 G
ghillman@dts.edu
HILLMAN, Kenna ...... 562-938-4016.. 48 K
khillman@lbcc.edu
HILLMAN, Luce .... 802-656-1079 462 D
luce.hillman@uvm.edu
HILLS, Fred .... 254-299-8602 438 G
fhills@mclennan.edu
HILLS, Megan .... 319-385-6391 167 F
megan.hills@iw.edu
HILLS, Warren, L ...... 269-387-3895 232 J
warren.l.hills@wmich.edu
HILLS, Wilfredo .... 787-743-7979 509 D
wihill@suagm.edu
HILLYARD, Harold ...... 361-354-2346 431 L
hhillyard@coastalbend.edu
HILLYER, Rebecca ...... 503-399-8677 372 A
rebecca.hillyer@chemeketa.edu
HILMEY, David .... 716-375-2603 312 F
dhilmey@sbu.edu
HILT, Michael .... 402-554-2232 269 C
mhilt@unomaha.edu
HILTNER, Erin .... 970-248-1908.. 78 F
ehiltner@coloradomesa.edu
HILTON, Adriel .... 504-286-5000 191 A
ahilton@suno.edu

HILTON, Adriel .... 724-830-1076 397 F
ahilton@setonhill.edu
HILTON, Don .... 254-267-7007 441 D
dhilton@rangercollege.edu
HILTON, III, Earl, M ...... 336-334-7686 341 C
hiltone@ncat.edu
HILTON, James, L ...... 734-764-9358 231 A
hilton@umich.edu
HILTON, Stacey .... 928-717-7775.. 17 B
stacey.hilton@yc.edu
HILTON, Warren .... 315-498-2214 310 C
HILTON-MORROW,
Wendy .... 309-794-7313 132 H
wendyhilton-morrow@augustana.edu
HILTS, Deb, B .... 607-431-4171 300 G
hiltsd@hartwick.edu
HILVO, Wendy, A ...... 920-923-8122 492 D
wahilvo37@marianuniversity.edu
HILYER, Billy, D .... 334-386-7414.... 5 D
bhilyer@faulkner.edu
HIMBER, Richard ...... 985-549-5322 192 E
richard.himber@selu.edu
HIMELFARB, Igor ...... 510-250-6113.. 48 G
ihimelfarb@lincolnuca.edu
HIMES, Christine ...... 312-567-3933 139 H
chimes@iit.edu
HIMMEL, Joy .... 757-683-4401 468 C
jhimmel@odu.edu
HIMMELBERGER,
Stacey, J .... 315-859-4416 300 F
shimmelb@hamilton.edu
HIMMELREICH, Ellen . 607-735-1190 298 G
ehimmelreich@elmira.edu
HIMMELSTEIN, Amos .... 323-259-1347.. 54 I
himmelstein@oxy.edu
HIMON, Kemia .... 410-857-2234 200 D
khimon@mcdaniel.edu
HIMSEL, Christian, R ...... 262-243-5700 491 E
christian.himsel@cuw.edu
HINCAPIE, Nelson ...... 305-237-3240 104 E
nhincapi@mdc.edu
HINCKLEY, R. Shane .... 979-458-1729 446 B
shane.hinckley@tamu.edu
HIND, Jonathan, T ...... 315-859-4116 300 F
jhind@hamilton.edu
HINDE, Liz .... 303-615-1444.. 81 L
ehinde@msudenver.edu
HINDE, RJ .... 865-974-0684 426 C
rhinde@utk.edu
HINDS, Thomas .... 412-924-1369 395 G
thinds@pts.edu
HINDS-BRUSH,
Kimberly .... 301-687-4121 203 F
kmhindsbrush@frostburg.edu
HINE, Cheryl .... 260-481-6129 159 H
hinec@pfw.edu
HINE, Christopher ...... 661-336-5040.. 47 A
christopher.hine@kccd.edu
HINE, Mark, L .... 434-592-3240 467 E
mhine@liberty.edu
HINEBAUGH, Kearstin . 301-387-3000 198 F
kearstin.hinebaugh@garrettcollege.edu
HINEMAN, Sheri .... 712-274-5335 168 C
hineman@morningside.edu
HINERMAN, Nate ...... 415-442-7000.. 44 B
HINES, CharMaine ...... 313-469-2720 232 B
chines1@wcccd.edu
HINES, Cory .... 325-649-8000 437 A
president@hputx.edu
HINES, Craig .... 312-662-4111 132 D
chines@adler.edu
HINES, Domonique ...... 229-500-2909 114 F
domonique.hines@asurams.edu
HINES, Florence .... 315-229-5226 313 F
fhines@stlawu.edu
HINES, Jacquelyn ...... 313-831-5200 223 G
jhines@etseminary.edu
HINES, Joseph .... 908-497-4317 283 E
joseph.hines@ucc.edu
HINES, Kenneth, D ...... 919-658-7755 340 E
dhines@umo.edu
HINES, Nancy .... 509-777-4638 485 D
nhines@whitworth.edu
HINES, Nancy, A .... 563-333-6377 169 D
hinesnancya@sau.edu
HINES, Rakesha .... 334-229-4357.... 4 B
rhines@alasu.edu
HINES, Rakesia .... 334-229-6810.... 4 B
rhines@alasu.edu
HINES, Ruth .... 857-701-1645 215 E
rhines@rcc.mass.edu
HINES, Scott .... 650-433-3855.. 55 K
shines@paloaltou.edu

HINES, Shanna .... 410-669-9200 200 B
shines@mica.edu
HINES, Susan .... 434-395-2921 467 F
hinessr@longwood.edu
HINES, Terri .... 719-598-0200.. 80 B
HINES, Wendy .... 828-565-4069 335 A
whines@haywood.edu
HINES-GAITHER,
Krishauna .... 213-477-2511.. 52 J
khinesgaither@msmu.edu
HINES-GAITHER,
Krishauna .... 336-316-2473 329 C
hinesgaitherkl@guilford.edu
HINEY, Delaine, S ...... 712-362-0428 166 H
dhiney@iowalakes.edu
HINGA, Beth, D .... 308-865-8541 268 J
hingabd@unk.edu
HINGELBERG, Julie ...... 313-664-7494 222 C
julieh@collegeforcreativestudies.edu
HINGORANI, Kamal ...... 334-229-4123.... 4 B
khingorani@alasu.edu
HINIKER, Justin .... 719-549-2195.. 79 G
justin.hiniker@csupueblo.edu
HINKEL, Nate .... 501-686-2951.. 21 G
nhinkel@uasys.edu
HINKLE, Adrian .... 405-789-7661 369 H
adrian.hinkle@swcu.edu
HINKLE, Christina ...... 949-582-4605.. 65 C
chinkle@saddleback.edu
HINKLE, Henry .... 913-288-7330 174 H
hhinkle@kckcc.edu
HINKLE, Jason .... 661-362-3420.. 38 E
jason.hinkle@canyons.edu
HINKLE, Lance .... 405-744-5237 367 G
lance.hinkle@okstate.edu
HINKLE, Sandy, L ...... 573-651-2250 258 J
shinkle@semo.edu
HINKLE, Sara .... 610-436-3511 394 F
shinkle@wcupa.edu
HINKLEY, Richard ...... 434-592-3077 467 E
rdhinkle@liberty.edu
HINKS, David .... 919-515-6500 341 E
dhinks@ncsu.edu
HINKSON, Avis .... 909-621-8017.. 57 K
avis.hinkson@pomona.edu
HINOJOSA, Felix .... 915-831-2623 435 B
fhinojo3@epcc.edu
HINOJOSA, Jason ...... 801-585-2677 459 D
jason.hinojosa@utah.edu
HINOJOSA, Joanne ...... 909-384-8595.. 60 F
jhinojosa@sbccd.cc.ca.us
HINOJOSA, Maggie ...... 956-665-2321 455 A
maggie.hinojosa@utrgv.edu
HINOJOSA-SEGURA,
Veronica .... 512-499-4271 454 A
vhinojosasegura@utsystem.edu
HINRICHSEN,
Jacqueline .... 402-826-2161 266 A
jackie.hinrichsen@doane.edu
HINSHAW, Dana .... 620-665-3322 174 D
hinshawd@hutchcc.edu
HINSHAW, Garrett, D .... 828-327-7000 332 H
ghinshaw@cvcc.edu
HINSHAW, Jeffrey ...... 310-660-3160.. 41 J
jhinshaw@elcamino.edu
HINSHAW, Lynn .... 828-898-3473 330 A
hinshaw@lmc.edu
HINSHAW, Melissa, M . 832-813-6535 438 E
melissa.m.hinshaw@lonestar.edu
HINSHAW, Stephanie ...... 800-280-0307 153 B
stephanie.hinshaw@ace.edu
HINSHAW, Steven ...... 937-393-3431 360 G
shinshaw@sscc.edu
HINSON, Brett .... 615-966-5642 420 B
brett.hinson@lipscomb.edu
HINSON, Cheyenne ...... 912-583-3297 116 D
chinson@bpc.edu
HINSON, David .... 336-917-5460 339 H
david.hinson@salem.edu
HINSON, Michael ...... 704-991-0300 338 A
mhinson4851@stanly.edu
HINSON, Natalie .... 910-788-6361 337 D
natalie.hinson@sccvnc.edu
HINTERBERGER, Karl .... 716-286-8323 309 F
khinterberger@niagara.edu
HINTERSTOISSER,
Tanja .... 802-651-5896 461 C
thinterstoisser@champlain.edu
HINTON, Aaron .... 704-406-4101 328 I
ahinton2@gardner-webb.edu
HINTON, Armenta ...... 717-736-4102 385 E
aehinton@hacc.edu
HINTON, Audra .... 501-374-6305.. 21 B
audra.hinton@shortercollege.edu

HINTON, Conner 504-816-8072 190 D chinton@nobts.edu
HINTON, Gregory, T 585-292-2190 306 K ghinton2@monroecc.edu
HINTON, Jeff 903-223-3005 447 C jeff.hinton@tamut.edu
HINTON, Mary, D 540-362-6321 467 A presoffc@hollins.edu
HINTON, Richard 406-447-4563 262 E rhinton@carroll.edu
HINTON, Samuel 803-793-5154 408 A hintons@denmarktech.edu
HINTON, Toby, R 770-534-6257 116 C thinton@brenau.edu
HINTON, Wendy 570-208-5900 386 G wendyhinton@kings.edu
HINTON-RIVERA, Jake 775-327-2116 270 G jake.hinton-rivera@gbcnv.edu
HINTZ, Alex 612-343-4400 241 O ajhintz@northcentral.edu
HINTZ, Carol 816-235-1621 260 D hintzc@umkc.edu
HINTZ, Debra 269-471-6124 220 H cio@andrews.edu
HINTZ, Sharon 908-835-2356 283 H hintz@warren.edu
HINTZE, Nate 207-725-4244 194 A nhintze@bowdoin.edu
HINZE, Jodey 281-649-3130 436 D jhinze@hbu.edu
HIONIDES, David 303-762-6980 80 G david.hionides@denverseminary.edu
HIOTT, Henry 843-321-1502 409 C hhiott@limestone.edu
HIPES, Barrett 212-799-5000 303 B
HIPOLITO, Melvin 808-984-3245 130 B mh2350@hawaii.edu
HIPOLITO, Veronica 480-732-7309 13 B veronica.hipolito@cgc.edu
HIPP, Joye, G 803-786-3178 407 E joyehipp@columbiasc.edu
HIPP, Julie 630-844-6503 133 A jhipp@aurora.edu
HIPPE, Adam 651-638-6941 233 J adam-hippe@bethel.edu
HIPPEN, Kristi 309-457-2327 144 E khippen@monmouthcollege.edu
HIPPISLEY, Andrew 316-978-6659 178 B andrew.hippisley@wichita.edu
HIPPS, Kathy 423-636-7320 425 E khipps@tusculum.edu
HIPPS, OSB, Norman 724-805-2322 397 D
HIRATA, Heather 808-932-7369 129 A hiratah@hawaii.edu
HIRDLER, Joy 707-965-6699 55 H jhirdler@puc.edu
HIRNING, Bernell 701-774-4231 346 C bernell.hirning@willistonstate.edu
HIRSCH, Alex 907-474-7931 10 B ahirsch@alaska.edu
HIRSCH, Andy 610-328-8534 398 B ahirsch1@swarthmore.edu
HIRSCH, Debra 517-371-5140 232 K hirschd@cooley.edu
HIRSCH, Jan 949-824-0505 69 C jdhirsch@uci.edu
HIRSCH, Michael 512-505-3125 437 B mlhirsch@htu.edu
HIRSCH, Sarah 949-258-7091 38 F shirsch3@occ.cccd.edu
HIRSCHFELD, Adam 614-251-4234 358 B hirschfa@ohiodominican.edu
HIRSCHFELD, Chloe 970-542-3126 81 M chloe.hirschfeld@morgancc.edu
HIRSCHHORN, Charles 310-665-6800 55 B
HIRSCHLER, Christopher 440-366-7171 355 B
HIRSCHLER, Dave 740-474-8896 358 A dhirschler@ohiochristian.edu
HIRSHEY, Jamie 816-654-7000 253 I
HIRSHMAN, Elliot 443-334-2125 202 C
HIRST, Martha, K 718-817-3120 300 A mhirst1@fordham.edu
HIRT, Samuel 540-261-8400 470 D samuel.hirt@svu.edu
HIRT, Sonia, A 706-542-8113 126 F sonia.hirt@uga.edu
HIRTLE, Christopher 413-572-5455 213 C chris@westfield.ma.edu
HISASHIMA, Karlee, C 808-956-8687 129 B karlee@hawaii.edu
HISCANO, Lisa 908-965-2358 283 E hiscano@ucc.edu
HISE, Jeremy 580-628-6200 366 J jeremy.hise@noc.edu
HISER, Larry, R 740-376-4665 355 E larry.hiser@marietta.edu
HISEY, Richard, M 617-747-2018 206 D rhisey@berklee.edu
HISLE, W. Lee 860-439-2650 87 F wlhis@conncoll.edu
HISLOP, Charlotte 619-298-1829 65 J
HISSONG, Wesley 315-786-6517 302 I whissong@sunyjefferson.edu
HITCHCOCK, Harold 937-778-7979 352 D
HITCHCOCK, Jayme 478-757-5146 127 D jhitchcock@wesleyancollege.edu
HITCHCOCK, Kristin 760-757-2121 52 G khitchcock@miracosta.edu
HITCHCOCK, Marina 570-561-1818 397 B
HITCHCOCK, Patrick 508-831-5577 220 C phitchcock@wpi.edu
HITCHCOCK, Richard 907-796-6493 10 C rhitchc1@alaska.edu
HITCHELL, Dan 860-297-4224 88 I dan.hitchell@trincoll.edu
HITCHMAN, Evan 315-268-4300 295 E ehitchma@clarkson.edu
HITE, Lisa 618-252-5400 149 E lisa.hite@sic.edu
HITE, Robert 415-458-3726 41 H
HITE, Stu 620-235-4624 176 H skhite@pittstate.edu
HITECHEW, Chris 423-354-2509 424 B clhitechew@northeaststate.edu
HITES, Michael, H 214-768-3805 443 G hites@smu.edu
HITT, Bridgett 601-635-6406 245 B bhitt@eccc.edu
HITT, Jennifer 508-793-7318 207 F jhitt@clarku.edu
HITT, Richard, J 863-784-7036 108 D richard.hitt@southflorida.edu
HITT-MAYO, Jennifer 901-321-3465 417 G jhitt@cbu.edu
HITTENMILLER, David 847-635-2619 146 E dhittenmiller@oakton.edu
HITTLE, Ann 509-452-5100 481 E ahittle@pnwu.edu
HITZEMAN, Adam 312-922-1884 143 D ahitzeman@maccormac.edu
HITZEMAN, Katrina 503-253-3443 374 E katrina.hitzeman@ocom.edu
HIVELY, Karla, R 304-457-6317 485 F hivelykr@ab.edu
HIX, Patty 803-754-4100 407 F
HIXON, Courtney 270-809-2146 184 A chixon@murraystate.edu
HIXON, Sharon 706-272-4594 118 A shixon@daltonstate.edu
HIXSON, Mindi 937-767-1286 347 E
HIYANE-BROWN, Kathi 360-383-3330 485 B presoffice@whatcom.edu
HJALTALIN, Lisa 509-434-5210 478 E lisa.hjaltalin@ccs.spokane.edu
HJALTALIN, Lisa 509-434-5275 478 C lisa.hjaltalin@ccs.spokane.edu
HJELLUM, Wilma 531-622-2723 266 G whjellum@mccneb.edu
HJERPE, Karen 724-938-4167 394 C hjerpe@calu.edu
HLADIS, Jirka 303-245-4702 81 N jirka@naropa.edu
HLAVACEK, Chris 919-761-2100 340 B chlavacek@sebts.edu
HLAVENKA, Lawrence 201-689-7057 274 I lhlavenka@bergen.edu
HLAVIN, Karen 847-543-2384 135 G adr016@clcillinois.edu
HLEBASKO, Julie 951-571-6332 59 B julie.hlebasko@mvc.edu
HLEBOWITSH, Peter 205-348-6052 7 G peter.hleb@ua.edu
HLINAK, Matthew, J 773-612-5797 137 A mhlinak@dom.edu
HLUBB, Emma 931-424-7366 426 F ehlubb@utsouthern.edu
HLUBB, James, R 931-424-7379 426 F jhlubb@utsouthern.edu
HLUCH, Dale, A 330-325-6191 357 D dhluch@neomed.edu
HLYNOSKY, Bob 406-243-5595 263 D robert.hlynosky@umontana.edu
HO, Co 714-992-7021 54 D cho@fullcoll.edu
HO, Henry 615-353-3231 424 A henry.ho@nscc.edu
HO, Katy, W 971-722-4005 375 C kho@pcc.edu
HO, Nan 925-424-1182 36 A nho@laspositascollege.edu
HO, Sam 408-223-6798 62 E sam.ho@sjeccd.edu
HO, Sandra 603-427-7600 271 J
HO, Shuk-Mei 501-686-7000 22 D shukmeiho@uams.edu
HO-A, Carla 303-492-3224 83 M carla.ho-a@colorado.edu
HOAG, David, A 863-638-7209 113 D david.hoag@warner.edu
HOAG, Jamie, D 508-793-2011 208 A jhoag@holycross.edu
HOAG, William 857-701-1380 215 E whoag@rcc.mass.edu
HOAGLAND, Amy 423-510-9675 421 D
HOAGLAND, Andrea 517-483-1077 226 D hoaglana@lcc.edu
HOAGLAND, Christopher 610-341-5934 383 A 0713mgr@follett.com
HOANG, Ann, D 973-596-5798 278 G ann.d.hoang@njit.edu
HOANG, Christina 714-816-0366 68 G christina.hoang@trident.edu
HOANG, Huu 602-787-7354 13 G huu.hoang@paradisevalley.edu
HOANG, Minh-Ha 619-260-4506 72 H mhoang@sandiego.edu
HOANG, SVD, Thang 563-876-3353 165 D hcthang@dwci.edu
HOANG POE, Linh 808-734-9570 129 E lhoang@hawaii.edu
HOARD, Phil 317-896-9324 161 D phoard@ubca.org
HOBAICA, Thomas 860-439-5429 87 F thobaica@conncoll.edu
HOBAN, Elizabeth 973-328-5160 276 A ehoban@ccm.edu
HOBAN, Patricia, K 503-375-5477 377 E phoban@willamette.edu
HOBART, Denise 330-733-2500 347 D denise.awfa@teachmetofly.com
HOBART, Paul 231-591-2376 223 H paulhobart@ferris.edu
HOBART, Will 361-825-2616 446 E will.hobart@tamucc.edu
HOBBS, Bill 301-696-3622 199 C hobbs@hood.edu
HOBBS, Brenna 541-440-4617 376 F brenna.hobbs@umpqua.edu
HOBBS, Clinton, G 478-757-5161 127 D chobbs@wesleyancollege.edu
HOBBS, David 503-943-7306 376 H hobbsd@up.edu
HOBBS, III, James, P 504-671-5510 187 I jhobbs@dcc.edu
HOBBS, Jeanie 817-598-6267 457 C jhobbs@wc.edu
HOBBS, Jennifer 212-229-5600 307 E hobbsj@newschool.edu
HOBBS, Jessica, W 910-630-7005 331 B jhobbs@methodist.edu
HOBBS, Klint 801-422-3035 458 A klint_hobbs@byu.edu
HOBBS, Mike 706-295-6328 119 C mhobbs@highlands.edu
HOBBS, Morgan 215-972-2199 392 P mhobbs@pafa.edu
HOBBS, Patrick, E 732-445-8610 281 B patrick.hobbs@rutgers.edu
HOBBS, Tameka, B 305-626-3955 100 B tameka.hobbs@fmuniv.edu
HOBBS, Tommy 205-929-3521 2 H thobbs@lawsonstate.edu
HOBBS, Valerie 503-253-3443 374 E valerie.hobbs@ocom.edu
HOBBS, William 559-730-3736 39 C williamh@cos.edu
HOBBS, III, William 305-430-1166 100 B william.hobbs@fmuniv.edu
HOBBY-MEARS, Michelle 949-480-4134 64 E mhobby@soka.edu
HOBERMAN, Chaim 516-255-4700 311 E
HOBERMAN, Evan 646-565-6000 322 C evan.hoberman@touro.edu
HOBERMAN, Evan 646-565-6000 322 B evan.hoberman@touro.edu
HOBGOOD, Kathy, B 864-656-1151 406 F kbhob@clemson.edu
HOBGOOD, Sarah, M 757-594-8763 465 A sarah.hobgood@cnu.edu
HOBIN, Caron, T 413-565-1333 205 I chobin@baypath.edu
HOBLER, Dean 419-998-3103 362 F dahobler@unoh.edu
HOBLET, Kent, H 662-325-1418 247 A hoblet@cvm.msstate.edu
HOBSON, Aaron 608-890-0158 494 D aaron.hobson@wisc.edu
HOBSON, Elizabeth 847-214-6945 137 D ehobson@elgin.edu
HOBSON, Jack 657-278-2935 31 E jhobson@fullerton.edu
HOBSON, Lynn, M 620-341-5267 173 C lhobson@emporia.edu
HOBSON, Paula Lee 607-431-4026 300 G hobsonp@hartwick.edu
HOBSON, Sheila 301-860-3451 203 D shobson@bowiestate.edu
HOBSON, Tricia 405-422-1235 368 I hobsont@redlandscc.edu
HOBYAK, Michael, S 215-785-0111 392 O
HOCH, Meredith 215-646-7300 384 G hoch-oescher.m@gmercyu.edu
HOCHMAN, Alex 415-422-2437 72 I ahochman@usfca.edu
HOCHNER, Rose 713-500-3824 455 D rose.hochner@uth.tmc.edu
HOCHSTEIN, Jessica 402-399-2664 265 H jhochstein@csm.edu
HOCHSTETLER, Salisa 715-394-8536 496 D sbuntham@uwsuper.edu
HOCK, Carrie 303-722-5724 81 K chock@lincolntech.edu
HOCKENBERRY, Frederick 301-846-2544 198 E fhockenberry@frederick.edu
HOCKENBURY, Ed 802-485-2230 461 H ehockenb@norwich.edu
HOCKENHULL, Ben 440-775-6727 357 G ben.hockenhull@oberlin.edu
HOCKER, Michael, B 956-296-1445 455 A michael.hocker@utrgv.edu
HOCKMAN, Joan 814-371-2090 399 B jhockman@triangle-tech.edu
HOCKMAN, Tanya, C 330-471-8287 355 D thockman@malone.edu
HOCOY, Dan 802-322-1600 461 D presidents.office@goddard.edu
HOCOY, Dan 816-604-2414 254 E dan.hocoy@mcckc.edu
HOCUTT, Kirby 806-742-3355 450 C kirby.hocutt@ttu.edu
HODA-KEARSE, Rebecca, A 315-565-3079 319 A rahodake@esf.edu
HODAPP, Maria 708-293-4558 150 H maria.hodapp@trnty.edu
HODEL, Laura 607-778-5028 317 A hodellj@sunybroome.edu
HODES, Max 510-845-5373 29 D
HODGDON, Gisele 802-828-2800 463 A
HODGE, Andrea 213-740-4225 73 C ahodge@usc.edu
HODGE, Angela 512-223-1102 429 J angela.hodge@austincc.edu
HODGE, Bill 715-788-7210 498 G bill.hodge@northwoodtech.edu
HODGE, Brad, K 215-670-9206 391 D bkhodge@peirce.edu
HODGE, Duane 937-328-6054 350 D hodged@clarkstate.edu
HODGE, Evelyn 334-229-4139 4 B ehodge@alasu.edu
HODGE, Frank 206-543-9132 484 A fhodge@uw.edu
HODGE, Harlan 314-367-8700 260 A harlan.hodge@uhsp.edu
HODGE, Jeremy 903-923-1671 457 I jhodge@wileyc.edu
HODGE, Johnesa 313-496-2796 232 B jdimick1@wcccd.edu
HODGE, Jonathan 512-448-8460 441 N jhodge1@stedwards.edu
HODGE, Julie 704-461-7006 326 I juliehodge@bac.edu
HODGE, Margaret 706-385-1069 124 C margaret.hodge@point.edu
HODGE, Matthew 301-405-4683 202 E hodge@umd.edu

HOGAN, Mary .... 910-672-1995 341 B
mhogan@uncfsu.edu
HOGAN, Matthew .... 718-522-2300 312 H
HOGAN, Melissa .... 847-330-4503 148 A
mhogan03@roosevelt.edu
HOGAN, Pashia .... 423-354-2425 424 B
phhogan@northeaststate.edu
HOGAN, Patrick, N .... 301-445-1927 202 D
phogan@usmd.edu
HOGAN, Paul .... 603-271-6484 272 C
phogan@ccsnh.edu
HOGAN, Susan, S .... 413-597-4204 220 A
shogan@williams.edu
HOGAN, Travis .... 303-360-4722.. 80 C
travis.hogan@ccaurora.edu
HOGAN, Whitney .... 207-725-3184 194 A
HOGANS, Karen .... 352-435-6358 103 U
hogansk@lssc.edu
HOGENCAMP, Kelly .... 909-607-2981.. 63 E
khogenca@scrippscollege.edu
HOGENSON, Liz .... 763-424-0902 239 D
lhogenson@nhcc.edu
HOGG, David, S .... 602-850-8000.. 15 D
HOGGARD, Justin .... 361-354-2200 431 L
jhoggard@coastalbend.edu
HOGGATT, Michael .... 405-682-1611 367 D
michael.d.hoggatt@occc.edu
HOGLE, Paul .... 216-791-5000 350 F
paul.hogle@cim.edu
HOGUE, Dale, A .... 719-333-2163 502 C
dale.hogue@afacademy.af.edu
HOGUE, Eric .... 303-963-3093.. 78 D
ehogue@ccu.edu
HOGUE, Laurel .... 660-543-4984 259 K
lhogue@ucmo.edu
HOGUE, Matthew, L .... 843-349-2813 407 B
dhogue@coastal.edu
HOGUE, Michael, D .... 909-558-1300.. 48 J
mhogue@llu.edu
HOGUE, Natasa .... 786-331-1000 104 H
library@maufl.edu
HOGUE, Terri .... 303-273-3000.. 79 A
thogue@mines.edu
HOGUE, Tiffany .... 254-710-3555 430 F
tiffany_hogue@baylor.edu
HOHAM, Lindsey .... 315-228-7438 296 C
lhoham@colgate.edu
HOHBERG, Tonian .... 213-624-1200.. 42 F
thohberg@fidm.edu
HOHERTZ, Cherie, L .... 972-721-5040 451 E
chohertz@udallas.edu
HOHL, Kathleen, M .... 414-410-4202 490 J
kghohl@stritch.edu
HOHMAN, Adam 260-982-5235 158W
arhohman@manchester.edu
HOHN, Daniel .... 303-797-5753.. 77 H
daniel.hohn@arapahoe.edu
HOHNHOLT, Chris .... 906-487-2313 227 D
cahohnho@mtu.edu
HOI, Samuel .... 410-225-2237 200 B
president@mica.edu
HOIE, Steffanie .... 619-260-7414.. 72 H
shoie@sandiego.edu
HOILAND, Eric .... 530-893-7528.. 27 F
hoilander@butte.edu
HOILAND, Erin .... 360-412-6149 482 D
ehoiland@stmartin.edu
HOILMAN, Sandra, K .... 828-448-6025 338 G
shoilman@wpcc.edu
HOIT, Marc, I .... 919-515-0141 341 E
mark_hoit@ncsu.edu
HOJAN-CLARK, Jane .... 212-853-0469 296 H
jh3574@columbia.edu
HOJSACK, Dana .... 619-849-2678.. 57 J
danahojsack@pointloma.edu
HOKANSON, SND,
Karen .... 617-735-9976 209 A
hokanson@emmanuel.edu
HOKE, Chris .... 701-252-3467 346 J
choke@uj.edu
HOKE, Franklin .... 212-327-8998 312 B
fhoke@rockefeller.edu
HOKE, Thomas .... 407-708-2224 108 B
hoket@seminolestate.edu
HOKOANA, Lui .... 808-984-3636 130 B
lhokoana@hawaii.edu
HOLADAY, Stephanie .... 304-326-1311 486 I
stephanie.holaday@salemu.edu
HOLAHAN, Barbara .... 516-686-7555 308 H
bholahan@nyit.edu
HOLAHAN, Cindy .... 262-524-7361 491 A
cholahan@carrollu.edu

HOLAK, Susan, L .... 718-982-2920 293 C
schoolofbusiness@csi.cuny.edu
HOLAN, Craig .... 618-650-2560 149 H
cholan@siue.edu
HOLANDA, Shelly .... 800-686-1883 222 B
sholanda@cleary.edu
HOLBECK, Michael .... 605-688-4455 416 A
michael.holbeck@sdstate.edu
HOLBERG, John .... 706-419-1565 117 G
john.holberg@covenant.edu
HOLBERT, Derek, A .... 304-457-6439 485 F
holbertda@ab.edu
HOLBROOK, Eric .... 701-483-2370 345 A
eric.l.holbrook@dickinsonstate.edu
HOLBROOK, Jamirae .... 606-539-4120 185 C
jamirae.holbrook@ucumberlands.edu
HOLBROOK, Jennifer .... 870-230-5275.. 19 H
holbroj@hsu.edu
HOLBROOK, Karen .... 941-359-4340 111 B
kholbrook@usf.edu
HOLBROOK, Peter .... 419-448-5864 361 C
holbrookpj@tiffin.edu
HOLCOMB, David .... 254-295-4184 453 A
dholcomb@umhb.edu
HOLCOMB, David .... 423-775-7136 417 D
dholcomb8093@bryan.edu
HOLCOMB, Debra .... 903-510-2380 451 D
debra.holcomb@tjc.edu
HOLCOMB, John .... 216-687-5548 350 G
j.p.holcomb@csuohio.edu
HOLCOMB, Mark, E .... 815-939-5236 146 F
mholcomb@olivet.edu
HOLCOMB, JR.,
Richard, S .... 734-647-5574 231 A
rsholcom@umich.edu
HOLCOMB, Robert .... 707-527-4615.. 63 C
rholcomb@santarosa.edu
HOLCOMB, Todd .... 319-296-4201 166 E
todd.holcomb@hawkeyecollege.edu
HOLCOMB-MCCOY,
Cheryl .... 202-885-3720.. 91 D
cholcomb@american.edu
HOLCOMBE, Bobby .... 864-424-8024 412 H
reholcom@mailbox.sc.edu
HOLCOMBE, Kara .... 503-554-2189 372 I
kholcombe@georgefox.edu
HOLDEMAN, Lisa, K .... 713-743-8408 451 F
lkholdeman@uh.edu
HOLDEMAN, Lisa, K .... 713-743-0945 451 G
lkholdeman@uh.edu
HOLDEN, Brad .... 541-278-5783 371 G
bholden@bluecc.edu
HOLDEN, Carol .... 520-515-3674.. 11 O
holdenc@cochise.edu
HOLDEN, Cheryl .... 509-542-4761 478 B
cholden@columbiabasin.edu
HOLDEN, Christy .... 719-846-5550.. 83 I
christy.holden@trinidadstate.edu
HOLDEN, Ginger .... 209-954-5040.. 61 H
gholden@deltacollege.edu
HOLDEN, Joan .... 773-508-2530 142 G
jholde1@luc.edu
HOLDEN, Joseph, M .... 714-966-8500.. 74 C
info@ves.edu
HOLDEN, Kimberly .... 706-771-4819 115 H
kimberly.holden@augustatech.edu
HOLDEN, Kurt, A .... 937-775-2056 364 D
kurt.holden@wright.edu
HOLDEN, Larry .... 615-327-6339 420 D
lholden@mmc.edu
HOLDEN, Leslie .... 540-365-4460 466 I
lholden@ferrum.edu
HOLDEN, Ronald .... 330-823-2138 362 E
holdenrf@mountunion.edu
HOLDEN, Wesley .... 772-546-5534 102 B
wesleyholden@hsbc.edu
HOLDER, Amy .... 931-393-1643 423 G
aholder@mscc.edu
HOLDER, Beth .... 910-521-6221 343 A
beth.holder@uncp.edu
HOLDER, Candace .... 336-386-3382 338 B
holderc@surry.edu
HOLDER, Connie .... 573-518-2119 255 G
cholder@mineralarea.edu
HOLDER, Debra .... 817-274-4284 430 G
dholder@bhcarroll.edu
HOLDER, Kenneth .... 251-405-7172.... 1 E
kholder@bishop.edu
HOLDER, Mitchell .... 660-359-3948 256 F
mholder@mail.ncmissouri.edu
HOLDERMAN, John .... 918-631-3092 371 C
john-holderman@utulsa.edu
HOLDERREAD, Brian, E 405-325-6006 370 J
bholderread@ou.edu

HOLDING, Frederick .... 910-962-1123 343 B
holdingf@uncw.edu
HOLEMAN, Gary .... 845-574-4770 312 C
gary.holeman@sunyrockland.edu
HOLFORD, Kenneth .... 219-989-2446 160 A
cholford@pnw.edu
HOLFTERY, Kerril .... 360-383-3000 485 B
HOLGARD, Austin, J .... 701-355-8297 347 A
ajholgard@umary.edu
HOLIDAY, Jana .... 978-468-7111 209 G
jholiday@gordonconwell.edu
HOLIFIELD, Brenda .... 870-780-1227.. 17 F
bholifield@smail.anc.edu
HOLIGROCKI, Rick .... 805-493-3528.. 29 E
rholigrocki@callutheran.edu
HOLL, Karolina .... 315-792-3179 323 G
kmholl@utica.edu
HOLL, Scott .... 314-252-3141 252 E
sholl@eden.edu
HOLLAAR, Jean .... 218-477-2070 239 A
jean.hollaar@mnstate.edu
HOLLADAY, Allison .... 570-321-4220 388 H
holladay@lycoming.edu
HOLLAND, Arnold .... 657-278-3158.. 31 E
aholland@fullerton.edu
HOLLAND, Beth .... 828-726-2200 332 E
bholland@cccti.edu
HOLLAND, Christopher . 808-932-7472 129 A
cjh2020@hawaii.edu
HOLLAND, Colleen .... 417-455-5588 251 H
colleenholland@crowder.edu
HOLLAND, JR., Earl, D . 410-621-2355 203 B
edholland1@umes.edu
HOLLAND, Frederick .... 888-775-1514.. 68 K
HOLLAND, Hailey .... 208-535-5622 130 I
hailey.holland@cei.edu
HOLLAND, Jeff .... 304-424-8229 490 A
jeff.holland@wvup.edu
HOLLAND, Jo .... 907-564-8342.... 9 F
jholland@alaskapacific.edu
HOLLAND, Joseph .... 401-739-5000 403 F
jholland@neit.edu
HOLLAND, Karen .... 330-569-5109 353 F
hollandk@hiram.edu
HOLLAND, Kevin .... 940-552-6291 456 F
kholland@vernoncollege.edu
HOLLAND, Kimberly .... 334-727-8881.... 7 D
kholland@tuskegee.edu
HOLLAND, Leslie .... 901-722-3238 422 I
lholland@sco.edu
HOLLAND, Linda .... 501-354-7565.. 23 D
holland@uaccm.edu
HOLLAND, Mario .... 405-466-3370 366 B
mario.holland@langston.edu
HOLLAND, Melissa .... 410-221-2001 203 A
mholland@umces.edu
HOLLAND, Richard .... 863-583-9050 110 A
HOLLAND, Sam .... 214-768-2880 443 G
sholland@smu.edu
HOLLAND, Sharon .... 301-295-3578 502 B
sharon.holland@usuhs.edu
HOLLAND, Taylor .... 501-977-2085.. 23 D
holland@uaccm.edu
HOLLAND, Tina .... 225-768-1710 186 H
tina.holland@franu.edu
HOLLAND, Tracey .... 845-437-7360 323 H
trholland@vassar.edu
HOLLAND, Vicki .... 704-878-3205 335 I
vholland@mitchellcc.edu
HOLLAND, Wentreal .... 312-922-1884 143 D
wholland@maccormac.edu
HOLLAND, Wesley .... 213-738-6705.. 66 A
registrar@swlaw.edu
HOLLANDER, Lisa .... 219-464-6882 162 C
lisa.hollander@valpo.edu
HOLLANDSWORTH,
Heather .... 540-365-4282 466 I
hhollandsworth@ferrum.edu
HOLLAR, Bruce .... 336-838-6558 338 H
bahollar052@wilkescc.edu
HOLLAWAY, Jamie .... 319-352-8418 170 F
jamie.hollaway@wartburg.edu
HOLLEMAN, Clate .... 662-472-9087 245 E
cholleman@holmescc.edu
HOLLEMON, John .... 434-223-7154 466 K
jhollemon@hsc.edu
HOLLENBAUGH, David . 724-805-2590 397 C
david.hollenbaugh@stvincent.edu
HOLLENBAUGH, David . 724-805-2590 397 D
david.hollenbaugh@stvincent.edu
HOLLENBECK, Nicole .... 480-750-4472.. 15 Q
nhollenbeck@tsoa.edu

HOLLENBECK, Peter .... 765-494-9709 159 G
phollenb@purdue.edu
HOLLENBURG, Amy .... 417-667-8181 251 E
ahollenburg@cottey.edu
HOLLENHORST, Steven . 360-650-2835 485 A
steve.hollenhorst@wwu.edu
HOLLER, Steven .... 503-251-0332 374 A
sholler@multnomah.edu
HOLLERAN, Meghan .... 660-263-4100 256 D
meghanh@macc.edu
HOLLERICH, Mary .... 612-330-1603 233 G
holleric@augsburg.edu
HOLLEY, Betty .... 937-971-2860 359 J
bholley@payneseminary.edu
HOLLEY, Chelsea .... 404-270-5279 126 A
chelsea.holley@spelman.edu
HOLLEY, Danielle, R .... 202-806-8000.. 92 E
danielle.holley@howard.edu
HOLLEY, John .... 256-306-2865.... 1 F
john.holley@calhoun.edu
HOLLEY, Stephanie .... 972-780-3600 453 C
stephanie.holley@untdallas.edu
HOLLEY, Steven .... 662-915-7200 248 F
vcaf@olemiss.edu
HOLLEY, Suzy .... 813-253-7116 102 A
sholley7@hccfl.edu
HOLLEY, Tracy, S .... 540-365-4216 466 I
tholley@ferrum.edu
HOLLIDAY, Deann .... 425-352-8324 477 F
dholliday@cascadia.edu
HOLLIDAY, Lisa .... 503-370-6300 377 E
HOLLIDAY, Lisa, C .... 503-370-6574 377 E
lcjones@willamette.edu
HOLLIDAY, Odell, P .... 252-451-8221 336 B
moholliday690@nashcc.edu
HOLLIDAY, Paul .... 213-356-5348.. 65 D
paul_holliday@sciarc.edu
HOLLIDAY, Shawn, P .... 580-327-8410 367 A
spholliday@nwosu.edu
HOLLIDAY, Theresa .... 913-288-7110 174 H
tholliday@kckcc.edu
HOLLIDAY, Wendy .... 801-626-6403 460 B
wendyholliday@weber.edu
HOLLIER, Larry, H .... 504-568-4800 189 C
lhholl@lsuhsc.edu
HOLLIFIELD, Jim .... 901-722-3264 422 I
jhollifield@sco.edu
HOLLIMAN-DOUGLAS,
Chassity .... 713-718-7948 436 E
c.hollimandouglas@hccs.edu
HOLLIMAN-GINKENS,
Stephanie .... 641-683-5751 166 F
stephanie.holliman-ginkens@
indianhills.edu
HOLLINGER, David .... 419-372-7477 348 F
holling@bgsu.edu
HOLLINGER-SMITH,
Linda .... 888-556-8226 134 D
HOLLINGSHEAD, Brad .. 863-680-4124 100 F
bhollingshead@flsouthern.edu
HOLLINGSHEAD,
Jennifer .... 848-445-1910 281 B
jh1509@echo.rutgers.edu
HOLLINGSWORTH,
Clifford .... 914-632-5400 306 J
chollingsworth@monroecollege.edu
HOLLINGSWORTH,
Guy, M .... 801-524-1928 458 F
ghollingsworth@ldsbc.edu
HOLLINGSWORTH,
Jeffrey, K .... 301-405-7700 202 E
hollings@umd.edu
HOLLINGSWORTH,
Kimberly .... 773-291-6313 135 B
khollingsworth@ccc.edu
HOLLINGSWORTH,
Nicole .... 831-582-3044.. 32 D
nhollingsworth@csumb.edu
HOLLINGSWORTH,
Rusty .... 270-789-5009 179 G
rhollingsworth@campbellsville.edu
HOLLINGSWORTH,
Stacey .... 601-635-6327 245 B
sholling@eccc.edu
HOLLINS, Cary .... 225-771-5662 190 K
cary_hollins@subr.edu
HOLLINS, Cassandra .... 205-929-2091.... 2 H
creneehollins@lawsonstate.edu
HOLLINS, Emily .... 540-665-4914 470 A
ehollins2@su.edu
HOLLINS, Jeannette .... 757-825-2810 474 F
hollinsj@tncc.edu
HOLLINS, Kayla .... 413-662-5585 212 F
kayla.hollins@mcla.edu

HOLTZCLAW, Rhonda ... 239-590-1037 109 G
rholtzcl@fgcu.edu
HOLTZMAN, Nathalia .... 718-997-2867 295 A
nathalia.holtzman@qc.cuny.edu
HOLUB, Tom ... 608-663-2303 491 F
tholub@edgewod.edu
HOLUBIK, Donna ... 734-487-0455 223 F
dholubik@emich.edu
HOLUP, Theresa ... 419-824-3809 355 C
tholup@lourdes.edu
HOLVEY BOWLES,
Joanna ... 315-228-7216 296 C
jholveybowles@colgate.edu
HOLWERDA, Jane ... 620-227-9359 173 A
jholwerda@dc3.edu
HOLWICK, Jana, W ... 770-426-2697 122 A
jana.holwick@life.edu
HOLYFIELD, Patrick ... 704-991-0235 338 A
pholyfield8286@stanly.edu
HOLZ, Marina ... 914-594-4110 308 J
mholz@nymc.edu
HOLZ, Richard ... 303-273-3000.. 79 A
rholz@mines.edu
HOLZ-CLAUSE, Mary ... 218-281-8343 243 B
mhclause@umn.edu
HOLZHEUSER,
Christina ... 361-825-3065 446 E
christina.holzheuser@tamucc.edu
HOLZMER, OSF,
M. Anita ... 260-399-7700 162 A
aholzmer@sf.edu
HOM-DIAMOND,
Hellen ... 860-297-2139.. 88 I
hellen.homdiamond@trincoll.edu
HOMAN, Elizabeth, S. 443-518-4073 199 D
ehoman@howardcc.edu
HOMAN, Fenecia ... 605-367-5462 416 B
fenecia.homan@southeasttech.edu
HOMAN, Judi ... 901-375-4400 421 A
judihoman@midsouthchristian.edu
HOMAN, Pamela ... 605-274-5016 413 G
pamela.homan@augie.edu
HOMAN, Vimla ... 708-524-6490 137 A
vhoman@dom.edu
HOMANY, Garry ... 216-397-1982 353 O
ghomany@jcu.edu
HOMARD, Jennifer ... 352-395-5493 107 G
jen.homard@sfcollege.edu
HOMER, Christine ... 303-273-3000.. 79 A
HOMER, Cory ... 973-300-2116 283 B
chomer@sussex.edu
HOMER, Erin ... 269-749-7644 229 G
ehomer@olivetcollege.edu
HOMER, Rollin ... 626-396-2263.. 26 G
rollin.homer@artcenter.edu
HOMER, Stephanie ... 503-338-2428 372 C
shomer@clatsopcc.edu
HOMES, Kijia ... 701-671-2221 346 B
kijia.homes@ndscs.edu
HOMFELDT, Mike ... 541-880-2244 373 B
homfeldt@klamathcc.edu
HOMOLKA, Karen, K ... 217-245-3094 139 A
khomolk@ic.edu
HOMSEY, David ... 518-631-9852 295 E
dhomsey@clarkson.edu
HONADEL, Tim ... 661-362-3699.. 38 H
tim.honadel@canyons.edu
HONAKER, Lisa ... 609-652-4505 283 A
lisa.honaker@stockton.edu
HONAN, David ... 607-255-7759 297 D
dmh12@cornell.edu
HONAN, Lisa ... 203-932-7264.. 89 F
lhonan@newhaven.edu
HONDA, Herminia ... 323-409-6301.. 50 D
hhonda@dhs.lacounty.gov
HONDA, Hirosuke ... 207-621-3216 196 E
hirosuke.honda@maine.edu
HONE, Shannon ... 701-845-7293 345 E
shannon.hone@vcsu.edu
HONEGAN, Rhonda ... 404-270-5075 126 A
rhonegan@spelman.edu
HONEMAN, Carrie ... 802-860-2757 461 C
choneman@champlain.edu
HONEYCUTT,
Andrew, E ... 714-772-3330.. 26 B
HONEYCUTT, Christie ... 704-991-0295 338 A
choneycutt7476@stanly.edu
HONEYCUTT, Del Rey ... 716-375-2310 312 F
dhoneycu@sbu.edu
HONEYCUTT, Katie ... 360-752-8490 477 C
khoneycutt@btc.edu
HONG, Barbara, S ... 956-326-2134 446 A
barbara.hong@tamiu.edu
HONG, Benjamin ... 909-671-4038.. 34 G
HONG, Emily ... 636-327-4645 255 E
music@midwest.edu
HONG, Luoluo ... 404-385-8772 119 D
vp_sewb@gatech.edu
HONG, Marcus ... 502-895-3411 183 E
mhong@lpts.edu
HONG, Molly, F ... 443-518-3823 199 D
mhong@howardcc.edu
HONG, Philip ... 706-542-5424 126 F
ph73816@uga.edu
HONG, Rebecca ... 310-338-7371.. 51 C
rebecca.hong@lmu.edu
HONG, Sung Wook ... 512-444-8082 448 B
whong@thsu.edu
HONG, Tran ... 951-343-3907.. 27 J
thong@calbaptist.edu
HONG, Z. George ... 718-817-0029 300 A
zhong4@fordham.edu
HONIGFORD, Kevin ... 317-921-4749 158 A
khonigford@ivytech.edu
HONIGFORD, Kevin ... 317-738-8026 155 A
khonigford@franklincollege.edu
HONMA, David ... 608-262-4766 494 D
david.honma@wisc.edu
HONNELL, Cherie ... 503-494-7878 374 F
acad@ohsu.edu
HONORA, Angela ... 504-816-5308 186 F
ahonora@dillard.edu
HONOREE, Nicole ... 504-568-2587 189 C
nhonor@lsuhsc.edu
HOO, Karlene ... 509-313-6117 479 E
hoo@gonzaga.edu
HOOD, Amanda ... 601-643-8619 244 G
amanda.hood@colin.edu
HOOD, Chester ... 850-599-3796 109 E
chester.hood@famu.edu
HOOD, David ... 973-655-4280 278 C
hoodd@montclair.edu
HOOD, Donna ... 828-395-1404 335 B
dhood@isothermal.edu
HOOD, Jim, W ... 336-316-2146 329 C
president@guilford.edu
HOOD, Marcia ... 229-500-2116 114 F
marcia.hood@asurams.edu
HOOD, Mattie ... 850-599-3203 109 E
mattie.hood@famu.edu
HOOD, Maya ... 619-849-2524.. 57 J
mhood@pointloma.edu
HOOD, Mike ... 903-233-4115 438 C
mikehood@letu.edu
HOOD, Scott, W ... 207-725-3256 194 A
shood@bowdoin.edu
HOOD, Steven ... 205-348-6010.... 7 G
HOOD, Tim ... 989-386-6602 227 E
thood@midmich.edu
HOOD, W.C. (Chip) ... 864-656-3414 406 F
chip@clemson.edu
HOOGEWERF, Arlene ... 616-526-8668 221 L
ahoogewe@calvin.edu
HOOK, Amy ... 617-353-2399 207 C
amyhook@bu.edu
HOOKE, Ruthanna ... 703-370-6600 475 F
HOOKER, John ... 352-395-5722 107 G
john.hooker@sfcollege.edu
HOOKER, Steven, P ... 619-594-6516.. 33 E
shooker@sdsu.edu
HOOKS, Deborah ... 850-484-2116 105 G
dhooks@pensacolastate.edu
HOOKS, Jeffery ... 269-783-2159 230 D
jhooks@swmich.edu
HOOKS, Phil ... 740-474-8896 358 A
phooks@ohiochristian.edu
HOOKS, Rebecca ... 704-216-3488 337 C
rebecca.hooks@rccc.edu
HOOLE, Thomas ... 978-934-3509 211 G
thomas_hoole@uml.edu
HOON, William ... 931-221-7330 416 H
hoonb@apsu.edu
HOOPER, Brooke ... 757-446-7439 465 H
hooperab@evms.edu
HOOPER, Bryan ... 850-201-8169 112 B
bryan.hooper@tcc.fl.edu
HOOPER, Christy ... 615-966-1000 420 B
christy.hooper@lipscomb.edu
HOOPER, Cynthia ... 713-623-2040 429 F
HOOPER, Dave ... 434-395-2099 467 F
hooperdv@longwood.edu
HOOPER, Elizabeth, A ... 253-535-7337 481 C
hooperea@plu.edu
HOOPER, Heath ... 706-292-3906 125 A
hhooper@shorter.edu
HOOPER, Joseph ... 831-656-3218 501 K
jphooper@nps.edu
HOOPER, Julie ... 510-642-6000.. 68 N
HOOPER, Mary, A ... 404-880-8363 116 I
mhooper@cau.edu
HOOPER, Peter ... 520-515-3692.. 11 O
hooperd@cochise.edu
HOOPER, Ryan ... 607-436-2317 316 C
ryan.hooper@oneonta.edu
HOOPER, Stephanie ... 304-336-8899 489 B
stephanie.hooper@westliberty.edu
HOOPER-PORTER,
Tracey ... 740-588-1377 364 H
tporter2@zanestate.edu
HOOPES, Jill ... 316-284-5326 171 I
jhoopes@bethelks.edu
HOOPES, Robbin ... 513-569-1511 350 C
robbin.hoopes@cincinnatistate.edu
HOOPES, Tom ... 913-360-7529 171 G
thoopes@benedictine.edu
HOOPS, Lisa ... 937-778-7955 352 D
lhoops@edisonohio.edu
HOOPS, Tony ... 316-284-5279 171 I
thoops@bethelks.edu
HOORMAN, Rachel ... 504-861-5881 190 A
rchoorma@loyno.edu
HOORNBEEK, Corbin ... 626-815-5328.. 26 K
choornbeek@apu.edu
HOORNBEEK, Corbin ... 651-631-5100 243 E
cmhoornbeek@unwsp.edu
HOOT, Dustin ... 414-847-3233 493 C
dustinhoot@miad.edu
HOOTEN, Jon ... 805-922-6966.. 24 L
jon.hooten@hancockcollege.edu
HOOVEN, Kamalesh, G . 408-847-4060.. 52 I
HOOVER, Amy, K ... 712-778-2466 265 J
amyhoover@creighton.edu
HOOVER, Braydon ... 540-432-4069 465 F
braydon.hoover@emu.edu
HOOVER, Curtis ... 212-752-1530 303 G
curtis.hoover@limcollege.edu
HOOVER, Diane ... 541-956-7011 375 G
dhoover@roguecc.edu
HOOVER, Donna, D ... 361-570-4332 452 C
hooverdd@uhv.edu
HOOVER, Douglas ... 724-938-4096 394 C
hoover@calu.edu
HOOVER, Jean, B ... 717-262-2007 402 D
jhoover@wilson.edu
HOOVER, John, F ... 202-685-3924 501 I
john.f.hoover.civ@ndu.edu
HOOVER, Josie ... 202-664-5682.. 94 D
jhoover@wesleyseminary.edu
HOOVER, Karelyn ... 909-274-4570.. 52 K
khoover@mtsac.edu
HOOVER, Kathleen ... 610-558-5560 390 G
hooverk@neumann.edu
HOOVER, Kelly ... 410-704-2516 204 B
khoover@towson.edu
HOOVER, Kevin ... 559-325-3600.. 28 F
khoover@chsu.edu
HOOVER, Linda ... 817-722-1628 437 H
linda.hoover@tku.edu
HOOVER, Lisa ... 214-637-3530 457 A
lhoover@wadecollege.edu
HOOVER, Myrna ... 850-644-6089 110 B
mhoover@fsu.edu
HOOVER, Nick ... 937-481-2369 363 H
nick_hoover@wilmington.edu
HOOVER, Robert ... 563-588-6338 164 C
robert.hoover@clarke.edu
HOOVER, Sandy ... 903-935-7963 435 A
shoover@etbu.edu
HOOVER, Sandy ... 903-923-2086 435 A
shoover@etbu.edu
HOOVER, Tom ... 318-257-2477 192 A
thoover@cloud.latech.edu
HOOVER, Zachary ... 605-668-1619 414 F
zachary.hoover@mountmarty.edu
HOOVER-ERBIG,
Andrea ... 757-455-3136 476 C
ahoover@vwu.edu
HOOYMAN, Jamie ... 660-562-1120 256 G
jhooyman@nwmissouri.edu
HOPE, Debra ... 402-472-7940 269 A
dhope1@unl.edu
HOPE, Deryle ... 864-503-5769 413 A
dhope@uscupstate.edu
HOPE, Henry ... 404-471-6355 114 E
hhope@agnesscott.edu
HOPE, John ... 251-981-3771.... 5 B
john.hope@columbiasouthern.edu
HOPE, Joseph, S ... 315-228-7422 296 C
jshope@colgate.edu
HOPE, Laura ... 909-652-6131.. 36 B
laura.hope@chaffey.edu
HOPE, Mindy ... 308-535-3773 266 J
hopem@mpcc.edu
HOPE, Oral ... 212-431-2300 308 I
oral.hope@nyls.edu
HOPE, Orielle ... 336-721-2600 339 H
orielle.hope@salem.edu
HOPES, Diana, L ... 972-549-6476 432 I
dhopes@collin.edu
HOPEWELL, Mitch ... 661-362-2683.. 51 E
mhopewell@masters.edu
HOPEY, Christopher, E . 978-837-5110 216 D
christopher.hopey@merrimack.edu
HOPKIN, Fran ... 435-797-8380 459 F
fran.hopkin@usu.edu
HOPKINS, Alex ... 816-654-7000 253 I
HOPKINS,
Alexander, M ... 713-798-4262 430 E
ahopkins@bcm.edu
HOPKINS, Barry ... 773-256-0734 143 C
bhopkins@jkmlibrary.org
HOPKINS, Barry ... 773-256-0734 143 E
bhopkins@jkmlibrary.org
HOPKINS, Boone, J ... 864-596-9050 407 G
boone.hopkins@converse.edu
HOPKINS, Brandon ... 312-553-3193 134M
bhopkins19@ccc.edu
HOPKINS, Carla ... 301-860-3939 203 D
alumni@bowiestate.edu
HOPKINS, Christi ... 620-242-0414 175 G
hopkinsc@mcpherson.edu
HOPKINS, David ... 903-675-6214 451 C
david.hopkins@tvcc.edu
HOPKINS, Dawn ... 302-857-6060.. 90 D
dhopkins@desu.edu
HOPKINS, Ebonnie ... 408-274-7900.. 62 F
ebonnie.hopkins@evc.edu
HOPKINS, Elijah ... 406-768-6371 262 I
ehopkins@fpcc.edu
HOPKINS,
Jamal-Dominique ... 803-376-5834 405 D
jhopkins@allenuniversity.edu
HOPKINS, Jeremy ... 919-365-7711 340 C
jeremy.hopkins@sfwbc.edu
HOPKINS, Jessica ... 618-537-6817 143 G
jlhopkins@mckendree.edu
HOPKINS, John, L ... 203-596-4652.. 88 E
jhopkins@post.edu
HOPKINS, Joseph ... 270-789-5000 179 G
HOPKINS, Kathryn ... 870-777-5722.. 23 C
HOPKINS, Kent, R ... 480-965-2408.. 11 A
kent.hopkins@asu.edu
HOPKINS, Kevin ... 785-594-8553 171 C
kevin.hopkins@bakeru.edu
HOPKINS, Michael ... 773-702-6490 151 B
mhopkins@uchicago.edu
HOPKINS, Randy ... 816-501-4659 257 K
randy.hopkins@rockhurst.edu
HOPKINS, Ronnie ... 803-780-1179 413 B
rhopkins@voorhees.edu
HOPKINS, Sarah ... 707-527-4831.. 63 C
shopkins@santarosa.edu
HOPKINS, Stacy ... 724-357-2230 393 G
stacy.hopkins@iup.edu
HOPKINS, T. Hampton . 704-355-5316 327 F
hampton.hopkins@carolinascollege.edu
HOPKINS, Timothy ... 815-455-8999 143 F
thopkins@mchenry.edu
HOPKINS, Vaughn, K ... 302-857-6822.. 90 D
vkhopkins@desu.edu
HOPKINS, Zachary ... 814-871-7202 383 H
hopkins013@gannon.edu
HOPKINS-GROSS, Anne 518-255-5214 318 F
hopkinam@cobleskill.edu
HOPKINS-POSELLE,
Denise ... 845-398-4052 314 D
dhopkins@stac.edu
HOPP, Csendi ... 360-992-2495 477 J
chopp@clark.edu
HOPP, Lisa ... 219-989-2823 160 A
ljhopp@pnw.edu
HOPP, Melissa ... 443-840-3176 198 D
mhopp@ccbcmd.edu
HOPPE, Elizabeth ... 909-706-3497.. 75 G
shoppe@westernu.edu
HOPPE, Heather ... 843-349-5238 409 A
heather.hoppe@hgtc.edu
HOPPE, James ... 617-824-8640 208 G
james_hoppe@emerson.edu
HOPPE, Marianne ... 406-265-3765 264 A
hoppe@msun.edu

HOUCK, Laurie .... 407-646-2124 106 L
lhouck@rollins.edu

HOUDE, Joe .... 858-653-6740.. 46 L
jhoude@jpcatholic.edu

HOUDEK, Rob .... 605-642-6562 415 F
rob.houdek@bhsu.edu

HOUDER, Nathalie .... 603-358-2014 274 A
nathalie.houder@keene.edu

HOUDYSCHELL,
Jendonnae .... 304-696-6704 488 N
houdyschell2@marshall.edu

HOUFER, Michael .... 651-747-4085 237 D
michael.houfer@century.edu

HOUFF, Bekah 260-982-5243 158W
rlhouff@manchester.edu

HOUGE, Melanie .... 406-791-5976 264 J
melanie.houge@uprovidence.edu

HOUGH, Andy .... 314-744-7623 255 H
andy.hough@mobap.edu

HOUGH, Brad .... 636-227-2100 254 C

HOUGH, Kendra .... 318-345-9187 188 A
khough@ladelta.edu

HOUGH, Samara .... 810-237-6648 231 C
samaralw@umich.edu

HOUGH, Tony .... 803-738-7695 409 E
hought@midlandstech.edu

HOUGHTON, Brian .... 808-675-3209 128 B
brian.houghton@byuh.edu

HOUGHTON, David .... 405-585-4400 367 B
david.houghton@okbu.edu

HOUK, Christopher .... 270-686-4241 179 F
chris.houk@brescia.edu

HOUK, Claire .... 785-827-5541 175 C

HOUK, Suzanne, N .... 724-458-2208 384 F
snhouk@gcc.edu

HOULIHAN, Janet, M ... 714-895-8307.. 38 E
jhoulihan@gwc.cccd.edu

HOULIHAN, Jill .... 501-760-4206.. 20 E
jill.houlihan@np.edu

HOULT, Kevin .... 256-782-5820.... 6 A
khoult@jsu.edu

HOULTON, Benjamin, Z 607-255-2241 297 D
calsdean@cornell.edu

HOUP, Trena .... 803-777-0460 412 A
thoup@sc.edu

HOUPHMAN, Shaya .... 773-463-7738 150 F

HOUPIS, James, L .... 530-741-6700.. 77 B

HOURIGAN,
Christopher, P .... 401-456-8998 404 A
chourigan@ric.edu

HOUSE, Andrew .... 410-293-1563 502 I
andrew.house@usna.edu

HOUSE, Dan .... 919-515-4211 341 E
dlhouse@ncsu.edu

HOUSE, Deandre .... 601-857-3353 245 D
deandre.house@hindscc.edu

HOUSE, H. Wayne .... 888-777-7675 479 D
hwhouse@faithiu.edu

HOUSE, Kamesia .... 910-672-1325 341 B
kmhouse@uncfsu.edu

HOUSE, Kandy .... 580-774-3260 369 I
kandy.house@swosu.edu

HOUSE, Karen .... 978-542-6120 213 B
karen.house@salemstate.edu

HOUSE, Stephanie .... 208-769-3368 132 A
stephanie.house@nic.edu

HOUSE, Vicki .... 325-670-1276 436 B
vhouse@hsutx.edu

HOUSEHOLDER, Mary .. 616-395-7413 224 H
householder@hope.edu

HOUSEKNECHT, Karen .. 207-602-2872 197 A
khouseknecht@une.edu

HOUSEKNECHT, Rick .... 215-702-4337 379 F
rhouseknecht@cairn.edu

HOUSEMAN, Jennifer .... 215-951-1070 386 I
houseman@lasalle.edu

HOUSENICK, Joseph .... 570-408-4630 402 B
joseph.housenick@wilkes.edu

HOUSER, Elijah .... 386-506-4417.. 98 A
elijah.houser@daytonastate.edu

HOUSER, Janet .... 303-458-1843.. 83 B
jhouser@regis.edu

HOUSER, John .... 575-562-2123 285 E
john.houser@enmu.edu

HOUSER, Katie .... 843-953-5606 407 D
houserkk@cofc.edu

HOUSER, Kay .... 910-788-6219 337 G
kay.houser@sccnc.edu

HOUSER, Kris .... 217-245-3832 139 A
kris.houser@ic.edu

HOUSER, Nate .... 785-594-8316 171 C
nate.houser@bakeru.edu

HOUSHMAND, Ali .... 856-256-4100 280 H
presidenthoushmand@rowan.edu

HOUSHOLDER, Suahil .. 765-641-4115 153 D
srhousholder@anderson.edu

HOUSLEY, Brooks .... 334-387-3877.... 4 C
brookshousley@amridgeuniversity.edu

HOUSLEY, Harold .... 903-875-7307 439 G
harold.housley@navarrocollege.edu

HOUSLEY, Heather, L ... 404-413-2070 120 C
heatherh@gsu.edu

HOUSLEY, La Royce .... 310-954-4191.. 52 J
ldodd@msmu.edu

HOUSMAN, Naomi .... 215-635-7300 384 D
nhousman@gratz.edu

HOUSMAN, Yosef .... 732-367-1060 275 B
yhousman@bmg.edu

HOUSTON, Angela .... 601-318-6231 249 B
lhouston@wmcarey.edu

HOUSTON, Annazette .... 813-253-7043 102 A
ahouston14@hccfl.edu

HOUSTON, Anne .... 610-330-5150 387 B
houstona@lafayette.edu

HOUSTON, Don .... 408-855-5428.. 75 C
don.houston@wvm.edu

HOUSTON, Doris .... 309-438-5677 140 C
dmhous2@ilstu.edu

HOUSTON, Doug .... 636-584-6732 252 D
doug.houston@eastcentral.edu

HOUSTON, Hope .... 781-891-2450 206 C
hhouston@bentley.edu

HOUSTON, Jason .... 509-328-4220 479 E
houston@gonzaga.edu

HOUSTON, Jean .... 707-765-1836.. 52 C

HOUSTON, Kathryn .... 816-235-6211 260 D
houstonk@umkc.edu

HOUSTON, Kristen .... 206-876-6100 483 A
khouston@theseattleschool.edu

HOUSTON, Michael .... 662-621-4853 244 E
mhouston@coahomacc.edu

HOUSTON, Michelle .... 631-499-7100 304 B
mhouston@libi.edu

HOUSTON, Michelle .... 309-672-5515 143 I
ahouston1@methodistcol.edu

HOUSTON, Nainsi .... 740-826-8260 356 H
nhouston@muskingum.edu

HOUSTON, Norma .... 919-962-1000 340 F

HOUSTON, Rachel .... 704-403-1228 327 B
rachel.houston@atriumhealth.org

HOUSTON, Raymond .... 914-606-6789 324 F
raymond.houston@sunywcc.edu

HOUSTON, Rick .... 978-867-4130 209 F
ric.houston@gordon.edu

HOUSTON, Sue .... 419-372-2211 348 F
shousto@bgsu.edu

HOUSTON, Vinson .... 256-782-5993.... 6 A
vhouston@jsu.edu

HOUSTON-BROWN,
Clive .... 909-469-7037.. 75 G
choustonbrown@westernu.edu

HOUTMAN, Anne .... 765-983-1211 154 H
earlhampresident@earlham.edu

HOVAN, Steve .... 724-357-2100 393 G
steven.hovan@iup.edu

HOVATER, Richard .... 910-323-5614 327 E
rhovater@ccbs.edu

HOVEKAMP, Tina .... 541-383-7295 371 I
thovekamp@cocc.edu

HOVELL, Ashley .... 651-255-6162 242 J
ahovell@unitedseminary.edu

HOVEN, Christina .... 716-286-8372 309 F
ccuttone@niagara.edu

HOVEN, Kierstin .... 218-755-4135 237 B
kierstin.hoven@bemidjistate.edu

HOVERSTEN, Mark .... 919-515-8347 341 E
mark_hoversten@ncsu.edu

HOVESTOL, Dan .... 406-586-3585 263 A
dan.hovestol@montanabiblecollege.edu

HOVEY, Ann .... 541-867-8541 374 D
ann.hovey@oregoncoast.edu

HOVEY, Jeff .... 314-977-8375 258 H
jeff.hovey@slu.edu

HOVEY, Mark .... 860-685-2337.. 90 A
mhovey@wesleyan.edu

HOVEY, Rebecca .... 413-585-2697 218 D
rhovey@smith.edu

HOW, John .... 406-994-2001 263 G
john.how@montana.edu

HOWAR, Julie .... 309-690-6909 138 I
julie.howar@icc.edu

HOWARD, Abby .... 575-646-2035 286 G

HOWARD, Alan .... 903-693-2023 440 E
ahoward@panola.edu

HOWARD, Amy .... 804-484-1600 471 E
amy.howard@richmond.edu

HOWARD, Angela .... 610-436-3515 394 F
ahoward@wcupa.edu

HOWARD, Ann .... 202-884-9608.. 94 A
howarda@trinitydc.edu

HOWARD, April .... 540-986-1800 463 F
ahoward@an.edu

HOWARD, Armando .... 718-270-6484 294 E
ahoward@mec.cuny.edu

HOWARD, Assuanta .... 718-730-7403 294 D
ahoward@lagcc.cuny.edu

HOWARD, Ayanna .... 614-292-2836 358 E
howard.1727@osu.edu

HOWARD, Barry .... 615-514-2787 421 H
bhoward@nossi.edu

HOWARD, Bobby .... 870-743-3000.. 20 F
robert.howard@northark.edu

HOWARD, Brandy .... 925-969-2048.. 40 H
bhoward@dvc.edu

HOWARD, Burt .... 218-335-4253 235 J

HOWARD, Carrie .... 724-503-1001 401 D
choward@washjeff.edu

HOWARD, Catherine .... 903-823-3285 445 C
catherine.howard@texarkanacollege.edu

HOWARD, Cedric .... 970-351-1890.. 84 D

HOWARD, Chad, E .... 479-248-7236.. 19 F
choward@ecollege.edu

HOWARD, Charles, L ... 215-898-8456 399 J
choward@upenn.edu

HOWARD, Chris .... 480-965-2820.. 11 A
chris.howard@asu.edu

HOWARD, Cindy .... 816-268-5424 256 E
choward@nts.edu

HOWARD, Daniel .... 601-925-3350 246 D
drhoward@mc.edu

HOWARD, David .... 601-979-6944 245 G
david.c.howard@jsums.edu

HOWARD, DeAndre .... 864-587-4632 411 F
howardd@smcsc.edu

HOWARD, Devon .... 817-202-6442 444 B
d.howard@swau.edu

HOWARD, Donna .... 443-885-4121 200 F
donna.howard@morgan.edu

HOWARD, Doug .... 615-460-6306 417 B
doug.howard@belmont.edu

HOWARD, Drew .... 863-680-4266 100 F
ahoward@flsouthern.edu

HOWARD, JR.,
Eddie, J .... 859-572-6447 184 B
howarde10@nku.edu

HOWARD, Erica .... 931-598-1229 422 F
eohoward@sewanee.edu

HOWARD, Ezra .... 662-621-4083 244 E
ehoward@coahomacc.edu

HOWARD, Garth, E .... 832-813-6737 438 E
garth.e.howard@lonestar.edu

HOWARD, Gary, E .... 859-858-3511 178 H
gary.howard@asbury.edu

HOWARD, Gene .... 205-726-2366.... 6 E
wehoward@samford.edu

HOWARD, Gregory .... 919-546-8610 339 I
gregory.howard@shawu.edu

HOWARD, Gregory .... 804-257-5717 475 G
gmhoward@vuu.edu

HOWARD, Hurstel .... 630-844-4889 133 A
hhoward@aurora.edu

HOWARD, Jay, R .... 317-940-9874 153 H
jrhoward@butler.edu

HOWARD, Jeff .... 910-521-6000 343 A

HOWARD, Jen .... 605-882-5284 414 D
jen.howard@lakeareatech.edu

HOWARD, Jessica .... 503-399-6591 372 A
jessica.howard@chemeketa.edu

HOWARD, John .... 303-273-3646.. 79 A
jkhoward@mines.edu

HOWARD, Jordan .... 620-768-2909 173 F
jordanh@fortscott.edu

HOWARD, Joseph, E .... 610-499-4000 401 I
jehoward1@widener.edu

HOWARD, Karleen .... 606-451-6905 182 D
karleen.howard@kctcs.edu

HOWARD, Katrina .... 912-427-5876 117 B
khoward@coastalpines.edu

HOWARD, LaMarcus .... 734-487-2470 223 F
lhoward7@emich.edu

HOWARD, Lelia .... 267-502-2680 378 I
lelia.howard@brynathyn.edu

HOWARD, Lonnie .... 409-880-8185 449 A
llhoward@lit.edu

HOWARD, Martin, J .... 617-353-2290 207 C
mjhoward@bu.edu

HOWARD, Mary Ann .... 478-757-5137 127 D
mhoward@wesleyancollege.edu

HOWARD, Michael .... 617-627-3331 219 A
michael.howard@tufts.edu

HOWARD, Michael, P .... 518-564-3140 318 C
mhowa001@plattsburgh.edu

HOWARD, Pamela .... 517-264-7165 230 C
phoward@sienaheights.edu

HOWARD, Predita .... 478-934-3092 122 D
predita.howard@mga.edu

HOWARD, Randy, B .... 386-226-6000.. 98 J
randy.howard@erau.edu

HOWARD, II, Ruben .... 847-635-1807 146 E
rhoward@oakton.edu

HOWARD, Stefanie .... 310-393-0411.. 56 C
stefanie_howard@rand.org

HOWARD, Tammy, L .... 217-443-8552 136 E
t.howard@dacc.edu

HOWARD, Valerie .... 919-962-2211 342 B

HOWARD, Vikki .... 218-335-4255 235 J
vikki.howard@lltc.edu

HOWARD, Yaffa .... 215-635-7300 384 D
yhoward@gratz.edu

HOWARD, Yelitza, M .... 956-326-2142 446 A
yelitza.howard@tamiu.edu

HOWARD-BOSTIC,
Chiquita .... 304-876-5056 489 A
chowardb@shepherd.edu

HOWARD-COSTER,
Claire .... 914-888-5355 305 H
choward@mercy.edu

HOWARD WHITE,
Demetria .... 601-977-7774 248 E
dhoward@tougaloo.edu

HOWARTH, James, R .... 860-465-4418.. 85 G
howarthja@easternct.edu

HOWARTH, Susan .... 270-745-2434 186 A
susan.howarth@wku.edu

HOWARTH-MOORE,
Adrienne .... 512-471-9104 454 C
adrienne.howarth-moore@austin.utexas.edu

HOWATT-NAB, Summer 805-893-5752.. 70 E
showatt-nab@ltsc.ucsb.edu

HOWDEN, Norman .... 214-860-2176 434 A
norman@dcccd.edu

HOWDEN, Tonya .... 269-294-4230 223 J
thowden@glenoaks.edu

HOWDYSHELL,
Cynthia, K .... 540-828-5314 464 C
chowdysh@bridgewater.edu

HOWE, Bob .... 212-636-6550 300 A
howe@fordham.edu

HOWE, Brian .... 620-792-9254 171 F
howeb@bartonccc.edu

HOWE, Derek .... 617-353-6540 207 C
dhowe@bu.edu

HOWE, Jennifer .... 404-894-1868 119 D
jennifer.howe@dev.gatech.edu

HOWE, Joseph .... 757-388-2604 469 H
jhowe@sentara.edu

HOWE, Kara .... 610-330-5090 387 B
howek@lafayette.edu

HOWE, Ken, D .... 985-549-2240 192 E
khowe@selu.edu

HOWE, Mark .... 951-343-4299.. 27 J
mhowe@calbaptist.edu

HOWE, Mark .... 518-464-8508 299 B
mhowe@excelsior.edu

HOWE, Melissa .... 617-747-2316 206 D
ootp@berklee.edu

HOWE, Mike .... 507-433-0621 240 A
mike.howe@riverland.edu

HOWE, Rex .... 740-377-2520 361 D

HOWE, Tiffany .... 605-718-2905 416 D
tiffany.howe@wdt.edu

HOWE, William .... 760-634-1771.. 28 G

HOWELL, Aaron .... 470-578-6000 121 J

HOWELL, Brad .... 704-527-9909 209 G
bhowell@gordonconwell.edu

HOWELL, Bradley .... 904-354-4800 209 G
bhowell@gcts.edu

HOWELL, Cabot .... 770-720-5551 124 E
cabot.howell@reinhardt.edu

HOWELL, Candace .... 843-349-7132 409 A
candace.howell@hgtc.edu

HOWELL, Candice .... 402-465-2401 267 J
chowell@nebrwesleyan.edu

HOWELL, Carson .... 435-283-7255 460 C

HOWELL, Charles .... 330-941-3265 364 G
clhowell01@ysu.edu

HOWELL, Daniel .... 978-478-3400 217 E
dhowell@northpoint.edu

HUDGENS, James .... 404-894-7325 119 D
james.hudgens@gtri.gatech.edu
HUDGENS, Kevin .... 719-502-2000.. 82 D
kevin.hudgens@pikespeak.edu
HUDGIK, Mark .... 413-552-2592 214 D
mhudgik@hcc.edu
HUDGIN, Denise .... 419-251-1324 355 G
denise.hudgin@mercycollege.edu
HUDGINS, Karen .... 904-819-6252.. 99 D
khudgins@flagler.edu
HUDGINS, Molly .... 636-949-4192 254 B
mhudgins@lindenwood.edu
HUDNELL, Jason .... 501-760-4374.. 20 E
jason.hudnell@np.edu
HUDOCK, Amy .... 843-722-5556 411 I
amy.hudock@tridenttech.edu
HUDON, Holly .... 603-428-2477 272 I
hhudon@nec.edu
HUDSON, Adair .... 864-488-4370 409 C
ahudson@limestone.edu
HUDSON, Allen .... 740-245-7841 363 A
ahudson@rio.edu
HUDSON, Andre .... 585-475-5127 312 A
HUDSON, Angela .... 501-686-2504.. 21 G
ahudson@uasys.edu
HUDSON, Ashley .... 503-777-7259 375 F
hashley@reed.edu
HUDSON, Barbara .... 256-840-4147.... 3 F
barbara.hudson@snead.edu
HUDSON, Blake .... 205-726-2704.... 6 E
rdhudson@samford.edu
HUDSON, Bo .... 918-293-4912 368 B
steven.w.hudson@okstate.edu
HUDSON, Bobby .... 615-230-3445 424 F
bobby.hudson@volstate.edu
HUDSON, Caprice .... 740-376-4000 355 E
HUDSON, Cindy .... 773-244-5691 145 F
cehudson2@northpark.edu
HUDSON, David, D .... 714-895-8104.. 38 E
dhudson@gwc.cccd.edu
HUDSON, David, J .... 434-243-0900 471 F
djh2t@virginia.edu
HUDSON, Dean, P .... 843-349-2739 407 B
dhudson@coastal.edu
HUDSON, Donald, M .... 609-652-4883 283 A
donald.hudson@stockton.edu
HUDSON, Edith .... 414-288-3633 492 E
edith.hudson@marquette.edu
HUDSON, El Pagnier .... 305-348-2190 109 H
elpagnier.hudson@fiu.edu
HUDSON, Elizabeth .... 617-373-2170 217 D
HUDSON, Garien .... 419-559-2525 361 B
ghudson01@terra.edu
HUDSON, Gregory .... 501-370-5295.. 21 A
gahudson@philander.edu
HUDSON, Holly .... 979-845-0544 446 B
studyabroad@tamu.edu
HUDSON, Janice, M .... 202-885-8601.. 94 D
jhudson@wesleyseminary.edu
HUDSON, Jennifer, M .... 713-646-1819 443 C
jhudson@stcl.edu
HUDSON, John .... 713-221-8664 452 B
hudsonj@uhd.edu
HUDSON, Karen .... 615-550-3165 427 F
karen.hudson@williamsoncc.edu
HUDSON, Krystiel .... 626-316-5324.. 63 D
mhudson@saybrook.edu
HUDSON, Lea Ann .... 404-471-6402 114 E
lhudson@agnesscott.edu
HUDSON, LeVetta .... 731-989-6769 418 H
lhudson@fhu.edu
HUDSON, Lori .... 304-336-8990 489 B
lori.hudson@westliberty.edu
HUDSON, Lyla .... 843-792-8721 409 D
hudsonly@musc.edu
HUDSON, Mac .... 352-638-9737.. 96 B
mhudson@beaconcollege.edu
HUDSON, Mark, A .... 217-581-7711 137 C
mahudson@eiu.edu
HUDSON, Matthew .... 417-447-8102 257 B
hudsonm@otc.edu
HUDSON, Mattie .... 256-352-8170.... 4 A
mattie.hudson@wallacestate.edu
HUDSON, Merissa .... 850-769-1551 101 O
mhudson@gulfcoast.edu
HUDSON, Michael, J .... 630-637-5661 145 E
mjhudson@noctrl.edu
HUDSON, Rob .... 719-502-3193.. 82 D
rob.hudson@pikespeak.edu
HUDSON, Robbie .... 540-231-5673 466 E
rhudson@vcom.vt.edu
HUDSON, Robert .... 903-434-8239 440 A
rhudson@ntcc.edu

HUDSON, Sean .... 773-907-4428 134 N
shudson52@ccc.edu
HUDSON, Sheila .... 707-864-7000.. 64 F
sheila.hudson@solano.edu
HUDSON, Shirley .... 972-524-3341 444 E
shirley.hudson@swcc.edu
HUDSON, Sid .... 405-224-3140 371 B
shudson@usao.edu
HUDSON, Stephanie .... 601-857-3280 245 D
stephanie.hudson@hindscc.edu
HUDSON, Stephanie .... 864-379-8718 408 F
hudson@erskine.edu
HUDSON, Thomas .... 601-979-2323 245 G
thomas.k.hudson@jsums.edu
HUDSON, Tijuana, R .... 803-535-5197 406 E
thudson@claflin.edu
HUDSON, Tim .... 931-221-7779 416 H
hudsont@apsu.edu
HUDSON, JR., William .... 850-599-3183 109 E
william.hudsonjr@famu.edu
HUDSON HOSEK,
Hilary .... 312-567-3012 139 H
hhudsonhosek@iit.edu
HUDSPETH, Donald .... 585-475-7077 312 A
don.hudspeth@croatia.rit.edu
HUDSPETH, Josie .... 541-885-1392 374 G
josie.hudspeth@oit.edu
HUDSPETH, William .... 770-426-2833 122 A
william.hudspeth2@life.edu
HUEBER, Charlie .... 830-792-7278 442 G
deanofstudents@schreiner.edu
HUEBNER, Casey .... 425-576-5807 480 D
casey.huebner@lwtech.edu
HUEBNER, Erinn .... 616-538-2330 224 B
ehuebner@gracechristian.edu
HUEBNER, Mj .... 269-337-7172 225 B
mj.huebner@kzoo.edu
HUEBNER, JR.,
Thomas .... 601-484-8618 246 B
thuebner@meridiancc.edu
HUEBNER, Tim .... 901-843-3653 422 C
huebner@rhodes.edu
HUEBOTTER, Chris .... 573-288-6542 251 I
chuebotter@culver.edu
HUEG, Kurt .... 650-949-7777.. 43 A
HUEG, Kurt .... 650-949-7394.. 43 A
huegkurt@foothill.edu
HUELSBECK, Tom, A .... 253-535-7200 481 C
tom.huelsbeck@plu.edu
HUENEMANN, Kurt .... 419-448-2351 353 D
keh@heidelberg.edu
HUENERFAUTH, Matt .... 585-475-5365 312 A
HUERTA, Homer, J .... 512-428-1385 441 N
homerh@stedwards.edu
HUERTA, Patricia .... 312-362-8601 136 F
phuerta@depaul.edu
HUERTA, Paul .... 312-341-4167 148 A
phuerta@roosevelt.edu
HUERTA, Yvette, V .... 915-831-2654 435 B
yhuerta@epcc.edu
HUERTAS, Carmelo, V .... 973-353-5581 281 C
carmelo.huertas@rutgers.edu
HUERTAS, Felix, R .... 787-743-7979 509 D
fhuertas@suagm.edu
HUERTAS, Roxanne .... 856-225-6532 281 A
roxanne.huertas@camden.rutgers.edu
HUERTAS GONZÁLEZ,
Félix, R .... 787-257-7373 509 B
fhuertas@uagm.edu
HUESER, Kyle .... 712-274-6400 170 H
kyle.hueser@witcc.edu
HUET, Yvette .... 704-687-8696 342 C
ymhuet@uncc.edu
HUETH, Jeremy .... 303-860-5600.. 83 L
HUEWITT, Kenneth .... 713-313-7011 448 D
HUEY, Keith .... 248-218-2124 229 I
khuey@rochesteru.edu
HUEY, Marcy .... 205-348-4132.... 7 G
mhuey@ua.edu
HUFF, Gary .... 512-448-8768 441 N
ghuff2@stedwards.edu
HUFF, Julie .... 334-844-5777.... 4 E
hilljul@auburn.edu
HUFF, Kim .... 803-535-1204 410 C
huffk@octech.edu
HUFF, Mary .... 502-272-8359 179 D
mhuff@bellarmine.edu
HUFF, Michael .... 256-824-6633.... 8 B
michael.huff@uah.edu
HUFF, Michael .... 216-987-4294 351 D
michael.huff@tri-c.edu
HUFF, Peter .... 630-829-6664 133 B
phuff@ben.edu

HUFF, Steven .... 801-863-8863 460 A
huff@uvu.edu
HUFF, Tim, T .... 405-744-2110 367 G
tim.huff@okstate.edu
HUFFAKER, Joshua .... 470-322-1200 422 G
jhuffaker@south.edu
HUFFAKER, Lindsi .... 870-633-4480.. 19 E
lhuffaker@eacc.edu
HUFFER, Sarah .... 434-200-3070 464 G
HUFFINE, David, M .... 404-378-8821 117 D
HUFFMAN, Barb .... 810-762-9680 225 F
bhuffman@kettering.edu
HUFFMAN, Ben .... 916-577-2200.. 76 C
bhuffman@jessup.edu
HUFFMAN, Donald .... 440-366-7397 355 B
HUFFMAN, Jodi .... 704-922-6250 334 E
huffman.jodi@gaston.edu
HUFFMAN, Keith .... 740-362-3380 355 H
khuffman@mtso.edu
HUFFMAN, Lisa .... 940-898-2204 451 A
lhuffman1@twu.edu
HUFFMAN, Mari, L .... 419-866-0261 361 A
mlhuffman@stautzenberger.com
HUFFMAN, Monica, R .... 660-543-4106 259 K
mhuffman@ucmo.edu
HUFFMAN, Rebecca .... 276-328-0139 471 G
reg5a@uvawise.edu
HUFFMAN, Robin .... 260-399-7700 162 A
rhuffman@sf.edu
HUFFMAN, Tammy, S .... 740-588-1212 364 H
thuffman@zanestate.edu
HUFFMAN, Xander .... 937-760-2410.. 66 F
xhuffman@sksm.edu
HUFFSTETLER, Aimee .... 215-646-7300 384 G
huffstetler.a@gmercyu.edu
HUFFSTETLER, Edward .... 304-384-5241 488 K
ehuffstetler@concord.edu
HUFFSTETLER, Jodie .... 704-355-3920 327 F
jodie.huffstetler@carolinascollege.edu
HUFFSTUTLER, Steven .... 618-650-5234 149 H
shuffst@siue.edu
HUFNAGEL, Michele, A .... 412-536-1096 386 H
michele.hufnagel@laroche.edu
HUFTALIN, Deneece .... 801-957-4226 460 D
deneece.huftalin@slcc.edu
HUFTON, Maren .... 805-756-6770.. 29 K
mhufton@calpoly.edu
HUG-ENGLISH, Cheryl .... 775-784-6122 270 K
cherylh@med.unr.edu
HUGANIR, Gail .... 717-815-1425 402 G
ghuganir@ycp.edu
HUGEE, Larita, L .... 410-651-6144 203 B
llhugee@umes.edu
HUGGINS, Deborah .... 718-997-4443 295 A
deborah.huggins@qc.cuny.edu
HUGGINS, Derrick, E .... 803-777-3150 412 A
dhuggins@mailbox.sc.edu
HUGGINS, Jennifer .... 815-802-8702 141 B
jhuggins@kcc.edu
HUGGINS, Jonathan .... 706-236-2217 116 A
jhuggins@berry.edu
HUGGINS, Michael .... 254-968-9781 445 F
mhuggins@tarleton.edu
HUGGINS, Michael .... 715-232-5904 496 C
hugginsm@uwstout.edu
HUGGINS, Regina, M .... 919-866-5408 338 E
rmhuggins@waketech.edu
HUGGINS, Sheldon .... 718-270-4858 294 E
shuggins@mec.cuny.edu
HUGGINS, Tim .... 864-977-7272 410 A
tim.huggins@ngu.edu
HUGHES, Alan .... 706-236-2202 116 A
rhughes@berry.edu
HUGHES, Andrew .... 775-673-7240 270 I
ahughes@tmcc.edu
HUGHES, Angela .... 865-694-6400 424 C
arhughes1@pstcc.edu
HUGHES, Blanche, M .... 970-491-1101.. 79 E
blanche.hughes@colostate.edu
HUGHES, Bonnie .... 506-865-8588 480 B
hughes_b@heritage.edu
HUGHES, Byron .... 865-974-3179 426 C
byron.hughes@utk.edu
HUGHES, JR., Byron, A .... 540-231-6272 475 D
bahughes@vt.edu
HUGHES, Carol .... 312-362-8592 136 F
chughe23@depaul.edu
HUGHES, Cathie .... 423-775-6596 421 I
HUGHES, Charles .... 318-342-3051 193 A
hughes@ulm.edu
HUGHES, Christopher .... 251-380-2292.... 6 H
chughes@shc.edu

HUGHES, Christy .... 812-866-7012 155 D
hughes@hanover.edu
HUGHES, Cory .... 410-290-7100 199 F
HUGHES, David .... 435-586-7735 459 E
hughes@suu.edu
HUGHES, Deborah .... 786-279-2643 290 B
dhughes@asa.edu
HUGHES, DeVetta .... 843-574-6199 411 I
devetta.hughes@tridenttech.edu
HUGHES, Dorothy .... 934-420-2166 320 C
hughesd@farmingdale.edu
HUGHES, Doug .... 509-544-8310 478 B
djhughes@columbiabasin.edu
HUGHES, Ed .... 901-334-5812 420 E
ehughes@memphisseminary.edu
HUGHES, Ernie, T .... 660-785-4133 259 J
ehughes@truman.edu
HUGHES, George .... 805-756-6650.. 29 K
grhughes@calpoly.edu
HUGHES, Glyn .... 804-484-1656 471 E
ghughes@richmond.edu
HUGHES, Greg .... 301-369-2314 197 F
ghughes@captechu.edu
HUGHES, Jacqueline .... 360-650-3000 485 A
HUGHES, James, J .... 617-287-5428 211 E
jamesj.hughes@umb.edu
HUGHES, James, L .... 410-706-1935 202 F
jhughes@umaryland.edu
HUGHES, Jamie .... 804-289-8053 471 E
jhughes3@richmond.edu
HUGHES, Jason .... 303-273-3892.. 79 A
jasonhughes@mines.edu
HUGHES, Jay .... 870-460-1127.. 22 E
hughesj@uamont.edu
HUGHES, Jeanell, N .... 216-687-7359 350 G
j.hughes20@csuohio.edu
HUGHES, Jennifer .... 903-589-7107 437 D
jguerra@jacksonville-college.edu
HUGHES, Jeremy .... 928-428-8300.. 12 H
jeremy.hughes@eac.edu
HUGHES, Jerry, M .... 660-543-4250 259 K
hughes@ucmo.edu
HUGHES, Jim .... 660-626-2391 249 C
HUGHES, Jim .... 620-235-4154 176 H
jhughes@pittstate.edu
HUGHES, Joe .... 208-459-5219 131 A
jhughes@collegeofidaho.edu
HUGHES, Joedon .... 405-736-0213 369 D
jhughes@rose.edu
HUGHES, Jonathan .... 870-245-5189.. 20 H
hughesj@obu.edu
HUGHES, Joseph .... 479-979-1228.. 24 A
jhughes@ozarks.edu
HUGHES, Joshua, A .... 419-289-5730 347 H
jhughe11@ashland.edu
HUGHES, Kevin, M .... 757-594-7160 465 A
kmhughes@cnu.edu
HUGHES, Kristin .... 413-585-2706 218 D
khughes@smith.edu
HUGHES, Laura .... 208-792-2224 131 F
lhughes@lcsc.edu
HUGHES, LeAnn .... 309-556-3031 140 E
lhughes@iwu.edu
HUGHES, Lecia .... 325-793-4998 439 A
hughes.lecia@mcm.edu
HUGHES, Lee .... 800-785-0585.. 39 F
lee.hughes@columbiacollege.edu
HUGHES, Louise .... 870-612-2013.. 23 B
louise.hughes@uaccb.edu
HUGHES, Mariah .... 207-974-4869 195 A
mhughes@emcc.edu
HUGHES, Mark .... 217-228-5432 147 C
m.hughes56@quincy.edu
HUGHES, Mark .... 860-297-2162.. 88 I
mark.hughes@trincoll.edu
HUGHES, Mark .... 512-245-2501 449 G
mh66@txstate.edu
HUGHES, Matthew .... 773-252-5310 146 D
matthew.hughes@oakpoint.edu
HUGHES, Matthew .... 850-718-2344.. 97 E
hughesm@chipola.edu
HUGHES, Megan .... 708-709-3536 147 A
mhughes3585@prairiestate.edu
HUGHES, Meghan .... 401-825-2188 403 D
meghanhughes@ccri.edu
HUGHES, Melany .... 308-432-6487 267 G
mhughes@csc.edu
HUGHES, Melissa .... 318-257-4205 192 A
mhughes@latech.edu
HUGHES, Melissa, P .... 864-592-4666 411 E
hughesm@sccsc.edu
HUGHES, Meriel .... 303-871-5731.. 84 C
meriel.hughes@du.edu

HUNT, Don .... 919-515-1491 341 E
dehunt2@ncsu.edu
HUNT, Donlad, E .... 530-752-5589.. 69 A
HUNT, Emily .... 806-651-5330 447 D
ehunt@wtamu.edu
HUNT, Faith .... 203-254-4000.. 87 G
fhunt@fairfield.edu
HUNT, Felicia .... 626-395-2923.. 29 B
fhunt@caltech.edu
HUNT, Gerri .... 336-342-4261 337 B
huntg0780@rockinghamcc.edu
HUNT, Gerry .... 405-208-5582 367 E
ghunt@okcu.edu
HUNT, Hollye .... 405-271-8001 370 J
hollye.hunt@ouhealth.com
HUNT, James .... 870-230-5134.. 19 H
huntj@hsu.edu
HUNT, James .... 850-644-4041 110 B
jhunt@fsu.edu
HUNT, Janette .... 727-341-3229 107 C
hunt.janette@spcollege.edu
HUNT, Jeff .... 303-963-3254.. 78 D
jhunt@ccu.edu
HUNT, Jennifer .... 765-641-4063 153 D
jehunt@anderson.edu
HUNT, Karen .... 563-387-1433 167 J
huntka01@luther.edu
HUNT, Katherine .... 352-854-2322.. 97 L
huntk@cf.edu
HUNT, Kristen, H .... 901-843-3730 422 C
huntk@rhodes.edu
HUNT, Laura .... 575-492-2161 288 I
lhunt@usw.edu
HUNT, Lee .... 276-739-2401 474 H
lhunt@vhcc.edu
HUNT, Lisa .... 910-521-6357 343 A
lisa.hunt@uncp.edu
HUNT, Lori .... 509-434-5060 478 C
lori.hunt@ccs.spokane.edu
HUNT, Mark .... 334-386-7140.... 5 D
mhunt@faulkner.edu
HUNT, Mary .... 860-231-5738.. 89 G
mhunt@usj.edu
HUNT, Michelle .... 760-750-8362.. 33 C
mihunt@csusm.edu
HUNT, Patrick, G .... 240-895-4307 201 F
pghunt@smcm.edu
HUNT, Philip .... 701-231-7987 345 D
philip.hunt@ndsu.edu
HUNT, Rusty .... 252-527-6223 335 E
rthunt78@lenoircc.edu
HUNT, Scott, H .... 801-422-6446 458 A
scott_hunt@byu.edu
HUNT, Shane .... 208-282-2601 131 E
shanehunt@isu.edu
HUNT, Shari .... 315-866-0300 301 B
huntsl@herkimer.edu
HUNT, Sherrica .... 251-405-7043.... 1 E
shunt@bishop.edu
HUNT, Sonia .... 937-376-6649 349 H
shunt@centralstate.edu
HUNT, Steve .... 310-434-4689.. 63 B
hunt_steve@smc.edu
HUNT, Steve .... 828-327-7000 332 H
shunt@cvcc.edu
HUNT, T. Jill .... 270-809-3763 184 A
thunt2@murraystate.edu
HUNT, Terry, L .... 520-621-3015.. 16 H
tlhunt@arizona.edu
HUNT, Thomas, M .... 805-437-3352.. 30 D
thomas.hunt@csuci.edu
HUNT, Tolif, R .... 319-273-3217 163 G
tolif.hunt@uni.edu
HUNT, Wendy .... 402-465-2135 267 J
whunt@nebrwesleyan.edu
HUNT-BULL, Nicholas .. 518-327-6223 310 G
nhuntbull@paulsmiths.edu
HUNTER, Aaron .... 503-399-5012 372 A
aaron.hunter@chemeketa.edu
HUNTER, Amy .... 413-585-2245 218 D
ahunter65@smith.edu
HUNTER, Andrea .... 336-256-0091 342 D
aghunter@uncg.edu
HUNTER, Ben .... 812-855-4296 156 B
bdhunter@iu.edu
HUNTER, Ben .... 208-885-6534 132 C
bhunter@uidaho.edu
HUNTER, Chip .... 509-335-3596 484 D
chip.hunter@wsu.edu
HUNTER, Derek .... 919-739-7020 338 F
mdhunter@waynecc.edu
HUNTER, Evie .... 215-489-4471 381 K
evelia.hunter@delval.edu
HUNTER, Gayle .... 386-752-1822.. 99 P
gayle.hunter@fgc.edu
HUNTER, Gerald, E .... 757-823-8011 468 B
gehunter@nsu.edu
HUNTER, Gill .... 859-622-8010 180 B
gill.hunter@eku.edu
HUNTER, Grant .... 402-984-8825 266 C
ghunter@hastings.edu
HUNTER, Jane .... 520-621-5168.. 16 H
jhunter2@arizona.edu
HUNTER, Jasmine .... 225-771-2552 191 C
jhunter@sulc.edu
HUNTER, Jeff, C .... 304-462-6113 488 M
jeff.hunter@glenville.edu
HUNTER, Jenna .... 253-879-3202 483 G
jhunter@pugetsound.edu
HUNTER, Jenna .... 828-669-8012 331 H
jenna.hunter@montreat.edu
HUNTER, Jessica, S ..... 570-326-3761 392 S
jhunter@pct.edu
HUNTER, Joanna .... 318-342-7942 193 A
jhunter@ulm.edu
HUNTER, Joseph .... 503-883-2202 373 E
jhunter3@linfield.edu
HUNTER, Kierstyn .... 413-236-2101 213 E
khunter@berkshirecc.edu
HUNTER, Kim .... 319-356-3155 163 F
kimberly-d-hunter@uiowa.edu
HUNTER, Kymm .... 803-705-4519 405 G
kymm.hunter@benedict.edu
HUNTER, Larry, T .... 614-236-6641 348 I
lhunter2@capital.edu
HUNTER, LeAnn .... 509-452-5100 481 E
lhunter@pnwu.edu
HUNTER, Lorna .... 410-778-7114 204 E
lhunter2@washcoll.edu
HUNTER, Lynn .... 781-239-3111 214 E
lhunter@massbay.edu
HUNTER, Marc .... 405-382-9950 369 E
m.hunter@sscok.edu
HUNTER, Mark .... 828-669-8012 331 H
mark.hunter@montreat.edu
HUNTER, Martin, J .... 410-543-6150 204 A
mjhunter@salisbury.edu
HUNTER, Patti .... 805-565-6076.. 75 I
phunter@westmont.edu
HUNTER, Rebecca .... 212-229-5620 307 E
hunterr@newschool.edu
HUNTER, Richie .... 541-346-3134 376 G
richieh@uoregon.edu
HUNTER, Sandra .... 252-638-7249 333 F
hunters@cravencc.edu
HUNTER, Sean .... 614-947-6103 352 J
sean.hunter@franklin.edu
HUNTER, Teressa .... 405-466-3274 366 B
teressa.hunter@langston.edu
HUNTER, Tiffany .... 937-328-6025 350 D
huntert@clarkstate.edu
HUNTER, Tiffany .... 602-787-6610.. 13 G
tiffany.hunter@paradisevalley.edu
HUNTER, Timothy .... 704-216-3694 337 C
timothy.hunter@rccc.edu
HUNTER, Tracie .... 310-434-4871.. 63 B
hunter_tracie@smc.edu
HUNTER, Vickie .... 614-287-2402 351 B
vhunter@cscc.edu
HUNTER, Will .... 843-661-1841 408 H
will.hunter@fmarion.edu
HUNTER, William .... 670-237-6719 503 G
william.hunter@marianas.edu
HUNTER-MCKINNEY,
Shaunna, E .... 434-223-6193 466 K
shunter@hsc.edu
HUNTHAUSEN,
Stephanie .... 406-447-6352 263 F
stephanie.hunthausen@helenacollege.edu
HUNTINGTON, Lucas .... 225-768-1732 186 H
lucas.huntington@franu.edu
HUNTINGTON, Robert ... 419-448-2202 353 D
president@heidelberg.edu
HUNTLEY, Brian .... 315-268-6723 295 E
bhuntley@clarkson.edu
HUNTLEY, Celestine ...... 954-201-7350.. 96 F
HUNTLEY, Deborah, R .. 989-964-4296 229 L
huntley@svsu.edu
HUNTLEY, Julie .... 918-495-7040 368 F
jhuntley@oru.edu
HUNTLEY, Kristy .... 403-205-3338 205 C
kristy.huntley@aic.edu
HUNTLEY, Miriam .... 910-410-1834 336 G
mbhuntley@richmondcc.edu
HUNTSINGER, Trish ...... 828-395-1297 335 B
thuntsinger@isothermal.edu
HUNTZ, Jude .... 913-758-6259 177 I
jude.huntz@stmary.edu
HUNZER, Kathleen .... 715-425-0720 496 A
kathleen.hunzer@uwrf.edu
HUNZIGER, Lucas .... 785-442-6180 174 C
lhunziger@highlandcc.edu
HUO,
Xiaoming (Sharon) ..... 931-372-3463 425 B
xhuo@tntech.edu
HUOPPI, Jennifer .... 860-465-4357.. 85 G
huoppij@easternct.edu
HUPFER, Mary, A .... 812-464-1627 162 B
mhupfer@usi.edu
HUPKE, Jennifer .... 219-989-2953 160 A
jhupke@pnw.edu
HUPP, Stephen .... 304-424-8273 490 A
stephen.hupp@wvup.edu
HUPPE, Alicia, L .... 972-377-1749 432 I
ahuppe@collin.edu
HUPPERT, Susan .... 515-271-1384 165 C
susan.huppert@dmu.edu
HURBANIS, Julie, T ...... 651-696-6475 236 C
jhurbani@macalester.edu
HURD, Amy .... 309-438-2187 140 C
arhurd@ilstu.edu
HURD, Anne, J .... 336-272-7102 329 B
anne.hurd@greensboro.edu
HURD, Brian .... 216-397-1974 353 O
bhurd@jcu.edu
HURD, Karen .... 315-312-3627 318 B
karen.hurd@oswego.edu
HURD, Nicole .... 610-330-5000 387 B
HURD, Phillip .... 713-743-8000 451 F
pwhurd@uh.edu
HURD, Roy .... 707-546-4000.. 42 A
rhurd@empcol.edu
HURD, Sherie .... 707-546-4000.. 42 A
shurd@empcol.edu
HURD-CRANK, Cathy .... 606-886-3863 181 A
cathy.hurdcrank@kctcs.edu
HURDA, Lisa .... 608-757-7704 497 D
lhurda@blackhawk.edu
HURDT, Emily .... 704-669-4321 333 C
hurdte@clevelandcc.edu
HURLBERT, Jeffrey, H ... 202-685-4344 501 I
jeffrey.h.hurlbert.mil@ndu.edu
HURLBUT, Bradford, D . 201-692-2170 276 I
hurlbut@fdu.edu
HURLBUT, Jeffrey .... 949-451-5546.. 65 B
jhurlbut@ivc.edu
HURLEY, Charles, T ...... 574-631-7495 161 G
hurley.32@nd.edu
HURLEY, Deanne .... 440-646-8320 363 C
dhurley@ursuline.edu
HURLEY,
Donald (Shane) .... 210-431-5531 440 D
dshurley@ollusa.edu
HURLEY, Elizabeth .... 617-521-2000 218 C
HURLEY, Jake .... 530-741-6976.. 77 D
jhurley@yccd.edu
HURLEY, James .... 617-627-4337 219 A
james.hurley@tufts.edu
HURLEY, James .... 254-968-9100 445 F
president@tarleton.edu
HURLEY, James .... 713-348-4057 441 K
james.hurley@rice.edu
HURLEY, Jeffrey .... 816-584-6226 257 E
jeffrey.hurley@park.edu
HURLEY, Kristin, M .... 301-447-5372 201 A
k.hurley@msmary.edu
HURLEY, Marycruz .... 417-626-1234 257 A
HURLEY, Nicole .... 239-938-7700 102 C
HURLEY, Rachel .... 937-529-2201 361 F
rehurley@united.edu
HURLEY, Roberta .... 864-597-4044 413 E
hurleyrl@wofford.edu
HURLEY, Ronald .... 201-200-3127 278 F
rhurley@njcu.edu
HURLEY, Sam .... 903-928-3288 451 C
shurley@tvcc.edu
HURLEY, Tim .... 804-862-6100 469 E
HURLEY, Wanda .... 601-635-2111 245 B
whurley@eccc.edu
HURLOW, Julia .... 765-998-4924 161 A
julia_hurlow@taylor.edu
HURN, Jeffrey .... 785-442-6077 174 C
jhurn@highlandcc.edu
HURN, Patricia, D .... 734-764-7185 231 A
phurn@umich.edu
HURRELL, Rockie .... 719-502-2007.. 82 D
rockie.hurrell@pikespeak.edu
HURREN, Lee .... 575-562-2443 285 E
HURSE, Jeremy .... 828-669-8012 331 H
jeremy.hurse@montreat.edu
HURSSEY, Elizabeth ...... 662-254-3531 247 C
ejhurssey@mvsu.edu
HURSSEY, Terrence ...... 662-254-3584 247 C
terrence.hurssey@mvsu.edu
HURST, Andrew .... 719-590-6797.. 80 B
ahurst@coloradotech.edu
HURST, Angela .... 334-420-4483.... 3 H
alhurst@trenholmstate.edu
HURST, Ashley .... 940-397-4461 439 F
ashley.hurst@msutexas.edu
HURST, Carl .... 570-941-6344 400 C
carl.hurst@scranton.edu
HURST, Corinne, C .... 703-323-3101 473 G
churst@nvcc.edu
HURST, Jamie .... 303-615-2044.. 81 L
jhurst7@msudenver.edu
HURST, Jason .... 704-669-6000 333 C
hurstj@clevelandcc.edu
HURST, Jeffrey, J .... 801-626-7256 460 B
jhurst@weber.edu
HURST, Kevin .... 972-860-4838 433 G
khurst@dcccd.edu
HURST, Mark .... 423-585-6876 424 G
mark.hurst@ws.edu
HURST, Travis .... 405-733-7917 369 D
thurst@rose.edu
HURT, Aaron .... 620-235-4680 176 H
ahurt@pittstate.edu
HURT, Aaron .... 317-940-9697 153 H
ahurt@butler.edu
HURT, Amelia .... 317-278-8415 157 B
amehurt@iupui.edu
HURT, Christi .... 919-962-2211 342 B
HURT, Robert .... 434-592-4898 467 E
rhurt1@liberty.edu
HURT, Shannon, M .... 757-683-7141 468 C
ssauerwa@odu.edu
HURTADO, John, E .... 979-845-1306 446 B
jehurtado@tamu.edu
HURTE, Vernon .... 410-704-2055 204 B
vhurte@towson.edu
HURTE, Vernon, J .... 515-294-1020 163 E
vhurte@iastate.edu
HURTIENNE,
Matthew, W .... 262-243-5700 491 E
matthew.hurtienne@cuw.edu
HURTIG, Julie .... 419-772-2032 358 D
j-hurtig@onu.edu
HURTIG, Julie, K .... 419-772-2032 358 D
j-hurtig@onu.edu
HURULA, Janet .... 505-224-4000 285 B
jhurula@cnm.edu
HURVITZ, Lori .... 504-865-5901 191 D
lhurvitz@tulane.edu
HURVITZ, Tate .... 619-644-7390.. 44 H
tate.hurvitz@gcccd.edu
HURWIT, Joshua, S .... 718-990-5699 313 B
hurwitj@stjohns.edu
HURWITCH, Stacie .... 518-354-5282 309 G
shurwitch@nccc.edu
HUSBAND, Carl .... 281-425-6396 438 B
chusband@lee.edu
HUSBAND, Eileen, K ...... 248-341-2184 228 H
ekhusban@oaklandcc.edu
HUSBAND-ARDOIN,
Madeline .... 337-482-6826 192 F
madeline.husband@louisiana.edu
HUSBANDS FEALING,
Kaye .... 404-385-2995 119 D
khf@gatech.edu
HUSELTON, Ken .... 412-323-4000 378 H
khuselton@manchesterbidwell.org
HUSH, Ken .... 620-341-5551 173 C
khush@emporia.edu
HUSHON, Kate .... 814-868-9900 383 C
kateh@erieit.edu
HUSIC, Diane .... 610-625-7100 390 D
husicd@moravian.edu
HUSKEY, Dontez .... 615-327-6185 420 D
dhuskey@mmc.edu
HUSKEY, Jeff .... 805-893-2181.. 70 E
jeff.huskey@recreation.ucsb.edu
HUSKEY, Melynda .... 360-650-3839 485 A
melynda.huskey@wwu.edu
HUSLIG, Lorie .... 940-898-3201 451 A
lhuslig@twu.edu
HUSMAN, John .... 626-398-2222.. 76 B
HUSMANN, Calvin, D ... 920-832-6517 492 B
calvin.d.husmann@lawrence.edu
HUSMANN, Mike .... 712-274-5310 168 C
husmann@morningside.edu

ICE, Richard 320-363-5503 234 I rice@csbsju.edu
ICENHOWER, Nathan 541-684-7221 371 H nicenhower@bushnell.edu
ICHIGAYA, Frank 925-473-7391 40 I fichigaya@losmedanos.edu
ICHSAN, Tony 509-527-5999 485 C ichsan@whitman.edu
ICKES, Jessica 321-674-7569 100 A jickes@fit.edu
IDE, Susan 248-218-2059 229 I side@rochesteru.edu
IDELL, Steven 903-565-5515 455 C sidell@uttyler.edu
IDETA, Lori 808-956-3290 129 B ideta@hawaii.edu
IDZERDA, Yves 406-994-7838 263 G idzerda@physics.montana.edu
IEVERS, Teresa 253-589-6039 478 A teresa.ievers@cptc.edu
IFERT JOHNSON, Danette 269-337-7162 225 B danette.johnson@kzoo.edu
IFRAH, Joseph 443-548-6037 201 B jifrah@nirc.edu
IGHODARO, Osaro, O 602-243-8036 14 C osaro.ighodaro@southmountaincc.edu
IGLEHART, Hope 770-593-2257 120 E
IGOE, Michael 209-588-5236 76 J igoem@yosemite.edu
IGONOR, Primrose 740-386-4125 355 F igonorp@mtc.edu
IGRAM, Lisa 562-903-4722 27 E lisa.igram@biola.edu
IGWIKE, Richard 504-816-4830 186 F rigwike@dillard.edu
IHEANYI-IGWE, Agametochukwu 541-684-7314 371 H aiheanyiigwe@bushnell.edu
IHEKWEAZU, Stanley, N 803-536-8392 410 H sihekwea@scsu.edu
IHEKWEAZU, Stanley, N 803-536-8860 410 H sihekwea@scsu.edu
IHRER, Kenneth 212-650-7400 293 B kihrer@ccny.cuny.edu
IHRIG, Stacy 515-574-1138 166 G ihrig@iowacentral.edu
IHRKE, Barbara 765-677-1578 157 F barbara.ihrke@indwes.edu
IKACH, Yugo 724-938-1589 394 C ikach@calu.edu
IKEGAMI, Robin 916-558-2226 51 B ikegamr@scc.losrios.edu
IKEM, Fidelis, M 601-979-2411 245 G fidelis.ikem@jsums.edu
IKHARO, Sadiq 510-466-7336 57 C sikharo@peralta.edu
IKNER, Martha Faye 773-995-3526 134 J mikner@csu.edu
ILA, Daryush 678-839-2630 127 A dila@westga.edu
ILER, Clifton 434-924-1424 471 F cliff.iler@virginia.edu
ILES, Linda 530-221-4275 63 G finaid@shasta.edu
ILIAKIS-DOHERTY, Sophia 360-417-6219 481 F sdoherty@pencol.edu
ILIC, Ashley 559-278-7303 31 D ailic@csufresno.edu
ILICETO, Thomas 212-229-5101 307 E ilicetot@newschool.edu
ILIEVA, Vessela, K 801-863-5183 460 A vessela.ilieva@uvu.edu
ILINCA, Ingrid 573-592-5358 261 F
ILINCA, Ingrid 573-592-5323 261 F ingrid.ilinca@westminster-mo.edu
ILLICH, Paul 402-323-3415 268 D pillich@southeast.edu
ILLIES, Diane 320-308-5572 240 D diane.illies@sctcc.edu
IM, Dou Ho 562-926-1023 58 A
IM, Douho 323-643-0301 25 L
IM, Manyul, E 203-576-4234 89 A manyulim@bridgeport.edu
IM, Sam 215-887-5511 401 G sim@wts.edu
IMAFUJI, Elizabeth 765-641-4441 153 D elimafuji@anderson.edu
IMASUEN, Edwin 252-536-7239 334 G eimasuen@halifaxcc.edu
IMBRACSIO, Nicola 612-728-5146 242 H nimbracs@smumn.edu
IMBRAGULIO, Lisa 205-726-4172 6 E lcimbrag@samford.edu
IMBRESCIA, Jeffrey, D 724-653-2200 382 C jimbrescia@dec.edu
IMBRESCIA, Julian 724-653-2213 382 C julian@dec.edu
IMBRIALE, William 718-409-5879 320 D wimbriale@sunymaritime.edu
IMBRIGLIO, Sarah 908-526-1200 280 C sarah.imbriglio@raritanval.edu
IMBROCK, Ryan 419-783-2302 351 J rimbrock@defiance.edu
IMEL, Travis 202-651-5064 92 B travis.imel@gallaudet.edu
IMES, Amber 480-994-9244 16 C amberi@swiha.edu
IMES, Jean 352-854-2322 97 L imesj@cf.edu
IMES, Josh 304-293-5355 489 E jmimes@mail.wvu.edu
IMES, Melissa, J 717-262-2000 402 D melissa.imes@wilson.edu
IMHOFF, Dan 608-822-2401 498 H dimhoff@swtc.edu
IMHOFF, Donna 216-987-5125 351 D donna.imhoff@tri-c.edu
IMHOFF, Maren, E 212-327-8682 312 B imhoff@rockefeller.edu
IMIG, Aaron 503-589-8105 372 G aimig@corban.edu
IMLER, Mary Elizabeth 815-740-2274 152 E mimler@stfrancis.edu
IMMLER, Eric 410-386-4639 200 D eimmler@mcdaniel.edu
IMPERATO, Pascal 718-270-1056 316 E pascal.imperato@downstate.edu
IMPERIALE, Michael, J 734-763-3472 231 A imperial@umich.edu
INABNIT, Lanny 704-403-3502 327 B lanny.inabnit@atriumhealth.org
INAFUKU, Derek 808-845-9123 129 G dinafuku@hawaii.edu
INAKE, Rachael 808-455-0676 130 A rinake@hawaii.edu
INBODY, Brian, L 620-432-0300 176 A binbody@neosho.edu
INCANDELA, Joe 805-893-8270 70 E incandela@research.ucsb.edu
INCERA, Vivian 956-665-8726 455 A vivian.incera@utrgv.edu
INCH, Edward 507-389-1111 238 L
INCH, Megan 336-841-9166 329 E minch@highpoint.edu
INCIARDI, Kristin 215-545-6400 391 D kinciardi@peirce.edu
INCITTI, Merri, S 304-367-4832 488 L merri.incitti@fairmontstate.edu
INFANTI, Steven, M 717-901-5146 385 G sinfanti@harrisburgu.edu
INFUSINO, Melissa 562-938-3217 48 K minfusino@lbcc.edu
INGALLS, Brett 919-573-5350 340 A bingalls@shepherds.edu
INGALLS, Dianne, J 603-646-3001 272 F dianne.j.ingalls@dartmouth.edu
INGALLS, Erica 303-404-5332 80 I erica.ingalls@frontrange.edu
INGALLS, Jenna 800-607-6377 60 C jingalls@samuelmerritt.edu
INGALLS SAUFLEY, Leigh 207-780-4141 196 J
INGARGIOLA, Janet 217-709-0920 142 A
INGBER, Marc 303-556-2870 84 B marc.ingber@ucdenver.edu
INGBRITSEN, Sherry 941-355-9080 98 E
INGE, Brittany 502-213-5155 181 H brittany.inge@kctcs.edu
INGERMAN, Bret 850-201-6082 112 B bret.ingerman@tcc.fl.edu
INGERSOLL, Christopher 407-823-6424 110 D christopher.ingersoll@ucf.edu
INGERSOLL, Julia 610-526-6132 385 F jingersoll@harcum.edu
INGLAND, Susan 620-417-1400 177 C susan.ingland@sccc.edu
INGLE, Karen 616-331-3688 224 D inglek@gvsu.edu
INGLE, III, Kenneth 704-216-3577 337 C ken.ingle@rccc.edu
INGLE, Kent 863-667-5002 108 I kingle@seu.edu
INGLES, Susan, L 414-410-4236 490 J slingles@stritch.edu
INGMIRE, Eric 785-442-6020 174 C eingmire@highlandcc.edu
INGMIRE, Mac 217-732-3168 142 D
INGMIRE, Randall 217-234-5253 141 H ringmire@lakelandcollege.edu
INGOLD, Rie 336-334-3520 342 D rieingold@uncg.edu
INGRAFFIA STRONG, Deborah 775-445-3334 271 A deborah.ingraffia@wnc.edu
INGRAHAM, Barry 207-768-2706 195 C bingraham@nmcc.edu
INGRAHAM, Jennifer 816-654-7000 253 I
INGRAHAM, Timothy 978-468-7111 209 G tingraham@gcts.edu
INGRAM, Amy 478-934-5204 122 D amy.ingram@mga.edu
INGRAM, Anna 903-434-8366 440 A aingram@ntcc.edu
INGRAM, Archinya 803-327-7402 407 A aingram@clintoncollege.edu
INGRAM, Beth 815-753-0493 145 H bingram@niu.edu
INGRAM, Beverly 318-487-7694 187 B beverly.ingram@lcuniversity.edu
INGRAM, Bill 501-420-1200 17 D bill.ingram@arkansasbaptist.edu
INGRAM, Brian, C 731-881-7069 426 E cingram@utm.edu
INGRAM, Casey 318-257-4917 192 A casey@latech.edu
INGRAM, Clark 603-880-8308 273 F
INGRAM, Clay 850-644-2525 110 B hcingram@fsu.edu
INGRAM, David 817-461-8741 429 C dingram@abu.edu
INGRAM, Donnie 803-327-7402 407 A dingram@clintoncollege.edu
INGRAM, Donnie, L 563-333-5826 169 D ingramdonniel@sau.edu
INGRAM, Geoff 951-785-2000 47 F gingram@lasierra.edu
INGRAM, Iris 714-480-7342 58 E ingram_iris@rsccd.edu
INGRAM, Iris, I 714-480-7340 58 F ingram_iris@rsccd.edu
INGRAM, J. Kevin 785-539-3571 175 F kingram@mccks.edu
INGRAM, John 412-536-1181 386 H john.ingram@laroche.edu
INGRAM, Joyce 850-412-5156 109 E joyce.ingram@famu.edu
INGRAM, Joyce 850-412-5146 109 E joyce.ingram@famu.edu
INGRAM, Krista 315-228-7797 296 C kingram@colgate.edu
INGRAM, Lashawanda, T 315-386-7128 319 E ingraml@canton.edu
INGRAM, Libby 501-686-6732 22 D leingram@uams.edu
INGRAM, Maleka 866-492-5336 243 G maleka.ingram@mail.waldenu.edu
INGRAM, Mark, T 205-934-0766 8 A mingram@uab.edu
INGRAM, Mary, H 256-352-7820 4 A mary.ingram@wallacestate.edu
INGRAM, Raymond 937-971-2862 359 J ringram@payneseminary.edu
INGRAM, SR., Roderick, L 330-325-6673 357 D ringram@neomed.edu
INGRAM, Shannon 410-669-9200 200 B singram@mica.edu
INGRAM, Trent 870-248-4000 18 H trent.ingram@blackrivertech.edu
INGRAM, William 615-460-6568 417 B william.ingram@belmont.edu
INGRAM-WALLACE, Brenda, J 610-921-7585 377 F bingramwallace@albright.edu
INGRASSIA, Catherine 804-828-8295 472 D cingrass@vcu.edu
INGS, Margaret Ann 617-824-8299 208 G margaret_ann_ings@emerson.edu
INGVALDSON, Stephanie 916-278-4868 33 A ingvaldson@csus.edu
INIGUEZ, Alicia 408-285-1761 12 D
INIGUEZ, Edmond 719-549-3206 82 I edmond.iniguez@pueblocc.edu
INIGUEZ, Maria 509-682-6400 484 H miniguez@wvc.edu
INKSTER, Kathy 606-546-1616 185 B kyinkster@unionky.edu
INLOW, Laura 618-468-3255 142 B linlow@lc.edu
INMAN, Barbara, L 757-727-5264 466 L barbara.inman@hamptonu.edu
INMAN, Don 630-942-2972 135 F inmand@cod.edu
INMAN, John, G 724-458-2176 384 F jginman@gcc.edu
INMAN, Kimberly 740-351-3554 360 E kinman@shawnee.edu
INMAN, Lisa 910-410-1734 336 G ldinman@richmondcc.edu
INMAN, Stan, D 801-585-5028 459 D sinman@sa.utah.edu
INMAN, Steve, G 814-868-8258 387 C sinman@mch1.org
INMAN, Tim 541-346-3440 376 G tbinman@uoregon.edu
INNERST, Sean 303-937-4420 77 J
INNIGER, Alyssa, K 507-344-7874 233 I alyssa.inniger@blc.edu
INNISS, Tasha 404-270-5897 126 A tinniss@spelman.edu
INOUYE, Carolyn 805-678-5803 74 A cinouye@vcccd.edu
INOUYE, Susan, K 808-956-8155 128 I susani@hawaii.edu
INOWAY-RONNIE, Eden 608-265-5975 494 D eden.inowayronnie@wisc.edu
INSKEEP, Kathryn 802-258-3101 462 B kathryn.inskeep@sit.edu
INTILLE, Amy 617-989-4885 219 D intillea@wit.edu
INTINE, Robert 847-578-8579 148 B robert.intine@rosalindfranklin.edu
INTROCASO, CDP, Candace 412-536-1204 386 H cintrocaso@laroche.edu
INYANG, Otu 817-272-2185 454 B otu.inyang@uta.edu
INZER, Monica, C 315-859-4421 300 F minzer@hamilton.edu
INZERILLA, Tina 925-424-1156 36 A tinzerilla@laspositascollege.edu
IOANNOU, Elaine 718-631-6222 295 B eioannou@qcc.cuny.edu
IOLI, Christine 412-809-5100 395 F ioli.christine@ptcollege.edu
IORG, Jeff 909-687-1701 43 G jeffiorg@gs.edu
IP, James 408-433-2280 36 I
IPACH, Nichole 805-437-8893 30 D nichole.ipach@csuci.edu
IPPOLITO, Vincent, T 240-500-2216 199 A vtippolito@hagerstowncc.edu
IRANI, Daraius 410-704-6363 204 B dirani@towson.edu
IRBY, Adam, W 336-322-2253 336 D adam.irby@piedmontcc.edu
IRBY, Bernice 803-934-3408 409 H birby@morris.edu
IRBY, Brandon 918-343-7771 369 A birby@rsu.edu
IRBY, Melissa 972-758-3831 432 I mirby@collin.edu
IRBY, Michele 573-651-5120 258 J mirby@semo.edu
IRELAND, Alan, G 336-750-2935 343 E irelandag@wssu.edu
IRELAND, Jim 620-792-9339 171 F irelandj@bartonccc.edu
IRELAND, Patricia 607-735-1804 298 G pireland@elmira.edu
IRELAND, R. Duane 979-845-4712 446 B rdireland@tamu.edu
IRELAND, Shonda 573-875-8700 251 A
IRELAND, Timothy 716-286-8342 309 F provost@niagara.edu
IREY, Sayumi 206-934-5353 482 H sayumi.irey@seattlecolleges.edu
IRICK, Shirley 718-270-5000 294 E sirick@mec.cuny.edu
IRIS, Michael 212-986-4343 291 A mki@berkeleycollege.edu
IRIS, Michael 973-278-5400 274 J mki@berkeleycollege.edu

JACHIM-MOORE, Darrell, K .... 585-292-2185 306 K djachim-moore@monroecc.edu
JACHNA, Timothy, J ..... 513-556-9808 361 I timothy.jachna@uc.edu
JACINTO, Marie .... 713-221-5806 452 B jacintom@uhd.edu
JACK, Adam .... 724-852-3211 401 E ajack@waynesburg.edu
JACK, Eric .... 205-934-8800.... 8 A ejack@uab.edu
JACK, Grilly .... 691-320-3795 503 B gjack@comfsm.fm
JACK, L, H .... 315-228-7407 296 C lhjack@colgate.edu
JACKANICZ, Jeffrey ..... 415-405-4061.. 34 A jjackanicz@sfsu.edu
JACKLIN, Lori .... 714-463-7541.. 51 D ljacklin@ketchum.edu
JACKLITSCH, Anthony ... 845-341-4715 310 D
JACKLOSKY, Robert ...... 718-405-3301 296 D robert.jacklosky@mountsaintvincent.edu
JACKMAN, Guy .... 305-595-9500.. 94 G finaid@amcollege.edu
JACKO, Mariusz .... 787-250-1912 507 C mjacko@intermetro.com
JACKSON, Adrian .... 210-486-2712 428 C ajackson202@alamo.edu
JACKSON, Aisha .... 831-459-1606.. 71 A vcit@ucsc.edu
JACKSON, Alan .... 318-274-6328 191 G jacksona@gram.edu
JACKSON, Alexander ..... 803-812-7354 412 E ja89@mailbox.sc.edu
JACKSON, Alicia .... 229-500-2156 114 F alicia.jackson@asurams.edu
JACKSON, SR., Alonzo, K .... 301-736-3631 200 A alonzo.jackson@msbbcs.edu
JACKSON, Amy .... 620-450-2135 176 I amyj@prattcc.edu
JACKSON, Andrea, D .... 202-806-0019.. 92 E adjackson@howard.edu
JACKSON, Angela .... 434-949-1004 474 D angela.jackson@southside.edu
JACKSON, Angela, B ..... 913-667-5700 172 G angela.jackson@cbts.edu
JACKSON, Anthony .... 225-771-5781 190 K anthony_jackson@subr.edu
JACKSON, Antonio .... 717-391-1364 398 E jacksona@stevenscollege.edu
JACKSON, Arrick, L ...... 218-477-4377 239 A arrick.jackson@mnstate.edu
JACKSON, Athena .... 713-743-9915 451 G anjackson7@uh.edu
JACKSON, Barcus .... 816-604-1180 254 E barcus.jackson@mcckc.edu
JACKSON, Bradley, A .... 513-585-0116 350 A bradley.jackson@thechristcollege.edu
JACKSON, Brenda .... 251-578-1313.... 3 D bjackson@rstc.edu
JACKSON, Brenda .... 910-695-3731 337 E jacksonbr@sandhills.edu
JACKSON, Brenda, W .... 504-586-5274 191 A bjackson@suno.edu
JACKSON, Brent .... 724-838-4215 397 F jbjackson@setonhill.edu
JACKSON, Brian, K .... 609-652-4900 283 A brian.jackson@stockton.edu
JACKSON, Bridgett .... 334-291-4972.... 1 H bridgett.jackson@cv.edu
JACKSON, Bryan .... 870-541-7858.. 20 B
JACKSON, Bryant .... 605-658-6199 415 E bryant.jackson@usd.edu
JACKSON, Carlissa .... 925-631-4754.. 59 I cj10@stmarys-ca.edu
JACKSON, Carlos, F ...... 734-763-4093 231 A carlosfj@umich.edu
JACKSON, Casanna .... 904-256-7267 102 G cjackso29@ju.edu
JACKSON, Chauncey ..... 440-375-7060 354 K chjackson@lec.edu
JACKSON, Cherise .... 618-468-5200 142 B chdjackson@lc.edu
JACKSON, Chris .... 213-615-7284.. 36 G cjackson4@thechicagoschool.edu
JACKSON, Christine ...... 563-876-3353 165 D cjackson@dwci.edu
JACKSON, Clarissa .... 865-694-6526 424 C
JACKSON, Corey .... 415-476-1000.. 70 D corey.jackson@ucsf.edu
JACKSON, Corey, A ...... 610-566-1776 402 C cjackson@williamson.edu
JACKSON, Cori .... 518-564-2280 318 C jacksoc@plattsburgh.edu
JACKSON, Courtney ...... 508-270-4005 214 E cjackson@massbay.edu
JACKSON, Craig .... 478-757-3508 116 F cjackson@centralgatech.edu
JACKSON, Craig .... 541-440-7729 376 F craig.jackson@umpqua.edu
JACKSON, Craig, R .... 909-558-4545.. 48 J cjackson@llu.edu
JACKSON, Cynthia .... 903-730-4890 437 E cstancil@jarvis.edu
JACKSON, Dalen, C .... 502-863-8300 179 B dalen.jackson@bsk.edu
JACKSON, Danielle .... 406-353-2607 262 B djackson@ancollege.edu
JACKSON, Darryl .... 256-372-4854.... 1 A darryl.jackson1@aamu.edu
JACKSON, JR., David ..... 850-599-3505 109 E david.jackson@famu.edu
JACKSON, David, H .... 941-309-0166 106 J djackson@ringling.edu
JACKSON, JR., David, H .... 919-530-6230 341 D djack189@nccu.edu
JACKSON, Deanne .... 573-341-4362 260 F registrar@mst.edu
JACKSON, Deborah, C .. 617-873-0112 207 E deborah.jackson@cambridgecollege.edu
JACKSON, Debra .... 661-654-3420.. 30 C djackson9@csub.edu
JACKSON, Deidra, A ..... 229-391-5001 114 D
JACKSON, Deirdre .... 910-630-7150 331 B dejackson@methodist.edu
JACKSON, Derek, A ...... 785-532-6453 175 A derekaj@ksu.edu
JACKSON, Dexter .... 334-214-4815.... 1 H dexter.jackson@cv.edu
JACKSON, Diana, K .... 510-231-5000.. 46 N diana.k.jackson@kp.org
JACKSON, Diane, V .... 803-793-5329 408 A guinyardjackson@denmarktech.edu
JACKSON, Dionne .... 765-658-4220 154 G dionnejackson@depauw.edu
JACKSON, Duane .... 501-370-5335.. 21 A djackson@philander.edu
JACKSON, Equilla .... 936-261-1890 445 E eqjackson@pvamu.edu
JACKSON, Erica .... 804-257-5848 475 G emjackson@vuu.edu
JACKSON, Ericka .... 313-577-1981 232 H emjackson@wayne.edu
JACKSON, Eugene .... 973-877-3276 276 G ejackson@essex.edu
JACKSON, Faith .... 201-200-2340 278 F fjackson@njcu.edu
JACKSON, Gary .... 662-325-3036 247 A gary@ext.msstate.edu
JACKSON, Gregory .... 256-372-8653.... 1 A gregory.jackson@aamu.edu
JACKSON, Heidi .... 308-635-6395 269 E jacksonh@wncc.edu
JACKSON, Hud .... 870-460-1058.. 22 E jacksonw@uamont.edu
JACKSON, J. Brooks ...... 319-335-8064 163 F brooks-jackson@uiowa.edu
JACKSON, Jackie .... 601-857-3352 245 D jackie.jackson@hindscc.edu
JACKSON, Jacob .... 425-235-5846 482 C jackson.jacob@rtc.edu
JACKSON, Jacqueline .... 443-412-2333 199 B jajackson@harford.edu
JACKSON, Jannett, N .... 510-466-7200.. 56 I
JACKSON, Jasmeial .... 609-984-1120 283 D jjackson@tesu.edu
JACKSON, Jean .... 919-760-8556 331 A jacksonj@meredith.edu
JACKSON, Jeffrey .... 785-670-1662 178 A jeffrey.jackson@washburn.edu
JACKSON, Jerry .... 606-539-4225 185 C jerry.jackson@ucumberlands.edu
JACKSON, Jillian .... 919-719-8860 339 I jillian.jackson@shawu.edu
JACKSON, Jim, C .... 580-581-2460 365 C jjackson@cameron.edu
JACKSON, John .... 916-577-2200.. 76 C jjackson@jessup.edu
JACKSON, John .... 540-231-8508 475 D johnj1@vt.edu
JACKSON, JR., John, L 215-898-4407 399 J dean@asc.upenn.edu
JACKSON, Julie .... 662-846-4151 245 A jjackson@deltastate.edu
JACKSON, Justin .... 973-408-3957 276 B jjackson@drew.edu
JACKSON, Justin .... 972-224-5481 443 E
JACKSON, Karen, K ...... 919-530-7477 341 D kkjackson@nccu.edu
JACKSON, Karina .... 443-412-2114 199 B kjackson@harford.edu
JACKSON, Kashanta ...... 662-846-4690 245 A kjackson@deltastate.edu
JACKSON, Katie .... 715-425-0720 496 A katie.jackson@uwrf.edu
JACKSON, Keith .... 304-293-4532 489 E keith.jackson@mail.wvu.edu
JACKSON, Keith .... 334-876-9238.... 2 D keith.jackson@wccs.edu
JACKSON, Kelly .... 970-339-6583.. 77 G kelly.jackson@aims.edu
JACKSON, Kelly .... 910-592-8081 337 D kjackson@sampsoncc.edu
JACKSON, Kelly .... 903-813-2468 429 I kjackson@austincollege.edu
JACKSON, Ken, L .... 208-496-1610 130 G jacksonken@byui.edu
JACKSON, Kenneth .... 219-989-2366 160 A kjackson@pnw.edu
JACKSON, Kevin, P .... 254-710-1314 430 F
JACKSON, Kevin, P .... 254-710-1616 430 F kevin_p_jackson@baylor.edu
JACKSON, Kim .... 509-793-2067 477 D kimj@bigbend.edu
JACKSON, Kimberly .... 252-940-6252 332 A kimberly.jackson@beaufortccc.edu
JACKSON, Kirk .... 918-335-6833 368 E kjackson@okwu.edu
JACKSON, LaTisha .... 501-370-5229.. 21 A ljackson@philander.edu
JACKSON, LaToya .... 916-660-7102.. 64 B ljackson7@sierracollege.edu
JACKSON, LaToya .... 646-313-8000 295 C latoya.jackson@guttman.cuny.edu
JACKSON, Laura .... 601-925-3865 246 D ljackson@mc.edu
JACKSON, Lauren .... 318-357-5961 192 D potterl@nsula.edu
JACKSON, Leah .... 318-357-4553 192 D jacksonl@nsula.edu
JACKSON, Leah .... 440-375-7200 354 K ljackson@lec.edu
JACKSON, Lee, M .... 773-907-4360 134 N ljackson410@ccc.edu
JACKSON, Lenora .... 404-270-5209 126 A lenoraj@spelman.edu
JACKSON, Lenora .... 931-221-7571 416 H jacksonlp@apsu.edu
JACKSON, Leon .... 928-724-6774.. 12 F lejackson@dinecollege.edu
JACKSON, Les .... 256-765-4357.... 8 E aljackson@una.edu
JACKSON, Linda .... 804-257-5807 475 G lrjackson@vuu.edu
JACKSON, Linda, Y .... 512-505-3006 437 B lyjackson@htu.edu
JACKSON, Lisa .... 972-524-3341 444 E lisa.jackson@swcc.edu
JACKSON, Lisa .... 225-743-8500 188 F ljackson@rpcc.edu
JACKSON, Lisa .... 301-985-7077 203 C lisa.jackson@umuc.edu
JACKSON, Madonna .... 269-294-4354 223 J mjackson271@glenoaks.edu
JACKSON, Marchon .... 301-314-2186 202 E marchon@umd.edu
JACKSON, Marcus .... 512-505-3005 437 B mwjackson@htu.edu
JACKSON, Margaret, W 931-363-9836 426 F mjacks93@utsouthern.edu
JACKSON, Marilyn .... 415-338-1293.. 34 A mjackson@sfsu.edu
JACKSON, Mark .... 610-519-4110 401 B m.w.jackson@villanova.edu
JACKSON, Mary Anne .... 816-235-1808 260 D jacksonmar@umkc.edu
JACKSON, McKenzie ...... 870-368-2313.. 20 I mckenzie.jackson@ozarka.edu
JACKSON, Mckenzie ...... 910-630-7108 331 B mjackson@methodist.edu
JACKSON, Melanie .... 850-729-5298 104 L jacks266@nwfsc.edu
JACKSON, Melodie, R ... 717-361-1404 383 B jacksonmr@etown.edu
JACKSON, Meredith .... 256-840-4163.... 3 F meredith.jackson@snead.edu
JACKSON, Micah .... 773-380-6780 133 C mjackson@bexleyseabury.edu
JACKSON, Michael .... 858-646-3100.. 62 L mjackson@sbpdiscovery.org
JACKSON, Michael, D ... 256-766-6610.... 5 F mjackson@hcu.edu
JACKSON, Monica .... 202-885-2155.. 91 D monica@american.edu
JACKSON, Myesha .... 619-216-6631.. 65 K mjackson@swccd.edu
JACKSON, Nan .... 850-484-1721 105 G njackson@pensacolastate.edu
JACKSON, Nancy .... 334-833-4482.... 5 H hcbookstore@hawks.huntingdon.edu
JACKSON, Natalie .... 419-372-0464 348 F njackson@bgsu.edu
JACKSON, Nicole .... 706-641-5245 117 F njackson@columbustech.edu
JACKSON, Paul .... 603-880-8308 273 F tmc@thomasmorecollege.edu
JACKSON, Paul .... 585-245-6128 317 E jackson@geneseo.edu
JACKSON, Peggy .... 870-612-2030.. 23 B peggy.jackson@uaccb.edu
JACKSON, Philip .... 870-972-3362.. 17 G pjackson@asusystem.edu
JACKSON, Raymond, L . 817-272-3186 454 B jackson@uta.edu
JACKSON, Richard .... 615-687-6892 416 F rjackson@abcnash.edu
JACKSON, Rickey .... 928-524-7350.. 14 L rickey.jackson@npc.edu
JACKSON, Robert .... 270-809-3763 184 A rjackson@murraystate.edu
JACKSON, Robert .... 574-372-5100 155 C jacksord@grace.edu
JACKSON, Robert .... 901-678-8324 426 A rjax@memphis.edu
JACKSON, Robert, D ...... 847-578-3248 148 B robert.jackson@rosalindfranklin.edu
JACKSON, Rodney .... 404-627-2681 116 B rodney.jackson@beulah.edu
JACKSON, Ronald .... 718-951-5352 293 A rcjackson@brooklyn.cuny.edu
JACKSON, Rose Mary ... 501-882-4407.. 17 H rmjackson@asub.edu
JACKSON, Ruth .... 207-859-4350 194 B ruth.jackson@colby.edu
JACKSON, Ruth .... 405-466-3424 366 B ruth.jackson@langston.edu
JACKSON, Sally .... 509-533-3123 478 E sally.jackson@sfcc.spokane.edu
JACKSON, Scarlett .... 863-638-7297 113 D scarlett.jackson@warner.edu
JACKSON, Shanna, L .... 615-353-3236 424 A shanna.jackson@nscc.edu
JACKSON, Sharon, S ..... 804-752-3747 469 B sjackson@rmc.edu
JACKSON, Shawn, L ...... 773-907-4450 134 N sljackson@ccc.edu
JACKSON, Sherri .... 904-256-7212 102 G sjackso@ju.edu
JACKSON, Sherry .... 865-354-3000 424 D jacksons3@roanestate.edu
JACKSON, Shirley, J ...... 202-806-7565.. 92 E sjackson@howard.edu
JACKSON, Smith .... 336-278-5837 328 H jacksons@elon.edu
JACKSON, Stacey, N ...... 248-246-2612 228 H snjackso@oaklandcc.edu
JACKSON, Stacy, N .... 313-447-3905 232 H stacy.jackson@wayne.edu
JACKSON, Stanley .... 410-455-1336 202 G jacksons@umbc.edu
JACKSON, Stephen, B .... 858-534-6514.. 70 C s7jackson@ucsd.edu
JACKSON, Tambra .... 317-274-2290 157 B tambjack@iupui.edu
JACKSON, Tammi .... 919-760-8516 331 A tdjacson@meredith.edu
JACKSON, Terell .... 256-551-3117.... 2 E terell.jackson@drakestate.edu
JACKSON, Tom .... 336-256-0543 341 C htjackson@ncat.edu
JACKSON, JR., Tom ...... 707-826-3311.. 30 A tom.jackson@humboldt.edu
JACKSON, Tony .... 504-520-7849 193 C
JACKSON, Tony .... 419-995-8200 360 B jackson.t1@rhodesstate.edu

JAMES, III, Frank .... 215-368-5000 389 G
fjames@missio.edu
JAMES, Gareth .... 404-727-6377 118 D
gjames7@emory.edu
JAMES, Glenn, E .... 210-829-3940 452 D
gjames@uiwtx.edu
JAMES, Gwendolyn .... 509-533-8883 478 D
gwendolyn.james@scc.spokane.edu
JAMES, Jacqueline .... 404-270-5111 126 A
jjames@spelman.edu
JAMES, Janet, C .... 972-238-6974 434 D
jjames@dcccd.edu
JAMES, Jason .... 360-676-2772 480 G
jlsjames@nwic.edu
JAMES, Jeff .... 412-397-2424 396 E
jamesj@rmu.edu
JAMES, Jeremy .... 334-556-2361.... 2 C
jjames@wallace.edu
JAMES, Jill .... 856-351-2910 282 I
jjames@salemcc.edu
JAMES, Karen .... 310-204-1666.. 58 K
JAMES, Karlon .... 405-466-3299 366 B
karlon.james@langston.edu
JAMES, Kelly .... 785-890-3641 176 E
kelly.james@nwktc.edu
JAMES, Kesha .... 205-929-6450.... 2 H
kjames@lawsonstate.edu
JAMES, Kevin, E .... 404-458-6085 123 B
JAMES, Kim .... 972-825-4634 444 C
kjames@sagu.edu
JAMES, Kimberly .... 860-773-1504.. 87 E
kjames@tunxis.edu
JAMES, Latoya .... 561-433-2330 108 H
JAMES, Lisa .... 719-502-2056.. 82 D
lisa.james@pikespeak.edu
JAMES, Lisa .... 256-726-7270.... 6 C
ljames@oakwood.edu
JAMES, Mark .... 806-874-3571 431 K
mark.james@clarendoncollege.edu
JAMES, Matricia .... 716-375-2000 312 F
mjames@sbu.edu
JAMES, Matthew .... 504-282-4455 190 D
JAMES, Matthew, D .... 304-696-2523 488 N
james65@marshall.edu
JAMES, Megan .... 601-974-1225 246 C
JAMES, Michael .... 620-947-3121 177 F
michaeljames@tabor.edu
JAMES, Michelle .... 412-536-1139 386 H
michelle.james@laroche.edu
JAMES, Mike .... 956-665-2451 455 A
mike.james@utrgv.edu
JAMES, Nancy .... 916-660-8300.. 64 B
njames3@sierracollege.edu
JAMES, Novia .... 520-383-0054.. 16 D
njames@tocc.edu
JAMES, Patrick .... 256-824-6942.... 8 B
patrick.james@uah.edu
JAMES, Patrick .... 312-629-6600 149 B
pjames@saic.edu
JAMES, Peggy .... 262-595-2101 495 D
james@uwp.edu
JAMES, Penny .... 402-354-7225 267 E
penny.james@methodistcollege.edu
JAMES, Regina .... 225-771-2552 191 C
rjames@sulc.edu
JAMES, Reuben .... 310-900-1600.. 39 H
JAMES, Robert .... 252-451-8308 336 B
rmjames752@nashcc.edu
JAMES, Ruben .... 310-900-1600.. 39 H
rjames@elcamino.edu
JAMES, Ruby, F .... 217-420-6029 144 D
rubyjames@millikin.edu
JAMES, Shashanta .... 269-387-6000 232 J
shanta.james@wmich.edu
JAMES, Shauna .... 256-765-4279.... 8 E
sljames@una.edu
JAMES, Shawneequa ..... 757-727-5486 466 L
shawneequa.james@hamptonu.edu
JAMES, Steve .... 916-691-7361.. 50 K
JAMES, Susan, M .... 757-822-1084 474 G
sjames@tcc.edu
JAMES, Sylvia .... 253-964-6710 481 H
JAMES, Timmy .... 256-331-5275.... 3 C
timmy.james@nwscc.edu
JAMES, Tracy .... 636-481-3187 253 G
tjames@jeffco.edu
JAMES, Vernon .... 719-549-3035.. 82 I
vernon.james@pueblocc.edu
JAMES, W. Brian .... 706-245-7226 118 C
bjames@ec.edu
JAMES BLACKWELL,
Leanna .... 413-565-1000 205 I
ljamesblackwell@baypath.edu

JAMES MILLER, Anna ... 559-453-3453.. 43 D
anna.miller@fresno.edu
JAMESON, Adrian .... 573-840-9106 259 I
adrianjameson@trcc.edu
JAMESON, Chandler ...... 559-325-3600.. 28 F
cjameson@chsu.edu
JAMESON, J, L .... 215-898-6796 399 J
ljameson@mail.med.upenn.edu
JAMESON, Naima .... 510-356-4760.. 77 E
JAMESON, Sean .... 914-395-2494 314 H
sjameson@sarahlawrence.edu
JAMESON, Susan .... 507-389-7211 240 F
susan.jameson@southcentral.edu
JAMGOCHIAN, Amy ...... 415-455-8088.. 53 B
JAMIESON, Cory .... 616-538-2330 224 B
cjamieson@gracechristian.edu
JAMIESON, Richard, J .. 216-368-3720 349 B
rjj@case.edu
JAMIESON, Steve .... 314-434-4044 251 F
steve.jamieson@covenantseminary.edu
JAMIESON-DRAKE,
David .... 919-684-0736 328 D
david.jamieson.drake@duke.edu
JAMISON, Calvin, D ...... 972-883-2213 454 D
cjamison@utdallas.edu
JAMISON, Hope .... 678-916-2682 115 G
hjamison@johnmarshall.edu
JAMISON, Leslie .... 609-343-5004 274 E
ljamison@atlantic.edu
JAMISON, Lucretzia ...... 773-451-3798 135 A
ljamison@ccc.edu
JAMISON, Matt .... 303-404-5103.. 80 I
matt.jamison@frontrange.edu
JAMISON, Matt .... 303-678-3845.. 80 I
matt.jamison@frontrange.edu
JAMISON, Pietra .... 717-871-7001 394 B
pietra.jamison@millersville.edu
JAMISON, Todd .... 507-222-4292 234 C
tjamison@carleton.edu
JAMISON, Wendy .... 319-398-5693 167 H
wendy.jamison@kirkwood.edu
JAMKHANDI,
Sudhakar, R .... 304-327-4000 488 J
sjamkhandi@bluefieldstate.edu
JAMOUS, Daniel .... 617-732-2885 216 B
daniel.jamous@mcphs.edu
JAMOUS, Danielly .... 401-739-5000 403 F
djamous@neit.edu
JAMSEN, Nina .... 909-537-7138.. 33 B
nina.jamsen@csusb.edu
JANAK, Justin .... 919-497-3290 330 E
jjanak@louisburg.edu
JANARO, Walter, A .... 540-636-2900 464 O
walter@christendom.edu
JANCHENKO, Michael ... 312-329-4495 144 F
michael.janchenko@moody.edu
JANDREAU, Jami .... 207-780-5250 196 J
jami.jandreau@maine.edu
JANELLE, Sherri .... 304-876-5043 489 A
sjanelle@shepherd.edu
JANELLE, William, P ..... 603-862-1903 273 H
william.janelle@unh.edu
JANESCH, Cynthia, D .... 570-577-3763 379 A
cindy.janesch@bucknell.edu
JANEWAY, Grey .... 423-869-6306 420 A
JANEZICH, Trent .... 218-293-6850 238 D
trent.janizech@minnesotanorth.edu
JANG, In Cheol .... 636-327-4645 255 E
ic.jang@midwest.edu
JANG, Michelle .... 714-533-1495.. 64 G
michelle@southbaylo.edu
JANG, Sung Shik .... 678-535-7771 118 F
sungjang@gcuniv.edu
JANICKI, Jeffrey .... 716-673-3424 316 A
jeffrey.janicki@fredonia.edu
JANIGA, Nicholas .... 914-594-4567 308 J
nicholas_janiga@nymc.edu
JANIS, Debra .... 715-425-4971 496 A
debra.janis@uwrf.edu
JANIS, Ely .... 413-662-5242 212 F
ely.janis@mcla.edu
JANIS, Robert, J .... 312-362-8762 136 F
bjanis@depaul.edu
JANIS, Sharon .... 605-455-6064 414 H
JANIS, Sofia, A .... 412-359-1000 399 D
sjanis@triangle-tech.edu
JANITZ, Suzanne .... 607-431-4244 300 G
janitzs@hartwick.edu
JANKE, Louise, L .... 608-785-8604 495 A
ljanke@uwlax.edu
JANKOWSKI, Kara, K ..... 920-748-8742 493 J
jankowskik@ripon.edu

JANKOWSKI, Mark .... 518-587-2100 320 B
mark.jankowski@esc.edu
JANKOWSKI NIEMCZURA,
Leslie .... 614-222-3225 351 A
ljankowski@ccad.edu
JANNEY, Cindy .... 507-389-1011 238 L
cynthia.janney@mnsu.edu
JANNEY, Dell Ann .... 573-288-6388 251 I
djanney@culver.edu
JANNEY, Justin .... 912-478-5224 120 A
jjjanney@georigasouthern.edu
JANOSIK, MaryAnn .... 847-925-6290 138 E
mjanosik@harpercollege.edu
JANOSKI-HAEHLEN,
Emily, M .... 330-972-6740 361 G
ejanoskihaehlen@uakron.edu
JANOSKY, Amanda .... 716-896-0700 324 A
ajanosky@villa.edu
JANOSKY, Janine, E ...... 773-838-7511 135 C
jjanosky@ccc.edu
JANOUSH, Andrea .... 601-857-3201 245 D
andrea.janoush@hindscc.edu
JANOW, Merit, E .... 212-854-4604 296 H
mj60@columbia.edu
JANOWIAK, Steve .... 219-464-5411 162 C
steven.janowiak@valpo.edu
JANOWSKI, Lori .... 212-772-4482 294 A
lori.janowski@hunter.cuny.edu
JANOYAN, Kerop .... 909-448-4748.. 71 C
kjanoyan@laverne.edu
JANS, Briget .... 832-842-3701 451 G
bajans@uh.edu
JANS, Roger .... 201-684-7231 280 B
rjans@ramapo.edu
JANSEN, Erica .... 808-518-4791 128 H
ericajansen@pacrim.edu
JANSEN, James, S .... 402-280-1804 265 J
jimjansen@creighton.edu
JANSEN, Shelley .... 970-943-2101.. 85 B
sjansen@western.edu
JANSMA, Dana .... 269-337-7210 225 B
dana.jansma@kzoo.edu
JANSMA, Pamela .... 303-556-2557.. 84 B
pamela.jansma@ucdenver.edu
JANSSEN, Emma .... 360-417-6503 481 F
ejanssen@pencol.edu
JANSSEN, Jill, M .... 815-599-3412 138 H
jill.janssen@highland.edu
JANSSEN, Michelle, L ... 765-361-6365 162 G
janssenm@wabash.edu
JANSSEN-ROBINSON,
Aimee .... 812-535-5219 160 E
a.janssen-robinson@smwc.edu
JANSSON, Jimilea .... 580-628-6771 366 J
jimilea.jansson@noc.edu
JANUARY, Shennell .... 703-445-9056 472 B
JANUSCH, Barry .... 360-475-7458 481 B
bjanusch@olympic.edu
JANUSZIEWICZ,
Jason, R .... 724-946-7119 401 F
januszjr@westminster.edu
JANZ, Curtis .... 479-788-7591.. 22 A
curtis.janz@uafs.edu
JANZ, Jeff .... 414-297-6043 498 B
janzjc@matc.edu
JANZ, Kenneth .... 507-457-2299 241 A
kjanz@winona.edu
JANZ, Mary .... 414-288-7208 492 E
mary.janz@marquette.edu
JANZEN, David .... 620-947-3121 177 F
JANZEN, Scott .... 574-296-6213 153 C
registrar@ambs.edu
JAQUES, Kate .... 916-484-8406.. 50 J
jaquesk@arc.losrios.edu
JAQUES-ROSS, Sarah .... 909-607-3370.. 37 F
sarah.jaques-ross@cgu.edu
JAQUEZ, Abraham .... 210-924-4338 430 D
abe.jaquez@bua.edu
JAQUILLARD, Jenny ...... 800-869-7223 124 G
jjaquill@scad.edu
JARA, Blanca .... 708-656-8000 145 B
blanca.jara@morton.edu
JARACZEWSKI, John ...... 864-592-4600 411 E
jaraczewski@sccsc.edu
JARAMILLO, Brooke .... 229-333-2100 127 F
brooke.jaramillo@wiregrass.edu
JARAMILLO, Ed .... 360-416-7719 483 D
ed.jaramillo@skagit.edu
JARAMILLO, John .... 312-341-3829 148 A
jjaramillo01@roosevelt.edu
JARAMILLO, John .... 949-582-4311.. 65 C
jjaramillo@saddleback.edu
JARAMILLO, Justin .... 303-315-1845.. 84 B
justin.jaramillo@ucdenver.edu

JARAMILLO, Lizeth .... 212-854-5561 290 H
ljaramil@barnard.edu
JARAMILLO, Luis .... 212-229-5611 307 E
jaramillo@newschool.edu
JARBOE, Dan .... 870-245-5591.. 20 H
jarboed@obu.edu
JARBOE, Marlena .... 540-453-2260 472 F
jarboem@brcc.edu
JARBOE, Shannon, K ...... 240-895-4309 201 F
skjarboe@smcm.edu
JARBOLA, Steven .... 570-558-2301 384 A
sjarbola@som.geisinger.edu
JARDINE, Daniel, D .... 607-587-4036 319 C
jardindd@alfredstate.edu
JARECKI, Amy .... 765-973-8525 156 D
ajarecki@iue.edu
JARECKI, Robin .... 928-226-4228.. 12 B
robin.jarecki@coconino.edu
JARES, Tim, E .... 308-865-8342 268 J
jareste@unk.edu
JARLEY, Paul .... 407-823-2181 110 D
pjarley@bus.ucf.edu
JARMAN, James .... 928-757-0827.. 14 H
jjarman@mohave.edu
JARMAN, Lois .... 304-876-5809 489 A
ljarman@shepherd.edu
JARMOND, Martin .... 310-206-6382.. 69 D
mjarmond@athletics.ucla.edu
JARMUL, Eileen .... 252-789-0219 335 F
eileen.jarmul@martincc.edu
JARMULOWICZ,
Linda, D .... 901-678-5800 426 A
ljrmlwcz@memphis.edu
JARMUS, Kristi .... 260-422-5561 156 A
kjarmus@indianatech.edu
JARNAGIN, Whitney ...... 423-585-2636 424 G
whitney.jarnagin@ws.edu
JARNIGAN, Renee .... 423-585-6960 424 G
renee.jarnigan@ws.edu
JAROCKI, Robert .... 516-572-9786 307 C
robert.jarocki@ncc.edu
JARONSKI, Ann .... 330-941-3737 364 G
atjaronski@ysu.edu
JAROSLAWICZ,
Mendel, M .... 516-239-9002 314 J
mjaroslawicaz@shoryoshuv.org
JARR, William .... 770-426-2632 122 A
wdjarr@life.edu
JARRAD, Ben .... 678-717-2332 126 G
ben.jarrad@ung.edu
JARRATT, Judy .... 806-785-9285 457 B
jarrattj@wbu.edu
JARRELL, Bruce, E .... 410-706-7002 202 F
bjarrell@umaryland.edu
JARRELL, Courtney .... 318-257-2377 192 A
cjarrell@latech.edu
JARRELL, Dan .... 907-745-3201.... 9 C
JARRELL, Emily .... 910-410-1724 336 G
ewjarrell@richmondcc.edu
JARRELL, James .... 443-997-6393 199 E
jjarrell@jhu.edu
JARRELL, Paul .... 503-842-8222 376 D
pauljarrell@tillamookbaycc.edu
JARRELL, Sheila .... 928-776-2107.. 17 B
sheila.jarrell@yc.edu
JARRETT, Courtney .... 540-665-4533 470 A
JARRETT, Courtney .... 540-535-3461 470 A
cjarrett1@su.edu
JARRETT, Erin .... 270-789-5070 179 G
edjarrett@campbellsville.edu
JARRETT, Gene Andrew 609-258-3000 279 E
JARRETT, Greg, A .... 260-982-5213 158 W
gajarrett@manchester.edu
JARRETT, James .... 863-680-4459 100 F
jjarrett@flsouthern.edu
JARRETT, Jeremiah .... 860-832-2648.. 85 F
jarrettj@ccsu.edu
JARRETT, Patrice .... 312-850-7125 135 E
pjarrett2@ccc.edu
JARRETT, Stephanie .... 707-527-4011.. 63 C
JARRETT BROMBERG,
Shelly .... 513-529-7135 356 A
jarretam@miamioh.edu
JARROUGE, Crystal .... 864-294-2164 408 I
crystal.jarrouge@furman.edu
JARSTFER, Amiel .... 419-289-5373 347 H
ajarstfe@ashland.edu
JARVI, Kennedi .... 540-831-6531 468 E
kjarvi@radford.edu
JARVIS, Anne .... 609-258-3170 279 E
ajarvis@princeton.edu
JARVIS, Cliff .... 573-875-7300 251 A
csjarvis@email.ccis.edu

JARVIS, Frances, H 617-228-2400 214 A
fjarvis@bhcc.mass.edu
JARVIS, Jeffrey, A 419-227-3141 362 F
jjarvis@unoh.edu
JARVIS, Jennifer 718-997-5000 295 A
JARVIS, Keith 307-532-8255 500 A
kjarvis@ewc.wy.edu
JARVIS, Michelle 317-940-8056 153 H
mjarvis@butler.edu
JARVIS, Robin 573-288-6536 251 I
rjarvis@culver.edu
JARVIS, Thomas, K 540-464-7700 475 C
jarvistk@vmi.edu
JARVIS-LETTMAN,
Michele 413-265-2249 208 B
jarvislettmanm@elms.edu
JARZYNA, Dave 260-665-4270 161 C
jarzynad@trine.edu
JASCR, Barb 920-924-3319 498 C
bjascor@morainepark.edu
JASHINSKI, Michelle, L 814-371-2090 399 B
mjashinski@triangle-tech.edu
JASINSKI, Jana 407-823-1113 110 D
jana.jasinski@ucf.edu
JASINSKI, John 417-836-5119 255 J
johnjasinski@missouristate.edu
JASKA, Jamie 254-659-7731 436 C
jjaska@hillcollege.edu
JASKEN, Julia 410-857-2222 200 D
presoffice@mcdaniel.edu
JASKO, Kristen 657-278-7240.. 31 E
kjasko@fullerton.edu
JASMAN, Troy 712-274-6400 170 H
troy.jasman@witcc.edu
JASON, Karen, W 508-531-2750 212 B
kjason@bridgew.edu
JASPER, Daniel 610-625-7882 390 D
jasperd@moravian.edu
JASPER, Kristin 405-703-8232 366 C
kristin.jasper@macu.edu
JASPER, Nate 413-265-2586 208 B
jaspern@elms.edu
JASPER-BUTLER,
Typhanie 504-865-2283 190 A
ttjasper@loyno.edu
JASPERSON, Kristen 715-394-8580 496 D
kjaspers@uwsuper.edu
JASS, Gwen 515-650-3198 163 C
gwenjass@theartofeducation.edu
JASSO DE LA GARZA,
Viridiana 903-923-2079 435 A
djassodelagarza@etbu.edu
JASTORFF, Michael 605-642-6279 415 F
michael.jastorff@bhsu.edu
JASUR, Angela 631-656-2102 299 G
angela.jasur@ftc.edu
JATTKOWSKI-HUDSON,
Anna, J 815-226-3392 147 J
ajattkowski-hudson@rockford.edu
JAUDES, Suzanne 314-529-9520 254 D
sjaudes@maryville.edu
JAUDON, Jon 706-712-8209 118 A
jjaudon@daltonstate.edu
JAUNARAJS, Imants 740-593-2909 358 L
jaunaraj@ohio.edu
JAUS, Rhonnie 212-229-5671 307 E
jausr@newschool.edu
JAVAHERIPOUR, G. H .. 209-575-6507.. 76 I
javaheripourg@yosemite.edu
JAVAHERIPOUR, G.H 209-575-6507.. 76 K
javaheripourg@yosemite.edu
JAVALUYAS,
Genevieve (Ivy) 562-988-2278.. 26 A
gjavaluyas@auhs.edu
JAVARIZ, Gerardo 787-890-2681 510 C
gerardo.javariz@upr.edu
JAVDEKAR, Chitra 781-239-2585 214 E
cjavdekar@massbay.edu
JAVIER, Byron 312-850-7126 135 E
bjavier@ccc.edu
JAVIER BRAVO, Milton 608-663-3371 491 F
milbravo@edgewood.edu
JAVIER-WONG, Beth 301-405-3336 202 E
bethjw@umd.edu
JAVINAR, Jan 808-689-2671 129 C
javinar@hawaii.edu
JAVOR, Seta 818-252-5101.. 76 D
seta.javor@woodbury.edu
JAWORSKI, Brian 503-375-7010 372 G
bjaworski@corban.edu
JAX, John 608-785-8567 495 A
jjax@uwlax.edu
JAY, Daniel 617-636-6714 219 A
daniel.jay@tufts.edu
JAY, Jodye 903-541-4099 437 D
jjay@jacksonville-college.edu
JAY, Leslie 718-997-5590 295 A
leslie.jay@qc.cuny.edu
JAYARAMAN, Ruki 714-816-0366.. 68 G
ruki.jayaraman@trident.edu
JAYARAMAN, Ruki 224-293-5746.. 10 F
rjayaraman@aiuniv.edu
JAYASURIYA, Kumara 507-537-6272 240 G
president@smsu.edu
JAYATHILAKE, Don 562-988-2278.. 26 A
djayathilake@auhs.edu
JAYAWARDHANA, Ray .. 607-255-1097 297 D
as_dean@cornell.edu
JAYNE, Billy Jo 315-279-5684 303 D
bjjayne@keuka.edu
JAYNE, Joe 413-577-1418 211 D
gift.planning@umass.edu
JAYNES, Cliff 817-735-2513 453 D
cliff.jaynes@unthsc.edu
JAYNES, Jamie 301-985-7000 203 C
jamie.jaynes@umuc.edu
JAYROE, Teresa 662-325-7069 247 A
tjayroe@colled.msstate.edu
JAZDZEWSKI, Rich, L 920-832-6574 492 B
richard.l.jazdzewski@lawrence.edu
JBARA, Craig 269-353-1263 225 C
cjbara@kvcc.edu
JEAN, Libby 269-749-7655 229 G
ljean@olivetcollege.edu
JEAN, Marc 785-442-6139 174 C
mjean@highlandcc.edu
JEAN, Martin, D 203-432-9681.. 90 B
martin.jean@yale.edu
JEAN, Paul 508-531-2660 212 B
paul.jean@bridgew.edu
JEAN-BAPTISTE,
Esmeralda 610-527-0200 396 G
ejeanbaptiste@rosemont.edu
JEAN-FRANCOIS, Tanya 781-768-7427 217 H
tanya.jean-francois@regiscollege.edu
JEAN-MARIE, Gaetane 856-256-4750 280 H
jeanmarie@rowan.edu
JEAN MARIE, Vivaldi 718-270-5031 294 E
vjean-marie@mec.cuny.edu
JEAN MICHEL, Jean, M 718-270-6431 294 E
jjean-michel@mec.cuny.edu
JEBALI, Lisa 978-837-5109 216 D
jebalil@merrimack.edu
JEBB, Cindy, R 201-684-7607 280 B
cjebb@ramapo.edu
JEDAMSKI, Bert 304-462-6181 488 M
bert.jedamski@glenville.edu
JEDNAK, P. Michael 860-486-4741.. 89 B
michael.jednak@uconn.edu
JEELANI, Shaik 334-725-2336.... 7 D
jeelanis@tuskegee.edu
JEFFCOAT, Holly 214-768-2400 443 G
hjeffcoat@smu.edu
JEFFERIES, Yvette 973-877-3006 276 G
jefferies@essex.edu
JEFFERS, Carrie 586-286-2187 226 F
jeffersc@macomb.edu
JEFFERS, Dixie 614-236-6551 348 I
djeffers@capital.edu
JEFFERS, Karen 479-788-7092.. 22 A
karen.jeffers@uafs.edu
JEFFERS, Latoya 718-518-4284 293 F
ljeffers@hostos.cuny.edu
JEFFERS, Linda 209-946-2125.. 71 E
ljeffers@pacific.edu
JEFFERSON, Adriene 772-462-7156 102 E
ajeffers@irsc.edu
JEFFERSON, Ann 510-849-8200.. 55 F
JEFFERSON, Diane 717-477-1616 394 D
dljeff@ship.edu
JEFFERSON, Doug 817-598-6247 457 C
djefferson@wc.edu
JEFFERSON, Jonathan 617-349-8621 210 H
jjeffer2@lesley.edu
JEFFERSON, Joy 757-727-5231 466 L
joy.jefferson@hamptonu.edu
JEFFERSON, Joy, L 757-683-3120 468 C
jljeffer@odu.edu
JEFFERSON, Kurt 502-585-9911 184 E
kjefferson@spalding.edu
JEFFERSON, Lauren 540-432-4234 465 F
lauren.jefferson@emu.edu
JEFFERSON, Lynda 803-780-1279 413 B
lyndaj@voorhees.edu
JEFFERSON, Mara 901-369-0835.. 93 H
JEFFERSON, Michael 707-965-7086.. 55 H
mjeffereson@puc.edu
JEFFERSON, Philip, N 704-894-2204 328 C
phjefferson@davidson.edu
JEFFERSON, Robin 804-342-3916 475 G
rljefferson@vuu.edu
JEFFERSON, Rod 856-351-2654 282 I
rjefferson@salemcc.edu
JEFFERSON, Shirley 802-831-1333 462 F
sjefferson@vermontlaw.edu
JEFFERSON, Willie 803-780-1049 413 B
williej@voorhees.edu
JEFFERSON EXUM,
Jelani 313-596-0210 230 H
jefferje1@udmercy.edu
JEFFERSON-GOMEZ,
Anita, R 937-708-5520 363 G
ajefferson-gomez@wilberforce.edu
JEFFERY, Charles 623-845-3692.. 13 E
charles.jeffery@gccaz.edu
JEFFERY, Kathryn, E 310-434-4200.. 63 B
jeffery_kathryn@smc.edu
JEFFORDS, Susan 503-725-5257 375 D
JEFFRESS, Danielle 559-453-7122.. 43 D
danielle.jeffress@fresno.edu
JEFFREY, Ann 510-642-6000.. 68 N
JEFFREY, Don 334-983-6556.... 7 C
djeffr@troy.edu
JEFFREY, Douglas 517-607-2538 224 G
djeffrey@hillsdale.edu
JEFFREY, Jeremy 870-541-7858.. 20 B
JEFFREY, Kim 806-874-3571 431 K
kim.jeffrey@clarendoncollege.edu
JEFFREY, Russell 512-313-4672 432 N
russell.jeffrey@concordia.edu
JEFFREYS, David 318-487-7769 187 B
david.jeffreys@lcuniversity.edu
JEFFREYS, Kimberlee 815-802-8472 141 B
kharpin@kcc.edu
JEFFRIE, Shellie 616-632-2130 221 A
jeffrmic@aquinas.edu
JEFFRIES, Ernest, E 540-887-7000 467 G
eejeffries@marybaldwin.edu
JEFFRIES, Eunice, M 248-341-2040 228 H
emjeffri@oaklandcc.edu
JEFFRIES, Jody 816-235-1086 260 D
jeffriesjd@umkc.edu
JEFFRIES, Mavonee 903-730-4890 437 E
mjeffries@jarvis.edu
JEFFRIES, Michael 781-283-3583 219 C
mjeffrie@wellesley.edu
JEFFRIES, Rick 863-669-2840 106 A
rjeffries@polk.edu
JEFFRIES, Sandy 949-451-5210.. 65 B
sjeffries@ivc.edu
JEFFRIES, Scott 214-333-5211 433 D
scottj@dbu.edu
JEFFRIES, William 570-504-7294 384 A
wjeffries@som.geisinger.edu
JEFFRIES-JACKSON,
Tamara 803-536-8103 410 H
thughes@scsu.edu
JEFFS, Kendle 307-754-6400 500 G
kendle.jeffs@nwc.edu
JEFFS, Monica 512-617-5700 432 B
JEFREMOW, George 212-217-4420 299 C
george_jefremow@fitnyc.edu
JEGER, Yehuda 718-268-4700 311 H
JEITSCHKO, Thomas 517-353-3220 227 C
jeitschko@msu.edu
JEKA, Mary, R 617-627-4220 219 A
mary.jeka@tufts.edu
JEKABSONS, Andrea 662-915-7211 248 F
JELENIK, Kristy 203-332-5078.. 86 E
kjelenik@housatonic.edu
JELINEK, Jaclyn 920-929-2127 498 C
jjelinek@morainepark.edu
JELINKOVA, Klara 617-495-1000 210 B
JELLERSON, George 804-862-6100 469 E
gjellerson@rbc.edu
JELLISON, Jody, L 413-545-4800 211 D
jjellison@cns.umass.edu
JELLUM, Lisa 706-204-2204 119 C
ljellum@highlands.edu
JEMISON, Keith 936-261-1387 445 E
ktjemison@pvamu.edu
JEMISON, William 315-268-6509 295 E
wjemison@clarkson.edu
JEMISON-POLLARD,
Dianne 713-313-7139 448 D
dianne.jemison-pollard@tsu.edu
JEMMOTT, Jill 203-576-4000.. 89 A
jjemott@bridgeport.edu
JENCKS, Doyle 580-477-7736 371 D
doyle.jencks@wosc.edu
JENDRASZAK, Stephen . 612-330-1182 233 G
jendra@augsburg.edu
JENE, Beverly 802-322-1650 461 D
beverly.jene@goddard.edu
JENEFSKY, Cyd 209-946-2300.. 71 E
cjenefsky@pacific.edu
JENEMANN, David 802-656-8209 462 D
david.jenemann@uvm.edu
JENERETTE, Kim 937-766-7866 349 C
kimjenerette@cedarville.edu
JENIOUS, Anita 615-322-4705 427 B
anita.jenious@vanderbilt.edu
JENKENS, A. Lawrence . 508-999-9286 211 F
lawrence.jenkens@umassd.edu
JENKINS, Anita 202-865-6660.. 92 E
ajenkins@huhosp.org
JENKINS, Anthony, L 410-951-1290 203 E
anjenkins@coppin.edu
JENKINS, April 917-493-4161 304 L
ajenkins@msmnyc.edu
JENKINS, Brandon, M .. 919-739-6841 338 F
bmjenkins@waynecc.edu
JENKINS, Brent 317-632-5553 158 V
bjenkins@lincolntech.edu
JENKINS, Bryan 919-807-7147 331 I
jenkinsb@nccommunitycolleges.edu
JENKINS, Cara 610-436-3513 394 F
cjenkins@wcupa.edu
JENKINS, Caren 304-462-6182 488 M
caren.jenkins@glenville.edu
JENKINS, Carri, P 801-422-1166 458 A
carri_jenkins@byu.edu
JENKINS, Celia 520-515-5491.. 11 O
jenkinsc@cochise.edu
JENKINS, Cheryl, S 919-760-8338 331 A
jenkinsc@meredith.edu
JENKINS, D. Scott 972-578-5579 432 I
sjenkins@collin.edu
JENKINS, David 229-931-2724 120 B
david.jenkins@gsw.edu
JENKINS, David, A 502-852-7997 185 E
d.jenkins@louisville.edu
JENKINS, DeAnna 214-333-5402 433 D
deannaj@dbu.edu
JENKINS, Diane 301-736-3631 200 A
djenkins@msbbcs.edu
JENKINS, Dinia 573-986-6191 258 J
djenkins@semo.edu
JENKINS, Dora 912-921-2900.. 93 H
JENKINS, Ernest 919-530-7639 341 D
ernest.jenkins@nccu.edu
JENKINS, Garry 612-625-4841 242 K
gjenkins@umn.edu
JENKINS, H. E 713-942-5079 453 H
jenkinhe@stthom.edu
JENKINS, Jacqueline 212-217-4000 299 C
jacqueline_jenkins1@fitnyc.edu
JENKINS, Jason 701-777-6345 344 H
jjenkins@nd.gov
JENKINS, Jo Ann 708-608-4199 144 G
jenkinsj52@morainevalley.edu
JENKINS, Joanna 215-965-4059 390 C
jjenkins@moore.edu
JENKINS, CSC, John, I . 574-631-3903 161 G
jenkins.1@nd.edu
JENKINS, Katrina 407-646-2115 106 L
kejenkins@rollins.edu
JENKINS, Keith 585-475-7404 312 A
kbjgpt@rit.edu
JENKINS, Keith 936-294-1759 449 E
rca_kej@shsu.edu
JENKINS, Kevin 870-307-7220.. 20 D
kevin.jenkins@lyon.edu
JENKINS, Latoya 410-651-6687 203 B
emse@umes.edu
JENKINS, Lidia 415-239-3267.. 37 C
ljenkins@ccsf.edu
JENKINS, Lucy 603-578-8900 272 B
ljenkins@ccsnh.edu
JENKINS, Malia 619-201-8728.. 60 G
malia.jenkins@sdcc.edu
JENKINS, Marjorie 864-455-7992 412 A
mjenkins@greenvillemed.sc.edu
JENKINS, Marjorie 864-455-7992 412 F
mjenkins@greenvillemed.sc.edu
JENKINS, Melanie 919-739-6731 338 F
mkjenkins@waynecc.edu
JENKINS, Melanie 435-283-7000 460 C
melanie.jenkins@snow.edu
JENKINS, Melanie 804-484-1581 471 E
mjenkin3@richmond.edu
JENKINS, Michelle 314-529-9625 254 D
mjenkins@maryville.edu

JENKINS, Mike 903-983-8188 437 G mjenkins@kilgore.edu
JENKINS, Nicole, T 434-924-3176 471 F nt4jw@virginia.edu
JENKINS, Pamela 671-734-1812 503 D pjenkins@piu.edu
JENKINS, Patricia 865-354-3000 424 D jenkinsp@roanestate.edu
JENKINS, Paul 603-899-4142 272 G jenkinsp@franklinpierce.edu
JENKINS, Pernell 334-229-4234 4 B pjenkins@alasu.edu
JENKINS, Rita, H 713-942-9505 436 F rjenkins@hgst.edu
JENKINS, Robert 909-384-8662 60 F rjenkins@sbccd.cc.ca.us
JENKINS, Robert 713-500-3334 455 D robert.jenkins@uth.tmc.edu
JENKINS, Rod 972-708-7369 434 F rod_jenkins@diu.edu
JENKINS, Rodney 928-776-2280 17 B rodney.jenkins@yc.edu
JENKINS, Rodney, C 803-536-7048 410 H rodney.jenkins@scsu.edu
JENKINS, Ronny 202-319-5492 91 G jenkinsr@cua.edu
JENKINS, Safia 504-286-5101 191 A sjenkins@suno.edu
JENKINS, Scott 402-643-7482 265 I finaid@cune.edu
JENKINS, Sherry 606-546-1701 185 B spartin2@unionky.edu
JENKINS, Simone 813-253-7449 102 A sjenkins41@hccfl.edu
JENKINS, Sonja 478-218-3308 116 F sjenkins@centralgatech.edu
JENKINS, Spencer 801-321-7101 459 C sjenkins@ushe.edu
JENKINS, Stancia, J 402-472-5270 268 I sjenkins@nebraska.edu
JENKINS, Stephanie 606-589-3086 181 A sjenkins0074@kctcs.edu
JENKINS, Stephen 541-737-4771 374 H
JENKINS, Steve 619-201-8716 60 G steve.jenkins@sdcc.edu
JENKINS, Steven 740-392-6868 356 G steven.jenkins@mvnu.edu
JENKINS, Sylvia 708-974-5201 144 G president@morainevalley.edu
JENKINS, Vanessa, C 757-823-8173 468 B vcjenkins@nsu.edu
JENKINS-EVANS, Janie 802-387-6814 461 E janiejenkinsevans@landmark.edu
JENKS, David 478-475-8630 122 D david.jenks@mga.edu
JENKS, Rick 815-921-4445 147 H r.jenks@rockvalleycollege.edu
JENKS, Wayne 919-761-2277 340 B wjenks@sebts.edu
JENNELLE, Stephanie 540-831-5411 468 E sjennelle@radford.edu
JENNESS, Jennier 701-845-7276 345 E jennifer.jenness@vcsu.edu
JENNETTE, Judy 252-789-0310 335 F judy.jennette@martincc.edu
JENNETTEN, Tory 309-677-2259 133 H tory@fsmail.bradley.edu
JENNINGS, Amani 732-987-2601 277 B ajennings@georgian.edu
JENNINGS, Arbolina, L 713-313-7661 448 D jennings_al@tsu.edu
JENNINGS, Barbara 641-844-5522 167 C barb.jennings@iavalley.edu
JENNINGS, Bill 541-880-2247 373 B jenningsb@klamathcc.edu
JENNINGS, Charla 870-743-3000 20 F charlam@northark.edu
JENNINGS, Charles 919-530-6198 341 D cjenni13@nccu.edu
JENNINGS, Chris 626-387-5763 26 K cjennings@apu.edu
JENNINGS, Chris 213-624-1200 42 F cjennings@fidm.edu
JENNINGS, David 646-378-6103 289 F david.jennings@nyack.edu
JENNINGS, Eli 808-518-4791 128 H elijennings@pacrim.edu
JENNINGS, Eva 510-748-2318 57 A ejennings@peralta.edu
JENNINGS, Jamie 541-880-2228 373 B jennings@klamathcc.edu
JENNINGS, Jarvis 423-585-6845 424 G jarvis.jennings@ws.edu
JENNINGS, Jody 864-977-7158 410 A jody.jennings@ngu.edu
JENNINGS, Linda 603-366-5260 271 K ljennings@ccsnh.edu
JENNINGS, Lynn 252-335-0821 333 E lynn_jennings@albemarle.edu
JENNINGS, Michael, E 864-294-2149 408 I michael.jennings3@furman.edu
JENNINGS, Robert 402-559-5899 269 B robert.jennings@unmc.edu
JENNINGS, Sarah, E 870-235-4040 21 E sejennings@saumag.edu
JENNINGS, Susan 423-697-2576 423 B susan.jennings@chattanoogastate.edu
JENNINGS, Thomas, W 540-458-8233 476 D tjennings@wlu.edu
JENNINGS, William 413-236-3003 213 E wjennings@berkshirecc.edu
JENNINGS-ROGGENSACK, Colleen 480-965-5062 11 A cjr@asu.edu
JENNISON, Barry 423-697-2614 423 B barry.jennison@chattanoogastate.edu
JENNUM, Joe 909-274-4630 52 K jjennum@mtsac.edu
JENRETTE, John 310-423-8294 35 M
JENS, Erik 301-243-2094 501 J erik.jens@dodiis.mil
JENSCHKE, Danielle 830-792-7217 442 G admissions@schreiner.edu
JENSEMA, Ryan 412-924-1384 395 G rjensema@pts.edu
JENSEN, Anna 812-856-2548 156 C anjensen@iu.edu
JENSEN, Anna, K 812-856-2548 156 B anjensen@iu.edu
JENSEN, Brenda 808-236-3533 128 E bjensen@hpu.edu
JENSEN, Carla 989-463-7421 220 F jensencr@alma.edu
JENSEN, Carlos 858-534-0096 70 C avcei@ucsd.edu
JENSEN, Christopher 270-745-5065 186 A christopher.jensen@wku.edu
JENSEN, Chuck 970-339-6509 77 G chuck.jensen@aims.edu
JENSEN, Dan 817-735-2500 453 D danny.jensen@unthsc.edu
JENSEN, Dawn 314-246-3119 261 D dawnjensen62@webster.edu
JENSEN, Douglas, J 701-224-5431 345 F douglas.j.jensen@bismarckstate.edu
JENSEN, Dustin 701-252-3467 346 J dustin.jensen@uj.edu
JENSEN, Eric 707-545-3647 27 A
JENSEN, Gail 951-487-3040 53 A gjensen@msjc.edu
JENSEN, Gail, M 402-280-3727 265 J gailjensen@creighton.edu
JENSEN, Grant 801-422-2290 458 A grant_jensen@byu.edu
JENSEN, Holly 520-626-5620 16 H hollyjensen@arizona.edu
JENSEN, Jamie 218-299-6882 238 K jaime.jensen@minnesota.edu
JENSEN, Jed 307-681-6100 500 F jjensen@sheridan.edu
JENSEN, Jeffrey, L 623-572-3451 144 C jjensen1@midwestern.edu
JENSEN, Jennifer 401-341-2209 404 D jennifer.jensen@salve.edu
JENSEN, Jennifer, M 610-758-3705 388 C jmj313@lehigh.edu
JENSEN, John 410-706-4358 202 F jjensen@umaryland.edu
JENSEN, John, A 540-458-8604 476 D jensenj@wlu.edu
JENSEN, Josh 440-775-5426 357 G jjensen@oberlin.edu
JENSEN, Kae 208-562-3336 131 C kaejensen@cwi.edu
JENSEN, Karen 907-474-7224 10 B kjensen@alaska.edu
JENSEN, Katie 425-388-9581 479 B kjensen@everettcc.edu
JENSEN, Kevin 607-255-9043 297 D finaid-director@cornell.edu
JENSEN, Kirsten 218-477-2175 239 A kirsten.jensen@mnstate.edu
JENSEN, Koll 760-878-8382 41 D kjensen@deepsprings.edu
JENSEN, Laura 970-491-5939 79 E l.jensen@colostate.edu
JENSEN, Laura 216-221-8584 357 C laura.jensen@thencc.edu
JENSEN, Lauren, J 616-526-6106 221 L lauren.jensen@calvin.edu
JENSEN, Laurie 320-308-5156 240 D laurie.jensen@sctcc.edu
JENSEN, Mary, K 540-432-4112 465 F mary.jensen@emu.edu
JENSEN, Megan 509-574-4635 485 E mjensen@yvcc.edu
JENSEN, Michael 208-562-3160 131 C michaeljensen2@cwi.edu
JENSEN, Michael, A 801-422-4327 458 A jensen@byu.edu
JENSEN, Michelle 785-833-4316 175 C kmichelj@kwu.edu
JENSEN, Nathan 714-432-5909 38 F njensen@occ.cccd.edu
JENSEN, Paul 708-456-0300 151 A pauljensen@triton.edu
JENSEN, Paul, E 215-895-2200 382 D jensenpe@drexel.edu
JENSEN, Riki 989-328-1220 227 G riki.jensen@montcalm.edu
JENSEN, Sam 734-481-5125 223 F ajensen2@emich.edu
JENSEN, Scott 316-978-3693 178 B scott.jensen@wichita.edu
JENSEN, Scott 435-879-4603 459 G scott.jensen@utahtech.edu
JENSEN, Sean 847-214-7195 137 D sjensen@elgin.edu
JENSEN, Sol 815-753-2253 145 H sjensen1@niu.edu
JENSEN, Steve, M 563-588-8000 165 K smjensen@emmaus.edu
JENSEN, Steven, M 330-471-8521 355 D sjensen@malone.edu
JENSEN, Trisha 801-832-2598 461 A tjensen@westminstercollege.edu
JENSEN, Tyler 307-675-0777 500 F tjensen@sheridan.edu
JENSEN, Valerie 408-855-5464 75 C valerie.jensen@missioncollege.edu
JENSEN, Vince 626-256-4673 37 D vjensen@coh.org
JENSON, John 671-735-2694 503 E jjenson@triton.uog.edu
JENSON, Todd 405-912-9475 368 H tjenson@ru.edu
JENT, Laura 931-540-2521 423 D ljent1@columbiastate.edu
JENUWINE, Daniel, J 248-341-2134 228 H djjenuwi@oaklandcc.edu
JEON, Isaac 323-643-0301 25 L
JEON, John 213-487-0150 41 I
JEONG, Jin O 770-232-2717 124 D jin.jeong@runiv.edu
JEONG, Sun Ki 678-535-7771 118 F blessjsk@yunhap.org
JEONG, Wooseob 620-341-5203 173 C wjeong1@emporia.edu
JEONG, Wooseob 620-341-5208 173 C wjeong1@emporia.edu
JEPPESEN, Vicki 715-675-3331 498 E jeppesen@ntc.edu
JERABEK, Megan 610-436-2205 394 F mjerabek@wcupa.edu
JERDAN, David 215-968-8184 379 B david.jerdan@bucks.edu
JERDINE, Kimberly 248-204-3943 226 E kosantows@ltu.edu
JEREMIAH, David 619-201-8995 65 F david.jeremiah@socalsem.edu
JEREMIAH, Jacob 847-638-1640 146 E jjeremia@oakton.edu
JEREZ, Sheryll 936-468-6186 444 H jerezs@sfasu.edu
JERGOVIC, Diana 626-395-6214 29 B jergovic@caltech.edu
JERIES, John 414-382-6344 490 G john.jeries@alverno.edu
JERMAN, Jerhett 435-879-4539 459 G jerhett.jerman@utahtech.edu
JERMIER, Jim 319-273-2487 163 G jim.jermier@uni.edu
JERMY, Charles, W 607-255-7393 297 D cwj1@cornell.edu
JERNIGAN, Andrew 229-931-2074 120 B andrew.jernigan@gsw.edu
JERNIGAN, Doug 601-484-8762 246 B djerniga@meridiancc.edu
JERNIGAN, Jazmin 318-797-5190 189 E jazmin.jernigan@lsus.edu
JERNIGAN, Monique 718-990-2514 313 B jernigam@stjohns.edu
JERNIGAN, Ron 505-566-3035 287 G jerniganr@sanjuancollege.edu
JEROME, Allison 808-735-4852 128 C ajerome@chaminade.edu
JEROME, Larry 315-364-3443 324 E ljerome@wells.edu
JEROME, Leslie 914-632-5400 306 J ljerome@monroecollege.edu
JEROME, Marc, M 718-933-6700 306 J mjerome@monroecollege.edu
JERRALDS, Aneshia 336-278-7300 328 H ajerralds@elon.edu
JERRY, Lisa 516-726-5799 502 G jerryl@usmma.edu
JERUE, JR., James 508-999-9216 211 F jjerue@umassd.edu
JERUE, James, M 401-456-8262 404 A jjerue@ric.edu
JERVIS, Kathryn 609-771-3140 275 J jervisk@tcnj.edu
JERZAK, Page 352-395-5817 107 G page.jerzak@sfcollege.edu
JESKE, Daniel, R 951-827-2304 70 B daniel.jeske@ucr.edu
JESME, Shannon 218-683-8577 239 E shannon.jesme@northlandcollege.edu
JESPERSEN, Christopher 706-864-1771 126 G christopher.jespersen@ung.edu
JESSE, III, John, J 402-280-3835 265 J johnjesse@creighton.edu
JESSEE, Amy 540-654-1055 471 B ajessee@umw.edu
JESSELL, Kenneth 305-348-2101 109 H kenneth.jessell@fiu.edu
JESSIE, Jason 334-222-6591 2 I jjessie@lbwcc.edu
JESSUP, Jim 916-577-2200 76 C jjessup@jessup.edu
JESSUP, Len 909-621-8025 37 F len.jessup@cgu.edu
JESSUP, Rhonda, E 919-658-7754 340 E rjessup@umo.edu
JESTEL, Mark 706-379-3111 128 A mjestel@yhc.edu
JESTER, Felicia 678-359-5733 120 D feliciaj@gordonstate.edu
JESTER, Vicki 404-880-8044 116 I vjester@cau.edu
JETER, Jeff 817-272-2101 454 B jeter@uta.edu
JETER, Pamela 253-583-8770 478 A pamela.jeter@cptc.edu
JETER-TWILLEY, Rhonda 301-860-3132 203 D rjeter@bowiestate.edu
JETHANI, Sonia 510-885-2784 31 C sonia.jethani@csueastbay.edu
JETT, Melissa 417-255-7955 256 A melissajett@missouristate.edu
JETT, Susan, P 864-424-8027 412 H jettsp@mailbox.sc.edu
JETT, Wendy 541-463-5803 373 C jettw@laneccfoundation.org
JETTER, Kim 215-702-4463 379 F kjetter@cairn.edu
JETTON, Barbara 479-308-2291 17 E barbara.jetton@acheedu.org
JEUNE, Christopher 732-224-2593 275 D cjeune@brookdalecc.edu
JEWELL, Christy 916-577-2200 76 C cjewell@jessup.edu
JEWELL, David 307-766-5760 500 H david.jewell@uwyo.edu
JEWELL, David, N 216-687-3673 350 G david.jewell@csuohio.edu
JEWELL, Nikki 269-965-3931 225 D jewelln@kellogg.edu
JEWELL, Scott 978-542-6139 213 B scott.jewel@salemstate.edu
JEWETT, John 386-752-1822 99 P john.jewett@fgc.edu
JEWETT, Matthew 805-678-5307 74 A mjewett@vcccd.edu
JEWSBURY, Evan 417-625-9805 255 I jewsbury-e@mssu.edu
JEWSBURY, Evan 918-595-7928 370 B evan.jewsbury@tulsacc.edu
JEZAK, Patricia 567-661-2650 359 H patricia_jezak@owens.edu

JOHNSON, Bryan .... 256-215-4311.... 1 G bmjohnson@cacc.edu
JOHNSON, Bryan .... 610-526-1582 378 D bryan.johnson@theamericancollege.edu
JOHNSON, Calvin, M .... 334-844-4546.... 4 E johncal@auburn.edu
JOHNSON, Candace ..... 936-261-1566 445 E cajohnson@pvamu.edu
JOHNSON, Cari .... 903-923-2043 435 A cjohnson@etbu.edu
JOHNSON, Carla .... 831-759-6006.. 44 J cjohnson@hartnell.edu
JOHNSON, Carlos .... 843-349-2876 407 B carlosj@coastal.edu
JOHNSON, Carmen .... 727-562-7802 111 F cjohnso2@law.stetson.edu
JOHNSON, Carol .... 906-227-2947 228 E carjohns@nmu.edu
JOHNSON, Carol .... 704-878-3225 335 I cjohnson@mitchellcc.edu
JOHNSON, Casie .... 507-453-2663 238 J cjohnson@southeastmn.edu
JOHNSON, Cassandra, M .... 903-927-3336 457 I cmjohnson@wileyc.edu
JOHNSON, Cassandra, M .... 903-927-3201 457 I cmjohnson@wileyc.edu
JOHNSON, Catherine .... 207-780-4141 196 J catherine.johnson@maine.edu
JOHNSON, Cathy .... 478-218-3309 116 F cajohnson@centralgatech.edu
JOHNSON, Chad .... 801-863-6182 460 A cjohnson@uvu.edu
JOHNSON, Chandrika ... 910-672-1258 341 B chjohnson01@uncfsu.edu
JOHNSON, Charlene ..... 803-780-1039 413 B cjohnson@voorhees.edu
JOHNSON, Charlene ..... 803-780-1234 413 B cjohnson@voorhees.edu
JOHNSON, Charles .... 912-260-4338 125 B charles.johnson@sgsc.edu
JOHNSON, III, Charles . 718-818-6470 314 B charles.johnson@edaff.com
JOHNSON, Charles, R .. 812-888-4208 162 E president@vinu.edu
JOHNSON, Charlotte ..... 870-584-1115.. 22 G cjohnson@cccua.edu
JOHNSON, Charlotte ..... 619-260-4588.. 72 H studentaffairs@sandiego.edu
JOHNSON, Cheryl .... 256-372-5835.... 1 A cheryl.johnson@aamu.edu
JOHNSON, Cheryl .... 650-738-7951.. 62 K johnsoncheryl@smccd.edu
JOHNSON, Chiara .... 251-380-2270.... 6 H wellnesscenter@shc.edu
JOHNSON, Chris .... 303-762-6924.. 80 G chris.johnson@denverseminary.edu
JOHNSON, Chris .... 202-319-4494.. 91 G johnsoncp@cua.edu
JOHNSON, Chris .... 315-443-1899 321 D cejohns@syr.edu
JOHNSON, Christine ..... 509-434-5006 478 C christine.johnson@ccs.spokane.edu
JOHNSON, Christine ..... 509-434-5006 478 D christine.johnson@ccs.spokane.edu
JOHNSON, Christine, L 859-858-3581 178 G christy.johnson@smsu.edu
JOHNSON, Christol ...... 214-860-2627 434 A christoljohnson@dcccd.edu
JOHNSON, Christopher 805-965-0581.. 62 M ckjohnson2@sbcc.edu
JOHNSON, Christopher 678-839-6467 127 A ckjohnson@westga.edu
JOHNSON, Christopher 940-898-3206 451 A cjohnson44@twu.edu
JOHNSON, Christy ...... 507-537-6215 240 G christy.johnson@smsu.edu
JOHNSON, Cindi Beth .. 651-255-6137 242 J cbjohnson@unitedseminary.edu
JOHNSON, Cindy .... 620-235-4175 176 H cynthia.johnson@pittstate.edu
JOHNSON, Cindy, K ..... 816-604-1011 254 E cindy.johnson@mcckc.edu
JOHNSON, Clint .... 816-604-6775 254 F clint.johnson@mcckc.edu
JOHNSON, Coleman ..... 806-743-2900 450 D coleman.johnson@ttuhsc.edu
JOHNSON, Connie .... 719-598-0200.. 80 B cjohnson@coloradotech.edu
JOHNSON, Cornelia ..... 302-857-1126.. 90 H cornelia@dtcc.edu
JOHNSON, Cornelius .... 214-860-2496 434 A cjohnson@dcccd.edu
JOHNSON, Cornelius, H .... 434-797-8454 472 H cornelius.johnson@danville.edu
JOHNSON, Craig .... 847-491-3741 146 C johnson-c@northwestern.edu
JOHNSON, Craig .... 320-222-5202 239 H craig.johnson@ridgewater.edu
JOHNSON, Cretia .... 740-386-4195 355 F johnsonc@mtc.edu
JOHNSON, Croslena ..... 864-646-1568 411 H cjohnso5@tctc.edu
JOHNSON, Cuthrell ...... 336-750-2233 343 E johnsonc@wssu.edu
JOHNSON, Cynthia .... 360-688-2290 482 D cjohnson@stmartin.edu
JOHNSON, Dacia .... 218-736-1512 238 K dacia.johnson@minnesota.edu
JOHNSON, Danette .... 804-524-5070 475 E dljohnson@vsu.edu
JOHNSON, Danette .... 865-539-5340 424 C djohnson11@pstcc.edu
JOHNSON, Daniel .... 803-812-7353 412 E johns943@mailbox.sc.edu
JOHNSON, Daniel .... 206-934-6709 482 H daniel.johnson@seattlecolleges.edu
JOHNSON, Daniel .... 701-662-1515 346 A dan.johnson@lrsc.edu
JOHNSON, Daniel .... 918-444-4211 366 G johnso89@nsuok.edu
JOHNSON, Daniel, W ... 414-443-8952 497 A daniel.johnson@wlc.edu
JOHNSON, Danny .... 714-895-8344.. 38 E djohnson@gwc.cccd.edu
JOHNSON, Dante .... 808-237-5145 128 D djohnson@hmi.edu
JOHNSON, Dara .... 765-455-9533 156 E darnjohn@iu.edu
JOHNSON, Daryl .... 651-793-1227 238 B daryl.johnson@metrostate.edu
JOHNSON, Dave .... 310-506-4798.. 56 H david.m.johnson@pepperdine.edu
JOHNSON, David .... 608-663-4343 491 F davjohnson@edgewood.edu
JOHNSON, David .... 716-338-1280 302 G davejohnson@mail.sunyjcc.edu
JOHNSON, David .... 314-838-8858 261 A djohnson@ugst.edu
JOHNSON, David .... 510-436-2501.. 57 C dmjohnson@peralta.edu
JOHNSON, David .... 812-855-8908 156 C vpem@indiana.edu
JOHNSON, David .... 256-824-6288..... 8 B david.johnson@uah.edu
JOHNSON, David .... 503-768-7766 373 D davidjohnson@lclark.edu
JOHNSON, David, B ...... 812-855-8908 156 B dj44@indiana.edu
JOHNSON, David, J .... 513-745-3202 364 F johnsond8@xavier.edu
JOHNSON, Dañáe .... 229-226-1621 126 B djohnson@thomasu.edu
JOHNSON, Deadre .... 202-885-2721.. 91 D deadrej@american.edu
JOHNSON, Dean, L .... 906-487-2668 227 D dean@mtu.edu
JOHNSON, Debbie .... 218-733-6904 238 A debra.johnson@lsc.edu
JOHNSON, Deborah ...... 484-365-7429 388 F dejohnson@lincoln.edu
JOHNSON, Deidre .... 410-951-2654 203 E deijohnson@coppin.edu
JOHNSON, Deirdra, G .. 410-334-2902 205 A djohnson@worwic.edu
JOHNSON, Delores .... 901-722-3397 422 I djohnson@sco.edu
JOHNSON, Denise .... 425-889-7829 481 A denise.johnson@northwestu.edu
JOHNSON, Derrick .... 559-244-2612.. 67 A derrick.johnson@fresnocitycollege.edu
JOHNSON, Deshawn ..... 248-204-2117 226 E djohnson@ltu.edu
JOHNSON, Diana .... 479-725-4681.. 20 G djohnson@nwacc.edu
JOHNSON, Donald .... 912-201-8000 125 D dojohnson@southuniversity.edu
JOHNSON, Donielle, R . 972-860-7372 433 I doniellejohnson@dcccd.edu
JOHNSON, Donna .... 318-383-5758 192 A donnaj@latech.edu
JOHNSON, Donte .... 804-751-9191 464 N djohnson@ccc-va.com
JOHNSON, Dorianne ..... 314-340-3534 253 E johnsdor@hssu.edu
JOHNSON, Doug .... 315-228-6624 296 C djohnson@colgate.edu
JOHNSON, Doug .... 785-460-5411 172 L doug.johnson@colbycc.edu
JOHNSON, Douglas, P . 207-581-1392 196 D douglasj@maine.edu
JOHNSON, Dreand .... 816-604-1206 254 E dreand.johnson@mcckc.edu
JOHNSON, Dreand .... 903-729-0256 451 C dreand.johnson@tvcc.edu
JOHNSON, Dustin .... 715-394-8122 496 D djohns75@uwsuper.edu
JOHNSON, E. Patrick .... 847-467-6993 146 C dean-epj@northwestern.edu
JOHNSON, Eartha .... 504-816-4723 186 F ejohnson@dillard.edu
JOHNSON, Edward .... 732-224-2899 275 D edjohnson@brookdalecc.edu
JOHNSON, Elizabeth ..... 203-596-4638.. 88 E ejohnson@post.edu
JOHNSON, Elizabeth ..... 208-732-6501 131 B ejohnson19@csi.edu
JOHNSON, Ellen, V ...... 814-332-3100 378 A
JOHNSON, Eric .... 815-224-0440 140 D eric_johnson@ivcc.edu
JOHNSON, Eric .... 907-260-7422.... 9 D
JOHNSON, Eric .... 813-253-7560 102 A ejohnson71@hccfl.edu
JOHNSON, Eric .... 906-227-2313 228 E ericjohn@nmu.edu
JOHNSON, Eric .... 617-627-5484 219 A eric.johnson@tufts.edu
JOHNSON, Eric, C .... 617-627-5484 219 A eric.johnson@tufts.edu
JOHNSON, Eric, P .... 218-299-3447 234 K johnson@cord.edu
JOHNSON, Eric, S .... 207-859-4460 194 B eric.johnson@colby.edu
JOHNSON, Eric, W .... 219-464-5310 162 C eric.johnson@valpo.edu
JOHNSON, Erica .... 901-572-2441 417 A erica.johnson@baptistu.edu
JOHNSON, Erica .... 406-657-1029 264 G erica.johnson@rocky.edu
JOHNSON, Erica .... 801-832-2206 461 A eljohnson@westminstercollege.edu
JOHNSON, Erica .... 717-262-2614 402 D erica.johnson@wilson.edu
JOHNSON, Erik .... 541-885-1151 374 G erik.johnson3@oit.edu
JOHNSON, Erin .... 865-981-8011 420 C erin.johnson@maryvillecollege.edu
JOHNSON, Erin, E .... 260-422-5561 156 A eejohnson@indianatech.edu
JOHNSON, Ethan .... 912-287-4027 117 B ejohnson@coastalpines.edu
JOHNSON, Ezra .... 952-446-4115 235 B johnsonez@crown.edu
JOHNSON, Feng-Ling ... 320-308-5272 240 C feng-ling.johnson@stcloudstate.edu
JOHNSON, Frances .... 517-264-7109 230 C fjohnso1@sienaheights.edu
JOHNSON, Frank .... 620-947-3121 177 F frankj@tabor.edu
JOHNSON, Franklin .... 804-524-1133 475 E fhjohnson@vsu.edu
JOHNSON, G. Michael . 816-654-7641 253 I mjohnson@kcumb.edu
JOHNSON, Gail .... 605-642-6054 415 F gail.johnson@bhsu.edu
JOHNSON, George .... 210-486-2174 428 C gjohnson@alamo.edu
JOHNSON, George, W .. 803-535-5077 406 E geojohnson@claflin.edu
JOHNSON, Glen .... 276-739-2467 474 H gjohnson@vhcc.edu
JOHNSON, Glenn .... 304-929-1495 486 J glennjohnson@ucwv.edu
JOHNSON, Greg .... 251-442-2269..... 8 C gjohnson@umobile.edu
JOHNSON, Greg, L .... 651-631-5363 243 E gljohnson@unwsp.edu
JOHNSON, Gregg .... 219-464-5325 162 C gregg.johnson@valpo.edu
JOHNSON, Gregg .... 412-392-3898 395 H gjohnson@pointpark.edu
JOHNSON, Gregory, J ... 812-461-5308 162 B gregory.johnson@usi.edu
JOHNSON, Hannah .... 662-685-4771 244 D hjohnson@bmc.edu
JOHNSON, Harper .... 719-255-3594.. 84 A hjohnson@uccs.edu
JOHNSON, Harrison, P . 601-979-2300 245 G harrison.p.johnson@jsums.edu
JOHNSON, Heather .... 847-628-2597 141 A hjohnson@judsonu.edu
JOHNSON, Heidi .... 217-333-1676 151 F johnso19@illinois.edu
JOHNSON, Hiluv .... 803-786-3856 407 E hjohnson@columbiasc.edu
JOHNSON, Holly .... 574-284-4581 160 F hjohnson@saintmarys.edu
JOHNSON, Imogene, G 740-368-3394 359 F igjohnson@owu.edu
JOHNSON, J. Mike .... 979-845-2345 446 B policechief@tamu.edu
JOHNSON, Jacqueline .. 731-881-3612 426 E jjohn253@utm.edu
JOHNSON, Jacy, R .... 515-294-5672 163 E jacyjohn@iastate.edu
JOHNSON, Jairus .... 662-476-5300 245 C jjohnson@eastms.edu
JOHNSON, James, F ..... 215-898-2173 399 J johnsonj@isc.upenn.edu
JOHNSON, Jamonicia ..... 662-243-2664 245 C jjohnson2@eastms.edu
JOHNSON, Janet, L .... 812-464-1924 162 B jljohnson@usi.edu
JOHNSON, Jared, W ..... 202-994-1135.. 92 C jaredw@gwu.edu
JOHNSON, Jasmin .... 209-476-7840.. 67 D jjohnson@clc.edu
JOHNSON, Jason .... 303-534-6270.. 79 D jason.johnson@colostate.edu
JOHNSON, Jason .... 580-774-7152 369 I jason.johnson@swosu.edu
JOHNSON, Jason .... 580-628-6240 366 J jason.johnson@noc.edu
JOHNSON, Jason .... 405-682-1611 367 D
JOHNSON, Jason, K ...... 662-252-8000 248 B jkjohnson@rustcollege.edu
JOHNSON, Jay .... 660-562-1277 256 G jayj@nwmissouri.edu
JOHNSON, Jeff .... 402-399-2607 265 H jjohnson@csm.edu
JOHNSON, Jeff .... 303-292-0015.. 80 F jjohnson@denvercollegeofnursing.edu
JOHNSON, Jeff .... 318-628-4342 187 H
JOHNSON, Jeff .... 850-718-2237.. 97 E johnsonj@chipola.edu
JOHNSON, Jeff .... 214-333-5759 433 D jeff@dbu.edu
JOHNSON, Jeffrey .... 570-348-6233 389 B jjohnson@marywood.edu
JOHNSON, Jeffrey, A .... 319-352-8659 170 F jeff.johnson@wartburg.edu
JOHNSON, Jeffrey, A .... 757-446-6100 465 H johnsonja@evms.edu
JOHNSON, Jeffrey, C .... 561-237-7333 103 W jjohnson@lynn.edu
JOHNSON, Jeffrey, W ... 515-294-4762 163 E jjohnsn@iastate.edu
JOHNSON, Jennifer ...... 870-763-3118.. 17 F jnjohnson@smail.anc.edu
JOHNSON, Jennifer ...... 503-768-6626 373 D jjj@lclark.edu
JOHNSON, Jennifer ...... 865-573-4517 419 E jjohnson@johnsonu.edu
JOHNSON, Jenny .... 731-989-6378 418 H jjohnson@fhu.edu
JOHNSON, Jesse .... 317-931-2387 154 D jwjohnson@cts.edu
JOHNSON, Jesse .... 205-940-7800..... 5 E
JOHNSON, Jessica .... 213-738-6705.. 66 A jejohnson@swlaw.edu
JOHNSON, Jessica .... 918-335-6854 368 E jjohnson@okwu.edu
JOHNSON, Jill, K .... 904-632-5016 101 A jill.johnson@fscj.edu
JOHNSON, Jill, R .... 864-587-4232 411 F johnsoj@smcsc.edu
JOHNSON, Jim .... 620-235-4389 176 H jjohnson@pittstate.edu
JOHNSON, Jodi .... 706-272-4475 118 A jjohnson@daltonstate.edu
JOHNSON, Joel .... 863-667-5400 108 I jkjohnson@seu.edu
JOHNSON, Joel, T .... 651-631-5312 243 E jtjohnson@unwsp.edu
JOHNSON, John .... 509-527-4996 485 C johnsonj@whitman.edu
JOHNSON, John, J .... 361-698-1269 434 H jjohnson@delmar.edu
JOHNSON, Johnnie .... 859-233-8261 185 A jjohnson@transy.edu

JOHNSON, Johnny 903-742-4910 457 I jfjohnson@wileyc.edu
JOHNSON, Jon 303-914-6444 82 L jon.johnson@rrcc.edu
JOHNSON, Jordan 205-348-2298 7 G jordan.m.johnson@ua.edu
JOHNSON, Jorine 425-889-5368 481 A jorine.johnson@northwestu.edu
JOHNSON, Joselyn 410-704-4453 204 B jmjohnson@towson.edu
JOHNSON, Joselyn 410-837-5714 204 C jjohnson@ubalt.edu
JOHNSON, Josh 763-544-9501 235 D
JOHNSON, Joshua 816-322-0110 250 E joshua.johnson@calvary.edu
JOHNSON, Joshua 408-852-2828 43 H jjohnson@gavilan.edu
JOHNSON, Joyce 951-639-5439 53 A jajohnso@msjc.edu
JOHNSON, Joyce, Y 478-825-4323 118 E johnsonj@fvsu.edu
JOHNSON, Joycelyn 225-771-2770 190 K joycelyn_johnson@subr.edu
JOHNSON, Juanita 850-599-3491 109 E juanita.johnson@famu.edu
JOHNSON, Judith 212-961-3399 290 F jjohnson@bankstreet.edu
JOHNSON, Julie 870-612-2165 23 B julie.johnson@uaccb.edu
JOHNSON, Julie 309-556-3134 140 E jjohns11@iwu.edu
JOHNSON, Julie 605-455-6011 414 H jjohnson@olc.edu
JOHNSON, Julie, A 352-273-6309 110 E johnson@cop.ufl.edu
JOHNSON, K-lee 610-225-5068 383 A kjohnso2@eastern.edu
JOHNSON, Kandi 601-477-5454 246 A kandi.johnson@jcjc.edu
JOHNSON, Karen 507-457-5300 241 A kjohnson@winona.edu
JOHNSON, Karen 903-813-2444 429 I kjohnson@austincollege.edu
JOHNSON, Karen 713-798-4951 430 E karenj@bcm.edu
JOHNSON, Karen, M 928-317-6000 11 B karen.johnson@azwestern.edu
JOHNSON, Karl 252-527-6223 335 E kejohnson27@lenoircc.edu
JOHNSON, Kathaerine 602-787-7106 13 G katharine.johnson@paradisevalley.edu
JOHNSON, Kathryn 916-900-2850 26 H kjohnson@asher.edu
JOHNSON, Kathy 508-565-1301 218 F kjohnson10@stonehill.edu
JOHNSON, Kathy, E 317-274-4500 157 B kjohnso@iupui.edu
JOHNSON, Kathy, J 605-642-6512 415 F kathy.johnson@bhsu.edu
JOHNSON, Kay 936-468-6550 444 H johnsondk6@sfasu.edu
JOHNSON, Keesha 501-337-5000 18 D kjohnson@asutr.edu
JOHNSON, Keith 205-453-6300 93 H
JOHNSON, Keith 701-671-2218 346 B keith.johnson@ndscs.edu
JOHNSON, Keith, V 423-439-4445 418 D johnsonk@etsu.edu
JOHNSON, Kelly 217-554-1678 136 E k.johnson43@dacc.edu
JOHNSON, Kelly 314-918-2617 252 E kjohnson@eden.edu
JOHNSON, Ken 903-233-3510 438 C kenjohnson@letu.edu
JOHNSON, Kendall 512-568-3300 93 H
JOHNSON, Kendall 210-202-3700 93 H
JOHNSON, Kenneth 850-644-9396 110 B ken.johnson@fsu.edu
JOHNSON, Kenneth 740-593-2247 358 L johnsok9@ohio.edu
JOHNSON, Kenyatta 229-500-2922 114 F kenyatta.johnson@asurams.edu
JOHNSON, Kerry 562-985-4128 32 A kerry.johnson@csulb.edu
JOHNSON, Kevin 620-341-5667 173 C kjohnson@emporia.edu
JOHNSON, Kevin, R 530-752-7225 69 A krjohnson@ucdavis.edu
JOHNSON, Kim 714-556-3610 73 G officevpem@vanguard.edu
JOHNSON, Kim, M 773-896-2400 134 K kjohnson@ctschicago.edu
JOHNSON, Kimberley 870-338-6474 23 A
JOHNSON, Kimberly 765-361-6209 162 G johnsonk@wabash.edu
JOHNSON, Kimberly 731-425-8826 423 F kjohnson75@jscc.edu
JOHNSON, Kimberly 541-346-1608 376 G johnskim@uoregon.edu
JOHNSON, Kimberly, T 301-447-5916 201 A kjohnson@msmary.edu
JOHNSON, Kintay 707-476-4293 58 I kinte-johnson@redwoods.edu
JOHNSON, Kristen 719-502-3363 82 D kristen.johnson@ppcc.edu
JOHNSON, Kristen 616-392-8555 233 B kristen@westernsem.edu
JOHNSON, Kristie 317-543-3093 159 B ksjohnson@martin.edu
JOHNSON, Kristina, M 614-292-2424 358 E president@osu.edu
JOHNSON, LaJoyya 214-860-2111 434 A lajoyya.johnson@dcccd.edu
JOHNSON, Larry 870-236-6901 19 D ljohnson@crc.edu
JOHNSON, Larry 646-313-8020 295 C president@guttman.cuny.edu
JOHNSON, Larry 202-685-2128 501 I johnsonl@ndu.edu
JOHNSON, Latesha, D 757-822-1054 474 G ldjohnson@tcc.edu
JOHNSON, Laura 906-217-4022 221 J lauralee.johnson@baycollege.edu
JOHNSON, Laura 704-216-6029 330 D ljohnson@livingstone.edu
JOHNSON, Laura, T 520-621-5150 16 H ltj@email.arizona.edu
JOHNSON, Lawrence, J 513-556-2322 361 I lawrence.johnson@uc.edu
JOHNSON, Le Keisha 210-567-2651 455 E johnsonld@uthscsa.edu
JOHNSON, Leanne 210-784-1320 447 B
JOHNSON, Leda 623-935-8868 13 C leda.johnson@estrellamountain.edu
JOHNSON, Lee 918-343-7541 369 A ljohnson@rsu.edu
JOHNSON, Lee 517-264-7108 230 C ljohnson@sienaheights.edu
JOHNSON, Lennor 760-355-6219 45 N lennor.johnson@imperial.edu
JOHNSON, Leslie 626-396-2200 26 G leslie.johnson@artcenter.edu
JOHNSON, Leslie 706-872-8072 119 C ljohnson@highlands.edu
JOHNSON, Leslie, R 217-786-2848 142 F leslie.johnson@llcc.edu
JOHNSON, Levester 309-438-5451 140 C ljohn13@ilstu.edu
JOHNSON, Lewis 850-599-3276 109 E lewis.johnson@famu.edu
JOHNSON, Linda 954-236-1282 109 F ljohnson@fau.edu
JOHNSON, Lindsay 618-833-3399 149 C lindsayj@shawneecc.edu
JOHNSON, Lisa 701-328-4143 344 G lisa.a.johnson@ndus.edu
JOHNSON, Lisa 253-879-2870 483 G ljohnson@pugetsound.edu
JOHNSON, Lisa 407-646-2391 106 L adjohnson@rollins.edu
JOHNSON, Lisa 239-745-4597 109 G ljohnson@fgcu.edu
JOHNSON, Lisa 336-506-4139 331 J lisa.johnson@alamancecc.edu
JOHNSON, Lisa 804-862-6100 469 E lsjohnson@rbc.edu
JOHNSON, Liz 512-448-8621 441 N ekjohnson@stedwards.edu
JOHNSON, Lori 574-284-4587 160 F ljohnson2@saintmarys.edu
JOHNSON, Lynn 970-491-1550 79 E lynn.johnson@colostate.edu
JOHNSON, Lynn 218-755-2068 237 B lynn.johnson@bemidjistate.edu
JOHNSON, Lynn 631-632-6151 316 D lynn.johnson@stonybrook.edu
JOHNSON, Lynn 503-883-2568 373 E ljohnson2@linfield.edu
JOHNSON, Lynne 907-796-6416 10 C lejohnson@alaska.edu
JOHNSON, M. Eric 615-322-2534 427 B eric.johnson@vanderbilt.edu
JOHNSON, Maggie 972-708-7358 434 F maggie_johnson@diu.edu
JOHNSON, Maleea, D 412-578-6227 380 A mdjohnson4833@carlow.edu
JOHNSON, Malkia, L 410-651-6449 203 B mljohnson3@umes.edu
JOHNSON, Malonda 740-351-3484 360 E mjohnson@shawnee.edu
JOHNSON, Marco 661-726-1911 68 L marco.johnson@uav.edu
JOHNSON, Marcus 702-651-4148 270 F marcus.johnson@csn.edu
JOHNSON, Maria 909-748-8333 72 E maria_johnson@redlands.edu
JOHNSON, Marianne, H 215-699-5700 387 G mjohnson@lsb.edu
JOHNSON, Marie 657-278-2638 31 E mariejohnson@fullerton.edu
JOHNSON, Marie, D 802-656-5700 462 D marie.johnson@uvm.edu
JOHNSON, Mark 510-466-7369 56 I
JOHNSON, Mark 704-894-2681 328 C majohnson@davidson.edu
JOHNSON, Mark 507-389-2555 238 L mark.johnson@mnsu.edu
JOHNSON, Marviene 304-327-4062 488 J mjohnson@bluefieldstate.edu
JOHNSON, Mary 919-760-8535 331 A mbjohnson@meredith.edu
JOHNSON, Matt 906-217-4134 221 J matt.c.johnson@baycollege.edu
JOHNSON, Matthew 708-444-4500 138 A
JOHNSON, McCartney 936-294-1594 449 E majohnson@shsu.edu
JOHNSON, Megan 302-622-8000 90 C mjohnson@dcad.edu
JOHNSON, Melanie 817-272-2099 454 B melanie.johnson@uta.edu
JOHNSON, Melisa 843-921-6980 410 B mjohnson@netc.edu
JOHNSON, Melissa 701-671-2520 346 B melissa.j.johnson@ndscs.edu
JOHNSON, Melvina 866-492-5336 243 G melvina.johnson@laureate.net
JOHNSON, Meredith, G 404-814-8813 126 F mgurley@uga.edu
JOHNSON, Micah 209-476-7840 67 D mjohnson@clc.edu
JOHNSON, Michael 713-743-8859 451 F cmj@uh.edu
JOHNSON, Michael 503-943-7930 376 H johnsomi@up.edu
JOHNSON, Michael 404-627-2681 116 B michael.johnson@beulah.edu
JOHNSON, Michael 903-468-8175 446 D michael.johnson@tamuc.edu
JOHNSON, Michael, A 205-929-1851 6 B majohnson@miles.edu
JOHNSON, Michael, C 214-860-2167 434 A mcjohnson@dcccd.edu
JOHNSON, Michael, D 407-823-2698 110 D michael.johnson@ucf.edu
JOHNSON, Michael, J 757-822-1768 474 G mjohnson@tcc.edu
JOHNSON, Michael, L 270-824-8567 182 A michael.johnson@kctcs.edu
JOHNSON, Michele 253-864-3100 481 H mjohnson@pierce.ctc.edu
JOHNSON, Michelle 254-710-1181 430 F michelle_m_johnson@baylor.edu
JOHNSON, Michelle 309-341-5258 134 A mljohnson@sandburg.edu
JOHNSON, Michelle 934-420-2369 320 C michelle.johnson@farmingdale.edu
JOHNSON, Michelle 605-688-5374 416 A michelle.johnson@sdstate.edu
JOHNSON, Michelle 414-229-7490 495 B john3453@uwm.edu
JOHNSON, Mike 713-743-8859 451 G cmj@uh.edu
JOHNSON, Mikki 559-442-4600 67 A mikki.johnson@fresnocitycollege.edu
JOHNSON, Mimi 334-420-4243 3 H mjohnson@trenholmstate.edu
JOHNSON, Mitchell 336-334-4822 334 F mjohnson@gtcc.edu
JOHNSON, Morgan 858-513-9240 16 I morgan.johnson@ashford.edu
JOHNSON, Nakikke 662-846-4646 245 A njohnson@deltastate.edu
JOHNSON, Nancy 952-885-5428 241 P njohnson@nwhealth.edu
JOHNSON, Natasha 225-743-8500 188 F njohnson@rpcc.edu
JOHNSON, Nathan 616-538-2330 224 B njohnson@gracechristian.edu
JOHNSON, Neil, A 303-867-1155 83 H johnson@taft.edu
JOHNSON, Nicole 805-546-3171 41 A nicole_johnson7@cuesta.edu
JOHNSON, Nicolette 972-883-2943 454 D nicolette.johnson@utdallas.edu
JOHNSON, Nikki 541-956-7109 375 G njohnson@roguecc.edu
JOHNSON, Nina 218-755-3760 237 B nina.johnson@bemidjistate.edu
JOHNSON, Pam 256-835-5456 2 B pjohnson@gadsdenstate.edu
JOHNSON, Pamela, D 937-766-7765 349 C johnsonp@cedarville.edu
JOHNSON, Pamela, L 701-788-5265 345 B pamela.l.johnson@mayvillestate.edu
JOHNSON, Patricia, A 610-758-3178 388 C paj214@lehigh.edu
JOHNSON, Patrick 240-567-5288 200 E patrick.johnson@montgomerycollege.edu
JOHNSON, Patrick, H 615-327-6061 420 D pjohnson@mmc.edu
JOHNSON, Paul 404-727-7707 118 D rpaul.johnson@emory.edu
JOHNSON, Paul, C 303-273-3000 79 A presoffice@mines.edu
JOHNSON, Paula, A 781-283-2237 219 C pjohnson@wellesley.edu
JOHNSON, Paula, J 858-534-2552 70 C pjjohnson@ucsd.edu
JOHNSON, Paulette, M 269-471-3275 220 H paulettej@andrews.edu
JOHNSON, Peggy, A 814-865-2631 391 F paj6@psu.edu
JOHNSON, Philip 906-487-7201 223 I philip.johnson@finlandia.edu
JOHNSON, Phill 334-244-3202 4 F pjohns23@aum.edu
JOHNSON, Phyllis 501-374-6305 21 B phyllis.johnson@shortercollege.edu
JOHNSON, Quenetta 252-985-5369 339 B qjohnson@ncwc.edu
JOHNSON, Quentin, R 434-949-1000 474 D quentin.johnson@southside.edu
JOHNSON, R 504-283-8822 186 F rjohnson@dillard.edu
JOHNSON, Rachel 916-660-8103 64 B rjohnson45@sierracollege.edu
JOHNSON, Rachel 320-589-6300 243 C rmjohnson@morris.umn.edu
JOHNSON, Ralph 301-891-4109 204 D rejohnson@wau.edu
JOHNSON, Ramon 502-597-6655 183 A ramon.johnson@kysu.edu
JOHNSON, Rana 812-237-8954 155 H rana.johnson@indstate.edu
JOHNSON, Randee 843-525-8250 411 G rjohnson@tcl.edu
JOHNSON, Raniyah 408-223-6768 62 F raniyah.johnson@evc.edu
JOHNSON, Rebecca 606-248-0256 182 F rebecca.parrott@kctcs.edu
JOHNSON, Rebecca, J 703-784-2105 501 H
JOHNSON, Regynold 773-291-6100 135 B
JOHNSON, Renita 704-922-6312 334 E johnson.renita@gaston.edu
JOHNSON, Richard 716-731-8850 309 E rajohnson@niagaracc.suny.edu
JOHNSON, Richard 870-236-6901 19 D rjohnson@crc.edu
JOHNSON, Richard 503-484-2257 374 F sphacad@ohsu.edu
JOHNSON, Richard, A 864-597-4090 413 E johnsonra@wofford.edu
JOHNSON, Rick 307-778-1135 500 D rjohnson@lccc.wy.edu
JOHNSON, Robby 580-349-2611 367 F
JOHNSON, Robert 928-524-7695 14 L robert.johnson@npc.edu
JOHNSON, Robert 973-972-4538 281 B rjohnson@njms.rutgers.edu
JOHNSON, Robert, E 413-782-1243 219 E robert.johnson@wne.edu
JOHNSON, Robert, E 913-667-5700 172 G rjohnson@cbts.edu
JOHNSON, Roberta, L 515-294-0109 163 E rljohns@iastate.edu
JOHNSON, Rochelle 208-459-5894 131 A rjohnson@collegeofidaho.edu
JOHNSON, Rodney 937-766-4114 349 C johnsonr@cedarville.edu

JOHNSON, Roger .... 540-261-8400 470 D
roger.johnson@svu.edu
JOHNSON, Ronald .... 843-574-6326 411 I
ronald.johnson@tridenttech.edu
JOHNSON, Ronald, A ... 502-597-5509 183 A
president@kysu.edu
JOHNSON, Ronnie, J .... 903-586-2501 430 C
ronnie.johnson@bmats.edu
JOHNSON, Rory .... 707-465-2300.. 58 I
rory-johnson@redwoods.edu
JOHNSON, Ruben .... 505-566-3279 287 G
johnsonr@sanjuancollege.edu
JOHNSON, Ruben .... 972-860-8161 433 H
rjohnson@dcccd.edu
JOHNSON, JR.,
Rushton, W .... 865-694-6552 424 C
rwjohnson2@pstcc.edu
JOHNSON, Russell, R ... 207-859-4776 194 B
margaret.mcfadden@colby.edu
JOHNSON, Ryan .... 501-205-8815.. 19 B
rjohnson@cbc.edu
JOHNSON, Samantha ... 334-808-6580.... 7 C
johnson@troy.edu
JOHNSON, Samantha ... 979-209-7281 430 I
samantha.johnson@blinn.edu
JOHNSON, Sandra, S ... 585-475-2267 312 A
ssjvsa@rit.edu
JOHNSON, Saphronia ... 770-426-2733 122 A
saphronia.johnson@life.edu
JOHNSON, Sara .... 218-683-8800 239 E
sara.johnson@northlandcollege.edu
JOHNSON, Sarah .... 419-448-3039 361 C
johnsonsat@tiffin.edu
JOHNSON, Scott .... 831-479-5663.. 27 G
scjohnso@cabrillo.edu
JOHNSON, Scott .... 714-449-7438.. 51 D
scottjohnson@ketchum.edu
JOHNSON, Scott .... 419-448-2280 353 D
sjohnson@heidelberg.edu
JOHNSON, Scott .... 336-838-6141 338 H
sajohnson366@wilkescc.edu
JOHNSON, Sean .... 707-664-4032.. 34 C
spjohnson@sonoma.edu
JOHNSON, Sean .... 701-252-3467 346 J
sean.johnson@uj.edu
JOHNSON, Sean .... 803-321-5166 409 I
sean.johnson@newberry.edu
JOHNSON, Seth .... 716-375-2382 312 F
sjohnson@sbu.edu
JOHNSON, Shalena .... 318-274-7720 191 G
johnsons@gram.edu
JOHNSON, Shannon ..... 541-556-1515 372 G
sjohnson@corban.edu
JOHNSON, Sharon .... 606-589-3321 182 F
sjohnson0265@kctcs.edu
JOHNSON, Sharon .... 314-516-6817 260 E
sharon_johnson@umsl.edu
JOHNSON, Sheila, G ..... 405-744-6321 367 G
sheila.johnson@okstate.edu
JOHNSON, Sheila, M ..... 727-376-6911 112 F
registrar@trinitycollege.edu
JOHNSON, Shelley .... 850-599-3017 109 E
shelley.johnson@famu.edu
JOHNSON, Sherrick .... 706-771-4008 115 H
sjohnson@augustatech.edu
JOHNSON, Sherrick, L . 706-771-4008 115 H
sjohnson@augustatech.edu
JOHNSON, Shirley .... 251-578-1313.... 3 D
sjohnson@rstc.edu
JOHNSON, Sonia .... 870-236-6901.. 19 D
sjohnson@crc.edu
JOHNSON, Sonja .... 910-362-7021 332 F
sjohnson@cfcc.edu
JOHNSON, Sonya .... 803-705-4815 405 G
sonya.johnson@benedict.edu
JOHNSON, Stacey .... 718-368-1193 304 B
sjohnson@libi.edu
JOHNSON, Stacy .... 248-689-8282 231 E
JOHNSON, Stephanie .... 607-735-1178 298 G
sjohnson@elmira.edu
JOHNSON, Stephanie ... 573-875-7357 251 A
sgjohnson@ccis.edu
JOHNSON, Stephanie ... 704-886-6500.. 93 H
JOHNSON, Stephen .... 626-812-3020.. 26 K
sjohnson@apu.edu
JOHNSON, Stephen .... 214-305-9500 427 G
scj98d@acu.edu
JOHNSON, Steve .... 913-360-7415 171 G
stevej@benedictine.edu
JOHNSON, Steve .... 504-280-6303 189 F
sgjohnso@uno.edu
JOHNSON, Steve .... 580-774-3016 369 I
steve.johnson@swosu.edu

JOHNSON, Steven .... 906-635-2160 226 C
sjohnson18@lssu.edu
JOHNSON, Steven, L .... 937-512-2525 360 F
president@sinclair.edu
JOHNSON, Susan .... 316-978-5587 178 B
susan.johnson@wichita.edu
JOHNSON, Susan, E ...... 651-631-5333 243 E
snjohnson@unwsp.edu
JOHNSON, Suzanne ...... 253-833-9111 480 A
sjohnson@greenriver.edu
JOHNSON, Tamara .... 312-662-4043 132 D
tajohnson@adler.edu
JOHNSON, Tamara .... 847-925-6103 138 E
jt03888@harpercollege.edu
JOHNSON, Tammy .... 304-696-3161 488 N
johnson73@marshall.edu
JOHNSON, Tara .... 229-500-2007 114 F
tara.johnson@asurams.edu
JOHNSON, Tardis .... 212-217-3082 299 C
tardis_johnson@fitnyc.edu
JOHNSON, Tasha .... 252-527-6223 335 E
tvjohnson90@lenoircc.edu
JOHNSON, Ted .... 858-822-5949.. 70 C
edjohnson@ucsd.edu
JOHNSON, Teisha .... 312-949-7407 139 B
tjohnson@ico.edu
JOHNSON, Terrence ...... 231-843-5874 232 I
tjohnson@westshore.edu
JOHNSON, Theodore ..... 630-889-6512 145 D
tjohnson@nuhs.edu
JOHNSON, Theresa .... 303-871-4912.. 84 C
theresa.johnson@du.edu
JOHNSON, Thomas .... 610-282-1100 382 A
thomas.johnson@desales.edu
JOHNSON, Thomas, A .. 409-882-3314 449 C
thomas.johnson@lsco.edu
JOHNSON, Tianna .... 507-457-1635 242 H
tpjohnso@smumn.edu
JOHNSON, Tiffany .... 870-972-3025.. 17 I
tijohnson@astate.edu
JOHNSON, Tiffany .... 512-313-4109 432 N
tiffany.johnson@concordia.edu
JOHNSON, Tim .... 918-495-7149 368 F
tjohnson@oru.edu
JOHNSON, Timothy .... 336-334-5636 342 D
tjjohns3@uncg.edu
JOHNSON, Timothy .... 843-953-5770 407 D
johnsonts@cofc.edu
JOHNSON, Timothy, R . 870-864-8421.. 21 C
JOHNSON, Toni .... 419-755-9028 357 B
tjohnson@ncstatecollege.edu
JOHNSON, Tonjanita ...... 205-348-8347.... 7 F
tjohnson@uasystem.edu
JOHNSON, Toya .... 312-850-7267 135 E
tjohnson616@ccc.edu
JOHNSON, Tracci .... 818-252-5114.. 76 D
tracci.johnson@woodbury.edu
JOHNSON, Tracci .... 734-973-3480 232 A
tjohnson29@wccnet.edu
JOHNSON, Tracy .... 704-216-6098 330 D
tjohnson@livingstone.edu
JOHNSON, Tracy .... 214-860-2033 434 A
tracy.johnson@dcccd.edu
JOHNSON, Tracy, L .... 310-825-4959.. 69 D
tjohnson@college.ucla.edu
JOHNSON, Travis, T ...... 803-536-8480 410 H
tjohns41@scsu.edu
JOHNSON, Trent .... 270-534-3302 182 G
trent.johnson@kctcs.edu
JOHNSON, Trent .... 270-534-3504 182 G
trent.johnson@kctcs.edu
JOHNSON, Tricia .... 303-404-5022.. 80 I
tricia.johnson@frontrange.edu
JOHNSON, Troy .... 334-244-3110..... 4 F
ljohns90@aum.edu
JOHNSON, Troy .... 817-272-5401 454 B
troy.johnson@uta.edu
JOHNSON, Trygve, D .... 616-395-7966 224 H
johnsont@hope.edu
JOHNSON, Valen, E .... 979-845-8817 446 B
vejohnson@tamu.edu
JOHNSON, Valerie .... 919-719-5061 339 I
valerie.johnson@shawu.edu
JOHNSON, Veronica ...... 773-947-6319 143 E
vjohnson@mccormick.edu
JOHNSON, Victoria, D .. 504-865-5591 191 D
victoria@tulane.edu
JOHNSON, Virginia .... 312-369-7504 136 C
vjohnson@colum.edu
JOHNSON, Vivian .... 937-529-2201 361 F
vjohnson@united.edu
JOHNSON, Wallace .... 909-384-8502.. 60 F
wjohnson@sbccd.cc.ca.us

JOHNSON, Walter .... 630-942-2800 135 F
JOHNSON, Walter .... 864-977-2007 410 A
walter.johnson@ngu.edu
JOHNSON, Wendy .... 225-743-8500 188 F
wjohnson@rpcc.edu
JOHNSON, Wesley .... 910-892-3178 329 D
JOHNSON, Wesley, T ... 407-582-1118 113 C
wjohnson55@valenciacollege.edu
JOHNSON, William, H .. 203-254-4000.. 87 G
wjohnson@fairfield.edu
JOHNSON, William, P .. 314-977-2788 258 H
william.johnson@slu.edu
JOHNSON, Willie .... 715-232-1151 496 C
johnsonw@uwstout.edu
JOHNSON, Zak .... 218-755-2226 237 B
zachary.johnson@bemidjistate.edu
JOHNSON-CASSULO,
Nancy .... 208-459-5680 131 A
njohnsoncassulo@collegeofidaho.edu
JOHNSON-COLEMAN,
Sasha .... 803-793-5197 408 A
johnson-coleman@denmarktech.edu
JOHNSON-CRAMER,
Michael .... 607-274-3341 302 E
mjohnsoncramer@ithaca.edu
JOHNSON-DEBAUFRE,
Melanie .... 973-408-3823 276 B
mjjohnso@drew.edu
JOHNSON GARCIA,
Michelle .... 305-628-6719 107 D
mjg@stu.edu
JOHNSON-HANKS,
Jennifer .... 510-642-6000.. 68 N
JOHNSON JONES,
Sylvia, M .... 847-543-2404 135 G
cps086@clcillinois.edu
JOHNSON-MALLARD,
Versie .... 330-672-8845 354 A
vjohns29@kent.edu
JOHNSON MATHERSON,
Akua, J .... 919-530-6204 341 D
amathers@nccu.edu
JOHNSON-MILLS,
Jessica .... 818-401-1151.. 39 F
jjohnsonmills@columbiacollege.edu
JOHNSON RAMEZ,
Teresa .... 540-375-2300 469 G
JOHNSON RENVALL,
Poppy .... 505-224-4435 285 B
pjohnsonrenvall@cnm.edu
JOHNSON-ROSS,
Debora .... 319-352-8284 170 F
debora.johnsonross@wartburg.edu
JOHNSON SHAHEED,
Karen .... 301-860-3555 203 D
kshaheed@bowiestate.edu
JOHNSON-SHAHEED,
Karen .... 301-860-3504 203 D
kshaheed@bowiestate.edu
JOHNSON SUSKI,
Katharine .... 515-294-0815 163 E
ksuski@iastate.edu
JOHNSON-VARNEY,
Suzanne .... 740-351-3410 360 E
svarney@shawnee.edu
JOHNSON-WALKER,
Heather .... 334-556-2397..... 2 C
hwalker@wallace.edu
JOHNSON-WEEKS,
Demetria .... 713-313-7940 448 D
weeks_dj@tsu.edu
JOHNSRUD, Jason .... 202-462-2101.. 93 A
johnsrud@iwp.edu
JOHNSSON,
Magnus, H .... 804-827-1363 472 D
johnssonm@vcu.edu
JOHNSTON, Alysia .... 620-223-2700 173 F
alysiaj@fortscott.edu
JOHNSTON, Amanda, J 210-805-5856 452 D
ajohnsto@uiwtx.edu
JOHNSTON, Angela .... 330-263-2141 350 H
ajohnston@wooster.edu
JOHNSTON, Ann .... 970-943-2493.. 85 B
afjohnston@western.edu
JOHNSTON, Barbara, A 972-985-3732 432 I
bjohnston@collin.edu
JOHNSTON, Brian, A .... 202-319-6425.. 91 G
johnston@cua.edu
JOHNSTON, Carol .... 213-477-2617.. 52 J
cjohnston@msmu.edu
JOHNSTON, Caroline .... 321-674-7400 100 A
cjohnston@fit.edu
JOHNSTON, Chad .... 318-678-6000 187 E
cjohnston@bpcc.edu

JOHNSTON,
Christine, D .... 309-457-2444 144 E
cjohnston@monmouthcollege.edu
JOHNSTON,
Christopher .... 708-209-3229 136 D
christopher.johnston@cuchicago.edu
JOHNSTON,
Christopher .... 216-987-5378 351 D
christopher.johnston@tri-c.edu
JOHNSTON, Cynthia ...... 843-349-7835 409 A
cynthia.johnston@hgtc.edu
JOHNSTON, David .... 707-468-3091.. 51 F
djohnston@mendocino.edu
JOHNSTON, Delaney ..... 812-221-1714 162 D
djohnston@vbc.edu
JOHNSTON, Dusty, R ... 940-552-6291 456 F
drj@vernoncollege.edu
JOHNSTON, Elizabeth ... 214-637-3530 457 A
ejohnston@wadecollege.edu
JOHNSTON, Elizabeth ... 412-237-8195 381 C
ejohnston@ccac.edu
JOHNSTON, Jacqueline 516-877-6004 288 L
jjohnston@adelphi.edu
JOHNSTON, James .... 940-397-4000 439 F
james.johnston@msutexas.edu
JOHNSTON, Jamie, M .. 770-720-9238 124 E
jmj@reinhardt.edu
JOHNSTON, Jason .... 207-768-9652 196 I
jason.johnston@maine.edu
JOHNSTON, Jennifer ..... 719-384-6841.. 82 C
jennifer.johnston@otero.edu
JOHNSTON, Jeremy .... 903-923-2010 435 A
jjohnston@etbu.edu
JOHNSTON, Jerome ...... 281-649-3467 436 D
jrjohnston@hbu.edu
JOHNSTON, Jerritt .... 218-235-2137 238 D
jerritt.johnston@minnesotanorth.edu
JOHNSTON, Jolie .... 701-662-1651 346 A
jolie.johnston@lrsc.edu
JOHNSTON, Judy .... 912-279-5705 117 C
jjohnston@ccga.edu
JOHNSTON, Julie, L ...... 530-251-8820.. 47 I
jjohnston@lassencollege.edu
JOHNSTON, Justin .... 585-343-0055 300 D
jmjohnston@genesee.edu
JOHNSTON, Kara .... 303-963-3320.. 78 D
kjohnston@ccu.edu
JOHNSTON, Kathy .... 636-481-3280 253 G
kjohnsto@jeffco.edu
JOHNSTON, Ken .... 312-567-5850 139 H
johnston@iit.edu
JOHNSTON, Kerri .... 978-934-3933 211 G
kerri_johnston@uml.edu
JOHNSTON, Kristen .... 316-677-1647 178 C
kjohnston@wsutech.edu
JOHNSTON, Kyle .... 518-891-2915 309 G
kyle.johnston@nccc.edu
JOHNSTON, Larry .... 301-846-2501 198 E
ljohnston@frederick.edu
JOHNSTON, Lisa .... 727-864-8206.. 98 G
johnstln@eckerd.edu
JOHNSTON, Marsha .... 314-838-8858 261 A
mjohnston@ugst.edu
JOHNSTON, Mary .... 618-842-3711 139 D
johnstonm@iecc.edu
JOHNSTON, Michael .... 850-484-1717 105 G
mjohnston@pensacolastate.edu
JOHNSTON, Michelle ...... 912-279-5705 117 C
president@ccga.edu
JOHNSTON, Pamela .... 850-201-6150 112 B
pamela.johnston@tcc.fl.edu
JOHNSTON, Phil .... 615-460-6964 417 B
phil.johnston@belmont.edu
JOHNSTON, Roxanne ..... 706-233-7464 125 A
rjohnston@shorter.edu
JOHNSTON, Ruth .... 575-646-9875 286 G
ruthj@nmsu.edu
JOHNSTON,
S. Claiborne .... 512-495-5000 454 C
dellmedschool@utexas.edu
JOHNSTON, Sal .... 562-907-4204.. 76 A
sjohnston@whittier.edu
JOHNSTON, Sandra .... 815-455-9793 143 F
sjohnston@mchenry.edu
JOHNSTON, Sharon .... 979-830-4115 430 I
sharon.johnston@blinn.edu
JOHNSTON, Susan .... 903-823-3260 445 C
susan.johnston@texarkanacollege.edu
JOHNSTON, Timothy ..... 530-242-7669.. 64 A
tjohnston@shastacollege.edu
JOHNSTON, Will .... 919-761-2284 340 B
wjohnston@sebts.edu
JOHNSTONE, Darin .... 213-613-2200.. 65 D
darin_johnstone@sciarc.edu

JONES, Janice .... 414-410-4687 490 J jezjones@stritch.edu
JONES, Jarian, R .... 678-535-7771 118 F library@gcuniv.edu
JONES, Jason .... 850-245-0466 109 D jason.jones@flbog.edu
JONES, Jeannette .... 830-372-6061 448 C jjones@tlu.edu
JONES, Jeff .... 909-687-1750.. 43 G jeffjones@gs.edu
JONES, Jeff .... 903-693-1112 440 E jjones@panola.edu
JONES, Jeffrey .... 610-399-2042 393 D jjones@cheyney.edu
JONES, Jennifer .... 479-575-7718.. 21 H jj073@uark.edu
JONES, Jennifer .... 920-465-2111 494 F jonesj@uwgb.edu
JONES, Jennifer .... 828-327-7000 332 H jjones555@cvcc.edu
JONES, Jennifer .... 315-684-6044 320 E jonesj@morrisville.edu
JONES, Jennifer, M .... 719-333-2877 502 C jennifer.jones@afacademy.af.edu
JONES, Jenny .... 859-246-6653 181 B jenny.jones@kctcs.edu
JONES, Jenny .... 512-542-7830 445 D jjones@tamus.edu
JONES, Jenny, B .... 662-472-9035 245 E jbailey@holmescc.edu
JONES, Jenny, L .... 404-880-8549 116 I jjones@cau.edu
JONES, Jeremy .... 541-962-3553 372 H jdjones1@eou.edu
JONES, Jessica .... 252-246-1221 339 A jjones@wilsoncc.edu
JONES, Jessie .... 573-592-5039 261 F jessica.jones@westminster-mo.edu
JONES, Jim .... 972-860-8058 433 H
JONES, Jimmy .... 903-657-6543 447 F jjones@tbi.edu
JONES, Joanne .... 912-260-4664 125 B joanne.jones@sgsc.edu
JONES, John .... 904-596-2304 112 E jjones@tbc.edu
JONES, John .... 316-978-7751 178 B john.jones@wichita.edu
JONES, John .... 765-677-2387 157 F john.jones@indwes.edu
JONES, John .... 256-372-5104.... 1 A john.jones@aamu.edu
JONES, John .... 817-598-6345 457 C jdjones@wc.edu
JONES, John .... 269-965-3931 225 D jonesjo@kellogg.edu
JONES, III, John, E .... 717-245-1322 382 B jonesjohn@dickinson.edu
JONES, John, P .... 520-621-1112.. 16 H jpjones@arizona.edu
JONES, III, John, R .... 205-996-0132.... 8 A jrjones3@uab.edu
JONES, John, S .... 772-546-5534 102 B johnjones@hsbc.edu
JONES, Johnny .... 501-374-6305.. 21 B johnny.jones@shortercollege.edu
JONES, Johnny .... 281-949-1800.. 93 H
JONES, Johnny .... 937-708-3747 363 G jjonesd@wilberforce.edu
JONES, Jon .... 417-268-6049 250 A jjones@gobbc.edu
JONES, Josefvon .... 336-506-4289 331 J jjones827@alamancecc.edu
JONES, Joseph .... 678-359-5468 120 D jjones1@gordonstate.edu
JONES, Joshua .... 309-677-1000 133 H jejones@bradley.edu
JONES, Joshua .... 901-678-5686 426 A jjjnes19@memphis.edu
JONES, Joshua .... 864-503-5093 413 A jjones3@uscupstate.edu
JONES, Joye .... 205-929-6442.... 2 H jjones@lawsonstate.edu
JONES, Julie .... 719-336-1923.. 81 J julie.jones@lamarcc.edu
JONES, Julie .... 215-895-1910 382 D jaj358@drexel.edu
JONES, K. Russell .... 479-968-0490.. 18 E rjones@atu.edu
JONES, Karen .... 607-777-4775 315 E kjones@binghamton.edu
JONES, Kathy .... 713-348-5460 441 K kjones@rice.edu
JONES, Katie .... 704-330-6758 333 B katie.jones@cpcc.edu
JONES, Katrina .... 716-338-1446 302 G katrinajones@mail.sunyjcc.edu
JONES, Keisha .... 336-249-8186 333 G keisha_jones@davidsondavie.edu
JONES, Keith .... 859-233-8181 185 A kjones@transy.edu
JONES, Kelly .... 802-586-7711 462 C kjones@sterlingcollege.edu
JONES, Ken .... 919-739-7027 338 F kwjones@waynecc.edu
JONES, Ken .... 405-425-5104 367 C ken.jones@oc.edu
JONES, Kenneth, E .... 615-329-8681 418 E kjones@fisk.edu
JONES, Kent .... 256-228-6001.... 3 B jonesk@nacc.edu
JONES, Kevin .... 518-736-3622 300 B kevin.jones@fmcc.suny.edu
JONES, Kevin .... 803-754-4100 407 F
JONES, Kim .... 530-895-6144.. 27 F joneski@butte.edu
JONES, Kim .... 270-831-9617 181 F kim.jones@kctcs.edu
JONES, Kim .... 270-824-8649 182 A kim.jones@kctcs.edu
JONES, Kim .... 910-755-7300 332 D
JONES, Kim .... 903-823-3004 445 C kimberly.jones@texarkanacollege.edu
JONES, Kimberly, W .... 305-626-3629 100 B kimberly.jones@fmuniv.edu
JONES, Kirk .... 315-386-7328 319 E jonesk@canton.edu
JONES, Kona .... 217-875-7211 147 G kona@richland.edu
JONES, Kristine .... 919-497-3217 330 E kjones@louisburg.edu
JONES, Lacretia .... 504-520-7593 193 C ljames6@xula.edu
JONES, Lance .... 386-752-1822.. 99 P christopher.jones@fgc.edu
JONES, Lance .... 303-458-3673.. 83 B ljones007@regis.edu
JONES, Larry .... 443-885-3465 200 F larry.jones@morgan.edu
JONES, Larry, C .... 719-333-4322 502 C larry.jones@afacademy.af.edu
JONES, Latia .... 786-331-1000 104 H ljones@maufl.edu
JONES, Laura, A .... 928-523-9084.. 14 J laura.jones@nau.edu
JONES, Laura, B .... 734-764-7423 231 A laurabj@umich.edu
JONES, Lee .... 281-931-7717 121 F
JONES, Lee .... 713-425-3100 432 C
JONES, Leonard .... 360-650-2953 485 A leonard.jones@wwu.edu
JONES, Leslie .... 313-883-8512 229 J jones.leslie@shms.edu
JONES, Leslie, M .... 504-398-2252 191 E lmjones@uhcno.edu
JONES, Levi .... 816-268-5414 256 E ljones@nts.edu
JONES, Lewis .... 256-726-8039.... 6 C ljones@oakwood.edu
JONES, Lisa .... 970-675-3210.. 78 P lisa.jones@cncc.edu
JONES, Lisa .... 845-257-3216 316 B jonesl@newpaltz.edu
JONES, Liz .... 706-368-7509 119 C lijones@highlands.edu
JONES, Logan .... 816-271-4476 256 C jones@missouriwestern.edu
JONES, Logan .... 231-591-2422 223 H loganjones@ferris.edu
JONES, Lucy .... 513-745-3825 364 F jonesl24@xavier.edu
JONES, Maggie .... 334-222-6591.... 2 I mjones@lbwcc.edu
JONES, Marcus .... 225-342-6950 191 F marcus.jones@ulsystem.edu
JONES, Marcus .... 318-357-6441 192 D
JONES, Margaret .... 914-422-4043 310 F mjones@pace.edu
JONES, Margie .... 909-869-3464.. 30 B mfjones@cpp.edu
JONES, Marian .... 704-378-1074 329 H myjones@jcsu.edu
JONES, Marie .... 828-641-0768 327 A jonesmf@brevard.edu
JONES, Marlon .... 216-421-7424 350 E mjjones@cia.edu
JONES, Marlynn .... 904-620-2513 111 A marlynn.jones@unf.edu
JONES, Martin .... 406-656-9950 263 B
JONES, Mary .... 805-289-6346.. 74 B mjones@vcccd.edu
JONES, OP, Mary .... 517-264-7109 230 C mjones@sienaheights.edu
JONES, Mary, O .... 845-575-3000 305 C mary.jones@marist.edu
JONES, Matthew .... 630-829-6135 133 B mjones@ben.edu
JONES, Matthew, W .... 601-857-3630 245 D matthew.jones@hindscc.edu
JONES, Mattie .... 317-543-3235 159 B mjones@martin.edu
JONES, Mautra .... 405-682-1611 367 D
JONES, Megan .... 732-571-3465 278 B mjones@monmouth.edu
JONES, Megan .... 423-323-0226 424 B majones@northeaststate.edu
JONES, Melanie .... 318-274-2217 191 G jonesm@gram.edu
JONES, Melanie, E .... 803-327-8012 413 F mjones@yorktech.edu
JONES, Melinda, L .... 901-678-2690 426 A mljones6@memphis.edu
JONES, Melissa .... 540-654-1923 471 B mjones6@umw.edu
JONES, Melissa, A .... 910-678-8474 334 C jonesma@faytechcc.edu
JONES, Meredith .... 580-559-5668 365 J mjones@ecok.edu
JONES, Michael .... 434-544-8538 470 K jones.mj@lynchburg.edu
JONES, Michael .... 321-674-8837 100 A jonesm@fit.edu
JONES, Michael .... 918-444-3211 366 G jones361@nsuok.edu
JONES, Michael .... 434-544-8300 470 K jones_mj@lynchburg.edu
JONES, Michael .... 518-292-8615 312 D jonesm4@sage.edu
JONES, Molly .... 513-618-1933 350 B mjones@ccms.edu
JONES, Monterrio .... 803-934-3226 409 H mjones@morris.edu
JONES, Nancy .... 714-241-6209.. 38 D njones@coastline.edu
JONES, Natalie .... 207-780-5113 196 J natalie.jones@maine.edu
JONES, III, Nathaniel .... 510-522-7221.. 57 A nathanieljones@peralta.edu
JONES, Ned .... 518-783-2423 314 K jones@siena.edu
JONES, Nedra, W .... 804-524-6706 475 E nwjones@vsu.edu
JONES, Nicholas, P .... 814-865-2505 391 F provost@psu.edu
JONES, Nicholaus .... 215-780-1417 397 E njones@salus.edu
JONES, Nicole .... 619-660-4302.. 44 G nicole.jones@gcccd.edu
JONES, Nicole .... 310-900-1600.. 39 H njones3@compton.edu
JONES, Niki .... 870-633-4480.. 19 E njones@eacc.edu
JONES, Nina .... 662-915-7690 248 F nina@olemiss.edu
JONES, Norm, E .... 615-329-8663 418 E nejones@fisk.edu
JONES, Olivia .... 919-530-7713 341 D ojones@nccu.edu
JONES, Orion .... 419-434-4544 362 D orion.jones@findlay.edu
JONES, Pamela .... 956-295-3622 448 E pamela.jones@tsc.edu
JONES, Para, M .... 330-494-6170 360 I pjones@starkstate.edu
JONES, Parago .... 303-329-6355.. 79 C dean@cstcm.edu
JONES, Pat .... 318-357-6441 192 D
JONES, Patrice .... 703-892-5100.. 93 H
JONES, Paul .... 478-825-6315 118 E president@fvsu.edu
JONES, Paul .... 414-288-5276 492 E paul.jones@marquette.edu
JONES, Pernell .... 903-813-2235 429 I pjones@austincollege.edu
JONES, Phil .... 772-546-5534 102 B philjones@hsbc.edu
JONES, Phyllis .... 314-838-8858 261 A pjones@ugst.edu
JONES, Polly .... 864-379-8833 408 F pjones@erskine.edu
JONES, Quincie .... 406-268-3723 264 B quincie.jones@gfcmsu.edu
JONES, Quinton .... 580-387-7000 366 E
JONES, R Clifford .... 256-726-7365.... 6 C rcjones@oakwood.edu
JONES, Randy, P .... 214-768-2146 443 G rpjones@smu.edu
JONES, Razel .... 615-963-5000 425 A
JONES, Rebecca .... 503-255-0332 374 A beccajones@multnomah.edu
JONES, Rebecca .... 314-367-8700 260 A rebecca.jones@uhsp.edu
JONES, Renee .... 310-665-6800.. 55 B rjones@otis.edu
JONES, Renee, S .... 302-857-6819.. 90 D rjones@desu.edu
JONES, Rhonda, W .... 252-493-7200 336 E
JONES, Robert .... 401-232-6027 403 B rjones10@bryant.edu
JONES, Robert .... 508-999-8552 211 F rjones@umassd.edu
JONES, Robert .... 903-823-3154 445 C robert.jones@texarkanacollege.edu
JONES, Robert .... 503-517-1862 377 D rjones@westernseminary.edu
JONES, Robert, H .... 864-656-3940 406 F provost@clemson.edu
JONES, Robert, J .... 217-333-6290 151 C rjjones@illinois.edu
JONES, Robert, J .... 217-333-6290 151 F chancellor@illinois.edu
JONES, Robert, T .... 434-297-7395 471 F rtj4q@virginia.edu
JONES, Robin .... 334-291-4927.... 1 H robin.jones@cv.edu
JONES, Robin .... 205-348-5490.... 7 G rjones@uasystem.edu
JONES, Robin .... 575-769-4111 285 C robin.jones@clovis.edu
JONES, Rockwell, F .... 740-368-3000 359 F rfjones@owu.edu
JONES, Roddrick .... 601-857-3357 245 D roddrick.jones2@hindscc.edu
JONES, Roger .... 434-544-8444 470 K jones@lynchburg.edu
JONES, Rosalyn .... 412-624-4200 400 A rosalyn.jones@pitt.edu
JONES, Sam .... 601-477-4047 246 A sam.jones@jcjc.edu
JONES, Samantha Major .... 828-835-4203 338 C sjones@tricountycc.edu
JONES, Samuel .... 601-979-2260 245 G samuel.jones@jsums.edu
JONES, Sandi .... 254-299-8433 438 G sjones@mclennan.edu
JONES, Sandra .... 800-462-7845.. 79 F
JONES, Sandra .... 229-253-4446 127 C syjones@valdosta.edu
JONES, Sarah, L .... 540-464-7667 475 C jonessl10@vmi.edu
JONES, Scott .... 864-388-8320 409 B sjones@lander.edu
JONES, Serene .... 212-280-1403 323 C sjones@uts.columbia.edu
JONES, Shannon .... 843-792-8839 409 D joneshan@musc.edu
JONES, Sharon .... 985-545-1500 188 B
JONES, Shawn .... 870-230-5072.. 19 H jonessh@hsu.edu
JONES, Shawn .... 626-914-8885.. 37 B sjones@citruscollege.edu
JONES, Shawntae .... 816-802-3434 253 H ssjones@kcai.edu
JONES, Sheba .... 312-662-4131 132 D sjones@adler.edu
JONES, Sheila .... 706-295-6366 119 C shjones@highlands.edu
JONES, Sheri .... 858-513-9240.. 16 I sheri.jones@ashford.edu
JONES, Sherri .... 402-472-2913 268 I sherri.jones@unl.edu
JONES, Sherri .... 402-472-2238 269 A sherri.jones@unl.edu
JONES, Sherry .... 214-860-2202 434 A sljones@dcccd.edu
JONES, Sherry .... 801-618-0438 458 H sjones@ameritech.edu
JONES, Sloan .... 678-407-5549 119 B sjones45@ggc.edu

JONES, Stacey 479-788-7302 22 A stacey.jones@uafs.edu
JONES, Stacy 706-542-3451 126 F stacy.jones@georgiacenter.uga.edu
JONES, Stanley 229-333-5732 127 C sjones@valdosta.edu
JONES, Stephanie 313-993-1549 230 H landerss@udmercy.edu
JONES, Stephanie 409-882-3314 449 C stephanie.jones@lsco.edu
JONES, Stephanie 610-579-6678 390 G joness@neumann.edu
JONES, Steve 817-202-6263 444 B joness@swau.edu
JONES, Steven 662-246-6204 246 E sjones@msdelta.edu
JONES, Steven, K 719-333-2469 502 C steven.jones@afacademy.af.edu
JONES, Steven, L 765-361-6450 162 G joness@wabash.edu
JONES, Stuart 413-748-3757 218 E sdjones@springfield.edu
JONES, Stuart 435-586-7775 459 E jones@suu.edu
JONES, Susan, M 864-250-8191 408 J susan.m.jones@gvltec.edu
JONES, Sven 703-284-1538 468 A sven.jones@marymount.edu
JONES, Tanya, P 301-860-3455 203 D tjones@bowiestate.edu
JONES, Tara 334-844-1052 4 E jonestg@auburn.edu
JONES, Tiffane 708-596-2000 149 D tjones@ssc.edu
JONES, Tim 501-279-4920 19 G tjones@harding.edu
JONES, Tim 501-812-2760 23 E htjones@uaptc.edu
JONES, Tim 334-493-3573 2 I twjones@lbwcc.edu
JONES, Tim 850-245-0466 109 D tim.jones@flbog.edu
JONES, Timothy Paul 502-897-4347 184 D tjones@sbts.edu
JONES, Tina, N 205-652-3497 9 B tnj@uwa.edu
JONES, Todd 515-964-6242 164 F tgjones@dmacc.edu
JONES, Todd 612-874-3759 236 E tjones@mcad.edu
JONES, Todd 304-734-6608 487 D todd.jones@bridgevalley.edu
JONES, Tony 816-802-3422 253 H tonyjones@kcai.edu
JONES, Tony 423-461-8981 421 E tpjones@milligan.edu
JONES, Tracie 810-762-9536 225 F tjones1@kettering.edu
JONES, Trina 757-569-6720 474 A tjones@pdc.edu
JONES, Trish 859-846-5784 183 G tjones@midway.edu
JONES, Ty 509-682-6435 484 H tjones@wvc.edu
JONES, Tyron 843-661-2803 408 G tyron.jones@fdtc.edu
JONES, V. Faye 502-852-7159 185 E veronnie.jones@louisville.edu
JONES, Valerie 281-290-3940 438 E valerie.jones@lonestar.edu
JONES, Vennette 212-592-2604 314 I vjones@sva.edu
JONES, Victoria 949-824-7209 69 C vljones@uci.edu
JONES, Walter 310-287-4244 50 C joneswc@wlac.edu
JONES, Walter, F 937-255-2321 501 A walter.jones@afit.edu
JONES, Wanda 901-843-3766 422 C jonesw@rhodes.edu
JONES, Ward 563-884-5271 169 C ward.jones@palmer.edu
JONES, Waunita, R 662-246-6390 246 E wroberts@msdelta.edu
JONES, Wayne 603-228-3000 273 I
JONES, JR., Wayne, E 603-862-2390 273 H academic.affairs@unh.edu
JONES, Wayne, R 573-341-4111 260 F wayne.jones@mst.edu
JONES, Wendy 325-674-2903 427 G jonesw@acu.edu
JONES, William 848-932-0184 281 B william.jones@rutgers.edu
JONES, Willie 504-284-5520 191 A wijones@suno.edu
JONES, Wittney 866-776-0331 54 E
JONES, Yasemin 212-217-4040 299 C yasemin_jones@fitnyc.edu
JONES, Yolanda 622-254-3528 247 C yjones@mvsu.edu
JONES, Yolanda 903-730-4890 437 E yjones@jarvis.edu
JONES, Zantrell, Y 803-323-2273 413 D jonesz@winthrop.edu
JONES, Zelma 770-824-5245 127 E zelma.jones@westgatech.edu
JONES BAIR, Meg 641-269-3000 166 D jonesme@grinnell.edu
JONES-BRANCH, Cherisse 870-972-3029 17 I crjones@astate.edu
JONES DAVIDSON, Leslie 704-216-6044 330 D
JONES-HALL, Jennifer, L 618-453-2461 149 G jennifer.jones-hall@siu.edu
JONES-HAZURE, Deidrea 504-284-5486 191 A dhazure@suno.edu
JONES-JAMES, Kimberly 225-490-1645 186 H kimberly.jones-james@franu.edu
JONES-JOHNSON, Knieba 314-977-7363 258 H knieba.jones-johnson@health.slu.edu
JONES LAMON, Jacqueline 516-877-4041 288 L lamon@adelphi.edu
JONES LEE, Ashley 801-618-0438 458 H ajoneslee@ameritech.edu
JONES-MALONE, Dionne 219-473-4305 154 A djonesmalone@ccsj.edu
JONES MILLER, Edna, D 407-582-3501 113 C ejonesmiller@valenciacollege.edu
JONES-MONROE, Katrieva 432-552-2879 456 C jones_kat@utpb.edu
JONES-O'BRIEN, Angela 215-717-6049 399 I ajonesobrien@uarts.edu
JONES SCOTT, Samaiyah 816-604-4114 255 B
JONES-THOMAS, Tabitha 225-768-1769 186 H tabitha.jones-thomas@franu.edu
JONKINS, DeRodrick 410-225-2285 200 B djonkins@mica.edu
JONSON, Elizabeth 318-427-4407 189 A ejonson@lsua.edu
JONSSON, Benjamin, R 719-333-3110 502 C benjamin.jonsson@afacademy.af.edu
JONSSON, Eulena 909-607-3884 63 E ejonsson@scrippscollege.edu
JOOF, Henan 213-763-7207 50 A joofh@lattc.edu
JOPPA, Daniel 308-635-6745 269 E joppad1@wncc.edu
JORAANSTAD, Pam 623-845-3773 13 E pam.joraanstad@gccaz.edu
JORDAHL, Susan 320-308-5908 240 D susan.jordahl@sctcc.edu
JORDAN, A. Dane 704-233-8026 344 E djordan@wingate.edu
JORDAN, Amber 706-295-6768 119 F ajordan@gntc.edu
JORDAN, Amy 413-549-4600 210 A akjss@hampshire.edu
JORDAN, Andy 803-508-7241 405 C jordana@atc.edu
JORDAN, Angela 623-845-4632 13 E angela.jordan@gccaz.edu
JORDAN, Antoine 410-778-2800 204 E
JORDAN, Autumn 251-626-3303 7 E ajordan@ussa.edu
JORDAN, Ben 256-395-2211 3 G benjordan@suscc.edu
JORDAN, Benjamin, R 901-321-4406 417 G ben.jordan@cbu.edu
JORDAN, Briana 602-285-7433 13 H briana.jordan@phoenixcollege.edu
JORDAN, C. Greer 414-955-8685 492 F gjordan@mcw.edu
JORDAN, Carla, C 229-333-5942 127 C ccjordan@valdosta.edu
JORDAN, Christopher 410-462-7445 197 E cjordan@bccc.edu
JORDAN, Chuck 870-777-5722 23 C chuck.jordan@uaht.edu
JORDAN, Cordell 405-947-4421 368 C
JORDAN, Corey 315-386-7319 319 E jordanc@canton.edu
JORDAN, Dave 443-334-2176 202 C djordan@stevenson.edu
JORDAN, David, M 404-712-8096 118 D david.m.jordan@emory.edu
JORDAN, Deborah 303-273-3884 79 A djordan@mines.edu
JORDAN, Dianna 479-308-2276 17 E dianna.jordan@acheedu.org
JORDAN, Douglas, K 718-793-2330 309 A
JORDAN, Edward, K 386-312-4151 107 A edwardjordan@sjrstate.edu
JORDAN, Elizabeth 573-681-5975 254 A jordane@lincolnu.edu
JORDAN, Elizabeth, P 302-295-1186 91 C elizabeth.p.jordan@wilmu.edu
JORDAN, Erika 617-353-9511 207 C enjordan@bu.edu
JORDAN, Holly 254-526-1128 431 E holly.jordan@ctcd.edu
JORDAN, Jeffrey, C 206-281-2123 482 K jordaj2@spu.edu
JORDAN, Jennifer 678-839-6423 127 A jjordan@westga.edu
JORDAN, Jeremy, S 215-204-3745 398 D jeremy.jordan@temple.edu
JORDAN, Jessica 415-257-1347 41 H jessica.jordan@dominican.edu
JORDAN, Joseph 919-962-3907 342 B jfjordan@email.unc.edu
JORDAN, Judy, G 615-547-1249 418 C jjordan@cumberland.edu
JORDAN, Julie 662-325-8929 247 A jordan@international.msstate.edu
JORDAN, Keith 678-331-4453 122 A keith.jordan@life.edu
JORDAN, Kevin 934-420-2622 320 C kevin.jordan@farmingdale.edu
JORDAN, LaFreeda 256-824-4600 8 B lafreeda.jordan@uah.edu
JORDAN, LaFreeda 256-824-6340 8 B lafreeda.jordan@uah.edu
JORDAN, Lashanda 601-979-2477 245 G lashanda.w.jordan@jsums.edu
JORDAN, Leo 931-431-9700 421 G ljordan@nci.edu
JORDAN, Linda 918-781-7258 365 B jordanl@bacone.edu
JORDAN, Lisa 304-336-8177 489 B lisa.jordan@westliberty.edu
JORDAN, Loretta 714-628-4933 58 G jordan_loretta@sccollege.edu
JORDAN, Lucille, A 603-578-8900 272 B ljordan@ccsnh.edu
JORDAN, Mary 320-308-5966 240 D mary.jordan@sctcc.edu
JORDAN, Matthew 818-947-2378 50 B jordanmt@lavc.edu
JORDAN, Michael 585-567-9228 301 G michael.jordan@houghton.edu
JORDAN, Peter, G 845-431-8980 298 B peter.jordan@sunydutchess.edu
JORDAN, Richard 806-414-9648 450 D richard.jordan@ttuhsc.edu
JORDAN, Robyn 318-342-5259 193 A jordan@ulm.edu
JORDAN, Sandra 615-226-3990 419 J
JORDAN, Shannon 724-532-6740 397 D shannon.jordan@stvincent.edu
JORDAN, Stacy 501-205-8817 19 B sjordan@cbc.edu
JORDAN, Thomas, T 607-746-4540 320 A jordantt@delhi.edu
JORDAN, Tracey 419-358-3377 348 E jordant@bluffton.edu
JORDAN, Travis 507-933-7574 235 E tjordan@gustavus.edu
JORDAN, Travis 828-227-2445 343 D jordant@wcu.edu
JORDAN, Tuajuanda, C 240-895-4410 201 F president@smcm.edu
JORDAN-COX, Courtnee, N 717-358-5843 383 G courtnee.jordan-cox@fandm.edu
JORDAN-GOODEN, Joyce 601-979-2323 245 G joyce.m.jordan-gooden@jsums.edu
JORDAN SHIVERS, Natasha 404-527-7793 121 I njordan@itc.edu
JORDAN-SMITH, Barbara 518-445-3398 289 B bjord@albanylaw.edu
JORDAN-WILLIAMS, Aletha, D 313-664-7475 222 C ajordan2@collegeforcreativestudies.edu
JORDANO, Mark 814-871-7438 383 H jordano001@gannon.edu
JORDON, Christina 863-638-2944 113 E jordoncm@webber.edu
JORDON, Michael 304-642-9203 486 D jordonm@dewv.edu
JORDON, Sandy 360-416-7923 483 D sandy.jordon@skagit.edu
JORE, Katie 715-346-3710 496 B kjore@uwsp.edu
JORE, Katie 715-346-3710 496 B
JORGE-CURTIS, Veronica 617-349-8636 210 H
JORGENS, Amy, G 402-323-3414 268 D ajorgens@southeast.edu
JORGENS, Cat 262-547-1211 491 A cjorgens@carrollu.edu
JORGENSEN, Harlan, R 712-707-7333 169 A harlan@nwciowa.edu
JORGENSEN, Lon 701-788-4787 345 B lonny.jorgensen@mayvillestate.edu
JORGENSEN, Michael 435-283-7262 460 C michael.jorgensen@snow.edu
JORGENSEN, Ronald, A 712-274-5142 168 C jorgensenr@morningside.edu
JORISSEN, Shari 866-492-5336 243 G shari.jorissen@mail.waldenu.edu
JORVIG, Erik 262-243-5700 491 E erik.jorvig@cuw.edu
JOSCHKO, Brian 309-677-1002 133 H bjoschko@bradley.edu
JOSE, Robert 617-373-7515 217 D
JOSEPH, Abson 765-677-2252 157 F abson.joseph@indwes.edu
JOSEPH, Alex 704-847-5600 340 D ajoseph@ses.edu
JOSEPH, Alexander 304-326-1272 486 I alexander.joseph@salemu.edu
JOSEPH, Amos 402-826-6760 266 A amos.joseph@doane.edu
JOSEPH, Candace 973-353-5500 281 C candace.joseph@rutgers.edu
JOSEPH, Cassandra 404-270-5067 126 A cassandra.joseph@spelman.edu
JOSEPH, Crystal 605-626-2529 415 H crystal.joseph@northern.edu
JOSEPH, Cynthia 562-907-4830 76 A cjoseph@whittier.edu
JOSEPH, Darnell 713-313-1826 448 D djoseph@tsu.edu
JOSEPH, Eric Anthony 503-255-0332 374 A president@multnomah.edu
JOSEPH, James, E 315-445-4279 303 F josepjae@lemoyne.edu
JOSEPH, Jann, L 678-407-5000 119 B president@ggc.edu
JOSEPH, Joanne 315-792-7295 320 F joanne.joseph@sunypoly.edu
JOSEPH, Laly 212-614-6153 310 H laly.joseph@mountsinai.org
JOSEPH, Laura 934-420-2003 320 C laura.joseph@farmingdale.edu
JOSEPH, Laurel 281-756-3513 428 E ljoseph@alvincollege.edu
JOSEPH, Marisa 718-368-5115 294 C marisa.joseph@kbcc.cuny.edu
JOSEPH, Mark 740-284-5870 352 I mjoseph@franciscan.edu
JOSEPH, Michael 312-369-7114 136 C mijoseph@colum.edu
JOSEPH, Michiko 808-689-2707 129 C msjoseph@hawaii.edu
JOSEPH, Nicole 208-282-2123 131 E rosenico@isu.edu
JOSEPH, Noson 718-601-3523 325 Q njoseph@ytariverdale.org
JOSEPH, Patricia 484-365-8152 388 F joseph@lincoln.edu
JOSEPH, Rabi 707-654-1782 32 C
JOSEPH, Sonya, F 407-582-7734 113 C sjoseph@valenciacollege.edu
JOSEPH, Stephen, M 724-287-8711 379 C steve.joseph@bc3.edu

JOSEPH, Susan 914-361-6221 307 A soojoseph@montefiore.org
JOSEPH, Susan 423-697-3136 423 B susan.joseph@chattanoogastate.edu
JOSEPH-KEMPLIN, Mitch 614-234-2341 356 E mjoseph-kemplin@mccn.edu
JOSEPHSON, David 973-655-6956 278 C josephsond@montclair.edu
JOSEY, Peige 334-222-6591 2 I pjosey@lbwcc.edu
JOSHEE, Jeet 562-985-8330 32 A jeet.joshee@csulb.edu
JOSHI, Chetan 301-314-7069 202 E cajoshi@umd.edu
JOSHUA, Donald 212-280-1462 323 C djoshua@uts.columbia.edu
JOSHUA, Kazi 509-527-5158 485 C joshuake@whitman.edu
JOSHUA, Querencia 281-756-3688 428 E qjoshua@alvincollege.edu
JOSHUA, Stefanie 212-592-2142 314 I sjoshua@sva.edu
JOSLEYN, Alyshia 206-546-4533 483 C ajosleyn@shoreline.edu
JOSLIN, Jennifer 417-873-6850 252 A jjoslin@drury.edu
JOSLIN, Michael 661-362-3260 38 H michael.joslin@canyons.edu
JOSLIN, Randall 530-251-8836 47 I rjoslin@lassencollege.edu
JOSLYN-GAUL, Danette 404-894-6088 119 D danette.joslyn-gaul@gatech.edu
JOSLYN-SIEMIATKOSKI, Dan 512-472-4133 442 H dan.joslyn-siemiatkoski@ssw.edu
JOSS, Jamie 321-674-7462 100 A jjoss@fit.edu
JOSSELL, Steven 662-621-4304 244 E sjossell@coahomacc.edu
JOSSERAND, Tamara 206-685-9926 484 A tmiche@uw.edu
JOSSERAND, Tamara, M 909-748-8840 72 E tamara_josserand@redlands.edu
JOST, Steve, A 301-860-4212 203 D sjost@bowiestate.edu
JOUGHIN, Sarah 207-581-3437 196 D joughin@maine.edu
JOURDAN, Dawn 301-405-8000 202 E djourdan@umd.edu
JOURDAN, Lee Ann 317-738-8755 155 A ljourdan@franklincollege.edu
JOURNET, Nancy 708-344-4700 142 E njournet@lincolntech.edu
JOUTZ, Marguerite 401-863-9212 403 A marguerite_joutz@brown.edu
JOUVENAS, Anthony 334-556-2474 2 C ajouvenas@wallace.edu
JOVANOVIC, Jasna 805-756-2033 29 K jjovanov@calpoly.edu
JOVEN, Robert 203-582-3468 88 F robert.joven@quinnipiac.edu
JOVICIC, Mila 310-204-1666 58 K
JOWERS, Angel 205-652-3547 9 B ajowers@uwa.edu
JOWERS, Rebecca 214-887-5366 434 G rjowers@dts.edu
JOY, Cory 727-376-6911 112 F anthony.abell@trinitycollege.edu
JOY, Lilia 270-831-9641 181 F lilia.joy@kctcs.edu
JOY, Steaven 731-426-7523 419 G sjoy@lanecollege.edu
JOYCE, Christine 317-632-5553 158 V cjoyce@lincolntech.edu
JOYCE, Christopher, J 781-891-2003 206 C cjoyce@bentley.edu
JOYCE, Daniel 215-951-1881 386 I joyced@lasalle.edu
JOYCE, SJ, Daniel, R 610-660-3291 397 A djoyce@sju.edu
JOYCE, Gerard 610-282-1100 382 A gerard.joyce@desales.edu
JOYCE, Kelly 215-895-1891 382 D kelly.a.joyce@drexel.edu
JOYCE, Kelly 812-866-7160 155 D joyce@hanover.edu
JOYCE, Kevin 914-674-7775 305 H kjoyce@mercy.edu
JOYCE, Kimberly 410-287-1022 198 A kjoyce@cecil.edu
JOYE, Teresa 510-430-3335 66 F tjoye@sksm.edu
JOYNER, Angela, M 540-831-5370 468 E ajoyner9@radford.edu
JOYNER, Chartarra 336-285-2941 341 C cmjoyne2@ncat.edu
JOYNER, Dondi 828-328-7349 330 B dondi.joyner@lr.edu
JOYNER, Duan 804-330-0111 464 K djoyner@centura.edu
JOYNER, Laurie, M 773-298-3000 148 I joyner@sxu.edu
JOYNER, Marie 973-408-3097 276 B mjoyner@drew.edu
JOYNER, Rashad 757-727-5474 466 L rashad.joyner@hamptonu.edu
JOYNER, Stephen 561-868-3033 105 C joyners@palmbeachstate.edu
JOYNER, SR., Stephen 704-330-1406 329 H sjoyner@jcsu.edu
JOYNER-GRAHAM, JoAnn 718-270-4832 294 E jjoyner@mec.cuny.edu
JOYNES, Stephanie, N 434-223-6325 466 K sjoynes@hsc.edu
JOYNES-STURGIS, Jicola, R 410-651-7821 203 B jrsturgis@umes.edu
JUÁREZ, Cesia 214-818-1386 433 A cjuarez@criswell.edu
JUÁREZ, JR., José (Beto), R 954-262-6101 104 M jjuarez@nova.edu
JUÁREZ, Luis 214-818-1345 433 A ljuarez@criswell.edu
JU, Randy, S 678-535-7771 118 F rju@gcuniv.edu
JU MILLER, Grace 765-998-4734 161 A grace_miller2@taylor.edu
JUARBE, Loraine 787-766-1912 507 C ljuarbe@inter.edu
JUARBE, Lorraine 787-763-6425 506 H ljuarbe@inter.edu
JUARBE REY, Myriam 787-720-4476 509 G asistenciaeconomica@mizpa.edu
JUAREZ, Anabel 972-273-3084 434 C
JUAREZ, Elisa 520-494-5426 11 M elisa.juarez@centralaz.edu
JUAREZ, III, Fred 956-326-2448 446 A fredjuarez@tamiu.edu
JUAREZ, Heather 575-835-5116 286 D heather.juarez@nmt.edu
JUAREZ, Raelene 209-588-5087 76 J juarezr@yosemite.edu
JUAREZ, Raelene 209-588-5107 76 J juarezr@yosemite.edu
JUAREZ, Reina 858-534-3755 70 C rjuarez@ucsd.edu
JUDAH, Courtney 541-506-6151 372 E cjudah@cgcc.edu
JUDD, Summer 731-989-6662 418 H sjudd@fhu.edu
JUDD, Tim 270-789-5027 179 G tmjudd@campbellsville.edu
JUDE, II, Willie 262-595-2591 495 D jude@uwp.edu
JUDGE, Gwenn 315-443-1870 321 D
JUDGE, Jeffrey 952-358-8585 239 C jeff.judge@normandale.edu
JUDGE, John 202-319-5160 91 G judge@cua.edu
JUDGE, Joseph 610-282-1100 382 A jjudge@follett.com
JUDGE, Kristin, O 215-572-2928 378 E judgek@arcadia.edu
JUDGE, Lisa 440-826-2106 348 C ljudge@bw.edu
JUDGE, Peter, J 803-323-2220 413 D judgep@winthrop.edu
JUDGE, Sheila 504-816-4370 186 F sjudge@dillard.edu
JUDGE CRIPE, Stephanie 317-940-9351 153 H sjudge@butler.edu
JUDKINS, Jason 760-245-4271 74 D jason.judkins@vvc.edu
JUDSON, Dan 617-559-8638 210 C djudson@hebrewcollege.edu
JUDSON, Frank 570-585-9444 381 A fjudson@clarkssummitu.edu
JUDY, Allison 308-635-6081 269 E judya2@wncc.edu
JUDY, Joyce, M 802-828-2800 463 A jmj10300@ccv.vsc.edu
JUELE, Lilia 845-574-4480 312 C ljuele@sunyrockland.edu
JUELG, Earl 832-246-0055 438 E butch@lonestar.edu
JUENGER, Mike 618-235-2700 150 B michael.juenger@swic.edu
JUERGENS, Kristin, A 414-464-9777 497 B juergens.kristin@wspp.edu
JUERGENS, Valorie 269-294-4329 223 J vjuergens@glenoaks.edu
JUKKALA, Clint, A 215-972-7623 392 P cjukkala@pafa.edu
JUKOSKI, Mary Ellen 860-215-9001 87 D mjukoski@threerivers.edu
JULAKA, Cheryl 303-333-4224 11 C
JULIA, Jake 847-491-2912 146 C jjulia@northwestern.edu
JULIAN, Charity 812-749-1235 159 E cjulian@oak.edu
JULIAN, Elizabeth, A 706-771-4049 115 H ejulian@augustatech.edu
JULIAN, JR., James 617-287-7050 211 C evp@umassp.edu
JULIAN, Janelle 314-719-8057 252 G jjulian@fontbonne.edu
JULIAN, Jeff 847-925-6183 138 E jjulian1@harpercollege.edu
JULIAN, Karen, M 651-962-6176 243 F kmjulian@stthomas.edu
JULIAN, Leisa 765-973-8348 156 D lejulian@iu.edu
JULIAN, Thom 440-775-8788 357 G thom.julian@oberlin.edu
JULIAN, Tijuana, S 417-873-7215 252 A tjulian@drury.edu
JULIANI, Justine 253-879-2720 483 G jjuliani@pugetsound.edu
JULICH, Daniel 863-638-7639 113 D daniel.julich@warner.edu
JULICH PEREZ, April 617-253-8095 215 G
JULIEN, Earlye, A 563-884-5476 169 C earlye.julien@palmer.edu
JULIEN, Logan 941-893-2864 106 J ljulien@ringling.edu
JULISON, James 815-455-8770 143 F jjulison@mchenry.edu
JULIUS, Greg 805-482-2755 59 G greg@stjohnsem.edu
JULIUS, James 760-757-2121 52 G jjulius@miracosta.edu
JUMP, Jonathon, D 765-361-6206 162 G jumpj@wabash.edu
JUMPER, Cynthia 806-743-3280 450 D cynthia.jumper@ttuhsc.edu
JUMPER, G. Robin 850-263-3261 95 P grjumper@baptistcollege.edu
JUNCO, Maite 646-664-9318 292 E maite.junco@cuny.edu
JUND, Ryan 208-732-6295 131 B rjund@csi.edu
JUNE, Robert 414-443-8867 497 A robert.june@wlc.edu
JUNE, Vincent 337-521-8959 188 G vincent.june@solacc.edu
JUNEAU-BUTLER, Allyson 801-649-5230 458 I admissions@midwifery.edu
JUNEK, Shauna 605-642-6203 415 F shauna.junek@bhsu.edu
JUNG, Alan 205-726-2716 6 E apjung@samford.edu
JUNG, Anne, S 518-861-2532 305 B ajung@mariacollege.edu
JUNG, Barnabas 951-763-0500 55 A
JUNG, Chanhwi 213-738-0712 64 G alexj@southbaylo.edu
JUNG, Chul Heon 562-926-1023 58 A ptsamedia@ptsa.edu
JUNG, Jackie 213-740-2311 73 B
JUNG, Sung, T 636-459-1960 255 E glica@midwest.edu
JUNG, Yoochang 323-643-0301 25 L
JUNG-MATHEWS, Anne, M 603-535-2458 274 B amjung@plymouth.edu
JUNGBLUT, Heather, L 563-588-7103 167 I heather.jungblut@loras.edu
JUNGERS, Christin 740-284-7220 352 I cjungers@franciscan.edu
JUNGHANS, Shawn 334-291-4955 1 H shawn.junghans@cv.edu
JUNGKUNTZ, David 360-752-8355 477 C djungkun@btc.edu
JUNIOR, Yolanda 937-512-4529 360 F yolanda.junior@sinclair.edu
JUNIOUS, Andrea 803-934-3989 409 H ajunious@morris.edu
JUNKER, OP, Gianna 615-297-7545 416 G srgianna@aquinascollege.edu
JUNKERMAN, Charles, L 650-723-6866 66 D clj@stanford.edu
JUNKIN, Chip 410-857-2256 200 D cjunkin@mcdaniel.edu
JUNN, Ellen 209-667-3201 33 D president@csustan.edu
JUNOD, Heather 407-882-0541 110 D heather.junod@ucf.edu
JUNOR, Bill 914-251-6460 318 E bill.junor@purchase.edu
JUNOR, Laura, J 202-685-4379 501 I laura.j.junor.civ@ndu.edu
JUNTUNEN, Cindy 701-777-2674 344 H cindy.juntunen@und.edu
JURADO, Roberto 626-585-7725 56 D
JURAN, Victor 651-690-6826 242 F vbjuran@stkate.edu
JURAS, Jennifer 415-703-9522 28 D jjuras@cca.edu
JURCZAK, Kirsten, J 217-443-8779 136 E k.jurczak@dacc.edu
JURGENS-TOEPKE, Pamela 630-515-6088 144 C pjurge@midwestern.edu
JURKOVIC, Frank 727-341-4732 107 C jurkovic.frank@spcollege.edu
JURNAK, Sheila 505-277-6331 288 C sjurnak@unm.edu
JURSZA-WILLIAMS, Tammy 607-871-2123 289 E jurszawilliams@alfred.edu
JUSINO, Lidis, L 787-284-1912 507 D ljusino@ponce.inter.edu
JUSKEVICE, Leigh 207-509-7208 196 B ljuskevice@unity.edu
JUSKIEWICZ, Scott 406-496-4523 264 C sjuskiewicz@mtech.edu
JUSSEAUME, Yvette 323-856-7721 25 M yjusseaume@afi.com
JUSSEL, Adam 414-229-4632 495 B jussel@uwm.edu
JUST, Eric 785-670-1860 178 A eric.just@washburn.edu
JUST, Molly 620-229-6371 177 D molly.just@sckans.edu
JUSTESEN, Bryan, H 208-356-1320 130 G justesenb@byui.edu
JUSTESON, Rebecca 530-898-6421 31 A rjusteson@csuchico.edu
JUSTICE, Brooke 270-901-1001 182 E brooke.palmer@kctcs.edu
JUSTICE, Della, M 850-263-3261 95 P dmjustice@baptistcollege.edu
JUSTICE, Elizabeth 405-585-4256 367 B elizabeth.justice@okbu.edu
JUSTICE, Gary 606-218-5306 185 F garyjustice@upike.edu
JUSTICE, Greg 260-481-6785 159 H justiceg@pfw.edu
JUSTICE, Jessica 606-546-1214 185 B jjustice@unionky.edu
JUSTICE, LaMica 601-977-7720 248 E ljustice@tougaloo.edu
JUSTICE, Lillian 310-660-6960 41 J ljustice@elcamino.edu
JUSTICE, Richard 317-299-0333 161 B richard@tcmi.org
JUSTICE, Shannon 843-921-6913 410 B sjustice@netc.edu
JUSTIN, Hardee 630-942-2800 135 F
JUSTINGER, Doreen 716-250-7500 291 H dajustinger@bryantstratton.edu
JUSTISON, Brian, K 217-424-6300 144 D bjustison@millikin.edu
JUSTNYA, Erin 806-743-3451 450 D erin.justyna@ttuhsc.edu
JUSZCZYK, Casey 815-479-7524 143 F cjuszczyk@mchenry.edu
JUTKIEWICZ, Richard 215-885-2360 389 A rjutkiewicz@manor.edu
JUUL, Kim 719-384-6948 82 C kim.juul@otero.edu
JUVERA, Kelly 520-515-3612 11 O juverak@cochise.edu

K

KA-TANDIA, Nogaye 607-962-9232 319 F nka1@corning-cc.edu

KAAI, Elmer 808-956-3816 129 B
elmerk@hawaii.edu
KAAKOUSH, Walid 847-756-4317 10 F
wkaakoush@aiuniv.edu
KAALBERG, Kyle 702-895-5427 270 J
kyle.kaalberg@unlv.edu
KAANE, Sophia 432-552-2373 456 C
kaane_s@utpb.edu
KAANOI, Aulani 808-739-8394 128 C
akaanoi@chaminade.edu
KAARI, Nancy 732-224-2887 275 D
nkaari@brookdalecc.edu
KAATZ, Forrest 575-461-4413 285 J
forrestk@mesalands.edu
KABALA, Heather 724-805-2960 397 D
heather.kabala@stvincent.edu
KABALA, Heather 724-805-2960 397 C
heather.kabala@stvincent.edu
KABANJE, David 402-486-2508 268 G
david.kabanje@ucollege.edu
KABETZKE, Donald 214-333-5477 433 D
donaldk@dbu.edu
KABOUREK, Chris 402-472-7102 268 I
ckabourek@nebraska.edu
KABUTO, Bobbie 718-997-5220 295 A
bobbie.kabuto@qc.cuny.edu
KACELI, Sali 215-702-4555 379 F
skaceli@cairn.edu
KACELI, Stephanie 215-702-4376 379 F
stephaniekaceli@cairn.edu
KACHANI, Soulaymane 212-854-1804 296 H
kachani@columbia.edu
KACHUR, John 412-434-6626 382 E
kachurj@duq.edu
KACSKOS, Janet, E 717-871-7870 394 B
janet.kacskos@millersville.edu
KACZMAR, Debra 831-770-6145 44 J
dkaczmar@hartnell.edu
KACZMAREK, Melissa 845-257-3454 316 B
kaczmarm@newpaltz.edu
KACZMAREK, Shannon 325-674-2036 427 G
srb04a@acu.edu
KACZVINSKY, Don 318-257-4805 192 A
dkaczv@latech.edu
KACZYNSKI, John, L 989-964-7481 229 L
jlkaczyn@svsu.edu
KADA, Solange 707-256-7186 53 E
skada@napavalley.edu
KADAKIA, Madhavi 937-775-2339 364 D
madhavi.kadakia@wright.edu
KADAMUS,
Benjamin, A 508-767-7505 205 F
ba.kadamus@assumption.edu
KADAN, Ohad 480-965-2468 11 A
ohad.kadan@asu.edu
KADDEN, Jerome, H 443-548-6064 201 B
jhk@nirc.edu
KADING, Linda 515-271-1465 165 C
linda.kading@dmu.edu
KADISH, Alan 212-463-0400 68 B
alan.kadish@touro.edu
KADISH, Alan 646-565-6136 322 B
alan.kadish@touro.edu
KADISH, Alan 646-565-6136 322 C
alan.kadish@touro.edu
KADISH, Alan, H 914-594-4600 308 J
alan_kadish@nymc.edu
KADOWAKI, Ted 562-985-7976 32 A
ted.kadowaki@csulb.edu
KADRMAS, Nicky 701-319-6660 345 A
nichole.r.kadrmas@dickinsonstate.edu
KAECHELE, Dana 847-574-5268 141 G
dkaechele@lfgsm.edu
KAEGI, Gina 480-858-9100 16 B
g.kaegi@scnm.edu
KAEHNE, Bruce 218-751-8670 241 Q
brucekaehne@oakhills.edu
KAELI, Dianne 617-277-3915 207 B
registrar@bgsp.edu
KAELKE, Christopher 217-641-4556 140 H
ckaelke@jwcc.edu
KAENZIG, Lisa 315-781-3467 301 D
kaenzig@hws.edu
KAESERMANN, Kathryn 414-297-6520 498 B
kaesermk@matc.edu
KAESTNER, Lynn 414-425-8300 494 A
lkaestner@shsst.edu
KAEUPER, Edie 415-239-3000 37 C
ekaeuper@ccsf.edu
KAEUPER, Edith 415-239-3301 37 C
ekaeuper@ccsf.edu
KAFER, Jyll 470-578-6000 121 J
KAFF, Pinches 718-854-2290 291 C
admin@bhsy.org
KAFSKY, Jennifer, L 828-641-0791 327 A
kafskyjl@brevard.edu
KAGAY, Laurie 615-879-2022 419 C
KAGDI, Huzefa 239-590-7390 109 G
hkagdi@fgcu.edu
KAGEL, Martin 706-542-4767 126 F
mkagel@uga.edu
KAHA, Myra 206-934-3706 482 F
myra.kaha@seattlecolleges.edu
KAHAN, Miriam 818-299-5500 74 I
mkahan@westcoastuniversity.edu
KAHANOV, Leamor 609-652-4514 283 A
leamor.kahanov@stockton.edu
KAHL, Jay 605-274-4190 413 G
jay.kahl@augie.edu
KAHL, Jenna 480-732-7093 13 B
jenna.kahl@cgc.edu
KAHLDEN, Dawn 817-598-6350 457 C
dkahlden@wc.edu
KAHLE, Lisa 607-753-5793 317 D
lisa.kahle@cortland.edu
KAHLEH, Saleim 281-649-3485 436 D
skahleh@hbu.edu
KAHLER, Dean 208-885-5690 132 C
dkahler@uidaho.edu
KAHLER, Jay, L 402-465-2169 267 J
jlk@nebrwesleyan.edu
KAHLER, Jeff 715-394-8473 496 D
jkahler@uwsuper.edu
KAHLER, Kari, L 231-995-1228 228 F
kkahler@nmc.edu
KAHLER, Lewis, J 315-792-5301 306 G
lkahler@mvcc.edu
KAHLER, Michael 213-382-1136 54 A
drmkahler@yahoo.com
KAHLER, William 619-239-0391 34 H
wkahler@cwsl.edu
KAHLIG, Charla 254-295-5436 453 A
ckahlig@umhb.edu
KAHN, Avi 718-382-8702 325 L
KAHN, Douglas 631-451-4578 320 G
kahnd@sunysuffolk.edu
KAHN, Erin 952-887-1384 241 P
ekahn@nwhealth.edu
KAHN, Hilary, E 317-274-7000 157 B
hkahn@iu.edu
KAHN, Jack 206-546-4552 483 C
jkahn@shoreline.edu
KAHN, Jay 404-413-2000 120 C
KAHN, Jeannine 225-342-6950 191 F
jeannine.kahn@ulsystem.edu
KAHN, Kenneth, B 216-687-3786 350 G
k.b.kahn@csuohio.edu
KAHN, Marc, J 702-895-1574 270 J
marc.kahn@unlv.edu
KAHN, Meghan, C 812-941-2174 157 D
mckahn@ius.edu
KAHN, Nora 323-259-1343 54 I
nkahn@oxy.edu
KAHN, Patricia 718-982-2350 293 C
patricia.kahn@csi.cuny.edu
KAHN, Steven 510-642-6000 68 N
KAHN-FOSS, Aimee, S 404-471-6423 114 E
akahnfoss@agnesscott.edu
KAHR, Audra, J 610-606-4630 380 C
ajhoffma@cedarcrest.edu
KAI, Carla 402-878-2380 266 D
carla.kai@littlepriest.edu
KAIDO, Shintaro 215-341-4051 382 D
shintaro.kaido@drexel.edu
KAIGLER, Port 314-367-8700 260 A
port.kaigler@uhsp.edu
KAIL, Pam 870-933-7903 17 G
pkail@asusystem.edu
KAILI, Tevita 808-675-3907 128 B
tevita.kaili@byuh.edu
KAIN, Aileen 610-667-3394 396 H
akain@scs.edu
KAIN, Douglas 209-384-6344 52 B
kain.d@mccd.edu
KAIN, Greg 309-298-1177 152 I
g-kain@wiu.edu
KAIN, Gregory 708-709-3579 147 A
gkain@prairiestate.edu
KAINE, Kryztofr 805-765-9300 39 E
KAINTH, Pritpal 516-876-3207 318 A
kainthp@oldwestbury.edu
KAINTZ, Jamie 610-807-9221 386 B
KAIRO, Moses, T 410-651-6072 203 B
mkairo@umes.edu
KAISER, Abby 605-668-1467 414 F
abby.kaiser@mountmarty.edu
KAISER, Carla 803-738-7610 409 E
kaiserc@midlandstech.edu
KAISER, Kenneth, H 215-204-6545 398 D
ken.kaiser@temple.edu
KAISER, Michelle 620-792-9232 171 F
kaiserm@bartonccc.edu
KAISER, Ryan 630-942-2800 135 F
KAISER-GOEBEL, Tracy 215-641-6612 390 A
tgoebel@mc3.edu
KAIVOLA, Karen 612-330-1024 233 G
kaivola@augsburg.edu
KAJIWARA, Robert 808-245-8236 129 H
kajiwara@hawaii.edu
KAKAC, Sharmila 618-842-3711 139 D
kakacs@iecc.edu
KAKOULIDIS, Sofia 516-463-6810 301 E
sofia.kakoulidis@hofstra.edu
KAKUGAWA-LEONG,
Alyson 808-932-7669 129 A
alyson@hawaii.edu
KAKUGAWA-LEONG,
Alyson, Y 808-932-7669 129 A
alyson@hawaii.edu
KALAFUT, Kimberly 815-740-3610 152 E
kkalafut@stfrancis.edu
KALAMAR, Wendy 610-282-1100 382 A
wendy.kalamar@desales.edu
KALANI, Manish 540-373-2200 465 G
mkalani@evcc.edu
KALAS, Ann 847-214-7228 137 D
aking@elgin.edu
KALASKY, Tom 540-458-8242 476 D
tkalasky@wlu.edu
KALATOZI, Nino 541-881-5578 376 E
nkalatozi@tvcc.cc
KALAVIK, James 267-502-2436 378 I
james.kalavik@brynathyn.edu
KALAYIL, Ann 312-369-3210 136 C
akalayil@colum.edu
KALB, Johanna 208-885-7988 132 C
jkalb@uidaho.edu
KALB, Melanie, T 740-368-3377 359 F
mtkalb@owu.edu
KALCIC, Adam, M 330-569-5437 353 F
kalcicam@hiram.edu
KALE, Kathy 408-554-5021 63 A
kkale@scu.edu
KALEEL, Joe, D 503-943-7523 376 H
kaleel@up.edu
KALEIWAHEA,
Kenneth, K 808-934-2508 129 F
kjakalei@hawaii.edu
KALER, Elizabeth 918-360-2737 365 B
kalere@bacone.edu
KALER, Eric, W 216-368-5094 349 B
eric.kaler@case.edu
KALER, Robin 217-333-5010 151 F
rkaler@illinois.edu
KALEVITCH, Maria, V 412-397-4020 396 E
kalevitch@rmu.edu
KALFAYAN, Stephanie 650-725-2788 66 D
kalfayan@stanford.edu
KALFSBEEK-GOETZ,
Jennifer 805-289-6380 74 B
jkgoetz@vcccd.edu
KALICH, Karrie 603-358-2885 274 A
kkalich@keene.edu
KALIL, Aida 787-850-9329 511 B
aida.kalil@upr.edu
KALINA, Susan 907-786-1988 10 A
smkalina@alaska.edu
KALINOWSKI, Joseph 508-793-7178 207 F
jkalinowski@clarku.edu
KALINOWSKI, Teresa 716-270-5112 299 A
kalinowski@ecc.edu
KALINSKY, Yosef 646-592-4068 325 R
kalinsky@yu.edu
KALIS, Michelle 860-231-5229 89 G
mkalis@usj.edu
KALISA, Marie-Chantal 402-472-3747 269 A
mkalisa2@unl.edu
KALITA, Tish 260-982-5025 158 W
nkalita@manchester.edu
KALK, Bruce 203-392-5468 85 H
kalkb1@southernct.edu
KALKA, Alicia 304-367-4754 488 L
alicia.kalka@fairmontstate.edu
KALKBRENNER,
Suzanne, K 518-629-4530 302 A
s.kalkbrenner@hvcc.edu
KALL, Andrew 617-587-5612 216 H
kalla@neco.edu
KALLEND, Jennifer 213-621-2200 38 G
KALLERGIS, Sophia, D 440-826-2180 348 C
skallerg@bw.edu
KALLIERIS, Nick, C 847-543-2476 135 G
nkallieris@clcillinois.edu
KALLMEYER, Alan 701-231-8978 345 D
alan.kallmeyer@ndsu.edu
KALLNER, Bobbie 207-602-2339 197 A
bkallner@une.edu
KALMANOFSKY, Amy 212-678-8826 303 A
amkalmanofsky@jtsa.edu
KALMANOWITZ, Osher 718-645-0536 306 F
dean@mirreryeshiva.org
KALMEY, Jon 814-866-8147 387 C
jkalmey@lecom.edu
KALNASY, Bonnie 216-687-4505 350 G
b.kalnasy@csuohio.edu
KALOGIANNIS, Natalie 707-664-2874 34 C
natalie.kalogiannis@sonoma.edu
KALOOSTIAN,
Damita, A 602-243-8021 14 C
damita.kaloostian@smcmail.maricopa.edu
KALOUSEK, Kay 909-706-8319 75 G
kaykalousek@westernu.edu
KALSCHEUR, S.J.,
Gregory 617-552-2393 207 A
gregory.kalscheur@bc.edu
KALSTROM, Sally 503-552-1616 374 B
skalstrom@nunm.edu
KALTCHEV, Matey 414-277-7544 493 D
kaltchev@msoe.edu
KALTENBAUGH,
Amanda 419-755-4723 357 B
akalten@ncstatecollege.edu
KALTENMARK, Michael 317-940-9672 153 H
mkaltenm@butler.edu
KALTMAN, Steven 954-262-7332 104 M
skaltman@nova.edu
KALUARACHCHI,
Jagath, J 435-797-2776 459 F
jagath.kaluarachchi@usu.edu
KALYN, Andrea 617-585-1200 217 A
andrea.kalyn@necmusic.edu
KALYNOVSKYI, Serhii 707-965-6218 55 H
skalynovskyi@puc.edu
KALYON, Dilhan 201-216-8911 282 L
dilhan.kalyon@stevens.edu
KAM, Moshe 973-596-6506 278 G
moshe.kam@njit.edu
KAMALESWARAN, Biju 831-502-8654 71 A
biju@ucsc.edu
KAMARA, Sheku 414-277-7416 493 D
kamara@msoe.edu
KAMARAH, Ehab 217-300-1144 151 F
ekamarah@illinois.edu
KAMAREI, Zahra 479-308-2200 17 E
KAMAT, Deborah 440-484-7027 363 C
deborah.kamat@ursuline.edu
KAMATANI, Kathy 732-224-2453 275 D
kkamatani@brookdalecc.edu
KAMBHAMPATI, Srini 248-204-3500 226 E
skambhamp@ltu.edu
KAMBOJ, Kaleem 312-939-0111 137 B
kaleem@eastwest.edu
KAMENETSKY, Shmuel 215-473-1212 398 C
talmudicalyeshiva@yahoo.com
KAMENETSKY, Sholom 215-477-1000 398 C
talmudicalyeshvia@yahoo.com
KAMERER, Caitlin 610-921-6608 377 F
ckamerer@albright.edu
KAMERON, Keith 815-836-5130 142 C
kameroke@lewisu.edu
KAMHI, Victoria 309-655-7100 148 G
victoria.kamhi@osfhealthcare.org
KAMI, Andrew 626-529-8500 55 E
KAMI, Andrew 714-997-6778 36 D
kami@chapman.edu
KAMIAB, Jane 336-770-3297 343 C
kamiabj@uncsa.edu
KAMICKER, Andrea 724-847-6610 384 B
amkamick@geneva.edu
KAMIMURA-JIMENEZ,
Mark 314-935-7535 261 B
mkamimura@wustl.edu
KAMIMURA-JIMENEZ,
Mark 314-935-3447 261 B
mkamimura@wustl.edu
KAMINSKI, Linda 509-574-4635 485 E
lkaminski@yvcc.edu
KAMINSKI, Lou 518-327-6488 310 G
lkaminski@paulsmiths.edu
KAMINSKI, Michael 213-624-1200 42 F
mkaminski@fidm.edu

KAMINSKI, Paul .... 562-938-4139.. 48 K
pkaminski@lbcc.edu
KAMINSKY, Margaret, I 585-292-3398 306 K
mkaminsky@monroecc.edu
KAMINSKY, Paul, A ..... 615-353-3615 424 A
paul.kaminsky@nscc.edu
KAMITSUKA, David .... 440-775-8410 357 G
david.kamitsuka@oberlin.edu
KAMMER, Dan .... 573-876-7273 259 F
dkammer@stephens.edu
KAMMER, Roy .... 651-213-4863 235 G
rkammer@hazeldenbettyford.edu
KAMMERER, Scott .... 260-399-7700 162 A
skammerer@creativedining.com
KAMMERZELL, Joan ...... 360-752-8436 477 C
jkammerzell@btc.edu
KAMMERZELL, Sharyl ... 509-335-5524 484 D
sharyl.kammerzell@wsu.edu
KAMMLER, David .... 937-767-1286 347 E
KAMOCHE, Njambi .... 847-925-6764 138 E
nkamoche@harpercollege.edu
KAMP, Cyndi .... 317-955-6103 159 A
ckamp@marian.edu
KAMPE, Jean .... 906-487-2827 227 D
kampej@mtu.edu
KAMPES, Craig .... 215-895-6680 382 D
cek35@drexel.edu
KAMPFSCHULTE, Darcy . 616-632-2894 221 A
kampfdar@aquinas.edu
KAMPHAUS, Lisa .... 412-536-1526 386 H
lisa.kamphaus@laroche.edu
KAMPMAN, Lia .... 920-403-3235 494 B
lia.kampman@snc.edu
KAMWITHI, Gina .... 419-755-4554 357 B
gkamwithi@ncstatecollege.edu
KANAK, Daniel .... 610-359-5135 381 J
dkanak@dccc.edu
KANAKIS, Chris .... 312-942-2831 148 C
chris_kanakis@rush.edu
KANALIS, Mike .... 724-938-5417 394 C
kanalis@calu.edu
KANARAS, Elizabeth ...... 610-902-8283 379 E
egk38@cabrini.edu
KANAREK, Berel .... 914-736-1500 310 B
KANAREK, E .... 914-736-1500 310 B
KANATANI, Kim .... 949-824-5517.. 69 C
kanatani@uci.edu
KANBAR, Hiam .... 831-242-5618 501 D
KANDEL-CISCO, Brooke 317-940-8000 153 H
KANDER, Ron .... 215-951-0252 398 G
kanderr@philau.edu
KANDLER, Mike .... 850-769-1551 101 O
mkandler@gulfcoast.edu
KANDUS-FISHER,
Christopher .... 617-747-2231 206 D
studentaffairs@berklee.edu
KANE, Andrew .... 609-258-3469 279 E
kane@princeton.edu
KANE, Barry, S .... 212-854-1458 296 H
barry@columbia.edu
KANE, Brian .... 402-643-4052 268 B
fr.brian-kane@sggs.edu
KANE, Brian .... 610-785-6265 396 H
bkane@scs.edu
KANE, Chris .... 610-690-5529 398 B
ckane1@swarthmore.edu
KANE, Christy .... 502-272-8424 179 D
ckane@bellarmine.edu
KANE, Colleen .... 715-422-5510 498 A
colleen.kane@mstc.edu
KANE, Daniel, C .... 207-768-9475 196 I
daniel.c.kane@maine.edu
KANE, Gina .... 315-781-3064 301 D
kane@hws.edu
KANE, Hillary .... 213-738-6825.. 66 A
hkane@swlaw.edu
KANE, Jane .... 908-709-7169 283 E
jane.kane@ucc.edu
KANE, Jennifer .... 904-620-2520 111 A
jkane@unf.edu
KANE, Jesse .... 718-270-6245 294 E
jkane@mec.cuny.edu
KANE, Joseph .... 607-735-1777 298 G
jkane@elmira.edu
KANE, Katherine, J .... 864-938-3913 410 E
kjkane@presby.edu
KANE, Kathleen .... 856-227-7200 275 F
kkane@camdencc.edu
KANE, Kerri .... 413-755-4115 215 F
kkane@stcc.edu
KANE, Kevin, M .... 610-499-4555 401 I
kmkane1@widener.edu

KANE, Kim .... 707-638-5280.. 68 B
kim.kane@tu.edu
KANE, Laura .... 580-581-5502 365 C
laurak@cameron.edu
KANE, Marie .... 210-485-0020 427 H
KANE, Matthew .... 904-256-8000 102 G
KANE, Micah .... 650-543-3744.. 52 A
bot@menlo.edu
KANE, Michael .... 650-738-4248.. 62 K
kanem@smccd.edu
KANE, Michael, J .... 859-858-3511 178 H
mike.kane@asbury.edu
KANE, Ryan .... 920-748-8115 493 J
KANE, Ryan, D .... 407-582-3421 113 C
rkane8@valenciacollege.edu
KANE, Sara, F .... 863-638-7602 113 D
sara.kane@warner.edu
KANE, Sylvia .... 714-556-3610.. 73 G
KANE, Tara .... 734-432-5429 226 G
tmkane@madonna.edu
KANE, Thomas .... 617-989-4590 219 D
kanet2@wit.edu
KANE, Thomas .... 781-891-2340 206 C
tkane@bentley.edu
KANE, Vicki .... 814-944-5643 402 J
vicki.kane@yti.edu
KANE, Wendy .... 432-685-4695 439 E
wkane@midland.edu
KANELOS, Gwen, E .... 708-209-3101 136 D
gwen.kanelos@cuchicago.edu
KANEPS, Katherine, D .... 610-330-5200 387 B
kanepsk@lafayette.edu
KANEVSKAYA, Svetlana 212-752-1530 303 G
svetlana.kanevskaya@limcollege.edu
KANEWISCHER, Amy .... 406-756-3366 262 H
akanewis@fvcc.edu
KANG, David .... 626-395-4724.. 29 B
dkang2@caltech.edu
KANG, Hyo Jeong .... 714-533-1495.. 64 G
hjkang@southbaylo.edu
KANG, Kathy, Y .... 310-739-0132.. 41 C
KANG, Mia .... 678-535-7771 118 F
academic@gcuniv.edu
KANG, Nichole .... 215-641-6300 390 A
nkang@mc3.edu
KANG, Richard .... 213-740-2311.. 73 B
KANG,
Seong-Yoon (David) .. 570-348-6211 389 B
dkang@marywood.edu
KANG, Soonhae .... 714-527-0691.. 42 D
KANG, Yunn .... 215-702-4461 379 F
ykang@cairn.edu
KANG, Yunn .... 215-702-4271 379 F
ykang@cairn.edu
KANGAS, Rick .... 218-322-2319 238 D
richard.kangas@minnesotanorth.edu
KANGETHE, Patrick .... 857-701-1552 215 E
pkangethe@rcc.mass.edu
KANIA, Dan .... 314-371-0236 257 H
KANIA, Ed .... 407-646-2117 106 L
ekania@rollins.edu
KANIATOBE, Phillip .... 505-984-6144 287 F
phillip.kaniatobe@sjc.edu
KANICH, Amy .... 814-886-6483 390 E
akanich@mtaloy.edu
KANIKKEBERG,
Dee Dee .... 208-885-6571 132 C
deedeek@uidaho.edu
KANIPES, Margaret .... 336-285-2030 341 C
mikanipe@ncat.edu
KANMORE, John .... 575-562-2511 285 E
john.kanmore@enmu.edu
KANN, Andrea .... 212-824-2208 300 H
akann@huc.edu
KANNAN, Govind .... 478-825-4613 118 E
govindak@fvsu.edu
KANNARKAT, Mily .... 757-446-8910 465 H
kannarmj@evms.edu
KANNE, Lynn .... 206-934-4072 482 G
lynn.kanne@seattlecolleges.edu
KANNENBERG, Karen ... 314-392-2337 255 H
karen.kannenberg@mobap.edu
KANNENWISCHER,
Susan .... 614-222-4001 351 A
skannenwischer@ccad.edu
KANOPKIN, Deena .... 617-559-8775 210 C
dkanopkin@hebrewcollege.edu
KANOY, David .... 910-362-7695 332 F
dkanoy@cfcc.edu
KANT, Keira .... 717-337-6324 384 C
kkant@gettysburg.edu

KANTARDJIEFF,
Katherine .... 831-582-4401.. 32 D
kkantardjieff@csumb.edu
KANTENWEIN, Heidi, L . 260-422-5561 156 A
hlkantenwein@indianatech.edu
KANTERMAN, Kathy .... 401-254-3531 404 C
kkanterman@rwu.edu
KANTNER, Joanne .... 815-825-9450 141 D
mkantner@kish.edu
KANTNER, John .... 904-620-2455 111 A
j.kantner@unf.edu
KANTNER, John .... 904-620-1360 111 A
j.kantner@unf.edu
KANTNER, Michael .... 856-256-4566 280 H
kantner@rowan.edu
KANTO, Kind .... 691-330-2620 503 B
kank@comfsm.fm
KANTOR, Ali .... 617-521-1038 218 C
ali.kantor@simmons.edu
KANTOR, Rebecca .... 303-315-6343.. 84 B
rebecca.kantor@ucdenver.edu
KANU, Andrew .... 804-524-5930 475 E
akanu@vsu.edu
KANWISCHER, Charlie .. 419-372-9395 348 F
ckanwis@bgsu.edu
KAO, Chi-Chang .... 650-723-2300.. 66 D
KAO, Lisa .... 559-278-6910.. 31 D
lisak@csufresno.edu
KAO, Patrick .... 415-422-5380.. 72 I
pk@usfca.edu
KAOPUIKI, Ryon 260-982-5000 158W
rdkaopuiki@manchester.edu
KAOUDIS, Kathryn .... 303-352-3356.. 80 D
kathy.kaoudis@ccd.edu
KAPASI, Zoher, F .... 843-792-3328 409 D
kapasi@musc.edu
KAPFHAMMER, Sean .... 410-777-2836 197 C
srkapfhammer@aacc.edu
KAPICA, Chris .... 626-577-1751.. 28 E
KAPIL, Deepika .... 503-517-1017 377 B
dkapil@warnerpacific.edu
KAPILESHWARI,
Sameer .... 336-334-5536 342 D
s_kapile@uncg.edu
KAPLA, Dale .... 906-227-2920 228 E
dkapla@nmu.edu
KAPLAN, Adam .... 424-901-9174.. 52 J
akaplan@msmu.edu
KAPLAN, Alan .... 608-263-8025 494 D
akaplan@uwhealth.org
KAPLAN, Judith .... 216-987-4613 351 D
judith.kaplan@tri-c.edu
KAPLAN, Keith, B .... 315-267-2141 318 D
kaplankb@potsdam.edu
KAPLAN, Leonard, I ...... 973-596-3638 278 G
leonard.i.kaplan@njit.edu
KAPLAN, Mark .... 352-392-4574 110 E
mark.kaplan@ufl.edu
KAPLAN, Richard .... 617-732-2808 216 B
richard.kaplan@mcphs.edu
KAPLAN, Ronald, S ...... 847-578-8538 148 B
ronald.kaplan@rosalindfranklin.edu
KAPLAN, Steven, H .... 203-932-7000.. 89 F
skaplan@newhaven.edu
KAPLINSKY, Yoheved ... 212-799-5000 303 B
KAPOUN, Jim .... 717-815-1353 402 G
jkapoun@ycp.edu
KAPP, Alisha .... 217-854-5110 133 F
alisha.kapp@blackburn.edu
KAPPANADZE,
Margaret .... 607-735-1867 298 G
mkappanadze@elmira.edu
KAPPEL, Jonathan .... 508-793-7505 207 F
jkappel@clarku.edu
KAPPEL, Stephanie .... 304-214-8801 487 J
skappel@wvncc.edu
KAPPES, Christiaan .... 412-321-8383 379 D
dean@bcs.edu
KAPRIVE, Mark .... 561-803-2542 105 B
mark_kaprive@pba.edu
KAPROU, Kiswendsida .. 973-877-3259 276 G
kaprou@essex.edu
KAPSAL, Sean .... 859-344-3698 184 G
kapsals@thomasmore.edu
KAPTAIN, Laurence .... 303-352-3559.. 84 B
laurence.kaptain@ucdenver.edu
KAPUR, Anup .... 609-771-2859 275 J
kapura@tcnj.edu
KAPUR, Sonia .... 503-552-1933 374 B
skapur@nunm.edu
KAPURCH, Jason .... 508-929-8045 213 D
jkapurch@worcester.edu

KARABURK, Hasan .... 703-941-2020 476 F
h.burk@wust.edu
KARACAL, Cem .... 618-650-2861 149 H
skaraca@siue.edu
KARAFA, Andy .... 716-673-3173 316 A
andy.karafa@fredonia.edu
KARAFIN, Diana, L .... 212-998-4426 309 D
diana.karafin@nyu.edu
KARAGEZIAN, Vardan ... 818-240-6900.. 25 O
karagezian@amsc.edu
KARAGOSIAN, Nico ...... 740-593-4764 358 L
nico@ohio.edu
KARAHADIAN, Milton ... 619-849-2649.. 57 J
miltonkarahadian@pointloma.edu
KARAKASHIAN, Ara ...... 201-360-4696 277 D
akarakashian@hccc.edu
KARAM, Robert .... 270-384-7309 183 D
karamr@lindsey.edu
KARAM, Vanessa .... 626-571-8811.. 73 D
vanessak@uwest.edu
KARAMAN, Ana .... 503-838-8137 377 C
karamana@wou.edu
KARANFIL, Tanju .... 864-656-7701 406 F
tkaranf@clemson.edu
KARANJA, Benson, M .. 404-627-2681 116 B
benson.karanja@beulah.edu
KARANJA, Peter .... 404-627-2681 116 B
peter.karanja@beulah.edu
KARAPANAGIOTIS,
Nicole .... 856-225-6574 281 A
nicole.karapanagiotis@rutgers.edu
KARAS, Jane, A .... 406-756-3801 262 H
jkaras@fvcc.edu
KARAS, Jennifer .... 303-871-6793.. 84 C
jkaras@du.edu
KARAS, Tara .... 941-487-5001 110 C
tkaras@ncf.edu
KARAS, Timothy .... 707-468-3071.. 51 F
tkaras@mendocino.edu
KARASEK, III,
Raymond, N .... 401-825-2298 403 D
mkarasek@ccri.edu
KARASINSKI, Tracy .... 401-825-2305 403 D
tkarasinski@ccri.edu
KARASS, Alan .... 706-507-8681 117 E
karass_alan@columbusstate.edu
KARATAN, Ece .... 828-262-7459 340 G
karatane@appstate.edu
KARAVOLAS, Susan ...... 518-694-7278 289 A
susan.karavolas@acphs.edu
KARBAN, Janel .... 920-498-5409 498 F
janel.karban@nwtc.edu
KARCH, Amanda .... 518-828-4181 296 G
amanda.karch@sunycgcc.edu
KARCH, Lisa .... 701-671-2112 346 B
lisa.karch@ndscs.edu
KARDAN, Sel .... 213-621-2200.. 38 G
KARDELL, Amy .... 301-243-2183 501 J
amy.kardell@dodiis.mil
KARDELL, Scott .... 531-622-2529 266 G
sakardell@mccneb.edu
KARDEN, Kala .... 909-607-9226.. 37 F
kala.karden@cgu.edu
KARDOW, Vivian, D ..... 409-772-2636 456 B
vdkardow@utmb.edu
KARGE, Sandy .... 909-384-8981.. 60 F
skarge@sbccd.cc.ca.us
KARGES, Teri .... 843-863-7050 406 C
tkarges@csuniv.edu
KARIC, Denis .... 313-962-7150 232 B
dkaric1@wcccd.edu
KARIM, Alema .... 401-456-9538 404 A
akarim@ric.edu
KARIM, Anwar .... 240-567-3212 200 E
anwar.karim@montgomerycollege.edu
KARIMBUX, Nadeem ..... 617-636-6636 219 A
nadeem.karimbux@tufts.edu
KARIOTIS, Angela .... 732-224-2109 275 D
akariotis@brookdalecc.edu
KARIUKI, Benson .... 903-730-4890 437 E
bkaruiku@jarvis.edu
KARIYA, Bruce .... 310-577-3000.. 76 H
bkariya@yosan.edu
KARL, Debbie .... 254-267-7009 441 D
dkarl@rangercollege.edu
KARLBERG,
Anne Marie .... 360-383-3302 485 B
amkarlberg@whatcom.edu
KARLESKINT, Kati .... 620-231-7000 176 H
kkarleskint@pittstate.edu
KARLGAARD, Joseph .... 713-348-4077 441 K
joe.karlgaard@rice.edu
KARLIN, Angela .... 785-864-4700 177 G
akarlin@ku.edu

KAVANAUGH, Kevin ..... 269-337-4400 233 A
KAVANAUGH, Maria, A 508-565-1331 218 F
mkavanaugh@stonehill.edu

KAVASCH, Kris .... 903-566-7044 455 C
kkavasch@uttyler.edu

KAVCSAK, Lynn, E .... 919-866-5696 338 E
lekavcsak@waketech.edu

KAVEH, Mostafa .... 612-626-3833 242 K
mos@umn.edu

KAWAGUCHI, Robbyn ... 510-666-8248.. 24 G
cao@aimc.edu

KAWAGUCHI, Robbyn ... 510-666-8248.. 24 G
studentservices@aimc.edu

KAWAHARA, Colleen ... 503-370-6031 377 E
kawahara@willamette.edu

KAWAI`AE`A, Keiki ..... 808-932-7360 129 A
keiki@hawaii.edu

KAWALL, Scott ...... 815-825-9837 141 D
skawall@kish.edu

KAWAMOTO, Judy .... 402-826-2161 266 A
judy.kawamoto@doane.edu

KAWANNA, JR.,
Ronald .... 708-596-2000 149 D
rkawanna@ssc.edu

KAWAR, Ferris .... 310-434-3911.. 63 B
kawar_ferris@smc.edu

KAWASAKI, Yuko .... 408-855-5579.. 75 C
yuko.kawasaki@missioncollege.edu

KAWELMACHER,
Jessica .... 760-384-6100.. 47 C

KAWOSA, Burhan .... 937-775-2136 364 D
burhan.kawosa@wright.edu

KAWSKI, Ryan .... 715-422-5300 498 A
ryan.kawski@mstc.edu

KAY, Carol .... 915-831-6725 435 B
ckay@epcc.edu

KAY, Catherine ..... 313-577-3049 232 H
catherine.kay@wayne.edu

KAY, Colin .... 973-761-9478 282 K
colin.kay@shu.edu

KAY, Gwen .... 518-320-3266 315 C
gwen.kay@suny.edu

KAY, Jessica ...... 609-626-3513 283 A
jessica.kay@stockton.edu

KAY, Peggy ...... 916-278-6862.. 33 A
peggy.kay@csus.edu

KAY, Peggy ...... 209-946-7358.. 71 E
pkay@pacific.edu

KAY, Scott .... 540-671-6981 464 O
scott.kay@christendom.edu

KAY COQUEMONT,
Kathryn .... 651-696-6220 236 C
kcoquemo@macalester.edu

KAY-WONG, Chelsea ... 808-932-7442 129 A
ckwong@hawaii.edu

KAYAL, Lisa .... 845-848-7824 298 A
lisa.kayal@dc.edu

KAYE, Alan .... 318-675-6124 189 D
alan.kaye@lsuhs.edu

KAYE, Johanna .... 503-554-2235 372 I
kayej@georgefox.edu

KAYE, Joyce .... 212-592-2011 314 I
jkaye3@sva.edu

KAYKAYOGLU, Ediz ... 509-963-1404 477 G
ediz.kaykayoglu@cwu.edu

KAYLOR, Debbie ...... 208-426-4351 130 F
debbiekaylor@boisestate.edu

KAYLOR, Sean, P ...... 845-575-3000 305 C
sean.kaylor@marist.edu

KAYNAMA, Shohreh, A . 410-704-6309 204 B
skaynama@towson.edu

KAYNARD, Meryl, R ..... 212-220-1237 292 G
mkaynard@bmcc.cuny.edu

KAYS, Brenda, S .... 903-983-8100 437 G
bkays@kilgore.edu

KAYSEN-LUZBETAK,
Angie .... 815-280-2885 140 I
akaysen@jjc.edu

KAZA, Sidd ...... 410-704-3701 204 B
skaza@towson.edu

KAZANECKI-KEMPTER,
Diane .... 934-420-2065 320 C
diane.kazanecki-kempter@farmingdale.
edu

KAZARIAN, Julie .... 508-929-8077 213 D
jkazarian@worcester.edu

KAZDA, Jim .... 609-258-3000 279 E
jkazda@princeton.edu

KAZDA, Kathleen .... 262-691-5464 499 A
kkazda@wctc.edu

KAZEN, James, D ...... 210-567-0390 455 E
kazen@uthscsa.edu

KAZEN, Tom .... 708-239-4866 150 H
thomas.kazen@trnty.edu

KAZER, Meredith, W ..... 203-254-4150.. 87 G
mkazer@fairfield.edu

KAZEROUNIAN, Kazem . 860-486-2221.. 89 B
kazem.kazerounian@uconn.edu

KAZMIR, Darin .... 361-582-2417 456 H
darin.kazmir@victoriacollege.edu

KAZUMA, Clement ...... 680-488-2471 504 A
clementk@palau.edu

KAZYAKA, Carrie ...... 619-297-9700.. 68 A
ckazyaka@tjsl.edu

KEADY, Thomas, J ...... 617-552-6795 207 A
thomas.keady@bc.edu

KEAL, Aaron, J .... 620-421-6700 175 D
aaronk@labette.edu

KEALA, David .... 808-675-3572 128 B
david.keala@byuh.edu

KEALEY, Jarrett .... 856-222-9311 280 E
jkealey@rcbc.edu

KEAN, Joy .... 970-943-2114.. 85 B
jkean@western.edu

KEAN, Linda .... 781-239-4284 205 G
kean@babson.edu

KEAN, Linda .... 252-328-1283 340 H
keanl@ecu.edu

KEANE, Cath .... 360-992-2071 477 J
ckeane@clark.edu

KEANE, Christopher ... 509-335-3574 484 D
chris.keane@wsu.edu

KEANE, James .... 508-854-4425 215 D
jkeane@qcc.mass.edu

KEANE, James .... 610-896-1023 385 H
jkeane@haverford.edu

KEANE, Timothy .... 619-260-4886.. 72 H
tkeane@sandiego.edu

KEARN, Tim .... 559-297-4500.. 46 C
tkearn@iot.edu

KEARNAN, Kelly .... 828-641-0360 327 A
kearnaka@brevard.edu

KEARNEY, Janice .... 870-575-8283.. 22 F
kearneyj@uapb.edu

KEARNEY, Jennifer ...... 813-988-5131.. 99 M
library@floridacollege.edu

KEARNEY, Joseph, D ... 414-288-1955 492 E
joseph.kearney@marquette.edu

KEARNEY, Kimberly ... 540-261-8542 470 D
kim.kearney@svu.edu

KEARNEY, Matt .... 573-651-2039 258 J
mkearney@semo.edu

KEARNS, Chris .... 406-994-2828 263 G
chris.kearns@montana.edu

KEARNS, Jennifer ...... 619-388-2759.. 61 A
jnkearns@sdccd.edu

KEARNS, Joanne .... 973-328-5044 276 A
jkearns@ccm.edu

KEARNS, Michelle ...... 801-863-8976 460 A
michelle.kearns@uvu.edu

KEARNS-BARRETT,
Marybeth .... 508-793-2448 208 A
mkearns@holycross.edu

KEAS, Lenora .... 361-698-1207 434 H
lkeas@delmar.edu

KEAST, Cindy .... 620-665-3565 174 D
keastc@hutchcc.edu

KEATING, Colleen ...... 518-454-5197 296 E
keatingc@strose.edu

KEATING, Frederick ...... 856-415-2100 280 F
fkeating@rcsj.edu

KEATING, Jeffery ...... 909-469-5205.. 75 G
keating@westernu.edu

KEATING, Joseph ...... 740-588-1396 364 H
jkeating@zanestate.edu

KEATING, Kathy .... 616-234-4953 224 C
kkeating@grcc.edu

KEATING, Lisa .... 617-989-4590 219 D
keatingl@wit.edu

KEATING, Lisa .... 518-458-5383 296 E
keatingl@strose.edu

KEATING, Scott .... 717-560-8211 387 D
skeating@lbc.edu

KEATING, Steven ...... 718-990-1511 313 B
keatings@stjohns.edu

KEATING, Tina .... 760-471-1316.. 72 G
tkeating@usk.edu

KEATING, Tina .... 760-471-1316.. 72 G
tkeating@usk.edu

KEATING POLSON,
Alicia .... 425-564-1000 477 B
presidentoffice@bellevuecollege.edu

KEATON, Alicia .... 407-823-2827 110 D
alicia.keaton@ucf.edu

KEATON, Michael ...... 215-571-4260 382 D
mjk458@drexel.edu

KEATON, Theodore ...... 803-376-5835 405 D
tkeaton@allenuniversity.edu

KEATY, Anthony .... 781-899-5500 217 F
akeaty@psjs.edu

KEBOS, Linus .... 692-625-3394 503 F

KEBREAB, Ermias ...... 530-754-9707.. 69 A
ekebreab@ucdavis.edu

KECHICHIAN,
Avedis (Avo) .... 909-448-4034.. 71 C
akechichian2@laverne.edu

KECK, Julie, L .... 740-695-9500 348 D
jkeck@belmontcollege.edu

KECK, Kathleen .... 518-327-6223 310 G
kkeck@paulsmiths.edu

KECK, Kay .... 269-965-3931 225 D
keckk@kellogg.edu

KECK, Michael .... 315-279-5327 303 D
msugalski@keuka.edu

KECK, III, Ray, M ...... 903-886-5014 446 D
ray.keck@tamuc.edu

KECKLEY, Kim .... 540-665-4841 470 A
kkeckley@su.edu

KEDROSKI, Cristie ...... 850-729-5210 104 L
kedroskc@nwfsc.edu

KEDSKI, Cathy .... 508-830-5042 213 A
ckedski@maritime.edu

KEDZIOR, Monica ...... 860-253-3026.. 86 B
mkedzior@asnuntuck.edu

KEE, Josh .... 870-235-4321.. 21 E
jrkee@saumag.edu

KEEBLER, Melissa ...... 412-536-1085 386 H
melissa.keebler@laroche.edu

KEEBLER, Patrick ...... 440-826-3745 348 C
pkeebler@bw.edu

KEECH, Brian, T .... 215-895-2244 382 D
brian.keech@drexel.edu

KEECH, Renee .... 860-465-4596.. 85 G
keechr@easternct.edu

KEECH, Roland .... 301-934-2251 198 C
rlkeech@csmd.edu

KEEDY, Thomas, E .... 765-361-6227 162 G
keedyt@wabash.edu

KEEFE, Andrea, B ...... 401-865-1534 403 G
aricci@providence.edu

KEEFE, Maureen ...... 617-879-7705 212 E
mkeefe@massart.edu

KEEFER, Jeffrey ...... 845-434-5750 321 B
jkeefer@sunysullivan.edu

KEEFER, Jessica ...... 303-384-2601.. 79 A
jkeefer@mines.edu

KEEFER, Maureen, H ... 412-397-6484 396 E
keefer@rmu.edu

KEEGAN, Bridget, M ... 402-280-4015 265 J
bmkeegan@creighton.edu

KEEGAN, Joe .... 518-354-5282 309 G
jkeegan@nccc.edu

KEEGAN, Lisa .... 570-577-1618 379 A
lak032@bucknell.edu

KEEGAN, Thomas ...... 360-416-7997 483 D
thomas.keegan@skagit.edu

KEEHN, Jay .... 513-861-6400 361 E
jay.keehn@myunion.edu

KEEL, Beverly .... 615-898-5150 421 C
beverly.keel@mtsu.edu

KEEL, Brooks, A ...... 706-721-2301 115 I
president@augusta.edu

KEEL, Darla .... 901-678-5755 426 A
darkeel@memphis.edu

KEEL, Dave .... 804-758-6731 474 C
dkeel@rappahannock.edu

KEELE, Kevin .... 213-624-1200.. 42 F
kkeele@fidm.edu

KEELER, Bruce .... 714-241-6257.. 38 C
bkeeler@coastline.edu

KEELER, Calvin .... 302-831-2524.. 91 A
ckeeler@udel.edu

KEELER-STROM,
Michela .... 402-844-7122 268 A
michela@northeast.edu

KEELEY, Brian .... 360-383-3375 485 B
bkeeley@whatcom.edu

KEELEY, Eileen, M ...... 704-894-2422 328 C
eikeeley@davidson.edu

KEELEY, Gloria .... 312-996-2860 151 D
gkeeley@uic.edu

KEELEY, Shawn .... 207-288-5015 194 C

KEELING, Amy .... 865-354-3000 424 D
keelinga@roanestate.edu

KEELING, Nicholas ...... 602-384-2555.. 11 H

KEELS, Carl .... 301-736-3631 200 A
drkeels@msbbcs.edu

KEELS, Carl, E .... 301-736-3631 200 A
drkeels@msbbcs.edu

KEELY, Brian .... 641-585-8791 170 E
keelyb@waldorf.edu

KEEN, Larry .... 910-678-8321 334 C
keenl@faytechcc.edu

KEEN, Ralph .... 312-413-2267 151 E
rkeen01@uic.edu

KEEN, Suzanne .... 909-621-8148.. 63 E
president@scrippscollege.edu

KEEN, Suzanne .... 315-859-4607 300 F
skeen@hamilton.edu

KEEN, William .... 706-507-8800 117 E

KEENAN, Claudine ...... 609-652-3593 283 A
claudine.keenan@stockton.edu

KEENAN, Erika .... 602-285-7842.. 13 H
erika.keenan@phoenixcollege.edu

KEENAN, Fran .... 603-578-8900 272 B

KEENAN, SJ, James, F . 617-552-3880 207 A
james.keenan.2@bc.edu

KEENAN, John .... 978-542-6400 213 B
john.keenan@salemstate.edu

KEENAN, Laurie ...... 518-464-8575 299 B
laurie@excelsior.edu

KEENAN, Mary .... 218-726-7009 243 A
mkeenan@d.umn.edu

KEENAN, Maura .... 215-780-1266 397 E
mkeenan@salus.edu

KEENAN, Ruth .... 281-998-6368 442 H
ruth.keenan@sjcd.edu

KEENAN, Sara .... 816-501-4815 257 K
sara.keenan@rockhurst.edu

KEENAN, Stuart .... 605-995-2647 414 A
stuart.keenan@dwu.edu

KEENAN, Timothy ...... 920-924-3420 498 C
tkeenan@morainepark.edu

KEENE, David .... 502-456-6504 184 F
dkeene@sullivan.edu

KEENE, Frances .... 540-231-8069 475 D
vpsa@vt.edu

KEENE, Jennifer ...... 714-744-2102.. 36 D
keene@chapman.edu

KEENE, Jennifer ...... 702-895-3401 270 J
jennifer.keene@unlv.edu

KEENE, John .... 973-353-3899 281 C
john.keene@rutgers.edu

KEENE, Kristen .... 615-898-2728 421 C
kristen.keene@mtsu.edu

KEENE, Vickie .... 276-498-5230 463 G
vkeene@acp.edu

KEENE, Vincent .... 276-326-4209 464 A
vkeene@bluefield.edu

KEENER, Barb .... 419-755-4539 357 B
bkeener@ncstatecollege.edu

KEENER, Gary, S ...... 540-863-2900 473 D
gkeener@mgcc.edu

KEENER, J. Michael ...... 678-466-4266 117 A
johnkeener@clayton.edu

KEENER, John .... 434-258-8061 469 A
jkeener@randolphcollege.edu

KEENER, John, F ...... 434-947-8367 469 A
jkeener@randolphcollege.edu

KEENER, Sarah .... 802-586-7711 462 C
skeener@sterlingcollege.edu

KEENER, Steve .... 214-818-1388 433 A
skeener@criswell.edu

KEENER, Sue .... 618-468-2001 142 F
skeener@lc.edu

KEENEY, Madonna .... 815-599-3449 138 H
madonna.keeney@highland.edu

KEENEY, Michael, S ... 843-953-5843 406 D
mkeeney@citadel.edu

KEENEY, Paul .... 701-355-8329 347 A
plkeeney@umary.edu

KEENUM, Mark, E ...... 662-325-3221 247 A
president@msstate.edu

KEENUM, Nancy .... 256-306-2850.... 1 F
nancy.keenum@calhoun.edu

KEERY, Nina .... 781-239-2463 214 E
nkeery@massbay.edu

KEESE, Russelle .... 502-597-5759 183 A
russelle.keese@kysu.edu

KEETER, Amanda ...... 512-313-3000 432 N
amanda.keeter@concordia.edu

KEETER, Tara .... 252-536-7223 334 G
tkeeter618@halifaxcc.edu

KEETON, Tim .... 913-971-3607 175 H
tkeeton@mnu.edu

KEEVE, Michael .... 757-823-8180 468 B
mokeeve@nsu.edu

KEEVY, Joline .... 912-358-4147 124 D
keevyj@savannahstate.edu

KEEVY, Lindsay .... 360-442-2667 480 E
lkeevy@lowercolumbia.edu

KELLY, Debra, D ... 716-880-2524 305 F debra.d.kelly@medaille.edu
KELLY, Dennis ... 937-481-2555 363 H dennis_kelly@wilmington.edu
KELLY, Diane ... 865-974-3265 426 C dianek@utk.edu
KELLY, Drew ... 610-526-6669 385 F dkelly@harcum.edu
KELLY, Drew ... 813-257-3122 113 B drew.kelly@ut.edu
KELLY, Ethan ... 601-366-8880 249 A ekelly@wbs.edu
KELLY, Francis, E ... 845-575-3000 305 C francis.kelly@marist.edu
KELLY, Georgetta ... 480-731-8103.. 13 A georgetta.kelly@domail.maricopa.edu
KELLY, Grayson ... 864-646-1548 411 H gkelly1@tctc.edu
KELLY, Heather, A ... 302-831-2021.. 91 A hkelly@udel.edu
KELLY, Inesha ... 773-481-8830 135 D ikelly1@ccc.edu
KELLY, Inesha ... 312-850-7090 135 E ikelly11@ccc.edu
KELLY, Inesha, B ... 773-291-6275 135 B ikelly1@ccc.edu
KELLY, Janet ... 478-218-3319 116 F jkelly@centralgatech.edu
KELLY, Jarrod ... 252-985-5261 339 B jkelly@ncwc.edu
KELLY, Jeffrey, M ... 443-352-4012 202 C jkelly@stevenson.edu
KELLY, Jeneen ... 914-323-5337 305 A jeneen.kelly@mville.edu
KELLY, Jennifer ... 617-451-0010 217 B
KELLY, Jennifer ... 808-518-4791 128 H jenniferkelly@pacrim.edu
KELLY, Jennifer ... 318-357-6441 192 D
KELLY, Jess, P ... 972-860-7141 433 I jesskelly@dcccd.edu
KELLY, John ... 617-735-9710 209 A kellyjo@emmanuel.edu
KELLY, John ... 870-512-7824.. 18 C john_kelly@asun.edu
KELLY, John ... 561-297-3450 109 F president@fau.edu
KELLY, Julia ... 215-489-2301 381 K julia.kelly@delval.edu
KELLY, Julie, A ... 860-444-8508 502 F julie.a.kelly@uscg.mil
KELLY, Kathleen ... 617-585-1154 217 A kathleen.kelly@necmusic.edu
KELLY, Kathleen ... 518-244-2030 312 D kellyk5@sage.edu
KELLY, Kathy ... 513-244-4418 356 F kathy.kelly@msj.edu
KELLY, Kelly ... 608-822-2305 498 H kkelly@swtc.edu
KELLY, Kevin ... 617-236-5402 209 D kkelly@fisher.edu
KELLY, Kevin ... 860-215-9325.. 87 D kkelly@threerivers.edu
KELLY, Kevin, P ... 410-269-5087 202 F kkelly@umaryland.edu
KELLY, Kirk ... 503-725-6246 375 D kkelly@pdx.edu
KELLY, Kristi ... 815-836-5538 142 C kellykj@lewisu.edu
KELLY, Laura ... 315-312-3151 318 B laura.kelly@oswego.edu
KELLY, Lee ... 718-997-4455 295 A lee.kelly@qc.cuny.edu
KELLY, Lee ... 904-725-0525.. 97 N
KELLY, Leslie, E ... 207-834-7522 196 G lesliek@maine.edu
KELLY, Liisa ... 910-843-5304 330 F lkelly@lumbeeriver.edu
KELLY, Lisa ... 732-906-2564 278 A lkelly@middlesexcc.edu
KELLY, Lynn ... 912-260-4324 125 B lynn.kelly@sgsc.edu
KELLY, Maisha ... 215-895-2000 382 D mk3883@drexel.edu
KELLY, Marie, C ... 508-565-1169 218 F mkelly1@stonehill.edu
KELLY, Marisa ... 617-573-8120 218 G mjkelly@suffolk.edu
KELLY, Maureen ... 708-534-5000 138 C mkelly7@govst.edu
KELLY, Michael ... 813-974-1442 111 B michaelskelly@usf.edu
KELLY, Michele ... 734-462-4400 230 B mkelly@schoolcraft.edu
KELLY, Mickie ... 828-669-8012 331 H mickie.kelly@montreat.edu
KELLY, Paige ... 276-739-2461 474 H pkelly@vhcc.edu
KELLY, Patricia ... 662-246-6417 246 E pkelly@msdelta.edu
KELLY, Patrick ... 304-336-8510 489 B patrick.kelly@westliberty.edu
KELLY, Peter ... 540-654-1464 471 B pkelly3@umw.edu
KELLY, Robert, D ... 503-943-7101 376 H rkelly1@up.edu
KELLY, Rosemary ... 910-678-8325 334 C kellyr@faytechcc.edu
KELLY, Ryan, J ... 517-750-1200 230 F jo776328@arbor.edu
KELLY, Sandra ... 803-777-2808 412 A sjkelly@mailbox.sc.edu
KELLY, Sandra, J ... 803-777-2808 412 A sandra-kelly@sc.edu
KELLY, Sara ... 585-395-2369 317 B skelly@brockport.edu
KELLY, Sarah, E ... 914-323-5304 305 A sarah.kelly@mville.edu
KELLY, Sarah, J ... 718-990-6161 313 B kellys@stjohns.edu
KELLY, Sarah, J ... 330-972-6134 361 G sarah30@uakron.edu
KELLY, Sean ... 210-458-6463 455 B sean.kelly@utsa.edu
KELLY, Stephanie ... 317-788-6099 161 F spkelly@uindy.edu
KELLY, Susan ... 617-287-7050 211 C skelly@umassp.edu
KELLY, Tami ... 281-998-6150 442 E
KELLY, Thomas, M ... 312-915-6400 142 G tkelly4@luc.edu
KELLY, Todd ... 719-549-2013.. 79 G todd.kelly@csupueblo.edu
KELLY, Tracy ... 716-338-1042 302 G tracykelly@mail.sunyjcc.edu
KELLY, Valerie, I ... 330-672-0020 354 A vkelly@kent.edu
KELLY, William, G ... 860-444-8285 502 F william.g.kelly@uscg.mil
KELLY BATES, Martha ... 847-578-8582 148 B martha.bates@rosalindfranklin.edu
KELLY-RILEY, Diane ... 208-885-5013 132 C dkr@uidaho.edu
KELLY-VERGONA, Barbara ... 973-957-0188 274 D registrar@acs350.org
KELM, Mary Helen ... 903-675-6338 451 C mary.kelm@tvcc.edu
KELMAN, Ari ... 530-752-7783.. 69 A
KELMER, JR., Kenneth, J ... 207-768-2715 195 C sm8407@bncollege.com
KELSAY, Missy ... 662-562-3319 247 E
KELSCH, Anne ... 701-777-3325 344 H anne.kelsch@und.edu
KELSCH, Tyler ... 303-546-3569.. 81 N tkelsch@naropa.edu
KELSER, Sandra, B ... 334-833-4409.... 5 H skelser@hawks.huntingdon.edu
KELSEY, Ashley, A ... 276-244-1283 463 H aakelsey@asl.edu
KELSEY, Barb ... 608-789-6199 499 B kelseyb@westerntc.edu
KELSEY, Cathie ... 303-765-3103.. 81 F ckelsey@iliff.edu
KELSEY, Katie, M ... 402-280-1715 265 J katiekelsey@creighton.edu
KELSEY, Mark, N ... 276-244-1285 463 H mkelsey@asl.edu
KELSEY, Ross ... 281-998-6150 442 E ross.kelsey@sjcd.edu
KELSO, Abby ... 360-867-6300 479 C kelso@evergreen.edu
KELSO, Amanda ... 919-684-2174 328 D amanda.kelso@duke.edu
KELSO, Anne-Marie ... 541-881-5838 376 E akelso@tvcc.cc
KELSO, Donovan ... 405-945-3243 368 C donovak@okstate.edu
KELTON, Emily ... 303-273-3148.. 79 A ekelton@mines.edu
KELTY, Edward ... 585-785-1300 299 E edward.kelty@flcc.edu
KELVEY, Bill ... 410-386-8214 197 G bkelvey@carrollcc.edu
KEM, Jack, D ... 913-684-3417 502 D
KEMENY, Paul, C ... 724-458-2025 384 F pckemeny@gcc.edu
KEMMELMEIER, Markus 775-784-6869 270 K markusk@unr.edu
KEMNETZ, Larry ... 773-252-6464 146 D larry.kemnetz@oakpoint.edu
KEMNITZ, Carl ... 760-750-4050.. 33 C ckemnitz@csusm.edu
KEMNITZ, Marcie ... 308-398-7400 265 C mkemnitz@cccneb.edu
KEMP, Arnold ... 312-899-1294 149 B akemp@saic.edu
KEMP, Darcy ... 413-755-4558 215 F dkemp@stcc.edu
KEMP, Dawn ... 317-632-5553 158 V dkemp@lincolntech.edu
KEMP, John ... 864-294-3717 408 I john.kemp@furman.edu
KEMP, Katie ... 847-317-8177 150 J katiek@tiu.edu
KEMP, Lisa ... 858-513-9240.. 16 I
KEMP, Nathan, R ... 309-341-7255 141 E nkemp@knox.edu
KEMP, Nicholas ... 352-365-3526 103 U kempn@lssc.edu
KEMP, Rick ... 480-517-8508.. 14 A rick.kemp@riosalado.edu
KEMP, Shirley ... 304-829-7485 486 B skemp@bethanywv.edu
KEMP, Stephen ... 515-292-9694 163 B stephen.kemp@antiochschool.edu
KEMP-CURTIS, Andrea .. 202-274-2303.. 94 C
KEMPE, Amy, P ... 401-825-2028 403 D apkempe@ccri.edu
KEMPE, Michael, A ... 330-325-6481 357 D mkempe@neomed.edu
KEMPEL, Leo, C ... 517-355-5114 227 C kempel@egr.msu.edu
KEMPER, Heather ... 501-279-4276.. 19 G hkemper@harding.edu
KEMPER, Kenneth, B ... 616-538-2330 224 B preskemper@gracechristian.edu
KEMPER, Lori, A ... 623-572-3202 144 C lorik@midwestern.edu
KEMPER, Steven ... 848-932-1395 281 B skemper@mgsa.rutgers.edu
KEMPF, Cory ... 715-394-8366 496 D ckempf1@uwsuper.edu
KEMPF, David ... 417-690-3448 250 K dkempf@cofo.edu
KEMPF, Kimberly ... 802-387-6723 461 E kimberlykempf@landmark.edu
KEMPNER, Brandon ... 505-454-3286 286 C bkempner@nmhu.edu
KEMPSTER, James ... 718-636-3471 311 A jkempster@pratt.edu
KEMPTON, Daniel ... 740-283-6228 352 I dkempton@franciscan.edu
KENAN, Tonya ... 910-275-6181 335 C tkenan@jamessprunt.edu
KENAUSIS, Veronica ... 203-837-9109.. 86 A kenausisv@wcsu.edu
KENCH, Brian ... 203-932-7115.. 89 F bkench@newhaven.edu
KENDALL, Anthony ... 513-487-1203 361 E anthony.kendall@myunion.edu
KENDALL, Curtis, L ... 540-828-5476 464 C ckendall@bridgewater.edu
KENDALL, David ... 574-535-7030 155 B davidk15@goshen.edu
KENDALL, Donna ... 781-891-3441 206 C dkendall@bentley.edu
KENDALL, Joel ... 580-774-3252 369 I joel.kendall@swosu.edu
KENDALL, Justin ... 620-862-5252 171 E justin.kendall@barclaycollege.edu
KENDALL, Kenny ... 315-470-7749 291 E kennethkendall@crouse.org
KENDALL, Maria, K ... 304-326-1234 486 I mkendall@salemu.edu
KENDALL, Mark ... 909-607-9660.. 57 K mark.kendall@pomona.edu
KENDALL, Rex ... 812-237-6100 155 H rkendall@indstatefoundation.org
KENDALL, Stephanie ... 617-573-8260 218 G skendall@suffolk.edu
KENDALL-LEKKA, Meitaka ... 692-625-3394 503 F mkendall@cmi.edu
KENDER, Joseph, P ... 610-660-2309 397 A jkender@sju.edu
KENDERDINE, Linda ... 410-706-5036 202 F lcassard@umaryland.edu
KENDI, Ibram, X ... 617-353-2230 207 C kendi@bu.edu
KENDIG, P. Tysen ... 860-486-6713.. 89 B tysen.kendig@uconn.edu
KENDJORIA, Barrett ... 864-656-4013 406 F bkendjo@clemson.edu
KENDRA-DILL, Zach ... 704-922-6223 334 E kendra-dill.zachary@gaston.edu
KENDREX, Bradley ... 480-461-7446.. 13 F bradley.kendrex@mesacc.edu
KENDREX, Bradley, S ... 480-732-7379.. 13 B bradley.kendrex@cgc.edu
KENDRICK, Bethany ... 620-421-6700 175 D bethanyk@labette.edu
KENDRICK, Curtis ... 607-777-4550 315 E kendrick@binghamton.edu
KENDRICK, David ... 847-635-1979 146 E dkendrick@oakton.edu
KENDRICK, Ebony ... 336-370-8632 326 J ekendrick@bennett.edu
KENDRICK, Frederick ... 814-871-5615 383 H kendrick003@gannon.edu
KENDRICK, Haley ... 704-406-3957 328 I hkendrick@gardner-webb.edu
KENDRICK, Kaetrena, D 803-323-2232 413 D kendrickk@winthrop.edu
KENDRICK, Kevin ... 334-229-6500.... 4 B kkendrick@alasu.edu
KENDRICK, Lorna ... 510-879-3347.. 60 C lkendrick@samuelmerritt.edu
KENDRICK, Marsha ... 405-703-8241 366 C marsha.kendrick@macu.edu
KENDRICK, Samantha ... 616-222-1428 222 F
KENERSON, Laura ... 401-874-5271 404 E lkenerson@uri.edu
KENFIELD, Mikal, C ... 218-299-3872 234 K kenfield@cord.edu
KENIMER, Ann, L ... 979-845-4016 446 B a-kenimer@tamu.edu
KENISTON, Joseph, C .. 315-229-1858 313 F jkeniston@stlawu.edu
KENISTON, Josh ... 603-646-0458 272 F josh.keniston@dartmouth.edu
KENISTON, Leonda ... 434-961-5380 474 B lkeniston@pvcc.edu
KENLEY, David ... 605-256-5270 415 G david.kenley@dsu.edu
KENLINE, Kelly ... 716-645-5344 315 F kellyd@buffalo.edu
KENMILLE, Cleo ... 406-275-4864 264 H cleo_kenmille@skc.edu
KENN, Jim ... 617-559-8688 210 C jkenn@hebrewcollege.edu
KENNA-SCHENK, Becca 360-951-3733 485 A becca.kenna-schenk@wwu.edu
KENNEALLY, Steve, P ... 724-847-6692 384 B spkennea@geneva.edu
KENNEBREW, Kara ... 281-998-6150 442 C kara.kennebrew@sjcd.edu
KENNEBREW, Kara ... 281-484-1900 442 E
KENNEDY, Aaron ... 575-461-4413 285 J aaronk@mesalands.edu
KENNEDY, Alejandra, S 864-656-9407 406 F alekenn@clemson.edu
KENNEDY, Angelica ... 513-569-1515 350 C angelica.kennedy@cincinnatistate.edu
KENNEDY, Calhoun, L ... 864-597-4200 413 E kennedycl@wofford.edu
KENNEDY, Carol, M ... 570-577-1511 379 A carol.kennedy@bucknell.edu
KENNEDY, Catherine, B 401-739-5000 403 F ckennedy@neit.edu
KENNEDY, Catherine, C ... 727-394-6202 107 C kennedy.catherine@spcollege.edu
KENNEDY, Charles, A ... 412-268-8836 380 B ckennedy@cmu.edu
KENNEDY, Charnequa .. 919-530-5294 341 D ckenne15@nccu.edu
KENNEDY, Chrisitne ... 312-942-5836 148 C christine_kennedy@rush.edu
KENNEDY, Christopher, M ... 843-661-1557 408 H ckennedy@fmarion.edu
KENNEDY, Colleen ... 773-371-5417 134 C ckennedy@ctu.edu
KENNEDY, Damon ... 432-685-4524 439 E dkennedy@midland.edu
KENNEDY, Dana ... 330-263-2317 350 H dakennedy@wooster.edu
KENNEDY, David ... 919-684-3363 328 D david.kennedy@duke.edu

KENNEDY, Deborah ...... 540-674-3690 473 F
dkennedy@nr.edu
KENNEDY, Dennis .... 518-629-8085 302 A
d.kennedy1@hvcc.edu
KENNEDY, Doug .... 304-236-7648 487 I
doug.kennedy@southernwv.edu
KENNEDY, Doug .... 304-896-7408 487 I
doug.kennedy@southernwv.edu
KENNEDY, Elizabeth ...... 816-271-4237 256 C
president@missouriwestern.edu
KENNEDY, Elizabeth ...... 802-485-2218 461 H
ekennedy@norwich.edu
KENNEDY, Ellen .... 413-236-1003 213 E
ekennedy@berkshirecc.edu
KENNEDY, Erica .... 216-397-4598 353 O
ekennedy@jcu.edu
KENNEDY, Gary .... 318-257-4287 192 A
kennedy@latech.edu
KENNEDY, Helen .... 724-422-2808 379 D
hkennedy@bcs.edu
KENNEDY, James .... 714-241-5708.. 58 G
kennedy_james@sac.edu
KENNEDY, James .... 714-241-5708.. 58 F
kennedy_james@sac.edu
KENNEDY, Jason .... 951-571-6931.. 59 B
jason.kennedy@mvc.edu
KENNEDY, Jay .... 617-747-2150 206 D
academicaffairs@berklee.edu
KENNEDY, Jeanne .... 252-527-6223 335 E
jmkennedy48@lenoircc.edu
KENNEDY, Jennifer ...... 734-432-5856 226 G
jkennedy@madonna.edu
KENNEDY, Jodi .... 912-478-1435 120 A
jmiddleton@georgiasouthern.edu
KENNEDY, Jody .... 662-329-7396 247 B
jwkennedy@muw.edu
KENNEDY, John .... 413-545-8500 211 D
jkennedy@admin.umass.edu
KENNEDY, John, M ...... 315-386-7513 319 E
kennedyjm@canton.edu
KENNEDY, Julia .... 704-463-1360 339 C
julia.kennedy@pfeiffer.edu
KENNEDY, Julie .... 205-929-6333.... 2 H
jkennedy@lawsonstate.edu
KENNEDY, Katherine, J 617-353-4745 207 C
kkennedy@bu.edu
KENNEDY, Kathleen ...... 504-520-7421 193 C
kkenned1@xula.edu
KENNEDY, Kathleen ...... 503-375-7585 372 G
kkennedy@corban.edu
KENNEDY, Kayla .... 785-462-3984 172 L
KENNEDY, Kelly .... 409-944-1303 435 F
kkennedy@gc.edu
KENNEDY, Kenneth ...... 417-625-9741 255 I
kennedy-k@mssu.edu
KENNEDY, Linda .... 949-480-4072.. 64 E
lkennedy@soka.edu
KENNEDY, Lola .... 803-376-5791 405 D
lkennedy@allenuniversity.edu
KENNEDY, Lola .... 803-321-5120 409 I
lola.kennedy@newberry.edu
KENNEDY, Lori, B .... 610-758-4665 388 C
lbk4@lehigh.edu
KENNEDY, Marcus .... 205-366-8817.... 7 A
mkennedy@stillman.edu
KENNEDY, Marina .... 415-503-6230.. 61 E
mkennedy@sfcm.edu
KENNEDY, Mary, M ...... 207-725-3067 194 A
mkennedy@bowdoin.edu
KENNEDY, Matthew ...... 732-255-0400 279 A
mkennedy@ocean.edu
KENNEDY, Melba .... 225-743-8500 188 F
mkennedy@rpcc.edu
KENNEDY, Melissa ...... 269-782-1241 230 D
mkennedy03@swmich.edu
KENNEDY, Mike .... 864-596-9390 407 G
mike.kennedy@converse.edu
KENNEDY, Missty .... 334-844-7771.... 4 E
kennem1@auburn.edu
KENNEDY, Missy .... 910-962-2049 343 B
kennedym@uncw.edu
KENNEDY, Natalia .... 301-687-4799 203 F
nkennedy@frostburg.edu
KENNEDY, Paul, W ...... 585-594-6469 311 L
kennedy_paul@roberts.edu
KENNEDY, Rachel, A 574-807-7462 153 G
rachel.kennedy@betheluniversity.edu
KENNEDY, Rebecca ...... 205-975-4041.... 8 A
rekenn@uab.edu
KENNEDY, Ron .... 434-592-5079 467 E
rkennedy@liberty.edu
KENNEDY, Ronphal .... 205-853-1200.... 2 G
rkenned5@jeffersonstate.edu

KENNEDY, Roxie .... 816-802-3358 253 H
rkennedy@kcai.edu
KENNEDY, Scott .... 949-451-5200.. 65 B
skennedy@ivc.edu
KENNEDY, Sean .... 856-256-5755 280 H
kennedyse@rowan.edu
KENNEDY, Shannon ...... 804-758-6701 474 C
KENNEDY, SSJ, Sheila .. 215-248-7104 380 G
kennedys@chc.edu
KENNEDY, Suzanne ...... 617-353-2230 207 C
skennedy@bu.edu
KENNEDY, Taurean .... 212-343-1234 306 C
tkennedy@mcny.edu
KENNEDY, Tiana .... 303-534-6290.. 79 D
tiana.kennedy@colostate.edu
KENNEDY, Timothy, R .. 507-933-6395 235 E
tkennedy@gustavus.edu
KENNEDY, II,
William "Rusty" .... 859-846-5456 183 G
wkennedy@midway.edu
KENNEDY-FLETCHER,
Jackie .... 812-855-7087 156 C
jacfletc@indiana.edu
KENNEDY-JONES,
Danielle .... 334-229-4202.... 4 B
botliaison@alasu.edu
KENNEDY-LORDE,
De Anne .... 718-270-1000 316 E
KENNEDY-PHILLIPS,
Lance, C .... 814-863-8721 391 F
lck7@psu.edu
KENNEDY-RATAJACK,
Kathy, S .... 302-356-2481.. 91 C
kathy.s.kennedy-ratajack@wilmu.edu
KENNEDY-WITTHAR,
Shawna, J .... 806-651-2227 447 D
switthar@wtamu.edu
KENNELL, Deena .... 308-432-6388 267 G
dkennell@csc.edu
KENNELL, Scott .... 734-432-5604 226 G
skennell@madonna.edu
KENNELL, Scott .... 570-320-2400 392 S
sek3@pct.edu
KENNER, Carole .... 609-771-2848 275 J
kennerc@tcnj.edu
KENNER, Rosaland .... 803-793-5196 408 A
kennerr@denmarktech.edu
KENNERKNECHT,
Megan .... 585-785-1277 299 E
megan.kennerknecht@flcc.edu
KENNERLY, A. Chris ...... 740-427-5160 354 I
kennerlyc@kenyon.edu
KENNERLY, JR.,
John, F .... 864-379-8788 408 F
kennerly@erskine.edu
KENNETT-HENSEL,
Pamela .... 504-280-6193 189 F
pkennett@uno.edu
KENNEY, Christopher ... 802-654-2200 462 A
ckenney@smcvt.edu
KENNEY, Eileen .... 918-595-8144 370 B
eileen.kenney@tulsacc.edu
KENNEY, Heather .... 904-646-2296 101 A
heather.a.kenney@fscj.edu
KENNEY, Jennie .... 303-273-3399.. 79 A
jkenney@mines.edu
KENNEY, Kristie .... 256-761-6233.... 7 B
kkenney@talladega.edu
KENNEY, Kristin .... 906-932-4231 224 A
kristink@gogebic.edu
KENNEY, Patrick, J ...... 480-727-2634.. 11 A
pkenney@asu.edu
KENNEY, Rob .... 815-802-8173 141 B
rkenney@kcc.edu
KENNEY, Steven, H ...... 985-448-4001 192 C
steven.kenney@nicholls.edu
KENNEY, Sue, B .... 443-334-2547 202 C
skenney@stevenson.edu
KENNEY, Tamara .... 607-871-2134 289 E
kenney@alfred.edu
KENNINGTON, Janet, S 410-334-2942 205 A
jkennington@worwic.edu
KENNON, Cheryl .... 817-257-6122 447 H
c.kennon@tcu.edu
KENNON, Susan .... 434-544-8218 470 K
kennon@lynchburg.edu
KENNY, Cathleen .... 718-636-3784 311 A
ckenny@pratt.edu
KENNY, Eddie .... 270-852-3146 183 B
ekenny@kwc.edu
KENNY, James .... 323-415-5374.. 49 D
kennyja@elac.edu

KENNY, John .... 702-254-7577 271 B
john.kenny@northwestcareercollege.
edu
KENNY, Michael .... 702-254-7577 271 B
stephanie.kenny@
northwestcareercollege.edu
KENNY, Patrick .... 702-254-7577 271 B
patrick.kenny@northwestcareercollege.
edu
KENNY, Stephanie ...... 702-254-7577 271 B
KENNY, Thomas .... 702-254-7577 271 B
thomas.kenny@northwestcareercollege.
edu
KENOLIO, Ellen .... 808-689-2755 129 C
kenolio@hawaii.edu
KENT, Allen .... 601-643-8314 244 G
allen.kent@colin.edu
KENT, Andrea .... 251-460-6261.... 9 A
akent@southalabama.edu
KENT, Angela .... 402-878-2380 266 D
angela.kent@littlepriest.edu
KENT, Cassy .... 585-785-1209 299 E
cassy.kent@flcc.edu
KENT, Christopher ...... 864-578-8770 410 G
ckent@sherman.edu
KENT, Jennifer .... 361-582-2560 456 H
jennifer.kent@victoriacollege.edu
KENT, Jonathan .... 607-871-2406 289 E
kentj@alfred.edu
KENT, K. Craig .... 434-924-9308 471 F
ck8aq@hscmail.mcc.virginia.edu
KENT, Kathryn .... 229-217-4206 125 G
kkent@southernregional.edu
KENT, Kimberly .... 563-884-5176 169 C
kent_k@palmer.edu
KENT, Rebekah .... 218-894-5172 237 C
rebekah.kent@clcmn.edu
KENT, Shayna .... 831-459-3966.. 71 A
skent1@ucsc.edu
KENT, Stephen .... 651-793-1910 238 B
stephen.kent@metrostate.edu
KENT, Tom .... 518-793-5250 319 D
kentt@sunyacc.edu
KENTON, Jay .... 503-838-8888 377 C
kentonj@wou.edu
KENTON, Katrina .... 513-244-4327 356 F
katrina.kenton@msj.edu
KENWORTHY, Anne ...... 901-321-4213 417 C
anne.kenworthy@cbu.edu
KENYON, Allie .... 559-638-0300.. 67 C
allie.kenyon@reedleycollege.edu
KENYON, Carl .... 814-944-5643 402 H
carl.kenyon@yti.edu
KENYON, Gina .... 815-752-8990 145 H
gkenyon@niu.edu
KENYON, Melaine .... 716-839-8290 297 F
mkenyon@daemen.edu
KENYON, Steven .... 508-678-2811 213 F
steve.kenyon@bristolcc.edu
KENZOR, Jennifer .... 812-877-8217 160 C
seddelme@rose-hulman.edu
KEOGH, Kristina .... 941-359-7582 106 J
kkeogh@ringling.edu
KEOGH, Lily .... 402-354-7263 267 E
lily.keogh@methodistcollege.edu
KEOGH GEORGE, Stacy 509-777-3851 485 D
sgeorge@whitworth.edu
KEOHANE, Ellen, J ...... 508-793-2477 208 A
ekeohane@holycross.edu
KEON, Thomas, L .... 219-989-2204 160 A
tkeon@pnw.edu
KEOPUHIWA, Thomas .. 808-734-9522 129 E
keopuhiw@hawaii.edu
KEOUGH, Diana .... 856-225-6053 281 A
diana.keough@camden.rutgers.edu
KEOUGH, Shawn .... 503-845-3579 373 G
shawn.keough@mtangel.edu
KEOUGH, Wendy .... 269-471-3611 220 H
keoughw@andrews.edu
KEOWN, Maureen .... 718-817-4160 300 A
mkeown@fordham.edu
KEPFORD, Joyce .... 605-688-4442 416 A
joyce.kepford@sdstate.edu
KEPHART, Joy .... 828-835-4212 338 C
jkephart@tricountycc.edu
KEPHART, Noah .... 515-964-0601 166 A
kephartn@faith.edu
KEPLEY, Bruce .... 812-258-9510 154 B
bkepley@cariscollege.edu
KEPPLE-MAMROS,
Deborah, J .... 515-964-6476 164 F
djkepplemamros@dmacc.edu
KEPPNER, Dana .... 217-641-4241 140 H
dkeppner@jwcc.edu

KERASTAMATIS,
Matthew .... 239-489-9283 100 G
matthew.kerastamatis@fsw.edu
KERBEL, Matthew .... 610-519-4553 401 B
matthew.kerbel@villanova.edu
KERBS, Kelsey .... 406-496-4377 264 C
kkerbs@mtech.edu
KERBS, Nancy .... 417-667-8181 251 E
nkerbs@cottey.edu
KERBY, Molly .... 270-745-6952 186 A
molly.kerby@wku.edu
KERBY, Steve .... 410-386-4686 200 D
skerby@mcdaniel.edu
KERCE, Walter .... 413-552-2155 214 D
wkerce@hcc.edu
KERCH, Matthew .... 205-348-9364.... 7 G
mkerch@ua.edu
KERDA, Stephen, J ...... 301-243-2167 501 J
stephen.kerda@dodiis.mil
KEREN, Hila .... 213-738-6755.. 66 A
hkeren@swlaw.edu
KERESTLY, Charles, E .. 325-942-2246 450 H
ed.kerestly@angelo.edu
KERFOOT, Adina .... 731-424-2603 423 F
akerfoot@jscc.edu
KERIN, Robert, J .... 717-361-1220 383 F
kerinr@etown.edu
KERKAERT, Debra .... 507-537-6093 240 G
deb.kerkaert@smsu.edu
KERLIN, Julie, M .... 404-413-1405 120 C
jkerlin1@gsu.edu
KERMAN, Lucy, E .... 215-895-2123 382 D
lucy.e.kerman@drexel.edu
KERMES, Anita .... 916-278-6980.. 33 A
anita.kermes@csus.edu
KERN, Alexander .... 617-373-2728 217 D
KERN, Allison .... 510-885-3000.. 31 C
allison.kern@csueastbay.edu
KERN, Jessica .... 606-759-7141 182 B
jessica.kern@kctcs.edu
KERN, Linda .... 770-538-4722 116 C
lkern@brenau.edu
KERN, Rhonda .... 763-433-1362 236 H
rhonda.kern@anokaramsey.edu
KERN, Tony .... 218-281-8257 243 B
akern@umn.edu
KERNAN, Maura .... 860-253-3006.. 86 B
mkernan@asnuntuck.edu
KERNER, Kelly, A .... 706-542-2002 126 F
kkerner@uga.edu
KERNER, Walter .... 212-217-3400 299 C
walter_kerner@fitnyc.edu
KERNICK, Rhonda .... 432-264-5100 436 H
rkernick@howardcollege.edu
KERNIN, Richard, P 716-286-8044 309 F
rpk@niagara.edu
KERNS, OSA, Bryan .. 978-837-5000 216 D
kernsb@merrimack.edu
KERNS, Connie .... 620-792-9273 171 F
kernsc@bartoncccc.edu
KERNS, Robert .... 301-387-3003 198 F
robert.kerns@garrettcollege.edu
KEROUAC, Luke .... 435-652-7513 459 G
luke.kerouac@utahtech.edu
KERR, Adrian .... 239-565-8100 100 G
adrian.kerr@fsw.edu
KERR, Alecia .... 412-536-1059 386 H
alecia.kerr@laroche.edu
KERR, Anne, B .... 863-680-4100 100 F
akerr@flsouthern.edu
KERR, Brian .... 212-237-8100 294 B
bkerr@jjay.cuny.edu
KERR, Brian .... 718-631-6262 295 H
bkerr@qcc.cuny.edu
KERR, Colleen .... 206-219-2415 484 D
colleen.kerr@wsu.edu
KERR, Courtney, A ...... 757-446-5798 465 H
kerrca@evms.edu
KERR, Dee Ann .... 651-641-8794 235 A
kerr@csp.edu
KERR, Elizabeth .... 716-896-0700 324 A
ekerr@villa.edu
KERR, Emily, C .... 706-886-6831 126 C
eraynor@tfc.edu
KERR, Jean .... 309-556-3212 140 F
jkerr@iwu.edu
KERR, Kathleen .... 315-312-3214 318 B
kathleen.kerr@oswego.edu
KERR, Kristi .... 860-439-5328.. 87 F
krandmet@conncoll.edu
KERR, Kristie .... 612-343-4741 241 O
kekerr@northcentral.edu

KERR, Mary Frances ..... 404-471-6325 114 E
mfkerr@agnesscott.edu
KERR, Mickey .... 254-295-4618 453 A
mkerr@umhb.edu
KERR, Peter .... 303-963-3163.. 78 D
pakerr@ccu.edu
KERR, Shelly, K .... 541-346-3227 376 G
skerr@uoregon.edu
KERR, Stephen .... 617-732-2093 216 B
stephen.kerr@mcphs.edu
KERR, Susan .... 478-445-1196 119 A
susan.kerr@gcsu.edu
KERR-MCCURRY, Norah 732-224-2628 275 D
nmccurry@brookdalecc.edu
KERRES, Johnna .... 563-336-3308 165 G
jkerres@eicc.edu
KERRICK, Ken .... 209-946-2251.. 71 E
kkerrick@pacific.edu
KERRIGAN, Adrian .... 516-572-0601 307 C
adrian.kerrigan@ncc.edu
KERRIGAN, Dana .... 610-989-1364 400 F
dkerrigan@vfmac.edu
KERRIGAN, John, E ...... 408-554-4968.. 63 A
jekerrigan@scu.edu
KERRIGAN, Noreen .... 718-430-2000 289 D
KERRIGAN, Rochelle ..... 773-252-6464 146 D
rochelle.kerrigan@oakpoint.edu
KERRUISH, Diane .... 847-214-7374 137 D
dkerruish@elgin.edu
KERRY, Bill .... 607-274-3353 302 E
wkerry@ithaca.edu
KERSCHNER, Joseph, E 414-955-8213 492 F
jkerschner@mcw.edu
KERSEY, Robert, N .... 843-953-5542 407 D
kerseyr@cofc.edu
KERSH, Rogan .... 336-758-3128 344 A
kersh@wfu.edu
KERSHAW, Josephine ... 870-743-3000.. 20 F
josephine.kershaw@northark.edu
KERSHNER, Scott, M .... 570-372-4220 398 A
kershner@susqu.edu
KERSTEN, Andrew .... 216-687-5580 350 G
a.e.kersten@csuohio.edu
KERSTEN, Belen .... 559-730-3794.. 39 C
belenk@cos.edu
KERSTEN, David, W .... 773-244-6235 145 F
dwkersten@northpark.edu
KERSTEN, James, B ...... 515-574-1132 166 G
kersten@iowacentral.edu
KERTSON, Brandon .... 916-306-1628.. 67 E
bkertson@sum.edu
KERTULIS-TARTAR,
Gina .... 706-272-4516 118 A
gkertulistartar@daltonstate.edu
KERTZ, Nancy, K .... 515-643-6615 168 B
nkertz@mercydesmoines.org
KERWICK, Sean .... 201-360-4023 277 D
skerwick@hccc.edu
KERWIN, David, M .... 206-543-4150 484 A
dkerwin@uw.edu
KERWIN, Kevin .... 559-791-2403.. 47 D
kevin.kerwin@portervillecollege.edu
KERWIN, Linda .... 716-827-2454 322 J
kerwinl@trocaire.edu
KERWIN, Linda, J .... 716-827-2454 322 J
kerwinl@trocaire.edu
KERWITZ, Ann .... 815-921-4001 147 H
a.kerwitz@rockvalleycollege.edu
KERYLOW, Tiffany .... 802-387-6725 461 E
tiffanykerylow@landmark.edu
KESARIS, Thomas .... 610-660-1836 397 A
tkesaris@sju.edu
KESAVADAS,
Thenkurussi .... 518-956-8170 315 D
tkesavadas@albany.edu
KESHVALA, Seelpa, H ... 281-290-1869 438 E
seelpa.h.keshvala@lonestar.edu
KESICKI, Michael .... 814-871-5873 383 H
kesicki001@gannon.edu
KESLER, David .... 734-462-4400 230 B
dkesler@schoolcraft.edu
KESLER, Laurie .... 662-720-7259 247 D
lgkesler@nemcc.edu
KESNER, Idalene, F ...... 812-855-8489 156 B
ikesner@indiana.edu
KESSEL, Monica .... 352-588-8646 107 B
monica.kessel@saintleo.edu
KESSELMAN, Harvey ...... 609-652-4521 283 A
harvey.kesselman@stockton.edu
KESSELMAN, Kevin, S .. 973-642-4935 278 G
kevin.kesselman@njit.edu
KESSINGER, David .... 618-664-7109 138 D
david.kessinger@greenville.edu
KESSINGER, Jason .... 812-288-8878 159 C
jkessinger@mid-america.edu
KESSLER, Brian .... 910-893-1776 327 C
kesslerb@campbell.edu
KESSLER, Emily .... 612-874-3777 236 E
ekessler@mcad.edu
KESSLER, Mary .... 812-488-2579 161 E
mk43@evansville.edu
KESSLER, Michael .... 701-231-7494 345 D
michael.r.kessler@ndsu.edu
KESSLER, Michoel .... 718-268-4700 311 H
KESSLER, Richard .... 212-580-0210 307 E
kesslerr@newschool.edu
KESSLER, Sheryl .... 215-972-7600 392 P
skessler@pafa.edu
KESSLER, Susan, B .... 386-312-4021 107 A
susankessler@sjrstate.edu
KESSLER-CLEARY,
Timothy .... 973-618-3484 275 E
tcleary@caldwell.edu
KESTENBAUM, Yoel ...... 845-782-1380 326 C
KESTER, John .... 910-410-1778 336 G
jikester@richmondcc.edu
KESTER, Kelly .... 360-383-3245 485 B
kkester@whatcom.edu
KESTER, Lori .... 303-273-3000.. 79 A
lkester@mines.edu
KESTERSON, Donald ..... 863-784-7132 108 D
donald.kesterson@southflorida.edu
KESTERSON, Ronald, L . 865-694-6608 424 C
rkesterson@pstcc.edu
KESTNER-RICKETTS,
Laura .... 309-794-7338 132 H
laurakestnerricketts@augustana.edu
KETCHESON, Kathi, A ... 503-725-3425 375 D
ketchesonk@pdx.edu
KETCHUM, Kendra .... 210-458-4011 455 B
kendra.ketchum@utsa.edu
KETELS, Margo .... 563-589-3765 170 C
mketels@dbq.edu
KETJEN, William .... 330-823-2293 362 E
ketjenwl@mountunion.edu
KETSDEVER, Andrew ..... 541-322-3100 374 H
andrew.ketsdever@osucascades.edu
KETTEMAN, P. Greg ...... 615-675-5312 427 D
gketteman@welch.edu
KETTENBEIL, Kenneth ... 313-593-5140 231 B
kketten@umich.edu
KETTERING, Rocky .... 706-507-8954 117 E
kettering_rocky@columbusstate.edu
KETTERING-LANE,
Denise .... 800-287-8822 153 F
kettede@bethanyseminary.edu
KETTERLING, Jayme ...... 208-732-6552 131 B
jketterling@csi.edu
KETTERLING, Kate .... 612-343-4442 241 O
kaketter@northcentral.edu
KETTERMAN, Beth .... 252-744-2212 340 H
kettermane@ecu.edu
KETTERMAN, Lynn .... 301-687-4090 203 F
lketterman@frostburg.edu
KETTINGER, Kevin .... 585-567-9350 301 G
kevin.kettinger@houghton.edu
KETTINGER, Kirk .... 585-594-6415 311 L
kettinger_kirk@roberts.edu
KETTLER, Karen .... 304-336-8070 489 B
kkettler@westliberty.edu
KETTLER, Ryan, J .... 615-772-1184 281 B
r.j.kettler@rutgers.edu
KETTLEWELL, Kelly .... 570-577-1604 379 A
kelly.kettlewell@bucknell.edu
KETTMANN, Nick .... 319-398-5563 167 H
nick.kettmann@kirkwood.edu
KETTNER, Valrey, V .... 701-231-9608 345 D
val.kettner@ndsu.edu
KEUFFEL, Elizabeth ...... 603-641-7203 273 C
ekeuffel@anselm.edu
KEUSS, Theresa .... 314-516-4602 260 E
keusst@umsl.edu
KEVARI, Jacob .... 951-571-6421.. 59 B
jacob.kevari@mvc.edu
KEVIL, Chris .... 318-675-4102 189 D
chris.kevil@lsuhs.edu
KEVIL, Tim .... 903-875-7443 439 G
tim.kevil@navarrocollege.edu
KEVORKIAN, Meline ...... 954-262-8523 104 M
melinek@nova.edu
KEVORKIAN,
Theresa, R .... 305-684-6020 320 E
kevorktr@morrisville.edu
KEW-FICKUS, Olivia ...... 615-343-2746 427 B
olivia.m.kew-fickus@vanderbilt.edu
KEY, Dan .... 641-844-5741 167 E
dan.key@iavalley.edu
KEY, Jacob .... 276-326-4211 464 A
jkey@bluefield.edu
KEY, Katari .... 414-382-6324 490 G
katari.key@alverno.edu
KEYEK-FRANSSEN,
Deborah .... 801-581-5057 459 D
deblkf@utah.edu
KEYES, Brian .... 417-865-2815 252 F
keyesb@evangel.edu
KEYES, Mandy .... 479-788-7086.. 22 A
mandy.keyes@uafs.edu
KEYES, Rusty .... 601-266-4986 248 H
rusty.keyes@usm.edu
KEYNTON, Robert, S ..... 704-687-8242 342 C
rkeynton@uncc.edu
KEYS, James, A .... 910-843-5304 330 F
jamesakeys@gmail.com
KEYS, Mattie .... 918-463-2931 365 I
mattie.keys@connorsstate.edu
KEYS, Staci .... 417-667-8181 251 E
skeys@cottey.edu
KEYS, Terrance .... 585-292-3432 306 K
tkeys@monroecc.edu
KEYS, Tracy .... 910-843-5304 330 F
finance@lumbeeriver.edu
KEYSER, Tom .... 541-885-1481 374 G
tom.keyser@oit.edu
KEYTACK, Ryan .... 518-388-6116 323 B
keytackr@union.edu
KEYTON, Debbie .... 870-512-7822.. 18 C
debbie_keyton@asun.edu
KEZEY, Katherine .... 802-828-2800 463 A
kap06170@ccv.vsc.edu
KHABARI, Ali .... 617-989-4590 219 D
khabaria@wit.edu
KHACHATRIAN, Gaiane . 510-925-4282.. 25 P
KHACHATRYAN,
Agun Anna .... 818-509-9970.. 43 F
KHACHATRYAN, Davit ... 949-451-5326.. 65 B
dkhachatryan@ivc.edu
KHADANGA, Dave .... 334-386-7113.... 5 D
dkhadanga@faulkner.edu
KHADEM, Farnaz .... 650-723-2300.. 66 D
KHADKA, Chandni .... 256-782-8304.... 6 A
ckhadka@jsu.edu
KHADVONGSINH,
Timothy .... 209-476-7840.. 67 D
tkhadvongsinh@clc.edu
KHAGRAM, Sanjeev .... 602-978-7203.. 11 A
sanjeev.khagram@thunderbird.asu.edu
KHAJARIAN, Seta .... 818-702-1036.. 56 H
seta.khajarian@pepperdine.edu
KHALDEN, Jeff .... 817-598-6485 457 C
jkhalden@wc.edu
KHALEDI, Morteza .... 817-272-3491 454 B
morteza.khaledi@uta.edu
KHALFANI, Akil .... 973-877-3219 276 G
khalfani@essex.edu
KHALILI, Kambiz .... 734-763-1291 231 A
kkhalili@umich.edu
KHALILI, Sheefteh .... 949-824-4911.. 69 C
skhalili@hs.uci.edu
KHAMIS, Hanan .... 508-999-8845 211 F
hkhamis@umassd.edu
KHAMKONGSAY, Ryan . 254-501-5817 446 C
rkhamkongsay@tamuct.edu
KHAMOUNA, Mo .... 308-367-5213 269 D
mkhamouna1@unl.edu
KHAN, Adil .... 636-227-2100 254 C
KHAN, Ali .... 402-559-4950 269 B
ali.khan@unmc.edu
KHAN, M. Rehan .... 502-852-7997 185 E
rehan.khan@louisville.edu
KHAN, M. Wasiullah ...... 312-939-0111 137 B
chancellor@eastwest.edu
KHAN, Ray .... 562-916-5055.. 56 G
KHAN, Raza .... 410-386-8222 197 G
rkhan@carrollcc.edu
KHAN, Rumaana, R .... 209-490-4591.. 24 H
rkhan@advancedcollege.edu
KHAN, Sadya .... 708-974-5283 144 G
khans46@morainevalley.edu
KHAN, Shafiq .... 404-880-6795 116 I
skhan@cau.edu
KHAN, Sobia .... 407-582-2929 113 C
skhan90@valenciacollege.edu
KHAN, Sobia .... 210-486-0947 428 D
skhan32@alamo.edu
KHAN-MARCUS,
Zaveeni .... 805-893-8411.. 70 E
zaveeni.khan-marcus@sa.ucsb.edu
KHANEJA, Gurvinder ...... 201-684-7766 280 B
gkhaneja@ramapo.edu
KHANNA, Pradeep .... 217-333-9525 151 F
pkhanna@illinois.edu
KHARGONEKAR,
Pramod .... 949-824-5796.. 69 C
pkhargon@uci.edu
KHARTABIL, Basim .... 407-708-4405 108 B
khartabilb@seminolestate.edu
KHASIDOVA, Albina ...... 212-776-7299 292 G
akhasidova@bmcc.cuny.edu
KHATOR, Renu .... 713-743-8820 451 F
rkhator@uh.edu
KHATOR, Renu .... 713-743-8820 451 G
rkhator@uh.edu
KHATRI, Achal .... 617-873-0235 207 E
achal.khatri@cambridgecollege.edu
KHATTAB, Ahmed .... 337-482-6166 192 F
khattab@louisiana.edu
KHAYUM, Mohammed .. 812-465-1617 162 B
mkhayum@usi.edu
KHELLA, Julie, T .... 562-907-4463.. 76 A
jkhella@whittier.edu
KHIDEKEL, Nelly .... 626-395-6454.. 29 B
nkhidekel@caltech.edu
KHOJA, Faiza .... 254-519-5724 446 C
fkhoja@tamuct.edu
KHOO-ROBINSON,
Cynthia .... 716-645-3313 315 F
ckr5@buffalo.edu
KHOR, Henry .... 909-895-7138.. 45 K
khor@huca.edu
KHOSLA, Pradeep, K .... 858-534-3135.. 70 C
chancellor@ucsd.edu
KHOSRAVANI, Mariam . 714-241-6159.. 38 D
mkhosravani@coastline.edu
KHOSRAVI, Ebrahim ..... 678-466-4400 117 A
ebrahimkhosravi@clayton.edu
KHOURY, Melik Peter ... 207-509-7221 196 B
mkhoury@unity.edu
KHOURY, Philip, S .... 617-253-0887 215 G
KHURANA, Rakesh .... 617-495-1555 210 B
deankhurana@fas.harvard.edu
KHURANA-BAUGH,
Nikki .... 845-569-3216 307 B
nikki.khurana-baugh@msmc.edu
KHUSHMAN, Aneesh .... 215-702-4843 379 F
akhushman@cairn.edu
KHUU, Jennifer .... 212-431-2816 308 I
jennifer.khuu@nyls.edu
KIA, Norman .... 575-769-4074 285 C
norman.kia@clovis.edu
KIAH, Jude .... 817-257-7820 447 H
j.kiah@tcu.edu
KIAMAN, Matthew .... 310-434-4397.. 63 B
kiaman_matthew@smc.edu
KIAN, David .... 561-297-3007 109 F
dkian@fau.edu
KIBBE, Melina, R .... 434-924-0311 471 F
erv2vm@virginia.edu
KIBBE, Sharon .... 785-442-6050 174 C
skibbe@highlandcc.edu
KIBBLE, Danny .... 317-940-8000 153 H
KIBBY, Dan .... 269-337-7175 225 B
dan.kibby@kzoo.edu
KIBLER, Michele .... 614-222-4009 351 A
mkibler@ccad.edu
KIBUI, Stephen .... 562-463-7099.. 58 M
skibui@riohondo.edu
KICKLIGHTER, Barry ...... 678-359-5680 120 D
bkicklighter@gordonstate.edu
KIDD, Anessa .... 334-876-9286.... 2 D
anessa.kidd@wccs.edu
KIDD, Beth Ann .... 903-675-6223 451 C
bkidd@tvcc.edu
KIDD, Jimmy .... 502-213-2446 181 H
jimmy.kidd@kctcs.edu
KIDD, Kevin .... 508-531-1255 212 B
k1kidd@bridgew.edu
KIDD, Lisa, L .... 920-923-8115 492 D
llkidd60@marianuniversity.edu
KIDD, Nim .... 512-424-2436 445 D
nim.kidd@tdem.texas.gov
KIDD, Quentin .... 757-594-8499 465 A
qkidd@cnu.edu
KIDD, Savalas .... 937-229-2131 362 C
skidd1@udayton.edu
KIDD, Windy .... 859-280-1237 183 C
wkidd@lextheo.edu
KIDDER, Micki .... 574-631-7505 161 G
mkidder@nd.edu
KIDDER, Micki .... 574-631-6526 161 G
mkidder@nd.edu
KIDDIE, Thomas .... 304-766-3170 489 D
tkiddie@wvstateu.edu

KIM, Sungah 203-582-6570 88 F sungah.kim2@quinnipiac.edu
KIM, Sunny 562-926-1023 58 A studentdean@ptsa.edu
KIM, Sylvia 702-651-3578 270 F sylvia.kim@csn.edu
KIM, Uriah, Y 510-649-2410 44 E ukim@gtu.edu
KIM, Won Eog 703-333-5904 476 G wekim@wuv.edu
KIM, Yoomin 703-425-4143 467 B
KIM, Young 719-549-3259 82 I young.kim@pueblocc.edu
KIM, Young, D 909-623-0302 59 H
KIM, Youngbin 215-884-8942 402 E youngbin.kim@woninstitute.edu
KIM, Yumi 714-222-1110 27 I
KIM, Yun 310-453-8300 41 K yun@emperors.edu
KIM-BEASLEY, Michelle 206-296-6070 483 B kimmi@seattleu.edu
KIM-LEE, Jennifer 848-445-3912 281 B jmkim@sas.rutgers.edu
KIM-RAUCHHOLZ, Mihamm 671-734-1812 503 D mkrauchholz@piu.edu
KIM-WONG, Chong 617-373-8345 217 D
KIMATA, Stephen, A 434-924-4241 471 F sak@virginia.edu
KIMBALL, Charles 312-369-7099 136 C ckimball@colum.edu
KIMBALL, Diane 617-868-9600 210 H
KIMBALL, Robert 616-331-2240 224 D kimbalro@gvsu.edu
KIMBARK, Kris 409-933-8131 432 H kkimbark@com.edu
KIMBER, Chawne 540-458-8746 476 D ckimber@wlu.edu
KIMBERLY, Casey 708-209-3003 136 D casey.kimberly@cuchicago.edu
KIMBLE, Robert 304-473-8438 490 E kimble.r@wvwc.edu
KIMBLE, Terri 901-761-9494 418 A tdowell-kimble@concorde.edu
KIMBLE, Thomas, D 757-446-5615 465 H kimbletd@evms.edu
KIMBLE, Treina 318-342-1004 193 A landrum@ulm.edu
KIMBRIEL, William 870-508-6107 18 B wkimbriel@asumh.edu
KIMBRO, Rachel 713-348-4824 441 K rtkimbro@rice.edu
KIMBROUGH, B. J 205-652-3531 9 B bkimbrough@uwa.edu
KIMBROUGH, B.J 205-652-3421 9 B bkimbrough@uwa.edu
KIMBROUGH, Qhamora 585-340-9588 296 B qkimbrough@crcds.edu
KIMBROUGH, III, Richard, D 210-829-6012 452 D rkimbrou@uiwtx.edu
KIMBROW, Kerrie 817-202-6736 444 B kkimbrow@swau.edu
KIMBROW, Terry 501-205-8904 19 B tkimbrow@cbc.edu
KIME, Kevin 814-886-6481 390 E kkime@mtaloy.edu
KIMERY, Millard 325-649-8173 437 A mkimery@hputx.edu
KIMLER, Robert 732-224-2355 275 D rkimler@brookdalecc.edu
KIMMEL, Amy 415-565-4837 69 B kimmela@uchastings.edus.edu
KIMMEL, Kate 631-656-2145 299 G kate.kimmel@ftc.edu
KIMMEL, Rhonda 262-595-2237 495 D rhonda.kimmel@uwp.edu
KIMMELMAN, Barbara 215-951-2612 398 G barbara.kimmelman@jefferson.edu
KIMMELMAN, Scott 772-462-7760 102 E skimmelm@irsc.edu
KIMMES, Nicole 207-221-4701 197 A nkimmes@une.edu
KIMMITT, Jonathan 918-631-2743 371 C jonathan-kimmitt@utulsa.edu
KIMPEL, Susan 731-989-6698 418 H skimpel@fhu.edu
KIMPLE, Kelley, C 305-626-3794 100 B kelley.kimple@fmuniv.edu
KIMREY, Phil 205-726-2736 6 E ppkimrey@samford.edu
KIN, Amanda, E 205-853-1200 2 G akin@jeffersonstate.edu
KIN, Jen 419-559-2388 361 B jkin01@terra.edu
KINANE, Michael, G 516-876-3162 318 A kinanem@oldwestbury.edu
KINARD, Mary 205-387-0511 1 D mary.kinard@bscc.edu
KINCAID, Heather 740-374-8716 363 F hkincaid@wscc.edu
KINCAID, Jennifer 812-855-7559 156 B oie@iu.edu
KINCAID, Kristine 602-285-7562 13 H kristine.kincaid@phoenixcollege.edu
KINCANNON, Laurie 254-442-5121 431 J laurie.kincannon@cisco.edu
KINCART, Joel, B 518-276-6247 311 J kincaj@rpi.edu
KINCH, Michael 516-299-2900 304 D michael.kinch@liu.edu
KINCHEN, Thomas, A 850-263-3261 95 P takinchen@baptistcollege.edu
KINCHENS, Eulish 229-931-2249 125 C ekinchens@southgatech.edu
KIND, Gene 970-542-3248 81 M gene.kind@morgancc.edu
KIND, Jule 765-677-2980 157 F jule.kind@indwes.edu
KIND-KEPPEL, Heather, M 847-578-3431 148 B heather.kindkeppel@rosalindfranklin.edu
KINDBERG, Maria 716-338-1143 302 G mariakindberg@mail.sunyjcc.edu
KINDER, Chad, L 580-774-3790 369 I chad.kinder@swosu.edu
KINDER, Sara 317-738-8080 155 A skinder@franklincollege.edu
KINDER, Terri 419-866-0291 361 A tkinder@stautzenberger.com
KINDL, Christine 724-938-5492 394 C kindl@calu.edu
KINDLE, Darin 952-829-4680 233 H darin.kindle@bethanygu.edu
KINDLE, Derek 608-262-3770 494 D derek.kindle@wisc.edu
KINDLER, Andreas 309-677-3107 133 H akindler@bradley.edu
KINDLER, Lisa 704-406-3923 328 I lkindler@gardner-webb.edu
KINDON, Victoria 434-395-2001 467 F kindonv@longwood.edu
KINEAVY, Jacqueline 973-684-6300 279 B jkineavy@pccc.edu
KINEAVY, John 617-573-8406 218 G jkineavy@suffolk.edu
KINEL, Janine, S 860-297-2255 88 I janine.kinel@trincoll.edu
KINERNEY, Donna 240-567-8827 200 E donna.kinerney@montgomerycollege.edu
KINERSON, Sara 802-635-1258 463 B sara.kinerson@northernvermont.edu
KING, Adrienne 419-530-2299 363 B adrienne.king@utoledo.edu
KING, Albert 419-289-5959 347 H aking@ashland.edu
KING, Alexander 218-679-2860 242 E
KING, Amy 312-261-3556 145 C aking19@nl.edu
KING, Andrew 207-780-5670 196 J andrew.king@maine.edu
KING, Angela 303-914-6417 82 L
KING, Angella 859-246-6696 181 B angie.king@kctcs.edu
KING, Anne 805-289-6503 74 B aking@vcccd.edu
KING, Art 646-312-4570 292 F art.king@baruch.cuny.edu
KING, B.J 423-439-5884 418 D kingbj@etsu.edu
KING, Bayard 212-217-4020 299 C bayard_king@fitnyc.edu
KING, JR., Berkley 502-597-6960 183 A berkley.king@kysu.edu
KING, Beth 304-637-1243 486 D kinge@dewv.edu
KING, Bill, L 972-758-3880 432 I bking@collin.edu
KING, Blythe 228-896-2503 246 F blythe.king@mgccc.edu
KING, Bob 210-999-8272 451 B bob.king@trinity.edu
KING, Brian 916-568-3021 50 I kingb@losrios.edu
KING, Brian 814-866-6641 387 C bking@lecom.edu
KING, Bruce 630-617-3407 137 E bruce.king@elmhurst.edu
KING, Bruce 510-215-4853 40 G bking@contracosta.edu
KING, Carolee 409-772-1904 456 B caaking@utmb.edu
KING, Caroline 941-907-2262 99 C caking@evergladesuniversity.edu
KING, Charles 501-370-5392 21 A cking@philander.edu
KING, Chris, A 412-397-4913 396 E kingc@rmu.edu
KING, Corey 920-465-2511 494 F kingc@uwgb.edu
KING, Corinna 515-263-2802 166 C cking@grandview.edu
KING, Craig 212-870-1238 309 C cking@nyts.edu
KING, Curt 978-542-6446 213 B curt.king@salemstate.edu
KING, Dan 218-679-2860 242 E
KING, Dana 309-694-5512 138 I dana.king@icc.edu
KING, Dana 706-622-5006 125 A dcking@shorter.edu
KING, Daniel 570-585-9208 381 A dking@clarkssummitu.edu
KING, Daniel, P 334-844-4810 4 E dpk0002@auburn.edu
KING, Darin 701-777-4237 344 G darin.r.king@ndus.edu
KING, David 301-447-6122 201 A king@msmary.edu
KING, David, S 252-334-2084 331 C david.king@macuniversity.edu
KING, Deborah 870-338-6474 23 A
KING, Del 404-727-7567 118 D dking2@emory.edu
KING, Denise 606-886-4755 181 A dking0024@kctcs.edu
KING, Dennis 785-628-4276 173 E dking@fhsu.edu
KING, Dianne 864-231-2000 405 F ldking@andersonuniversity.edu
KING, Dottie 812-535-5296 160 E president@smwc.edu
KING, Elizabeth, H 316-978-3510 178 B elizabeth.king@wichita.edu
KING, Elle 336-249-8186 333 G elle_king@davidsondavie.edu
KING, Emily 702-651-7511 270 F emily.king@csn.edu
KING, Emily 540-458-8700 476 D eking@wlu.edu
KING, Eric 972-524-3341 444 E eric.king@swcc.edu
KING, Evelyn 205-366-8851 7 A eking@stillman.edu
KING, JR., Frank, C 218-477-4000 239 A frank.king@mnstate.edu
KING, Fred, L 304-293-3449 489 E fred.king@mail.wvu.edu
KING, Garrett 580-774-3267 369 I garrett.king@swosu.edu
KING, Gillian, M 315-859-4105 300 F gking@hamilton.edu
KING, Glenn 334-876-9420 2 D glenn.king@wccs.edu
KING, Greg 309-556-3248 140 E gking@iwu.edu
KING, Greg 423-236-2975 422 H gking@southern.edu
KING, Gregory 330-823-2282 362 E kinggl@mountunion.edu
KING, Herbert, L 828-898-8785 330 A kingl@lmc.edu
KING, Jason 850-484-1337 105 G jking@pensacolastate.edu
KING, Jason 512-499-4465 454 A jking@utsystem.edu
KING, Jeff 630-892-6431 133 A jking@aurora.edu
KING, Jeff 615-230-3461 424 F jeff.king@volstate.edu
KING, Jerry 903-675-6211 451 C jking@tvcc.edu
KING, Jody 718-522-9073 290 B
KING, Joel 308-398-7315 265 C joelking@cccneb.edu
KING, John 806-720-7211 438 F john.king@lcu.edu
KING, John 541-552-6261 376 A kingjo@sou.edu
KING, John, E 832-813-6663 438 E john.e.king@lonestar.edu
KING, John, J 401-254-3093 404 C jjking@rwu.edu
KING, Jovanna, J 864-656-0663 406 F jovanna@clemson.edu
KING, Julie 803-786-3650 407 E juking@columbiasc.edu
KING, Jyne 708-239-4770 150 H jyne.king@trnty.edu
KING, Karen 828-898-3446 330 A kingk@lmc.edu
KING, Karen, D 423-439-5654 418 D kingk@etsu.edu
KING, Katherine 949-480-4161 64 E kking@soka.edu
KING, Kathryn 859-985-3924 179 E kingk2@berea.edu
KING, Kelvin 334-844-8888 4 E kfk0014@auburn.edu
KING, Kevin 760-384-6367 47 C kevin.king@cerrocoso.edu
KING, Khristian, J 716-673-3398 316 A khristian.king@fredonia.edu
KING, Kimberly 239-280-2484 95 M kimberly.king@avemaria.edu
KING, Kristie 731-661-5202 425 F kking@uu.edu
KING, Kristine 360-923-8724 482 D kking@stmartin.edu
KING, Kwanna 307-766-5272 500 H regirtrar@uwyo.edu
KING, Laura 715-232-2857 496 C kingla@uwstout.edu
KING, Leslie 770-426-2713 122 A lesliek@life.edu
KING, Leslie 718-518-4377 293 F lking@hostos.cuny.edu
KING, Linda 903-886-5013 446 D linda.king@tamuc.edu
KING, Linda 252-493-7220 336 E lking@email.pittcc.edu
KING, Makini 816-235-1727 260 D kingml@umkc.edu
KING, Marsha, M 260-399-7700 162 A mking@sf.edu
KING, Mary 940-552-6291 456 F mking@vernoncollege.edu
KING, Meade, B 540-464-7287 475 C mking@vmiaa.org
KING, Meredith 508-793-7739 207 F meking@clarku.edu
KING, Michael 913-360-7633 171 G mking@benedictine.edu
KING, Mike 812-535-5273 160 E mking2@smwc.edu
KING, Mikki 567-268-6022 361 C kingmr@tiffin.edu
KING, Mindy 715-346-2321 496 B mking@uwsp.edu
KING, Natalie 831-582-3609 32 D nmking@csumb.edu
KING, Natasha 912-287-5827 117 B nking@coastalpines.edu
KING, Nathan 828-669-8012 331 H nathan.king@montreat.edu
KING, Nathaniel 702-992-2806 270 H nathaniel.king@nsc.edu
KING, Nina, E 919-684-2431 328 D nina.king@duke.edu
KING, Paula Kay 765-973-8331 156 D pkayking@iue.edu
KING, Peter, D 843-661-1286 408 H pking@fmarion.edu
KING, Phillip 206-546-4651 483 C pking@shoreline.edu
KING, Phyllis 561-803-2807 105 B phyllis_king@pba.edu
KING, Phyllis 414-229-6175 495 B pking@uwm.edu
KING, Piper 505-438-8884 287 J cfo@acupuncturecollege.edu
KING, Queen 661-654-2251 30 C qking@csub.edu
KING, Robert 773-995-2002 134 J rking31@csu.edu
KING, Robert 810-762-3000 231 C rwking@umich.edu
KING, Robert 724-738-2199 394 E robert.king@sru.edu

KIRKPATRICK, Lisa, L ... 512-448-8408 441 N
lisak@stedwards.edu
KIRKPATRICK, Mac ... 864-338-8090 409 B
mkirkpatrick@lander.edu
KIRKPATRICK, Michael . 800-895-7411 463 H
mkirkpatrick@asl.edu
KIRKPATRICK, Ron ... 951-571-6100.. 59 B
KIRKSEY, Jason ... 405-744-9154 367 G
jason.kirksey@okstate.edu
KIRKSEY, Matthew ... 330-494-6170 360 I
mkirksey@starkstate.edu
KIRKWOOD,
William, G ... 423-439-4210 418 D
kirkwood@etsu.edu
KIRLEIS, Kathleen ... 617-287-5100 211 E
kathleen.kirleis@umb.edu
KIRMER, Lisa ... 620-343-4600 173 D
lkirmer@fhtc.edu
KIRMSE, David ... 415-422-2057.. 72 I
dkirmse@usfca.edu
KIRNBAUER, Thomas ... 718-862-7312 304 K
tkirnbauer@manhattan.edu
KIRON, Gopu ... 570-504-7929 387 A
kirong@lackawanna.edu
KIRSCH, Breanne ... 712-279-5451 163 H
breanne.kirsch@briarcliff.edu
KIRSCH, OSB, Myron ... 724-805-2111 397 C
myron.kirsch@email.stvincent.edu
KIRSCH, OSB, Myron ... 724-805-2111 397 D
myron.kirsch@stvincent.edu
KIRSCH, Nicole ... 605-642-6111 415 F
nicole.kirsch@bhsu.edu
KIRSCH, Ramona, R ... 540-362-6214 467 A
kirschrr@hollins.edu
KIRSCHBAUM, Steven ... 563-588-6326 164 C
steven.kirschbaum@clarke.edu
KIRSCHEN, Alyse ... 714-449-7835.. 51 D
akirschen@ketchum.edu
KIRSCHLING, Jane, M .. 410-706-6741 202 F
kirschling@son.umaryland.edu
KIRSCHMANN, Anne ... 414-847-3238 493 C
annekirschmann@miad.edu
KIRSCHNER, Kelly ... 727-864-8880.. 98 G
kirschkm@eckerd.edu
KIRST, Thomas ... 541-485-1780 374 C
thomaskirst@newhope.edu
KIRSTEN, Jan ... 732-255-0400 279 A
jkirsten@ocean.edu
KIRTLEY, Adam, M ... 509-522-4449 485 C
kirtleam@whitman.edu
KIRTMAN, Janet ... 212-346-1700 310 F
jkirtman@pace.edu
KIRTMAN, Lisa ... 657-278-5901.. 31 E
lkirtman@fullerton.edu
KIRVES, Carol ... 270-707-3751 181 G
carol.kirves@kctcs.edu
KIRWAN, Kristin ... 413-594-2761 208 B
kirwank@elms.edu
KIRWIN, Luanne ... 617-373-2520 217 D
KIS, Daphne ... 504-662-1946 193 B
KISCADEN, Elizabeth, J 402-280-2700 265 J
elizabethkiscaden@creighton.edu
KISER, Joe ... 276-328-0143 471 G
jbk5b@uvawise.edu
KISER, Liz ... 252-399-6453 326 H
epkiser@barton.edu
KISER, Rus ... 701-483-2340 345 A
rus.kiser@dickinsonstate.edu
KISH, Anne ... 406-683-7492 263 E
anne.kish@umwestern.edu
KISH, Joy ... 828-689-1140 330 H
jkish@mhu.edu
KISH, Kelley ... 704-233-8194 344 E
k.kish@wingate.edu
KISH, Kelly ... 858-822-4382.. 70 C
kkish@ucsd.edu
KISH-JOHANSEN, Deb .. 813-253-7860 102 A
dkishjohansen@hccfl.edu
KISHBAUGH, Tara ... 540-432-4665 465 F
dean-sean@emu.edu
KISHEN, Ron ... 215-895-8800 400 B
KISHIDA, Katsumi ... 908-737-0349 277 F
kkishida@kean.edu
KISHPAUGH, Jason ... 423-869-6277 420 A
jason.kishpaugh@lmunet.edu
KISHPAUGH, Melva ... 540-654-1084 471 B
mkishpau@umw.edu
KISLER, Jeffrey ... 215-717-6420 399 I
jkisler@uarts.edu
KISLOSKI, Roger ... 903-463-8777 435 H
kisloskir@grayson.edu
KISONGO, Ibuchwa ... 763-424-0806 239 D
ikisongo@nhcc.edu

KISPERT, Craig ... 623-233-7547 176 F
craig.kispert@ottawa.edu
KISS, Boglarka ... 805-289-6232.. 74 B
bkiss@vcccd.edu
KISS, John, Z ... 336-334-5241 342 D
jzkiss@uncg.edu
KISS, Michelle ... 562-951-4700.. 29 J
mkiss@calstate.edu
KISSEBERTH, Sara ... 419-358-3484 348 E
kisseberths@bluffton.edu
KISSEL, Chuck ... 657-278-4101.. 31 E
ckissel@fullerton.edu
KISSINGER, Sue ... 715-346-3361 496 B
skissing@uwsp.edu
KISSLER, Lance ... 509-359-4257 478 H
lkissler@ewu.edu
KISSLING, Catherine ... 847-574-5224 141 G
ckissling@lfgsm.edu
KIST, Emily ... 517-265-5161 220 D
ekist@adrian.edu
KIST-KLINE, Gail, E ... 513-585-1414 350 A
gail.kistkline@thechristcollege.edu
KISTLER, Eric ... 843-863-7933 406 C
ekistler@csuniv.edu
KISTNER, Frances ... 508-373-5749 216 B
frances.kistner@mcphs.edu
KISTNER, Janet ... 850-644-6876 110 B
jkistner@fsu.edu
KISTNER, Warren ... 309-556-3237 140 E
wkistner@iwu.edu
KISTULENTZ, Steven ... 352-588-7218 107 B
steven.kistulentz@saintleo.edu
KISUNZU, Cheryl ... 301-891-4000 204 D
ckisunzu@wau.edu
KIT, Stephanie ... 865-974-5435 426 C
smkit@utk.edu
KITALONG,
Christopher, U ... 680-488-2746 504 A
ckitalong@gmail.com
KITAS, Chris ... 724-357-4077 393 G
ckitas@iup.edu
KITCH, Rhonda, K ... 607-255-3203 297 D
registrar@cornell.edu
KITCHEN, Augusta ... 803-780-1159 413 B
akitchen@voorhees.edu
KITCHEN, David ... 281-283-2255 452 A
kitchen@uhcl.edu
KITCHEN, Todd ... 216-987-2004 351 D
KITCHENS, Caroline ... 479-968-0242.. 18 E
ckitchens@atu.edu
KITCHENS, Joann ... 701-662-1502 346 A
joann.kitchens@lrsc.edu
KITCHENS, Penny ... 478-553-2060 123 D
pkitchens@oftc.edu
KITCHIN, Steven, H ... 401-739-5000 403 F
skitchin@neit.edu
KITCHINGS, Maribeth ... 601-974-1002 246 C
kitchme@millsaps.edu
KITE, Brian ... 310-825-7891.. 69 D
bkite@tft.ucla.edu
KITE, Eddie ... 903-675-6359 451 C
eddie.kite@tvcc.edu
KITE, Michelle ... 269-782-1302 230 D
mkite@swmich.edu
KITE, Terry ... 636-481-3273 253 G
tkite@jeffco.edu
KITHAKYE, Mumbe ... 405-744-7979 367 G
mumbe.kithakye@okstate.edu
KITHCART, Jane ... 845-687-5111 322 K
kithcarj@sunyulster.edu
KITHCART, Shawn ... 617-849-8814 210 H
KITLEY, Barry, S ... 336-841-9363 329 E
bkitley@highpoint.edu
KITTEL, Jane ... 262-691-5214 499 A
jkittel@wctc.edu
KITTELSON, Laura ... 763-576-4039 237 A
laura.kittelson@anokatech.edu
KITTLE, Daniel ... 605-995-2601 414 A
dan.kittle@dwu.edu
KITTNER, Missy ... 254-299-8514 438 G
mkittner@mclennan.edu
KITTREDGE, Cynthia, B . 512-472-4133 442 H
cynthia.kittredge@ssw.edu
KITTRELL-MIKELL,
Deborah ... 478-289-2368 118 B
dkittrell@ega.edu
KITTS, Kenneth, D ... 256-765-4211.... 8 E
kkitts@una.edu
KITTS, Tristin ... 540-857-6323 475 A
tkitts@virginiawestern.edu
KITZINGER, Denis ... 603-880-8308 273 F
dkitzinger@thomasmorecollege.edu

KITZINGER, Sara ... 603-566-5017 273 F
skitzinger@thomasmorecollege.edu
KIWUS, Christopher ... 540-231-6291 475 D
chkiwus@vt.edu
KIYAR, Baris ... 812-855-6413 156 B
bkiyar@iu.edu
KIZART, ClauDean ... 757-822-1074 474 G
ckizart@tcc.edu
KJELLEREN, Donald, J .. 413-597-2312 220 A
dfk1@williams.edu
KLAAS, Brian ... 816-235-1333 260 D
klaasb@umkc.edu
KLAAS, Daniel ... 770-689-4965 114 J
dklass@aii.edu
KLAASSEN, Sara ... 816-322-0110 250 E
sara.klaassen@calvary.edu
KLABE, Kimberly, S ... 301-447-5377 201 A
klabe@msmary.edu
KLAEHN, Scott ... 651-450-3462 237 H
sklaehn@inverhills.edu
KLAFFKE, David ... 360-383-3016 485 B
dklaffke@whatcom.edu
KLAHR, Sabine, C ... 801-587-8888 459 D
s.klahr@utah.edu
KLANDERUD, Jessica ... 859-985-3783 179 E
klanderudj@berea.edu
KLANG, Becca ... 406-377-9401 262 G
bklang@dawson.edu
KLAPER, Rebecca ... 414-382-1713 495 B
rklaper@uwm.edu
KLAPPENBACK, Kirby ... 402-643-7192 265 I
kirby.klappenback@cune.edu
KLARE, Diana, G ... 719-333-2180 502 C
diane.klare@afacademy.af.edu
KLASEK, Angie ... 402-466-4774 266 A
angie.klasek@doane.edu
KLASEN, James ... 617-588-1344 206 B
jklasen@bfit.edu
KLASKOW, Sam ... 810-762-7870 225 F
sklaskow@kettering.edu
KLATT, Ed ... 248-476-1122 227 B
eklatt@msp.edu
KLATT, Lori ... 360-867-5185 479 C
klattl@evergreen.edu
KLATT, Sara ... 712-274-6400 170 H
sara.klatt@witcc.edu
KLAUBER, SR.,
James, S ... 240-500-2233 199 A
jklauber@hagerstowncc.edu
KLAUS, Amanda ... 732-571-3653 278 B
aklaus@monmouth.edu
KLAUS, Chad, L ... 609-258-5498 279 E
klaus@princeton.edu
KLAUS, Courtney ... 785-242-5200 176 F
courtney.klaus@ottawa.edu
KLAUS, Larry, S ... 989-774-3081 221 M
klaus1ls@cmich.edu
KLAUS, Sky ... 575-234-9414 287 I
skyklaus@senmc.edu
KLAUSLI, Julia ... 703-416-1441 465 E
jklausli.ips@divinemercy.edu
KLAUSMEYER, Robert ... 573-875-7304 251 A
rklausmeyer@ccis.edu
KLAVER, Lenny ... 660-359-3948 256 F
lklaver@mail.ncmissouri.edu
KLAVER, Tzipora ... 305-944-0035 114 B
KLAWE, Maria, M ... 909-921-8120.. 44 K
klawe@hmc.edu
KLAWUNN, Margaret ... 805-893-3651.. 70 E
margaret.klawunn@sa.ucsb.edu
KLEBBA, Megan ... 913-367-5340 171 G
KLEBE, Kelli ... 719-255-3779.. 84 A
kklebe@uccs.edu
KLEE-TIESMAN,
Kerry, J ... 517-750-1200 230 F
ke497810@arbor.edu
KLEEMAN, Kathryn ... 217-206-4847 151 E
kklee1@uis.edu
KLEICH, Tammie ... 308-635-6072 269 E
kleicht@wncc.edu
KLEIMAN, Adriana ... 213-615-7295.. 36 G
akleiman@thechicagoschool.edu
KLEIN, Andrew ... 317-274-4417 156 C
chancllr@iupui.edu
KLEIN, Andrew, R ... 317-274-5555 157 B
anrklein@iupui.edu
KLEIN, Barb ... 641-648-4611 167 D
barb.klein@iavalley.edu
KLEIN, Barbara ... 641-844-8502 167 C
barb.klein@iavalley.edu
KLEIN, Bart ... 816-501-4780 257 K
bart.klein@rockhurst.edu

KLEIN, Cynthia ... 412-809-5100 395 F
klein.cynthia@ptcollege.edu
KLEIN, Daniel ... 617-559-8637 210 C
dklein@hebrewcollege.edu
KLEIN, David ... 818-333-3558.. 53 J
david@nyfa.edu
KLEIN, Deborah ... 805-553-4013.. 73 I
dklein@vcccd.edu
KLEIN, Erick, P ... 651-631-5141 243 E
epklein@unwsp.edu
KLEIN, Erin ... 701-252-3467 346 J
eklein@uj.edu
KLEIN, Gary ... 507-457-1489 242 H
gklein@smumn.edu
KLEIN, Janette ... 660-543-4159 259 K
jklein@ucmo.edu
KLEIN, Jill ... 909-621-8129.. 57 E
pitzerpresident@pitzer.edu
KLEIN, Jim ... 502-456-6508 184 F
jklein@sullivan.edu
KLEIN, Jude ... 518-580-5819 315 A
jsklein@skidmore.edu
KLEIN, June ... 650-433-3849.. 55 K
jklein@paloaltou.edu
KLEIN, Kenneth, S ... 619-239-0391.. 34 H
kklein@cwsl.edu
KLEIN, Kim ... 717-477-1604 394 D
kmklei@ship.edu
KLEIN, Leslie, G ... 410-358-3144 204 F
KLEIN, Lori ... 907-796-6540.. 10 C
laklein@alaska.edu
KLEIN, Lori ... 907-796-6057.. 10 C
laklein@alaska.edu
KLEIN, Mendel ... 718-384-5460 325 I
KLEIN, Michael ... 215-204-1927 398 D
mike.klein@temple.edu
KLEIN, Michelle, W ... 504-866-7426 190 E
finance@nds.edu
KLEIN, Nate ... 319-363-1323 168 D
nklein@mtmercy.edu
KLEIN, Patti ... 651-523-2421 235 F
pklein01@hamline.edu
KLEIN, Peg ... 401-841-3665 501 L
margaret.klein@usnwc.edu
KLEIN, Phil ... 304-214-8967 487 J
pklein@wvncc.edu
KLEIN, Sara ... 201-216-3543 282 L
sara.klein@stevens.edu
KLEIN, Steve ... 503-352-2822 375 B
kleinsk@pacificu.edu
KLEIN, Terry ... 715-645-7048 498 G
terry.klein@northwoodtech.edu
KLEIN-WILLIAMS,
Marcella ... 805-678-5262.. 74 A
mkleinwilliams@vcccd.edu
KLEINE, Patricia, A ... 715-836-2320 494 E
kleinepa@uwec.edu
KLEINE, Todd ... 708-524-6570 137 A
tdkleine@dom.edu
KLEINER, Zev ... 347-394-1036 291 B
zkleiner@ateret.net
KLEINHEKSEL, Scott ... 509-527-5968 485 C
kleinhsc@whitman.edu
KLEINJAN, Barb ... 605-882-5284 414 D
barb.kleinjan@lakeareatech.edu
KLEINJAN, Brent ... 701-255-3285 346 I
bkleinjan@uttc.edu
KLEINKAUFMAN, Dovid 718-327-7600 325 A
info@yofr.org
KLEINMAN, Daniel, L ... 617-353-2230 207 C
dlklein@bu.edu
KLEINMAN, Kent ... 401-454-6406 404 B
kkleinman@risd.edu
KLEINSCHMIDT, Robert . 609-586-4800 277 H
kleinscr@mccc.edu
KLEINSMITH, Warren ... 609-626-3532 283 A
warren.kleinsmith@stockton.edu
KLEISER, Richele ... 559-325-3600.. 28 F
rkleiser@chsu.edu
KLEITSCH, II, Andrew ... 919-536-7200 334 A
kleistcha@durhamtech.edu
KLEMANN, Jim ... 406-657-1124 264 G
james.klemann@rocky.edu
KLEMANN, Jim ... 701-252-3467 346 J
jklemann@uj.edu
KLEMANN, M. Adam ... 330-471-8308 355 D
aklemann@malone.edu
KLEMENS, Kristina ... 262-595-2004 495 D
klemens@uwp.edu
KLEMIUK, Christy ... 817-515-6960 445 A
christy.klemiuk@tccd.edu
KLEMM, Aaron ... 909-869-3047.. 30 B
amklemm@cpp.edu

KLEN, Joseph, R ... 765-361-6052 162 G
klenj@wabash.edu
KLENKLEN, Andy ... 202-885-8696.. 94 D
aklenklen@wesleyseminary.edu
KLENZ, Jackie, L ... 414-410-4222 490 J
jlklenz@stritch.edu
KLEPARSKI, Tracy ... 217-351-2206 146 G
tkleparski@parkland.edu
KLEPETAR, Adam ... 413-236-2140 213 E
aklepetar@berkshirecc.edu
KLEPFER, Jennifer ... 352-854-2322.. 97 L
klepferj@cf.edu
KLEPONIS, Catherine ... 610-436-2695 394 F
ckleponis@wcupa.edu
KLEPONIS, Stephen ... 610-526-6017 385 F
skleponis@harcum.edu
KLEPPER, Scott ... 405-789-7661 369 H
scott.klepper@swcu.edu
KLESENSKI-RISPOLI,
Deborah ... 212-217-4045 299 C
deborah_klesenski@fitnyc.edu
KLESENSKI-RISPOLI,
Deborah ... 212-217-4040 299 C
deborah_klesenski@fitnyc.edu
KLESS, Teresa, M ... 401-825-2003 403 D
tkless@ccri.edu
KLETT, Breanna, M ... 562-903-4751.. 27 E
breanna.m.klett@biola.edu
KLETTNER, Kurt ... 304-424-8000 490 A
kurt.klettner@wvup.edu
KLETZER, Lori ... 831-459-3885.. 71 A
cpevc@ucsc.edu
KLEVENO, Robert ... 951-222-8000.. 59 D
robert.kleveno@rcc.edu
KLEVER, Mark ... 530-938-5927.. 39 D
mklever@siskiyous.edu
KLEWICKI, Lisa ... 703-416-1441 465 E
lklewicki.ips@divinemercy.edu
KLEYN, Henk ... 616-432-3400 229 H
henk.kleyn@prts.edu
KLIEGER, Claire ... 610-328-8352 398 B
career@swarthmore.edu
KLIER, John ... 405-325-2621 370 J
klier@ou.edu
KLIETHERMES, Aaron ... 573-897-5000 259 E
KLIEVER, Amanda ... 541-917-4204 373 F
klievea@linnbenton.edu
KLIEWER, Jan ... 580-774-3084 369 I
jan.kliewer@swosu.edu
KLIEWER, Miriam ... 620-947-3121 177 F
miriamkliewer@tabor.edu
KLIEWER, Ray ... 509-313-6827 479 E
kliewer@gonzaga.edu
KLIEWER, Wayne ... 620-947-3121 177 F
waynekliewer@tabor.edu
KLIGMAN, Linda ... 610-807-9221 386 B
lindakligman@iirp.edu
KLIGMAN, Linda, B ... 267-975-2254 386 B
lindakligman@iirp.edu
KLIM, Karin ... 609-896-5167 280 D
kklim@rider.edu
KLIMCZYK, Karen ... 219-464-5015 162 C
karen.klimczyk@valpo.edu
KLIMKEWICZ, Patricia ... 518-629-7887 302 A
p.klimkewicz@hvcc.edu
KLIMKOWSKI,
Ann Francis ... 419-885-3211 355 C
aklimkowski@lourdes.edu
KLIMOFF, Dodi ... 215-635-7300 384 D
dklimoff@gratz.edu
KLIMPT, Kelly ... 281-756-3539 428 E
kklimpt@alvincollege.edu
KLIN, Celia ... 607-777-2145 315 E
cklin@binghamton.edu
KLINE, Amy ... 570-674-6330 389 H
akline@misericordia.edu
KLINE, Chad ... 731-286-3259 423 E
kline@dscc.edu
KLINE, Christina ... 971-722-4607 375 C
christina.kline@pcc.edu
KLINE, Christopher ... 815-838-0500 142 C
klinech@lewisu.edu
KLINE, David ... 651-846-1703 240 E
david.kline@saintpaul.edu
KLINE, Elizabeth ... 740-588-4116 364 H
ekline@zanestate.edu
KLINE, John ... 714-816-0366.. 68 G
john.kline@trident.edu
KLINE, John ... 847-585-2014.. 10 F
jkline@aiuniv.edu
KLINE, Kenneth ... 315-268-6689 295 E
kjkline@clarkson.edu
KLINE, Kevin ... 419-755-4521 357 B
kkline@ncstatecollege.edu
KLINE, Laura ... 610-921-7293 377 F
lckline@albright.edu
KLINE, Loni, N ... 570-326-3761 392 S
lnk6@pct.edu
KLINE, Richard ... 440-375-7512 354 K
rkline@lec.edu
KLINE, Thomas ... 262-551-6036 491 B
tkline@carthage.edu
KLINEDINST, Robert ... 301-696-3611 199 C
klinedinst@hood.edu
KLINEPETER, Pamela ... 606-326-2254 180 I
pamela.klinepeter@kctcs.edu
KLING, Rory ... 785-890-3641 176 E
rory.kling@nwktc.edu
KLINGELE, Nora ... 217-228-5432 147 C
n.klingele29@quincy.edu
KLINGEMANN, John ... 325-942-2162 450 B
john.klingemann@angelo.edu
KLINGENBERG, Erin ... 701-845-7300 345 E
erin.klingenberg@vcsu.edu
KLINGENSMITH, Dan ... 865-981-8278 420 C
dan.klingensmith@maryvillecollege.edu
KLINGER, Donna, J ... 301-447-5657 201 A
d.j.klinger@msmary.edu
KLINGER, Joe ... 708-456-0300 151 A
joeklinger@triton.edu
KLINGER, John ... 314-505-7384 251 D
klingerj@csl.edu
KLINGER-KANTOR, Lisa 914-893-4028 288 K
lklingerkantor@ajr.edu
KLINGLER, Samantha ... 309-298-2457 152 I
sj-klingler@wiu.edu
KLINGSHIRN, Connie ... 419-267-1329 357 E
cklingshirn@northweststate.edu
KLINKENBERG, Laurel ... 217-641-4500 140 H
lklinkenberg@jwcc.edu
KLINKHAMMER,
Barbara ... 215-951-2899 398 G
barbara.klinkhammer@jefferson.edu
KLINKHAMMER,
Nathan ... 503-725-3000 375 D
KLIPFEL, India ... 605-225-1634 414 I
india.klipfel@presentation.edu
KLIPPENSTEIN,
Stacy, S ... 928-757-0800.. 14 H
sklippenstein@mohave.edu
KLOBERDANZ, Jennifer 815-280-2414 140 I
jkloberd@jjc.edu
KLOBERDANZ, Mark ... 515-271-4526 165 F
mark.kloberdanz@drake.edu
KLOBY, Kathryn ... 320-308-3151 240 C
kathryn.kloby@stcloudstate.edu
KLOCEK, David ... 276-376-3445 471 G
dmk8e@uvawise.edu
KLOCEK, Juliana ... 952-830-3868 241 R
juliana.klocek@rasmussen.edu
KLOCKE, Astrid ... 928-523-6235.. 14 J
astrid.klocke@nau.edu
KLOCKO, Tim ... 816-942-8400 249 H
tim.klocko@avila.edu
KLOEPPEL, Brian ... 828-227-7398 343 D
bkloeppel@wcu.edu
KLOFT, Craig ... 563-589-3251 170 C
ckloft@dbq.edu
KLOKE, Rafeeka ... 360-383-3330 485 B
rkloke@whatcom.edu
KLOMMHAUS, Kylee ... 641-782-1455 170 B
klommhaus@swcciowa.edu
KLONOFF, Elizabeth ... 407-823-5538 110 D
elizabeth.klonoff@ucf.edu
KLONOSKI, Edward ... 860-515-3888.. 85 D
eklonoski@charteroak.edu
KLOOS, Lori ... 320-308-5017 240 D
lkloos@sctcc.edu
KLOS, Laura ... 314-367-8700 260 A
laura.klos@uhsp.edu
KLOS, Ryan ... 815-455-8562 143 F
rklos@mchenry.edu
KLOSS, Michelle ... 410-386-8411 197 G
mkloss@carrollcc.edu
KLOSTERMANN, Jill ... 618-545-3081 141 C
jklostermann@kaskaskia.edu
KLOSTERMEYER,
William ... 904-620-1327 111 A
wkloster@unf.edu
KLOTMAN, Mary, E ... 919-684-2455 328 D
mary.klotman@duke.edu
KLOTMAN, Paul ... 713-798-4800 430 E
president@bcm.edu
KLOTZ, Ann Marie ... 303-444-0202.. 81 N
KLOTZ, Joy ... 213-252-5100.. 24 C
joy.klotz@faculty.alu.edu
KLOTZ, Kristen ... 520-621-9181.. 16 H
kbklotz@arizona.edu
KLOTZBACH, Daniel, P . 773-298-3019 148 I
klotzbach@sxu.edu
KLOTZBIER, Ed ... 209-201-6693.. 70 A
eklotzbier@ucmerced.edu
KLUCINEC, John ... 603-456-2656 273 A
jklucinec@magdalen.edu
KLUCK, Annette ... 662-915-7474 248 F
askluck@olemiss.edu
KLUCKING, Joel ... 509-963-2323 477 G
joel.klucking@cwu.edu
KLUG, Jane ... 605-642-6080 415 F
jane.klug@bhsu.edu
KLUG, Theodore, A ... 507-354-8221 236 D
klugta@mlc-wels.edu
KLUGE, Cindy ... 414-229-4586 495 B
ckluge@uwm.edu
KLUIN, Richard ... 605-367-5692 416 B
rich.kluin@southeasttech.edu
KLUNDT, Matthew ... 319-385-6262 167 F
matt.klundt@iw.edu
KLUTTZ, Kelly ... 704-216-3779 337 C
kelly.kluttz@rccc.edu
KLUTTZ-LEACH,
Camille ... 617-373-7433 217 D
KLUVER, Erica, L ... 515-263-2816 166 C
ekluver@grandview.edu
KLUVER, Kirk, R ... 319-335-2516 163 F
kirk-kluver@uiowa.edu
KLYMENKO, Anthony ... 201-559-6100 277 A
klymenkoa@felician.edu
KLYMENKO, Priscilla ... 201-559-6037 277 A
klymenkop@felician.edu
KLYN, Jeremy ... 708-239-4854 150 H
jeremy.klyn@trnty.edu
KLYN DE NOVELO,
Jessica ... 641-628-7600 164 B
klynj@central.edu
KLYNE, Dov ... 718-774-5050 321 G
dklyne@optonline.net
KMIECH, Joseph ... 715-425-3658 496 A
joseph.kmiech@uwrf.edu
KNAAPEN, Laura ... 920-424-2368 495 C
knaapen@uwosh.edu
KNAB, Drew ... 414-229-3494 495 B
knab@uwm.edu
KNABE, Alexis ... 907-474-2600.. 10 B
asknabe@alaska.edu
KNABE, Alexis ... 907-474-6533.. 10 B
asknabe@alaska.edu
KNAFF, Mary ... 423-697-3371 423 B
mary.knaff@chattanoogastate.edu
KNAP, Andrew ... 630-617-5682 137 E
andrew.knap@elmhurst.edu
KNAPE, Beth ... 409-839-2054 449 A
bknape1@lit.edu
KNAPP, Brian, R ... 517-750-1200 230 F
bknapp@arbor.edu
KNAPP, IV, Clair, W ... 260-982-5245 158W
cwknapp@manchester.edu
KNAPP, Corinne ... 530-898-6325.. 31 A
clknapp@csuchico.edu
KNAPP, David ... 360-383-3000 485 B
KNAPP, Jake ... 916-568-3101.. 50 I
knappj@losrios.edu
KNAPP, Jeffrey ... 518-458-5374 296 E
knappj@strose.edu
KNAPP, Jennifer ... 315-312-2285 318 B
jennifer.knapp@oswego.edu
KNAPP, Jennifer ... 615-353-3117 424 A
jennifer.knapp@nscc.edu
KNAPP, John ... 724-503-1001 401 D
jknapp@washjeff.edu
KNAPP, Katherine ... 713-221-5055 452 B
knappk@uhd.edu
KNAPP, Kenyon ... 434-582-2697 467 E
kcknapp@liberty.edu
KNAPPER, William ... 308-635-6002 269 E
knapperw@wncc.edu
KNAPSACK, Bailey ... 607-735-1773 298 G
bknapsack17@elmira.edu
KNARESBORO, Laura ... 928-317-6000.. 11 B
laura.knaresboro@azwestern.edu
KNARR, Rob ... 513-936-1724 362 A
robert.knarr@uc.edu
KNAUER, Cheryl ... 410-857-2294 200 D
cknauer@mcdaniel.edu
KNAUS, Kathy ... 720-890-8922.. 81 H
financial@itea.edu
KNAUS, Kelli ... 440-646-8316 363 C
kknaus@ursuline.edu
KNAUSS, Hollie ... 610-282-1100 382 A
hollie.knauss@desales.edu
KNAUSS, Tina ... 712-325-3230 167 G
tknauss@iwcc.edu
KNAUTZ, Arcetta ... 414-251-5203 495 B
knautz@uwm.edu
KNEALING, Todd ... 712-279-5402 163 H
todd.knealing@briarcliff.edu
KNEAS, Kristi, A ... 717-361-1555 383 B
kneask@etown.edu
KNECHT, Doug ... 212-875-4400 290 F
dknecht@bankstreet.edu
KNECHT, Mike ... 270-831-9625 181 F
mike.knecht@kctcs.edu
KNEDLER, Jacque ... 402-280-2166 265 J
jacqueknedler@creighton.edu
KNEEBONE, Elaine ... 870-230-5820.. 19 H
kneebone@hsu.edu
KNEELAND, Ben ... 585-594-6140 311 L
kneeland_benjamin@roberts.edu
KNEESKERN, Scott ... 419-334-8400 361 B
KNELLY, Kennith ... 518-564-3622 318 C
kknel001@plattsburgh.edu
KNEPFLE, Chuck ... 503-725-5249 375 D
knepfle@pdx.edu
KNEPP, M. Dustin ... 936-468-2066 444 H
mdknepp@sfasu.edu
KNEPP, Marcia ... 301-387-3056 198 F
marcia.knepp@garrettcollege.edu
KNEPPE, Janiece ... 303-914-6553.. 82 L
janiece.kneppe@rrcc.edu
KNEPPER, Karla ... 937-512-4561 360 F
karla.knepper@sinclair.edu
KNERR, Amanda ... 812-237-3993 155 H
amanda.knerr@indstate.edu
KNERR, Amanda, R ... 765-285-8011 153 E
amanda.knerr@bsu.edu
KNERR, Christopher ... 413-565-1000 205 I
cknerr@baypath.edu
KNERR, Douglas ... 810-762-3234 231 C
dknerr@umich.edu
KNESER, Greg ... 319-352-8443 170 F
greg.kneser@wartburg.edu
KNESER, Greg ... 419-824-3759 355 C
gkneser@lourdes.edu
KNETL, Brian ... 616-234-4000 224 C
KNETSCHE, Kelly ... 859-238-5500 179 H
kelly.knetsche@centre.edu
KNETTER, Michael, M ... 608-265-9953 494 D
mike.knetter@supportuw.org
KNEUPPER, Julie ... 210-431-6584 440 D
jkneupper@ollusa.edu
KNICELEY, Allen ... 704-669-4037 333 C
kniceleya@clevelandcc.edu
KNIERIM, Maria-Louisa 314-529-9330 254 D
mknierim@maryville.edu
KNIEWEL, Marla ... 402-354-7036 267 E
marla.kniewel@methodistcollege.edu
KNIFE, Christopher ... 352-873-5808.. 97 L
knifec@cf.edu
KNIFFEN, Robyn ... 402-399-2435 265 H
rkniffen@csm.edu
KNIFFIN, Mary ... 513-745-4275 364 F
kniffinm@xavier.edu
KNIGGE, Dalynn ... 732-412-7397 281 A
knigge@rutgers.edu
KNIGGE, Dalynn ... 732-584-6365 281 B
knigge@rutgers.edu
KNIGGE, Dalynn ... 732-584-6365 281 C
knigge@rutgers.edu
KNIGGE, David ... 605-626-2537 415 H
david.knigge@northern.edu
KNIGHT, Aaron ... 281-922-3403 442 E
aaron.knight@sjcd.edu
KNIGHT, Alexis ... 985-448-7939 187 J
alexis.knight@fletcher.edu
KNIGHT, Allison, P ... 757-446-5255 465 H
knightap@evms.edu
KNIGHT, Antonia ... 716-286-8204 309 F
abk@niagara.edu
KNIGHT, Ashley ... 773-325-4852 136 F
aknight@depaul.edu
KNIGHT, Aubrey, L ... 815-740-5047 152 E
aknight@stfrancis.edu
KNIGHT, Bobbie ... 205-929-1428.... 6 B
bknight@miles.edu
KNIGHT, Brenda ... 239-489-9056 100 G
bknight3@fsw.edu
KNIGHT, Cecilia ... 618-634-3271 149 C
ceciliak@shawneecc.edu
KNIGHT, Cindi ... 304-647-6299 489 C
cknight@osteo.wvsom.edu
KNIGHT, Cynthia ... 985-545-1500 188 B
KNIGHT, Danita ... 404-471-6000 114 E
dknight@agnesscott.edu

© COPYRIGHT HIGHER EDUCATION PUBLICATIONS, INC. 2022

KNIGHT, Derric .... 906-635-6244 226 C
dknight@lssu.edu
KNIGHT, Gabe .... 563-441-4201 165 J
gknight@eicc.edu
KNIGHT, Gary, E .... 803-705-4559 405 G
gary.knight@benedict.edu
KNIGHT, Gina, R .... 252-335-4822 341 A
grknight@ecsu.edu
KNIGHT, Jack .... 540-568-5242 467 C
knigh2jf@jmu.edu
KNIGHT, Jaime .... 508-531-2337 212 B
j2knight@bridgew.edu
KNIGHT, James .... 828-689-1122 330 H
jknight@mhu.edu
KNIGHT, John, C .... 423-585-6882 424 G
john.knight@ws.edu
KNIGHT, Joseph .... 601-484-8779 246 B
jknight5@meridiancc.edu
KNIGHT, Lance .... 404-364-8542 123 G
lknight@oglethorpe.edu
KNIGHT, Leonard .... 760-245-4271.. 74 D
leonard.knight@vvc.edu
KNIGHT, Patricia .... 757-727-5447 466 L
patricia.knight@hamptonu.edu
KNIGHT, Sandra .... 857-701-1290 215 E
sknight@rcc.mass.edu
KNIGHT, Sandra .... 617-879-7906 212 E
sknight@massart.edu
KNIGHT, Saskia .... 949-753-4774.. 71 D
KNIGHT, Stephanie .... 352-638-9730.. 96 B
sknight@beaconcollege.edu
KNIGHT, Stephanie, L .. 214-768-4242 443 G
slknight@smu.edu
KNIGHT, Tamara .... 804-751-9191 464 N
tknight@ccc-va.com
KNIGHT, Tim .... 870-245-5528.. 20 H
knightt@obu.edu
KNIGHT, Tirzah .... 918-335-6252 368 E
tknight@okwu.edu
KNIGHT, Tracey .... 870-245-5401.. 20 H
knightte@obu.edu
KNIGHT, Victoria .... 573-592-5245 261 F
victoria.knight@westminster-mo.edu
KNIGHT, Wendy, S .... 844-642-2338 168 F
knightw@nicc.edu
KNIGHT, Wesley .... 573-288-6420 251 I
wknight@culver.edu
KNIGHT-MANUEL,
Michelle .... 303-871-2509.. 84 C
michelle.knight-manuel@du.edu
KNIGHTEN, Valeri .... 214-818-1347 433 A
vknighten@criswell.edu
KNIGHTON, Denise .... 662-915-7792 248 F
denisek@olemiss.edu
KNIGHTON, Diana .... 205-929-1442.... 6 B
dknighton@miles.edu
KNIGHTON, Jeffery .... 678-359-5018 120 D
jknighton@gordonstate.edu
KNIGHTON, JR.,
Lewis, J .... 864-656-3184 406 F
knightl@clemson.edu
KNIGHTS, Chad .... 703-323-3387 473 G
cknights@nvcc.edu
KNIGHTS, John, E .... 407-582-5197 113 C
jknights@valenciacollege.edu
KNIPE, Mike .... 612-343-3541 241 O
mjknipe@northcentral.edu
KNIPE, Sheri .... 319-208-5015 169 I
sknipe@scciowa.edu
KNIPFEL, Shirley, J .... 515-294-1781 163 E
sknipfel@iastate.edu
KNIPPEL, Dianne .... 661-722-6300.. 26 E
dknippel@avc.edu
KNISLEY, Emilia .... 513-875-3344 349 K
emilia.knisley@chatfield.edu
KNISLEY, Erica .... 512-404-4870 429 K
eknisley@austinseminary.edu
KNISLEY, Joel .... 828-232-5121 342 A
jknisley@unca.edu
KNISLEY, Patrick .... 212-217-4320 299 C
patrick_knisley@fitnyc.edu
KNISPEL, Todd .... 620-432-0384 176 A
tknispel@neosho.edu
KNISS, Fred, L .... 540-432-4105 465 F
fred.kniss@emu.edu
KNISS, Rob .... 806-742-3681 450 C
rob.kniss@ttu.edu
KNITIG, Sherri .... 785-890-3641 176 E
sherri.knitig@nwktc.edu
KNOBBE, Amy .... 402-481-8847 265 B
amy.knobbe@bryanhealthcollege.edu
KNOBLICH, Julie .... 620-792-9275 171 F
knoblichj@bartonccc.edu

KNOCH, Karen .... 336-727-7102 329 B
karen.knoch@greensboro.edu
KNODEL, Becky .... 701-252-3467 346 J
bknodel@uj.edu
KNODEL, Becky, L .... 701-252-3467 346 J
KNODLE-BRAGIEL, Lisa 503-883-2214 373 E
lbragiel@linfield.edu
KNOEPPEL, Robert, C ... 813-974-3400 111 B
rkc3@usf.edu
KNOETTGEN, Amber ..... 785-243-1435 172 J
aknoettgen@cloud.edu
KNOETTGEN, Suzi .... 785-243-1435 172 J
sknoettgen@cloud.edu
KNOLL, Eric .... 314-367-8700 260 A
eric.knoll@uhsp.edu
KNOLL, Joseph .... 617-824-8112 208 G
joseph_knoll@emerson.edu
KNOLL, Molly, H .... 641-422-4404 168 E
knollmol@niacc.edu
KNOLL-FINN, MJ .... 212-998-4553 309 D
mjknollfinn@nyu.edu
KNOLLE, Jon .... 831-646-3030.. 52 H
jknolle@mpc.edu
KNOLLENBERG, Dustin . 217-234-5253 141 H
dknollenberg@lakelandcollege.edu
KNOLTON, Cristina, C .. 213-738-5774.. 66 A
cknolton@swlaw.edu
KNOOR, Robert .... 616-957-6039 221 K
rknoor@calvinseminary.edu
KNOP, Joachim, W .... 202-994-6506.. 92 C
knop@gwu.edu
KNOPF, Lydia .... 714-879-3901.. 45 J
lknopf@hiu.edu
KNORR, Dan .... 570-389-4655 393 E
dknorr@bloomu.edu
KNORR, Justin .... 309-268-8143 138 F
justin.knorr@heartland.edu
KNOTT, Betsy .... 740-376-4480 355 E
emk004@marietta.edu
KNOTT, Blythe .... 503-768-7296 373 D
blythe@lclark.edu
KNOTT, Catherine .... 812-866-7087 155 D
knott@hanover.edu
KNOTT, Dana .... 614-287-2461 351 B
dknott@cscc.edu
KNOTT, Dana .... 937-769-1881 347 F
dknott@antioch.edu
KNOTT, Gail .... 800-658-4308 266 J
knottg@mpcc.edu
KNOTT, Gail .... 308-535-3605 266 J
knottg@mpcc.edu
KNOTT, Greg .... 217-333-9334 151 C
gknott63@uillinois.edu
KNOTT, Gregory .... 217-333-9334 151 F
gknott63@uillinois.edu
KNOTT, Kevin .... 217-351-2239 146 G
kknott@parkland.edu
KNOTTS, Brad .... 812-749-1215 159 E
bknotts@oak.edu
KNOTTS, Brice .... 304-293-4874 489 E
brice.knotts@mail.wvu.edu
KNOTTS, Chantaye .... 256-469-7333.... 5 I
deaninst@hbc1.edu
KNOTTS, Debby .... 505-277-9000 288 C
debby@unm.edu
KNOTTS, Gibbs .... 843-953-6792 407 D
knottshg@cofc.edu
KNOTTS, Joshua .... 801-618-0438 458 H
jknotts@ameritech.edu
KNOWLES, Ann .... 864-522-2000 408 I
ann.knowles@prismahealth.org
KNOWLES, Bill .... 405-382-9272 369 E
b.knowles@sscok.edu
KNOWLES, James, M ... 409-984-6432 449 D
knowlejm@lamarpa.edu
KNOWLES, Matteel .... 864-250-8177 408 J
matteel.knowles@gvltec.edu
KNOWLES, Melody, D .. 703-370-6600 475 F
KNOWLES, Monica .... 360-992-2904 477 J
mknowles@clark.edu
KNOWLES, Sada .... 405-425-5803 367 C
sada.knowles@oc.edu
KNOWLES, Tamece .... 305-348-7882 109 H
knowles@fiu.edu
KNOWLTON, Eloise .... 508-767-7487 205 F
eknowlton@assumption.edu
KNOWLTON, James .... 510-642-5316.. 68 N
athletic.director@berkeley.edu
KNOX, Brenda .... 918-610-0027 365 H
bknox@communitycarecollege.edu
KNOX, Cecilia .... 301-546-1580 201 D
knoxca@pgcc.edu

KNOX, Craig .... 850-201-8660 112 B
adminservices@tcc.fl.edu
KNOX, Danny .... 859-233-8287 185 A
dknox@transy.edu
KNOX, George .... 919-546-8527 339 I
george.knox@shawu.edu
KNOX, Jan .... 336-334-4822 334 F
jhknox@gtcc.edu
KNOX, Linda, B .... 219-989-3169 160 A
lbknox@pnw.edu
KNOX, Lindsay .... 503-554-2242 372 I
lknox@georgefox.edu
KNOX, Lindsay .... 503-538-8383 372 I
KNOX, Lisa .... 574-284-5318 160 F
lknox@saintmarys.edu
KNOX, Michael, J .... 806-651-2050 447 D
mknox@wtamu.edu
KNOX, Ryan .... 309-248-8189 138 F
ryan.knox@heartland.edu
KNOX, Sasha .... 619-388-3307.. 60 I
sknox@sdccd.edu
KNOX, Tracey .... 970-521-6643.. 82 B
tracey.knox@njc.edu
KNOX, Wayne .... 512-505-3003 437 B
wknox@htu.edu
KNUCKLES, Jill .... 970-248-1426.. 78 F
jknuckle@coloradomesa.edu
KNUCKLES, Leator .... 410-238-9000.. 93 H
KNUDSEN, J. Todd .... 315-568-3146 309 H
tknudsen@northeastcollege.edu
KNUDSEN, Jeffrey .... 802-831-1285 462 F
jknudsen@vermontlaw.edu
KNUDSEN, Ross .... 208-376-7731 130 E
rknudsen@boisebible.edu
KNUDSEN, Thomas .... 805-493-3031.. 29 E
tknudsen@callutheran.edu
KNUDSON, Christopher 319-352-8580 170 F
chris.knudson@wartburg.edu
KNUDSON, Kari .... 701-224-5604 345 F
kari.l.knudson@bismarckstate.edu
KNUDTSON, Matt .... 573-642-3361 261 F
KNUFFMAN, Nathan .... 919-843-4080 342 B
nknuffman@unc.edu
KNUPPEL, Lisa .... 714-432-5575.. 38 F
lknuppel@occ.cccd.edu
KNUREK, Charles .... 860-253-3037.. 86 B
cknurek@asnuntuck.edu
KNUST, Alyse .... 217-424-3769 144 D
aknust@millikin.edu
KNUTEL, Phil .... 617-747-2558 206 D
pknutel@berklee.edu
KNUTEL, Phillip .... 781-239-4225 205 G
pknutel@babson.edu
KNUTH, Doug .... 775-784-6900 270 K
dknuth@unr.edu
KNUTH, Julie, J 260-982-5214 158W
jjknuth@manchester.edu
KNUTSEN, Maren .... 414-847-3243 493 C
marenknutson@miad.edu
KNUTSEN, Mark .... 423-697-4785 423 B
mark.knutsen@chattanoogastate.edu
KNUTSON, Jennifer .... 605-331-6611 416 C
jennifer.knutson@usiouxfalls.edu
KNUTSON, Jonathan .... 218-855-8027 237 C
jonathan.knutson@clcmn.edu
KNUTSON, Karen .... 320-363-5922 234 I
kknutson@csbsju.edu
KNUTSON, Ryan .... 406-994-4545 263 G
ryan.knutson2@montana.edu
KNUTSON, Stephanie .... 608-789-6083 499 B
knutsons@westerntc.edu
KNUTSON, Todd .... 605-331-6813 416 C
todd.knutson@usiouxfalls.edu
KNYSAK, Elsa .... 414-955-4516 492 F
eknysak@mcw.edu
KO, Jeanne .... 212-472-1500 309 B
jeanne.ko@nysid.edu
KO, Kristina .... 202-554-0578 231 A
kdko@umich.edu
KO, Lester, D .... 717-245-1102 382 B
kole@dickinson.edu
KO, Shinsaeng .... 404-727-0825 118 D
shinsaeng.ko@emory.edu
KO, Yoo, K .... 571-730-4750 255 E
wdc@midwest.edu
KOAN, Mark .... 480-731-8895.. 13 A
mark.koan@domail.maricopa.edu
KOBALLA, JR.,
Thomas, R .... 678-547-6333 122 C
koballa_tr@mercer.edu
KOBAYASHI, Frank .... 916-484-8202.. 50 J
kobayaf@arc.losrios.edu

KOBEK PEZZAROSSI,
Caroline .... 202-559-5370.. 92 B
caroline.pezzarossi@gallaudet.edu
KOBERNUSZ, Bob .... 605-995-7128 414 E
bob.kobernusz@mitchelltech.edu
KOBES, Patricia .... 845-574-4280 312 C
pkobes@sunyrockland.edu
KOBETT, Beth .... 443-334-2545 202 C
bkobett@stevenson.edu
KOBETZ, Erin .... 305-243-6185 112 K
ekobetz@miami.edu
KOBLE, Sonya .... 701-224-5434 345 F
sonya.koble@bismarckstate.edu
KOBLER, Soheila .... 973-618-3724 275 E
skobler@caldwell.edu
KOBRINSKY, Natasha ... 310-665-6837.. 55 B
nkobrinsky@otis.edu
KOBRYN, Jessica .... 904-826-8553.. 99 D
jkobryn@flagler.edu
KOBUS, Gloria .... 404-894-9396 119 D
gloria.kobus@business.gatech.edu
KOBUS, James .... 641-673-1046 170 I
james.kobus@wmpenn.edu
KOBYLESKI, Kammie .... 928-776-2032.. 17 B
kammie.kobyleski@yc.edu
KOBYLSKI, Gerald .... 845-938-5608 502 H
gerald.kobylski@westpoint.edu
KOBYLSKI, Janet .... 570-208-5900 386 G
janetkobylski@kings.edu
KOCAK, Taskin .... 203-582-7829.. 88 F
taskin.kocak@quinnipiac.edu
KOCER, Ken .... 605-668-1589 414 F
kkocer@mountmarty.edu
KOCH, Amy .... 317-955-6021 159 A
akoch@marian.edu
KOCH, Bill .... 252-328-6166 340 H
kochb@ecu.edu
KOCH, Brad .... 610-328-8325 398 B
bkoch2@swarthmore.edu
KOCH, Colleen .... 352-273-7500 110 E
kochc@ufl.edu
KOCH, Don .... 618-634-3289 149 C
donk@shawneecc.edu
KOCH, Doug .... 573-651-2207 258 J
dskoch@semo.edu
KOCH, Greg .... 770-960-1298 121 F
gkoch@ict.edu
KOCH, Jennifer .... 303-492-2277.. 83M
jennifer.koch@colorado.edu
KOCH, Jiang Fei .... 503-338-2522 372 C
amclean@clatsopcc.edu
KOCH, Jo Ann .... 770-216-2960 121 F
jkoch@ict.edu
KOCH, John, C .... 607-777-6757 315 E
jkoch@binghamton.edu
KOCH, Jon .... 262-691-5227 499 A
jkoch18@wctc.edu
KOCH, Kathie .... 312-369-7436 136 C
kkoch@colum.edu
KOCH, Kevin .... 781-762-1211 209 C
kkoch@fmc.edu
KOCH, Matthew .... 919-890-7500.. 93 H
KOCH, Paul .... 563-333-6212 169 D
kochpaulc@sau.edu
KOCH, Paul .... 831-459-2931.. 71 A
plkoch@ucsc.edu
KOCH, Sheena .... 270-707-3921 181 G
bkshopkinsville@bncollege.com
KOCH, Thomas, L .... 520-621-2448.. 16 H
tlkoch@arizona.edu
KOCHANOWSKI,
Sharon .... 863-297-1000 106 A
skochanowski@polk.edu
KOCHER, Andrew .... 317-788-3493 161 F
akocher@uindy.edu
KOCHER, Craig, T .... 804-289-8500 471 E
ckocher@richmond.edu
KOCHER, Rebecca .... 937-327-7426 364 C
kocherr@wittenberg.edu
KOCHIS, Brad, A .... 740-392-6868 356 G
brad.kochis@mvnu.edu
KOCHIS, Stephen, J .... 845-575-3000 305 C
stephen.kochis@marist.edu
KOCHKA, Michael, D .... 304-457-6356 485 F
kochkamd@ab.edu
KOCHMAN, Laura .... 215-965-4000 390 C
KOCIAN, Bryce .... 979-532-6315 457 H
brycek@wcjc.edu
KOCIAN, Justin .... 402-494-2311 267 D
jkocian@thenicc.edu
KOCIELA, Ryan .... 724-772-5520 379 C
ryan.kociela@bc3.edu

KOOISTRA, Fred .... 616-988-1000 222 D
fred.k@compass.edu
KOOK, Tom .... 563-588-8000 165 K
tkook@emmaus.edu
KOOMER, Ajoy .... 714-872-5695.. 51 E
akoomer@ketchum.edu
KOON, Chi .... 718-270-6107 294 E
chi@mec.cuny.edu
KOONCE, David .... 740-593-0370 358 L
koonce@ohio.edu
KOONCE, JR.,
George, E .... 923-923-7676 492 D
gkoonce@marianuniversity.edu
KOONG, Kia .... 334-727-8705.... 7 D
kkoong@tuskegee.edu
KOONTZ, Megan .... 866-680-2756 458 I
academicdean@midwivery.edu
KOONTZ, Megan .... 866-680-2756 458 I
graduatedean@midwifery.edu
KOONTZ, Nikki .... 435-586-5400 459 E
nikkikoontz@suu.edu
KOONTZ, Stephanie .... 330-244-4943 363 E
skoontz@walsh.edu
KOOP, Christiaan .... 929-265-2145 308 F
ckoop@nycda.edu
KOOPMAN, Daniel .... 541-888-2525 376 B
daniel.koopman@socc.edu
KOOPMAN, Joseph .... 440-943-7600 360 D
frkoopman@yahoo.com
KOOPMANN, Ann .... 402-466-4774 266 A
ann.koopmann@doane.edu
KOOPMANS, Ken .... 517-607-2609 224 G
kkoopmans@hillsdale.edu
KOOREN, Lisa .... 209-478-0800.. 45 L
lkooren@humphreys.edu
KOOTI, John .... 717-477-1435 394 D
jgkooti@ship.edu
KOOTTUNGAL, Yvette .. 305-899-3600.. 96 A
ybrown@barry.edu
KOOZER, Maggie .... 212-580-0210 307 E
koozerm@newschool.edu
KOPACH,
Christopher, M .... 520-241-6482.. 16 H
ckopach@arizona.edu
KOPAS, Michael .... 914-251-6916 318 E
michael.kopas@purchase.edu
KOPAS, William .... 954-262-4412 104 M
wk128@nsu.nova.edu
KOPEC, Heather .... 305-284-2667 112 K
hkopec@miami.edu
KOPEL, Tina .... 718-368-5109 294 C
KOPERA, Jacob .... 716-286-8305 309 F
jkopera@niagara.edu
KOPERA, Ken .... 864-646-1770 411 H
kkopera@tctc.edu
KOPERSKI, Mike .... 415-442-7082.. 44 B
mkoperski@ggu.edu
KOPISCHKE, Connie ..... 612-455-3420 234 A
connie.kopischke@bcsmn.edu
KOPKOWSKI, Renee ..... 404-894-0870 119 D
renee.kopkowski@gatech.edu
KOPLIN, Manuela .... 408-274-6700.. 62 E
KOPLINSKI, Sarah .... 217-854-3231 133 F
KOPP, Corey .... 406-265-4113 264 A
KOPP, Courtney, A .... 515-574-1020 166 G
kopp@iowacentral.edu
KOPP, David .... 305-899-3708.. 96 A
dkopp@barry.edu
KOPP, Nicole .... 715-675-3331 498 E
koppn@ntc.edu
KOPP, Richard .... 215-751-8876 381 H
dkopp@ccp.edu
KOPP, Sacha, E .... 509-313-4200 479 E
sonya.kopp@columbiasouthern.edu
KOPP, Sonya .... 251-981-3771.... 5 B
sonya.kopp@columbiasouthern.edu
KOPP, Will, E .... 740-368-3108 359 F
wekopp@owu.edu
KOPP-MILLER, Barbara . 419-530-4488 363 B
barbara.kopp-miller@utoledo.edu
KOPPEL, Michael .... 202-885-8610.. 94 D
mkoppel@wesleyseminary.edu
KOPPELL, Jonathan ...... 973-655-4212 278 C
koppellj@montclair.edu
KOPPEN, Jason .... 928-774-3890.. 12 N
jkoppen@indianbible.org
KOPPI, Stefan .... 508-831-5260 220 C
skoppi@wpi.edu
KOPPISCH, Andrew ...... 928-523-8893.. 14 J
andy.koppisch@nau.edu
KOPPY, Katie .... 320-625-5114 239 G
katie.koppy@pine.edu
KOPROWSKI, John ...... 307-766-1121 500 H

KOPS, Christopher, P .. 414-955-8704 492 F
ckops@mcw.edu
KOPSTAIN, Eric .... 615-875-8617 427 B
eric.kopstain@vanderbilt.edu
KOPTEROS, Michelle .... 312-658-5100 150 E
KORALESKY, Barron .. 413-597-3072 220 A
bk4@williams.edu
KORB, Kristi .... 417-667-8181 251 E
kkorb@cottey.edu
KORB-NICE, Jobe, S ... 206-281-2564 482 K
jobe@spu.edu
KORBEL, Linda .... 847-635-1952 146 E
lkorbel@oakton.edu
KORBER, William ...... 787-622-8000 509 H
jdavila@pupr.edu
KORD, JoLanna .... 620-341-6829 173 C
jkord@emporia.edu
KORDEK, Nicholas, M . 315-655-7230 292 B
nmkordek@cazenovia.edu
KORDENBROCK,
William, R .... 906-487-2200 227 D
billk@mtu.edu
KORELL, Patrick .... 307-532-8330 500 A
pkorell@ewc.wy.edu
KORENEK, Rebecca ...... 409-747-2210 456 E
bbkorene@utmb.edu
KORENGEL, Jacqueline . 912-443-4150 124 I
jkorengel@savannahtech.edu
KORETOFF, Lisa, A ..... 336-334-4822 334 F
lakoretoff@gtcc.edu
KORETSKY, Carla, M .. 269-387-4360 232 J
carla.koretsky@wmich.edu
KORETZKY, Gary ...... 607-255-7200 297 D
gak36@cornell.edu
KOREY, Christopher, A . 843-953-7178 407 D
koreyc@cofc.edu
KORF, Abraham .... 305-673-5664 114 C
rabbikorf@hotmail.com
KORF, Benzion .... 305-653-8770 114 C
bkorf@lecfl.com
KORGAN, Kate, H ...... 702-895-0446 270 J
kate.korgan@unlv.edu
KORINKE, Kim .... 805-378-1463.. 73 I
kkorinke@vcccd.edu
KORIR, Albert .... 417-873-7509 252 A
akorir@drury.edu
KORITARI, Andi .... 312-261-3317 145 C
andi.koritari@nl.edu
KORKLAN, Michael ...... 816-604-1000 255 B
michael.korklan@mcckc.edu
KORMAN, Caryn .... 312-996-7125 151 D
caryn1@uic.edu
KORMAN, Thomas, P .. 517-750-1200 230 F
tkorman@arbor.edu
KORMANAK, Steve ...... 608-757-7766 497 D
skormanak@blackhawk.edu
KORN, Megan .... 918-595-7846 370 B
megan.korn@tulsacc.edu
KORN, Nicholas .... 513-562-6280 347 G
nicholas.korn@artacademy.edu
KORN, Randi .... 617-349-8596 210 H
lijiri@lesley.edu
KORNBERG, Judith ...... 804-828-6786 472 D
kornbergjf@vcu.edu
KORNBERG, Mindy .... 206-685-4730 484 A
mindyk@uw.edu
KORNBLUH, Mark ...... 313-577-2200 232 H
kornbluh@wayne.edu
KORNBLUTH, Jerry ..... 516-572-7664 307 C
jerry.kornbluth@ncc.edu
KORNBLUTH, Sally ..... 919-684-2631 328 D
sally.kornbluth@duke.edu
KORNEGAY, Joy .... 919-739-7091 338 F
jmkornegay@waynecc.edu
KORNER, Christoph ...... 818-394-3325.. 76 D
christoph.korner@woodbury.edu
KORNFELD, Julie .... 212-854-2691 296 H
jk3924@columbia.edu
KORNFUEHRER, Dana . 512-313-3000 432 N
dana.kornfuehrer@concordia.edu
KORNISH, Dina, M ...... 570-348-6211 389 B
dkornish@marywood.edu
KORNKVEN, Kelly, J ... 701-788-4816 345 B
kelly.kornkven@mayvillestate.edu
KORNOWA, Alicia ...... 269-387-2000 232 J
alicia.kornowa@wmich.edu
KORNS, Linda .... 409-839-2022 449 A
ldkorns@lit.edu
KORNUTA, Halyna ...... 310-204-1666.. 58 K
KORONKIEWICZ, Talia . 815-455-8584 143 F
tkoronkiewicz@mchenry.edu
KOROS, Shadrack ...... 678-422-4100.. 93 H

KORPELA, Doreen ...... 906-487-7201 223 I
doreen.korpela@finlandia.edu
KORSAKOV, Stephan .. 212-966-0300 308 A
KORSCHINOWSKI,
Claire .... 253-589-5516 478 A
claire.korschinowski@cptc.edu
KORST, Summer .... 206-878-3710 480 C
skorst@highline.edu
KORT, Sarah .... 402-460-2194 265 C
sarakort@cccneb.edu
KORTCAMP, Bryan ...... 661-362-2687.. 51 E
bkortcamp@masters.edu
KORTE, Andrea .... 910-695-3767 337 E
kortea@sandhills.edu
KORTEPETER, Mark .... 301-295-9440 502 B
mark.kortepeter@usuhs.edu
KORTLEVER, Jaima .... 360-438-4576 482 D
jkortlever@stmartin.edu
KORTOKRAX, Sandy .. 419-995-8200 360 B
kortokrax.s@rhodesstate.edu
KORUS, Daniel .... 361-698-1065 434 H
dkorus@delmar.edu
KORVER, Bill .... 910-323-5614 327 E
president@ccbs.edu
KORZA, Lynn .... 413-265-2454 208 B
korzal@elms.edu
KORZENDORFER, Kate . 781-768-7340 217 H
kate.korzendorfer@regiscollege.edu
KOSAKOWSKI, Jennifer 609-652-4939 283 A
jennifer.kosakowski@stockton.edu
KOSAKOWSKI, Sheryl .. 413-565-1000 205 I
skosakowski@baypath.edu
KOSARUE, Lori .... 517-264-5161 220 D
lkosarue@adrian.edu
KOSBOTH, Michele ...... 440-775-6392 357 G
mkosboth@oberlin.edu
KOSCHMANN, Mark .... 651-641-8278 235 A
koschmann@csp.edu
KOSCHMEDER,
Douglas, D .... 319-352-8761 170 F
doug.koschmeder@wartburg.edu
KOSCHWANEZ, Jeanne . 760-795-6840.. 52 G
jkoschwanez@miracosta.edu
KOSCIW, Dennis .... 850-718-2244.. 97 C
kosciwd@chipola.edu
KOSHI, Deanne .... 808-245-8226 129 H
deannesy@hawaii.edu
KOSHI-LUM, Jessica .. 425-235-2352 482 C
jkoshilum@rtc.edu
KOSHLAND, Cathy ...... 510-643-7384.. 68 N
ckoshland@berkeley.edu
KOSHMIDER, III,
John, W .... 330-471-8326 355 D
jkoshmider@malone.edu
KOSHORK, Lori .... 206-726-5027 478 F
lkoshork@cornish.edu
KOSHUT, Thomas, M ... 256-824-6100.... 8 B
tom.koshut@uah.edu
KOSHY, Chetna .... 713-348-2287 441 K
chetna.koshy@rice.edu
KOSIEK, Timothy .... 708-974-5388 144 G
kosiekt2@morainevalley.edu
KOSIEK, Timothy, J .... 708-709-3702 147 A
tkosiek@prairiestate.edu
KOSIK, Jamie, F .... 304-293-7202 489 D
jamie.kosik@mail.wvu.edu
KOSINA, Joseph .... 631-451-4881 320 G
kosinaj@sunysuffolk.edu
KOSINE, Brandon ...... 307-268-2550 499 T
bkosine@caspercollege.edu
KOSINSKI, Mark .... 203-285-2077.. 86 D
mkosinski@gatewayct.edu
KOSINSKI, Ross, J ...... 630-515-6479 144 C
rkosin@midwestern.edu
KOSINSKY, James, A ... 708-209-3519 136 D
jim.kosinsky@cuchicago.edu
KOSKI, Janet .... 906-227-2420 228 E
jakoski@nmu.edu
KOSKI, Lynne .... 308-635-6792 269 E
koskil1@wncc.edu
KOSKI, Mary .... 309-794-7208 132 H
marykoski@augustana.edu
KOSKOFF, Max .... 607-871-2601 289 E
koskoff@alfred.edu
KOSKY, John .... 434-924-5948 471 F
jak3fa@virginia.edu
KOSKY, Kristy .... 740-695-9500 348 D
kskoky@belmontcollege.edu
KOSLOSKY, Jill .... 307-637-1154 500 D
jkoslosk@lccc.wy.edu
KOSLOW MARTIN, Jodi 708-456-0300 151 A
jodikoslowmartin@triton.edu
KOSOBUCKI, Dave ...... 858-695-8587 155 F
dkosobucki@horizonuniversity.edu

KOSS, Kim .... 706-721-0140 115 I
kkoss@augusta.edu
KOSS, Michelle .... 586-286-2172 226 F
kossm26@macomb.edu
KOSS, Susan .... 217-443-8814 136 E
s.koss@dacc.edu
KOSSES, Jennifer ...... 617-989-4486 219 D
kossesj@wit.edu
KOST, Patricia, L ...... 216-368-2165 349 B
patricia.kost@case.edu
KOSTECKI, David ...... 808-356-5256 128 E
dkostecki@hpu.edu
KOSTECKI, James ...... 630-942-3821 135 F
kosteckij@cod.edu
KOSTELIS, Kimberly ... 860-832-2228.. 85 F
kimberly.kostelis@ccsu.edu
KOSTEN, Linda .... 303-871-7922.. 84 C
linda.kosten@du.edu
KOSTENBAUDER, Molly 407-708-2483 108 B
kostenbauderm@seminolestate.edu
KOSTER, Ed .... 402-761-8224 268 C
ekoster@southeast.edu
KOSTER, Jill .... 785-833-4332 175 C
jill.koster@kwu.edu
KOSTIC, Jennifer .... 937-512-4191 360 F
jennifer.kostic@sinclair.edu
KOSTIC, Ljubisa .... 619-388-6591.. 60 H
lkostic@sdccd.edu
KOSTIHOVA, Marcela .. 651-523-2252 235 F
mkostihova01@hamline.edu
KOSTJUK, Todd .... 661-362-2734.. 51 E
tkostjuk@masters.edu
KOSTYUKOV, Victoria . 718-522-9073 290 B
vkostyukov@asa.edu
KOT, Valerie, A .... 832-813-6809 438 E
valerie.a.kot@lonestar.edu
KOTCAMP, Butch .... 740-351-3429 360 E
bkotcamp@shawnee.edu
KOTCH, Amanda .... 618-842-3711 139 D
kotcha@iecc.edu
KOTECKI, Kathy .... 406-657-1660 263 H
kkotecki@msubillings.edu
KOTH, Jason .... 212-592-2259 314 I
jkoth@sva.edu
KOTH, Kent .... 206-296-2329 483 B
kothk@seattleu.edu
KOTHANDARAMAN,
Prabakar .... 315-312-3168 318 E
pk@oswego.edu
KOTHMANN, Angie ...... 228-493-5300 247 F
akothmann@prcc.edu
KOTLAS, Maureen ...... 301-405-3960 202 E
mkotlas@umd.edu
KOTLER, A. Malkiel ..... 732-367-1060 275 B
KOTLER, Yitzchok, S .... 732-367-1060 275 B
KOTLIKOFF, Michael, I . 607-255-2364 297 D
provost@cornell.edu
KOTLINSKI, Michael, J . 717-337-6363 384 C
mkotlinski@gettysburg.edu
KOTOISUVA, Agnes ...... 692-625-3394 503 F
KOTORI, Chiaki .... 570-321-4029 388 H
kotori@lycoming.edu
KOTOWICZ, Keith, A ... 414-847-3301 493 C
keithkotowicz@miad.edu
KOTOWSKI, Amy .... 516-364-0808 308 C
akotowski@nycollege.edu
KOTOWSKI, Kelli .... 740-597-1819 358 L
kotowskk@ohio.edu
KOTT, Micheal .... 708-656-8000 145 B
micheal.kott@morton.edu
KOTTAS, Kathy .... 620-786-1107 171 F
kottask@bartonccc.edu
KOTTENSTETTE, Kathy . 970-675-3237.. 78 P
kathy.kottenstette@cncc.edu
KOTTER, David .... 303-963-3336.. 78 D
dkotter@ccu.edu
KOTTICH, Sarah .... 402-399-2427 265 H
skottich@csm.edu
KOTTON, Stevenson .... 692-625-3394 503 F
skotton@cmi.edu
KOTTRE, Chris .... 805-581-1233.. 42 C
ckottre@eternitybiblecollege.com
KOTULA, Nadia .... 813-258-6151 102 A
nkotula@hccfl.edu
KOTWICKI, Lee .... 941-363-7218 109 C
kotwicl@scf.edu
KOTZ, David, F .... 603-646-2404 272 F
david.f.kotz@dartmouth.edu
KOTZ, Kim .... 716-896-0700 324 A
kkotz@villa.edu
KOUA, Deb .... 515-965-7025 164 F
dkkoua@dmacc.edu

KOUANCHAO, Ketmani . 626-585-7560.. 56 D
kkouanchao@pasadena.edu
KOUBA, Mary Beth ...... 325-670-1679 436 B
marybeth.kouba@hsutx.edu
KOUBEK, Richard, J ..... 906-487-2200 227 D
koubek@mtu.edu
KOUGH, Katherine .... 717-262-2006 402 D
kkough@wilson.edu
KOUKOL, June .... 617-333-2091 208 D
jkoukol@curry.edu
KOULIK, Chet .... 845-451-1347 297 E
chet.koulik@culinary.edu
KOULOS, Elleni, R .... 909-448-4178.. 71 C
ekoulos@laverne.edu
KOUMAS, Sokratis .... 508-999-8859 211 F
skoumas@umassd.edu
KOUPLEN, Angela .... 918-631-3075 371 C
angela-kouplen@utulsa.edu
KOUREMETIS, Michael .. 617-731-3500 210 D
KOUROPOVA, Patricia .. 213-427-2200.. 35 L
KOURY, Regina .... 856-225-2828 281 A
regina.koury@rutgers.edu
KOVAC, Celia .... 540-458-8794 476 D
ckovac@wlu.edu
KOVAC, Jason .... 503-594-3390 372 B
jason.kovac@clackamas.edu
KOVAC, John .... 412-346-2100 395 D
jkovac@pia.edu
KOVAC, Matt .... 724-287-8711 379 C
matt.kovac@bc3.edu
KOVACH, Amy .... 740-392-6868 356 G
amy.kovach@mvnu.edu
KOVACH, Jacalyn, E ...... 330-325-6369 357 D
jkovach1@neomed.edu
KOVACICH, Christine, L 330-325-6551 357 D
ckovacich@neomed.edu
KOVACS, Andrea, E .... 203-773-8550.. 85 C
KOVACS, Anita .... 850-484-1728 105 G
akovacs@pensacolastate.edu
KOVACS, Charles .... 941-359-7650 106 J
ckovacs@ringling.edu
KOVACS, Edward .... 610-526-6080 385 F
ekovacs@harcum.edu
KOVACS, Gene .... 850-245-0466 109 D
gene.kovacs@flbog.edu
KOVALCHICK, Mary ...... 610-799-1957 388 B
mkovalchick@lccc.edu
KOVALESKI, John .... 251-461-1622.... 9 A
jkovales@southalabama.edu
KOVATCH, Julie .... 503-338-2429 372 C
jkovatch@clatsopcc.edu
KOVATCH, Richard, A .... 434-982-5166 471 F
rak3e@virginia.edu
KOVIC, Hong Yu .... 860-215-9259.. 87 D
hkovic@threerivers.edu
KOVITZ, Jenn .... 541-383-7599 371 I
jkovitz@cocc.edu
KOVOLSKI, Chris .... 610-519-7450 401 B
chris.kovolski@villanova.edu
KOWAL, John .... 518-562-4110 295 F
john.kowal@clinton.edu
KOWALESKI, Curtis, J .. 507-933-7499 235 E
curtk@gustavus.edu
KOWALESKI, Mary, A ... 989-964-4041 229 L
makowale@svsu.edu
KOWALEWSKI, John, L . 801-626-7212 460 B
jkowalewski@weber.edu
KOWALEWSKY, Lyn ...... 989-358-7280 220 G
kowalewl@alpenacc.edu
KOWALKOWSKI, Brian .. 800-567-2344 491 C
bkowalkowski@menominee.edu
KOWALLIS, Brandon ...... 801-957-6342 460 D
brandon.kowallis@slcc.edu
KOWALSKI, Brian .... 609-652-4494 283 A
brian.kowalski@stockton.edu
KOWALSKI, Marion .... 631-687-4561 313 C
mkowalski@sjcny.edu
KOWALSKI, Melanie ...... 570-504-1583 387 A
kowalskim@lackawanna.edu
KOWALSKI, Patrick .... 513-556-2413 361 I
kowalspk@ucmail.uc.edu
KOWALSKI-BRAUN, Marlene .... 616-331-2555 224 D
kowalskm@gvsu.edu
KOWALSKY, Margaret ... 570-208-5986 386 G
margaretkowalsky@kings.edu
KOWATSCH, Adrijana ..... 859-442-1177 181 D
adrijana.kowatsch@kctcs.edu
KOWEEK, Joan .... 518-828-4181 296 G
joan.koweek@sunycgcc.edu
KOWERT, Baylee, L .... 903-813-3000 429 I
bkowert@austincollege.edu
KOX, Amy .... 920-498-6908 498 F
amy.kox@nwtc.edu
KOYZIS, Pamela, D ...... 626-395-8075.. 29 B
pamela.koyzis@caltech.edu
KOZACHYN, Karen .... 610-359-5362 381 J
kkozachy@dccc.edu
KOZAK, Greg .... 847-543-2974 135 G
gkozak@clcillinois.edu
KOZAK, Laura, A .... 410-706-8138 202 F
lkozak@umaryland.edu
KOZAR, John .... 412-624-4845 400 A
jjk118@pitt.edu
KOZEL, Nik .... 215-895-0268 382 D
kozel@drexel.edu
KOZIKOWSKI, Kenneth, M .... 617-228-2322 214 A
kkozikow@bhcc.edu
KOZIL, Cindy, T .... 508-541-1552 208 E
ckozil@dean.edu
KOZIMOR, Renee .... 847-635-1761 146 E
rkozimor@oakton.edu
KOZISEK, Kelly, L .... 541-737-4261 374 H
kelly.kozisek@oregonstate.edu
KOZISEK, Sue .... 402-421-7410 267 C
director@myotherapy.edu
KOZLIK, Cathy .... 802-468-1285 462 H
cathy.kozlik@castleton.edu
KOZLOWSKI, Dorothy ... 773-325-2191 136 F
dkozlows@depaul.edu
KOZLOWSKI, Michael ... 607-871-2595 289 E
kozlowski@alfred.edu
KOZMA, Laura .... 305-284-3965 112 K
lkozma@miami.edu
KOZOJED, Bob, J .... 701-788-4872 345 B
bob.kozojed@mayvillestate.edu
KOZUMA, Hikaru .... 215-898-6081 399 J
kozuma@upenn.edu
KRACHT, Peter .... 412-383-2499 400 A
pkracht@upress.pitt.edu
KRAEGEL, Irene .... 616-526-7016 221 L
ibk2@calvin.edu
KRAEMER, David .... 212-678-8075 303 A
dakraemer@jtsa.edu
KRAEMER, Joseline .... 570-422-3906 393 F
jkraemer@esu.edu
KRAETSCH, Angela .... 805-756-2171.. 29 K
akraetsc@calpoly.edu
KRAFFT, Susan .... 479-788-7019.. 22 A
susan.krafft@uafs.edu
KRAFT, Damon .... 785-833-4332 175 C
kraft@kwu.edu
KRAFT, Erin .... 847-851-5468.. 80 B
ekraft@coloradotech.edu
KRAFT, Jeff .... 317-916-7812 158 A
jkraft6@ivytech.edu
KRAFT, John .... 912-478-0779 120 A
jkraft@georgiasouthern.edu
KRAFT, Paul .... 907-796-6100.. 10 C
KRAFT, Walter .... 734-487-6895 223 F
wkraft@emuch.edu
KRAFTICK, Chris .... 606-539-4540 185 C
chris.kraftick@ucumberlands.edu
KRAGENBRING, James, J .... 816-414-3700 255 F
KRAGNESS, Jon .... 218-736-1595 238 K
jon.kragness@minnesota.edu
KRAGT, Nicole .... 269-337-7203 225 B
nicole.kragt@kzoo.edu
KRAGULJEVIC, Nev .... 401-598-1000 403 E
nev.kraguljevic@jwu.edu
KRAHE, Stacey .... 954-492-5353.. 97 G
skrahe@citycollege.edu
KRAHL, Tracy .... 312-362-5577 136 F
tkrahl@depaul.edu
KRAJESKI, Lark .... 617-573-8460 218 G
lkrajeski@suffolk.edu
KRAJEWSKI, Heather, L 434-223-7258 466 K
hkrajewski@hsc.edu
KRAJEWSKI, Laura .... 804-289-8841 471 E
lkrajews@richmond.edu
KRAJEWSKI, Rex .... 978-762-4000 215 B
rkrajews@northshore.edu
KRAJEWSKI, Scott .... 612-330-1471 233 G
krajewsk@augsburg.edu
KRAJNIAK, Chris, A .... 262-554-2010 493 A
chriskrajniak@gmail.com
KRAKER, Karen .... 909-667-4486.. 38 A
kkraker@claremontlincoln.edu
KRAKOW, Anne, Z .... 610-660-1905 397 A
akrakow@sju.edu
KRAL, Gwen, L .... 507-354-8221 236 D
kralgl@mlc-wels.edu
KRALEVICH, Richard, C 410-777-2195 197 C
rckralevich@aacc.edu
KRALL, Jason .... 412-578-6659 380 A
jkrall@carlow.edu
KRALL, Jessica .... 760-384-6362.. 47 C
jessica.krall@cerrocoso.edu
KRALL, Jim .... 479-524-7145.. 20 C
jkrall@jbu.edu
KRALL-LANOUE, Aimee 312-553-3216 134 M
akralllanoue@ccc.edu
KRAMER, Alan .... 229-391-4928 114 D
akramer@abac.edu
KRAMER, Alice .... 989-463-7111 220 F
krameram@alma.edu
KRAMER, Chip .... 804-706-5063 473 B
akramer@jtcc.edu
KRAMER, Esther .... 262-646-6530 493 F
ekramer@nashotah.edu
KRAMER, John .... 319-296-4307 166 E
john.kramer@hawkeyecollege.edu
KRAMER, Kevin .... 925-424-1275.. 36 A
kmkramer@laspositascollege.edu
KRAMER, Kirk .... 810-989-5503 230 A
kkramer@sc4.edu
KRAMER, Lance .... 612-455-3420 234 A
lance.kramer@bcsmn.edu
KRAMER, Laurie .... 617-373-2333 217 D
KRAMER, Linda .... 507-354-8221 236 D
kramerlm@mlc-wels.edu
KRAMER, Lisa .... 415-442-7889.. 44 B
lkramer@ggu.edu
KRAMER, Lisa .... 815-772-7218 145 A
KRAMER, Mark .... 757-825-2815 474 F
kramerm@tncc.edu
KRAMER, Marla .... 570-321-4037 388 H
kramer@lycoming.edu
KRAMER, Matt .... 612-624-9022 242 K
kramerm@umn.edu
KRAMER, Monica .... 623-572-3490 144 C
mkrame1@midwestern.edu
KRAMER, Monte .... 402-471-2505 267 F
mkramer@nscs.edu
KRAMER, Pamela .... 239-687-5305.. 95 L
pkramer@avemarialaw.edu
KRAMER, Patrick .... 806-742-1780 450 A
KRAMER, Patrick .... 806-742-1780 450 C
patrick.kramer@ttu.edu
KRAMER, Scott, E .... 270-852-3122 183 B
scottkr@kwc.edu
KRAMER, Sean .... 440-375-7166 354 K
skramer@lec.edu
KRAMER, Sharon .... 617-747-6959 206 D
institutionalassessment@berklee.edu
KRAMER, Terry .... 781-239-2431 214 E
tkramer@massbay.edu
KRAMER, Thomas, E ..... 757-594-8671 465 A
tkramer@cnu.edu
KRAMER, Zachary .... 480-727-0300.. 11 A
zachery.a.kramer@asu.edu
KRAMER-JEFFERSON, Kate .... 301-846-2409 198 E
kkramerjefferson@frederick.edu
KRAMER-LUCAS, Laura . 903-468-8181 446 D
laura.kramer-lucas@tamuc.edu
KRAMER-MAZER, Beth .. 914-893-4029 288 K
bkramermazer@ajr.edu
KRAMERIUS, Charity ...... 310-544-6483.. 60 B
charity.kramerius@usw.salvationarmy.org
KRAMERIUS, Premek .... 310-544-6419.. 60 B
premek.kramerius@usw.salvationarmy.org
KRAMISH, Bob .... 510-204-0714.. 37 A
bkramish@cdsp.edu
KRAMKA, James, S .... 615-322-2591 427 B
jim.kramka@vanderbilt.edu
KRAMP, Joseph .... 239-432-6778 100 G
jkramp@fsw.edu
KRAMPF, Allison .... 718-779-1430 310 I
akrampf@plazacollege.edu
KRAMSCHUSTER, Kate .. 715-232-4071 496 C
kramschusterk@uwstout.edu
KRANTZ, Aaron .... 509-865-8574 480 B
krantz_a@heritage.edu
KRANTZ, Jennifer .... 414-847-3331 493 C
jenniferkrantz@miad.edu
KRAPOHL, Robert .... 870-307-7206.. 20 D
robert.krapohl@lyon.edu
KRAPP, Elizabeth, M .... 215-670-9210 391 D
emkrapp@peirce.edu
KRASNER, David .... 631-656-2139 299 G
david.krasner@ftc.edu
KRASNOW, Aaron .... 480-965-8537.. 11 A
aaron.krasnow@asu.edu
KRASSNER DAWSON, Holly .... 707-256-7000.. 53 E
KRATKY, Rita .... 406-874-6199 262 K
kratkyr@milescc.edu
KRATOCHVIL, Bob .... 925-473-7301.. 40 I
bkratochvil@losmedanos.edu
KRATOCHVIL, Christopher .... 402-559-8490 269 B
ckratoch@unmc.edu
KRATZ, David .... 212-966-0300 308 A
president@nyaa.edu
KRATZER, Michelle, B .. 859-858-3511 178 H
michelle.kratzer@asbury.edu
KRAUS, Allen .... 614-287-2412 351 B
akraus3@cscc.edu
KRAUS, Katie .... 563-589-3161 170 C
kkraus@dbq.edu
KRAUS, Leah .... 919-530-7423 341 D
leah.kraus@nccu.edu
KRAUS, Leslyn .... 530-734-7993.. 69 A
lakraus@ucdavis.edu
KRAUS, Robert .... 701-777-3196 344 H
robert.j.kraus@und.edu
KRAUSE, Aric .... 860-548-2404 311 J
krausa2@rpi.edu
KRAUSE, Carolyn .... 513-861-6400 361 E
carolyn.krause@myunion.edu
KRAUSE, Deborah .... 314-918-2620 252 E
dkrause@eden.edu
KRAUSE, Judy .... 626-529-8500.. 55 E
KRAUSE, Karen .... 817-272-3561 454 B
kkrause@uta.edu
KRAUSE, Mark, C .... 310-983-3741.. 69 D
mkrause@conet.ucla.edu
KRAUSE, Nicolle .... 219-980-7753 157 A
nihanson@iu.edu
KRAUSE, Paul, A .... 866-326-7635 297 D
pkrause@cornell.edu
KRAUSE, Susan .... 928-350-2100.. 15 O
KRAUSE, Teresa .... 213-487-2211.. 26 C
KRAUSE, Traci .... 612-659-6472 238 C
traci.krause@minneapolis.edu
KRAUSE-HANSON, Ann 262-691-5207 499 A
akrausehanson@wctc.edu
KRAUSS, Clay .... 253-566-6005 483 F
ckrauss@tacomacc.edu
KRAUSZ, Yitzchok .... 845-784-4020 325 K
KRAUTHAMER, Barbara 413-545-4169 211 D
barbara@grad.umass.edu
KRAUTHEIMER, Daniel .. 912-443-3395 124 I
dkrautheimer@savannahtech.edu
KRAVITZ, Connie .... 847-543-2210 135 G
ckravitz@clcillinois.edu
KRAVITZ, Cynthia .... 330-941-3001 364 G
cakravitz@ysu.edu
KRAWCHYK, Peter .... 302-831-4703.. 91 A
krawchyk@udel.edu
KRAWCZYK, Tammy .... 541-567-1800 371 G
tkrawczyk@bluecc.edu
KRAYNAK, Carrie .... 724-964-8811 391 A
ckraynak@ncstrades.edu
KRCIC, Zeco .... 718-997-2803 295 A
zeco.krcic@qc.cuny.edu
KREASSIG, Kurt .... 757-352-4372 469 D
kkreassig@regent.edu
KREBILL, Scott, L .... 517-750-1200 230 F
skrebill@arbor.edu
KREBS, John .... 215-885-2360 389 A
jkrebs@manor.edu
KREBS, John, T .... 215-885-2360 389 A
jkrebs@manor.edu
KREBS, Julianne .... 937-393-3431 360 G
jkrebs@sscc.edu
KREBS, Stephanie, R .... 813-257-3020 113 B
srkrebs@ut.edu
KREBSBACH, David .... 701-328-4116 344 G
david.krebsbach@ndus.edu
KREBSBACH, Kim .... 701-766-4415 344 F
KREBSBACH, Paul .... 310-206-6063.. 69 D
pkrebsbach@dentistry.ucla.edu
KREFT, Rachel .... 708-444-4500 138 A
KREGEL, Kevin .... 319-335-0256 163 F
kevin-kregel@uiowa.edu
KREGEL, Kevin .... 319-335-3565 163 F
kevin-kregel@uiowa.edu
KREHBIEL, Lee .... 479-788-7304.. 22 A
lee.krehbiel@uafs.edu
KREHL, Stephanie .... 870-733-6790.. 18 A
slkrehl@asumidsouth.edu
KREIDER, Paul .... 304-293-7119 489 E
paul.kreider@mail.wvu.edu

KREIDLER, Kathleen 713-500-3968 455 D kathleen.kreidler@uth.tmc.edu
KREIKEMEIER, Kat 402-437-2624 268 D kkreikemeier@southeast.edu
KREILICK, Amy 419-559-2121 361 B akreilick01@terra.edu
KREISER, Valerie 610-740-3785 380 C valerie@cedarcrest.edu
KREISS, Andrew 309-556-3031 140 E akreiss@iwu.edu
KREITZER, Charles 703-993-1000 466 J
KREITZER, Ilene 516-773-5000 502 G kreitzeri@usmma.edu
KREJCI, Teresa 815-836-5200 142 C hkrejci@lewisu.edu
KREJECKY, Lisa 434-528-5276 476 B
KREMER, Anne 515-271-3181 165 F anne.kremer@drake.edu
KREMER, Cheryl, E 717-245-1098 382 B kremerc@dickinson.edu
KREMER, Ed 913-288-7111 174 H ekremer@kckcc.edu
KREMER, Jacalyn 978-665-3833 212 C jkremer@fitchburgstate.edu
KREMER, Peter, W 502-272-8334 179 D pkremer@bellarmine.edu
KRENGEL, Jennifer 415-458-3785 41 H jennifer.krengel@dominican.edu
KRENKEL, Kelly 305-821-3333 100 C kkrenkel@fnu.edu
KRENTZ, Shelby 859-815-7648 181 D shelby.krentz@kctcs.edu
KRENTZMAN, Lily, A 508-565-1105 218 F lkrentzman@stonehill.edu
KRESCH, Dov 845-426-3110 325 M
KRESKEN, Jonathan 843-953-1411 406 D jkresken@citadel.edu
KRESL, Molly 707-826-3776 30 A molly.kresl@humboldt.edu
KRESS, Anne, M 703-323-3000 473 G
KRESS, Cathann 614-292-6164 358 E kress.98@osu.edu
KRESS, Jeffrey 212-678-8065 303 A jekress@jtsa.edu
KRESS, Lisa, P 785-864-3911 177 G lpkress@ku.edu
KRESS, Ruth 812-357-6561 160 G rkress@saintmeinrad.edu
KRETA, Mary 406-243-6234 263 D mary.kreta@umontana.edu
KRETSCHMAR, Lani 413-205-3202 205 C lani.kretschmar@aic.edu
KRETSCHMER, Mark 805-421-5919 67 J mkretschmer@thomasaquinas.edu
KRETSCHMER, Thomas 815-455-8675 143 F tkretschmer@mchenry.edu
KRETZ, Bryan 402-363-5689 269 F bckretz@york.edu
KREUSER, Ryan 715-394-8538 496 D rkreuser@uwsuper.edu
KREUTZER, Steven 973-748-9000 275 C steven_kreutzer@bloomfield.edu
KREUZER, Charlene 507-457-5090 241 A ckreuzer@winona.edu
KREVH, Janet 216-397-4349 353 O jkrevh@jcu.edu
KREYE, Judy 330-244-4757 363 E jkreye@walsh.edu
KREYMER, Diana 718-518-4300 293 F
KREYNIS, Ilona 408-498-5104 73 A ikreynis@cogswell.edu
KRHIN, Daniel, J 920-748-8394 493 J krhind@ripon.edu
KRIARAS, Dimitrios 602-384-2555 11 H
KRIBS, Rick, A 812-888-4176 162 E rkribs@vinu.edu
KRICK, Keenon 209-575-6714 76 K krickk@mjc.edu
KRIDLI, Ghassan 313-593-5290 231 B gkridli@umich.edu
KRIEB, Dennis 618-468-4300 142 B dkrieb@lc.edu
KRIEBS, John 641-844-5670 167 E john.kriebs@iavalley.edu
KRIEG, John 360-650-7405 485 A john.krieg@wwu.edu
KRIEG, Lisa, M 412-268-5399 380 B krieg@andrew.cmu.edu
KRIEGE, Bill 816-501-4855 257 K bill.kriege@rockhurst.edu
KRIEGER, Andrea 850-484-1477 105 G akrieger@pensacolastate.edu
KRIEGER, Jill, M 412-397-5279 396 E krieger@rmu.edu
KRIEGER, Marcos 570-372-4292 398 A kriegerm@susqu.edu
KRIEPS, Kevin 219-473-4330 154 A kkrieps@ccsj.edu
KRIER, Jacob, C 507-344-7519 233 I jake.krier@blc.edu
KRIESE, Theresa 605-995-2621 414 A theresa.kriese@dwu.edu
KRIGEL, Belinda 256-233-8100 4 D belinda.krigel@athens.edu
KRIKORIAN, Greg 410-778-7752 204 E gkrikorian2@washcoll.edu
KRILEY, Taylor 785-628-4664 173 E tlkriley2@fhsu.edu
KRIMMEL, Jon 626-815-4570 26 K
KRIMPELBEIN, Kristi 715-232-2149 496 C krimpelbeink@uwstout.edu
KRINJECK, Ashley 814-262-6442 393 A akrinjeck@pennhighlands.edu
KRIPP, Andrew 860-723-0000 85 E
KRISE, Thomas, W 671-735-2990 503 E tkrise@triton.uog.edu
KRISHNAIAH, Raghu 602-557-3501 16 L raghu.krishnaiah@phoenix.edu
KRISHNAMOORTI, Ramanan 713-743-4307 451 G rkrishna@uh.edu
KRISHNAMURTHY, Sushma 318-342-1041 193 A krishnamurthy@ulm.edu
KRISHNAN, Kris 562-902-3399 65 H kriskrishnan@scuhs.edu
KRISHNAN, Ramayya 412-268-2159 380 B rk2x@andrew.cmu.edu
KRISHNASWAMY, Vidya 972-377-1575 432 I vkrishnaswamy@collin.edu
KRISHNASWAMY, Vidya 972-860-8152 433 H vkrishnaswamy@dcccd.edu
KRISIAK, Jeff 570-504-1760 387 A krisiakj@lackawanna.edu
KRISLOV, Marvin 212-346-1097 310 F president@pace.edu
KRISS, George 618-545-3099 141 C gkriss@kaskaskia.edu
KRISSOFF BOEHM, Lisa 508-531-2809 212 B lkrissoffboehm@bridgew.edu
KRISTENSEN, Douglas, A 308-865-8208 268 J kristensend@unk.edu
KRISTJANSSON-NELSON, Kyja 218-477-2815 239 A kyja.nelson@mnstate.edu
KRISTOF-BROWN, Amy 319-335-0866 163 F amy-kristof-brown@uiowa.edu
KRITSCHER, Matthew 510-723-6743 35 Q mkritscher@chabotcollege.edu
KRITSKY, Gene 513-244-4401 356 F gene.kritsky@msj.edu
KRIZ, Christine 540-868-7094 473 C ckriz@lfcc.edu
KROBOTH, Patricia, D 412-624-3270 400 A pkroboth@pitt.edu
KROEGER, Danielle, T 919-209-2027 335 D dlkroeger@johnstoncc.edu
KROEGER, William 812-888-4227 162 E
KROENKE, Paul 309-677-2325 133 H pkroenke@bradley.edu
KROETCH, Jennifer 303-914-6020 82 L
KROFT, Allison 219-464-5333 162 C allison.kroft@valpo.edu
KROGDAHL, Renate 888-820-1484 64 D renate.krogdahl@sofia.edu
KROGH, Mary Anne 605-688-5178 416 A maryanne.krogh@sdstate.edu
KROGOL, Jacob 313-317-1546 224 F jakrogol@hfcc.edu
KROGULL, Steve 479-718-3314 21 H skrogull@uark.edu
KROH, Lynne 417-862-9533 252 H enroll@globaluniversity.edu
KROHN, Lisa 712-274-5100 168 C krohn@morningside.edu
KROL, Miroslaw 248-392-9995 230 G mkrol@orchardlakeschools.com
KROL, Naz 814-866-8152 387 C nkrol@lecom.edu
KROLAK, Steven 812-941-2470 157 D skrolak@ius.edu
KROLICK, Sandy 505-747-2191 287 C sandyk@nnmc.edu
KROLL, Ann 510-723-7637 36 A akroll@clpccd.edu
KROLL, Dana 262-551-5706 491 B dkroll@carthage.edu
KROLL, Jason 201-200-3111 278 F jkroll@njcu.edu
KROLOFF, Reed 312-567-3000 139 H
KROMER, Neil 906-487-7207 223 I neil.kromer@finlandia.edu
KROMHOLTZ, Bryan 510-883-7151 41 G bkromholtz@dspt.edu
KROMPF, Steven 703-425-4143 467 B
KRONBERG, Sheila 608-663-3288 491 F skronberg@edgewood.edu
KRONENBERGER, Judy 513-862-5010 353 C judy.kronenberger@email.gscollege.edu
KRONENBITTER, Jennifer 607-753-2221 317 D jennifer.kronenbitter@cortland.edu
KRONFELD, Michelle 608-796-3025 496 L mlkronfeld@viterbo.edu
KRONISER, Maria 412-365-1862 380 F mkroniser@chatham.edu
KRONK-WARNER, Elizabeth 801-581-6571 459 D elizabeth.warner@law.utah.edu
KROOT, Irwin 212-229-5671 307 E krooti@newschool.edu
KROPF, Kevin 417-873-7524 252 A kkropf@drury.edu
KROPP, Kevin 518-828-4181 296 G kevin.kropp@sunycgcc.edu
KROPP-ANDERSON, Pamela 207-941-7107 194 D kroppandersonp@husson.edu
KROSKIE, Hanna 502-863-7947 180 E hanna_kroskie@georgetowncollege.edu
KROTINGER, Nicole 802-485-2126 461 H nkroting@norwich.edu
KROUSE, Alisa 713-963-8979 125 D akrouse@southuniversity.edu
KROUSE, Andrew 903-565-5658 455 C akrouse@uttyler.edu
KROUSE, Anne, M 610-499-4214 401 I amkrouse@widener.edu
KROVI, Ravi 801-626-6006 460 B rkrovi@weber.edu
KRPIC, Diana 914-694-4283 295 G dkrpic@riversidehealth.org
KRSTIC, Miroslav 858-534-5556 70 C mkrstic@ucsd.edu
KRUCKEBERG, Tara 626-395-8661 29 B tkruckeb@caltech.edu
KRUCKEL, Kerry 516-299-2513 304 C kerry.kruckel@liu.edu
KRUCKENBERG, Erica 620-947-3121 177 F
KRUEGER, Brian 920-424-3466 495 C
KRUEGER, Carr 801-422-3760 458 A carr@byu.edu
KRUEGER, Cole 701-858-3062 345 C cole.krueger@minotstateu.edu
KRUEGER, Conrad 210-486-0915 428 D ckrueger@alamo.edu
KRUEGER, Dave 406-265-4157 264 A david.krueger@msun.edu
KRUEGER, Dee 217-786-2778 142 F debra.krueger@llcc.edu
KRUEGER, Jamie 517-629-1000 220 E jkrueger@albion.edu
KRUEGER, Joni 605-274-4015 413 G joni.krueger@augie.edu
KRUEGER, Kate 315-268-2320 295 E kkrueger@clarkson.edu
KRUEGER, Laura 480-423-6116 14 B laura.krueger@scottsdalecc.edu
KRUEGER, Mablene 312-341-3500 148 A
KRUEGER, Matthew 218-855-8115 237 C matthew.krueger@clcmn.edu
KRUEGER, Paul 214-768-3051 443 G dean@engr.smu.edu
KRUEGER, Paul, R 605-394-2484 415 I paul.krueger@sdsmt.edu
KRUEGER, Severa 920-923-8091 492 D smkrueger36@marianuniversity.edu
KRUEGER, Todd 252-335-0821 333 E todd_krueger@albemarle.edu
KRUEMMLING, Brooke 215-780-1364 397 E bkruemmling@salus.edu
KRUG, Anita, K 312-567-3000 139 H
KRUG, Cherie 301-387-3100 198 F cherie.krug@garrettcollege.edu
KRUG, Kirstin 918-595-7924 370 B kirstin.krug@tulsacc.edu
KRUGER, Jennifer 712-325-3200 167 G
KRUGER, Jenny 712-325-3326 167 G jkruger@iwcc.edu
KRUGER, Matt 651-450-3701 237 H mkruger@inverhills.edu
KRUGER, Michael 817-257-7727 447 H michael.kruger@tcu.edu
KRUGER, Michael, J 704-688-4233 248 A mkruger@rts.edu
KRUIZENGA, Alicia 714-564-6970 58 F kruizenga_alicia@sac.edu
KRUKONES, James 216-397-4762 353 O jkrukones@jcu.edu
KRUKOVITZ, Robyn, M 570-348-6231 389 B rmkrukovitz@marywood.edu
KRULAK, Todd 205-726-4036 6 E tkrulak@samford.edu
KRULICH, Jon 218-935-0417 244 A jon.krulich@wetcc.edu
KRULL, Kimberly 316-322-3100 172 B kim.krull@butlercc.edu
KRULY, Genevieve 716-826-1200 322 J krulyg@trocaire.edu
KRUMBACH, Carol 562-467-5053 35 O ckrumbach@cerritos.edu
KRUMBACH, Jillian 402-354-7129 267 E jillian.krumbach@methodistcollege.edu
KRUMER, Walter 718-522-9073 290 B wkrumer@asa.edu
KRUMHANSL, Ezra 502-585-9911 184 E ekrumhansl@spalding.edu
KRUMM, Brenda, L 620-432-0364 176 A bkrumm@neosho.edu
KRUMM, Javier 951-785-2295 47 F jkrumm@lasierra.edu
KRUMMEN SCHRAVEN, Ginger, B 920-433-6631 490 H ginger.krummen@bellincollege.edu
KRUMMENACHER, Alan 512-404-4803 429 K akrummenacher@austinseminary.edu
KRUMPELMAN, Jacqui 330-363-6347 348 B jacqui.krumpelman@aultman.com
KRUMWEIDE, Darrin 323-466-6663 44 A
KRUPA, Cynthia 563-674-6633 169 B ckrupa@orion.edu
KRUPIN, Maria 845-451-1385 297 E maria.krupin@culinary.edu
KRUPITSKIY, Anna 201-360-4070 277 D akrupitskiy@hccc.edu
KRUPKA, Moshe, D 646-565-6277 322 B moshe.krupka@touro.edu
KRUPKA, Moshe, D 646-565-6277 322 C moshe.krupka@touro.edu
KRUPNICK-WALSH, Kayla 415-442-7228 44 B kkrupnick@ggu.edu
KRUPP, David 808-235-7416 130 C krupp@hawaii.edu
KRUPP, Jason 727-341-3339 107 C krupp.jason@spcollege.edu
KRUPPA, Karen 617-973-1141 218 G kkruppa@suffolk.edu
KRUPPS, Gina 309-341-5264 134 A gkrupps@sandburg.edu
KRUPPSTADT, Tom 877-476-8674 435 G
KRUPSKI, Eric, A 617-422-7298 217 B ekrupski@nesl.edu
KRUSCHINSKA, Kurt 313-577-6748 232 H registrar@wayne.edu
KRUSE, Amy 320-629-5129 239 G amy.kruse@pine.edu
KRUSE, Beckie 262-243-5700 491 E beckie.kruse@cuw.edu
KRUSE, Derek 507-786-3636 242 I kruse6@stolaf.edu
KRUSE, Heather 602-285-7229 13 H heather.kruse@phoenixcollege.edu
KRUSE, Janetta 817-598-6391 457 C jkruse@wc.edu
KRUSE, Jerry, E 217-545-3625 149 G jkruse@siumed.edu
KRUSE, Krystal 515-271-1447 165 C krystal.kruse@dmu.edu
KRUSE, Liz 563-588-6300 164 C liz.kruse@clarke.edu
KRUSE, Thomas, D 563-588-4948 167 I tom.kruse@loras.edu
KRUSE, Tracy, L 402-844-7056 268 A tracyk@northeast.edu
KRUSEMARK, Diane 630-752-5009 152 K diane.krusemark@wheaton.edu

KRUSEMARK, Stacy, L .. 605-256-5127 415 G
stacy.krusemark@dsu.edu
KRUSEMARK, Stephanie .... 303-765-3106.. 81 F
skrusemark@iliff.edu
KRUSLING, James .... 415-442-7248.. 44 B
jkrusling@ggu.edu
KRUSNIAK, Bryan .... 660-626-2364 249 C
bkrusniak@atsu.edu
KRUTKA, Holly .... 307-766-1121 500 H
KRUTSCH, Jackie .... 479-308-2295.. 17 E
jackie.krutsch@acheedu.org
KRUZANSKY, Charles .. 518-434-4157 297 D
albany_office@cornell.edu
KRYLOWICZ, Brian .... 413-748-3345 218 E
bkrylowicz@springfield.edu
KRYSIAK, JR., Richard . 937-229-3766 362 C
rkrysiak1@udayton.edu
KRYSIAK BITTAR, S. Mary .... 561-723-4424 107 E
mkrysiakbittar@svdp.edu
KRYSL, Gina .... 402-844-7277 268 A
gkrysl@northeast.edu
KRYSTYNIAK, Becky ..... 763-433-1216 236 H
rebecca.krystyniak@anokaramsey.edu
KRYZHANOVSKAYA, Tatyana .... 718-522-9073 290 B
tkryzhanovskaya@asa.edu
KRZAK, Chris .... 732-987-2785 277 B
ckrzak@georgian.edu
KRZANIK, Jacki .... 413-662-5421 212 F
j.krzanik@mcla.edu
KRZANOWSKI, Roseanne .... 860-231-5647.. 89 G
rkrzanowski@usj.edu
KRZMARZICK, Tony .... 724-830-1052 397 F
tkrzmarzick@setonhill.edu
KRZYWICKI, Michael .... 570-408-4952 402 B
michael.krzywicki@wilkes.edu
KSACHIKIAN, Sam .... 818-988-2300.. 53 F
KTUL, Kathy .... 252-492-2061 338 D
ktul@vgcc.edu
KUAN, Jeffrey .... 909-447-2552.. 37 H
jkuan@cst.edu
KUAN TSU, Christina ... 212-854-2024 290 H
ckuantsu@barnard.edu
KUBA, Jodie, M .... 808-956-7251 129 B
jodiek@hawaii.edu
KUBA, Shawn .... 304-473-8560 490 E
kuba_s@wvwc.edu
KUBACKI, Matthew .... 718-420-4324 324 B
matthew.kubacki@wagner.edu
KUBAJAK, Jacob .... 660-944-2832 251 B
jacob@conception.edu
KUBAT, Robert, A .... 814-863-3681 391 F
rak28@psu.edu
KUBATZKE, Trevor, A .... 269-927-8600 226 B
tkubatzke@lakemichigancollege.edu
KUBE, Marcia .... 402-481-8845 265 B
marcia.kube@bryanhealthcollege.edu
KUBEL, Jane .... 650-508-3516.. 54 G
jkubel@ndnu.edu
KUBERSKI, Christina .... 815-599-3513 138 H
chris.kuberski@highland.edu
KUBES, Nathan .... 970-943-3084.. 85 B
nkubes@western.edu
KUBIAK, Cathy .... 616-234-3971 224 C
cathykubiak@grcc.edu
KUBIAK, Sheryl .... 313-577-4400 232 H
ao1692@wayne.edu
KUBIK, Rachel .... 714-432-5834.. 38 F
rkubik@occ.cccd.edu
KUBINAK, Lois, A .... 610-921-7612 377 F
lkubinak@albright.edu
KUBISTA, Ray .... 360-752-8312 477 C
rkubista@btc.edu
KUBITSKEY, Beth .... 810-766-6878 231 C
kubitske@umich.edu
KUBO, Takeo .... 408-288-3733.. 62 G
takeo.kubo@sjcc.edu
KUBUS, Tom .... 585-271-3657 312 E
tom.kubus@stbernards.edu
KUCER, MSA, Peter, S .. 860-632-3063.. 88 B
pkucer@holyapostles.edu
KUCERA, Karil .... 507-786-3129 242 I
kucera@stolaf.edu
KUCERA, Kevin .... 734-487-8892 223 F
kkucera@emich.edu
KUCHARSKI, Joanna ..... 212-650-7865 293 B
jkucharski@ccny.cuny.edu
KUCHESKY, Anicia .... 617-322-3513 210 F
anicia_kuchesky@laboure.edu
KUCHIBHOTLA, Anand .. 844-872-8680.. 72 J
KUCHIBHOTLA, Mamatha .... 844-872-8680.. 72 J
KUCHTA, Christopher, J .... 708-709-3950 147 A
ckuchta@prairiestate.edu
KUCIC, Terry .... 814-371-2090 399 D
tkucic@triangle-tech.edu
KUCIK, Maggie .... 317-955-6213 159 A
mkucik@marian.edu
KUCZMA, Justin .... 585-785-1454 299 E
justin.kuczma@flcc.edu
KUDLA-POLAY, Zoe ...... 309-341-5230 134 A
zkudla@sandburg.edu
KUE, Mailee .... 401-232-6448 403 B
mkue@bryant.edu
KUEBLER, Daniel .... 740-284-5268 352 I
dkuebler@franciscan.edu
KUEBLER, Jared .... 805-525-4417.. 67 J
jkuebler@thomasaquinas.edu
KUECKER, Aaron .... 708-239-4839 150 H
aaron.kuecker@trnty.edu
KUEHL, Bill .... 803-321-5276 409 I
bill.kuehl@newberry.edu
KUEHL, Katie .... 651-290-6328 241 N
katie.kuehl@mitchellhamline.edu
KUEHLER, Robert .... 303-837-2112.. 83 L
robert.kuehler@cu.edu
KUEHNER, Holly .... 850-872-3804 101 O
hkuehner@gulfcoast.edu
KUEHNL, Kody .... 614-947-6104 352 J
kody.kuehnl@franklin.edu
KUEHNLE, Melissa .... 863-784-7251 108 D
melissa.kuehnle@southflorida.edu
KUENNEN, Connie .... 844-642-2338 168 F
kuennenc@nicc.edu
KUENSTNER, Debby ...... 781-283-5770 219 C
dkuenstner@wellesley.edu
KUENTZEL, Jeffrey .... 313-577-3398 232 H
jkuentzel@wayne.edu
KUETHER, Eva .... 414-297-6897 498 B
kuethere@matc.edu
KUETHER, Shawna .... 920-424-0283 495 C
KUFFEL, Cesalee .... 989-275-5000 225 H
cesalee.kuffel@kirtland.edu
KUFFEL, Lorne .... 205-348-7200.... 7 G
lkuffel@ua.edu
KUFFREY, Casey .... 770-484-1204 122 B
casey.kuffrey@lutherrice.edu
KUFUOR, Edward .... 718-522-9071 290 B
ekufuor@asa.edu
KUGLER, Angela .... 425-558-0299 478 G
KUGLER, Jeffrey .... 717-477-1451 394 D
jwkugler@ship.edu
KUGLER, Sharon .... 203-432-1128.. 90 B
sharon.kugler@yale.edu
KUHAJDA, Kimberlee, A .... 440-826-2251 348 C
kkuhajda@bw.edu
KUHAR, Marilyn .... 617-228-3290 214 A
mkkuhar@bhcc.mass.edu
KUHL, Jaromy .... 850-474-2688 111 E
jkuhl@uwf.edu
KUHL, Sue .... 303-861-1151.. 80 E
skuhl@concorde.edu
KUHLENGEL HORVATH, Tina .... 352-392-2171 110 E
tinah@housing.ufl.edu
KUHLHORST, Michelle, L .... 260-399-7700 162 A
mkuhlhorst@sf.edu
KUHLMAN, Ann .... 203-432-9686.. 90 B
ann.kuhlman@yale.edu
KUHLMAN, Gregory ...... 718-951-5174 293 A
kuhlman@brooklyn.cuny.edu
KUHLMAN, Kathy .... 636-481-3131 253 G
kkuhlman@jeffco.edu
KUHLMANN, Diana, E .. 620-341-5173 173 C
dkuhlman@emporia.edu
KUHN, Ashley .... 239-489-9352 100 G
ashley.kuhn@fsw.edu
KUHN, Bill .... 952-446-4162 235 B
kuhnb@crown.edu
KUHN, Bradley .... 562-368-3139.. 65 H
bradleykuhn@scuhs.edu
KUHN, Chuck .... 616-988-1000 222 D
chuck.k@compass.edu
KUHN, Darlene .... 205-726-2727.... 6 E
dfkuhn@samford.edu
KUHN, David .... 307-742-3776 500 K
dkuhn@wyotech.edu
KUHN, Helen .... 217-245-3013 139 A
registrar@ic.edu
KUHN, Jens-Uwe .... 805-965-0581.. 62 M
jkuhn@sbcc.edu
KUHN, Joel, A .... 260-422-5561 156 A
jakuhn@indianatech.edu
KUHN, Karl, A .... 920-565-1000 492 A
kuhnka@lakeland.edu
KUHN, Kathryn, A .... 414-955-6501 492 F
kkuhn@mcw.edu
KUHN, Lisa .... 410-386-8032 197 G
lkuhn@carrollcc.edu
KUHN, Paul .... 732-247-5241 278 E
pkuhn@nbts.edu
KUHN, Rachel .... 773-371-5415 134 C
rkuhn@ctu.edu
KUHN, Wiebke .... 507-222-4916 234 C
wkuhn@carleton.edu
KUHN-SCHNELL, Tamara .... 217-786-2353 142 F
tammy.schnell@llcc.edu
KUHNER, Matthew .... 585-271-3657 312 E
matthew.kuhner@stbernards.edu
KUHNLENZ, Whitney .... 781-891-2630 206 C
wkuhnlenz@bentley.edu
KUHR, Brittanie .... 419-783-2411 351 J
bkuhr@defiance.edu
KUHR, Werner .... 303-384-2312.. 79 A
wkuhr@mines.edu
KUIPER, Forrest .... 907-474-7681.. 10 B
fjkuiper@alaska.edu
KUIPERS, David .... 229-931-2004 125 C
dkuipers@southgatech.edu
KUJAWA, Lisa, R .... 248-204-2403 226 E
lkujawa@ltu.edu
KUJAWA, Tricia, A .... 217-786-2211 142 F
tricia.kujawa@llcc.edu
KUKLINSKI, Danny .... 414-410-4839 490 J
dpkuklinski@stritch.edu
KUKREJA, Sunil .... 253-879-3207 483 G
kukreja@pugetsound.edu
KUKULIES, Emily Ann .. 808-845-9219 129 G
kukulies@hawaii.edu
KULA, Stan .... 973-300-2100 283 B
skula@sussex.edu
KULAGA, Jon .... 740-474-8896 358 A
KULBECK, Jennifer .... 925-631-8223.. 59 I
jak12@stmarys-ca.edu
KULESZA, Darrell .... 508-541-1864 208 E
dkulesza@dean.edu
KULESZA, Randy .... 814-866-8423 387 C
rkulesza@lecom.edu
KULESZO, Michelle .... 585-395-2622 317 B
kuleszo@brockport.edu
KULICK, Steven, W .... 315-445-4560 303 F
kulicksw@lemoyne.edu
KULIK, Dmitry .... 202-462-2101.. 93 A
kulik@iwp.edu
KULIS, Carol .... 858-653-3000.. 29 F
ckulis@calmu.edu
KULKA, Maria .... 269-782-1472 230 D
mkulka01@swmich.edu
KULKE, Erik .... 262-551-5916 491 B
ekulke@carthage.edu
KULL, Christian .... 607-962-9430 319 F
ckull1@corning-cc.edu
KULL, Edward .... 718-817-1000 300 A
ekull@fordham.edu
KULL, F. Jon .... 603-646-1552 272 F
f.jon.kull@dartmouth.edu
KULP, Amanda .... 904-620-1944 111 A
amanda.kulp@unf.edu
KULP, Holly .... 570-208-5900 386 G
hollykulp@kings.edu
KULP, Julie .... 610-625-7942 390 D
kulpj@moravian.edu
KULTAN-PFAUTZ, Natissa .... 610-341-5936 383 A
nkultan@eastern.edu
KUM, Byung-Dal .... 714-995-9988.. 47 E
KUMAR, Anish .... 412-324-6991 400 A
ank3640@pitt.edu
KUMAR, Manish .... 773-583-4050 145 G
KUMAR, Mukul .... 617-746-1990 210 E
mukul.kumar@hult.edu
KUMAR, Neeraj .... 312-341-3587 148 A
nkumar@roosevelt.edu
KUMAR, Neeraj .... 917-493-4445 304 L
nkumar@msmnyc.edu
KUMAR, Poonam .... 409-880-7398 449 B
poonam.kumar@lamar.edu
KUMAR, R. Thulasi .... 540-231-1428 475 D
tkumar@vt.edu
KUMAR, Rajesh .... 914-674-7798 305 H
rkumar@mercy.edu
KUMAR, Rakesh .... 312-658-5100 150 E
rakesh.kumar@tbiil.edu
KUMAR, Sanjeev .... 605-688-4161 416 A
sanjeev.kumar@sdstate.edu
KUMAR, Senthil .... 352-588-8351 107 B
senthil.kumar@saintleo.edu
KUMAR, Sunil .... 410-516-3355 199 E
provost@jhu.edu
KUMAR, Vijay .... 215-898-7244 399 J
kumar@seas.upenn.edu
KUMLER, Kurt .... 412-391-4100 395 H
kkumler@pointpark.edu
KUMM, David .... 402-643-7222 265 I
david.kumm@cune.edu
KUMMERMAN, Howard . 714-484-7126.. 54 C
hkummerman@cypresscollege.edu
KUMOR, Beth .... 510-649-2540.. 44 E
KUMP, Lee .... 814-863-1274 391 F
lrk4@psu.edu
KUMP, Melissa .... 406-496-4108 264 C
mkump@mtech.edu
KUN, Josh .... 213-740-5389.. 73 C
musicdean@thornton.usc.edu
KUNA, Monica .... 215-968-8003 379 B
monica.kuna@bucks.edu
KUNCE, Kim, M .... 708-709-3684 147 A
kkunce@prairiestate.edu
KUNCE, Rachel .... 216-791-5000 350 F
rachel.kunce@cim.edu
KUNDELL, Ken, F .... 410-543-6043 204 A
kfkundell@salisbury.edu
KUNDINGER, Amy .... 920-403-4223 494 B
amy.kundinger@snc.edu
KUNE, Natacha, F .... 206-543-1240 484 A
fookune@uw.edu
KUNERT, Charles .... 503-552-1742 374 B
ckunert@nunm.edu
KUNES, Melissa, J .... 814-867-0647 391 F
mjk5@psu.edu
KUNG, Bethany, E .... 202-994-6046.. 92 C
bcobb@gwu.edu
KUNJUMMEN, Raju .... 563-588-8000 165 K
rkunjummen@emmaus.edu
KUNKA, Jennifer .... 843-661-1520 408 H
jkunka@fmarion.edu
KUNKEL, JoAnn .... 605-658-3622 415 E
joann.kunkel@usd.edu
KUNKEL, Karl .... 608-785-8113 495 A
kkunkel@uwlax.edu
KUNKEL, Roberta .... 408-274-7900.. 62 F
roberta.kunkel@evc.edu
KUNKEL, Thomas .... 920-403-3165 494 B
tom.kunkel@snc.edu
KUNKEL, Tony .... 320-308-3064 240 C
abkunkel@stcloudstate.edu
KUNKEL-JORDAN, Laurie .... 414-382-6300 490 G
laurie.kunkel-jordan@alverno.edu
KUNKO, Bill .... 575-492-2501 286 E
bkunko@nmjc.edu
KUNKO, Tina .... 575-492-2782 286 E
tkunko@nmjc.edu
KUNO, Phyllis .... 701-349-5407 346 G
phylliskuno@trinitybiblecollege.edu
KUNOVICH, Sheri .... 214-768-1285 443 G
kunovich@smu.edu
KUNSMAN, Kip .... 410-777-2961 197 C
kakunsman@aacc.edu
KUNST, Malia .... 619-388-7834.. 61 B
mkunst@sdccd.edu
KUNTZ, Bliss .... 402-486-2514 268 G
bliss.kuntz@ucollege.edu
KUNTZ, Dave .... 406-243-5659 263 D
dave.kuntz@umontana.edu
KUNTZ, David .... 216-987-4790 351 D
david.kuntz@tri-c.edu
KUNTZ, F. Douglas .... 570-321-4116 388 H
kuntz@lycoming.edu
KUNTZ, Jason .... 717-391-7322 398 E
kuntz@stevenscollege.edu
KUNTZ, Jim .... 215-335-0800 388 E
KUNTZ, John .... 973-300-2252 283 B
jkuntz@sussex.edu
KUNTZ, Kristi .... 217-333-6677 151 F
kakuntz@illinois.edu
KUNTZ, Nicole .... 570-321-4081 388 H
kuntzn@lycoming.edu
KUNTZ, Twyla .... 701-349-5438 346 G
twyla@trinitybiblecollege.edu
KUNTZ, Wayne .... 228-897-4361 246 F
wayne.kuntz@mgccc.edu
KUNZ, Amy, S .... 808-956-7161 128 I
amykunz@hawaii.edu
KUNZ, Erin .... 701-788-5240 345 B
erin.kunz@mayvillestate.edu

KUNZ, Jason .... 410-837-4482 204 C
jkunz.ubpolice@ubalt.edu

KUNZ, Leonard .... 908-852-1400 275 H
kunzl01@centenaryuniversity.edu

KUNZINGER, Michael ... 434-582-7390 467 E
mmkunzin@liberty.edu

KUO, David .... 215-871-6690 395 A
davidku@pcom.edu

KUO, David .... 215-871-7128 395 A
davidku@pcom.edu

KUO, Grace, R .... 806-414-9277 450 D
grace.kuo@ttuhsc.edu

KUO, Kent .... 541-737-3525 374 H
kent.kuo@oregonstate.edu

KUO, Ling Ling .... 626-571-8811.. 73 D
linglingk@uwest.edu

KUO, Zheng-jie .... 510-763-7787.. 24 F

KUPEC, Matthew .... 618-453-7250 149 G
siuad@siu.edu

KUPERMAN, Eli .... 732-367-1060 275 B
ekuperman@bmg.edu

KUPERMAN, Tina .... 562-908-3405.. 58 M
tkuperman@riohondo.edu

KUPERMAN, Tina .... 310-900-1600.. 39 H

KUPERSMITH, Peter, A . 215-489-2254 381 K
peter.kupersmith@delval.edu

KUPFERMAN,
Francine, S .... 617-228-2316 214 A
fskupfer@bhcc.edu

KUPIEC, Suzanne .... 908-737-4804 277 F
skupiec@kean.edu

KUPO, Leilani .... 775-784-4898 270 K
lkupo@unr.edu

KUPPER, Jodi .... 402-471-2505 267 F
jkupper@nscs.edu

KUPPINGER, Karen .... 585-389-2100 307 D
kkuppin9@naz.edu

KUPRES, Megan .... 269-687-4810 230 D
mkupres@swmich.edu

KURACINA, William .... 903-886-5166 446 D
william.kuracina@tamuc.edu

KURAPATI, Raaj .... 901-678-2121 426 A
kurapati@memphis.edu

KURDA, Linda .... 907-543-4502.. 10 B
lrcurda@alaska.edu

KURIMAY, Mary Beth ... 610-436-6931 394 F
mkurimay@wcupa.edu

KURKER-STEWART,
Nicole .... 860-768-5101.. 89 E
kurkerste@hartford.edu

KUROKAWA, Linda .... 760-757-2121.. 52 G
lkorokawa@miracosta.edu

KUROWSKI, Gail .... 231-995-1283 228 F
gkurowski@nmc.edu

KURPIUS, David, D .... 573-882-6686 260 C
kurpius@missouri.edu

KURR, Brigitte .... 918-610-0027 365 H
bkurr@communitycarecollege.edu

KURTH, Ann .... 203-737-6785.. 90 B
ann.kurth@yale.edu

KURTINITIS, Sandra, L . 443-840-1015 198 D
skurtinitis@ccbcmd.edu

KURTZ, Andrew .... 419-372-0623 348 F
kurtz@bgsu.edu

KURTZ, Diane, L .... 517-750-1200 230 F
dkurtz@arbor.edu

KURTZ, James, E .... 651-696-6711 236 C
jkurtz2@macalester.edu

KURTZ, Josef .... 617-735-9979 209 A
kurtzj@emmanuel.edu

KURTZ, Rick .... 507-389-7369 240 F
rick.kurtz@southcentral.edu

KURTZ, Steve .... 208-769-7835 132 A
steve.kurtz@nic.edu

KURTZ, Terri .... 361-572-6463 456 H
terri.kurtz@victoriacollege.edu

KURTZ, Terry .... 440-775-8692 357 G
terry.kurtz@oberlin.edu

KURTZ-SHAW, Brad .... 208-467-8539 132 B
bradshaw@nnu.edu

KURZY, Tracy .... 626-256-4673.. 37 D
tkurzy@coh.org

KURZYNA, Mary .... 201-216-9901 276 C
mary.kurzyna@eicollege.edu

KUSCH, Bruce, C .... 801-524-8113 458 F
bkusch@ldsbc.edu

KUSCH, Jennifer .... 414-955-4860 492 F
jkusch@mcw.edu

KUSER, Janet .... 617-236-5458 209 D
jkuser@fisher.edu

KUSH, Lynn, A .... 215-871-6815 395 A
lynnku@pcom.edu

KUSHMIDER, Kristin ..... 303-724-8488.. 84 B
kristin.kushmider@ucdenver.edu

KUSHNER, Cynthia .... 440-366-7610 355 B

KUSHNER, Mikhel, A .... 410-706-1852 202 F
mikhel.kushner@umaryland.edu

KUSHNER, Tiffany .... 908-852-1400 275 H
kushnert@centenaryuniversity.edu

KUSKA, Sharon .... 402-472-9237 269 A
skuska1@unl.edu

KUSKOWSKI, David .... 864-656-5297 406 F
dkuskow@clemson.edu

KUSPA, Adam .... 713-798-1060 430 E
akuspa@bcm.edu

KUSS, Charlotte .... 850-729-4935 104 L
kussc@nwfsc.edu

KUSUMI, Kenro .... 480-965-8065.. 11 A
kenro.kusumi@asu.edu

KUTA RESKE, Teresa .... 413-265-2355 208 B
resket@elms.edu

KUTATELADZE, Andrei .. 303-871-2995.. 84 C
akutatel@du.edu

KUTCH, Jason .... 219-464-5684 162 C
jason.kutch@valpo.edu

KUTCHER, Gene .... 609-895-5152 280 D
ekutcher@rider.edu

KUTCHMAN, Michael .... 814-472-3035 396 I
mkutchman@francis.edu

KUTHY, Anna .... 270-686-4277 179 F
anna.kuthy@brescia.edu

KUTI, Morakinyo .... 937-376-6598 349 H
mkuti@centralstate.edu

KUTINAC, Linda .... 575-674-2201 284 P
lkutinac@burrell.edu

KUTLENIOS, Rose, M ... 304-336-8108 489 B
rose.kutlenios@westliberty.edu

KUTNEY, Joshua, P .... 920-565-1000 492 A
kutneyjp@lakeland.edu

KUTZKE, Mike .... 320-222-5218 239 H
mike.kutzke@ridgewater.edu

KUVAAS, Laura .... 320-222-6090 239 H
laura.kuvaas@ridgewater.edu

KUYKENDALL, Brad ...... 915-532-3737 457 E

KUYKENDALL, John ...... 317-788-3778 161 F
kuykendallj@uindy.edu

KUYKENDALL, John ...... 870-575-8498.. 22 F
kuykendallj@uapb.edu

KUYKENDALL, John ...... 870-575-8489.. 22 F
kuykendallj@uapb.edu

KUYKENDALL, John ...... 843-863-7026 406 C
jkuykendall@csuniv.edu

KUYKENDALL, Michelle 208-467-8521 132 B
mlkuykendall@nnu.edu

KUYKENDALL, Robin .... 575-769-4994 285 C
robin.kuykendall@clovis.edu

KUZMA, Marta .... 203-432-2606.. 90 B
marta.kuzma@yale.edu

KUZNACIC, Katharine ... 262-472-1918 496 E

KVAAL, Kim .... 253-879-3204 483 G
kkvaal@pugetsound.edu

KVIGNE, Eric .... 530-752-1247.. 69 A
epkvigne@ucdavis.edu

KWAI, Joshladd .... 216-687-3910 350 G
j.kwai@csuohio.edu

KWAK, Kun .... 909-623-0302.. 59 H

KWAK, Kyueil .... 678-889-8029 118 F
kkwak@gcuniv.edu

KWAK, Nojin .... 716-645-2368 315 F
vpinted@buffalo.edu

KWAN, Billy .... 212-472-1500 309 B
libraryinfo@nysid.edu

KWANBUNBUMPEN,
Ada .... 204-286-5244 191 A
akwanbunbumpen@suno.edu

KWANDRANS, Karen .... 716-286-8559 309 F
kwandrans@niagara.edu

KWANG CHUNG, Sae ... 714-222-1110.. 27 I

KWASIGROH, Catherine 731-661-5281 425 F
ckwasigroh@uu.edu

KWASITSU, Lishi .... 503-517-1023 377 B
lkwasitsu@warnerpacific.edu

KWENDA, Maxwell .... 509-313-6948 479 E
kwenda@gonzaga.edu

KWESKIN, Amy, B .... 314-935-9842 261 B
amy.b.kweskin@wustl.edu

KWIATEK, Brandon .... 610-799-1120 388 B
bkwiatek@lccc.edu

KWIATKOWSKI, Amy ..... 415-955-2100.. 25 A
akwiatkowski@alliant.edu

KWIATKOWSKI,
Anthony .... 773-907-4784 134 N
akwiatkowski@ccc.edu

KWIATKOWSKI, Christa 304-367-4796 488 L
christa.kwiatkowski@fairmontstate.edu

KWIATKOWSKI,
Randall, D .... 719-333-4144 502 C
randall.kwiatkowski@afacademy.af.edu

KWIECIEN, Garth .... 510-531-4911.. 57 C
gkwiecien@peralta.edu

KWIECIEN, Garth .... 415-452-7768.. 37 C
gkwiecien@ccsf.edu

KWIECINSKA, Karolina .. 860-297-4203.. 88 I
karolina.kwiecinska@trincoll.edu

KWILINSKI, Kathie .... 206-934-7965 482 H
kathie.kwilinski@seattlecolleges.edu

KWINTERA, Tony .... 219-473-4246 154 A

KWIST, Sabrina, T .... 925-473-7314.. 40 I
skwist@losmedanos.edu

KWOFIE, Winnie .... 510-885-4149.. 31 C
winnie.kwofie@csueastbay.edu

KWOLEK, Katherine ...... 617-585-0200 206 E
katherine.kwolek@the-bac.edu

KWOLEK, Kathryn .... 617-587-5662 216 H
kwolekk@neco.edu

KWON, Jenny .... 415-565-4627.. 69 B
kwonjenny@uchastings.edu

KWONG, Davina .... 202-651-5005.. 92 B
davina.kwong@gallaudet.edu

KYLE, Eric .... 417-447-7602 257 B
kylee@otc.edu

KYLE, James, R .... 619-596-2766.. 26 I
jkyle@ata.edu

KYLE, Jean .... 507-433-0568 240 A
jean.kyle@riverland.edu

KYLE, Katherine .... 678-407-5770 119 B
kkyle@ggc.edu

KYLE, Michael .... 507-786-3025 242 I
kylem@stolaf.edu

KYLE, Randy .... 651-641-3456 236 A
rkyle001@luthersem.edu

KYLE, Roberta .... 508-929-8811 213 D
rkyle@worcester.edu

KYNARD, Olivia, L .... 413-538-7000 214 D
okynard@hcc.edu

KYNOR, James .... 719-589-7075.. 83 I
james.kynor@trinidadstate.edu

KYOORE, Jude .... 636-481-3210 253 G
jkyoore@jeffco.edu

KYPRIANE, Schemanun 530-464-3544.. 60 A
mky@spots.edu

KYPUROS, Javier .... 903-566-7267 455 C
jkypuros@uttyler.edu

KYRIAKIDES, Michelle .. 516-463-6060 301 E
michelle.kyriakides@hofstra.edu

KYTE, Murray, E .... 989-837-4986 228 G
kytem@northwood.edu

KYTE, Rachel .... 617-627-4172 219 A
rachel.kyte@tufts.edu

KYTE, Richard, L .... 608-796-3704 496 L
rlkyte@viterbo.edu

L

LA, Mibong .... 973-684-5877 279 B
mla@pccc.edu

LA BARBERA,
Christopher .... 781-239-3114 214 E
clabarbera@massbay.edu

LA BELLE, Brian .... 312-488-6062.. 36 G
blabelle@thechicagoschool.edu

LA BELLE-HAMER,
Nettie .... 907-474-5837.. 10 B
nalabellehamer@alaska.edu

LA CHAPELLE,
Jacqueline .... 337-550-1282 189 B
jlachape@lsue.edu

LA CRETA, James .... 781-736-2231 207 D
jlacreta@brandeis.edu

LA MAZZA, Bernadette . 480-732-7019.. 13 B
bernadette.la.mazza@cgc.edu

LA PIERRE, Mary .... 518-562-4125 295 F
mary.lapierre@clinton.edu

LA POINT, Kristine, L ... 773-975-1295 493 A
krisbob1@cs.com

LA ROCCA, Chris .... 252-492-2061 338 D
laroccac@vgcc.edu

LA ROCQUE, Monique .. 207-893-6643 195 I
mlarocque@sjcme.edu

LA TORRA, Grace .... 206-876-6100 483 A
glatorra@theseattleschool.edu

LABA, Laura .... 847-543-2200 135 G
llaba@clcillinois.edu

LABADIE, Nicole .... 574-284-4000 160 F

LABADIE, Nicole .... 713-525-3129 453 H
labadin@stthom.edu

LABADIE, Tracy .... 269-488-4223 225 C
tlabadie@kvcc.edu

LABAN, Danielle .... 312-261-3162 145 C
dlaban@nl.edu

LABANG, Yaw .... 903-593-8311 448 A
ylabang@texascollege.edu

LABARBERA, Paul .... 845-758-7940 290 G
labarbera@bard.edu

LABARR, Carrie .... 315-268-6480 295 E
clabarr@clarkson.edu

LABAT, Nichole .... 985-545-1500 188 B

LABATTE, Rhonda .... 605-698-3966 415 C
rlabatte@swcollege.edu

LABAUGH, Amy, R .... 208-496-1155 130 G
labaugha@byui.edu

LABAY, Theodore .... 251-405-7240.... 1 E
tlabay@bishop.edu

LABBADIA, Ashley .... 860-343-5861.. 86 G
alabbadia@mxcc.edu

LABBERTON, Mark, A ... 626-584-5201.. 43 E

LABE, Geoffey .... 610-896-1806 385 H
glabe@haverford.edu

LABELL, Yitzi .... 301-649-7077 205 B
ylabell@yeshiva.edu

LABENSKI, Paula .... 570-740-0388 388 G
plabenski@luzerne.edu

LABKOWSKI, Zalman .... 718-774-3430 292 D

LABOE, Mark .... 773-325-4004 136 F
mlaboe@depaul.edu

LABOE, Timothy .... 313-883-8556 229 J
laboe.timothy@shms.edu

LABONTE, Angela .... 603-342-3041 272 E
alabonte@ccsnh.edu

LABONTE, Gene, R .... 978-542-6542 213 B
gene.labonte@salemstate.edu

LABONTE, Jason .... 631-656-2113 299 G
jason.labonte@ftc.edu

LABONTE, Kim .... 618-650-2789 149 F
klabont@siue.edu

LABOR, Jennifer .... 918-465-1828 365 K
jlabor@eosc.edu

LABORDE, Bridget .... 985-545-1500 188 B

LABOSIER, Jeremy .... 562-906-4532.. 27 E
jeremy.labosier@biola.edu

LABOSSIERE, James ..... 845-368-7210 314 F

LABOUNTY, Jennifer ..... 714-992-7085.. 54 D
jlabounty@fullcoll.edu

LABOY, Gloryber .... 787-751-0160 505 C
glaboy@cmpr.pr.gov

LABOY FUSTER, Rafael . 787-720-4476 509 G
relacionespublicas@mizpa.edu

LABRAKE, Matthew .... 201-360-4038 277 D
mlabrake@hccc.edu

LABRANCHE, Michael .... 504-398-2241 191 E
mlabranche@uhcno.edu

LABRIE, John .... 508-793-7623 207 F
jlabrie@clarku.edu

LABRIE, Lori, A .... 713-313-7040 448 D
labrie_la@tsu.edu

LABRIOLA, Elisabeth, S 860-439-2064.. 87 F
elisabeth.labriola@conncoll.edu

LABRON, Wendy .... 617-735-9778 209 A
labronw@emmanuel.edu

LABROSSE, Tonya, B .... 603-535-2846 274 B
tblabrosse@plymouth.edu

LABROZZI, Ryan .... 304-637-1253 486 D
labrozzir@dewv.edu

LABRY, Daniel .... 877-476-8674 435 G

LABS, Jeff .... 715-365-4406 498 D
jlabs@nicoletcollege.edu

LABUDE, Mark .... 318-342-1040 193 A
labude@ulm.edu

LACAGNINO, Sara, N .... 908-709-7007 283 E
lacagnino@ucc.edu

LACASCIO, Joe .... 508-286-3405 219 F
lacascio_joe@wheatoncollege.edu

LACEFIELD, Aretha .... 870-575-8491.. 22 F
lacefielda@uapb.edu

LACEFIELD, Hyla .... 650-306-3460.. 62 I
lacefieldh@smccd.edu

LACEY, Doris .... 256-469-7333.... 5 I
finaid@hbc1.edu

LACEY, Kasi .... 573-592-5269 261 F
kasi.lacey@westminster-mo.edu

LACEY, Kristin .... 864-596-9031 407 G
kristin.lacey@converse.edu

LACEY, Mark .... 904-632-3319 101 A
mark.lacey@fscj.edu

LACEY, Pete .... 810-989-5561 230 A
placey@sc4.edu

LACEY, Roshae .... 601-877-6333 244 B
rlacey@alcorn.edu

LACH, Carolyn .... 773-244-5506 145 F
clach@northpark.edu

LALLEY, Bobbi ... 301-688-4670 501 I
bobbi.lalley@dodiis.mil
LALLO, Christian ... 410-225-2300 200 B
clallo@mica.edu
LALLY, Jay ... 321-674-8953 100 A
jlally@fit.edu
LALLY, Kim, B ... 937-229-3902 362 C
klally1@udayton.edu
LALLY, Mary ... 617-573-8436 218 G
mlally@suffolk.edu
LALLY, Shiela ... 617-236-4422 209 D
slally@fisher.edu
LALONDE, Catherine ... 518-327-6056 310 G
clalonde@paulsmiths.edu
LALONDE, Joseph, C ... 337-550-1470 189 B
jlalonde@lsue.edu
LALONDE, Matthew ... 518-255-5215 318 F
lalondmm@cobleskill.edu
LALOVIC-HAND, Mira ... 856-256-4146 280 H
lalovic-hand@rowan.edu
LALTRELLO, Rob ... 678-872-8088 119 C
rlaltrel@highlands.edu
LALUMENDRE, Rob ... 815-939-5350 146 F
rlalumen@olivet.edu
LALUZERNE, Joe ... 619-849-2317.. 57 J
jlaluzer@pointloma.edu
LALUZERNE,
Shannon, S ... 920-923-7661 492 D
slaluzerne@marianuniversity.edu
LAM, Clement ... 408-855-5332.. 75 C
clement.lam@wvm.edu
LAM, Felix ... 212-650-8173 293 B
flam@ccny.cuny.edu
LAM, Kenneth ... 201-692-7035 276 I
kenneth_lam@fdu.edu
LAM, Mariam ... 951-827-5672.. 70 B
mariam.lam@ucr.edu
LAM, Ming-huei ... 323-357-6234.. 49 D
lamm2@elac.edu
LAM, Philip ... 212-517-3929 315 B
p.lam@sia.edu
LAM, Sarah ... 315-792-5321 306 G
slam@mvcc.edu
LAMA, Diane ... 914-367-8344 313 E
diane.lama@dunwoodie.edu
LAMACK, Mary ... 580-559-5702 365 J
mlamack@ecok.edu
LAMAGNA, Dan ... 570-504-1579 387 A
lamagnad@lackawanna.edu
LAMANNA, Richard ... 718-289-5355 292 H
richard.lamanna@bcc.cuny.edu
LAMANQUE, Andrew ... 510-742-2315.. 54 J
alamanque@ohlone.edu
LAMAR, Melissa ... 860-773-1407.. 87 E
mlamar@tunxis.edu
LAMAR, Sharmaine ... 610-690-5675 398 B
slamar1@swarthmore.edu
LAMARAND, Donita, M 757-446-6009 465 H
lamaradm@evms.edu
LAMARCH, Jessica ... 906-217-4086 221 J
jessica.lamarch@baycollege.edu
LAMARCHE, Gilles ... 770-426-2674 122 A
gilles.lamarche@life.edu
LAMARCHE, Paul ... 609-258-4999 279 E
lamarche@princeton.edu
LAMARRE-LAURENT,
Valerie ... 530-752-1011.. 69 A
LAMB, Barry, P ... 217-786-2334 142 F
barry.lamb@llcc.edu
LAMB, Colin ... 620-276-9683 173 H
colin.lamb@gcccks.edu
LAMB, Cory ... 641-683-5141 166 F
cory.lamb@indianhills.edu
LAMB, Craig ... 585-345-6975 300 D
crlamb@genesee.edu
LAMB, Craig ... 704-216-3500 337 C
craig.lamb@rccc.edu
LAMB, David ... 215-368-5000 389 G
dlamb@missio.edu
LAMB, Duane ... 205-348-8092.... 7 G
dlamb@fa.ua.edu
LAMB, Jeffrey, N ... 714-564-6080.. 58 F
lamb_jeffrey@sac.edu
LAMB, Jennifer ... 276-326-4397 464 A
jlamb@bluefield.edu
LAMB, Jon ... 734-462-4400 230 B
jlamb@schoolcraft.edu
LAMB, Joseph, E ... 937-255-6565 501 A
joseph.lamb@afit.edu
LAMB, Keith ... 940-397-4291 439 F
keith.lamb@msutexas.edu
LAMB, Kelly ... 816-331-5700 257 F
LAMB, Kevin, D ... 859-238-5367 179 H
kevin.lamb@centre.edu
LAMB, Kyle ... 731-989-6020 418 H
klamb@fhu.edu
LAMB, Linda ... 315-866-0300 301 B
lamblc@herkimer.edu
LAMB, Margaret ... 619-388-6957.. 60 H
mlamb@sdccd.edu
LAMB, Mary ... 707-468-3071.. 51 F
mlamb@mendocino.edu
LAMB, Marybeth ... 508-531-1353 212 B
marybeth.lamb@bridgew.edu
LAMB, Melissa ... 912-427-5840 117 B
mlamb@coastalpines.edu
LAMB, Michael ... 316-978-3804 178 B
mike.lamb@wichita.edu
LAMB, Molly ... 217-206-8622 151 E
mehle01s@uis.edu
LAMB, Stephen, R ... 706-446-3147 115 I
stelamb@augusta.edu
LAMB, Susan ... 925-969-2001.. 40 H
slamb@dvc.edu
LAMBA, Sandy ... 707-864-7000.. 64 F
sandy.lamba@solano.edu
LAMBA, Sangeeta ... 973-972-4823 281 B
lambasa@njms.rutgers.edu
LAMBDIN, Brandon ... 423-746-5337 425 C
bslambdin@tnwewsleyan.edu
LAMBERSON, Diane ... 281-649-3090 436 D
dlamberson@hbu.edu
LAMBERSON, Jeffrey ... 843-953-7962 406 D
jlamber6@citadel.edu
LAMBERSON, Shannon . 817-531-5817 450 F
sklamberson@txwes.edu
LAMBERT, Alli ... 802-656-0518 462 D
alli.lambert@uvm.edu
LAMBERT, Ame ... 503-725-4410 375 D
alamber2@pdx.edu
LAMBERT, Angela ... 304-327-4480 488 J
alambert@bluefieldstate.edu
LAMBERT, Angelena ... 916-558-2201.. 51 B
lambera@scc.losrios.edu
LAMBERT, Anne ... 713-525-2160 453 H
lambera@stthom.edu
LAMBERT, Barry ... 254-968-9227 445 F
blambert@tarleton.edu
LAMBERT, Bill ... 909-274-4215.. 52 K
wlambert@mtsac.edu
LAMBERT, Buddy ... 918-540-6451 366 F
georgml@neo.edu
LAMBERT, Charla ... 516-367-6890 296 A
LAMBERT, Chip ... 276-326-4603 464 A
clambert@bluefield.edu
LAMBERT, Chris ... 757-352-4091 469 D
clambert@regent.edu
LAMBERT, Christopher .. 267-341-3309 385 I
clambert@holyfamily.edu
LAMBERT, Cindy ... 806-874-3571 431 K
cindy.lambert@clarendoncollege.edu
LAMBERT, David ... 740-377-2520 361 D
david.lambert@tsbc.edu
LAMBERT, Dewayne ... 985-545-1500 188 B
LAMBERT, Elizabeth ... 607-735-1822 298 G
elambert@elmira.edu
LAMBERT, Eric ... 219-980-6821 157 A
erilambe@iu.edu
LAMBERT, Ian ... 313-664-1474 222 C
ilambert@collegeforcreativestudies.edu
LAMBERT, James ... 802-468-6052 462 H
james.lambert@castleton.edu
LAMBERT, James ... 540-261-4122 470 D
james.lambert@svu.edu
LAMBERT, James ... 419-372-9970 348 F
jlamber@bgsu.edu
LAMBERT, Jay ... 361-570-4290 452 C
lambertj1@uhv.edu
LAMBERT, Joni ... 251-580-2100.... 1 I
joni.lambert@coastalalabama.edu
LAMBERT, Kathy ... 919-508-2028 344 D
kplambert@peace.edu
LAMBERT, Kelley ... 276-326-4260 464 A
klambert@bluefield.edu
LAMBERT, Kevin ... 606-589-3305 182 F
kevin.lambert@kctcs.edu
LAMBERT, III, Lake ... 812-866-7056 155 D
lambert@hanover.edu
LAMBERT, Lee, D ... 520-206-4747.. 15 E
llambert@pima.edu
LAMBERT, Lori, A ... 513-745-3203 364 F
lambert@xavier.edu
LAMBERT, Olga ... 630-829-6291 133 B
olambert@ben.edu
LAMBERT, Robyn ... 573-288-6640 251 I
rlambert@culver.edu
LAMBERT, Shari ... 734-973-3345 232 A
shlambert@wccnet.edu
LAMBERT, Stacey ... 617-327-6777 219 G
stacey_lambert@williamjames.edu
LAMBERT, Steven ... 217-854-3231 133 F
LAMBERT, Tamatha ... 478-471-2700 122 D
tamatha.lambert@mga.edu
LAMBERT, Toni ... 434-949-1017 474 D
toni.lambert@southside.edu
LAMBERT-JONES,
Rythee ... 301-405-5649 202 E
rljones7@umd.edu
LAMBERT-THOMAS,
Kimberly ... 713-221-8166 452 B
thomaski@uhd.edu
LAMBERTH, Lucy ... 601-484-8776 246 B
lmorgan1@meridiancc.edu
LAMBERTON, Jill ... 765-361-6154 162 G
lambertj@wabash.edu
LAMBETH, Gregory ... 208-885-6716 132 C
lambeth@uidaho.edu
LAMBKIN, Leslie ... 816-322-0110 250 E
leslie.lambkin@calvary.edu
LAMBLEY, Jennifer ... 605-367-5990 416 B
jennifer.lambley@southeasttech.edu
LAMBORN, Kim ... 314-367-8700 260 A
kim.lamborn@uhsp.edu
LAMBORN, Kim ... 503-251-5798 377 A
klamborn@uws.edu
LAMBOY, Camille ... 787-743-7979 509 D
calamboy@suagm.edu
LAMBOY, Edwin ... 212-650-5471 293 B
elamboy@ccny.cuny.edu
LAMBRECHT, Anne, K ... 989-463-7225 220 F
lambrechtak@alma.edu
LAMBRECHT, Jess ... 920-465-2222 494 F
lambrej@uwgb.edu
LAMBRECHT,
Jessica, N ... 920-565-1000 492 A
lambrechtjn@lakeland.edu
LAMBRECHT, John ... 708-456-0300 151 A
johnlambrecht@triton.edu
LAMBRECHTSEN, Karen 916-577-2200.. 76 C
klambrechtsen@jessup.edu
LAMBRIGHT, Jonathan .. 912-358-4172 124 H
lambrij@savannahstate.edu
LAMBROPOULOS,
Despina ... 978-556-3614 215 C
dlambropoulos@necc.mass.edu
LAMBRUNO, Joyce ... 270-707-3844 181 G
joyce.lambruno@kctcs.edu
LAMELZA, George ... 417-447-2664 257 B
lamelzag@otc.edu
LAMERS, Chet ... 920-498-5723 498 F
chet.lamers@nwtc.edu
LAMICA, Lauren ... 413-545-3016 211 D
llamica@finaid.umass.edu
LAMICA, Thomas ... 805-922-6966.. 24 L
thomas.lamica@hancockcollege.edu
LAMIMAN, Lynne ... 972-708-7536 434 F
LAMIQUIZ, Jason ... 509-453-0374 481 G
jason.lamiquiz@perrytech.edu
LAMM, Edward ... 920-403-3007 494 B
edward.lamm@snc.edu
LAMM, Gary ... 254-295-4545 453 A
glamm@umhb.edu
LAMMERS, Jenna ... 618-545-3044 141 C
jlammers@kaskaskia.edu
LAMMERS, Shelley ... 402-844-7282 268 A
shelley@northeast.edu
LAMMONS, Anthony ... 951-343-4309.. 27 J
alammons@calbaptist.edu
LAMONS, Jerisia ... 270-706-8841 181 C
jlamons0001@kctcs.edu
LAMONT, Becky ... 812-488-2680 161 E
bl164@evansville.edu
LAMONTAGNE, Ramona 815-836-5291 142 C
lamontra@lewisu.edu
LAMOTT, Eric, E ... 651-641-8729 235 A
lamott@csp.edu
LAMOUREUX, Leila ... 781-239-4702 205 G
llamoureux@babson.edu
LAMOUREUX, AA,
Richard, E ... 508-767-7033 205 F
re.lamoureux@assumption.edu
LAMPE, Lawrence, P ... 513-556-2201 361 I
lampelp@ucmail.uc.edu
LAMPE, Paul ... 636-584-6581 252 D
paul.lampe@eastcentral.edu
LAMPEREZ, Eddie ... 480-423-6300.. 14 B
eddie.lamperez@scottsdalecc.edu
LAMPERT, Jackie ... 701-766-4415 344 F
LAMPERT-SHEPEL,
Elina ... 212-463-0400 322 C
elina.lampert-shepel@touro.edu
LAMPHERE, Scott ... 617-243-2115 210 G
slamphere@lasell.edu
LAMPHIER, Denise ... 641-628-5279 164 B
lamphierd@centrla.edu
LAMPING, Patrick ... 859-442-4175 181 D
patrick.lamping@kctcs.edu
LAMPKIN, Patricia, M ... 847-491-5360 146 C
pml@northwestern.edu
LAMPKIN, Reggie ... 706-867-4518 126 G
reggie.lampkin@ung.edu
LAMPKIN-WILLIAMS,
Ann ... 313-593-5090 231 B
lampkin@umich.edu
LAMPKIN-WILLIAMS,
Ann ... 313-593-5321 231 B
lampkin@umich.edu
LAMPLEY, Dearl ... 615-790-4419 423 D
dlampley@columbiastate.edu
LAMPLEY, Katherine ... 781-891-2243 206 C
klampley@bentley.edu
LAMPMAN, Claudia ... 907-786-1619.. 10 A
cblampman@alaska.edu
LAMPONE, Nick ... 715-675-3331 498 E
lamponen@ntc.edu
LAMPSON, Dawayne ... 715-682-1399 493 G
dlampson@northland.edu
LAMSMA, Matt ... 509-313-4100 479 E
lamsma@gonzaga.edu
LAMUNYON, Craig ... 909-869-3898.. 30 B
cwlamunyon@cpp.edu
LANA, Peter ... 585-389-2344 307 D
plana0@naz.edu
LANAGAN, Keni ... 865-981-8308 420 C
keni.lanagan@maryvillecollege.edu
LANCASTER, Amy, E ... 864-597-4430 413 E
lancasterae@wofford.edu
LANCASTER, Brad ... 717-337-6377 384 C
blancast@gettysburg.edu
LANCASTER, Brian ... 620-223-2700 173 F
brianl@fortscott.edu
LANCASTER, David ... 304-424-8346 490 A
david.lancaster@wvup.edu
LANCASTER, Dennis ... 417-255-7900 256 A
dennislancaster@missouristate.edu
LANCASTER, Dennis ... 417-255-7900 255 J
dennislancaster@missouristate.edu
LANCASTER, James ... 323-953-4000.. 49 E
lancasj@lacitycollege.edu
LANCASTER, Jennifer ... 718-489-5323 312 H
jlancaster@sfc.edu
LANCASTER, Kelly ... 406-604-4300 262 C
klancaster@apollos.edu
LANCASTER, Kim ... 270-745-4346 186 A
kim.lancaster@wku.edu
LANCASTER, Kimberley . 561-790-9006 105 C
lancastk@palmbeachstate.edu
LANCASTER, Loren ... 406-874-6171 262 K
lancasterl@milescc.edu
LANCASTER, Mary Beth 251-809-1500.... 1 I
mary.lancaster@coastalalabama.edu
LANCASTER, Paula, E ... 989-774-6995 221 M
lanca1pe@cmich.edu
LANCASTER, Rich ... 484-365-7252 388 F
rlancaster@lincoln.edu
LANCASTER, Robin ... 501-882-4545.. 17 H
rglancaster@asub.edu
LANCE, Amanda ... 870-777-5722.. 23 C
amanda.lance@uaht.edu
LANCE, Cindy ... 870-777-5722.. 23 C
cindy.lance@uaht.edu
LANCE, Tina ... 540-834-1906 472 J
tlance@germanna.edu
LAND, Christopher ... 508-289-2900 220 B
cland@whoi.edu
LAND, Elizabeth ... 504-280-6723 189 F
eland@uno.edu
LAND, Kelly ... 706-778-8500 124 B
LAND, Matt ... 260-665-4143 161 C
landm@trine.edu
LAND, Roderic ... 801-957-4024 460 D
roderic.land@slcc.edu
LANDA, Carrie ... 617-353-3569 207 C
clanda@bu.edu
LANDA, Keith ... 914-251-6435 318 E
keith.landa@purchase.edu
LANDA, Michelle ... 844-922-8228.. 91 E
LANDAETA, Rafael ... 254-459-5601 445 F
rlandaeta@tarleton.edu
LANDAU, Joshua ... 717-815-6632 402 G
jlandau@ycp.edu

LANDEN, Alexander .... 734-487-6469 223 F
alanden@emich.edu
LANDEN, Jenny .... 505-428-1837 287 H
jenny.landen@sfcc.edu
LANDEN, Marcia .... 601-266-4119 248 H
marcia.landen@usm.edu
LANDEN, Robyn .... 307-268-2362 499 T
rlanden@caspercollege.edu
LANDENBERGER, Lacey 316-295-5407 173 G
lacey_landenberger@friends.edu
LANDENBERGER,
Rebecca .... 906-217-4266 221 J
becky.landenberger@baycollege.edu
LANDENBERGER, Toni .. 402-228-8286 268 D
tlandenberger@southeast.edu
LANDENBURGER,
Marguerite .... 540-665-4618 470 A
mlandenb@su.edu
LANDER, Janice .... 303-273-3266.. 79 A
jslander@mines.edu
LANDER, Laura .... 903-730-4890 437 E
llander@jarvis.edu
LANDEROS, Ramiro ...... 714-744-7865.. 36 D
landeros@chapman.edu
LANDERS, Ben .... 865-251-1800 422 G
blanders@south.edu
LANDERS, Joanne ...... 973-290-4720 282 G
jlanders@steu.edu
LANDERS, Mary, G ...... 336-256-2014 342 D
mglander@uncg.edu
LANDERS, Michael ...... 903-875-7488 439 G
michael.landers@navarrocollege.edu
LANDERS, Tyler, R ...... 262-243-5700 491 E
tyler.landers@cuw.edu
LANDETA, Lynne .... 818-677-3689.. 32 E
lynne.landeta@csun.edu
LANDEVER, Gwen ...... 913-758-6243 177 I
gwen.landever@stmary.edu
LANDGAARD, Jodi ...... 507-372-3403 239 B
jodi.landgaard@mnwest.edu
LANDGRAF, Tanya ...... 712-749-2212 164 A
landgraft@bvu.edu
LANDGREN, Peter ...... 513-556-6703 361 I
peter.landgren@uc.edu
LANDING, Haydee .... 787-725-8120 505 J
hlandiing0030@eap.edu
LANDIS, Amy .... 303-273-3871.. 79 A
amylandis@mines.edu
LANDIS, Bethany, L ...... 517-750-1200 230 F
blandis@arbor.edu
LANDIS, David .... 620-278-4235 177 E
dlandis@sterling.edu
LANDIS, Kristi .... 712-324-5061 168 H
klandis@nwicc.edu
LANDIS, Michelle ...... 928-344-7526.. 11 B
michelle.landis@azwestern.edu
LANDIS, Sarah .... 540-828-5334 464 C
slandis@bridgewater.edu
LANDIS, Susan .... 540-665-4513 470 A
slandis@su.edu
LANDISS, Leslie .... 615-966-6194 420 B
leslie.landiss@lipscomb.edu
LANDOWSKI, Anthony .. 608-757-7726 497 D
alandowski@blackhawk.edu
LANDPHAIR, Juliette ..... 540-654-1656 471 B
jlandpha@umw.edu
LANDRAU-ESPINOSA,
Barbara .... 787-993-8856 510 E
barbara.landrau@upr.edu
LANDREMAN, Lisa ...... 503-370-6139 377 E
llandreman@willamette.edu
LANDRETH, Paige ...... 405-945-3200 368 C
paige.n.landreth@okstate.edu
LANDRIEU, Josefina ..... 651-793-1272 238 F
josefina.landrieu@metrostate.edu
LANDRIEU, Madeleine .. 504-861-5550 190 A
landrieu@loyno.edu
LANDRITH, James ...... 864-231-2000 405 F
wlandrith@andersonuniversity.edu
LANDRUM, Kay .... 817-598-6499 457 C
klandrum@wc.edu
LANDRUM, Zalika ...... 773-602-5116 135 A
zlandrum@ccc.edu
LANDRY, Abbie .... 318-357-4403 192 D
landry@nsula.edu
LANDRY, Brett .... 972-721-5276 451 E
cobdean@udallas.edu
LANDRY, Debborah ...... 918-444-2060 366 G
landryd@nsuok.edu
LANDRY, Fred .... 318-869-5136 186 C
flandry@centenary.edu
LANDRY, Patrick .... 337-482-6402 192 F
pml@louisiana.edu

LANDRY, Stephen .... 973-761-7386 282 K
stephen.landry@shu.edu
LANDRY-THOMAS,
Kerii .... 225-771-2142 191 C
klandry-thomas@sulc.edu
LANDS, Jon .... 850-478-8496 105 F
jlands@pcci.edu
LANDSAW, Christy .... 918-444-2192 366 G
landsaw@nsuok.edu
LANDWER, Allan, J ...... 325-670-5894 436 B
alandwer@hsutx.edu
LANDWERMEYER,
Elizabeth .... 817-515-3049 445 A
elizabeth.landwermeyer@tccd.edu
LANDY, Margo .... 415-338-3982.. 34 A
margolandy@sfsu.edu
LANE, Austin, A .... 618-453-2341 149 G
austin.lane@siu.edu
LANE, Betsy .... 760-355-6525.. 45 N
betsy.lane@imperial.edu
LANE, Beverly .... 614-885-5585 359 K
bslane@pcj.edu
LANE, Bradley .... 206-934-4100 482 E
bradley.lane@seattlecolleges.edu
LANE, Bradley .... 206-934-3881 482 G
bradley.lane@seattlecolleges.edu
LANE, Charles, E .... 352-392-9122 110 E
charlielane@ufl.edu
LANE, David .... 865-354-3000 424 D
lanedr@roanestate.edu
LANE, Dean .... 202-462-2101.. 93 A
dlane@iwp.edu
LANE, Deborah .... 865-573-4517 419 E
dlane@johnsonu.edu
LANE, Diane, L .... 217-362-6416 144 D
dlane@millikin.edu
LANE, Edwin, H .... 816-415-7587 261 G
lanee@william.jewell.edu
LANE, Gower .... 845-451-1309 297 E
gower.lane@culinary.edu
LANE, Illana, R .... 215-637-7700 385 I
LANE, Jason, E .... 513-529-6317 356 A
laneje4@miamioh.edu
LANE, Jill .... 678-466-4194 117 A
jilllane@clayton.edu
LANE, John .... 713-221-8292 452 B
lanej@uhd.edu
LANE, Jon .... 940-397-4241 439 F
jon.lane@msutexas.edu
LANE, Kelsi-Leandra .... 315-445-4194 303 F
lanekl@lemoyne.edu
LANE, Kimberly, A ...... 864-833-8379 410 E
kalane@presby.edu
LANE, Kristi .... 218-855-8054 237 C
kristi.lane@clcmn.edu
LANE, Krystle .... 918-463-2931 365 I
kdlane@connorsstate.edu
LANE, LaTia .... 773-291-6100 135 B
LANE, Mark .... 706-721-0211 115 I
LANE, Mary Ellen ...... 508-856-4018 212 A
maryellen.lane@umassmed.edu
LANE, Michael, J .... 765-285-2191 153 E
michael.lane@bsu.edu
LANE, Michelle .... 361-354-2275 431 L
malane1@coastalbend.edu
LANE, Nancy .... 760-744-1150.. 56 B
nlane@palomar.edu
LANE, Natalie .... 307-382-1673 500 I
nlane@westernwyoming.edu
LANE, Nathan .... 561-803-2754 105 B
nathan_lane@pba.edu
LANE, Nathan .... 561-803-2318 105 B
nathan_lane@pba.edu
LANE, Nicole .... 559-278-0860.. 31 D
nicolel@csufresno.edu
LANE, Phillip .... 618-985-2828 140 G
philliplane@jalc.edu
LANE, Rick .... 217-206-6678 151 E
rlane3@uis.edu
LANE, Robert, J .... 515-961-1417 169 G
bob.lane@simpson.edu
LANE, Rona .... 212-237-8000 294 B
LANE, Roy .... 202-274-6410.. 94 B
LANE, Sean .... 256-824-6200.... 8 B
sean.lane@uah.edu
LANE, Shamica .... 252-335-3251 341 A
sdlane@ecsu.edu
LANE, Stephanie .... 707-826-3132.. 30 A
sml19@humboldt.edu
LANE, Thomas, A ...... 785-532-6237 175 A
talane@ksu.edu
LANE, Tracy .... 252-246-1202 339 A
tlane@wilsoncc.edu

LANE, Troy .... 865-974-6631 426 C
tlane15@utk.edu
LANE RASMUS, Fran, R 253-535-7141 481 C
lanerafr@plu.edu
LANEEL TANNER, Beth . 732-247-5241 278 E
btanner@nbts.edu
LANESSKOG, Stig ...... 909-621-8026.. 37 E
stig.lanesskog@claremont.edu
LANEY, Brenda .... 816-501-4122 257 K
brenda.laney@rockhurst.edu
LANEY, Candy .... 406-874-6165 262 K
laneyc@milescc.edu
LANEY, Jennifer .... 207-216-4399 195 F
LANFEAR, Jeffery ...... 773-325-8308 136 F
jlanfear@depaul.edu
LANFORD, Coty .... 540-863-2861 473 D
clanford@mgcc.edu
LANFORD, Julie .... 864-587-4233 411 F
lanfordj@smcsc.edu
LANG, Angela .... 740-374-8716 363 F
alang1@wscc.edu
LANG, Bob .... 970-248-1754.. 78 F
bllang@coloradomesa.edu
LANG, Christopher ...... 660-543-4673 259 K
crlang@ucmo.edu
LANG, Heather .... 971-722-4008 375 F
heather.lang@pcc.edu
LANG, Jennifer, R ...... 718-780-0679 291 G
jennifer.lang@brooklaw.edu
LANG, Jessica .... 646-312-3870 292 F
jessica.lang@baruch.cuny.edu
LANG, Katherine .... 580-559-5424 365 J
klang@ecok.edu
LANG, Lisa .... 901-435-1200 419 I
lisa_lang@loc.edu
LANG, Lisa, K .... 502-597-6414 183 A
lisa.lang@kysu.edu
LANG, Mandy .... 715-422-5446 498 A
mandy.lang@mstc.edu
LANG, Mary, K .... 330-569-5137 353 F
langmk@hiram.edu
LANG, Mindy .... 212-353-4212 297 C
lang@cooper.edu
LANG, Nathan .... 785-628-5304 173 E
ndlang@fhsu.edu
LANGAN, Brooke ...... 570-422-3619 393 F
blangan1@esu.edu
LANGAN, Elena .... 631-761-7100 322 C
elangan@tourolaw.edu
LANGAN, Frances ...... 570-945-8000 386 F
fran.langan@keystone.edu
LANGAN, Nicole .... 570-945-8274 386 F
nicole.langan@keystone.edu
LANGDON, Dawn ...... 315-781-3784 301 D
langdon@hws.edu
LANGDON, Dawn ...... 304-243-2304 490 F
finaid@wheeling.edu
LANGDON, Deb .... 740-389-4636 355 F
langdond@mtc.edu
LANGDON, Heather, H . 828-262-2093 340 G
langdonhh@appstate.edu
LANGDON, James ...... 608-262-4048 494 C
jlangdon@uwsa.edu
LANGDON, Nikolette .... 502-213-2400 181 H
nikolette.langdon@kctcs.edu
LANGDON, Steven, D .. 573-334-6825 258 I
slangdon@sehcollege.edu
LANGE, Denice .... 480-285-1761.. 12 D
LANGE, Don .... 817-272-3571 454 B
donlange@uta.edu
LANGE, Janet .... 309-677-2374 133 H
lange@fsmail.bradley.edu
LANGE, Jeff .... 309-438-3383 140 C
jwlange@ilstu.edu
LANGE, Karen, M ...... 651-962-6120 243 F
kmlange@stthomas.edu
LANGE, Mark .... 608-262-3253 494 C
mark.lange@business.wisconsin.edu
LANGE, Paul .... 800-553-4674 155 F
plange@horizonuniversity.edu
LANGE, Richard .... 915-215-4300 450 E
richard.lange@ttuhsc.edu
LANGE, Robert, A ...... 423-439-4641 418 D
langer@etsu.edu
LANGE, Robert, J ...... 757-594-7015 465 A
robert.lange@cnu.edu
LANGE, Shane .... 815-224-0219 140 D
shane_lange@ivcc.edu
LANGE, Steven .... 320-629-5155 239 G
steve.lange@pine.edu
LANGE, Tom, J .... 715-831-7285 497 E
tlange8@cvtc.edu

LANGE, Tyana .... 660-785-7468 259 J
tyana@truman.edu
LANGE, Tyler .... 206-616-5631 484 A
langet2@uw.edu
LANGELL, John .... 330-325-6255 357 D
LANGEMEIER, Ryan ..... 507-379-3335 240 A
ryan.langemeier@riverland.edu
LANGEN, Jill .... 989-729-3350 221 B
jill.langen@baker.edu
LANGENBERG, Todd .... 410-704-4679 204 B
tlangenberg@towson.edu
LANGENEGGER, Joyce .. 979-209-8991 430 I
joyce.langenegger@blinn.edu
LANGENMAYR,
Kimberly .... 516-323-3952 306 I
klangenmayr@mollloy.edu
LANGER, Katherine ...... 803-323-4746 413 D
langerk@winthrop.edu
LANGER, Manfred ...... 740-377-2520 361 D
manfred.langer@tsbc.edu
LANGER, Patricia ...... 651-696-6211 236 C
planger@macalester.edu
LANGEVIN, OP,
Dominic .... 202-495-3820.. 93 D
dean@dhs.edu
LANGEVIN, Duetta ...... 909-274-4230.. 52 K
dlangevin@mtsac.edu
LANGEVIN, Patrice ...... 909-607-2226.. 57 E
patrice_langevin@pitzer.edu
LANGFORD, Chris ...... 503-253-3443 374 E
clangford@ocom.edu
LANGFORD, Curt .... 806-742-3641 450 C
curt.langford@ttu.edu
LANGFORD, Debra .... 304-876-5216 489 A
dlangfor@shepherd.edu
LANGFORD, Jeremy, W 312-915-6159 142 G
jlangford@luc.edu
LANGFORD, Joel, C ...... 770-720-5585 124 C
jcl@reinhardt.edu
LANGFORD, Russ .... 417-862-9533 252 H
rlangford@globaluniversity.edu
LANGGUTH, Jay .... 859-344-3375 184 G
langguj@thomasmore.edu
LANGHAM, Gay .... 601-643-8307 244 G
gay.langham@colin.edu
LANGHAM, Julie .... 706-771-4180 115 H
jlangham@augustatech.edu
LANGHART, Alex .... 662-915-1101 248 F
langhart@olemiss.edu
LANGHART, Maura ...... 662-915-2760 248 F
mmwakefi@olemiss.edu
LANGIN, Cynthia, P ...... 516-463-6809 301 E
cynthia.langin@hofstra.edu
LANGKILDE, Tracy .... 814-865-9591 391 F
tll30@psu.edu
LANGLANDS, Bryan ...... 502-863-8153 180 E
bryan_langlands@georgetowncollege.
edu
LANGLEY, Anne .... 860-486-4035.. 89 B
anne.langley@uconn.edu
LANGLEY, Clint .... 334-214-4853.... 1 H
clint.langley@cv.edu
LANGLEY, Dorothy ...... 903-730-4890 437 E
dlangley@jarvis.edu
LANGLEY, Jessie .... 252-985-5177 339 B
jlangley@ncwc.edu
LANGLEY, Rebekah ...... 252-334-2076 331 C
rebekah.langley@macuniversity.edu
LANGLEY, Seth .... 718-270-7763 316 E
seth.langley@downstate.edu
LANGLEY, Terrell .... 870-575-7187.. 22 F
langleyt@uapb.edu
LANGLEY, Terrell .... 541-917-4999 373 F
langlet@linnbenton.edu
LANGLEY, Trinette, B .... 252-399-6626 326 H
tboone@barton.edu
LANGLEY-TURNBAUGH,
Samantha .... 859-572-7528 184 B
langleys1@nku.edu
LANGLOIS, Mary Ann ... 716-888-2103 291 M
langloim@canisius.edu
LANGOLF, Judi .... 810-762-9585 225 F
jlangolf@kettering.edu
LANGONI, Kerri .... 505-566-3515 287 C
langonik@sanjuancollege.edu
LANGREHR, Andrew ...... 314-539-5364 258 C
alangrehr@stlcc.edu
LANGRIDGE, Nick ...... 540-568-3197 467 C
langrinl@jmu.edu
LANGROCK, Adela ...... 802-443-3440 461 G
alangroc@middlebury.edu
LANGSTON, Carol .... 870-307-7075.. 20 D
carol.langston@lyon.edu

LANGSTON, Emily .... 410-972-3303 201 E
emily.langston@sjc.edu
LANGSTON, James .... 209-476-7840.. 67 D
jlangston@clc.edu
LANGSTON, Jessica .... 918-463-2931 365 I
jessica.langston@connorsstate.edu
LANGSTON, Marissa ..... 850-644-3035 110 B
m.langston@fsu.edu
LANGSTON, Randall ...... 660-543-4811 259 K
rlangston@ucmo.edu
LANGSTRAAT, Jim .... 503-352-1621 375 B
jim.langstraat@pacificu.edu
LANGSTRAAT, Nate .... 360-383-3350 485 B
nlangstraat@whatcom.edu
LANGTEAU, Paula .... 605-229-8405 414 I
presidentsoffice@presentation.edu
LANGVARDT, Guy .... 213-740-2311.. 73 B
LANGWAY, Zach .... 401-863-3189 403 A
zach_langway@brown.edu
LANGWELL, Teri .... 806-457-4200 435 D
tlangwell@fpctx.edu
LANGWORTHY, Judy .... 716-673-3109 316 A
judy.langworthy@fredonia.edu
LANHAM, Chuck .... 360-650-3917 485 A
chuck.lanham@wwu.edu
LANHAM, Heather .... 937-778-7803 352 D
hlanham@edisonohio.edu
LANHAM, Jeff .... 740-245-7485 363 A
jlanham@rio.edu
LANHAM, Terri .... 270-686-4548 182 C
terri.lanham@kctcs.edu
LANHAM, Tracey, M ..... 239-513-1122 102 C
tlanham@hodges.edu
LANIER, Lisa .... 912-871-1606 123 F
llanier@ogeecheetech.edu
LANIER, Mark .... 910-962-3030 343 B
lanierm@uncw.edu
LANIER, Stephen, M ..... 313-577-5600 232 H
stephen.lanier@wayne.edu
LANIER-SHIPP,
Elizabeth .... 314-516-4753 260 E
laniershippe@umsl.edu
LANKISCH, Karen .... 513-556-5400 362 B
karen.lankisch@uc.edu
LANN, Jennifer .... 802-387-6764 461 E
jlann@landmark.edu
LANNEN, Daniel .... 610-282-1100 382 A
daniel.lannen@desales.edu
LANNERS, Brandon .... 607-255-6224 297 D
bl738@cornell.edu
LANNING, Brek .... 828-565-4027 335 A
bwlanning@haywood.edu
LANNING, Crystal .... 715-425-3246 496 A
crystal.lanning@uwrf.edu
LANNING, Stephanie .... 785-670-1574 178 A
stephanie.lanning@washburn.edu
LANOUE, David .... 870-235-4004.. 21 E
davidlanoue@saumag.edu
LANPHER, Jim .... 803-754-4100 407 F
LANSAW, Anna .... 410-209-2378 197 E
alansaw@bccc.edu
LANSING, Carolyn .... 518-243-4471 290 K
LANSING, Corey .... 231-439-6349 228 D
clansing@ncmich.edu
LANSING, Travis .... 801-957-4009 460 D
travis.lansing@slcc.edu
LANSIQUOT,
Beverley, A .... 340-692-4117 512 B
beverley.lansiquot@uvi.edu
LANTER, Jennifer .... 920-735-2520 497 F
lanter@fvtc.edu
LANTHIER, Eric .... 617-243-2433 210 G
elanthier@lasell.edu
LANTHIER-BANDY,
Julie .... 760-744-1150.. 56 B
jlanthierbandy@palomar.edu
LANTIS, Glenda .... 541-318-3753 371 I
glantis@cocc.edu
LANTRIP, Jennifer .... 812-749-1217 159 E
jlantrip@oak.edu
LANTZ, Dana .... 330-941-2216 364 G
cdlantz@ysu.edu
LANTZ, David .... 301-387-3011 198 F
david.lantz@garrettcollege.edu
LANTZ, Mary Jan .... 409-944-1281 435 F
mlantz@gc.edu
LANXON, Julie .... 531-622-2203 266 G
jlanxon@mccneb.edu
LANYON, Scott .... 612-625-2809 242 K
slanyon@umn.edu
LANZA, Michael .... 718-951-5220 293 A
mlanza@brooklyn.cuny.edu

LANZA-GALINDO,
Oscar, R .... 617-228-3240 214 A
oscar.lanzagalindo@bhcc.edu
LANZEROTTI, Robert ..... 309-794-7374 132 H
robertlanzerotti@augustana.edu
LANZI, Lesley .... 518-736-3622 300 B
lesley.lanzi@fmcc.suny.edu
LANZO, Caryn .... 216-802-3143 350 G
c.lanzo@csuohio.edu
LAO, Lixing .... 703-323-5690 476 A
LAOYZA, Matt .... 507-389-5308 238 L
matthew.laoyza@mnsu.edu
LAPAYOVER, Alan .... 215-576-0800 396 B
alapayover@rrc.edu
LAPERLE, Kimberly .... 508-856-8992 212 A
kimberlymuri.laperle@umassmed.edu
LAPHAM, Steve .... 301-891-0103 204 D
slapham@wau.edu
LAPIANA, William, P .... 212-431-2840 308 I
william.lapiana@nyls.edu
LAPIDUS, Richard, S .... 978-665-3101 212 C
rlapidus@fitchburgstate.edu
LAPIER, Terrance .... 407-265-8383.. 96 H
LAPIER, Terrence .... 561-381-4990.. 96 G
LAPIKAS, Ken .... 814-724-0700 387 H
klapikas@laurel.edu
LAPIKAS, Sonya, L .... 724-589-2172 398 F
slapikas@thiel.edu
LAPINSKI, Scott .... 432-552-2629 456 C
lapinski_s@utpb.edu
LAPLANT, James, T .... 229-245-6517 127 C
jtlaplant@valdosta.edu
LAPLANTE, Brian .... 518-445-2381 289 B
blapl@albanylaw.edu
LAPLANTE, Jane .... 701-858-3855 345 C
jane.laplante@minotstateu.edu
LAPLANTE, Kim .... 920-498-5487 498 F
kim.laplante@nwtc.edu
LAPLANTE, Melissa .... 603-342-3086 272 E
mlaplante@ccsnh.edu
LAPLANTE, Mike .... 970-943-7038.. 85 B
mlaplante@western.edu
LAPOINTE, Lacey .... 817-735-5126 453 D
lacey.lapointe@unthsc.edu
LAPOINTE, Laurence .... 860-465-5113.. 85 G
lapointel@easternct.edu
LAPOINTE, Michael .... 219-980-7106 157 A
mslapoin@iun.edu
LAPOINTE, Robert .... 312-567-7135 139 H
lapointe@iit.edu
LAPORTE, Christopher .. 860-773-1362.. 87 E
claporte@tunxis.edu
LAPORTE, Laura .... 518-736-3622 300 B
llaporte@fmcc.suny.edu
LAPORTE, Sandra .... 312-567-5199 139 H
laporte@iit.edu
LAPOS, Christopher ...... 570-389-4740 393 E
clapos@bloomu.edu
LAPOTASKY, Michael .... 215-596-8800 400 B
LAPP, Beverly, K .... 574-296-6267 153 C
bklapp@ambs.edu
LAPP, Katherine, N .... 617-495-1524 210 B
katie_lapp@harvard.edu
LAPP, Tina .... 614-350-5748 353 I
LAPPAS, Thomas .... 585-389-4648 307 D
tlappas4@naz.edu
LAPPIE, Joseph, D .... 563-333-6150 169 D
lappiejosephd@sau.edu
LAPPIN, Julie, M .... 909-537-5002.. 33 B
jlappin@csusb.edu
LAPPLE, James, H .... 212-327-8371 312 B
james.lapple@rockefeller.edu
LAPPS, Brian .... 615-366-4438 423 A
brian.lapps@tbr.edu
LAPRADE, Shane .... 508-565-1970 218 F
slaprade@stonehill.edu
LAPRISE, Coleen .... 207-741-5715 195 D
claprise@smccme.edu
LAPRISE, John .... 423-585-6829 424 G
john.laprise@ws.edu
LAPSLEY, Jacqueline, E 609-497-7815 279 D
academic.dean@ptsem.edu
LAQUEY, Karen .... 325-649-8805 437 A
klaquey@hputx.edu
LARA, Dan .... 541-867-8506 374 D
dan.lara@oregoncoast.edu
LARA, Gabriel .... 847-543-2288 135 G
glara3@clcillinois.edu
LARA, Larry .... 714-992-7025.. 54 D
llara@fullcoll.edu
LARA, Maria .... 650-306-3125.. 62 I
lara@smccd.edu

LARA, Rosa .... 717-720-4010 393 C
rlara@passhe.edu
LARA, Veronica .... 512-448-8575 441 N
vlara@bncollege.com
LARANGE, Shannon .... 413-775-1410 214 C
larange@gcc.mass.edu
LARAY SEALEY,
Alphonso .... 804-257-5742 475 G
LARDIZABAL, Alana .... 541-552-8110 376 A
lardizaba@sou.edu
LARDNER, Emily .... 206-878-3710 480 C
elardner@highline.edu
LARDNER, Patrick .... 803-777-2036 412 A
lardnerp@mailbox.sc.edu
LARDY, Greg .... 701-231-7660 345 D
gregory.lardy@ndsu.edu
LARDY, Greg .... 701-231-7426 345 D
gregory.lardy@ndsu.edu
LAREY, Franklin .... 309-556-3061 140 E
flarey@iwu.edu
LAREZ, Joseph .... 509-961-4674 480 B
larez_j@heritag.edu
LARGE, Laura .... 512-448-8411 441 N
llarge@stedwards.edu
LARGE, Ron .... 509-313-6767 479 E
large@gonzaga.edu
LARGEN, Kristin, K .... 563-589-0200 170 G
klargen@wartburgseminary.edu
LARGENT, Mark, A .... 517-353-5380 227 C
largent@msu.edu
LARGENT, Trudy .... 510-466-7252.. 57 C
tlargent@peralta.edu
LARIC, Katie .... 303-761-2482.. 80 G
katie.laric@denverseminary.edu
LARIMORE, Ashley .... 315-279-5500 303 D
alarimore@keuka.edu
LARIMORE, Jennifer .... 715-425-4603 496 A
jennifer.larimore@uwrf.edu
LARIOS, Daphne .... 509-542-4562 478 B
klarios@columbiabasin.edu
LARIOS, Jose .... 828-669-8012 331 H
jlarios14@montreat.edu
LARIOS, Liza .... 718-631-6356 295 B
llarios@qcc.cuny.edu
LARIVE, Cynthia .... 831-459-2058.. 71 A
chancellor@ucsc.edu
LARIVEE, Lisa .... 802-322-1644 461 D
lisa.larivee@goddard.edu
LARKAN, Kara .... 210-999-7479 451 B
klarkans@trinity.edu
LARKIN, Anne .... 508-856-4250 212 A
anne.larkin@umassmed.edu
LARKIN, Conal .... 607-778-5257 317 A
larkincl@sunybroome.edu
LARKIN, DeAndra .... 810-232-2087 228 B
deandra.larkin@mcc.edu
LARKIN, Lora .... 661-395-4011.. 47 B
llarkin@bakersfieldcollege.edu
LARKIN, SSJ,
Mary Josephine .... 215-248-7055 380 G
mjlarkin@chc.edu
LARKIN, Sheila .... 334-291-4949.... 1 H
sheila.larkin@cv.edu
LARKIN, Sue .... 757-455-3210 476 C
slarkin@vwu.edu
LARMON, Brandy .... 662-329-7299 247 B
bhlarmon@muw.edu
LARMORE, Mark .... 614-292-6446 358 E
larmore.6@osu.edu
LAROBINA, Michael, D . 203-371-7859.. 88 H
larobinam@sacredheart.edu
LAROCCA, Cherie, K ...... 504-278-6273 188 E
clarocca@nunez.edu
LAROCHE, Adrienne .... 207-741-5994 195 D
alaroche@smccme.edu
LAROCHE, OP, Victor ... 504-520-7593 193 C
vlaroche@xula.edu
LAROCQUE, Edward, A . 260-399-7700 162 A
elarocque@sf.edu
LAROCQUE,
Monique, M .... 207-581-3143 196 D
mlarocque@maine.edu
LAROCQUE, Sandra .... 701-477-7913 346 H
slarocqu@tm.edu
LAROI, Heather .... 608-265-3195 494 C
hlaroi@uwsa.edu
LAROSA, Joe .... 716-926-8925 301 C
jlarosa@hilbert.edu
LAROSE, Jesse .... 970-675-1149.. 78 P
jesse.larose@cncc.edu
LAROSEE, Howie .... 617-879-7938 212 E
hlarosee@massart.edu
LARRABEE, Ashley .... 361-825-3020 446 E
ashley.larrabee@tamucc.edu

LARRAT, Paul .... 401-874-5003 404 E
larrat@uri.edu
LARRIVEE, Linda .... 508-929-8333 213 D
llarrivee@worcester.edu
LARROUSSE, William ...... 267-502-6034 378 I
william.larrousse@brynathyn.edu
LARRY, Latasha .... 773-291-6210 135 B
llarry4@ccc.edu
LARSEN, Carlton .... 423-869-6484 420 A
carl.larsen@lmunet.edu
LARSEN, Christoffer ...... 785-227-3380 171 H
larsencl@bethanylb.edu
LARSEN, Curt .... 801-957-4186 460 D
curt.larsen@slcc.edu
LARSEN, Cynde .... 608-822-2642 498 H
clarsen@swtc.edu
LARSEN, Daniel .... 630-466-7900 152 H
dlarsen@waubonsee.edu
LARSEN, David .... 253-833-9111 480 A
dlarsen@greenriver.edu
LARSEN, Dawn .... 269-965-3931 225 D
larsend@kellogg.edu
LARSEN, Jennifer .... 402-559-4837 269 B
jlarsen@unmc.edu
LARSEN, Jon-Erik .... 503-352-7221 375 B
jon-erik@pacificu.edu
LARSEN, Kaerielle .... 973-761-9205 282 K
kaerielle.larsen@shu.edu
LARSEN, Kelly Jo .... 918-444-2120 366 G
larsenk@nsuok.edu
LARSEN, Kerstin .... 609-258-9289 279 E
klarsen@princeton.edu
LARSEN, Kevin, W .... 252-334-2009 331 C
kevin.larsen@macuniversity.edu
LARSEN, Marci .... 435-283-7013 460 C
marci.larsen@snow.edu
LARSEN, Matt .... 701-231-5614 345 D
matt.larsen@ndsu.edu
LARSEN, Patricia .... 301-243-2121 501 J
patricia.larsen@odni.gov
LARSEN, Rachel .... 916-691-7207.. 50 K
larsenr@crc.losrios.edu
LARSEN, Sarah .... 713-743-7948 451 G
sclarsen@uh.edu
LARSEN, Susan .... 575-562-2211 285 E
susan.larsen@enmu.edu
LARSEN, Whitney, M .... 540-261-8530 470 D
whitney.larsen@svu.edu
LARSON, Barb .... 308-398-7359 265 C
blarson@cccneb.edu
LARSON, Brittany .... 651-793-1411 238 B
brittany.tweed@metrostate.edu
LARSON, Bruce .... 360-650-3319 485 A
bruce.larson@wwu.edu
LARSON, Carol .... 719-549-2439.. 79 G
carol.larson@csupueblo.edu
LARSON, Craig .... 763-424-0733 239 D
clarson@nhcc.edu
LARSON, Dan .... 541-737-3626 374 H
dan.larson@oregonstate.edu
LARSON, Daniel .... 320-308-5980 240 D
daniel.larson@sctcc.edu
LARSON, David .... 864-231-2000 405 F
dlarson@andersonuniversity.edu
LARSON, Debra .... 618-537-6816 143 G
dlarson@mckendree.edu
LARSON, Debra, S .... 530-898-6101.. 31 A
dslarson@csuchico.edu
LARSON, Denise .... 570-955-1479 387 A
larsond@lackawanna.edu
LARSON, Doreen .... 937-778-7801 352 D
dlarson@edisonohio.edu
LARSON, Elena .... 916-278-6845.. 33 A
larsone@csus.edu
LARSON, Ellen .... 315-228-7750 296 C
elarson@colgate.edu
LARSON, Erik .... 570-961-0700 387 A
larsone@lackawanna.edu
LARSON, Gary .... 630-752-5990 152 K
gary.larson@wheaton.edu
LARSON, George .... 918-465-1750 365 K
glarson@eosc.edu
LARSON, Greg .... 239-590-1500 109 G
LARSON, Heidi .... 701-252-3467 346 J
hlarson@uj.edu
LARSON, Jamie .... 409-880-7126 449 B
jamie.larson@lamar.edu
LARSON, Jan .... 605-995-2614 414 A
jan.larson@dwu.edu
LARSON, Jason .... 480-314-2102.. 16 A
LARSON, Jeff .... 503-883-2562 373 E
jelarson@linfield.edu

Index of Key Administrators LARSON – LAVERGNE 749

LARSON, Jennifer .... 701-845-7401 345 E jennifer.larson@vcsu.edu
LARSON, Jens .... 509-359-6584 478 H jlarson@ewu.edu
LARSON, Jon, H .... 732-255-0330 279 A jlarson@ocean.edu
LARSON, Kristin .... 906-635-2453 226 C klarsen1@lssu.edu
LARSON, Laura .... 651-633-4311 242 J llarson@unitedseminary.edu
LARSON, Levi .... 863-667-5000 108 I lalarson1@seu.edu
LARSON, Lisa .... 207-974-4691 195 A llarson@emcc.edu
LARSON, Lori .... 218-736-1514 238 K lori.larson@minnesota.edu
LARSON, Marie .... 414-847-3214 493 C marielarson@miad.edu
LARSON, Molly, B .... 715-682-1205 493 G mlarson@northland.edu
LARSON, Paul, V .... 805-565-6286.. 75 I plarson@westmont.edu
LARSON, R. Alan .... 434-799-2271 470 F
LARSON, Rebecca .... 630-752-5566 152 K rebecca.a.larson@wheaton.edu
LARSON, Robert .... 718-390-3100 324 B
LARSON, Robert .... 503-255-0332 374 A rlarson@multnomah.edu
LARSON, Ruth .... 315-470-4716 319 A rlarson@esf.edu
LARSON, Samantha ...... 712-325-3341 167 G slarson@iwcc.edu
LARSON, Sandra .... 847-578-3400 148 B sandra.larson@rosalindfranklin.edu
LARSON, Scott .... 806-720-7266 438 F scott.larson@lcu.edu
LARSON, Shane .... 712-325-3402 167 G
LARSON, Shane .... 970-945-8691.. 78 H
LARSON, Susan, J .... 218-299-3001 234 K larson@cord.edu
LARSON, Thomas, R ..... 423-652-4765 419 F trlarson@king.edu
LARUE, Clint .... 405-425-5191 367 C clint.larue@oc.edu
LARUE, Shanda .... 270-686-4252 179 F shanda.larue@brescia.edu
LARUE, Wesley .... 901-678-2732 426 A wtlarue@memphis.edu
LASAKOW, Paul, H .... 757-822-1527 474 G plasakow@tcc.edu
LASCEK, Natalie .... 717-396-7833 392 Q nlascek@pcad.edu
LASCH, Chris .... 480-750-4470.. 15 Q clasch@tsoa.edu
LASCH, Jackie, D .... 407-582-3302 113 C jlasch@valenciacollege.edu
LASCHER, Sandra .... 520-494-5526.. 11 M sandra.lascher@centralaz.edu
LASH, Chris .... 847-628-1565 141 A christopher.lash@judsonu.edu
LASH, Jonathan .... 413-559-5521 210 A jlpr@hampshire.edu
LASHER, Marie .... 603-456-2656 273 A mlasher@magdalen.edu
LASHER, Robert, W .... 603-646-3095 272 F robert.w.lasher@dartmouth.edu
LASHLEY, Edwin, L ...... 410-543-6222 204 A ellashley@salisbury.edu
LASHLEY, Janeisa .... 410-337-6000 198 G janeisa.lashley@goucher.edu
LASHLEY, Jeffery .... 660-263-4100 256 D jeffl@macc.edu
LASHLEY, Kent .... 405-733-7306 369 D klashley@rose.edu
LASHLEY, Marsha .... 660-831-4115 256 B lashleym@moval.edu
LASHLEY, Maudry .... 718-270-4995 294 E mlashley@mec.cuny.edu
LASHUA, Chad .... 906-932-4231 224 A chadl@gogebic.edu
LASHURE, Faith .... 630-466-7900 152 H flashure@waubonsee.edu
LASINSKI, Jon .... 907-796-6497.. 10 C jlasinski@alaska.edu
LASITER, Paul .... 406-243-4662 263 D paul.lasiter@umontana.edu
LASITS, Mary .... 260-422-5560 156 A mlasits@indianatech.edu
LASKER, Y. Mayer .... 718-377-0777 311 B
LASKEY, Dina .... 541-888-7400 376 B dina.laskey@socc.edu
LASKIN, Emily .... 626-396-2455.. 26 G emily.laskin@artcenter.edu
LASKOFSKI, Mike .... 703-993-4573 466 J mlaskofs@gmu.edu
LASKOWSKI, Anne .... 860-685-2006.. 90 A alaskowski@wesleyan.edu
LASKY, Sarah .... 716-851-1994 299 A lasky@ecc.edu
LASLEY, Kyle .... 719-336-1519.. 81 J kyle.lasley@lamarcc.edu
LASLEY, Steven, T .... 615-460-6404 417 B steve.lasley@belmont.edu
LASPISA, Matt .... 845-434-5750 321 B mlaspisa@sunysullivan.edu
LASSETTER, Jane, H ...... 801-422-7198 458 A jane_lassetter@byu.edu
LASSETTER, Jerry .... 919-761-2266 340 B jlassetter@sebts.edu
LASSIAL, Erin .... 315-386-7608 319 E lassiale@canton.edu
LASSITER, Carllos .... 903-813-2228 429 I classiter@austincollege.edu
LASSITER, Catherine ...... 919-866-7106 338 E cblassiter@waketech.edu
LASSITER, Colleen .... 706-233-7319 125 A classiter@shorter.edu
LASSITER, Donald, L ..... 910-630-7081 331 B lassiter@methodist.edu
LASSITER, Elbert, J .... 336-633-0009 336 F ejlassiter@randolph.edu
LASSITER, Ingrid .... 404-270-5383 126 A ilassite@spelman.edu
LASSITER, John .... 706-295-6511 119 F jlassiter@gntc.edu
LASSITER, Keith .... 704-233-8098 344 E k.lassiter@wingate.edu
LASSITER, Teresa, C ..... 252-335-8740 341 A tclassiter@ecsu.edu
LASSITER, Timothy .... 252-862-1351 336 H tmlassiter6983@roanokechowan.edu
LASSITER-COUNTS, Leigh .... 501-450-1373.. 19 I lassiter-counts@hendrix.edu
LASSNER, David .... 808-956-8207 129 B david@hawaii.edu
LASSNER, David, K .... 808-956-8207 128 I david@hawaii.edu
LASSNER, Jennifer .... 319-335-2123 163 F jennifer-lassner@uiowa.edu
LASSO, Megan .... 406-994-4391 263 G megan.lasso@montana.edu
LAST, Brad .... 435-652-7858 459 G brad.last@utahtech.edu
LAST, Brett .... 734-487-3044 223 F blast@emich.edu
LASTER, Braylin .... 731-426-7500 419 G
LASTRA, Lauren .... 805-969-3626.. 55 I llastra@pacifica.edu
LASTRA, Sarai .... 787-743-7979 509 D
LASZCZ, Amy .... 504-671-5456 187 I alaszc@dcc.edu
LATA, Fran .... 303-373-2008.. 83 D flata@rvu.edu
LATARTE, Allison .... 608-263-5658 494 D
LATCOVICH, Mark, A .... 440-943-7600 360 D mal@dioceseofcleveland.org
LATHAM, Adrienne .... 615-329-8632 418 E alatham@fisk.edu
LATHAM, Amy .... 662-562-3201 247 E a_latham@northwestms.edu
LATHAM, Chris .... 256-233-8291.... 4 D chris.latham@athens.edu
LATHAM, Heather .... 410-626-2511 201 E heather.latham@sjc.edu
LATHAM, Jessica .... 910-898-9617 336 A lathamj@montgomery.edu
LATHAM, Linda .... 336-734-7412 334 D llatham@forsythtech.edu
LATHAM, Lindsay, S .... 336-272-7102 329 B lindsay.latham@greensboro.edu
LATHAM, Mike .... 252-451-8327 336 B dmlatham118@nashcc.edu
LATHAM, Sarah .... 401-863-9400 403 A sarah_latham@brown.edu
LATHAM, Scott .... 713-942-5036 453 H slatham@stthom.edu
LATHAM, Sheila .... 701-858-4145 345 C sheila.latham@minotstateu.edu
LATHAM, William .... 202-274-5210.. 94 B william.latham@udc.edu
LATHROP, Amanda .... 805-756-2328.. 29 K lathrop@calpoly.edu
LATHROP, Jessica .... 608-262-2326 494 C jlathrop@uwsa.edu
LATHROP, Justin .... 863-667-5000 108 I jjlathrop@seu.edu
LATHROP, Sam .... 217-228-5432 147 C lathrsa@quincy.edu
LATIF, Niaz .... 219-989-3251 160 A nlatif@pnw.edu
LATIF, Saima .... 213-624-1200.. 42 F slatif@fidm.edu
LATIMER, Cassandra, H 717-264-2784 402 D cassandra.latimer@wilson.edu
LATIMER, Linda .... 423-439-1000 418 D trustees@etsu.edu
LATIMER, Tanisha .... 864-250-8107 408 J tanisha.latimer@gvltec.edu
LATIMER, William .... 215-248-7021 380 G
LATINO, Niki .... 303-871-2712.. 84 C niki.latino@du.edu
LATINO-NEWMAN, Tracy .... 916-278-6989.. 33 A tracy.newman@csus.edu
LATIOLAIS, Scott .... 253-589-5546 478 A scott.latiolais@cptc.edu
LATONA, Erin .... 712-324-5066 168 H elatona@nwicc.edu
LATOUF, Christina .... 646-660-6114 292 F christina.latouf@baruch.cuny.edu
LATOUR, Bill .... 217-641-4290 140 H blatour@jwcc.edu
LATOUR, Jennifer, B ..... 757-594-8589 465 A jennifer.latour@cnu.edu
LATOUR, Mickey .... 870-972-2085.. 17 I mlatour@astate.edu
LATSCH, Wolfram .... 206-221-4308 484 A latsch@uw.edu
LATSHAW, Todd, M ...... 717-867-6330 388 A latshaw@lvc.edu
LATTA, Bruce, J .... 410-293-1801 502 I latta@usna.edu
LATTA, Dustin, W .... 904-276-6800 107 A dustinlatta@sjrstate.edu
LATTA, Jonathan .... 209-946-2211.. 71 E jlatta@pacific.edu
LATTA, Michael .... 812-877-8975 160 C mlatta@rose-hulman.edu
LATTIMER, Heather .... 408-924-3600.. 34 B heather.lattimer@sjsu.edu
LATTIMORE, Mark .... 478-825-6296 118 E lattimorem@fvsu.edu
LATTIMORE, Vergel, L .. 704-636-6823 329 F vlattimore@hoodseminary.edu
LATTING, John .... 404-727-6036 118 D john.latting@emory.edu
LATTY, Erika .... 207-509-7297 196 B elatty@unity.edu
LATZ, II, Gil, I .... 614-688-1178 358 E latz.9@osu.edu
LAU, Bradley, A .... 503-554-2316 372 I blau@georgefox.edu
LAU, Eric .... 505-277-1444 288 C elau@unm.edu
LAU, Lawrence .... 310-577-3000.. 76 H lau@yosan.edu
LAU, Margaret .... 805-922-6966.. 24 L mlau@hancockcollege.edu
LAU, Pam .... 217-351-2542 146 G plau@parkland.edu
LAU, Terence .... 530-898-6272.. 31 A tjlau@csuchico.edu
LAUB, Joe .... 212-484-1108 294 B jlaub@jjay.cuny.edu
LAUBE, Philip .... 740-826-8101 356 H plaube@muskingum.edu
LAUBER, Brian .... 567-661-7588 359 H brian_lauber@owens.edu
LAUBER, David .... 630-752-5054 152 K david.lauber@wheaton.edu
LAUBER, Ray .... 620-341-5077 173 C rlauber@emporia.edu
LAUD, Sher-Ron .... 252-398-6500 328 A
LAUDENSLAGER, Kristen .... 610-606-4666 380 C kristin.laudenslager@cedarcrest.edu
LAUDER, Frank .... 617-873-0137 207 E francis.lauder@cambridgecollege.edu
LAUDERDALE, Wendy ... 985-549-2239 192 E wlauderdale@selu.edu
LAUDERMILK, Erin .... 620-278-4340 177 E elaudermilk@sterling.edu
LAUDNER, Kevin .... 719-255-4490.. 84 A klaudner@uccs.edu
LAUEN, Wendy .... 815-479-7528 143 F wlauen@mchenry.edu
LAUER, Andrew, J .... 646-592-4410 325 R andrewlauer@yu.edu
LAUER, Betty .... 508-854-2765 215 D blauer@qcc.mass.edu
LAUER, Bonnie .... 570-740-0734 388 G blauer@luzerne.edu
LAUER, Casey, S .... 785-532-2578 175 A cslauer@ksu.edu
LAUER, Joel .... 210-436-3791 442 A jlauer@stmarytx.edu
LAUER, Karla .... 941-752-5694 109 C lauerk@scf.edu
LAUFFER, Shannon .... 515-650-3198 163 C shannonlauffer@theartofeducation.edu
LAUG, Adam .... 641-269-3200 166 D laugadam@grinnell.edu
LAUGHEAD, Ross .... 210-485-0059 427 H rlaughead@alamo.edu
LAUGHLIN, Jennifer ...... 214-638-0484 437 F jenlaughlin@kdstudio.com
LAUGHLIN, Karen, L ..... 850-644-2740 110 B klaughlin@admin.fsu.edu
LAUGHLIN, Laura .... 601-266-1000 248 H
LAUGHLIN, Michael .... 618-664-6817 138 D michael.laughlin@greenville.edu
LAUGHLIN, Robert .... 504-941-8211 189 C rlaugh@lsuhsc.edu
LAUGHLIN, Ronda .... 360-752-8334 477 C rlaughlin@btc.edu
LAUGHLIN, Russ .... 817-202-6462 444 B laughlinr@swau.edu
LAUGHLIN, Teresa .... 760-744-1150.. 56 B tlaughlin@palomar.edu
LAUGHRAN, Patrick .... 508-626-4357 212 D plaughran@framingham.edu
LAUMBATTUS, Doug ..... 217-234-5253 141 H dlaumbattus@lakelandcollege.edu
LAUNDERVILLE, OSB, Dale .... 320-363-3389 242 G dlaunderville@csbsju.edu
LAUNTZ, Timothy .... 814-641-3192 386 E launtzt@juniata.edu
LAUR, Dave .... 906-217-4031 221 J dave.laur@baycollege.edu
LAURDSEN, Lindsay ..... 801-426-8234 459 B ucdhlibrarian@gmail.com
LAUREANO, José .... 732-906-2509 278 A jlaureano@middlesexcc.edu
LAURENCE, David .... 928-776-7666.. 17 B david.laurence@yc.edu
LAURENT, Timothy .... 319-363-1323 168 D tlaurent@mtmercy.edu
LAURENZ, Jamie .... 575-562-2312 285 E jamie.laurenz@enmu.edu
LAURENZI, Kellie, L ...... 412-397-5201 396 E laurenzi@rmu.edu
LAURIE, Sean .... 516-323-4820 306 I slaurie@molloy.edu
LAURITA, Brandi .... 419-434-4663 362 D laurita@findlay.edu
LAURITSEN, Brittany ..... 218-755-4022 237 B brittany.lauritsen@bemidjistate.edu
LAURITSEN, Jessica ...... 763-488-2605 237 G jessica.lauritsen@hennepintech.edu
LAURSEN, Tod .... 315-792-7400 320 F tod.laursen@sunypoly.edu
LAUTERBACH, Lisa .... 734-487-1118 223 F counseling.services@emich.edu
LAUX, Beth .... 310-506-4532.. 56 H beth.laux@pepperdine.edu
LAUX, Donald .... 406-238-7293 264 G donald.laux@rocky.edu
LAUZON CLABO, Laurie .... 313-577-4138 232 H fx1599@wayne.edu
LAVAL, Jennifer .... 559-442-8206.. 67 A jennifer.laval@fresnocitycollege.edu
LAVALLEY, David .... 203-672-6646.. 85 C dlavalley@albertus.edu
LAVALLEY, Kenneth, J .. 603-862-4343 273 H ken.lavalley@unh.edu
LAVASZ, Michelle .... 323-343-3280.. 32 B mlavasz@calstatela.edu
LAVEIST, Thomas .... 504-988-5397 191 D tal@tulane.edu
LAVENDER, Bernadette .. 770-426-2633 122 A bernadette.lavender@life.edu
LAVENDER, Carol .... 281-649-3300 436 D clavender@hbu.edu
LAVENDER, Michael, K . 828-652-0681 335 H michaell@mcdowelltech.edu
LAVERDURE, Andrea ..... 701-477-7862 346 H
LAVERGNE, April .... 504-278-6425 188 E

© COPYRIGHT HIGHER EDUCATION PUBLICATIONS, INC. 2022

LAVERGNE, Joseph .... 337-421-6951 188 H
joseph.lavergne@sowela.edu
LAVERGNE, Paul .... 718-429-6600 323 I
paul.lavergne@vaughn.edu
LAVERY, Hugh, J .... 215-955-6834 398 G
hugh.lavery@jefferson.edu
LAVES, Beth .... 270-745-5308 186 A
beth.laves@wku.edu
LAVIAL, Pierre .... 772-466-4822.. 95 N
pierre.lavial@aviator.edu
LAVIENA, Adiary .... 787-850-9363 511 B
adiary.laviena@upr.edu
LAVIGNE, Brent .... 574-807-7120 153 G
brent.lavigne@betheluniversity.edu
LAVIGNE, Robert, W ...... 508-213-2217 217 C
robert.lavigne@nichols.edu
LAVIGUEUR, Michelle ... 760-744-1150.. 56 B
mlavigueur@palomar.edu
LAVIN, Gabrielle .... 215-965-4027 390 C
glavin@moore.edu
LAVIN, Lindsie .... 413-565-1000 205 I
llavin@baypath.edu
LAVIN, Luke .... 406-756-3839 262 H
llavin@fvcc.edu
LAVIN, Theresa .... 303-352-6625.. 80 D
theresa.lavin@ccd.edu
LAVINDER,
Katherine, W .... 610-758-4159 388 C
kwl211@lehigh.edu
LAVINE, Deborah .... 336-770-1333 343 C
lavined@uncsa.edu
LAVINE, Natasha .... 404-756-4000 115 E
LAVOIE, Chuck .... 802-468-1250 462 H
chuck.lavoie@castleton.edu
LAVOIE, Donna .... 314-977-2244 258 H
donna.lavoie@slu.edu
LAVONDRA, Lacey .... 773-602-5000 135 A
LAVORGNA, Josh .... 845-341-4565 310 D
josh.lavorgna@sunyorange.edu
LAVOY, Joan .... 218-935-0417 244 A
joan.lavoy@wetcc.edu
LAW, Amir .... 213-763-7000.. 50 A
LAW, Cameron .... 916-278-5556.. 33 A
c.law@csus.edu
LAW, David .... 323-685-6196.. 67 I
davidlaw@toa.edu
LAW, Donna .... 435-865-8182 459 E
law@suu.edu
LAW, Mike .... 503-253-3443 374 E
mlaw@ocom.edu
LAW, Renee .... 954-201-7482.. 96 F
rlaw@broward.edu
LAW, Rhea .... 813-974-2011 111 B
LAW, Scott .... 515-271-3860 165 F
scott.law@drake.edu
LAW, Shirley .... 646-313-8000 295 C
shirley.law@guttman.cuny.edu
LAW, Theresa .... 505-454-3198 286 C
tlaw@nmhu.edu
LAWDERMILT, Sherry .... 218-755-2832 237 B
sherry.lawdermilt@bemidjistate.edu
LAWERANCE, Adrea ...... 406-243-4911 263 D
adrea.lawerance@umontana.edu
LAWHORN, Janice .... 928-428-8509.. 12 H
janice.lawhorn@eac.edu
LAWHORNE, Jeffrey, L .. 540-464-7156 475 C
lawhornejl@vmi.edu
LAWKIS, Nicholas .... 251-460-7277.... 9 A
nlawkis@southalabama.edu
LAWLER, Ann .... 563-441-4173 165 J
alawler@eicc.edu
LAWLER, Hannah .... 310-434-3472.. 63 B
lawler_hannah@smc.edu
LAWLER, John .... 518-276-6266 311 J
lawlej4@rpi.edu
LAWLER, Margaret .... 217-854-5519 133 F
LAWLER, Michael, J ...... 509-452-5100 481 E
president@pnwu.edu
LAWLER-SAGARIN,
Kimberly .... 630-617-3202 137 E
ksagarin@elmhurst.edu
LAWLESS, Jacob .... 248-218-2080 229 I
jlawless@rochesteru.edu
LAWLESS, Kimberly .... 814-865-2526 391 F
klr5825@psu.edu
LAWLESS, Perry .... 985-448-4417 192 C
perry.lawless@nicholls.edu
LAWLESS-ANDRIC,
Dana .... 330-672-1980 354 A
dlawless@kent.edu
LAWLOR, IHM, Antoine 610-647-4400 385 K
LAWLOR, Dave .... 510-879-9273.. 60 C
dlawlor@samuelmerritt.edu
LAWLOR, Michael .... 916-691-7215.. 50 K
lawlorm@crc.losrios.edu
LAWLOR, Michael .... 215-204-8580 398 D
michael.lawlor@temple.edu
LAWLOR, Sarah .... 406-447-4515 262 E
slawlor@carroll.edu
LAWRENCE, Alvin .... 352-392-1575 110 E
alaw@ufl.edu
LAWRENCE, Barbara ...... 336-316-2196 329 C
blawrenc@guilford.edu
LAWRENCE, Barbara, J . 609-896-5395 280 D
blawrence@rider.edu
LAWRENCE, Cherrelle ... 252-492-2061 338 D
lawrencec@vgcc.edu
LAWRENCE, Courtney ... 701-255-3285 346 I
clawrence@uttc.edu
LAWRENCE, Craig, D .... 205-929-3427.... 2 H
clawrence@lawsonstate.edu
LAWRENCE, Dan .... 303-360-4740.. 80 C
dan.lawrence@ccaurora.edu
LAWRENCE, Dana, J ..... 972-438-6932 440 G
LAWRENCE, David .... 616-233-2595 222 H
david.lawrence@davenport.edu
LAWRENCE, David, A .... 740-245-7032 363 A
lawrence@rio.edu
LAWRENCE, Deborah .... 317-955-6208 159 A
dlawrence@marian.edu
LAWRENCE, Derrick ...... 605-698-3966 415 C
dlawrence@swcollege.edu
LAWRENCE, Diana .... 502-456-6506 184 F
dlawrence@sullivan.edu
LAWRENCE, Gail .... 325-235-7333 448 F
gail.lawrence@tstc.edu
LAWRENCE, Gary .... 805-893-3781.. 70 E
gary@ucen.ucsb.edu
LAWRENCE, Jamie .... 270-789-5227 179 G
jwlawrence@campbellsville.edu
LAWRENCE, Jason .... 860-231-5700.. 89 G
jmlawrence@usj.edu
LAWRENCE, Jennifer ..... 318-678-6000 187 E
jelawrence@bpcc.edu
LAWRENCE, John, D ...... 515-294-5390 163 E
jdlaw@iastate.edu
LAWRENCE, Kalista .... 812-535-5102 160 E
kalista.lawrence@smwc.edu
LAWRENCE, Kendra .... 504-520-7388 193 C
klawren4@xula.edu
LAWRENCE, Kevin .... 757-388-2862 469 H
klawrence@sentara.edu
LAWRENCE, Lara .... 660-263-3900 250 G
laralawrence@cccb.edu
LAWRENCE, Leila .... 215-751-8000 381 H
llawrence@ccp.edu
LAWRENCE, Leslie .... 518-276-6287 311 J
lawrel@rpi.edu
LAWRENCE, Mark .... 757-352-4295 469 D
marklaw@regent.edu
LAWRENCE, Maureen .... 718-522-2300 312 H
LAWRENCE, Melanie ..... 404-727-1886 118 D
melanie.lawrence@emory.edu
LAWRENCE, Mya .... 618-468-6030 142 B
mylawrence@lc.edu
LAWRENCE, Octavia ...... 270-534-3244 182 G
octavia.lawrence@kctcs.edu
LAWRENCE, Paul .... 412-624-6620 400 A
plawrence@cfo.pitt.edu
LAWRENCE, Ross .... 406-874-6172 262 K
lawrencer@milescc.edu
LAWRENCE, Seth .... 740-245-7033 363 A
slawrence@rio.edu
LAWRENCE, Sharee .... 478-825-6282 118 E
lawrencs@fvsu.edu
LAWRENCE, ShirDonna . 319-335-3565 163 F
LAWRENCE, Tena .... 701-252-3467 346 J
tlawrenc@uj.edu
LAWRENCE, Tom .... 864-646-1429 411 H
tlawrenc@tctc.edu
LAWRENCE, Tonya .... 662-605-3413 245 E
tlawrence@holmescc.edu
LAWRENCE, Torrey .... 208-885-6448 132 C
tlawrence@uidaho.edu
LAWRENCE KEANE,
Loretta .... 212-217-4700 299 C
loretta_keane@fitnyc.edu
LAWRIE, Jeanne .... 863-638-2918 113 E
LAWRIE, Joshua .... 419-372-2011 348 F
jlawrie@bgsu.edu
LAWRIE, Kelly .... 419-772-1853 358 D
k-lawrie@onu.edu
LAWS, David .... 423-869-6418 420 A
david.laws@lmunet.edu
LAWS,
Donna Jean (DJ) .... 864-656-5616 406 F
djlaws@clemson.edu
LAWS, Frank .... 601-968-8978 244 C
flaws@belhaven.edu
LAWS, Georgianna .... 972-780-3600 453 C
georgianna.laws@untdallas.edu
LAWS, Mishelle .... 562-985-8356.. 32 A
mishelle.laws@csulb.edu
LAWS, Paige .... 870-633-4480.. 19 E
plaws@eacc.edu
LAWS, Tyler .... 502-863-8182 180 E
tyler_laws@georgetowncollege.edu
LAWSON, Abby .... 803-934-3298 409 H
alawson@morris.edu
LAWSON, Andrea .... 805-756-2511.. 29 K
alawso07@calpoly.edu
LAWSON, Angela .... 615-230-3576 424 F
angela.lawson@volstate.edu
LAWSON, Ann, O .... 330-471-8542 355 D
alawson@malone.edu
LAWSON, Carey .... 337-457-6135 189 B
clawson@lsue.edu
LAWSON, Cassandra .... 415-452-7689.. 37 C
clawson@ccsf.edu
LAWSON, Cynthia .... 212-229-8970 307 E
lawsonc@newschool.edu
LAWSON, Dan .... 419-289-5244 347 H
dlawson@ashland.edu
LAWSON, Daniel, L .... 415-422-4222.. 72 I
lawson@usfca.edu
LAWSON, Darren, P ...... 864-242-5100 405 H
LAWSON, Deneen .... 864-242-5100 405 H
LAWSON, Diana .... 616-331-7100 224 D
lawsond1@gvsu.edu
LAWSON, Donald .... 864-424-8040 412 H
lawsondr@mailbox.sc.edu
LAWSON, Earl .... 831-582-3062.. 32 D
elawson@csumb.edu
LAWSON, Ernest .... 336-334-4822 334 F
elawson@gtcc.edu
LAWSON, Greg .... 510-659-6438.. 54 J
glawson@ohlone.edu
LAWSON, Jake .... 918-463-2931 365 I
jacob.lawson@connorsstate.edu
LAWSON, Jason .... 270-789-5031 179 G
jklawson@campbellsville.edu
LAWSON, Jill .... 606-387-3236 182 D
jill.lawson@kctcs.edu
LAWSON, John .... 847-925-6330 138 E
jlawson@harpercollege.edu
LAWSON, Kelvin .... 904-281-9800 109 E
kelvin.lawson@famu.edu
LAWSON, Kenneth .... 360-416-7732 483 D
kenneth.lawson@skagit.edu
LAWSON, Laura .... 848-932-3517 281 B
ljlawson@sebs.rutgers.edu
LAWSON, Melanie .... 713-313-7762 448 D
lawson_mw@tsu.edu
LAWSON, Michael, S .... 919-761-2100 340 B
mlawson@sebts.edu
LAWSON, Patricia .... 312-893-7120 137 F
plawson@erikson.edu
LAWSON, Patricia, P ..... 804-523-5375 473 A
plawson@reynolds.edu
LAWSON, Peter .... 541-880-2363 373 B
lawson@klamathcc.edu
LAWSON, Regina, G ...... 336-758-6066 344 A
lawsonrg@wfu.edu
LAWSON, Sarah .... 317-813-2300 157 G
LAWSON, Sarah .... 309-298-2515 152 I
sm-lawson2@wiu.edu
LAWSON, Steve .... 859-985-3050 179 E
lawsonst@berea.edu
LAWSON, Thomas .... 661-255-1050.. 28 I
tlawson@calarts.edu
LAWSON, Tonia .... 850-872-3843 101 O
tlawson@gulfcoast.edu
LAWSON, Valerie, S ...... 276-376-4523 471 G
vas7k@uvawise.edu
LAWSON, Victoria .... 206-221-6075 484 A
lawson@uw.edu
LAWSON, Von .... 951-487-3440.. 53 A
vlawson@msjc.edu
LAWSON, Zach .... 918-540-6234 366 F
zachary.lawson@neo.edu
LAWSON-BORDERS,
Gracie .... 202-806-7694.. 92 E
gracie.lawsonborders@howard.edu
LAWTER, JR., Vernon .... 352-746-6721.. 97 L
lawterv@cf.edu
LAWTON, Elizabeth .... 603-366-5299 271 K
elawton@ccsnh.edu
LAWTON, Jack .... 315-445-4444 303 F
lawtonjd@lemoyne.edu
LAWTON, Jennifer .... 508-793-7478 207 F
jlawton@clarku.edu
LAWTON, Margaret, M .. 843-377-2423 406 B
mlawton@charlestonlaw.edu
LAWTON-RAUH,
Amy, L .... 864-656-9867 406 F
apfa@clemson.edu
LAWYER, Becky .... 952-885-5458 241 P
blawyer@nwhealth.edu
LAWYER, Mary .... 518-783-4288 314 K
mlawyer@siena.edu
LAXTON, Cassi .... 806-457-4200 435 D
claxton@fpctx.edu
LAY, Bethany .... 931-540-2837 423 D
blay@columbiastate.edu
LAY, Brian, K .... 734-384-4188 227 F
blay@monroeccc.edu
LAYCOCK, Sharon .... 318-487-5443 187 G
sharonlaycock@cltcc.edu
LAYE, Don .... 229-430-3577 114 G
dlaye@albanytech.edu
LAYER, Paul .... 907-450-8019.... 9 I
pwlayer@alaska.edu
LAYISH, Michael, D ...... 781-239-4022 205 G
mlayish@babson.edu
LAYMAN, Amy, T .... 717-358-4263 383 G
amy.layman@fandm.edu
LAYMAN, Leslie .... 773-907-4059 134 N
llayman1@ccc.edu
LAYMAN, Sarah .... 405-224-3140 371 B
slayman@usao.edu
LAYMON, Steven, E .... 540-362-6000 467 A
laymonse@hollins.edu
LAYNE, Barbara .... 978-542-8036 213 B
barbara.layne@salemstate.edu
LAYNE, Donnell .... 951-571-6118.. 59 B
donnell.layne@mvc.edu
LAYNE, Kenneth .... 606-589-3091 182 F
klayne0003@kctcs.edu
LAYNE, Michael .... 909-384-8987.. 60 F
mlayne@sbccd.cc.ca.us
LAYNE, Preston .... 276-523-7491 473 E
playne@mecc.edu
LAYNE, Rebecca .... 540-665-4500 470 A
LAYNE, Ron .... 910-246-4109 337 E
layner@sandhills.edu
LAYTHAM, D. Brent ...... 410-864-4202 202 A
blaytham@stmarys.edu
LAYTON, Bruce .... 847-491-5680 146 C
b-layton@northwestern.edu
LAYTON, Casey .... 503-594-6000 372 B
casey.layton@clackamas.edu
LAYTON, Christopher .... 281-873-0262 432 J
c.layton@commonwealth.edu
LAYTON, Dave, B .... 724-847-6508 384 B
dblayton@geneva.edu
LAYTON, Heather .... 978-630-9154 215 A
hlayton@mwcc.mass.edu
LAYTON, III,
William, C .... 207-859-4342 194 B
bill.layton@colby.edu
LAZARO, Helena, C .... 323-259-2500.. 54 I
LAZARUS, Natalia .... 310-656-8070.. 50 H
LAZDINS, Maira .... 415-703-9500.. 28 D
LAZENBY, Mark .... 949-824-4469.. 69 C
mark.lazenby@uci.edu
LAZIC, Boris .... 617-573-8415 218 G
blazic@suffolk.edu
LAZO, Ryan .... 970-247-7080.. 80 H
alumni@fortlewis.edu
LAZU, Carlos .... 787-850-9804 511 B
carlos.lazu@upr.edu
LAZZARI, John (JW) ..... 775-445-3259 271 A
john.lazzari@wnc.edu
LE, Hao .... 713-313-7950 448 D
hao.le@tsu.edu
LE, Hung, V .... 310-506-4307.. 56 H
hung.le@pepperdine.edu
LE, Michael, S .... 707-826-5489.. 30 A
michael.le@humboldt.edu
LE, Trang Thithuy .... 714-995-9988.. 47 E
LE, Vy .... 510-659-6201.. 54 J
vle@ohlone.edu
LE-CHAN, Trang .... 718-260-5352 294 F
tle-chan@citytech.cuny.edu
LE GUEN-SCHMIDT,
Daniel .... 763-488-2525 237 G
daniel.leguen-schmidt@hennepintech.edu
LE MASTERS, Philip ...... 325-793-3898 439 A
plemasters@mcm.edu

LEE, Dennis 916-558-2402.. 51 B
leed@scc.losrios.edu
LEE, Dennis 229-227-2414 125 G
dlee@southernregional.edu
LEE, Dewain 812-866-7078 155 D
leed@hanover.edu
LEE, Don 714-222-1110.. 27 I
LEE, Dongjin 510-639-7879.. 54 K
LEE, Donna 407-646-2185 106 L
dalee@rollins.edu
LEE, Donny 501-279-4187.. 19 G
dlee@harding.edu
LEE, Doug 724-852-3212 401 E
dlee@waynesburg.edu
LEE, Douglas 319-335-0444 163 F
douglas-lee@uiowa.edu
LEE, Elise 814-860-5106 387 C
elee@lecom.edu
LEE, Elwyn, C 832-842-5090 451 G
eclee@uh.edu
LEE, George, L 501-916-5347.. 22 C
gllee@ualr.edu
LEE, Grace 415-442-7859.. 44 B
glee@ggu.edu
LEE, Grace, J 310-739-0132.. 41 C
LEE, Hannah 213-381-0081.. 46 I
library@irus.edu
LEE, Harkmore 323-343-4907.. 32 B
hlee55@calstatela.edu
LEE, Hee Cheol 636-327-4645 255 E
hclee@midwest.edu
LEE, Herbert 831-459-1349.. 71 A
vpaa@ucsc.edu
LEE, Ho Yeon 678-552-1066 118 F
hoyeon@gcuniv.edu
LEE, Holly 580-628-6274 366 J
holly.lee@noc.edu
LEE, Howoo 770-831-9500 126 E
LEE, Hyejoo 703-629-1281 472 C
studentdean@vacu.edu
LEE, HyeKyung 303-360-4737.. 80 C
hyekyung.lee@ccaurora.edu
LEE, Ilsoo 213-293-1771.. 75 F
LEE, James 760-252-2411.. 26 L
jlee@barstow.edu
LEE, James 617-873-0236 207 E
james.lee@cambridgecollege.edu
LEE, James, A 713-467-4501 443 H
LEE, James, D 808-675-3289 128 B
james.lee@byuh.edu
LEE, James, S 626-448-0023.. 46 K
president@itsla.edu
LEE, Jason 937-766-7674 349 C
jasonlee@cedarville.edu
LEE, Jean 201-216-3667 282 L
jean.lee@stevens.edu
LEE, Jenna 940-898-3031 451 A
jlee11@twu.edu
LEE, Jinsam 213-246-4174.. 35 B
LEE, Joanne 406-496-4769 264 C
jlee@mtech.edu
LEE, Joe 325-674-2000 427 G
joe.lee@acu.edu
LEE, Joel 336-256-1440 342 D
jslee5@uncg.edu
LEE, Johanna 315-386-7879 319 E
leej@canton.edu
LEE, John 703-812-4757 467 D
jlee@leland.edu
LEE, Jonathan 210-486-1097 428 D
jlee@alamo.edu
LEE, Jonathan 310-233-4471.. 49 F
leej@lahc.edu
LEE, Jong Yong 310-913-0075 255 E
muca@midwest.edu
LEE, JongOh 909-447-6305.. 37 H
jolee@cst.edu
LEE, Joni, C 501-916-5698.. 22 C
jclee@ualr.edu
LEE, Jooman 510-639-7879.. 54 K
LEE, Joseph 251-380-3865.... 6 H
jlee@shc.edu
LEE, Joseph 651-213-4006 235 G
LEE, Juanita 701-224-2597 345 F
juanita.lee@bismarckstate.edu
LEE, Judy 718-818-6470 314 B
jlee@edaff.com
LEE, Julian 626-455-0312.. 58 J
LEE, Ka Yee, C 773-702-8810 151 B
kayeelee@uchicago.edu
LEE, Kang Won 714-592-7878.. 45 A
kwlee@haven.edu
LEE, Karen 630-752-5004 152 K
karen.lee@wheaton.edu
LEE, Karen 808-845-9225 129 G
karenlee@hawaii.edu
LEE, Karen 313-993-1544 230 H
leekm@udmercy.edu
LEE, Karyn 626-316-5331.. 63 D
klee2@saybrook.edu
LEE, Katrina 919-739-6736 338 F
kklee@waynecc.edu
LEE, Kelley 562-804-1239.. 45 C
kelleyl@healthcarecareercollege.edu
LEE, Kelvin, H 302-831-2136.. 91 A
khl@udel.edu
LEE, Ken 406-496-4249 264 C
klee5@mtech.edu
LEE, Kenneth 603-645-9691 273 E
k.lee7@snhu.edu
LEE, Kenya, N 646-312-3322 292 F
kenya.lee@baruch.cuny.edu
LEE, Kirk, D 972-377-1793 432 I
kdlee@collin.edu
LEE, Kyongbum 617-627-4323 219 A
kyongbum.lee@tufts.edu
LEE, Kyu, H 253-752-2020 479 D
klee@faithiu.edu
LEE, Kyu Hae 562-926-1023.. 58 A
office@ptsa.edu
LEE, Kyuboem 215-368-5000 389 G
klee@missio.edu
LEE, Kyung Hun 678-535-7771 118 F
khlee@gmail.com
LEE, Larry 320-308-3917 240 C
larry.lee@stcloudstate.edu
LEE, LeBlanc 210-486-0560 428 D
lleblanc7@alamo.edu
LEE, Lenetta 484-365-7222 388 F
llee@lincoln.edu
LEE, Lily 240-567-5272 200 E
lily.lee@montgomerycollege.edu
LEE, Lisa 212-410-8007 308 D
llee@nycpm.edu
LEE, Lisa 713-348-6312 441 K
lisahlee@rice.edu
LEE, IV, Luther, G 785-670-1745 178 A
luther.lee@washburn.edu
LEE, Mai Soua 559-730-3826.. 39 C
maisoual@cos.edu
LEE, Malisa 559-278-4639.. 31 D
malisal@csufresno.edu
LEE, Marion 210-690-9000 436 A
mlee2@hallmarkuniversity.edu
LEE, Mary W, L 630-515-7311 144 C
mleexx@midwestern.edu
LEE, Matt 225-578-2111 188 J
LEE, Matthew 225-578-3202 188 K
mlee@lsu.edu
LEE, Matthew 913-722-0272 174 G
matt.lee@kansaschristian.edu
LEE, Meesun 714-525-0088.. 44 C
LEE, Miae 888-777-7675 479 D
koreaninfo@faithiu.edu
LEE, Michael 509-542-4399 478 B
mlee@columbiabasin.edu
LEE, Michael 641-683-5295 166 F
michael.lee@indianhills.edu
LEE, Michael 717-477-1211 394 D
mjlee@ship.edu
LEE, Michael, J 216-368-4306 349 B
michael.j.lee6@case.edu
LEE, Michele 864-424-8038 412 H
michele@mailbox.sc.edu
LEE, Michelle 910-362-7777 332 F
mlee@cfcc.edu
LEE, Min 714-525-0088.. 44 C
gmu@gm.edu
LEE, Ming-Tung (Mike) 707-664-2156.. 34 C
LEE, Miwon 323-643-0301.. 25 L
LEE, Myung Chul 562-926-1023.. 58 A
mclee@ptsa.edu
LEE, Natasha 510-849-8200.. 55 F
LEE, Norice 575-674-2346 284 P
nlee@burrell.edu
LEE, Norman 315-294-8412 292 A
norman.lee@cayuga-cc.edu
LEE, Ok-Hee 218-477-2095 239 A
okheelee@mnstate.edu
LEE, Ouk Sub 703-712-7073 476 E
olee@wtsva.edu
LEE, Patricia, A 843-355-4127 413 C
leepa@wiltech.edu
LEE, Patrick 210-486-3282 428 B
plee18@alamo.edu
LEE, Paula 225-216-8732 187 D
leep@mybrcc.edu
LEE, Randolph 860-297-2413.. 88 I
randolph.lee@trincoll.edu
LEE, Rebecca 270-901-1019 182 E
rebecca.lee@kctcs.edu
LEE, Rebekah 610-917-1425 400 D
purchasing@valleyforge.edu
LEE, Richard 607-436-2517 316 C
richard.lee@oneonta.edu
LEE, Richard 910-678-8327 334 C
leeri@faytechcc.edu
LEE, Samuel 951-372-7199.. 59 C
samuel.lee@norcocollege.edu
LEE, Sang Meyng 562-926-1023.. 58 A
sangmeynglee@msn.com
LEE, Sanghoon 323-643-0301.. 25 L
president@aeu.edu
LEE, Sara 216-368-2000 349 B
hirschfeld.lee@case.edu
LEE, Sarah, K 972-549-6417 432 I
sklee@collin.edu
LEE, Staci 760-921-5512.. 56 A
staci.lee@paloverde.edu
LEE, Stephen 570-484-2087 393 E
slee@lockhaven.edu
LEE, Stephen 435-652-7651 459 G
stephen.lee@utahtech.edu
LEE, Steven 757-446-5221 465 H
leect@evms.edu
LEE, Sunny 510-642-6000.. 68 N
LEE, Susan 406-791-5318 264 J
susan.lee@uprovidence.edu
LEE, Taehoon 909-623-0302.. 59 H
LEE, Teresa 785-670-1538 178 A
teresa.lee@washburn.edu
LEE, Terri, S 919-209-2125 335 D
tslee@johnstoncc.edu
LEE, Theresa 865-974-4337 426 C
artscidean@utk.edu
LEE, Tiffany 562-944-0351.. 27 E
tiffany.lee@biola.edu
LEE, Tiffany 484-365-7608 388 F
tlee@lincoln.edu
LEE, Timothy 315-445-4300 303 F
leetm@lemoyne.edu
LEE, Tony 310-825-1633.. 69 D
tlee@ucpd.ucla.edu
LEE, Traci 480-314-2102.. 16 A
LEE, Treva, A 504-520-7653 193 C
tlee@xula.edu
LEE, Trisha 907-796-6294.. 10 C
tclee@alaska.edu
LEE, Trudy 573-651-2332 258 J
tglee@semo.edu
LEE, Tyjaun 816-604-4205 254 E
tyjaun.lee@mcckc.edu
LEE, Tyjaun 816-604-4203 255 B
tyjaun.lee@mcckc.edu
LEE, Valerie 276-523-2400 473 E
vlee@mecc.edu
LEE, Vina 845-672-0550 299 D
LEE, W. P. Andrew 214-648-8712 456 D
wpandrew.lee@utsouthwestern.edu
LEE, Yung-Jae 415-458-3786.. 41 H
yung-jae.lee@dominican.edu
LEE, Zelda 803-535-5348 406 E
zlee@claflin.edu
LEE-BARBER, Jill 404-413-1655 120 C
jleebarber@gsu.edu
LEE-CHUVALA, Christa .. 610-341-1544 383 A
christa.lee-chuvala@eastern.edu
LEE HUMPHREYS,
Carol 888-820-1484.. 64 D
carol.humphreys@sofia.edu
LEE-LEWIS, Sherri 310-434-4419.. 63 B
lee-lewis_sherri@smcv.edu
LEE MURPHY, Karen 954-201-7350.. 96 F
LEE SANG, Brian 202-885-6108.. 91 D
leesang@american.edu
LEE-YUAN, Mona 516-739-1545 308 E
clinicdirector@nyctcm.edu
LEEBRON TUTELMAN,
Elizabeth 215-204-8660 398 D
elizabeth.leebron@temple.edu
LEECK, Henry 618-437-5321 147 F
leeckh@rlc.edu
LEEDER, Mike 229-931-2222 120 B
mike.leeder@gsw.edu
LEEDY, David 212-659-0741 303 E
dleedy@tkc.edu
LEEDY, David 212-659-7290 303 E
dleedy@tkc.edu
LEEDY, Debbie 623-845-4770.. 13 E
debbie.leedy@gccaz.edu
LEEK, Danielle, R 804-371-3000 473 A
dleek@reynolds.edu
LEEMAN, Julia 847-585-2267.. 10 F
jleeman@careered.com
LEEMAN BARTZIS,
Opal 517-353-8920 227 C
bartziso@msu.edu
LEENHOUTS, Dave 636-922-8740 258 A
dleenhouts@stchas.edu
LEENHOUTS, James 828-898-8730 330 A
leenhoutsj@lmc.edu
LEEPER, Karla 706-721-7406 115 I
kleeper@augusta.edu
LEEPER, Lonnie 765-641-4168 153 D
lleeper@anderson.edu
LEEPORT, Patrick 218-755-2957 237 B
patrick.leeport@bemidjistate.edu
LEER, Raysa 202-274-5000.. 94 B
LEES, David 215-991-2015 386 I
leesp@lasalle.edu
LEES, Jill 812-855-7621 156 C
jmlees@iu.edu
LEES, Melissa 410-617-6769 199 G
mklees@loyola.edu
LEFAUVE, Linda, M 704-894-2124 328 C
lilefauve@davidson.edu
LEFEBVRE, Carol 706-721-8611 115 I
clefebvr@augusta.edu
LEFEBVRE, Ray 617-287-5000 211 E
raymond.lefebvre@umb.edu
LEFEVER, Annette, M 315-294-8508 292 A
alefev4@cayuga-cc.edu
LEFEVER, Shirley 316-978-3301 178 B
shirley.lefever@wichita.edu
LEFEVRE, Lisa 970-521-6615.. 82 B
lisa.lefevre@njc.edu
LEFEW, Susan 304-357-4713 486 J
susanlefew@ucwv.edu
LEFFEL, Lisa 414-443-8796 497 A
lisa.leffel@wlc.edu
LEFFELMAN, Jeremy 218-755-4222 237 B
jeremy.leffelman@bemidjistate.edu
LEFFLER, Lyvier 972-686-7878 441 G
LEFLER, Jennifer 952-358-8200 239 C
jennifer.lefler@normandale.edu
LEFNER, Monica 254-298-8282 445 B
LEFRANC-MORALES,
Ricardo 787-622-8000 509 H
lefranc@iraarch.com
LEFRANCOIS, Paul, R ... 864-488-4527 409 C
plefrancois@limestone.edu
LEFTHERIS, Julie 850-245-0466 109 D
julie.leftheris@flbog.edu
LEFTON, Toni 303-273-3000.. 79 A
tlefton@mines.edu
LEFTWICH, Hannah 405-425-5907 367 C
hannah.leftwich@oc.edu
LEFTWICH, Lukas 812-855-0973 156 C
lleftwic@indiana.edu
LEFTWICH, Lukas, D 812-855-0973 156 B
lleftwic@indiana.edu
LEGASPI, Lorenze 619-388-2990.. 61 A
llegaspi@sdccd.edu
LEGAULT, Greg 785-227-3380 171 H
legaultg@bethanylb.edu
LEGG, Hal, S 607-436-2748 316 C
hal.legg@oneonta.edu
LEGG, Jamie, W 910-630-7028 331 B
jlegg@methodist.edu
LEGGETT, Terri 252-789-0204 335 F
terri.leggett@martincc.edu
LEGGETTE COLLINS,
Priscilla 315-386-7315 319 E
leggettep@canton.edu
LEGRAND, Tom 864-488-8274 409 C
tslegrand@limestone.edu
LEGRANDE, Tomika 804-827-8737 472 D
tplegrande@vcu.edu
LEGRO, Jeffrey 804-289-8153 471 E
jlegro@richmond.edu
LEHFELDT, Elizabeth 216-687-5559 350 G
e.lehfeldt@csuohio.edu
LEHKER, Michael 956-665-2291 455 A
michael.lehker@utrgv.edu
LEHMACHER, Andrea 847-635-1806 146 E
alehmacher@oakton.edu
LEHMAN, Amy 831-479-6285.. 27 G
amlehman@cabrillo.edu
LEHMAN, Andrea, L 330-569-5441 353 F
lehmanal@hiram.edu

LEHMAN, Andrew 717-720-4030 393 C
alehman@passhe.edu
LEHMAN, Andrew 610-436-6966 394 F
alehman@wcupa.edu
LEHMAN, Ann 716-375-2435 312 F
alehman@sbu.edu
LEHMAN, Brennan 660-562-1187 256 G
blehman@nwmissouri.edu
LEHMAN, DeWayne 617-287-5302 211 E
dewayne.lehman@umb.edu
LEHMAN, Ed 540-432-4390 465 F
lehmanem@emu.edu
LEHMAN, John, B 906-487-1832 227 D
jblehman@mtu.edu
LEHMAN, Katherine 678-466-4000 117 A
spiveyexecdir@clayton.edu
LEHMAN, Sandra 801-957-4227 460 D
sandra.lehman@slcc.edu
LEHMAN, Tracey, A 541-885-1291 374 G
tracey.lehman@oit.edu
LEHMAN, William, H 262-554-2010 493 A
bill@encptech.com
LEHMAN-SEXTON, Amy 831-479-6100.. 27 G
LEHMANN, Candace 407-971-5124 108 B
lehmannc@seminolestate.edu
LEHMKUHL, Dennis 859-341-5800 184 G
LEHMKUHL, James 937-778-8600 352 D
jlehmkuhl@edisonohio.edu
LEHMKUHL, James 937-778-8600 352 D
LEHMPUHL, David 719-549-2340.. 79 G
david.lehmpuhl@csupueblo.edu
LEHN, Kathy, M 218-477-2243 239 A
kathleen.lehn@mnstate.edu
LEHNER, Eric, J 757-479-3706 472 A
elehner@vbts.edu
LEHNER, Jennifer 800-818-6136.. 55 K
jlehner@paloaltou.edu
LEHNERTZ, Rod 319-335-3565 163 F
rodney-lehnertz@uiowa.edu
LEHNERTZ, Tracy 507-457-1694 242 H
tlehnert@smumn.edu
LEHOCKY, John, F 847-970-4810 152 F
jlehocky@usml.edu
LEHOCZKY, Maria 863-669-2896 106 A
mlehoczky@polk.edu
LEHOTAK, Ed 402-557-7050 265 A
ed.lehotak@bellevue.edu
LEHR, David 434-395-4952 467 F
lehrdl@longwood.edu
LEHR, Randy 916-660-7900.. 64 B
rlehr1@sierracollege.edu
LEHRBERGER, Paula 610-526-6197 385 F
plehrberger@harcum.edu
LEHRBERGER, Paula 610-499-1226 401 I
pjlehrberger@widener.edu
LEHRE, Elaine 906-248-8422 221 I
elehre@bmcc.edu
LEHRER, Ilana 646-592-4313 325 R
ilana.lehrer@yu.edu
LEHRFELD, David 971-236-9231 372 D
LEHRIAN, Amanda 863-674-6010 100 G
alehrian@fsw.edu
LEHRLING, Tony 580-745-2186 369 F
tlehrling@se.edu
LEHRMAN, Susan 856-256-5225 280 H
lehrman@rowan.edu
LEHUA, Connie 415-485-9361.. 39 B
clehua@marin.edu
LEHWALD, Annie 816-501-4276 257 K
anne.lehwald@rockhurst.edu
LEI, Lei 973-353-1169 281 B
llei@business.rutgers.edu
LEI, Lei 973-353-1169 281 C
llei@business.rutgers.edu
LEIB, Michael 510-659-6518.. 54 J
mleib@ohlone.edu
LEIBER, Lee 713-798-1103 430 E
lleiber@bcm.edu
LEIBOLD, Susanne 563-588-6580 164 C
susanne.leibold@clarke.edu
LEICHLITER, Kirk 970-351-2446.. 84 D
kirk.leichliter@unco.edu
LEICHTY, Jeff, S 260-422-5561 156 A
jsleichty@indianatech.edu
LEID, Mark 509-368-6700 484 D
mark.leid@wsu.edu
LEIDICH, David 610-861-1622 390 D
leidich@moravian.edu
LEIDIG, Julie 703-450-2517 473 G
jleidig@nvcc.edu
LEIDINGER, Angela 803-737-0695 406 F
angiel@clemson.edu
LEIFELD, Robert, A 712-362-0439 166 H
rleifeld@iowalakes.edu
LEIFERMAN, Jeremy 218-726-8178 243 A
jsleifer@d.umn.edu
LEIGH, Anthony, J 334-833-4528.... 5 H
aleigh@hawks.huntingdon.edu
LEIGH, Bradley, K 419-372-2238 348 F
bleigh@bgsu.edu
LEIGH, Century 702-254-7577 271 B
century.leigh@northwestcareercollege.edu
LEIGH, Debra 320-308-5998 240 D
debra.leigh@sctcc.edu
LEIGH, Nathan 907-796-6496.. 10 C
nleigh1@alaska.edu
LEIGH, Sara 724-480-3624 381 G
sara.leigh@ccbc.edu
LEIGH, Stephanie 202-885-2121.. 91 D
leighse@american.edu
LEIGH, Tara 570-321-4000 388 H
LEIGHTON, Robyn 207-454-1024 195 E
rleighton@wccc.me.edu
LEIJA, Shirley 210-486-3608 428 B
sleija@alamo.edu
LEIKER, Jeff 620-252-7147 172 K
leiker.jeff@coffeyville.edu
LEIKER, Meg 619-265-0107.. 57 I
mleiker@platt.edu
LEIKER, Robert, D 619-265-0107.. 57 I
rleiker@platt.edu
LEIMBACH, Bill 410-337-6298 198 G
bleimbach@goucher.edu
LEIMBACH, Bill 410-386-4866 200 D
bleimbach@mcdaniel.edu
LEIMBEK, Melissa 763-424-0713 239 D
mleimbek@nhcc.edu
LEINEN, Jared 402-363-5675 269 F
jaleinen@york.edu
LEINEN, Margaret 858-534-2827.. 70 C
mleinen@ucsd.edu
LEINEN, Seinquis 701-231-8698 345 D
seinquis.leinen@ndsu.edu
LEINGANG, Dan 701-224-5525 345 F
daniel.leingang@bismarckstate.edu
LEININGER, Jeffrey 708-209-3470 136 D
jeff.leininger@cuchicago.edu
LEIPOLD, Bil 848-932-3922 281 C
bil.leipold@rutgers.edu
LEIS, Lyn 914-674-7802 305 H
lleis@mercy.edu
LEISETH, Jon 218-299-3448 234 K
leiseth@cord.edu
LEISINGER, Scott, C 319-352-8480 170 F
scott.leisinger@wartburg.edu
LEIST, Stephen 757-455-2131 476 C
sleist@vwu.edu
LEIST, Terry 406-994-4361 263 G
tleist@montana.edu
LEITCHMAN, Lauren 213-738-6710.. 66 A
lawdean@swlaw.edu
LEITSON, Cynthia 216-987-3510 351 D
cynthia.leitson@tri-c.edu
LEITZEL, Thomas, C 863-784-7110 108 D
leitzelt@southflorida.edu
LEIVA, Laura, E 504-861-5419 190 A
leleiva@loyno.edu
LEIVA, Pathy 607-436-2407 316 C
pathy.leiva@oneonta.edu
LEJEUNE, Olivia 978-921-4242 216 F
olivia.lejeune@montserrat.edu
LEJMAN, Michael 870-733-6782.. 18 A
mjlejman@asumidsouth.edu
LEJTER MORALES, Nelly 646-565-6430 322 B
nlejter@touro.edu
LEJUEZ, Carl 631-632-6265 316 D
provost@stonybrook.edu
LELAND, Chris 405-733-7350 369 D
cleland@rose.edu
LELAND, John, E 937-229-2114 362 C
john.leland@udri.udayton.edu
LELCHOOK, Heather 970-667-4611.. 77 G
heather.lelchook@aims.edu
LELIK, Mary, K 919-515-6434 341 E
mklelik@ncsu.edu
LEMAHIEU, Keith 219-864-2400 159 D
klemahieu@midamerica.edu
LEMAIRE, Gail 201-692-7083 276 I
lemaire@fdu.edu
LEMAITRE, Ludo 434-947-8288 469 A
llemaitre@randolphcollege.edu
LEMASTER, Chuck 254-267-7060 441 D
clemaster@rangercollege.edu
LEMASTER, J. Michael .. 937-258-8251 353 N
mlemaster@icb.edu
LEMASTER, J. Michael .. 937-258-8251 353 N
admissions@icb.edu
LEMASTERS, Christopher 434-947-8131 469 A
LEMASTERS, Laura 360-992-2268 477 J
llemasters@clark.edu
LEMAY, C. Aaron 409-266-2006 456 B
calemay@utmb.edu
LEMAY, Jerret 315-312-2136 318 B
jerret.lemay@oswego.edu
LEMBKE, Roberta 507-786-3097 242 I
lembke@stolaf.edu
LEMBURG, Mary 713-718-8505 436 E
mary.lemburg@hccs.edu
LEMELLE, Martin 410-225-2352 200 B
martin@martinlemelle.com
LEMERE, Brian, J 864-597-4068 413 E
lemerebj@wofford.edu
LEMEROND, James 920-693-1871 497 H
james.lemerond@gotoltc.edu
LEMERT, Louie, S 620-417-1202 177 C
louie.lemert@sccc.edu
LEMERY, Cynthia 518-327-6399 310 G
clemery@paulsmiths.edu
LEMERY, Monya 512-863-1538 444 F
lemerym@southwestern.edu
LEMHENEY, A.J 484-664-3614 390 F
ajlemheney@muhlenberg.edu
LEMIEN, Laura 603-366-5347 271 K
llemien@ccsnh.edu
LEMIEUX, Frederick 337-475-5508 192 B
flemieux@mcneese.edu
LEMIEUX, Frederick 337-475-5690 192 B
flemieux@mcneese.edu
LEMING, Crystal 785-670-1470 178 A
crystal.leming@washburn.edu
LEMING, Heidi 615-366-4482 423 A
heidi.leming@tbr.edu
LEMIRE, Joe 336-278-5555 328 H
jlemire2@elon.edu
LEMIRE, Mark 315-792-7100 320 F
mark.lemire@sunypoly.edu
LEMKE, Dustin, E 813-253-7210 102 A
dlemke@hccfl.edu
LEMKE, Henry 479-308-6060.. 17 E
henry.lemke@acheedu.org
LEMKE, Jeffrey, C 507-344-7373 233 I
jeff.lemke@blc.edu
LEMLER, Brad 325-649-8149 437 A
blemler@hputx.edu
LEMMA, Dawit 301-314-8291 202 E
dlemma@umd.edu
LEMMENES, Morghan 563-333-6210 169 D
lemmenesmorghan@sau.edu
LEMOINE, Francene 318-357-5805 192 D
lemoinef@nsula.edu
LEMOINE, Katherine 504-278-6491 188 E
klemoine@nunez.edu
LEMOINE, Lynn 651-695-7668 241 N
lynn.lemoine@mitchellhamline.edu
LEMOINE, Mary 318-473-6537 189 A
mlemoine@lsua.edu
LEMOINE, Patrice, A 860-297-2086.. 88 I
patrice.lemoine@trincoll.edu
LEMON, Deborah, A 812-856-3731 156 B
dalemon@iu.edu
LEMON, Jake 860-486-2337.. 89 B
jlemon@foundation.uconn.edu
LEMON, Jason, E 513-556-5318 361 I
jason.lemon@uc.edu
LEMON, Julie 608-785-9890 499 B
lemonj@westerntc.edu
LEMON, Latrina 804-289-8064 471 E
healthcenter@richmond.edu
LEMON, Patty 360-688-2101 482 D
plemon@stmartin.edu
LEMON, Paul 276-326-4215 464 A
plemon@bluefield.edu
LEMONIS, Samuel 601-857-3204 245 D
splemonis@hindscc.edu
LEMONIUS, Garfield 412-392-4304 395 H
glemonius@pointpark.edu
LEMONS, Marlow 310-660-3200.. 41 J
mlemons@elcamino.edu
LEMOS, Marcie 916-577-2200.. 76 C
mlemos@jessup.edu
LEMPINEN-LEEDY, Nance 352-395-5256 107 G
nance.lempinen-leedy@sfcollege.edu
LEMUEL, Robert, L 989-964-4393 229 L
lemuel@svsu.edu
LEMURA, Linda, M 315-445-4120 303 F
president14@lemoyne.edu
LEMUS, Maria De Jesus 773-371-5453 134 C
mlemus@ctu.edu
LENAGHAN, Andrew 815-836-5015 142 C
lenaghan@lewisu.edu
LENAGHAN, Janet, A 516-463-5676 301 E
janet.lenaghan@hofstra.edu
LENARES, Nicole 508-849-3363 205 E
nlenares@annamaria.edu
LENDOF, Delmy 718-636-3639 311 A
dlendof@pratt.edu
LENDVED, Alex 715-422-5300 498 A
LENER, Jason, A 724-946-7313 401 F
lenerja@westminster.edu
LENFEST, Richard 413-572-5405 213 C
rlenfest@westfield.ma.edu
LENGA, Kirk 818-333-3558.. 53 J
kirk.lenga@nyfa.edu
LENGNICK, Todd 305-919-5305 109 H
todd.lengnick@fiu.edu
LENGSFELD, Corinne 303-871-4843.. 84 C
clengsfe@du.edu
LENHART, Lisa 330-972-6961 361 G
lenhar1@uakron.edu
LENIG, Joni 931-540-2520 423 D
jlenig@columbiastate.edu
LENIHAN, David 787-840-2575 508 G
dlenihan@psm.edu
LENIO, Jim 866-492-5336 243 G
jim.lenio@mail.waldenu.edu
LENKER, Caitlin 717-867-6231 388 A
lenker@lvc.edu
LENN, Michael 608-262-1234 494 D
mlenn@wisc.edu
LENNEMAN, Marc 406-447-4869 262 E
mlenneman@carroll.edu
LENNERTON, Mark 718-289-5655 292 H
mark.lennerton@bcc.cuny.edu
LENNEY, Raina 202-885-5936.. 91 D
lenney@american.edu
LENNO, Chip 831-582-4700.. 32 D
clenno@csumb.edu
LENNO, Matthew 410-704-2332 204 B
mlenno@towson.edu
LENNON, Craig 203-576-4273.. 89 A
clennon@bridgeport.edu
LENNON, John 845-848-4061 298 A
john.lennon@dc.edu
LENO, Melissa 218-733-5903 238 A
melissa.leno@lsc.edu
LENOIR, Nina 714-997-6622.. 36 D
lenoir@chapman.edu
LENORE, Shani 314-529-9359 254 D
slenore@maryville.edu
LENOTRE, Alain 713-692-0077 433 B
acervantes@ciaml.com
LENSER, Leslie, A 615-460-6456 417 B
leslie.lenser@belmont.edu
LENSING, Peggy 563-387-1015 167 J
lensinpe@luther.edu
LENSON, Jacob, G 219-989-3120 160 A
lenson@pnw.edu
LENT, Tina 209-954-5151.. 61 H
tlent@deltacollege.edu
LENTINE, Ellen 484-664-3958 390 F
ellenlentine@muhlenberg.edu
LENTINI, James, P 516-323-3200 306 I
jlentini@molloy.edu
LENTINO, Nicholas 860-727-6765.. 87 H
nlentino@goodwin.edu
LENTZ, Brannon 334-514-8607.... 2 F
brannon.lentz@istc.edu
LENTZ, Kathryn 918-495-7163 368 F
klentz@oru.edu
LENTZ, Tracy 212-757-1190 289 H
tlentz@aami.edu
LENZ, Brenda 414-288-7172 492 E
brenda.lenz@marquette.edu
LENZ, Mary 320-762-4648 236 G
maryl@alextech.edu
LENZ, Phillip, R 724-946-6216 401 F
lenzpr@westminster.edu
LENZ-FISHER, Tyler 262-595-2239 495 D
lenzfish@uwp.edu
LENZMEIER, Brian, A 712-749-2103 164 A
lenzmeier@bvu.edu
LENZO, Diana, D 607-778-5100 317 A
lenzodd@sunybroome.edu
LEO, Donald 706-542-1653 126 F
donleo@engr.uga.edu

© COPYRIGHT HIGHER EDUCATION PUBLICATIONS, INC. 2022

LEO, Laurie .... 585-594-6861 310 A
leo_laurie@roberts.edu
LEO, Laurie .... 585-594-6861 311 L
leo_laurie@roberts.edu
LEO, Sydney .... 617-262-5000 206 E
LEOMITI, Sonny .... 684-699-9155 503 A
s.leomiti@amsamoa.edu
LEON, Dante .... 386-506-4153.. 98 A
dante.leon@daytonastate.edu
LEON, Deborah .... 215-635-7300 384 D
dleon@gratz.edu
LEON, Frances .... 860-906-5002.. 86 C
fleon@ccc.commnet.edu
LEON, Gabriela .... 281-756-3524 428 E
gleon@alvincollege.edu
LEON, Jairo .... 909-537-3647.. 33 B
jairo.leon@csusb.edu
LEON, Linda, J .... 330-471-8442 355 D
lleon2@malone.edu
LEON, Nelson .... 212-752-1530 303 G
nelson.leon@limcollege.edu
LEON, Tony .... 559-297-4500.. 46 C
tleon@iot.edu
LEON, Victor .... 505-224-3028 285 B
vleon@cnm.edu
LEON GUERRERO,
Arline, E .... 671-735-2218 503 E
arlinelg@triton.uog.edu
LEON GUERRERO,
Deborah, D .... 671-735-2585 503 E
deborah@triton.uog.edu
LEON GUERRERO,
Rachael, T .... 671-735-2170 503 E
rachaeltlg@triton.uog.edu
LEON-JORDAN,
Jordania .... 262-595-2010 495 D
leonjord@uwp.edu
LEONARD, Alice .... 866-294-3974 154 E
alice.leonard@ccr.edu
LEONARD, Andy .... 704-461-6200 326 I
andyleonard@bac.edu
LEONARD, Anne .... 718-260-5497 294 F
aleonard@citytech.cuny.edu
LEONARD, Bethany .... 262-695-6520 499 A
bleonard3@wctc.edu
LEONARD, Bryan .... 217-245-3048 139 A
bryan.leonard@ic.edu
LEONARD, Courtney ..... 563-588-6585 164 C
courtney.leonard@clarke.edu
LEONARD, Daniel, S ..... 303-282-3427.. 83 E
father.leonard@archden.org
LEONARD, David, M ..... 540-458-8752 476 D
dleonard@wlu.edu
LEONARD, J. Rich .... 919-865-5878 327 C
leonardjr@campbell.edu
LEONARD, Jesse, W ..... 814-641-3162 386 E
leonarj@juniata.edu
LEONARD, Joe .... 202-806-6100.. 92 E
joe.leonard@howard.edu
LEONARD, Jordahn .... 573-629-3058 253 D
jordahn.leonard@hlg.edu
LEONARD, Katie .... 570-702-8925 386 D
kleonard@johnson.edu
LEONARD, Kelly .... 865-981-8246 420 C
kelly.leonard@maryvillecollege.edu
LEONARD, Kevin .... 618-650-5047 149 H
kleonar@siue.edu
LEONARD, Kim .... 913-722-0272 174 G
LEONARD, Lindsey .... 319-352-8526 170 F
lindsey.leonard@wartburg.edu
LEONARD, Lou .... 412-365-1842 380 F
l.leonard@chatham.edu
LEONARD, Marjolie .... 631-632-6280 316 D
marjolie.leonard@stonybrook.edu
LEONARD,
Mary Kathleen .... 814-871-7430 383 H
leonard010@gannon.edu
LEONARD, Patti .... 916-558-2552.. 51 B
leonarp@scc.losrios.edu
LEONARD, Raychelle ..... 928-724-6683.. 12 F
rleonard@dinecollege.edu
LEONARD, Robert .... 256-824-2233.... 8 B
robert.leonard@uah.edu
LEONARD, Robert .... 252-492-2061 338 D
leonardr@vgcc.edu
LEONARD, Roberta .... 724-589-2024 398 F
rleonard@thiel.edu
LEONARD, Sanejo .... 916-306-1628.. 67 E
sleonard@sum.edu
LEONARD, Steve .... 317-738-8316 155 A
sleonard@franklincollege.edu
LEONARD, Tammy .... 214-388-5466 434 E
tleonard@dallasinstitute.edu

LEONARD, Tammy .... 972-721-5336 451 E
tleonard@udallas.edu
LEONARD, Trish .... 602-639-7500.. 12 L
LEONARD, Vee .... 239-590-1101 109 G
vleonard@fgcu.edu
LEONARD, William, J .... 610-361-5217 390 G
leonardw@neumann.edu
LEONE, Cataldo .... 617-358-6621 207 C
cleone@bu.edu
LEONE, Gerard .... 617-287-7050 211 C
gleone@umassp.edu
LEONE, John .... 518-828-4181 296 G
john.leone@sunycgcc.edu
LEONE, Thomas, A .... 410-706-7032 202 F
tleone@police.umaryland.edu
LEONETTI, Marc .... 401-254-3843 404 C
mleonetti@rwu.edu
LEONHART, Alex .... 717-396-7833 392 Q
aleonhart@pcad.edu
LEONI, Amy .... 740-284-7214 352 I
aleoni@franciscan.edu
LEONOR, JR.,
Samuel, E .... 951-785-2090.. 47 F
sleonor@lasierra.edu
LEOPARD, Tim .... 205-348-4530.... 7 G
tleopard@fa.ua.edu
LEOPOLD, Emily .... 617-588-1347 206 B
eleopold@bfit.edu
LEOPOLD, Joseph .... 727-341-3719 107 C
leopold.joseph@spcollege.edu
LEOPOLD, Lillian .... 619-482-6564.. 65 K
lleopold@swccd.edu
LEOTE, Jean .... 508-548-1400 220 B
LEOUSIS, Kim .... 251-442-2290.... 8 C
kleousis@umobile.edu
LEPAGE, Aimee .... 206-934-4386 482 G
aimee.lepage@seattlecolleges.edu
LEPAGE, Sharon .... 808-440-4263 128 C
slepage@chaminade.edu
LEPHART, Scott, M .... 859-323-1100 185 D
scott.lephart@uky.edu
LEPICK, Vicki .... 808-518-4791 128 H
vickilepick@pacrim.edu
LEPLEY, Suzanne .... 269-337-7177 225 B
suzanne.lepley@kzoo.edu
LEPORE, Lisa, M .... 410-546-6213 204 A
lmlepore@salisbury.edu
LEPOWSKY, Steven .... 860-679-2808.. 89 B
slepowsky@uchc.edu
LEPPER, Charles .... 801-957-4285 460 D
charles.lepper@slcc.edu
LEPRE, Carolyn, R .... 410-543-6011 204 A
crlepre@salisbury.edu
LERCH, Derek .... 530-283-0202.. 42 E
dlerch@frc.edu
LERER, Nava .... 516-877-3236 288 L
lerer@adelphi.edu
LEROY, Francois .... 859-572-7976 184 B
leroy@nku.edu
LEROY, Lindsay .... 910-962-2684 343 B
leroyl@uncw.edu
LEROY, Richard, S .... 805-437-1662.. 30 D
richard.leroy@csuci.edu
LERWICK, Scott .... 208-376-7731 130 E
slerwick@boisebible.edu
LESA, Elsie .... 684-699-2722 503 A
e.lesa@amsamoa.edu
LESANE, II, Cornell, B .. 508-793-3622 208 A
clesane@holycross.edu
LESANE, Steven .... 919-546-8534 339 I
slesane@shawu.edu
LESCARBEAU, Lisa .... 413-662-5205 212 F
lisa.lescarbeau@mcla.edu
LESCAULT, JR.,
Maurice, A .... 434-971-3291 501 G
maurice.a.lescault.civ@army.mil
LESCHES, Elchonon .... 718-363-2034 321 G
bmotzal@gmail.com
LESEN, Beth .... 562-985-5587.. 32 A
beth.lesen@csulb.edu
LESESNE, David, L .... 804-752-7305 469 B
davidlesesne@rmc.edu
LESH, Aja .... 626-815-6000.. 26 K
alesh@apu.edu
LESHER, Nicole .... 949-376-6000.. 47 G
nlesher@lcad.edu
LESHIN, Laurie .... 818-354-2286.. 29 B
laurie.a.leshin@jpl.nasa.gov
LESHINSKIE, Eric .... 480-423-6310.. 14 B
eric.leshinskie@scottsdalecc.edu
LESHINSKIE, Eric .... 480-731-8000.. 13 A
eric.leshinskie@domail.maricopa.edu

LESHKEVICH, Peter .... 734-973-3729 232 A
pleshkev@wccnet.edu
LESHKOWICH,
Ann Marie .... 508-793-2335 208 A
aleshkow@holycross.edu
LESHOK, Laura .... 734-462-4400 230 B
lleshok@schoolcraft.edu
LESIAK, Erin .... 308-398-7406 265 C
erinlesiak@cccneb.edu
LESKO, Katie .... 518-438-5963 305 B
klesko@mariacollege.edu
LESKOVAR, Jack .... 608-663-6901 491 F
jleskovar@edgewood.edu
LESLEY, Kimberly .... 215-965-8582 390 C
klesley@moore.edu
LESLIE, Bethany .... 330-823-8440 362 E
lesliebe@mountunion.edu
LESLIE, Brian .... 321-674-8899 100 A
bleslie@fit.edu
LESLIE, Colleen, M .... 617-253-7086 215 G
LESLIE, Howard .... 973-278-5400 291 A
hdl@berkeleycollege.edu
LESLIE, Howard .... 973-278-5400 274 J
hdl@berkeleycollege.edu
LESLIE, Jon .... 303-492-2537.. 83 M
jon.leslie@colorado.edu
LESLIE, Julie .... 419-251-1598 355 G
julie.leslie@mercycollege.edu
LESLIE, Ken .... 802-635-1315 463 B
ken.leslie@northernvermont.edu
LESLIE, Kyle .... 716-375-2143 312 F
kleslie@sbu.edu
LESLIE, Robin .... 704-463-3442 339 C
robin.leslie@pfeiffer.edu
LESMEISTER, Heather .... 417-625-9365 255 I
lesmeister-h@mssu.edu
LESPERANCE, Dawn .... 208-792-2318 131 F
sdlesperance@lcsc.edu
LESPERANCE, Katherine 920-465-2464 494 F
lesperka@uwgb.edu
LESPERANCE, Wayne .... 603-428-2908 272 I
wlesperance@nec.edu
LESSANE JENKINS,
Wanda .... 910-672-1145 341 B
wljenkins@uncfsu.edu
LESSARD, Kelley .... 508-830-5014 213 A
klessard@maritime.edu
LESSARD, Richard .... 617-732-2880 216 B
richard.lessard@mcphs.edu
LESSEIG, Lisa .... 912-279-5737 117 C
llesseig@ccga.edu
LESSEM, Louis, A .... 313-577-2268 232 H
louis.lessem@wayne.edu
LESSER, Cheryl .... 603-427-7600 271 J
LESSER, Mary .... 828-328-7078 330 B
mary.lesser@lr.edu
LESSITER, Julie .... 318-795-4238 189 E
julie.lessiter@lsus.edu
LESSNE, Eric .... 203-392-6050.. 85 H
lessnee1@southernct.edu
LESSNER, Kimberly .... 903-510-2383 451 D
kles@tjc.edu
LESTER, Cancee .... 936-591-9075 440 E
clester@panola.edu
LESTER, Cynthia, Y .... 678-891-2705 120 C
clester6@gsu.edu
LESTER, Dennis .... 831-656-3432 501 K
dennis.lester@nps.edu
LESTER, Dyan, E .... 276-964-7677 474 E
dyan.lester@sw.edu
LESTER, Gillian .... 212-854-2675 296 H
glester@law.columbia.edu
LESTER, Jason .... 561-803-2402 105 B
jason_lester@pba.edu
LESTER, Jason .... 561-803-2000 105 B
jason_lester@pba.edu
LESTER, Jay .... 304-792-7098 487 I
LESTER, John .... 912-478-6397 120 A
jlester@georgiasouthern.edu
LESTER, John .... 334-670-3923.... 7 C
jlester@troy.edu
LESTER, Karen, K .... 218-477-2062 239 A
lesterka@mnstate.edu
LESTER, Melinda .... 888-532-7282.. 56 E
LESTER, Mike .... 812-221-1714 162 D
mikelester@vbc.edu
LESTER, Mike .... 507-285-7254 240 B
mike.lester@rctc.edu
LESTER, Richard, K .... 617-253-7704 215 G
LESTER, Ron .... 405-491-6356 369 G
rlester@snu.edu
LESTER, Tammy .... 252-451-8371 336 B
ttlester342@nashcc.edu

LESUEUR, Mary .... 662-252-8000 248 B
mlesueur@rustcollege.edu
LESZKO, Dennis .... 203-837-8214.. 86 A
leszkod@wcsu.edu
LETANG, Alick .... 203-392-5652.. 85 H
letanga1@southernct.edu
LETCHER, Owen .... 925-485-5277.. 35 P
oletcher@clpccd.org
LETCHWORTH, Deemie . 601-643-8403 244 G
deemie.letchworth@colin.edu
LETCHWORTH, Megan .. 928-350-1006.. 15 O
megan.letchworth@prescott.edu
LETELLIER, Lisa .... 580-559-5173 365 J
lletellier@ecok.edu
LETELLIER, Travis .... 605-658-3424 415 E
travis.letellier@usd.edu
LETENDRE, Donald, E ... 319-335-8794 163 F
donald-letendre@uiowa.edu
LETENDRE, Linell, A .... 719-333-4270 502 C
linell.letendre@afacademy.af.edu
LETH-STEENSEN, Ted .... 413-565-1000 205 I
tlethsteensen@baypath.edu
LETIZIA, Katelyn .... 716-926-8942 301 C
kletizia@hilbert.edu
LETO, Leah .... 201-761-6102 282 H
lleto@saintpeters.edu
LETOURNEAU, Diana .... 315-268-7608 295 E
dletourn@clarkson.edu
LETT, Erika, L .... 828-398-7900 331 K
erikallett@abtech.edu
LETT-BREWINGTON,
La Wanza .... 757-683-4109 468 C
llettbre@odu.edu
LETTER, Leon .... 734-384-4282 227 F
lletter@monroeccc.edu
LETTIERE, Barbara .... 610-647-4400 385 K
blettiere@immaculata.edu
LETTINI, Gabriella .... 510-430-3335.. 66 F
glettini@sksm.edu
LETTINI, Pat .... 516-876-3191 318 A
lettinip@oldwestbury.edu
LETTKO, James .... 518-464-8500 299 B
jlettko@excelsior.edu
LETURMY, Aimee .... 781-891-2297 206 C
aleturmy@bentley.edu
LEUENBERGER, Deniz ... 508-531-1201 212 B
dleuenberger@bridgew.edu
LEUGERS, Lucinda .... 928-692-3041.. 14 H
lleugers@mohave.edu
LEUMA, Elizabeth .... 684-699-2722 503 A
e.leuma@amsamoa.edu
LEUNER, Jean .... 334-244-3658.... 4 F
jleuner@aum.edu
LEUNG, David .... 818-767-0888.. 76 D
david.leung@woodbury.edu
LEUNG, Katheryn .... 626-917-9482.. 36 H
kleung@cesna.edu
LEUNG, Paul Lap .... 713-221-5896 452 B
leungpa@uhd.edu
LEUNG-ROGALA,
Bridget .... 508-849-3490 205 E
blrogala@annamaria.edu
LEVA, Gennaro, J .... 215-204-2452 398 D
levagj@temple.edu
LEVAN, Gretchen, L .... 610-917-1478 400 D
gllevan@valleyforge.edu
LEVAN, Kent, G .... 314-977-7143 258 H
kent.levan@slu.edu
LEVAN, Stephanie .... 843-863-7382 406 C
slevan@csuniv.edu
LEVANDA, Eric .... 334-833-4335.... 5 H
elevanda@hawks.huntingdon.edu
LEVANDER, Caroline ..... 717-348-4228 441 K
clevande@rice.edu
LEVARIO GUTIERREZ,
Estela .... 775-337-5647 270 I
elevario@tmcc.edu
LEVAS, Frances .... 617-731-3500 210 D
flevas@hchc.edu
LEVASSEUR, Katherine .. 802-224-3000 462 G
katherine.levasseur@vsc.edu
LEVEL, Alvin, E .... 502-597-5815 183 A
alvin.level@kysu.edu
LEVEN, Carol .... 212-217-4700 299 C
carol_leven@fitnyc.edu
LEVEN, Scott .... 417-447-6985 257 B
levens@otc.edu
LEVENGOOD, Tina .... 603-646-9257 272 F
tina.levengood@dartmouth.edu
LEVENS, Michael, P .... 248-689-8282 231 E
mlevens@walshcollege.edu
LEVEQUE, Karen .... 312-362-8091 136 F
kleveque@depaul.edu

LEWIS, Paul, W .... 417-865-2815 249 G lewisp@evangel.edu
LEWIS, Paul, W .... 417-268-1014 249 G lewisp@evangel.edu
LEWIS, Paula .... 740-376-4701 355 E lewisp@marietta.edu
LEWIS, Pericles .... 203-432-2550.. 90 B
LEWIS, Pericles .... 203-432-2517.. 90 B pericles.lewis@yale.edu
LEWIS, Phil .... 304-384-6292 488 K plewis@concord.edu
LEWIS, Rachel .... 801-957-4563 460 D rachel.lewis@slcc.edu
LEWIS, Ranny .... 954-486-7728 112 J rlewis@uftl.edu
LEWIS, Raynold .... 508-929-8883 213 D rlewis1@worcester.edu
LEWIS, Rebecca .... 817-272-3365 454 B rebeccal@uta.edu
LEWIS, Rebecca, B .... 423-439-6155 418 D bakerr@etsu.edu
LEWIS, Rhiannon .... 415-503-6291.. 61 E rlewis@sfcm.edu
LEWIS, Rob .... 214-333-5821 433 D robertl@dbu.edu
LEWIS, Robin .... 606-326-2423 180 I robin.lewis@kctcs.edu
LEWIS, Ronald, J .... 605-342-0317 414 C president@jwc.edu
LEWIS, Ryan .... 870-245-5128.. 20 H lewisr@obu.edu
LEWIS, Shelia .... 818-575-6800.. 68 C shelia.lewis@tuw.edu
LEWIS, Shirley .... 707-864-7000.. 64 F shirley.lewis@solano.edu
LEWIS, Stacy .... 415-422-5540.. 72 I lewiss@usfca.edu
LEWIS, Stephanie .... 909-384-8534.. 60 F slewis@sbccd.cc.ca.us
LEWIS, Stephen .... 606-589-3111 182 F kent.lewis@kctcs.edu
LEWIS, Susan .... 325-674-2024 427 G lewiss@acu.edu
LEWIS, Susan .... 541-506-6047 372 E slewis@cgcc.edu
LEWIS, Tammy .... 718-951-5024 293 A tlewis@brooklyn.cuny.edu
LEWIS, Ted .... 304-327-4161 488 J tlewis@bluefieldstate.edu
LEWIS, Tiffany .... 765-677-2102 157 F tiffany.lewis@indwes.edu
LEWIS, Tracie, O .... 336-285-4491 341 C tolewis@ncat.edu
LEWIS, Trevor .... 305-626-3750 100 B trevor.lewis@fmuniv.edu
LEWIS, Trevor, C .... 215-898-1135 399 J lewistc@upenn.edu
LEWIS, Walter .... 518-587-2100 320 B walter.lewis@esc.edu
LEWIS, JR., Wayne, D .. 585-567-9310 301 G wayne.lewis@houghton.edu
LEWIS, Whitney .... 404-364-8309 123 G wlewis@oglethorpe.edu
LEWIS, Wick .... 520-452-2619.. 11 O lewisw@cochise.edu
LEWIS, Zach .... 480-517-8418.. 14 A zach.lewis@riosalado.edu
LEWIS, Zachary .... 314-367-8700 260 A zachary.lewis@uhsp.edu
LEWIS-BHOLA, Prudence .... 305-626-3180 100 B prudence.bhola@fmuniv.edu
LEWIS-GUMP, Kelly ...... 248-645-3300 222 G kgump@cranbrook.edu
LEWIS-JASPER, Vera ...... 409-944-1496 435 F vlewis@gc.edu
LEWMAN, Marguerite .... 530-251-8834.. 47 I mlewman@lassencollege.edu
LEWTER, John, A .... 731-881-7710 426 E jlewter@utm.edu
LEWTER, Richard .... 804-758-6840 474 C rlewter@rappahannock.edu
LEWTON-YATES, Jennifer .... 601-974-1327 246 C yatesjl@millsaps.edu
LEY, David .... 907-745-3201.... 9 C dley@akbible.edu
LEY-SOTO, Javier .... 305-237-3694 104 E jleysoto@mdc.edu
LEYBA, John .... 706-864-1958 126 G john.leyba@ung.edu
LEYBA-RUIZ, Teresa ..... 623-845-3010.. 13 E teresa.leyba-ruiz@gccaz.edu
LEYK, Mary .... 320-222-5210 239 H mary.leyk@ridgewater.edu
LEYKAM, Scott, R .... 503-943-8420 376 H leykam@up.edu
LEYSHON, Lisa .... 208-282-3111 131 E leyslisa@isu.edu
LEYVA-PUEBLA, Ricardo .... 206-934-3890 482 G ricardo.leyvapuebla@seattlecolleges.edu
LEZHEO, Kao .... 206-934-3851 482 G kao.lezheo@seattlecolleges.edu
LE'I, Emilia .... 684-699-2722 503 A e.lei@amsamoa.edu
LI, Chien-pin .... 936-294-2204 449 E cxl085@shsu.edu
LI, Dai .... 209-667-3204.. 33 D dli4@csustan.edu
LI, Haipeng .... 209-228-7632.. 70 A hli58@ucmerced.edu
LI, Joanne .... 305-348-2751 109 H joli@fiu.edu
LI, Joanne .... 402-554-2419 269 C joli@unomaha.edu
LI, Kathy .... 312-658-5100 150 E
LI, Kuiyuan .... 850-473-7716 111 E kli@uwf.edu
LI, Lin .... 615-963-5000 425 A
LI, Luchen .... 410-337-6000 198 G luchen.li@goucher.edu
LI, Luyan .... 773-878-8756 148 F
LI, Penny .... 888-820-1484.. 64 D penny.li@sofia.edu
LI, Peter .... 361-593-4340 447 A peter.li@tamuk.edu
LI, Rui .... 309-677-4457 133 H rli2@fsmail.bradley.edu
LI, Rui .... 610-430-4959 394 F rli@wcupa.edu
LI, Sharon, F .... 415-422-2790.. 72 I lis@usfca.edu
LI, Xiaofan .... 312-567-3135 139 H lix@iit.edu
LI, Xiaohong .... 661-763-7978.. 67 F xli@taftcollege.edu
LI, Xiaonong .... 661-763-7978.. 67 F xli@taftcollege.edu
LI, Xun .... 954-776-4476 103 B xli@keiseruniversity.edu
LI, Yan .... 425-352-8633 477 F yli@cascadia.edu
LI, Yi .... 212-237-8801 294 B yili@jjay.cuny.edu
LI, Zhan .... 203-254-4070.. 87 G zli2@fairfield.edu
LI-BUGG, Cherry .... 714-808-4787.. 54 B clibugg@nocccd.edu
LI-ROSI, AnaMaria .... 239-280-7398.. 95 M anamaria.lirosi@avemaria.edu
LIANG, Bruce .... 860-679-7214.. 89 B bruce.liang@uconn.edu
LIANG, Bruce .... 860-679-7214.. 89 B bliang@uchc.edu
LIANG, Heng .... 707-621-7000.. 41 F
LIANG, John Paul .... 713-780-9777 428 H jpliang@acaom.edu
LIANG, Mark .... 714-564-6040.. 58 F liang_mark@sac.edu
LIANG, Sara .... 608-663-2277 491 F sliang@edgewood.edu
LIANTONIO, Richard ..... 913-253-5036 177 A richard.liantonio@spst.edu
LIAO, Min-Ken .... 864-294-2248 408 I minken.liao@furman.edu
LIAO-TROTH, Matthew .. 727-341-3323 107 C liaotroth.matthew@spcollege.edu
LIAUTAUD, Danielle ...... 973-720-2121 283 I liautaudd@wpunj.edu
LIAUTAUDWATKINS, Danielle .... 215-751-8000 381 H dliautaudwatkins@ccp.edu
LIBBY, Betsy .... 207-755-5250 194 J blibby@cmcc.edu
LIBBY, Grace .... 860-913-2264.. 87 H glibby@goodwin.edu
LIBBY, Olivia .... 570-577-1674 379 A olivia.libby@bucknell.edu
LIBEN-NOWELL, David .. 507-222-4300 234 C dln@carleton.edu
LIBENGOOD, Desiree .... 612-343-4796 241 O dslibeng@northcentral.edu
LIBERATI, Dennis .... 267-295-2314 401 C dliberati@walnuthillcollege.edu
LIBERATORI, Ellen, A ... 607-746-4612 320 A liberaem@delhi.edu
LIBERATOSCIOLI, Daniel .... 267-295-2316 401 C president@walnuthillcollege.edu
LIBERATOSCIOLI, Peggy .... 267-295-2315 401 C pl@walnuthillcollege.edu
LIBERIO, Lydia, G .... 213-252-5100.. 24 C lliberio@alu.edu
LIBERMAN, Ira .... 718-438-1002 306 A yliberman@yeshivanet.com
LIBERTINI, Christopher . 845-848-4069 298 A christopher.libertini@dc.edu
LIBERTO, Salvadore ...... 251-460-7725.... 9 A sliberto@southalabama.edu
LIBERTO, Terri .... 412-536-1813 386 H terri.liberto@laroche.edu
LIBERTY, Bob .... 254-526-1310 431 E bob.liberty@ctcd.edu
LIBERTY, Cynthia .... 336-770-3333 343 C libertyc@uncsa.edu
LIBERTY, Paul .... 703-993-8860 466 J pliberty@gmu.edu
LIBET, Alice, Q .... 843-792-4930 409 D libeta@musc.edu
LIBUTTI, Dean .... 401-874-4408 404 E dean@uri.edu
LIBUTTI, Ken, L .... 561-868-3236 105 C libuttik@palmbeachstate.edu
LIBUTTI, Steven, K .... 732-235-8064 281 B steven.libutti@cinj.rutgers.edu
LICARI, Frank .... 702-990-4433 271 D flicari@roseman.edu
LICARI, Michael .... 931-221-7011 416 H
LICATA, Christine, M .... 585-475-2953 312 A cmlnbt@rit.edu
LICATA, Julian .... 218-755-4606 237 B julian.licata@bemidjistate.edu
LICHT, Daniel .... 914-395-2301 314 H dlicht@sarahlawrence.edu
LICHT, William .... 920-206-2320 492 C william.licht@mbu.edu
LICHTBLAU, Jobey .... 710-231-7672 345 D jobey.lichtblau@ndsu.edu
LICHTENSTEIN, Mark .... 315-470-4748 319 A malichte@esf.edu
LICHTERMAN, Hilary, L 206-296-6305 483 B hlichterman@seattleu.edu
LICHTI, Benjamin .... 316-284-5349 171 I blichti@bethelks.edu
LICHTMAN, Jeffrey .... 212-463-0400 322 C jeff.lichtman@touro.edu
LICHTVELD, Maureen .... 412-624-3001 400 A mlichtve@pitt.edu
LICKTEIG, Denise .... 402-872-2379 267 H dlickteig@peru.edu
LIDAYWA, Lora .... 309-298-1819 152 I lj-lidaywa@wiu.edu
LIDDELL, Tammy .... 206-296-6052 483 B liddellt@seattleu.edu
LIDDELL, Wendy .... 509-248-7100 479 G
LIDDICOAT, Al .... 805-756-2844.. 29 K aliddico@calpoly.edu
LIDDY, Colette .... 973-618-3209 275 E cliddy@caldwell.edu
LIDERS, Gunta .... 585-275-5373 323 E gliders@orpa.rochester.edu
LIDGUS, Jonathan .... 314-516-5911 260 E lidgusj@umsl.edu
LIDINGTON, Siobhan ..... 203-773-8550.. 85 C slidington@albertus.edu
LIDSTONE, Rena .... 409-772-5714 456 B rllidsto@utmb.edu
LIDTKE, Suzanne .... 262-547-1211 491 A slidtke@carrollu.edu
LIDY, Paul .... 217-362-6410 144 D plidy@millikin.edu
LIDZ, Carmen .... 213-891-2034.. 49 C carmen@laccd.edu
LIEBEGOTT, Kris .... 570-955-1530 387 A liebegott@lackawanna.edu
LIEBENGOOD, Kelly .... 903-233-3372 438 C kellyliebengood@letu.edu
LIEBER, Barbara .... 217-641-4535 140 H blieber@jwcc.edu
LIEBERMAN, Devorah, A .... 909-448-4900.. 71 C dlieberman@laverne.edu
LIEBERMAN, Matthew ... 646-565-6067 322 C matthew.lieberman@touro.edu
LIEBERMAN, Matthew ... 646-565-6067 322 B matthew.lieberman@touro.edu
LIEBERT, Jane .... 913-758-6126 177 I jane.liebert@stmary.edu
LIEBESKIND, Lanny, S .. 404-727-6604 118 D chemll1@emory.edu
LIEBHABER, Karen .... 870-248-4000.. 18 H karenl@blackrivertech.edu
LIEBHABER, Sharon ...... 215-635-7300 384 D sharon.liebhaber@gmail.com
LIEBLICH, Kathleen ...... 516-876-3242 318 A lieblichk@oldwestbury.edu
LIEBLING, Mark .... 231-995-1342 228 F mliebling@nmc.edu
LIEBOWITZ, Debra, J .... 203-582-7576.. 88 F debra.liebowitz@qu.edu
LIEBOWITZ, Ronald, D . 781-736-2000 207 D president@brandeis.edu
LIEBSCH, Anita .... 303-963-3365.. 78 D aliebsch@ccu.edu
LIEBURN, Scott .... 920-924-6459 498 C slieburn@morainepark.edu
LIECHTI, Brian .... 828-771-3006 344 B bliechti@warren-wilson.edu
LIECHTY, Benjamin, A .. 765-455-9595 156 E baliecht@iuk.edu
LIECHTY, Dan .... 574-535-7563 155 B dankl@goshen.edu
LIECHTY, Jeanne, M ..... 574-535-7401 155 B jeannem@goshen.edu
LIECHTY, Spencer .... 716-883-7000 291 M
LIEDERBACH, Mark .... 919-761-2100 340 B mliederbach@sebts.edu
LIEDTKA, Theresa .... 423-425-4506 426 D theresa-liedtka@utc.edu
LIEDTKE, Richard, W .... 785-670-1812 178 A richard.liedtke@washburn.edu
LIEF, Charles, G .... 303-245-4804.. 81 N president@naropa.edu
LIEF, Nathan, P .... 651-696-6140 236 C nlief@macalester.edu
LIEN, Helen .... 256-824-5485.... 8 B helen.lien@uah.edu
LIEN, Thuy .... 858-513-9240.. 16 I thuy.lien@ashford.edu
LIERZ, Rachel .... 913-469-8500 174 F rachellierz@jccc.edu
LIESEN, Joseph .... 573-288-6480 251 I jliesen@culver.edu
LIESEN, Kristen .... 217-228-5432 147 C liesekr@quincy.edu
LIESTMAN, Daniel .... 509-865-8520 480 B liestman_d@heritage.edu
LIETO, Mary .... 914-923-2690 310 F mlieto@pace.edu
LIETZ, Cynthia .... 602-496-0600.. 11 A clietz@asu.edu
LIFKA, David .... 607-254-8621 297 D lifka@cornell.edu
LIFSEY, Britt .... 678-359-5108 120 D brittl@gordonstate.edu
LIFTON, Richard, P .... 212-327-8080 312 B rickl@rockefeller.edu
LIGAS, Mark .... 203-254-4025.. 87 G mligas@fairfield.edu
LIGE, Matthew .... 734-487-1222 223 F mlige@emich.edu
LIGEIKIS, David .... 607-778-5575 317 A ligeikisd@sunybroome.edu
LIGHT, Aaron .... 417-447-8802 257 B lighta@otc.edu
LIGHT, Brad .... 336-334-4355 342 D uncg@bkstore.com
LIGHT, Cathy, A .... 626-395-6304.. 29 B clight@caltech.edu
LIGHT, Logan .... 501-279-4332.. 19 G hlight@harding.edu
LIGHT, Susan .... 315-228-7444 296 C slight@colgate.edu
LIGHT, Wesley .... 717-477-1121 394 D wwlight@ship.edu
LIGHTCAP, Rhonda .... 516-671-0379 324 C rlightcap@webb.edu
LIGHTCAP, Stephen .... 215-717-6375 399 I slightcap@uarts.edu
LIGHTFOOT, Carolyn, A 281-425-6455 438 B clightfoot@lee.edu
LIGHTFOOT, David .... 434-832-7643 472 G lightfootd@centralvirginia.edu
LIGHTFOOT, Kevin .... 254-299-8389 438 G klightfoot@mclennan.edu
LIGHTFOOT, Stacy, G .... 423-425-4141 426 D stacy-lightfoot@utc.edu
LIGHTNER, Joseph .... 903-586-2518 437 D

LIGHTNER, Michael ...... 303-860-5600.. 83 L
lightner@cu.edu
LIGHTNER, Robin .... 513-745-5660 362 A
robin.lightner@uc.edu
LIGHTSEY, Pamela .... 773-256-3000 143 H
LIGHTY, JoAnn .... 208-426-1450 130 F
joannlighty@boisestate.edu
LIGMAN, Scott .... 509-527-2395 484 C
scott.ligman@wallawalla.edu
LIGON, Jay .... 318-257-4321 192 A
ligon@latech.edu
LIGON, Theresa .... 713-780-9777 428 H
tligon@acaom.edu
LIGUORI, Gary .... 401-874-9330 404 E
gliguori@uri.edu
LIKELY, Nygil .... 269-927-8752 226 B
nlikely@lakemichigancollege.edu
LIKEN, Fiona, B .... 706-542-6020 126 F
fliken@uga.edu
LIKENS, Erin .... 601-643-8316 244 G
erin.likens@colin.edu
LIKINS, Michelle .... 706-754-7819 123 C
mlikins@northgatech.edu
LIKNESS, Tabitha .... 605-668-1603 414 F
tabitha.likness@mountmarty.edu
LILES, Jeffrey .... 419-824-3829 355 C
jliles@lourdes.edu
LILFORD, Grant .... 912-583-3103 116 D
glilford@bpc.edu
LILIENTHAL, Ronda .... 615-248-1245 425 D
rlilienthal@trevecca.edu
LILJEGREN, Donna .... 630-947-8914 133 A
dliljegren@aurora.edu
LILJEGREN, Lisa .... 262-243-5700 491 E
lisa.liljegren@cuw.edu
LILLARD, Justin .... 501-977-2033.. 23 D
lillard@uaccm.edu
LILLARD, Laura .... 423-648-2675 422 D
llillard@richmont.edu
LILLARD, Tom .... 540-831-6172 468 E
tlillard@radford.edu
LILLBACK, Peter, A .... 215-572-3811 401 G
plillback@wts.edu
LILLEBO, Troy .... 816-235-6585 260 D
lillebot@umkc.edu
LILLEHAUGEN, Sandi .... 701-662-1543 346 A
sandra.lillehaugen@lrsc.edu
LILLEY, Lisa .... 256-331-5368.... 3 C
lisa.lilley@nwscc.edu
LILLIE, Deb .... 319-385-6210 167 F
deb.lillie@iw.edu
LILLQUIST, Erik .... 973-275-4811 282 K
erik.lillquist@shu.edu
LILLY, Flavius .... 410-706-7767 202 F
flilly@umaryland.edu
LILLY, Larissa .... 425-889-5319 481 A
larissa.lilly@northwestu.edu
LILLY, Ryan .... 865-981-8033 420 C
bookstore@marylvillecollege.edu
LIM, Adriene .... 301-405-1668 202 E
LIM, Bob .... 408-924-1000.. 34 B
LIM, Choong .... 808-735-4831 128 C
clim@chaminade.edu
LIM, David .... 213-386-0080.. 45 D
LIM, Paul, J .... 213-385-2322.. 76 E
paul1911@wmu.edu
LIM, Paul, S .... 213-385-2322.. 76 E
sunglim@wmu.edu
LIM, Rosy .... 323-731-2383.. 55 G
rosylim@psuca.edu
LIM, Sulgi .... 413-597-3036 220 A
sl3@williams.edu
LIM, Teik, C .... 973-596-3102 278 G
president.lim@njit.edu
LIM, Xieng .... 425-739-8264 480 D
xieng.lim@lwtech.edu
LIM-TEPPER, Noriko ...... 415-338-1948.. 34 A
noriko@sfsu.edu
LIMA, Alex .... 305-377-8817.. 95 K
alex.lima@atlantisuniversity.edu
LIMA, Kristin .... 503-491-6991 373 H
kristin.lima@mhcc.edu
LIMAS MARTINEZ,
Maricela .... 323-259-2500.. 54 I
mlimas@oxy.edu
LIMAYEM, Moez .... 813-974-4281 111 B
mlimayem@usf.edu
LIMAYEM, Moez .... 904-620-2500 111 A
mlimayem@unf.edu
LIMBACH, Patrick, A ..... 513-558-0026 361 I
pat.limbach@uc.edu
LIMBAUGH, James, M . 310-287-4325.. 50 C
limbaujm@wlac.edu
LIMOGES, Brian .... 605-658-3308 415 E
brian.limoges@usd.edu
LIMON, Gissella .... 312-850-7168 135 E
glimon7@ccc.edu
LIMPER, Leslie .... 503-352-2871 375 B
limp5635@pacificu.edu
LIMTUATCO, Edwin, E ... 671-735-5560 503 C
edwin.limtuatco@guamcc.edu
LIN, Anne, Y .... 718-990-6275 313 B
lina1@stjohns.edu
LIN, Chia-Yen .... 619-260-4598.. 72 H
linc@sandiego.edu
LIN, Janice .... 219-464-5333 162 C
janice.lin@valpo.edu
LIN, Jerry .... 409-880-8760 449 B
jerry.lin@lamar.edu
LIN, Kathleen .... 626-571-5110.. 48 I
kathleenlin@les.edu
LIN, Shu-Chiang .... 512-444-8082 448 B
sclin@thsu.edu
LIN, Stephanie .... 480-750-4470.. 15 Q
slin@tsoa.edu
LIN, Yi-Chun Tricia .... 203-392-6864.. 85 H
lyny4@southernct.edu
LIN-COOK, Wendy .... 973-655-4259 278 C
lincookw@montclair.edu
LIN-KIRK, Haven .... 213-740-6267.. 73 C
raddean@usc.edu
LINAM, Gail .... 214-333-5372 433 D
gaill@dbu.edu
LINAMEN, Larry .... 951-552-8744.. 27 J
llinamen@calbaptist.edu
LINARD, Stephanie .... 850-729-6466 104 L
linards@nwfsc.edu
LINCE, Amy .... 989-386-6601 227 E
alince@midmich.edu
LINCOLN, Holly .... 636-481-3230 253 G
hlincoln@jeffco.edu
LINCOLN, Jonathan .... 973-720-2858 283 I
lincolnj@wpunj.edu
LINCOLN, Michael .... 973-278-5400 274 J
mil@berkeleycollege.edu
LINCOLN, Michael .... 212-986-4343 291 A
mil@berkeleycollege.edu
LINCOLN, Timothy .... 512-404-4873 429 K
tlincoln@austinseminary.edu
LIND, Elise .... 218-293-6850 238 D
elise.lind@minnesotanorth.edu
LIND, Josh .... 715-232-1233 496 C
lindjo@uwstout.edu
LIND, Kellie .... 707-965-6507.. 55 H
klind@puc.edu
LIND, Paul .... 970-339-6422.. 77 G
paul.lind@aims.edu
LIND, Sonja .... 909-537-3204.. 33 B
sonja.lind@csusb.edu
LIND, Steven .... 415-442-6622.. 44 B
slind@ggu.edu
LIND, Werner .... 276-326-4267 464 A
wlind@bluefield.edu
LIND, William .... 843-953-5011 406 D
wlind@citadel.edu
LIND-AYRES, Justin .... 612-330-1746 233 G
lindayre@augsburg.edu
LIND-GONZALEZ,
Patricia .... 934-420-2298 320 C
lindgop@farmingdale.edu
LINDAHL, Roberta, D .... 503-943-7321 376 H
lindahl@up.edu
LINDAUER, Jeff, R .... 716-888-2121 291 M
lindauej@canisius.edu
LINDBERG, Brad .... 641-269-3250 166 D
lindbergb@grinnell.edu
LINDBERGH, Tracy .... 480-858-9100.. 16 B
t.lindbergh@scnm.edu
LINDBLAD, Gary .... 562-903-4770.. 27 E
gary.lindblad@biola.edu
LINDBLAD, Jill .... 405-682-1611 367 D
jillian.c.lindblad@occc.edu
LINDBLOM, Timothy ..... 256-782-8488.... 6 A
tlindblom@jsu.edu
LINDBURG, Jaci .... 402-554-2020 269 C
jlindburg@nebraska.edu
LINDEBORG, Ruth .... 610-526-5157 378 J
rlindebo@brynmawr.edu
LINDELL, Andrea .... 866-492-5336 243 G
andrea.lindell@mail.waldenu.edu
LINDELL, Calvin, O .... 606-474-3273 180 G
colindell@kcu.edu
LINDELL, Melissa, M .... 315-268-6716 295 E
mlindell@clarkson.edu
LINDEMANN, Susan, K . 269-337-7308 225 B
susan.lindemann@kzoo.edu
LINDEN, Eric .... 646-565-6000 322 B
eric.linden@touro.edu
LINDEN, Erika .... 515-271-1526 165 C
erika.linden@dmu.edu
LINDEN, Kristin .... 310-338-2868.. 51 C
kristen.linden@lmu.edu
LINDEN, Stephen, M .... 248-232-4674 228 H
smlinden@oaklandcc.edu
LINDENBERG, Beren ..... 305-809-3109.. 97 M
beren.lindenberg@cfk.edu
LINDENFELD, Laura ...... 631-632-7403 316 D
laura.lindenfeld@stonybrook.edu
LINDENMAYER,
Kathleen .... 203-837-8266.. 86 A
lindenmayerk@wcsu.edu
LINDENMEYR, Adele ..... 610-519-4606 401 B
adele.lindenmeyr@villanova.edu
LINDER, Meloney .... 701-777-2038 344 H
meloney.linder@und.edu
LINDERMAN, Regan ...... 209-667-3440.. 33 D
rlinderman@csustan.edu
LINDERS, Annette .... 623-845-3377.. 13 E
annette.linders@gccaz.edu
LINDGREN, Robert, R ... 804-752-7211 469 B
rlindgren@rmc.edu
LINDHOLM, Mary, C ..... 512-232-2959 454 C
lindholm@austin.utexas.edu
LINDLEY, Holly .... 650-433-3881.. 55 K
hlindley@paloaltou.edu
LINDLEY, Kelli .... 208-467-8352 132 B
kalindley@nnu.edu
LINDLEY, Korey .... 949-451-5435.. 65 B
klindley@ivc.edu
LINDLEY, Lori .... 814-871-7522 383 H
lindley001@gannon.edu
LINDLEY, Steve .... 507-786-3521 242 I
lindley@stolaf.edu
LINDNER, Amy .... 315-792-3355 323 G
aklindne@utica.edu
LINDNER, Angela .... 352-273-1102 110 E
alindner@aa.ufl.edu
LINDNER, Bill .... 850-644-7572 110 B
blindner@fsu.edu
LINDNER, JoEllen .... 717-477-1235 394 D
jrlindner@ship.edu
LINDO-ARDILA, Gabriel 706-355-5035 115 C
glindoardila@athenstech.edu
LINDOERFER, Brian ...... 303-735-0716.. 83 M
brian.lindoerfer@colorado.edu
LINDON, Jennifer .... 606-487-3100 181 E
jennifer.lindon@kctcs.edu
LINDON-BURGETT,
Dana .... 405-733-7433 369 D
dlindon@rose.edu
LINDOW, Claudio .... 718-262-5337 295 D
clindow@york.cuny.edu
LINDOW, Tracy .... 901-722-3230 422 I
tlindow@sco.edu
LINDQUIST, Cynthia, A . 701-766-4055 344 F
president@littlehoop.edu
LINDQUIST, Kelsey .... 510-436-1245.. 45 H
lindquist@hnu.edu
LINDQUIST, Kimberly ... 734-384-4101 227 F
klindquist@monroeccc.edu
LINDQUIST, Robert .... 256-824-2882.... 8 B
robert.lindquist@uah.edu
LINDQUIST, Vern, L ...... 217-786-2885 142 F
vern.lindquist@llcc.edu
LINDQUIST, Will .... 816-415-7655 261 G
lindquistw@william.jewell.edu
LINDSAY, Charles, W ... 607-735-1790 298 G
clindsay@elmira.edu
LINDSAY, D. Michael ... 765-998-5000 161 A
president@taylor.edu
LINDSAY, Dawn, S .... 410-777-1177 197 C
dslindsay@aacc.edu
LINDSAY, Deb .... 561-732-4424 107 E
dlindsay@svdp.edu
LINDSAY, Dennis .... 541-684-7253 371 H
dlindsay@bushnell.edu
LINDSAY, Jenny .... 610-647-4400 385 K
jlindsay2@immaculata.edu
LINDSAY, Jonathan .... 410-337-6000 198 G
jonathan.lindsay@goucher.edu
LINDSAY, Kristen, R ..... 419-434-5898 362 D
kristen.lindsay@findlay.edu
LINDSAY, Marsha, N .... 412-809-5293 395 F
lindsay.marsha@ptcollege.edu
LINDSAY, Shawn .... 660-263-3900 250 G
shawnlindsay@cccb.edu
LINDSAY, Terry .... 229-500-2000 114 F
LINDSETH, Jenna .... 715-425-4972 496 A
jenna.lindseth@uwrf.edu
LINDSEY, Ashley .... 617-573-8667 218 G
alindsey@suffolk.edu
LINDSEY, Connie .... 773-947-6300 143 E
clindsey@mccormick.edu
LINDSEY, Delario .... 703-908-7863 468 A
delario.lindsey@marymount.edu
LINDSEY, Heidie .... 337-482-6272 192 F
hlindsey@louisiana.edu
LINDSEY, Jill .... 540-545-7324 470 A
jlindsey@su.edu
LINDSEY, John .... 918-781-7200 365 B
lindseyj@bacone.edu
LINDSEY, Jonathan .... 602-274-1885.. 15 C
jlindsey@pihma.edu
LINDSEY, Jordan .... 503-375-7156 372 G
jlindsey@corban.edu
LINDSEY, Patrick, O ..... 313-577-4228 232 H
patrick.lindsey@wayne.edu
LINDSEY, Rochelle .... 404-752-5223 123 A
rlindsey@msm.edu
LINDSEY, Shannon .... 785-628-5326 173 E
sdlindsey@fhsu.edu
LINDSEY, Steve .... 602-557-7537.. 16 L
steve.lindsey@phoenix.edu
LINDSEY, Terryl .... 918-293-5388 368 B
terryl.lindsey@okstate.edu
LINDSEY, JR.,
Trumanue .... 612-659-6474 238 C
trumanue.lindsey@minneapolis.edu
LINDSEY, Valarie .... 773-252-5318 146 D
valarie.lindsey@oakpoint.edu
LINDSKOOG, Marie ...... 765-455-9468 156 E
mlindsko@iuk.edu
LINDSTAEDT, William .... 415-502-2422.. 70 D
bill.lindstaedt@ucsf.edu
LINDSTEDT, John .... 508-856-2198 212 A
john.lindstedt@umassmed.edu
LINDSTROM, Chris .... 207-581-1640 196 D
chris.lindstrom@maine.edu
LINDSTROM, Derrick ..... 612-659-6030 238 C
derrick.lindstrom@minneapolis.edu
LINDSTROM, Lauren ..... 530-752-4663.. 69 A
lelindstrom@ucdavis.edu
LINDSTROM, Lynne ...... 563-884-5313 169 C
lynne.lindstrom@palmer.edu
LINDSTROM, Peter .... 303-352-6785.. 80 D
peter.lindstrom@ccd.edu
LINDSTROM, Ryan .... 801-863-8303 460 A
lindstry@uvu.edu
LINDSTROM, Yvonne .... 313-578-0328 230 H
lindstym@udmercy.edu
LINEBACK, Carla .... 802-258-3266 462 B
carla.lineback@worldlearning.org
LINEBERGER,
Susanne, B .... 386-312-4050 107 A
susannelineberger@sjrstate.edu
LINEBERRY, Gene, T ..... 859-323-6630 185 D
gt.lineberry@uky.edu
LINEBURG, Robert .... 540-831-5228 468 E
rlineburg@radford.edu
LINEGAR, Malinda .... 308-432-6399 267 G
mlinegar@csc.edu
LINEHAN, Stephen .... 781-899-5500 217 F
rev.linehan@psjs.edu
LINEMAN, Hope .... 570-389-4000 393 E
hlineman@bloomu.edu
LINFANTE, Patrick .... 973-761-9328 282 K
patrick.linfante@shu.edu
LINFORD, Jon, F .... 208-496-1123 130 G
linfordj@byui.edu
LINGEN, Scott .... 701-224-5441 345 F
scott.lingen@bismarckstate.edu
LINGENFELTER, Monica 304-876-5286 489 A
mlingenf@shepherd.edu
LINGER, Frederick, S .... 740-427-5250 354 I
lingerf@kenyon.edu
LINGLE, Earl, W .... 336-841-9552 329 E
elingle@highpoint.edu
LINGLE, Richard .... 816-279-7000 249 D
richard.lingle@abtu.edu
LINGNER, Jackie .... 321-674-8053 100 A
jlingner@fit.edu
LINGO, Amy .... 502-852-6411 185 E
amy.lingo@louisville.edu
LINGO, Bradley, J .... 757-352-4411 469 D
blingo@regent.edu
LINK, Christine, A .... 626-914-8821.. 37 B
clink@citruscollege.edu
LINK, Eric .... 701-777-2049 344 H
eric.link@und.edu
LINK, James .... 805-525-4417.. 67 J
jlink@thomasaquinas.edu
LINK, Jeff .... 828-726-2242 332 E
jlink@cccti.edu

LINK, John 314-968-6982 261 D johnlink24@webster.edu
LINK, Kathryn 508-548-1400 220 B
LINK, Laura 612-874-3700 236 E llink@mcad.edu
LINK, Lisa 616-222-1426 222 F lisa.link@cornerstone.edu
LINK, Matthew 253-879-3244 483 G mlink@pugetsound.edu
LINK, Robert 419-434-4528 362 D link@findlay.edu
LINK, Stephen 202-687-1747 92 D spl8@georgetown.edu
LINK, Tonya 701-355-8245 347 A tmlink@umary.edu
LINK, Whitney 701-671-2507 346 B whitney.link@ndscsd.edu
LINKER, Maureen 313-593-5621 231 B mlinker@umich.edu
LINKER, Maureen 313-593-5445 231 B mlinker@umich.edu
LINKS, Jonathan 410-516-6880 199 E jlinks1@jhu.edu
LINMAN, Eric 503-255-0332 374 A elinman@multnomah.edu
LINN, Andrew 901-678-4825 426 A ablinn@memphis.edu
LINN, Brooke 503-552-1716 374 B blinn@nunm.edu
LINN, Jean 716-614-6787 309 E jlinn@niagaracc.suny.edu
LINN, Joseph 785-628-4277 173 E jlinn@fhsu.edu
LINN, Maria 803-323-3806 413 D linnm@winthrop.edu
LINN, Richard, T 716-827-4351 322 J linnr@trocaire.edu
LINN-ADDISON, Margaret 303-964-3657 83 B mlinnaddison@regis.edu
LINNELL, Michael 701-858-3065 345 C michael.linnell@minotstateu.edu
LINNEMAN, Scott 360-650-3446 485 A scott.linneman@wwu.edu
LINNERTZ, Amber 402-826-8674 266 A amber.linnertz@doane.edu
LINNEWEBER, Travis, W 765-658-4175 154 G travislinneweber@depauw.edu
LINO, Paulette 510-723-2665 35 Q plino@chabotcollege.edu
LINSEBIGLER, Tommie 406-275-4985 264 H tommie_linsebigler@skc.edu
LINSENMEYER, Machelle 304-793-6871 489 C alinsenmeyer@osteo.wvsom.edu
LINSEY, Troy 678-513-5202 121 L tlinsey@laniertech.edu
LINSON, Marci 417-690-2636 250 K linson@cofo.edu
LINSON, Robert 202-885-6013 91 D rlinson@american.edu
LINSTRA, Ralph 434-582-2427 467 E rlinstra@liberty.edu
LINTNER, Tim 803-641-3564 412 B tlintner@usca.edu
LINTON, Greg 865-573-4517 419 E glinton@johnsonu.edu
LINTON, Richard, H 785-532-6221 175 A rhlinton@ksu.edu
LINTZ, Brian 410-386-8249 197 G blintz@carrollcc.edu
LINVILLE, Allison 406-756-3668 262 H alinville@fvcc.edu
LINVILLE, Joe 304-896-7366 487 I joe.linville@southernwv.edu
LINZEY, Scott 912-525-5000 124 G slinzey@scad.edu
LINZY, Charlene, A 585-292-2363 306 K clinzy@monroecc.edu
LION, Ben 325-942-2047 450 B
LION, Benjamin 314-392-2211 255 H benjamin.lion@mobap.edu
LIOSATOS, Alex 920-565-1000 492 A liosatosa@lakeland.edu
LIOTTA, Robert 301-295-9172 502 B robert.liotta@usuhs.edu
LIPAN, Petruta 314-977-3571 258 H petruta.lipan@slu.edu
LIPE, Kaiwipuni 808-956-2697 129 B kaiwipun@hawaii.edu
LIPECKA, Evy 773-256-3000 143 H
LIPHART, Kristin 920-693-1854 497 H kristin.liphart@gotoltc.edu
LIPITZ, Jon 410-225-2516 200 B jlipitz@mica.edu
LIPITZ, Michael 312-996-2695 151 D mlipitz@uic.edu
LIPIZ GONZALEZ, Elaine 714-992-7088 54 D elipizgonzalez@fullcoll.edu
LIPKIN, Len 215-717-6380 399 I llipkin@uarts.edu
LIPMAN, Howard 305-348-6298 109 H howard.lipman@fiu.edu
LIPP, Evan 703-284-5906 468 A elipp@marymount.edu
LIPP, Jacob 713-226-5585 452 B lippp@uhd.edu
LIPPARD, Rodney 501-450-5202 23 K rlippard@uca.edu
LIPPARD, Rodney 803-641-3460 412 B rodneyl@usca.edu
LIPPE, Diane 954-262-4932 104 M lipped@nova.edu
LIPPENS, Susan 419-720-6670 359 L susan.lippens@proskills.edu
LIPPERT, Patricia, A 812-488-2152 161 E pl23@evansville.edu
LIPPERT, Robert 559-453-2189 43 D robert.lippert@fresno.edu
LIPPIELLO, Stephen 412-536-1047 386 H steve.lippiello@laroche.edu
LIPPINCOTT, Tammy 610-282-1100 382 A tammy.lippincott@desales.edu
LIPPMAN, Fred 954-262-1508 104 M flippman@nsu.nova.edu
LIPPMAN, Stuart 646-565-6726 322 B stuart.lippman@touro.edu
LIPPMAN, Stuart 646-565-6726 322 C stuart.lippman@touro.edu
LIPSCHUETZ, Angie 415-817-4205 34 A alipschuetz@sfsu.edu
LIPSCOMB, Benjamin 585-567-9374 301 G benjamin.lipscomb@houghton.edu
LIPSCOMB, Darren 215-751-8131 381 H dlipscomb@ccp.edu
LIPSCOMB, Natasha 704-216-3622 337 C natasha.lipscomb@rccc.edu
LIPSETT, Jack 856-227-7200 275 F jlipsett@camdencc.edu
LIPSETT, Teresa 787-743-7979 509 D ut_tlipsett@suagm.edu
LIPSKIER, Hershel 973-267-9404 279 G info@rca.edu
LIPSTREU, Tiffany 614-823-1414 359 G tlipstreu@otterbein.edu
LIPTAK, Kathy 304-384-6303 488 K liptakka@concord.edu
LIPTAK, Victoria 617-585-0200 206 E
LIRLEY, Sean 719-336-1543 81 J sean.lirley@lamarcc.edu
LIS, Robert 215-895-1526 382 D rel33@drexel.edu
LISCHWE, Sheila, T 864-656-1661 406 F slischw@clemson.edu
LISCIO, Gina 315-792-7288 320 F gina.liscio@sunypoly.edu
LISCO, Heather 812-258-9510 154 B financialaid@cariscollege.edu
LISEA, Scott 805-565-6170 75 I slisea@westmont.edu
LISHEN, Wendy 301-295-1667 502 B wendy.lishen@usuhs.edu
LISHNER, Ryan 303-233-4697 79 B
LISING, Jennifer 215-489-2969 381 K jennifer.lising@delval.edu
LISK, Patti 540-423-9824 472 J plisk@germanna.edu
LISKOWICZ, Bob 570-941-7620 400 C bob.liskowicz@scranton.edu
LISLE, Tara 432-264-5646 436 H tlisle@howardcollege.edu
LISNER, Lydia 804-627-5300 464 B lydia_lisner@bshsi.org
LISONBEE, Stephen 435-586-5418 459 E lisonbee@suu.edu
LISS, Donna 660-785-4163 259 J dliss@truman.edu
LISS, Joshua 267-341-3100 385 I jliss@holyfamily.edu
LISS, Joshua, E 215-637-7700 385 I
LISS, Tony 212-650-8261 293 B tliss@ccny.cuny.edu
LIST, Allison 631-687-5198 313 C alist@sjcny.edu
LIST, Edith 618-374-5068 147 B edith.list@principia.edu
LISTAU, Lynsey 850-484-2128 105 G llistau@pensacolastate.edu
LISTER, Philip 505-224-4000 285 B plister@cnm.edu
LISTER, Tommy 626-584-5338 43 E tommylister@fuller.edu
LISTERMAN, Robin 704-463-3062 339 C robin.listerman@pfeiffer.edu
LISTON, Brenda 614-947-6532 352 J brenda.liston@franklin.edu
LISTWAK, Jeffrey 570-372-4128 398 A listwak@susqu.edu
LISTWAK, Jeffrey, A 412-397-5263 396 E listwak@rmu.edu
LITA SARMIENTO, Maria 201-360-5444 277 D msarmiento2@hccc.edu
LITANT, Josiah 507-453-1420 238 J josiah.litant@southeastmn.edu
LITCHMAN, Jennifer, B 410-706-3477 202 F jlitchman@umaryland.edu
LITHERLAND, Steve, E 757-822-1944 474 G slitherland@tcc.edu
LITHGOW, C. Vince 505-747-5050 287 C vince.lithgow@nnmc.edu
LITKE, Russ 419-995-8342 360 B litke.r@rhodesstate.edu
LITMAN, Kay 610-372-4721 396 A klitman@racc.edu
LITOLFF, Edwin 318-274-6401 191 G litolffe@gram.edu
LITSITSA, Anna 650-433-3807 55 K alitsitsa@paloaltou.edu
LITT, Eleni 212-229-8947 307 E litte@newschool.edu
LITT, Jacquelyn, S 848-932-3047 281 B jlitt@echo.rutgers.edu
LITTEN, Lyndsi 559-737-4892 39 C lyndsil@cos.edu
LITTERER, Denise 419-372-2081 348 F denisel@bgsu.edu
LITTKY, Dennis 401-752-2640 403 C
LITTLE, Andrew, P 410-777-2227 197 C aplittle1@aacc.edu
LITTLE, Bernard 630-466-7900 152 H blittle@waubonsee.edu
LITTLE, Chris 530-895-2400 27 F littlech@butte.edu
LITTLE, Christopher 765-983-1400 154 H littlch@earlham.edu
LITTLE, Christopher 765-983-1400 154 H littlech@earlham.edu
LITTLE, Crystal 619-594-5901 33 E little@sdsu.edu
LITTLE, F. Shanon 707-664-2358 34 C
LITTLE, Jennifer 541-349-7487 371 H jlittle@bushnell.edu
LITTLE, Jill, M 586-445-7576 226 F littlej@macomb.edu
LITTLE, Joseph 606-368-6058 178 D josephlittle@alc.edu
LITTLE, Lara 704-463-3353 339 C lara.little@pfeiffer.edu
LITTLE, Laura 570-702-8946 386 D llittle@johnson.edu
LITTLE, Leeann 918-335-6234 368 E llittle@okwu.edu
LITTLE, Mark 704-290-5245 337 F mlittle@spcc.edu
LITTLE, Michael 678-466-4477 117 A michaellittle@clayton.edu
LITTLE, Michael 678-466-4478 117 A michaellittle@clayton.edu
LITTLE, Pamela 919-866-5805 338 E pmlittle@waketech.edu
LITTLE, Rebecca, K 812-888-4220 162 E rlittle@vinu.edu
LITTLE, Scott 601-968-5956 244 C slittle@belhaven.edu
LITTLE, Shay 912-478-2795 120 A slittle@georgiasouthern.edu
LITTLE-BERRY, Terri 850-599-3183 109 E ruthie.littleberry@famu.edu
LITTLE-HERRING, Sandy 478-757-2579 122 D sandy.littleherring@mga.edu
LITTLE-PALMER, Tanya 770-689-5088 429 F tlittle-palmer@aii.edu
LITTLE WHITEMAN, Iona 701-627-4738 346 D ilittl@nhsc.edu
LITTLEBEAR, Richard 406-477-6215 262 F rlbear@cdkc.edu
LITTLEFIELD, Elizabeth, S 804-523-5181 473 A blittlefield@reynolds.edu
LITTLEJOHN, Quincina 973-748-9000 275 C quincina_littlejohn@bloomfield.edu
LITTLEJOHN, Sylvia 803-738-7764 409 E littlejohns@midlandstech.edu
LITTLES, Kathy 415-575-6105 29 A
LITTLETON, Robert, A 423-652-6022 419 F ralittle@king.edu
LITTLETON STEIB, Larissa 504-762-3000 187 I llsteib@dcc.edu
LITTON, Paul, J 573-882-6042 260 C littonp@missouri.edu
LITTON, Reuben, J 719-333-3143 502 C reuben.litton@afacademy.af.edu
LITTRELL, Johnny 931-540-2840 423 D jlittrell@columbiastate.edu
LITTRELL, Meghann 513-732-5327 362 B meghann.littrell@uc.edu
LITVACK, Steven, B 201-489-5836 277 E
LITWACK, Kim 414-229-4189 495 B litwack@uwm.edu
LITWILLER, Andy 309-268-8461 138 F andy.litwiller@heartland.edu
LITWILLER, Hannah 620-241-0723 172 H hannah.litwiller@centralchristian.edu
LITWIN, Daveen, H 603-646-3780 272 F daveen.h.litwin@dartmouth.edu
LITZ, Kerri 410-225-2277 200 B klitz@mica.edu
LITZIN, Louise 928-724-6633 12 F louise@dinecollege.edu
LIU, Bei 408-733-1878 71 B
LIU, Chris 816-235-1301 260 D y.liu@umkc.edu
LIU, Eric 641-472-7000 168 A bliu@miu.edu
LIU, Fengshan 302-857-6421 90 D fliu@desu.edu
LIU, Frank 626-917-9482 36 H frankliu@cesna.edu
LIU, Monika 415-452-5730 37 C mliu@ccsf.edu
LIU, Samuel 626-571-5110 48 I samuelliu@les.edu
LIU, Shuang 410-777-1868 197 C sliu4@aacc.edu
LIU, Susan 626-448-0023 46 K
LIU, Tina 626-917-9482 36 H tinaliu@cesna.edu
LIU, Xiaoqing 618-453-4321 149 G xiaoqing.liu@siu.edu
LIU, Ying 561-297-2719 109 F yingliu@fau.edu
LIU, Yun Lin (Cynthia) 631-499-7100 304 B clin@libi.edu
LIU, Yuxiang 646-592-6008 325 R yuxiang.liu@yu.edu
LIU, Yuxing 512-454-1188 429 B info@aoma.edu
LIVANU, Andrei 909-218-3253 25 J
LIVELY, Alisa 304-473-8431 490 E lively_a@wvwc.edu
LIVELY, Amanda 478-538-3160 125 E alively@southeasterntech.edu
LIVELY, David 847-491-2094 146 C david.lively@northwestern.edu
LIVENGOOD, Matthew 816-995-2901 257 I matthew.livengood@researchcollege.edu
LIVENGOOD, Tamella 231-995-1242 228 F
LIVERMAN, Deborah, L 617-715-5329 215 G
LIVESAY, Dennis 906-487-2259 227 D dlivesay@mtu.edu
LIVESAY, Wes 210-567-2760 455 E livesay@uthscsa.edu
LIVINGOOD, Susannah, B 405-325-5065 370 J slivingood@ou.edu
LIVINGSTON, Brandon 509-533-4864 478 C brandon.livingston@ccs.spokane.edu
LIVINGSTON, Carolyn 507-222-4248 234 C clivingston@carleton.edu
LIVINGSTON, Danena, R 410-651-6172 203 B drlivingston@umes.edu

LOGAN, Linda 269-749-6669 229 G
llogan@olivetcollege.edu
LOGAN, Logan 334-683-2362 3 A
llogan@marionmilitary.edu
LOGAN, Mark 562-860-2451 35 O
mlogan@cerritos.edu
LOGAN, Matt 601-403-1111 247 F
mlogan@prcc.edu
LOGAN, Melissa 412-924-1373 395 G
mlogan@pts.edu
LOGAN, Michael, F 336-334-4104 342 D
mflogan@uncg.edu
LOGAN, Mikaela 276-376-3430 471 G
mra4p@uvawise.edu
LOGAN, Mike 712-274-6400 170 H
mike.logan@witcc.edu
LOGAN, Steven 903-510-2127 451 D
steven.logan@tjc.edu
LOGAN, Traci 617-587-5711 216 H
logant@neco.edu
LOGAN-BENNETT, Lorie 410-704-2386 204 B
lloganbennett@towson.edu
LOGAN BRAYSHAW, Laurie 505-424-2305 285 H
llogan@iaia.edu
LOGGINS, Jeffery 662-254-3325 247 C
jloggins@mvsu.edu
LOGGINS, Ron 402-375-7030 267 I
rologgi1@wc.edu
LOGSDON, Phillip 859-985-3886 179 E
logsdonp@berea.edu
LOGSDON, Seana 518-587-2100 320 B
LOGUE, Jean 918-444-2230 366 G
loguej@nsuok.edu
LOH, Albert 510-628-8028 48 G
aloh@lincolnuca.edu
LOHAN-BREMER, Maureen 845-257-3256 316 B
lbremerm@newpaltz.edu
LOHDEN, Bethany, L 636-584-6503 252 D
bethany.lohden@eastcentral.edu
LOHER, Steven 314-889-1493 252 G
sloher@fontbonne.edu
LOHMANN, Janet 207-725-3228 194 A
jlohmann@bowdoin.edu
LOHR, Joel 860-509-9502 88 A
jlohr@hartfordinternational.edu
LOHR, Nathan 317-788-3349 161 F
lohrn@uindy.edu
LOHREY, Adam 937-481-2266 363 H
adam_lohrey@wilmington.edu
LOHSE, MaryPat 617-349-8669 210 H
mlohse@lesley.edu
LOHT, Shawn 504-671-5055 187 I
sloht@dcc.edu
LOILAND, Sharon 701-777-3178 344 H
sharon.loiland@und.edu
LOIODICE, Melissa 413-236-1022 213 E
mloiodice@berkshirecc.edu
LOISEAU, Marvin 617-588-1368 206 B
mloiseau@bfit.edu
LOJOWSKY, MacAdam 707-468-3081 51 F
mlojowsky@mendocino.edu
LOKE, Vernon 509-359-4564 478 H
vloke@ewu.edu
LOKEN, Lana 605-995-2851 414 A
lana.loken@dwu.edu
LOKENI, Lokeni 684-699-2722 503 A
l.lokeni@amsamoa.edu
LOKKEN, Pamela, S 314-935-5752 261 B
lokken@wustl.edu
LOKMAN, Lawrence, H 814-863-1028 391 F
lhl11@psu.edu
LOKUTA, Sharon 260-422-5561 156 A
slokuta@indianatech.edu
LOLL, Andrea 618-544-8657 139 C
lolla@iecc.edu
LOLLAND, Sonja 530-741-6793 77 B
slolland@yccd.edu
LOLLATHIN, Eric 740-245-7438 363 A
ericl@rio.edu
LOMAX, Courtney 570-408-5891 402 B
courtney.lomax@wilkes.edu
LOMBARD, Anne, E 315-470-6658 319 A
aelombard@esf.edu
LOMBARD-SIMS, Danielle 501-603-1315 22 D
dlombardsims@uams.edu
LOMBARDI, Alisha 509-313-5799 479 E
lombardi@gonzaga.edu
LOMBARDI, Annie 845-398-4016 314 D
alombard@stac.edu
LOMBARDI, Mark 314-529-9330 254 D
president@maryville.edu

LOMBARDI, Phillip 401-232-6374 403 B
plombard@bryant.edu
LOMBARDI, Ryan, T 607-255-7595 297 D
ryan.lombardi@cornell.edu
LOMBARDO, Hilaree 815-282-7900 148 E
hilaree.j.lombardo@osfhealthcare.org
LOMBARDO, Joann 860-486-5519 89 B
joann.lombardo@uconn.edu
LOMBARDO, John 631-851-6225 320 G
lombarj@sunysuffolk.edu
LOMBARDO, Kristina 904-826-8583 99 D
klombardo@flagler.edu
LOMBARDO, Michael 503-777-7542 375 F
lombardm@reed.edu
LOMBARDO, Roberto 386-506-3159 98 A
roberto.lombardo@daytonastate.edu
LOMBARDO, Tony 225-578-0552 188 K
lauramorrow@lsu.edu
LOMBARDO, Tony 225-578-2111 188 J
LOMBARDO-BEAVER, Natalie 814-234-7755 397 H
LOMBELLA, James, P 860-773-1419 87 E
jlombella@acc.commnet.edu
LOMBERA, Crystal 408-727-1060 46 A
LOMELI, Nestor 559-925-3135 75 A
nestorlomeli@whccd.edu
LOMIDZE, Kote 202-464-6973 462 B
kote.lomidze@worldlearning.org
LOMONACO, Barbara 859-238-5200 179 H
LOMONACO, Barbara 401-454-6655 404 B
blomonac@risd.edu
LONDON, Allen, S 478-301-4169 122 C
london_a@mercer.edu
LONDON, April 847-866-3902 138 B
LONDON, Ingrid 972-883-2270 454 D
ingrid.london@utdallas.edu
LONDON, Lauren 734-487-1055 223 F
llondon2@emich.edu
LONDON, Manuel 631-632-8304 316 D
manuel.london@stonybrook.edu
LONDON, Michael, E 415-422-4400 72 I
melondon@usfca.edu
LONDON, Nubian 626-529-8500 55 E
LONDON, Samuel 256-726-7223 6 C
slondon@oakwood.edu
LONDON, Stephanie 479-788-7697 22 A
stephanie.london@uafs.edu
LONDON, Tim 812-237-6311 155 H
tim.london@indstate.edu
LONDRAVILLE, Erin 315-268-7810 295 E
elondrav@clarkson.edu
LONDRE, Tristan 660-359-3948 256 F
tlondre@mail.ncmissouri.edu
LONE HILL, Karen 605-455-6100 414 H
klonehill@olc.edu
LONERGAN, Dennis 718-862-7349 304 K
dennis.lonergan@manhattan.edu
LONERGAN, Elizabeth 315-786-2252 302 I
elonergan@sunyjefferson.edu
LONEY, Teresa, A 816-604-1517 254 E
teresa.loney@mcckc.edu
LONG, Adam 864-503-5863 413 A
calong@uscupstate.edu
LONG, Adina 336-734-7272 334 D
along@forsythtech.edu
LONG, Andrew 520-494-5418 11 M
andrew.long@centralaz.edu
LONG, Angi 920-832-6579 492 B
angi.long@lawrence.edu
LONG, Blake 662-720-7448 247 D
bdlong@nemcc.edu
LONG, Bobby 803-321-5282 409 I
bobby.long@newberry.edu
LONG, Brenda 706-233-7461 125 A
blong@shorter.edu
LONG, Brenda, J 252-222-6151 332 G
longb@carteret.edu
LONG, Bridget, T 617-495-3401 210 B
bridget_long@gse.harvard.edu
LONG, Brittney 402-399-2454 265 H
blong@csm.edu
LONG, Bruce 972-241-3371 433 E
blong@dallas.edu
LONG, Carol 310-434-4762 63 B
long_carol@smc.edu
LONG, Carol 503-375-6623 377 E
clong@willamette.edu
LONG, Christina 620-665-3521 174 D
longc@hutchcc.edu
LONG, Christopher, P 517-355-4597 227 C
cplong@msu.edu
LONG, Curt 563-588-6657 164 C
curt.long@clarke.edu

LONG, Cynthia 563-884-5157 169 C
cynthia.long@palmer.edu
LONG, Dallas 309-438-3139 140 C
dlong@ilstu.edu
LONG, Daniel 334-347-2623 2 A
dlong@escc.edu
LONG, Daniel 313-664-7675 222 C
dlong@collegeforcreativestudies.edu
LONG, Doreen 603-428-2303 272 I
dlong@nec.edu
LONG, Dustin 910-272-3566 337 A
dulong@robeson.edu
LONG, Emily 612-330-1558 233 G
long10@augsburg.edu
LONG, Gerard, E 210-562-6285 455 E
longg@uthscsa.edu
LONG, Gretchen 413-597-2125 220 A
glong@williams.edu
LONG, James 316-295-5527 173 G
james_long@friends.edu
LONG, James 559-453-3439 43 D
james.long@fresno.edu
LONG, Jan 951-785-3531 47 F
jlong@lasierra.edu
LONG, Janet, R 610-499-4105 401 I
jrlong@widener.edu
LONG, II, JD 314-935-5582 261 B
jlongii@wustl.edu
LONG, Jeanine 229-227-2668 125 G
jlong@southernregional.edu
LONG, Jeff 575-562-2221 285 E
jeff.long@enmu.edu
LONG, Jeff 601-403-1041 247 F
jlong@prcc.edu
LONG, Jeffery, R 808-956-3965 128 I
jeffery.long@hawaii.edu
LONG, Jessica 336-757-7416 334 D
jlong@forsythtech.edu
LONG, Jodi 352-395-5680 107 G
jodi.long@sfcollege.edu
LONG, John 847-214-7220 137 D
jlong@elgin.edu
LONG, John 302-931-2200 91 A
jwl@udel.edu
LONG, Juliet 541-956-7279 375 G
jlong@roguecc.edu
LONG, Justin 239-985-8361 100 G
justin.long@fsw.edu
LONG, Karen, S 518-276-6216 311 J
longks@rpi.edu
LONG, Kelly 970-491-5932 79 E
kelly.long@colostate.edu
LONG, Kenneth 231-777-0560 228 C
kenneth.long@muskegoncc.edu
LONG, Kenneth, A 570-422-3201 393 F
kenlong@esu.edu
LONG, Kevin 240-567-7972 200 E
kevin.long@montgomerycollege.edu
LONG, Laurel 256-824-2285 8 B
laurel.long@uah.edu
LONG, Lauren 703-993-2909 466 J
llong3@gmu.edu
LONG, Leann 423-585-6772 424 G
leann.long@ws.edu
LONG, Linda 713-942-9505 436 F
llong@hgst.edu
LONG, Lisa 265-761-6215 7 B
lelong@talladega.edu
LONG, Marcus 605-668-1514 414 F
marcus.long@mountmarty.edu
LONG, Matt 972-708-7340 434 F
helpdesk@diu.edu
LONG, Matthew 707-778-3930 63 C
mlong@santarosa.edu
LONG, Michele 215-392-2938 395 B
mlong@pitc.edu
LONG, Nathan 626-316-5310 63 D
nlong@saybrook.edu
LONG, Nicholas 212-924-5900 321 C
LONG, Nicholas, K 989-774-3334 221 M
fas@cmich.edu
LONG, Nigel 410-888-9048 200 C
nlong@muih.edu
LONG, Rebecca 740-245-7376 363 A
rlong@rio.edu
LONG, Samuel, C 517-321-0242 224 E
slong@glcc.edu
LONG, Shawn 470-578-3132 121 J
slong70@kennesaw.edu
LONG, Sheryl 336-721-2774 339 H
sheryl.long@salem.edu
LONG, Susan 501-686-5731 22 D
longsusanl@uams.edu

LONG, Tamara 325-674-2949 427 G
tnb99a@acu.edu
LONG, Terry 660-562-1706 256 G
tlong@nwmissouri.edu
LONG, Todd 419-559-2360 361 B
tlong08@terra.edu
LONG, Valerie 870-368-2006 20 I
valerie.long@ozarka.edu
LONG-COFFEE, Michelle 310-287-4597 50 C
longcofm@wlac.edu
LONGACRE, Jeffrey 301-295-1917 502 B
jeffrey.longacre@usuhs.edu
LONGACRE, Kyle 215-641-6300 390 A
klongacre@mc3.edu
LONGACRE, Teri, E 713-743-4669 451 G
elkins@uh.edu
LONGAKER, Frank 540-444-4101 470 J
flongaker@ufairfax.edu
LONGAKER, Frank, E 540-986-1800 463 F
frank@an.edu
LONGBELLA, Jody 218-894-5128 237 C
jody.longbella@clcmn.edu
LONGBRAKE, John 805-893-2191 70 E
john.longbrake@ucsb.edu
LONGENECKER, Penni 717-947-6093 392 R
pelongen@pacollege.edu
LONGHOFER, Kristi 661-946-2274 74 G
LONGHTA, Karie, L 217-786-2263 142 F
karie.longhta@llcc.edu
LONGIE, Candace 701-477-7862 346 H
clongie@tm.edu
LONGJOHN, Gerald 616-222-1423 222 F
gerald.longjohn@cornerstone.edu
LONGLEY, Katie 413-265-2322 208 B
longleyk@elms.edu
LONGLEY, Ross 479-308-2356 17 E
ross.longleu@arcomedu.org
LONGMIRE, Carla 205-247-8927 7 A
clongmirer@stillman.edu
LONGMIRE, Kolleen 615-514-2787 421 H
klongmire@nossi.edu
LONGMUIR, Marcus 212-229-5300 307 E
longmuim@newschool.edu
LONGO, Jose Miguel 315-792-7165 320 F
longojm@sunypoly.edu
LONGO, Laura 732-224-2259 275 D
llongo@brookdalecc.edu
LONGO, Rick 718-636-3514 311 A
rlongo@pratt.edu
LONGO, Timothy 434-924-7166 471 F
tjl8x@virginia.edu
LONGORIA, Estrellita 610-957-6113 398 B
elongor1@swarthmore.edu
LONGORIA, Hossiella 305-899-3950 96 A
hlongoria@barry.edu
LONGRIDGE, George 717-391-6947 398 E
longridge@stevenscollege.edu
LONGSDORF, Brittany 207-753-6906 193 D
blongsdo@bates.edu
LONGWORTH, Rhonda 734-487-3200 223 F
rkinney@emich.edu
LONGYEAR, JR., George, E 203-436-4899 90 B
george.longyear@yale.edu
LONON, Justin 214-378-1601 433 F
justin.lonon@dcccd.edu
LONOWSKI, Jerrold 575-624-8421 286 F
lonowsk@nmmi.edu
LONTOC, Arlene 510-464-3219 57 B
alontoc@peralta.edu
LOO, Chih 256-824-2243 8 B
chih.loo@uah.edu
LOO, Lisa 480-965-4550 11 A
lisaloo@asu.edu
LOOMER, Peter, M 210-567-3160 455 E
loomer@uthscsa.edu
LOOMER, Tim 805-565-6832 75 I
tloomer@westmont.edu
LOOMIS, Ryan 406-447-6944 263 F
ryan.loomis@helenacollege.edu
LOOMIS, Susan 207-326-2345 195 G
susan.loomis@mma.edu
LOOMIS HUBBELL, Loren 203-392-5722 85 H
loomishubbl1@southernct.edu
LOONAN, John 843-953-3669 407 D
loonanjf@cofc.edu
LOONEY, David 252-940-6455 332 A
david.looney@beaufortccc.edu
LOONEY, Erin 423-614-8200 419 H
elooney@leeuniversity.edu
LOONEY, Joseph, D 719-333-1309 502 C
joseph.looney@afacademy.af.edu

LORENZEN, Chris .... 307-268-3088 499 T
christopher.lorenzen@caspercollege.edu

LORENZET, Steven .... 631-665-1600 322 C
slorenze@touro.edu

LORENZO, Janice .... 787-891-0925 506 I
jalorenzo@aguadilla.inter.edu

LORENZO, Susan .... 650-738-4253.. 62 K
lorenzo@smccd.edu

LORENZONI, Paul .... 718-678-8485 305 H
plorenzoni@mercy.edu

LORETO, David, P .... 716-878-4017 317 C
loretodp@buffalostate.edu

LORGAN, Jason .... 530-752-9075.. 69 A
jplorgan@ucdavis.edu

LORGE-GROVER,
Christina .... 715-422-5526 498 A
christina.lorgegrover@mstc.edu

LORIA, Anne .... 716-250-7500 291 H
alloria@bryantstratton.edu

LORICK, Piper .... 803-750-2510.. 93 H

LORIMER, David, W ...... 606-693-5000 182 H
dlorimer@kmbc.edu

LORIMER, Steve, A .... 606-693-5000 182 H
slorimer@kmbc.edu

LORIMER, Steve, E .... 606-693-5000 182 H
slorimer@kmbc.edu

LORIMER, Thomas .... 606-693-5000 182 H
tlorimer@kmbc.edu

LORINCZOVA, Klaudia .. 315-279-5699 303 D
klorincz@keuka.edu

LORING, Trish .... 603-271-6484 272 C
tloring@ccsnh.edu

LORING, Trish .... 603-271-6984 272 C
tloring@ccsnh.edu

LORIUS, Billie Jo .... 701-328-4107 344 G
billiejo.lorius@ndus.edu

LORTA, Danielle .... 510-780-4500.. 48 D
dlorta@lifewest.edu

LORTON-ROWLAND,
Julie .... 317-921-4715 158 A
jlorton@ivytech.edu

LORTZ, Peter .... 206-934-3701 482 F
peter.lortz@seattlecolleges.edu

LOSASSO, Joseph .... 609-652-4235 283 A
joe.losasso@stockton.edu

LOSCHIAVO, Linda .... 718-817-3570 300 A
loschiavo@fordham.edu

LOSCHIAVO, Melissa ..... 770-426-2741 122 A
melissa.loschiavo@life.edu

LOSO, Chris .... 860-231-5323.. 89 G
closo@usj.edu

LOSS, Jeffrey .... 570-577-1911 379 A
jeffrey.loss@bucknell.edu

LOSTON WILLIAMS,
Adena .... 210-486-2900 428 C
aloston@alamo.edu

LOTANO, Vincent .... 908-709-7046 283 E
vincent.lotano@ucc.edu

LOTHRINGER,
Robert, L .... 214-768-3531 443 G
rlothringer@smu.edu

LOTITO, Tom .... 757-382-9900.. 93 H

LOTRIONTE, John, D .... 901-321-3550 417 G
jlotrion@cbu.edu

LOTSU, Adamma .... 773-291-6100 135 B

LOTT, Cari .... 620-242-0400 175 G

LOTT, Colleen .... 303-722-5724.. 81 K
clott@lincolntech.edu

LOTT, Ileo .... 847-635-1660 146 E
ilott@oakton.edu

LOTT, Jesse .... 315-655-7161 292 B
jlott@cazenovia.edu

LOTT, Stephanie .... 785-532-6220 175 A
slott@ksu.edu

LOTTO, Benjamin .... 845-437-7437 323 H
lotto@vassar.edu

LOTURCO, Jennifer .... 212-217-4000 299 C
jennifer_loturco@fitnyc.edu

LOTZ, Cindy .... 309-556-3536 140 E
clotz@iwu.edu

LOTZ, Erin .... 928-350-2307.. 15 O
elotz@prescott.edu

LOTZ, Hailey .... 850-484-1714 105 G
hlotz@pensacolastate.edu

LOTZE, Conrad .... 304-724-3700 485 G
clotze@apus.edu

LOTZER, Gina .... 651-641-3456 236 A
glotzer001@luthersem.edu

LOU, Kris .... 503-370-5328 377 E
klou@willamette.edu

LOUALLEN, Cheryl .... 937-481-2337 363 H
cheryl_louallen@wilmington.edu

LOUCHOUARN, Patrick . 979-845-4016 446 B
loup@tamu.edu

LOUCKS, Susan .... 718-940-5564 313 C
sloucks@sjcny.edu

LOUDEN, Jennifer .... 410-617-2861 199 G
jhlouden@loyola.edu

LOUDEN, Sandy .... 731-352-4095 417 C
loudens@bethelu.edu

LOUDER, Corey .... 660-626-2203 249 C
clouder@atsu.edu

LOUDERMILK, Jennifer . 706-295-1715 119 F
jloudermilk@gntc.edu

LOUDERMILK, Jessica .. 210-784-1612 447 B
jloudermilk@tamusa.edu

LOUDIN, Rose Ellen ..... 304-473-8600 490 E
loudin_r@wvwc.edu

LOUFEK, Michelle .... 321-433-7765.. 98 F
loufekm@easternflorida.edu

LOUGEE, Wendy, P .... 612-624-1807 242 K
wlougee@umn.edu

LOUGHLIN, Stephen, J . 585-271-3657 312 E
stephen.loughlin@stbernards.edu

LOUGHMAN, Ann .... 518-262-5435 289 C
loughma@amc.edu

LOUGHREN, Joseph ..... 718-997-5910 295 A
joseph.loughren@qc.cuny.edu

LOUIMA, Gariot .... 765-983-1208 154 H
louimga@earlham.edu

LOUIMA, Gariot .... 937-767-6082 347 E
glouima@antiochcollege.edu

LOUIS, Germaine .... 703-993-1918 466 J
chhsdean@gmu.edu

LOUIS, Lindsay .... 508-213-2372 217 C
lindsay.louis@nichols.edu

LOUIS, Louisana .... 727-341-3640 107 C
louis.louisana@spcollege.edu

LOUIS, Michael .... 314-505-7301 251 D
louism@csl.edu

LOUIS, Naomi .... 937-328-6031 350 D
louisn@clarkstate.edu

LOUNDER, Lee .... 406-265-3711 264 A
lee.lounder@msun.edu

LOUNSBERY, Monica .... 562-985-4691.. 32 A
monica.lounsbery@csulb.edu

LOURO, Jeffrey .... 508-999-8171 211 F
jlouro@umassd.edu

LOUTHAN, Christa .... 405-744-7420 367 G
christa.louthan@okstate.edu

LOUTHAN, Katherine ..... 314-529-9671 254 D
mlouthan@maryville.edu

LOUTTIT, Julianne, E .... 724-287-8711 379 C
juli.louttit@bc3.edu

LOUTTIT, Kristen .... 724-938-4404 394 C
louttit@calu.edu

LOVAS, Judy .... 973-300-2100 283 B
jlovas@sussex.edu

LOVATO, Heather .... 575-769-4039 285 C
heather.lovato@clovis.edu

LOVATO, Stella .... 210-486-0903 428 D
slovato@alamo.edu

LOVATO, Stella .... 210-486-0000 428 D
slovato@alamo.edu

LOVATO, Todd .... 505-428-1217 287 H
todd.lovato@sfcc.edu

LOVE, Andrea .... 225-771-2552 191 C
alove@sulc.edu

LOVE, Brandolyn .... 843-355-4131 413 C
loveb@wiltech.edu

LOVE, Brian .... 803-705-4479 405 G
brian.love@benedict.edu

LOVE, Casey .... 504-862-8315 191 D
mkane1@tulane.edu

LOVE, Cindy .... 919-516-5082 339 G
clove@st-aug.edu

LOVE, Deborah .... 336-517-2247 326 J
deborah.love@bennett.edu

LOVE, Eric .... 574-631-2859 161 G
elove1@nd.edu

LOVE, Jamica, N .... 540-464-7789 475 C
lovejn@vmi.edu

LOVE, Jan .... 404-727-6324 118 D
jlove3@emory.edu

LOVE, Jennifer .... 325-942-2116 450 B
jenny.love@angelo.edu

LOVE, Kathy, S .... 912-443-3024 124 I
klove@savannahtech.edu

LOVE, Latanya, J .... 713-500-6054 455 D
latanya.d.jones@uth.tmc.edu

LOVE, Maleeka, T .... 919-497-3278 330 E
mlove@louisburg.edu

LOVE, Marla .... 607-255-1115 297 D
dean_of_students@cornell.edu

LOVE, Paula .... 903-730-4890 437 E
plove@jarvis.edu

LOVE, Sydney .... 601-857-3350 245 D
sydney.love@hindscc.edu

LOVE, Vanessa .... 412-391-4100 395 H
vlove@pointpark.edu

LOVE-SMITH, Ashley ..... 310-206-6361.. 69 D
alovesmith@volunteer.ucla.edu

LOVE-VAUGHN,
Devonia .... 318-257-2532 192 A
dlvaughn@latech.edu

LOVEDAY, Joyce .... 253-589-5500 478 A
joyce.loveday@cptc.edu

LOVEDAY, Travis, C ...... 865-694-6415 424 C
tcloveday@pstcc.edu

LOVEJOY, Jonathan, C . 210-832-5668 452 D
lovejoy@uiwtx.edu

LOVEJOY, Mike .... 469-348-2500 432 M

LOVELACE, Amber .... 256-395-2211.... 3 G
alovelace@suscc.edu

LOVELACE, Rhonda .... 501-370-5297.. 21 A
rlovelace@philander.edu

LOVELACE, Vanessa ..... 717-290-8723 387 F
vlovelace@lancasterseminary.edu

LOVELADY, III, Artis ..... 832-252-4617 431 M
artis@cbshouston.edu

LOVELAND, David, A .... 607-746-4013 320 A
lovelada@delhi.edu

LOVELESS, Debra .... 937-327-6131 364 C
registrar@wittenberg.edu

LOVELESS, Jill .... 304-214-8856 487 J
jloveless@wvncc.edu

LOVELESS, Stephanie ... 706-368-7736 119 C
sloveless@highlands.edu

LOVELL, Dave .... 800-553-4674 155 F
dlovell@horizonindy.org

LOVELL, Diana .... 580-774-3766 369 I
diana.lovell@swosu.edu

LOVELL, Donna .... 650-723-2300.. 66 D
dlovell@stanford.edu

LOVELL, Janet .... 706-754-7833 123 C
jlovell@northgatech.edu

LOVELL, Janice .... 615-248-1563 425 D
jelovell@trevecca.edu

LOVELL, Kenya .... 386-481-2275.. 96 D
lovellk@cookman.edu

LOVELL, Matthew, D ..... 812-877-8318 160 C
lovellmd@rose-hulman.edu

LOVELL, Michael, R ...... 414-288-7223 492 E
michael.lovell@marquette.edu

LOVELL, Sharon .... 540-568-2705 467 C
lovellse@jmu.edu

LOVELL, Wendy, W .... 540-458-8412 476 D
wwlovell@wlu.edu

LOVELY, Christine .... 530-752-1011.. 69 A

LOVELY, Courtney .... 561-803-2337 105 B
courtney_lovely@pba.edu

LOVERIN, David .... 559-730-3722.. 39 C
davidl@cos.edu

LOVETT, Julie .... 817-257-7132 447 H
j.n.lovett@tcu.edu

LOVETT, Lisa .... 303-492-4129.. 83 M
lisa.lovett@colorado.edu

LOVETT, Myra .... 318-342-1266 193 A
mlovett@ulm.edu

LOVETT, Patricia .... 270-686-4332 179 F
patricia.lovett@brescia.edu

LOVETT, Winda .... 719-884-5000.. 82 A
wglovett@nbc.edu

LOVETTE-COLYER,
Michael .... 619-260-4251.. 72 H
mlovettecolyer@sandiego.edu

LOVIK, Eric .... 540-831-5099 468 E
elovik@radford.edu

LOVIN, Eddie .... 615-547-1231 418 C
elovin@cumberland.edu

LOVIN, Eddie .... 662-846-4150 245 A
elovin@deltastate.edu

LOVINS, Greg .... 910-672-1151 341 B
glovins@uncfsu.edu

LOVITT, Del .... 913-469-8500 174 F
dlovitt@jccc.edu

LOVITT, Timmothy .... 425-388-9142 479 B
tlovitt@everettcc.edu

LOVORN, Beth .... 228-497-7685 246 F
beth.lovorn@mgccc.edu

LOVORN, Michael .... 507-457-6620 242 H
mlovorn@smumn.edu

LOVSETH, Stephanie ..... 618-374-5215 147 B
stephanie.lovseth@principia.edu

LOVSTUEN, Brenda, C .. 319-895-4292 164 E
blovstuen@cornellcollege.edu

LOW, Avrum Yehuda ..... 718-600-8897 325 G

LOW,
Catherine Yu-Ling ...... 808-371-5443 128 G
cfo@orientalmedicine.edu

LOW, Daniel .... 626-398-2222.. 76 B

LOW, George, S .... 678-407-5200 119 B
gslow@ggc.edu

LOW, Greg .... 949-794-9090.. 66 C
glow@stanbridge.edu

LOW, Hershel .... 718-600-8897 325 G

LOW, Rochel .... 718-600-8897 325 G

LOW, Ryan .... 207-581-5846 196 C
ryan.low@maine.edu

LOW, Tom .... 510-845-5373.. 29 D

LOW, Wai Hoa .... 808-521-2288 128 G
whlow@orientalmedicine.edu

LOWDEN, Jay .... 530-740-1703.. 77 D
jlowden@yccd.edu

LOWDEN, Kyle .... 217-854-5781 133 F

LOWDEN, Paul .... 616-732-1194 222 H
plowden@davenport.edu

LOWDEN, Rob .... 317-278-7533 156 B
rlowden@iu.edu

LOWDEN, Rob .... 317-278-7533 156 C
rlowden@iu.edu

LOWDER, Diane, M .... 804-752-7218 469 B
dianelowder@rmc.edu

LOWDER, Michael .... 405-789-7661 369 H
michael.lowder@swcu.edu

LOWDERMILK,
Robert, S .... 336-342-4261 337 B
lowdermilkb@rockinghamcc.edu

LOWE, Brenda .... 806-720-7307 438 F
brenda.lowe@lcu.edu

LOWE, Carmen .... 617-627-4239 219 A
carmen.lowe@tufts.edu

LOWE, Carrie Beth .... 865-573-4517 419 E
cblowe@johnsonu.edu

LOWE, Charles .... 973-720-2200 283 I
lowec1@wpunj.edu

LOWE, Charm .... 864-592-4624 411 E
lowec@sccsc.edu

LOWE, JR., Eugene, Y .. 847-491-8409 146 C
eyljr@northwestern.edu

LOWE, Grant .... 706-419-1360 117 G
grant.lowe@covenant.edu

LOWE, James .... 765-285-2805 153 E
jlowe@bsu.edu

LOWE, James, R .... 860-486-0566.. 89 B
jim.lowe@uconn.edu

LOWE, Jeanette .... 706-595-0166 115 H
jlowe@augustatech.edu

LOWE, Jody .... 662-915-7911 248 F
jplowe@olemiss.edu

LOWE, John-Martin .... 402-552-3001 269 B
jjlowe@unmc.edu

LOWE, Joshua .... 919-889-0114 339 I
joshua.lowe@shawu.edu

LOWE, Judy .... 423-697-2686 423 B
judy.lowe@chattanoogastate.edu

LOWE, Kathy .... 707-638-5200.. 68 B

LOWE, Kristen, M .... 585-292-2114 306 K
klowe5@monroecc.edu

LOWE, Larry .... 803-705-4573 405 G
larry.lowe@benedict.edu

LOWE, Mark, E .... 314-747-0515 261 B
lowe@wustl.edu

LOWE, Melinda .... 662-241-6088 247 B
mslowe@muw.edu

LOWE, Monica .... 815-802-8964 141 B
mlowe@kcc.edu

LOWE, Nathan .... 541-962-3098 372 H
nlowe@eou.edu

LOWE, Pamela .... 847-578-8786 148 B
pamela.lowe@rosalindfranklin.edu

LOWE, Patricia .... 617-552-3334 207 A
patricia.lowe@bc.edu

LOWE, Rick, D .... 910-630-7027 331 B
rlowe@methodist.edu

LOWE, Rosemary .... 870-762-3182.. 17 F
rlowe@smail.anc.edu

LOWE, Scott .... 208-426-5439 130 F
scottlowe@boisestate.edu

LOWE, Sharon .... 419-289-5035 347 H
slowe3@ashland.edu

LOWE, Shelley .... 517-367-8221 222 H
shelley.lowe@davenport.edu

LOWE, Stephen, R .... 815-939-5231 146 F
slowe@olivet.edu

LOWE, Susan .... 276-964-7304 474 E

LOWE, Susan, L .... 276-964-7304 474 E
susan.lowe@sw.edu

LOWE, Tiffany, P .... 254-710-6978 430 F
tiffany_lowe@baylor.edu

LOWE, William .... 918-781-7277 365 B
lowew@bacone.edu
LOWE-SCHNEIDER,
Katy .... 812-866-7081 155 D
lowe@hanover.edu
LOWE-WINCENTSEN,
Dawn .... 206-546-4774 483 C
dlowe-wincentsen@shoreline.edu
LOWELL, Hillary .... 406-683-7151 263 E
hillary.lowell@umwestern.edu
LOWELL, Randy .... 864-424-8046 412 H
lowell@mailbox.sc.edu
LOWENBERG, Ron ...... 714-895-8373.. 38 E
rlowenberg@gwc.cccd.edu
LOWENSTEIN,
Daniel, H .... 415-476-4451.. 70 D
lowenstein@ucsf.edu
LOWENTHAL, Benjamin 410-704-2151 204 B
blowenthal@towson.edu
LOWENTHAL, Tina .... 626-395-2758.. 29 B
tina.lowenthal@caltech.edu
LOWERY, Andrew .... 706-302-5624 121 K
alowery@lagrange.edu
LOWERY, Carla .... 662-329-7197 247 B
cmlowery@muw.edu
LOWERY, Christina ...... 207-780-5240 196 J
christina.smith1@maine.edu
LOWERY, David .... 601-318-6445 249 B
dlowery@wmcarey.edu
LOWERY, Jonathan ...... 317-955-6621 159 A
jlowery@marian.edu
LOWERY, Kathryn .... 601-266-6775 248 H
kathryn.lowery@usm.edu
LOWERY, LaRonda .... 910-272-3305 337 A
lalowery@robeson.edu
LOWERY, LaTanya .... 432-552-2020 456 C
lowery_l@utpb.edu
LOWERY, Randall .... 912-358-4350 124 H
loweryr@savannahstate.edu
LOWERY, Shelly, L .... 563-333-6347 169 D
loweryshellyl@sau.edu
LOWERY-HART,
Russell, D .... 806-371-5123 428 F
rdloweryhart@actx.edu
LOWHAM, Elizabeth ...... 559-278-6502.. 31 D
elowham@mail.fresnostate.edu
LOWIN, Clinton .... 210-826-7595 457 B
lowinc@wbu.edu
LOWKS, Tammy, A .... 740-368-3002 359 F
talowks@owu.edu
LOWMAN, Anthony .... 856-256-5300 280 H
lowman@rowan.edu
LOWMAN, Sara .... 713-348-2457 441 K
lowman@rice.edu
LOWN, Maris .... 908-709-7006 283 E
maris.lown@ucc.edu
LOWNES, Chris .... 803-822-3583 409 E
lownesc@midlandstech.edu
LOWNES-JACKSON,
Millicent .... 615-963-7127 425 A
mlownes@tnstate.edu
LOWNEY, John .... 336-334-7500 341 C
LOWRANCE, Jeff .... 704-330-6666 333 B
jeff.lowrance@cpcc.edu
LOWREY, James, S .... 336-841-9283 329 E
jlowrey@highpoint.edu
LOWREY, Jason, H .... 507-344-7378 233 I
jason.lowrey@blc.edu
LOWREY, Will .... 662-685-4771 244 D
wlowrey@bmc.edu
LOWRIE, Kalie .... 325-649-8007 437 A
klowrie@hputx.edu
LOWRY, Alexander .... 978-867-4276 209 F
alexander.lowry@gordon.edu
LOWRY, Grace .... 570-372-4157 398 A
lowryg@susqu.edu
LOWRY, John .... 615-966-3000 420 B
john.lowry@lipscomb.edu
LOWRY, Lee .... 813-253-7671 102 A
llowry2@hccfl.edu
LOX, Curt .... 904-620-2810 111 A
c.lox@unf.edu
LOY, Marty .... 715-346-3169 496 B
mloy@uwsp.edu
LOYA, Landon .... 814-443-2522 393 A
lloya@pennhighlands.edu
LOYA, Leanne .... 307-268-2662 499 T
leanne.loya@caspercollege.edu
LOYA, Leanne .... 307-268-2111 499 T
leanne.loya@caspercollege.edu
LOYACK, John, R .... 484-254-2121 378 C
john.loyack@alvernia.edu
LOYD, James .... 706-649-1449 117 F
jloyd@columbustech.edu

LOYD, James .... 256-306-2784.... 1 F
james.loyd@calhoun.edu
LOYD, Jo Lynn .... 972-279-6511 428 G
jloyd@amberton.edu
LOYD, Kristen, J .... 812-877-8484 160 C
loyd1@rose-hulman.edu
LOYD, Nicholas .... 256-824-6257.... 8 B
nicholas.loyd@uah.edu
LOYD, Nicole, L .... 610-861-1502 390 D
loydn@moravian.edu
LOYD, Sage .... 870-460-1422.. 22 E
coons@uamont.edu
LOYD-PAIGE, Michelle .. 616-526-8703 221 L
lopa@calvin.edu
LOYET, Deborah .... 330-325-6258 357 D
dloyet@neomed.edu
LOYET, Michelle .... 314-246-7762 261 D
michelleloyet46@webster.edu
LOYKE, Christopher ...... 423-869-6661 420 A
christopher.loyke@lmunet.edu
LOYNAZ, Oscar .... 305-237-5006 104 E
oloynaz@mdc.edu
LOYOLA, David .... 956-380-8196 441 L
dloyola@riogrande.edu
LOZADA, Edwin, C .... 787-780-0070 504 E
elozada@caribbean.edu
LOZADA, Fuji, P .... 704-894-2035 328 C
erlozada@davidson.edu
LOZADA, Zaida .... 787-704-1020 505 B
zlozada@columbiacentral.edu
LOZADA-CRUZ, Isabel .. 787-480-2380 505 A
ilozada@sanjuan.pr
LOZANO, Franz .... 707-654-1032.. 32 C
flozano@csum.edu
LOZANO, Javier .... 210-805-3015 452 D
lozano@uiwtx.edu
LOZANO, Ruth, V .... 214-768-4708 443 G
rlozano@smu.edu
LOZANO, Sara .... 956-872-6116 443 B
smcardoz@southtexascollege.edu
LOZANO CUELLAR,
Christian .... 415-338-1111.. 34 A
christianlozano@sfsu.edu
LOZIER, Chris .... 812-535-5186 160 E
chris.lozier@smwc.edu
LOZIER, Susan .... 404-894-3300 119 D
susan.lozier@cos.gatech.edu
LOZINA, Mary .... 914-674-7651 305 H
mlozina@mercy.edu
LOZOYA, Karna .... 202-319-5100.. 91 G
lozoya@cua.edu
LOZOYA, Lynnette .... 909-599-5433.. 48 E
llozoya@lifepacific.edu
LU, Arthur .... 315-792-7116 320 F
xinjian.lu@sunypoly.edu
LU, Elissa .... 508-793-7513 207 F
ellu@clarku.edu
LU, Flora .... 831-459-5852.. 71 A
floralu@ucsc.edu
LU, Kuang Kai .... 323-731-2383.. 55 G
rex@psuca.edu
LU, Michael, C .... 510-664-4219.. 68 N
mclu@berkeley.edu
LU, Zhaoxue .... 503-253-3443 374 E
zlu@ocom.edu
LUAN, Jing .... 650-358-6880.. 62 H
luan@smccd.edu
LUBA, Kristen .... 646-564-6774 289 F
kristen.luba@nyack.edu
LUBARSKY, David, A ...... 916-734-0751.. 69 A
dalubarsky@ucdavis.edu
LUBAS, Rebecca .... 509-963-1981 477 G
rebecca.lubas@cwu.edu
LUBBEN, Richard .... 559-730-3735.. 39 C
richardl@cos.edu
LUBBERS, Tony .... 660-543-8266 259 K
lubbers@ucmo.edu
LUBELL, David .... 607-431-4031 300 G
lubelld@hartwick.edu
LUBELL, Ellen .... 212-410-8479 308 D
elubell@nycpm.edu
LUBER, Tia .... 719-255-3726.. 84 A
tluber@uccs.edu
LUBHAN, Dawn .... 507-453-2738 238 J
dawn.lubhan@southeastmn.edu
LUBIENICKI, Teresa ...... 313-883-8654 229 J
lubienicki.teresa@shms.edu
LUBIG, Joe .... 906-227-1880 228 E
jlubig@nmu.edu
LUBIN, James .... 212-686-9244 289 G
LUBINGER, Bill .... 216-368-4443 349 B
william.lubinger@case.edu

LUBINSKY, Hindy .... 718-787-1602 322 C
hindy.lubinsky@touro.edu
LUBNOW, Jeff .... 973-328-5155 276 A
jlubnow@ccm.edu
LUBS, Shawna .... 661-362-3639.. 38 H
shawna.lubs@canyons.edu
LUCAL, Mary .... 865-974-1909 426 C
mlucal@utk.edu
LUCAS, Bryan .... 817-257-7682 447 H
b.lucas@tcu.edu
LUCAS, Carol, A .... 516-877-3154 288 L
lucas@adelphi.edu
LUCAS, Cathy .... 910-221-2224 330 G
clucas@manna.edu
LUCAS, Christina .... 601-426-6346 248 C
clucas@southeasternbaptist.edu
LUCAS, Daniel .... 850-474-3380 111 E
dlucas@uwf.edu
LUCAS, Danita .... 605-995-7195 414 E
danita.lucas@mitchelltech.edu
LUCAS, Garriell .... 336-744-0900 327 D
financialaid@carolina.edu
LUCAS, Hakim, J .... 804-257-5835 475 G
hjlucas@vuu.edu
LUCAS, Janet .... 209-946-2392.. 71 E
jlucas@pacific.edu
LUCAS, Jaron .... 478-825-6514 118 E
lucasj01@fvsu.edu
LUCAS, Jeanne .... 785-227-3380 171 H
lucasja@bethanylb.edu
LUCAS, Jennifer .... 906-487-2400 227 D
jpjung@mtu.edu
LUCAS, Jennifer, R .... 717-337-6211 384 C
jlucas@gettysburg.edu
LUCAS, Joan .... 662-325-8131 247 A
jlucas@legal.msstate.edu
LUCAS, John .... 608-262-8287 494 D
jplucas@wisc.edu
LUCAS, John .... 336-334-5702 342 D
jslucas@uncg.edu
LUCAS, John .... 540-231-4000 466 E
jrlucas@vt.vcom.edu
LUCAS, Julie .... 617-253-3952 215 G
LUCAS, Karen .... 617-449-7070 219 B
LUCAS, Karen, E .... 570-422-2844 393 F
klucas@esu.edu
LUCAS, Kendall .... 619-849-2680.. 57 J
kendalllucas@pointloma.edu
LUCAS, Kylie .... 620-421-6700 175 D
kyliel@labette.edu
LUCAS, Lisa .... 901-321-3259 417 G
llucas@cbu.edu
LUCAS, Lynn .... 440-449-4433 363 C
lynn.lucas@ursuline.edu
LUCAS, Mark .... 785-227-3380 171 H
lucas@bethanylb.edu
LUCAS, Matt .... 765-677-2408 157 F
matt.lucas@indwes.edu
LUCAS, Michelle .... 717-796-1800 389 F
mlucas@messiah.edu
LUCAS, Pam, A .... 214-860-2097 434 A
plucas@dcccd.edu
LUCAS, Paul, M .... 724-287-8711 379 C
paul.lucas@bc3.edu
LUCAS, Richard .... 404-880-6040 116 I
rlucas@cau.edu
LUCAS, Scott .... 316-677-9535 178 C
slucas@wsutech.edu
LUCAS, Sharron .... 913-758-6102 177 I
sharron.lucas@stmary.edu
LUCAS, Sheri .... 614-222-3220 351 A
slucas@ccad.edu
LUCAS, Yerodin .... 570-340-6042 389 B
ylucas@marywood.edu
LUCAS-ROSS, Jennifer .. 239-687-5351.. 95 L
jlross@avemarialaw.edu
LUCAS-YOUMANS,
Tasha .... 386-481-2181.. 96 D
youmanst@cookman.edu
LUCCHI, Addison .... 913-971-3567.. 82 A
amlucchi@mnu.edu
LUCCI, David .... 970-204-5363.. 80 I
david.lucci@frontrange.edu
LUCCI, Elaine .... 724-266-3838 399 F
elucci@tsm.edu
LUCE, Greg .... 215-968-8225 379 B
greg.luce@bucks.edu
LUCE, Russ .... 480-732-7177.. 13 B
russ.luce@cgc.edu
LUCERO, Cori .... 209-228-4440.. 70 A
clucero2@ucmerced.edu
LUCERO, David .... 505-454-5312 285 I
dlucero@luna.edu

LUCERO, Gabe .... 307-742-3776 500 K
glucero@wyotech.edu
LUCERO, Joseph .... 615-514-2787 421 H
LUCERO, Kenneth .... 505-747-5034 287 C
ken.lucero@nnmc.edu
LUCERO, Louis .... 661-722-6300.. 26 E
llucero@avc.edu
LUCERO, Marie .... 510-649-2437.. 44 E
mlucero@gtu.edu
LUCERO-MAZEI,
Vanessa .... 248-645-3300 222 G
vmazei@cranbrook.edu
LUCETTE, Kisha .... 706-821-8495 123 I
klucette@paine.edu
LUCHAU, Michael .... 575-527-7604 287 A
mluchau@nmsu.edu
LUCHKO, Nicholas .... 610-282-1100 382 A
nicholas.luchko@desales.edu
LUCIA, Joseph, P .... 215-204-8231 398 D
joseph.lucia@temple.edu
LUCIANI, Michael .... 802-387-6713 461 E
mluciani@landmark.edu
LUCIANO, Jack .... 910-755-7336 332 D
lucianoj@brunswickcc.edu
LUCIANO, Jennifer, K ... 201-200-2220 278 F
jluciano@njcu.edu
LUCIDO, Michael .... 314-977-8173 258 H
michael.lucido@slu.edu
LUCIO, Nickolas .... 559-442-8225.. 67 A
nickolas.lucio@fresnocitycollege.edu
LUCIUS, Ellen .... 419-448-3413 361 C
luciuse@tiffin.edu
LUCIUS, Shannon .... 662-329-7135 247 B
smlucius@muw.edu
LUCK, Deborah, S .... 336-633-0272 336 F
dsluck@randolph.edu
LUCK, Garrett .... 847-317-8118 150 J
gmluck@tiu.edu
LUCK, Janice, J .... 610-921-7824 377 F
jluck@albright.edu
LUCK, Jessica, E .... 540-828-5720 464 C
jluck@bridgewater.edu
LUCK, Tonya .... 910-898-9631 336 A
luckt@montgomery.edu
LUCKER, Lucy .... 860-231-5220.. 89 G
llucker@usj.edu
LUCKETT, Jenni .... 503-352-3006 375 B
jluckett@pacificu.edu
LUCKETT, Matt .... 270-824-1757 182 A
matt.luckett@kctcs.edu
LUCKEY, JR.,
William, T .... 270-384-8001 183 D
luckeyw@lindsey.edu
LUCKING, Rachel .... 508-626-4615 212 D
rlucking@framingham.edu
LUCKY, Jana .... 318-357-4503 192 D
luckyj@nsula.edu
LUCY, Cecil .... 815-280-6647 140 I
clucy@jjc.edu
LUCY, John .... 904-596-2507 112 E
jlucy@tbc.edu
LUDDEN, Mary .... 617-373-6417 217 D
LUDDY, Jennifer .... 781-280-3200 214 G
LUDDY, Jennifer .... 617-984-1657 217 G
jluddy@quincycollege.edu
LUDEMA, James .... 616-526-6000 221 L
jdl42@calvin.edu
LUDEMAN, Randall .... 218-755-3750 237 B
randall.ludeman@bemidjistate.edu
LUDEMAN, Randy .... 218-755-3750 237 B
LUDES, James .... 401-341-2397 404 D
jim.ludes@salve.edu
LUDESCHER,
Sandra, M .... 563-589-3223 170 C
sludescher@dbq.edu
LUDLUM, Beth .... 202-885-8616.. 94 D
bludlum@wesleyseminary.edu
LUDWICK, Richard .... 713-525-2160 453 H
president@stthom.edu
LUDWIG, Adam .... 715-232-1121 496 C
ludwiga@uwstout.edu
LUDWIG, Allison .... 718-430-2000 289 D
LUDWIG, Amy .... 479-394-7622.. 23 F
aludwig@uarichmountain.edu
LUDWIG, Mary .... 515-574-1145 166 G
ludwig@iowacentral.edu
LUDWIG, Wendi .... 715-675-3331 498 E
ludwig@ntc.edu
LUEBBERING, Kevin ...... 417-447-8188 257 B
luebberk@otc.edu
LUEBKE, Miriam .... 651-651-8825 235 A
luebke@csp.edu

LUECKE, Chris .... 435-797-2452 459 F
chris.luecke@usu.edu
LUECKE, Julie .... 608-663-2372 491 F
jluecke@edgewood.edu
LUEDTKE-JONES, Sarah 651-641-3434 236 A
sluedtkejones001@luthersem.edu
LUEKEN, Joel .... 605-394-2352 415 I
joel.lueken@sdsmt.edu
LUEKENGA, Chris .... 970-943-2616.. 85 B
cluekenga@western.edu
LUEKENGA, Julie .... 303-718-5307.. 77 G
julie.luekenga@aims.edu
LUEKING, Angela .... 406-496-4106 264 C
alueking@mtech.edu
LUELLEN, Mark .... 434-243-2249 471 F
mml2r@virginia.edu
LUELLMAN, Becky .... 605-668-1464 414 F
becky.luellman@mountmarty.edu
LUER, Mark, S .... 618-650-5153 149 H
mluer@siue.edu
LUESSE, Amy .... 952-446-4122 235 B
luessea@crown.edu
LUETH, Brian .... 269-488-4777 225 C
blueth@kvcc.edu
LUETH, Erica, S .... 253-535-7385 481 C
erica.lueth@plu.edu
LUETKEHANS, Lara ..... 724-357-2219 393 G
lara.luetkehans@iup.edu
LUEVANO, Margaret, Y . 512-471-7885 454 C
mluevano@austin.utexas.edu
LUFF, Libby .... 615-514-2787 421 H
lfunke@nossi.edu
LUFF, Paula .... 765-285-5344 153 E
pcluff@bsu.edu
LUFKIN, Daniel .... 817-515-4501 445 A
daniel.lufkin@tccd.edu
LUFKIN, MB .... 603-358-2181 274 A
mb.lufkin@keene.edu
LUFKINS, Lorraine ...... 218-935-0417 244 A
lorraine.lufkins@wetcc.edu
LUFT, John, P .... 717-796-1800 389 F
jluft@messiah.edu
LUFT, Megan .... 717-477-1123 394 D
mnluft@ship.edu
LUGDON, Shannon ...... 207-834-7800 196 G
shannon.lugdon@maine.edu
LUGER, Todd .... 619-574-6909.. 55 D
tluger@pacificcollege.edu
LUGIOYO, Brian .... 206-281-2208 482 K
lugioyob@spu.edu
LUGO, Daniel, G .... 704-337-2216 339 D
president@queens.edu
LUGO, Efrain .... 787-620-2040 504 B
elugo@aupr.edu
LUGO, Eric .... 646-660-6095 292 F
eric.lugo@baruch.cuny.edu
LUGO, Monica .... 907-852-1860.... 9 H
monica.lugo@ilisagvik.edu
LUGO, Nilsa, L .... 787-850-9337 511 B
nilsa.lugo@upr.edu
LUGO CARDONA,
Jennifer .... 787-250-0000 510 B
jennifer.lugo1@upr.edu
LUHTA, Brad .... 440-375-7585 354 K
bluhta@lec.edu
LUI, Joyce .... 408-288-3177.. 62 G
joyce.lui@sjcc.edu
LUIKART, Nancy .... 563-288-6073 165 I
nluikart@eicc.edu
LUING, Kevin, L .... 973-278-5400 291 A
kevin@berkeleycollege.edu
LUING, Kevin, L .... 973-278-5400 274 J
kevin@berkeleycollege.edu
LUING, Tim .... 973-278-5400 274 J
tim@berkeleycollege.edu
LUING, Tim .... 212-986-4343 291 A
tim@berkeleycollege.edu
LUIS, Timothy .... 614-885-5585 359 K
tluis@pcj.edu
LUJAN, Annette .... 719-846-5679.. 83 I
annette.lujan@trinidadstate.edu
LUJAN, Jarett .... 361-593-3269 447 A
jarett.lujan@tamuk.edu
LUJAN, Linda .... 719-336-1511.. 81 J
linda.lujan@lamarcc.edu
LUKAC, Dan .... 513-244-4617 356 F
dan.lukac@msj.edu
LUKACH, Matt .... 701-777-4409 344 H
matt.lukach@und.edu
LUKACSKO, Debbie ..... 201-684-7535 280 B
dlukacsk@ramapo.edu
LUKAS, Sofia .... 678-450-0550 121 F
slukas@ict.edu

LUKAS, Veronica .... 718-281-5196 295 B
vlukas@qcc.cuny.edu
LUKASIEWICZ, Mark ..... 516-463-5213 301 E
mark.lukasiewicz@hofstra.edu
LUKASKIEWICZ, Robert . 860-297-2279.. 88 I
robert.lukaskiewicz@trincoll.edu
LUKE, Amy .... 807-956-9704 129 B
aluke@hawaii.edu
LUKE, Amy, M .... 808-956-8207 128 I
aluke@hawaii.edu
LUKE, Don, J .... 570-326-3761 392 S
dluke@pct.edu
LUKE, Emily .... 304-829-7630 486 B
eluke@bethanywv.edu
LUKE, Kristie .... 580-745-2176 369 F
kluke@se.edu
LUKE, Kristin .... 931-393-1930 423 G
kluke@mscc.edu
LUKE, Learie, B .... 803-536-7903 410 H
lluke@scsu.edu
LUKE, Sarah .... 207-801-5670 194 C
sluke@coa.edu
LUKE, Victoria .... 308-367-5204 269 D
vluke1@unl.edu
LUKENS, Michael .... 559-278-5001.. 31 D
mlukens@csufresno.edu
LUKER, Betsy .... 205-652-3892.... 9 B
bcompton@uwa.edu
LUKES, Don .... 812-855-4206 156 C
dlukes@iu.edu
LUKES, Donald, S .... 812-855-4206 156 B
dlukes@iu.edu
LUKIDIS, Lambrini ...... 312-369-8695 136 C
llukidis@colum.edu
LUKKES, Nathan .... 605-773-3455 415 D
nathan.lukkes@sdbor.edu
LUKOWSKI, Kristin ..... 810-762-9748 225 F
klukowski@kettering.edu
LUKSA, Jennifer .... 570-674-6224 389 H
jluksa@misericordia.edu
LUKSENBURG, Dana ..... 800-371-6105.. 14 I
dana@nationalparalegal.edu
LULING, Jennifer .... 267-341-3479 385 I
jluling@holyfamily.edu
LUM, Jeannie .... 808-735-4761 128 C
jeannie.lum@chaminade.edu
LUM, Jennifer, T .... 626-395-5940.. 29 B
jennifer.lum@caltech.edu
LUMAN, Karl .... 601-366-8880 249 A
kluman@wbs.edu
LUMPKIN, Collier .... 336-721-2600 339 H
collier.lumpkin@salem.edu
LUMPKIN, Melissa ...... 205-726-4459.... 6 E
mlumpki1@samford.edu
LUMPKIN, Myra .... 810-762-9743 225 F
mlumpkin@kettering.edu
LUMPKIN, Robert .... 773-291-6100 135 B
LUMPKINS, Peter .... 706-865-2134 126 D
plumpkins@truett.edu
LUMSDEN, Mark .... 321-674-8493 100 A
mlumsden@fit.edu
LUMZY, Arthur .... 972-780-3600 453 C
arthur.lumzy@untdallas.edu
LUNA, Andrew .... 931-221-6184 416 H
lunaa@apsu.edu
LUNA, Cyndie .... 559-442-4600.. 67 A
cyndie.luna@fresnocitycollege.edu
LUNA, David .... 520-515-5485.. 11 O
lunad@cochise.edu
LUNA, Edna, G .... 931-363-9824 426 F
eluna7@utsouthern.edu
LUNA, Faye .... 520-515-3649.. 11 O
lunaf@cochise.edu
LUNA, Javier .... 760-355-6448.. 45 N
javier.luna@imperial.edu
LUNA, Joy .... 951-552-8967.. 27 J
jluna@calbaptist.edu
LUNA, Kimberly .... 432-552-2805 456 C
luna_k@utpb.edu
LUNA, Mickey .... 314-977-3948 258 H
mickey.luna@slu.edu
LUNA, Miranda .... 503-883-2200 373 E
mluna@linfield.edu
LUNA, Naelys .... 561-297-2056 109 F
ndiaz10@fau.edu
LUNA, Olga .... 787-766-1912 507 C
oluna@inter.edu
LUNA, Olga .... 787-758-6260 506 H
oluna@inter.edu
LUNA, Raul .... 509-453-0374 481 G
raul.luna@perrytech.edu
LUNA, Reyes .... 909-869-3983.. 30 B
rjluna@cpp.edu

LUNA, Victoria .... 210-341-1366 440 B
LUNAK, Miles .... 218-733-7600 238 A
brad.vieths@lsc.edu
LUNBECK, Jo .... 501-660-1030.. 17 G
jlunbeck@asusystem.edu
LUNCEFORD, Daniel ..... 575-835-5961 286 D
dan.lunceford@nmt.edu
LUND, Alisha .... 541-888-7055 376 B
alisha.lund@socc.edu
LUND, Annette .... 801-863-3000 460 A
annette.lund@uvu.edu
LUND, Brenda .... 360-438-4307 482 D
blund@stmartin.edu
LUND, Christopher ...... 412-359-1000 399 D
clund@triangle-tech.edu
LUND, James .... 760-480-8474.. 75 H
jlund@wscal.edu
LUND, Josh .... 909-651-4089.. 48 J
jlund@llu.edu
LUND, Lisa .... 989-328-1284 227 G
lisal@montcalm.edu
LUND, Robin .... 210-486-4134 428 A
rlund4@alamo.edu
LUND, Vanessa .... 406-656-9950 263 B
LUNDAY, Bobbi, J .... 701-662-1501 346 A
bobbi.lunday@lrsc.edu
LUNDAY, Tammy .... 605-688-4157 416 A
tammy.lunday@sdstate.edu
LUNDBERG, Alessandra 860-932-4170.. 87 C
alundberg@qvcc.edu
LUNDBERG, Erik .... 734-615-4445 231 A
lerikl@umich.edu
LUNDBERG, Phil .... 503-253-3443 374 E
phil.lundberg@ocom.edu
LUNDBERG, Stacey ..... 218-335-4222 235 J
stacey.lundberg@lltc.edu
LUNDBLAD, Jeffrey, K .. 773-244-5542 145 F
jlundblad@northpark.edu
LUNDBURG, Wesley ..... 619-388-7834.. 61 B
wlundburg@sdccd.edu
LUNDE, Beth .... 757-789-1789 472 I
blunde@tcc.edu
LUNDE, Beth, E .... 757-822-1711 474 G
blunde@tcc.edu
LUNDE-STOCKERO,
Beth .... 906-487-3310 227 D
blunde@mtu.edu
LUNDEEN, Kate .... 414-382-6103 490 G
kate.lundeen@alverno.edu
LUNDGREN, Angie .... 336-734-7157 334 D
alundgren@forsythtech.edu
LUNDGREN, Jennifer ... 816-235-1107 260 D
lundgrenj@umkc.edu
LUNDGREN, LouAnne ... 505-224-3936 285 B
llundgren1@cnm.edu
LUNDQUIST, Harvey ..... 907-260-7422.... 9 D
LUNDQUIST, Lisa, M .... 678-547-6308 122 C
lundquist_lm@mercer.edu
LUNDQUIST, Lynn .... 651-641-8232 235 A
lundquist@csp.edu
LUNDSTROM, Joel .... 712-792-8308 164 F
jtlundstrom@dmacc.edu
LUNDSTROM, Marc ...... 435-879-4669 459 G
marc.lundstrom@utahtech.edu
LUNDY, Jennifer .... 724-838-4236 397 F
jlundy@setonhill.edu
LUNDY, Jennifer, R ..... 814-871-7000 383 H
lundy005@gannon.edu
LUNDY, Rae .... 903-927-3296 457 I
rlundy@wileyc.edu
LUNDY, Rae .... 903-923-3296 457 I
rlundy@wileyc.edu
LUNDY, Thackston ...... 312-261-3690 145 C
thackston.lundy@nl.edu
LUNG, Melissa .... 614-236-6011 348 I
LUNN, Ardelia, M .... 334-727-8147.... 7 D
alunn@tuskegee.edu
LUNSFORD, Justin, P ... 260-982-5280 158W
jplunsford@manchester.edu
LUNT, Andrew .... 575-538-6181 288 J
andrew.lunt@wnmu.edu
LUNTSFORD, Becky ..... 850-474-2449 111 E
rluntsford@uwf.edu
LUOMA, Jeffrey .... 203-773-8573.. 85 C
jluoma@albertus.edu
LUOMA, Jeffrey, E ...... 203-773-8550.. 85 C
LUOMA, Nichol .... 480-965-5282.. 11 A
nichol.luoma@asu.edu
LUONG, Carmen .... 718-482-5511 294 D
carmenl@lagcc.cuny.edu
LUONGO, Ann Marie .... 516-323-3200 306 I
presidents-office@molloy.edu

LUPACHINO, Keri .... 860-832-2204.. 85 F
lupachinok@ccsu.edu
LUPER, Brian .... 848-445-6950 281 B
bluper@oit.rutgers.edu
LUPIANI, Blanca, M .... 979-845-4274 446 B
blupiani@tamu.edu
LUPIEN, Todd .... 575-624-8110 286 F
todd@nmmi.edu
LUPTAK, Marcia .... 847-214-6917 137 D
mluptak@elgin.edu
LUPTON, Brendan .... 847-970-4891 152 F
blupton@usml.edu
LUPTON, Sarah, C ...... 540-375-2068 469 G
lupton@roanoke.edu
LUPU, Peter .... 623-845-3747.. 13 E
peter.lupu@gccaz.edu
LUQUETTE, Heidi .... 503-842-8222 376 D
heidiluquette@tillamookbaycc.edu
LUQUIRE, Heath .... 704-991-0122 338 A
rluquire5455@stanly.edu
LURIA, Valerie .... 718-960-8000 293 E
valerie.luria@lehman.cuny.edu
LURZ, Carol .... 910-938-6343 333 D
lurzc@coastalcarolina.edu
LUSHBAUGH, Jeffery .... 609-777-3083 283 D
jlushbaugh@tesu.edu
LUSHNIAK, Boris, D ..... 301-405-2437 202 E
lushniak@umd.edu
LUSK, Brian .... 540-831-6327 468 E
blusk@radford.edu
LUSK, Carol .... 615-966-5256 420 B
carol.lusk@lipscomb.edu
LUSK, D. Claude .... 806-291-3436 457 B
luskc@wbu.edu
LUSK, Kent 312-553-5628 134M
klusk1@ccc.edu
LUSK, Laurel .... 330-244-4762 363 E
llusk@walsh.edu
LUSSIER, Michel .... 207-741-5519 195 D
mlussier@smccme.edu
LUSSON, Keith .... 312-369-7645 136 C
klusson@colum.edu
LUSTER, Pamela, T ...... 619-388-2721.. 61 A
pluster@sdccd.edu
LUSTER, Stacey .... 508-929-8022 213 D
sluster@worcester.edu
LUSTER-TEASLEY,
Stephanie .... 336-334-7500 341 C
LUTAT, Daniel .... 712-362-0491 166 H
dlutat@iowalakes.edu
LUTCHEN, Kenneth, R ... 617-353-2800 207 C
klutch@bu.edu
LUTER, Gary, S .... 813-258-7283 113 B
gluter@ut.edu
LUTES, David .... 703-284-5993 468 A
david.lutes@marymount.edu
LUTES, Nicholas .... 253-680-7123 477 A
nlutes@batestech.edu
LUTGEN, Roxanne .... 715-675-3331 498 E
lutgen@ntc.edu
LUTGRING, Ray .... 812-488-2589 161 E
rl5@evansville.edu
LUTHE, Brad .... 620-450-2170 176 I
bradl@prattcc.edu
LUTHER, Kathleen .... 314-505-7258 251 D
lutherk@csl.edu
LUTHER, Raminder ...... 978-542-6000 213 B
raminder.luther@salemstate.edu
LUTNER, Rachel .... 216-687-2223 350 G
r.lutner@csuohio.edu
LUTON, Sally .... 315-498-2466 310 C
lutons@sunyocc.edu
LUTRICK, Candace ...... 972-825-4650 444 C
clutrick@sagu.edu
LUTRICK, Donny .... 972-825-4824 444 C
dlutrick@sagu.edu
LUTTJEBOER, Jared ..... 219-864-2400 159 D
jluttjeboer@midamerica.edu
LUTTON, Margaret, K .... 817-515-5140 445 A
margaret.lutton@tccd.edu
LUTTRELL, Cindy .... 919-866-5005 338 E
clluttrell@waketech.edu
LUTUS, Peter, E .... 302-356-6920.. 91 C
peter.e.lutus@wilmu.edu
LUTZ, JR., Ben .... 865-573-4517 419 E
blutz@johnsonu.edu
LUTZ, Bob .... 561-803-2552 105 B
bob_lutz@pba.edu
LUTZ, Brock .... 517-607-2561 224 G
blutz@hillsdale.edu
LUTZ, Bryan .... 740-753-6489 353 G
lutzb@hocking.edu

LUTZ, Carrie .... 812-237-8764 155 H
carrie.lutz@indstate.edu
LUTZ, Cathleen, A ...... 570-321-4069 388 H
lutz@lycoming.edu
LUTZ, John, M .... 615-875-8895 427 B
john.lutz@vanderbilt.edu
LUTZ, Julie .... 706-865-2134 126 D
jlutz@truett.edu
LUTZ, Kimberley .... 843-661-8005 408 G
kimberley.lutz@fdtc.edu
LUTZ, Nate, K .... 612-874-3780 236 G
nate_lutz@mcad.edu
LUTZ, Renee .... 610-758-3383 388 C
e00421@lehigh.edu
LUTZ, Todd .... 254-519-5708 446 C
todd.lutz@tamuct.edu
LUTZ DAVIDSON,
Stacy .... 765-983-1744 154 H
davidst@earlham.edu
LUU, Han .... 575-758-8914 286 A
LUU, SCC, Marie .... 973-957-0188 274 D
studentservices@acs350.org
LUVIS-NÚÑEZ,
Agustina .... 787-763-6700 505 K
decanatura@se-pr.edu
LUX, J.D .... 317-916-7977 158 A
jdlux@ivytech.edu
LUX, Jace .... 270-745-4295 186 A
jace.lux@wku.edu
LUXNER, Catherine .... 570-961-4703 389 B
luxner@marywood.edu
LUXTON, Andrea, T ...... 269-471-3100 220 H
aluxton@andrews.edu
LUZOD, Meghan .... 248-645-3301 222 G
mluzod@cranbrook.edu
LUZURIAGA, Katherine . 508-856-6282 212 A
katherine.luzuriaga@umassmed.edu
LUZURIAGA VOIGHT,
Suzana, H .... 513-556-0364 361 I
susana.luzuriaga@uc.edu
LUZZI, David .... 617-373-4160 217 D
dluzzi@northeastern.edu
LY, Geisce .... 415-267-6521.. 37 C
jly@ccsf.edu
LY, Geisce .... 415-267-6521.. 37 C
gly@ccsf.edu
LY, Janet .... 714-533-1495.. 64 G
janetly@southbaylo.edu
LY, Michael .... 714-867-5009.. 64 H
mcly@southcoastcollege.com
LY, Pearl .... 619-388-2801.. 61 A
ply@sdccd.edu
LY, Vi .... 323-953-4000.. 49 E
lyvk@lacitycollege.edu
LYALL, Rachel .... 610-861-1304 390 D
lyallr@moravian.edu
LYBECKER, Donna .... 208-282-2592 131 H
lybedonn@isu.edu
LYBYER, Debra .... 208-792-2313 131 F
dlybyer@lcsc.edu
LYDEN MURPHY,
Diane .... 315-443-5582 321 D
dlmurphy@syr.edu
LYDING, Linnea .... 602-489-5300.. 10 G
linnea.lyding@arizonachristian.edu
LYDUM, Randi .... 503-838-8094 377 C
lydumr@wou.edu
LYKE, Alan, D .... 719-884-5000.. 82 A
adlyke@nbc.edu
LYKE, Heather, R .... 412-648-8230 400 A
lykeh@pitt.edu
LYKINS, Karen .... 931-372-3636 425 B
klykins@tntech.edu
LYKINS, Karen .... 931-372-3084 425 B
klykins@tntech.edu
LYLE, David .... 740-284-5177 352 I
dlyle@franciscan.edu
LYLES, Kerrin .... 908-737-5170 277 F
lylesk@kean.edu
LYLES, Marcus .... 202-806-6100.. 92 E
marcus.lyles@howard.edu
LYLES, Vell .... 301-846-2429 198 E
vlyles@frederick.edu
LYMAN, Barbara, G ..... 845-257-3280 316 B
provost@newpaltz.edu
LYMAN, Daniel .... 716-286-8788 309 F
dlyman@niagara.edu
LYMAN, Katie .... 319-398-4947 167 H
katie.lyman@kirkwood.edu
LYMANSTALL, Judy ...... 419-783-2300 351 J
jlymanstall@defiance.edu
LYN, Janice .... 985-448-4563 192 C
janice.lyn@nicholls.edu
LYN, Rodney .... 404-413-1133 120 C
ryn1@gsu.edu

LYNCH, Alicia .... 515-271-1457 165 C
alicia.lynch@dmu.edu
LYNCH, Andrea .... 626-256-4673.. 37 D
alynch@coh.org
LYNCH, Andrea .... 609-586-4800 277 H
lyncha@mccc.edu
LYNCH, Bruce, G .... 717-361-1300 383 B
lynchbg@etown.edu
LYNCH, Chad .... 531-622-2929 266 G
celynch@mccneb.edu
LYNCH, Christopher ..... 951-827-6374.. 70 B
christopher.lynch@ucr.edu
LYNCH, Christopher ..... 405-974-2328 370 H
clynch6@uco.edu
LYNCH, Darlene .... 219-980-6614 157 A
darlynch@iun.edu
LYNCH, Deborah .... 407-708-2147 108 B
lynchd@seminolestate.edu
LYNCH, Diane .... 973-761-9175 282 K
diane.lynch@shu.edu
LYNCH, Dianne .... 573-876-7210 259 F
president@stephens.edu
LYNCH, Erica .... 651-638-6543 233 J
e-lynch@bethel.edu
LYNCH, Jacqueline ...... 708-456-0300 151 A
jacquelinelynch@triton.edu
LYNCH, James .... 912-279-5713 117 C
jlynch@ccga.edu
LYNCH, James .... 315-792-5316 306 G
jlynch@mvcc.edu
LYNCH, James .... 508-588-9100 214 F
jlynch@massasoit.mass.edu
LYNCH, Jim .... 912-260-4419 125 B
jim.lynch@sgsc.edu
LYNCH, Joanna .... 502-213-2410 181 H
joanna.morris@kctcs.edu
LYNCH, Joe .... 717-337-6518 384 C
jlynch@gettysburg.edu
LYNCH, Joseph .... 717-871-7821 394 B
joseph.lynch@millersville.edu
LYNCH, Katherine .... 845-574-4743 312 C
katie.lynch@sunyrockland.edu
LYNCH, Katie .... 415-338-7264.. 34 A
katielynch@sfsu.edu
LYNCH, Kelly .... 781-239-4220 205 G
klynch@babson.edu
LYNCH, Laura .... 912-279-4548 117 C
llynch@ccga.edu
LYNCH, Lindsay .... 918-293-5423 368 B
lindsay.lynch@okstate.edu
LYNCH, Malkia .... 757-340-2121 464 L
mlynch@centura.edu
LYNCH, Marilyn, K ...... 972-860-4181 433 G
mklynch@dcccd.edu
LYNCH, Marlon, C .... 517-355-1855 227 C
lynchmc@msu.edu
LYNCH, Michael .... 678-916-2661 115 G
mlynch@johnmarshall.edu
LYNCH, Michael .... 781-239-4528 205 G
mlynch4@babson.edu
LYNCH, Molly .... 703-257-6664 473 G
mlynch@nvcc.edu
LYNCH, Nancy .... 608-262-0866 494 D
nancy.lynch@wisc.edu
LYNCH, Patricia .... 336-334-9725 342 D
pmlynch2@uncg.edu
LYNCH, Patrick .... 870-307-7227.. 20 D
patrick.lynch@lyon.edu
LYNCH, Richard .... 972-708-7340 434 F
dick_lynch@diu.edu
LYNCH, Stacy .... 318-345-9322 188 A
stacyainsworth@ladelta.edu
LYNCH, Stephanie, J .... 202-687-4560.. 92 D
sjl28@georgetown.edu
LYNCH, Stephen, J ...... 401-865-2233 403 G
sjlynch@providence.edu
LYNCH, Timothy .... 718-631-6344 295 H
tlynch@qcc.cuny.edu
LYNCH, Timothy, G ...... 718-982-2400 293 C
president@csi.cuny.edu
LYNCH, Timothy, G ...... 734-764-0304 231 A
timlynch@umich.edu
LYNCH, Valerie .... 217-234-5250 141 H
vlynch@lakelandcollege.edu
LYNCH, Viron .... 941-359-7518 106 J
vlynch@ringling.edu
LYNCH, Viron .... 615-963-5000 425 A
LYNCH, Wayne .... 716-614-5980 309 E
wlynch@niagaracc.suny.edu
LYNCH, Will .... 912-344-2964 120 A
wlynch@georgiasouthern.edu

LYNCH GADALETA,
Margaret, A .... 401-456-8387 404 A
mlynchgadaleta@ric.edu
LYNCH-SOSA, Jill .... 402-472-7488 269 A
jlynch-sosa@nebraskamed.com
LYNDON, Laura .... 510-436-1658.. 45 H
lyndon@hnu.edu
LYNDS, Daniel .... 760-744-1150.. 56 B
dlynds@palomar.edu
LYNETT, Christopher .... 617-243-2211 210 G
clynett@lasell.edu
LYNHAM, Sandra .... 207-741-5923 195 D
slynham@smccme.edu
LYNN, Brent .... 806-291-3672 457 B
lynnb@wbu.edu
LYNN, David .... 405-425-5645 367 C
david.lynn@oc.edu
LYNN, Jeff .... 256-234-6346... 1 G
jlynn@cacc.edu
LYNN, Jolene .... 816-423-4671 166 B
jlynn1@graceland.edu
LYNN, Laura .... 866-492-5336 243 G
laura.lynn@mail.waldenu.edu
LYNN, Mac .... 504-526-4745 190 C
macl@nationsu.edu
LYNN, Marvin .... 503-725-4697 375 D
marvinlynn@pdx.edu
LYNN, Steve .... 803-777-2128 412 A
lynns@mailbox.sc.edu
LYNN, Terence .... 215-641-6300 390 A
tlynn@mc3.edu
LYNN, Vicki .... 501-450-1494.. 19 I
lynn@hendrix.edu
LYNN, Vivian .... 732-255-0400 279 A
vlynn@ocean.edu
LYNNE, Chris .... 602-557-5760.. 16 L
chris.lynne@phoenix.edu
LYON, Brett .... 712-274-5234 168 C
lyon@morningside.edu
LYON, Brooke .... 256-782-5449... 6 A
bbell@jsu.edu
LYON, Greg .... 414-443-8551 497 A
greg.lyon@wlc.edu
LYON, James .... 706-721-8106 115 I
jlyon@augusta.edu
LYON, Jason .... 423-425-4662 426 D
jason-lyon@utc.edu
LYON, Jonathan .... 978-837-5280 216 D
lyonj@merrimack.edu
LYON, L. Andrew .... 714-997-6930.. 36 D
lyon@chapman.edu
LYON, Larry .... 504-282-4455 190 D
LYON, Larry .... 254-710-3588 430 F
larry_lyon@baylor.edu
LYON, Leah .... 580-559-5259 365 J
llyon@ecok.edu
LYON, Mary Eileen ...... 616-331-2221 224 D
lyonme@gvsu.edu
LYON, Matthew .... 865-585-5318 420 A
matthew.lyon@lmunet.edu
LYON, Melissa .... 714-895-8284.. 38 E
mlyon@gwc.cccd.edu
LYON, Misty .... 757-822-7042 474 G
mlyon@tcc.edu
LYON, Mollie .... 515-271-1400 165 C
mollie.lyon@dmu.edu
LYON, Rachele .... 541-888-7259 376 B
rachele.lyon@socc.edu
LYON, Wade .... 620-417-1064 177 C
wade.lyon@sccc.edu
LYONS, Becky .... 406-657-2168 263 H
blyons@msubillings.edu
LYONS, Bridget .... 540-665-4646 470 A
blyons@su.edu
LYONS, Bruce .... 410-455-1000 202 G
blyons@umbc.edu
LYONS, Charles, F ...... 716-878-3026 317 C
lyonscf@buffalostate.edu
LYONS, Cheryl, C .... 501-450-3140.. 23 K
clyons@uca.edu
LYONS, Christine .... 229-226-1621 126 B
LYONS, Cindy .... 434-947-8722 469 A
clyons@randolphcollege.edu
LYONS, Cindy, S .... 858-534-5448.. 70 C
cglyons@ucsd.edu
LYONS, Florence .... 229-500-2805 114 F
florence.lyons@asurams.edu
LYONS, Heather .... 425-640-1088 479 A
LYONS, Heather .... 910-695-3701 337 E
lyonsh@sandhills.edu
LYONS, James .... 408-551-1691.. 63 A
jlyons@scu.edu

LYONS, Jason, C .... 757-594-8175 465 A
jason.lyons@cnu.edu
LYONS, Jered .... 301-891-4481 204 D
jlyons@wau.edu
LYONS, Jeri Annette .... 970-351-1890.. 84 D
jeri.lyons@unco.edu
LYONS, Joseph .... 804-524-6453 475 E
jlyons@vsu.edu
LYONS, Kendall .... 214-818-1311 433 A
klyons@criswell.edu
LYONS, Laura .... 808-956-5971 129 B
lelyons@hawaii.edu
LYONS, Leah, T .... 615-898-2534 421 C
leah.lyons@mtsu.edu
LYONS, Marybeth .... 315-792-7505 320 F
smbl@sunypoly.edu
LYONS, Matt .... 202-664-5703.. 94 D
mlyons@wesleyseminary.edu
LYONS, Melanie, N ...... 616-526-7745 221 L
mnl2@calvin.edu
LYONS, Michael .... 781-239-3000 214 E
LYONS, Patrick, G ...... 973-761-9498 282 K
patrick.lyons@shu.edu
LYONS, Paul .... 909-580-9661.. 34 E
LYONS, Phillip .... 936-294-1634 449 E
icc_pml@shsu.edu
LYONS, Richard, K ...... 510-643-2027.. 68 N
lyons@haas.berkeley.edu
LYONS, Sarah .... 218-733-5975 238 A
sarah.lyons@lsc.edu
LYONS, Sarah .... 800-567-2344 491 C
salyons@menominee.edu
LYONS, Shane .... 304-293-5621 489 E
shlyons@mail.wvu.edu
LYONS, Shawn .... 859-233-8551 185 A
slyons@transy.edu
LYONS, Steve .... 218-723-6167 234 J
slyons@css.edu
LYONS, Tricia .... 781-239-5840 205 E
plyons@babson.edu
LYSIAK, Amber .... 503-251-5747 377 A
alysiak@uws.edu
LYSNE, Josh, D .... 218-299-3645 234 K
jlysne@cord.edu
LYSNE, Marit .... 507-222-4080 234 C
mlysne@carleton.edu
LYSTRUP, Noah .... 408-848-4702.. 43 H
nlystrup@gavilan.edu
LYTHGOE, Maren .... 801-524-8103 458 F
mlythgoe@ldsbc.edu
LYTLE, Anne .... 212-772-4246 294 A
alytle@hunter.cuny.edu
LYTLE, Daniel .... 715-233-5358 497 E
dlytle@cvtc.edu
LYTLE, Dixie .... 361-354-2211 431 L
dalytle@coastalbend.edu
LYTLE, James, R .... 570-586-2400 381 A
jlytle@clarkssummitu.edu
LYTLE, Jesse .... 610-896-1000 385 H
jlytle@haverford.edu
LYTLE, Roy .... 505-566-3990 287 C
lytler@sanjuancollege.edu
LYTTLE, Darylnet .... 757-683-3132 468 C
dlyttle@odu.edu
LYTTLE, Kasey .... 602-489-5300.. 10 G
kasey.lyttle@arizonachristian.edu
LYZUN, Nancy .... 317-940-8029 153 H
nlyzun@butler.edu
L'ALLIER, Kristi .... 763-424-0725 239 D
k.l'allier@nhcc.edu
L'AMOREAUX, Neal .... 330-972-7535 361 G
neal@uakron.edu
L'ECUYER, John .... 304-243-2090 490 F
jlecuyer@wheeling.edu
L'ESPERANCE, Mark ...... 540-568-6572 467 C
lesperme@jmu.edu

M

MA, Cynthia .... 408-532-5567.. 34 F
MA, David .... 972-265-5744 451 E
wma@udallas.edu
MA, Elise .... 516-739-1545 308 E
elise.ma@nyctcm.edu
MA, Jennifer .... 510-464-3420.. 57 B
jenniferma@peralta.edu
MA, Patricia .... 215-965-4069 390 C
pma@moore.edu
MA, Qing .... 626-289-7719.. 24 K
qma@amu.edu
MA, Steven .... 941-782-5946 387 C
sma@lecom.edu
MA, Wei .... 928-532-6164.. 14 L
wei.ma@npc.edu

MA, Wonsuk ... 918-495-6868 368 F wma@oru.edu
MA, Yue ... 773-298-5516 148 I ma@sxu.edu
MAAS, Lyndsay ... 805-965-0581.. 62 M lmmaas@sbcc.edu
MAAS, Paula ... 646-909-2358 307 E maasp@newschool.edu
MAAS, Tammy ... 307-778-1258 500 D tmaas@lccc.wy.edu
MAASJO, Brian ... 212-772-4852 294 A bm514@hunter.cuny.edu
MAASS, Kern ... 504-865-3039 190 A kdmaass@loyno.edu
MABE, Scotty ... 910-410-1684 336 G samabe@richmondcc.edu
MABERY, Dan ... 918-444-2017 366 G mabery@nsuok.edu
MABERY, Mary, V ... 504-526-4745 190 C registrar@nationsu.edu
MABEUS, Amy ... 319-385-6478 167 F amy.mabeus@iw.edu
MABILE, Katherine ... 985-448-4109 192 C katherine.mabile@nicholls.edu
MABOKELA, Reitumetse 217-333-1828 151 F mabokela@illinois.edu
MAC PHERSON, Garry .. 805-893-3132.. 70 E gmacpherson@ucsb.edu
MACADE, Joseph ... 870-307-7229.. 20 D joseph.macade@lyon.edu
MACALESTER, Tom ... 704-461-6721 326 I tommacalester@bac.edu
MACALINTAL, Debbie ... 617-353-3608 207 C dtavares@bu.edu
MACALUSO, Dan ... 325-674-2000 427 G dan.macaluso@acu.edu
MACAPINLAC, Jonas ... 671-735-2944 503 E jmac@triton.uog.edu
MACAPINLAC, Jonas, D 671-735-2944 503 E jmac@triton.uog.edu
MACARTHUR, John ... 661-362-2210.. 51 E jmacarthur@masters.edu
MACARTHUR, John ... 989-463-7241 220 F macarthurjr@alma.edu
MACARTHUR, Sharon ... 718-990-6360 313 B macarths@stjohns.edu
MACAULAY, Barbara ... 508-373-5897 216 B barbara.macaulay@mcphs.edu
MACAULAY, Jennifer, M ... 508-565-1238 218 F jmacaulay@stonehill.edu
MACCARONE, Ellen ... 509-313-4244 479 E maccarone@gonzaga.edu
MACCARONE, Ellen, M . 509-313-6136 479 E maccarone@gonzaga.edu
MACCARTHY, Stephen, J ... 215-898-8724 399 J smaccar@upenn.edu
MACCARTNEY, Danielle . 314-246-7516 261 D dmaccartney@webster.edu
MACCARTNEY, Teresa ... 404-962-3016 127 B teresa.maccartney@usg.edu
MACCHI, Thomas, J ... 215-572-2942 378 E macchit@arcadia.edu
MACCHIARELLA, Sue, A 386-226-7740.. 98 J macchis1@erau.edu
MACCHIAVELLI, Raul, E 787-832-4040 511 C decanodirector.cca@upr.edu
MACCLAREN, Jon ... 802-387-6721 461 E jmacclaren@landmark.edu
MACCLAREN, Jon, A ... 802-387-6721 461 E jonmacclaren@landmark.edu
MACCORMACK, Jennifer ... 206-616-7933 484 A jmaccorm@uw.edu
MACCUISH, Spencer ... 805-581-1233.. 42 C smaccuish@eternitybiblecollege.com
MACCULLOCH, Heather . 646-312-5045 292 F heather.macculloch@baruch.cuny.edu
MACDONALD, Amy ... 919-866-5076 338 E ajmacdonald@waketech.edu
MACDONALD, Ashley ... 207-454-1020 195 E amacdonald@wccc.me.edu
MACDONALD, Beth ... 701-228-2277 345 G beth.macdonald@dakotacollege.edu
MACDONALD, Brian ... 610-282-1100 382 A brian.macdonald@desales.edu
MACDONALD, David, E 419-772-2200 358 D d-macdonald@onu.edu
MACDONALD, Donna, K ... 407-582-5602 113 C dmacdonald8@valenciacollege.edu
MACDONALD, Elizabeth 636-949-4396 254 B emacdonald@lindenwood.edu
MACDONALD, Gregory . 610-330-5069 387 B macdonag@lafayette.edu
MACDONALD, Heather ... 708-344-4700 142 E hmacdonald@lincolntech.edu
MACDONALD, Ian ... 518-458-5396 296 E macdonai@strose.edu
MACDONALD, Jody ... 207-974-4633 195 A jmacdonald@emcc.edu
MACDONALD, Kent ... 989-837-4203 228 G president@northwood.edu
MACDONALD, Kerry ... 802-828-8613 462 E kerry.macdonald@vcfa.edu
MACDONALD, Laura ... 732-571-7563 278 B lembrey@monmouth.edu
MACDONALD, Lauren ... 925-631-4232.. 59 I lmm24@stmarys-ca.edu
MACDONALD, Lisa ... 781-239-3147 214 E lmacdonald@massbay.edu
MACDONALD, Paul ... 843-661-1134 408 H pmacdonald@fmarion.edu
MACDONALD, Randall, M ... 863-680-4165 100 F rmacdonald1@flsouthern.edu
MACDONALD, Sam ... 303-329-6355.. 79 C
MACDONALD, Sarah ... 410-626-2514 201 E skmacdonald@sjc.edu
MACDONALD, Shauna, M ... 610-519-4895 401 B shauna.macdonald@villanova.edu
MACDONALD, Thomas . 617-254-2610 218 A thomas.macdonald@sjs.edu
MACDONALD, William .. 218-299-4358 234 K macdonal@cord.edu
MACDONALD-DENNIS, Christopher ... 413-662-5300 212 F christopher.macdonald-dennis@mcla.edu
MACDONNELL, Lisa ... 313-993-1455 230 H macdonnl@udmercy.edu
MACDONNELL, Tony ... 703-416-1441 465 E campusministry@divinemercy.edu
MACE, Christina, M ... 570-340-6058 389 B cmace@marywood.edu
MACE, Darryl ... 610-796-8300 378 C darryl.mace@alvernia.edu
MACE, Drema ... 304-647-6380 489 C dmace@osteo.wvsom.edu
MACE, Melissa ... 314-529-6857 254 D mmace@maryville.edu
MACE, Melissa ... 816-271-4200 256 C mace@missouriwestern.edu
MACEK, Kate ... 216-421-8019 350 E kemacek@cia.edu
MACELI, Peter ... 914-633-2466 302 C pmaceli@iona.edu
MACEMORE, Kristen ... 336-838-6122 338 H khmacemore969@wilkescc.edu
MACEO, Thandabantu, B ... 317-738-8785 155 A tmaceo@franklincollege.edu
MACERA, Anthony ... 757-822-1071 474 G amacera@tcc.edu
MACEY, David ... 405-974-5605 370 H dmacey@uco.edu
MACFARLAND, Joseph . 410-626-2511 201 E joseph.macfarland@sjc.edu
MACFARLANE, Colin ... 386-822-7256 111 F cmacfarl@stetson.edu
MACFARLANE, Lisa ... 603-862-1234 273 H lisa.macfarlane@unh.edu
MACGILLIVRAY, Diane, N ... 617-373-2520 217 D
MACGILVRAY, Phyllis ... 864-455-6707 412 F phyllis.macgilvray@prismahealth.org
MACGREGOR, Mariam .. 817-257-7088 447 H mariam.macgregor@tcu.edu
MACGREGOR, Teresa ... 904-256-8000 102 G tmacgre@ju.edu
MACH, Thomas ... 937-766-7770 349 C macht@cedarville.edu
MACHA, Barry ... 940-397-6225 439 F barry.macha@msutexas.edu
MACHACEK, Jennifer, L 920-748-8185 493 J machacekj@ripon.edu
MACHADO, Alyson ... 808-544-1126 128 E amachado@hpu.edu
MACHADO, Daniel ... 845-368-7200 314 F
MACHADO, Jessica ... 540-654-1266 471 B jmachado@umw.edu
MACHADO, Jorge, E ... 305-760-7500 103 V
MACHADO, Miguel ... 713-798-4951 430 E
MACHAMER, Ann ... 408-223-6728.. 62 E ann.machamer@sjeccd.edu
MACHAMER, Claire ... 336-770-3293 343 C machamerc@uncsa.edu
MACHANDE, Ken ... 540-654-1457 471 B kmachand@umw.edu
MACHARYAS, Jeff ... 315-684-6646 320 E macharjp@morrisville.edu
MACHEN, Chase ... 903-463-8608 435 H machenc@grayson.edu
MACHEN, Paul ... 210-486-2252 428 C
MACHERY, Edouard ... 412-624-1052 400 A machery@pitt.edu
MACHIA, Michael ... 580-628-6291 366 J michael.machia@noc.edu
MACHIRA, Mary, A ... 801-626-6839 460 B marymachira@weber.edu
MACHLIS, OBM, Gedalyah ... 718-232-7800 325 D
MACHLIS, Gedelyah ... 718-232-7800 325 D
MACHUCA, José, E ... 787-257-7373 509 B jemachuca@uagm.edu
MACHUCA, Yesenia ... 787-710-8999 505 D yesenia.machuca@dewey.edu
MACHUGA, Steve, B ... 860-685-2138.. 90 A smachuga@wesleyan.edu
MACIAS, Benjamin ... 626-914-8611.. 37 B bmacias@citruscollege.edu
MACIAS, Cecilia ... 210-436-3767 442 A cmacias15@stmarytx.edu
MACIAS, Julia ... 314-935-7661 261 B julia.macias@wustl.edu
MACIAS, Sandra ... 650-961-9300.. 55 K smacias@paloaltou.edu
MACIAS, Steve ... 212-650-7551 293 B smacias@ccny.cuny.edu
MACIAS, Tom ... 760-757-2121.. 52 G tmacias@miracosta.edu
MACIAS, Trinidad ... 210-805-2539 452 D trmacias@uiwtx.edu
MACIEL, Anthony ... 760-757-2121.. 52 G amaciel@miracosta.edu
MACIEL, Anthony ... 949-582-4882.. 65 C amaciel@saddleback.edu
MACIK-FREY, Marilyn ... 985-448-4170 192 C marilyn.macik-frey@nicholls.edu
MACINTOSH, Amanda ... 626-584-5201.. 43 E mandymacintosh@fuller.edu
MACINTYRE, Rich ... 215-248-7138 380 G macintyre@chc.edu
MACK, Alicia Graf ... 212-799-5000 303 B
MACK, Anthony ... 213-283-4258.. 36 G amack2@thechicagoschool.edu
MACK, Craig ... 617-732-2929 216 B craig.mack@mcphs.edu
MACK, Deana ... 724-847-6538 384 B dmmack@geneva.edu
MACK, Dwayne ... 859-985-3369 179 E mackd@berea.edu
MACK, Henry ... 229-500-2197 114 F henry.mack@asurams.edu
MACK, Jeffrey ... 229-500-2197 114 F jeffrey.mack@asurams.edu
MACK, John ... 414-425-8300 494 A jmack@shsst.edu
MACK, Joseph ... 607-431-4209 300 G mackj@hartwick.edu
MACK, Kari ... 845-687-5214 322 K mackk@sunyulster.edu
MACK, Kimberly ... 252-536-7273 334 G kmack@halifaxcc.edu
MACK, Qing Lin ... 860-253-3041.. 87 E qmack@acc.commnet.edu
MACK, Rachel ... 859-251-4700 180 C rachel.mack@frontier.edu
MACK, Rob ... 617-627-3323 219 A robert.mack@tufts.edu
MACK, Sherri ... 724-287-8711 379 C sherri.mack@bc3.edu
MACK, Susan ... 513-585-0365 350 A susan.mack@thechristcollege.edu
MACKAY, Cynthia ... 603-342-3054 272 E cmackay@ccsnh.edu
MACKAY, Janet ... 970-675-3276.. 78 P janet.mackay@cncc.edu
MACKAY, Jeff ... 503-883-2278 373 E jmackay@linfield.edu
MACKAY, Jeff ... 503-883-2436 373 E jmackay@linfield.edu
MACKE, Aaron, M ... 651-962-6470 243 F ammacke@stthomas.edu
MACKEITH, Peter ... 479-575-2702.. 21 H mackeith@uark.edu
MACKEN, Jen ... 303-914-6303.. 82 L jen.macken@rrcc.edu
MACKENZIE, Ellen ... 410-955-3540 199 E emacken1@jhu.edu
MACKENZIE, Lorie ... 315-229-5600 313 F lmackenzie@stlawu.edu
MACKENZIE, Lorie, R ... 315-229-5600 313 F lmackenzie@stlawu.edu
MACKERSIE, Chris ... 517-483-1813 226 D mackersc@lcc.edu
MACKESY, Francis, J ... 904-620-2800 111 A f.mackesy@unf.edu
MACKEY, Carl ... 936-468-2222 444 H carl.mackey@sfasu.edu
MACKEY, Geoffrey ... 724-266-3838 399 F gmackey@tsm.edu
MACKEY, George ... 501-374-6305.. 21 B gmackey@shortercollege.edu
MACKEY, Josh ... 928-523-6144.. 14 J joshua.mackey@nau.edu
MACKEY, Matt ... 716-614-6733 309 E mmackey@niagaracc.suny.edu
MACKEY, Roberta ... 850-729-5337 104 L mackeyr@nwfsc.edu
MACKEY, Stephen ... 831-582-4749.. 32 D smackey@csumb.edu
MACKEY, Tonja ... 903-823-3028 445 C tonja.mackey@texarkanacollege.edu
MACKEY, Will, E ... 719-884-5000.. 82 A wemackey@nbc.edu
MACKIE, Jennifer ... 805-765-9300.. 39 E
MACKIE-MASON, Jeffrey ... 510-642-3773.. 68 N jmmason@berkeley.edu
MACKILLOP, Jane ... 718-960-4681 293 E jane.mackillop@lehman.cuny.edu
MACKIN, Brian ... 336-944-6206 342 D bwmackin@uncg.edu
MACKIN, Gail ... 509-963-1403 477 G gail.mackin@cwu.edu
MACKINNON, Fern ... 978-934-4660 211 G fern_mackinnon@uml.edu
MACKINNON, George ... 414-955-2850 492 F gmackinnon@mcw.edu
MACKINNON, Joseph ... 508-362-2131 214 B jmackinnon@capecod.edu
MACKINNON, Neil, J ... 706-721-4014 115 I nmackinnon@augusta.edu
MACKINNON, Thomas .. 570-941-7723 400 C thomas.mackinnon@scranton.edu
MACKINTOSH, Kathryn . 781-283-2335 219 C kmackint@wellesley.edu
MACKLER, Dan ... 818-333-3558.. 53 J dan@nyfa.edu
MACKLIN, Charles ... 425-388-9990 479 B cmacklin@everettcc.edu
MACKLIN, Lisa ... 404-727-1535 118 D lisa.macklin@emory.edu
MACKSEY, Alisa ... 507-457-1469 242 H amacksey@smumn.edu
MACLAINE, Julie, A ... 740-588-1201 364 H jmaclaine@zanestate.edu
MACLAREN, James, M .. 717-867-6211 388 A maclaren@lvc.edu
MACLEAN, Mark ... 715-394-8052 496 D mmaclean@uwsuper.edu
MACLEAN, Sean ... 714-556-3610.. 73 G
MACLENNAN, Kevin ... 303-492-1394.. 83 M kevin.maclennan@colorado.edu
MACLEOD, Jason ... 716-829-7673 298 C macleodj@dyc.edu
MACLEOD, Melissa, A .. 724-458-2050 384 F mamacleod@gcc.edu
MACLEOD, Robert ... 813-974-6015 111 B rmacleod@usf.edu
MACLEOD WALLS, Elizabeth ... 816-415-5026 261 G macleodwallse@william.jewell.edu
MACLURE, Maureen ... 401-598-4470 403 E maureen.maclure@jwu.edu
MACMASTER, Donald ... 989-358-7246 220 G macmastd@alpenacc.edu
MACMILLAN, John ... 831-459-3014.. 71 A jomacmil@ucsc.edu
MACMILLAN FOX, Rebecca ... 305-284-2648 112 K rfox@miami.edu
MACMILLION-WILLIAMS, Jacqueline ... 617-228-3476 214 A jrwillia@bhcc.edu
MACMULLIN, Annette ... 978-837-5000 216 D
MACNEIL, Jacqueline ... 727-864-7856.. 98 G macneijm@eckerd.edu
MACNEILL, Andrew ... 619-388-2799.. 61 A amacneil@sdccd.edu

Index of Key Administrators MACNEILL – MAHAN 767

MACNEILL, Shirley .... 409-984-6365 449 D
macneisb@lamarpa.edu
MACNEW, James .... 267-341-3261 385 I
jmacnew@holyfamily.edu
MACNOW, Andrea .... 203-285-2000.. 86 D
MACON, Kenneth .... 334-523-3670.. 93 H
MACON, Kyle .... 931-393-1623 423 G
kmacon@mscc.edu
MACOPSON, Elmer, R ... 828-652-0603 335 H
elmerm@mcdowelltech.edu
MACPHERSON, Andrew . 319-398-5669 167 H
andrew.macpherson@kirkwood.edu
MACPHERSON,
Heidi, R .... 585-395-2361 317 B
hmacpherson@brockport.edu
MACRAE, Gaylene .... 509-533-7000 478 D
MACRAE, Pamela .... 207-621-3255 196 E
pamela.macrae@maine.edu
MACRO, Venessa .... 515-271-3710 165 F
venessa.macro@drake.edu
MACTAGGART, Julie ..... 563-589-3619 170 C
jmactaggart@dbq.edu
MACUR, Kenneth, M ..... 716-880-2202 305 F
kenneth.m.macur@medaille.edu
MACVEY, Mark .... 760-480-8474.. 75 H
mmacvey@wscal.edu
MACY, Dawn .... 657-278-7450.. 31 E
dmacy@fullerton.edu
MACZKIEWICZ,
Keith, A .... 203-254-4000.. 87 G
kmaczkiewicz@fairfield.edu
MADAIO, Carolyn .... 718-990-6302 313 B
madaioc@stjohns.edu
MADAN, Vibhas .... 215-895-2124 382 D
madanv@drexel.edu
MADANAT, Hala .... 619-594-3754.. 33 E
hmadanat@sdsu.edu
MADAR, Sandra .... 330-829-6129 362 E
madarsi@mountunion.edu
MADAS, Yesenia .... 732-224-2215 275 D
ymadas@brookdalecc.edu
MADDAHI,
Dariush (David) .... 888-243-2493.. 53 G
MADDEN, Christopher .. 214-648-0702 456 D
christopher.madden@utsouthwestern.edu
MADDEN, Danielle .... 202-884-9525.. 94 A
maddend@trinitydc.edu
MADDEN, Dean, R .... 603-646-4091 272 F
dean.r.madden@dartmouth.edu
MADDEN, Fred, H .... 856-415-2272 280 F
fmadden@rcsj.edu
MADDEN, Jennifer .... 503-883-2252 373 E
jrmadden@linfield.edu
MADDEN, Kimberly .... 240-629-7810 198 E
kmadden@frederick.edu
MADDEN, Margaret .... 518-783-2307 314 K
mmadden@siena.edu
MADDEN, Mary Lou ..... 907-796-6050.. 10 C
mlmadden@alaska.edu
MADDEN, Meggan .... 618-374-5155 147 B
meggan.madden@principia.edu
MADDEN, Paul .... 740-351-3270 360 E
pmadden@shawnee.edu
MADDEN, Richard .... 931-363-9844 426 F
rmadden3@utsouthern.edu
MADDEN, Sally, J .... 847-578-3266 148 B
sally.madden@rosalindfranklin.edu
MADDEN, Susan .... 240-567-5274 200 E
susan.madden@montgomerycollege.edu
MADDEN, Susan .... 917-493-4115 304 L
smadden@msmnyc.edu
MADDEN, Vicky, L .... 606-474-3118 180 G
vmadden@kcu.edu
MADDIPATLA,
Krishna, A .... 540-373-2200 465 G
kmaddipatla@evcc.edu
MADDIRALA, James, S . 340-693-1013 512 B
james.maddirala@uvi.edu
MADDOX, Dallas .... 718-990-5249 313 B
maddoxd@stjohns.edu
MADDOX, Gregory, H ... 713-313-7889 448 D
maddox_gh@tsu.edu
MADDOX, Kelley, L .... 770-534-6270 116 C
kmaddox@brenau.edu
MADDOX, Kim .... 479-979-1201.. 24 A
kmaddox@ozarks.edu
MADDOX, Natasha .... 606-759-7141 182 B
natasha.maddox@kctcs.edu
MADDOX, Nedra .... 704-669-4142 333 C
maddox@clevelandcc.edu
MADDOX, Nicole .... 706-880-8243 121 K
nmaddox@lagrange.edu
MADDOX, Rob, W .... 240-895-3000 201 F
rwmaddox@smcm.edu
MADDOX, Tangella .... 917-493-4456 304 L
tmaddox@msmnyc.edu
MADDOX, Timothy .... 252-527-6223 335 E
tdmaddox07@lenoircc.edu
MADDOX-POWELL,
Gloria .... 817-515-5259 445 A
gloria.maddox-powell@tccd.edu
MADDUX, Pat .... 563-588-6366 164 C
pat.maddux@clarke.edu
MADDUX, Susan .... 864-294-2140 408 I
susan.maddux@furman.edu
MADDY, Angela .... 620-792-9226 171 F
maddya@bartonccc.edu
MADDY, Luther .... 208-792-2400 131 F
lmmaddy@lcsc.edu
MADELONE LINCOLN,
Laura .... 607-436-2526 316 C
laura.lincoln@oneonta.edu
MADER, Mary .... 603-641-7174 273 C
mmader@anselm.edu
MADER, Pamela .... 909-621-8856.. 57 E
pamela_mader@pitzer.edu
MADERA, Merilee .... 304-336-8436 489 B
merilee.madera@westliberty.edu
MADERA, Pablo .... 413-265-2278 208 B
maderap@elms.edu
MADERO, Flor .... 325-942-2031 450 B
flor.madero@angelo.edu
MADHIRI, Nicholas .... 817-202-6209 444 B
nmadhiri@swau.edu
MADIA, Sherrie .... 267-341-3348 385 I
smadia@holyfamily.edu
MADIGAN, David .... 617-373-4517 217 D
MADIGAN, Dennis, J .... 617-873-0689 207 E
dennis.madigan@cambridgecollege.edu
MADIGAN, James .... 617-373-3376 217 D
MADIGAN, Karen .... 216-221-8584 357 C
karen.madigan@thencc.edu
MADIGAN, Kay .... 330-652-9919 352 E
kaymadigan@eticollege.edu
MADIGAN, Kaye .... 320-762-4684 236 G
kayem@alextech.edu
MADISON, JR., Chet .... 916-278-6851.. 33 A
MADISON, Maria .... 718-736-3738 207 D
mtm@brandeis.edu
MADISON, Renee .... 315-228-7288 296 C
rmadison@colgate.edu
MADISON, Sean .... 817-515-1002 445 A
sean.madison@tccd.edu
MADISON-CANNON,
Sabrina .... 541-346-1000 376 G
smadison@uoregon.edu
MADLOCK, Calvin .... 510-466-5398.. 57 C
cmadlock@peralta.edu
MADLOCK, Krystal .... 319-352-8434 170 F
krystal.madlock@wartburg.edu
MADOR, Jonathan, M ... 336-841-9370 329 E
jmador@highpoint.edu
MADORE, Brenda .... 432-264-5051 436 H
bmadore@howardcollege.edu
MADORE, Keith .... 860-253-3041.. 86 B
kmadore@asnuntuck.edu
MADORE, Keith .... 860-253-3041.. 87 E
kmadore@acc.commnet.edu
MADORIN, Jeanne .... 336-334-5167 342 D
j_madori@uncg.edu
MADRAMOOTOO,
Narinedat .... 916-484-8108.. 50 J
madramn@arc.losrios.edu
MADRIAN, Brigitte .... 801-422-4122 458 A
brigitte_madrian@byu.edu
MADRID, Carlos .... 671-735-2156 503 E
madridc@triton.uog.edu
MADRID, Shawn, P ...... 505-747-5432 287 C
MADRID, Sol .... 619-388-3549.. 60 I
smadrid@sdccd.edu
MADRIGAL, Alexandra .. 973-803-5000 279 C
amadrigal@pillar.edu
MADRIGAL, Daniel .... 909-607-2760.. 44 K
dmadrigal@hmc.edu
MADRIGAL, Richard ...... 949-359-0045.. 29 C
MADSEN, Jan, E .... 402-280-2131 265 J
janmadsen@creighton.edu
MADSEN, Monte .... 210-688-3101 431 I
MADSEN, Patrick .... 704-687-0784 342 C
pmadsen@uncc.edu
MADSEN, Reva .... 210-688-3101 431 I
MADSEN, Ruthanne ...... 617-824-8600 208 G
ruthanne_madsen@emerson.edu
MADSEN, Thor .... 816-414-3700 255 F
academicdean@mbts.edu
MADSEN-SMITH, Amy ... 563-244-7021 165 H
amadsen-smith@eicc.edu
MADSON, Brieanna .... 801-818-8900 458 M
bmadson@provocollege.edu
MADSON, Greg .... 406-791-5359 264 J
gregory.madson@uprovidence.edu
MADSON, Gregory .... 406-791-5359 264 J
gregory.madson@uprovidence.edu
MADURAMENTE, Althea 718-368-5996 294 C
althea.maduramente@kbcc.cuny.edu
MAEA, Cheri .... 540-834-1980 472 J
cmaea@germanna.edu
MAEDA, Daryl, J .... 303-492-8477.. 83 M
daryl.maeda@colorado.edu
MAEDER, Deb .... 402-481-8065 265 B
deb.maeder@bryanhealthcollege.edu
MAENE, Sara .... 304-876-5112 489 A
smaene@shepherd.edu
MAENNLE, Erin .... 828-689-1435 330 H
erinmaennle1@mhu.edu
MAENZA, Amanda .... 610-861-1342 390 D
maenzaa@moravian.edu
MAESTAS, Ashley, A ..... 719-587-7011.. 77 F
MAESTAS, Belen .... 719-587-7321.. 77 F
bmaestas@adams.edu
MAESTAS, Michael .... 785-864-2277 177 G
mvm1@ku.edu
MAESTAS, Reynaldo ...... 505-454-3323 286 C
reynaldo@nmhu.edu
MAESTAS, Stacy .... 307-778-1240 500 D
smaestas@lccc.wy.edu
MAFFEI, Melody .... 209-667-3623.. 33 D
mmaffei@csustan.edu
MAFFIA, Robert .... 201-216-3542 282 L
robert.maffia@stevens.edu
MAGALDI, Kim .... 601-692-7475 429 B
MAGALDI, Thomas, G .. 646-888-6639 304 H
magaldit@mskcc.org
MAGALLON, Eric .... 626-914-8624.. 37 B
emagallon@citruscollege.edu
MAGANA, Elbi .... 818-677-2121.. 32 E
elbi.magana@csun.edu
MAGAZU, Daniel .... 508-626-4539 212 D
dmagazu@framingham.edu
MAGAZU, Jessica .... 678-331-4276 122 A
jessica.magzu@life.edu
MAGAZZU, Tammi .... 781-768-7291 217 H
MAGBIE-CARR, Shawna 704-886-6500.. 93 H
MAGDZIARZ, Wayne ..... 312-915-6403 142 G
wmagdzi@luc.edu
MAGEE, Colin .... 270-824-8674 182 A
colin.magee@kctcs.edu
MAGEE, Derrick, N .... 919-530-7420 341 D
dmagee@nccu.edu
MAGEE, Edward .... 304-558-0281 488 I
edward.magee@wvhepc.edu
MAGEE, Francy .... 570-372-4134 398 A
mageef@susqu.edu
MAGEE, Jeanette .... 323-241-5274.. 49 I
mageejm@lasc.edu
MAGEE, Jennifer .... 214-637-3530 457 A
jmagee@wadecollege.edu
MAGEE, Michael .... 610-785-2213 396 H
mmagee@scs.edu
MAGEE, Mike .... 415-649-7658.. 52 F
MAGEEHON, Ali .... 541-888-7417 376 B
ali.mageehon@socc.edu
MAGENAU, Keller .... 805-678-5116.. 74 A
kmagenau@vcccd.edu
MAGENNIS, Joe .... 401-598-4467 403 E
joe.magennis@jwu.edu
MAGERS, Ron .... 304-243-8162 490 F
rmagers@wheeling.edu
MAGET, Douglas .... 212-854-5204 290 H
dmaget@barnard.edu
MAGGARD, Bryan .... 337-482-5393 192 F
athleticdirector@louisiana.edu
MAGGARD, Ginger .... 620-862-5252 171 E
MAGGARD, Trent .... 620-862-5252 171 E
trent.maggard@barclaycollege.edu
MAGGART, Christina ..... 765-641-4111 153 D
clmaggart@anderson.edu
MAGGI, Liz .... 415-565-4686.. 69 B
maggiliz@uchastings.edu
MAGGIO, Evelyn .... 718-270-5103 294 E
emaggio@mec.cuny.edu
MAGGIO, Marielena .... 216-368-2519 349 B
mxm346@case.edu
MAGGIONI, Susan .... 781-239-2461 214 E
smaggioni@massbay.edu
MAGGIORE, Ray .... 516-876-2031 318 A
maggiorer@oldwestbury.edu
MAGGITTI, Patrick, G ... 610-519-4521 401 B
patrick.maggitti@villanova.edu
MAGID, Julie .... 317-274-2275 157 B
jmagid@iupui.edu
MAGID, Karen .... 512-505-6479 437 B
kmagid@htu.edu
MAGILL, M. Elizabeth ... 215-898-7221 399 J
president@upenn.edu
MAGINNIS, JR.,
Edward .... 301-405-4939 202 E
maginnis@umd.edu
MAGLARAS,
Constantinos .... 212-854-4240 296 H
cm479@columbia.edu
MAGLOIRE, Yves, M ..... 516-628-5007 318 A
magloirey@oldwestbury.edu
MAGLONE, Alyssa .... 618-393-2982 139 C
maglonea@iecc.edu
MAGNER, Brent .... 402-363-5657 269 F
bnmagner@york.edu
MAGNER, Kevin .... 714-867-5009.. 64 H
kjmagner@southcoastcollege.com
MAGNER, Michael .... 978-837-5019 216 D
magnerm@merrimack.edu
MAGNONI, Dee .... 848-932-7129 281 B
dee.magnoni@rutgers.edu
MAGNUS, Keith, B .... 317-940-9385 153 H
kmagnus@butler.edu
MAGNUSON, Amy .... 850-644-8866 110 B
amagnuson@admin.fsu.edu
MAGNUSON, Chad, M . 863-680-3092 100 F
cmagnuson@flsouthern.edu
MAGNUSON, Kelly, J ... 320-222-6094 239 H
kelly.magnuson@ridgewater.edu
MAGNUSON, Kendyl ..... 760-744-1150.. 56 B
kmagnuson@palomar.edu
MAGNUSSON, Selena ... 706-295-6866 119 F
smagnusson@gntc.edu
MAGO, Pedro .... 304-293-4157 489 E
pedro.mago@mail.wvu.edu
MAGORIAN, Cortney ..... 916-660-7391.. 64 B
cmagorian@sierracollege.edu
MAGORIAN, Kathy .... 605-668-1535 414 F
kathy.magorian@mountmarty.edu
MAGRAS, Aly .... 910-630-7005 331 B
MAGRETTA, Dawn .... 734-462-4400 230 B
dmagrett@schoolcraft.edu
MAGRO, Edward .... 401-232-6528 403 B
emagro@bryant.edu
MAGRO, Kate .... 561-803-2661 105 B
MAGUET, Kathryn, L ..... 570-577-3700 379 A
kathryn.maguet@bucknell.edu
MAGUINA HELLER,
Marie .... 563-589-3115 170 C
MAGUIRE, Brian, L .... 719-333-1707 502 C
brian.maguire@afacademy.af.edu
MAGUIRE, Celia .... 972-438-6932 440 G
MAGUIRE, Mary .... 916-278-7255.. 33 A
maguirem@csus.edu
MAGUIRE, Rachel .... 502-456-0058 184 F
rmaguire@sullivan.edu
MAGUIRE, Robert .... 973-278-5400 274 J
robert-maguire@berkeleycollege.edu
MAGUIRE, Robert .... 973-278-5400 291 A
robert-maguire@berkeleycollege.edu
MAGURK, Michael .... 518-327-6465 310 G
mmagurk@paulsmiths.edu
MAGUSIAK, Henry .... 724-738-4898 394 E
henry.magusiak@sru.edu
MAH, Grace .... 617-228-2182 214 A
gmmah@bhcc.edu
MAHADY, Sarah .... 812-535-5143 160 E
sarah.mahady@smwc.edu
MAHAFFEY, Patricia ...... 858-534-4378.. 70 C
pmahaffey@ucsd.edu
MAHAFFY, Kevin .... 312-329-4134 144 F
kevin.mahaffy@moody.edu
MAHALINGAM,
Shankar .... 256-824-6474.... 8 B
shankar.mahalingam@uah.edu
MAHAN, Christine, P .... 610-341-1706 383 A
cmahan@eastern.edu
MAHAN, Forest, E .... 803-508-7247 405 C
mahanf@atc.edu
MAHAN, Karl .... 806-720-7122 438 F
karl.mahan@lcu.edu
MAHAN, Kim, B .... 806-371-5050 428 F
kbmahan@actx.edu
MAHAN, Lisa .... 317-738-8020 155 A
lmahan@franklincollege.edu
MAHAN, Mickie .... 417-455-5533 251 H
mickiemahan@crowder.edu

MAHANY, Patrick .... 310-665-6995 .. 55 B
pmahany@otis.edu

MAHAR, Alissa .... 503-594-3009 372 B
alissa.mahar@clackamas.edu

MAHAR, Eddie .... 903-785-7661 440 F
emahar@parisjc.edu

MAHAR, Kate .... 530-242-7769 .. 64 A
kmahar@shastacollege.edu

MAHARAJ, Peter, S ..... 619-388-6939 .. 60 H
pmaharaj@sdccd.edu

MAHARAS, Marian .... 303-404-5285 .. 80 I
marian.maharas@frontrange.edu

MAHATO, Jennifer ...... 408-864-8209 .. 42 K
mahatojennifer@fhda.edu

MAHDAVI, Pardis .... 406-243-4689 263 D
pardis.mahdavi@umontana.edu

MAHDY, Ahmed .... 361-825-3881 446 E
ahmed.mahdy@tamucc.edu

MAHDY, Ahmed .... 361-825-5777 446 E
ahmed.mahdy@tamucc.edu

MAHER, Brian .... 212-986-4343 291 A
bdm@berkeleycollege.edu

MAHER, Brian .... 973-278-5400 274 J
bdm@berkeleycollege.edu

MAHER, Brian .... 605-773-3455 415 B
brian.maher@sdbor.edu

MAHER,
Elizabeth (Beth) .... 510-464-3221 .. 57 B
emaher@peralta.edu

MAHER, Hannah .... 309-457-2286 144 E
hmaher@monmouthcollege.edu

MAHER, CM, James ..... 716-286-8350 309 F
president@niagara.edu

MAHER, Jason .... 503-777-7774 375 F
maherj@reed.edu

MAHER, Jeffrey .... 207-725-3178 194 A
jmaher@bowdoin.edu

MAHER, Jerelyn .... 309-676-7611 133 H
jmaher2@fsmail.bradley.edu

MAHER, Jim, M .... 989-964-2222 229 L
jmmaher@svsu.edu

MAHER, John .... 304-696-4748 488 N
maherj@marshall.edu

MAHER, Judith .... 724-805-2581 397 D
judith.maher@stvincent.edu

MAHER, Nicole .... 775-327-8290 270 G
nicole.maher@gbcnv.edu

MAHER, Shannon .... 212-217-4330 299 C
shannon_maher@fitnyc.edu

MAHER, Tracy .... 701-854-8039 346 F
tracy.maher@sittingbull.edu

MAHER, Walter .... 210-829-3939 452 D
maher@uiwtx.edu

MAHER, William, J 716-888-2986 291M
maherw@canisius.edu

MAHFOOD, Stephanie .. 314-246-8610 261 D
smahfood03@webster.edu

MAHINDRA, Ankush .. 310-665-6916 .. 55 B
amahindra@otis.edu

MAHINDRA, Ankush ..... 310-665-6800 .. 55 B
amahindra@otis.edu

MAHITAB, Frank .... 478-825-6754 118 E
mahitabf@fvsu.edu

MAHLBERG, Raye ...... 918-610-0027 365 H
rmahlberg@communitycarecollege.edu

MAHLE-GRISEZ, Lisa .. 513-556-5400 362 B
cmahler@welch.edu

MAHLER, Craig .... 615-675-5292 427 C
cmahler@welch.edu

MAHLMANN, Jaclyn ... 361-825-2321 446 E
jaclyn.mahlmann@tamucc.edu

MAHLMEISTER,
Kenneth, J .... 718-990-5883 313 B
mahlmeik@stjohns.edu

MAHMOOD, Asma .... 919-530-5036 341 D
amahmood@nccu.edu

MAHMOOD, Ghazanfar . 209-490-4591 .. 24 H
gmahmood@advancedcollege.edu

MAHMUD, Faisal ..... 703-993-1000 466 J
mojdeh.mahn@canyons.edu

MAHN, Mojdeh .... 661-362-3346 .. 38 H
mojdeh.mahn@canyons.edu

MAHON, Cathy .... 843-953-5432 407 D
mahonc@cofc.edu

MAHON,
Gwendolyn, M .... 973-972-4892 281 B
mahongm@shp.rutgers.edu

MAHON, James .... 718-960-8675 293 E
james.maho@lehman.cuny.edu

MAHONE-LEIWS,
Gerald .... 254-526-1166 431 E
gerald.mahone-lewis@ctcd.edu

MAHONEY, Angela ...... 336-770-3317 343 C
mahoneya@uncsa.edu

MAHONEY, Erin, A ...... 765-658-4278 154 G
emahoney@depauw.edu

MAHONEY, Jackie ...... 518-694-7305 289 A
jackie.mahoney@acphs.edu

MAHONEY, Joanie ...... 315-470-6681 319 A
jmahoney@esf.edu

MAHONEY, JR., John ... 617-552-3100 207 A
john.mahoney.2@bc.edu

MAHONEY, Kathryn ..... 303-352-6165 .. 80 D
kathryn.mahoney@ccd.edu

MAHONEY, Kevin, B ..... 215-662-2203 399 J
kevin.mahoney@uphs.upenn.edu

MAHONEY, Kim .... 907-786-1110 .. 10 A
kmahone1@alaska.edu

MAHONEY, Leo .... 440-366-7218 355 B
president@sfsu.edu

MAHONEY, Lynn .... 415-338-1381 .. 34 A
president@sfsu.edu

MAHONEY, Melissa ...... 804-862-6100 469 E
mmahoney@rbc.edu

MAHONEY, Peter, E ..... 330-569-5416 353 F
mahoneype@hiram.edu

MAHONEY, Regina .... 910-678-8527 334 C
mahoneyr@faytechcc.edu

MAHONEY, Thomas ..... 609-771-2734 275 J
tmahoney@tcnj.edu

MAHONEY, Trina .... 208-885-4387 132 C
tmahoney@uidaho.edu

MAHONEY, Yemi .... 765-973-8474 156 D
ymahoney@iu.edu

MAHONY, Daniel, F ..... 618-536-3471 149 F
president@siu.edu

MAHONY, James .... 517-264-3525 220 D
jmahony@adrian.edu

MAHOWALD, Rose .... 310-660-3111 .. 41 J
rmahowald@elcamino.edu

MAI, Brent .... 904-620-2615 111 A
brent.mai@unf.edu

MAI, Christy .... 502-863-8031 180 E
christy_mai@georgetowncollege.edu

MAI, Uyen .... 909-274-4121 .. 52 K
umai@mtsac.edu

MAIDEN, Michael ...... 732-263-5285 278 B
mmaiden@monmouth.edu

MAIENSHEIN,
Richard, W .... 215-887-5511 401 E
rmaienshein@wts.edu

MAIER, Kim .... 608-822-2463 498 H
kmaier@swtc.edu

MAIER, Mark .... 517-607-2648 224 G
mmaier@hillsdale.edu

MAIER-O'SHEA,
Kathryn .... 773-244-5582 145 F
kmaier@northpark.edu

MAIKISCH, MaryAnn ... 973-290-4000 282 G
MAILE, Kristin .... 914-395-2560 314 H
kmaile@sarahlawrence.edu

MAILEY, Sharon .... 304-876-5344 489 A
smailey@shepherd.edu

MAILLEY, Kimberly ..... 718-940-5987 313 C
kmailley@sjcny.edu

MAIMONE, Charles ..... 919-515-2155 341 E
camaimon@ncsu.edu

MAIN, Jean .... 860-773-1494 .. 87 E
jmain@tunxis.edu

MAIN, Jean .... 860-343-5751 .. 86 G
jmain@tunxis.edu

MAIN, Nathan .... 269-927-8169 226 B
nmain@lakemichigancollege.edu

MAIN, Sherry .... 949-824-0061 .. 69 C
sherry@uci.edu

MAINE, Kate .... 706-864-1950 126 G
kate.maine@ung.edu

MAINUS, Michael ...... 520-383-0061 .. 16 D
mmainus@tocc.edu

MAIO, James .... 315-792-5401 306 G
jmaio@mvcc.edu

MAISBERGER, Lauren ... 620-901-6218 171 A
maisberger@allencc.edu

MAISENBACHER,
Melissa .... 863-667-5010 108 I
mamaisenbacher@seu.edu

MAISON, Amy .... 229-225-3977 125 G
amaison@southernregional.edu

MAISTO, Jeremy, A ..... 717-867-6215 388 A
maisto@lvc.edu

MAITLAND, Gillian ...... 315-786-2234 302 I
gmaitland@sunyjefferson.edu

MAITLEN, Caitlyn .... 641-782-1453 170 A
maintlen@swcciowa.edu

MAIZE, David .... 210-883-1000 452 D
maize@uiwtx.edu

MAJAK, Julieta .... 845-257-3295 316 B
majakj@newpaltz.edu

MAJCHRZAK, Monika ... 503-847-2626 377 A
mohernandez@uws.edu

MAJEBE, Mary Cissy ... 828-225-3993 328 B
president@daoisttraditions.edu

MAJEED, Hameedah ..... 281-756-3584 428 E
hmajeed@alvincollege.edu

MAJEKOBAJE, Abolade . 503-847-2601 377 A
bmajekobaje@uws.edu

MAJESKI, Mark .... 541-917-4245 373 F
majeskm@linnbenton.edu

MAJETTE, Yolanda ...... 252-398-6249 328 A
majety@chowan.edu

MAJEWSKI, Deborah ... 508-999-9293 211 F
dmajewski@umassd.edu

MAJEWSKI, John .... 805-893-4327 .. 70 E
majewski@ltsc.ucsb.edu

MAJEWSKI, Marc .... 415-338-2596 .. 34 A
majewski@sfsu.edu

MAJEWSKI, Michelle, E 920-923-7617 492 D
mmajewski@marianuniversity.edu

MAJID, Anouar .... 206-221-4447 197 A
amajid@une.edu

MAJKA, David, R .... 412-397-5443 396 E
majka@rmu.edu

MAJOCHA, Kristen ..... 724-938-5891 394 C
majocha@calu.edu

MAJOCHA, Kristen ...... 308-865-8209 268 J
majochak@unk.edu

MAJOR, Blair .... 252-789-0323 335 F
bm07738@martincc.edu

MAJOR, Carla .... 504-762-3003 187 I
cmajor@dcc.edu

MAJOR, Carrie .... 865-251-1800 422 G
cmajor@south.edu

MAJOR, Debbie .... 602-274-1885.. 15 C
dmajor@pihma.edu

MAJOR, Heather .... 215-572-2900 378 E
majorh@arcadia.edu

MAJORS, Cristina ...... 615-550-3170 427 F
cris@williamsoncc.edu

MAJZNER, Kathy .... 561-803-2080 105 B
kathy_majzner@pba.edu

MAKARECHI, Pejman ... 215-503-7841 398 G
pejman.makarechi@jefferson.edu

MAKAROFF, JR.,
Christopher, A .... 513-529-4432 356 A
makaroca@miamioh.edu

MAKATCHE, Jaime ...... 620-242-0487 175 G
makatchej@mcpherson.edu

MAKDISI, John .... 305-474-2418 107 D
jmakdisi@stu.edu

MAKEVICH, John .... 760-757-2121 .. 52 G
jmakevich@miracosta.edu

MAKHIJA, Anil, K .... 614-292-7899 358 E
makhija.1@osu.edu

MAKI, David, W .... 906-227-1262 228 E
dmaki@nmu.edu

MAKI, Kristen .... 508-856-1870 212 A
kristen.maki@umassmed.edu

MAKI, Laura .... 209-575-6173 .. 76 K
makil@mjc.edu

MAKI, William .... 651-201-1732 236 F
MAKI-SCHRAMM,
Roger .... 248-476-1122 227 B
rmaki-schramm@msp.edu

MAKIN, Linda .... 801-863-8457 460 A
linda.makin@uvu.edu

MAKIN, Richard, C ...... 814-359-2793 380 E
MAKINEN, Bryan .... 859-622-2421 180 B
bryan.makinen@eku.edu

MAKINSTER, Jamie ..... 315-781-3304 301 D
makinster@hws.edu

MAKIYA, George .... 832-562-1782 153 B
george.makiya@ace.edu

MAKOW, Grace .... 213-884-4133 .. 24 C
gmakow@ajrca.edu

MAKOWSKI, Susan ..... 609-896-5250 280 D
smakowski@rider.edu

MAKREZ ALLEN,
Heather .... 978-934-4809 211 G
heather_makrezallen@uml.edu

MAKRIS, Sara .... 866-492-5336 243 G
sara.makris@laureate.net

MAKSOUD, Jane .... 212-614-6110 310 H
MAL, Frances .... 973-748-9000 275 C
frances_mal@bloomfield.edu

MAL, Mirlen, A .... 401-865-2430 403 G
mmal@providence.edu

MALAFA, Jeanette ...... 217-652-6467 152 I
j-malafa@wiu.edu

MALAGIERE, Kenneth .. 732-255-0400 279 A
kmalagiere@ocean.edu

MALAGON, Blanca ..... 305-284-2605 112 K
bmalagon@miami.edu

MALAGON, Kelli Jo ...... 213-252-5100 .. 24 C
kmalagon@alu.edu

MALAKLOU, M Shadee 859-985-3953 179 E
malakloum@berea.edu

MALANDRA, Theresa .... 215-951-1619 386 I
malandrat1@lasalle.edu

MALASKI, Donna .... 269-965-3931 225 D
malaskid@kellogg.edu

MALASPINA, Margaret . 860-906-5096 .. 86 C
mmalaspina@capitalcc.edu

MALAT, Heide .... 651-690-6805 242 F
hlmalat@stkate.edu

MALATESTA, Addy ...... 570-408-4020 402 B
adelene.malatesta@wilkes.edu

MALATESTA,
Matthew, J .... 518-388-6026 323 B
malatesm@union.edu

MALAVE, Cesar, O ...... 979-845-2217 446 B
dean@qatar.tamu.edu

MALAVE, Tania .... 787-850-9387 511 B
tania.malave@upr.edu

MALAVE-LASSO, Mara . 787-480-2418 505 A
mamalave@sanjuan.pr

MALAVET, Carmen ..... 787-840-2575 508 G
cmalavet@psm.edu

MALAY, Jacqueline ..... 507-457-5525 241 A
jmalay@winona.edu

MALBAURN, Scott ...... 541-552-8484 376 A
malbaurns@sou.edu

MALBROUGH, Russell . 631-451-4630 320 G
malbror@sunysuffolk.edu

MALCOLM, Amir .... 973-353-3569 281 C
am2777@afc.rutgers.edu

MALCOLM, Everett ...... 904-819-6239 .. 99 D
emalcolm@flagler.edu

MALCOLM, Jacquelyn .. 651-201-1800 236 F
MALCOLM, John .... 617-824-8544 208 G
john_malcolm@emerson.edu

MALCOLM, Kathy ...... 309-796-5038 133 D
malcolmk@bhc.edu

MALCOLM, Laura .... 269-471-3591 220 H
mlaura@andrews.edu

MALCOLM, Lorna, A ..... 212-220-801 .. 292 G
lmalcolm@bmcc.cuny.edu

MALCOLM, Molly Beth . 512-223-7683 429 J
mollybeth.malcolm@austincc.edu

MALCOM-PIQUEUX,
Lindsey, E .... 626-395-1567 .. 29 B
malcom@caltech.edu

MALCZYK, Ben .... 801-524-1958 458 F
benjamin.malczyk@ensign.edu

MALDAR, Mustafa ...... 832-230-5555 439 H
maldar@na.edu

MALDONADO, Amelia ... 787-850-9327 511 B
amelia.maldonado1@upr.edu

MALDONADO, Candice . 325-481-8300 436 H
cdraper@howardcollege.edu

MALDONADO, Carlos ... 760-773-2566.. 39 A
cmaldonado@collegeofthedesert.edu

MALDONADO, Cesar ... 713-718-5059 436 E
cesar.maldonado@hccs.edu

MALDONADO, Gilda .... 619-388-2817.. 61 A
gmaldona@sdccd.edu

MALDONADO,
Gretchen .... 909-607-9671.. 63 E
gmaldona@scrippscollege.edu

MALDONADO, Heather . 315-279-5000 303 D
MALDONADO, Ileana .... 787-725-8120 505 J
imaldonado@eap.edu

MALDONADO, Israel .... 718-270-3161 316 E
israel.maldonado@downstate.edu

MALDONADO, José, E . 787-751-0178 509 A
maldonadoj5@uagm.edu

MALDONADO, Leticia ... 650-949-7777.. 43 A
MALDONADO,
Maria del Carmen .... 787-751-0160 505 C
mcmaldon@cmpr.pr.gov

MALDONADO, Marisela 281-649-3186 436 H
momaldonado@hbu.edu

MALDONADO, Michelle 570-941-7520 400 C
michelle.maldonado@scranton.edu

MALDONADO, Orlando . 787-751-0160 505 C
omaldonado@cmpr.pr.gov

MALDONADO, Victor ... 787-878-5475 506 J
vmaldonado@arecibo.inter.edu

MALDONADO, Víctor ... 787-815-0000 510 D
victor.maldonado1@upr.edu

MALDONADO, Wanda ... 787-758-4417 510 B
rector.rcm@upr.edu

MALDONADO, Wanda ... 787-758-2525 511 D
wanda.maldonado1@upr.edu

MALDONADO, Yesenia . 630-889-6546 145 D
ymaldonado@nuhs.edu

MALDONADO-RIVERA, Irving ... 787-743-3038 508 L imaldonado@sanjuanbautista.edu
MALE, Taylor ... 989-328-1275 227 G taylor.male@montcalm.edu
MALECHA, Ryan ... 731-989-6022 418 H rmalecha@fhu.edu
MALEK RICHARD, Christine, S ... 904-620-3983 111 A christine.malek.richard@unf.edu
MALEKPOUR, Susan ... 865-354-3000 424 D malekpours@roanestate.edu
MALEKZADEH, Ali ... 312-341-3800 148 A amalekzadeh@roosevelt.edu
MALEPEAI-RHODES, Alexis ... 208-562-3505 131 C alexisrhodes@cwi.edu
MALESZEWSKI, Joseph . 850-412-5479 109 E joseph.maleszewski@famu.edu
MALESZWESKI, Amanda ... 518-956-8050 315 D amaleszweski@albany.edu
MALEY, Beth ... 859-344-3356 184 G maleyb@thomasmore.edu
MALEY, Brian ... 513-745-3315 364 F maley@xavier.edu
MALEY, David, C ... 607-274-3480 302 E maley@ithaca.edu
MALFITANO, Gregory, J ... 561-237-7277 103 W gmalfitano@lynn.edu
MALHAS, Faris ... 901-321-3405 417 G fmalhas@cbu.edu
MALHOTRA, Devinder ... 651-201-1638 236 F devinder.malhotra@minnstate.edu
MALHOTRA, Manoj ... 216-368-1156 349 B manoj.malhotra@case.edu
MALHOTRA, Monica ... 661-654-2124.. 30 C mmalhotra1@csub.edu
MALHOTRA, Rishab ... 312-567-3909 139 H rmalhot1@iit.edu
MALIA, Marcia ... 352-588-8242 107 B marcia.malia@saintleo.edu
MALICKEL, Jolly ... 610-399-2032 393 D jmalickel@cheyney.edu
MALIEKAL, Jose ... 585-395-2394 317 B jmalieka@brockport.edu
MALIG, Jannet ... 562-860-2451.. 35 O jmalig@cerritos.edu
MALIGO, Pedro ... 402-826-8221 266 A pedro.maligo@doane.edu
MALIK, Abigail ... 502-863-8209 180 E abigail_malik@georgetowncollege.edu
MALIK, Nish ... 415-405-4105.. 34 A nish@sfsu.edu
MALIK, Samira ... 484-365-7236 388 F smalik@lincoln.edu
MALIK, Zafar, A ... 312-939-0111 137 B zafar@eastwest.edu
MALIN, Burke ... 650-685-6616.. 44 I bmalin@gurnick.edu
MALIN, Jennifer, L ... 620-417-2102 177 C jennifer.malin@sccc.edu
MALINA, Joel, M ... 607-255-9029 297 D joel.malina@cornell.edu
MALINAK, Steven ... 724-503-1001 401 D smalinak@washjeff.edu
MALINOWSKI, Frank ... 229-500-2000 114 F
MALINOWSKI, Gayle ... 802-468-1389 462 H gayle.malinowski@castleton.edu
MALINOWSKI-FERRARY, Sarah ... 201-761-6239 282 H smalinowski@saintpeters.edu
MALISCH, Susan, M ... 773-508-7750 142 G smalisc@luc.edu
MALIWESKY, Martin ... 614-287-2501 351 B mmaliwes@cscc.edu
MALKOWSKI, Keith, J ... 989-774-7226 221 M malko1kj@cmich.edu
MALLABO, Jose ... 470-639-0543 122 H jose.mallabo@morehouse.edu
MALLARD, Cindy ... 731-352-4000 417 C mallardc@bethel.edu
MALLARD, Jessica ... 806-651-2777 447 D jmallard@wtamu.edu
MALLAS, Dave ... 818-947-2508.. 50 B mallasdc@lavc.edu
MALLERY, Mary ... 718-951-5611 293 A mary.mallery@brooklyn.cuny.edu
MALLET, Colleen ... 845-437-5276 323 H comallet@vassar.edu
MALLETT, Chris ... 617-373-6440 217 D
MALLETT, Justin ... 660-562-1517 256 G jmallett@nwmissouri.edu
MALLETT, Robyn ... 773-508-7063 142 G rmallett@luc.edu
MALLETTE, Constance ... 336-750-2703 343 E mallettec@wssu.edu
MALLETTE, Wesley ... 951-827-1012.. 70 B wesley.mallette@ucr.edu
MALLIE, Andre ... 619-260-5951.. 72 H amallie@sandiego.edu
MALLIOS, Peter ... 301-405-9675 202 E mallios@umd.edu
MALLO, Krista ... 727-376-6911 112 F krista.mallo@trinitycollege.edu
MALLOL, Ramon ... 787-765-3560 505 H ramon@edpuniversity.edu
MALLORY, Brian ... 843-521-4137 412 C malloryb@uscb.edu
MALLORY, Caroline ... 812-237-3683 155 H caroline.mallory@indstate.edu
MALLORY, Jeffrie ... 724-805-2770 397 C jeffrie.mallory@stvincent.edu
MALLORY, Jeffrie ... 724-805-2770 397 D jeffrie.mallory@stvincent.edu
MALLORY, Kristen ... 909-621-8267.. 37 G kristen.mallory@cmc.edu
MALLORY, Kristin, L ... 410-334-2813 205 A kmallory@worwic.edu
MALLORY, Lisa ... 404-756-4700 115 E lmallory@atlm.edu
MALLORY, Robert ... 417-625-9574 255 I mallory-r@mssu.edu
MALLORY, Tesia ... 937-529-2201 361 F tmallory@united.edu
MALLOY, Dannel, P ... 207-973-3220 196 C dannel.malloy@maine.edu
MALLOY, Gary ... 843-953-5118 406 D malloyg1@citadel.edu
MALLOY, SR., Quincy ... 910-630-7005 331 B qmalloy@methodist.edu
MALLOY, Sarah, L ... 479-575-6224.. 21 H slmalloy@uark.edu
MALLOY, Stephanie ... 419-998-8854 362 F branding@unoh.edu
MALM, Amy ... 202-651-5005.. 92 B amy.malm@gallaudet.edu
MALM, Loren ... 765-285-1034 153 E lmalm@bsu.edu
MALMBERG, Kyle ... 678-593-3119 124 C kyle.malmberg@point.edu
MALMBERG, Stephanie . 607-778-5404 317 A malmbergsm@sunybroome.edu
MALMGREN, Jodi ... 507-786-3375 242 I malmgren@stolaf.edu
MALONE, Alanna ... 425-235-2426 482 C amalone@rtc.edu
MALONE, Amber ... 618-546-2221 139 C malone@iecc.edu
MALONE, Anne, B ... 412-924-1379 395 G amalone@pts.edu
MALONE, Barbara ... 903-463-8730 435 H maloneb@grayson.edu
MALONE, Brian ... 505-277-8900 288 C bmalone@unm.edu
MALONE, Christopher ... 934-420-2337 320 C malonecj@farmingdale.edu
MALONE, David ... 616-526-6072 221 L dbm9@calvin.edu
MALONE, Derek ... 256-765-4768.... 8 E dmalone3@una.edu
MALONE, Elbert, R ... 803-536-8213 410 H malone@scsu.edu
MALONE, Greg ... 314-246-8249 261 D gregmalone44@webster.edu
MALONE, Gregory ... 216-987-2340 351 D gregory.malone@tri-c.edu
MALONE, Helen ... 614-292-6446 358 E malone.175@osu.edu
MALONE, Judith ... 781-891-2016 206 C jmalone@bentley.edu
MALONE, Katie ... 231-348-6698 228 D kmalone@ncmich.edu
MALONE, Katie ... 612-381-3062 235 C kmalone@dunwoody.edu
MALONE, Laurie ... 513-936-1537 362 A laurie.malone@uc.edu
MALONE, Marc ... 620-276-9597 173 H marc.malone@gcccks.edu
MALONE, Matt ... 620-241-0723 172 H matthew.malone@centralchristian.edu
MALONE, Maureen ... 610-527-0200 396 G maureen.malone@rosemont.edu
MALONE, Michael ... 740-826-8086 356 H mmalone@muskingum.edu
MALONE, Michael, F ... 413-545-5270 211 D mmalone@umass.edu
MALONE, Mike ... 479-575-5606.. 21 H mikem@uark.edu
MALONE, Pamela ... 528-587-2100 320 B pamela.malone@esc.edu
MALONE, Tamra ... 562-777-4085.. 27 E tamra.j.malone@biola.edu
MALONE, Todd, M ... 773-508-3075 142 G tmalon1@luc.edu
MALONE, Travis ... 757-455-3256 476 C tmalone@vwu.edu
MALONE, JR., Walter ... 502-776-1443 184 C wmalone@simmonscollegeky.edu
MALONE-COLON, Linda 757-727-5400 466 L linda.malone-colon@hamptonu.edu
MALONE-HADDOX, Kimberly ... 615-871-2260.. 93 H
MALONEY, Barry, M ... 508-929-8020 213 D bmaloney@worcester.edu
MALONEY, Caroline ... 760-674-7640.. 39 A cmaloney@collegeofthedesert.edu
MALONEY, Catherine ... 617-405-5953 217 G cmaloney@quincycollege.edu
MALONEY, Cory ... 740-283-6944 352 I cmaloney@franciscan.edu
MALONEY, Edward, J ... 202-687-9858.. 92 D ejm@georgetown.edu
MALONEY, Heather ... 513-745-5710 362 A heather.maloney@uc.edu
MALONEY, Kimberly ... 732-255-0400 279 A kmalony@ocean.edu
MALONEY, MyKellann .. 732-923-4770 278 B mmalone@monmouth.edu
MALONEY, Rebecca, S . 504-866-7426 190 E rmaloney@nds.edu
MALONEY, Shari ... 320-762-4466 236 G sharim@alextech.edu
MALONEY, Vinnie ... 803-786-3871 407 E vmaloney@columbiasc.edu
MALOOF, Eric ... 210-999-7824 451 B emaloof@trinity.edu
MALOTKY, Daniel ... 336-272-7102 329 B dmalotky@greensboro.edu
MALOTT, Michelle ... 765-973-8201 156 D mimalott@iue.edu
MALOTT, Richard ... 763-433-1204 236 H richard.malott@anokaramsey.edu
MALOTT, Richard ... 763-433-1204 237 A richard.malott@anokaramsey.edu
MALOY, Frances, J ... 518-388-6739 323 B maloyf@union.edu
MALSIN, Amy ... 212-229-5667 307 E malsina@newschool.edu
MALTA, Anthony ... 318-342-3547 193 A malta@ulm.edu
MALTBY, Marc ... 270-686-4544 182 C marc.maltby@kctcs.edu
MALTER, Dave ... 215-635-7300 384 D admissions@gratz.edu
MALTINO, Frank ... 732-906-2505 278 A fmaltino@middlesexcc.edu
MALVEAUX, Gregory ... 240-567-8077 200 E greg.malveaux@montgomerycollege.edu
MALVEAUX, Julianne ... 323-343-6960.. 32 B julianne.malveaux@calstatela.edu
MALY, Lonn ... 651-641-8203 235 A maly@csp.edu
MALY, Mike ... 312-341-3769 148 A mmaly@roosevelt.edu
MALYN, Justin ... 816-235-5294 260 D malynj@umkc.edu
MAMA, Robin ... 732-571-3607 278 B rmama@monmouth.edu
MAMAN, Yair ... 212-463-0400 322 C yair.maman@touro.edu
MAMAY, Fred ... 973-300-2119 283 B fmamay@sussex.edu
MAMEROW, Geoff ... 814-863-8721 391 F gpm15@psu.edu
MAMISEISHVILI, Kate ... 479-575-3208.. 21 H kmamisei@uark.edu
MAMMEN, Tanya ... 641-673-2123 170 I tanyamammen@wmpenn.edu
MAMMENGA, Brenda ... 605-626-2433 415 H brenda.mammenga@northern.edu
MAMMENGA, Jon ... 605-274-5530 413 G jon.mammenga@augie.edu
MANAGAWANG, Mya, M ... 617-287-5000 211 E mya.mangawang@umb.edu
MANALLA, Christine ... 504-568-2072 189 C cmanal@lsuhsc.edu
MANAUTOU, Teresa ... 787-864-2222 507 B teresa.manautou@guayama.inter.edu
MANAZIR, Theodore ... 802-728-1275 463 D tmanazir@vtc.edu
MANCE, Nick, J ... 618-235-2700 150 B nick.mance@swic.edu
MANCEOR, Thomas ... 313-993-1508 230 H tmanceor@udmercy.edu
MANCERA, Maria ... 909-621-8148.. 63 E mmancera@scrippscollege.edu
MANCHESTER, Rob ... 478-387-4705 119 E rmanches@gmc.edu
MANCHESTER, Shannon, M ... 518-255-5687 318 F manchesm@cobleskill.edu
MANCHESTER-MOLAK, Ann ... 401-865-2055 403 G ammolak@providence.edu
MANCHIN, Mark, A ... 304-462-6100 488 M mark.manchin@glenville.edu
MANCINI, Abigail ... 617-868-9600 210 H
MANCINI, Amy ... 402-562-1267 265 C amandamancini@cccneb.edu
MANCINI, Michael ... 609-984-1105 283 D mmancini@tesu.edu
MANCINI, Michael ... 609-984-1124 283 D mmancini@tesu.edu
MANCINI, Mike ... 574-520-4415 157 C mmancini@iusb.edu
MANCINI, Sarah ... 216-881-1700 358 K smancini@ohiotech.edu
MANCINI, Tracy ... 252-222-6140 332 G mancinit@carteret.edu
MANCINI-BROWN, Darlene ... 860-512-3660.. 86 F dmancini-brown@manchestercc.edu
MANCINO, Mary, S ... 610-861-5415 391 B msinibaldi@northampton.edu
MANCOSH, Bridget ... 412-392-3992 395 H bmancosh@pointpark.edu
MANCUSO, Frani ... 570-941-6200 400 C frani.mancuso@scranton.edu
MANCUSO, Karl ... 215-785-0111 392 O
MANCUSO, Matthew ... 712-325-3434 167 G mmancuso@iwcc.edu
MAND, Claire ... 608-663-3228 491 F cmand@edgewood.edu
MANDA, Vinay ... 918-495-6245 368 F vmanda@oru.edu
MANDAN, Gaurav ... 206-296-6000 483 B gmandan@seattleu.edu
MANDAYAM, Shreekanth, A ... 512-245-2314 449 G elu13@txstate.edu
MANDEL, Gregory, M ... 215-204-2381 398 D gregory.mandel@temple.edu
MANDEL, Jeffrey ... 570-389-4311 393 E jmandel@bloomu.edu
MANDEL, Jennifer ... 207-602-2980 197 A jmandel2@une.edu
MANDEL, Maud, S ... 413-597-4233 220 A msm8@williams.edu
MANDELKERN, Michael 714-432-5786.. 38 F mmandelkern@occ.cccd.edu
MANDEVILLE, Steve ... 314-529-6849 254 D shmandeville@maryville.edu
MANDEVILLE-GAMBLE, Steven ... 951-827-3221.. 70 B steven.mandeville-gamble@ucr.edu
MANDIJA, Brelanda ... 313-577-2027 232 H bmandija@wayne.edu
MANDOLFO, Carleen ... 415-338-2204.. 34 A mandolfo@sfsu.edu
MANDRELL, Jon, D ... 815-835-6344 149 A jon.d.mandrell@svcc.edu
MANDUJANO, Hazel ... 310-665-6976.. 55 B hmandujano@otis.edu
MANDY, Lisa ... 408-864-8403.. 42 K mandylisa@deanza.edu
MANERI, Wendy ... 315-568-3262 309 H wmaneri@northeastcollege.edu
MANESS, Virginia ... 813-988-5131.. 99 M admissions@floridacollege.edu
MANEVAL, Rhonda, E ... 412-578-6115 380 A remaneval@carlow.edu
MANEY, Beth ... 515-244-3146 312 D maneye@sage.edu
MANFERDINI, Elena ... 213-613-2200.. 65 D elena_manferdini@sciarc.edu
MANFRA, Matthew ... 732-987-2478 277 B mmanfra@georgian.edu
MANFREDA, Teresa ... 732-224-2638 275 D tmanfreda@brookdalecc.edu
MANFREDI, Stefan ... 253-566-5000 483 F

MANGAN, Jane 704-894-2878 328 C
jamangan@davidson.edu
MANGAN, William 608-663-2862 491 F
wmangan@edgewood.edu
MANGANARO, Marc 816-271-4200 256 C
MANGAROVA, Nelly 510-592-9688 61 D
nelly.mangarova@npu.edu
MANGELS, Andrew, P 413-545-1581 211 D
amangels@admin.umass.edu
MANGELSDORF,
Sarah, C 585-275-8356 323 E
sarah.mangelsdorf@rochester.edu
MANGELSON, Mike 801-618-0438 458 H
mmangelson@ameritech.edu
MANGHAM, Kirk 757-490-1241 463 E
kmangham@auto.edu
MANGIACAPRA,
Vincent, P 203-932-7058 89 F
vmangiacapra@newhaven.edu
MANGINE, John, J 814-332-4356 378 A
jmangine@allegheny.edu
MANGINO, Christine 718-631-6222 295 B
cmangino@qcc.cuny.edu
MANGIONE, Amy 518-445-2361 289 B
amang@albanylaw.edu
MANGIONE, Lisa 864-250-8461 408 J
lisa.mangione@gvltec.edu
MANGIONE, Terri, L 310-338-3756 51 C
terri.mangione@lmu.edu
MANGLONA, Roland 671-735-5545 503 C
roland.manglona@guamcc.edu
MANGLONA-PROPST,
Daisy 670-237-6792 503 G
daisy.propst@marianas.edu
MANGOLD, Maria 406-243-5600 263 D
maria.mangold@umontana.edu
MANGOLD, Nancy 510-885-3291 31 C
nancy.mangold@csueastbay.edu
MANGOLD, Thomas 401-841-7886 501 L
thomas.mangold@usnwc.edu
MANGUAL, Julio, A 787-766-1717 509 C
jumangual@uagm.edu
MANGUM, Genita, D 717-736-4144 385 A
gdmangum@hacc.edu
MANGUM, Linda 336-285-3769 341 C
lmangum@ncat.edu
MANGUM, Sarah 530-752-2427 69 A
semangum@ucdavis.edu
MANGUM, Steve 865-974-5061 426 C
smangum@utk.edu
MANGUM, Todd 215-386-5000 389 G
tmangum@missio.edu
MANGUM, Vincent 404-756-4006 115 E
vmangum@atlm.edu
MANGUM, William 770-426-2833 122 A
william.mangum@life.edu
MANGUS, Christy 269-782-1473 230 D
cmangus@swmich.edu
MANHARDT, Joseph 207-741-5598 195 D
jmanhardt@smccme.edu
MANI, Nandita, S 413-545-6740 211 D
nsmani@umass.edu
MANIAGO, Vanessa 702-968-2872 271 D
vmaniago@roseman.edu
MANIATIS, Marc 203-932-7200 89 F
mmaniatis@newhaven.edu
MANICKAM, Joseph 620-327-8233 174 B
joseph.manickam@hesston.edu
MANIER, Tracy, L 512-448-8602 441 N
tracym@stedwards.edu
MANIGAULT, Kimberly 412-237-3001 381 C
kmanigault@ccac.edu
MANIGO, Jocelyn 610-436-3238 394 F
jmanigo@wcupa.edu
MANIGO, Venis 803-777-4115 412 A
venis.manigo@sc.edu
MANILAY, Jol 209-946-2236 71 E
jmanilay@pacific.edu
MANION, Amy 262-695-3459 499 A
amanion@wctc.edu
MANION, Andrew, P 608-663-2240 491 F
amanion@edgewood.edu
MANION, Christine 414-297-6508 498 B
manionc@matc.edu
MANION, Sheila, M 314-977-2306 258 H
sheila.manion@slu.edu
MANIS, Christopher 619-388-6546 60 H
cmanis@sdccd.edu
MANIS, Salia 417-873-7543 252 A
smanis@drury.edu
MANISCALCO, Steven 607-436-2735 316 C
steven.maniscalco@oneonta.edu
MANJONE, Joe 251-981-3771 5 B
joe.manjone@columbiasouthern.edu

MANKEY, Richanne, C 419-783-2300 351 J
rmankey@defiance.edu
MANKO, Tammy, P 724-357-2235 393 G
tammy.manko@iup.edu
MANKOWICH, James 205-929-3498 2 H
jmankowich@lawsonstate.edu
MANLEY, Colleen 315-229-5988 313 F
cmanley@stlawu.edu
MANLEY, James 845-451-1760 297 E
james.manley@culinary.edu
MANLEY, Jennifer 360-596-5305 483 E
jmanley@spscc.edu
MANLEY, John 252-335-3266 341 A
jhmanley@ecsu.edu
MANLEY, Lisa 860-913-2078 87 H
lmanley@goodwin.edu
MANLEY, William, J 570-961-4503 389 B
wmanley@marywood.edu
MANLEY-ROOK,
Stephanie 252-493-7383 336 E
sgmrook@email.pittcc.edu
MANN, Andrea 678-225-7507 395 A
andreama1@pcom.edu
MANN, Barbara 678-407-5818 119 B
bmann@ggc.edu
MANN, Brian 813-253-7022 102 A
bmann@hccfl.edu
MANN, Carola 863-583-9050 110 A
MANN, Christy 870-512-7867 18 C
christy_mann@asun.edu
MANN, Daniel 217-333-9299 151 F
danmann@illinois.edu
MANN, Donna 509-828-1348 478 H
dmann@ewu.edu
MANN, Douglas, F 423-775-7201 417 D
dmann7365@bryan.edu
MANN, Eric 251-626-3303 7 E
emann@ussa.edu
MANN, Erin 615-230-3214 424 F
erin.mann@volstate.edu
MANN, Henry, J 614-292-5711 358 E
mann.414@osu.edu
MANN, Janet 202-687-1307 92 D
mannj2@georgetown.edu
MANN, Laura 507-457-5069 241 A
lmann@winona.edu
MANN, Lisa 828-251-6867 342 A
mann@unca.edu
MANN, Lynde 256-228-6001 3 B
mannl@nacc.edu
MANN, Steve 732-247-5241 278 E
smann@nbts.edu
MANN, Terri, L 915-831-5012 435 B
tmann1@epcc.edu
MANN, Thomas 401-232-6977 403 B
tmann@bryant.edu
MANN, Tommy 239-432-7336 100 G
tmann2@fsw.edu
MANNARA, Kevin 585-385-8196 313 A
kmannara@sjfc.edu
MANNELLA, Stephen 610-436-2242 394 F
smannella@wcupa.edu
MANNERING,
Susan, M 302-225-6232 90 I
manners@gbc.edu
MANNINEN, Kevin 906-487-7371 223 I
kevin.manninen@finlandia.edu
MANNING, Amelia 603-314-1416 273 E
a.manning@snhu.edu
MANNING, Beth 810-762-3150 231 C
bmanning@umich.edu
MANNING, Carmen, K 715-836-3671 494 E
manninck@uwec.edu
MANNING, Colleen 713-646-1729 443 C
cmanning@stcl.edu
MANNING, Danielle 508-793-7443 207 F
damanning@clarku.edu
MANNING, Dawn 252-493-7633 336 E
dmanning@email.pittcc.edu
MANNING, Dianne 413-662-5249 212 F
dianne.manning@mcla.edu
MANNING, Gaye 870-574-4509 21 F
gmanning@sautech.edu
MANNING, Heidi 712-749-2243 164 A
manningh@bvu.edu
MANNING, Jessica 214-305-9454 427 G
jxm15c@acu.edu
MANNING, Jessica 325-942-2021 450 B
jessica.manning@angelo.edu
MANNING, John, F 617-495-4601 210 B
jmanning@law.harvard.edu
MANNING, Karen 910-695-3995 337 E
manningk@sandhills.edu

MANNING, Mark 315-498-2268 310 C
m.r.manning@sunyocc.edu
MANNING, Mike 765-674-6901 157 F
mike.manning@indwes.edu
MANNING, Noel, T 704-406-4631 328 I
ntmanning@gardner-webb.edu
MANNING, R. Douglas 714-564-6900 58 F
manning_r-douglas@sac.edu
MANNING, Robert 217-228-5432 147 C
manniro@quincy.edu
MANNING, Scott 570-372-4256 398 A
manning@susqu.edu
MANNING, Stephanie 870-235-4399 21 E
sdmanning@saumag.edu
MANNING, Sylvia, O 323-563-5854 36 E
sylviamanning@cdrewu.edu
MANNING, Tina 912-427-5814 117 B
tmanning@coastalpines.edu
MANNING, Veronica 870-512-7890 18 C
veronica_manning@asun.edu
MANNING, Vivian 360-992-2104 477 J
vmanning@clark.edu
MANNINO, Sam 502-459-3535 184 F
smannino@sullivan.edu
MANNISTO, Richard 414-443-8788 497 A
rich.mannisto@wlc.edu
MANNIX, Kristin 507-281-7770 240 B
kristin.mannix@rctc.edu
MANNO, Kim 740-366-9135 349 D
manno.18@osu.edu
MANNO, Mariann, M 508-856-2323 212 A
admissions@umassmed.edu
MANNS, Jennifer 970-207-4500 84 E
jenniferm@uscareerinstitute.edu
MANNS, Jill, R 260-982-5050 158W
jrmanns@manchester.edu
MANOGIN, Toni, L 225-771-2273 190 K
toni_manogin@sus.edu
MANOLIS, Lilly 617-327-6777 219 G
lilly_manolis@williamjames.edu
MANOR, Mel 850-474-2007 111 E
jmanor@uwf.edu
MANOR, Scott 954-771-0376 103 S
smanor@knoxseminary.edu
MANORD, Wayne 256-352-8116 4 A
wayne.manord@wallacestate.edu
MANORE, David 315-792-7280 320 F
david.manore@sunypoly.edu
MANRING, Noah, D 573-882-0693 260 C
manringn@missouri.edu
MANRIQUE, Santos 620-231-3690 173 F
santosm@fortscott.edu
MANRIQUEZ, Chris 310-243-3655 31 B
cmanriquez@csudh.edu
MANROSE, Mark 310-665-6851 55 B
mmanrose@otis.edu
MANRY, J. Mark 248-218-2120 229 I
mmanry@rochesteru.edu
MANRY, Mark 248-218-2120 229 I
mmanry@rochesteru.edu
MANRY, Robert 785-628-4298 173 E
rjmanry@fhsu.edu
MANSBACH, Jessica 312-915-6000 142 G
mthibeau@luc.edu
MANSDOERFER,
Stephen 800-995-3159 262 A
MANSDORF, Geri 646-592-4550 325 R
geri.mansdorf@yu.edu
MANSELL, Chrisa 662-846-4050 245 A
cmansell@deltastate.edu
MANSER,
Jacqueline, M 330-490-7117 363 E
jmanser@walsh.edu
MANSFIELD, Amy 616-698-7111 222 H
MANSFIELD, Darla 903-677-8822 451 C
dmansfield@tvcc.edu
MANSFIELD, Jerry 614-234-5800 356 E
jerry.mansfield@mchs.com
MANSFIELD,
Michael, P 207-236-8581 195 H
mmansfield@mainemedia.edu
MANSFIELD, Sylvell 404-225-4712 115 F
smansfield@atlantatech.edu
MANSKI, Marion 203-576-4815 89 A
mmanski@bridgeport.edu
MANSO, Jose, R 212-694-1000 291 F
jmanso@boricuacollege.edu
MANSON, Rachel 484-365-7807 388 F
rmanson@lincoln.edu
MANSON, Robert 714-564-6247 58 F
manson_robert@sac.edu
MANSOUR, Deena 406-243-2713 263 D
deena.mansour@umontana.edu

MANSOUR, Nick 602-222-9300 10 I
nmansour@arizonacollege.edu
MANSOUR, Ruchana 347-394-1036 291 B
rmansour@ateret.net
MANSUETO, Anthony 214-860-2693 434 A
anthony.mansueto@dcccd.edu
MANSUR, Jay 859-858-2305 178 G
MANTEL, Dorota, A 718-990-2089 313 B
pienkosd@stjohns.edu
MANTELLA,
Philomena, V 616-331-2100 224 D
president@gvsu.edu
MANTER, Debbie 972-708-7340 434 F
alumni@diu.edu
MANTERNACH, Dean 402-354-7058 267 E
dean.manternach@methodistcollege.edu
MANTHA, Jordan 913-971-3676 175 H
jhmantha@mnu.edu
MANTHE, Theodore, E 507-344-7745 233 I
ted.manthe@blc.edu
MANTHEY, James 816-604-4062 255 B
MANTHEY, Tom 406-657-2085 263 H
tom.manthey@msubillings.edu
MANTLO, Ryan 910-362-7042 332 F
rmantlo@cfcc.edu
MANTOCK, Todd 918-270-6451 368 G
todd.mantock@ptstulsa.edu
MANTON, Mark, H 303-329-6355 79 C
MANTONI, Thomas 610-282-1100 382 A
thomas.mantoni@desales.edu
MANTOOTH, Brooks, E 620-665-3497 174 D
mantoothb@hutchcc.edu
MANTOOTH, James, D 731-881-7053 426 E
jdmantooth@utm.edu
MANTOOTH, Liz 910-362-7067 332 F
lmantooth@cfcc.edu
MANTOVANI, Theresa 407-265-8383 96 H
MANTRANA, Manuel 214-860-3633 434 B
manuelmantrana@dcccd.edu
MANTZ, Erika 603-862-1567 273 H
erika.mantz@unh.edu
MANTZ, Tim 610-902-8765 379 E
tm10760@cabrini.edu
MANUEL, Barbara 276-739-2432 474 H
bmanuel@vhcc.edu
MANUEL, Beulah 301-891-4184 204 D
bmanuel@wau.edu
MANUEL, Bryan 864-646-1763 411 H
bmanuel1@tctc.edu
MANUEL, Elizabeth 304-558-0655 488 I
elizabeth.manuel@wvhepc.edu
MANUEL, Marilyn, G 504-286-5020 191 A
mmanuel@suno.edu
MANUEL, Mark 859-246-6673 181 B
mark.manuel@kctcs.edu
MANUEL, Mary 661-362-3184 38 H
mary.manuel@canyons.edu
MANUEL, Nicole 337-521-8898 188 G
nicole.manuel@solacc.edu
MANUEL, Thomas, E 859-238-5361 179 H
thomas.manuel@centre.edu
MANUEL, Todd 225-578-9000 188 K
MANUEL, Warde 734-764-9416 231 A
wardemanuelad@umich.edu
MANUKIN, Jeff 724-222-5330 391 E
MANULI, Nunziatina, A 718-990-2401 313 B
manulin@stjohns.edu
MANWARING, Kristine 801-422-5281 458 A
kristine_manwaring@byu.edu
MANZANAREZ,
Magdaleno 575-538-6229 288 J
magdaleno.manzanarez@wnmu.edu
MANZANERA, Ignacio 770-426-2873 122 A
ignacio.manzanera@life.edu
MANZANO, Anna 310-665-6951 55 B
amanzano@otis.edu
MANZANO, David 575-835-6997 286 D
david.manzano@nmt.edu
MANZANO, Florentino 818-947-2691 50 B
manzanf@lavc.edu
MANZANO, Lester, J 773-508-7067 142 G
lmanzan@luc.edu
MANZKE, Robert 715-346-3738 496 B
rmanzke@uwsp.edu
MANZO, Dana 352-638-9751 96 B
dmanzo@beaconcollege.edu
MANZO, Pablo 916-856-3400 50 I
manzop@losrios.edu
MAO, Jenny 206-934-3712 482 F
jenny.mao@seattlecolleges.edu
MAPIRA, Happiness 614-251-7641 358 B
mapirah@ohiodominican.edu

MARKOFF, Eliane .... 781-891-3102 206 C
emarkoff@bentley.edu
MARKOVICH, Monica ... 574-239-8405 155 E
mmarkovich@hcc-nd.edu
MARKOVICH, Trevor, L . 517-629-0440 220 E
tlmarkovich@albion.edu
MARKOVITCH, Matthew 707-524-1849.. 63 C
mmarkovitch@santarosa.edu
MARKOW, David .... 802-828-8535 462 E
david.markow@vcfa.edu
MARKOWITT, Xenia ...... 646-909-3647 307 E
markowix@newschool.edu
MARKOWITZ, Carol ...... 504-865-3149 190 A
carol@loyno.edu
MARKOWITZ, Sheila ..... 620-341-5211 173 C
smarkowi@emporia.edu
MARKS, Andrea .... 210-567-7103 455 E
marksa@uthscsa.edu
MARKS, Andy .... 219-473-4323 154 A
amarks@ccsj.edu
MARKS, David .... 201-879-7999 274 I
dmarks1@bergen.edu
MARKS, Dennis .... 503-883-2602 373 E
dmarks@linfield.edu
MARKS, Erica .... 845-257-3240 316 B
markse@newpaltz.edu
MARKS, Farah .... 434-947-8056 469 A
fmarks@randolphcollege.edu
MARKS, Jeffrey .... 760-750-4062.. 33 C
jmarks@csusm.edu
MARKS, John .... 414-382-6360 490 G
john.marks@alverno.edu
MARKS, Laurie .... 414-229-3161 495 B
lmarks@uwm.edu
MARKS, Mary Beth .... 504-280-7014 189 F
mmarks1@uno.edu
MARKS, Michelle .... 303-556-2400.. 84 B
chancellor@ucdenver.edu
MARKS, Nick .... 603-822-5434 273 I
nicholas.marks@granite.edu
MARKS, Patrice .... 908-526-1200 280 C
patrice.marks@raritanval.edu
MARKS, Rachelle .... 410-778-7710 204 E
rmarks2@washcoll.edu
MARKS, Rick .... 325-794-4411 431 J
rick.marks@cisco.edu
MARKSON, Sephora ..... 510-649-2400.. 44 E
MARKULY, Mark .... 206-296-5330 483 B
markulym@seattleu.edu
MARKUM, Michael .... 254-298-8291 445 B
mmarkum@templejc.edu
MARKUSON, Chad .... 218-477-2401 239 A
chad.markuson@mnstate.edu
MARKUSON, Lori .... 847-465-0575 145 C
lori.markuson@nl.edu
MARKWORTH, Ruth ...... 414-425-8300 494 A
rmarkworth@shsst.edu
MARLAIRE, Colin .... 866-776-0331.. 54 E
cmarlaire@ncu.edu
MARLAIRE, Colin .... 866-776-0331.. 54 E
MARLAIRE, Natalyn, M . 715-852-1399 497 E
nmarlaire@cvtc.edu
MARLER, Eric .... 808-675-3708 128 B
eric.marler@byuh.edu
MARLETTE, Marnie, S ... 336-841-4683 329 E
mmarlett@highpoint.edu
MARLEY, Chad .... 307-778-1346 500 D
cmarley@lccc.wy.edu
MARLIN, John .... 973-328-5090 276 A
jmarlin@ccm.edu
MARLOW, Amber .... 715-634-4790 491 L
marlowa@lco.edu
MARLOW, Dan .... 816-279-7000 249 D
dan@abtu.edu
MARLOW, J.J .... 712-274-5424 168 C
marlow@morningside.edu
MARLOW, Mike .... 928-523-5353.. 14 J
mike.marlow@nau.edu
MARLOW, Peter .... 619-260-7460.. 72 H
petermarlow@sandiego.edu
MARLOW, Thomas, J ... 718-390-4352 313 B
marlowt@stjohns.edu
MARLOWE,
Channing, H .... 205-391-2256.... 3 E
cmarlowe@sheltonstate.edu
MARLOWE, June .... 314-991-6245 134 D
jmarlowe@chamberlain.edu
MARLOWE, Wendy, C ... 252-451-8243 336 B
wcmarlowe937@nashcc.edu
MARMARELLI, Beth .... 313-593-5542 231 B
bethmar@umich.edu
MARMO, Michelle .... 717-391-7213 398 E
marmo@stevenscollege.edu

MARMOLEJO, William .. 818-710-2955.. 49 H
marmolwa@piercecollege.edu
MARMOLEJO GOMEZ,
Angela .... 575-492-2573 286 E
amarmolejo@nmjc.edu
MARNEY, Dylan .... 573-288-6351 251 I
dmarney@culver.edu
MARNEY, Katherine ...... 573-288-6478 251 I
kmarney@culver.edu
MARNICH, Darlene .... 412-392-3474 395 H
dmarnich@pointpark.edu
MAROHL, Matthew .... 507-786-3092 242 I
marohl@stolaf.edu
MAROLDO, Brian .... 516-686-7449 308 H
bmaroldo@nyit.edu
MARONEY,
Christopher, S .... 315-684-6465 320 E
maronecs@morrisville.edu
MARONEY, Dustin .... 520-494-5237.. 11 M
dustin.maroney@centralaz.edu
MAROUN, Sarah .... 518-891-2915 309 G
smaroun@nccc.edu
MAROZICK, Jeff .... 415-485-9467.. 39 B
jmarozick@marin.edu
MARPLES, Sarah .... 818-833-3558.. 53 J
sarah.marples@nyfa.edu
MARQUARDT,
Benjamin .... 315-858-0945 301 F
MARQUARDT,
Christopher .... 315-229-5250 313 F
cmarquardt@stlawu.edu
MARQUARDT, Robert .... 405-585-5504 367 B
robert.marquardt@okbu.edu
MARQUARDT, Shelly .... 714-547-9625.. 28 C
smarquardt@calcoast.edu
MARQUES, Ashley .... 843-747-1279 411 C
amarques@sec.edu
MARQUES, Jeffrey .... 413-775-1700 214 C
marquesj@gcc.mass.edu
MARQUES, Joan .... 818-394-3391.. 76 D
joan.marques@woodbury.edu
MARQUEZ, Andrew .... 520-792-1506 457 B
andrew.marquez@wbu.edu
MARQUEZ, Angela .... 303-360-4824.. 80 C
angela.marquez@ccaurora.edu
MARQUEZ, Celia .... 408-848-4800.. 43 H
MARQUEZ, Dianne .... 575-492-2841 286 E
dmarquez@nmjc.edu
MARQUEZ, Jacqueline .. 781-283-2687 219 C
jm100@wellesley.edu
MARQUEZ, Krishna .... 787-746-1400 505 L
kmarquez@huertas.edu
MARQUEZ, Loren, L ...... 757-455-3338 476 C
lmarquez@vwu.edu
MARQUEZ, Mat .... 212-659-3604 303 E
mat_marquez@tkc.edu
MARQUEZ, Monica .... 559-325-5257.. 66 H
monica.marquez@cloviscollege.edu
MARQUEZ, Nelson .... 863-734-1509 113 E
marqueznj@webber.edu
MARQUEZ, Nora .... 650-433-3865.. 55 K
nmarquez@paloaltou.edu
MARQUEZ, Patricia .... 619-260-7795.. 72 H
pmarquez@sandiego.edu
MARQUEZ, Raymond ...... 805-482-2755.. 59 G
rmarquez@stjohnsem.edu
MARQUEZ, Vanessa ...... 925-631-4107.. 59 I
vgm2@stmarys-ca.edu
MARQUEZ-HUDSON,
Christine .... 303-615-0065.. 81 L
cmarqu37@msudenver.edu
MARQUINEZ,
Romualdo .... 904-632-3374 101 A
rmarquin@fscj.edu
MARQUIS, Jenifer .... 252-633-2039 333 F
marquisj@cravencc.edu
MARR, Jay, D .... 502-456-6506 184 F
jmarr@sullivan.edu
MARR, Jena .... 405-422-1265 368 I
jena.marr@redlandscc.edu
MARR, Kelly .... 603-206-8004 272 A
kmarr@ccsnh.edu
MARR, Ronda .... 209-946-2206.. 71 E
rmarr@pacific.edu
MARR, Ryan "Bud" .... 515-643-6679 168 B
rmarr@mercydesmoines.org
MARR, Shannon .... 406-771-4408 264 B
shannon.marr1@gfcmsu.edu
MARRA, Chelsea .... 315-786-6544 302 I
cmarra@sunyjefferson.edu
MARRA, Michele, L .... 740-376-4718 355 E
mm011@marietta.edu
MARRANT, Dale .... 913-234-0612 172 I
dale.marrant@cleveland.edu

MARRAPESE, Patricia .... 607-777-2510 315 E
pmarra@binghamton.edu
MARRERO, Antonio .... 718-951-5000 293 A
MARRERO, Argelio .... 860-906-5125.. 86 C
amarrero@capitalcc.edu
MARRERO, Kyle .... 912-478-5211 120 A
kmarrero@georgiasouthern.edu
MARRERO, Luis, A .... 787-766-1717 509 C
lumarrero@uagm.edu
MARRERO, Rafael .... 787-780-0070 504 E
rmarrero@caribbean.edu
MARRERO, Rene .... 787-841-2000 508 H
rene_marrero@pucpr.edu
MARRERO, Tara .... 510-531-4911.. 57 C
MARRERO, Wilma .... 787-765-1915 507 G
wmarrero@opto.inter.edu
MARRERO CARRER,
Darwin, J .... 787-764-0000 511 F
darwin.marrero@upr.edu
MARRERO DIAS, Rafael 787-783-4125 511 F
rafael.marrero@upr.edu
MARRERO-HERNÁNDEZ,
Angel .... 787-993-8852 510 E
angel.marrero@upr.edu
MARRETT, Clifford .... 860-465-0306.. 85 G
marrettc@easternct.edu
MARRI, Anand .... 765-285-5452 153 E
armarri@bsu.edu
MARRIN, John .... 308-635-6001 269 E
marrinj1@wncc.edu
MARRINER, Nigel, R ...... 716-878-4811 317 C
marrinnr@buffalostate.edu
MARRIOTT, Carol .... 585-343-0055 300 D
cmarriott@genesee.edu
MARRIOTT, Jean .... 410-386-8121 197 G
jmarriott@carrollcc.edu
MARRIOTT, Karin .... 951-487-3060.. 53 A
kmarriott@msjc.edu
MARRIOTT, Martin .... 920-206-2310 492 C
marty.marriott@mbu.edu
MARRIOTT, Taylor .... 785-442-6051 174 C
tmarriott@highlandcc.edu
MARROCCO, Susan .... 941-752-5201 109 C
marrocs@scf.edu
MARROCHELLO, Drew ... 617-353-4631 207 C
marroand@bu.edu
MARRON, Victoria .... 281-425-6501 438 B
vmarron@lee.edu
MARROW, Cary .... 806-894-9611 443 A
cmarrow@southplainscollege.edu
MARRS, Chris .... 979-691-2069 430 I
chris.marrs@blinn.edu
MARRS, III, Ezell, F ..... 317-917-3388 159 B
emarrs@martin.edu
MARRS, Sherrie .... 606-218-5261 185 F
sherriemarrs@upike.edu
MARSALA, Ebony .... 617-552-3300 207 A
ebony.marsala@bc.edu
MARSALEK, Lisa .... 419-783-2587 351 J
lmarsalek@defiance.edu
MARSALIS, Joyce .... 865-354-3000 424 D
marsalisje@roanestate.edu
MARSALIS, Wynton .... 212-799-5000 303 B
MARSCHIK, Celia .... 631-632-7035 316 D
celia.marschik@stonybrook.edu
MARSCHKE, Robyn .... 719-255-3640.. 84 A
rmarschk@uccs.edu
MARSDEN, Janet .... 740-427-5158 354 I
marsden1@kenyon.edu
MARSDEN, John, P .... 859-846-5310 183 G
jmarsden@midway.edu
MARSELIAN, Zareh .... 805-493-3119.. 29 E
marselia@callutheran.edu
MARSH, Anne .... 540-828-8024 464 C
atmarsh@bridgewater.edu
MARSH, Barry .... 843-349-7557 409 A
barry.marsh@hgtc.edu
MARSH, Bonnie .... 724-439-4900 387 H
bmarsh@laurel.edu
MARSH, Brent .... 662-915-7705 248 F
MARSH, Brittany .... 361-570-4350 452 C
marshb2@uhv.edu
MARSH, Cecilia .... 660-359-3948 256 F
cmarsh@mail.ncmissouri.edu
MARSH, Clay, B .... 304-293-1024 489 E
cbmarsh@hsc.wvu.edu
MARSH, Dawn, E .... 517-264-7190 230 C
dmarsh1@sienaheights.edu
MARSH, Douglas, K ...... 574-631-4200 161 G
marsh.14@nd.edu
MARSH, Eric .... 585-785-1293 299 E
eric.marsh@flcc.edu
MARSH, III, F. Chapin . 954-453-9228.. 34 I

MARSH, Geoff .... 562-903-4744.. 27 E
geoff.marsh@biola.edu
MARSH, Geoff .... 810-762-9640 225 F
gmarsh@kettering.edu
MARSH, James, G .... 254-710-2467 430 F
jim_marsh@baylor.edu
MARSH, Janet .... 517-607-2240 224 G
jmarsh@hillsdale.edu
MARSH, Jed .... 609-258-7860 279 E
jmarsh@princeton.edu
MARSH, Jerry .... 570-702-8927 386 D
jmarsh@johnson.edu
MARSH, Jolee .... 910-678-8217 334 C
marshj@faytechcc.edu
MARSH, Marilyn .... 215-324-0746 383 A
mmarsh@eastern.edu
MARSH, Marlee .... 803-786-3932 407 E
mmarsh@columbiasc.edu
MARSH, Maureen .... 410-516-8132 199 E
mmarsh9@jhu.edu
MARSH, Nicole, Y .... 510-379-4053.. 48 G
librarian@lincolnuca.edu
MARSH, Sonja, B .... 937-255-6565 501 A
sonja.marsh@afit.edu
MARSH, Wendy .... 503-517-1220 377 B
wmarsh@warnerpacific.edu
MARSH-PEEK, Angela ... 269-488-4793 225 C
amarshpeek@kvcc.edu
MARSHAK, Sofia .... 425-235-2464 482 C
smarshak@rtc.edu
MARSHALECK, Allison .. 610-341-4375 383 A
amarshal@eastern.edu
MARSHALL, Alycia .... 215-751-8160 381 H
amarshall@ccp.edu
MARSHALL, Alycia .... 410-777-2776 197 C
aamarshall@aacc.edu
MARSHALL, Amy .... 510-986-6984.. 57 B
amarshall@peralta.edu
MARSHALL, Amy .... 706-886-6831 126 C
amarshall@tfc.edu
MARSHALL, Amy .... 716-673-3188 316 A
amy.marshall@fredonia.edu
MARSHALL, Ave .... 404-270-5288 126 A
amarshall@spelman.edu
MARSHALL, Ben .... 813-253-7125 102 A
rmarshall10@hccfl.edu
MARSHALL, Bleuzette .... 513-556-6262 361 I
bleuzette.marshall@uc.edu
MARSHALL, Bryon .... 609-586-4800 277 H
marshalb@mccc.edu
MARSHALL, Cameron .... 434-223-6148 466 K
cmarshall@hsc.edu
MARSHALL, Charles ...... 606-368-6061 178 D
charlesmarshall@alc.edu
MARSHALL, Charles ...... 919-962-1219 342 B
charles.marshall@unc.edu
MARSHALL, Chebon ..... 661-255-1050.. 28 I
cmarshall@calarts.edu
MARSHALL, Christina ... 714-997-6517.. 36 D
cmarsh@chapman.edu
MARSHALL,
Christopher .... 813-529-2640 501 J
christopher.g.marshall4.civ@mail.mil
MARSHALL, Connie ...... 423-279-7632 424 B
cmarshall@northeaststate.edu
MARSHALL, Courtney ... 316-978-3830 178 B
courtney.marshall@wichita.edu
MARSHALL, Darren .... 801-957-4782 460 D
darren.marshall@slcc.edu
MARSHALL, Dave .... 218-235-2135 238 D
dave.marshall@minnesotanorth.edu
MARSHALL, David .... 909-537-5032.. 33 B
dmarshall@csusb.edu
MARSHALL, David .... 912-358-3202 124 H
marshalld@savannahstate.edu
MARSHALL, David, B .... 805-893-2785.. 70 E
david.marshall@ucsb.edu
MARSHALL, Debbie .... 858-695-8587 155 F
dmarshall@horizonuniversity.edu
MARSHALL, Donna .... 252-638-7220 333 F
marshalldo@cravencc.edu
MARSHALL, Ella .... 843-383-8060 407 C
emarshall@coker.edu
MARSHALL, Erica, A ..... 260-359-4290 155 G
emarshall@huntington.edu
MARSHALL, Eugene ...... 757-727-5651 466 L
eugene.marshall@hamptonu.edu
MARSHALL, Filomela .... 609-633-6460 283 D
pmarshall@tesu.edu
MARSHALL, Gabriel ...... 315-312-3214 318 B
gabriel.marshall@oswego.edu
MARSHALL, Isiah .... 757-823-8648 468 B
imarshall@nsu.edu

MARTIN, Joshua ... 508-854-7513 215 D
jmartin@qcc.mass.edu
MARTIN, Joshua ... 972-825-4821 444 C
jmartin@sagu.edu
MARTIN, Joshua ... 740-264-5591 352 B
jmartin@egcc.edu
MARTIN, Juanita, K ... 330-972-7082 361 G
juanita@uakron.edu
MARTIN, Kameelah, L .. 843-953-0675 407 D
martinkl2@cofc.edu
MARTIN, Karen ... 419-289-5604 347 H
kmarti44@ashland.edu
MARTIN, Karla ... 740-264-5591 352 B
kmartin@egcc.edu
MARTIN, Kathleen, A ... 413-748-3070 218 E
kmartin5@springfield.edu
MARTIN, Kathryn ... 573-629-3016 253 D
kathryn.martin@hlg.edu
MARTIN, Kathy ... 540-375-2262 469 G
kmartin@roanoke.edu
MARTIN, Keith ... 918-343-7706 369 A
kmartin@rsu.edu
MARTIN, Keith ... 713-743-1449 451 G
kmartin@uh.edu
MARTIN, Kelsey, A ... 580-327-8478 367 A
kamartin@nwosu.edu
MARTIN, Kenneth, M ... 717-815-1211 402 G
kmartin@ycp.edu
MARTIN, Kevin ... 215-407-0584 392 P
kmartin@pafa.edu
MARTIN, Kevin ... 337-475-5887 192 B
kmartin@mcneese.edu
MARTIN, Kimberly ... 731-352-7646 417 C
martink@bethelu.edu
MARTIN, Kristina ... 617-585-1725 217 A
kristina.martin@necmusic.edu
MARTIN, Lara ... 561-237-7459 103 W
lmartin@lynn.edu
MARTIN, Larry ... 657-278-4380.. 31 E
larrymartin@fullerton.edu
MARTIN, Laura ... 304-877-6428 486 A
financialaid@abc.edu
MARTIN, Leah ... 651-641-8300 235 A
lmartin@csp.edu
MARTIN, Leandra ... 913-722-0272 174 G
leandra.martin@kansaschristian.edu
MARTIN, Linda ... 505-224-4000 285 B
lmartin@cnm.edu
MARTIN, Linda ... 206-934-5300 482 H
MARTIN, Linda, C ... 931-363-9802 426 F
lcmartin@utsouthern.edu
MARTIN, Linda, C ... 865-974-3843 426 B
lcmartin@tennessee.edu
MARTIN, Lisa ... 254-710-2611 430 F
lisa_m_martin@baylor.edu
MARTIN, Lisa ... 864-941-8393 410 D
martin.l@ptc.edu
MARTIN, Lizbeth ... 650-508-3503.. 54 G
president@ndnu.edu
MARTIN, Lori ... 225-578-2031 188 K
lkemp1@lsu.edu
MARTIN, Machelle ... 916-278-6078.. 33 A
martin.machelle@csus.edu
MARTIN, Maegan ... 580-477-7875 371 D
maegan.martin@wosc.edu
MARTIN, Marc ... 510-780-4500.. 48 D
mmartin@lifewest.edu
MARTIN,
Marty (Dewey) ... 314-246-7560 261 D
deweymartin21@webster.edu
MARTIN, Mary ... 541-506-6028 372 E
mmartin@cgcc.edu
MARTIN, Maureen ... 734-647-6000 231 A
mmartin@umich.edu
MARTIN, Melissa ... 607-778-5210 317 A
martinmm2@sunybroome.edu
MARTIN, Micah ... 704-406-2135 328 I
mmartin8@gardner-webb.edu
MARTIN, Michael ... 707-654-1000.. 32 C
MARTIN, Michael ... 216-397-4199 353 O
mmartin@jcu.edu
MARTIN, Michael, V ... 239-590-1055 109 G
president@fgcu.edu
MARTIN, Michelle ... 478-825-6436 118 E
michelle.martin@fvsu.edu
MARTIN, Michelle ... 972-580-7600 430 G
mmartin@bhcarroll.edu
MARTIN, Natalie ... 501-202-6200.. 18 G
MARTIN, Natasha ... 206-398-4039 483 B
nmartin@seattleu.edu
MARTIN, Pat ... 610-328-8451 398 B
pmartin1@swarthmore.edu

MARTIN, Paul, W ... 518-276-8711 311 J
martip@rpi.edu
MARTIN, Paula ... 618-537-6952 143 G
phmartin@mckendree.edu
MARTIN, Rafael, O ... 972-883-3550 454 D
rafael.martin@utdallas.edu
MARTIN, Randy ... 870-972-2093.. 17 I
rmartin@astate.edu
MARTIN, Renee ... 318-626-6730 189 E
sm8267@bncollege.com
MARTIN, Renee ... 303-963-3384.. 78 D
rmartin@ccu.edu
MARTIN, Robert ... 505-424-2301 285 H
rmartin@iaia.edu
MARTIN, Robyn ... 520-515-3688.. 11 O
martinrc@cochise.edu
MARTIN, Ronald ... 773-843-7553 135 C
rmartin@ccc.edu
MARTIN, Roneida ... 847-543-2641 135 G
rmartin@clcillinois.edu
MARTIN, Rosa, L ... 706-821-8365 123 I
rmartin@paine.edu
MARTIN, Rosemary ... 816-604-1587 254 E
rosemary.martin@mcckc.edu
MARTIN, Russell ... 864-941-8669 410 D
martin.r@ptc.edu
MARTIN, Sandra, E ... 870-235-4041.. 21 E
sandrasmith@saumag.edu
MARTIN, Sarah ... 509-533-3680 478 E
sarah.martin@sfcc.spokane.edu
MARTIN, Sean ... 860-439-2058.. 87 F
sean.martin@conncoll.edu
MARTIN, Shaelagh ... 215-368-5000 389 G
smartin@missio.edu
MARTIN, Shane ... 206-296-2595 483 B
martins@seattleu.edu
MARTIN, Sharon, L ... 304-293-9091 489 E
sharon.martin@mail.wvu.edu
MARTIN, Shaun ... 503-338-2393 372 C
smartin@clatsopcc.edu
MARTIN, Sherry ... 910-272-3343 337 A
smartin@robeson.edu
MARTIN, Stacey ... 325-670-1253 436 B
smartin@hsutx.edu
MARTIN, Staci ... 903-983-8651 437 G
smartin@kilgore.edu
MARTIN, Stephanie ... 903-463-8735 435 H
martins@grayson.edu
MARTIN, Steve ... 336-770-3322 343 C
martinw@uncsa.edu
MARTIN, Steve ... 850-478-8496 105 F
smartin@pcci.edu
MARTIN, Steven, J ... 419-772-2277 358 D
s-martin.11@onu.edu
MARTIN, Susan ... 352-588-8117 107 B
susan.martin04@saintleo.edu
MARTIN, Susan, G ... 617-228-2135 214 A
susan.martin@bhcc.edu
MARTIN, Terrence ... 252-246-1251 339 A
tmartin@wilsoncc.edu
MARTIN, Terry ... 479-575-3836.. 21 H
MARTIN, Theodore, D .. 913-684-0014 502 D
MARTIN, Thomas, J ... 413-345-1247 211 D
thojmartin@umass.edu
MARTIN, Thomas, K ... 972-758-3817 432 I
tmartin@collin.edu
MARTIN, Timothy, J ... 515-574-1097 166 G
martin@iowacentral.edu
MARTIN, Timothy, R ... 508-767-7373 205 F
timartin@assumption.edu
MARTIN, Tod ... 501-279-4403.. 19 G
registrar@harding.edu
MARTIN, Todd ... 660-263-4100 256 D
toddmartin@macc.edu
MARTIN, Tom ... 859-622-2334 180 B
tom.martin@eku.edu
MARTIN, Tom ... 361-593-2139 447 A
katdm00@tamuk.edu
MARTIN, Tony, L ... 336-386-3222 338 B
martint@surry.edu
MARTIN, Tracey ... 281-949-1800.. 93 H
MARTIN, Traci ... 410-337-6191 198 G
tmartin@goucher.edu
MARTIN, Tracy ... 602-489-5300.. 10 G
tracy.martin@arizonachristian.edu
MARTIN, Travis ... 734-936-3683 231 A
travislm@umich.edu
MARTIN, Traycee, F ... 229-333-5710 127 C
tmartin@valdosta.edu
MARTIN, Troy ... 617-745-3865 208 F
troy.martin@enc.edu
MARTIN, Troy ... 801-863-8183 460 A
troy.martin@uvu.edu

MARTIN, Vicki ... 803-778-7825 406 A
martinva@cctech.edu
MARTIN, Vicki, J ... 414-297-6320 498 B
martinv@matc.edu
MARTIN, Victor ... 253-879-3902 483 G
vmartin@pugetsound.edu
MARTIN, Walter ... 919-866-5385 338 E
wmartin@waketech.edu
MARTIN, Wayne ... 973-754-7192 279 B
wmartin@pccc.edu
MARTIN, Wes ... 978-869-1122 439 B
MARTIN, Willadean ... 972-860-4817 433 G
wmartin@dcccd.edu
MARTIN-BROWN,
Karen ... 352-371-2833.. 98 D
director@dragonrises.edu
MARTIN-MEJIA, Ana ... 303-340-7567.. 80 C
ana.martin@ccaurora.edu
MARTIN-OSORIO,
Carol, J ... 615-353-3268 424 A
carol.martin-osorio@nscc.edu
MARTIN PARISIEN,
Terri ... 701-477-7862 346 H
tparisien@tm.edu
MARTIN-REND, Jill ... 814-653-8265 379 C
jill.martin-rend@bc3.edu
MARTIN SCOUFIELD,
Ali ... 216-687-2048 350 G
a.martinscoufield@csuohio.edu
MARTIN THORNTON,
Renee ... 951-222-8048.. 59 D
renee.martin-thornton@rcc.edu
MARTIN TSE, Jennifer ... 315-464-4604 316 F
registrar@upstate.edu
MARTIN-VEGA,
Louis, A ... 919-515-2311 341 E
louis_martin-vega@ncsu.edu
MARTINDALE, Judy ... 801-863-8932 460 A
judy.martindale@uvu.edu
MARTINDALE, Trey ... 615-494-8909 421 C
trey.martindale@mtsu.edu
MARTINE, Jason ... 407-618-5900.. 93 H
MARTINE, Jason ... 407-926-2000.. 93 H
MARTINEAU, Jim ... 503-594-3271 372 B
jmartineau@clackamas.edu
MARTINEAU,
Michael, D ... 801-581-7481 459 D
mike.martineau@utah.edu
MARTINELLE, Lorraine .. 413-572-8014 213 C
lmartinelle@westfield.ma.edu
MARTINELLI, Deena ... 203-287-3031.. 88 D
MARTINELLI, Diana ... 304-293-5746 489 E
diana.martinelli@mail.wvu.edu
MARTINELLI, Joseph ... 973-275-2733 282 K
joseph.martinelli@shu.edu
MARTINELLI,
Rosemaria ... 512-471-2694 454 C
rmartinelli@austin.utexas.edu
MARTINELLI-FERNANDEZ,
Susan ... 309-298-1828 152 I
martinelli-fernandez@wiu.edu
MARTINES, Ian ... 210-436-3996 442 A
imartines@stmarytx.edu
MARTINES, James ... 702-651-7488 270 F
james.martines@csn.edu
MARTINEZ, Abelardo ... 787-758-2525 511 D
abelardo.martinez@upr.edu
MARTINEZ, Adrienne ... 303-615-1333.. 81 L
amart475@msudenver.edu
MARTINEZ, Aime ... 305-348-2000 109 H
MARTINEZ, Alicia ... 860-701-5000.. 88 C
martinez_a@mitchell.edu
MARTINEZ, Amy ... 559-934-2203.. 74 L
amymartinez@whccd.edu
MARTINEZ, Angel ... 787-279-1912 506 L
amartinezc@bayamon.inter.edu
MARTINEZ, Art ... 512-499-4296 454 A
amartinez@utsystem.edu
MARTINEZ, Auris ... 787-878-5475 506 J
amartinez@arecibo.inter.edu
MARTINEZ, Brenda ... 510-466-7203.. 57 C
bmartinez@peralta.edu
MARTINEZ, Bunny ... 505-922-2889 285 G
MARTINEZ, Carla ... 714-895-8705.. 38 E
cmartinez@gwc.cccd.edu
MARTINEZ, Carlos ... 817-531-4959 450 F
cmartinez@txwes.edu
MARTINEZ, Carlos ... 210-458-4011 455 B
carlos.martinez.cos@utsa.edu
MARTINEZ, Chanel ... 213-427-2200.. 35 L
MARTINEZ, Charles ... 512-471-7255 454 C
dean.education@austin.utexas.edu
MARTINEZ, Christina ... 806-742-0012 450 C
christina.martinez@ttu.edu

MARTINEZ, Connie ... 210-486-3960 428 B
cacovio@alamo.edu
MARTINEZ, Cristina ... 787-257-0000 510 F
cristina.martinezlebron@upr.edu
MARTINEZ, Cynthia ... 909-607-0121.. 37 I
cynthia_martinez@kgi.edu
MARTINEZ, Debra ... 517-353-3922 227 C
oie.debramartinez@msu.edu
MARTINEZ, Diana ... 630-942-3007 135 F
martinezd59@cod.edu
MARTINEZ, Diana ... 602-285-7821.. 13 H
dr.martinez@phoenixcollege.edu
MARTINEZ, Diana, S ... 210-458-8000 455 B
diana.martinez1@utsa.edu
MARTINEZ, Edward ... 505-454-2500 285 I
MARTINEZ, Edward ... 631-451-4176 321 A
martineze@sunysuffolk.edu
MARTINEZ, Elena, M ... 956-326-2433 446 A
emartinez@tamiu.edu
MARTINEZ, Elias, L ... 512-245-1555 449 G
elm170@txstate.edu
MARTINEZ, Elizabeth ... 505-438-8884 287 J
librarians@acupuncturecollege.edu
MARTINEZ, Elizabeth ... 787-841-2000 508 H
elizabeth_martinez@pucpr.edu
MARTINEZ, Ernie ... 559-265-5711.. 67 A
ernie.martinez@fresnocitycollege.edu
MARTINEZ, Federico ... 305-629-2929 107 F
MARTINEZ, Gayle ... 505-454-2534 285 I
MARTINEZ, Geraldine ... 575-528-7244 287 A
gerri66@nmsu.edu
MARTINEZ, German ... 609-497-7779 279 D
facilities-security@ptsem.edu
MARTINEZ, Gilbert ... 815-836-5442 142 C
gmartinez9@lewisu.edu
MARTINEZ, Glenn ... 210-458-4011 455 B
glenn.martinez@utsa.edu
MARTINEZ, Graciela ... 361-698-1192 434 H
gmartinez@delmar.edu
MARTINEZ, Hector ... 787-284-1912 507 D
hmartin@ponce.inter.edu
MARTINEZ, Hector ... 787-284-1912 507 D
hemart@ponce.inter.edu
MARTINEZ, Jacqueline .. 212-938-5500 319 B
jmartinez@sunyopt.edu
MARTINEZ, Janice, A ... 787-765-1915 507 G
jamartinez@opto.inter.edu
MARTINEZ, Jeffrey ... 909-748-8400.. 72 E
jeff_martinez@redlands.edu
MARTINEZ, Jenny, S ... 650-723-2300.. 66 D
MARTINEZ, Jerry ... 979-532-6965 457 H
martinezje@wcjc.edu
MARTINEZ, Jerry ... 979-230-3215 431 A
jerry.martinez@brazosport.edu
MARTINEZ, Jesse ... 208-885-7716 132 C
jessem@uidaho.edu
MARTINEZ, Jesus ... 787-738-2161 511 A
jesus.martinez5@upr.edu
MARTINEZ, Joaquin ... 443-840-1021 198 D
jmartinez@ccbcmd.edu
MARTINEZ, Jose ... 510-592-9688.. 61 D
jose.martinez@npu.edu
MARTINEZ, JR.,
Jose, F ... 210-832-3294 452 D
jfmartin@uiwtx.edu
MARTINEZ, Juan ... 787-894-2828 511 G
juan.martinez8@upr.edu
MARTINEZ, Juan ... 334-683-2333.... 3 A
jmartinez@marionmilitary.edu
MARTINEZ, Juan ... 716-851-1257 299 A
martinez@ecc.edu
MARTINEZ, Julie ... 815-836-5288 142 C
jmartinez38@lewisu.edu
MARTINEZ, Kara ... 806-716-4600 443 A
kmartinez@southplainscollege.edu
MARTINEZ, Karla ... 773-878-8756 148 F
MARTINEZ, Kate ... 646-745-8328 290 H
kmartine@barnard.edu
MARTINEZ, Kimberly ... 303-861-1151.. 80 E
kmartinez@concorde.edu
MARTINEZ, Kristen ... 617-236-5400 209 D
kmartinez@fisher.edu
MARTINEZ, Kymm ... 651-962-6486 243 F
kymm.martinez@stthomas.edu
MARTINEZ, Lisette ... 215-955-6000 398 G
MARTINEZ, Lissette ... 619-260-4659.. 72 H
lissettemartinez@sandiego.edu
MARTINEZ, Loretta ... 505-277-5035 288 C
lpmartinez@salud.unm.edu
MARTINEZ, Lorna ... 787-766-1717 509 C
lomartinez@uagm.edu
MARTINEZ, Luis, E ... 786-331-1000 104 H
lmartinez@maufl.edu

MASON-GARNER,
Felicia .... 803-780-1259 413 B
fgarner@voorhees.edu
MASON-KINSEY,
Natalie, L .... 818-677-2077.. 32 E
natalie.masonkinsey@csun.edu
MASOUM, Nazi .... 949-794-9090.. 66 C
nazim@stanbridge.edu
MASRI, Safwan, M .... 212-854-8716 296 H
smm1@columbia.edu
MASS, Emily .... 772-462-7361 102 E
emass@irsc.edu
MASS, Gregory .... 973-596-5745 278 G
gregory.mass@njit.edu
MASS-FEARY, Maureen . 585-785-1364 299 E
maureen.massfeary@flcc.edu
MASSA, Gary, R .... 513-745-3335 364 F
massag@xavier.edu
MASSA, James .... 914-968-6200 313 E
bishop.james.massa@archny.org
MASSAGEE, Danielle ..... 719-365-8291.. 83 K
danielle.massagee@uchealth.org
MASSAGUE, Joan .... 646-888-6639 304 H
j-massague@ski.mskcc.org
MASSANELLI, Randy ..... 479-575-7964.. 21 H
jrmassan@uark.edu
MASSARI, Lydia, I .... 787-751-0178 509 A
ac_lmassari@uagm.edu
MASSARO, Chris, J .... 615-898-2450 421 C
chris.massaro@mtsu.edu
MASSARO, Megan .... 212-678-3000 321 H
mrm2276@tc.columbia.edu
MASSARO, Patrick .... 315-386-7838 319 E
massarop@canton.edu
MASSE, Tracy .... 716-839-8504 297 F
tmasse@daemen.edu
MASSELL, Laura .... 802-654-0532 463 A
lxm09190@ccv.vsc.edu
MASSENBURG, Gregg ... 252-246-1386 339 A
gmassenburg@wilsoncc.edu
MASSENBURG,
Shirley, B .... 504-520-5229 193 C
sbmoses@xula.edu
MASSENGALE, Rick .... 870-743-3000.. 20 F
rick.massengale@northark.edu
MASSERINI, John .... 928-523-2672.. 14 J
john.masserini@nau.edu
MASSEY, Anne .... 413-545-9853 211 D
dean@isenberg.umass.edu
MASSEY, April .... 202-274-5194.. 94 B
amassey@udc.edu
MASSEY, Beverly .... 254-442-5116 431 J
beverly.massey@cisco.edu
MASSEY, Carissa .... 717-396-7833 392 Q
cmassey@pcad.edu
MASSEY, Jeff .... 318-473-6423 189 A
jmassey@lsua.edu
MASSEY, John, D .... 817-921-8640 444 D
jmassey@swbts.edu
MASSEY, Jonathan .... 734-764-1315 231 A
drjrm@umich.edu
MASSEY, Julie .... 920-403-3014 494 B
julie.massey@snc.edu
MASSEY, Kristine .... 972-273-3283 434 C
kmassey@dcccd.edu
MASSEY, Laura .... 971-722-7700 375 C
laura.massey@pcc.edu
MASSEY, Michael .... 919-209-2087 335 D
mtmassey@johnstoncc.edu
MASSEY, Rachel .... 504-280-4436 189 F
rdmassey@uno.edu
MASSEY, Tanya .... 806-742-2661 450 C
tanya.massey@ttu.edu
MASSEY-GARRETT,
Tamara .... 334-244-3754.... 4 F
tmassey2@aum.edu
MASSEY-SAMPSON,
Lamonte, J .... 704-216-6933 330 D
sampson@livingstone.edu
MASSIAH-ARTHUR,
Lesley, A .... 718-817-3023 300 A
massiah@fordham.edu
MASSIE, Charles .... 541-880-2339 373 B
massie@klamathcc.edu
MASSINGILL, Judson .... 713-683-3817 442 F
MASSINGILL, Linda .... 713-683-3817 442 F
MASSINI, Stephen, M ... 717-531-6614 391 F
smm83@psu.edu
MASSIS-SANCHEZ,
Judith .... 718-997-5725 295 A
judith.massis-sanchez@qc.cuny.edu
MASSMAN, Joseph .... 816-654-7105 253 I
jmassman@kcumb.edu

MASSOGLIA, Mike .... 336-734-7177 334 D
mmassoglia@forsythtech.edu
MASSOT, Devon .... 407-646-1943 106 L
dmassot@rollins.edu
MASSRI, Al .... 479-619-2202.. 20 G
amassri@nwacc.edu
MAST, Gabriel .... 360-416-7797 483 D
gabriel.mast@skagit.edu
MAST, Maura, B .... 718-817-4700 300 A
mmast@fordham.edu
MAST, Russell, F .... 606-783-2870 183 H
r.mast@moreheadstate.edu
MASTASCUSA, Martin .... 610-526-5266 378 J
mmastasc@brynmawr.edu
MASTEL, Chad, L .... 651-641-8815 235 A
MASTELLER, John, Q .... 805-421-5930.. 67 J
jmasteller@thomasaquinas.edu
MASTER, Sarah, L .... 818-364-7788.. 49 G
mastersl@lamission.edu
MASTERS, Bradley .... 318-345-9239 188 A
bmasters@ladelta.edu
MASTERS, Carolynn .... 401-456-8014 404 A
cmasters@ric.edu
MASTERS, Deborah, C .. 415-338-1681.. 34 A
dmasters@sfsu.edu
MASTERS, Hannah .... 417-667-8181 251 E
hmasters@cottey.edu
MASTERS, Joshua .... 360-792-6050 481 B
MASTERS, Kathy .... 318-342-1022 193 A
masters@ulm.edu
MASTERS, Mark .... 559-323-2100.. 61 G
mmasters@sjcl.edu
MASTERS, Michael .... 706-272-4461 118 A
mmasters@daltonstate.edu
MASTERS, Nicole .... 269-965-3931 225 D
mastersn@kellogg.edu
MASTERS, Peggy .... 256-824-2771.... 8 B
peggy.masters@uah.edu
MASTERSON, Ana .... 928-692-3016.. 14 H
amasterson@mohave.edu
MASTERSON, Dan .... 785-227-3380 171 H
masterson@bethanylb.edu
MASTERSON, Doug .... 601-266-4714 248 H
doug.masterson@usm.edu
MASTERSON, Joshua ...... 502-863-7035 180 E
joshua_masterson@georgetowncollege.edu
MASTERSON, Julie, J .... 417-836-5335 255 J
juliemasterson@missouristate.edu
MASTERSON, JR.,
Thomas, J 989-774-1850 221M
maste1tj@cmich.edu
MASTIN, Lorie .... 360-867-5371 479 C
mastinl@evergreen.edu
MASTON, Tammy .... 716-829-7810 298 C
mastont@dyc.edu
MASTRANGELO, Ryan .... 207-778-7048 196 F
ryan.mastrangelo@maine.edu
MASTRO, Denise .... 619-298-1829.. 65 J
MASUCCI, Michele, M ... 215-204-6875 398 D
michele.masucci@temple.edu
MASUDA, Danielle .... 808-735-4718 128 C
danielle.masuda@chaminade.edu
MASZAROS, Sue .... 615-460-5496 417 B
sue.maszaros@belmont.edu
MASZCZAK, Melissa, A 609-777-5660 283 D
mmaszczak@tesu.edu
MATA, Carolyn .... 404-364-8320 123 G
cmata@oglethorpe.edu
MATA, Daniel .... 208-376-7731 130 E
dmata@boisebible.edu
MATA, Luis .... 615-244-5848 422 E
MATA, Margot .... 830-591-7223 443 I
mhmata@swtjc.edu
MATA, Sara .... 316-942-4291 176 B
matas@newmanu.edu
MATANYI, Eric .... 708-209-3255 136 D
eric.mantanyi@cuchicago.edu
MATAS, Francine .... 805-969-3626.. 55 I
fmatas@pacifica.edu
MATAVA, Robert, J .... 703-658-4304 464 O
rmatava@christendom.edu
MATCHAN, Steven .... 626-585-7489.. 56 D
sxmatchan@pasadena.edu
MATCHETT, Laura .... 231-995-1704 228 F
lmatchett@nmc.edu
MATCHIN, Patricia .... 575-624-8203 286 F
matchin@nmmi.edu
MATEJCIK, Mark, M ...... 216-916-7515 354 A
mmatejci@kent.edu
MATEN, Lionel .... 662-915-7705 248 F
lmaten@olemiss.edu

MATEO, Aurorisa .... 787-743-7979 509 D
amateo@suagm.edu
MATEO, Frances .... 623-845-3147.. 13 E
frances.mateo@gccaz.edu
MATERRE, Denise, W .... 413-585-2025 218 D
dmaterre@smith.edu
MATES, Ilene .... 610-436-2128 394 F
emates@wcupa.edu
MATETZSCHK-CAMPBELL,
Judy .... 512-404-4830 429 K
jmatetzschk-campbell@austinseminary.edu
MATHAI, Cynthia .... 503-517-1810 377 D
cmathai@westernseminary.edu
MATHEMA,
Shubhashish .... 603-542-7744 272 D
smathema@ccsnh.edu
MATHENA, Cindy .... 605-394-4800 414 G
MATHENEY, H. Scott ..... 630-617-3025 137 E
hscottm@elmhurst.edu
MATHENY, Chris .... 920-735-5731 497 F
matheny@fvtc.edu
MATHENY, Jacqueline .. 716-827-2450 322 J
mathenyj@trocaire.edu
MATHENY, Samuel .... 215-871-6170 395 A
samuelmat@pcom.edu
MATHENY, Stephen .... 828-395-1293 335 B
smatheny@isothermal.edu
MATHER, Claudia .... 855-239-1886 171 F
matherc@bartonccc.edu
MATHERLY, Barron .... 919-962-1091 342 B
matherly@unc.edu
MATHERLY, Cheryl, A .... 610-758-2981 388 C
cam716@lehigh.edu
MATHERN, Rebecca .... 541-737-4331 374 H
rebecca.mathern@oregonstate.edu
MATHES, Cassie .... 423-425-4363 426 D
cassie-mathes@utc.edu
MATHES, Hannah .... 309-268-8019 138 F
hannah.mathes@heartland.edu
MATHES, Kevin .... 570-577-1446 379 A
kmathes@bucknell.edu
MATHESON, Regina, M .. 563-333-5838 169 D
mathesonreginam@sau.edu
MATHEW, Roy .... 915-747-5117 454 E
rmathew@utep.edu
MATHEWS, Angela .... 507-786-3231 242 I
mathews@stolaf.edu
MATHEWS, Becky .... 785-833-4303 175 C
becky.mathews@kwu.edu
MATHEWS, Bruce .... 808-932-7036 129 A
bmathews@hawaii.edu
MATHEWS, Christopher 952-446-4202 235 B
mathewsc@crown.edu
MATHEWS, Darren .... 941-309-4058 106 J
dmathews@ringling.edu
MATHEWS, Gary .... 512-404-4806 429 K
gmathews@austinseminary.edu
MATHEWS, Georgia .... 478-289-2112 118 B
gmathews@ega.edu
MATHEWS, Jennifer .... 508-565-1915 218 F
jmathews@stonehill.edu
MATHEWS, John .... 215-968-8211 379 B
john.mathews@bucks.edu
MATHEWS, Josh .... 503-517-1876 377 D
jmathews@westernseminary.edu
MATHEWS, Karen .... 937-376-6076 349 H
kmathews@centralstate.edu
MATHEWS, Kimberly .... 714-564-6224.. 58 F
mathews_kimberly@sac.edu
MATHEWS, Lakeisha ...... 410-837-4030 204 C
lmathews@ubalt.edu
MATHEWS, Marc .... 859-233-8100 185 A
mmathews@transy.edu
MATHEWS, Mark .... 419-995-8200 360 B
mathews.m@rhodesstate.edu
MATHEWS, Marsha .... 865-882-4517 424 D
mathewsmr@roanestate.edu
MATHEWS, Michael .... 918-495-6812 368 F
mmathews@oru.edu
MATHEWS, Michael .... 303-333-4224.. 11 C
MATHEWS, Mike .... 971-722-2831 375 C
mike.mathews@pcc.edu
MATHEWS, Rajan, G ...... 646-378-6153 289 F
president@nyack.edu
MATHEWS, Rebecca .... 781-292-2376 209 E
rmathews@olin.edu
MATHEWS, Robert .... 920-498-5701 498 F
robert.mathews@nwtc.edu
MATHEWSON, Dan, B ... 864-597-4560 413 E
mathewsondb@wofford.edu
MATHIA, Sarah .... 785-227-3380 171 H
mathiaak@bethanylb.edu

MATHIAS, Duane, A ...... 719-884-5000.. 82 A
damathias@nbc.edu
MATHIAS, James .... 360-676-2772 480 G
jlmathias@nwic.edu
MATHIAS, Jim, N .... 410-651-7789 203 B
jnmathias@umes.edu
MATHIAS, Michael .... 301-687-4120 203 F
mbmathias@frostburg.edu
MATHIESEN, Gaylan .... 218-739-3375 236 B
gmathiesen@lbs.edu
MATHIEU, Dickens .... 860-297-2253.. 88 I
dickens.mathieu@trincoll.edu
MATHIEU, Rick .... 704-337-2701 339 D
mathieur@queens.edu
MATHIS, Clay, P .... 361-593-5400 447 A
clay.mathis@tamuk.edu
MATHIS, Jennifer .... 870-759-4139.. 24 B
jmathis@williamsbu.edu
MATHIS, Jennifer, M ..... 864-388-8307 409 B
jmathis@lander.edu
MATHIS, Jim .... 307-742-3776 500 K
jmathis@wyotech.edu
MATHIS, Kassie .... 334-347-2623.... 2 A
kmathis@escc.edu
MATHIS, Malissa .... 501-916-3110.. 22 C
mktrantham@ualr.edu
MATHIS, Maureen .... 610-660-1306 397 A
mmathis@sju.edu
MATHIS, Mia .... 410-888-9048 200 C
MATHIS, Michael .... 817-735-0224 453 D
michael.mathis@unthsc.edu
MATHIS, Michele, W ..... 336-322-2237 336 D
michele.mathis@piedmontcc.edu
MATHIS, Molly .... 256-765-4343.... 8 E
mjmathis@una.edu
MATHIS, RJ .... 478-825-6316 118 E
rj.mathis@fvsu.edu
MATHIS, Sharale .... 413-552-2226 214 D
smathis@hcc.edu
MATHIS, Shawn .... 501-450-1333.. 19 I
mathis@hendrix.edu
MATHIS, Terence .... 903-988-7520 437 G
tmathis@kilgore.edu
MATHIS, Teri .... 229-391-5045 114 D
terimathis@abac.edu
MATHIS, William .... 419-372-8603 348 F
wmathis@bgsu.edu
MATHISEN, Germaine .... 834-842-3446 451 G
glmathisen@uh.edu
MATHISON, Karyssa ...... 253-566-5169 483 F
kmathison@tacomacc.edu
MATHOV, Sara .... 503-251-5739 377 A
smathov@uws.edu
MATHUR, Ambika .... 210-458-5264 455 B
ambika.mathur@utsa.edu
MATIAS, Audeliz .... 518-587-2100 320 B
MATIC, Katharina .... 717-245-1010 382 B
matick@dickinson.edu
MATICH, Michael .... 734-432-5441 226 G
mmatich@madonna.edu
MATIIA, Mike, M .... 717-337-6530 384 C
mmattia@gettysburg.edu
MATIKA, Susan .... 908-709-7548 283 E
matika@ucc.edu
MATITIA, Abraham .... 440-943-5300 360 A
MATKIN, H. Neil .... 972-758-3800 432 I
nmatkin@collin.edu
MATLEY, Stephen .... 619-684-8800.. 53 K
smatley@newschoolarch.edu
MATLIN, David .... 808-956-7301 129 B
athdir@hawaii.edu
MATLOCK, Debra .... 312-996-7084 151 D
mdebra@uic.edu
MATLOCK, Haley .... 580-559-5697 365 J
hmatlock@ecok.edu
MATLOCK, Monica .... 907-563-7575.... 9 E
monica.matlock@alaskacareercollege.edu
MATNEY, Ross .... 540-674-3613 473 F
rmatney@nr.edu
MATONAK, Jessica, M . 724-287-8711 379 C
jessica.matonak@bc3.edu
MATOS, Anthony, D ...... 540-568-6764 467 C
matosad@jmu.edu
MATOS, Awilda .... 787-834-9595 508 O
amatos@uaa.edu
MATOS, Bethany .... 559-934-2217.. 74 L
bethanymatos@whccd.edu
MATOS, Carol .... 917-493-4450 304 L
cmatos@msmnyc.edu
MATOS, Dania .... 510-642-6000.. 68 N
vcei@berkeley.edu

MAVRINAC, Mary Ann .. 585-275-4461 323 E
maryann.mavrinac@rochester.edu
MAVROS, Jeff .... 309-438-2181 140 C
jmavros@ilstu.edu
MAW, Elizabeth .... 415-561-6555.. 58 B
MAWUNTU, Valencia .... 269-471-3484 220 H
valencia@andrews.edu
MAX, Rosemary .... 248-370-4730 229 F
rmax@oakland.edu
MAX, Sheryl .... 816-995-2842 257 I
sheryl.max@researchcollege.edu
MAXEINER, Amy .... 309-796-5043 133 D
maxeinera@bhc.edu
MAXEY, Angie .... 713-525-3546 453 H
gonzalea@stthom.edu
MAXEY, Evie .... 864-231-2000 405 F
emaxey@andersonuniversity.edu
MAXEY, JoAnn .... 501-686-2515.. 21 G
jmaxey@uasys.edu
MAXEY, Larry .... 619-388-5940.. 61 A
lmaxey@sdccd.edu
MAXEY, Susan .... 606-783-2317 183 H
s.maxey@moreheadstate.edu
MAXFIELD, John .... 303-963-3228.. 78 D
jmaxfield@ccu.edu
MAXFIELD, Sylvia ...... 401-865-1224 403 E
maxfield@providence.edu
MAXIE, Donell .... 662-254-3577 247 C
donell.maxie@mvsu.edu
MAXIE, Leslie .... 502-272-7150 179 D
lmaxie@bellarmine.edu
MAXIM, Raven .... 757-789-1774 472 I
rmaxim@es.vccs.edu
MAXSON, Amanda ...... 901-843-3885 422 C
registrar@rhodes.edu
MAXSON, Kathi .... 605-718-2401 416 D
katherine.maxson@wdt.edu
MAXSON, Ryan .... 760-750-8161.. 33 C
rmaxson@csusm.edu
MAXWELL, Ben .... 864-587-4251 411 F
maxwellb@smcsc.edu
MAXWELL, Brandon, T . 404-687-4522 117 D
maxwellb@ctsnet.edu
MAXWELL, Cathy .... 303-292-0015.. 80 F
cmaxwell@denvercollegeofnursing.edu
MAXWELL, Chris .... 706-245-7226 118 C
cmaxwell@ec.edu
MAXWELL, Dan .... 713-743-5388 451 F
dmmaxwell@uh.edu
MAXWELL, Daniel .... 713-743-5390 451 F
dmmaxwell@uh.edu
MAXWELL, Drew .... 414-847-3317 493 C
drewmaxwell@miad.edu
MAXWELL, James .... 423-869-6298 420 A
james.maxwell@lmunet.edu
MAXWELL, James .... 972-524-3341 444 E
jamxw@swcc.edu
MAXWELL, Jewerl .... 765-998-5204 161 A
jewerl_maxwell@taylor.edu
MAXWELL, Jewerl .... 978-867-4118 209 F
jewerl.maxwell@gordon.edu
MAXWELL, Kate .... 410-827-5802 198 B
kmaxwell@chesapeake.edu
MAXWELL, Logan .... 903-463-2646 435 H
maxwelll@grayson.edu
MAXWELL, Lonnicia .... 512-432-1400 443 F
MAXWELL, Mardell ...... 832-842-9058 451 G
mrmaxwell@uh.edu
MAXWELL, OSB,
Maximilian .... 724-805-2679 397 C
maximilian.maxwell@stvincent.edu
MAXWELL, Noel .... 907-745-3201.... 9 C
nmaxwell@akbible.edu
MAXWELL, Sharon ...... 630-844-5630 133 A
smaxwell@aurora.edu
MAXWELL, Sharon ...... 214-818-1353 433 A
smaxwell@criswell.edu
MAXWELL, Tanisha .... 925-473-7421.. 40 I
tmaxwell@losmedanos.edu
MAXWELL-DOHERTY,
Melissa .... 805-493-3330.. 29 E
revmmmd@callutheran.edu
MAY, Barbara .... 574-284-4575 160 F
bmay@saintmarys.edu
MAY, Barbara .... 320-363-5401 242 G
bmay@csbsju.edu
MAY, Barbara .... 320-363-5401 234 I
bmay@csbsju.edu
MAY, Bryan .... 803-778-7841 406 A
maybw@cctech.edu
MAY, Caleb .... 785-539-3571 175 F
caleb.may@mccks.edu

MAY, Cathryn .... 601-635-6238 245 B
cmay@eccc.edu
MAY, Charles, A .... 573-882-7744 260 C
mayc@missouri.edu
MAY, Christopher, V .... 314-977-3167 258 H
christopher.may@slu.edu
MAY, David, J .... 603-862-2727 273 H
david.may@unh.edu
MAY, Erin .... 402-466-4774 266 A
erin.may@doane.edu
MAY, Gary, S .... 530-752-2065.. 69 A
chancellor@ucdavis.edu
MAY, Ginny, A .... 248-218-2018 229 I
gmay@rochesteru.edu
MAY, Joanna .... 413-584-2700 218 D
MAY, Joe, D .... 214-378-1601 433 F
jmay@dcccd.edu
MAY, Karen .... 314-340-3880 253 E
mayk@hssu.edu
MAY, Larry .... 865-981-8113 420 C
larry.may@maryvillecollege.edu
MAY, Libby .... 603-645-9698 273 E
l.may@snhu.edu
MAY, MaryAnn .... 334-699-2266.... 1 B
mmay@acom.edu
MAY, Michael .... 724-738-4573 394 E
michael.may@sru.edu
MAY, Mindy .... 937-766-7855 349 C
mkmay@cedarville.edu
MAY, Nathanael .... 316-295-5849 173 G
nathanael_may@friends.edu
MAY, Nina .... 609-586-4800 277 H
mayn@mccc.edu
MAY, Nita .... 903-434-8113 440 A
nmay@ntcc.edu
MAY, Robert, E .... 276-739-2436 474 H
rmay@vhcc.edu
MAY, Ronald .... 253-964-6736 481 H
rmay@pierce.ctc.edu
MAY, Sarah, E .... 478-301-2413 122 C
may_se@mercer.edu
MAY, Susan .... 618-985-2828 140 G
susanmay@jalc.edu
MAY, Tammie .... 816-604-4018 254 E
tammie.may@mcckc.edu
MAY, Travis .... 602-243-8191.. 14 C
travis.may@southmountaincc.edu
MAY, Walter, P .... 770-720-5540 124 E
wpm@reinhardt.edu
MAY-RICCIUTI, Heather . 304-829-7335 486 B
hricciuti@bethanywv.edu
MAYAN, Kathy .... 410-386-8110 197 G
kmayan@carrollcc.edu
MAYBANK, Denise, B ... 646-664-8759 292 E
denise.maybank@cuny.edu
MAYCUNICH, Marc ..... 906-217-4300 221 J
marc.maycunich@baycollege.edu
MAYDEN, Sharrie .... 702-895-0970 270 J
sharrie.mayden@unlv.edu
MAYDEW, Mary Jo ...... 413-538-2512 216 G
mjmaydew@mtholyoke.edu
MAYEA, Bethany .... 810-989-5537 230 A
blmayea@sc4.edu
MAYER, Charles .... 336-249-8186 333 G
cmayer@davidsondavie.edu
MAYER, Connie .... 518-445-2393 289 B
cmaye@albanylaw.edu
MAYER, Deidra .... 409-880-7870 449 B
demayer@lamar.edu
MAYER, Fritz .... 303-871-6338.. 84 C
frederick.mayer@du.edu
MAYER, Jamie .... 325-942-2116 450 B
jamie.akin@angelo.edu
MAYER, Jason .... 425-235-5555 482 C
jmayer@rtc.edu
MAYER, Kathy .... 608-262-1605 494 C
kmayer@uwsa.edu
MAYER, Kerry .... 707-476-4326.. 58 I
kerry-mayer@redwoods.edu
MAYER, Louis .... 201-216-8761 282 L
louis.mayer@stevens.edu
MAYER, Lynn .... 202-319-5220.. 91 G
mayer@cua.edu
MAYER, Patrick .... 606-451-6702 182 D
patrick.mayer@kctcs.edu
MAYER, Rob .... 704-847-5600 340 D
rmayer@ses.edu
MAYER, Susan .... 623-845-3849.. 13 E
susan.mayer@gccaz.edu
MAYER, Thomas .... 803-793-5197 408 A
mayert@denmarktech.edu
MAYERS, Brock .... 804-257-5875 475 G
bmayers@vuu.edu

MAYERS, Kendra .... 804-342-3939 475 G
kmayers@vuu.edu
MAYERSKI, Christopher 570-408-7890 402 B
christopher.mayerski@wilkes.edu
MAYES, David .... 501-882-8986.. 17 H
dmmayes@asub.edu
MAYES, John, A .... 203-432-8049.. 90 B
john.mayes@yale.edu
MAYES, LaVerne .... 215-871-6560 395 A
lavernema@pcom.edu
MAYES, Nathan .... 660-284-4800 253 F
MAYEUX, Liza .... 225-490-1664 186 H
liza.mayeux@franu.edu
MAYFIELD, Amanda, B . 860-439-2088.. 87 F
amanda.mayfield@conncoll.edu
MAYFIELD, Charles ..... 660-562-1138 256 G
mayfield@nwmissouri.edu
MAYFIELD, Donny ...... 423-746-5253 425 C
dmayfield@tnwesleyan.edu
MAYFIELD, Janet .... 314-392-2355 255 H
mayfij@mobap.edu
MAYFIELD, Pamela ..... 254-867-3118 448 F
pamela.mayfield@tstc.edu
MAYFIELD, Tracey ...... 562-985-4047.. 32 A
tracey.mayfield@csulb.edu
MAYFIELD-BURFORD,
Rosetta .... 901-321-3119 417 G
rmayfie1@cbu.edu
MAYFIELD MULLEN,
Jana .... 805-565-6144.. 75 I
jmayfield@westmont.edu
MAYHER, Michael, E ... 440-525-7255 354 L
mmayher@lakelandcc.edu
MAYHEW, Sam .... 423-439-4286 418 D
mayhew@etsu.edu
MAYHEW, Susan, L ..... 276-498-5201 463 G
slmayhew@acp.edu
MAYLE, Chad, A .... 304-457-6410 485 F
mayleca@ab.edu
MAYLE, Tony .... 740-376-3287 355 E
aam006@marietta.edu
MAYMI-SUGRANES,
Hector .... 309-298-2762 152 I
hj-sugranes@wiu.edu
MAYNARD, Charmel ..... 305-284-9587 112 K
cmaynard@miami.edu
MAYNARD, Christopher 281-283-3000 452 A
maynard@uhcl.edu
MAYNARD, Craig .... 309-467-6305 137 G
cmaynard@eureka.edu
MAYNARD, Francyenne 972-273-3015 434 C
fmaynard@dcccd.edu
MAYNARD, Gene .... 916-348-4689.. 42 B
gmaynard@epic.edu
MAYNARD, Kimberly, L 304-896-7345 487 I
kimberly.maynard@southernwv.edu
MAYNARD, Thurmond ... 301-696-3546 199 C
maynard@hood.edu
MAYNARD, Wendy ...... 508-830-5036 213 A
wmaynard@maritime.edu
MAYNARD-ERRAMI,
Nickcole .... 434-947-8704 469 A
nmaynard@randolphcollege.edu
MAYNARD-ERRAMI,
Nickcole .... 434-381-6478 470 H
nmaynarderrami@sbc.edu
MAYNARD NELSON,
Jeanette .... 612-767-7043 233 E
jeanette@alfredadler.edu
MAYNARD-REID,
Pedrito .... 509-527-2028 484 C
pedrito.maynard-reid@wallawalla.edu
MAYNC, Tania .... 213-740-2311.. 73 B
tmaze@barton.edu
MAYNE, Kevin .... 802-387-6716 461 E
kevinmayne@landmark.edu
MAYNES, Leslie .... 515-271-2011 165 F
leslie.maynes@drake.edu
MAYO, Christy .... 616-234-5722 231 D
christy.mayo@vai.edu
MAYO, Dan .... 252-493-7531 336 E
dmayo@email.pittcc.edu
MAYO, Daniel, J .... 909-384-4400.. 60 F
dmayo@sbccd.cc.ca.us
MAYO, Jacqueline ...... 704-403-1326 327 B
jacqueline.mayo@atriumhealth.org
MAYO, Jennifer .... 919-739-6721 338 F
jbmayo@waynecc.edu
MAYO, Julia .... 503-517-1856 377 D
jmayo@westernseminary.edu
MAYO, Karen .... 859-246-6525 181 B
karen.mayo@kctcs.edu
MAYO, Kathy .... 252-249-1851 336 C
kmayo@pamlicocc.edu

MAYO, Kelly .... 847-491-3741 146 C
tgsdean@northwestern.edu
MAYO, Michelle, L ...... 919-530-7149 341 D
mlmayo@nccu.edu
MAYO, Michelle, P ...... 585-292-2370 306 K
mmayo@monroecc.edu
MAYO, Rachel .... 831-786-4710.. 27 G
ramayo@cabrillo.edu
MAYOR, Ryan .... 651-846-1305 240 E
ryan.mayer@saintpaul.edu
MAYOR-GLENN,
Jennifer, A .... 801-972-3596 459 D
j.mayer-glenn@partners.utah.edu
MAYORAL, Eliza .... 480-245-7930.. 12 O
eliza.mayoral@ibcs.edu
MAYORAL, James .... 716-878-6332 317 C
mayoraj@buffalostate.edu
MAYORGA, Luanne ..... 815-455-8581 143 F
lmayorga@mchenry.edu
MAYRAND, Leslie .... 325-486-6247 450 B
leslie.mayrand@angelo.edu
MAYROSE, James .... 716-878-5550 317 C
mayrosj@buffalostate.edu
MAYS, Beth, A .... 410-777-2480 197 C
bamays@aacc.edu
MAYS, Carey, J .... 512-464-8822 441 N
careym@stedwards.edu
MAYS, Cathy .... 434-381-6448 470 K
cdmays@sbc.edu
MAYS, Elizabeth .... 714-772-3330.. 26 B
MAYS, Florence .... 803-822-3419 409 E
maysf@midlandstech.edu
MAYS, Jordan .... 618-985-3741 140 G
jordanmays@jalc.edu
MAYS, Justin .... 678-466-5544 117 A
justinmays@clayton.edu
MAYS, Justin .... 417-667-8181 251 E
jmays@cottey.edu
MAYS, Lisa .... 937-433-3410 352 G
lmays@fortiscollege.edu
MAYS, Nathaniel .... 617-349-8539 210 H
nmays@lesley.edu
MAYS, Susan .... 615-550-3161 427 F
susan@williamsoncc.edu
MAYS, Theresa .... 334-420-4296.... 3 H
tmays@trenholmstate.edu
MAYS, Thomas .... 301-546-7594 201 D
maysto@pgcc.edu
MAYS-JACKSON, Debra 601-979-2323 245 G
debra.mays-jackson@jsums.edu
MAYSE, Tiffany .... 859-572-5806 184 B
masyset@nku.edu
MAYSENT, Patty .... 858-249-5534.. 70 C
pmaysent@ucsd.edu
MAZA, Antonio .... 703-416-1441 465 E
amaza@divinemercy.edu
MAZA, Octavio .... 786-331-1000 104 H
octavio.maza@maufl.edu
MAZA-DUERTO,
Aristides .... 786-331-1000 104 H
amaza@maufl.edu
MAZA-DUERTO,
Jenice, C .... 786-331-1000 104 H
jmaza@maufl.edu
MAZACHEK, JuliAnn .... 940-397-4000 439 F
juliann.mazachek@msutexas.edu
MAZARIEGOS, John .... 847-947-5086 145 C
jmazariegos@nl.edu
MAZARIS, AJ .... 336-721-2600 339 H
aj.mazaris@salem.edu
MAZDRA, Brad .... 575-527-7519 287 A
bmazdra@nmsu.edu
MAZE, Tom .... 252-399-6533 326 H
tmaze@barton.edu
MAZEIKA, Michael ...... 413-572-8541 213 C
mmazeika@westfield.ma.edu
MAZELIN, Mark .... 937-766-4155 349 C
mazelinm@cedarville.edu
MAZER, Joe .... 865-974-3031 426 C
joemazer@utk.edu
MAZER, Vickie .... 410-857-2437 200 D
vmazer@mcdaniel.edu
MAZIAR, Christine, M .. 574-631-2749 161 G
maziar.1@nd.edu
MAZIAR, Lucia .... 860-444-8517 502 F
lucia.maziar@uscga.edu
MAZIARZ, Jordanna .... 973-655-3533 278 C
maziarzj@montclair.edu
MAZIARZ, Marcela ...... 609-777-5654 283 D
mmaziarz@tesu.edu
MAZICH, OSB,
Edward, M .... 724-805-2592 397 D
edward.mazich@stvincent.edu
MAZO, Carlos, E .... 305-456-0289 113 G

MCCANDLESS, Ann .... 724-287-8711 379 C ann.mccandless@bc3.edu
MCCANDLESS, Michael . 209-384-6185.. 52 B mccandless.m@mccd.edu
MCCANDLESS, Raymond .... 419-434-4565 362 D mccandless@findlay.edu
MCCANN, Bonnie .... 614-947-6017 352 J bonnie.mccann@franklin.edu
MCCANN, Elizabeth ...... 949-582-4481.. 65 C emccann@saddleback.edu
MCCANN, Erin .... 201-761-7362 282 H emccann@saintpeters.edu
MCCANN, Jonathan ...... 202-885-1000.. 91 D jmccann@american.edu
MCCANN, Maggie .... 225-768-1783 186 H maggie.mccann@franu.edu
MCCANN, Mitch .... 805-922-6966.. 24 L mitch.mccann@hancockcollege.edu
MCCANN, Paul, A .... 217-581-2979 137 C pmccann@eiu.edu
MCCANN, Terry .... 715-232-3076 496 C mccannte@uwstout.edu
MCCARDLE, Elizabeth .... 386-752-1822.. 99 P elizabeth.mccardle@fgc.edu
MCCAREY, Christine ...... 508-362-2131 214 B cmccarey@capecod.edu
MCCARGO, Donavan ..... 610-683-4000 394 A
MCCARGO, Donavan ..... 610-683-1396 394 A mccargo@kutztown.edu
MCCARLEY, Brian .... 417-893-7143 258 K bmccarley@sbuniv.edu
MCCARLEY, Erin .... 503-842-8222 376 D erinmccarley@tillamookbaycc.edu
MCCARN, Sarah .... 912-525-5000 124 G smccarn@scad.edu
MCCARRAGHER, Timothy, M .... 330-972-5976 361 G mccarra@uakron.edu
MCCARRELL, Kyle .... 708-239-4797 150 H kyle.mccarrell@trnty.edu
MCCARRELL, Ronnie ..... 864-587-4229 411 F mccarrellr@smcsc.edu
MCCARREN, Gerard .... 973-275-2111 282 K gerard.mccarren@shu.edu
MCCARRICK, Ashley ...... 914-594-4900 308 J amccarri@nymc.edu
MCCARRICK, Richard, G .... 914-594-4503 308 J richard_mccarrick@nymc.edu
MCCARRIE, Ashley .... 267-502-2400 378 I
MCCARRON, Anne .... 414-382-6068 490 G anne.mccarron@alverno.edu
MCCARRON, Cathy .... 508-362-2131 214 B
MCCARRY, Tim .... 325-670-1434 436 B facilities@hsutx.edu
MCCARTAN, Brian .... 206-616-2021 484 A bpmcc@uw.edu
MCCARTER, Iika .... 662-329-7106 247 B itmccarter@muw.edu
MCCARTHY, Alison .... 860-773-1487.. 87 E amccarthy@tunxis.edu
MCCARTHY, Amanda ..... 585-245-5514 317 E mccarthya@geneseo.edu
MCCARTHY, Anne .... 402-375-7215 267 I anmccar1@wsc.edu
MCCARTHY, Barbara ...... 914-773-3741 310 F bmccarthy@pace.edu
MCCARTHY, Brendan .... 904-256-7550 102 G bmccart3@ju.edu
MCCARTHY, Brian .... 480-858-9100.. 16 B b.mccarthy1@scnm.edu
MCCARTHY, Carlie .... 530-283-0202.. 42 E cmccarthy@frc.edu
MCCARTHY, Casey, J .... 218-755-3888 237 B casey.mccarthy@bemidjistate.edu
MCCARTHY, Charles ..... 610-604-7700.. 93 H
MCCARTHY, Colby .... 973-408-3112 276 B finaid@drew.edu
MCCARTHY, Cynthia ..... 732-987-2254 277 B cmccarthy@georgian.edu
MCCARTHY, Daniel .... 985-549-2055 192 E dmccarthy@selu.edu
MCCARTHY, David, M .... 301-447-5333 201 A dmccarth@msmary.edu
MCCARTHY, Dennis, K .. 805-421-5914.. 67 J dmccarthy@thomasaquinas.edu
MCCARTHY, Dominica .. 972-860-4689 433 G dmccarthy@dcccd.edu
MCCARTHY, Douglas ..... 602-285-7245.. 13 H douglas.mccarthy@phoenixcollege.edu
MCCARTHY, Faith .... 530-221-4275.. 63 G fmccarthy@shasta.edu
MCCARTHY, Faith .... 530-221-4275.. 63 G registrar@shasta.edu
MCCARTHY, James .... 978-921-4242 216 F jim.mccarthy@montserrat.edu
MCCARTHY, John .... 740-593-9336 358 L mccarthj@ohio.edu
MCCARTHY, John, C ..... 202-319-5259.. 91 G mccartjc@cua.edu
MCCARTHY, Joseph, J .. 412-624-0790 400 A jjmcc@pitt.edu
MCCARTHY, Kate .... 530-898-6650.. 31 A kmccarthy@csuchico.edu
MCCARTHY, Kate .... 802-635-1458 463 B kathleen.mccarthy@northernvermont.edu
MCCARTHY, Katherine, M .... 315-470-4945 319 A kmccar10@esf.edu
MCCARTHY, Kevin .... 315-568-3267 309 H kmccarthy@northeastcollege.edu
MCCARTHY, Kevin .... 803-508-7337 405 C mccarthk@atc.edu
MCCARTHY, Kevin .... 704-330-6907 333 B kevin.mccarthy@cpcc.edu
MCCARTHY, Kristin, C .. 617-422-7418 217 B kmccarthy@nesl.edu
MCCARTHY, Marsha ...... 908-737-7100 277 F mmccarth@kean.edu
MCCARTHY, Maureen .... 765-285-1042 153 E mmcarthy@bsu.edu
MCCARTHY, Maureen .... 215-968-8058 379 B maureen.mccarthy@bucks.edu
MCCARTHY, Megan .... 270-686-4255 179 F megan.mccarthy@brescia.edu
MCCARTHY, Melissa ..... 401-874-2599 404 E mcmel@uri.edu
MCCARTHY, SJ, Michael .... 617-552-6509 207 A michael.mccarthy@bc.edu
MCCARTHY, Michael, R 978-556-3924 215 C mmccarthy1@necc.mass.edu
MCCARTHY, Michelle .... 607-587-3917 319 C mccartma@alfredstate.edu
MCCARTHY, Patricia ...... 724-357-7544 393 G mccarthy@iup.edu
MCCARTHY, Patrick ...... 619-594-1643.. 33 E pmccarthy@sdsu.edu
MCCARTHY, Piper .... 775-445-3270 271 A piper.mccarthy@wnc.edu
MCCARTHY, Rosemary .. 412-536-1173 386 H rosemary.mccarthy@laroche.edu
MCCARTHY, Ryan .... 718-960-1117 293 E ryan.mccarthy@lehman.cuny.edu
MCCARTHY, Sherry .... 712-279-3158 169 E sherry.mccarthy@stlukescollege.edu
MCCARTHY, William ...... 973-353-3292 281 C wm307@scj.rutgers.edu
MCCARTNEY, Jill .... 740-427-5811 354 I mccartney1@kenyon.edu
MCCARTNEY, Kathleen .. 413-585-2100 218 D kmccartney@smith.edu
MCCARTY, Alison .... 781-239-2506 214 E amccarty1@massbay.edu
MCCARTY, III, Gerald .... 734-384-4183 227 F gmccarty@monroeccc.edu
MCCARTY, Kevin .... 512-617-5700 432 B
MCCARTY, Kevin .... 512-245-5500 449 G km20@txstate.edu
MCCARTY, Lori .... 706-272-4462 118 A lmccarty@daltonstate.edu
MCCARTY, Michael .... 502-897-4720 184 D mmccarty@sbts.edu
MCCARTY, Nolan .... 609-258-4796 279 E
MCCARTY, Philips, R .... 212-217-4100 299 C philips_mccarty@fitnyc.edu
MCCARTY, Rich, M .... 203-576-2354.. 89 A rmccarty@bridgeport.edu
MCCARVER, Viva .... 419-372-8421 348 F vivam@bgsu.edu
MCCARVILLE, Jeanie ...... 515-965-7120 164 F jamccarville1@dmacc.edu
MCCARY, Jennifer, Q .... 419-372-2147 348 F jmccary@bgsu.edu
MCCASKEY, Mary .... 931-372-3503 425 B mamccaskey@tntech.edu
MCCASKILL, John .... 803-535-1264 410 C mccaskilljm@octech.edu
MCCASKILL, Sharrell ..... 202-651-5642.. 92 B sharrell.mccaskill@gallaudet.edu
MCCASLAND, Shannon . 970-339-6563.. 77 G shannon.mccasland@aims.edu
MCCASLIN, Blake .... 423-745-7504 425 C bmccaslin@tnwesleyan.edu
MCCASLIN, Jaime .... 814-871-7330 383 H mccaslin007@gannon.edu
MCCASLIN, James .... 270-901-1112 182 E james.mccaslin@kctcs.edu
MCCASLIN, Julie .... 423-746-5214 425 C jmccaslin@tnwesleyan.edu
MCCASLIN, Sharon .... 314-889-4567 252 G smccaslin@fontbonne.edu
MCCAUGHAN, Amanda . 651-641-8739 235 A mccaughan@csp.edu
MCCAULEY, David, W ... 304-473-8322 490 E mccauley@wvwc.edu
MCCAULEY, Dennis .... 215-968-8394 379 B dennis.mccauley@bucks.edu
MCCAULEY, Juli .... 806-743-2848 450 C juli.mccauley@ttuhsc.edu
MCCAULEY, Justin .... 508-531-1277 212 B jmccauley@bridgew.edu
MCCAULEY, Justin .... 402-878-2380 266 D justin.mccauley@littlepriest.edu
MCCAULEY, Laurie .... 734-763-3311 231 A mccauley@umich.edu
MCCAULEY, Linda .... 404-727-7976 118 D linda.mccauley@emory.edu
MCCAULEY, Linda .... 559-737-6194.. 39 C lindam@cos.edu
MCCAULEY, Michele ...... 269-749-7141 229 G mmccauley@olivetcollege.edu
MCCAULLEY, Michelle .. 573-875-8700 251 A
MCCAUSLAND, Bill .... 813-974-1868 111 B mccausland@usf.edu
MCCAUSLAND, Rachel .. 610-359-5131 381 J rmccausland@dccc.edu
MCCAUSLIN, Christine .. 301-447-8399 201 A mccauslin@msmary.edu
MCCAW, Ian .... 434-582-2100 467 E ijmccaw@liberty.edu
MCCAW, Shawn .... 314-889-4686 252 G smccaw@fontbonne.edu
MCCAY, Megan .... 601-266-4059 248 H megan.mccay@usm.edu
MCCHORD, Jennifer, J .. 859-858-3511 178 H jennifer.mcchord@asbury.edu
MCCHURCH, Bob .... 309-796-5013 133 D mcchurchb@bhc.edu
MCCLAIN, Carol, M ...... 803-934-3430 409 H cmcclain@morris.edu
MCCLAIN, Elizabeth ..... 479-308-2286.. 17 E elizabeth.mcclain@acheedu.org
MCCLAIN, Elman .... 773-244-5222 145 F memcclain@northpark.edu
MCCLAIN, James, W ..... 870-838-2910.. 17 F jmcclain@smail.anc.edu
MCCLAIN, Janet .... 617-585-0200 206 E janet.mcclain@the-bac.edu
MCCLAIN, Jeremy .... 601-266-5017 248 H jeremy.mcclain@usm.edu
MCCLAIN, Lisa, L .... 504-520-7593 193 C lmcclain@xula.edu
MCCLAIN, Michael .... 803-981-7126 413 F mmclain@yorktech.edu
MCCLAIN, Rance .... 479-308-2382.. 17 E rance.mcclain@arcomedu.org
MCCLAIN, Samantha, E 515-574-1080 166 G mcclain@iowacentral.edu
MCCLAIN, Stephenie ..... 210-567-2503 455 E mcclains@uthscsa.edu
MCCLANAHAN, Barry .... 803-321-5206 409 I barry.mcclanahan@newberry.edu
MCCLANAHAN, Denise . 434-961-5275 474 B dmcclanahan@pvcc.edu
MCCLANAHAN, Elizabeth .... 540-231-2265 475 D elizabeth.mcclanahan@vtf.org
MCCLANAHAN, Keith .... 870-762-3151.. 17 F kmcclanahan@smail.anc.edu
MCCLANE, Curtis .... 423-775-6596 421 I cmcclane@ogs.edu
MCCLAREN, Jack .... 480-461-7057.. 13 F jack.mcclaren@mesacc.edu
MCCLARNON, Ryan .... 317-738-8758 155 A rmclarnon@franklincollege.edu
MCCLAY, Liam .... 352-395-5199 107 G liam.mcclay@sfcollege.edu
MCCLEARN, Keith .... 706-419-1209 117 G keith.mcclearn@covenant.edu
MCCLEARY, Jillian .... 563-884-5726 169 C jillian.mccleary@palmer.edu
MCCLEARY, Tim .... 406-638-3121 262 J baaxpaa@lbhc.edu
MCCLELLAN, Amy .... 937-393-3431 360 G
MCCLELLAN, Amy .... 937-393-3431 360 G amcclellan@sscc.edu
MCCLELLAN, Mia .... 619-482-6542.. 65 K mmcclellan@swccd.edu
MCCLELLAN, Michael .... 909-652-6020.. 36 B michael.mcclellan@chaffey.edu
MCCLELLAN, Scott .... 206-296-2104 483 B mcclells@seattleu.edu
MCCLELLAN, Teri .... 352-392-5201 107 G teri.mcclellan@sfcollege.edu
MCCLELLAND, Jeremy ... 214-860-2351 434 A jmcclelland@dcccd.edu
MCCLELLAND, Karin ...... 925-631-4013.. 59 I klm14@stmarys-ca.edu
MCCLELLAND, Paul .... 740-826-8468 356 H paulm@muskingum.edu
MCCLELLON, Leslie, R .. 313-670-9300 191 B lmcclellon@susla.edu
MCCLENAGAN, Cindy, M .... 806-291-3410 457 B cindym@wbu.edu
MCCLENAHAN, Lindsey 415-422-6423.. 72 I lmcclenahan@usfca.edu
MCCLENDON, Dawn ...... 541-278-5937 371 G ddifuria@bluecc.edu
MCCLENDON, Karen ..... 916-686-8602.. 29 G
MCCLENDON, Mark ...... 405-208-5088 367 E mbmcclendon@okcu.edu
MCCLENDON, Michael .. 918-631-2742 371 C michael-mcclendon@utulsa.edu
MCCLENDON, Vivienne . 281-283-3931 452 A mcclendonv@uhcl.edu
MCCLENNEY, Elizabeth .. 540-375-2293 469 G mcclenney@roanoke.edu
MCCLENNY, Bradley ..... 903-463-8749 435 H mcclennyb@grayson.edu
MCCLINTICK, Wes .... 208-885-7994 132 C mcclintick@uidaho.edu
MCCLINTOCK, Angela ... 314-838-8858 261 A amcclintock@ugst.edu
MCCLINTOCK, Elizabeth, A .... 412-578-6018 380 A eamcclintock@carlow.edu
MCCLINTOCK, Grace ..... 831-459-4300.. 71 A grace@ucsc.edu
MCCLINTOCK, Jonathan 314-838-8858 261 A jmcclintock@ugst.edu
MCCLINTOCK, Melvin, A .... 240-895-4309 201 F mamcclintock@smcm.edu
MCCLINTOCK, Patty ...... 812-237-2305 155 H patty.mcclintock@indstate.edu
MCCLINTOCK-COMEAUX, Marta .... 724-938-5246 394 C mcclintock@calu.edu
MCCLINTON, Angela ..... 281-646-1109 430 H angela.mcclinton@thebibleseminary.edu
MCCLINTON, Flandus ... 225-771-5550 190 J flandus_mcclinton@sus.edu
MCCLINTON, Flandus .. 225-771-5550 190 K flandus_mcclinton@sus.edu
MCCLINTON, Leon .... 405-744-9164 367 G leon.mcclinton@okstate.edu
MCCLINTON, Lisa, R ..... 252-335-8792 341 A lrmcclinton@ecsu.edu
MCCLINTON, Martin ...... 239-432-6798 100 G martin.mcclinton@fsw.edu
MCCLOSKEY, Erin .... 814-472-3938 396 I emccloskey@francis.edu
MCCLOSKEY, James, M . 302-356-6880.. 91 C james.m.mccloskey@wilmu.edu
MCCLOSKEY, JR., John, R .... 484-254-2121 378 C john.mccloskey@alvernia.edu
MCCLOSKEY, Marybeth . 934-420-2107 320 C mcclosm@farmingdale.edu
MCCLOUD, Alyssa .... 973-761-9107 282 K alyssa.mccloud@shu.edu
MCCLOUD, Amber .... 806-291-3430 457 B amber.mccloud@wbu.edu
MCCLOUD, Barbara, L ... 630-515-7687 144 C bmcclo@midwestern.edu
MCCLOUD, Clarence ..... 386-506-6301.. 98 A clarence.mccloud@daytonastate.edu
MCCLOUD, Mark .... 731-881-3715 426 E mmcclou5@utm.edu
MCCLOUD, Mickey .... 913-469-8500 174 F mccloud@jccc.edu
MCCLOY, Eric .... 610-341-1372 383 A eric.mccloy@eastern.edu
MCCLUNG, bruce, d ...... 336-334-5789 342 D bdmcclun@uncg.edu
MCCLUNG, Kiwana .... 337-482-6464 192 F kiwana.mcclung@louisiana.edu

MCCRAY, Kenjuana 910-678-0058 334 C mccrayk@faytechcc.edu
MCCRAY, Lonnie 318-670-6000 191 B
MCCRAY, Suzanne 479-575-4883 21 H smccray@uark.edu
MCCRAY, Sylvia 215-574-9600 385 J sylvia.mccray@hussiancollege.edu
MCCRAY-ROBERTS, Patty 253-566-5050 483 F pmccray-roberts@tacomacc.edu
MCCREA, Douglas 609-896-5196 280 D dmccrea@rider.edu
MCCREA, Larry 816-604-1000 254 F
MCCREADY, Randall 412-624-7180 400 A mccready@pitt.edu
MCCREARY, Micah, L 732-247-5241 278 E mmccreary@nbts.edu
MCCREARY, William 419-530-3990 363 B william.mccreary@utoledo.edu
MCCREE, Bernard, L 610-683-4032 394 A mccree@kutztown.edu
MCCREIGHT, Christopher, J 330-569-6094 353 F mccreightcj@hiram.edu
MCCREIGHT, Megan 719-365-8292 83 K megan.mccreight@uchealth.org
MCCREIGHT, Robert 785-738-9031 176 C rmccreight@ncktc.edu
MCCRILLIS, Neal, R 312-413-1468 151 D nealrm@uic.edu
MCCROHAN, Betty, A 979-532-6304 457 H bettym@wcjc.edu
MCCRORY, Heidi, H 864-294-2475 408 I heidi.mccrory@furman.edu
MCCROSKEY, Lorie, L 336-633-1118 336 F llmccroskey@randolph.edu
MCCROW, Rich 661-395-4694 47 B rmccrow@bakersfieldcollege.edu
MCCUBBIN, Todd, A 573-882-6017 260 C mccubbint@missouri.edu
MCCUDDEN, Suzanne 253-833-9111 480 A smccudden@greenriver.edu
MCCUE, Cindy 934-420-2319 320 C cynthia.mccue@farmingdale.edu
MCCUE, Jennie 949-582-4500 65 C jmccue@saddleback.edu
MCCUEN, Jan 714-997-6862 36 D mccuen@chapman.edu
MCCUIEN-SMITH, Cassandra 501-450-3173 23 K cmccuien@uca.edu
MCCUISTION, Kim 682-703-7067 445 F mccuistion@tarleton.edu
MCCULLA, Justin 937-328-7819 350 D mccullaj@clarkstate.edu
MCCULLAR, Bryan, L 785-833-4398 175 C bryan.mccullar@kwu.edu
MCCULLEY, Becky 214-633-4805 456 D becky.mcculley@utsouthwestern.edu
MCCULLEY, Heather 530-226-4943 64 C hmcculley@simpsonu.edu
MCCULLEY, Justin 276-964-2555 474 E justin.mcculley@sw.edu
MCCULLOCH, Dennis 701-845-7425 345 E dennis.mcculloch@vcsu.edu
MCCULLOCH, Greg 618-252-5400 149 E greg.mcculloch@sic.edu
MCCULLOCH, Sonja 912-260-4402 125 B sonja.mcculloch@sgsc.edu
MCCULLOH, Edna 330-490-7191 363 E emcculloh@walsh.edu
MCCULLOH, Julie, A 509-313-6591 479 E mccullohj@gonzaga.edu
MCCULLOH, Thayne, M 509-313-6102 479 E president@gonzaga.edu
MCCULLOUCH, Amanda 614-234-5800 356 E
MCCULLOUGH, Catherine 802-728-1247 463 D cmccullough@vtc.edu
MCCULLOUGH, Cheryl, J 803-327-7402 407 A cmccullough@clintoncollege.edu
MCCULLOUGH, Dona 312-662-4000 132 D
MCCULLOUGH, Jonathan, W 903-434-8115 440 A jmccullough@ntcc.edu
MCCULLOUGH, Karen 785-628-4260 173 E kmccullo@fhsu.edu
MCCULLOUGH, Laura 606-759-7141 182 B laura.mccullough@kctcs.edu
MCCULLOUGH, Laura 912-478-5234 120 A lmccullough@georgiasouthern.edu
MCCULLOUGH, Laura 304-205-6611 487 D laura.mccullough@bridgevalley.edu

MCCULLOUGH, Phenicia 657-278-4637 31 E pmccullough@fullerton.edu
MCCULLOUGH, Richard 850-644-1085 110 B president@fsu.edu
MCCULLOUGH, Robert, R 216-368-5445 349 B robert.mccullough@case.edu
MCCULLOUGH, Robyne 410-951-6546 203 E rmccullough@coppin.edu
MCCULLOUGH, Scott 507-529-2789 240 B scott.mccullough@rctc.edu
MCCULLOUGH, Tami 262-472-6704 496 E mccullot@uww.edu
MCCULLOUGH, Telara 509-527-5941 485 C mccullt@whitman.edu
MCCULLUM, BJ 217-234-5253 141 H bmccullum@lakelandcollege.edu
MCCULLY, Clare 617-724-6399 216 E cmccully@mghihp.edu
MCCUNE, Jennifer 661-654-3405 30 C jmccune@csub.edu
MCCUNE, Kathryn 606-539-4316 185 C kathryn.mccune@ucumberlands.edu
MCCUNE, LB 810-762-9629 225 F lbmccune@kettering.edu
MCCUNE, Rebekah 605-668-5126 414 F rebekah.mccune@mountmarty.edu
MCCUNE, Roger 304-485-5487 486 H
MCCURDY, Alison 323-343-2000 32 B amccurd@calstatela.edu
MCCURDY, Clantha 617-391-6098 211 B cmccurdy@dhe.mass.edu
MCCURDY, Dean 317-921-4882 158 A dmccurdy1@ivytech.edu
MCCURDY, Debra, L 410-462-7799 197 E dlmccurdy@bccc.edu
MCCURDY, Eugene, M 608-796-3921 496 L emmccurdy@viterbo.edu
MCCURDY, Katie 850-872-3814 101 O kmccurdy2@gulfcoast.edu
MCCURDY, Scott 903-923-2107 435 A smccurdy@etbu.edu
MCCURLEY, Lisa 603-427-7600 271 J
MCCURREN, Cynthia 810-762-3420 231 C mccurrec@umich.edu
MCCURRY, David 864-503-5509 413 A dmccurry@uscupstate.edu
MCCURRY, Elizabeth 985-448-4521 192 C liz.mccurry@nicholls.edu
MCCURRY, Faith 803-535-1230 410 C mccurryf@octech.edu
MCCURRY, Michael 202-885-8600 94 D mmccurry@wesleyseminary.edu
MCCURRY, Rickey 702-895-2810 270 J rickey.mccurry@unlv.edu
MCCURRY, Roslyn 770-229-3404 125 F roslyn.mccurry@sctech.edu
MCCURTY, Kenyetta 334-387-3877 4 C kenyettamccurty@amridgeuniversity.edu
MCCUSKEY, Beth 765-494-4600 159 G
MCCUTCHEON, Andy 661-362-3387 38 H andy.mccutcheon@canyons.edu
MCCUTCHEON, John 805-893-8320 70 E jmccutch@athletics.ucsb.edu
MCDADE, Joseph 518-832-7795 319 D mcdadej@sunyacc.edu
MCDADE, Kate 216-987-4710 351 D kate.mcdade@tri-c.edu
MCDADE, Lucinda 909-625-8767 37 F lucinda.mcdade@cgu.edu
MCDAID, James 617-879-7960 212 E jmcdaid@massart.edu
MCDANIEL, Allison 210-297-9664 430 A
MCDANIEL, Amy 636-481-3465 253 G amcdanie@jeffco.edu
MCDANIEL, Anna, M 352-273-6324 110 E annammcdaniel@ufl.edu
MCDANIEL, Antonio 919-530-5422 341 D antonio.mcdaniel@nccu.edu
MCDANIEL, Becky 620-235-4769 176 H remcdaniel@pittstate.edu
MCDANIEL, Brienne 678-359-5133 120 D briennem@gordonstate.edu
MCDANIEL, Cleve 575-835-5606 286 D cleve.mcdaniel@nmt.edu
MCDANIEL, Clifton 817-461-8741 429 C cmcdaniel@abu.edu
MCDANIEL, Cynthia 973-748-9000 275 C cindy_mcdaniel@bloomfield.edu
MCDANIEL, Diane 765-677-2436 157 F diane.mcdaniel@indwes.edu

MCDANIEL, Donna 903-823-3220 445 C donna.mcdaniel@texarkanacollege.edu
MCDANIEL, Gary 402-643-7233 265 I gary.mcdaniel@cune.edu
MCDANIEL, Juley 620-223-2700 173 F juleym@fortscott.edu
MCDANIEL, Kristina, D 573-840-9695 259 I kristinamcdaniel@trcc.edu
MCDANIEL, Laura 701-231-8330 345 D laura.mcdaniel@ndsu.edu
MCDANIEL, Mick, R 607-844-8222 321 I mcdanim@tompkinscortland.edu
MCDANIEL, Phil 703-993-1000 466 J
MCDANIEL, Samual, G 210-829-6035 452 D sgmcdani@uiwtx.edu
MCDANIEL, Sonya 770-962-7580 121 B smcdaniel@gwinnetttech.edu
MCDANIEL, Wendy 479-394-7622 23 F wmcdaniel@uarichmountain.edu
MCDANIEL ANSCHUTZ, Mary 620-341-5223 173 C mmcdanie@emporia.edu
MCDANIEL-SMITH, Nicole, L 302-356-6928 91 C nicole.l.mcdaniel-smith@wilmu.edu
MCDANIELS, Preselfannie 601-979-2455 245 G preselfannie.w.mcdaniels@jsums.edu
MCDANIELS, Rob, M 573-882-9370 260 C mcdanielsr@missouri.edu
MCDANIELS WILSON, Cathy 614-236-6114 348 I cmcdanielswilson@capital.edu
MCDAVID, Cristina, C 304-696-2248 488 N mcdavidc@marshall.edu
MCDAY, Lakesha 828-251-6500 342 A lmcday@unca.edu
MCDAYTER, Ghislaine 570-577-1453 379 A ghislaine.mcdayter@bucknell.edu
MCDEAVITT, James 713-798-4951 430 E
MCDEDE, Savanna 858-566-1200 41 E smcdede@disd.edu
MCDERMOTT, Anastacia, M 563-588-7056 167 I anastacia.mcdermott@loras.edu
MCDERMOTT, Anne 401-341-2140 404 D anne.mcdermott@salve.edu
MCDERMOTT, Brian 907-564-8323 9 F bmcdermott@alaskapacific.edu
MCDERMOTT, Brian 308-398-7387 265 C bmcdermott@cccneb.edu
MCDERMOTT, Christine 315-568-3105 309 H cmcdermott@northeastcollege.edu
MCDERMOTT, Colleen 920-424-1210 495 C mcdermot@uwosh.edu
MCDERMOTT, David 617-287-7050 211 C dmcdermott@umassp.edu
MCDERMOTT, Joan 415-422-6623 72 I jmcdermott2@usfca.edu
MCDERMOTT, John, R 563-588-7132 167 I john.mcdermott@loras.edu
MCDERMOTT, Kathleen 607-735-1802 298 G kmcdermott@elmira.edu
MCDERMOTT, Loren 914-323-5299 305 A loren.mcdermott@mville.edu
MCDERMOTT, Madonna, K 651-962-6750 243 F mkmcdermott@stthomas.edu
MCDERMOTT, Marty 231-777-0462 228 C marty.mcdermott@muskegoncc.edu
MCDERMOTT, Patrice 410-455-3150 202 G mcdermot@umbc.edu
MCDERMOTT, Patrick 941-377-4880 104 D pmcdermott@meridian.edu
MCDERMOTT, Randi 208-426-1493 130 F randimcdermott@boisestate.edu
MCDERMOTT, Teresa 360-475-7480 481 B tmcdermott@olympic.edu
MCDERMOTT, Tom 410-516-8028 199 E tmcderm1@jhu.edu
MCDERMOTT, Virginia, M 336-841-9384 329 E vmcdermo@highpoint.edu
MCDERMOTT, Walter, M 434-223-6112 466 K wmcdermott@hsc.edu
MCDEVITT, Richard, K 704-406-2361 328 I rmcdevitt@gardner-webb.edu
MCDEVITT, Steven 603-641-7574 273 C smcdevitt@anselm.edu
MCDOLE, Daphne 512-505-3034 437 B dmcdole@htu.edu
MCDONAGH, David, L 646-888-6639 304 H mcdonagd@sloankettering.edu

MCDONALD, Angela, R 610-660-1265 397 A amcdonal@sju.edu
MCDONALD, Ann 508-626-4993 212 D amcdonald3@framingham.edu
MCDONALD, Barbara 218-723-6041 234 J president@css.edu
MCDONALD, Bridgette 678-466-5400 117 A bridgettemcdonald@clayton.edu
MCDONALD, Carleigh 415-703-9500 28 D c.mcdonald@cca.edu
MCDONALD, Cathy 785-594-8362 171 C cathy.mcdonald@bakeru.edu
MCDONALD, Charles 518-292-1725 312 D mcdonc@sage.edu
MCDONALD, Christie, M 989-837-4454 228 G mcdonald@northwood.edu
MCDONALD, Christopher 949-582-4960 65 A cmcdonald@socccd.edu
MCDONALD, Clay 636-227-2100 254 C
MCDONALD, Damita 410-532-5546 201 C dmcdonald1@ndm.edu
MCDONALD, Danielle 813-974-6677 111 B dmcdonald@usf.edu
MCDONALD, Dave 503-838-8919 377 C mcdonald@wou.edu
MCDONALD, Deborah 502-776-1443 184 C dmcdonald@simmonscollegeky.edu
MCDONALD, Deborah 845-938-5706 502 H admissions@westpoint.edu
MCDONALD, Dennis 417-865-2815 252 F mcdonaldd@evangel.edu
MCDONALD, Donna 703-445-9056 472 B
MCDONALD, Dotty 337-550-1357 189 B dmcdonal@lsue.edu
MCDONALD, Elizabeth 323-860-0789 50 E
MCDONALD, Eric 864-587-4200 411 F mcdonalde@smcsc.edu
MCDONALD, Francis, X 508-830-5001 213 A fmcdonald@maritime.edu
MCDONALD, Frank 212-346-1800 310 F fmcdonald@pace.edu
MCDONALD, Glen 850-872-3805 101 O gmcdonald@gulfcoasast.edu
MCDONALD, Hannah 254-501-5454 446 C h.mcdonald@tamuct.edu
MCDONALD, James 508-830-5096 213 A jmcdonald@maritime.edu
MCDONALD, Jan 864-977-7151 410 A jan.mcdonald@ngu.edu
MCDONALD, Jennifer 714-241-6163 38 D jmcdonald@coastline.edu
MCDONALD, John 773-298-3364 148 I mcdonald@sxu.edu
MCDONALD, Jomar 312-662-4000 132 D
MCDONALD, Joseph, M 518-461-2534 305 B jmcdonald01@mariacollege.edu
MCDONALD, Joy 973-353-5953 281 C joymcd@newark.rutgers.edu
MCDONALD, Karen 214-887-5221 434 G kmcdonald@dts.edu
MCDONALD, Ken 314-434-4044 251 F ken.mcdonald@covenantseminary.edu
MCDONALD, Kevin, G 434-243-2079 471 F kgm8km@virginia.edu
MCDONALD, Kim 540-665-4500 470 A
MCDONALD, Leander 701-255-3285 346 I president@uttc.edu
MCDONALD, Lori 949-214-3074 40 E lori.mcdonald@cui.edu
MCDONALD, Lori, K 801-581-7793 459 D lmcdonald@sa.utah.edu
MCDONALD, Lynn 478-553-2059 123 D ljmcdonald@oftc.edu
MCDONALD, Lynn, J 478-275-6589 123 E
MCDONALD, Martha 949-451-5624 65 B mmcdonald@ivc.edu
MCDONALD, Mary 478-471-2700 122 D mary.mcdonald@mga.edu
MCDONALD, Mary Rae 575-538-6238 288 J maryrae.mcdonald@wnmu.edu
MCDONALD, Michael 239-590-7212 109 G mmcdonal@fgcu.edu
MCDONALD, Michelle 901-572-2500 417 A michelle.mcdonald@baptistu.edu
MCDONALD, Molly 408-554-6993 63 A mmcdonald@scu.edu
MCDONALD, Nicholas 978-837-3597 216 D mcdonaldn@merrimack.edu
MCDONALD, Nicholas 757-455-3242 476 C nmcdonald@vwu.edu

MCGEE, Christina .... 913-288-7489 174 H
chmcgee@kckcc.edu
MCGEE, Darryl .... 731-425-2550 419 G
dmcgee@lanecollege.edu
MCGEE, Ed .... 434-832-7742 472 G
mcgee@centralvirginia.edu
MCGEE, Glenn .... 203-479-4192.. 89 F
gmcgee@newhaven.edu
MCGEE, Glenn .... 336-917-5557 339 H
glenn.mcgee@salem.edu
MCGEE, Gregory, R .... 859-858-3511 178 H
gregory.mcgee@asbury.edu
MCGEE, Isaiah, R .... 803-535-5679 406 E
imcgee@claflin.edu
MCGEE, James .... 404-756-4443 115 E
MCGEE, James .... 708-534-4900 138 C
jmcgee@govst.edu
MCGEE, John .... 770-426-2805 122 A
john.mcgee@life.edu
MCGEE, John .... 816-322-0110 250 E
john.mcgee@calvary.edu
MCGEE, Keith .... 601-877-6678 244 B
kmcgee@alcorn.edu
MCGEE, Laura .... 847-925-6686 138 E
lmcgee@harpercollege.edu
MCGEE, Lucy .... 800-895-7411 463 H
lmcgee@asl.edu
MCGEE, Marjorie .... 352-854-2322.. 97 L
mcgeem@cf.edu
MCGEE, Melandie .... 985-545-1500 188 B
MCGEE, Michael .... 828-328-7127 330 B
michael.mcgee@lr.edu
MCGEE, Michael .... 409-933-8324 432 H
mmcgee5@com.edu
MCGEE, Robby .... 910-362-7191 332 F
rmcgee@cfcc.edu
MCGEE, Shannon .... 229-333-5706 127 C
slmcgee@valdosta.edu
MCGEE, Sharon .... 423-439-1000 418 D
MCGEE, Sharon, J .... 423-439-4221 418 D
mcgees@etsu.edu
MCGEE, Summer .... 336-721-2605 339 H
summer.mcgee@salem.edu
MCGEE, Summer, J .... 203-479-4104.. 89 F
smcgee@newhaven.edu
MCGEE, Tammy .... 612-381-3370 235 C
tmcgee@dunwoody.edu
MCGEE, Tara .... 401-598-5160 403 E
tara.mcgee@jwu.edu
MCGEE, Tim .... 217-245-3060 139 A
timothy.mcgee@ic.edu
MCGEE, Tom .... 815-479-7764 143 F
tmcgee@mchenry.edu
MCGEE-YUROFF, Carrie 203-857-7000.. 87 B
cmcgee-yuroff@norwalk.edu
MCGEHEE, Janice .... 208-562-3163 131 C
janicemcgehee@cwi.edu
MCGEHEE, JR.,
Robert, E .... 501-686-5454.. 22 D
rem@uams.edu
MCGETTIGAN,
Mary Kay .... 215-951-1632 386 I
mcgettigan@lasalle.edu
MCGHEE, JR.,
James, D .... 804-752-3736 469 B
jamesmcghee@rmc.edu
MCGHEE, Lisa .... 870-763-3174.. 17 F
lmcghee@smail.anc.edu
MCGHEE, Marianne, S .. 804-523-5810 473 A
mmcghee@reynolds.edu
MCGHEE, Megan .... 615-248-1627 425 D
mmcghee@trevecca.edu
MCGHEE, Sandra, W ..... 540-375-2287 469 G
mcghee@roanoke.edu
MCGHEE, Tanya .... 252-444-0739 333 F
mcgheet@cravencc.edu
MCGHEE, Tony .... 276-964-5668 474 E
tony.mcghee@sw.edu
MCGILL, Angela .... 972-881-5151 432 I
amcgill@collin.edu
MCGILL, Antoinette .... 510-780-4500.. 48 D
amcgill@lifewest.edu
MCGILL, Bret .... 256-306-2861.... 1 F
bret.mcgill@calhoun.edu
MCGILL, Diana .... 859-572-5860 184 B
mcgill@nku.edu
MCGILL, Elizabeth, A .... 570-348-6231 389 B
emcgill@marywood.edu
MCGILL, Jason, T .... 402-280-5750 265 J
jasonmcgill@creighton.edu
MCGILL, Lawrence .... 410-888-9048 200 C
lmcgill@muih.edu

MCGILL, Peggy .... 305-289-1121.. 98 B
peggy@dolphins.org
MCGILL, Shaniece .... 626-316-5342.. 63 D
MCGILL, Shawna .... 575-769-4954 285 C
shawna.mcgill@clovis.edu
MCGILL, Sheila .... 405-466-2957 366 B
srmcgill@langston.edu
MCGILL, Shelia, R .... 405-466-3283 366 B
srmcgill@langston.edu
MCGILLICUDDY, Maren 207-509-7136 196 B
mmcgillicuddy@unity.edu
MCGILLICUDDY,
Suzanne .... 212-217-3800 299 C
suzanne_mcgillicuddy@fitnyc.edu
MCGILLIS, Bill .... 619-260-2982.. 72 H
wmcgillis@sandiego.edu
MCGILLOWAY,
Samantha .... 978-762-4000 215 B
smcgillo@northshore.edu
MCGILVRAY, Richard .... 716-827-4338 322 J
mcgilvrayr@trocaire.edu
MCGING, Christine .... 651-779-3368 237 D
christine.mcging@century.edu
MCGINLEY, Christina ... 215-968-8224 379 B
christina.mcginley@bucks.edu
MCGINLEY, Lynn .... 409-772-8909 456 B
lmmcginl@utmb.edu
MCGINLEY, William ...... 440-826-8014 348 C
wmcginle@bw.edu
MCGINNESS, Colleen .... 517-607-2304 224 G
cmcginness@hillsdale.edu
MCGINNIS, Blake .... 870-759-4170.. 24 B
bmcginnis@williamsbu.edu
MCGINNIS, Brianna ...... 410-386-8304 197 G
bmcginnis@carrollcc.edu
MCGINNIS, Carrie .... 270-809-3437 184 A
cmcginnis2@murraystate.edu
MCGINNIS, Erik .... 704-463-3001 339 C
erik.mcginnis@pfeiffer.edu
MCGINNIS, Gia, G .... 410-617-2489 199 G
ggrier@loyola.edu
MCGINNIS, Grace .... 708-709-3519 147 A
gmcginnis@prairiestate.edu
MCGINNIS, Katherine .... 808-932-7446 129 A
kfmcginn@hawaii.edu
MCGINNIS, Michael ...... 814-472-3004 396 I
mmcginnis@francis.edu
MCGINNIS, Sharon, R .. 910-938-6231 333 D
mcginniss@coastalcarolina.edu
MCGINNIS GONZALEZ,
Sherri .... 312-996-2398 151 D
smcginn@uic.edu
MCGINNISH, Paul .... 651-638-6094 233 J
paul-mcginnis@bethel.edu
MCGINNISS, Michael ..... 215-951-1360 386 I
mcginnis@lasalle.edu
MCGINTY, Evelyn, J ...... 936-261-1725 445 E
ejmcginty@pvamu.edu
MCGINTY, Rachel .... 845-848-4034 298 A
rachel.mcginty@dc.edu
MCGIVERN, Martha .... 312-362-8998 136 F
martha.mcgivern@depaul.edu
MCGIVNEY, R, J .... 860-768-4401.. 89 E
rmcgivney@hartford.edu
MCGIVNEY-BURELLE,
Jean .... 208-282-4143 131 E
jeanmcgivneyburel@isu.edu
MCGLADDERY, Ryan ...... 805-581-1233.. 42 C
rmcgladdery@eternitybiblecollege.com
MCGLADE, Catharine, A 718-817-4339 300 A
cmcglade@fordham.edu
MCGLADE, Jackie .... 304-243-2281 490 F
jmcglade@wheeling.edu
MCGLAMERY, Angie ...... 912-681-5500 123 F
arosengart@ogeecheetech.edu
MCGLAMERY, Matt .... 970-247-7065.. 80 H
mcglamery_m@fortlewis.edu
MCGLAMERY, Orien, S .. 970-247-7317.. 80 H
mcglamery_o@fortlewis.edu
MCGLASHAN, Holland .. 352-854-2322.. 97 L
mcglashh@cf.edu
MCGLAUFLIN, Nicole .... 712-279-5494 163 H
nicole.mcglauflin@briarcliff.edu
MCGLINCHEY, Tom .... 714-879-3901.. 45 J
tmcglinchey@hiu.edu
MCGLOTHLIN, Jason .... 276-498-5247 463 G
jmcglothlin@acp.edu
MCGLOTHLIN,
Michael, G .... 276-498-4190 463 G
mmcglothlin@acp.edu
MCGLYNN, Mia .... 215-646-7300 384 G
mcglynn.m@gmercyu.edu
MCGODMAN, Kandi ...... 916-348-4689.. 42 B
kmcgodman@epic.edu

MCGOFF, Michael, F .... 607-777-2143 315 E
mmcgoff@binghamton.edu
MCGOLDRICK, Rowena . 860-515-3751.. 85 D
rmcgoldrick@charteroak.edu
MCGOLDRICK, Sean ...... 775-784-6514 270 K
smcgoldrick@unr.edu
MCGONIGLE, Erin .... 410-455-2691 202 G
emcgonigle@umbc.edu
MCGONIGLE, Gregory ... 404-727-4429 118 D
gregory.mcgonigle@emory.edu
MCGONIGLE, Mary .... 610-519-4070 401 B
mary.mcgonigle@villanova.edu
MCGONIGLE, Robert ..... 570-208-5875 386 G
rbmcgoni@kings.edu
MCGORRY, Marian .... 610-359-5394 381 J
mmcgorry@dccc.edu
MCGORRY, Sue .... 610-282-1100 382 A
sue.mcgorry@desales.edu
MCGOVERN, Julie .... 707-468-3164.. 51 F
jmcgovern@mendocino.edu
MCGOVERN, Kathy .... 610-896-1089 385 H
kmcgovern@haverford.edu
MCGOVERN, Kevin .... 617-879-5982 216 B
kevin.mcgovern@mcphs.edu
MCGOVERN, Michael ..... 718-933-6700 306 J
MCGOWAN, Annie .... 979-458-2905 446 B
al-mcgowan@tamu.edu
MCGOWAN, Christina ... 203-254-4000.. 87 G
cmcgowan@fairfield.edu
MCGOWAN, John .... 205-348-5610.... 7 G
john.mcgowan@ua.edu
MCGOWAN, John .... 585-345-6999 300 D
jmmcgowan@genesee.edu
MCGOWAN, Joumana .... 626-914-8881.. 37 B
jmcgowan@citruscollege.edu
MCGOWAN, Katie .... 610-526-6062 385 F
cmcgowan@harcum.edu
MCGOWAN, Kevin .... 239-687-5335.. 95 L
kmcgowan@avemarialaw.edu
MCGOWAN, Kyle .... 208-282-3198 131 E
mcgokyle@isu.edu
MCGOWAN, Kyle, D .... 615-322-6850 427 B
kyle.mcgowan@vanderbilt.edu
MCGOWAN, Mary, M ..... 585-385-8066 313 A
mmcgowan@sjfc.edu
MCGOWAN, Matthew .... 617-984-1700 217 G
MCGOWAN, Michelle .... 770-534-6265 116 C
mmcgowan@brenau.edu
MCGOWAN, Michelle .... 229-271-4045 125 C
mmcgowan@southgatech.edu
MCGOWAN, Paul .... 617-552-3055 207 A
paul.mcgowan.2@bc.edu
MCGOWAN, Stephanie .. 201-559-3551 277 A
mcgowans@felician.edu
MCGRADY, Patricia .... 973-957-0188 274 D
treasurer@acs350.org
MCGRADY, Ronald, L .... 330-325-6799 357 D
rmcgrady@neomed.edu
MCGRADY, Tracy .... 417-447-8152 257 B
mcgradyt@otc.edu
MCGRAIL, James .... 603-862-0927 273 G
james.mcgrail@usnh.edu
MCGRAN, Don .... 904-819-6200.. 99 D
dmcgran@flagler.edu
MCGRANE, Wendy .... 417-625-9801 255 I
mcgrane-w@mssu.edu
MCGRANN, Michael .... 718-940-5741 313 C
mmgrann@sjcny.edu
MCGRATH, Beth .... 201-216-3389 282 L
cos.mcgrath@stevens.edu
MCGRATH, Bill .... 239-992-4624.. 96 E
MCGRATH, Cheryl .... 617-824-8328 208 G
cheryl_mcgrath@emerson.edu
MCGRATH, Christina ..... 719-549-3308.. 82 I
christina.mcgrath@pueblocc.edu
MCGRATH, Elizabeth ..... 563-588-6414 164 C
beth.mcgrath@clarke.edu
MCGRATH, Frank .... 239-687-5331.. 95 L
fmcgrath@avemarialaw.edu
MCGRATH, Greg .... 802-485-2225 461 H
gmcgrath@norwich.edu
MCGRATH, Heather .... 660-543-4900 259 K
hmcgrath@ucmo.edu
MCGRATH, James .... 517-371-5140 232 K
mcgrathj@cooley.edu
MCGRATH, Jane .... 312-362-5765 136 F
jmcgrath@depaul.edu
MCGRATH, John, J .... 518-786-0855 306 D
jmcgrath@mildred-elley.edu
MCGRATH, Karen .... 607-431-4130 300 G
mcgrathk@hartwick.edu
MCGRATH, Kat .... 518-608-8374 299 B
kmcgrath@excelsior.edu

MCGRATH, Mark .... 267-331-2853 380 G
mcgrathm@chc.edu
MCGRATH, Matthew ...... 585-785-1471 299 E
matthew.mcgrath@flcc.edu
MCGRATH, Nicole .... 203-932-7077.. 89 F
nmcgrath@newhaven.edu
MCGRATH, Riley, C ...... 715-836-5521 494 E
mcgratrc@uwec.edu
MCGRATH, Thomas .... 508-565-1086 218 F
tmcgrath@stonehill.edu
MCGRATH, Tim .... 714-895-8178.. 38 E
tmcgrath@gwc.cccd.edu
MCGRATH-ROTHENBERG,
Alexis .... 914-674-7607 305 H
arothenberg@mercy.edu
MCGRAW, Bryan .... 630-752-5928 152 K
bryan.mcgraw@wheaton.edu
MCGRAW, Christopher .. 404-962-3263 127 B
chris.mcgraw@usg.edu
MCGRAW, Darryl .... 919-508-2418 344 D
ddmcgraw@peace.edu
MCGRAW, Larry .... 325-670-1269 436 B
mcgraw@hsutx.edu
MCGRAW, Matthew .... 540-863-2866 473 D
mmcgraw@mgcc.edu
MCGRAW, Packy .... 518-694-7257 289 A
packy.mcgraw@acphs.edu
MCGREAL, Kristy .... 708-974-5335 144 G
mcgrealc2@morainevalley.edu
MCGREEVEY, Michael .... 614-890-3000 359 G
mmcgreevey@otterbein.edu
MCGREEVY, Bill .... 619-644-7141.. 44 H
bill.mcgreevy@gcccd.edu
MCGREEVY, Jeanette .... 605-256-5663 415 G
jeanette.mcgreevy@dsu.edu
MCGREEVY, John, T ..... 574-631-6631 161 G
jmcgreev@nd.edu
MCGREGOR, Alyson, J . 864-455-7000 412 F
alyson.mcgregor@prismahealth.org
MCGREGOR, Cynthia .... 619-482-6371.. 65 K
cmcgregor@swccd.edu
MCGREGOR, Justin .... 901-843-3874 422 C
mcgregorj@rhodes.edu
MCGREGOR, Mike .... 812-749-1392 159 E
mmcgregor@oak.edu
MCGREGOR, Tiffany ...... 610-361-2487 390 G
mcgregot@neumann.edu
MCGREW, Cindy .... 650-543-3996.. 52 A
cmcgrew@menlo.edu
MCGREW, Martha .... 505-277-2321 288 C
mmcgrew@salud.unm.edu
MCGREW, Mary Beth .... 412-383-5337 400 A
mbm77@pitt.edu
MCGREW, Michelle .... 843-953-7408 407 D
mmcgrew@cofc.edu
MCGRIFF, Elizabeth .... 415-565-4600.. 69 B
mcgriffelizabeth@uchastings.edu
MCGRUDER, Janell, J ... 309-341-7492 141 E
jmcgruder@knox.edu
MCGRUDER, Juan .... 404-261-1441 123 G
MCGUCKIN, Tammy ...... 262-595-2571 495 D
mcguckin@uwp.edu
MCGUFFEE, James .... 901-321-3482 417 G
jmcguffee@cbu.edu
MCGUFFEY, Amy .... 937-327-6342 364 C
amcguffey@wittenberg.edu
MCGUFFEY, Michael, J . 304-696-3648 488 N
mcguffey@marshall.edu
MCGUFFIN, Kurt .... 731-881-7661 426 E
rmcguffi@utm.edu
MCGUFFIN CAWLEY,
James .... 216-368-6842 349 B
jxc41@case.edu
MCGUINNESS, Maureen 940-565-2648 453 B
moe@unt.edu
MCGUINNESS, Paul ...... 708-235-7308 138 C
pmcguinness@govst.edu
MCGUINNESS, Scott ..... 724-503-1001 401 D
smcguinness@washjeff.edu
MCGUINNESS, Tom .... 207-786-8210 193 D
tmcguinn@bates.edu
MCGUIRE, Ann .... 440-646-6033 363 C
ann.mcguire@ursuline.edu
MCGUIRE, Bud .... 903-233-3000 438 C
MCGUIRE, Cassandra ... 206-934-3881 482 G
cassandra.mcguire@seattlecolleges.edu
MCGUIRE, Christine, W 617-353-9814 207 C
chmcguir@bu.edu
MCGUIRE, David, T .... 435-586-7755 459 E
mcguire@suu.edu
MCGUIRE, Jack .... 315-267-2131 318 D
mcguirjp@potsdam.edu

MCGUIRE, Jamie .... 902-403-3166 494 B
jamie.mcguire@snc.edu
MCGUIRE, Jamie .... 336-838-6482 338 H
jdmcguire271@wilkescc.edu
MCGUIRE, Kathleen ...... 508-541-1615 208 E
kmcguire@dean.edu
MCGUIRE, Kristen .... 410-617-2701 199 G
kcmcguire@loyola.edu
MCGUIRE, Larry .... 309-677-2919 133 H
lmcguire@bradley.edu
MCGUIRE, Maureen ...... 509-313-6137 479 E
mcguirem@gonzaga.edu
MCGUIRE, Michael .... 303-871-3518.. 84 C
mmcguire@du.edu
MCGUIRE, Patricia, A ... 202-884-9050.. 94 A
mcguirep@trinitydc.edu
MCGUIRE, Rachel, L ..... 641-422-4104 168 E
rachel.mcguire@niacc.edu
MCGUIRE, Rachel, L ..... 641-422-4104 168 E
mcguirac@niacc.edu
MCGUIRE, Ruth, A .... 651-631-5343 243 E
ramcguire@unwsp.edu
MCGUIRE, Shirley .... 415-422-6136.. 72 I
mcguire@usfca.edu
MCGUIRE, Sue .... 828-898-2561 330 A
mcguirer@lmc.edu
MCGUIRE, Tara, S .... 402-280-3973 265 J
taramcguire@creighton.edu
MCGUIRE, Venus .... 214-698-0461 434 A
ecc5100@dcccd.edu
MCGUIRE-WELCH,
Majorie .... 641-782-1425 170 B
welch@swcciowa.edu
MCGUIRK, Ryan .... 303-273-3062.. 79 A
mcguirk@mines.edu
MCGUIRT, Tony .... 864-294-2448 408 I
tony.mcguirt@furman.edu
MCGURGAN, Melissa .... 480-285-1761.. 12 D
MCGURIMAN, Timothy . 610-660-1357 397 A
tmcgurim@sju.edu
MCGURK, Mark .... 915-747-5113 454 E
mmcgurk@utep.edu
MCGURL, Mike .... 570-702-8938 386 D
mmcgurl@johnson.edu
MCGURN, Joseph, P ..... 740-283-6278 352 I
jmcgurn@franciscan.edu
MCGUTHRY, John, W ... 909-869-6442.. 30 B
jwmcguthry@cpp.edu
MCHALE, Brendan .... 217-351-2409 146 G
jmchale@parkland.edu
MCHALE, JR., William .. 717-358-3870 383 G
william.mchale@fandm.edu
MCHARRIS, Michael ..... 315-792-5489 306 G
mmcharris@mvcc.edu
MCHENRY, Beau .... 850-484-1146 105 G
bmchenry@pensacolastate.edu
MCHENRY, Erin .... 949-582-4481.. 65 C
emchenry@saddleback.edu
MCHENRY, Jason .... 317-738-8151 155 A
jmchenry@franklincollege.edu
MCHENRY, John .... 760-384-6148.. 47 C
john.mchenry@cerrocoso.edu
MCHENRY, Patrick .... 706-507-8800 117 E
MCHONE-CHASE, Sarah 630-844-5443 133 A
smchone-chase@aurora.edu
MCHORNEY, Mark .... 630-829-6150 133 B
mmchorney@ben.edu
MCHUGH, Chris .... 563-588-8000 165 K
cmchugh@emmaus.edu
MCHUGH, Elizabeth ...... 360-867-6808 479 C
mchughe@evergreen.edu
MCHUGH, John .... 704-748-5213 334 E
mchugh.john@gaston.edu
MCHUGH, John .... 804-828-0033 472 D
mchughj2@vcu.edu
MCHUGH, Michael .... 215-965-4028 390 C
MCHUGH, Patti .... 610-341-5812 383 A
pmchugh@eastern.edu
MCHUGH, Shelley .... 402-465-2123 267 J
smchugh@nebrwesleyan.edu
MCHUGH, Tracy .... 630-889-6605 145 D
tmchugh@nuhs.edu
MCHUGH, Tracy .... 630-889-6607 145 D
tmchugh@nuhs.edu
MCILDUFF, Stacy .... 518-381-1322 319 G
mcildusm@sunysccc.edu
MCILHENNEY, Daniel .... 610-436-2627 394 F
dmcilhenny@wcupa.edu
MCILROY, Julia .... 208-885-6123 132 C
juliam@uidaho.edu
MCILVANE, Amy .... 770-426-2648 122 A
mcilvane@life.edu
MCILWAIN, Dana .... 702-254-7577 271 B

MCILWAIN, Holly, J ...... 740-283-6340 352 I
hmcilwain@franciscan.edu
MCILWAINE, Tammi ...... 704-991-0311 338 A
tmcilwaine7455@stanly.edu
MCILWRAITH, Andy ...... 321-674-8935 100 A
andy@fit.edu
MCINERNEY, Todd .... 203-932-7031.. 89 F
tmcinerney@newhaven.edu
MCINNIS, Deena .... 601-857-3749 245 D
deena.mcinnis@hindscc.edu
MCINNIS, Emily .... 205-652-3587.... 9 B
ejm@uwa.edu
MCINNIS, James, P .... 601-643-8488 244 G
jp.mcinnis@colin.edu
MCINNIS, Kyle, J .... 401-865-1777 403 G
kmcinnis@providence.edu
MCINNIS, Maurie .... 631-632-6265 316 D
president@stonybrook.edu
MCINNIS, Robert, L ...... 704-216-6400 330 D
rmcinnis@livingstone.edu
MCINNIS, Talmadge ...... 704-922-6480 334 E
mcinnis.talmadge@gaston.edu
MCINNIS, W. Dale .... 910-410-1806 336 G
wdmcinnis@richmondcc.edu
MCINNIS, Wayne .... 972-780-3600 453 C
wayne.mcinnis@untdallas.edu
MCINTEE, Justin .... 714-556-3610.. 73 G
justin.mcintee@vanguard.edu
MCINTIRE, Kelsey .... 706-754-7768 123 C
kmcintire@northgatech.edu
MCINTIRE, Molly .... 407-582-5588 113 C
mmcintire1@valenciacollege.edu
MCINTOSH, Angela .... 937-766-3200 349 C
mcintosh@cedarville.edu
MCINTOSH, Carolyn ..... 212-752-1530 303 G
carolyn.mcintosh@limcollege.edu
MCINTOSH, Charles ...... 352-854-2322.. 97 L
mcintosc@cf.edu
MCINTOSH,
Christopher .... 608-265-0769 494 D
cpm@athletics.wisc.edu
MCINTOSH, Dawn .... 661-722-6300.. 26 E
dmcintosh1@avc.edu
MCINTOSH, Derek .... 606-539-4472 185 C
derek.mcintosh@ucumberlands.edu
MCINTOSH, Gary .... 425-889-7790 481 A
gary.mcintosh@northwestu.edu
MCINTOSH, Gayle .... 253-879-3905 483 G
gmcintosh@pugetsound.edu
MCINTOSH, Glenn .... 248-370-4200 229 F
mcintosh@oakland.edu
MCINTOSH, John .... 256-331-5323.... 3 C
jmcintosh@nwscc.edu
MCINTOSH, Joshua .... 207-786-6219 193 D
jmcintos@bates.edu
MCINTOSH, Julie .... 419-434-4062 362 D
mcintosh@findlay.edu
MCINTOSH, Katy .... 714-556-3610.. 73 G
katy.mcintosh@vanguard.edu
MCINTOSH, Keith, W .... 804-289-8771 471 E
kmcintosh@richmond.edu
MCINTOSH, Laurel .... 479-308-2212.. 17 E
laurel.mcintosh@arcomedu.org
MCINTOSH, Paulett .... 301-546-0854 201 D
mcintopd@pgcc.edu
MCINTOSH, Tanisha ...... 352-315-4383.. 96 B
tmcintosh@beaconcollege.edu
MCINTOSH-DOTY,
Mikail .... 512-313-3000 432 N
mikail.doty@concordia.edu
MCINTURF, Rob .... 940-369-7053 453 B
robert.mcinturf@unt.edu
MCINTYRE, Andrew .... 503-552-1775 374 B
amcintyre@nunm.edu
MCINTYRE, Crystal .... 603-271-6484 272 C
MCINTYRE, Ellen .... 865-974-2201 426 C
emcinty2@utk.edu
MCINTYRE, Helen, M .... 205-934-8132.... 8 A
hmcintyre@uab.edu
MCINTYRE, Jacqueline .. 516-364-0808 308 C
jmcintyre@nycollege.edu
MCINTYRE, James .... 615-460-6053 417 B
james.mcintyre@belmont.edu
MCINTYRE, Janene .... 619-421-6700.. 65 K
MCINTYRE, John .... 910-221-2224 330 G
jmcintyre@manna.edu
MCINTYRE, Kevin .... 806-743-7425 450 D
kevin.mcintyre@ttuhsc.edu
MCINTYRE, Laura Lee ... 541-346-1000 376 G
llmcinty@uoregon.edu
MCINTYRE, Sean .... 740-245-7974 363 A
smcintyre@rio.edu

MCINTYRE, Sherry .... 832-813-6828 438 E
sherry.mcintyre@lonestar.edu
MCIVOR, John .... 630-844-3830 133 A
jmcivor@aurora.edu
MCKAIN, Betty, J .... 269-387-4728 232 J
betty.mckain@wmich.edu
MCKAIN, Joshua .... 617-236-8854 209 D
jmckain@fisher.edu
MCKAIN, Mishele .... 218-751-8670 241 Q
mishelemckain@oakhills.edu
MCKANNA, Nate .... 214-887-5041 434 G
nmckanna@dts.edu
MCKAY, Ashley, M .... 812-941-2075 157 D
atronc01@ius.edu
MCKAY, Bill .... 509-542-5531 478 B
bmckay@columbiabasin.edu
MCKAY, Cheryl, A .... 573-341-7060 260 F
cherylan@mst.edu
MCKAY, Kerri .... 313-664-7441 222 C
kmckay@collegeforcreativestudies.edu
MCKAY, Kimber .... 406-243-4689 263 D
kimber.mckay@umontana.edu
MCKAY, Kimber .... 406-243-2571 263 D
kimber.mckay@umontana.edu
MCKAY, Kimberly .... 432-335-6683 440 C
kmckay@odessa.edu
MCKAY, Rebecca .... 256-761-6306.... 7 B
rmckay@talladega.edu
MCKAY, Richard .... 281-998-6150 442 E
richard.mckay@sjcd.edu
MCKAY JOHNSON,
Rebecca .... 903-566-7351 455 C
rjohnson@uttyler.edu
MCKAYLE, Camille, A ... 340-693-1200 512 B
cmckayl@uvi.edu
MCKEACHNIE, Brett .... 801-863-8940 460 A
mckeacbr@uvu.edu
MCKEAN, Molly .... 603-641-7020 273 C
mmckean@anselm.edu
MCKECHNIE, Janna .... 701-858-3373 345 C
janna.mckechnie@minotstateu.edu
MCKEE, Andy .... 260-356-4200 155 G
amckee@huntington.edu
MCKEE, Andy .... 260-399-7700 162 A
amckee@sf.edu
MCKEE, Diann, E .... 812-237-2372 155 H
diann.mckee@indstate.edu
MCKEE, Erin .... 712-325-3204 167 G
emckee@iwcc.edu
MCKEE, John, C .... 409-747-9080 456 B
jcmckee@utmb.edu
MCKEE, Joseph .... 662-621-4168 244 E
jmckee@coahomacc.edu
MCKEE, Kelli, J .... 724-847-6526 384 B
kelli.mckee@geneva.edu
MCKEE, Larry .... 856-351-2605 282 I
lmckee@salemcc.edu
MCKEE, Lori .... 575-646-8306 286 G
lomckee@nmsu.edu
MCKEE, Lori, L .... 419-755-4828 357 B
lmckee@ncstatecollege.edu
MCKEE, Marites .... 808-687-7014 128 E
mmckee@hpu.edu
MCKEE, Mark .... 419-448-2194 353 D
mmckee@heidelberg.com
MCKEE, Martin .... 214-887-5000 434 G
mmckee@dts.edu
MCKEE, Mike .... 386-752-1822.. 99 P
mike.mckee@fgc.edu
MCKEE, Nancy, C .... 850-245-0466 109 D
nancy.mckee@flbog.edu
MCKEE, Suzanne .... 334-683-2347.... 3 A
smckee@marionmilitary.edu
MCKEE, William .... 615-547-1311 418 C
bmckee@cumberland.edu
MCKEEGAN, John, N .... 814-886-6411 390 E
jmckeegan@mtaloy.edu
MCKEEN, Jerry .... 515-964-6514 164 F
jemckeen@dmacc.edu
MCKEEVER, Diane, M ... 312-942-6950 148 C
diane_m_mckeever@rush.edu
MCKEEVER, Shawna ...... 562-951-4500.. 31 C
smckeever@calstate.edu
MCKEIGUE, Elizabeth ... 978-542-6762 213 B
elizabeth.mckeigue@salemstate.edu
MCKEITHAN, Justin ...... 205-940-6302 332 A
justin.mckeithan@beaufortccc.edu
MCKEITHEN, Susan, P .. 719-884-5000.. 82 A
spmckeithen@nbc.edu
MCKELLIP, Mark .... 419-251-8989 355 G
mark.mckellip@mercycollege.edu
MCKELVEY, Brandon ..... 407-582-3046 113 C
jmckelvey@valenciacollege.edu

MCKELVEY, Donovan .... 404-458-6085 123 B
MCKELVEY, Jessica .... 713-348-4966 441 K
jm8@rice.edu
MCKELVEY, Kathryn ...... 419-267-1327 357 E
kmckelvey@northweststate.edu
MCKENDREE, Lynda ...... 713-525-2151 453 H
mckendla@stthom.edu
MCKENNA, Brian .... 864-941-8324 410 D
mckenna.b@ptc.edu
MCKENNA, Courtney .... 617-989-4590 219 D
mckennac4@wit.edu
MCKENNA, Crichton ..... 207-453-5019 195 B
cmckenna@kvcc.me.edu
MCKENNA, Doug .... 703-993-2434 466 J
cmckenn@gmu.edu
MCKENNA, James .... 508-830-5016 213 A
jmckenna@maritime.edu
MCKENNA, Kevin .... 914-395-2510 314 H
kmckenna@sarahlawrence.edu
MCKENNA, Kristen, P ... 617-228-2416 214 A
kpmckenn@bhcc.edu
MCKENNA, Lynn, C ...... 413-545-6272 211 D
lmckenna@admin.umass.edu
MCKENNA, Matthew ...... 216-421-7384 350 E
mkmckenna@cia.edu
MCKENNA, Michele ...... 603-456-2656 273 A
mmmckenna@magdalen.edu
MCKENNA, Timothy, J .. 319-273-3241 163 G
tim.mckenna@uni.edu
MCKENNA, Tori .... 860-439-2314.. 87 F
tori.mckenna@conncoll.edu
MCKENNA-JONES, Amy 573-518-2146 255 G
mjones@mineralarea.edu
MCKENZIE, Alicia .... 508-213-2020 217 C
alicia.mckenzie@nichols.edu
MCKENZIE, Amber .... 509-533-3122 478 D
amber.mckenzie@ccs.spokane.edu
MCKENZIE, Amber .... 509-533-3122 478 C
amber.mckenzie@ccs.spokane.edu
MCKENZIE, Amber .... 509-533-3122 478 E
amber.mckenzie@ccs.spokane.edu
MCKENZIE, Andre .... 718-990-1892 313 B
mckenzia@stjohns.edu
MCKENZIE, Bruce .... 937-778-7855 352 D
bmckenzie@edisonohio.edu
MCKENZIE, Chris .... 252-399-6314 326 H
cdmckenzie@barton.edu
MCKENZIE, Connie, L ... 757-965-8500 465 H
mckenzcl@evms.edu
MCKENZIE, Deborah ..... 803-705-4589 405 G
deborah.mckenzie@benedict.edu
MCKENZIE, Helen, R ..... 814-866-8130 387 C
hmckenzie@lecom.edu
MCKENZIE, JoAnn .... 404-727-6052 118 D
jmckenz@emory.edu
MCKENZIE, Justin .... 484-365-8134 388 F
cio@lincoln.edu
MCKENZIE, Laura .... 208-282-2979 131 E
mckelaur@isu.edu
MCKENZIE, Mary Beth .. 978-665-3123 212 C
memckenzie@fitchburgstate.edu
MCKENZIE, Michael ...... 828-262-2130 340 G
mckenziemj@appstate.edu
MCKENZIE, Rene .... 541-956-7129 375 G
rmckenzie@roguecc.edu
MCKENZIE, Sarah .... 334-808-6128.... 7 C
smckenzie93530@troy.edu
MCKENZIE, Steve .... 707-476-4385.. 58 I
MCKENZIE, Vandeen ..... 575-646-6014 286 G
vmckenzi@nmsu.edu
MCKEON, Margaret .... 215-871-6826 395 A
margaremc@pcom.edu
MCKEON, Michael .... 518-442-5435 315 D
mmckeon@albany.edu
MCKEOWN, Joshua, S .. 315-312-2118 318 B
joshua.mckeown@oswego.edu
MCKEOWN, Robert .... 716-614-6201 309 E
mckeown@niagaracc.suny.edu
MCKERNAN, Sarah .... 620-341-5551 173 C
smckerna@emporia.edu
MCKERNAN-WALLEY,
Jillian .... 315-229-5512 313 F
jmckwall@stlawu.edu
MCKERNON, Bill .... 620-341-5331 173 C
wmckerna@emporia.edu
MCKETHAN, Lisa, H ..... 254-710-3817 430 F
lisa_mckethan@baylor.edu
MCKIBBON, Chris .... 402-844-7015 268 A
chris@northeast.edu
MCKIBBON, Craig .... 952-806-3910 241 R
MCKIE, Angi .... 319-335-3531 163 F
angi-mckie@uiowa.edu

MCKIERNAN GONZALEZ,
Eileen .... 859-985-3181 179 E
mckiernan-gonzaleze@berea.edu

MCKIM, Heather ...... 970-248-1950.. 78 F
hmckim@coloradomesa.edu

MCKINDRA, Freeman ... 731-426-7500 419 G
rmkinion@cedarville.edu

MCKINION, Randall ... 937-766-7986 349 C
rmkinion@cedarville.edu

MCKINLEY, Bob .... 817-598-6256 457 C
bmckinley@wc.edu

MCKINLEY, Colleen ... 562-860-2451.. 35 O
cmckinley@cerritos.edu

MCKINLEY, Kristin, L ... 920-832-6532 492 B
kristin.l.mckinley@lawrence.edu

MCKINLEY, Robert ... 210-485-0020 427 H

MCKINLEY, Ronald ...... 510-466-7200.. 56 I

MCKINLEY, Ronald ...... 510-981-2800.. 56 J

MCKINLEY, Tracy ...... 817-598-6408 457 C
tdmckinley@wc.edu

MCKINNEY, Amy ...... 209-588-5100.. 76 J

MCKINNEY, Anya .... 865-251-1800 422 G
library@south.edu

MCKINNEY, Bryan ...... 870-245-5513.. 20 H
mckinneyb@obu.edu

MCKINNEY, Bryan ...... 870-245-5250.. 20 H
mckinneyb@obu.edu

MCKINNEY, Jason ... 315-279-5434 303 D
jmckinney@keuka.edu

MCKINNEY, Jermaine ... 386-481-2358.. 96 D
mckinneyj@cookman.edu

MCKINNEY, Jill .... 317-940-8312 153 C
jsmckinn@butler.edu

MCKINNEY, Joan, C ... 270-789-5214 179 G
jmckinney@campbellsville.edu

MCKINNEY, Kirsten ... 540-432-4107 465 F
kirsten.mckinney@emu.edu

MCKINNEY, Mica .... 435-797-1156 459 F
mica.mckinney@usu.edu

MCKINNEY, Michael ... 724-589-2600 398 F
mmckinney@thiel.edu

MCKINNEY, Mitchell, S 330-972-6433 361 G
mmckinney@uakron.edu

MCKINNEY, Monica ... 919-760-8056 331 A
mckinneym@meredith.edu

MCKINNEY, Nancy ...... 803-732-5355 409 E
mckinneyn@midlandstech.edu

MCKINNEY, Nick ... 509-777-4596 485 D
nmckinney@whitworth.edu

MCKINNEY, Paul ...... 662-325-7428 247 A
kpm137@msstate.edu

MCKINNEY, Rebekah ... 417-255-7949 256 A
rebekahmckinney@missouristate.edu

MCKINNEY, Robert ...... 337-482-5308 192 F
mckinney@louisiana.edu

MCKINNEY, Roger ...... 866-492-5336 243 G
roger.mckinney@laureate.net

MCKINNEY, Ronnie ...... 334-244-3668.... 4 F
ronnie@aum.edu

MCKINNEY, Scott .... 304-473-8041 490 E
mckinney.s@wvwc.edu

MCKINNEY, Scott .... 330-672-0347 354 A
smckinne@kent.edu

MCKINNEY, Shortie ... 978-934-4460 211 G
shortie_mckinney@uml.edu

MCKINNEY, Teresa ... 713-313-7011 448 D

MCKINNEY, Teresa, F ... 423-425-4141 426 D
teresa-mckinney@utc.edu

MCKINNISS, Mike ...... 805-565-6819.. 75 I
mmckinniss@westmont.edu

MCKINNON, Brad .... 256-766-6610.... 5 F
bmckinnon@hcu.edu

MCKINNON, Charles ... 770-962-7580 121 B
cmckinnon@gwinnetttech.edu

MCKINNON, Georgia ... 980-495-3978 329 A

MCKINNON, Laura ...... 817-515-4521 445 A
laura.mckinnon@tccd.edu

MCKINNON, Will .... 801-863-8922 460 A
will.mckinnon@uvu.edu

MCKINNON-HOWE,
Leah .... 617-585-1284 217 A
leah.mckinnon-howe@necmusic.edu

MCKINNY, Terry .... 864-488-8907 409 C
atmckinney@limestone.edu

MCKINSEY-MABRY,
Kimberly .... 585-292-2121 306 K
kmckinseymabry@monroecc.edu

MCKINZIE, Jena ...... 830-372-8155 448 C
jmckinzie@tlu.edu

MCKIRDY, Pam .... 434-791-5618 463 L
pmckirdy@averett.edu

MCKISSON, Kevin ...... 281-998-6150 442 D
kevin.mckisson@sjcd.edu

MCKISSON, Kevin ...... 281-669-4711 442 B
kevin.mckisson@sjcd.edu

MCKISSON, Kevin ...... 281-998-6150 442 E
kevin.mckisson@sjcd.edu

MCKISSON, Kevin, R ... 281-669-4711 442 C
kevin.mckisson@sjcd.edu

MCKITTRICK,
Christopher .... 732-571-7517 278 B
cmckittr@monmouth.edu

MCKITTRICK, Jerry ... 314-744-5345 255 H
mckittrickj@mobap.edu

MCKLOSKEY, Brian ... 412-237-3056 381 C
bmckloskey@ccac.edu

MCKNIGHT, Ariel ...... 724-832-1050 399 E
amcknight@triangle-tech.edu

MCKNIGHT, Carla, L ... 407-582-1756 113 C
cmcknight5@valenciacollege.edu

MCKNIGHT, Colleen ... 301-846-2446 198 E
cmcknight@frederick.edu

MCKNIGHT, Cynthia ... 440-684-6102 363 C
cmcknigh@ursuline.edu

MCKNIGHT, Elizabeth ... 423-354-2541 424 B
epmcknight@northeaststate.edu

MCKNIGHT, John ...... 610-896-1232 385 H
jmcknight@haverford.edu

MCKNIGHT, Justin ... 608-796-3808 496 L
jsmcknight@viterbo.edu

MCKNIGHT, Natalie ...... 617-353-2852 207 C
njmck@bu.edu

MCKNIGHT, Oscar .... 419-289-5065 347 H
omcknigh@ashland.edu

MCKNIGHT, Sandra ... 216-987-4832 351 D
sandra.mcknight@tri-c.edu

MCKNIGHT, Scott ...... 210-233-1102 432 A

MCKNIGHT, Steven, H ... 571-858-3000 475 D
shm@vt.edu

MCKNIGHT, Tanner ... 870-633-4480.. 19 E
tmcknight@eacc.edu

MCKNIGHT-TUTEIN,
Gillian .... 303-352-3059.. 80 D
gillian.mcknight-tutein@ccd.edu

MCKONE, Kevin .... 601-643-8369 244 G
kevin.mckone@colin.edu

MCKOWN, Denise ...... 432-685-6839 439 E
dmckown@midland.edu

MCKOWN, Johnette ...... 254-299-8601 438 G
jmckown@mclennan.edu

MCKOY, Cynthia ...... 910-879-5566 332 B
cmckoy@bladencc.edu

MCKOY, Sheila, S ...... 415-422-5555.. 72 I
ssmithmckoy@usfca.edu

MCLAIN, Andrea ...... 617-984-1713 217 G
amclain@quincycollege.edu

MCLAIN, Chris ...... 425-739-8265 480 D
chris.mclain@lwtech.edu

MCLAIN, Joe .... 712-749-2386 164 A
joe@bvu.edu

MCLAIN, Kimberly ... 607-778-5024 317 A
mclainkb@sunybroome.edu

MCLAIN, Mandy ...... 336-725-8344 327 G
mclainm@carolinau.edu

MCLAIN, Rebecca ...... 704-922-6352 334 E
mclain.rebecca@gaston.edu

MCLALLEN, Peter ...... 626-398-2222.. 76 B

MCLAMB, Alvin .... 803-327-7402 407 A
amclamb@clintoncollege.edu

MCLANE, Margaret ... 518-485-3334 296 E
mclanem@strose.edu

MCLANEY, Carl .... 323-563-4854.. 36 E
carlmclaney@cdrewu.edu

MCLAREN, Alison, J ... 513-585-0032 350 A
alison.mclaren@thechristcollege.edu

MCLAREN, Donna ...... 585-594-6114 311 L
mclaren_donna@roberts.edu

MCLARIO, Lisa .... 770-381-7200 120 F

MCLARTY, Meridith ... 972-860-4823 433 G
mmclarty@dcccd.edu

MCLARY, Laura ...... 540-362-7433 467 A
mclaryla@hollins.edu

MCLAUCHLAN, Craig ... 309-438-7018 140 C
ccmclau@ilstu.edu

MCLAUGHLIN, Adam ... 319-385-6490 167 F
adam.mclaughlin@iw.edu

MCLAUGHLIN, Amy ... 315-684-6038 320 E
mclaugai@morrisville.edu

MCLAUGHLIN, Annette ... 718-817-4350 300 A
lmclaughlin9@fordham.edu

MCLAUGHLIN, Ashley ... 601-977-7870 248 E
amclaughlin@tougaloo.edu

MCLAUGHLIN,
Bryan, S .... 402-280-2386 265 J
bmclaughlin@creighton.edu

MCLAUGHLIN, Cate ... 617-521-2000 218 C

MCLAUGHLIN, Chris ... 541-962-3516 372 H
cjmclaughlin@eou.edu

MCLAUGHLIN,
David, B .... 419-207-5555 347 H
dmclaugh@ashland.edu

MCLAUGHLIN, Denise ... 845-848-7803 298 A
denise.mclaughlin@dc.edu

MCLAUGHLIN, Edward ... 267-341-3031 385 I
emclaughlin2@holyfamily.edu

MCLAUGHLIN,
Edward, K .... 804-828-6692 472 D
athleticsdir@vcu.edu

MCLAUGHLIN,
Francis, X .... 718-817-4300 300 A
mclaughlin@fordham.edu

MCLAUGHLIN, Jennifer . 215-335-0800 388 E
jmcloughlin@lincolntech.edu

MCLAUGHLIN, Joyce ... 978-934-4237 211 G
joyce_mclaughlin@uml.edu

MCLAUGHLIN, Keith ... 708-656-8000 145 B
keith.mclaughlin@morton.edu

MCLAUGHLIN, Kerry ... 718-933-6700 306 J
kmclaughlin@monroecollege.edu

MCLAUGHLIN, Kevin ... 216-791-5000 350 F
kevin.mclaughlin@cim.edu

MCLAUGHLIN, Laura, L 217-581-7264 137 C
lmclaughlin@eiu.edu

MCLAUGHLIN,
Laurie, L .... 612-626-1499 242 K
mclau001@umn.edu

MCLAUGHLIN, LaVerne 229-500-3468 114 F
laverne.mclaughlin@asurams.edu

MCLAUGHLIN, Lisa ... 701-854-8023 346 F
lisa.mclaughlin@sittingbull.edu

MCLAUGHLIN, Mark ... 610-785-6216 396 H
mmclaughlin@scs.edu

MCLAUGHLIN, Mark ... 513-745-3409 364 F
mclaughlin@xavier.edu

MCLAUGHLIN,
Maureen .... 215-248-7137 380 G
mclaughlinm1@chc.edu

MCLAUGHLIN, Mireille . 617-333-2967 208 D
mireille.mclaughlin@curry.edu

MCLAUGHLIN, Robert ... 775-241-4445 269 G

MCLAUGHLIN, Robert ... 713-798-4613 430 E
rmclaughlin@bcm.edu

MCLAUGHLIN, Sean, M 614-823-1576 359 G
smclaughlin@otterbein.edu

MCLAUGHLIN,
Steven, W .... 404-894-6825 119 D
swm@gatech.edu

MCLAUGHLIN, Tim ...... 850-478-8496 105 F
tmclaughlin@pcci.edu

MCLAUGHLIN, William . 585-785-1561 299 E
william.mclaughlin@flcc.edu

MCLAUGHLIN VIGNIER,
Loretta .... 973-720-2104 283 I
mclaughlinvignierl@wpunj.edu

MCLAUGHLIN VIGNIER,
Loretta, C .... 973-720-3636 283 I
mclaughlinvignierl@wpunj.edu

MCLAUGHLIN-VOLPE,
Tracy .... 617-873-0150 207 E
tracy.mclaughlin@cambridgecollege.
edu

MCLEAN, Amber ...... 906-635-2382 226 C
amclean@lssu.edu

MCLEAN, Angela ...... 406-449-9131 263 C
amclean@montana.edu

MCLEAN, Beverly ...... 925-631-4600.. 59 I
bam12@stmarys-ca.edu

MCLEAN, Brandon ...... 402-844-7102 268 A
brandon@northeast.edu

MCLEAN, Connie ...... 309-796-5369 133 D
mcleanc@bhc.edu

MCLEAN, David ...... 970-491-3366.. 79 E
david.mclean@colostate.edu

MCLEAN, Jake ...... 309-341-7303 141 E
jrmclean@knox.edu

MCLEAN, Janna ...... 574-807-7191 153 G
janna.mclean@betheluniversity.edu

MCLEAN, Jennifer ... 570-326-3761 392 S
jmclean@pct.edu

MCLEAN, Kirk ...... 202-319-6065.. 91 G
mclean@cua.edu

MCLEAN, Mark ...... 985-448-7925 187 J
mark.mclean@fletcher.edu

MCLEAN, Monique ... 202-884-9097.. 94 A
mcleanmo@trinitydc.edu

MCLEAN, Natalie ...... 336-517-2334 326 J
nmclean@bennett.edu

MCLEAN, Pat ...... 417-690-3441 250 K
mclean@cofo.edu

MCLEAN, Robert ...... 443-997-8767 199 E
bobmclean@jhu.edu

MCLEAN, Selvin ...... 321-674-7715 100 A
smclean@fit.edu

MCLEAN, William ... 804-289-6010 471 E
wmclean2@richmond.edu

MCLEER, Karen ...... 608-342-1081 495 E
mcleerk@uwplatt.edu

MCLELLAN, Amy ...... 415-442-5285.. 44 B
amclellan@ggu.edu

MCLELLAND, Brandy ... 210-784-1204 447 B
brandy.mclelland@tamusa.edu

MCLEMAN, Laura ...... 810-762-3000 231 C
lauramcl@umflint.edu

MCLEMORE, Daniel ... 409-880-7886 449 B

MCLEMORE, Kareem ... 302-857-6351.. 90 D
kmclemore@desu.edu

MCLEMORE, Larry ...... 619-660-4064.. 44 G
larry.mclemore@gcccd.edu

MCLEMORE, Larry ...... 719-336-1516.. 81 F
larry.mclemore@lamarcc.edu

MCLENDON, James ... 314-935-5923 261 B
james.mclendon@wustl.edu

MCLENDON, Matthew ... 205-348-5666.... 7 G
mbmclendon@ua.edu

MCLENDON, Sandra ... 864-644-5354 411 E
smclendon@swu.edu

MCLENNAN, Dale ... 978-232-2101 209 B
dmclenna@endicott.edu

MCLEOD, Brian ...... 989-837-4329 228 G
mcleodb@northwood.edu

MCLEOD, Crystal ...... 906-487-2538 227 D
cpmcleod@mtu.edu

MCLEOD, Dale, A ...... 973-596-3140 278 G
dale.a.mcleod@njit.edu

MCLEOD, Dwight ...... 660-626-2842 249 C
dmcleod@atsu.edu

MCLEOD, Gregory ...... 252-823-5166 334 B
mcleodg@edgecombe.edu

MCLEOD, Joetta ...... 701-627-4738 346 D

MCLEOD, Michael ...... 718-990-1428 313 B
mcleodm@stjohns.edu

MCLEOD, Michael ...... 209-228-4055.. 70 A
mmcleod@ucmerced.edu

MCLEOD, Michael, J ... 516-877-3177 288 L
mcleod@adelphi.edu

MCLEOD, Steve ...... 706-864-1915 126 G
steve.mcleod@ung.edu

MCLERAN, Laura ...... 319-335-3549 163 F
laura-mcleran@uiowa.edu

MCLESKEY, Stephanie . 828-689-1128 330 H
smcleskey@mhu.edu

MCLODA, Todd ...... 309-438-7602 140 C
tamclod@ilstu.edu

MCLOUD, Debbie ...... 479-575-2159.. 21 D
dmcloud@uark.edu

MCLOUD-SCHINGEN,
Kelli .... 918-631-2713 371 C
kelli-mcloud-schingen@utulsa.edu

MCLOUGHLIN, Eileen ... 518-276-6426 311 J
mcloue@rpi.edu

MCLOUGHLIN, Nial ... 480-947-6644.. 15 B

MCLOUGHLIN, II,
Paul, J .... 315-228-7425 296 C
pmcloughlin@colgate.edu

MCLOUGHLIN, Suzanne 516-876-3109 318 A
mcloughlins@oldwestbury.edu

MCLOUTH, Rusty ...... 816-501-2941 249 H
rusty.mclouth@avila.edu

MCMACKIN, Carolyn ... 336-734-7382 334 D
cmcmackin@forsythtech.edu

MCMAHAN, Carla ...... 864-977-7092 410 A
carla.mcmahan@ngu.edu

MCMAHAN, Chantel ... 360-752-8320 477 E
cmcmahan@btc.edu

MCMAHAN, Craig, T ... 478-301-2992 122 C
mcmahan_ct@mercer.edu

MCMAHAN, David ...... 321-674-8000 100 A
dmcmahan@fit.edu

MCMAHAN, Kerrin ...... 323-415-4135.. 49 D
mcmahakm@elac.edu

MCMAHAN,
Maureen, E .... 260-399-7700 162 A
mmcmahan@sf.edu

MCMAHAN, Mendi ...... 214-333-5119 433 D
mendi@dbu.edu

MCMAHAN, Oliver, L ... 423-478-7037 421 J
omcmahan@ptseminary.edu

MCMAHAN, Robert, K ... 810-762-9782 225 F
mcmahan@kettering.edu

MCMAHAN, Shari ...... 509-359-6362 478 E
smcmahan2@ewu.edu

MCNULTY, Timothy .... 412-268-7778 380 B
tpm@andrew.cmu.edu
MCNUTT, Jill .... 608-663-3369 491 F
jmcnutt@edgewood.edu
MCNUTT, Kraig .... 214-887-5141 434 G
kmcnutt@dts.edu
MCPARTLAND, Terence . 203-672-6647.. 85 C
tmcpartland@albertus.edu
MCPARTLON, Shannon . 313-664-7460 222 C
smcpartlon@collegeforcreativestudies.edu
MCPHAIL, Amber .... 256-824-6775.... 8 B
amber.mcphail@uah.edu
MCPHAIL, Christine ...... 919-516-4000 339 G
MCPHAIL, Craig .... 828-898-2483 330 A
mcphail@lmc.edu
MCPHAIL, Julie .... 319-656-2447 169 F
MCPHAIL, Mark .... 503-883-2270 373 E
mmcphail@linfield.edu
MCPHAIL, P. Curtis ...... 864-597-4261 413 E
mcphailpc@wofford.edu
MCPHATTER, Anna .... 443-885-3922 200 F
anna.mcphatter@morgan.edu
MCPHATTER, Renee ...... 202-994-0679.. 92 C
rmcphatt@gwu.edu
MCPHEARSON, Petra, R 731-881-7800 426 E
prencher@utm.edu
MCPHEE, Debra .... 212-636-6616 300 A
dmcphee1@fordham.edu
MCPHEE, Myra, M .... 305-626-3626 100 B
myra.mcphee@fmuniv.edu
MCPHEE, Sidney, A ...... 615-898-2623 421 C
sidney.mcphee@mtsu.edu
MCPHEETERS, Andrew .. 503-768-7936 373 D
mcpheete@lclark.edu
MCPHERON, Lisa .... 714-992-7014.. 54 D
mcpheron@fullcoll.edu
MCPHERSON, Brisco ...... 405-224-3140 371 B
bmcpherson@usao.edu
MCPHERSON, Christopher, A .... 304-336-8274 489 B
christopher.mcpherson@westliberty.edu
MCPHERSON, John .... 765-285-5600 153 E
jmcphers@bsu.edu
MCPHERSON, Kevin ...... 312-488-6051.. 36 G
kmcpherson1@tcsedsystem.edu
MCPHERSON, Michael .. 305-809-3280.. 97 M
michael.mcpherson@cfk.edu
MCPHERSON, Michael .. 940-565-5206 453 B
michael.mcpherson@unt.edu
MCPHERSON, Michael, A .... 940-565-5206 453 B
michael.mcpherson@unt.edu
MCPHERSON, Nancy ..... 816-268-5402 256 E
nmcpherson@nts.edu
MCPHERSON, Robert .... 713-743-5003 451 G
bmcph@uh.edu
MCPHERSON, Robert, H .... 832-743-5003 451 G
bmcph@uh.edu
MCPHERSON, Tim .... 423-648-2421 422 D
tmcpherson@richmont.edu
MCPHERSON, Timothy .. 816-268-5430 256 E
tmcpherson@nts.edu
MCPHERSON, William ... 903-983-8657 437 G
wmcpherson@kilgore.edu
MCPHERSON MYERS, Penny .... 856-256-4086 280 H
mcphersonp@rowan.edu
MCPHILLIPS, Michael ... 740-351-3046 360 E
mmcphillips@shawnee.edu
MCQUADE, Eileen .... 805-565-6117.. 75 I
mcquade@westmont.edu
MCQUARIE, Audra .... 602-557-6151.. 16 L
audra.mcquarie@phoenix.edu
MCQUARTERS, Alfred .... 503-491-6422 373 H
alfred.mcquarters@mhcc.edu
MCQUEEN, Candice .... 615-966-1787 420 B
candice.mcqueen@lipscomb.edu
MCQUEEN, Chandra ...... 214-768-4767 443 G
chandram@smu.edu
MCQUEEN, Deborah ...... 919-530-7887 341 D
dmcquee2@nccu.edu
MCQUEEN, Mary .... 361-698-1317 434 H
mmcqueen2@delmar.edu
MCQUEEN, Rebecca ...... 270-852-3289 183 B
rmcqueen@kwc.edu
MCQUEENEY, Christopher .... 315-568-3352 309 H
cmcqueeney@northeastcollege.edu
MCQUERRY, Marcia ...... 405-585-5100 367 B
marcia.mcquerry@okbu.edu
MCQUILKIN, Scott .... 509-777-3200 485 D
president@whitworth.edu
MCQUILLAN, Shawn, A 412-365-1591 380 F
s.mcquillan@chatham.edu
MCQUILLEN, Troy .... 319-398-5569 167 H
troy.mcquillen@kirkwood.edu
MCQUINN, Nathan .... 251-380-3089.... 6 H
nmcquinn@shc.edu
MCQUINN, Robert .... 847-467-2469 146 C
r-mcquinn@northwestern.edu
MCRAE, Amanda .... 205-652-3579.... 9 B
amcrae@uwa.edu
MCRAE, Kevin .... 406-449-9154 263 C
kmcrae@montana.edu
MCRAE, Mary, S .... 972-378-8790 432 I
mmcrae@collin.edu
MCRAE, Rod .... 478-471-2989 122 D
rod.mcrae@mga.edu
MCRAE-BRUNSON, Marcela, C .... 870-235-4025.. 21 E
mdbrunson@saumag.edu
MCREE, Matt .... 706-245-3115 118 C
mmcree@ec.edu
MCRELL, Michael .... 620-341-5214 173 C
mcrellmi@emporia.edu
MCREYNOLDS, Alisha ... 501-686-7001.. 22 D
mcreynoldsalisham@uams.edu
MCREYNOLDS, Julie ..... 618-453-7935 149 G
jcima@siu.edu
MCREYNOLDS, Karla ..... 573-288-6544 251 I
kmcreynolds@culver.edu
MCREYNOLDS, Shawn .. 276-223-4810 475 B
smcreynolds@wcc.vccs.edu
MCRINA, Rhonda .... 319-296-4463 166 E
rhonda.mcrina@hawkeyecollege.edu
MCSHAN, Braxton .... 504-816-4669 186 F
bmcshan@dillard.edu
MCSHAY, James .... 301-314-8430 202 E
jmcshay@umd.edu
MCSHEFFERY, Ed .... 724-938-4299 394 C
mcsheffery@calu.edu
MCSHERRY, Bernard ..... 201-200-2020 278 F
bmcsherry@njcu.edu
MCSPADDEN, Daniel, L 513-745-3756 364 F
mcspaddend@xavier.edu
MCSTOWE, Dana .... 845-848-4122 298 A
dana.mcstowe@dc.edu
MCSWAIN, Ann .... 573-681-5400 254 A
mcswaina@lincolnu.edu
MCSWAIN, Roderick ...... 251-405-7013.... 1 E
rmcswain@bishop.edu
MCSWEEN, Amanda ...... 806-743-6431 450 D
amanda.mcsween@ttuhsc.edu
MCTIERNAN, Kerri-Ann . 516-572-7537 307 C
kerriann.mctiernan@ncc.edu
MCTIERNAN, Susan ...... 401-254-3444 404 C
smctiernan@rwu.edu
MCTYIER, James (Jay) .. 812-941-2454 157 D
jmctyier@ius.edu
MCVAY, Janine .... 413-565-1000 205 I
jmcvay@baypath.edu
MCVAY, John .... 509-527-2121 484 C
john.mcvay@wallawalla.edu
MCVEAN, Aaron .... 650-358-6803.. 62 H
mcveana@smccd.edu
MCVEY, Bernadette .... 973-761-9655 282 K
bernadette.mcvey@shu.edu
MCVEY, Greg .... 352-395-5536 107 G
greg.mcvey@sfcollege.edu
MCVEY, Josh .... 575-461-4413 285 J
joshm@mesalands.edu
MCVICKER, Libby .... 618-395-7777 139 C
mcvickero@iecc.edu
MCWAINE, DeRhonda ... 281-998-6150 442 C
derhonda.mcwaine@sjcd.edu
MCWELL, Andre .... 712-274-5318 168 C
mcwell@morningside.edu
MCWHORTER, Shirlyon, J .... 305-348-2785 109 H
shirlyon.mcwhorter@fiu.edu
MCWHORTER, Thomas . 213-740-5445.. 73 C
faodean@usc.edu
MCWHORTER, Todd .... 502-895-3411 183 E
tmcwhorter@lpts.edu
MCWILLIAMS, Brendan . 617-735-9986 209 A
mcwilliamsb@emmanuel.edu
MCWILLIAMS, Diana ..... 972-686-7878 441 G
MCWILLIAMS, Gene ...... 610-558-5504 390 G
genemcw@neumann.edu
MCWILLIAMS, Joe .... 208-496-7010 130 G
mcwilliamsj@byui.edu
MCWILLIAMS, Josette, A .... 207-581-1512 196 D
josette.mcwilliams@maine.edu
MCWILLIAMS, Mindy .... 202-687-8041.. 92 D
mcwillie@georgetown.edu
MCWILLIAMS, Rachel ... 252-985-5343 339 B
rmcwilliams@ncwc.edu
MCWILLIAMS, Stephen, T .... 610-519-4095 401 B
stephen.mcwilliams@villanova.edu
MCWILLIAMS, Susan .... 207-228-8258 196 J
susan.mcwilliams@maine.edu
MCWORTHY, Chance .... 319-363-1323 168 D
cmcworthy@mtmercy.edu
MEA, William .... 614-236-6872 348 I
wmea@capital.edu
MEAD, Ann Marie .... 609-896-5000 280 D
amead@rider.edu
MEAD, Bryan .... 903-923-2229 435 A
bmead@etbu.edu
MEAD, Craig .... 907-786-1480.. 10 A
MEAD, Molly .... 816-235-6595 260 D
meadmo@umkc.edu
MEAD, Shawnboda .... 662-915-2933 248 F
sdmead@olemiss.edu
MEADE, Elizabeth .... 610-606-4612 380 C
president@cedarcrest.edu
MEADE, Melissa .... 360-596-5364 483 E
mmeade@spscc.edu
MEADE, OSB, Pachomius .... 660-944-2950 251 B
pachomius@conception.edu
MEADE, Philip .... 212-343-1234 306 C
pmeade@mcny.edu
MEADE, Ronald, L .... 606-451-6823 182 D
ron.meade@kctcs.edu
MEADER, Eric .... 207-755-5348 194 J
emeader@cmcc.edu
MEADERDS, Genesis ..... 541-962-3496 372 H
gmeaderds@eou.edu
MEADOR, Cherie .... 708-974-5633 144 G
meadorc@morainevalley.edu
MEADOR, Earl .... 318-371-3035 188 C
earlmeador@nltcc.edu
MEADOR, Ryan .... 816-604-1076 254 E
ryan.meador@mcckc.edu
MEADOWS, Aaron .... 843-953-5049 406 D
smeadows@citadel.edu
MEADOWS, Courtney .... 618-395-1169 139 F
meadowsc@iecc.edu
MEADOWS, David, D .... 814-641-0714 386 E
meadowd@juniata.edu
MEADOWS, David, J .... 412-578-8842 380 A
djmeadows@carlow.edu
MEADOWS, Ed .... 850-484-1700 105 G
emeadows@pensacolastate.edu
MEADOWS, Leslie .... 334-244-3657.... 4 F
lmeadows@aum.edu
MEADOWS, Melissa ...... 760-252-2411.. 26 L
mmeadows@barstow.edu
MEADOWS, Ricky .... 252-638-4550 333 F
meadowsr@cravencc.edu
MEADOWS, Steve .... 304-384-5180 488 K
meadows@concord.edu
MEADOWS, Terry .... 479-788-7891.. 22 A
terry.meadows@uafs.edu
MEADS, Lisa .... 252-335-0821 333 E
lisa_meads@albemarle.edu
MEAGER, Kevin .... 419-227-3141 362 F
klmeager@unoh.edu
MEAGHER, Jo-Ann .... 978-630-9101 215 A
j_meagher@mwcc.mass.edu
MEAGHER, Kathy .... 301-387-3095 198 F
kathy.meagher@garrettcollege.edu
MEAGHER, Paula, G ..... 915-831-4530 435 B
pmeagher@epcc.edu
MEALER, Donna .... 731-286-3312 423 E
mealer@dscc.edu
MEALIE, Monica .... 225-771-3282 190 K
monica_mealie@subr.edu
MEALY, Stephanie .... 414-277-7224 493 D
MEANEY, Dorothy .... 617-627-2979 219 A
dorothy.meaney@tufts.edu
MEANEY, Heather, L ..... 518-381-1250 319 G
meaneyhl@sunysccc.edu
MEANEY, Kevin .... 910-962-3241 343 B
meaneykm@uncw.edu
MEANOR, Michael .... 570-706-8659 181 C
michaelj.meanor@kctcs.edu
MEANOR, Nicole .... 470-578-7629 121 J
nmeanor@kennesaw.edu
MEANS, Amanda .... 216-373-6470 357 F
ameans@ndc.edu
MEANS, John .... 661-336-5036.. 47 A
jmeans@kccd.edu
MEANY, David .... 509-359-6335 478 H
dmeany@ewu.edu
MEARA, Mark .... 856-222-9311 280 E
mmeara@rcbc.edu
MEARES, Scott .... 361-825-2107 446 E
scott.meares@tamucc.edu
MEARIG, Sayaka .... 541-485-1780 374 C
sayakamearig@newhope.edu
MEARNS, Geoffrey, S .... 765-285-5555 153 E
gsmearns@bsu.edu
MEARS, Jamie .... 806-665-8801 431 K
jamie.mears@clarendoncollege.edu
MEASAMER, Ronnie .... 919-718-7409 333 A
rmeasamer@cccc.edu
MEASE, Ervin, J .... 610-799-1112 388 B
emease@lccc.edu
MECHAM, Melissa .... 206-239-4500 477 I
MECHAM, Melissa, E .... 206-239-4500 477 I
MECHE, Eddie .... 225-342-6950 191 F
eddie.meche@ulsystem.edu
MECHE, Lance .... 972-825-4802 444 C
lmeche@sagu.edu
MECHLER, Heather, S ... 505-918-7302 288 C
hsmechler@unm.edu
MECKEL, David .... 415-703-9561.. 28 D
dmeckel@cca.edu
MECKLEY, Phil .... 785-833-4354 175 C
pmeckley@kwu.edu
MEDA, Pat .... 626-529-8261.. 55 E
pmeda@pacificoaks.edu
MEDASTIN, Jean-Jacques .... 937-376-6302 349 H
jmedastin@centralstate.edu
MEDBERY, Russell .... 603-526-3870 271 H
rmedbery@colby-sawyer.edu
MEDBURY, Doug .... 425-235-2352 482 C
dmedbury@rtc.edu
MEDDERS, Elizabeth ...... 817-735-2483 453 D
elizabeth.medders@unthsc.edu
MEDDERS, Mike, W ...... 903-566-7393 455 C
mmedders@uttyler.edu
MEDEARIS, Cheryl .... 605-856-5880 415 A
cheryl.medearis@sintegleska.edu
MEDEARIS, Jessica .... 763-433-1103 236 H
jessica.medearis@anokaramsey.edu
MEDEIROS, Madeline .... 805-546-3123.. 41 A
mmedeiro@cuesta.edu
MEDEL, Michael .... 805-965-0581.. 62 M
medel@sbcc.edu
MEDEMA, Pamela, S ..... 815-835-6378 149 A
pamela.s.medema@svcc.edu
MEDENBLIK, Julius, T .. 616-957-6024 221 K
jmedenblik@calvinseminary.edu
MEDER, Cheri .... 719-587-8368.. 77 F
cmeder@adams.edu
MEDFORD, Lienne .... 864-596-9082 407 G
lienne.medford@converse.edu
MEDFORD, Lienne, F .... 864-596-9082 407 G
lienne.medford@converse.edu
MEDFORD, Mike .... 404-687-4576 117 D
medfordm@ctsnet.edu
MEDI, Srini .... 480-557-2000.. 16 L
srini.medi@phoenix.edu
MEDICO, Karim .... 570-408-5512 402 B
karim.medico@wilkes.edu
MEDINA, Allyson, M .... 210-829-6000 452 D
ammedin4@uiwtx.edu
MEDINA, Barbara, M .... 505-747-2100 287 C
barbara.medina@nnmc.edu
MEDINA, Barbara, M .... 505-747-2147 287 C
barbara.medina@nnmc.edu
MEDINA, Celia .... 787-815-0000 510 D
celia.medina@upr.edu
MEDINA, Edgar .... 312-369-7688 136 C
emedina@colum.edu
MEDINA, Griselda .... 432-552-2700 456 C
medina_g@utpb.edu
MEDINA, Heather .... 609-652-4831 283 A
heather.medina@stockton.edu
MEDINA, Herbert, A ...... 503-943-7105 376 H
medinah@up.edu
MEDINA, Kathryn .... 510-723-6751.. 35 Q
kmedina@chabotcollege.edu
MEDINA, Kimberly .... 970-248-1958.. 78 F
kmedina@coloradomes.edu
MEDINA, Lisa .... 760-750-4840.. 33 C
lmmedina@csusm.edu
MEDINA, Maribel .... 213-891-2188.. 49 C
medinams@laccd.edu
MEDINA, Maxiel .... 212-410-8486 308 D
mmedina@nycpm.edu
MEDINA, Nancy .... 847-925-6675 138 E
mn18357@harpercollege.edu

MELLING, Alice .... 206-934-3693 482 F
alice.melling@seattlecolleges.edu
MELLINGER, Keith .... 540-654-1052 471 B
kmelling@umw.edu
MELLO, Catherine .... 402-559-4385 269 B
catherine.mello@unmc.edu
MELLO, Heath, M .... 402-472-7156 268 I
hmello@nebraska.edu
MELLO, James .... 740-284-5369 352 I
jmello@franciscan.edu
MELLO, Lynne .... 401-254-3436 404 C
lmello@rwu.edu
MELLON, Aimee .... 205-665-6540.... 8 D
amellon@montevallo.edu
MELLON, James, P .... 808-932-7467 129 A
mellon@hawaii.edu
MELLOR, Kariena .... 253-589-5588 478 A
kariena.mellor@cptc.edu
MELLOR, Tracey .... 617-747-6600 206 D
studyabroad@berklee.edu
MELLOTT, David, M ...... 317-931-2303 154 D
dmellott@cts.edu
MELLOTT, Ramona, N ... 928-523-7145.. 14 J
ramona.mellott@nau.edu
MELMED, Shlomo .... 310-423-8294.. 35 M
MELNICK, Patrick .... 216-221-8584 357 C
patrick.melnick@thencc.edu
MELNYK, Bernadette ..... 614-292-4844 358 E
melnyk.15@osu.edu
MELO, Amberr .... 409-880-7011 449 B
MELO, Aselia .... 916-691-7066.. 50 K
meloa@crc.losrios.edu
MELO, Diane .... 661-824-2977.. 53 H
dmelo@ntps.edu
MELOAN, Andrea .... 816-415-7831 261 G
meloana@william.jewell.edu
MELOHUSKY, Lisa .... 716-673-3649 316 A
lisa.melohusky@fredonia.edu
MELOY, Michelle .... 856-225-2724 281 A
mlmeloy@rutgers.edu
MELROE LEHRMAN,
Bethany .... 605-995-2706 414 A
bethany.melroe@dwu.edu
MELSON, Richard, J ..... 417-328-5281 258 K
MELSON, Vollie, D .... 410-777-1494 197 C
vmelson@aacc.edu
MELTON, Alisha, M .... 731-881-7015 426 E
amelton6@utm.edu
MELTON, Angela .... 402-471-2505 267 F
amelton@nscs.edu
MELTON, Brice .... 828-327-7000 332 H
bmelton@cvcc.edu
MELTON, Chad, W .... 517-750-1200 230 F
cmelton@arbor.edu
MELTON, Cindy .... 601-925-3250 246 D
cmelton@mc.edu
MELTON, David, V .... 617-364-3510 206 F
dmelton@boston.edu
MELTON, Ellen, C .... 512-233-1400 441 N
ellencm@stedwards.edu
MELTON, Judi .... 214-329-4447 429 L
judi.melton@bgu.edu
MELTON, Judy .... 828-652-0645 335 H
judym@mcdowelltech.edu
MELTON, Julie .... 217-875-7211 147 G
jmelton@richland.edu
MELTON, Leslie, J .... 740-368-3152 359 F
ljdelerm@owu.edu
MELTON, Mark, A .... 919-516-4029 339 G
mamelton@st-aug.edu
MELTON, Matthew .... 423-614-8115 419 H
mmelton@leeuniversity.edu
MELTON, Randy, G .... 517-750-1200 230 F
ra766788@arbor.edu
MELTON, Ryan .... 541-684-7470 371 H
rmelton@bushnell.edu
MELTON, JR., Samuel .. 662-254-3434 247 C
smelton@mvsu.edu
MELTON, Steve .... 828-297-3811 332 E
smelton@cccti.edu
MELTON, Susan, B .... 252-862-1228 336 H
sbmelton1310@roanokechowan.edu
MELTON, Toni .... 901-381-3939 427 C
toni@visible.edu
MELTZER, Carolyn .... 323-442-6411.. 73 C
deanksom@usc.edu
MELUSKY, Marie, B ...... 814-472-3126 396 I
mmelusky@francis.edu
MELVILLE, John .... 252-638-7260 333 F
melvillej@cravencc.edu
MELVIN, Christopher .... 618-235-2700 150 B
christopher.melvin@swic.edu

MELVIN, Dana .... 724-653-2216 382 C
dmelvin@dec.edu
MELVIN, Julienne .... 440-775-8460 357 G
jmelvin@oberlin.edu
MELVIN, Kari .... 301-846-2442 198 E
kmelvin@frederick.edu
MELVIN, Lee, H .... 716-645-5970 315 F
leemelvi@buffalo.edu
MELVIN, Marilee, A ...... 630-752-5517 152 K
marilee.melvin@wheaton.edu
MELVIN, Matt .... 785-864-4381 177 G
mattmelvin@ku.edu
MELZER, Deborah .... 410-617-5171 199 G
dcmelzer@loyola.edu
MELZER, Libby .... 614-234-5213 356 E
emelzer@mccn.edu
MEMANI, Krishna, K ..... 610-330-5000 387 B
MEMMOTT, Brian .... 208-496-4829 130 G
memmottb@byui.edu
MENA, Clara .... 203-285-2123.. 86 D
cmena@gatewayct.edu
MENA, Robert .... 213-738-6716.. 66 A
studentaffairs@swlaw.edu
MENA, Salvador .... 848-932-8576 281 B
salvador.mena@rutgers.edu
MENA, Terry .... 773-442-4600 145 G
t-mena2@neiu.edu
MENADIER, Judy .... 352-854-2322.. 97 L
menadiej@cf.edu
MENARD, Jennifer .... 508-678-2811 213 F
jennifer.menard@bristolcc.edu
MENARD, Richard, R ..... 401-841-7004 501 L
richard.menard@usnwc.edu
MENARD, Tim .... 218-281-8585 243 B
menar021@umn.edu
MENARD, William .... 401-739-5000 403 F
bmenard@neit.edu
MENCARELLI, Brent, T .. 574-372-5100 155 C
mencarb@grace.edu
MENCARINI, Steven ...... 336-316-2465 329 C
mencarinism@guilford.edu
MENCER, Curt .... 404-752-1500 123 A
cmencer@msm.edu
MENCH, Matthew .... 865-974-5321 426 C
mmench@utk.edu
MENCHACA, Patricia ..... 760-744-1150.. 56 B
pmenchaca@palomar.edu
MENDELSOHN, Loren ... 212-650-7271 293 B
lmend@ccny.cuny.edu
MENDELSON, Eleonor ... 831-476-9424.. 42 I
admissions@fivebranches.edu
MENDENHALL, James .... 918-463-2931 365 I
james.mendenhall@connorsstate.edu
MENDES, Godfrey .... 614-947-6027 352 J
godfrey.mendes@frankli.edu
MENDES, Steve .... 203-857-7011.. 87 B
smendes@norwalk.edu
MENDES, Susy .... 212-237-8449 294 B
smendes@jjay.cuny.edu
MENDEZ, Angel .... 787-878-5475 506 J
amendez@arecibo.inter.edu
MENDEZ, Ariel .... 303-797-5647.. 77 H
ariel.mendez@arapahoe.edu
MENDEZ, Boamari .... 787-701-5100 505 B
bmendez@columbiacentral.edu
MENDEZ, Celia .... 787-257-0000 510 F
celia.mendez@upr.edu
MENDEZ, David .... 787-743-7979 509 D
edmendez@suagm.edu
MENDEZ, Elisaida .... 216-421-7463 350 E
emendez@cia.edu
MENDEZ, Ernesto .... 509-521-4599 478 B
emendez@columbiabasin.edu
MENDEZ, Ignacio .... 218-679-2860 242 E
MENDEZ, Jeanette .... 405-744-5627 367 G
jeanette.mendez@okstate.edu
MENDEZ, José, F .... 787-751-0178 509 B
jmendez@uagm.edu
MENDEZ, Jose, F .... 787-751-2262 509 A
jmendez@uagm.edu
MENDEZ, Jose, F .... 787-766-1717 509 C
jmendez@uagm.edu
MENDEZ, Magaly .... 787-815-0000 510 D
magaly.mendez@upr.edu
MENDEZ, Mike .... 651-423-8319 237 E
mike.mendez@dctc.edu
MENDEZ, Pedro .... 209-575-6332.. 76 K
mendezp@mjc.edu
MENDEZ, Rafael .... 787-257-0000 510 F
MENDEZ, Sheri .... 775-784-4252 270 K
smendez@unr.edu

MENDEZ CASTILLO,
Milagros .... 787-767-2040 511 F
milagros.mendez@upr.edu
MENDEZ ESCUDERO,
Margarita .... 787-250-0000 510 B
margarita.mendez@upr.edu
MENDEZ-GRANT,
Monica .... 940-898-3700 451 A
mmendezgrant@twu.edu
MENDEZ-HERNANDEZ,
Santiago .... 787-296-1101 207 E
santiago.mendez-hernandez@cambridgecollege.edu
MENDIETA, Erick .... 787-834-9595 508 O
emendieta@uaa.edu
MENDIETA, Juan .... 305-237-7611 104 E
jmendiet@mdc.edu
MENDINI, Shauna .... 435-865-8185 459 E
mendini_s@suu.edu
MENDIOLA, Denise, M . 671-735-5640 503 C
denise.mendiola4@guamcc.edu
MENDIOLA, Francisco .. 691-320-2480 503 B
mendiolaf@comfsm.fm
MENDIOLA, Marcos .... 505-224-4000 285 B
mmendiola5@cnm.edu
MENDIOLA, Mark .... 671-735-2260 503 E
mendiolam@triton.uog.edu
MENDOLA, Richard, A .. 404-727-6861 118 D
rich.mendola@emory.edu
MENDOLARO,
Angela, J .... 407-582-3011 113 C
amendolaro@valenciacollege.edu
MENDONCA, James .... 401-456-8888 404 A
jmendonca@ric.edu
MENDONCA, Maribel .... 956-380-8102 441 L
mmendonca@riogrande.edu
MENDOZA, Eric .... 408-864-8402.. 42 K
mendozaeric@deanza.edu
MENDOZA, Gaylyn .... 682-465-9279 441 D
gmendoza@rangercollege.edu
MENDOZA, Graciano .... 408-848-4715.. 43 H
MENDOZA, Graciano .... 831-755-6995.. 44 J
gmendoza@hartnell.edu
MENDOZA, Graciano .... 650-306-3274.. 62 I
mendozag@smccd.edu
MENDOZA, Johnny .... 800-785-0585.. 39 F
MENDOZA, Jorge .... 218-335-4218 235 J
jorge.mendoza@lltc.edu
MENDOZA, Kimberlee ... 806-291-1100 457 B
mendozak@wbu.edu
MENDOZA, Mark .... 605-394-4800 414 G
MENDOZA, Mynor .... 760-252-2411.. 26 L
mmendoza@barstow.edu
MENDOZA, Pablo .... 678-696-2462 126 G
pablo.mendoza@ung.edu
MENDOZA, Patricia .... 714-432-5562.. 38 F
pmendoza31@occ.cccd.edu
MENDOZA, Raul .... 787-891-0925 506 I
rmendoza@aguadilla.inter.edu
MENDOZA, Stephanie ... 415-503-6280.. 61 E
security@sfcm.edu
MENDOZA, Sylvia, F .... 201-360-4201 277 D
smendoza@hccc.edu
MENDOZA, Tracey .... 210-829-3837 452 D
temendo2@uiwtx.edu
MENDOZA-BAUTISTA,
Maria .... 920-748-8190 493 J
mendoza-bautistam@ripon.edu
MENDOZA-MILLER,
Marylou .... 559-278-2032.. 31 D
maryloum@csufresno.edu
MENDOZA PLASCENCIA,
Oscar .... 916-691-7669.. 50 K
mendozo@crc.losrios.edu
MENDOZA-WELCH,
Maxine .... 903-886-5851 446 D
maxine.mmendo@tamu.edu
MENEAR, Shelley .... 301-387-3037 198 F
shelley.menear@garrettcollege.edu
MENEELY, Emily .... 252-334-2020 331 C
emily.meneely@macuniversity.edu
MENEELY, J. Andy .... 252-334-2087 331 C
andy.meneely@macuniversity.edu
MENEELY, Josh .... 412-731-6000 396 D
jmeneely@rpts.edu
MENELEY, Theresa .... 713-221-8612 452 B
meneleyt@uhd.edu
MENENDEZ,
Jacqueline, R .... 305-284-5505 112 K
jmenendez@miami.edu
MENENDEZ, Megan .... 303-867-1155.. 83 H
menendez@taft.edu
MENENDEZ, Mirizza ...... 305-442-9223 104 G
mmenendez@mru.edu

MENENDEZ, Rasel .... 310-287-4379.. 50 C
menendrm2@wlac.edu
MENESES, Eloise .... 610-341-5800 383 A
emeneses@eastern.edu
MENEZES, Jill .... 217-206-6651 151 E
jmene1@uis.edu
MENGEL, David .... 513-745-3101 364 F
mengel@xavier.edu
MENGEL, Stanley .... 312-862-3217.. 68 G
stanley.mengel@kirkland.com
MENGHINI, Becci .... 919-843-0594 342 B
becci_menghini@unc.edu
MENGHINI, Jared .... 570-408-3837 402 B
jared.menghini@wilkes.edu
MENGLER, Thomas, M. . 210-436-3722 442 A
tmengler@stmarytx.edu
MENICE, Paul .... 207-786-6254 193 D
pmenice@bates.edu
MENIFEE, Delorean, J ... 570-372-4293 398 A
menifee@susqu.edu
MENIFIELD, Charles ..... 973-353-5093 281 C
charles.menifield@rutgers.edu
MENJARES, Pete .... 714-556-3610.. 73 G
MENJARES, Pete .... 714-556-3610.. 73 G
officeoftheprovost@vanguard.edu
MENJARES, Pete, C .... 206-281-2114 482 K
president@spu.edu
MENJIVAR, Claudia, I ... 650-574-6146.. 62 J
menjivarc@smccd.edu
MENK, David, A .... 507-933-6539 235 E
dmenk@gustavus.edu
MENKE, Adriana .... 305-237-0656 104 E
amenke@mdc.edu
MENKE, David .... 206-878-3710 480 C
dmenke@highline.edu
MENKE, Donna .... 800-658-4308 266 J
menked@mpcc.edu
MENKE, Scott .... 262-595-2076 495 D
menke@uwp.edu
MENN, Esther .... 773-256-0721 143 C
emenn@lstc.edu
MENNEKE, Beth, R .... 314-505-7761 251 D
mennekeb@csl.edu
MENNELL, Betsy .... 801-626-6002 460 B
betsymennell@weber.edu
MENNELLA, Hillary .... 562-860-2451.. 35 O
hmennella@cerritos.edu
MENNICKE, Sue .... 717-358-7187 383 G
sue.mennicke@fandm.edu
MENON, Sanjay, T .... 318-797-5234 189 E
sanjay.menon@lsus.edu
MENON, Sathyapal .... 415-442-7080.. 44 B
smenon@ggu.edu
MENON, Shaily .... 203-932-7257.. 89 F
smenon@newhaven.edu
MENSA-WILMOT, Kojo .. 470-578-6000 121 J
MENSAH, Ernesta .... 323-860-0789.. 50 E
MENSCH, Deserie .... 254-519-5722 446 C
d.mensch@tamuct.edu
MENSCHING, Ron .... 630-889-6606 145 D
rmensching@nuhs.edu
MENSE, Tobias .... 334-244-3838.... 4 F
tmense@aum.edu
MENTA, Vijay .... 802-443-2929 461 G
vmenta@middlebury.edu
MENTZER, Stacy .... 515-574-1148 166 G
mentzer_s@iowacentral.edu
MENZ, Harald .... 304-829-7915 486 B
hmenz@bethanywv.edu
MENZEL, Carol, A .... 410-334-2946 205 A
cmenzel@worwic.edu
MENZEMER, Craig, C ..... 330-972-7911 361 G
ccmenze@uakron.edu
MENZER, Paul .... 540-887-7058 467 G
pmenzer@marybaldwin.edu
MENZIES, April .... 303-404-5393.. 80 I
april.menzies@frontrange.edu
MENZIES, Victoria .... 408-288-3119.. 62 G
victoria.menzies@sjcc.edu
MEONSKE, Kali, A .... 330-325-6492 357 D
kmeonske@neomed.edu
MEOZ, Ben .... 503-768-7757 373 D
bcmeoz@lclark.edu
MEOZ, Emily .... 360-992-2505 477 J
emeoz@clark.edu
MERANDA, Seth .... 402-643-7220 265 I
seth.meranda@cune.edu
MERAR, Roland .... 670-234-5498 503 G
roland.merrar@marianas.edu
MERCADEL, Robert .... 504-520-7396 193 C
rmercade@xula.edu
MERCADO, Claudia .... 847-925-6622 138 E
cmercado@harpercollege.edu

MESSPLAY, Paul .... 540-654-1410 471 B
pmesspla@umw.edu
MESTAN, Michael .... 315-568-3100 309 H
mmestan@northeastcollege.edu
MESTETH, Leslie .... 605-455-6033 414 H
lmesteth@olc.edu
MESTLER, Nathan, M .... 480-245-7993.. 12 O
nathan.mestler@ibcs.edu
MESTRES, Ibrahim .... 787-780-0070 504 E
imestres@caribbean.edu
MESYEF, Masha .... 801-649-5230 458 I
marketing@midwifery.edu
MESYEF, Masha .... 866-680-2756 458 I
fundraising@midwifery.edu
MESYEF, Masha .... 866-680-2756 458 I
MESYEF, Whitney .... 866-680-2756 458 I
financialaid@midwifery.edu
METAJ, Dee .... 317-278-5644 157 B
metaj@iupui.edu
METALLO, Laura .... 413-748-3120 218 E
lmetallo@springfield.edu
METCALF, Amanda .... 304-367-4241 488 L
amanda.metcalf@fairmontstate.edu
METCALF, Courtney .... 620-223-2700 173 F
courtneym@fortscott.edu
METCALF, Gary .... 559-453-2089.. 43 D
gary.metcalf@fresno.edu
METCALF, Kyle .... 603-578-8900 272 B
METCALF, Linda .... 817-531-7530 450 F
lmetcalf@txwes.edu
METCALFE, Allen .... 508-830-5063 213 A
ametcalfe@maritime.edu
METE, T.J .... 772-466-4822.. 95 N
tj.mete@aviator.edu
METESH, John, J .... 406-496-4159 264 C
jmetesh@mtech.edu
METH, Clifford .... 646-565-6133 322 C
yehudah.meth2@touro.edu
METH, Clifford .... 646-565-6133 322 B
yehudah.meth2@touro.edu
METHVIN, Jennifer .... 501-882-8956.. 17 H
jlmethvin@asub.edu
METIANU, Mihaela .... 561-297-3049 109 F
mmetianu@fau.edu
METILLY, Paul .... 617-254-2610 218 A
paul.metilly@sjs.edu
METIVIER SCOTT,
Shelly .... 508-999-8407 211 F
shelly.scott@umassd.edu
METRAKOS, Nicholas .... 617-731-3500 210 D
nmetrakos@hchc.edu
METRESS, Heather, B .... 706-721-5052 115 I
hmetress@augusta.edu
METS, Lisa, A .... 727-864-8221.. 98 G
metsla@eckerd.edu
METSGAR, Christopher . 651-450-3520 237 H
cmetsgar@inverhills.edu
METTEN, Michelle .... 618-252-5400 149 E
michelle.metten@sic.edu
METTILLE, Teege .... 262-524-7221 491 A
tmettill@carrollu.edu
METTLACH, Deborah ...... 314-362-6289 253 A
deborah.mettlach@
barnesjewishcollege.edu
METTS, Amanda .... 252-399-6315 326 H
ahmetts@barton.edu
METTS, Deanna .... 931-372-3045 425 B
dmetts@tntech.edu
METZ, Bernice .... 712-279-5400 163 H
bernice.metz@briarcliff.edu
METZ, Catherine, A .... 765-361-6418 162 G
metzc@wabash.edu
METZ, Christine .... 516-562-3403 298 F
cmetz@northwell.edu
METZ, Lisa, B .... 973-761-9215 282 K
lisa.metz@shu.edu
METZ, Nick .... 315-781-3304 301 D
nmetz@hws.edu
METZ, Roxanne .... 949-582-4824.. 65 C
rmetz@saddleback.edu
METZ, Susan .... 201-216-5245 282 L
susan.metz@stevens.edu
METZ, Terry .... 651-523-2160 235 F
tmetz01@hamline.edu
METZ, Tim .... 323-860-1129.. 53 D
tmetz@mi.edu
METZ, Tim .... 828-227-3046 343 D
tdmetz@wcu.edu
METZGAR, Jennifer .... 607-274-3177 302 E
jmetzgar@ithaca.edu
METZGAR, Johanna ...... 650-723-2300.. 66 D
METZGAR, Kim .... 724-805-2601 397 D
kim.metzgar@stvincent.edu

METZGER, Amanda .... 585-385-8005 313 A
ametzger@sjfc.edu
METZGER, Carl .... 407-823-5555 110 D
carl.metzger@ucf.edu
METZGER, Carol .... 513-556-1299 361 I
metzgecs@ucmail.uc.edu
METZGER, David, D .... 757-683-4865 468 C
dmetzger@odu.edu
METZGER, Elizabeth ...... 505-277-5111 288 C
emetzger@unm.edu
METZGER, Jeff .... 419-251-6122 355 G
jeff.metzger@mercycollege.edu
METZGER, Liz .... 812-237-3088 155 H
liz.metzger@indstate.edu
METZGER, Matthew, R .. 574-372-5100 155 C
metzgemr@grace.edu
METZGER, Michael, D ... 716-673-3109 316 A
michael.metzger@fredonia.edu
METZGER, Nan .... 414-930-3338 493 E
metzgern@mtmary.edu
METZGER, Peggy .... 707-826-4321.. 30 A
mam7001@humboldt.edu
METZGER, Rob .... 757-490-1241 463 E
rmetzger@auto.edu
METZGER, Thomas .... 702-968-2013 271 D
tmetzger@roseman.edu
METZGER, Tina .... 804-627-5300 464 B
METZINGER, Harry .... 856-222-9311 280 E
hmetzinger@rcbc.edu
METZINGER, Michelle ... 913-758-6115 177 I
michelle.metzinger@stmary.edu
METZLER, Christopher .. 717-299-7794 398 E
metzler@stevenscollege.edu
METZO, Vincent .... 212-924-5900 321 C
vmetzo@swedishinstitute.edu
MEULEMANS, Nicole ...... 651-423-8403 237 E
nicole.meulemans@dctc.edu
MEULLENET, JF .... 479-575-2034.. 21 H
jfmeull@uark.edu
MEUNKS, Chris .... 573-897-5000 259 E
MEURS, Kate .... 919-515-2191 341 E
MEUSCHKE, Daylene ...... 661-362-5329.. 38 H
daylene.meuschke@canyons.edu
MEUWISSEN, Daniel, J . 651-962-5100 243 F
djmeuwissen@stthomas.edu
MEWIN, Jon .... 510-885-2775.. 31 C
jon.medwin@csueastbay.edu
MEYER, Adam .... 212-799-5000 303 B
MEYER, AJ .... 937-327-6471 364 C
meyera@wittenberg.edu
MEYER, Alexis .... 414-955-8246 492 F
alemeyer@mcw.edu
MEYER, Angela .... 573-651-2292 258 J
admeyer@semo.edu
MEYER, Ann .... 312-329-4417 144 F
ann.meyer@moody.edu
MEYER, Barbara .... 402-375-7221 267 I
bameyer1@wsc.edu
MEYER, Brenda .... 785-227-3380 171 H
meyerbm@bethanylb.edu
MEYER, Carrie .... 765-998-4554 161 A
crmeyer@taylor.edu
MEYER, Chris .... 405-733-7913 369 D
cmeyer@rose.edu
MEYER, Christine .... 304-876-5526 489 A
cmeyer@shepherd.edu
MEYER, Christopher, G . 559-278-3936.. 31 D
cmeyer@csufresno.edu
MEYER, David .... 816-414-3700 255 F
dmeyer@mbts.edu
MEYER, David, D .... 504-865-5930 191 D
meyer@tulane.edu
MEYER, Dulcie .... 315-781-3082 301 D
dmeyer@hws.edu
MEYER, Eddie .... 860-727-6906.. 87 H
emeyer@goodwin.edu
MEYER, Ellie .... 256-260-2441.... 1 F
ellie.meyer@calhoun.edu
MEYER, Eric, T .... 512-471-3821 454 C
dean@ischool.utexas.edu
MEYER, Fredric, B .... 507-284-3268 234 F
MEYER, Fredric, B .... 507-538-0554 234 E
MEYER, Gary .... 414-288-6350 492 E
gary.meyer@marquette.edu
MEYER, Gregg, A .... 508-531-1237 212 B
gmeyer@bridgew.edu
MEYER, Heidi .... 612-625-2008 242 K
meyer119@umn.edu
MEYER, Hilary .... 708-456-0300 151 A
hilarymeyer@triton.edu
MEYER, Jacque .... 513-244-4232 356 F
jacque.meyer@msj.edu

MEYER, Jay .... 847-543-2717 135 G
jmeyer@clcillinois.edu
MEYER, Jean, C .... 610-526-1466 378 D
jean.meyer@theamericancollege.edu
MEYER, Jennifer .... 818-785-2726.. 35 K
jennifer.meyer@casalomacollege.edu
MEYER, Jill .... 414-277-7365 493 D
MEYER, John .... 414-443-8910 497 A
john.meyer@wlc.edu
MEYER, John, D .... 239-513-1122 102 C
jmeyer@hodges.edu
MEYER, John, E .... 507-354-8221 236 D
meyerjd@mlc-wels.edu
MEYER, Kathy .... 701-483-2535 345 A
kathleen.meyer@dickinsonstate.edu
MEYER, Katie .... 270-706-8443 181 C
cmeyer0015@kctcs.edu
MEYER, Kelli, A .... 203-576-4487.. 89 A
kmeyer@bridgeport.edu
MEYER, Kelsey .... 314-367-8700 260 A
kelsey.meyer@uhsp.edu
MEYER, Kimberly, J ...... 574-807-7021 153 G
kimberly.meyer@betheluniversity.edu
MEYER, Kyle, P .... 402-559-7428 269 B
kpmeyer@unmc.edu
MEYER, Lakeisha .... 570-577-1188 379 A
ldm010@bucknell.edu
MEYER, Larry .... 859-572-6117 184 B
meyerl3@nku.edu
MEYER, LeAnn .... 406-243-5211 263 D
leann.meyer@umontana.edu
MEYER, Marilyn, S .... 801-863-6797 460 A
marilyn.meyer@uvu.edu
MEYER, Mathys .... 606-218-5467 185 F
mathysmeyer@upike.edu
MEYER, Matthew .... 919-807-7155 331 I
meyerm@nccommunitycolleges.edu
MEYER, Merry .... 845-758-7005 290 G
sm568@bncollege.com
MEYER, Michael .... 808-844-2308 129 G
mmeyer@hawaii.edu
MEYER, Michele .... 407-691-1754 106 L
mmeyer@rollins.edu
MEYER, Patricia .... 513-745-1996 364 F
meyerp@xavier.edu
MEYER, Rich .... 434-381-6110 470 H
rmeyer@sbc.edu
MEYER, Richard .... 314-246-7429 261 D
richardmeyer33@webster.edu
MEYER, Rick .... 909-599-5433.. 48 E
rmeyer@lifepacific.edu
MEYER, Robert .... 907-564-8890.... 9 F
rmeyer@alaskapacific.edu
MEYER, Scott .... 701-252-3467 346 J
scott.meyer@uj.edu
MEYER, Sheree .... 916-278-6502.. 33 A
meyers@csus.edu
MEYER, Steve .... 307-742-3776 500 K
smeyer@wyotech.edu
MEYER, Susan .... 320-308-5473 240 D
smeyer@sctcc.edu
MEYER, Ted .... 615-966-1107 420 B
ted.meyer@lipscomb.edu
MEYER, Terry .... 701-328-2963 344 G
terry.meyer@ndus.edu
MEYER, Thomas .... 816-604-5250 254 E
thomas.meyer@mcckc.edu
MEYER, Thomas .... 816-604-5250 254 G
thomas.meyer@mcckc.edu
MEYER, Thomas, W .... 816-604-6544 254 F
thomas.meyer@mcckc.edu
MEYER-BERNSTEIN,
Elizabeth .... 843-953-2298 407 D
meyerbernstein@cofc.edu
MEYER-LEE, Elaine .... 410-337-6000 198 G
elaine.myer-lee@goucher.edu
MEYER REIMER,
Kathryn .... 574-535-7443 155 B
kathymr@goshen.edu
MEYERAAN, Susan .... 319-352-8315 170 F
susan.meyeraan@wartburg.edu
MEYERAND, Beth .... 608-262-5246 494 D
memeyerand@wisc.edu
MEYERS, Allison .... 215-885-2360 389 A
ameyers@manor.edu
MEYERS,
Harry (Matt), M .... 610-892-1543 393 B
matt.meyers@pit.edu
MEYERS, Luke .... 518-580-5744 315 A
lmeyers@skidmore.edu
MEYERS, Mark, M .... 412-397-6801 396 E
meyersm@rmu.edu
MEYERS, Ruth .... 510-204-0720.. 37 A
rmeyers@cdsp.edu

MEYERS, Shelly .... 864-488-8207 409 C
smeyers@limestone.edu
MEYERS, Simmuelle ...... 610-359-5199 381 J
smeyers@dccc.edu
MEYERS, Will .... 716-896-0700 324 A
wjmeyer@villa.edu
MEZA, Jane .... 402-559-6825 269 B
jmeza@unmc.edu
MEZA, Jane, L .... 402-559-6825 269 C
jmeza@unomaha.edu
MEZA, Jose .... 787-257-0000 510 F
jose.meza1@upr.edu
MEZA, Jose, I .... 787-769-9965 510 F
jose.meza1@upr.edu
MEZA, Norma .... 562-804-1239.. 45 C
normam@healthcarecareercollege.edu
MEZA PEREIRA, Jose, I 787-276-0226 510 B
jose.meza@upr.edu
MEZEY, Nancy .... 732-263-5631 278 B
nmezey@monmouth.edu
MEZIERE, Kevin .... 858-653-6740.. 46 L
kmeziere@jpcatholic.com
MEZQUITA, Jennifer ...... 978-762-4005 215 B
jmezquit@northshore.edu
MEZQUITA, Jennifer ...... 978-556-3720 215 C
jmezquita@necc.mass.edu
MEZWA, Duane .... 248-370-2452 229 F
mezwa@oakland.edu
MHLANGA, Fortune .... 615-327-6111 420 D
fmhlanga@mmc.edu
MIAN, Mahreen, N .... 904-620-2371 111 A
mahreen.mian@unf.edu
MIANO, Heather .... 540-831-5401 468 E
hmiano@radford.edu
MIAOULIS, Ioannis .... 401-254-3201 404 C
imiaoulis@rwu.edu
MIARKA-GRZELAK,
Anna .... 518-562-4171 295 F
anna.miarka-grzelak@clinton.edu
MICCO, Melissa, A .... 412-397-5264 396 E
micco@rmu.edu
MICELI, Anthony .... 313-664-7814 222 C
amiceli@collegeforcreativestudies.edu
MICELI, Christy .... 312-629-6706 149 B
cmiceli@saic.edu
MICELI, Paul .... 781-899-5500 217 F
MICELI, Paul, E .... 781-899-5500 217 F
rev.miceli@psjs.edu
MICHAEL, Cynthia .... 937-376-6304 349 H
cmichael@centralstate.edu
MICHAEL, Jody .... 810-762-0048 228 B
jody.michael@mcc.edu
MICHAEL, Josh .... 937-766-7849 349 C
jmichael@cedarville.edu
MICHAEL, Leoni .... 214-333-5261 433 D
leoni@dbu.edu
MICHAEL, Nicky .... 918-683-4581 365 B
michaeln@bacone.edu
MICHAEL, Rebecca .... 831-646-5506.. 52 H
rmichael@mpc.edu
MICHAEL,
Talamantes, J .... 915-831-2302 435 B
mtalam10@epcc.edu
MICHAEL, Thomas, R ... 217-581-6014 137 C
trmichael@eiu.edu
MICHAEL, Timothy .... 313-577-2313 232 H
tmichael@wayne.edu
MICHAELIDES, Anthony 661-362-3253.. 38 H
anthony.michaelides@canyons.edu
MICHAELIS, Joel .... 402-323-3427 268 D
jmichaelis@southeast.edu
MICHAELS, Dennis .... 845-687-5169 322 K
michaeld@sunyulster.edu
MICHAELS, George, H .. 805-893-2378.. 70 E
george.michaels@id.ucsb.edu
MICHAELS, Jackie .... 816-501-4555 257 K
jackie.michaels@rockhurst.edu
MICHAELS, Jeff, A .... 717-477-1171 394 D
jamich@ship.edu
MICHAELS, Lynda .... 570-389-4061 393 E
lmichael@bloomu.edu
MICHAELSEN, Kevin .... 919-760-8565 331 A
michaelsen@meredith.edu
MICHALAK, Mary Jane . 317-921-4882 158 A
mmichalak@ivytech.edu
MICHALAK, Russell .... 302-225-6227.. 90 I
michalr@gbc.edu
MICHALENKO, John, A . 412-397-6483 396 E
michalenko@rmu.edu
MICHALKE, Kirsten .... 218-683-8800 239 E
kirsten.michalke@northlandcollege.edu
MICHALKO, Nancy .... 801-957-4247 460 D
nancy.michalko@slcc.edu

Index of Key Administrators MICHALOWSKI – MILKOWSKI 793

MICHALOWSKI, Sam .... 201-692-2060 276 I
ir_sam@fdu.edu
MICHALSEN, Kara .... 520-795-0787.. 10 J
academicdean@asaom.edu
MICHALSKI, Gregory .... 904-632-3017 101 A
g.michalski@fscj.edu
MICHALSKI, Monica ..... 718-489-5272 312 H
mmichalski@sfc.edu
MICHALSKI, Tim .... 361-570-4107 452 C
michalskit@uhv.edu
MICHAUD, Carolyn .... 508-830-5034 213 A
cmichaud@maritime.edu
MICHAUD, Lisa .... 207-834-7607 196 G
lisa.michaud@maine.edu
MICHAUX, Wayne .... 706-880-8911 121 K
wmichaux@lagrange.edu
MICHEAU, Devere, P .... 910-938-6321 333 D
micheaud@coastalcarolina.edu
MICHEL, Alice .... 831-459-2882.. 71 A
globallearning@ucsc.edu
MICHEL, Bill .... 773-702-2673 151 B
wmichel@uchicago.edu
MICHEL, Brian .... 716-614-6472 309 E
brmichel@niagaracc.suny.edu
MICHEL, Tabatha .... 404-413-5057 120 C
tmichele@gsu.edu
MICHELBACH,
Andrea, N .... 253-535-7447 481 C
michelan@plu.edu
MICHELS, Kallie, B .... 734-764-3526 231 A
kallie@umich.edu
MICHELSON, Melissa .... 650-543-3844.. 52 A
melissa.michelson@menlo.edu
MICHTAVY, Lesley .... 209-588-5100.. 76 J
michtavyl@yosemite.edu
MICIAK, Alan .... 216-397-4281 353 O
president@jcu.edu
MICK, Christina .... 931-372-3331 425 B
cmick@tntech.edu
MICKELL, Hillary .... 650-740-4008 217 D
MICKELSON, Sally .... 702-968-2004 271 D
smickelson@roseman.edu
MICKENS, Kendrick .... 610-359-5340 381 J
kmickens@dccc.edu
MICKENS, Telishia .... 409-944-1285 435 F
tmickens@gc.edu
MICKEY, Marty .... 312-261-3050 145 C
mmickey@nl.edu
MICKEY, Travis .... 336-272-7102 329 B
travis.mickey@greensboro.edu
MICKEY-BOGGS, Shari .. 217-333-3101 151 F
smboggs@illinois.edu
MICKLE, Angelia .... 937-766-7720 349 C
amickle@cedarville.edu
MICKLER, Michael .... 845-752-3000 323 A
mm@uts.edu
MICKLES, Muriel .... 434-832-7656 472 G
micklesm@centralvirginia.edu
MICKLES, Ryan .... 434-528-5276 476 B
MICKOOL, Richard .... 937-525-3811 364 C
rmickool@wittenberg.edu
MICKOOL, Rick .... 401-709-8479 404 B
rmickool@risd.edu
MIDCAP, Richard .... 301-387-3056 198 F
richard.midcap@garrettcollege.edu
MIDDAUGH,
Jessica, M .... 607-871-2108 289 E
middaugh@alfred.edu
MIDDENDORF, Terry ..... 651-523-2302 235 F
tmiddendorf@hamline.edu
MIDDENDORF, Tom ...... 615-248-1258 425 D
tmiddendorf@trevecca.edu
MIDDENTS, Jeffrey .... 202-885-1000.. 91 D
middents@american.edu
MIDDLEKAUFF, Paul ..... 212-659-0736 303 E
pmiddlekauff@tkc.edu
MIDDLETON, Angela ..... 817-272-2771 454 B
middleton@uta.edu
MIDDLETON, Caylie ...... 410-455-1000 202 G
educationabroad@umbc.edu
MIDDLETON, David .... 412-924-1390 395 G
dmiddleton@pts.edu
MIDDLETON, Dewayne .. 601-849-0302 244 G
dewayne.middleton@colin.edu
MIDDLETON, John .... 573-882-6857 260 B
middletonjr@missouri.edu
MIDDLETON, John, R .... 573-882-1288 260 C
middletonjr@missouri.edu
MIDDLETON, Kristi .... 859-622-1597 180 B
kristi.middleton@eku.edu
MIDDLETON, Lauren ..... 860-439-2666.. 87 F
lmiddlet@conncoll.edu
MIDDLETON, Leslie ...... 765-658-4194 154 G
lesliemiddleton@depauw.edu
MIDDLETON, Lyle .... 501-205-8830.. 19 B
lmiddleton@cbc.edu
MIDDLETON, Marci .... 706-396-7596 123 I
mmiddleton@paine.edu
MIDDLETON,
Melinda, L .... 812-877-8259 160 C
middleto@rose-hulman.edu
MIDDLETON, Michael ... 212-772-4622 294 A
soedean@hunter.cuny.edu
MIDDLETON, Natavia ..... 727-398-8288 107 C
middleton.natavia@spcollege.edu
MIDDLETON, Tracy .... 803-705-4594 405 G
tracy.middleton@benedict.edu
MIDEI, Ron .... 954-262-5224 104 M
ronmidei@nsu.nova.edu
MIDGETT, Pam .... 940-397-4182 439 F
pam.midgett@msutexas.edu
MIDGLEY, Ed .... 973-655-3450 278 C
midgleye@montclair.edu
MIDGLEY, Michael, T .... 512-223-7579 429 J
midgley@austincc.edu
MIDKIFF, Kittridge .... 270-686-4508 182 C
kitt.midkiff@kctcs.edu
MIDKIFF, Lindsay .... 870-633-4480.. 19 E
lindsay.midkiff@eacc.edu
MIDKIFF, Lori, A .... 304-929-5472 487 G
lmidkiff@newriver.edu
MIDKIFF, Michael .... 831-646-3073.. 52 H
mmidkiff@mpc.edu
MIDKIFF, Robert .... 570-577-1561 379 A
robert.midkiff@bucknell.edu
MIDKIFF, Scott, F .... 540-231-4227 475 D
midkiff@vt.edu
MIEDREICH, Lukas .... 934-420-2103 320 C
miedrelh@farmingdale.edu
MIEDZIONOSKI, Paul ... 978-556-3921 215 C
pmiedzionoski@necc.mass.edu
MIELE, Tony .... 480-423-6414.. 14 B
anthony.miele@scottsdalecc.edu
MIELKE, Cindi .... 815-599-3491 138 H
cindi.mielke@highland.edu
MIELSCH, Emily .... 409-747-1431 456 B
ejmielsc@utmb.edu
MIENE, Peter .... 507-457-5017 241 A
pmiene@winona.edu
MIERA, Jeff .... 310-660-3593.. 41 J
jmiera@elcamino.edu
MIERA, Joseph .... 702-895-5116 270 J
joe.miera@unlv.edu
MIERS, Michael .... 508-849-3326 205 E
mmiers@annamaria.edu
MIERTSCHIN, Charla ..... 507-457-5299 241 A
cmiertschin@winona.edu
MIESO, Rob .... 408-864-8330.. 42 K
miesorob@deanza.edu
MIESS, Robert, D .... 701-788-4885 345 B
robert.miess@mayvillestate.edu
MIGEL, April .... 224-293-5876.. 10 F
amigel@aiuniv.edu
MIGHTY, Hugh, E .... 202-806-5677.. 92 E
hugh.mighty@howard.edu
MIGHTY, Nathalia .... 214-329-4447 429 L
nathalia.mighty@bgu.edu
MIGLER, Jerry .... 701-228-5403 345 G
jerome.migler@dakotacollege.edu
MIGLIO, Joseph .... 617-873-0490 207 E
joseph.miglio@cambridgecollege.edu
MIGLIO, Sarah .... 630-752-5153 152 K
sarah.miglio@wheaton.edu
MIGLIORINO, Nicholas . 845-398-4084 314 D
nmiglior@stac.edu
MIGNARDOT, Henry ...... 505-424-2326 285 H
henry.mignardot@iaia.edu
MIGUEL, George .... 520-383-0023.. 16 D
gmiguel@tocc.edu
MIGUEL, Joann .... 520-383-0025.. 16 D
jmiguel@tocc.edu
MIGYANKO,
Stephanie, M .... 724-439-4900 387 H
smigyanko@laurel.edu
MIHAL, Matt .... 570-674-6166 389 H
mmihal@misericordia.edu
MIHAL, Ruthie .... 704-609-1542 327 F
ruthie.mihal@carolinascollege.edu
MIHALIC, Angela .... 214-648-2168 456 D
angela.mihalic@utsouthwestern.edu
MIHALKO, Taras .... 570-674-6246 389 H
tmihalko@misericordia.edu
MIHALY, Zachariah .... 203-773-6923.. 85 C
zmihaly@albertus.edu
MIHELIC, Jerry .... 580-559-5350 365 J
jmihelic@ecok.edu
MIHELICH, John .... 701-777-7589 344 H
john.mihelich@und.edu
MIHEVC, Jake .... 315-792-5653 306 G
jmihevc@mvcc.edu
MIHLON, Mildred .... 201-559-6000 277 A
MIHM-HEROLD,
Wendy, A .... 844-642-2338 168 F
mihm-heroldw@nicc.edu
MIHOPOULOS,
Elizabeth .... 510-436-1071.. 45 H
mihopoulos@hnu.edu
MIHOPULOS, Sheryl, L . 516-877-3365 288 L
mihopulos@adelphi.edu
MIHULKA, Don .... 417-625-9807 255 I
mihulka-d@mssu.edu
MIKE, Nena .... 691-370-3191 503 B
nenam@comfsm.fm
MIKEMAN, Cindy .... 405-736-0315 369 D
cmikeman@rose.edu
MIKESELL, Jennifer .... 517-796-8482 225 A
mikeseljennifes@jccmi.edu
MIKHAIL, Michael, B .... 312-996-2671 151 D
mmikhail@uic.edu
MIKHAIL, Mona .... 626-812-3013.. 26 K
mmikhail@apu.edu
MIKHAIL, Peter .... 408-727-1060.. 46 A
MIKHAIL, Peter .... 702-567-1920 270 D
MIKIC, Borjana .... 413-585-7007 218 D
bmikic@smith.edu
MIKKELSEN, Chris .... 952-358-8121 239 C
chris.mikkelsen@normandale.edu
MIKKELSEN, Nicole .... 701-224-5427 345 F
nicole.mikkelsen@bismarckstate.edu
MIKLUSAK, Courtney .... 619-239-0391.. 34 H
cmiklusak@cwsl.edu
MIKNAVICH, Marie .... 315-792-5467 306 G
mmiknavich@mvcc.edu
MIKOL, Donna .... 610-282-1100 382 A
donna.mikol@desales.edu
MIKOS, Shari .... 312-329-6651.. 36 G
smikos@tcsedsystem.edu
MIKOTA, G. Michael ..... 864-592-4616 411 E
mikotam@sccsc.edu
MIKSA, Anthony, R .... 423-585-6770 424 G
tony.miksa@ws.edu
MIKTARIAN, Christine .. 559-243-7182.. 66 G
christine.miktarian@scccd.edu
MIKULIK, Kerri .... 325-942-2041 450 B
kerri.mikulik@angelo.edu
MIKUS, Robert, L .... 717-867-6863 388 A
mikus@lvc.edu
MILAM, B. Hofler .... 336-758-3121 344 A
bhm@wfu.edu
MILAM, Dale .... 509-527-2608 484 C
dale.milam@wallawalla.edu
MILAM, Elizabeth .... 864-656-3431 406 F
milamm@clemson.edu
MILAM, John .... 540-868-7249 473 C
jmilam@lfcc.edu
MILAM, Linda .... 918-781-7275 365 B
milaml@bacone.edu
MILAN, Jordan .... 715-394-8213 496 D
jmilan@uwsuper.edu
MILANICH, Timothy, R . 216-368-4306 349 B
timothy.milanich@case.edu
MILANO, Angela .... 916-484-8050.. 50 J
milanoa@arc.losrios.edu
MILANO-HIGHTOWER,
Alyssa .... 360-442-2241 480 E
amilanohightower@lowercolumbia.edu
MILAS, T. Patrick .... 732-247-5241 278 E
MILASINOVIC, Milan ..... 216-221-8584 357 C
milan.milasinovic@thencc.edu
MILAVEC, Ellizabeth ...... 585-275-2121 323 E
MILAZZO, Theresa .... 404-727-7404 118 D
theresa.milazzo@emory.edu
MILBERG, Craig .... 503-370-6561 377 E
cmilberg@willamette.edu
MILBERG, William .... 212-229-5901 307 E
milbergw@newschool.edu
MILBOURNE, Lauren ..... 805-922-6966.. 24 L
lauren.milbourne@hancockcollege.edu
MILBRETT, Juanita .... 507-389-5860 238 L
juanita.milbrett@mnsu.edu
MILBURN, Jaime, E ...... 740-368-3206 359 F
jemilbur@owu.edu
MILBURN, Jen .... 717-477-1904 394 D
jsmilburn@ship.edu
MILBURN, John .... 661-362-3245.. 38 H
john.milburn@canyons.edu
MILBURN DOAN,
Natalie .... 740-368-2000 359 F
nmdoan@owu.edu
MILBY, John .... 864-294-2111 408 I
john.milby@furman.edu
MILBY, Kevin, S .... 859-238-5534 179 H
kevin.milby@centre.edu
MILBY, Megan, H .... 859-238-5516 179 H
megan.milby@centre.edu
MILCZARSKI, Vivian ...... 845-569-3523 307 B
vivian.milczarski@msmc.edu
MILDENHALL, Joseph ... 602-639-7500.. 12 L
MILEHAM, Trisha .... 219-464-5099 162 C
trisha.mileham@valpo.edu
MILEK, Joseph .... 814-863-2521 391 F
jmm9228@psu.edu
MILEM, Jeffrey .... 805-893-3917.. 70 E
jmilem@education.ucsb.edu
MILES, Arletha .... 914-773-3856 310 F
lmiles@pace.edu
MILES, Belinda, S .... 914-606-6707 324 F
belinda.miles@sunywcc.edu
MILES, Byron .... 208-535-5387 130 I
byron.miles@cei.edu
MILES, Catherine .... 225-771-6231 190 K
catherine_miles@sus.edu
MILES, David, A .... 201-692-2227 276 I
dmiles@fdu.edu
MILES, Deborah .... 912-279-5750 117 C
dmiles@ccga.edu
MILES, Donald .... 814-472-3029 396 I
dmiles@francis.edu
MILES, Donna .... 405-224-3140 371 B
dmiles@usao.edu
MILES, Doug .... 479-575-8409.. 21 H
dmiles@uark.edu
MILES, Elizabeth .... 503-253-3443 374 E
elizabeth.miles@ocom.edu
MILES, Jennifer, P .... 512-505-3040 437 B
jpmiles@htu.edu
MILES, Jenny .... 601-857-3250 245 D
jenny.miles@hindscc.edu
MILES, Jessica .... 217-443-8769 136 E
j.miles@dacc.edu
MILES, John, D .... 770-720-9102 124 E
john.miles@reinhardt.edu
MILES, Keith .... 850-599-3413 109 E
keith.miles@famu.edu
MILES, Kim .... 941-377-4880 104 D
kmiles@meridian.edu
MILES, Leon .... 319-471-6260 414 B
lmiles@ilt.edu
MILES, Lloyd .... 301-985-7237 203 C
lloyd.miles@umuc.edu
MILES, Martin .... 757-727-5635 466 L
martin.miles@hamptonu.edu
MILES, Mary Elizabeth .. 502-852-6688 185 E
maryelizabeth.miles@louisville.edu
MILES, Michelle .... 304-769-0011 490 B
mmiles@wvjc.edu
MILES, Reginald, H .... 507-786-3334 242 I
miles3@stolaf.edu
MILES, Sarah, L .... 508-831-4180 220 C
smiles@wpi.edu
MILES, Thomas .... 773-702-9495 151 B
tmiles@law.uchicago.edu
MILES, Tom .... 478-445-2090 119 A
tom.miles@gcsu.edu
MILES, Travis .... 660-785-4242 259 J
tmiles@truman.edu
MILES, Vickie .... 334-670-3732.... 7 C
vmiles@troy.edu
MILEWICZ, Mark .... 910-521-6630 343 A
mark.milewicz@uncp.edu
MILEY, Melinda .... 843-953-5426 407 D
mileym@cofc.edu
MILI, Fatma .... 616-331-2400 224 D
milif@gvsu.edu
MILICI, JR., Roger, A ... 212-636-6545 300 A
milici@fordham.edu
MILIONI, Barbara .... 417-268-6008 250 A
bmilioni@gobbc.edu
MILIONI, Emily .... 417-268-6068 250 A
emilioni@gobbc.edu
MILIONI, Mark, L .... 417-268-6008 250 A
mmilioni@gobbc.edu
MILIOTIS, David .... 507-457-1421 242 H
dmilioti@smumn.edu
MILJEVICH, Greg .... 715-365-4486 498 D
gmiljevich@nicoletcollege.edu
MILKE, Natalie .... 319-399-8275 164 D
nmilke@coe.edu
MILKOVICH, Patrice ...... 619-575-6176.. 65 K
pmilkovich@swccd.edu
MILKOWSKI, Rose .... 312-629-6182 149 B
rmilkowski@saic.edu

MILKOWSKI, Tracy 414-847-3239 493 C tracymilkowski@miad.edu
MILLAR, Janet 661-654-3366 30 C jmillar@csub.edu
MILLARD, Cristi 801-957-4145 460 D cristi.millard@slcc.edu
MILLARD, David 805-546-3205 41 A david_millard1@cuesta.edu
MILLARD, Jill 704-290-5887 337 F jmillard@spcc.edu
MILLARD, Jim 252-638-7266 333 F millardj@cravencc.edu
MILLARD, Kent 937-529-2201 361 F kmillard@united.edu
MILLARD, Rachel 316-295-5719 173 G millard@friends.edu
MILLARD, Sandy 919-209-2011 335 D sbmillard@johnstoncc.edu
MILLAS, Nikoletta 610-896-1032 385 H nmillas@haverford.edu
MILLEA, Matthew, J 315-470-6649 319 A mjmillea@esf.edu
MILLEN, Jonathan 207-283-0171 197 A jmillen@une.edu
MILLEN, Michelle, L 972-548-6677 432 I mmillen@collin.edu
MILLENBAH, Kelly, F 517-355-0234 227 C millenba@msu.edu
MILLENBINE, Donnie 618-437-5321 147 F millenbined@rlc.edu
MILLENDER, Angelia 651-779-3368 237 D angelia.millender@century.edu
MILLER, JR., A.T 402-554-4832 269 C atmiller@unomaha.edu
MILLER, Adam 509-527-5778 485 C millera@whitman.edu
MILLER, Al 251-442-2357 8 C amiller@umobile.edu
MILLER, Alexander 740-587-0810 351 K
MILLER, Allyson 214-333-2212 433 D allysonm@dbu.edu
MILLER, Alyce 818-710-4332 49 H millerae@piercecollege.edu
MILLER, Amanda 909-448-4574 71 C amiller@laverne.edu
MILLER, Amber, D 213-740-2531 73 C dean@dornsife.usc.edu
MILLER, Amy 616-732-1157 222 H amy.miller@davenport.edu
MILLER, Amy 931-372-3634 425 B almiller@tntech.edu
MILLER, Andrea 940-565-2095 453 B andrea.miller@unt.edu
MILLER, Andrew 719-549-3353 82 I andrew.miller@pueblocc.edu
MILLER, Andrew, M 269-337-7542 225 B andrew.miller@kzoo.edu
MILLER, III, Andy 601-366-8880 249 A amiller@wbs.edu
MILLER, Angela 601-718-5900 93 H
MILLER, Angela 502-456-6771 184 F anmiller@sullivan.edu
MILLER, Angela 225-578-6801 188 K aemiller@lsu.edu
MILLER, Angela 937-512-2526 360 F angela.miller5594@sinclair.edu
MILLER, Angela, M 608-342-1555 495 E millerang@uwplatt.edu
MILLER, Angie 970-675-3235 78 P angela.miller@cncc.edu
MILLER, Anita 617-287-5000 211 E anita.miller@umb.edu
MILLER, Anita 580-477-2000 371 D
MILLER, Ann 440-826-3308 348 C amiller@bw.edu
MILLER, Anthony 763-424-0822 239 D amiller@nhcc.edu
MILLER, Anthony 540-545-7257 470 A amiller@su.edu
MILLER, April, D 606-783-2857 183 H ad.miller@moreheadstate.edu
MILLER, Ave 770-962-7580 121 B amiller@gwinnetttech.edu
MILLER, B.J 202-685-2906 501 I bj.miller.civ@ndu.edu
MILLER, Barbara, K 320-308-5447 240 C barbara.miller@stcloudstate.edu
MILLER, Baruch 718-269-4080 292 C
MILLER, Becky 913-360-7410 171 G beckymiller@benedictine.edu
MILLER, Becky 812-298-2361 158 A rmiller@ivytech.edu
MILLER, Bert 580-559-5760 365 J bmiller@ecok.edu
MILLER, Bethany 859-622-0269 180 B bethany.miller@eku.edu
MILLER, Bethany 562-906-4522 27 E bethany.miller@biola.edu
MILLER, Bethany, L 651-696-6265 236 C bmille14@macalester.edu
MILLER, Betsy 575-538-6119 288 J betsy.miller@wnmu.edu
MILLER, Bill 830-372-8120 448 C bmiller@tlu.edu
MILLER, Blanca 309-671-2909 143 I bmiller@methodistcol.edu
MILLER, Bo 601-968-8777 244 C bmiller@belhaven.edu
MILLER, Bob 610-526-7878 378 J rmiller03@brynmawr.edu
MILLER, Bobby 304-691-1700 488 N miller12@marshall.edu
MILLER, Brad 570-320-2400 392 S brad.miller@pct.edu
MILLER, Brandon 918-444-4677 366 G mille218@nsuok.edu
MILLER, Brett 304-473-8462 490 E miller_bt@wvwc.edu
MILLER, Brian 562-906-4572 27 E brian.miller@biola.edu
MILLER, Brian 616-732-1195 222 H bmiller@davenport.edu
MILLER, Brian 414-277-6947 493 D
MILLER, Brian 408-855-5247 75 C brian.miller@missioncollege.edu
MILLER, Brian 315-781-3548 301 D bmiller@hws.edu
MILLER, Brian 252-493-7421 336 E bmiller@email.pittcc.edu
MILLER, Brian, E 219-989-2994 160 A mill1817@pnw.edu
MILLER, Bridget 267-620-4834 378 E millerb@arcadia.edu
MILLER, Brittney 325-942-2248 450 B brittney.miller@angelo.edu
MILLER, Caitlin 450-620-2122 176 I caitlinm@prattcc.edu
MILLER, Cameron 419-866-0261 361 A
MILLER, Carey 412-365-1552 380 F cmiller8@chatham.edu
MILLER, Carey 307-754-6114 500 G carey.miller@nwc.edu
MILLER, Carolann 631-656-2134 299 G carolann.miller@ftc.edu
MILLER, Carolyn 318-670-6000 191 B
MILLER, Catherine 203-857-3342 87 B cmiller@norwalk.edu
MILLER, Chad, N 651-631-5100 243 E cnmiller@unwsp.edu
MILLER, Chana 908-354-6057 284 M
MILLER, Chandra 580-559-5262 365 J chalmil@ecok.edu
MILLER, Charles 337-521-8990 188 G charles.miller@solacc.edu
MILLER, Cheryl 503-552-1510 374 B cmiller@nunm.edu
MILLER, Chris 847-317-7036 150 J cmiller@tiu.edu
MILLER, Chris 760-744-1150 56 B cmiller@palomar.edu
MILLER, Chris 623-845-3841 13 E c.miller@gccaz.edu
MILLER, Chris 864-656-2161 406 F lcmille@clemson.edu
MILLER, Chris, E 570-326-3761 392 S cmiller@pct.edu
MILLER, Christi 806-291-3526 457 B millerc@wbu.edu
MILLER, Christine 850-474-2628 111 E cmiller6@uwf.edu
MILLER, Cindy 314-838-8858 261 A cmiller@ugst.edu
MILLER, Cindy 419-824-3752 355 C cmiller@lourdes.edu
MILLER, Clinton 423-417-3550 93 H
MILLER, Clinton 901-251-7100 93 H
MILLER, Colin 612-343-4400 241 O
MILLER, Corry 814-824-2000 389 E
MILLER, Cory 952-886-7569 241 P cmiller@nwhealth.edu
MILLER, Dale 518-381-1280 319 G millerdj@sunysccc.edu
MILLER, Daniel 406-994-4410 263 G danmiller@montana.edu
MILLER, Daniel, P 570-321-4139 388 H millerda@lycoming.edu
MILLER, Darlene 973-877-3101 276 G dmiller@essex.edu
MILLER, David 205-226-4723 5 A wdmiller@bsc.edu
MILLER, David 316-978-5821 178 B david.miller@wichita.edu
MILLER, David 606-546-1291 185 B dkmiller@unionky.edu
MILLER, David 623-845-3707 13 E david.miller@gccaz.edu
MILLER, David 312-362-8720 136 F miller@cdm.depaul.edu
MILLER, David, L 865-974-9080 426 B davidmiller@tennessee.edu
MILLER, Davin 706-721-5426 115 I davmiller@augusta.edu
MILLER, Davlon 816-235-1225 260 D d.miller@umkc.edu
MILLER, Dawn 612-330-1216 233 G millerd1@augsburg.edu
MILLER, Dawn 337-482-6471 192 F dawn.miller@louisiana.edu
MILLER, Deb 904-620-1416 111 A deb.miller@unf.edu
MILLER, Deborah 410-617-2020 199 G dherman@loyola.edu
MILLER, Deborah, L 419-772-2464 358 D d-miller@onu.edu
MILLER, Delana 831-479-6100 27 G demiller@cabrillo.edu
MILLER, Denise 540-828-5611 464 C dmiller2@bridgewater.edu
MILLER, Derek 334-699-2266 1 B dmiller@southeasthealth.org
MILLER, Diane 419-530-5529 363 B diane.miller@utoledo.edu
MILLER, Dianna 956-721-5232 438 A dmiller@laredo.edu
MILLER, Dion 718-482-5741 294 D dmiller@lagcc.cuny.edu
MILLER, Don 562-908-3402 58 M dmiller@riohondo.edu
MILLER, Don 314-514-3103 147 B don.miller@principia.edu
MILLER, Don, M 336-322-2154 336 D don.miller@piedmontcc.edu
MILLER, Doug 417-626-1234 257 A miller.doug@occ.edu
MILLER, Doug 713-348-6770 441 K doug.miller@rice.edu
MILLER, Drew 936-294-1786 449 E adm007@shsu.edu
MILLER, Drew 936-294-1720 449 E adm007@shsu.edu
MILLER, E. John 701-231-7933 345 D ej.miller@ndsu.edu
MILLER, Elizabeth 560-860-2451 35 O emiller@cerritos.edu
MILLER, Elizabeth 562-860-2451 35 O emiller@cerritos.edu
MILLER, Elizabeth 920-403-3117 494 B elizabeth.miller@snc.edu
MILLER, Elizabeth, K 651-638-6215 233 J e-miller@bethel.edu
MILLER, Emily, A 606-474-3212 180 G emilyamiller@kcu.edu
MILLER, Emma 228-896-2506 246 F emma.miller@mgccc.edu
MILLER, Eric 724-847-6634 384 B emiller@geneva.edu
MILLER, Erika 830-372-8077 448 C emiller@tlu.edu
MILLER, Fayneese, S 651-523-2202 235 F president@hamline.edu
MILLER, Frank 314-286-3390 257 H fdmiller@ranken.edu
MILLER, Fred 828-669-8012 331 H registrar@montreat.edu
MILLER, Gabriela 651-846-1792 240 E gabriela.miller@saintpaul.edu
MILLER, Gary, L 330-972-7869 361 G president@uakron.edu
MILLER, George, C 901-722-3217 422 I gmiller@sco.edu
MILLER, III, George, E 757-823-8015 468 B gemiller@nsu.edu
MILLER, Glen 503-399-6520 372 A glen.miller@chemeketa.edu
MILLER, Glenn 816-268-5400 256 E gamiller@mmsmidwest.com
MILLER, Glynis 512-223-7850 429 J glynis.miller@austincc.edu
MILLER, Grant 208-467-8059 132 B gtmiller@nnu.edu
MILLER, Gregory, J 330-471-8121 355 D gmiller@malone.edu
MILLER, Gretchen 260-665-4312 161 C millerg@trine.edu
MILLER, Gretchen 414-229-3067 495 B gemiller@uwm.edu
MILLER, JR., H. Samuel 828-227-7147 343 D sammiller@wcu.edu
MILLER, Harmony 661-722-6300 26 E hmiller8@avc.edu
MILLER, Heather 662-846-4311 245 A hmiller@deltastate.edu
MILLER, Heather, C 704-233-8632 344 E h.miller@wingate.edu
MILLER, J. Scott 801-422-2779 458 A scott_miller@byu.edu
MILLER, Jacqueline 704-216-6080 330 D
MILLER, Jaime 334-844-5972 4 E jmiller@auburn.edu
MILLER, Jaime, M 708-709-3513 147 A jmmiller@prairiestate.edu
MILLER, James 630-637-5513 145 E jlmiller@noctrl.edu
MILLER, James 601-635-6267 245 B jmiller@eccc.edu
MILLER, James 435-652-7625 459 G james.miller@utahtech.edu
MILLER, James, A 256-824-2482 8 B james.miller@uah.edu
MILLER, Jamie, J 617-373-2000 217 D
MILLER, Jan 205-652-3675 9 B jmiller@uwa.edu
MILLER, Jan 205-652-3421 9 B jmiller@uwa.edu
MILLER, Jason 419-289-5621 347 H jmille70@ashland.edu
MILLER, Jean 309-438-8321 140 C jmmill5@ilstu.edu
MILLER, Jeanette 206-934-3727 482 F jeanette.miller@seattlecolleges.edu
MILLER, Jeff 314-529-9353 254 D jeffmiller@maryville.edu
MILLER, Jeff 320-222-5218 239 H jeff.miller@ridgewater.edu
MILLER, Jeff 970-247-7525 80 H jkmiller2@fortlewis.edu
MILLER, Jeff 937-512-3889 360 F jeff.miller@sinclair.edu
MILLER, Jeffrey 435-586-7700 459 E
MILLER, Jeffrey, A 412-396-5081 382 E millerjeff@duq.edu
MILLER, Jeffrey, D 402-559-2704 269 B jeffrey.miller@unmc.edu
MILLER, Jen 602-787-6607 13 G jen.miller@paradisevalley.edu
MILLER, Jennifer 440-375-7379 354 K jemiller@lec.edu
MILLER, Jeremy 740-857-1311 360 C jmiller@rosedale.edu
MILLER, Jerry 707-524-1506 63 C jmiller@santarosa.edu
MILLER, Jerry, L 724-847-6639 384 B glmiller@geneva.edu
MILLER, Jessica 724-357-2621 393 G jemiller@iup.edu
MILLER, Jim 412-396-6000 382 E
MILLER, Jim, D 540-464-7251 475 C millerjd@vmi.edu
MILLER, Jo Ann 770-426-2819 122 A joann.miller@life.edu
MILLER, Joannie 541-888-7298 376 B joannie.miller@socc.edu
MILLER, Jodi 410-516-6330 199 E jodimiller@jhu.edu
MILLER, John 256-840-4195 3 F john.miller@snead.edu
MILLER, John 802-831-1334 462 F jmiller@vermontlaw.edu
MILLER, Jonathan 413-597-2502 220 A jm30@williams.edu
MILLER, Jonathan, L 978-556-3818 215 C jmiller@necc.mass.edu
MILLER, Joseph 773-244-6232 145 F jmiller2@northpark.edu
MILLER, Joseph 361-825-5967 446 E joseph.miller@tamucc.edu
MILLER, Joseph, C 803-323-2191 413 D millerjc@winthrop.edu

MILLER, Joshua .... 205-665-6245 .... 8 D millerjd@montevallo.edu
MILLER, Julie, H .... 313-577-2034 232 H julie.h.miller@wayne.edu
MILLER, Julie, L .... 317-940-9714 153 H jlmille5@butler.edu
MILLER, June, B .... 301-447-5188 201 A jmiller@msmary.edu
MILLER, Justin .... 941-487-4649 110 C jumiller@ncf.edu
MILLER, Kara .... 248-218-2038 229 I kmiller@rochesteru.edu
MILLER, Karen .... 507-223-7252 239 B karen.miller@mnwest.edu
MILLER, Karen .... 404-639-0999 122 H karen.miller@morehouse.edu
MILLER, Karen .... 270-824-8680 182 A karen.miller@kctcs.edu
MILLER, Karen .... 216-987-3471 351 D karen.miller@tri-c.edu
MILLER, Karen, A .... 770-216-2960 121 F kam@ict.edu
MILLER, Kari .... 209-667-3111 .. 33 D kkmiller@csustan.edu
MILLER, Karissa .... 941-359-7970 106 J karissa@ringling.edu
MILLER, Karla .... 256-372-4871 .... 1 A karla.miller@aamu.edu
MILLER, Kate .... 817-272-1021 454 B kate.miller@uta.edu
MILLER, Kate, M .... 651-286-7541 243 E kmmiller7@unwsp.edu
MILLER, Kathryn .... 863-583-9050 110 A
MILLER, Kathryn .... 615-230-3343 424 F kathryn.miller@volstate.edu
MILLER, SSJ, Kathryn ... 215-248-7167 380 G kmiller@chc.edu
MILLER, Katie .... 615-248-1325 425 D klmiller@trevecca.edu
MILLER, Katie .... 252-335-0821 333 E kathryn_miller@albemarle.edu
MILLER, Kausha .... 859-246-6417 181 B kausha.miller@kctcs.edu
MILLER, KC .... 480-994-9244 .. 16 C kc@swiha.edu
MILLER, Keila .... 606-487-3287 181 E keila.miller@kctcs.edu
MILLER, Keith .... 864-250-8175 408 J keith.miller@gvltec.edu
MILLER, Kelly .... 217-581-2223 137 C kpmiller@eiu.edu
MILLER, Kelly, M .... 317-788-3437 161 F kmiller@uindy.edu
MILLER, Kelly, M .... 361-825-2621 446 E kelly.miller@tamucc.edu
MILLER, Kelsey .... 410-778-7745 204 E kmiller8@washcoll.edu
MILLER, Ken .... 407-646-2999 106 L kmiller@rollins.edu
MILLER, Kenneth .... 740-857-1311 360 C kmiller@rosedale.edu
MILLER, Kevin .... 847-866-3920 138 B kevin.miller@garrett.edu
MILLER, Kevin .... 434-223-6161 466 K kmiller@hsc.edu
MILLER, Kevin, D .... 973-408-3109 276 B theoadm@drew.edu
MILLER, Kevin, D .... 973-408-3646 276 B kmiller@drew.edu
MILLER, Kevin, J .... 716-878-5601 317 C millerkj@buffalostate.edu
MILLER, Kevyn .... 480-517-8076 .. 14 A kevyn.miller@riosalado.edu
MILLER, Khadijah, O .... 757-823-2864 468 B komiller@nsu.edu
MILLER, Kim .... 419-995-8200 360 B miller.k9@rhodesstate.edu
MILLER, Kimela .... 575-835-5881 286 D kimela.miller@nmt.edu
MILLER, Kris .... 615-966-5722 420 B kris.miller@lipscomb.edu
MILLER, Kristen .... 603-342-3002 272 E kmiller@ccsnh.edu
MILLER, Kristine .... 435-797-3646 459 F kristine.miller@usu.edu
MILLER, Kyren .... 701-224-2450 345 F kyren.miller@bismarckstate.edu
MILLER, Lance .... 620-276-9789 173 H lance.miller@gcccks.edu
MILLER, Larry .... 410-706-7776 202 F larry.miller@umaryland.edu
MILLER, Larry .... 864-250-8058 408 J larry.miller@gvltec.edu
MILLER, Laura, M .... 717-796-1800 389 F lmiller@messiah.edu
MILLER, Laurence .... 724-357-2229 393 G llmiller@iup.edu
MILLER, Leigh-Anna .... 918-456-5511 366 G bennet09@nsuok.edu
MILLER, Libby .... 865-471-3200 417 E lmiller@cn.edu
MILLER, Lindsay .... 605-658-6250 415 E lindsay.miller@usd.edu
MILLER, Lisa .... 561-237-7000 103 W lmiller@lynn.edu
MILLER, Lisa .... 620-450-2185 176 I lisam@prattcc.edu
MILLER, Lisa .... 708-210-5767 149 D lmiller@ssc.edu
MILLER, Lisa .... 318-342-5441 193 A lmiller@ulm.edu
MILLER, Lisa .... 516-323-3046 306 I lmiller@molloy.edu
MILLER, Lor, M .... 844-642-2338 168 F millerd1533@nicc.edu
MILLER, Lori .... 215-702-4335 379 F lmiller@cairn.edu
MILLER, Mandrake .... 706-245-7226 118 C mandrake.miller@ec.edu
MILLER, Marc .... 478-471-2724 122 D marc.miller@mga.edu
MILLER, Marc .... 870-230-5377 .. 19 H millermd@hsu.edu
MILLER, Marc, L .... 520-621-1498 .. 16 H marc.miller@law.arizona.edu
MILLER, Marcia, K .... 316-284-5315 171 I mmiller@bethelks.edu
MILLER, Maria .... 440-775-6747 357 G maria.miller@oberlin.edu
MILLER, Mark .... 740-376-4811 355 E mark.miller@marietta.edu
MILLER, Mark .... 620-862-5252 171 E
MILLER, Mark .... 318-869-5117 186 C mmiller@centenary.edu
MILLER, Martin, J .... 724-287-8711 379 C martin.miller@bc3.edu
MILLER, Matt .... 724-287-8711 379 C matt.miller@bc3.edu
MILLER, Matt .... 989-386-6600 227 E mmiller@midmich.edu
MILLER, Matthew .... 903-875-7422 439 G matt.miller@navarrocollege.edu
MILLER, Megan .... 434-395-2064 467 F millermp@longwood.edu
MILLER, Megan, M .... 603-526-3409 271 H megan.miller@colby-sawyer.edu
MILLER, Megan, M .... 978-542-7537 213 B megan.miller@salemstate.edu
MILLER, Melinda .... 615-248-1650 425 D mmiller@trevecca.edu
MILLER, Melinda, A .... 315-386-7085 319 E millerm@canton.edu
MILLER, Melvin .... 803-705-4461 405 G melvin.miller@benedict.edu
MILLER, Merlin, R .... 660-562-1836 256 G merlin@nwmissouri.edu
MILLER, Michael .... 817-257-7577 431 B michael.miller@tcu.edu
MILLER, Michael .... 805-893-2118 .. 70 E mikemiller@ucsb.edu
MILLER, Michael .... 239-280-2401 .. 95 M michael.miller@avemaria.edu
MILLER, Michael .... 617-420-1820 218 B
MILLER, Michael .... 484-664-3300 390 F michaelmiller@muhlenberg.edu
MILLER, Michael, J .... 718-289-5548 292 H michael.miller@bcc.cuny.edu
MILLER, Mike .... 805-893-2118 .. 70 E mikemiller@ucsb.edu
MILLER, Mike .... 512-245-8441 449 G wmm30@txstate.edu
MILLER, Mindy .... 704-637-4394 327 H mmmiller17@catawba.edu
MILLER, Miryom, R .... 845-434-5240 326 G mmiller@ygzm.edu
MILLER, Mitch .... 608-757-7659 497 D mmiller80@blackhawk.edu
MILLER, Mollie .... 513-569-1898 350 C mollie.miller@cincinnatistate.edu
MILLER, Molly .... 614-947-6541 352 J molly.miller@franklin.edu
MILLER, Monica .... 620-327-4221 174 B
MILLER, Nancy .... 307-754-6243 500 G nancy.miller@nwc.edu
MILLER, Natasha .... 240-965-2469 197 F nmiller@captechu.edu
MILLER, Nora, R .... 662-329-7100 247 B nrmiller@muw.edu
MILLER, Pamela .... 605-274-0770 413 G pamela.miller@augie.edu
MILLER, Pat .... 517-629-0318 220 E pmiller@albion.edu
MILLER, Pat .... 405-912-9015 368 H pmiller@ru.edu
MILLER, Patrick .... 903-813-2307 429 I pmiller@austincollege.edu
MILLER, Paul .... 662-243-1902 245 C pmiller@eastms.edu
MILLER, Paul .... 336-278-5882 328 H millerp@elon.edu
MILLER, Paul .... 603-358-2119 274 A paul.miller@keene.edu
MILLER, Paul .... 215-222-4200 401 C pmiller@walnuthillcollege.edu
MILLER, Pearlie .... 334-876-9341 .... 2 D pearlie.miller@wccs.edu
MILLER, Pete .... 423-354-2448 424 B pwmiller@northeaststate.edu
MILLER, Peter .... 516-671-7373 324 C pmiller@webb.edu
MILLER, Phil .... 803-754-4100 407 F
MILLER, Phillip .... 610-527-0200 396 G phillip.miller@rosemont.edu
MILLER, Phillip, G .... 412-397-6914 396 E millerp@rmu.edu
MILLER, Randall .... 304-260-4380 487 C rmiller@blueridgectc.edu
MILLER, Rebecca .... 707-654-1000 .. 32 C
MILLER, Renata .... 212-650-8836 293 B remiller@ccny.cuny.edu
MILLER, Richard .... 718-613-8590 316 E richard.miller@downstate.edu
MILLER, Richard .... 855-702-7434 186 B
MILLER, Richard .... 423-636-7300 425 E rmiller@tusculum.edu
MILLER, Rita .... 508-531-1295 212 B rmiller@bridgew.edu
MILLER, Rob .... 913-758-6160 177 I rob.miller@stmary.edu
MILLER, Robert .... 270-809-3399 184 A rmiller47@murraystate.edu
MILLER, Robert .... 423-323-0212 424 B rdmiller@northeaststate.edu
MILLER, JR., Robert, L . 908-852-1400 275 H robert.miller@centenaryuniversity.edu
MILLER, Robert, P .... 302-356-2477 .. 91 C robert.p.miller@wilmu.edu
MILLER, Robert, R .... 540-828-5383 464 C rmiller@bridgewater.edu
MILLER, Rod .... 501-450-1423 .. 19 I miller@hendrix.edu
MILLER, Rodney, E .... 316-978-3389 178 B rodney.miller@wichita.edu
MILLER, Rodney, E .... 706-419-1190 117 G miller@covenant.edu
MILLER, Ronald .... 201-447-7157 274 I rmiller1@bergen.edu
MILLER, Ronda .... 517-483-1452 226 D miller53@lcc.edu
MILLER, Roy .... 865-573-4517 419 E rmiller@johnsonu.edu
MILLER, Russell, L .... 281-283-2295 452 A millerr@uhcl.edu
MILLER, Ryan .... 716-829-7822 298 C millerr@dyc.edu
MILLER, Ryan .... 979-830-4282 430 I ryan.miller@blinn.edu
MILLER, Ryan .... 561-586-0121 101 P
MILLER, Ryan, M .... 540-458-8148 476 D rmiller@wlu.edu
MILLER, Sandy, A .... 716-888-8222 291 M mille267@canisius.edu
MILLER, Sarah .... 913-971-3838 175 H smmiller@mnu.edu
MILLER, Sarah .... 661-722-6300 .. 26 E
MILLER, Sarah .... 803-812-7337 412 E semiller@mailbox.sc.edu
MILLER, Saul .... 805-493-3225 .. 29 E similler@callutheran.edu
MILLER, Scott .... 308-398-7355 265 C scottmiller@cccneb.edu
MILLER, Scott .... 580-774-3187 369 I scott.miller@swosu.edu
MILLER, Scott .... 724-938-4000 394 C
MILLER, Scott .... 307-855-2113 499 U smiller@cwc.edu
MILLER, Scott, D .... 757-455-3215 476 C president@vwu.edu
MILLER, Shae .... 417-328-7210 258 K shaemiller@sbuniv.edu
MILLER, Shannon .... 408-924-4300 .. 34 B shannon.miller@sjsu.edu
MILLER, Shari .... 631-444-2139 316 D shari.miller@stonybrookmedicine.edu
MILLER, Shari, K .... 716-673-3438 316 A shari.miller@fredonia.edu
MILLER, Sharyne .... 910-962-7261 343 B millersa@uncw.edu
MILLER, Shawn .... 315-379-3820 319 E millers@canton.edu
MILLER, Shawn .... 425-352-8135 477 F smiller@cascadia.edu
MILLER, Shealynn .... 336-725-8344 327 G
MILLER, Simone .... 662-472-9144 245 E smiller@holmescc.edu
MILLER, Simone .... 909-469-5608 .. 75 G simone.miller@westernu.edu
MILLER, ESQ, Sonya, A 305-626-3678 100 B sonya.miller@fmuniv.edu
MILLER, Staci .... 662-246-6314 246 E smiller@msdelta.edu
MILLER, Stephanie .... 256-215-4251 .... 1 G stmiller01@cacc.edu
MILLER, Stephanie .... 405-682-7897 367 D smiller@occc.edu
MILLER, Stephen .... 812-941-2101 157 D sfmiller@ius.edu
MILLER, Stephen .... 240-684-2037 203 C stephen.miller@umuc.edu
MILLER, Steve .... 925-631-4970 .. 59 I scmiller@stmarys-ca.edu
MILLER, Steve .... 513-745-5736 362 A steve.miller2@uc.edu
MILLER, Steven .... 601-266-5001 248 H steven.g.miller@usm.edu
MILLER, Steven .... 848-932-8714 281 B stmiller@rutgers.edu
MILLER, Stormy, C .... 415-485-9601 .. 39 B smiller@marin.edu
MILLER, Susan .... 219-989-5300 160 A stmiller@pnw.edu
MILLER, Susan .... 610-436-2442 394 F smiller2@wcupa.edu
MILLER, Svetlana .... 516-629-6260 324 C lmiller@webb.edu
MILLER, Tabitha .... 252-789-0246 335 F tabitha.miller@martincc.edu
MILLER, Tamsin .... 865-882-4640 424 D miller@roanestate.edu
MILLER, Tara .... 641-648-4611 167 D tara.miller@iavalley.edu
MILLER, Terri .... 517-884-0841 227 C ticklet@msu.edu
MILLER, Tia .... 603-862-0700 273 G tia.miller@usnh.edu
MILLER, Tiffany .... 310-287-4521 .. 50 C millerts@wlac.edu
MILLER, Timothy, M .... 540-568-3685 467 C millertm@jmu.edu
MILLER, Tina .... 602-787-7081 .. 13 G tina.miller@paradisevalley.edu
MILLER, Tina .... 906-248-8437 221 I tinamiller@bmcc.edu
MILLER, Tod .... 775-445-4282 271 A todm@unr.edu
MILLER, Tony, W .... 205-665-6020 .... 8 D tmiller7@montevallo.edu
MILLER, Tracy .... 734-462-4400 230 B tmiller@schoolcraft.edu
MILLER, Troy .... 717-815-1218 402 G tmiller15@ycp.edu
MILLER, Troy .... 215-248-7004 380 G millert@chc.edu
MILLER, Tyrus .... 949-824-5133 .. 69 C humanitiesdean@uci.edu
MILLER, Valerie .... 740-593-9853 358 L millerv@ohio.edu
MILLER, Van .... 940-668-3333 439 I vmiller@nctc.edu
MILLER, Victoria .... 619-388-2699 .. 61 A vmiller@sdccd.edu
MILLER, Vince .... 229-333-5941 127 C vincemiller@valdosta.edu
MILLER, Vince .... 208-282-1045 131 E millvinc@isu.edu
MILLER, Vincia .... 704-216-6009 330 D
MILLER, Wayne, C .... 606-783-2158 183 H w.miller@moreheadstate.edu
MILLER, Wendy .... 847-214-7308 137 D wmiller@elgin.edu

MILLER, Wendy .... 415-239-3370.. 37 C
wmiller@ccsfs.edu
MILLER, William .... 904-256-7030 102 G
wmiller5@ju.edu
MILLER, William .... 605-668-1514 414 F
bill.miller@mountmarty.edu
MILLER, Yolanda, D ...... 662-621-4101 244 E
ymiller@coahomacc.edu
MILLER-CALVERT,
Deborah .... 562-938-3032.. 48 K
dmiller-calvert@lbcc.edu
MILLER DIVINE,
Christine .... 678-407-5437 119 B
cmillerdivine@ggc.edu
MILLER-GALAZ,
Michelle .... 559-791-2432.. 47 D
michelle.miller@portervillecollege.edu
MILLER-GONZALEZ,
Emily, B .... 732-263-5393 278 B
emillerg@monmouth.edu
MILLER-HERNANDEZ,
Leangela .... 559-730-3795.. 39 C
leangelam@cos.edu
MILLER-LUGO, Karl ...... 210-458-4011 455 B
karl.miller-lugo@utsa.edu
MILLER-MCCOLLUM,
Keyunda .... 919-546-8539 339 I
keyunda.miller@shawu.edu
MILLER-MCNEILL,
Laurie .... 914-606-6804 324 F
laurie.millermcneill@sunywcc.edu
MILLER-SCANDLE,
Tabbi, L .... 570-348-6211 389 B
tlmillerscandle@marywood.edu
MILLER-SCHACHINGER,
Susanne .... 616-234-5825 231 D
susanne.miller@vai.edu
MILLER-SCHUSTER,
Danielle .... 309-438-5451 140 C
dnmille@ilstu.edu
MILLER-THORN, Jill ...... 631-656-2122 299 G
jill.millerthorn@ftc.edu
MILLER-WIETECHA,
Lynn .... 248-204-2383 226 E
lmillerwi@ltu.edu
MILLER-YOW, Ronnie ... 501-370-5344.. 21 A
rmiller-yow@philander.edu
MILLER-YOW, Ronnie ... 501-370-5297.. 21 A
rmiller-yow@philander.edu
MILLERBERG, Reid .... 808-675-3514 128 B
reid.millerberg@byuh.edu
MILLESON, Nyla .... 417-873-7294 252 A
nmilleson@drury.edu
MILLET, Matthew, B ...... 412-397-6405 396 E
millet@rmu.edu
MILLET, Michelle .... 607-274-1364 302 E
mmillet@ithaca.edu
MILLET, Peter, E .... 615-327-6015 420 D
pmillet@mmc.edu
MILLICAN, Joni .... 903-223-3054 447 C
businessoffice@tamut.edu
MILLICAN, Tony .... 931-393-1613 423 G
tmillican@mscc.edu
MILLIER, Deborah .... 706-245-7226 118 C
dmillier@ec.edu
MILLIGAN, Ammon .... 509-793-2291 477 D
ammonm@bigbend.edu
MILLIGAN, Aretha .... 901-843-3241 422 C
milligana@rhodes.edu
MILLIGAN, Barry .... 937-775-2953 364 D
barry.milligan@wright.edu
MILLIGAN, Kevin .... 210-829-3127 452 D
kmilliga@uiwtx.edu
MILLIGAN, Kristen .... 760-776-7428.. 39 A
kmilligan@collegeofthedesert.edu
MILLIGAN, Tina .... 757-524-2135 476 C
tmilligan@vwu.edu
MILLIGAN, Troy .... 405-422-1206 368 I
milligant@redlandscc.edu
MILLIKEN, James, B .... 512-499-4201 454 A
chancellor@utsystem.edu
MILLIKEN, Michelle ...... 910-592-8081 337 D
mmilliken@sampsoncc.edu
MILLIKEN, Roberta .... 740-774-7221 358 L
millikenr@ohio.edu
MILLIKEN, Ronald, P ..... 207-778-7105 196 F
milliken@maine.edu
MILLIKEN, Stephanie ..... 270-534-3394 182 G
stephanie.milliken@kctcs.edu
MILLIKIN, Mary .... 918-343-7605 369 A
mmillikin@rsu.edu
MILLIMAN, Robert, W ... 316-284-5239 171 I
rmilliman@bethelks.edu

MILLION, Christina, C .. 404-413-2190 120 C
cmillion@gsu.edu
MILLION, Kimberly .... 317-788-3488 161 F
0224mgr@follett.com
MILLIRON, Mark, D ...... 858-642-8000.. 53 I
mmilliron@nu.edu
MILLIRON, Maureen ..... 239-687-5303.. 95 L
mmmilliron@avemarialaw.edu
MILLISON, Jeffrey .... 703-323-5690 476 A
MILLNER, Kate .... 701-224-5666 345 F
katharine.millner@bismarckstate.edu
MILLNER, Musco .... 315-792-3046 323 G
mumillne@utica.edu
MILLNER, Tanya, C .... 410-777-2332 197 C
tcmillner@aacc.edu
MILLORA, Lisa .... 408-924-1000.. 34 B
MILLS, Alicia .... 508-831-5000 220 C
MILLS, Allison .... 217-786-2290 142 F
allison.mills@llcc.edu
MILLS, Andrea .... 615-966-5737 420 B
andrea.mills@lipscomb.edu
MILLS, Bethany .... 662-325-3344 247 A
bjb142@msstate.edu
MILLS, Brian .... 541-681-7304 371 H
bmills@bushnell.edu
MILLS, Caroline .... 864-294-2191 408 I
caroline.mills@furman.edu
MILLS, Chavonda, J ...... 678-407-5602 119 B
cmills9@ggc.edu
MILLS, Cheri .... 502-776-1443 184 C
cmills@simmonscollegeky.edu
MILLS, Cheryll .... 757-789-1730 472 I
cmills@es.vccs.edu
MILLS, Chloe, P .... 412-397-6839 396 E
millsc@rmu.edu
MILLS, Chris .... 610-896-1039 385 H
cmills@haverford.edu
MILLS, Christopher .... 410-287-1034 198 A
cmills@cecil.edu
MILLS, Colleen .... 603-888-1311 273 B
MILLS, Diana .... 410-334-2884 205 A
dmills@worwic.edu
MILLS, Edward .... 916-278-6060.. 33 A
emills@csus.edu
MILLS, F. Joe .... 931-221-7444 416 H
millsj@apsu.edu
MILLS, JR., Gordon .... 251-460-7859..... 9 A
gmills@southalabama.edu
MILLS, Jacala .... 802-387-6732 461 E
jacalamills@landmark.edu
MILLS, Jennifer .... 509-248-7100 479 G
MILLS, Joe .... 304-336-5189 489 B
jmills@westliberty.edu
MILLS, John .... 606-368-6121 178 D
johnmills@alc.edu
MILLS, Joseph, B .... 540-375-2310 469 G
mills@roanoke.edu
MILLS, Juline .... 413-572-5300 213 C
MILLS, Juline .... 413-572-8691 213 C
jmills@westfield.ma.edu
MILLS, Kathy .... 315-787-4005 299 F
MILLS, Kelley, L .... 513-745-3503 364 F
millsk9@xavier.edu
MILLS, Kevin .... 209-932-3014.. 71 E
kmills@pacific.edu
MILLS, Leslie .... 361-825-2628 446 E
leslie.mills@tamucc.edu
MILLS, Lillian .... 512-471-4607 454 C
lillian.mills@mccombs.utexas.edu
MILLS, Mark .... 215-898-1453 399 J
millsme@upenn.edu
MILLS, Martin .... 512-245-2501 449 G
mm79@txstate.edu
MILLS, Marvin, J .... 240-567-5371 200 E
marvin.mills@montgomerycollege.edu
MILLS, Matthew .... 913-253-5060 177 A
matthew.mills@spst.edu
MILLS, Michael .... 240-567-6001 200 E
michael.mills@montgomerycollege.edu
MILLS, Michael .... 940-397-4590 439 F
michael.mills@msutexas.edu
MILLS, Pamela .... 718-960-8764 293 E
pamela.mills@lehman.cuny.edu
MILLS, Rebecca .... 802-651-5965 461 C
rmills@champlain.edu
MILLS, Richard, G .... 603-646-0459 272 F
richard.g.mills@dartmouth.edu
MILLS, Sandra .... 513-487-1104 361 E
sandra.mills@myunion.edu
MILLS, Shala .... 845-257-3550 316 B
millss@newpaltz.edu
MILLS, Susan .... 951-328-3738.. 59 A
susan.mills@rccd.edu

MILLS, Thomas .... 817-515-1011 445 A
thomas.mills@tccd.edu
MILLS, William, R .... 617-552-8661 207 A
william.mills@bc.edu
MILLS-DICK, Melissa ..... 413-559-5316 210 A
memdv@hampshire.edu
MILLS-LEMIRE, Denise .. 218-733-7600 238 A
denise.mills-lemire@lsc.edu
MILLSAP, Pamela .... 409-984-6211 449 D
millsappa@lamarpa.edu
MILLSAPPS, Michael ...... 970-339-6376.. 77 G
michael.millsapps@aims.edu
MILLSAPS, Brooke .... 828-771-3015 344 B
bmillsaps@warren-wilson.edu
MILLUNCHICK, Joanna . 812-856-1079 156 C
iuldean@indiana.edu
MILLWOOD, Kent .... 864-231-2049 405 F
kmillwood@andersonuniversity.edu
MILNE, Arryn .... 410-864-4075 202 A
amilne@stmarys.edu
MILNE, Erica .... 406-377-9419 262 G
emilne@dawson.edu
MILNE, Erin .... 413-662-5049 212 F
erin.milne@mcla.edu
MILNE, Sheila .... 252-399-6326 326 H
smilne@barton.edu
MILNER, Andrea .... 517-265-5161 220 D
amilner@adrian.edu
MILNER, Devika, M ...... 305-284-6858 112 K
dmilner@miami.edu
MILNER, Eric .... 401-341-2218 404 D
eric.milner@salve.edu
MILNER, Melissa .... 719-587-8171.. 77 F
mmilner@adams.edu
MILO, Elaine .... 978-542-8031 213 B
elaine.milo@salemstate.edu
MILO, Jennifer .... 760-750-7108.. 33 C
jmilo@csusm.edu
MILOCH, Kim .... 940-898-3500 451 A
kmiloch@twu.edu
MILON, Ronald, A .... 212-217-3070 299 C
ronald_milon@fitnyc.edu
MILONE-NUZZO, Paula .. 617-726-8002 216 E
pmilone-nuzzo@mghihp.edu
MILOWSKI, Nicholas, B 718-817-4975 300 A
nmilowski@fordham.edu
MILROY, Melodie .... 406-657-1022 264 G
melodie.milroy@rocky.edu
MILSTEAD, MaLea .... 256-331-5297.... 3 C
mmilstead@nwscc.edu
MILTENBERGER, Chad .. 509-758-1711 484 B
chad.miltenberger@wwcc.edu
MILTENBERGER, Lori .... 219-464-5005 162 C
lori.miltenberger@valpo.edu
MILTER, Rebecca .... 678-916-2621 115 G
rmilter@johnmarshall.edu
MILTON, Alice .... 205-929-6306.... 2 H
amilton@lawsonstate.edu
MILTON, James .... 704-636-6580 329 F
jmilton@hoodseminary.edu
MILTON, John .... 661-362-2287.. 51 E
jmilton@masters.edu
MILTON, Mia .... 734-487-0250 223 F
mmilton@emich.edu
MILTON, Shawntee .... 760-245-4271.. 74 D
shawntee.milton@vvc.edu
MILTON, Shirlette .... 713-313-7551 448 D
milton_sg@tsu.edu
MILTON, Vikki .... 850-718-2371.. 97 E
miltonv@chipola.edu
MILZ, George .... 713-646-1864 443 C
gmilz@stcl.edu
MIMA, Rebecca .... 330-490-7090 363 E
rmima@walsh.edu
MIMMS, Lee .... 817-552-3700 437 H
lmimms@tku.edu
MIMS, Charles .... 251-981-3771..... 5 B
charles.mims@columbiasouthern.edu
MIMS, Christina .... 254-562-3848 439 G
christina.mims@navarrocollege.edu
MIMS, Dana, M .... 570-577-3171 379 A
dana.mims@bucknell.edu
MIMS, Jane .... 210-784-1000 447 B
jane.mims@tamusa.edu
MIMS, Lonette .... 919-335-1020 338 E
lemims@waketech.edu
MIMS, Melissa, O .... 803-323-2143 413 D
mimsm@winthrop.edu
MIMS, Nina .... 731-989-6916 418 H
nmims@fhu.edu
MIMS, Ronda 304-443-9170 106M
rmims@sabercollege.edu

MIN, John .... 949-480-4171.. 64 E
min@soka.edu
MIN, Ki Wook .... 510-639-7879.. 54 K
MIN, Sang Ki .... 239-590-7050 109 G
samin@fgcu.edu
MIN, Sarah .... 323-731-2383.. 55 G
sarahmin@psuca.edu
MINA, Jean .... 847-578-8378 148 B
jean.mina@rosalindfranklin.edu
MINARD, Jeff .... 972-708-7340 434 F
vp-operations@diu.edu
MINARD, Tiffany .... 859-441-4500 181 D
tiffany.minard@kctcs.edu
MINARD, Tiffany .... 859-815-7683 181 D
tiffany.minard@kctcs.edu
MINCE, Rosalie .... 410-386-8195 197 G
rmince@carrollcc.edu
MINCER, Amy .... 402-872-2239 267 H
amincer@peru.edu
MINCH, Kevin, M .... 660-785-4105 259 J
kminch@truman.edu
MINCHEFF, Daniel .... 920-498-5444 498 F
daniel.mincheff@nwtc.edu
MINCHELLO, Carla .... 508-626-4534 212 D
cminchello@framingham.edu
MINCKS, Kathy .... 907-564-8272.... 9 F
kmincks.akpacprop@gci.net
MINDEN, Courtney .... 781-239-5589 205 G
cminden@babson.edu
MINDER, Janice .... 605-773-3455 415 D
janice.minder@sdbor.edu
MINE, Jodi .... 808-934-2742 129 F
mine@hawaii.edu
MINEHART, Heather ...... 760-252-2411.. 26 L
hminehart@barstow.edu
MINEHART, James .... 419-448-2160 353 D
jminehar@heidelberg.edu
MINELLA, Rosenda .... 505-224-4000 285 B
rnaranjo9@cnm.edu
MINEO, Steve .... 912-525-5000 124 G
smineo@scad.edu
MINER, Anna, D .... 603-526-3655 271 H
anna.miner@colby-sawyer.edu
MINER, Brenda .... 479-394-7622.. 23 F
bminer@uarichmountain.edu
MINER, Dylan AT .... 517-884-1323 227 C
dminer@msu.edu
MINER, Jack, D .... 513-556-3379 361 I
minerjd@ucmail.uc.edu
MINER, Jerry .... 309-341-7150 141 E
jminer@knox.edu
MINER, Judy, C .... 650-949-6100.. 42 J
minerjudy@fhda.edu
MINER, Melvin .... 701-255-3285 346 I
mminer@uttc.edu
MINER, Molly .... 860-231-5365.. 89 G
mminer@usj.edu
MINER, Seth .... 575-646-1879 286 G
miners@nmsu.edu
MINERD, Matthew, K .... 724-237-3708 379 D
mminerd@bcs.edu
MINFORD, Joell .... 412-392-3422 395 H
jminford@pointpark.edu
MING, Amanda .... 248-476-1122 227 B
aming@msp.edu
MINGE, Jeanine .... 910-962-3876 343 B
mingej@uncw.edu
MINGEE, Sheila .... 217-709-0923 142 A
smingee@lakeviewcol.edu
MINGO, Rhonda .... 864-596-9140 407 G
rhonda.mingo@converse.edu
MINGO, Shadana .... 903-593-8311 448 A
smingo@texascollege.edu
MINGO, Susan .... 207-454-1001 195 E
smingo@wccc.me.edu
MINGO, Tracey .... 912-358-4162 124 H
mingot@savannahstate.edu
MINGO, Tracey .... 912-478-5413 120 A
tmingo@georgiasouthern.edu
MINHAS, Omer .... 847-578-8394 148 B
omer.minhas@rosalindfranklin.edu
MINICH, Mike .... 952-996-1389 233 H
mike.minich@bethfel.org
MINICK, Amy .... 773-702-5033 150 G
aminick@ttic.edu
MINICK, Thomas .... 610-790-2862 378 C
thomas.minick@alvernia.edu
MINICOLA, Steven .... 215-573-0251 399 J
minicola@upenn.edu
MINIER, Jesenia .... 203-837-8277.. 86 A
minierj@wcsu.edu
MINIER, Matt .... 502-897-4205 184 D
mrminier@sbts.edu

Index of Key Administrators MININGER – MITCHELL 797

MININGER, Marcus ...... 219-864-2400 159 D
mmininger@midamerica.edu
MINK, Rose .... 901-751-8453 420 G
rmink@mabts.edu
MINKOFF, Scott .... 215-635-7300 384 D
sminkoff@gratz.edu
MINNEMA, Linnea .... 205-726-2735.... 6 E
lminnema@samford.edu
MINNER, Mandy .... 302-831-1234.. 91 A
aminner@udel.edu
MINNER, Sam .... 505-454-3269 286 C
president_office@nmhu.edu
MINNICH, Matthew .... 216-421-8028 350 E
mminnich@cia.edu
MINNICH, Sharon .... 717-720-4100 393 C
sminnich@passhe.edu
MINNICH, William .... 650-738-4484.. 62 K
minnichw@smccd.edu
MINNICH SPUHLER,
Donna .... 973-720-3258 283 I
minnichspuhlerd@wpunj.edu
MINNICK, Ann, M .... 651-696-6036 236 C
aminnick@macalester.edu
MINNICK, Charlie .... 858-513-9240.. 16 I
charlie.minnick@ashford.edu
MINNIEFIELD, Angela ... 323-563-4800.. 36 E
angelaminniefield@cdrewu.edu
MINNIEFIELD,
Angela, L .... 323-563-4897.. 36 E
angelaminniefield@cdrewu.edu
MINNIS, Stephen, D ..... 913-360-7400 171 G
sminnis@benedictine.edu
MINNIS, Tia, A .... 804-524-3283 475 E
tminnis@vsu.edu
MINNITE, Lorraine .... 856-225-2526 281 A
minnite@camden.rutgers.edu
MINNITI, Lea .... 513-745-3711 364 F
minnitil@xavier.edu
MINNIX, Gena .... 512-472-4133 442 H
gena.minnix@ssw.edu
MINNIX, Katy .... 573-897-5120 259 E
katy.minnix@statetechmo.edu
MINOR, Chelsea .... 815-226-4022 147 J
MINOR, Diana .... 909-537-3428.. 33 B
diana.minor@csusb.edu
MINOR, Frankie .... 401-874-2899 404 E
frankie@uri.edu
MINOR, James, T .... 618-650-2475 149 H
jtminor@siue.edu
MINOR, Jeremy .... 918-647-1200 365 D
jrminor@carlalbert.edu
MINOR, Jessica .... 864-242-5100 405 H
MINOR, Karen .... 770-533-7030 121 L
kminor@laniertech.edu
MINOR, Leslie .... 661-763-7871.. 67 F
lminor@taftcollege.edu
MINOR, Lloyd .... 650-723-2300.. 66 D
lminor@stanford.edu
MINOR, Scott .... 916-631-8363.. 29 G
MINOR, Tamra .... 716-286-8354 309 F
tminor@niagara.edu
MINOR, Timothy, A ...... 919-962-1000 340 F
MINOR, Tracey .... 601-977-7879 248 E
tminor@tougaloo.edu
MINSON, Patrick .... 516-686-7718 308 H
patrick.minson@nyit.edu
MINSTER, Brian .... 610-225-5010 383 A
brian.minster@eastern.edu
MINTER, Douglas .... 630-466-7900 152 H
dminter@waubonsee.edu
MINTER, Michelle .... 609-258-6110 279 E
mminter@princeton.edu
MINTER, Toni .... 972-780-3600 453 C
toniminter@my.unt.edu
MINTO, James .... 718-270-3128 316 E
james.minto@downstate.edu
MINTO, Robert .... 614-508-7246 353 M
rminto@hondros.edu
MINTON, J. Ernest .... 785-532-7137 175 A
eminton@ksu.edu
MINTON, Jessie .... 314-935-0000 261 B
minton@wustl.edu
MINTZ, Zev .... 732-370-1560 274 H
MINUS, Daryl .... 434-949-1012 474 D
daryl.minus@southside.edu
MIOFSKY, Christopher .. 303-871-3111.. 84 C
christopher.miofsky@du.edu
MIRABAL, Gloria .... 787-743-4041 505 B
gmirabal@columbiacentral.edu
MIRABAL, Jonathan ...... 908-852-1400 275 H
jonathan.mirabal@centenaryuniversity.edu
MIRABAL, Lawrence ...... 505-424-2316 285 H
lmirabal@iaia.edu
MIRAMONTEZ, Daniel ... 619-388-7333.. 61 B
dmiramon@sdccd.edu
MIRANDA, Alex .... 714-895-8180.. 38 E
amiranda42@gwc.cccd.edu
MIRANDA, Candida .... 312-567-3134 139 H
miranda@iit.edu
MIRANDA, Charles .... 934-420-2297 320 C
mirandc@farmingdale.edu
MIRANDA, Cynthia .... 787-780-0070 504 E
cmiranda@caribbean.edu
MIRANDA, Jen .... 904-620-2526 111 A
j.miranda@unf.edu
MIRANDA,
Katherine, M .... 330-325-6483 357 D
kmiranda@neomed.edu
MIRANDA, Kenneth, M . 607-254-1150 297 D
kmm446@cornell.edu
MIRANDA, Leanda .... 617-824-8453 208 G
leanda_miranda@emerson.edu
MIRANDA, Leslie .... 877-722-3285 124 G
lmiranda@scad.edu
MIRANDA, Mark .... 732-571-3593 278 B
mmiranda@monmouth.edu
MIRANDA, Rick .... 562-860-2451.. 35 O
ermiranda@cerritos.edu
MIRANDA, Rick .... 949-451-5679.. 65 B
rmiranda@ivc.edu
MIRANDA, Rick .... 970-491-6614.. 79 D
rick.miranda@colostate.edu
MIRANDA, Sabrina .... 209-575-6067.. 76 K
mirandasa@mjc.edu
MIRANDA, Yolanda .... 787-743-3038 508 L
ymiranda@sanjuanbautista.edu
MIRELEZ, Yvette .... 830-591-7318 443 I
yvetteh@swtjc.edu
MIRENBERG, Mark .... 718-522-9073 290 B
mmirenberg@asa.edu
MIRIJANIAN, Nara .... 586-498-4124 226 F
mirijanian225@macomb.edu
MIRMIRAN, Amir .... 903-566-7104 455 C
amirmiran@uttyler.edu
MIRMIRANI, Maj .... 740-593-1479 358 L
mirmirani@ohio.edu
MIRNICS, Karoly .... 402-559-5720 269 B
karoly.mirnics@unmc.edu
MIRSHAB, Bahman .... 248-204-3050 226 E
bmirshab@ltu.edu
MIRTSCHINK, Steven .... 770-426-2851 122 A
smirtsch@life.edu
MIRUS, Kevin .... 608-246-6478 497 I
kmirus@madisoncollege.edu
MIRUS, Tarrah, N .... 404-413-2275 120 C
tmirus@gsu.edu
MISAK, David .... 580-774-3275 369 I
david.misak@swosu.edu
MISAK, Doug .... 580-774-3750 369 I
doug.misak@swosu.edu
MISALE, Lauren .... 508-793-7795 207 F
lmisale@clarku.edu
MISCHKE, Carly .... 310-506-6738.. 56 H
carly.mischke@pepperdine.edu
MISERENDINO, Peter ..... 203-287-3026.. 88 D
paier.admin@snet.net
MISEY, Monica .... 414-425-8300 494 A
mmisey@shsst.edu
MISHLER, Jeremy .... 231-591-2345 223 H
jeremymishler@ferris.edu
MISHRA, Aneil .... 810-762-3160 231 C
mishra@umich.edu
MISHRA, Ashu .... 916-691-7090.. 50 K
mishraa@crc.losrios.edu
MISHRA, Sharda, D ...... 615-327-6156 420 D
smishra@mmc.edu
MISHRA, Tara .... 479-788-7002.. 22 A
tara.mishra@uafs.edu
MISIAK, Mark, J .... 315-267-3133 318 D
misiakmj@potsdam.edu
MISIANO, Chris .... 434-592-3144 467 E
cjmisiano@liberty.edu
MISJUNS, Sue .... 434-592-3004 467 E
smisjuns@liberty.edu
MISKELL, Anita .... 812-749-1240 159 E
amiskell@oak.edu
MISKOVIC, Maja .... 708-209-3554 136 D
maja.miskovic@cuchicago.edu
MISKUS, Lynn .... 219-473-4310 154 A
lmiskus@ccsj.edu
MISKY, Allison .... 860-727-2117.. 87 H
amisky@goodwin.edu
MISRA, Aidtya, V .... 607-255-5070 297 D
am2374@cornell.edu
MISRA, Christopher, P . 413-545-9339 211 D
chris.misra@umass.edu
MISRA, Ravi, P .... 414-955-4403 492 F
rmisra@mcw.edu
MISS, Stephen .... 704-461-6802 326 I
stephenmiss@bac.edu
MISSEL, Thomas .... 716-375-2303 312 F
tmissel@sbu.edu
MISSOURI, Joshua .... 254-519-5760 446 C
jmissouri@tamuct.edu
MISTUR, Mark .... 330-672-2917 354 A
mmistur1@kent.edu
MITCHELL, Adrienne ...... 414-955-4145 492 F
abmitchell@mcw.edu
MITCHELL, Andrew, J ... 757-446-5199 465 H
mitcheaj@evms.edu
MITCHELL, Angela .... 540-831-6297 468 E
amitchell90@radford.edu
MITCHELL, Anne, L .... 317-274-2306 157 B
amitch29@iupui.edu
MITCHELL, Anne, M ...... 401-254-3207 404 C
amitchell@rwu.edu
MITCHELL, Annette .... 937-229-4122 362 C
amitchell2@udayton.edu
MITCHELL, Arden .... 863-680-3943 100 F
amitchell@flsouthern.edu
MITCHELL, Ashley .... 503-517-1819 377 D
amitchell@westernseminary.edu
MITCHELL, Beth .... 315-445-4310 303 F
mitchell@lemoyne.edu
MITCHELL, Betsy .... 626-395-6148.. 29 B
betsy.mitchell@caltech.edu
MITCHELL, Brad .... 415-442-7000.. 44 B
MITCHELL, Brandi .... 919-209-2035 335 D
bnmitchell@johnstoncc.edu
MITCHELL, Brenda .... 704-216-6222 330 D
bmitchell@livingstone.edu
MITCHELL, Brenda .... 301-546-3088 201 D
mitchebs@pgcc.edu
MITCHELL, Brenda .... 334-244-3464.... 4 F
bmitche8@aum.edu
MITCHELL, Brooke .... 704-233-8060 344 E
bmclaugh@wingate.edu
MITCHELL, Bryan .... 404-756-2733 115 E
bmitchell@atlm.edu
MITCHELL, Carl .... 910-678-8373 334 C
mitchelc@faytechcc.edu
MITCHELL, Carlton .... 903-233-3482 438 C
carltonmitchell@letu.edu
MITCHELL, Cathy .... 575-392-4510 286 E
cmitchell@nmjc.edu
MITCHELL, Charles .... 409-882-3367 449 C
charles.mitchell@lsco.edu
MITCHELL, Chase .... 435-283-7340 460 C
chase.mitchell@snow.edu
MITCHELL, Chris .... 501-205-8919.. 19 B
cmitchell@cbc.edu
MITCHELL, SR.,
Chris, A .... 757-226-5030 469 D
policeprofessionalstandards@cbn.org
MITCHELL, Chrisie .... 845-431-8976 298 B
chrisie.mitchell@sunydutchess.edu
MITCHELL, Clayton .... 215-503-7268 398 G
clayton.mitchell@jefferson.edu
MITCHELL, Clifton .... 229-226-1621 126 B
cmitchell@thomasu.edu
MITCHELL, Connie .... 803-754-4100 407 F
MITCHELL, Cordelia .... 501-374-6305.. 21 B
cordelia.mitchell@shortercollege.edu
MITCHELL, Courtney ...... 443-412-2379 199 B
cmitchell@harford.edu
MITCHELL, Craig .... 206-517-4541 482 J
cmitchell@sieam.edu
MITCHELL, Damon .... 314-529-9252 254 D
dmitchell@maryville.edu
MITCHELL, Darren .... 815-753-9679 145 H
dmitchell12@niu.edu
MITCHELL, David .... 415-503-6218.. 61 E
dlmitchell@sfcm.edu
MITCHELL, David, B ...... 301-405-5726 202 E
dmitche5@umd.edu
MITCHELL, Dawn .... 318-357-5960 192 D
dawnmitchell@nsula.edu
MITCHELL, Debbie .... 828-766-1273 335 G
dmitchell@mayland.edu
MITCHELL, Delmer .... 217-222-8020 147 C
MITCHELL, Dennis .... 480-461-7213.. 13 F
dennis.mitchell@mesacc.edu
MITCHELL, Dennis .... 212-854-7161 296 H
dmitchell@columbia.edu
MITCHELL, Dennis, A .... 212-854-1754 296 H
MITCHELL, Donna .... 740-245-7303 363 A
mitchell@rio.edu
MITCHELL, Emilie .... 916-691-7142.. 50 K
mitchee@crc.losrios.edu
MITCHELL, Erica .... 901-321-3318 417 G
erica.mitchell@cbu.edu
MITCHELL, Erik, T .... 858-534-2230.. 70 C
MITCHELL, III,
Ernest, L .... 731-426-7604 419 G
emitchell@lanecollege.edu
MITCHELL, Glendon, G . 801-587-3784 459 D
gmitchell@purchasing.utah.edu
MITCHELL, Gloria .... 903-927-3304 457 I
gemitchell@wileyc.edu
MITCHELL,
Gwendolyn, F .... 803-536-8212 410 H
gmitche3@scsu.edu
MITCHELL, Heather .... 850-201-6067 112 B
heather.mitchell@tcc.fl.edu
MITCHELL, Jada .... 678-466-4076 117 A
jadamitchell@clayton.edu
MITCHELL, James .... 517-483-1673 226 D
mitch94@lcc.edu
MITCHELL, James, M .... 334-876-9230.... 2 D
james.mitchell@wccs.edu
MITCHELL, Janekia .... 256-439-6852.... 2 B
jmitchell@gadsdenstate.edu
MITCHELL, Jaymi .... 252-493-7254 336 E
jlmitchell645@my.pittcc.edu
MITCHELL, Jennifer .... 229-732-5946 114 I
jennifermitchell@andrewcollege.edu
MITCHELL, Joan .... 801-274-3280 460 E
jmitchell@wgu.edu
MITCHELL, Joann .... 215-898-6630 399 J
joannm@upenn.edu
MITCHELL, Joanne .... 310-665-6963.. 55 B
jmitchell@otis.edu
MITCHELL, Jon .... 731-352-4280 417 C
MITCHELL, Joseph, M .. 304-457-6242 485 F
mitchelljm@ab.edu
MITCHELL, Joshua .... 610-769-1322 388 B
jmitchell10@lccc.edu
MITCHELL, Joshua .... 262-547-1211 491 A
jmitchell@carrollu.edu
MITCHELL, Jud .... 870-574-4726.. 21 F
jmitchel@sautech.edu
MITCHELL, Judy .... 815-280-2207 140 I
jmitchel@jjc.edu
MITCHELL, Karen .... 615-230-3505 424 F
karen.mitchell@volstate.edu
MITCHELL, Katharyne .... 831-459-2919.. 71 A
kmitch@ucsc.edu
MITCHELL, Kathryn .... 661-722-6300.. 26 E
kmitchell18@avc.edu
MITCHELL, Keith .... 580-581-2211 365 C
kmitchel@cameron.edu
MITCHELL, Ken, H .... 919-209-2112 335 D
khmitchell@johnstoncc.edu
MITCHELL, Kerrie .... 575-492-2560 286 E
kmitchell@nmjc.edu
MITCHELL, Kerry .... 623-845-3693.. 13 E
kerry.mitchell@gccaz.edu
MITCHELL, Kim .... 502-456-6508 184 F
kmitchell@sullivan.edu
MITCHELL, Kimberly, A . 309-655-2230 148 G
kim.mitchell@osfhealthcare.org
MITCHELL, Lori .... 540-674-3790 473 F
lmitchell@nr.edu
MITCHELL, Maria .... 610-372-4721 396 A
mmitchell@racc.edu
MITCHELL, Mark .... 540-338-1776 468 D
MITCHELL, Marquita ...... 214-379-5412 440 H
mmitchell@pqc.edu
MITCHELL, Melanie .... 508-793-2011 208 A
MITCHELL, Melissa .... 308-432-6221 267 G
mmitchell@csc.edu
MITCHELL, Melynda .... 505-346-2348 288 B
MITCHELL, Michael .... 251-460-6172.... 9 A
mmitchell@southalabama.edu
MITCHELL, Michele .... 601-403-1440 247 F
mmitchell@prcc.edu
MITCHELL, Michelle .... 731-352-4239 417 C
mitchellm@bethelu.edu
MITCHELL, Mitch .... 812-288-8878 159 C
mmitchell@mid-america.edu
MITCHELL, Mitch .... 336-750-3356 343 E
mitchellja@wssu.edu
MITCHELL, Nancy .... 636-584-6617 252 D
nancy.mitchell@eastcentral.edu
MITCHELL, Naomi .... 318-345-9150 188 A
nmitchell@ladelta.edu
MITCHELL, Pamela .... 860-512-2605.. 86 F
pmitchell1@manchestercc.edu
MITCHELL, Paula .... 915-831-6375 435 B
pmitche8@epcc.edu

MITCHELL, JR., Randolph .... 904-470-8128.. 98 I
randolph.mitchell@ewc.edu
MITCHELL, JR., Robert . 504-816-4864 186 F
rvmitchell@dillard.edu
MITCHELL, Robin .... 563-288-6103 165 I
rmitchell@eicc.edu
MITCHELL, Roland .... 225-578-2156 188 K
rwmitch@lsu.edu
MITCHELL, Sandra .... 651-690-6649 242 F
slmitchell224@stkate.edu
MITCHELL, Scott .... 815-226-4026 147 J
smitchell@rockford.edu
MITCHELL, Scott .... 510-809-1444.. 46 B
MITCHELL, Sharon, L .... 716-645-2720 315 F
smitch@buffalo.edu
MITCHELL, Sheila .... 731-661-5953 425 F
smitchell@uu.edu
MITCHELL, Stephen .... 517-265-5161 220 D
smitchell@adrian.edu
MITCHELL, Steve .... 903-823-3269 445 C
steven.mitchell@texarkanacollege.edu
MITCHELL, Tedd, L .... 806-742-0012 450 A
MITCHELL, Tedd, L .... 806-742-0012 450 C
tedd.mitchell@ttuhsc.edu
MITCHELL, Terrence ...... 724-938-4000 394 C
MITCHELL, Thomas, J .... 352-392-5407 110 E
tmitchell@uff.ufl.edu
MITCHELL, Thomas, R .... 956-326-2240 446 A
tmitchell@tamiu.edu
MITCHELL, Todd .... 336-334-5831 342 D
todd_mitchell@uncg.edu
MITCHELL, Tracy .... 706-865-2134 126 D
tmitchell@truett.edu
MITCHELL, Trapper .... 608-342-1183 495 E
mitchellt@uwplatt.edu
MITCHELL, Venita .... 434-791-5627 463 L
vmitchell@averett.edu
MITCHELL, Vicki .... 740-588-1386 364 H
vmitchell@zanestate.edu
MITCHELL, Victor .... 860-314-4709.. 87 E
vmitchell@tunxis.edu
MITCHELL, William .... 508-588-9100 214 F
wamitchell@massasoit.mass.edu
MITCHELL, JR., Zane, W .... 812-465-7137 162 B
zwmitchell@usi.edu
MITCHELL-COOK, Amy .. 850-857-6014 111 E
amitchellcook@uwf.edu
MITCHELL-HOLDER, Sandra .... 317-924-1331 154 D
MITCHEM, Brandi .... 478-445-2313 116 F
bmitchem@centralgatech.edu
MITCHUM, M.G .... 843-574-6995 411 I
mg.mitchum@tridenttech.edu
MITCHUSSON, Karen .... 870-733-6847.. 18 A
kmitchusson@asumidsouth.edu
MITHANI, Amynah .... 667-208-7545 199 E
amithan1@jhu.edu
MITJANS, Dolores .... 787-882-2065 508 N
dmitjans@unitecpr.edu
MITNICK, Eric .... 508-985-1169 211 F
emitnick@umassd.edu
MITRA, Sabyasachi .... 352-392-2398 110 E
sabymitra@warrington.ufl.edu
MITSLER, Julee .... 636-949-4913 254 B
jmitsler@lindenwood.edu
MITTELSTAEDT, John ..... 937-229-3349 362 C
jmittelstaedt1@udayton.edu
MITTEN, Richard .... 646-312-2076 292 F
richard.mitten@baruch.cuny.edu
MITTEN, Trae .... 573-651-2524 258 J
lmitten@semo.edu
MITTLEMAN, Michael, H .... 215-780-1280 397 E
president@salus.edu
MITTLER, Tiina .... 626-852-8047.. 37 B
ttittler@citruscollege.edu
MITTMAN, Paul, A .... 480-858-9100.. 16 B
p.mittman@scnm.edu
MITTON, Gregory, S ..... 484-664-3175 390 F
gregmitton@muhlenberg.edu
MITTON, Lynda .... 816-960-2008 250 J
dean@cityvision.edu
MITTS, Maryann .... 417-667-8181 251 E
mmitts@cottey.edu
MITTUCH, Maggie, A .... 253-879-3673 483 G
mmittuch@pugetsound.edu
MITZEL, Andrew .... 208-426-1429 130 F
andrewmitzel@boisestate.edu
MITZEL, Bobbi .... 307-675-0703 500 F
rmitzel@sheridan.edu

MITZEL, Thomas, M ...... 270-852-3104 183 B
tom.mitzel@kwc.edu
MIX, Julie, L .... 253-535-7101 481 C
mixjl@plu.edu
MIX, Kerry .... 409-839-2048 449 A
kmix@lit.edu
MIXON, Clarinda .... 251-578-1313.... 3 D
cmixon@rstc.edu
MIXON, Lonnie .... 407-303-8192.. 95 A
lonnie.mixon@ahu.edu
MIXSON, Frank .... 562-860-2451.. 35 O
fmixson@cerritos.edu
MIYAKE, Christina .... 212-563-6647 323 A
c.lmiyake@uts.edu
MIYARES, Javier .... 952-806-3910 241 R
MIYASHIRO, James .... 619-260-7690.. 72 H
publicsafety@sandiego.edu
MIYASHIRO, Jane .... 310-660-3401.. 41 J
jmiyashiro@elcamino.edu
MIYASHIRO, Ross .... 310-660-3472.. 41 J
rmiyashiro@elcamino.edu
MIZAK, Pat .... 941-893-2858 106 J
pmizak@ringling.edu
MIZE, Kyle, C .... 325-649-8049 437 A
kmize@hputx.edu
MIZELL, Claire .... 903-510-2939 451 D
cmiz@tjc.edu
MIZELL, Hunter .... 843-863-7000 406 C
hmizell@csuniv.edu
MIZELL, Nathan .... 252-789-0232 335 F
nathan.mizell@martincc.edu
MIZZY, Danianne .... 973-655-4301 278 C
mizzyd@montclair.edu
MIÑANA, Rogelio .... 215-571-3194 382 D
rogelio.minana@drexel.edu
MLLER, Justin (Jay) ...... 859-257-3887 185 D
justin.miller1@uky.edu
MLODZIK, Leigh .... 515-961-1699 169 G
leigh.mlodzik@simpson.edu
MLYNSKI, Melissa .... 217-206-7148 151 E
mmlyn2@uis.edu
MMEJE, Kenechukwu (K.C.) ...... 214-768-2821 443 G
kmmeje@smu.edu
MMONU, Ambrosia .... 512-617-5700 432 B
MNOOKIN, Jennifer .... 608-262-9946 494 D
chancellor@wisc.edu
MNOOKIN, Jennifer, L .. 310-825-8202.. 69 D
mnookin@law.ucla.edu
MO, Huanbiao .... 404-413-1082 120 C
hmo@gsu.edu
MOAK, Marvin .... 601-629-6805 245 D
memoak@hindscc.edu
MOANANU, Letupu .... 684-699-2722 503 A
l.moananu@amsamoa.edu
MOATS, Kyle .... 417-836-5244 255 J
kylemoats@missouristate.edu
MOATS, Scott .... 651-638-6125 233 J
scm44939@bethel.edu
MOBELINI, Deronda .... 606-487-3409 181 E
deronda.mobelini@kctcs.edu
MOBERG, Christopher, R .... 989-774-2481 221 M
mober1cr@cmich.edu
MOBERLY, Jonathon ...... 402-643-7430 265 I
jonathon.moberly@cune.edu
MOBERLY, Richard .... 402-472-1256 269 A
moberly@unl.edu
MOBLEY, Johnnie .... 206-934-6070 482 F
johnnie.mobley@seattlecolleges.edu
MOBLEY, Karen .... 912-871-1638 123 F
kmobley@ogeecheetech.edu
MOBLEY, Katie .... 802-654-0505 463 A
kjf06010@ccv.vsc.edu
MOBLEY, Wade .... 763-544-9501 235 D
MOBLEY SMITH, Miriam .... 808-932-8120 129 A
miriamms@hawaii.edu
MOBRAY, Todd .... 620-792-9245 171 F
mobrayt@bartonccc.edu
MOCCIA, Mario .... 575-646-7630 286 G
moccia@nmsu.edu
MOCK, James .... 662-252-8000 248 B
jmock@rustcollege.edu
MOCK, Kenrick .... 907-786-1956.. 10 A
kjmock@alaska.edu
MOCK, Lisa .... 701-228-5432 345 G
lisa.mock@dakotacollege.edu
MOCK, Robert, C .... 410-651-6101 203 B
rcmock@umes.edu
MOCNIK, Joe .... 785-532-7492 175 A
mocnik@ksu.edu

MOCTEZUMA, Edgar ..... 713-522-7911 453 H
mocteze@stthom.edu
MODENA, Shawn .... 478-825-6100 118 E
modenas@fvsu.edu
MODERO, Thomas .... 646-565-6163 322 B
thomas.modero@touro.edu
MODERO, Thomas .... 646-565-6163 322 C
thomas.modero@touro.edu
MODESTOU, Jennifer, A .... 319-335-0705 163 F
jennifer-modestou@uiowa.edu
MODIC, Jeannette, L ..... 240-895-2260 201 F
jlmodic@smcm.edu
MODICA, Joseph .... 909-748-8692.. 72 E
joseph_modica@redlands.edu
MODICA, Joseph, B .... 610-341-5826 383 A
jmodica@eastern.edu
MODICA, Kathy .... 870-864-7107.. 21 C
kmodica@southark.edu
MODISETTE, Jan .... 903-589-7300 437 D
jmodisette@jacksonville-college.edu
MODLIN, Andrew, S ...... 336-841-9605 329 E
amodlin@highpoint.edu
MODLIN, Eli, J .... 410-548-3316 204 A
ejmodlin@salisbury.edu
MODLIN, Jason .... 252-985-5404 339 B
jmodlin@ncwc.edu
MODROVSKY, Amanda . 570-408-5534 402 B
amanda.modrovsky@wilkes.edu
MODRY-CARON, Irah .... 260-481-6375 159 H
modryi@pfw.edu
MOE, Keri, L .... 915-831-6526 435 B
kmoe@epcc.edu
MOE, Rolin .... 650-738-7149.. 62 K
moer@smccd.edu
MOEBIUS, Kim .... 510-430-3335.. 66 F
kmoebius@sksm.edu
MOEDER, Brenda .... 660-543-4515 259 K
moeder@ucmo.edu
MOEGGENBERG, Rich .... 517-607-2250 224 G
rmoeggenberg@hillsdale.edu
MOEHLING, Carolyn ...... 848-932-8662 281 B
cmoehling@echo.rutgers.edu
MOELLER, Darin .... 712-274-6400 170 H
darin.moeller@witcc.edu
MOELLER, Lon, D .... 386-226-6000.. 98 J
moellerl@erau.edu
MOELLER, Marcus .... 405-692-3102 366 C
marcus.moeller@macu.edu
MOELLER, Mike .... 717-464-7050 387 E
MOELLER, Molly .... 515-271-7497 165 C
molly.moeller@dmu.edu
MOENCH, Loren .... 308-635-6144 269 E
moenchl1@wncc.edu
MOENKHAUS, Kevin, P 515-271-3902 165 F
kevin.moenkhaus@drake.edu
MOENTMANN, Elise, M 503-943-7341 376 H
moentman@up.edu
MOERKERKE, Abby .... 406-657-2246 263 H
abby.moerkerke@msubfoundation.com
MOERMAN, LeeAnn .... 712-722-6002 165 E
leeann.moerman@dordt.edu
MOERSCHBAECHER, Joseph, M .... 504-568-4804 189 C
jmoers@lsuhsc.edu
MOES, James, R .... 816-604-3048 255 A
james.moes@mcckc.edu
MOESSNER, Phil .... 320-308-3190 240 C
pmmoessner@stcloudstate.edu
MOETZ, John .... 386-481-2510.. 96 D
moetzj@cookman.edu
MOFFATT, Amy .... 410-704-3974 204 B
amoffatt@towson.edu
MOFFATT, Tammy, L ..... 603-646-2811 272 F
tammy.l.moffatt@dartmouth.edu
MOFFATT-LIMOGES, Pamela .... 401-739-5000 403 F
pmoffatt-limoges@neit.edu
MOFFETT, Brad .... 423-614-8310 419 H
bmoffett@leeuniveristy.edu
MOFFETT, Janelle .... 301-689-4493 203 F
jamoffett@frostburg.edu
MOFFETT, Jared, E .... 202-274-6858.. 94 B
jared.moffett@udc.edu
MOFFETT, Leigh Ann .... 214-768-4047 443 G
leighannm@smu.edu
MOFFITT, Amy .... 515-574-1144 166 G
moffitt_a@iowacentral.edu
MOFFITT, Brittany .... 480-245-7994.. 12 O
brittany.moffitt@ibcs.edu
MOFFITT, Jamie, H .... 541-346-3003 376 G
jmoffitt@uoregon.edu
MOFFITT, Jill .... 206-220-8515 483 B
jmoffitt@seattleu.edu

MOFFITT, Kimberly .... 410-455-2376 202 G
kmoffitt@umbc.edu
MOFFITT, Lisa .... 615-327-3927 419 D
moffitt@guptoncollege.edu
MOFFITT, Mark .... 614-823-1108 359 G
mmoffitt@otterbein.edu
MOFFITT, Michael .... 765-674-6901 157 F
michael.moffitt@indwes.edu
MOFFITT, Thomas, J ..... 610-566-1776 402 C
tmoffitt@williamson.edu
MOGA, Paul, D .... 800-443-9266 502 C
paul.moga@afacademy.af.edu
MOGARD, Naomi .... 320-223-7510 242 A
MOGFORD, Jon, E .... 979-436-0205 446 B
jmogford@tamu.edu
MOHAJIR, Terry .... 407-823-2261 110 D
adoffice@athletics.ucf.edu
MOHAM, Carren .... 620-327-8207 174 B
carren.moham@hesston.edu
MOHAMED, Rafik .... 909-537-5024.. 33 B
rafik.mohamed@csusb.edu
MOHAMED, Rafik .... 909-537-5500.. 33 B
rafik.mohamed@csusb.edu
MOHAMMAD, Esam .... 316-323-6426 172 B
emohammad@butlercc.edu
MOHAMMAD, Kareem .. 262-547-1211 491 A
MOHAMMAD, Yatty ...... 402-878-2380 266 D
ymohammad@littlepriest.edu
MOHAMMADI, Amir ...... 724-738-2002 394 E
amir.mohammadi@sru.edu
MOHAMMADI, Jamshid 312-567-7516 139 H
mohammadi@iit.edu
MOHAMMADI, Rameen 315-312-2232 318 B
rameen.mohammadi@oswego.edu
MOHANAN, M.K .... 269-387-5865 232 J
mk.mohanan@wmich.edu
MOHANTY, Lisa .... 800-375-9878.. 68 G
lisa.mohanty@trident.edu
MOHAPATRA, Prasant ... 530-754-7764.. 69 A
pmohapatra@ucdavis.edu
MOHEBBI, Vargha .... 480-425-6903.. 14 B
vargha.mohebbi@scottsdalecc.edu
MOHIYEDDINI, Sohila .. 714-533-1495.. 64 G
soh@southbaylo.edu
MOHLENHOFF, Deb .... 607-844-8222 321 I
mohlend@tompkinscortland.edu
MOHLER, Benjamin .... 859-256-3100 180 H
ben.mohler@kctcs.edu
MOHLER, JR., R. Albert .... 502-897-4121 184 D
mohler@sbts.edu
MOHLER, Rigg .... 703-416-1441 465 E
rmohler@divinemercy.edu
MOHLER, Robin .... 517-629-0960 220 E
rmohler@albion.edu
MOHNEY, David .... 908-737-4770 277 F
dmohney@kean.edu
MOHR, Caitilin .... 434-961-5278 474 B
cmohr@pvcc.edu
MOHR, James, R .... 724-946-7116 401 F
mohrjr@westminister.edu
MOHR, Jannine, R .... 970-491-6270.. 79 E
jannine.mohr@colostate.edu
MOHR, Jim .... 509-434-5120 478 C
james.mohr@ccs.spokane.edu
MOHR, Karl .... 530-752-2063.. 69 A
kfmohr@ucdavis.edu
MOHR, Lisa .... 320-308-5486 240 D
lisa.mohr@sctcc.edu
MOHR, Sandra .... 617-587-5608 216 H
mohrs@neco.edu
MOHR, Thomas .... 208-795-4266 131 D
MOHR, Thomas .... 936-294-4719 449 E
MOHRBACHER, Robert .. 360-623-8552 477 H
bob.mohrbacher@centralia.edu
MOHRE, Trudy .... 517-264-7185 230 C
tmohre@sienaheights.edu
MOHRFELD, Maggie ...... 816-501-2430 249 H
MOHRMANN, Helen .... 512-579-5036 454 A
hmohrmann@utsystem.edu
MOHSEN, Bashir .... 201-216-9901 276 C
bashir.mohsen@eicollege.edu
MOIN, Angel, L .... 651-631-5493 243 E
almoin@unwsp.edu
MOIR, Chris .... 216-987-3492 351 D
chris.moir@tri-c.edu
MOIR, Joe .... 207-768-9649 196 I
joseph.moir@maine.edu
MOISEY, Neil .... 406-265-3726 264 A
neil.moisey@msun.edu
MOIST, Kirk, L .... 715-833-6224 497 E
kmoist@cvtc.edu

MONTENEGRO-SPENCER,
Delmy .... 909-389-3355.. 60 E
dspencer@craftonhills.edu
MONTERO, Grecia .... 609-771-3132 275 J
montero@tcnj.edu
MONTERO, Joel ...... 787-720-1022 504 D
admisiones@atlanticu.edu
MONTERO, Michele, M 225-578-2306 188 K
mmorr12@lsu.edu
MONTERO-RIVERA,
Anderson .... 787-620-2040 504 B
amontero@aupr.edu
MONTEROSO,
Catherine .... 304-336-8004 489 B
cmonteroso@westliberty.edu
MONTES, Angel .... 213-356-5321.. 65 D
angel_montes@sciarc.edu
MONTES, Anibal .... 787-844-8181 511 E
anibal.montes@upr.edu
MONTES, Ineabelle .... 787-844-8181 511 E
ineabelle.montes@upr.edu
MONTES, Nathania ...... 630-942-3324 135 F
nmontes@mendocino.edu
MONTES, Porfirio ...... 787-863-2390 507 A
porfirio.montes@fajardo.inter.edu
MONTES, Rebecca ...... 707-468-3009.. 51 F
rmontes@mendocino.edu
MONTES, Sofia .... 956-665-3650 455 A
sofia.montes@utrgv.edu
MONTES, Susan, R .... 305-284-6021 112 K
smontes@miami.edu
MONTES DE OCA,
Dillon .... 678-839-5000 127 A
dmontes@westga.edu
MONTES-HELU, Mario . 520-383-0076.. 16 D
mmontes@tocc.edu
MONTESINO,
María del C .... 787-720-1022 504 D
recaudaciones@atlanticu.edu
MONTEZ, Daniel ...... 956-447-6635 443 B
dmontez@southtexascollege.edu
MONTEZ, Nicholas ...... 619-482-6306.. 65 K
nmontez@swccd.edu
MONTEZ, Zeyra .... 254-526-1302 431 E
zeyra.montez@ctcd.edu
MONTGOMERY,
Adrienne .... 513-745-3302 364 F
montgomerya10@xavier.edu
MONTGOMERY, Alan .... 772-462-7860 102 E
jmontgom@irsc.edu
MONTGOMERY,
Alisa, L .... 336-322-2213 336 D
alisa.montgomery@piedmontcc.edu
MONTGOMERY,
Angela, L .... 215-895-1516 382 D
alm525@drexel.edu
MONTGOMERY, Arlene . 757-727-5251 466 L
arlene.montgomery@hamptonu.edu
MONTGOMERY,
Beronda .... 641-269-3100 166 D
montgomb@grinnell.edu
MONTGOMERY, Cassie . 806-345-5600 428 F
c0353116@actx.edu
MONTGOMERY, Christy . 985-545-1500 188 B
MONTGOMERY, Cindy . 229-226-1621 126 B
cmontgomery@thomasu.edu
MONTGOMERY, Daron .. 603-641-7107 273 C
dmontgomery@anselm.edu
MONTGOMERY, Don .... 928-757-0821.. 14 H
dmontgomery@mohave.edu
MONTGOMERY,
Edward, B .... 269-387-2351 232 J
edward.montgomery@wmich.edu
MONTGOMERY, Erin ... 863-298-6837 106 A
emontgomery@polk.edu
MONTGOMERY, Jeff ...... 937-393-3431 360 G
jlmontgo@sscc.edu
MONTGOMERY, John .. 951-343-4963.. 27 J
jmontgomery@calbaptist.edu
MONTGOMERY, John ... 734-432-5447 226 G
jmontgomery@madonna.edu
MONTGOMERY, John .. 575-562-4002 285 E
john.montgomery@enmu.edu
MONTGOMERY,
Joseph, D .... 330-823-2295 362 E
montgojd@mountunion.edu
MONTGOMERY, Justin .. 541-962-3517 372 H
jmontgomery4@eou.edu
MONTGOMERY,
Kara, H .... 724-946-7363 401 F
montgokh@westminster.edu
MONTGOMERY, Keisha . 803-705-4601 405 G
keisha.montgomery@benedict.edu

MONTGOMERY,
Laura, M .... 630-752-5227 152 K
laura.montgomery@wheaton.edu
MONTGOMERY, Lisa .... 312-567-3777 139 H
montgomeryl@iit.edu
MONTGOMERY, Lisa ... 843-792-2691 409 D
montgoml@musc.edu
MONTGOMERY,
Maraina .... 503-943-7821 376 H
montgomm@up.edu
MONTGOMERY, Mark .. 610-526-1518 378 D
mark.montgomery@
theamericancollege.edu
MONTGOMERY, Mark .. 315-792-7100 320 F
martha.montgomery@cisco.edu
MONTGOMERY, Martha 254-442-5114 431 J
martha.montgomery@cisco.edu
MONTGOMERY, Nancy . 949-451-5273.. 65 B
nmontgomery@ivc.edu
MONTGOMERY, Robby . 575-835-5816 286 D
robby.montgomery@nmt.edu
MONTGOMERY, Robert . 248-232-4808 228 H
rjmontgo@oaklandcc.edu
MONTGOMERY, Royal .. 954-763-9840.. 95 J
library@atom.edu
MONTGOMERY,
Tamara, F .... 225-771-2200 190 J
tamara_montgomery@subr.edu
MONTGOMERY,
Tamara, F .... 225-771-2200 190 K
tamara_montgomery@subr.edu
MONTGOMERY, Tina .... 936-261-1000 445 E
tlmontgomery@pvamu.edu
MONTGOMERY,
Toni-Marie .... 847-491-7552 146 C
t-montgomery@northwestern.edu
MONTGOMERY, Tony ... 662-476-5025 245 C
tmontgomery@eastms.edu
MONTGOMERY,
Walter, C .... 336-322-2185 336 D
walter.montgomery@piedmontcc.edu
MONTGOMERY, Wayne . 202-274-6065.. 94 B
wmont@umd.edu
MONTGOMERY, Wendy 301-405-6279 202 E
wmont@umd.edu
MONTGOMERY RICE,
Valerie .... 404-752-1740 123 A
vmrice@msm.edu
MONTI, Joseph .... 407-644-1408 106 L
jmonti@rollins.edu
MONTICELLO, Anthony . 908-737-4843 277 F
amontice@kean.edu
MONTIEL, Arthuro ...... 956-488-5808 443 B
amontiel@southtexascollege.edu
MONTIEL, Mauricio .. 305-237-7563 104 E
mmontie3@mdc.edu
MONTILEAUX, Kateri .. 605-455-6142 414 H
kmontileaux@olc.edu
MONTILLA, Elaine ..... 212-817-7300 293 D
emontilla@gc.cuny.edu
MONTILLA, Hector .... 787-834-9595 508 O
h.montilla@uaa.edu
MONTILLA, Lisannie ... 240-567-5264 200 E
lisannie.montilla@montgomerycollege.
edu
MONTOYA, Carlos .... 925-473-7341.. 40 I
cmontoya@losmedanos.edu
MONTOYA, David ...... 760-744-1150.. 56 B
dmontoya@palomar.edu
MONTOYA, Denise ..... 505-426-2240 286 C
montoyad@nmhu.edu
MONTOYA, Hayley ...... 209-228-4400.. 70 A
MONTOYA, Indosa ..... 218-935-0417 244 A
indosa.montoya@wetcc.edu
MONTOYA, Jimi ...... 505-747-2139 287 C
jimi.montoya@nnmc.edu
MONTOYA, Krystle .... 505-224-4000 285 B
klucero3@cnm.edu
MONTOYA, Mitzi .... 505-277-6471 288 C
mitzimontoya@unm.edu
MONTOYA, Sharon ... 928-428-8289.. 12 H
sharon.montoya@eac.edu
MONTOYA, Valerie .... 505-346-2351 288 B
valerie.montoya@bie.edu
MONTPLAISIR, Daniel .. 909-869-4789.. 30 B
dmontplaisir@cpp.edu
MONTREAL, Steven, R . 262-243-5700 491 E
steven.montreal@cuw.edu
MONTROSE, Lee .... 910-410-1813 336 G
ljmontrose@richmondcc.edu
MONTROSS, Julia, H .. 989-774-3332 221 M
montr1jh@cmich.edu
MONTROY, Brett .... 478-445-5004 119 A
MONTS, William .... 864-231-2000 405 F
wmonts@andersonuniversity.edu

MONYPENY, Derek .... 760-366-3791.. 40 K
dmonypeny@cmccd.edu
MONZU, Mariano ...... 615-248-7795 425 D
mmonzu@trevecca.edu
MOO-YOUNG, Keith .... 518-276-2244 311 J
mooyoh2@rpi.edu
MOODY, Anissa .... 609-896-5157 280 D
amoody@rider.edu
MOODY, Bryan .... 847-578-3206 148 B
bryan.moody@rosalindfranklin.edu
MOODY, Jeff, T .... 866-294-3974 154 E
jeff.moody@ccr.edu
MOODY, Kay .... 866-294-3974 154 E
kay.moody@ccr.edu
MOODY, Kelly .... 212-678-3755 321 H
ksm2182@tc.columbia.edu
MOODY, Krystal .... 903-927-3312 457 I
kmoody@wileyc.edu
MOODY, Kyle .... 620-241-0723 172 H
kyle.moody@centralchristian.edu
MOODY, Michelle, L .... 757-594-8819 465 A
mlmoody@cnu.edu
MOON, Alan .... 903-693-1113 440 E
amoon@panola.edu
MOON, Beverly .... 662-846-4834 245 A
bmoon@deltastate.edu
MOON, Daniel .... 309-677-2380 133 H
dmoon@bradley.edu
MOON, Harry, K ...... 954-262-0510 104 M
hmoon@nova.edu
MOON, Hyon, J .... 949-480-4139.. 64 E
hmoon@soka.edu
MOON, Josh .... 920-465-2069 494 F
moonj@uwgb.edu
MOON, Lisa .... 866-492-5336 243 G
lisa.moon@mail.waldenu.edu
MOON, Lisa, T .... 804-257-5605 475 C
ltmoon@vuu.edu
MOON, Melanie ...... 607-735-1748 298 G
mmoon@elmira.edu
MOON, Pat .... 256-766-6610... 5 F
pmoon@hcu.edu
MOON, Rose .... 828-726-2269 332 E
rmoon@cccti.edu
MOON, Sandra .... 502-895-3411 183 E
smoon@lpts.edu
MOON, Sarah .... 585-785-1373 299 E
sarah.moon@flcc.edu
MOON, Shin .... 212-431-2117 308 I
shin.moon@nyls.edu
MOON, Sunny .... 323-343-2739.. 32 B
sunny.moon@calstatela.edu
MOON, Susan .... 573-288-6441 251 I
smoon@culver.edu
MOON JOHNSON,
Joshua .... 916-484-8925.. 50 J
johnso2j@arc.losrios.edu
MOONEY, Debra .... 513-745-3204 364 F
mooney@xavier.edu
MOONEY, Denise .... 617-353-9814 207 C
dmooney@bu.edu
MOONEY, Dewanna .. 706-886-6831 126 C
dmooney@tfc.edu
MOONEY, Kim .... 603-899-4128 272 G
president@franklinpierce.edu
MOONEY, Laura ..... 413-662-5411 212 F
laura.mooney@mcla.edu
MOONEY, Lisa ..... 434-395-2074 467 F
mooneylj@longwood.edu
MOONEY, Sandra .... 281-649-3256 436 D
smooney@hbu.edu
MOONEY, SiGn ...... 812-855-1432 156 C
simoon@iu.edu
MOONEY, Thelma .... 936-294-4289 449 E
mooney@shsu.edu
MOONEY BURNS,
Mary .... 816-501-4199 257 K
mary.burns@rockhurst.edu
MOONEYHAN, Allen .. 870-512-7864.. 18 C
allen_mooneyhan@asun.edu
MOONFLOWER, Nandi 206-239-4500 477 I
moored@evangel.edu
MOONO, Steady ..... 518-381-1304 319 G
moonosh@sunysccc.edu
MOONZWE, Isaac ..... 706-855-8233.. 93 H
MOORADIAN, Jody ... 401-341-2268 404 D
jody.mooradian@salve.edu
MOORADIAN, Todd ... 502-852-4812 185 E
tamoor10@louisville.edu
MOORE, Al .... 205-387-0511... 1 D
al.moore@bscc.edu
MOORE, Alan ...... 828-652-6021 335 H
MOORE, Alfred ...... 336-316-2151 329 C
moorea2@guilford.edu

MOORE, Alicia .... 541-383-7211 371 I
amoore@cocc.edu
MOORE, Amy .... 304-734-6676 487 D
amy.moore@bridgevalley.edu
MOORE, Andrew .... 303-273-3925.. 79 A
amoore@mines.edu
MOORE, Angela ...... 334-386-7299.... 5 D
almoore@faulkner.edu
MOORE, Angela .... 719-384-6857.. 82 C
angela.moore@otero.edu
MOORE, Angela .... 417-667-8181 251 E
amore@cottey.edu
MOORE, Anne, C ...... 704-687-0145 342 C
amoor168@uncc.edu
MOORE, Annette ...... 636-584-6704 252 D
annette.moore@eastcentral.edu
MOORE, Anthony ..... 909-274-4365.. 52 K
amoore@mtsac.edu
MOORE, Barbara ..... 914-251-6018 318 E
barbara.moore@purchase.edu
MOORE, Barbara, E ... 207-859-4254 194 B
barbara.moore@colby.edu
MOORE, Beata .... 913-758-3033 502 D
MOORE, Becca .... 706-419-1262 117 G
becca.moore@covenant.edu
MOORE, III, Berrien .. 405-325-3095 370 J
berrien@ou.edu
MOORE, Beth .... 513-862-3188 353 C
beth.moore@email.gscollege.edu
MOORE, Beverly, Y ... 713-486-2251 455 D
beverly.y.moore@uth.tmc.edu
MOORE, Billy .... 662-846-4200 245 A
bmoore@deltastate.edu
MOORE, Bonnie ..... 217-238-8260 141 H
bmoore71258@lakelandcollege.edu
MOORE, Brad .... 505-224-4423 285 B
bmoore28@cnm.edu
MOORE, Brad, D ...... 336-278-5492 328 H
bmoore6@elon.edu
MOORE, Brandon ..... 951-639-5426.. 53 A
bmoore@msjc.edu
MOORE, Brian .... 845-569-3275 307 B
brian.moore@msmc.edu
MOORE, Brooks .... 812-237-3890 155 H
brooks.moore@indstate.edu
MOORE, Brooks ...... 979-458-6144 446 B
rbm@tamus.edu
MOORE, Bryan .... 309-467-6377 137 G
bmoore@eureka.edu
MOORE, Caitlin ...... 352-323-3677 103 U
moorec@lssc.edu
MOORE, Candice ...... 501-279-4316.. 19 G
ckmoore@harding.edu
MOORE, Carl, S .... 443-518-1000 199 D
cmoore@howardcc.edu
MOORE, Cassandra ... 757-240-2404 469 F
cassandra.moore@rivhs.com
MOORE, Cassandra, S .. 410-777-2151 197 C
csmoore@aacc.edu
MOORE, Chad .... 785-227-3380 171 H
moorecd@bethanylb.edu
MOORE, Charles ...... 904-256-7062 102 G
cmoore@ju.edu
MOORE, Charlette .... 501-812-2299.. 23 E
cmoore@uaptc.edu
MOORE, Chipper ...... 575-527-7592 287 A
chipmoor@nmsu.edu
MOORE, Chris .... 760-744-1150.. 56 B
cmoore@palomar.edu
MOORE, Chris .... 740-351-3082 360 E
cmoore@shawnee.edu
MOORE, Christine .... 602-285-7454.. 13 H
christine.moore@phoenixcollege.edu
MOORE, Christopher, A 617-353-2704 207 C
mooreca@bu.edu
MOORE, Christy ..... 318-678-6000 187 F
cmoore@bpcc.edu
MOORE, Chuck ...... 850-201-6085 112 B
chuck.moore@tcc.fl.edu
MOORE, Dane .... 417-268-1000 249 G
moored@evangel.edu
MOORE, Danielle ..... 740-695-9500 348 D
dmoore@belmontcollege.edu
MOORE, Dannie ..... 859-622-5830 180 B
dannie.moore@eku.edu
MOORE, Danny, B .... 252-398-6448 328 A
moored@chowan.edu
MOORE, David .... 714-516-4590.. 36 C
dmoore@chapman.edu
MOORE, David .... 740-593-2958 358 L
moored3@ohio.edu
MOORE, David, P .... 256-824-6540.... 8 B
david.moore@uah.edu

MOORE, Derek 870-875-7262 21 C dmoore@southark.edu
MOORE, Derek 575-392-5004 286 E dmoore@nmjc.edu
MOORE, Derek 731-661-5212 425 F dmoore@uu.edu
MOORE, Diane 636-949-4901 254 B dmoore@lindenwood.edu
MOORE, Dinah 413-565-1000 205 I
MOORE, Dorothy 919-739-7010 338 F dpmoore@waynecc.edu
MOORE, Elizabeth 202-651-5160 92 B elizabeth.moore@gallaudet.edu
MOORE, Elizabeth 415-703-8266 69 B mooreelizabeth@uchastings.edu
MOORE, Erika 724-266-3838 399 F emoore@tsm.edu
MOORE, Erin 580-349-1588 367 F emoor17@opsu.edu
MOORE, Faye 570-586-2400 381 A fmoore@clarkssummitu.edu
MOORE, Gene 937-376-6657 349 H gmoore@centralstate.edu
MOORE, Gina 803-705-4605 405 G gina.moore@benedict.edu
MOORE, Hallie 216-791-5000 350 F hallie.moore@cim.edu
MOORE, Heidi 208-535-5339 130 I heidi.moore@cei.edu
MOORE, Honour 215-635-7300 384 D hmoore@gratz.edu
MOORE, Ida, M 520-626-6205 16 H imoore@arizona.edu
MOORE, Inez 951-222-8000 59 D
MOORE, Jackie 715-682-1811 493 G jmoore@northland.edu
MOORE, James 304-473-8042 490 E moore_j@wvwc.edu
MOORE, JR., James, H 217-333-0810 151 C jimmoore@uif.uillinois.edu
MOORE, James, L 614-688-3704 358 E moore.1408@osu.edu
MOORE, Jamillah 415-338-2032 34 A moorej@sfsu.edu
MOORE, Jan 912-688-6026 123 F jmoore@ogeecheetech.edu
MOORE, Janice, R 717-871-5156 394 B janice.moore@millersville.edu
MOORE, Jason, A 513-569-1756 350 C arrick.moore@cincinnatistate.edu
MOORE, Jeff 309-298-1931 152 I jm-moore2@wiu.edu
MOORE, Jeffrey 407-823-2573 110 D jeffrey.moore@ucf.edu
MOORE, Jennifer 479-308-6040 17 E jennifer.moore@acheedu.org
MOORE, Jennifer 662-329-8543 247 B jnmoore@muw.edu
MOORE, Jennifer 828-225-3993 328 B
MOORE, Joanne 310-338-5800 51 C joanne.moore@lmu.edu
MOORE, John 585-475-2154 312 A jfmfms@rit.edu
MOORE, John 248-689-8282 231 E jmoore1@walshcollege.edu
MOORE, John, C 858-822-4358 70 C due@ucsd.edu
MOORE, Johnny, M 870-512-7851 18 C johnny_moore@asun.edu
MOORE, Joseph 630-752-5729 152 K joseph.moore@wheaton.edu
MOORE, Joseph 315-786-2364 302 I jmoore@sunyjefferson.edu
MOORE, Joshua 740-753-6523 353 G moorej@hocking.edu
MOORE, Joy 617-552-4459 207 A joy.moore@bc.edu
MOORE, Julie 903-233-4445 438 C juliemoore@letu.edu
MOORE, Karen 816-604-1311 254 E karen.moore@mcckc.edu
MOORE, Kate, B 812-941-2189 157 D kabmoore@ius.edu
MOORE, Keith, D 801-585-1766 459 D diazmoore@utah.edu
MOORE, Keith, E 757-455-3354 476 C kmoore@vwu.edu
MOORE, Kevin 785-248-1075 176 F kevin.moore@ottawa.edu
MOORE, Kimberly 850-201-6061 112 B kim.moore@tcc.fl.edu
MOORE, Kimberly 513-529-1877 356 A moorek4@miamioh.edu
MOORE, Kirby 336-334-4822 334 F khmoore1@gtcc.edu
MOORE, Kyle 717-947-6068 392 R kmmoore2@pacollege.edu
MOORE, Kyle 307-766-4898 500 H
MOORE, Lara 541-962-3773 372 H lmoore@eou.edu
MOORE, Larry 954-486-7728 112 J financialaid@uftl.edu
MOORE, Laura 414-297-6661 498 B moorel52@matc.edu
MOORE, Laura, J 419-372-9464 348 F ljmoore@bgsu.edu
MOORE, Lauryn 315-792-3111 323 G
MOORE, LeAnn 620-241-0723 172 H leann.moore@centralchristian.edu
MOORE, Lesa 251-442-2207 8 C lmoore@umobile.edu
MOORE, Leslie 507-786-3294 242 I moore8@stolaf.edu
MOORE, Lew 501-279-4347 19 G lmoore@harding.edu
MOORE, Lew Rita 513-861-6400 361 E lewrita.moore@myunion.edu
MOORE, Lisa 904-632-3326 101 A lisa.moore@fscj.edu
MOORE, Lisa, J 904-632-3326 101 A lisa.moore@fscj.edu
MOORE, Lizzy 310-434-4307 63 B moore_lizzy@smc.edu
MOORE, Lynn 781-239-2752 214 E lmoore@massbay.edu
MOORE, Mable, J 504-520-5287 193 C mamoore@xula.edu
MOORE, Marcie 740-588-1229 364 H mmoore3@zanestate.edu
MOORE, Marian 281-487-1170 447 G mmoore@txchiro.edu
MOORE, Mark 256-551-3136 2 E mark.moore@drakestate.edu
MOORE, Marshall 502-410-6200 180 D mmoore@galencollege.edu
MOORE, Mary 410-287-1053 198 A mmoore@cecil.edu
MOORE, Mary, C 317-788-6150 161 F moore@uindy.edu
MOORE, Mary Pat 319-296-4255 166 E mary.moore@hawkeyecollege.edu
MOORE, Mary-Rita 708-456-0300 151 A maryritamoore@triton.edu
MOORE, Matthew 937-512-2960 360 F matthew.moore157@sinclair.edu
MOORE, Melinda 409-772-2180 456 B melmoore@utmb.edu
MOORE, Melissa 731-661-5408 425 F mmoore@uu.edu
MOORE, Melody 410-386-8217 197 G mmoore@carrollcc.edu
MOORE, Michael 865-573-4517 419 E mmoore@johnsonu.edu
MOORE, Michael, A 231-843-5900 232 I mamoore@westshore.edu
MOORE, Michael, K 501-686-2533 21 G mmoore@uasys.edu
MOORE, Mike 949-480-4155 64 E mmoore@soka.edu
MOORE, Mitchell, L 540-665-1298 470 A mmoore7@su.edu
MOORE, Molly 605-394-5236 415 I molly.moore@sdsmt.edu
MOORE, Monica 239-489-9378 100 G monica.moore@fsw.edu
MOORE, Nathan 706-542-9167 126 F nathan.moore25@uga.edu
MOORE, Nicki 315-228-7783 296 C nwmoore@colgate.edu
MOORE, Pamela 870-575-8545 22 F moorep@uapb.edu
MOORE, Pamela 215-641-5571 384 G moore.pamela@gmercyu.edu
MOORE, Patrice 504-671-6535 187 I pmoore@dcc.edu
MOORE, Patrick 909-621-8275 63 E pmoore@scrippscollege.edu
MOORE, Patrick 803-536-8570 410 H pmoore6@scsu.edu
MOORE, Paul 575-769-4179 285 C paul.moore@clovis.edu
MOORE, Penta 601-974-1001 246 C moorep@millsaps.edu
MOORE, Phil 860-727-6941 87 H pmoore@goodwin.edu
MOORE, Philip 215-635-7300 384 D pmoore@gratz.edu
MOORE, Quincy 936-261-5256 445 E qcmoore@pvamu.edu
MOORE, R. Bartley 202-687-0454 92 D rbm9@georgetown.edu
MOORE, Randall 617-358-0300 207 C rcmoore@bu.edu
MOORE, Randolph, G 808-956-8213 129 B bor@hawaii.edu
MOORE, Regina 870-248-4000 18 H regina.moore@blackrivertech.edu
MOORE, Renee 865-694-6604 424 C rmoore@pstcc.edu
MOORE, Rob 417-836-5262 255 J robmoore@missouristate.edu
MOORE, Robert 575-624-7001 285 F robert.moore@roswell.enmu.edu
MOORE, Robert, G 719-389-6693 78 E rmoore@coloradocollege.edu
MOORE, Robin 402-323-3497 268 D rmoore@southeast.edu
MOORE, Roger 501-882-8835 17 H rlmoore@asub.edu
MOORE, Rose Marie 405-422-1262 368 I rosemarie.moore@redlandscc.edu
MOORE, Rudell 937-708-5734 363 G rmoore@wilberforce.edu
MOORE, Russell 303-492-2890 83 M rmoore@colorado.edu
MOORE, Rustin 614-688-8749 358 E moore.66@osu.edu
MOORE, Ryan 402-481-8336 265 B ryan.moore@bryanhealthcollege.edu
MOORE, Sandra 510-215-4908 40 G smoore@contracosta.edu
MOORE, Sandra 803-535-1237 410 C mooresj@octech.edu
MOORE, Sara 212-517-3929 315 B s.moore@sothebysinstitute.com
MOORE, Sarah 541-885-1023 374 G sarah.moore@oit.edu
MOORE, Scott 559-278-0333 31 D scottm@csufresno.edu
MOORE, Shamus 580-774-3001 369 I shamus.moore@swosu.edu
MOORE, Shaun, A 248-370-4414 229 F samoore@oakland.edu
MOORE, Shelby 713-646-1884 443 C smoore@stcl.edu
MOORE, Shelly 724-480-3492 381 G shelly.moore@ccbc.edu
MOORE, Sheri 925-424-1002 36 A slmoore@laspositascollege.edu
MOORE, Stacey 803-327-8014 413 F smoore@yorktech.edu
MOORE, Stephan 410-951-3582 203 E stmoore@coppin.edu
MOORE, Steve 248-218-2430 229 I smoore4@rochesteru.edu
MOORE, Stuart 307-382-1618 500 I smoore@westernwyoming.edu
MOORE, Susan 314-367-8700 260 A susan.moore@uhsp.edu
MOORE, Susan 585-245-5502 317 E moores@geneseo.edu
MOORE, Susan 910-272-3345 337 A smoore@robeson.edu
MOORE, Tamara 213-738-6602 66 A tmoore@swlaw.edu
MOORE, Tammy 563-588-6374 164 C tammy.moore@clarke.edu
MOORE, Taniel 973-877-3435 276 G tmoore37@essex.edu
MOORE, Tanya 919-962-6229 342 B tanya_moore@unc.edu
MOORE, Teresa 515-274-4111 413 G teresa.moore@augie.edu
MOORE, Teresa 903-813-2451 429 I temoore@austincollege.edu
MOORE, Terrell 240-965-2452 197 F tmoore@captechu.edu
MOORE, Thad 410-778-7231 204 E tmoore2@washcoll.edu
MOORE, Thomas, F 304-457-6238 485 F mooretf@ab.edu
MOORE, Timothy 617-353-0750 207 C mooretj@bu.edu
MOORE, Timothy 847-214-7137 137 D tmoore@elgin.edu
MOORE, Timothy 772-462-4701 102 E timmoore@irsc.edu
MOORE, Timothy 518-255-5323 318 F mooretw@cobleskill.edu
MOORE, Tina 217-234-5346 141 H tmoore@lakelandcollege.edu
MOORE, Tom 641-422-4192 168 E tommy.moore@niacc.edu
MOORE, Tom 870-972-2985 17 I tmoore@astate.edu
MOORE, Tomeka, L 601-877-6710 244 B tmoore1@alcorn.edu
MOORE, Tony 936-261-9370 445 E tamoore@pvamu.edu
MOORE, Tony 252-940-6416 332 A tony.moore@beaufortccc.edu
MOORE, Tony 503-399-6505 372 A tony.moore@chemeketa.edu
MOORE, Tonya 770-454-9270 93 H
MOORE, Tonya 678-359-5719 120 D tmoore@gordonstate.edu
MOORE, Torrey 662-246-6331 246 E tmoore@msdelta.edu
MOORE, Towana 540-568-6434 467 C mooreth@jmu.edu
MOORE, Tracey 501-420-1240 17 D tracey.moore@arkansasbaptist.edu
MOORE, Traci 256-726-7353 6 C tmoore@oakwood.edu
MOORE, Vicki 319-895-4378 164 E vmoore@cornellcollege.edu
MOORE, Virginia 304-357-4957 486 J virginiamoore@ucwv.edu
MOORE, Warren 252-527-6223 335 E wcmoore39@lenoircc.edu
MOORE, Wes 214-333-5331 433 D wesm@dbu.edu
MOORE, William 229-500-2027 114 F william.moore@asurams.edu
MOORE, Zachery 814-865-6563 391 F zpm100@psu.edu
MOORE-BOHANNON, Anita 630-466-7900 152 H amoorebohannon@waubonsee.edu
MOORE-GARCIA, Beverly 305-237-8902 104 E bmoorega@mdc.edu
MOORE JOHNSON, Monica 662-621-4156 244 E mmjohnson@coahomacc.edu
MOORE-JONES, Yolanda, V 919-536-7201 334 A jonesym@durhamtech.edu
MOORE ROBERSON, Heather 814-332-3100 378 A
MOORE-THOMAS, Cheryl 410-617-2451 199 G cmoore4@loyola.edu
MOOREFIELD, Jennifer 864-250-6482 408 J jennifer.moorefield@gvltec.edu
MOORHEAD, Cari, A 603-862-3007 273 H cari.moorhead@unh.edu
MOORHEAD, Jill 614-222-3291 351 A jmoorhead@ccad.edu
MOORMAN, Annorah 817-257-6519 447 H a.moorman@tcu.edu
MOORMAN, Nate 706-245-7226 118 C nmoorman@ec.edu
MOORMON, Josh 818-333-3558 53 J josh.mormon@nyfa.edu
MOORTI, Sujata 802-443-5735 461 G smoorti@middlebury.edu
MOORWOOD, Woody 626-815-3855 26 K wmoorwood@apu.edu
MOOS, Michael, R 920-923-8103 492 D mrmoos83@marianuniversity.edu
MOOSALLY, Michelle 713-221-8254 452 B moosallym@uhd.edu
MOOT, Bradley 212-678-8035 303 A brmoot@jtsa.edu
MOOTHART, Kathy 319-385-6209 167 F kathy.moothart@iw.edu
MOOTISPAW, Angel 937-393-3431 360 G amootispaw@sscc.edu
MOOTS, Russ 919-365-7711 340 C russmoots@sfwbc.edu
MOOTZ, Allison, C 215-885-2360 389 A amootz@manor.edu
MOQTADERI, Emily 718-951-5074 293 A emily.moqtaderi@brooklyn.cuny.edu
MORA, Cecilio 559-934-2430 74 K ceciliomora@whccd.edu
MORA, Claudia, I 512-232-0884 454 C claudia.mora@jsg.utexas.edu
MORA, Fabiola 818-364-7644 49 G morafp@lamission.edu

MORA, Flora 808-984-3517 130 B
fmora@hawaii.edu
MORA, Michelle 818-240-1000.. 43 J
mmora@glendale.edu
MORA, Priscilla 805-965-0581.. 62 M
mora@sbcc.edu
MORA, Priscilla 805-378-4121.. 73 I
pmora@vcccd.edu
MORA, Vanessa 787-815-0000 510 D
vanessa.mora@upr.edu
MORA-ALVAREZ,
Gabriela 626-968-1328.. 47 J
MORA-HERAS, Karen 787-998-8997 508 K
kmora@eeapr.org
MORADILLOS-DELGADO,
Alicia 787-834-9595 508 O
amora@uaa.edu
MORALE, Mary 937-708-5663 363 G
mmorale@wilberforce.edu
MORALES, Adelina, C 325-942-2073 450 B
adelina.morales@angelo.edu
MORALES, Alaina 920-403-3290 494 B
alaina.morales@snc.edu
MORALES, Anna Marie 773-481-8612 135 D
amorales115@ccc.edu
MORALES, Aurea 718-963-4112 291 F
amorales@boricuacollege.edu
MORALES, Awilda 787-761-0640 510 A
oficialderegistroacademico@utcpr.edu
MORALES, Betsy 787-265-3807 511 C
decasac@uprm.edu
MORALES, Carlos 817-515-5024 445 A
carlos.morales@tccd.edu
MORALES, David 409-984-6304 449 D
moralesdp@lamarpa.edu
MORALES, David 801-274-3280 460 E
david.morales@wgu.edu
MORALES, Emily 630-844-7836 133 A
emorales@aurora.edu
MORALES, Erica 713-221-8443 452 B
moralese@uhd.edu
MORALES, Eulanie 562-475-5148.. 65 H
eulaniemorales@scuhs.edu
MORALES, Farisa 818-364-7848.. 49 G
moralef@lamission.edu
MORALES, Gaddiel 787-844-8181 511 E
gaddiel.morales@upr.edu
MORALES, Gary 787-264-1912 507 E
gary_morales_rodriguez@intersg.edu
MORALES, Gilbert 314-968-7424 261 D
moralesg@webster.edu
MORALES, Héctor, M 787-766-1717 509 C
hemorales@uagm.edu
MORALES, Ileana 787-878-5475 506 J
imorales@arecibo.inter.edu
MORALES, James 435-797-1712 459 F
james.morales@usu.edu
MORALES, Jessica 575-538-6139 288 J
jessica.morales@wnmu.edu
MORALES, Juan 719-549-2082.. 79 G
juan.morales@csupueblo.edu
MORALES, Julia 575-538-6238 288 J
julia.morales@wnmu.edu
MORALES, Karen, G 787-841-2000 508 H
karen_morales@pucpr.edu
MORALES, Karla 620-417-1011 177 C
karla.moralesesc@sccc.edu
MORALES, Kathy 954-453-9228.. 34 I
MORALES, Kristie 407-265-8383.. 96 H
MORALES, Lilliam 787-850-9376 511 B
lilliam.morales@upr.edu
MORALES, Melissa 210-784-1446 447 B
mmorales@tamusa.edu
MORALES, Nancy 787-882-2065 508 N
nmorales@unitecpr.edu
MORALES, Nora 361-354-2239 431 L
moralesn@coastlbend.edu
MORALES, Ofelia, A 303-492-8223.. 83 M
ofelia.morales@colorado.edu
MORALES, Patricia 949-824-6701.. 69 C
patricia.morales@uci.edu
MORALES, Rachel 207-780-5758 196 J
rachel.morales@maine.edu
MORALES, Ray 212-678-8000 303 A
ramorales@jtsa.edu
MORALES, Robert 805-965-0581.. 62 M
moralesr@sbcc.edu
MORALES, Rosalie 787-780-0070 504 E
rmorales@caribbean.edu
MORALES, Sigfredo 787-834-9595 508 O
smorales@uaa.edu
MORALES, Sulmarie 787-264-1912 507 E
smorales@intersg.edu
MORALES, Taina 732-906-2524 278 A
tmorales@middlesexcc.edu
MORALES, Tamara 787-765-3560 505 H
tmorales@edpuniversity.edu
MORALES, Tomas 909-537-5002.. 33 B
president_morales@csusb.edu
MORALES CRUZ, OP,
Oscar 787-786-3030 509 E
omorales@ucb.edu.pr
MORALES-DIAZ,
Enrique 413-572-8580 213 C
emoralesdiaz@westfield.ma.edu
MORALES ELIZONDO,
Jacqueline 312-939-0111 137 B
jacquelinem@eastwest.edu
MORALES-MATIAS,
Marjorie 787-890-2681 510 C
marjorie.morales1@upr.edu
MORALES-ORTIZ,
Javier 440-826-2452 348 C
jmorales@bw.edu
MORALES-RODRIGUEZ,
Sandra, M 787-857-3600 506 K
smmorales@br.inter.edu
MORALES TORRES,
Jessica, A 787-764-0000 511 F
jessica.morales1@upr.edu
MORAMARCO, Jacques 310-453-8300.. 41 K
jacques@emperors.edu
MORAN, Allen 510-883-2083.. 41 G
amoran@dspt.edu
MORAN, Anne 206-296-2810 483 B
morana@seattleu.edu
MORAN, Awilda 787-720-1022 504 D
recursos@atlanticu.edu
MORAN, Bradley 907-474-7210.. 10 B
sbmoran@alaska.edu
MORAN, Brandon 631-656-2157 299 G
brandon.moran@ftc.edu
MORAN, Chris 308-865-8191 268 J
morancl@unk.edu
MORAN, Demetria 401-456-8031 404 A
dmoran@ric.edu
MORAN, Eileen, P 940-565-3687 453 B
eileen.moran@unt.edu
MORAN, Ellen, L 412-624-7355 400 A
emoran@pitt.edu
MORAN, James 203-576-4773.. 89 A
jmoran@bridgeport.edu
MORAN, Jason, E 814-641-3419 386 E
moranj@juniata.edu
MORAN, Jessina 209-381-6410.. 52 B
MORAN, Kathy 518-464-8784 299 B
kmoran@excelsior.edu
MORAN, Laura, P 615-353-3217 424 A
laura.moran@nscc.edu
MORAN, Mark 425-869-6843 420 A
mark.moran@lmunet.edu
MORAN, III, Martin, O 301-447-5223 201 A
m.o.moran@msmary.edu
MORAN, Mike 478-289-2377 118 B
mmoran@ega.edu
MORAN, Patrick 307-766-5586 500 H
pmoran5@uwyo.edu
MORAN, Paul 570-208-5948 386 G
pjmoran@kings.edu
MORAN, Raymond 775-784-1641 270 K
rmoran@unr.edu
MORAN, Robert 718-862-7449 304 K
robert.moran@manhattan.edu
MORAN, Sheri 239-513-1122 102 C
MORAN, Troy 319-296-4457 166 E
troy.moran@hawkeyecollege.edu
MORAN, Virginia 760-245-4271.. 74 D
virginia.moran@vvc.edu
MORAN-REPINSKI,
Kelly 724-938-4000 394 C
MORANO, Kevin, A 713-500-5890 455 D
kevin.a.morano@uth.tmc.edu
MORANO, Nancy 914-633-2494 302 C
nmorano@iona.edu
MORANSKI, Karen 707-664-3222.. 34 C
MORANT, Lapari 662-476-5443 245 C
lmorant@eastms.edu
MORANT-WILSON,
Nada 803-938-3893 412 G
morantna@uscsumter.edu
MORAROS, Nikolaos 210-590-5695 457 B
morarosn@wbu.edu
MORAVEC, Todd 518-564-2072 318 C
moraveta@plattsburgh.edu
MORAVEC, Todd, A 518-564-2072 318 C
moraveta@plattsburgh.edu
MORAVITZ, Judy 909-667-4411.. 38 A
jmoravitz@claremontlincoln.edu
MORAWIEC, SCJ,
Zbigniew 414-425-8300 494 A
zmorawiec@shsst.edu
MORAY, Yvonne 212-472-1500 309 B
resumes@nysid.edu
MORBER, Timothy, T 330-471-8279 355 D
tmorber@malone.edu
MORDACI, John 585-389-2834 307 D
jmordac9@naz.edu
MORDEN, Erik 909-384-8671.. 60 F
emorden@sbccd.cc.ca.us
MOREA, John 757-822-1932 474 G
jmorea@tcc.edu
MOREAU, Bill 503-256-3180 377 A
bmoreau@uws.edu
MOREAU, Joe 650-949-6120.. 42 K
moreaujoe@fhda.edu
MOREAU, Joseph 650-949-6119.. 42 J
moreaujoe@fhda.edu
MOREAU, Scott 630-752-5933 152 K
scott.moreau@wheaton.edu
MORECI, Rick 773-325-4283 136 F
rmoreci@depaul.edu
MOREFIELD, Bill, R 423-318-2735 424 G
bill.morefield@ws.edu
MOREHEAD, David 254-710-4072 430 F
david_morehead@baylor.edu
MOREHEAD, Jere, W 706-542-1214 126 F
president@uga.edu
MOREHEAD, Krystal 704-379-6800.. 93 H
MOREHOUSE, Karissa 209-384-6199.. 52 B
MOREHOUSE, Troy 207-941-7109 194 D
morehouset@husson.edu
MOREIRA, Antonio, R 410-455-6576 202 G
moreira@umbc.edu
MOREIRA, Dyanna 401-341-2915 404 D
dyanna.moreira@salve.edu
MOREJON, Anthony 308-432-7033 267 G
amorejon@csc.edu
MORELAND, Anna 610-519-4651 401 B
anna.moreland@villanova.edu
MORELAND, Jeremy, L 800-995-3159 262 A
MORELAND, Kristen 317-921-4858 158 A
kmoreland@ivytech.edu
MORELAND, Milton, C 859-238-5220 179 H
milton.moreland@centre.edu
MORELAND, Susan 970-893-9542.. 77 G
sus.moreland@aims.edu
MORELL, Christina 434-924-8958 471 F
cm5c@virginia.edu
MORELLI, Colby 360-867-6205 479 C
morellic@evergreen.edu
MORELLI, Maria 978-232-2060 209 B
mmorelli@endicott.edu
MORELLO, Chanell 828-327-7000 332 H
cmorello@cvcc.edu
MORELLO, Joseph 650-738-4293.. 62 K
morelloj@smccd.edu
MORELOCK, Luann 309-655-7353 148 G
MORELOS, Alfredo 318-274-1010 191 G
sm107@bncollege.com
MORENA, Pat 212-650-7997 293 B
pmorena@ccny.cuny.edu
MORENCY, Maurice 212-752-1530 303 G
maurice.morency@limcollege.edu
MORENO, Camille 916-691-7541.. 50 K
morenoc@crc.losrios.edu
MORENO, Cynthia 773-838-7699 135 C
cmoreno38@ccc.edu
MORENO, Edward, J 210-486-3803 428 B
emoreno131@alamo.edu
MORENO, Judith 207-755-5265 194 J
jmoreno@cmcc.edu
MORENO, Kathy 432-837-8443 449 F
kam15ki@sulross.edu
MORENO, Laura 785-227-3380 171 H
morenoc@bethanylb.edu
MORENO, Linda 773-298-3379 148 I
moreno@sxu.edu
MORENO, Marissa 281-425-6384 438 B
mmoreno@lee.edu
MORENO, Melissa 650-738-4111.. 62 K
morenomelissa@smccd.edu
MORENO, Melissa 805-683-8292.. 62 M
melissa.moreno@sbcc.edu
MORENO, Nancy 713-798-8200 430 E
nmoreno@bcm.edu
MORENO, Patricia 281-873-0262 432 J
p.moreno@commonwealth.edu
MORENO, Valerie 503-517-3999 375 F
vmoreno@reed.edu
MORENO ORAMA,
Fernando 787-841-2000 508 H
fernando_moreno@pucpr.edu
MORENO-RIAÑO,
Gerson 616-222-1428 222 F
president@cornerstone.edu
MORENZ, Tim 217-854-5759 133 F
tim.morenz@blackburn.edu
MORERA-GONZÁLEZ,
Angel 787-993-8871 510 E
angel.morera1@upr.edu
MORESCHI, Robert, W 540-464-7212 475 C
moreschirw@vmi.edu
MORESCHI, Tracy, L 503-255-0332 374 A
tmoreschi@multnomah.edu
MOREST, Vanessa 914-606-6712 324 F
vanessa.morest@sunywcc.edu
MORETON, April, L 651-286-7773 243 E
almoreton@unwsp.edu
MORETZ, Patsy 334-387-3877.... 4 C
patsymoretz@amridgeuniversity.edu
MOREY, Ann, N 818-677-3266.. 32 E
ann.morey@csun.edu
MOREY, Casey 207-509-7298 196 B
cmorey@unity.edu
MOREY, Debby 404-727-4583 118 D
dmorey@emory.edu
MOREY, Joshua 951-343-4235.. 27 J
jmorey@calbaptist.edu
MOREY, Megan 413-597-4217 220 A
mmorey@williams.edu
MOREY, Robin 404-727-8561 118 D
robin.morey@emory.edu
MORGAN, Adrienne 585-275-7814 323 E
morgan.levy@rochester.edu
MORGAN, Adrienne 585-275-2121 323 E
MORGAN, Amanda 864-388-8971 409 B
amorgan@lander.edu
MORGAN, Andrew 903-434-8166 440 A
amorgan@ntc.edu
MORGAN, Annie 866-492-5336 243 G
ann.morgan@mail.waldenu.edu
MORGAN, Anthony, M 570-577-3333 379 A
amm051@bucknell.edu
MORGAN, Barb 910-630-7005 331 B
bamorgan@methodist.edu
MORGAN, Betsy 608-785-8042 495 A
bmorgan@uwlax.edu
MORGAN, Brandee 405-945-3315 368 C
brandee.morgan@okstate.edu
MORGAN, Brian 304-696-2424 488 N
brian.morgan@marshall.edu
MORGAN, Bruce 910-630-7005 331 B
bmorgan@methodist.edu
MORGAN, Bruce, A 423-775-7233 417 D
bruce.morgan@bryan.edu
MORGAN, Camella 253-833-9111 480 A
cmorgan@greenriver.edu
MORGAN, Carlene, J 919-516-4084 339 G
cjmorgan@st-aug.edu
MORGAN, Cassie 912-478-5421 120 A
cnmorgan@georgiasouthern.edu
MORGAN, Catherine, A 423-439-4300 418 D
morganca1@etsu.edu
MORGAN, Cathy 916-577-2200.. 76 C
cmorgan@jessup.edu
MORGAN, Chris 951-343-4369.. 27 J
cmorgan@calbaptist.edu
MORGAN, Chris 717-361-1407 383 B
morganc@etown.edu
MORGAN, David 765-361-6382 162 G
morgand@wabash.edu
MORGAN, David, A 423-775-7597 417 D
morganda@bryan.edu
MORGAN, Derek 303-273-3288.. 79 A
dmorgan@mines.edu
MORGAN, Derrick 972-780-3600 453 C
derrick.morgan@untdallas.edu
MORGAN, Dorothy 706-368-7707 119 C
dmorgan@highlands.edu
MORGAN, Elizabeth 909-621-8101.. 37 G
elizabeth.morgan@cmc.edu
MORGAN, Elizabeth 413-748-3301 218 E
emorgan2@springfield.edu
MORGAN, Eric 931-221-6163 416 H
morgane@apsu.edu
MORGAN, Gilbert 443-885-3658 200 F
gilbert.morgan@morgan.edu
MORGAN, Ginny 510-841-9230.. 76 F
vmorgan@wi.edu
MORGAN, Gus 423-461-8968 421 E
gmorgan@milligan.edu
MORGAN, Hal, D 602-557-1270.. 16 L
hal.morgan@phoenix.edu

MORRIS, Kathryn, A ..... 315-229-5892 313 F
kmorris@stlawu.edu
MORRIS, Keith .... 610-861-6362 391 B
kmorris@northampton.edu
MORRIS, Kelli .... 256-326-2602.... 1 F
kelli.morris@calhoun.edu
MORRIS, Kellie .... 207-755-5294 194 J
kmorris@cmcc.edu
MORRIS, Kevin .... 281-922-3479 442 E
kevin.morris@sjcd.edu
MORRIS, Kevin .... 936-294-1794 449 E
kmorris@shsu.edu
MORRIS, Kizzy .... 610-399-2279 393 D
kmorris@cheyney.edu
MORRIS, Kyle .... 307-742-3776 500 K
kmorris@wyotech.edu
MORRIS, Larry .... 405-491-6314 369 G
MORRIS, Laura, M .... 302-295-1179.. 91 C
laura.m.morris@wilmu.edu
MORRIS, Lauren, B .... 312-996-7000 151 D
MORRIS, Lawrence, J ... 202-319-5100.. 91 G
morrisl@cua.edu
MORRIS, Loren, L .... 620-665-3523 174 D
morrisl@hutchcc.edu
MORRIS, Matthew .... 417-836-5233 255 J
mattmorris@missuristate.edu
MORRIS, Michael .... 805-437-8881.. 30 D
michael.morris@csuci.edu
MORRIS, Miranda .... 605-256-5112 415 G
miranda.morris@dsu.edu
MORRIS, Nora .... 763-433-1632 236 H
nora.morris@anokaramsey.edu
MORRIS, Nora .... 763-433-1632 237 A
nora.morris@anokaramsey.edu
MORRIS, Paul .... 435-652-7504 459 G
paul.morris@utahtech.edu
MORRIS, Regina .... 573-840-9606 259 I
rmorris@trcc.edu
MORRIS, Renea .... 303-871-2711.. 84 C
renea.morris@du.edu
MORRIS, Robert .... 815-280-2884 140 I
romorris@jjc.edu
MORRIS, Sara, R .... 716-888-2120 291 M
morriss@canisius.edu
MORRIS, Sheila .... 405-382-9501 369 E
s.morris@sscok.edu
MORRIS, Stephanie .... 716-286-8539 309 F
smorris@niagara.edu
MORRIS, Steve .... 270-789-5017 179 G
srmorris@campbellsville.edu
MORRIS, Steve .... 606-546-1201 185 B
smorris@unionky.edu
MORRIS, Tama .... 704-337-2363 339 D
morrist@queens.edu
MORRIS, Thomas .... 256-824-6316.... 8 B
tommy.morris@uah.edu
MORRIS, Thomas .... 304-896-7407 487 I
tom.morris@southernwv.edu
MORRIS, Tracy .... 304-293-2021 489 E
tracy.morris@mail.wvu.edu
MORRIS, Trevor .... 806-291-3636 457 B
morrist@wbu.edu
MORRIS, Vicky .... 252-399-6330 326 H
vamorris@barton.edu
MORRIS, Vicky, A .... 252-399-6330 326 H
vamorris@barton.edu
MORRIS, Wendy .... 410-857-2247 200 D
wmorris@mcdaniel.edu
MORRIS-SHEPARD,
Fenita, T .... 919-530-6105 341 D
fmorris7@nccu.edu
MORRIS-WOOD, Alex ... 352-638-9777.. 96 B
amorriswood@beaconcollge.edu
MORRISETT, J. Gregory 212-255-8587 297 D
techdean@cornell.edu
MORRISETTE, Joanna .... 919-739-6725 338 F
jmmorrisette@waynecc.edu
MORRISON, Aaron .... 978-927-0585 209 B
MORRISON, Alison .... 202-379-7808.. 93 H
MORRISON, Amy .... 425-739-8200 480 D
amy.morrison@lwtech.edu
MORRISON, Andrew .... 740-588-1388 364 H
amorrison@zanestate.edu
MORRISON, Angel .... 785-460-5484 172 L
MORRISON, Cammie ..... 856-225-2949 281 A
cammor@camden.rutgers.edu
MORRISON, Chris .... 937-229-1000 362 C
MORRISON, Dan .... 848-932-4371 281 B
dan.morrison@rutgers.edu
MORRISON, Darrell .... 816-271-4226 256 C
morrison@missouriwestern.edu
MORRISON, Debbie .... 231-439-6306 228 D
d.morrison@follett.com

MORRISON, Edwina ...... 406-449-9150 263 C
emorrison@montana.edu
MORRISON,
Hassel Andre .... 507-786-3503 242 I
morrison@stolaf.edu
MORRISON, Heather ..... 802-468-1212 462 H
heather.morrison@castleton.edu
MORRISON, Ian .... 504-865-5210 191 D
imorrison@tulane.edu
MORRISON, Jacob .... 509-359-6564 478 H
jmorrison10@ewu.edu
MORRISON, Jason .... 870-574-4501.. 21 F
jmorriso@sautech.edu
MORRISON, Jean .... 617-353-2230 207 C
morrison@bu.edu
MORRISON, Jennifer ..... 870-307-7425.. 20 D
jennifer.morrison@lyon.edu
MORRISON, Jennifer .... 503-244-0726 371 E
jennifermorrison@achs.edu
MORRISON, Jennifer, K 508-767-7007 205 F
jemorrison@assumption.edu
MORRISON, Jessica ..... 559-730-3755.. 39 C
jessicamo@cos.edu
MORRISON, Julia .... 707-476-4172.. 58 I
julia-morrison@redwoods.edu
MORRISON, Julie .... 623-845-4761.. 13 E
julie.morrison@gccaz.edu
MORRISON, Julie .... 734-973-5010 232 A
jmorriso@wccnet.edu
MORRISON, Laura .... 252-335-0821 333 E
laura_morrison@albemarle.edu
MORRISON, Lisa .... 712-325-3287 167 G
lmorrison@iwcc.edu
MORRISON, Marjorie ..... 216-987-4529 351 D
marjorie.morrison@tri-c.edu
MORRISON, Melanie ..... 650-433-3895.. 55 K
mmorrison@paloaltou.edu
MORRISON, Michael ..... 980-495-3978 329 A
MORRISON, Michael, L 812-888-5736 162 E
mmorrison@vinu.edu
MORRISON, Monica ..... 225-743-8500 188 F
mmorrison@rpcc.edu
MORRISON, Nancy, J .... 212-998-4924 309 D
nancy.morrison@nyu.edu
MORRISON,
Rebecca, L .... 414-955-4949 492 F
rmorriso@mcw.edu
MORRISON, Rod .... 419-448-2391 353 D
rmorriso@heidelberg.edu
MORRISON, Roderick ... 253-566-5178 483 F
rmorrison@tacomacc.edu
MORRISON, Rodney ..... 302-831-0746.. 91 A
rodmo@udel.edu
MORRISON, Roxanne ... 619-260-7579.. 72 H
roxannemorrison@sandiego.edu
MORRISON, Sarah .... 740-366-9209 349 D
morrison.415@cotc.edu
MORRISON, Sarah, B ... 276-656-0322 473 H
sbmorrison@patrickhenry.edu
MORRISON, Scott .... 775-445-4401 271 A
scott.morrison@wnc.edu
MORRISON, Thomas, A 812-855-6992 156 C
morrisot@iu.edu
MORRISON, Thomas, A 812-855-6992 156 B
morrisot@iu.edu
MORRISON, Tiffany ...... 312-850-7070 135 E
tmorrison2@ccc.edu
MORRISON, Valerie, A . 904-620-2900 111 A
n00140121@unf.edu
MORRISON, William ..... 508-588-9100 214 F
wmorrison@massasoit.mass.edu
MORRISON-FRONCKOWIAK,
Lisa, T .... 716-878-6210 317 C
morrislt@buffalostate.edu
MORRISON-MONGER,
Heather .... 865-524-8079 419 A
heather.monger@huhs.edu
MORRISON-SHETLAR,
Alison .... 434-544-8200 470 K
president@lynchburg.edu
MORRISON-WILLAIMS,
Suzanne .... 954-492-5353.. 97 G
smw@citycollege.edu
MORRISS, Andrew, P .... 216-272-9187 446 B
amorriss@tamu.edu
MORRISSEY, Ann, M ..... 401-874-4402 404 E
morrissey@uri.edu
MORRISSEY, Dale, S .... 770-720-5506 124 E
dsm1@reinhardt.edu
MORRISSEY, James ...... 313-577-2001 232 H
hb2698@wayne.edu
MORRISSEY, Kelly, A .... 401-333-7173 403 D
kamorrissey@ccri.edu

MORRISSEY, Sharon ..... 804-819-4972 472 E
smorrissey@vccs.edu
MORRISSEY, Shawn ...... 508-856-2265 212 A
shawn.morrissey@umassmed.edu
MORRO, Robert .... 610-519-4589 401 B
robert.morro@villanova.edu
MORROBEL-SOSA,
Anny .... 608-262-8839 494 C
amorrobel@uwsa.edu
MORRONE, Anastasia ... 812-856-8010 156 C
amorrone@iu.edu
MORRONE,
Anastasia (Stacy) .... 812-856-8010 156 B
amorrone@iu.edu
MORRONE, Anthony ..... 702-992-2156 270 H
finaid@nsc.edu
MORROW, Andrea .... 567-661-7104 359 H
andrea_morrow@owens.edu
MORROW, Barbara, A ... 314-340-5763 253 E
morrowb@hssu.edu
MORROW, Bill, J .... 302-857-1245.. 90 H
bmorrow@dtcc.edu
MORROW, David .... 267-295-2357 401 C
dmorrow@walnuthillcollege.edu
MORROW, Donnie .... 828-835-4287 338 C
dmorrow@tricountycc.edu
MORROW, Eric .... 254-968-9141 445 F
morrow@tarleton.edu
MORROW, Erik .... 512-472-4133 442 H
emorrow@ssw.edu
MORROW, Frances .... 330-490-7312 363 E
fmorrow@walsh.edu
MORROW, Jeff .... 509-574-4691 485 E
jmorrow@yvcc.edu
MORROW, Marjann .... 325-574-7608 457 G
mmorrow@wtc.edu
MORROW, Michael .... 651-523-1660 236 A
mmorrow001@luthersem.edu
MORROW, Nick .... 904-620-1537 111 A
nick.morrow@unf.edu
MORROW, Rebecca ...... 304-793-6591 489 C
rmorrow@osteo.wvsom.edu
MORROW, Wanda .... 713-646-1825 443 C
wmorrow@stcl.edu
MORSCHES, Michael ..... 708-974-5310 144 G
morschesm@morainevalley.edu
MORSE, Alicia .... 410-777-2587 197 C
ammorse@aacc.edu
MORSE, Andrew .... 319-273-2570 163 G
andrew.morse@uni.edu
MORSE, Cary .... 508-853-2300 215 D
csmorse@qcc.mass.edu
MORSE, Charles, C .... 508-831-5540 220 C
cmorse@wpi.edu
MORSE, Julie .... 517-750-1200 230 F
MORSE, MaryKate .... 503-554-6150 372 I
mkmorse@georgefox.edu
MORSE, Micael .... 903-589-7114 437 D
mmorse@jacksonville-college.edu
MORSE, Saul .... 518-608-8472 299 B
smorse@excelsior.edu
MORSE, Susan .... 740-427-5926 354 I
morses@kenyon.edu
MORSE, Terry .... 410-706-2456 202 F
tmorse@umaryland.edu
MORSE, Victoria .... 507-222-5367 234 C
vmorse@carleton.edu
MORSMAN, Elaine .... 607-587-4061 319 C
morsmaem@alfredstate.edu
MORTALI, Jill, M .... 603-646-3007 272 F
jill.m.mortali@dartmouth.edu
MORTAZAVI, Mansour .. 870-575-7140.. 22 F
mortazavim@uapb.edu
MORTELA, Cecilia .... 805-267-1690.. 48 A
cecilia.mortela@lauruscollege.edu
MORTENSEN, Alan .... 217-234-5253 141 H
amortens@lakelandcollege.edu
MORTENSEN, Brad, L ... 801-626-6001 460 B
bmortensen@weber.edu
MORTENSEN, John .... 435-797-1110 459 F
john.mortensen@usu.edu
MORTENSEN, Norm .... 304-734-6680 487 D
norm.mortensen@bridgevalley.edu
MORTENSEN, Stacey ..... 701-627-4738 346 D
smorte@nhsc.edu
MORTENSON, Gary .... 254-710-1161 430 F
gary_mortenson@baylor.edu
MORTENSON, Lindsey .. 734-764-8320 231 A
lmortens@umich.edu
MORTENSON, Shuree .... 605-773-3455 415 D
shuree.mortenson@sdbor.edu
MORTIMER, Gayle .... 620-862-5252 171 E
gayle.mortimer@barclaycollege.edu

MORTIMER, Ian .... 585-475-6637 312 A
ijmoem@rit.edu
MORTIMER, Jarron .... 919-516-4000 339 G
MORTLEY, Preston .... 323-241-5059.. 49 I
mortlepc@lasc.edu
MORTON, Ben .... 907-786-1214.. 10 A
bmorton4@alaska.edu
MORTON, Bradley .... 973-684-6626 279 B
bmorton@pccc.edu
MORTON, Brandon .... 303-722-5724.. 81 K
bmorton@lincolntech.edu
MORTON, Brandon .... 972-273-3392 433 G
bmorton@dcccd.edu
MORTON, Cassandra .... 909-748-8391.. 72 E
cassandra_morton@redlands.edu
MORTON, Christina ...... 412-392-4207 395 H
cmorton@pointpark.edu
MORTON, Doug .... 919-515-8851 341 E
dgmorton@ncsu.edu
MORTON, Jack .... 512-936-8202 453 B
jack.morton@untsystem.edu
MORTON, James, P .... 910-362-7555 332 F
jpmorton634@mail.cfcc.edu
MORTON, Jen .... 207-221-4361 197 A
jmorton@une.edu
MORTON, Jordan .... 661-362-2234.. 51 E
jmorton@masters.edu
MORTON, Josh .... 605-274-4316 413 G
josh.morton@augie.edu
MORTON, Lindsay .... 707-965-6613.. 55 H
lmorton@puc.edu
MORTON, Matt .... 949-376-6000.. 47 G
mmorton@lcad.edu
MORTON, Pierre .... 603-899-4000 272 G
MORTON, Pierre .... 603-899-4045 272 G
mortonp@franklinpierce.edu
MORTON, Sally, C .... 480-965-4087.. 11 A
scmorton@asu.edu
MORTON, Skylor .... 610-519-4154 401 B
skylor.morton@villanova.edu
MORTON, Tracy, L .... 757-446-5800 465 H
mortontl@evms.edu
MORTON, Vincent .... 512-245-2124 449 G
vm05@txstate.edu
MORTSON, Stephanie ... 216-421-7320 350 E
smmortson@cia.edu
MORVANT, Mark, C .... 405-325-6553 370 J
mmorvant@ou.edu
MORVICE, Michael .... 714-432-5741.. 38 F
mmorvice@occ.cccd.edu
MORY, Scott, M .... 412-268-2136 380 B
mory@cmu.edu
MOSBO BALLESTRO,
Julie .... 979-862-1239 446 B
jmosbo@tamu.edu
MOSBURG, Calleb, N .... 580-327-8415 367 A
cnmosburg@nwosu.edu
MOSBY, Christel .... 602-639-7500.. 12 L
MOSBY, Gary .... 913-288-7305 174 H
gmosby@kckcc.edu
MOSBY, John .... 206-878-3710 480 C
jmosby@highline.edu
MOSBY, Karen .... 847-866-3900 138 B
MOSBY, Todd .... 812-749-1300 159 E
tmosby@oak.edu
MOSBY-WILSON,
Shatiqua, A .... 504-286-5030 191 A
swilson@suno.edu
MOSCA, Caroline .... 518-471-3079 314 C
MOSCA, David .... 443-367-0035 202 D
dmosca@usmd.edu
MOSCATELLO, Anjanie .. 336-334-5494 342 D
agbledso@uncg.edu
MOSCATO, Robin, A ..... 609-258-3330 279 E
moscato@princeton.edu
MOSCHELLA, Jayne .... 972-438-6932 440 G
jmoschella@parker.edu
MOSCHENROSS, Sarah . 641-269-3702 166 D
moschenr@grinnell.edu
MOSCHINA, Justin .... 949-214-3613.. 40 E
justin.mochina@cui.edu
MOSCOVITZ, Yechezkel . 718-269-4080 292 C
MOSELEY, John .... 573-681-5042 254 A
moseleyj@lincolnu.edu
MOSEMAN, Dennis .... 774-243-3489 216 B
dennis.moseman@mcphs.edu
MOSER, Brett .... 701-252-3467 346 J
brett.moser@uj.edu
MOSER, Drew .... 765-998-5384 161 A
drmoser@taylor.edu
MOSER, Gary .... 707-654-1224.. 32 C
gmoser@csum.edu

MUCH, Kari .... 507-389-1455 238 L
karen.much@mnsu.edu
MUCHANE, Mary, W ..... 704-894-2644 328 C
mamuchane@davidson.edu
MUCHANE, Mur .... 336-758-4016 344 A
mmuchane@wfu.edu
MUCHIRI, Rosalind .... 301-860-4335 203 D
rmuchiri@bowiestate.edu
MUCKERHEIDE, Erin ..... 320-363-5011 234 I
MUDD, Michael, A .... 508-929-8746 213 D
mmudd@worcester.edu
MUDD, Summer .... 702-895-5381 270 J
summer.mudd@unlv.edu
MUDGE, Suzanne .... 210-784-2500 447 B
smudge@tamusa.edu
MUECK, Robert .... 410-626-6931 201 E
robert.mueck@sjc.edu
MUEGGE, Dave .... 417-836-4040 255 J
davemuegge@missouristate.edu
MUELLENBACH, Joanne 559-325-3600.. 28 F
jmuellenbach@chsu.edu
MUELLER, II, Alfred, G . 610-558-5508 390 G
muellera@neumann.edu
MUELLER, Brian .... 602-639-7500.. 12 L
MUELLER, Carl, D .... 414-410-4376 490 J
cd2mueller@stritch.edu
MUELLER, Don .... 562-860-2451.. 35 O
dmueller@cerritos.edu
MUELLER, Edward, A .... 603-862-3272 273 H
edward.mueller@unh.edu
MUELLER, Erin, R .... 773-298-3319 148 I
emueller@sxu.edu
MUELLER, Janis .... 810-762-9500 225 F
jmueller1@kettering.edu
MUELLER, Jennifer .... 320-308-3023 240 C
jjmueller@stcloudstate.edu
MUELLER, Jeremy .... 618-985-2828 140 G
jeremymueller@jalc.edu
MUELLER, Joanna .... 605-668-1514 414 F
joanna.mueller@mountmarty.edu
MUELLER, Joe, B .... 307-675-0501 500 F
jbmueller@sheridan.edu
MUELLER, SJ, Joseph ... 510-549-5040.. 63 A
jmueller@scu.edu
MUELLER, Kate .... 714-241-6160.. 38 D
kmueller@coastline.edu
MUELLER, Lloyd .... 503-338-2412 372 C
lmueller@clatsopcc.edu
MUELLER, Michael .... 956-665-2121 455 A
michael.mueller@utrgv.edu
MUELLER, Michelle .... 734-477-8976 232 A
mimueller@wccnet.edu
MUELLER, OSU, Pam ... 270-686-4319 179 F
pam.mueller@brescia.edu
MUELLER, Shelia .... 412-536-1180 386 H
sheila.mueller@laroche.edu
MUELLER, Stacy .... 513-244-4524 356 F
stacy.mueller@msj.edu
MUELLER, Steven, P ..... 949-214-3386.. 40 E
steve.mueller@cui.edu
MUELLER, Teri .... 405-425-5104 367 C
teri.mueller@oc.edu
MUELLER, Tony .... 909-748-8288.. 72 E
tony_mueller@redlands.edu
MUELLER, Valerie .... 252-335-0821 333 E
valerie_mueller50@albemarle.edu
MUENCH, Kim .... 414-382-6091 490 G
kim.muench@alverno.edu
MUENKS, Kathy .... 573-681-5050 254 A
muenksk@lincolnu.edu
MUFFICK, Ron .... 406-496-4316 264 C
rmuffick@mtech.edu
MUGG, Heather .... 404-727-9326 118 D
hmugg@emory.edu
MUGGEO, Louis .... 845-398-4174 314 D
lmuggeo@stac.edu
MUGGLI, Darrin .... 913-360-7961 171 G
dmuggli@benedictine.edu
MUGRIDGE, Rebecca ..... 518-442-3568 315 D
rmugridge@albany.edu
MUHA, Beth .... 202-885-2451.. 91 D
bmuha@american.edu
MUHA, David .... 609-771-2132 275 J
muhad@tcnj.edu
MUHA, Mark .... 616-977-5300 222 F
mark.muha@cornerstone.edu
MUHA, Mark .... 847-317-4061 150 J
mmuha@tiu.edu
MUHA, Priscilla .... 707-654-1275.. 32 C
pmuha@csum.edu
MUHAMMAD,
Darrick, D .... 313-496-2650 232 B
dmuhamm1@wcccd.edu
MUHAMMAD, Randal .... 773-281-4700 132 G
MUHAMMAD, Toni .... 803-376-5780 405 D
tmuhammad@allenuniversity.edu
MUHL, Erica .... 617-266-1400 206 D
MUHLEMAN, Aimee .... 309-796-5505 133 D
muhlemana@bhc.edu
MUHLFELDER, Leslie, F 610-330-5060 387 B
muhlfell@lafayette.edu
MUHSIN, Karen .... 504-671-6138 187 I
kmuhsi@dcc.edu
MUHVIC, Marie .... 203-365-4824.. 88 H
muhvicm@sacredheart.edu
MUHVIC, Marie .... 417-873-7879 252 A
MUI, Eva Marie, L .... 671-735-8889 503 C
evamarie.mui@guamcc.edu
MUIR, Bernard .... 650-723-2300.. 66 D
MUIR, Eleanor .... 717-796-1800 389 F
emuir@messiah.edu
MUIR, Janette .... 703-993-8891 466 J
jmuir@gmu.edu
MUIR, Nick .... 402-375-7107 267 I
nimuir1@wsc.edu
MUIR, Thorton .... 770-426-2624 122 A
tmuir@life.edu
MUJICA, Andrea, J .... 641-422-4438 168 E
andrea.mujica@niacc.edu
MUJUMDAR, Sudesh .... 812-465-1681 162 B
smujumda@usi.edu
MUJUMDAR, Sudesh .... 912-358-4190 124 H
mujumdar@savannahstate.edu
MUKHERJEE,
Avinandan .... 304-696-3716 488 N
mukherjeea@marshall.edu
MUKHERJEE, Mohini .... 848-932-7015 281 B
mohinim@global.rutgers.edu
MUKOOZA,
Margaret, N .... 803-934-3439 409 H
mmukooza@morris.edu
MULADORE, James, G .. 989-964-4190 229 L
jgm@svsu.edu
MULARKEY, Terry, J ..... 954-262-7555 104 M
tmularkey@nova.edu
MULAT, Fitsum .... 562-903-4752.. 27 E
fitsum.mulat@biola.edu
MULCAIRE, Carrie .... 831-479-3566.. 27 G
camulcai@cabrillo.edu
MULDER, Lori .... 616-395-7817 224 H
mulderl@hope.edu
MULDER, Mark, R .... 253-535-7251 481 C
muldermr@plu.edu
MULDOON, Kevin .... 215-572-4076 378 E
muldoonk@arcadia.edu
MULDOWNEY, Jennifer . 617-243-2000 210 G
jmuldowney@lasell.edu
MULET, Mariel .... 323-343-3040.. 32 B
mmulet@calstatela.edu
MULFORD, Joe .... 320-629-5140 239 G
joe.mulford@pine.edu
MULFORD, Shannon, L 417-268-6037 250 A
smulford@gobbc.edu
MULGRAV, Shalonda ..... 912-358-3059 124 H
mulgravs@savannahstate.edu
MULHALL, Lawrence, P 864-833-8300 410 E
lmulhall@presby.edu
MULHERIN, April, C ...... 207-778-7081 196 F
april.mulherin@maine.edu
MULHERN, John .... 480-461-7627.. 13 F
john.mulhern@mesacc.edu
MULHERN, Maureen ...... 845-398-4067 314 D
mmulhern@stac.edu
MULHERN,
Michelle, M .... 330-325-6259 357 D
mmulhern@neomed.edu
MULHOLLAND,
Angela, B .... 843-953-5502 407 D
mulhollandab@cofc.edu
MULHOLLAND, Anne ..... 308-632-6933 268 F
amulholland@summitcc.edu
MULHOLLAND,
Colleen, S .... 319-273-2717 163 G
colleen.mulholland@uni.edu
MULIK, Jim .... 425-640-1610 479 A
james.mulik@edcc.edu
MULKA, Christine .... 616-988-3626 226 A
cmulka@kuyper.edu
MULL, Diane .... 803-754-4100 407 F
MULL, D'Andra .... 352-392-1265 110 E
dmull@ufsa.ufl.edu
MULL, Stephen, D .... 434-924-8612 471 F
sdm9rg@virginia.edu
MULLAHY, Michael .... 617-725-4140 218 G
mmullahy@suffolk.edu
MULLALLY, Sandra .... 734-487-1116 223 F
smullall@emich.edu
MULLALY, Victoria .... 312-752-2080 145 C
vmullaly@nl.edu
MULLANEY, Carol .... 574-631-1293 161 G
cmullaney@nd.edu
MULLANEY, Tom .... 651-285-4219 236 A
tmullaney001@luthersem.edu
MULLANEY, William, P . 607-962-9232 319 F
president@corning-cc.edu
MULLEN, Avery .... 718-368-5136 294 C
avery.mullen@kbcc.cuny.edu
MULLEN, Bill .... 706-233-7336 125 A
bmullen@shorter.edu
MULLEN, Eric .... 616-234-3673 224 C
emullen@grcc.edu
MULLEN, Greg .... 864-656-2222 406 F
gmullen@clemson.edu
MULLEN, Jacqueline ...... 662-325-2513 247 A
jmullen@saffairs.msstate.edu
MULLEN, Jason .... 410-827-5930 198 B
jmullen@chesapeake.edu
MULLEN, Jeff .... 501-977-2125.. 23 D
mullen@uaccm.edu
MULLEN, John .... 785-227-3380 171 H
mullenj@bethanylb.edu
MULLEN, Kate .... 518-327-6480 310 G
kmullen@paulsmiths.edu
MULLEN, Ken .... 209-946-2345.. 71 E
kmullen@pacific.edu
MULLEN, Laurie .... 410-704-2084 204 B
lmullen@towson.edu
MULLEN, Megan .... 585-224-3222 320 B
megan.mullen@esc.edu
MULLEN, Michael .... 610-361-5222 390 G
mullenm@neumann.edu
MULLEN, Michael, C .... 260-422-5561 156 A
mcmullen@indianatech.edu
MULLEN, Steven .... 716-851-1294 299 A
mullens@ecc.edu
MULLENIX,
Elizabeth, R .... 513-529-6721 356 A
provost@miamioh.edu
MULLENS, Deborah, K .. 304-473-8181 490 E
mullens_d@wvwc.edu
MULLENS, Mary .... 781-280-3200 214 G
MULLENS, Michelle ...... 405-789-6400 369 G
mmullens@snu.edu
MULLENS, Rob, A .... 541-346-5455 376 G
athleticdirector@uoregon.edu
MULLER, Brook .... 704-687-0090 342 C
brookmuller@uncc.edu
MULLER, Dalia, A .... 716-645-3020 315 F
daliamul@buffalo.edu
MULLER, David .... 212-241-8716 302 B
MULLER, Eugene .... 212-752-1530 303 G
eugene.muller@limcollege.edu
MULLER, Jacquelyn, P . 724-458-3302 384 F
jpmuller@gcc.edu
MULLER, Joseph .... 860-253-3055.. 86 B
jmuller@asnuntuck.edu
MULLER, Kathy, A .... 712-362-0433 166 H
kmuller@iowalakes.edu
MULLER, Kim .... 806-651-2345 447 D
kmuller@wtamu.edu
MULLER, Kimberly .... 906-635-2170 226 C
kmuller@lssu.edu
MULLER, Marcus .... 320-589-6011 243 C
mull0262@morris.umn.edu
MULLER, Nicole .... 518-783-2342 314 K
nmuller@siena.edu
MULLER, Stephen .... 434-582-3459 467 E
swmuller@liberty.edu
MULLER, Susan .... 815-836-5245 142 C
smuller1@lewisu.edu
MULLER, Tammy .... 828-327-7000 332 H
tmuller@cvcc.edu
MULLER, Wade .... 541-278-5971 371 G
wmuller@bluecc.edu
MULLER-BORER,
Barbara .... 252-744-2546 340 H
mullerborerb@ecu.edu
MULLIGAN, Barbara ...... 845-569-3112 307 B
barbara.mulligan@msmc.edu
MULLIGAN, Jason .... 815-394-5061 147 J
jmulligan@rockford.edu
MULLIGAN, Leah .... 936-294-1047 449 E
lrw001@shsu.edu
MULLIGAN, Maura .... 617-989-4232 219 D
mulliganm@wit.edu
MULLIGAN, Rob .... 916-608-6736.. 51 A
mulligr@flc.losrios.edu
MULLIGAN, Tricia .... 914-633-2601 302 C
tmullligan@iona.edu
MULLIGAN-NGUYEN,
Erin .... 361-825-5785 446 E
erin.mulligan-nguyen@tamucc.edu
MULLIKEN, Ken, R .... 920-923-7604 492 D
mulliken@marianuniversity.edu
MULLIKIN, Demeri, C ... 563-588-7407 167 I
demeri.mullikin@loras.edu
MULLIKIN, Heath .... 864-644-5015 411 D
hmullikin@swu.edu
MULLIKIN, Jadeline, A . 671-735-5527 503 C
jadeline.mullikin@guamcc.edu
MULLIN, Allyson .... 610-796-8317 378 C
allyson.mullin@alvernia.edu
MULLIN, Beth .... 334-291-4964.... 1 H
beth.mullin@cv.edu
MULLIN, Chris .... 978-934-4232 211 G
christopher_mullin@uml.edu
MULLIN, James .... 320-363-2882 242 G
sjpresident@csbsju.edu
MULLIN, Joseph .... 630-942-4278 135 F
mullin@cod.edu
MULLIN, Mark, E .... 573-341-4175 260 F
memullin@mst.edu
MULLIN-SAWICKI,
Gretchen .... 727-341-3002 107 C
mullins.gretchen@spcollege.edu
MULLINAX, Kenneth ..... 334-229-4104.... 4 B
kmullinax@alasu.edu
MULLINEAUX, J .... 707-527-4011.. 63 C
MULLINS, April .... 276-223-4897 475 B
amullins@wcc.vccs.edu
MULLINS, Beth .... 731-286-3358 423 E
lamullins@dscc.edu
MULLINS, Brian .... 859-622-2821 180 B
brian.mullins@eku.edu
MULLINS, Cathy .... 603-358-2281 274 A
catherine.mullins@keene.edu
MULLINS, Corey .... 276-326-4316 464 A
cmullins@bluefield.edu
MULLINS, Greg .... 360-867-6243 479 C
mullinsg@evergreen.edu
MULLINS, Joseph, W ... 770-720-5946 124 E
jwm@reinhardt.edu
MULLINS, Kathryn .... 616-234-4000 224 C
MULLINS, Kerry .... 908-852-1400 275 H
kerry.mullins@centenaryuniversity.edu
MULLINS, Megan .... 304-877-6428 486 A
officeofpresident@abc.edu
MULLINS, Rachel .... 501-977-2174.. 23 D
mullins@uaccm.edu
MULLINS, Stephanie, B 205-934-5121.... 8 A
smullins@uab.edu
MULLINS, Steve .... 714-879-3901.. 45 J
smullins@hiu.edu
MULLINS, Turan .... 314-529-9434 254 D
tmullins@maryville.edu
MULLION, Carrie .... 760-921-5440.. 56 A
carrie.mullion@paloverde.edu
MULLIS, Ben .... 478-275-6589 123 E
MULLIS, Chad .... 615-494-7647 421 C
chad.mullis@mtsu.edu
MULLIS, Christina .... 513-875-3344 349 K
christina.mullis@chatfield.edu
MULLIS,
Clarence (Tres) .... 717-337-6498 384 C
tmullis@gettysburg.edu
MULLIS, Jay .... 478-274-7879 123 E
jmullis@oftc.edu
MULLIS, Kimberly .... 252-940-6203 332 A
kimberly.mullis@beaufortccc.edu
MULLIS, Riann .... 620-432-0377 176 A
rmullis@neosho.edu
MULLNER, Joel, W .... 412-578-6119 380 A
jwmullner@carlow.edu
MULLOWNEY, Bill, J ..... 407-582-3411 113 C
bmullowney@valenciacollege.edu
MULREADY, Maritza ..... 716-286-8350 309 F
mmulready@niagara.edu
MULREADY, Stephen .... 860-768-4243.. 89 E
mulready@hartford.edu
MULROONEY, James .... 860-832-2660.. 85 F
mulrooneyj@ccsu.edu
MULROY, Kevin .... 323-259-2542.. 54 I
kmulroy@oxy.edu
MULROY-BOWDEN,
Linda, A .... 608-342-1845 495 E
mulroy@uwplatt.edu
MULROY-DEGENHART,
Carmella .... 814-865-7611 391 F
qum11@psu.edu
MULRYAN, Michael ...... 714-879-3901.. 45 J
mdmulryan@hiu.edu

MURPHY, OSB, Isaac ... 603-641-7010 273 C
imurphy@anselm.edu
MURPHY, James, H ...... 573-341-4292 260 F
murphyj@mst.edu
MURPHY, Jenni .... 916-278-4433.. 33 A
jmurphy@csus.edu
MURPHY, Jennifer ...... 318-840-3566.. 88 B
jmurphy@holyapostles.edu
MURPHY, Jessica, C ... 972-883-3536 454 D
ugdean@utdallas.edu
MURPHY, Jim .... 973-748-9000 275 C
jim_murphy@bloomfield.edu
MURPHY, John .... 210-458-3026 455 B
john.murphy@utsa.edu
MURPHY, John .... 203-837-8395.. 86 A
murphyj@wcsu.edu
MURPHY, John .... 317-921-4243 158 A
jmmurphy@ivytech.edu
MURPHY, Joshua .... 603-703-8484 272 K
jmurphy@ccsnh.edu
MURPHY, Justin .... 812-749-1373 159 E
jmurphy@oak.edu
MURPHY, Kathy .... 256-549-8200.... 2 B
MURPHY, Kelly .... 406-756-3801 262 H
kmurphy@fvcc.edu
MURPHY, Kelsey, L ..... 724-847-6643 384 B
klmurphy@geneva.edu
MURPHY, Kerry .... 606-783-2888 183 I
k.murphy@moreheadstate.edu
MURPHY, Kevin .... 239-304-7827.. 95 M
kevin.murphy@avemaria.edu
MURPHY, Kevin .... 607-735-1729 298 C
kmurphy@elmira.edu
MURPHY, Kevin .... 934-420-3578 320 C
murphykw@farmingdale.edu
MURPHY, Kyle .... 706-867-2720 126 G
kyle.murphy@ung.edu
MURPHY, Laura .... 508-929-8649 213 D
lmurphy@worcester.edu
MURPHY, Leah .... 712-324-5061 168 H
lmurphy@nwicc.edu
MURPHY, Lillie .... 225-743-8500 188 F
lmurphy@rpcc.edu
MURPHY, Linda .... 574-232-2408 158 U
MURPHY, Lynda .... 940-898-3405 451 A
lmurphy@twu.edu
MURPHY, M. Patrick .... 336-278-7640 328 H
murphyp@elon.edu
MURPHY, Mark .... 402-465-2254 267 J
mam@nebrwesleyan.edu
MURPHY, Mary .... 612-343-4406 241 O
mlmurphy@northcentral.edu
MURPHY, Mary Joan .... 212-854-2091 290 H
mmurphy@barnard.edu
MURPHY, Maryanne .... 215-972-7600 392 P
MURPHY, Maureen ...... 301-934-7625 198 C
mmurphy@csmd.edu
MURPHY, Mehegan ..... 585-785-1469 299 E
mehegan.murphy@flcc.edu
MURPHY, Michael ...... 508-678-2811 213 F
michael.murphy@bristolcc.edu
MURPHY, Michael ...... 845-398-4118 314 D
mmurphy@stac.edu
MURPHY, Miguel .... 305-237-7740 104 E
mmurphy3@mdc.edu
MURPHY, Mollie .... 202-685-3951 501 I
murphyma@ndu.edu
MURPHY, Moses .... 802-656-8830 462 D
moses.murphy@uvm.edu
MURPHY, Patrick ...... 570-961-2513 389 B
prmurphy@marywood.edu
MURPHY, Patty .... 305-284-3276 112 K
pattymurphy@miami.edu
MURPHY, Paul .... 805-922-6966.. 24 L
pmurphy@hancockcollege.edu
MURPHY, Paul .... 617-726-0422 216 E
pwmurphy@mghihp.edu
MURPHY, Paul .... 937-512-2518 360 F
paul.murphy@sinclair.edu
MURPHY, Penny .... 217-234-5253 141 H
pmurphy52829@lakelandcollege.edu
MURPHY, Pollie .... 757-727-5201 466 L
pollie.muphy@hamptonu.edu
MURPHY, Pollie .... 757-727-5237 466 L
pollie.murphy@hamptonu.edu
MURPHY, Sarah .... 402-354-7000 267 E
sarah.murphy@methodistcollege.edu
MURPHY, Scott .... 888-556-8226 134 D
MURPHY, Sean .... 213-738-6762.. 66 A
it@swlaw.edu
MURPHY, Shakarie ...... 501-450-3183.. 23 K
smurphy7@uca.edu

MURPHY, Shar .... 530-257-6181.. 47 I
smurphy@lassencollege.edu
MURPHY, Stephen ...... 203-432-4486.. 90 B
stephen.murphy@yale.edu
MURPHY, Susan .... 706-379-3111 128 A
samurphy@yhc.edu
MURPHY, Susan .... 361-825-2852 446 E
susan.murphy@tamucc.edu
MURPHY, Tara .... 781-283-2378 219 C
tm100@wellesley.edu
MURPHY, Taylor .... 910-630-7485 331 B
tamurphy@methodist.edu
MURPHY, Thomas ...... 516-876-3215 318 A
murphyt@oldwestbury.edu
MURPHY, Thomas ...... 305-284-6650 112 K
thomas.murphy@miami.edu
MURPHY, Thomas, H .... 215-898-7581 399 J
tom.murphy@isc.upenn.edu
MURPHY, Tim .... 254-442-5133 431 J
tim.murphy@cisco.edu
MURPHY, Todd .... 610-436-3102 394 F
tmurphy@wcupa.edu
MURPHY, Todd .... 714-432-5896.. 38 F
todd.murphy@mail.cccd.edu
MURPHY, Traci .... 716-839-8587 297 I
tmurphy@daemen.edu
MURPHY, Velissa ...... 606-886-7332 181 A
vmurphy0001@kctcs.edu
MURPHY, Vicky .... 903-813-2431 429 I
vmurphy@austincollege.edu
MURPHY, William ...... 617-552-1272 207 A
william.murphy@bc.edu
MURPHY, William ...... 845-574-4362 312 C
wmurphy@sunyrockland.edu
MURPHY ALEXANDER,
Coleen .... 845-758-7431 290 G
murphy@bard.edu
MURPHY-MORRIS,
Jayne, I .... 973-290-4245 282 G
jmmorris@steu.edu
MURPHY-NORRIS,
Carmel .... 540-453-2237 472 F
murphynorrisc@brcc.edu
MURR, Christopher ..... 512-245-3975 449 G
cm18@txstate.edu
MURRAH, Matt .... 214-333-5160 433 D
matt@dbu.edu
MURRAY, Aaron .... 850-729-5260 104 L
murraya8@nwfsc.edu
MURRAY, Abby .... 773-442-5216 145 G
a-murray3@neiu.edu
MURRAY, Ashley .... 919-508-2209 344 D
ammurray@peace.edu
MURRAY, Benjamin ..... 612-238-4526 242 H
bmurray@smumn.edu
MURRAY, Bob .... 231-591-2850 223 H
robertmurray@ferris.edu
MURRAY, Carol .... 406-338-5441 262 D
c_murray@bfcc.edu
MURRAY,
Christopher, D .... 406-994-2513 263 G
chris.murray@msuaf.org
MURRAY, Damon .... 704-922-2242 334 E
murray.damon@gaston.edu
MURRAY, David .... 616-234-3535 224 C
commdept@grcc.edu
MURRAY, David .... 415-703-9533.. 28 D
dmurray@cca.edu
MURRAY, Deborah ...... 423-614-8118 419 H
debmurray@leeuniversity.edu
MURRAY, Dennis, J ..... 845-575-3000 305 C
dennis.murray@marist.edu
MURRAY, Edwin .... 504-568-4810 189 C
emurr1@lsuhsc.edu
MURRAY, Eric .... 425-352-8810 477 F
emurray@cascadia.edu
MURRAY, Erika, S ...... 678-916-2603 115 G
emurray@johnmarshall.edu
MURRAY, Ginger .... 217-234-5253 141 H
gmurray@lakelandcollege.edu
MURRAY, Jay .... 203-837-8286.. 86 A
murrayj@wcsu.edu
MURRAY, Jennifer ...... 251-981-3771.... 5 B
jennifer.murray@columbiasouthern.edu
MURRAY, Jennifer ...... 315-781-3740 301 D
jmurray@hws.edu
MURRAY, Jennifer ...... 315-267-2492 318 D
murrayjm@potsdam.edu
MURRAY, Jill, A .... 570-504-1575 387 A
murrayj@lackawanna.edu
MURRAY, Joddy .... 618-453-2466 149 G
cola.dean@siu.edu
MURRAY, John, D ...... 305-899-3021.. 96 A
jdmurray@barry.edu

MURRAY, Jonathan ...... 706-225-5300.. 93 H
MURRAY, Julie, N ...... 785-864-3131 177 G
jnmurray@ku.edu
MURRAY, Kailea .... 315-792-3409 323 G
kemurray1@utica.edu
MURRAY, Karen .... 914-594-4882 308 J
karen_murray@nymc.edu
MURRAY, Kim .... 434-381-6202 470 H
kmurray@sbc.edu
MURRAY, Lynne .... 785-594-8308 171 C
president@bakeru.edu
MURRAY, Maggie .... 336-342-4261 337 B
murraym7639@rockinghamcc.edu
MURRAY, Melissa ...... 802-656-2925 462 D
melissa.murray@uvm.edu
MURRAY, Michelle ...... 508-793-2414 208 A
mmurray@holycross.edu
MURRAY, Michelle ...... 215-646-7300 384 G
murray.m@gmercyu.edu
MURRAY, Nancy .... 978-665-3530 212 C
nmurray5@fitchburgstate.edu
MURRAY, Peter, J ...... 410-706-2461 202 F
pmurray@umaryland.edu
MURRAY, Richard ...... 808-932-7644 129 A
ramurray@hawaii.edu
MURRAY, Richard ...... 914-633-2013 302 C
rmurray@iona.edu
MURRAY, Richard, M .... 626-395-4951.. 29 A
murray@caltech.edu
MURRAY, Rick .... 508-259-2512 220 B
rickmurray@whoi.edu
MURRAY, Rita .... 212-517-0416 305 D
rmurray@mmm.edu
MURRAY, Robert .... 845-398-4125 314 D
rmurray@stac.edu
MURRAY, Rodney, B ... 215-596-8789 400 B
r.murray@usciences.edu
MURRAY, Sally .... 617-333-2929 208 D
sally.murray@curry.edu
MURRAY, Sarah, A ...... 859-238-5376 179 H
sarah.murray@centre.edu
MURRAY, Sean .... 888-491-8686.. 75 E
seanmurray@westcliff.edu
MURRAY, Shailagh, J .. 212-854-3229 296 H
sjm2245@columbia.edu
MURRAY, Shannon ...... 925-631-4105.. 59 I
srm30@stmarys-ca.edu
MURRAY, Sharon .... 518-292-1753 312 D
murras2@sage.edu
MURRAY, Susan .... 619-388-4010.. 60 I
smurray001@sdccd.edu
MURRAY, Suzette .... 630-466-7900 152 H
smurray@waubonsee.edu
MURRAY, Thomas ...... 773-508-2398 142 G
tmurray3@luc.edu
MURRAY, Timothy, S ... 845-575-3000 305 C
tim.murray@marist.edu
MURRAY, Tom, L ...... 405-789-7661 369 H
tom.murray@swcu.edu
MURRAY, Tracey, L ..... 410-951-3980 203 B
tmurray@coppin.edu
MURRAY, Valerie, M .... 412-397-6423 396 E
murrayv@rmu.edu
MURRAY-HANSEN,
Ashley .... 402-465-2129 267 J
amurray3@nebrwesleyan.edu
MURRAY-LUKE,
Shanna .... 601-318-6668 249 B
smurray-luke@wmcarey.edu
MURRELL, Terry .... 712-274-6400 170 H
terry.murrell@witcc.edu
MURRET, Patricia ...... 504-865-5448 190 A
pmurret@loyno.edu
MURREY, Brett .... 903-468-8687 446 E
brett.murrey@tamuc.edu
MURRMAN, OSB,
Warren .... 724-805-2331 397 D
warren.murrman@gmail.com
MURRY, Christopher ... 307-382-1701 500 I
cmurry@westernwyoming.edu
MURRY, Kim .... 620-901-6221 171 A
murry@allencc.edu
MURRY, Melanie .... 901-678-2155 426 A
mmurry@memphis.edu
MURRY, Nichole .... 850-599-3270 109 E
nichole.murry@famu.edu
MURRY-HIBBLER,
LeKeisha .... 662-562-3271 247 E
MURTAGH, Michael ... 309-298-1808 152 I
mk-murtagh@wiu.edu
MURTAUGH, Peter, T ... 314-286-4813 257 H
ptmurtaugh@ranken.edu
MURTHA, Bernie .... 607-274-7764 302 E
bmurtha@ithaca.edu

MURTHA, James .... 603-428-2284 272 I
jmurtha@nec.edu
MURTHA, Katie .... 212-799-5000 303 B
MURTHA, Mitch .... 610-359-5141 381 J
MURTHY, Jayathi .... 541-737-2111 374 H
pres.office@oregonstate.edu
MURTHY, Jayathi, Y ... 310-825-2938.. 69 D
jmurthy@seas.ucla.edu
MURTHY, Raj .... 405-744-3555 367 G
cio@okstate.edu
MURTON, Rosey .... 850-641-5021 110 B
rmurton@fsu.edu
MURUGAN, Suresh ...... 202-274-5986.. 94 B
suresh.murugan@udc.edu
MURUGESAN, Hayley ... 619-398-4902.. 45 F
hmurugesan@hightechhigh.org
MURVIN, Keith, E ...... 301-546-0606 201 D
murvinek@pgcc.edu
MUSA, Karen, V .... 469-365-1961 432 I
kmusa@collin.edu
MUSAL, Edward .... 914-251-6923 318 E
edward.musal@purchase.edu
MUSCARELLA, Susan ... 510-845-5373.. 29 D
susan@cjc.edu
MUSCAT, Anthony ...... 316-978-6513 178 B
anthony.muscat@wichita.edu
MUSCAT, Bernadette, T .. 559-278-4468.. 31 D
bmuscat@csufresno.edu
MUSCAT, Tracy .... 313-664-7864 222 C
tmuscat@collegeforcreativestudies.edu
MUSCENTE, Catherine .. 516-323-4710 306 I
cmuscente@molloy.edu
MUSE, Bill .... 918-463-2931 365 I
wmuse@connorsstate.edu
MUSE, Doug .... 870-612-2167.. 23 B
douglas.muse@uaccb.edu
MUSE, Douglas .... 870-612-2167.. 23 B
douglas.muse@uaccb.edu
MUSE, Justin .... 540-365-4501 466 I
jmuse@ferrum.edu
MUSE, Kevin .... 716-884-9120 291 I
kmmuse@bryantstratton.edu
MUSE, Van .... 909-389-3205.. 60 E
wmuse@sbccd.cc.ca.us
MUSEL, Matt .... 507-457-8733 242 H
mmusel@smumn.edu
MUSEUS DABAY,
Katherine .... 219-464-5093 162 C
katherine.museusdabay@valpo.edu
MUSGROVE, Jeff .... 573-875-7663 251 A
jmusgrove@ccis.edu
MUSGROVE, Jeffery ...... 512-516-8703 125 D
jmusgrove@southuniversity.edu
MUSGROVE, Joel .... 540-986-1800 463 F
jmusgrove@an.edu
MUSGROVE, Joel .... 520-971-5623 470 J
jmusgrove@ufairfax.edu
MUSHEL, Jessica .... 845-569-3591 307 B
jessica.mushel@msmc.edu
MUSHENO, Joseph ...... 570-702-8933 386 B
jmusheno@johnson.edu
MUSHO, Suzanne .... 516-686-1456 308 H
smusho@nyit.edu
MUSHONG, Karen ...... 616-331-3490 224 D
mushongk@gvsu.edu
MUSHONGA, Shane ...... 972-524-3341 444 E
shane.mushonga@swcc.edu
MUSIAL, David .... 503-251-5775 377 A
dmusial@uws.edu
MUSIC, Casey .... 606-886-3863 181 A
casey.music@kctcs.edu
MUSICH, Michelle ...... 828-766-1262 335 E
mmusich@mayland.edu
MUSICH, Nita, R .... 812-465-1634 162 B
nita.musich@usi.edu
MUSICK, Charles .... 276-964-7647 474 E
charles.musick@sw.edu
MUSIL, Carol, M .... 216-368-2544 349 B
carol.musil@case.edu
MUSILA, Frida .... 305-760-7500 103 V
MUSILLI, Laura .... 304-336-8226 489 B
laura.musilli@westliberty.edu
MUSKAT, Yael .... 646-592-4200 325 R
ymuskat@yu.edu
MUSKAVITCH, John, W 909-389-3269.. 60 E
jmuskavitch@craftonhills.edu
MUSKOPF, Sandra ...... 407-438-6000 108 L
MUSNICKI, Sundi .... 206-546-6973 483 C
smusnicki@shoreline.edu
MUSOLF, Shelly, R ...... 260-422-5561 156 A
srmusolf@indianatech.edu

NAIR, Ajay ... 215-572-2900 378 E
presidentnair@arcadia.edu
NAIR, Murali ... 734-487-0077 223 F
mnair@emich.edu
NAIR, Raghunath ... 512-432-1400 443 F
NAIR, Sukumaran ... 214-768-2856 443 G
nair@smu.edu
NAIRN, Jason ... 814-472-3001 396 I
jnairn@francis.edu
NAIRN, Roderick ... 303-315-2102.. 84 B
roderick.nairn@ucdenver.edu
NAIRN, Tori ... 606-368-6134 178 D
torinairn@alc.edu
NAISH, Cheri ... 951-487-3409.. 53 A
cnaish@msjc.edu
NAJAM, Adil ... 617-358-7238 207 C
anajam@bu.edu
NAJARIAN, David ... 704-637-4335 327 H
dnajaria@catawba.edu
NAJARRO, Evelyn ... 954-453-9228.. 34 I
NAJDUCH, Kimberly ... 540-365-4275 466 I
knajduch@ferrum.edu
NAJIM, Michel ... 833-468-2467.. 26 F
NAKADA-ALM,
Christina ... 253-460-4464 483 F
cnakada-alm@tacomacc.edu
NAKADOMARI, Therese 808-689-2414 129 C
therese@hawaii.edu
NAKAGAWA, Deborah ... 808-956-0321 129 D
debn@hawaii.edu
NAKAMA, Debra ... 808-984-3515 130 B
debran@hawaii.edu
NAKAMURA, Aaron ... 509-527-2656 484 C
aaron.nakamura@wallawalla.edu
NAKAMURA, Mayumi ... 804-752-3607 469 B
mayuminakamura@rmc.edu
NAKAMURA, Tim ... 760-568-3352.. 39 A
tnakamura@collegeofthedesert.edu
NAKANO, Mark, E ... 714-463-7504.. 51 D
mnakano@ketchum.edu
NAKASONE, Nancy, K ... 808-689-2521 129 C
nancynak@hawaii.edu
NAKATA, Glen ... 260-481-6804 159 H
gnakata@pfw.edu
NAKHLEH, Luay ... 713-348-4009 441 K
nakhleh@rice.edu
NAKONECHNYI, Alex ... 513-244-4264 356 F
alex.nakonechnyi@msj.edu
NAKUTIS, Kristine ... 931-221-1400 416 H
nakutisk@apsu.edu
NALEPA, Laurie ... 818-947-2498.. 50 B
nalepal@lavc.edu
NALESKI, Greg ... 202-319-6904.. 91 G
naleski@cua.edu
NALETTE, Kevin, J ... 785-532-6221 175 A
nalette@ksu.edu
NALLY, Angela, D ... 765-658-4800 154 G
angelanally@depauw.edu
NALYWAYKO, Serge ... 845-451-1409 297 E
serge.nalywayko@culinary.edu
NAMUO, Clyne ... 602-285-7433.. 13 H
clyne.namuo@phoenixcollege.edu
NANCE, Agnieszka ... 504-862-3348 191 D
anance@tulane.edu
NANCE, Catherine ... 904-264-2172 106 K
catherine.nance@iws.edu
NANCE, Cynthia ... 479-575-4504.. 21 H
cnance@uark.edu
NANCE, Damon ... 951-372-7041.. 59 C
damon.nance@norcocollege.edu
NANCE, Donna ... 817-531-6579 450 F
dnance@txwes.edu
NANCE, Jason, P ... 214-768-3775 443 G
nance@smu.edu
NANCE, Kristy ... 910-775-4347 343 A
kristy.nance@uncp.edu
NANCE, Summer ... 864-488-8251 409 C
snance@limestone.edu
NANCE, Teresa, A ... 610-519-4077 401 B
terry.nance@villanova.edu
NANNEN, Tampa, J ... 903-510-3324 451 D
tnan@tjc.edu
NANNERY, Tracy ... 716-250-7500 291 H
tbnannery@bryantstratton.edu
NANNEY, Ana ... 985-448-7940 187 J
ana.nanney@fletcher.edu
NANNEY, Cat ... 321-674-7371 100 A
cnanney@fit.edu
NANNEY, Chris ... 704-669-4062 333 C
nanney@clevelandcc.edu
NANNI, Louis, M ... 574-631-6123 161 G
nanni.3@nd.edu

NANTZ, Samantha ... 606-546-1207 185 B
snantz@unionky.edu
NAPARLO, Michael ... 732-224-2395 275 D
mnaparlo@brookdalecc.edu
NAPIER, Audrey ... 334-229-4316.... 4 B
anapier@alasu.edu
NAPIER, Katherine ... 404-752-1500 123 A
knapier@msm.edu
NAPIER, Stacey ... 512-664-9043 454 A
snapier@utsystem.edu
NAPOLEON, Jose ... 954-500-2987.. 95 O
NAPOLEON, Nawa'a ... 808-734-9517 129 E
nawaa@hawaii.edu
NAPOLES, Gerald, F ... 832-813-6648 438 E
gerald.f.napoles@lonestar.edu
NAPOLI, Brandon ... 831-479-5040.. 27 G
brnapoli@cabrillo.edu
NAPOLI, Kim ... 208-459-5147 131 A
knapoli@collegeofidaho.edu
NAPOLILLO, Steven, R . 401-865-2677 403 G
snapolil@providence.edu
NAPPER, Stan ... 281-649-3232 436 D
snapper@hbu.edu
NAQUIN, Rose ... 504-520-7301 193 C
xubooks@xula.edu
NARCISSE,
Margaretta, S ... 913-253-5097 177 A
margaretta.narcisse@spst.edu
NARDI, Elizabeth ... 815-394-4379 147 J
enardi@rockford.edu
NARDI, Peter, A ... 410-293-1585 502 I
nardi@usna.edu
NARDIN, Gail ... 212-752-1530 303 G
gail.nardin@limcollege.edu
NARDINO, Carol ... 802-387-6877 461 E
cnardino@landmark.edu
NARDO, Rachel ... 435-797-3046 459 F
rachel.nardo@usu.edu
NARDONE, Christopher 518-828-4181 296 G
christopher.nardone@sunycgcc.edu
NARDONE, Mary, S ... 617-552-0346 207 A
mary.nardone@bc.edu
NARDONE, Paul ... 570-674-8130 389 H
pnardone@misericordia.edu
NARDUCCI, Julie ... 951-785-2578.. 47 F
jnarducc@lasierra.edu
NARI, Jen ... 408-852-2880.. 43 H
jnari@gavilan.edu
NARKIEWICZ, Geralyn .. 906-635-2228 226 C
gnarkiewicz@lssu.edu
NARMONTAS, Steven ... 413-782-1778 219 E
steven.narmontas@wne.edu
NARVAEZ, Ivonne ... 850-201-8457 112 B
ivonne.narvaez@tcc.fl.edu
NARVAEZ, Maria ... 213-477-2908.. 52 J
mnarvaez@msmu.edu
NARVEKAR, Medha ... 215-898-7005 399 J
narvekar@upenn.edu
NARYKA, Marisa ... 507-457-1781 242 H
mnaryka@smumn.edu
NAS, Paula ... 810-424-5486 231 C
pnas@umflint.edu
NASE, Christina ... 856-415-2297 280 F
cnase@rcsj.edu
NASH, Amy ... 724-938-5570 394 C
nash@calu.edu
NASH, Bob ... 714-241-6143.. 38 D
bnash@coastline.edu
NASH, Brian ... 712-324-5061 168 H
bnash@nwicc.edu
NASH, Gail ... 731-989-6072 418 H
gnash@fhu.edu
NASH, Julie ... 978-934-4191 211 G
julie_nash@uml.edu
NASH, Katie ... 608-265-1988 494 D
katie.nash@wisc.edu
NASH, Kylie ... 256-372-5230.... 1 A
kylie.nash@aamu.edu
NASH, Laura ... 203-254-4000.. 87 G
lnash@fairfield.edu
NASH, Leon ... 231-439-6443 228 D
lnash3@ncmich.edu
NASH, Lillian ... 301-405-2583 202 E
lnash1@umd.edu
NASH, Meghann ... 409-944-1238 435 F
mnash@gc.edu
NASH, Mika ... 610-527-0200 396 G
mika.nash@rosemont.edu
NASH, Milton ... 240-567-7794 200 E
milton.nash@montgomerycollege.edu
NASH, Myranda ... 828-641-0089 327 A
nashmh@brevard.edu

NASH, Peggy ... 812-535-5296 160 E
peggy.nash@smwc.edu
NASH, Robert ... 870-235-4075.. 21 E
robertnash@saumag.edu
NASH, Robert, B ... 509-420-4545 481 D
bob@gather4him.net
NASH, Stephen ... 972-708-7573 434 F
admissions-director@diu.edu
NASH, Steve ... 269-471-3284 220 H
snash@andrews.edu
NASH, Timothy, G ... 989-837-4129 228 G
tgnash@northwood.edu
NASH, Victoria ... 262-691-5495 499 A
vnash@wctc.edu
NASH, Whitney ... 912-478-5322 120 A
wnash@georgiasouthern.edu
NASH, William ... 256-782-8351.... 6 A
bnash@jsu.edu
NASHUA, Loy ... 562-938-4398.. 48 K
lnashua@lbcc.edu
NASIM, Aashir ... 804-828-8947 472 D
anasim@vcu.edu
NASON, Bradley, A ... 406-657-1018 264 G
nasonb@rocky.edu
NASON, Stephen, S ... 207-509-7284 196 B
snason@unity.edu
NASORI, Renee ... 619-644-7000.. 44 H
renee.nasori@gcccd.edu
NASR, Nabil ... 585-475-5106 312 A
nasr@rit.edu
NASSAR, Sayed ... 248-370-3781 229 F
nassar@oakland.edu
NASSE, Jeffrey ... 954-201-7350.. 96 F
NASSER, Abdul ... 310-900-1600.. 39 H
skibui@compton.edu
NASSER, Dawn, S ... 217-443-8755 136 E
d.nasser@dacc.edu
NASSER, Edward, D ... 520-621-5449.. 16 H
enasser@arizona.edu
NASSER, Helen ... 718-368-5597 294 C
helen.nasser@kbcc.cuny.edu
NASSER, Ryn ... 919-613-5577 328 D
ryn.nasser@duke.edu
NASSIM, Sami ... 401-341-2480 404 D
sami.nassim@salve.edu
NASSOUR, Kelly ... 956-665-3844 455 A
kelly.nassour@utrgv.edu
NAST, Paul ... 479-524-7296.. 20 C
pnast@jbu.edu
NATAF, Daniel, D ... 410-777-2407 197 C
ddnataf@aacc.edu
NATAL, Daniel ... 484-794-9787 378 C
daniel.natal@alvernia.edu
NATALE, Joel, A ... 610-558-5635 390 G
natalej@neumann.edu
NATALI, Glenn ... 724-480-3361 381 G
glenn.natali@ccbc.edu
NATALI, Jeanne, B ... 757-822-7193 474 G
jnatali@tcc.edu
NATALI, Tony ... 574-807-7259 153 G
tony.natali@betheluniversity.edu
NATALICCHIO, Gino, Q . 407-563-6501.. 95 C
NATALIZIO, Nicholas ... 407-563-6501.. 95 C
NATALY, Mark ... 508-678-2811 213 F
mark.nataly@bristolcc.edu
NATARAJAN, Tara ... 765-983-1318 154 H
natarta@earlham.edu
NATELBORG,
Christopher ... 503-491-6422 373 H
christopher.natelborg@mhcc.edu
NATH, Mary Kay ... 319-399-8100 164 D
NATHAN, Sean ... 808-734-9124 129 E
smnathan@hawaii.edu
NATHAN, Susan ... 603-626-9267 273 E
s.nathan@snhu.edu
NATHAN, Vini ... 334-844-5771.... 4 E
provost@auburn.edu
NATHANSON, Andrea ... 413-755-4889 215 F
anathanson@stcc.edu
NATHANSON, Mike ... 352-435-5027 103 U
nathansm@lssc.edu
NATION, Ramie ... 785-594-4530 171 C
ramie.nation@bakeru.edu
NATION, Travis ... 206-296-2002 483 B
nationt@seattleu.edu
NATIVIDAD, Rory ... 562-860-2451.. 35 O
rnatividad@cerritos.edu
NATTER, Gretchen ... 717-337-6490 384 C
gnatter@gettysburg.edu
NATTINGER, Ann ... 414-955-8495 492 F
anatting@mcw.edu
NATZEL, Kasie, L ... 989-774-1012 221 M
natze1kl@cmich.edu

NAUGHTON, Blake ... 970-491-6281.. 79 E
blake.naughton@colostate.edu
NAUGHTON, John ... 614-251-6654 358 B
naughtoj@ohiodominican.edu
NAUGHTON, John ... 614-251-4721 358 B
naughtoj@ohiodominican.edu
NAUGLE, Deemie ... 214-333-5291 433 D
deemie@dbu.edu
NAUGLE, Lori ... 419-372-0113 348 F
lnaugle@bgsu.edu
NAULT, Ray ... 386-822-8946 111 F
renault@stetson.edu
NAULU, Elaine ... 541-485-1780 374 C
elainenaulu@newhope.edu
NAUMAN, Barbara ... 401-825-1023 403 D
bnauman@ccri.edu
NAUMAN, Josh ... 503-554-2564 372 I
jnauman@georgefox.edu
NAUMANN, Cheryl ... 602-557-1742.. 16 L
cheryl.naumann@phoenix.edu
NAURIGHT, John ... 301-447-5068 201 A
j.nauright@msmary.edu
NAUSI KUMORU,
Demiana ... 692-625-3394 503 F
dkumoru@cmi.edu
NAUTA-RODRIGUEZ,
Debra ... 202-319-5515.. 91 G
nautarodriguez@cua.edu
NAVA, Esmeralda ... 626-396-2267.. 26 G
esmeralda.nava@artcenter.edu
NAVA, Rachael ... 510-987-0500.. 68 M
rachael.nava@ucop.edu
NAVA, Robert ... 909-537-5004.. 33 B
rjnava@csusb.edu
NAVA, Robert ... 218-477-4308 239 A
robert.nava@mnstate.edu
NAVARI, Shelley ... 802-865-2132 461 C
snavari@champlain.edu
NAVARRE, Michael ... 801-975-5094 460 D
michael.navarre@slcc.edu
NAVARRETE, Adrian ... 914-633-2245 302 C
anavarrete@iona.edu
NAVARRETTE, Jay ... 559-791-2365.. 47 D
jay.navarrette@portervillecollege.edu
NAVARRO, Brenden ... 315-279-5295 303 D
bnavarro@keuka.edu
NAVARRO, Jim ... 956-872-3085 443 B
jnavar53@southtexascollege.edu
NAVARRO, JoAnn ... 607-777-3060 315 E
jnavarro@binghamton.edu
NAVARRO, Kristina, M . 608-342-9187 495 E
navarrok@uwplatt.edu
NAVARRO, Pablo, A ... 305-223-4561 106 N
rector@sjvcs.edu
NAVARRO, Renee ... 415-476-7700.. 70 D
renee.navarro@ucsf.edu
NAVARRO, Richard ... 909-869-3905.. 30 B
ranavarro@cpp.edu
NAVARRO, Sarina ... 559-638-0299.. 67 C
sarina.navarro@reedleycollege.edu
NAVARRO, Yolanda ... 305-821-3333 100 C
ynavarro@fnu.edu
NAVARRO-CASTELLANOS,
Norma ... 918-595-7362 370 B
norma.navarrocastellanos@tulsacc.edu
NAVARRO-FIGUEROA,
Mayra ... 787-993-8887 510 E
mayra.navarro@upr.edu
NAVARRO FLOYD,
Shawnda ... 972-860-8201 433 H
NAVARRO-LECA, Nancy 510-659-7376.. 54 J
nnavarro@ohlone.edu
NAVARRO-NICOSIA,
Sylvia ... 934-420-2529 320 C
sylvia.nicosia@farmingdale.edu
NAVARRO SULLIVAN,
Lynnette ... 951-571-6103.. 59 B
lynnette.sullivan@rccd.edu
NAVAS, Gabrielle ... 850-629-3250.. 93 H
NAVE, Felecia, M ... 601-877-6111 244 B
president20@alcorn.edu
NAVE, Jeffery, W ... 504-282-4455 190 D
jnave@nobts.edu
NAVIA, Christine ... 414-288-4121 492 E
christine.navia@marquette.edu
NAVIA, Christine ... 608-263-7876 494 C
cnavia@uwsa.edu
NAVIA, Pedro ... 269-471-3181 220 H
navia@andrews.edu
NAVIN, John, C ... 419-772-2070 358 D
j-navin@onu.edu
NAVRAN, Darius ... 303-797-5822.. 77 H
darius.navran@arapahoe.edu

Index of Key Administrators NAWOICHIK – NELSON 811

NAWOICHIK, Michael ... 978-867-4500 209 F mike.nawoichik@gordon.edu
NAWROCKI, Ann .... 610-796-8428 378 C ann.nawrocki@alvernia.edu
NAWROT, Lisa .... 218-477-5892 239 A nawrot@mnstate.edu
NAYLON, Karen, C .... 336-888-6388 329 E kcoffman@highpoint.edu
NAYLOR, Ben .... 845-574-4215 312 C bnaylor@sunyrockland.edu
NAYLOR, Mary .... 910-362-7193 332 F menaylor80@mail.cfcc.edu
NAYLOR-JOHNSON, Darrell .... 912-525-5000 124 G dnaylorj@scad.edu
NAYOR, Greg, J .... 716-839-8520 297 F gnayor@daemen.edu
NAZAR, Kelsey .... 913-469-8500 174 F knazar@jccc.edu
NAZARENKO, Larissa ... 714-432-5536.. 38 F lnazarenko@occ.cccd.edu
NAZARENKO, Nadezhda (Nadia) .... 281-756-3723 428 E nnazarenko@alvincollege.edu
NAZARENKO, Tatiana ... 805-565-6070.. 75 I tnazarenko@westmont.edu
NAZARIO, Evelyn .... 562-951-4455.. 29 J enazario@calstate.edu
NAZARIO-COLON, Ricardo .... 828-227-3251 343 D rnazariocolon@wcu.edu
NAZARIO TORRES, Juan, C .... 787-620-2040 504 B jcnazario@aupr.edu
NAZWORTH, Susan .... 806-894-9611 443 A snazworth@southplainscollege.edu
NCUBE, Lisa .... 773-244-5287 145 F lncube@northpark.edu
NDAO, Yacine .... 323-860-0789.. 50 E
NDIAYE, Momar .... 860-832-2050.. 85 F mndiaye@ccsu.edu
NDUBUISI, Chioma .... 323-343-2600.. 32 B chioma.ndubuisi@calstatela.edu
NDURA, Elavie .... 707-826-4503.. 30 A en82@humboldt.edu
NEAD, Catherine .... 630-617-3628 137 E catherine.nead@elmhurst.edu
NEAL, A. Sierra .... 803-774-3361 406 A nealas@cctech.edu
NEAL, Adam .... 540-375-2285 469 G neal@roanoke.edu
NEAL, Brenda .... 304-260-4380 487 C bneal@blueridgectc.edu
NEAL, Dan .... 617-989-4790 219 D neald@wit.edu
NEAL, Donna, V .... 252-493-7309 336 E dneal@email.pittcc.edu
NEAL, Gordon, W .... 434-223-6262 466 K gneal@hsc.edu
NEAL, James, G .... 626-264-8880.. 71 F
NEAL, Kathleen .... 860-768-4408.. 89 E kaneal@hartford.edu
NEAL, Kurtis, R .... 325-942-2168 450 B kurtis.neal@angelo.edu
NEAL, Linda, R .... 407-582-2510 113 C lneal@valenciacollege.edu
NEAL, Lisa .... 308-865-8442 268 J neall@unk.edu
NEAL, Mike .... 913-469-8500 174 F mneal26@jccc.edu
NEAL, Nicole .... 740-351-3140 360 E nneal@shawnee.edu
NEAL, Pat .... 208-562-2336 131 C patneal@cwi.edu
NEAL, Phillip, W .... 270-901-1111 182 E phil.neal@kctcs.edu
NEAL, Rodney .... 909-558-4543.. 48 J rneal@llu.edu
NEAL, Ryan .... 864-231-2000 405 F rneal@andersonuniversity.edu
NEAL, Thomas, M .... 714-547-9625.. 28 C tneal@calcoast.edu
NEAL, Tom .... 714-546-7600.. 38 D tneal14@coastline.edu
NEAL, W. Anthony .... 903-927-3381 457 I wneal@wileyc.edu
NEAL, Zach .... 501-279-4332.. 19 G zneal@harding.edu
NEALON, Michael .... 313-845-9835 224 F manealon@hfcc.edu
NEALON, Michele .... 213-615-2700.. 36 G mnealon@thechicagoschool.edu
NEAME, Simon .... 206-543-1760 484 A sneame@uw.edu
NEARY, Michele .... 317-940-9535 153 H mneary@butler.edu
NEAU, George .... 916-306-1628.. 67 E chancellor@sum.edu
NEAU, Matthew .... 317-738-8100 155 A mneau@franklincollege.edu
NEAULT, Lynn .... 619-644-7570.. 44 F lynn.neault@gcccd.edu
NEAVES, Mitchell .... 340-693-1040 512 B mneaves@uvi.edu
NEBEKER, Jennifer .... 701-774-4267 346 C jennifer.nebeker@willistonstate.edu
NEBEKER, Kenley .... 701-774-4563 346 C kenley.nebeker@willistonstate.edu
NEBEL, Andriea .... 402-552-3373 265 G nebel@clarksoncollege.edu
NEBEN, Jason .... 949-214-3349.. 40 E jason.neben@cui.edu
NEBESKY, Michael .... 864-656-2067 406 F mnebesky@clemson.edu
NEBLETT, Tommy .... 617-266-1400 206 D conservatoryadmissions@berklee.edu
NEDDER, Stephen .... 401-456-8200 404 A snedder@ric.edu
NEDELL, Thomas .... 617-373-2240 217 D
NEDLEY, Neil .... 530-422-7927.. 74 F nnedley@yahoo.com
NEE, Kelly, A .... 617-353-2127 207 C kellynee@bu.edu
NEECE, Taylor .... 951-343-4871.. 27 J tneece@calbaptist.edu
NEECE-FIELDER, Kasey . 210-458-4819 455 B kasey.neece-fielder@utsa.edu
NEEDHAM, Matthew, R . 336-633-0210 336 F mrneedham@randolph.edu
NEEDHAM, Michele .... 630-466-7900 152 H mneedham@waubonsee.edu
NEEDLER, Kent .... 314-434-4044 251 F kent.needler@covenantseminary.edu
NEEDLES, Philip .... 215-641-6510 390 A pneedles@mc3.edu
NEEDY, Bryan .... 502-456-6504 184 F bneedy@sullivan.edu
NEEDY, Kim .... 479-575-3054.. 21 H needy@uark.edu
NEEF, Jennifer .... 217-333-0820 151 F jneef@illinois.edu
NEEL, Buster .... 207-621-3300 196 E buster.neel@maine.edu
NEEL, Monica .... 410-337-6562 198 G monica.neel@goucher.edu
NEEL, Paul, E .... 574-807-7035 153 G paul.neel@betheluniversity.edu
NEELEY, Dewayne .... 618-664-7139 138 D dewayne.neeley@greenville.edu
NEELEY, Lisa .... 707-864-7000.. 64 F lisa.neeley@solano.edu
NEELEY, Phillip .... 352-588-8363 107 B phillip.neely@saintleo.edu
NEELY, Elaine .... 203-591-7418.. 88 E eneely@post.edu
NEELY, JR., James .... 313-831-5200 223 G jneely@etseminary.edu
NEELY, Jocelyn .... 937-708-5745 363 G jneely@wilberforce.edu
NEELY, Kevin .... 503-725-2042 375 D kneely@pdx.edu
NEELY, Patricia .... 276-326-4477 464 A pneely@bluefield.edu
NEELY, Robert .... 949-359-0045.. 29 C
NEELY, Winfred .... 312-329-4042 144 F winfred.neely@moody.edu
NEELY-SMITH, Shane .... 386-752-1822.. 99 P shane.neely-smith@fgc.edu
NEEM, Barbara .... 781-899-5500 217 F bneem@psjs.edu
NEEMANN, Brenda .... 402-481-8692 265 B brenda.neemann@bryanhealthcollege.edu
NEER, Stephen .... 312-261-3031 145 C stephen.neer@nl.edu
NEESAM, Jaci .... 415-422-6712.. 72 I neesam@usfca.edu
NEESAM, Jaci, E .... 415-422-6762.. 72 I neesam@usfca.edu
NEESE, John, M .... 325-670-1273 436 B jneese@hsutx.edu
NEESMITH, Debra .... 704-216-3460 337 C debra.neesmith@rccc.edu
NEF, Dennis, L .... 559-278-2636.. 31 D dennisn@csufresno.edu
NEFF, Charles .... 419-289-5624 347 H cneff@ashland.edu
NEFF, Graham .... 864-656-0128 406 F neffg@clemson.edu
NEFF, Joan .... 304-293-4813 489 E joan.neff@mail.wvu.edu
NEFF, Jon .... 319-398-7195 167 H jon.neff@kirkwood.edu
NEFF, Kathryn .... 573-518-2378 255 G kneff@mineralarea.edu
NEFF-HENDERSON, Laura .... 941-351-5100 106 J lneffhen@ringling.edu
NEFF-SHARUM, Emily ..... 910-775-4409 343 A emily.neffsharum@uncp.edu
NEGLIA, Michael, S ...... 904-620-2923 111 A mneglia@unf.edu
NEGRÓN, Dennis .... 423-236-2813 422 H negron@southern.edu
NEGRÓN, Gisela .... 787-751-0178 509 A gnegron@uagm.edu
NEGRETE, Elizabeth .... 818-947-2361.. 50 B negretme@lavc.edu
NEGRETE, Michael .... 510-879-9275.. 60 C mnegrete@samuelmerritt.edu
NEGRETE, Nick .... 310-665-6967.. 55 B nnegrete@otis.edu
NEGRON, Frankie .... 787-761-0640 510 A decanoadministracion@utcpr.edu
NEGRON, Olga .... 787-832-6000 506 B onegron@icprjc.edu
NEGRON, Rafael .... 787-780-0070 504 E rnegron@caribbean.edu
NEGRON, Zaima .... 787-754-7597 506 H zynegron@inter.edu
NEGRON, Zyma .... 787-766-1912 507 C zynegron@inter.edu
NEGRON-BERRIOS, Juan, A .... 787-857-3600 506 K janegron@br.inter.edu
NEGRON-COLON, Wigdalys .... 787-780-5134 508 C
NEGRON DELGADO, Juan Luis .... 787-841-2000 508 H juan_negron@pucpr.edu
NEHMER, Matthew .... 805-765-9300.. 39 E
NEHRENZ, Guy .... 954-262-1213 104 M gnehrenz@nova.edu
NEHRING, Kellie .... 619-260-4700.. 72 H knehring@sandiego.edu
NEHRING, Matt .... 719-587-7504.. 77 F matt.nehring@adams.edu
NEIBAUER, Todd .... 231-995-1671 228 F tneibauer@nmc.edu
NEIBERG, Maryke .... 508-373-5707 216 B maryke.neiberg@mcphs.edu
NEIDERHISER, Jonathan .... 605-331-6667 416 C jonathan.neiderhiser@usiouxfalls.edu
NEIDERMYER, Gindy ..... 715-232-4053 496 C neidermyerg@uwstout.edu
NEIDUSKI, Rebecca .... 319-352-8450 170 F president@wartburg.edu
NEIDY, Jon .... 309-677-2510 133 H neidy@fsmail.bradley.edu
NEIGER, Brad, L .... 801-422-3567 458 A neiger@byu.edu
NEIHOUSE, Kristina ...... 305-809-3504.. 97 M kristina.neihouse@cfk.edu
NEIKIRK, Mark .... 859-572-1449 184 B neikirkm1@nku.edu
NEIL, Jennifer .... 208-426-2927 130 F jenniferneil1@boisestate.edu
NEILING, Francine .... 863-680-4119 100 F fneiling@flsouthern.edu
NEILL, Erin .... 619-201-8957.. 65 F erin.neill@socalsem.edu
NEILL, Jim .... 718-270-7482 316 E jim.neill@downstate.edu
NEILL, Ushma, S .... 646-888-2011 304 H neillu@mskcc.org
NEILS, Kathleen, A .... 603-862-2421 273 H kathy.neils@unh.edu
NEILSEN, Steve .... 951-343-4614.. 27 J sneilsen@calbaptist.edu
NEILSON, Eric, G .... 312-503-0340 146 C egneilson@northwestern.edu
NEILSON, Jonathan, B .. 651-603-6315 235 A neilson@csp.edu
NEILSON, Leanne .... 805-493-3145.. 29 E neilson@callutheran.edu
NEIMAN, Sabrina .... 406-477-6215 262 F
NEINER, Catherine .... 404-413-1835 120 C cneiner1@gsu.edu
NEISES, Marlene .... 414-382-6017 490 G marlene.neises@alverno.edu
NEISES, Sarah .... 920-424-2147 495 C neises@uwosh.edu
NEISLER, Gretchen .... 865-974-3177 426 C gneisler@utk.edu
NEITZEL, Kathy .... 920-565-1000 492 A neitzelk@lakeland.edu
NEITZEL, Lynn .... 608-743-4508 497 D lneitzel@blackhawk.edu
NEITZEL, Margaret .... 206-296-2332 483 B fielderm@seattleu.edu
NELANT, Dan .... 317-805-1788 486 I dan.nelant@salemu.edu
NELEN, Carla .... 814-886-6411 390 E cnelen@mtaloy.edu
NELHUEBEL, Robin, M . 757-240-2200 469 F robin.nelhuebel@rivhs.com
NELKENBAUM, Avrohom Yaakov .... 718-645-0536 306 F nelk@thejnet.com
NELL, Sharon, D .... 512-448-8620 441 N sharonn@stedwards.edu
NELLE, Nora .... 215-517-2659 378 E nellen@arcadia.edu
NELLER, Irene .... 805-565-6016.. 75 I ineller@westmont.edu
NELLESEN, Gary .... 909-274-4850.. 52 K gnellesen@mtsac.edu
NELLIS, Ginny .... 802-258-3283 462 B ginny.nellis@worldlearning.org
NELLIS, Leah .... 765-455-9441 156 E lmnellis@iu.edu
NELMS, Jalete .... 205-226-4981.... 5 A jjnelms@bsc.edu
NELMS, Kristi .... 217-854-5594 133 F kristi.nelms@blackburn.edu
NELMS, Lauren .... 757-455-3352 476 C lnelms@vwu.edu
NELONS, Dee .... 253-680-7143 477 A dnelons@batestech.edu
NELSEN, Jeff, A .... 515-574-1115 166 G nelsen@iowacentral.edu
NELSEN, Kyle .... 402-375-7274 267 I kynelse1@wsc.edu
NELSEN, Melissa .... 402-375-7209 267 I menelse1@wsc.edu
NELSEN, Robert, S .... 916-278-7737.. 33 A nelsen@csus.edu
NELSON, Adam .... 781-239-2664 214 E anelson@massbay.edu
NELSON, Alex .... 310-233-4312.. 49 F nelsonaw@lahc.edu
NELSON, Allan .... 302-857-1707.. 90 H anelso11@dtcc.edu
NELSON, Andrew .... 515-433-5020 164 F adnelson@dmacc.edu
NELSON, Andy .... 712-274-5148 168 C nelsona@morningside.edu
NELSON, Angela .... 414-955-4708 492 F annelson@mcw.edu
NELSON, Annella .... 318-675-7013 189 D annella.nelson@lsuhs.edu
NELSON, Anthony, C .... 919-530-6175 341 D acnelson@nccu.edu
NELSON, April .... 580-477-7896 371 D april.nelson@wosc.edu
NELSON, Ben .... 415-649-7658.. 52 F
NELSON, Beth .... 281-756-3509 428 E bnelson@alvincollege.edu
NELSON, Brandi .... 701-662-1509 346 A brandi.nelson@lrsc.edu
NELSON, Breck .... 618-664-7111 138 D breck.nelson@greenville.edu
NELSON, Brent .... 239-489-9039 100 G bnelson@fsw.edu
NELSON, Brian .... 612-381-3042 235 C bnelson@dunwoody.edu
NELSON, Camille .... 808-956-6363 129 B nelsonca@hawaii.edu
NELSON, Carol .... 909-274-5431.. 52 K cnelson@mtsac.edu
NELSON, Cassidy .... 678-839-6426 127 A cassidy@westga.edu
NELSON, Chris .... 701-777-2786 344 H chris.nelson@und.edu
NELSON, Christopher .... 757-388-2900 469 H cnelson@sentara.edu
NELSON, Christopher ... 956-872-6715 443 B cnelson@southtexascollege.edu
NELSON, Daniel .... 651-638-6241 233 J dc-nelson@bethel.edu
NELSON, David .... 704-637-4414 327 H davidnelson@catawba.edu

NELSON, David .... 312-662-4151 132 D
dnelson@adler.edu
NELSON, David .... 352-733-1700 110 E
nelsodr@ufl.edu
NELSON, Denise .... 619-849-2477.. 57 J
denisenelson@pointloma.edu
NELSON, Dexter .... 405-208-5000 367 E
danelson@okcu.edu
NELSON, Diane .... 415-422-2444.. 72 I
dlnelson3@usfca.edu
NELSON, Dirk .... 806-651-3501 447 D
jdnelson@wtamu.edu
NELSON, Douglas .... 909-869-3419.. 30 B
dnelson1@cpp.edu
NELSON, Eboni, S .... 860-570-5127.. 89 B
eboni.nelson@uconn.edu
NELSON, Eric .... 805-565-6003.. 75 I
enelson@westmont.edu
NELSON, Eric .... 267-341-3205 385 I
enelson@holyfamily.edu
NELSON, Evelyn, C 561-237-7816 103W
enelson@lynn.edu
NELSON, Fred .... 605-642-6848 415 F
fred.nelson@bhsu.edu
NELSON, Gena, C .... 315-267-2330 318 D
nelsongc@potsdam.edu
NELSON, Glen .... 208-282-3540 131 E
nelsglen@isu.edu
NELSON, Glen .... 831-582-3397.. 32 D
gnelson@csumb.edu
NELSON, Greg .... 415-884-3100.. 39 B
gnelson@marin.edu
NELSON, Gwynth, R ...... 803-536-8767 410 H
gnelson3@scsu.edu
NELSON, Hart .... 314-539-5311 258 C
hartnelson@stlcc.edu
NELSON, Holly .... 503-399-5145 372 A
holly.nelson@chemeketa.edu
NELSON, James .... 816-584-6548 257 E
james.nelson@park.edu
NELSON, James, H .... 606-693-5000 182 H
jnelson@kmbc.edu
NELSON, Jamie .... 360-442-2134 480 E
jrnelson@lowercolumbia.edu
NELSON, Janet .... 703-632-1976 501 J
NELSON, Jay .... 763-576-4054 236 H
jnelson@anokatech.edu
NELSON, Jay .... 763-576-4054 237 A
jnelson@anokatech.edu
NELSON, Jeff .... 218-235-2193 238 D
jeff.nelson@minnesotanorth.edu
NELSON, Jennifer .... 770-975-4000 116 H
jnelson@chattahoocheetech.edu
NELSON, Jesselyn .... 517-355-6560 227 C
nelso343@msu.edu
NELSON, Jessica .... 801-585-5950 459 D
jessica.nelson@utah.edu
NELSON, Jillian .... 309-438-2592 140 C
jyoun11@ilstu.edu
NELSON, Jim .... 479-619-2282.. 20 G
jnelson3@nwacc.edu
NELSON, Jim .... 304-327-4000 488 J
jnelson@bluefieldstate.edu
NELSON, Joan .... 713-348-4759 441 K
joan.m.nelson@rice.edu
NELSON, Johnathan, K . 606-783-5158 183 H
j.nelson@moreheadstate.edu
NELSON, Karen .... 706-419-1288 117 G
karen.nelson@covenant.edu
NELSON, Karen .... 724-653-2191 382 C
knelson@dec.edu
NELSON, Karen .... 901-751-8453 420 G
NELSON, Karen, L .... 617-585-0200 206 E
karen.nelson@the-bac.edu
NELSON, Karson .... 252-744-3784 340 H
nelsonkars21@ecu.edu
NELSON, Kathleen .... 973-684-6333 279 B
knelson@pccc.edu
NELSON, Kathy .... 937-328-6006 350 D
nelsonk@clarkstate.edu
NELSON, Kim .... 701-671-2131 346 B
kim.j.nelson@ndscs.edu
NELSON, Kim .... 507-433-0664 240 A
kimberly.nelson@riverland.edu
NELSON, Kimberly .... 410-951-3816 203 E
kinelson@coppin.edu
NELSON, Kirk .... 225-768-1793 186 H
timothy.nelson@franu.edu
NELSON, Kristy .... 989-686-9422 223 E
kristynelson@delta.edu
NELSON, KT .... 531-622-2739 266 G
ktnelson@mccneb.edu

NELSON, Kurt, D .... 570-577-1183 379 A
kurt.nelson@bucknell.edu
NELSON, Lindsey, C ...... 207-859-4622 194 B
lindsey.nelson@colby.edu
NELSON, Lisa .... 570-740-0732 388 G
lnelson@luzerne.edu
NELSON, Louis .... 434-924-3728 471 F
ln6n@virginia.edu
NELSON, Louise, C ...... 310-206-1355.. 69 D
lnelson@conet.ucla.edu
NELSON, Maisie .... 606-546-1583 185 B
mnelson@unionky.edu
NELSON, Mandy .... 208-426-1294 130 F
mandynelson@boisestate.edu
NELSON, Margaret .... 718-289-5608 292 H
margaret.nelson@bcc.cuny.edu
NELSON, Mark .... 607-255-8791 297 D
mwn2@cornell.edu
NELSON, Mark .... 218-646-3756 238 K
mark.nelson@minnesota.edu
NELSON, Mark .... 303-797-5654.. 77 H
mark.nelson@arapahoe.edu
NELSON, Mark .... 252-940-6213 332 A
mark.nelson@beaufortccc.edu
NELSON, Matt .... 425-889-5331 481 A
matt.nelson@northwestu.edu
NELSON, Michele .... 973-313-6053 282 K
michele.nelson@shu.edu
NELSON, Michele .... 262-691-5520 499 A
mnelson58@wctc.edu
NELSON, Michelle .... 262-691-3484 499 A
mnelson63@wctc.edu
NELSON, Mike .... 256-765-4440.... 8 E
mnelson7@una.edu
NELSON, Nancy .... 414-227-3123 495 B
nln@uwm.edu
NELSON, Paul .... 630-829-6000 133 B
NELSON, Peter, C .... 312-996-3259 151 D
nelson@uic.edu
NELSON, Phil .... 909-469-5661.. 75 G
pnelson@westernu.edu
NELSON, Randy .... 605-575-6585 416 C
randy.nelson@usiouxfalls.edu
NELSON, Rencelly .... 691-320-2480 503 B
rencelly@comfsm.fm
NELSON, Rhonda, L ...... 701-788-4208 345 B
rhonda.nelson@mayvillestate.edu
NELSON, Ryan .... 218-477-5869 239 A
ryan.nelson@mnstate.edu
NELSON, Sandra .... 717-901-5117 385 G
snelson@harrisburgu.edu
NELSON, Sandra, H ...... 773-256-0676 143 C
sandra.nelson@lstc.edu
NELSON, Sarah .... 715-425-3500 496 A
sarah.nelson@uwrf.edu
NELSON, Sasha .... 970-682-1118.. 78 P
sasha.nelson@cncc.edu
NELSON, Scott Bernard 503-883-2498 373 E
scott.nelson@linfield.edu
NELSON, Sean .... 608-262-1311 494 C
snelson@uwsa.edu
NELSON, Seth .... 757-560-0040 408 F
seth.nelson@erskine.edu
NELSON, Shad .... 361-593-2454 447 A
shad.nelson@tamuk.edu
NELSON, Shannan .... 605-274-5330 413 G
shannan.nelson@augie.edu
NELSON, Stacy .... 707-965-6221.. 55 H
snelson@puc.edu
NELSON, Steve .... 504-568-4009 189 C
snelso1@lsuhsc.edu
NELSON, Steven .... 201-692-2477 276 I
snelson@fdu.edu
NELSON, Susie .... 503-375-7117 372 G
snelson@corban.edu
NELSON, Suzanne .... 267-502-2482 378 I
suzanne.nelson@brynathyn.edu
NELSON, Suzy .... 617-253-8566 215 G
NELSON, Tammy .... 207-768-2747 195 C
tnelson@nmcc.edu
NELSON, Tim .... 301-891-4046 204 D
tnelson@wau.edu
NELSON, Tony .... 931-372-3234 425 B
tnelson@tntech.edu
NELSON, Trista .... 269-294-4293 223 J
tnelson@glenoaks.edu
NELSON, Veronica .... 775-289-3589 270 G
veronica.nelson@gbcnv.edu
NELSON, W. Ken .... 909-558-7658.. 48 J
knelson@llu.edu
NELSON, Wesley .... 704-461-6545 326 I
wesleynelson@bac.edu

NELSON, Wilbert .... 602-285-7174.. 13 H
wilbert.nelson@phoenixcollege.edu
NELSON, William, L ...... 800-867-2243.. 55 C
wnelson@pacific-college.edu
NELSON FISHER, Anne . 218-855-8221 237 C
anne.nelsonfisher@clcmn.edu
NELSON MOELLER,
Rachel .... 610-330-5810 387 B
moellerr@lafayette.edu
NELSON NASH, Denise 909-607-7180.. 63 E
dnelnash@scrippscollege.edu
NELSON WINGER,
Elyse .... 617-627-6024 219 A
elyse.nelson_winger@tufts.edu
NEMAZIE, Dave .... 410-228-9250 203 A
nemazie@umces.edu
NEMBHARD, Harriet ...... 319-335-5766 163 F
harriet-nembhard@uiowa.edu
NEMEC, Mark, R .... 203-254-4000.. 87 G
mnemec@fairfield.edu
NEMECZ, Attila .... 252-940-6387 332 A
attila.nemecz@beaufortccc.edu
NEMELKA, Ian .... 435-797-1000 459 F
ian.nemelka@usu.edu
NEMER, Robert, J .... 330-972-7442 361 G
rjn@uakron.edu
NEMETI, Jami .... 417-862-9533 252 H
jnemeti@globaluniversity.edu
NEMIRE, Ruth, E .... 305-760-7500 103 V
NEMITZ, James, W .... 304-647-6200 489 C
jnemitz@osteo.wvsom.edu
NEPIL, John .... 303-282-3423.. 83 E
father.nepil@archden.org
NEPPER, Terry, S .... 806-651-2747 447 D
tnepper@wtamu.edu
NEPPL, Susan .... 952-885-5387 241 P
sneppl@nwhealth.edu
NEPTUNE, Miriam .... 212-854-0408 290 H
mneptune@barnard.edu
NEPTUNE RIVERA,
Vivian .... 787-999-9531 511 F
vneptune@law.upr.edu
NERE, Jeremy .... 715-394-8306 496 D
jnere@uwsuper.edu
NERGER, Janice, L .... 970-491-6974.. 79 E
janice.nerger@colostate.edu
NERIA, Angela .... 620-235-4603 176 H
aneria@pittstate.edu
NERIANI, Kelly .... 937-328-6075 350 D
nerianik@clarkstate.edu
NERO, Christopher .... 701-228-5461 345 G
christopher.nero@dakotacollege.edu
NERONHA, Christopher 401-865-2774 403 G
cneronha@providence.edu
NESBARY, Dale, K .... 231-777-0311 228 C
dale.nesbary@muskegoncc.edu
NESBIT, Jim .... 937-298-3399 354 J
jim.nesbit@kc.edu
NESBIT, Ryan, A .... 706-542-1361 126 F
rnesbit@uga.edu
NESBIT, Vanessa, D .... 302-857-6351.. 90 D
vnesbit@desu.edu
NESBITT, Chris .... 704-216-3756 337 C
chris.nesbitt@rccc.edu
NESBITT, Joan .... 414-229-3013 495 B
nesbitjm@uwm.edu
NESBITT, Joan, M .... 573-341-4111 260 F
nesbittj@mst.edu
NESBITT, Mason .... 661-362-2360.. 51 E
mnesbitt@masters.edu
NESBITT, Sean .... 970-945-8691.. 78 H
NESBITT, Shawna .... 214-648-2168 456 D
shawna.nesbitt@utsouthwestern.edu
NESBITT, Stephanie, R .. 315-792-5292 323 G
srnesbit@utica.edu
NESBITT, Thomas .... 518-244-4623 312 D
nesbit@sage.edu
NESBY, Robin .... 718-951-5000 293 A
NESHEIM, Jeff .... 303-797-5075.. 77 H
jeffrey.nesheim@arapahoe.edu
NESHEIM-KAUFFMAN,
Rhonda, K .... 641-422-4232 168 E
rhonda.nesheim-kauffman@niacc.edu
NESMITH, Mark, A .... 304-326-1473 486 I
mnesmith@salemu.edu
NESS, Claudia, L .... 509-527-5040 485 C
nesscl@whitman.edu
NESS, Deborah .... 708-209-3115 136 D
deb.ness@cuchicago.edu
NESS, Eric .... 570-389-4000 393 E
eness@bloomu.edu
NESS, Eric .... 570-389-4517 393 E
eness@bloomu.edu

NESS, Jaclyn .... 414-288-4464 492 E
jaclyn.ness@marquette.edu
NESS, Melvin, M .... 646-565-6015 322 B
melvin.ness@touro.edu
NESS, Mevin, M .... 646-565-6015 322 C
melvin.ness@touro.edu
NESS, Phil .... 419-448-2384 353 D
philness@heidelberg.edu
NESS, Shanda .... 323-259-2500.. 54 I
sness@oxy.edu
NESSELBUSH, Danielle . 716-829-8337 298 C
nesselbd@dyc.edu
NESSELRODE, Brian ...... 904-819-6206.. 99 D
bness@flagler.edu
NESTER, Joel .... 434-791-7252 463 L
jnester@averett.edu
NESTER, Keri .... 912-583-3287 116 D
knester@bpc.edu
NESTER, Michael .... 856-227-7200 275 F
mnester@camdencc.edu
NESTER, Stefanie, E ...... 610-799-1740 388 B
snester2@lccc.edu
NESTOR, David, A .... 802-656-3380 462 D
david.nestor@uvm.edu
NESTOR, Mark .... 617-573-8000 218 G
NESTOR, Mark .... 215-596-8910 400 B
m.nestor@usciences.edu
NESWICK, Judi .... 712-274-5178 168 C
neswickj@morningside.edu
NETHERCOTT, Nancy ..... 904-264-2172 106 K
NETHERTON, James, S . 478-301-2710 122 C
netherton_js@mercer.edu
NETLAND, John, T .... 731-661-5355 425 F
jnetland@uu.edu
NETTER, Matt .... 973-618-3605 275 E
mnetter@caldwell.edu
NETTLES, Evelyn .... 615-963-7004 425 A
enettles1@tnstate.edu
NETTLES, Lafawn .... 270-384-8170 183 D
nettlesl@lindsey.edu
NETTLES, Lindsey, M .... 843-953-5254 406 D
lnettles@citadel.edu
NETTLES, Stephen .... 858-513-9240.. 16 I
stephen.nettles@ashford.edu
NETTLETON, Kim .... 606-783-2337 183 H
k.nettleton@moreheadstate.edu
NETZER, Michael .... 443-840-4777 198 D
mnetzer@ccbcmd.edu
NETZHAMMER, Mel ...... 360-546-9581 484 D
mel.netzhammer@vancouver.wsu.edu
NEU, Denise .... 281-290-2621 438 E
denise.neu@lonestar.edu
NEUBAUER, Janelle ...... 484-664-3120 390 F
janelleneubauer@muhlenberg.edu
NEUBAUER, Jennifer ...... 217-333-1471 151 C
jln5@illinois.edu
NEUBERGER,
Boruch, Y .... 443-548-6060 201 B
byn@nirc.edu
NEUBRANDER,
Johanna .... 423-354-5106 424 B
jlneubrander@northeaststate.edu
NEUBRANDER, Judy ..... 309-438-2174 140 C
jlneubr@ilstu.edu
NEUBRANDER, Leanna . 407-303-7753.. 95 A
leanna.neubrander@ahu.edu
NEUENDORF, Andrew ... 515-964-6270 164 F
ajneuendorf@dmacc.edu
NEUENSCHWANDER,
Mary .... 610-606-4609 380 C
mary.neuenschwander@cedarcrest.edu
NEUFELD, Iris .... 419-358-3322 348 E
neufeldi@bluffton.edu
NEUFELD, Kenley .... 805-965-0581.. 62 M
neufeld@sbcc.edu
NEUFELDT, Ellen, J ...... 760-750-4040.. 33 C
pres@csusm.edu
NEUFIND, Nate .... 402-399-2658 265 H
nneufind@csm.edu
NEUHARD, Ian .... 904-632-3030 101 A
ineuhard@fscj.edu
NEUHAUSER, Crystal .... 603-899-1159 272 G
neuhauserc@franklinpierce.edu
NEUHOLD-RAVIKUMAR,
Patti .... 405-974-2311 370 H
pneuhold@uco.edu
NEUMAN, Dave .... 267-341-3642 385 I
dneuman10@holyfamily.edu
NEUMAN, Kevin .... 715-346-3875 496 B
kneuman@uwsp.edu
NEUMAN, Yisroel .... 732-367-1060 275 B
NEUMANN, Bruce .... 262-691-5226 499 A
bneumann6@wctc.edu

NGUYEN, Vannee, C ..... 850-474-2175 111 E
vcao@uwf.edu
NGWAFU, Peter .... 229-500-2279 114 F
peter.ngwafu@asurams.edu
NHIRA, Tafadzwa .... 410-238-9000.. 93 H
NICA, Claude .... 310-665-6870.. 55 B
cnica@otis.edu
NICE, Jason .... 530-898-3276.. 31 A
jnice@csuchico.edu
NICE-WEBB, Kiva .... 573-592-6213 261 F
kiva.webb@westminster-mo.edu
NICELY, Kathleen .... 415-864-7326.. 61 E
knicely@sfcm.edu
NICELY, Nancy .... 303-871-4948.. 84 C
nancy.nicely@du.edu
NICELY, Nancy .... 303-871-4848.. 84 C
nancy.nicely@du.edu
NICELY, Tim .... 540-453-2371 472 F
nicelyt@brcc.edu
NICHOL, Charlene .... 330-672-2210 354 A
cnicho22@kent.edu
NICHOL, Kristi .... 816-654-7107 253 I
knichol@kcumb.edu
NICHOLAS, Angela .... 434-961-5245 474 B
anicholas@pvcc.edu
NICHOLAS, David, R ..... 530-221-4275.. 63 G
sbcadm@shasta.edu
NICHOLAS, Donna, R ... 530-221-4275.. 63 G
donna@shasta.edu
NICHOLAS, Jason .... 906-227-2379 228 E
janichol@nmu.edu
NICHOLAS, Jim .... 530-895-6154.. 27 F
nicholaswi@butte.edu
NICHOLAS, Jonah .... 925-485-5253.. 35 P
jnicholas@clpccd.org
NICHOLAS, Kedrick .... 337-475-5610 192 B
knicholas@mcneese.edu
NICHOLAS, Kutchak, D . 202-685-3835 501 I
nicholas.d.kutchak.civ@ndu.edu
NICHOLAS, Marc .... 334-556-2223.... 2 C
mnicholas@wallace.edu
NICHOLAS, Mark .... 508-626-4670 212 D
mnicholas1@framingham.edu
NICHOLAS-EDWARDS,
Brenita .... 740-392-6868 356 G
brenita.nicholas@mvnu.edu
NICHOLES, Miriam .... 312-369-8576 136 C
mnicholes@colum.edu
NICHOLL, Matthew .... 617-266-1400 206 D
pwd@berklee.edu
NICHOLLS, Gregory, K .. 610-660-1090 397 A
gnicholl@sju.edu
NICHOLLS, Jennifer ...... 802-383-6608 461 C
jnicholls@champlain.edu
NICHOLS, Aaron, F .... 802-656-3425 462 D
aaron.nichols@uvm.edu
NICHOLS, Andrew, W ... 808-956-8965 129 B
nicholsa@hawaii.edu
NICHOLS, Becky .... 816-501-2428 249 H
rebecca.nichols@avila.edu
NICHOLS, Brian .... 859-257-3609 185 D
bnichols@uky.edu
NICHOLS, Carolee .... 910-843-5304 330 F
carolee.rhea@gmail.com
NICHOLS, Daniel .... 202-885-2534.. 91 D
dnichols@american.edu
NICHOLS, Denise .... 757-727-5221 466 L
denise.nichols@hamptonu.edu
NICHOLS, Eric .... 410-617-2000 199 G
ernichols@loyola.edu
NICHOLS, III, George ... 610-526-1301 378 D
george.nichols@theamericancollege.edu
NICHOLS, Gregory, A ... 785-309-3182 177 B
greg.nichols@salinatech.edu
NICHOLS, Jason .... 708-656-8000 145 B
NICHOLS, Jennifer .... 704-922-6231 334 E
nichols.jennifer@gaston.edu
NICHOLS, Jim .... 434-592-3655 467 E
jmnichols1@liberty.edu
NICHOLS, Jody .... 715-425-3982 496 A
jody.nichols@uwrf.edu
NICHOLS, Joel, A .... 651-962-5000 243 F
NICHOLS, Jonothan .... 801-524-1991 458 F
jon.nichols@ensign.edu
NICHOLS, Keegan .... 479-968-0276.. 18 E
knichols@atu.edu
NICHOLS, Kelly .... 205-934-4488.... 8 A
nicholsk@uab.edu
NICHOLS, Lanell .... 325-942-2012 450 B
lanell.nichols@angelo.edu
NICHOLS, Laurie .... 805-437-8425.. 30 D
laurie.nichols@csuci.edu
NICHOLS, Laurie .... 605-642-6111 415 F
laurie.nichols@bhsu.edu
NICHOLS, Lesley .... 617-824-8281 208 G
lesley_nichols@emerson.edu
NICHOLS, Linda .... 337-482-6491 192 F
linda.nichols@louisiana.edu
NICHOLS, Linda .... 307-268-2220 499 T
lnichols@caspercollege.edu
NICHOLS, Nichole .... 636-227-2100 254 C
NICHOLS, Pat .... 805-421-5937.. 67 J
pnichols@thomasaquinas.edu
NICHOLS, Randall .... 207-725-3474 194 A
rnichols@bowdoin.edu
NICHOLS, Reginald .... 781-280-3536 214 G
NICHOLS, Richard .... 903-510-2200 451 D
richard.nichols@tjc.edu
NICHOLS, Ronald .... 540-674-3639 473 F
rnichols@nr.edu
NICHOLS, Sam .... 501-450-1340.. 19 I
nichols@hendrix.edu
NICHOLS, Shane .... 847-866-3866 138 B
shane.nichols@garrett.edu
NICHOLS, Sheila .... 850-484-1428 105 G
snichols@pensacolastate.edu
NICHOLS, Steve .... 417-269-3045 251 G
steve.nichols@coxcollege.edu
NICHOLS, Teresa .... 904-620-2100 111 A
teresa.nichols@unf.edu
NICHOLS, Teresa .... 620-229-0012 177 D
teresa.nichols@sckans.edu
NICHOLS, Timothy .... 406-243-2541 263 D
timothy.nichols@umontana.edu
NICHOLS, Tracy .... 940-397-4277 439 F
tracy.nichols@msutexas.edu
NICHOLS, Warren .... 409-933-8271 432 H
wnichols@com.edu
NICHOLS, William .... 724-847-6544 384 B
wjnichol@geneva.edu
NICHOLSON,
Ann-Henley .... 609-497-3673 279 D
NICHOLSON, Ashley ..... 203-332-5013.. 86 E
anicholson@commnet.edu
NICHOLSON, Debra .... 620-276-9575 173 H
debra.nicholson@gcccks.edu
NICHOLSON, Emily .... 518-485-3818 296 E
nicholse@strose.edu
NICHOLSON, Eugene ..... 919-516-4000 339 G
enicholas@st-aug.edu
NICHOLSON,
Jacqueline .... 585-475-2615 312 A
jknatle@rit.edu
NICHOLSON, Jennifer ... 904-264-2172 106 K
susan.massey@iws.edu
NICHOLSON, Judd .... 202-687-4402.. 92 D
nicholsonj@georgetown.edu
NICHOLSON, Karen .... 718-862-7374 304 K
karen.nicholson@manhattan.edu
NICHOLSON, Kim .... 765-677-2131 157 F
kim.nicholson@indwes.edu
NICHOLSON, Kristal ...... 903-875-7361 439 G
kristal.nicholson@navarrocollege.edu
NICHOLSON, Marie .... 828-689-1151 330 H
mnicholson@mhu.edu
NICHOLSON, Molly .... 704-878-4362 335 I
mnicholson@mitchellcc.edu
NICHOLSON, Robin .... 319-235-3516 163 A
robin.nicholson@unitypoint.org
NICHOLSON, Sylvia ...... 336-517-2102 326 J
snicholson@bennett.edu
NICHOLSON, Tim .... 828-835-4261 338 C
tnicholson@tricountycc.edu
NICHOLSON, Vickie .... 251-578-1313.... 3 D
vickien@rstc.edu
NICHOLSON, Wendy ..... 718-482-5140 294 D
wnicholson@lagcc.cuny.edu
NICHOLSON-SWEVAL,
Fedearia, A .... 330-972-5899 361 G
fn@uakron.edu
NICK, Sara, J .... 715-833-6275 497 E
snick1@cvtc.edu
NICKEL, Graig .... 785-864-9525 177 G
g491n194@ku.edu
NICKEL, Jamie .... 866-766-0331.. 54 E
jnickel@ncu.edu
NICKELL, Ashley .... 434-947-8029 469 A
anickell@randolphcollege.edu
NICKELL, Barbara, J ..... 785-833-4390 175 C
bmarsh@kwu.edu
NICKELL, Christopher ... 937-433-3410 352 G
NICKELL, Jane Ellen ...... 814-332-2800 378 A
jnickell@allegheny.edu
NICKELL, Julie .... 713-798-4951 430 E
nickell@bcm.edu
NICKELL, Roberta .... 620-901-6214 171 A
nickell@allencc.edu
NICKELL, Tom .... 314-574-3104 147 B
tom.nickell@principia.edu
NICKELS, Ken .... 309-796-5048 133 D
nickelsk@bhc.edu
NICKELS, Lisa .... 415-503-6231.. 61 E
lnickels@sfcm.edu
NICKELS, Taylor .... 844-922-8228.. 91 E
NICKENS, Tawanna .... 217-351-2390 146 G
tnickens@parkland.edu
NICKERSON, Becky .... 402-280-3118 265 J
beckynickerson@creighton.edu
NICKERSON, Floyd, W .. 972-599-3159 432 I
fnickerson@collin.edu
NICKERSON, Jon .... 607-587-4750 319 C
nickerjd@alfredstate.edu
NICKERSON, Lauren ..... 559-278-4240.. 31 D
NICKERSON, Matt .... 435-865-1955 459 E
nickerson@suu.edu
NICKERSON, Molly .... 660-284-4800 253 F
NICKERSON, Nathaniel . 203-432-1345.. 90 B
nathaniel.nickerson@yale.edu
NICKERSON, Sherita ..... 325-674-6802 427 G
sherita.nickerson@acu.edu
NICKITAS, Donna .... 856-225-2248 281 A
snc-dean@rutgers.edu
NICKLAUS, Mark, B ...... 920-748-8186 493 J
nicklausm@ripon.edu
NICKLAUS, Megan .... 719-389-6424.. 78 E
mnicklaus@coloradocollege.edu
NICKLE, Mary Anne ...... 641-236-2202 167 C
maryanne.nickle@iavalley.edu
NICKLESS, Peter .... 315-568-3310 309 H
pnickless@northeastcollege.edu
NICKLOW, John, W .... 504-280-6723 189 F
president@uno.edu
NICKNAIR-KEON, Julie . 603-526-3621 271 H
julie.nicknairkeon@colby-sawyer.edu
NICKODEMUS, Matt ...... 435-652-7542 459 G
matt.nickodemus@utahtech.edu
NICKOLS, Sharon .... 217-333-6677 151 F
nickrich@illinois.edu
NICKS, Leanna .... 336-841-9313 329 E
lnicks@highpoint.edu
NICKSA, Gary, W .... 617-353-2290 207 C
nicksa@bu.edu
NICOL, Amanda .... 419-434-5928 362 D
amanda.nicol@findlay.edu
NICOL, Patricia .... 617-824-8123 208 G
patricia_nicol@emerson.edu
NICOLA, Ramani .... 305-273-4499.. 96 I
ramani.nicola@cbt.edu
NICOLAI, Michael .... 312-629-9411 149 B
mnicolai@saic.edu
NICOLET, Todd .... 919-962-3192 342 B
todd_nicolet@unc.edu
NICOLETTI, Marian .... 585-475-7298 312 A
mmnadm@rit.edu
NICOLOV, Pressian .... 310-434-4765.. 63 B
nicolov_pressian@smc.edu
NICOSIA, Mark, A .... 610-499-4566 401 I
manicosia@widener.edu
NICOSIA, Patricia .... 830-703-4836 449 F
pnicosia@sulross.edu
NICOTERA, Phillip .... 713-718-7628 436 E
phillip.nicotera@hccs.edu
NICULESCU, Jeremy ...... 503-777-7560 375 F
niculescuj@reed.edu
NIDO, Nellie .... 407-823-5346 110 D
nellie.nido@ucf.edu
NIECE, Matthew .... 208-426-1604 130 F
matthewniece@boisestate.edu
NIEDERHAUSER,
Victoria .... 865-974-7584 426 C
vniederh@utk.edu
NIEDGE, Erin .... 406-874-6211 262 K
niedgee@milescc.edu
NIEDWIECKI,
Anthony, S .... 651-290-7510 241 N
anthony.niedwiecki@mitchellhamline.edu
NIEDZWIECKI, Michael . 718-933-6700 306 J
mniedzwiedi@monroecollege.edu
NIEHAUS, John, D .... 608-342-7658 495 E
niehausjo@uwplatt.edu
NIEHAUS, Paige .... 813-253-7260 102 A
pniehaus@hccfl.edu
NIEKRO, Catherine .... 828-328-7360 330 B
cat.niekro@lr.edu
NIELSEN, Cody .... 717-245-1931 382 B
nielsenc@dickinson.edu
NIELSEN, David .... 860-512-3108.. 86 F
dnielsen@manchestercc.edu
NIELSEN, Glenn .... 314-505-7201 251 D
nielseng@csl.edu
NIELSEN, Jason .... 831-459-3457.. 71 A
jnielsen@ucsc.edu
NIELSEN, Kelly, A .... 920-748-8852 493 J
nielsenk@ripon.edu
NIELSEN, Leila .... 651-493-3622 233 F
campusdirector@acupunctureschoolusa.com
NIELSEN, Lisa .... 831-459-4344.. 71 A
lmnielse@ucsc.edu
NIELSEN, Mary, F .... 414-277-7216 493 D
nielsen@msoe.edu
NIELSEN, Melore .... 206-220-8040 483 B
admissions@seattleu.edu
NIELSEN, Melore .... 206-296-2000 483 B
mnielsen@seattleu.edu
NIELSEN, Paul, D .... 412-268-7740 380 B
nielsen@sei.cmu.edu
NIELSEN, Richard, P ..... 801-375-5125 459 A
rick.nielsen@rm.edu
NIELSEN, Scott .... 775-327-2098 270 G
scott.nielsen@gbcnv.edu
NIELSON, Eric .... 208-732-6267 131 B
enielson@csi.edu
NIELSON, Kathy .... 978-837-5000 216 D
NIELSON, Lauren .... 770-426-2832 122 A
lauren.nielsen@life.edu
NIELSON, Robert .... 435-283-7037 460 C
rob.nielson@snow.edu
NIEMAN, Donald .... 607-777-2070 315 E
dnieman@binghamton.edu
NIEMAN, James .... 773-256-0728 143 C
jnieman@lstc.edu
NIEMAN, Paul .... 818-710-4121.. 49 H
niemanp@piercecollege.edu
NIEMANN, Jessica .... 402-552-3325 265 G
niemannjessica@clarksoncollege.edu
NIEMEIER, Brian .... 951-552-8637.. 27 J
bniemeier@calbaptist.edu
NIEMEYER, Heath .... 661-654-3579.. 30 C
hniemeyer@csub.edu
NIEMEYER, Wendy .... 620-331-4100 174 E
wniemeyer@indycc.edu
NIEMI, Nancy .... 508-626-4575 212 D
nniemi@framingham.edu
NIEMIEC, Brian .... 724-805-2457 397 C
brian.niemiec@stvincent.edu
NIEMIEC, Brian .... 724-805-2457 397 D
brian.niemiec@stvincent.edu
NIEMIEC, Catherine .... 602-274-1885.. 15 C
cniemiec@pihma.edu
NIEMIEC, Kristin .... 414-955-8272 492 F
kniemiec@mcw.edu
NIENABER, Annie .... 718-780-7505 291 G
annie.nienaber@brooklaw.edu
NIERAETH, Nancy .... 253-879-3100 483 G
NIERMANN, Scott, K ...... 865-354-3000 424 D
niermannsk@roanestate.edu
NIES, Charles .... 209-228-7620.. 70 A
cnies@ucmerced.edu
NIESE, Vicki, J .... 419-772-2057 358 D
v-niese@onu.edu
NIESPO, Molly .... 630-617-3047 137 E
molly.niespo@elmhurst.edu
NIETO-PHILLIPS, John .. 812-855-2076 156 C
jnietoph@indiana.edu
NIETSCHE, Nichole .... 802-387-6711 461 E
registrar@landmark.edu
NIEUWENHUIS,
Michelle .... 520-206-2692.. 15 E
mnieuwenhuis@pima.edu
NIEVES, Danily .... 787-882-2065 508 N
NIEVES, Deborah, E ...... 787-850-9303 511 B
deborah.nieves1@upr.edu
NIEVES, Gladys, T .... 787-765-3560 505 H
gnieves@edpuniversity.edu
NIEVES, Ivette .... 787-279-1912 506 L
inieves@bayamon.inter.edu
NIEVES, Maggie .... 440-775-5579 357 G
maggie.nieves@oberlin.edu
NIEVES, Reynaldo .... 787-766-1717 509 C
rnieves@uagm.edu
NIEVES, Yolanda .... 787-856-0845 505 B
ynieves@columbiacentral.edu
NIEVES GARCIA,
Daulan .... 787-720-4476 509 G
NIEVES OSLÁN,
Lisa, M .... 787-250-0000 510 B
lisa.nieves@upr.edu

NOORI, Edris .... 315-866-0300 301 B
nooried@herkimer.edu
NORCIA MARSHALL, Lisa .... 201-200-2335 278 F
lnorcia@njcu.edu
NORCINI, Heather .... 610-341-5890 383 A
hnorcini@eastern.edu
NORCROSS, Celia .... 413-236-1601 213 E
cnorcross@berkshirecc.edu
NORCROSS, Craig .... 215-489-2276 381 K
craig.norcross@delval.edu
NORCROSS, Paul, W ..... 315-464-4361 316 F
norcrossp@upstate.edu
NORCROSS, William ...... 413-662-5529 212 F
william.norcross@mcla.edu
NORD, Elonda .... 701-662-1513 346 A
elonda.nord@lrsc.edu
NORD, Elonda .... 701-665-4639 346 A
elonda.nord@lrsc.edu
NORDBERG, Erik .... 731-881-7070 426 E
enordber@utm.edu
NORDBY, Chelsea .... 503-847-2619 377 A
cnordby@uws.edu
NORDBY, Shawn .... 402-461-5344 266 E
snordby@marylanning.org
NORDEEN, Mark .... 307-855-2140 499 U
mark.nordeen@cwc.edu
NORDICK, Pat .... 218-299-6821 238 K
pat.nordick@minnesota.edu
NORDIN, Becky .... 612-659-6712 238 C
becky.nordin@minneapolis.edu
NORDIN, Thom .... 763-433-1424 236 H
thom.nordin@anokaramsey.edu
NORDLAND, Jeffrey ...... 585-245-5606 317 E
nordland@geneseo.edu
NORDMANN, Andrea .... 817-257-5520 447 H
a.nordmann@tcu.edu
NORDONE, Ronald .... 610-282-1100 382 A
ronald.nordone@desales.edu
NORDSTROM, Amanda . 906-524-8111 225 G
anordstrom@kbocc.edu
NORDSTROM, Autumn .. 540-362-6332 467 A
nordstromam@hollins.edu
NORDSTROM, Steve ..... 615-966-5002 420 B
steve.nordstrom@lipscomb.edu
NORDT, Lee, C .... 254-710-3361 430 F
lee_nordt@baylor.edu
NORDYKE, Alan .... 660-543-4089 259 K
nordyke@ucmo.edu
NORELLI, Melinda, C ... 908-709-7509 283 E
melinda.norelli@ucc.edu
NOREN, Patricia .... 516-572-7396 307 C
patricia.noren@ncc.edu
NOREUIL, Margaret ...... 608-663-2820 491 F
mnoreuil@edgewood.edu
NORGARD, Kelsey .... 361-570-4869 452 C
norgardkn@uhv.edu
NORIEGA, David .... 619-876-4260.. 68 J
NORIN, Casandra .... 620-417-1161 177 C
casandra.norin@sccc.edu
NORISE, Hershey .... 773-602-5484 135 A
hnorise@ccc.edu
NORITA, Mark .... 760-750-4679.. 33 C
mnorita@csusm.edu
NORLAND, Gretchen ..... 785-227-3380 171 H
norlandg@bethanylb.edu
NORLEN, Tracy, C .... 206-281-2977 482 K
tcnorlen@spu.edu
NORLIEN, Cheryl, A ..... 320-222-5638 239 H
cheryl.norlien@ridgewater.edu
NORMAN, Antony .... 606-783-2002 183 H
adnorman@moreheadstate.edu
NORMAN, Carolyn .... 916-660-7202.. 64 B
cnorman6@sierracollege.edu
NORMAN, Cheryl, R ..... 651-631-5247 243 E
crnorman@unwsp.edu
NORMAN, David .... 903-813-2499 429 I
dnorman@austincollege.edu
NORMAN, Donald .... 559-453-2287.. 43 D
donald.norman@fresno.edu
NORMAN, Elizabeth ...... 325-670-1222 436 B
enorman@hsutx.edu
NORMAN, Emily .... 402-844-7151 268 A
enorman1@northeast.edu
NORMAN, Josh, L .... 217-581-6077 137 C
jlnorman@eiu.edu
NORMAN, Kathleen .... 918-540-6312 366 F
kathleen.norman@neo.edu
NORMAN, Linda .... 615-343-8876 427 B
linda.norman@vanderbilt.edu
NORMAN, Lindsay .... 706-236-2209 116 A
lnorman@berry.edu
NORMAN, Margie, A .... 903-813-2247 429 I
mnorman@austincollege.edu
NORMAN, Peter, E .... 815-599-3465 138 H
pete.norman@highland.edu
NORMAN, Rashawn ...... 775-784-6516 270 K
norman@unr.edu
NORMAN, Robert .... 701-858-3058 345 C
robert.norman.1@minotstateu.edu
NORMAN, Stan .... 870-759-4101.. 24 B
snorman@williamsbu.edu
NORMAN, Steve .... 719-549-2108.. 79 G
steve.norman@csupueblo.edu
NORMAN, Terry, W .... 608-796-3900 496 L
twnorman@viterbo.edu
NORMAN, Tom .... 507-389-1268 238 L
thomas.norman-1@mnsu.edu
NORMAN-MARZELLA, Nancy .... 410-287-1541 198 A
nnormormanmarzella@cecil.edu
NORMAND, Jason .... 318-427-4442 189 A
jason@lsua.edu
NORMANDIN, Karen ...... 207-453-5129 195 B
president@kvcc.me.edu
NORMANDY, Elizabeth .. 910-521-6180 343 A
elizabeth.normandy@uncp.edu
NORMANN, Karen, R .... 484-664-3496 390 F
karennormann@muhlenberg.edu
NORMENT, Arielle .... 215-751-8737 381 H
anorment@ccp.edu
NORMENT, Heather .... 843-383-8010 407 C
NORMORE, Clinton .... 660-626-2827 249 C
cnormore@atsu.edu
NORNHOLM, Rick .... 619-594-1889.. 33 E
rnornholm@sdsu.edu
NORNHOLM, Rick .... 619-594-1889.. 33 E
nornholm@sdsu.edu
NORONHA, Gloria .... 617-327-6777 219 G
gloria_noronha@williamjames.edu
NORQUIST, Bruce, R .... 312-329-4192 144 F
bruce.norquist@moody.edu
NORQUIST, Michelle ..... 616-988-3660 226 A
mnorquist@kuyper.edu
NORRED, Jonathan .... 706-649-5601 117 F
jnorred@columbustech.edu
NORRIS, Adam .... 504-280-6939 189 F
amnorris@uno.edu
NORRIS, Benjamin .... 301-687-4212 203 F
bnnorris@frostburg.edu
NORRIS, Brenda .... 218-477-2070 239 A
brenda.norris@mnstate.edu
NORRIS, David .... 512-621-4850 429 H
dnorris@escoffier.edu
NORRIS, JR., Davy .... 318-257-3798 192 A
dnorris@latech.edu
NORRIS, Debbie .... 601-925-3260 246 D
dnorris@mc.edu
NORRIS, Dena .... 816-604-1527 254 E
dena.norris@mcckc.edu
NORRIS, Emily .... 502-585-9911 184 E
enorris@spalding.edu
NORRIS, Heather .... 828-262-2070 340 G
hulburthm@appstate.edu
NORRIS, Helen .... 714-744-7848.. 36 D
hnorris@chapman.edu
NORRIS, Jeffery, S .... 434-223-6123 466 K
jnorris@hsc.edu
NORRIS, Jessica .... 314-529-9332 254 D
jessica.norris@maryville.edu
NORRIS, Jo Anna .... 202-319-6913.. 91 G
norrisj@cua.edu
NORRIS, John .... 704-330-1448 329 H
jnorris@jcsu.edu
NORRIS, Joye .... 417-836-4127 255 J
joyenorris@missouristate.edu
NORRIS, Katherine .... 630-637-5100 145 E
klnorris@noctrl.edu
NORRIS, Katie .... 870-368-2045.. 20 I
katie.norris@ozarka.edu
NORRIS, Kyle .... 712-852-5224 166 H
knorris@iowalakes.edu
NORRIS, Mark, M .... 574-372-5100 155 C
norrismm@grace.edu
NORRIS, Marly .... 415-482-1944.. 41 H
marly.norris@dominican.edu
NORRIS, Michael, C ...... 563-884-5469 169 C
michael.norris@palmer.edu
NORRIS, Nancy, E .... 828-448-3150 338 G
nnorris@wpcc.edu
NORRIS, Pamela .... 202-994-6255.. 92 C
pamnorris@gwu.edu
NORRIS, Paul .... 209-667-3868.. 33 D
pnorris@csustan.edu
NORRIS, Robert, F .... 630-752-5559 152 K
bob.norris@wheaton.edu
NORRIS, Shawn .... 225-752-4233 187 A
admissions@iticollege.edu
NORRIS, Taylor .... 828-398-7200 331 K
taylorrnorris@abtech.edu
NORRIS, Tenille, C .... 909-384-8958.. 60 F
tnorris@sbccd.cc.ca.us
NORRIS, Terry .... 702-651-5813 270 F
terry.norris@csn.edu
NORRIS, Tiffany .... 205-226-4600.... 5 A
tdnorris@bsc.edu
NORRIS, Todd .... 574-284-4610 160 F
tnorris@saintmarys.edu
NORRIS HALL, Sarah .... 206-543-6277 484 A
sahall@uw.edu
NORRIS-PAULISON, Robin .... 828-694-1746 332 C
r_paulison@blueridge.edu
NORSTROM, Carolyn .... 317-208-5311 159 F
NORTH, Donald .... 225-771-2552 191 C
dnorth@sulc.edu
NORTH, Doug .... 641-782-1459 170 B
north@swcciowa.edu
NORTH, Jon, D .... 913-971-3600 175 H
jonnorth@mnu.edu
NORTH, Joshua .... 540-828-5376 464 C
jnorth@bridgewater.edu
NORTH, Keith .... 406-657-1078 264 G
keith.north@rocky.edu
NORTH, Linda .... 334-745-6437.... 3 G
lnorth@suscc.edu
NORTH, Matthew .... 412-396-4075 382 E
northm@duq.edu
NORTH, Mike .... 865-228-2303 424 C
mnorth@pstcc.edu
NORTH, Paula .... 918-293-5240 368 B
paula.north@okstate.edu
NORTH, Sharon .... 251-578-1313.... 3 D
snorth@rstc.edu
NORTH, Stephanie .... 503-244-0726 371 E
NORTH, Stephanie, M .. 304-336-8311 489 B
northsm@westliberty.edu
NORTH, Stephen .... 337-521-8914 188 G
stephen.north@solacc.edu
NORTHAM, Andrea .... 507-457-5024 241 A
anortham@winona.edu
NORTHAM, Jennifer ...... 509-526-4794 485 C
northajl@whitman.edu
NORTHCUT, Kathryn ..... 573-341-7276 260 F
northcut@mst.edu
NORTHCUTT, David .... 706-419-1214 117 G
david.northcutt@covenant.edu
NORTHCUTT, Larry .... 903-923-2117 435 A
lnorthcutt@etbu.edu
NORTHCUTT, Melissa ... 337-475-5581 192 B
mnorthcutt@mcneese.edu
NORTHERN, Orathai ...... 863-292-3645 106 A
onorthern@polk.edu
NORTHINGTON, Adrienne .... 919-739-7007 338 F
awnorthington@waynecc.edu
NORTHOVER, Michael .. 971-722-8508 375 C
michael.northover@pcc.edu
NORTHROP, Dale .... 530-422-7913.. 74 F
dnorthropsr@weimar.org
NORTHRUP, Cody .... 575-624-8316 286 F
northrup@nmmi.edu
NORTHUP, Connie .... 913-288-7112 174 H
cnorthup@kckcc.edu
NORTON, Andrew .... 323-860-0789.. 50 E
NORTON, Andrew .... 215-702-4318 379 F
anorton@cairn.edu
NORTON, Beth .... 423-697-4792 423 B
NORTON, Daniel .... 601-266-4344 248 H
daniel.norton@usm.edu
NORTON, David, P .... 352-392-9271 110 E
dpnorton@ufl.edu
NORTON, Holly .... 309-649-6050 150 D
holly.norton@src.edu
NORTON, Jamie .... 260-665-4847 161 C
nortonj@trine.edu
NORTON, Karen .... 617-228-2177 214 A
kmnorton@bhcc.mass.edu
NORTON, Karen, M .... 617-228-2177 214 A
kmnorton@bhcc.mass.edu
NORTON, Krista .... 405-733-7317 369 D
knorton@rose.edu
NORTON, Lib .... 843-921-6902 410 B
lnorton@netc.edu
NORTON, Lisa .... 707-638-5200.. 68 B
lisa.norton@tu.edu
NORTON, Lisa, M .... 812-877-8892 160 C
olson@rose-hulman.edu
NORTON, M. Grant .... 509-335-4505 484 D
mg_norton@wsu.edu
NORTON, Michael, E .... 515-294-5352 163 E
mnorton@iastate.edu
NORTON, Mitzi .... 312-662-4002 132 D
mnorton@adler.edu
NORTON, Noelle .... 619-260-4545.. 72 H
norton@sandiego.edu
NORTON, Pamela .... 620-341-5413 173 C
pnorton1@emporia.edu
NORTON, Patrick .... 504-862-8698 191 D
pjn@tulane.edu
NORTON, Robert .... 517-607-2687 224 G
rnorton@hillsdale.edu
NORTON, Robin .... 859-344-3386 184 G
nortonr@thomasmore.edu
NORTON, Roger, L .... 845-575-3000 305 C
roger.norton@marist.edu
NORTON, Sally .... 269-471-3307 220 H
sallyn@andrews.edu
NORTON, Steve .... 309-341-5227 134 A
snorton@sandburg.edu
NORTON, Timothy .... 386-506-3658.. 98 A
timothy.norton@daytonastate.edu
NORVELL, Amanda .... 609-771-2724 275 J
norvell@tcnj.edu
NORWOOD, John .... 918-463-2931 365 I
john.norwood@connorsstate.edu
NORWOOD, Kristie ...... 757-727-5617 466 L
kristie.norwood@hamptonu.edu
NORWOOD, Melvin ...... 336-750-3203 343 E
norwoodm@wssu.edu
NORWOOD, Robert ...... 479-524-7466.. 20 C
rnorwood@jbu.edu
NORWOOD, Scott .... 254-267-7062 441 D
snorwood@rangercollege.edu
NORWOOD, Tierra .... 252-451-8233 336 B
tanorwood386@nashcc.edu
NOSAL, Julie .... 630-617-3440 137 E
julien@elmhurst.edu
NOSEEP, Willie .... 307-855-2149 499 U
wnoseep@cwc.edu
NOSEGBE, Isibor, J ...... 703-891-1787 470 G
ijnosegbe@standardcollege.edu
NOSEL, Cathy .... 304-637-1339 486 D
noselc@dewv.edu
NOSEWORTHY, John, H .... 507-266-4861 234 E
noseworthy.john@mayo.edu
NOSSETT, Mary .... 812-749-1213 159 E
mnossett@oak.edu
NOSTROM, Kim .... 607-436-2563 316 C
kim.nostrom@oneonta.edu
NOSTRUM, Rian .... 701-231-7890 345 D
rian.nostrum@ndsu.edu
NOTA, Alyssa .... 775-682-5888 270 K
alyssa.nota@usac.edu
NOTA, Michele .... 401-874-2242 404 E
mnota@uri.edu
NOTARIAN, Matthew, F 330-569-5453 353 F
notarianmf@hiram.edu
NOTESTEIN, Mary .... 319-385-6204 167 F
mary.notestein@iw.edu
NOTHERN, Nick .... 620-432-0381 176 A
nnothern@neosho.edu
NOTHSTINE, Kellie .... 910-893-1534 327 C
nothstine@campbell.edu
NOTIS, Chana .... 845-362-3053 290 I
cnotis@byts.edu
NOTT, Phillip .... 706-865-2134 126 D
pnott@truett.edu
NOTTKE, Janine .... 906-487-7267 223 I
janine.nottke@finlandia.edu
NOURSE, Chris .... 740-245-7228 363 A
cnourse@rio.edu
NOVA, Autumn-Carol ... 646-378-6158 289 F
autumn.nova@nyack.edu
NOVAK, Amy, C .... 563-333-6213 169 D
novakamy@sau.edu
NOVAK, Dale .... 402-643-7416 265 I
dale.novak@cune.edu
NOVAK, Debbie .... 970-945-8691.. 78 H
dnovak@coloradomtn.edu
NOVAK, Elizabeth .... 734-462-4400 230 B
enovak@schoolcraft.edu
NOVAK, Greg .... 314-792-6221 253 J
gregnovak@kenrick.edu
NOVAK, Jeffrey .... 608-262-6982 494 D
novak4@wisc.edu
NOVAK, John .... 219-980-6905 157 A
jmnovak@iun.edu

OBERHELMAN, Don 805-756-1407 29 K
obe@calpoly.edu
OBERHELMAN,
Steven, M 979-862-6797 446 B
s-oberhelman@tamu.edu
OBERLANDER, Cyril 707-826-3441 30 A
cyril.oberlander@humboldt.edu
OBERLANDER, Cyril 707-826-5877 30 A
cyril.oberlander@humboldt.edu
OBERLANDER, Janell 307-681-6201 500 F
joberlander@sheridan.edu
OBERLEITNER, Melinda 337-482-5611 192 F
melinda.oberleitner@louisiana.edu
OBERLIN, Kevin 864-242-5100 405 H
OBERMAN, Anne 320-363-5999 234 I
aoberman@csbsju.edu
OBERMARK, Julie 618-545-3015 141 C
jobermark@kaskaskia.edu
OBERMEISTER,
Tuvia, M 718-377-0777 311 B
OBERMILLER, Edwin, H 503-943-8009 376 H
obermill@up.edu
OBERMILLER, Laureen 202-250-2176 92 B
laureen.obermiller@gallaudet.edu
OBERMUELLER, Joe 605-575-2063 416 C
joe.obermueller@usiouxfalls.edu
OBERQUELL, Christian 406-265-3761 264 A
coberquell@msun.edu
OBERSTE, Christy 501-812-2243 23 E
coberste@uaptc.edu
OBERSTEIN, Leonard 410-484-7200 201 B
loberstein@nirc.edu
OBERSTEIN, Ron 510-780-4500 48 D
roberstein@lifewest.edu
OBERT, Brian 308-345-8109 266 J
obertb@mpcc.edu
OBI, Stacey, L 864-592-4618 411 E
obis@sccsc.edu
OBILADE, Sandra, O 270-686-4209 179 F
sandra.obilade@brescia.edu
OBIOMON, Pamela 936-261-9956 445 E
phobiomon@pvamu.edu
OBISESAN, Thomas, O 202-806-2550 92 E
tobisesan@howard.edu
OBLANDER,
Frances, W 912-650-5684 125 D
foblander@southuniversity.edu
OBLAS, David 610-282-1100 382 A
david.oblas@desales.edu
OBOURN, Milo 585-395-2034 317 B
mobourn@brockport.edu
OBPTANDE, Rachel 615-226-3990 419 J
OBRECHT, John 303-273-3000 79 A
jobrecht@mines.edu
OBRYCKI, Marybeth 973-290-4460 282 G
mobrycki@steu.edu
OBSNIUK, Karen 734-432-5648 226 G
kobsniuk@madonna.edu
OBSTA, Kim 361-572-6410 456 H
kim.obsta@victoriacollege.edu
OCAMPO, Carlota 202-884-9209 94 A
ocampoc@trinitydc.edu
OCAMPO, Kathy 928-314-9559 11 B
katheline.ocampo@azwestern.edu
OCAMPO, Renata 817-202-6320 444 B
r.ocampo@swau.edu
OCASIO, Arcadio 787-257-0000 510 F
arcadio.ocasio@upr.edu
OCASIO, Luz 787-765-1915 507 G
locasio@opto.inter.edu
OCASIO, Orializ 787-764-0000 511 F
orializ.ocasio@upr.edu
OCCHIOGROSSO,
Gabrielle 718-405-3225 296 D
gabrielle.occhiogrosso@
mountsaintvincent.edu
OCCHIOGROSSO,
Paul, F 212-650-8276 293 B
pocchiogrosso@ccny.cuny.edu
OCCHIPINTI, Laurie 978-630-9350 215 A
locchipinti@mwcc.mass.edu
OCEGUEDA, Isela 714-546-7600 38 D
OCEGUERA, Gustavo 951-372-7885 59 C
gustavo.oceguera@norcocollege.edu
OCHES, Eric 781-891-2937 206 C
roches@bentley.edu
OCHIE, Charles 229-500-2221 114 F
charles.ochie@asurams.edu
OCHOA, Briana 619-934-0797 61 C
OCHOA, Eduardo, M 831-582-3532 32 D
emochoa@csumb.edu
OCHOA, Gabriela 312-658-5100 150 E
OCHOA, Gerardo 503-883-2617 373 E
gochoa@linfield.edu
OCHOA, Hector 619-594-6881 33 E
provost@sdsu.edu
OCHOA, Marcia 831-459-2769 71 A
oakesprovost@ucsc.edu
OCHOA, Marilyn 732-906-4252 278 A
mochoa@middlesexcc.edu
OCHOA, Micaela 925-229-6850 40 F
mochoa@4cd.edu
OCHOA, Vanessa 323-265-8721 49 D
ochoavj@elac.edu
OCHOA, William, R 510-464-3592 57 B
wrochoa@peralta.edu
OCHS, Jon 765-998-5301 161 A
jnochs@taylor.edu
OCHSNER, David 512-863-1258 444 F
ochsnerd@southwestern.edu
OCHSNER, Tom, J 402-465-2212 267 J
tjo@nebrwesleyan.edu
OCONNELL, Amy 401-598-2346 403 E
amy.oconnell@jwu.edu
ODDO, Jennifer 330-941-3001 364 G
joddo01@ysu.edu
ODE, Joshua, J 989-964-7331 229 L
jjode@svsu.edu
ODEGARD, Esther 714-628-4931 58 G
odegard_esther@sccollege.edu
ODEH, Omar 478-445-6804 119 A
omar.odeh@gcsu.edu
ODEJIMI,
Kristina Bethea 207-725-3490 194 A
ODEN, JR., Joe 304-766-3019 489 D
odenjr@wvstateu.edu
ODEN, John 585-567-9338 301 G
john.oden@houghton.edu
ODEN, Lorette 309-298-2228 152 I
ls-oden@wiu.edu
ODENTHAL, Paul 541-737-0123 374 H
ODENWALD, Joseph 269-782-1270 230 D
president@swmich.edu
ODI, Henry, U 610-758-5923 388 C
huo0@lehigh.edu
ODIN, Eric 212-217-4030 299 C
eric_odin@fitnyc.edu
ODOM, David 402-363-5732 269 F
dodom@york.edu
ODOM, James 870-762-3154 17 F
jodom@smail.anc.edu
ODOM, Julia, L 701-654-1000 32 C
ODOM, Lisa 706-295-6928 119 F
lodom@gntc.edu
ODOM, Megan 530-898-5253 31 A
modom@csuchico.edu
ODOM, Shawn 336-750-3372 343 E
odoms@wssu.edu
ODOM, Stanyell 410-455-2632 202 G
stanyell_odom@umbc.edu
ODOM, Tammy 479-394-7622 23 F
todom@uarichmountain.edu
ODOMS, Lauren 843-921-6903 410 B
lodoms@netc.edu
ODU, Michael 619-388-7800 61 B
ODUCADO, Joey 691-320-2480 503 B
joducado@comfsm.fm
ODUKE, SJ, Charles 315-445-4110 303 F
odukeco@lemoyne.edu
ODUSAMI, Kim 978-762-4000 215 B
kodusami@northshore.edu
OECHSLIN, Brad 540-362-6000 467 A
boechslin@hollins.edu
OEHLER, David 816-604-2385 254 H
david.oehler@mcckc.edu
OEHLER, Elizabeth 830-792-7303 442 G
eoehler@schreiner.edu
OEHLER, Robert 608-363-2200 490 I
oehlerr@beloit.edu
OEHLERKING, Kelly 605-718-2931 416 D
kelly.oehlerking@wdt.edu
OEHLERT, Priscilla 713-226-5552 452 B
oehlertp@uhd.edu
OEHM, Cathy 785-532-5469 175 A
cathyo@ksu.edu
OELFKE, Melanie 903-813-2433 429 I
moelfke@austincollege.edu
OELSCHLAGER,
Sharon, G 412-396-5028 382 E
goedert@duq.edu
OEN, Ray 425-602-3000 476 H
OERLY-BENNETT,
Sandra, K 304-293-5242 489 E
sybennett@mail.wvu.edu
OERTEL, Ryan 414-443-8825 497 A
ryan.oertel@wlc.edu
OESER, Sara 615-966-5085 420 B
sara.oeser@lipscomb.edu
OEST, Danielle 608-249-6611 491 H
OESTER, Stephanie 541-881-5806 376 E
soester@tvcc.cc
OESTERLE, Lisa 660-596-7251 259 D
loesterle@sfccmo.edu
OESTMANN, Eric 941-224-5502 354 K
eoestmann@lec.edu
OESTREICH, Melanie, R 610-917-2003 400 D
mroestreich@valleyforge.edu
OFE, Suellen, S 334-833-4515 5 H
ofe@hawks.huntingdon.edu
OFFBECK, Sean 907-260-7422 9 D
OFFENBACH, Janice 559-638-0300 67 C
janice.offenbach@reedleycollege.edu
OFFER, Patricia 312-893-7113 137 F
poffer@erikson.edu
OFFERMANN, Joseph 815-280-2211 140 I
joffermann@jjc.edu
OFFICER, Danielle 212-237-8185 294 B
dofficer@jjay.cuny.edu
OFODILE, Caroline 201-447-9242 274 I
cofodile@bergen.edu
OFORLEA, Veronica 714-564-6277 58 F
oforlea_veronica@sac.edu
OGATA, Amanda 559-651-2500 61 I
OGAWA, Tim 617-228-2051 214 A
togawa@bhcc.mass.edu
OGBAA, Clara 203-392-5760 85 H
ogbaac1@southernct.edu
OGBONNA, Kelechi, C 804-828-3006 472 D
kcunegbuogbo@vcu.edu
OGBURN, Anna, H 662-329-7148 247 B
ahogburn@muw.edu
OGDEN, Alix, R 401-825-2387 403 D
aogden@ccri.edu
OGDEN, Denise 912-921-2900 93 H
OGDEN, Kristen 434-832-7618 472 G
ogdenk@centralvirginia.edu
OGDEN, Matt 414-847-3223 493 C
mattogden@miad.edu
OGDEN, Molly 315-228-7475 296 C
mogden@colgate.edu
OGDEN, Patricia 858-513-9240 16 I
patricia.ogden@ashford.edu
OGDEN, Patricia 912-358-4412 124 H
ogdenp@savananhstate.edu
OGDEN, Patrick 302-831-4135 91 A
pogden@udel.edu
OGDEN, Rachel 814-860-5118 387 C
rogden@lecom.edu
OGEA, Angelique 337-475-5154 192 B
aogea@mcneese.edu
OGEA, Reggie, R 504-282-4455 190 D
rogea@nobts.edu
OGEKA, Alex 610-683-4112 394 A
ogeka@kuf.org
OGG, Laurie 707-664-2036 34 C
laurie.ogg@sonoma.edu
OGIBA, Shawn 212-229-5300 307 E
ogibas@newschool.edu
OGILVIE, Craig 406-994-4145 263 G
craig.ogilvie@montana.edu
OGILVIE, Susan 253-272-1126 480 F
sogilvie@ncad.edu
OGLE, Billy 530-283-0202 42 E
wogle@frc.edu
OGLE, Chad 859-572-6371 184 B
oglec1@nku.edu
OGLE, Christophor, M 920-748-8111 493 J
oglec@ripon.edu
OGLE, Josh 541-956-7039 375 G
jogle@roguecc.edu
OGLE, Kaci 256-782-5405 6 A
kogle@jsu.edu
OGLESBEE, Ariane 509-777-4320 485 D
aoglesbee@whitworth.edu
OGLESBEE, Gina 936-468-2203 444 H
oglesbeegs@sfasu.edu
OGLESBY, Lamar 848-932-4179 281 B
lo170@ored.rutgers.edu
OGLESBY, Lamar 848-932-4179 281 C
lo170@ored.rutgers.edu
OGLESBY, Leisa 318-675-7629 189 D
leisa.oglesby@lsuhs.edu
OGLESBY, Michelle 706-754-7880 123 C
michelle.oglesby@northgatech.edu
OGLESBY, Willie 215-955-6648 398 G
willie.oglesby@jefferson.edu
OGORZALEK, Karen 309-457-2113 144 E
kareno@monmouthcollege.edu
OGREN, Kathy 909-748-8072 72 E
kathy_ogren@redlands.edu
OGRODNIK, Eugene, C 412-362-8500 395 E
pims5808@aol.com
OGUL, David 619-644-7840 44 H
david.ogul@gcccd.edu
OGULLUKIAN, Tania 212-924-5900 321 C
togullukian@swedishinstitute.edu
OGUNMAKIN, Dolapo 678-466-4181 117 A
dolapoogunmakin@clayton.edu
OGUNMOKUN, Oyinada 692-625-7982 503 F
oogunmokun@cmi.edu
OGUNTOLA, Andy 863-292-3627 106 A
aoguntola@polk.edu
OGUNYEMI, Daniel 417-447-7617 257 B
ogunyemd@otc.edu
OH, Abraham 909-895-7138 45 K
abraham@huca.edu
OH, Boo Un 951-372-8080 45 G
hisuniv@yahoo.com
OH, David, K 213-293-1771 75 F
OH, Ellen 650-725-3104 66 D
ellenoh@stanford.edu
OH, Henry 856-256-4320 280 H
oh@rowan.edu
OH, Janet, S 818-677-3277 32 E
janetoh@csun.edu
OH, Jinny 626-350-1500 28 H
OH, Joha 213-381-0081 46 I
ojo@irus.edu
OH, John 323-422-1453 434 F
john_oh@diu.edu
OH, John 972-708-7340 434 F
OH, Myeong Hwan 636-327-4645 255 E
mhoh@midwest.edu
OH, Seonhee 714-683-1402 27 C
OHL-GIGLIOTTI,
Christine, A 240-500-2526 199 A
caohl-gigliotti@hagerstowncc.edu
OHLES, Janet 610-861-1540 390 D
ohlesj@moravian.edu
OHLIN, Jens, D 607-255-3527 297 D
law.dean@cornell.edu
OHLSCHWAGER, Kristi 620-227-9201 173 A
kohlschwager@dc3.edu
OHLSEN, Erin, C 407-582-3001 113 C
eohlsen@valenciacollege.edu
OHLSON, Vicky 334-293-4568 1 C
vicky.ohlson@accs.edu
OHMAN, Jessica 316-322-3231 172 B
johman@butlercc.edu
OHMER, Douglas 605-626-2400 415 H
doug.ohmer@northern.edu
OHMER, Todd 734-487-4190 223 F
tohmer@emich.edu
OHMS, Collin 314-434-4044 251 F
collin.ohms@covenantseminary.edu
OHNECK, Claudia 870-733-6701 18 A
crohneck@asumidsouth.edu
OHNESORGE, Karen 785-242-5200 176 F
karen.ohnesorge@ottawa.edu
OHNSTAD, Gina 509-527-5768 485 C
ohnstagz@whitman.edu
OHOTNICKY, John 508-793-7561 207 F
jrohotnicky@clarku.edu
OHOTNICKY, Julianne 413-585-4940 218 D
johotnic@smith.edu
OIKELOME, Gloria 215-641-6470 390 A
goikelome@mc3.edu
OIKELOME, Gloria 215-489-2349 381 K
gloria.oikelome@delval.edu
OISHI, Kendra 808-956-8213 129 B
bor@hawaii.edu
OISHI, Kendra, T 808-956-8213 128 I
bor@hawaii.edu
OJADA, Joanna 212-616-7200 301 A
OJEDA, Alex 818-778-5764 50 B
OJEDA, Andrea 201-216-9901 276 C
andrea.ojeda@eicollege.edu
OJEDA, Christa 312-949-7020 139 B
cojeda@ico.edu
OJEDA, Jessica 787-786-3030 509 E
jojeda@ucb.edu.pr
OJEDA, Jorge 626-568-8850 49 B
OJEDA, Juan 773-878-7980 148 F
jojeda@staugustine.edu
OJEDA, Marivel 210-436-3141 442 A
mojeda@stmarytx.edu
OJEDA, Vanessa 787-665-7910 505 B
vojeda@columbiacentral.edu

OJEISEKHOBA, John, O 562-903-4877.. 27 E
john.o.ojeisekhoba@biola.edu
OJENNUS, Deanna 509-777-4860 485 D
dojennus@whitworth.edu
OJEWUYI, Olusegun 618-453-3267 149 G
sojewuyi@siu.edu
OJO, Akinlolu 913-588-5200 177 G
aojo@kumc.edu
OJO, Olabisi 229-500-2309 114 F
olabisi.ojo@asurams.edu
OJO-OHIKUARE, Renee 973-877-3491 276 G
rojoohik@essex.edu
OKADA, David, S 671-735-2902 503 E
dsokada@triton.uog.edu
OKADA, David, S 671-735-2372 503 E
dsokada@triton.uog.edu
OKADA, Mary, Y 671-735-5700 503 C
gccpresident@guamcc.edu
OKAGAKI, Lynn 302-831-2101.. 91 A
okagaki@udel.edu
OKAMOTO, Mark 559-325-3600.. 28 F
mokamoto@chsu.edu
OKAMOTO, Matt 530-754-9868.. 69 A
mwokamoto@ucdavis.edu
OKAMURA, Grant 808-455-0462 130 A
okamurag@hawaii.edu
OKANDA, Fred, M 252-335-3036 341 A
fmokanda@ecsu.edu
OKAY, Kathleen 973-300-2131 283 B
kokay@sussex.edu
OKECH, Jane 802-656-4627 462 D
jane.okech@uvm.edu
OKEEFFE, Jennifer 617-243-2065 210 G
jokeeffe@lasell.edu
OKEKE, Charles 702-651-7425 270 F
charles.okeke@csn.edu
OKELLO, Candace, C 724-946-7110 401 F
okelloca@westminster.edu
OKERE, Erica 859-371-9393 179 C
eokere@beckfield.edu
OKESON, Jeff 859-323-1884 185 D
okeson@uky.edu
OKESSON, Gregg 859-858-2261 178 G
OKESSON, Gregg 859-858-3581 178 G
OKINAGA, Carrie 808-956-2211 129 B
carrieok@hawaii.edu
OKINAGA, Carrie, K 808-956-2211 128 I
carrieok@hawaii.edu
OKKER, Patricia 941-487-4100 110 C
patokker@ncf.edu
OKOLI, Daniel, T 928-523-8871.. 14 J
daniel.okoli@nau.edu
OKORIE, Ferdinand 773-371-5400 134 C
fokorie@ctu.edu
OKORIE, CMP,
Ferdinand 773-371-5423 134 C
fokorie@ctu.edu
OKORONKWO,
Josephine 504-286-5361 191 A
jokoronkwo@suno.edu
OKUDA, Alex, H 949-480-4159.. 64 E
aokuda@soka.edu
OKUN, Logan 252-222-6240 332 G
okunl@carteret.edu
OLADIPUPO, Adebisi 443-885-3372 200 F
adebisi.oladipupo@morgan.edu
OLAKA, Musa 936-261-1533 445 E
mwolaka@pvamu.edu
OLALDE, Patricia 312-369-7248 136 C
polalde@colum.edu
OLAN, David 212-817-7232 293 D
dolan@gc.cuny.edu
OLANDER, Keith 218-894-5163 237 C
keith.olander@clcmn.edu
OLANDER, Renee, E 757-363-4108 468 C
rolander@odu.edu
OLATUNJI, Bunmi 615-322-7311 427 B
OLATUNJI, Ciricie 504-520-5470 193 C
colatunj@xula.edu
OLAVARRIA, Lourdes 787-891-0925 506 I
lolavarr@aguadilla.inter.edu
OLCOTT, Sarah 507-457-2516 241 A
solcott@winona.edu
OLD, Philip, K 831-656-2511 501 K
philip.old@nps.edu
OLD COYOTE, Shaleen 406-638-3110 262 J
oldcoyotes@lbhc.edu
OLD CROW, William 406-638-3185 262 J
oldcrowb@lbhc.edu
OLDENBURGER, Tad 972-708-7340 434 F
tad_oldenburger@diu.edu
OLDENKAMP, Mike 712-324-5061 168 H
mikeo@nwicc.edu

OLDFIELD, Annemarie 575-624-7160 285 F
annemarie.oldfield@roswell.enmu.edu
OLDFIELD, Curt 309-649-6200 150 D
curt.oldfield@src.edu
OLDFIELD, Jessica 937-395-8006 354 J
jessica.oldfield@ketteringhealth.org
OLDFIELD, Melody, K 541-737-3871 374 H
university.marketing@oregonstate.edu
OLDHAM, Deborah 601-484-8636 246 B
doldham@meridiancc.edu
OLDHAM, Philip, B 931-372-3241 425 B
poldham@tntech.edu
OLDS, Amy 502-597-5509 183 A
amy.olds@kysu.edu
OLDS, Bill 925-631-4542.. 59 I
wlo1@stmarys-ca.edu
OLDS, Carole 719-502-3249.. 82 D
carole.olds@pikespeak.edu
OLDS, Scott 707-638-5200.. 68 B
OLDS, Terlynn 706-880-8631 121 K
tolds@lagrange.edu
OLDS, Wendy 218-846-3810 238 K
wendy.olds@minnesota.edu
OLEGERIIL, Jay 680-488-2471 504 A
jayo@palau.edu
OLEKSIW, Steven 718-625-2200 291 G
steven.oleksiw@brooklaw.edu
OLEN, Simcha 718-252-6333 325 P
OLENIK DORMAN, Lisa 334-833-4465.... 5 H
ldorman@hawks.huntingdon.edu
OLER, Greg 301-405-5636 202 E
goler@umd.edu
OLES, Brian 508-565-1914 218 F
boles@stonehill.edu
OLES, Brian, M 508-565-1914 218 F
boles@stonehill.edu
OLESON, Kathryn, C 503-777-7257 375 F
koleson@reed.edu
OLEVSKY, Eugene 619-594-6329.. 33 E
eolvesky@sdsu.edu
OLEVSON, Jennifer 808-237-5144 128 D
jolevson@hmi.edu
OLEWINE, Gary, D 610-799-1658 388 B
golewine@lccc.edu
OLGE, Rich 209-667-3203.. 33 D
rogle@csustan.edu
OLGUIN, Javier, E 972-860-5306 433 I
javiereolguin@dcccd.edu
OLIAN, Judy, D 203-582-8700.. 88 F
judy.olian@quinnipiac.edu
OLIHA-DONALDSON,
Hannah 763-433-1186 236 H
hannah.oliha@anokaramsey.edu
OLIKONG, Deikola 680-488-2471 504 A
olikongd@gmail.com
OLIN, Bradley 831-479-6406.. 27 G
brolin@cabrillo.edu
OLIN, Joanna 413-585-2108 218 D
jolin@smith.edu
OLIN, Mike 610-330-5917 387 B
olinm@lafayette.edu
OLING-SISAY, Mary 415-955-2100.. 25 A
moling-sisay@alliant.edu
OLING-SISAY, Mary 760-750-8034.. 33 C
molingsisay@csusm.edu
OLINGER, Gerard, J 574-631-7394 161 G
golinger@nd.edu
OLINGER, Ronald, J 913-360-7413 171 G
rolinger@benedictine.edu
OLINTO, Angela, V 773-702-7950 151 B
aolinto@uchicago.edu
OLIPHINT, Melody 806-743-7382 450 D
melody.oliphint@ttuhsc.edu
OLISZCZAK, Jennifer 603-578-8900 272 B
joliszczak@ccsnh.edu
OLISZCZAK, Peter 623-845-4634.. 13 E
peter.oliszczak@gccaz.edu
OLIVA, Gil 316-295-5128 173 G
gilberto_oliva@friends.edu
OLIVA, Joseph, E 718-990-6421 313 B
olivaj@stjohns.edu
OLIVA, Julia 718-289-5100 292 H
julia.oliva@bcc.cuny.edu
OLIVA, Mary 312-329-4112 144 F
mary.oliva@moody.edu
OLIVA, Robert 718-489-5372 312 H
roliva@sfc.edu
OLIVARES, Carlos, J 787-279-2220 506 L
colivares@bayamon.inter.edu
OLIVAREZ, Delma 888-882-8201 455 A
OLIVAREZ, Juan, R 616-234-4000 224 C
president@grcc.edu

OLIVAS, Julian 806-742-1482 450 C
julian.olivas@ttu.edu
OLIVE, David, W 276-326-4466 464 C
david.olive@bluefield.edu
OLIVE, Derek 270-745-2409 186 A
derek.olive@wku.edu
OLIVEIRA, Cassia 870-307-7355.. 20 D
cassia.oliveira@lyon.edu
OLIVEIRA, Jason, G 973-275-2385 282 K
jason.oliveira@shu.edu
OLIVEIRA, Marcio 301-405-5190 202 E
marcio@umd.edu
OLIVEIRA, Sandra, J 401-865-2602 403 G
solivei6@providence.edu
OLIVENCIA, Yanitza 787-834-9595 508 O
yolivencia@uaa.edu
OLIVER, Astrid 970-247-7507.. 80 H
oliver_a@fortlewis.edu
OLIVER, Bernard 678-407-5603 119 B
beoliver@ggc.edu
OLIVER, Brande' 248-204-2308 226 E
boliver@ltu.edu
OLIVER, Christine 401-598-1000 403 E
christine.oliver@jwu.edu
OLIVER, Courtney 606-546-1281 185 B
coliver@unionky.edu
OLIVER, Dawn 912-871-8544 123 F
doliver@ogeecheetech.edu
OLIVER, Debra 937-708-5748 363 G
doliver@wilberforce.edu
OLIVER, Denita 256-215-4293.... 1 G
doliver@cacc.edu
OLIVER, Diana 301-846-2437 198 E
doliver@frederick.edu
OLIVER, Dominick 412-924-1460 395 G
doliver@pts.edu
OLIVER, Donald, E 605-342-0317 414 C
dojos@msn.com
OLIVER, Donna, H 904-470-8004.. 98 I
donna.oliver@ewc.edu
OLIVER, Ebigaly 787-878-5475 506 J
eoliver@arecibo.inter.edu
OLIVER, Erica 973-803-5000 279 C
eoliver@pillar.edu
OLIVER, Jorge 718-636-3671 311 A
joliver6@pratt.edu
OLIVER, Jose, L 787-798-3001 509 F
jose.oliver@uccaribe.edu
OLIVER, Justin 757-925-6302 474 A
joliver@pdc.edu
OLIVER, Kenneth 217-228-5432 147 C
oliveke@quincy.edu
OLIVER, Kenneth 785-833-4342 175 C
ken.oliver@kwu.edu
OLIVER, Lonetta 309-694-5477 138 I
lonetta.oliver@icc.edu
OLIVER, Malcom, K 607-777-4351 283 D
moliver@tesu.edu
OLIVER, Matthew 800-686-1883 222 B
moliver@cleary.edu
OLIVER, Meghan 802-485-2125 461 H
moliver@norwich.edu
OLIVER, Michael 734-462-4400 230 B
moliver@schoolcraft.edu
OLIVER, Parker 931-598-1586 422 F
pwoliver@sewanee.edu
OLIVER, Patricia Belton 713-743-2400 451 G
poliver@uh.edu
OLIVER, Richard 417-865-2815 252 F
oliverr@evangel.edu
OLIVER, Robin 740-593-1000 358 L
roliver@ohio.edu
OLIVER, Roxanne 614-234-2870 356 E
roliver@mccn.edu
OLIVER,
Samuel (Dub), W 731-661-5180 425 F
doliver@uu.edu
OLIVER, Sarah, E 563-333-6424 169 D
oliversarahe@sau.edu
OLIVER, Sharon, J 919-530-5313 341 D
soliver@nccu.edu
OLIVER, Sharon, M 207-581-1585 196 D
smoliver@maine.edu
OLIVER, Shawn 609-497-7814 279 D
shawn.oliver@ptsem.edu
OLIVER, Tamara 607-844-8222 321 I
tmo@tompkinscortland.edu
OLIVER, Tanya, W 252-862-1267 336 H
toliver@roanokechowan.edu
OLIVER, Tom 217-228-5432 147 C
oliveth@quincy.edu
OLIVER, Tony 435-586-7700 459 E

OLIVER, Zachary 808-237-5140 128 D
zoliver@hmi.edu
OLIVER-STANLEY,
Aisha 212-998-1212 309 D
OLIVER-VERONESI,
Robin, E 814-865-6555 391 F
reo133@psu.edu
OLIVERAS, Esther 212-217-5546 299 C
esther_oliveras@fitnyc.edu
OLIVERAS, Ivette 787-840-2575 508 G
ivoliveras@psm.edu
OLIVERAS, Jose 787-844-8181 511 E
jose.oliveras2@upr.edu
OLIVERAS, Marilyn 787-284-1912 507 D
molivera@ponce.inter.edu
OLIVERI, Dee 949-582-4500.. 65 C
doliveri@saddleback.edu
OLIVERI, Mary, A 570-961-7855 387 A
oliverim@lackawanna.edu
OLIVERIO, Robert 602-489-5300.. 10 G
robert.oliverio@arizonachristian.edu
OLIVEROS, Claire 916-691-7487.. 50 K
claire.oliveros@crc.losrios.edu
OLIVEROS, Jon 847-397-0300 132 E
OLIVIA, Elizabeth 903-510-2362 451 E
eoli@tjc.edu
OLIVIERI-LENAHAN,
Elizabeth 914-633-2360 302 C
eolivieri@iona.edu
OLIVO, Christiane 970-542-3191.. 81 M
christiane.olivo@morgancc.edu
OLIVO, Cynthia 626-585-7074.. 56 D
cdolivo@pasadena.edu
OLKOWSKI, Mark 920-465-5045 494 F
olkowskm@uwgb.edu
OLLE-LAJOIE, Maureen 715-425-3799 496 A
maureen.olle-lajoie@uwrf.edu
OLLER, Jeremy 405-974-5347 370 H
joller@uco.edu
OLLIFF, Kenneth 314-977-2925 258 H
knneth.a.olliff@slu.edu
OLLIFF, Martin 334-983-6556.... 7 C
molliff@troy.edu
OLLIFF, Martin 334-983-6556.... 7 C
OLLINGER, Nancy 610-902-8276 379 E
nancy.ollinger@cabrini.edu
OLMANSON, Angela 415-457-8811.. 39 B
aolmanson@marin.edu
OLMER, Sudarat (Pon) 860-632-3067.. 88 B
polmer@holyapostles.edu
OLMOS, Amanda 888-491-8686.. 75 E
OLMOS, Ernesto, F 806-371-5456 428 F
efolmos@actx.edu
OLMSTADT, William 318-675-5449 189 D
will.olmstadt@lsuhs.edu
OLMSTEAD, Karen, L 410-548-3374 204 A
klolmstead@salisbury.edu
OLMSTEAD, Patrick 818-401-1041.. 39 F
polmstead@columbiacollege.edu
OLMSTEAD, Steve 918-293-3812 368 B
steve.olmstead@okstate.edu
OLNEY, Kent 815-939-5231 146 F
kolney@olivet.edu
OLOWUDE, Brian 805-893-4411.. 70 E
brian.olowude@sa.ucsb.edu
OLOYEDE, Oluwatayo 904-264-2172 106 K
oluwatayo.oloyede@iws.edu
OLPHIE, Elizabeth, W 229-333-7837 127 C
ewolphie@valdosta.edu
OLSEN, Ann, E 502-272-8133 179 D
aolsen@bellarmine.edu
OLSEN, Catharine 219-989-2370 160 A
catharine.olsen@pnw.edu
OLSEN, Chris 208-496-9510 130 K
olsenc@byui.edu
OLSEN, Christopher 812-237-2309 155 H
chris.olsen@indstate.edu
OLSEN, Elisa, L 832-813-6205 438 E
elisa.l.olsen@lonestar.edu
OLSEN, Jane 320-308-4958 240 C
jolsen@stcloudstate.edu
OLSEN, Jeff 713-942-3466 453 H
jolsen@stthom.edu
OLSEN, Jennifer 334-347-2623.... 2 A
jolsen@escc.edu
OLSEN, Katie 973-328-5058 276 A
kolsen@ccm.edu
OLSEN, Keith 402-599-7927 269 B
keith.olsen@unmc.edu
OLSEN, Levi 585-343-0055 300 D
ltolsen@genesee.edu
OLSEN, Linda 502-863-8000 180 E

OLSEN, Mandy ... 866-492-5336 243 G miranda.olsen@mail.waldenu.edu
OLSEN, Melissa ... 775-673-7025 270 I maolsen@tmcc.edu
OLSEN, Micah ... 307-681-6007 500 F molsen@sheridan.edu
OLSEN, Michelle, D ... 417-836-5274 255 J molsen@missouristate.edu
OLSEN, Morgan, R ... 480-727-9920.. 11 A morgan.r.olsen@asu.edu
OLSEN, Nancy ... 218-879-0715 237 F nancy.olsen@fdltcc.edu
OLSEN, Natalie ... 402-280-1798 265 J natalieolsen@creighton.edu
OLSEN, Pete ... 831-645-1362.. 52 H polsen@mpc.edu
OLSEN, Steven, M ... 716-878-4113 317 C olsensw@buffalostate.edu
OLSEN, Taimi ... 864-656-4542 406 F taimio@clemson.edu
OLSHINE FRASIER, Rachel ... 903-233-4410 438 C rachelolshine@letu.edu
OLSON, Adam ... 813-988-5131.. 99 M olsona@floridacollege.edu
OLSON, Alexandra ... 847-735-5231 141 F aolson@lakeforest.edu
OLSON, Barry ... 269-387-2152 232 J barry.olson@wmich.edu
OLSON, Barry ... 919-513-3402 341 E barry_olson@ncsu.edu
OLSON, Ben ... 907-745-3201.... 9 C bolson@akbible.edu
OLSON, Bob ... 904-276-6775 107 A bobolson@sjrstate.edu
OLSON, Camron, M ... 641-422-4281 168 E camron.olson@niacc.edu
OLSON, Cari ... 701-858-3323 345 C cari.olson@minotstateu.edu
OLSON, Chris ... 912-478-5357 120 A cgolson@georgiasouthern.edu
OLSON, Cynthia ... 612-381-8124 235 C colson@dunwoody.edu
OLSON, David ... 910-962-3102 343 B olsond@uncw.edu
OLSON, Deborah ... 863-784-7275 108 D deborah.olson@southflorida.edu
OLSON, Dustin ... 303-273-3000.. 79 A dolson1@mines.edu
OLSON, Ellen ... 815-921-4402 147 H e.olson@rockvalleycollege.edu
OLSON, Ellie ... 612-330-1169 233 G eolson@augsburg.edu
OLSON, Ernest ... 309-438-1946 140 C ewolson@ilstu.edu
OLSON, Gary, A ... 716-839-8210 297 F golson@daemen.edu
OLSON, Heidi, L ... 320-222-5209 239 H heidi.olson@ridgewater.edu
OLSON, James ... 225-578-3202 188 K jmolson@lsu.edu
OLSON, Jayden ... 701-774-4546 346 C jayden.olson@willistonstate.edu
OLSON, Jeffery, D ... 651-638-6241 233 J jeff-olson@bethel.edu
OLSON, John ... 425-388-9555 479 B jolson@everettcc.edu
OLSON, Jon ... 507-457-5021 241 A jon.olson@winona.edu
OLSON, Joshua ... 906-487-1217 227 D jolson@mtu.edu
OLSON, Keith ... 304-327-4247 488 J kolson@bluefieldstate.edu
OLSON, Kelly ... 715-836-2327 494 E olsonke@uwec.edu
OLSON, Kim ... 920-996-2933 497 F olsonk@fvtc.edu
OLSON, Kirsten, G ... 805-437-3784.. 30 D kirsten.olson@csuci.edu
OLSON, Kris ... 218-299-3024 234 K krisolson@cord.edu
OLSON, Kristin ... 562-938-4095.. 48 K kolson@lbcc.edu
OLSON, Lane ... 916-348-4689.. 42 B lolson@epic.edu
OLSON, Mary Ellen ... 920-403-3181 494 B maryellen.olson@snc.edu
OLSON, Matthew ... 781-280-3802 214 G olsonm@middlesex.mass.edu
OLSON, Megan ... 907-786-1764.. 10 A msolson5@alaska.edu
OLSON, Mike ... 480-314-2102.. 16 A
OLSON, Missy ... 541-440-7865 376 F missy.olson@umpqua.edu
OLSON, Nancy ... 507-537-6544 240 G nancy.olson@smsu.edu
OLSON, Paul ... 701-252-3467 346 J paul.olson@uj.edu
OLSON, Robert ... 253-833-9111 480 A rolson@greenriver.edu
OLSON, Robin ... 614-251-4700 358 B olsonr@ohiodominican.edu
OLSON, Roger, T ... 218-299-3682 234 K rolson@cord.edu
OLSON, Sara ... 402-465-2159 267 J solson@nebrwesleyan.edu
OLSON, Sara ... 863-680-3965 100 F solson@flsouthern.edu
OLSON, Scott ... 480-245-7993.. 12 O scott.olson@ibcs.edu
OLSON, Scott, R ... 507-457-5003 241 A solson@winona.edu
OLSON, Sharon ... 562-985-5585.. 32 A sharon.olson@csulb.edu
OLSON, Stephen ... 765-998-5119 161 A stolson@taylor.edu
OLSON, Todd ... 319-363-1323 168 D
OLSON, Tomoko ... 281-998-6146 442 B tomoko.olson@sjcd.edu
OLSON, Wendy ... 509-777-4313 485 D wolson@whitworth.edu
OLSON, Zac ... 541-552-7672 376 A
OLSON-BUCHANAN, Julie ... 559-278-2482.. 31 D julieo@csufresno.edu
OLSON-KOPP, Kim ... 608-796-3267 496 L kmolsonkopp@viterbo.edu
OLSON-LOY, Sandra ... 320-589-6013 243 C olsonloy@morris.umn.edu
OLSON-NIKUNEN, Shari, L ... 602-243-8035.. 14 C shari.olson@southmountaincc.edu
OLSON-STRILZUK, Alicia ... 952-851-0066 233 D fadept@academycollege.edu
OLSTEIN, Binyamin ... 847-982-2500 138 G olstein@htc.edu
OLSZEWSKI, Gabriel, G 860-297-2119.. 88 I gabriel.olszewski@trincoll.edu
OLSZEWSKI, Kristen ... 215-489-2946 381 K kristen.olszewski@delval.edu
OLSZEWSKI, Ryan ... 330-569-5332 353 F ryan.olszewski@abm.com
OLTROGGE, Michael ... 402-494-2311 267 D moltrogge@thenicc.edu
OLUFSEN, Chantel ... 319-399-8662 164 D colufsen@coe.edu
OLUWOLE SOBOYEJO, Winston ... 508-831-4694 220 C wsoboyejo@wpi.edu
OLVER, Kristen ... 262-646-6519 493 F kolver@nashotah.edu
OLVER, Thomas ... 989-386-6675 227 E tolver@midmich.edu
OLVERA, Tina ... 323-466-6663.. 44 A
OLWELL, David ... 360-688-2731 482 D dolwell@stmartin.edu
OMAE, Masa ... 619-388-3207.. 60 I momae@sdccd.edu
OMAN, Megan, E ... 603-526-3451 271 H megan.oman@colby-sawyer.edu
OMANN, Bernie ... 320-308-2122 240 C bomann@stcloudstate.edu
OMAR, Sohair ... 203-575-8281.. 86 H somar@nv.edu
OMARY, M. Bishr ... 848-445-9833 281 B bishr.omary@rutgers.edu
OMBRELLO, Joseph ... 906-227-1188 228 E jombrell@nmu.edu
OMEN, Shieleen ... 218-679-2860 242 E
OMENITSCH, Katie ... 202-884-9301.. 94 A omenitschka@trinitydc.edu
OMER, Aftab ... 707-765-1836.. 52 C
OMER, Nicole ... 801-957-4209 460 D nicole.omer@slcc.edu
OMINSKY, Paul ... 609-258-6688 279 E pominsky@princeton.edu
OMOJOKUN, Emmanuel ... 804-524-5322 475 E eomojokun@vsu.edu
OMOLE, Nike ... 954-453-9228.. 34 I
OMOTO, Allen ... 909-621-8218.. 57 E dean_faculty@pitzer.edu
OMURA, Kanae ... 626-571-8811.. 73 D kanaeo@uwest.edu
ONABANJO, Rae ... 210-458-4011 455 B
ONAPITO, Amanda ... 847-317-7034 150 J aonapito@tiu.edu
ONDER, David ... 828-565-4077 335 A donder@haywood.edu
ONDERKO, Daniel ... 903-566-7277 455 C donderko@uttyler.edu
ONDRIZEK, Megan, M . 305-284-3667 112 K m.ondrizek@umiami.edu
ONDRUS LEWIS, Sherri 602-787-6500.. 13 G sherri.ondrus@paradisevalley.edu
ONEBEAR, Lindsay ... 701-766-4415 344 F
ONG, Meaghan ... 314-719-3661 252 G mong@fontbonne.edu
ONG, Teresa ... 650-949-7794.. 43 A ongteresa@fhda.edu
ONGARO, Guilio ... 714-997-6672.. 36 D ongaro@chapman.edu
ONGERI, Elimelda ... 336-285-3508 341 C eongeri@ncat.edu
ONI, Andrew ... 440-775-5787 357 G andrew.oni@oberlin.edu
ONISHI, Joni, Y ... 808-934-2514 129 F jonishi@hawaii.edu
ONNEN, Kendi ... 309-467-6303 137 G registrar@eureka.edu
ONO, Mika ... 909-748-6297.. 72 E mika_ono@redlands.edu
ONO, Santa, J ... 734-764-6270 231 A
ONORATO, Suzanne ... 860-486-0744.. 89 B suzanne.onorato@uconn.edu
ONSUREZ GAUNA, Valerie ... 575-492-2780 286 E vgauna@nmjc.edu
ONTIVEROS, Juan ... 512-232-4191 454 C juan.ontiveros@austin.utexas.edu
ONTL, Lynn ... 518-255-5225 318 F ontll@cobleskill.edu
ONUNWOR, Enyinda ... 651-846-1542 240 E enyinda.onunwor@saintpaul.edu
ONUSKO, Mark ... 216-397-1756 353 O monusko@jcu.edu
ONWUACHI-WILLIG, Angela ... 617-353-3112 207 C aow@bu.edu
ONWUNLI, Agatha ... 850-599-3115 109 E agatha.onwunli@famu.edu
ONYEAGHALA, Raphael 507-537-6218 240 G raphael.onyeaghala@smsu.edu
OOMMEN, Jose ... 740-397-9000 356 G jose.oommen@mvnu.edu
OOTEN, Tim ... 304-896-7658 487 I tim.ooten@southernwv.edu
OOTEN, Timothy, D ... 304-896-7658 487 I tim.ooten@southernwv.edu
OPARAH, Chinyere ... 415-422-6136.. 72 I jcoparah@usfca.edu
OPATZ, Patrick ... 651-779-3346 237 D patrick.opatz@century.edu
OPAVA, William ... 617-236-8812 209 D wopava@fisher.edu
OPDYCKE, Anita ... 312-567-7553 139 H aopdycke@iit.edu
OPFER, Ryan ... 530-226-4153.. 64 C ropfer@simpsonu.edu
OPGENORTH, Timothy .. 414-229-4541 495 B opgenort@uwm.edu
OPITZ, Brian, R ... 724-287-8711 379 C brian.opitz@bc3.edu
OPITZ, Don ... 312-362-6426 136 F dopitz@depaul.edu
OPITZ, Donald, D ... 724-458-2143 384 F opitzdd@gcc.edu
OPOCYZNSKI, Shaul ... 718-268-4700 311 H
OPOKU, Michael ... 763-433-1272 236 H michael.opoku@anokaramsey.edu
OPPATT, Ron ... 864-231-2000 405 F roppatt@andersonuniversity.edu
OPPENHEIM, Marc, E ... 516-463-6795 301 E marc.oppenhein@hofstra.edu
OPPENHEIMER, Phillip, R ... 209-946-2561.. 71 E poppenhe@pacific.edu
OPPERMAN, Amanda ... 415-561-6555.. 58 B
OPPERMAN, Lynne ... 214-828-8201 446 B lopperman@tamu.edu
OPPERMAN, Mary ... 607-255-3621 297 D mary.opperman@cornell.edu
OPPMANN, Andrew, J .. 615-898-7800 421 C andrew.oppmann@mtsu.edu
OPSATA, Rebecca ... 510-464-3213.. 57 B ropsata@peralta.edu
OQUENDO, Carmen ... 787-250-1912 507 C coquendo@metro.inter.edu
OQUENDO, Diane ... 646-660-6154 292 F diane.oquendo@baruch.cuny.edu
ORACION, Donna ... 575-624-7403 285 F donna.oracion@roswell.enmu.edu
ORANGE, Taur, D ... 212-217-4170 299 C taur_orange@fitnyc.edu
ORANGE, Thomas ... 716-880-2000 305 F
ORANJE, Tammy ... 925-473-7518.. 40 I toranje@losmedanos.edu
ORANSKY, Elissa ... 949-451-5472.. 65 B eoransky@ivc.edu
ORANTE, Newin ... 650-738-4333.. 62 K oranten@smccd.edu
ORAVECZ, Joseph ... 508-531-1276 212 B joravecz@bridgew.edu
ORAVETZ, Teresa ... 203-332-5014.. 86 E toravetz@hcc.commnet.edu
ORBILLE LAFFERTY, Iris ... 858-513-9240.. 16 I iris.lafferty@ashford.edu
ORCHARD, James ... 612-330-1744 233 G orchard@augsburg.edu
ORCHARD, Milissa ... 651-641-8278 235 A morchard@csp.edu
ORCHARD, Sue ... 360-442-2301 480 E sorchard@lowercolumbia.edu
ORCUTT, Jill ... 209-201-8531.. 70 A jorcutt2@ucmerced.edu
ORD, Anna, S ... 757-352-4673 469 D annashi@regent.edu
ORDAZ, Jason ... 505-424-2348 285 H jason.ordaz@iaia.edu
ORDONEZ, Bonnie ... 412-809-5336 395 F ordonez.bonnie@ptcollege.edu
ORDONEZ, Lisa, D ... 858-822-0830.. 70 C lordonez@ucsd.edu
ORDONEZ, Milton ... 562-985-4162.. 32 A milton.ordonez@csulb.edu
OREDEIN, Ade ... 270-852-8607 182 C ade.oredein@kctcs.edu
OREE, Jim ... 803-774-3331 406 A oreeej@cctech.edu
OREIRO, David ... 360-676-2772 480 G doreiro@nwic.edu
ORELLANA, Alicia ... 713-692-0077 433 B aorellana@ciaml.com
ORELLANA, Evelyn ... 661-942-6204.. 34 J
ORELLANA, Victoria ... 201-360-4121 277 D vorellana@hccc.edu
OREM, Christopher, D .. 540-568-7208 467 C oremcd@jmu.edu
OREMUS, Karen ... 803-323-2323 413 D oremusk@winthrop.edu
ORENDER, Patricia ... 386-752-1822.. 99 P patricia.orender@fgc.edu
ORENDORFF, Jay ... 415-338-2862.. 34 A jayo@sfsu.edu
ORENGO, Juan ... 787-856-0945 505 B jorengo@columbiacentral.edu
ORENGO-ORTEGA, Orlando ... 787-993-0000 510 E orlando.orengo@upr.edu
ORF, Michael ... 417-255-7272 256 A michaelorf@missouristate.edu
ORF, Robert, W ... 603-535-2461 274 B rorf@plymouth.edu
ORIHUELA, Omar ... 619-482-6360.. 65 K oorihuela@swccd.edu
ORIHUELA, Ruthanne ... 303-556-3595.. 80 D ruthanne.orihuela@ccd.edu
ORIO, Julie, J ... 415-422-2823.. 72 I orioj@usfca.edu
ORIOLO, Michael ... 315-866-0300 301 B orioloma@herkimer.edu
ORITZ, Fernando ... 509-313-4054 479 E oritz2@gonzaga.edu
ORKIN, Michael ... 510-466-7308.. 57 C morkin@peralta.edu
ORKISZEWSKI, Paul ... 828-262-2801 340 G orkiszewskip@appstate.edu
ORLANDO, Karen ... 949-451-5511.. 65 B korlando@ivc.edu
ORLANDO, Matthew ... 207-725-3804 194 A morlando@bowdoin.edu
ORLANDO, Michael ... 517-264-7601 230 C morlando@sienaheights.edu
ORLANDO, Steve ... 352-846-3903 110 E sfo@ufl.edu
ORLASKE, Michelle ... 269-782-1486 230 D mbogue@swmich.edu

OSBURN, Darren 636-922-8533 258 A dosburn@stchas.edu
OSBURN, Monica 919-515-2423 341 E monica_osburn@ncsu.edu
OSBURN, Toby 337-562-4249 192 B tosburn@mcneese.edu
OSBURN, Wade 731-989-6067 418 H wosburn@fhu.edu
OSCHERWITZ, Dayna 214-768-2210 443 G oscherwi@smu.edu
OSEGUEDA, Roberto 915-747-5680 454 E osegueda@utep.edu
OSEGUERA, Tonantzin 657-278-7755 31 E toseguera@fullerton.edu
OSEI, Akwasi 302-857-6625 90 D aosei@desu.edu
OSGOOD, Jeanne 651-638-6035 233 J j-osgood@bethel.edu
OSGOOD, Jeffery 610-738-0492 394 F josgood@wcupa.edu
OSGOOD, Russell, K 314-935-4042 261 B rosgood@wustl.edu
OSGOOD, Schuyler 212-752-1530 303 G schuyler.osgood@limcollege.edu
OSGUTHORPE, Rich 801-422-4331 458 A rich_osguthorpe@byu.edu
OSHIER, Mark 317-940-8000 153 H
OSHIRO, Cathie 620-792-9234 171 F oshiroc@bartonccc.edu
OSHIRO, James 808-689-2663 129 C joshiro6@hawaii.edu
OSHIRO, Julie 818-299-5500 74 I
OSHIRO, Wayde 808-455-0378 130 A waydeo@hawaii.edu
OSHMAN, Melissa 909-389-3309 60 E moshman@craftonhills.edu
OSHRY, Yehuda 845-426-3110 325 M
OSIER, Adam 763-544-9501 235 D
OSIKA, Elizabeth 317-955-6095 159 A eosika@marian.edu
OSIRIS, Charles, E 805-437-3218 30 D charles.osiris@csuci.edu
OSKEY, Lance, D 717-245-3131 502 E lance.d.oskey.mil@mail.mil
OSKVIG, Bryant 202-885-1000 91 D revo@american.edu
OSLER, Cheri 509-533-7311 478 D cheri.osler@scc.spokane.edu
OSMAN, Md 213-262-3939 46 H
OSMOND, Tatiana 207-454-1094 195 E tosmond@wccc.me.edu
OSMOTHERLY, Jason 800-658-4308 266 J osmotherlyj@mpcc.edu
OSOFSKY, Hari 312-503-0491 146 C hariosofsky@law.northwestern.edu
OSOFSKY, Hari, M 814-863-1521 391 F hmo8@psu.edu
OSORIO, Jonhathan 808-956-0980 129 B osorio@hawaii.edu
OSORIO, Jorge, J 718-990-7990 313 B osorioj@stjohns.edu
OSORIO, Kelly 413-236-1641 213 E kosorio@berkshirecc.edu
OSORIO, Michael 408-274-7900 62 F michael.osorio@evc.edu
OSOWA, Sarah, R 401-865-2202 403 G sosowa@providence.edu
OSOWICZ, Lauren 270-686-6415 179 F lauren.osowicz@brescia.edu
OSOWSKI, Anne 843-953-1431 407 D osowskia@cofc.edu
OSSEIRAN-HANNA, Khatmeh 724-357-5661 393 G osseiran@iup.edu
OSSOWSKI, John 315-792-3216 323 G jdossows@utica.edu
OSTASH, Heather 760-384-6249 47 C hostash@cerrocoso.edu
OSTENDORF, Mari 206-221-5748 484 A ostendor@uw.edu
OSTENDORFF, Stephen 516-323-3000 306 I
OSTENDORFF, Stephen 212-875-4402 290 F sostendorff@bankstreet.edu
OSTER, Ben Zion 323-937-3763 76 G boster@yoec.edu
OSTER, JoAnna 607-729-1581 297 G joster@davisny.edu
OSTER-AALAND, Laura 701-231-7052 345 D laura.oster-aaland@ndsu.edu
OSTERBERG, Rick 781-292-2431 209 E rick.osterberg@olin.edu
OSTERBIND, Kelly 251-461-7643 9 A osterbind@southalabama.edu
OSTERGREN, Jennifer 760-750-4311 33 C jostergren@csusm.edu
OSTERHOUT, Benjamin, R 717-361-3749 383 B osterhoutb@etown.edu
OSTERHOUT, Colin 907-796-6576 10 C ctosterhout@alaska.edu
OSTERLUND, Linda 303-458-4100 83 B losterla@regis.edu
OSTERMAN, Michael 509-527-4975 485 C ostermmg@whitman.edu
OSTERTHUN, Stu 402-323-3401 268 D sosterthun@southeast.edu
OSTGAARD, Kolleen 916-484-8569 50 J ostgaak@arc.losrios.edu
OSTLER, Jon 435-283-7361 460 C jon.ostler@snow.edu
OSTLING, Suzanne 540-863-2925 473 D sostling@mgcc.edu
OSTLUND, Scott 847-866-3900 138 B
OSTOLAZA, Magda, E 787-257-7373 509 B ue_mostolaza@uagm.edu
OSTRANDER, Rick 805-565-6000 75 I rostrander@westmont.edu
OSTROM, Lee 208-282-7903 132 C ostrom@uidaho.edu
OSTROM, Rennolds 714-516-5434 36 D rostrom@chapman.edu
OSTROSKY, Jay 617-850-1261 210 D jostrosky@hchc.edu
OSTROTH, Amy 434-381-6330 470 H aostroth@sbc.edu
OSTROWICKI, Jacqueline, M 402-472-7130 268 I jostrowicki@nebraska.edu
OSTROWSKI, Jason 208-732-6225 131 B jostrowski@csi.edu
OSTROWSKI, Julie 704-923-8438 334 E ostrowski.julie@gaston.edu
OSTROWSKI, Michael 931-598-1661 422 F mtostrow@sewanee.edu
OSTROWSKI, Radek 864-656-5274 406 F rostrow@clemson.edu
OSTWINKLE, Chris 815-280-6635 140 I costwink@jjc.edu
OSWALD, Cecelia 484-323-3183 385 K coswald@immaculata.edu
OSWALD, Clark 316-284-5233 171 I coswald@bethelks.edu
OSWALD, Debra 937-512-3007 360 F debra.oswald@sinclair.edu
OSWALD, Scott 251-981-3771 5 B scott.oswald@columbiasouthern.edu
OSWALD, Sharon 662-325-2580 247 A soswald@cobilan.msstate.edu
OSWALD, Vicki 605-367-8355 416 B vicki.oswald@southeasttech.edu
OSWALT, Natalie 903-693-2095 440 E noswalt@panola.edu
OSWELL, Michelle 215-893-5265 381 I michelle.oswell@curtis.edu
OSZUST, Renee 248-341-2153 228 H raoszust@oaklandcc.edu
OTÓN-OLIVIERI, Patricia 787-751-1912 507 F poton@juris.inter.edu
OTERO, George 787-257-0000 510 F george.otero@upr.edu
OTHMAN, Saib 773-298-3900 148 I sothman@sxu.edu
OTHUON, Alberto 610-372-4721 396 A aothuon@racc.edu
OTIENO, Tom 859-622-1405 180 B tom.otieno@eku.edu
OTIS, Brian 203-932-7000 89 F
OTIS, Brian 860-486-5960 89 B botis@foundation.uconn.edu
OTIZ ALVAREZ, Luis 787-841-2000 508 H capellania@pucpr.edu
OTRADOVEC, George 800-567-2344 491 C gotradovec@menominee.edu
OTSTOT, Kylie 602-489-5300 10 G kylie.otstot@arizonachristian.edu
OTT, Alexander 718-289-5939 292 H alexander.ott@bcc.cuny.edu
OTT, Amy 803-535-1222 410 C otta@octech.edu
OTT, Daniel 540-432-4984 465 F dean-thpa@emu.edu
OTT, Geoffrey 863-667-5182 108 I gdott@seu.edu
OTT, Kevin 559-791-2232 47 D kevin.ott@portervillecollege.edu
OTT, Kim, A 928-523-1894 14 J kimberly.ott@nau.edu
OTT, Luisa 520-494-5283 11 M luisa.ott@centralaz.edu
OTT, Sandra 501-450-5015 23 K sott@uca.edu
OTT ROWLANDS, Sue 434-947-8140 469 A sottrowlands@randolphcollege.edu
OTTAWAY, Mallory 504-398-2110 191 E mottaway@uhcno.edu
OTTE, Bobbi 406-657-1086 264 G otteb@rocky.edu
OTTE, Jennifer 402-363-5718 269 F jaotte@york.edu
OTTEMAN, Marcie, M 989-774-3312 221 M alumni@cmich.edu
OTTEN, Daren 760-366-5289 40 K dotten@cmccd.edu
OTTEN, Laura 215-951-1118 386 I otten@lasalle.edu
OTTEN, Val 303-871-2647 84 C val.otten@du.edu
OTTER, Kelly 202-687-7169 92 D otter@georgetown.edu
OTTEY, Jacqueline 201-447-7204 274 I jottey@bergen.edu
OTTINGER, Marie 334-386-7512 5 D mottinger@faulkner.edu
OTTINGER, Michael 505-566-3081 287 G ottingerm@sanjuancollege.edu
OTTINO, Julio, M 847-491-3195 146 C jm-ottino@northwestern.edu
OTTMAN, Ray 479-788-7110 22 A ray.ottman@uafs.edu
OTTMAN, Stephanie 918-495-7392 368 F sottman@oru.edu
OTTO, Alicia 913-758-6327 177 I alicia.otto@stmary.edu
OTTO, Andy 785-242-2500 176 F andy.otto@ottawa.edu
OTTO, Andy 800-995-3159 262 A
OTTO, Dieter 734-487-0306 223 F dotto@emich.edu
OTTO, Lori 269-749-7642 229 G lotto@olivetcollege.edu
OTTO, Richard, H 312-461-0600 132 F ifitzgerald@aaart.edu
OTTO, Ryan 540-375-5249 469 G otto@roanoke.edu
OTTO, Tyson 660-359-3948 256 F totto@mail.ncmissouri.edu
OTTOBONI, John 408-554-5359 63 A jottoboni@scu.edu
OTTOSSON, John 641-673-1076 170 I ottossonj@wmpenn.edu
OTTS, Cynthia 816-584-6273 257 E cynthia.otts@park.edu
OTU, Emmanual 262-598-2973 495 D otu@uwp.edu
OTUAFI, Quincey 801-832-2222 461 A qotuafi@westminstercollege.edu
OTUYA, Etuwe 678-323-7700 93 H
OTWELL, Ginger 870-230-5458 19 H otwellg@hsu.edu
OTWELL, Michelle 386-386-7380 5 D motwell@faulkner.edu
OTWORTH, Pamela 740-351-3208 360 E potworth@shawnee.edu
OTY, Karla 580-581-7962 365 C koty@cameron.edu
OTYENOH, Kimberly 540-665-5436 470 A kotyenoh@su.edu
OUBRÉ, Linda 562-907-4201 76 A president@whittier.edu
OUDSHOORN, Michael 336-841-9000 329 E moudshoo@highpoint.edu
OUECHANI, Maryam 314-367-8700 260 A maryam.ouechani@uhsp.edu
OUELLETTE, Alicia 518-445-3305 289 B aouel@albanylaw.edu
OUELLETTE, Andrew 574-239-8305 155 E aouellette@hcc-nd.edu
OUELLETTE, Calen 360-992-2677 477 J couellette@support.clark.org
OUELLETTE, Dallas 301-387-3097 198 F dallas.ouellette@garrettcollege.edu
OUELLETTE, Nicole 803-778-7820 406 A ouellettend@cctech.edu
OUELLETTE-SCHRAMM, Jen 507-433-0812 240 A jen.ouellette-schramm@riverland.edu
OUERT, Mike 406-994-5411 263 G mrouert@montana.edu
OUILLET, Pierre-Yves 858-534-3390 70 C pouillet@ucsd.edu
OUIMET, Maurice 802-468-1491 462 H maurice.ouimet@castleton.edu
OUKAYAN, Tzoler 818-240-1000 43 J toukayan@glendale.edu
OULAMINE, Saadia 267-256-0200 93 H
OULD, Jennifer 773-947-6307 143 E jould@mccormick.edu
OURADA, Stephanie 402-461-7733 266 C stephanie.ourada@hastings.edu
OURS, Alan 912-279-5762 117 C aours@ccga.edu
OURSO, Mark 225-214-1955 186 H mark.ourso@franu.edu
OUSLEY, Allisha 678-422-4100 93 H
OUTAR, O'Neil 401-454-6532 404 B ooutar@risd.edu
OUTEN, Jason 828-835-4229 338 C jouten@tricountycc.edu
OUTING, Donald, A 610-758-2128 388 C dao417@lehigh.edu
OUTLAW, Steve 850-201-7000 112 B steve.outlaw@tcc.fl.edu
OUTLEY, Patrice 318-274-2288 191 G outleyp@gram.edu
OUTON, Peggy, M 412-397-6000 396 E outon@rmu.edu
OVADIA, Steve 718-482-6022 294 D sovadia@lagcc.cuny.edu
OVEDIA, Nicole, R 561-237-7237 103 W novedia@lynn.edu
OVERBEE, Peyton 919-735-5151 338 F
OVERBY, David 605-688-4988 416 A david.overby@sdstate.edu
OVERCASH, Shannon 508-541-1841 208 E sovercash@dean.edu
OVERDORF, Daniel 865-573-4517 419 E doverdorf@johnsonu.edu
OVEREND, Gregory 203-932-7430 89 F goverend@newhaven.edu
OVERHOLSER, Toni 937-328-8070 350 D overholsert@clarkstate.edu
OVERHOLTZER, Michael, H 646-888-6639 304 H overhom1@mskcc.org
OVERLAND, Royce 320-564-5007 239 B royce.overland@mnwest.edu
OVERLAUR, Kevin, J 229-245-4357 127 C kjoverlaur@valdosta.edu
OVERMYER-VELAZQUEZ, Mark 959-200-3766 89 B mark.velazquez@uconn.edu
OVEROCKER, Quintin 828-641-0020 327 A overocqm@brevard.edu
OVERPECK, Jonathan, T 734-764-2550 231 A overpeck@umich.edu
OVERSTREET, Darryl 580-559-5582 365 J doverstt@ecok.edu
OVERSTREET, Kirk 618-985-2828 140 G kirkoverstreet@jalc.edu
OVERSTREET, Mana 615-732-7893 421 B m.overstreet@mtsa.edu
OVERSTREET, Tammie 423-236-2759 422 H toverstreet@southern.edu
OVERTON, Chrystal 580-477-7702 371 D chrystal.overton@wosc.edu
OVERTON, Karen 919-497-3212 330 E finaid@louisburg.edu
OVERTON, Kirby 419-434-4439 362 D overton@findlay.edu
OVERTON, Milton 470-578-6033 121 J
OVERTON, Travis, E 843-349-2168 407 B toverton@coastal.edu
OVERTON-HEALY, Julia 585-385-8143 313 A joverton-healy@sjfc.edu
OVERTURF, Mitzi 501-332-0230 18 D moverturf@asutr.edu
OVERVOORDE, Paul 651-696-6460 236 C overvoorde@macalester.edu
OVESON, Kip, R 320-222-6930 239 H kip.oveson@ridgewater.edu
OVEZOV, Dovran 832-230-5548 439 H dovran@na.edu
OVIEDO, Sonya 209-575-7738 76 K oviedos@mjc.edu
OVITT, Kimberly 503-494-0992 374 F ovitt@ohsu.edu
OVUERAYE, Loretta 305-237-7296 104 E oovueray@mdc.edu
OWCZARCZAK, Kathleen 716-884-9120 291 I kowczarczak@bryantstratton.edu

O'CONNOR, Brian ...... 406-994-5016 263 G
boconnor@montana.edu
O'CONNOR, Christi ...... 323-953-4000.. 49 E
oconnoca@lacitycollege.edu
O'CONNOR, Daniel, P .. 713-743-4002 451 G
doconnor2@uh.edu
O'CONNOR, Debra .... 516-323-4110 306 I
doconnor@molloy.edu
O'CONNOR, Deirdre, M 570-577-3141 379 A
deirdre.oconnor@bucknell.edu
O'CONNOR, Diane .... 518-694-7232 289 A
diane.oconnor@acphs.edu
O'CONNOR, Diane .... 215-641-6416 390 A
doconnor@mc3.edu
O'CONNOR, Edward, R . 816-654-7000 253 I
eoconnor@kcumb.edu
O'CONNOR, Ellen, M ... 215-955-6835 398 G
ellen.oconnor@jefferson.edu
O'CONNOR, Gregory ..... 934-420-2170 320 C
oconnor@farmingdale.edu
O'CONNOR, Heidi .... 978-468-7111 209 G
hoconnor@gcts.edu
O'CONNOR, Isabel .... 619-388-2755.. 61 A
ioconnor@sdccd.edu
O'CONNOR, James .... 563-884-5294 169 C
james.oconnor@palmer.edu
O'CONNOR, James .... 334-844-3500.... 4 E
jmo0024@auburn.edu
O'CONNOR, Jasi .... 218-299-3549 234 K
oconnor@cord.edu
O'CONNOR, Jen .... 785-864-2640 177 G
jen.occonor@ku.edu
O'CONNOR, Jeremiah ... 508-793-2564 208 A
joconnor@holycross.edu
O'CONNOR, Julie, A ..... 414-425-8300 494 A
joconnor@shsst.edu
O'CONNOR, Kevin .... 949-582-4788.. 65 C
koconnor@saddleback.edu
O'CONNOR, Kevin .... 800-658-4308 266 J
oconnork@mpcc.edu
O'CONNOR, Lisa, G ..... 203-582-8549.. 88 F
lisa.o'connor@quinnipiac.edu
O'CONNOR, Maria .... 216-397-4268 353 O
moconnor@jcu.edu
O'CONNOR, Mary .... 203-837-8460.. 86 A
oconnorma@wcsu.edu
O'CONNOR, Maureen ... 650-433-3895.. 55 K
moconnor@paloaltou.edu
O'CONNOR, Michael .... 815-802-8908 141 B
moconnor@kcc.edu
O'CONNOR, Mike, K .... 920-832-6561 492 B
mike.k.oconnor@lawrence.edu
O'CONNOR, Patricia ..... 559-278-7392.. 31 D
poconnor@csufresno.edu
O'CONNOR, Patrick ...... 617-879-7878 212 E
poconnor@massart.edu
O'CONNOR, Patrick, W 201-684-7500 280 B
poconnor@ramapo.edu
O'CONNOR, Rob .... 501-450-1225.. 19 I
o'connor@hendrix.edu
O'CONNOR, Robert .... 315-781-3535 301 D
oconnor@hws.edu
O'CONNOR, Shawn .... 507-433-0564 240 A
shawn.o'connor@riverland.edu
O'CONNOR, Tennille, I . 727-816-3116 105 E
oconnot@phsc.edu
O'CONNOR, Teri .... 214-887-5065 434 G
toconnor@dts.edu
O'CONNOR, Timothy ..... 212-327-8080 312 B
toconnor@rockefeller.edu
O'DANIEL, Jennifer .... 512-863-1691 444 F
odanielj@southwestern.edu
O'DAY, Steven, P .... 903-813-3001 429 I
soday@austincollege.edu
O'DELL, April .... 802-865-5734 461 C
o'dell@champlain.edu
O'DELL, Cynthia .... 219-980-6509 157 A
codell@iun.edu
O'DELL, Ryan .... 608-663-6796 491 F
rodell@edgewood.edu
O'DELL, Tammy .... 931-393-1745 423 G
todell@mscc.edu
O'DONNELL, Alicia .... 402-461-7488 266 C
aodonnell@hastings.edu
O'DONNELL, James ...... 480-965-3956.. 11 A
jod@asu.edu
O'DONNELL, Kathleen ... 207-778-7094 196 F
katie.odonnell@maine.edu
O'DONNELL, Loraine .... 716-829-8141 298 C
kavinokytheater@dyc.edu
O'DONNELL, Niall .... 540-636-2900 464 O
niall.odonnell@christendom.edu
O'DONNELL, SSJ,
Patricia .... 215-248-7125 380 G
podonnel@chc.edu
O'DONNELL, Patrick ...... 562-860-2451.. 35 O
podonnell@cerritos.edu
O'DONNELL, Timothy ... 540-654-1252 471 B
todonnel@umw.edu
O'DONNELL,
Timothy, T .... 540-636-2900 464 O
president@christendom.edu
O'DONNELL-RUNDLETT,
Marylou .... 617-353-5315 207 C
modonnel@bu.edu
O'DONOVAN, Stephen .. 254-526-1114 431 E
admissions.registrar@ctcd.edu
O'DOWD, Ann, M .... 402-280-2293 265 J
annodowd@creighton.edu
O'DOWD, Diane, K .... 949-824-0622.. 69 C
dkodowd@uci.edu
O'DRISCOLL, Daniel ..... 401-254-3510 404 C
dodriscoll@rwu.edu
O'DRISCOLL, Dean .... 509-452-5100 481 E
dodriscoll@pnwu.edu
O'DRISCOLL, Sue .... 540-545-7399 470 A
sodrisco09@su.edu
O'FARRELL, Billie .... 727-569-1401 112 F
bskinner@trinitycollege.edu
O'FARRELL, Kevin, F .... 813-527-6620 105 E
ofarrek@phsc.edu
O'FARRELL, Mark, T ..... 727-376-6911 112 F
mofarrell@trinitycollege.edu
O'FLYNN, Greg .... 305-809-3184.. 97 M
greg.oflynn@cfk.edu
O'GEARY, Amy .... 252-492-2061 338 D
ogearya@vgcc.edu
O'GRADY, Elaine .... 845-569-3190 307 B
elaine.ogrady@msmc.edu
O'GRADY, Tina .... 415-575-6143.. 29 A
O'GUINN, Dave .... 812-855-8188 156 C
vpsa@indiana.edu
O'GUINN, M. Dave .... 812-855-8188 156 B
mdoguinn@iu.edu
O'GWYNN, Chris .... 334-844-5061.... 4 E
ogwynca@auburn.edu
O'GWYNN, Marty .... 864-977-2093 410 A
marty.o'gwynn@ngu.edu
O'HALLORAN,
Bernadette (BJ) .... 626-584-5238.. 43 E
bjohalloran@fuller.edu
O'HALLORAN,
Teresa, E .... 715-836-2387 494 E
ohallote@uwec.edu
O'HANION, Kimberly .... 480-212-1704.. 15 R
O'HARA, Bradley .... 604-482-5510 132 D
bohara@adler.edu
O'HARA, Elin .... 518-564-5187 318 C
oharaea@plattsburgh.edu
O'HARA, Jamie .... 401-454-6709 404 B
johara01@risd.edu
O'HARA, Kate .... 508-678-2811 213 F
kate.o'hara@bristolcc.edu
O'HARA, Kate .... 508-678-2811 213 F
O'HARA, Matt .... 831-459-2328.. 71 A
mdohara@ucsc.edu
O'HARA, Patrick .... 773-702-1234 151 B
O'HARA, Shawn .... 336-506-4136 331 J
shawn.ohara@alamancecc.edu
O'HARA, Timothy .... 315-464-7345 316 F
oharati@upstate.edu
O'HARA O'CONNOR,
Erin .... 850-644-3071 110 B
eoconnor@law.fsu.edu
O'HARE, Katie .... 617-323-6662 219 G
katie_ohare@williamjames.edu
O'HARE, Lauren .... 201-761-6272 282 H
lohare@saintpeters.edu
O'HERRON, Mike .... 815-965-8616 147 I
moherron@rockfordcareercollege.edu
O'HORA UHNAK,
Marilyn .... 315-781-3734 301 D
uhnak@hws.edu
O'KANE, Barbara .... 303-384-2561.. 79 A
bokane@mines.edu
O'KANE, Gail .... 612-659-6299 238 C
gail.okane@minneapolis.edu
O'KEEFE, Carolyn .... 909-537-5240.. 33 B
carolynokeefe@csusb.edu
O'KEEFE, Claire .... 239-687-5423.. 95 L
cokeefe@avemarialaw.edu
O'KEEFE, Claire .... 239-687-5300.. 95 L
O'KEEFE, Colleen .... 201-684-7494 280 B
cokeefe3@ramapo.edu
O'KEEFE, Dean, R .... 508-565-1667 218 F
dokeefe@stonehill.edu
O'KEEFE, Erin .... 203-932-7000.. 89 F
O'KEEFE, John, L .... 610-330-5803 387 B
okeefej@lafayette.edu
O'KEEFE, Laurie .... 401-598-1000 403 E
laurie.okeefe@jwu.edu
O'KEEFE, Louise .... 256-824-2445.... 8 B
louise.okeefe@uah.edu
O'KEEFE, Matt, J .... 785-532-5590 175 A
mjokeefe@ksu.edu
O'KEEFE, Michael .... 781-768-7000 217 H
O'KEEFE, Mildred .... 516-876-3247 318 A
okeefem@oldwestbury.edu
O'KEEFE, Natalie .... 417-328-1815 258 K
nokeefe@sbuniv.edu
O'KEEFE, Robert .... 414-930-3201 493 E
okeefer@mtmary.edu
O'KEEFE, Steve .... 618-985-3741 140 G
steveokeefe@jalc.edu
O'KELLY, Kimberly, B ... 715-836-4325 494 E
weigelkb@uwec.edu
O'LEARY, Erin .... 912-525-5000 124 G
eoleary@scad.edu
O'LEARY, Heather .... 617-573-8302 218 G
holeary@suffolk.edu
O'LEARY, Heather, S .... 212-752-1530 303 G
heather.oleary@limcollege.edu
O'LEARY, Janet .... 206-239-4500 477 I
O'LEARY, Kara .... 574-284-4578 160 F
koleary@saintmarys.edu
O'LEARY, Kathryn .... 919-497-3260 330 E
koleary@louisburg.edu
O'LEARY, Katy .... 860-509-9528.. 88 A
koleary@hartfordinternational.edu
O'LEARY, Michael .... 304-434-8000 487 E
michael.o_leary@easternwv.edu
O'LINGER, Jennifer .... 256-551-3125.... 2 E
jennifer.o'linger@drakestate.edu
O'LYNN, Robert, G .... 606-474-3230 180 G
rolynn@kcu.edu
O'MAHONEY, Angel ...... 310-393-0411.. 56 C
O'MALLEY, Barbara .... 909-706-7055.. 75 G
domalley@westernu.edu
O'MALLEY, Bert .... 713-798-6205 430 E
berto@bcm.edu
O'MALLEY, Jeff .... 409-880-2248 449 B
jeffrey.omalley@lamar.edu
O'MALLEY, Marjorie ...... 617-879-7045 212 E
momalley@massart.edu
O'MALLEY, Michael ...... 512-245-2150 449 G
mo20@txstate.edu
O'MALLEY, Nora .... 630-617-3178 137 E
nora.omalley@elmhurst.edu
O'MALLEY, Richard .... 979-830-4054 430 I
richard.omalley@blinn.edu
O'MALLEY, Sean, M ...... 856-225-6159 281 A
omallese@camden.rutgers.edu
O'MALLEY, Stephanie ... 303-871-2784.. 84 C
stephanie.omalley@du.edu
O'MARA, Kevin .... 718-270-4628 316 E
kevin.o'mara@downstate.edu
O'MARA, Kevin .... 910-893-1380 327 C
komara@campbell.edu
O'MARA CARVER,
Maureen .... 215-871-6704 395 A
maureenca@pcom.edu
O'MEALEY, Ryan .... 515-650-3198 163 C
ryanomealey@theartofeducation.edu
O'MEARA, James .... 956-326-2680 446 A
james.omeara@tamiu.edu
O'MEARA, KerryAnn ...... 301-405-2335 202 E
komeara@umd.edu
O'MEARA, Mary Ellen .. 740-427-5112 354 I
omearam@kenyon.edu
O'MEARA, Ron .... 229-225-5200 125 G
romeara@southernregional.edu
O'NEAL, Adam .... 870-633-4480.. 19 E
aoneal@eacc.edu
O'NEAL, Aleshia .... 402-363-5690 269 F
ajoneal@york.edu
O'NEAL, Angela, D .... 518-629-8172 302 A
a.oneal@hvcc.edu
O'NEAL, Benjamin .... 317-738-8303 155 A
boneal@franklincollege.edu
O'NEAL, Bryan .... 312-329-4057 144 F
bryan.oneal@moody.edu
O'NEAL, Christian .... 501-916-6433.. 22 C
cxoneal@ualr.edu
O'NEAL, Debbie .... 417-873-7527 252 A
doneal@drury.edu
O'NEAL, Dennis, L .... 254-710-3871 430 F
dennis_oneal@baylor.edu
O'NEAL, Ginger, H .... 252-335-0821 333 E
goneal@albemarle.edu
O'NEAL, Justin .... 660-596-7282 259 D
joneal@sfccmo.edu
O'NEAL, Kate .... 213-356-5386.. 65 D
kate_oneal@sciarc.edu
O'NEAL, Montrice .... 225-771-3922 190 K
dos@subr.edu
O'NEAL, Patricia, Y ...... 708-534-4132 138 C
poneal2@govst.edu
O'NEAL, Robert .... 803-535-5549 406 E
roneal@claflin.edu
O'NEAL, Sharon .... 843-525-8248 411 G
soneal@tcl.edu
O'NEAL, Stephanie .... 918-631-2200 371 C
stephanie-oneal@utulsa.edu
O'NEIL, Alysha, M .... 573-341-4122 260 F
O'NEIL, Brian .... 410-777-2373 197 C
boneil1@aacc.edu
O'NEIL, Danielle .... 603-862-1073 273 H
danielle.oneil@unh.edu
O'NEIL, Faith .... 434-797-8458 472 H
faith.oneil@danville.edu
O'NEIL, Jill .... 605-688-6092 416 A
jill.oneil@sdstate.edu
O'NEIL, Laura, L .... 607-777-2131 315 E
loneil@binghamton.edu
O'NEIL, Patricia, S .... 312-942-5600 148 C
poneil@rush.edu
O'NEILL, Charles .... 724-830-1144 397 F
oneill@setonhill.edu
O'NEILL, Colleen .... 480-423-6177.. 14 B
colleen.oneill@scottsdalecc.edu
O'NEILL, Daniel .... 978-762-4000 215 B
daoneill@northshore.edu
O'NEILL, Dianne, M ...... 301-369-2325 197 F
dmoneill@captechu.edu
O'NEILL, F. Shawn .... 201-684-7550 280 B
soneill@ramapo.edu
O'NEILL, Joan, E .... 203-432-5461.. 90 B
joan.oneill@yale.edu
O'NEILL, Katy .... 410-617-6801 199 G
mconeill@loyola.edu
O'NEILL, Kelsey .... 605-394-1203 415 I
kelsey.oneill@sdsmt.edu
O'NEILL, Kevin .... 270-534-3206 182 G
kevin.oneill@kctcs.edu
O'NEILL, Kim .... 360-650-3524 485 A
O'NEILL, Mary .... 410-617-6811 201 C
moneill5@ndm.edu
O'NEILL, Stephen .... 507-786-3062 242 I
oneill@stolaf.edu
O'NEILL, Walter .... 616-554-5827 222 H
woneill1@davenport.edu
O'NEILL, William .... 402-559-1952 269 B
woneill@unmc.edu
O'QUINN, Robin .... 918-463-2931 365 I
robin.oquinn@connorsstate.edu
O'REAR, Randy, G .... 254-295-4500 453 A
rorear@umhb.edu
O'REILLY, Andrew .... 310-258-5693.. 51 C
andrew.oreilly@lmu.edu
O'REILLY, Lillian .... 718-951-5114 293 A
loreilly@brooklyn.cuny.edu
O'REILLY, Maureen, A ... 603-641-7084 273 C
moreilly@anselm.edu
O'REILLY, Paul .... 805-421-5974.. 67 J
president@thomasaquinas.edu
O'REILLY, Paul, J .... 805-525-4417.. 67 J
poreilly@thomasaquinas.edu
O'REILLY, Tricia .... 510-841-9230.. 76 F
toreilly@wi.edu
O'RILEY, Jane .... 318-670-9401 191 B
joriley@susla.edu
O'RIORDAN, Steven ...... 978-934-3185 211 G
steven_oriordan@uml.edu
O'RORKE, Kevin .... 530-242-7621.. 64 A
kororke@shastacollege.edu
O'ROURKE, Brian .... 219-464-5616 162 C
brian.orourke@valpo.edu
O'ROURKE, Brian .... 908-526-1200 280 C
brian.o'rourke@raritanval.edu
O'ROURKE, Brian, J ..... 864-656-5658 406 F
orourke@clemson.edu
O'ROURKE, Catherine ... 212-217-3800 299 C
catherine_orourke@fitnyc.edu
O'ROURKE, Deidre .... 716-827-4348 322 J
orourked@trocaire.edu
O'ROURKE, Elizabeth .... 401-874-9512 404 E
lorourke@uri.edu
O'ROURKE, Erin .... 413-577-2112 211 D
eorourke@umass.edu
O'ROURKE, John .... 413-565-1000 205 I
jorourke@baypath.edu

O'ROURKE, Kevin .... 718-489-5496 312 H
korourke@sfc.edu
O'ROURKE, Kim .... 540-231-6232 475 D
orourkek@vt.edu
O'ROURKE, Krysti .... 631-656-2163 299 G
krysti.orourke@ftc.edu
O'ROURKE, Mary, C ..... 443-518-4778 199 D
O'ROURKE, Maureen .... 617-353-3123 207 C
morourke@bu.edu
O'ROURKE, Patrick .... 303-492-5852.. 83 M
evc-coo@colorado.edu
O'ROURKE, Patty .... 412-281-2600 395 C
porourke@pci.edu
O'ROURKE, Sheila, N .... 973-618-3341 275 E
sorourke@caldwell.edu
O'RYAN, Kelly .... 802-387-6362 461 E
kellyoryan@landmark.edu
O'SHEA, David .... 480-517-8689.. 14 A
david.oshea@riosalado.edu
O'SHEA, Maureen .... 508-362-2131 214 B
moshea@capecod.edu
O'SHEA, William .... 503-352-1419 375 B
osheawa@pacificu.edu
O'SHIELDS, Shannon .... 714-879-3901.. 45 J
soshields@hiu.edu
O'SICK, Kathryn .... 518-743-2277 319 D
osickk@sunyacc.edu
O'SULLIVAN, Connor ..... 832-813-6294 438 E
connor.osullivan@lonestar.edu
O'SULLIVAN, Daniel, W 410-293-1582 502 I
osulliva@usna.edu
O'SULLIVAN, Eileen ...... 508-531-2921 212 B
eosullivan@bridgew.edu
O'SULLIVAN, Gerard ..... 215-885-2360 389 A
provost@manor.edu
O'SULLIVAN, Gerry .... 215-884-8942 402 E
academicdean@woninstitute.edu
O'SULLIVAN, Grace ...... 480-727-1924.. 11 A
grace.osullivan@asu.edu
O'SULLIVAN, Joseph .... 314-516-6800 260 E
osullivanj@umsl.edu
O'SULLIVAN, Kevin .... 914-633-2120 302 C
kosullivan@iona.edu
O'SULLIVAN, Margaret . 718-270-2487 316 E
margaret.o'sullivan@downstate.edu
O'SULLIVAN, Patrick ..... 805-756-7244.. 29 K
posulliv@calpoly.edu
O'SULLIVAN, Rachel ..... 256-233-8100.... 4 D
rachel.osullivan@athens.edu
O'SULLIVAN, Trecia ...... 646-717-9742 300 C
osullivan@gts.edu
O'TOOL, Nick .... 402-572-3650 265 F
O'TOOLE, Beth .... 605-331-6797 416 C
elisabeth.otoole@usiouxfalls.edu
O'TOOLE, Jason .... 620-441-5246 172 M
jason.otoole@cowley.edu
O'TOOLE, Jennifer, A .... 412-578-8725 380 A
jaotoole@carlow.edu
O'TOOLE, Kayla .... 701-228-5479 345 G
kayla.otoole@dakotacollege.edu
O'TOOLE, Selina .... 203-932-7337.. 89 F
sotoole@newhaven.edu

P

PAASCH, Robert .... 312-369-7878 136 C
rpaasch@colum.edu
PAAVOLA, Cindy, L .... 906-227-2720 228 E
cipaavol@nmu.edu
PAAVOLA, Michelle .... 802-656-8821 462 D
michelle.paavola@uvm.edu
PABÓN-BATLLE, Luis .... 787-993-8868 510 E
luis.pabon4@upr.edu
PABÓN PAGÁN, Jose ... 787-766-1399 510 B
jose.pagan@upr.edu
PABON, Peter .... 845-848-4065 298 A
peter.pabon@dc.edu
PABON-RODRIGUEZ,
Edith, C .... 787-751-1912 507 F
epabon@juris.inter.edu
PAC, Becca .... 508-849-3406 205 E
rpac@annamaria.edu
PACACHA, Edith .... 772-462-7340 102 E
epacacha@irsc.edu
PACATTE, Bob .... 325-649-8609 437 A
bpacatte@hputx.edu
PACE, Anthony, J .... 570-326-3761 392 S
ajp25@pct.edu
PACE, Bobby .... 303-360-4940.. 80 C
bobby.pace@ccaurora.edu
PACE, Christy .... 870-460-1020.. 22 E
pacec@uamont.edu
PACE, Danielle .... 843-921-6932 410 B
mpace@netc.edu
PACE, Dean .... 601-318-6486 249 B
dpace@wmcarey.edu
PACE, Derek .... 601-635-2111 245 B
dpace@eccc.edu
PACE, Duane .... 423-614-8104 419 H
dpace@leeuniversity.edu
PACE, Elizabeth .... 423-614-8637 419 H
epace@leeuniversity.edu
PACE, Gay .... 870-460-1140.. 22 E
pace@uamont.edu
PACE, Harold .... 336-758-5000 344 A
hpace@wfu.edu
PACE, James, C .... 229-333-5959 127 C
jcpace@valdosta.edu
PACE, Jarrod .... 972-825-5469 444 C
japace@sagu.edu
PACE, Jessica .... 903-693-2044 440 E
jpace@panola.edu
PACE, Jessica .... 903-693-2000 440 E
jpace@panola.edu
PACE, JoeAnn .... 757-493-6000.. 93 H
PACE, Katrina .... 601-925-7645 246 D
kpace@mc.edu
PACE, Kris .... 816-501-4865 257 K
kristine.pace@rockhurst.edu
PACE, Kris .... 816-501-4862 257 K
kris.pace@rockhurst.edu
PACE, Lisa, L .... 843-953-4823 406 D
lisa.pace@citadel.edu
PACE, Marissa .... 404-270-5160 126 A
mpace@spelman.edu
PACE, Roger .... 619-260-4059.. 72 H
pace@sandiego.edu
PACE, Tom .... 864-455-7912 412 F
thomas.pace@prismahealth.org
PACENTI, Elena .... 619-684-8802.. 53 K
epacenti@newschoolarch.edu
PACETTI-DONELSON,
Vandy .... 251-626-3303.... 7 E
vpacettidonelson@ussa.edu
PACHECO, Andrea .... 505-467-6809 288 A
registrar@swc.edu
PACHECO, Andree .... 310-900-1600.. 39 H
PACHECO, Benito .... 505-454-3127 286 C
bmpacheco@nmhu.edu
PACHECO, Caryn .... 580-581-2295 365 C
carynp@cameron.edu
PACHECO, Christine ...... 870-235-5483.. 21 E
christinepacheco@saumag.edu
PACHECO, Edwin, R ...... 401-456-9866 404 A
epacheco@ric.edu
PACHECO, Jennifer .... 508-531-1221 212 B
jennifer.pacheco@bridgew.edu
PACHECO, Lisa .... 619-201-8993.. 65 F
lisa.pacheco@socalsem.edu
PACHECO, Michael .... 606-218-5216 185 F
michaelpacheco@upike.edu
PACHECO, Michelle ...... 303-340-7511.. 80 C
michelle.pacheco@ccaurora.edu
PACHECO, Philicia .... 508-678-2811 213 F
philicia.pacheco@bristolcc.edu
PACHECO, Richard, M .. 913-971-3299 175 H
rmpacheco@mnu.edu
PACHECO, Robert .... 817-515-5289 445 A
robert.pacheco@tccd.edu
PACHECO DUNN,
Tanhena .... 845-257-3164 316 B
pachecot@newpaltz.edu
PACHECO DUNN,
Tanhena .... 845-257-3172 316 B
pachecot@newpaltz.edu
PACHMAN, Tracey .... 610-660-3140 397 A
tpachman@sju.edu
PACHOLEC, Mark .... 716-270-5612 299 A
pacholec@ecc.edu
PACHUAU,
Lalsangkima .... 859-858-3581 178 G
PACHUTA, Stephen .... 304-293-2521 489 E
stephen.pachuta@hsc.wvu.edu
PACIERO, Christine ...... 847-376-7057 146 E
cpaciero@oakton.edu
PACIONE, Anne, R .... 718-990-5800 313 B
roccoa@stjohns.edu
PACK, Andrew .... 215-717-6147 399 I
apack@uarts.edu
PACK, Andrew .... 503-517-1898 377 D
apack@westernseminary.edu
PACK, Daniel .... 423-425-2256 426 D
daniel-pack@utc.edu
PACK, Gary .... 402-552-2209 265 G
packgary@clarksoncollege.edu
PACK, Jodi .... 903-434-8114 440 A
jpack@ntcc.edu
PACK, Lee .... 828-398-7482 331 K
leerpack@abtech.edu
PACK, Robert .... 423-439-4815 418 D
packr@etsu.edu
PACKARD, Brandi .... 918-610-0027 365 H
bpackard@communitycarecollege.edu
PACKARD, Francine ...... 330-821-5320 362 E
packarfr@mountunion.edu
PACKARD, Kathrin .... 816-531-5223 251 C
PACKARD, Matthew, W . 850-857-6070 111 E
mpackard@uwf.edu
PACKARD, Ryan .... 678-466-5499 117 A
ryanpackard@clayton.edu
PACKER, Chris .... 540-261-8400 470 D
chris.packer@svu.edu
PACKER, Lauren .... 717-358-4107 383 G
lauren.packer@fandm.edu
PACTOL, Monica .... 916-608-6503.. 51 A
pactolm@flc.losrios.edu
PACURARI, Nicholas ..... 423-775-7217 417 D
npacurari5211@bryan.edu
PAD, Rebecca .... 313-664-7641 222 C
rpad@collegeforcreativestudies.edu
PADASH, Ali .... 916-608-6648.. 51 A
padasha@flc.losrios.edu
PADDEN, Carol, A .... 858-534-6073.. 70 C
deansocsci@ucsd.edu
PADDOCK, Ericka .... 909-389-3457.. 60 E
epaddock@craftonhills.edu
PADDOCK, Jean .... 330-363-6347 348 B
jean.paddock@aultman.com
PADDOCK, Suzanne ...... 315-866-0300 301 B
paddocksm@herkimer.edu
PADEN, Catherine .... 603-899-4000 272 G
provostoffice@franklinpierce.edu
PADEN, Matt .... 615-966-1904 420 B
matt.paden@lipscomb.edu
PADEN, Quincy .... 312-662-4141 132 D
qpaden@adler.edu
PADGETT, Brett .... 773-702-1234 151 B
PADGETT, Mila .... 803-641-3230 412 B
milap@usca.edu
PADILLA, Ailin .... 787-264-1912 507 E
ailin_padilla@intersg.edu
PADILLA, Carlos .... 931-393-1846 423 G
cpadilla@mscc.edu
PADILLA, Diana .... 559-486-1166.. 24 I
dpadilla@agapeschools.org
PADILLA, Jose .... 562-907-4211.. 76 A
jpadilla@whittier.edu
PADILLA, Jose, D .... 219-464-5115 162 C
president@valpo.edu
PADILLA, Lymaries .... 787-725-6500 504 F
lpadilla@albizu.edu
PADILLA, Maria .... 508-362-2131 214 B
mpadilla@capecod.edu
PADILLA, Mark .... 307-382-1690 500 I
mpadilla@westernwyoming.edu
PADILLA, Mayra .... 510-215-3880.. 40 G
mpadilla@contracosta.edu
PADILLA, Pamela .... 940-369-8289 453 B
pam.padilla@unt.edu
PADILLA, Pamela .... 940-565-2000 453 B
PADILLA, JR., Ramon ... 865-974-0637 426 B
rpadilla@tennessee.edu
PADILLA, Rene, L .... 402-280-4745 265 J
renepadilla@creighton.edu
PADILLA, Sherrie .... 808-932-7451 129 A
sherriep@hawaii.edu
PADILLA, Vivian, A .... 787-786-3030 509 E
vpadilla@ucb.edu.pr
PADILLA JACKSON,
Olivia .... 505-224-4413 285 B
opadillajackson@cnm.edu
PADILLA-WALKER,
Laura .... 801-422-9053 458 A
laura_walker@byu.edu
PADLAN, Jennifer .... 814-332-2312 378 A
jmangus@allegheny.edu
PADLEY, B. Paul .... 713-348-4703 441 K
padley@rice.edu
PADMA, Ji Hyang .... 760-634-1771.. 28 G
PADMANABHAN,
Anand .... 718-817-1000 300 A
anandp@fordham.edu
PADMARAJU,
Lakshmikara .... 217-581-7568 137 C
lpadmaraju@eiu.edu
PADOVANI, John, J .... 607-746-4632 320 A
padovajj@delhi.edu
PADUNTIN, Jack .... 626-529-8008.. 55 E
PAEPLOW, Randall, K .... 863-784-7083 108 D
randall.paeplow@southflorida.edu
PAETSCH, Claudia .... 414-288-5629 492 E
claudia.paetsch@marquette.edu
PAEZ, Karen .... 971-722-4406 375 C
karen.paez@pcc.edu
PAEZ, Leticia .... 915-747-8268 454 E
lpaez@utep.edu
PAEZ-FIGUEROA, Jose .. 908-709-7084 283 E
paez@ucc.edu
PAFFENROTH, Kim .... 914-637-2743 302 C
kpaffenroth@iona.edu
PAFFRATH, Dennis .... 410-706-1101 202 F
dpaffrath@umaryland.edu
PAGAN, Andres .... 787-765-1915 507 G
apagan@opto.inter.edu
PAGAN, Carlos, H .... 787-844-8181 511 E
carlos.pagan6@upr.edu
PAGAN, Damaris .... 787-765-1915 507 G
dpagan@opto.inter.edu
PAGAN, Luis .... 787-993-8869 510 E
luis.pagan3@upr.edu
PAGAN, Robert .... 718-960-8048 293 E
robert.pagan@lehman.cuny.edu
PAGAN, William .... 848-445-5067 281 C
william.pagan@rutgers.edu
PAGAN, William .... 848-445-5067 281 B
william.pagan@rutgers.edu
PAGAN, William .... 848-445-5067 281 A
william.pagan@rutgers.edu
PAGAN, Yolanda .... 787-891-0925 506 I
ypagan@ns.inter.edu
PAGANELLI, John .... 508-531-1328 212 B
jpaganelli@bridgew.edu
PAGANO, Amy, E .... 724-458-3850 384 F
aepagano@gcc.edu
PAGANO, Diane, P .... 386-312-4267 107 A
dianepagano@sjrstate.edu
PAGANO, Jeffrey, M ...... 716-839-8254 297 F
jpagano@daemen.edu
PAGANO, Michael, A ...... 312-413-3375 151 D
mapagano@uic.edu
PAGANO, Neil .... 312-369-8218 136 C
npagano@colum.edu
PAGANO SOTO,
Juan, C .... 787-765-4210 504 I
PAGE, Antony .... 305-348-1118 109 H
antony.page@fiu.edu
PAGE, Dawn .... 760-366-3791.. 40 K
dawnpage@cmccd.edu
PAGE, Eric, J .... 860-701-6117 502 F
eric.j.page@uscg.mil
PAGE, Erika .... 909-554-3814.. 54 H
PAGE, JR., Hugh, R ..... 574-631-5716 161 G
hpage@nd.edu
PAGE, James .... 203-287-3031.. 88 D
PAGE, Jennifer .... 850-973-1603 104 K
pagej@nfc.edu
PAGE, Jonathan, E .... 434-395-4808 467 F
pageje@longwood.edu
PAGE, Kelli .... 209-946-2987.. 71 E
kpage@pacific.edu
PAGE, LeAnne .... 910-892-3178 329 D
lpage@heritagebiblecollege.edu
PAGE, Michael .... 919-530-5402 341 D
mpage@nccu.edu
PAGE, Michelle .... 320-589-6402 243 C
pagem@morris.umn.edu
PAGE, Natalie .... 773-298-3000 148 I
PAGE, Phillip .... 617-873-0256 207 E
phillip.page@cambridgecollege.edu
PAGE, Randy .... 864-242-5100 405 H
PAGE, Richard, L .... 802-656-3114 462 D
richard.page@uvm.edu
PAGE, Robert .... 912-260-4201 125 B
robert.page@sgsc.edu
PAGE, Roberta .... 724-738-2021 394 E
roberta.page@sru.edu
PAGE, Scott .... 503-494-8050 374 F
faclog@ohsu.edu
PAGE, Susan .... 708-456-0300 151 A
susanpage@triton.edu
PAGE, Yolanda .... 504-816-4368 186 F
ypage@dillard.edu
PAGE-SMITH, Julie .... 231-843-5949 232 I
jsmith@westshore.edu
PAGE-STADLER, Jaime .. 920-424-2181 495 C
pagestad@uwosh.edu
PAGEL, Andrew, T .... 210-829-3933 452 D
apagel@uiwtx.edu
PAGEL, Jessica, L .... 253-535-7414 481 C
jessica.pagel@plu.edu
PAGEL, Myshie, M .... 915-831-2394 435 B
mpagel@epcc.edu

PAGEL, Richard 714-432-5024 38 F
rpagel@occ.cccd.edu

PAGLICCI, Michael 716-839-8492 297 F
mpaglicc@daemen.edu

PAGNATTARO, Marisa, A 706-583-0690 126 F
pagnatta@uga.edu

PAGOTTO, Louise 808-734-9565 129 E
pagotto@hawaii.edu

PAGUIO, Arnold 510-723-6608 35 Q
apaguio@chabotcollege.edu

PAHL, Jennifer, K 989-964-4011 229 L
jkpahl@svsu.edu

PAHLEN, Kayla 218-281-6510 243 B
knott043@crk.umn.edu

PAHNKE, Thomas 262-547-1211 491 A
tpahnke@carrollu.edu

PAHNO, Kari 918-836-6886 370 A
kari.pahno@spartan.edu

PAI, Edward 310-233-4044 49 F
paie@lahc.edu

PAICE, Elizabeth 574-520-4560 157 C
epaice@iusb.edu

PAIGE, Brian 616-526-6758 221 L
bp28@calvin.edu

PAIGE, Diane 704-290-5278 337 F
dpaige@spcc.edu

PAIGE, Edward Adam 864-646-1362 411 H
epaige@tctc.edu

PAIGE, Michael 978-232-2259 209 B
mpaige@endicott.edu

PAIGE, Peter 518-262-5376 289 C
paigep@amc.edu

PAIGE, Shelia 706-821-8364 123 I
spaige@paine.edu

PAIGE, Sonji 617-327-6777 219 G
sonji_paige@williamjames.edu

PAIGE, Timothy 401-232-6011 403 B
tpaige@bryant.edu

PAIKOWSKI, Gary 903-463-8707 435 H
paikowskig@grayson.edu

PAINE, Andrew 714-879-3901 45 J
arpaine@hiu.edu

PAINE, Brenda 248-689-8282 231 E
bpaine@walshcollege.edu

PAINE, Clarke, C 717-358-3991 383 G
clarke.paine@fandm.edu

PAINE, Dorie 573-341-4218 260 F
pained@mst.edu

PAINE, Josh 706-583-2552 115 C
jpaine@athenstech.edu

PAINE, Wilson 540-365-4211 466 I
wpaine@ferrum.edu

PAINLEY, Candice, K 330-569-5120 353 F
painleyck@hiram.edu

PAINLEY, Peggy, A 330-569-5190 353 F
painleypa@hiram.edu

PAINO, Troy 540-654-1301 471 B
president@umw.edu

PAINTER, Amanda 864-206-2701 411 E
paintera@sccsc.edu

PAINTER, Claire 405-974-5563 370 H
cpainter1@uco.edu

PAINTER, Jami 217-244-8247 151 C
painterj@uillinois.edu

PAINTER, Michelle 760-245-4271 74 D
michelle.painter@vvc.edu

PAINTER, Noel 386-822-7010 111 F
npainter@stetson.edu

PAINTER, Sherry 901-435-1383 419 I
sherry_painter@loc.edu

PAINTER, Virginia, R 304-696-4621 488 N
painterv@marshall.edu

PAISANT, Julie 408-924-2250 34 B
julie.paisant@sjsu.edu

PAISANT, Karen 504-280-6259 189 F
kmpaisan@uno.edu

PAIT, Kevin 910-775-6260 343 A
kevin.pait@uncp.edu

PAIXAO, Francis 609-586-4800 277 H
paixaof@mccc.edu

PAIZ, Teresa 408-288-3791 62 G
teresa.paiz@sjcc.edu

PAIZIS, Kassie 863-680-3883 100 F
kpaizis@flsouthern.edu

PAJAKOWSKI, John 574-239-8354 155 E
jpajakowski@hcc-nd.edu

PAJE-MANALO, Leila, L 603-862-3491 273 H
leila.paje-manalo@unh.edu

PAJEWSKI, Donald 414-410-4413 490 J
dpajewski@stritch.edu

PAJIC MONGIARDO, Natasa 859-233-8213 185 A
npajic@transy.edu

PAK, David, Y 703-425-4143 467 B

PAK, G. Sujin 617-353-3052 207 C
gspak@bu.edu

PAK, Rene, K 213-740-2111 73 C
renepak@president.usc.edu

PAK, Su, Y 212-662-7100 323 C
spak@uts.columbia.edu

PAKHMANOV, Laura 201-761-6412 282 H
lpakhmanov@saintpeters.edu

PAKOWSKI, Lawrence 863-297-5282 106 A
lpakowski@polk.edu

PALACE-NEININGER, Christine 585-785-1438 299 E
christine.palace-neininger@flcc.edu

PALACIO, Michelle 305-348-1757 109 H
michelle.palacio@fiu.edu

PALACIOS, Carol 305-377-8817 95 K
carol.palacios@atlantisuniversity.edu

PALACIOS, Francisco, E 671-735-5501 503 C
francisco.palacios1@guamcc.edu

PALACIOS, Luz, M 787-786-3030 509 E
lpalacios@ucb.edu.pr

PALACIOS, Omar 305-377-8817 95 K
omar.palacios@atlantisuniversity.edu

PALACIOS, Rosanne 956-326-2178 446 A
rosanne.palacios@tamiu.edu

PALACIOS ROBLEDO, Monica 956-326-2856 446 A
monica.robledo@tamiu.edu

PALACIOUS, Casey 954-637-2268 108 C

PALAGANO, Nicole 973-748-9000 275 C
nicole_palagano@bloomfield.edu

PALAGONIA, Michael 802-635-1205 463 B
michael.palagonia@northernvermont.edu

PALAKAL, Mathew, J 317-278-7689 157 B
mpalakal@iupui.edu

PALAN, Kay, M 205-348-8901 7 G
kay.palan@culverhouse.ua.edu

PALEL, Dipte 310-660-3444 41 J
dpatel@elcamino.edu

PALEN, Andrew 262-695-6247 499 A
apalen@wctc.edu

PALEN, Chiyo 618-664-6643 138 D
chiyo.palen@greenville.edu

PALEN, Lisa 203-575-8100 86 H
lpalen@nv.edu

PALENCIA, Oscar 202-885-8664 94 D
opalencia@wesleyseminary.edu

PALENSKE, Jamie 785-309-3114 177 B
jamie.palenske@salinatech.edu

PALERMO, Kirk, M 830-591-7350 443 I
kmpalermo@swtjc.edu

PALERMO, Wendi 225-922-2800 187 C
wendipalermo@lctcs.edu

PALICH, Alitha 919-497-3325 330 E
apalich@louisburg.edu

PALICIA, Deborah 973-278-5400 274 J
dlp@berkeleycollege.edu

PALICIA, Deborah 973-278-5400 291 A
dlp@berkeleycollege.edu

PALINKAS, Robert 847-491-8100 146 C
robert.palinkas@northwestern.edu

PALIS, Jeffrey, M 336-841-9636 329 E
jpalis@highpoint.edu

PALIS, Michael 856-225-6077 281 A
palis@camden.rutgers.edu

PALIWAL, Rupendra 401-232-6000 403 B
rpaliwal@bryant.edu

PALKO, Kenneth 216-373-5296 357 F
kpalko@ndc.edu

PALLADINO, Elena 413-585-2105 218 D
epalladino@smith.edu

PALLADINO, Joan 203-837-9500 86 A
palladino@wcsu.edu

PALLADINO, Joan 203-837-9600 86 A
palladinoj@wcsu.edu

PALLADINO, Michael 973-748-9000 275 C
michael_palladino@bloomfield.edu

PALLADINO, Richard 914-633-2351 302 C
rpalladino@iona.edu

PALLADINO, Robert 740-283-6506 352 I
rpalladino@franciscan.edu

PALLANTI, Theresa 708-974-5532 144 G
pallantit@morainevalley.edu

PALLARES, Amalia 312-355-1308 151 D
amalia@uic.edu

PALLAVICINI, Maria 209-946-2011 71 E

PALLEMONI, Sushil 361-698-1131 434 H
spallemoni@delmar.edu

PALLIN, Jeff 408-855-5179 75 C
jeffrey.pallin@missioncollege.edu

PALLITO, Andrew 802-828-2800 463 A
aap10150@ccv.vsc.edu

PALLOT, Brooke 305-899-1188 96 A
bpallot@barry.edu

PALLOTO, Mike 805-289-6486 74 B
mpallotto@vcccd.edu

PALM, Daniel 928-523-2461 14 J
daniel.palm@nau.edu

PALM, Daniel 520-621-5854 16 H
dpalm@arizona.edu

PALM, Donald 804-524-5654 475 E
dpalm@vsu.edu

PALM, Matt 419-448-2020 353 D
mpalm@heidelberg.edu

PALMA, Eric 833-637-0866 46 J
epalma@itu.edu

PALMA, Eugene 516-877-3505 288 L
palma@adelphi.edu

PALMA, Yazmin 305-273-4499 96 I
yazmin@cbt.edu

PALMER, Alexis 801-863-8681 460 A
palmeral@uvu.edu

PALMER, Andrew 859-257-5068 185 D
andrew.palmer8@uky.edu

PALMER, Andrew 706-425-3117 115 C
apalmer@athenstech.edu

PALMER, Aparna 303-678-3620 80 I
aparna.palmer@frontrange.edu

PALMER, April 239-489-9067 100 G
apalmer1@fsw.edu

PALMER, Blake, E 972-265-5765 451 E
bepalmer@udallas.edu

PALMER, Brian 206-934-4547 482 F
brian.palmer@seattlecolleges.edu

PALMER, Collin 419-530-5740 363 B
collin.palmer@utoledo.edu

PALMER, Dale, J 404-413-3434 120 C
dpalmer@gsu.edu

PALMER, Daniel 937-775-2199 364 D
daniel.palmer@wright.edu

PALMER, Daniel 605-677-5011 415 E
daniel.palmer@usd.edu

PALMER, David 843-863-7930 406 C
dpalmer@csuniv.edu

PALMER, David 315-655-7777 292 B
dwpalmer@cazenovia.edu

PALMER, Doug 671-735-2862 503 E
palmerd@triton.uog.edu

PALMER, Douglas 573-288-6323 251 I
president@culver.edu

PALMER, Gregory 603-428-2397 272 I
gpalmer@nec.edu

PALMER, Gregory 361-698-1302 434 H
gpalmer3@delmar.edu

PALMER, James, M 936-261-2175 445 E
jmpalmer@pvamu.edu

PALMER, Janice 860-832-1791 85 F
palmerj@ccsu.edu

PALMER, Jason 254-295-4698 453 A
jbpalmer@umhb.edu

PALMER, Jennifer 909-687-1500 43 G
jenniferpalmer@gs.edu

PALMER, Joyce 315-792-5477 306 G
jpalmer2@mvcc.edu

PALMER, Julio 787-841-2000 508 H
jpalmer@pucpr.edu

PALMER, Kaitlin 605-642-6942 415 F
kaitlin.palmer@bhsu.edu

PALMER, Katherine 914-323-5168 305 A
katherine.palmer@mville.edu

PALMER, Kerry 334-670-3365 7 C
kjpalmer@troy.edu

PALMER, Kevin 573-875-7329 251 A
kpalmer@ccis.edu

PALMER, Kris, R 660-284-4800 253 F

PALMER, Kristi, L 317-274-8230 157 B
klpalmer@iupui.edu

PALMER, Larry 304-243-4453 490 F
lpalmer@wheeling.edu

PALMER, Laurel, S 269-337-7282 225 B
laurel.palmer@kzoo.edu

PALMER, Martha 660-284-4800 253 F

PALMER, Meredith 973-408-3976 276 B
mpalmer@drew.edu

PALMER, Natalie 215-641-6553 390 A
npalmer@mc3.edu

PALMER, Phomika 202-274-5000 94 B
phomika.palmer@udc.edu

PALMER, Rita 405-789-7661 369 H
rita.palmer@swcu.edu

PALMER, Robert 405-789-7661 369 H
robert.palmer@swcu.edu

PALMER, Ronnie 203-596-4531 88 E
rpalmer@post.edu

PALMER, Sally 216-421-7311 350 E
spalmer@cia.edu

PALMER, Sandra 718-281-5731 295 B
spalmer@qcc.cuny.edu

PALMER, Sidney, L 208-496-4622 130 G
palmers@byui.edu

PALMER, Steven, C 269-387-4465 232 J
steven.palmer@wmich.edu

PALMER, Susan, M 320-363-5298 234 I
spalmer@csbsju.edu

PALMER, Trent 765-641-4104 153 D
trpalmer@anderson.edu

PALMER, William 816-415-7871 261 G
palmerw@william.jewell.edu

PALMERI, Marian 570-208-5900 386 G
mkpalmer@kings.edu

PALMERSHEIM, Rhonda, K 651-641-8894 235 A
rbehm@csp.edu

PALMESE, Giuseppe, R 856-256-5300 280 H
palmese@rowan.edu

PALMIERI, Becky 518-587-2100 320 B
becky.palmieri@esc.edu

PALMISANO, Victoria 608-663-6859 491 F
vpalmisano@edgewood.edu

PALMORE, Erik 314-246-8648 261 D
palmoeri@webster.edu

PALMOUR, Mack 843-208-8118 412 C
mpalmour@uscb.edu

PALOK, Debra 623-845-3536 13 E
debra.palok@gccaz.edu

PALOMAS, Farah 619-934-0797 61 C

PALOMBO, Vincent 419-755-4740 357 B
vpalombo@ncstatecollege.edu

PALOMINO, Paulina 323-265-8977 49 D
palomipp@elac.edu

PALOMINO, Sophia 702-254-7577 271 B

PALOMO, Giovanni 212-517-3929 315 B
g.palomo@sothebysinstitute.com

PALOZZOLO, Connie 661-362-5006 38 H
connie.palozzolo@canyons.edu

PALSER, Stacia 402-472-1201 268 I
spalser@nebraska.edu

PALSIC, Abigail 303-458-4202 83 B
apalsic@regis.edu

PALSMA, Jason 712-274-6400 170 H
jason.palsma@witcc.edu

PALTER-GILL, Dianne 978-762-4000 215 B
dpalterg@northshore.edu

PALTZA, David 303-373-2008 83 D
dpaltza@rvu.edu

PALU-AY, Lyssa 617-879-7782 212 E
lpaluay@massart.edu

PALUCKI BLAKE, Laura 909-607-8191 44 K
lpblake@hmc.edu

PALUMBO, Angelina 928-523-6700 14 J
angelina.palumbo@nau.edu

PALUMBO, Carmine 478-289-2046 118 B
cpalumbo@ega.edu

PALUMBO, John 602-275-7133 15 P
john.palumbo@rsiaz.edu

PALUMBO, Jonathan 361-825-5542 446 E
jon.palumbo@tamucc.edu

PALUMBO, Katey 508-929-8835 213 D
kpalumbo2@worcester.edu

PALUMBO, Mark 770-593-2257 120 E

PALUS, Christine 610-519-8024 401 B
christine.palus@villanova.edu

PAMARAN, Sabina 831-656-2033 501 K
sabina.pamaran@nps.edu

PAMPEL, Robert 314-977-9301 258 H
robert.pampel@slu.edu

PAMPLIN, Hope 713-221-8001 452 B
pamplinh@uhd.edu

PAN, Angela 818-364-7723 49 G
panaj@lamission.edu

PANACEK, Susan 848-445-4674 281 B
susan.panacek@rutgers.edu

PANAMA, Annie 684-699-2722 503 A
a.panama@amsamoa.edu

PANAPA, Alofagia 684-699-2722 503 A
a.panapa@amsamoa.edu

PANARELLA, Pamela 610-409-3163 400 E
ppanarella@ursinus.edu

PANAS, Tom 773-838-7968 135 C
tpanas@ccc.edu

PANAYOTOVA, Evelina 610-790-1905 378 C
evelina.panayotova@alvernia.edu

PANCAKE, Candy 812-749-1372 159 E
cpancake@oak.edu

PARK, Sunny .... 806-720-7507 438 F sunny.park@lcu.edu
PARK, Un Yeong .... 508-999-8658 211 F upark@umassd.edu
PARK, Yong Hee .... 714-533-1495.. 64 G yhpark@southbaylo.edu
PARK, Young Hae .... 202-559-0434.. 92 B younghae.park@gallaudet.edu
PARKE, Millicent .... 478-471-2859 122 D millicent.parke@mga.edu
PARKER, Amie .... 207-621-3448 196 E amie.parker@maine.edu
PARKER, Amy, E .... 407-582-1238 113 C aparker@valenciacollege.edu
PARKER, Andrew .... 765-677-1989 157 F andrew.parker@indwes.edu
PARKER, Annette .... 507-389-7211 240 F annette.parker@southcentral.edu
PARKER, Anthony .... 562-860-2451.. 35 O aparker@cerritos.edu
PARKER, Anthony .... 903-593-8311 448 A aparker@texascollege.edu
PARKER, Ava, L .... 561-868-3501 105 C parkera@palmbeachstate.edu
PARKER, Brian .... 330-923-9959 352 H
PARKER, Candy .... 337-421-6565 188 H
PARKER, Cassandra ...... 202-274-5669.. 94 B cparker@udc.edu
PARKER, Cassandra ...... 334-727-8655.... 7 D cparker@tuskegee.edu
PARKER, Catherine .... 248-218-2154 229 I cparker@rochesteru.edu
PARKER, Charlie .... 253-840-8419 481 H cparker@pierce.ctc.edu
PARKER, Charlie .... 253-964-6500 481 H cparker@pierce.ctc.edu
PARKER, Chip .... 417-873-7504 252 A cparker@drury.edu
PARKER, Chris .... 870-733-6047.. 18 A crparker@asumidsouth.edu
PARKER, Cindy .... 401-598-1345 403 E cindy.parker@jwu.edu
PARKER, Craig .... 502-897-4131 184 D cparker@sbts.edu
PARKER, Dale .... 757-423-2095 466 H
PARKER, Dana .... 513-558-9964 362 B dana.parker@uc.edu
PARKER, Darnell .... 508-286-8200 219 F
PARKER, Darrell .... 864-488-4617 409 C dparker@limestone.edu
PARKER, Debra .... 419-434-5478 362 D parker@findlay.edu
PARKER, Devahn .... 619-934-0797.. 61 C
PARKER, Edith .... 319-384-1503 163 F edith-parker@uiowa.edu
PARKER, Franklin .... 312-658-5100 150 E
PARKER, Hannia .... 916-558-2088.. 51 B parkerh@scc.losrios.edu
PARKER, Heath .... 334-442-4000 466 E hparker@auburn.vcom.edu
PARKER, Heather .... 352-588-8200 107 B
PARKER, Hilary .... 609-258-5574 279 E haparker@princeton.edu
PARKER, Ingrid .... 312-662-4037 132 D iparker@adler.edu
PARKER, Jack .... 321-433-7090.. 98 F parkerj@easternflorida.edu
PARKER, Janet .... 312-355-4565 151 D japarker@uic.edu
PARKER, Janet .... 910-892-3178 329 D jparker@heritagebiblecollege.edu
PARKER, Janice, C .... 312-658-5100 150 E janice.parker@tbiil.edu
PARKER, Jeanette .... 270-789-5075 179 G jjparker@campbellsville.edu
PARKER, Jerry .... 515-271-2835 165 F jerry.parker@drake.edu
PARKER, Joe .... 970-491-3350.. 79 E joe.parker@colostate.edu
PARKER, JoeAnn .... 919-466-4400.. 93 H
PARKER, John .... 619-388-3538.. 60 I jparker002@sdccd.edu
PARKER, John .... 570-561-1818 397 B
PARKER, Juli .... 508-910-4582 211 F juli.parker@umassd.edu
PARKER, Julia .... 601-643-8308 244 G julia.parker@colin.edu
PARKER, Karen .... 508-678-2811 213 F karen.parker@bristolcc.edu
PARKER, Kathleen .... 320-363-2121 242 G kparker@csbsju.edu
PARKER, Kathy .... 320-363-2121 234 I kparker@csbsju.edu
PARKER, Katie .... 202-495-3830.. 93 D secretary@dhs.edu
PARKER, Keith .... 561-732-4424 107 E kparker@svdp.edu
PARKER, Kelly .... 818-345-9245.. 39 F kparker@columbiacollege.edu
PARKER, Kyle, D .... 479-308-2272.. 17 E kyle.parker@acheedu.org
PARKER, Larry .... 607-735-1930 298 G lparker@elmira.edu
PARKER, Laura .... 310-794-2304.. 69 D lparker@support.ucla.edu
PARKER, III, Lee .... 804-289-8405 471 E lparker@richmond.edu
PARKER, Linda, M .... 518-388-6578 323 B parkerl@union.edu
PARKER, Mae .... 641-269-4631 166 D parkerma@grinnell.edu
PARKER, Mark .... 405-208-5315 367 E mparker@okcu.edu
PARKER, Mary .... 352-392-1365 110 E maryparker@ufl.edu
PARKER, Mary Jo .... 713-221-8471 452 B parkerm@uhd.edu
PARKER, Micah .... 712-707-7292 169 A micah.parker@nwciowa.edu
PARKER, Michelle, G ..... 928-523-6500.. 14 J michelle.parker@nau.edu
PARKER, Neal .... 425-388-9392 479 B nparker@everettcc.edu
PARKER, Patsy .... 580-772-6611 369 I
PARKER, Patsy .... 580-774-3284 369 I patsy.parker@swosu.edu
PARKER, Pennie .... 407-646-2636 106 L pparker@rollins.edu
PARKER, Philip, J .... 608-342-1235 495 E parkerp@uwplatt.edu
PARKER, Pippin .... 212-229-5859 307 E parkerp@newschool.edu
PARKER, Ramona .... 254-968-1694 445 F rparker1@tarleton.edu
PARKER, Rob .... 504-568-2412 189 C rspark@lsuhsc.edu
PARKER, Robert .... 818-364-7772.. 49 G parkerr@lamission.edu
PARKER, Robert .... 915-747-8171 454 E rmparker@utep.edu
PARKER, JR., Robert, D .... 217-383-4114 151 F rcparker@illinois.edu
PARKER, JR., Robert, J 518-388-6180 323 B parkerr@union.edu
PARKER, Robyn .... 626-316-5330.. 63 D rparker2@saybrook.edu
PARKER, Ron .... 979-230-3480 431 A ron.parker@brazosport.edu
PARKER, Sara .... 707-256-7000.. 53 E
PARKER, Sarah .... 740-374-8716 363 F sparker@wscc.edu
PARKER, Saundra .... 312-850-7176 135 E sparker66@ccc.edu
PARKER, Scott, B .... 701-430-2108 345 B scott.b.parker@mayvillestate.edu
PARKER, Sonya .... 865-354-3000 424 D parkers@roanestate.edu
PARKER, Sonya, L .... 270-824-8586 182 A sonya.parker@kctcs.edu
PARKER, Steven .... 218-755-4121 237 B steven.parker@bemidjistate.edu
PARKER, Taylor .... 716-954-7680 298 C parkert@dyc.edu
PARKER, Terry .... 863-583-9050 110 A
PARKER, Timothy .... 510-907-2432.. 60 C tparker@samuelmerritt.edu
PARKER, Tonya .... 478-757-4028 127 D tparker@wesleyancollege.edu
PARKER, Vic .... 601-857-3961 245 D victor.parker@hindscc.edu
PARKER AMES, Gwen ..... 646-564-6742 289 F gwen.ames@nyack.edu
PARKER-COLLIER, Kathy .... 417-455-5773 251 H kathycollier@crowder.edu
PARKER-DER BOGHOSSIAN, John .... 952-358-8358 239 C john.parker-derboghossian@normandale.edu
PARKER-JONES, Tonya . 619-934-0797.. 61 C
PARKER-KELLY, Darlene .... 323-563-9340.. 36 E darleneparkerkelly@cdrewu.edu
PARKER-LOW, Joan .... 207-859-1131 196 A joan.parkerlow@thomas.edu
PARKHILL, Jason .... 207-859-4000 194 B
PARKHURST, Abbie ...... 540-828-5782 464 C aparkhur@bridgewater.edu
PARKHURST, Cindy .... 951-785-2982.. 47 F cparkhurst@lasiera.edu
PARKHURST, Jennifer ... 626-256-4673.. 37 D jparkhurst@coh.org
PARKIN, Michael .... 440-775-8410 357 G michael.parkin@oberlin.edu
PARKINSON, Elizabeth .. 614-688-2048 358 E parkinson.107@osu.edu
PARKINSON, III, Henry, C .... 978-665-3160 212 C hparkinson@fitchburgstate.edu
PARKINSON, Richard .... 815-772-7218 145 A rcpark@morrisontech.edu
PARKINSON, Tracy .... 828-689-1237 330 H tracy_parkinson@mhu.edu
PARKMAN, Julie .... 315-386-7119 319 E parkman@canton.edu
PARKS, Amy .... 216-987-5137 351 D amy.parks@tri-c.edu
PARKS, Amy .... 216-987-6130 351 D amy.parks@tri-c.edu
PARKS, Ann .... 660-263-4100 256 D annp@macc.edu
PARKS, Charlotte .... 662-915-3120 248 F cpparks@olemiss.edu
PARKS, Daniel, A .... 909-869-2373.. 30 B daparks@cpp.edu
PARKS, David .... 304-473-8011 490 E parks.d@wvwc.edu
PARKS, Earl .... 202-651-5494.. 92 B earl.parks@gallaudet.edu
PARKS, Elysa .... 270-707-3761 181 G eparks0023@kctcs.edu
PARKS, Jana .... 785-594-4595 171 C jana.parks@bakeru.edu
PARKS, JaNice .... 202-885-8687.. 94 D jparks@wesleyseminary.edu
PARKS, Jason .... 318-484-2184 192 D parksj@nsula.edu
PARKS, Jason .... 951-372-7017.. 59 C jason.parks@norcocollege.edu
PARKS, Jeffrey .... 281-756-3631 428 E jparks@alvincollege.edu
PARKS, Jo-Lynne .... 303-546-3570.. 81 N jparks@naropa.edu
PARKS, Jordan .... 503-943-7101 376 H parksjo@up.edu
PARKS, Julie .... 616-234-4000 224 C
PARKS, Kaela .... 971-722-4868 375 C kaela.parks@pcc.edu
PARKS, Karen .... 386-481-2975.. 96 D parksk@cookman.edu
PARKS, Lisa .... 541-956-7446 375 G lparks@roguecc.edu
PARKS, Matt .... 815-753-2095 145 H mparks2@niu.edu
PARKS, Matthew .... 212-659-7200 303 E mparks@tkc.edu
PARKS, Michael .... 210-567-2791 455 E parksm@uthscsa.edu
PARKS, Patricia .... 714-816-0366.. 68 G patricia.parks@trident.edu
PARKS, Rodney .... 336-278-6677 328 H rparks4@elon.edu
PARKS, Tawana .... 503-517-4057 375 F tawanap@reed.edu
PARKS, Vanasia Conley 423-425-4467 426 D vanasia-parks@utc.edu
PARKS, Wendy, E .... 630-942-2755 135 F parksw@cod.edu
PARKS, Whitney .... 660-248-6221 250 H wparks@centralmethodist.edu
PARKS-PARTON, Toni ... 217-234-5252 141 H tparks@lakelandcollege.edu
PARLACOSKI, Julie .... 732-987-2219 277 B jparlacoski@georgian.edu
PARLANGE, Marc .... 401-874-1000 404 E
PARLE, Joseph, D .... 832-252-4659 431 M joe.parle@cbshouston.edu
PARLETT, Ray, M .... 585-567-9333 301 G ray.parlett@houghton.edu
PARLETT-SWEENEY, Mary .... 518-782-6988 314 K mparlett-sweeney@siena.edu
PARLOW, Matt .... 714-744-7690.. 36 D parlow@chapman.edu
PARMAR, Rene .... 718-960-6777 293 E rene.parmar@lehman.cuny.edu
PARMENTER, Robert ...... 707-468-3051.. 51 F rparmenter@mendocino.edu
PARMS, Jericho .... 802-828-8600 462 E jericho.parms@vcfa.edu
PARNELL, Katherine, T . 828-641-0826 327 A parnelkt@brevard.edu
PARNELL, Kathleen .... 410-617-1350 199 G kmparnell@loyola.edu
PARNELL, Lori .... 478-553-2050 123 D
PARNELL, Michael .... 330-823-4840 362 E parnelmi@mountunion.edu
PARNELL, Patrick, M .... 417-836-4127 255 J patrickparnell@missouristate.edu
PARNELL, Philip .... 903-675-6220 451 C philip.parnell@tvcc.edu
PARNELL, Sean .... 907-786-1437.. 10 A uaa_chancellor@alaska.edu
PAROLIN, Peter .... 307-766-4110 500 H honors@uwyo.edu
PARR, Adrian .... 541-346-3631 376 G aparr@uoregon.edu
PARR, Ashleigh, F .... 843-953-5348 407 D parra@cofc.edu
PARRA, Alejandra .... 305-348-3062 109 H alejandra.parra@fiu.edu
PARRA, Alicia, F .... 954-322-4460 102 I aliciafernandaparra@jmvu.edu
PARRA, Dan .... 614-222-3208 351 A dparra@ccad.edu
PARRA, Jonallie .... 209-946-3288.. 71 E jparra@pacific.edu
PARRELLA, Michael .... 208-885-4933 132 C mpp@uidaho.edu
PARRELLA, Michael .... 208-885-6681 132 C mpp@uidaho.edu
PARRENT, Condoa .... 817-515-6532 445 A condoa.parrent@tccd.edu
PARRENT, Jay .... 270-824-8571 182 A jay.parrent@kctcs.edu
PARRENT, Rick .... 615-230-3321 424 F rick.parrent@volstate.edu
PARREÑAS SHIMIZU, Celine .... 831-459-0111.. 71 A artsdean@ucsc.edu
PARRILL, Jacqueline ..... 740-366-9407 349 D parrill.9@osu.edu
PARRILL-BAKER, Abby .. 901-678-2119 426 A aparrill@memphis.edu
PARRILLA, Arlene .... 787-863-2390 507 A arlene.parrilla@fajardo.inter.edu
PARRIOTT, Karen .... 307-532-8264 500 A kparriott@ewc.wy.edu
PARRIS, Marcia .... 610-647-4400 385 K mparris@immaculata.edu
PARRISH, Austen .... 949-824-0066.. 69 C aparrish@law.uci.edu
PARRISH, Austen, L ...... 812-855-8885 156 C austparr@indiana.edu
PARRISH, Chelsie .... 715-394-8584 496 D candera@uwsuper.edu
PARRISH, David, K .... 308-632-6933 268 F dparrish@summitcc.edu
PARRISH, Gretchen .... 336-342-4261 337 B parrishg@rockinghamcc.edu
PARRISH, J. Michael .... 718-982-2440 293 C provost@csi.cuny.edu
PARRISH, John, M .... 310-338-2775.. 51 C john.parrish@lmu.edu
PARRISH, Lorena .... 202-706-6840.. 94 D lparrish@wesleyseminary.edu
PARRISH, Lyndon .... 269-782-1321 230 D lparrish@swmich.edu
PARRISH, Patricia .... 270-384-8030 183 D parrishp@lindsey.edu
PARRISH, Sid .... 803-321-5263 409 I sid.parrish@newberry.edu
PARRISH-ONUKWULI, Kenya .... 251-405-7052.... 1 E konukwuli@bishop.edu
PARRONDO, Robert .... 305-237-0623 104 E rparrond@mdc.edu
PARROTT, Autumn .... 248-645-3300 222 G aparrott@cranbrook.edu
PARROTT, Mike .... 843-208-8040 412 C rparrot@uscb.edu
PARROTT, Roger .... 601-968-5919 244 C president@belhaven.edu
PARROTT, Steve .... 662-325-7790 247 A sparrott@its.msstate.edu
PARRY, Jessica .... 812-855-0717 156 C jjparry@iu.edu
PARRY, John .... 970-491-3939.. 79 E john.parry@colostate.edu
PARRY, Mary Jane .... 315-792-5510 306 G mparry@mvcc.edu

PATTERSON, Elizabeth .. 903-223-6722 447 C
elizabeth.patterson@tamut.edu
PATTERSON, Emily, A ... 316-978-3030 178 B
emily.patterson@wichita.edu
PATTERSON, Eric .... 214-654-9075 202 B
PATTERSON, Felicia, L .. 410-777-2718 197 C
flpatterson@aacc.edu
PATTERSON,
Franklin, E .... 386-481-2020.. 96 D
pattersonf@cookman.edu
PATTERSON, Hahna ...... 207-221-4418 197 A
hpatterson@une.edu
PATTERSON, Howard .... 903-566-7350 455 C
hpatterson@uttyler.edu
PATTERSON, Jackie .... 215-780-1397 397 E
jpatterson@salus.edu
PATTERSON, James ...... 860-738-6482.. 87 A
jpatterson@nwcc.edu
PATTERSON,
Jana Lynn, F .... 336-278-7200 328 H
patters@elon.edu
PATTERSON, Jen .... 507-433-0610 240 A
jennifer.patterson@riverland.edu
PATTERSON, Jennifer .... 614-236-6502 348 I
jpatterson@capital.edu
PATTERSON, Joanna ..... 866-492-5336 243 G
joanna.patterson@laureate.net
PATTERSON, John, A .... 478-301-5537 122 C
patterson_ja@mercer.edu
PATTERSON, Joseph ..... 239-280-1595.. 95 M
joseph.patterson@avemaria.edu
PATTERSON, Karen .... 904-620-2700 111 A
karen.patterson@unf.edu
PATTERSON, Kenneth .... 937-481-2241 363 H
kenn.patterson@wilmington.edu
PATTERSON, Kim .... 254-299-8606 438 G
kpatterson@mclennan.edu
PATTERSON, Kimbraly .. 864-592-4819 411 E
pattersonk@sccsc.edu
PATTERSON, Mark .... 805-437-3283.. 30 D
mark.patterson@csuci.edu
PATTERSON, Michael .... 410-225-2422 200 B
mpatters@mica.edu
PATTERSON, Michael .... 415-503-6237.. 61 E
mpatterson@sfcm.edu
PATTERSON, Michelle ... 865-354-3000 424 D
pattersonm@roanestate.edu
PATTERSON, Myrna ...... 808-845-9103 129 G
mpatters@hawaii.edu
PATTERSON, Nancy ...... 423-697-2630 423 B
nancy.patterson@chattanoogastate.edu
PATTERSON, Pamela, L 703-993-1000 466 J
PATTERSON, Patty .... 954-492-5353.. 97 G
ppatterson@citycollege.edu
PATTERSON, Paul, M .... 334-844-3209.... 4 E
pmp0003@auburn.edu
PATTERSON, Robert, H . 804-752-3605 469 B
robertpatterson@rmc.edu
PATTERSON, Ron, K ...... 256-765-5159.... 8 E
rpatterson1@una.edu
PATTERSON, Rubin .... 202-806-6700.. 92 E
rubin.patterson@howard.edu
PATTERSON, Sarah .... 575-492-2575 286 E
spatterson@nmjc.edu
PATTERSON, Shannon .. 706-771-4013 115 H
sbentley@augustatech.edu
PATTERSON, Sharon, E . 626-395-3937.. 29 B
sharon.patterson@caltech.edu
PATTERSON, Stacey ...... 865-974-4048 426 B
stacey.patterson@tennessee.edu
PATTERSON, Steven ...... 703-323-3554 473 G
spatterson@nvcc.edu
PATTERSON, Thomas .... 334-387-3877.... 4 C
thomaspatterson@amridgeuniversity.
edu
PATTERSON, Tim .... 864-977-7032 410 A
tim.patterson@ngu.edu
PATTERSON, Tracy .... 901-843-3856 422 C
pattersont@rhodes.edu
PATTERSON, Van .... 409-944-1205 435 F
vpatterson@gc.edu
PATTERSON, Vicki .... 832-252-4624 431 M
vicki.patterson@cbshouston.edu
PATTERSON, Zachary .... 559-730-3906.. 39 C
zacharyp@cos.edu
PATTERSON HARRIS,
Emily .... 405-466-3265 366 B
patterson.harris@okstate.edu
PATTILLO, Nicolas .... 479-788-7166.. 22 A
npattillo@uafs.edu
PATTISAPU, Krishna ...... 303-678-3768.. 80 I
krishna.pattisapu@frontrange.edu
PATTISON, Margaret ..... 313-578-0327 230 H
peggy.pattison@udmercy.edu
PATTIT, Katherina .... 320-308-4866 240 C
katherina.pattit@stcloudstate.edu
PATTON, Chad .... 434-949-1038 474 D
chad.patton@southside.edu
PATTON, Dave, K .... 989-774-3632 221 M
aaoffice@cmich.edu
PATTON, Julia, G .... 610-917-2004 400 D
jgpatton@valleyforge.edu
PATTON, Kerry .... 203-582-3087.. 88 F
kerry.patton2@quinnipiac.edu
PATTON, Laurie, L .... 802-443-5400 461 G
president@middlebury.edu
PATTON, Laurie, S .... 740-368-3026 359 F
lspatton@owu.edu
PATTON, Linda .... 404-270-5048 126 A
lpatton@spelman.edu
PATTON, Paul, E .... 606-218-5262 185 F
pep@upike.edu
PATTON, Stephen .... 706-865-2134 126 D
spatton@truett.edu
PATTON, Venetria .... 217-333-1529 151 F
vkpatton@illinois.edu
PATTON, Wendy .... 541-506-6000 372 E
PATTON-OSTRANDER,
Kelley, A .... 518-580-5814 315 A
kostrand@skidmore.edu
PATTY, Stacy .... 806-720-7652 438 F
stacy.patty@lcu.edu
PATWARY, Mohsin .... 718-270-6217 294 E
mohsin@mec.cuny.edu
PATZ, Thomas .... 317-738-8183 155 A
tpatz@franklincollege.edu
PATZER, Troy .... 509-527-2586 484 C
troy.patzer@wallawalla.edu
PAUGH, Jennifer .... 734-423-2139 227 A
PAUGH, Jessica .... 541-440-7847 376 F
jessica.paugh@umpqua.edu
PAUGH, Mark .... 352-854-2322.. 97 L
paughm@cf.edu
PAUKEN, Evan .... 269-488-4215 225 C
epauken@kvcc.edu
PAUKEN, Megan .... 269-488-4755 225 C
mpauken@kvcc.edu
PAUKEN, Patrick .... 419-372-2226 348 F
paukenp@bgsu.edu
PAUKEN, Patrick .... 419-372-2550 348 F
paukenp@bgsu.edu
PAUL, Alyson .... 706-864-1900 126 G
alyson.paul@ung.edu
PAUL, Brandie .... 931-363-9879 426 F
bpaul7@utsouthern.edu
PAUL, Brandon .... 954-731-8880.. 97 O
PAUL, Christine .... 805-493-3220.. 29 E
clpaul@callutheran.edu
PAUL, David, W .... 801-422-4887 458 A
davidwpaul@byu.edu
PAUL, Elizabeth, L .... 585-389-2004 307 D
epaul3@naz.edu
PAUL, Jina .... 402-552-3100 265 G
pauljina@clarksoncollege.edu
PAUL, Kara .... 406-447-4401 262 E
kpaul@carroll.edu
PAUL, Kelli .... 949-794-9090.. 66 C
kpaul@stanbridge.edu
PAUL, Kohle .... 770-962-7580 121 B
kpaul@gwinnetttech.edu
PAUL, Mary .... 619-849-2215.. 57 J
marypaul@pointloma.edu
PAUL, Michaelynn .... 509-527-2145 484 C
michaelynn.paul@wallawalla.edu
PAUL, Minnu .... 910-630-7225 331 B
mpaul@methodist.edu
PAUL, Phyllis, M .... 330-941-3625 364 G
pmpaul@ysu.edu
PAUL, Rachelle .... 201-761-7302 282 H
rpaul2@saintpeters.edu
PAUL, Robert, H .... 314-516-8403 260 E
paulro@umsl.edu
PAUL, Sheilah .... 718-270-4936 294 E
spaul@mec.cuny.edu
PAUL, Theresa, C .... 828-227-3812 343 D
tcpaul@wcu.edu
PAUL, Tonya, D .... 419-772-3106 358 D
t-paul@onu.edu
PAULE, Romeo .... 415-949-7308.. 43 A
pauleromeo@foothill.edu
PAULE, Sara .... 765-983-1431 154 H
paulesa@earlham.edu
PAULETTI, Giovanni ...... 314-367-8700 260 A
giovanni.pauletti@uhsp.edu
PAULEY, Ann .... 202-884-9725.. 94 A
pauleya@trinitydc.edu
PAULEY, Jennifer .... 740-351-3530 360 E
jpauley@shawnee.edu
PAULICK, Joe .... 305-348-4196 109 H
joseph.paulick@fiu.edu
PAULINE, Rose Lee .... 215-951-1014 386 I
pauline@lasalle.edu
PAULINO, Avianny .... 787-761-0640 510 A
promocion@utcpr.edu
PAULK, Chavis .... 205-247-8151.... 7 A
cpaulk@stillman.edu
PAULOSKI, SP, Pam .... 773-371-5420 134 C
presoffice@ctu.edu
PAULS, Kelly .... 620-241-0723 172 H
kelly.pauls@centralchristian.edu
PAULS, Rebecca .... 304-829-7633 486 B
rpauls@bethanywv.edu
PAULSEN, Derek .... 859-622-2906 180 B
derek.paulsen@eku.edu
PAULSEN, Elizabeth, P .. 608-757-7769 497 D
lpaulsen@blackhawk.edu
PAULSEN, Jenny .... 813-974-8944 111 B
jpaulsen@usf.edu
PAULSEN, Josh .... 972-600-2818.. 26 H
jpaulsen@asher.edu
PAULSON, Alicia .... 507-372-3464 239 B
alicia.paulson@mnwest.edu
PAULSON, Cheri .... 781-239-3845 205 G
cpaulson@babson.edu
PAULSON, Erik .... 212-752-1530 303 G
erik.paulson@limcollege.edu
PAULSON, J. Robert ...... 563-387-1001 167 J
jbobpaulson@gmail.com
PAULSON, Janis .... 888-775-1514.. 68 K
PAULSON, Kimberly .... 715-634-4790 491 L
kpaulson@lco.edu
PAULSON, Veronica .... 605-626-2537 415 H
veronica.paulson@northern.edu
PAULUS, Bill .... 612-624-1091 242 K
paulu038@umn.edu
PAULUS, Michael .... 206-281-2414 482 K
paulusm@spu.edu
PAULY, Karen .... 704-330-6976 333 B
karen.pauly@cpcc.edu
PAULY, Katelyn .... 518-861-2565 305 B
kpauly@mariacollege.edu
PAUNAN, Crystal .... 630-953-3660 134 E
PAUSTIAN, Pamela, E .... 205-975-9376..... 8 A
paustian@uab.edu
PAUSTIAN, Tony .... 515-633-2439 164 F
adpaustian@dmacc.edu
PAUXTIS, Cody .... 760-384-6369.. 47 C
cody.pauxtis@cerrocoso.edu
PAVALKO, Eliza .... 812-855-9973 156 C
vpfaa@indiana.edu
PAVAN, Ron .... 615-547-1348 418 C
rpavan@cumberland.edu
PAVAN, Tammi .... 615-547-1228 418 C
tpavan@cumberland.edu
PAVEK, Annette .... 320-762-4411 236 G
annettep@alextech.edu
PAVELCHIK, Adam, D .... 507-354-8221 236 D
pavelcad@mlc-wels.edu
PAVELL, Cynthia .... 310-506-6023.. 56 H
cynthia.pavell@pepperdine.edu
PAVEY, Katheryne .... 251-405-7089.... 1 E
kpavey@bishop.edu
PAVEZA, Gregory .... 773-995-4517 134 J
PAVIK, Nicholas .... 661-362-3630.. 38 H
nick.pavik@canyons.edu
PAVILONIS, Brigid .... 508-830-5012 213 A
bpavilonis@maritime.edu
PAVLAT, Penny .... 906-217-4099 221 J
pavlatp@baycollege.edu
PAVLIK, Angie .... 440-943-7600 360 D
apavlik@dioceseofcleveland.org
PAVLIK, Kimberly .... 561-912-1211.. 99 C
kpavlik@evergladesuniversity.edu
PAVLIS, Tim .... 203-436-9358.. 90 B
timothy.pavlis@yale.edu
PAVLOU, Paul, A .... 713-743-3562 451 G
papavlou@uh.edu
PAVLOW, Joseph .... 908-526-1200 280 C
joseph.pavlow@raritanval.edu
PAVON, Tracie .... 515-961-1630 169 G
tracie.pavon@simpson.edu
PAVONE, Scott .... 610-790-2959 378 C
scott.pavone@alvernia.edu
PAVUK, Michael .... 315-858-0945 301 F
paulesa@earlham.edu
PAVY, Anna .... 270-789-5059 179 G
ampavy@campbellsville.edu
PAWAR, Ashlesha .... 678-839-6449 127 A
apawar@westga.edu
PAWELEK, Kathy .... 361-593-2849 447 A
kathy.pawelek@tamuk.edu
PAWELL, Liz .... 909-469-5202.. 75 G
lpawell@westernu.edu
PAWLAK, Erin .... 716-896-0700 324 A
epawlak@villa.edu
PAWLAK, Katherine .... 863-680-3964 100 F
kpawlak@flsouthern.edu
PAWLAK, Kurt .... 740-264-5591 352 B
kpawlak@egcc.edu
PAWLIK, Amy .... 309-268-8249 138 F
amy.munson-pawlik@heartland.edu
PAWLIKOWSKI,
Deborah, J .... 973-290-4184 282 G
dpawlikowski@steu.edu
PAWLO - JOHNSTONE,
Jennifer .... 410-337-6181 198 G
jennifer.pawlojohnstone@goucher.edu
PAXSON, Christina, H ... 401-863-2234 403 A
christina_paxson@brown.edu
PAXSON, Sherrie .... 505-566-3490 287 G
paxsons@sanjuancollege.edu
PAXTON, Bobby .... 804-287-6591 471 E
bpaxton@richmond.edu
PAXTON, Ellen .... 269-399-7700 162 A
epaxton@sf.edu
PAYAN-CATAÑO,
Sandra .... 773-481-8765 135 D
spayancatano@ccc.edu
PAYANZO COTTON,
Anna .... 856-222-9311 280 E
ftietz@rcbc.edu
PAYAWAL, Pamela .... 323-860-0789.. 50 E
PAYBA, Shane .... 808-984-3496 130 B
payba@hawaii.edu
PAYLO, Keith .... 412-392-3862 395 H
kpaylo@pointpark.edu
PAYLOR, Becca .... 704-233-8828 344 E
b.paylor@wingate.edu
PAYNE, Alyssa .... 816-322-0110 250 E
student.deans@calvary.edu
PAYNE, Amanda .... 618-252-5400 149 E
amanda.payne@sic.edu
PAYNE, Andre .... 803-570-0028 408 A
paynea@denmarktech.edu
PAYNE, Brian, K .... 757-683-4757 468 C
bpayne@odu.edu
PAYNE, Candice .... 817-257-6104 447 H
candice.payne@tcu.edu
PAYNE, Charles, M .... 973-353-1750 281 C
charles.payne@rutgers.edu
PAYNE, Crystal .... 757-340-2121 464 L
registrarcvab@centura.edu
PAYNE, Dalry, B .... 269-471-3100 220 H
dalry@andrews.edu
PAYNE, David .... 801-734-6789 459 A
david.payne@rm.edu
PAYNE, Dawn .... 806-742-3627 450 C
dawn.payne@ttu.edu
PAYNE, Don .... 303-762-6900.. 80 G
academicdean@denverseminary.edu
PAYNE, Donna, G .... 585-275-2758 323 E
donna.payne@rochester.edu
PAYNE, George, M .... 240-567-2582 200 E
george.payne@montgomerycollege.edu
PAYNE, Gloria, E .... 252-335-3595 341 A
gepayne@ecsu.edu
PAYNE, Harvey .... 703-416-1441 465 E
hpayne@divinemercy.edu
PAYNE, Heather .... 954-492-5353.. 97 G
hpayne@citycollege.edu
PAYNE, James, E .... 915-747-7781 454 E
jpayne2@utep.edu
PAYNE, Janet .... 570-321-4151 388 H
payne@lycoming.edu
PAYNE, John .... 801-422-9099 458 A
john_payne@byu.edu
PAYNE, John, F .... 671-735-5565 503 C
john.payne2@guamcc.edu
PAYNE, Karen, E .... 937-529-2201 361 F
kepayne@united.edu
PAYNE, Kathy .... 215-489-2372 381 K
kathy.payne@delval.edu
PAYNE, Kent .... 847-214-7552 137 D
kpayne@elgin.edu
PAYNE, Laura .... 432-837-8744 449 F
lbutler@sulross.edu
PAYNE, Leslie .... 573-288-6395 251 I
lpayne@culver.edu
PAYNE, Maggie .... 701-349-5798 346 G
mpayne@trinitybiblecollege.edu
PAYNE, Maribeth .... 573-840-9007 259 I
mpayne@trcc.edu

PAYNE, Mary .... 515-271-1452 165 C
mary.payne@dmu.edu
PAYNE, Matthew .... 701-349-5415 346 G
mattpayne@trinitybiblecollege.edu
PAYNE, Melissa .... 319-398-5584 167 H
melissa.payne@kirkwood.edu
PAYNE, Molly .... 617-732-2218 216 B
molly.payne@mcphs.edu
PAYNE, Neal .... 704-406-4278 328 I
npayne@gardner-webb.edu
PAYNE, Nikita, T .... 334-293-4603.... 1 C
nikita.payne@accs.edu
PAYNE, Nikki .... 314-529-6864 254 D
npayne@maryville.edu
PAYNE, Paige .... 406-447-6927 263 F
paige.payne@helenacollege.edu
PAYNE, Pamela .... 915-831-6511 435 B
ppayne1@epcc.edu
PAYNE, Sean .... 912-871-8559 123 F
spayne@ogeecheetech.edu
PAYNE, Stephen, C .... 202-319-5139.. 91 G
paynesl@cua.edu
PAYNE, Stephen, D .... 269-471-6534 220 H
stephen@andrews.edu
PAYNE, Tamara .... 205-853-1200.... 2 G
tlpayne@jeffersonstate.edu
PAYNE, Tara .... 603-513-1356 273 I
tara.payne@granite.edu
PAYNE, Taylor .... 217-732-3168 142 D
PAYNE, Thomas .... 931-372-3372 425 B
tpayne@tntech.edu
PAYNE, Tyran .... 928-771-6132.. 17 B
tyran.payne@yc.edu
PAYNE, Wesley, A .... 573-840-9698 259 I
wpayne@trcc.edu
PAYNE, William .... 775-784-6604 270 K
bpayne@cabnr.unr.edu
PAYNE CERVERA,
Brandi .... 307-778-1218 500 D
bcervera@lccc.wy.edu
PAYNTER, Alan .... 315-781-3729 301 D
paynter@hws.edu
PAYNTER, Chris .... 704-330-6531 333 B
chris.paynter@cpcc.edu
PAYNTER, Sharon .... 252-328-9480 340 H
paynters@ecu.edu
PAYOVICH, Nathan .... 708-974-5330 144 G
payovichn@morainevalley.edu
PAYSON, Valerie .... 254-526-1472 431 E
valerie.payson@ctcd.edu
PAYTON, Amanda .... 937-376-6611 349 H
apayton@centralstate.edu
PAYTON, Andy .... 812-488-2000 161 E
apayton@methodisttemple.church
PAYTON, Annie .... 256-372-4747.... 1 A
annie.payton@aamu.edu
PAYTON, Karl .... 903-233-3142 438 C
karlpayton@letu.edu
PAYTON, Kizzy .... 225-216-8404 187 D
paytonk2@mybrcc.edu
PAYTON, Leanna .... 870-460-1245.. 22 E
payton@uamont.edu
PAYTON, Montrez .... 256-372-5555.... 1 A
montrez.payton@aamu.edu
PAYTON STEWART,
Floristina .... 504-520-7381 193 C
flpayton@xula.edu
PAZ, Gabriel .... 717-867-6302 388 A
paz@lvc.edu
PAZ, Harold .... 631-444-2800 316 D
harold.paz@stonybrookmedicine.edu
PAZ, Veronica .... 210-366-2701 441 C
vpaz@questcollege.edu
PAZ-AMOR, Windy .... 908-526-1200 280 C
windy.paz-amor@raritanval.edu
PAZDRO, Michael, A .... 989-964-4841 229 L
mapazdro@svsu.edu
PEABODY, William .... 845-437-7267 323 H
wipeabody@vassar.edu
PEACE, Derryle .... 903-886-5764 446 D
derryle.peace@tamuc.edu
PEACE, Donald .... 864-231-2000 405 F
dpeace@andersonuniversity.edu
PEACE, Matthew .... 386-752-1822.. 99 P
matthew.peace@fgc.edu
PEACH, Kyle .... 618-262-8641 139 G
peachk@iecc.edu
PEACOCK, Benjamin ..... 972-860-4643 433 G
bpeacock@dcccd.edu
PEACOCK, Caleb .... 423-478-7703 421 J
cpeacock@ptseminary.edu
PEACOCK, Corey .... 307-268-2249 499 T
michael.peacock@caspercollege.edu
PEACOCK, Jackye .... 619-849-2631.. 57 J
jpeacock@pointloma.edu
PEACOCK, Katie .... 425-739-8455 480 D
katie.peacock@lwtech.edu
PEACOCK, Melissa .... 360-676-2772 480 G
mpeacock@nwic.edu
PEACOCK, Ross .... 440-775-6927 357 G
ross.peacock@oberlin.edu
PEACOCK, Starr .... 334-387-3877.... 4 C
starrfain@amridgeuniversity.edu
PEACOCK, Steve .... 612-330-1583 233 G
peacock@augsburg.edu
PEACOCK-LANDRUM,
Linda, G .... 920-465-2163 494 F
peacockl@uwgb.edu
PEAK, Douglas, C .... 817-515-3076 445 A
douglas.peak@tccd.edu
PEAK, Lisa .... 502-410-6200 180 D
PEAL, Darryl, A .... 859-572-6630 184 B
peald1@nku.edu
PEARCE, Amanda .... 859-238-5200 179 H
PEARCE, Amy .... 314-773-0083 250 C
apearce@brookes.edu
PEARCE, Arthur, B .... 229-333-5832 127 C
apearce@valdosta.edu
PEARCE, Chris .... 336-734-7570 334 D
cpearce@forsythtech.edu
PEARCE, David .... 660-543-4365 259 K
dpearce@ucmo.edu
PEARCE, Jared .... 641-673-2107 170 I
pearcej@wmpenn.edu
PEARCE, Jeff .... 405-422-1246 368 I
PEARCE, Jennifer .... 276-944-6968 466 F
jpearce@ehc.edu
PEARCE, Julie, L .... 818-677-2366.. 32 E
julie.pearce@csun.edu
PEARCE, Kelley .... 256-549-8376.... 2 B
kpearce@gadsdenstate.edu
PEARCE, Kim .... 952-214-0945 241 P
kpearce@nwhealth.edu
PEARCE, Rick .... 309-268-8100 138 F
rick.pearce@heartland.edu
PEARCE, Rick .... 229-226-1621 126 B
rpearce@thomasu.edu
PEARCE, Steve .... 770-229-3293 125 F
steve.pearce@sctech.edu
PEARCY, Shelly .... 231-591-3825 223 H
shellypearcy@ferris.edu
PEARD, Patricia .... 207-581-5841 196 C
patricia.peard@maine.edu
PEARIGEN, Rob .... 601-974-1001 246 C
rob.pearigen@millsaps.edu
PEARL, Danita .... 937-708-5704 363 G
dpearl@wilberforce.edu
PEARLE, Kathleen .... 508-678-2811 213 F
kathleen.pearle@bristolcc.edu
PEARLMAN, Russ, B ..... 402-280-5104 265 J
russellpearlman@creighton.edu
PEARON, Jill .... 574-520-4872 157 C
PEARSALL, Joel, K .... 208-467-8521 132 B
president@nnu.edu
PEARSALL, Jonathan ..... 617-824-8426 208 G
jonathan_pearsall@emerson.edu
PEARSALL, Kim .... 863-669-2309 106 A
kpearsall@polk.edu
PEARSALL, Roland .... 617-236-8879 209 D
rpearsall@fisher.edu
PEARSE, David .... 956-295-3517 448 E
david.pearse@tsc.edu
PEARSE, Kelly .... 262-524-7124 491 A
kgilling@carrollu.edu
PEARSEY, Lindsey, K .... 812-855-3870 156 B
lpearsey@iu.edu
PEARSON, Andrew, L .... 540-828-5410 464 C
apearson@bridgewater.edu
PEARSON, Annie .... 405-422-1486 368 I
annie.pearson@redlandscc.edu
PEARSON, Barry .... 914-251-6020 318 E
barry.pearson@purchase.edu
PEARSON, Bryan, J .... 814-886-6424 390 E
bpearson@mtaloy.edu
PEARSON, Christie .... 214-768-7432 443 G
cmpearson@smu.edu
PEARSON,
Christopher, A .... 810-762-3000 231 C
pear@umich.edu
PEARSON, Craig .... 641-472-1186 168 A
cpearson@miu.edu
PEARSON, David .... 951-343-4298.. 27 J
dpearson@calbaptist.edu
PEARSON, David, L .... 515-574-1234 166 G
pearson@iowacentral.edu
PEARSON, Doug, R .... 478-301-2685 122 C
pearson_dr@mercer.edu
PEARSON, Jan .... 706-233-7236 125 A
jpearson@follett.com
PEARSON, Janice, L ..... 559-323-2100.. 61 G
jpearson@sjcl.edu
PEARSON, Karen, L ...... 208-467-8663 132 B
klpearson@nnu.edu
PEARSON, Kelsey .... 315-268-6620 295 E
kmperason@clarkson.edu
PEARSON, Mary .... 435-865-8270 459 E
pearsonm@suu.edu
PEARSON, Matt .... 707-778-3608.. 63 C
mpearson@santarosa.edu
PEARSON, Meg .... 518-564-3150 318 C
mpear009@plattsburgh.edu
PEARSON, Sandy .... 415-485-3200.. 41 H
sandy.pearson@dominican.edu
PEARSON, Sarah, R ...... 207-786-6247 193 D
spearson@bates.edu
PEARSON, Shelley .... 817-515-8004 445 A
shelley.pearson@tccd.edu
PEARSON, Sonya .... 702-651-7980 270 F
sonya.pearson@csn.edu
PEARSON, Stacy .... 509-335-5524 484 D
stacy.pearson@wsu.edu
PEARSON, Susan .... 509-527-4265 484 B
susan.pearson@wwcc.edu
PEARSON, Susan .... 865-354-3000 424 D
pearsonc@roanestate.edu
PEARSON, Tammi .... 909-274-4220.. 52 K
tpearson@mtsac.edu
PEARSON, Terri .... 580-477-7918 371 D
PEARSON, Tracey .... 910-630-7122 331 B
tpearson@methodist.edu
PEARSON, Vanessa .... 610-330-5000 387 B
PEARSON, Virgil .... 314-340-5300 253 E
pearsonv@hssu.edu
PEARSON, Vonda .... 651-255-6115 242 J
vpearson@unitedseminary.edu
PEARSON, Yvette, E ...... 972-883-4566 454 D
yepearson@utdallas.edu
PEARSON-WHARTON,
Stacey .... 570-372-4238 398 A
pearsonwharton@susqu.edu
PEART, Gwendolyn .... 704-334-6882 327 J
gpeart@charlottechristian.edu
PEART, Sandra, J .... 804-287-6086 471 E
speart@richmond.edu
PEASE, Isabel .... 904-620-2115 111 A
isabel.pease@unf.edu
PEASE, Patrick, P .... 319-273-2518 163 G
patrick.pease@uni.edu
PEASLEE, Deidra .... 651-846-1364 240 E
deidra.peaslee@saintpaul.edu
PEASTER, Carl .... 303-404-5799.. 80 I
carl.peaster@frontrange.edu
PEASTER, Rita .... 405-744-5000 367 G
rita.peaster@okstate.edu
PEAT, Kareem .... 718-817-3112 300 A
kpeat@fordham.edu
PEAVEY, Donna, B .... 504-282-4455 190 D
dpeavey@nobts.edu
PEAVLER, Karen .... 859-622-7836 180 B
karen.peavler@eku.edu
PEAVY, Kristi .... 478-757-5200 127 D
kpeavy@wesleyancollege.edu
PEAVY, Liesa .... 770-216-2960 121 F
lpeavy@ict.edu
PEAVY, Terence .... 212-217-3801 299 C
terence_peavy@fitnyc.edu
PECCHIA, John, P .... 845-575-3000 305 C
john.pecchia@marist.edu
PECCIA, Veronica .... 845-437-5331 323 H
PECENY, Mark .... 505-277-7381 288 C
markpec@unm.edu
PECHA, David, M .... 580-327-8528 367 A
dmpecha@nwosu.edu
PECHAN, Gwen .... 904-819-6359.. 99 D
gpechan@flagler.edu
PECHENKINA, Ekaterina 718-997-5210 295 A
ekaterina.pechenkina@qc.cuny.edu
PECK, David .... 626-815-4503.. 26 K
dpeck@apu.edu
PECK, David, R .... 208-496-3963 130 G
peckdr@byui.edu
PECK, Edward .... 216-397-4218 353 O
epeck@jcu.edu
PECK, James .... 414-955-4700 492 F
jpeck@mcw.edu
PECK, Jane .... 781-768-7307 217 H
jane.peck@regiscollege.edu
PECK, Kendall, D .... 208-496-1123 130 G
peckk@byui.edu
PECK, Kierstan .... 320-629-5100 239 G
PECK, Sherry .... 614-236-6534 348 I
speck@capital.edu
PECK, Susan .... 252-335-0821 333 E
susan_peck@albemarle.edu
PECK, Travis .... 918-343-6816 369 A
tpeck@rsu.edu
PECKA, Kenneth .... 509-777-3292 485 D
kpecka@whitworth.edu
PECKHAM, Karissa .... 203-582-7644.. 88 F
karissa.peckham@quinnipiac.edu
PECKHAM, Michael .... 920-403-3360 494 B
mike.peckham@snc.edu
PECKSKAMP, Terra .... 313-228-7374 296 C
tpeckskamp@colgate.edu
PECOR, Sarah, A .... 262-243-5700 491 E
sarah.pecor@cuw.edu
PECORA, Krystn, E .... 860-444-8444 502 F
krystn.e.pecora@uscg.mil
PECORARO, Heather ..... 508-767-7355 205 F
hl.pecoraro@assumption.edu
PECORD, Melanie .... 618-985-2828 140 G
melaniepecord@jalc.edu
PECOTA, Samuel, R ...... 707-654-1000.. 32 C
PECTOL, James, B .... 423-585-6823 424 G
james.pectol@ws.edu
PEDAWI, Evonne .... 517-884-4234 227 C
pedawi@cga.msu.edu
PEDDLE, Ronald .... 602-206-8220 272 A
rpeddle@ccsnh.edu
PEDE, Michael .... 315-792-5411 306 G
mpede@mvcc.edu
PEDE, Mike .... 713-743-9551 451 G
mlpede@uh.edu
PEDEN, Gary, S .... 315-470-6588 319 A
gspeden@esf.edu
PEDEN CHRISTODOULOU,
Jean .... 516-463-6815 301 E
jean.pedenchristodoulou@hofstra.edu
PEDERSEN, Andrew .... 701-671-2314 346 B
andrew.pedersen.1@ndscs.edu
PEDERSEN, Dan .... 815-753-9676 145 H
dpedersen2@niu.edu
PEDERSEN, Eric .... 435-652-7977 459 G
eric.pedersen@utahtech.edu
PEDERSEN, Henrik .... 848-445-4795 281 B
hpederse@soe.rutgers.edu
PEDERSEN, Jon .... 405-744-9805 367 G
jon.pederson@okstate.edu
PEDERSEN, Joy, M .... 805-756-6749.. 29 K
jmpeders@calpoly.edu
PEDERSEN, Karen, L ...... 785-532-5644 175 A
karenpedersen@ksu.edu
PEDERSEN, Mary .... 970-491-6614.. 79 E
mary.pedersen@colostate.edu
PEDERSEN, Matthew, D 801-863-8320 460 A
mpedersen@uvu.edu
PEDERSEN, Patricia, E .. 203-436-8518.. 90 B
patty.pedersen@yale.edu
PEDERSEN, Ryan .... 925-473-7404.. 40 I
rpedersen@losmedanos.edu
PEDERSON, Joshua .... 507-344-7840 233 I
jpederson@blc.edu
PEDERSON, Mark .... 765-677-2117 157 F
mark.pederson@indwes.edu
PEDERSON, Paula .... 218-736-1559 238 K
paula.pederson@minnesota.edu
PEDESCLEAUX, Desiree . 404-270-5696 126 A
dpedescl@spelman.edu
PEDNEAU, Judy .... 276-326-4461 464 A
jpedneau@bluefield.edu
PEDONE, Melissa, D .... 321-682-4176 113 C
mpedone@valenciacollege.edu
PEDRAJA, Luis .... 508-854-4203 215 D
lpedraja@qcc.mass.edu
PEDRAZA, Jonathan, N . 262-691-5308 499 A
jpedraza2@wctc.edu
PEDRAZA-GUEVARA,
Omar, A .... 787-751-1912 507 F
opedraza@juris.inter.edu
PEDRICK, Jim .... 319-385-6218 167 F
jim.pedrick@iw.edu
PEDRICK, Laura .... 414-229-3203 495 B
lpedrick@uwm.edu
PEDRO, David .... 508-910-9070 211 F
dpedro@umassd.edu
PEDRO, Joan .... 281-283-3501 452 A
pedro@uhcl.edu
PEDROTTY, Danielle ...... 215-489-4975 381 K
danielle.pedrotty@delval.edu

PEDROTTY, Kate .... 318-869-5715 186 C
kpedrotty@centenary.edu
PEE, Charles, M .... 803-934-3294 409 H
cpee@morris.edu
PEEBLES, Lee .... 401-739-5000 403 F
lpeebles@neit.edu
PEED, Stephen .... 207-326-2451 195 G
stephen.peed@mma.edu
PEEK, Patricia .... 718-817-1000 300 A
peek@fordham.edu
PEEK-ASA, Corinne .... 858-534-3526.. 70 C
cpeekasa@ucsd.edu
PEEL, Bill .... 214-932-1112 438 C
billpeel@letu.edu
PEEL, Chermae .... 432-552-3744 456 C
peel_c@utpb.edu
PEEL, Debra .... 575-527-7745 287 A
dpeel@nmsu.edu
PEEL, Henry .... 239-489-9011 100 G
hpeel@fsw.edu
PEEL, Joe .... 318-257-3267 192 A
jpeel@latech.edu
PEELE, Tracy, E .... 252-862-1316 336 H
tepeele2452@roanokechowan.edu
PEELER, Jody .... 740-284-5216 352 I
jpeeler@franciscan.edu
PEELER, Mark, L .... 864-379-8850 408 F
mlp@erskine.edu
PEEPLES, Jim .... 706-778-8500 124 B
jpeeples@piedmont.edu
PEEPLES, Matilda .... 404-297-9522 119 G
PEEPLES, Terry, G .... 870-245-5169.. 20 H
peeplest@obu.edu
PEEPLES, Tim .... 336-278-5613 328 H
peeples@elon.edu
PEERY, Tracy .... 276-944-6112 466 F
tpeery@ehc.edu
PEETERS, Clare .... 212-678-8808 303 A
clpeeters@jtsa.edu
PEETHALA, Sudha .... 503-255-0332 374 A
sudhapeethala@multnomah.edu
PEETZ, Ralf .... 718-982-2440 293 C
ralf.peetz@csi.cuny.edu
PEEVY, Andrea .... 985-549-3275 192 E
apeevy@selu.edu
PEEVY, DeWayne .... 773-325-7503 136 F
dpeevy@depaul.edu
PEFFER, Deb .... 313-593-5100 231 B
dkpeffer@umich.edu
PEFFER, G. Anthony ..... 203-857-7309.. 87 B
gpeffer@norwalk.edu
PEGAH, Kris .... 941-351-7220 106 J
kpegah@ringling.edu
PEGAH, Mahmoud .... 941-359-7633 106 J
mpegah@ringling.edu
PEGGRAM, Rosemary ... 806-291-3414 457 B
peggramr@wbu.edu
PEGRAM, Mike .... 402-761-8270 268 D
mpegram@southeast.edu
PEGUES, Antonius .... 318-670-6000 191 B
PEGUES, Lisa .... 914-694-4225 295 G
lpegues@riversidehealth.org
PEGUES, Wanda .... 662-252-8000 248 B
wpegues@rustcollege.edu
PEHRSSON,
Dale-Elizabeth .... 724-938-4400 394 C
PEIFER, Bruce .... 903-927-3293 457 I
bpeifer@wileyc.edu
PEIFFER, Cyndi .... 641-673-1040 170 I
peifferc@wmpenn.edu
PEIFFER, Kelly .... 215-885-2360 389 A
admissions@manor.edu
PEIFFER, Kelly .... 215-885-2360 389 A
kpeiffer@manor.edu
PEIFFER, Mark .... 515-271-1475 165 C
mark.peiffer@dmu.edu
PEIPERL, Maury .... 703-993-1860 466 J
mpeiperl@gmu.edu
PEIRANO, Molly .... 803-777-3854 412 A
peirano@mailbox.sc.edu
PEKLO, Emily .... 402-354-7274 267 E
emily.peklo@methodistcollege.edu
PEKRUL, William, A ...... 507-354-8221 236 D
pekrulwa@mlc-wels.edu
PELA, Carolyn .... 602-489-5300.. 10 G
carolyn.pela@arizonachristian.edu
PELAEZ, Bares .... 305-348-1957 109 H
bronwen.bares@fiu.edu
PELAEZ, Michelle .... 813-257-3319 113 B
mpelaez@ut.edu
PELAYO, Lula .... 210-808-4765 502 B
lula.pelayo@usuhs.edu
PELAYO, Martha .... 562-860-2451.. 35 O
mpelayo@cerritos.edu
PELAZZA, Todd, A .... 203-254-4090.. 87 G
tapelazza@fairfield.edu
PELCH, Aaron .... 601-974-1194 246 C
aaron.pelch@millsaps.edu
PELCHAT, Christopher .. 509-533-3429 478 E
chris.pelchat@sfcc.spokane.edu
PELCHER, Mary .... 989-317-4760 229 K
mpelcher@sagchip.edu
PELCZARSKI, Danielle ... 802-485-3174 461 H
dpelczar@norwich.edu
PELESKO, John, A .... 302-831-0740.. 91 A
pelesko@udel.edu
PELESKY, Timothy .... 301-687-3240 203 F
tdpelesky@frostburg.edu
PELHAM, Stephanie .... 973-408-3961 276 B
spelham@drew.edu
PELIA, Clarissa .... 907-852-1820.... 9 H
clarissa.pelia@ilisagvik.edu
PELIZZA, John .... 518-244-2051 312 D
pelizj@sage.edu
PELKEY, David .... 360-596-5231 483 E
dpelkey@spscc.edu
PELL, John .... 509-777-3257 485 D
jpell@whitworth.edu
PELL, John .... 212-772-4146 294 A
jpell@hunter.cuny.edu
PELLAZGU, Eleni .... 973-278-5400 274 J
eleni-pellazgu@berkeleycollege.edu
PELLEGRIN, Nathan .... 510-466-7210.. 57 C
npellegrin@peralta.edu
PELLEGRINI, Larry .... 570-674-6307 389 H
lpellegrini@misericordia.edu
PELLEGRINO, Karen .... 610-660-1305 397 A
kpellegr@sju.edu
PELLERIN, Angela .... 318-797-5219 189 E
angela.pellerin@lsus.edu
PELLERIN, Jody .... 319-398-5409 167 H
jody.pellerin@kirkwood.edu
PELLERIN, Virginia .... 504-520-7229 193 C
vpelleri@xula.edu
PELLETIER, Andrew .... 203-332-8516.. 86 E
apelletier@housatonic.edu
PELLETIER, Corey .... 207-859-1106 196 A
pelletierc@thomas.edu
PELLETIER, Debra .... 207-834-7844 196 G
debra.pelletier1@maine.edu
PELLETIER, Jo-Ann, M .. 508-678-2811 213 F
jo-ann.pelletier@bristolcc.edu
PELLICANO, Gregory, J 215-898-7958 399 J
gpell@upenn.edu
PELLINEN, Brian .... 978-921-4242 216 F
brian.pellinen@montserrat.edu
PELLOT, Robert .... 212-938-5720 319 B
rpellot@sunyopt.edu
PELLY, Michael .... 714-997-6982.. 36 D
pelly@chapman.edu
PELONIA, Nikki .... 978-762-4000 215 B
npelonia@northshore.edu
PELOQUIN, Andy .... 503-517-1815 377 D
apeloquin@westernseminary.edu
PELOQUIN, Elayne .... 434-544-8230 470 K
peloquin_em@lynchburg.edu
PELOQUIN-DODD,
Mary, T .... 919-515-2143 341 E
mary_peloquin-dodd@ncsu.edu
PELOSI, Lisa .... 401-598-1848 403 E
lisa.pelosi@jwu.edu
PELOSO, Elizabeth, D ... 215-746-0234 399 J
epeloso@upenn.edu
PELTIER, Beverly .... 706-771-4023 115 H
bpeltier@augustatech.edu
PELTIER, Eileen .... 860-253-3032.. 86 B
epeltier@commnet.edu
PELTIER, Eileen .... 860-253-3032.. 87 E
epeltier@acc.commnet.edu
PELTIER, Matt .... 423-652-4740 419 F
mspeltie@king.edu
PELTON, Jeremy .... 502-897-4200 184 D
jpelton@sbts.edu
PELTON, Mark .... 478-445-5075 119 A
mark.pelton@gcsu.edu
PELTON, Vanessa .... 805-965-0581.. 62 M
pelton@sbcc.edu
PELTS, Dody .... 479-979-1422.. 24 A
dpelts@ozarks.edu
PELTZ, Kristen, S .... 660-562-1348 256 G
kpeltz@nwmissouri.edu
PELTZ, Mark .... 641-269-4940 166 D
peltzm@grinnell.edu
PELUSO, Constance .... 718-631-6297 295 B
cpeluso@qcc.cuny.edu
PELUSO, Kerry .... 850-644-8664 110 B
kpeluso@fsu.edu
PELUSO, W. Mark .... 802-443-5249 461 G
wpeluso@middlebury.edu
PELUSO-VERDEND,
Gary .... 918-270-6405 368 G
gary.peluso@ptstulsa.edu
PELUSZAK, Kris .... 215-503-1956 398 G
kris.peluszak@jefferson.edu
PEMBERTON, Barbara ... 870-245-5541.. 20 H
pembertonb@obu.edu
PEMBERTON,
Cynthia, L .... 208-792-2216 131 F
clpemberton@lcsc.edu
PEMBERTON, Paul .... 218-935-0417 244 A
paul.pemberton@wetcc.edu
PEMMASANI, Jyothi ...... 540-373-2200 465 G
jpemmasani@evcc.edu
PEMSTEIN, Debra, R ..... 845-758-7405 290 G
pemstein@bard.edu
PENA, Agusto, E .... 336-334-4442 342 D
aepenaes@uncg.edu
PENA, Amy, C .... 210-486-1209 428 D
apena259@alamo.edu
PENA, Andrew, M .... 915-831-6325 435 B
apena20@epcc.edu
PENA, Daniel .... 517-264-7146 230 C
dpena@sienaheights.edu
PENA, Denise .... 714-556-3610.. 73 G
PENA, Elizabeth .... 830-758-5023 449 F
epena@sulross.edu
PENA, JR., Federico ...... 402-826-8260 266 A
fred.pena@doane.edu
PENA, Fernando .... 415-338-7211.. 34 A
fernandopena@sfsu.edu
PENA, Hector .... 787-725-6500 504 F
hpena@albizu.edu
PENA, Jesus .... 610-683-4700 394 A
pena@kutztown.edu
PENA, Juanita .... 719-549-2943.. 79 G
juanita.pena@csupueblo.edu
PENA, Mauro .... 909-389-3327.. 60 E
mpena@craftonhills.edu
PENA, Meghan .... 325-942-2083 450 B
meghan.pena@angelo.edu
PENA, Michelle .... 661-395-4318.. 47 B
michelle.pena@bakersfieldcollege.edu
PENA, Milly .... 914-251-6010 318 E
milly.pena@purchase.edu
PENA, Philip .... 515-961-1398 169 G
philip.pena@simpson.edu
PENALBA, Richelle .... 714-432-5869.. 38 F
rpenalba@occ.cccd.edu
PENALOZA, Carlos .... 808-455-0215 130 A
carlospe@hawaii.edu
PENALOZA, Lorena .... 831-459-1848.. 71 A
campuscounsel@ucsc.edu
PENALVA, Andrew .... 317-921-7931 158 B
apenalva@ivytech.edu
PENALVER, Eduardo, M 206-296-6000 483 B
PENAS, Angela, D .... 786-331-1000 104 H
apena@maufl.edu
PENCE, Barry .... 563-884-5866 169 C
barry.pence@palmer.edu
PENCE, Dana .... 281-756-3501 428 E
dpence@alvincollege.edu
PENCE, Heather .... 770-528-4545 116 H
PENCE, Kory .... 918-335-6879 368 E
kpence@okwu.edu
PENCE, Maggie .... 605-626-2416 415 H
maggie.pence@northern.edu
PENCE, Mike .... 512-404-4819 429 K
mpence@austinseminary.edu
PENCHI, Zulma .... 787-257-0000 510 F
zulma.penchi@upr.edu
PENCYLA, Michelle .... 708-216-3354 142 G
mpencyla@luc.edu
PENDER, Moriah .... 706-233-7417 125 A
mpender@shorter.edu
PENDERGAST, Jayme ..... 770-426-2858 122 A
jayme.pendergast@life.edu
PENDERGAST, Kate .... 860-768-2403.. 89 E
pendergas@hartford.edu
PENDERGAST, Kiley, M 518-783-2302 314 K
kpendergast@siena.edu
PENDERGAST, Marcy ..... 518-629-7230 302 A
m.pendergast@hvcc.edu
PENDERGRASS, Toni ..... 505-566-3209 287 G
pendergrasst@sanjuancollege.edu
PENDERS, Brooke .... 860-768-4288.. 89 E
penders@hartford.edu
PENDHARKAR, Daya .... 813-253-7091 102 A
dpendharkar@hccfl.edu
PENDLETON, C. Jay ...... 813-257-3147 113 B
cpendleton@ut.edu
PENDLETON,
Christopher .... 540-261-8400 470 D
chris.pendleton@svu.edu
PENDLETON, Gail .... 510-981-2804.. 56 J
gpendleton@peralta.edu
PENDLETON, Jody .... 972-279-6511 428 G
jpendleton@amberton.edu
PENDLETON, Laura .... 509-452-5100 481 E
lpendleton@pnwu.edu
PENDLETON, Laurence .. 615-963-7925 425 A
laurence.pendleton@tnstate.edu
PENDLETON, Lorraine ... 540-891-3033 472 J
lpendleton@germanna.edu
PENDLEY, Catherine ...... 919-365-7711 340 C
catherine.pendley@sfwbc.edu
PENDSE, Ravi .... 734-763-7590 231 A
rpendse@umich.edu
PENER, Lita .... 219-980-6853 157 A
lmpener@iu.edu
PENFIELD, Randall, D ... 336-334-3944 342 D
rdpenfie@uncg.edu
PENG, Hsin (Gina) .... 310-233-4356.. 49 F
penghw@lahc.edu
PENG, Willie .... 657-278-2866.. 31 E
wpeng@fullerton.edu
PENGRA, Matt .... 407-679-0100 101 J
mpengra@fullsail.com
PENICK, William .... 951-785-2100.. 47 F
wpenick@lasierra.edu
PENINGER, Heather ...... 704-403-1638 327 B
heather.peninger@atriumhealth.org
PENISTEN, Douglas .... 918-444-4000 366 G
penisten@nsuok.edu
PENIX, Doug .... 859-442-1634 181 D
doug.penix@kctcs.edu
PENKALA, Robert .... 586-445-7636 226 F
penkalar@macomb.edu
PENKE, Ann .... 920-565-1000 492 A
penkea@lakeland.edu
PENLAND, Jennifer .... 304-876-5222 489 A
jpenland@shepherd.edu
PENLEY, Julie .... 915-731-6715 435 B
jpenley@epcc.edu
PENLEY, Rashelle .... 828-726-2218 332 E
rpenley@cccti.edu
PENN, Jamilyn .... 206-878-3710 480 C
jpenn@highline.edu
PENNA, Anthony .... 617-552-3475 207 A
anthony.penna@bc.edu
PENNAVARIA,
Katherine .... 717-299-7754 398 E
pennavaria@stevenscollege.edu
PENNELLA, Heather .... 661-654-6098.. 30 C
hpennella@csub.edu
PENNER, Julie .... 815-836-5667 142 C
pennerju@lewisu.edu
PENNER, Marlene .... 574-535-7507 155 B
marlenemp@goshen.edu
PENNEY, Bill .... 352-395-5160 107 G
bill.penney@sfcollege.edu
PENNEY, Samantha .... 812-237-8479 155 H
samantha.penney@indstate.edu
PENNIMAN, Sarah .... 717-361-1428 383 B
pennimans@etown.edu
PENNINGTON, Amy ...... 479-968-0407.. 18 E
apennington@atu.edu
PENNINGTON, Evan ...... 816-604-1000 255 B
evan.pennington@mcckc.edu
PENNINGTON, Kevin .... 252-399-6343 326 H
kpennington@barton.edu
PENNINGTON,
Kimberly .... 828-328-7473 330 B
kimberly.pennington@lr.edu
PENNINGTON, Laura .... 276-739-2538 474 H
lpennington@vhcc.edu
PENNINGTON,
Sandra, L .... 801-375-5125 459 A
sandy.pennington@rm.edu
PENNINGTON, Sherry ... 417-667-8181 251 E
spennington@cottey.edu
PENNINI, Susan, W .... 617-333-2165 208 D
spennini@curry.edu
PENNOCK, Kimberly ..... 508-999-8073 211 F
kpennock@umassd.edu
PENNY, Anthony .... 508-793-7769 207 F
apenny@clarku.edu
PENNY, Lee .... 843-953-5520 407 D
pennyll@cofc.edu
PENNY, Rick .... 440-525-7320 354 L
rpenny@lakelandcc.edu
PENPRASE, Bryan, E ..... 949-480-4184.. 64 E
bpenprase@soka.edu

PERKINS, Mark .... 307-778-1113 500 D
mperkins@lccc.wy.edu
PERKINS, Mary .... 847-214-7414 137 D
mperkins@elgin.edu
PERKINS, Meredith .... 212-217-3500 299 C
meredith_perkins@fitnyc.edu
PERKINS, Michele, D .... 603-428-2222 272 I
mperkins@nec.edu
PERKINS, Mike .... 707-476-4331.. 58 I
mike-perkins@redwoods.edu
PERKINS, Myrna .... 620-792-9201 171 F
perkinsm@bartonccc.edu
PERKINS, Peter .... 607-753-2518 317 D
peter.perkins@cortland.edu
PERKINS, Priscilla, L .... 413-782-1531 219 E
priscilla.perkins@wne.edu
PERKINS, Ryan .... 870-762-3146.. 17 F
rperkins@smail.anc.edu
PERKINS, Susan, L .... 212-650-7947 293 B
sperkins@ccny.cuny.edu
PERKINS, Ungina .... 704-922-2310 334 E
perkins.ungina@gaston.edu
PERKINS-HOLTSCLAW, Kala .... 423-869-7089 420 A
k.perkins-holtsclaw@lmunet.edu
PERKINS JASPER, Erica 909-607-3138.. 37 G
erica.jasper@cms.claremont.edu
PERKINSON, Greg .... 541-552-6319 376 A
perkinsog@sou.edu
PERKOWSKI, Henry .... 212-678-3016 321 H
hp2125@tc.columbia.edu
PERLAKY, Steve .... 269-387-8584 232 J
stephen.perlaky@wmich.edu
PERLAS, Char .... 530-938-5200.. 39 D
cperlas@siskiyous.edu
PERLIONI, Jason .... 443-997-2370 199 E
perlioni@jhu.edu
PERLMAN, Andrew .... 617-573-8155 218 G
aperlman@suffolk.edu
PERLMAN, Bruce, J .... 505-277-1092 288 C
bperlman@unm.edu
PERLMAN, Lynn .... 617-277-3915 207 B
perlmanl@bgsp.edu
PERLMAN, Susan .... 301-243-2153 501 J
susan.perlman@dodiis.mil
PERLMUTTER, David .... 806-742-3385 450 C
david.perlmutter@ttu.edu
PERLMUTTER, David, H 314-362-6827 261 B
perlmutterd@wustl.edu
PERLOW, Yehoshua .... 718-438-2727 326 D
PERLOW, Yisroel .... 718-438-2727 326 D
PERLUS, Jessamyn .... 607-255-3559 297 D
jgp66@cornell.edu
PERMAN, Jay, A .... 301-445-1901 202 D
jperman@usmd.edu
PERMAN, Matthew .... 212-659-7200 303 E
mperman@tkc.edu
PERMENTER, Selma .... 817-272-2101 454 B
PERNA, Laura .... 215-898-4032 399 J
lperna@gse.upenn.edu
PERNELL-MCGEE, Anthony .... 440-775-5364 357 G
apernell@oberlin.edu
PERNICELLO, Collene ... 215-572-2840 378 E
pernicelloc@arcadia.edu
PERNOT, Laurent .... 312-369-7606 136 C
lpernot@colum.edu
PEROG, Cheryl .... 518-255-5211 318 F
perogcj@cobleskill.edu
PEROO, Rama .... 620-441-5587 172 M
rama.peroo@cowley.edu
PEROW, Lauren, A .... 814-641-3302 386 E
perowl@juniata.edu
PEROZZI, Brett .... 801-626-6008 460 B
brettperozzi@weber.edu
PEROZZI, Thomas .... 847-574-5168 141 G
tperozzi@lfgsm.edu
PERR, Yechiel, I .... 718-327-7600 325 A
info@yofr.org
PERRAULT, Jeanette .... 563-589-0200 170 G
PERREAULT, Amy .... 207-778-7256 196 F
amy.f.perreault@maine.edu
PERREAULT, Melanie .... 410-704-4498 204 B
mperreault@towson.edu
PERRELLI, John .... 410-337-6527 198 G
john.perrelli@goucher.edu
PERRES, Irving .... 718-232-7800 325 D
PERRET, Geraldine .... 973-618-3536 275 E
gperret@caldwell.edu
PERRETTA, Betty .... 972-721-5000 451 E
bboop@udallas.edu
PERRI, Christine .... 619-216-6668.. 65 K
cperri@swccd.edu
PERRI, Jason .... 716-851-1421 299 A
perri@ecc.edu
PERRI, Mary Lynn .... 440-646-8329 363 C
mperri@ursuline.edu
PERRIEN, Shane .... 402-941-6171 267 B
perrien@midlandu.edu
PERRIER, Sarah .... 412-392-8184 395 H
sperrier@pointpark.edu
PERRIGO, Ryan .... 906-353-8400 225 G
rperrigo@kbocc.edu
PERRIN, Amy .... 847-214-7217 137 D
aperrin@elgin.edu
PERRIN, Brent .... 509-452-5100 481 E
bperrin@pnwu.edu
PERRIN, Brian .... 617-236-8880 209 D
bperrin@fisher.edu
PERRIN, David, H .... 801-581-8537 459 D
david.perrin@health.utah.edu
PERRIN, Gregory .... 512-448-8452 441 N
gperrin@stedwards.edu
PERRIN, Nicholas .... 847-317-8001 150 J
jmyers@tiu.edu
PERRIN, Thomas .... 334-833-4236..... 5 H
cao@hawks.huntingdon.edu
PERRIN, Tim .... 310-506-4266.. 56 H
tim.perrin@pepperdine.edu
PERRINE, Richard .... 603-897-8206 273 B
rperrine@rivier.edu
PERRINE, Zach .... 870-612-2014.. 23 B
zach.perrine@uaccb.edu
PERRINO, James, J .... 516-877-3385 288 L
jperrino@adelphi.edu
PERRINS, Robert, J .... 310-954-4015.. 52 J
rperrins@msmu.edu
PERRON, Evelyn, R .... 603-206-8121 272 A
eperron@ccsnh.edu
PERRON, Pam .... 978-478-3400 217 E
pperron@northpoint.edu
PERRON, Sloane .... 508-849-3344 205 E
sperron@annamaria.edu
PERROTTA, Kimberly .... 603-206-8072 272 A
kperrotta@ccsnh.edu
PERROTTA, Steve .... 603-513-1341 273 I
steve.perrotta@granite.edu
PERROTTA, Steven .... 603-888-1311 273 B
sperrotta@rivier.edu
PERRY, Al .... 810-762-0417 228 B
al.perry@mcc.edu
PERRY, Belvin .... 386-481-2856.. 96 D
portera@cookman.edu
PERRY, Brandon .... 865-573-4517 419 E
bperry@johnsonu.edu
PERRY, Brea .... 812-855-0447 156 C
blperry@indiana.edu
PERRY, Bruce .... 410-455-1687 202 G
bperry1@umbc.edu
PERRY, Bryan .... 815-753-1000 145 H
bperry3@niu.edu
PERRY, Carol .... 336-342-4261 337 B
perry4145@rockinghamcc.edu
PERRY, Catherine .... 508-999-8648 211 F
catherine.perry@umassd.edu
PERRY, Christine .... 518-828-4181 296 G
christine.perry@sunycgcc.edu
PERRY, Dan .... 512-245-2396 449 G
d_p93@txstate.edu
PERRY, Danny .... 334-420-4277..... 3 H
dperry@trenholmstate.edu
PERRY, David .... 801-832-2584 461 A
dperry@westminstercollege.edu
PERRY, Dwight, A .... 312-329-4114 144 F
dwight.perry@moody.edu
PERRY, Eddie .... 253-912-2368 481 H
eperry@pierce.ctc.edu
PERRY, Garth .... 520-621-0075.. 16 H
perryg@arizona.edu
PERRY, James .... 678-664-0520 127 E
james.perry@westgatech.edu
PERRY, Janet .... 970-207-4500.. 84 E
janetp@uscareerinstitute.edu
PERRY, Jason, P .... 801-581-8514 459 D
jason.perry@utah.edu
PERRY, Jennifer .... 903-886-5666 446 D
jennifer.perry@tamuc.edu
PERRY, Jennifer, E .... 805-437-3694.. 30 D
jennifer.perry@csuci.edu
PERRY, John .... 708-534-4480 138 C
jperry@govst.edu
PERRY, Justin .... 561-799-8579 109 F
justin.perry@fau.edu
PERRY, KayDee .... 269-749-7324 229 G
kperry@olivetcollege.edu
PERRY, Kedrick .... 504-865-2306 190 A
kbperry@loyno.edu
PERRY, Kimberly .... 360-752-8333 477 C
kperry@btc.edu
PERRY, Laura .... 315-268-6760 295 E
lperry@clarkson.edu
PERRY, Linda .... 719-846-5541.. 83 I
linda.perry@trinidadstate.edu
PERRY, Lori .... 660-263-4100 256 D
lorip@macc.edu
PERRY, Maria .... 215-884-8942 402 E
cfo@woninstitute.edu
PERRY, Marlene .... 281-873-0262 432 J
m.perry@commonwealth.edu
PERRY, Matthew .... 281-283-3661 452 A
perrym@uhcl.edu
PERRY, Melissa .... 386-312-4088 107 A
melissaperry@sjrstate.edu
PERRY, Meredith .... 423-425-4431 426 D
meredith-perry@utc.edu
PERRY, Michael .... 321-674-7127 100 A
perrymj@fit.edu
PERRY, Michael .... 815-226-4067 147 J
mperry@rockford.edu
PERRY, Michele .... 805-553-4915.. 73 I
sperry@vcccd.edu
PERRY, Mike .... 317-274-7200 157 B
perrymike@iupui.edu
PERRY, Missy .... 864-941-8666 410 D
perry.m@ptc.edu
PERRY, Nancy .... 410-386-8231 197 G
nperry@carrollcc.edu
PERRY, Nate .... 937-229-1000 362 C
PERRY, III, Nathaniel ... 615-329-8604 418 E
nperry@fisk.edu
PERRY, Pamela .... 319-895-4176 164 E
pperry@cornellcollege.edu
PERRY, Pamela .... 312-850-7344 135 E
pperry18@ccc.edu
PERRY, Paul .... 231-995-1114 228 F
pperry@nmc.edu
PERRY, Rhonda .... 217-206-7796 151 E
rrperry@uillinois.edu
PERRY, Robert .... 617-879-7269 212 E
rperry@massart.edu
PERRY, Roderick, D .... 317-278-5247 157 B
perryrd@iupui.edu
PERRY, Rodger .... 704-669-4032 333 C
perryr@clevelandcc.edu
PERRY, Rubye .... 334-727-8350..... 7 D
rperry@tuskegee.edu
PERRY, Stephanie, D .... 276-328-0240 471 G
sdh9y@uvawise.edu
PERRY, Stuart .... 320-363-5047 234 I
sperry@csbsju.edu
PERRY, Stuart .... 320-363-5047 242 G
sperry@csbsju.edu
PERRY, Ted .... 740-474-8896 358 A
tperry@ohiochristian.edu
PERRY, Terri .... 812-888-4103 162 E
tperry@vinu.edu
PERRY, Thomas, D .... 740-376-4408 355 E
tom.perry@marietta.edu
PERRY, Tiffani .... 662-252-8000 248 B
tperry@rustcollege.edu
PERRY, Todd .... 208-885-7179 132 C
tperry@uidaho.edu
PERRY, Tom .... 479-524-7122.. 20 C
tperry@jbu.edu
PERRY, Tom .... 740-376-4408 355 E
perryt@marietta.edu
PERRY, Tracy .... 734-384-4261 227 F
tperry@monroeccc.edu
PERRY, Walter .... 215-242-7989 380 G
perryw@chc.edu
PERRY-CONLEY, Tonia .. 609-586-4800 277 H
conleyt@mccc.edu
PERRY KEITH, Colleen . 302-225-6260.. 90 I
keithcp@gbc.edu
PERRY-MCCLURE, Kyleigh, M .... 606-474-3200 180 G
kmperrymcclure@kcu.edu
PERRY WOOTEN, Lynn . 617-521-2070 218 C
PERRYMAN, Nancy, S .. 309-655-4119 148 G
nancy.s.perryman@osfhealthcare.org
PERRYMAN, Tiffany .... 601-643-8411 244 G
tiffany.perryman@colin.edu
PERSALES, David .... 210-999-7011 451 B
PERSAUD, Axel .... 301-405-6473 202 E
apersaud@umd.edu
PERSAUD, June .... 973-877-3412 276 G
persaud@essex.edu
PERSHAD, Lutisha .... 203-285-2524.. 86 D
PERSICO, IHM, Mary .... 570-348-6231 389 B
persico@marywood.edu
PERSINGER, Bill .... 931-221-6309 416 H
persingerb@apsu.edu
PERSKY, Laura .... 914-323-5188 305 A
laura.persky@mville.edu
PERSON, Andy .... 516-299-2851 304 D
andy.person@liu.edu
PERSON, Andy .... 516-299-2851 304 C
andy.person@liu.edu
PERSON, Gretchen .... 615-322-2457 427 B
religiouslife@vanderbilt.edu
PERSON, Paul .... 501-370-5211.. 21 A
pperson@philander.edu
PERSONS, Alexis .... 507-433-0508 240 A
alexis.persons@riverland.edu
PERSONS, Amanda .... 315-386-7333 319 E
hewle105@canton.edu
PERSSON, Brittany .... 718-780-7975 291 G
brittany.persson@brooklaw.edu
PERTL, Brian, G .... 920-832-6614 492 B
brian.g.pertl@lawrence.edu
PERTZ, Sara .... 715-852-1305 497 E
spertz@cvtc.edu
PERTZBORN, Kathleen .. 413-542-5502 205 D
kpertzborn@amherst.edu
PERUSKI, David .... 972-548-6884 432 I
dperuski@collin.edu
PERUSO, Jennifer .... 610-647-4400 385 K
jperuso@immaculata.edu
PERUZZOTTI, Robert .... 860-701-5016.. 88 C
peruzzotti_r@mitchell.edu
PERVIER, Curt .... 432-685-4677 439 E
cpervier@midland.edu
PERVINE, Robert .... 270-809-3744 184 A
rpervine@murraystate.edu
PERZESKI, Donna, M .... 216-916-7506 354 A
dperzesk@kent.edu
PESARCHICK, Robert, A 610-785-6204 396 H
rpesarchick@scs.edu
PESCARMONA, Denee .... 760-795-6805.. 52 G
dpescarmona@miracosta.edu
PESCE, Lucy, A .... 718-990-3004 313 B
pescel@stjohns.edu
PESCH, Linda .... 507-223-1325 239 B
linda.pesch@mnwest.edu
PESCINSKI, Robert .... 908-526-1200 280 C
robert.pescinski@raritanval.edu
PESCOVITZ, Ora .... 248-370-3500 229 F
pescovitz@oakland.edu
PESHECK, Philip .... 605-642-6297 415 F
philip.pesheck@bhsu.edu
PESHON MCGARRY, Mari .... 916-608-6500.. 51 A
PESKA, Scott .... 630-466-7900 152 H
speska@waubonsee.edu
PESKO, Rebecca .... 252-249-1851 336 C
rpesko@pamlicocc.edu
PESOLA, Steven .... 413-662-5073 212 F
steven.pesola@mcla.edu
PESSIA, Mary Beth .... 617-824-8525 208 G
marybeth_pessia@emerson.edu
PESSIER, Julian .... 631-632-6720 316 D
julian.pessier@stonybrook.edu
PESTA, Donna .... 518-255-5624 318 F
pestadh@cobleskill.edu
PESTANA, JP .... 617-824-8655 208 G
jp_pestana@emerson.edu
PESTELLO, Fred, P .... 314-977-7777 258 H
president@slu.edu
PESTER, Megan .... 660-359-3948 256 F
mpester@mail.ncmissouri.edu
PESTUN, Jeff .... 616-395-7670 224 H
pestun@hope.edu
PETAK, Katty .... 402-399-2411 265 H
vpetak@csm.edu
PETE, James .... 678-466-4000 117 A
jamespete@clayton.edu
PETE, Kendall .... 540-831-5095 468 E
kkpete@radford.edu
PETEET, Allison .... 602-489-5300.. 10 G
allison.peteet@arizonachristian.edu
PETEK, Kate .... 312-939-0111 137 B
katepetek@eastwest.edu
PETER, Beth, C .... 651-641-8795 235 A
peter@csp.edu
PETER, Florence, L .... 692-625-0635 503 F
fpeter@cmi.edu
PETER, Jennifer .... 402-280-2735 265 J
jenniferpeter@creighton.edu
PETER, Pam .... 315-443-1870 321 D
PETER, Troy .... 217-228-5432 147 C
peterff@quincy.edu

PETRITES, Cindy .... 414-288-3062 492 E
cynthia.petrites@marquette.edu
PETRITIS, Paul .... 413-662-5543 212 F
paul.petritis@mcla.edu
PETRIZZO, Louis, J .... 631-451-4235 320 G
petrizl@sunysuffolk.edu
PETROCHUK, Michael ... 330-244-4764 363 E
mpetrochuk@walsh.edu
PETROKA, Louise, A ..... 203-285-2145.. 86 D
lpetroka@gatewayct.edu
PETRONE, Eileen .... 412-536-1115 386 H
eileen.petrone@laroche.edu
PETRONSKY, LeeAnn .... 716-926-8963 301 C
lpetronsky@hilbert.edu
PETROS, William, P ..... 304-293-5212 489 E
wpetros@hsc.wvu.edu
PETROSIAN, Anahid ...... 956-872-8339 443 B
anahid@southtexascollege.edu
PETROSINO, Linda .... 607-274-3265 302 E
lpetrosino@ithaca.edu
PETROSKE, Destiny .... 360-676-2772 480 G
dpetroske@nwic.edu
PETROSKI, Mike .... 561-237-7007 103 W
mpetroski@lynn.edu
PETROSKY, Fawn .... 724-938-4453 394 C
petrosky@calu.edu
PETROSKY, Joseph, L ... 248-232-4179 228 H
jlpetros@oaklandcc.edu
PETROSYAN, Narine ...... 510-925-4282.. 25 P
narinep@aua.am
PETROSYAN, Varduhi .... 510-925-4282.. 25 P
vpetrosi@aua.am
PETROSYAN, Violetta .... 304-357-4758 486 J
violettapetrosyan@ucwv.edu
PETROVA, Elena .... 706-721-0211 115 I
epetrova@augusta.edu
PETROVICH, Jason .... 219-464-6858 162 C
jason.petrovich@valpo.edu
PETRUCCI, Michele, L ... 724-357-2295 393 G
michelep@iup.edu
PETRULAKIS, Karen ...... 781-283-2207 219 C
kpetrula@wellesley.edu
PETRUS, Laura .... 423-425-4111 426 D
PETRUS, Robin .... 607-778-5201 317 A
petrusre@sunybroome.edu
PETRUSHA, Cynthia .... 707-476-4170.. 58 I
cynthia-petrusha@redwoods.edu
PETRUZELLA, Gerol .... 413-662-5570 212 F
g.petruzella@mcla.edu
PETRUZZELLI,
Barbara, W .... 845-569-3663 307 B
barbara.petruzzelli@msmc.edu
PETSCHE, Carolyn .... 815-599-3577 138 H
carolyn.petsche@highland.edu
PETSCHENKO, Lisa .... 630-953-3694 134 E
lpetschenko@chamberlain.edu
PETTA, Tim .... 360-992-2408 477 J
tpetta@clark.edu
PETTAZZONI, Jodi, E .... 336-334-5535 342 D
jepettaz@uncg.edu
PETTEGREW, Melinda ... 816-501-4689 257 K
melinda.pettegrew@rockhurst.edu
PETTENGER, Wade, W .. 417-862-9533 252 H
wpettenger@globaluniversity.edu
PETTENGILL, Keri-Beth . 804-594-1576 473 B
kpettengill@jtcc.edu
PETTI, Doris .... 212-752-1530 303 G
doris.petti@limcollege.edu
PETTI, Julie .... 518-320-1100 315 C
julie.petti@suny.edu
PETTIBON, II,
Joseph, P .... 979-845-4016 446 B
jpp2@tamu.edu
PETTID, Cathy .... 402-554-3523 269 C
cpettid@unomaha.edu
PETTIE, Brian .... 870-512-7829.. 18 C
brian_pettie@asun.edu
PETTIFER, Geoffrey .... 609-626-6023 283 A
geoffrey.pettifer@stockton.edu
PETTIGREW, Jason .... 605-229-8350 414 I
jason.pettigrew@presentation.edu
PETTINGILL, Jayn .... 510-845-5373.. 29 D
jayn@cjc.edu
PETTINGILL, Sara, Y ..... 502-272-8401 179 D
spettingill@bellarmine.edu
PETTIS, Carl .... 334-229-4232.... 4 B
cpettis@alasu.edu
PETTIS, Curtis .... 937-376-6201 349 H
cpettis@centralstate.edu
PETTIS, Sean .... 413-755-4029 215 F
skpettis@stcc.edu
PETTIS-WALDEN,
Karen, M .... 804-523-5029 473 A
kpettis-walden@reynolds.edu

PETTIT, Frederick .... 570-208-5881 386 G
frederickpettit@kings.edu
PETTIT, Martin, A .... 607-746-4702 320 A
pettitma@delhi.edu
PETTIT, Paul, E .... 214-887-5102 434 G
ppettit@dts.edu
PETTIT, Stephen, D .... 864-242-5100 405 H
PETTITT, Julie .... 406-657-2888 263 H
julie.pettitt@msubillings.edu
PETTITT, Robert .... 801-375-5125 459 A
robert.pettitt@rm.edu
PETTRY, Michael .... 757-455-3230 476 C
mpettry@vwu.edu
PETTY, Adriana .... 574-284-4861 160 F
apetty@saintmarys.edu
PETTY, Blake .... 404-364-8400 123 G
bpetty@oglethorpe.edu
PETTY, Bradley .... 325-942-2191 450 B
bradley.petty@angelo.edu
PETTY, Davion, L .... 803-536-8067 410 H
dpetty@scsu.edu
PETTY, Jamie .... 706-802-5105 119 C
jpetty@highlands.edu
PETTY, Jenny .... 406-243-2522 263 D
jenny.petty@umontana.edu
PETTY, Leslie .... 608-246-6100 497 I
lpetty1@madisoncollege.edu
PETTY, Marcia, L .... 202-994-6710.. 92 C
cpetty@gwu.edu
PETTY, Mark .... 605-658-6220 415 E
mark.petty@usd.edu
PETTY, Marshall .... 217-854-5559 133 F
PETTY, Monica .... 202-885-8612.. 94 D
mpetty@wesleyseminary.edu
PETTY, Nadine .... 603-862-1234 273 H
nadine.petty@unh.edu
PETTY, Ryan .... 312-341-3500 148 A
rpetty01@roosevelt.edu
PETTY, Theresa .... 712-274-6400 170 H
theresa.petty@witcc.edu
PETTY, Warren .... 202-806-1316.. 92 E
warren.petty@howard.edu
PETTY, Warren .... 201-216-5218 282 L
warren.petty@stevens.edu
PETTY, William, J .... 864-488-8344 409 C
wpetty@limestone.edu
PETULA, Eileen, E .... 570-577-3347 379 A
eep005@bucknell.edu
PETZKE, Greg .... 704-378-1190 329 H
gpetzke@jcsu.edu
PETZNICK, Michelle, L . 641-422-4205 168 E
petznmic@niacc.edu
PETZOLD, Terri .... 270-852-3183 183 B
terri.petzold@kwc.edu
PEWE, Rich .... 517-607-2518 224 G
rpewe@hillsdale.edu
PEWITT, Shawn .... 313-577-3390 232 H
dv3831@wayne.edu
PEYER, Patrick .... 815-921-4092 147 H
p.peyer@rockvalleycollege.edu
PEYTON, Janice, L .... 713-313-7885 448 D
janice.peyton@tsu.edu
PEZMAN, Chris .... 713-743-9370 451 G
cwpezman@uh.edu
PEZZI, Eileen .... 315-464-7853 316 F
pezzie@upstate.edu
PEZZULLO, Laurie .... 516-572-7832 307 C
laurie.pezzullo@ncc.edu
PEZZUTO, John .... 413-796-2323 219 E
john.pezzuto@wne.edu
PEÑA, Amy, F .... 505-747-2140 287 C
amy.pena@nnmc.edu
PEÑA, Damien, A .... 805-289-6113.. 74 B
dpena@vcccd.edu
PEÑA RIVERA, Norma .. 787-764-0000 511 F
norma.pena1@upr.edu
PFAFF, Caryl .... 715-634-4790 491 L
cpfaff@lco.edu
PFAFF, Mimi .... 303-751-8700.. 78 A
pfaff@belrea.edu
PFAHL, Michael .... 567-661-7270 359 H
michael_pfahl@owens.edu
PFANG, Raymond .... 210-486-3921 428 B
tpfang@alamo.edu
PFANNENSTIEL, Matt .... 785-227-3380 171 H
pfannenstielmm@bethanylb.edu
PFANNENSTIEL, Myra ... 316-942-4291 176 B
pfannenstielm@newmanu.edu
PFANNESTIEL, Todd ...... 315-792-3122 323 G
tjpfanne@utica.edu
PFAUTZ, Nadine .... 617-745-3812 208 F
nadine.pfautz@enc.edu

PFEFER, Mark, T .... 913-234-0796 172 I
mark.pfefer@cleveland.edu
PFEIFER, Aimee .... 843-805-5507 407 D
pfeiferad@cofc.edu
PFEIFER, Chuck .... 620-276-9521 173 H
chuck.pfeifer@gcccks.edu
PFEIFER, Darin .... 215-895-2164 382 D
dfp28@drexel.edu
PFEIFER, Gene, R .... 507-344-7315 233 I
gene.pfeifer@blc.edu
PFEIFER, Justin .... 316-677-1020 178 C
jpfeifer@wsutech.edu
PFEIFER, Tad .... 308-535-3684 266 J
pfeifert@mpcc.edu
PFEIFER, Terry .... 785-628-4259 173 E
tpfeifer@fhsu.edu
PFEIFFENBERGER,
Colleen .... 513-244-4296 356 F
colleen.pfeiffenberger@msj.edu
PFEIFFER, Larisa .... 301-934-7627 198 C
ljpfeiffer@csmd.edu
PFEIFFER, Patricia, A .... 919-739-7000 338 F
pfeiffer@waynecc.edu
PFEIFFER, Tamarah .... 785-749-8404 174 A
PFISTER, Matthew .... 712-274-6400 170 H
matthew.pfister1@witcc.edu
PFLANZ, Mary .... 913-621-8764 173 B
mpflanz@donnelly.edu
PFLAUM, Kathy .... 785-670-2312 178 A
kathy.pflaum@washburn.edu
PFLEGER, Heather .... 201-559-6000 277 A
PFLEGER, Heather .... 610-892-1500 393 B
heather.pfleger@pit.edu
PFLIPSEN, Andrew .... 320-308-5382 240 D
andrew.pflipsen@sctcc.edu
PFLIPSEN, Andrew, J .... 701-788-4770 345 B
andrew.pflipsen@mayvillestate.edu
PFLUGER, Stacy .... 870-543-5961.. 21 D
spfluger@seark.edu
PFOHL, Jody .... 563-588-6315 164 C
jody.pfohl@clarke.edu
PFRIENDER, Cindy .... 352-854-2322.. 97 L
prfriendc@cf.edu
PFUHL, Adam .... 651-255-6117 242 J
apfuhl@unitedseminary.edu
PHAGAN, Kathy .... 770-533-6906 121 L
kphagan@laniertech.edu
PHAGAN, Tiffany, D ...... 386-748-1364.. 98 J
phagant@erau.edu
PHAKITTHONG,
Rachelle .... 715-833-6411 497 E
rphakitthong@cvtc.edu
PHALEN, Ann .... 215-646-7300 384 G
phalen.a@gmercyu.edu
PHAM, Chelsy .... 209-954-5300.. 61 H
chelsy.pham@deltacollege.edu
PHAM, Chelsy .... 831-755-6700.. 44 J
PHAM, Hong .... 916-691-7793.. 50 K
phamh@crc.losrios.edu
PHAM, John .... 210-283-6994 452 D
jopham@uiwtx.edu
PHAM, SVD, Linh .... 563-876-3353 165 D
lpham@dwci.edu
PHAM, Michael .... 206-878-3710 480 C
mpham@highline.edu
PHAM, Ni .... 303-867-1155.. 83 H
pham@taft.edu
PHAM, Thinh .... 805-482-2755.. 59 G
tdpham@stjohnsem.edu
PHAM, Thomas .... 910-893-1415 327 C
tpham@campbell.edu
PHAM, Tom, C .... 617-984-1699 217 G
tpham@quincycollege.edu
PHAM, Tonga .... 716-645-5265 315 F
tongapha@buffalo.edu
PHAN, Nga .... 760-410-5334.. 72 F
nphan@usa.edu
PHAN, Tony .... 563-425-5200 170 D
phant43@uiu.edu
PHARES, Jason .... 304-462-6141 488 M
jason.phares@glenville.edu
PHARO, SCN, Diane ..... 812-357-6598 160 G
dpharo@saintmeinrad.edu
PHARR, Angela, D .... 770-720-5503 124 E
adp@reinhardt.edu
PHARR, Julie .... 336-386-3452 338 B
pharrj@surry.edu
PHARR, Kathy, R .... 706-542-0054 126 F
pharr@uga.edu
PHARR, Kathy, R .... 706-542-8090 126 F
pharr@uga.edu
PHARR, Maria .... 704-290-5251 337 F
mpharr@spcc.edu

PHARRIS, Heather .... 863-680-4754 100 F
hpharris@flsouthern.edu
PHAYRE, Allison .... 360-475-7108 481 B
aphayre@olympic.edu
PHEASANT, Joel, C ...... 814-641-5334 386 E
pheasaj@juniata.edu
PHELAN, Daniel, J .... 517-787-0800 225 A
phelandanielj@jccmi.edu
PHELAN, Sherry, A ...... 573-840-9689 259 I
sphelan@trcc.edu
PHELAN, Thomas, J ..... 719-333-2516 502 C
thomas.phelan@afacademy.af.edu
PHELAN JOHNSON,
Marcia .... 860-297-2041.. 88 I
marcia.johnson@trincoll.edu
PHELON, Kerry .... 860-701-5000.. 88 C
PHELPS, Barry .... 270-831-9678 181 F
barry.phelps@kctcs.edu
PHELPS, Bill .... 870-245-5567.. 20 H
phelpswr@obu.edu
PHELPS, Brad .... 501-660-1008.. 17 G
bphelps@asusystem.edu
PHELPS, Corey, C .... 405-325-0100 370 J
corey.phelps@ou.edu
PHELPS, Craig .... 660-626-2391 249 C
cphelps@atsu.edu
PHELPS, Deborah .... 620-442-0430 172 M
deborah.phelps@cowley.edu
PHELPS, Esther .... 330-337-6403 347 B
ephelps@awc.edu
PHELPS, Gary, L .... 330-471-8127 355 D
gphelps@malone.edu
PHELPS, Hilary .... 860-343-5879.. 86 G
hphelps@mxcc.edu
PHELPS, Jean .... 718-262-2285 295 D
phelps@york.cuny.edu
PHELPS, Jodi .... 910-521-6863 343 A
jodi.phelps@uncp.edu
PHELPS, Joel .... 518-828-4181 296 G
joel.phelps@sunycgcc.edu
PHELPS, Kathy .... 239-304-7074.. 95 M
kathy.phelps@avemaria.edu
PHELPS, Laura .... 904-256-7042 102 G
lphelps5@ju.edu
PHELPS, Lena .... 863-784-7303 108 D
lena.phelps@southflorida.edu
PHELPS, Sherri .... 870-245-5410.. 20 H
phelpss@obu.edu
PHENICIE,
Christopher, N .... 864-488-4549 409 C
cphenicie@limestone.edu
PHIFER-MCGHEE,
Kimberly, C .... 919-530-7593 341 D
kpmcghee@nccu.edu
PHILIE, Lauren .... 802-635-1240 463 B
PHILION, Thomas .... 312-853-4780 148 A
tphilion@roosevelt.edu
PHILIP, Matthew .... 206-296-5870 483 B
hr@seattleu.edu
PHILIP, Mintu .... 718-517-7772 314 B
mphilip@edaff.com
PHILIPOSE, Sandy .... 903-813-2455 429 I
sphilipose@austincollege.edu
PHILIPP, Diane .... 517-607-2333 224 G
dphilipp@hillsdale.edu
PHILIPP, Jason .... 651-779-5834 237 D
jason.philipp@century.edu
PHILIPP, Shirin .... 617-349-9600 210 H
philipp@lesley.edu
PHILIPPA, Elaine .... 262-595-3215 495 D
laine@uwp.edu
PHILIPS, JR., Billy, U ... 806-743-1338 450 D
billy.philips@ttuhsc.edu
PHILIPSON, Randolph ... 504-314-7157 191 D
rphilipson@tulane.edu
PHILLEY, Tim .... 918-495-6970 368 F
tphilley@oru.edu
PHILLIP, Thomas, G ...... 262-243-5700 491 E
thomas.phillip@cuw.edu
PHILLIPS, Alan .... 281-756-3514 428 E
aphillips@alvincollege.edu
PHILLIPS, Allison .... 336-838-6491 338 H
alphillips068@wilkescc.edu
PHILLIPS, Amanda .... 760-636-7962.. 39 A
afphillips@collegeofthedesert.edu
PHILLIPS, Amanda .... 724-653-2195 382 C
aphillips@dec.edu
PHILLIPS, Amber .... 978-478-3400 217 E
aphillips@northpoint.edu
PHILLIPS, Andre .... 608-262-3237 494 D
andre.phillips@wisc.edu
PHILLIPS, Andrew, T .... 410-293-1583 502 I
aphillip@usna.edu

PICKENS, Joe 386-312-4111 107 A
joepickens@sjrstate.edu
PICKENS, Laura 724-589-2009 398 F
lpickens@thiel.edu
PICKENS, Ronda 580-387-7261 366 E
rpickens@mscok.edu
PICKENS-OPOKU, Ali 651-779-5784 237 D
ali.pickens-opoku@century.edu
PICKERELL, Jennifer, K 618-537-6805 143 G
jkpickerell@mckendree.edu
PICKERILL, Ted, O 513-529-6225 356 A
pickerto@miamioh.edu
PICKERING, Amanda 315-268-3994 295 E
apickeri@clarkson.edu
PICKERING, Bob 918-631-2356 371 C
bob-pickering@utulsa.edu
PICKERING, David, J 815-928-5577 146 F
dpickrng@olivet.edu
PICKERING, Jeff 919-209-2000 335 D
jlpickering@johnstoncc.edu
PICKERING, Larry 228-897-3912 246 F
adam.pickering@mgccc.edu
PICKERING, Robert, P 843-953-5096 406 D
robert.pickering@citadel.edu
PICKETT, Dakiesha 404-756-4442 115 E
dpickett@atlm.edu
PICKETT, Himie 301-736-3631 200 A
himie.pickett@msbbcs.edu
PICKETT, Jean 817-257-7465 447 H
j.pickett@tcu.edu
PICKETT, Regina 281-283-2626 452 A
pickett@uhcl.edu
PICKETT, Todd 562-903-4754 27 E
todd.pickett@biola.edu
PICKHARDT, Paul 920-565-1000 492 A
pickhardtp@lakeland.edu
PICKRON-DAVIS,
Marcine 215-871-6178 395 A
marcinepi@pcom.edu
PICKRUM, Vita, C 302-857-6064 90 D
vpickrum@desu.edu
PICO, Claudio 619-574-6909 55 D
cpico@pacificcollege.edu
PICONE, Deborah 212-686-9244 289 G
PIDDINGTON, Josh, R 856-415-2270 280 F
jpiddington@rcsj.edu
PIEART, Nicole 847-735-6137 141 F
npieart@lakeforest.edu
PIECORA, Annette 914-674-7337 305 H
apiecora@mercy.edu
PIECZYNSKI,
William, C 508-213-2162 217 C
william.pieczynski@nichols.edu
PIEDIMONTE, Giovanni 504-988-3291 191 D
gpiedimonte@tulane.edu
PIEDRA, Daynet 956-867-8721 441 F
PIEDRAS, Alex, H 515-263-6017 166 C
apiedras@grandview.edu
PIEHLER, Keith 207-941-7875 194 D
piehlerk@husson.edu
PIEHLER, Michael 252-726-6841 342 B
mpiehler@email.unc.edu
PIEKOS, Mark 815-455-8593 143 F
mpiekos@mchenry.edu
PIEKUTOWSKI,
Michelle 412-268-5523 380 B
mpie@andrew.cmu.edu
PIENTA-LETT, Diane 973-300-2226 283 B
dpienta-lett@sussex.edu
PIEPER, Michael 701-777-6862 344 H
michael.pieper@und.edu
PIEPER-OLSON,
Heather 320-363-5964 234 I
hpieperolso@csbsju.edu
PIERACCINI,
Alessandra 410-704-2512 204 B
apieraccini@towson.edu
PIERATT, William 575-674-2201 284 P
dpieratt@burrell.edu
PIERCE, Amanda, K 757-594-8851 465 A
amanda.pierce@cnu.edu
PIERCE, Bess 423-869-6752 420 A
bess.pierce@lmunet.edu
PIERCE, Brynn 541-383-7402 371 I
bpierce@cocc.edu
PIERCE, Charles 248-370-3279 229 F
capierce@oakland.edu
PIERCE, Emily 617-244-1682 219 G
emily_pierce@williamjames.edu
PIERCE, Evan, F 716-286-8327 309 F
epierce@niagara.edu
PIERCE, Fred 906-635-2674 226 C
fpierce@lssu.edu
PIERCE, Frederic 607-753-2232 317 D
fred.pierce@cortland.edu
PIERCE, Greg 601-266-5006 248 H
greg.pierce@usm.edu
PIERCE, Guy 305-821-3333 100 C
gpierce@fnu.edu
PIERCE, Jana 541-440-7791 376 F
jana.pierce@umpqua.edu
PIERCE, Janelle 770-962-7580 121 B
jpierce@gwinnetttech.edu
PIERCE, Jason 709-379-3111 128 A
jpierce@yhc.edu
PIERCE, Jason 210-436-3716 442 A
jpierce7@stmarytx.edu
PIERCE, Jason, L 937-229-2601 362 C
jpierce2@udayton.edu
PIERCE, Jeff 828-262-3190 340 G
piercewj@appstate.edu
PIERCE, Jennifer 856-351-2642 282 I
jpierce@salemcc.edu
PIERCE, Jerry, D 318-357-6588 192 D
pierce@nsula.edu
PIERCE, Jessica, A 504-398-2190 191 E
jpierce@uhcno.edu
PIERCE, Jill, A 207-859-4807 194 B
jill.pierce@colby.edu
PIERCE, Joan 608-785-9915 499 B
piercej@westerntc.edu
PIERCE, John 828-251-6742 342 A
jpierce@unca.edu
PIERCE, Jonathan 503-883-2553 373 E
jdpierce@linfield.edu
PIERCE, Kellee 406-657-1166 264 G
piercek@rocky.edu
PIERCE, Kenneth 512-245-9650 449 G
krp91@txstate.edu
PIERCE, Kristen 617-745-3586 208 F
kristen.pierce@enc.edu
PIERCE, Latoya 716-375-2394 312 F
lpierce@sbu.edu
PIERCE, Lori, J 734-764-0151 231 A
ljpierce@umich.edu
PIERCE, Malisa 918-270-6409 368 G
malisa.pierce@ptstulsa.edu
PIERCE, Mario 203-332-5015 86 E
mpierce@housatonic.edu
PIERCE, Marisa 972-273-3135 434 C
marisapierce@dcccd.edu
PIERCE, Marisa 425-640-1697 479 A
marisa.pierce@edcc.edu
PIERCE, Mark 518-736-3622 300 B
mark.pierce@fmcc.suny.edu
PIERCE, Melody, C 336-334-7696 341 C
mcpierce@ncat.edu
PIERCE, Michael 562-903-4777 27 E
michael.pierce@biola.edu
PIERCE, Robert 'Bob' 205-348-4769 7 G
bpierce@advance.ua.edu
PIERCE, Sean 718-997-4881 295 A
sean.pierce@qc.cuny.edu
PIERCE, Sharon 612-659-6300 238 C
sharon.pierce@minneapolis.edu
PIERCE, Sonja 812-288-8878 159 C
spierce@mid-america.edu
PIERCE, Stephen 540-338-1776 468 D
admissions@phc.edu
PIERCE, Travis, L 906-487-2682 227 D
tlp@mtu.edu
PIERCE, Victoria 864-231-2000 405 F
vpierce@andersonuniversity.edu
PIERCE, William 419-530-5359 363 B
william.pierce@utoledo.edu
PIERCE, Yolanda 202-806-0744 92 E
yolanda.pierce@howard.edu
PIERMATTEI,
Dianne, M 413-542-2352 205 D
dmpiermattei@amherst.edu
PIERNER, Tracy, P 608-757-7770 497 D
tpierner@blackhawk.edu
PIEROTTI, Laura 201-559-3504 277 A
pierottil@felician.edu
PIERRE, David, A 718-990-2616 313 B
pierred@stjohns.edu
PIERRE, Devona 727-302-6653 107 C
pierre.devona@spcollege.edu
PIERRE, John, K 225-771-2552 191 C
jpierre@sulc.edu
PIERRE, Markey 318-813-5151 189 D
markey@lsuhs.edu
PIERRRE-LOUIS,
Paul-Arthur 919-716-5503 339 I
pa.pierre-louis@shawu.edu
PIERS, Sheri 207-893-6634 195 I
spiers@sjcme.edu
PIERSALL, Vicki 503-554-2161 372 I
vpiersall@georgefox.edu
PIERSOL, Jonathan 404-962-3300 127 B
jonathan.piersol@usg.edu
PIERSON, Ann 618-374-5030 147 B
ann.pierson@principia.edu
PIERSON, Carrie 217-424-3999 144 D
cpierson@millikin.edu
PIERSON, Connie 410-455-3055 202 G
krach@umbc.edu
PIERSON, Edwin 979-845-9999 446 B
epierson@tamu.edu
PIERSON, Gary 970-943-2049 85 B
gpierson@western.edu
PIERSON, James 412-365-1615 380 F
j.pierson@chatham.edu
PIERSON, Katricia 417-455-5534 251 H
president@crowder.edu
PIERSON, Lynn 570-577-1292 379 A
lynn.pierson@bucknell.edu
PIERSON, Megan 650-723-2300 66 D
PIERSON, Molly 785-670-1065 178 A
molly.pierson@washburn.edu
PIERSON, Scott 715-232-5365 496 C
piersons@uwstout.edu
PIESCO, Ryan 617-745-3849 208 F
ryan.piesco@enc.edu
PIESTER, Kenneth 661-362-2293 51 E
kpiester@masters.edu
PIETERSE, Carousel 281-646-1109 430 H
carousel.pieterse@thebibleseminary.edu
PIETREWICZ, Brian 505-277-5930 288 C
bpietrewicz@unm.edu
PIETRO, Kimberly 716-829-7556 298 C
pietrok@dyc.edu
PIETROK, Mark 503-768-7065 373 D
pietrok@lclark.edu
PIETROPAULO, Jason 865-251-1800 422 G
jpietropaulo@south.edu
PIETROWSKI, Michael 505-565-1082 218 F
mpietrowski@stonehill.edu
PIETRUSZKIEWICZ,
Christopher, M 812-488-2151 161 E
prezp@evansville.edu
PIETRYKOWSKI, Chet 406-791-5283 264 J
chet.pietrykowski@uprovidence.edu
PIETRYKOWSKI,
Robert, J 954-262-7893 104 M
rpietrykowski@nova.edu
PIETRZAK, Dale, R 812-888-4141 162 E
dpietrzak@vinu.edu
PIETSCH, Amy 920-735-2594 497 F
pietsch@fvtc.edu
PIETTE, Kylie 231-591-2089 223 H
kyliepiette@ferris.edu
PIETZ, Kady 601-528-8446 246 F
kady.pietz@mgccc.edu
PIFER, Kenneth 503-943-7337 376 H
pifer@up.edu
PIFER, Kenneth 503-370-6104 377 E
kpifer@willamette.edu
PIFKO, Melissa, K 713-500-3268 455 D
melissa.pifko@uth.tmc.edu
PIGA, John 781-891-2148 206 C
jpiga@bentley.edu
PIGATTI, Kimberly 708-596-2000 149 D
kpigatti@ssc.edu
PIGG, Eddie 334-745-6437 3 G
epigg@suscc.edu
PIGG, Tom 731-424-3520 423 F
tpigg@jscc.edu
PIGGOTT, Robyn 508-999-8002 211 F
robyn.piggott@umassd.edu
PIGNATELLO, Robert 973-443-8422 276 I
pignatello@fdu.edu
PIGNATORE, Amy 724-287-8711 379 C
amy.pignatore@bc3.edu
PIGORS, Aaron 219-980-7203 157 A
apigors@iu.edu
PIGOTT, Miguel 860-512-2815 86 F
mpigott@manchestercc.edu
PIGZA, Jennifer 925-631-4755 59 I
jpigza@stmarys-ca.edu
PIKE, Cynthia 603-342-3063 272 E
cpike@ccsnh.edu
PIKE, Dale 540-231-7108 475 D
dalepike@vt.edu
PIKE, Thomas 301-243-2112 501 J
thomas.pike@dodiis.mil
PIKLA, Christina 210-999-8898 451 B
cpikla@trinity.edu
PIKOWSKY, Reta 404-894-4181 119 D
reta.pikowsky@registrar.gatech.edu
PILARSKI, Jason 414-382-6151 490 G
jason.pilarski@alverno.edu
PILCH, Michael 215-489-2261 381 K
michael.pilch@delval.edu
PILCHER, Jeff 208-885-6155 132 C
jpilcher@uidaho.edu
PILCHICK, Yochanan 718-232-7800 325 D
PILCO, Joel 760-634-1771 28 G
PILE, Judy 501-202-7433 18 G
PILE, Sherry 502-272-8056 179 D
spile@bellarmine.edu
PILEGGI, Christopher 718-429-6600 323 I
chris.pileggi@vaughn.edu
PILGER, Dale 810-762-9525 225 F
dpilger@kettering.edu
PILGRIM, Antolina, E 229-333-5708 127 C
anedwards@valdosta.edu
PILGRIM, David 231-591-3946 223 H
davidpilgrim@ferris.edu
PILGRIM, Jacqui 617-422-7401 217 B
jpilgrim@nesl.edu
PILGRIM, Scott 864-388-8698 409 B
spilgrim@lander.edu
PILIECI, Kim 616-538-2330 224 B
kpilieci@gracechristian.edu
PILIERI, Thais 718-270-6986 294 E
tpilieri@mec.cuny.edu
PILIPZECK, Beth 215-596-8970 400 B
b.pilipz@usciences.edu
PILITSIS, Julie 561-297-3000 109 F
jpilitsis@health.fau.edu
PILKINGTON, Annette 303-273-3498 79 A
apilking@mines.edu
PILLANS, Elizabeth 903-875-7370 439 G
elizabeth.pillans@navarrocollege.edu
PILLAR, James 732-571-3585 278 B
jpillar@monmouth.edu
PILLARELLI, Tina 734-384-4332 227 F
tpillarelli@monroeccc.edu
PILLAY, Sasi 509-335-8017 484 D
sasi.k.pillay@wsu.edu
PILLING, Peter, E 212-854-4774 296 H
pp2542@columbia.edu
PILLING, Terry 701-355-8240 347 A
tgpilling@umary.edu
PILLO, Pam 203-365-7560 88 H
pillop@sacredheart.edu
PILLOW, Peggy 501-205-8834 19 B
ppillow@cbc.edu
PILLSBURY, Brooke 503-244-0726 371 E
brookepillsbury@achs.edu
PILLY, Prashanth 772-462-7152 102 E
ppilly@irsc.edu
PILON, Maryann 845-569-3332 307 B
maryannpilon@msmc.edu
PILON, Simone 617-266-1400 206 D
PILTZ, Anthony 406-657-1020 264 G
piltza@rocky.edu
PIMBER, Lisa 800-371-6105 14 I
lisa@nationalparalegal.edu
PIMENTAL, Michael, V 401-341-2443 404 D
michael.pimental@salve.edu
PIMENTEL, Art 530-661-5710 77 C
apimente@yccd.edu
PIMENTEL, Chad 603-862-0960 273 G
chad.pimentel@usnh.edu
PIMENTEL, Dorothy 209-575-6963 76 I
pimenteld@yosemite.edu
PIMENTEL, Enrique, L 787-723-4481 504 J
enrique.pimentel@ceaprc.edu
PIMENTEL, George 731-424-3520 423 F
gpimentel@jscc.edu
PIMENTEL, Marissa 408-554-4607 63 A
mpimentel@scu.edu
PIMENTEL, Pamela 530-661-5700 77 C
PIMENTEL, Robert 559-442-8257 67 A
robert.pimentel@fresnocitycollege.edu
PINA, Anthony 309-438-2111 140 C
aapina@ilstu.edu
PINA, Jason 212-998-1212 309 D
PINAR, Kemale 507-457-2394 241 A
kpinar@winona.edu
PINAULT, Christopher 401-341-2355 404 D
christopher.pinault@salve.edu
PINCHBACK, Christal 919-546-8210 339 I
cpinchback@shawu.edu
PINCHBACK, G. Keith 870-338-6474 23 A
PINCHBACK, Rebekah 248-218-2096 229 I
rpinchback@rochesteru.edu
PINCHOUCK, Lee 386-752-1822 99 P
lee.pinchouck@fgc.edu
PINCIKOWSKI, Scott 301-696-3475 199 C
pincikowski@hood.edu

PLANEK, John .... 815-836-5937 142 C
planekjo@lewisu.edu
PLANEY, Steve .... 724-480-3395 381 G
steve.planey@ccbc.edu
PLANK, Jennifer .... 772-546-5534 102 B
PLANK, Linda .... 214-820-3361 430 F
linda_plank@baylor.edu
PLANT, Alicia .... 404-627-2681 116 B
alicia.plant@beulah.edu
PLANT, Alisa .... 225-578-6144 188 K
alisaplant1@lsu.edu
PLANT, Maureen .... 301-447-5621 201 A
mplant@msmary.edu
PLANTE, Dawn, M .... 440-525-7327 354 L
dplante@lakelandcc.edu
PLANTEFABER, Lisa .... 413-572-5733 213 C
lplantefaber@westfield.ma.edu
PLANTY, Teresa .... 315-268-3852 295 E
tplanty@clarkson.edu
PLANTZ, Robert .... 570-585-9258 381 A
rplantz@clarkssummitu.edu
PLANTZ-MASTERS,
Shari .... 303-458-4272.. 83 B
splantzmasters@regis.edu
PLASBERG, Pam .... 540-636-2900 464 O
pam.plasberg@christendom.edu
PLASENCIO, Eric .... 915-532-3737 457 E
PLASSE, Michelle .... 310-338-7332.. 51 C
michelle.plasse@lmu.edu
PLASSMANN, Florenz .... 740-593-2850 358 L
plassmann@ohio.edu
PLASTERS, Shana .... 336-272-7102 329 B
shana.plasters@greensboro.edu
PLATANIA, Jennifer .... 336-278-5938 328 H
jplatania@elon.edu
PLATE, William, M .... 435-797-1356 459 F
william.plate@usu.edu
PLATING, John .... 706-419-1663 117 G
john.plating@covenant.edu
PLATT, David, E .... 512-471-3518 454 C
david.platt@austin.utexas.edu
PLATT, Judy, T .... 617-353-5940 207 C
juplatt@bu.edu
PLATT, Kathleen .... 912-358-4144 124 H
plattk@savannahstate.edu
PLATTE, Chelsea .... 231-348-6621 228 D
cplatte1@ncmich.edu
PLATUKUS, Graceann ... 570-740-0355 388 G
gplatukus@luzerne.edu
PLATZEK, Russell .... 718-262-2140 295 D
rplatzek@york.cuny.edu
PLAWECKI, Jeffrey .... 317-274-4553 157 B
jplaweck@iupui.edu
PLAZA, Erica .... 920-498-6969 498 F
erica.plaza@nwtc.edu
PLAZEK, David .... 802-635-1348 463 B
PLEAS, Dawn, E .... 620-229-6336 177 D
dawn.pleas@sckans.edu
PLEAS, Dorothy, J .... 630-637-5156 145 E
djpleas@noctrl.edu
PLEASANT, Audra .... 501-279-4145.. 19 G
apleasant@harding.edu
PLEASANT, Jamie .... 404-880-6359 116 I
jpleasant@cau.edu
PLEASANT, Klint .... 248-218-2058 229 I
kpleasant@rochesteru.edu
PLEASANT, Klint, A .... 248-218-2058 229 I
kpleasant@rochesteru.edu
PLEASANT, Lori .... 850-973-9469 104 K
pleasantl@nfc.edu
PLEASANT, Rachel .... 706-778-8500 124 B
johnroberts@piedmont.edu
PLEASANT, Rickie .... 513-562-6273 347 G
ricky.pleasant@artacademy.edu
PLEASANT-DOINE,
Sheia, I .... 904-819-6435.. 99 D
spleasant@flagler.edu
PLEDGER, Barbara .... 607-436-2010 316 C
barbara.pledger@oneonta.edu
PLEGGENKUHLE, Jesse . 563-425-5666 170 D
pleggenkuhlej@uiu.edu
PLEHN, Michael, T .... 202-685-3540 501 I
michael.t.plehn.mil@ndu.edu
PLEMMONS, Donna .... 501-450-1351.. 19 I
plemmons@hendrix.edu
PLENDL, Jackie .... 712-274-6400 170 H
jackie.plendl@witcc.edu
PLENSKI, Sandra .... 415-581-8863.. 69 B
plenskis@uchastings.edu
PLENTY CHIEF, Melissa 701-255-3285 346 I
mplentychief@uttc.edu
PLESSEL, Kristin .... 262-472-1918 496 E

PLESSINGER, Brian .... 860-738-6409.. 87 A
bplessinger@nwcc.edu
PLETA, Jeffrey .... 724-503-1001 401 D
jpleta@washjeff.edu
PLETT, Angie .... 620-278-2173 177 E
PLINER, Lauren .... 215-953-5999.. 93 H
PLINER, Susan .... 315-781-3354 301 D
pliner@hws.edu
PLINSKE, Kathleen, A ... 407-582-3400 113 C
kplinske@valenciacollege.edu
PLINSKE, Paul .... 719-549-2730.. 79 G
paul.plinske@csupueblo.edu
PLISCO, Mary .... 404-835-6135 422 D
mplisco@richmont.edu
PLOECKELMAN,
Rebecca .... 414-277-7129 493 D
ploeckel@msoe.edu
PLOEGER, Robin .... 918-631-3170 371 C
robin-ploeger@utulsa.edu
PLOEHN, Harry .... 252-328-9600 340 H
ploehnh17@ecu.edu
PLOESSL, Donna .... 205-665-6360.... 8 D
dploessl@montevallo.edu
PLONSKY, Christine, A . 512-471-4780 454 C
cp@utexas.edu
PLOSKONKA, James ..... 216-987-5177 351 D
james.ploskonka@tri-c.edu
PLOTKIN, David .... 503-594-3020 372 B
david.plotkin@clackamas.edu
PLOTKOWSKI, Paul .... 616-331-6260 224 D
plotkowp@gvsu.edu
PLOTNER, Amy .... 315-312-3702 318 B
amy.plotner@oswego.edu
PLOTT, Richard .... 903-790-4890 437 E
rplott@jaravis.edu
PLOUFF, Chris .... 317-788-3213 161 F
plouffc@uindy.edu
PLOUFFE, Audrey .... 406-275-4969 264 H
audrey_plouffe@skc.edu
PLOUFFE, Jeffrey .... 401-874-4198 404 E
jeffplouffe@uri.edu
PLOURD, Samantha .... 413-755-4333 215 F
seplourd@stcc.edu
PLOUTZ-SNYDER, Lori .. 734-764-5210 231 A
lorips@umich.edu
PLOWFIELD, Lisa .... 410-704-2132 204 B
lplowfield@towson.edu
PLOWMAN, Donde .... 865-974-2445 426 C
chancellor@utk.edu
PLUEARD, Kelley .... 541-440-7690 376 F
kelley.plueard@umpqua.edu
PLUEMER, Julie .... 608-822-2369 498 H
jpluemer@swtc.edu
PLUMB, Hylon .... 717-396-7833 392 Q
hplumb@pcad.edu
PLUMB, Richard, G .... 925-631-4203.. 59 I
rplumb@stmarys-ca.edu
PLUMB, Sylvia .... 802-626-6459 463 B
sylvia.plumb@northernvermont.edu
PLUMLEY, Brittany .... 315-228-7418 296 C
bplumley@colgate.edu
PLUMLEY, Susan .... 304-327-4182 488 J
splumley@bluefieldstate.edu
PLUMMER, AJ .... 319-895-4331 164 E
aplummer@cornellcollege.edu
PLUMMER, Dale, H .... 610-566-1776 402 C
dplummer@williamson.edu
PLUMMER, David, C ..... 956-872-5575 443 B
davidp@southtexascollege.edu
PLUMMER, Dianne .... 508-541-1574 208 E
dplummer@dean.edu
PLUMMER, Eric .... 540-831-5500 468 E
eplummer@radford.edu
PLUMMER, Keith .... 215-702-4358 379 F
kplummer@cairn.edu
PLUMMER, Laura .... 915-532-3737 457 E
lplummer@westerntech.edu
PLUMMER, Lisa .... 610-282-1100 382 A
lisa.plummer@desales.edu
PLUMMER, Meredith .... 760-366-5284.. 40 K
mplummer@cmccd.edu
PLUMMER, Troy, A .... 515-263-6050 166 C
tplummer@grandview.edu
PLUNK, Kelly .... 870-584-1104.. 22 G
kplunk@cccua.edu
PLUNKETT, Chris .... 319-385-6204 167 F
chris.plunkett@iw.edu
PLUNKETT, Gary .... 760-773-2581.. 39 A
gplunkett@collegeofthedesert.edu
PLUNKETT, John .... 636-949-4973 254 B
jplunkett@lindenwood.edu
PLUNKETT, Mary Rob ... 706-864-1625 126 G
maryrob.plunkett@ung.edu

PLURETTI, Anthony .... 610-499-4202 401 I
ampluretti@widener.edu
PLUSCHT, Patrick .... 940-565-4936 453 B
patrick.pluscht@unt.edu
PLUTCHOK, Moshe .... 718-438-5476 324 H
PLUTINO, Maria, S .... 585-385-7258 313 A
mplutino@sjfc.edu
PLYMALE, Chad .... 585-567-9480 301 G
chad.plymale@houghton.edu
POAGE, Alison .... 512-472-4133 442 H
alison.poage@ssw.edu
POAGE, Miranda .... 432-685-6754 439 E
mpoage@midland.edu
POARCH, Mark .... 828-726-2211 332 E
mpoarch@cccti.edu
POATS, Lillian, B .... 713-313-1133 448 D
poats_lb@tsu.edu
POATS, Lillian, B .... 713-313-7978 448 D
poats_lb@tsu.edu
POCHARD, Brad .... 864-294-3406 408 I
brad.pochard@furman.edu
POCHE, Reggie .... 504-278-6277 188 E
rpoche1@nunez.edu
POCHOCKI, Wendy, E ... 630-637-5808 145 E
wepochocki@noctrl.edu
POCIUS, Adam .... 719-549-2263.. 79 G
adam.pocius@csupueblo.edu
POCK, Arnyce .... 301-295-9945 502 B
arnyce.pock@usuhs.edu
POCTA, Beth .... 210-341-1366 440 B
bpocta@ost.edu
POCZATEK, Evelyn .... 312-947-1987 148 C
evelyn_poczatek@rush.edu
PODELL, David .... 781-239-3101 214 E
dpodell@massbay.edu
PODESCHI, Amanda .... 217-424-3506 144 D
apodeschi@millikin.edu
PODESCHI, RJ .... 217-424-6285 144 D
rjpodeschi@millikin.edu
PODESTÁ, Guido .... 608-262-9833 494 D
gpodesta@wisc.edu
PODESZWA, Stephen .... 413-737-7000 205 C
PODHRADSKY, Ashley .. 605-256-5821 415 G
ashley.podhradsky@dsu.edu
PODOL, Edward .... 480-858-9100.. 16 B
e.podol@scnm.edu
PODOLSKY, Daniel, K ... 214-648-2508 456 D
julia.kanellos@utsouthwestern.edu
PODVIN, John .... 585-276-5945 323 E
john.podvin@rochester.edu
POE, Evelyn .... 484-365-7461 388 F
epoe@lincoln.edu
POE, Katrina .... 662-325-2383 247 A
knp3@msstate.edu
POE, Scott .... 304-424-8212 490 A
scott.poe@wvup.edu
POE, Shawna .... 217-854-5506 133 F
shawna.poe@blackburn.edu
POEHLER, M.J .... 816-802-3393 253 H
mpoehler@kcai.edu
POEHLERT, Edward .... 760-757-2121.. 52 G
epoehlert@miracosta.edu
POEHLMAN, Lauren .... 518-327-6291 310 G
lpoehlman@paulsmiths.edu
POELKER, Scott .... 843-574-6198 411 I
scott.poelker@tridenttech.edu
POELMA, John .... 228-897-4373 246 F
john.poelma@mgccc.edu
POELVOORDE, Tracy, L. 309-779-7710 150 I
tracy.poelvoorde@trinitycollegeqc.edu
POESE, Debra .... 240-567-7269 200 E
debra.poese@montgomerycollege.edu
POFF, G. Elaine, N 954-262-7261 104M
poff@nova.edu
POFF, Robert, C .... 812-941-2331 157 D
rcpoff@ius.edu
POFF, Samantha .... 843-747-1279 411 C
spoff@sec.edu
POGGENDORF,
Brenda, P .... 540-375-2270 469 G
poggendorf@roanoke.edu
POGLIANO, Kit .... 858-534-6654.. 70 C
kpogliano@ucsd.edu
POGLIANO, Kit .... 858-822-5738.. 70 C
altea@ucsd.edu
POGODZINSKI, Joel .... 414-288-1671 492 E
joel.pogodzinski@marquette.edu
POHL, Charles, A .... 215-503-6988 398 G
charles.pohl@jefferson.edu
POHL, Don, J .... 314-286-3653 257 H
POHL, Jonathan .... 860-832-1945.. 85 F
pohlj@ccsu.edu

POHL, Mark .... 574-372-5100 155 C
pohlma@grace.edu
POHL, Mark, A .... 574-372-5100 155 C
pohlma@grace.edu
POHLMAN, Jean .... 513-487-1126 361 E
jean.pohlman@myunion.edu
POHLMAN, Scott, A .... 330-569-5478 353 F
pohlmansa@hiram.edu
POHLMEIER, Brandi .... 605-336-6588 415 B
bpohlmeier@kairos.edu
POHLSON, Scott .... 605-658-6261 415 E
scott.pohlson@usd.edu
POHRTE, Shannon .... 847-214-7595 137 D
spohrte@elgin.edu
POIANI, Eileen .... 201-761-6022 282 H
epoiani@saintpeters.edu
POIGER, Uta .... 617-373-5173 217 D
POINDEXTER, Jeanne ... 423-417-3550.. 93 H
POINDEXTER, Jeanne ... 864-250-7000.. 93 H
POINDEXTER, Kathi .... 586-498-4170 226 F
poindexterk@macomb.edu
POINDEXTER, Kim .... 816-604-5230 254 G
kim.poindexter@mcckc.edu
POINDEXTER, Kimberly 816-604-6639 254 F
kim.poindexter@mcckc.edu
POINTER, Monica .... 678-715-2200.. 93 H
POINTS, Emily .... 309-694-8501 138 I
emily.points@icc.edu
POIRIER, Bill .... 603-862-3530 274 B
POIRIER, Bill .... 603-862-3530 273 H
bill.poirier@unh.edu
POIRIER, Bill .... 603-862-1800 273 G
bill.poirier@unh.edu
POIRIER, J. Nicolas .... 315-568-3197 309 H
npoirier@northeastcollege.edu
POIRIER, Tim .... 215-489-2297 381 K
timothy.poirier@delval.edu
POISSON, Craig .... 413-748-3333 218 E
cpoisson@springfield.edu
POISSON, Frances .... 978-232-2001 209 B
fpoisson@endicott.edu
POITRA, Peggy .... 218-879-0803 237 F
poitra@fdltcc.edu
POJMANN, Wendy .... 518-786-5003 314 K
wpojmann@siena.edu
POKIDAYLO, Regina .... 718-779-1430 310 I
rpokidaylo@plazacollege.edu
POKORNOWSKI, Alex ... 701-777-2664 344 H
alexander.pokornowski@und.edu
POKOT, Elena .... 262-472-7790 496 E
pokote@uww.edu
POKPHANH, Roberta .... 785-864-3617 177 G
pokphanh@ku.edu
POKRANDT, Rachel .... 541-440-4622 376 F
rachel.pokrandt@umpqua.edu
POLACEK, Cheryl .... 406-638-3660 262 J
birdhatc@lbhc.edu
POLAK, Debra .... 707-468-3068.. 51 F
dpolak@mendocino.edu
POLAKOW-SURANSKY,
Shael .... 212-875-4595 290 F
ssuransky@bankstreet.edu
POLANIECKI, Andrew .... 574-239-8315 155 E
apolaniecki@hcc-nd.edu
POLASKI, Tamara, R ..... 515-294-0983 163 E
tra@iastate.edu
POLATAJKO, Mark, M .. 330-672-2422 354 A
mpolataj@kent.edu
POLCYN, Steve .... 909-687-1550.. 43 G
stevepolycn@gs.edu
POLCZYNSKI, Mimi .... 618-545-3363 141 C
mpolczynski@kaskaskia.edu
POLDEN, Kelly .... 806-651-2125 447 D
kpolden@wtamu.edu
POLE, Rhonda .... 605-995-2902 414 A
rhonda.pole@dwu.edu
POLEC, Angela, M .... 215-951-1849 386 I
poleca@lasalle.edu
POLECHEK, Jeff .... 205-726-2711.... 6 E
jpoleche@samford.edu
POLEN, Melissa .... 541-956-7075 375 G
mpolen@roguecc.edu
POLESKI, Dana .... 434-381-6379 470 H
dpoleski@sbc.edu
POLETO, Rachel, A .... 301-546-0546 201 D
poletora@pgcc.edu
POLETTI, Ed .... 215-972-2053 392 P
epoletti@pafa.edu
POLETTI, Sara .... 412-365-2754 380 F
s.poletti@chatham.edu
POLFLIET, Nathan .... 507-537-6285 240 G
nathan.polfliet.2@smsu.edu

POPEJOY, Lori, L 573-882-0277 260 C
popejoyl@health.missouri.edu
POPELKA, David, M 515-294-7007 163 E
dpopelka@iastate.edu
POPENFOOSE, Joel 847-628-1595 141 A
joel.popenfoose@judsonu.edu
POPENUCK, Betty 253-879-2925 483 G
epopenuck@pugetsound.edu
POPESCU, Adriana 805-756-2622.. 29 K
popescu@calpoly.edu
POPHAM, Don 636-922-8636 258 A
dpopham@stchas.edu
POPHAM, Heidi 706-295-6928 119 F
hpopham@gntc.edu
POPHRISTIC, Vojislava 856-256-4850 280 H
pophristic@rowan.edu
POPHRISTIC, Vojislava 215-596-8800 400 B
POPIELARCZYK, Zsa 773-907-4450 134 N
zpopiela@ccc.edu
POPIOLEK, Marcus 541-885-0192 374 G
marcus.popiolek@oit.edu
POPKEY, Megan 920-498-7186 498 F
megan.popkey@nwtc.edu
POPKO, Susan 408-551-3085.. 63 A
spopko@scu.edu
POPLAR, Andre' 248-341-2037 228 H
alpoplar@oaklandcc.edu
POPLIN, Lori 704-991-0116 338 A
lpoplin0217@stanly.edu
POPLIN, Michelle 704-991-0208 338 A
mpoplin4375@stanly.edu
POPLOWSKI, Kira 212-237-8628 294 B
kpoplowski@jjay.cuny.edu
POPOVICH, Donna, B 813-253-6237 113 B
dpopovich@ut.edu
POPOVICI, Alexandru 914-961-8313 314 E
alpopovici@svots.edu
POPP, Melissa, D 636-584-6703 252 D
melissa.popp@eastcentral.edu
POPP, Stephen 616-949-5300 222 F
stephen.popp@cornerstone.edu
POPP, Tari 269-471-3613 220 H
tari@andrews.edu
POPP-FINCH, Rochelle 772-462-7476 102 E
rfinch@irsc.edu
POPPA, Joseph 914-347-3910 324 F
joseph.poppa@sunywcc.edu
POPPENBERGER, Ross 928-344-7521.. 11 B
ross.poppenberger@azwestern.edu
POPPLEWELL, Venus 270-384-8189 183 D
popplewellv@lindsey.edu
POPPO, Kristin 607-587-3913 319 C
poppokr@alfredstate.edu
POPPRE, Beth 480-219-6046 249 C
bpoppre@atsu.edu
PORCA, Sanela 803-641-3340 412 B
sanelap@usca.edu
PORCARO, Anna 316-978-7787 178 B
anna.porcaro@wichita.edu
PORCELLA, Adam 215-702-4502 379 F
aporcella@cairn.edu
PORCENA, Yves-Rose 404-471-6450 114 E
yporcena@agnesscott.edu
PORCHE, Demetrius 504-568-4106 189 C
dporch@lsuhsc.edu
PORCHE, Saadia 323-953-4000.. 49 E
porchest@lacitycollege.edu
PORE, Karen 910-893-1266 327 C
kpore@campbell.edu
PORELL, Ryan 401-456-8094 404 A
rporell@ric.edu
PORFIDO, Nancy 609-343-5095 274 E
porfido@atlantic.edu
PORGES, David 909-869-4121.. 30 B
dwporges@cpp.edu
PORPILIA, Amy 864-231-2000 405 F
aporpilia@andersonuniversity.edu
PORRAS, Jose 575-624-8023 286 F
porras@nmmi.edu
PORRAS, Precious 708-524-6629 137 A
pporras@dom.edu
PORRIER, Jennifer 802-224-3001 462 G
jen.porrier@vsc.edu
PORTEE, Charlene 334-229-5053.... 4 B
dportee@alasu.edu
PORTEE, Kevin 803-705-4321 405 G
kevin.portee@benedict.edu
PORTELA, Stanley 787-752-4540 510 F
stanley.portela@upr.edu
PORTELA IRIGOYEN,
Celso, E 787-725-8120 505 J
cportela@centro.eap.edu
PORTELLEZ, Humberto 757-683-4425 468 C
hportell@odu.edu
PORTEOUS, Alexander 207-780-4497 196 J
alexander.porteous@maine.edu
PORTEOUS, Andrew 605-331-6801 416 C
andrew.porteous@usiouxfalls.edu
PORTER, Alexander 657-278-2115.. 31 E
porter@fullerton.edu
PORTER, Andrea 806-651-2037 447 D
aporter@wtamu.edu
PORTER, Bonisha 757-823-8141 468 B
bdtporter@nsu.edu
PORTER, Brandon 262-551-5941 491 B
bporter@carthage.edu
PORTER, Byron 540-261-4931 470 D
byron.porter@svu.edu
PORTER, Chong, U 916-734-9402.. 69 A
chong.porter@ucdmc.ucdavis.edu
PORTER, Christopher 540-857-6697 475 A
cporter@virginiawestern.edu
PORTER, Chrystal 617-243-2083 210 G
cporter@lasell.edu
PORTER, Cindy, L 914-323-5135 305 A
cindy.porter@mville.edu
PORTER, Clifford 757-823-8323 468 B
cporter@nsu.edu
PORTER, Connie 713-718-6477 436 E
connie.porter@hccs.edu
PORTER, Dale 520-515-5432.. 11 O
porterd@cochise.edu
PORTER, Dana 205-226-4912.... 5 A
dmporter@bsc.edu
PORTER, David, S 401-874-2370 404 E
dporter@uri.edu
PORTER, Elizabeth 206-543-2586 484 A
lawdean@uw.edu
PORTER, Esther 704-406-3502 328 I
eporter1@gardner-webb.edu
PORTER, Hugh, E 503-788-6604 375 F
hporter@reed.edu
PORTER, J. Davidson 504-314-2188 191 D
jporter6@tulane.edu
PORTER, James, P 801-422-3963 458 A
james_porter@byu.edu
PORTER, Jared, L 859-858-3511 178 H
jared.porter@asbury.edu
PORTER, Jeffry 717-871-4829 394 B
jeffry.porter@millersville.edu
PORTER, Jennifer 617-735-9772 209 A
porterj@emmanuel.edu
PORTER, Jennifer 248-218-2152 229 I
jporter1@rochesteru.edu
PORTER, John, R 636-949-4900 254 B
jporter@lindenwood.edu
PORTER, Kathleen 239-489-9091 100 G
kathleen.porter@fsw.edu
PORTER, Katlyn 740-588-1374 364 H
kporter2@zanestate.edu
PORTER, Lori 607-753-2201 317 D
lori.porter@cortland.edu
PORTER, Marie 757-455-3400 476 C
mporter@vwu.edu
PORTER, Mark 401-254-3667 404 C
mporter@rwu.edu
PORTER, Miacia 615-327-6806 420 D
mfporter@mmc.edu
PORTER, Michelle, C 605-342-0317 414 C
mporter@jwc.edu
PORTER, Molly 619-849-2628.. 57 J
mollyporter@pointloma.edu
PORTER, Monica 574-520-4872 157 C
moport@iusb.edu
PORTER, Nadine 240-567-5386 200 E
nadine.porter@montgomerycollege.edu
PORTER, Narda 276-328-0116 471 G
nnb3h@uvawise.edu
PORTER, Nicosha 214-860-2476 434 A
nporter@dcccd.edu
PORTER, Paul 260-399-7700 162 A
pporter@sf.edu
PORTER, Rhonda 229-500-2153 114 F
rhonda.porter@asurams.edu
PORTER, Robyn 712-325-3413 167 G
rporter@iwcc.edu
PORTER, Russell 254-501-5823 446 C
porter@tamuct.edu
PORTER, Ryan 425-889-6310 481 A
ryan.porter@northwestu.edu
PORTER, Seth 719-255-3115.. 84 A
sporter9@uccs.edu
PORTER, Stephen 816-268-5462 256 E
sporter@nts.edu
PORTER, Susie, S 801-585-5693 459 D
s.porter@utah.edu
PORTER, Todd 212-799-5000 303 B
PORTER, Wilma, B 248-232-4640 228 H
wbporter@oaklandcc.edu
PORTER BRANNON,
Towuanna 757-825-2700 474 F
PORTER-UTLEY, Kristen 508-626-4582 212 D
kporterutley@framingham.edu
PORTERFIELD,
Deana, L 585-594-6100 310 A
presidentsoffice@roberts.edu
PORTERFIELD,
Deana, L 585-594-6100 311 L
presidentsoffice@roberts.edu
PORTERFIELD, Julie 918-595-8191 370 B
julie.porterfield@tulsacc.edu
PORTERFIELD, Kent 509-313-4115 479 E
porterfield@gonzaga.edu
PORTERVINT, Bernice 602-872-7957.. 14 C
bernice.portervint@southmountaincc.edu
PORTILLO, Pedro 817-515-4591 445 A
pedro.portillo@tccd.edu
PORTMAN, Alan 636-529-0000 258 B
aportman@slchc.edu
PORTNER, Matthew 419-289-5251 347 H
mportner@ashland.edu
PORTNOY, Lauren 610-896-4984 385 H
lportnoy@haverford.edu
PORTNOY, Robert, N 402-472-7450 269 A
rportnoy1@unl.edu
PORTO, JR., Jeff 209-667-3131.. 33 D
jporto1@csustan.edu
PORTUGAL, Elsen 501-623-2272.. 19 C
PORTWINE, Ronald, E 989-964-2064 229 L
report@svsu.edu
PORTWOOD, Craig 478-387-4900 119 E
aportwood@gmc.edu
PORTZ, Margaret, A 610-758-5794 388 C
mak5@lehigh.edu
PORZUCEK, Sarah 716-839-8210 297 F
sporzuce@daemen.edu
POSCOVER, Randi 314-367-8700 260 A
randi.poscover@uhsp.edu
POSENER, Paul 910-775-4253 343 A
paul.posener@uncp.edu
POSER, Susan 516-463-6800 301 E
president@hofstra.edu
POSEY, Doneisha 317-916-7819 158 A
dposey17@ivytech.edu
POSEY, Evan 770-484-1204 122 B
evan.posey@lutherrice.edu
POSEY, Jamie 423-585-6894 424 G
jamie.posey@ws.edu
POSEY, Jamie, C 832-813-6776 438 E
jamie.c.posey@lonestar.edu
POSEY, Jim 229-931-2302 120 B
jim.posey@gsw.edu
POSEY, Monica 513-569-1515 350 C
monica.posey@cincinnatistate.edu
POSHEK, Joseph 949-451-5650.. 65 B
jposhek@ivc.edu
POSILLICO, Joseph 516-686-7925 308 H
joseph.posillico@nyit.edu
POSING, Mary 815-802-8202 141 B
mposing@kcc.edu
POSLER, Brian 440-375-7200 354 K
president@lec.edu
POSLUSNY, Matthew 919-760-8514 331 A
mposlusny@meredith.edu
POSNER, Kenneth 352-588-8992 107 B
kenneth.posner@saintleo.edu
POSNER, Marc 714-484-7006.. 54 C
mposner@cypresscollege.edu
POSNER, Mark 651-638-6383 233 J
m-posner@bethel.edu
POSPISIL, KC 512-313-3000 432 N
kc.pospisil@concordia.edu
POSS, Joe 509-313-6215 479 E
poss@gonzaga.edu
POSSEHL, Kristin 605-367-4753 416 B
kristin.possehl@southeasttech.edu
POST, Beth 518-580-5750 315 A
bpost@skidmore.edu
POST, Jack 856-227-7200 275 F
jpost@camdencc.edu
POST, Julie 678-664-0530 127 E
president@westgatech.edu
POST, Kari 802-387-6790 461 E
karipost@landmark.edu
POST, Michael, A 540-828-8014 464 C
mpost@bridgewater.edu
POST, Scott 501-760-4123.. 20 E
scott.post@np.edu
POST, Todd 815-802-8602 141 B
tpost@kcc.edu
POST, Tracee 806-651-2100 447 D
tpost@wtamu.edu
POSTEL, Gregory, C 419-530-2211 363 B
gregory.postel@utoledo.edu
POSTEMA, Miles, J 231-591-3894 223 H
milespostema@ferris.edu
POSTER, Michael, C 563-333-6032 169 D
postermichaelc@sau.edu
POSTI, Sarah 412-578-2093 380 A
seposti@carlow.edu
POSTLEWAIT, Mariah 717-396-7833 392 Q
mpostlewait@pcad.edu
POSTMA, James 530-226-4129.. 64 C
jpostma@simpsonu.edu
POSTMA, Jana 616-988-3650 226 A
jpostma@kuyper.edu
POSTMA, Kurt 616-538-2330 224 B
kpostma@gracechristian.edu
POSTMA, Laura 906-248-8420 221 I
lpostma@bmcc.edu
POSTMUS, Judy, L 410-706-7794 202 F
postmus@ssw.umaryland.edu
POSTON, Linda 717-691-6006 389 F
poston@messiah.edu
POSTON, Robin 214-768-6175 443 G
rposton@smu.edu
POSTON, Robin 901-678-5739 426 A
rposton@memphis.edu
POSTUPACK,
Mary Frances 570-422-7920 393 F
mpostupack@esu.edu
POTASH, David 773-481-8175 135 D
dpotash@ccc.edu
POTEAU, Youseline 305-626-3631 100 B
youseline.poteau@fmuniv.edu
POTEET, Jim 913-722-0272 174 G
jim.poteet@kansaschristian.edu
POTEET, Tanya, J 614-236-6408 348 I
tpoteet@capital.edu
POTEET, Tony 901-678-2619 426 A
ppoteet@memphis.edu
POTEETE-YOUNG,
Lanette 847-628-1097 141 A
lpoteete-young@judsonu.edu
POTEMKIN, Alex 817-515-7463 445 A
alexis.potemkin@tccd.edu
POTEMKIN, Dmitri 909-447-2501.. 37 H
dpotemkin@cst.edu
POTEMPA, John 708-534-4515 138 C
jpotempa@govst.edu
POTERALA, Michael, R 301-405-4945 202 E
poterala@umd.edu
POTH, Kelly, G 253-535-7139 481 C
kpoth@plu.edu
POTILLO, Jean 603-206-8081 272 A
jpotillo@ccsnh.edu
POTTEIGER, Jeffrey 616-331-7207 224 D
potteigj@gvsu.edu
POTTENGER, Tatum 828-328-1741 330 B
tatum.pottenger@lr.edu
POTTER, Aron 620-252-7005 172 K
potter.aron@coffeyville.edu
POTTER, Bryce 207-326-2276 195 G
bryce.potter@mma.edu
POTTER, Cathryn, C 848-932-7520 281 B
cpotter@ssw.rutgers.edu
POTTER, Cheryl, J 704-406-4269 328 I
cpotter@gardner-webb.edu
POTTER, Corrie 650-723-2300.. 66 D
cjpotter@stanford.edu
POTTER, Cory 434-797-8576 472 H
cory.potter@danville.edu
POTTER, Danielle 423-510-9675 421 D
POTTER, Douglas, E 704-847-5600 340 D
dpotter@ses.edu
POTTER, Gia 606-218-5211 185 F
giapotter@upike.edu
POTTER, James 618-453-6732 149 G
jim.potter@siu.edu
POTTER, James 406-265-3727 264 A
potterj@msun.edu
POTTER, Jennifer 609-626-3492 283 A
jennifer.potter@stockton.edu
POTTER, Joan 806-414-9680 450 D
joan.potter@ttuhsc.edu
POTTER, Jonathan 848-932-7500 281 B
jonathan.potter@rutgers.edu
POTTER, Karen 864-646-1507 411 H
kpotter2@tctc.edu

POTTER, Katy .... 620-241-0723 172 H katharyn.potter@centralchristian.edu
POTTER, Keith .... 541-684-7439 371 H kpotter@bushnell.edu
POTTER, Lawrence .... 202-274-6591.. 94 B lawrence.potter@udc.edu
POTTER, Mark .... 312-553-2500 134 L mdpotter@ccc.edu
POTTER, Mike .... 425-739-8387 480 D mike.potter@lwtech.edu
POTTER, Monifa, J .... 340-693-1151 512 B mpotter@uvi.edu
POTTER, R. Neal .... 850-263-3261.. 95 P rnpotter@baptistcollege.edu
POTTER, Rachel .... 540-887-7134 467 G rpotter@marybaldwin.edu
POTTER, Ralph .... 502-570-6357 181 B ralph.potter@kctcs.edu
POTTER, Rhyannon .... 757-683-3407 468 C rpotter@follett.com
POTTER, Sarah .... 802-224-3000 462 G sarah.potter@vsc.edu
POTTER, Terry .... 303-315-5830.. 84 B terence.potter@ucdenver.edu
POTTER-HENDERSON, Leslie .... 509-574-4984 485 E lpotter-henderson@yvcc.edu
POTTHARST, Kris .... 504-520-5441 193 C kpotthar@xula.edu
POTTHOFF, Dennis .... 702-992-2525 270 H dennis.potthoff@nsc.edu
POTTINGER, Trecia .... 440-775-8450 357 G trecia.pottinger@oberlin.edu
POTTLE, Russ .... 508-929-8257 213 D rpottle@worcester.edu
POTTS, Charlie .... 507-933-7526 235 E cpotts@gustavus.edu
POTTS, Christopher .... 503-399-8111 372 A chris.potts@chemeketa.edu
POTTS, Colin .... 573-341-4138 260 F provost@mst.edu
POTTS, Jonathan, E ...... 412-397-5291 396 E potts@rmu.edu
POTTS, Mandy .... 920-924-6326 498 C apotts2@morainepark.edu
POTTS, OP, Mary Esther .... 615-297-7545 416 G srmesther@aquinascollege.edu
POTTS, Molly .... 706-864-1800 126 G molly.potts@ung.edu
POTTS, Nacole .... 828-641-0325 327 A pottsna@brevard.edu
POTTS, Natalie .... 773-442-5412 145 G n-potts@neiu.edu
POTTS, Stephane .... 217-443-8749 136 E s.potts@dacc.edu
POTTS, Steven .... 310-506-4749.. 56 H steve.potts@pepperdine.edu
POTTS, Teresa .... 805-493-3139.. 29 E tpotts@callutheran.edu
POTTS, Tiffany .... 724-357-2218 393 G tcoffen@iup.edu
POTTS, Tim .... 260-481-0739 159 H pottst@pfw.edu
POTVIN, David .... 601-968-5904 244 C dpotvin@belhaven.edu
POTVIN, David .... 601-968-5900 244 C dpotvin@belhaven.edu
POTVIN-GIORDANO, Claudine .... 518-629-7451 302 A c.potvingiordano@hvcc.edu
POU, Laure .... 423-425-5742 426 D laure-pou@utc.edu
POUDRIER-AARONSON, Lucinda .... 508-999-8145 211 F laaronson@umassd.edu
POUERIET-DE LA CRUZ, Zacarias .... 787-480-2392 505 A zpoueriet@sanjuan.pr
POULAKIDAS, Jennifer .. 310-794-6808.. 69 D jpoulakidas@support.ucla.edu
POULIN, Krystal .... 207-288-5015 194 C
POULIOT, Cory .... 617-627-2661 219 A cory.pouliot@tufts.edu
POULLARD, Theresa ...... 909-469-5560.. 75 G tpoullard@westernu.edu
POULLETTE, Sam, G ..... 920-565-1000 492 A poullettesg@lakeland.edu
POULOS, Peter, G .... 216-368-4286 349 B peter.poulos@case.edu
POULSON, Tamara, N ... 757-961-4307 465 H robinstn@evms.edu
POULSON-JONES, Danielle .... 417-865-2815 252 F poulsonjonesd@evangel.edu
POULTER, Patricia, S .... 501-450-5073.. 23 K ppoulter@uca.edu
POULTON, Chris .... 515-650-3198 163 C chrispoulton@theartofeducation.edu
POUNCEY, Craig .... 251-580-2100.... 1 I craig.pouncey@coastalalabama.edu
POUNCIL, Matais .... 408-270-6451.. 62 F matais.pouncil@evc.edu
POUNDS, Leonard .... 954-262-4869 104 M lpounds@nova.edu
POURCHIER, Jeffrey, M 770-720-5824 124 E jmp@reinhardt.edu
POURCHOT, Jeri .... 425-388-9572 479 B jpourchot@everettcc.edu
POURCIAUX, Courtney . 573-288-6390 251 I cpourciaux@culver.edu
POURIER, Marilyn .... 605-455-6045 414 H mpourier@olc.edu
POUSS, Matthew .... 301-447-5202 201 A pouss@msmary.edu
POWE, F. Douglas .... 202-664-5706.. 94 D dpowe@wesleyseminary.edu
POWELEIT, Deborah ...... 513-569-1550 350 C deborah.poweleit@cincinnatistate.edu
POWELL, Allynn .... 301-314-7237 202 E acpowell@umd.edu
POWELL, Anna .... 870-777-5722.. 23 C anna.powell@uaht.edu
POWELL, Arthur, B .... 973-353-3530 281 C powellab@newark.rutgers.edu
POWELL, Austen .... 817-202-6275 444 B aupowell@swau.edu
POWELL, Brett .... 254-710-3454 430 F brett_powell@baylor.edu
POWELL, Brian .... 714-997-6779.. 36 D powell@chapman.edu
POWELL, Brian, M .... 724-458-2992 384 F bmpowell@gcc.edu
POWELL, Bryan .... 360-596-5283 483 E bpowell@spscc.edu
POWELL, Chyenne .... 713-313-7011 448 D
POWELL, Cody, J .... 513-529-7070 356 A powellcj@miamioh.edu
POWELL, Curtis, N .... 518-276-6302 311 J powelc2@rpi.edu
POWELL, Daniel .... 210-486-4097 428 A dpowell52@alamo.edu
POWELL, Darrin .... 270-706-8406 181 C darrin.powell@kctcs.edu
POWELL, Deborah .... 301-846-2479 198 E dpowell@frederick.edu
POWELL, Denise .... 912-538-3162 125 E dpowell@southeasterntech.edu
POWELL, Devon .... 708-596-2000 149 D dpowell@ssc.edu
POWELL, Emily .... 325-574-7629 457 G epowell@wtc.edu
POWELL, Gregory, S ..... 903-693-2022 440 E gpowell@panola.edu
POWELL, Hattie .... 903-886-5140 446 D hattie.powell@tamuc.edu
POWELL, James .... 308-432-6203 267 G jpowell@csc.edu
POWELL, James .... 419-289-5350 347 H jpowell1@ashland.edu
POWELL, Jason .... 540-365-4376 466 I jpowell@ferrum.edu
POWELL, Jeffrey, A .... 701-788-4697 345 B jeffrey.powell@mayvillestate.edu
POWELL, Jill .... 336-750-3284 343 E powellj@wssu.edu
POWELL, Jocelyn .... 478-825-1018 118 E
POWELL, Joel .... 916-691-7427.. 50 K powellj@crc.losrios.edu
POWELL, John .... 304-205-6607 487 D john.powell@bridgevalley.edu
POWELL, Justina-Jupiter .... 619-574-6909.. 55 D jjupiter-powell@pacificcollege.edu
POWELL, Kara .... 626-584-5547.. 43 E kpowell@fuller.edu
POWELL, Karon .... 423-236-2895 422 H kpowell@southern.edu
POWELL, Kevin .... 804-524-5691 475 E manager525@nebook.com
POWELL, Logan .... 401-863-7940 403 A logan_powell@brown.edu
POWELL, Lynn .... 484-365-8051 388 F lpowell@lincoln.edu
POWELL, Margherite ..... 305-474-6965 107 D mpowell@stu.edu
POWELL, Marilyn .... 866-492-5336 243 G marilyn.powell@mail.waldenu.edu
POWELL, Marleen .... 910-592-8081 337 D mpowell@sampsoncc.edu
POWELL, Michael .... 724-357-4820 393 G mpowell@iup.edu
POWELL, Michael, C ..... 757-822-1783 474 G mpowell@tcc.edu
POWELL, Mitch .... 256-765-4319.... 8 E mpowell7@una.edu
POWELL, Monica .... 318-869-5016 186 C mpowell@centenary.edu
POWELL, Nicole .... 904-470-8837.. 98 I nicole.powell@ewc.edu
POWELL, Reese .... 601-318-6170 249 B rpowell@wmcarey.edu
POWELL, Sam .... 619-849-2334.. 57 J sampowell@pointloma.edu
POWELL, Shawn .... 575-624-7111 285 F shawn.powell@roswell.enmu.edu
POWELL, Stephanie, E .. 850-263-3261.. 95 P sepowell@baptistcollege.edu
POWELL, Stephen .... 740-753-7080 353 G powells25816@hocking.edu
POWELL, Susan, E .... 601-979-2241 245 G susan.e.powell@jsums.edu
POWELL, Theresa, A ..... 215-204-6556 398 D theresa.powell@temple.edu
POWELL, Theresa, D ..... 405-466-3201 366 B theresa.graves@langston.edu
POWELL, Timothy, M .... 559-251-4215.. 28 B tpowell@calchristiancollege.edu
POWELL, Tremaine .... 423-697-4471 423 B tremaine.powell@chattanoogastate.edu
POWELL BRASWELL, Gwendolyn .... 269-471-6530 220 H ogc@andrews.edu
POWELL LOGAN, Kelly . 717-901-5171 385 G klogan@harrisburgu.edu
POWER, Anne .... 402-375-7245 267 I anpower1@wsc.edu
POWER, Jane .... 252-493-7630 336 E jpower@email.pittcc.edu
POWER, Mark .... 479-575-5064.. 21 H mepower@uark.edu
POWER, Nadeena .... 706-385-1017 124 C nadeena.power@point.edu
POWER, Sandy .... 606-759-7141 182 B sandy.power@kctcs.edu
POWER-BARNES, Marie, R .... 609-984-4839 283 D mpowerbarnes@tesu.edu
POWERS, Amanda, C .... 662-329-7333 247 B amandacpowers@muw.edu
POWERS, Amber .... 215-576-0800 396 B apowers@rrc.edu
POWERS, Andrew .... 740-593-1911 358 L powersa@ohio.edu
POWERS, Anjanette .... 662-846-4406 245 A apowers@deltastate.edu
POWERS, Christa .... 214-333-5842 433 D christa@dbu.edu
POWERS, Christopher ... 513-244-4278 356 F chris.powers@msj.edu
POWERS, Colleen .... 914-674-7707 305 H cpowers5@mercy.edu
POWERS, David .... 206-296-5300 483 B powersda@seattleu.edu
POWERS, Douglas .... 707-621-7000.. 41 F
POWERS, Heidi .... 208-467-8011 132 B heidipowers@nnu.edu
POWERS, Helen .... 803-777-3971 412 A hefields@mailbox.sc.edu
POWERS, Jeff .... 256-216-3314.... 4 D jeff.powers@athens.edu
POWERS, Joshua .... 973-720-2122 283 I powersj@wpunj.edu
POWERS, Kathleen .... 716-851-1017 299 A mcgrifpowers@ecc.edu
POWERS, Kelly .... 401-341-2641 404 D kellyj.powers@salve.edu
POWERS, Keri .... 508-531-1324 212 B keri.powers@bridgew.edu
POWERS, Kristina .... 650-543-3787.. 52 A kristina.powers@menlo.edu
POWERS, Lindsey .... 870-508-6204.. 18 B lpowers@asumh.edu
POWERS, Lisa, M .... 814-865-7517 391 F lmr8@psu.edu
POWERS, Lynn .... 386-312-4116 107 A lynnpowers@sjrstate.edu
POWERS, Mark, R .... 508-626-4545 212 D mpowers@framingham.edu
POWERS, Michael .... 724-357-3062 393 G michael.powers@iup.edu
POWERS, Miranda .... 651-638-8776 233 J m-powers@bethel.edu
POWERS, Nancy .... 419-473-2700 351 I npowers@daviscollege.edu
POWERS, Peter, K .... 717-691-6013 389 F ppowers@messiah.edu
POWERS, Rebecca .... 215-753-3664 380 G powersr@chc.edu
POWERS, Richard .... 864-592-4774 411 E powersr@sccsc.edu
POWERS, Sandee .... 618-537-6957 143 G sjpowers@mckendree.edu
POWERS, Sandra, F ...... 252-335-3228 341 A sfpowers@ecsu.edu
POWERS, Sarah .... 405-208-5032 367 E sepowers@okcu.edu
POWERS, Sherry .... 859-622-1175 180 B sherry.powers@eku.edu
POWERS, Shonda .... 606-539-3546 185 C shonda.powers@ucumberlands.edu
POWERS, Susan .... 812-237-2307 155 H susan.powers@indstate.edu
POWERS, Susan .... 315-268-6542 295 E spowers@clarkson.edu
POWERS, Susie .... 859-846-5340 183 G spowers@midway.edu
POWERS, Tammy .... 928-428-8308.. 12 H tammy.powers@eac.edu
POWERS, Tanya .... 206-878-3710 480 C tpowers@highline.edu
POWERS, Tyrone .... 410-777-7496 197 C tpowers@aacc.edu
POWERS, Wendy .... 509-335-4561 484 D w.powers-schilling@wsu.edu
POWICKI, Mike .... 402-375-7520 267 I mipowic1@wsc.edu
POWLEY, Mary, R .... 585-385-8057 313 A mpowley@sjfc.edu
POWNALL, Phillip .... 904-819-6460.. 99 D ppownall@flagler.edu
POYNTER, Barry .... 859-622-5012 180 B barry.poynter@eku.edu
POYNTER, Mary .... 606-451-6622 182 D mary.poynter@kctcs.edu
POYZER, Bryan .... 701-671-2872 346 B bryan.poyzer@ndscs.edu
POZANC, Lisa .... 507-453-2402 238 J lpozanc@southeastmn.edu
POZZA, Amy .... 804-627-5300 464 B amy_pozza@bshsi.org
PRABA, Rashmi .... 619-594-5211.. 33 E rpraba@sdsu.edu
PRABHAKARAN, Bharath .... 513-556-4357 361 I bharath.prabhakaran@uc.edu
PRABHU, Sunil .... 909-469-5550.. 75 G sprabhu@westernu.edu
PRABHU, Veena .... 323-343-4606.. 32 B vprabhu@calstatela.edu
PRACHAND, Amit .... 847-467-5067 146 C a-prachand@northwestern.edu
PRADO, Guillermo .... 305-243-2748 112 K gprado@miami.edu
PRAET, Diane, M .... 313-993-3313 230 H praetdm@udmercy.edu
PRAJER, Stephen .... 336-917-5405 339 H stephen.prajer@salem.edu
PRAKASH, Anupma .... 907-474-7096.. 10 B aprakash@alaska.edu
PRAKASH, Channapatana .... 334-725-2334.... 7 D cprakash@tuskegee.edu
PRAKASH, Neeta .... 954-637-2268 108 C nprakash@sfbc.edu
PRALL, Andrew .... 630-844-5252 133 A aprall@aurora.edu
PRANGE, Raphaella .... 217-424-6395 144 D rpalmer@millikin.edu
PRANGER, Henriette ...... 617-732-2283 216 B henriette.pranger@mcphs.edu
PRANKE, Greg .... 712-279-5435 163 H greg.pranke@briarcliff.edu
PRAPAVESSI, Despina ... 925-969-2689.. 40 H dprapavessi@dvc.edu
PRASAD, Rashmi .... 660-785-4346 259 J rprasad@truman.edu
PRASAD, Shankar .... 401-863-3184 403 A shankar_prasad@brown.edu
PRASLOVA, Ludmilla ...... 714-556-3610.. 73 G ludmilla.praslova@vanguard.edu

PRASNICKI, David .... 800-444-1839 475 C
dpras@vmiaa.org
PRASTACOS, Gregory .... 201-216-8366 282 L
gregory.prastacos@stevens.edu
PRATER, Chanda, F ...... 270-852-3104 183 B
cprater@kwc.edu
PRATER, Michael .... 574-520-4319 157 C
maprater@iusb.edu
PRATER, Sarah, E .... 574-372-5100 155 C
praterse@grace.edu
PRATER, Wendi .... 337-475-5126 192 B
wprater@mcneese.edu
PRATER, Wesley .... 253-589-5813 478 A
wesley.prater@cptc.edu
PRATHER, Anthony .... 812-855-3312 156 C
prather@iu.edu
PRATHER, Curtis .... 703-370-6600 475 F
PRATHER, Darla .... 785-594-4340 171 C
darla.prather@bakeru.edu
PRATHER, Kanidrus ...... 706-225-5300.. 93 H
PRATHER, Kerry, N .... 317-738-8009 155 A
kprather@franklincollege.edu
PRATHER, Sean .... 925-424-1690.. 36 A
sprather@laspositascollege.edu
PRATHER, Tammy .... 662-243-1928 245 C
tprather@eastms.edu
PRATHER-JOHNSON,
Nancy, N .... 757-822-1191 474 G
nprather@tcc.edu
PRATS, John, C .... 305-474-6871 107 D
jprats2@stu.edu
PRATT, Allison .... 540-831-5408 468 E
apratt6@radford.edu
PRATT, Barbara .... 908-835-2355 283 H
pratt@warren.edu
PRATT, Bernard .... 302-857-7635.. 90 D
bpratt@desu.edu
PRATT, Christy .... 574-631-7305 161 G
cpratt3@nd.edu
PRATT, Dale .... 970-351-1890.. 84 D
dale.pratt@unco.edu
PRATT, Elizabeth .... 408-288-3142.. 62 G
elizabeth.pratt@sjcc.edu
PRATT, Gary, L .... 785-532-6520 175 A
gpratt@ksu.edu
PRATT, H. Wes .... 417-836-3736 255 J
wpratt@missouristate.edu
PRATT, Mary Jo .... 918-683-4581 365 B
PRATT, Michael .... 205-652-3565.... 9 B
mpratt@uwa.edu
PRATT, Michele .... 989-686-9822 223 E
michelepratt@delta.edu
PRATT, Rob .... 423-585-6952 424 G
robert.pratt@ws.edu
PRATT, Robert, C .... 517-750-1200 230 F
bpratt@arbor.edu
PRATT, Sally .... 213-740-8867.. 73 C
pratt@usc.edu
PRATT, Tot .... 636-584-6733 252 D
tot.pratt@eastcentral.edu
PRATT, Vallarie .... 706-712-8244 118 A
vpratt@daltonstate.edu
PRATT-CLARKE, Menah . 540-231-7500 475 D
inclusive@vt.edu
PRATT-COOK, Patricia ... 651-690-6560 242 F
pcprattcook867@stkate.edu
PRATTE, John .... 318-342-1235 193 A
pratte@ulm.edu
PRATTELLA, Todd .... 914-674-7844 305 H
tprattella@mercy.edu
PRAWIRA, Pepy .... 510-356-4760.. 77 E
PREAS, Ethan, D .... 903-468-8781 446 D
derek.preas@tamuc.edu
PREAST, Lori .... 252-493-7700 336 E
lpreast@email.pittcc.edu
PREASTLY, Jacqueline ... 225-771-6276 190 J
jacqueline_preastly@subr.edu
PREASTLY,
Jacqueline, G .... 225-771-5808 190 K
jacqueline_preastly@subr.edu
PREBENDA, Aaron .... 410-334-2993 205 A
aprebenda@worwic.edu
PREBLE, Lucas .... 307-332-2930 500 J
lpreble@wyomingcatholic.edu
PRECHT, Erica .... 337-521-6985 188 G
erica.precht@solacc.edu
PRECHTER, Patricia ...... 504-398-2213 191 E
pprechter@uhcno.edu
PRECISE, Leigh .... 740-362-3121 355 H
lprecise@mtso.edu
PRECISE, Natalie .... 417-873-7874 252 A
nprecise@drury.edu

PREDOEHL, Dan .... 949-582-4313.. 65 C
dpredoehl@saddleback.edu
PREGEANT, Gene, E ...... 985-549-5888 192 E
gpregeant@selu.edu
PREGITZER, Michael ...... 757-352-4411 469 D
mpregitzer@regent.edu
PREGLIASCO, Collin .... 916-691-7367.. 50 K
preglic@crc.losrios.edu
PREHN, James .... 312-915-6400 142 G
jprehn@luc.edu
PREIMESBERGER, Paul . 218-855-8163 237 C
paul.preimesberger@clcmn.edu
PREISMEYER, Kim .... 601-709-0966 244 C
kpreismeyer@belhaven.edu
PREISS, Lori .... 910-962-3855 343 B
preissl@uncw.edu
PRELLER, Aprile .... 703-284-6541 468 A
aprile.preller@marymount.edu
PRELOCK, Patricia, A .... 802-656-1417 462 D
patricia.prelock@med.uvm.edu
PREMO, Jason .... 989-686-9584 223 E
jasonpremo@delta.edu
PRENDERGAST,
Jason-Anthony, K .... 305-626-3138 100 B
jason.prendergast@fmuniv.edu
PRENDERGAST, John .... 215-951-1993 386 I
prendergastj1@lasalle.edu
PRENDERGAST,
Thomas .... 419-755-4712 357 B
tprendergast@ncstatecollege.edu
PRENEVOST, Jason .... 253-460-4462 483 F
jprenevost@tacomacc.edu
PRENKERT, Robby .... 574-807-7143 153 G
robby.prenkert@betheluniversity.edu
PRENTICE, Dean .... 918-495-6143 368 F
dprentice@oru.edu
PRENTICE, Deborah ...... 609-258-3026 279 E
predebb@princeton.edu
PRENTICE, Marilyn .... 847-214-7992 137 D
mprentice@elgin.edu
PREOCANIN, Shelley ..... 812-866-7056 155 D
preocanins@hanover.edu
PRERO, Chana .... 305-944-0035 114 B
PRESCOTT, Angel .... 270-707-3801 181 G
angel.prescott@kctcs.edu
PRESCOTT, Barbara ...... 318-357-6171 192 D
prescottb@nsula.edu
PRESCOTT, Charles .... 865-938-8186 418 B
charles.prescott@thecrowncollege.edu
PRESCOTT, Jay, B .... 515-263-2890 166 C
jprescott@grandview.edu
PRESCOTT, Patricia, M .. 516-671-0439 324 C
pprescott@webb.edu
PRESCOTT, Romeyn .... 518-736-3622 300 B
rprescott@fmcc.edu
PRESENT, Melissa .... 212-678-8820 303 A
mepresent@jtsa.edu
PRESENT, Wendy .... 928-776-2132.. 17 B
wendy.present@yc.edu
PRESLEY, Brian .... 276-244-1267 463 H
bpresley@asl.edu
PRESLEY, David .... 205-726-4494.... 6 E
dapresle@samford.edu
PRESNELL, Deena .... 509-313-6803 479 E
presnell@gonzaga.edu
PRESNELL, Mark .... 847-491-3707 146 C
mark.presnell@northwestern.edu
PRESS, Daniel .... 408-554-4455.. 63 A
dpress@scu.edu
PRESSER, Art .... 865-524-8079 419 A
arthur.presser@huhs.edu
PRESSER, Matthew .... 914-888-5364 305 H
mpresser@mercy.edu
PRESSEY, Natalie .... 212-229-5660 307 E
presseyn@newschool.edu
PRESSIMONE,
J. Michael .... 216-373-5238 357 F
jmpressimone@ndc.edu
PRESSLEY, Diana .... 409-772-8205 456 B
dipressl@utmb.edu
PRESSLEY, Leslie .... 704-922-6366 334 E
pressley.leslie@gaston.edu
PRESSLEY, Pamela .... 510-231-5000.. 46 N
pamela.c.pressley@kp.org
PRESSMAN, Avrohom .... 570-346-1747 402 F
PRESSON, Dewayne ...... 314-838-8858 261 A
ithelpdesk@ugst.edu
PRESSON, Kim .... 256-782-8142..... 6 A
kpresson@jsu.edu
PRESTA, Natalie .... 775-404-5536.. 42 E
npresta@frc.edu
PRESTAGE, Fheryl, J ..... 713-718-8708 436 E
fheryl.prestage@hccs.edu

PRESTAMO, Anne .... 305-348-5726 109 H
anne.prestamo@fiu.edu
PRESTON, Alison, T ...... 512-475-7255 454 C
apreston@utexas.edu
PRESTON, April .... 615-366-4404 423 A
april.preston@tbr.edu
PRESTON, Colin .... 714-484-7355.. 54 C
cpreston@cypresscollege.edu
PRESTON, David .... 918-335-6265 368 E
dpreston@okwu.edu
PRESTON, Deborah .... 609-586-4800 277 H
prestond@mccc.edu
PRESTON, Don .... 479-248-7236.. 19 F
dpreston@ecollege.edu
PRESTON, Elaine, C ...... 405-466-3202 366 B
elaine.preston@langston.edu
PRESTON, James .... 312-329-4140 144 F
james.preston@moody.edu
PRESTON, James .... 559-925-3146.. 75 A
jamespreston@whccd.edu
PRESTON, Jennifer .... 270-831-9804 181 F
jennifer.preston@kctcs.edu
PRESTON, Jon .... 470-578-5572 121 J
jonpreston@kennesaw.edu
PRESTON, Jon .... 678-839-6445 127 A
jpreston@westga.edu
PRESTON, Joseph .... 901-321-3509 417 G
jpreston@cbu.edu
PRESTON, Lisa .... 212-229-5667 307 E
lisa.preston@newschool.edu
PRESTON, Mindy .... 903-823-3198 445 C
mindy.preston@texarkanacollege.edu
PRESTON, Natalie .... 406-657-2300 263 H
natalie.preston@msubillings.edu
PRESTON, Patrick .... 508-362-2131 214 B
ppreston@capecod.edu
PRESTON, Travis .... 661-255-1050.. 28 I
tpreston@calarts.edu
PRESTON-NELSON,
Amanda .... 209-954-5022.. 61 H
amanda.preston-nelson@deltacollege.edu
PRESUTTI, Katherine ..... 860-768-4296.. 89 E
deacon@hartford.edu
PRETLOW, Lester .... 706-721-2621 115 I
lpretlow@augusta.edu
PRETORIUS, Joseph, A . 260-359-4134 155 G
jpretorius@huntington.edu
PRETTI, Janet .... 208-732-6327 131 B
jpretti@csi.edu
PRETTOL, Ken .... 972-708-7340 434 F
financial-aid@diu.edu
PREUSCH, Dana .... 816-268-5400 256 E
dpreusch@nts.edu
PREUSS, Timothy .... 402-643-7364 265 I
timothy.preuss@cune.edu
PREVATTE, Tenette .... 910-678-7353 334 C
prevattt@faytechcc.edu
PREVAUX, Steven, D .... 813-974-7777 111 B
prevaux@usf.edu
PREVITE, Pete .... 904-825-4681.. 99 D
pprevite@flagler.edu
PREVO, Jerry .... 434-582-2950 467 E
president@liberty.edu
PREVOST, Emily .... 254-295-4023 453 A
eprevost@umhb.edu
PREVOST, Suzanne, S ... 205-348-1040..... 7 G
sprevost@ua.edu
PREVOST-SHULTZ,
Justin .... 773-244-6263 145 F
jprevost@northpark.edu
PREWITT, Michael .... 304-696-3765 488 N
prewitta@marshall.edu
PREWITT, Steve .... 615-966-5804 420 B
steve.prewitt@lipscomb.edu
PREZANT, Robert .... 203-392-5350.. 85 H
prezantr1@southenct.edu
PREZIOSI, Kristine .... 928-350-2306.. 15 O
kpreziosi@prescott.edu
PRIBBENOW, Brad .... 218-739-3375 236 B
bpribbenow@lbs.edu
PRIBBENOW, Dean .... 630-617-3063 137 E
dpribbenow@elmhurst.edu
PRIBBENOW, Paul, C .... 612-330-1212 233 G
president@augsburg.edu
PRIBULSKY,
Christopher .... 814-262-3824 393 A
cpribulsky@pennhighlands.edu
PRIBYL, Becky .... 605-626-2640 415 H
becky.pribyl@northern.edu
PRIBYL, Kim .... 319-399-8686 164 D
kpribyl@coe.edu
PRICCI, Erica .... 570-955-1461 387 A
priccie@lackawanna.edu

PRICE, Abbie .... 478-757-3714 127 D
aprice@wesleyancollege.edu
PRICE, Adrienne .... 909-274-5417.. 52 K
aprice@mtsac.edu
PRICE, Alan .... 805-965-0581.. 62 M
aprice3@sbcc.edu
PRICE, Amanda .... 636-949-4477 254 B
aprice@lindenwood.edu
PRICE, Amy .... 920-832-7164 492 B
amy.price@lawrence.edu
PRICE, Amy, S .... 812-468-2000 162 B
asprice@usi.edu
PRICE, Angie, C .... 423-775-7269 417 D
aprice6832@bryan.edu
PRICE, Antonia .... 717-477-1251 394 D
afprice@ship.edu
PRICE, Barrington .... 708-524-5930 137 A
bprice@dom.edu
PRICE, Berkeley .... 310-660-3715.. 41 J
bprice@elcamino.edu
PRICE, Bill .... 540-231-4025 466 E
bprice@vcom.vt.edu
PRICE, Bryan .... 540-458-8316 476 D
bprice@wlu.edu
PRICE, Carol .... 207-307-3900 193 E
cprice@beal.edu
PRICE, Cecil, D .... 336-758-5218 344 A
price@wfu.edu
PRICE, Cynthia, J .... 206-281-2179 482 K
cprice@spu.edu
PRICE, Danny .... 706-368-5644 116 A
dprice@berry.edu
PRICE, Dave .... 541-994-4166 374 D
dave.price@oregoncoast.edu
PRICE, David .... 214-777-6433 440 I
PRICE, David .... 405-682-1611 367 D
david.n.price@occc.edu
PRICE, Dawne .... 402-494-2311 267 D
dprice@thenicc.edu
PRICE, Deidre .... 850-729-6448 104 L
priced@nwfsc.edu
PRICE, Derrick .... 304-327-4191 488 J
dprice@bluefieldstate.edu
PRICE, Donna .... 276-739-2412 474 H
dprice@vhcc.edu
PRICE, Donna .... 276-964-7287 474 E
donna.price@sw.edu
PRICE, Donna .... 931-221-7907 416 H
priced@apsu.edu
PRICE, Douglas .... 918-595-7853 370 B
douglas.price@tulsac.edu
PRICE, III, Emmett, G ... 617-266-1400 206 D
epriceiii@berklee.edu
PRICE, Gary .... 386-481-2906.. 96 D
priceg@cookman.edu
PRICE, Greg .... 334-670-3507..... 7 C
wgprice@troy.edu
PRICE, James, B .... 610-436-3063 394 F
jprice@wcupa.edu
PRICE, Jason .... 806-457-4200 435 D
jprice@fpctx.edu
PRICE, Jennifer .... 941-309-4381 106 J
jprice1@ringling.edu
PRICE, Jennifer .... 904-470-8844.. 98 I
j.price@ewc.edu
PRICE, Jennifer .... 518-262-5679 289 C
pricej@amc.edu
PRICE, Jerry .... 714-997-6721.. 36 D
jprice@chapman.edu
PRICE, Jill .... 859-622-1937 180 B
jill.price@eku.edu
PRICE, JoEllen .... 713-718-8891 436 E
joellen.price@hccs.edu
PRICE, Karen .... 704-461-6859 326 I
karenprice@bac.edu
PRICE, Keiko .... 404-727-2912 118 D
keiko.price@emory.edu
PRICE, Leigh .... 912-478-5211 120 A
llprice@georgiasouthern.edu
PRICE, Linda, L .... 812-877-8165 160 C
price@rose-hulman.edu
PRICE, Lisa .... 618-634-3200 149 C
lisap@shawneecc.edu
PRICE, Marianne .... 267-341-3204 385 I
mprice@holyfamily.edu
PRICE, Maribeth, H .... 605-394-1763 415 I
maribeth.price@sdsmt.edu
PRICE, Megan .... 864-388-8019 409 B
mprice@lander.edu
PRICE, Mercedes .... 703-993-5160 466 J
mprice21@gmu.edu
PRICE, Michael .... 952-446-4161 235 B
pricem@crown.edu

PROVOST, Adrienne 352-395-5958 107 G adrienne.provost@sfcollege.edu
PROVOST, David, J 802-443-5699 461 G dprovost@middlebury.edu
PROVOST, Laura 603-342-3020 272 E lprovost@ccsnh.edu
PROVOST, Mark 715-833-6670 497 E mprovost@cvtc.edu
PRSHA, Matthew, G 314-516-6100 260 E mprsha@umsl.edu
PRUCHNICKI, Jennifer 580-581-2209 365 C jpruchni@cameron.edu
PRUDE, Regina 615-687-6901 416 F rprude@abcnash.edu
PRUDEN, Karen, H 757-823-8160 468 B khpruden@nsu.edu
PRUDENTI, A. Gail 516-463-4068 301 E gail.prudenti@hofstra.edu
PRUDHOMME, Harvey, J 503-370-6576 377 E hprudhom@willamette.edu
PRUD'HOMME, Sabrina 541-522-7672 376 A
PRUD'HOMME, Sabrina 541-552-6060 376 A prudhomms@sou.edu
PRUETT, Karen 706-880-8977 121 K kpruett@lagrange.edu
PRUETT, Robert, R 919-658-7760 340 E rpruett@umo.edu
PRUETT, Teresa 276-964-7365 474 E teresa.pruett@sw.edu
PRUETT, Timothy 419-783-2317 351 J tpruett@defiance.edu
PRUETT, Tyler 510-879-9232 60 C tpruett@samuelmerritt.edu
PRUIS, Angela 817-722-1636 437 H angela.pruis@tku.edu
PRUITT, Beverly 305-284-2842 112 K b.pruitt@miami.edu
PRUITT, Christine 254-267-7057 441 D cpruitt@rangercollege.edu
PRUITT, Courtney 903-988-7536 437 G cpruitt@kilgore.edu
PRUITT, Dwain, C 864-597-4056 413 E pruittdc@wofford.edu
PRUITT, Glenell 903-730-4890 437 E gpruitt@jarvis.edu
PRUITT, Jason 470-239-3103 126 G jason.pruitt@ung.edu
PRUITT, Jolene 626-316-5340 63 D jpruitt@saybrook.edu
PRUITT, Jonathan 919-962-1000 340 F
PRUITT, Jonathan, C 512-499-4560 454 A jpruitt@utsystem.edu
PRUITT, Judy 612-343-4491 241 O japruitt@northcentral.edu
PRUITT, Karl 205-929-6348 2 H kpruitt@lawsonstate.edu
PRUITT, Kylie 615-248-1253 425 D kpruitt1@trevecca.edu
PRUITT, Leah, L 864-587-4225 411 F pruittl@smcsc.edu
PRUITT, Michael 562-985-4296 32 A michael.pruitt@csulb.edu
PRUITT, Pamela 609-896-5000 280 D ppruitt@rider.edu
PRUITT, Samory, T 205-348-8376 7 G samory.pruitt@ua.edu
PRUITT, Steven 561-237-7834 103 W spruitt@lynn.edu
PRUNCHUNAS, Edward 310-423-8294 35 M
PRUNEDA, Eli 913-360-7500 171 G epruneda@benedictine.edu
PRUNTY, Bonnie, S 607-274-3376 302 E bprunty@ithaca.edu
PRUS, Mark 607-753-2207 317 D mark.prus@cortland.edu
PRUSKI, Thomas 202-706-6843 94 D tpruski@wesleyseminary.edu
PRUSS, Julie, A 585-395-2361 317 B jpruss@brockport.edu
PRUTSOS, Bryce 760-252-2411 26 L bprutsos@barstow.edu
PRUZANSKY, Aron 732-363-7110 284 B
PRYBUTOK, Victor 940-565-3957 453 B victor.prybutok@unt.edu
PRYER, Ashley 910-521-6000 343 A
PRYJMAK, Myron 718-409-7306 320 D mpryjmak@sunymaritime.edu
PRYLO, Caelynn 518-743-2329 319 D pryloc@sunyacc.edu
PRYOR, Adam 785-227-3380 171 H pryoraw@bethanylb.edu
PRYOR, Ann 843-953-2060 407 D pryoral@cofc.edu
PRYOR, Carranza 318-675-5406 189 D carranza.pryor@lsuhs.edu
PRYOR, Charles 646-313-8000 295 C charles.pryor@guttman.cuny.edu
PRYOR, Joanna 316-942-4291 176 B pryorj@newmanu.edu
PRYOR, Julie 256-686-5850 93 H
PRYOR, Julie 205-453-6300 93 H
PRYOR, Kim 336-342-4261 337 B pryork@rockinghamcc.edu
PRYOR, Marcus 704-991-0278 338 A mpryor7642@stanly.edu
PRYOR, Monique 718-489-5520 312 H mpryor@sfc.edu
PRYOR, Raymond 570-208-5828 386 G rgpryor@kings.edu
PRYOR, Sandra 770-962-7580 121 B spryor@gwinnetttech.edu
PRYOR, Tammy, L 828-694-1705 332 C t_pryor@blueridge.edu
PRYOR, Walter 773-995-2462 134 J wpryor@csu.edu
PRYOR-BENNETT, Julie 203-837-8111 86 A pryorbennettj@wcsu.edu
PRYOR HARRIS, Holli 312-567-3167 139 H pryor@iit.edu
PRZEKOP, Lisa 805-893-3641 70 E lisa.przekop@sa.ucsb.edu
PRZEKURAT, Paris 405-422-1442 368 I przekuratp@redlandscc.edu
PRZYBORSKI, Carol 412-321-8383 379 D office@bcs.edu
PRZYGODA, Melitha 203-392-5405 85 H przygodam1@southernct.edu
PRZYMUS, Beth 402-562-1284 265 C bprzymus@cccneb.edu
PRZYWARA, Ann Marie 518-580-5765 315 A aprzywar@skidmore.edu
PSAILA, Marisa 585-475-4932 312 A mxpdar@rit.edu
PSARRIS, Kleanthis 718-951-5966 293 A kpsarris@brooklyn.cuny.edu
PSOTKA, Brenda 412-809-5307 395 F psotka.brenda@ptcollege.edu
PUC, Gina 413-662-5201 212 F g.puc@mcla.edu
PUCCIO O'BRIEN, Erica 617-879-7716 212 E erica.puccio@massart.edu
PUCHTER, Carolee 262-646-6514 493 F cpuchter@nashotah.edu
PUCKETT, Adam 503-554-2911 372 I apuckett@georgefox.edu
PUCKETT, Carrie 269-387-4286 232 J carrie.puckett@wmich.edu
PUCKETT, Christopher 303-315-6619 84 B chris.puckett@ucdenver.edu
PUCKETT, Clifton 678-872-8006 119 C cpuckett@highlands.edu
PUCKETT, Holly 434-200-5302 464 G holly.puckett@centracollege.edu
PUCKETT, Jacob 575-624-7491 285 F jacob.puckett@roswell.enmu.edu
PUCKETT, Jeffrey 616-395-7413 224 H puckett@hope.edu
PUCKETT, Joan 812-888-4480 162 E jpuckett@vinu.edu
PUCKETT, Katherine 601-857-3624 245 D kbpuckett@hindscc.edu
PUENTE, Rachel 312-329-4189 144 F rachel.puente@moody.edu
PUFF, Derek 716-286-8055 309 F dpuff@niagara.edu
PUFFER, Lois 606-487-3503 181 E lois.puffer@kctcs.edu
PUFFETT, Anne 563-425-5229 170 D puffetta@uiu.edu
PUGEL, Joe 515-964-6200 164 F joe.pugel@dmacc.edu
PUGEL, Mary, E 336-758-3005 344 A mpugel@wfu.edu
PUGH, Benjamin 225-771-5021 190 K benjamin_pugh@subr.edu
PUGH, Coleen 316-978-3095 178 B coleen.pugh@wichita.edu
PUGH, David, N 770-689-4795 114 J
PUGH, Henry 617-243-2221 210 G hpugh@lasell.edu
PUGH, Holly 804-627-5300 464 B holly_pugh@bshsi.org
PUGH, Jason 601-928-6234 246 F jason.pugh@mgccc.edu
PUGH, Judy, M 857-701-1280 215 E jpugh@rcc.mass.edu
PUGH, Megan 828-251-6585 342 A mpugh1@unca.edu
PUGH, S Douglas 804-828-1062 472 D sdpugh@vcu.edu
PUGH, Sandi 559-297-4500 46 C spugh@iot.edu
PUGH-BASSETT, Lovell 856-227-7200 275 F lpughbassett@camdencc.edu
PUGLIESE, Heidi 207-326-4311 195 G
PUGLIESE, Michael 405-609-6622 365 F
PUGLIESI, Karen 928-523-2230 14 J karen.pugliesi@nau.edu
PUGLISI, Michael, J 276-944-6662 466 F mpuglisi@ehc.edu
PUHAK, Robert 973-353-3246 281 C rpuhak@rutgers.edu
PUHALA, Kimberly 508-286-3621 219 F puhala_kimberly@wheatoncollege.edu
PUJOL, Joe 573-651-2408 258 J jpujol@semo.edu
PUJOLS, Yeurys 201-360-4628 277 D ypujols@hccc.edu
PULAVARTI, Srinivas 404-727-6123 118 D srinivas.pulavarti@emory.edu
PULCINI, Brad, T 740-368-3943 359 F btpulcin@owu.edu
PULEO, David 256-824-6337 8 B provost@uah.edu
PULEO, David 662-915-7407 248 F dpuleo@olemiss.edu
PULIAFICO, Venus 216-368-4530 349 B venus.puliafico@case.edu
PULIDO, Jairo 787-250-1912 507 C jpulido@metro.inter.edu
PULIDO, Maria 509-453-0374 481 G maria.pulido@perrytech.edu
PULIDO, Miguel 209-667-3509 33 D mpulido5@csustan.edu
PULIDO LEON, Jose, M 775-784-4936 270 K jpulidoleon@unr.edu
PULINKALA, Ivan 470-578-6789 121 J ipulinka@kennesaw.edu
PULLEN, Huston 904-620-2479 111 A huston.pullen@unf.edu
PULLEN, Terri 513-862-7761 353 C terri.pullen@email.gscollege.edu
PULLEY, Alyssa 660-562-1571 256 G apulley@nwmissouri.edu
PULLEY, D. J 601-318-6048 249 B djpulley@wmcarey.edu
PULLIAM, Camden 816-414-3700 255 F cpulliam@mbts.edu
PULLIAM, Cheryl 704-355-5093 327 F cheryl.pulliam@carolinascollege.edu
PULLIAM, Jeff 870-543-5950 21 D jpulliam@seark.edu
PULLIAM, Joni, L 315-792-3344 323 G jpulliam@utica.edu
PULLIAM, Shane 307-268-2633 499 T shane.pulliam@caspercollege.edu
PULLIN, Daniel, W 817-257-7511 447 H d.pullin@tcu.edu
PULLIS, Stephen 313-883-8768 229 J pullis.stephen@shms.edu
PULLIZA, Carmen 787-743-7979 509 D cpulliza@suagm.edu
PULLLIAM, Cathy 434-797-8538 472 H cathy.pulliam@danville.edu
PULLO, SR., John, F 570-945-8000 386 F
PULS, Darrell 509-420-4545 481 D dean@gather4him.net
PULSE, II, Jeffrey 260-452-2273 154 F jeffrey.pulse@ctsfw.edu
PULSIFER, Joy 231-591-2612 223 H joypulsifer@ferris.edu
PULSIPHER, Scott, D 801-274-3280 460 E spulsipher@wgu.edu
PULTZ, Stephen, F 619-260-4506 72 H spultz@sandiego.edu
PULVER, Shayne 615-226-3990 419 J
PUMA, Lynn, M 716-878-5509 317 C pumalm@buffalostate.edu
PUMARIEGA, Madeline 305-237-3221 104 E mpumarie@mdc.edu
PUMPHREY, Robert 212-563-6647 323 A it@uts.edu
PUMROY, B.J 402-461-7331 266 C bj.pumroy@hastings.edu
PUNCHELLO, Cathy 609-984-1180 283 D registrar@tesu.edu
PUNIELLO, Jennifer 508-678-2811 213 F jennifer.puniello@bristolcc.edu
PUNSALAN-MANLIMOS, Catherine 206-296-6000 483 B
PUPILLO, Melinda 309-794-7478 132 H melindapupillo@augustana.edu
PURCELL, Anthony, B 205-934-2297 8 A bpurcell@uab.edu
PURCELL, Chris 412-365-1482 380 F c.purcell@chatham.edu
PURCELL, Howard, B 617-587-5678 216 H purcellh@neco.edu
PURCELL, Margaret 205-391-2387 3 E mpurcell@sheltonstate.edu
PURCELL, Meredith 815-802-8510 141 B mpurcell@kcc.edu
PURCELL, Satch 949-794-9090 66 C spurcell@stanbridge.edu
PURCELL, Sebastian 607-753-2192 317 D sebastian.purcell@cortland.edu
PURCELL, Stacy, R 757-446-6002 465 H purcellsr@evms.edu
PURDOM, Kirk 662-915-7375 248 F kirk@olemiss.edu
PURDY, Elaine 225-490-1616 186 H elaine.purdy@franu.edu
PURDY, Jill 308-865-8421 268 J purdyj@unk.edu
PURDY, Kim 479-619-4399 20 G kpurdy@nwacc.edu
PURDY, Lillian 318-487-7110 187 B lillian.purdy@lcuniversity.edu
PURDY, Matt 270-809-3375 184 A mpurdy1@murraystate.edu
PURDY, Ryan 308-535-3720 266 J purdyr@mpcc.edu
PURDY, Von 502-776-1443 184 C vpurdy@simmonscollegeky.edu
PURGASON, Angie 336-342-4261 337 B purgasona@rockinghamcc.edu
PURGASON, Ashley 817-272-6107 454 B purgason@uta.edu
PURGASON, Devin 336-734-7230 334 D dpurgason@forsythtech.edu
PURI, Ishwar 213-740-6709 73 C vpres@usc.edu
PURINTON, Jeff 870-972-2100 17 I
PURNELL, Carol 773-291-6100 135 B
PURNELL, Jay 619-388-3537 60 I jpurnell@sdccd.edu
PURRENHAGE, Ingrid, L 727-816-3418 105 E purreni@phsc.edu
PURRI, Patti 815-836-5983 142 C purripa@lewisu.edu
PURRINGTON, Kristen 603-366-5265 271 K kpurrington@ccsnh.edu
PURSER, Lori 254-526-1486 431 E lori.purser@ctcd.edu
PURSES, Jeanna 440-375-7405 354 K jpurses@lec.edu
PURSLEY, Dana 740-587-0810 351 K
PURSWANI, Elizabeth 410-462-8508 197 E epurswani@bccc.edu
PURTLE, Dorothy 913-722-0272 174 G institutional.research@kansaschristian.edu
PURTLE, Dwight 913-568-6126 174 G dpurtle@sbcglobal.net
PURTLEBAUGH, Charlene 407-277-0311 99 C cpurtlebaugh@evergladesuniversity.edu
PURVIANCE, Chris 509-313-5858 479 E purviance@gonzaga.edu
PURVIS, Donald 940-397-4214 439 F donald.purvis@msutexas.edu
PURVIS, Jonathan 317-940-9913 153 H jpurvis@butler.edu
PURVIS, Kathy 254-968-9070 445 F kpurvis@tarleton.edu
PURYEAR, Roberta (Robbi) 713-743-8780 451 F rdpuryea@uh.edu
PUSCHNER, Birgit 517-355-6509 227 C puschner@msu.edu
PUSECKER, Kathleen, L 240-895-4388 201 F klpusecker@smcm.edu
PUSECKER, Paul, A 240-895-4413 201 F papusecker@smcm.edu
PUSEY, Audrey 561-297-3542 109 F apusey@fau.edu
PUSHIA, Suzanna 843-355-4115 413 C pushias@wiltech.edu

QUINN, Pegeen .... 312-369-6891 136 C
pquinn@colum.edu
QUINN, Sarah, F .... 610-660-1230 397 A
squinn@sju.edu
QUINN, Shaman .... 307-754-6232 500 G
shaman.quinn@nwc.edu
QUINN, Susan .... 707-524-1598.. 63 C
squinn@santarosa.edu
QUINN, Susan .... 585-389-2501 307 D
squinn2@naz.edu
QUINN, Teresa .... 845-437-5370 323 H
tequinn@vassar.edu
QUINN, Thomas .... 989-275-5000 225 H
tom.quinn@kirtland.edu
QUINN, Wade .... 919-739-7086 338 F
dwquinn@waynecc.edu
QUINN-BARRON,
Heather .... 503-777-7705 375 F
quinnbarron@reed.edu
QUINN BUSSEY,
Consuelo .... 706-821-8262 123 I
cquinn@paine.edu
QUINNAN, Timothy ...... 404-835-6132 422 D
tquinnan@richmont.edu
QUINNELL, Katherine .... 254-968-9937 445 F
quinnell@tarleton.edu
QUINONES, Carlos, A ... 787-710-8999 505 D
QUINONES, Ivelisse ...... 706-580-0168 114 I
ivelissequinones@andrewcollege.edu
QUINONES, Patricia ..... 909-274-4109.. 52 K
pquinones@mtsac.edu
QUINONES, Roberto ..... 562-408-6969.. 24 H
rquinones@advancedcollege.edu
QUINONES, Weyna .... 787-815-0000 510 D
QUINONES, Yesenia ..... 787-844-8181 511 E
yesenia.quinones1@upr.edu
QUINONEZ, Julie, R ..... 419-530-6213 363 B
julie.quinonez@utoledo.edu
QUINONEZ, Virginia ..... 312-329-6623.. 36 G
vquinonez@thechicagoschool.edu
QUINTAL, Rollande ...... 508-849-3340 205 E
rquintal@annamaria.edu
QUINTANA, Anita .... 509-452-5100 481 E
aquintana@pnwu.edu
QUINTANA, Elena .... 312-662-4021 132 D
equintana@adler.edu
QUINTANA, Javier .... 787-279-1912 506 L
jquintana@bayamon.inter.edu
QUINTANA, Jen .... 719-549-2764.. 79 G
jennifer.quintana@csupueblo.edu
QUINTANA, Rebecca ..... 787-780-0070 504 E
rquintana@caribbean.edu
QUINTANA, Sara .... 802-865-5417 461 C
squintana@champlain.edu
QUINTANA HESS,
Jessica, A .... 570-321-4318 388 H
hess@lycoming.edu
QUINTANILLA, Hector ... 817-531-4405 450 F
hquintanilla@txwes.edu
QUINTENZ, Briana .... 217-424-3758 144 D
bquintenz@millikin.edu
QUINTERO, Amanda, M 805-437-3285.. 30 D
amanda.quintero@csuci.edu
QUINTERO, Sandra .... 657-278-5366.. 31 E
squintero@fullerton.edu
QUINTUS, Rebecca .... 419-434-4549 362 D
quintus@findlay.edu
QUINTYNE, Renee .... 845-398-4207 314 D
rquintyn@stac.edu
QUIONEZ, Angelica ...... 415-422-6796.. 72 I
anquinonez@usfca.edu
QUIRE, Heather .... 413-662-5231 212 F
heather.quire@mcla.edu
QUIRION, Alison .... 562-977-6006.. 43 C
alison.quirion@fremont.edu
QUIRK, Lea Ann .... 405-585-5413 367 B
leaann.quirk@okbu.edu
QUIRK, Walter .... 530-226-4503.. 64 C
rquirk@simpsonu.edu
QUIRK-BAILEY, Sheila .. 309-694-5550 138 I
sheila.quirk-bailey@icc.edu
QUIROGA, Jacqueline ... 470-578-6000 121 J
QUIROLGICO, Ray .... 626-396-2325.. 26 G
ray.quirolgico@artcenter.edu
QUIROS, Ondrea, M ..... 915-831-6615 435 B
oquiros@epcc.edu
QUIROZ, Jaime .... 562-860-2451.. 35 O
jquiroz@cerritos.edu
QUIROZ, Sally .... 806-291-3702 457 B
sally.quiroz@wbu.edu
QUIS, Steve .... 619-388-7876.. 61 B
squis@sdccd.edu
QUISTORF, Mark, W ..... 414-410-4016 490 J
mwquistorf@stritch.edu
QUIÑONES, Mickey ...... 804-289-8549 471 E
mguinones@richmond.edu
QUIÑONES SANTIAGO,
Nelson .... 787-250-0000 510 B
nelson.qui±ones2@upr.edu
QUMSIEH, Miriam .... 281-283-3005 452 A
qumsieh@uhcl.edu
QUOCK, Dan .... 509-542-4803 478 B
dquock@columbiabasin.edu
QURESHI, Elena .... 734-432-5574 226 G
equreshi@madonna.edu
QURESHI, Omar .... 510-356-4760.. 77 E
QVARNSTROM, Jeanne . 432-837-8395 449 F
jqvarnstrom@sulross.edu

R

RAAB, Jennifer, J .... 212-772-4242 294 A
jennifer.raab@hunter.cuny.edu
RAAB, Keith .... 541-737-2241 374 H
financial.aid@oregonstate.edu
RAAB, Maryrose .... 315-792-7215 320 F
maryrose.raab@sunypoly.edu
RAAB, Ron .... 512-448-8441 441 N
RABAGO, Cristine .... 650-543-3782.. 52 A
crabago@menlo.edu
RABB, Sydni .... 254-442-5113 431 J
sydni.rabb@cisco.edu
RABBANY, Sina, Y .... 516-463-6672 301 E
sina.y.rabbany@hofstra.edu
RABBITT, Kara, M .... 973-720-2621 283 I
rabbittk@wpunj.edu
RABE, Josh .... 217-228-5432 147 C
rabejo@quincy.edu
RABELO, Marlyn .... 973-661-0600 276 E
mrabelo@eastwick.edu
RABENOLD, Scott, A ..... 512-471-4124 454 C
srabenold@utexas.edu
RABERN, Don .... 719-255-3543.. 84 A
drabern@uccs.edu
RABI, Moses .... 202-932-8988.. 91 F
RABIDEAU, Shelly, S .... 317-940-8423 153 H
srabidea@butler.edu
RABINOVICH, Sheryl .... 213-624-1200.. 42 F
srabinovich@fidm.edu
RABINOWITZ, Celia, E .. 603-358-2736 274 A
celia.rabinowitz@keene.edu
RABINOWITZ, David, B 973-290-4084 282 G
drabinowitz@steu.edu
RABINOWITZ, Eli .... 718-377-0777 311 B
erabinowitz@myrcb.org
RABITOY, Eric .... 626-914-8788.. 37 B
erabitoy@citruscollege.edu
RABITOY, Linda .... 909-667-4433.. 38 A
lrabitoy@claremontlincoln.edu
RABLE, Michelle .... 419-372-8932 348 F
marable@bgsu.edu
RABY, Don Butch .... 601-403-1300 247 F
braby@prcc.edu
RABY, James .... 803-641-3569 412 B
jamesr@usca.edu
RABY, Melissa .... 209-588-5132.. 76 J
rabym@yosemite.edu
RABY, Sherry .... 252-249-1851 336 C
sraby@pamlicocc.edu
RABY, Susan .... 315-312-2260 318 B
susan.raby@oswego.edu
RABY, Tracy .... 256-233-8106.... 4 D
tracy.raby@athens.edu
RACCANELLO, Paul .... 415-485-3223.. 41 H
paul.raccanello@dominican.edu
RACE, Debbie .... 828-262-2050 340 G
racedw@appstate.edu
RACE, Tammera .... 941-487-4405 110 C
trace@ncf.edu
RACER, Jennifer .... 866-776-0331.. 54 E
jracer@ncu.edu
RACER, Jennifer .... 419-755-4040 357 B
racer.5@osu.edu
RACHAL, Michael .... 504-865-2486 190 A
rachal@loyno.edu
RACHEL, Cherie .... 479-575-4808.. 21 H
clrachel@uark.edu
RACHITA, David, A .... 281-283-2568 452 A
rachita@uhcl.edu
RACHOUH, Susan .... 201-216-3518 282 L
susan.rachouh@stevens.edu
RACICOT, Philip .... 603-358-2811 274 A
philip.racicot@keene.edu
RACINE, Christa .... 973-408-3650 276 B
cracine@drew.edu
RACIOPPI, Gerald .... 732-255-0315 279 A
gracioppi@ocean.edu
RACKI, James .... 508-854-7496 215 D
jracki@qcc.mass.edu
RACKLEY, Jeanette .... 910-275-6111 335 C
jrackley@jamessprunt.edu
RACKLEY, Michael .... 954-545-4500 108 C
registrar@sfbc.edu
RACKLEY, Tammy .... 704-878-3215 335 I
trackley@mitchellcc.edu
RACKLIFFE, Jerry, J ...... 404-413-3004 120 C
jracklif@gsu.edu
RACOVITA, Laura .... 423-236-2638 422 H
racovita@southern.edu
RADAK, Lisa .... 808-734-9569 129 E
lradak@hawaii.edu
RADAKOVICH, Dan .... 305-284-1768 112 K
drad@miami.edu
RADANDE, Katie, W ...... 610-758-4735 388 C
kaw8@lehigh.edu
RADCLIFF, Christine ..... 361-593-3528 447 A
christine.radcliff@tamuk.edu
RADCLIFFE, Shelby .... 503-370-6397 377 E
sradcliffe@willamette.edu
RADCLIFFE, Timothy ..... 740-392-6868 356 G
timothy.radcliffe@mvnu.edu
RADDEN, Michael .... 256-233-8146.... 4 D
michael.radden@athens.edu
RADEMACHER, Eric .... 513-556-3304 361 I
eric.rademacher@uc.edu
RADEMAKER, II, Jim .... 616-331-6775 224 D
rademakj@gvsu.edu
RADEMAKER, Scot .... 985-448-4325 192 C
scot.rademaker@nicholls.edu
RADER, Darian .... 336-506-4056 331 J
derader420@alamancecc.edu
RADER, Patrick .... 202-250-2491.. 92 B
patrick.rader@gallaudet.edu
RADER, Sherri .... 309-649-6255 150 D
sherri.rader@src.edu
RADFORD, Marilyn .... 270-384-8022 183 D
radfordm@lindsey.edu
RADFORD, Mitchell .... 828-641-0095 327 A
radformr@brevard.edu
RADFORD-POPP, Amy .... 269-749-7718 229 G
aradfordpopp@olivetcollege.edu
RADHAKRISHNAN,
Rashmi .... 215-572-2900 378 E
radhakrishnanr@arcadia.edu
RADICE, Brad .... 205-726-4373.... 6 E
bjradice@samford.edu
RADING, Michael .... 410-462-7410 197 E
mrading@bccc.edu
RADISH, Ross .... 215-596-8800 400 B
r.radish@usciences.edu
RADKE, Cheryl .... 623-245-4600.. 16 F
cradke@uticuti.edu
RADKE, Jordan .... 719-389-7270.. 78 E
jradke@coloradocollege.edu
RADKE, Kristi .... 510-659-6534.. 54 J
kradke@ohlone.edu
RADKE, Suzette .... 712-749-2044 164 A
radkes@bvu.edu
RADNEY, Ron .... 209-228-2257.. 70 A
rradney@ucmerced.edu
RADO, George .... 703-591-7042 466 G
grado@fxua.edu
RADSON, Darrell .... 630-829-6018 133 B
dradson@ben.edu
RADT, Jennifer .... 513-732-5221 362 B
jennifer.radt@uc.edu
RADTKE, Elizabeth .... 651-523-2959 235 F
bradtke@hamline.edu
RADTKE, Sarah .... 630-844-5113 133 A
sradtke@aurora.edu
RADULESCU, Eugen .... 713-348-6725 441 K
eugen@rice.edu
RADWAN, Ahmed, Y ...... 315-792-3853 323 G
aradwan@utica.edu
RADWAN, Theresa .... 727-562-7858 111 F
tradwan@law.stetson.edu
RADWANSKI, Steven, E 609-652-4915 283 A
steven.radwanski@stockton.edu
RADWINE, Sam .... 213-884-4133.. 24 D
RADZIESKI, Laurel .... 610-568-1442 378 C
laurel.radzieski@alvernia.edu
RADZIESKI, Laurel .... 570-961-7810 387 A
radzieskil@lackawanna.edu
RADZYMINSKI, Sharon . 956-665-3495 455 A
sharon.radzyminski@utrgv.edu
RAE, Janelle .... 502-585-9911 184 E
jrae@spalding.edu
RAE, Lisa .... 802-258-3149 462 B
lisa.rae@worldlearning.org
RAE, Patrick .... 585-785-1355 299 E
patrick.rae@flcc.edu
RAE, Rosemarie .... 510-642-6000.. 68 N
RAEBEL, Christopher .... 414-277-7302 493 D
RAEBER, Michael .... 706-542-0006 126 F
mraeber@uga.edu
RAEFIELD, Julie .... 541-956-7319 375 G
jraefield@roguecc.edu
RAEHLL, Meghan .... 614-947-6579 352 J
meghan.raehll@franklin.edu
RAEKER-REBEK, Mary ... 866-492-5336 243 G
mary.raeker-rebek@mail.waldenu.edu
RAEL, Sylvia .... 970-248-1029.. 78 F
srael@coloradomesa.edu
RAETHER, Julie .... 402-354-7256 267 E
julianne.raether@methodistcollege.edu
RAFALSON, Lisa .... 716-829-8489 298 C
rafalson@dyc.edu
RAFANELLO, Allyson .... 319-273-7153 163 G
allyson.rafanello@uni.edu
RAFANELLO, Nicholas .. 319-273-2333 163 G
nicholas.rafanello@uni.edu
RAFELD, Jessica .... 920-403-3071 494 B
jessica.rafeld@snc.edu
RAFFAELLE, David .... 623-845-3676.. 13 E
david.raffaelle@gccaz.edu
RAFFAELLE, Ryne .... 585-475-2055 312 A
ryne.raffaelle@rit.edu
RAFFAELLI, Kellie .... 906-487-2920 227 D
kraffael@mtu.edu
RAFFELD, Beth .... 413-585-2020 218 D
braffeld@smith.edu
RAFFENSPERGER,
Thomas .... 413-572-5233 213 C
traffensperger@westfield.ma.edu
RAFFERTY, Kaydee .... 603-897-8511 273 B
krafferty@rivier.edu
RAFFETTO, William .... 281-998-6150 442 D
william.raffetto@sjcd.edu
RAFFETY, Matt .... 406-683-7201 263 E
matt.raffety@umwestern.edu
RAFI, Fawad .... 610-683-4000 394 A
RAFN, H. Jeffrey .... 920-498-5411 498 F
jeff.rafn@nwtc.edu
RAFO, Michael .... 239-590-7729 109 G
mrafo@fgcu.edu
RAFTERY, Andrea .... 419-251-1314 355 G
andrea.raftery@mercycollege.edu
RAFTERY, Katherine, G . 516-367-6890 296 A
RAGAISIS, James .... 281-476-1806 442 C
james.ragaisis@sjcd.edu
RAGAN, Deirdre .... 843-953-3708 406 D
dragan@citadel.edu
RAGAN, Jody .... 515-961-1517 169 G
jody.ragan@simpson.edu
RAGAN, Mckenzie .... 229-732-5956 114 I
mckenzieragan@andrewcollege.edu
RAGAN, McKenzie .... 229-732-5956 114 I
mckenzieragan@andrewcollege.edu
RAGAN, Nola .... 605-698-3966 415 C
nragan@swcollege.edu
RAGAN, Ron, E .... 785-864-4882 177 G
ronragan@ku.edu
RAGER, Tim .... 425-259-8701 479 B
trager@everettcc.edu
RAGHAVAN, Padma ...... 615-322-6067 427 B
padma.raghavan@vanderbilt.edu
RAGLAND, Janet .... 903-790-4890 437 E
dragland@jarvis.net
RAGLAND, Janet .... 903-233-3815 438 C
janetragland@letu.edu
RAGLAND, Lori .... 618-437-5321 147 F
ragland@rlc.edu
RAGLAND, Margaret ..... 575-461-4413 285 J
margaretr@mesalands.edu
RAGLAND, Matthew ..... 334-244-3138.... 4 F
mragland@aum.edu
RAGLE, Cynthia .... 812-888-5127 162 E
cragle@vinu.edu
RAGLIN, Candace .... 502-597-6502 183 A
candace.raglin@kysu.edu
RAGLIN, David .... 847-970-4919 152 F
draglin@usml.edu
RAGNO, John .... 212-517-0400 305 D
jragno@mmm.edu
RAGNO, Kerry, S .... 757-822-1187 474 G
kragno@tcc.edu
RAGO-CRAFT, Zaneta .... 732-263-5505 278 B
zragocra@monmouth.edu
RAGSDALE, Caroyln ...... 217-353-2383 146 G
cragsdale@parkland.edu

RAMIREZ, Raymond ...... 559-442-8200.. 67 A
raymond.ramirez@fresnocitycollege.edu
RAMIREZ, Rhonda .... 510-879-9217.. 60 C
rramirez@samuelmerritt.edu
RAMIREZ, Robert .... 940-898-3142 451 A
rramirez9@twu.edu
RAMIREZ, Robert .... 516-572-7781 307 C
robert.ramirez@ncc.edu
RAMIREZ, Rodolfo .... 530-422-7923.. 74 F
rramirez@weimar.edu
RAMIREZ, Ronald .... 760-750-4211.. 33 C
rramirez@csusm.edu
RAMIREZ, Rosemary .... 520-494-5471.. 11 M
rosemary.ramirez@centralaz.edu
RAMIREZ, Ruben .... 805-922-6966.. 24 L
rubenc.ramirez@hancockcollege.edu
RAMIREZ, Sam .... 361-825-2765 446 E
samuel.ramirez@tamucc.edu
RAMIREZ, Sandra .... 281-998-2648 442 B
sandra.ramirez@sjcd.edu
RAMIREZ, Steve, D .... 512-233-1464 441 N
steveramirez@stedwards.edu
RAMIREZ, Sylvia .... 787-832-6000 506 B
sramirez@icprjc.edu
RAMIREZ, Sylvia .... 608-243-4587 497 I
sframirez@madisoncollege.edu
RAMIREZ, Wilmer .... 303-783-3137.. 80 G
wilmer.ramirez@denverseminary.edu
RAMIREZ, Yvonne .... 718-430-2000 289 D
RAMIREZ-CARLO, III,
Bolivar .... 787-620-2040 504 B
bramirez@aupr.edu
RAMIREZ-FIGUEROA,
Jose .... 787-620-2040 504 B
jramirez@aupr.edu
RAMIREZ-GELPI, Sofia .. 805-922-6966.. 24 L
sgelpi@hancockcollege.edu
RAMIREZ-PEREZ,
Felicia .... 480-732-7093.. 13 B
felicia.ramirez-perez@cgc.edu
RAMIREZ-PEREZ,
Felicia .... 602-285-7422.. 13 H
felicia.a.ramirez-perez@phoenixcollege.edu
RAMIREZ-RIVERA,
Rafael .... 787-878-5475 506 J
rramirez@arecibo.inter.edu
RAMIREZ ZUNIGA,
Jorge .... 202-646-1337.. 93 B
RAMJEE, Anju .... 304-829-7311 486 B
aramjee@bethanywv.edu
RAMKARAN, Arshaw ..... 212-650-5824 293 B
aramkaran@ccny.cuny.edu
RAMKUMAR,
S. Manian .... 585-475-5955 312 A
smrmet@rit.edu
RAMLER, Tom .... 903-434-8175 440 A
tramler@ntcc.edu
RAMLI, Phi .... 213-738-6818.. 66 A
accounting@swlaw.edu
RAMM, Jennifer .... 254-295-5527 453 A
jennifer.ramm@umhb.edu
RAMMER, Brian .... 920-465-2226 494 F
rammerb@uwgb.edu
RAMMING, Ronald, S ... 918-463-2931 365 I
rronald@connorsstate.edu
RAMON, Deanna Rene .. 580-349-1556 367 F
rene.ramon@opsu.edu
RAMON, Ralph .... 325-574-7625 457 G
rramon@wtc.edu
RAMONES, Eric .... 408-741-2060.. 75 D
eric.ramones@wvm.edu
RAMONES, Eric .... 408-741-2060.. 75 C
eric.ramones@wvm.edu
RAMONES, Eric .... 408-741-2060.. 75 B
eric.ramones@wvm.edu
RAMOS, Alberto .... 603-535-5000 274 B
RAMOS, Andrea .... 213-738-5574.. 66 A
aramos@swlaw.edu
RAMOS, Anthony .... 847-214-7257 137 D
aramos@elgin.edu
RAMOS, Antonio .... 787-284-1912 507 D
aramos@ponce.inter.edu
RAMOS, Cerese .... 386-506-3562.. 98 A
cerese.ramos@daytonastate.edu
RAMOS, Cerese .... 386-506-3240.. 98 A
cerese.ramos@daytonastate.edu
RAMOS, Chelsea .... 718-289-5153 292 H
chelsea.ayala@bcc.cuny.edu
RAMOS, Cynthia .... 602-285-7404.. 13 H
cynthia.ramos@phoenixcollege.edu
RAMOS, Daisy .... 787-738-2161 511 A
daisy.ramos@upr.edu
RAMOS, Derek .... 620-276-9559 173 H
derek.ramos@gcccks.edu
RAMOS, Edith .... 787-878-6000 506 B
eramos@icprjc.edu
RAMOS, Efrain .... 787-891-0925 506 I
eramos@aguadilla.inter.edu
RAMOS, Elizabeth .... 908-965-6090 283 E
ramos@ucc.edu
RAMOS, Erica .... 203-857-7301.. 87 B
eramos@commnet.edu
RAMOS, Ernesto, V .... 787-751-0160 505 C
eramos@cmpr.pr.gov
RAMOS, Gladys .... 787-738-2161 511 A
gladys.ramos@upr.edu
RAMOS, Hilda .... 312-341-2005 148 A
RAMOS, Idalmy .... 787-264-1912 507 E
iramos@intersg.edu
RAMOS, Irma .... 714-808-4810.. 54 B
iramos@nocccd.edu
RAMOS, Ismael .... 787-738-2161 511 A
ismael.ramos1@upr.edu
RAMOS, Jennifer .... 954-262-2134 104 M
jennifer.ramos@nova.edu
RAMOS, Joahana .... 787-844-8181 511 E
joahana.ramos@upr.edu
RAMOS, JR., Joe, W ..... 808-564-5843 129 B
joe.w.ramos@hawaii.edu
RAMOS, Joseph .... 619-388-6411.. 60 H
jramos@sdccd.edu
RAMOS, Kenneth, S ...... 713-677-7440 446 B
kramos@tamu.edu
RAMOS, Mandy .... 863-638-7129 113 D
mandy.ramos@warner.edu
RAMOS, Miguel .... 713-718-7444 436 E
miguel.ramos@hccs.edu
RAMOS, Nancy, L .... 401-254-3455 404 C
nramos@rwu.edu
RAMOS, Patricia .... 310-434-3311.. 63 B
ramos_patricia@smc.edu
RAMOS, Patricia .... 718-631-6262 295 B
RAMOS, Reynaldo .... 978-542-7321 213 B
reynaldo.ramos@salemstate.edu
RAMOS, Richard, O .... 515-961-1536 169 G
rich.ramos@simpson.edu
RAMOS, Rosabel .... 956-326-3088 446 A
rosabel.ramos@tamiu.edu
RAMOS, Sergio .... 915-831-6413 435 B
sramos7@epcc.edu
RAMOS, Sofia .... 863-667-5000 108 I
svramos@seu.edu
RAMOS, Somar .... 787-764-0000 511 F
somar.ramos@upr.edu
RAMOS, Vanessa .... 787-725-6500 504 F
varamos@albizu.edu
RAMOS, Victor .... 717-871-7500 394 B
victor.ramos@millersville.edu
RAMOS, Yolanda .... 432-685-4733 439 E
yramos@midland.edu
RAMOS-DIAZ, Mirna ...... 509-452-5100 481 E
mramosdiaz@pnwu.edu
RAMOS RUIZ, Anuchka 787-728-1515 512 A
anuchka.ramos@sagrado.edu
RAMOS-VARGAS,
Luz, N .... 787-798-3001 509 F
luz.ramos@uccaribe.edu
RAMOUTAR, Prakash ..... 509-527-2402 484 C
prakash.ramoutar@wallawalla.edu
RAMPAUL, Andre .... 212-757-1190 289 H
arampaul@aami.edu
RAMPELLO, Frank .... 934-420-2104 320 C
rampelf@farmingdale.edu
RAMPERSAD, Dave .... 334-386-7100.... 5 D
drampersad@faulkner.edu
RAMPP, Carrie .... 717-358-4161 383 G
carrie.rampp@fandm.edu
RAMS, Richard .... 626-914-8534.. 37 B
rrams@citruscollege.edu
RAMSAMMY, Jillian .... 352-854-2322.. 97 L
jillian.ramsammy@cf.edu
RAMSAMMY, Roger, A .. 518-629-4530 302 A
r.ramsammy@hvcc.edu
RAMSARAN, Dave .... 570-372-4127 398 A
ramsaran@susqu.edu
RAMSAY, Carl .... 870-574-4546.. 21 F
cramsay@sautech.edu
RAMSAY, Darlene .... 573-341-4584 260 F
ramsayd@mst.edu
RAMSAY, Kerr, C .... 336-841-9148 329 E
kramsay@highpoint.edu
RAMSAY, Lara .... 509-777-4347 485 D
lramsay@whitworth.edu
RAMSAY, Tim .... 616-632-2076 221 A
ramsatim@aquinas.edu
RAMSBURG, David .... 304-357-4766 486 J
davidramsburg@ucwv.edu
RAMSDELL, Keith .... 419-289-5397 347 H
kramsdel@ashland.edu
RAMSDELL, Kerry .... 978-232-2225 209 B
kramsdel@endicott.edu
RAMSDELL, Nancy, M .. 508-929-8605 213 D
nramsdell@worcester.edu
RAMSDELL, Twyla .... 651-213-4180 235 G
tramsdell@hazeldenbettyford.edu
RAMSDEN-MEIER,
Joanna .... 319-226-2004 163 A
joanna.ramsden-meier@allencollege.edu
RAMSEL, Janelle .... 303-964-5387.. 83 B
jramsel@regis.edu
RAMSEY, Andrea, B ...... 330-471-8328 355 D
aramsey@malone.edu
RAMSEY, III, James ..... 919-488-8500 330 C
RAMSEY, Jason, M .... 814-332-2761 378 A
jramsey@allegheny.edu
RAMSEY, Kathy .... 785-462-3984 172 L
RAMSEY, Kim .... 318-797-5234 189 E
kim.ramsey@lsus.edu
RAMSEY, Kyle, H .... 630-515-6165 144 C
kramse@midwestern.edu
RAMSEY, Mae .... 540-362-6519 467 A
mramsey@hollins.edu
RAMSEY, Marty .... 828-227-7335 343 D
mramsey@wcu.edu
RAMSEY, Matthew .... 913-360-7387 171 G
mramsey@benedictine.edu
RAMSEY, Nate .... 773-947-6309 143 E
nramsey@mccormick.edu
RAMSEY, Patricia .... 718-270-5000 294 E
6thpresident@mec.cuny.edu
RAMSEY, Rachel .... 518-337-4318 296 E
ramseyr@strose.edu
RAMSEY, Richard .... 207-454-1067 195 E
rramsey@wccc.me.edu
RAMSEY, Ruth .... 415-257-1393.. 41 H
ruth.ramsey@dominican.edu
RAMSEY, Stacey .... 309-438-8642 140 C
srramse@ilstu.edu
RAMSEY, Traci .... 972-881-5847 432 I
tramsey@collin.edu
RAMSEY, Vickie .... 530-251-8852.. 47 I
vramsey@lassencollege.edu
RAMSEY-HAMACHER,
Paige .... 352-588-8489 107 B
paige.ramsey.hamacher@saintleo.edu
RAMSEY-MARTIN,
Shanequa .... 804-751-9191 464 N
sramseymartin@ccc-va.com
RAMSEYER, Rob .... 316-295-5433 173 G
rob_ramseyer@friends.edu
RAMSLAND, Katherine .. 610-282-1100 382 A
katherine.ramsland@desales.edu
RAMSOONDAR-CUEVAS,
Meera .... 917-507-0070 293 B
mramsoondarcuevas@ccny.cuny.edu
RAMSTAD, Erik .... 218-299-4923 234 K
eramstad@cord.edu
RAMZAH, Hassan .... 402-472-4467 269 A
hassan.ramzah@unl.edu
RAMÍREZ, Rafael .... 787-763-4203 506 H
rramirez@inter.edu
RANABARGAR, Kerry .... 620-432-0301 176 A
kranabargar@neosho.edu
RANALLI, Carlee, K .... 240-500-2228 199 A
ckranalli@hagerstowncc.edu
RANALLO-HIGGINS,
Frederick .... 215-884-8942 402 E
fred.ranallo.higgins@woninstitute.edu
RANCATI, Chrisanne ..... 704-637-4322 327 H
crancati20@catawba.edu
RANCK, Lorrie .... 408-855-5182.. 75 C
lorrie.ranck@missioncollege.edu
RAND, Jonathan .... 617-879-7263 212 E
jrand@massart.edu
RAND, Patricia .... 813-253-7995 102 A
prand@hccfl.edu
RAND, Paul, M .... 773-702-0689 151 B
prand@uchicago.edu
RANDALL, Anne .... 508-421-3804 207 F
anrandall@clarku.edu
RANDALL, Brandy .... 248-370-3169 229 F
brandall@oakland.edu
RANDALL, Briana .... 206-685-4139 484 A
brianakr@uw.edu
RANDALL, Caroline .... 505-984-6976 287 F
caroline.randall@sjc.edu
RANDALL, David .... 617-253-4052 215 G
RANDALL, Jody .... 806-743-2181 450 D
jody.randall@ttuhsc.edu
RANDALL, John .... 949-214-3358.. 40 E
john.randall@cui.edu
RANDALL, Kelli, V .... 704-216-6195 330 D
krandall@livingstone.edu
RANDALL, Meridith .... 714-892-7711.. 38 E
RANDALL, Monte .... 918-549-2806 365 G
mrandall@cmn.edu
RANDALL, Nancy .... 704-233-8065 344 E
nrandall@wingate.edu
RANDALL, Regina .... 614-287-5343 351 B
rrandal2@cscc.edu
RANDALL, Robin .... 413-538-2023 216 G
rrandall@mtholyoke.edu
RANDALL, Stacey .... 630-466-7900 152 H
srandall@waubonsee.edu
RANDALL, Taylor, R ...... 801-581-3074 459 D
taylor.randall@eccles.utah.edu
RANDALL, Wesley .... 940-565-2628 453 B
wesley.randall@unt.edu
RANDALL-LEE,
Valerie, J .... 410-677-0022 204 A
vjrandall-lee@salisbury.edu
RANDAZZA, Paula .... 603-897-8303 273 B
prandazza@rivier.edu
RANDAZZA, Scott .... 404-471-6000 114 E
RANDAZZO, Jennifer .... 563-884-5141 169 C
jennifer.randazzo@palmer.edu
RANDAZZO, Maria .... 315-445-4195 303 F
randazmc@lemoyne.edu
RANDERS, Mary .... 503-370-6928 377 E
mranders@willamette.edu
RANDERS, Mary .... 903-813-2370 429 I
mranders@austincollege.edu
RANDHAWA, Sabah ...... 360-650-3480 485 A
president@wwu.edu
RANDICK, Nicole .... 612-861-7554 233 E
nicole.randick@alfredadler.edu
RANDLE, Jonathan .... 601-925-3849 246 D
randle@mc.edu
RANDLES,
Christopher, M .... 217-351-2513 146 G
crandles@parkland.edu
RANDO, Robert, A .... 937-775-3409 364 D
robert.rando@wright.edu
RANDOLPH, Adrian .... 847-491-3276 146 C
weinberg-dean@northwestern.edu
RANDOLPH, Amber .... 973-353-5541 281 C
amber.randolph@rutgers.edu
RANDOLPH, Brennan .... 812-535-1152 160 E
brennan.randolph@smwc.edu
RANDOLPH, Chris, N ... 304-457-6368 485 F
randolphcn@ab.edu
RANDOLPH, Robert .... 417-447-7851 257 B
randolphr@otc.edu
RANDOLPH, Tamela ...... 573-651-2163 258 J
trandolph@semo.edu
RANDOLPH, Trent .... 256-331-5260.... 3 C
trentrandolph@nwscc.edu
RANDS, Melissa .... 612-874-3700 236 E
mrands@mcad.edu
RANES, Rodney .... 618-842-3711 139 D
ranesr@iecc.edu
RANESES, Jade .... 808-518-4791 128 H
jaderaneses@pacrim.edu
RANEY, Candace .... 918-465-1723 365 K
craney@eosc.edu
RANEY, Megan .... 816-271-4206 256 C
mraney@missouriwestern.edu
RANFT, Annette, L .... 334-844-4030.... 4 E
alr0076@auburn.edu
RANGEL, Jessica .... 817-735-2000 453 D
RANGEL,
Mary Margaret .... 214-768-4740 443 G
marymargaret@smu.edu
RANGEL, Robert .... 817-257-7933 447 H
r.rangel@tcu.edu
RANGOS, Mike .... 248-370-4423 229 F
mrangos@oakland.edu
RANGUETTE, Renea, L .. 608-757-7700 497 D
rranguette@blackhawk.edu
RANK, Carin .... 413-559-5385 210 A
croo@hampshire.edu
RANKIN, Darrin .... 903-790-4890 437 E
drankin@jarvis.net
RANKIN, James .... 605-394-2257 415 I
jim.rankin@sdsmt.edu
RANKIN, Janet .... 617-253-7559 215 G
RANKIN, Julie .... 405-585-4522 367 B
julie.rankin@okbu.edu
RANKIN, Stephanie, A .. 717-361-1569 383 B
rankins@etown.edu

RAY, Joshua .... 801-618-0438 458 H
jray@ameritech.edu
RAY, Judy, K .... 336-841-9201 329 E
jray@highpoint.edu
RAY, Karen .... 256-551-5227 .... 2 E
karen.ray@drakestate.edu
RAY, Ken .... 813-253-7054 102 A
kray6@hccfl.edu
RAY, Leigh, A .... 931-372-3320 425 B
lray@tntech.edu
RAY, Mandy .... 978-542-7253 213 B
mandy.ray@salemstate.edu
RAY, Marty .... 617-627-3300 219 A
marty.ray@tufts.edu
RAY, Michelle, B .... 202-462-2101 .. 93 A
hr@iwp.edu
RAY, Morgan .... 919-278-2673 339 I
morgan.ray@shawu.edu
RAY, Nancy .... 704-334-6882 327 J
nray@charlottechristian.edu
RAY, Natalie .... 251-578-1313 .... 3 D
nray@rstc.edu
RAY, Nicholas, T ...... 812-941-2411 157 D
nicray@ius.edu
RAY, Nick .... 317-274-0015 156 F
nicray@iu.edu
RAY, Nick .... 574-520-4463 157 C
nicray@iu.edu
RAY, Nick .... 219-980-7202 157 A
nicray@iu.edu
RAY, Pamela .... 850-644-8643 110 B
pray2@fsu.edu
RAY, Phillip .... 979-458-6421 445 D
pray@tamus.edu
RAY, Sandy .... 850-484-1213 105 G
scesaretti@pensacolastate.edu
RAY, Shanna .... 615-966-5833 420 B
shanna.ray@lipscomb.edu
RAY, JR., Stephen, G .. 773-896-2400 134 K
creagan@tusculum.edu
RAY, Thomas .... 408-864-8510 .. 42 K
raythomas@deanza.edu
RAY, Tiffany .... 540-891-3037 472 J
tray@germanna.edu
RAY, Tracey .... 610-436-1104 394 F
tray2@wcupa.edu
RAY, Vivyen .... 973-328-5037 276 A
vray@ccm.edu
RAYBURN, James, E .... 817-554-5950 439 C
jrayburn@messengercollege.edu
RAYBURN, Jill .... 864-977-7256 410 A
jill.rayburn@ngu.edu
RAYBURN, T. Monroe .. 202-319-5765 .. 91 G
rayburn@cua.edu
RAYFIELD, Stuart ...... 404-962-3040 127 B
stuart.rayfield@usg.edu
RAYFORD, Austin ...... 662-252-8000 248 B
arayford@rustcollege.edu
RAYMER, John .... 617-405-5987 217 G
jraymer@quincycollege.edu
RAYMOND, Annette .... 973-748-9000 275 C
annette_raymond@bloomfield.edu
RAYMOND, SR.,
John, R .... 414-955-8225 492 F
jraymond@mcw.edu
RAYMOND,
Katherine, M .... 718-260-4981 294 E
kmraymond@citytech.cuny.edu
RAYMOND, Lisa .... 508-289-3557 220 B
lraymond@whoi.edu
RAYMOND, Sarah ...... 406-496-4384 264 C
sraymond@mtech.edu
RAYMOND, Tiffany ...... 315-364-3352 324 E
traymond@wells.edu
RAYMOND, Wendy, E .. 610-896-1021 385 H
president@haverford.edu
RAYMUNDO, Laurie .... 671-735-2184 503 E
lraymundo@triton.uog.edu
RAYNER, Jill .... 706-864-1688 126 G
jill.rayner@ung.edu
RAYNOR, Jamie .... 828-227-3052 343 D
jtraynor@wcu.edu
RAYNOR, Samantha .... 336-256-0190 342 D
slraynor@uncg.edu
RAYNOR, Timothy ...... 203-576-4168 .. 89 A
traynor@bridgeport.edu
RAYNOR, Vanessa ...... 919-719-2284 339 I
rraynor@shawu.edu
RAYO, Agustín .... 617-253-2559 215 G
RAYOME, Megan .... 406-293-2721 262 H
mrayome@fvcc.edu
RAZA, Ahsan .... 212-870-1228 309 C
araza@nyts.edu

RAZA, Syed .... 256-761-6200 .... 7 B
sqraza@talladega.edu
RAZAFIMANJATO, Laza . 501-370-5252.. 21 A
rlaza@philander.edu
RAZDAN,
Anshuman (AR) .... 541-346-2090 376 G
razdan@uoregon.edu
RAZI, Nahid .... 619-644-7799 .. 44 H
nahid.razi@gcccd.edu
RAZICK, Danagene .... 843-661-1142 408 H
drazick@fmarion.edu
RAZZA, Paul .... 336-770-3264 343 C
razzap@uncsa.edu
RAZZI, A. Wade ...... 843-577-5245 405 E
REA, Allyson .... 434-961-5223 474 B
area@pvcc.edu
REA, Jen .... 970-675-3229.. 78 P
jennifer.rea@cncc.edu
REA, Jessica .... 513-529-5919 356 A
reajt@miamioh.edu
REABACK, Roslyn ...... 203-932-7263.. 89 F
rreaback@newhaven.edu
REABOLD, Beth ...... 480-818-0388 467 G
bsreabold@marybaldwin.edu
READ, Caitlyn .... 540-568-5152 467 C
readcl@jmu.edu
READ, Carole .... 757-789-1733 472 I
cread@es.vccs.edu
READ, Charles .... 678-466-4369 117 A
charlesread@clayton.edu
READ, Melissa .... 508-541-1654 208 E
mread@dean.edu
READ, Russel .... 336-734-7651 334 D
rread@forsythtech.edu
READE, Christopher ...... 617-266-1400 206 D
creade@berklee.edu
READNOUR, Warren .... 501-450-5007.. 23 K
wreadnour@uca.edu
REAGAN, Casey .... 423-636-7300 425 E
creagan@tusculum.edu
REAGAN, Emily .... 512-471-4945 454 C
emily.reagan@utexas.edu
REAGAN, Jackie .... 580-774-3166 369 I
jackie.reagan@swosu.edu
REAGAN, Katherine, M .. 423-869-6389 420 A
katherine.reagan@lmunet.edu
REAGAN, Krystal ...... 618-985-2828 140 G
krystalreagan@jalc.edu
REAGAN, Melinda ...... 972-279-6511 428 G
mreagan@amberton.edu
REAGEN, Nate .... 515-271-2949 165 F
nate.reagen@drake.edu
REAGIN, Cam .... 803-641-3399 412 B
camr@usca.edu
REAGINS-LILLY, Soncia 512-471-1133 454 C
vpsa@austin.utexas.edu
REAGLE, Mike .... 270-745-2037 186 A
mike.reagle@wku.edu
REAL, Yannick .... 562-860-2451.. 35 O
yreal@cerritos.edu
REAL BIRD, Sunny Day 406-657-2144 263 H
sunnyday.realbird@msubillings.edu
REALIVASQUEZ,
Yvonne .... 432-837-8008 449 F
yrealivasquez@sulross.edu
REAM, Debbie .... 213-477-2505.. 52 J
dream@msmu.edu
REAMER, Amy .... 910-962-4075 343 B
reamera@uncw.edu
REAMER, OFM, Mark .. 518-783-2938 314 K
mreamer@siena.edu
REAMS, Amelia .... 229-219-3198 127 C
alharmon@valdosta.edu
REAMS, Angie .... 319-335-1162 163 F
angela-reams@uiowa.edu
REAMS, John, D .... 706-233-7203 125 A
jreams@shorter.edu
REAMS, Thomas ...... 801-689-2160 458 K
treams@nightingale.edu
REAMY, Brian .... 301-295-1080 502 B
brian.reamy@usuhs.edu
REAMY, Sara .... 503-554-2118 372 I
sreamy@georgefox.edu
REARDON, Amy .... 310-544-6484.. 60 B
amy.reardon@usw.salvationarmy.org
REARDON, Cheryl .. 319-335-0056 163 F
cheryl-reardon@uiowa.edu
REARDON, Diana ...... 803-774-3354 406 A
reardondl@cctech.edu
REARDON, Emily ...... 508-213-2275 217 C
emily.reardon@nichols.edu
REARDON, Greg ...... 951-343-4245.. 27 J
greardon@calbaptist.edu

REARDON, Mary ...... 512-381-7253 429 H
mreardon@escoffier.edu
REARDON, Patrick ...... 256-824-2530.... 8 B
patrick.reardon@uah.edu
REARDON, Penny, E .... 540-828-5395 464 C
preardon@bridgewater.edu
REARDON, Richard ...... 802-468-1234 462 H
richard.reardon@castleton.edu
REARDON, Texas ...... 903-693-2024 440 E
treardon@panola.edu
REARDON, Tim .... 401-739-5000 403 F
treardon@neit.edu
REARDON HENRY,
Melissa .... 973-720-2242 283 I
reardonhenrym@wpunj.edu
REASH, Brenda .... 252-222-6262 332 G
reashb@carteret.edu
REASONER, Carroll .... 319-335-2841 163 F
carroll-reasoner@uiowa.edu
REASOR, Erin .... 606-589-3054 182 F
erin.wilson@kctcs.edu
REAUME, Vicki .... 734-487-2410 223 F
vreaume@emich.edu
REAVES, Ken .... 678-872-8511 119 C
kreaves@highlands.edu
REAVES, Ken .... 863-667-5408 108 I
kmreasves@seu.edu
REAVES, Nicole .... 919-532-5705 338 E
nreaves1@waketech.edu
REBEOR, Sara .... 315-312-2246 318 B
sara.rebeor@oswego.edu
REBER, Christopher, M 201-360-4003 277 D
creber@hccc.edu
REBHOLZ, Nancy ...... 309-671-5112 143 I
nrebholz@methodistcol.edu
REBMAN, Johanna .... 815-836-5050 142 C
jrebman@lewisu.edu
REBOLI, Annette ...... 856-361-2800 280 H
reboli@rowan.edu
REBOUCHE', Rachel ...... 215-204-9674 398 D
rachel.rebouche@temple.edu
REBURN, Tom .... 218-477-2549 239 A
tom.reburn@mnstate.edu
RECA, Michael, F ...... 609-896-5080 280 D
reca@rider.edu
RECALDE, Tina .... 619-388-2789.. 61 A
trecalde@sdccd.edu
RECCHIA, Karen .... 318-678-6000 187 E
krecchia@bpcc.edu
RECHTSCHAFFEN,
Joyce, A .... 202-220-1364 279 E
jrechtsc@princeton.edu
RECINOS, Alba .... 714-808-4796.. 54 B
arecinos@nocccd.edu
RECINOS, Diane .... 973-278-5400 274 J
dr@berkeleycollege.edu
RECINOS, Diane .... 212-986-4343 291 A
dr@berkeleycollege.edu
RECKER, Amy .... 531-622-2743 266 G
arecker@mccneb.edu
RECKER, Mary, A ...... 937-229-4354 362 C
mpoirier1@udayton.edu
RECORDS, Stefany ...... 713-221-8636 452 B
recordss@uhd.edu
RECTOR, David .... 660-785-7607 259 J
daverec@truman.edu
RECTOR, David .... 425-739-8287 480 D
david.rector@lwtech.edu
RECTOR, Eric .... 540-365-4427 466 I
erector@ferrum.edu
RECTOR, Ray .... 509-359-6612 478 H
rrector@ewu.edu
RECTOR, Rob .... 417-447-4852 257 B
rectorr@otc.edu
RECZEK, Lauren ...... 716-827-2487 322 I
reczekl@trocaire.edu
RECZNIK, Joel, S ...... 740-284-5236 352 I
jrecznik@franciscan.edu
REDD, Annie .... 804-524-5070 475 E
aredd@vsu.edu
REDD, Annie, C .... 804-524-3340 475 E
aredd@vsu.edu
REDD, Brett .... 661-395-4605.. 47 B
brett.redd@bakersfieldcollege.edu
REDD, Hugh .... 540-261-8400 470 D
hugh.redd@svu.edu
REDD, Leslie .... 904-256-7882 102 G
lredd@ju.edu
REDD, Randy .... 901-751-8453 420 G
rredd@mabts.edu
REDD, Rea .... 724-852-3254 401 E
rredd@waynesburg.edu
REDD, Scott .... 703-996-4054 248 A
sredd@rts.edu

REDDER, Vince .... 605-995-2631 414 A
vince.redder@dwu.edu
REDDERSON, Jeff, P .... 864-294-3262 408 I
jeff.redderson@furman.edu
REDDI, Lakshmi .... 575-646-2914 286 G
lnr@nmsu.edu
REDDICK, Chenita, R .... 410-651-8045 203 B
crreddick@umes.edu
REDDICK, Don .... 815-939-5111 146 F
dreddick@olivet.edu
REDDICK, Rinardo ...... 914-606-6313 324 F
rinardo.reddick@sunywcc.edu
REDDING, Brandi, D .... 302-295-1161.. 91 C
brandi.d.redding@wilmu.edu
REDDING, Gregory .... 765-361-6310 162 G
reddingg@wabash.edu
REDDING, Melanie .... 423-585-2690 424 G
melanie.redding@ws.edu
REDDING, Victor ...... 775-784-4031 270 K
vredding@unr.edu
REDDING LAPUZ,
Danni .... 650-738-4121.. 62 K
reddinglapuzd@smccd.edu
REDDINGER, Amy ...... 906-217-4068 221 J
amy.reddinger@baycollege.edu
REDDINGTON, Cynthia . 757-240-2229 469 F
cynthia.reddington@rivhs.com
REDDIX, Rhoda .... 225-214-6966 186 M
rhoda.reddix@franu.edu
REDDY, Howard, J ...... 850-474-3306 111 E
hreddy@uwf.edu
REDDY, Indra, K .... 979-458-7200 446 B
ireddy@tamu.edu
REDDY, John .... 757-352-4704 469 D
jreddy@regent.edu
REDDY, Kirti .... 510-723-6641.. 35 Q
kreddy@chabotcollege.edu
REDDY, Michael .... 415-476-1323.. 70 D
michael.reddy@ucsf.edu
REDDY, Narem .... 678-466-4100 117 A
naremreddy@clayton.edu
REDDY, Robert .... 617-373-3190 217 G
REDDY, Venkat ...... 719-255-3436.. 84 A
chancellor@uccs.edu
REDEKER, Kerri ...... 949-376-6000.. 47 G
kredeker@lcad.edu
REDEKER, Maureen .... 435-586-7700 459 E
maureenredeker@suu.edu
REDEKOP, Steven ...... 559-453-3451.. 43 D
steven.redekop@fresno.edu
REDFEARN,
Christopher .... 701-252-3467 346 J
chris.redfearn@uj.edu
REDFERN, Paul .... 315-229-5845 313 F
predfern@stlawu.edu
REDFIELD, Chaunta .... 317-955-6044 159 A
credfield@marian.edu
REDING, Jody .... 806-720-7154 438 F
jody.reding@lcu.edu
REDING, Roger .... 806-894-9611 443 A
rreding@southplainscollege.edu
REDINGER, Matthew .. 406-791-5302 264 J
matthew.redinger@uprovidence.edu
REDINGTON, Joseph .... 570-674-6756 389 H
jredington@misericordia.edu
REDINGTON, Lyn ...... 208-282-2315 131 E
redilyn@isu.edu
REDLINGER,
Lawrence, J .... 972-883-6188 454 D
redling@utdallas.edu
REDMAN, Cynthia ...... 773-256-3000 143 H
credman@meadville.edu
REDMAN, Donald, L .... 717-338-3036 399 H
dredman@uls.edu
REDMAN, Jay .... 248-204-2317 226 E
jredman@ltu.edu
REDMAN, Laurel ...... 480-517-8000.. 14 A
laurel.redman@riosalado.edu
REDMAN, Paul .... 217-333-1166 151 F
predman@illinois.edu
REDMON, Allen .... 254-519-5446 446 C
allen.redmon@tamuct.edu
REDMOND, Angie ...... 641-844-5712 167 E
angie.redmond@iavalley.edu
REDMOND, James ...... 805-267-1690.. 48 A
REDMOND, Jeff .... 805-267-1690.. 48 A
jeff.redmond@lauruscollege.edu
REDMOND, Michael, J .. 303-458-4995.. 83 B
mredmond@regis.edu
REDMOND, Rachel ...... 607-735-1817 298 G
rredmond@elmira.edu
REDMOND, Rodney .... 301-934-2251 198 C
ryredmond@csmd.edu

REEVES, Joey .... 912-478-8607 120 A
jreeves@georgiasouthern.edu
REEVES, Lisa .... 803-376-6007 405 D
lreeves@allenuniversity.edu
REEVES, Lisa .... 214-887-5025 434 G
lreeves@dts.edu
REEVES, Mark .... 678-839-5079 127 A
mreeves@westga.edu
REEVES, Michelle .... 706-880-8249 121 K
mreeves@lagrange.edu
REEVES, Richard, J .... 302-831-2021.. 91 A
rjreeves@udel.edu
REEVES, Shane .... 845-938-2000 502 H
janine.gizzi@westpoint.edu
REEVES, Tracey .... 352-395-5507 107 G
tracey.reeves@sfcollege.edu
REGA, Elizabeth .... 909-469-5460.. 75 G
erega@westernu.edu
REGALADO, Juan .... 909-448-4448.. 71 C
jregalado@laverne.edu
REGAN, Anna .... 732-255-0400 279 A
aregan@ocean.edu
REGAN, Brendan .... 623-845-3449.. 13 E
brendan.regan@gccaz.edu
REGAN, Joseph, P .... 312-341-2110 148 A
jregan@roosevelt.edu
REGAN, Kathleen .... 315-781-3309 301 D
regan@hws.edu
REGAN, Rich .... 312-341-3500 148 A
rregan01@roosevelt.edu
REGAN, Sheila .... 336-342-4261 337 B
regans@rockinghamcc.edu
REGE, Karen .... 443-412-2145 199 B
krege@harford.edu
REGE, Karen, M .... 443-412-2145 199 B
krege@harford.edu
REGE, Robert .... 214-648-3050 456 D
robert.rege@utsouthwestern.edu
REGE, Vidyanidhi .... 508-678-2811 213 F
vidyanidhi.rege@bristolcc.edu
REGEHR, Nanci .... 480-517-8314.. 14 A
nanci.regehr@riosalado.edu
REGEHR, Shellie .... 620-901-6299 171 A
sregehr@allencc.edu
REGENCIO, Eugenia .... 973-596-3068 278 G
eugenia.regencio@njit.edu
REGER, Tim .... 515-263-6136 166 C
treger@grandview.edu
REGIER, Elaine .... 405-945-9104 368 C
elaine.regier@okstate.edu
REGIER, Jeanette .... 816-322-0110 250 E
jeanette.regier@calvary.edu
REGIER, Philip, R .... 480-965-2457.. 11 A
phil.regier@asu.edu
REGINA, Henrique .... 808-488-8570 457 B
hregina@wbu.edu
REGIS, Chris, C .... 214-768-1178 443 G
cregis@smu.edu
REGIST TOMLINSON,
Tara .... 718-960-2416 293 E
tara.registtomlinson@lehman.cuny.edu
REGISTER, Kimberly ...... 831-459-5837.. 71 A
ksregist@ucsc.edu
REGISTER, Kimberly ...... 770-412-4586 125 F
kimberly.register@sctech.edu
REGISTER, Patrick .... 831-459-4404.. 71 A
jpregister@ucsc.edu
REGISTER, Tammy .... 307-382-1606 500 I
tregister@westernwyoming.edu
REGISTRAR, Brian .... 928-523-9011.. 14 J
REGJO, Kathryn .... 970-945-8691.. 78 H
REGN, Todd .... 201-200-2453 278 F
tregn@njcu.edu
REGNER, Cecile .... 857-701-1270 215 E
cregner@rcc.mass.edu
REGNER, Cecile .... 857-701-1272 215 E
cregner@rcc.mass.edu
REGNER, Cecile .... 857-701-1270 215 E
cregner@rcc.mass.edu
REGNERUS, Arlene .... 312-341-3500 148 A
REGUEIRO, Maria, C ...... 305-821-3333 100 C
mregueiro@fnu.edu
REGUERIN, Pablo, G ...... 530-752-1011.. 69 A
REGULSKA, Joanna .... 530-752-6376.. 69 A
jregulska@ucdavis.edu
REHAK, Patricia .... 361-354-2728 431 L
prehak@coastalbend.edu
REHBEIN, Matt .... 615-966-6043 420 B
matt.rehbein@lipscomb.edu
REHFELD, Andrew .... 212-674-5300 300 H
REHFELD, Peggy .... 773-298-3503 148 I
rehfeld@sxu.edu

REHFELD, Renee .... 830-372-6803 448 C
rrehfeld@tlu.edu
REHM, David .... 570-674-6403 389 H
drehm@misericordia.edu
REHM, Julie .... 216-523-7275 350 G
j.rehm@csuohio.edu
REHM, Mark .... 325-942-2555 450 B
mark.rehm@angelo.edu
REHM, Matthew .... 740-362-3136 355 H
mrehm@mtso.edu
REHN, Andrea .... 562-907-4200.. 76 A
arehn@whittier.edu
REHN, Andrea .... 518-244-2466 312 D
rscdean@sage.edu
REHN, Lynn .... 410-228-9250 203 A
lrehn@umces.edu
REHNELT, Wayne .... 562-860-2451.. 35 O
wrehnelt@cerritos.edu
REIBER, Carl .... 912-478-5258 120 A
creiber@georgiasouthern.edu
REICH, Amy, R .... 516-463-7580 301 E
amy.reich@hofstra.edu
REICH, Evan .... 843-574-6368 411 I
evan.reich@tridenttech.edu
REICH, Jacqueline .... 845-575-3000 305 C
jacqueline.reich@marist.edu
REICH, Jacqueline .... 215-248-7148 380 G
reichj@chc.edu
REICH, Lewis .... 901-722-3220 422 I
lreich@sco.edu
REICH, Patricia .... 610-330-5017 387 B
reichp@lafayette.edu
REICH, Tyler .... 503-375-6586 377 E
treich@willamette.edu
REICH PAULSEN,
Sharon .... 802-656-8585 462 D
sharon.reich.paulsen@uvm.edu
REICHARD, Jacob .... 620-223-2700 173 F
jacobr@fortscott.edu
REICHARD, Joshua .... 423-775-6596 421 I
REICHARD, Joshua .... 423-775-6596 421 I
jreichard@ogs.edu
REICHARDT, Eike .... 610-799-1756 388 B
ereichardt@lccc.edu
REICHEL, Scott .... 970-339-6513.. 77 G
scott.reichel@aims.edu
REICHERT, Brett .... 678-839-4780 127 A
breicher@westga.edu
REICHERT, Greg .... 608-785-8672 495 A
greichert@uwlax.edu
REICHERT, Linda, A ...... 570-326-3761 392 S
lar22@pct.edu
REICHERT, Tom .... 803-777-4105 412 A
reichert@sc.edu
REICHMAN, Harold .... 305-944-0035 114 B
REICHMUTH, Geri .... 303-292-0015.. 80 F
greichmuth@denvercollegeofnursing.
edu
REICHNER, Phil .... 843-953-3721 406 D
preichne@citadel.edu
REID, Adam .... 240-567-4264 200 E
adam.reid@montgomerycollege.edu
REID, Alicia .... 718-270-6406 294 E
areid@mec.cuny.edu
REID, Austin .... 803-321-5229 409 I
austin.reid@newberry.edu
REID, OP, Barbara, E ..... 773-371-5420 134 C
president@ctu.edu
REID, Brian .... 617-573-8144 218 G
bmreid@suffolk.edu
REID, Carol .... 678-664-0533 127 E
carol.reid@westgatech.edu
REID, Charise .... 216-421-7312 350 E
clreid@cia.edu
REID, Chris, B .... 540-458-4070 476 D
creid@wlu.edu
REID, Colette .... 757-881-5100.. 93 H
REID, Dawn .... 310-233-4287.. 49 F
reidd@lahc.edu
REID, Diana .... 860-512-2909.. 86 F
dreid@manchestercc.edu
REID, Donna, M .... 718-522-9073 290 B
dreid@asa.edu
REID, Greg .... 281-756-3561 428 E
greid@alvincollege.edu
REID, Gregory .... 973-748-9000 275 C
greg_reid@bloomfield.edu
REID, Heidi .... 913-758-6172 177 I
heidi.reid@stmary.edu
REID, James .... 325-942-2264 450 B
james.reid@angelo.edu
REID, Jodi .... 360-442-2421 480 E
jreid@lowercolumbia.edu

REID, Jodyann .... 954-545-4500 108 C
academics@sfbc.edu
REID, Jonathan .... 518-562-4124 295 F
jonathan.reid@clinton.edu
REID, Karl .... 617-373-2000 217 D
REID, Kayleigh .... 248-204-2000 226 E
kreid@ltu.edu
REID, Kelly .... 601-403-1489 247 F
kareid@prcc.edu
REID, Keni .... 808-675-3701 128 B
ken.reid@byuh.edu
REID, La Verne, M .... 919-530-5349 341 D
lreid@nccu.edu
REID, Lee .... 540-887-7212 467 G
lreid@marybaldwin.edu
REID, III, Lenzy .... 706-355-5124 115 C
lreid@athenstech.edu
REID, Letissa .... 860-486-2943.. 89 B
letissa.reid@uconn.edu
REID, Mark .... 308-865-8265 268 J
reidm@unk.edu
REID, Mark .... 206-281-2624 482 K
mreid@spu.edu
REID, Michael, B .... 352-294-1601 110 E
michael.reid@ufl.edu
REID, Michael, L .... 406-683-7151 263 E
michael.reid@umwestern.edu
REID, Michele .... 269-965-3931 225 D
reidm@kellogg.edu
REID, Sean, F .... 401-865-2155 403 G
sean.reid@providence.edu
REID, Shannon .... 603-230-3504 271 I
sreid@ccsnh.edu
REID, Steve .... 254-710-3601 430 F
stephen_reid@baylor.edu
REID, III, Wilbur .... 865-573-4517 419 E
wreid@johnsonu.edu
REID ALSTON, Melissa . 336-315-7800.. 93 H
REID-BUNCH, Jan .... 731-286-3200 423 E
REID-MARTINEZ,
Kathaleen .... 918-495-7855 368 F
kreid-martinez@oru.edu
REIDY, Francis .... 352-588-8246 107 B
fran.reidy@saintleo.edu
REIDY, Robert, C .... 650-723-6324.. 66 D
rcr@stanford.edu
REIDY-FOX, Kelly .... 773-298-3780 148 I
fox@sxu.edu
REIF, L. Rafael .... 617-253-0148 215 G
president@mit.edu
REIF, Richard .... 918-444-5900 366 G
reif01@nsuok.edu
REIFENHEISER, Paul ..... 607-844-8222 321 I
pr022@tompkinscortland.edu
REIFERT, Steve .... 231-591-2800 223 H
stevereifert@ferris.edu
REIG, Michael .... 215-248-7069 380 G
reigm@chc.edu
REIGEL, Heidi .... 410-857-2226 200 D
hreigel@mcdaniel.edu
REIGHARD, Erica .... 814-262-6440 393 A
ereighard@pennhighlands.edu
REIGHLEY, Twila .... 517-884-4367 227 C
reighley@msu.edu
REIGLE, Kim .... 828-689-1233 330 H
kreigle@mhu.edu
REIHER, William .... 692-625-5427 503 F
wreiher@cmi.edu
REIHL, Raeann .... 865-981-8355 420 C
raeann.reihl@maryvillecollege.edu
REIHMAN, Greg .... 610-758-3025 388 C
grr3@lehigh.edu
REIKOFSKI, Diane .... 402-844-7055 268 A
diane@northeast.edu
REILAND, Kathleen .... 714-484-7231.. 54 C
kreiland@cypresscollege.edu
REILAND, Mandi .... 281-998-6150 442 B
mandi.reiland@sjcd.edu
REILLEY, Mary Clare ...... 914-633-2686 302 C
mreilley@iona.edu
REILLO, Lissette .... 787-891-0925 506 I
lreillo@aguadilla.inter.edu
REILLY, Carolyn .... 706-368-6397 116 A
creilly@berry.edu
REILLY, Charles .... 202-250-2934.. 92 B
charles.reilly@gallaudet.edu
REILLY, Colleen .... 713-718-7307 436 E
colleen.reilly@hccs.edu
REILLY, David .... 973-748-9000 275 C
david_reilly1@bloomfield.edu
REILLY, Edward .... 507-457-5300 241 A
ereilly@winona.edu

REILLY, John, J .... 330-972-7753 361 G
jreilly@uakron.edu
REILLY, JR., John, J .... 303-556-2400.. 84 B
REILLY, Karen .... 269-782-1220 230 D
kreilly@swmich.edu
REILLY, Karen .... 218-736-1508 238 K
karen.reilly@minnesota.edu
REILLY, Keith .... 703-284-1614 468 A
sm669@marymount.edu
REILLY, Kerin .... 212-686-9244 289 G
kreilly@aada.edu
REILLY, Kevin, P .... 540-365-4407 466 I
kpreilly@ferrum.edu
REILLY, Lisa .... 304-829-7244 486 B
lreilly@bethanywv.edu
REILLY, M. B .... 513-556-1824 361 I
reillymb@ucmail.uc.edu
REILLY, Marianne .... 718-862-7891 304 K
mreilly01@manhattan.edu
REILLY, Mary Beth .... 732-224-2806 275 D
mreilly@brookdalecc.edu
REILLY, Matthew .... 617-243-2468 210 G
mreilly@lasell.edu
REILLY, Patricia .... 617-627-2000 219 A
patricia.reilly@tufts.edu
REILLY, Ronald .... 816-604-4125 255 B
ronald.reilly@mcckc.edu
REILLY, Seamus .... 309-341-5214 134 A
sreilly@sandburg.edu
REILLY, Tim .... 706-712-8228 118 A
treilly@daltonstate.edu
REILLY, William, T .... 704-894-2765 328 C
wireilly@davidson.edu
REIM, Melanie .... 212-217-7665 299 C
melanie_reim@fitnyc.edu
REIMAN, Brock .... 330-363-6347 348 B
brock.reiman@aultman.com
REIMAN, Dennis .... 203-392-5004.. 85 H
reimand1@southernct.edu
REIMAN, Tricia .... 972-708-7552 434 F
tricia_reiman@diu.edu
REIMANN, Rick .... 518-587-2100 320 B
rick.reimann@esc.edu
REIMER, Denise .... 608-243-4484 497 I
dmreimer@madisoncollege.edu
REIMER, Martin .... 641-648-4611 167 D
martin.reimer@iavalley.edu
REIMER, Martin .... 360-538-4009 479 F
martin.reimer@ghc.edu
REIMER, Rachel .... 515-271-1424 165 C
rachel.reimer@dmu.edu
REIMONDO, Sue .... 859-985-3212 179 E
reimondos@berea.edu
REINA, John .... 845-257-3685 316 B
reinaj@newpaltz.edu
REINA, Michelle .... 254-295-4015 453 A
mreina@umhb.edu
REINACHER, Deanna ...... 619-216-6673.. 65 K
dreinacher@swccd.edu
REINCKE, Nancy .... 515-271-2161 165 F
nancy.reincke@drake.edu
REINEKE, Juliann .... 419-434-4662 362 D
juliann.reineke@findlay.edu
REINEKE, Sandra .... 208-885-3165 132 C
sreineke@uidaho.edu
REINER, Christian .... 435-586-7783 459 E
christianreiner@suu.edu
REINER, Michael, D .... 402-280-2337 265 J
michaelreiner@creighton.edu
REINERT, Brett .... 618-468-2700 142 B
breinert@lc.edu
REINERT, Duane .... 660-944-2852 251 B
dreinert@conception.edu
REINETTE ANDREWS,
Mary .... 610-527-0200 396 G
randrews@rosemont.edu
REINHARD, Herb .... 229-333-5462 127 C
hreinhar@valdosta.edu
REINHARD, Patrick .... 914-694-4415 295 G
preinhard@riversidehealth.org
REINHARDT, Beth .... 217-641-4541 140 H
breinhardt@jwcc.edu
REINHARDT, John .... 217-641-4201 140 H
jreinhardt@jwcc.edu
REINHART, Adam .... 806-291-1124 457 B
reinharta@wbu.edu
REINHART, Rose .... 724-946-7935 401 F
reinhar@westminster.edu
REINI, Aaron .... 218-293-6850 238 D
aaron.reini@minnesotanorth.edu
REINIG, Amanda .... 757-455-3116 476 C
areinig@vwu.edu

REX, Barbara, A .... 805-437-3282.. 30 D
barbara.rex@csuci.edu
REX, Judith .... 610-861-5533 391 B
jrex@northampton.edu
REX, Lisa Youngkin ...... 610-330-5060 387 B
rexl@lafayette.edu
REX, Scott .... 541-552-6745 376 A
rexs@sou.edu
REX SMITH, Amy .... 601-968-8933 244 C
arexsmith@belhaven.edu
REXFORD, Nathan .... 530-938-5336.. 39 D
REXROAD, Diane .... 843-377-2145 406 B
drexroad@charlestonlaw.edu
REY, Chuck .... 803-323-2129 413 D
reyc@winthrop.edu
REY, Holly .... 815-479-7573 143 F
hrey@mchenry.edu
REY, Janeil .... 716-673-3311 316 A
janeil.rey@fredonia.edu
REY, Rosamil .... 787-279-1912 506 L
rrey@bayamon.inter.edu
REY ROMERO, Carlos ... 575-835-5675 286 D
carlos.romero@nmt.edu
REYELL, Sarah .... 518-564-5062 318 C
sarah.reyell@plattsburgh.edu
REYES, Amy, S .... 570-321-4134 388 H
reyes@lycoming.edu
REYES, Arjay, A .... 671-735-5558 503 C
arjay.reyes@guamcc.edu
REYES, Carlos .... 530-242-7760.. 64 A
creyes@shastacollege.edu
REYES, Debra .... 575-538-6174 288 J
debra.reyes@wnmu.edu
REYES, Esmeralda .... 903-586-2518 437 D
reyese27@jacksonville-college.edu
REYES, Esmeralda .... 903-586-7110 437 D
reyese27@jacksonville-college.edu
REYES, Ginger .... 805-437-8521.. 30 D
ginger.reyes@csuci.edu
REYES, Ginny .... 785-227-3380 171 H
reyesg@bethanylb.edu
REYES, Idania .... 310-660-3483.. 41 J
ireyes@elcamino.edu
REYES, Ivelisse .... 787-850-9332 511 B
ivelisse.reyes1@upr.edu
REYES, Javier .... 312-996-7000 151 D
REYES, Jean .... 305-899-3000.. 96 A
jreyes@barry.edu
REYES, Jennifer .... 201-447-7456 274 I
jreyes@bergen.edu
REYES, Jorge .... 207-454-1011 195 E
jreyes@wccc.me.edu
REYES, Joseph .... 831-755-6950.. 44 J
jreyes@hartnell.edu
REYES, Karen .... 831-479-3503.. 27 G
kareyes@cabrillo.edu
REYES, Kasie, C .... 757-683-4576 468 C
kliles@odu.edu
REYES, Kyle .... 801-863-6158 460 A
kyle.reyes@uvu.edu
REYES, Livette .... 787-894-2828 511 G
livette.reyes@upr.edu
REYES, Lorenzo .... 505-566-3742 287 G
reyesl@sanjuancollege.edu
REYES, Marcos .... 787-725-6500 504 F
mreyes@albizu.edu
REYES, Maria .... 562-985-8051.. 32 A
maria.reyes@csulb.edu
REYES, Maria .... 602-285-7434.. 13 H
maria.reyes@phoenixcollege.edu
REYES, Melissa .... 949-753-4774.. 71 D
REYES, Nora .... 480-461-7444.. 13 F
nora.reyes@mesacc.edu
REYES, Otoniel .... 203-582-3660.. 88 F
otoniel.reyes@qu.edu
REYES, Rafael .... 212-870-1213 309 C
rreyes@nyts.edu
REYES, Ray .... 619-660-4206.. 44 G
ray.reyes@gcccd.edu
REYES, Raymond .... 509-313-6550 479 E
reyes@gonzaga.edu
REYES, Robert, G .... 214-860-2664 434 A
rreyes@dcccd.edu
REYES, Rosana .... 570-740-0336 388 G
rreyes@luzerne.edu
REYES, Saul .... 352-854-2322.. 97 L
reyess@cf.edu
REYES, Tony .... 817-202-6232 444 B
treyes@swau.edu
REYES-CUBIDES,
William .... 408-288-3785.. 62 G
william.reyescubides@sjcc.edu
REYES-GIL, Yanira .... 787-751-1912 507 F
yreyes@juris.inter.edu
REYES-GUEVARA,
Yolanda .... 210-486-4195 428 A
yreyes@alamo.edu
REYES-RIVERA, Felix ..... 787-620-2040 504 B
fereyes@aupr.edu
REYMALDO, Randy .... 818-677-2128.. 32 E
randy.reynaldo@csun.edu
REYMANN, Linda .... 443-352-4203 202 C
lreymann@stevenson.edu
REYNA, Angel .... 559-675-4800.. 67 B
REYNA, Brenda .... 210-341-1366 440 B
registrar@ost.edu
REYNA, Cynthia .... 870-864-7130.. 21 C
creyna@southark.edu
REYNA, Elosia .... 806-651-0000 447 D
REYNA, Juan Carlos ..... 619-388-3132.. 60 I
jreyna001@sdccd.edu
REYNA, Oscar .... 361-825-5934 446 E
oscar.reyna@tamucc.edu
REYNARD, Betty .... 409-984-6100 449 D
betty.reynard@lamarpa.edu
REYNARD, Michelle .... 216-397-1659 353 O
mreynard@jcu.edu
REYNHOUT, Ken .... 651-641-3247 236 A
kreynhout001@luthersem.edu
REYNOLDS, Allison .... 846-208-8263 412 C
ar60@uscb.edu
REYNOLDS, Amy .... 330-672-2950 354 A
areyno24@kent.edu
REYNOLDS, Beth .... 607-274-3683 302 E
breynolds@ithaca.edu
REYNOLDS, Brad .... 706-865-2134 126 D
breynolds@truett.edu
REYNOLDS, Braden, B .. 719-333-8697 502 C
braden.reynolds@afacademy.af.edu
REYNOLDS, Burt .... 307-382-1621 500 I
breynolds@westernwyoming.edu
REYNOLDS, Chip .... 770-297-4511 121 L
creynolds@laniertech.edu
REYNOLDS, Chris .... 309-677-2670 133 H
reynolds@fsmail.bradley.edu
REYNOLDS, Clara .... 978-934-3567 211 G
clara_reynolds@uml.edu
REYNOLDS, Cristin .... 601-266-4466 248 H
cristin.reynolds@usm.edu
REYNOLDS, Curtis .... 352-392-1336 110 E
curtrey@ufl.edu
REYNOLDS, Daisy .... 214-818-1360 433 A
dreynolds@criswell.edu
REYNOLDS, Dan .... 662-325-0519 247 A
daniel.reynolds@msstate.edu
REYNOLDS, Debbie .... 530-895-2378.. 27 F
reynoldsde@butte.edu
REYNOLDS, Dennis .... 713-743-7896 451 G
der@uh.edu
REYNOLDS, Derrick .... 606-546-1272 185 B
dreynolds@unionky.edu
REYNOLDS, Diane, L ..... 804-828-3430 472 D
dlreynol@vcu.edu
REYNOLDS, Don .... 334-386-7240.... 5 D
dreynolds2@faulkner.edu
REYNOLDS, Ed .... 940-565-3000 453 B
ed.reynolds@unt.edu
REYNOLDS, Edward .... 318-670-6000 191 B
REYNOLDS,
Elizabeth, P .... 304-293-4245 489 E
liz.reynolds@mail.wvu.edu
REYNOLDS, Ellen .... 401-874-5155 404 E
ellenreynolds@uri.edu
REYNOLDS, Ellen, M ..... 401-874-1000 404 E
REYNOLDS, James .... 217-424-6208 144 D
jimreynolds@millikin.edu
REYNOLDS, James .... 708-456-0300 151 A
jimreynolds@triton.edu
REYNOLDS, Jamie .... 334-727-8011.... 7 D
jreynolds@tuskegee.edu
REYNOLDS, John .... 626-624-4673.. 50 G
REYNOLDS, Joseph .... 775-784-3226 270 E
REYNOLDS, Karen .... 727-341-3370 107 C
reynolds.karen@spcollege.edu
REYNOLDS, Karl .... 918-343-7819 369 A
kreynolds@rsu.edu
REYNOLDS, Katie .... 985-867-2284 190 I
reynoldsk@sjasc.edu
REYNOLDS, Katie .... 443-412-2190 199 B
kreynolds@harford.edu
REYNOLDS, Kayla .... 314-367-8700 260 A
kayla.reynolds@uhsp.edu
REYNOLDS, Kevin .... 859-344-3346 184 G
reynolk@thomasmore.edu
REYNOLDS, Kevin .... 503-725-3886 375 D
reynoldsk@pdx.edu
REYNOLDS, Kristin .... 269-783-2110 230 D
kreynolds02@swmich.edu
REYNOLDS, Lana .... 405-382-9200 369 E
l.reynolds@sscok.edu
REYNOLDS, Laura .... 201-692-7036 276 I
laura_reynolds@fdu.edu
REYNOLDS, Lucas .... 660-263-3900 250 G
lucasreynolds@cccb.edu
REYNOLDS, Mark, A ...... 410-706-7461 202 F
mreynolds@umaryland.edu
REYNOLDS, Marlene ...... 419-372-9824 348 F
mreyno@bgsu.edu
REYNOLDS, Mary Beth . 304-696-2987 488 N
reynoldm@marshall.edu
REYNOLDS, Matthew .... 209-478-0800.. 45 L
REYNOLDS, Michael ..... 704-233-8252 344 E
m.reynolds@wingate.edu
REYNOLDS, Michael, C 334-844-4367.... 4 E
reynom2@auburn.edu
REYNOLDS, Michaela ... 325-942-2335 450 B
0295mgr@follett.com
REYNOLDS, Michelle ..... 410-951-3939 203 E
mreynolds@coppin.edu
REYNOLDS, Michelle ..... 573-840-9077 259 I
michellereynolds@trcc.edu
REYNOLDS, Nancy, W .. 270-686-4244 179 F
nancy.reynolds@brescia.edu
REYNOLDS, Phillip .... 334-699-2266.... 1 B
preynolds@acom.edu
REYNOLDS, Randall .... 615-460-6443 417 B
randall.reynolds@belmont.edu
REYNOLDS, Russell .... 585-385-8025 313 A
rreynolds@sjfc.edu
REYNOLDS, Sean, B ...... 847-491-7326 146 C
sean.reynolds@northwestern.edu
REYNOLDS, Sharon, S .. 606-783-2527 183 H
sb.reynolds@moreheadstate.edu
REYNOLDS,
Stephanie, C .... 315-792-5456 306 G
sreynolds@mvcc.edu
REYNOLDS, Thomas ...... 318-357-4577 192 D
reynoldst@nsula.edu
REYNOLDS, Thomas ...... 440-525-7064 354 L
treynolds17@lakelandcc.edu
REYNOLDS, Thomas, L . 704-687-7248 342 C
tlreynol@uncc.edu
REYNOLDS, Tiffany .... 239-590-1005 109 G
treynold@fgcu.edu
REYNOLDS, Torry .... 336-757-7478 334 D
treynolds@forsythtech.edu
REYNOLDS, Travis .... 308-865-8308 268 J
reynoldstj@unk.edu
REYNOLDS-CASPER,
ReGina .... 620-792-9364 171 F
reynoldsr@bartonccc.edu
REYNOLDS-STUMP,
Krista .... 518-262-2929 289 C
reynolk1@amc.edu
REYNOLDSON, Jason ... 712-274-5116 168 C
reynoldsonj@morningside.edu
REYNOSO, Bernardo ..... 559-442-4600.. 67 A
bernardo.reynoso@fresnocitycollege.
edu
REYNOSO, Ivan .... 213-427-2200.. 35 L
REZA, Fawzia .... 800-280-0307 153 B
fawzia.reza@ace.edu
REZAC, Barb .... 605-668-1292 414 F
barbara.rezac@mountmarty.edu
REZAEI, Roksana .... 801-832-2003 461 A
rrezaei@westminstercollege.edu
REZAIE, Jaleh .... 919-530-7395 341 D
jrezaie@nccu.edu
REZAK, Mary .... 509-335-5593 484 D
mary.rezak@wsu.edu
REZEK, Jon .... 252-328-1936 340 H
rezekjo17@ecu.edu
REZENDES, Elizabeth .... 203-932-7131.. 89 F
erezendes@newhaven.edu
REZENDES, Robert .... 508-678-2811 213 F
robert.rezendes@bristolcc.edu
REZENE, Deborah .... 503-255-0332 374 A
deborahrezene@multnomah.edu
RHAMES, Ronald .... 803-738-7600 409 E
rhamesr@midlandstech.edu
RHEA, Amanda .... 704-978-4441 335 I
ahrea@mitchellcc.edu
RHEA, Kai .... 504-520-5839 193 C
krhea1@xula.edu
RHEA, Kenneth .... 585-389-2606 307 D
krhee9@naz.edu
RHEA, Kristy, K .... 540-828-5471 464 C
krhea@bridgewater.edu
RHEAD, Lori .... 608-363-2630 490 I
rheadl@beloit.edu
RHEAULT, Wendy .... 847-578-3238 148 B
wendy.rheault@rosalindfranklin.edu
RHEAUME, Steve .... 603-535-2266 274 B
srheaume@plymouth.edu
RHEE, Edmund, K .... 678-535-7771 118 F
dredkrhee@gcuniv.edu
RHEE, Jinny .... 562-985-1512.. 32 A
jinny.rhee@csulb.edu
RHEE, Kenneth .... 978-837-5000 216 D
RHEE, Michael .... 212-431-2893 308 I
michael.rhee@nyls.edu
RHEE, Thomas .... 703-629-1281 472 C
president@vacu.edu
RHEIN, John .... 610-430-4163 394 F
jrhein@wcupa.edu
RHEINECKER, Connie ... 704-216-3485 337 C
connie.rheinecker@rccc.edu
RHEINECKER, Matthew . 734-432-5832 226 G
mrheinecker@madonna.edu
RHI-KLEINERT, Susan ... 818-710-2289.. 49 H
rhiks@piercecollege.edu
RHIE, Suok .... 714-525-0088.. 44 C
cfo@gm.edu
RHIM, Chonhee .... 323-265-8625.. 49 D
rhimcl@elac.edu
RHINE, Christine .... 610-647-4400 385 K
crhine@immaculata.edu
RHINE, Lisa .... 928-445-7300.. 17 B
lisa.rhine@yc.edu
RHINE, Randy .... 308-432-6201 267 G
rrhine@csc.edu
RHINIER, William .... 717-947-6181 392 R
wrhinier2@pacollege.edu
RHOADES, Dena .... 661-336-5141.. 47 A
drhoades@kccd.edu
RHOADES, Jeff .... 419-448-2977 353 D
jrhoade1@heidelberg.edu
RHOADES, Jeffrey .... 707-527-4811.. 63 C
jrhoades@santarosa.edu
RHOADES, IV, Mack ...... 254-710-1234 430 F
mack_rhoadesiv@baylor.edu
RHOADES, Margot .... 704-461-6733 326 I
margotrhoades@bac.edu
RHOADS, Jeffrey .... 480-461-7565.. 13 F
jeffrey.rhoads@mesacc.edu
RHOADS, Troy .... 309-298-1834 152 I
te-rhoads@wiu.edu
RHODA, Christopher ..... 207-859-1124 196 A
chris@thomas.edu
RHODE, Carolyn .... 336-506-4128 331 J
carolyn.rhode@alamancecc.edu
RHODEN, Brenda .... 256-761-6204.... 7 B
brhoden@talladega.edu
RHODEN, Deborah .... 256-840-4137.... 3 F
deborah.rhoden@snead.edu
RHODEN, Rob .... 757-826-1883 463 J
rrhoden@ascent.edu
RHODES, Anthony, P .... 212-592-2071 314 I
tonyrhodes@sva.edu
RHODES, II,
C. Edwards .... 601-877-6138 244 B
crhodes@alcorn.edu
RHODES, Courtenay ...... 813-253-6230 113 B
RHODES, David .... 217-424-6340 144 D
djrhodes@millikin.edu
RHODES, David .... 570-945-8112 386 F
david.rhodes@keystone.edu
RHODES, David, J .... 212-592-2350 314 I
drhodes@sva.edu
RHODES, Dawn, M .... 410-706-2802 202 F
drhodes@umaryland.edu
RHODES, Heather .... 281-459-7106 442 D
heather.rhodes@sjcd.edu
RHODES, Jason, F .... 410-543-6031 204 A
jfrhodes@salisbury.edu
RHODES, Jennifer .... 425-388-9509 479 B
jrhodes@everettcc.edu
RHODES, John .... 410-225-2201 200 B
jrhodes@mica.edu
RHODES, Karen .... 864-578-8770 410 G
krhodes@sherman.edu
RHODES, Kathy .... 206-934-3796 482 F
kathy.rhodes@seattlecolleges.edu
RHODES, Lisa .... 714-620-1005.. 40 A
lrhodes@concorde.edu
RHODES, Lisa .... 601-766-6422 246 F
lisa.rhodes@mgccc.edu
RHODES, Michelle .... 616-331-3234 224 D
rhodesmi@gvsu.edu
RHODES, Myki .... 618-235-2700 150 B
myki.rhodes@swic.edu

RHODES, Neisha 209-667-3201 33 D
nrhodes@csustan.edu
RHODES, Quent 585-292-2804 306 K
qrhodes@monroecc.edu
RHODES, Rhosetta 509-777-4536 485 D
rrhodes@whitworth.edu
RHODES, Richard, M 512-223-7598 429 J
rrhodes@austincc.edu
RHODES, Robert 325-674-2024 427 G
rlr12a@acu.edu
RHODES, Tammy 256-765-4100 8 E
tdrhodes@una.edu
RHODES, Tim 606-783-2000 183 H
t.rhodes@moreheadstate.edu
RHODES, Tim 405-325-4122 370 J
timrhodes@ou.edu
RHODES, Valerie 972-708-7340 434 F
RHODES, Vincent, A 757-446-7070 465 H
rhodesva@evms.edu
RHODIN, Benjamin 201-200-3156 278 F
brhodin@njcu.edu
RHONEMUS, Sarita, A 304-327-4334 488 J
sarhonemus@bluefieldstate.edu
RHORER, Maile 660-248-6651 250 H
mrhorer@centralmethodist.edu
RHUE, Monika 704-371-6741 329 H
mrhue@jcsu.edu
RHUE, Phanalphie 336-273-4431 326 J
phanalphie.rhue@bennett.edu
RHYAND, Matt 614-236-6011 348 I
RHYNE, Teresa, L 757-455-3345 476 C
trhyne@vwu.edu
RHYNE, Whitney 239-433-6943 100 G
whitney.rhyne@fsw.edu
RHYNEDANCE, George 516-726-6048 502 G
rhynedanceg@usmma.edu
RHYNER, Robyn 315-786-2350 302 I
rrhyner@sunyjefferson.edu
RHYNHART, Hans 860-486-4806 89 B
hans.rhynhart@uconn.edu
RHYNHOLD, Daniel 646-592-6370 325 R
rhynhold@yu.edu
RIAL, Scott 847-543-2652 135 G
srial@clcillinois.edu
RIANO, Alexa 201-360-4002 277 D
ariano@hccc.edu
RIBAKOW, Larry 443-548-6056 201 B
lribakow@nirc.edu
RIBAUDO, Anthony 773-252-6464 146 D
RIBBLE, Jared 505-387-7490 286 B
jribble@navajotech.edu
RIBEIRO, Solange 612-767-7055 233 E
solange.ribeiro@alfredadler.edu
RIBELIN, David 803-778-7858 406 A
ribelindt@cctech.edu
RIBINSON, Gregory 615-963-5000 425 A
RIBNER, Jason 503-917-5005 374 B
jribner@nunm.edu
RICAFRENTE, Tina 619-876-4250 68 J
tricafrente@usuniversity.edu
RICARDI, Richard 508-849-3367 205 E
rricardi@annamaria.edu
RICARDINO CSAPO,
Jorge 303-273-3503 79 A
ycsapo@mines.edu
RICCA, Beth 201-684-7455 280 B
bricca@ramapo.edu
RICCA, Beth, M 732-571-3580 278 B
bricca@monmouth.edu
RICCARDI, Mark, T 304-724-3700 485 G
mriccardi@apus.edu
RICCI, Heidi 763-488-2549 237 G
heidi.ricci@hennepintech.edu
RICCI, Micheal 508-213-2277 217 C
michael.ricci@nichols.edu
RICCIARDI, Jennifer, H 617-573-8470 218 G
jricciardi@suffolk.edu
RICCOBONO, Steve 718-636-3787 311 A
sriccobo@pratt.edu
RICE, Adrian 212-410-8429 308 D
arice@nycpm.edu
RICE, Alaina, M 620-417-1061 177 C
alaina.rice@sccc.edu
RICE, Amy 208-467-8609 132 B
arice@nnu.edu
RICE, Angela 434-592-6327 467 E
amrice3@liberty.edu
RICE, Becca 765-285-1147 153 E
rapolcz@bsu.edu
RICE, Billie Jo 661-395-4936 47 B
brice@bakersfieldcollege.edu
RICE, Brian 937-393-3431 360 G
brice@sscc.edu
RICE, Carolyn 828-398-7105 331 K
carolynhrice@abtech.edu
RICE, Chris 504-865-3579 190 A
crice@loyno.edu
RICE, Condoleezza 650-723-2300 66 D
RICE, Cynthia, E 410-706-3171 202 F
crice@umaryland.edu
RICE, Deborah 707-826-5135 30 A
deborah.rice@humboldt.edu
RICE, Edward 870-574-4504 21 F
erice@sautech.edu
RICE, Fred 920-924-3291 498 C
frice@morainepark.edu
RICE, Gale 314-889-1479 252 G
grice@fontbonne.edu
RICE, Heather 256-228-6001 3 B
riceh@nacc.edu
RICE, James, W 320-222-7474 239 H
jim.rice@ridgewater.edu
RICE, Jennifer, K 301-405-5252 202 E
jkr@umd.edu
RICE, Jonah 618-252-5400 149 E
jonah.rice@sic.edu
RICE, Josh 423-648-6129 422 D
jrice@richmont.edu
RICE, Josh 404-835-6129 422 D
jrice@richmont.edu
RICE, Julie 317-299-0333 161 B
julie@tcmi.org
RICE, Kathy 740-389-4636 355 F
ricek@mtc.edu
RICE, Kevin 585-395-2408 317 B
krice@brockport.edu
RICE, Larry 918-343-7612 369 A
lrice@rsu.edu
RICE, Laura 626-316-5351 63 D
lrice1@saybrook.edu
RICE, Leah, B 859-846-5308 183 G
lbarth@midway.edu
RICE, Leila 978-837-5997 216 D
ricelc@merrimack.edu
RICE, Louisa 715-836-5276 494 E
ricelc@uwec.edu
RICE, Malcolm 256-824-2613 8 B
malcolm.rice@uah.edu
RICE, Martin 765-677-2939 157 F
martin.rice@indwes.edu
RICE, Monica 620-242-0432 175 G
ricem@mcpherson.edu
RICE, Peter 201-684-7500 280 B
price@ramapo.edu
RICE, Priscilla 215-968-8450 379 B
priscilla.rice@bucks.edu
RICE, Rachel 207-768-9447 196 I
rachel.rice@maine.edu
RICE, Raymond, J 207-768-9525 196 I
raymond.rice@maine.edu
RICE, Rolondus, R 662-252-8000 248 B
rrice@rustcollege.edu
RICE, Scott 217-333-0560 151 F
serice@uillinois.edu
RICE, Sherwin 910-879-5646 332 B
srice@bladencc.edu
RICE, Vance 662-325-6731 247 A
mvr50@msstate.edu
RICE, Whit 256-352-8406 4 A
whit.rice@wallacestate.edu
RICE-SPEARMAN, Lori 806-743-2900 450 D
lori.ricespearman@ttuhsc.edu
RICELLI, Iliana 901-333-5000 424 E
iricelli@southwest.tn.edu
RICH, Andrew 212-650-5967 293 B
arich@ccny.cuny.edu
RICH, Carson, D 252-335-3229 341 A
cdrich@ecsu.edu
RICH, Frank 432-335-6507 440 C
frich@odessa.edu
RICH, Jason 518-783-2302 314 K
jrich@siena.edu
RICH, Jeffrey 808-544-0200 128 E
RICH, Julie 801-626-6232 460 B
jrich@weber.edu
RICH, Kathy 781-280-3501 214 G
richk@middlesex.mass.edu
RICH, Laura 910-893-4364 327 C
richl@campbell.edu
RICH, Marcus 252-985-5176 339 B
mritch@ncwc.edu
RICH, Robbie 706-379-3111 128 A
crich@yhc.edu
RICH, Scott 620-278-4213 177 E
srich@sterling.edu
RICH, Steven 617-236-8800 209 D
srich@fisher.edu
RICH, Teresa 509-574-4667 485 E
thollandrich@yvcc.edu
RICH, Trena 909-623-6116 75 G
trich@westernu.edu
RICH, Virginia 973-618-3516 275 E
vrich@caldwell.edu
RICH, Wendall 801-626-7443 460 B
wrich@weber.edu
RICH FREDERICKS,
Jacquie 970-351-2399 84 D
RICHARD, Ann-Marie 212-517-2771 315 B
a.richard@sia.edu
RICHARD, Daryl 203-582-8651 88 F
daryl.richard@quinnipiac.edu
RICHARD, Deborah 407-708-2487 108 B
richardd@seminolestate.edu
RICHARD, Guy 770-852-8884 248 A
grichard@rts.edu
RICHARD, Mark 205-665-6612 8 D
mrichard11@montevallo.edu
RICHARD, Mark 256-840-4110 3 F
mark.richard@snead.edu
RICHARD, Patricia 775-784-4805 270 K
prichard@unr.edu
RICHARD, Reed 409-984-6252 449 D
richardrj@lamarpa.edu
RICHARD, Renee 216-987-4865 351 D
renee.richard@tri-c.edu
RICHARD, Robert 337-482-6923 192 F
bookstore@louisiana.edu
RICHARD, Ryan, W 318-257-3693 192 A
richard@latech.edu
RICHARD, Stephen 757-446-7165 465 H
richarsw@evms.edu
RICHARD, Travis 336-334-7973 341 C
tarichard1@ncat.edu
RICHARD, Valerie 704-403-3507 327 B
valerie.richard@atriumhealth.org
RICHARDS, Caroline, B 404-880-6146 116 I
crichards@cau.edu
RICHARDS, Chris 207-561-1619 196 D
christopher.michael.richards@maine.edu
RICHARDS, David 559-453-7195 43 D
david.richards@fresno.edu
RICHARDS, David, E 402-554-2640 269 C
derichards@unomaha.edu
RICHARDS, Debbie 304-424-8201 490 A
debbie.richards@wvup.edu
RICHARDS, Debra 480-212-1704 15 R
RICHARDS, Faith 605-455-6029 414 H
frichards@olc.edu
RICHARDS, Geoffrey 512-499-4336 454 A
grichards@utsystem.edu
RICHARDS, Heraldo 615-963-5620 425 A
hrichards@tnstate.edu
RICHARDS, Jeremy 503-883-2259 373 E
jrichards2@linfield.edu
RICHARDS, Jerry 920-924-3184 498 C
jrichards2@morainepark.edu
RICHARDS, Joe 330-494-6170 360 I
jrichards@starkstate.edu
RICHARDS, John 808-734-9518 129 E
john.richards@hawaii.edu
RICHARDS, Kathy, A 906-227-1237 228 E
kathrich@nmu.edu
RICHARDS, Katie, J 701-788-4675 345 B
katie.richards.2@mayvillestate.edu
RICHARDS, Lee 740-362-3344 355 H
lrichards@mtso.edu
RICHARDS, Lisa 508-565-1085 218 F
lrichards@stonehill.edu
RICHARDS, Lois, M 561-683-1400 94 F
admin@anho.edu
RICHARDS, Mandy 770-533-7012 121 L
mrichards@laniertech.edu
RICHARDS, Marilyn 919-546-8529 339 I
marilyn.richards@shawu.edu
RICHARDS, Mark 206-543-7632 484 A
provost@uw.edu
RICHARDS, Mark, A 801-524-8107 458 F
mrichards@ldsbc.edu
RICHARDS, Marvin 805-969-3626 55 I
mrichards@pacifica.edu
RICHARDS, Maryanne 508-830-5039 213 A
mrichards@maritime.edu
RICHARDS, Matthew 207-741-5927 195 D
mrichards@smccme.edu
RICHARDS, Melissa 315-859-4019 300 F
mfrichar@hamilton.edu
RICHARDS, Michael 505-272-1175 288 C
mrichards@salud.unm.edu
RICHARDS, Michael, J 515-281-3934 163 D
RICHARDS, Michelle 801-618-0438 458 H
mrichards@ameritech.edu
RICHARDS, Patricia 706-542-2846 126 F
plr333@uga.edu
RICHARDS, Paula 559-297-4500 46 C
prichards@iot.edu
RICHARDS, Rashna 901-843-2430 422 C
richardr@rhodes.edu
RICHARDS, Regina 303-556-2400 84 B
RICHARDS, Rosalie 386-822-7256 111 F
rrichar1@stetson.edu
RICHARDS, Rosann 973-353-5943 281 C
rcarey@newark.rutgers.edu
RICHARDS, Samantha 843-574-6771 411 I
samantha.richards@tridenttech.edu
RICHARDS, Sandra, K 800-328-2660 95 P
skrichards@baptistcollege.edu
RICHARDS, Scott 412-396-5140 382 E
richards@duq.edu
RICHARDS, Seth 732-987-2541 277 B
srichards@georgian.edu
RICHARDS, Steve 320-762-4692 236 G
stever@alextech.edu
RICHARDS, Steven, N 540-863-2880 473 D
srichards@mgcc.edu
RICHARDS, Terri 386-738-6682 111 F
trichard@stetson.edu
RICHARDS, Terry 410-837-4772 204 C
trichards@ubalt.edu
RICHARDS, Tom, F 573-882-2612 260 B
richardstf@umsystem.edu
RICHARDS, Tracey 610-799-1779 388 B
trichards1@lccc.edu
RICHARDS, Troy 212-217-7665 299 C
troy_richards@fitnyc.edu
RICHARDS, Virginia 925-473-1350 40 I
vrichards@losmedanos.edu
RICHARDS, Virginia 317-805-1783 486 I
vrichards@salemu.edu
RICHARDS, Wendi 207-509-7100 196 B
RICHARDSON, Aaron 601-979-3704 245 G
aaron.richardson@jsums.edu
RICHARDSON,
Andre, S 903-730-4890 437 E
arichardson@jarvis.edu
RICHARDSON, Andrea 334-285-5177 2 F
andrea.richardson@istc.edu
RICHARDSON, Ann 206-934-4567 482 F
ann.richardson@seattlecolleges.edu
RICHARDSON,
Antoine, D 816-333-1577 250 F
RICHARDSON, Autumn 256-766-6610 5 F
arichardson@hcu.edu
RICHARDSON, Barbara 520-586-1981 11 O
richardsonbarbara@cochise.edu
RICHARDSON,
Belinda, M 724-287-8711 379 C
belinda.richardson@bc3.edu
RICHARDSON,
Bernard, L 202-806-7280 92 E
brichardson@howard.edu
RICHARDSON, Beverly 501-375-9845 21 A
brichardson@philander.edu
RICHARDSON, Bonita L 412-237-4413 381 C
brichardson@ccac.edu
RICHARDSON, Brenda 912-478-4636 120 A
brendarichardson@georgiasouthern.edu
RICHARDSON, Brittany 504-816-4797 186 F
brichardson@dillard.edu
RICHARDSON, Casie 270-824-8575 182 A
casie.richardson@kctcs.edu
RICHARDSON, Charles 256-372-5092 1 A
charles.richardson@aamu.edu
RICHARDSON,
Christopher 804-355-0671 470 I
crichardson@upsem.edu
RICHARDSON, Cinzia 973-720-2976 283 I
richardsonc@wpunj.edu
RICHARDSON, Dale 636-481-3501 253 G
drichar6@jeffco.edu
RICHARDSON, David 256-726-7398 6 C
drichardson@oakwood.edu
RICHARDSON, David, E 352-392-0780 110 E
der@ufl.edu
RICHARDSON, Dawn, J 972-377-1015 432 I
drichardson@collin.edu
RICHARDSON, Debra 406-683-7530 263 E
debra.richardson@umwestern.edu
RICHARDSON, Denise 510-531-4911 57 C
drichardson@peralta.edu

RICHARDSON, Edie .... 830-372-8016 448 C
erichardson@tlu.edu
RICHARDSON, Elizabeth .... 570-422-3139 393 F
erichard10@esu.edu
RICHARDSON, Ellis .... 413-236-1011 213 E
erichardson@berkshirecc.edu
RICHARDSON, Erica ...... 903-675-6371 451 C
erica.richardson@tvcc.edu
RICHARDSON, Florence 301-295-3045 502 B
florence.richardson@usuhs.edu
RICHARDSON, Gary ...... 712-707-7052 169 A
gary.richardson@nwciowa.edu
RICHARDSON, Greer ..... 215-951-1806 386 I
richards@lasalle.edu
RICHARDSON, Greg, C . 606-474-3250 180 G
greg@kcu.edu
RICHARDSON, Guy, L ... 601-923-1650 248 A
grichardson@rts.edu
RICHARDSON, James .... 509-682-6400 484 H
jrichardson@wvc.edu
RICHARDSON, Jane ...... 207-236-8581 195 H
RICHARDSON, Jennifer . 518-454-2023 296 E
richardj@strose.edu
RICHARDSON, Jim .... 575-624-7443 285 F
jim.richardson@roswell.enmu.edu
RICHARDSON, John ...... 706-771-4111 115 H
jhrichar@augustatech.edu
RICHARDSON, Josiah ... 907-745-3201.... 9 C
RICHARDSON, Julie ...... 813-259-6586 102 A
jrichardson58@hccfl.edu
RICHARDSON, Julie ...... 413-782-3111 219 E
julie.richardson@wne.edu
RICHARDSON, K. Scott . 724-287-8711 379 C
scott.richardson@bc3.edu
RICHARDSON, Karen ..... 609-258-6150 279 E
karenr@princeton.edu
RICHARDSON, Kathy, B 724-946-7130 401 F
richarkb@westminster.edu
RICHARDSON, Keith ..... 215-646-7300 384 G
richardson.k@gmercyu.edu
RICHARDSON, Krista .... 419-995-8312 360 B
richardson.k@rhodesstate.edu
RICHARDSON, L. Song . 719-389-6700.. 78 E
RICHARDSON, Lara, K .. 803-938-3890 412 G
painterl@uscsumter.edu
RICHARDSON, Lisa, A .. 727-816-3404 105 E
richarl@phsc.edu
RICHARDSON, Lyneene 515-643-6659 168 B
lrichardson@mercydesmoines.org
RICHARDSON, Lynne ..... 914-633-2256 302 C
lrichardson@iona.edu
RICHARDSON, Mary ..... 229-430-3588 114 G
mrichardson@albanytech.edu
RICHARDSON, Matthew 304-293-0111 489 E
m.richardson@mail.wvu.edu
RICHARDSON, Melanie . 360-438-4367 482 D
mrichardson@stmartin.edu
RICHARDSON, Melissa . 503-594-3300 372 B
melissa.richardson@clackamas.edu
RICHARDSON, Nicholas 718-420-4124 324 B
nrichard@wagner.edu
RICHARDSON, Ray .... 253-680-7000 477 A
RICHARDSON, Raymond .... 806-720-7230 438 F
raymond.richardson@lcu.edu
RICHARDSON, Rebecca 707-545-3647.. 27 A
becca@berginu.edu
RICHARDSON, Robert ... 317-955-6789 159 A
rrichardson@marian.edu
RICHARDSON, Robin ..... 401-232-6000 403 B
rarich@bryant.edu
RICHARDSON, Sarah, D .... 402-280-2703 265 J
sarahrichardson@creighton.edu
RICHARDSON, Sarah Catherine .... 931-424-4073 426 F
scrich@utsouthern.edu
RICHARDSON, Scott ..... 607-587-3992 319 C
richarsa@alfredstate.edu
RICHARDSON, Stephen . 312-329-4243 144 F
stephen.richardson@moody.edu
RICHARDSON, Steven ... 801-626-6001 460 B
stevenrichardson1@weber.edu
RICHARDSON, Sydney .. 336-734-7764 334 D
srichardson@forsythtech.edu
RICHARDSON, Tammi ... 660-263-4100 256 D
tamerarichardson@macc.edu
RICHARDSON, TaNeal ... 432-264-5072 436 H
trichardson@howardcollege.edu
RICHARDSON, Ted .... 865-251-1800 422 G
trichardson@south.edu
RICHARDSON, Terry ..... 276-944-6231 466 F
trichard@ehc.edu
RICHARDSON, Theodore .... 321-674-8123 100 A
trichardson@fit.edu
RICHARDSON, Thomas, J .... 717-871-7085 394 B
tom.richardson@millersville.edu
RICHARDSON, Timothy . 281-283-3044 452 A
richardsont@uhcl.edu
RICHARDSON, Todd ..... 812-855-2239 156 C
ctr@iu.edu
RICHARDSON, Vanessa 575-674-2396 284 P
vrichardson@burrell.edu
RICHARDSON, Victoria . 256-469-7333.... 5 I
librn@hbc1.edu
RICHARDSON, William "Rusty" .... 615-547-1257 418 C
rrichardson@cumberland.edu
RICHARDSON-DEAN, Tonya .... 903-670-2615 451 C
tonya.dean@tvcc.edu
RICHARDSON-ECHOLS, Mya .... 678-466-5478 117 A
tomiiyarichardson@clayton.edu
RICHART, Maria .... 585-475-5479 312 A
mjroce@rit.edu
RICHE, Cindy .... 206-934-3930 482 F
cindy.riche@seattlecolleges.edu
RICHE, Cindy .... 206-934-3930 482 E
cindy.riche@seattlecolleges.edu
RICHERSON, Melissa .... 805-546-3129.. 41 A
melissa_richerson@cuesta.edu
RICHES, Jonathan, S .... 610-292-9852 396 C
jonathan.riches@reseminary.edu
RICHEY, Angie .... 909-599-5433.. 48 E
arichey@lifepacific.edu
RICHEY, Anthony .... 334-244-3571.... 4 F
arichey@aum.edu
RICHEY, Barbara .... 509-359-7099 478 H
brichey@ewu.edu
RICHEY, Deborah .... 518-629-4552 302 A
d.richey@hvcc.edu
RICHEY, James, H .... 321-433-7000.. 98 F
richeyj@easternflorida.edu
RICHEY, Jim .... 903-510-2468 451 D
jric@tjc.edu
RICHEY, Lance, B .... 260-399-7700 162 A
lrichey@sf.edu
RICHEY, Patrick .... 585-389-2020 307 D
prichey1@naz.edu
RICHIE, Darren .... 863-638-2953 113 E
richieda@webber.edu
RICHIE, Darren .... 803-754-4100 407 F
RICHIE, Natalie .... 360-442-2500 480 E
nrichie@lowercolumbia.edu
RICHMAN, Aaron .... 231-773-9131 228 C
RICHMAN, Erin .... 904-256-6984 101 A
erin.richman@fscj.edu
RICHMAN, Lawrence ..... 916-339-7371.. 53 C
RICHMAN, Susan .... 781-891-2660 206 C
srichman@bentley.edu
RICHMOND, Jayne, E .... 401-874-5505 404 E
jrichmond@uri.edu
RICHMOND, John, W ... 940-565-4092 453 B
john.richmond@unt.edu
RICHMOND, Kenyetta ... 336-757-7242 334 D
krichmond@forsythtech.edu
RICHMOND, Kerry .... 570-321-4202 388 H
richmond@lycoming.edu
RICHMOND, LÆTanya, B .... 413-585-4940 218 D
lrichmon@smith.edu
RICHMOND, Michael .... 209-946-2777.. 71 E
mrichmond@pacific.edu
RICHMOND, Michael .... 425-739-8428 480 D
michael.richmond@lwtech.edu
RICHMOND, Nicola ...... 520-206-4414.. 15 E
ncrichmond@pima.edu
RICHMOND, Peggy .... 603-358-2273 274 A
mrichmon@keene.edu
RICHMOND, Randale ..... 330-672-3120 354 A
rrichmo2@kent.edu
RICHMOND, Sevanna .... 866-323-0233.. 58 D
RICHNER, Gabriel .... 417-862-9533 252 H
RICHTER, Carmen .... 256-765-5215.... 8 E
crichter@una.edu
RICHTER, Jeffrey .... 610-282-1100 382 A
jeff.richter@desales.edu
RICHTER, Jerome, J ...... 701-355-8072 347 A
jjrichter@umary.edu
RICHTER, Sheila, W ...... 814-824-2287 389 E
srichter@mercyhurst.edu
RICHTERMEYER, Sandra .... 978-934-2850 211 G
sandra_richtermeyer@uml.edu
RICHTMAN, Meg .... 319-385-6212 167 F
meg.richtman@iw.edu
RICK, Adam .... 517-607-2645 224 G
arick@hillsdale.edu
RICK, Jennifer .... 216-397-1905 353 O
jrick@jcu.edu
RICKARD, Keilan .... 404-727-7457 118 D
grickar@emory.edu
RICKARD, Walter .... 718-636-3771 311 A
wrickard@pratt.edu
RICKARDS, Brenden .... 856-415-2106 280 F
brickar1@rcsj.edu
RICKARDS, Laura .... 732-255-0400 279 A
lrickards@ocean.edu
RICKEL, Brian .... 916-691-7171.. 50 K
rickelb@crc.losrios.edu
RICKELS, Clarissa .... 541-888-2525 376 B
clarissa.rickels@socc.edu
RICKENBACKER, Millicent .... 903-593-8311 448 A
mrickenbacker@texascollege.edu
RICKENBAKER, Monique .... 803-705-4655 405 G
monique.rickenbaker@benedict.edu
RICKENBERG, Cassie .... 419-267-1319 357 E
crickenberg@northweststate.edu
RICKENBERG, Jason ..... 419-267-1258 357 E
jrickenberg@northweststate.edu
RICKER, Charlie .... 812-877-8470 160 C
ricker@rose-hulman.edu
RICKER, Deborah .... 301-696-3623 199 C
ricker@hood.edu
RICKER, Frances .... 303-369-5151.. 82 H
fran.ricker@plattcolorado.edu
RICKER, Jean .... 781-292-2343 209 E
jean.ricker@olin.edu
RICKER-GILBERT, Alexander .... 904-256-7401 102 G
aricker1@ju.edu
RICKERT, Benjamin .... 828-694-1860 332 C
b.rickert@blueridge.edu
RICKERT, Christina .... 715-346-0123 496 B
RICKETT, R. Brian .... 501-422-4042 250 C
brickett@brookes.edu
RICKETTS, Lloyd .... 609-771-2186 275 J
ricketts@tcnj.edu
RICKETTS, Nsombi, B ... 718-687-5350 311 A
nrickett@pratt.edu
RICKEY, Ron .... 413-254-2520 208 B
rickeyron@elms.edu
RICKLES, Jeff .... 601-968-8875 244 C
jrickles@belhaven.edu
RICKMAN, Blake .... 479-788-7029.. 22 A
blake.rickman@uafs.edu
RICKMAN, Richard .... 229-333-5886 127 C
RICKS, Chris .... 757-569-6722 474 A
cricks@pdc.edu
RICKS, Melissa, K .... 479-248-7236.. 19 F
mricks@ecollege.edu
RICKS, Naima, K .... 973-290-4219 282 G
nricks@steu.edu
RICKS, Ruchelle .... 252-862-1246 336 H
rricks@roanokechowan.edu
RICKSECKEER, Anne .... 575-439-3717 286 H
anricks@nmsu.edu
RICKUS, Jenna .... 765-494-4600 159 G
RICO, Camilla .... 360-417-6442 481 F
crico@pencol.edu
RICO, Debra .... 413-737-7000 205 C
RICO, Jorge .... 817-202-6400 444 B
ricoj@swau.edu
RICO-GUTIERREZ, Luis, C .... 515-294-7427 163 E
lrico@iastate.edu
RICORDATI, Timothy ..... 630-617-3089 137 E
timothy.ricordati@elmhurst.edu
RICZKER, Nickey .... 716-338-1035 302 G
nickeyriczker@mail.sunyjcc.edu
RICZKER, Nicolette .... 716-338-1035 302 G
nickeyriczker@mail.sunyjcc.edu
RIDD-YOUNG, Kristi ..... 866-680-2756 458 I
president@midwifery.edu
RIDDELL, William .... 209-476-7840.. 67 D
w.riddell@clc.edu
RIDDELL, William .... 209-476-7840.. 67 D
wriddell@clc.edu
RIDDICK, Althea, A .... 252-335-8787 341 A
aariddick@ecsu.edu
RIDDICK, Iman .... 202-462-2101.. 93 A
iriddick@iwp.edu
RIDDICK, Rich .... 308-635-6067 269 E
riddickr@wncc.edu
RIDDICK, Romy .... 609-258-3000 279 E
RIDDICK, Vera, E .... 757-683-3689 468 C
vriddick@odu.edu
RIDDLE, Alan .... 716-375-2068 312 F
ariddle@sbu.edu
RIDDLE, Brian, T .... 724-589-2130 398 F
briddle@thiel.edu
RIDDLE, Catherine .... 518-262-3593 289 C
riddlec@amc.edu
RIDDLE, Christy .... 662-846-4336 245 A
criddle@deltastate.edu
RIDDLE, Joyce, E .... 304-462-6184 488 M
joyce.riddle@glenville.edu
RIDDLE, Kelley .... 575-538-6513 288 J
kelley.riddle@wnmu.edu
RIDDLE, Laura .... 601-276-2000 248 D
RIDDLE, Laura .... 870-633-4480.. 19 E
lriddle@eacc.edu
RIDDLE, Tiffany .... 509-777-4542 485 D
triddle@whitworth.edu
RIDEAUX, JR., Laarry ... 816-604-3044 255 A
larry.rideaux@mcckc.edu
RIDEAUX, Larry .... 816-604-3046 254 E
larry.rideaux@mcckc.edu
RIDEN, Ronda .... 918-338-8000 369 A
rriden@rsu.edu
RIDENER, Barbara .... 908-737-5326 277 F
bridener@kean.edu
RIDENOUR, Nancy .... 314-362-6289 253 A
nancy.ridenour@barnesjewishcollege.edu
RIDEOUT, Junior .... 910-879-5661 332 B
jrideout@bladencc.edu
RIDEOUT, Kathy .... 585-275-8902 323 E
kathy_rideout@urmc.rochester.edu
RIDER, Abigail .... 401-874-2433 404 E
arider@uri.edu
RIDER, David, R .... 201-200-2070 278 F
drider@njcu.edu
RIDER, Elizabeth, A ...... 717-361-1193 383 B
president@etown.edu
RIDER, Jeff .... 870-759-4194.. 24 B
jrider@williamsbu.edu
RIDER, Pamela, S .... 605-342-0317 414 C
registrar@jwc.edu
RIDER, Paul .... 515-263-2917 166 C
prider@grandview.edu
RIDGE, Matthew .... 336-249-8186 333 G
mridge5374@davidsondavie.edu
RIDGE, Sean .... 865-573-4517 419 E
sridge@johnsonu.edu
RIDGEDELL, Ken, W .... 985-549-3856 192 E
kridgedell@selu.edu
RIDGES, Jarvis .... 404-270-5003 126 A
jarvis.ridges@spelman.edu
RIDGEWAY-HAGERMAN, Melissa .... 815-965-8616 147 I
RIDGWAY, Dan .... 216-649-7525 354 A
dridgway@kent.edu
RIDGWAY, Kristi .... 650-574-6161.. 62 J
RIDGWAY, Timothy .... 605-357-1309 415 E
med@usd.edu
RIDLER, Chris .... 253-589-5529 478 A
chris.ridler@cptc.edu
RIDLEY, Rodney .... 484-254-2124 378 C
rodney.ridley@alvernia.edu
RIDLEY, Tim .... 661-654-2066.. 30 C
tridley1@csub.edu
RIDLEY, Wadell .... 610-660-1223 397 A
wridley@sju.edu
RIDPATH, Kathy, T .... 540-674-3601 473 F
kridpath@nr.edu
RIDPATH, Lance .... 304-647-6424 489 C
lridpath@osteo.wvsom.edu
RIDPATH, Lisa .... 540-857-6310 475 A
lridpath@virginiawestern.edu
RIDPATH, Tanya .... 540-375-2323 469 G
ridpath@roanoke.edu
RIDSDALE, Carol .... 303-329-6355.. 79 C
RIEBE, Thomas .... 317-921-4562 158 A
triebe@ivytech.edu
RIECKER, Robin .... 315-866-0300 301 B
rieckerra@herkimer.edu
RIEDEL, Eric .... 651-779-3200 237 D
RIEDEL CARNEY, Elizabeth .... 651-690-6836 242 F
eacarney@stkate.edu
RIEDL-FARREY, Cathy, J .... 608-342-1435 495 E
riedlfac@uwplatt.edu

RIPPEE, Rusty .... 870-460-1018.. 22 E
rippee@uamont.edu
RIPPETOE, Heather .... 615-353-3636 424 A
heather.rippetoe@nscc.edu
RIPPEY, Sharon, T .... 315-859-4672 300 F
srippey@hamilton.edu
RIPPINGER, Timothy ..... 414-288-4771 492 E
timothy.rippinger@marquette.edu
RIPPLE, Jacob .... 620-227-9349 173 A
jripple@dc3.edu
RIPPS, Linda .... 914-893-4031 288 K
lripps@ajr.edu
RIQUELME, Joseph .... 202-885-1000.. 91 D
jriquelme@american.edu
RIQUEZ, Elizabeth .... 646-312-1390 292 F
elizabeth.riquez@baruch.cuny.edu
RISAL, Pri .... 903-468-6041 446 D
pri.risal@tamuc.edu
RISBOSKIN, John .... 570-961-7828 387 A
risboskinj@lackawanna.edu
RISCH, Thomas .... 870-972-3333.. 17 I
trisch@astate.edu
RISCHBIETER, Natalie .... 478-471-2732 122 D
natalie.rischbieter@mga.edu
RISCHE, Barbara .... 805-756-6001.. 29 K
brische@calpoly.edu
RISCO, Carlos .... 405-744-6651 367 G
carlos.risco@okstate.edu
RISDON-JACKSON,
Sharlene .... 909-607-7855.. 37 I
srisdon@kgi.edu
RISELEY, Leanne .... 808-455-0440 130 A
leannech@hawaii.edu
RISEMAN, Stacy .... 508-793-2741 208 A
sriseman@holycross.edu
RISHWORTH, Christie ... 401-456-8520 404 A
crishworth@ric.edu
RISINGER, Jeff .... 979-845-7995 446 B
jrisinger@tamu.edu
RISINGER, Jeff .... 614-292-6446 358 E
risinger.22@osu.edu
RISKEDAHL, Laura .... 319-399-8023 164 D
lriskedahl@coe.edu
RISLEY, Levi .... 479-308-2225.. 17 E
levi.resley@acheedu.org
RISMILLER, Lisa, S .... 937-229-4087 362 C
lrismiller1@udayton.edu
RISNER, Kevin .... 419-434-4200 364 B
RISO, Christina .... 215-646-7300 384 G
riso.c@gmercyu.edu
RISO, Kelly-Rue .... 802-728-1211 463 D
kriso@vtc.edu
RISSE, Duane .... 719-502-2403.. 82 D
duane.risse@pikespeak.edu
RISSE, Duane .... 303-404-5111.. 80 I
duane.risse@frontrange.edu
RISSEL, Timothy, O .... 570-326-3761 392 S
tor1@pct.edu
RISSER, Deanna, A .... 574-296-6212 153 C
darisser@ambs.edu
RISSER, Paige .... 574-520-4445 157 C
parisser@iusb.edu
RISSLER, Heather, M .... 641-422-4319 168 E
heather.rissler@niacc.edu
RISSLER, Jacob .... 800-658-4308 266 J
risslerj@mpcc.edu
RITACCO, Kevin .... 508-854-4200 215 D
kritacco@qcc.mass.edu
RITAYIK, Mary .... 845-257-3344 316 B
ritayikm@newpaltz.edu
RITCHEY, Brandon .... 740-474-8896 358 A
britchey@ohiochristian.edu
RITCHEY, Fred, L .... 903-233-4210 438 C
fredritchey@letu.edu
RITCHEY, Mary Kaye ..... 706-886-6831 126 C
mritchey@tfc.edu
RITCHEY, Philip .... 662-685-4771 244 D
pritchey@bmc.edu
RITCHEY, William, V ...... 757-594-7047 465 A
bill.ritchey@cnu.edu
RITCHIE, Chad .... 912-583-3167 116 D
critchie@bpc.edu
RITCHIE, Courtney, S ... 540-828-5605 464 C
critchie@bridgewater.edu
RITCHIE, David .... 765-998-5397 161 A
dvritchie@taylor.edu
RITCHIE, Gloria .... 412-809-5100 395 F
ritchie.gloria@ptcollege.edu
RITCHIE, Meghan .... 510-204-0733.. 37 A
mritchie@cdsp.edu
RITCHIE, Michael .... 610-282-1100 382 A
michael.ritchie@desales.edu

RITCHIE, Tangi .... 419-448-3580 361 C
ritchiet@tiffin.edu
RITCHIE-MITCHELL,
Kedecia .... 972-773-8300.. 93 H
RITEA, Steve .... 310-825-4796.. 69 D
sritea@stratcomm.ucla.edu
RITENOUR, Lisa, L .... 330-972-6084 361 G
lritenour@uakron.edu
RITER, Jayme, S .... 716-878-4301 317 C
riterjs@buffalostate.edu
RITO, Edward .... 786-534-0500.. 99 J
RITSCHDORFF, John ...... 845-575-3000 305 C
john.ritschdorff@marist.edu
RITSCHEL-TRIFILO,
Trish .... 806-291-3745 457 B
trifilot@wbu.edu
RITTENHOUSE, Mary ..... 308-367-4124 269 D
mrittenhouse2@uni.edu
RITTENHOUSE, Niki ...... 860-253-3044.. 86 B
nrittenhouse@asnuntuck.edu
RITTER, Barbara .... 904-256-7859 102 G
britter1@ju.edu
RITTER, Gary .... 314-977-2495 258 H
gary.ritter@slu.edu
RITTER, Gretchen .... 315-443-1870 321 D
RITTER, Joe .... 606-693-5000 182 H
finaid@kmbc.edu
RITTER, Julia, M .... 213-740-5389.. 73 C
kaufman.dean@usc.edu
RITTER, Julie .... 717-338-3007 399 H
jritter@uls.edu
RITTER, Kristy .... 520-515-4516.. 11 O
ritterk@cochise.edu
RITTER, Mark .... 864-503-5939 413 A
mritter@uscupstate.edu
RITTER, Michael .... 863-638-2968 113 E
rittermj@webber.edu
RITTER, Pamela, S .... 423-439-4242 418 D
ritterp@etsu.edu
RITTER, Scott .... 608-246-6791 497 I
sritter@madisoncollege.edu
RITTER, Ted, L .... 804-257-5734 475 G
tlritter@vuu.edu
RITTER, Will .... 336-272-7102 329 B
will.ritter@greensboro.edu
RITTER SMITH, Karl .... 425-388-9211 479 B
kritter@everettcc.edu
RITTERBROWN,
Michael .... 818-240-1000.. 43 J
michaelr@glendale.edu
RITTERBUSCH, Kristen ... 217-641-4314 140 H
kritterbusch@jwcc.edu
RITTLE, Dennis .... 479-619-4191.. 20 G
drittle@nwacc.edu
RITTLE, Joel .... 312-261-3915 145 C
jrittle@nl.edu
RITVALSKY, Zachary ..... 717-560-8200 387 D
zritvalsky@lbc.edu
RITZ, David .... 317-632-5553 158 V
dritz@lincolntech.edu
RITZ, Robert, L .... 434-592-4800 467 E
rlritz@liberty.edu
RITZERT, Marcy .... 740-826-8044 356 H
mritzert@muskingum.edu
RITZLINE, Pamela .... 330-490-7446 363 E
pritzline@walsh.edu
RITZMAN, Elizabeth ...... 708-524-6520 137 A
eritzman@dom.edu
RIVALEAU, Susan, A ..... 843-953-4973 407 D
rivaleaus@cofc.edu
RIVARA, Sara .... 503-491-7469 373 H
sara.rivara@mhcc.edu
RIVARD, Dawn .... 715-682-1812 493 G
drivard@northland.edu
RIVARD, Mary .... 940-552-6291 456 F
mrivard@vernoncollege.edu
RIVARD, Timothy .... 781-239-2631 214 E
trivard@massbay.edu
RIVARD, TJ .... 765-973-8243 156 D
trivard@iue.edu
RIVAS, Frank .... 787-894-2828 511 G
frank.rivas@upr.edu
RIVAS, Josh .... 209-476-7840.. 67 D
jrivas@clcm.net
RIVAS, Robert .... 432-335-6311 440 C
rrivas@odessa.edu
RIVAS, Rolando .... 704-461-6561 326 I
rolandorivas@bac.edu
RIVAS, Rosalinda .... 951-571-6965.. 59 B
rosalinda.rivas@mvc.edu
RIVAS, Sandra .... 951-571-6214.. 59 B
sandra.rivas@mvc.edu

RIVAS, Tony, A .... 727-816-3403 105 E
rivast@phsc.edu
RIVAULT, Mike .... 985-549-5861 192 E
mike.rivault@selu.edu
RIVEIRE STUMPF,
Patricia .... 812-855-2560 156 C
priveire@iu.edu
RIVELAND, Bruce .... 425-739-8164 480 D
bruce.riveland@lwtech.edu
RIVENBARK, Derotha ..... 918-463-2931 365 I
derotha.rivenbark@connorsstate.edu
RIVENBURG, Kevin .... 518-694-7183 289 A
kevin.rivenburg@acphs.edu
RIVENES, Teresa .... 541-440-4624 376 F
teresa.rivenes@umpqua.edu
RIVERA, Albert .... 609-258-3000 279 E
arivera@princeton.edu
RIVERA, Alexieyi .... 787-879-5270 510 D
alexieyi.rivera@upr.edu
RIVERA, Alfredo .... 787-891-0925 506 I
arivera@aguadilla.inter.edu
RIVERA, Ana, Y .... 787-276-8240 510 F
ana.rivera2@upr.edu
RIVERA, Anitra .... 573-341-4632 260 F
RIVERA, Ann .... 716-896-0700 324 A
riveraar@villa.edu
RIVERA, Ann .... 716-926-8854 301 C
arrivera@hilbert.edu
RIVERA, Annelis .... 787-480-2372 505 A
armarquez@sanjuan.pr
RIVERA, Anthony .... 787-279-1912 506 L
arivera@bayamon.inter.edu
RIVERA, Anthony, C ..... 419-772-2190 358 D
a-rivera@onu.edu
RIVERA, Arcilia .... 787-864-2222 507 B
arcilia.rivera@guayama.inter.edu
RIVERA, JR., Augustin .. 361-698-1098 434 H
ariverajr@delmar.edu
RIVERA, Beatriz .... 787-250-1912 507 C
brivera@metro.inter.edu
RIVERA, Carlos .... 718-319-7968 293 F
carivera@hostos.cuny.edu
RIVERA, Carlos, E .... 787-725-8120 505 J
planificacion@eap.edu
RIVERA, Carmen .... 787-725-6500 504 F
crivera@albizu.edu
RIVERA, Carmen .... 787-250-1912 507 C
crivera@metro.inter.edu
RIVERA, Carmen .... 787-850-9301 511 B
carmen.rivera19@upr.edu
RIVERA, Carmen, J .... 787-743-7979 509 D
ut_crivera@suagm.edu
RIVERA, Deborah .... 787-480-2455 505 A
derivera@sanjuan.pr
RIVERA, Edwin .... 787-279-1912 506 L
edrivera@bayamon.inter.edu
RIVERA, Eileen .... 787-864-2222 507 B
eileen.rivera@guayama.inter.edu
RIVERA, Elean .... 760-252-2411.. 26 L
erivera@barstow.edu
RIVERA, Eleric .... 787-738-2161 511 A
eleric.rivera@upr.edu
RIVERA, Elizabeth .... 718-289-5114 292 H
elizabeth.rivera@bcc.cuny.edu
RIVERA, Elsandra .... 787-738-2161 511 A
elsandra.rivera@upr.edu
RIVERA, Enid .... 787-786-3030 509 E
erivera@ucb.edu.pr
RIVERA, Epifanio .... 787-725-6500 504 F
RIVERA, Epifanio .... 787-725-6500 504 F
epirivera@albizu.edu
RIVERA, Eric .... 443-352-4307 202 C
ericrivera9@stevenson.edu
RIVERA, Francisco .... 787-765-1915 507 G
frivera@opto.inter.edu
RIVERA, Frank .... 949-451-5237.. 65 B
frivera@ivc.edu
RIVERA, George .... 787-250-1912 507 C
griverar@metro.inter.edu
RIVERA, Ginady .... 787-284-1912 507 D
girivera@ponce.inter.edu
RIVERA, Gisselle .... 787-834-9595 508 O
grivera@uaa.edu
RIVERA, Guillermo .... 305-463-7210.. 98 C
RIVERA, Hannah .... 859-256-3132 180 H
hannah.rivera@kctcs.edu
RIVERA, Jaime .... 787-852-1430 506 A
jaimerivera@hccpr.edu
RIVERA, Janice .... 787-789-4251 504 D
jrivera@atlanticu.edu
RIVERA, Jim .... 617-353-9200 207 C
seo@bu.edu

RIVERA, Johana .... 718-368-6646 294 C
johana.rivera@kbcc.cuny.edu
RIVERA, Jorge .... 973-761-9355 282 K
jorge.rivera@shu.edu
RIVERA, Jose .... 413-755-4260 215 F
jarivera@stcc.edu
RIVERA, Jose .... 661-722-6300.. 26 E
jrivera102@avc.edu
RIVERA, Jose, A .... 787-751-1912 507 F
jrivera@juris.inter.edu
RIVERA, Jose, O .... 915-747-8535 454 E
jrivera@utep.edu
RIVERA, Julian, J .... 610-989-1276 400 F
jrivera@vfmac.edu
RIVERA, Laura, E .... 787-766-1717 509 C
larivera@uagm.edu
RIVERA, Leonard .... 361-698-2404 434 H
lrivera@delmar.edu
RIVERA, Lisette .... 787-250-1912 507 C
lriverao@metro.inter.edu
RIVERA, Liza .... 347-964-8600 291 F
lrivera@boricuacollege.edu
RIVERA, Lizbeth .... 787-743-7979 509 D
lizrivera@suagm.edu
RIVERA, Luis .... 787-765-3560 505 H
luisrivera@edpuniversity.edu
RIVERA, Maria, G .... 787-864-2222 507 B
mariagisela.rivera@guayama.inter.edu
RIVERA, Marie, L .... 787-723-4481 504 J
marie.rivera@ceaprc.edu
RIVERA, Marielis, E ...... 787-257-7373 509 B
mrivera966@uagm.edu
RIVERA, María .... 787-765-3560 505 H
marivera@edpuniversity.edu
RIVERA, Maximina .... 908-737-6800 277 F
mrivera@kean.edu
RIVERA, Mayra .... 787-765-3560 505 H
mrivera@edpuniversity.edu
RIVERA, Michelle .... 787-891-0925 506 I
mrivera@aguadilla.inter.edu
RIVERA, Mildred .... 787-798-3001 509 F
mildred.rivera@uccaribe.edu
RIVERA, Mildred, Y ...... 787-257-7373 509 B
myrivera@suagm.edu
RIVERA, Mildred, Y ...... 787-766-1717 509 C
myrivera@uagm.edu
RIVERA, Mildred, Y ...... 787-743-7979 509 D
myrivera@suagm.edu
RIVERA, Mishelle .... 787-841-2000 508 H
mishelle_rivera@pucpr.edu
RIVERA, Monica .... 718-951-5693 293 A
monica@brookly.cuny.edu
RIVERA, Nelida .... 787-763-4633 507 C
nerivera@inter.edu
RIVERA, Nydia .... 787-765-3560 505 H
nrivera@edpuniversity.edu
RIVERA, Olga .... 787-753-6335 506 B
orivera@icprjc.edu
RIVERA, Pedro .... 787-878-5475 506 J
pirivera@arecibo.inter.edu
RIVERA, Pedro .... 717-299-6947 398 E
RIVERA, Peter .... 979-830-4189 430 I
peter.rivera@blinn.edu
RIVERA, Rafael .... 914-961-8313 314 E
rafael@svots.edu
RIVERA, Raymond .... 972-860-8228 433 H
rrivera@dcccd.edu
RIVERA, Rey .... 623-935-8010.. 13 C
rey.rivera@estrellamountain.edu
RIVERA, Rosa, M .... 856-225-6100 281 A
rosarive@camden.rutgers.edu
RIVERA, Serafin .... 787-279-2250 506 L
sriverat@bayamon.inter.edu
RIVERA, Sergio .... 210-486-3892 428 B
srivera@alamo.edu
RIVERA, Susan .... 301-405-1691 202 E
smrivera@umd.edu
RIVERA, Suzanne, M .... 651-696-6207 236 C
president@macalester.edu
RIVERA, Vanessa .... 787-725-6500 504 F
vrivera@albizu.edu
RIVERA, Veronica .... 530-938-5233.. 39 D
vrivera@siskiyous.edu
RIVERA, Vicki .... 269-956-3931 225 D
riverav@kellogg.edu
RIVERA, Wendy .... 818-364-7779.. 49 G
riverawc@lamission.edu
RIVERA, Yamaris .... 215-392-6741 395 B
yrivera@pitc.edu
RIVERA, Yolanda .... 787-758-2525 511 D
yolanda.rivera3@upr.edu
RIVERA, Yvette .... 787-284-1912 507 D
yriveram@ponce.inter.edu

ROBERTS, James .... 570-674-6758 389 H
jroberts@misericordia.edu
ROBERTS, Jay .... 828-771-2083 344 B
jroberts@warren-wilson.edu
ROBERTS, Jeff .... 931-372-3365 425 B
jjroberts@tntech.edu
ROBERTS, Jeffrey .... 619-594-5142.. 33 E
jroberts@sdsu.edu
ROBERTS, Jerilyn, C ..... 605-394-6729 415 I
jerilyn.roberts@sdsmt.edu
ROBERTS, Jerry .... 972-825-4870 444 C
jroberts@sagu.edu
ROBERTS, Jim .... 315-792-5649 306 G
jroberts@mvcc.edu
ROBERTS, John .... 903-593-8311 448 A
jroberts@texascollege.edu
ROBERTS, Jonathan .... 501-279-4257.. 19 G
jroberts@harding.edu
ROBERTS, Joy .... 816-235-1700 260 D
robertsme@umkc.edu
ROBERTS, Juanita .... 334-727-8894.... 7 D
jroberts@tuskegee.edu
ROBERTS, Julia .... 910-788-6327 337 G
julia.roberts@sccnc.edu
ROBERTS, Julian .... 212-228-1888 311 I
ROBERTS, Justin, L ...... 314-516-7673 260 E
robertsju@umsl.edu
ROBERTS, Kelli .... 417-873-6349 252 A
kroberts001@drury.edu
ROBERTS, Kevin .... 574-372-5100 155 C
robertkw@grace.edu
ROBERTS, Kyle .... 651-255-6108 242 J
kroberts@unitedseminary.edu
ROBERTS, Lance .... 605-394-2256 415 I
lance.roberts@sdsmt.edu
ROBERTS, LaShawnda .. 319-385-6241 167 F
lashawnda.roberts@iw.edu
ROBERTS, Leigh .... 203-285-2143.. 86 D
lroberts@gatewayct.edu
ROBERTS, LeShawn ...... 407-831-9816.. 97 F
ROBERTS, Lonnie .... 912-427-5816 117 B
lroberts@coastalpines.edu
ROBERTS, Mandy .... 918-647-1214 365 D
mroberts@carlalbert.edu
ROBERTS, Marie .... 601-635-6375 245 B
mroberts@eccc.edu
ROBERTS, Mark, A .... 770-720-5503 124 E
mar@reinhardt.edu
ROBERTS, Marlene .... 715-675-3331 498 E
robertsm@ntc.edu
ROBERTS, Mary .... 478-471-2441 122 D
mary.roberts3@mga.edu
ROBERTS, Matt .... 843-953-5546 407 D
robertsmj1@cofc.edu
ROBERTS, Matthew .... 423-652-4780 419 F
mroberts@king.edu
ROBERTS, Melissa .... 601-266-5390 248 H
melissa.b.roberts@usm.edu
ROBERTS, Michael .... 907-773-4462 134 N
mroberts39@ccc.edu
ROBERTS, Michael, H ... 843-349-2282 407 B
mroberts@coastal.edu
ROBERTS, Michelle, A .. 662-846-4000 245 A
mroberts@deltastate.edu
ROBERTS, Mike .... 801-422-4164 458 A
mike.roberts@byu.edu
ROBERTS, Nancy .... 610-606-4640 380 C
nroberts@cedarcrest.edu
ROBERTS, Nathan .... 816-383-7100 256 C
nroberts4@missouriwestern.edu
ROBERTS, Nathan .... 785-320-4589 175 E
nathanroberts@manhattantech.edu
ROBERTS, Nathan .... 337-482-6678 192 F
nathan@louisiana.edu
ROBERTS, Pamela .... 605-773-3455 415 D
pamela.roberts@sdbor.edu
ROBERTS, Patricia .... 210-436-3308 442 A
proberts6@stmarytx.edu
ROBERTS, Patrick, S ..... 330-471-8411 355 D
proberts@malone.edu
ROBERTS, Patty, J .... 318-869-5747 186 C
pjrobert@centenary.edu
ROBERTS, Paul, G .... 773-508-3163 142 G
prober2@luc.edu
ROBERTS, Phyllis .... 276-964-7588 474 E
phyllis.roberts@sw.edu
ROBERTS, Quinton .... 567-661-7418 359 H
quinton_roberts2@owens.edu
ROBERTS, Randy .... 620-235-4878 176 H
reroberts@pittstate.edu
ROBERTS, Ruth .... 972-825-4656 444 C
rroberts@sagu.edu
ROBERTS, Ruth .... 215-596-8800 400 B

ROBERTS, Ryan .... 616-949-5300 222 F
ryan.roberts@cornerstone.edu
ROBERTS, Samona .... 770-216-2960 121 F
sroberts@ict.edu
ROBERTS, Sarah .... 615-353-3275 424 A
sarah.roberts@nscc.edu
ROBERTS, Severin .... 573-876-7207 259 F
ROBERTS, Shearon .... 504-520-5747 193 C
srobert7@xula.edu
ROBERTS, Sherri .... 870-543-5952.. 21 D
sroberts@seark.edu
ROBERTS, Sonja .... 404-756-4012 115 E
sroberts@atlm.edu
ROBERTS, Stephanie ..... 912-427-5835 117 B
sroberts@coastalpines.edu
ROBERTS, Stephanie ..... 304-326-1310 486 I
sroberts@salemu.edu
ROBERTS, Stevie .... 972-524-3341 444 E
stevie.roberts@swcc.edu
ROBERTS, Teresa .... 417-626-1234 257 A
roberts.teresa@occ.edu
ROBERTS, Thomas .... 601-643-8351 244 G
tommy.roberts@colin.edu
ROBERTS, Thomas .... 785-243-1435 172 J
ROBERTS, Tom .... 239-590-7806 109 G
troberts@fgcu.edu
ROBERTS, Tracy .... 270-809-3380 184 A
troberts@murraystate.edu
ROBERTS, Valerie .... 530-938-5309.. 39 D
robertsv@siskiyous.edu
ROBERTS, Wendy .... 256-260-2475.... 1 F
wendy.roberts@calhoun.edu
ROBERTS, William .... 201-692-2629 276 I
william_roberts@fdu.edu
ROBERTS, William .... 301-295-1166 502 B
william.roberts@usuhs.edu
ROBERTS, William, N ... 406-275-4825 264 H
nick_roberts@skc.edu
ROBERTS-BRESLIN, Jan 617-824-8912 208 G
jan_roberts_breslin@emerson.edu
ROBERTS-CAMPS, Traci 209-946-2343.. 71 E
trobertscamps@pacific.edu
ROBERTSHAW, Mia .... 415-485-9304.. 39 B
mrobertshaw@marin.edu
ROBERTSON, Alan, D ... 850-599-3270 109 E
alan.robertson@famu.edu
ROBERTSON, Anne .... 773-702-8512 151 B
awrx@uchicago.edu
ROBERTSON, Brenda ...... 972-780-3600 453 C
brenda.robertson@untdallas.edu
ROBERTSON, Bruce .... 920-403-3045 494 B
bruce.robertson@snc.edu
ROBERTSON, Charlene . 617-732-2786 216 B
charlene.robertson@mcphs.edu
ROBERTSON, Cheryl ..... 713-221-8256 452 B
robertsonc@uhd.edu
ROBERTSON, Chuck ...... 601-477-4277 246 A
chuck.robertson@jcjc.edu
ROBERTSON, Clyde .... 504-286-5006 191 A
crobertson@suno.edu
ROBERTSON, Craig, L .. 618-537-6856 143 G
ROBERTSON, Dalana ..... 615-322-5179 427 B
dalana.robertson@vanderbilt.edu
ROBERTSON, Derrick .... 859-572-5744 184 B
robertsond5@nku.edu
ROBERTSON, Don .... 270-809-6839 184 A
drobertson@murraystate.edu
ROBERTSON, Donna ...... 201-692-2196 276 I
donnamjr@fdu.edu
ROBERTSON, Emily .... 704-406-3249 328 I
erobertson@gardner-webb.edu
ROBERTSON, Ian .... 608-262-3482 494 D
engr-dean@wisc.edu
ROBERTSON, J. D .... 435-652-7576 459 G
jd.robertson@utahtech.edu
ROBERTSON, Jacob, M 951-552-8677.. 27 J
jmrobertson@calbaptist.edu
ROBERTSON, Jeff .... 479-968-0498.. 18 E
jrobertson@atu.edu
ROBERTSON, Jeff .... 660-543-4030 259 K
jrobertson@ucmo.edu
ROBERTSON, Jen .... 603-428-2418 272 I
jrobertson@nec.edu
ROBERTSON, Jennifer .... 407-582-6150 113 C
jrobertson@valenciacollege.edu
ROBERTSON, Jill .... 303-273-3207.. 79 A
jirobert@is.mines.edu
ROBERTSON, Jim .... 845-574-4466 312 C
jrobert7@sunyrockland.edu
ROBERTSON, Joel .... 423-652-4724 419 F
jcrobert@king.edu
ROBERTSON, John .... 972-860-7709 433 F
jrobertson@dcccd.edu

ROBERTSON,
John Howard .... 601-477-4109 246 A
john.robertson@jcjc.edu
ROBERTSON, Jon, H ...... 561-237-7701 103 W
jrobertson@lynn.edu
ROBERTSON, Jordan ..... 612-343-4440 241 O
ROBERTSON, Julie .... 360-992-2076 477 J
jrobertson@clark.edu
ROBERTSON, Keona ...... 281-425-6327 438 B
krobertson@lee.edu
ROBERTSON, Kristy ...... 276-328-0220 471 G
kej5c@uvawise.edu
ROBERTSON, Lillian ...... 706-295-6328 119 C
lrobertson@highlands.edu
ROBERTSON,
M.G. (Pat) .... 757-352-4036 469 D
lfinn@regent.edu
ROBERTSON, Marjorie .. 580-745-2000 369 F
ROBERTSON,
Michael, J .... 214-768-1148 443 G
robertsonm@smu.edu
ROBERTSON,
Michael, N .... 901-722-3226 422 I
mike.robertson@sco.edu
ROBERTSON,
Michelle, L .... 570-577-3775 379 A
mlr040@bucknell.edu
ROBERTSON, Nyk .... 620-341-5551 173 C
nrobert7@emporia.edu
ROBERTSON, Paul .... 520-383-0079.. 16 D
probertson@tocc.edu
ROBERTSON, Prince ..... 309-556-3111 140 E
probert1@iwu.edu
ROBERTSON, Rachel ..... 801-587-9889 459 D
rachel.robertson@utah.edu
ROBERTSON, Samantha 603-271-6484 272 C
ROBERTSON,
Stacey, M .... 610-499-4101 401 I
smrobertson@widener.edu
ROBERTSON, Sue .... 630-889-6527 145 D
srobertson@nuhs.edu
ROBERTSON, Tim .... 402-872-2411 267 H
trobertson@peru.edu
ROBERTSON, Tracee ..... 940-397-8948 439 F
tracee.robertson@msutexas.edu
ROBERTSON, Trey .... 601-928-6306 246 F
trey.robertson@mgccc.edu
ROBERTSON, Valerie ..... 360-596-5240 483 E
vrobertson1@spscc.edu
ROBERTSON, William ... 915-747-8200 454 E
robertson@utep.edu
ROBERTSON-JAMES,
Candace .... 215-951-1430 386 I
robertsonjames@lasalle.edu
ROBEY, Jason .... 314-434-4044 251 F
jason.robey@covenantseminary.edu
ROBICHAUD, Betin .... 508-213-2292 217 C
betin.robichaud@nichols.edu
ROBICHAUD, David .... 508-531-2731 212 B
drobichaud@bridgew.edu
ROBICHAUD, Jeanette .. 978-665-4646 212 C
jrobic15@fitchburgstate.edu
ROBICHAUD, Keith .... 617-333-2210 208 D
krobicha0804@curry.edu
ROBICHEAUX, Wendi ..... 337-521-8932 188 G
wendi.robicheaux@solacc.edu
ROBIDOUX, Patricia ..... 909-607-0107.. 37 I
probidoux@kgi.edu
ROBIE, Candra .... 970-675-3356.. 78 P
candra.robie@cncc.edu
ROBILOTTO, Philip .... 410-706-2378 202 F
probilotto@umaryland.edu
ROBIN, Jennifer .... 203-392-5356.. 85 H
robinj2@southernct.edu
ROBIN, Tracy .... 212-229-1671 307 E
robint@newschool.edu
ROBIN, Wayne .... 508-767-7095 205 F
w.robin@assumption.edu
ROBINETT, Laura .... 402-941-6523 267 B
robinett@midlandu.edu
ROBINETTE, Kyrsten ..... 614-236-6011 348 I
ROBINETTE, Timothy ..... 276-326-4618 464 A
trobinette@bluefield.edu
ROBINS, Anthony, G .... 412-397-6482 396 E
robins@rmu.edu
ROBINS, Diana .... 215-571-3439 382 D
dlr76@drexel.edu
ROBINS, Michael .... 408-741-2187.. 75 C
michael.robins@wvm.edu
ROBINS, Michael .... 831-477-3521.. 27 G
mirobins@cabrillo.edu
ROBINS, Rochelle .... 213-884-4133.. 24 D
rrobins@ajrca.edu

ROBINSON, Alexandra .. 212-817-7112 293 D
arobinson@gc.cuny.edu
ROBINSON, Anafe .... 818-610-6515.. 49 H
robinsa@piercecollege.edu
ROBINSON, Andrea .... 507-222-5465 234 C
arobinson@carleton.edu
ROBINSON, Andrew ...... 402-554-3750 269 C
ROBINSON, Andrew ...... 478-471-4394 121 C
anrobinson@helms.edu
ROBINSON,
Andristine, M .... 301-546-7422 201 D
robinsam1@pgcc.edu
ROBINSON, Angela .... 229-430-3500 114 G
arobinson@albanytech.edu
ROBINSON, Angela .... 309-672-5513 143 I
arobinson@methodistcol.edu
ROBINSON, Ann .... 716-566-7836 297 F
arobinso@daemen.edu
ROBINSON, April .... 205-726-2803.... 6 E
alrobins@samford.edu
ROBINSON, April .... 863-297-1020 106 A
arobinson@polk.edu
ROBINSON, Ashley .... 601-979-2291 245 G
ashley.n.robinson@jsums.edu
ROBINSON, Barry .... 360-383-3000 485 B
ROBINSON, Beverly ...... 972-825-4798 444 C
brobinson@sagu.edu
ROBINSON, Breck .... 707-826-6212.. 30 A
breck.robinson@humboldt.edu
ROBINSON, Brian .... 916-608-6849.. 51 A
robinsb@flc.losrios.edu
ROBINSON, Brigette ..... 517-990-1386 225 A
robinsobrigetta@jccmi.edu
ROBINSON, Carlos .... 405-466-3428 366 B
carlos.m.robinson@langston.edu
ROBINSON, Carrie .... 215-670-9328 391 D
cnrobinson@peirce.edu
ROBINSON,
Cassandra, M .... 301-860-4000 203 D
crobinson@bowiestate.edu
ROBINSON, Chad .... 970-943-3123.. 85 B
crobinson@western.edu
ROBINSON, Charles, F . 479-575-3836.. 21 H
ROBINSON, Charles, F . 510-987-9800.. 68 M
charles.robinson@ucop.edu
ROBINSON, Cheryl .... 407-582-3457 113 C
crobinson@valenciacollege.edu
ROBINSON, Chris .... 870-575-7950.. 22 F
robinsonec@uapb.edu
ROBINSON, Chris .... 606-218-5226 185 F
chrisrobinson@upike.edu
ROBINSON, Christina ... 860-832-2364.. 85 F
christinarobinson@ccsu.edu
ROBINSON, Christine ... 704-687-5385 342 C
crobinson@uncc.edu
ROBINSON,
Christopher .... 315-268-3986 295 E
crobinso@clarkson.edu
ROBINSON,
Christopher, D .... 336-246-3900 338 H
cdrobinson877@wilkescc.edu
ROBINSON, Collis .... 859-985-3611 179 E
robinsonc@berea.edu
ROBINSON, Courtney ... 512-505-3035 437 B
crrobinson@htu.edu
ROBINSON, Dave .... 641-269-9990 166 D
daver@grinnell.edu
ROBINSON, David .... 510-642-7791.. 68 N
dmrobinson@berkeley.edu
ROBINSON, David .... 212-650-8357 293 B
drobinson2@ccny.cuny.edu
ROBINSON, David, W ... 503-494-4460 374 F
provost@ohsu.edu
ROBINSON, Dawnelle ... 256-331-5310.... 3 C
dawnelle.robinson@nwscc.edu
ROBINSON,
Debra A, G .... 573-341-6154 260 F
debrar@mst.edu
ROBINSON, OSB,
Denis .... 812-357-6522 160 G
drobinson@saintmeinrad.edu
ROBINSON, Derek .... 307-382-1896 500 I
derek@westernwyoming.edu
ROBINSON, Edward .... 202-274-2300.. 94 C
library@potomac.edu
ROBINSON, Elwood, L . 336-750-2042 343 E
robinsonel@wssu.edu
ROBINSON, Erin .... 941-893-2856 106 J
erobinso@ringling.edu
ROBINSON, Foster .... 360-752-8571 477 C
frobinson@btc.edu
ROBINSON, Freddie ...... 804-257-5783 475 G
frobinson@vuu.edu

RODEN, Tyler .... 256-352-8440.... 4 A
tyler.roden@wallacestate.edu
RODENBORN, Steven ... 401-341-3127 404 D
steven.rodenborn@salve.edu
RODER, Claire .... 715-858-1806 497 E
croder3@cvtc.edu
RODERICK, Daniel .... 508-793-7578 207 F
droderick@clarku.edu
RODERICK, Lori .... 309-794-7182 132 H
loriroderick@augustana.edu
RODGER, Andrea .... 360-650-4478 485 A
andrea.rodger@wwu.edu
RODGERS, Ardie .... 405-733-7434 369 D
arodgers@rose.edu
RODGERS, Chris, T ..... 402-280-2455 265 J
chrisrodgers@creighton.edu
RODGERS, Christopher . 718-817-4755 300 A
chrodgers@fordham.edu
RODGERS, Colette .... 718-780-0382 291 G
colette.rodgers@brooklaw.edu
RODGERS, Corey .... 949-451-5409.. 65 B
crodgers@ivc.edu
RODGERS, Denise, V .... 973-972-3645 281 B
rodgerdv@ca.rutgers.edu
RODGERS, Frederick, B 607-871-2958 289 E
rodgers@alfred.edu
RODGERS, Micah .... 850-973-1604 104 K
rodgersm@nfc.edu
RODGERS, Michael .... 270-686-4503 182 C
mike.rodgers@kctcs.edu
RODGERS, Mike .... 325-649-8055 437 A
mrodgers@hputx.edu
RODGERS, Rob, G .... 412-383-0358 400 A
rgr5@pitt.edu
RODGERS, Ronda .... 509-542-4802 478 B
rrodgers@columbiabasin.edu
RODGERS, Ruth .... 317-955-6321 159 A
rrodgers@marian.edu
RODGERS, Scott, M ..... 601-984-5009 248 G
srodgers@umc.edu
RODGERS, Victor .... 717-221-1361 385 A
vrodgers@hacc.edu
RODIBAUGH, Jon .... 585-475-4485 312 A
jprrar@rit.edu
RODKIN, Dan .... 352-395-4171 107 G
dan.rodkin@sfcollege.edu
RODMAN, Gary, S .... 920-748-8343 493 J
rodmang@ripon.edu
RODMAN, Michael .... 617-627-3024 219 A
michael.rodman@tufts.edu
RODNING, Janet, M ..... 770-720-5954 124 E
jmr@reinhardt.edu
RODOCKER, Jason, L ... 540-458-8753 476 D
jrodocker@wlu.edu
RODRIGUE, STD,
Joshua, J .... 504-866-7426 190 E
jrodrigue@nds.edu
RODRIGUE, Kelly, J ..... 985-448-4154 192 C
kelly.rodrigue@nicholls.edu
RODRIGUE, Morris, J ... 909-274-4230.. 52 K
mrodrigue@mtsac.edu
RODRIGUES, Helena ..... 520-621-1684.. 16 H
hrodrigu@arizona.edu
RODRIGUES, Leon .... 651-641-3209 236 A
lrodrigues001@luthersem.edu
RODRIGUES, Nishanth .. 662-915-7206 248 F
nr@olemiss.edu
RODRIGUES, Usha, R ... 706-542-0415 126 F
rodrig@uga.edu
RODRIGUEZ, Abel .... 787-834-9595 508 O
arodriguez@uaa.edu
RODRIGUEZ, Adam .... 361-485-4570 452 C
rodriguezag2@uhv.edu
RODRIGUEZ, Adrian ..... 361-825-3404 446 E
adrian.rodriguez@tamucc.edu
RODRIGUEZ, Agustin .... 787-758-2525 511 D
agustin.rodriguez1@upr.edu
RODRIGUEZ, Aida, E .... 787-852-1430 506 A
arodriguez@hccpr.edu
RODRIGUEZ, Alba .... 478-301-2136 122 C
rodriguez_a@mercer.edu
RODRIGUEZ, Alexander 978-556-3626 215 C
arodriguez@necc.mass.edu
RODRIGUEZ, Alfred ..... 210-999-7201 451 B
alfred.rodriguez@trinity.edu
RODRIGUEZ, Alina .... 305-377-8817.. 95 K
alina.rodriguez@atlantisuniversity.edu
RODRIGUEZ, Alma .... 805-289-6360.. 74 B
arodriguez@vcccd.edu
RODRIGUEZ, Alma .... 956-882-7657 455 A
alma.rodriguez@utrgv.edu
RODRIGUEZ, Amanda ... 650-723-2300.. 66 D
RODRIGUEZ, Anastacia . 303-352-6564.. 80 D
anastacia.rodriguez@ccd.edu
RODRIGUEZ, Anastasia . 410-651-6230 203 B
awrodriquez@umes.edu
RODRIGUEZ, Andy .... 970-248-1337.. 78 F
arodrigu@coloradomesa.edu
RODRIGUEZ, Annabelle 956-781-6800 441 M
RODRIGUEZ, Arlene ...... 781-280-3200 214 G
RODRIGUEZ, Arlene ...... 508-362-2131 214 B
RODRIGUEZ, Armando . 787-841-2000 508 H
armando_rodriguez@pucpr.edu
RODRIGUEZ, Art .... 507-222-4190 234 C
adrodriguez@carleton.edu
RODRIGUEZ, Arturo ...... 805-965-0581.. 62 M
amrodriguez19@sbcc.edu
RODRIGUEZ,
Barbara, L .... 505-277-0735 288 C
kkachirisky@unm.edu
RODRIGUEZ, Beatriz ..... 908-709-7448 283 E
rodriguez@ucc.edu
RODRIGUEZ, Brenda ..... 512-245-3219 449 G
br25@txstate.edu
RODRIGUEZ, Carlos ..... 847-970-4846 152 F
crodriguez@usml.edu
RODRIGUEZ, Carlos ..... 323-343-3929.. 32 B
carlos.rodriguez@calstatela.edu
RODRIGUEZ, Carlos ..... 215-780-1400 397 E
crodriguez@salus.edu
RODRIGUEZ, Carmen ... 787-878-5475 506 J
clrodri@arecibo.inter.edu
RODRIGUEZ, Carmen ... 909-384-8592.. 60 F
marodrig@sbccd.cc.ca.us
RODRIGUEZ, Carmen ... 305-629-2929 107 F
crodriguez@sanignaciouniversity.edu
RODRIGUEZ, Carmen ... 787-780-0070 504 E
crodriguez@caribbean.edu
RODRIGUEZ,
Carmen, B .... 787-850-9380 511 B
carmen.rodriguez17@upr.edu
RODRIGUEZ, Claribel ... 787-621-2835 504 B
crodriguez@aupr.edu
RODRIGUEZ, Claudia .... 787-761-0640 510 A
asistenciaeconomica@utcpr.edu
RODRIGUEZ, Clemente . 713-348-6000 441 K
crod@rice.edu
RODRIGUEZ, Daron ...... 303-753-6046.. 83 C
drodriguez@rmcad.edu
RODRIGUEZ, David .... 949-359-0045.. 29 C
RODRIGUEZ, Dawn, M . 813-974-7297 111 B
dmrodriguez@usf.edu
RODRIGUEZ, Delia .... 815-479-7588 143 F
drodriguez462@mchenry.edu
RODRIGUEZ, Desiree .... 504-865-3849 190 A
desiree@loyno.edu
RODRIGUEZ, Diriee, Y .. 787-743-7979 509 D
dyrodriguez@suagm.edu
RODRIGUEZ, Edgar .... 787-841-2000 508 H
edrodrios@pucpr.edu
RODRIGUEZ, Edgar .... 617-989-4590 219 D
rodrigueze9@wit.edu
RODRIGUEZ, Eduardo ... 509-542-4408 478 B
erodriguez@columbiabasin.edu
RODRIGUEZ, Elisandra . 787-840-2575 508 G
erodriguez@psm.edu
RODRIGUEZ, Elisha ...... 212-678-8206 321 H
erodriguez@tc.columbia.edu
RODRIGUEZ, Elizabeth .. 561-683-1400.. 94 F
lrodriguez@anho.edu
RODRIGUEZ, Elsa .... 787-753-6335 506 B
e_rodriguez@icprjc.edu
RODRIGUEZ, Emilio ...... 909-537-3944.. 33 B
emilio@csusb.edu
RODRIGUEZ, Emilio ...... 626-568-8850.. 49 B
emilio@lacm.edu
RODRIGUEZ, Enerida .... 787-738-2161 511 A
enerida.rodriguez@upr.edu
RODRIGUEZ, Ericka ...... 787-844-8181 511 E
ericka.rodriguez@upr.edu
RODRIGUEZ, Evelyn ..... 787-850-9305 511 B
evelyn.rodriguez3@upr.edu
RODRIGUEZ,
Francisco, C .... 213-891-2201.. 49 C
chancellor@email.laccd.edu
RODRIGUEZ, Gilberto ... 641-472-1170 168 A
grodriguez@miu.edu
RODRIGUEZ, Ginger ..... 219-473-4227 154 A
grodriguez@ccsj.edu
RODRIGUEZ, Glendali ... 715-232-2421 496 C
rodriguezg@uwstout.edu
RODRIGUEZ,
Guadalupe .... 360-442-2444 480 E
grodriguez@lowercolumbia.edu
RODRIGUEZ, Henberto . 787-884-6000 506 B
hrodriguez@icprjc.edu
RODRIGUEZ, Israel .... 787-743-7979 509 D
ut_irodriguez@suagm.edu
RODRIGUEZ, Israel .... 562-977-6017.. 43 C
israel.rodriguez@fremont.edu
RODRIGUEZ, Israel .... 209-476-7840.. 67 D
irodriguez@clc.edu
RODRIGUEZ, Jalibeth ... 787-841-2000 508 H
jalibeth_rodriguez@pucpr.edu
RODRIGUEZ, James ...... 661-654-2219.. 30 C
jlrodriguez@csub.edu
RODRIGUEZ, Janeth ..... 909-652-6620.. 36 B
janeth.rodriguez@chaffey.edu
RODRIGUEZ, Janeth ..... 909-652-6541.. 36 B
janeth.rodriguez@chaffey.edu
RODRIGUEZ, Janeth ..... 909-652-6620.. 36 B
janeth.rodriguez@chaffey.edu
RODRIGUEZ, Javier ...... 815-838-0500 142 C
RODRIGUEZ, Javier ...... 702-895-3670 270 J
javier.rodriguez@unlv.edu
RODRIGUEZ, Jerry .... 915-215-4040 450 E
jerry.rodriguez@ttuhsc.edu
RODRIGUEZ, Jesus, R ... 956-295-3399 448 E
jroberto.rodriguez@tsc.edu
RODRIGUEZ, Jorge .... 973-618-3320 275 E
jrrodiguez@caldwell.edu
RODRIGUEZ, Jose .... 973-618-3534 275 E
jlrodiguez@caldwell.edu
RODRIGUEZ, Jose .... 718-489-5315 312 H
jrodriguez2300@sfc.edu
RODRIGUEZ, Jose .... 909-621-8774.. 57 K
jose.rodriguez@pomona.edu
RODRIGUEZ, Jose, A .... 787-279-1912 506 L
jarodriguez@bayamon.inter.edu
RODRIGUEZ, Jose, C ... 972-860-7603 433 I
jcrodriguez@dcccd.edu
RODRIGUEZ, Josefina .. 787-257-0000 510 F
josefina.rodriguez@upr.edu
RODRIGUEZ, Juan .... 787-878-5475 506 J
jcrodrig@arecibo.inter.edu
RODRIGUEZ, Julian ...... 210-486-4815 428 A
jrodriguez6@alamo.edu
RODRIGUEZ, Kathy .... 760-757-2121.. 52 G
krodriguez@miracosta.edu
RODRIGUEZ, Katrina ..... 320-308-3111 240 C
katrina.rodriguez@stcloudstate.edu
RODRIGUEZ, Kevin .... 210-924-4338 430 D
RODRIGUEZ, Laura .... 423-585-6798 424 G
laura.rodriguez@ws.edu
RODRIGUEZ, Laurie ...... 406-447-5465 262 E
lrodriguez@carroll.edu
RODRIGUEZ, Leslie ...... 708-524-6821 137 A
lrodriguez@dom.edu
RODRIGUEZ, Lora .... 972-721-5322 451 E
lbrodriguez@udallas.edu
RODRIGUEZ, Louie, F .. 951-827-5802.. 70 B
gsoedean@ucr.edu
RODRIGUEZ, Lucia, M . 915-831-2848 435 B
lrodr258@epcc.edu
RODRIGUEZ, Luis, R .... 787-850-9204 511 B
luis.rodriguez40@upr.edu
RODRIGUEZ, Magaly .... 787-850-9361 511 B
magaly.rodriguez1@upr.edu
RODRIGUEZ, Marcos ..... 661-395-4221.. 47 B
marcos.rodriguez@bakersfieldcollege.
edu
RODRIGUEZ, Maria, E .. 410-462-7791 197 E
mrodriguez@bccc.edu
RODRIGUEZ,
Maria-Judith .... 858-752-4963 347 F
mjrodriguez@antioch.edu
RODRIGUEZ, Maribel .... 312-553-2500 134 L
mrodriguez@ccc.edu
RODRIGUEZ, Mario ...... 916-568-3058.. 50 I
rodrigm3@losrios.edu
RODRIGUEZ, Marisela .. 956-721-5820 438 A
marisela.rodriguez@laredo.edu
RODRIGUEZ,
Marissa, A .... 210-283-5096 452 D
marodr33@uiwtx.edu
RODRIGUEZ, Mark .... 216-987-5459 351 D
mark.rodriguez@tri-c.edu
RODRIGUEZ, Mary Ann 361-582-2560 456 H
maryann.rodriguez@victoriacollege.edu
RODRIGUEZ, Mary Ann 909-607-9060.. 37 F
mary-ann.rodriguez@cgu.edu
RODRIGUEZ, Mauricio .. 913-758-6173 177 I
mauricio.rodriguez@stmary.edu
RODRIGUEZ, Mayra ...... 787-743-7979 509 D
mrodrigu@suagm.edu
RODRIGUEZ, Melba ...... 812-866-7011 155 D
rodriguez@hanover.edu
RODRIGUEZ, Monica ..... 510-215-3958.. 40 G
mrodriguez@contracosta.edu
RODRIGUEZ, Nannette .. 531-622-2733 266 G
nmrodriguez@mccneb.edu
RODRIGUEZ, Narce .... 503-352-1457 375 B
nrodrigu@pacificu.edu
RODRIGUEZ,
Narcedalia .... 503-357-1457 375 B
nrodrigu@pacificu.edu
RODRIGUEZ, Natalie ..... 213-738-6801.. 66 A
academicadmin@swlaw.edu
RODRIGUEZ, Nate .... 620-901-6240 171 A
rodriguez@allencc.edu
RODRIGUEZ, Nilda .... 914-422-4213 310 F
nrodriguez@pace.edu
RODRIGUEZ, Norelis .... 787-704-1020 505 B
norodriguez@columbiacentral.edu
RODRIGUEZ, Norma ...... 562-860-2451.. 35 O
nrodriguez@cerritos.edu
RODRIGUEZ, Oscar .... 361-354-2338 431 L
omrodriguez1@coastalbend.edu
RODRIGUEZ, Oscar .... 910-678-8413 334 C
rodriguo@faytechcc.edu
RODRIGUEZ, Pedro .... 203-287-3031.. 88 D
RODRIGUEZ, Peter .... 713-348-5928 441 K
peter.l.rodriguez@rice.edu
RODRIGUEZ, Rafael .... 212-998-4401 309 D
RODRIGUEZ, Rafael, J .. 787-766-1717 509 C
rjrodriguez@uagm.edu
RODRIGUEZ, Ray .... 801-618-0438 458 H
rrodriguez@ameritech.edu
RODRIGUEZ, Rene .... 512-232-2780 454 C
renerod@austin.utexas.edu
RODRIGUEZ,
Reuban, B .... 804-828-8940 472 D
rbrodriguez@vcu.edu
RODRIGUEZ, Ricardo .... 817-531-4249 450 F
rrodriguez@txwes.edu
RODRIGUEZ, Ricardo .... 787-751-0178 509 A
ricrodriguez@uagm.edu
RODRIGUEZ, Richard .... 559-323-2100.. 61 G
rrodriguez@sjcl.edu
RODRIGUEZ, Rodney ..... 956-872-8366 443 B
rodrodriguez@southtexascollege.edu
RODRIGUEZ, Ron .... 209-667-3709.. 33 D
rrodriguez36@csustan.edu
RODRIGUEZ, Rosa .... 651-779-5786 237 D
rosa.rodriguez@century.edu
RODRIGUEZ, Sandra ..... 505-747-2194 287 C
sandra.rodriguez@nnmc.edu
RODRIGUEZ, Segundo .. 787-758-2525 511 D
segundo.rodriguez@upr.edu
RODRIGUEZ, Seph .... 909-272-6947.. 36 G
seph.rodriguez@tcsedsystem.edu
RODRIGUEZ, Sherri ...... 818-947-2726.. 50 B
rodrigsa@lavc.edu
RODRIGUEZ, Silvio .... 305-237-7445 104 E
srodrig2@mdc.edu
RODRIGUEZ, Sonia .... 585-475-2395 312 A
smrfa@rit.edu
RODRIGUEZ, Steven ..... 949-214-3003.. 40 E
steven.rodriguez@cui.edu
RODRIGUEZ, Teresita .... 310-434-4774.. 63 B
rodriguez_teresita@smc.edu
RODRIGUEZ, Theresa ... 507-222-4290 234 C
trodriguez@carleton.edu
RODRIGUEZ, Tiffany ..... 503-244-0726 371 E
tiffanyrodriguez@achs.edu
RODRIGUEZ, Velia .... 559-730-3775.. 39 C
veliar@cos.edu
RODRIGUEZ, Venessa ... 607-778-5220 317 A
rodriguezvl1@sunybroome.edu
RODRIGUEZ, Veronica .. 773-583-4050 145 G
RODRIGUEZ, Vince .... 714-546-7600.. 38 D
RODRIGUEZ, Wanda ..... 787-257-0000 510 F
wanda.rodriguez@upr.edu
RODRIGUEZ, William .... 773-508-8890 142 G
wrodriguez1@luc.edu
RODRIGUEZ, Yanelis .... 414-410-4003 490 J
yrodriguez@stritch.edu
RODRIGUEZ-ANDUJAR,
Glorimar .... 787-780-5134 508 C
RODRIGUEZ ANTONE,
Megan .... 650-306-3418.. 62 I
rodriguezm@smccd.edu
RODRIGUEZ-CHARDAVOYNE,
Esther .... 718-518-4308 293 F
erodriguez@hostos.cuny.edu
RODRIGUEZ DAVILA,
Soniemi .... 787-960-4787 510 B
soniemi.rodriguez@upr.edu
RODRIGUEZ-FARRAR,
Hanna .... 315-228-5150 296 C
hrf@colgate.edu

RODRIGUEZ-GONZALEZ, Christina .... 361-593-2132 447 A christina.rodriguez-gonzalez@tamuk.edu
RODRIGUEZ-GREGORY, Lisa .... 732-906-2550 278 A lgregory@middlesexcc.edu
RODRIGUEZ HOWELL, Daniel .... 787-850-9341 511 B daniel.rodriguez32@upr.edu
RODRIGUEZ JAMES, Heather .... 256-726-7250.... 6 C hjames@oakwood.edu
RODRIGUEZ JOHNSON, Fatima, L .... 716-888-2118 291 M rodrig23@canisius.edu
RODRIGUEZ LABOY, Juan, A .... 787-841-2000 508 H juan_rodriguez@pucpr.edu
RODRIGUEZ-LAMAS, Barbara .... 407-708-2768 108 B lamasb@seminolestate.edu
RODRIGUEZ MARTINEZ, Melanie .... 787-720-4476 509 G biblioteca@mizpa.edu
RODRIGUEZ-MOLINA, Nilda, E .... 787-480-2439 505 A nilrodriguez@sanjuan.pr
RODRIGUEZ REYES, Zulyn .... 787-764-0000 511 F zulyn.rodriguez@upr.edu
RODRIGUEZ-RIVERA, Carlos .... 787-250-0000 510 B carlos.rodriguez107@upr.edu
RODRIGUEZ-ROIG, Aida .... 787-850-9374 510 B aida.rodriguez1@upr.edu
RODRIGUEZ ROIG, Aida, I .... 787-850-9375 511 B aida.rodriguez1@upr.edu
RODRIGUEZ-SUAREZ, Francisco .... 217-333-1330 151 F paco70@illinois.edu
RODRIGUEZ-VARGAS, Claribel .... 787-621-2835 504 B crodriguez@aupr.edu
RODRIGUEZ-VINCENTY, Carmen, J .... 787-480-2438 505 A crodriguez03@sanjuan.pr
RODRIQUEZ, Madelyn .. 570-389-4937 393 E mrodrig2@bloomu.edu
RODRIQUEZ, Nicky, M . 866-294-3974 154 E nicky.rodriquez@ccr.edu
RODRÍGUEZ, Havidán ... 518-956-8030 315 D presmail@albany.edu
RODRÍGUEZ, Inocencio 787-815-0000 510 D inocencio.rodriguez@upr.edu
RODRÍGUEZ, Mayra ..... 787-892-5115 507 E mayra_rodriguez@sangerman.inter.edu
RODRÍGUEZ, Nestor ..... 787-993-8898 510 E nestor.rodriguez1@upr.edu
RODRÍGUEZ-DÁVILA, Soniemi .... 787-751-3601 510 B soniemi.rodriguez@upr.edu
RODRÍGUEZ MONTALBAN, Ramón .... 787-725-6500 504 F rmontalban@albizu.edu
RODRÍGUEZ OCASIO, Ruben .... 787-764-0000 511 F ruben.rodriguezocasio@upr.edu
RODRÍGUEZ-RIVERA, Rafael, E .... 787-751-1600 507 F rrodriguez@juris.inter.edu
ROE, Alexandria .... 608-265-0551 494 C aroe@uwsa.edu
ROE, Elizabeth, P .... 330-471-8626 355 D eproe@malone.edu
ROE, Laurie .... 541-956-7133 375 G lroe@roguecc.edu
ROE, Lesa .... 214-752-8585 453 B chancellor@unt.edu
ROE, Michael .... 845-431-8018 298 B michael.roe@sunydutchess.edu
ROE, Robert, M .... 989-774-3933 221 M roe1rm@cmich.edu
ROEBUCK, Alissa .... 931-393-1682 423 G aroebuck@mscc.edu
ROEBUCK, Paris .... 910-775-4577 343 A paris.roebuck@uncp.edu
ROEBUCK, Randy .... 316-677-9437 178 C rroebuck@wsutech.edu
ROECKER, Pamela .... 781-768-7147 217 H pamela.roecker@regiscollege.edu
ROECKER-PHELPS, Carolyn .... 937-229-3334 362 C cphelps1@udayton.edu
ROEDEL, Glenn .... 215-780-1296 397 E groedel@salus.edu
ROEDEL, Mark .... 903-233-3296 438 C markroedel@letu.edu
ROEDER, Lynn, M .... 252-328-9297 340 H roederl@ecu.edu
ROEGER, Tyler .... 847-214-7696 137 D troeger@elgin.edu
ROEHM, Michelle .... 336-758-5000 344 A
ROEHRICK, Randy .... 952-995-1525 237 G randy.roehrick@hennepintech.edu
ROELFS, Melinda .... 620-235-4206 176 H mroelfs@pittstate.edu
ROELKE, Scott .... 651-423-8297 237 E scott.roelke@dctc.edu
ROELKE, Scott .... 651-450-3330 237 H sroelke@inverhills.edu
ROELLKE, Christopher .. 386-822-7250 111 F croellke@stetson.edu
ROELOFS, Lyle, D .... 859-985-3522 179 E roelofsl@berea.edu
ROEMER, Lara .... 309-341-5219 134 A lroemer@sandburg.edu
ROEMER, Nils .... 972-883-2984 454 D nroemer@utdallas.edu
ROEMER, Nils .... 972-883-4376 454 D nroemer@utdallas.edu
ROEPKE, Holly .... 805-493-3833.. 29 E roepke@callutheran.edu
ROEPKE, Melinda .... 419-755-4848 357 B mroepke@ncstatecollege.edu
ROESCHENTHALER, Robert .... 740-264-5591 352 B rroeschenthaler@egcc.edu
ROESLER, Eric .... 715-346-3975 496 B eric.roesler@uwsp.edu
ROESNER, Rebecca .... 309-556-3220 140 E rroesner@iwu.edu
ROESSEL, Charles .... 928-724-6669.. 12 F cmroessel@dinecollege.edu
ROESSLEIN, Tim .... 314-256-8865 249 F roesslein@ai.edu
ROEST, Michael .... 415-503-6309.. 61 E mroest@sfcm.edu
ROETHEL, Bryan .... 804-862-6100 469 E broethel@rbc.edu
ROETHEMEYER, Robert, V .... 260-452-2146 154 F robert.roethemeyer@ctsfw.edu
ROETHER, Diane .... 940-668-4338 439 I droether@nctc.edu
ROETHLER, Don .... 701-224-5485 345 F donald.roethler@bismarckstate.edu
ROETTGER, Linda .... 219-464-5958 162 C linda.roettger@valpo.edu
ROEWER, Anita .... 815-455-8737 143 F aroewer@mchenry.edu
ROGALSKI, Kathryn .... 920-498-5401 498 F kathryn.rogalski@nwtc.edu
ROGELSTAD, Todd .... 701-845-7209 345 E todd.rogelstad@vcsu.edu
ROGER-GORDON, A. Patrick .... 212-346-1295 310 F arogergordon@pace.edu
ROGERS, Amy .... 570-321-4135 388 H rogers@lycoming.edu
ROGERS, Andre .... 803-754-4100 407 F
ROGERS, Audra .... 620-450-2113 176 I audrar@prattcc.edu
ROGERS, B. Keith .... 702-895-3201 270 J
ROGERS, Benjamin .... 512-245-4822 449 G br16@txstate.edu
ROGERS, Brandon .... 253-589-5727 478 A brandon.rogers@cptc.edu
ROGERS, Brian .... 503-494-8362 374 F cdrcadmin@ohsu.edu
ROGERS, Bridget .... 212-659-7209 303 E brogers@tkc.edu
ROGERS, Carrie .... 218-299-3000 234 K
ROGERS, Chris .... 541-867-8549 374 D chris.rogers@oregoncoast.edu
ROGERS, Christina .... 212-659-7200 303 E crogers@tkc.edu
ROGERS, Christine .... 602-383-8228.. 16 G crogers@uat.edu
ROGERS, Christopher ... 847-970-4833 152 F crogers@usml.edu
ROGERS, Chuck .... 804-289-8603 471 E crogers2@richmond.edu
ROGERS, Cindy, A .... 972-860-8187 433 H car3810@dcccd.edu
ROGERS, Cody .... 907-474-6026.. 10 B cbrogers@alaska.edu
ROGERS, Craig .... 706-776-0104 124 B crogers@piedmont.edu
ROGERS, Craig, L .... 270-789-5057 179 G crogers@campbellsville.edu
ROGERS, Danny .... 719-846-5619.. 83 I danny.rogers@trinidadstate.edu
ROGERS, David .... 602-384-2555.. 11 H dave.rogers@bryanuniversity.edu
ROGERS, David, E .... 315-684-6044 320 E rogersde@morrisville.edu
ROGERS, Deborah .... 585-340-9588 296 B drogers@crcds.edu
ROGERS, Donnita .... 405-466-3262 366 B ddrogers@langston.edu
ROGERS, Duke .... 785-227-3380 171 H rogersk@bethanylb.edu
ROGERS, Elsa, P .... 239-513-1122 102 C erogers@hodges.edu
ROGERS, Emily .... 912-478-7288 120 A erogers@georgiasouthern.edu
ROGERS, Eric .... 570-342-8000 383 F
ROGERS, Falonda .... 513-569-1759 350 C falonda.rogers@cincinnatistate.edu
ROGERS, Frederick .... 803-508-7272 405 C rogersf@atc.edu
ROGERS, Gail .... 423-746-5202 425 C grogers@tnwesleyan.edu
ROGERS, Gary .... 816-322-0110 250 E gary.rogers@calvary.edu
ROGERS, Hannah .... 706-233-7327 125 A hrogers@shorter.edu
ROGERS, Heather .... 270-901-1116 182 E heather.rogers@kctcs.edu
ROGERS, Holly .... 518-738-8500 299 B
ROGERS, Irina .... 205-453-6300.. 93 H
ROGERS, J.R .... 707-965-6411.. 55 H jrogers@puc.edu
ROGERS, Jack .... 724-938-4961 394 C rogers@calu.edu
ROGERS, James .... 212-327-8506 312 B jrogers@mail.rockefeller.edu
ROGERS, Jan .... 229-500-3056 114 F jan.rogers@asurams.edu
ROGERS, Janet .... 765-998-5330 161 A jnrogers@taylor.edu
ROGERS, Jason .... 615-460-6441 417 B jason.rogers@belmont.edu
ROGERS, Jaye .... 765-641-4442 153 D jlrogers2@anderson.edu
ROGERS, Jevita .... 719-255-3460.. 84 A jrogers3@uccs.edu
ROGERS, Jolene, R .... 712-362-0431 166 H jrogers@iowalakes.edu
ROGERS, Josh .... 928-536-6227.. 14 L joshua.rogers@npc.edu
ROGERS, Julian .... 216-368-1723 349 B julian.rogers@case.edu
ROGERS, Karen, L .... 334-844-5384.... 4 E klr0008@auburn.edu
ROGERS, Kathleen, R ... 617-521-2276 218 C kathleen.rogers@simmons.edu
ROGERS, Katrina, S .... 805-898-2924.. 42 G krogers@fielding.edu
ROGERS, Kelly .... 815-280-2217 140 I krogers@jjc.edu
ROGERS, Kent .... 406-756-3919 262 H krogers@fvcc.edu
ROGERS, Kim .... 618-437-5321 147 F rogers@rlc.edu
ROGERS, Kim .... 580-559-5677 365 J kimmrog@ecok.edu
ROGERS, Kimberly, R ... 510-215-3806.. 40 G krogers@contracosta.edu
ROGERS, Lalita .... 318-670-9223 191 B lrogers@susla.edu
ROGERS, Larson .... 617-588-1318 206 B lrogers@bfit.edu
ROGERS, Lynn .... 518-782-6654 314 K lrogers@siena.edu
ROGERS, Mark .... 478-274-7871 123 E mwrogers@oftc.edu
ROGERS, Melissa .... 901-321-3545 417 G cbu@bkstr.com
ROGERS, Michael .... 202-274-5986.. 94 B michael.rogers@udc.edu
ROGERS, Michelle, L .... 909-748-8138.. 72 E michelle_rogers@redlands.edu
ROGERS, Mike .... 209-946-2569.. 71 E mrogers@pacific.edu
ROGERS, Nancy, B .... 812-237-7900 155 H nancy.rogers@indstate.edu
ROGERS, Nashitka .... 662-252-8000 248 B nrogers@rustcollege.edu
ROGERS, Patricia, L .... 218-733-7600 238 A patricia.rogers@lsc.edu
ROGERS, Patrick .... 802-635-1417 463 B patrick.rogers@northernvermont.edu
ROGERS, Phil .... 208-459-5282 131 A progers@collegeofidaho.edu
ROGERS, Philip .... 252-328-6212 340 H chancelloroffice@ecu.edu
ROGERS, Piper .... 801-832-2139 461 A progers@westminstercollege.edu
ROGERS, Randy .... 336-386-3466 338 B rogersrj@surry.edu
ROGERS, Ray .... 512-245-2645 449 G r_r836@txstate.edu
ROGERS, Rickey .... 870-245-5221.. 20 H rogersr@obu.edu
ROGERS, Rodney, K .... 419-372-2211 348 F rrogers@bgsu.edu
ROGERS, Russell .... 201-216-5688 282 L russell.rogers@stevens.edu
ROGERS, Sandra .... 630-889-6461 145 D srogers@nuhs.edu
ROGERS, Scott .... 509-542-4834 478 B srogers@columbiabasin.edu
ROGERS, Sonya .... 251-981-3771.... 5 B sonya.rogers@columbiasouthern.edu
ROGERS, Stephanie ...... 318-670-9244 191 B srogers@susla.edu
ROGERS, Steve .... 541-440-4625 376 F steve.rogers@umpqua.edu
ROGERS, Susan .... 845-431-8952 298 B susan.rogers1@sunydutchess.edu
ROGERS, Tammy .... 706-880-8344 121 K trogers@lagrange.edu
ROGERS, Tamy .... 214-333-5158 433 D tamyr@dbu.edu
ROGERS, Tarsha, M ...... 252-335-3327 341 A tmrogers@ecsu.edu
ROGERS, Terri .... 417-328-1520 258 K tlrogers@sbuniv.edu
ROGERS, Terri .... 580-745-2510 369 F trogers@se.edu
ROGERS, Thomas .... 502-935-6853 181 H thomas.rogers@kctcs.edu
ROGERS, Timothy .... 315-866-0300 301 B rogerstd@herkimer.edu
ROGERS, Toby .... 806-720-7627 438 F toby.rogers@lcu.edu
ROGERS, Tracy .... 719-587-7990.. 77 F tracy_rogers@adams.edu
ROGERS, Victor .... 316-295-5812 173 G victor_rogers@friends.edu
ROGERS-ADKINSON, Diana .... 570-389-4308 393 E drogers@bloomu.edu
ROGERS-LOWERY, Constance .... 704-645-4803 327 H clowery@catawba.edu
ROGG, Michael .... 660-596-7172 259 D mrogg@sfccmo.edu
ROGGEMAN, Pamela .... 602-557-1476.. 16 L pamela.roggeman@phoenix.edu
ROGGIE, Edie .... 315-786-2200 302 I eroggie@sunyjefferson.edu
ROGGOW, Michael ...... 508-588-9100 214 F mroggow@massasoit.mass.edu
ROGSTAD, Leanne .... 763-488-2465 237 G leanne.rogstad@hennepintech.edu
ROHALL, David .... 740-654-6711 358 L rohall@ohio.edu
ROHAN, Robert, C .... 240-500-2367 199 A rcrohan@hagerstowncc.edu
ROHANI, Mushka .... 425-640-1647 479 A mushka.rohani@edcc.edu
ROHDE, Jeffrey .... 310-506-6347.. 56 H jeffrey.rohde@pepperdine.edu
ROHDE, Monika .... 516-686-7615 308 H monika.rohde@nyit.edu
ROHDE, Scott .... 860-685-2809.. 90 A srohde@wesleyan.edu
ROHDER-TONELLI, Kelly .... 815-280-2915 140 I krohder@jjc.edu
ROHLEDER, John .... 651-779-3496 237 D john.rohleder@century.edu
ROHLENA, Andrea .... 712-274-6400 170 H andrea.rohlena@witcc.edu
ROHLENA, Mark .... 540-636-2900 464 O mark.rohlena@christendom.edu

ROHLFING, Alexis .... 603-880-8308 273 F
arohlfing@thomasmorecollege.edu
ROHLFING, Andrea .... 312-369-7694 136 C
arohlfing@colum.edu
ROHLMAN, Jessica .... 501-977-2004.. 23 D
rohlman@uaccm.edu
ROHMAN, Chad .... 708-524-6816 137 A
crohman@dom.edu
ROHMANN, LeeAnn ...... 661-940-9300.. 45 E
ROHMANN, LeeAnn ...... 831-424-6767.. 35 N
ROHN, Marisa .... 330-494-6170 360 I
mrohn@starkstate.edu
ROHNER, Christy .... 270-686-4243 179 F
christy.rohner@brescia.edu
ROHNER, Tom .... 312-662-4141 132 D
trohner@adler.edu
ROHR, Denise .... 513-569-4972 350 C
denise.rohr@cincinnatistate.edu
ROHR, Margie .... 973-290-4054 282 G
mrohr@steu.edu
ROHR ADAMS, Betsy ..... 315-386-7951 319 E
rohradams@canton.edu
ROHRBACK, Jane, T ..... 248-204-3177 226 E
jrohrback@ltu.edu
ROHRBAUGH,
Suzanne, Y .... 336-633-0218 336 F
syrohrbaugh@randolph.edu
ROHRER, Brad .... 305-284-3961 112 K
brohrer@miami.edu
ROHRER, Thelma 260-982-5327 158W
tsrohrer@manchester.edu
ROHRMAN, Patrick .... 252-940-6426 332 A
patrick.rohrman@beaufortccc.edu
ROHWER, Debbie .... 940-565-3514 453 B
debbie.rohwer@unt.edu
ROIDT, Joseph .... 605-995-2625 414 A
joseph.roidt@dwu.edu
ROIG, Katy .... 619-260-7404.. 72 H
kroig@sandiego.edu
ROJAS, Balbina, J .... 787-766-1717 509 C
barojas@uagm.edu
ROJAS, Carlos .... 787-840-2575 508 G
crojas@psm.edu
ROJAS, Daniela .... 402-399-2603 265 H
drojas@csm.edu
ROJAS, Eddy, M .... 651-962-6720 243 F
eddy.rojas@stthomas.edu
ROJAS, Eddy, M .... 937-229-4632 362 C
erojas1@udayton.edu
ROJAS, Felipe, E .... 304-336-8474 489 B
felipe.rojas@westliberty.edu
ROJAS, Frank .... 626-624-4673.. 50 G
ROJAS, Frank .... 413-565-1000 205 I
ROJAS, Gilbert .... 801-274-3280 460 E
gilbert.rojas@wgu.edu
ROJAS, Jason .... 860-297-4166.. 88 I
jason.rojas@trincoll.edu
ROJAS, Jesus .... 912-525-5000 124 G
jrojas@scad.edu
ROJAS, Legier .... 787-798-3001 509 F
legier.rojas@uccaribe.edu
ROJAS, Liliana .... 415-422-6707.. 72 I
lrojas3@usfca.edu
ROJAS, Lisa .... 731-425-8835 423 F
lrojas@jscc.edu
ROJAS, Maria .... 620-225-0186 173 A
mrojas@dc3.edu
ROJAS, Raquel .... 787-765-1915 507 G
rrojas@opto.inter.edu
ROJAS, Robyn, D .... 405-325-3337 370 J
rrojas@ou.edu
ROJAS, Rodney .... 213-613-2200.. 65 D
rodney_rojas@sciarc.edu
ROJAS-MORA, Norma ... 661-395-4382.. 47 B
norma.rojas@bakersfieldcollege.edu
ROJCEWICZ, Peter .... 805-969-3626.. 55 I
projcewicz@pacifica.edu
ROKAVEC, Gregg .... 570-577-7439 379 A
gregg.rokavec@bucknell.edu
ROKSANDIC, Stevo .... 614-234-1644 356 E
sroksandic@mchs.com
ROLAND, David, E .... 706-233-7505 125 A
droland@shorter.edu
ROLAND, Harriet, A ...... 803-533-3790 410 H
rolandha@scsu.edu
ROLAND, Julia .... 218-477-2777 239 A
julia.roland@mnstate.edu
ROLAND, Karin, P .... 229-245-3825 127 C
kroland@valdosta.edu
ROLAND, Kirc, J .... 360-442-2471 480 E
kroland@lowercolumbia.edu
ROLAND, Meg .... 541-917-4999 373 F
rolandm@linnbenton.edu
ROLAND, Shane .... 478-471-2414 122 D
shane.roland@mga.edu
ROLAND, Troy .... 801-883-8336 458 B
ROLDAN, Rebecca .... 310-506-7596.. 56 H
rebecca.roldan@pepperdine.edu
ROLDAN, Richard .... 419-372-7937 348 F
rrolda@bgsu.edu
ROLEN, Aneisa, L .... 865-694-6403 424 C
alrolen@pstcc.edu
ROLEN, Chris .... 408-741-2055.. 75 C
chris.rolen@wvm.edu
ROLEN, Dalton Chris .... 408-741-2055.. 75 B
chris.rolen@wvm.edu
ROLEN, Scott .... 541-917-4420 373 F
rolens@linnbenton.edu
ROLEY, V. Vance .... 808-956-8377 129 B
vroley@hawaii.edu
ROLEY, V. Vance .... 808-956-8377 129 B
vance.roley@hawaii.edu
ROLFE, Alexander .... 503-554-2414 372 I
ROLFE, Kim .... 509-526-3011 485 C
rolfekb@whitman.edu
ROLFES, Katherine .... 337-521-8906 188 G
katherine.rolfes@solacc.edu
ROLFS, Megan .... 309-268-8129 138 F
megan.rolfs@heartland.edu
ROLFS, Trevor .... 620-792-9378 171 F
rolfst@bartonccc.edu
ROLING, Barbara .... 563-589-0332 170 G
broling@wartburgseminary.edu
ROLL, Debbie .... 907-564-8220.... 9 F
droll@alaskapacific.edu
ROLL, Todd .... 608-342-1245 495 E
rollt@uwplatt.edu
ROLLAND, Erik .... 909-869-2400.. 30 B
erolland@cpp.edu
ROLLE, Anthony .... 401-277-5489 404 E
anthony_rolle@uri.edu
ROLLE, Jo-Ann .... 718-270-5110 294 E
jrolle@mec.cuny.edu
ROLLE, Kevin, A .... 334-229-6500.... 4 B
krolle@alasu.edu
ROLLE, Rudolph 260-982-5444 158W
rhrolle@manchester.edu
ROLLEFSON, Kathy .... 641-585-8681 170 E
kathy.rollefson@waldorf.edu
ROLLER, Steven, A .... 617-228-2394 214 A
sroller@bhcc.mass.edu
ROLLERSON,
Terrance, J .... 651-628-3306 243 E
tjrollerson@unwsp.edu
ROLLING, Kristin .... 608-246-6677 497 I
krolling1@madisoncollege.edu
ROLLING, Matthew .... 402-643-4052 268 B
fr.matthew-rolling@sggs.edu
ROLLINGS, David .... 803-323-2191 413 D
rollingsd@winthrop.edu
ROLLINGS, Grenna .... 972-860-8181 433 H
grollings@dcccd.edu
ROLLINO, Richard .... 307-332-2930 500 J
rick.rollino@wyomingcatholic.edu
ROLLINS, Adam .... 423-869-6421 420 A
adam.rollins@lmunet.edu
ROLLINS, Alison .... 301-295-3357 502 B
alison.rollins@usuhs.edu
ROLLINS, Alyssa .... 503-838-8000 377 C
ROLLINS, Charlene .... 512-505-3060 437 B
csrollins@htu.edu
ROLLINS, Cheryl .... 443-885-4429 200 F
cheryl.rollins@morgan.edu
ROLLINS, Kate .... 402-354-7264 267 E
kate.rollins@methodistcollege.edu
ROLLINS, Kathy .... 864-379-6546 408 F
rollins@erskine.edu
ROLLINS, Maxwell .... 843-863-7956 406 C
mrollins@csuniv.edu
ROLLINS, Pam .... 334-420-4253.... 3 H
prollins@trenholmstate.edu
ROLLINS, Paul .... 276-376-3452 471 G
pmb6bn@uvawise.edu
ROLLINS, Stephen .... 907-786-1825.. 10 A
srollins@alaska.edu
ROLLINS, Tina .... 757-727-5371 466 L
tina.rollins@hamptonu.edu
ROLLINS, Tyler .... 916-691-7052.. 50 K
rollint@crc.losrios.edu
ROLLISON, Jeffrey .... 610-647-4400 385 K
jrollison@immaculata.edu
ROLLMAN,
Catherine, A .... 804-752-7270 469 B
crollman@rmc.edu
ROLLOFF, Mary, K .... 920-433-6639 490 H
mary.rolloff@bellincollege.edu
ROLLOR, Michael .... 410-706-1875 202 F
mrollor@umaryland.edu
ROLLS, Dickie .... 620-252-7053 172 K
rolls.dickie@coffeyville.edu
ROLLS, Niccole .... 301-696-3717 199 C
rolls@hood.edu
ROLNICK, Harriet, M ..... 213-738-6690.. 66 A
scale@swlaw.edu
ROLOFF, ReBecca, K ..... 651-690-6525 242 F
broloff@stkate.edu
ROLON, Reynaldo .... 787-279-1912 506 L
rrolon@bayamon.inter.edu
ROLPH, Marc .... 601-815-5133 248 G
mrolph@umc.edu
ROLSTON, Stacey .... 608-890-0960 494 C
stacey.rolston@uwss.wisconsin.edu
ROMÁN, Brenda .... 787-878-5475 506 J
broman@arecibo.inter.edu
ROMÁN ROA, Dennis .... 787-728-1515 512 A
dennis.roman@sagrado.edu
ROM, Curt .... 479-575-5900.. 21 H
crom@uark.edu
ROM, Kjetil .... 541-881-5746 376 E
krom@tvcc.cc
ROM, Matthew, C .... 405-325-6400 370 J
rom@ou.edu
ROMAGNI, Elizabeth ...... 901-321-3306 417 G
elizabeth.romagni@cbu.edu
ROMAGNI, Joanne .... 423-425-1743 426 D
joanne-romagni@utc.edu
ROMAGNOLI, Janice ...... 615-655-7274 292 B
jaromagnoli@cazenovia.edu
ROMALI, Reagan .... 310-233-4051.. 49 F
romalir@lahc.edu
ROMAN, Alberto, J .... 323-265-8663.. 49 D
vanhalkm@elac.edu
ROMAN, Allison .... 616-234-5536 231 D
alli.roman@vai.edu
ROMAN, Andrew .... 251-981-3771.... 5 B
andrew.roman@columbiasouthern.edu
ROMAN, Angela .... 231-591-2674 223 H
angelaroman@ferris.edu
ROMAN, Aris .... 787-891-0925 506 I
aroman@aguadilla.inter.edu
ROMAN, Irene .... 954-322-1612.. 99 E
ROMAN, Jennifer .... 214-329-4447 429 L
jennifer.roman@bgu.edu
ROMAN, Juan, E .... 787-841-2000 508 H
jroman@pucpr.edu
ROMAN, Judith .... 787-780-0070 504 E
judroman@caribbean.edu
ROMAN, Kristen .... 608-262-4527 494 D
kristen.roman@wisc.edu
ROMAN, Vladimir .... 787-763-6425 506 H
vroman@inter.edu
ROMAN, Yosmeriz .... 856-225-6664 281 A
yosmeriz.roman@camden.rutgers.edu
ROMAN, Yosmeriz .... 513-556-1100 361 I
yosmeriz.roman@uc.edu
ROMAN-LAGUNAS,
Victoria .... 219-980-6707 157 A
viroman@iu.edu
ROMANCZUK, Jeffrey .... 704-499-9200.. 93 H
ROMANDINI, Russ .... 513-618-1930 350 B
rromandini@ccms.edu
ROMANELLI, Ralph .... 718-631-6262 295 B
ROMANELLI, Tina .... 919-760-8554 331 A
cromanelli@meredith.edu
ROMANO, Angela .... 845-431-8097 298 B
angela.romano@sunydutchess.edu
ROMANO, Carol .... 301-295-9002 502 B
carol.romano@usuhs.edu
ROMANO, Cenia, K .... 787-884-3838 504 C
vpacademico@atenascollege.edu
ROMANO, Christopher .. 201-684-7309 280 B
cromano@ramapo.edu
ROMANO, Fred, D .... 630-515-7435 144 C
froman@midwestern.edu
ROMANO, Joan .... 617-989-4908 219 D
romanoj3@wit.edu
ROMANO, Linda .... 718-990-2023 313 B
romanol@stjohns.edu
ROMANO, Matthew .... 803-786-3770 407 E
mromano@columbiasc.edu
ROMANO, Nicole .... 302-356-6846.. 91 C
nicole.romano@wilmu.edu
ROMANO, Sandra .... 340-692-4254 512 B
sromano@live.uvi.edu
ROMANO, Susan .... 585-245-5731 317 E
romano@geneseo.edu
ROMANO, Victor .... 305-899-3756.. 96 A
vromano@barry.edu
ROMANO, Wendy, W .... 215-871-6300 395 A
wendyr@pcom.edu
ROMANOSKY, Neil .... 740-593-2705 358 L
romanosky@ohio.edu
ROMANT, Stacy .... 414-288-3654 492 E
stacy.romant@marquette.edu
ROMAY, Melanie .... 215-717-6380 399 I
mromay@uarts.edu
ROMBALSKI, Patrick .... 617-792-3636 134 D
prombalski@chamberlain.edu
ROME, Alan, K .... 440-943-7600 360 D
akrome@dioceseofcleveland.org
ROME, Alan, K .... 440-943-7600 360 D
cpl@dioceseofcleveland.org
ROME, Dennis .... 773-442-5420 145 G
d-rome@neiu.edu
ROME, JoAnne .... 413-552-2259 214 D
jrome@hcc.edu
ROME, Michael .... 281-649-3772 436 D
merome@hbu.edu
ROMEO, Jamie .... 860-701-3530.. 88 C
romeo_j@mitchell.edu
ROMEO, Matt .... 203-582-8990.. 88 F
matt.romeo@qu.edu
ROMEO TARTE, Mary .... 313-664-7451 222 C
mrtarte@collegeforcreativestudies.edu
ROMER, Charles .... 386-312-4074 107 A
charlesromer@sjrstate.edu
ROMER-NIEMIEC, Ellen . 773-371-5445 134 C
eromer-niemiec@ctu.edu
ROMERO, Angel, F .... 787-765-1915 507 G
aromero@opto.inter.edu
ROMERO, Bianca .... 909-448-4693.. 71 C
bromero@laverne.edu
ROMERO, Cecilia .... 505-747-5477 287 C
cromero@nnmc.edu
ROMERO, Christina .... 714-564-6091.. 58 F
romero_christina@sac.edu
ROMERO, Clarence .... 505-454-3369 286 C
clromero@nmhu.edu
ROMERO, Clorinda .... 575-758-8914 286 A
clorindar@midwiferycollege.edu
ROMERO, Cynthia .... 757-446-7414 465 H
romerocc@evms.edu
ROMERO, Eileen .... 914-594-4495 308 J
eileen_romero@nymc.edu
ROMERO, Elizabeth .... 951-827-2750.. 70 B
elizabeth.romero@ucr.edu
ROMERO, Henrietta .... 505-454-3405 286 C
hromero@nmhu.edu
ROMERO, Herminio .... 787-622-8000 509 H
hromero@pupr.edu
ROMERO, Jessica .... 787-894-2828 511 G
jessica.romero1@upr.edu
ROMERO, Jose .... 787-864-2222 507 B
jose.romero@guayama.inter.edu
ROMERO, Julie .... 505-984-6075 287 F
julie.romero@sjc.edu
ROMERO, Lizbeth .... 787-878-5475 506 J
lromero@arecibo.inter.edu
ROMERO, Lyndsi .... 620-241-0723 172 H
lyndsi.romero@centralchristian.edu
ROMERO, Manuel .... 212-220-1238 292 G
mromero@bmcc.cuny.edu
ROMERO, Monica .... 619-388-5025.. 61 A
mdromero@sdccd.edu
ROMERO, Narda .... 914-674-7841 305 H
nromero@mercy.edu
ROMERO, Nehemias .... 626-968-1328.. 47 J
ROMERO, Ramona, E .... 609-258-2511 279 E
ramonar@princeton.edu
ROMERO, Reyna .... 713-221-8460 452 B
romeror@uhd.edu
ROMERO, Roxane .... 602-384-2555.. 11 H
roxane.romero@bryanuniversity.edu
ROMERO, Sally .... 970-943-2150.. 85 B
sromero@western.edu
ROMERO, Victor .... 432-837-8085 449 F
vromero@sulross.edu
ROMERO, Victoria .... 909-621-8149.. 63 E
vromero@scrippscollege.edu
ROMERO, Yaritza .... 210-688-3101 431 I
ROMERO-ALDAZ,
Patrick .... 303-458-4086.. 83 B
promeroaldaz@regis.edu
ROMERO-BEGLEY,
Carlita .... 559-325-3600.. 28 F
cromerobegley@chsu.edu
ROMERO-CURIEL,
Monica .... 907-852-1844.... 9 H
monica.romero-cruiel@ilisagvik.edu
ROMEU, Patricia .... 212-592-2389 314 I
promeu@sva.edu

ROMIG, Kenneth, J .... 724-946-7141 401 F
romigkj@westminster.edu
ROMIG, Phillip .... 303-273-3866.. 79 A
promig3@mines.edu
ROMINE, Rebecca .... 601-965-7021 244 C
rromine@belhaven.edu
ROMIOUS, Angila .... 424-207-3753.. 55 B
aromious@otis.edu
ROMKEY, Matthew .... 515-643-6663 168 B
mromkey@mercydesmoines.org
ROMNEY, Brett .... 602-366-9699.. 16 L
brett.romney@phoenix.edu
ROMNEY, Jake .... 208-496-3947 130 G
romneyri@byui.edu
ROMO, Anthony .... 559-651-2500.. 61 I
ROMO, Nanette .... 520-515-5399.. 11 O
romon@cochise.edu
ROMO, Paul .... 623-845-3051.. 13 E
paul.romo@gccaz.edu
ROMRELL, Danae .... 208-496-7543 130 G
romrelld@byui.edu
RONAN, Donald .... 937-769-1800 347 F
dronan@antioch.edu
RONCA, Paul, L .... 804-523-5239 473 A
pronca@reynolds.edu
RONCOLATO, David .... 814-332-5318 378 A
droncola@allegheny.edu
RONDA, Rene, S .... 787-743-7979 509 D
rsronda@suagm.edu
RONDEAU, RET.,
Ann Elisabeth .... 831-656-2511 501 K
ann.rondeau@nps.edu
RONDEAU,
Christopher, M .... 937-255-3636 501 A
christopher.rondeau@afit.edu
RONDEAU, Heather ...... 320-762-4589 236 G
heather.rondeau@alextech.edu
RONDEAU, Janet .... 518-244-2214 312 D
rondej@sage.edu
RONDENO, Joshua .... 504-280-1154 189 F
jrondeno@uno.edu
RONDINELLI, Diane ...... 904-826-0084.. 72 F
drondinelli@usa.edu
RONDON, Marvin .... 910-592-8081 337 D
mrondon@sampsoncc.edu
RONE, Angela .... 502-272-8100 179 D
arone@bellarmine.edu
RONEY, Kristen .... 808-932-7332 129 A
ksroney@hawaii.edu
RONEY, Kristen .... 808-932-7272 129 A
ksroney@hawaii.edu
RONEY, Kylee .... 217-362-6423 144 D
kroney@millikin.edu
RONEY, Linda .... 214-333-5147 433 D
linda@dbu.edu
RONK, Chris .... 336-725-8344 327 G
ronkc@carolinau.edu
RONKOSKI, Bob .... 636-922-8604 258 A
rronkoski@stchas.edu
RONNEBURG, Debra ..... 208-282-2602 131 E
ronndebr@isu.edu
RONNFELDT, Derek ...... 253-833-9111 480 A
dronnfeldt@greenriver.edu
RONNING, Jon .... 615-868-6503 421 B
RONNING LINDGREN,
Rachel .... 805-493-3690.. 29 E
rronning@callutheran.edu
ROOD, Denine .... 320-629-5126 239 G
denine.rood@pine.edu
ROOD, Robert .... 716-839-8503 297 F
rrood@daemen.edu
ROOD, TJ (Garrett) .... 812-237-6311 155 H
garrett.rood@indstate.edu
ROOF, Karin .... 843-953-4871 406 D
kroof1@citadel.edu
ROOF, Rick .... 434-582-2177 467 E
raroof@liberty.edu
ROOF, Steven, E .... 304-367-4363 488 L
steven.roof@fairmontstate.edu
ROOFNER, Perry, F ...... 412-397-5256 396 E
roofner@rmu.edu
ROOHANI, Ben .... 312-850-7154 135 E
broohani@ccc.edu
ROOHPARVAR,
Shahrooz .... 931-221-7883 416 H
roohparvars@apsu.edu
ROOK, Steve .... 501-332-0230.. 18 D
srook@asutr.edu
ROOK, Tony .... 252-618-6669 334 B
rookt@edgecombe.edu
ROOKE, Michael .... 860-738-6300.. 87 A
mrooke@nwcc.edu
ROOKER, Darrin .... 315-568-3063 309 H
drooker@northeastcollege.edu
ROOKER, Suzanne .... 580-477-7944 371 D
suzanne.rooker@wosc.edu
ROOKS, Bryan .... 970-248-1252.. 78 F
brooks@coloradomesa.edu
ROOKS, Stephanie .... 770-962-7580 121 B
srooks@gwinnetttech.edu
ROOKSBY, Jacob .... 509-313-3700 479 E
rooksby@lawschool.gonzaga.edu
ROONEY, CM, Aidan ..... 718-990-6570 313 B
rooneya@stjohns.edu
ROONEY, Anna-Marie ... 858-784-8469.. 63 F
ROONEY, Gerard, J .... 585-385-8010 313 A
grooney@sjfc.edu
ROONEY, John .... 402-643-4052 268 B
fr.john-rooney@sggs.edu
ROONEY, Larry .... 802-485-2499 461 H
lrooney@norwich.edu
ROONEY, Melinda .... 410-626-2540 201 E
melinda.rooney@sjc.edu
ROONEY, Paul .... 407-582-1100 113 C
prooney@valenciacollege.edu
ROONEY, Thomas 561-237-7181 103W
trooney@lynn.edu
ROOPNARINE, Darshini 315-445-4661 303 F
roopnatd@lemoyne.edu
ROOS, David .... 435-222-1252.. 83 D
droos@rvu.edu
ROOS, Jannicke .... 617-746-1990 210 E
jannicke.roos@hult.edu
ROOS, Johan .... 617-619-1900 210 E
johan.roos@hult.edu
ROOSA, Mark, S .... 310-506-4252.. 56 H
mark.roosa@pepperdine.edu
ROOSE, Craig .... 641-628-7632 164 B
roosec@central.edu
ROOSE, Robert .... 989-358-7200 220 G
rooser@alpenacc.edu
ROOSEVELT, Mark .... 505-984-6098 287 F
mroosevelt@sjc.edu
ROOT, David .... 606-539-4406 185 C
david.root@ucumberlands.edu
ROOT, Deborah .... 870-245-5510.. 20 H
rootd@obu.edu
ROOT, Jeff .... 870-245-4186.. 20 H
rootj@obu.edu
ROOT, John .... 512-245-2585 449 G
jr28@txstate.edu
ROOT, Mark, J .... 574-807-7219 153 G
rootm1@betheluniversity.edu
ROOT, Rennie, A .... 563-588-7775 167 I
rennie.root@loras.edu
ROOT, Shannon, A .... 210-832-2161 452 D
sroot@uiwtx.edu
ROOTH, Gerald, T .... 301-447-5003 201 A
rooth@msmary.edu
ROOTS, Keith, D .... 757-594-0581 465 A
keith.roots@cnu.edu
ROOTS, Rochelle .... 361-991-9403 444 G
rroots@stark.edu
ROPELLA, Kristina .... 414-288-5460 492 E
kristina.ropella@marquette.edu
ROPER, Amy .... 803-793-5149 408 A
ropera@denmarktech.edu
ROPER, Chris .... 304-358-2000 486 E
ROPER, Craig .... 618-545-3137 141 C
croper@kaskaskia.edu
ROPER, David .... 843-349-6532 407 B
droper@coastal.edu
ROPER, Emily .... 936-294-2395 449 E
rcr039@shsu.edu
ROPER, Gary .... 575-234-9205 287 I
groper@senmc.edu
ROPER, Gina .... 541-881-5577 376 E
groper@tvcc.cc
ROPER, Lari .... 843-349-3658 409 A
laura.roper@hgtc.edu
ROPER, Melinda .... 805-493-3553.. 29 E
mroper@callutheran.edu
ROPER, Teri .... 501-882-8967.. 17 H
tlroper@asub.edu
ROPER-DOTEN, Emily .... 781-292-2201 209 E
emily.roper-doten@olin.edu
ROPETI, Siamaua .... 684-699-2722 503 A
s.ropeti@amsamoa.edu
RORABAUGH, Jim .... 307-532-8336 500 A
jrorabaugh@ewc.wy.edu
RORK, Jeannette .... 570-372-4242 398 A
rork@susqu.edu
RORRER, Caleb .... 336-342-4261 337 B
rorrerm8871@rockinghamcc.edu
ROSA, Belinda .... 787-743-7979 509 D
ac_brosa@suagm.edu
ROSA, Carmen .... 203-576-4652.. 89 A
carosa@bridgeport.edu
ROSA, Jerry .... 718-518-6561 293 F
jrosa@hostos.cuny.edu
ROSA, Jessie .... 334-244-3712.... 4 F
jrosa@aum.edu
ROSA, Maria .... 270-809-4225 184 A
mrosa1@murraystate.edu
ROSA, Peter .... 203-837-8376.. 86 A
rosap@wcsu.edu
ROSA, Sandra .... 787-279-1912 506 L
srosa@bayamon.inter.edu
ROSA, Veronica .... 603-358-2425 274 A
veronica.rosa@keene.edu
ROSA-NUNEZ,
Waleska, Y .... 787-480-2386 505 A
wrosa01@sanjuan.pr
ROSAASEN, Orlynn .... 701-777-3823 344 H
orlynn.rosaasen@und.edu
ROSACCO, Claire .... 216-987-4804 351 D
claire.rosacco@tri-c.edu
ROSADO, Akilah .... 212-875-4596 290 F
arosado@bankstreet.edu
ROSADO, Alexander .... 787-878-5475 506 J
alrosado@arecibo.inter.edu
ROSADO, Christine .... 908-852-1440 275 H
christine.rosado@centenaryuniversity.edu
ROSADO, Clarisa, Z ...... 787-850-9345 511 B
clarisa.rosado2@upr.edu
ROSADO, Ernie .... 251-981-3771.... 5 B
ernie.rosado@columbiasouthern.edu
ROSADO, Inia .... 787-878-5475 506 J
irosado@arecibo.inter.edu
ROSADO, Martin .... 787-884-6000 506 B
mrosado@icprjc.edu
ROSADO, Reinaldo .... 787-284-1912 507 D
rrosado@ponce.inter.edu
ROSADO, Renee .... 413-205-3248 205 C
renee.rosado@aic.edu
ROSADO-BERRIOS,
Carmen, C .... 787-857-3600 506 K
crosado@br.inter.edu
ROSADO-LOPEZ,
Eleane .... 787-857-3600 506 K
erosado@br.inter.edu
ROSALES, Ilian .... 619-934-0797.. 61 C
ROSANDICH,
Thomas, J .... 251-626-3303.... 7 E
president@ussa.edu
ROSARIO, Lisanette ...... 718-518-4311 293 F
lrosario@hostos.cuny.edu
ROSARIO, Lucy .... 787-284-1912 507 D
lrsario@ponce.inter.edu
ROSARIO, Yolanda .... 787-746-1400 505 L
yrosario@huertas.edu
ROSARIO, Yoleidy .... 941-309-4023 106 J
yrosario@ringling.edu
ROSARIO, Yvette .... 718-960-8755 293 E
yvette.rosario@lehman.cuny.edu
ROSARIO DELGADO,
Victor .... 787-758-5297 511 F
victor.rosario1@upr.edu
ROSARIO-NIEVES, Ilia ... 787-841-2000 508 H
irosario@pucpr.edu
ROSARIO-PEREZ,
Glorivee .... 787-738-4660 510 B
glorivee.rosario@upr.edu
ROSARIO PEREZ,
Glorivee .... 787-738-4660 511 A
glorivee.rosario@upr.edu
ROSARIO-RODRIGUEZ,
Elizabeth .... 787-480-2444 505 A
erosario03@sanjuan.pr
ROSARIO-ROSARIO,
Yolanda .... 787-725-6500 504 F
yrosario@albizu.edu
ROSAS, Alisha .... 909-652-6502.. 36 B
alisha.rosas@chaffey.edu
ROSAS, Erudina .... 787-832-6000 506 B
erosas@icprjc.edu
ROSAS, Mirna .... 480-423-6754.. 14 B
mirna.rosas@scottsdalecc.edu
ROSAS, Olivia .... 909-384-8992.. 60 F
rrosas@sbccd.cc.ca.us
ROSASCHI, Catherine .... 703-416-1441 465 E
registrar@divinemercy.edu
ROSATI, David, M .... 617-333-2302 208 D
david.rosati@curry.edu
ROSATI, Ross .... 612-625-5516 242 K
rosat002@umn.edu
ROSAY, Andre .... 907-786-4852.. 10 A
arosay@alaska.edu
ROSBERG, Gerald, M ..... 212-854-9967 296 H
gerry.rosberg@columbia.edu
ROSBURY-HENNE,
Marcia .... 978-630-9337 215 A
mrosburyhenne@mwcc.mass.edu
ROSCH, Laura .... 417-208-0632 253 I
lrosch@kcumb.edu
ROSCH, Laura, M .... 630-515-6147 144 C
lrosch@midwestern.edu
ROSDAIL, Lisa .... 803-938-3794 412 G
lrosdai@uscsumter.edu
ROSE, Adam .... 501-450-3247.. 23 K
arose@uca.edu
ROSE, Alisha, D .... 901-678-2230 426 A
arose3@memphis.edu
ROSE, Allison .... 773-602-5000 135 A
ROSE, Billy .... 256-352-8110.... 4 A
billy.rose@wallacestate.edu
ROSE, Breanna .... 828-652-6021 335 H
ROSE, Calandra .... 580-349-1302 367 F
ROSE, Camille .... 970-521-6952.. 82 B
camille.rose@njc.edu
ROSE, Carey .... 254-298-8326 445 B
carey.rose@templejc.edu
ROSE, Carlene .... 603-524-3207 271 K
crose@ccsnh.edu
ROSE, Carrie, J .... 724-458-2134 384 F
rosecj@gcc.edu
ROSE, III, Charles, H ... 419-772-2205 358 D
c-rose.5@onu.edu
ROSE, Clayton .... 207-725-3221 194 A
crose@bowdoin.edu
ROSE, Dan, C .... 860-701-6798 502 F
dan.c.rose@uscga.edu
ROSE, Deatrea .... 620-235-6556 176 H
drose@pittstate.edu
ROSE, Dianna .... 831-755-6700.. 44 J
ROSE, Don .... 620-665-3597 174 D
rosed@hutchcc.edu
ROSE, Emily .... 310-825-4606.. 69 D
erose@conet.ucla.edu
ROSE, Eric, D .... 201-216-8724 282 L
eric.rose@stevens.edu
ROSE, Greg .... 813-253-7015 102 A
jrose44@hccfl.edu
ROSE, Gregory .... 724-925-4071 401 H
roseg@westmoreland.edu
ROSE, Gregory, S .... 740-725-6218 358 E
rose.9@osu.edu
ROSE, Jennie .... 785-628-4231 173 E
jrose.cw@ad.fhsu.edu
ROSE, John .... 212-772-4242 294 A
john.rose@hunter.cuny.edu
ROSE, Julie .... 607-587-3979 319 C
roseja@alfredstate.edu
ROSE, Justin .... 217-206-6333 151 E
jrose22@uis.edu
ROSE, Kevin .... 903-434-8186 440 A
krose@ntcc.edu
ROSE, Laura .... 201-216-5000 282 L
lrose2@stevens.edu
ROSE, Lawrence, D .... 909-537-3703.. 33 B
lrose@csusb.edu
ROSE, JR., LeRoy .... 401-598-1000 403 E
leroy.rosejr@jwu.edu
ROSE, Lesa .... 207-330-7743 194 H
rosele@mchp.edu
ROSE, Lisa .... 310-434-4402.. 63 B
rose_lisa@smc.edu
ROSE, Mark .... 754-312-2898 103 R
ROSE, Matt .... 276-523-2400 473 E
mrose@mecc.edu
ROSE, Melissa .... 304-243-2233 490 F
mrose@wheeling.edu
ROSE, Randall .... 276-964-7278 474 E
randall.rose@sw.edu
ROSE, JR., Robert .... 703-333-5904 476 G
rrose@wuv.edu
ROSE, Ryan .... 620-432-0348 176 A
rarose@neosho.edu
ROSE, Samantha .... 334-290-3265.... 2 F
samantha.rose@istc.edu
ROSE, Sarah .... 703-908-7839 468 A
srose@marymount.edu
ROSE, Saxton .... 336-631-1226 343 C
roses@uncsa.edu
ROSE, Shawn .... 970-521-6601.. 82 B
shawn.rose@njc.edu
ROSE, Stephanie .... 401-254-3036 404 C
sm551@bncollege.com
ROSE, Steven .... 973-684-5900 279 B
srose@pccc.edu

ROSE-SEWELL, Quincy .. 719-549-3175.. 82 I
quincy.rose-sewell@pueblocc.edu
ROSEBERRY, David .... 206-934-4427 482 G
david.roseberry@seattlecolleges.edu
ROSEBORO, Donyell ...... 910-962-4084 343 B
roseborod@uncw.edu
ROSEBORO-BARNES,
Edwina .... 803-981-7162 413 F
eroseboro@yorktech.edu
ROSEBURR-OLOTU,
Dene .... 405-974-5946 370 H
droseburrolotu@uco.edu
ROSEBY, Yolanda .... 503-517-1024 377 B
yroseby@warnerpacific.edu
ROSEDALE, Jeff .... 914-323-5277 305 A
jeff.rosedale@mville.edu
ROSEL, Evangeline .... 845-938-2022 502 H
ROSEMOND, Michelle ... 678-407-5153 119 B
mrosemond@ggc.edu
ROSEN, Aaron .... 202-885-8674.. 94 D
arosen@wesleyseminary.edu
ROSEN, Alesha .... 301-846-2630 198 E
arosen@frederick.edu
ROSEN, Julie .... 602-386-4103.. 10 G
julie.rosen@arizonachristian.edu
ROSEN, Libby .... 785-594-6451 171 C
lrosen@stormontvail.org
ROSEN, Mike, S .... 713-743-8155 451 G
msrosen@uh.edu
ROSEN, Richard .... 207-326-2241 195 G
richard.rosen@mma.edu
ROSEN, Sara .... 404-413-6555 120 C
srosen@gsu.edu
ROSEN, Scott .... 757-479-3706 472 A
ROSEN, Steven, T .... 626-256-4673.. 37 D
srosen@coh.org
ROSEN-METSCH, Lisa ..... 212-854-6321 296 H
lm2892@columbia.edu
ROSENBAUM, Irving 954-262-1507 104M
irv@nova.edu
ROSENBAUM, Philip ..... 610-896-1290 385 H
prosenba@haverford.edu
ROSENBAUM,
Thomas, F .... 626-395-6301.. 29 B
tfr@caltech.edu
ROSENBERG, Alannah ... 949-582-4854.. 65 C
aorrison@saddleback.edu
ROSENBERG, Chaim ...... 718-854-2290 291 C
ROSENBERG, David ...... 845-731-3700 326 F
ROSENBERG, Elynn ...... 516-239-9002 314 J
ROSENBERG, Eric .... 973-720-2684 283 I
rosenberge@wpunj.edu
ROSENBERG, Randall .... 314-977-3827 258 H
randall.rosenberg@slu.edu
ROSENBERG, Sol .... 718-854-2290 291 C
ROSENBERG, Travis ...... 435-652-7522 459 G
travis.rosenberg@utahtech.edu
ROSENBERG, Warren .... 914-831-0219 296 F
wrosenberg@cw.edu
ROSENBERGER,
Benjamin .... 610-372-4721 396 A
brosenberger@racc.edu
ROSENBERGER, Jeanne 408-554-4366.. 63 A
jrosenberger@scu.edu
ROSENBERGER,
Jennifer .... 503-847-2548 377 A
jrosenberger@uws.edu
ROSENBLATT, Mark ...... 312-996-3500 151 D
mrosenbl@uic.edu
ROSENBLITH,
Suzane, N .... 716-645-6640 315 F
rosenbli@buffalo.edu
ROSENBLOOM, Stuart ... 312-461-0600 132 F
srosenbloom@aaart.edu
ROSENBLUM, Eliyohu ... 718-854-2290 291 C
ROSENBOOM, David ..... 661-255-1050.. 28 I
david@calarts.edu
ROSENBOOM, Sharon .... 712-722-6740 165 E
sharon.rosenboom@dordt.edu
ROSENBURGI, Melissa . 207-941-7175 194 D
ROSENBURY, Laura, A .. 352-273-0600 110 E
rosenbury@law.ufl.edu
ROSENCRANTS, Lydia ... 901-321-3315 417 G
lrosencr@cbu.edu
ROSENDAHL, Matt .... 218-726-6562 243 A
libaskus@d.umn.edu
ROSENFELD, Alan .... 808-689-2351 129 C
alan3@hawaii.edu
ROSENFELD, Chaim ...... 845-731-3700 326 F
ROSENFELD, Haley .... 781-736-8406 207 D
haleyrosenfeld@brandeis.edu
ROSENFELD, Sholom .... 718-774-5050 321 G
oholeitorah@aol.com

ROSENGART, Sharon ..... 973-720-3019 283 I
rosengarts@wpunj.edu
ROSENGARTEN, Jeffrey . 646-565-6239 322 B
jeffrey.rosengarten@touro.edu
ROSENGARTEN, Jeffrey . 646-565-6239 322 C
jeffrey.rosengarten@touro.edu
ROSENGARTEN, Lewis .. 607-753-4808 317 D
lewis.rosengarten@cortland.edu
ROSENGRANT, Bruce ..... 719-587-7846.. 77 F
brosengrant@adams.edu
ROSENOW, Thomas, C . 530-898-5556.. 31 A
trosenow@csuchico.edu
ROSENSAFT, Jean, B .... 212-824-2209 300 H
jrosensaft@huc.edu
ROSENSTEIN, Ilena ...... 860-768-4418.. 89 E
rosenstei@hartford.edu
ROSENSTEIN, Ilene .... 213-740-7711.. 73 C
irosenst@usc.edu
ROSENSTIEL, Todd .... 503-725-9554 375 D
rosensti@pdx.edu
ROSENSTOCK, Jeffrey .... 718-997-4995 295 A
jeffrey.rosenstock@qc.cuny.edu
ROSENTEL, Edward .... 850-729-5368 104 L
rosentee@nwfsc.edu
ROSENTHAL, Adam 954-262-5379 104M
jar1248@nova.edu
ROSENTHAL, Alisa, J .... 804-752-7268 469 B
alisarosenthal@rmc.edu
ROSENTHAL, Amy .... 269-471-3411 220 H
rosenthala@andrews.edu
ROSENTHAL, Austin ...... 918-444-2202 366 G
rosentha@nsuok.edu
ROSENTHAL, Bruce .... 859-344-3650 184 G
rosentb@thomasmore.edu
ROSENTHAL, Crystal ..... 949-854-8002.. 40 E
ROSENTHAL, Elijah .... 848-932-1994 281 B
elijah.rosenthal@ruf.rutgers.edu
ROSENTHAL, Eric .... 610-861-5565 391 B
erosenthal@northampton.edu
ROSENTHAL, Julie .... 303-373-2008.. 83 D
jrosenthal@rvu.edu
ROSENTHAL, Keith, M .. 415-485-9528.. 39 B
kmrosenthal@marin.edu
ROSENTHAL, Ken .... 818-677-2561.. 32 E
ken.rosenthal@csun.edu
ROSENTHAL, Lauren ..... 718-933-6700 306 J
lrosenthal@monroecollege.edu
ROSENTHAL, Lori .... 617-243-2074 210 G
lrosenthal@lasell.edu
ROSENTHAL,
Roseanne, K .... 312-225-6288 152 G
rrosenthal@vandercook.edu
ROSENTHAL, Susan .... 305-899-3050.. 96 A
srosenthal@barry.edu
ROSET, Alex .... 844-922-8228.. 91 E
ROSETTI, Crystal .... 909-607-7894.. 37 E
crystal.rosetti@claremont.edu
ROSETTI, Patricia, H ..... 570-961-4596 389 B
rosetti@marywood.edu
ROSEVEAR, Scott, G ..... 570-577-3647 379 A
scott.rosevear@bucknell.edu
ROSEVEARE, Mark .... 864-592-4763 411 E
rosevearem@sccsc.edu
ROSFELD, Stephen .... 513-556-6177 361 I
stephen.rosfeld@uc.edu
ROSHAU, Kristine .... 541-383-7407 371 I
kroshau@cocc.edu
ROSIER, Emily, J .... 304-457-6278 485 F
rosierej@ab.edu
ROSINSKI, David .... 413-782-3111 219 E
david.rosinski@wne.edu
ROSINSKI-KAUS,
Donna .... 732-255-0400 279 A
drosinski-kaus@ocean.edu
ROSIUS, Davius .... 863-638-2920 113 E
rosius@webber.edu
ROSKO, Thomas .... 831-656-2441 501 K
ROSKY, Bruce .... 818-610-6543.. 49 H
roskybr@piercecollege.edu
ROSMAN, Andrew 954-262-5064 104M
arosman1@nova.edu
ROSMANN, Vicki .... 713-780-9777 428 H
vrosman@acaom.edu
ROSNICK, Jonathan ...... 724-503-1001 401 D
ROSOFF, Nancy .... 215-572-2921 378 E
rosoffn@arcadia.edu
ROSOWSKY, David, V ... 785-532-5110 175 A
rosowsky@ksu.edu
ROSPLOCK, Valerie, R ... 607-735-1174 298 G
vrosplock@elmira.edu
ROSS, Aaron .... 419-289-5048 347 H
aross23@ashland.edu

ROSS, Amanda .... 315-268-6633 295 E
aross@clarkson.edu
ROSS, Angela .... 804-523-5029 473 A
aross@reynolds.edu
ROSS, Anissa .... 870-460-1036.. 22 E
ross@uamont.edu
ROSS, Beth .... 617-735-9701 209 A
ross@emmanuel.edu
ROSS, Casey .... 405-208-5979 367 E
crosspetherick@okcu.edu
ROSS, Cheryl .... 858-822-2797.. 70 C
caross@ucsd.edu
ROSS, Christine, C .... 434-223-6056 466 K
cross@hsc.edu
ROSS, Clint .... 928-774-3890.. 12 N
cross@indianbible.org
ROSS, Corey .... 517-750-1200 230 F
co126092@arbor.edu
ROSS, Crissy .... 513-569-1699 350 C
crissy.ross@cincinnatistate.edu
ROSS, David .... 501-279-4930.. 19 G
dross@harding.edu
ROSS, David .... 972-708-7340 434 F
ROSS, David, J .... 813-253-7680 102 A
dross26@hccfl.edu
ROSS, Desi .... 601-484-8823 246 B
dross1@meridiancc.edu
ROSS, Donald, E 561-237-7782 103W
dross@lynn.edu
ROSS, Elizabeth (Liz) .... 865-694-6444 424 C
eross@pstcc.edu
ROSS, Eric .... 660-263-4100 256 D
ericr@macc.edu
ROSS, III, Frank, E .... 317-940-9570 153 H
feross@butler.edu
ROSS, Gabe .... 916-568-3056.. 50 I
rossg@losrios.edu
ROSS, Gary .... 401-841-7501 501 L
gary.ross@usnwc.edu
ROSS, Gary, L .... 315-228-7401 296 C
gross@colgate.edu
ROSS, Gloria .... 662-254-3558 247 C
gloria.ross@mvsu.edu
ROSS, Hannah .... 802-443-5229 461 G
hross@middlebury.edu
ROSS, James .... 732-255-0400 279 A
jross@ocean.edu
ROSS, James, A .... 734-384-4259 227 F
jross@monroeccc.edu
ROSS, Jason .... 864-977-7026 410 A
jason.ross@ngu.edu
ROSS, Jeannie .... 620-862-5252 171 E
jeannie.ross@barclaycollege.edu
ROSS, Jeannine .... 207-859-1105 196 A
sfs@thomas.edu
ROSS, Jeffery .... 816-235-6212 260 D
umkccontracts@umkc.edu
ROSS, Jennifer .... 718-522-9073 290 B
jross@asa.edu
ROSS, Jennifer, A .... 260-422-5561 156 A
jaross@indianatech.edu
ROSS, Jeremy, B .... 423-439-5353 418 D
rossjb@etsu.edu
ROSS, Jerry, P .... 530-898-6116.. 31 A
ROSS, Jill .... 540-674-3600 473 F
jross@nr.edu
ROSS, Jim .... 252-249-1851 336 C
jross@pamlicocc.edu
ROSS, Joey .... 714-879-3901.. 45 J
jaross@hiu.edu
ROSS, Julia .... 540-231-9752 475 D
rjulie@vt.edu
ROSS, Julie, S .... 617-627-3360 219 A
j.ross@tufts.edu
ROSS, Keith, L .... 314-392-2355 255 H
president@mobap.edu
ROSS, Kendall .... 479-424-5140.. 22 A
kendall.ross@uafs.edu
ROSS, Kevin .... 714-532-7751.. 36 D
kross@chapman.edu
ROSS, Kevin, M 561-237-7823 103W
kross@lynn.edu
ROSS, Kristen .... 281-929-4653 442 E
kristen.ross@sjcd.edu
ROSS, Laura .... 407-708-2511 108 B
rossl@seminolestate.edu
ROSS, Laura .... 314-529-6893 254 D
lross@maryville.edu
ROSS, Lauren .... 937-512-2164 360 F
lauren.ross@sinclair.edu
ROSS, Leigh, A .... 601-984-2620 248 G
laross@umc.edu

ROSS, Lori, A .... 513-556-3483 361 I
rossla@ucmail.uc.edu
ROSS, Mari .... 704-687-7400 342 C
mari.ross@uncc.edu
ROSS, Matthew .... 717-815-1359 402 G
mross@ycp.edu
ROSS, Megan .... 507-285-7206 240 B
megan.ross@rctc.edu
ROSS, Mikki .... 806-742-2121 450 C
mikki.ross@ttu.edu
ROSS, Neil .... 785-320-4554 175 E
neilross@manhattantech.edu
ROSS, Pam .... 864-231-2000 405 F
pross@andersonuniversity.edu
ROSS, Patricia, A .... 801-585-7832 459 D
p.ross@utah.edu
ROSS, Paul .... 602-285-7855.. 13 H
paul.ross@phoenixcollege.edu
ROSS, JR., Quinton, T .. 334-229-4202..... 4 B
president.ross@alasu.edu
ROSS, Ramsey .... 850-729-5358 104 L
ramseyr@nwfsc.edu
ROSS, Reginald .... 973-720-6225 283 I
rossr@wpunj.edu
ROSS, Rick .... 360-417-6533 481 F
rross@pencol.edu
ROSS, Robin .... 828-327-7000 332 H
rross@cvcc.edu
ROSS, Sadie .... 518-587-2100 320 B
sadie.ross@esc.edu
ROSS, Sharon .... 914-961-8313 314 E
sross@svots.edu
ROSS, Sheila .... 414-277-7238 493 D
ross@msoe.edu
ROSS, Susan .... 304-367-4098 488 L
susan.ross@fairmontstate.edu
ROSS, Susan .... 570-321-4204 388 H
ross@lycoming.edu
ROSS, Tausha .... 513-875-3344 349 K
ROSS, Teri .... 330-494-6170 360 I
tross@starkstate.edu
ROSS, Thelma .... 301-546-0766 201 D
rosstl1@pgcc.edu
ROSS, Trevor .... 360-475-7120 481 B
tross@olympic.edu
ROSS, William .... 814-332-2316 378 A
wross@allegheny.edu
ROSS-SCOTT, Carol .... 607-778-5199 317 A
rossca@sunybroome.edu
ROSS STAMPS,
Clara, R .... 502-597-6786 183 A
clara.stamps@kysu.edu
ROSSBACH, Janet .... 646-660-6097 292 F
janet.rossbach@baruch.cuny.edu
ROSSELL, Anita .... 724-222-5330 391 E
arossell@penncommercial.edu
ROSSELLI, David .... 254-710-2561 430 F
dave_rosselli@baylor.edu
ROSSELLO, Jay .... 210-458-4105 455 B
jay.rossello@utsa.edu
ROSSER, Charice .... 252-536-7207 334 G
crosser@halifaxcc.edu
ROSSER, Edward .... 615-329-8775 418 E
erosser@fisk.edu
ROSSER, Edward .... 404-756-4000 115 E
ROSSER, Keith .... 315-268-7258 295 E
krosser@clarkson.edu
ROSSER, Virginia, J ...... 419-372-9865 348 F
jrosser@bgsu.edu
ROSSER-MIMS, Dionne . 334-448-5112.... 7 C
drosser-mims@troy.edu
ROSSETTI, Erin .... 802-626-6417 463 B
ROSSETTI, Gina .... 773-298-3598 148 I
rossetti@sxu.edu
ROSSI, Jaclyn .... 716-286-8761 309 F
jrossi@niagara.edu
ROSSI, Jamal .... 585-274-1010 323 E
jrossi@esm.rochester.edu
ROSSI, Janelle .... 707-664-2158.. 34 C
ROSSI, John, J .... 626-256-4673.. 37 D
jrossi@coh.org
ROSSI, Louis .... 302-831-1880.. 91 A
rossi@udel.edu
ROSSI, Reagan .... 208-459-5855 131 A
rrossi@collegeofidaho.edu
ROSSI, Renee .... 904-256-7458 102 G
rrossi@ju.edu
ROSSI-LONG, Jennifer .. 610-436-2501 394 F
jlong@wcupa.edu
ROSSIGNOL, Paul .... 505-438-8884 287 J
paul@acupuncturecollege.edu
ROSSITER, Andrew .... 808-923-9741 129 B
andrewro@hawaii.edu

ROSSITER, Sherry ... 740-593-4129 358 L bursar@ohio.edu
ROSSITER-SMITH, Carla, M ... 727-816-3190 105 E
ROSSITTO, Paul ... 860-832-1617 .. 85 F rossitto@ccsu.edu
ROSSMANN, Doralyn ... 406-994-6978 263 G doralyn@montana.edu
ROSSMILLER, Sheila ... 715-675-3331 498 E rossmiller@ntc.edu
ROSSMILLER, Zach ... 406-243-6556 263 D zachary.rossmiller@umontana.edu
ROSSON, Michael ... 718-368-5144 294 C mrosson@kbcc.cuny.edu
ROST, Jamie, D ... 407-582-5412 113 C jrost@valenciacollege.edu
ROSTAD, Jerry ... 701-239-6668 344 G jerry.rostad@ndus.edu
ROSTAR, Jimmy ... 252-328-1275 340 H rostarj@ecu.edu
ROSTER, Ellen ... 651-846-1324 240 E ellen.roster@saintpaul.edu
ROSTRON, Stephanie ... 937-502-3734 363 G srostron@wilberforce.edu
ROSU, Gabriela ... 480-732-7012 .. 13 B gabriela.rosu@cgc.edu
ROSZMAN, Deborah ... 419-448-3513 361 C roszmandl@tiffin.edu
ROTELLA, Christopher .. 516-572-9786 307 C christopher.rotella@ncc.edu
ROTGER, Mariolga ... 787-850-9364 511 B mariolga.rotger@upr.edu
ROTGER, Mariolga ... 787-850-9324 511 B mariolga.rotger@upr.edu
ROTH, Adam ... 203-582-3325 .. 88 F adam.roth@quinnipiac.edu
ROTH, Amy ... 513-875-3344 349 K amy.roth@chatfield.edu
ROTH, Ben ... 217-786-2773 142 F ben.roth@llcc.edu
ROTH, Beth ... 815-740-3216 152 E broth@stfrancis.edu
ROTH, Cindi ... 304-284-4040 489 E croth@mail.wvu.edu
ROTH, Deb ... 620-327-8279 174 B deb.roth@hesston.edu
ROTH, Don, F ... 530-754-5418 .. 69 A droth@ucdavis.edu
ROTH, Dori ... 620-327-4221 174 B
ROTH, Frank, A ... 610-758-3572 388 C far4@lehigh.edu
ROTH, James ... 405-208-5440 367 E jaroth@okcu.edu
ROTH, Jason ... 702-968-1633 271 D jroth@roseman.edu
ROTH, Jeff ... 310-206-8041 .. 69 D jroth@ponet.ucla.edu
ROTH, Jessica ... 650-508-3640 .. 54 G jroth@ndnu.edu
ROTH, John ... 510-231-5000 .. 46 N john.roth@kp.org
ROTH, John, C ... 718-940-5616 313 C jroth@sjcny.edu
ROTH, Marilyn, A ... 617-228-3338 214 A maroth@bhcc.edu
ROTH, Martin, S ... 304-357-4713 486 J
ROTH, Megan ... 325-674-2885 427 G mkr15a@acu.edu
ROTH, Merianne ... 817-257-5063 447 H m.roth@tcu.edu
ROTH, Michael ... 707-527-6939 .. 63 C mroth@santarosa.edu
ROTH, Michael, S ... 860-685-3500 .. 90 A mroth@wesleyan.edu
ROTH, Mike ... 503-589-8152 372 G mroth@corban.edu
ROTH, Neil ... 304-473-8312 490 E roth@wvwc.edu
ROTH, Rachel ... 973-618-3236 275 E rroth@caldwell.edu
ROTH, JR., Toby ... 989-774-3871 221 M rothj1t@cmich.edu
ROTH NICKS, Rebecca . 706-880-8088 121 K rroth@lagrange.edu
ROTHAMER, Russ ... 970-339-6300 .. 77 G russ.rothamer@aims.edu
ROTHAUS, Richard, M .. 989-774-3931 221 M provost@cmich.edu
ROTHBERG, Jacob ... 914-736-1500 310 B
ROTHE, Justy ... 217-532-2181 141 H jrothe@lakelandcollege.edu
ROTHELL, Cynthia ... 540-373-2200 465 G crothell@evcc.edu
ROTHENBERG, Jeffrey ... 317-338-3879 160 H
ROTHENBERGER, Sara .. 860-439-2834 .. 87 F srothenb@conncoll.edu
ROTHENBUHLER, Eric ... 314-246-7154 261 D erothenbuhler@webster.edu
ROTHFELS, Nigel ... 414-229-6041 495 B rothfels@uwm.edu
ROTHMAN, Jay, O ... 608-262-2321 494 C
ROTHMEYER, Melissa ... 415-955-2100 .. 25 A
ROTHMEYER, Michelle .. 815-825-9807 141 D mrothmeyer@kish.edu
ROTHROCK, Dan ... 253-272-1126 480 F
ROTHROCK, Dan ... 253-272-1126 480 F drothrock@ncad.edu
ROTHSCHILD, Dovid, N 516-255-4700 311 E rdnr@mlb.edu
ROTHSCHILD, Martha, D ... 410-777-2701 197 C mdrothschild@aacc.edu
ROTHSTEIN, Carol ... 615-353-3326 424 A carol.rothstein@nscc.edu
ROTHSTEIN, Gary ... 931-540-2558 423 D grothstein@columbiastate.edu
ROTHWELL, Suzanne ... 573-875-7563 251 A srothwell@ccis.edu
ROTICH, Herbert, K ... 517-750-1200 230 F hrotich@arbor.edu
ROTKIEWICZ, Melissa, S ... 413-545-0333 211 D mlr@uhs.umass.edu
ROTOLO, Rene, M ... 718-960-8539 293 E rene.rotolo@lehman.cuny.edu
ROTONDO, Denise, M .. 716-888-2160 291 M rotondod@canisius.edu
ROTONDO, Mark ... 617-873-0675 207 E mark.rotondo@cambridgecollege.edu
ROTROFF, Kristi ... 419-267-1271 357 E krotroff@northweststate.edu
ROTT, Cynthia ... 701-231-7458 345 D cynthia.rott@ndsu.edu
ROTTENBERG, Aaron ... 718-854-2290 291 C
ROTTHOFF, Kurt ... 973-761-9102 282 K kurt.rotthoff@shu.edu
ROTTMAN, Courtney ... 214-648-2288 456 D courtney.rottman@utsouthwestern.edu
ROTTWEILER, James, D 520-515-5498 .. 11 O jdr@cochise.edu
ROTUNDO, Michael, R . 906-227-2327 228 E mrotundo@nmu.edu
ROTUNNI, Lisa, M ... 909-869-2474 .. 30 B lmrotunni@cpp.edu
ROTZ, Ben ... 918-766-4357 368 E brotz@okwu.edu
ROUBIDOUX, Nikol ... 503-352-2777 375 B ncroubidoux@pacificu.edu
ROUBINEK, Darren ... 816-501-2422 249 H darren.roubinek@avila.edu
ROUGEAU, Vincent, D .. 508-793-2011 208 A
ROUGHTON, Dean ... 252-335-0821 333 E dean_roughton@albemarle.edu
ROUGHTON, Dean ... 252-335-0821 333 E
ROUGHTON, Keith ... 912-478-0747 120 A kroughton@georgiasouthern.edu
ROUILLARD, Jansen ... 325-793-4801 439 A rouillard.jansen@mcm.edu
ROULETTE, Barbara, W . 240-500-2233 199 A bwroulette@hagerstowncc.edu
ROUND, Sara ... 816-415-5984 261 G rounds@william.jewell.edu
ROUNDS, Dayle, G ... 609-497-7991 279 D dayle.rounds@ptsem.edu
ROUNDS, Michael ... 785-864-4419 177 G m528r913@ku.edu
ROUNDS, Michael, J ... 610-565-0999 402 C mrounds@williamson.edu
ROUNDS, Susan ... 707-621-7000 .. 41 F
ROUNDS, Tyra ... 313-993-1046 230 H roundstc@udmercy.edu
ROUNDTREE, Leslie, A . 773-995-2411 134 J lroundtr@csu.edu
ROUNDTREE, Naomi ... 541-383-7233 371 I nroundtree@cocc.edu
ROUNTREE, Hazel ... 575-461-4413 285 J hazelr@mesalands.edu
ROUNTREE, Jeffrey, W .. 540-479-1892 471 B jeff.rountree@umwf.org
ROUNTREE, Mike ... 478-289-2093 118 B rountree@ega.edu
ROURKE, David ... 415-338-1822 .. 34 A drourke@sfsu.edu
ROURKE, SJ, Paul ... 203-254-4000 .. 87 G prourke@fairfield.edu
ROUS, Philip ... 410-455-2598 202 G rous@umbc.edu
ROUSE, Art ... 252-328-6060 340 H rousew@ecu.edu
ROUSE, Douglas ... 908-709-7113 283 E douglas.rouse@ucc.edu
ROUSE, Kevin ... 828-327-7000 332 H krouse@cvcc.edu
ROUSE, Lawrence, L ... 252-493-7200 336 E llrouse@email.pitcc.edu
ROUSE, Linda ... 954-262-1408 104 M lrouse@nova.edu
ROUSE, Matthew ... 562-903-4769 .. 27 E matt.rouse@biola.edu
ROUSE, Nina ... 920-403-4427 494 B nina.rouse@snc.edu
ROUSE, Patrick ... 586-498-4119 226 F rousep933@macomb.edu
ROUSE-MAINOR, Sheri . 912-358-3053 124 H mainors@savannahstate.edu
ROUSER, Jessica ... 313-993-3354 230 H rouserjm@udmercy.edu
ROUSH, Chris, G ... 203-582-3641 .. 88 F chris.roush@quinnipiac.edu
ROUSH, Clark, A ... 402-363-5610 269 F croush@york.edu
ROUSH, Jeffrey ... 785-227-3380 171 H roushjs@bethanylb.edu
ROUSH, Matt ... 248-204-2210 226 E mroush@ltu.edu
ROUSH, Rebecca ... 910-695-3704 337 E roushr@sandhills.edu
ROUSH, Richard, T ... 814-865-2541 391 F rtr10@psu.edu
ROUSSE, Wade ... 337-475-5588 192 B wrousse1@mcneese.edu
ROUSSEAU, Karen ... 413-205-3056 205 C karen.rousseau@aic.edu
ROUSSEAU, Melissa ... 616-526-7920 221 L mr55@calvin.edu
ROUSSEL, Hart ... 657-278-5429 .. 31 E hroussel@fullerton.edu
ROUSU, Matthew ... 570-372-4186 398 A rousu@susqu.edu
ROUTBORT, Julia, C ... 518-580-5555 315 A jroutbor@skidmore.edu
ROUTENBERG, robbie ... 585-245-5020 317 E routenberg@geneseo.edu
ROUTH, David ... 919-962-0329 342 B drouth@email.unc.edu
ROUTHIER, Stacy ... 860-231-5661 .. 89 G srouthier@usj.edu
ROUTT, Thalethia ... 859-257-9293 185 D thalethia.routt@uky.edu
ROVARIS, SR., Dereck .. 225-578-2111 188 J
ROVARIS, SR., Dereck, J ... 240-895-4363 201 F djrovaris@smcm.edu
ROVARIS, Jill ... 415-476-1281 .. 70 D jill.rovaris@ucsf.edu
ROVARIS, Jill ... 408-554-4501 .. 63 A jrovaris@scu.edu
ROVINELLI HELLER, Nina ... 860-570-3649 .. 89 B nina.heller@uconn.edu
ROVIRA-ALVAREZ, Jorge ... 787-993-8860 510 E jorge.rovira@upr.edu
ROVNER, Amy ... 206-546-6937 483 C arovner@shoreline.edu
ROW, Darren ... 507-457-6971 242 H drow@smumn.edu
ROW, Joy ... 936-639-1301 429 A jrow@angelina.edu
ROWAN, Bernard ... 773-995-2439 134 J trowanii@csu.edu
ROWAN, Carl ... 703-993-3840 466 J crowan2@gmu.edu
ROWAN, John ... 318-473-6446 189 A jrowan@lsua.edu
ROWANE, Michael ... 814-866-8118 387 C mrowane@lecom.edu
ROWE, Alan ... 229-333-7816 127 C carowe@valdosta.edu
ROWE, Brian ... 931-393-1544 423 G browe@mscc.edu
ROWE, David ... 414-297-8854 498 B rowed1@matc.edu
ROWE, Dayna ... 405-422-1467 368 I dayna.rowe@redlandscc.edu
ROWE, Jimmy ... 859-846-4357 183 G james.rowe@midway.edu
ROWE, Katherine, A ... 757-221-1693 465 B president@wm.edu
ROWE, Michael ... 304-877-6428 486 A business@abc.edu
ROWE, Mindy, S ... 610-917-1415 400 D msrowe@valleyforge.edu
ROWE, Nicholas ... 978-867-4299 209 F nicholas.rowe@gordon.edu
ROWE, Nicole ... 906-932-4231 224 A nicoler@gogebic.edu
ROWE, Rebecca ... 218-855-8145 237 C rebecca.rowe@clcmn.edu
ROWE, Sherri ... 509-359-4273 478 H sherrir@ewu.edu
ROWE, Steven ... 773-995-4412 134 J srowe21@csu.edu
ROWE, Tim ... 304-877-6428 486 A academicvp@abc.edu
ROWE, Tim ... 304-877-6428 486 A registrar@abc.edu
ROWE-ALLEN, Ophelie .. 203-932-7176 .. 89 F orallen@newhaven.edu
ROWE-JONES, Kelly ... 606-218-5273 185 F kellyrowe@upike.edu
ROWELL, Jeren ... 816-268-5401 256 E jrowell@nts.edu
ROWELL, Sam ... 423-354-5207 424 B ssrowell@northeaststate.edu
ROWEN, Cate ... 413-585-3021 218 D crowen@smith.edu
ROWH, Brett ... 918-825-6021 369 A browh@rsu.edu
ROWH, Mark, C ... 540-674-3617 473 F mrowh@nr.edu
ROWLAND, Barbara ... 217-228-5432 147 C rowlaba@quincy.edu
ROWLAND, Diane ... 207-581-1865 196 D
ROWLAND, Jerome ... 404-458-6085 123 B
ROWLAND, Jim ... 918-540-6301 366 F jrowland@neo.edu
ROWLAND, Leo ... 909-748-8717 .. 72 E leo_rowland@redlands.edu
ROWLAND, Linda ... 706-864-1358 126 G linda.rowland@ung.edu
ROWLAND, IV, Roy ... 863-667-5081 108 I rrowland@seu.edu
ROWLAND, Sally ... 661-362-3638 .. 38 H sally.rowland@canyons.edu
ROWLAND, Sheri ... 850-201-6250 112 B sheri.rowland@tcc.fl.edu
ROWLANDS, Jodi ... 610-799-1342 388 B jrowlands@lccc.edu
ROWLEY, Becky ... 505-428-1201 287 H becky.rowley@sfcc.edu
ROWLEY, Chris ... 503-375-7168 372 G crowley@corban.edu
ROWLEY, Don ... 765-677-2313 157 F don.rowley@indwes.edu
ROWLEY, Sarah, L ... 248-341-2081 228 H slrowley@oaklandcc.edu
ROWLEY, Sue ... 415-274-2200 .. 24 E srowley@academyart.edu
ROWSER, Mayola ... 314-454-7055 253 A mayola.rowser@barnesjewishcollege.edu
ROWZEE, Julie ... 601-635-2111 245 B jrowzee@eccc.edu
ROXBURGH, Russell ... 631-656-2147 299 G russell.roxburgh@ftc.edu
ROXBURY, Tiese ... 810-762-3000 231 C troxbury@umich.edu
ROXWORTHY, Emily ... 213-821-4035 .. 73 C sdadean@usc.edu
ROY, Alisa ... 704-922-6202 334 E roy.alisa@gaston.edu
ROY, Jocelyn ... 859-371-9393 179 C jroy@beckfield.edu
ROY, Judy, K ... 260-422-5561 156 A jkroy@indianatech.edu
ROY, Justin ... 617-322-3551 210 F justin_roy@laboure.edu
ROY, Kevin ... 413-748-3252 218 E kroy@springfieldcollege.edu
ROY, Lara ... 612-874-3778 236 E lara_roy@mcad.edu
ROY, Lisa ... 207-326-4715 195 G lisa.roy@mma.edu
ROY, Lisa, M ... 207-834-7504 196 G roylisa@maine.edu
ROY, Marc ... 856-351-2680 282 I mroy@salemcc.edu
ROY, Matthew ... 508-910-9052 211 F mroy@umassd.edu
ROY, Melissa ... 845-574-4758 312 C mroy@sunyrockland.edu

ROY, Michael, D .... 802-443-5490 461 G
mdroy@middlebury.edu
ROY, Omaira .... 508-286-3544 219 F
roy_omaira@wheatoncollege.edu
ROY, Rani .... 718-862-7755 304 K
rani.roy@manhattan.edu
ROY, Tracey .... 218-322-2409 238 D
tracey.roy@minnesotanorth.edu
ROY, Wesley .... 401-598-1000 403 E
wesley.roy@jwu.edu
ROYAL, Angela .... 573-288-6334 251 I
aroyal@culver.edu
ROYAL, Christina .... 413-552-2700 214 D
croyal@hcc.edu
ROYAL, Mary .... 801-832-2496 461 A
mroyal@westminstercollege.edu
ROYAL, Rebecca .... 973-684-6868 279 B
rroyal@pccc.edu
ROYALS, Stephanie .... 478-289-2039 118 B
sroyals@ega.edu
ROYCE, Richard, A .... 516-671-2356 324 C
rroyce@webb.edu
ROYCE-DAVIS,
Joanna, C .... 253-535-7206 481 C
roycedjc@plu.edu
ROYCE-DAVIS,
Joanna, C .... 253-535-7191 481 C
roycedjc@plu.edu
ROYE, Shauna .... 202-495-3837.. 93 D
sroye@dhs.edu
ROYE, Terry .... 281-425-6862 438 B
troye@lee.edu
ROYEEN, Charlotte .... 312-942-7120 148 C
charlotte_l_royeen@rush.edu
ROYER, Dara, J .... 315-443-8338 321 D
djroyer@syr.edu
ROYER, James .... 504-671-5477 187 I
jroyer@dcc.edu
ROYER, Jeffrey .... 513-231-2223 348 A
jroyer@athenaeum.edu
ROYER, Randy .... 913-288-7188 174 H
rroyer@kckcc.edu
ROYER, Roma .... 602-429-4947.. 15 D
rroyer@ps.edu
ROYER, Tina .... 209-476-7840.. 67 D
troyer@clc.edu
ROYER ENGLE,
Ro-Anne .... 765-285-3734 153 E
raroyer@bsu.edu
ROYKO, Barry .... 216-987-0205 351 D
barry.royko@tri-c.edu
ROYO, Sebastian .... 508-793-7673 207 F
provost@clarku.edu
ROYSE, Tammy, J .... 812-941-2499 157 D
tjroyse@ius.edu
ROYSTON, Mimi .... 413-205-3448 205 C
mimi.royston@aic.edu
ROYSTON,
Rosemary, R .... 706-379-3111 128 A
rosemary@yhc.edu
ROYZMAN, Anna .... 212-799-5000 303 B
ROZADA, Mayra .... 787-891-0925 506 I
mrozada@aguadilla.inter.edu
ROZBORSKI, Joanne .... 850-484-1708 105 G
jrozborski@pensacolastate.edu
ROZEBOOM, David .... 828-689-1212 330 H
david_rozeboom@mhu.edu
ROZEK, Charles, E .... 216-368-4390 349 B
cer2@case.edu
ROZELL, Mark .... 703-993-8171 466 J
mrozell@gmu.edu
ROZELLE-STONE,
A. Rebecca .... 701-777-3302 344 H
adrian.rozelle@und.edu
ROZENEK, Carl .... 814-864-6666 384 E
ROZEWSKI, Mark .... 203-392-5456.. 85 H
rozewskim1@southernct.edu
ROZHON, Tamara .... 562-902-3304.. 65 H
tamararozhon@scuhs.edu
ROZLER, Tracy .... 716-896-0700 324 A
trozler@villa.edu
ROZOWSKI, Casey .... 715-836-5368 494 E
rozowscm@uwec.edu
RUANE, Matthew .... 845-905-4613 297 E
matthew.ruane@culinary.edu
RUANO, Maritza .... 630-942-2800 135 F
RUANO, Sylvia .... 909-274-5480.. 52 K
sruano@mtsac.edu
RUARK, Brian .... 973-378-2665 282 K
brian.ruark@shu.edu
RUARK, Matthew .... 270-852-3120 183 B
matthewru@kwc.edu
RUARTE, Daniel .... 909-599-5433.. 48 E
druarte@lifepacific.edu

RUBACK, Chad .... 847-578-8589 148 B
chad.ruback@rosalindfranlin.edu
RUBALCABA, Jacquelyn 559-325-5271.. 66 H
jacquelyn.rubalcaba@cloviscollege.edu
RUBALCAVA, Elva .... 657-278-5403.. 31 E
erubalcava@fullerton.edu
RUBEMEYER, Susan .... 636-922-8360 258 A
srubemeyer@stchas.edu
RUBEN, Brent, D .... 848-932-7092 281 B
bruben@rutgers.edu
RUBIEN, Ira, L .... 610-758-4487 388 C
ilr212@lehigh.edu
RUBIN, Adam .... 618-985-3741 140 G
adamrubin@jalc.edu
RUBIN, Beno .... 757-822-5196 474 G
brubin@tcc.edu
RUBIN, Beth .... 910-814-4377 327 C
brubin@campbell.edu
RUBIN, David .... 603-428-2509 272 I
drubin@nec.edu
RUBIN, James .... 602-787-6546.. 13 G
james.rubin@paradisevalley.edu
RUBIN, Joshua .... 718-436-2122 321 F
RUBIN, Kyle .... 906-487-1888 227 D
ktrubin@mtu.edu
RUBIN, Laura, C .... 617-228-2465 214 A
laura.rubin@bhcc.edu
RUBIN, Lisa .... 770-426-2725 122 A
lrubin@life.edu
RUBIN, Lucas .... 212-966-4014 293 A
lrubin@brooklyn.cuny.edu
RUBIN, Moshe .... 515-239-9002 314 J
myrubin@shoryoshuv.org
RUBIN, Nancy, G .... 330-569-3211 353 F
rubinng@hiram.edu
RUBIN, Rachel .... 860-486-2337.. 89 B
rachel.rubin@uconn.edu
RUBIN, Steve .... 719-219-9636.. 78 C
srubin@cavt.edu
RUBINO, David .... 814-866-6641 387 C
drubino@lecom.edu
RUBINO, Joseph .... 410-293-1549 502 I
rubino@usna.edu
RUBINO, Karen, M .... 401-456-8849 404 A
krubino@ric.edu
RUBINO, Lorraine .... 631-632-4385 316 D
lorraine.rubino@stonybrook.edu
RUBINO, Michael, H .... 508-767-7156 205 F
rubino@assumption.edu
RUBINSTEIN, James .... 623-572-3395 144 C
jrubinstein@midwestern.edu
RUBINSTEIN, Mark .... 603-271-6484 272 C
RUBINSTEIN, Mark .... 603-230-3501 271 I
mrubinstein@ccsnh.edu
RUBIO, Amy .... 210-341-1366 440 B
arubio@ost.edu
RUBIO, Dave .... 909-384-8640.. 60 F
drubio@sbccd.cc.ca.us
RUBIO, Don .... 323-669-7555.. 49 D
derubio@lasd.org
RUBIO, Joan .... 714-463-7550.. 51 D
jrubio@ketchum.edu
RUBIO, Sara .... 310-233-4033.. 49 F
rubiosv@lahc.edu
RUBLE, Megan .... 507-933-7526 235 E
mruble@gustavus.edu
RUBLE, Michelle .... 301-934-7508 198 C
mmruble@csmd.edu
RUBRITZ, Gerald .... 814-886-6460 390 E
grubritz@mtaloy.edu
RUBY, Ashley .... 301-387-3733 198 F
ashley.ruby@garrettcollege.edu
RUBY, Kirsten, A .... 217-333-3070 151 C
RUCKEL, Stephanie .... 612-330-1550 233 G
ruckels@augsburg.edu
RUCKER, Alan, M .... 606-783-5367 183 H
a.rucker@moreheadstate.edu
RUCKER, Cleo .... 615-322-7311 427 B
RUCKER, Marty, K .... 423-585-6983 424 G
marty.rucker@ws.edu
RUCKER, Nolan .... 303-751-8700.. 78 A
rucker@belrea.edu
RUCKER, Paul .... 206-685-9223 484 A
uwalumni@uw.edu
RUCKER, Robert, E .... 662-685-4771 244 D
erucker@bmc.edu
RUCKERT, Jason .... 386-226-7330.. 98 J
jason.ruckert@erau.edu
RUCKH, Eric .... 618-650-2712 149 H
eruckh@siue.edu
RUCKS, Lucas .... 206-546-4516 483 C
lrucks@shoreline.edu

RUDA, Ryan .... 620-276-9533 173 H
ryan.ruda@gcccks.edu
RUDATSIKIRA,
Emmanuel .... 269-471-6648 220 H
rudatsikira@andrews.edu
RUDAWSKY, Donald, J .. 954-262-5392 104 M
rudawsky@nova.edu
RUDD, Robert .... 215-596-8800 400 B
RUDDELL, Lori .... 208-792-2216 131 F
lruddell@lcsc.edu
RUDDEN, David .... 847-214-7925 137 D
drudden@elgin.edu
RUDE, Jen, L .... 253-535-7464 481 C
rudejl@plu.edu
RUDEAU, William .... 609-771-2187 275 J
rudeau@tcnj.edu
RUDECOFF,
Christine, A .... 315-684-6055 320 E
rudecoc@morrisville.edu
RUDIGER, Jennifer .... 715-232-5161 496 C
rudigerj@uwstout.edu
RUDIN, Mark, J .... 903-886-5011 446 D
mark.rudin@tamuc.edu
RUDINSKAYER, Yelena . 718-429-6600 323 I
yelena.rudinskayer@vaughn.edu
RUDISILL, Mark .... 630-942-4306 135 F
rudisillm@cod.edu
RUDNICK, Virginia .... 315-294-8842 292 A
vrudnick@cayuga-cc.edu
RUDNYTZKY, Nick .... 215-885-2360 389 A
nrudnytzky@manor.edu
RUDOLPH, Alan, S .... 970-491-7194.. 79 E
alan.rudolph@colostate.edu
RUDOLPH, Angela .... 304-724-5000 486 C
angela@rjpccpa.com
RUDOLPH, Cassius .... 212-870-1244 309 C
crudolph@nyts.edu
RUDOLPH, Hillel .... 305-944-0035 114 B
RUDOLPH, Leena .... 580-559-5206 365 J
leeerud@ecok.edu
RUDOLPH-SHABINSKY,
Ivan .... 845-848-4023 298 A
i.rudolph-shabinsky@dc.edu
RUDOVSKY, Michele .... 650-378-6733.. 62 J
rudovskym@smccd.edu
RUDOWSKY, Catherine . 361-825-2643 446 E
catherine.rudowsky@tamucc.edu
RUDY, James .... 714-432-5017.. 38 F
jrudy7@occ.cccd.edu
RUE, Cynthia .... 239-454-5000 106 E
crue@picollege.edu
RUE, Derek .... 201-327-8877 276 F
drue@eastwick.edu
RUE, Penny .... 336-758-5943 344 A
rue@wfu.edu
RUEFF, Alicia .... 561-732-4424 107 E
arueff@svdp.edu
RUEFLE, Colleen .... 412-536-1069 386 H
colleen.ruefle@laroche.edu
RUEGG, Texas .... 903-233-4381 438 C
texasruegg@letu.edu
RUEGGER, Jacqueline ... 718-933-6700 306 J
jruegger@monroecollege.edu
RUELAS, AnnMarie .... 714-484-7369.. 54 C
aruelas@cypresscollege.edu
RUELAS, George .... 951-827-1012.. 70 B
RUELLE, Joan .... 336-278-6572 328 H
jruelle@elon.edu
RUELLE, Maggie .... 903-510-2724 451 D
mrue@tjc.edu
RUEPPEL, Cary .... 315-655-7012 292 B
carueppel@cazenovia.edu
RUESCH, Sherry .... 435-652-7551 459 G
sherry.ruesch@utahtech.edu
RUESS, Valerie .... 317-924-1331 154 D
RUFF, Corey .... 325-674-2665 427 G
clr06a@acu.edu
RUFF, Haskell .... 470-639-0999 122 H
haskell.ruff@morehouse.edu
RUFF, Joy, C .... 305-237-2090 104 E
jruff@mdc.edu
RUFF, Margaret .... 903-785-7661 440 F
mruff@parisjc.edu
RUFF, III, Raymond, H . 864-597-4171 413 E
ruffrh@wofford.edu
RUFF, Sydney .... 802-387-7223 461 E
sydneyruff@landmark.edu
RUFF, Tina .... 775-673-7135 270 I
truff@tmcc.edu
RUFF, Tina, B .... 919-536-7200 334 A
rufft@durhamtech.edu
RUFFIN, Derrick .... 212-924-5900 321 C

RUFFIN, Finee .... 601-477-4082 246 A
finee.ruffin@jcjc.edu
RUFFIN, Reginald .... 205-929-1100.... 6 B
rruffin@miles.edu
RUFFING, Charles, W .... 920-923-7166 492 D
cwruffing23@marianuniversity.edu
RUFFING, Rebecca .... 315-866-0300 301 B
ruffingrj@herkimer.edu
RUFFRAGE, Jo .... 315-792-7172 320 F
ruffraj@sunypoly.edu
RUFINO, Paul .... 856-415-2173 280 F
prufino@rcsj.edu
RUFLETH, Ernest .... 318-257-5500 192 A
erufleth@latech.edu
RUFO, Joseph .... 315-470-6622 319 A
jlrufo@esf.edu
RUFTY, Beverly .... 704-878-3249 335 I
brufty@itchellcc.edu
RUGEMER, Ellen .... 410-857-2203 200 D
erugemer@mcdaniel.edu
RUGER, Theodore, W ... 215-898-7061 399 J
deanruger@law.upenn.edu
RUGG, Rebecca .... 312-996-2006 151 D
rugg@uic.edu
RUGGERI, Tom .... 434-961-5229 474 B
truggeri@pvcc.edu
RUGGIERO, Bruno .... 985-448-4262 192 C
bruno.ruggiero@nicholls.edu
RUGGIRELLO, John .... 860-727-6907.. 87 H
jruggirello@goodwin.edu
RUGGLES, Jennifer .... 216-368-1723 349 B
jor15@case.edu
RUGGLES, Reed .... 701-355-8150 347 A
raruggles@umary.edu
RUGH, Susan .... 801-422-2742 458 A
susan_rugh@byu.edu
RUGLESS, Katrina .... 606-218-5291 185 F
katrinarugless@upike.edu
RUGON, Kim .... 504-286-5000 191 A
krugon@suno.edu
RUHL, Chris .... 317-208-5311 159 F
RUHL, Christopher, A .... 765-494-4600 159 G
RUHLAND, David .... 715-425-4105 496 A
david.ruhland@uwrf.edu
RUHLANDT, Karin .... 315-443-3949 321 D
kruhland@syr.edu
RUHMAN, Douglas .... 406-275-4763 264 H
douglas_ruhman@skc.edu
RUITER, Kathy .... 217-854-5525 133 F
kathleen.ruiter@blackburn.edu
RUIZ, Agustin .... 408-554-4000.. 63 A
RUIZ, Alex .... 951-827-5045.. 70 B
alex.ruiz@ucr.edu
RUIZ, Alfredo .... 269-471-6979 220 H
jaruiz@andrews.edu
RUIZ, Andrew .... 806-894-9611 443 A
aruiz@southplainscollege.edu
RUIZ, Angel, J .... 787-863-2390 507 A
angel.ruiz@fajardo.inter.edu
RUIZ, Angela .... 504-398-2271 191 E
aruiz@uhcno.edu
RUIZ, Carey .... 270-789-5177 179 G
cdruiz@campbellsville.edu
RUIZ, Christina .... 417-328-1826 258 K
cruiz@sbuniv.edu
RUIZ, Deb .... 480-988-8118.. 13 B
deborah.ruiz@cgc.edu
RUIZ, Dora .... 310-289-5123.. 68 E
dora.ruiz@wcui.edu
RUIZ, Ediltrudys .... 718-960-8421 293 E
ediltrudys.ruiz@lehman.cuny.edu
RUIZ, Elaine .... 787-798-3001 509 F
elaine.ruiz@uccaribe.edu
RUIZ, Eric .... 815-740-5070 152 E
eruiz@stfrancis.edu
RUIZ, Israel, A .... 787-840-2575 508 G
iruiz@psm.edu
RUIZ, Jesus .... 847-543-2113 135 G
jruiz20@clcillinois.edu
RUIZ, Joaquin .... 520-626-8527.. 16 H
jruiz@email.arizona.edu
RUIZ, OP, John Martin 202-495-3821.. 93 D
jruiz@dhs.edu
RUIZ, Joseph .... 361-698-1374 434 H
jruiz156@delmar.edu
RUIZ, Lauri .... 713-221-5771 452 B
ruizla@uhd.edu
RUIZ, Lucy .... 559-243-7105.. 66 G
lucy.ruiz@scccd.edu
RUIZ, Luis, A .... 787-766-1717 509 C
um_lruiz@uagm.edu
RUIZ, Luis, E .... 787-250-1912 507 C
leruiz@metro.inter.edu

RUIZ, Manuel 717-477-1161 394 D mruiz@ship.edu
RUIZ, Miguel 713-221-8564 452 B ruizm@uhd.edu
RUIZ, Phyllis 201-216-5213 282 L phyllis.ruiz@stevens.edu
RUIZ, Rafael 787-257-0000 510 F rafael.ruiz@upr.edu
RUIZ, Robert 805-565-7164 75 I rruiz@westmont.edu
RUIZ, Ruben 708-656-8000 145 B ruben.ruiz@morton.edu
RUIZ, Ryan 513-233-2223 348 A rruiz@athenaeum.edu
RUIZ, Sina 903-875-7376 439 G sina.ruiz@navarrocollege.edu
RUIZ, Trisha 713-525-2101 453 H ruizt@stthom.edu
RUIZ DE FIISCHLER, Carmen 787-764-0000 511 F carmen.ruiz14@upr.edu
RUIZ-ESPARZA, Emir 620-947-3121 177 F emirruizesparza@tabor.edu
RUIZ ESPARZA, Emir 215-702-4353 379 F eesparza@cairn.edu
RULAND, Heather 978-630-9361 215 A hruland@mwcc.mass.edu
RULE, Dave 425-602-3000 476 H drule@bastyr.edu
RULE, Nik 641-673-2168 170 I ruleng@wmpenn.edu
RULLAN TORO, Agustin 787-265-3878 510 B agustin.rullan@upr.edu
RULLAN TORO, Agustin 787-832-4040 511 C rector.uprm@upr.edu
RULNEY, Lisa 520-621-5977 16 H lisa.rulney@arizona.edu
RULOFSON, Eric 307-268-2492 499 T eric.rulofson@caspercollege.edu
RUMANO, Moses 316-295-5867 173 G moses_rumano@friends.edu
RUMERY, Joyce, V 207-581-1655 196 D rumery@maine.edu
RUMIANO, Sara 530-898-5270 31 A srumiano@csuchico.edu
RUMLEY, Timothy 616-538-2330 224 B trumley@gracechristian.edu
RUMMEL, Justin 570-372-4314 398 A rummelj@susqu.edu
RUMPCA, Susan 218-855-8038 237 C susan.rumpca@clcmn.edu
RUMPF, Troy 307-778-1142 500 D trumpf@lccc.wy.edu
RUMPLER, Laura 208-769-3316 132 A lkrumpler@nic.edu
RUMPZA, Kathy 612-659-6222 238 C kathy.rumpza@minneapolis.edu
RUMPZA, Matthew, D 651-696-6551 236 C mrumpza@macalester.edu
RUMSEY, Tyler 928-776-2332 17 B tyler.rumsey@yc.edu
RUND, James, A 480-965-2200 11 A james.rund@asu.edu
RUNDELL, Isabel 317-896-9324 161 D irundell@ubca.org
RUNDELL, Jay, A 740-362-3121 355 H jrundell@mtso.edu
RUNDLE, David 607-735-1780 298 G drundle@elmira.edu
RUNDLE, Sarah 931-598-1553 422 F serundle@sewanee.edu
RUNDQUIST, Andy 651-523-2800 235 F
RUNDQUIST, Brad 701-777-4589 344 H bradley.rundquist@und.edu
RUNDSTROM, Amy, L 308-865-8501 268 J rundstromal@unk.edu
RUNELL HALL, Marcella 413-538-2550 216 G mhall@mtholyoke.edu
RUNESTAD, Eric, J 507-222-5411 234 C erunestad@carleton.edu
RUNEY, Mim, L 401-598-1000 403 E mim.runey@jwu.edu
RUNFELDT, John 973-877-3078 276 G runfeldt@essex.edu
RUNGAITIS, Stacy 760-744-1150 56 B srungaitis@palomar.edu
RUNGE, Carol 717-871-7871 394 B carol.runge@millersville.edu
RUNGE, Christina 414-955-8487 492 F chrunge@mcw.edu
RUNGE, Denise 907-786-1050 10 A provost@alaska.edu
RUNGE, Marschall, S 734-647-9351 231 A mrunge@umich.edu
RUNGE, Nate 715-830-5563 497 E nrunge1@cvtc.edu
RUNIEWICZ, Michael, J 314-935-8976 261 B michael_runiewicz@wustl.edu
RUNION, Trish 785-539-3571 175 F trunion@mccks.edu
RUNKLE, Dan 563-589-3599 170 C drunkle@dbq.edu
RUNKLE, Gita 562-463-7359 58 M grunkle@riohondo.edu
RUNKSMEIER, Lori 860-465-5091 85 G runksmeierl@easternct.edu
RUNNELS, Greg 574-239-8312 155 E grunnels@hcc-nd.edu
RUNNING, Patrick 320-762-4483 236 G patrickr@alextech.edu
RUNSER, Beth 704-461-6573 326 I bethrunser@bac.edu
RUNYAN, Lisa 937-775-5595 364 D lisa.runyan@wright.edu
RUNYON, Darla, J 660-562-1532 256 G drunyon@nwmissouri.edu
RUNYON, David 717-901-5137 385 G drunyon@harrisburgu.edu
RUNYON, Jean 970-204-8100 80 I jean.runyon@frontrange.edu
RUNYON, Tim 417-626-1234 257 A
RUOFF, Christy 818-785-2726 35 K christy.ruoff@casalomacollege.edu
RUPE, Jolene, K 785-539-3571 175 F jrupe@mccks.edu
RUPE, Manuel, R 989-774-2544 221 M med@cmich.edu
RUPE-HAROLD, Nicole 304-357-4747 486 J nicolerupe@ucwv.edu
RUPERT, Kimberly 517-750-1200 230 F krupert@arbor.edu
RUPERT, Molly 530-226-4135 64 C mrupert@simpsonu.edu
RUPLEY, Larissa 254-710-6972 430 F larissa_rupley@baylor.edu
RUPP, Lisa 541-463-5561 373 C ruppl@lanecc.edu
RUPP, Sharon, L 864-424-8014 412 H ruppsl@mailbox.sc.edu
RUPP, Sheila 989-356-9021 220 G
RUPPRECHT, Stephen 610-902-8417 379 E smr438@cabrini.edu
RURSCH, Keri 309-794-7721 132 H kerirursch@augustana.edu
RUSAK, Katie 313-664-7861 222 C krusak@collegeforcreativestudies.edu
RUSCH, Dan 704-825-6264 334 E rusch.dan@gaston.edu
RUSCH, Kathleen, M 414-464-9777 497 B rusch.kathleen@wspp.edu
RUSCH-CURL, Kari 651-450-3692 237 H krusch-curl@inverhills.edu
RUSCH-CURL, Kari 952-358-8776 239 C kari.rusch-curl@normandale.edu
RUSCHE, Ernst 231-348-6624 228 D erusche@ncmich.edu
RUSCHIVAL, Michael 303-292-0015 80 F mruschival@denvercollegeofnursing.edu
RUSCHMAN, Doug 513-745-3185 364 F ruschman@xavier.edu
RUSCITTI, Jerry 847-317-8020 150 J jruscitit@tiu.edu
RUSCZYK, George 570-484-2317 393 E grusczyk@lockhaven.edu
RUSE, Elaine 330-941-3399 364 G eruse@ysu.edu
RUSEN, Barbara 848-932-4712 281 B brusen@docs.rutgers.edu
RUSH, Amber 870-368-2008 20 I arush@ozarka.edu
RUSH, Bonnie, R 785-532-5660 175 A brush@vet.ksu.edu
RUSH, Bryan 334-844-5390 4 E sbr0024@auburn.edu
RUSH, Cherylyn, L 215-951-1948 386 I rush@lasalle.edu
RUSH, Christopher 714-712-7900 46 F
RUSH, Denise 617-585-0200 206 E denise.rush@the-bac.edu
RUSH, Dennis 845-569-3492 307 B dennis.rush@msmc.edu
RUSH, James 662-476-5386 245 C jrush@eastms.edu
RUSH, Janet 402-363-5661 269 F jgrush@york.edu
RUSH, John, H 563-588-8000 165 K jrush@emmaus.edu
RUSH, John, P 662-325-9306 247 A rush@devalumni.msstate.edu
RUSH, Katy 563-441-4046 165 J krush@eicc.edu
RUSH, Keith 225-769-8820 188 I
RUSH, Kimberly 601-581-3506 246 B krush5@meridiancc.edu
RUSH, Lauri 202-651-5005 92 B lauri.rush@gallaudet.edu
RUSH, Leslie 307-766-1121 500 H
RUSH, Mark, E 540-458-8904 476 D rushm@wlu.edu
RUSH, Michele 863-583-9050 110 A
RUSH, Pat 708-596-2000 149 D prush@ssc.edu
RUSH, Patrick 708-596-2000 149 D prush@ssc.edu
RUSH, Rosalee 209-667-3131 33 D
RUSH, Tonyalle, V 662-562-3219 247 E
RUSH-WALLACE, MaryAnn 610-799-1155 388 B mrushwallace@lccc.edu
RUSHER, Bryan 501-812-2256 23 E brusher@uaptc.edu
RUSHFORTH, Brenda 909-621-8175 57 K brenda.rushforth@pomona.edu
RUSHI, Purva 708-456-0300 151 A purvarushi@triton.edu
RUSHING, Cheri 618-985-3741 140 G cherirushing@jalc.edu
RUSHING, Dorrie 713-646-1898 443 C drushing@stcl.edu
RUSHING, Ken 904-264-2172 106 K krushing@iwsfla.org
RUSHING, Linda 870-364-6414 22 E rushingl@uamont.edu
RUSHING, Mark 479-575-5555 21 H markr@uark.edu
RUSHING, Ray 254-867-4893 448 F ray.rushing@tstc.edu
RUSHLOW, Jennifer 802-831-1136 462 F jrushlow@vermontlaw.edu
RUSHMER, Bernadette 570-674-8028 389 H brushmer@misericordia.edu
RUSHNAWITZ, P 248-968-3360 233 C
RUSHTON, Jennifer 706-379-3111 128 A jlrushton@yhc.edu
RUSILOSKI, Benjamin 215-489-2946 381 K president@delval.edu
RUSINEK, Ken 207-985-7976 194 F
RUSKIN, Susan 323-856-7741 25 M sruskin@afi.com
RUSLANDER, Barbara 518-861-2516 305 B bruslander@mariacollege.edu
RUSS, Christina 425-640-1683 479 A christina.russ@edcc.edu
RUSS, Roy 304-793-6819 489 C rruss@osteo.wvsom.edu
RUSS, Shelly 802-728-1303 463 D sruss@vtc.edu
RUSS-WILSON, Traci, L 704-894-2201 328 C trruss@davidson.edu
RUSSEK, Lori 361-593-2678 447 A lori.russek@tamuk.edu
RUSSEL, Caskey 360-650-7493 485 A russel51@wwu.edu
RUSSEL, Michael 817-257-7926 447 H m.russel@tcu.edu
RUSSEL, Philip 215-951-2814 398 G philip.russel@jefferson.edu
RUSSELBURG, Morgan 270-686-4285 179 F morgan.russelburg@brescia.edu
RUSSELL, Adam 206-934-3848 482 G adam.russell@seattlecolleges.edu
RUSSELL, Adrina 910-670-2116 341 B arussell@uncfsu.edu
RUSSELL, Agnes, M 616-988-3656 226 A arussell@kuyper.edu
RUSSELL, Andrew 315-792-7317 320 F andrew.russell@sunypoly.edu
RUSSELL, April 419-448-2202 353 D arussell@heidelberg.edu
RUSSELL, Avis 202-274-5400 94 B avis.russell@udc.edu
RUSSELL, Babs 770-947-7260 127 E babs.russell@westgatech.edu
RUSSELL, Bryan 270-745-5818 186 A bryan.russell@wku.edu
RUSSELL, Bryce 212-812-4041 308 F brussell@nycda.edu
RUSSELL, Carol, G 513-556-6169 361 I russecg@ucmail.uc.edu
RUSSELL, Craig 501-279-5000 19 G crussell@harding.edu
RUSSELL, Danny 740-362-3322 355 H drussell@mtso.edu
RUSSELL, Darcy 785-594-8312 171 C darcy.russell@bakeru.edu
RUSSELL, David, R 573-875-7200 251 A
RUSSELL, Denise 614-236-6196 348 I drussell@capital.edu
RUSSELL, Jarad 423-614-6001 419 H jrussell@leeuniversity.edu
RUSSELL, Jeffrey 608-262-5823 494 D jrussell@dcs.wisc.edu
RUSSELL, Jennie 314-838-8858 261 A jrussell@ugst.edu
RUSSELL, Jennifer 202-685-4094 501 I jennifer.russell@ndu.edu
RUSSELL, Jill, T 717-867-6076 388 A russell@lvc.edu
RUSSELL, Jim 914-323-5236 305 A james.russell@mville.edu
RUSSELL, Joanna, S 503-223-5100 376 C jrussell@sumnercollege.edu
RUSSELL, Joanne 718-368-5661 294 C joanne.russell@kbcc.cuny.edu
RUSSELL, Josh 408-274-7900 62 F josh.russell@evc.edu
RUSSELL, Joyce 610-519-4331 401 B joyce.russell@villanova.edu
RUSSELL, Judith 352-273-2505 110 E jcrussell@ufl.edu
RUSSELL, Julie 208-376-7731 130 E jrussell@boisebible.edu
RUSSELL, Justin 912-583-3161 116 D drussell@bpc.edu
RUSSELL, Keith 503-399-5184 372 A keith.russell@chemeketa.edu
RUSSELL, Kelly 559-278-2182 31 D kellyr@csufresno.edu
RUSSELL, Kenneth 616-949-5300 222 F kenneth.russell@cornerstone.edu
RUSSELL, Kevin 601-968-8746 244 C krussell@belhaven.edu
RUSSELL, Kimberly 940-898-3863 451 A krussell9@twu.edu
RUSSELL, Kristie 740-245-7191 363 A krussell@rio.edu
RUSSELL, Leigh 252-493-7354 336 E lrussell@email.pittcc.edu
RUSSELL, Lois 334-229-4431 4 B lrussell@alasu.edu
RUSSELL, Mark, A 419-772-2011 358 D m-russell.7@onu.edu
RUSSELL, Mary Jane 802-654-2000 462 A ir@smcvt.edu
RUSSELL, Matt 704-334-6882 327 J mrussell@charlottechristian.edu
RUSSELL, Michael 804-819-4995 472 E mrusssell@vccs.edu
RUSSELL, Michelle 856-222-9311 280 E mrussell@rcbc.edu
RUSSELL, Pam 304-485-5487 486 H
RUSSELL, Pat 206-239-4500 477 I
RUSSELL, Patrice 603-641-7202 273 C prussell@anselm.edu
RUSSELL, Robb 562-947-8755 65 H robbrussell@scuhs.edu
RUSSELL, Robert 605-626-7770 415 H robert.russell@northern.edu
RUSSELL, Robin 540-231-6601 475 D busdean@vt.edu
RUSSELL, Scott 515-650-3198 163 C scottrussell@theartofeducation.edu
RUSSELL, Sharron 501-450-1348 19 I russell@hendrix.edu
RUSSELL, Susan 575-538-6118 288 J susan.garland@wnmu.edu
RUSSELL, Tamara 502-213-2171 181 H tamara.russell@kctcs.edu
RUSSELL, Tammy 269-294-4243 223 J trussell@glenoaks.edu
RUSSELL, Thad 559-791-2307 47 D thad.russell@portervillecollege.edu
RUSSELL, Tikola 718-631-6314 295 B trussell@qcc.cuny.edu
RUSSELL, Todd 985-867-2266 190 I trussell@sjasc.edu

© COPYRIGHT HIGHER EDUCATION PUBLICATIONS, INC. 2022

RUSSELL, Tommiann, R 315-267-2162 318 D
russeltr@potsdam.edu
RUSSELL, Traci 206-934-5661 482 F
traci.russell@seattlecolleges.edu
RUSSELL, William 860-632-3050.. 88 B
busoffice@holyapostles.edu
RUSSELL-EDWARDS,
Juanita 601-877-6122 244 B
juanita@alcorn.edu
RUSSELL-STOKES,
Morgan 804-289-8032 471 E
mrussell@richmond.edu
RUSSIAKY, Rachael 864-977-7190 410 A
rachael.russiaky@ngu.edu
RUSSIN, Gabrielle 914-961-8313 314 E
grussin@svots.edu
RUSSIN, Ted 845-905-4427 297 E
ted.russin@culinary.edu
RUSSO, Colleen 801-618-0438 458 H
crusso@ameritech.edu
RUSSO, Diana 718-636-3467 311 A
dmartucc@pratt.edu
RUSSO, Elizabeth 315-279-5273 303 D
drusso@keuka.edu
RUSSO, Greg 619-574-6909.. 55 D
grusso@pacificcollege.edu
RUSSO, Kelly 724-439-4900 387 H
RUSSO, Kelly 724-983-0700 387 I
RUSSO, Lisa 213-613-2200.. 65 D
lisarusso@sciarc.edu
RUSSO, Maria 518-454-5121 296 E
russom@strose.edu
RUSSO, Michael 860-832-1904.. 85 F
michael.russo@ccsu.edu
RUSSO, Paul 646-592-4720 325 R
paul.russo@yu.edu
RUSSO, Richard 510-642-2700.. 68 N
russo@berkeley.edu
RUSSO, Rick 510-642-6000.. 68 N
extension-dean@berkeley.edu
RUSSO, Ronald 504-762-3005 187 I
rrusso@dcc.edu
RUSSO, Sandra 347-532-6300 322 C
sandra.russo2@touro.edu
RUSSO, Thomas 417-873-7413 252 A
trusso@drury.edu
RUSSOM, Vaughn, N 715-394-8327 496 D
vrussom@uwsuper.edu
RUSSOMANNO,
Catherine 609-896-5121 280 D
RUSSOMANNO,
David, J 317-274-0802 157 B
drussoma@iupui.edu
RUSSOS, Milton, A 904-442-2950 101 A
mrussos@fscj.edu
RUST, Jodi 620-227-9322 173 A
jrust@dc3.edu
RUST, Melissa 501-686-2532.. 21 G
mrust@uasys.edu
RUSTAD, Dan 507-222-4890 234 C
drustad@carleton.edu
RUSTGI, Anil 212-854-1754 296 H
RUSTICUS, Lisa 616-988-3653 226 A
lrusticus@kuyper.edu
RUTENBAR, Rob, A 412-624-9019 400 A
rutenbar@pitt.edu
RUTENBECK, Jeff 215-572-2900 378 E
rutenbeckj@arcadia.edu
RUTH, Alice, A 603-646-2445 272 F
alice.a.ruth@dartmouth.edu
RUTH, Andrea 610-225-5054 383 A
aruth@eastern.edu
RUTH, Anna 727-864-7966.. 98 G
ruthar@eckerd.edu
RUTH, Dave, A 610-861-5458 391 B
druth@northampton.edu
RUTH, Gary 304-887-1795 464 A
gruth@bluefield.edu
RUTH, John 212-353-4247 297 C
jruth@cooper.edu
RUTH, Kevin, J 844-283-2246.. 93 C
RUTH, Matthew 540-432-4118 465 F
matthew.ruth@emu.edu
RUTH, Ted 573-341-7619 260 F
truth@mst.edu
RUTHENBECK, Julie, J 325-942-2255 450 B
julie.ruthenbeck@angelo.edu
RUTHER, Elliott 513-569-1451 350 C
elliott.ruther@cincinnatistate.edu
RUTHER, Elliott, V 513-569-1451 350 C
elliott.ruther@cincinnatistate.edu
RUTHERFORD, David 561-868-3450 105 C
rutherfd@palmbeachstate.edu

RUTHERFORD, Jason 903-988-7517 437 G
jrutherford@kilgore.edu
RUTHERFORD, John 406-447-6935 263 F
john.rutherford@helenacollege.edu
RUTHERFORD, John, D 214-648-0400 456 D
john.rutherford@utsouthwestern.edu
RUTHERFORD, Lisa, H 413-542-5645 205 D
lrutherford@amherst.edu
RUTHERFORD,
Marcella, M 954-262-1963 104 M
rmarcell@nova.edu
RUTHERFORD, Matthew 315-268-4443 295 E
mrutherf@clarkson.edu
RUTHERFORD, Michael 978-934-3657 211 G
michael_rutherford@uml.edu
RUTHERFORD, Paul 304-327-4403 488 J
prutherford@bluefieldstate.edu
RUTHERFORD, Tom 626-398-2222.. 76 B
RUTHERFORD, Whitney 850-729-5253 104 L
rutherf2j@nwfsc.edu
RUTHERMAN, Kathy 270-852-3143 183 B
kruthrman@kwc.edu
RUTKOWSKE, Snow 312-567-3677 139 H
srutkowske@iit.edu
RUTKOWSKI, Leslie, A 315-470-6655 319 A
larutkow@esf.edu
RUTKOWSKI, Sandra 419-824-3762 355 C
srutkowski@lourdes.edu
RUTKOWSKI, Stephen 973-278-5400 291 A
sru@berkeleycollege.edu
RUTKOWSKI, Stephen 973-278-5400 274 J
sru@berkeleycollege.edu
RUTLAND, Jason 864-231-2000 405 F
jrutland@andersonuniversity.edu
RUTLAND, Katie 912-424-3645 117 B
krutland@coastalpines.edu
RUTLEDGE, Brian 601-984-1010 248 G
brutledge@umc.edu
RUTLEDGE, Catherine 484-365-8087 388 F
crutledge@lincoln.edu
RUTLEDGE, Debi 248-218-2192 229 I
drutledge@rochesteru.edu
RUTLEDGE, Jacqueline 817-531-6571 450 F
jrutledge@txwes.edu
RUTLEDGE, James 662-846-4004 245 A
jrutledge@deltastate.edu
RUTLEDGE, Janet 410-455-1781 202 G
jrutledge@umbc.edu
RUTLEDGE, Melissa, B 540-378-5120 469 G
rutledge@roanoke.edu
RUTLEDGE, Peter 706-542-7140 126 F
borut@uga.edu
RUTLEDGE, Scott 765-285-5818 153 E
scott.rutledge@bsu.edu
RUTLEDGE, Valerie 423-425-4249 426 D
valerie-rutledge@utc.edu
RUTSTEIN-RILEY, Amy 617-349-8401 210 H
arutstei@lesley.edu
RUTT, Charles, D 660-543-4370 259 K
rutt@ucmo.edu
RUTT, Douglas, L 314-505-7566 251 D
ruttd@csl.edu
RUTTEN, Chris 402-844-7051 268 A
christopherr@northeast.edu
RUTTEN, Matthew 218-299-3514 234 K
mrutten@cord.edu
RUTTER, Evan 909-621-8153.. 37 G
evan.rutter@cmc.edu
RUTTER, Jeff 602-489-5300.. 10 G
jeff.rutter@arizonachristian.edu
RUTTER, Jeff 540-458-8590 476 D
jrutter@wlu.edu
RUTTER, Sandy 423-697-4475 423 B
sandy.rutter@chattanoogastate.edu
RUTTLER, Megan 856-468-5000 280 F
RUUD, William, N 740-376-4701 355 E
wnr001@marietta.edu
RUYLE, Dianna 217-854-5772 133 F
dianna.ruyle@blackburn.edu
RUYS, Jasmine 661-362-3466.. 38 H
jasmine.ruys@canyons.edu
RUYS, Steve 661-362-3545.. 38 H
steve.ruys@canyons.edu
RUZEK, Nicole 434-243-5150 471 F
nar7r@virginia.edu
RUZICH, Steve 708-596-2000 149 D
sruzich@ssc.edu
RUZICKA, Jim 402-465-2323 267 J
jruzicka@nebrwesleyan.edu
RYALL, Eric 770-729-8400 115 A
RYALL, Patrick 503-768-7294 373 D
ryall@lclark.edu

RYALS, Tara 334-699-2266.. 1 B
tryals@acom.edu
RYAN, Andrew, J 859-238-5572 179 H
andrew.ryan@centre.edu
RYAN, Barry 661-726-1911.. 68 L
RYAN, CSC, Brogan 570-208-5900 386 G
broganryan@kings.edu
RYAN, Caroll 562-988-2278.. 26 A
cryan@auhs.edu
RYAN, Carrie 336-278-5584 328 H
cryan2@elon.edu
RYAN, Casey, J 215-596-8800 400 B
RYAN, Christine 716-827-2467 322 J
ryanc@trocaire.edu
RYAN, Clay, M 205-348-5863.... 7 F
cryan@uasystem.edu
RYAN, Colleen 703-526-6932 468 A
colleen.ryan@marymount.edu
RYAN, Dana 775-445-4284 271 A
dana.ryan@wnc.edu
RYAN, Dana 775-445-4431 271 A
dana.ryan@wnc.edu
RYAN, Dennis 757-340-2121 464 L
RYAN, Diane 928-717-7644.. 17 D
diane.ryan@yc.edu
RYAN, Duane 575-562-2112 285 E
duane.ryan@enmu.edu
RYAN, Ed 408-554-4533.. 63 A
eryan@scu.edu
RYAN, Erik 617-873-0106 207 E
erik.ryan@cambridgecollege.edu
RYAN, Gail, L 313-577-6595 232 H
gail.ryan@wayne.edu
RYAN, Greg 714-992-7092.. 54 D
gryan@fullcoll.edu
RYAN, Helen, G 502-272-8052 179 D
hryan@bellarmine.edu
RYAN, James 617-585-0200 206 E
james.ryan@the-bac.edu
RYAN, James, E 434-924-3337 471 F
jer6p@virginia.edu
RYAN, James, P 203-582-7229.. 88 F
james.ryan@quinnipiac.edu
RYAN, Jason 802-635-1240 463 B
RYAN, Jennifer 785-833-4351 175 C
jennifer.ryan@kwu.edu
RYAN, Jessica 508-213-2027 217 C
jessica.ryan@nichols.edu
RYAN, Jessica Nicole 215-898-5000 399 J
jesryan@upenn.edu
RYAN, Joseph 859-846-5321 183 G
jryan@midway.edu
RYAN, Joseph 707-864-7000.. 64 F
joseph.ryan@solano.edu
RYAN, Julie, A 928-523-9658.. 14 J
julie.ryan@nau.edu
RYAN, Kathleen 508-541-1515 208 E
kryan@dean.edu
RYAN, Kathleen 617-732-5042 216 B
kathleen.ryan@mcphs.edu
RYAN, Kathleen 614-823-1250 359 G
kryan@otterbein.edu
RYAN, Kelly, A 812-941-2200 157 D
ryanka@ius.edu
RYAN, Kevin, A 540-464-7132 475 C
ryanka@vmi.edu
RYAN, Kim 617-628-5000 219 A
kim.ryan@tufts.edu
RYAN, Kimberly 973-300-2267 283 B
kryan@sussex.edu
RYAN, Kyle 781-899-5500 217 F
kryan@psjs.edu
RYAN, Larry 505-313-7626 288 C
larry.ryan@unmfund.org
RYAN, Lauren 216-421-8073 350 E
lnryan@cia.edu
RYAN, Marianne, P 773-508-2657 142 G
mryan21@luc.edu
RYAN, Mark 619-849-2489.. 57 J
markryan@pointloma.edu
RYAN, Maura, A 574-631-9488 161 G
mryan11@nd.edu
RYAN, Megan 484-664-3204 390 F
meganryan@muhlenberg.edu
RYAN, Monica 409-880-8307 449 B
mryan@lamar.edu
RYAN, Nicole 845-398-4163 314 D
nryan@stac.edu
RYAN, Pat 503-842-8222 376 D
patryan@tillamookbaycc.edu
RYAN, Patrick 716-270-2869 299 A
ryanp@ecc.edu

RYAN, Patrick 973-720-3326 283 I
ryanp@wpunj.edu
RYAN, Patrick 518-381-1210 319 G
ryanpc@sunysccc.edu
RYAN, Paula 641-628-5198 164 B
ryanp@central.edu
RYAN, Peter 662-325-3742 247 A
ryan@cvm.msstate.edu
RYAN, Rebecca 773-244-5623 145 F
rryan@northpark.edu
RYAN, Rochelle 508-565-1646 218 F
rryan@stonehill.edu
RYAN, Rosaleen 831-646-4035.. 52 H
rryan@mpc.edu
RYAN, Scott 817-272-3181 454 E
sdryan@uta.edu
RYAN, Sean, J 502-272-8376 179 D
sryan@bellarmine.edu
RYAN, Sharon 708-524-6299 137 A
sryan1@dom.edu
RYAN, Susan 386-822-7181 111 F
sryan@stetson.edu
RYAN, Thomas 504-865-2304 190 A
tfryan@loyno.edu
RYAN, Thomas, J 856-225-6361 281 A
tomryan@camden.rutgers.edu
RYAN, Tim 845-452-9600 297 E
tim.ryan@culinary.edu
RYAN, Tim 415-452-5352.. 37 C
tryan@ccsf.edu
RYAN, Timothy, M 207-725-3247 194 A
tryan@bowdoin.edu
RYAN, Tom 727-864-8305.. 98 G
ryantj@eckerd.edu
RYAN, Virginia 212-853-0702 290 H
vryan@barnard.edu
RYAN, Zoe 215-898-5000 399 J
hello@ica.upenn.edu
RYAN-BENDER, Anna 215-248-7993 380 G
aryan@chc.edu
RYAN BULONE, Mary 419-473-2700 351 I
mryan@daviscollege.edu
RYAN HOFFMAN,
Maureen 802-387-4767 461 E
RYAN RODRIGUEZ,
Christina 714-895-8128.. 38 E
cryanrodriguez@gwc.cccd.edu
RYAN VAN ZEE,
Marynel 507-222-4917 234 C
mryanvanzee@carleton.edu
RYANT, Marion 299-500-3027 114 F
marion.ryant@asurams.edu
RYBAK, Chuck 920-465-2336 494 F
rybakc@uwgb.edu
RYBALOV, Lana 215-392-0371 395 E
lrybalov@pitc.edu
RYBERG, Bill 253-566-5336 483 F
bryberg@tacomacc.edu
RYBERG, Mary 757-455-5707 476 C
mryberg@vwu.edu
RYBIN KOOB, Amanda 303-245-4664.. 81 N
arybinkoob@naropa.edu
RYCHEL, William, E 305-628-6775 107 D
wrychel@stu.edu
RYCHLEC, Timothy 713-221-5869 452 B
rychlect@uhd.edu
RYCKERT, Clay 270-534-3184 182 G
clay.ryckert@kctcs.edu
RYCRAFT, Rickianne 951-639-5420.. 53 A
rrycraft@msjc.edu
RYCYNA, Mary 216-397-4921 353 O
mrycyna@jcu.edu
RYDER, Collette, L 212-327-8054 312 B
cryder@rockefeller.edu
RYDER, Ellen 415-422-2558.. 72 I
eryder@usfca.edu
RYDER, Michelle 703-284-1667 468 A
michelle.ryder@marymount.edu
RYDER, Tina 301-447-5038 201 A
ryder@msmary.edu
RYDL, Chareny, L 979-845-3158 446 B
chareny@tamu.edu
RYDSTROM, Rebecca 202-651-5005.. 92 B
rebecca.rydstrom@gallaudet.edu
RYE, Leah 518-381-1490 319 G
ryeleah@sunysccc.edu
RYERSON, Crystal 704-216-3806 337 C
crystal.ryerson@rccc.edu
RYKEN, Amy 253-879-2810 483 G
aryken@pugetsound.edu
RYKEN, Philip, G 630-752-5002 152 K
philip.ryken@wheaton.edu
RYLAARSDAM, David 616-957-6032 221 K
drylaars@calvinseminary.edu

ST. JOHN, Mike 405-382-9201 369 E m.stjohn@sscok.edu
ST. JULIEN, Tanya 337-521-8941 188 G tanya.stjulien@solacc.edu
ST. LEGER, Gabrielle 215-951-1018 386 I
ST. LEGER, Trish 314-228-7224 296 C tstleger@colgate.edu
SAINT-LOUIS, Moise 508-999-9208 211 F msaintlouis@umassd.edu
ST. LOUIS, Shelly 518-891-2915 309 G mstlouis@nccc.edu
ST. ONGE, Katherine 850-729-5364 104 L stongek@nwfsc.edu
ST. ONGE, Stephen 707-826-3451 30 A srs706@humboldt.edu
ST. PIERRE, Beverly 413-565-1000 205 I bstpierre@baypath.edu
ST. PIERRE, Gail, S 207-786-6120 193 D gstpierr@bates.edu
ST. PIERRE, Traci 207-780-4771 196 J tracy.st@maine.edu
ST. ROMAIN, Claire 337-482-0925 192 F cstromain@louisiana.edu
ST. ROMAIN, Karen 248-689-8282 231 E kstromain@walshcollege.edu
SAINT-VICTOR, Nicole 708-239-4560 150 H nicole.saint-victor@trnty.edu
SAINTJONES, Jerome 256-372-4863 1 A jerome.saintjones@aamu.edu
SAINZ, Jose 540-654-1261 471 B jsainz@umw.edu
SAIRS, Reuben 740-857-1311 360 C rsairs@rosedale.edu
SAITTA, Tom 336-272-7102 329 B thomas.saitta@greensboro.edu
SAJADIAN, Dalila, A 641-422-4103 168 E sajaddal@niacc.edu
SAJDAK, Jeff 616-957-6042 221 K js036@calvinseminary.edu
SAJKO, Brian 412-237-3008 381 C bsajko@ccac.edu
SAKAGAWA, Tamara 863-292-3744 106 A tsakagawa@polk.edu
SAKAGUCHI, Ron 503-494-8801 374 F sodcontactus@ohsu.edu
SAKAI, Hiro 949-480-4008 64 E sakai@soka.edu
SAKALLA, Khaled 205-940-7800 5 E ksakalla@fortisinstitute.edu
SAKAMAKI, Yuri 661-654-3675 30 C ysakamaki@csub.edu
SAKAMOTO, June 415-703-8291 69 B sakamotoj@uchastings.edu
SAKELLARIOU, Dimitris 626-395-3208 29 B dimitris@caltech.edu
SAKRAIDA, Nicole 541-956-7166 375 G nsakraida@roguecc.edu
SAKS, Deborah 916-558-2407 51 B saksd@scc.losrios.edu
SAKS, Greg 657-278-5287 31 E gsaks@fullerton.edu
SAKS, Michael 848-445-7952 281 B chair@math.rutgers.edu
SAKSENA, P.N 803-323-2186 413 D saksenapn@winthrop.edu
SALA, Andrea 310-660-3670 41 J asala@elcamino.edu
SALA, Pete 315-443-5439 321 D pesala@syr.edu
SALADIN, Lisa 843-792-3031 409 D saladinl@musc.edu
SALADIN, Shawn 956-665-3651 455 A shawn.saladin@utrgv.edu
SALAFSKY, David, B 520-621-8297 16 H salafsky@arizona.edu
SALAK, Carly 402-844-7045 268 A csalak@northeast.edu
SALAMON, Joseph 718-851-8721 325 B
SALAMY, James 315-866-0300 301 B salamyjr@herkimer.edu
SALAND, Emily, V 845-575-3000 305 C emily.saland@marist.edu
SALAS, Alexandra 610-359-5057 381 J asalas@dccc.edu
SALAS, ESQ, Alexandria 210-283-6977 452 D ansalas@uiwtx.edu
SALAS, Carmen 773-371-5484 134 C csalas@ctu.edu
SALAS, Leslie 760-744-1150 56 B lsalas@palomar.edu
SALAS, Richard 515-271-1709 165 C rich.salas@dmu.edu
SALASEK, Aaron 651-450-3611 237 H asalasek@inverhills.edu
SALASKI, Kori 608-796-3185 496 L kfsalaski@viterbo.edu
SALAY, Lawrence 203-285-2046 86 D lsalay@gatewayct.edu
SALAYANDIA, Destinee 575-624-7155 285 F destinee.salayandia@roswell.enmu.edu
SALAZ, Alicia 541-346-3053 376 G asalaz@uoregon.edu
SALAZ, Mark 520-494-5250 11 M mark.salaz@centralaz.edu
SALAZAR, Abraham 325-793-4611 439 A salazar.abraham@mcm.edu
SALAZAR, Carolyn 410-386-4814 200 D csalazar@mcdaniel.edu
SALAZAR, David 414-251-5896 495 B salazada@uwm.edu
SALAZAR, Freddie 575-769-4143 285 C freddie.salazar@clovis.edu
SALAZAR, Greg 505-454-2500 285 I
SALAZAR, Jamie 405-491-6310 369 G jsalazar@snu.edu
SALAZAR, S.J., Jose-Luis 718-817-4503 300 A jsalazar8@fordham.edu
SALAZAR, Linda 505-454-2500 285 I
SALAZAR, Nicole 520-621-7739 16 H hinzen@arizona.edu
SALAZAR, Rosalinda 956-882-7665 455 A rosalinda.salazar@utrgv.edu
SALAZAR, Stacey 410-225-2541 200 B ssalazar@mica.edu
SALAZAR, Susie, B 210-436-3722 442 A ssalazar1@stmarytx.edu
SALAZAR, Toni 254-298-8808 445 B toni.salazar@templejc.edu
SALAZAR, Tony 303-860-5600 83 L tony.salazar@cu.edu
SALAZAR, Veronikha 870-230-5231 19 H salazav@hsu.edu
SALAZAR, Victor, G 210-431-4149 440 D vmsalazar@ollusa.edu
SALAZAR MENDEZ, Veronica 210-458-4011 455 B veronica.salazar.vpba@utsa.edu
SALAZAR-VALENTINE, Marcia 419-372-8185 348 F marcias@bgsu.edu
SALB, Ephraim 845-406-4308 325 C rabbisalb@kessertorah.org
SALBATO, Michael 719-846-5653 83 I michael.salbato@trinidadstate.edu
SALCEDO, Richard 661-654-3491 30 C rsalcedo5@csub.edu
SALCIDO, Steven, M 916-278-6060 33 A steven.salcido@csus.edu
SALDANA, Michelle 310-954-4327 52 J msaldana@msmu.edu
SALDANA, Momo 517-796-8626 225 A saldanamoniquea@jccmi.edu
SALDIVAR, Patricia 956-295-3426 448 E patricia.saldivar@tsc.edu
SALE, Rachel 956-872-2576 443 B rsale@southtexascollege.edu
SALEM, Joseph 919-660-5800 328 D joseph.salem@duke.edu
SALEM, Susan 310-954-4112 52 J ssalem@msmu.edu
SALEMME, Kevin 978-837-5377 216 D kevin.salemme@merrimack.edu
SALERNO, Cheryl 918-335-6887 368 E csalerno@okwu.edu
SALERNO, Dena 570-372-4302 398 A salerno@susqu.edu
SALERNO, Denise 252-638-7225 333 F horned@cravencc.edu
SALERNO, Janice 215-885-2360 389 A jsalerno@manor.edu
SALERNO, Kerry 781-235-1200 205 G
SALERNO, Sarah 781-239-2782 214 E ssalerno@massbay.edu
SALGADO, Gloriana 787-765-1915 507 G gsalgado@opto.inter.edu
SALGADO, Juan 773-777-7900 135 D jsalgado@ccc.edu
SALGADO, Juan 312-553-2500 134 L jsalgado@ccc.edu
SALGADO, Nicole 619-660-4654 44 G nicole.salgado@gcccd.edu
SALGADO, Rafael 787-279-1912 506 L rsalgado@bayamon.inter.edu
SALGADO, Sergio 507-344-7310 233 I ssalgado@blc.edu
SALGUERO, Jossie 787-766-1912 506 H jsalguer@inter.edu
SALHOTRA, Poonam 713-221-8066 452 B gulatip@uhd.edu
SALIBA, Matt 863-638-2947 113 E salibam@webber.edu
SALIBA, Therese 360-867-6854 479 C salibat@evergreen.edu
SALIBA EL HABRE, Arlene 352-254-4119 112 D
SALII, Uroi, N 680-488-2471 504 A usalii@palau.edu
SALIMAN, Todd 303-860-5600 83 L officeofthepresident@cu.edu
SALINAS, Antonio 575-439-3601 286 H antsalin@nmsu.edu
SALINAS, Christy 626-395-3651 29 B cssalina@caltech.edu
SALINAS, Felix 210-486-4788 428 A fsalinas26@alamo.edu
SALINAS, Horacio 956-764-5798 438 A hsalinas@laredo.edu
SALINAS, Jesse 559-453-5570 43 D jesse.torres@fresno.edu
SALINAS, Laura 530-541-4660 47 H salinas@ltcc.edu
SALINAS, Lelia 956-872-7209 443 B lelias1@southtexascollege.edu
SALINAS, Nick 914-395-2570 314 H nsalinas@sarahlawrence.edu
SALINAS, Romelia 909-274-5659 52 K rsalinas@mtsac.edu
SALINAS, Sergio 559-324-6483 66 H sergio.salinas@cloviscollege.edu
SALINAS, Stacy 845-848-7818 298 A stacy.salinas@dc.edu
SALINAS-HOVAR, Marta 956-665-7304 455 A marta.salinashovar@utrgv.edu
SALISBURY, Jason 712-279-5227 163 H jason.salisbury@briarcliff.edu
SALISBURY, Jon 831-479-6187 27 G josalisb@cabrillo.edu
SALISBURY, Kevin, S 401-333-7316 403 D ksalisbury@ccri.edu
SALISBURY, Micheal 325-942-2595 450 B micheal.salisbury@angelo.edu
SALISBURY, Susan 860-297-4281 88 I susan.salisbury@trincoll.edu
SALIUS, Erin 617-358-3977 207 C esalius@bu.edu
SALKA, William 860-465-5246 85 G salkaw@easternct.edu
SALKIN, Patricia 646-565-6522 322 C patricia.salkin@touro.edu
SALKIN, Patricia, E 646-565-6522 322 B patricia.salkin@touro.edu
SALLAM, Miriam 559-737-4842 39 C mirams@cos.edu
SALLAN, Veena 270-686-4639 182 C veena.sallan@kctcs.edu
SALLEE, Emily 816-584-6779 257 E emily.sallee@park.edu
SALLEE, Holly, E 618-537-6824 143 G hesallee@mckendree.edu
SALLEE-JUSTESEN, Dawn 503-491-6422 373 H dawn.sallee-justesen@mhcc.edu
SALLEH-BARONE, Normah 708-974-5209 144 G salleh-barone@morainevalley.edu
SALLIS, Archer 662-476-8414 245 C jsallis@eastms.edu
SALLUSTIO, Joseph 909-667-4494 38 A jsallustio@claremontlincoln.edu
SALMAN, Fatma 860-512-2602 86 F
SALMAN, Juli 505-426-2155 286 C jesalman@nmhu.edu
SALMEIER, Michael 276-326-4355 464 A msalmeier@bluefield.edu
SALMO, Jim 608-796-3074 496 L jgsalmo@viterbo.edu
SALMON, Lorraine 845-687-5093 322 K salmonl@sunyulster.edu
SALMON, Michael, G 212-517-0563 305 D msalmon@mmm.edu
SALMON, Pamela 315-792-3011 323 G pjsalmon@utica.edu
SALOCKS, Stephen 617-254-2610 218 A rector@sjs.edu
SALOIS, Brad 785-827-5541 175 C
SALOME, JoAnn 575-835-5955 286 D joann.salome@nmt.edu
SALOMON, Danielle 310-954-4371 52 J dsalomon@msmu.edu
SALOMON, Mattisyahu 732-367-1060 275 B
SALOMON, Nasser 909-580-9661 34 E
SALOMONE, Giuseppe 215-895-1050 382 D registrar@drexel.edu
SALOMONSON, Kristen 231-591-3801 223 H kristensalomonson@ferris.edu
SALON, Mabel 530-752-9795 69 A masalon@ucdavis.edu
SALOVEY, Peter 203-432-2550 90 B peter.salovey@yale.edu
SALSBURY, Lysa 208-885-9358 132 C lsalsbur@uidaho.edu
SALTANOVICH, Julia 518-262-5522 289 C saltanj@amc.edu
SALTER, Les 770-533-6901 121 L lsalter@laniertech.edu
SALTER, Sid 662-325-7454 247 A ss51@msstate.edu
SALTERS, Gregory, A 305-626-3713 100 B gregory.salters@fmuniv.edu
SALTIEL, Henry 718-482-6120 294 D hsaltiel@lagcc.cuny.edu
SALTON, Susan 814-332-4793 378 A ssalton@allegheny.edu
SALTONSTALL, Margot 928-523-6990 14 J
SALTSMAN, Brian 607-871-2671 289 E saltsman@alfred.edu
SALTSMAN, Terry 931-372-3200 425 B tsaltsman@tntech.edu
SALVAGE, Lynn 718-818-6470 314 B lsalvage@edaff.com
SALVATORE, Michael 908-737-7032 277 F msalvato@kean.edu
SALVATORIELLO, Vincent 610-398-5300 388 D vsalvatoriello@lincolntech.edu
SALVESEN, Guy 858-646-3100 62 L gsalvesen@sbpdiscovery.org
SALVINI, Tonia 785-830-2753 174 A tsalvini@haskell.edu
SALVO, Robyn 732-263-5228 278 B rsalvo@monmouth.edu
SALVUCCI, Rachael 304-296-8282 490 C
SALYER, Greg 720-496-1370 81 C
SALYERS, Vince 414-410-4397 490 J vlsalyers@stritch.edu
SALZAMEDA, Bridget 714-992-7044 54 D bsalzameda@fullcoll.edu
SALZBRUNN, Kimberly 630-637-5454 145 E ksalzbrunn@noctrl.edu
SALZMAN, Christine 908-709-7485 283 E csalzman@follett.com
SALZMANN, Nick 847-628-2492 141 A nsalzmann@judsonu.edu
SAM, David 847-214-7374 137 D dsam@elgin.edu
SAM, Mary 218-855-8159 237 C mary.sam@clcmn.edu
SAM, Penselyn 691-320-2480 503 B petse@comfsm.fm
SAMAHA, Ahmed 803-641-3411 412 B ahmeds@usca.edu
SAMAHA, Mamoun 833-637-0866 46 J msamaha@itu.edu
SAMAIE, Parissa 323-242-5536 49 I samaiep@lasc.edu
SAMAN, Sarmad 508-678-2811 213 F sarmad.saman@bristolcc.edu
SAMANGO, Melissa 610-526-6196 385 F msamango@harcum.edu
SAMANIEGO, Sue 970-675-3216 78 P sue.samaniego@cncc.edu
SAMANT, Ajay 309-438-2251 140 C asamant@ilstu.edu
SAMARDZIJA, Michael 909-558-8544 48 J msamardzija@llu.edu
SAMBAMURTHY, Vallabh 608-262-7867 494 D vsambamurthy@wisc.edu
SAMBDMAN, Cory, W 563-333-6336 169 D 1312mgr@follett.com
SAMBLE, Brian 610-330-5000 387 B
SAMHAT, Nayef, H 864-597-4010 413 E president@wofford.edu
SAMMAKIA, Bahgat 607-777-4818 315 E bahgat@binghamton.edu
SAMMARCO, Erica, C 716-888-2100 291 M sammarce@canisius.edu

SANDERS, Brian .... 314-406-8845 250 C
brpsanders@gmail.com
SANDERS, Brian .... 209-575-6058.. 76 K
sandersb@mjc.edu
SANDERS, Bryce .... 318-487-7020 187 B
bryce.sanders@lcuniversity.edu
SANDERS, Cameron ...... 520-494-5289.. 11 M
cameron.sanders@centralaz.edu
SANDERS, Cheryl .... 361-698-2250 434 H
cgarner6@delmar.edu
SANDERS, Cindy .... 203-576-4226.. 89 A
cisander@bridgeport.edu
SANDERS, Clifton .... 801-957-4182 460 D
clifton.sanders@slcc.edu
SANDERS, Connie .... 303-605-5587.. 81 L
csande29@msudenver.edu
SANDERS, Dale, B .... 573-884-0798 260 C
sandersdb@missouri.edu
SANDERS, David .... 312-850-7031 135 E
dsanders67@ccc.edu
SANDERS, Diane, F .... 843-349-2848 407 B
diane@coastal.edu
SANDERS, Emily .... 585-582-8206 298 E
emilysanders@elim.edu
SANDERS, Erica, L .... 734-647-0102 231 A
yale@umich.edu
SANDERS, George .... 239-433-8026 100 G
gsanders@fsw.edu
SANDERS, Gregory .... 440-525-7097 354 L
gsanders3@lakelandcc.edu
SANDERS, Gwendolyn ... 252-335-3226 341 A
gsanders@ecsu.edu
SANDERS, J.C .... 405-224-3140 371 B
jcsanders@usao.edu
SANDERS, James .... 404-270-5674 126 A
jsande14@spelman.edu
SANDERS, Janet .... 318-487-7752 187 B
janet.sanders@lcuniversity.edu
SANDERS, Jenny .... 870-574-4530.. 21 F
jsanders@sautech.edu
SANDERS, Joe .... 432-552-2740 456 C
sanders_j@utpb.edu
SANDERS, Judy .... 501-977-2016.. 23 D
sanders@uaccm.edu
SANDERS, Karen .... 386-506-3050.. 98 A
karen.sanders@daytonastate.edu
SANDERS, Karen .... 361-570-4850 452 C
sanderkg1@uhv.edu
SANDERS, Karen, A .... 217-786-2784 142 F
karen.sanders@llcc.edu
SANDERS, Kenneth .... 315-279-5000 303 D
ksander@keuka.edu
SANDERS, Kim .... 252-862-1308 336 H
kasanders7800@roanokechowan.edu
SANDERS, Kristie .... 912-871-1937 123 F
ksanders@ogeecheetech.edu
SANDERS, LaSha .... 678-359-5015 120 D
lashas@gordonstate.edu
SANDERS, Lisa .... 931-433-9350 423 G
lsanders@mscc.edu
SANDERS, Lisa, K .... 618-537-6865 143 G
lksanders@mckendree.edu
SANDERS, Liz .... 312-362-5289 136 F
lsander3@depaul.edu
SANDERS, Mae .... 931-393-1520 423 G
msanders@mscc.edu
SANDERS, Mark .... 318-342-7135 466 E
msanders@vlm.vcom.edu
SANDERS, Megan .... 303-384-2617.. 79 A
sanders@mines.edu
SANDERS, Melanie .... 662-243-1979 245 C
msanders@eastms.edu
SANDERS, Melinda .... 501-332-0303.. 18 D
msanders@asutr.edu
SANDERS, Nancy, A ...... 815-282-7900 148 E
nancysanders@sacn.edu
SANDERS, Nicholas .... 843-377-1104 406 B
nsanders@charlestonlaw.edu
SANDERS, Phillip .... 614-287-5127 351 B
psanders@cscc.edu
SANDERS, Rebecca .... 903-510-2084 451 D
rsan2@tjc.edu
SANDERS, Robert .... 407-646-2292 106 L
rsanders@rollins.edu
SANDERS, Salvatore, A . 330-941-3091 364 G
sasanders@ysu.edu
SANDERS, Sara .... 319-335-2625 163 F
sara-sanders@uiowa.edu
SANDERS, Shalonda ..... 229-333-5356 127 F
shalonda.sanders@wiregrass.edu
SANDERS, Sonia, P ...... 502-597-6063 183 A
sonia.sanders@kysu.edu
SANDERS, Susan .... 310-243-3301.. 31 B
ssanders@csudh.edu
SANDERS, Thomas .... 903-923-2075 435 A
tsanders@etbu.edu
SANDERS, Tom .... 330-337-6403 347 B
prdept@awc.edu
SANDERS, Tricia .... 218-281-8326 243 B
sand0803@umn.edu
SANDERS, Tyler .... 909-687-1759.. 43 G
tylersanders@gs.edu
SANDERS, William, H .... 412-268-5090 380 B
sanders@andrew.cmu.edu
SANDERS-FUNNYE,
Sharon .... 847-543-2383 135 G
ssandersfunnye@clcillinois.edu
SANDERS-MCMURTRY,
Kijua .... 413-538-2800 216 G
kijuasm@mtholyoke.edu
SANDERSON, Carla .... 888-556-8226 134 D
SANDERSON, Erika .... 509-527-2615 484 C
erika.sanderson@wallawalla.edu
SANDERSON,
Francie, W .... 919-866-5944 338 E
fwsanderson@waketech.edu
SANDERSON, Jordan .... 228-897-4378 246 F
jordan.sanderson@mgccc.edu
SANDERSON, Karri .... 402-465-2411 267 J
ksanders@nebrwesleyan.edu
SANDERSON, Lex .... 818-401-1032.. 39 F
lsanderson@columbiacollege.edu
SANDERSON, Robyn ...... 864-231-2000 405 F
rsanderson@andersonuniversity.edu
SANDERSON-TOBLER,
Karri .... 402-466-2371 267 J
SANDFORD, Art .... 805-678-5198.. 74 A
asandford@vcccd.edu
SANDFORT, Jodi .... 206-406-7369 484 A
jrs1@uw.edu
SANDIDGE, Christa .... 208-467-8941 132 B
csandidge@nnu.edu
SANDIFER, Joyce .... 504-520-5230 193 C
jsandife@xula.edu
SANDIFER, William, A .. 803-812-7302 412 E
sandifea@mailbox.sc.edu
SANDIFER, Willie .... 903-730-4890 437 E
wsandifer@jarvis.edu
SANDIGO, Laura .... 928-317-6000.. 11 B
laura.sandigo@azwestern.edu
SANDIGO, Laura .... 928-344-7699.. 11 B
laura.sandigo@azwestern.edu
SANDLER, Elysha .... 516-239-9002 314 J
esandler@shoryoshuv.org
SANDLER, Jennifer .... 206-878-3710 480 C
jsandler@highline.edu
SANDLER, Mike .... 303-860-5600.. 83 L
michael.sandler@cu.edu
SANDLES, Sherry .... 817-531-4401 450 F
slsandles@txwes.edu
SANDLIN, Betsy .... 931-598-1254 422 F
bsandlin@sewanee.edu
SANDLIN, Terrie .... 541-956-7283 375 G
tsandlin@roguecc.edu
SANDMANN, Laura .... 580-387-7000 366 E
lsandmann@mscok.edu
SANDNER, Michael .... 860-509-9525.. 88 A
msandner@hartfordinternational.edu
SANDNESS, Debra .... 701-224-5524 345 F
debra.sandness@bismarckstate.edu
SANDOE, Timothy .... 717-780-2648 385 A
tlsandoe@hacc.edu
SANDONATO, Judith ...... 617-353-2230 207 C
jsandona@bu.edu
SANDOR, Kathy .... 540-654-1648 471 B
kunderwo@umw.edu
SANDOVAL, Amada .... 914-395-2590 314 H
asandoval@sarahlawrence.edu
SANDOVAL, April .... 928-226-4217.. 12 B
april.sandoval@coconino.edu
SANDOVAL, April .... 336-334-4822 334 F
adsandoval@gtcc.edu
SANDOVAL, Barbara, A . 360-650-7614 485 A
barbara.sandoval@wwu.edu
SANDOVAL, Belinda ...... 909-748-8164.. 72 E
belinda_sandoval@redlands.edu
SANDOVAL, Brian .... 775-784-4805 270 K
SANDOVAL, Darlene ...... 505-984-6058 287 F
darlene.sandoval@sjc.edu
SANDOVAL, Deanna .... 303-867-1155.. 83 H
sandoval@taft.edu
SANDOVAL, Derek .... 830-591-7372 443 I
mdsandoval@swtjc.edu
SANDOVAL, Eric .... 575-674-2214 284 P
esandoval@burrell.edu
SANDOVAL, John .... 719-549-2535.. 79 G
john.sandoval@csupueblo.edu
SANDOVAL, Natalie .... 432-837- ... 449 F
natalie.sandoval@sulross.edu
SANDOVAL, Nichole ...... 906-227-1000 228 E
SANDOVAL, Nikki .... 301-985-7000 203 C
nikki.sandoval@umuc.edu
SANDOVAL, Paul .... 520-626-6309.. 16 H
sandovar@arizona.edu
SANDOVAL, Rudy .... 254-501-3007 431 E
rudolfo.sandoval@ctcd.edu
SANDOVAL, Yuliana ...... 707-468-3110.. 51 F
ysandoval@mendocino.edu
SANDOVAL, Yvonne .... 928-776-2307.. 17 B
yvonne.sandoval@yc.edu
SANDOVAL DANCS,
Jennifer .... 909-621-8111.. 37 G
jennifer.sandoval-dancs@cmc.edu
SANDRIN, Todd, R .... 602-543-4506.. 11 A
todd.sandrin@asu.edu
SANDS, Charles .... 951-343-4213.. 27 J
csands@calbaptist.edu
SANDS, Rosita .... 312-369-7291 136 C
rsands@colum.edu
SANDS, Timothy, D ...... 540-231-6231 475 D
president@vt.edu
SANDS WISE, Jonathan 502-863-8009 180 E
jonathan_sandswise@
georgetowncollege.edu
SANDSTROM, Lynne ..... 707-826-4031.. 30 A
les37@humboldt.edu
SANDT, Jennifer, A .... 410-334-2911 205 A
jsandt@worwic.edu
SANDU, Terri, B .... 440-366-4215 355 B
SANDUM TUNE, Rachel 937-327-7411 364 C
rtune@wittenberg.edu
SANDY, Michael .... 508-531-6183 212 B
michael.sandy@bridgew.edu
SANDY, Paula .... 716-851-1868 299 A
sandy@ecc.edu
SANELLI, Brittany .... 720-890-8922.. 81 H
vicepres@itea.edu
SANFILIPPO, Marjorie ... 727-864-7562.. 98 G
sanfilmd@eckerd.edu
SANFILIPPO, Rick .... 610-526-4600 385 F
rsanfilippo@harcum.edu
SANFORD, Debra .... 703-330-8400.. 93 H
SANFORD, Delacy .... 904-470-8290.. 98 I
dsanford@ewc.edu
SANFORD, Eric .... 316-295-5787 173 G
eric_sanford@friends.edu
SANFORD, Glenn .... 281-283-3300 452 A
sanford@uhcl.edu
SANFORD, Jennifer .... 707-826-3236.. 30 A
jls7003@humboldt.edu
SANFORD, Jessica .... 765-983-1432 154 H
sanfoje@earlham.edu
SANFORD, Jonathan, J . 972-721-5203 451 E
president@udallas.edu
SANFORD, Julie .... 601-984-6200 248 G
jrsanford@umc.edu
SANFORD, Larry .... 410-228-9250 203 A
lsanford@umces.edu
SANFORD, Mark .... 313-579-6931 232 B
msanfor1@wcccd.edu
SANFORD, Matthew .... 607-431-4460 300 G
sanfordm@hartwick.edu
SANFORD, Sara .... 617-735-1420 216 B
sara.sanford@mcphs.edu
SANFORD, Susan, H ..... 315-470-6604 319 A
shsanfor@esf.edu
SANFTNER, Alexis .... 512-444-8082 448 B
registrar@thsu.edu
SANGER, Jeff .... 641-628-5161 164 B
sangerj@central.edu
SANGER, Tchad .... 831-459-5604.. 71 A
cpsanger@ucsc.edu
SANGHA, Gurminder ..... 559-265-5763.. 67 A
gurminder.sangha@fresnocitycollege.
edu
SANGHVI, Kamlesh .... 708-974-5522 144 G
sanghvik@morainevalley.edu
SANGHVI, Kunali .... 844-283-2246.. 93 C
SANGREY-BILLY, Cory ... 406-395-4875 264 I
csangrey@stonechild.edu
SANIAL, Greg .... 616-331-2188 224 D
sanialg@gvsu.edu
SANJUAN, Alfredo .... 214-860-2064 434 A
aesanjuan@dcccd.edu
SANJURJO, Zenaida ...... 787-891-0925 506 I
zsanjurjo@aguadilla.inter.edu
SANKEY, Andrea .... 936-261-1209 445 E
arsankey@pvamu.edu
SANKEY, Lorinda .... 402-643-7385 265 I
lorinda.sankey@cune.edu
SANKO, Jerry .... 620-450-2193 176 I
jerrys@prattcc.edu
SANKS GUIDRY,
Beverly .... 909-469-5341.. 75 G
bguidry@westernu.edu
SANNEY, Stephen .... 419-447-6442 361 C
SANNS, Aaron .... 208-496-1109 130 G
sannsa@byui.edu
SANON, Malissa .... 512-863-1342 444 F
sanonm@southwestern.edu
SANREGRET, Suzanne ... 906-487-3070 227 D
srsangre@mtu.edu
SANSBURY, Timothy ...... 954-771-0376 103 S
tsansbury@knoxseminary.edu
SANSING, Perry .... 662-915-7014 248 F
psansing@olemiss.edu
SANSOLA, Steve .... 845-575-3000 305 C
steve.sansola@marist.edu
SANSOM, Allison .... 541-880-2223 373 B
sansom@klamathcc.edu
SANSOM, Erikka .... 304-829-7717 486 B
esansom@bethanywv.edu
SANSOM, Melvin .... 251-442-2390.... 8 C
msansom@umobile.edu
SANSOM, Randall .... 213-427-2200.. 35 L
SANT, Anne, M .... 508-565-1343 218 F
asant@stonehill.edu
SANTA, Brittany, F .... 812-855-3603 156 B
bfsanta@iu.edu
SANTA MARIA,
Diane, M .... 713-500-2187 455 D
diane.m.santamaria@uth.tmc.edu
SANTAMARIA, Anthony . 973-290-4338 282 G
asantamaria@steu.edu
SANTAMARIA, Danielle . 401-598-1000 403 E
danielle.santamaria@jwu.edu
SANTAMARIA, Meghan . 610-625-7788 390 D
santamariam@moravian.edu
SANTAMOURIS, Beverly 502-852-6272 185 E
bgsant01@louisville.edu
SANTANA, Evelyn .... 610-526-6006 385 F
esantana@harcum.edu
SANTANA, Jesse .... 562-985-8511.. 32 A
jesse.santana@csulb.edu
SANTANA, Jocelyn .... 218-736-1500 238 K
SANTANA, Juan .... 787-738-2161 511 A
juan.santana6@upr.edu
SANTANA, Leslie .... 310-289-5123.. 68 E
leslie.santana@wcui.edu
SANTANA, Martha, M ... 516-876-3000 318 A
SANTANA, Pedro .... 309-671-2753 143 I
psantana@methodistcol.edu
SANTANA-BRAVO,
Maydel .... 305-348-1555 109 H
santanam@fiu.edu
SANTANA MARINO,
Julio .... 787-725-6500 504 F
jsantana@albizu.edu
SANTANDREA, Mona .... 512-472-6736 429 K
msantandrea@austinseminary.edu
SANTANDREA, Mona .... 512-404-4823 429 K
msantandrea@austinseminary.edu
SANTANGELO, Chloe .... 716-926-8772 301 C
csantangelo@hilbert.edu
SANTANGELO,
Victoria, R .... 718-990-1363 313 B
santangv@stjohns.edu
SANTANIELLO, Emily ..... 860-253-3092.. 86 B
esantaniello@asnuntuck.edu
SANTAROSA, Michael ... 801-832-2186 461 A
msantarosa@westminstercollege.edu
SANTAW, Carrie .... 352-638-9705.. 96 B
csantaw@beaconcollege.edu
SANTEE, Wendi .... 864-379-8701 408 F
santee@erskine.edu
SANTELLANO, Claudia ... 509-527-2632 484 C
claudia.santellano@wallawalla.edu
SANTERRE, Kim .... 770-228-7365 125 F
kim.santerre@sctech.edu
SANTESTEBAN, David .... 559-638-0300.. 67 C
david.santesteban@reedleycollege.edu
SANTIAGO, Alma, L ...... 787-841-2000 508 H
alsantiago@pucpr.edu
SANTIAGO, Antonio ...... 203-437-9637.. 86 H
asantiago@nv.edu
SANTIAGO, Barbara, I ... 787-850-9386 511 B
barbara.santiago2@upr.edu
SANTIAGO, Carlos .... 617-994-6901 211 B
commissioner@dhe.mass.edu
SANTIAGO, Carol .... 787-620-2040 504 B
csantiago@aupr.edu

SATTERFIELD, Jay .... 731-989-6058 418 H
jsatterfield@fhu.edu
SATTERFIELD, Kathleen . 909-706-3505.. 75 G
ksatterfield@westernu.edu
SATTERFIELD, Lisa .... 828-398-2500 422 G
lsatterfield@south.edu
SATTERFIELD, Rachel .... 919-684-5055 328 D
rachel.satterfield@duke.edu
SATTERFIELD, Sherri ..... 704-233-8810 344 E
s.satterfield@wingate.edu
SATTERFIELD, Sonya ..... 334-229-6802.... 4 B
ssatterfield@alasu.edu
SATTERFIELD, Tanya ..... 662-915-7692 248 F
tnsatter@olemiss.edu
SATTERLEE, Kevin .... 208-282-3440 131 E
SATTERLEE, Richard ...... 717-815-1460 402 G
rsatterlee@ycp.edu
SATTERLUND, Alysson .. 858-534-4371.. 70 C
asatterlund@ucsd.edu
SATTERLY, Eric .... 502-272-8098 179 D
esatterly@bellarmine.edu
SATTERLY, Rob .... 970-675-3231.. 78 P
robert.satterly@cncc.edu
SATTERLY, Tom .... 970-491-0006.. 79 E
tom.satterly@colostate.edu
SATTERWHITE, Dawn ..... 919-761-2209 340 B
dsatterwhite@sebts.edu
SATTERWHITE, Robin .... 806-716-2200 443 A
rsatterwhite@southplainscollege.edu
SATZ, Debra .... 650-723-9784.. 66 D
SATZER, Neeley, V .... 304-457-6260 485 F
satzernv@ab.edu
SAUCEDA, John .... 312-329-4388 144 F
john.sauceda@moody.edu
SAUCEDA, Mary .... 303-605-7350.. 81 L
msauce11@msudenver.edu
SAUCEDA, Mary .... 214-768-3016 443 G
msauceda@smu.edu
SAUCEDA, Steve .... 575-492-4713 286 E
ssauceda@nmjc.edu
SAUCEDO, Federico ...... 818-240-1000.. 43 J
fsaucedo@glendale.edu
SAUCEDO, Lorena .... 253-566-5139 483 F
SAUCHUK, Stacy, R .... 610-917-2002 400 D
srsauchuk@valleyforge.edu
SAUCIER, Jason .... 207-741-5544 195 D
jsaucier@smccme.edu
SAUDER, Dustin .... 402-486-2507 268 G
dustin.sauder@ucollege.edu
SAUDER, Vinita .... 402-486-2500 268 G
vinita.sauder@ucollege.edu
SAUDERS, Charlette, R . 574-372-5100 155 C
saudercr@grace.edu
SAUDERS, Robert, R ..... 509-359-6015 478 H
rsauders@ewu.edu
SAUER, Dietrich .... 928-226-4204.. 12 B
dietrich.sauer@coconino.edu
SAUER, Greg .... 802-485-2170 461 H
gsauer@norwich.edu
SAUER, Jenni .... 434-381-6231 470 H
jsauer@sbc.edu
SAUER, Marty, R .... 630-637-5801 145 E
mrsauer@noctrl.edu
SAUERBREI, Aaron .... 319-277-2490 166 E
aaron.sauerbrei@hawkeyecollege.edu
SAUERBRUNN, Kayla .... 618-634-3203 149 C
kaylas@shawneecc.edu
SAUERBURGER, Kate .... 314-792-7435 253 J
sauerburger@kenrick.edu
SAUERS, Darlene .... 724-838-4210 397 F
sauers@setonhill.edu
SAUL, Amy .... 610-861-1508 390 D
saula@moravian.edu
SAUL, D. Eric .... 610-989-1230 400 F
esaul@vfmac.edu
SAUL, Shelby .... 918-540-6260 366 F
shelby.saul@neo.edu
SAUL, Sheryl .... 651-846-1384 240 E
sheryl.saul@saintpaul.edu
SAULNIER, Timothy ...... 540-654-2468 471 B
tsaulnie@umw.edu
SAULS, Jina, M .... 276-244-1232 463 H
jsauls@asl.edu
SAULS, Steve .... 229-333-2100 127 F
SAULSBERRY, Jean .... 901-435-1727 419 I
jean_saulsberry@loc.edu
SAULSBERRY, Keith ...... 334-556-2470.... 2 C
ksaulsberry@wallace.edu
SAULSBERRY,
Lynette, M .... 478-289-2169 118 B
lsaulsberry@ega.edu
SAULSBERRY, Pamela ... 318-342-1445 193 A
saulsberry@ulm.edu

SAULSBERRY, Raquel .... 901-321-3480 417 G
rlogansa@cbu.edu
SAUMBY, Sydney .... 361-698-1080 434 H
ssaumby@delmar.edu
SAUNDERS, Aleister ...... 215-895-6203 382 D
aleister.j.saunders@drexel.edu
SAUNDERS, Amber .... 318-371-3035 188 C
ambersaunders@nltcc.edu
SAUNDERS, Catherine ... 812-535-5225 160 E
catherine.saunders@smwc.edu
SAUNDERS,
Christopher .... 615-353-3066 424 A
christopher.saunders@nscc.edu
SAUNDERS, Dee .... 503-552-1946 374 B
dsaunders@nunm.edu
SAUNDERS, Gary .... 336-506-4152 331 J
gary.saunders@alamancecc.edu
SAUNDERS, Greer .... 804-819-4906 472 E
gsaunders@vccs.edu
SAUNDERS, Jennifer ...... 801-957-5009 460 D
jennifer.saunders@slcc.edu
SAUNDERS, Kara, C ...... 716-645-5725 315 F
kcs23@buffalo.edu
SAUNDERS, Kathleen .... 716-827-2445 322 J
saundersk@trocaire.edu
SAUNDERS, Keith .... 319-335-0553 163 F
keith-saunders@uiowa.edu
SAUNDERS, Kevin .... 515-271-1984 165 F
kevin.saunders@drake.edu
SAUNDERS, Lee .... 719-549-2708.. 79 G
lee.saunders@csupueblo.edu
SAUNDERS, Martha, D .. 850-474-2200 111 E
msaunders@uwf.edu
SAUNDERS, Melissa ...... 507-222-5500 234 C
msaunders@carleton.edu
SAUNDERS, Michael ..... 206-934-6020 482 F
michael.saunders@seattlecolleges.edu
SAUNDERS, Robin .... 413-565-1000 205 I
SAUNDERS, Scott, D ..... 716-673-3171 316 A
scott.saunders@fredonia.edu
SAUNDERS, Sharon ...... 281-649-3206 436 D
ssaunders@hbu.edu
SAUNDS, Lindsay .... 706-419-1279 117 G
lindsay.saunds@covenant.edu
SAURBIER, Ann .... 304-336-8060 489 B
ann.saurbier@westliberty.edu
SAURI, Mariana .... 562-804-1239.. 45 C
marianas@healthcarecareercollege.edu
SAUTER, Maranah .... 706-880-8201 121 K
msauter@lagrange.edu
SAUTER, Ramona .... 408-554-4397.. 63 A
rsauter@scu.edu
SAUVIGNON, Carine ..... 508-588-9100 214 F
csauvigno@massasoit.mass.edu
SAVAGE, Daina .... 717-396-7833 392 Q
dsavage@pcad.edu
SAVAGE, David .... 706-754-7815 123 C
david.savage@northgatech.edu
SAVAGE, Deana .... 432-685-4515 439 E
docsavage@midland.edu
SAVAGE, Devin .... 312-567-3615 139 H
dsavage@iit.edu
SAVAGE, James .... 337-482-6434 192 F
james.savage@louisiana.edu
SAVAGE, Jess .... 970-247-7180.. 80 H
jlsavage@fortlewis.edu
SAVAGE, Jinny .... 570-348-6241 389 B
jsavage@marywood.edu
SAVAGE, Lauren .... 970-247-6073.. 80 H
lasavage@fortlewis.edu
SAVAGE, Mary .... 860-439-2251.. 87 F
mary.savage@conncoll.edu
SAVAGE, Pam .... 314-744-5331 255 H
savagep@mobap.edu
SAVAGE, Richard, N ..... 724-458-2033 384 F
savagern@gcc.edu
SAVAGE, Ron .... 617-747-2025 206 D
rsavage@berklee.edu
SAVAGE, Scott .... 419-289-5401 347 H
ssavage2@ashland.edu
SAVAGE, Shauna .... 406-496-4422 264 C
ssavage@mtech.edu
SAVAIANO, Patrick .... 760-744-1150.. 56 B
psavaiano@palomar.edu
SAVELSKI, Mariano .... 856-256-4052 280 H
savelski@rowan.edu
SAVIA, Anthony .... 301-860-3470 203 D
asavia@bowiestate.edu
SAVIET, Nathaniel .... 201-879-3676 274 I
nsaviet@bergen.edu
SAVILLE, Vicki .... 704-330-6224 333 B
vicki.saville@cpcc.edu
SAVIN, Stuart .... 717-464-7050 387 E

SAVINO, Jeffrey .... 814-472-3006 396 I
jsavino@francis.edu
SAVITT-KING, Robin ..... 413-782-1243 219 E
robin.savitt-king@wne.edu
SAVIZKY, Ruben .... 212-353-4372 297 C
ruben.savizky@cooper.edu
SAVOCA, Marianna .... 631-632-6810 316 D
marianna.savoca@stonybrook.edu
SAVOIE, E. Joseph .... 337-482-6203 192 F
president@louisiana.edu
SAVOIE, Michael, P ...... 229-249-4894 127 C
mpsavoie@valdosta.edu
SAVOIT, Taina, J .... 337-475-5065 192 B
tsavoit@mcneese.edu
SAVONA, Richard .... 302-622-8000.. 90 C
rsavona@dcad.edu
SAVORY, Paul .... 800-462-7845.. 79 F
SAVRON, Doris .... 602-557-9021.. 16 L
doris.savron@phoenix.edu
SAVU, Vasemaca .... 692-625-3394 503 F
vsavu@cmi.edu
SAVUKINAS, Robert .... 831-242-5828 501 D
SAWA, Glen .... 218-335-4200 235 J
SAWADOGO, Annette ...... 906-487-7554 223 I
SAWATSKY, Kelly .... 917-493-4077 304 L
ksawatsky@msmnyc.edu
SAWATZKY, Radonna ...... 580-774-3783 369 I
radonna.sawatzky@swosu.edu
SAWERS, Kimberly, M .. 206-281-2445 482 K
ksawers@spu.edu
SAWHILL ESPE, Betsy ... 207-768-9515 196 I
besty.sawhill@maine.edu
SAWTELLE, III,
James (Jimmy), R ...... 318-487-5443 187 G
jsawtelle@cltcc.edu
SAWYER, Brenda .... 928-314-9515.. 11 B
brenda.sawyer@azwestern.edu
SAWYER, Caroline .... 704-463-3026 339 C
caroline.sawyer@pfeiffer.edu
SAWYER, Donald, C ...... 203-582-8964.. 88 F
donald.sawyer@quinnipiac.edu
SAWYER, Gretchen .... 775-674-7686 270 I
gsawyer@tmcc.edu
SAWYER, James, O .... 586-445-7241 226 F
sawyerj@macomb.edu
SAWYER, Jane .... 626-529-8500.. 55 E
SAWYER, Jenny, L .... 502-852-4957 185 E
jsawyer@louisville.edu
SAWYER, John .... 301-243-2097 501 J
john.sawyer@dodiis.mil
SAWYER, Jonathan, C .. 202-319-5619.. 91 G
sawyerj@cua.edu
SAWYER, Julie .... 918-444-2210 366 G
sawyerjk@nsuok.edu
SAWYER, Katherine .... 847-635-1718 146 E
ksawyer@oakton.edu
SAWYER, Lisa .... 256-215-4536.... 1 G
lsawyer@cacc.edu
SAWYER, Lisa .... 661-362-3314.. 38 H
lisa.sawyer@canyons.edu
SAWYER, Masonne .... 336-734-7343 334 D
msawyer@forsythtech.edu
SAWYER, Mike .... 660-543-4750 259 K
msawyer@ucmo.edu
SAWYER, Nichole .... 207-454-1040 195 E
nsawyer@wccc.me.edu
SAWYER, Sarah .... 207-974-4828 195 A
ssawyer@emcc.edu
SAWYER, Scott .... 832-842-8705 451 G
ssawyer@uh.edu
SAWYER, Terrence .... 410-617-2201 199 G
officeofthepresident@loyola.edu
SAWYERS, Tamberly ...... 423-697-3359 423 B
tammy.sawyers@chattanoogastate.edu
SAX, Christina .... 410-888-9048 200 C
csax@muih.edu
SAXBY, Christopher ...... 239-590-7924 109 G
csaxby@fgcu.edu
SAXBY, Rushelle, D ...... 252-862-1248 336 H
rsaxby@roanokechowan.edu
SAXENA, Peter .... 585-594-6800 310 A
SAXENA, Pradeep .... 585-594-6430 311 L
saxenap@roberts.edu
SAXENIAN, AnnaLee .... 510-642-9980.. 68 N
anno@ischool.berkeley.edu
SAXON, Lance .... 920-206-2342 492 C
lance.saxon@mbu.edu
SAXON-PRICE, Melissa . 570-702-8956 386 D
msaxonprice@johnson.edu
SAXTON, Rebecca .... 816-995-2800 257 I
SAXTON, Todd .... 217-641-4555 140 H
tsaxton@jwcc.edu

SAYAVONG, Phoumy ..... 410-981-5014.. 56 J
psayavong@peralta.edu
SAYE, Shaydean .... 406-657-1051 264 G
shaydean.saye@rocky.edu
SAYED, Ellen, N .... 414-955-4852 492 F
esayed@mcw.edu
SAYEGH, Sharlene .... 562-985-5428.. 32 A
sharlene.sayegh@csulb.edu
SAYERS, David .... 954-545-4500 108 C
cfo@sfbc.edu
SAYERS, David .... 803-321-3353 409 I
david.sayers@newberry.edu
SAYLER, David, A .... 513-529-7286 356 A
saylerda@miamioh.edu
SAYLER, Michelle .... 701-858-3367 345 C
michelle.sayler@minotstateu.edu
SAYLOR, JR., Allen, C .. 229-391-5001 114 D
SAYLOR, Andrea .... 517-264-3100 220 D
asaylor@adrian.edu
SAYLOR, Jessica, M ...... 701-349-5444 346 G
jsaylor@trinitybiblecollege.edu
SAYLOR, Laura .... 513-244-3263 356 F
laura.saylor@msj.edu
SAYLOR, Laurie .... 813-253-7152 102 A
lsaylor@hccfl.edu
SAYLOR, Nicole .... 865-974-2196 426 C
ensaylor@utk.edu
SAYLORS, Tony .... 870-248-4000.. 18 H
tony.saylors@blackrivertech.edu
SAYRE, Cris .... 773-602-3403 135 A
csayre@ccc.edu
SAYRE, Matt .... 541-552-6273 376 A
sayrem@sou.edu
SAYRS, Elizabeth .... 740-593-1935 358 L
sayrs@ohio.edu
SBALBI,
Anthony (Tony) .... 413-755-4336 215 F
atsbalbi@stcc.edu
SBRISCIA, Amanda .... 413-552-2747 214 D
asbriscia@hcc.edu
SCACCIA, Jeff, P .... 864-833-8205 410 E
jpscaccia@presby.edu
SCAGLIONE, Agnes .... 201-692-2596 276 I
agnes@fdu.edu
SCALA, Kerry, L .... 603-862-1355 273 H
kerry.scala@unh.edu
SCALBERG, Daniel .... 503-255-0332 374 A
dscalberg@multnomah.edu
SCALERO, Michael .... 201-216-5475 282 L
mscalero@stevens.edu
SCALES, Barbara .... 931-393-1500 423 G
bscales@mscc.edu
SCALES, Jane .... 800-686-1883 222 B
jscales@cleary.edu
SCALES, Lea Ann .... 978-630-9320 215 A
lscales2@mwcc.mass.edu
SCALES, Michael, D ...... 215-204-3121 398 D
michael.scales@temple.edu
SCALES, Roger .... 316-295-5551 173 G
roger_scales@friends.edu
SCALF, Candace .... 817-554-5950 439 C
cscalf@messengercollege.edu
SCALLY, Alethea .... 505-984-6182 287 F
alethea.scally@sjc.edu
SCALZO, Denise .... 718-862-7178 304 K
dscalzo01@manhattan.edu
SCANDALIS, Thomas .... 509-452-5100 481 E
tscandalis@pnwu.edu
SCANDRETT, Nic .... 712-279-1761 163 H
nic.scandrett@briarcliff.edu
SCANLAN, Michael .... 216-397-1596 353 O
mscanlan@jcu.edu
SCANLAN, Therese, A ... 773-252-5311 146 D
president@oakpoint.edu
SCANLON, Jennifer .... 207-725-3578 194 A
SCANLON, John .... 201-360-4771 277 D
jscanlon@hccc.edu
SCANLON, Tom .... 617-732-2775 216 B
tom.scanlon@mcphs.edu
SCANNELL, Janet .... 507-222-4077 234 C
jscannell@carleton.edu
SCANTLIN, Chelsye .... 417-967-5466 259 H
SCAPPATICCI, Jason ...... 860-906-5085.. 86 C
jscappaticci@capitalcc.edu
SCARANO, John .... 216-397-4701 353 O
jscarano@jcu.edu
SCARANO, Martin .... 603-862-2116 273 H
marty.scarano@unh.edu
SCARANTINO, Laura ...... 410-706-2562 202 F
lscarantino@umaryland.edu
SCARBORO, Gina .... 912-650-5640 125 D
gscarboro@southuniversity.edu

SCHENK, Stacy, L .... 814-886-6357 390 E
sschenk@mtaloy.edu
SCHENKELBERGER,
Chad .... 231-995-3150 228 F
cschenkelberger@nmc.edu
SCHENKER, Mark .... 203-432-2920.. 90 B
mark.schenker@yale.edu
SCHENONE, Esther .... 530-467-3544.. 60 A
librarian@spots.edu
SCHENONE, Michael ...... 925-473-7375.. 40 I
mschenone@losmedanos.edu
SCHEPP, Robina, C .... 212-346-1281 310 F
rschepp@pace.edu
SCHEPPS, Laura .... 609-586-4800 277 H
scheppsl@mccc.edu
SCHER, Anne .... 510-879-9231.. 60 C
ascher@samuelmerritt.edu
SCHERCZINGER, Carol .. 704-216-3923 337 C
carol.scherczinger@rccc.edu
SCHERER, John .... 910-962-4027 343 B
schererj@uncw.edu
SCHERER, Laurie, K ...... 410-543-6070 204 A
lkscherer@salisbury.edu
SCHERI, Jennifer, C ...... 815-224-0428 140 D
jennifer_scheri@ivcc.edu
SCHERLE, Jackie .... 812-354-6610 160 G
jscherle@saintmeinrad.edu
SCHERLING, Sarah .... 303-963-3483.. 78 D
sscherling@ccu.edu
SCHERMERHORN, Don . 251-343-8200.... 6 D
SCHERR, Linda .... 732-906-4663 278 A
lscherr@middlesexcc.edu
SCHERRENS,
Maurice, W .... 803-321-5102 409 I
mscherrens@newberry.edu
SCHERRY, Rejoice .... 607-962-9000 319 F
SCHERTLER, Dayna .... 806-651-2340 447 D
dschertler@wtamu.edu
SCHERTZ, Taira .... 314-485-8475 255 H
taira.schertz@mobap.edu
SCHERWATZKY, Steven . 978-837-5000 216 D
scherwatzkys@merrimack.edu
SCHERZER, Karen .... 812-357-6522 160 G
kscherzer@saintmeinrad.edu
SCHETTLER, Martha, A .. 330-569-5205 353 F
schettlerma@hiram.edu
SCHEUERMANN, Joe ..... 504-671-5452 187 I
jscheu@dcc.edu
SCHEUFENS, William .... 337-475-5711 192 B
wscheufens@mcneese.edu
SCHEWE, Andrew .... 202-250-2942.. 92 B
andrew.schewe@gallaudet.edu
SCHEXNIDER-FIELDS,
Ingenue, S .... 504-520-6209 193 C
itschexn@xula.edu
SCHIAVETTA, Michael ... 212-261-1701 308 H
michael.schiavetta@nyit.edu
SCHIAZZA, Douglas, J .. 413-597-4747 220 A
dschiazz@williams.edu
SCHICK, Avi .... 732-985-6533 279 F
SCHICK, Eric .... 918-631-3245 371 C
eric-schick@utulsa.edu
SCHICK, Jennifer .... 616-331-2231 224 D
schickj@gvsu.edu
SCHIDLOVSKY,
Nicholas .... 315-858-0945 301 F
SCHIEBER, Amy, K .... 660-944-2847 251 B
aschieber@conception.edu
SCHIEBER, Jeanette .... 660-944-2839 251 B
admissions@conception.edu
SCHIEL, Melynie .... 760-366-3791.. 40 K
SCHIER, DJ (Donald) .... 716-896-0700 324 A
dschier@villa.edu
SCHIFF, Emanuel .... 845-356-1980 311 C
SCHIFFER, Jason, D ...... 610-758-4200 388 C
jds517@lehigh.edu
SCHIFFER, Peter .... 203-432-2647.. 90 B
peter.schiffer@yale.edu
SCHIFFGENS, Hope .... 412-536-1266 386 H
hope.schiffgens@laroche.edu
SCHIFFKE, Heather .... 503-552-1750 374 B
hschiffke@nunm.edu
SCHIFFMAN, Robyn ...... 630-942-2865 135 F
SCHILKE, Richard .... 254-519-5435 446 C
rschilke@tamuct.edu
SCHILL, Matt .... 402-554-3041 269 C
mschill@unomaha.edu
SCHILL, Michael, H .... 847-491-7456 146 C
nupresident@northwestern.edu
SCHILL, Sara .... 276-376-3432 471 G
srp4b@uvawise.edu
SCHILLER-SMITH, Ali ..... 410-337-6000 198 G
ali.schiller-smith@goucher.edu

SCHILLI, Kara .... 636-949-4349 254 B
kschilli@lindenwood.edu
SCHILLING, Dee .... 909-706-3526.. 75 G
dschilling@westernu.edu
SCHILLING, JoAnna .... 714-484-7308.. 54 C
jschilling@cypresscollege.edu
SCHILLINGER, Don, N .. 318-257-3712 192 A
dschill@latech.edu
SCHILT, Louis, J .... 480-212-1704.. 15 R
louis@sessions.edu
SCHILTZ, Thomas .... 440-775-5574 357 G
tom.schiltz@oberlin.edu
SCHIMER, Maria, R .... 330-325-6356 357 D
maria@neomed.edu
SCHIMMEL, Kari .... 309-694-5590 138 I
kari.schimmel@icc.edu
SCHIMPF, Kelly .... 856-351-2247 282 I
kaschimpf@salemcc.edu
SCHINDLER, Brooke ...... 715-675-3331 498 E
schindler@ntc.edu
SCHINDLER, Kerry .... 254-659-7821 436 C
kschindler@hillcollege.edu
SCHINSTOCK, OSB,
Victor .... 660-944-2992 251 B
victor@conception.edu
SCHIPANI, Pamela .... 860-486-2060.. 89 B
p.schipani@uconn.edu
SCHIPPERS, Dave .... 248-689-8282 231 E
dschippe@walshcollege.edu
SCHIRER-SUTER, Myron 978-867-4419 209 F
myron.schirer-suter@gordon.edu
SCHIRLING, Michael ..... 802-656-2212 462 D
michael.schirling@uvm.edu
SCHIRMER, James .... 909-448-4997.. 71 C
jschirmer@laverne.edu
SCHISSLER, John .... 330-490-7263 363 E
jschissler@walsh.edu
SCHISSLER, Kathy .... 303-914-6214.. 82 L
kathy.schissler@rrcc.edu
SCHIWIETZ,
Michelle, B .... 214-887-5002 434 G
mschiwietz@dts.edu
SCHLACHTER, John .... 812-357-6142 160 G
jschlachter@saintmeinrad.edu
SCHLAFER, Tammy .... 315-470-4769 319 A
tsschlaf@esf.edu
SCHLAG, Kevin .... 808-675-3444 128 B
kevin.schlag@byuh.edu
SCHLAG, Paul, A .... 937-376-6668 349 H
pschlag@centralstate.edu
SCHLAK, Tim, M .... 412-397-6868 396 E
schlak@rmu.edu
SCHLAM, Elisheva .... 646-565-6420 322 B
elisheva.schlam@touro.edu
SCHLAM, Elisheva .... 646-565-6420 322 C
elisheva.schlam@touro.edu
SCHLAPP, Andrew .... 316-978-3001 178 B
andy.schlapp@wichita.edu
SCHLARB, Mary .... 607-753-2209 317 D
mary.schlarb@cortland.edu
SCHLATER, Nicole .... 315-498-2581 310 C
schlaten@sunyocc.edu
SCHLATHER,
Mary Margaret .... 304-724-5000 486 C
srschlather@cdu.edu
SCHLATTER, Andy .... 802-440-4439 461 B
aschlatter@bennington.edu
SCHLECT, Brenda .... 208-882-1566 131 H
bschlect@nsa.edu
SCHLECT, Christopher ... 208-882-1566 131 H
cschlect@nsa.edu
SCHLEEF, Debra .... 540-654-1505 471 B
dschleef@umw.edu
SCHLEGEL, Alice .... 509-542-4823 478 B
aschlegel@columbiabasin.edu
SCHLEGEL, Len .... 518-388-6607 323 B
schlegel@union.edu
SCHLEGEL, Natalie .... 781-891-3474 206 C
nschlegel@bentley.edu
SCHLEIBAUM, Michelle . 914-606-6505 324 F
michelle.schleibaum@sunywcc.edu
SCHLEICH, Tamatha ...... 309-649-6632 150 D
tamatha.schleich@src.edu
SCHLEICHER, Julie .... 781-239-3053 214 E
jschleicher@massbay.edu
SCHLEICHER, Rolf .... 818-710-4142.. 49 H
schleir@piercecollege.edu
SCHLEICHERT, Cat .... 503-491-6995 373 H
catherine.schleichert@mhcc.edu
SCHLEMEYER, Lynn .... 575-646-1837 286 G
vlynns@nmsufoundation.org
SCHLENBECKER,
Darlene .... 847-925-6008 138 E
dschlenb@harpercollege.edu

SCHLENKER, Steven ...... 215-702-4340 379 F
sschlenker@cairn.edu
SCHLERETH, Jonathan ... 314-529-9236 254 D
jschlereth2@maryville.edu
SCHLESINGER, Ed .... 410-516-7134 199 E
tschles4@jhu.edu
SCHLESINGER, Kenneth 718-960-8577 293 E
kenneth.schlesinger@lehman.cuny.edu
SCHLESINGER, Marissa 253-566-5022 483 F
mschlesinger@tacomacc.edu
SCHLESINGER, Patrick .. 510-642-2866.. 68 N
pschlesinger@berkeley.edu
SCHLESINGER, Philip .... 706-272-2985 118 A
pschlesinger@daltonstate.edu
SCHLEY, Alisa, S .... 715-833-6266 497 E
ahoepner1@cvtc.edu
SCHLICHT, Terri .... 913-469-8500 174 F
tschlich@jccc.edu
SCHLICHTEMEIER, Kent . 949-854-8002.. 40 E
SCHLICKMANN, Paul .... 203-254-4000.. 87 G
pschlickmann@fairfield.edu
SCHLIMGEN, Matt .... 317-931-2382 154 D
mschlimgen@cts.edu
SCHLIMGEN, Todd .... 605-668-1363 414 F
todd.schlimgen@mountmarty.edu
SCHLOER, Wolfgang ...... 404-413-2530 120 C
wschloer@gsu.edu
SCHLOESSER, Brad .... 507-389-7263 240 F
brad.schloesser@southcentral.edu
SCHLOESSER, Deann ..... 507-933-7495 235 E
dmschloesser@gustavus.edu
SCHLOSSER, Peter .... 480-965-9801.. 11 A
sclosser@asu.edu
SCHLOSSMAN, Paul ...... 818-240-1000.. 43 J
pschloss@glendale.edu
SCHLOTTHAUER, Scott .. 405-744-5984 367 G
scott.schlotthauer@okstate.edu
SCHLUETER, Jennifer .... 614-437-1061 351 A
jschlueter@ccad.edu
SCHLUETER, Margie ...... 763-433-1119 237 A
margie.schlueter@anokaramsey.edu
SCHLUETER, Margie ...... 763-433-1119 236 H
margie.schlueter@anokaramsey.edu
SCHLUP, Amy .... 580-559-5225 365 J
aschlup@ecok.edu
SCHLUTER, Valerie .... 225-768-1795 186 H
valerie.schluter@franu.edu
SCHLUTERMAN, Karen .. 479-979-1224.. 24 A
kschlut@ozarks.edu
SCHMADER, Kelly, J ...... 310-206-4181.. 69 D
kschmader@facnet.ucla.edu
SCHMAEFF, Robert .... 865-524-8079 419 A
rschmaeff@huhs.edu
SCHMAHL, Georgina ...... 210-431-5510 440 D
gschmahl@ollusa.edu
SCHMAILZL, Randy .... 531-622-2415 266 G
rschmailzl@mccneb.edu
SCHMALFUSS, Amy .... 585-594-6254 311 L
schmalfuss_amy@roberts.edu
SCHMALHOFER,
Beverly .... 717-361-1422 383 B
schmalhoferb@etown.edu
SCHMALL, Steve .... 507-285-7214 240 B
steve.schmall@rctc.edu
SCHMALZEL, Katryn ...... 303-273-3260.. 79 A
kschmalz@mines.edu
SCHMAND, Kathleen ...... 615-898-2773 421 C
kathleen.schmand@mtsu.edu
SCHMELCZER, Moshe .... 773-463-7738 150 F
menahel@telshe.edu
SCHMELING, James .... 202-685-3924 501 I
schmeling@ndufoundation.org
SCHMELTZER, Tracy ...... 919-739-6877 338 F
tmschmeltzer@waynecc.edu
SCHMELZ, Kim .... 608-822-2379 498 H
kschmelz@swtc.edu
SCHMELZ, Mark .... 541-346-2987 376 G
mschmelz@uoregon.edu
SCHMELZER, Joy .... 978-542-6416 213 B
joy.schmelzer@salemstate.edu
SCHMELZER, Judy .... 954-201-7458.. 96 F
jschmelzer@broward.edu
SCHMID, Albertha .... 531-622-2354 266 G
acschmid@mccneb.edu
SCHMIDEK, Celine .... 408-554-4982.. 63 A
cschmidek@scu.edu
SCHMIDT, Amanda .... 706-385-1065 124 C
amanda.schmidt@point.edu
SCHMIDT, Amber .... 605-256-5079 415 G
amber.schmidt@dsu.edu
SCHMIDT, Amy .... 507-453-2700 238 J
SCHMIDT, Barbara, T .... 516-323-3015 306 I
bschmidt@molloy.edu

SCHMIDT, Betsy .... 317-738-8054 155 A
bschmidt@franklincollege.edu
SCHMIDT, Bradley .... 316-284-5349 171 I
bschmidt@bethelks.edu
SCHMIDT, Casey .... 360-623-8614 477 H
casey.schmidt@centralia.edu
SCHMIDT, Christine ...... 540-636-2900 464 O
finaid@christendom.edu
SCHMIDT, Christopher .. 270-384-8136 183 D
schmidtc@lindsey.edu
SCHMIDT, Curt .... 612-659-6902 238 C
curt.schmidt@minneapolis.edu
SCHMIDT, Dan .... 701-224-5735 345 F
daniel.j.schmidt@bismarckstate.edu
SCHMIDT, Denise .... 973-328-5245 276 A
dschmidt@ccm.edu
SCHMIDT, Dirk .... 406-874-6201 262 K
schmidtd@milescc.edu
SCHMIDT, Dobby .... 505-428-1226 287 H
dobby.schmidt@sfcc.edu
SCHMIDT, Gary .... 937-775-3771 364 D
gary.schmidt@wright.edu
SCHMIDT, Gordon .... 516-686-3802 308 H
gordon.schmidt@nyit.edu
SCHMIDT, Howard .... 540-338-1776 468 D
SCHMIDT, Jacqueline .... 904-646-2300 101 A
jacqueline.schmidt@fscj.edu
SCHMIDT, James, C ...... 715-836-2327 494 E
jschmidt@uwec.edu
SCHMIDT, Jeffrey .... 410-704-3414 204 B
jschmidt@towson.edu
SCHMIDT, Jenae, A .... 651-696-6214 236 C
schmidtj@macalester.edu
SCHMIDT, Jens .... 310-204-1666.. 58 K
SCHMIDT, Jill, L .... 563-333-6278 169 D
schmidtjillI@sau.edu
SCHMIDT, Joanna .... 817-257-5294 447 H
joanna.schmidt@tcu.edu
SCHMIDT, John .... 334-670-3100.... 7 C
SCHMIDT, Karen .... 713-718-8596 436 E
karen.schmidt2@hccs.edu
SCHMIDT, Karol .... 480-517-8767.. 14 A
karol.schmid@riosalado.edu
SCHMIDT, Lynn .... 765-641-4388 153 D
lmschmidt@anderson.edu
SCHMIDT, Martin, A ..... 518-276-6211 311 J
president@rpi.edu
SCHMIDT, Maynard .... 845-341-4205 310 D
maynard.schmidt@sunyorange.edu
SCHMIDT, Mike .... 770-533-6914 121 L
mschmidt@laniertech.edu
SCHMIDT, Paul .... 864-503-5036 413 A
pschmidt@uscupstate.edu
SCHMIDT, Rachel .... 216-687-5594 350 G
r.m.schmidt@csuohio.edu
SCHMIDT, Robert .... 203-576-4792.. 89 A
rschmidt@bridgeport.edu
SCHMIDT, Shana .... 715-833-6410 497 E
sschmidt42@cvtc.edu
SCHMIDT, Shannon .... 215-641-6347 390 A
sschmidt@mc3.edu
SCHMIDT, Sierra .... 813-988-5131.. 99 M
schmidts@floridacollege.edu
SCHMIDT, Steven, P ...... 330-325-6290 357 D
sschmidt@neomed.edu
SCHMIDT, Stuart, J .... 920-565-1023 492 A
schmidtsj@lakeland.edu
SCHMIDT, Sue .... 307-532-8207 500 A
sschmidt@ewc.wy.edu
SCHMIDT, Tania .... 507-457-2800 241 A
tschmidt@winona.edu
SCHMIDT, Thao .... 360-992-2628 477 J
tschmidt@clark.edu
SCHMIDT, Toby .... 208-467-8107 132 B
tjschmidt@nnu.edu
SCHMIDTKE, Rachel ...... 812-866-7031 155 D
schmidtke@hanover.edu
SCHMIEDE, Angela .... 650-543-3905.. 52 A
angela.schmiede@menlo.edu
SCHMIEDEL, Mary, E .... 202-687-3911.. 92 D
schmiedm@georgetown.edu
SCHMIEG, Rose, A .... 540-665-5534 470 A
rschmieg@su.edu
SCHMIEISING, David .... 740-283-6513 352 I
dschmiesing@franciscan.edu
SCHMIESING, Ann .... 303-492-5537.. 83 M
ann.schmiesing@colorado.edu
SCHMIESING, Ryan .... 614-292-5881 358 E
schmiesing.3@osu.edu
SCHMILL, Stuart .... 617-258-5514 215 G
SCHMISSEUR, John .... 931-393-7123 426 C
jschmiss@utsi.edu

Index of Key Administrators SCHMIT – SCHOONMAKER 881

SCHMIT, Matt ... 563-336-3300 165 G mschmit@eicc.edu
SCHMIT, Matt ... 563-441-4125 165 J mschmit@eicc.edu
SCHMIT, Michaeline ... 920-498-7106 498 F michaeline.schmit@nwtc.edu
SCHMIT, Roxy ... 605-642-6129 415 F roxy.schmit@bhsu.edu
SCHMIT, Shelly, M ... 641-422-4211 168 E schmishe@niacc.edu
SCHMITT, Barbara ... 570-208-5868 386 G barbaraschmitt@kings.edu
SCHMITT, Deborah ... 574-520-4398 157 C dsschmit@iusb.edu
SCHMITT, Deborah, F ... 716-851-1270 299 A schmitt@ecc.edu
SCHMITT, Karen, R ... 608-757-7737 497 D kschmitt3@blackhawk.edu
SCHMITT, Loraine ... 971-722-4398 375 C loraine.schmitt@pcc.edu
SCHMITT, Mark ... 315-464-4538 316 F schmittm@upstate.edu
SCHMITT, Mark ... 520-515-5478.. 11 O schmittm@cochise.edu
SCHMITT, Pamela ... 410-293-1595 502 I daa@usna.edu
SCHMITT, Phil ... 863-667-5437 108 I pjschmitt@seu.edu
SCHMITT, Stacy, C ... 336-318-0025 336 F scschmitt@randolph.edu
SCHMITTENDORF, Susan ... 716-270-5139 299 A ascschmittendorfs@ecc.edu
SCHMITTLEIN, David, C 617-253-2804 215 G
SCHMITTMANN, Beate .. 515-294-3220 163 E schmittb@iastate.edu
SCHMITZ, Andrea, M ... 920-565-1000 492 A schmitzam@lakeland.edu
SCHMITZ, Cody ... 815-753-1747 145 H cschmitz@niu.edu
SCHMITZ, Donna ... 701-252-3467 346 J dschmitz@uj.edu
SCHMITZ, Michelle ... 320-308-2151 240 C maschmitz@stcloudstate.edu
SCHMITZ, Polly ... 914-323-5118 305 A polly.schmitz@mville.edu
SCHMITZ, Stevie ... 406-657-1134 264 G schmitzs@rocky.edu
SCHMITZ, Timothy, J ... 864-597-4000 413 E schmitztj@wofford.edu
SCHMITZ, Todd, J ... 812-856-1214 156 B schmitz@iu.edu
SCHMOHL, C. Pat ... 508-751-7942 215 D pschmohl@qcc.mass.edu
SCHMOKE, Kurt, L ... 410-837-4866 204 C president@ubalt.edu
SCHMOLL, Claire, B ... 207-786-6100 193 D cschmoll@bates.edu
SCHMOLL, Kevin ... 618-650-3324 149 H kschmol@siue.edu
SCHMOYER, Andrea ... 773-878-8756 148 F
SCHMUDE, Michelle ... 570-504-9691 384 A mschmude@som.geisinger.edu
SCHMUDLACH, Scott, D ... 507-354-8221 236 D schmudsd@mlc-wels.edu
SCHNABEL, William ... 907-474-7730.. 10 B weschnabel@alaska.edu
SCHNACK, Darcy ... 845-938-4379 502 H darcy.schnack@westpoint.edu
SCHNACK, Laura, L ... 309-794-7533 132 H lauraschnack@augustana.edu
SCHNACK, RJ ... 785-628-4470 173 E rschnack@fhsu.edu
SCHNACKENBERG, Scott ... 845-431-8682 298 B scott.schnackenberg@sunydutchess.edu
SCHNAIDMAN, Yaakov . 570-346-1747 402 F
SCHNAPP, Derek ... 217-206-7823 151 E schnapp.derek@uis.edu
SCHNARR, Grant ... 267-502-4844 378 I grant.schnarr@brynathyn.edu
SCHNEBLY, Sharon ... 360-438-4555 482 D sschnebly@stmartin.edu
SCHNECK, Colleen ... 859-622-6301 180 B colleen.schneck@eku.edu
SCHNECK, Kara ... 801-863-8825 460 A kschneck@uvu.edu
SCHNEEBERGER, Charity, J ... 610-917-1563 400 D cjschneeberger@valleyforge.edu
SCHNEFKE, Emilee ... 314-421-0949 259 G eschnefke@siba.edu
SCHNEIDER, Amye ... 620-792-9302 171 F schneidera@bartonccc.edu
SCHNEIDER, Angela ... 510-885-3973.. 31 C angela.schneider@csueastbay.edu
SCHNEIDER, Austin ... 858-653-6740.. 46 L aschneider@jpcatholic.com
SCHNEIDER, Betsy ... 636-922-8473 258 A bschneider@stchas.edu
SCHNEIDER, Brandt, L .. 806-743-4040 450 D brandt.schneider@ttuhsc.edu
SCHNEIDER, Catherine .. 310-476-9777.. 25 N catherine.schneider@aju.edu
SCHNEIDER, David ... 614-823-1240 359 G dschneider@otterbein.edu
SCHNEIDER, Eric, F ... 704-233-8675 344 E e.schneider@wingate.edu
SCHNEIDER, Helen ... 410-617-2995 199 G hschneider@loyola.edu
SCHNEIDER, Jed, S ... 315-445-4500 303 F schneij@lemoyne.edu
SCHNEIDER, Jeffrey, K .. 417-690-2222 250 K jschneider@cofo.edu
SCHNEIDER, Jeremy ... 909-448-4065.. 71 C jschneider@laverne.edu
SCHNEIDER, Jody ... 715-833-6238 497 E jschneider69@cvtc.edu
SCHNEIDER, John ... 925-631-4363.. 59 I jrs6@stmarys-ca.edu
SCHNEIDER, Karen ... 707-664-4004.. 34 C karen.schneider@sonoma.edu
SCHNEIDER, Ken ... 973-720-3122 283 I schneiderk@wpunj.edu
SCHNEIDER, Kenneth ... 201-692-2531 276 I k.schneider@fdu.edu
SCHNEIDER, Marc ... 770-426-2700 122 A marcs@life.edu
SCHNEIDER, Mark ... 610-409-3000 400 E mschneider@ursinus.edu
SCHNEIDER, Martin ... 845-431-8968 298 B martin.schneider@sunydutchess.edu
SCHNEIDER, Michael, A ... 309-341-7216 141 E mschneid@knox.edu
SCHNEIDER, Michael, P ... 620-242-0405 175 G schneidm@mcpherson.edu
SCHNEIDER, Ray ... 419-372-7595 348 F rayschn@bgsu.edu
SCHNEIDER, S. Jane ... 979-845-6917 446 B jane-schneider@tamu.edu
SCHNEIDER, Scott ... 563-326-5319 165 J sjschneider@eicc.edu
SCHNEIDER, Scott ... 580-581-2226 365 C sschneid@cameron.edu
SCHNEIDER, Steven ... 315-792-7200 320 F steve@sunypoly.edu
SCHNEIDER, Tamara, J . 417-690-2470 250 K schneider@cofo.edu
SCHNEIDER, Tamera ... 646-664-8910 292 E tamera.schneider@cuny.edu
SCHNEIDER, Tara ... 614-251-4642 358 B schneidt@ohiodominican.edu
SCHNEIDER, Terrance ... 678-407-5333 119 B tschneid@ggc.edu
SCHNEIDER, Tina ... 419-995-8326 360 B tschneider@lima.ohio-state.edu
SCHNEIDER, Tom ... 727-864-8409.. 98 G schneite@eckerd.edu
SCHNEIDER, Tracy ... 970-542-3127.. 81 M tracy.schneider@morgancc.edu
SCHNEIDER BINGHAM, Stacy Lee ... 845-437-5285 323 H stbingham@vassar.edu
SCHNEIDER HASSELER, Susan ... 740-826-8115 356 H hasseler@muskingum.edu
SCHNEIDERMAN, Edward, S ... 718-933-6700 306 J eschneiderman@monroecollege.edu
SCHNEIER, JR., Edward 518-828-4181 296 G
SCHNEIKART-LUEBBE, Christine ... 316-942-4291 176 B luebbec@newmanu.edu
SCHNELL, Elizabeth, R .. 248-341-2035 228 H erschnel@oaklandcc.edu
SCHNELL, Julie ... 479-397-7622.. 23 F jschnell@uarichmountain.edu
SCHNELL, Kara ... 413-369-4044 208 C schnell@csld.edu
SCHNELL, Santiago ... 574-631-6456 161 G sschnel2@nd.edu
SCHNELL, Sarah ... 651-690-8754 242 F sbschnell@stkate.edu
SCHNELLER, Beverly ... 708-534-4980 138 C bschneller@govst.edu
SCHNELLER, Heather ... 706-729-2300 115 I hschneller@augusta.edu
SCHNELLMAN, Rick ... 520-626-1657.. 16 H schnell@arizona.edu
SCHNEPPER, Rachel ... 860-685-2763.. 90 A rschnepper@wesleyan.edu
SCHNETZLER, Greta ... 415-476-8005.. 70 D greta.schnetzler@ucsf.edu
SCHNICK, Chris ... 480-732-7274.. 13 B chris.schnick@cgc.edu
SCHNIER, Kurt ... 209-228-4400.. 70 A
SCHNIREL, Adam, M ... 951-827-4210.. 70 B adam.schnirel@ucr.edu
SCHNIRRING, Marsha ... 323-259-2542.. 54 I mschnirring@oxy.edu
SCHNITKEY, Dawn ... 517-750-1200 230 F
SCHNITKEY, Dawn, I ... 517-750-1200 230 F danderso@arbor.edu
SCHNITTKER, Dennis ... 850-644-1360 110 B dschnitt@fsu.edu
SCHNITTKER, Doug ... 309-438-8493 140 C drschni@ilstu.edu
SCHNITZER, Carol, N ... 518-580-5849 315 A cschnitz@skidmore.edu
SCHNOOR, Alexis ... 714-556-3610.. 73 G alexis.schnoor@vanguard.edu
SCHNOOR, Barry ... 540-665-4543 470 A bschnoor@su.edu
SCHNOOR, Neal ... 605-626-2521 415 H nsupresident@northern.edu
SCHNORENBERG, Sandi ... 507-389-2111 238 L sandi.schnorenberg@mnsu.edu
SCHNOWSKE, Betsy ... 815-479-7534 143 F bschnowske@mchenry.edu
SCHNYDERS, Christina, M ... 330-471-8119 355 D cschnyders@malone.edu
SCHOBER, Kristen ... 716-896-0700 324 A kschober@villa.edu
SCHOBER, Michael ... 212-229-5727 307 E schober@newschool.edu
SCHOCHET, Ezra, B ... 323-937-3763.. 76 G eschochet@yoec.edu
SCHOCK, Pam ... 559-453-7115.. 43 D pam.schock@fresno.edu
SCHODOWSKI, Francis, G ... 803-786-3927 407 E fschodowski@columbiasc.edu
SCHOEN, David ... 716-286-8001 309 F schoen@niagara.edu
SCHOEN, Karen ... 313-845-9849 224 F kschoen@hfcc.edu
SCHOENBERG, Lynn ... 386-822-7473 111 F lschoenb@stetson.edu
SCHOENBERGER, Susan ... 860-509-9519.. 88 A sschoenberger@hartfordinternational.edu
SCHOENBORN, Stephanie ... 210-458-4249 455 B
SCHOENECKE, Marvin ... 870-759-4128.. 24 B mschoenecke@williamsbu.edu
SCHOENECKER, Kathleen ... 559-925-3349.. 75 A kathleenschoenecker@whccd.edu
SCHOENECKER, Timothy ... 618-650-3823 149 H tschoen@siue.edu
SCHOENFELD, Amy, R ... 718-990-5076 313 B schoenfa@stjohns.edu
SCHOENFELD, Jennifer . 785-460-4684 172 L jennifer.schoenfeld@colbycc.edu
SCHOENFELD, Michael . 919-681-3788 328 D michael.schoenfeld@duke.edu
SCHOENFELDER, Louis . 605-995-2191 414 A louie.schoenfelder@dwu.edu
SCHOENGOOD, Matthew, G ... 212-817-7400 293 D mschoengood@gc.cuny.edu
SCHOENHALS, Dillon ... 580-349-1549 367 F dillon.schoenhals@opsu.edu
SCHOENING, Lisa ... 213-624-1200.. 42 F lschoening@fidm.edu
SCHOEPFLIN, Rennie ... 323-343-5969.. 32 B rschoep@calstatela.edu
SCHOEPHOERSTER, Richard ... 216-687-2576 350 G r.schoephoerster@csuohio.edu
SCHOFIELD, Janelle ... 304-929-1044 487 G jschofield@newriver.edu
SCHOFIELD, Matthew ... 607-777-4526 315 E mschofie@binghamton.edu
SCHOFIELD, Rich ... 301-387-3119 198 F rich.schofield@garrettcollege.edu
SCHOFIELD, Sean ... 484-664-3170 390 F seanschofield@muhlenberg.edu
SCHOFIELD, Sherri ... 906-248-8424 221 I sschofield@bmcc.edu
SCHOFIELD, William ... 559-243-7243.. 66 G wil.schofield@scccd.edu
SCHOH, Eric ... 507-457-5210 241 A eschoh@winona.edu
SCHOKNECHT, Patricia .. 207-786-6260 193 D pschokne@bates.edu
SCHOLER, Steven, A ... 402-280-2180 265 J stevenscholer@creighton.edu
SCHOLES, Heidi ... 641-673-1084 170 I scholesh@wmpenn.edu
SCHOLES, Scott ... 970-542-3111.. 81 M scott.scholes@morgancc.edu
SCHOLL, Bill ... 414-288-4739 492 E william.scholl@marquette.edu
SCHOLL, Bridget ... 315-498-2516 310 C b.k.scholl@sunyocc.edu
SCHOLL, Daniel ... 605-688-5642 416 A daniel.scholl@sdstate.edu
SCHOLL, Heather ... 847-214-7177 137 D hscholl@elgin.edu
SCHOLL, Jenifer ... 561-237-7811 103 W jscholl@lynn.edu
SCHOLTEN, Melissa ... 507-537-6071 240 G melissa.scholten@smsu.edu
SCHOLTEN, Patrick ... 781-891-2679 206 C pscholten@bentley.edu
SCHOLTING, Linda ... 402-826-8201 266 A linda.scholting@doane.edu
SCHOLTZ, Martin ... 319-335-2453 163 F marty-scholtz@uiowa.edu
SCHOLZ, Ben ... 201-761-6085 282 H bscholz@saintpeters.edu
SCHOLZ, Daniel, J ... 414-410-4006 490 J djscholz@stritch.edu
SCHOLZ, Karl ... 608-262-1304 494 D provost@provost.wisc.edu
SCHOLZ, Ted ... 213-615-7231.. 36 G tscholz@thechicagoschool.edu
SCHOLZ, Teresa Maria Linda ... 515-646-3203 286 G vpeid@nmsu.edu
SCHOMAKER, Alan ... 504-865-2719 190 A aschomak@loyno.edu
SCHOMBURG, Jeff ... 210-431-5073 442 A jschomburg@stmarytx.edu
SCHOMMER, Beth ... 715-425-0662 496 A beth.schommer@uwrf.edu
SCHON, Jennifer ... 712-707-7078 169 A jennifer.schon@nwciowa.edu
SCHONBERG, Bianca ... 281-283-2740 452 A schonberg@uhcl.edu
SCHONBERG, Cicely ... 216-791-5000 350 F cicely.schonberg@cim.edu
SCHONBERG, Karl, K ... 315-229-5993 313 F kschonberg@stlawu.edu
SCHONBERGER, Alfred .. 718-302-7500 326 A
SCHONE, Jeffrey, L ... 507-354-8221 236 D schonejl@mlc-wels.edu
SCHONFELD, Leah, S ... 843-953-6922 406 D leah.schonfeld@citadel.edu
SCHOO, Diana ... 636-922-8387 258 A dschoo@stchas.edu
SCHOOF, Aaron, D ... 773-244-5564 145 F aschoof@northpark.edu
SCHOOK, Jessie ... 859-256-3100 180 H
SCHOOLCRAFT, Tracy ... 717-477-1371 394 D tascho@ship.edu
SCHOOLEY, Jerri ... 817-531-4404 450 F jschooley@txwes.edu
SCHOON, Michelle ... 620-441-6584 172 M michelle.schoon@cowley.edu
SCHOON, Perry ... 309-438-0650 140 C pschoon@ilstu.edu
SCHOONMAKER, Linda . 509-793-2002 477 D lindas@bigbend.edu
SCHOONMAKER, Lori ... 304-367-4111 488 L lori.schoonmaker@fairmontstate.edu
SCHOONMAKER, Martha ... 240-567-2007 200 E martha.schoonmaker@montgomerycollege.edu
SCHOONMAKER, Nancy 765-677-2605 157 F nancy.schoonmaker@indwes.edu
SCHOONMAKER, Stephen ... 714-484-7285.. 54 C sschoonmaker@cypresscollege.edu

SCHOONMAKER, Stephen ..... 714-484-7313.. 54 C sschoonmaker@cypresscollege.edu
SCHOONVELD, Tim ..... 616-395-7698 224 H schoonveld@hope.edu
SCHOPEN, Annamarie ... 847-214-7185 137 D aschopen@elgin.edu
SCHOPF, Gloria ..... 732-263-5417 278 B gschopf@monmouth.edu
SCHORNACK, Julie, A ... 714-463-7503.. 51 D jschornack@ketchum.edu
SCHORNACK, Kent, A ... 515-263-2986 166 C kschornack@grandview.edu
SCHORR, Timothy ..... 608-796-3774 496 L tbschorr@viterbo.edu
SCHORZMAN, Cindy, M ..... 530-752-7842.. 69 A cshorzman@ucdavis.edu
SCHOTT, Chris ..... 919-739-7040 338 F cpschott@waynecc.edu
SCHOTT, Elizabeth ..... 239-477-3514 100 G eschott@fsw.edu
SCHOTTO, Margaret ..... 410-706-5523 202 F mschotto@umaryland.edu
SCHOVANEC, Lawrence . 806-742-2121 450 C lawrence.schovanec@ttu.edu
SCHRACK, Fae ..... 610-799-1172 388 B fschrack@lccc.edu
SCHRADER, Claudia, V . 718-368-5109 294 C president@kbcc.cuny.edu
SCHRADER, Kacey ..... 386-752-1822.. 99 P kacey.schrader@fgc.edu
SCHRADER, Sarah ..... 209-575-6122.. 76 K schraders@mjc.edu
SCHRADER, Shari ..... 810-424-5448 231 C sjschrad@umich.edu
SCHRAEDER, Michael ... 214-638-0484 437 F mschraeder@kdstudio.com
SCHRAEDER, Peter, J .... 773-508-3500 142 G pschrae@luc.edu
SCHRAGE, Charles ..... 217-206-7395 151 E schrage.charles@uis.edu
SCHRAGE, Jim ..... 661-362-3222.. 38 H jim.schrage@canyons.edu
SCHRAM, Jacqueline, S 574-372-5100 155 C schramjs@grace.edu
SCHRAM, Mandy ..... 218-679-2860 242 E
SCHRAM, Michelle ..... 716-338-1092 302 G michellsschram@mail.sunyjcc.edu
SCHRAMM, Christine, M ..... 937-229-2229 362 C cschramm1@udayton.edu
SCHRAMM, Dorothy ..... 610-861-5421 391 B dschramm@northampton.edu
SCHRAMM, Jamie ..... 920-459-6611 494 F schrammj@uwgb.edu
SCHRAMM, Jamie ..... 920-683-4711 494 F schrammj@uwgb.edu
SCHRAMMEL, Debra, S . 215-670-9270 391 D dsschrammel@peirce.edu
SCHRAN, Liz ..... 207-893-7892 195 I eschran@sjcme.edu
SCHRANTZ, John ..... 937-481-2432 363 H john_schrantz@wilmington.edu
SCHRANZ, William ..... 402-643-7246 265 I bill.schranz@cune.edu
SCHRAUTH, Jodi, S ..... 920-923-7615 492 D jsschrauth11@marianuniversity.edu
SCHRECK, Jayne ..... 309-457-2129 144 E jayne@monmouthcollege.edu
SCHREFFLER, Ahaji ..... 215-895-1704 382 D ahaji@drexel.edu
SCHREIBER, Meredith ... 503-399-2535 372 A meredith.schreiber@chemeketa.edu
SCHREIBER, Michael ..... 646-592-4226 325 R michael.schreiber@yu.edu
SCHREIBER, Nancy ..... 401-341-2222 404 D nancy.schreiber@salve.edu
SCHREIBER, Pam ..... 206-543-2430 484 A pschreib@uw.edu
SCHREIBER, Rachel ..... 212-229-8950 307 E schreibr@newschool.edu
SCHREIBMAN, Andi ..... 925-424-1585.. 36 A aschreibman@laspositascollege.edu
SCHREIER, Barry ..... 319-335-7294 163 F barry-schreier@uiowa.edu
SCHREIER, Julie ..... 646-592-4305 325 R julie.schreier@yu.edu
SCHREINER, Holly ..... 320-308-3102 240 C hjschreiner@stcloudstate.edu
SCHREINER, Steven ..... 718-862-7303 304 K sschreiner01@manhattan.edu
SCHREINER, Susan ..... 360-538-4051 479 F susan.schreiner@ghc.edu
SCHREYER, Robert ..... 609-586-4800 277 H schreyer@mccc.edu
SCHRINER, Brian ..... 305-348-3181 109 H brian.schriner@fiu.edu
SCHROCK, Lindsey ..... 740-283-6456 352 I lschrock@franciscan.edu
SCHROCK, Lynford ..... 740-857-1311 360 C lschrock@rosedale.edu
SCHRODER, Adam ..... 850-478-8496 105 F aschroder@pcci.edu
SCHRODER, Sharon ..... 253-566-5064 483 F sschroder@tacomacc.edu
SCHROEDER, Alicia ..... 937-512-5369 360 F alicia.schroeder@sinclair.edu
SCHROEDER, Alisha ..... 406-265-4191 264 A alisha.schroeder@msun.edu
SCHROEDER, Ashley ..... 402-481-8698 265 B ashley.schroeder@bryanhealthcollege.edu
SCHROEDER, Blair ..... 325-674-2000 427 G blair.schroeder@acu.edu
SCHROEDER, Brian ..... 973-803-5000 279 C brschroeder@pillar.edu
SCHROEDER, Bryon ..... 432-837-8339 449 F bxs16zg@sulross.edu
SCHROEDER, Courtney . 713-221-8097 452 B lundgrenc@uhd.edu
SCHROEDER, Cynthia .... 636-949-4318 254 B cschroeder@lindenwood.edu
SCHROEDER, David ..... 203-931-2959.. 89 F dschroeder@newhaven.edu
SCHROEDER, David, E .. 973-803-5000 279 C dschroeder@pillar.edu
SCHROEDER, Dennis, J 818-364-7650.. 49 G schroedj@lamission.edu
SCHROEDER, Fritz ..... 410-516-8631 199 E fschroed@jhu.edu
SCHROEDER, Guy ..... 316-978-3450 178 B guy.schroeder@wichita.edu
SCHROEDER, James ..... 214-637-3530 457 A jschroeder@wadecollege.edu
SCHROEDER, Jennifer ... 785-243-1435 172 J jschroeder@cloud.edu
SCHROEDER, Jennifer ... 217-424-3927 144 D jrschroeder@millikin.edu
SCHROEDER, Jennifer ... 903-886-5160 446 D jennifer.schroeder@tamuc.edu
SCHROEDER, Joe ..... 815-939-5267 146 F schroed@olivet.edu
SCHROEDER, Karen ..... 800-287-8822 153 F schroka@bethanyseminary.edu
SCHROEDER, Kay ..... 940-668-3302 439 I kschroeder@nctc.edu
SCHROEDER, Kristi ..... 319-208-5100 169 I kschroeder@scciowa.edu
SCHROEDER, Lori ..... 707-654-1000.. 32 C
SCHROEDER, Mark ..... 734-432-5662 226 G maschroeder@madonna.edu
SCHROEDER, Matt ..... 419-530-1448 363 B matt.schroeder@utoledo.edu
SCHROEDER, Michael ... 314-529-9673 254 D mschroeder@maryville.edu
SCHROEDER, Neil ..... 210-829-6000 452 D nschroed@uiwtx.edu
SCHROEDER, Nick ..... 828-327-7000 332 H nschroeder@cvcc.edu
SCHROEDER, Rachel ..... 336-734-7646 334 D rschroeder@forsythtech.edu
SCHROEDER, Ross ..... 979-830-4118 430 I ross.schroeder@blinn.edu
SCHROEDER, Ryan ..... 912-478-6068 120 A rshroeder@georgiasouthern.edu
SCHROEDER, Samantha 906-248-8456 221 I sschroeder@bmcc.edu
SCHROEDER, Stephanie 205-226-4600.... 5 A
SCHROEDER, Tracy ..... 617-353-1155 207 C tas@bu.edu
SCHROEDER-BIEK, Julie ..... 574-284-4333 160 F jsbiek@saintmarys.edu
SCHROEDER-GREEN, Suzanna ..... 440-646-8178 363 C sschroeder@ursuline.edu
SCHROEPFER, Nick ..... 651-641-8278 235 A schroepfer@csp.edu
SCHROER, Jessica ..... 636-949-4920 254 B jschroer@lindenwood.edu
SCHROER, Tara ..... 785-460-5487 172 L tara.schroer@colbycc.edu
SCHROER, Timothy ..... 507-786-3615 242 I schroert@stolaf.edu
SCHROF, Robert ..... 302-857-6200.. 90 D rschrof@desu.edu
SCHROT, Sheree ..... 231-591-3725 223 H shereeschrot@ferris.edu
SCHROTH, Keith ..... 504-568-5135 189 C kschro@lsuhsc.edu
SCHROYER, Heath ..... 337-475-5563 192 B hschroyer@mcneese.edu
SCHRUM, Mindi-Kim .... 505-566-3261 287 G schrumm@sanjuancollege.edu
SCHUBERT, Beth ..... 804-752-7270 469 B bethschubert@rmc.edu
SCHUBERT, Leighton .... 979-830-4243 430 I leighton.schubert@blinn.edu
SCHUBERT, Marianne, A ..... 336-758-5273 344 A schubem@wfu.edu
SCHUBERT, Melissa, B . 562-903-4555.. 27 E melissa.b.schubert@biola.edu
SCHUBERT, Phil ..... 325-674-2412 427 G schubert@acu.edu
SCHUBERT, Ryan ..... 309-671-5147 143 I rschubert@methodistcol.edu
SCHUCH, Debra ..... 717-299-7408 398 E schuch@stevenscollege.edu
SCHUCHARDT, Bob ..... 913-758-6111 177 I robert.schuchardt@stmary.edu
SCHUCHARDT, Maureen ..... 913-758-6182 177 I maureen.schuchardt@stmary.edu
SCHUCK, Emily ..... 740-376-4712 355 E schucke@marietta.edu
SCHUCK, John ..... 856-227-7200 275 F jschuck@camdencc.edu
SCHUCKER, Julie ..... 716-614-6251 309 E jschucker@niagaracc.suny.edu
SCHUELER, Leah ..... 909-469-5238.. 75 G lschueler@westernu.edu
SCHUELLER, Kenneth ... 660-543-4721 259 K schueller@ucmo.edu
SCHUELLER, Tina ..... 325-793-3819 439 A schueller.tina@mcm.edu
SCHUEMANN, Kahler, B ..... 269-387-2360 232 J kahler.schuemann@wmich.edu
SCHUERMER, David, A . 270-824-8633 182 A david.schuermer@kctcs.edu
SCHUESSLER, Jennifer .. 678-839-5640 127 A jschuess@westga.edu
SCHUESSLER VELOZ, Nicole, A ..... 619-260-7408.. 72 H nschuessler@sandiego.edu
SCHUETZ, Bill ..... 435-283-7000 460 C
SCHUH, Jane ..... 701-231-6542 345 D jane.schuh@ndsu.edu
SCHUH, Mary Paula ..... 859-572-5122 184 B schuh@nku.edu
SCHUILING, Kerri ..... 906-227-2242 228 E kschuili@nmu.edu
SCHUKEI, Chris ..... 402-461-7341 266 C cschukei@hastings.edu
SCHULANG, Jamie ..... 215-780-1333 397 E jschulang@salus.edu
SCHULER, Gwendollyn .. 512-448-8404 441 N
SCHULING, Kristen ..... 402-280-2717 265 J kristenschuling@creighton.edu
SCHULIST, Mike ..... 262-650-4844 491 A mschulis@carrollu.edu
SCHULL, David ..... 303-963-3283.. 78 D dschull@ccu.edu
SCHULL, Gail ..... 541-880-2202 373 B schull@klamathcc.edu
SCHULLER, Aimee ..... 330-823-2755 362 E schullal@mountunion.edu
SCHULLER, Jennifer ..... 440-375-7255 354 K jschuller@lec.edu
SCHULMAN, Avrohom .. 908-354-6057 284 M
SCHULMAN, Jeffrey, L .. 802-656-3075 462 D jeffrey.schulman@uvm.edu
SCHULT, Jordan ..... 715-675-3331 498 E schult@ntc.edu
SCHULTE, Brandy ..... 660-831-4108 256 B schulteb@moval.edu
SCHULTE, Cynthia ..... 641-844-5602 167 C cindy.schulte@iavalley.edu
SCHULTE, Karissa ..... 970-542-3140.. 81 M karissa.schulte@morgancc.edu
SCHULTE, Kristi ..... 940-397-4427 439 F kristi.schulte@msutexas.edu
SCHULTE, Mary ..... 618-468-3300 142 B mschulte@lc.edu
SCHULTE, Megan ..... 419-434-4505 362 D megan.schulte@findlay.edu
SCHULTE, Patricia ..... 503-338-2425 372 C pschulte@clatsopcc.edu
SCHULTE, Priscilla ..... 907-228-4548.. 10 C pmschulte@alaska.edu
SCHULTE, Sarah, H ..... 906-487-2318 227 D shschult@mtu.edu
SCHULTE, Sheila ..... 706-867-2844 126 G sheila.schulte@ung.edu
SCHULTE, Stacey ..... 573-681-5030 254 A schultes@lincolnu.edu
SCHULTE, Tim ..... 660-831-4148 256 B schultet@moval.edu
SCHULTE, Vickie ..... 618-437-5321 147 F schultev@rlc.edu
SCHULTES, Debra ..... 201-684-7311 280 B dschulte@rampao.edu
SCHULTHEIS, Luke, D ... 201-692-7080 276 I luke@fdu.edu
SCHULTHEIS, Stephen ... 478-471-2494 122 D stephen.schultheis@mga.edu
SCHULTZ, Amber ..... 309-298-3100 152 I a-schultz2@wiu.edu
SCHULTZ, Ann ..... 859-441-4500 181 D ann.schultz@kctcs.edu
SCHULTZ, Barry ..... 901-572-2772 417 A barry.schultz@baptistu.edu
SCHULTZ, Bethany ..... 208-467-8353 132 B bhaglund@nnu.edu
SCHULTZ, Bruce ..... 907-786-6108.. 10 A brschultz@alaska.edu
SCHULTZ, Clayton ..... 919-573-5350 340 A cschultz@shepherds.edu
SCHULTZ, Craig ..... 608-757-6322 497 D cschultz31@blackhawk.edu
SCHULTZ, Diana, C ..... 239-513-1122 102 C dschultz2@hodges.edu
SCHULTZ, Eric ..... 605-882-5284 414 D eric.schultz@lakeareatech.edu
SCHULTZ, Greg ..... 440-934-3101 357 I gschultz@ohiobusinesscollege.edu
SCHULTZ, Jennifer, A ... 815-835-6405 149 A jennifer.a.schultz@svcc.edu
SCHULTZ, Jessica ..... 309-794-7331 132 H jessicaschultz@augustana.edu
SCHULTZ, Jessica ..... 763-657-2401 237 G jessica.schultz@hennepintech.edu
SCHULTZ, Joseph, P ..... 607-777-2187 315 E jschultz@binghamton.edu
SCHULTZ, Katherine ..... 303-492-6937.. 83 M katherine.schultz@colorado.edu
SCHULTZ, Lynda, K ..... 920-923-8793 492 D lkschultz@marianuniversity.edu
SCHULTZ, Marie ..... 951-827-6302.. 70 B marie.schultz@ucr.edu
SCHULTZ, Mark ..... 510-592-9688.. 61 D mark.schultz@npu.edu
SCHULTZ, Melissa ..... 734-462-4400 230 B mschultz@schoolcraft.edu
SCHULTZ, Michael ..... 903-233-4441 438 C michaelschultz@letu.edu
SCHULTZ, Michelle ..... 937-775-3469 364 D michelle.schultz@wright.edu
SCHULTZ, Myron ..... 701-224-5512 345 F myron.schultz@bismarckstate.edu
SCHULTZ, Peter, G ..... 858-784-8469.. 63 F
SCHULTZ, Roger, D ..... 434-592-4032 467 E rschultz@liberty.edu
SCHULTZ, Roger, W ..... 951-487-3002.. 53 A rschultz@msjc.edu
SCHULTZ, Scott ..... 515-965-7123 164 F sfschultz@dmacc.edu
SCHULTZ, Whitney ..... 707-527-4011.. 63 C
SCHULTZ, William ..... 651-641-8211 235 A schultz@csp.edu
SCHULTZ, Yvonne ..... 740-392-6868 356 G yvonne.schultz@mvnu.edu
SCHULTZ-HUXMAN, Susan ..... 540-432-4100 465 F susan.huxman@emu.edu
SCHULTZE, Christine ..... 303-329-6355.. 79 C
SCHULZ, Amy ..... 916-660-7800.. 64 B aschulz1@sierracollege.edu
SCHULZ, Amy ..... 317-738-8319 155 A aschulz@franklincollege.edu
SCHULZ, Andrew ..... 520-621-7886.. 16 H apschulz@arizona.edu
SCHULZ, Christa ..... 360-416-7974 483 D christa.schulz@skagit.edu
SCHULZ, Greg ..... 626-914-8821.. 37 B gschulz@citruscollege.edu
SCHULZ, Karyn ..... 410-837-4141 204 C kschulz@ubalt.edu
SCHULZ, Kathy, L ..... 201-216-5667 282 L kathy.schulz@stevens.edu

SCHULZ, Kirk .... 509-335-4200 484 D
presidentsoffice@wsu.edu
SCHULZ, Phyllis .... 212-817-7460 293 D
pschulz@gc.cuny.edu
SCHULZ, Robert .... 619-594-5901.. 33 E
rschulz@sdsu.edu
SCHULZ, Scott .... 623-845-3692.. 13 E
scott.schulz@gccaz.edu
SCHULZ, Scott .... 218-726-7171 243 A
sschulz1@d.umn.edu
SCHULZ, Scott .... 440-826-6970 348 C
saschulz@bw.edu
SCHULZ, Steven, D .... 641-422-4000 168 E
steve.schulz@niacc.edu
SCHULZ, Tara .... 563-884-5828 169 C
tara.schulz@palmer.edu
SCHULZ, William .... 866-492-5336 243 G
william.schulz@mail.waldenu.edu
SCHULZE, Edee .... 805-565-6028.. 75 I
eschulze@westmont.edu
SCHULZE, Janet, Y .... 610-660-2311 397 A
jschulze@sju.edu
SCHULZE, Lori, A .... 920-748-8310 493 J
schulzel@ripon.edu
SCHULZE, Rob .... 802-635-1305 463 B
rob.schulze@northernvermont.edu
SCHULZE, Robin, G .... 716-645-2711 315 F
cas-dean@buffalo.edu
SCHUMACHER, Bett ...... 413-538-2179 216 G
bkschumacher@mtholyoke.edu
SCHUMACHER, Brenda . 531-622-2406 266 G
bschumacher@mccneb.edu
SCHUMACHER,
Bryan, J .... 605-394-5102 415 I
bryan.schumacher@sdsmt.edu
SCHUMACHER,
Daniel, J .... 715-836-5858 494 E
schumadj@uwec.edu
SCHUMACHER, Denny .. 217-245-3012 139 A
dennis.schumacher@ic.edu
SCHUMACHER, Eric ...... 610-399-2599 393 D
eschumacher@cheyney.edu
SCHUMACHER, Gail ...... 708-237-5050 146 B
gschumacher@nc.edu
SCHUMACHER,
Karlyn, M .... 920-748-8750 493 J
schumacherka@ripon.edu
SCHUMACHER, Kathryn 414-930-3445 493 E
schumack@mtmary.edu
SCHUMACHER, Lane .... 509-542-4595 478 B
lschumacher@columbiabasin.edu
SCHUMACHER, Laura .... 407-708-4576 108 B
schumacherl@seminolestate.edu
SCHUMACHER, Lauren .. 708-237-5050 146 B
lwschumacher@nc.edu
SCHUMACHER,
Lawrence .... 708-237-5050 146 B
lschumacher@nc.edu
SCHUMACHER, Leisa .... 714-564-6975.. 58 F
schumacher_leisa@sac.edu
SCHUMACHER, Lillian ... 419-448-3413 361 C
schumacherlb@tiffin.edu
SCHUMACHER,
Mary Jeanne .... 812-357-6501 160 G
mschumacher@saintmeinrad.edu
SCHUMACHER, Ron ...... 419-559-2326 361 B
president@terra.edu
SCHUMACHER, Sara ..... 304-260-4380 487 C
SCHUMACHER, Sara ..... 828-694-1809 332 C
sp_schumacher@blueridge.edu
SCHUMACHER, Scott ... 979-830-4172 430 I
scott.schumacher@blinn.edu
SCHUMAKER, Ashley, L 757-683-3159 468 C
aschumak@odu.edu
SCHUMAN, Alan, M ...... 410-386-8495 197 G
aschuman@carrollcc.edu
SCHUMAN, Jacqueline .. 617-287-5000 211 E
jacqueline.schuman@umb.edu
SCHUMAN, Shmuel ...... 847-982-2500 138 G
schuman@htc.edu
SCHUMANN, Lisa .... 216-421-7405 350 E
lschumann@cia.edu
SCHUMANN, Patricia, J 304-766-3020 489 D
pschumann@wvstateu.edu
SCHUMARD-SHELTON,
Lisa .... 217-234-5270 141 H
lschumard-shelton@lakelandcollege.
edu
SCHUMM, Jillian .... 407-646-2120 106 L
jschumm@rollins.edu
SCHUMOCK, Glen .... 312-996-7240 151 D
schumock@uic.edu
SCHUMWAY, Michael ... 812-357-6539 160 G
mschumway@saintmeinrad.edu
SCHUPBACH, Jason ...... 215-895-1621 382 D
jss422@drexel.edu
SCHUPPERT, Cindy .... 503-352-3191 375 B
schuppec@pacificu.edu
SCHURMAN, Ryan .... 402-552-3390 265 G
schurmanryan@clarksoncollege.edu
SCHUSTER, Danny .... 347-619-9074 326 B
SCHUSTER, Heather ...... 312-662-4035 132 D
hschuster@adler.edu
SCHUSTER, Julian, Z .... 314-246-8242 261 D
julianschuster@webster.edu
SCHUSTER, Leslie .... 401-456-9723 404 A
lschuster@ric.edu
SCHUSTER, Mark, A ...... 888-576-3348.. 46 M
SCHUSTER, Sheldon, M 909-607-0107.. 37 I
sheldon_schuster@kgi.edu
SCHUSTER-MATLOCK,
Tracy .... 563-333-6049 169 D
schustertracy@sau.edu
SCHUSTER-WEBB,
Karen .... 513-487-1102 361 E
karen.webb@myunion.edu
SCHUTH, Kristen .... 585-345-6898 300 D
keschuth@genesee.edu
SCHUTT, Michelle .... 413-775-1000 214 C
SCHUTT, Stephen, D ..... 847-735-5100 141 F
presiden@lakeforest.edu
SCHUTTE, Kelli .... 816-415-7665 261 G
schuttek@william.jewell.edu
SCHUTTS, Katrina .... 850-474-2766 111 E
kschutts@uwf.edu
SCHUTZ, Christine .... 208-459-5524 131 A
cschutz@collegeofidaho.edu
SCHUVER, Debbie .... 213-624-1200.. 42 F
dschuver@fidm.edu
SCHUYLER, Lori, G .... 804-289-8781 471 E
lschuyle@richmond.edu
SCHWAB, Corinne .... 502-597-6557 183 A
corinne.schwab@kysu.edu
SCHWAB, Glenn .... 512-863-1697 444 F
schwabg@southwestern.edu
SCHWAB, Sheri .... 919-515-4559 341 E
slschwab@ncsu.edu
SCHWAB, Tracy .... 734-973-3349 232 A
tschwab@wccnet.edu
SCHWABE, Annette .... 850-644-1841 110 B
aschwabe@fsu.edu
SCHWABROW, Lynsey .. 262-472-1801 496 E
schwabrl@uww.edu
SCHWAGER, Paul, H ..... 843-805-5507 407 D
schwagerph@cofc.edu
SCHWAIG, Kathy, S ...... 470-578-6425 121 J
kschwaig@kennesaw.edu
SCHWAIGER, Patsy .... 513-244-4371 356 F
patsy.schwaiger@msj.edu
SCHWAN, Anna .... 605-626-2415 415 H
anna.schwan@northern.edu
SCHWANDT, Jehana .... 320-222-5986 239 H
jehana.schwandt@ridgewater.edu
SCHWANTES, Randy ...... 209-946-7613.. 71 E
rschwantes@pacific.edu
SCHWARTZ, Adam .... 515-294-2770 163 E
director@ameslab.gov
SCHWARTZ, Ann .... 512-313-3000 432 N
ann.schwartz@concordia.edu
SCHWARTZ, Anthony .... 518-381-1256 319 G
schwaraj@sunysccc.edu
SCHWARTZ, Brian .... 303-373-2008.. 83 D
bschwartz@rvu.edu
SCHWARTZ, Celeste, M 215-641-6492 390 A
cschwartz@mc3.edu
SCHWARTZ, Corene .... 909-652-6242.. 36 B
cory.schwartz@chaffey.edu
SCHWARTZ, Daniel .... 650-723-2300.. 66 D
daniel.schwartz@stanford.edu
SCHWARTZ, David .... 845-783-9901 323 F
utamds@gmail.com
SCHWARTZ, David, J ..... 248-370-3465 229 F
schwart3@oakland.edu
SCHWARTZ, Elimelech .. 845-352-3431 325 O
SCHWARTZ, Ernest .... 718-384-5460 325 I
SCHWARTZ, Gary .... 718-960-6093 293 E
gary.schwartz@lehman.cuny.edu
SCHWARTZ, Hayim .... 718-268-4700 311 H
SCHWARTZ, Jana .... 602-787-7668.. 13 G
jana.schwartz@paradisevalley.edu
SCHWARTZ, Jeff .... 941-893-2857 106 J
jschwartz@ringling.edu
SCHWARTZ, Jennifer ...... 317-955-6056 159 A
jschwartz@marian.edu
SCHWARTZ, Jennifer ...... 805-922-6966.. 24 L
jennifer.schwartz@hancockcollege.edu
SCHWARTZ, Jessica .... 715-833-6256 497 E
jschwartz31@cvtc.edu
SCHWARTZ, Jonathan .... 713-221-8001 452 B
schwartzj@uhd.edu
SCHWARTZ, Judith .... 718-270-4817 294 E
jschwartz@mec.cuny.edu
SCHWARTZ, Justin .... 814-865-7537 391 F
jzs622@psu.edu
SCHWARTZ, Lance, W .. 507-344-7427 233 I
lance.schwartz@blc.edu
SCHWARTZ, Mary Beth . 803-327-8042 413 F
mbschwartz@yorktech.edu
SCHWARTZ, Matthew ..... 850-474-3455 111 E
mschwartz@uwf.edu
SCHWARTZ, Matthew, J 812-888-4386 162 E
mschwartz@vinu.edu
SCHWARTZ, Melissa ...... 707-765-1836.. 52 C
SCHWARTZ, Michael, H 916-739-7151.. 71 E
SCHWARTZ, Niki .... 479-968-0399.. 18 E
lschwartz@atu.edu
SCHWARTZ, Paul .... 816-235-1366 260 D
schwartzpn@umkc.edu
SCHWARTZ, Philip .... 518-243-4471 290 K
schwartp@ellismedicne.org
SCHWARTZ, Rebecca ..... 801-626-8740 460 B
rebeccaschwartz1@weber.edu
SCHWARTZ, Robert .... 414-930-3110 493 E
schwartr@mtmary.edu
SCHWARTZ, Robert .... 206-296-2348 483 B
schwartr@seattleu.edu
SCHWARTZ, Saara .... 305-348-2401 109 H
saara.schwartz@fiu.edu
SCHWARTZ, Sandor .... 718-963-1212 303 C
kyrs@thejnet.com
SCHWARTZ, Shari .... 940-565-4616 453 B
shari.schwartz@unt.edu
SCHWARTZ, Shuly .... 212-678-8072 303 A
shschwartz@jtsa.edu
SCHWARTZ, Steven, J ... 970-247-7196.. 80 H
schwartz_s@fortlewis.edu
SCHWARTZ, Teresa .... 636-481-3284 253 G
tschwart@jeffco.edu
SCHWARTZ, Zach .... 617-585-1103 217 A
zach.schwartz@necmusic.edu
SCHWARTZE GRISHAM,
Mary .... 432-837-8203 449 F
mschwartze@sulross.edu
SCHWARTZKOPF,
Hayley .... 760-757-2121.. 52 G
hschwartzkopf@miracosta.edu
SCHWARZ, Arthur .... 817-202-6259 444 B
schwarz.arthur@swau.edu
SCHWARZ, Brian .... 952-829-2411 233 H
brian.schwarz@bethfel.org
SCHWARZ, Felipe .... 978-837-5459 216 D
schwarzf@merrimack.edu
SCHWARZ, Jonathan, D 617-324-7019 215 G
SCHWARZ, Justin .... 617-217-9050 206 A
jschwarz@baystate.edu
SCHWARZ, Justin .... 304-243-2359 490 F
jschwarz@wheeling.edu
SCHWARZ, Sara .... 303-273-3604.. 79 A
sschwarz@mines.edu
SCHWARZ, Sarah .... 503-725-5037 375 D
schwarzs@psuf.org
SCHWARZ, Thomas .... 973-408-3100 276 B
president@drew.edu
SCHWARZ, Todd .... 208-732-6325 131 B
tschwarz@csi.edu
SCHWARZMANN, Alex .. 706-721-0211 115 I
aschwarzmann@augusta.edu
SCHWASS, Anthony .... 906-487-7260 223 I
anthony.schwass@finlandia.edu
SCHWEBEL, Lisa .... 718-951-4771 293 A
lisas@brooklyn.cuny.edu
SCHWEERS, Rob .... 575-294-6142 163 E
rob@iastate.edu
SCHWEERS, Valerie .... 210-999-8536 451 B
vschweer@trinity.edu
SCHWEIBENZ,
Donna, L .... 215-204-8106 398 D
donna.schweibenz@temple.edu
SCHWEIKERT, Kristina .. 517-265-5161 220 D
kschweikert@adrian.edu
SCHWEINLE, Amy .... 605-658-6600 415 E
amy.schweinle@usd.edu
SCHWEITZER, Cameron 909-687-1455.. 43 G
cameronschweitzer@gs.edu
SCHWEITZER,
Connie, J .... 989-964-4160 229 L
schw@svsu.edu
SCHWEITZER, Kelli .... 402-826-8573 266 A
kelli.schweitzer@doane.edu
SCHWEITZER, Mark .... 313-577-7742 232 H
mark.schweitzer@med.wayne.edu
SCHWEITZER, Steven, J 800-287-8822 153 F
schwest@bethanyseminary.edu
SCHWELLENBACH,
Jordan .... 660-248-3391 250 H
jschwellenbach@centralmethodist.edu
SCHWELM, Anne .... 610-902-8260 379 E
aschwelm@cabrini.edu
SCHWEMMIN, Kevin ..... 435-797-3588 459 F
kevin.schwemmin@usu.edu
SCHWEN, Cari .... 406-447-6920 263 F
cari.schwen@helenacollege.edu
SCHWENKE, Stacy .... 906-227-2456 228 E
stschwen@nmu.edu
SCHWENNICKE, Antje ... 757-233-8806 476 C
aschwennicke@vwu.edu
SCHWERTNER, Melanie . 325-574-6503 457 G
mschwertner@wtc.edu
SCHWICKERATH,
Chad, R .... 773-896-2400 134 K
SCHWIDERSKI, Erika ..... 309-694-8825 138 I
erika.schwiderski@icc.edu
SCHWIEBERT, Ryan .... 919-866-5108 338 E
rlschwiebert@waketech.edu
SCHWINN, Debra, A ...... 561-803-2004 105 B
debra_schwinn@pba.edu
SCHWITZ, Frank .... 770-426-2637 122 A
fschwitz@life.edu
SCHWYN, Melinda .... 517-265-5161 220 D
mschwyn2@adrian.edu
SCIALABBA, Dawn .... 814-641-3171 386 E
scialad@juniata.edu
SCIALDONE, Robert .... 657-278-2025.. 31 E
rscialdone@fullerton.edu
SCIAME, Joseph, A .... 718-990-1941 313 B
sciamej@stjohns.edu
SCIAME-GIESECKE, Sue 812-855-4613 156 B
sgieseck@iuk.edu
SCIAME-GIESECKE,
Susan .... 812-855-4848 156 C
SCIAME-GIESECKE,
Susan .... 765-455-9221 156 E
sgieseck@iuk.edu
SCIBETTA, Nicholas ...... 412-268-6449 380 B
nscibett@andrew.cmu.edu
SCIBONA, Karen .... 903-983-8101 437 G
kscibona@kilgore.edu
SCIFO, Joseph .... 847-635-1784 146 E
jscifo@oakton.edu
SCINTA, Tony .... 702-992-2626 270 H
tony.scinta@nsc.edu
SCIPIO, Lisa .... 912-358-4000 124 H
scipiol@savannahstate.edu
SCIPIO, Patrick .... 803-378-5813 408 A
scipiop@denmarktech.edu
SCISSUM GUNN, Karyn 562-985-4128.. 32 A
karyn.scissumgunn@csulb.edu
SCIUTO, Jim .... 925-631-4238.. 59 I
jsciuto@stmarys-ca.edu
SCLAROFF, Stan .... 617-353-2401 207 C
sclaroff@bu.edu
SCOBEE, Georgia .... 225-216-8608 187 D
scobeeg@mybrcc.edu
SCOBEE, Roland .... 719-502-4926.. 82 D
roland.scobee@pikespeak.edu
SCOBEE, Scot .... 417-836-5102 255 J
sscobee@missouristate.edu
SCOCCO, Joan .... 732-224-2349 275 D
jscocco@brookdalecc.edu
SCOFIELD, Dorie .... 913-722-0272 174 G
dorie.scofield@kansaschristian.edu
SCOFIELD, Elizabeth ...... 215-951-1913 386 I
scofield@lasalle.edu
SCOFIELD, Jeff .... 808-735-4871 128 C
jeff.scofield@chaminade.edu
SCOGGINS, Amy .... 229-227-2687 125 G
ascoggins@southernregional.edu
SCOGGINS, Matthew ..... 865-974-2444 426 C
scoggins@utk.edu
SCOGIN, Breanne .... 559-278-8570.. 31 D
bscogin@csufresno.edu
SCOGIN, Brooke .... 817-257-7281 447 H
b.scogin@tcu.edu
SCOGIN, Matthew, A ..... 616-395-7780 224 H
president@hope.edu
SCOLA, Anthony, L .... 773-244-5570 145 F
ascola@northpark.edu
SCOLARI, Laurie .... 650-949-7823.. 43 A
scolarilaurie@foothill.edu
SCOLARO, Diane .... 802-485-2358 461 H
dscolaro@norwich.edu
SCOLES, Samantha .... 740-392-6868 356 G
samantha.scoles@mvnu.edu

SCOPELLITI, Theresa ..... 570-961-7840 387 A
scopellitit@lackawanna.edu

SCORDINO, Anthony ..... 914-606-6521 324 F
anthony.scordino@sunywcc.edu

SCORZA, Jason .... 201-692-7364 276 I
scorza@fdu.edu

SCOTMAN, Paula .... 404-527-7761 121 I
pscotman@itc.edu

SCOTT, Adrian .... 803-327-7402 407 A
ascott@clintoncollege.edu

SCOTT, Adrian, L .... 803-536-8542 410 H
ascott64@scsu.edu

SCOTT, Alexander .... 718-982-2396 293 C
alexander.scott@csi.cuny.edu

SCOTT, Allison .... 704-216-3632 337 C
allison.scott@rccc.edu

SCOTT, Amy .... 309-677-3538 133 H
alscott@fsmail.bradley.edu

SCOTT, Andrea .... 503-554-2142 372 I
scotta@georgefox.edu

SCOTT, Andrew .... 415-565-4812.. 69 B
scottandrewf@uchastings.edu

SCOTT, Angie .... 304-637-1983 486 D
scotta3@dewv.edu

SCOTT, Anne .... 931-540-2851 423 D
ascott12@columbiastate.edu

SCOTT, Annie .... 860-343-5767.. 86 G
ascott@mxcc.edu

SCOTT, Autumn .... 309-341-5422 134 A
anscott@sandburg.edu

SCOTT, Brad .... 218-550-2539 238 D
bradley.scott@minnesotanorth.edu

SCOTT, Carl .... 325-793-4919 439 A
scott.carl@mcm.edu

SCOTT, Carolyn .... 352-435-6308 103 U
scottc@lssc.edu

SCOTT, Carolyn .... 888-980-9151 470 J

SCOTT, Carolyn .... 540-986-1800 463 F

SCOTT, Charles .... 304-896-7420 487 I
chad.scott@southernwv.edu

SCOTT, Charles .... 212-817-7736 293 D
cscott@gc.cuny.edu

SCOTT, Charles .... 918-495-6228 368 F
cscott@oru.edu

SCOTT, Cheryl .... 775-673-8239 270 I
clscott@tmcc.edu

SCOTT, Cheryl .... 661-395-4840.. 47 B
cheryl.scott@bakersfieldcollege.edu

SCOTT, Christina .... 479-979-1244.. 24 A
cscott@ozarks.edu

SCOTT, Christopher .... 210-784-2038 447 B
christopher.scott@tamusa.edu

SCOTT, Christopher, D .. 815-772-7218 145 A
cdscott@morrisontech.edu

SCOTT, Christopher, D .. 413-755-4961 215 F
cdscott@stcc.edu

SCOTT, Clifford .... 617-266-2030 216 H
scottc@neco.edu

SCOTT, Daniel .... 831-755-6888.. 44 J
dscott@hartnell.edu

SCOTT, Daniel .... 210-446-6719 456 E

SCOTT, Dave .... 626-584-5269.. 43 E
dscott@fuller.edu

SCOTT, Dave .... 360-416-7600 483 D
dave.scott@skagit.edu

SCOTT, Dave, L .... 626-584-5269.. 43 E
dscott@fuller.edu

SCOTT, David .... 850-474-3003 111 E
dscott@uwf.edu

SCOTT, David .... 719-632-7626.. 81 I
dscott@intellitec.edu

SCOTT, David .... 361-825-2661 446 E
david.scott@tamucc.edu

SCOTT, Dawn, M .... 262-524-7297 491 A
dscott@carrollu.edu

SCOTT, Deborah .... 830-792-7355 442 G
dlscott@schreiner.edu

SCOTT, Deloria .... 270-707-3823 181 G
deloria.scott@kctcs.edu

SCOTT, Derek .... 402-280-2780 265 J
derekscott@creighton.edu

SCOTT, Doneka .... 919-515-4392 341 E
doneka@ncsu.edu

SCOTT, Donna .... 512-404-4807 429 K
dscott@austinseminary.edu

SCOTT, Douglas .... 484-646-4250 394 A
dscott@kutztown.edu

SCOTT, Ed .... 850-263-3261.. 95 P
eescott@baptistcollege.edu

SCOTT, Elaine .... 408-554-4600.. 63 A
escott@scu.edu

SCOTT, Emily .... 336-272-7102 329 B
emily.scott@greensboro.edu

SCOTT, Emily, M .... 336-272-7102 329 B
emily.scott@greensboro.edu

SCOTT, Eric .... 662-216-3429 248 B
escott@rustcollege.edu

SCOTT, Eric .... 512-472-4133 442 H
eric.scott@ssw.edu

SCOTT, Garry .... 217-234-5253 141 H
gscott12070@lakelandcollege.edu

SCOTT, Gray .... 940-898-3042 451 A
grayscott@twu.edu

SCOTT, Gregory .... 865-524-8079 419 A
gregory.scott@huhs.edu

SCOTT, Harriette .... 508-588-9100 214 F
hdudley1@massasoit.mass.edu

SCOTT, Jamal .... 630-466-7900 152 H
jscott@waubonsee.edu

SCOTT, James .... 707-638-5200.. 68 B

SCOTT, Jan, L .... 727-816-3424 105 E
scottj@phsc.edu

SCOTT, Jeannie, J .... 210-283-5002 452 D
scott@uiwtx.edu

SCOTT, Jennifer .... 651-638-6519 233 J
jscott@bethel.edu

SCOTT, Jeremy .... 954-637-2268 108 C
admissions@sfbc.edu

SCOTT, Jim .... 509-434-5325 478 E
jim.scott@ccs.spokane.edu

SCOTT, Jonathan, H ...... 229-928-1273 120 B
jonathan.scott@gsw.edu

SCOTT, Joseph .... 501-882-4411.. 17 H
jlscott@asub.edu

SCOTT, Joyce .... 870-543-4917.. 21 D
jscott@seark.edu

SCOTT, Joylynn .... 423-236-2801 422 H
jmichals@southern.edu

SCOTT, Katelyn .... 325-793-4608 439 A
scott.katelyn@mcm.edu

SCOTT, Kathleen, E .... 937-255-3636 501 A
kathleen.scott@afit.edu

SCOTT, Katie, E .... 937-255-3636 501 A
kathleen.scott@afit.edu

SCOTT, Kelly .... 970-675-3211.. 78 P
kelly.scott@cncc.edu

SCOTT, Kendall .... 918-360-9703 365 B
scottk@bacone.edu

SCOTT, Kimberly .... 508-999-8600 211 F
kimberly.scott@umassd.edu

SCOTT, Lana .... 580-477-7719 371 D
lana.scott@wosc.edu

SCOTT, Laura .... 707-864-7000.. 64 F
laura.scott@solano.edu

SCOTT, Laura, A .... 603-271-6484 272 C
lascott@ccsnh.edu

SCOTT, Linda .... 608-263-9725 494 D
ldscott@wisc.edu

SCOTT, Linda .... 559-486-1166.. 24 I
lscott@agapeschools.org

SCOTT, Linda .... 804-524-5304 475 E
lscott@vsu.edu

SCOTT, Lisa, N .... 408-848-4711.. 43 H
lscott@gavilan.edu

SCOTT, Lori .... 318-487-7401 187 B
lori.scott@lcuniversity.edu

SCOTT, Marc .... 740-351-3439 360 E
mscott@shawnee.edu

SCOTT, Marcia .... 805-546-3119.. 41 A
mscott@cuesta.edu

SCOTT, Matthew .... 413-205-3015 205 C
matthew.scott@aic.edu

SCOTT, Megan .... 425-889-5205 481 A
president@northwestu.edu

SCOTT, Megan, J .... 920-832-6587 492 B
megan.j.scott@lawrence.edu

SCOTT, Melody, K .... 330-471-8502 355 D
mscott@malone.edu

SCOTT, Michael .... 580-559-5649 365 J
mscott@ecok.edu

SCOTT, Michael .... 415-405-3943.. 34 A
mjscott@sfsu.edu

SCOTT, Michael .... 978-478-3400 217 E
mscott@northpoint.edu

SCOTT, Michael, S .... 410-543-6456 204 A
msscott@salisbury.edu

SCOTT, Michelle, T .... 240-567-5276 200 E
michellet.scott@montgomerycollege.edu

SCOTT, Mike .... 817-257-7858 447 H
m.scott@tcu.edu

SCOTT, Natalie .... 845-574-4289 312 C
natalie.scott@sunyrockland.edu

SCOTT, Patricia, A .... 410-706-7347 202 F
pscott@umaryland.edu

SCOTT, Patty .... 541-888-7401 376 B
pscott@socc.edu

SCOTT, Paul .... 912-443-5500 124 I
pscott@savannahtech.edu

SCOTT, Phyllis .... 305-899-3900.. 96 A
pscott@barry.edu

SCOTT, Raegina .... 270-824-8593 182 A
raegina.scott@kctcs.edu

SCOTT, Randa .... 512-313-3000 432 N
randa.scott@concordia.edu

SCOTT, Randolph .... 850-474-3295 111 E
rscott1@uwf.edu

SCOTT, Ray .... 662-720-7302 247 D
jrscott@nemcc.edu

SCOTT, Renae .... 208-282-2499 131 E
renaescott@isu.edu

SCOTT, Renay .... 575-646-7607 286 G
rmscott@nmsu.edu

SCOTT, Renee .... 325-793-3803 439 A
scott.renee@mcm.edu

SCOTT, Richard .... 269-965-3931 225 D
scottr@kellogg.edu

SCOTT, Richard .... 801-957-3334 460 D
richard.scott@slcc.edu

SCOTT, Rob .... 770-426-2603 122 A
rob.scott@life.edu

SCOTT, Robin .... 603-342-3016 272 E
rscott@ccsnh.edu

SCOTT, Samantha .... 626-350-1500.. 28 H

SCOTT, Sandi .... 715-232-1181 496 C
duexs@uwstout.edu

SCOTT, Sara .... 937-481-2307 363 H
sara_scott@wilmington.edu

SCOTT, Sarah .... 301-447-7415 201 A
sscott@msmary.edu

SCOTT, Sean, M .... 619-239-0391.. 34 H
sscott@cwsl.edu

SCOTT, Sharron .... 802-224-3000 462 G
sharron.scott@vsc.edu

SCOTT, Shawne .... 443-394-3339.. 93 H

SCOTT, Sheila .... 434-528-5276 476 B

SCOTT, Sherrill, B .... 731-426-7522 419 G
sbscott@lanecollege.edu

SCOTT, Stacie .... 608-363-2250 490 I
scottst@beloit.edu

SCOTT, Susan, W .... 601-266-5000 248 H
susan.w.scott@usm.edu

SCOTT, Susanne .... 718-951-5000 293 A
sscott@brooklyn.cuny.edu

SCOTT, Tabatha .... 501-374-6305.. 21 B
tabatha.scott@shortercollege.edu

SCOTT, Tawana .... 864-877-1598 410 A
tawana.scott@ngu.edu

SCOTT, Taylor .... 401-709-8671 404 B
tscott01@risd.edu

SCOTT, Terri .... 208-459-5328 131 A
tscott@collegeofidaho.edu

SCOTT, Thomas .... 208-769-5906 132 A
ttscott@nic.edu

SCOTT, Timothy, P .... 979-845-4016 446 B
t-scott@tamu.edu

SCOTT, Todd .... 760-245-4271.. 74 D
todd.scott@vvc.edu

SCOTT, Trayvean .... 318-274-2374 191 G
scotttr@gram.edu

SCOTT, Vann .... 256-840-4188.... 3 F
vann.scott@snead.edu

SCOTT, William, J .... 260-399-7700 162 A
bscott@sf.edu

SCOTT, Xavier, M .... 606-783-5466 183 H
x.scott@moreheadstate.edu

SCOTT, Zaldwaynaka (Z) .... 773-995-2400 134 J
zscott21@csu.edu

SCOTT-BRAND, Tammy . 312-850-4584 135 E
tscott-brand@ccc.edu

SCOTT-GILMORE, Jennifer .... 601-857-3395 245 D
jennifer.scottgilmore@hindscc.edu

SCOTT-JOHNSON, Pamela .... 732-571-3405 278 B
pscottjo@monmouth.edu

SCOTT LEE, Kristalyn ..... 205-665-6001.... 8 D
klee8@montevallo.edu

SCOTTI, Frank .... 714-463-7540.. 51 D
fscotti@ketchum.edu

SCOTTO, Kathleen .... 732-235-4812 281 B
kathleen.scotto@rutgers.edu

SCOUREY, Joy .... 509-335-9711 484 D
scourey@wsu.edu

SCOVILLE, Jan .... 715-732-3888 498 F
jan.scoville@nwtc.edu

SCOVILLE, Kathy .... 518-244-2053 312 D
scovik@sage.edu

SCOVILLE, Shawn .... 541-737-3288 374 H

SCOZZAFAVA, Samuel .. 315-443-4027 321 D
sjscozza@syr.edu

SCRANAGE, Kimberly .... 678-839-5000 127 A
kscranage@westga.edu

SCREMENTI, Lori .... 773-244-5770 145 F
lmscrementi@northpark.edu

SCREWS, Jacqueline ...... 334-291-4981.... 1 H
jackie.screws@cv.edu

SCRIBNER, Andrea .... 518-736-3622 300 B
andrea.scribner@fmcc.suny.edu

SCRIBNER, Heidi, M ..... 951-827-1012.. 70 B

SCRICCA, Cherie .... 508-793-7194 207 F
titleix@clarku.edu

SCRIMENTI, Santo, A .... 240-567-5361 200 E
santo.scrimenti@montgomerycollege.edu

SCRIVEN, Darryl .... 315-268-6544 295 E
dscriven@clarkson.edu

SCRIVEN, Gloria .... 803-934-3216 409 H
gscriven@morris.edu

SCRIVENER, Carley .... 715-232-2346 496 C
scrivenerc@uwstout.edu

SCRIVNER, Joseph .... 205-366-8838.... 7 A
jscrivner@stillman.edu

SCROGGINS, Beth .... 503-838-8000 377 C
scrogginsb@wou.edu

SCROGGINS, Don .... 575-769-4909 285 C
don.scroggins@clovis.edu

SCROGGINS, Melinda .... 559-251-4215.. 28 B
financialaid@calchristiancollege.edu

SCROGGINS, Sarah .... 636-584-6553 252 D
sarah.scroggins@eastcentral.edu

SCROGGINS, William, T .... 909-274-4250.. 52 K
bscroggins@mtsac.edu

SCROGIN, Tara .... 402-559-9005 269 B
tscrogin@unmc.edu

SCRONCE, Tamara .... 775-784-1733 270 K
tamaras@unr.edu

SCRUGGS, Adina .... 423-775-7121 417 D
ascruggs8899@bryan.edu

SCRUGGS, Jeff .... 478-218-3333 116 F
jscruggs@centralgatech.edu

SCUILETTI, Linda .... 919-718-7417 333 A
lscuiletti@cccc.edu

SCULLY, Amy .... 803-691-3879 409 E
scullya@midlandstech.edu

SCULLY, Beverly .... 860-701-7795.. 88 C
scully_b@mitchell.edu

SCULLY, Dale .... 559-453-7154.. 43 D
dale.scully@fresno.edu

SCULLY, Jonathan .... 413-265-2519 208 B
scullyj@elms.edu

SCULLY, Joseph, F .... 856-256-4127 280 H
scullyj@rowan.edu

SCULLY, Mary Ann .... 410-617-2301 199 G
mascully@loyola.edu

SCULLY, Pamela .... 910-678-8232 334 C
scullyp@faytechcc.edu

SCULLY, Serena .... 304-367-4151 488 L
serena.scully@fairmontstate.edu

SCURALLI, Joseph .... 973-405-2111 274 J
jss@berkeleycollege.edu

SCURALLI, Joseph .... 212-986-4343 291 A
jss@berkeleycollege.edu

SCURALLI, Joseph .... 973-405-2111 291 A
jss@berkeleycollege.edu

SCUTO, Donna, L .... 716-878-6700 317 C
scutodl@buffalostate.edu

SEABERRY, Ben .... 408-531-6144.. 62 E
ben.seaberry@sjeccd.edu

SEABERRY, Ben .... 559-243-7321.. 66 G
ben.seaberry@scccd.edu

SEABERT, Denise .... 559-278-4004.. 31 D
dseabert@csufresno.edu

SEABOLD, Brian .... 201-216-8722 282 L
brian.seabold@stevens.edu

SEABOLD, Daniel, E .... 516-463-5411 301 E
daniel.e.seabold@hofstra.edu

SEABOLT, Kerry .... 706-865-2134 126 D
klseabolt@truett.edu

SEABROOK-WRIGHT, Gloria .... 803-934-3257 409 H
gwright@morris.edu

SEABROOKS, Joseph .... 972-860-8250 433 H
jseabrooks@dcccd.edu

SEACH, Kerri .... 248-204-4108 226 E
kseach@ltu.edu

SEAGA, Andrew .... 305-237-7581 104 E
aseaga@mdc.edu

SEIFERT, Charles, E ...... 806-743-4200 450 D
charles.seifert@ttuhsc.edu
SEIFERT, David .... 716-270-5348 299 A
seifertd@ecc.edu
SEIFERT, Trevor .... 501-450-3117.. 23 K
tseifert1@uca.edu
SEIFERT, Tricia .... 406-994-3127 263 G
tricia.seifert@montana.edu
SEIG, Mary Theresa .... 218-755-3874 237 B
marytheresa.seig@bemidjistate.edu
SEIGAR, Marc .... 419-530-7840 363 B
marcus.seigar@utoledo.edu
SEIGART, Denise .... 570-422-3425 393 F
dseigart@esu.edu
SEIGH, William, R .... 206-726-5002 478 F
provost@cornish.edu
SEIJAS, Octavio .... 413-265-2462 208 B
seijaso@elms.edu
SEIL, Tim .... 716-926-8884 301 C
tseil@hilbert.edu
SEILER, Brian .... 931-372-3004 425 B
bseiler@tntech.edu
SEILER, David .... 512-863-1809 444 F
seilerd@southwestern.edu
SEILER, OP,
Marie Hannah .... 615-297-7545 416 G
srmhannah@aquinascollege.edu
SEILER, Matthew .... 443-352-5314 202 C
mseiler@stevenson.edu
SEIMEARS, Matt .... 541-962-3511 372 H
mseimears@eou.edu
SEIMERS, Jeff .... 907-260-7422.... 9 D
SEINFELD, Laura .... 516-299-4122 304 D
laura.seinfeld@liu.edu
SEIPPEL, Danielle .... 608-822-2317 498 H
dseippel@swtc.edu
SEITZ, Albert .... 508-830-6681 213 A
aseitz@maritime.edu
SEITZ, Greg .... 256-782-5368.... 6 A
gseitz@jsu.edu
SEITZ, Tim .... 440-826-8029 348 C
tseitz@bw.edu
SEITZER, Joan, M .... 410-827-5808 198 B
jseitzer@chesapeake.edu
SEIXAS, Karyn .... 626-395-6161.. 29 B
karyn@caltech.edu
SEJDINAJ, John .... 812-855-7114 156 B
vpcfo@iu.edu
SEKAS, Kimberly .... 262-595-2500 495 D
sekask@uwp.edu
SEKELSKY, Mary Jo ...... 810-424-5448 231 C
maryjoss@umich.edu
SEKER, Remzi .... 269-387-8294 232 J
remzi.seker@wmich.edu
SEKERAK, Robert .... 814-471-0013 393 A
rsekerak@pennhighlands.edu
SEKI, Bill, H .... 213-738-5743.. 66 A
bseki@swlaw.edu
SEKUL, Michelle .... 228-497-7647 246 F
michelle.sekul@mgccc.edu
SEKULICH, Brad .... 704-687-7747 342 C
sekulich@uncc.edu
SELANDER, Nora, J .... 360-870-6453 479 C
nora.j.selander@evergreen.edu
SELASSIE-OKPE,
O'KenZoe .... 650-738-4100.. 62 K
selassieokpeo@smccd.edu
SELBY, David, K .... 317-788-3386 161 F
selbyd@uindy.edu
SELBY, Rosemary .... 478-553-2055 123 D
rselby@oftc.edu
SELBY, Steve .... 714-992-7081.. 54 D
sselby@fullcoll.edu
SELBY, Tami .... 308-432-7030 267 G
tselby@csc.edu
SELDEN, Pete .... 918-595-7976 370 B
peter.selden@tulsacc.edu
SELDEN, Sally .... 843-953-5007 406 D
sselden@citadel.edu
SELDES, Suzanne .... 772-462-7265 102 E
sseldes@irsc.edu
SELESKY, Melissa .... 848-445-1961 281 B
selesky@rutgers.edu
SELF, Megan .... 970-339-6210.. 77 G
megan.self@aims.edu
SELF, Michael .... 573-681-5074 254 A
selfm@lincolnu.edu
SELF, Rosemary .... 662-472-9079 245 E
rself@holmescc.edu
SELF, Sarah .... 865-354-3000 424 D
selfs1@roanestate.edu
SELF, Sharmistha .... 936-294-1254 449 E
sxs257@shsu.edu
SELF, Sheila .... 918-444-2120 366 G
selfsj@nsuok.edu
SELF-DAVIS, LeAnn .... 731-989-6931 418 H
ldavis@fhu.edu
SELIG, C. Wood .... 757-683-3369 468 C
wselig@odu.edu
SELIGER, Jared .... 319-226-2015 163 A
jared.seliger@allencollege.edu
SELIGMAN, Joel .... 802-656-7878 462 D
joel.seligman@uvm.edu
SELIGMAN, Richard, P .. 626-395-6073.. 29 B
richard.seligman@caltech.edu
SELIN, Mark .... 920-403-3055 494 B
mark.selin@snc.edu
SELINKO, Katy .... 312-662-4235 132 D
kselinko@adler.edu
SELKIRK, Sara, E .... 816-654-7214 253 I
sselkirk@kcumb.edu
SELL, Justin .... 605-688-6388 416 A
justin.sell@sdstate.edu
SELL, Susan .... 701-231-8011 345 D
susan.sell@ndsu.edu
SELL MATZKE, Jen .... 320-308-0121 240 C
SELLARS, Frances .... 360-676-2772 480 G
fsellars@nwic.edu
SELLARS, Telly .... 606-883-7371 181 A
telly.sellars@kctcs.edu
SELLAS, Carlos .... 787-840-2575 508 G
csellas@psm.edu
SELLAS, Erik .... 563-884-5400 169 C
erik.sellas@palmer.edu
SELLEN, Mary, K .... 757-594-7130 465 A
mary.sellen@cnu.edu
SELLERS, Darlene .... 406-265-3527 264 A
sellersd@msun.edu
SELLERS, Emma .... 434-791-7116 463 L
elugar@averett.edu
SELLERS, Jeff .... 501-420-1206.. 17 D
jeff.sellers@arkansasbaptist.edu
SELLERS, Karen .... 401-841-6547 501 L
karen.sellers@usnwc.edu
SELLERS, Lauren .... 704-272-5331 337 F
lsellers@spcc.edu
SELLERS, Linda .... 254-442-5151 431 J
linda.sellers@cisco.edu
SELLERS, Martin .... 423-869-6815 420 A
martin.sellers@lmunet.edu
SELLERS, Matt .... 662-562-3292 247 E
msellers@northwestms.edu
SELLERS, Meghann .... 407-708-2010 108 B
sellersm@seminolestate.edu
SELLERS, Suzanne .... 940-898-3748 451 A
ssellers1@twu.edu
SELLERS, Terrie .... 912-408-3024 124 I
tsellers@savannahtech.edu
SELLERS, Timothy .... 315-279-5685 303 D
tsellers@keuka.edu
SELLERS BATTLE,
Crystal .... 814-641-3173 386 E
battlec@juniata.edu
SELLMAN, Carol .... 510-436-1265.. 45 H
sellman@hnu.edu
SELLMANN, James, D ... 671-735-2805 503 E
jsellman@triton.uog.edu
SELLS, Ben, R .... 870-245-5400.. 20 H
sellsb@obu.edu
SELLS, Deanna .... 573-334-6825 258 I
dsells@sehcollege.edu
SELLS, Debra, K .... 615-898-2440 421 C
debra.sells@mtsu.edu
SELLS, Tamatha .... 864-941-8363 410 D
sells.t@ptc.edu
SELMAN, Brenda, V .... 573-884-9153 260 C
selmanb@missouri.edu
SELMO, Barbara .... 617-349-8267 210 H
bselmo@lesley.edu
SELMON, John .... 231-777-0265 228 C
john.selmon@muskegoncc.edu
SELNER TAN, Anya .... 619-849-2209.. 57 J
aselnert@pointloma.edu
SELORIO, Conrad .... 562-860-2451.. 35 O
cselorio@cerritos.edu
SELTZER, Jill .... 832-230-5540 439 H
jseltzer@na.edu
SELTZER-STITT, Jennifer 801-957-4753 460 D
jen.seltzerstitt@slcc.edu
SELVA, Kenia .... 512-492-3011 429 B
registrar@aoma.edu
SELVA, Marci .... 916-558-2337.. 51 B
selvam@scc.losrios.edu
SELVAGGIO, Donna .... 516-773-5000 502 G
selvaggiod@usmma.edu
SELWITZ, Jason .... 360-596-5409 483 E
jselwitz@spscc.edu
SEMAH, Charles .... 732-431-1600 283 C
SEMAN, Elizabeth .... 864-294-3474 408 I
liz.seman@furman.edu
SEMANIE, Victoria, V ...... 410-864-4000 202 A
SEMANOFF, Matthew .... 406-243-5637 263 D
matthew.semanoff@umontana.edu
SEMENIUK, CM,
Gregory .... 716-286-8400 309 F
gsemeniuk@niagara.edu
SEMENZA, Michael, L ...... 401-341-2465 404 D
semenzam@salve.edu
SEMERARO, Steve .... 619-961-4259.. 68 A
ssemeraro@tjsl.edu
SEMICH, Robert .... 740-264-5591 352 B
rsemich@egcc.edu
SEMLAK, William .... 309-438-5276 140 C
wdsemlak@ilstu.edu
SEMLEY, Lorelle .... 508-793-2769 208 A
lsemley@holycross.edu
SEMMEL, Abraham .... 718-268-4700 311 H
SEMMEL, Ralph .... 443-778-5190 199 E
ralph.semmel@jhuapl.edu
SEMMES, John .... 757-446-5676 465 H
semmesoj@evms.edu
SEMMLERSMITH, Sarah 906-487-7239 223 I
sarah.semmlersmith@finlandia.edu
SEMONES, Andy .... 229-225-3932 125 G
csemones@southernregional.edu
SEMPKOWSKI, Dan .... 732-987-2699 277 B
dsempkowski@georgian.edu
SEMPREBON, Gina .... 413-565-1000 205 I
gsemprebon@baypath.edu
SEN, Aparna .... 425-739-8100 480 D
aparna.sen@lwtech.edu
SENA, Al .... 505-277-6644 288 C
asena5@unm.edu
SENA, Ali .... 559-453-2236.. 43 D
ali.sena@fresno.edu
SENA, Johanna .... 617-989-4590 219 D
senaj@wit.edu
SENA, Maria .... 505-454-3269 286 C
misena@nmhu.edu
SENAPATIRATNE, Tim ... 651-255-6144 242 J
tsenapatiratne@unitedseminary.edu
SENCIL, Sabrina .... 916-691-7144.. 50 K
sencils@crc.losrios.edu
SENDERHAUF, Terye .... 360-417-6322 481 F
tsenderhauf@pencol.edu
SENDLER, Karen .... 646-745-8310 290 H
ksendler@barnard.edu
SENDZE, Monique .... 530-898-3700.. 31 A
msendze@csuchico.edu
SENECAL, Molly .... 916-608-6688.. 51 A
senacam@flc.losrios.edu
SENECAUT, Tim .... 620-235-4776 176 H
tsenecaut@pittstate.edu
SENEGAL, Pamela, G .... 336-322-2100 336 D
pamela.senegal@piedmontcc.edu
SENEQUE, Guy .... 516-877-3650 288 L
seneque@adelphi.edu
SENESE, Jeffrey .... 352-588-8242 107 B
jeffrey.senese@saintleo.edu
SENESE, Richard .... 888-227-3552 234 B
SENESE, Vera .... 347-577-4031 293 E
elvira.senese@lehman.cuny.edu
SENFT, James .... 847-543-2975 135 G
jsenft@clcillinois.edu
SENG, Victoria, S .... 731-881-7855 426 E
vseng@utm.edu
SENGUPTA, Ayesha .... 641-472-7000 168 A
asengupta@miu.edu
SENGUPTA, Shivaji .... 347-964-8600 291 F
ssengupta@boricuacollege.edu
SENIOR, Ann Marie .... 609-984-1151 283 D
amsenior@tesu.edu
SENIOR, Timothy, C .... 610-785-6200 396 H
bsenior@scs.edu
SENKBEIL, Peter .... 949-214-3201.. 40 E
peter.senkbeil@cui.edu
SENKER, Richard .... 813-253-7144 102 A
rsenker@hccfl.edu
SENN, Kate .... 270-534-3143 182 G
catherine.senn@kctcs.edu
SENN, Sarah .... 334-699-2266.... 1 B
ssenn@acom.edu
SENNER, Denise .... 208-467-8061 132 B
dsenner@nnu.edu
SENNETT, Peter .... 978-630-9160 215 A
psennett@mwcc.mass.edu
SENNYEY, Pongracz, J .. 540-464-7573 475 C
sennyeypj@vmi.edu
SENSABAUGH,
Kathleen .... 540-568-4346 467 C
sensabkb@jmu.edu
SENSENIG, Melvin .... 610-921-7708 377 F
msensenig@albright.edu
SENSENIG, Victor .... 410-778-7201 204 E
vsensenig2@washcoll.edu
SENSER, Randie .... 212-247-3434 304 J
rsenser@mandl.edu
SENSI, Patricia .... 732-224-2234 275 D
psensi@brookdalecc.edu
SENSIBAUGH,
Cyndee, K .... 304-367-4933 487 H
cyndee.sensibaugh@pierpont.edu
SENTEL, Tetine, L .... 808-956-6300 129 B
tsentell@hawaii.edu
SENTER, Jim .... 915-747-5347 454 E
jsenter@utep.edu
SENTER, Timothy, C .... 662-862-8460 245 F
tcsenter@iccms.edu
SENTER, William .... 830-372-6550 448 C
wsenter@tlu.edu
SENTZ, Justin .... 717-477-1507 394 D
jasentz@ship.edu
SEO, Bocheon .... 213-381-0081.. 46 I
SEO, EunJa .... 714-525-0088.. 44 C
library@gm.edu
SEO, Hillary .... 515-294-3540 163 E
hseo@iastate.edu
SEO, Sang Bae .... 636-327-4645 255 E
seoul@midwest.edu
SEPANIC, Michael, J .... 856-225-6026 281 A
msepanic@camden.rutgers.edu
SEPEHRI, Mohamad .... 202-274-7050.. 94 B
mohamad.sepehri@udc.edu
SEPLOW, Suzanne .... 310-825-3401.. 69 D
suzanne@orl.ucla.edu
SEPPALA, Julie .... 906-487-2642 227 D
jhseppal@mtu.edu
SEPSEY, Katlyn .... 864-294-2405 408 I
katlyn.sepsey@furman.edu
SEPULVEDA, Dolores .... 787-891-0925 506 I
dsepulve@aguadilla.inter.edu
SEPULVEDA, Pamela .... 562-860-2451.. 35 O
psepulveda@cerritos.edu
SEQUEIRA, Gerald .... 626-914-8517.. 37 B
gsequeira@citruscollege.edu
SERAFIMOV, Val .... 417-873-7262 252 A
vserafimov@drury.edu
SERAFIN, Julie .... 304-558-4128 488 I
julie.serafin@wvhepc.edu
SERAFIN, Renata .... 210-486-4689 428 A
rserafin@alamo.edu
SERAFINO, Candice, J ...... 413-545-6253 211 D
serafino@acad.umass.edu
SERBAN, Andreea .... 714-438-4698.. 38 C
aserban@cccd.edu
SERBANTES, Jessica, A 210-829-6030 452 D
serbante@uiwtx.edu
SERBER, Michael .... 214-648-9569 456 D
michael.serber@utsouthwestern.edu
SERBY-WILKENS, Anja .. 757-455-3215 476 C
aserbywilkens@vwu.edu
SERCK, Steve .... 704-406-2707 328 I
sserck@gardner-webb.edu
SERENA, Joe .... 209-384-6000.. 52 B
SERFASS, Chad, A .... 724-946-7338 401 F
serfasca@westminster.edu
SERGE, Susan .... 307-681-6082 500 F
sserge@sheridan.edu
SERGEANT, SR., Glenn . 501-975-8536.. 21 A
gsergeant@philander.edu
SERGENT, Ann .... 419-559-2147 361 B
asergent01@terra.edu
SERGEYEVA, Larisa .... 714-564-6806.. 58 F
sergeyeva_larisa@sac.edu
SERGI, Joseph .... 301-985-7000 203 C
joseph.sergi@umgc.edu
SERGIO, Tiffany .... 310-233-4208.. 49 F
sergiot@lahc.edu
SERIO, Tricia, R .... 413-545-6223 211 D
tserio@umass.edu
SERJOIE, Ara .... 336-316-2320 329 C
serjoiea@guilford.edu
SERLING, Kitty .... 816-276-4309 257 I
c.serling@researchcollege.edu
SERMONS, Lydia .... 404-681-3643 126 A
SERNA, Carlos .... 562-860-2451.. 35 O
cserna@cerritos.edu
SERNA, Edward, A .... 803-323-2225 413 D
president@winthrop.edu
SERNA, Falone .... 805-493-3049.. 29 E
fserna@callutheran.edu

SHAFFER, John .... 304-829-7394 486 B
jshaffer@bethanywv.edu
SHAFFER, Jon, L .... 618-453-2301 149 G
jshaffer@siu.edu
SHAFFER, Martin, B ...... 845-575-3000 305 C
martin.shaffer@marist.edu
SHAFFER, Shelley ..... 304-876-5236 489 A
sshaff06@shepherd.edu
SHAFFER, Tonaya .... 717-815-1271 402 G
tshaffer1@ycp.edu
SHAFFER, Virginia ..... 630-752-5623 152 K
virginia.shaffer@wheaton.edu
SHAFFER, Virginia .... 620-901-6235 171 A
shaffer@allencc.edu
SHAFFER, W. Michael .. 706-721-4413 115 I
wshaffer@augusta.edu
SHAFFER,
William (Bill) .... 202-884-9135.. 94 A
shafferw@trinitydc.edu
SHAFFER LILIENTHAL,
Robin .... 641-844-5730 167 C
robin.lilienthal@iavalley.edu
SHAFFER LILIENTHAL,
Robin .... 641-844-5730 167 E
robin.lilienthal@iavalley.edu
SHAFFER-WALSH, Rory .631-687-2658 313 C
rshaffer-walsh@sjcny.edu
SHAFFETT, John .... 912-583-3230 116 D
jshaffett@bpc.edu
SHAFIZADEH, Kevan .916-278-6366.. 33 A
kevan@csus.edu
SHAFKOWITZ, Marshall 479-619-8600.. 20 G
mshafkowitz@nwacc.edu
SHAFTEL, Matthew ...... 740-593-1808 358 L
shaftel@ohio.edu
SHAGER, Dorian .... 765-658-4267 154 G
dshager@depauw.edu
SHAH, Avani .... 651-403-4132 240 E
avani.shah@saintpaul.edu
SHAH, Gaurav .... 781-891-3467 206 C
gshah@bentley.edu
SHAH, Kashif .... 708-974-5348 144 G
shah@morainevalley.edu
SHAH, Preyal .... 212-431-2357 308 I
pshah@nyls.edu
SHAH, Swapnal .... 800-280-0307 153 B
swapnal.shah@ace.edu
SHAH-GORDON, Ruta .. 718-420-4254 324 B
rshahgor@wagner.edu
SHAHEDIPOUR-SANDVIK,
Shadi .... 315-792-7100 320 F
sshahedipour-sandvik@sunypoly.edu
SHAHEDIPOUR-SANDVIK,
Shadi .... 518-320-1100 315 C
shadi.sandvik@suny.edu
SHAHEED-SONUBI,
Taheera .... 716-851-1773 299 A
shaheed@ecc.edu
SHAHEEN, Lisa .... 212-686-9244 289 G
SHAHID, Abdus .... 503-838-9331 377 C
shahida@wou.edu
SHAHID, Charles .... 937-376-6332 349 H
cshahid@centralstate.edu
SHAHID, Charles .... 937-376-6081 349 H
cshahid@centralstate.edu
SHAHID-BELLOT,
Robyn .... 857-701-1494 215 E
rshahid-bellot@rcc.mass.edu
SHAHIN, Hamdi .... 201-559-6076 277 A
shahinh@felician.edu
SHAHIN, Wisam .... 908-709-7024 283 E
wisam.shahin@ucc.edu
SHAHISAMAN,
Mohammad .... 951-493-6753.. 77 A
mshahisaman@yacollege.edu
SHAHRABI, Kamal ..... 585-475-2411 312 A
kxscada@rit.edu
SHAHROKHI, Hossein .. 713-221-8542 452 B
shahrokhi@uhd.edu
SHAIN, Daniel .... 856-225-6144 281 A
dshain@camden.rutgers.edu
SHAIN, Sue .... 978-556-3710 215 C
sshain@necc.mass.edu
SHAIN, Yeruchim .... 732-431-1600 283 C
taofnj@gmail.com
SHAKE, Miranda .... 217-709-0927 142 A
mshake@lakeviewcol.edu
SHAKESPEARE,
Christine .... 212-346-1200 310 F
SHAKIBA, Trevor ..... 918-333-6151 368 E
llittle@okwu.edu
SHAKIR, Salah .... 859-846-6248 183 G
sshakir@midway.edu

SHAKYA, Miroj .... 626-571-8811... 73 D
mirojs@uwest.edu
SHALHOUB, Robert .. 973-379-2044 379 D
finance@archpitt.org
SHALLEY, Heather ..... 312-329-4272 144 F
heather.shalley@moody.edu
SHALLO, Denisa .... 815-455-8726 143 F
dshallo@mchenry.edu
SHAMAH, Irwin .... 347-394-1036 291 B
ishamah@ateret.net
SHAMBARGER, Angela .207-221-4554 197 A
ashambarger@une.edu
SHAMBAUGH, Jeannine 330-363-6347 348 B
jeannine.shambaugh@aultman.com
SHAMBLIN, Mesha ... 304-710-3401 487 F
shamblinm@mctc.edu
SHAMBURGER,
Katherine .... 318-869-5280 186 C
kshamburger@centenary.edu
SHAMBURGER,
Kenyatta .... 501-370-5329... 21 A
kshamburger@philander.edu
SHAMES, Shauna ..... 856-225-2974 281 A
shauna.shames@rutgers.edu
SHAMS, Arian .... 714-300-0300... 65 E
ashams@scitech.edu
SHAMS, Nazila .... 714-300-0300... 65 E
nshams@scitech.edu
SHAMS, Parviz .... 714-300-0300... 65 E
pshams@scitech.edu
SHAMSUD-DIN, Ayasha 503-552-1608 374 B
ashamsud-din@nunm.edu
SHANAFELT, Rebecca .. 727-816-3288 105 E
shanafr@phsc.edu
SHANAHAN, Alanna ...... 215-898-9828 399 J
athdir@upenn.edu
SHANAHAN, Brian ..... 607-871-2144 289 E
shanahan@alfred.edu
SHANAHAN, Brian ..... 585-389-2473 307 D
bshanah0@naz.edu
SHANAHAN, Jenny ..... 508-531-2764 212 B
jshanahan@bridgew.edu
SHANAHAN, Kristina .... 706-295-6332 119 C
kshanaha@highlands.edu
SHANAHAN, Michael .. 805-965-0581... 62 M
SHANDA, Mark .. 859-257-1707 185 D
mark.shanda@uky.edu
SHANDERSON, Laurie .. 309-672-5515 143 I
lshanderson@methodistcol.edu
SHANDLEY, Emily .... 203-432-2337... 90 B
emily.shandley@yale.edu
SHANDLEY, Janet ... 206-296-5904 483 B
janshan@seattleu.edu
SHANDOR, Britnee .... 404-297-9522 119 G
SHANE, Suzanne .... 631-632-6110 316 D
suzanne.shane@stonybrook.edu
SHANER, Megan, C ...... 919-209-2201 335 D
mlshaner@johnstoncc.edu
SHANG, Ying .... 260-422-5561 156 A
yshang@indianatech.edu
SHANHOLTZ, Cathy .... 540-665-5561 470 A
cshanhol2@su.edu
SHANK, Christy .... 254-526-1291 431 E
christy.shank@ctcd.edu
SHANK, Derek .... 520-494-5527... 11 M
derek.shank@centralaz.edu
SHANK, Jennifer .... 931-372-3016 425 B
jshank@tntech.edu
SHANK, Matthew .... 703-284-1598 468 A
matthew.shank@marymount.edu
SHANK, Sherri .... 704-233-8025 344 E
s.shank@wingate.edu
SHANK, Steve .... 704-233-8691 344 E
sh.shank@wingate.edu
SHANK, Theresa, M ... 240-500-2476 199 A
tmshank@hagerstowncc.edu
SHANKER, Anil .... 615-327-6460 420 D
ashanker@mmc.edu
SHANKLE, Nicole .... 812-381-6002 162 E
nshankle@vinu.edu
SHANKLIN, Iris .... 404-756-4916 115 E
ishanklin@atlm.edu
SHANKMAN,
Kimberly, C .... 913-360-7413 171 G
kshankman@benedictine.edu
SHANKS, Alisa .... 303-963-3378... 78 D
ashanks@ccu.edu
SHANKS, Brian .... 512-245-2319 449 G
bs26@txstate.edu
SHANKS, Cindy .... 918-595-8291 370 B
cindy.shanks@tulsacc.edu
SHANLEY, OP, Brian, J 718-990-6301 313 B
pres@stjohns.edu

SHANMUGARATNAM,
Carol .... 781-283-2308 219 C
cshanmug@wellesley.edu
SHANNON, Crystal ..... 219-980-6961 157 A
crshanno@iun.edu
SHANNON, David .... 405-878-6000 367 B
david.shannon@okbu.edu
SHANNON, David, R .... 731-989-6001 418 H
dshannon@fhu.edu
SHANNON, Erin .... 217-353-2683 146 G
eshannon@parkland.edu
SHANNON, Henry, D ... 909-652-6100... 36 B
henry.shannon@chaffey.edu
SHANNON, John .... 260-665-4224 161 C
shannonj@trine.edu
SHANNON, Kelly .... 612-238-4515 242 H
kshannon@smumn.edu
SHANNON, Kim .... 864-388-8885 409 B
kshannon@lander.edu
SHANNON, Linda, A ..... 718-990-6578 313 B
shannonl@stjohns.edu
SHANNON, Michael ..... 404-894-4615 119 D
michael.shannon@gatech.edu
SHANNON, Nathan ..... 215-572-5511 401 G
nshannon@wts.edu
SHANNON, Peggy ..... 619-594-4464... 33 E
pshannon@sdsu.edu
SHANNON, S. Scott ..... 315-470-6537 319 A
sshannon@esf.edu
SHANNON, Sarah ..... 406-994-3784 263 G
sarah.shannon1@montana.edu
SHANNON, Susan, K .... 717-796-1800 389 F
sshannon@messiah.edu
SHANTON, David ..... 646-660-6067 292 F
david.shanton@baruch.cuny.edu
SHAO, Chris .... 254-968-1944 445 F
shao@tarleton.edu
SHAO, Lawrence .... 724-738-2093 394 E
lawrence.shao@sru.edu
SHAO, Rodrick .... 830-372-8000 448 C
rshao@tlu.edu
SHAO, Yu-Ling .... 410-704-4011 204 B
yulingshao@towson.edu
SHAPAZIAN, Heather .... 617-228-2298 214 A
hjshapaz@bhcc.edu
SHAPE, Ronald .... 605-721-5214 414 G
rshape@national.edu
SHAPIRO, Claire, R ...... 901-843-3750 422 C
shapiro@rhodes.edu
SHAPIRO, Dan .... 831-582-3878... 32 D
dshapiro@csumb.edu
SHAPIRO, David, W ...... 717-867-6060 388 A
shapiro@lvc.edu
SHAPIRO, Jeff .... 973-877-3142 276 G
shapiro@essex.edu
SHAPIRO, Joe .... 657-278-3724... 31 E
jbshapiro@fullerton.edu
SHAPIRO, Phil .... 207-602-2157 197 A
pshapiro@une.edu
SHAPIRO, Steven ..... 617-349-8458 210 H
sshapir3@lesley.edu
SHAPOVAL, Sandy ..... 918-270-6459 368 G
sandy.shapoval@ptstulsa.edu
SHAPPLEY, Ben .... 662-696-2312 247 D
bshappley@nemcc.edu
SHARAR, Scott .... 319-352-8318 170 F
scott.sharar@wartburg.edu
SHARBAUGH, Tim, L .... 724-357-3011 393 G
timothy.sharbaugh@iup.edu
SHARER, C. Gregory ..... 607-753-4721 317 D
greg.sharer@cortland.edu
SHARER, Mark .... 570-577-3914 379 A
mark.sharer@bucknell.edu
SHARIAT, Vahid .... 714-816-0366... 68 G
vahid.shariat@trident.edu
SHARIF, Zaki .... 937-376-6007 349 H
zsharif@centralstate.edu
SHARKEY, Brian .... 563-884-5306 169 C
brian.sharkey@palmer.edu
SHARKEY, Fredricka ..... 501-852-2659... 23 K
fsharkey@uca.edu
SHARKEY, Kevin .... 724-738-3333 394 E
kevin.sharkey@sru.edu
SHARMA, Gulshan ..... 409-772-2436 456 B
gusharma@utmb.edu
SHARMA, Malhar .... 203-576-2348... 89 A
msharma@bridgeport.edu
SHARMA, Pam .... 304-214-8891 487 J
psharma@wvncc.edu
SHARMA, Salil .... 626-350-1500... 28 H
SHARMA, Sanjay ..... 802-656-3175 462 D
sanjay.sharma@uvm.edu

SHARMA, Saroj .... 949-824-3235... 69 C
saroj.sharma@uci.edu
SHARMA, Sushil .... 903-334-6629 447 C
ssharma@tamut.edu
SHARMA,
Venkatanarayanan .... 973-720-2432 283 I
sharmav@wpunj.edu
SHARMAN, Kara .... 903-983-8102 437 G
ksharman@kilgore.edu
SHARNSKY, Brittany ..... 210-805-5832 452 I
sharnsky@uiwtx.edu
SHARON, Daniel ..... 914-632-5400 306 J
dsharon@monroecollege.edu
SHARP, Andrew .... 601-477-4198 246 A
andrew.sharp@jcjc.edu
SHARP, Chris .... 806-371-5008 428 F
chris.sharp@actx.edu
SHARP, David .... 870-245-5181... 20 H
sharpd@obu.edu
SHARP, Debbie .... 940-668-4213 439 I
dsharp@nctc.edu
SHARP, Deltha .... 870-612-2057... 23 B
deltha.sharp@uaccb.edu
SHARP, Donna .... 918-724-6444 365 B
sharpd@bacone.edu
SHARP, Jan, T .... 865-539-7182 424 C
jtsharp@pstcc.edu
SHARP, Jason .... 620-421-6700 175 D
jasons@labette.edu
SHARP, Jason, R .... 651-631-5045 243 E
jrsharp@unwsp.edu
SHARP, John .... 979-458-6000 445 D
chancellor@tamus.edu
SHARP, Jordan .... 559-453-7104... 43 D
jordan.sharp@fresno.edu
SHARP, Jordon .... 435-652-7544 459 G
jordon.sharp@utahtech.edu
SHARP, Kimberly ..... 601-925-3278 246 D
ksharp@mc.edu
SHARP, Kirk .... 620-223-2700 173 F
kirks@fortscott.edu
SHARP, Lara .... 413-755-4576 215 F
llsharp@stcc.edu
SHARP, Leslie .... 404-385-7590 119 D
leslie.sharp@gatech.edu
SHARP, Linda .... 573-876-7277 259 F
lsharp@stephens.edu
SHARP, Nick .... 417-690-2224 250 K
sharp@cofo.edu
SHARP, Nicole .... 812-749-1225 159 E
nsharp@oak.edu
SHARP, Randy .... 808-675-3499 128 B
randy.sharp@byuh.edu
SHARP, Valerie .... 417-865-2815 252 F
sharpv@evangel.edu
SHARP-MCHENRY,
Lepaine .... 617-521-2000 218 C
SHARPE, Allen .... 803-732-5211 409 E
sharpea@midlandstech.edu
SHARPE, Anna .... 706-233-4080 116 A
asharpe@berry.edu
SHARPE, Dolores ..... 810-762-5698 228 B
dolores.sharpe@mcc.edu
SHARPE, Jessica .... 336-272-7102 329 B
jessica.sharpe@greensboro.edu
SHARPE, Kelli .... 615-963-1232 425 A
SHARPE, Michael .... 912-358-3132 124 H
sharpem@savannahstate.edu
SHARPE, Norean, R ... 718-990-6800 313 B
sharpen@stjohns.edu
SHARPE, Paul .... 956-882-8221 455 A
paul.sharpe@utrgv.edu
SHARPE, Ron .... 989-275-5000 225 H
ron.sharpe@kirtland.edu
SHARPHORN, Dan ..... 512-499-4462 454 A
dsharphorn@utsystem.edu
SHARPLES, Stacey ..... 941-752-5256 109 C
sharpls@scf.edu
SHARPNACK, Patricia .. 440-684-6032 363 C
psharpnack@ursuline.edu
SHARRAR, Tricia .... 402-280-4076 265 J
sharrar@creighton.edu
SHARRARD, Aurora .. 412-624-5122 400 A
asharrard@pitt.edu
SHARRATT, Emily .... 541-962-3866 372 H
esharratt@eou.edu
SHATTUCK, Anne ..... 603-862-2415 273 H
anne.shattuck@unh.edu
SHATTUCK, Larry ..... 410-532-5551 201 C
lshattuck@ndm.edu
SHATTUCK, Leslie ..... 425-739-8236 480 D
leslie.shattuck@lwtech.edu

SHAUB, Larry .... 610-796-5600 378 C
larry.shaub@alvernia.edu
SHAUGHNESSY, Anne ... 617-824-8525 208 G
anne_shaughnessy@emerson.edu
SHAUGHNESSY, Joseph 781-768-7133 217 H
joseph.shaughnessy@regiscollege.edu
SHAUGHNESSY, Josette 915-831-6330 435 B
jshaugh2@epcc.edu
SHAULIS, Maria .... 712-560-7414 163 H
maria.shaulis@briarcliff.edu
SHAUNAK, Sudershan .. 760-757-2121.. 52 G
sshaunak@miracosta.edu
SHAVER, Bryan, D .... 304-293-6600 489 E
bryan.shaver@mail.wvu.edu
SHAVER, Deborah .... 208-885-4627 132 C
dshaver@uidaho.edu
SHAVER, Joseph, E .... 304-326-1481 486 I
jshaver@salemu.edu
SHAVER, Savannah .... 704-637-4394 327 H
smshaver15@catawba.edu
SHAW, Anne, C .... 910-938-6322 333 D
shawa@coastalcarolina.edu
SHAW, Arnitria .... 309-694-5561 138 I
arnitria.shaw@icc.edu
SHAW, Becky .... 413-585-4940 218 D
rshaw@smith.edu
SHAW, Bobbi .... 816-584-6202 257 E
bobbi.shaw@park.edu
SHAW, Carolyn .... 316-978-3010 178 B
carolyn.shaw@wichita.edu
SHAW, Carolyn .... 661-362-3482.. 38 H
carolyn.shaw@canyons.edu
SHAW, Carrie .... 970-943-3085.. 85 B
cshaw@western.edu
SHAW, Carrie .... 425-235-2415 482 C
cshaw@rtc.edu
SHAW, Chester .... 708-974-5360 144 G
schawc6@morainevalley.edu
SHAW, Chris .... 972-780-3600 453 C
christopher.shaw@untdallas.edu
SHAW, Dameon .... 662-254-3790 247 C
dameon.shaw@mvsu.edu
SHAW, David .... 662-325-3742 247 A
david.shaw@msstate.edu
SHAW, D'Wayne .... 903-983-8130 437 G
dshaw@kilgore.edu
SHAW, Jack .... 304-876-5496 489 A
jshaw@shepherd.edu
SHAW, Jaclyn .... 210-458-6859 455 B
jaclyn.shaw@utsa.edu
SHAW, Jason .... 325-793-4882 439 A
shaw.jason@mcm.edu
SHAW, Jeffrey, L .... 314-340-3632 253 E
shawj@hssu.edu
SHAW, Jen .... 352-588-7096 107 B
jen.shaw@saintleo.edu
SHAW, Jerone .... 662-621-4085 244 E
jshaw@coahomacc.edu
SHAW, Karen, A .... 585-262-1501 306 K
kshaw@monroecc.edu
SHAW, Karen, L .... 423-652-4798 419 F
klshaw@king.edu
SHAW, Ken .... 423-236-2800 422 H
shawk@southern.edu
SHAW, Kerrie, S .... 757-446-5841 465 H
shawks@evms.edu
SHAW, Kristi 620-441-5206 172M
kristi.shaw@cowley.edu
SHAW, Linda .... 415-239-3303.. 37 C
lshaw@ccsf.edu
SHAW, Lisa-Anne .... 954-322-1612.. 99 E
SHAW, Matthew .... 765-285-5277 153 E
mcshaw2@bsu.edu
SHAW, Melissa .... 706-295-2912 119 F
mshaw@gntc.edu
SHAW, Nicole .... 940-668-7731 439 I
SHAW, JR., Richard, H . 650-723-2300.. 66 D
SHAW, Rick .... 661-722-6300.. 26 E
rshaw@avc.edu
SHAW, Robert, S .... 570-348-6245 389 B
rsshaw@marywood.edu
SHAW, Suzanne .... 417-836-5139 255 J
suzanneshaw@missouristate.edu
SHAW, Timothy .... 972-883-5291 454 D
tim.shaw@utdallas.edu
SHAW, Tina .... 256-378-2010.... 1 G
tshaw5@cacc.edu
SHAW, Vickie .... 912-478-5468 120 A
vshaw@georgiasouthern.edu
SHAW HORTON,
Sheilah .... 781-283-2322 219 C
shorton2@wellesley.edu
SHAW-NEVINS, Andrea . 954-262-8208 104M
andrshaw@nova.edu
SHAW THOMAS, Amy ... 512-499-4257 454 A
athomas@utsystem.edu
SHAWANOKASIC,
Norman .... 800-567-2344 491 C
nshawanokasic@menominee.edu
SHAWCROFT, Sally .... 970-542-3151.. 81M
sally.shawcroft@morgancc.edu
SHAWHAN, Jordan .... 906-487-7348 223 I
SHAWN, Donna, S .... 913-627-4171 174 H
dshawn@kckcc.edu
SHAWNEY, Lisa .... 978-921-4242 216 F
lisa.shawney@montserrat.edu
SHAWVER, Jeffrey .... 304-647-6325 489 C
jshawver@osteo.wvsom.edu
SHAWVER, Todd .... 570-389-5297 393 E
tshawver@bloomu.edu
SHAY, Lisa .... 212-353-4309 297 C
lisa.shay@cooper.edu
SHAY, William .... 323-563-4840.. 36 E
williamshay@cdrewu.edu
SHAYLER, Todd .... 517-629-0305 220 E
tmshayler@albion.edu
SHCHEGOL, Alex .... 718-522-9073 290 B
SHEA, Bob .... 336-334-5200 342 D
r_shea@uncg.edu
SHEA, Catherine .... 303-492-7896.. 83M
catherine.shea@colorado.edu
SHEA, Diane .... 617-732-1604 209 A
shead@emmanuel.edu
SHEA, James, P .... 701-355-8100 347 A
SHEA, Karen .... 207-893-7733 195 I
kshea@sjcme.edu
SHEA, Kevin, J .... 617-552-3252 207 A
k.shea@bc.edu
SHEA, McKennon .... 336-841-9856 329 E
mckennon@highpoint.edu
SHEA, Rich, J .... 814-886-6474 390 E
rshea@mtaloy.edu
SHEA, Robert .... 617-243-2426 210 G
rshea@lasell.edu
SHEA, Rose .... 508-793-2011 208 A
SHEA, Staci .... 781-768-7000 217 H
staci.shea@regiscollege.edu
SHEAHAN, Thomas, C .. 617-373-2000 217 D
SHEALEY, Monika .... 856-256-5440 280 H
shealey@rowan.edu
SHEAN, Andy .... 770-729-8400 115 A
SHEAR, Stephen .... 813-253-7014 102 A
sshear2@hccfl.edu
SHEARD, Reed, L .... 805-565-7171.. 75 I
rsheard@westmont.edu
SHEARER, Jonathan ...... 630-617-6146 137 E
jonathan.shearer@elmhurst.edu
SHEARER, Liz .... 410-704-2451 204 B
lshearer@towson.edu
SHEARER, Pam .... 601-318-6561 249 B
pshearer@wmcarey.edu
SHEARES ASHBY,
Valerie .... 410-455-2274 202 G
president@umbc.edu
SHEARON, Randall .... 919-739-7029 338 F
shearon@waynecc.edu
SHEARS, III, George ...... 704-334-6882 327 J
gshears@charlottechristian.edu
SHEARS, Mitchell .... 601-979-2321 245 G
mitchell.m.shears@jsums.edu
SHEARS, Stacey .... 510-981-2820.. 56 J
sshears@peralta.edu
SHEATHER, Simon, J .... 859-257-8939 185 D
simon.sheather@uky.edu
SHEATS, Karen, A .... 302-356-6867.. 91 C
karen.a.sheats@wilmu.edu
SHEBLE, Mary Ann .... 248-232-4512 228 H
masheble@oaklandcc.edu
SHEDD, Dawn .... 281-998-6150 442 C
dawn.shedd@sjcd.edu
SHEDD, Jessica .... 504-314-2898 191 D
jshedd@tulane.edu
SHEDD, Louis .... 205-391-2359.... 3 E
lshedd@sheltonstate.edu
SHEDLETSKY, Nikki .... 502-585-9911 184 E
nshedletsky@spalding.edu
SHEDRICK, Karen, R ..... 601-877-6111 244 B
karen@alcorn.edu
SHEEHAN, Heather .... 701-224-5465 345 F
heather.sheehan@bismarckstate.edu
SHEEHAN, Jaime .... 657-278-3040.. 31 E
jsheehan@fullerton.edu
SHEEHAN, John .... 260-399-7700 162 A
jsheehan@sf.edu
SHEEHAN, Kimberly ...... 419-824-3826 355 C
ksheehan@lourdes.edu
SHEEHAN, Meaghan ...... 617-984-1700 217 G
SHEEHAN, Mike .... 530-752-0339.. 69 A
mtsheehan@ucdavis.edu
SHEEHAN, Patricia .... 617-353-4720 207 C
sheehanp@bu.edu
SHEEHAN, Patrick .... 608-262-3927 494 D
patrick.sheehan@wisc.edu
SHEEHAN, Ryan .... 570-941-6480 400 C
ryan.sheehan@scranton.edu
SHEEHAN, Stephanie .... 423-236-2373 422 H
ssheehan@southern.edu
SHEEHAN, Tim .... 801-957-2001 460 D
tim.scheehan@slcc.edu
SHEEHAN, William .... 660-248-6214 250 H
wsheehan@centralmethodist.edu
SHEEHY, Clark .... 417-328-1785 258 K
csheehy@sbuniv.edu
SHEEHY, Colette .... 434-924-3349 471 F
cc@virginia.edu
SHEEHY, Connor .... 207-755-5273 194 J
csheehy@cmcc.edu
SHEEHY, Matthew .... 781-736-4642 207 D
sheehy@brandeis.edu
SHEEHY, Rich .... 914-694-2200 305 A
SHEEKS, Gina .... 706-507-8730 117 E
sheeks_gina@columbusstate.edu
SHEELER, Kristina, H .... 317-278-3161 157 B
ksheeler@iupui.edu
SHEELEY, Jonathan .... 920-206-2395 492 C
jonathan.sheeley@mbu.edu
SHEELEY, Megan .... 845-688-1946 322 K
sheeleym@sunyulster.edu
SHEER, Lauren .... 512-609-8046 456 B
lesheer@utmb.edu
SHEERAN, Robert, M ..... 513-745-2072 364 F
sheeran@xavier.edu
SHEERAZI, Saji .... 718-281-5144 295 B
ssheerazi@qcc.cuny.edu
SHEESLEY, Debra, K ..... 717-361-1492 383 B
sheesleyd@etown.edu
SHEESLEY, Erica .... 716-664-5100 302 F
ericasheesley@jbc.edu
SHEETS, Amanda .... 419-755-9041 357 B
asheets@ncstatecollege.edu
SHEETS, Helene .... 419-824-3965 355 C
hsheets@lourdes.edu
SHEETS, James .... 617-745-3832 208 F
james.sheets@enc.edu
SHEETS, Julie .... 573-518-2262 255 G
jsheets@mineralarea.edu
SHEETS, Tamara .... 740-351-3207 360 E
tsheets@shawnee.edu
SHEETS, Tammy .... 276-944-6117 466 F
tsheets@ehc.edu
SHEETZ, Kraig, E .... 301-447-5535 201 A
k.e.sheetz@msmary.edu
SHEETZ, Ruth .... 717-871-7884 394 B
ruth.sheetz@millersville.edu
SHEETZ, Tracey .... 724-938-4404 394 C
sheetz@calu.edu
SHEETZ, Tracey .... 724-503-1001 401 D
tsheetz@washjeff.edu
SHEFCHIK, Thomas, J .. 920-433-4306 490 H
thomas.shefchik@bellincollege.edu
SHEFET, Oren .... 516-876-3053 318 A
shefeto@oldwestbury.edu
SHEFFIELD, Bethany, D 814-641-3101 386 E
sheffib@juniata.edu
SHEFFIELD,
Christopher, R .... 716-286-8405 309 F
crs@niagara.edu
SHEFFIELD, Jenna .... 336-721-2619 339 H
jenna.sheffield@salem.edu
SHEFFIELD, Lindsey ...... 251-460-6052.... 9 A
bsheffield@southalabama.edu
SHEFFIELD, Mary .... 308-630-6571 269 E
sheffie6@wncc.edu
SHEFFIELD, Tracey .... 504-762-3031 187 I
tsheff@dcc.edu
SHEFFIELD, Vonne .... 478-301-2500 122 C
sheffield_v@mercer.edu
SHEFMAN, Pamela .... 281-283-3061 452 A
shefman@uhcl.edu
SHEFTON, Elizabeth ...... 843-661-1210 408 H
eshefton@fmarion.edu
SHEHATA, Erika .... 610-399-2053 393 D
eshehata@cheyney.edu
SHEHDAN, David .... 919-934-3051 335 D
SHEHEANE, Dene .... 404-385-1354 119 D
sheheane@gatech.edu
SHEHEE, Amy .... 704-687-0301 342 C
ashehee@uncc.edu
SHEHU, Katelyn, L .... 651-962-6142 243 F
sheh9359@stthomas.edu
SHEIKH, Ammad .... 540-464-7560 475 C
sheikhas@vmi.edu
SHEIL, Astrid .... 540-545-7253 470 A
asheil@su.edu
SHEILLEY, Holly .... 859-233-8548 185 A
hsheilley@transy.edu
SHEIN, David .... 845-758-7454 290 G
shein@bard.edu
SHEKHAR, Anantha .... 412-648-8975 400 A
as1@pitt.edu
SHELANGOSKIE, Susan 517-264-7667 230 C
sshelang@sienaheights.edu
SHELBURNE, Nathan ..... 254-710-7240 430 F
nathan_shelburne@baylor.edu
SHELBY, Aaron .... 765-361-6488 162 G
shelbya@wabash.edu
SHELBY, Dorie, A .... 517-750-1200 230 F
dshelby@arbor.edu
SHELBY, Jane .... 907-786-4708.. 10 A
njshelby@alaska.edu
SHELBY, Kristin .... 618-634-3240 149 C
kristins@shawneecc.edu
SHELBY, Paula .... 803-705-4809 405 G
paula.shelby@benedict.edu
SHELBY, Robert .... 812-488-5268 161 E
rs262@evansville.edu
SHELDAHL, Tania .... 928-776-2128.. 17 B
tania.sheldahl@yc.edu
SHELDON, Al .... 541-956-7440 375 G
asheldon@roguecc.edu
SHELDON, Debbie, L ..... 906-487-3112 227 D
dlassila@mtu.edu
SHELDON, Jane .... 308-865-8427 268 J
sheldonj@unk.edu
SHELDON, Karen .... 859-371-9393 179 C
ksheldon@beckfield.edu
SHELDON, Michael .... 207-221-4591 197 A
msheldon@une.edu
SHELDON, Richard .... 212-774-0778 305 D
rsheldon@mmm.edu
SHELDON, Todd .... 402-363-5601 269 F
tlsheldon@york.edu
SHELL, Chandrea .... 423-461-8756 421 E
chshell@milligan.edu
SHELL, Christina .... 734-487-2382 223 F
cshell@emich.edu
SHELL, Martin .... 650-723-4186.. 66 D
mshell@stanford.edu
SHELL, Michael .... 502-213-2184 181 H
michael.shell@kctcs.edu
SHELLA, Andrew .... 419-559-2450 361 B
ashella01@terra.edu
SHELLABARGER,
Heather .... 937-529-2201 361 F
hshellabarger@united.edu
SHELLABARGER,
Roxanne .... 423-648-2416 422 D
rshellabarger@richmont.edu
SHELLAWAY, Ruby, Z ... 615-322-5155 427 B
ruby.shellaway@vanderbilt.edu
SHELLBERG, David .... 541-278-5850 371 G
dshellberg@bluecc.edu
SHELLEDY, David, C ..... 210-567-8850 455 E
shelledyy@uthscsa.edu
SHELLEY, Camille .... 914-674-7131 305 H
cshelley@mercy.edu
SHELLEY, Jennifer .... 812-866-7091 155 D
shelley@hanover.edu
SHELLEY, Jennifer, A .... 812-941-2280 157 D
jashelle@iu.edu
SHELLEY, Joseph .... 315-859-4169 300 F
jshelley@hamilton.edu
SHELLEY, MargE .... 913-469-8500 174 F
mshelley@jccc.edu
SHELLEY, Marshall .... 303-762-6919.. 80 G
marshall.shelley@denverseminary.edu
SHELLEY, Melanie .... 405-208-5982 367 E
mshelley@okcu.edu
SHELLEY, Staci .... 352-588-7560 107 B
staci.shelley@saintleo.edu
SHELLEY, Staci .... 866-492-5336 243 G
staci.shelley@laureate.net
SHELLLEY, Joe .... 315-859-4169 300 F
jshelley@hamilton.edu
SHELMERDINE,
Kathleen .... 239-687-5300.. 95 L
SHELNUTT, Sarah .... 913-234-0672 172 I
sarah.shelnutt@cleveland.edu
SHELPMAN, JR., David . 561-586-0121 101 P

SHELSTAD, Kyle 612-351-0631 235 I kshelstad@ipr.edu
SHELTON, Alexa 860-215-9000.. 87 D
SHELTON, Alice 317-955-6022 159 A ashelton@marian.edu
SHELTON, Austin 671-735-2918 503 E shelton@uog.edu
SHELTON, Brad 541-346-2090 376 G shelton@uoregon.edu
SHELTON, Charlita 509-313-4356 479 E sheltonc@gonzaga.edu
SHELTON, Cheryl 810-762-0553 228 B cheryl.shelton@edtech.mcc.edu
SHELTON, Christie 256-782-5540... 6 A cshelton@jsu.edu
SHELTON, Courtney 800-280-0307 153 B courtney.shelton@ace.edu
SHELTON, Courtney 864-278-6281 411 F sheltonc@smcsc.edu
SHELTON, Cynthia 901-435-1674 419 I cynthia_shelton@loc.edu
SHELTON, Edward 636-649-5807 252 D edward.shelton@eastcentral.edu
SHELTON, Garrett, L 757-683-4848 468 C gshelton@odu.edu
SHELTON, Joey 601-974-1226 246 C sheltonjj@millsaps.edu
SHELTON, Julie 931-363-9895 426 F jshelt48@utsouthern.edu
SHELTON, Julie 205-348-7917.... 7 G jshelton@fa.ua.edu
SHELTON, Kristi 217-228-5432 147 C sheltkr@quincy.edu
SHELTON, Leslie 281-649-3306 436 D lshelton@hbu.edu
SHELTON, Marc 503-554-2869 372 I mshelton@georgefox.edu
SHELTON, Mark 508-793-2371 208 A mshelton@holycross.edu
SHELTON, Michelle 610-499-4239 401 I mmshelton@widener.edu
SHELTON, Myles 409-944-1200 435 F mshelton@gc.edu
SHELTON, Nellie, R 864-833-8213 410 E nshelton@presby.edu
SHELTON, Patricia 503-375-7020 372 G pshelton@corban.edu
SHELTON, Rick 315-792-7100 320 F richard.shelton@sunypoly.edu
SHELTON, Robby 931-363-9890 426 F rshelt19@utsouthern.edu
SHELTON, Ryan 219-980-6793 157 A rydshelt@iun.edu
SHELTON, Shawna 509-533-4566 478 E shawna.shelton@sfcc.spokane.edu
SHELTON, Terri, L 336-256-0232 342 D shelton@uncg.edu
SHELTON, Tina 773-896-2400 134 K
SHELTON, TJ 216-368-2000 349 B tes123@case.edu
SHEMMER, Rosalie 312-899-5100 149 B
SHEMTOV, Ellie 914-893-4030 288 K librarian@ajr.edu
SHEMWELL, Bridget 870-762-3174.. 17 F bshemwell@smail.anc.edu
SHEMWELL, James 870-762-3191.. 17 F jshemwell@smail.anc.edu
SHEN, Chi 502-597-6083 183 A chi.shen@kysu.edu
SHEN, Mark 626-571-5110.. 48 I mys2016@les.edu
SHEN-AUSTIN, Christina 202-250-2419.. 92 B christina.shen-austin@gallaudet.edu
SHENBERGER, Amy 940-565-2354 453 B amy.shenberger@unt.edu
SHENETTE, John 336-758-5000 344 A shenetjj@wfu.edu
SHENETTE, John 336-758-4623 344 A shenettj@wfu.edu
SHENK, Hans 740-857-1311 360 C hshenk@rosedale.edu
SHENNAN, Andrew 781-283-3583 219 C ashennan@wellesley.edu
SHENNOY, Anitha 559-325-3600.. 28 F ashennoy@chsu.edu
SHENODA, Matthew 401-454-6444 404 B mshenoda@risd.edu
SHEPARD, Anne 301-546-7527 201 D sheparaf@pgcc.edu
SHEPARD, Barry 412-809-5338 395 F shepard.barry@ptcollege.edu
SHEPARD, Brian 408-498-5135.. 73 A bshepard@cogswell.edu
SHEPARD, Jenni 706-865-2134 126 D jshepard@truett.edu
SHEPARD, Jeremy 617-217-9218 206 A jshepard@baystate.edu
SHEPARD, Joseph 575-538-6238 288 J joseph.shepard@wnmu.edu
SHEPARD, Kathy, J 717-728-2261 380 D kathyshepard@centralpenn.edu
SHEPARD, Kirsten 800-686-1883 222 B kshepard@cleary.edu
SHEPARD, Nicole 912-583-3298 116 D nshepard@bpc.edu
SHEPARD, Thom 650-433-3814.. 55 K tshepard@paloaltou.edu
SHEPARD, William 734-487-0296 223 F bill.shepard@emich.edu
SHEPARD RAWLINS, Cindy 540-231-5419 466 E crawlins@vcom.vt.edu
SHEPARDSON, J. Andrew 781-891-2161 206 C ashepardson@bentley.edu
SHEPELOV, Sergey 503-491-7411 373 H sergey.shepelov@mhcc.edu
SHEPHARD, Landon, P 407-582-4877 113 C lshephard@valenciacollege.edu
SHEPHERD, Janet 319-208-5053 169 I jshepherd@scciowa.edu
SHEPHERD, Jennifer, A 603-646-2223 272 F jennifer.a.shepherd@dartmouth.edu
SHEPHERD, Jerry 765-677-1903 157 F jerry.shepherd@indwes.edu
SHEPHERD, Justin 404-727-0692 118 D justin.shepherd@emory.edu
SHEPHERD, Karen 510-845-5373.. 29 D
SHEPHERD, Katharine 802-656-3424 462 D katharine.shepherd@uvm.edu
SHEPHERD, Kirby 903-586-2518 437 D
SHEPHERD, Lewis 870-245-5302.. 20 H shepherdl@obu.edu
SHEPHERD, Margaret 206-399-1496 484 A mshep@uw.edu
SHEPHERD, Misty 407-823-2339 110 D misty.shepherd@ucf.edu
SHEPHERD, Sara 252-334-2010 331 C sara.shepherd@macuniversity.edu
SHEPHERD, Stacy 318-371-3035 188 C stacyshepherd@nltcc.edu
SHEPHERD, Steve 417-690-2569 250 K shepherd@cofo.edu
SHEPHERD, Sue 330-363-6347 348 B admissions@aultmancollege.edu
SHEPPARD, Andy 229-226-1621 126 B asheppard@thomasu.edu
SHEPPARD, Anna 218-935-0417 244 A anna.sheppard@wetcc.edu
SHEPPARD, Deana 903-510-2261 451 D deana.sheppard@tjc.edu
SHEPPARD, Kirsten 865-273-8991 420 C kirsten.sheppard@maryvillecollege.edu
SHEPPARD, Matt 952-446-4190 235 B
SHEPPARD, Ray 910-879-5542 332 B rsheppard@bladencc.edu
SHEPSON, Paul 631-632-8781 316 D paul.shepson@stonybrook.edu
SHEPTAK, Juliann 724-287-8711 379 C julie.sheptak@bc3.edu
SHER, Anna 831-459-4302.. 71 A asher@ucsc.edu
SHER, Ephraim, Y 845-434-5240 326 G esher@ygzm.edu
SHERADIN, Pamela 315-364-3260 324 E psheradin@wells.edu
SHERAM, Norma 903-675-6211 451 C nsheram@tvcc.edu
SHERAR, Megan 419-289-5943 347 H msherar@ashland.edu
SHERBEYN, Aaron 217-234-5253 141 H asherbeyn@lakelandcollege.edu
SHERBURNE, Gwen 651-523-2804 235 F gsherburne@hamline.edu
SHERER, Sara 330-823-2761 362 E sherersj@mountunion.edu
SHERER, Todd 404-727-5550 118 D ttshere@emory.edu
SHERF, Thomas 215-702-4848 379 F tsherf@cairn.edu
SHERFESEE, Kimberly, B 843-349-2138 407 B ksherf@coastal.edu
SHERIDAN, Andrea 512-475-6089 454 C andrea.sheridan@austin.utexas.edu
SHERIDAN, Chris 216-368-2774 349 B chris.sheridan@case.edu
SHERIDAN, Kevin, P 262-243-5700 491 E kevin.sheridan@cuw.edu
SHERIDAN, Mark 806-742-1832 450 C mark.sheridan@ttu.edu
SHERIDAN, Terence 334-387-3877.... 4 C terencesheridan@amridgeuniversity.edu
SHERIDAN, Tricia 850-484-1796 105 G tkruse@pensacolastate.edu
SHERIFF, Brad 573-651-2570 258 J bsheriff@semo.edu
SHERIFF, Christopher 717-728-2433 380 D christophersheriff@centralpenn.edu
SHERIFF, Omar 708-596-2000 149 D osheriff@ssc.edu
SHERIFF, Sarah, M 717-245-1787 382 B sheriffs@dickinson.edu
SHERKAWY, Yasser 281-495-0078 436 G
SHERLIN, Joe, H 423-439-4210 418 D sherlin@etsu.edu
SHERLOCK, Rick 419-448-2171 353 D rsherloc@heidelberg.edu
SHERMAN, Alison 401-709-8417 404 B asherman@risd.edu
SHERMAN, Ann 530-898-6231.. 31 A asherman@csuchico.edu
SHERMAN, Brian 318-798-4117 189 E brian.sherman@lsus.edu
SHERMAN, Courtney 920-465-2033 494 F shermanc@uwgb.edu
SHERMAN, Curt 402-643-7369 265 I curt.sherman@cune.edu
SHERMAN, Daniel 713-500-3270 455 D daniel.sherman@uth.tmc.edu
SHERMAN, Douglas, H 401-739-5000 403 F dsherman@neit.edu
SHERMAN, Erin, L 210-486-4932 428 A esherman6@alamo.edu
SHERMAN, Glen 973-720-2761 283 I shermang@wpunj.edu
SHERMAN, Heather 610-921-2381 377 F
SHERMAN, Holly 507-433-0606 240 A holly.sherman@riverland.edu
SHERMAN, Hugh 740-593-1804 358 L president@ohio.edu
SHERMAN, James 518-564-3824 318 C sher9195@plattsburgh.edu
SHERMAN, Jeffrey 660-248-6390 250 H jsherm01@centralmethodist.edu
SHERMAN, Jennifer 719-549-3362.. 82 I jennifer.sherman@pueblocc.edu
SHERMAN, Jill 502-895-3411 183 E jsherman@lpts.edu
SHERMAN, Joshua 817-722-1647 437 H joshua.sherman@tku.edu
SHERMAN, JR 239-489-9414 100 G j.r.sherman@fsw.edu
SHERMAN, Julee 660-248-6203 250 H jsherman@centralmethodist.edu
SHERMAN, Lori Ann 906-524-8414 225 G lsherman@kbocc.edu
SHERMAN, Malia 559-278-6777.. 31 D msherman@csufresno.edu
SHERMAN, Mike 330-941-7281 364 G msherman02@ysu.edu
SHERMAN, Moshe 212-463-0400 322 C michael.sherman2@touro.edu
SHERMAN, Peter 218-477-2667 239 A peter.sherman@mnstate.edu
SHERMAN, Peter 970-943-3000.. 85 B psherman@western.edu
SHERMAN, Renee 207-621-3041 196 E renee.sherman@maine.edu
SHERMAN, Robin 207-581-5401 196 D robin.sherman@maine.edu
SHERMAN, Rush 502-863-8000 180 E
SHERMAN, Rush 502-585-9911 184 E rsherman@spalding.edu
SHERMAN, Scott 503-375-7044 372 G ssherman@corban.edu
SHERMAN, Sherry 828-766-1317 335 G ssherman@mayland.edu
SHERMAN, Stasia 660-248-6239 250 H ssherman@centralmethodist.edu
SHERMAN, Suzanne 941-487-4225 110 C sherman@ncf.edu
SHERMAN, Suzette 505-424-2309 285 H suzette.sherman@iaia.edu
SHERMAN, Timothy 770-612-2170.. 93 H
SHERMAN HECKLER, Wendy, R 614-823-1556 359 G wshermanheckler@otterbein.edu
SHERR, Karin, K 619-961-4240.. 68 A ksherr@tjsl.edu
SHERRICK, Rebecca, L 630-844-5476 133 A sherrick@aurora.edu
SHERRILL, Andrea 270-745-5360 186 A andrea.sherrill@wku.edu
SHERRILL, Audrey 704-922-6217 334 E sherrill.audrey@gaston.edu
SHERRILL, Erin 404-504-1993 123 G esherrill@oglethorpe.edu
SHERRILL, Jason 517-607-2564 224 G jsherrill@hillsdale.edu
SHERRILL, Mary Ellen 828-328-1741 330 B maryellen.sherrill@lr.edu
SHERRILL, Regina, B 256-765-4705.... 8 E rbsherrill@una.edu
SHERRILL, Zach 405-789-7661 369 H zachary.sherrill@swcu.edu
SHERROD, Jeff 615-879-2022 419 C
SHERROD, Jeffrey 615-879-2022 419 C
SHERROD, Marc 918-836-6886 370 A marc.sherrod@spartan.edu
SHERROD, Marc 815-965-8616 147 I
SHERROD, Shalunda 256-726-7340.... 6 C ssherrod@oakwood.edu
SHERRON, Catherine 859-344-3387 184 G catherine.sherron@thomasmore.edu
SHERRY, Rebecca 815-802-8830 141 B rsherry@kcc.edu
SHERRY, Suzanne 804-706-5201 473 B ssherry@jtcc.edu
SHERSTAD, Brian, P 616-538-2330 224 B bsherstad@gracechristian.edu
SHERWOOD, David, G 262-646-6534 493 F dsherwood@nashotah.edu
SHERWOOD, Emily, S 574-807-7023 153 G emily.sherwood@betheluniversity.edu
SHERWOOD, Jim 978-934-3313 211 G james_sherwood@uml.edu
SHERWOOD, Kim 316-322-3227 172 B ksherwood@butlercc.edu
SHERWOOD, Mary Frances 337-421-6926 188 H mary.sherwood@sowela.edu
SHERWOOD, Sarah, K 508-767-7343 205 F sk.sherwood@assumption.edu
SHERWOOD, Scott, J 719-884-5000.. 82 A sjsherwood@nbc.edu
SHERWOOD, Timothy 443-412-2244 199 B sherwota@harford.edu
SHERZER, Melinda 515-271-1461 165 C melinda.miller@dmu.edu
SHETH, Ruchi 972-721-5395 451 E rsheth@udallas.edu
SHETH, Sam 540-373-2200 465 G ssheth@evcc.edu
SHETLEY, Shane 620-862-5252 171 E
SHETTY, Devdas 202-274-5220.. 94 B devdas.shetty@udc.edu
SHEUCRAFT, Derrek, G 615-353-3272 424 A derrek.sheucraft@nscc.edu
SHEVCHUK, Angela 651-846-1477 240 E angela.shevchuk@saintpaul.edu
SHEVLIN, Katie 434-924-4159 471 F khr7f@virginia.edu
SHEW, Rick 828-759-4635 332 E rshew@cccti.edu
SHEWMAKER, Jennifer 325-674-2700 427 G jws02b@acu.edu
SHEWMAKER, Stephen 325-674-2317 427 G sbs02a@acu.edu
SHEYBANI, Shayan 678-331-4571 122 A shayan.sheybani@life.edu
SHI, Charlie 925-685-1230.. 40 H cshi@dvc.edu
SHIAVO, Donna 508-531-2106 212 B dschiavo@bridgew.edu
SHIBATA, Keri Kei 574-631-5559 161 G kshibata@nd.edu
SHIBER, Cheryl 908-709-7511 283 E cheryl.shiber@ucc.edu
SHIBLEY, Robert, G 716-829-3981 315 F rshibley@buffalo.edu
SHIDELER, Lorri, P 814-641-3605 386 E shidell@juniata.edu
SHIDEMANTLE, Ronald 304-327-4096 488 J rshidemantle@bluefieldstate.edu
SHIEH, Charles 863-683-2975 113 E shiehcs@webber.edu
SHIELDS, Christa 414-382-6000 490 G

SHORT, Brian .... 608-246-6055 497 I
bpshort@madisoncollege.edu
SHORT, Curt .... 773-380-6780 133 C
SHORT, JR., David ...... 409-880-8060 449 B
david.short@lamar.edu
SHORT, Emily .... 615-230-3441 424 F
emily.short@volstate.edu
SHORT, Jeffery .... 931-393-1590 423 G
jshort@mscc.edu
SHORT, Jeremy .... 440-826-2908 348 C
jshort@bw.edu
SHORT, John .... 301-687-4068 203 F
jtshort@frostburg.edu
SHORT, Kristi .... 919-718-7426 333 A
kshort@cccc.edu
SHORT, Kyla .... 918-343-7792 369 A
kshort@rsu.edu
SHORT, Liz .... 304-829-7281 486 B
lshort@bethanywv.edu
SHORT, Lora Beth .... 229-217-4135 125 G
lshort@southernregional.edu
SHORT, Mark .... 704-330-6689 333 B
mark.short@cpcc.edu
SHORT, Matt .... 918-293-5222 368 B
matt.short@okstate.edu
SHORT, Paula, M .... 713-743-5227 451 F
pmshort@uh.edu
SHORT, Rosanna .... 623-935-8941.. 13 C
rosanna.short@estrellamountain.edu
SHORT, William .... 407-646-2619 106 L
wshort@rollins.edu
SHORTBULL,
Thomas, H .... 605-455-6022 414 H
tshortb@olc.edu
SHORTER, Shavonne ..... 540-654-1213 471 B
sshorter@umw.edu
SHORTHILL, Berkeley .... 530-226-4980.. 64 C
bshorthill@simpsonu.edu
SHORTT, Pamela .... 336-734-7224 334 D
pshortt@forsythtech.edu
SHOSTACK, Michelle ..... 848-932-7167 281 B
shostack@rutgers.edu
SHOTTS, Gary .... 614-885-5585 359 K
gshotts@pcj.edu
SHOTTS, Lesley .... 256-551-5206.... 2 E
lesley.shotts@drakestate.edu
SHOUBA, Derek .... 219-473-4305 154 A
dshouba@ccsj.edu
SHOULSON, Jeffrey ...... 860-486-4037.. 89 B
jeffrey.shoulson@uconn.edu
SHOUN, Stan .... 314-286-4807 257 H
shshoun@ranken.edu
SHOUP, Angela .... 214-905-3001 454 D
angela.shoup@utdallas.edu
SHOUP, John .... 951-343-4205.. 27 J
jshoup@calbaptist.edu
SHOUSE, Aimee .... 254-968-9429 445 F
ashouse@tarleton.edu
SHOUSE, Amy .... 304-724-5000 486 C
ashouse@cdu.edu
SHOW, Elizabeth .... 301-387-3053 198 F
elizabeth.show@garrettcollege.edu
SHOWALTER, Jennifer ... 615-248-7735 425 D
jdshowalter@trevecca.edu
SHOWALTER, Jewel ...... 740-857-1311 360 C
jshowalter@rosedale.edu
SHOWALTER, Matthew .. 740-857-1311 360 C
mshowalter@rosedale.edu
SHOWALTER,
Rodney, J .... 540-338-1776 468 D
ie@phc.edu
SHOWERS, Kimberly ..... 985-545-1500 188 B
SHOWERS, Shane .... 315-568-3125 309 H
sshowers@northeastcollege.edu
SHOWERS, William ...... 412-809-5268 395 F
showers.william@ptcollege.edu
SHOWS, Alicia .... 601-276-3706 248 D
showsa@smcc.edu
SHOWS, Deidre .... 601-318-6583 249 B
dede.shows@wmcarey.edu
SHOWS-PEREZ, Cindy .. 337-482-6497 192 F
cperez@louisiana.edu
SHRADER, Matt .... 763-417-8250 234 D
mshrader@centralseminary.edu
SHRADER, Theresa ...... 410-532-5155 201 C
tshrader@ndm.edu
SHREFLER, Christy, L ... 440-826-2231 348 C
chking@bw.edu
SHRESTHA, Prabesh ..... 320-222-5219 239 H
prabesh.shrestha@ridgewater.edu
SHRESTHA, Shakil .... 510-628-8020.. 48 G
shakil@lincolnuca.edu

SHREVE, Daryl .... 413-236-1661 213 E
dshreve@berkshirecc.edu
SHREVE, Jeremy .... 828-328-7334 330 B
jeremy.shreve@lr.edu
SHREVE, Jeremy .... 919-658-7776 340 E
jshreve@umo.edu
SHREVE, Paula .... 219-473-7770 154 A
SHREVE, Teresa .... 205-348-7829.... 7 G
tshreve@fa.ua.edu
SHREVES, Shawn .... 432-685-4690 439 E
sshreves@midland.edu
SHREWSBURY, Carrie ... 724-266-3838 399 F
cshrewsbury@tsm.edu
SHREWSBURY,
Charlene, P .... 765-658-5555 154 G
cpbrown@depauw.edu
SHRIEVE-HAWKINS,
Stephanie, E .... 415-338-7567.. 34 A
shrieve@sfsu.edu
SHRIMPTON, Michael .... 417-873-7352 252 A
mshrimpton@drury.edu
SHRIVASTAV, Rahul ...... 812-855-4613 156 B
SHRIVASTAV, Rahul ...... 812-855-4848 156 C
SHROCK, Joel .... 641-784-5115 166 B
jshrock1@graceland.edu
SHROFF, Nilufer, K ...... 609-258-8732 279 E
nshroff@princeton.edu
SHROPSHIRE, Doug ...... 508-531-1207 212 B
dshropshire@bridgew.edu
SHROPSHIRE, James ..... 641-269-4600 166 D
shropshi@grinnell.edu
SHROPSHIRE, Marty ..... 336-386-3453 338 B
shropshirem@surry.edu
SHROPSHIRE, Phyllis ... 770-426-2759 122 A
pwilliams@life.edu
SHROPSHIRE, Sandra .... 208-282-2997 131 E
shrosand@isu.edu
SHROPSHIRE, Sonel ..... 302-857-6060.. 90 D
sshropshire@desu.edu
SHRUCK, Meghan .... 402-363-5701 269 F
mshruck@york.edu
SHRUM, Kayse .... 405-744-6384 367 G
osupres@okstate.edu
SHRUM, Kelly .... 724-805-2820 397 D
kelly.shrum@stvincent.edu
SHTAMLER, Victoriya .... 718-522-9073 290 B
vshtamler@asa.edu
SHTROMBERG, Alisa ..... 425-739-8389 480 D
alisa.shtromberg@lwtech.edu
SHUBERT, Lisa, A .... 507-344-7324 233 I
lisa.shubert@blc.edu
SHUBERT, Stephen ...... 810-762-0501 228 B
stephen.shubert@mcc.edu
SHUDAK, Nicholas .... 402-375-7379 267 I
nishuda1@wsc.edu
SHUEY, Heather, M ...... 570-326-3761 392 S
hms27@pct.edu
SHUEY, Jill .... 716-286-8029 309 F
jshuey@niagara.edu
SHUEY, Lisa .... 419-559-2342 361 B
lshuey03@terra.edu
SHUEY, Timothy .... 704-406-4280 328 I
tshuey@gardner-webb.edu
SHUFFITT, Jason .... 512-313-3000 432 N
jason.shuffitt@concordia.edu
SHUFORD, Beverly, C ... 361-570-4811 452 C
shufordb@uhv.edu
SHUFORD, Eddie .... 828-652-0652 335 H
eddieshuford@mcdowelltech.edu
SHUGART, Michael .... 405-682-1611 367 D
mshugart@occc.edu
SHUGATS-CUMMINGS,
Alissa .... 716-614-6293 309 E
acummings@niagaracc.suny.edu
SHUKLA, Amit .... 206-296-5505 483 B
SHULER, Hal .... 910-410-1807 336 G
whshuler@richmondcc.edu
SHULL, Libby .... 864-833-8477 410 E
esshull@presby.edu
SHULL, Roger .... 806-894-9611 443 A
rshull@southplainscollege.edu
SHULMAN, Brian .... 973-275-2168 282 K
brian.shulman@shu.edu
SHULMAN, David, J ...... 206-568-4387 482 I
SHULMAN, Joshua .... 562-368-3146.. 65 H
joshuashulman@scuhs.edu
SHULMAN, Yaakov .... 732-367-1060 275 B
yshulman@bmg.edu
SHULSE, Brian .... 760-872-2000.. 41 D
bdshulse@deepsprings.edu
SHULTES, Kenneth, E .... 717-245-1247 382 B
shultes@dickinson.edu

SHULTS, Christopher .... 212-220-1400 292 G
cshults@bmcc.cuny.edu
SHULTS, Kari .... 918-595-8845 370 B
kari.shults@tulsacc.edu
SHULTZ, Bridget .... 641-422-4325 168 E
bridget.shultz@niacc.edu
SHULTZ, Dee .... 970-339-6434.. 77 G
dee.shultz@aims.edu
SHULTZ, John .... 913-758-6329 177 I
john.shultz@stmary.edu
SHULTZ, Kara .... 570-389-4308 393 E
kshultz@bloomu.edu
SHULTZ, Kari .... 423-236-2484 422 H
kshultz@southern.edu
SHULTZ, Megan .... 515-961-1611 169 G
megan.shultz@simpson.edu
SHULTZ, Norah .... 619-594-6881.. 33 E
nshultz@sdsu.edu
SHULTZ, Sarah .... 732-263-5191 278 B
sshultz@monmouth.edu
SHULTZ, JR., Walter, J . 570-326-3761 392 S
walter.shultz@pct.edu
SHUMACHER, Carrie ...... 406-768-6312 262 I
cshumacher@fpcc.edu
SHUMACK, Gareth .... 516-876-3210 318 A
shumackg@oldwestbury.edu
SHUMAKER, Carrie .... 313-593-5454 231 B
shumakr@umich.edu
SHUMAKER, Carrie .... 313-593-5000 231 B
shumakr@umich.edu
SHUMAKER, Deb .... 989-275-5000 225 H
deb.shumaker@kirtland.edu
SHUMAKER, Ryan .... 619-388-2737.. 61 A
rshumaker@sdccd.edu
SHUMAN, Jeff .... 860-253-3018.. 86 B
jshuman@asnuntuck.edu
SHUMAN, Kelli .... 336-278-5560 328 H
kshuman2@elon.edu
SHUMAN, Michaeline ... 570-372-4325 398 A
shumanm@susqu.edu
SHUMAN, Richard .... 713-525-6974 453 H
shumanr@stthom.edu
SHUMAN, Victoria .... 304-793-6898 489 C
vshuman@osteo.wvsom.edu
SHUMATE, Bonnie .... 207-307-3900 193 E
bshumate@beal.edu
SHUMATE, David .... 480-245-7993.. 12 O
david.shumate@ibcs.edu
SHUMPERT, Barry .... 865-225-2365 424 C
bshumpert@pstcc.edu
SHUMPERT, Shanon ..... 410-516-8075 199 E
shanonshumpert@jhu.edu
SHUMWAY, Aaron .... 808-675-4971 128 B
aaron.shumway@byuh.edu
SHUMWAY, Karen .... 972-780-3600 453 C
karen.shumway@untdallas.edu
SHUPALA, Christine ...... 956-665-4025 455 A
christine.shupala@utrgv.edu
SHUPE, John .... 845-257-3335 316 B
shupej@newpaltz.edu
SHUPP, Benjamin .... 410-293-6332 502 I
shupp@usna.edu
SHUPP, Kevin .... 843-661-1360 408 H
kevin.shupp@fmarion.edu
SHUPP, Leslie .... 843-661-1161 408 H
leslie.shupp@fmarion.edu
SHUR, Luba .... 401-598-5155 403 E
luba.shur@jwu.edu
SHURANCE, Mike .... 949-214-3363.. 40 E
mike.shurance@cui.edu
SHURER, Brooke .... 919-760-8429 331 A
shurerb@meredith.edu
SHURLEY, Britton .... 270-534-3243 182 G
britton.shurley@kctcs.edu
SHURTLEFF, Amanda .... 941-359-7531 106 J
ashurtle@ringling.edu
SHURTLEFF, Courtney ... 508-286-3425 219 F
shurtleff_courtney@wheatoncollege.edu
SHUSHOK, Frank .... 540-375-2200 469 G
fshushok@roanoke.edu
SHUSKO, Robin .... 301-624-2858 198 E
rshusko@frederick.edu
SHUTE, Paula .... 239-304-2955.. 95 M
paula.shute@avemaria.edu
SHUTT, Barbara, C .... 207-859-5415 194 B
barbara.shutt@colby.edu
SHUTTER, Jamie, L ...... 573-884-8383 260 C
shutterj@health.missouri.edu
SHUTTERLY, Martin ...... 561-803-2200 105 B
SHUTTERS, Debi .... 336-841-9000 329 E
SHUTTLEWORTH,
Dennis, K .... 937-255-6565 501 A
dennis.shuttleworth@afit.edu

SHYNN, David .... 562-777-4066.. 27 E
david.shynn@biola.edu
SIACA, Aleyda .... 787-766-1717 509 C
siacaa1@uagm.edu
SIAHMAKOUN, Azad ..... 812-877-8400 160 C
siahmako@rose-hulman.edu
SIAMPOS, Christa .... 314-421-0949 259 G
csiampos@siba.edu
SIBENALLER, Jim .... 773-508-7665 142 G
jsibena@luc.edu
SIBENALLER-WOODALL,
Beth .... 712-324-5061 168 H
beths@nwicc.edu
SIBERT, Kimberley .... 740-366-9233 349 D
ksibert@cotc.edu
SIBERT, Sonja .... 775-327-2355 270 G
sonja.sibert@gbcnv.edu
SIBERT, William .... 607-255-6240 297 D
controller@cornell.edu
SIBLEY, David .... 312-467-2260.. 36 G
dsibley@thechicagoschool.edu
SIBLEY, Dedra .... 321-433-7060.. 98 F
sibleyd@easternflorida.edu
SIBLEY, Scott .... 508-541-1898 208 E
ssibley@dean.edu
SIBSON, Thomas .... 215-951-1080 386 I
SIBUMA, Bernadette ...... 781-239-2481 214 E
bsibuma@massbay.edu
SICARD, OP, Kenneth ... 401-865-2153 403 G
nkelley@providence.edu
SICARD, Rex, E .... 785-243-1435 172 J
rsicard@cloud.edu
SICIENSKY, Emily .... 931-540-2704 423 D
esiciensky@columbiastate.edu
SICILIANO, Stephen, N . 231-995-1373 228 F
ssiciliano@nmc.edu
SIDAOUI, Mouwafac ...... 650-543-3940.. 52 A
mouwafac.sidaoui@menlo.edu
SIDAROUS, Mallory .... 618-650-4628 149 H
msidaro@siue.edu
SIDBERRY, Gregory ...... 954-486-7728 112 J
gsidberry@uftl.edu
SIDBURY, Ben .... 704-233-8019 344 E
b.sidbury@wingate.edu
SIDDALL, David .... 641-784-5138 166 B
davids1@graceland.edu
SIDDALL, Jared, M .... 610-917-1433 400 D
jmsiddall@valleyforge.edu
SIDDARAJU, Raj .... 309-649-6387 150 D
raj.siddaraju@src.edu
SIDDENS, Nancy .... 217-732-3168 142 D
SIDDIQI, Aamir .... 414-229-4716 495 B
siddiqi@uwm.edu
SIDDIQI, Muddassir ..... 713-718-6041 436 E
muddassir.siddiqi@hccs.edu
SIDERAS, John, F .... 216-368-4340 349 B
john.sideras@case.edu
SIDERS, Angie .... 765-455-9515 156 E
asiders@iuk.edu
SIDERS, Austin .... 812-465-1080 162 B
austin.siders@usi.edu
SIDES, Bobbie .... 803-321-5102 409 I
bobbie.sides@newberry.edu
SIDES, Courtney, M ...... 361-570-4354 452 C
sidesc@uhv.edu
SIDES, Emilee .... 870-733-6722.. 18 A
essides@asumidsouth.edu
SIDES, Tevian .... 325-574-7640 457 G
tevian.sides@wtc.edu
SIDHU, Elda .... 702-895-5185 270 J
elda.sidhu@unlv.edu
SIDLE, Meg .... 606-218-5290 185 F
margaretsidle@upike.edu
SIDLE, Stuart .... 914-674-7517 305 H
ssidle@mercy.edu
SIDLER, Sherri .... 312-362-6695 136 F
ssidler@depaul.edu
SIDLER, Sherri .... 312-362-6727 136 F
ssidler@depaul.edu
SIDMORE, Malaika .... 603-526-1870 271 H
malaika.sidmore@colby-sawyer.edu
SIDNEY, Mary .... 530-898-3865.. 31 A
msidney@csuchico.edu
SIDORAN, Laura .... 321-632-1111.. 98 F
SIDORKIN, Alexander .... 916-278-3326.. 33 A
sidorkin@csus.edu
SIEBEN, Jeffrey .... 609-497-7789 279 D
jeffrey.sieben@ptsem.edu
SIEBENECK, Paula .... 419-995-8458 360 B
siebeneck.p@rhodesstate.edu
SIEBENMORGEN, Tom .. 501-450-1333.. 19 I
siebenmorgen@hendrix.edu

SIEBENS, Libby 509-682-6436 484 H lsiebens@wvc.edu

SIEBENS, Mackie 845-758-7472 290 G msiebens@bard.edu

SIEBERT, Alex 513-562-8749 347 G asiebert@artacademy.edu

SIEBERT, Dave 847-735-5042 141 F siebert@lakeforest.edu

SIEBERT, Florence, E 920-565-1000 492 A siebertfe@lakeland.edu

SIEBERT, Katy 913-621-8713 173 B ksiebert@donnelly.edu

SIEBERT, Mary Anne 501-450-1372 19 I siebert@hendrix.edu

SIEBERT, Todd 618-664-6739 138 D todd.siebert@greenville.edu

SIEBUHR, Bryan 303-273-3092 79 A bsiebuhr@mines.edu

SIEBUHR, Shantee 903-463-8693 435 H siebuhrs@grayson.edu

SIECZKIEWICZ, Robert 570-372-4329 398 A sieczkiewicz@susqu.edu

SIEDERS, Laura 906-487-7359 223 I

SIEGA-RIZ, Anna Maria 413-545-1079 211 D asiegariz@umass.edu

SIEGEL, Christine 203-254-4000 87 G csiegel@fairfield.edu

SIEGEL, Kyle 508-831-5000 220 C

SIEGEL, Se-Ah 617-349-8563 210 H

SIEGELIN, Christa 765-998-5109 161 A chsiegelin@taylor.edu

SIEGFRIED, Jessica 435-283-7169 460 C jessica.siegfried@snow.edu

SIEGFRIED, Kenneth 812-488-2237 161 E es405@evansville.edu

SIEGLE, Suzanne 248-689-8282 231 E ssiegle@walshcollege.edu

SIEMANN, Thomas 510-666-8248 24 G academicdirector@aimc.edu

SIEMEN, Duane 407-823-3010 110 D duane.siemen@ucf.edu

SIEMENS, Henrietta 559-453-7100 43 D henrietta.siemens@fresno.edu

SIEMINSKI, Randy, B 315-386-7335 319 E sieminski@canton.edu

SIEMS, Blaire 641-683-5115 166 F blaire.siems@indianhills.edu

SIENA, Steven 516-628-5558 318 A sienas@oldwestbury.edu

SIEREVELD, Sarah 318-342-5244 193 A ssiereveld@ulm.edu

SIERKOWSKI, Dave 219-464-6906 162 C dave.sierkowski@valpo.edu

SIERRA, Miguel 407-708-2492 108 B sierram@seminolestate.edu

SIES, Susan 410-386-8325 197 G ssies@carrollcc.edu

SIESING, Gina 610-526-5270 378 J gsiesing@brynmawr.edu

SIETSEMA, Adriane 641-648-4611 167 D adriane.sietsema@iavalley.edu

SIEVEN, Lauren 657-278-4320 31 E lasieven@fullerton.edu

SIEVERDING, John 605-770-0700 414 E john.sieverding@mitchelltech.edu

SIEVERS, Alex 812-888-4386 162 E asievers@vinu.edu

SIEVERS, Sylvia, J 864-833-8757 410 E sjsievers@presby.edu

SIEVING, Allison 253-964-6531 481 H asieving@pierce.ctc.edu

SIFERT, Jaclyn 641-585-8148 170 E jaclyn.sifert@waldorf.edu

SIFFRING, Ed 402-643-7450 265 I ed.siffring@cune.edu

SIFRI, Tatiana 630-637-5161 145 E tsifri@noctrl.edu

SIFTAR, Michael 918-595-8123 370 B michael.siftar@tulsacc.edu

SIFUENTES, Aldo 909-384-8940 60 F usifuentes@sbccd.cc.ca.us

SIGALA, Al 503-491-7548 373 H al.sigala@mhcc.edu

SIGANDER, Max 503-517-1397 377 B msigander@warnerpacific.edu

SIGANOS, Dina 813-868-8160 99 C dsiganos@evergladesuniversity.edu

SIGAUKE, Erica 603-428-2293 272 I esigauke@nec.edu

SIGER, Rick 412-268-5751 380 B rsiger@andrew.cmu.edu

SIGG, Ryan 620-901-6248 171 A sigg@allencc.edu

SIGGERS, Lauretta 617-873-0170 207 E lauretta.siggers@cambridgecollege.edu

SIGISMOND, Dee 209-384-6068 52 B

SIGLER, Christy 615-898-2185 421 C christy.sigler@mtsu.edu

SIGLER, Haley 540-458-8400 476 D siglerh@wlu.edu

SIGLER, Tim, M 919-573-5350 340 A tsigler@shepherds.edu

SIGMON, Georgia 252-493-7834 336 E gsigmon@email.pittcc.edu

SIGMON, JR., Kenneth, E 336-334-7600 341 C kesigmon@ncat.edu

SIGMUND, Nicole 724-805-2701 397 C nicole.sigmund@stvincent.edu

SIGMUND, Nicole 724-805-2701 397 D nicole.sigmund@stvincent.edu

SIGNOR, Mary 212-998-6807 309 D mary.signor@nyu.edu

SIGNORELLO, John 973-761-9615 282 K john.signorello@shu.edu

SIGWING, Marty 620-242-0400 175 G sigwingm@mcpherson.edu

SII, Shelley 626-571-5110 48 I shelley@les.edu

SIKAHEMA, Leland 808-675-4819 128 B leland.sikahema@byuh.edu

SIKER, Malika 414-955-4493 492 F msiker@mcw.edu

SIKER, Nancy 414-847-3343 493 C nancysiker@miad.edu

SIKES, Bruce 479-667-4046 18 E bsikes1@atu.edu

SIKES, Steddon, L 402-363-5668 269 F slsikes@york.edu

SIKKENGA, Jeff 419-289-5413 347 H jsikkenga@ashbrook.org

SIKKINK, Jenae 641-628-5138 164 B jenisonj@central.edu

SIKORSKY, Charles 703-416-1441 465 E csikorsky@divinemercy.edu

SILAGYI, Tyler 716-338-1188 302 G tylersilagyi@mail.sunyjcc.edu

SILANSKIS, Theresa 410-837-6838 204 C tsilanskis@ubalt.edu

SILAS, Monique 205-929-6350 2 H msilas@lawsonstate.edu

SILBER, Daniel 706-778-8500 124 B dsilber@piedmont.edu

SILBER, Eric 512-313-3000 432 N eric.silber@concordia.edu

SILBER, Jeffrey, A 607-255-2016 297 D jas9@cornell.edu

SILBERMAN, Gerald, L 717-361-3737 383 B silbermang@etown.edu

SILBERQUIT, Paul 410-334-2829 205 A psilberquit@worwic.edu

SILBERSTEIN, Dara, J 607-777-2815 315 E lael@binghamton.edu

SILBERSTEIN, Jeffrey 212-659-9091 302 B jeffrey.silberstein@mssm.edu

SILCOX, Steve 269-927-7060 226 B ssilcox@lakemichigancollege.edu

SILECCHIA, Anthony 419-434-5708 362 D anthony.silecchia@findlay.edu

SILENTWALKER, Mary 505-424-2307 285 H mary.silentwalker@iaia.edu

SILER, Keri, S 407-582-2867 113 C ksiler@valenciacollege.edu

SILER, Lisa 870-633-4480 19 E lsiler@eacc.edu

SILER, Ryan 920-403-3146 494 B ryan.siler@snc.edu

SILICIANO, John, A 607-255-6230 297 D jas83@cornell.edu

SILIS, Mark 617-253-3292 215 G

SILK, Daniel 706-542-5813 126 F dsilk@police.uga.edu

SILK, Elizabeth 708-524-6461 137 A esilk@dom.edu

SILK, Mary, L 692-625-4410 503 F msilk@cmi.edu

SILKA, Christina 419-824-3617 355 C dsilka@lourdes.edu

SILKAITIS, Carin 907-796-6531 10 C cdsilkaitis@alaska.edu

SILL, Nancy 209-575-6128 76 K silln@mjc.edu

SILLIMAN, Stephen 615-248-1237 425 D sesilliman@trevecca.edu

SILLIMON, Laird 209-476-7840 67 D lgsillimon@clc.edu

SILLIMON, Laird, G 209-476-7840 67 D lgsillimon@clc.edu

SILLS, Veronica 336-334-7500 341 C

SILMAN, Shawn 281-459-7673 442 D shawn.silman@sjcd.edu

SILTMAN, Kent 217-245-3004 139 A kent.siltman@ic.edu

SILVA, Adelina 210-485-0153 427 H asilva@alamo.edu

SILVA, Alan 317-955-6000 159 A ajsilva@marian.edu

SILVA, Alyson 954-262-5258 104 M asilva1@nova.edu

SILVA, Andria 407-646-2268 106 L asilva2@rollins.edu

SILVA, Belinda 916-577-2200 76 C bsilva@jessup.edu

SILVA, Betsy 605-642-6551 415 F betsy.silva@bhsu.edu

SILVA, David 210-458-4011 455 B davidr.silva@utsa.edu

SILVA, David, J 978-542-6246 213 B david.silva@salemstate.edu

SILVA, Efrain 760-355-6249 45 N efrain.silva@imperial.edu

SILVA, Elizabeth 619-260-2888 72 H registrar@sandiego.edu

SILVA, Eneida 787-850-9390 511 B eneida.silva@upr.edu

SILVA, Jack 401-454-6480 404 B jsilva@risd.edu

SILVA, Jessica, L 401-456-8047 404 A jsilva@ric.edu

SILVA, Joseph 916-686-7400 29 G

SILVA, Joseph 505-277-2241 288 C jsilva23@unm.edu

SILVA, Mariza 312-922-1884 143 D msilva@maccormac.edu

SILVA, Maureen 540-828-5450 464 C msilva@bridgewater.edu

SILVA, Rebecca 575-234-9213 287 I rsilva@senmc.edu

SILVA, Rito 361-593-3105 447 A rito.silva@tamuk.edu

SILVA, Sonia 661-654-6113 30 C ssilva7@csub.edu

SILVA, Stella 512-245-5580 449 G ss23@txstate.edu

SILVA, Stephanie 510-436-1405 45 H ssilva@hnu.edu

SILVA, Tammy 508-999-8486 211 F tsilva@umassd.edu

SILVA, Tammy, A 508-999-8486 211 F tsilva@umassd.edu

SILVA, Tina 307-268-2547 499 T tina.silva@caspercollege.edu

SILVA-BREEN, Bill 651-641-3527 236 A wsilvabr@luthersem.edu

SILVA-BROWN, Jennifer 417-873-7213 252 A jsilvabrown@drury.edu

SILVA-DIAZ, Debora, H 787-758-2525 511 D

SILVANO, Brian 949-794-9090 66 C bsilvano@stanbridge.edu

SILVAS, Kassie 208-769-3300 132 A

SILVER, Bret 973-408-3227 276 B bsilver@drew.edu

SILVER, Edward 201-692-7071 276 I edsilver@fdu.edu

SILVER, Frank 828-652-0634 335 H franksil@mcdowelltech.edu

SILVER, Jonathan 646-717-9705 300 C silver@gts.edu

SILVER, Stephen 530-898-6116 31 A ssilver@calstate.edu

SILVERBLATT, Pamela, S 646-664-2977 292 E pamela.silverblatt@cuny.edu

SILVERHEELS, Sumana 716-878-4500 317 C silvers@buffalostate.edu

SILVERI, Annamaria 313-993-1170 230 H silveran@udmercy.edu

SILVERIO, Alain 212-410-8046 308 D asilverio@nycpm.edu

SILVERMAN, David 323-469-3300 25 G

SILVERMAN, Jennifer 310-338-4404 51 C jennifer.silverman@lmu.edu

SILVERMAN, Lori 510-659-6191 54 J lsilverman@ohlone.edu

SILVERMAN, Scott 310-434-4370 63 B silverman_scott@smc.edu

SILVERMAN, Stephen 561-297-3357 109 F silverman@fau.edu

SILVERS, Dominic 570-577-1911 379 A dominic.silvers@bucknell.edu

SILVERS, Laurie 305-284-4025 112 K

SILVERS, Liz 828-726-2375 332 E lsilvers@cccti.edu

SILVESTER, Katherine 518-783-2321 314 K ksilvester@siena.edu

SILVESTRI, Mary Ann 508-541-1602 208 E msilvestri@dean.edu

SILVESTRI, Timothy 484-664-3178 390 F timothysilvestri@muhlenberg.edu

SILVESTRO, Michael 973-761-9138 282 K michael.silvestro1@shu.edu

SILVEY, Greg 660-831-4028 256 B silveyg@moval.edu

SILVIS, Kathryn 412-536-1297 386 H kathryn.silvis@laroche.edu

SILVIS, Shera, L 843-377-4904 406 B ssilvis@charlestonlaw.edu

SILVIS, Victor 843-640-7578 406 B vsilvis@charlestonlaw.edu

SILVYN, Jeffrey 520-206-4678 15 E jsilvyn@pima.edu

SILY, Michel 305-899-3781 96 A msily@barry.edu

SIM, Hyun Bo 714-517-1945 27 C

SIM, Stephen 920-565-1000 492 A

SIMARD, Denise 518-564-3066 318 C simardda@plattsburgh.edu

SIMARI, Robert 913-588-1698 177 G rsimari@kumc.edu

SIMCOX, Mary Grace 717-947-6090 392 R mrsimcox@pacollege.edu

SIMCOX, Nate 610-359-5190 381 J nsimcox@dccc.edu

SIMENTAL, Yolanda 909-384-8927 60 F ysimental@sbccd.cc.ca.us

SIMER, Lauren 864-250-8484 408 J lauren.simer@gvltec.edu

SIMFUKWE, David 904-470-8174 98 I dsimfukwe@ewc.edu

SIMIEN, Tammy 504-568-3250 189 C tsimie@lsuhsc.edu

SIMINOE, Judith, P 320-308-2122 240 C jpsiminoe@stcloudstate.edu

SIMIO, Frank 212-636-6265 300 A simio@fordham.edu

SIMION, Karen 691-320-2480 503 B ksimion@comfsm.fm

SIMIONE, Lauren, E 302-831-1408 91 A lemurray@udel.edu

SIMKINS, Kathy 406-683-7566 263 E kathy.simkins@umwestern.edu

SIMMELINK, Tara 253-535-8787 481 C tara.simmelink@plu.edu

SIMMERS, Susan 406-657-2155 263 H susan.simmers@msubillings.edu

SIMMONDS, Donna 812-237-2215 155 H donna.simmonds@indstate.edu

SIMMONDS, Thomas 914-674-7473 305 H tsimmonds1@mercy.edu

SIMMONS, Alexis 217-443-8865 136 E a.simmons@dacc.edu

SIMMONS, Angela, D 843-208-8120 412 C

SIMMONS, Bette, M 973-328-5171 276 A bsimmons@ccm.edu

SIMMONS, Brian 803-754-4100 407 F

SIMMONS, Cara 706-542-7575 126 F caraj@uga.edu

SIMMONS, Charlotte 405-974-2538 370 H csimmons@uco.edu

SIMMONS, Christopher 919-668-6285 328 D chris.simmons@duke.edu

SIMMONS, Clay 940-565-4142 453 B clay.simmons@unt.edu

SIMMONS, Dale, H 530-226-4143 64 C dsimmons@simpsonu.edu

SIMMONS, Dan 580-745-2839 369 F dsimmons@se.edu

SIMMONS, David 706-253-4504 116 H dsimmons@chattahoocheetech.edu

SIMMONS, Debra, J 903-790-4890 437 E dsimmons@jarvis.edu

SIMMONS, Dionne 661-253-7897 28 I dsimmons@calarts.edu

SIMMONS, Douglas 603-314-1775 216 B douglas.simmons@mcphs.edu

SIMMONS, Elaine 620-792-9214 171 F simmonse@bartonccc.edu

SIMMONS, Elizabeth 508-830-6683 213 A esimmons@maritime.edu

SIMMONS, Elizabeth, H 858-534-3130 70 C evc@ucsd.edu

SIMMONS, Gregory ...... 410-455-1452 202 G gsimmons@umbc.edu
SIMMONS, Gwen ...... 417-690-3411 250 K simmons@cofo.edu
SIMMONS, Hezekiah ... 585-385-8000 313 A
SIMMONS, Jacqueline, A ...... 812-855-3312 156 B simmonja@iu.edu
SIMMONS, Jamar ...... 504-816-4026 186 F jsimmons@dillard.edu
SIMMONS, Jay ...... 913-253-5010 177 A jay.simmons@spst.edu
SIMMONS, Jay ...... 484-365-7526 388 F jsimmons@lincoln.edu
SIMMONS, Jeffrey, A ... 301-447-5266 201 A simmons@msmary.edu
SIMMONS, Jennie, M ... 910-788-6271 337 G jennie.simmons@sccnc.edu
SIMMONS, Kelly, M ...... 708-524-5921 137 A ksimmons@dom.edu
SIMMONS, Kitty ...... 951-785-2397.. 47 F ksimmons@lasierra.edu
SIMMONS, Kya ...... 516-876-3000 318 A
SIMMONS, Laura ...... 704-290-5261 337 F lsimmons@spcc.edu
SIMMONS, Laura ...... 828-694-1807 332 C lm_simmons@blueridge.edu
SIMMONS, Martha ...... 719-544-0677.. 82 I martha.simmons@pueblocc.edu
SIMMONS, Mary ...... 407-888-8689.. 99 N msimmons@fcim.edu
SIMMONS, Mary ...... 570-408-7836 402 B mary.simmons@wilkes.edu
SIMMONS, Max ...... 405-682-1611 367 D msimmons@occc.edu
SIMMONS, Michelle ...... 765-252-5473 158 A msimmons@ivytech.edu
SIMMONS, Miranda ...... 912-583-3176 116 D msimmons1@bpc.edu
SIMMONS, Naree ...... 610-861-1330 390 D simmonsn@moravian.edu
SIMMONS, Pamela ...... 585-594-6853 311 L simmons_pamela@roberts.edu
SIMMONS, Rasheeda ...... 318-670-6000 191 B
SIMMONS, Regina ...... 704-463-3404 339 C regina.simmons@pfeiffer.edu
SIMMONS, Renita, W .... 718-951-5137 293 A rwsimmons@brooklyn.cuny.edu
SIMMONS, Roy ...... 304-205-6708 487 D roy.simmons@bridgevalley.edu
SIMMONS, Ruth, J ...... 936-261-2111 445 E rjsimmons@pvamu.edu
SIMMONS, Shanni, E .... 812-888-4026 162 E ssimmons@vinu.edu
SIMMONS, Shannon ...... 478-445-5149 119 A shannon.simmons@gcsu.edu
SIMMONS, Sherry ...... 262-695-3481 499 A ssimmons9@wctc.edu
SIMMONS, Steve ...... 803-508-7270 405 C simmonss@atc.edu
SIMMONS, Tami ...... 704-378-1024 329 H tsimmons@jcsu.edu
SIMMONS, Tanya ...... 804-524-5087 475 E tsimmons@vsu.edu
SIMMONS, Tera ...... 256-549-8200.... 2 B
SIMMONS, Thomas, E ... 419-772-2450 358 D t-simmons@onu.edu
SIMMONS, Todd, H ...... 336-285-2606 341 C thsimmons@ncat.edu
SIMMONS, Tonja ...... 478-476-5167 116 F tsimmons@centralgatech.edu
SIMMONS, Toye ...... 713-221-8061 452 B simmonsto@uhd.edu
SIMMONS, Traci ...... 503-491-6422 373 H traci.simmons@mhcc.edu
SIMMONS, Tracy ...... 916-739-7198.. 71 E tsimmons@pacific.edu
SIMMONS, Victoria ...... 818-240-1000.. 43 J vsimmons@glendale.edu
SIMMONS COFFEY, Ashley ...... 904-819-6218.. 99 D acoffey@flagler.edu
SIMMONS-HENRY, Linda ...... 903-593-8311 448 A lsimmons-henry@texascollege.edu
SIMMS, Laurene ...... 202-250-2587.. 92 B laurene.simms@gallaudet.edu
SIMMS, Marcie ...... 740-351-3392 360 E msimms@shawnee.edu
SIMMS, Marcie ...... 304-696-4634 488 N marcie.simms@marshall.edu
SIMMS, Mary Helen ...... 318-371-3035 188 C maryhelensimms@nltcc.edu
SIMMS, Michele ...... 859-442-1690 181 D michele.simms@kctcs.edu
SIMMS, Pat ...... 501-332-0245.. 18 D pats@asutr.edu
SIMMS, Rebecca ...... 859-246-6761 181 B rebecca.simms@kctcs.edu
SIMMS, Shalei ...... 516-876-3000 318 A
SIMON, Bashe ...... 718-252-7800 322 C barbara.simon@touro.edu
SIMON, Bashe ...... 212-463-0400 322 B simonb@touro.edu
SIMON, Constance ...... 313-831-5200 223 G csimon@etseminary.edu
SIMON, Dan ...... 916-388-2800.. 35 C
SIMON, Darica ...... 225-216-8171 187 D simond@mybrcc.edu
SIMON, David, F ...... 215-871-6819 395 A simond@pcom.edu
SIMON, David, R ...... 920-565-1000 492 A simondr@lakeland.edu
SIMON, Donald, E ...... 718-933-6700 306 J dsimon@monroecollege.edu
SIMON, Elizabeth ...... 646-564-6727 289 F elizabeth.simon@nyack.edu
SIMON, Eric ...... 410-857-2207 200 E esimon@mcdaniel.edu
SIMON, Jacob ...... 419-448-3421 361 C simonja@tiffin.edu
SIMON, Jason ...... 620-223-2700 173 F jasons@fortscott.edu
SIMON, Jason, F ...... 940-565-2085 453 B jason.simon@unt.edu
SIMON, Jennifer ...... 406-496-4307 264 C jsimon@mtech.edu
SIMON, Marisa ...... 574-239-8339 155 E mvillano@hcc-nd.edu
SIMON, Michael ...... 810-762-5640 228 B michael.simon@mcc.edu
SIMON, Michael ...... 936-633-5200 429 A msimon@angelina.edu
SIMON, Tia ...... 832-230-5156 439 H tsimon1@na.edu
SIMON, Tim ...... 402-486-2600 268 G tim.simon@ucollege.edu
SIMON, Tina, L ...... 419-372-2700 348 F tsimon@bgsu.edu
SIMONCELLI, Andrew .... 985-448-4131 192 C andrew.simoncelli@nicholls.edu
SIMONDS, Ken ...... 760-366-5297.. 40 K ksimonds@cmccd.edu
SIMONDS, Kurt ...... 971-722-5573 375 C kurt.simonds@pcc.edu
SIMONDS, Richard ...... 713-221-5711 452 B simondsr@uhd.edu
SIMONE, Carmen ...... 701-228-5431 345 C carmen.simone@dakotacollege.edu
SIMONE, John ...... 609-586-4800 277 H simonej@mccc.edu
SIMONE, Lucian ...... 203-285-2223.. 86 D lsimone@gatewayct.edu
SIMONE, Nadia ...... 626-571-8811.. 73 D nadias@uwest.edu
SIMONEAUX, Wendy ...... 225-578-8878 189 C wsimo1@lsuhsc.edu
SIMONETTI, Joseph ...... 773-995-3689 134 J jsimonet@csu.edu
SIMONI, Mary ...... 518-276-6575 311 J msimoni@rpi.edu
SIMONIAN, Yasmen ...... 801-626-7117 460 B ysimonian@weber.edu
SIMONICH, Staci ...... 541-737-2331 374 H staci.simonich@oregonstate.edu
SIMONS, Austin ...... 269-965-3931 225 D simonsa2@kellogg.edu
SIMONS, Danita ...... 605-718-2436 416 D danita.simons@wdt.edu
SIMONS, Doug, A ...... 808-956-8566 129 B dsimons@hawaii.edu
SIMONS, Earl, G ...... 718-262-3795 295 D esimons@york.cuny.edu
SIMONS, Ernest ...... 252-493-7243 336 E esimons@email.pittcc.edu
SIMONS, Eunika ...... 803-705-4661 405 G eunika.simons@benedict.edu
SIMONS, Horace ...... 614-837-4088 363 D simonsh@valorcollege.edu
SIMONS, Jill ...... 870-972-3574.. 17 I jsimons@astate.edu
SIMONS, Kenneth, B ..... 414-955-4575 492 F ksimons@mcw.edu
SIMONS, Kyle ...... 605-331-6743 416 C kyle.simons@usiouxfalls.edu
SIMONS, Lisa ...... 817-598-6263 457 C lsimons@wc.edu
SIMONS, TOR, Matthew ...... 814-472-3001 396 I msimons@francis.edu
SIMONS, Michael, A ...... 718-990-6601 313 B simonsm@stjohns.edu
SIMONS, Shino ...... 626-812-3061.. 26 K ssimons@apu.edu
SIMONS, Tina ...... 256-840-4115.... 3 F tina.simons@snead.edu
SIMONS, Valerie ...... 303-860-5600.. 83 L valerie.simons@cu.edu
SIMONSEN, Jaime ...... 651-201-1669 236 F jaime.simonsen@minnstate.edu
SIMONSON, Erik ...... 218-733-5915 238 A erik.simonson@lsc.edu
SIMONSON, Jocelyn ...... 718-780-7592 291 G jocelyn.simonson@brooklaw.edu
SIMONSON, Richelle ...... 614-222-3211 351 A rsimonson@ccad.edu
SIMONSON, William ...... 586-286-2110 226 F simonsonb@macomb.edu
SIMOS-VALDEZ, Imelda 661-395-4406.. 47 B imelda.valdez@bakersfieldcollege.edu
SIMOWITZ, Aaron ...... 503-370-6840 377 E asimowitz@willamette.edu
SIMPKINS, Alice, M ...... 706-396-8111 123 I asimpkins@paine.edu
SIMPKINS, Felix ...... 708-709-3518 147 A fsimpkins@prairiestate.edu
SIMPKINS, Latrisa ...... 251-578-1313.... 3 D lsimpkins@rstc.edu
SIMPKINS, Will ...... 303-605-5590.. 81 L wsimpkin@msudenver.edu
SIMPLICIO, Sean, S ...... 510-325-7089 467 G sssimplicio@marybaldwind.edu
SIMPSON, Amanda ...... 760-252-2411.. 26 L asimpson@barstow.edu
SIMPSON, Amy ...... 606-248-0484 182 F amy.simpson@kctcs.edu
SIMPSON, Andy, L ...... 651-631-5239 243 E alsimpson@unwsp.edu
SIMPSON, Angela ...... 606-589-3025 182 F angela.simpson@kctcs.edu
SIMPSON, Anita ...... 580-628-6237 366 J anita.simpson@noc.edu
SIMPSON, Betsy ...... 303-963-3350.. 78 D bsimpson@ccu.edu
SIMPSON, Brett ...... 504-864-7787 190 A bsimpson@loyno.edu
SIMPSON, Caroline ...... 304-724-3700 485 G csimpson@apus.edu
SIMPSON, JR., Charles, L ...... 919-516-4249 339 G clsimpson@st-aug.edu
SIMPSON, Chocoletta ... 320-308-5123 240 C chocoletta.simpson@stcloudstate.edu
SIMPSON, Christopher . 402-557-7095 265 A
SIMPSON, Colleen ...... 303-404-5481.. 80 I colleen.simpson@frontrange.edu
SIMPSON, Colleen ...... 920-498-5418 498 F colleen.simpson@nwtc.edu
SIMPSON, Cynthia ...... 734-432-5684 226 G cssimpson@madonna.edu
SIMPSON, Cynthia, F ... 718-990-6333 313 B simpsoc1@stjohns.edu
SIMPSON, Dionne ...... 619-596-2766.. 26 I dsimpson@ata.edu
SIMPSON, Donald ...... 318-342-3312 193 A dsimpson@ulm.edu
SIMPSON, Jaime ...... 215-885-2360 389 A jsimpson@manor.edu
SIMPSON, Jamie ...... 402-941-6200 267 B simpson@midlandu.edu
SIMPSON, Jeanna ...... 417-667-8181 251 E jbrauer@cottey.edu
SIMPSON, Jeff ...... 334-241-5412.... 7 C simpsonj@troy.edu
SIMPSON, Jeff ...... 801-422-5330 458 A jeff.simpson@byu.edu
SIMPSON, Jennifer ...... 229-225-5072 125 G jsimpson@southernregional.edu
SIMPSON, Kisha ...... 252-638-7203 333 F bectonk@cravencc.edu
SIMPSON, Kurt ...... 815-599-3501 138 H kurt.simpson@highland.edu
SIMPSON, Lynne ...... 405-466-3294 366 B lynne.simpson@langston.edu
SIMPSON, Mark ...... 512-475-7310 454 C mark.simpson@austin.utexas.edu
SIMPSON, Mark ...... 866-931-4300 257 J mark.simpson@rockbridge.edu
SIMPSON, Matthew ...... 417-447-2648 257 B simpsonm@otc.edu
SIMPSON, Matthew ...... 508-849-3462 205 E msimpson@annamaria.edu
SIMPSON, Michael, E ... 518-564-2155 318 C simpsome@plattsburgh.edu
SIMPSON, Philip ...... 321-433-5078.. 98 F simpsonp@easternflorida.edu
SIMPSON, Ralph ...... 512-505-3041 437 B rssimpson@htu.edu
SIMPSON, Rich ...... 951-343-4579.. 27 J rsimpson@calbaptist.edu
SIMPSON, Stacy ...... 618-634-3375 149 C stacys@shawneecc.edu
SIMPSON, Stephanie, A 330-569-6185 353 F simpsonsa@hiram.edu
SIMPSON, Steven, M .... 248-232-4175 228 H smsimpso@oaklandcc.edu
SIMPSON, Sun-Kyung .. 845-368-7201 314 F
SIMPSON, Suzanne ...... 256-824-6686.... 8 B suzanne.simpson@uah.edu
SIMPSON, Tammi ...... 301-696-3573 199 C simpson@hood.edu
SIMPSON, Teresa ...... 361-570-4236 452 C simpsonte@uhv.edu
SIMPSON-LOGG, Anastasia ...... 707-468-3102.. 51 F asimpson@mendocino.edu
SIMS, Andrea ...... 909-274-4525.. 52 K asims16@mtsac.edu
SIMS, Angela ...... 505-224-4000 285 B asims9@cnm.edu
SIMS, Angela, D ...... 585-340-9680 296 B asims@crcds.edu
SIMS, Bradford, L ...... 301-369-2541 197 F president@captechu.edu
SIMS, Dale ...... 903-923-2147 435 A dsims@etbu.edu
SIMS, Damon, R ...... 814-865-0909 391 F drs37@psu.edu
SIMS, Dana ...... 503-847-2597 377 A dsims@uws.edu
SIMS, Darryl ...... 920-424-1034 495 C sims@uwosh.edu
SIMS, David ...... 478-471-2780 122 D david.sims@mga.edu
SIMS, Douglas ...... 702-651-3627 270 F douglas.sims@csn.edu
SIMS, Frank, L ...... 615-329-8500 418 E
SIMS, Geoffrey ...... 201-360-4045 277 D gsims@hccc.edu
SIMS, Haley ...... 804-828-1645 472 D hgsims@vcu.edu
SIMS, Hillel ...... 857-701-1501 215 E hsims@rcc.mass.edu
SIMS, Hunter ...... 325-649-8115 437 A hsims@hputx.edu
SIMS, Janet ...... 910-410-1889 336 G jmsims@richmondcc.edu
SIMS, Jaquelyn ...... 310-660-3119.. 41 J jsims@elcamino.edu
SIMS, Jeanetta ...... 405-974-2000 370 H jsims7@uco.edu
SIMS, Joel ...... 406-268-3719 264 B joel.sims@gfcmsu.edu
SIMS, Kavaris ...... 405-466-3623 366 B kavaris.sims@langston.edu
SIMS, Kavaris ...... 405-466-2231 366 B
SIMS, Leslie ...... 304-424-8221 490 A leslie.sims@wvup.edu
SIMS, Lisa ...... 601-477-4107 246 A lisa.sims@jcjc.edu
SIMS, Melinda ...... 405-382-9604 369 E m.sims@sscok.edu
SIMS, Michael ...... 201-200-3113 278 F msims@njcu.edu
SIMS, Ni'Cole ...... 503-594-3220 372 B nicole.sims@clackamas.edu
SIMS, Patricia ...... 256-551-3117.... 2 E patricia.sims@drakestate.edu
SIMS, Patrick ...... 336-770-3262 343 C simsp@uncsa.edu
SIMS, Quanda, D ...... 803-934-3422 409 H qdsims@morris.edu
SIMS, Ronshekua ...... 229-333-2100 127 F
SIMS, Sandra ...... 303-384-2008.. 79 A ssims@mines.edu
SIMS, Scott ...... 317-931-2328 154 D ssims@cts.edu
SIMS, Shannon ...... 325-649-8069 437 A ssims@hputx.edu
SIMS, Steve ...... 724-266-3838 399 F ssims@tsm.edu

SKELLY, Theresa .... 978-921-4242 216 F
theresa.skelly@montserrat.edu
SKERIK, Maryellen .... 630-637-5678 145 E
mjskerik@noctrl.edu
SKERRETT-LLANOS,
Carmen .... 787-993-8870 510 E
carmen.skerrett@upr.edu
SKEVAKIS, Anthony ...... 410-704-2270 204 B
askevakis@towson.edu
SKIDMORE, Alan .... 304-766-3261 489 D
askidmore@wvstateu.edu
SKIDMORE, Ashley .... 815-836-5212 142 C
skidmoas@lewisu.edu
SKIDMORE, Charlene .... 515-271-2999 165 F
charlene.skidmore@drake.edu
SKIDMORE, Daniel, L ... 315-445-4759 303 F
skidmodl@lemoyne.edu
SKIDMORE, Heather ...... 304-424-8210 490 A
heather.skidmore@wvup.edu
SKIDMORE, Tom .... 317-921-4909 158 A
tskidmore2@ivytech.edu
SKILES, Adam, L .... 260-359-4130 155 G
askiles@huntington.edu
SKILES, Jesse .... 304-462-6221 488 M
jesse.skiles@glenville.edu
SKILL, Thomas, D .... 937-229-3511 362 C
tskill1@udayton.edu
SKILLETT, Jenei .... 402-826-8253 266 A
jenei.skillett@doane.edu
SKINKLE, Lee .... 417-328-1601 258 K
lskinkle@sbuniv.edu
SKINNER, Alysun .... 252-399-6300 326 H
alskinner@barton.edu
SKINNER, Bruce .... 573-651-5103 258 J
bskinner@semo.edu
SKINNER, Celette .... 214-648-5499 456 D
celette.skinner@utsouthwestern.edu
SKINNER, Daniel .... 973-748-9000 275 C
daniel_skinner@bloomfield.edu
SKINNER, Deborah .... 641-784-5110 166 B
dskinner@graceland.edu
SKINNER, Denese .... 806-371-5252 428 F
denese.skinner@actx.edu
SKINNER, Donal .... 740-593-2723 358 L
dcs@ohio.edu
SKINNER, Erik .... 916-660-7600.. 64 B
eskinner2@sierracollege.edu
SKINNER, Georgia .... 404-627-2681 116 B
georgia.skinner@beulah.edu
SKINNER, Gregory .... 757-524-5595 476 C
gskinner@vwu.edu
SKINNER, James .... 580-774-3788 369 I
james.skinner@swosu.edu
SKINNER, Kendra .... 573-651-2274 258 J
ksskinner@semo.edu
SKINNER, Lee .... 504-865-5720 191 D
leeskinner@tulane.edu
SKINNER, Loren .... 409-772-6615 456 B
leskinne@utmb.edu
SKINNER, Noah .... 415-581-8873.. 69 B
skinnernoah@uchastings.edu
SKINNER, Patti .... 231-843-5869 232 I
pskinner@westshore.edu
SKINNER, Robert .... 304-473-8557 490 E
skinner_b@wvwc.edu
SKINNER, Sara .... 269-927-6851 226 B
skinner@lakemichigancollege.edu
SKINNER, Thomas .... 619-260-7974.. 72 H
tskinner@sandiego.edu
SKIPPER, Curt .... 601-635-2111 245 B
cskipper@eccc.edu
SKIPPER, Eric .... 843-208-8000 412 C
eskipper@uscb.edu
SKIPWORTH, Rachel ..... 704-687-7683 342 C
dskipwor@uncc.edu
SKIPWORTH, Stan .... 909-621-8033.. 37 E
stan.skipworth@claremont.edu
SKIRA, Aaron .... 937-775-3208 364 D
aaron.skira@wright.edu
SKLAR, Jay .... 314-434-4044 251 F
jay.sklar@covenantseminary.edu
SKLEDER, Anne, A .... 770-534-6110 116 C
askleder@brenau.edu
SKLENKA, Angela .... 813-974-5711 111 B
asklenka@usf.edu
SKLUT, John .... 509-313-3175 479 E
sklut@gonzaga.edu
SKLUT, John .... 509-313-3715 479 E
sklut@gonzaga.edu
SKOGLUND,
Elizabeth, A .... 410-543-6161 204 A
easkoglund@salisbury.edu
SKOGLUND, Kirk .... 816-501-4813 257 K
kirk.skoglund@rockhurst.edu

SKOLOSH, Tori .... 865-573-4517 419 E
tskolosh@johnsonu.edu
SKOMP, Elizabeth .... 386-822-7515 111 F
eskomp@stetson.edu
SKONER, Peter, R .... 814-472-3085 396 I
pskoner@francis.edu
SKOPEK, Tracy .... 903-983-8123 437 G
tskopek@kilgore.edu
SKORA, Sue .... 847-925-6921 138 E
sskora@harpercollege.edu
SKOUDIS, Ed .... 301-654-7267 202 B
SKOWRONSKI, Eric .... 716-673-3177 316 A
eric.skowronski@fredonia.edu
SKOWYRA, Jamie .... 508-213-2131 217 C
jamie.skowyra@nichols.edu
SKRABUT, Stan .... 508-541-1774 208 E
sskrabut@dean.edu
SKREEN, Janel .... 360-442-2273 480 E
jskreen@lowercolumbia.edu
SKROCKI, Kyle .... 802-387-6887 461 E
kyleskrocki@landmark.edu
SKULLEY, Kathryn .... 303-360-4954.. 80 C
kathryn.skulley@ccaurora.edu
SKURZEWSKI-SERVANT,
Missy .... 715-422-5356 498 A
missy.skurzewskiservant@mstc.edu
SKVARLA, Jennifer .... 815-836-5201 142 C
skvarlje@lewisu.edu
SLABACH, Frederick, G . 817-531-4401 450 F
fslabach@txwes.edu
SLABAUGH, David .... 864-644-5558 411 D
dslabaugh@swu.edu
SLABAUGH, Dawnie .... 530-938-5822.. 39 D
slabaugh@siskiyous.edu
SLABODEN, Carolyn ...... 781-283-2216 219 C
cslaboden@wellesley.edu
SLABODEN, Scott .... 508-793-3644 208 A
sslabode@holycross.edu
SLABU, Claudia .... 360-442-2216 480 E
cslabu@lowercolumbia.edu
SLABY, Greg .... 216-421-7940 350 E
gslaby@cia.edu
SLACK, Judy .... 800-553-4674 155 F
jslack@horizonuniversity.edu
SLACK, Lynn .... 412-391-7021 401 A
lslack@vti.edu
SLADE, David .... 706-236-2229 116 A
dslade@berry.edu
SLADE, Heather .... 805-969-3626.. 55 I
hslade@pacifica.edu
SLADE, Jason .... 231-995-1995 228 F
jslade@nmc.edu
SLADE, Lisa .... 203-332-5017.. 86 E
lslade@housatonic.edu
SLADEN, Ian .... 215-895-2185 382 D
ian.sladen@drexel.edu
SLADEN, Sue .... 610-409-3175 400 E
ssladen@ursinus.edu
SLAFF, Sara .... 410-704-4003 204 B
sslaff@towson.edu
SLAFKOSKY, Mary .... 616-632-2453 221 A
mvs002@aquinas.edu
SLAGAN, Stephanie .... 760-921-5421.. 56 A
stephanie.slagan@paloverde.edu
SLAGAN, Stephanie .... 760-921-5524.. 56 A
stephanie.slagan@paloverde.edu
SLAGELL, Jeff .... 662-846-4441 245 A
jslagell@deltastate.edu
SLAGER, Joan .... 859-251-4563 180 C
joan.slager@frontier.edu
SLAGER, Karen .... 815-802-8110 141 B
kslager@kcc.edu
SLAGHT, Charles .... 559-730-3821.. 39 C
charless@cos.edu
SLAGLE, Roger .... 828-689-1306 330 H
rslagle@mhu.edu
SLAGTER, Cynthia .... 616-526-6551 221 L
cslagter@calvin.edu
SLANGAN, Rebecca .... 570-504-9620 384 A
rslangan@som.geisinger.edu
SLANIA, Heather .... 410-225-2311 200 B
hslania@mica.edu
SLATE, Julie .... 585-292-2224 306 K
jslate@monroecc.edu
SLATE, Kristine .... 903-233-4332 438 C
kristineslate@letu.edu
SLATE, Selina .... 706-886-6831 126 C
sslate@tfc.edu
SLATER, Alicia .... 845-575-3000 305 C
alicia.slater@marist.edu
SLATER, Bernata .... 650-358-6795.. 62 H
slaterb@smccd.edu

SLATER, Emilee .... 559-325-5012.. 66 H
emilee.slater@cloviscollege.edu
SLATER, Erin .... 804-752-7305 469 B
erinslater@rmc.edu
SLATER, Glenn .... 814-234-7755 397 H
SLATER, Ian .... 617-745-3717 208 F
ian.slater@enc.edu
SLATER, Ian .... 765-677-2138 157 F
ian.slater@indwes.edu
SLATER, Joseph .... 931-372-3172 425 B
jslater@tntech.edu
SLATER, Kara .... 616-395-7836 224 H
slater@hope.edu
SLATER, Lori .... 417-873-7267 252 A
lslater002@drury.edu
SLATER, Nikki .... 325-670-1130 436 B
nikki.slater@hsutx.edu
SLATER, Richard .... 773-291-6100 135 B
SLATER, Tracy .... 207-216-4439 195 F
tslater@yccc.edu
SLATER, Troy .... 231-348-6610 228 D
tslater@ncmich.edu
SLATER, William .... 615-675-5255 427 D
wslater@welch.edu
SLATER, Willie .... 404-880-6037 116 I
wslater@cau.edu
SLATER, Willie .... 334-724-4880.... 7 D
wslater@tuskegee.edu
SLATTERY, Christopher . 508-830-5060 213 A
cslattery@maritime.edu
SLATTERY, Katheryn ...... 815-836-5275 142 C
slatteka@lewisu.edu
SLAUGHTER, Amanda ... 574-807-7168 153 G
amanda.slaughter@betheluniversity.edu
SLAUGHTER, Arnie .... 859-572-5538 184 B
slaughtera@nku.edu
SLAUGHTER, Clinton ..... 707-476-4242.. 58 I
clinton-slaughter@redwoods.edu
SLAUGHTER, Clinton ..... 661-362-3298.. 38 H
clinton.slaughter@canyons.edu
SLAUGHTER, Clinton .... 530-895-2366.. 27 F
slaughtercl@butte.edu
SLAUGHTER, Craig .... 740-427-5430 354 I
slaughterc@kenyon.edu
SLAUGHTER, John .... 254-267-7024 441 D
jslaughter@rangercollege.edu
SLAUGHTER, Lauren ..... 308-398-7548 265 C
laurenslaughter@cccneb.edu
SLAUGHTER,
Matthew, J .... 603-646-2460 272 F
matthew.j.slaughter@dartmouth.edu
SLAUGHTER, Mildred ..... 361-593-2834 447 A
mildred.slaughter@tamuk.edu
SLAUGHTER, Shirley ..... 510-981-2840.. 56 J
sslaughter@peralta.edu
SLAUGHTER, Sonya ...... 312-939-0111 137 B
sonya@eastwest.edu
SLAUGHTER ALLISON,
Michelle .... 619-961-4222.. 68 A
mallison@tjsl.edu
SLAVEN-LEE, Pamela ..... 843-271-7222.. 92 C
pamelaslavenlee@gwu.edu
SLAVENS, Joseph .... 503-255-0332 374 A
joeslavens@multnomah.edu
SLAVIN, Cheryl .... 212-824-2294 300 H
cslavin@huc.edu
SLAVIN, Dennis .... 646-660-6504 292 F
dennis.slavin@baruch.cuny.edu
SLAVIN, Joan, L .... 714-850-4800.. 67 G
slavin@taftu.edu
SLAVIN, Ken .... 210-486-0883 428 D
kslavin4@alamo.edu
SLAVIN, Lisa .... 781-239-2501 214 E
lslavin@massbay.edu
SLAVIN, Marc .... 510-628-8013.. 48 G
mslavin@lincolnuca.edu
SLAWIK, Nora .... 651-779-3338 237 D
nora.slawik@century.edu
SLAWSON, Linda .... 903-923-2137 435 A
lslawson@etbu.edu
SLAY, Carlquista .... 256-372-5601.... 1 A
carlquista.slay@aamu.edu
SLAYMAKER, Valerie ...... 651-213-4746 235 G
vslaymaker@hazeldenbettyford.edu
SLAYTER, Misty .... 318-487-5443 187 G
mistyslayter@cltcc.edu
SLAYTON, Mark .... 480-947-6644.. 15 B
SLAZER, Mary .... 985-545-1500 188 B
SLEASMAN, Brent, C ..... 419-434-4201 364 B
president@winebrenner.edu
SLEDGE, Dennis .... 229-430-2837 114 G
dsledge@albanytech.edu

SLEE, Joshua .... 610-282-1100 382 A
joshua.slee@desales.edu
SLEIGH-LAYMAN, Staci . 509-963-2111 477 G
SLEIGHT, Garth .... 406-874-6212 262 K
sleightg@milescc.edu
SLEJKO, Christa .... 972-273-3010 434 C
cslejko@dcccd.edu
SLEMMER, Duane .... 280-467-8039 132 B
dlslemmer@nnu.edu
SLENKER, Robert .... 229-931-2074 120 B
robert.slenker@gsw.edu
SLEPITZA, Ron .... 816-501-3750 249 H
ron.slepitza@avila.edu
SLEPPPY,
Christopher, G .... 317-921-4882 158 B
SLEVA, Michael .... 616-451-3511 222 H
msleva@davenport.edu
SLEZAK, Cyrill .... 801-863-6205 460 A
cslezak@uvu.edu
SLIDER, Chancey .... 318-473-6578 189 A
cslider@lsua.edu
SLIFE, JR., Harry .... 808-743-2952 450 D
harry.slife@ttuhsc.edu
SLIMAN, David .... 601-266-6633 248 H
david.sliman@usm.edu
SLINGER, Ron .... 406-874-6165 262 K
president@milescc.edu
SLINKARD, Tiffany .... 417-455-5636 251 H
tiffanyslinkard@crowder.edu
SLIWA, William .... 773-821-2215 134 J
wsliwa@csu.edu
SLIWINSKI, Laura .... 858-513-9240.. 16 I
laura.sliwinski@ashford.edu
SLIWOSKI, Richard, F ... 804-828-9647 472 D
rfsliwoski@vcu.edu
SLIZEWSKI, James .... 215-489-2220 381 K
james.slizewski@delval.edu
SLIZEWSKI, Jim .... 215-489-2220 381 K
james.slizewski@delval.edu
SLOAN, Daniel .... 530-226-4125.. 64 C
dsloan@simpsonu.edu
SLOAN, Jon, R .... 504-526-4745 190 C
jonroy@nationsu.edu
SLOAN, Kelly .... 816-271-4465 256 C
SLOAN, Mary Anne .... 765-430-0600 158 A
msloan26@ivytech.edu
SLOAN, Noel .... 806-742-4250 450 C
noel.a.sloan@ttu.edu
SLOAN, Robert .... 281-649-3450 436 D
rsloan@hbu.edu
SLOAN, Stacey .... 303-751-8700.. 78 A
sloan@belrea.edu
SLOAN, Tim .... 801-524-1986 458 F
tim.sloan@ldsbc.edu
SLOAN, Todd .... 203-582-7525.. 88 F
todd.sloan@quinnipiac.edu
SLOAN LATTA, Marcia .. 419-434-5722 362 D
latta@findlay.edu
SLOANE, Todd .... 585-585-1836 299 E
todd.sloane@flcc.edu
SLOAS, Ike .... 901-843-3880 422 C
sloasi@rhodes.edu
SLOBERT, Yantee .... 585-385-8423 313 A
yslobert@sjfc.edu
SLOCKETT, Deena .... 407-303-7747.. 95 A
deena.slockett@ahu.edu
SLOCUM, Cameron .... 214-648-6404 456 D
cameron.slocum@utsouthwestern.edu
SLOCUM, Jeff .... 315-655-7192 292 B
jslocum@cazenovia.edu
SLOCUM, Stacy, S .... 585-385-8388 313 A
sslocum@sjfc.edu
SLOKA, Sandra, L .... 815-740-5026 152 E
ssloka@stfrancis.edu
SLOMOVITS, Mendel ..... 732-414-2834 284 K
SLON, Dennis .... 703-908-7600 468 A
dennis.slon@marymount.edu
SLONE, Amanda, J .... 606-218-5016 185 F
amandjslone@upike.edu
SLONE, Greta .... 606-886-3863 181 A
gslone0020@kctcs.edu
SLONE, Katrina .... 606-368-6091 178 D
katrinaslone@alc.edu
SLONE, Tammy, L .... 937-766-7987 349 C
slonet@cedarville.edu
SLONIKER, Steven .... 509-574-4676 485 E
ssloniker@yvcc.edu
SLOOP, John, M .... 615-322-7360 427 B
john.m.sloop@vanderbilt.edu
SLOPER, Aaron .... 503-883-2240 373 E
asloper@linfield.edu
SLOSS, Brian .... 715-346-4617 496 B
bsloss@uwsp.edu

Index of Key Administrators

SLOTA – SMITH 897

SLOTA, Danielle 206-878-3710 480 C
dslota@highline.edu
SLOTNICK, Ruth 508-531-2783 212 B
ruth.slotnick@bridgew.edu
SLOTTERBACK, Carissa 612-720-4048 400 A
cslotterback@pitt.edu
SLOVER, Todd 603-513-1379 273 I
todd.slover@granite.edu
SLOWE, Ashley 215-965-4000 390 C
SLOWENSKY, Joseph 714-744-7882 36 D
jslowens@chapman.edu
SLOWINSKI, Jason 303-273-3000 79 A
jslowinski@mines.edu
SLOWINSKI, Mandy 715-346-4771 496 B
mandy.slowinski@uwsp.edu
SLUDER, Dusti 850-484-2232 105 G
dsluder@pensacolastate.edu
SLUDER, Jesse 805-289-6235 74 B
jsluder@vcccd.edu
SLUDER, Richard, D 615-898-2324 421 C
richard.sluder@mtsu.edu
SLUDER, Robin 423-478-7727 421 J
rsluder@ptseminary.edu
SLUIS, Kimberly 630-637-5152 145 E
kasluis@noctrl.edu
SLUPIK, Monida 916-348-4689 42 B
mslupik@epic.edu
SLUSARSKI, Diane 585-475-5567 312 A
dcsrgs@rit.edu
SLUSSER, Jeney 941-309-4033 106 J
jslusser@ringling.edu
SLYKHUIS, David 229-333-5925 127 C
dslykhuis@valdosta.edu
SLYTER, Alexis 417-873-7848 252 A
aslyter@drury.edu
SMAGLO, Stephanie 757-233-8757 476 C
ssmaglo@vwu.edu
SMAIL, John 704-687-0966 342 C
jsmail@uncc.edu
SMAJIC, Alen 315-792-5331 306 G
asmajic@mvcc.edu
SMALARZ, Matthew 215-885-2360 389 A
msmalarz@manor.edu
SMALE, Heather 207-454-1025 195 E
hsmale@wccc.me.edu
SMALE, Maura, A 212-817-7060 293 D
msmale@gc.cuny.edu
SMALL, Blake 425-889-5235 481 A
blake.small@northwestu.edu
SMALL, Brent 575-562-2194 285 E
brent.small@enmu.edu
SMALL, Brent 502-897-4721 184 D
bsmall@sbts.edu
SMALL, Charles 219-464-6894 162 C
charles.small@valpo.edu
SMALL, Chiyedza 718-270-6458 294 E
csmall@mec.cuny.edu
SMALL, Christine 760-384-6219 47 C
christine.small@cerrocoso.edu
SMALL, Cindy 406-265-3787 264 A
csmall@msun.edu
SMALL, Darlene 843-383-8039 407 C
dsmall@coker.edu
SMALL, Elizabeth 508-793-3759 208 A
esmall@holycross.edu
SMALL, Erika, E 843-349-2071 407 B
esmall@coastal.edu
SMALL, Jessica 575-562-2118 285 F
jessica.small@enmu.edu
SMALL, Jessica 575-562-2218 285 E
jessica.small@enmu.edu
SMALL, Jonathan 781-768-7335 217 H
jonathan.small@regiscollege.edu
SMALL, Jonathan 504-247-1758 191 D
jsmall4@tulane.edu
SMALL, LaTrice 501-420-1242 17 D
latrice.small@arkansasbaptist.edu
SMALL, Natissia 314-516-5128 260 E
smalln@umsl.edu
SMALL, Sonya 252-451-8261 336 B
sysmall345@nashcc.edu
SMALL, Steven, L 972-883-2355 454 D
small@utdallas.edu
SMALL, Tyvi 865-974-6270 426 C
tsmall@utk.edu
SMALL KELLOGG,
Rebecca 315-786-6549 302 I
rsmallkellogg@sunyjefferson.edu
SMALLEN, Stephanie 423-746-5213 425 C
ssmallen@tnwesleyan.edu
SMALLIDGE, Dianne 617-732-1528 216 B
dianne.smallidge@mcphs.edu
SMALLING, Scott, J 315-268-6473 295 E
ssmallin@clarkson.edu
SMALLING, Steven 315-268-4368 295 E
sssmalli@clarkson.edu
SMALLING, Susan 507-786-3350 242 I
smalling@stolaf.edu
SMALLS, Shanté, P 718-990-2936 313 B
smallss@stjohns.edu
SMALLWOOD, Dawn 631-632-6350 316 D
dawn.smallwood@stonybrook.edu
SMALLWOOD, Will 937-766-2211 349 C
SMARR, Debbie 903-415-2592 435 H
smarrd@grayson.edu
SMARRELLA, Tony 530-226-4607 64 C
tsmarrella@simpsonu.edu
SMART, III, Clifton, M 417-836-8500 255 J
president@missouristate.edu
SMART, Gary 406-771-5140 264 B
gary.smart@gfcmsu.edu
SMART, Monica 325-670-1595 436 B
monica.j.smart@hsutx.edu
SMART, Robert 616-331-2281 224 D
smartr@gvsu.edu
SMART, Rod 760-355-6113 45 N
rod.smart@imperial.edu
SMART, William 615-297-7545 416 G
smartb@aquinascollege.edu
SMATRESK, Neal 940-565-4307 453 B
president@unt.edu
SMEDLEY, David 973-877-3468 276 G
dsmedley@essex.edu
SMEDLEY, Lori 312-362-8610 136 F
SMEDLEY, Susan 660-543-4640 259 K
smedley@ucmo.edu
SMEED, Shane 816-584-6202 257 E
shane.smeed@park.edu
SMELIANSKY, Julia 212-686-9244 289 G
SMELKINSON, Michael 443-518-4522 199 D
msmelkinson@howardcc.edu
SMENT, Nicole 608-262-0110 494 C
nsment@uwsa.edu
SMETANIUK, Mira 904-264-2172 106 K
SMID, Terry 563-425-5359 170 D
smidt@uiu.edu
SMIDT, Niki 605-658-5641 415 E
niki.smidt@usd.edu
SMIETANA, Rebecca 901-722-3241 422 I
rsmietana@sco.edu
SMIGIELSKI, Kristin 217-351-2535 146 G
ksmigielski@parkland.edu
SMILEY, Ellen 318-274-3228 191 G
smileye@gram.edu
SMILEY, Joseph 727-712-5851 107 C
smiley.joseph@spcollege.edu
SMILEY, Justin 760-744-1150 56 B
jsmiley@palomar.edu
SMIT, Cori 817-257-5157 447 H
cori.smit@tcu.edu
SMITH, Adam, D 717-361-1161 383 B
smithadam1@etown.edu
SMITH, Addie 805-565-6024 75 I
addsmith@westmont.edu
SMITH, Adrian 212-343-1234 306 C
asmith@mcny.edu
SMITH, Adriana, K 864-938-3777 410 E
adsmith@presby.edu
SMITH, Alan 256-549-8601 2 B
asmith@gadsdenstate.edu
SMITH, Alan 435-797-0634 459 F
al.smith@usu.edu
SMITH, Alexa 917-493-4477 304 L
asmith@msmnyc.edu
SMITH, Alexandra 262-547-1211 491 A
SMITH, Alicia 732-987-2454 277 B
asmith@georgian.edu
SMITH, Alisa 419-824-3963 355 C
asmith@lourdes.edu
SMITH, Alison 330-672-3709 354 A
alisonjs@kent.edu
SMITH, Allen, D 785-827-5541 175 C
allen.smith@kwu.edu
SMITH, Altrice 804-706-5079 473 B
asmith@jtcc.edu
SMITH, Amanda 972-883-6154 454 D
als072000@utdallas.edu
SMITH, Amanda 815-921-3102 147 H
a.smith@rockvalleycollege.edu
SMITH, Amanda 806-874-3571 431 K
amanda.smith@clarendoncollege.edu
SMITH, Amber 806-291-3425 457 B
smitha@wbu.edu
SMITH, Amber 317-788-2412 161 F
smitha008@uindy.edu
SMITH, Amber 252-638-7226 333 F
smitham@cravencc.edu
SMITH, Amy 651-962-5000 243 F
SMITH, Amy 205-226-4699 5 A
acsmith3@bsc.edu
SMITH, Amy 513-745-5615 362 A
amy.smith@uc.edu
SMITH, Amy, E 716-926-8877 301 C
asmith@hilbert.edu
SMITH, Ana 520-515-3636 11 O
smitha@cochise.edu
SMITH, Andrew 859-257-8779 185 D
drewsmith02@uky.edu
SMITH, Andrew 423-775-7218 417 D
asmith2831@bryan.edu
SMITH, Andrew 865-471-3243 417 E
asmith@cn.edu
SMITH, Angela 229-928-1373 120 B
angela.smith@gsw.edu
SMITH, Angi 423-585-2680 424 G
angi.smith@ws.edu
SMITH, Angie 812-877-8436 160 C
smith21@rose-hulman.edu
SMITH, Ann, T 859-238-5459 179 H
ann.smith@centre.edu
SMITH, Anne 910-362-7028 332 F
awsmith427@mail.cfcc.edu
SMITH, Annie 864-424-8055 412 H
alsmith@mailbox.sc.edu
SMITH, April 936-468-4048 444 H
alsmith@sfasu.edu
SMITH, Ariel 478-471-4394 121 C
SMITH, Ashley 704-378-1237 329 H
apsmith2@jcsu.edu
SMITH, Astria 214-768-4738 443 G
astrias@smu.edu
SMITH, Atheria 510-981-2800 56 J
atheriasmith@peralta.edu
SMITH, Barbra 256-761-6415 7 B
bsmith@talladega.edu
SMITH, Becky 614-823-1420 359 G
rsmith@otterbein.edu
SMITH, Benny 828-227-3083 343 D
bennysmith@wcu.edu
SMITH, Beth 845-938-3808 502 H
beth.smith@westpoint.edu
SMITH, Beverly 770-720-5523 124 E
beverly.smith@reinhardt.edu
SMITH, Beverly, R 804-237-5467 475 G
brsmith@vuu.edu
SMITH, Bill 818-345-7921 39 F
bsmith@columbiacollege.edu
SMITH, Bill 870-972-2169 17 I
billsmith@astate.edu
SMITH, Bill 401-232-6078 403 B
bsmith8@bryant.edu
SMITH, Bill, H 703-812-4757 467 D
bsmith@leland.edu
SMITH, Blake 865-981-8264 420 C
blake.smith@maryvillecollege.edu
SMITH, Bonnie 850-718-2451 97 E
smithb@chipola.edu
SMITH, Brad 214-329-4447 429 L
brad.smith@bgu.edu
SMITH, Brad, D 304-696-3977 488 N
president@marshall.edu
SMITH, Brad, D 937-766-7872 349 C
smthb@cedarville.edu
SMITH, Brad, K 608-743-4596 497 D
bsmith32@blackhawk.edu
SMITH, Bradford 601-973-5015 244 C
bmsmith@belhaven.edu
SMITH, Bradley, D 574-807-7255 153 G
bradley.smith@betheluniversity.edu
SMITH, Brian 701-858-3210 345 C
brian.smith.2@minotstateu.edu
SMITH, Brian 716-888-2785 291 M
smith@canisius.edu
SMITH, Brian 443-997-5661 199 E
brismith@jhu.edu
SMITH, Brian 803-938-3707 412 G
bcsmith2@uscsumter.edu
SMITH, Brian, D 972-241-3371 433 E
bsmith@dallas.edu
SMITH, Brian, T 734-764-7270 231 A
btsm@umich.edu
SMITH, Brien, N 330-941-3103 364 G
bnsmith06@ysu.edu
SMITH, Brittain 508-793-2011 208 A
bsmith@holycross.edu
SMITH, Brooksie 812-749-1271 159 E
bsmith@oak.edu
SMITH, Bruce 256-761-6225 7 B
bcsmith@talladega.edu
SMITH, Bruce 303-871-6103 84 C
bruce.smith@du.edu
SMITH, Bryan 270-706-8616 181 C
bryan.smith@kctcs.edu
SMITH, Bryan 419-448-2045 353 D
bsmith3@heidelberg.edu
SMITH, Bryan, F 850-599-3183 109 E
bryanf.smith@famu.edu
SMITH, Bryanna, E 360-442-2100 480 E
bsmith@lowercolumbia.edu
SMITH, Buffy 651-962-8010 243 F
bsmith@stthomas.edu
SMITH, Burton, C 540-365-4221 466 I
bcsmith@ferrum.edu
SMITH, C. Drew 870-230-5466 19 H
smithc@hsu.edu
SMITH, Cade 256-824-2274 8 B
cade.smith@uah.edu
SMITH, Carl 760-245-4271 74 D
carl.smith@vvc.edu
SMITH, Carlton 918-587-6789 370 G
carlton.smith@tws.edu
SMITH, Carol 303-273-3911 79 A
cesmith@mines.edu
SMITH, Carol 559-297-4500 46 C
clsmith@iot.edu
SMITH, Carol, L 765-658-4580 154 G
clsmith@depauw.edu
SMITH, Carola 805-965-0581 62 M
smith@sbcc.edu
SMITH, Carola 805-965-0581 62 M
smithc@sbcc.edu
SMITH, Carolyn 713-798-7640 430 E
carolyns@bcm.edu
SMITH, Carolyn, A 304-697-7550 486 F
csmith@huntingtonjuniorcollege.edu
SMITH, Caryn 847-947-5229 145 C
clsmith@nl.edu
SMITH, Ceil 856-351-2644 282 I
csmith@salemcc.edu
SMITH, Chad 605-336-6588 415 B
casmith@kairos.edu
SMITH, Chantel 415-422-5555 72 I
csmith28@usfca.edu
SMITH, Charity 501-375-9845 21 A
cosmith@philander.edu
SMITH, Charles 334-727-8448 7 D
csmith1@tuskegee.edu
SMITH, Charles 256-761-6205 7 B
csmith@talladega.edu
SMITH, Charles 910-678-8484 334 C
smithch@faytechcc.edu
SMITH, Charles, M 979-209-8272 430 I
charlesm@blinn.edu
SMITH, JR.,
Charles, W 816-414-3700 255 F
csmith@mbts.edu
SMITH, Charmaine, I 340-692-4070 512 B
hsmithc@uvi.edu
SMITH, Charmian 516-572-7376 307 C
charmian.smith@ncc.edu
SMITH, Chelsea 936-294-4155 449 E
cxs027@shsu.edu
SMITH, Cheryl 413-265-2253 208 B
smithc911@elms.edu
SMITH, Chris 719-549-2611 79 G
chris.smith@csupueblo.edu
SMITH, Chris 630-844-6143 133 A
csmith@aurora.edu
SMITH, Chris 901-334-5835 420 E
csmith@memphisseminary.edu
SMITH, Christa 785-670-1873 178 A
christa.smith@washburn.edu
SMITH, Christala 580-745-3185 369 F
clsmith@se.edu
SMITH, Christie 585-245-5571 317 E
csmith@geneseo.edu
SMITH, Christine 678-466-5406 117 A
christinesmith@clayton.edu
SMITH, Christine 423-425-4646 426 D
chris-smith@utc.edu
SMITH, Christopher 646-564-6731 289 F
christopher.smith@nyack.edu
SMITH, Christopher 870-777-5722 23 C
christopher.smith@uaht.edu
SMITH, Christopher 740-427-5415 354 I
smith5@kenyon.edu
SMITH, Cindy 432-264-5034 436 H
csmith@howardcollege.edu
SMITH, Cindy 256-469-7333 5 I
admin@hbc1.edu

SMITH, Cindy .... 412-281-2600 395 C
csmith@pci.edu
SMITH, Claire .... 210-999-8841 451 B
csmith9@trinity.edu
SMITH, Colleen, A .... 928-266-4217.. 12 B
colleen.smith@coconino.edu
SMITH, Connie .... 209-476-7840.. 67 D
csmith@clcm.net
SMITH, Connie .... 207-581-1371 196 I
csmith@maine.edu
SMITH, Connie .... 207-581-1372 196 D
csmith@maine.edu
SMITH, Connor .... 214-333-5365 433 D
connors@dbu.edu
SMITH, Cortney .... 918-647-1213 365 D
clsmith@carlalbert.edu
SMITH, Courtney .... 859-233-8124 185 A
cesmith@transy.edu
SMITH, Courtney .... 601-877-6147 244 B
clsmith@alcorn.edu
SMITH, Courtney .... 973-313-6203 282 K
courtney.smith@shu.edu
SMITH, Craig .... 406-768-5555 262 I
csmith@fpcc.edu
SMITH, Crystal .... 973-596-3690 278 G
crystal.s.smith@njit.edu
SMITH, Crystal, M .... 301-546-0180 201 D
smithcm@pgcc.edu
SMITH, Cynthia .... 301-687-4328 203 F
colsmith@frostburg.edu
SMITH, D. Gordon .... 801-422-6384 458 A
smithg@law.byu.edu
SMITH, Dale, T .... 914-831-0311 296 F
dsmith@cw.edu
SMITH, Dan .... 414-443-8800 497 A
dan.smith@wlc.edu
SMITH, Dane .... 202-885-8663.. 94 D
dsmith@wesleyseminary.edu
SMITH, Daniel .... 864-242-5100 405 H
SMITH, Darby .... 903-927-3300 457 I
dsmith3@wileyc.edu
SMITH, Darnell .... 210-784-5500 447 B
dsmith@tamusa.edu
SMITH, Darren, A .... 407-582-3015 113 C
dsmith335@valenciacollege.edu
SMITH, Darron .... 931-372-3149 425 B
darronsmith@tntech.edu
SMITH, Daryl .... 716-829-7623 298 C
smithd@dyc.edu
SMITH, David .... 518-783-2432 314 K
dsmith@siena.edu
SMITH, David .... 310-568-5538.. 56 H
david.smith@pepperdine.edu
SMITH, Davis .... 919-532-5770 338 E
dbsmith9@waketech.edu
SMITH, Dayle .... 310-338-7504.. 51 C
dayle.smith@lmu.edu
SMITH, Dean .... 504-568-5960 189 C
dgsmith@lsuhsc.edu
SMITH, Dean .... 919-687-3600 328 D
dean.j.smith@duke.edu
SMITH, Deanna .... 601-484-8895 246 B
dsmith40@meridiancc.edu
SMITH, Debbi .... 516-877-3522 288 L
smith8@adelphi.edu
SMITH, Deborah .... 281-998-6150 442 D
SMITH, Denise .... 914-633-2067 302 C
dsmith@iona.edu
SMITH, Denise .... 567-661-7250 359 H
denise_smith4@owens.edu
SMITH, Denise, D .... 804-662-3196 471 E
ddsmith@richmond.edu
SMITH, Denise, S .... 765-973-8560 156 D
dss3@iu.edu
SMITH, Dennis .... 530-226-4754.. 64 C
dsmith@simpsonu.edu
SMITH, Dennis .... 252-335-0821 333 E
dennis_smith@albemarle.edu
SMITH, Deron .... 615-966-6280 420 B
dsmith2@lipscomb.edu
SMITH, Derrek .... 256-233-8274.... 4 D
derrek.smith@athens.edu
SMITH, Devin .... 402-643-7328 265 I
devin.smith@cune.edu
SMITH, Diana .... 303-762-6886.. 80 G
diana.smith@denverseminary.edu
SMITH, Diane .... 931-372-3554 425 B
dianesmith@tntech.edu
SMITH, Dolores .... 951-639-5230.. 53 A
dolsmith@msjc.edu
SMITH, Donald .... 623-845-3070.. 13 E
don.smith@gccaz.edu
SMITH, Donald .... 215-641-6534 390 A
dsmith4@mc3.edu
SMITH, Donald, L .... 270-745-6256 186 A
donald.smith@wku.edu
SMITH, Donna .... 601-925-3313 246 D
dsmith@mc.edu
SMITH, Donna .... 701-777-4172 344 H
donna.smith@und.edu
SMITH, Donovan .... 706-886-6831 126 C
dsmith@tfc.edu
SMITH, Dorothy .... 706-233-7299 125 A
djsmith@shorter.edu
SMITH, Doug .... 508-565-1344 218 F
dougsmith@stonehill.edu
SMITH, Doug .... 910-695-3811 337 E
smithd@sandhills.edu
SMITH, Douglas .... 716-839-8237 297 F
dsmith@daemen.edu
SMITH, Douglas .... 765-361-6011 162 G
smithd@wabash.edu
SMITH, Drew .... 248-689-8282 231 E
dsmith4@walshcollege.edu
SMITH, Dwayne .... 203-332-5224.. 86 E
dsmith@housatonic.edu
SMITH, Dwayne .... 813-974-3151 111 B
mdsmith8@usf.edu
SMITH, III, Dwight .... 832-813-6603 438 E
dwight.smith@lonestar.edu
SMITH, E. Ashley .... 713-718-7514 436 E
edgar.smith2@hccs.edu
SMITH, Ed .... 615-550-3160 427 F
ed.smith@williamsoncc.edu
SMITH, Elaine .... 865-471-3208 417 E
esmith@cn.edu
SMITH, Elaine, L .... 516-833-8181 288 L
elsmith@adelphi.edu
SMITH, Elizabeth, F .... 603-646-3999 272 F
elizabeth.f.smith@dartmouth.edu
SMITH, Elmer, R .... 770-216-2960 121 F
ers@ict.edu
SMITH, Emmett .... 252-538-4317 334 G
esmith956@halifaxcc.edu
SMITH, Eric .... 315-464-5763 316 F
smither@upstate.edu
SMITH, Eric .... 270-789-5202 179 G
epsmith@campbellsville.edu
SMITH, Eric .... 304-357-4358 486 J
ericsmith@ucwv.edu
SMITH, Eric, D .... 805-922-6966.. 24 L
ericd.smith@hancockcollege.edu
SMITH, Ericka .... 702-895-3958 270 J
ericka.smith@unlv.edu
SMITH, Erika, J .... 860-439-2010.. 87 F
esmith25@connoll.edu
SMITH, Erin .... 318-797-5324 189 E
erin.smith@lsus.edu
SMITH, Erin .... 828-898-3416 330 A
smithe@lmc.edu
SMITH, Erin .... 214-333-5770 433 D
erins@dbu.edu
SMITH, Erin, T .... 724-946-7327 401 F
smithet@westminster.edu
SMITH, Eva .... 425-640-1394 479 A
esmith@edcc.edu
SMITH, JR., Frank, M .... 502-776-1443 184 C
fsmith@simmonscollegeky.edu
SMITH, Fred .... 410-706-8337 202 F
fsmith@umaryland.edu
SMITH, Frederick .... 201-200-3474 278 F
fsmith@njcu.edu
SMITH, Frederick .... 507-933-8809 235 E
fredericksmith@gustavus.edu
SMITH, Fritz .... 562-907-4951.. 76 A
fritz@whittier.edu
SMITH, Gabie .... 336-278-6490 328 H
gsmith@elon.edu
SMITH, Garrett .... 480-461-7211.. 13 F
garrett.smith@mesacc.edu
SMITH, Gary .... 716-827-2507 322 J
smithg@trocaire.edu
SMITH, Gavin .... 206-546-4792 483 C
gavinsmith@shoreline.edu
SMITH, Gene .... 910-755-7302 332 D
smithgene@brunswickcc.edu
SMITH, Gene, D .... 614-292-2477 358 E
smith.5407@osu.edu
SMITH, George .... 207-879-8955 194 E
gsmith@idsva.edu
SMITH, Gerritt .... 937-328-6062 350 D
smithg@clarkstate.edu
SMITH, Gigi .... 843-792-2228 409 D
smithgi@musc.edu
SMITH, Glenn .... 801-832-2826 461 A
gsmith@westminstercollege.edu
SMITH, Glenn, C .... 503-552-1514 374 B
gsmith@nunm.edu
SMITH, Grace .... 310-434-4454.. 63 B
smith_grace@smc.edu
SMITH, Greg .... 256-824-2542.... 8 B
greg.smith@uah.edu
SMITH, Greg .... 704-922-6476 334 E
smith.greg@gaston.edu
SMITH, Greg .... 973-408-3580 276 B
gsmith2@drew.edu
SMITH, Gregory .... 662-720-7164 247 D
gcsmith@nemcc.edu
SMITH, Gregory .... 714-449-7456.. 51 D
gsmith@ketchum.edu
SMITH, Gregory .... 610-399-2240 393 D
gsmith@cheyney.edu
SMITH, Gregory, A .... 619-388-6589.. 60 H
gsmith@sdccd.edu
SMITH, Harris .... 505-277-2112 288 C
hdsmith@unm.edu
SMITH, Heidi .... 714-816-0366.. 68 G
heidilinn.smith@trident.edu
SMITH, Hilary, B .... 618-537-6981 143 G
hbsmith@mckendree.edu
SMITH, Holly .... 870-612-2003.. 23 B
holly.smith@uaccb.edu
SMITH, Holly .... 870-512-7841.. 18 C
holly_smith@asun.edu
SMITH, Holly .... 812-488-2241 161 E
hh98@evansville.edu
SMITH, Holly .... 253-964-6287 481 H
hsmith@pierce.ctc.edu
SMITH, Howard .... 620-235-4113 176 H
smith@pittstate.edu
SMITH, Ian .... 740-427-5181 354 I
smith18@kenyon.edu
SMITH, Idelia .... 413-552-2228 214 D
ismith@hcc.edu
SMITH, Ivan .... 301-934-7724 198 C
ilsmith1@csmd.edu
SMITH, J. Cole .... 315-443-4341 321 D
colesmit@syr.edu
SMITH, J. Malcolm .... 269-337-7209 225 B
malcolm.smith@kzoo.edu
SMITH, Jackie .... 208-732-6304 131 B
jksmith1@csi.edu
SMITH, Jaclyn .... 312-369-7571 136 C
jsmith2@colum.edu
SMITH, Jake .... 608-263-2985 494 D
soas@soas.wisc.edu
SMITH, James .... 740-392-6868 356 G
james.smith@mvnu.edu
SMITH, James .... 334-241-5436.... 7 C
jesmith@troy.edu
SMITH, James .... 214-860-2232 434 A
jhsmith@dcccd.edu
SMITH, James, M .... 734-487-2211 223 F
president@emich.edu
SMITH, Jamie .... 602-557-5757.. 16 L
jamie.smith@phoenix.edu
SMITH, Jamie, M .... 941-752-5587 109 C
smithj4@scf.edu
SMITH, Janet .... 423-869-6287 420 A
janet.smith@lmunet.edu
SMITH, Janet, F .... 931-540-2510 423 D
janet.smith@columbiastate.edu
SMITH, Janet, M .... 724-946-7139 401 F
smithjm@westminster.edu
SMITH, Jared .... 704-355-4305 327 F
robert.smith2@carolinascollege.edu
SMITH, Jared .... 716-375-2622 312 F
jasmith@sbu.edu
SMITH, Jarret, L .... 540-828-5469 464 C
jlsmith@bridgewater.edu
SMITH, Jasmine .... 479-788-7241.. 22 A
jasmine.smith@uafs.edu
SMITH, Jason .... 269-687-5642 230 D
jsmith07@swmich.edu
SMITH, Jason .... 409-944-1356 435 F
jsmith@gc.edu
SMITH, Jason .... 903-823-3198 445 C
jason.smith@texarkanacollege.edu
SMITH, Jason .... 870-248-4000.. 18 H
jason.smith@blackrivertech.edu
SMITH, Jason .... 469-614-3800 451 C
jason.smith@tvcc.edu
SMITH, Jason, S .... 832-842-9064 451 F
jsmith10@uh.edu
SMITH, Jason, S .... 832-842-9064 451 G
jsmith10@uh.edu
SMITH, Jay Dee .... 360-417-6403 481 F
jsmith@pencol.edu
SMITH, Jeannette .... 413-662-5231 212 F
jeannette.smith@mcla.edu
SMITH, Jeannette .... 901-333-4737 424 E
jgsmith@southwest.tn.edu
SMITH, Jeff .... 941-487-4353 110 C
jsmith@ncf.edu
SMITH, Jeffrey .... 305-809-3149.. 97 M
jeffrey.smith6@cfk.edu
SMITH, Jeffrey .... 907-260-7422.... 9 D
SMITH, Jeffrey .... 404-225-4634 115 F
jsmith@atlantatech.edu
SMITH, JR., Jeffrey .... 617-732-1652 209 A
smithj4@emmanuel.edu
SMITH, Jeffrey, N .... 716-645-4592 315 F
jeff@buffalo.edu
SMITH, Jenelle .... 251-578-1313.... 3 D
jsmith@rstc.edu
SMITH, Jeniece .... 815-599-3421 138 H
jeniece.smith@highland.edu
SMITH, Jennie .... 570-422-3732 393 F
jsmith239@esu.edu
SMITH, Jennie .... 570-422-3798 393 F
jsmith239@esu.edu
SMITH, Jennifer .... 847-925-6523 138 E
jsmith5@harpercollege.edu
SMITH, Jennifer .... 212-229-5300 307 E
jennifer.smith@newschool.edu
SMITH, Jennifer, A .... 253-535-7811 481 C
jennifer.smith@plu.edu
SMITH, Jennifer, B .... 270-745-6824 186 A
jennifer.breiwa.smith@wku.edu
SMITH, Jerry .... 928-344-7535.. 11 B
jerry.smith@azwestern.edu
SMITH, Jerry .... 617-266-1400 206 D
SMITH, Jesse .... 661-255-1050.. 28 I
jsmith@calarts.edu
SMITH, Jesse, R .... 601-477-4100 246 A
jesse.smith@jcjc.edu
SMITH, Jessi, L .... 719-255-3963.. 84 A
jsmith20@uccs.edu
SMITH, Jessica .... 212-228-1888 311 I
SMITH, Jessica .... 276-326-4473 464 A
jsmith@bluefield.edu
SMITH, Jill .... 859-257-8907 185 D
jhsmith@uky.edu
SMITH, Jim .... 918-293-5234 368 B
jim.smith10@okstate.edu
SMITH, Joe .... 509-313-6801 479 E
smithj@gonzaga.edu
SMITH, Joel .... 607-746-4522 320 A
smithjm@delhi.edu
SMITH, Joel .... 308-432-6345 267 G
jsmith@csc.edu
SMITH, John .... 515-271-2969 165 F
john.smith@drake.edu
SMITH, John .... 309-298-1888 152 I
jw-smith@wiu.edu
SMITH, John, W .... 309-298-1888 152 I
jw-smith@wiu.edu
SMITH, John, W .... 931-372-6338 425 B
jwsmith@tntech.edu
SMITH, Johnny .... 252-493-7915 336 E
jmsmith@email.pittcc.edu
SMITH, Joianne, L .... 847-635-1801 146 E
joismith@oakton.edu
SMITH, Jordan .... 270-809-5706 184 A
jsmith3@murraystate.edu
SMITH, Josh .... 530-541-4660.. 47 H
SMITH, Joshua .... 714-592-7878.. 45 A
jsmith@haven.edu
SMITH, Joshua .... 606-337-1164 180 A
joshua.smith@ccbbc.edu
SMITH, Joyya .... 617-223-4423 218 G
jsmith19@suffolk.edu
SMITH, Judy .... 814-824-3650 389 E
jsmith@mercyhurst.edu
SMITH, Julie .... 540-654-1614 471 B
jsmith23@umw.edu
SMITH, Julie .... 503-725-3773 375 D
smithju@pdx.edu
SMITH, Juliet .... 410-822-5400 198 B
jsmith@chesapeake.edu
SMITH, Justin .... 541-917-4214 373 F
smithju@linnbenton.edu
SMITH, Kalith .... 217-786-2414 142 F
kalith.smith@llcc.edu
SMITH, Karan .... 252-249-1851 336 C
ksmith@pamlicocc.edu
SMITH, Karen .... 410-827-5704 198 B
ksmith@chesapeake.edu

SMITH, Robert .... 806-720-7111 438 F
robert.smith@lcu.edu
SMITH, Robert, F .... 610-989-1458 400 F
rsmith@vfmac.edu
SMITH, Robert, R .... 520-621-7777.. 16 H
rrsmith@arizona.edu
SMITH, Robert, T .... 229-333-5950 127 C
rtsmith@valdosta.edu
SMITH, Robert, W .... 252-334-2018 331 C
bob.smith@macuniversity.edu
SMITH, Roberta, J .... 309-298-2446 152 I
rj-smith3@wiu.edu
SMITH, Rochelle .... 256-782-8122.... 6 A
rdsmith@jsu.edu
SMITH, Rochelle .... 314-977-2921 258 H
rochelle.smith@slu.edu
SMITH, Rodney .... 816-415-7848 261 G
smithr@william.jewell.edu
SMITH, Ron .... 904-997-2997 101 A
ron.smith@fscj.edu
SMITH, Ronald .... 904-646-2300 101 A
ron.smith@fscj.edu
SMITH, Rory .... 708-608-4405 144 G
smithr543@morainevalley.edu
SMITH, Rosa .... 301-546-8307 201 D
smithrd@pgcc.edu
SMITH, Roy .... 440-934-3101 357 I
rsmith@ohiobusinesscollege.edu
SMITH, Roy .... 864-592-4905 411 E
smithr@sccsc.edu
SMITH, Royce .... 406-994-6654 263 G
royce.smith@montana.edu
SMITH, Rueben, C .... 213-891-2366.. 49 C
smithrc@laccd.edu
SMITH, Rusty .... 434-544-8880 470 K
smith.ar@lynchburg.edu
SMITH, Ruth .... 618-634-3347 149 C
ruths@shawneecc.edu
SMITH, Ruth, S .... 407-582-1601 113 C
rsmith257@valenciacollege.edu
SMITH, Ryan .... 309-438-2135 140 C
rlsmith@ilstu.edu
SMITH, Ryan .... 707-965-7362.. 55 H
ryesmith@puc.edu
SMITH, Ryan .... 740-245-7204 363 A
rsmith@rio.edu
SMITH, Sam .... 402-363-5621 269 F
samsmith@york.edu
SMITH, Samantha .... 912-871-4779 123 F
ssmith@ogeecheetech.edu
SMITH, Samantha .... 409-882-3083 449 C
samantha.smith@lsco.edu
SMITH, Samuel, J .... 301-295-3028 502 B
samuel.smith@usuhs.edu
SMITH, Sandra, B .... 540-674-3600 473 F
ssmith@nr.edu
SMITH, Sandy .... 760-366-5296.. 40 K
ssmith@cmccd.edu
SMITH, Scott .... 906-635-6672 226 C
ssmith58@lssu.edu
SMITH, Scott .... 423-636-7300 425 E
scsmith@tusculum.edu
SMITH, Scott, A .... 803-786-3672 407 E
scsmith@columbiasc.edu
SMITH, Scott, F .... 305-899-3085.. 96 A
sfsmith@barry.edu
SMITH, Sean .... 805-565-6063.. 75 I
sesmith@westmont.edu
SMITH, Selina .... 301-687-4187 203 F
ssmith@frostburg.edu
SMITH, Sharon .... 404-965-8118.. 10 F
ssmith2@aiuniv.edu
SMITH, Sharon, E .... 616-632-2902 221 A
smithsha@aquinas.edu
SMITH, Shawn .... 217-732-3168 142 D
SMITH, Shawn .... 865-573-4517 419 E
ssmith@johnsonu.edu
SMITH,
Shawn Michelle .... 312-899-5100 149 B
SMITH, Sheila .... 615-329-8710 418 E
shsmith@fisk.edu
SMITH, Shelley .... 256-840-4128..... 3 F
shelley.smith@snead.edu
SMITH, Shelley .... 601-968-5940 244 C
sasmith@belhaven.edu
SMITH, Shelly .... 304-263-0979 487 A
SMITH, Sinclair .... 215-596-8800 400 B
SMITH, Sonya .... 845-437-7583 323 H
SMITH, Stacey .... 509-777-4388 485 D
skammsmith@whitworth.edu
SMITH, Stacey .... 901-435-1351 419 I
stacey_smith@loc.edu
SMITH, Stanley .... 334-347-2623.... 2 A
ssmith@escc.edu
SMITH, Stephanie .... 337-421-6966 188 H
stephanie.smith@sowela.edu
SMITH, Stephanie .... 312-362-7552 136 F
ssmit185@depaul.edu
SMITH, Stephanie .... 928-523-3937.. 14 J
stephanie.smith@nau.edu
SMITH, Stephanie .... 606-546-1259 185 B
sasmith@unionky.edu
SMITH, Stephanie .... 916-558-2120.. 51 B
smithsa@scc.losrios.edu
SMITH, Stephanie .... 415-551-9287.. 28 D
stephanie.smith@cca.edu
SMITH, Stephen .... 253-566-5055 483 F
ssmith@tacomacc.edu
SMITH, Steve .... 865-974-6600 426 C
stevensmith@utk.edu
SMITH, Steve .... 205-652-3576..... 9 B
sdsmith@uwa.edu
SMITH, Steve .... 507-389-5022 238 L
steven.smith@mnsu.edu
SMITH, Steve .... 432-264-5019 436 H
sismith@howardcollege.edu
SMITH, Steven .... 970-521-6657.. 82 B
steven.smith@njc.edu
SMITH, Steven .... 775-682-5613 270 K
ssmith@unr.edu
SMITH, Steven .... 915-831-6472 435 B
ssmith54@epcc.edu
SMITH, Steven .... 304-424-8000 490 A
steven.smith@wvup.edu
SMITH, Steven, E .... 516-877-3304 288 L
stsmith@adelphi.edu
SMITH, Steven, J .... 413-565-1000 205 I
ssmith@baypath.edu
SMITH, Steven, N .... 262-243-5700 491 E
steve.smith@cuw.edu
SMITH, Steven, P .... 989-837-4294 228 G
smithsp@northwood.edu
SMITH, Stuart, A .... 859-858-3511 178 H
stuart.smith@asbury.edu
SMITH, Sue .... 812-372-1623 158 A
sgsmith@ivytech.edu
SMITH, Susanne .... 614-947-6160 352 J
suzanne.smith@franklin.edu
SMITH, Suzanne .... 605-274-5010 413 G
suzanne.smith@augie.edu
SMITH, Suzanne .... 503-255-0332 374 A
ssmith@multnomah.edu
SMITH, Suzanne, R .... 229-928-1361 120 B
suzanne.smith@gsw.edu
SMITH, Tabitha .... 276-328-0131 471 G
tabitha.smith@uvawise.edu
SMITH, Tacci .... 828-771-3800 344 B
tsmith@warren-wilson.edu
SMITH, Tamara, J .... 770-720-5659 124 E
tjs@reinhardt.edu
SMITH, Tammy .... 540-674-3600 473 F
tsmith@nr.edu
SMITH, Tammy .... 716-338-1054 302 G
tammysmith@mail.sunyjcc.edu
SMITH, Tara .... 501-686-2923.. 21 G
tsmith@uasys.edu
SMITH, Tara .... 419-434-4035 362 D
travis@findlay.edu
SMITH, Tariva .... 678-323-7700.. 93 H
SMITH, Tawanikka .... 718-482-5590 294 D
tsmith@lagcc.cuny.edu
SMITH, Teresa .... 410-778-7204 204 E
tsmith23@washcoll.edu
SMITH, Teresa .... 207-453-5155 195 B
tsmith@kvcc.me.edu
SMITH, Teresa, A .... 856-227-7200 275 F
tasmith@camdencc.edu
SMITH, Teresa, L .... 714-879-3901.. 45 J
tlsmith@hiu.edu
SMITH, Terri .... 661-763-7817.. 67 F
tsmith@taftcollege.edu
SMITH, Terry .... 732-247-5241 278 E
tsmith@nbts.edu
SMITH, Terry .... 713-646-1708 443 C
tsmith@stcl.edu
SMITH, Thomas .... 202-319-5115.. 91 G
artsandsciences@cua.edu
SMITH, Thomas .... 314-392-2264 255 H
smitht@mobap.edu
SMITH, Thomas .... 865-573-4517 419 E
tsmith@johnsonu.edu
SMITH, Thomas, J .... 616-234-3951 224 C
tsmith@grcc.edu
SMITH, Tierra .... 813-253-7160 102 A
tsmith175@hccfl.edu
SMITH, Tiffany .... 816-322-0110 250 E
tiffany.smith@calvary.edu
SMITH, Tiffany .... 580-581-2612 365 C
tismith@cameron.edu
SMITH, Tim .... 205-226-4650..... 5 A
tsmith@bsc.edu
SMITH, Todd .... 207-859-1111 196 A
todd.smith@thomas.edu
SMITH, Todd .... 713-831-7225 453 H
tsmith1@stthom.edu
SMITH, Tracee .... 601-877-3966 244 B
tracee@alcorn.edu
SMITH, Tracy, D .... 501-882-8806.. 17 H
tdsmith@asub.edu
SMITH, Travis .... 561-433-2330 108 H
SMITH, Travis .... 315-386-7300 319 E
smitht@canton.edu
SMITH, Travis, A .... 920-433-6621 490 H
travis.smith@bellincollege.edu
SMITH, Trent .... 620-276-9510 173 H
trent.smith@gcccks.edu
SMITH, Treva .... 706-867-2761 126 G
treva.smith@ung.edu
SMITH, Trevor .... 480-461-7631.. 13 F
trevor.smith@mesacc.edu
SMITH, Tricia, G .... 410-548-3999 204 A
tgarveysmith@salisbury.edu
SMITH, Trish .... 417-255-7900 256 A
trishsmith@missouristate.edu
SMITH, Trisha .... 202-884-9000.. 94 A
smithtri@trinitydc.edu
SMITH, Tyne .... 641-673-1703 170 I
smitht@wmpenn.edu
SMITH, Val .... 626-316-5391.. 63 D
lsmith6@saybrook.edu
SMITH, Valerie, A .... 610-328-8314 398 B
vsmith1@swarthmore.edu
SMITH, Vayta .... 707-527-4508.. 63 C
vsmith@santarosa.edu
SMITH, Vernon .... 304-724-3700 485 G
vsmith@apus.edu
SMITH, Vincent .... 541-552-7672 376 A
SMITH, Virginia .... 405-945-3214 368 C
virginia.smith@okstate.edu
SMITH, W. Randy .... 614-292-5881 358 E
smith.70@osu.edu
SMITH,
Walter (Tommy), T 260-470-2668 158W
wtsmith@manchester.edu
SMITH, Wanda .... 305-237-2377 104 E
wsmith2@mdc.edu
SMITH, Wayne .... 845-341-4261 310 D
wayne.smith@sunyorange.edu
SMITH, Wendall .... 610-896-1000 385 H
w1smith@haverford.edu
SMITH, Wendy .... 305-284-4101 112 K
wendy.smith@miami.edu
SMITH, Wendy, J .... 530-226-4128.. 64 C
wsmith@simpsonu.edu
SMITH, Wendy, M .... 307-065-0412 500 F
wsmith@sheridan.edu
SMITH, Wesley .... 804-523-2296 473 A
wsmith@reynolds.edu
SMITH, Whitney .... 479-575-5158.. 21 H
wesmith@uark.edu
SMITH, William .... 760-921-5428.. 56 A
william.smith@paloverde.edu
SMITH, William .... 860-444-8201 502 F
william.smith@uscg.mil
SMITH, William .... 610-861-5301 391 B
wsmith@northampton.edu
SMITH, William, C .... 508-565-1347 218 F
wsmith1@stonehill.edu
SMITH, III, William, C . 601-984-1010 248 G
wcsmith3@umc.edu
SMITH, Willie, E .... 225-216-8403 187 D
chancellorsoffice@mybrcc.edu
SMITH, Yolanda .... 617-628-5000 219 A
yolanda.smith@tufts.edu
SMITH, Zachary .... 336-334-3004 342 D
zrsmith3@uncg.edu
SMITH, Zachary, K .... 805-756-5790.. 29 K
zks@calpoly.edu
SMITH, Zelotes .... 415-458-3793.. 41 H
zelotes.smith@dominican.edu
SMITH-CLAY, Deborah .. 859-371-9393 179 C
dclay@beckfield.edu
SMITH-COX, Cathy, L ... 276-964-7338 474 E
cathy.smith-cox@sw.edu
SMITH DICKERSON,
Janet .... 909-621-8355.. 37 E
janet.dickerson@claremont.edu
SMITH-DUNBAR, Hope . 803-641-3786 412 B
hopes@usca.edu
SMITH-GANTT, Alicia .... 713-522-7911 453 H
smithgaj@stthom.edu
SMITH-HOWELL,
Deborah .... 402-554-4849 269 C
dsmith-howell@unomaha.edu
SMITH-HUPP, Karen ..... 301-934-2251 198 C
kshupp@cmd.edu
SMITH-IRVING, Brandi .. 713-221-8681 452 B
smithirvingb@uhd.edu
SMITH-JACKSON,
Tonya .... 336-334-7965 341 C
tlsmithj@ncat.edu
SMITH-JOACHIM,
Vergina .... 501-337-5000.. 18 D
vsmith@asutr.edu
SMITH-MACKLIN,
Alexius .... 412-578-6137 380 A
asmacklin@carlow.edu
SMITH MOORE, Karen .. 718-960-8000 293 E
karen.smithmoore@lehman.cuny.edu
SMITH-PATTERSON,
Trina .... 817-515-7059 445 A
trina.patterson@tccd.edu
SMITH ROWE, Angela ... 617-451-0010 217 B
SMITH-SIMMONS,
Margie .... 317-274-8149 157 B
smithsim@iupui.edu
SMITH-WARD, Lori, A .. 606-474-3121 180 G
lsmithward@kcu.edu
SMITHCAMP, Ronnette .. 831-479-6306.. 27 G
rosmithc@cabrillo.edu
SMITHEE, Deanna .... 812-535-5299 160 E
deanna.smithee@smwc.edu
SMITHER, Edward .... 803-754-4100 407 F
SMITHERS, Marc .... 585-567-9220 301 G
marc.smithers@houghton.edu
SMITHHART, Dana .... 936-633-3213 429 A
dsmithhart@angelina.edu
SMITHSON, Misty .... 620-947-3121 177 F
mistys@tabor.edu
SMOCK, Jordan .... 857-701-1230 215 E
jsmock@rcc.mass.edu
SMOKE, Gladden .... 864-596-9041 407 G
gladden.smoke@converse.edu
SMOKER, Emily .... 717-391-7206 398 E
smoker@stevenscollege.edu
SMOKER, Gail .... 765-973-8254 156 D
gsmoker@iue.edu
SMOKOWSKI, Peter ...... 617-353-2148 207 C
psmokows@bu.edu
SMOLEN, Jean .... 215-489-2278 381 K
jean.smolen@delval.edu
SMOLEN, Jodi .... 718-820-4917 322 C
jodi.smolen@touro.edu
SMOLENSKY, Marjorie .. 309-341-5463 134 A
msmolensky@sandburg.edu
SMOLICH, James .... 916-446-1275.. 48 F
SMOLOS, Jennifer .... 661-362-3116.. 38 H
jennifer.smolos@canyons.edu
SMOLOVA, Alona .... 757-683-3080 468 C
asmolova@odu.edu
SMOLOW, Bobbie .... 914-395-2476 314 H
bsmolow@sarahlawrence.edu
SMOLOWITZ, Janice ..... 973-655-3714 278 C
smolowitzj@montclair.edu
SMOOT, Althea .... 937-971-2867 359 J
asmoot@payneseminary.edu
SMOOT, Lori .... 410-334-2898 205 A
lsmoot@worwic.edu
SMOROL, Bobbi, H .... 315-792-3128 323 G
bsmorol@utica.edu
SMOTHERS, JR.,
Roderick .... 501-370-5317.. 21 A
smothersrj@philander.edu
SMOTHERS, SR.,
Roderick, L .... 501-370-5275.. 21 A
rsmothers@philander.edu
SMOTHERS, Traci .... 504-762-3004 187 I
tsmoth@dcc.edu
SMUCKER, April .... 419-372-2620 348 F
aprils@bgsu.edu
SMUDER, Kristin .... 813-253-7180 102 A
ksmuder@hccfl.edu
SMULSON, Erik .... 202-687-8496.. 92 D
ems62@georgetown.edu
SMUNIEWSKI, Kevin ..... 843-792-5944 409 D
smuniewk@musc.edu
SMURDON, Melissa, J . 317-940-8200 153 H
msmurdon@butler.edu
SMYDRA, Tara .... 402-844-7361 268 A
taras@northeast.edu

SOEHNER, Catherine, B 801-581-5071 459 D
catherine.soehner@utah.edu
SOENS, Brandee .... 406-896-5998 263 H
brandee.soens@msubillings.edu
SOFFA, Kari .... 661-362-5417.. 38 H
kari.soffa@canyons.edu
SOFO, Dianna .... 732-987-2287 277 B
dsofo@georgian.edu
SOFRANKO, Greg .... 724-938-4274 394 C
sofranko@calu.edu
SOFT, Max .... 406-656-9950 263 B
msoft@yellowstonechristian.edu
SOFTY, Charles .... 516-572-7701 307 C
charles.softy@ncc.edu
SOHARU, Rajni Etka ..... 518-276-6028 311 J
soharr@rpi.edu
SOHN, Christopher .... 937-766-2789 349 C
chrissohn@cedarville.edu
SOHN, Eugene .... 718-518-4154 293 F
esohn@hostos.cuny.edu
SOHNLE, Steven .... 732-235-8421 281 B
steven.sohnle@rutgers.edu
SOHOLT, Pam, B .... 701-788-4823 345 B
pam.soholt@mayvillestate.edu
SOIFER, Yitzchok .... 845-362-3053 290 I
ysoifer@byts.edu
SOIGNIER, Taryn .... 318-257-2235 192 A
taryns@latech.edu
SOINE, Aeleah .... 925-631-4139.. 59 I
ahs3@stmarys-ca.edu
SOKENU, Julius .... 805-553-4052.. 73 H
SOKENU, Julius .... 805-378-1407.. 73 I
jsokenu@vcccd.edu
SOKIA, Ashley .... 801-957-4493 460 D
ashley.sokia@slcc.edu
SOKOL, Moshe .... 718-820-4800 322 C
moshe.sokol@touro.edu
SOKOL, Stacey .... 804-862-6100 469 E
ssokol@rbc.edu
SOKOLL, Shane .... 512-313-4207 432 N
shane.sokoll@concordia.edu
SOKOLOSKI, Leo .... 570-389-4775 393 E
lsokoloski@bloomu.edu
SOKOLOSKY, Laura .... 414-425-8300 494 A
lsokolosky@shsst.edu
SOLA, Peter, L .... 651-631-5349 243 E
plsola@unwsp.edu
SOLA-PERKINS, Bianca . 708-456-0300 151 A
biancasolaperkins@triton.edu
SOLANDER, Sondra, K .. 620-432-0303 176 A
ssolander@neosho.edu
SOLANO, Maria .... 213-477-2536.. 52 J
msolano@msmu.edu
SOLAZZO, Daniel .... 513-732-5204 362 B
solazzds@ucmail.uc.edu
SOLAZZO, James .... 843-349-2717 407 B
jsolazzo@coastal.edu
SOLBACH, Robin .... 732-987-2681 277 B
rsolbach@georgian.edu
SOLBACH, Robin .... 732-987-2757 277 B
rsolbach@georgian.edu
SOLBERG, Eric .... 630-829-6497 133 B
esolberg@ben.edu
SOLBERG, Eric, J .... 713-500-3596 455 D
eric.j.solberg@uth.tmc.edu
SOLBERG, Janet .... 402-280-2731 265 J
janetsolberg@creighton.edu
SOLBERG, Laura .... 352-588-8218 107 B
laura.solberg@saintleo.edu
SOLDAT, Kaylin .... 503-943-7134 376 H
soldat@up.edu
SOLDWISCH, Sandie, S 815-282-7909 148 G
sandie.soldwisch@osfhealthcare.org
SOLDZ, Stephen .... 617-277-3915 207 B
soldzs@bgsp.edu
SOLE, Mary, L .... 407-823-5496 110 D
mary.sole@ucf.edu
SOLECKI, Amanda .... 410-287-1003 198 A
asolecki@cecil.edu
SOLEIM, Heather, M ...... 218-477-4060 239 A
heather.soleim@mnstate.edu
SOLEM, Thomas .... 701-777-0561 344 H
thomas.solem@und.edu
SOLEMBRINO, Karie ...... 410-572-8741 205 A
ksolembrino@worwic.edu
SOLEMSAAS, Rachel, H 808-934-2504 129 F
rsolems@hawaii.edu
SOLER, Ariackna .... 650-738-4350.. 62 K
solerariackna@smccd.edu
SOLER-MCDINE, Suzett . 646-592-4232 325 R
ssoler@yu.edu
SOLERNOU, Sheila .... 203-285-2393.. 86 D
ssolernou@gatewayct.edu

SOLEY, Mary Ann .... 773-907-4754 134 N
msoley@ccc.edu
SOLHEIM, Derek, N .... 319-352-8425 170 F
derek.solheim@wartburg.edu
SOLIBAKKE, Karl .... 715-682-1202 493 G
ksolibakke@northland.edu
SOLIMAN, Phebe .... 973-328-5056 276 A
psoliman@ccm.edu
SOLIMAN, Sam .... 970-521-6606.. 82 B
sam.soliman@njc.edu
SOLINSKI, Karen .... 404-880-6623 116 I
ksolinski@cau.edu
SOLINSKI, Patrick .... 405-682-1611 367 D
patrick.t.solinski@occc.edu
SOLIS, Amy .... 701-627-4738 346 D
asolis@nhsc.edu
SOLIS, Carlos .... 512-245-1799 449 G
crs218@txstate.edu
SOLIS, Federico .... 956-764-5955 438 A
fsolis@laredo.edu
SOLIS, Francisco .... 210-486-0063 428 D
fsolis@alamo.edu
SOLIS, Gerard .... 813-974-1680 111 B
gsolis@usf.edu
SOLIS, Jamie .... 909-448-4441.. 71 C
jsolis@laverne.edu
SOLIS, Mary .... 915-747-6087 454 E
mavitia@utep.edu
SOLIS, Ricardo, J .... 956-872-5051 443 B
SOLIS, Santiago .... 570-422-3463 393 F
ssolis@esu.edu
SOLIS, Shannon .... 559-638-0300.. 67 C
shannon.solis@reedleycollege.edu
SOLIS, Vanessa .... 915-215-4300 450 E
vanessa.solis@ttuhsc.edu
SOLIS, Vincent .... 979-230-3000 431 A
SOLIZ, Gina, M .... 315-228-7431 296 C
gsoliz@colgate.edu
SOLIZ, Michele .... 812-237-8111 155 H
michele.soliz@indstate.edu
SOLIZ, Sandra .... 713-525-3116 453 H
solizs@stthom.edu
SOLIZ, Ty .... 432-685-6467 439 E
asoliz@midland.edu
SOLKO-OLLIFF, Carol ... 785-628-4176 173 E
csolko@fhsu.edu
SOLLARS, David .... 785-670-2045 178 A
david.sollars@washburn.edu
SOLLBERGER, Robyn .... 270-789-5305 179 G
rlsollberger@campbellsville.edu
SOLLENBERGER,
Mitchel .... 313-593-5030 231 B
msollenb@umich.edu
SOLLOSI, Nancy, B .... 336-334-4822 334 F
nbsollosi@gtcc.edu
SOLMAN, Amy, L .... 724-847-4081 384 B
alsolman@geneva.edu
SOLOCHEK, Beverly ...... 212-217-4000 299 C
beverly_solochek@fitnyc.edu
SOLOMON, Adam .... 404-669-2097 124 C
adam.solomon@point.edu
SOLOMON, Ian, H .... 434-924-0812 471 F
ihs8m@virginia.edu
SOLOMON, Ishmael .... 724-805-2564 397 C
ishmael.solomon@stvincent.edu
SOLOMON, Jeffrey, S .... 508-831-5288 220 C
solomon@wpi.edu
SOLOMON, Jeremy .... 781-239-2637 214 E
jsolomon@massbay.edu
SOLOMON, Jerome .... 408-498-5154.. 73 A
jsolomon@cogswell.edu
SOLOMON, Jessica .... 334-347-2623.... 2 A
jsolomon@escc.edu
SOLOMON, Kate .... 973-618-3352 275 E
ksolomon@caldwell.edu
SOLOMON, Kevin .... 479-968-0343.. 18 E
ksolomon@atu.edu
SOLOMON, Mark .... 609-895-5653 280 D
masolomon@rider.edu
SOLOMON, Michael, J .. 734-764-4401 231 A
mjsolo@umich.edu
SOLOMON, Robert, L ... 216-368-2532 349 B
robert.l.solomon@case.edu
SOLOMON, Ronald .... 225-216-8267 187 D
solomonr@mybrcc.edu
SOLOMON, Samuel .... 781-736-8539 207 D
sasolomon@brandeis.edu
SOLOMON, Shoshana ... 973-267-9404 279 G
shoshanasolomon@rca.edu
SOLOMON, Sigrid, B .... 937-481-2270 363 H
sigrid_solomon@wilmington.edu
SOLOMON, Stephanie ... 850-558-4516 112 B
stephanie.solomon@tcc.fl.edu

SOLOMON, Steven .... 850-201-6549 112 B
steven.solomon@tcc.fl.edu
SOLOMON, William .... 772-462-7656 102 E
wsolomon@irsc.edu
SOLOMONSON, Mike .... 928-532-6141.. 14 L
michael.solomonson@npc.edu
SOLOMOU, Costas .... 585-245-5619 317 E
solomou@geneseo.edu
SOLORZANO PARADA,
Javier .... 419-251-1597 355 G
javier.solorzanoparada@mercycollege.edu
SOLOW BOUWER,
Linda .... 707-654-1000.. 32 C
SOLOWAY, Seth .... 914-251-6196 318 E
seth.soloway@purchase.edu
SOLT, Michael .... 562-985-5306.. 32 A
michael.solt@csulb.edu
SOLTIS, Bryan .... 860-727-2217.. 87 H
bsoltis@goodwin.edu
SOLTIS, Corinne .... 206-934-6739 482 H
corinne.soltis@seattlecolleges.edu
SOLTIS, Robert, P .... 317-940-8960 153 H
rsoltis@butler.edu
SOLTISH, Michael .... 845-431-8921 298 B
soltish@sunydutchess.edu
SOLTZ-KNOWLTON,
Bonnie .... 860-528-4111.. 87 H
bknowlton@goodwin.edu
SOM, Andrew .... 707-654-1085.. 32 C
asom@csum.edu
SOMAN, Sherril .... 616-331-6821 224 D
somans@gvsu.edu
SOMER, Regina .... 402-461-2422 265 C
reginasomer@cccneb.edu
SOMERLAD, Tracy .... 910-755-7422 332 D
somerladt@brunswickcc.edu
SOMERLAD, Tracy, L ..... 910-755-7300 332 D
SOMERO, Marty .... 970-351-2502.. 84 D
marty.somero@unco.edu
SOMERS, Charles .... 215-641-6538 390 A
csomers@mc3.edu
SOMERS, Christine .... 570-674-6314 389 H
csomers@misericordia.edu
SOMERS, Clayton .... 919-962-6331 342 B
clayton@unc.edu
SOMERS, Kevin .... 870-743-3000.. 20 F
ksomers@northark.edu
SOMERS, Micki .... 870-743-3000.. 20 F
msomers@northark.edu
SOMERVILLE, Dione ...... 567-661-7200 359 H
dione_somerville@owens.edu
SOMERVILLE, Mark .... 781-292-2509 209 E
mark.somerville@olin.edu
SOMERVILLE, Mary .... 303-556-4587.. 84 B
mary.somerville@ucdenver.edu
SOMERVILLE, Sandi ...... 951-719-2994.. 58 C
SOMERVILLE, Tim .... 951-719-2994.. 58 C
doc@golfcollege.edu
SOMMER, Jacquelyn ...... 513-562-6262 347 G
jacquelynsommer@icloud.com
SOMMERER, Shaun .... 660-219-6115 249 C
ssommerer@atsu.edu
SOMMERFELD, Janee .... 253-833-9111 480 A
jsommerfeld@greenriver.edu
SOMMERFELD, Marvin .. 913-758-6230 177 I
marvin.sommerfeld@stmary.edu
SOMMERS, Brittany .... 216-687-2277 350 G
b.sommers52@csuohio.edu
SOMMERS, Donald .... 212-960-5200 325 R
dsommers@yu.edu
SOMMERS, Greg .... 972-273-3518 434 C
gsommers@dcccd.edu
SOMMERS, Holly .... 404-727-2507 118 D
hsomme2@emory.edu
SOMMERS, Janet, B .... 651-631-5201 243 E
jbsommers@unwsp.edu
SOMMERS, Kari .... 312-369-7223 136 C
klsommers@colum.edu
SOMMERS, Mary .... 308-865-8520 268 J
sommersm@unk.edu
SOMMERS, Rhoda .... 937-328-6060 350 D
sommersr@clarkstate.edu
SOMMERS, Shirley .... 585-389-2958 307 D
ssommer4@naz.edu
SOMMERS, William .... 717-262-2002 402 D
william.sommers@wilson.edu
SOMMERVILLE,
John, M .... 651-631-5392 243 E
jmsommerville@unwsp.edu
SOMMERVILLE, Linda ... 916-577-2200.. 76 C
lsommerville@jessup.edu
SOMNARAIN, Emry .... 305-821-3333 100 C
esomnarain@fnu.edu

SOMOZA, Amarilis .... 305-443-9170 106 M
asomoza@sabercollege.edu
SOMPOLSKI, Robert .... 847-635-1690 146 E
somplski@oakton.edu
SON, Chang Ho .... 714-527-0691.. 42 D
SONBOL, Dena .... 651-290-6398 241 N
dena.sonbol@mitchellhamline.edu
SONDAG, Lynn .... 415-485-3269.. 41 H
lynn.sondag@dominican.edu
SONDBERG, Brittany ..... 336-272-7102 329 B
brittany.sondberg@greensboro.edu
SONDEJ, Julia .... 626-316-5374.. 63 D
jsondej@saybrook.edu
SONDER, Henk, E .... 401-456-9577 404 A
hsonder@ric.edu
SONDEY, Brian .... 845-574-4237 312 C
brian.sondey@sunyrockland.edu
SONDEY, Joann .... 914-831-0288 296 F
jsondey@cw.edu
SONDEY, Stephen .... 973-720-2862 283 I
sondeys@wpunj.edu
SONE, Marling .... 718-260-4999 294 F
msone@citytech.cuny.edu
SONENBERG, Joyce .... 925-631-4522.. 59 I
jsonenberg@stmarys-ca.edu
SONG, A Li .... 516-364-0808 308 C
asong@nycollege.edu
SONG, Bokhee .... 636-327-4645 255 E
dbo@midwest.edu
SONG, Connie .... 513-231-2223 348 A
csong@athenaeum.edu
SONG, Edward .... 323-953-4000.. 49 E
songeb@lacitycollege.edu
SONG, Hee Sook .... 678-535-7771 118 F
joysong@gcuniv.edu
SONG, Jae, M .... 636-327-4645 255 E
midwest47@daum.net
SONG, Jae Pil .... 636-327-4645 255 E
jp@midwest.edu
SONG, James .... 636-327-4645 255 E
js8083@gmail.com
SONG, Landon .... 636-327-4645 255 E
miri@midwest.edu
SONG, Landon .... 636-327-4645 255 E
ks@midwest.edu
SONG, Sarah .... 818-947-2606.. 50 B
songsj@lavc.edu
SONG, Sokha .... 909-274-7500.. 52 K
SONG, Sui .... 925-424-1634.. 36 A
ssong@laspositascollege.edu
SONG, Sumie .... 773-244-5571 145 F
ssong@northpark.edu
SONG, Violet .... 512-492-3060 429 B
vsong@aoma.edu
SONGAO, Tracey .... 253-589-5595 478 A
tracey.songao@cptc.edu
SONGBIRD, Brooke .... 816-654-7000 253 I
SONGCO, Ken .... 408-855-5037.. 75 C
kenneth.songco@missioncollege.edu
SONGER, Nancy .... 801-581-8221 459 D
nancy.songer@utah.edu
SONGER, Zacchary .... 617-670-4539 209 D
zsonger@fisher.edu
SONI, Ash .... 812-855-8489 156 C
soni@indiana.edu
SONI, Varun .... 213-740-6110.. 73 C
vasoni@usc.edu
SONKAYNAR, Zehra .... 707-527-4431.. 63 C
zsonkaynar@santarosa.edu
SONNENBERG, Jeffrey .. 847-586-4364.. 10 F
jsonnenberg@aiuniv.edu
SONNENBLICK, Carol ... 718-552-1180 294 F
csonnenblick@citytech.cuny.edu
SONNENSTEIN, Mark .... 718-933-6700 306 J
ssonnenstein@monroecollege.edu
SONNTAG, Dave .... 509-313-6192 479 E
sonntagd@gonzaga.edu
SONNTAG, Michael .... 803-938-3826 412 G
sonntagm@uscsumter.edu
SONODA, Kazuhiro .... 509-865-8584 480 B
sonoda_k@heritage.edu
SONOFF, Thomas .... 503-594-1698 372 B
thomas.sonoff@clackamas.edu
SONRICKER, Nicholas ... 716-851-1282 299 A
sonrickern@ecc.edu
SONSTEBY, Jill .... 651-638-6254 233 J
jks44888@bethel.edu
SONTAG, Michael .... 513-244-4766 356 F
michael.sontag@msj.edu
SONTY, Vijay .... 215-751-8526 381 H
vsonty@ccp.edu
SOO, Billy .... 617-552-3260 207 A
billy.soo@bc.edu

SPANG, Zane 406-477-6215 262 F zspang@cdkc.edu
SPANGLER, Anthony 313-664-7462 222 C aspangler@collegeforcreativestudies.edu
SPANGLER, Chris 215-242-7764 380 G spanglerc@chc.edu
SPANGLER, Denise 706-542-6446 126 F dspangle@uga.edu
SPANGLER, Mary 913-288-7161 174 H mspangler@kckcc.edu
SPANGLER, Michael 702-651-4959 270 F michael.spangler@csn.edu
SPANGLER, Stephanie 203-432-4446 90 B stephanie.spangler@yale.edu
SPANN, Alyssa 931-363-9827 426 F aevans91@utsouthern.edu
SPANN, B. Steven 615-327-3927 419 D spann@guptoncollege.edu
SPANN, Charles 404-225-4016 115 F cspann@atlantatech.edu
SPANN, Emily 618-985-3741 140 G emilyspann@jalc.edu
SPANN, Robert, T 248-522-3512 228 H rtspann@oaklandcc.edu
SPANN, Sammy 419-530-7963 363 B sammy.spann@utoledo.edu
SPANN, Stephen, J 713-743-0875 451 G sjspann@uh.edu
SPANN-PACK, Robin 601-979-2015 245 G robin.m.spann-pack@jsums.edu
SPANNAGEL, Ashlee 319-208-5193 169 I aspannagel@scciowa.edu
SPANO, Anthony 813-397-2125 145 C aspano@nl.edu
SPARACINO, Ann 570-702-8929 386 D asparacino@johnson.edu
SPARACINO, Debra 864-656-2171 406 F dcspara@clemson.edu
SPARGEN, Dan 402-399-2600 265 H dspargen@csm.edu
SPARKMAN, Calvin 951-343-4356 27 J csparkman@calbaptist.edu
SPARKS, Brad 618-235-2700 150 B bradley.sparks@swic.edu
SPARKS, Carolyn, B 864-597-4160 413 E sparkscb@wofford.edu
SPARKS, Cheryl, T 432-264-5030 436 H csparks@howardcollege.edu
SPARKS, Edie 209-946-2011 71 E
SPARKS, Edie 617-573-8000 218 G edie.sparks@suffolk.edu
SPARKS, Jerry 740-474-8896 358 A jesparks@ohiochristian.edu
SPARKS, John 618-634-3230 149 C johns@shawneecc.edu
SPARKS, Kenton 610-341-4383 383 A ksparks@eastern.edu
SPARKS, Laura 212-353-4240 297 C sparks@cooper.edu
SPARKS, Maria 518-464-8768 299 B msparks@excelsior.edu
SPARKS, Rick 540-231-7951 475 D rasparks@vt.edu
SPARKS, Sonny 662-472-9015 245 E sparks@holmescc.edu
SPARKS, Sonny 662-472-9015 245 E ssparks@holmescc.edu
SPARKS, Stacey 828-689-1307 330 H ssparks@mhu.edu
SPARKS, Steve 252-222-6087 332 G sparkss@carteret.edu
SPARKS, Terrell 801-878-1494 271 D tsparks@roseman.edu
SPARLING, Jennifer 760-366-5294 40 K jsparling@cmccd.edu
SPARPANA, Eileen 906-217-4023 221 J eileen.sparpana@baycollege.edu
SPARROW, Anita 860-512-3223 86 F asparrow@manchestercc.edu
SPATAFORA, Grace 802-443-5431 461 G spatafor@middlebury.edu
SPATAFORE, Lisa 267-341-3477 385 I lspatafore@holyfamily.edu
SPATAFORE, Marisa 408-864-8672 42 K spataforemarisa@deanza.edu
SPATARO, Keith 650-543-3853 52 A kspataro@menlo.edu
SPATARO-WILSON, Jennifer, A 540-665-5412 470 A jspataro@su.edu
SPATES, Gerald 336-285-2736 341 C gspates@ncat.edu
SPATZ, Dan 541-506-6034 372 E dspatz@cgcc.edu
SPAULDING, Angela 806-651-2730 447 D aspaulding@wtamu.edu
SPAULDING, Brad 218-751-8670 241 Q bradspaulding@oakhills.edu
SPAULDING, II, Henry, W 740-392-6868 356 G hspauldi@mvnu.edu
SPAULDING, Melinda 713-313-1361 448 D melinda.spaulding@tsu.edu
SPAYD, Ann 315-787-4005 299 F ann.spayd@flhcon.edu
SPAZIANI, Gina 617-879-7053 212 E gspaziani@massart.edu
SPEAKMAN, Jennifer 614-236-7127 348 I jspeakman@capital.edu
SPEAKMAN, Thomas 215-489-4343 381 K thomas.speakman@delval.edu
SPEAKMAN, Wendy, S 260-359-4228 155 G wspeakman@huntington.edu
SPEAKS, Michael, A 315-443-0790 321 D maspeaks@syr.edu
SPEAR, Brenda 602-489-5300 10 G brenda.spear@arizonachristian.edu
SPEARIN, Rod 248-645-3300 222 G rspearin@cranbrook.edu
SPEARMAN, Ashlee 503-517-1056 377 B aspearman@warnerpacific.edu
SPEARMAN, Elicia 203-582-7722 88 F elicia.spearman@quinnipiac.edu
SPEARMAN, Howard, J 815-921-4008 147 H h.spearman@rockvalleycollege.edu
SPEARS, Ashley 814-871-5592 383 H spears005@gannon.edu
SPEARS, Christian 304-696-5408 488 N spearsc@marshall.edu
SPEARS, Curtis, L 210-431-3917 440 D cspears@ollusa.edu
SPEARS, Jacqueline, D 913-307-7381 175 A jdspears@ksu.edu
SPEARS, Linda, C 615-963-5281 425 A lspears@tnstate.edu
SPEARS, Marty 501-279-4335 19 G mspears@harding.edu
SPEARS, Matthew 503-589-8154 372 G mspears@corban.edu
SPEARS, Sylvia 617-824-8500 208 G sylvia_spears@emerson.edu
SPEARS-BOYD, Amy 931-540-2509 423 D aspears@columbiastate.edu
SPEAS, Philip, E 606-693-5000 182 H pspeas@kmbc.edu
SPECHT, Andy 805-922-6966 24 L aspecht@hancockcollege.edu
SPECHT, Darlene 408-288-3725 62 G darlene.specht@sjcc.edu
SPECHT, Mark, A 610-566-1776 402 C mspecht@williamson.edu
SPECHT, Neva, J 828-262-3078 340 G spechtnj@appstate.edu
SPECK, Christie 707-864-7000 64 F christie.speck@solano.edu
SPECTAR, Jem, M 814-269-2090 400 A spectar@pitt.edu
SPECTER, Robert, M 202-319-5606 91 G specter@cua.edu
SPECTOR, Carol 617-824-8586 208 G carol_spector@emerson.edu
SPEED, Coleen 318-274-3338 191 G speedc@gram.edu
SPEED, Heather 719-549-3082 82 I heather.speed@pueblocc.edu
SPEED, Melissa 276-498-5237 463 G mspeed@acp.edu
SPEED, Sam 318-257-4917 192 A sspeed@latech.edu
SPEEG, Samantha 601-643-8318 244 G samantha.speeg@colin.edu
SPEELMAN, Diana 814-866-6641 387 C dspeelman@lecom.edu
SPEER, Brian 704-406-4269 328 I bspeer@gardner-webb.edu
SPEER, Jennifer 615-868-6503 421 B
SPEER, Roger 623-245-4600 16 F rspeer@uti.edu
SPEERSCHNEIDER, Kim 518-831-2528 305 B kspeerschneider@mariacollege.edu
SPEHN, Steven 507-222-4271 234 C sspehn@carleton.edu
SPEIDEL, Daniel 603-897-8576 273 B dspeidel@rivier.edu
SPEIRS, Lane 605-668-1525 414 F lane.speirs@mountmarty.edu
SPEISSER, Nancy 757-493-6946 125 D nspeisser@southuniversity.edu
SPELL, Ashley 312-499-4184 149 B aspell@saic.edu
SPELL, Bomani 850-599-3183 109 E bomani.spell@famu.edu
SPELL, Paul 601-477-4223 246 A paul.spell@jcjc.edu
SPELLECY, Sean 503-251-5727 377 A sspellecy@uws.edu
SPELLMAN, Denise 504-816-4864 186 F dspellman@dillard.edu
SPELLMAN, Marcia 617-559-8642 210 C mspellman@hebrewcollege.edu
SPELLS, Doretha, J 757-727-5213 466 L doretha.spells@hamptonu.edu
SPELLS, Kaschia 252-246-1214 339 A kspells@wilsoncc.edu
SPELLS, Renee 803-793-5174 408 A spellsr@denmarktech.edu
SPELLS-FENTY, Rhonda 301-546-7014 201 D spellsrx@pgcc.edu
SPELMAN, Amy 309-298-1914 152 I ae-spelman@wiu.edu
SPENCE, Charles 434-592-3503 467 E cpspence@liberty.edu
SPENCE, Cody 601-635-2111 245 B cspence@eccc.edu
SPENCE, Harlan 603-862-0322 273 H harlan.spence@unh.edu
SPENCE, Jeff 334-347-2623 2 A jspence@escc.edu
SPENCE, Jeffrey 920-565-1000 492 A
SPENCE, Jon 417-268-1000 249 G
SPENCE, Jon 417-865-2815 252 F spencej@evangel.edu
SPENCE, Jon, N 913-971-3279 175 H jnspence@mnu.edu
SPENCE, Juanita, M 252-335-3586 341 A jmidgette@ecsu.edu
SPENCE, Laura 802-586-7711 462 C lspence@sterlingcollege.edu
SPENCE, Penny 816-926-4400 253 C
SPENCE, Thomas 615-460-6417 417 B thom.spence@belmont.edu
SPENCE, Weymouth 301-891-4128 204 D wspence@wau.edu
SPENCELEY, Laura 315-312-2102 318 B laura.spenceley@oswego.edu
SPENCER, A. Clayton 207-786-6100 193 D cspencer@bates.edu
SPENCER, Arlene 518-736-3622 300 B aspencer@fmcc.suny.edu
SPENCER, Chad, A 704-894-2000 328 C
SPENCER, Christine 410-837-6134 204 C cspencer@ubalt.edu
SPENCER, Cindy 417-667-8181 251 E cspencer@cottey.edu
SPENCER, Deborah 860-231-5390 89 G dspencer@usj.edu
SPENCER, Dorsey 315-228-7425 296 C dspencer@colgate.edu
SPENCER, Estelle, H 413-205-3461 205 C estelle.spencer@aic.edu
SPENCER, Gene 610-409-3064 400 E gspencer@ursinus.edu
SPENCER, Janett 256-306-2628 1 F janet.spencer@calhoun.edu
SPENCER, Jed 801-626-6586 460 B jedspencer@weber.edu
SPENCER, Jeremy 508-626-4500 212 D jspencer1@framingham.edu
SPENCER, Joel 303-329-6355 79 C finaid@cstcm.edu
SPENCER, JR., John 304-327-4118 488 J jspencer@bluefieldstate.edu
SPENCER, John, D 817-515-5079 445 A john.spencer@tccd.edu
SPENCER, Joseph, F 419-434-4791 362 D spencer@findlay.edu
SPENCER, Julie 424-207-3763 55 B jspencer@otis.edu
SPENCER, Keith 417-667-8181 251 E kspencer@cottey.edu
SPENCER, Kyle 406-656-9950 263 B kspencer@yellowstonechristian.edu
SPENCER, Lena 620-441-2701 172 M lena.spencer@cowley.edu
SPENCER, Lisa 304-647-6369 489 C lspencer@osteo.wvsom.edu
SPENCER, Lori 662-846-4794 245 A lspencer@deltastate.edu
SPENCER, Lydia 901-843-3850 422 C spencerl@rhodes.edu
SPENCER, Mary Ellen 865-694-6517 424 C mespencer@pstcc.edu
SPENCER, MonSher 281-649-3646 436 D mspencer@hbu.edu
SPENCER, Nichole 706-771-4035 115 H nichole.spencer@augustatech.edu
SPENCER, Rick, E 630-637-5209 145 E respencer@noctrl.edu
SPENCER, Ruth 845-431-8673 298 B ruth.spencer@sunydutchess.edu
SPENCER, Samantha 252-940-6223 332 A samantha.spencer@beaufortccc.edu
SPENCER, Scott 412-392-3876 395 H sspencer@pointpark.edu
SPENCER, Shanan 304-876-5276 489 A sspencer@shepherd.edu
SPENCER, Shannon 828-771-3747 344 B sspencer@warren-wilson.edu
SPENCER, Shannon, M 419-772-2036 358 D s-spencer@onu.edu
SPENCER, Shawn 678-225-7340 395 A shawnsp@pcom.edu
SPENCER, Susan 660-263-4100 256 D susanspencer@macc.edu
SPENCER, Suzette 240-567-0000 200 E suzette.spencer@montgomerycollege.edu
SPENCER, Tammy 352-365-3502 103 U spencert@lssc.edu
SPENCER, Terri 303-368-7462 82 E tspencer@pmi.edu
SPENCER, Thomas, E 573-882-9500 260 C spencerte@missouri.edu
SPENCER, Tina 702-254-7577 271 B tina.spencer@northwestcareercollege.edu
SPENCER, Travis 908-852-1400 275 H travis.spencer@centenaryuniversity.edu
SPENCER, Yvette 205-226-7720 5 A yspencer@bsc.edu
SPENCER-MONTEIRO, Carol 508-999-8705 211 F cspencer@umassd.edu
SPENGLER, Gregory, C 410-706-1264 202 F gspengler@umaryland.edu
SPENNER, Anne 816-235-1576 260 D spennerae@umkc.edu
SPENSLEY, Nicole 803-641-3338 412 B nicolesp@usca.edu
SPERANZA-REEDER, Mary 651-641-3472 236 A msperanzareeder001@luthersem.edu
SPERDUTO, John 610-558-5611 390 G sperdutj@neumann.edu
SPERGER, Herb 610-785-6284 396 H hsperger@scs.edu
SPERICO, Jodie 516-877-3118 288 L jsperico@adelphi.edu
SPERICO, Jodie 516-299-4079 304 C jodie.sperico@liu.edu
SPERLING, Chad 218-793-2436 239 E chad.sperling@northlandcollege.edu
SPERLING, Mark 219-980-6887 157 A masperli@iun.edu
SPERLING, Michael 845-905-4616 297 E michael.sperling@culinary.edu
SPERLING, Michael 704-991-0357 338 A msperling0559@stanly.edu
SPERLING, Susan, S 510-723-6641 35 Q ssperling@chabotcollege.edu
SPERON, Sarah 925-631-4150 59 I ses2@stmarys-ca.edu
SPEROS, Michael 916-278-6655 33 A msperos@csus.edu
SPEROW, William 478-757-5253 127 D wsperow@wesleyancollege.edu
SPERRAZZA, Alexander 570-422-3110 393 F asperrazza@esu.edu
SPERRING, Tiffany 614-222-6183 351 A tsperring@ccad.edu
SPERRY, Amber 402-375-7370 267 I amsperr1@wsc.edu
SPERRY, Sarah 412-396-5894 382 E sperrys@duq.edu
SPESERT, Douglas 310-360-8888 27 D
SPETH, Megan 540-887-7323 467 G mspeth@marybaldwin.edu
SPETKA, Rosemary, V 315-792-5495 306 G rspetka@mvcc.edu
SPETS, Steve 906-932-4231 224 A

SQUIRES, Keith .... 801-585-0804 459 D
keith.squires@utah.edu
SQUIRES, Kyle .... 480-965-2147.. 11 A
squires@asu.edu
SQUIRES, Robert .... 360-650-4446 485 A
robert.squires@wwu.edu
SQUIRES, Stephanie ..... 201-761-6195 282 H
ssquires@saintpeters.edu
SQUIRES, Thomas .... 315-792-5445 306 G
tsquires@mvcc.edu
SRAMEK, Jennifer .... 361-698-1703 434 H
jsramek@delmar.edu
SRAY, Heidi, J .... 724-847-6551 384 B
hjsray@geneva.edu
SRBA, Karen, V .... 304-724-3700 485 G
kvendouern-srba@apus.edu
SRECKOVIC, Melissa ...... 810-762-3000 231 C
msreck@umich.edu
SRIDHAR, Nigamanth ... 216-687-3588 350 G
n.sridhar1@csuohio.edu
SRIDHARAN, Priya .... 323-259-2523.. 54 I
sridharan@oxy.edu
SRIHARI, Hari .... 607-777-2871 315 E
srihari@binghamton.edu
SRIHARI, Hari .... 607-777-2336 315 E
srihari@binghamton.edu
SRIKANTA, Deepa .... 517-884-1079 227 C
srikanta@msu.edu
SRIKANTH, Rajini .... 617-287-5600 211 E
rajini.srikanth@umb.edu
SRINIVASAN, Balaji .... 773-795-2901 151 B
balajis@uchicago.edu
SRIRAMAN, Vedaraman 512-245-1217 449 G
vs04@txstate.edu
SRONCE, Robin .... 870-235-4300.. 21 E
robinsronce@saumag.edu
SROUFE, Darren .... 812-357-6331 160 G
dsroufe@saintmeinrad.edu
SRYGLEY, David, B .... 504-526-4745 190 C
davidsrygley@gmail.com
ST-GERMAIN, Pierre ...... 401-874-2698 404 E
pst-germain@uri.edu
STAAB, Eric .... 503-768-7053 373 D
ericstaab@lclark.edu
STAAB, Susan, K .... 815-282-7900 148 E
susanstaab@sacn.edu
STAAL, Todd .... 616-988-1000 222 D
todd.s@compass.edu
STAATS, Raymond .... 252-638-7202 333 F
staatsr@cravencc.edu
STABILE, Carol .... 541-346-5414 376 G
cstabile@uoregon.edu
STABILE, Joseph .... 914-633-2207 302 C
jstabile@iona.edu
STABINGER, John .... 843-953-3706 406 D
jstabing@citadel.edu
STACEY, Elizabeth .... 314-529-9364 254 D
estacey@maryville.edu
STACEY, Eric .... 651-690-8778 242 F
emstacey@stkate.edu
STACEY, Joann .... 608-796-3843 496 L
jmstacey@viterbo.edu
STACEY, Kathleen .... 734-487-0021 223 F
kstacey@emich.edu
STACEY, Marsha .... 605-394-4800 414 G
STACEY, Simon .... 410-455-2164 202 G
spstacey@umbc.edu
STACHE, Kris .... 563-589-0274 170 G
kstache@wartburgseminary.edu
STACHOWIAK, Bonni .... 714-966-6307.. 73 G
STACHOWIAK, Sage, C . 203-392-5200.. 85 H
stachowiaks1@southernct.edu
STACHOWSKI,
Mary Albertine .... 716-896-0700 324 A
smalbertine@villa.edu
STACHURA, Hubert .... 631-656-2157 299 G
hubert.stachura@ftc.edu
STACK, Brendan .... 718-260-5604 294 F
bstack@citytech.cuny.edu
STACK, Dana .... 619-388-7579.. 61 B
dstack@sdccd.edu
STACK, Gilbert .... 212-752-1530 303 G
gilbert.stack@limcollege.edu
STACK, John .... 305-348-7266 109 H
john.stack@fiu.edu
STACK, Kim .... 401-874-4777 404 E
kstack@uri.edu
STACK, Patrick .... 314-968-6921 261 D
stackpa@webster.edu
STACK, Robert .... 863-837-5962 106 A
bstack@polk.edu

STACK LOMBARDO,
Jessie .... 585-245-5721 317 E
stack@geneseo.edu
STACKHOUSE, LaToya ... 229-931-2442 120 B
latoya.stackhouse@gsw.edu
STACKHOUSE TAETZSCH,
Cindra .... 630-752-5049 152 K
cindra.taetzsch@wheaton.edu
STACKMAN, Robert .... 561-297-2313 109 F
STACKMAN, William, B . 573-882-0157 260 C
william.stackman@missouri.edu
STACKMAN, William, B . 573-882-5397 260 C
bill.stackman@missouri.edu
STACKPOLE, Richard ..... 513-732-5278 362 B
richard.stackpole@uc.edu
STACKPOOLE, Roger ..... 508-286-8200 219 F
STACKS, Pamela .... 408-924-2488.. 34 B
pamela.stacks@sjsu.edu
STACY, Jason .... 803-777-6383 412 A
stacyj@mailbox.sc.edu
STACY, Jeanne .... 225-216-8591 187 D
stacyj@mybrcc.edu
STACY, Mark, W .... 585-395-5149 317 B
mstacy@brockport.edu
STADICK, Anna .... 262-595-2167 495 D
stadick@uwp.edu
STADLER, Al .... 417-455-5712 251 H
alstadler@crowder.edu
STADLER, Megan .... 315-786-6500 302 I
mstadler@sunyjefferson.edu
STADLER, Rose .... 510-436-1089.. 45 H
stadler@hnu.edu
STAEBLER, Ned .... 313-577-2164 232 H
nedstaebler@wayne.edu
STAEHLE, Andrea .... 760-862-1326.. 39 A
astaehle@collegeofthedesert.edu
STAFFA, Adam .... 206-546-4101 483 C
astaffa@shoreline.edu
STAFFORD, Ben .... 409-984-6354 449 D
staffordbk@lamarpa.edu
STAFFORD, Courtney ..... 615-550-3171 427 F
courtney.stafford@williamsoncc.edu
STAFFORD, Derek, S ...... 336-841-9433 329 E
dstaffor@highpoint.edu
STAFFORD, Gina .... 423-425-4363 426 D
gina-stafford@utc.edu
STAFFORD, Heather .... 316-978-6837 178 B
heather.stafford@wichita.edu
STAFFORD, Joanne .... 405-733-7373 369 D
joannestafford@rose.edu
STAFFORD, Kyle .... 918-540-6201 366 F
kyle.j.stafford@neo.edu
STAFFORD, Laura .... 419-372-2079 348 F
llstaff@bgsu.edu
STAFFORD, Mark .... 501-812-2248.. 23 E
mstafford@uaptc.edu
STAFFORD, Michael .... 713-718-5051 436 E
michael.stafford@hccs.edu
STAFFORD,
Michael Dale .... 713-780-9777 428 H
mstafford@acaom.edu
STAFFORD, Pam .... 606-759-7141 182 B
pam.stafford@kctcs.edu
STAFFORD, Ronnie .... 843-921-6953 410 B
rstafford@netc.edu
STAFFORD, Vanessa ...... 614-781-1085 352 F
vstafford@felbrycollege.edu
STAGE, Andrew .... 607-735-1719 298 G
astage@elmira.edu
STAGER, Karl .... 281-756-3594 428 E
kstager@alvincollege.edu
STAGGERS, Leroy .... 803-934-3211 409 H
lstaggers@morris.edu
STAHL, C.J .... 215-972-2059 392 P
cstahl@pafa.edu
STAHL, Frank .... 620-450-2238 176 I
franks@prattcc.edu
STAHL, Robert .... 516-463-6745 301 E
robert.stahl@hofstra.edu
STAHL, Stephen, D .... 440-826-2762 348 C
sstahl@bw.edu
STAHL, Ted .... 816-235-1625 260 D
stahlt@umkc.edu
STAHLE, Noel .... 641-673-1010 170 I
stahlen@wmpenn.edu
STAHLEY, Timothy .... 970-521-6655.. 82 B
timothy.stahley@njc.edu
STAHMER, Cynthia .... 810-762-3488 231 C
stahmer@umich.edu
STAHR, Jason, A .... 314-516-4934 260 E
stahrj@umsl.edu
STAIGER, Jennifer, L ..... 301-447-8387 201 A
staiger@msmary.edu

STAIHAR, Karla .... 503-357-6151 375 B
karlas@pacificu.edu
STAKE, Amy .... 301-846-2460 198 E
astake@frederick.edu
STAKER, Julie .... 319-399-8500 164 D
jstaker@coe.edu
STAKES, Robert, L .... 915-747-5683 454 E
rlstakes@utep.edu
STALDER, Michele .... 907-455-2850.. 10 B
mestalder@alaska.edu
STALDER, Rob .... 662-621-4050 244 E
rstalder@coahomacc.edu
STALEY, Avery .... 828-328-1741 330 B
avery.staley@lr.edu
STALEY, Joseph, L .... 281-283-2018 452 A
staleyj@uhcl.edu
STALEY, Marc, E .... 419-772-2462 358 D
m-staley@onu.edu
STALEY, Mark .... 503-251-2844 377 A
mstaley@uws.edu
STALEY, Michael .... 231-591-2635 223 H
michaelstaley@ferris.edu
STALEY, Priscilla, A .... 214-860-2038 434 A
pstaley@dcccd.edu
STALICK, Theresa .... 360-442-2583 480 E
tstalick@lowercolumbia.edu
STALL, Beth .... 214-860-2374 434 A
sbstall@dcccd.edu
STALL-RYAN, CHC,
Jamie, J .... 860-444-8481 502 F
jamie.j.stall-ryan@uscg.mil
STALLBAUMER,
Rosemary .... 619-260-4722.. 72 H
rstallbaumer@sandiego.edu
STALLIARD, SR.,
George .... 541-463-5310 373 C
stalliardg@lanecc.edu
STALLING, Undria .... 404-639-0999 122 H
undria.stalling@morehouse.edu
STALLING, Undria .... 470-639-0484 122 H
undria.stalling@morehouse.edu
STALLINGS, Amanda ...... 817-257-4684 447 H
a.stallings@tcu.edu
STALLINGS, Laura .... 503-352-2191 375 B
laurastallings@pacificu.edu
STALLINGS, Samaria ...... 781-239-3175 214 E
sstallings@massbay.edu
STALLINGS, Sean .... 609-771-1855 275 J
stalling@tcnj.edu
STALLINGS, Tamya .... 870-508-6166.. 18 B
tstallings@asumh.edu
STALLMAN, Amber .... 607-777-6569 315 E
stallman@binghamton.edu
STALLMAN, Christine ..... 607-255-4125 297 D
cms353@cornell.edu
STALLMAN, Jeanne .... 541-552-6221 376 A
stallman@sou.edu
STALLMAN, Scott .... 612-381-3326 235 C
sstallman@dunwoody.edu
STALLMANN, Diane .... 773-298-3089 148 I
stallmann@sxu.edu
STALLONES, Jared .... 970-351-2817.. 84 D
jared.stallones@unco.edu
STALLWORTH, Charles .. 205-929-1156.... 6 B
cstallworth@miles.edu
STALLWORTH, Janice ..... 405-682-7502 367 D
janice.d.stallworth@occc.edu
STALLWORTH, Melissa . 251-578-1313.... 3 D
melstallworth@rstc.edu
STALNAKER, Ron .... 912-478-5491 120 A
rstalnaker@georgiasouthern.edu
STALNAKER, Samantha . 817-515-1795 445 A
samantha.stalnaker@tccd.edu
STALTER, Ann, M .... 937-775-3133 364 D
ann.stalter@wright.edu
STAMAN, Brad .... 307-532-8206 500 A
bstaman@ewc.wy.edu
STAMBAUGH, Barbara .. 717-358-3981 383 G
barbara.stambaugh@fandm.edu
STAMBAUGH, Emily .... 650-543-3933.. 52 A
emily.stambaugh@menlo.edu
STAMBAUGH, Jeff .... 940-397-4088 439 F
jeff.stambaugh@msutexas.edu
STAMEY, Jamie .... 704-894-2678 328 C
jastamey@davidson.edu
STAMEY, Jodi .... 919-508-2362 344 D
jstamey@peace.edu
STAMM, Timothy .... 504-671-5482 187 I
tstamm@dcc.edu
STAMMEL, Andrew .... 607-436-2830 316 C
andrew.stammel@oneonta.edu
STAMOS, Michael .... 949-824-1046.. 69 C
mstamos@uci.edu

STAMP, Diane, L .... 540-568-6895 467 C
stampdl@jmu.edu
STAMPALIA,
Jacqueline, B .... 518-276-8007 311 J
stampj@rpi.edu
STAMPER, Richard, E .... 812-877-8956 160 C
stamper1@rose-hulman.edu
STAMPINO, Maria .... 305-284-2006 112 K
mgstampino@miami.edu
STAMPS, Luke .... 405-585-4426 367 B
luke.stamps@okbu.edu
STAN RAICU, Daniela ... 312-362-5460 136 F
dstan@cs.depaul.edu
STANAITIS, Judi .... 610-558-5544 390 G
stanaitj@neumann.edu
STANBROUGH,
Beverly, J .... 248-522-3811 228 H
bjstanbr@oaklandcc.edu
STANCHER, Amber .... 715-342-3114 498 A
amber.stancher@mstc.edu
STANCIL, Jennifer .... 804-289-8261 471 E
jlittle@richmond.edu
STANCILL, Jane .... 919-962-1000 340 F
STANCIU, Hope .... 330-490-7142 363 E
hstanciu@walsh.edu
STANDBERRY,
Cassandra .... 804-862-6100 469 E
cstandberry@rbc.edu
STANDER, Karina .... 701-858-3993 345 C
karina.stander@minotstateu.edu
STANDERFER, Mary ...... 479-394-7622.. 23 F
mstanderfer@uarichmountain.edu
STANDERFORD, Chris ... 906-227-2092 228 E
cstander@nmu.edu
STANDIFER, Alton, M ... 706-542-9167 126 F
alton@uga.edu
STANDIFIRD, Stephen ... 309-677-3167 133 H
president@bradley.edu
STANDIFORD, Chris, L . 509-313-4210 479 E
standiford@gonzaga.edu
STANDISH, Christopher 860-768-5938.. 89 E
standish@hartford.edu
STANDO, Michelle .... 734-462-4400 230 B
mstando@schoolcraft.edu
STANDRIDGE, Michelle . 502-585-9911 184 E
mstandridge@spalding.edu
STANEK, Chris .... 541-552-8786 376 A
stanek@sou.edu
STANEK, Marin .... 303-735-5525.. 83 M
marin.stanek@colorado.edu
STANEK, Mark .... 503-589-8167 372 G
mstanek@corban.edu
STANELLE, Brett .... 478-445-5800 119 A
brett.stanelle@gcsu.edu
STANFIELD, Alan .... 770-233-6139 125 F
alan.stanfield@sctech.edu
STANFIELD, Andrea .... 678-839-6370 127 A
astanfie@westga.edu
STANFIELD, Kaitlyn .... 662-862-8232 245 F
kgstanfield@iccms.edu
STANFILL, Adrienne .... 716-286-8339 309 F
aestanfill@niagara.edu
STANFILL, Sandy .... 731-968-5722 423 F
sstanfill@jscc.edu
STANFILL, William .... 417-667-8181 251 E
bstanfill@cottey.edu
STANFORD, Clark .... 319-335-7274 163 F
clark-stanford@uiowa.edu
STANFORD, Clark .... 312-996-1040 151 D
cmstan60@uic.edu
STANFORD, Erica .... 662-560-5216 247 E
STANFORD, Kathy .... 503-552-2009 374 B
kstanford@nunm.edu
STANFORD, Roger .... 608-785-9210 499 B
stanfordr@westerntc.edu
STANFORD, Shawana ...... 706-583-2760 115 C
sstanford@athenstech.edu
STANFORD, Shontell ...... 404-527-7790 121 I
sstanford@itc.edu
STANFORD, Stephen .... 904-632-3142 101 A
s.stanford@fscj.edu
STANG, Kristin .... 657-278-8811.. 31 E
kstang@fullerton.edu
STANG, Megan, M .... 909-869-3768.. 30 B
mmstang@cpp.edu
STANG, Thomas .... 281-542-2042 442 C
thomas.stang@sjcd.edu
STANGE, Von .... 319-335-3000 163 F
von-stange@uiowa.edu
STANGER, Winn .... 801-626-6876 460 B
wstanger@weber.edu
STANGLE, James, R .... 563-333-6060 169 D
stanglejamesr@sau.edu

STAUFFER, II, Ronald, E 570-577-3305 379 A ron.stauffer@bucknell.edu
STAUSS, Jodi 218-793-2539 239 E jodi.stauss@northlandcollege.edu
STAUSS, Michelle 973-618-3555 275 E mstauss@caldwell.edu
STAVA, Jackson 206-281-2175 482 K stavaj@spu.edu
STAVENGA, Mink 619-482-6569 65 K mstavenga@swccd.edu
STAVITSKY, Alan 775-784-6656 270 K ags@unr.edu
STAVRIANOUDAKIS, Nick 209-575-6835 76 K stavrianoudakisn@mjc.edu
STEAD, John 661-362-2202 51 E jstead@masters.edu
STEADMAN, Allison 843-661-1685 408 H asteadman@fmarion.edu
STEADMAN, Jacqui 423-461-8686 421 E jrsteadman@milligan.edu
STEADMAN, Meredith 919-962-1000 340 F
STEADMAN, Sheryl 801-832-2168 461 A ssteadman@westminstercollege.edu
STEARNS, Ana 716-685-9631 309 H astearns@northeastcollege.edu
STEARNS, Diane 254-968-9992 445 F dstearns@tarleton.edu
STEARNS, Gail 714-628-7260 36 D stearns@chapman.edu
STEARNS, Jill 805-546-3118 41 A jill_stearns@cuesta.edu
STEARNS, Keith 805-546-3228 41 A keith_stearns@cuesta.edu
STEARNS, Marc 215-503-0155 398 G marc.stearns@jefferson.edu
STEARNS, Stephanie, L 704-406-4236 328 I sstearns@gardner-webb.edu
STEARNS, Susan, M 515-263-2955 166 C sstearns@grandview.edu
STEARNS MOORE, Kai 714-808-4829 54 B kstearnsmoore@nocccd.edu
STEBBINS, Chad 417-625-9736 255 I stebbins-c@mssu.edu
STEBBINS, Gerald 304-829-7640 486 B gstebbins@bethanywv.edu
STEBBINS, Tim 202-462-2101 93 A tstebbins@iwp.edu
STEC, Gina 413-236-2110 213 E gstec@berkshirecc.edu
STECKBAUER, Jill 715-422-5322 498 A jill.steckbauer@mstc.edu
STECKLEIN, Brian 801-626-6787 460 B bstecklein@weber.edu
STECKLER, Mary 714-564-6839 58 F steckler_mary@sac.edu
STEDMAN, Bruce 413-203-6797 208 C stedman@csld.edu
STEDMAN, Nicole 352-392-6622 110 E nstedman@ufl.edu
STEEB, David 314-367-8700 260 A david.steeb@uhsp.edu
STEED, Deedra 870-368-2002 20 I dsteed@ozarka.edu
STEED, Jennifer 817-722-1644 437 H jennifer.steed@tku.edu
STEED, Laura 209-946-2325 71 E lsteed@pacific.edu
STEEL, Diane, M 559-323-2100 61 G dsteel@sjcl.edu
STEEL, Virginia 310-825-1201 69 D vsteel@library.ucla.edu
STEELANT, Wim, F 330-941-3009 364 G wfsteelant@ysu.edu
STEELE, Brett 310-206-6469 69 D brett@arts.ucla.edu
STEELE, Cherie 253-589-6010 478 A cherie.steele@cptc.edu
STEELE, Christopher 410-455-6841 202 G csteele@umbc.edu
STEELE, Courtney 251-405-7135 1 E csteele@bishop.edu
STEELE, Danielle 478-757-3501 116 F dsteele@centralgatech.edu
STEELE, David 423-425-1785 426 D david-steele@utc.edu
STEELE, Diane 913-758-6102 177 I steeled@stmary.edu
STEELE, Donna 731-989-6001 418 H dsteele@fhu.edu
STEELE, Doug 208-792-2211 131 F dlsteele@lcsc.edu
STEELE, Gail, T 340-693-1008 512 B gsteele@uvi.edu
STEELE, Jeffrey 586-498-4090 226 F steelej40@macomb.edu
STEELE, Jennifer 256-378-4900 1 G jsteele@cacc.edu
STEELE, Joanne 914-633-2691 302 C jsteele@iona.edu
STEELE, Kandis 334-395-8800 125 D ksteele@southuniversity.edu
STEELE, Kemper 434-961-6585 474 B ksteele@pvcc.edu
STEELE, Laura, L 714-879-3901 45 J llsteele@hiu.edu
STEELE, Leslie 615-547-1268 418 C lsteele@cumberland.edu
STEELE, Linda, M 614-947-6583 352 J linda.steele@franklin.edu
STEELE, Michael 308-535-3723 266 J steelem@mpcc.edu
STEELE, Mike 657-278-4447 31 E misteele@fullerton.edu
STEELE, Misty 405-224-3140 371 B msteele@usao.edu
STEELE, Mitzi, B 540-375-2249 469 G steele@roanoke.edu
STEELE, Molly, M 540-458-8595 476 D msteele@wlu.edu
STEELE, Pamela 540-568-7402 467 C steelepr@jmu.edu
STEELE, Rachel 662-862-8032 245 F resteele@iccms.edu
STEELE, Rich 704-687-5747 342 C rich.steele@uncc.edu
STEELE, Sarah 910-893-1460 327 C steeles@campbell.edu
STEELE, Sarah Jill 812-888-4502 162 E ssteele@vinu.edu
STEELE, Scott 859-985-3490 179 E steeles@berea.edu
STEELE, Sherri 412-244-3240 386 A
STEELE, Stephanie 269-927-8861 226 B ssteele@lakemichigancollege.edu
STEELE, Steven 970-223-2669 81 D ssteele@ibmc.edu
STEELE, Tyler 605-256-5318 415 G tyler.steele@dsu.edu
STEELE, Valerie 212-217-4530 299 C valerie_steele@fitnyc.edu
STEELE, Vicki 614-251-4706 358 B steelev@ohiodominican.edu
STEELE-FIGUEREDO, David, M 818-252-5101 76 D president@woodbury.edu
STEELE-MIDDLETON, Amanda 302-831-2727 91 A amsteele@udel.edu
STEELE-MOSES, Susan 225-490-1674 186 H susan.steele-moses@franu.edu
STEELEY, Jodie 559-489-2226 67 A jodie.steeley@fresnocitycollege.edu
STEELMAN, Joseph 770-720-5603 124 E joseph.steelman@reinhardt.edu
STEELMAN, Kelly, L 806-371-5311 428 F k051162@actx.edu
STEELMAN, Megan 303-273-3640 79 A msteelman@mines.edu
STEELMAN, Stephanie 601-968-8783 244 C ssteelman@belhaven.edu
STEELMAN, Toddi, R 919-613-8135 328 D toddi.steelman@duke.edu
STEELY, Jeff 404-413-2000 120 C jsteely@gsu.edu
STEELY, Kelly 208-562-2508 131 C kellysteely@cwi.edu
STEEN, Brant 215-497-8791 379 B brant.steen@bucks.edu
STEEN, Carrie 417-255-7255 256 A carriesteen@missouristate.edu
STEEN, Clayton 518-587-2100 320 B clayton.steen@esc.edu
STEEN, Franklin 646-565-6533 322 C franklin.steen@touro.edu
STEEN, Franklin 646-565-6533 322 B franklin.steen@touro.edu
STEEN, James 281-649-3208 436 D jsteen@hbu.edu
STEENIS, Paul, R 309-341-7145 141 E psteenis@knox.edu
STEENSON, Greg 651-690-8825 242 F gpsteenson@stkate.edu
STEENSON, Molly 412-268-2000 380 B steenson@cmu.edu
STEENWYK, Thomas, L 616-526-6549 221 L steeto@calvin.edu
STEEVES, Brian 612-626-6300 242 K stee0168@umn.edu
STEFANAKOS, Irene 617-732-2866 216 B irene.stefanakos@mcphs.edu
STEFANIA, Danielle 718-780-0305 291 G danielle.stefania@brooklaw.edu
STEFANICK, Susan, A 609-896-5065 280 D stefanic@rider.edu
STEFANKO, Lisa 412-392-4727 395 H lstefanko@pointpark.edu
STEFANONI, Andra 620-235-4124 176 H astefanoni@pittstate.edu
STEFANOVIC, Tijana 610-526-5632 378 J tstefano@brynmawr.edu
STEFANOWICZ, Michael 802-654-3000 462 A admissions@smcvt.edu
STEFFAN, Eileen 412-809-5211 395 F steffan.eileen@ptcollege.edu
STEFFEN, Colleen 716-827-4342 322 J steffenc@trocaire.edu
STEFFEN, Kaitlyn 218-733-7612 238 A kaitlyn.steffen@lsc.edu
STEFFEN, Leticia 719-549-2533 79 G leticia.steffen@csupueblo.edu
STEFFEN, Lloyd, H 610-758-3877 388 C lhs1@lehigh.edu
STEFFEN, Wayne 559-453-3677 43 D wayne.steffen@fresno.edu
STEFFENS, Aaron 563-387-1439 167 J stefaa01@luther.edu
STEFFENSEN, Lisa 865-354-3000 424 D steffensenl@roanestate.edu
STEFFES, Thomas 607-735-1720 298 G tsteffes@elmira.edu
STEFFY, Christina 610-468-1465 378 C christina.steffy@alvernia.edu
STEG HASKETT, Allie 970-351-1886 84 D allie.steghaskett@unco.edu
STEGALL, Kelly 704-290-5247 337 F kstegall@spcc.edu
STEGER, Paul 314-246-7505 261 D psteger@webster.edu
STEGGALL, Kelli 218-755-2504 237 B kelli.steggall@bemidjistate.edu
STEGLICH, Leila 703-330-8400 93 H
STEGMAIER, Mary, A 573-882-6008 260 C stegmaierm@missouri.edu
STEGNER, Joe 208-334-2315 132 C jstegner@uidaho.edu
STEHLIK, Michael 402-826-6796 266 A micheal.stehlik@doane.edu
STEHOUWER, Kristin 989-837-4224 228 G stehouwer@northwood.edu
STEIDEL, Michael 412-268-2082 380 B ms44@andrew.cmu.edu
STEIER, Kenneth 646-981-4500 322 C kenneth.steier@touro.edu
STEIGER, Gavin 512-245-3451 449 G g_s339@txstate.edu
STEIGER, Gretchen 252-249-1851 336 C
STEIGLEMAN, Carolyn 610-282-1100 382 A carolyn.steigleman@desales.edu
STEILBERG, OP, John 314-256-8861 249 F steilberg@ai.edu
STEIN, Barbara 617-627-3333 219 A barbara.stein@tufts.edu
STEIN, Beki 610-796-8202 378 C beki.stein@alvernia.edu
STEIN, Cynthia 818-766-8151 40 B cstein@concorde.edu
STEIN, David 718-232-7800 325 D dstein@yks.edu
STEIN, David, B 210-805-3591 452 D dbstein@uiwtx.edu
STEIN, Diane 818-364-7867 49 G steindb@lamission.edu
STEIN, Douglas, H 614-885-5585 359 K dstein@pcj.edu
STEIN, Ellen 646-312-4685 292 F ellen.stein@baruch.cuny.edu
STEIN, Jeff 336-278-7304 328 H jstein@elon.edu
STEIN, John 404-894-7444 119 D john.stein@gatech.edu
STEIN, Kathy 432-837-8770 449 F kstein@sulross.edu
STEIN, Lindy 414-847-3240 493 C lindystein@miad.edu
STEIN, Marni, B 801-274-3280 460 E marni.stein@wgu.edu
STEIN, Melanie 607-274-3113 302 E mstein2@ithaca.edu
STEIN, N 732-364-1220 274 G
STEIN, Rebecca 215-898-7733 399 J rstein2@upenn.edu
STEIN, Robert 607-871-2171 289 E rstein@alfred.edu
STEIN, Scott 772-462-7691 102 E sstein@irsc.edu
STEIN, Sonya 518-327-6119 310 G sstein@paulsmiths.edu
STEIN, Steve 408-420-2224 71 A ststein@ucsc.edu
STEIN, Wayne 321-433-5150 98 F steinw@easternflorida.edu
STEINACKER, Kathy 815-939-5359 146 F ksteinac@olivet.edu
STEINBACK, Robin 951-571-6160 59 A robin.steinback@mvc.edu
STEINBACK, Robin, L 951-571-6160 59 B robin.steinback@mvc.edu
STEINBERG, Aaron 718-868-2300 290 J
STEINBERG, Abbie 641-422-4313 168 E abbie.steinberg@niacc.edu
STEINBERG, Bettie, M 516-562-1159 298 F bsteinbe@northwell.edu
STEINBERG, Bryan 610-647-4400 385 K bsteinberg@immaculata.edu
STEINBERG, Dean 608-262-2322 494 C dstensberg@uwsa.edu
STEINBERG, James 202-663-5628 199 E jimsteinberg@jhu.edu
STEINBERG, Kurt, T 978-921-4242 216 F kurt.steinberg@montserrat.edu
STEINBERG, Nicole 215-965-8561 390 C nsteinberg@moore.edu
STEINBERG, Scott 207-221-4208 197 A ssteinberg@une.edu
STEINBERG, Stacey 414-847-3261 493 C staceysteinberg@miad.edu
STEINBERGER, Eric 419-559-2228 361 B esteinberger@terra.edu
STEINCAMP, Hugo 520-494-5044 11 M hugo.steincamp@centralaz.edu
STEINER, Earle 217-442-7232 136 E e.steiner@dacc.edu
STEINER, Fred 313-845-9621 224 F fred@hfcc.edu
STEINER, Frederick 215-898-3425 399 J fsteiner@design.upenn.edu
STEINER, Glen, D 708-209-3328 136 D glen.steiner@cuchicago.edu
STEINER, Gregory, G 276-944-6763 466 F gsteiner@ehc.edu
STEINER, James, D 563-589-3210 170 C jsteiner@dbq.edu
STEINER, John 856-227-7200 275 F jsteiner@camdencc.edu
STEINER, Karen 303-404-5111 80 I karen.steiner@frontrange.edu
STEINER, Karl, V 410-455-5827 202 G steinerk@umbc.edu
STEINER, Kimberly 276-964-7389 474 E kim.steiner@sw.edu
STEINER, Lori 316-942-4291 176 B steinerl@newmanu.edu
STEINER, Michael 863-667-5000 108 I masteiner@seu.edu
STEINER, Michael 660-562-1197 256 G msteine@nwmissouri.edu
STEINER, Michele 916-608-6500 51 A
STEINER, Michelle 703-284-1538 468 A michelle.steiner@marymount.edu
STEINER, Mick 330-569-5239 353 F steinerm@hiram.edu
STEINER, Sheila 206-281-2761 482 K steiners1@spuu.edu
STEINER, Ted 216-373-5387 357 F tsteiner@ndc.edu
STEINERT, Brandon 620-792-9307 171 F steinertb@bartonccc.edu
STEINFORD, Jennifer 251-981-3771 5 B jennifer.steinford@columbiasouthern.edu
STEINGRABER, Thor 818-677-4400 32 E thor.steingraber@csun.edu
STEINHART, Elisheva 305-944-0035 114 B
STEINHAUS, Paul 412-365-1606 380 F psteinhaus@chatham.edu
STEINHILBER, Steven 770-484-1204 122 B steven.steinhilber@lutherrice.edu
STEINHOFF, Cynthia, K 410-777-2483 197 C ckstEinhoff@aacc.edu

STETZ, Katherine .... 312-567-3080 139 H
kstetz@iit.edu
STETZER, Ed .... 630-752-5918 152 K
ed.stetzer@wheaton.edu
STEUBER, Jason .... 352-854-2322.. 97 L
steuberj@cf.edu
STEVA, Erin .... 773-995-5400 134 J
esteva@csu.edu
STEVENS, Alysia .... 509-865-8618 480 B
stevens_a@heritage.edu
STEVENS, Andrea .... 502-895-3411 183 E
astevens@lpts.edu
STEVENS, Andrea, N ..... 662-329-7431 247 B
anstevens@muw.edu
STEVENS, Andrew .... 303-373-2008.. 83 D
astevens@rvu.edu
STEVENS, Ann .... 512-471-4141 454 C
ann.stevens@austin.utexas.edu
STEVENS, April .... 906-487-7309 223 I
april.stevens@finlandia.edu
STEVENS, Bren .... 304-357-4911 486 J
brenstevens@ucwv.edu
STEVENS, Carrie .... 785-242-5200 176 F
carrie.stevens@ottawa.edu
STEVENS, Cathleen, M .. 585-389-2001 307 D
csteven9@naz.edu
STEVENS, David .... 603-545-4392 271 K
dstevens@ccsnh.edu
STEVENS, Debbie .... 641-673-2173 170 I
stevensd@wmpenn.edu
STEVENS, Elizabeth .... 651-690-8600 242 F
ejstevens@stkate.edu
STEVENS, Eric, A .... 660-263-3900 250 G
STEVENS, Gladstone ...... 410-864-3602 202 A
gstevens@stmarys.edu
STEVENS, Greg .... 509-434-5037 478 E
greg.stevens@ccs.spokane.edu
STEVENS, Greg, L .... 509-434-5037 478 C
greg.stevens@ccs.spokane.edu
STEVENS, Holly, L .... 423-652-4784 419 F
hlstevens@king.edu
STEVENS, Jared .... 620-227-9355 173 A
jstevens@dc3.edu
STEVENS, Jeff .... 607-587-3101 319 C
stevenjs@alfredstate.edu
STEVENS, Jeffrey .... 315-464-4927 316 F
stevejef@upstate.edu
STEVENS, John .... 435-283-7017 460 C
john.stevens@snow.edu
STEVENS, Kara .... 413-565-1000 205 I
kstevens@baypath.edu
STEVENS, Karl .... 775-327-2184 270 G
karl.stevens@gbcnv.edu
STEVENS, Kristina .... 860-486-0723.. 89 B
kristina.stevens@uconn.edu
STEVENS, Kristine, A .... 816-654-7000 253 I
STEVENS, Leslie .... 701-228-5613 345 G
leslie.stevens@dakotacollege.edu
STEVENS, RSM,
Maryanne .... 402-399-2435 265 H
mstevens@csm.edu
STEVENS, Meg .... 434-791-5700 463 L
mstevens@averett.edu
STEVENS, Megan .... 201-216-5000 282 L
msteven5@stevens.edu
STEVENS, Michael .... 802-316-6702 463 B
STEVENS, Michele .... 806-457-4200 435 D
mstevens@fpctx.edu
STEVENS, Nick .... 785-864-4914 177 G
nickstevens@ku.edu
STEVENS, Pam .... 304-876-5287 489 A
pstevens@shepherd.edu
STEVENS, Pamela .... 937-395-8601 354 J
pamela.stevens@kc.edu
STEVENS, Randy .... 909-558-4558.. 48 J
rstevens@llu.edu
STEVENS, Richie .... 304-876-5370 489 A
rstevens@shepherd.edu
STEVENS, Rob .... 309-341-5457 134 A
rstevens@sandburg.edu
STEVENS, Robert .... 203-932-7435.. 89 F
rstevens@newhaven.edu
STEVENS, Sarah, E .... 812-461-5357 162 B
sestevens@usi.edu
STEVENS, Scott .... 903-923-2178 435 A
sstevens@etbu.edu
STEVENS, Scott .... 802-860-2751 461 C
stevens@champlain.edu
STEVENS, Stephanie ...... 610-399-2437 393 D
sstevens@cheyney.edu
STEVENS, Sylvia .... 513-481-1337 363 H
sylvia_stevens@wilmington.edu
STEVENS, Tanisha .... 314-516-5695 260 E
smithtn@umsl.edu
STEVENS, Timothy .... 646-592-6005 325 R
timothy.stevens@yu.edu
STEVENS, Tristan .... 715-634-4790 491 L
tstevens2@lco.edu
STEVENS, Tristan .... 715-634-4790 491 L
tstevens@lco.edu
STEVENS TAYLOR,
Calley .... 610-606-4666 380 C
cstaylor@cedarcrest.edu
STEVENSON, Andre, P .. 252-335-3678 341 A
apstevenson@ecsu.edu
STEVENSON, Barbra ...... 870-338-6474.. 23 A
STEVENSON, Bill .... 479-524-7119.. 20 C
wstevens@jbu.edu
STEVENSON, Cameron .. 760-750-4063.. 33 C
cstevenson@csusm.edu
STEVENSON, Courtney .. 646-313-8000 295 C
courtney.stevenson@guttman.cuny.edu
STEVENSON, Duncan .... 253-964-6612 481 H
dstevenson@pierce.ctc.edu
STEVENSON, J. Edward . 408-288-3197.. 62 G
je.stevenson@sjcc.edu
STEVENSON, Jaclyn ..... 518-828-4181 296 G
jaclyn.stevenson@sunycgcc.edu
STEVENSON, James, W . 904-997-2931 101 A
james.stevenson@fscj.edu
STEVENSON, Jennifer .... 940-565-2702 453 B
jennifer.stevenson@unt.edu
STEVENSON, Joy .... 816-235-6234 260 D
stevensonjoy@umkc.edu
STEVENSON, Karen .... 724-266-3838 399 F
karen.stevenson@tsm.edu
STEVENSON, Karen, L ... 615-353-3430 424 A
karen.stevenson@nscc.edu
STEVENSON, Keith .... 217-234-5253 141 H
kstevenson50021@lakelandcollege.edu
STEVENSON,
Kimberley, N .... 252-335-3699 341 A
knstevenson@ecsu.edu
STEVENSON, Kimberly .. 615-327-6759 420 D
kstevenson@mmc.edu
STEVENSON, Leslie, W . 804-289-8141 471 E
lsteven2@richmond.edu
STEVENSON, Mark .... 563-588-8000 165 K
mstevenson@emmaus.edu
STEVENSON, Marshall .. 410-651-6083 203 B
mfstevensonjr@umes.edu
STEVENSON, Martha ..... 610-683-4484 394 A
stevenson@kutztown.edu
STEVENSON,
Martha Ann .... 205-226-4648.... 5 A
mstevens@bsc.edu
STEVENSON,
Michael, P .... 815-835-6466 149 A
michael.p.stevenson@svcc.edu
STEVENSON, Paula .... 954-545-4500 108 C
library@sfbc.edu
STEVENSON, Raymond . 610-436-2828 394 F
rstevenson@wcupa.edu
STEVENSON, Robert ..... 209-575-6081.. 76 K
stevensonr@mjc.edu
STEVENSON, Scott, J .... 404-727-3323 118 D
sjsteve@emory.edu
STEVENSON, Tamara ..... 801-832-2454 461 A
tstevenson@westminstercollege.edu
STEVENSON, Tara .... 904-826-8508.. 99 D
tstevenson@flagler.edu
STEVENSON, Terri .... 704-216-6272 330 D
STEVENSON, Valerie, O . 904-620-2920 111 A
vstevens@unf.edu
STEVENSON DUMAS,
Laura .... 904-819-6200.. 99 D
lstevenson@flagler.edu
STEVER, Matthew .... 585-785-1281 299 E
matthew.stever@flcc.edu
STEVICK, David .... 585-567-9607 301 G
david.stevick@houghton.edu
STEWARD, Agnes .... 253-840-8403 481 H
asteward@pierce.ctc.edu
STEWARD, III, Donald .. 845-687-5191 322 K
stewardd@sunyulster.edu
STEWARD, Gary .... 405-974-5528 370 H
gsteward@uco.edu
STEWARD, Kyle .... 662-325-3221 247 A
ksteward@pres.msstate.edu
STEWARD, Terry .... 225-771-3136 191 C
tsteward@sulc.edu
STEWART, Alandrea .... 314-340-3391 253 E
stewarta@hssu.edu
STEWART, Alex .... 909-687-1602.. 43 G
alexstewart@gs.edu
STEWART, Amy .... 865-524-8079 419 A
STEWART, Andrea .... 870-575-8475.. 22 F
stewarta@uapb.edu
STEWART, Anna .... 724-938-4400 394 C
stewart_a@calu.edu
STEWART, Barbara, A .... 408-554-4396.. 63 A
bstewart@scu.edu
STEWART,
Basil Andrew .... 413-782-1288 219 E
basil.stewart@wne.edu
STEWART, Beth .... 828-398-7633 331 K
bethstewart@abtech.edu
STEWART, Betty .... 972-338-1600 453 C
betty.stewart@untdallas.edu
STEWART, Brad, J .... 240-567-1312 200 E
brad.stewart@montgomerycollege.edu
STEWART, Bryan .... 305-237-4064 104 E
bstewar2@mdc.edu
STEWART, Caren .... 561-586-0121 101 P
STEWART, Carol, A .... 520-382-2491.. 16 H
carolstewart@arizona.edu
STEWART,
Chauncine, R .... 323-241-5225.. 49 I
stewarcr@lasc.edu
STEWART, Chavonne ...... 404-627-2681 116 B
chavonne.stewart@beulah.edu
STEWART, Chris .... 423-236-2356 422 H
cbstewart@southern.edu
STEWART, Christine ...... 410-337-6000 198 G
christine.stewart@goucher.edu
STEWART, Christy .... 618-985-3741 140 G
christystewart@jalc.edu
STEWART, Claire .... 402-472-2526 269 A
cstewart@unl.edu
STEWART, Connie .... 989-328-1249 227 G
connies@montcalm.edu
STEWART, Connie .... 731-286-7714 423 E
cstewart@dscc.edu
STEWART, Darla .... 806-720-7482 438 F
darla.stewart@lcu.edu
STEWART, David .... 217-234-5263 141 H
dstewart@lakelandcollege.edu
STEWART, David .... 304-293-6955 489 E
david.stewart@mail.wvu.edu
STEWART, David, R .... 651-638-6225 233 J
d-stewart@bethel.edu
STEWART, Dawn .... 614-823-3529 359 G
dstewart@otterbein.edu
STEWART, Dawn .... 614-890-3000 359 G
dstewart@otterbein.edu
STEWART, Deborah .... 802-828-2800 463 A
das07200@ccv.vsc.edu
STEWART, DeShaunta ..... 972-860-7156 433 I
STEWART, Donette .... 864-503-5280 413 A
dstewart@uscupstate.edu
STEWART, Dorothy .... 313-993-1028 230 H
stewardm@udmercy.edu
STEWART, Douglas .... 601-877-2419 244 B
stewartd@alcorn.edu
STEWART, Elizabeth, D . 570-577-3108 379 A
eds019@bucknell.edu
STEWART, Grace .... 970-675-3218.. 78 P
grace.stewart@cncc.edu
STEWART, Gregory .... 405-208-6365 367 E
gstewart@okcu.edu
STEWART, H.D .... 828-898-8823 330 A
stewarth@lmc.edu
STEWART, Hansen .... 815-921-4043 147 H
h.stewart@rockvalleycollege.edu
STEWART, Jane .... 313-664-1533 222 C
jstewart@collegeforcreativestudies.edu
STEWART, Janeen, K ..... 319-352-8331 170 F
janeen.stewart@wartburg.edu
STEWART, Jen .... 608-663-6813 491 F
jstewart@edgewood.edu
STEWART, Jennifer .... 417-873-6919 252 A
jstewart012@drury.edu
STEWART, Jennifer .... 314-968-7105 261 D
jstewart15@webster.edu
STEWART, Jimmy .... 318-678-6000 187 E
jistewart@bpcc.edu
STEWART, Jocelyn .... 323-343-3050.. 32 B
jocelyn.stewart@calstatela.edu
STEWART, John .... 803-780-1200 413 B
jstewart@voorhees.edu
STEWART, III, John, W .. 205-665-6001.... 8 D
presidentsoffice@montevallo.edu
STEWART, Julie .... 303-340-5234.. 80 C
julie.stewart@ccaurora.edu
STEWART, Karla .... 701-777-3511 344 H
karla.stewart@und.edu
STEWART, Kaylan .... 731-989-6651 418 H
kstewart@fhu.edu
STEWART, Keegan .... 806-720-7129 438 F
keegan.stewart@lcu.edu
STEWART, Kevin .... 951-571-6291.. 59 B
kevin.stewart@mvc.edu
STEWART, Kiesha .... 718-368-5034 294 C
kiesha.stewart@kbcc.cuny.edu
STEWART, Lana .... 308-345-8110 266 J
stewartl@mpcc.edu
STEWART, Larry .... 248-218-2023 229 I
lstewart@rochesteru.edu
STEWART, Leah .... 859-572-6437 184 B
stewartl1@nku.edu
STEWART, Leesa .... 802-322-1652 461 D
leesa.stewart@goddard.edu
STEWART, Lisa .... 850-599-3730 109 E
lisa.stewart@famu.edu
STEWART, Lisa .... 832-252-0758 431 M
lisa.stewart@cbshouston.edu
STEWART, Makena .... 704-290-5840 337 F
mstewart@spcc.edu
STEWART, Malek .... 610-527-0200 396 G
malek.stewart@rosemont.edu
STEWART, Mark .... 718-270-2740 316 E
mark.stewart@downstate.edu
STEWART, Marshall, M . 573-882-2394 260 C
stewartmars@missouri.edu
STEWART, Michael .... 310-289-5123.. 68 E
mike.stewart@wcui.edu
STEWART, Michael .... 478-471-2710 122 D
michael.stewart@mga.edu
STEWART, Michelle, C .. 312-935-4232 140 F
mstewart@icsw.edu
STEWART, Mindy .... 703-812-4757 467 D
mstewart@leland.edu
STEWART, Morrisia .... 863-638-7244 113 D
morrisia.stewart@warner.edu
STEWART, Muriel .... 218-935-0417 244 A
muriel.stewart@wetcc.edu
STEWART, Nathan .... 262-551-5931 491 B
nstewart@carthage.edu
STEWART, Nydia .... 847-578-8482 148 B
nydia.stewart@rosalindfranklin.edu
STEWART, Patrick .... 409-880-2279 449 B
stewarts@lamar.edu
STEWART, Paul .... 904-620-3978 111 A
p.stewart@unf.edu
STEWART, Peter .... 207-326-2181 195 G
peter.stewart@mma.edu
STEWART, Rachel .... 231-777-0461 228 C
rachel.stewart@muskegoncc.edu
STEWART, Raedorah ...... 202-885-8671.. 94 D
rcstewart@wesleyseminary.edu
STEWART, Reginald, C .. 714-997-6815.. 36 D
regstewart@chapman.edu
STEWART, Robert .... 617-552-2671 207 A
bobstewart@theq.follett.com
STEWART, Ronnie .... 706-886-6831 126 C
rstewart@tfc.edu
STEWART, Ross .... 206-281-2900 482 K
rstewart@spu.edu
STEWART, Scott .... 616-949-5300 222 F
scott.stewart@cornerstone.edu
STEWART, Sean .... 510-659-6173.. 54 J
sstewart@ohlone.edu
STEWART, Sheilynda ..... 406-466-3577 366 B
sheilynda.stewart@langston.edu
STEWART, Standish .... 216-987-4596 351 D
standish.stewart@tri-c.edu
STEWART, Thomas .... 413-538-7000 214 D
tstewart@hcc.edu
STEWART, Tish .... 662-472-9080 245 E
tstewart@holmescc.edu
STEWART, Todd, M .... 270-745-5276 186 A
todd.stewart@wku.edu
STEWART, Tommy .... 901-761-9494 418 A
tstewart@concorde.edu
STEWART, Toyia, K .... 312-341-2137 148 A
tkstewart@roosevelt.edu
STEWART, Trevor .... 209-575-6530.. 76 I
stewartt@yosemite.edu
STEWART, Tynelle .... 585-275-7532 323 E
tstewar4@ur.rochester.edu
STEWART, Vicki, L .... 717-815-1287 402 G
vstewart@ycp.edu
STEWART, Wendy .... 760-757-2121.. 52 G
wstewart@miracosta.edu
STEWART, Wendy .... 253-833-9111 480 A
wstewart@greenriver.edu
STEWART, Wes .... 713-500-4963 455 D
william.w.stewart@uth.tmc.edu
STEWART GONZALEZ,
Lori .... 502-852-6153 185 E
lori.gonzalez@louisville.edu

STOMBERGER, Mary ..... 970-491-6817.. 79 E
mary.stromberger@colostate.edu
STOMPER, Jeffrey .... 847-543-2531 135 G
stomper@clcillinois.edu
STONE, Andrea .... 606-783-5272 183 H
a.fryman@moreheadstate.edu
STONE, Andrew .... 480-461-7479.. 13 F
andrew.stone@mesacc.edu
STONE, Angie .... 256-331-5475.... 3 C
angies@nwscc.edu
STONE, Benjamin .... 414-425-8300 494 A
bstone@shsst.edu
STONE, Cedric .... 501-370-5360.. 21 A
cstone@philander.edu
STONE, Cody .... 406-994-2205 263 G
cstone@montana.edu
STONE, David .... 401-841-3569 501 L
david.stone@usnwc.edu
STONE, David, A .... 248-370-2762 229 F
dstone@oakland.edu
STONE, Dawn .... 989-358-7293 220 G
stoned@alpenacc.edu
STONE, Denise .... 503-255-0332 374 A
dstone@multnomah.edu
STONE, Elizabeth .... 202-559-5079.. 92 B
elizabeth.stone@gallaudet.edu
STONE, Emily .... 925-969-2113.. 40 H
estone@dvc.edu
STONE, Greg .... 918-595-7723 370 B
greg.stone@tulsacc.edu
STONE, Gwendalyn .... 276-964-2555 474 E
gwendalyn.stone@sw.edu
STONE, Jeff .... 916-577-2200.. 76 C
jstone@jessup.edu
STONE, Jenna .... 315-268-3790 295 E
jestone@clarkson.edu
STONE, Jennifer .... 315-228-6928 296 C
jstone@colgate.edu
STONE, John .... 661-362-2271.. 51 E
jstone@masters.edu
STONE, Karen, J .... 904-620-2828 111 A
kstone@unf.edu
STONE, Laird .... 208-732-6201 131 B
csitrustees@csi.edu
STONE, Lisa .... 602-489-5300.. 10 G
lisa.stone@arizonachristian.edu
STONE, Mark .... 979-458-6450 445 D
mstone@tamus.edu
STONE, Melissa .... 313-436-9131 231 B
mjmstone@umich.edu
STONE, Meredith .... 541-888-7353 376 B
mstone@socc.edu
STONE, Patrick .... 508-362-2131 214 B
STONE, Rhonda .... 870-248-4000.. 18 H
rhonda.stone@blackrivertech.edu
STONE, Robert .... 626-256-4673.. 37 D
rstone@coh.org
STONE, Rowena .... 417-836-5051 255 J
rowenastone@missouristate.edu
STONE, Sammy .... 229-931-2394 125 C
sstone@southgatech.edu
STONE, Staci, L .... 256-782-5690.... 6 A
slstone@jsu.edu
STONE, Sue .... 229-226-1621 126 B
sstone@thomasu.edu
STONE, Susan .... 859-251-4700 180 C
susan.stone@frontier.edu
STONE, Tia .... 256-331-5279.... 3 C
tstone@nwscc.edu
STONE, Ty .... 423-472-7141 423 C
tstone@clevelandstatecc.edu
STONE-MOYE, Shelly, T 336-322-2163 336 D
shelly.stone-moye@piedmontcc.edu
STONE RICHMOND,
Sally .... 540-458-8710 476 D
srichmond@wlu.edu
STONEBROOK, Kenneth 801-957-4004 460 D
kenneth.stonebrook@slcc.edu
STONECIPHER,
Amanda, G .... 812-941-2420 157 D
agstonec@ius.edu
STONEHAM, Edrel .... 361-582-2516 456 H
edrel.stoneham@victoriacollege.edu
STONEHILL, Amy .... 541-776-9942 375 A
amy.s@pacificbible.edu
STONEKING, Dawn, M .. 812-464-1932 162 B
dstoneking@usi.edu
STONER, Cathy .... 574-533-7000 155 B
cgstoner@goshen.edu
STONER, Keith .... 419-755-4810 357 B
kstoner@ncstatecollege.edu
STONER, Kevin .... 845-687-5092 322 K
stonerk@sunyulster.edu

STONER, Melinda, J ..... 402-280-4021 265 J
registrar@creighton.edu
STONER, Melissa .... 425-352-8667 477 F
mstoner@cascadia.edu
STONER, Tamara, L ...... 302-857-6001.. 90 D
tstoner@desu.edu
STONEROCK, Krista .... 740-474-8896 358 A
kstonerock@ohiochristian.edu
STONEY, BeEtta, L .... 785-532-6221 175 A
bestoney@ksu.edu
STOOKEY, Stephen .... 806-291-1161 457 B
stookeys@wbu.edu
STOOKSBERRY, Robert . 210-436-3301 442 A
stooksberry@stmarytx.edu
STOOPS, Melinda .... 617-552-3280 207 A
melinda.stoops@bc.edu
STOOS, Barbara .... 419-251-1702 355 G
barbara.stoos@mercycollege.edu
STOOTHOFF, Lisa .... 913-621-8726 173 B
lstoothoff@donnelly.edu
STOPHER, Brenda .... 812-856-1907 156 C
brstoph@iu.edu
STOPHER, Brenda .... 470-578-3225 121 J
bstopher@kennesaw.edu
STOPPEL, Chris .... 303-273-3064.. 79 A
cstoppel@mines.edu
STOPPENBRINK, Norm . 614-837-4088 363 D
stoppenbrinkn@valorcollege.edu
STOPPER, Suzanne, T ... 570-326-3761 392 S
sstoppe2@pct.edu
STOPPLE, Jeffrey .... 805-893-2385.. 70 E
jstopple@ltsc.ucsb.edu
STORER, Andrew .... 906-487-2440 227 D
storer@mtu.edu
STORER, Andrew, J .... 906-487-2352 227 D
storer@mtu.edu
STOREY, Amy .... 315-279-5201 303 D
astorey@keuka.edu
STOREY, Bruce .... 309-796-5129 133 D
storeyb@bhc.edu
STOREY, Karen .... 906-635-2418 226 C
kstorey@lssu.edu
STOREY, Xavier .... 540-863-2824 473 D
xstorey@mgcc.edu
STOREY GROVES,
Margaret .... 802-443-5196 461 G
mgroves@middlebury.edu
STOREY LEE, Candice ... 615-343-1107 427 B
STORIE, Barbara .... 817-722-1742 437 H
barbara.storie@tku.edu
STORIE, Cheryl .... 240-582-5680 203 C
financial-affairs@umuc.edu
STORIE, Monique .... 671-735-2333 503 E
mstorie@triton.uog.edu
STORIN LINITZ, Karen .. 617-975-9324 209 A
linitzk@emmanuel.edu
STORLAZZI, Caesar, T .. 203-432-0371.. 90 B
caesar.storlazzi@yale.edu
STORM, JR., Chris, K ... 516-877-3165 288 L
cstorm@adelphi.edu
STORM, Maryam .... 818-708-9232.. 49 A
STORMER, Kevin .... 812-866-6839 155 D
stormer@hanover.edu
STORMS, Amy .... 417-626-1234 257 A
storms.amy@occ.edu
STORMS, Andy .... 417-626-1234 257 A
storms.andy@occ.edu
STORMS, Melanie .... 352-588-7805 107 B
melanie.storms@saintleo.edu
STORRAR, Scott .... 734-487-3591 223 F
sstorrar@emich.edu
STORRS, Debbie .... 336-334-5495 342 D
dastorrs@uncg.edu
STORRS, Regina, M .... 313-593-5020 231 B
rstorrs@umich.edu
STORSVED, John, R ...... 217-581-6025 137 C
jrstorsved@eiu.edu
STORTI, Kelly .... 484-254-2121 378 C
kelly.storti@alvernia.edu
STORY, Lachel .... 601-266-6485 248 H
lachel.story@usm.edu
STORY, Lisa, L .... 712-324-5061 168 H
lstory@nwicc.edu
STORY, Pamela .... 845-848-6039 298 A
pamela.story@dc.edu
STORY, Quinisha .... 770-394-8300 114 J
STORY, Sarah .... 830-372-8053 448 C
sstory@tlu.edu
STORY, Shelley .... 512-863-1281 444 F
storys@southwestern.edu
STORY-HUFFMAN, Ru .... 229-931-2259 120 B
ru.story-huffman@gsw.edu

STORZ, Eddie .... 303-360-4788.. 80 C
eddie.storz@ccaurora.edu
STOSS, Kate .... 765-285-1847 153 E
kpstoss@bsu.edu
STOTE, Kim .... 518-587-2100 320 B
STOTLER, Vanessa .... 805-289-6410.. 74 B
vstotler@vcccd.edu
STOTO, Robert .... 609-896-5140 280 D
stoto@rider.edu
STOTT, Roger, F .... 443-518-4463 199 D
rstott@howardcc.edu
STOTTS, Bob .... 270-789-5017 179 G
restotts@campbellsville.edu
STOTTS, James .... 404-880-8992 116 I
jstotts@cau.edu
STOTTS, Joshua .... 734-432-5749 226 G
jstotts@madonna.edu
STOTTS, Mark .... 814-864-6666 384 E
marks@glit.edu
STOUDT, Jennifer .... 610-921-7511 377 F
jstoudt@albright.edu
STOUDT, Rebecca .... 570-271-6766 384 A
rstoudt@som.geisinger.edu
STOUDT, Ryan .... 989-463-7162 220 F
stoudtrr@alma.edu
STOUFFER, Vicki .... 269-749-7535 229 G
vstouffer@olivetcollege.edu
STOUFFER, Wendy, D ... 479-575-6870.. 21 H
wstouff@uark.edu
STOUGH, Edward .... 304-829-7000 486 B
estough@bethanywv.edu
STOUP, Gregory .... 530-895-2266.. 27 F
stoupgr@butte.edu
STOUP, Russ .... 618-634-3276 149 C
russs@shawneecc.edu
STOUPAS, Leslie .... 805-889-0169.. 17 A
STOUT, Alden .... 316-942-4291 176 B
stouta@newmanu.edu
STOUT, Christine .... 248-689-8282 231 E
cstout@walshcollege.edu
STOUT, David, M .... 732-224-2204 275 D
dstout@brookdalecc.edu
STOUT, Gary .... 817-531-6552 450 F
gstout@txwes.edu
STOUT, Jane .... 773-995-2548 134 J
jstout@csu.edu
STOUT, Michael .... 336-334-4822 334 F
mcstout@gtcc.edu
STOUT, Rebecca .... 706-771-4089 115 H
rebecca.stout@augustatech.edu
STOUT, Ross .... 503-370-6911 377 E
rstout@willamette.edu
STOUTE, Steve .... 312-362-7571 136 F
sstoute@depaul.edu
STOUTE, Steve, K .... 716-888-2100 291 M
steves8@canisius.edu
STOVALL, Alethea .... 402-481-3804 265 B
alethea.stovall@bryanhealthcollege.edu
STOVALL, Alfred, J .... 662-252-8000 248 B
ajstovall@rustcollege.edu
STOVALL, Chris .... 940-397-4273 439 F
chris.stovall@msutexas.edu
STOVALL, Holly .... 817-515-5905 445 A
holly.stovall@tccd.edu
STOVALL, Jerry .... 229-931-2562 125 C
jstovall@southgatech.edu
STOVALL, Keith .... 601-643-8376 244 G
keith.stovall@colin.edu
STOVALL, Kristen .... 903-983-8144 437 G
kstovall@kilgore.edu
STOVALL, Shana .... 303-352-3310.. 80 D
shana.stovall@ccd.edu
STOVALL, Terri, H .... 817-921-8680 444 D
tstovall@swbts.edu
STOVER, Caitlin, M .... 508-767-7698 205 F
cm.stover@assumption.edu
STOVER, Corey .... 605-455-6000 414 H
STOVER, Dennis .... 877-954-1500 420 F
STOVER, Janice .... 620-441-5247 172 M
janice.stover@cowley.edu
STOVER, Mark .... 818-677-2271.. 32 E
mark.stover@csun.edu
STOVER, Meredith, A .... 781-239-4015 205 G
stoverm@babson.edu
STOVER, Patrick, J .... 979-845-4747 446 B
vcdean@ag.tamu.edu
STOVER, Ronalda, S ..... 803-778-6688 406 A
stoverrs@cctech.edu
STOVER, Stacey .... 734-462-4400 230 B
sstover@schoolcraft.edu
STOW, Becka .... 816-604-4016 255 B
becka.stow@mcckc.edu

STOWASSER, Melissa ... 843-574-6312 411 I
melissa.stowasser@tridenttech.edu
STOWE, Brook .... 718-522-9073 290 B
bstowe@asa.edu
STOWE, Cindy .... 501-686-5557.. 22 D
cstowe@uams.edu
STOWE, Lentz .... 252-940-6306 332 A
lentz.stowe@beaufortccc.edu
STOWE, Melissa .... 205-387-0511.... 1 D
melissa.stowe@bscc.edu
STOWE, William .... 903-983-8602 437 G
wstowe@kilgore.edu
STOWELL, Jessica .... 904-819-6322.. 99 D
jstowell@flagler.edu
STOWELL, Jessica .... 540-831-5783 468 E
jstowell1@radford.edu
STOWELL, Michael .... 864-977-7004 410 A
mike.stowell@ngu.edu
STOWERS, Chris .... 850-729-6468 104 L
stowersc@nwfsc.edu
STOWERS, Ray, E .... 479-308-2285.. 17 E
ray.stowers@arcomedu.org
STOWERS, Rebecca .... 574-372-5100 155 C
stowerri@grace.edu
STOWIK, Stanley .... 401-232-6240 403 B
sstowik@bryant.edu
STOYNOFF, Stephen ...... 507-389-1242 238 L
stephen.stoynoff@mnsu.edu
STRABALA, Cecilia .... 480-377-4555.. 14 A
cecilia.strabala@riosalado.edu
STRABLE, Kim .... 336-272-7102 329 B
kim.strable@greensboro.edu
STRACHAN, Dana .... 561-803-2000 105 B
dana_strachan@pba.edu
STRACHAN, Jacquelyn .. 954-486-7728 112 J
jstrachan@uftl.edu
STRACK, Ashkhen .... 860-773-1489.. 87 E
astrack@tunxis.edu
STRACK, Jason .... 269-471-6571 220 H
strack@andrews.edu
STRADER, Scott .... 813-974-9232 111 B
scottstrader@usf.edu
STRAHAN, Jennifer .... 908-737-3232 277 F
jestraha@kean.edu
STRAHAN, Samantha .... 256-372-5500..... 1 A
samantha.strahan@aamu.edu
STRAHN-KOLLER,
Brooke .... 319-398-4969 167 H
brooke.strahn-koller@kirkwood.edu
STRAIT, Dana .... 574-284-4556 160 F
dstrait@saintmarys.edu
STRAIT, LuAnn .... 605-882-5284 414 D
straitl@lakeareatech.edu
STRAITS, Jeffrey .... 202-885-8684.. 94 D
jstraits@wesleyseminary.edu
STRAKA, Richard .... 507-389-6621 238 L
richard.straka@mnsu.edu
STRAKA, Ronald .... 952-446-4127 235 B
strakar@crown.edu
STRALEY, Cassandra ...... 614-236-6116 348 I
cstraley@capital.edu
STRANG, Kathy .... 866-492-5336 243 G
katherine.strang@laureate.net
STRANGE, Adiaha .... 704-334-6882 327 J
astrange@charlottechristian.edu
STRANGE, Alan .... 219-864-2400 159 D
astrange@midamerica.edu
STRANGE, Kendra .... 864-578-8770 410 G
kstrange@sherman.edu
STRANGE, Tammy .... 303-273-3281.. 79 A
tstrange@mines.edu
STRANGE LEWIS,
Sharon .... 202-238-2446.. 92 E
STRANGE-MARTIN,
Nicole .... 334-229-4250..... 4 B
nystrange@alasu.edu
STRANO, Kimberly .... 845-257-3215 316 B
lavoiek@newpaltz.edu
STRASBERG, David .... 323-650-7777.. 48 C
STRASNER, Sam .... 479-498-6045.. 18 E
sstrasner@atu.edu
STRASSER, Nora .... 316-295-5818 173 G
strasser@friends.edu
STRASSFELD, Brenda ..... 212-463-0400 322 C
brenda.strassfeld@touro.edu
STRATFORD, Denis .... 617-724-6340 216 E
dgstratford@mghihp.edu
STRATHEARN, Becky ...... 716-896-0700 324 A
bstrathearn@villa.edu
STRATIGAKOS,
Despina, M .... 716-645-6200 315 F
dms58@buffalo.edu
STRATTON, Chuck .... 573-840-9079 259 I
cstratton@trcc.edu

Index of Key Administrators STRATTON – STROW 913

STRATTON, Gary .... 865-573-4517 419 E
gstratton@johnsonu.edu
STRATTON, Gary, R .... 502-597-6912 183 A
gary.stratton@kysu.edu
STRATTON, Micheal, T .. 478-445-5497 119 A
micheal.stratton@gcsu.edu
STRATTON, Timothy ...... 218-726-6018 243 A
tstratto@umn.edu
STRAUB, Katherine, H ... 570-372-4318 398 A
straubk@susqu.edu
STRAUB, Keri, B .... 717-361-6412 383 B
straubk@etown.edu
STRAUB, Peter .... 609-652-4548 283 A
peter.straub@stockton.edu
STRAUB, Steve .... 920-735-5717 497 F
straub@fvtc.edu
STRAUBE, Lori .... 269-337-4400 233 A
STRAUCH, Pierre .... 203-287-3018.. 88 D
paier.admin@snet.net
STRAUGHAN, Robert, D 540-458-8602 476 D
straughanr@wlu.edu
STRAUGHN, Greg .... 325-674-2209 427 G
gbs00a@acu.edu
STRAUGHN, Marcia ...... 325-674-2000 427 G
STRAUS, Julie .... 573-288-6314 251 I
jstraus@culver.edu
STRAUSE, Sandra .... 610-372-4721 396 A
sstrause@racc.edu
STRAUSS, Andrew, L ..... 937-229-3795 362 C
astrauss1@udayton.edu
STRAUSS, Daniel .... 727-394-6217 145 D
dstrauss@nuhs.edu
STRAUSS, David, J .... 313-577-1010 232 H
davidstrauss@wayne.edu
STRAUSS, Jason .... 510-841-9230.. 76 F
jstrauss@wi.edu
STRAUSS, Kate .... 714-772-3330.. 26 B
vpadmin@anaheim.edu
STRAUSS, Rob .... 214-768-7505 443 G
rstrauss@smu.edu
STRAUT COLLARD,
Susan .... 718-940-5689 313 C
sstautcollard@sjcny.edu
STRAUTS, Erin .... 708-656-8000 145 B
STRAWN, Chuck .... 206-281-2845 482 K
cstrawn@spu.edu
STRAWN, Cindy .... 903-566-7214 455 C
cstrawn@uttyler.edu
STRAWN, Douglas .... 330-337-6403 347 B
alumni@awc.edu
STRAWN, Kelley .... 503-370-6017 377 E
kstrawn@willamette.edu
STRAWN, Scott .... 405-491-6306 369 G
sstrawn@snu.edu
STRAWSER, Joyce, A ..... 973-761-9225 282 K
joyce.strawser@shu.edu
STRAYER, Colleen .... 419-530-2516 363 B
colleen.strayer@utoledo.edu
STRAYHORN, Terrell ..... 804-354-5210 475 G
tstrayhorn@vuu.edu
STREATER, Kristen, L .... 972-881-5891 432 I
kstreater@collin.edu
STREBE, Chet, A .... 715-675-3331 498 E
strebe@ntc.edu
STRECKER, Deborah .... 610-896-1142 385 H
dstrecke@haverford.edu
STRECKER, Julie .... 515-650-3198 163 C
juliestrecker@theartofeducation.edu
STRECKER, Michael, J ... 504-865-5210 191 D
mstreck@tulane.edu
STREED, Scott .... 218-855-8063 237 C
scott.streed@clcmn.edu
STREEK, Dan .... 203-596-4500.. 88 E
STREET, Brandon .... 435-586-5420 459 E
brandonstreet@suu.edu
STREET, Peggy .... 276-244-1227 463 H
pstreet@asl.edu
STREET, Scott .... 409-984-6292 449 D
scott.street@lamarpa.edu
STREET, Tearanny .... 718-489-2016 312 H
tstreet@sfc.edu
STREETER, Holly .... 319-425-5340 170 D
streeterh@uiu.edu
STREETER, Montrose ...... 252-398-6209 328 A
mastreeter@chowan.edu
STREETER-FERRARI,
Michelle .... 937-775-3766 364 D
michelle.streeter@wright.edu
STREETMAN, Craig .... 423-652-4158 419 F
wcstreetman@king.edu
STREFF, Fredrick, M ...... 540-674-3637 473 F
fstreff@nr.edu
STREGE, Ron .... 507-457-5631 241 A
rstrege@winona.edu
STREHLE-HENSON,
Elvira, U .... 303-492-7481.. 83 M
elvira.henson@colorado.edu
STREICH, Eric .... 508-213-2398 217 C
eric.streich@nichols.edu
STREICH, Jessica, A ...... 865-694-6565 424 C
jastreich@pstcc.edu
STREICH, Kelsi .... 303-384-2538.. 79 A
kstreich@mines.edu
STREIT, Tina .... 320-363-5165 234 I
tstreit@csbsju.edu
STREMIECKI, Kat .... 765-860-1732 158 A
kstremiecki@ivytech.edu
STREMPEL, Eileen .... 310-206-9593.. 69 D
strempel@schoolofmusic.ucla.edu
STREUFERT, Billie .... 605-274-4123 413 G
billie.streufert@augie.edu
STREY, Mary, M .... 641-628-5233 164 B
streym@central.edu
STREY, Tara .... 320-222-5211 239 H
tara.strey@ridgewater.edu
STRICHERZ, Shanda, L . 605-336-6588 415 B
shandas@kairos.edu
STRICKLAND, Ann .... 251-580-2255.... 1 I
ann.strickland@coastalalabama.edu
STRICKLAND, Beth .... 229-732-5947 114 I
bethstrickland@andrewcollege.edu
STRICKLAND, Brooke ..... 334-556-2418.... 2 C
bstrickland@wallace.edu
STRICKLAND,
Carolyn, R .... 570-326-3671 392 S
cstrickl@pct.edu
STRICKLAND, Ceimone . 678-466-4288 117 A
ceimonestrickland@clayton.edu
STRICKLAND, Claire, I .. 207-581-1593 196 D
cpratt@maine.edu
STRICKLAND, Donna ..... 910-521-6565 343 A
donna.strickland@uncp.edu
STRICKLAND,
Earnestine .... 512-505-3082 437 B
eestrickland@htu.edu
STRICKLAND, JR.,
Elliott .... 570-326-3761 392 S
estrickl@pct.edu
STRICKLAND, Frank ...... 229-391-5060 114 D
fstrickland@abac.edu
STRICKLAND, Gary .... 912-443-5794 124 I
gstrickland@savannahtech.edu
STRICKLAND, Glenn ...... 850-973-1616 104 K
stricklandg@nfc.edu
STRICKLAND, James ..... 601-925-3354 246 D
jstrickland@mc.edu
STRICKLAND, Jason ...... 910-788-6403 337 G
jason.strickland@sccnc.edu
STRICKLAND, Jay .... 870-612-2020.. 23 B
jay.strickland@uaccb.edu
STRICKLAND, Jeff .... 770-533-6912 121 L
jstrickland@laniertech.edu
STRICKLAND, Jennifer .. 225-490-1679 186 H
jennifer.strickland@franu.edu
STRICKLAND, Joy .... 740-392-6868 356 G
joy.strickland@mvnu.edu
STRICKLAND, Kristine ... 985-448-7922 187 J
kristine.strickland@fletcher.edu
STRICKLAND, Mark .... 727-394-6110 107 C
strickland.mark@spcollege.edu
STRICKLAND, Michele .. 478-553-2097 123 D
mstrickland@oftc.edu
STRICKLAND, Michelle . 478-275-6589 123 E
STRICKLAND, Michelle . 478-553-2097 123 D
mstrickland@oftc.edu
STRICKLAND, Olan, C ... 850-263-3261.. 95 P
ocstrickland@baptistcollege.edu
STRICKLAND, Ora .... 304-348-0231 109 H
ora.strickland@fiu.edu.edu
STRICKLAND, Rose, A .. 850-263-3261.. 95 P
rastrickland@baptistcollege.edu
STRICKLAND, Shelley ... 478-445-5004 119 A
STRICKLAND, Sidney .... 215-327-8084 312 B
strickland@rockefeller.edu
STRICKLAND, Timothy .. 252-493-7330 336 E
tstrickland@email.pittcc.edu
STRICKLEN, Mac .... 740-593-2627 358 L
strickle@ohio.edu
STRICKLER, Andrew ...... 860-439-2200.. 87 F
andrew.strickler@conncoll.edu
STRICKLIN, Jan .... 503-352-2890 375 B
jstricklin@pacificu.edu
STRICKLIN, Michelle ..... 706-233-7898 125 A
pstricklin@shorter.edu
STRICKLIN, Scott .... 352-375-4683 110 E
scotts@gators.ufl.edu
STRICKMAN, Tamiko ...... 734-615-8669 231 A
tstrickm@umich.edu
STRIEDTER, Georg .... 949-824-7685.. 69 C
chair@uci.edu
STRIEF, Kristi, L .... 844-642-2338 168 F
striefk@nicc.edu
STRIEFEL, Ed .... 701-483-2407 345 A
edward.c.striefel@dickinsonstate.edu
STRIEKER, Mark .... 217-228-5432 147 C
striema@quincy.edu
STRIGENS, Lora .... 414-288-1693 492 E
lora.strigens@marquette.edu
STRIKE, Frank .... 703-993-2513 466 J
fstrike@gmu.edu
STRIMPLE, Karen .... 620-252-7061 172 K
strimple.karen@coffeyville.edu
STRINGER, Brenda .... 256-228-6001.... 3 B
stringerb@nacc.edu
STRINGER, Calandra ..... 850-201-8775 112 B
calandra.stringer@tcc.fl.edu
STRINGER, Christopher . 609-984-1100 283 D
cstringer@tesu.edu
STRINGER, Cindy .... 254-647-3120 441 D
1224mgr@theg.follett.com
STRINGER, Gregory .... 575-835-5253 286 D
gregory.stringer@nmt.edu
STRINGER, Jamie .... 865-354-3000 424 D
stringer@roanestate.edu
STRINGER, Jen .... 510-642-6000.. 68 N
STRINGER, Martin .... 714-628-4816.. 58 G
stringer_martin@sccollege.edu
STRINGER, Mike .... 714-997-6527.. 36 D
stringer@chapman.edu
STRINGER, Tammy .... 770-531-3130 116 C
tstringer1@brenau.edu
STRINGFELLOW,
Heather .... 801-832-2749 461 A
hstringfellow@westminstercollege.edu
STRINGFELLOW, Kurt .... 229-226-1621 126 B
stringfellow@thomasu.edu
STRINGHAM, Heidi .... 435-893-2256 460 C
heidi.stringham@snow.edu
STRIPE PORTILLO,
Jennifer .... 213-615-7264.. 36 G
jstripe@thechicagoschool.edu
STRIPLIN, Thomas .... 304-434-8000 487 E
STRIPLING, Helen .... 734-384-4103 227 F
hstripling@monroeccc.edu
STRIPLING, Scott .... 281-646-1109 430 H
scott.stripling@thebibleseminary.edu
STRIPP, Greg, J .... 541-346-5551 376 G
stripp@uoregon.edu
STRITIKUS, Tom .... 970-247-7100.. 80 H
tstritikus@fortlewis.edu
STRITTMATTER, Scott .... 574-520-5533 157 C
sstrittm@iusb.edu
STROBEL, Corbin .... 620-665-3537 174 D
strobelc@hutchcc.edu
STROBEL, Jennifer .... 213-615-7269.. 36 G
jstrobel@thechicagoschool.edu
STROBEL, Kathy .... 724-287-8711 379 C
kathleen.strobel@bc3.edu
STROBEL, Ricky .... 909-623-0302.. 59 H
STROBEL, Scott, A .... 203-432-1430.. 90 B
STROBLE, Elizabeth, J ... 314-968-6996 261 D
stroble@webster.edu
STROBLE, Jennifer .... 770-426-2762 122 A
jennifer.stroble@life.edu
STRODE, Clint .... 209-667-3795.. 33 D
cstrode@csustan.edu
STRODEMIER, Tammy ... 360-623-8625 477 H
tammy.strodemier@centralia.edu
STRODER, Miriam .... 423-636-7300 425 E
mstroder@tusculum.edu
STRODER, Yvonne .... 618-537-6949 143 G
STROFFOLINO, John ...... 540-423-9853 472 J
jstroffolino@germanna.edu
STROHBEEN, Jodi .... 712-274-5133 168 C
strohbeenj@morningside.edu
STROHECKER, Carol .... 612-625-3350 242 K
stro@umn.edu
STROHMEYER, Donna ..... 254-968-9484 445 F
dstrohm@tarleton.edu
STROHSCHEIN, Lesley .. 913-288-7211 174 H
lstrohschein@kckcc.edu
STROJNY, Duane .... 517-371-5140 232 K
strojnyd@cooley.edu
STROKER, Robert, T ...... 215-204-5004 398 D
robert.stroker@temple.edu
STROLLO, Ronald, A ...... 330-941-2385 364 G
rastrollo@ysu.edu
STROLLO HOLBROOK,
Toni .... 407-646-2355 106 L
tsholbrook@rollins.edu
STROM, Brian, J .... 973-972-4400 281 B
bstrom@rbhs.rutgers.edu
STROM, Jordan .... 785-539-3571 175 F
jstrom@mccks.edu
STROM, Laura, A .... 618-650-3330 149 H
lstrom@siue.edu
STROM, Mark .... 478-387-4887 119 E
mstrom@gmc.edu
STROM, Stephen .... 231-348-6660 228 D
sstrom@ncmich.edu
STROM, Steven .... 845-451-1552 297 E
steve.strom@culinary.edu
STROM, Valerie .... 661-654-2243.. 30 C
vstrom@csub.edu
STROMAN, Devin .... 575-624-7012 285 F
devin.stroman@roswell.enmu.edu
STROMAN, Jay .... 813-974-2011 111 B
STROMBECK, Stephen .... 916-577-2200.. 76 C
sstrombeck@jessup.edu
STROMBERG, Lori .... 308-635-6703 269 E
stromber@wncc.edu
STROMBOM, Mari .... 970-491-4752.. 79 E
mari.strombom@colostate.edu
STROMME, Karen .... 218-726-7143 243 A
kstromme@d.umn.edu
STRONACH, Jeanne .... 619-594-8712.. 33 E
jstronac@sdsu.edu
STRONG, Allan .... 802-656-4280 462 D
allan.strong@uvm.edu
STRONG, Arlene .... 312-261-3522 145 C
astrong5@nl.edu
STRONG, Elizabeth, C .... 417-836-6368 255 J
elizabethstrong@missouristate.edu
STRONG, Ella .... 606-487-3091 181 E
ella.strong@kctcs.edu
STRONG, Jennifer .... 843-355-4111 413 C
strongj@wiltech.edu
STRONG, Kerra .... 641-673-1014 170 I
strongk@wmpenn.edu
STRONG, III,
L. Thomas .... 504-282-4455 190 D
tstrong@nobts.edu
STRONG, Michael, A ..... 330-972-6593 361 G
mstrong@uakron.edu
STRONG, Mike .... 909-389-3210.. 60 E
mstrong@craftonhills.edu
STRONG, Shawn .... 573-897-5000 259 E
STRONG, Whitney .... 617-537-6456 143 G
wbstrong@mckendree.edu
STRONG-LEEK, Linda ..... 610-896-1014 385 H
lgriffin@haverford.edu
STROTHER, Jennielle ..... 512-313-5468 432 N
jennielle.strother@concordia.edu
STROTHER, Mary .... 617-373-2000 217 D
STROTHER, Nina .... 662-862-8242 245 F
njstrother@iccms.edu
STROUD, Dusk .... 252-527-6223 335 E
dostroud89@lenoircc.edu
STROUD, George, H .... 717-245-1639 382 B
stroudg@dickinson.edu
STROUD, Ian .... 715-425-4123 496 A
ian.stroud@uwrf.edu
STROUD, John .... 646-313-8000 295 C
john.stroud@guttman.cuny.edu
STROUD, Kerci, M .... 401-454-6380 404 B
kstroud@risd.edu
STROUD, Lewis .... 252-222-6021 332 G
stroudl@carteret.edu
STROUD, Misty .... 408-288-3734.. 62 G
misty.stroud@sjcc.edu
STROUD, Toney .... 304-696-6295 488 N
stroudh@marshall.edu
STROUP, Carrie, D .... 330-471-8538 355 D
cstroup@malone.edu
STROUP, Chandler .... 907-564-8299.... 9 F
cstroup@alaskapacific.edu
STROUP, Joshua .... 636-584-6646 252 D
joshua.stroup@eastcentral.edu
STROUP-BENHAM,
Christine .... 303-315-2835.. 84 B
christine.stroup-benham@ucdenver.edu
STROUSE, Natalie .... 216-373-5298 357 F
nstrouse@ndc.edu
STROUSS, Elaine .... 724-480-3494 381 G
elaine.strouss@ccbc.edu
STROUT, Sarah .... 508-929-8119 213 D
sstrout@worcester.edu
STROW, Brian .... 561-803-2473 105 B
brian_strow@pba.edu

© COPYRIGHT HIGHER EDUCATION PUBLICATIONS, INC. 2022

STROYAN, Todd .... 817-722-1623 437 H
todd.stroyan@tku.edu
STRUBBERG, Megen ..... 636-584-6723 252 D
megen.strubberg@eastcentral.edu
STRUBY, Shannon .... 402-354-7104 267 E
shannon.struby@methodistcollege.edu
STRUCK, Monica .... 701-483-2136 345 A
monica.struck@dickinsonstate.edu
STRUDLER, Keith .... 973-655-5214 278 C
strudlerk@montclair.edu
STRUDWICK, Daniel ...... 217-228-5432 147 C
strudda@quincy.edu
STRUEBEL, Philip .... 716-851-1588 299 A
struebel@ecc.edu
STRUNK, Brian .... 606-546-1276 185 B
bstrunk@unionky.edu
STRUNK, Lauren .... 717-245-1663 382 B
strunkl@dickinson.edu
STRUNK, Mary .... 518-783-2314 314 K
strunk@siena.edu
STRUPP, Kindra, L .... 812-464-1755 162 B
kstrupp@usi.edu
STRUPPA, Daniele, C ..... 714-997-6611.. 36 D
struppa@chapman.edu
STRUSOWSKI, Lisa .... 302-857-1124.. 90 H
lstrusow@dtcc.edu
STRUTTON, Jill .... 281-649-3321 436 D
jstrutton@hbu.edu
STRYBOS, John .... 361-698-1243 434 H
jstrybos@delmar.edu
STRYKER, Joann .... 406-247-5752 263 H
joann.stryker@msubillings.edu
STRYKER, Joanne .... 401-454-6177 404 B
jstryker@risd.edu
STRYKER, Quinn .... 402-826-8285 266 A
quinn.stryker@doane.edu
STRZEPEK, Jason .... 978-468-7111 209 G
jstrzepek@gordonconwell.edu
STUARD, Avis .... 504-520-7583 193 C
astuard@xula.edu
STUART, Barbara .... 802-586-7711 462 C
bstuart@sterlingcollege.edu
STUART, Cheryl .... 937-775-2556 364 D
cheryl.stuart@wright.edu
STUART, Christian .... 269-471-3310 220 H
christians@andrews.edu
STUART, Cledis, D .... 870-235-4046... 21 E
cdstuart@sauniag.edu
STUART, Dana .... 262-524-7200 491 A
dstuart@carrollu.edu
STUART, D'Anne .... 575-646-2431 286 G
dstuart@nmsu.edu
STUART, Eddie .... 910-962-3626 343 B
stuarte@uncw.edu
STUART, Forrest .... 610-330-5055 387 B
stuartf@lafayette.edu
STUART, G. Rob .... 216-987-4757 351 D
g.rob.stuart@tri-c.edu
STUART, Julia .... 910-755-7300 332 D
STUART, Nancy, M .... 860-768-4846.. 89 E
nstuart@hartford.edu
STUART, JR.,
Robert, M .... 225-578-3811 188 K
rstuart@lsufoundation.org
STUART, Stephanie .... 217-351-2200 146 G
sstuart@parkland.edu
STUART, Susan .... 913-288-7265 174 H
sstuart@kckcc.edu
STUART, Thomas .... 816-415-5973 261 G
stuartt@william.jewell.edu
STUART-CARRUTHERS,
Christine .... 956-364-4328 448 F
christine.stuart-carruthers@tstc.edu
STUBBERT, Amanda ...... 206-281-2587 482 K
amandas@spu.edu
STUBBLEFIELD,
Claudine .... 304-724-3700 485 G
cstubblefield@apus.edu
STUBBLEFIELD, George . 916-577-2200.. 76 C
gstubblefield@jessup.edu
STUBBLEFIELD, Jay .... 423-869-7000 420 A
robert.stubblefield@lmunet.edu
STUBBLEFIELD,
Michael, A .... 225-771-3890 190 K
michael_stubblefield@subr.edu
STUBBLEFIELD,
Shannon .... 760-775-2121.. 52 G
sstubblefield@miracosta.edu
STUBBS, Brent .... 912-443-3015 124 I
bstubbs@savannahtech.edu
STUBBS, Fany .... 203-857-7025.. 87 B
fstubbs@ncc.commnet.edu
STUBBS, Janice .... 954-201-6464.. 96 F

STUBBS, Leah .... 502-863-8030 180 E
leah_stubbs@georgetowncollege.edu
STUBBS, Robert .... 303-492-3750.. 83 M
robert.stubbs@colorado.edu
STUBBS, Sandra .... 256-372-5230.... 1 A
sandra.stubbs@aamu.edu
STUBBS, Sidney, J .... 334-833-4416..... 5 H
oir@hawks.huntingdon.edu
STUBBS, Veronica .... 601-928-6288 246 F
veronica.stubbs@mgccc.edu
STUCHELL, Tina .... 330-823-2844 362 E
stuchetm@mountunion.edu
STUCKENBRUCK, Emily . 715-675-3331 498 E
stuckenbruck@ntc.edu
STUCKEY, Carol .... 617-732-2114 216 B
carol.stuckey@mcphs.edu
STUCKEY, Jon, C .... 717-796-5065 389 F
jstuckey@messiah.edu
STUCKEY, Lanette .... 217-709-0920 142 A
lstuckey@lakeviewcol.edu
STUCKEY, Mike .... 740-389-4636 355 F
stuckeym@mtc.edu
STUCKEY, Sheila, A .... 502-597-6867 183 A
sheila.stuckey@kysu.edu
STUCKY, Alan .... 940-565-2468 453 B
alan.stucky@untsystem.edu
STUCKY, Duane .... 618-536-3475 149 F
dustucky@siu.edu
STUCKY, Tommy .... 770-426-2616 122 A
tommy.stucky@life.edu
STUDEBAKER, Brian ...... 320-589-6035 243 C
bstude@morris.umn.edu
STUDEBAKER, Kim .... 775-674-7502 270 I
kstudebaker@tmcc.edu
STUDEBAKER, Melissa .. 260-399-7700 162 A
mstudebaker@sf.edu
STUDER, Dominique ...... 646-768-5300 300 E
STUDER, Garet .... 425-388-9328 479 B
gstuder@everettcc.edu
STUDER, Mary Ann .... 419-783-2553 351 J
mstuder@defiance.edu
STUDINGER, Robert ...... 303-352-3193.. 80 D
bob.studinger@ccd.edu
STUDINKA, Diane .... 760-744-1150.. 56 B
sstudinka@palomar.edu
STUEBING, David .... 757-455-8709 476 C
dstuebing@vwu.edu
STUEBNER, Susan, D ..... 603-526-3451 271 H
sue.stuebner@colby-sawyer.edu
STUEMPFLE, Kristin, J .. 717-337-6011 384 C
kstuempf@gettysburg.edu
STUFFLEBEAN, Ernie ..... 816-415-5969 261 G
stuffle@william.jewell.edu
STUFLICK, William .... 425-388-9212 479 B
wstuflick@everettcc.edu
STUHR-MOOTZ,
Kristin, J .... 414-955-8208 492 F
kmootz@mcw.edu
STUIFBERGEN,
Alexa, M .... 512-471-4100 454 C
astuifbergen@mail.utexas.edu
STULL, David .... 415-503-6230.. 61 E
emoon@sfcm.edu
STULTS, Randy .... 205-387-0511..... 1 D
randy.stults@bscc.edu
STULTZ, Laura .... 205-226-4877..... 5 A
lstultz@bsc.edu
STULTZ, Shelley .... 316-322-3152 172 B
sstultz@butlercc.edu
STUM, Beth .... 409-772-9866 456 B
estum@utmb.edu
STUMB, IV, Paul .... 615-547-1223 418 C
pstumb@cumberland.edu
STUMBLINGBEAR,
Barbara .... 785-749-8460 174 A
barbara.stumblingbea@bie.edu
STUMBO, Christine .... 606-368-6125 178 D
christinestumbo@alc.edu
STUMBRIS, Steven, V .... 570-577-3791 379 A
steven.stumbris@bucknell.edu
STUMNE, James .... 651-779-3918 237 D
james.stumne@century.edu
STUMO, Karl, A .... 218-299-3004 234 K
kstumo@cord.edu
STUMP, Chellye .... 334-347-2623..... 2 A
cstump@escc.edu
STUMP, Sandy .... 610-921-7205 377 F
sstump@albright.edu
STUMP-KURNICK,
Linda, J .... 352-392-5445 110 E
lstump@ufl.edu
STUMPF, Michelle .... 814-262-6436 393 A
mstumpf@pennhighlands.edu

STUMPFF, Lindsay .... 641-782-1555 170 B
stumpff@swcciowa.edu
STUOPIS,
Cecilia Warpinski .... 617-253-1716 215 G
STURDIVANT, Alvin .... 206-296-6066 483 B
STURE, Linda .... 907-563-7575..... 9 E
linda.sture@alaskacareercollege.edu
STURGE-APPLE,
Melissa .... 585-275-3540 323 E
melissa.sturge-apple@rochester.edu
STURGEON, David .... 231-777-0465 228 C
david.sturgeon@muskegoncc.edu
STURGEON, Judy .... 217-854-5536 133 F
STURGEON, Kathy, R ..... 217-443-8805 136 E
k.sturgeon@dacc.edu
STURGILL, David .... 859-246-6896 181 B
david.sturgill@kctcs.edu
STURGIS, Tina .... 585-275-2121 323 E
STURM, Emily .... 903-586-2518 437 D
STURM, Joel .... 212-410-8047 308 D
jsturm@nycpm.edu
STURM, Neal, M .... 973-443-8689 276 I
sturm@fdu.edu
STURM-SMITH, Melissa 515-271-2835 165 F
melissa.sturm-smith@drake.edu
STURRUP, Daniel, H ...... 207-581-1799 196 D
dsturrup@maine.edu
STURTZ, Carma .... 641-628-5269 164 B
sturtzc@central.edu
STUTES, Ann, B .... 806-291-1066 457 B
stutesa@wbu.edu
STUTZ, Brian .... 402-826-2161 266 A
brian.stutz@doane.edu
STUTZ, Melissa .... 307-778-1217 500 D
mstutz@lccc.wy.edu
STUTZMAN, Karl .... 574-296-6280 153 C
kstutzman@ambs.edu
STUTZMAN,
Timothy, W .... 540-432-4197 465 F
timothy.stutzman@emu.edu
STVAN, Kenneth, J .... 315-470-6689 319 A
kjstvan@esf.edu
STYLES, Jared .... 606-337-4524 180 A
registrar@ccbbc.edu
STYRON, Ken .... 251-981-3771..... 5 B
ken.styron@columbiasouthern.edu
STYRON, Kent .... 254-968-9898 445 F
wkstyron@tarleton.edu
STYSKAL, Michael .... 410-293-6301 502 I
styskal@usna.edu
SU, Dan .... 903-468-3048 446 D
dan.su@tamuc.edu
SU, John, J .... 414-288-3476 492 E
john.su@marquette.edu
SU, Nancy .... 212-217-3640 299 C
nancy_su@fitnyc.edu
SU, Susan .... 516-739-1545 308 E
records@nyctcm.edu
SUARA, Zulfat, A .... 615-327-6815 420 D
zsuara@mmc.edu
SUAREZ, Angelica .... 714-432-5577... 38 F
angelica.suarez@occ.cccd.edu
SUAREZ, Francisco .... 787-841-2000 508 H
fsuarez@pucpr.edu
SUAREZ, Maria .... 805-922-6966.. 24 L
maria.suarez@hancockcollege.edu
SUAREZ-ESPINAL,
Cynthia .... 718-289-5914 292 H
cynthia.suarez-espinal@bcc.cuny.edu
SUAREZ-OROZCO,
Marcelo, M .... 617-287-6800 211 E
marcelo.orozco@umb.edu
SUAZO, Karelie .... 787-701-5100 505 B
ksuazo@columbiacentral.edu
SUAZO, Mark .... 660-543-4560 259 K
suazo@ucmo.edu
SUBASI, Munevver .... 321-674-7486 100 A
msubasi@fit.edu
SUBBARAO, Italo .... 601-318-6572 249 B
isubbarao@wmcarey.edu
SUBBASWAMY,
Kumble, R .... 413-545-2211 211 D
chancellor@umass.edu
SUBE, Bob .... 805-678-5821... 74 A
bsube@vcccd.edu
SUBHANI, Ali .... 972-516-5036 432 I
asubhani@collin.edu
SUBLETTE, Garrett .... 325-674-2655 427 G
jgs99a@acu.edu
SUBLETTE, Gaylah .... 660-626-2860 249 C
gsublette@atsu.edu
SUBOCZ, Sue .... 866-492-5336 243 G
susan.subocz@mail.waldenu.edu

SUBRAHMANYAM,
Kaveri .... 904-620-2560 111 A
ksubrah@unf.edu
SUBRAMANIAM,
Chandra .... 818-677-2455.. 32 E
chandra.subramaniam@csun.edu
SUBRAMANIAM, Chelvi 310-233-4041.. 49 F
subramt@lahc.edu
SUBRAMANIAM, Ram ... 650-949-7472.. 43 A
subramaniamram@foothill.edu
SUBRAMANIAM, Ram ... 650-940-7472.. 43 A
subramaniamram@fhda.edu
SUBRAMANIAN, Ashok . 928-523-1237.. 14 J
ashok.subramanian@nau.edu
SUBREENDUTH, Sharon 912-478-5648 120 A
ssubreenduth@georgiasouthern.edu
SUCH, Tami .... 239-489-9296 100 G
tami.such@fsw.edu
SUCH, Tami .... 701-788-4711 345 B
tami.such@mayvillestate.edu
SUCHAN, Jennifer .... 515-294-8381 163 E
jsuchan@iastate.edu
SUCHANEK, Michael ...... 318-487-7000 187 B
bubba.suchanek@lcuniversity.edu
SUCHANIC, Angela, C ... 302-356-6924.. 91 C
angela.c.suchanic@wilmu.edu
SUCKOW, Melissa, A .... 630-515-3015 144 C
msucko@midwestern.edu
SUDA, Delight .... 671-734-1812 503 D
dsuda@piu.edu
SUDAK, Sarah .... 615-898-5342 421 C
sarah.sudak@mtsu.edu
SUDBECK, Kristine .... 402-494-2311 267 D
ksudbeck@thenicc.edu
SUDDICK, Lori .... 847-543-2200 135 G
lsuddick@clcillinois.edu
SUDEIKIS, Barbara .... 269-965-3931 225 D
sudeikisb@kellogg.edu
SUDERMAN, Julie .... 630-617-3012 137 E
julie.suderman@elmhurst.edu
SUDHAKAR, Samuel ..... 909-537-5100.. 33 B
ssudhakar@csusb.edu
SUDIA, Tanya .... 706-721-3771 115 I
tsudia@augusta.edu
SUDLER, Clifton .... 609-343-5126 274 E
csudler@atlantic.edu
SUDLOW, Jennifer .... 215-572-4483 378 E
sudlowj@arcadia.edu
SUDMEYER, Alecia .... 207-509-7166 196 B
asudmeyer@unity.edu
SUDTELGTE, Beau .... 563-425-5959 170 D
sudtelgteb121@uiu.edu
SUEBERT, Jack .... 305-809-3195.. 97 M
jack.seubert@cfk.edu
SUELFLOW, Sara, C .... 651-696-6307 236 C
suelflow@macalester.edu
SUEME, Zana .... 314-392-2230 255 H
zana.sueme@mobap.edu
SUERTH, Matthew, P .... 815-224-0550 140 D
matt_suerth@ivcc.edu
SUESS, Jack, J .... 410-455-2582 202 G
jack@umbc.edu
SUEYOSHI, Amy .... 415-338-1694.. 34 A
sueyoshi@sfsu.edu
SUFFRIDGE, Diane .... 415-257-0131.. 41 H
diane.suffridge@dominican.edu
SUGALSKI, Noelle .... 302-857-1072.. 90 H
nsugalsk@dtcc.edu
SUGANO, Adam .... 310-825-5713.. 69 D
asugano@ponet.ucla.edu
SUGARMAN, Barry .... 866-492-5336 243 G
barry.sugarman@laureate.net
SUGGS, Amber .... 618-634-3236 149 C
ambers@shawneecc.edu
SUGGS, Benny .... 919-515-3375 341 E
benny_suggs@ncsu.edu
SUGGS, Thomas .... 704-272-5363 337 F
tsuggs@spcc.edu
SUGHRUE, Helen .... 843-574-6649 411 I
helen.sughrue@tridenttech.edu
SUGIHARA, Fumio .... 413-549-4600 210 A
fsad@hampshire.edu
SUGIHARA, Fumio .... 413-559-6042 210 A
fsad@hampshire.edu
SUGIMOTO, Lara .... 808-845-9235 129 G
larahs@hawaii.edu
SUH, Joseph .... 213-738-0712.. 64 G
hhsuh@southbaylo.edu
SUHLER, Mitzi .... 620-278-2173 177 E
SUHO, Stephen .... 928-317-6000.. 11 B
stephen.suho@azwestern.edu
SUHR, Marin .... 402-461-7326 266 C
mnsuhr@hastings.edu

SUI, Dan ... 540-231-3270 475 D
dsui20@vt.edu
SUIB, Steven, L ... 860-486-4623.. 89 B
steven.suib@uconn.edu
SUISALA, Frederick, R .. 684-699-2722 503 A
f.suisala@amsamoa.edu
SUIT, Teresa ... 256-233-8167.... 4 D
teresa.suit@athens.edu
SUITE, Denzil ... 206-543-4972 484 A
djsuite@uw.edu
SUJECKI, Gailmarie ... 516-403-5906 324 C
gsujecki@webb.edu
SUKENIC, Harvey ... 617-559-8757 210 C
hsukenic@hebrewcollege.edu
SUKHABUT, Jules ... 808-735-4856 128 C
jules.sukhabut@chaminade.edu
SUKHATME, Vikas, P .... 404-727-5631 118 D
vsukhatme@emory.edu
SUKHRAM, Diana, P ..... 516-628-5603 318 A
sukhramd@oldwestbury.edu
SUKUMARAN, Beena .... 513-529-0538 356 A
sukumab@miamioh.edu
SULAIMAN, Karina ... 888-820-1484.. 64 D
karina.sulaiman@sofia.edu
SULAIMAN HARA,
Sadika ... 415-485-9375.. 39 B
ssulaimanhara@marin.edu
SULESKI, Andrew ... 530-895-2353.. 27 F
suleskian@butte.edu
SULFRIDGE, Jay ... 606-337-1114 180 A
jsulfridge@ccbbc.edu
SULIOL, Shaun ... 691-320-2480 503 B
SULKIN, Tracy ... 217-333-6677 151 F
tsulkin@illinois.edu
SULLEY, Jaclynn ... 715-634-4790 491 L
jsulley@lco.edu
SULLINS, Dori ... 815-455-8559 143 F
dsullens@mchenry.edu
SULLIVAN, Adelfa ... 702-992-2119 270 H
adelfa.sullivan@nsc.edu
SULLIVAN, Amy ... 270-534-3169 182 G
amy.sullivan@kctcs.edu
SULLIVAN, Andrew, J ... 401-865-2610 403 G
andrew.sullivan@providence.edu
SULLIVAN, Anne, R ... 212-854-4038 296 H
asullivan@columbia.edu
SULLIVAN, Barry ... 903-875-7355 439 G
barry.sullivan@navarrocollege.edu
SULLIVAN, Bobbi ... 515-961-1372 169 G
bobbi.sullivan@simpson.edu
SULLIVAN, Brian ... 513-325-4599 362 B
brian.sullivan@uc.edu
SULLIVAN, Brian, T ... 607-871-2494 289 E
sullivan@alfred.edu
SULLIVAN, Brigitte ... 410-225-2209 200 B
bsullivan01@mica.edu
SULLIVAN, Bryce ... 615-460-6437 417 B
bryce.sullivan@belmont.edu
SULLIVAN, Carole ... 614-508-7277 353 M
SULLIVAN, Casey ... 800-785-0585.. 39 F
SULLIVAN, Cheryl ... 256-726-7026.... 6 C
csullivan@oakwood.edu
SULLIVAN, Cheryl ... 559-243-7112.. 66 G
cheryl.sullivan@scccd.edu
SULLIVAN, Chris ... 936-633-5216 429 A
csullivan@angelina.edu
SULLIVAN, Chris ... 206-934-5566 482 G
chris.sullivan@seattlecolleges.edu
SULLIVAN, Crystal, C ... 937-229-3369 362 C
csulllivan1@udayton.edu
SULLIVAN, Dan ... 919-658-7748 340 E
dsullivan@umo.edu
SULLIVAN, David ... 910-678-8485 334 C
sullivad@faytechcc.edu
SULLIVAN, Deb ... 563-336-3300 165 G
djsullivan@eicc.edu
SULLIVAN, Debbie ... 336-917-5329 339 H
debbie.sullivan@salem.edu
SULLIVAN, Elizabeth ..... 201-761-7106 282 H
esullivan@saintpeters.edu
SULLIVAN, Eric ... 314-446-7239 253 E
sullivae@hssu.edu
SULLIVAN, Erin ... 860-215-9297.. 87 D
esullivan@threerivers.edu
SULLIVAN, Gerald ... 706-867-2543 126 G
gerald.sullivan@ung.edu
SULLIVAN, Glenn, D ... 502-451-0815 184 F
glennds@sullivan.edu
SULLIVAN, Heather ... 410-704-5074 204 B
hsullivan@towson.edu
SULLIVAN, Heather ... 617-262-5000 206 E
SULLIVAN, Jack ... 973-328-5252 276 A
jsullivan@ccm.edu
SULLIVAN, Jake ... 617-353-2292 207 C
jakesull@bu.edu
SULLIVAN, James ... 423-775-7306 417 D
james@bryan.edu
SULLIVAN, James, J ..... 570-340-6063 389 B
jimsullivan@marywood.edu
SULLIVAN, Jeff ... 715-874-4608 497 E
jsullivan25@cvtc.edu
SULLIVAN, Jennifer ... 706-721-3278 115 I
jensullivan@augusta.edu
SULLIVAN, Jessica ... 570-372-4425 398 A
sullivanjessica@susqu.edu
SULLIVAN, Joan, D ... 781-768-7212 217 H
joan.sullivan@regiscollege.edu
SULLIVAN, Joanne ... 845-398-4379 314 D
jsulliva@stac.edu
SULLIVAN, John ... 727-864-8331.. 98 G
sullivjf@eckerd.edu
SULLIVAN, John, M ... 508-286-3484 219 F
sullivan_john@wheatoncollege.edu
SULLIVAN, Julie ... 408-554-4100.. 63 A
jhsullivan@scu.edu
SULLIVAN, Justin ... 251-288-6000.. 93 H
SULLIVAN, Justin ... 415-476-5761.. 70 D
justin.sullivan@ucsf.edu
SULLIVAN, Kathleen ... 845-848-7804 298 A
kathleen.sullivan@dc.edu
SULLIVAN, Kevin ... 919-502-0965 339 I
kevin.sullivan@shawu.edu
SULLIVAN, Kristen ... 401-598-2931 403 E
kristen.sullivan@jwu.edu
SULLIVAN, Kristopher ... 508-831-5000 220 C
SULLIVAN, Lamont ... 864-977-0177 410 A
lamont.sullivan@ngu.edu
SULLIVAN, Laura ... 715-319-7181 498 G
laura.sullivan@northwoodtech.edu
SULLIVAN, Lauren ... 715-833-6500 497 E
lsullivan9@cvtc.edu
SULLIVAN, Leslie ... 269-749-7638 229 G
lsullivan@olivetcollege.edu
SULLIVAN, Linda ... 310-434-3427.. 63 B
sullivan_linda@smc.edu
SULLIVAN, Lisa ... 413-538-3093 216 G
provostsoffice@mtholyoke.edu
SULLIVAN, Lisa, M ... 504-394-7744 191 E
SULLIVAN, Lisa, M ... 909-621-8122.. 44 K
sullivan@hmc.edu
SULLIVAN, Maggie ... 401-456-8216 404 A
msullivan@ric.edu
SULLIVAN, Margaret ... 251-460-7616.... 9 A
msullivan@southalabama.edu
SULLIVAN, Maria ... 508-565-1402 218 F
msullivan7@stonehill.edu
SULLIVAN, Marianne ... 508-999-8984 211 F
msullivan@umassd.edu
SULLIVAN, Mark, J ... 607-746-4533 320 A
sullivmj@delhi.edu
SULLIVAN, Martha ... 540-857-7311 475 A
msullian@virginiawestern.edu
SULLIVAN, Matthew ... 608-663-2235 491 F
msullivan@edgewood.edu
SULLIVAN, Maya ... 651-793-1508 238 B
maya.sullivan@metrostate.edu
SULLIVAN, Megan, M ... 617-353-2230 207 C
msullvan@bu.edu
SULLIVAN, Melanie, R .. 401-865-2723 403 G
oir@providence.edu
SULLIVAN, Melissa ... 207-699-5043 194 G
msullivan@meca.edu
SULLIVAN, Michael ... 607-778-5040 317 A
sullivanmj4@sunybroome.edu
SULLIVAN, Michael, A .. 607-746-4538 320 A
sullivmt@delhi.edu
SULLIVAN, Monty ... 225-922-1643 187 C
montysullivan@lctcs.edu
SULLIVAN, Neil, G ... 937-229-2165 362 C
nsullivan1@udayton.edu
SULLIVAN, Nicole ... 636-949-4900 254 B
nsullivan@lindenwood.edu
SULLIVAN, Patrick ... 413-545-4630 211 D
psulliva@umass.edu
SULLIVAN, Renee ... 203-773-4474.. 85 C
rsullivan@albertus.edu
SULLIVAN, Rob ... 214-333-5671 433 D
roberts@dbu.edu
SULLIVAN, Rusty ... 816-604-5277 254 E
rusty.sullivan@mcckc.edu
SULLIVAN, Sarah ... 708-524-6298 137 A
ssullivan@dom.edu
SULLIVAN, Scott ... 914-606-6284 324 F
scott.sullivan@sunywcc.edu
SULLIVAN, Sean ... 708-456-0300 151 A
seansullivan@triton.edu
SULLIVAN, Sean ... 206-685-8153 484 A
sdsull@uw.edu
SULLIVAN, Sean, M ... 202-319-5286.. 91 G
sullivansm@cua.edu
SULLIVAN, Serena ... 252-940-6326 332 A
serena.sullivan@beaufortccc.edu
SULLIVAN, Sharon ... 704-637-4741 327 H
slsulliv@catawba.edu
SULLIVAN, Shayna ... 707-333-9623.. 24 J
SULLIVAN, Slade ... 325-674-2485 427 G
sullivans@acu.edu
SULLIVAN, Slade ... 325-674-2485 427 G
sls02h@acu.edu
SULLIVAN, Stephanie .... 770-426-2636 122 A
stephanie.sullivan@life.edu
SULLIVAN, Stephen ... 254-710-8332 430 F
stephen_sullivan@baylor.edu
SULLIVAN, Stuart ... 540-654-2031 471 B
ssulliva@umw.edu
SULLIVAN, Susan ... 978-762-4000 215 B
susulliv@northshore.edu
SULLIVAN, Suzanne ... 601-968-8881 244 C
ssullivan@belhaven.edu
SULLIVAN, Terry ... 419-448-5148 361 C
tsullivan@tiffin.edu
SULLIVAN, OSB,
Thomas ... 660-944-2875 251 B
brothomas@conception.edu
SULLIVAN, Thomas, B .. 512-448-8727 441 N
toms@stedwards.edu
SULLIVAN, Todd ... 928-523-3731.. 14 J
todd.sullivan@nau.edu
SULLIVAN, Tracy ... 708-235-2179 138 C
tsullivan@govst.edu
SULLIVAN-GONZALEZ,
Douglass ... 662-915-7294 248 F
dsg@olemiss.edu
SULLIVAN-TORREZ, Kat 916-484-8403.. 50 J
sullivk@arc.losrios.edu
SULLIVANT, Stan ... 870-338-6474.. 23 A
SULLY, John ... 216-397-1965 353 O
jsully@jcu.edu
SULMASY, Glenn, M ..... 508-213-2215 217 C
president@nichols.edu
SULPRIZIO, Tony ... 617-266-1400 206 D
SULTAN, Farooq ... 541-605-0520 374 G
farooq.sultan@oit.edu
SULTAN, Omer ... 713-563-2287 456 A
SULZBACH, J. Bonnie ... 443-412-2119 199 B
bsulzbach@harford.edu
SUMAS, Keith, P ... 404-413-0783 120 C
ksumas1@gsu.edu
SUMAYA, Isabel ... 661-654-2381.. 30 C
isumaya@csub.edu
SUMEREL, Michelle ... 662-862-8050 245 F
jmsumerel@iccms.edu
SUMLIN, Rene ... 334-683-2378.... 3 A
renesumlin@marionmilitary.edu
SUMLIN, Robert, D ... 334-683-2305.... 3 A
dsumlin@marionmilitary.edu
SUMME, Sean ... 816-501-3756 249 H
sean.summe@avila.edu
SUMMER, Sharon ... 336-770-1312 343 C
summers@uncsa.edu
SUMMER, Todd ... 619-594-7539.. 33 E
todd.summer@sdsu.edu
SUMMERFIELD, Sarah ... 813-253-7304 102 A
ssummerfield@hccfl.edu
SUMMERLIN,
Christopher, A ... 210-805-5863 452 D
csummerl@uiwtx.edu
SUMMERS, Amanda ... 281-425-6533 438 B
asummers@lee.edu
SUMMERS, Brian ... 901-321-3370 417 G
bsummers@cbu.edu
SUMMERS, Chris ... 404-364-8355 123 G
csummers@oglethorpe.edu
SUMMERS, II, Dan ... 207-509-7100 196 B
SUMMERS, Eric ... 985-549-5250 192 E
esummers@selu.edu
SUMMERS, James (Zip) 214-376-1000 440 H
jsummers@pq.edu
SUMMERS, Jeffrey ... 859-846-5358 183 G
jgsummers@midway.edu
SUMMERS, Jessica, J ... 417-836-6105 255 J
jessicaheinz@missouristate.edu
SUMMERS, Karen ... 704-330-6429 333 B
karen.summers@cpcc.edu
SUMMERS,
Kimberly Kay ... 210-567-0313 455 E
summers@uthscsa.edu
SUMMERS, JR., LeRoy . 706-821-8232 123 I
lsummers@paine.edu
SUMMERS, Lori Ann ..... 803-321-5617 409 I
loriann.summers@newberry.edu
SUMMERS, Matthew, A . 304-637-1990 486 D
summersm@dewv.edu
SUMMERS,
Meredeth, D ... 336-316-2131 329 C
summersm@guilford.edu
SUMMERS, Michael, D . 757-822-1088 474 G
msummers@tcc.edu
SUMMERS, Mike ... 610-330-5338 387 B
summersm@lafayette.edu
SUMMERS, Ragan ... 904-470-8231.. 98 I
ragan.summers@ewc.edu
SUMMERS, Richard ... 601-984-1018 248 G
rsummers@umc.edu
SUMMERS, Robert ... 615-898-2116 421 C
robert.summers@mtsu.edu
SUMMERS, Robert, P .... 870-633-4480.. 19 E
rsummers@eacc.edu
SUMMERS, Sarah ... 317-738-8017 155 A
ssummers@franklincollege.edu
SUMMERS, Scott ... 901-321-3237 417 G
ssummers@cbu.edu
SUMMERS, Shauna ... 617-879-7761 212 E
ssummers@massart.edu
SUMMERS, Stuart ... 208-282-3620 131 E
summstua@isu.edu
SUMMERS, Tiffany ... 615-230-3551 424 F
tiffany.summers@volstate.edu
SUMMERS, Vicky ... 501-450-5200.. 23 K
vsummers@uca.edu
SUMMERSELL, Charley . 518-587-2100 320 B
charley.summersell@esc.edu
SUMMEY, Chris ... 423-636-7300 425 E
csummey@tusculum.edu
SUMMIT, Jennifer ... 415-338-1141.. 34 A
jsummit@sfsu.edu
SUMMITT, April ... 951-785-2210.. 47 F
asummitt@lasierra.edu
SUMNER, Amber ... 706-295-6869 119 F
asumner@gntc.edu
SUMNER, Carol, A ... 806-742-7025 450 C
carol.a.sumner@ttu.edu
SUMNER, Dana ... 919-760-8341 331 A
sumnerd@meredith.edu
SUMNER, Jean, R ... 478-301-5571 122 C
sumner_jr@mercer.edu
SUMNER, Kenneth ... 973-655-4280 278 C
sumnerk@montclair.edu
SUMNER, Wesley, D ... 321-674-6218 100 A
wsumner@fit.edu
SUMPTER, Jeppie ... 270-745-6911 186 A
jeppie.sumpter@wku.edu
SUMPTER,
Johnathan, M ... 972-721-4045 451 E
jmsumpter@udallas.edu
SUMSION, Jared, M ..... 801-863-7291 460 A
jared.sumsion@uvu.edu
SUMTER, Takita ... 803-323-2160 413 D
sumtert@winthrop.edu
SUN, Bruce ... 651-493-3622 233 F
coo@acupunctureschoolusa.com
SUN, Chloe ... 626-571-5110.. 48 I
chloesun@les.edu
SUN, Grace ... 404-756-8927 123 A
gsun@msm.edu
SUN, Grace ... 610-861-1536 390 D
sung@moravian.edu
SUN, Hala ... 213-381-0081.. 46 I
hsun.irus@irus.edu
SUN, Joseph, S ... 215-517-2383 378 E
sunj@arcadia.edu
SUN, Justin ... 415-503-6217.. 61 E
jsun@sfcm.edu
SUN, Marcus ... 626-584-5203.. 43 E
marcussun@fuller.edu
SUN, Zhen ... 512-444-8082 448 B
bookkeeper@thsu.edu
SUNAHARA, Wayne ... 808-845-9135 129 G
waynens@hawaii.edu
SUNATA, Cem ... 805-756-6016.. 29 K
csunata@calpoly.edu
SUNCHILD, Jolin ... 406-395-4875 264 I
jsunchild@stonechild.edu
SUND, Andrew, C ... 509-865-8600 480 B
sund_a@heritage.edu
SUNDA-MEYA,
Anderson ... 504-520-7652 193 C
asundame@xula.edu
SUNDARAM, Bala ... 617-287-6055 211 E
bala.sundaram@umb.edu
SUNDARAM, Sridhar .... 657-278-0000.. 31 E
ssundaram@fullerton.edu

SUNDAY, Richard, S ..... 212-217-3760 299 C
richard_sunday@fitnyc.edu
SUNDBERG, Lori .... 847-735-5030 141 F
lsundberg@lakeforest.edu
SUNDBERG, Lori .... 319-398-5501 167 H
lori.sundberg@kirkwood.edu
SUNDBY, David .... 714-997-6668.. 36 D
sundby@chapman.edu
SUNDEEN, Kendra, L .... 651-628-3240 243 E
klsundeen@unwsp.edu
SUNDERLAND, Paul ...... 618-664-6577 138 D
paul.sunderland@greenville.edu
SUNDERLAND, JR., Richard .... 304-724-3700 485 G
rsunderland@apus.edu
SUNDERLAND, Terri ..... 618-664-7031 138 D
terri.sunderland@greenville.edu
SUNDERMAN, Rick .... 614-947-6605 352 J
rick.sunderman@franklin.edu
SUNDERMANN, Brigitte 970-255-2700.. 78 F
bsunderm@coloradomesa.edu
SUNDERMEIER, Elisabeth .... 816-802-3376 253 H
esundermeier@kcai.edu
SUNDGREN, Donald, E . 434-982-5834 471 F
des5j@virginia.edu
SUNDQUIST, Jeffery ..... 831-646-4036.. 52 H
jsundquist@mpc.edu
SUNDSTROM, Sandy ..... 503-777-7224 375 F
sundstrom@reed.edu
SUNG, Daniel .... 833-637-0866.. 46 J
dsung@itu.edu
SUNIGA, Eduardo .... 989-686-9276 223 E
eduardosuniga@delta.edu
SUNLEAF, Arthur, W ..... 563-588-7959 167 I
arthur.sunleaf@loras.edu
SUNNY, Heidi, L .... 859-858-3511 178 H
heidi.sunny@asbury.edu
SUNNYGARD, John ...... 270-745-4857 186 A
john.sunnygard@wku.edu
SUNNYGARD, John ...... 303-807-9956.. 84 B
john.sunnygard@ucdenver.edu
SUNQUIST, Scott, W ..... 978-468-7111 209 G
sunquist@gcts.edu
SUNSER, James .... 585-345-6812 300 D
presidentsoffice@genesee.edu
SUPAK, Brian .... 254-298-8609 445 B
brian.supak@templejc.edu
SUPLER, Robin .... 954-262-4349 104 M
rsupler@nsu.nova.edu
SUPOWITZ, Paul, A ...... 412-624-2901 400 A
psupowit@pitt.edu
SUPPES, Lindsey .... 315-294-8557 292 A
lsuppes@cayuga-cc.edu
SUPPLE, Matthew .... 301-314-7781 202 E
msupple@umd.edu
SUPPLEE, JR., Jack ...... 859-257-8288 185 D
supplee@uky.edu
SUPPLEE, Janice .... 937-766-7470 349 C
suppleej@cedarville.edu
SUPURGECI, Jonna .... 605-668-1298 414 F
jsupurgeci@mountmarty.edu
SUR, Sarah Gilman .... 808-235-7435 130 C
sgilman@hawaii.edu
SURA, Marissa .... 616-632-2843 221 A
mks007@aquinas.edu
SURATT, Huyuni .... 212-817-7530 293 D
hsuratt@gc.cuny.edu
SURENDER, Sheelu, M . 316-978-5337 178 B
sheelu.surender@wichita.edu
SURESH-MENON, Durga .... 617-989-4590 219 D
sureshmenond@wit.edu
SURGINER, Holly .... 254-299-8631 438 G
hsurginer@mclennan.edu
SURLS, Courtney .... 202-885-1334.. 91 D
surls@american.edu
SUROVIEC, Alice .... 706-236-1756 116 A
asuroviec@berry.edu
SURPRENANT, Aimee .... 540-231-7581 475 D
asurprenant@vt.edu
SURRATT, Christopher .. 513-558-3784 361 I
surratck@ucmail.uc.edu
SURRATT, David, A .... 405-325-3161 370 J
dsurratt@ou.edu
SURRATT, Jacob .... 336-734-7733 334 D
jsurratt@forsythtech.edu
SURRELL, Jane .... 906-227-2596 228 E
jasurrel@nmu.edu
SURRELL, Matt .... 662-472-9178 245 E
msurrell@holmescc.edu
SURRIDGE, Mary, K ...... 773-244-5710 145 F
president@northpark.edu
SURRY, Daniel, W .... 334-844-8348.... 4 E
dws0015@auburn.edu
SUSA, Angela .... 715-422-5320 498 A
angela.susa@mstc.edu
SUSANA, Gil .... 619-961-4316.. 68 A
gsusana@tjsl.edu
SUSANKA, Joseph .... 307-322-2930 500 J
jsusanka@wyomingcatholic.edu
SUSANTO-ONG, Yuliana .... 502-597-7014 183 A
yuliana.susanto@kysu.edu
SUSHINSKY, David, M .. 240-895-3381 201 F
dmsushinsky@smcm.edu
SUSKI-LENCZEWSKI, Anna .... 860-832-1757.. 85 F
lenczewskia@mail.ccsu.edu
SUSMANN, Phillip .... 802-485-2213 461 H
susmann@norwich.edu
SUSMARSKI, Aaron, E .. 814-860-5101 387 C
asusmarski@lecom.edu
SUSMILCH, Tyler .... 503-538-8383 372 I
tsusmilch@georgefox.edu
SUSSENBACH, Michelle 618-664-7025 138 D
michelle.sussenbach@greenville.edu
SUSSMAN, Ronny .... 818-883-9002.. 73 F
SUTARDJI, Anne .... 510-592-9688.. 61 D
anne.sutardji@npu.edu
SUTER, Charlene .... 585-292-2500 306 K
csuter@monroecc.edu
SUTER, Cynthia .... 802-485-2035 461 H
csuter@norwich.edu
SUTERA, Tom .... 360-532-9020 479 F
tom.sutera@ghc.edu
SUTHERLAND, Cierra .... 734-432-5665 226 G
csutherland@madonna.edu
SUTHERLAND, David .... 218-879-0816 237 F
dsutherland@fdltcc.edu
SUTHERLAND, David .... 501-450-1254.. 19 I
sutherlandd@hendrix.edu
SUTHERLAND, John ..... 706-729-2260 115 I
jsutherland@augusta.edu
SUTHERLAND, Kathleen 973-408-3100 276 B
ksutherl@drew.edu
SUTHERLAND, Richard . 989-358-7368 220 G
sutherlr@alpenacc.edu
SUTHERLAND, Ron .... 765-998-5118 161 A
rnsutherl@taylor.edu
SUTHERLIN, John .... 318-342-1413 193 A
sutherlin@ulm.edu
SUTLIFF, Deborah, A .... 603-829-6027 133 B
dsutliff@ben.edu
SUTLIFF, Michael .... 714-432-5122.. 38 F
msutliff@occ.cccd.edu
SUTLIFFE, Nicole .... 202-651-5346.. 92 B
nicole.sutliffe@gallaudet.edu
SUTLIVE, Vins, H .... 859-858-3511 178 H
vins.sutlive@asbury.edu
SUTTER, Brian .... 712-325-3328 167 G
bsutter@iwcc.edu
SUTTER, Frankie .... 910-592-8081 337 D
fsutter@sampsoncc.edu
SUTTERFIELD, Shirley ... 251-442-2414.... 8 C
ssutterfield@umobile.edu
SUTTLE, J. Lloyd .... 203-432-4453.. 90 B
j.suttle@yale.edu
SUTTMEIER, Bruce .... 503-768-7100 373 D
cas@lclark.edu
SUTTON, Angela .... 504-865-5653 191 D
asutton1@tulane.edu
SUTTON, Chad .... 334-222-6591.... 2 I
jmh@lbwcc.edu
SUTTON, Chuck .... 423-636-7300 425 E
csutton@tusculum.edu
SUTTON, Cynthia .... 314-392-2291 255 H
suttonc@mobap.edu
SUTTON, David .... 863-669-2929 106 A
dosutton@polk.edu
SUTTON, Deborah .... 252-527-6223 335 E
dssutton14@lenoircc.edu
SUTTON, Dennis .... 910-275-6137 335 C
dsutton@jamessprunt.edu
SUTTON, Duncan .... 310-265-6155.. 60 B
duncan.sutton@usw.salvationarmy.org
SUTTON, Gary .... 843-208-8059 412 C
suttong2@uscb.edu
SUTTON, Gentry .... 863-638-1426 113 D
gentry.sutton@warner.edu
SUTTON, Jalesa .... 919-546-8388 339 I
jalesa.sutton@shawu.edu
SUTTON, Jama .... 865-774-5800 424 G
jama.sutton@ws.edu
SUTTON, Jayne .... 402-472-7131 268 I
jsutton@nebraska.edu
SUTTON, Jeff .... 254-295-5044 453 A
jsutton@umhb.edu
SUTTON, Jennifer .... 256-765-5558.... 8 E
jballard1@una.edu
SUTTON, Judith .... 304-485-5487 486 H
jsutton@msc.edu
SUTTON, Lawrence .... 724-805-2402 397 D
lawrence.sutton@stvincent.edu
SUTTON, Nancy .... 217-353-2113 146 G
nsutton@parkand.edu
SUTTON, Pamela .... 512-223-7598 429 J
psutton@austincc.edu
SUTTON, R. Anderson ... 808-956-8818 129 B
rasutton@hawaii.edu
SUTTON, Renee .... 910-275-6103 335 C
rsutton@jamessprunt.edu
SUTTON, Rick .... 334-699-2266.... 1 B
rosutton@acom.edu
SUTTON, Scott .... 828-339-4296 337 H
scotts@southwesterncc.edu
SUTTON, Shan, C .... 520-621-0717.. 16 H
ssutton@arizona.edu
SUTTON, Shannon .... 309-298-2073 152 I
sm-sutton@wiu.edu
SUTTON, Stephanie .... 330-494-6170 360 I
ssutton@starkstate.edu
SUTTON, Steve .... 510-642-6727.. 68 N
studentaffairs@berkeley.edu
SUTTON, Susan, R .... 865-882-4658 424 D
suttonsr@roanestate.edu
SUTTON, Todd .... 336-790-8607 342 D
tasutton@uncg.edu
SUTTON GERBER, Ronette .... 910-521-6268 343 A
ronette.gerber@uncp.edu
SUTTON-LOVETT, Tommy .... 800-517-0857 355 A
SUTTON NOSS, Melinda .... 214-768-4564 443 G
msnoss@smu.edu
SUTTON-SMITH, Leslie . 973-655-4376 278 C
suttonsmithl@montclair.edu
SUTYAK, John .... 540-365-4493 466 I
jsutyak@ferrum.edu
SUTZKO, Christopher .... 570-208-5874 386 G
christophersutzko@kings.edu
SUWALSKY, SJ, David .. 314-977-7065 258 H
david.suwalsky@slu.edu
SUZUKI, Anne .... 480-732-7028.. 13 B
anne.suzuki@cgc.edu
SUZUKI, Takeo .... 423-425-4759 426 D
takeo-suzuki@utc.edu
SU'ESU'E, Jessie .... 684-699-2722 503 A
j.suesue@amsamoa.edu
SVEHLIK, Edward, T ..... 304-293-2545 489 E
ted.svehlik@mail.wvu.edu
SVEI, Yehuda .... 215-477-1000 398 C
talmudicalyeshiva@yahoo.com
SVENDSEN, Ryan .... 602-222-9300.. 10 I
SVETE, Lee .... 276-944-6660 466 F
lsvete@ehc.edu
SVINARICH, Kathryn ..... 810-762-7885 225 F
ksvinari@kettering.edu
SVOBODA, Angela, M ... 512-448-8622 441 N
asvoboda@stedwards.edu
SVONAVEC, Stephen ..... 478-275-6769 122 D
stephen.svonavec@mga.edu
SWAFFORD, Jeanna, C . 731-881-7629 426 E
jswafford@utm.edu
SWAFFORD, Jenny .... 423-775-7580 417 D
jswafford6722@bryan.edu
SWAFFORD, Melissa ..... 216-987-3195 351 D
melissa.swafford@tri-c.edu
SWAGER, Sarah .... 406-243-5225 263 D
sarah.swager@umontana.edu
SWAGERTY, John .... 785-833-4323 175 C
john.swagerty@kwu.edu
SWAGGER, Russell .... 715-634-4790 491 L
rswagger@lco.edu
SWAHA, Chuck .... 540-231-7670 466 E
cswaha@vcom.vt.edu
SWAILS, Nicholas .... 970-675-3265.. 78 P
nicholas.swails@cncc.edu
SWAIM, Charles .... 309-694-8584 138 I
charles.swaim@icc.edu
SWAIN, Bill, F .... 302-295-1216.. 91 C
bill.f.swain@wilmu.edu
SWAIN, Colleen .... 903-565-5898 455 C
cswain@uttyler.edu
SWAIN, Heather, C .... 517-355-2262 227 C
swainh@msu.edu
SWAIN, Jackie .... 406-275-4859 264 H
jackie_swain@skc.edu
SWAIN, Jeffrey, D .... 305-626-3674 100 B
jeffrey.swain@fmuniv.edu
SWAIN, Jennifer, L .... 607-735-1894 298 G
jswain@elmira.edu
SWAIN, Ruth .... 541-956-7484 375 G
rswain@roguecc.edu
SWAIN, Sarah .... 910-893-1236 327 C
swain@campbell.edu
SWAIN, Scott .... 216-373-5306 357 F
sswain@ndc.edu
SWAIN, Scott, R .... 407-278-4557 248 A
sswain@rts.edu
SWAIN-GILLIARD, LaTashia, H .... 410-651-6668 203 B
lswaingilliard@umes.edu
SWAINE, Richard .... 419-383-3443 363 B
richard.swaine@utoledo.edu
SWALES, Tammy .... 315-279-5000 303 D
SWALLOW, John, R .... 262-551-5858 491 B
jswallow@carthage.edu
SWALLOW, Steve .... 937-529-2201 361 F
slswallow@united.edu
SWALLOW, Steven .... 937-529-2201 361 F
slswallow@united.edu
SWAN, Joel .... 256-761-6318.... 7 B
jswan@talladega.edu
SWAN, John .... 916-577-2200.. 76 C
jswan@jessup.edu
SWAN, Lilymae .... 313-993-3323 230 H
swanls@udmercy.edu
SWAN, Lisa .... 262-646-6509 493 F
lswan@nashotah.edu
SWAN, Lorretta .... 903-510-2349 451 D
lswa@tjc.edu
SWAN, S. Tomeka .... 410-287-1892 198 A
tswan@cecil.edu
SWANAGAN, Diana .... 706-233-7301 125 A
dswanagan@shorter.edu
SWANGER, Rachel .... 310-393-0411.. 56 C
rachel_swanger@rand.org
SWANGLER, Jennifer ..... 701-777-6374 344 H
jennifer.swangler@und.edu
SWANK, Angela, P .... 919-209-2024 335 D
apswank@johnstoncc.edu
SWANK, Jamie, R .... 724-847-6136 384 B
jrswank@geneva.edu
SWANK, Justin .... 724-503-1001 401 D
jswank@washjeff.edu
SWANKER, Susanne ...... 413-205-3216 205 C
susanne.swanker@aic.edu
SWANN, Ed .... 251-626-3303.... 7 E
eswann@ussa.edu
SWANN, Jerilyn .... 865-981-8167 420 C
jerilyn.swann@maryvillecollege.edu
SWANN, Jerilyn .... 865-981-8167 420 C
jerilyn.swann@maryvillecollege.edu
SWANN, Laura .... 256-549-8263.... 2 B
lswann@gadsdenstate.edu
SWANN, Victoria .... 212-854-6933 290 H
vswann@barnard.edu
SWANSON, Adam .... 228-897-4377 246 F
adam.swanson@mgccc.edu
SWANSON, Annette .... 567-661-7510 359 H
annette_swanson@owens.edu
SWANSON, Barry .... 716-338-1015 302 G
barryswanson@mail.sunyjcc.edu
SWANSON, Barry .... 859-257-9101 185 D
barry.swanson@uky.edu
SWANSON, Brian, R ..... 909-869-2261.. 30 B
bswanson@cpp.edu
SWANSON, Chris .... 541-683-5141 373 A
cswanson@gutenberg.edu
SWANSON, Christina .... 815-455-8692 143 F
cswanson@mchenry.edu
SWANSON, Christopher 815-836-5393 142 C
swansoch@lewisu.edu
SWANSON, Cynthia .... 269-471-3288 220 H
swansonc@andrews.edu
SWANSON, Darlene ...... 815-928-5541 146 F
dswanso2@olivet.edu
SWANSON, Darren .... 320-363-5810 234 I
dswanson@csbsju.edu
SWANSON, Dennis .... 708-534-4110 138 C
dswanson99@govst.edu
SWANSON, Dennis .... 910-521-6365 343 A
dennis.swanson@uncp.edu
SWANSON, Emily .... 801-832-2013 461 A
eswanson@westminstercollege.edu
SWANSON, Greg .... 910-630-7050 331 B
gswanson@methodist.edu
SWANSON, Janine .... 209-946-2062.. 71 E
jswanson@pacific.edu

SYLVESTER, Kenneth ..... 810-766-3383 231 C
kenms@umich.edu

SYLVESTER, Samantha .. 337-521-9043 188 G
samantha.sylvester@solacc.edu

SYLVESTER-CAESAR,
Jemma .... 713-221-2791 452 B
caesarj@uhd.edu

SYLVIA, Hillary .... 508-999-8531 211 F
hillary.sylvia@umassd.edu

SYLVIA, Lynn .... 910-362-7679 332 F
lbsylvia845@mail.cfcc.edu

SYLWESTER, Breana ...... 541-383-7260 371 I
bsylwester@cocc.edu

SYMICEK, Alan .... 715-425-4655 496 A
alan.symicek@uwrf.edu

SYMONDS, Lisa .... 518-891-2915 309 G
lsymonds@nccc.edu

SYMS, Deirdre .... 586-445-7862 226 F
symsd@macomb.edu

SYNAKOWSKI, Edmund 307-766-5353 500 H
esynakow@uwyo.edu

SYNAN, Sharon .... 706-245-7226 118 C
ssynan@ec.edu

SYNDAB, Ricky .... 803-780-1025 413 B
rsyndab@voorhees.edu

SYNDER, Brittany .... 305-809-3233.. 97 M
brittany.snyder@cfk.edu

SYNDER, Deanna .... 816-604-4507 254 E
deanna.synder@mcckc.edu

SYNDER, Tamara .... 352-638-9764.. 96 B
tsnyder@beaconcollege.edu

SYNER, Alicia .... 304-205-6746 487 D
alicia.syner@bridgevalley.edu

SYNODI, George, S .... 203-832-7273.. 89 F
gsynodi@newhaven.edu

SYNODINOS, Dimitrios . 323-953-4000.. 49 E
synodid@lacitycollege.edu

SYOEN, Elise .... 423-869-6433 420 A
elise.syoen@lmunet.edu

SYPNIEWSKI, Holly .... 601-974-1000 246 C
sypnih@millsaps.edu

SYPNIEWSKI, Holly .... 717-815-1216 402 G
hsypniewski@ypc.edu

SYRMOS, Vassilis, L ..... 808-956-5006 128 I
syrmos@hawaii.edu

SYRMOS, Vassilis, L ..... 808-956-5006 129 B
syrmos@hawaii.edu

SYRMOS, Vassilis, L ..... 808-956-5006 128 I
syrmos@hawaii.edu

SYVERSON, Janet .... 503-375-7119 372 G
jsyverson@corban.edu

SYVERTSON, Krisi .... 406-353-2607 262 B
ksyvertson@ancollege.edu

SYVERUD, Kent .... 315-443-2235 321 D
chancellor@syr.edu

SZABAT, Sandy .... 505-438-8884 287 J
sandy@acupuncturecollege.edu

SZABO, Jennifer .... 240-629-7927 198 E
jszabo@frederick.edu

SZABO, Mihaela .... 304-336-8270 489 B
mszabo@westliberty.edu

SZABO, Shari .... 863-680-4900 100 F
sszabo@flsouthern.edu

SZAFRAN, Zvi .... 315-386-7204 319 E
president@canton.edu

SZAJ, Christine .... 651-290-6362 241 N
christine.szaj@mitchellhamline.edu

SZAKALY, CSC,
Anthony .... 508-565-1343 218 F
aszakaly@stonehill.edu

SZAKAS, Joseph, S .... 207-621-3198 196 E
szakas@maine.edu

SZALDA, Katie .... 518-782-6767 314 K
kszalda@siena.edu

SZANI, Phyllis .... 201-200-3350 278 F
pszani@njcu.edu

SZANTON, Sarah .... 410-502-2361 199 E
sarah.szanton@jhu.edu

SZAREK, Michael .... 201-559-6047 277 A
szarekm@felician.edu

SZARLETA, Ellen .... 219-980-6698 157 A
eszarlet@iun.edu

SZAROLETTA, Betti .... 906-524-8301 225 G
betti.szaroletta@kbocc.edu

SZARVAS, Tibor .... 318-797-5371 189 E
tibor.szarvas@lsus.edu

SZARZYNSKI, Lori .... 414-382-6329 490 G
lori.szarzynski@alverno.edu

SZATARAY, Balint .... 209-946-2654.. 71 E
bsztaray@pacific.edu

SZATKO, Judi .... 402-280-2709 265 J
judiszatko@creighton.edu

SZCZEPANEK,
Charlene, L .... 401-456-8130 404 A
cszczepanek@ric.edu

SZCZERBACKI, David .... 617-333-2233 208 D
dszczerbacki@curry.edu

SZCZYS, Patricia .... 860-465-0252.. 85 G
szczysp@easternct.edu

SZE TO, Pau Ping .... 215-572-5511 401 G
pszeto@wts.edu

SZEFINSKI, Colleen .... 201-761-6416 282 H
cszefinski@saintpeters.edu

SZEJKO, Thomas .... 724-503-1001 401 D
tszejko@washjeff.edu

SZELEST, Bruce .... 518-956-8058 315 D
bszelest@albany.edu

SZELISTOWSKI, Warren 410-532-5110 201 C
wszelistowski@ndm.edu

SZENTMIKLOSI, Jill, M . 407-582-4142 113 C
jszentmiklosi@valenciacollege.edu

SZEP, Chris Ann .... 410-287-1028 198 A
caszep@cecil.edu

SZEPIWDYCZ, Valerie ... 617-585-1139 217 A
valerie.szepiwdycz@necmusic.edu

SZESZYCKI, Donald, J ... 319-335-3565 163 F
donald-szeszycki@uiowa.edu

SZKODNEY, Robert .... 908-526-1200 280 C
bob.szkodny@raritanval.edu

SZKREDKA, Slawomir ... 805-482-2755.. 59 G
sszkredka@stjohnsem.edu

SZMYT, Anne-Marie ...... 413-585-2262 218 D
aszmyt@smith.edu

SZOLYGA, Chris .... 608-249-6611 491 H

SZOSTAK, Maja .... 607-778-5001 317 A
szostakmm@sunybroome.edu

SZPARAGOWSKI,
George .... 610-785-6205 396 H
gszparagowski@scs.edu

SZROMBA, Matthew, P . 920-923-8505 492 D
mpszromba93@marianuniversity.edu

SZTAJN, Paola .... 919-515-5900 341 E
psztajn@ncsu.edu

SZUCS, Peter .... 503-491-6904 373 H
peter.szucs@mhcc.edu

SZUKALSKI, SVD,
John, A .... 563-876-3353 165 D
jszukalski@dwci.edu

SZUPKA, Jennifer .... 803-774-3339 406 A
szupkajl@cctech.edu

SZUR, Katalin .... 212-237-8041 294 B
kszur@jjay.cuny.edu

SZWEDKO, Emmalee ...... 801-832-2553 461 A
eszwedko@westminstercollege.edu

SZYMANSKI, Lynda ...... 563-387-1005 167 J
szymly01@luther.edu

SZYMANSKI, Nicholas .. 330-263-2198 350 H
nszymanski@wooster.edu

SZYMKOWICZ,
Caitlin, B .... 413-585-4944 218 D
cszymkowicz@smith.edu

SZYMURSKI, Tish .... 770-720-5527 124 E
pss@reinhardt.edu

T

TA, Jennie .... 626-350-1500.. 28 H

TA, Minh-hoa .... 626-656-2101.. 73 D
mhta@uwest.edu

TAAFAKI, Irene, J .... 692-625-3394 503 F

TABACHOW, Daisy .... 407-303-9203.. 95 A
daisy.tabachow@ahu.edu

TABAK, Lorie .... 713-798-6649 430 E
tabak@bcm.edu

TABAK, Rachel .... 716-896-0700 324 A
rtabak@villa.edu

TABAN, Faruk .... 832-230-5350 439 H
faruk@na.edu

TABATABAI, Habib .... 405-974-2865 370 H
htabatabai@uco.edu

TABB, Brian .... 612-455-3420 234 A
brian.tabb@bcsmn.edu

TABB, Iris .... 314-340-3541 253 E
tabbi@hssu.edu

TABB, Winston, G .... 410-516-8328 199 E
wtabb@jhu.edu

TABER, Charles, S .... 785-532-6224 175 A
ctaber@ksu.edu

TABER, Samara .... 907-474-5526.. 10 B
setaber@alaska.edu

TABER DOUGHTY,
Teresa .... 817-272-2591 454 B
teresa.doughty@uta.edu

TABERNER, Ian .... 617-585-0200 206 E
ian.taberner@the-bac.edu

TABERSKI, Michael .... 585-245-5618 317 E
mtaberski@geneseo.edu

TABING, Karla .... 618-985-3741 140 G
karlatabing@jalc.edu

TABOADA, Heidi, A .... 361-593-3964 447 A
heidi.taboada@tamuk.edu

TABOR, Anne .... 207-973-1090 194 D
tabora@husson.edu

TABOR, Tammy .... 620-276-9508 173 H
tammy.tabor@gcccks.edu

TABRON-GIDDINGS,
Jasmine .... 570-208-5898 386 G
jasminetabron@kings.edu

TACCONE, Al .... 760-757-2121.. 52 G
ataccone@miracosta.edu

TACCONI, Selah .... 281-425-6352 438 B
stacconi@lee.edu

TACK, Eric .... 678-466-4085 117 A
erictack@clayton.edu

TACKETT, Lake .... 304-697-7550 486 F
ltackett@huntingtonjuniorcollege.edu

TACZANOWSKY, Amy .... 724-589-2155 398 F
ataczanowsky@thiel.edu

TADAO, Tchuzie .... 680-488-2471 504 A
tchuziet@gmail.com

TADEO, Joseph .... 352-588-8244 107 B
joseph.tadeo@saintleo.edu

TADEO ORBIK, Kelly .... 402-280-1293 265 J
kellytadeoorbik@creighton.edu

TADEPALLI, Raghu .... 336-278-6000 328 H
rtadepalli@elon.edu

TADEPALLI, Raghu .... 336-278-6647 328 H

TADESSE, Berhanu .... 657-278-8748.. 31 E
btadesse@fullerton.edu

TADLOCK, Katherine ..... 740-593-2860 358 L
tadlockk@ohio.edu

TADLOCK, Martin .... 727-873-4151 111 B
mtadlock@mail.usf.edu

TADTMAN, Jeff .... 620-223-2700 173 F
jeffta@fortscott.edu

TAFOYA, Christina .... 760-862-1364.. 39 A
chtafoya@collegeofthedesert.edu

TAFOYA, Michelle .... 213-738-5500.. 66 A
housing@swlaw.edu

TAFOYA, Yvette .... 562-860-2451.. 35 O
ytafoya@cerritos.edu

TAFT, Tamara Jo .... 701-845-7227 345 E
tammyjo.taft@vcsu.edu

TAGA, Brendon .... 360-475-7474 481 B
btaga@olympic.edu

TAGAREL, Lyndsay .... 734-462-4400 230 B
ltagarel@schoolcraft.edu

TAGAWA, Helen .... 510-809-1444.. 46 B

TAGGART, Julie .... 614-222-6171 351 A
jtaggart@ccad.edu

TAGGART, Sean .... 541-956-7061 375 G
staggart@roguecc.edu

TAGGART, Thomas .... 904-256-7000 102 G
ttaggar@ju.edu

TAGLIARENI, Jim .... 336-599-1181 336 D
jim.tagliareni@piedmontcc.edu

TAHA, Dianne .... 516-726-5837 502 G
tahad@usmma.edu

TAHMASSEBI, Debbie .... 801-832-2585 461 A
dtahmassebi@westminstercollege.edu

TAICHMAN, Russell .... 205-934-4720.... 8 A
taichman@uab.edu

TAILLON, Gretchen .... 603-342-3003 272 E
gtaillon@ccsnh.edu

TAILOR, Bhavna .... 201-327-8877 276 F
btailor@eastwick.edu

TAILOR, Bhavna .... 973-661-0600 276 E
btailor@eastwick.edu

TAIRA, Lora .... 217-234-5253 141 H
ltaira@lakelandcollege.edu

TAIT, Michelle .... 828-898-8785 330 A
taitm@lmc.edu

TAIT, Tamara .... 866-680-2756 458 I
studentlife@midwifery.edu

TAITANO, Carlos .... 671-735-2600 503 E
ctaitano@triton.uog.edu

TAKAC, Jeff .... 478-301-2687 122 C
takac_j@mercer.edu

TAKACS, Audrey .... 586-445-7314 226 F
takacsa@macomb.edu

TAKACS, Sarolta, A .... 718-982-2315 293 C
humanitiessocsci@csi.cuny.edu

TAKAGISHI-ALMEIDA,
Michelle .... 213-738-6886.. 66 A
publicservice@swlaw.edu

TAKAHASHI, Jack .... 800-754-1009 493 B

TAKAHASHI, Lucy .... 909-621-8142.. 57 K
lucy.takahashi@pomona.edu

TAKAHASHI, Sandra ..... 208-535-5372 130 I
sandra.takahashi@cei.edu

TAKAHASHI, Tomoko ..... 949-480-4047.. 64 E
ttakahashi@soka.edu

TAKAHASHI, Victor .... 916-278-6241.. 33 A
vtakahas@csus.edu

TAKAI, Helio .... 718-636-3570 311 A
htakai@pratt.edu

TAKAKI, Leslie .... 503-251-2840 377 A
ltakaki@uws.edu

TAKATA, George .... 559-638-0300.. 67 C
george.takata@reedleycollege.edu

TAKATA, Warren .... 425-235-2352 482 C
wtakata@rtc.edu

TAKAYAMA-PEREZ,
Amy .... 843-953-5339 407 D
takayamaperezal@cofc.edu

TAKAYAMA-PEREZ,
Amy, A .... 843-953-5339 407 D
takayamaperezal@cofc.edu

TAKEDA, Sharon .... 916-278-3922.. 33 A
sharon.takeda@csus.edu

TAKEDA-TINKER, Becky 303-534-6290.. 79 D
becky.takeda-tinker@colostate.edu

TAKES, Faith, A .... 518-786-0855 306 D
faith.takes@mildred-elley.edu

TAKSAR, Stephen .... 413-572-8424 213 C

TALAVERA, Karla .... 661-255-1050.. 28 I
talavera@calarts.edu

TALAVINIA, Phillip .... 419-358-3226 348 E
talaviniap@bluffton.edu

TALBERT, Charles .... 773-907-4864 134 N
ctalbert@ccc.edu

TALBERT, Cynthia .... 850-474-2636 111 E
ctalbert@uwf.edu

TALBERT, Katie .... 828-898-2489 330 A
talbertk@lmc.edu

TALBERT, Kelly .... 208-426-3844 130 F
kellytalbert@boisestate.edu

TALBOT, Bill .... 607-844-8222 321 I
bt021@tompkinscortland.edu

TALBOT, Reuben .... 970-675-3238.. 78 P
reuben.talbot@cncc.edu

TALBOT, Scott .... 214-887-5191 434 G
stalbot@dts.edu

TALBOTT,
Everett Shane .... 615-230-3357 424 F
everett.talbott@volstate.edu

TALBOTT, Jeffrey .... 909-748-8888.. 72 E
jeff_talbott@redlands.edu

TALBOTT, Robert .... 650-543-3714.. 52 A
rtalbott@menlo.edu

TALBOTT, Sherry .... 540-828-5369 464 C
stalbott@bridgewater.edu

TALENTINO, Andrea ...... 585-389-2010 307 D
atalent0@naz.edu

TALESH, Rameen, A ...... 949-824-5181.. 69 C
rtalesh@uci.edu

TALIENTO, Tamela, K .... 931-431-9700 421 G
ttaliento@nci.edu

TALLARIDA, Ronald, J .. 856-256-5413 280 H
tallarida@rowan.edu

TALLERICO, Betty, L ...... 724-458-3790 384 F
bltallerico@gcc.edu

TALLEY, Braque .... 256-372-8164.... 1 A
braque.talley@aamu.edu

TALLEY, Chestley .... 903-730-4890 437 E
ctalley@jarvis.edu

TALLEY, Lauren .... 770-533-7034 121 L
larmour@laniertech.edu

TALLEY, Lee .... 856-256-4775 280 H
talleyl@rowan.edu

TALLEY, Nina .... 937-481-2299 363 H
nina_talley@wilmington.edu

TALLMAN, Jessica .... 718-687-5765 311 A
jtallman@pratt.edu

TALLMAN, Lawrence, J . 304-457-6247 485 F
tallmanlj@ab.edu

TALLO, Angela .... 315-781-3545 301 D
tallo@hws.edu

TALLON, Philip .... 281-649-3403 436 D
ptallon@hbu.edu

TALOSI, Mary .... 928-776-2359.. 17 B
mary.talosi@yc.edu

TALTON, Angela, L .... 626-256-4673.. 37 D
altalton@coh.org

TALWAR, Malvika .... 607-844-8222 321 I
mt056@tompkinscortland.edu

TAM, Sunny .... 508-626-4769 212 D
stam@framingham.edu

TAM, Victor .... 707-527-4246.. 63 C
vtam@santarosa.edu

TAMADA, Mike .... 503-788-6613 375 F
tamadam@reed.edu

TAUBENFELD, Aviva ...... 914-251-6550 318 E aviva.taubenfeld@purchase.edu
TAUBER, Hendy .... 323-937-3763.. 76 G htauber@yoec.edu
TAUBER, Yitzchok, M ... 845-425-9565 305 E
TAUBMAN, Mark, B ... 585-275-0017 323 E mark_taubman@urmc.rochester.edu
TAUILIILI, Shanell .... 684-699-2722 503 A s.tauiliili@amsamoa.edu
TAUPIER, Andrea, S ..... 413-748-3609 218 E ataupier@springfield.edu
TAURIAC, Jesse .... 617-243-2173 210 G jtauriac@lasell.edu
TAUSSI, Lee .... 845-398-4013 314 D altaussi@stac.edu
TAVARE, Kristel .... 715-858-1833 497 E ktavare@cvtc.edu
TAVARES, Kim .... 513-529-5990 356 A kim.tavares@miamioh.edu
TAVARES, Rosemary ..... 201-200-2595 278 F rtavares@njcu.edu
TAVARES, Shirley, A ..... 787-725-8120 505 J investigacion@eap.edu
TAVARES, Stephen .... 860-465-4521.. 85 G tavaresst@easternct.edu
TAVAREZ, Elisabeth, W . 845-575-3000 305 C elisabeth.tavarez@marist.edu
TAVAREZ, Jason .... 805-565-6633.. 75 I jtavarez@westmont.edu
TAVE, Stephen .... 815-967-7329 147 I stave@rockfordcareercollege.edu
TAVELLI, Nancy, J .... 509-527-5297 485 C tavelln@whitman.edu
TAVERA, Deborah, T ..... 610-660-1276 397 A dtavera@sju.edu
TAVERNER, Melissa, P . 870-307-7030.. 20 D president@lyon.edu
TAVERNIER, Sharon ...... 315-386-7616 319 E taverniers@canton.edu
TAWFEEQ, Dante .... 718-982-2729 293 C dante.tawfeeq@csi.cuny.edu
TAWNEY, Amy .... 210-567-2590 455 E tawney@uthscsa.edu
TAWNEY, Andrea .... 915-215-4850 450 E andrea.tawney@ttuhsc.edu
TAXTER, Marianne .... 619-265-0107.. 57 I mtaxter@platt.edu
TAYEH, Raja .... 402-826-6776 266 A raja.tayeh@doane.edu
TAYLOE, John .... 252-398-1232 328 A tayloj@chowan.edu
TAYLOR, Adam .... 864-388-8195 409 B ataylor@lander.edu
TAYLOR, Alison .... 501-450-3377.. 23 K ataylor45@uca.edu
TAYLOR, Allana .... 703-284-1530 468 A allana.taylor@marymount.edu
TAYLOR, Allen .... 304-696-6195 488 N taylor@marshall.edu
TAYLOR, Allison .... 281-646-1109 430 H allison.taylor@thebibleseminary.edu
TAYLOR, Allison, S .... 402-280-3189 265 J allisontaylor@creighton.edu
TAYLOR, Amanda .... 202-885-3827.. 91 D ataylor@american.edu
TAYLOR, Amanda .... 864-379-6606 408 F taylor@erskine.edu
TAYLOR, Amy .... 203-392-6800.. 85 H taylora28@southernct.edu
TAYLOR, Andrea .... 617-358-3045 207 C tayloran@bu.edu
TAYLOR, Andy .... 712-749-2226 164 A taylora@bvu.edu
TAYLOR, Angela .... 757-388-5133 469 H ataylor@sentara.edu
TAYLOR, Ann .... 765-361-6186 162 G taylora@wabash.edu
TAYLOR, Ann .... 314-516-5109 260 E taylorann@umsl.edu
TAYLOR, Anna .... 770-233-5560 125 F anna.taylor@sctech.edu
TAYLOR, AnnMarie .... 561-803-2500 105 B annmarie_taylor@pba.edu
TAYLOR, April .... 912-201-8000 125 D ataylor@southuniversity.edu
TAYLOR, Audra .... 254-442-5117 431 J audra.taylor@cisco.edu
TAYLOR, Baishakhi ...... 413-585-4900 218 D btaylor44@smith.edu
TAYLOR, Beck, A .... 205-726-2727.... 6 E president@samford.edu
TAYLOR, Bill .... 408-741-2642.. 75 D bill.taylor@westvalley.edu
TAYLOR, Blythe .... 252-399-6541 326 H mbtaylor@barton.edu
TAYLOR, Bonnie .... 404-270-5132 126 A bonnie.taylor@spelman.edu
TAYLOR, Bradley, G ...... 336-841-9548 329 E btaylor@highpoint.edu
TAYLOR, Brandy .... 912-871-1616 123 F btaylor@ogeecheetech.edu
TAYLOR, Brett .... 949-854-8002.. 40 E
TAYLOR, Brian .... 660-263-3900 250 G briantaylor@cccb.edu
TAYLOR, Briana .... 903-223-3079 447 C briana.taylor@tamut.edu
TAYLOR, Cameron, P .... 202-441-0058 118 D cameron.taylor@emory.edu
TAYLOR, Carmen .... 308-398-7335 265 C carmentaylor@cccneb.edu
TAYLOR, Cathy .... 618-650-2345 149 H cattayl@siue.edu
TAYLOR, Cathy .... 847-214-7238 137 D ctaylor@elgin.edu
TAYLOR, Cathy .... 615-460-6781 417 B cathy.taylor@belmont.edu
TAYLOR, Cathy, N .... 618-650-5176 149 H cattayl@siue.edu
TAYLOR, Celya .... 870-230-5358.. 19 H taylorc@hsu.edu
TAYLOR, Charles .... 817-735-0268 453 D charles.taylor@unthsc.edu
TAYLOR, Charlie, M ...... 205-348-5205..... 7 F ctaylor@uasystem.edu
TAYLOR, Cherie, O .... 713-646-1856 443 C ctaylor@stcl.edu
TAYLOR, Chris .... 937-775-4240 364 D chris.taylor@wright.edu
TAYLOR, Christie .... 202-806-6100.. 92 E christie.taylor@howard.edu
TAYLOR, Christine, H .... 405-325-3546 370 J christine.taylor@ou.edu
TAYLOR, Christopher .... 843-661-8231 408 G christopher.taylor@fdtc.edu
TAYLOR, Courtney .... 765-641-4020 153 D cktaylor@anderson.edu
TAYLOR, Courtney .... 419-372-2211 348 F
TAYLOR, Craig .... 251-981-3771..... 5 B craig.taylor@columbiasouthern.edu
TAYLOR, Daniel .... 231-591-3707 223 H danieltaylor@ferris.edu
TAYLOR, Daniel .... 360-623-8364 477 H dan.taylor@centralia.edu
TAYLOR, Daniel .... 304-358-2000 486 E dtaylor@future.edu
TAYLOR, Darrell .... 304-896-7432 487 I darrell.taylor@southernwv.edu
TAYLOR, David, A .... 718-289-5598 292 H david.taylor@bcc.cuny.edu
TAYLOR, David, F .... 336-758-5000 344 A taylordf@wfu.edu
TAYLOR, Dean .... 617-420-1820 218 B
TAYLOR, Debbie .... 864-231-2000 405 F dtaylor@andersonuniversity.edu
TAYLOR, Debora, W .... 512-448-8450 441 N deboraw@stedwards.edu
TAYLOR, Des'mon .... 773-508-3300 142 G dtaylor20@luc.edu
TAYLOR, Donald, B .... 313-993-1455 230 H dontaylor@udmercy.edu
TAYLOR, Dub .... 803-376-5723 405 D dtaylor@allenuniversity.edu
TAYLOR, Dustin .... 740-374-8716 363 F dtaylor@wscc.edu
TAYLOR, Ed .... 206-616-7175 484 A edtaylor@uw.edu
TAYLOR, Edward .... 608-663-2333 491 F etaylor@edgewood.edu
TAYLOR, Ellen .... 509-335-3165 484 D ellen.taylor@wsu.edu
TAYLOR, Endalyn .... 336-770-3207 343 C taylore@uncsa.edu
TAYLOR, Faye .... 732-247-5241 278 E ftaylor@nbts.edu
TAYLOR, G. Christine ... 205-348-2053..... 7 G christine.taylor@ua.edu
TAYLOR, JR., G. Don ... 540-231-3270 475 D taylorgd@vt.edu
TAYLOR, Gail .... 231-591-3888 223 H gailtaylor@ferris.edu
TAYLOR, Gene .... 410-532-5324 201 C gtaylor@ndm.edu
TAYLOR, Gene .... 785-532-6912 175 A ksuad@ksu.edu
TAYLOR, Geoffrey .... 912-525-5000 124 G gtaylor@scad.edu
TAYLOR, Gina .... 321-433-7000.. 98 F taylorg@easternflorida.edu
TAYLOR, Ginny .... 513-244-4432 356 F ginny.taylor@msj.edu
TAYLOR, Giselle .... 913-971-3381 175 H
TAYLOR, Goldie .... 404-752-1500 123 A gtaylor@msm.edu
TAYLOR, Greg .... 910-898-9605 336 A taylorg@montgomery.edu
TAYLOR, Greg .... 307-742-3776 500 K gtaylor@wyotech.edu
TAYLOR, Gregory .... 914-251-6485 318 E gregory.taylor@purchase.edu
TAYLOR, Harold, A .... 800-443-9266 502 C harold.taylor@afacademy.af.edu
TAYLOR, Harold, A .... 719-333-8972 502 C harold.taylor@afacademy.af.edu
TAYLOR, Heather .... 616-331-9517 224 D taylorh1@gvsu.edu
TAYLOR, Heather .... 304-829-7408 486 B htaylor@bethanywv.edu
TAYLOR, Helen .... 318-797-5374 189 E helen.taylor@lsus.edu
TAYLOR, Hunter .... 252-398-6505 328 A tayloh1@chowan.edu
TAYLOR, Ivy, R .... 662-252-2491 248 B irtaylor@rustcollege.edu
TAYLOR, J. Kevin .... 805-756-1757.. 29 K jktaylor@calpoly.edu
TAYLOR, J. Kevin .... 805-756-1503.. 29 K jktaylor@calpoly.edu
TAYLOR, Jack, A .... 808-956-3063 129 B jat9@hawaii.edu
TAYLOR, Jacob .... 814-472-3009 396 I jtaylor@francis.edu
TAYLOR, Jaime, R .... 409-880-8405 449 B jtaylor81@lamar.edu
TAYLOR, James .... 410-777-2318 197 C jmtaylor@aacc.edu
TAYLOR, James .... 470-578-6033 121 J jtayl378@kennesaw.edu
TAYLOR, James .... 801-626-6055 460 B jamestaylor8@weber.edu
TAYLOR, James, E .... 202-646-1337.. 93 B
TAYLOR, Jana .... 918-557-5356 365 B taylorj@bacone.edu
TAYLOR, Janet .... 815-921-4324 147 H j.taylor@rockvalleycollege.edu
TAYLOR, Janie .... 817-461-8741 429 C jtaylor@abu.edu
TAYLOR, Jay .... 704-216-7116 337 C jay.taylor@rccc.edu
TAYLOR, Jeannie .... 800-280-0307 153 B jeannie.taylor@ace.edu
TAYLOR, Jeff .... 910-275-6342 335 C jtaylor@jamessprunt.edu
TAYLOR, Jeffrey .... 814-777-7213 383 H taylor030@gannon.edu
TAYLOR, Jennifer .... 931-372-3897 425 B jennifertaylor@tntech.edu
TAYLOR, Jennifer .... 575-674-2281 284 P jetaylor@burrell.edu
TAYLOR, Jessica, L .... 503-255-0332 374 A jltaylor@multnomah.edu
TAYLOR, John .... 541-888-7428 376 B jtaylor@socc.edu
TAYLOR, John .... 714-432-5935.. 38 F jtaylor174@occ.cccd.edu
TAYLOR, John .... 719-587-7382.. 77 F jhtaylor@adams.edu
TAYLOR, Joseph .... 804-342-1484 475 G jdtaylor@vuu.edu
TAYLOR, Joy .... 703-993-5270 466 J jtaylo16@gmu.edu
TAYLOR, Juanyce .... 601-984-1010 248 G jdtaylor@umc.edu
TAYLOR, Judith, M .... 240-567-7337 200 E judith.taylor@montgomerycollege.edu
TAYLOR, Julie .... 360-992-2101 477 J jtaylor@clark.edu
TAYLOR, Julie, Y .... 256-765-4680..... 8 E jayates@una.edu
TAYLOR, Justin .... 785-833-4444 175 C justin.taylor@kwu.edu
TAYLOR, Karina .... 414-297-8425 498 B taylorkl@matc.edu
TAYLOR, Kathryn .... 618-664-6833 138 D kathy.taylor@greenville.edu
TAYLOR, Kathy .... 504-816-4304 186 F ktaylor@dillard.edu
TAYLOR, Kathy .... 918-631-2051 371 C kathy-taylor@utulsa.edu
TAYLOR, Keith .... 814-871-7609 383 H ktaylor@gannon.edu
TAYLOR, Kelley, G .... 334-844-4794..... 4 E taylokg@auburn.edu
TAYLOR, Kelli, W .... 910-630-7157 331 B ktaylor@methodist.edu
TAYLOR, Kenneth .... 870-230-5216.. 19 H taylorke@hsu.edu
TAYLOR, Kent .... 575-624-8235 286 F kent@nmmi.edu
TAYLOR, Kevin .... 718-862-7825 304 K ktaylor02@manhattan.edu
TAYLOR, Kevin .... 303-615-1223.. 81 L ktaylo79@msudenver.edu
TAYLOR, Kevin, L .... 864-242-5100 405 H
TAYLOR, Kim .... 773-702-7749 151 B kimtaylor@uchicago.edu
TAYLOR, Kim .... 513-569-1236 350 C kim.taylor@cincinnatistate.edu
TAYLOR, Kimberly .... 859-323-7311 185 D kta254@uky.edu
TAYLOR, Kimberly .... 518-292-1854 312 D taylok3@sage.edu
TAYLOR, Kirsten .... 217-786-2258 142 F kirsten.taylor@llcc.edu
TAYLOR, Kristy .... 740-389-4636 355 F taylork@mtc.edu
TAYLOR, Kyle .... 217-420-6717 144 D kataylor@millikin.edu
TAYLOR, Kyle .... 405-789-7661 369 H kyle.taylor@swcu.edu
TAYLOR, Ladd .... 601-928-6299 246 F ladd.taylor@mgccc.edu
TAYLOR, Laura .... 706-290-2163 116 A lataylor@berry.edu
TAYLOR, Lauren, M .... 205-726-2956..... 6 E lmtaylor@samford.edu
TAYLOR, Lee .... 334-387-3877..... 4 C leetaylor@amridgeuniversity.edu
TAYLOR, Leslie .... 970-491-1128.. 79 E leslie.taylor@colostate.edu
TAYLOR, Leslie, W .... 501-686-8998.. 22 D taylorlesliew@uams.edu
TAYLOR, Linda .... 610-499-1039 401 I lmtaylor@widener.edu
TAYLOR, Lindsey .... 706-236-2207 116 A ltaylor@berry.edu
TAYLOR, Lois, J .... 740-412-0687 358 A lotaylor@ohiochristian.edu
TAYLOR, Lora .... 910-938-6211 333 D taylorl@coastalcarolina.edu
TAYLOR, Loralyn .... 740-593-1059 358 L taylorl4@ohio.edu
TAYLOR, Lori .... 501-812-2224.. 23 E ltaylor@uaptc.edu
TAYLOR, Lucretia .... 316-978-5177 178 B lucretia.taylor@wichita.edu
TAYLOR, Marcia .... 302-857-7823.. 90 D mtayor@desu.edu
TAYLOR, Marcia .... 918-781-7271 365 B taylorm@bacone.edu
TAYLOR, Marcia, M .... 989-774-3341 221M class@cmich.edu
TAYLOR, Marcie .... 765-641-4495 153 D mjtaylor@anderson.edu
TAYLOR, Margaret .... 315-786-2250 302 I mtaylor@sunyjefferson.edu
TAYLOR, Margaret, W ... 870-575-8733.. 22 F taylorm@uapb.edu
TAYLOR, Maria .... 704-233-8126 344 E m.taylor@wingate.edu
TAYLOR, Marilyn .... 520-621-3876.. 16 H taylorm@arizona.edu
TAYLOR, Mark .... 513-529-9203 356 A mataylor@miamioh.edu
TAYLOR, Martha, M .... 334-844-4438..... 4 E taylomm@auburn.edu
TAYLOR, Mary .... 208-535-5303 130 I mary.taylor@cei.edu
TAYLOR, Mary .... 330-325-6728 357 D mtaylor4@neomed.edu
TAYLOR, Mary .... 828-898-8763 330 A taylorm@lmc.edu
TAYLOR, MaryAnn .... 607-274-3111 302 E mataylor@ithaca.edu
TAYLOR, Matthew, A ..... 410-651-7800 203 B mataylor3@umes.edu
TAYLOR, Melanie .... 562-903-4800.. 27 E melanie.taylor@biola.edu
TAYLOR, Michael .... 617-449-7037 219 B michael.taylor@urbancollege.edu
TAYLOR, Mike .... 330-263-2143 350 H mitaylor@wooster.edu

TEMPLETON, Erin 864-596-9099 407 G
erin.templeton@converse.edu
TEMPLETON, Jenna 412-365-1168 380 F
jtempleton@chatham.edu
TEMPLETON, Joanna 516-877-3909 288 L
jtempleton@adelphi.edu
TEMPLETON, Kelli 509-420-4545 481 D
kelli@gather4him.net
TEMPLETON, Lisa 541-737-0123 374 H
TEMPLETON, Lisa 541-737-2676 374 H
ecampus@oregonstate.edu
TEMPLETON, Mary 334-670-3189 7 C
mtempleton@troy.edu
TEMPLETON, Mary, A 318-675-7652 189 D
mary.templeton@lsuhs.edu
TEMPLIN, Kelly 979-458-6000 445 D
ktemplin@tamus.edu
TEN NAPEL, Karmen 712-274-5191 168 C
tennapel@morningside.edu
TENA, Lydia 915-831-8818 435 B
lpere121@epcc.edu
TENA, Theresa 916-691-7252 50 K
theresa.tena@crc.losrios.edu
TENBUS, Eric 478-445-4441 119 A
eric.tenbus@gcsu.edu
TENCHER, Donald, E 401-456-8007 404 A
dtencher@ric.edu
TENCZAR, Bob 909-537-5007 33 B
robert.tenczar@csusb.edu
TENENBAUM, Elchonon 707-638-5507 68 B
rabbi@tu.edu
TENER, Brent, B 615-343-1422 427 B
b.tener@vanderbilt.edu
TENG, Anthony 949-582-4895 65 C
ateng@saddleback.edu
TENGLIN, Ingrid, K 773-244-5601 145 F
itenglin@northpark.edu
TENGLUND, Ann 716-375-2378 312 F
ateng@sbu.edu
TENHOUSE, Mike 217-641-4558 140 H
mtenhouse@jwcc.edu
TENIENTE, Yvonne 805-922-6966 24 L
yteniente@hancockcollege.edu
TENIENTE-MATSON,
Cynthia 210-784-1600 447 B
cmatson@tamusa.edu
TENNANT, Cassie 989-463-7156 220 F
tennant@alma.edu
TENNANT, Leslie, A 724-480-3552 381 G
leslie.tennant@ccbc.edu
TENNANT, Otto 270-789-5034 179 G
otennant@campbellsville.edu
TENNENT, Timothy, C 859-858-2202 178 G
TENNERELLI, Logan 559-323-2100 61 G
ltennerelli@sjcl.edu
TENNEY, David 713-348-8036 441 K
dtenney@rice.edu
TENNEY, Randall 304-473-8099 490 E
tenney_r@wvwc.edu
TENNIE, Jameia 336-285-4110 341 C
jatennie@ncat.edu
TENNIS, Jeffrey 951-343-4330 27 J
jtennis@calbaptist.edu
TENNISON, Allen 612-343-4762 241 O
datennis@northcentral.edu
TENNY, Elissa 312-899-5100 149 B
president@saic.edu
TENORIO, Jessica 918-495-6553 368 F
jtenorio@oru.edu
TENTES, Theresa 650-738-4331 62 K
tentes@smccd.edu
TENUTA, Bob 815-455-8585 143 F
btenuta@mchenry.edu
TEPPER, Steven, J 480-965-6536 11 A
steven.tepper@asu.edu
TER MOLEN, Matthew 315-443-9161 321 D
termolen@syr.edu
TERCERO, Lorinda 432-552-2673 456 C
tercero_l@utpb.edu
TERDIMAN, David 201-684-7179 280 B
dterdima@ramapo.edu
TEREF, Steven 773-907-4361 134 N
steref@ccc.edu
TEREFFE, Welela 713-794-5599 456 A
TERENZIO, Marion 518-255-5111 318 F
terenzma@cobleskill.edu
TERESA, Daniel 831-755-6840 44 J
dteresa@hartnell.edu
TERESH, Tonia 619-388-7270 61 B
tteresh@sdccd.edu
TERESH, Tonia 530-741-6705 77 D
tteresh@yccd.edu
TERESH, Tonia 530-741-6700 77 B

TERHAAR, Jody, L 320-363-5601 234 I
jterhaar@csbsju.edu
TERHARK, Troy 715-836-2637 494 E
TERHUNE, James 610-328-8365 398 B
jterhun1@swarthmore.edu
TERHUNE, Jason 262-646-6518 493 F
jterhune@nashotah.edu
TERHUNE, Jason 626-646-6518 493 F
jterhune@nashotah.edu
TERKLA, Dawn, G 617-627-2177 219 A
dawn.terkla@tufts.edu
TERMOTT, Kenneth 732-247-5241 278 E
ktermott@nbts.edu
TERMUHLEN, Paula 269-337-4400 233 A
TERO, Kevin 405-974-2410 370 H
ktero@uco.edu
TERP, Douglas, C 207-859-4774 194 B
douglas.terp@colby.edu
TERPIS, Katherine 575-646-3279 286 G
kterpis@nmsu.edu
TERPSTRA, Joylita, W 423-478-7731 421 J
jterpstra@ptseminary.edu
TERPSTRA, Phil 620-276-9554 173 H
philip.terpstra@gcccks.edu
TERRANCE, Teah 585-385-8198 313 A
tterrance@sjfc.edu
TERRANOVA, Joanne 504-280-6155 189 F
jterrano@uno.edu
TERRAZAS, Denise 951-372-7016 59 C
denise.terrazas@norcocollege.edu
TERRAZAS, Lissete 575-492-2122 288 I
lterrazas@usw.edu
TERRAZAS, Susan 909-706-2476 75 G
sterrazas@westernu.edu
TERRELL, Beth, M 260-399-7700 162 A
bterrell@sf.edu
TERRELL, David, R 765-285-2201 153 E
drterrell@bsu.edu
TERRELL, Jonathan 985-448-7079 192 C
jonathan.terrell@nicholls.edu
TERRELL, Mark 814-866-6641 387 C
mterrell@lecom.edu
TERRELL, Mark, A 252-399-6528 326 H
materrell@barton.edu
TERRELL, Rita 512-492-3032 429 B
rterrell@aoma.edu
TERRELL-JORDAN, Ola 229-500-2000 114 F
TERRELL LEACH,
Monica 910-672-1111 341 B
TERRELL-POWELL,
Yvonne 425-640-1456 479 A
yvonneterrellpowell@edcc.edu
TERRILL, Brian 410-209-2270 197 E
bterrill@bccc.edu
TERRIO, Dan, M 509-527-4981 485 C
terrio@whitman.edu
TERRIO, Paul 612-238-4552 242 H
pterrio@smumn.edu
TERRONEZ, Danny 979-532-6465 457 H
terronezd@wcjc.edu
TERRY, Carolyn 240-567-4366 200 E
carolyn.terry@montgomerycollege.edu
TERRY, Catherine 615-966-1964 420 B
catherine.terry@lipscomb.edu
TERRY, Chihoko 910-410-1821 336 G
ckterry@richmondcc.edu
TERRY, Christopher 607-735-1938 298 G
cterry@elmira.edu
TERRY, Colin 303-273-3000 79 A
cterry@mines.edu
TERRY, Cynthia 205-934-8152 8 A
cterry@uab.edu
TERRY, Daniel Scott 304-637-1273 486 D
terrys@dewv.edu
TERRY, Denise, A 574-372-5100 155 C
terryda@grace.edu
TERRY, Edward 828-726-2202 332 E
eterry@cccti.edu
TERRY, Emily 252-398-6204 328 A
evterry@chowan.edu
TERRY, Gina 864-250-8157 408 J
gina.terry@gvltec.edu
TERRY, James 573-876-2363 259 F
jterry@stephens.edu
TERRY, James, E 304-696-2486 488 N
terry@marshall.edu
TERRY, Kim 405-682-1611 367 D
TERRY, Laura, C 423-439-4210 418 D
terryl@etsu.edu
TERRY, Linda 512-223-7503 429 J
lkluck@austincc.edu

TERRY, SR.,
Matthew, L 972-524-3341 444 E
terry.matthew@swcc.edu
TERRY, Melissa, D 503-554-2101 372 I
terrym@georgefox.edu
TERRY, Neil, W 806-651-2042 447 D
nterry@wtamu.edu
TERRY, Phil 317-788-3211 161 F
terryp@uindy.edu
TERRY, Sabrina 910-362-7040 332 F
sjterry@mail.cfcc.edu
TERRY, Sandra 678-331-4368 122 A
sandra.terry@life.edu
TERRY, Scott 304-357-4363 486 J
scottterry@ucwv.edu
TERRY, Toni 205-652-3528 9 B
tterry@uwa.edu
TERRY-JACKSON,
Tonishea 773-602-5000 135 A
TERRY-SHARP,
Kathleen 901-321-4299 417 G
katerry@cbu.edu
TERRYN, Dottie 850-872-3801 101 O
dterryn@gulfcoast.edu
TERWILLIGER, Brandi 208-885-3008 132 C
brandit@uidaho.edu
TESAR, Kathleen 212-799-5000 303 B
TESKE, April 618-634-3200 149 C
aprilt@shawneecc.edu
TESKE, Paul 303-315-2805 84 B
paul.teske@ucdenver.edu
TESKE, Yolanda, K 252-334-2029 331 C
yolanda.teske@macuniversity.edu
TESLUK, Paul 781-891-2399 206 C
ptesluk@bentley.edu
TESORIERO, Cristine 516-876-3033 318 A
tesorieroc@oldwestbury.edu
TESSIER, Dorita 509-527-2646 484 C
dorita.tessier@wallawalla.edu
TESSIER, Michael, A 812-488-2956 161 E
mt28@evansville.edu
TESSIER-LAVIGNE,
Marc 650-723-2481 66 D
president@stanford.edu
TESSLER, Chani 773-973-0241 138 G
tessler@htc.edu
TESSLER, Faith 213-884-4133 24 D
ftessler@ajrca.edu
TESSLER, Lisa 845-437-5439 323 H
litessler@vassar.edu
TESSMAN, Brock 406-449-9129 263 C
btessman@montana.edu
TESTA, Ashley 412-536-1194 386 H
ashley.testa@laroch.edu
TESTA, Michael 610-892-1548 393 B
mtesta@pit.edu
TESTA, Taylor 518-681-5604 319 D
testat@sunyacc.edu
TESTANI, Joe 585-275-2366 323 E
j.testani@rochester.edu
TESTI, Andrea 541-881-5761 376 E
atesti@tvcc.cc
TESTORI, Peter 413-565-1000 205 I
ptestori@baypath.edu
TETEN, Ryan, L 308-865-8995 268 J
tetenrl@unk.edu
TETER, Ayana 412-924-1398 395 G
ateter@pts.edu
TETI, Polly 215-242-7777 380 G
tetip@chc.edu
TETLOW, Tania 718-817-3000 300 A
president@fordham.edu
TETREAULT, Jules 203-392-5556 85 H
tetreaultj4@southernct.edu
TETREAULT, Patricia, L 570-941-7767 400 C
patricia.tetreault@scranton.edu
TETTEH, Edem 856-222-9311 280 E
etetteh@rcbc.edu
TETZLAFF, Christian 770-533-6966 121 L
ctetzlaff@laniertech.edu
TEUFEL, Kyla 951-222-8649 59 D
kyla.oconnor@rcc.edu
TEVAGA, Laura 808-675-3669 128 B
laura.tevaga@byuh.edu
TEVES, Erin 859-846-5494 183 G
eteves@midway.edu
TEVES, Frances 909-869-3503 30 B
fteves@cpp.edu
TEW, Keith 252-399-6361 326 H
ktew@barton.edu
TEW, Michael 734-487-3200 223 F
mtew@emich.edu
TEWART, Terri 505-428-1836 287 H
terri.tewart@sfcc.edu

TEWELL, Jodie 620-276-9533 173 H
jodie.tewell@gcccks.edu
TEWES, Matt 402-465-2102 267 J
mtewes@nebrwesleyan.edu
TEXIDOR, Migdalia 787-250-1912 507 C
mtexidor@metro.inter.edu
TEXTER, Lynne 215-951-1147 386 I
TEYMOURTASH,
Janet, L 415-422-5898 72 I
janet@usfca.edu
TEZENO, Albert 972-599-3151 432 I
atezeno@collin.edu
THACHENKARY,
Sebastian 414-277-7141 493 D
thachenkary@msoe.edu
THACKER, Allison 713-348-4818 441 K
invest@rice.edu
THACKER, Linda 314-529-9308 254 D
lthacker@maryville.edu
THACKER, Samantha 517-264-7172 230 C
sthacker@sienaheights.edu
THACKER, Scott 386-822-8808 111 F
sthacker@stetson.edu
THACKER, Tiffany 606-218-5953 185 F
tiffanythacker@upike.edu
THACKERAY, Rosemary 801-422-4919 458 A
rosemary_thackeray@byu.edu
THADEN, Mark 540-654-2160 471 B
mthad2zw@umw.edu
THAKOR, Anjan 314-935-6344 261 B
thakor@wustl.edu
THAKURIAH,
Piyushimita 848-932-2714 281 B
mhanniga@ejb.rutgers.edu
THALACKER, Karen 319-352-8225 170 F
karen.thalacker@wartburg.edu
THAMES, Brenda, A 310-660-3111 41 J
rmahowald@elcamino.edu
THAMES, James, H 214-887-5013 434 G
jthames@dts.edu
THAMES, Judith 317-813-2301 157 G
jthames@ibcindianapolis.edu
THANGAM, Siva 201-216-5558 282 L
sthangam@stevens.edu
THANKI, Sandip 702-992-2618 270 H
sandip.thanki@nsc.edu
THANNICKAL, Steve 918-495-7371 368 F
sthannickal@oru.edu
THAO-SCHUCK, May 651-690-6511 242 F
mthaoschuck644@stkate.edu
THARAKUNNEL, Kurian 708-456-0300 151 A
kuriantharakunnel@triton.edu
THARCHIN, Jinpa 925-473-7342 40 I
jtharchin@losmedanos.edu
THARP, Brent 912-478-5444 120 A
btharp@georgiasouthern.edu
THARP, Glen 602-242-6265 11 E
glen.tharp@brooklinecollege.edu
THARP, Holly 309-457-2426 144 E
htharp@monmouthcollege.edu
THARP, Karen 931-598-1270 422 F
kmtharp@sewanee.edu
THARP, Katie 630-844-5449 133 A
ktharp@aurora.edu
THARPE, Barbara 615-327-6827 420 D
btharpe@mmc.edu
THARPE, Brad 909-621-8519 57 E
brad_tharpe@pitzer.edu
THARRINGTON, Sally 434-949-1061 474 D
sally.tharrington@southside.edu
THARRINGTON,
Sterling 910-892-3178 329 D
stharrington@heritagebiblecollege.edu
THATCHER, Derek 740-366-9453 349 D
thatcher.42@cotc.edu
THATCHER, Kathleen 406-657-2204 263 H
kathleen.thatcher@msubillings.edu
THATCHER, Rene 315-323-1550 313 F
rene@stlawu.edu
THAXTON, Deron 318-473-6409 189 A
dthaxton@lsua.edu
THAYER, Jainen 641-269-9800 166 D
thayerja@grinnell.edu
THAYER, Laura 509-359-6901 478 H
lthayer3@ewu.edu
THAYER, Scott, W 909-384-4470 60 F
sthayer@sbccd.cc.ca.us
THAYER, Tammy 608-246-6451 497 I
tthayer2@madisoncollege.edu
THE, Cheryl 817-202-6323 444 B
cthe@swau.edu
THE, James 817-202-6719 444 B
jthe@swau.edu

THOMAS, Kevin .... 360-992-2936 477 J
kthomas@clark.edu
THOMAS, Kevin, P .... 501-852-0272.. 23 K
kpthomas@uca.edu
THOMAS, Kimberly .... 219-989-2853 160 A
thoma744@pnw.edu
THOMAS, Kirby .... 863-680-4113 100 F
kthomas@flsouthern.edu
THOMAS, LaQuitta .... 214-567-5901 190 J
laquitta_thomas@sualumni.org
THOMAS, Lenier .... 212-870-1253 309 C
lthomas@nyts.edu
THOMAS, Leslie .... 503-768-7689 373 D
lthomas@lclark.edu
THOMAS, Linda .... 540-568-4213 467 C
thoma7lm@jmu.edu
THOMAS, Lisa .... 231-995-1043 228 F
lthomas@nmc.edu
THOMAS, London .... 864-388-8310 409 B
lthomas@lander.edu
THOMAS, Lori .... 732-987-2275 277 B
lthomas@georgian.edu
THOMAS, Marcia .... 501-623-2272.. 19 C
THOMAS, Marcia, R .... 312-460-0600 132 F
mthomas@aaart.edu
THOMAS, Marcus .... 501-279-4332.. 19 G
mathomas@harding.edu
THOMAS, Margo .... 386-822-7480 111 F
mthomas20@stetson.edu
THOMAS, Maria .... 515-650-3198 163 C
mariathomas@theartofeducation.edu
THOMAS, Mariah .... 860-512-3214.. 86 F
THOMAS, Mariette .... 504-864-7550 190 A
mlthoma1@loyno.edu
THOMAS, Mark .... 618-664-7041 138 D
mark.thomas@greenville.edu
THOMAS, Mark .... 863-638-7228 113 D
mark.thomas@warner.edu
THOMAS, Mark .... 863-638-2345 113 D
mark.thomas@warner.edu
THOMAS, Mark .... 608-246-6301 497 I
mthomasjr@madisoncollege.edu
THOMAS, Mary Beth ..... 617-735-9766 209 A
thomasmb@emmanuel.edu
THOMAS, Maxcie .... 870-575-7029.. 22 F
thomasm@uapb.edu
THOMAS, Melissa .... 503-554-2218 372 I
mthomas@georgefox.edu
THOMAS, Meshia .... 804-257-5851 475 G
clthomas@vuu.edu
THOMAS, Michael .... 410-986-3220 197 E
mdthomas@bccc.edu
THOMAS, Michael .... 310-506-4181.. 56 H
michael.j.thomas@pepperdine.edu
THOMAS, Michael, A ...... 949-214-3201.. 40 E
michael.thomas@cui.edu
THOMAS, Michael, D ...... 802-443-5551 461 G
thomas@middlebury.edu
THOMAS, Mike, R .... 618-235-2700 150 B
michael.thomas@swic.edu
THOMAS, Natalie .... 703-329-9100.. 93 H
THOMAS, Nathan .... 309-677-3140 133 H
nthomas@fsmail.bradley.edu
THOMAS, Nichole .... 315-268-3854 295 E
nthomas@clarkson.edu
THOMAS, Nishanth .... 973-803-5000 279 C
nthomas@pillar.edu
THOMAS, Oliver .... 336-285-2436 341 C
omthomas@ncat.edu
THOMAS, Patricia .... 334-229-4406.... 4 B
pthomas@alasu.edu
THOMAS, Patricia .... 412-323-4000 378 H
pthomas@manchesterbidwell.org
THOMAS, Patricia, A ..... 202-274-7257.. 94 B
pthomas@udc.edu
THOMAS, Paul .... 337-482-2976 192 F
paul.thomas@louisiana.edu
THOMAS, R. Brent .... 620-341-5278 173 C
rthomas2@emporia.edu
THOMAS, Rachel .... 504-520-5732 193 C
rthomas18@xula.edu
THOMAS,
Randi Malcolm .... 513-529-4151 356 A
thomasrm@miamioh.edu
THOMAS, Ray .... 616-988-3677 226 A
rthomas@kuyper.edu
THOMAS, Rebecca .... 859-233-8121 185 A
rthomas@transy.edu
THOMAS, Renard .... 661-362-3469.. 38 H
renard.thomas@canyons.edu
THOMAS, Renee .... 276-223-4752 475 B
rthomas@wcc.vccs.edu
THOMAS, Richard .... 304-293-7173 489 E
richard.thomas@mail.wvu.edu
THOMAS, Rick .... 414-277-7300 493 D
THOMAS, Rikki .... 757-727-5250 466 L
rikki.thomas@hamptonu.edu
THOMAS, Robbin .... 225-771-2552 191 C
rthomas@sulc.edu
THOMAS, Rosalyn .... 417-873-6827 252 A
rthomas005@drury.edu
THOMAS, Rosemary, M 304-637-1337 486 D
thomasr@dewv.edu
THOMAS, Roy .... 410-951-4231 203 E
rothomas@coppin.edu
THOMAS, Ryan .... 760-480-8474.. 75 H
rthomas@wscal.edu
THOMAS, Ryan .... 518-743-2200 319 D
thomasr@sunyacc.edu
THOMAS, S. Marjorie ... 941-487-4504 110 C
smthomas@ncf.edu
THOMAS, Sam .... 901-251-7100.. 93 H
THOMAS, Samantha .... 214-768-3603 443 G
thomassa@smu.edu
THOMAS, Sandi .... 760-252-2411.. 26 L
sthomas@barstow.edu
THOMAS, Sandra .... 580-745-3172 369 F
sthomas@se.edu
THOMAS, Sapada .... 662-252-8093 248 B
sthomas@rustcollege.edu
THOMAS, Shannon .... 952-995-1626 237 G
shannon.thomas@hennepintech.edu
THOMAS, Shawn .... 806-291-3750 457 B
shawn.thomas@wbu.edu
THOMAS, Shiloa .... 610-526-1000 378 D
shiloa.thomas@theamericancollege.edu
THOMAS, Shirman .... 615-898-2516 421 C
shirman.thomas@mtsu.edu
THOMAS, Stacey .... 765-455-9391 156 E
stathoma@iuk.edu
THOMAS, Stacy .... 276-739-2429 474 H
sthomas@vhcc.edu
THOMAS, Steve .... 432-685-4520 439 E
steve@midland.edu
THOMAS, Steven .... 360-417-6235 481 F
sthomas@pencol.edu
THOMAS, Susan, L .... 660-785-4100 259 J
suethomas@truman.edu
THOMAS, Suzanne .... 843-792-1533 409 D
thomass@musc.edu
THOMAS, Tamara .... 909-558-4481.. 48 J
tthomas@llu.edu
THOMAS, Teresa .... 903-875-7315 439 G
teresa.thomas@navarrocollege.edu
THOMAS, Teresa, W ...... 615-898-2603 421 C
teresa.thomas@mtsu.edu
THOMAS, Teri .... 479-979-1448.. 24 A
tthomas@ozarks.edu
THOMAS, Terri .... 607-436-2020 316 C
terri.thomas@oneonta.edu
THOMAS, Terry .... 816-501-4250 257 K
terry.thomas@rockhurst.edu
THOMAS, Timothy .... 315-792-5611 306 G
tthomas@mvcc.edu
THOMAS, Todd .... 423-652-6045 419 F
tthomas@king.edu
THOMAS, Tommy .... 423-869-6216 420 A
tommy.thomas@lmunet.edu
THOMAS, Tony .... 718-951-3118 293 A
tony.thomas@brooklyn.cuny.edu
THOMAS, Toyarna, Y ..... 804-342-3565 475 G
tythomas@vuu.edu
THOMAS, Tracy .... 217-732-3168 142 D
THOMAS, Tyrone .... 843-355-4152 413 C
thomast@wiltech.edu
THOMAS, Vadim .... 518-276-8531 311 J
thomav@rpi.edu
THOMAS, Valerie .... 410-455-3142 202 G
valerie.thomas@umbc.edu
THOMAS, Vanessa .... 909-384-8904.. 60 F
vthomas@sbccd.cc.ca.us
THOMAS, Vanessa .... 701-766-4415 344 F
THOMAS, Victoria .... 812-288-8878 159 C
vthomas@mid-america.edu
THOMAS, Victoria Lee .. 860-723-0011.. 85 E
thomasv@ct.edu
THOMAS, Von .... 402-643-3651 265 I
von.thomas@cune.edu
THOMAS, Wanda, S .... 318-675-5190 189 D
wanda.thomas@lsuhs.edu
THOMAS, Wayne .... 423-636-7300 425 E
wthomas@tusculum.edu
THOMAS, Wendy .... 410-777-1309 197 C
wcthomas2@aacc.edu
THOMAS, Wilbert, L ...... 757-727-5356 466 L
bill.thomas@hamptonu.edu
THOMAS, Willie .... 423-472-7141 423 C
wthomas01@clevelandstatecc.edu
THOMAS-ANDERSON,
Tricia .... 972-860-7396 433 I
triciathomas-anderson@dcccd.edu
THOMAS-STARCK,
Jennifer .... 781-283-3532 219 C
jthomass@wellesley.edu
THOMAS-WILLIAMS,
Regina .... 912-443-5708 124 I
rthomas@savannahtech.edu
THOMAS-WOOD,
Roberta .... 864-578-8770 410 G
rthomas@sherman.edu
THOMASEE, David .... 850-873-3582 101 O
dthomasee@gulfcoast.edu
THOMASON, Anne .... 309-341-7491 141 E
athomason@knox.edu
THOMASON, Brian .... 714-744-7099.. 36 D
bthomason@chapman.edu
THOMASON, Chris .... 205-652-3898.... 9 B
cthomason@uwa.edu
THOMASON,
Christopher .... 501-686-2940.. 21 G
cthomason@uasys.edu
THOMASON, Daniel .... 405-491-6339 369 G
danny.thomason@snu.edu
THOMASON, Justin .... 989-837-4151 228 G
thomaso@northwood.edu
THOMASON, Mary .... 817-554-5950 439 C
mthomason@messengercollege.edu
THOMASON, Troy .... 407-628-6317 106 L
tthomason@rollins.edu
THOMBS, Dennis .... 817-735-5439 453 D
dennis.thombs@unthsc.edu
THOME, Jennifer .... 419-267-1223 357 E
jthome@northweststate.edu
THOMEN, Karlee .... 217-709-0920 142 A
kthomen@lakeviewcol.edu
THOMES, Chris .... 386-506-4499.. 98 A
chris.thomes@daytonastate.edu
THOMPSON, A. Renee .. 609-835-6000.. 93 H
THOMPSON, Adam .... 510-780-4500.. 48 D
athompson@lifewest.edu
THOMPSON, Adelia, P .. 757-594-7002 465 A
adelia.thompson@cnu.edu
THOMPSON, Al .... 715-346-2481 496 B
al.thompson@uwsp.edu
THOMPSON, Alanna ...... 256-306-2601.... 1 F
alanna.thompson@calhoun.edu
THOMPSON, Albert .... 757-822-1715 474 G
bthompson@tcc.edu
THOMPSON, Alex .... 507-457-5584 241 A
alexandra.thompson@winona.edu
THOMPSON, Alfreda ..... 601-635-2111 245 B
athompson@eccc.edu
THOMPSON, Allen .... 360-867-6851 479 C
allen.thompson@evergreen.edu
THOMPSON, Allison, L . 318-342-6917 193 A
althompson@ulm.edu
THOMPSON, Amanda .... 937-393-3431 360 G
athompson@sscc.edu
THOMPSON, Amber .... 254-710-3828 430 F
amber_thompson@baylor.edu
THOMPSON, Ameer .... 650-306-3322.. 62 I
thompsona@smccd.edu
THOMPSON, Amy .... 937-775-3035 364 D
amy.thompson@wright.edu
THOMPSON, Amy .... 718-940-5713 313 C
althompson@sjcny.edu
THOMPSON, Angela ...... 817-257-5028 447 H
angela.thompson@tcu.edu
THOMPSON, Ann, M ...... 717-361-1395 383 B
thompsonann@etown.edu
THOMPSON, Annette ..... 210-283-5091 452 D
athompson@uiwtx.edu
THOMPSON, April .... 814-332-4356 378 A
THOMPSON, April .... 607-753-2011 317 D
april.thompson@cortland.edu
THOMPSON, Ash .... 706-542-2273 126 F
contact@uhs.uga.edu
THOMPSON, B. J .... 919-718-7375 333 A
bthompson@cccc.edu
THOMPSON, Bart .... 225-578-3231 188 K
bthompson@lsu.edu
THOMPSON, Blake .... 601-925-3200 246 D
bthompson@mc.edu
THOMPSON, Bobbie ...... 706-379-3111 128 A
rthompson@yhc.edu
THOMPSON, Bradley ..... 901-751-8453 420 G
bthompson@mabts.edu
THOMPSON, Brenda ...... 512-863-1956 444 F
thompso2@southwestern.edu
THOMPSON, Brian, L ..... 904-819-6249.. 99 D
bthompson@flagler.edu
THOMPSON, Carey .... 717-337-6582 384 C
carthomp@gettysburg.edu
THOMPSON, Carleen .... 520-206-4637.. 15 E
cthompson57@pima.edu
THOMPSON, Casey .... 229-333-2210 127 F
THOMPSON, Cesarina ... 860-768-4648.. 89 E
cthompson@hartford.edu
THOMPSON, Chad .... 650-738-7035.. 62 K
thompsonc@smccd.edu
THOMPSON, Cheryl .... 505-387-7432 286 B
cthompson@navajotech.edu
THOMPSON, Chet .... 724-480-3558 381 G
chet.thompson@ccbc.edu
THOMPSON, Chris .... 919-761-2100 340 B
cthompson@sebts.edu
THOMPSON, Chris .... 803-705-4730 405 G
chris.thompson@benedict.edu
THOMPSON,
Christopher, J .... 651-962-5966 243 F
cjthompson@stthomas.edu
THOMPSON, Chuck .... 909-621-8026.. 37 E
chuck.thompson@claremont.edu
THOMPSON, Cindy .... 816-235-1511 260 D
thompsoncym@umkc.edu
THOMPSON, Clare .... 563-884-5611 169 C
clare.thompson@palmer.edu
THOMPSON, Cora .... 912-358-4145 124 H
thompsonc@savannahstate.edu
THOMPSON,
Corinne, B .... 802-656-7898 462 D
corinne.thompson@uvm.edu
THOMPSON, Cory .... 703-323-4220 473 G
cthompson@nvcc.edu
THOMPSON, Cory .... 404-297-9522 119 G
THOMPSON, Courtney .. 931-372-3500 425 B
cothompson@tntech.edu
THOMPSON, Craig .... 208-282-2120 131 E
thomcra2@isu.edu
THOMPSON, Craig, B ... 646-888-6639 304 H
thompsonc@mskcc.org
THOMPSON, Cynthia .... 217-206-4762 151 E
thompson.cynthia@uis.edu
THOMPSON, Danielle ... 904-632-3356 101 A
danielle.thompson@fscj.edu
THOMPSON, Darryl, D .. 502-597-6149 183 A
darryl.thompson1@kysu.edu
THOMPSON, Dave .... 714-546-7600.. 38 D
THOMPSON, David .... 256-782-5455.... 6 A
dthompson@jsu.edu
THOMPSON, David .... 214-860-2342 434 A
davidthompson@dcccd.edu
THOMPSON, Dawn, G ... 503-777-7502 375 F
dthomp@reed.edu
THOMPSON, Deborah ... 252-794-4861 335 F
deborah.thompson@martincc.edu
THOMPSON,
Deborah, L .... 904-819-6302.. 99 D
dthompson@flagler.edu
THOMPSON,
Deborah, L .... 269-337-7318 225 B
debbie.roberts@kzoo.edu
THOMPSON, Deidre ...... 408-727-1060.. 46 A
THOMPSON, Desiree ..... 207-454-1021 195 E
dthompson@wccc.me.edu
THOMPSON, Dewayne .. 423-614-8160 419 H
dthompson@leeuniversity.edu
THOMPSON, Dixie .... 865-974-2475 426 C
dixielee@utk.edu
THOMPSON, Doug .... 507-933-7538 235 E
thompson@gustavus.edu
THOMPSON, Dreama ..... 740-283-6264 352 I
dthompson@franciscan.edu
THOMPSON, Edward, J . 516-323-4600 306 I
ethompson@molloy.edu
THOMPSON, Elizabeth .. 423-869-6844 420 A
elizabeth.thompson@lmunet.edu
THOMPSON, Elizabeth .. 352-245-4119 112 D
elizabeth.thompson@taylorcollege.edu
THOMPSON,
Elizabeth, B .... 832-813-6507 438 E
elizabeth.b.thompson@lonestar.edu
THOMPSON, Erik .... 410-337-6000 198 G
erik.thompson@goucher.edu
THOMPSON, Gabrielle ... 315-786-6560 302 I
gthompson@sunyjefferson.edu
THOMPSON, Garrett ...... 480-222-9219.. 16 B
g.thompson@scnm.edu
THOMPSON, Gerene, M 727-816-3264 105 E
thompsg@phsc.edu

THORNTON, Laura .... 770-537-5720 127 E
laura.thornton@westgatech.edu
THORNTON, Linda .... 507-222-4171 234 C
lthornto@carleton.edu
THORNTON, Marie .... 808-237-5140 128 D
mthornton@hmi.edu
THORNTON, Matha .... 585-385-8229 313 A
mthornton@sjfc.edu
THORNTON, Philip .... 317-788-3360 161 F
pthornton@uindy.edu
THORNWALL-ROGERS,
Stacy .... 717-299-7723 398 E
thornwallrogers@stevenscollege.edu
THORP, Karen, L .... 434-381-6136 470 H
kthorp@sbc.edu
THORP, Michael .... 717-815-2240 402 G
mthorp@ycp.edu
THORPE, Abigail .... 718-933-6700 306 J
athorpe@monroecollege.edu
THORPE, Alayne .... 269-471-3405 220 H
alayne@andrews.edu
THORPE, Alayne .... 269-471-6581 220 H
alayne@andrews.edu
THORPE, Christine .... 908-737-5902 277 F
chthorpe@kean.edu
THORPE, Denise .... 412-924-1421 395 G
dthorpe@pts.edu
THORPE, Derrick .... 336-744-0900 327 D
derrick.thorpe@carolina.edu
THORPE, Graham .... 215-702-4307 379 F
gthorpe@cairn.edu
THORPE, Hillory .... 212-924-5900 321 C
hthorpe@swedishinstitute.edu
THORPE, Jennifer .... 573-875-7668 251 A
jcthorpe1@ccis.edu
THORPE, LaKeisha .... 215-242-7751 380 G
thorpel@chc.edu
THORPE, Matthew .... 864-644-5141 411 D
mthorpe@swu.edu
THORPE, Paul .... 610-341-5865 383 A
pwthorpe@eastern.edu
THORPE, Stephen, W ..... 610-499-4117 401 I
swthorpe@mail.widener.edu
THORPE, Terry .... 229-928-1360 120 B
terry.thorpe@gsw.edu
THORSEN, Michelle .... 425-640-1428 479 A
mthorsen@edcc.edu
THORSETT, Stephen .... 503-370-6209 377 E
president@willamette.edu
THORSON, Carola .... 218-755-2040 237 B
carola.thorson@bemidjistate.edu
THORSON, Carola .... 937-327-6360 364 C
thorsonc@wittenberg.edu
THORSON, Kip .... 507-372-3460 239 B
kip.thorson@mnwest.edu
THORSON, Phil .... 320-308-5396 240 C
pthorson@stcloudstate.edu
THORSTAD, Todd, M ..... 320-222-5572 239 H
todd.thorstad@ridgewater.edu
THORTON, Ree'shemah 510-531-4911.. 57 C
rthorton@peralta.edu
THORTON, Toni .... 703-878-2800.. 93 H
THOTA, Vykuntapathi ..... 804-524-5024 475 E
vthota@vsu.edu
THOURSON, Peter .... 541-485-1780 374 C
peterthourson@newhope.edu
THRAILKILL, James .... 619-260-4558.. 72 H
jthrailkill@sandiego.edu
THRAILKILL, Krystal ...... 479-394-7622.. 23 F
kthrailkill@uarichmountain.edu
THRANE, Linda .... 713-348-6281 441 K
thrane@rice.edu
THRASH, Carrie .... 740-374-8716 363 F
cthrash@wscc.edu
THRASH, Rhone .... 304-829-7299 486 B
rthrash@bethanywv.edu
THRASHER, Lee .... 251-405-7072.... 1 E
lthrasher@bishop.edu
THRASHER, Melissa .... 734-487-4400 223 F
mthrashe@emich.edu
THREATT, Norda .... 256-761-6119.... 7 B
nthreatt@talladega.edu
THREET, Ali .... 435-652-7514 459 G
ali.threet@utahtech.edu
THREET, Dwight .... 910-695-3831 337 E
threetd@sandhills.edu
THRELKELD, Aubry .... 978-232-2408 209 B
athrelke@endicott.edu
THRIFT, Jack .... 858-653-3000.. 29 F
THRO, Donna .... 314-256-8886 249 F
thro@ai.edu
THRO, William, E .... 859-257-2936 185 D
william.thro@uky.edu

THROCKMORTON,
Hunter .... 903-510-2586 451 D
jthr@tjc.edu
THROCKMORTON, Julie 412-809-5161 395 F
throckmorton.julie@ptcollege.edu
THRONSON, Jodean ...... 651-779-5837 237 D
jodean.thronson@century.edu
THROOP, Victoria .... 337-550-1410 189 B
vthroop@lsue.edu
THROWER, Jabe .... 870-850-4821.. 21 D
jthrower@seark.edu
THRUMAN, Michelle ...... 815-588-3575 138 H
michelle.thruman@highland.edu
THRUSH, Anne, R .... 989-774-3166 221 M
pybus1a@cmich.edu
THUER, Rachel .... 856-225-6005 281 A
rmt84@camden.rutgers.edu
THUESON, Mike, B .... 208-496-2316 130 G
thuesonm@byui.edu
THULIN, Andrew .... 805-756-2161.. 29 K
athulin@calpoly.edu
THUM, Dennis, L .... 605-331-6777 416 C
dennis.thum@usiouxfalls.edu
THUM, Scott, W .... 260-422-5561 156 A
swthum@indianatech.edu
THUMM MOORE, Kelly . 303-722-5724.. 81 K
kmoore@lincolntech.edu
THUNDER HAWK, Jodi . 701-854-8058 346 F
jodi.thunderhawk@sittingbull.edu
THUNELL, Meagan .... 801-626-7496 460 B
meaganthunell@weber.edu
THUOT, Christopher ...... 315-498-2920 310 C
THURBER, Darla .... 501-760-4113.. 20 E
darla.thurber@np.edu
THURINGER, Chris .... 859-257-2000 185 D
chris.thuringer@uky.edu
THURLOW, David .... 802-831-1064 462 F
dthurlow@vermontlaw.edu
THURMAN, Connie .... 319-398-5466 167 H
connie.thurman@kirkwood.edu
THURMAN, Connie .... 309-344-2518 134 A
THURMAN, David .... 206-254-1904 217 D
THURMAN, Erik, J .... 651-962-6691 243 F
erik.thurman@stthomas.edu
THURMAN, Jacquelyn ..... 315-755-0411 302 I
jthurman@sunyjefferson.edu
THURMAN, Jill .... 765-998-5123 161 A
jill_thurman@taylor.edu
THURMAN, Kathy .... 615-898-5792 421 C
kathy.thurman@mtsu.edu
THURMAN, Katie .... 731-989-6672 418 H
knixon@fhu.edu
THURMAN, Kerri, L .... 217-443-8850 136 E
k.thurman@dacc.edu
THURMAN, Kevin .... 573-431-4593 255 G
kthurman@mineralarea.edu
THURMAN, JR.,
Robert, D .... 314-773-0083 250 C
rthurman@brookesbible.org
THURMER, Anne .... 218-299-6506 238 K
anne.thurmer@minnesota.edu
THURMOND, Pat .... 866-492-5336 243 G
patricia.thurmond@mail.waldenu.edu
THURSTON, Katie, S ...... 256-824-6042.... 8 B
katie.thurston@uah.edu
THURSTON, Michael ...... 413-585-3000 218 D
mthursto@smith.edu
THUSWALDNER, Gregor 509-777-3755 485 D
gthuswaldner@whitworth.edu
THYNNE, Sara .... 336-506-4186 331 J
sara.thynne@alamancecc.edu
THYREEN, Timothy, R .... 724-852-7777 401 E
thyreen@waynesburg.edu
TIAGI, Olesia .... 914-632-5400 306 J
otiagi@monroecollege.edu
TIAHRT, Cheryl .... 605-658-6026 415 E
cheryl.tiahrt@usd.edu
TIAPO, Bernadette .... 607-436-2513 316 C
bernadette.tiapo@oneonta.edu
TIAPO, Bernadette .... 607-436-2830 316 C
bernadette.tiapo@oneonta.edu
TIBBETTS, Bill .... 612-343-4181 241 O
wetibbet@northcentral.edu
TIBBITT, Julie .... 202-651-5005.. 92 B
julie.tibbitt@gallaudet.edu
TIBBITTS, Laura .... 512-463-1808 448 G
laura.tibbitts@tsus.edu
TIBBS, Terri .... 864-833-2820 410 E
TIBERI, Tom, R .... 716-645-2171 315 F
tiberi@buffalo.edu
TIBERIO, Amy .... 401-254-5450 404 C
atiberio@rwu.edu

TIBOR, Alexis .... 701-355-8028 347 A
ajtibor@umary.edu
TICE, Jared .... 704-637-4410 327 H
jrtice18@catawba.edu
TICE, Jessica .... 304-558-0699 488 I
jessica.tice@wvhepc.edu
TICHENOR, Kristin .... 617-989-4590 219 D
TICHENOR, Kristin, R .... 508-831-6720 220 C
tichenor@wpi.edu
TICK, Michael .... 315-443-7671 321 D
mtick1@syr.edu
TIDEMAN, Susan .... 816-415-7550 261 G
tidemans@william.jewell.edu
TIDWELL, Brandon .... 309-794-7141 132 H
brandontidwell@augustana.edu
TIDWELL, Jackson .... 337-482-1000 192 F
TIDWELL, James, H .... 502-597-8104 183 A
james.tidwell@kysu.edu
TIDWELL, Sarah .... 281-425-6384 438 B
stidwell@lee.edu
TIE, Peter .... 408-433-2280.. 36 I
TIEFENTHALER, Jay .... 515-964-6612 164 F
jmtiefenthaler3@dmacc.edu
TIEKEN, Scott, K .... 812-877-8604 160 C
tieken1@rose-hulman.edu
TIENSVOLD, Melissa ..... 406-275-4978 264 H
melissa_tiensvold@skc.edu
TIERCE, Meghan .... 559-730-3745.. 39 C
meghant@cos.edu
TIERNAN, Bernadette ..... 973-720-2463 283 I
tiernanb@wpunj.edu
TIERNEY, Joan .... 815-280-2661 140 I
jtierney@jjc.edu
TIERNEY, Kathleen .... 610-526-5364 378 J
ktierney01@brynmawr.edu
TIET, Kien .... 626-350-1500.. 28 H
TIETJE, Brian .... 361-825-6045 446 E
brian.tietje@tamucc.edu
TIETJEN, Carl .... 585-275-2008 323 E
carl_tietjen@urmc.rochester.edu
TIETJEN, Rick .... 845-451-1380 297 E
rick.tietjen@culinary.edu
TIETZ, Leah Jo .... 406-449-9156 263 C
ltietz@montana.edu
TIETZ, Ryan, M .... 260-452-2135 154 F
ryan.tietz@ctsfw.edu
TIFFANY, Beth .... 518-388-6286 323 B
TIFFANY, Heather .... 805-421-5922.. 67 J
htiffany@thomasaquinas.edu
TIFFIN, Doug .... 972-708-7340 434 F
president@diu.edu
TIFFT, Allison .... 918-595-7923 370 B
allison.tifft@tulsacc.edu
TIGER, Andrew .... 325-942-2337 450 B
andrew.tiger@angelo.edu
TIGER, Carolyn .... 610-282-1100 382 A
carolyn.tiger@desales.edu
TIGHE, Charles .... 732-987-2612 277 B
ctighe@georgian.edu
TIGHE, Roger .... 254-442-5034 431 J
roger.tighe@cisco.edu
TIGNER, Terrell .... 816-604-3175 255 A
terrell.tigner@mcckc.edu
TIGNOR, Mia .... 772-462-7590 102 E
mtignor@irsc.edu
TIKALSKY, Paul, J .... 405-744-5140 367 G
paul.tikalsky@okstate.edu
TILDEN, Kevin .... 949-214-3127.. 40 E
kevin.tilden@cui.edu
TILDEN, Marsha, A .... 740-368-3163 359 F
matilden@owu.edu
TILDON, Maria .... 443-997-9930 199 E
maria.tildon@jhu.edu
TILGHMAN, Justin .... 252-527-6880 335 E
jgtilghman38@lenoircc.edu
TILL, Kimberly, B .... 214-887-5061 434 G
ktill@dts.edu
TILL, Matt .... 954-771-0376 103 S
mtill@knoxseminary.edu
TILLE, James .... 253-752-2020 479 D
TILLEMAN, Suzanne .... 406-243-6195 263 D
suzanne.tilleman@umontana.edu
TILLEN, Dawn .... 270-824-1830 182 A
dawn.tillen@kctcs.edu
TILLET, Kerri, T .... 413-545-3464 211 D
ktillet@umass.edu
TILLEY, Blake .... 636-481-3104 253 G
btilley@jeffco.edu
TILLEY, Genoria .... 225-216-8292 187 D
tilleyg@mybrcc.edu
TILLEY, Laurie .... 918-595-7884 370 B
laurie.tilley@tulsacc.edu

TILLINGHAST, David ...... 508-531-6140 212 B
dtillinghast@bridgew.edu
TILLIS, Antonio .... 856-225-6095 281 A
chancellor@camden.rutgers.edu
TILLMAN, Harry, J .... 757-446-7073 465 H
tillmahj@evms.edu
TILLMAN, Mark .... 904-256-7282 102 G
mtillma3@ju.edu
TILLMAN, Shalita .... 909-384-8659.. 60 F
scunningh@sbccd.cc.ca.us
TILLOTSON, James, R ... 515-964-0601 166 A
tillotsonj@faith.edu
TILLOTSON, Jeanette ..... 607-778-5195 317 A
tillotsonjo@sunybroome.edu
TILLOTSON, Kanetra ...... 504-520-5276 193 C
ktillots@xula.edu
TILSON, Heather .... 505-454-3562 286 C
htilson@nmhu.edu
TILSON, Vincent .... 704-233-8011 344 E
tilson@wingate.edu
TILSTRA, Doug .... 509-527-2511 484 C
doug.tilstra@wallawalla.edu
TILTON, Abigail .... 940-898-3326 451 A
atilton@twu.edu
TILTON, James .... 401-863-2721 403 A
james_tilton@brown.edu
TILTON, Penny .... 605-995-2119 414 A
penny.tilton@dwu.edu
TIMBERMAN, Amy .... 812-877-8006 160 C
timberm1@rose-hulman.edu
TIMBERS, Tammy .... 301-860-5000 203 D
ttimbers@bowiestate.edu
TIMBY, Tracy .... 215-968-8225 379 B
tracy.timby@bucks.edu
TIMKO, Michael, A .... 724-503-1001 401 D
mtimko@washjeff.edu
TIMLIN, Kevin .... 573-986-6863 258 J
kjtimlin@semo.edu
TIMLIN, Laynee, H .... 757-455-2137 476 C
etimlin@vwu.edu
TIMM, Randy .... 619-594-5221.. 33 E
deanofstudents@sdsu.edu
TIMMER, Amy .... 517-371-5140 232 K
timmera@cooley.edu
TIMMER, JR., James ..... 616-526-6037 221 L
jrt3@calvin.edu
TIMMER, Jeff .... 708-293-4597 150 H
jeff.timmer@trnty.edu
TIMMERMAN, Beth, J ... 989-774-2317 221 M
timme1bj@cmich.edu
TIMMERMAN, Candace . 402-375-7034 267 I
catimme1@wsc.edu
TIMMERMAN, David ...... 262-551-5813 491 B
dtimmerman@carthage.edu
TIMMERMAN, Melanie .. 740-392-6868 356 G
melanie.timmerman@mvnu.edu
TIMMERMAN, Melanie .. 740-392-6868 356 G
mtimmerman@mvnu.edu
TIMMERMANS, Dana ..... 714-992-7094.. 54 D
dtimmermans@fullcoll.edu
TIMMINS, Paul .... 541-346-1000 376 G
ptimmins@uoregon.edu
TIMMIS, Jerry .... 215-887-5511 401 G
jtimmis@wts.edu
TIMMONS,
Charles (Chip) .... 765-361-6054 162 G
timmonsc@wabash.edu
TIMMONS, Daren .... 803-641-3458 412 B
darent@usca.edu
TIMMONS, George .... 518-828-4181 296 G
george.timmons@sunycgcc.edu
TIMMONS, J Michael ... 575-835-5237 286 D
mike.timmons@nmt.edu
TIMMONS, Noelle .... 212-966-0300 308 A
TIMMONS, Tim .... 708-239-4787 150 H
tim.timmons@trnty.edu
TIMMS, David .... 916-577-2200.. 76 C
dtimms@jessup.edu
TIMMS, Samara .... 619-849-2722.. 57 J
stimms@pointloma.edu
TIMONER, OP, Gerard .. 202-495-3820.. 93 D
TIMPSON, Natalie .... 714-895-8992.. 38 E
ntimpson@gwc.cccd.edu
TIMS, Tiffany .... 740-753-6589 353 G
timst@hocking.edu
TIMSON, Joe .... 816-802-3419 253 H
jtimson@kcai.edu
TIMUR, Aysegul .... 239-590-1069 109 G
atimur@fgcu.edu
TINDALL, Amanda .... 502-213-2255 181 H
amanda.tindall@kctcs.edu
TINDALL, David .... 810-762-7981 225 F
dtindall@kettering.edu

TOLSON, Shannon .... 870-759-4101.. 24 B
TOLSTOY, Maya .... 206-221-0908 484 A
envdean@uw.edu
TOLY, Noah .... 616-526-6102 221 L
njt8@calvin.edu
TOM, Keith .... 360-676-2772 480 G
kjtom@nwic.edu
TOM, Marlene, K .... 415-422-2350.. 72 I
mktom@usfca.edu
TOM, Shelley .... 480-994-9244.. 16 C
tshelley@swiha.edu
TOM, Steven .... 866-492-5336 243 G
steven.tom@laureate.net
TOM, Vicki .... 510-436-1520.. 45 H
tom@hnu.edu
TOM-MIURA, Allison ..... 310-287-4431.. 50 C
tommiua@wlac.edu
TOMA, Brooke .... 518-743-2237 319 D
tomab@sunyacc.edu
TOMANEK, Jody .... 308-535-3624 266 J
tomanekj@mpcc.edu
TOMANENG, Rowena .... 408-288-3725.. 62 G
TOMANIO, David .... 516-876-3000 318 A
TOMANY, Claudia .... 320-308-2126 240 C
claudia.tomany@stcloudstate.edu
TOMAR, Myrriah .... 575-835-5438 286 D
myrriah.tomar@nmt.edu
TOMAS, Alejandria .... 510-464-3218.. 57 B
atomas@peralta.edu
TOMAS, Brad .... 706-419-1659 117 G
brad.tomas@covenant.edu
TOMAS, Don, L .... 828-339-4242 337 H
d_tomas@southwesterncc.edu
TOMASELLI, Gordon, F . 718-430-2000 289 D
TOMASELLO, Ronald ..... 856-227-7200 275 F
rtomasello@camdencc.edu
TOMASZEWSKI, Lynn ..... 215-568-4012 390 C
TOMASZKIEWICZ, Ed ..... 815-226-3372 147 J
etomaszkiewicz@rockford.edu
TOMASZKIEWICZ, Teri .. 630-844-5511 133 A
ttomaszk@aurora.edu
TOMBARGE, Chuck .... 612-625-8510 242 K
tombarge@umn.edu
TOMBARI, Chris .... 303-361-7361.. 80 C
chris.tombari@ccaurora.edu
TOMBERLIN, Daniel, D . 423-478-7713 421 J
dtomberlin@ptseminary.edu
TOMBES, Robert, M ...... 804-827-5600 472 D
rtombes@vcu.edu
TOMBLESON, Shelly ..... 719-336-1572.. 81 J
shelly.tombleson@lamarcc.edu
TOMBLIN, Debra .... 334-244-3250.... 4 F
dtomblin@aum.edu
TOMBLIN, John, S .... 316-978-5234 178 B
john.tomblin@wichita.edu
TOMCZAK, Patricia .... 217-228-5432 147 C
tomczpa@quincy.edu
TOMCZAK, Timothy .... 585-345-6831 300 D
tptomczak@genesee.edu
TOMCZYK, Christie .... 304-357-4944 486 J
christinetomczyk@ucwv.edu
TOMEK, Beverly .... 361-570-4200 452 C
tomekb@uhv.edu
TOMEK, Mary .... 804-333-6738 474 C
mtomek@rappahannock.edu
TOMES, Shawn .... 270-852-3203 183 B
stomes@kwc.edu
TOMESCU, Cosmin .... 212-592-2718 314 I
ctomescu@sva.edu
TOMFOHRDE, Tammy ...... 423-869-6465 420 A
tammy.tomfohrde@lmunet.edu
TOMHAVE, Brian .... 909-599-5433.. 48 E
btomhave@lifepacific.edu
TOMLIN, Kathy, H .... 540-464-7323 475 C
tomlinkh@vmi.edu
TOMLIN, Ross, L .... 503-842-8222 376 D
rosstomlin@tillamookbaycc.edu
TOMLINSON, Ann .... 310-660-3593.. 41 J
atomlinson@elcamino.edu
TOMLINSON, Doug .... 972-883-2141 454 D
douglas.tomlinson@utdallas.edu
TOMLINSON, Elise .... 907-796-6300.. 10 C
emtomlinson@alaska.edu
TOMLINSON, Jan .... 740-364-9510 349 D
tomlinson.88@cotc.edu
TOMLINSON, Jason .... 940-898-3505 451 A
jtomlinson1@twu.edu
TOMLINSON, Jennifer ... 407-582-1908 113 C
jtomlinson2@valenciacollege.edu
TOMLINSON, Jessica ...... 207-699-5016 194 G
jtomlinson@meca.edu
TOMLINSON, Jon .... 740-474-8896 358 A
jtomlinson@ohiochristian.edu

TOMLINSON, Karen .... 706-864-1948 126 G
karen.tomlinson@ung.edu
TOMLINSON, Kathryn ..... 229-259-5178 127 F
kathryn.tomlinson@wiregrass.edu
TOMLINSON, Leslie ...... 256-331-8040.... 3 C
ltomlinson@nwscc.edu
TOMLINSON, Rob .... 573-840-9649 259 I
rtomlinson@trcc.edu
TOMLINSON, Sandra .... 386-752-1822.. 99 P
sandra.tomlinson@fgc.edu
TOMLINSON, Susan .... 806-742-1828 450 C
susan.tomlinson@ttu.edu
TOMLINSON, Tim .... 865-938-8186 418 B
tim.tomlinson@thecrowncollege.edu
TOMLINSON, Virginia .... 509-963-2001 477 G
virginia.tomlinson@cwu.edu
TOMLINSON-CLARKE,
Saundra .... 848-932-0815 281 B
saundra.tomlinson-clarke@gse.rutgers.edu
TOMLJANOVICH,
Marc, I .... 717-871-4435 394 B
marc.tomljanovich@millersville.edu
TOMMASINO, Joseph ... 631-665-1600 322 B
joseph.tommasino@touro.edu
TOMMASINO, Joseph ... 631-665-1600 322 C
joseph.tommasino@touro.edu
TOMMEY, Dale .... 870-574-4512.. 21 F
dtommey@sautech.edu
TOMOSER, T. Paul .... 402-280-3026 265 J
ptomoser@creighton.edu
TOMOVA, Maggy .... 407-823-1911 110 D
maggy.tomova@ucf.edu
TOMPKINS,
Anthony (Tony) .... 913-288-7150 174 H
ttompkins@kckcc.edu
TOMPKINS, OSB,
John-Mary .... 724-805-2771 397 D
johnmary.tompkins@stvincent.edu
TOMPKINS, Kevin .... 252-492-2061 338 D
tompkinsk@vgcc.edu
TOMPKINS, Michael ...... 845-758-7523 290 G
tompkins@bard.edu
TOMPKINS, Page .... 603-678-4888 274 C
TOMPKINS, Patrick .... 757-789-1748 472 I
ptompkins@es.vccs.edu
TOMPKINS, Ricky .... 479-619-4325.. 20 G
rtompkins1@nwacc.edu
TOMPOS, Mike .... 651-523-2800 235 F
TOMS, David, E .... 401-456-8803 404 A
dtoms@ric.edu
TOMS, Debbie .... 605-718-2958 416 D
deborah.toms@wdt.edu
TOMSETH, Michelle .... 503-883-2434 373 E
mtomseth@linfield.edu
TOMSHINSKY, Ida .... 305-821-3333 100 C
itomshinsky@fnu.edu
TOMSO, Gregory .... 850-474-3177 111 E
gtomso@uwf.edu
TOMSON, Nathan, C ...... 989-964-2048 229 L
nctomson@svsu.edu
TONCHE, Carlos .... 718-862-7313 304 K
ctonche01@manhattan.edu
TONCIC, JR.,
Andrew, A .... 724-458-2170 384 F
aatoncic@gcc.edu
TONDER, Rick .... 701-777-4270 344 G
rick.tonder@ndus.edu
TONDIGLIA, Dean .... 330-672-3111 354 A
u347@police.kent.edu
TONDREAU, Rebecca .... 401-598-1000 403 E
rebecca.tondreau@jwu.edu
TONEV, Simon, T .... 610-330-5783 387 B
tonevs@lafayette.edu
TONEY, Carl .... 714-879-3901.. 45 J
cntoney@hiu.edu
TONEY, Glenn .... 706-245-7226 118 C
gtoney@ec.edu
TONEY, Pamela .... 800-462-7845.. 79 F
TONEY, RJ .... 970-943-2312.. 85 B
rjtoney@western.edu
TONG, Hui .... 425-235-2352 482 C
htong@rtc.edu
TONG, Ray .... 909-687-1513.. 43 G
raytong@gs.edu
TONG, Vincent .... 203-332-5220.. 86 E
vtong@gcc.commnet.edu
TONG, Vincent, P .... 203-285-2415.. 86 D
vtong@gatewayct.edu
TONG-CHING WU, Tom 508-531-2324 212 B
twu@bridgew.edu
TONI, Keith .... 508-678-2811 213 F
keith.toni@bristolcc.edu

TONKOWICH, Jonathan 307-332-2930 500 J
jtonkowich@wyomingcatholic.edu
TONN, Derek .... 541-888-7182 376 B
derek.tonn@socc.edu
TONNESON, Julie, A ...... 612-626-9278 242 K
tonne001@umn.edu
TONONO, Hiroko .... 949-480-4116.. 64 E
htonono@soka.edu
TOOEY, Mary, J .... 410-706-2693 202 F
mjtooey@hshsl.umaryland.edu
TOOHEY, Megan .... 716-645-4095 315 F
metoohey@buffalo.edu
TOOKE-RAWLINS, Dixie 540-231-6059 466 E
dtrawlins@vcom.vt.edu
TOOKE-RAWLINS, Dixie 540-231-4000 466 E
dtrawlins@vcom.vt.edu
TOOLE, Genesis .... 623-845-3000.. 13 E
genesis.toole@gccaz.edu
TOOLE, Michael .... 419-530-8000 363 B
michael.toole@utoledo.edu
TOOLE, Raymond, L ...... 610-359-5330 381 J
rtoole@dccc.edu
TOOLIN, Cynthia .... 860-796-3468.. 88 B
ctoolin@holyapostles.edu
TOOMES, Christopher ... 409-772-3565 456 B
cwtoomes@utmb.edu
TOOMEY, Christopher ... 213-740-1638.. 73 C
ctoomey@usc.edu
TOOMEY, Richard .... 978-665-4619 212 C
rtoomey1@fitchburgstate.edu
TOOMSEN, Corbett .... 414-847-3335 493 C
corbetttoomsen@miad.edu
TOON, Kellie .... 865-694-6523 424 C
kltoon@pstcc.edu
TOONE, Rachel .... 828-669-8012 331 H
rachel.toone@montreat.edu
TOONG, Kenneth, K .... 413-545-1504 211 D
ktoong@mail.aux.umass.edu
TOOSI, Mori .... 863-837-5937 106 A
mtoosi@polk.edu
TOOTOONCHI, Ahmad .. 731-881-7225 426 E
atootoon@utm.edu
TOPASNA, Yolonda, T .. 671-735-6013 503 C
yolonda.topasna@guamcc.edu
TOPHAM, Susan .... 619-388-6922.. 60 H
stopham@sdccd.edu
TOPIC, Miloš .... 616-331-2035 224 D
topicm@gvsu.edu
TOPLIFF, Donald, R ...... 325-942-2165 450 B
don.topliff@angelo.edu
TOPOL, Eric .... 858-784-8469.. 63 F
TOPOLSKI, Virginia .... 201-559-6055 277 A
topolskiv@felician.edu
TOPOUSIS, Dana .... 530-752-9841.. 69 A
dtopousis@ucdavis.edu
TOPP, Joelle .... 517-371-5140 232 K
toppj@cooley.edu
TOPPE, Michele .... 503-725-4422 375 D
toppem@pdx.edu
TOPPER, Curt .... 215-489-2928 381 K
curt.topper@delval.edu
TOPPIN, Ian .... 404-225-4502 115 F
itoppin@atlantatech.edu
TOPPLE, Dianne .... 518-828-4181 296 G
dianne.topple@sunycgcc.edu
TOPSHE, Joyce .... 860-685-3757.. 90 A
jtopshe@wesleyan.edu
TORABI, Shouka .... 949-582-4565.. 65 C
storabi@saddleback.edu
TORAIN, Martarash .... 919-516-4000 339 G
TORAIN, Mirian .... 301-546-5259 201 D
torainml@pgcc.edu
TORAIN, Wes .... 256-306-2965..... 1 F
wes.torain@calhoun.edu
TORBET, Linda .... 734-384-4245 227 F
ltorbet@monroeccc.edu
TORBITZKY, Nichole ...... 636-949-4651 254 B
ntorbitzky@lindenwood.edu
TORCHIA, Richard .... 215-572-2131 378 E
torchia@arcadia.edu
TORDELLA, Tina .... 304-243-2081 490 F
ttordella@wheeling.edu
TORELLO, Tom .... 518-445-3208 289 B
ttore@albanylaw.edu
TORGERSON, Jane .... 817-257-7940 447 H
j.torgerson@tcu.edu
TORGUSON, Kirsten .... 909-607-9313.. 37 I
kirsten_torguson@kgi.edu
TORIBIO, Rica .... 805-969-3626.. 55 I
rtoribio@pacifica.edu
TORINO, Frank .... 212-659-7200 303 E
ftorino@tkc.edu

TORMEY, Susan .... 315-498-2764 310 C
tormeys@sunyocc.edu
TORNABENE, Meredith . 315-445-4185 303 F
tornabmm@lemoyne.edu
TORNO, Keith .... 616-222-3000 226 A
itdirector@kuyper.edu
TORNOE, Monica .... 512-404-4832 429 K
mtornoe@austinseminary.edu
TORNQUIST, Kristi .... 605-688-5106 416 A
kristi.tornquist@sdstate.edu
TORNQUIST, Susan .... 541-737-6943 374 H
susan.tornquist@oregonstate.edu
TORNQUIST, Wade .... 734-487-0042 223 F
wtornquis@emich.edu
TORO, Dan .... 619-849-2571.. 57 J
dtoro@pointloma.edu
TORO, Sofia .... 909-607-8587.. 37 I
storo@kgi.edu
TORO, Sofia .... 909-607-0121.. 37 I
sofia_toro@kgi.edu
TORO, Zulma, R .... 860-832-3000.. 85 F
toro@ccsu.edu
TORO-ZAPATA, Rogelio 787-264-1912 507 E
rtoro@intersg.edu
TOROK, Kate, M .... 585-385-3801 313 A
ktorok@sjfc.edu
TOROS, Orkun .... 972-883-4735 454 D
ont130030@utdallas.edu
TOROSYAN, Roben .... 508-531-2435 212 B
roben.torosyan@bridgew.edu
TORRADO PEREZ,
Nellie .... 787-764-0000 511 F
nellie.torrado@upr.edu
TORRANCE, Peggy, L .... 218-299-3339 234 K
torrance@cord.edu
TORRE, Douglas .... 516-367-6869 296 A
TORRE, Patrick .... 203-932-7224.. 89 F
ptorre@newhaven.edu
TORRE, Scott .... 201-761-7403 282 H
storre@saintpeters.edu
TORREGOSA, Marivic ..... 956-326-2574 446 A
mtorregosa@tamiu.edu
TORREGROSSA, Tom .... 318-342-5353 193 A
torregrossa@ulm.edu
TORRENCE, Michael ...... 931-393-1682 423 G
mtorrence@mscc.edu
TORRENS, Michael .... 435-797-0220 459 F
michael.torrens@usu.edu
TORRES, Abigail .... 787-878-5475 506 J
atorres@arecibo.inter.edu
TORRES, Ana, D .... 787-834-9595 508 O
atorres@uaa.edu
TORRES, Angela .... 787-751-1912 507 F
atorres@juris.inter.edu
TORRES, Anna .... 860-512-3382.. 86 F
atorres1@manchestercc.edu
TORRES, Anna .... 330-941-3675 364 G
amtorres@ysu.edu
TORRES,
Antoinette (Toni) .... 212-353-4251 297 C
atorres@cooper.edu
TORRES, Aurelio .... 956-364-4255 448 F
aurelio.torres@tstc.edu
TORRES, Betania .... 863-667-5463 108 I
btorres@seu.edu
TORRES, Carmelo .... 787-751-0178 509 A
ctorresr@uagm.edu
TORRES, Carmelo .... 787-751-0178 509 C
ctorresr@uagm.edu
TORRES, Carmen, Z ...... 787-841-2000 508 H
admisiones@pucpr.edu
TORRES, Cathy .... 305-809-3250.. 97M
cathy.torres@cfk.edu
TORRES, Chanda .... 407-823-5001 110 D
chanda.torres@ucf.edu
TORRES, Cristobal .... 305-899-3836.. 96 A
ctorres@barry.edu
TORRES, Damaris .... 787-840-2575 508 G
dtorres@psm.edu
TORRES, Danille .... 503-768-7186 373 D
diversityinclusion@lclark.edu
TORRES, Darlin .... 787-250-1912 507 C
djtorres@metro.inter.edu
TORRES, Diana .... 213-740-2111.. 73 C
TORRES, Donna, K .... 225-578-2111 188 J
TORRES, Edwin .... 310-954-4348.. 52 J
eotorres@msmu.edu
TORRES, Eliseo, S .... 505-277-0952 288 C
cheo@unm.edu
TORRES, Evelyn .... 787-882-2065 508 N
etorres@unitecpr.edu
TORRES, Evelyn .... 787-264-1912 507 E
evetorre@intersg.edu

TRAN, Mai-Anh, L .... 847-866-3904 138 B
maianh.tran@garrett.edu

TRAN, Martin .... 814-254-0564 381 B
mtran@pa.gov

TRAN, My Linh .... 773-907-4770 134 N
mtran@ccc.edu

TRAN, Paul .... 480-732-7307.. 13 B
paul.tran@cgc.edu

TRAN, Sheena .... 714-628-4836.. 58 G
tran_sheena@sccollege.edu

TRAN, Song-Ho .... 408-288-3137.. 62 G
ho.tran@evc.edu

TRAN, Song-Ho .... 408-274-7900.. 62 F
ho.tran@evc.edu

TRAN-JOHNSON, Jenny 515-271-3094 165 F
jennifer.tran@drake.edu

TRANA, Paul .... 402-872-2298 267 H
ptrana@peru.edu

TRANA, Steve .... 402-486-2502 268 G
steve.trana@ucollege.edu

TRANQUADA, Jim .... 323-259-2990.. 54 I
jtranqua@oxy.edu

TRANSIT, Shannon .... 248-204-2316 226 E
stransit@ltu.edu

TRANT, Sid, J .... 205-348-8345.... 7 F
sjtrant@uasystem.edu

TRAPA, Peter .... 801-585-7671 459 D
peter.trapa@utah.edu

TRAPANICK,
Benjamin, J .... 508-626-4505 212 D
btrapanick@framingham.edu

TRAPP, Daniel .... 313-883-8540 229 J
trapp.daniel@shms.edu

TRAPP, Kristi .... 866-492-5336 243 G
kristi.trapp@laureate.net

TRAPP, Rodney .... 202-274-5930.. 94 B
rodney.trapp@udc.edu

TRASKA, Anthony .... 216-687-2020 350 G
a.traska@csuohio.edu

TRAUBE, Dave .... 304-696-3170 488 N

TRAUBE, David .... 304-357-0014 486 J
davidtraube@ucwv.edu

TRAUGH, Cecelia .... 212-875-4668 290 F
ctraugh@bankstreet.edu

TRAUPMAN-CARR,
Carol .... 610-861-1348 390 D
traupman-carrc@moravian.edu

TRAUSCH, Diane, M ...... 312-261-3230 145 C
diane.trausch@nl.edu

TRAUTMAN, Karla .... 605-688-4792 416 A
karla.trautman@sdstate.edu

TRAUTMAN, Stewart ...... 352-854-2322.. 97 L
trautmas@cf.edu

TRAUTWEILER,
Courtney .... 471-667-8181 251 E
ctrautweiler@cottey.edu

TRAUTWEIN, Paul .... 310-434-4204.. 63 B
trautwein_paul@smc.edu

TRAVENICK, Ron .... 707-638-5342.. 68 B
ron.travenick@tu.edu

TRAVENY, Carol .... 267-502-2547 378 I
carol.traveny@brynathyn.edu

TRAVER, Michele .... 810-762-0242 228 B
michele.traver@mcc.edu

TRAVERNICHT, Marcia .. 585-475-7292 312 A
mstwml@rit.edu

TRAVERS, Brian .... 978-542-6265 213 B
btravers@salemstate.edu.edu

TRAVERS, Nan .... 518-587-2100 320 B
nan.travers@esc.edu

TRAVERSE, Marshall ..... 425-558-0299 478 G

TRAVERSIE, Stephanie .. 605-882-5472 414 D
stephanie.traversie@lakeareatech.edu

TRAVERSO, Susan .... 724-589-2100 398 F
straverso@thiel.edu

TRAVIS, Antonio .... 404-756-4023 115 E
atravis@atlm.edu

TRAVIS, Artie .... 301-687-4311 203 F
altravis@frostburg.edu

TRAVIS, Brittany .... 718-779-1499 310 I
btravis@plazacollege.edu

TRAVIS, David .... 715-425-3700 496 A
david.travis@uwrf.edu

TRAVIS, Frederick .... 641-472-1209 168 A
ftravis@miu.edu

TRAVIS, Jody .... 520-494-5081.. 11 M
jody.travis@centralaz.edu

TRAVIS, Rick .... 662-325-2646 247 A
travis@ps.msstate.edu

TRAVIS, Scott .... 616-395-7251 224 H
travis@hope.edu

TRAVIS, Theresa .... 610-499-4123 401 I
ttravis@widener.edu

TRAVIS, Thomas .... 804-862-6100 469 E

TRAVIS-TEAGUE,
Dianne .... 805-969-3626.. 55 I
dtravis-teague@pacifica.edu

TRAVISANO, Jacqueline 305-284-6100 112 K
jtravisano@miami.edu

TRAWICK, Michelle .... 402-554-2596 269 C
mtrawick@unomaha.edu

TRAWICK, Rebecca .... 909-652-6493.. 36 B
rebecca.trawick@chaffey.edu

TRAWICK, Travis, H ...... 817-921-8833 444 D
ttrawick@swbts.edu

TRAXLER, Pete .... 907-796-6139.. 10 C
pbtraxler@alaska.edu

TRAXLER, Rebecca .... 937-775-7032 364 D
rebecca.traxler@wright.edu

TRAXLER, Roxy .... 507-389-7470 240 F
roxy.traxler@southcentral.edu

TRAXLER, Roxy .... 507-389-7200 240 F
roxy.traxler@southcentral.edu

TRAXLER, Suzanne .... 715-232-2501 496 C
traxlers@uwstout.edu

TRAYLOR, Angela .... 502-895-3411 183 E
atraylor@lpts.edu

TRAYNOR, Thomas, L .... 937-775-4859 364 D
thomas.traynor@wright.edu

TRAYWICK, Deaver .... 828-251-6001 342 A
traywick@unca.edu

TREACY, Margaret .... 845-569-3355 307 B
margaret.treacy@msmc.edu

TREACY, Patrick .... 708-974-5555 144 G
treacyp@morainevalley.edu

TREADWAY, Barbara ...... 402-399-2474 265 H
btreadway@csm.edu

TREADWAY, Chris .... 304-558-0265 487 B
treadway@wvctcs.edu

TREADWAY, Kristen .... 614-287-2647 351 B
ktreadway@cscc.edu

TREADWELL, Andrew .... 772-336-6205 102 E
atreadwe@irsc.edu

TREADWELL, Melinda ... 603-358-2000 274 A
president@keene.edu

TREADWELL, Orlando ... 202-274-5050.. 94 B

TREAGER-HUBER,
Carey .... 317-921-4882 158 A
ctreagerhuber@ivytech.edu

TREANOR, Ellen .... 657-278-4475.. 31 E
etreanor@fullerton.edu

TREANOR, Laura .... 812-888-4262 162 E
provost@vinu.edu

TREANOR, William, M .. 202-662-9030.. 92 D
wtreanor@georgetown.edu

TREAT, Tod .... 509-682-6605 484 H
ttreat@wvc.edu

TREBER, Karen, A .... 410-548-2330 204 A
katreber@salisbury.edu

TRECARTIN, JR., Ralph . 707-965-6211.. 55 H
president@puc.edu

TREDENNICK, Linda ...... 509-313-6790 479 E
tredennick@gonzaga.edu

TREDO, Jeffrey, P .... 716-884-9120 291 I
jptredo@bryantstratton.edu

TREDUP, Fred .... 702-895-3201 270 J

TREECE, Richard .... 661-763-7768.. 67 F
rtreece@taftcollege.edu

TREEN, Debbie .... 206-726-5020 478 F
dtreen@cornish.edu

TREES, April .... 314-977-2500 258 H
april.trees@slu.edu

TREFF, Shaya .... 732-370-3360 284 L

TREFF, Yisroel Meir ...... 732-370-3360 284 L

TREFT, Paul .... 712-274-5221 168 C
treft@morningside.edu

TREFZ, Steve, A .... 605-336-6588 415 B
strefz@kairos.edu

TREIB, Chris, A .... 724-847-6787 384 B
catreib@geneva.edu

TREICHEL, Johnny .... 806-874-3571 431 K
johnny.treichel@clarendoncollege.edu

TREJO, Alanna .... 805-437-2757.. 30 D
alanna.trejo@csuci.edu

TREJO, Sam .... 909-387-1642.. 60 F
strejo@sbccd.cc.ca.us

TREJOS-CASTILLO,
Elizabeth .... 806-742-3667 450 C
elizabeth.trejos@ttu.edu

TREKELL, Eric .... 425-388-9273 479 B
etrekell@everettcc.edu

TRELLES, Sofia .... 305-348-2797 109 H
sofia.trelles@fiu.edu

TREMBLAY, Britni .... 785-243-1435 172 J
btremblay@cloud.edu

TREMBLAY, Matthew ...... 858-784-8469.. 63 F

TREMBLAY, Pamela ...... 706-880-8313 121 K
ptremblay@lagrange.edu

TREMBLAY, Paul .... 212-410-8142 308 D
ptremblay@nycpm.edu

TREMBLAY, Rocky .... 203-285-2185.. 86 D
rtremblay@gatewayct.edu

TREMBLE, Gayle .... 843-355-4133 413 C
trembleg@wiltech.edu

TREML, Colleen .... 216-397-1595 353 O
ctreml@jcu.edu

TREMPER, Michael .... 315-268-6789 295 E
mtremper@clarkson.edu

TRENKLE, Catheryne ..... 970-521-6619.. 82 B
catheryne.trenkle@njc.edu

TRENKLE, Lizza .... 254-659-7601 436 C
ltrenkle@hillcollege.edu

TRENT, Dietra, Y .... 703-993-8730 466 J
dtrent@gmu.edu

TRENT, Malissa .... 423-354-2521 424 B
mbtrent@northeaststate.edu

TRENT-BROWN, Sonja .. 616-395-6829 224 H
trentbrown@hope.edu

TRENTACOSTE, Peter ..... 225-578-5388 188 K
pjt@lsu.edu

TRENTHEM, Richard ...... 901-843-3890 422 C
trenthem@rhodes.edu

TRENUM, Gary .... 301-687-3174 203 F
gtrenum@frostburg.edu

TREPAC, Letisha .... 309-268-8109 138 F
letisha.trepac@heartland.edu

TREPAL, Michael, J .... 212-410-8067 308 D
mtrepal@nycpm.edu

TREROTOLA,
Michael, R .... 718-817-3185 300 A
trerotola@fordham.edu

TRESSEL, James, P .... 330-941-3101 364 G
jptressel@ysu.edu

TRESSELT, Thomas .... 212-353-4119 297 C

TRESSLER-GELOK,
Thomas .... 718-390-3420 324 B
thomas.gelok@wagner.edu

TRESSLER-GELOK,
Thomas .... 718-390-3100 324 B

TRETHEWEY, Angela ..... 530-898-4015.. 31 A
atrethewey@csuchico.edu

TRETTER, April .... 502-272-7329 179 D
atretter@bellarmine.edu

TREUNER, Mary .... 660-596-7249 259 D
mtreuner@sfccmo.edu

TREUTING, Mary .... 318-473-6482 189 A
maryt@lsua.edu

TREVARTHEN, Josie, B . 931-424-2055 426 F
jtrev@utsouthern.edu

TREVATHAN, Enna .... 408-848-4866.. 43 H
etrevathan@gavilan.edu

TREVENA, Emma .... 201-216-9901 276 C
emma.trevena@eicollege.edu

TREVETT-SMITH,
Matthew .... 302-831-2027.. 91 A
mtrevett@udel.edu

TREVIER, Tim .... 815-226-4107 147 J
ttrevier@rockford.edu

TREVINO, Beth .... 618-374-5202 147 B
beth.trevino@principia.edu

TREVINO, Cori .... 940-898-3273 451 A
ctrevino@twu.edu

TREVINO, Crispin .... 361-593-4036 447 A
crispin.trevino@tamuk.edu

TREVINO, Cynthia .... 806-291-3401 457 B
trevinoc@wbu.edu

TREVINO, Leonard .... 412-365-1650 380 F
ltrevino@chatham.edu

TREVINO, Monica .... 405-224-3140 371 B
mtrevino@usao.edu

TREVINO, Nicole, G .... 512-428-1037 441 N
nicoleg@stedwards.edu

TREVINO, Nicole, G .... 512-428-1037 441 N
nicoleg@stewards.edu

TREVINO, Oscar .... 802-831-1348 462 F
otrevino@vermontlaw.edu

TREVIS, Michael .... 310-660-3101.. 41 J
mtrevis@elcamino.edu

TREVISAN, Michael .... 509-335-4853 484 D
trevisan@wsu.edu

TREVISANELLO, Lisa ...... 352-591-5385.. 97 D
lisa@chiu.edu

TREVOR, Tyler .... 406-449-9145 263 C
ttrevor@montana.edu

TREVOR, Will .... 518-445-2311 289 B
wtrev@albanylaw.edu

TREWARTHA, Robert ...... 651-423-8275 237 E
robert.trewartha@dctc.edu

TREWARTHA, Robert ...... 651-423-8275 237 H
robert.trewartha@dctc.edu

TREXLER, Lisa .... 704-669-4042 333 C
trexlerl847@clevelandcc.edu

TREZEVANT, Latitia .... 803-822-3597 409 E
trezevantl@midlandstech.edu

TREZZA, Frank .... 240-567-5031 200 E
frank.trezza@montgomerycollege.edu

TRI, Sandjaya .... 714-535-3886.. 64 G
santri@southbaylo.edu

TRIANA, Alisha .... 765-983-1211 154 H
trianal@earlham.edu

TRIANTIS, Alexander ..... 410-234-9214 199 E
atriantis@jhu.edu

TRIBBLE, SR.,
Jeffery, L .... 404-687-4586 117 D
tribblej@ctsnet.edu

TRIBBLE, Kenyetta .... 925-551-6204.. 40 H
ktribble@dvc.edu

TRIBLEY, Walter .... 307-675-0505 500 F

TRICE, Matt .... 229-430-6618 114 G
mtrice@albanytech.edu

TRICHE, Casie .... 985-448-4077 192 C
casie.triche@nicholls.edu

TRICK, Michael .... 412-268-3697 380 B
trick@cmu.edu

TRIER, Vicki .... 406-247-3003 263 H
vicki.trier@msubillings.edu

TRIERWEILER, John, K . 585-475-4727 312 A
jktcmo@rit.edu

TRIETLEY, Rick .... 608-796-3001 496 L
rctrietley@viterbo.edu

TRIEZENBERG,
Steven, J .... 616-234-5708 231 D

TRIGALO, Ophir .... 312-567-3290 139 H
trigalo@iit.edu

TRIGG, Latokia .... 864-592-4158 411 E
triggl@sccsc.edu

TRIGO, Fabiola .... 787-766-1717 509 C
ftrigo@uagm.edu

TRIGONIS, Marina .... 760-471-1316.. 72 G
mkaravokiris@usk.edu

TRIGUEROS, Williams ... 214-887-5207 434 G
wtrigueros@dts.edu

TRIHUS, Meg .... 972-708-7379 434 F
dean-students@diu.edu

TRIMARCHI, Valarie ...... 912-201-8007 125 D
vtrimarchi@southuniversity.edu

TRIMBLE, Ashtin .... 309-796-5143 133 D
trimblea@bhc.edu

TRIMBLE, Dani .... 360-442-2622 480 E
dtrimble@lowercolumbia.edu

TRIMBLE, Jodene .... 208-535-5489 130 I
jodene.trimble@cei.edu

TRIMBLE, LaDonna .... 661-722-6300.. 26 E
ltrimble@avc.edu

TRIMBLE, Lisa .... 307-778-1603 500 D
lisatrimble@lcccfoundation.edu

TRIMBLE, Michele .... 406-874-6305 262 K
trimblem@milescc.edu

TRIMBOLI, Dana .... 718-262-2350 295 D
dtrimboli@york.cuny.edu

TRIMBOLI, James .... 716-614-6202 309 E
trimboli@niagaracc.suny.edu

TRINH, Caitlin .... 860-768-2430.. 89 E
ctrinh@hartford.edu

TRINH, Steven .... 650-574-6161.. 62 J

TRINH, SVD, Vinh .... 563-876-3353 165 D
vtrinh@dwci.edu

TRINIDAD, Angel .... 787-878-5475 506 J
atrinidad@arecibo.inter.edu

TRINIDAD, Vanessa .... 787-884-6000 506 B
vtrinidad@icprjc.edu

TRINIDAD, Ysabel, D ..... 909-869-3019.. 30 B
ydtrinidad@cpp.edu

TRINKLEIN, Andrea, J ... 407-823-4663 110 D
andrea.trinklein@ucf.edu

TRINN, Dune .... 858-653-3000.. 29 F
dtrinn@calmu.edu

TRINOSKEY, Jessica ..... 317-955-6730 159 A
jtrinoskey@marian.edu

TRIOLO, John .... 718-631-6320 295 B
jtriolo@qcc.cuny.edu

TRIONE, Lindsey .... 910-962-3030 343 B
trionel@uncw.edu

TRIPATHI, Satish, K ...... 716-645-2901 315 F
president@buffalo.edu

TRIPLETT, Jennifer .... 660-359-3948 256 F
jtriplett@mail.ncmissouri.edu

TRIPLETT, Jennifer .... 865-981-8201 420 C
jennifer.triplett@maryvillecollege.edu

TRIPLETT, Kevin .... 865-471-4369 417 E
ktriplett@cn.edu

TRIPODI, Michael, A .... 201-684-6975 280 B
mtripodi@rmapo.edu

TUCKER, G.L .... 218-846-3765 238 K
gl.tucker@minnesota.edu
TUCKER, Gardiner .... 970-351-2001.. 84 D
gardiner.tucker@unco.edu
TUCKER, Gary, R .... 517-750-1200 230 F
garyt@arbor.edu
TUCKER, Jameel .... 610-526-6092 385 F
jtucker@harcum.edu
TUCKER, James .... 518-327-6286 310 G
jtucker@paulsmiths.edu
TUCKER, Jamilah .... 419-267-1225 357 E
jtucker@northweststate.edu
TUCKER, John .... 501-760-4229.. 20 E
john.tucker@np.edu
TUCKER, John, D .... 619-298-1829.. 65 J
jtucker@ssu.edu
TUCKER, Karen .... 630-752-5060 152 K
karen.tucker@wheaton.edu
TUCKER, Katie .... 337-550-1202 189 B
ktucker@lsue.edu
TUCKER, Ken .... 205-652-3527.... 9 B
ktucker@uwa.edu
TUCKER, Lakeisha .... 803-536-8584 410 H
ltucker3@scsu.edu
TUCKER, Laura .... 703-416-1441 465 E
ltucker@divinemercy.edu
TUCKER, Mark .... 479-936-5171.. 20 G
mtucker8@nwacc.edu
TUCKER, Mark .... 336-386-3217 338 B
tuckerm@surry.edu
TUCKER, Megan .... 802-295-8822 463 A
mjt09050@ccv.vsc.edu
TUCKER, Melanie, V ...... 865-981-8111 420 C
melanie.tucker@maryvillecollege.edu
TUCKER, Michael .... 765-641-4295 153 D
matucker@anderson.edu
TUCKER, Murl .... 714-547-9625.. 28 C
mtucker@calcoast.edu
TUCKER, Nate .... 423-473-1190 419 H
ntucker@leeuniversity.edu
TUCKER, Patrick .... 860-832-1786.. 85 F
ptucker@ccsu.edu
TUCKER, Robert .... 325-670-1498 436 B
robert.tucker@hsutx.edu
TUCKER, Sandra .... 386-481-2106.. 96 D
tuckers@cookman.edu
TUCKER, Sarah .... 304-558-0265 488 I
tucker@wvctcs.org
TUCKER, Sarah .... 304-558-0699 488 I
sarah.tucker@wvhepc.edu
TUCKER, Sarah, A .... 304-558-0265 487 B
tucker@wvctcs.edu
TUCKER, Shawna .... 580-349-1534 367 F
shawna.tucker@opsu.edu
TUCKER, Sheryl .... 405-744-6368 367 G
sheryl.tucker@okstate.edu
TUCKER, Stacy .... 602-412-9003.. 16 L
stacy.tucker@phoenix.edu
TUCKER, Stacy .... 913-288-7239 174 H
stucker@kckcc.edu
TUCKER, Tommy .... 870-307-7324.. 20 D
thomas.tucker@lyon.edu
TUCKER, William, T ...... 631-451-4760 320 G
tuckerw@sunysuffolk.edu
TUCKER, Zack .... 501-882-4491.. 17 H
zatucker@asub.edu
TUCKMAN, Eric .... 626-289-7719.. 24 K
TUDELA, Virginia, C ...... 671-735-5590 503 C
virginia.tudela@guamcc.edu
TUDINI, Kathryn, E .... 716-645-2258 315 F
katietud@buffalo.edu
TUDOR, Amanda .... 859-985-3316 179 E
tudora@berea.edu
TUDOR, Colin .... 909-607-3679.. 37 E
colin.tudor@claremont.edu
TUDOR, David .... 859-276-4357 184 F
dtudor@sullivan.edu
TUDOR, Jarrod .... 740-654-6711 358 L
tudorg@ohio.edu
TUDOR, Kristen .... 916-278-7737.. 33 A
khtudor@csus.edu
TUDOR, Lauren .... 412-365-2731 380 F
l.tudor@chatham.edu
TUDOR, Lisa .... 239-489-9350 100 G
ltudor@fsw.edu
TUDOR, Marie .... 314-392-2348 255 H
marie.tudor@mobap.edu
TUDOR, Robert .... 304-876-5294 489 A
rtudor@shepherd.edu
TUDOR-LOCKE, Catrine . 704-687-7917 342 C
ctudorlo@uncc.edu

TUDORIE,
Ionut Alexandru .... 914-961-8313 314 E
iatudorie@svots.edu
TUDRYN, Jonathan .... 413-755-4420 215 F
jtudryn@stcc.edu
TUEDIO, James, A .... 209-667-3531.. 33 D
jtuedio@csustan.edu
TUELL, David .... 865-471-2020 417 E
dtuell@cn.edu
TUELLER, David .... 801-422-3861 458 A
david_tueller@byu.edu
TUELLER, Steve, W .... 808-675-3705 128 B
steve.tueller@byuh.edu
TUESCHER-GILLE, Heidi 608-342-1125 495 E
tuescheh@uwplatt.edu
TUFAU-AFRIYIE,
Michelle .... 508-854-2300 215 D
mtufau@qcc.mass.edu
TUFEL, Peter .... 212-686-9244 289 G
TUFELE, Fa'amamata ..... 907-852-1763.... 9 H
registration@ilisagvik.edu
TUFENKJAN, Mark .... 323-343-4510.. 32 B
mtufenk@calstatela.edu
TUGGLE, Andrew .... 530-226-4140.. 64 C
atuggle@simpsonu.edu
TUIA, Jennifer .... 360-596-5369 483 E
jtuia@spscc.edu
TUITASI, Michael .... 310-434-4389.. 63 B
tuitasi_michael@smc.edu
TUITASI, Sifagatogo ...... 684-699-2722 503 A
s.tuitasi@amsamoa.edu
TUITE, Jayme .... 724-222-5330 391 E
jtuite@penncommercial.edu
TUITE, Marie .... 408-924-1200.. 34 B
marie.tuite@sjsu.edu
TUITT, Franklin, A .... 860-486-2422.. 89 B
franklin.tuitt@uconn.edu
TUKEL, Oya, I .... 973-596-6262 278 G
oya.i.tukel@njit.edu
TULAFONO-ASI, Grace .. 684-699-2722 503 A
g.tulafono@amsamoa.edu
TULBERG, Clark .... 805-421-5938.. 67 J
ctulberg@thomasaquinas.edu
TULINO, Michael .... 520-206-4625.. 15 E
mtulino@pima.edu
TULLEY, Nickolas, B ..... 240-895-3149 201 F
nbtulley@smcm.edu
TULLEY, Ronald .... 419-434-4445 362 D
rtulley@findlay.edu
TULLIER, Michael .... 334-724-4553.... 7 D
mtullier@tuskegee.edu
TULLIS, Josh .... 574-631-0407 161 G
jtullis@nd.edu
TULLOS, Andrea, D .... 334-953-5613 501 B
TULLOS, Casey .... 704-687-7501 342 C
kctullos@uncc.edu
TULLOS, Charlotte .... 510-841-1905.. 27 B
ctullos@bst.edu
TULLOS, Kristen .... 903-223-3053 447 C
ktullos@tamut.edu
TULLY, Amy, H .... 817-257-2787 447 H
a.h.tully@tcu.edu
TULLY, Greg, J .... 815-772-7218 145 A
gtully@morrisontech.edu
TULLY, John, J .... 610-566-1776 402 C
jtully@williamson.edu
TULLY-DARTEZ,
Stephanie .... 870-862-8131.. 21 C
stully-dartez@southark.edu
TUMA, Tiffany .... 919-516-4101 339 G
tctuma@st-aug.edu
TUMBLIN, Tom .... 859-858-3581 178 G
TUMEO, Michael, D .... 214-768-2808 443 G
mtumeo@smu.edu
TUMER, Irem .... 541-737-3467 374 H
TUMEY, Terrance .... 559-278-3178.. 31 D
TUMIEL, John .... 207-221-4665 197 A
jtumiel@une.edu
TUMIEL, John .... 207-221-4628 197 A
jtumiel@une.edu
TUMILTY, Meredith .... 847-543-2946 135 G
mtumilty@clcillinois.edu
TUMINEZ, Astrid .... 801-863-3000 460 A
president@uvu.edu
TUMLINSON, Karen .... 641-628-5276 164 B
tumlinsonk@central.edu
TUNE, Kathie .... 434-791-7106 463 L
ktune@averett.edu
TUNG, Freddy .... 708-235-2127 138 C
ftung@govst.edu
TUNG, Lisa .... 617-879-7335 212 E
ltung@massart.edu

TUNGSETH,
Margaret, A .... 563-588-4992 167 I
margaret.tungseth@loras.edu
TUNHEIM, Kathi .... 507-933-6540 235 E
ktunheim@gustavus.edu
TUNK, Chana .... 973-267-9404 279 G
TUNNICLIFFE, Erin .... 617-747-3096 206 D
etunnicliffe@berklee.edu
TUNNING, Michael .... 563-884-5865 169 C
michael.tunning@palmer.edu
TUPPER, Rick .... 605-274-4499 413 G
rick.tupper@augie.edu
TUPUA, Tiare .... 684-699-2722 503 A
t.tupua@amsamoa.edu
TUPUOLA, Tafaimamao . 684-699-2722 503 A
t.tupuola@amsamoa.edu
TURBEVILLE, Donna ...... 910-788-6203 337 G
donna.turbeville@sccnc.edu
TURBEVILLE, Frank .... 405-974-2753 370 H
fturbeville@uco.edu
TURBEVILLE, John .... 315-470-6660 319 A
jturbev@esf.edu
TURBIDE, Gerard .... 315-364-3358 324 E
gturbide@wells.edu
TURBIVILLE, Alice .... 610-957-6040 398 B
aturbiv1@swarthmore.edu
TURCHETTA, Greg .... 239-489-9061 100 G
gregory.turchetta@fsw.edu
TURCHI, Marissa .... 610-526-5151 378 J
mturchi@brynmawr.edu
TURCOTT, Scott .... 765-677-2246 157 F
scott.turcott@indwes.edu
TURCOTTE, Amanda ...... 859-233-8111 185 A
aturcotte@transy.edu
TURCOTTE, Jim .... 601-925-3809 246 D
turcotte@mc.edu
TURCOTTE, Katie .... 540-654-1372 471 B
kturcott@umw.edu
TURDO, Michael, A .... 860-444-8286 502 F
michael.j.turdo@uscg.mil
TUREK, John, G .... 714-879-3901.. 45 J
jgturek@hiu.edu
TUREK, Margaret .... 650-325-5621.. 59 J
margaret.turek@stpsu.edu
TUREN, Chris .... 310-879-0554.. 66 B
TURGEON, Pennie .... 516-686-7744 308 H
pturgeon@nyit.edu
TURICO, Michael .... 602-538-9396.. 10 E
TURK, David .... 903-813-2408 429 I
dturk@austincollege.edu
TURK, David, F .... 646-378-6153 289 F
david.turk@nyack.edu
TURK, Laura .... 540-831-5248 468 E
lturk@radford.edu
TURK, Matthew .... 773-834-2493 150 G
TURK, Stella .... 845-257-3105 316 B
turks@newpaltz.edu
TURK FIECOAT,
Heather .... 775-682-8081 270 K
hturk@unr.edu
TURKS, Stacie .... 209-946-2225.. 71 E
sturks@pacific.edu
TURLEY, Jo Lynn .... 660-596-7222 259 D
jturley@sfccmo.edu
TURLEY, Patty .... 802-224-3000 462 G
patricia.turley@vsc.edu
TURLEY, Scott .... 479-575-6601.. 21 H
lturley@uark.edu
TURLEY-AMES, Kandi .... 208-282-3053 131 E
turlkand@isu.edu
TURLINGTON, Lisa .... 910-592-8081 337 D
lturlington@sampsoncc.edu
TURMAN, Paul, D .... 402-471-2505 267 F
pturman@nscs.edu
TURMAN, Thad .... 254-459-5336 445 F
tturman@tarleton.edu
TURNAGE, Craig, A ...... 936-468-3407 444 H
turnagecraig@sfasu.edu
TURNAGE, Richard .... 501-686-7000.. 22 D
rhturnage@uams.edu
TURNAGE, Tyrone .... 252-493-7777 336 E
tturnage@email.pittcc.edu
TURNBOW, Eboni .... 707-826-3504.. 30 A
eboni.turnbow@humboldt.edu
TURNBULL, Kadeem, C 410-651-7606 203 B
kcturnbull@umes.edu
TURNER, Amanda .... 850-484-1618 105 G
amturner@pensacolastate.edu
TURNER, Andrea .... 812-749-1248 159 E
aturner@oak.edu
TURNER, Angela .... 434-797-8438 472 H
angela.turner@danville.edu

TURNER, Avery .... 610-647-4400 385 K
aturner@immaculata.edu
TURNER, B, P .... 334-387-3877.... 4 C
businessoffice@amridgeuniversity.edu
TURNER, Brooke .... 850-973-1674 104 K
turnerb@nfc.edu
TURNER, Dawn .... 252-985-5124 339 B
dturner@ncwc.edu
TURNER, Debra .... 706-737-1431 115 I
debturner@augusta.edu
TURNER, Deidra .... 817-515-1280 445 A
deidra.turner@tccd.edu
TURNER, Donna, A .... 252-246-1240 339 A
daturner@wilsoncc.edu
TURNER, Donnell .... 617-243-2125 210 G
dturner@lasell.edu
TURNER, Elaine .... 404-727-7631 118 D
elaine.turner@emory.edu
TURNER, Eric, M .... 617-243-2071 210 G
eturner@lasell.edu
TURNER, Fraser, S .... 773-508-7591 142 G
fturner1@luc.edu
TURNER, Ginny Rae ...... 678-839-6592 127 A
vturner@westga.edu
TURNER, Heather .... 803-376-5801 405 D
hturner@allenuniversity.edu
TURNER, Ireland .... 316-322-3144 172 B
iturner@butlercc.edu
TURNER, J. Fidel .... 404-880-6126 116 I
jturner@cau.edu
TURNER, Janet, K .... 503-943-7311 376 H
turnerj@up.edu
TURNER, Jeffrey .... 573-681-5087 254 A
turnerj@lincolnu.edu
TURNER, Jere .... 603-206-8165 272 A
jturner@ccsnh.edu
TURNER, John .... 979-830-4316 430 I
john.turner@blinn.edu
TURNER, Jonna .... 580-581-2218 365 C
jbrown@cameron.edu
TURNER, June .... 760-921-5558.. 56 A
june.turner@paloverde.edu
TURNER, K. B .... 601-979-7036 245 G
kb.turner@jsums.edu
TURNER, Kara .... 443-885-3126 200 F
kara.turner@morgan.edu
TURNER, Kay .... 718-817-1000 300 A
kturner27@fordham.edu
TURNER, Keith .... 218-733-6940 238 A
keith.turner@lsc.edu
TURNER, Kim .... 806-742-3220 450 A
TURNER, Kirsten .... 859-257-1911 185 D
kirsten.turner@uky.edu
TURNER, Kyle .... 303-964-5724.. 83 B
kturner005@regis.edu
TURNER, Kyle .... 806-720-7779 438 F
kyle.turner@lcu.edu
TURNER, LaTonya .... 317-955-6427 159 A
lturner@marian.edu
TURNER, Louise .... 406-586-3585 263 A
louise.turner@montanabiblecollege.edu
TURNER, Marietta .... 217-351-2505 146 G
mturner@parkland.edu
TURNER, Mary .... 606-368-6014 178 D
maryturner@alc.edu
TURNER, Matt .... 304-558-4016 488 I
matt.turner@wvhepc.edu
TURNER, Michael .... 843-953-5145 406 D
mturner7@citadel.edu
TURNER, Michael, C ...... 334-387-3877.... 4 C
mcturner@amridgeuniversity.edu
TURNER, Monica .... 575-769-4948 285 C
monica.sanchez@clovis.edu
TURNER, Morgan .... 530-283-0202.. 42 E
mturner@frc.edu
TURNER, Natalie, T .... 502-597-6373 183 A
natalie.turner@kysu.edu
TURNER, Nicole .... 401-254-3886 404 C
nturner@rwu.edu
TURNER, Paaige, K .... 765-285-6000 153 E
pkturner@bsu.edu
TURNER, Pamela .... 502-213-2110 181 H
pamela.turner@kctcs.edu
TURNER, Paul 954-262-8082 104M
TURNER, Phyllis .... 903-233-4170 438 C
phyllisturner@letu.edu
TURNER, Preston .... 731-425-2619 423 F
pturner@jscc.edu
TURNER, R. Elaine .... 352-392-1961 110 E
returner@ufl.edu
TURNER, R. Gerald .... 214-768-3300 443 G
cleggl@smu.edu

UHAL, Len .... 563-876-3353 165 D
luhal@dwci.edu

UHDE, Alicia .... 701-224-5764 345 F
alicia.uhde@bismarckstate.edu

UHER, Bill .... 505-681-6279 288 C
bill.uher@unmfund.org

UHL, Carolyn .... 920-403-3964 494 B
carolyn.uhl@snc.edu

UHLENKAMP, James 563-588-6533 164 C
james.uhlenkamp@clarke.edu

UHLER, Jill .... 803-508-7247 405 C
uhlerj@atc.edu

UHLIR, Jim .... 715-232-2188 496 C
uhlirj@uwstout.edu

UHRICH, James .... 323-259-2506.. 54 I
juhrich@oxy.edu

UHRICH, Kathryn .... 951-827-3101.. 70 B
cnasdean@ucr.edu

UILK, Kristen .... 605-256-5121 415 G
kristen.uilk@dsu.edu

UKACHUKWU, Victoria . 908-412-3590 283 E
victoria.ukachukwu@ucc.edu

ULATE, David .... 650-949-6905.. 42 J
ulatedavid@fhda.edu

ULATOWSKI, Lydia .... 716-614-6450 309 E
ulatowsk@niagaracc.suny.edu

ULBRICH, Casandra . 313-593-5393 231 B
culbrich@umich.edu

ULIANA, Marla .... 818-364-7729.. 49 G
ulianamr@lamission.edu

ULII, Diedra .... 808-675-3474 128 B
diedra.ulii@byuh.edu

ULLAND, Greg .... 701-252-3467 346 J
gulland@uj.edu

ULLMANN, Brian ...... 301-314-1482 202 E
ullmann@umd.edu

ULLMANN, Jeffrey .... 816-604-1062 254 E
jeffrey.ullmann@mcckc.edu

ULLOA HEATH,
Julie, U .... 671-735-5517 503 C
julie.ulloaheath@guamcc.edu

ULLOM, Carine .... 785-248-2510 176 F
carine.ullom@ottawa.edu

ULLOM, Lynn .... 304-336-8200 489 B
ullomlyn@westliberty.edu

ULLRICH, Cindy ...... 979-230-3415 431 A
cindy.ullrich@brazosport.edu

ULMEN, Dan .... 406-265-3755 264 A
dulmen@msun.edu

ULMER, Robert, R ..... 702-895-0628 270 J
robert.ulmer@unlv.edu

ULOZAS, Catherine, B .. 215-895-6685 382 D
catherine.b.ulozas@drexel.edu

ULREY, Burke .... 828-641-0259 327 A
ulreydb@brevard.edu

ULRICH, James .... 847-317-8061 150 J
jfulrich@tiu.edu

ULRICH, Jesse .... 515-576-7201 166 G
ulrich@iowacentral.edu

ULRICH, Mary .... 575-527-7526 287 A
mulrich@nmsu.edu

ULRICH, Melanie ..... 303-273-3056.. 79 A
mulrich@mines.edu

ULRICHSEN, Borre .. 509-313-6455 479 E
ulrichsen@gonzaga.edu

ULSES, Randy .... 513-556-3511 361 I
ulsesrj@ucmail.uc.edu

UMALI, Arzie .... 816-235-5577 260 D
umalia@umkc.edu

UMAN, Deborah .... 801-626-6424 460 B
deborahuman@weber.edu

UMANS, Dorothy .... 240-567-3820 200 E
dorothy.umans@montgomerycollege.
edu

UMBERGER, Jennifer .... 570-389-5150 393 E
jumberger@bloomu.edu

UMEHIRA, Ron .... 808-455-0228 130 A
umehira@hawaii.edu

UMEZU, Kodo .... 510-809-1444.. 46 B
kumezu@hawaii.edu

UMFRESS, Jason, W ... 912-279-5970 117 C
jumfress@ccga.edu

UMIDI, Joseph .... 757-352-4404 469 D
joseumi@regent.edu

UMONTUEN, Nicholas . 615-329-8763 418 E
numontuen@fisk.edu

UMPHREY, Monique ..... 512-223-7598 429 J
rumstattd@mbts.edu

UMSTATTD, Rustin ... 816-414-3700 255 F
rumstattd@mbts.edu

UNAEZE, Felix .... 912-358-4337 124 H
unaezef@savannahstate.edu

UNBEHAGEN, Leonard .. 504-278-6438 188 E
lunbehagen@nunez.edu

UNDA, Viviana .... 310-660-3515.. 41 J
vunda@elcamino.edu

UNDERBAKKE,
Richard, G .... 304-929-5493 487 G
runderbakke@newriver.edu

UNDERCOFLER,
Jennifer .... 914-251-6707 318 E
jennifer.undercofler@purchase.edu

UNDERHILL, Terri .... 304-357-4980 486 J
terriunderhill@ucwv.edu

UNDERWOOD, Alex .. 520-621-3432.. 16 H
aunderwood@arizona.edu

UNDERWOOD, Anita .... 646-378-3090 289 F
anita.underwood@nyack.edu

UNDERWOOD, Chloris . 954-486-7728 112 J
cunderwood@uftl.edu

UNDERWOOD,
George, T .... 865-539-7401 424 C
gtunderwood@pstcc.edu

UNDERWOOD, Jeanette 972-775-7250 439 G
jeanette.underwood@navarrocollege.
edu

UNDERWOOD, Jeffrey . 323-343-3793.. 32 B
jeffrey.underwood@calstatela.edu

UNDERWOOD, Jeremy . 865-251-1800 422 G
junderwood@south.edu

UNDERWOOD,
Kathy, A .... 702-895-0283 270 J
kathyunderwood@unlv.edu

UNDERWOOD, Kim ...... 618-985-3741 139 C
underwoodk@iecc.edu

UNDERWOOD, Mark .... 830-591-7286 443 I
meunderwood@swtjc.edu

UNDERWOOD, Matt ... 254-485-4469 441 D
munderwood@rangercollege.edu

UNDERWOOD,
Michelle, W .... 229-931-2627 120 B
michelle.underwood@gsw.edu

UNDERWOOD, Ruth .... 478-289-2134 118 B
runderwood@ega.edu

UNDERWOOD, Tara ... 478-471-2734 122 D
tara.underwood@mga.edu

UNDERWOOD, Tiffani .. 276-656-0281 473 H
tunderwood@patrickhenry.edu

UNDERWOOD,
Timothy, J .... 304-462-6432 488 M
timothy.underwood@glenville.edu

UNDERWOOD,
William, D .... 478-301-2500 122 C
underwood_wd@mercer.edu

UNEBASAMI,
Michael, T .... 808-956-6280 129 D
mune@hawaii.edu

UNGAR, Samuel, D .... 718-384-5460 325 I
sunger@clcillinois.edu

UNGER, Bradley ..... 847-543-2477 135 G
bunger@clcillinois.edu

UNGER, Jacob .... 845-362-3053 290 I
junger@byts.edu

UNGER, Karen .... 845-758-7434 290 G
kunger@bard.edu

UNGER, Leigh .... 562-908-3415.. 58 M
lunger@riohondo.edu

UNGER, Maggie .... 952-446-4323 235 B
ungerm@crown.edu

UNGER, Sue .... 630-889-6565 145 D
sunger@nuhs.edu

UNGERANK, Stephanie . 501-882-8842.. 17 H
ssungerank@asub.edu

UNGERER, Dorothy ... 413-755-4438 215 F
daungerer@stcc.edu

UNIS, Corry, D .... 203-254-4000.. 87 G
cunis@fairfield.edu

UNKE, James, M ...... 507-354-8221 236 D
unkejm@mlc-wels.edu

UNNAVA, H. Rao ...... 530-752-4600.. 69 A
runnava@ucdavis.edu

UNRATH, Karen .... 973-300-2112 283 B
kunrath@sussex.edu

UNREIN, Ashley .... 970-521-6741.. 82 B
ashley.unrein@njc.edu

UNRUH, David, L ..... 215-895-1261 382 D
dlu23@drexel.edu

UNRUH, Nancy .... 620-276-9571 173 H
nancy.unruh@gcccks.edu

UNSWORTH, John, M ... 434-924-7849 471 F
jmu2m@virginia.edu

UNTARTO, SSPS,
Aprilia .... 563-876-3353 165 D
auntarto@dwci.edu

UNZICKER, Ted .... 208-792-2223 131 F
tounzicker@lcsc.edu

UPAH, Jesse .... 319-399-8000 164 D
jupah@coe.edu

UPCHURCH, Bart .... 903-823-3246 445 C
bart.upchurch@texarkanacollege.edu

UPCHURCH, Luke ..... 704-923-8405 334 E
upchurch.luke@gaston.edu

UPCHURCH, Luke ..... 704-922-6513 334 E
upchurch.luke@gaston.edu

UPCHURCH, Oliver Lee . 606-218-5940 185 F
oliverupchurch@upike.edu

UPCHURCH, Rick ...... 601-968-8942 244 C
rupchurch@belhaven.edu

UPCHURCH, Robert .... 205-652-3533.... 9 B
rupchurch@uwa.edu

UPDIKE, Jeremy .... 507-923-4210 233 G
updike@augsburg.edu

UPHOLD, Kimberly .... 253-680-7025 477 A
kuphold@batestech.edu

UPLINGER, Matthew .... 920-206-2318 492 C
matthew.uplinger@mbu.edu

UPNEJA, Arun .... 617-358-6744 207 C
aupneja@bu.edu

UPSHAW, Tyler .... 352-395-8516 107 B
tyler.upshaw@saintleo.edu

UPTON, Ed .... 817-921-8846 444 D
eupton@swbts.edu

UPTON, Michael .... 662-862-8035 245 F
maupton@iccms.edu

UQDAH, Aesha .... 502-852-6585 185 E
aesha.uqdah@louisville.edu

URAN, Mike, T .... 320-308-2116 240 C
mturan@stcloudstate.edu

URBAITIS, Carol, S .... 585-785-1212 299 E
carol.urbaitis@flcc.edu

URBAN, Brooke .... 716-880-2000 305 F
URBAN, Chad, H ...... 843-577-5245 405 E
URBAN, David, J ...... 615-898-2764 421 C
david.urban@mtsu.edu

URBAN, Kristi .... 979-830-4141 430 I
kristi.urban@blinn.edu

URBAN, Nathan, N .... 610-758-3605 388 C
nnu220@lehigh.edu

URBANCZYK, Allison ... 219-464-5212 162 C
allison.urbanczyk@valpo.edu

URBANEK, Philip ..... 251-405-7006.... 1 E
purbanek@bishop.edu

URBANEK-MUELLER,
Mary .... 314-256-8855 249 F
urbanek@ai.edu

URBANO, George .... 863-297-1086 106 A
gurbano@polk.edu

URDAN, Joely, B ...... 414-229-4730 495 B
jurdan@uwm.edu

URDANETA, Marta .... 903-434-8367 440 A
murdaneta@ntcc.edu

URDIALES, Juan .... 323-260-8133.. 49 D
urdialjr@elac.edu

URDIALEZ, Christine ... 210-366-2701 441 C
curdialez@questcollege.edu

URETSKY, Stewart ..... 781-736-4403 207 D
suretsky@brandeis.edu

UREÑA, Maria .... 787-852-1430 506 A
murena@hccpr.edu

URICK, Cindy .... 610-372-4721 396 A
curick@racc.edu

URICK, Michael ...... 724-805-2654 397 C
michael.urick@stvincent.edu

URICK, Mike .... 724-537-4597 397 D
mike.urick@stvincent.edu

URIEGAS, Samantha ... 956-872-6763 443 D
sbmunoz@southtexascollege.edu

URLA, Jacqueline ..... 413-545-2869 211 D
jurla@umass.edu

URQUIDEZ,
Kasandra, K .... 520-621-3705.. 16 H
kurquidez@arizona.edu

URQUIOLA, Angel ...... 305-821-3333 100 C
aurquiola@fnu.edu

URRABAZO, Gloria ..... 210-528-7047 440 D
gaurrabazo@ollusa.edu

URSCHEL, Kris .... 574-284-4542 160 F
kurschel@saintmarys.edu

URSO, David .... 540-453-2376 472 F
ursod@brcc.edu

URSUY, Andrea .... 989-686-9222 223 E
alnadols@delta.edu

URSUY, Andrea, L ..... 989-686-9222 223 E
alnadols@delta.edu

URTZ, Anastasia .... 315-498-7271 310 C
urtza@sunyocc.edu

URTZ, Mike .... 607-753-4953 317 D
mike.urtz@cortland.edu

URY, Erica .... 573-334-6825 258 I
eury@sehcollege.edu

USATCH, Jeri .... 518-255-5227 318 F
usatchj@cobleskill.edu

USCHER, Nancy .... 702-895-4210 270 J
nancy.uscher@unlv.edu

USDAN, Stuart .... 205-348-6250.... 7 G
susdan@ches.ua.edu

USHER, Diane .... 401-254-3039 404 C
dusher@rwu.edu

USHER, John .... 251-460-6140.... 9 A
jusher@southalabama.edu

USINA, Phyllis .... 707-527-4547.. 63 C
pusina@santarosa.edu

UTASH, Sheree .... 316-677-9400 178 C
sutash@wsutech.edu

UTECH, Tracy .... 313-577-9278 232 H
tracy.utech@wayne.edu

UTER, Joe .... 202-806-6131.. 92 E
UTHOFF, Jay, L .... 563-387-1012 167 J
uthoffja@luther.edu

UTLEY, Danya .... 501-882-4509.. 17 H
dlutley@asub.edu

UTPADEL, Justin ...... 715-232-2200 496 C
utpadelj@uwstout.edu

UTSCHIG, Theresa .... 414-930-3000 493 C
utschigt@mtmary.edu

UTSUKI, Melissa ...... 626-914-8872.. 37 B
mutsuki@citruscollege.edu

UTT, Heather .... 580-349-1399 367 F
heather.utt@opsu.edu

UTTECH, Kristin ...... 608-246-6336 497 I
kuttech@madisoncollege.edu

UTTER, Alan .... 870-972-2030.. 17 I
autter@astate.edu

UTZIG, Michael .... 518-783-2914 314 K
mutzig@siena.edu

UVERO, Marilyn .... 562-988-2278.. 26 A
muvero@auhs.edu

UWONO, Dee .... 808-956-2299 129 B
deeuwono@hawaii.edu

UWONO, Dee, E .... 808-956-7077 128 I
deeuwono@hawaii.edu

UY, Danielle .... 314-977-2506 258 H
danielle.uy@slu.edu

UYENO, Sandra .... 808-956-7038 129 D
uyeno@hawaii.edu

UZMAN, James .... 713-221-8488 452 B
uzmana@uhd.edu

UZNANSKI, Laurel ..... 360-867-6366 479 E
uznanski@evergreen.edu

UZORUO, Petra .... 409-984-6151 449 D
petra.uzoruo@lamarpa.edu

UZZELL, Janet, F ...... 202-994-7377.. 92 C
janetuzzell@gwu.edu

UZZI, Jeannine .... 207-780-4485 196 J
jeannine.uzzi@maine.edu

U'REN, Brian .... 859-858-2298 178 G

V

VABRE, Bert .... 201-761-7834 282 H
bvabre@saintpeters.edu

VACA, Alex .... 816-531-5223 251 C
VACCARELLI, Rebecca ... 212-799-5000 303 B
VACCARO, Anne .... 718-862-7409 304 K
anne.vaccaro@manhattan.edu

VACCARO, Paul .... 508-849-3482 205 E
pvaccaro@annamaria.edu

VACEK, Heather .... 610-861-1516 390 D
vacekh@moravian.edu

VACEK, Heather, H .... 717-290-8701 387 F
VACEK, Kris .... 816-501-4819 257 K
kris.vacek@rockhurst.edu

VACHA-HAASE, Tammi . 903-886-5514 446 D
tammi.vacha-haase@tamuc.edu

VACIK, Stephen .... 601-857-3352 245 D
stephen.vacik@hindscc.edu

VAD, Aron .... 417-862-9533 252 H
VADEN, David .... 716-250-7500 291 H
dvaden@bryantstratton.edu

VADGAMA, Jadutt ...... 323-563-9397.. 36 E
jayvadgama@cdrewu.edu

VAGLIENTI, Kendra .... 972-860-4332 433 G
kvaglienti@dcccd.edu

VAGNERINI, Beverly ... 910-962-7422 343 G
vagnerinib@uncw.edu

VAHEY, Karen .... 516-686-7742 308 H
karen.vahey@nyit.edu

VAHLKAMP, Laura ...... 618-545-3070 141 C
lvahlkamp@kaskaskia.edu

VAIDYA, Ashish .... 859-572-5123 184 B
vaidya@nku.edu

VAIDYA, Sameer .... 817-531-4840 450 F
svaidya@txwes.edu

VAN KLEY, Eric ... 641-628-5422 164 B vankleye@central.edu
VAN KOOTEN, Rick ... 812-855-2392 156 C rvankoot@indiana.edu
VAN KOOY, Samantha .. 856-415-2276 280 F svankooy@rcsj.edu
VAN KUIKEN, Jerome .. 918-335-6802 368 E jvankuiken@okwu.edu
VAN LEHN, Darren ... 541-956-7144 375 G dvanlehn@roguecc.edu
VAN LEIDEN, Melissa ... 785-594-8306 171 C melissa.vanleiden@bakeru.edu
VAN LIERE, Lori ... 419-866-0261 361 A lori.vanliere@sctoday.edu
VAN LIEW, Chris ... 206-296-2003 483 B vanliew@seattleu.edu
VAN LOO, Scott ... 937-766-7700 349 C vanloos@cedarville.edu
VAN LOON, Ruth Anne 513-556-4628 361 I ruth.anne.vanloon@uc.edu
VAN LUNEN, Bonnie ... 757-683-3516 468 C bvanlune@odu.edu
VAN MAARTH, Robin ... 303-329-6355.. 79 C clinicdirector@cstcm.edu
VAN METER, Eric ... 605-995-2919 414 A eric.vanmeter@dwu.edu
VAN NESS, Clare ... 530-898-5674.. 31 A croby@csuchico.edu
VAN NEST, Douglas ... 740-392-6868 356 G douglas.vannest@mvnu.edu
VAN NEST, Lisa, L ... 740-392-6868 356 G lisa.vannest@mvnu.edu
VAN NIEJENHUIS, Nate 712-722-6401 165 E natevn@dordt.edu
VAN NOORT, Kimberly . 919-843-8347 340 F kpvannoort@northcarolina.edu
VAN NORMAN, Karen ... 973-761-9076 282 K karen.vannorman@shu.edu
VAN NORT, Ella ... 213-624-1200.. 42 F evanort@fidm.edu
VAN NOSTRAND, Chris 619-239-0391.. 34 H cvannostrand@cwsl.edu
VAN NOSTRAND, Robert ... 934-420-2700 320 C foundation@farmingdale.edu
VAN NOY, Karla ... 785-749-8467 174 A kvannoy@haskell.edu
VAN NOY, Vielane ... 435-222-1256.. 83 D vvannoy@rvu.edu
VAN OMMEREN, Andrew ... 712-707-7000 169 A andrew.vanommeren@nwciowa.edu
VAN OMMEREN, Ryan .. 805-493-3211.. 29 E rvommere@callutheran.edu
VAN OOT, Amy ... 860-701-5019.. 88 C vanoot_a@mitchell.edu
VAN ORMAN, Kit ... 315-364-3317 324 E kit@wells.edu
VAN PATTEN, Paul, G .. 615-898-2613 421 C greg.vanpatten@mtsu.edu
VAN PELT, Donna ... 515-294-1280 163 E dvanpelt@foundation.iastate.edu
VAN PUFFELEN, Sara Kaitlin ... 706-419-1439 117 G sarak.vanpuffelen@covenant.edu
VAN RENSBURG, Deryck ... 310-506-5689.. 56 H deryck.rensburg@pepperdine.edu
VAN RENSELAAR, Erik .. 401-739-5000 403 F evanrenselaar@neit.edu
VAN RIJN, Paul ... 610-917-1450 400 D p_vanrijn@valleyforge.edu
VAN RIPER, Lisa, K ... 309-341-7760 141 E lkvanriper@knox.edu
VAN ROOYEN, Pieter ... 313-883-8623 229 J vanrooyen.pieter@shms.edu
VAN SICKLE, Fred ... 607-254-7150 297 D fmv7@cornell.edu
VAN SLOOTEN, Jessica 906-217-4054 221 J jessica.vanslooten@baycollege.edu
VAN STRATEN, Amy ... 920-831-4355 497 F vanstrat@fvtc.edu
VAN TASSEL, Kristin ... 785-227-3380 171 H vantasselk@bethanylb.edu
VAN TASSELL, TOR, Malachi ... 814-472-3001 396 I mvantassell@francis.edu
VAN TIL, Seth, J ... 724-458-3887 384 F sjvantil@gcc.edu
VAN VLERAH, Abby, L . 260-982-5132 158W alvanvlerah@manchester.edu
VAN VLIET, Krystyn ... 617-253-3315 215 G
VAN VOORHIS, Sue, N . 612-625-8098 242 K vanvo002@umn.edu

VAN WAGNER, Molly ... 715-425-3195 496 A molly.van-wagner@uwrf.edu
VAN WAGNER, Thomas 301-243-2211 501 J thomas.vanwagner@dodiis.mil
VAN WAGONER, Randall, J ... 315-792-5333 306 G rvanwagoner@mvcc.edu
VAN WICKLIN, Robert .. 716-375-2331 312 F bvanwick@sbu.edu
VAN WINKLE, Ken ... 575-646-9874 286 G kvanwink@nmsu.edu
VAN WINKLE, Ken ... 575-646-2036 286 H kvanwink@nmsu.edu
VAN WINKLE, Robin ... 541-440-4668 376 F robin.vanwinkle@umpqua.edu
VAN WOERT, Timothy .. 802-865-6499 461 C tvanwoert@champlain.edu
VAN WORMER, Laura, A ... 330-569-5249 353 F vanwormerla@hiram.edu
VAN WYK, Natalie ... 610-361-5418 390 G vanwykn@neumann.edu
VAN WYLEN, David, G . 616-395-7317 224 H vanwylend@hope.edu
VAN WYNGARDEN, Doug ... 708-239-4828 150 H doug.vanwyngarden@trnty.edu
VAN ZEE, Carolina ... 909-537-7576.. 33 B quinterc@csusb.edu
VAN ZEELAND, Kathy ... 414-930-3552 493 E vanzeek@mtmary.edu
VANABLE, Peter ... 315-443-2543 321 D pvanable@syr.edu
VANACORE, Gina ... 940-565-2282 453 B gina.vanacore@unt.edu
VANAKEN, Troy ... 630-617-3100 137 E president@elmhurst.edu
VANASSE, Dennis ... 508-849-3372 205 E dvanasse@annamaria.edu
VANASSE, Janelle ... 907-564-8220... 9 F jvanasse@alaskapacific.edu
VANATTA, Debbie ... 419-434-4558 362 D vanatta@findlay.edu
VANBEBBER, James ... 903-886-5996 446 D james.vanbebber@tamuc.edu
VANBEEK, Gennie ... 503-883-2238 373 E gvanbeek@linfield.edu
VANBOCKSTAELE, Elisabeth ... 215-762-4359 382 D elisabeth.vanbockstaele@drexelmed.edu
VANBUREN, Tiffany ... 276-739-2425 474 H tvanburen@vhcc.edu
VANBUREN, Tina ... 610-799-1510 388 B tvanburen@lccc.edu
VANCAMP, Connie ... 412-809-5309 395 F vancamp.connie@ptcollege.edu
VANCE, Gina, K ... 928-523-6747.. 14 J gina.vance@nau.edu
VANCE, Gina, M ... 724-946-7110 401 F vancegm@westminster.edu
VANCE, Justin ... 208-562-3449 131 C justinvance@cwi.edu
VANCE, Karen ... 814-865-3917 391 F ksv21@psu.edu
VANCE, Kristie ... 828-689-1353 330 H kvance@mhu.edu
VANCE, Lara ... 859-622-3436 180 B lara.vance@eku.edu
VANCE, Laura ... 828-641-0354 327 A lvancebc@gmail.com
VANCE, Mickey ... 601-635-6338 245 B mvance@eccc.edu
VANCE, Samantha ... 334-291-4974.... 1 H samantha.vance@cv.edu
VANCE, Shawn ... 225-771-2552 191 C svance@sulc.edu
VANCE, Shonna ... 903-730-4890 437 E svance@jarvis.edu
VANDAL, Mike ... 701-477-7862 346 H mvandal@tm.edu
VANDALEN, Wendy ... 985-867-2273 190 I vandalenw@sjasc.edu
VANDALOVSKY, Emily .. 201-879-7066 274 I evandalovsky@bergen.edu
VANDAVEER, Karen ... 406-496-4392 264 C kvandaveer@mtech.edu
VANDE YACHT, Daniel .. 920-465-2111 494 F vandeyad@uwgb.edu
VANDE ZANDE, Carleen ... 608-262-5089 494 C cvandezande@uwsa.edu
VANDEL, Laurie ... 406-496-4119 264 C lvandel@mtech.edu

VANDEMEULEBROEKE, Leon ... 973-761-9454 282 K leon.vandemeulebroeke@shu.edu
VANDEN BOOGAARD, Brad ... 806-874-3571 431 K brad.vandenboogaard@clarendoncollege.edu
VANDEN BOUT, David, A ... 512-232-0677 454 C cnsdean@austin.utexas.edu
VANDEN HOUTEN, Art .. 904-819-6274.. 99 D vandena@flagler.edu
VANDENAVOND, Steve . 906-227-2190 228 E svanden@nmu.edu
VANDENAVOND, Steve . 906-227-6767 228 E svanden@nmu.edu
VANDENBERG, Christine ... 908-852-1400 275 H christine.vandenberg@centenaryuniversity.edu
VANDENBERG, Matthew, P ... 864-833-2820 410 E
VANDENBERG, Theresa 712-279-1633 163 H theresa.vandenberg@briarcliff.edu
VANDENBOSCH, Kathryn ... 608-262-4930 494 D kate.vandenbosch@cals.wisc.edu
VANDENELZEN, Brad ... 715-346-3693 496 B
VANDER FEEN, Aimee .. 605-331-6602 416 C aimee.vanderfeen@usiouxfalls.edu
VANDER HART, Mark, D ... 219-864-2400 159 D mvanderhart@midamerica.edu
VANDER HEIDEN, Michael ... 920-498-6306 498 F michael.vanderheiden@nwtc.edu
VANDER HOEK, Nancy . 605-229-8545 414 I nancy.vanderhoek@presentation.edu
VANDER HOOVEN, James, L ... 978-632-0001 215 A jvanderhooven@mwcc.mass.edu
VANDER MAAS, Brittany ... 256-766-6610.... 5 F bvandermaas@hcu.edu
VANDER STOEP, Scott, D ... 616-395-7903 224 H vanderstoep@hope.edu
VANDER VALK, Frank ... 518-587-2100 320 B frank.vandervalk@esc.edu
VANDER VEEN, Lincoln 206-296-6116 483 B vanderv1@seattleu.edu
VANDER VEER, Lisa ... 815-939-5256 146 F lvanderv@olivet.edu
VANDER WAL, Jennifer 605-688-4491 416 A jennifer.vanderwal@sdstate.edu
VANDER WEELE, Dennis, A ... 845-368-7206 314 F dennis.vanderweele@use.salvationarmy.org
VANDER WERF, Dave ... 712-722-6020 165 E dave.vanderwerff@dordt.edu
VANDERBILT, Jonas ... 903-927-3291 457 I jvanderbilt@wileyc.edu
VANDERBILT, Robin ... 937-298-3399 354 J robin.vanderbilt@kc.edu
VANDERBILT, William ... 616-395-7850 224 H vanderbilt@hope.edu
VANDERBURGH, Paul, M ... 937-229-2345 362 C pvanderburgh1@udayton.edu
VANDERGHEYNST, Jean 508-999-8539 211 F jvandergheynst@umassd.edu
VANDERGIFF, Ronda ... 360-438-4356 482 D rvandergriff2@stmartin.edu
VANDERGRIFF, Rhonda 573-334-6825 258 I rvandergriff@sehcollege.edu
VANDERGRIFT, Donna .. 856-222-9311 280 E dvandergrift@rcbc.edu
VANDERGRIFT, Paul ... 919-516-4014 339 G pvandergrift@st-aug.edu
VANDERHEIDE, Peter ... 801-863-8818 460 A peter.vanderheide@uvu.edu
VANDERHILL, Dan ... 517-750-1200 230 F danv@arbor.edu
VANDERHOOF, Doug ... 620-241-0723 172 H doug.vanderhoof@centralchristian.edu
VANDERHOOF, Karen ... 973-328-5012 276 A kvanderhoof@ccm.edu
VANDERHOOF, Lara ... 620-241-0723 172 H lara.vanderhoof@centralchristian.edu
VANDERKAR, Caroline .. 805-756-2945.. 29 K cmoore36@calpoly.edu
VANDERMARK, Sarah ... 435-652-7500 459 G sarah.vandermark@utahtech.edu

VANDERMAUSE, Roxanne, K ... 314-516-7067 260 E vandermauserk@umsl.edu
VANDERMOLEN, Geoff ... 616-957-6045 221 K gav016@calvinseminary.edu
VANDERPOOL, Molly ... 765-973-8415 156 D moberry@iue.edu
VANDERPUYE, Archibald, W ... 512-505-3076 437 B awvanderpuye@htu.edu
VANDERSAL, Denise ... 412-651-1671 322 B denise.vandersal@touro.edu
VANDERSANDEN, Susan ... 608-663-2355 491 F svandersanden@edgewood.edu
VANDERSLICE, Ronna, J ... 580-581-2250 365 C rvanderslice@cameron.edu
VANDERSPOEL, James .. 906-932-4231 224 A jimv@gogebic.edu
VANDERVEEN, Kathleen 616-331-2662 224 D vandervk@gvsu.edu
VANDERVEEN, Sara ... 269-927-8611 226 B svanderveen@lakemichigancollege.edu
VANDERWOUDE, Geoffrey ... 315-386-7844 319 E vanderwoudeg@canton.edu
VANDERWOUDE, Katrina ... 213-891-2036.. 49 C vanderka@laccd.edu
VANDERZANDEN, Ann Marie ... 515-294-7184 163 E vanderza@iastate.edu
VANDERZEE, Lenore ... 315-386-7109 319 E vanderzeel@canton.edu
VANDERZWAAG, George ... 585-275-4301 323 E george.vanderzwaag@rochester.edu
VANDEURSEN, Marianne ... 908-835-2430 283 H vandeursen@warren.edu
VANDEUSEN, Scott ... 718-990-6240 313 B vandeuss@stjohns.edu
VANDEVEN, Alissa ... 573-651-2206 258 J avandeven@semo.edu
VANDEVILLE, Denise ... 906-487-7379 223 I denise.vandeville@finlandia.edu
VANDEWALKER, Richard ... 409-984-6520 449 D vandewalkerre@lamarpa.edu
VANDEWEERT, Lisa ... 616-632-2885 221 A lhv001@aquinas.edu
VANDEWEERT, Lisa ... 269-337-7410 225 B lisa.vandeweert@kzoo.edu
VANDIJK, Cindee ... 319-385-6495 167 F cindee.vandijk@iw.edu
VANDORIN, Robert, K .. 989-774-3068 221M careers@cmich.edu
VANDORN, Cody ... 805-756-1131.. 29 K cvandorn@calpoly.edu
VANDUSER, Trisha ... 817-735-2508 453 D trisha.vanduser@unthsc.edu
VANDUYN, Janet, A ... 570-561-1818 397 B
VANDYKE, Candice ... 845-687-5000 322 K vandykec@sunyulster.edu
VANDYKE, Diane ... 215-461-1143 390 A dvandyke@mc3.edu
VANDYKE, John ... 541-885-1452 374 G john.vandyke@oit.edu
VANDYKE, Ross ... 254-710-3555 430 F ross_vandyke@baylor.edu
VANECEK, Frank ... 802-485-2898 461 H vanecek@norwich.edu
VANEGAS, Jorge, A ... 979-845-1230 446 B jvanegas@tamu.edu
VANEMAN, Christopher 864-596-9038 407 G chris.vaneman@converse.edu
VANG, Chia ... 414-229-1101 495 B vangcy@uwm.edu
VANG, Koue ... 916-484-8484.. 50 J vangk@arc.losrios.edu
VANG, Mary ... 651-403-4147 240 E mary.vang@saintpaul.edu
VANG, Tou ... 828-448-6041 338 G tvang5@wpcc.edu
VANG, Touger ... 910-898-9651 336 A vangt@montgomery.edu
VANGEL, Darcy ... 508-213-2111 217 C darcy.vangel@nichols.edu
VANGELE, Jim ... 650-738-4455.. 62 K vangelej@smccd.edu
VANGILDER, JT ... 785-539-3571 175 F jt.vangilder@mccks.edu

VAUGHN, Andy .... 415-955-2001.. 25 A
VAUGHN, Bryan .... 903-886-5865 446 D
bryan.vaughn@tamuc.edu
VAUGHN, Caitlin .... 615-547-1307 418 C
cvaughn@cumberland.edu
VAUGHN, Chris .... 917-493-4486 304 L
cme@msmnyc.edu
VAUGHN, Debbie .... 931-598-1431 422 F
dsvaughn@sewanee.edu
VAUGHN, Evan .... 843-383-8082 407 C
VAUGHN, Gary .... 806-291-3549 457 B
vaughng@wbu.edu
VAUGHN, James .... 405-224-3140 371 B
jvaughn@usao.edu
VAUGHN, Katie .... 501-882-8826.. 17 H
klvaughn@asub.edu
VAUGHN, Kellie .... 270-789-5173 179 G
kpvaughn@campbellsville.edu
VAUGHN, Lamont .... 773-442-4044 145 G
l-vaughn@neiu.edu
VAUGHN, Laura .... 865-882-4553 424 D
vaughnlp@roanestate.edu
VAUGHN, Patricia .... 336-757-7381 334 D
pvaughn@forsythtech.edu
VAUGHN, Patti .... 617-585-0200 206 E
patti.vaughn@the-bac.edu
VAUGHN, Ronald, L .... 813-253-6201 113 B
president@ut.edu
VAUGHN, Sheila .... 508-362-2131 214 B
VAUGHN, Tanika .... 303-360-4914.. 80 C
tanika.vaughn@ccaurora.edu
VAUGHN, Tonya .... 662-620-5121 245 F
tlvaughn@iccms.edu
VAUGHN, Woodrow .... 256-726-7306.... 6 C
wvaughn@oakwood.edu
VAUGHN-TUCKER,
Daenel .... 318-487-5443 187 G
dvaughntucker@cltcc.edu
VAUGHT, Patrick .... 423-869-6241 420 A
patrick.vaught@lmunet.edu
VAUGHT, Wayne .... 801-863-8048 460 A
wvaught@uvu.edu
VAULTZ, Patrica .... 504-520-5237 193 C
pvaultz@xula.edu
VAUPEL, Christian, P .... 718-990-2781 313 B
vaupelc@stjohns.edu
VAVRA, Deborah .... 979-830-4241 430 I
dvavra@blinn.edu
VAZ, Pam .... 508-286-3485 219 F
vaz_pamela@wheatoncollege.edu
VAZ, Tammy .... 203-287-3036.. 88 D
paier.vaz@snet.net
VAZQUEZ, Airlyn .... 787-882-2065 508 N
avazquez@unitecpr.edu
VAZQUEZ, Carlo .... 412-237-3108 381 C
cvazquez@ccac.edu
VAZQUEZ, David .... 760-245-4271.. 74 D
david.vasquez@vvc.edu
VAZQUEZ, David .... 239-590-1121 109 G
dvazquez@fgcu.edu
VAZQUEZ, Dharma .... 787-758-2525 511 D
dharma.vazquez@upr.edu
VAZQUEZ, Edwin .... 787-738-2161 511 A
edwin.vazquez4@upr.edu
VAZQUEZ, Emsley .... 787-840-2575 508 G
evazquez@psm.edu
VAZQUEZ, Estrella .... 787-725-8120 505 J
evazquez@biblioteca.eap.edu
VAZQUEZ, Felice .... 908-737-7000 277 F
fvazquez@kean.edu
VAZQUEZ, Fermin .... 305-237-1152 104 E
fvazque2@mdc.edu
VAZQUEZ, Héctor .... 787-765-3560 505 H
hectorvazquez@edpuniversity.edu
VAZQUEZ, Harry .... 787-779-2500 504 K
VAZQUEZ, Heber .... 787-834-9595 508 O
heberv@uaa.edu
VAZQUEZ, Ingrid .... 787-850-9374 511 B
ingrid.vazquez1@upr.edu
VAZQUEZ, Ismael .... 787-864-2222 507 B
ismael.vazquez@guayama.inter.edu
VAZQUEZ, Jose .... 347-964-8600 291 F
jvazquez@boricuacollege.edu
VAZQUEZ, Juan .... 559-730-3700.. 39 C
juanv@cos.edu
VAZQUEZ, Katherine .... 787-738-2161 511 A
katherine.vazquez1@upr.edu
VAZQUEZ, Maria .... 787-725-8120 505 J
mvazquez0060@eap.edu
VAZQUEZ, Maria .... 531-622-2430 266 G
mvazquez@mccneb.edu
VAZQUEZ, Nelly .... 787-738-2161 511 A
nelly.vazquez1@upr.edu
VAZQUEZ, Obed .... 925-969-2423.. 40 H
ovazquez@dvc.edu
VAZQUEZ, Patricia .... 617-745-3851 208 F
patty.vazquez@enc.edu
VAZQUEZ, Respicio .... 847-214-7760 137 D
rvazquez@elgin.edu
VAZQUEZ, Robert .... 719-336-6653.. 81 J
robert.vazquez@lamarcc.edu
VAZQUEZ, Rosabel .... 787-620-2040 504 B
rvazquez@aupr.edu
VAZQUEZ, Rosalyn .... 518-861-2580 305 B
rvazquez@mariacollege.edu
VAZQUEZ, Sheila .... 787-622-8000 509 H
svazquez@pupr.edu
VAZQUEZ, Silvio, E .... 630-752-5562 152 K
silvio.vazquez@wheaton.edu
VAZQUEZ, Vilmaris .... 787-878-5475 506 J
vvazquez@arecibo.inter.edu
VAZQUEZ, Vivian .... 787-758-2525 511 D
vivian.vazquez4@upr.edu
VAZQUEZ-MARTINEZ,
Ernesto .... 787-622-8000 509 H
evazquezjr@pupr.edu
VAZQUEZ MEDINA,
Edwin .... 787-890-2681 510 C
edwin.vazquez7@upr.edu
VAZSONYI, Nicholas .... 864-656-3084 406 F
vazsony@clemson.edu
VEACH, Jason .... 816-268-5436 256 E
jveach@nts.edu
VEAL, Don-Terry .... 443-885-3035 200 F
don-terry.veal@morgan.edu
VEALE, Natasha .... 336-272-7102 329 B
natasha.veale@greensboro.edu
VEARA, Dennis .... 248-218-2018 229 I
dveara@rochesteru.edu
VEASLEY, Quintin .... 202-274-7254.. 94 B
quintin.veasley@udc.edu
VEATCH, John .... 818-667-2305.. 32 E
john.veatch@csun.edu
VEATCH, Laird .... 901-678-5395 426 A
lfveatch@memphis.edu
VEAZ, María, G .... 787-257-7373 509 B
m_veaz@uagm.edu
VEAZEY, Brooke .... 205-358-8543.... 8 D
bbrownlo@montevallo.edu
VECCHIARELLO,
Michelle .... 603-206-8002 272 A
mvecchiarello@ccsnh.edu
VECCHIO, Paul .... 607-871-2193 289 E
vecchio@alfred.edu
VECCHIO, Terry .... 508-854-4294 215 D
tvecchio@qcc.mass.edu
VECCHIONE, Tom .... 209-932-3042.. 71 E
tvecchione@pacific.edu
VEDDER, Kevin .... 931-372-3034 425 B
kvedder@tntech.edu
VEDDER, Lori .... 810-762-3444 231 C
lvedder@umich.edu
VEEDER, Heather .... 509-359-2681 478 H
hveeder@ewu.edu
VEEDER, Samantha .... 585-275-3226 323 E
sveeder2@finaid.rochester.edu
VEEGER, Anne .... 401-874-4408 404 E
veeger@uri.edu
VEGA, Aixa .... 787-834-9595 508 O
avega@uaa.edu
VEGA, Aymee .... 787-766-1717 509 C
avega@uagm.edu
VEGA, Cesar .... 760-355-6235.. 45 N
cesar.vega@imperial.edu
VEGA, Debra .... 928-317-6000.. 11 B
debra.vega@azwestern.edu
VEGA, Erlinda .... 787-264-1912 507 E
linvega@intersg.edu
VEGA, Esther, Z .... 787-850-9187 511 B
esther.vega@upr.edu
VEGA, Fabian .... 713-718-2445 436 E
fabian.vega@hccs.edu
VEGA, Francesca .... 415-476-4749.. 70 D
francesca.vega@ucsf.edu
VEGA, Fredrick .... 787-250-1912 507 C
fvega@intermetro.com
VEGA, Gregory .... 619-660-4030.. 44 G
gregory.vega@gcccd.edu
VEGA, Javier .... 212-592-2031 314 I
jvega@sva.edu
VEGA, Jesus .... 805-289-6507.. 74 B
jesusvega@vcccd.edu
VEGA, Lina .... 787-704-1020 505 B
lvega@columbiacentral.edu
VEGA, Magdalena .... 787-878-6000 506 B
mvega@icprjc.edu
VEGA, Manfredo .... 787-620-2040 504 B
mvega@aupr.edu
VEGA, Matt .... 731-989-6310 418 H
mvega@fhu.edu
VEGA, Michelle .... 909-607-0821.. 37 I
michelle_vega@kgi.edu
VEGA, Natalie .... 303-273-3569.. 79 A
nvega@mines.edu
VEGA, Victor .... 734-973-5185 232 A
vvega@wccnet.edu
VEGA, Waleska .... 787-761-0640 510 A
presidencia@utcpr.edu
VEGA, Zaida .... 787-766-1717 509 C
zvega@uagm.edu
VEGA-GEBOYEAUX,
Mario .... 787-993-8866 510 E
mario.vega3@upr.edu
VEGA-LA SERNA,
Jennifer .... 559-730-3823.. 39 C
jenniferl@cos.edu
VEGERANO, George .... 702-567-1920 270 D
gvegerano@lvcollege.edu
VEIL, Shari .... 402-472-3041 269 A
veil@unl.edu
VEIL-EHNERT, Jillain .... 218-299-3556 234 K
ehnert@cord.edu
VEILLEUX, John, M .... 989-774-3197 221 M
ucomm@cmich.edu
VEIT, Kathy .... 650-723-2300.. 66 D
VEIT, Kenneth, J .... 215-871-6770 395 A
kenv@pcom.edu
VEIT, Linda .... 315-464-4513 316 F
veitl@upstate.edu
VEITCH, Dionne .... 814-824-3315 389 E
dveitch@mercyhurst.edu
VELA, Cesar .... 956-721-5142 438 A
cvela@laredo.edu
VELA, Eddie .... 530-898-6171.. 31 A
evela@csuchico.edu
VELA, Jason .... 307-675-0889 500 F
jvela@sheridan.edu
VELA, III, Manuel .... 956-326-1300 446 A
manuel_vela@tamiu.edu
VELA, Robert .... 210-486-0959 427 H
rvela63@alamo.edu
VELA, Robert .... 361-593-3209 447 A
rvela@tamuk.edu
VELA, Robert, H .... 210-486-0959 428 D
rvela63@alamo.edu
VELASCO, Amy .... 805-756-2982.. 29 K
aevelasc@calpoly.edu
VELASCO, Anna .... 858-653-6740.. 46 L
avelasco@jpcatholic.edu
VELASCO, Ariana .... 530-661-5700.. 77 C
VELASCO, Debbie .... 612-767-7064 233 E
debbie.velasco@alfredadler.edu
VELASCO, Enrique .... 408-288-3762.. 62 G
enrique.velasco@sjcc.edu
VELASCO, Steven, C .... 805-893-2434.. 70 E
steven.velasco@ucsb.edu
VELASCO, Ulises .... 707-467-1037.. 51 F
uvelasco@mendocino.edu
VELASQUEZ, Ashleigh .... 708-293-4624 150 H
ashleigh.velasquez@trnty.edu
VELASQUEZ, Crystal .... 432-685-4675 439 E
crystalv@midland.edu
VELASQUEZ, Josephine 505-747-2162 287 C
josephine.velasquez@nnmc.edu
VELAZQUEZ, Carine .... 847-866-3900 138 B
VELAZQUEZ, Ginger .... 217-333-9634 151 F
gmayol@uillinois.edu
VELAZQUEZ, Jonathan .. 787-279-1912 506 L
jvelazquez@bayamon.inter.edu
VELAZQUEZ, Leida .... 787-864-2222 507 B
leida.velazquez@guayama.inter.edu
VELAZQUEZ, Marisol .... 787-864-2222 507 B
marisol.velazquez@guayama.inter.edu
VELAZQUEZ, Marisol .... 708-656-8000 145 B
marisol.velazquez@morton.edu
VELAZQUEZ, Monica, A 972-599-3144 432 I
mvelazquez@collin.edu
VELAZQUEZ, Raisa .... 888-820-1484.. 64 D
raisa.velazquez@sofia.edu
VELAZQUEZ, Tania .... 631-451-4475 320 G
velazqt@sunysuffolk.edu
VELAZQUEZ, Tania .... 631-451-4475 321 A
velazqt@sunysuffolk.edu
VELAZQUEZ-OLIVER,
Yoel, A .... 787-725-6500 504 F
yvelazquez@albizu.edu
VELDHEER, Kristine .... 773-371-5460 134 C
kveldheer@ctu.edu
VELDKAMP, David .... 407-278-4484 248 A
dveldkamp@rts.edu
VELEZ, Ada .... 787-878-5475 506 J
avelez@arecibo.inter.edu
VELEZ, Angel .... 787-250-1912 507 C
avelez@metro.inter.edu
VELEZ, Arlene .... 787-725-6500 504 F
arvelez@albizu.edu
VELEZ, Ashley .... 787-841-2000 508 H
avelez@pucpr.edu
VELEZ, Carlos .... 319-399-8000 164 D
cvelez@coe.edu
VELEZ, Carlos .... 802-443-5745 461 G
velezbla@middlebury.edu
VELEZ, Daniel .... 616-331-2025 224 D
velezd@gvsu.edu
VELEZ, Glenis .... 787-710-8999 505 D
glenis.velez@dewey.edu
VELEZ, Joel .... 787-841-2000 508 H
joel_velez@pucpr.edu
VELEZ, Larissa .... 214-648-2668 456 D
larissa.velez@utsouthwestern.edu
VELEZ, Rosa .... 787-264-1912 507 E
rosa_velez@intersg.edu
VELEZ, Vanessa .... 787-844-8181 511 E
vanessa.velez@upr.edu
VELEZ, Wanda .... 646-378-6181 289 F
wanda.velez@nyack.edu
VELEZ, Wilda .... 787-743-4041 505 B
wilda.velez@columbiacentral.edu
VELEZ AROCHO,
Jorge, I .... 787-841-2000 508 H
jivelezarocho@pucpr.edu
VELEZ-LUCE, Melissa .... 773-244-4796 145 F
mvelezluce@northpark.edu
VELEZ RIVERA,
Bienvenido .... 787-265-3822 511 C
decano.ingenieria@upr.edu
VELEZ-RUBIO, Miguel ... 787-993-8850 510 E
miguel.velez@upr.edu
VELEZ-RUBIO, Miguel ... 787-993-8850 510 B
rectoria.uprb@upr.edu
VELEZ-VENDRELL,
Norma .... 210-486-4516 428 A
nvelez-vendrell@alamo.edu
VELGUTH, Peter .... 989-317-4629 227 E
pvelguth@midmich.edu
VELIKY, Dawn .... 252-536-7227 334 G
rveliky004@halifaxcc.edu
VELKAVRH, Nick .... 562-907-4245.. 76 A
nvelkavrh@whittier.edu
VELKOFF, Townsend .... 570-321-4258 388 H
velkoff@lycoming.edu
VELLANOWETH, Rene .... 323-343-2000.. 32 B
rvellan@calstatela.edu
VELLECA, Kim .... 405-682-7595 367 D
kimberly.a.velleca@occc.edu
VELLIOS, Kathryn .... 908-709-7062 283 E
kathryn.vellios@ucc.edu
VELLUZZI, Nicholas .... 509-527-3685 484 B
nicholas.velluzzi@wwcc.edu
VELONI, Mary .... 888-777-7675 479 D
mveloni@faithiu.edu
VELORIA, Ruth .... 602-557-1544.. 16 L
ruth.veloria@phoenix.edu
VELTRI, Linda .... 541-684-7338 371 H
lveltri@bushnell.edu
VELTSOS, Jennifer .... 507-389-1334 238 L
jennifer.veltsos@mnsu.edu
VELVEL, Lawrence, R .... 978-681-0800 216 A
velvel@mslaw.edu
VELZY, Kevin .... 315-312-5555 318 B
kevin.velzy@oswego.edu
VEMALA, Prasad .... 412-397-3538 396 E
vemala@rmu.edu
VENABLE, James, E .... 901-722-3260 422 I
jvenable@sco.edu
VENABLE, Margaret .... 706-272-4436 118 A
mvenable@daltonstate.edu
VENABLE, Margo .... 856-227-7200 275 F
mvenable@camdencc.edu
VENCAK, Denise .... 718-990-1435 313 B
vencakd@stjohns.edu
VENCILL, Jason .... 276-964-7251 474 E
jason.vencill@sw.edu
VENDERLEY, Emily .... 260-481-6322 159 H
emily.venderley@pfw.edu
VENDIOLA, Rudy .... 360-676-2772 480 G
rvendiola@nwic.edu
VENDITTELLI, Deborah .. 734-462-4400 230 B
dventitt@schoolcraft.edu
VENDRELY, Ann .... 574-535-7503 155 B
dean@goshen.edu

Index of Key Administrators
VENDRICK – VIGIL 939

VENDRICK, Baxter 757-594-8987 465 A baxter.vendrick@cnu.edu
VENEGAS, Clare 972-721-5179 451 E cvenegas@udallas.edu
VENEGAS, Kristan 909-448-4930.. 71 C kvenegas2@laverne.edu
VENEGAS, Valerie, A 714-892-7711.. 38 E vvenegas@gwc.cccd.edu
VENEKLASE, Dave 616-732-1195 222 H dveneklase@davenport.edu
VENEMA, Cornelis 219-864-2400 159 D cvenema@midamerica.edu
VENERO, Sherri 715-682-1841 493 G svenero@northland.edu
VENERO, Sherri 715-682-1824 493 G svenero@northland.edu
VENETO, Dominic 904-256-7715 102 G dveneto@ju.edu
VENEZIA, Shannon 281-290-3776 438 E shannon.venezia@lonestar.edu
VENKAT, Rama 702-895-1094 270 J rama.venkat@unlv.edu
VENKATACHALAM, Venky 605-658-6517 415 E venky.venkatachalam@usd.edu
VENKATARAMAN, Latha 212-854-2255 296 H lv2117@columbia.edu
VENKATARAMANAN, Munirpallam, A 812-855-9011 156 C vpfs@indiana.edu
VENKATESH, Karthik 866-492-5336 243 G karthik.venkatesh@laureate.net
VENKATESWARAN, Anuradha 937-708-5633 363 G a1venkateswaran@wilberforce.edu
VENSKE, Nathan 269-965-3931 225 D vensken@kellogg.edu
VENTI, Kimberly, A 716-888-8220 291 M ventik@canisius.edu
VENTIMIGLIA, Phil 404-413-4701 120 C pventimiglia@gsu.edu
VENTO, Jaclyn 516-628-5021 318 A ventoj@oldwestbury.edu
VENTO-CIFELLI, Lauren 732-571-3562 278 B lvento@monmouth.edu
VENTURA, Bryan 714-484-7717.. 54 C bventura@cypresscollege.edu
VENTURA, Elizabeth, E 301-243-2045 501 J elizabeth.ventura@dodiis.mil
VENTURA, Heidi 615-248-1529 425 D hrventura@trevecca.edu
VENTURA, Jamey 802-635-1285 463 B jamey.ventura@northernvermont.edu
VENTURA, Valerie 617-573-8120 218 G vventura@suffolk.edu
VENTURA, Yoav 626-264-8880.. 71 F
VENTURA-MENDOZA, Oscar 703-284-5711 468 A oscar.ventura-mendoza@marymount.edu
VENUGOPALAN, Devarajan 414-323-9790 495 B dv@uwm.edu
VENUTI, John, A 804-828-1210 472 D javenuti@vcu.edu
VENUTO, Mary Clare 856-225-6756 281 A maryclare.venuto@rutgers.edu
VER BERKMOES, John 616-945-5300 222 F john.verberkmoes@cornerstone.edu
VER STEEG, Jennie, E 515-643-6612 168 B jversteeg@mercydesmoines.org
VERA, David 617-449-7070 219 B
VERA, Janet 714-484-7177.. 54 C jvera@cypresscollege.edu
VERA-DIAZ, Fuensanta 617-587-5685 216 H vera_diazf@neco.edu
VERA-MORALES, Sheila 787-480-2451 505 A svera01@sanjuan.pr
VERBECK, Susan 308-635-6101 269 E sverbeck@wncc.edu
VERBOSH, Kyle, W 717-871-7871 394 B kyle.verbosh@millersville.edu
VERCH, Christopher 507-457-1709 242 H cverch@smumn.edu
VERCHER, Kathy 318-678-6000 187 E kvercher@bpcc.edu
VERCHER, Kevin 318-473-6497 189 A kvercher@lsua.edu
VERDERAME, Michael 847-982-2500 138 G verderame@htc.edu
VERDERBER, Carl 845-752-3000 323 A carlv@uts.edu
VERDICCHIO, James 914-323-6001 314 H jverdicchio@sarahlawrence.edu
VERDIN, Regina 931-393-1828 423 G rverdin@mscc.edu
VERDUCE, Cynthia, P 260-422-5561 156 A cpverduce@indianatech.edu
VERDUGO, Jason 651-523-2035 235 F jverdugo@hamline.edu
VERDUZCO, Oscar 509-574-4937 485 E overduzco@yvcc.edu
VERES, Joe 602-639-7500.. 12 L
VERES, Karen 610-861-5344 391 B kveres@northampton.edu
VERES, Madalina 215-596-8800 400 B
VERGARA, Derek 714-432-5741.. 38 F dvergara2@occ.cccd.edu
VERGNETTI, Stephenie 570-702-8944 386 D svergnetti@johnson.edu
VERHASSELT, Holly 706-867-3281 126 G holly.verhasselt@ung.edu
VERHELST, Jason 608-245-2102 497 I jverhelst@madisoncollege.edu
VERHOEVEN, Martin 707-621-7000.. 41 F
VERHOFF, Monica 419-448-2452 353 D mverhoff@heidelberg.edu
VERKAMP, Brian 904-620-2018 111 A brian.verkamp@unf.edu
VERKAMP, Brian 270-809-2154 184 A bverkamp@murraystate.edu
VERKENNES, Joseph 734-384-4207 227 F jverkennes@monroeccc.edu
VERKRUYSE, Peter 217-732-3168 142 D pverkruyse@lincolnchristian.edu
VERKUILEN, Lena 815-965-8616 147 I
VERLANIC, Amy 406-496-4289 264 C averlanic@mtech.edu
VERLENGIA, Andrew 515-271-3077 165 F andrew.verlengia@drake.edu
VERMA, Neena 617-353-2230 207 C neenav@bu.edu
VERMEER ELLIOTT, Julie 712-707-7200 169 A julie.elliott@nwciowa.edu
VERMEULEN, Jeffrey 717-815-6601 402 G jvermuel@ycp.edu
VERMEYCHUK, Janice 609-771-2483 275 J vermeyj@tcnj.edu
VERMILLION, Laurel 701-854-8014 346 F laurel.vermillion@sittingbull.edu
VERMUND, Sten 203-785-2867.. 90 B sten.vermund@yale.edu
VERNAZA, Karinna 814-871-7912 383 H vernaza001@gannon.edu
VERNI, Christine 716-286-8124 309 F cverni@niagara.edu
VERNON, Andrea 406-243-5159 263 D andrea.vernon@umontana.edu
VERNON, Brian 203-837-8851.. 86 A vernonb@wcsu.edu
VERNON, David 973-655-4227 278 C vernond@montclair.edu
VERNON, Jim 970-829-4982.. 77 G jim.vernon@aims.edu
VERNON, Marc, T 757-825-2851 474 F vernonm@tncc.edu
VERNON, Marcel 603-228-3000 273 I
VERNON, Marcel 603-862-1234 273 H
VERNON, Sonja 513-721-7944 353 B svernon@gbs.edu
VERNON WHITE, Marisa 440-366-7622 355 B
VERON, Fabrice 302-831-6658.. 91 A fveron@udel.edu
VERRECCHIA, Lynn 508-793-2011 208 A
VERRET, C. Reynold 504-520-7541 193 C president@xula.edu
VERRICO, Tara, M 724-847-6532 384 B tmverric@geneva.edu
VERRILL, Tom 423-236-2816 422 H tverrill@southern.edu
VERSCHUYL, Molly 425-739-8223 480 D molly.verschuyl@lwtech.edu
VERSLUYS, Susan 512-472-4133 442 H susan.versluys@ssw.edu
VERSTANDIG, Kimberly 860-439-2408.. 87 F kimberly.verstandig@conncoll.edu
VERSTEEG, Deanna 605-274-4191 413 G deanna.versteeg@augie.edu
VERTA, Larissa, M 610-799-1517 388 B lverta@lccc.edu
VERTHEIN, Matt 602-243-8072.. 13 H matthew.verthein@phoenixcollege.edu
VERTIN, Diane 218-723-6012 234 J dvertin@css.edu
VERTREES, Larry 314-719-8024 252 G lvertrees@fontbonne.edu
VERWOERD, Fred 706-419-1129 117 G fred.verwoerd@covenant.edu
VERYSER, Joseph, C 248-204-2818 226 E jveryser@ltu.edu
VERZINSKI, Becky 301-860-3501 203 D bverzinski@bowiestate.edu
VERZYL, Scott 803-777-7700 412 A verzyl@mailbox.sc.edu
VESCIO, Sara, L 716-888-8285 291 M vescio11@canisius.edu
VESEI, Charles 440-826-3579 348 C cvesei@bw.edu
VESELY, Mark 910-521-6375 343 A mark.vesely@uncp.edu
VESELY, Pamela 828-898-8734 330 A veselyp@lmc.edu
VESHI, Susan 508-213-2227 217 C susan.veshi@nichols.edu
VESPASIAN, Bill 828-835-4211 338 C bvespasian@tricountycc.edu
VESPER, Josh 308-635-6185 269 E vesperj@wncc.edu
VESPERMAN, Katie 608-663-3224 491 F kvesperman@edgewood.edu
VESS, Paula 704-669-4101 333 C vessp750@clevelandcc.edu
VESSELLA, Thomas 562-988-2278.. 26 A tvessella@auhs.edu
VEST, Ann 502-456-6509 184 F avest@sullivan.edu
VEST, Daniel 772-462-7357 102 E dvest@irsc.edu
VEST, Eric 479-619-4345.. 20 G evest@nwacc.edu
VEST, Kevin 903-510-2178 451 D kevin.vest@tjc.edu
VEST, Margie 540-831-5008 468 E mbvest@radford.edu
VEST, Patricia Zurita 909-621-8503.. 57 K patricia.vest@pomona.edu
VEST, Rick 334-514-5070.... 2 F rick.vest@istc.edu
VESTAL, Amber 406-994-2343 263 G amber.vestal1@montana.edu
VESTER, Jonathan, S 252-451-8364 336 B jsvester529@nashcc.edu
VETERI, Kathleen 646-745-8361 290 H kveteri@barnard.edu
VETETO, Steve 303-779-6431.. 43 G stephenveteto@gs.edu
VETRANO, Dawn 718-779-1499 310 I dvetrano@plazacollege.edu
VETSCH, Angela 320-589-6173 243 C vetscham@morris.umn.edu
VETTER, Charlene, J 716-878-4436 317 C vettercj@buffalostate.edu
VETTER, Christopher 503-589-8180 372 G cvetter@corban.edu
VETTER, Kay 502-852-3551 185 E kay.vetter@louisville.edu
VETTER, Phyllis, J 801-585-7002 459 D phyllis.vetter@legal.utah.edu
VETTER, Shaun 559-934-2234.. 74 K shaunvetter@whccd.edu
VEUM, David 218-739-3375 236 B dveum@lbs.edu
VEVE, Mia 210-567-2648 455 E veve@uthscsa.edu
VEVERKA, Wolf 618-468-3130 142 B mveverka@lc.edu
VEYL, Traci 205-226-4676.... 5 A tlveyl@bsc.edu
VEYL, Traci 209-384-6034.. 52 B traci.veyl@mccd.edu
VEZINA, Michelle 859-344-3380 184 G vezinam@thomasmore.edu
VIA, Sandra 540-365-4394 466 I svia@ferrum.edu
VIAL, Theodore, M 303-765-3166.. 81 F tvial@iliff.edu
VIALA, Linda 212-686-9244 289 G
VIANDEN, Becky 608-785-8515 495 A bvianden@uwlax.edu
VIANO, Gavin 508-286-5699 219 F viano_gavin@wheatoncollege.edu
VIAR, David 818-240-1000.. 43 J dviar@glendale.edu
VIATOR, Lisa 806-742-3674 450 C lisa.viator@ttu.edu
VIAUD, Cindy 713-525-2162 453 H viaudc@stthom.edu
VIBBERTS, Richard 860-528-4111.. 87 H rvibberts@goodwin.edu
VIBOCH, Paul 304-263-6262 486 G pviboch@martinsburgcollege.edu
VIBROCK, Randy, G 662-329-7436 247 B rgvibrock@muw.edu
VICARS, Ron 276-523-7478 473 E rvicars@mecc.edu
VICE, David 916-900-2850.. 26 H dvice@asher.edu
VICENTE, Edward 787-279-1912 506 L evicente@bayamon.inter.edu
VICHALES, Kevin 210-832-2198 452 D vichcales@uiwtx.edu
VICHOREK, Jestina 218-733-7677 238 A jestina.vichorek@lsc.edu
VICK, Dustin 205-453-6300.. 93 H
VICKER, Kevin 816-584-6517 257 E kevin.vicker@park.edu
VICKERMAN, Pat 309-438-8901 140 C pvicker@ilstu.edu
VICKERS, Haley 580-559-5203 365 J hvickers@ecok.edu
VICKERS, Kelly, G 706-886-6831 126 C registrar@tfc.edu
VICKERS, LouAnn 503-838-8888 377 C vickersl@wou.edu
VICKERS, Neil, W 512-223-1098 429 J nvickers@austincc.edu
VICKERS, Selwyn, M 205-934-1111.... 8 A smv@uab.edu
VICKERS, Suzanne 850-644-1019 110 B svickers@fsu.edu
VICKERS, Tonya 912-871-7295 123 F tvickers@ogeecheetech.edu
VICKERY, Joseph 334-386-7274.... 5 D jvickery@faulkner.edu
VICTOR, Paula, T 562-903-6000.. 27 E paula.victor@biola.edu
VICTORINE, Jon 978-934-5060 211 G jon_victorine@uml.edu
VICTORINO, Christine 951-827-7883.. 70 B christine.victorino@ucr.edu
VICTORY, Gregory, J 919-660-1050 328 D gregory.victor@duke.edu
VIDAL, Betsy 787-704-1020 505 B bvidal@columbiacentral.edu
VIDAL, Karyn, J 561-202-6333 102 F
VIDAL-RODRIGUEZ, Angela 219-464-5255 162 C angela.vidalrodriguez@valpo.edu
VIDLER, Lynn 719-255-4550.. 84 A lvidler@uccs.edu
VIDMAR, Tony 254-968-9890 445 F tvidmar@tarleton.edu
VIDRINE, Tammy 225-768-1773 186 H tammy.vidrine@franu.edu
VIEIRA, Elvira 973-877-3062 276 G vieira@essex.edu
VIEIRA, Stephen 615-366-4451 423 A stephen.vieira@tbr.edu
VIELBIG, Matthew 425-235-7836 482 C mvielbig@rtc.edu
VIEN, Michele 518-694-7216 289 A michele.vien@acphs.edu
VIENNE, Charlie 936-294-1840 449 E cvienne@shsu.edu
VIENNE, Kristy 936-294-2274 449 E klv002@shsu.edu
VIENS, Donna 407-563-6501.. 95 C
VIENS, Rob 425-564-3158 477 B rob.viens@bellevuecollege.edu
VIERA, Eddie 561-868-3390 105 C vierae@palmbeachstate.edu
VIERA, Javier, A 847-866-3900 138 B
VIERNA, Natalie 501-374-6305.. 21 B natalie.vierna@shortercollege.edu
VIERTEL, Cynthia, S 920-748-8312 493 J viertelc@ripon.edu
VIESCA, Veronica 432-552-2663 456 C viesca_v@utpb.edu
VIETEN, Shaun 323-860-1137.. 53 D shaunv@mi.edu
VIEWEG, Johannes 954-262-1506 104 M jvieweg@nova.edu
VIG, Megan 701-788-5254 345 B megan.vig@mayvillestate.edu
VIGESAA, Linda 503-491-6928 373 H linda.vigesaa@mhcc.edu
VIGGERS, Victoria 915-831-6465 435 B vviggers@epcc.edu
VIGIL, Amanda 719-846-5551.. 83 I amanda.vigil@trinidadstate.edu

Index of Key Administrators VITO – WADDELL 941

VITO, Christine .... 704-499-9200.. 93 H
VITO, Christine .... 304-760-1700.. 93 H
VITRANO, Judy .... 504-314-2783 191 D
jvitrano@tulane.edu
VITTEK, Jeremy .... 740-695-9500 348 D
jvittek@belmontcollege.edu
VITTONE, Jason .... 800-995-3159 262 A
VITUCCI, Tom .... 954-262-7304 104 M
tomv@nova.edu
VITZELIO, Tom .... 951-571-6383.. 59 B
tom.vitzelio@mvc.edu
VIVANCO, Nayeli .... 617-746-1990 210 E
nayeli.vivanco@hult.edu
VIVEIROS, Derek .... 508-678-2811 213 F
derek.viveiros@bristolcc.edu
VIVIAN, Miranda .... 520-515-5489.. 11 O
mirandav@cochise.edu
VIVIAN, Richard .... 773-256-0710 143 C
richard.vivian@lstc.edu
VIVIANO-BRODERICK,
Tamara .... 352-854-2322.. 97 L
vivianot@cf.edu
VIZOSO, Elisabet .... 305-237-2222 104 E
evizoso@mdc.edu
VIZZIELLO, Daniella .... 203-582-7806.. 88 F
daniella.vizziello@quinnipiac.edu
VLACH, Erin .... 614-222-4000 351 A
evlach@ccad.edu
VLADESCU, Bogdana .... 914-674-7697 305 H
bvladescu@mercy.edu
VLAHAKIS, Stacy .... 312-261-3724 145 C
svlahakis@nl.edu
VLAHOS, John .... 408-741-4606.. 75 D
john.vlahos@westvalley.edu
VLAHOS, John .... 408-741-4606.. 75 C
john.vlahos@westvalley.edu
VLASIE, Schemamonk .... 530-467-3544.. 60 A
fv@spots.edu
VLASIK, Tonya .... 414-930-3627 493 E
vlasikt@mtmary.edu
VO, Alexander .... 212-812-4090 308 F
avo@nycda.edu
VO, Thoa Hoang .... 972-860-4604 433 G
tvo@dcccd.edu
VO-KUMAMOTO, Tram . 949-582-4625.. 65 C
tvokumamoto@saddleback.edu
VOAKLANDER, Ben .... 515-964-6375 164 F
bjvoaklander@dmacc.edu
VOCK, Jean .... 702-895-3571 270 J
jean.vock@unlv.edu
VODDEN, Jessica .... 423-439-1000 418 D
VODICKA, Kate .... 216-987-2283 351 D
kate.vodicka@tri-c.edu
VOEGERL, Michael .... 575-835-5060 286 D
michael.voegerl@nmt.edu
VOELCKER, Aaron .... 714-628-4990.. 58 G
voelcker_aaron@sccollege.edu
VOELKEL, Tyson .... 979-847-8700 446 B
tvoelkel@tamu.edu
VOELLER, Steve .... 602-827-2558.. 16 H
sjvoeller@arizona.edu
VOGAN, Randall .... 314-516-5478 260 E
vogan@umsl.edu
VOGEL, David .... 713-718-8208 436 E
david.vogel@hccs.edu
VOGEL, Janet .... 330-569-5353 353 F
vogelj@hiram.edu
VOGEL, Joanne .... 480-965-2200.. 11 A
joanne.vogel@asu.edu
VOGEL, Justin .... 859-344-3307 184 G
vogelc@thomasmore.edu
VOGEL, Richard .... 934-420-2189 320 C
richard.vogel@farmingdale.edu
VOGEL, Ronald .... 323-343-4600.. 32 B
rvogel@calstatela.edu
VOGEL, Tanya .... 202-994-8273.. 92 C
tvogel@gwu.edu
VOGEL, Terri .... 660-562-1153 256 G
tvogel@nwmissouri.edu
VOGELSANG, Ashton, J 570-961-4547 389 B
ajvogelsang@marywood.edu
VOGELWEID, Eric .... 573-882-2011 260 B
vogelweidej@umsystem.edu
VOGLER, Janelle .... 913-469-8500 174 F
jvogler@jccc.edu
VOGT, Elizabeth .... 940-565-2628 453 B
elizabeth.vogt@unt.edu
VOGT, Erica .... 239-513-1122 102 C
evogt@hodges.edu
VOGT, Kara .... 402-471-2505 267 F
kvogt@nscs.edu
VOGT, Marlene .... 815-479-7559 143 F
mvogt@mchenry.edu
VOGT, Peter .... 651-638-6659 233 J
p-vogt@bethel.edu
VOGT, Randy .... 559-243-7245.. 66 G
randy.vogt@scccd.edu
VOGT, Tracy .... 734-384-4230 227 F
tvogt@monroeccc.edu
VOGTMAN, Jena .... 715-319-7181 498 G
jena.vogtman@northwoodtech.edu
VOHRA, Amin .... 209-490-4591.. 24 H
avohra@advancedcollege.edu
VOIGHT, Robyn .... 903-463-8648 435 H
voightr@grayson.edu
VOIGT, Duane .... 408-554-4331.. 63 A
dvoigt@scu.edu
VOIGT, Julie .... 910-695-3715 337 E
voigtj@sandhills.edu
VOIGTS, Adam .... 515-271-3112 165 F
adam.voigts@drake.edu
VOIGTS, Sheryl .... 859-858-3511 178 H
sheryl.voigts@asbury.edu
VOISIN, Dexter .... 216-368-2270 349 B
drv22@case.edu
VOISS, S.J., James .... 414-288-6453 492 E
james.voiss@marquette.edu
VOITEK, Desiree .... 570-208-8505 386 G
desireevoitek@kings.edu
VOKES, Rebecca .... 231-591-2025 223 H
rebeccavokes@ferris.edu
VOKOUN, Cori .... 402-446-8459 267 J
csv@sampson-construction.com
VOLAK, Renee .... 201-692-2730 276 I
renee_volak@fdu.edu
VOLAKIS, John .... 305-348-0273 109 H
john.volakis@fiu.edu
VOLBRECHT, Adam .... 414-443-8689 497 A
adam.volbrecht@wlc.edu
VOLDEN, Eric .... 620-417-1105 177 C
eric.volden@sccc.edu
VOLDEN, Eric, D .... 620-417-1563 177 C
eric.volden@sccc.edu
VOLDEN, Lora .... 907-786-1266.. 10 A
llvolden@alaska.edu
VOLETY, Aswani, K .... 910-962-3030 343 B
voletyak@uncw.edu
VOLIBER, Delores .... 501-420-1238.. 17 D
delores.voliber@arkansasbaptist.edu
VOLIN, John .... 207-581-1547 196 D
VOLINO, Milissa .... 607-735-1890 298 G
mvolino@elmira.edu
VOLIS, Yelena .... 212-463-0400 322 B
yelena.volis@touro.edu
VOLK, Mari .... 701-224-5580 345 F
mari.volk@bismarckstate.edu
VOLK, Michael, S .... 616-554-5695 222 H
mvolk@davenport.edu
VOLKINBURG,
Heather Van .... 562-938-4623.. 48 K
hvanvolkinburg@lbcc.edu
VOLKMANN, Jeff .... 202-885-3500.. 91 D
volkmann@american.edu
VOLKMER, James .... 402-472-7677 269 A
james.volkmer@unl.edu
VOLKMER, James, S .... 402-472-7677 269 A
james.volkmer@unl.edu
VOLL, William .... 914-923-2772 310 F
wvoll@pace.edu
VOLLAN, Beth .... 605-688-4697 416 A
beth.vollan@sdstate.edu
VOLLAS VISCARIELLO,
Andrianni .... 848-932-7899 281 B
andrianni.viscariello@ruf.rutgers.edu
VOLLENDORF, Lisa .... 518-587-2100 320 B
VOLLER, Julie .... 480-461-7178.. 13 F
julie.voller@mesacc.edu
VOLLER, Julie .... 602-285-7558.. 13 H
julie.voller@phoenixcollege.edu
VOLLMER, Sara .... 701-224-5639 345 F
sara.vollmer@bismarckstate.edu
VOLLMER, Tiffany .... 620-441-5234 172 M
tiffany.vollmer@cowley.edu
VOLNA, Michael, D .... 612-625-9529 242 K
volna001@umn.edu
VOLNICK, Stacy .... 561-297-6319 109 F
svolnick@fau.edu
VOLOSHIN, Irina .... 206-296-2802 483 B
voloshii@seattleu.edu
VOLPATTI, Mark .... 219-464-5215 162 C
mark.volpatti@valpo.edu
VOLPE, Greg .... 856-222-9311 280 E
gvolpe@rcbc.edu
VOLPE, Jonathan .... 440-366-4051 355 B
VOLPI, Karla .... 575-234-9216 287 I
kvolpi@senmc.edu
VOLPI, Kirsten .... 303-273-3000.. 79 A
kvolpi@mines.edu
VOLRATH, David .... 828-641-0573 327 A
volratdl@brevard.edu
VOLTMER, Jill .... 816-271-4438 256 C
jvoltmer3@missouriwestern.edu
VON, Mary .... 503-352-7299 375 B
maryvon@pacificu.edu
VON ARB, David .... 515-643-6708 168 B
dvonarb@mercydesmoines.org
VON HEIN, Michele .... 401-598-1000 403 E
michele.vonhein@jwu.edu
VON LINDERN, Aaron ... 208-562-3322 131 C
aaronvonlindern@cwi.edu
VON NORDECK,
Marianne .... 410-516-8068 199 E
mvonnordeck@jhu.edu
VON VOGT, Lance .... 916-577-2200.. 76 C
lvonvogt@jessup.edu
VONDER HEIDE, Dan .... 773-508-6093 142 G
dvonder@luc.edu
VONDRAK, Jane, M .... 216-368-5094 349 B
jane.vondrak@case.edu
VONDRASEK, Tammy .... 507-453-2639 238 J
tvondrasek@southeastmn.edu
VONHANDORF, Teri .... 859-442-4173 181 D
teri.vonhandorf@kctcs.edu
VONREICHBAUER, Lisa . 231-591-2838 223 H
lisavonreichbauer@ferris.edu
VOORHEES, Derek .... 208-376-7731 130 E
dvoorhees@boisebible.edu
VOORHEES, Herschel .... 940-565-4911 453 B
herschel.voorhees@unt.edu
VOORHEES, Sinead .... 509-777-4604 485 D
svorhees@whitworth.edu
VORACHEK-WARREN,
Mara .... 636-922-8291 258 A
mvorachek-warren@stchas.edu
VORARITSKUL, Micah ... 423-614-8081 419 H
mvoraritskul@leeuniversity.edu
VORDERSTRASSE,
Allison .... 413-545-5093 211 D
dean@nursing.umass.edu
VORE, Mary Ellen .... 585-389-2906 307 D
mvore9@naz.edu
VORES, Andy .... 617-266-1400 206 D
avores@berklee.edu
VORFELD, Patti .... 603-899-4108 272 G
vorfeldr@franklinpierce.edu
VORKINK, Gerilynn .... 801-422-8985 458 A
gerilynn_vorkink@byu.edu
VORKINK, Keith .... 801-422-2640 458 A
kvorkink@byu.edu
VORMWALD, Sean .... 315-498-2847 310 C
vormwals@sunyocc.edu
VOROS, Tamiko .... 760-634-1771.. 28 G
VOROUS, Theresa .... 863-784-7123 108 D
theresa.vorous@southflorida.edu
VORSKY, Frances .... 518-454-5196 296 E
vorskyf@strose.edu
VORTHERMS, Kristie .... 605-367-5688 416 B
kristie.vortherms@southeasttech.edu
VOS, Dale .... 810-989-5671 230 A
dvos@sc4.edu
VOSBERG, Sarah .... 608-342-7636 495 E
vosbergsara@uwplatt.edu
VOSBURGH, Danielle .... 931-598-1446 422 F
dlvosbur@sewanee.edu
VOSBURGH, Tracy .... 540-231-5396 475 D
tracyv@vt.edu
VOSEVICH, Kathi .... 636-949-4564 254 B
kvosevich@lindenwood.edu
VOSEVICH, Mary, S .... 859-257-5929 185 D
mary.vosevich@uky.edu
VOSKANIAN, Vince .... 818-333-3558.. 53 J
vince@nyfa.edu
VOSS, Brian .... 864-656-8135 406 F
bdvoss@clemson.edu
VOSS, Bryan .... 414-847-3277 493 C
brianvoss@miad.edu
VOSS, Karl .... 570-577-3293 379 A
karl.voss@bucknell.edu
VOSS, Kenneth, L .... 314-516-6987 260 E
vossk@umsl.edu
VOSS, Lori .... 608-262-5936 494 D
lori.voss@wisc.edu
VOSS, Michael .... 480-461-7315.. 13 F
michael.voss@mesacc.edu
VOSS PLAXTON,
Catherine .... 408-924-6051.. 34 B
catherine.vossplaxton@sjsu.edu
VOTH, Aaron .... 320-363-5074 234 I
avoth001@csbsju.edu
VOTIPKA, Andrew .... 252-985-5101 339 B
avotipka@ncwc.edu
VOTTO, Stacy .... 860-832-3715.. 85 F
stacy.votto@ccsu.edu
VOUK, Mladen .... 919-515-2117 341 E
vouk@ncsu.edu
VOURNELIS, April, J .... 203-576-4914.. 89 A
vourneli@bridgeport.edu
VOUTSINAS, Mickie .... 305-899-3087.. 96 A
mvoutsinas@barry.edu
VOVES, Mary .... 509-359-4210 478 H
mvoves@ewu.edu
VOWELS, Kelly, J .... 913-360-7418 171 G
kvowels@benedictine.edu
VOWELS, Robert .... 313-993-1700 230 H
robert.vowels@udmercy.edu
VOYLES, Brad .... 706-419-1107 117 G
VOYTEK, Robert .... 928-226-4208.. 12 B
bob.voytek@coconino.edu
VRANCILA, Alin .... 503-255-0332 374 A
alinvrancila@multnomah.edu
VRANICH, Tracey .... 213-740-2211.. 73 C
vranich@usc.edu
VRBKA, Natalie .... 402-552-3100 265 G
vrbkanatalie@clarksoncollege.edu
VREELAND, Diana .... 906-227-2925 228 E
dvreelan@nmu.edu
VREKA, Mimoza .... 617-449-7070 219 B
mimoza.vreka@urbancollege.edu
VRIESMAN, Douglas .... 616-538-2330 224 B
dvriesman@gracechristian.edu
VROMAN, Mona, O .... 315-267-2120 318 D
vromanmo@potsdam.edu
VU, Cory, N .... 530-752-1730.. 69 A
jgcampbell@ucdavis.edu
VU, Dustin, L .... 563-588-7108 167 I
dustin.vu@loras.edu
VU, Mishu .... 657-278-7675.. 31 E
mishuvu@fullerton.edu
VU, Nancy .... 619-961-4325.. 68 A
nancyv@tjsl.edu
VU, Tony .... 303-860-5600.. 83 L
tony.vu@cu.edu
VU, Tuan .... 718-636-4551 311 A
tuanvu@pratt.edu
VUCELICH, Tom .... 412-809-5291 395 F
vucelich.tom@ptcollege.edu
VUI, Wendy .... 253-879-2732 483 G
wvu@pugetsound.edu
VUJNOVIC, Alison .... 918-495-7119 368 F
avujnovic@oru.edu
VUKOVICH, Matthew .... 605-688-6580 416 A
matthew.vukovich@sdstate.edu
VULLO, Russell .... 478-301-2409 122 C
vullo_ra@mercer.edu
VULLO, Stephanie .... 718-780-0605 291 G
stephanie.vullo@brooklaw.edu
VUORI, Kristiina .... 858-646-3100.. 62 L
kvuori@sbpdiscovery.org
VYSKOCIL, Cindy .... 949-582-4699.. 65 A
cvyskocil@socccd.edu
VYSKOCIL, Michelle .... 989-275-5000 225 H
michelle.vyskocil@kirtland.edu

W

WAACK, Jason .... 636-949-4738 254 B
jwaack@lindenwood.edu
WACASTER, David .... 704-406-4269 328 I
dswacaster@gardner-webb.edu
WACHLER, Brad .... 636-949-4777 254 B
bwachler@lindenwood.edu
WACHOWSKI, Robert .... 773-325-7762 136 F
bwachows@depaul.edu
WACHTER, Renee .... 715-394-8221 496 D
rwachter@uwsuper.edu
WACHTFOGEL, Marc .... 515-271-1400 165 C
WACHTOR, Kathryn .... 708-974-5344 144 G
wachtork@morainevalley.edu
WACK, Mary, F .... 509-335-8044 484 D
mwack@wsu.edu
WACKER, Robbyn, R .... 320-308-2122 240 C
presidentsoffice@stcloudstate.edu
WACTAWSKI-WENDE,
Jean .... 716-829-5374 315 F
jww@buffalo.edu
WACTOR, Tracy .... 864-646-1840 411 H
twactor@tctc.edu
WADA, Frank, Y .... 310-825-1443.. 69 D
fwada@registrar.ucla.edu
WADDELL, Adicia .... 504-520-7537 193 C
awaddell@xula.edu
WADDELL, James .... 313-831-5200 223 G
jwaddell@etseminary.edu

WADDELL, Jenetta .... 662-685-4771 244 D
jwaddell@bmc.edu
WADDELL, Kristin .... 501-202-7933.. 18 G
registrar@bhclr.edu
WADDELL, Stan, M ...... 412-268-1263 380 B
swaddell@cmu.edu
WADDLE, Brian .... 281-425-6336 438 B
bwaddle@lee.edu
WADDLE, Chris .... 402-461-2400 265 C
cwaddle@cccneb.edu
WADDLE, Valerie .... 281-649-3406 436 D
vwaddle@hbu.edu
WADE, Adam .... 919-718-7526 333 A
awade@cccc.edu
WADE, Alton .... 901-321-4102 417 G
awade2@cbu.edu
WADE, Angela .... 314-273-0744 253 A
angela.wade@barnesjewishcollege.edu
WADE, Argyle .... 608-263-5700 494 D
dean@studentlife.wisc.edu
WADE, Bernadette .... 914-674-7596 305 H
bwade@mercy.edu
WADE, Chandra .... 773-947-6285 143 E
cwade@mccormick.edu
WADE, Charles .... 810-762-0409 228 B
chuck.wade@mcc.edu
WADE, Courtney .... 413-597-4139 220 A
cwade@williams.edu
WADE, Damon, R .... 919-530-6682 341 D
dwade26@nccu.edu
WADE, Doug .... 503-517-1043 377 B
dswade@warnerpacific.edu
WADE, Elisabeth .... 707-664-2880.. 34 C
WADE, Eugene, V .... 626-966-4576.. 56 F
gene@agu.edu
WADE, Gourjoine .... 830-372-8060 448 C
gwade@tlu.edu
WADE, Gwen .... 404-880-8290 116 I
gwade@cau.edu
WADE, H. Keith .... 863-638-2940 113 E
wadehk@webber.edu
WADE, Ian .... 603-897-8615 273 B
iwade1@rivier.edu
WADE, Jason .... 541-346-2905 376 G
jwade@uoregon.edu
WADE, Jennifer, G .... 901-843-3850 422 C
goodloe@rhodes.edu
WADE, John .... 510-215-3804.. 40 G
jwade@contracosta.edu
WADE, John .... 847-635-2602 146 E
jwade@oakton.edu
WADE, Juli .... 860-486-2713.. 89 B
juli.wade@uconn.edu
WADE, Kevin, J .... 252-335-3271 341 A
kjwade@ecsu.edu
WADE, Kyle .... 864-587-4387 411 F
wadek@smcsc.edu
WADE, Landon .... 253-879-3651 483 G
lwade@pugetsound.edu
WADE, Lisa .... 901-722-3265 422 I
lwade@sco.edu
WADE, Noreen .... 516-572-7780 307 C
noreen.wade@ncc.edu
WADE, Raymond .... 417-447-4818 257 B
wader@otc.edu
WADE, Tamara .... 706-507-8800 117 E
WADE, Veronica .... 206-934-5216 482 H
veronica.wade@seattlecolleges.edu
WADE, William .... 662-621-4126 244 E
wwade@coahomacc.edu
WADE JOHNSON,
Regina .... 314-719-3627 252 G
rwadejohnson@fontbonne.edu
WADE SMITH, Michael . 814-865-4700 391 F
WADLEY, Melissa .... 405-744-6384 367 G
melissa.wadley@okstate.edu
WADLEY, Sue .... 740-366-1351 349 D
WADLINGTON, Corey ... 270-534-3413 182 G
corey.wadlington@kctcs.edu
WADLINGTON, Derek .... 717-264-2062 402 D
derek.wadlington@wilson.edu
WADSWORTH, Andrea .. 413-236-3001 213 E
awadsworth@berkshirecc.edu
WADSWORTH, Michael . 248-370-3352 229 F
wadsworth@oakland.edu
WADY, Andrea .... 972-686-7878 441 G
WAECHTER, Carolyn ..... 563-876-3353 165 D
waechter@dwci.edu
WAER, Amy, L .... 979-436-9051 446 B
waer@tamu.edu
WAERS, Stephen .... 706-385-1348 124 C
stephen.waers@point.edu

WAGEMESTER, Doug ..... 319-398-4909 167 H
dwageme@kirkwood.edu
WAGENBLAST, Thomas . 973-290-4265 282 G
twagenblast@steu.edu
WAGENER, Melanee ...... 513-244-4381 356 F
melanee.wagener@msj.edu
WAGENHEIM,
Christopher .... 717-396-7833 392 Q
cwagenheim@pcad.edu
WAGER, Lisa .... 212-217-4700 299 C
lisa_wager@fitnyc.edu
WAGERS, Karen, C .... 859-280-1236 183 C
kwagers@lextheo.edu
WAGES, Charlene .... 843-661-1140 408 H
cwages@fmarion.edu
WAGES, Kelli, E .... 419-434-6954 362 D
wages@findlay.edu
WAGESTER,
Kimberly, A .... 989-774-7388 221 M
wages1ka@cmich.edu
WAGGENER, Anna .... 301-243-2123 501 J
anna.waggener@dodiis.mil
WAGGONER, Earl .... 303-963-3485.. 78 D
ewaggoner@ccu.edu
WAGGONER, Jon, G ..... 334-844-4866.... 4 E
waggojg@auburn.edu
WAGGONER, Julia .... 715-682-1279 493 G
jwaggoner@northland.edu
WAGGONER, Randy, S . 882-354-3000 424 D
waggonerrs@roanestate.edu
WAGGONER, Reneau .... 502-213-3637 181 H
reneau.waggoner@kctcs.edu
WAGGONER, Todd .... 417-862-9533 252 H
twaggoner@globaluniversity.edu
WAGGONER, Wes, K .... 214-768-2110 443 G
wwaggoner@smu.edu
WAGLEY, Spencer .... 903-675-6282 451 C
spencer.wagley@tvcc.edu
WAGNAC, Evens .... 973-877-3040 276 G
wagnac@essex.edu
WAGNER, Alexander ...... 617-349-8509 210 H
alex.wagner@lesley.edu
WAGNER, Anthony, E ... 864-656-2421 406 F
wagnera@clemson.edu
WAGNER, Craig .... 715-422-5308 498 A
craig.wagner@mstc.edu
WAGNER, Dan .... 605-995-2145 414 A
dan.wagner@dwu.edu
WAGNER, Daniel .... 419-755-4817 357 B
dwagner@ncstatecollege.edu
WAGNER, Daniel, O ...... 419-755-4817 357 B
dwagner@ncstatecollege.edu
WAGNER, Darren .... 856-256-4728 280 H
wagnerda@rowan.edu
WAGNER, David .... 715-394-8070 496 D
dwagne13@uwsuper.edu
WAGNER, David, H .... 336-334-7880 341 C
dhwagner@ncat.edu
WAGNER, Deanna .... 614-236-6904 348 I
dwagner1453@capital.edu
WAGNER, OSB,
Francis DeSales .... 812-357-6611 160 G
fwagner@saintmeinrad.edu
WAGNER, Jeff .... 320-308-2286 240 C
jswagner@stcloudstate.edu
WAGNER, Jodi .... 509-527-2772 484 C
jodi.wagner@wallawalla.edu
WAGNER, Katherine ...... 516-572-7487 307 C
katherine.wagner@ncc.edu
WAGNER, Kevin, J .... 740-826-6129 356 H
kevinw@muskingum.edu
WAGNER, Kimberly .... 260-481-6103 159 H
kimberly.wagner@pfw.edu
WAGNER, Kimberly .... 847-214-7124 137 D
kwagner@elgin.edu
WAGNER, Kurt .... 732-571-4401 278 B
kwagner@monmouth.edu
WAGNER, Kyle .... 843-921-6901 410 B
kwagner@netc.edu
WAGNER, Lea .... 800-323-5692 347 G
lea.wagner@artacademy.edu
WAGNER, Linda .... 305-628-6699 107 D
lwagner@stu.edu
WAGNER, Marci, K .... 724-450-4089 384 F
mkwagner@gcc.edu
WAGNER, Mark .... 312-329-4131 144 F
mark.wagner@moody.edu
WAGNER, Mary .... 803-777-7700 412 A
mary.wagner@sc.edu
WAGNER, Megan .... 863-667-5205 108 I
mmwagner@seu.edu
WAGNER, Michael, F ... 413-597-4421 220 A
mfw1@williams.edu

WAGNER, Mike .... 309-556-3561 140 E
mwagner@iwu.edu
WAGNER, Nicholas, J ... 989-964-2468 229 L
njwagner@svsu.edu
WAGNER, Patrick .... 828-641-0322 327 A
wagnerpw@brevard.edu
WAGNER, Rich .... 612-381-3099 235 C
rwagner@dunwoody.edu
WAGNER, Richard, T .... 240-895-3421 201 F
rtwagner@smcm.edu
WAGNER, Robert .... 212-563-6647 323 A
r.wagner@uts.edu
WAGNER, Robert .... 607-274-5843 302 E
rwagner1@ithaca.edu
WAGNER, Robert .... 435-797-0945 459 F
robert.wagner@usu.edu
WAGNER, Robin .... 717-337-7000 384 C
rowagner@gettysburg.edu
WAGNER, Russell .... 361-825-2352 446 E
russell.wagner@tamucc.edu
WAGNER, Sam .... 814-886-6465 390 E
swagner@mtaloy.edu
WAGNER, Sharon .... 513-244-4273 356 F
sharon.wagner@msj.edu
WAGNER, Stuart .... 208-769-3300 132 A
WAGNER, Susan .... 520-795-0787.. 10 J
financialaid@asaom.edu
WAGNER, Todd .... 618-545-3259 141 C
twagner@kaskaskia.edu
WAGNER, Tonya .... 608-796-3376 496 L
tmwagner@viterbo.edu
WAGNER, Tracy, A .... 941-309-4376 106 J
twagner@ringling.edu
WAGNER DAVIS,
Jennifer (J.J.) .... 434-924-3252 471 F
jwd3n@virginia.edu
WAGNER-FOSSEN,
Dena .... 406-771-4312 264 B
dfossen@gfcmsu.edu
WAGNER-SCHULTZ,
Jessica .... 715-634-4790 491 L
jwschultz@lco.edu
WAGNON, Bill .... 601-635-6242 245 B
bwagnon@eccc.edu
WAGNON, Shelley .... 313-993-1588 230 H
wagnonsm@udmercy.edu
WAGNON, Stan .... 405-974-2500 370 H
swagnon1@uco.edu
WAGONER, Dale .... 510-723-6618.. 35 Q
dwagoner@chabotcollege.edu
WAGONER, Jessica, M . 909-869-3147.. 30 B
jmwagoner@cpp.edu
WAGONER, Natalie .... 301-687-4406 203 F
nmwagoner@frostburg.edu
WAGONER, Zandra, L ... 909-448-4446.. 71 C
zwagoner@laverne.edu
WAGSTAFF, Jennifer ..... 434-791-5624 463 L
jwagstaff@averett.edu
WAHFELDT, Tracy .... 217-373-3789 146 G
twahlfeldt@parkland.edu
WAHL, Lynette .... 651-523-3000 235 F
lwahl@hamline.edu
WAHL, Shawn, T .... 417-836-5247 255 J
shawnwahl@missouristate.edu
WAHL, Todd .... 812-749-1242 159 E
twahl@oak.edu
WAHLBECK, Paul, J ...... 202-994-6130.. 92 C
ccasdean@gwu.edu
WAHLROOS-RITTER,
Ingalill .... 818-252-5185.. 76 D
ingalill.wahlroos-ritter@woodbury.edu
WAHLS, Dustha .... 217-234-5210 141 H
dwahls@lakelandcollege.edu
WAHLS, Kathryn .... 605-394-2348 415 I
kathryn.wahls@sdsmt.edu
WAHLSTROM, David, A 617-989-4552 219 D
wahlstromd@wit.edu
WAHLSTROM, Tomi ...... 251-626-3303.... 7 E
twahlstrom@ussa.edu
WAHLSTROM HELGREN,
Elizabeth .... 312-567-6917 139 H
ewahlstr@iit.edu
WAHLUND, Tina .... 707-476-4100.. 58 I
WAHR, David .... 567-661-7401 359 H
david_wahr@owens.edu
WAHR, Linda .... 312-329-2213 144 F
linda.wahr@moody.edu
WAIAMAU-ARIOTA,
Kawika .... 425-235-2352 482 C
kwaiamau-ariota@rtc.edu
WAIBEL, Janet .... 573-882-2011 260 B
waibelj@umsystem.edu
WAIDE, Michael .... 304-376-4284 487 H
michael.waide@pierpont.edu

WAIDE, Michael, P .... 304-367-4284 487 H
michael.waide@pierpont.edu
WAIKART, Elise .... 801-626-5050 460 B
elisewaikart@weber.edu
WAINWRIGHT,
Christopher .... 386-506-3162.. 98 A
christopher.wainwright@daytonastate.edu
WAINWRIGHT, Philip .... 404-727-7504 118 D
pwainwr@emory.edu
WAINWRIGHT,
William, S .... 985-545-1500 188 B
WAINZ, Laura .... 314-246-7546 261 D
lwainz@webster.edu
WAIT, Julianna, M .... 757-594-7385 465 A
julianna.wait@cnu.edu
WAITE, Dan .... 848-932-7787 281 B
dwaite@global.rutgers.edu
WAITE, Dan .... 848-932-7787 281 C
dwaite@global.rutgers.edu
WAITE, Lucy .... 716-896-0700 324 A
lwaite@villa.edu
WAITE, Michelle .... 402-472-2116 269 A
mwaite1@unl.edu
WAITE, Peter .... 801-626-8957 460 B
pwaite@weber.edu
WAITE, Zauyah .... 413-559-5751 210 A
zwaite@hampshire.edu
WAITHAKA, Maina .... 847-970-4904 152 F
mwaithaka@usml.edu
WAITS, Jennifer .... 972-881-5174 432 I
jwaits@collin.edu
WAITS, Laura .... 713-221-5026 452 B
waitsl@uhd.edu
WAITSMAN, Eileen .... 410-462-7785 197 E
ewaitsman@bccc.edu
WAITZ, Emily .... 952-885-5417 241 P
ewaitz@nwhealth.edu
WAITZ, Ian, A .... 617-253-0218 215 G
WAIWAIOLE, Evelyn ...... 254-298-8766 445 B
evelyn.waiwaiole@templejc.edu
WAJDA, Phillip, J .... 518-388-6131 323 B
wajdap@union.edu
WAJERT, Susan .... 419-251-1314 355 G
susan.wajert@mercycollege.edu
WAKEFIELD, Larry, S .... 478-757-2083 127 D
lwakefield@wesleyancollege.edu
WAKEFIELD, Sarah .... 425-235-2285 482 C
swakefield@rtc.edu
WAKEM, Jake .... 651-641-8228 235 A
wakem@csp.edu
WAKEMAN, Roger, F ..... 315-859-4506 300 F
rwakeman@hamilton.edu
WAKIMOTO, Roger .... 310-825-7943.. 69 D
rwakimoto@conet.ucla.edu
WAKSDAHL, Robert, B .. 715-394-8017 496 D
rwaksdah@uwsuper.edu
WALBORN, Ronald .... 646-378-6171 289 F
ronald.walborn@nyack.edu
WALBURG, Wendy .... 320-629-5100 239 G
WALCERZ, Douglas .... 281-425-6440 438 B
dwalcerz@lee.edu
WALCHER, Sheldon .... 847-543-2551 135 G
swalcher@clcillinois.edu
WALCHESKI, Michael .... 651-603-6184 235 A
walcheski@csp.edu
WALCHLE, John .... 740-392-6868 356 G
john.walchle@mvnu.edu
WALCK, Barbara .... 716-614-5902 309 E
bwalck@niagaracc.suny.edu
WALCOTT, Ronald .... 706-542-6392 126 F
rwalcott@uga.edu
WALCROFT, Marie, B .... 215-699-5700 387 G
mwalcroft@lsb.edu
WALCZYK, Christine ...... 619-298-1829.. 65 J
WALD, Cara .... 561-803-2174 105 B
cara_wald@pba.edu
WALDBILLIG, Amy .... 513-569-1414 350 C
amy.waldbillig@cincinnatistate.edu
WALDEN, Barbara .... 989-275-5000 225 H
barb.walden@kirtland.edu
WALDEN, Daniel, W ...... 760-245-4271.. 74 D
daniel.walden@vvc.edu
WALDEN, David .... 315-859-4340 300 F
dwalden@hamilton.edu
WALDEN, Kyle .... 301-243-2150 501 J
kyle.walden@dodiis.mil
WALDEN, Lisa .... 505-277-7494 288 C
lwalden@unm.edu
WALDEN, Michelle .... 910-678-8372 334 C
waldenm@faytechcc.edu
WALDEN, Stacey .... 906-248-3354 221 I

WALLA, Bob .... 660-543-4001 259 K
walla@ucmo.edu
WALLACE, Ainsely .... 207-780-4461 196 J
ainsley.wallace@maine.edu
WALLACE, Alan .... 256-549-8317.... 2 B
awallace@gadsdenstate.edu
WALLACE, Andrea .... 912-279-5931 117 C
awalace@ccga.edu
WALLACE, Andrew .... 212-772-5462 294 A
aw4559@hunter.cuny.edu
WALLACE, Angela .... 815-455-8904 143 F
awallace90@mchenry.edu
WALLACE, Auguster ...... 662-254-3088 247 C
akeys@mvsu.edu
WALLACE, Bentley .... 870-864-7213.. 21 C
bwallace@southark.edu
WALLACE, Beth, D .... 864-597-4371 413 E
wallaceed@wofford.edu
WALLACE, Brent .... 903-510-2969 451 D
brent.wallace@tjc.edu
WALLACE, Chad .... 765-641-4374 153 D
cewallace@anderson.edu
WALLACE, Cheryl .... 908-526-1200 280 C
cheryl.wallace@raritanval.edu
WALLACE, Christina .... 910-938-6247 333 D
wallacec@coastalcarolina.edu
WALLACE, Christine ...... 810-762-9575 225 F
cwallace@kettering.edu
WALLACE, Darcie .... 770-426-2925 122 A
darcie.wallace@life.edu
WALLACE, David .... 270-534-3859 182 G
david.wallace@kctcs.edu
WALLACE, David .... 909-607-8095.. 57 K
david.wallace@pomona.edu
WALLACE, Debbie .... 870-543-5996.. 21 D
dwallace@seark.edu
WALLACE, Deborah .... 310-243-3750.. 31 B
dwallace@csudh.edu
WALLACE, Denise .... 850-599-3591 109 E
denise.wallace@famu.edu
WALLACE, Donald .... 760-921-5499.. 56 A
donald.wallace@paloverde.edu
WALLACE, Douglas, J ... 864-833-8312 410 E
dwallace@presby.edu
WALLACE, Elaine .... 954-262-1407 104 M
ewallace@nova.edu
WALLACE, Eric, C .... 806-356-3682 428 F
ecwallace@actx.edu
WALLACE, G. Brent ...... 940-668-4230 439 I
bwallace@nctc.edu
WALLACE, Glenn .... 912-525-5000 124 G
gwallace@scad.edu
WALLACE, Greg .... 617-879-7000 212 E
greg.wallace@massart.edu
WALLACE, Harold .... 931-221-6274 416 H
wallaceh@apsu.edu
WALLACE, JR., James .. 219-980-6601 157 A
jamewall@iun.edu
WALLACE, Janice .... 870-633-4480.. 19 E
jwallace@eacc.edu
WALLACE, Jeff .... 765-998-5396 161 A
jfwallace@taylor.edu
WALLACE, Jeremy .... 303-963-3237.. 78 D
jerwallace@ccu.edu
WALLACE, Jerry .... 910-893-1880 327 C
wallace@campbell.edu
WALLACE, Jerry .... 434-797-8400 472 H
jerry.wallace@danville.edu
WALLACE, John, M .... 412-624-5749 400 A
johnw@pitt.edu
WALLACE, Joseph .... 740-284-5860 352 I
jwallace@franciscan.edu
WALLACE, Justin .... 661-362-3788.. 38 H
justin.wallace@canyons.edu
WALLACE, Kim .... 303-404-5671.. 80 I
kim.wallace@frontrange.edu
WALLACE, Kim .... 303-404-5316.. 81 J
kim.wallace@frontrange.edu
WALLACE, Kimberly ...... 239-590-1087 109 G
kwilliam@fgcu.edu
WALLACE, Kristen .... 662-252-8000 248 B
kwallace@rustcollege.edu
WALLACE, Laurie .... 314-744-5321 255 H
wallace@mobap.edu
WALLACE, Leigh .... 229-217-4143 125 G
lwallace@southernregional.edu
WALLACE, Lynn .... 610-526-1327 378 D
lynn.wallace@theamericancollege.edu
WALLACE, Matthew, L .. 603-931-4369 274 B
mlwallace@plymouth.edu
WALLACE, Mike, J .... 408-554-4981.. 63 A
mjwallace@scu.edu
WALLACE, Miriam .... 941-487-4360 110 C
mwallace@ncf.edu
WALLACE, Nancy .... 716-888-2768 291 M
wallacen@canisius.edu
WALLACE, Patrick .... 856-225-6095 281 A
WALLACE, Paula .... 912-525-5000 124 G
pwallace@scad.edu
WALLACE, Robert .... 903-657-6543 447 F
rwallace@tbi.edu
WALLACE, Robert .... 718-982-2355 293 C
robert.wallace@csi.cuny.edu
WALLACE, Robert .... 650-723-2300.. 66 D
WALLACE, Robert .... 304-766-4114 489 D
wallacer@wvstateu.edu
WALLACE, Sally .... 404-413-0046 120 C
swallace@gsu.edu
WALLACE, Sam, G .... 318-257-2769 192 A
wallace@latech.edu
WALLACE, Scott .... 706-737-1411 115 I
scwallace@augusta.edu
WALLACE, Steve .... 501-977-2086.. 23 D
wallace@uaccm.edu
WALLACE, Suzanne .... 608-663-8334 491 F
suzwallace@edgewood.edu
WALLACE, Tamara .... 540-831-6374 468 E
twallace8@radford.edu
WALLACE, Tami .... 615-230-3573 424 F
tami.wallace@volstate.edu
WALLACE, Tania .... 870-368-2010.. 20 I
tania.wallace@ozarka.edu
WALLACE, Thomas .... 661-654-2161.. 30 C
twallace4@csub.edu
WALLACE, Tracy .... 229-430-3867 114 G
twallace@albanytech.edu
WALLACE, Zachary .... 503-352-2205 375 B
zwallace@pacificu.edu
WALLACK, Jessica .... 253-589-5734 478 A
jessica.wallack@cptc.edu
WALLAERT, Kerry .... 706-880-8112 121 K
kwallaert@lagrange.edu
WALLEN, Jillian .... 402-280-5061 265 J
jillianwallen@creighton.edu
WALLENMEYER, Mark ... 479-619-4310.. 20 G
mwallenmeyer@nwacc.edu
WALLER, Cynthia, G ..... 615-353-3645 424 A
cynthia.waller@nscc.edu
WALLER, Edward .... 281-283-3100 452 A
waller@uhcl.edu
WALLER, J. Kerry .... 706-778-8500 124 B
WALLER, J.J .... 912-525-5000 124 G
jwaller@scad.edu
WALLER, Janet .... 256-824-7777.... 8 B
janet.waller@uah.edu
WALLER, Karen .... 615-230-3500 424 F
karen.waller@volstate.edu
WALLER, Lorie .... 919-739-6757 338 F
loriew@waynecc.edu
WALLER, Louise .... 434-395-2358 467 F
wallermw@longwood.edu
WALLER, Matthew .... 479-575-5949.. 21 H
mwaller@uark.edu
WALLER, Michelle .... 318-473-6443 189 A
cwaller001@lsua.edu
WALLER, Rhonda .... 336-278-5185 328 H
rwaller3@elon.edu
WALLER, Stephen .... 661-395-4642.. 47 B
swaller@bakersfieldcollege.edu
WALLER-RANDLES,
Jill, A .... 559-323-2100.. 61 G
jrandles@sjcl.edu
WALLESHAUSER,
Linda, M .... 716-888-2244 291 M
walleshl@canisius.edu
WALLETT, Robert .... 215-248-7163 380 G
wallett@chc.edu
WALLEY, Jennifer .... 559-251-4215.. 28 B
jwalley@calchristiancollege.edu
WALLEY, Jim .... 601-477-4173 246 A
jim.walley@jcjc.edu
WALLEY, Katrina .... 575-769-4034 285 C
katrina.walley@clovis.edu
WALLEY, Trent .... 559-251-4215.. 28 B
twalley@calchristiancollege.edu
WALLHAUSSER, Karl ..... 606-546-1424 185 B
kwallhausser@unionky.edu
WALLIN, Cynthia .... 434-832-7707 472 G
wallinc@centralvirginia.edu
WALLIN, Gail .... 254-519-8025 446 C
gwallin@tamuct.edu
WALLIN, John .... 603-862-1234 273 H
john.wallin@unh.edu
WALLIN, Jon .... 540-261-4095 470 D
jon.wallin@svu.edu
WALLIN, Jonathan .... 540-261-8400 470 D
jon.wallin@svu.edu
WALLIN, Julie .... 917-493-4595 304 L
jwallin@msmnyc.edu
WALLIN, Kimberly .... 701-231-7411 345 D
kimberly.wallin@ndsu.edu
WALLING, Lisa .... 931-526-3660 418 F
lisaq.walling@fortisinstitute.edu
WALLINGA, Willem .... 617-670-4457 209 D
wwallinga@fisher.edu
WALLINGTON, Jamison 323-668-7555.. 25 I
WALLINGTON-HARRIS,
Danielle .... 773-907-6834 134 N
dwallington-harris@ccc.edu
WALLIS, Don .... 419-755-4210 357 B
wallis.10@osu.edu
WALLIS, Donna .... 931-372-3492 425 B
dwallis@tntech.edu
WALLIS, Matthew .... 817-257-5808 447 H
matthew.wallis@tcu.edu
WALLIS, Sherry, L .... 660-263-3900 250 G
sherrywallis@cccb.edu
WALLMAN, Eric .... 407-582-2814 113 C
ewallman@valenciacollege.edu
WALLMAN, Marc .... 701-231-8640 345 D
marc.wallman@ndsu.edu
WALLNER, Heidi .... 715-346-2926 496 B
hwallner@uwsp.edu
WALLNER, Steve .... 262-595-2451 495 D
wallner@uwp.edu
WALLS, Caitlin .... 907-319-8755.... 9 H
caitlin.walls@ilisagvik.edu
WALLS, Eric, R .... 210-562-6201 455 E
wallse@uthscsa.edu
WALLS, Harry .... 661-362-2620.. 51 E
hwalls@masters.edu
WALLS, Keith .... 610-921-6619 377 F
kwalls@albright.edu
WALLS, Maryanna .... 301-962-5111 205 B
mwalls@yeshiva.edu
WALLS, Randy .... 417-865-2815 249 G
wallsr@evangel.edu
WALLS, Renee .... 870-230-5640.. 19 H
wallsr@hsu.edu
WALLS-MCKAY,
Maureen, J .... 434-395-2409 467 F
wallsmckaymj@longwood.edu
WALMSLEY, Fran .... 215-713-4171 390 G
walmesf@neumann.edu
WALPIN, Edward .... 505-984-6050 287 F
edward.walpin@sjc.edu
WALPOLE, Tommy .... 318-342-5419 193 A
walpole@ulm.edu
WALROND, LaKeesha ... 212-870-1222 309 C
lwalrond@nyts.edu
WALSH, Bernadette .... 610-359-5040 381 J
bwalsh@dccc.edu
WALSH, Beth .... 630-752-5072 152 K
beth.walsh@wheaton.edu
WALSH, Brendan .... 845-451-1616 297 E
brendan.walsh@culinary.edu
WALSH, Carolyn .... 815-479-7837 143 F
cwalsh97@mchenry.edu
WALSH, Christopher ..... 410-777-2528 197 C
clwirth@aacc.edu
WALSH, Clifton .... 915-747-6636 454 E
cwalsh@utep.edu
WALSH, Daniel .... 773-244-5236 145 F
dewalsh@northpark.edu
WALSH, Debra .... 323-469-3300.. 25 G
dwalsh@amda.edu
WALSH, Elizabeth, K ...... 610-660-1000 397 A
lkwalsh@sju.edu
WALSH, Eric .... 603-524-3207 271 K
ewalsh@ccsnh.edu
WALSH, Gayle .... 803-712-7301 412 E
gwalsh@mailbox.sc.edu
WALSH, Jack .... 724-266-3838 399 F
jwalsh@tsm.edu
WALSH, James .... 209-946-2011.. 71 E
WALSH, Jay .... 217-244-2119 151 C
jaywalsh@uillinois.edu
WALSH, Jennifer .... 808-544-0216 128 E
provost@hpu.edu
WALSH, Jennifer .... 516-877-4687 288 L
jenwalsh@adelph.edu
WALSH, Jill .... 484-664-3165 390 F
jillwalsh@muhlenberg.edu
WALSH, Joe .... 205-665-6520.... 8 D
walshj@montevallo.edu
WALSH, Julie .... 845-257-2632 316 B
walshj@newpaltz.edu
WALSH, Kate, D .... 607-255-5106 297 D
kmw33@cornell.edu
WALSH, Kenneth .... 703-993-1000 466 J
WALSH, Kimberly, A ...... 563-588-7417 167 I
kimberly.walsh@loras.edu
WALSH, Konrad .... 336-734-7495 334 D
kwalsh@forsythtech.edu
WALSH, Lenore, J .... 516-876-4974 318 A
walshle@oldwestbury.edu
WALSH, Mark .... 813-974-2660 111 B
mwalsh@usf.edu
WALSH, Mary .... 785-864-4999 177 G
marywalsh@ku.edu
WALSH, Megan .... 716-375-2447 312 F
mwalsh@sbu.edu
WALSH, Meghan .... 414-382-6089 490 G
meghan.walsh@alverno.edu
WALSH, Melissa .... 215-345-1500 381 K
melissa.walsh@delval.edu
WALSH, Michael .... 518-631-9846 295 E
mwalsh@clarkson.edu
WALSH, Michael .... 508-531-2840 212 B
m6walsh@bridgew.edu
WALSH, Michelle .... 845-437-7452 323 H
miwalsh@vassar.edu
WALSH, Molly .... 215-951-1650 386 I
WALSH, Patrick .... 541-684-7244 371 H
pwalsh@bushnell.edu
WALSH, CSC, Peter .... 503-943-7130 376 H
walshp@up.edu
WALSH, Susan .... 541-552-6114 376 A
walsh@sou.edu
WALSH, Susan, E .... 609-258-6207 279 E
swalsh@princeton.edu
WALSH, Suzanne, E ...... 336-273-4431 326 J
suzanne.walsh@bennett.edu
WALSH, Tammy, S .... 941-359-7505 106 J
twalsh@ringling.edu
WALSH, Teresa .... 732-255-0400 279 A
twalsh@ocean.edu
WALSH, Tim .... 386-226-6000.. 98 J
walsht10@erau.edu
WALSH-DAVIS,
Nicholas .... 818-785-2726.. 35 K
nicholas.walsh-davis@casalomacollege.edu
WALSH FITZPATRICK,
Mary .... 518-445-2377 289 B
mfitz@albanylaw.edu
WALSHOK, Mary, L .... 858-534-3411.. 70 C
mwalshok@ucsd.edu
WALSINGHAM, Kelli ..... 850-873-3514 101 O
kwalsingham@gulfcoast.edu
WALSTAD, Annette .... 406-447-5434 262 E
awalstad@carroll.edu
WALSTEAD, Brenda .... 360-992-2474 477 J
bwalstead@clark.edu
WALSTON, Angie .... 252-399-6313 326 H
amwalston@barton.edu
WALSTON, Dustin .... 910-275-6252 335 C
dwalston@jamessprunt.edu
WALSTON, Tim .... 660-785-4248 259 J
tdwalston@truman.edu
WALTENBERGER, Don ... 641-683-5154 166 F
don.waltenberger@indianhills.edu
WALTER, Ally, P .... 515-574-1140 166 G
walter@iowacentral.edu
WALTER, Almar .... 614-287-2735 351 B
awalter3@cscc.edu
WALTER, Elizabeth .... 660-263-3900 250 G
elizabethwalter@cccb.edu
WALTER, Jim .... 706-355-5120 115 C
jwalter@athenstech.edu
WALTER, Joey .... 850-201-6038 112 B
joey.walter@tcc.fl.edu
WALTER, Josh .... 503-768-7921 373 D
jwalter@lclark.edu
WALTER, Kelly, A .... 617-353-3530 207 C
kwalter@bu.edu
WALTER, Kristy .... 617-243-2147 210 G
kwalter@lasell.edu
WALTER, Margaret .... 530-752-2300.. 69 A
matrout@ucdavis.edu
WALTER, Mary Beth ...... 937-327-7517 364 C
walterm@wittenberg.edu
WALTER, Robyn .... 636-584-6601 252 D
robyn.walter@eastcentral.edu
WALTER, Shulem .... 718-855-4092 311 F
swalter@rcosy.org
WALTER, Willis, W .... 804-524-6869 475 E
wwalter@vsu.edu
WALTERREIT, Jay .... 989-358-7215 220 G
walterrj@alpenacc.edu

WARD, Heather .... 316-322-3121 172 B
hmward@butlercc.edu
WARD, Heather .... 919-962-1051 342 B
heather.ward@unc.edu
WARD, IV, James .... 207-581-2201 196 D
jsward@maine.edu
WARD, Jamie .... 417-455-5636 251 H
jamieward@crowder.edu
WARD, Jeff .... 617-732-2896 216 B
jward@mcphs.edu
WARD, Jenifer, K .... 563-387-1001 167 J
president@luther.edu
WARD, John .... 610-683-4253 394 A
ward@kutztown.edu
WARD, John, A .... 513-529-4634 356 A
wardja2@miamioh.edu
WARD, Joseph .... 435-797-1195 459 F
joe.ward@usu.edu
WARD, Joy, K .... 216-368-4437 349 B
joy.ward@case.edu
WARD, Kathy .... 501-882-8831.. 17 H
kward@asub.edu
WARD, Kris .... 575-624-8319 286 F
wardk@nmmi.edu
WARD, Laurie .... 301-696-3803 199 C
ward@hood.edu
WARD, Lawrence, P ..... 781-239-5346 205 B
lward@babson.edu
WARD, Leslie Colis ...... 802-828-8631 462 E
leslie.ward@vcfa.edu
WARD, Luke .... 847-317-8192 150 J
lsward@tiu.edu
WARD, Lynne .... 801-321-7157 459 C
lward@utahsbr.edu
WARD, Marcus, D .... 601-877-6296 244 B
mdward@alcorn.edu
WARD, Mark .... 563-589-3115 170 C
ward@ncat.edu
WARD, Matthew .... 805-493-3481.. 29 E
mward@callutheran.edu
WARD, Michael .... 314-362-9155 253 A
michael.ward@barnesjewishcollege.edu
WARD, Michael .... 973-408-3000 276 B
mward@drew.edu
WARD, Michael .... 336-838-6489 338 H
mrward284@wilkescc.edu
WARD, Michael, S .... 334-833-4463.. 5 H
mward@hawks.huntingdon.edu
WARD, Mike .... 270-686-9572 179 F
mike.ward@brescia.edu
WARD, Monica .... 770-426-2611 122 A
monica.ward@life.edu
WARD, Patricia .... 510-666-8248.. 24 G
pward@aimc.edu
WARD, Paul, J .... 214-768-3233 443 G
paulw@smu.edu
WARD, Randall .... 617-364-3510 206 F
rward@boston.edu
WARD, Rhonda .... 740-725-4017 355 F
wardr@mtc.edu
WARD, Robert .... 714-564-6319.. 58 F
ward_robert@sac.edu
WARD, Robert, A .... 585-385-8310 313 A
bward@sjfc.edu
WARD, Roger, J .... 410-706-2477 202 F
rward@umaryland.edu
WARD, Rose Marie ...... 513-556-4335 361 I
wardrm@ucmail.uc.edu
WARD, Russ .... 609-759-7141 182 B
russ.ward@kctcs.edu
WARD, Ryan .... 406-586-3585 263 A
ryan.ward@montanabiblecollege.edu
WARD, Scott .... 231-843-5802 232 I
scward@westshore.edu
WARD, Shenika .... 910-695-3952 337 E
wards@sandhills.edu
WARD, Stephen .... 330-672-8533 354 A
sward52@kent.edu
WARD, Steve .... 605-658-3600 415 E
steve.ward@usd.edu
WARD, Susan .... 208-496-7720 130 G
wards@byui.edu
WARD, Suzanne .... 870-584-1403.. 22 G
sward@cccua.edu
WARD, Tamica .... 925-424-1542.. 36 A
tward@laspositascollege.edu
WARD, Tara .... 818-364-7780.. 49 G
wardtht@lamission.edu
WARD, Theresa .... 518-454-2147 296 E
wardt@strose.edu
WARD, Thomas .... 212-563-6647 323 A
ward@uts.edu
WARD, JR., Thomas, J 516-877-3131 288 L
tward@adelphi.edu

WARD, Tim .... 718-862-7307 304 K
tim.ward@manhattan.edu
WARD, Tony .... 334-727-8364.... 7 D
tward@tuskegee.edu
WARD, Tony .... 605-455-6057 414 H
tward@olc.edu
WARD, Tracy .... 951-343-4552.. 27 J
tward@calbaptist.edu
WARD, Tracy .... 910-275-6376 335 C
tward@jamessprunt.edu
WARD, Vicki .... 979-830-4347 430 I
vicki.ward@blinn.edu
WARD, Virginia .... 617-427-7293 209 G
vward@gordonconwell.edu
WARD, Wanda, E .... 217-265-0451 151 F
weward@illinois.edu
WARD, William .... 360-867-6115 479 C
wardw@evergreen.edu
WARD-JOHNSON,
Frances .... 336-334-7806 341 C
fward@ncat.edu
WARD-PERADOZA,
Marianne .... 512-448-8446 441 N
mperadoz@stedwards.edu
WARD-ROOF, Jeanine .. 231-591-3578 223 H
jeaninewardroof@ferris.edu
WARDE, Robin, T .... 401-232-6253 403 B
rwarde@bryant.edu
WARDEN, Chris .... 510-659-7382.. 54 J
cwarden@ohlone.edu
WARDEN, Joel .... 718-522-2300 312 H
WARDEN, Ken .... 479-788-7721.. 22 A
ken.warden@uafs.edu
WARDINSKY, Ken .... 208-769-3377 132 A
kmwardinsky@nic.edu
WARDLAW, Debra .... 803-786-3723 407 E
dwardlaw@columbiasc.edu
WARDLE, Marianne ...... 307-766-1121 500 H
WARDWELL, Melissa ... 717-871-7655 394 B
melissa.wardwell@millersville.edu
WARDZALA, Ellen .... 419-559-2408 361 B
ewardzala01@terra.edu
WARE, Amy .... 901-321-3331 417 G
aware1@cbu.edu
WARE, Bob .... 870-222-5360.. 22 E
wareb@uamont.edu
WARE, Charles .... 832-252-2424 431 M
charles.ware@cbshouston.edu
WARE, Larry .... 304-647-6220 489 C
lware@osteo.wvsom.edu
WARE, Lisa .... 864-587-4295 411 F
warel@smcsc.edu
WARE, Mamie .... 770-426-2718 122 A
mamie.ware@life.edu
WARE, Paige .... 214-768-3754 443 G
pware@smu.edu
WARE, Peggy, J .... 309-341-7211 141 E
pjware@knox.edu
WARE, Shelby .... 903-233-4070 438 C
shelbyware@letu.edu
WARE, Shunda .... 843-525-8307 411 H
sware@tcl.edu
WARE, Thomas .... 606-759-7141 182 B
thomas.ware@kctcs.edu
WARE, Thomas .... 601-936-5555 245 D
thomas.ware@hindscc.edu
WARE, Tony .... 661-362-3236.. 38 H
tony.ware@canyons.edu
WARE-CARLTON,
Rachel, J .... 920-565-1000 492 A
carltonrj@lakeland.edu
WARE-JACKSON,
Wynnona .... 301-546-7596 201 D
warewd@pgcc.edu
WARE JOSEPH, Caran . 303-765-3111.. 81 F
cwarejoseph@iliff.edu
WARE-ROBERTS,
Vonnie .... 405-466-2999 366 B
vonnie.w.roberts@langston.edu
WAREJAYE, Hollie ...... 773-907-4456 134 N
hwarejaye@ccc.edu
WARFEL, Robert .... 513-745-2000 364 F
warfelr@xavier.edu
WARFIELD, Aimee, S .. 518-381-1207 319 G
warfieas@sunysccc.edu
WARFIELD, Jaime .... 509-777-4665 485 D
jwarfield@whitworth.edu
WARFIELD, Shaneice .. 323-259-2500.. 54 I
WARFIELD, Tara .... 706-233-7362 125 A
twarfield@shorter.edu
WARGO, David, A .... 724-847-5678 384 B
dawargo@geneva.edu
WARGO, Melissa .... 828-227-3082 343 D
wargo@wcu.edu

WARHOLAK, Terri .... 314-367-8700 260 A
terri.warholak@uhsp.edu
WARING, Jennifer .... 215-248-7150 380 G
sm8127@bncollege.com
WARING BERRY,
Williette .... 803-535-1202 410 C
waringw@octech.edu
WARK, Maureen .... 978-921-4242 216 F
maureen.wark@montserrat.edu
WARK, Mike .... 253-964-6232 481 H
mwark@pierce.ctc.edu
WARK, Ryan .... 907-796-6100.. 10 C
mrwark@alaska.edu
WARKENTIN, Bettina ... 615-547-1374 418 C
bwarkentin@cumberland.edu
WARLEY, Russell, L .... 812-877-8046 160 C
warley@rose-hulman.edu
WARMACK, Dwaun, J .. 803-535-5412 406 E
WARMANN, Cheryl ..... 847-635-1719 146 E
cwarmann@oakton.edu
WARN, Dara .... 480-947-6644.. 15 B
dara.warn@pennfoster.edu
WARNEKE, Kent .... 402-844-7244 268 A
kent@northeast.edu
WARNER, Amy, C .... 317-274-7400 157 B
awarner@iupui.edu
WARNER, Angela .... 314-529-9300 254 D
awarner@maryville.edu
WARNER, Ann .... 337-475-5820 192 B
awarner@mcneese.edu
WARNER, OP,
Cecilia Anne .... 615-297-7545 416 G
president@aquinascollege.edu
WARNER, Charles .... 740-351-3468 360 E
cwarner@shawnee.edu
WARNER, Corrina .... 706-721-2161 115 I
cwarner1@augusta.edu
WARNER, Dan .... 610-758-3100 388 C
daw318@lehigh.edu
WARNER, David .... 240-500-2231 199 A
cdwarner@hagerstowncc.edu
WARNER, Gail .... 760-355-6275.. 45 N
gail.warner@imperial.edu
WARNER, Jack, R .... 401-456-8100 404 A
WARNER, Janice .... 732-987-2314 277 B
jwarner@georgian.edu
WARNER, Jason .... 214-768-4379 443 G
jasonw@smu.edu
WARNER, John .... 214-648-9794 456 D
john.warner@utsouthwestern.edu
WARNER, Kathleen ..... 410-888-9048 200 C
kwarner@muih.edu
WARNER, Kyle .... 989-463-7359 220 F
warnerka@alma.edu
WARNER, Linda .... 913-288-7194 174 H
lwarner@kckcc.edu
WARNER, Lynn .... 518-442-3300 315 D
lwarner@albany.edu
WARNER, Maleese ...... 707-527-4828.. 63 C
mwarner@santarosa.edu
WARNER, Ryan .... 740-351-3127 360 E
rwarner@shawnee.edu
WARNER, Sandra .... 913-469-8500 174 F
swarner@jccc.edu
WARNER, Somerset ..... 801-818-8900 458 M
swarner@provocollege.edu
WARNER, Susan, T ..... 440-826-2476 348 C
swarner@bw.edu
WARNER, Timothy, R .. 650-723-4567.. 66 D
trw@stanford.edu
WARNER-SAADAT, Val . 760-757-2121.. 52 G
vwarnersaadat@miracosta.edu
WARNES, Jamie, E ..... 716-878-4822 317 C
warnesje@buffalostate.edu
WARNES, Taylor .... 218-879-0820 237 F
taylor.warnes@fdltcc.edu
WARNICK, Benjamin ... 508-588-9100 214 F
bwarnick@massasoit.mass.edu
WARNICK, Lorin, D ..... 607-253-3771 297 D
ldw3@cornell.edu
WARNICK, Mark .... 870-240-4000.. 18 H
mark.warnick@blackrivertech.edu
WARNOCK, Bonnie ..... 432-837-8201 449 F
bwarnock@sulross.edu
WARNOCK, JR.,
Douglas, W .... 719-333-4153 502 C
douglas.warnock@afacademy.af.edu
WARR, Annie .... 831-582-3595.. 32 D
awarr@csumb.edu
WARR, Jason .... 303-765-3185.. 81 F
jwarr@iliff.edu
WARREM, Beth .... 619-594-7985.. 33 E
bwarrem@sdsu.edu

WARREN, Aileen .... 402-559-8992 269 C
aileen.warren@unmc.edu
WARREN, Amy .... 360-709-2015 483 E
awarren@spscc.edu
WARREN, Ann .... 310-233-4250.. 49 F
warrenal@lahc.edu
WARREN, Ashley .... 432-335-6411 440 C
awarren@odessa.edu
WARREN, A'Lelianne ... 704-216-3617 337 C
alelianne.warren@rccc.edu
WARREN, Bradley ...... 706-721-2856 115 I
bradwarren@augusta.edu
WARREN, Carolyn ...... 901-722-3215 422 I
cwarren@sco.edu
WARREN, Charlotte, J .. 217-786-2273 142 F
charlotte.warren@llcc.edu
WARREN, Cher .... 601-484-8614 246 B
cwarren@meridiancc.edu
WARREN, Cleve .... 904-357-8896 101 A
clwarren@fscj.edu
WARREN, Daniel .... 912-449-7534 125 B
daniel.warren@sgsc.edu
WARREN, Derrick .... 225-771-5380 190 K
derrick_warren@sus.edu
WARREN, Ester .... 434-592-6468 467 E
ejwarren@liberty.edu
WARREN, Franklin ...... 336-517-2254 326 J
fwarren@bennett.edu
WARREN, Geelyn .... 270-534-3461 182 G
geelyn.warren@kctcs.edu
WARREN, Jacquelyn ... 314-516-6877 260 E
warrenja@umsl.edu
WARREN, Jason, D ..... 270-827-1867 181 F
jason.warren@kctcs.edu
WARREN, Joan, D ...... 212-779-5000 303 B
WARREN, Kathi, D ...... 713-348-6090 441 K
kdwarren@rice.edu
WARREN, Katie .... 507-786-3316 242 I
warren2@stolaf.edu
WARREN, Kayla .... 260-665-4105 161 C
warrenk@trine.edu
WARREN, Kelly .... 806-291-1022 457 B
warrenk@wbu.edu
WARREN, Kerry .... 256-216-5343.... 4 D
kerry.warren@athens.edu
WARREN, Layne .... 804-862-6100 469 E
lwarren@rbc.edu
WARREN, Leslie .... 906-227-2920 228 B
lwarren@nmu.edu
WARREN, Leslie, A ..... 906-227-2117 228 E
lwarren@nmu.edu
WARREN, Marty .... 903-923-2314 435 A
mswarren@etbu.edu
WARREN, Mary .... 601-643-8442 244 G
mary.warren@colin.edu
WARREN, Matt .... 918-631-4602 371 C
matt-warren@utulsa.edu
WARREN, Michelle ..... 218-935-0417 244 A
michelle.warren@wetcc.edu
WARREN, Mike .... 601-925-3204 246 D
mjwarren@mc.edu
WARREN, Monica ...... 615-297-7545 416 G
WARREN, Pamela, C ... 920-923-8530 492 D
pcwarren17@marianuniversity.edu
WARREN, Reuben ...... 334-725-2314.... 7 D
rwarren@tuskegee.edu
WARREN, Robert .... 909-706-8424.. 75 C
rjwarren@westernu.edu
WARREN, Russ .... 724-266-3838 399 F
rwarren@tsm.edu
WARREN, Samantha ... 207-621-3024 196 B
samantha.warren@maine.edu
WARREN, Samantha, C 207-621-3024 196 C
samantha.warren@maine.edu
WARREN, Sara .... 410-225-2264 200 B
swarren@mica.edu
WARREN, Shannon ..... 304-645-6382 489 C
swarren@osteo.wvsom.edu
WARREN, Shauna ...... 773-896-2400 134 K
shauna.warren@ctschicago.edu
WARREN, Sydney ...... 270-686-6417 179 F
sydney.warren@brescia.edu
WARREN, Thomas ...... 207-941-7786 194 D
warrent@husson.edu
WARREN, Timothy ...... 615-963-5000 425 A
WARREN, Todd, W ..... 504-865-3434 190 A
twwarren@loyno.edu
WARREN, Trina .... 314-367-8700 260 A
trina.warren@uhsp.edu
WARREN, William ...... 631-632-6313 316 D
william.warren@stonybrook.edu
WARREN, William, J ... 801-581-6773 459 D
william.warren@utah.edu

WATSON, Billy ... 706-233-7315 125 A
wwatson@shorter.edu
WATSON, Bret ... 650-949-7777.. 43 A
WATSON, Bret ... 650-949-7777.. 43 A
watsonbret@fhda.edu
WATSON, Brett ... 760-480-8474.. 75 H
bwatson@wscal.edu
WATSON, Brian ... 217-234-5253 141 H
bwatson@lakelandcollege.edu
WATSON, Camille ... 800-818-6136.. 55 K
cwatson@paloaltou.edu
WATSON, Christopher ... 847-491-4100 146 C
christopher-watson@northwestern.edu
WATSON, Christopher ... 903-730-4890 437 E
cwatson@jarvis.edu
WATSON, Cynthia, A ... 202-685-3924 501 I
WATSON, Darius ... 573-681-5216 254 A
watsond@lincolnu.edu
WATSON, David ... 937-529-2201 361 F
dwatson@united.edu
WATSON, Donna ... 914-395-2204 314 H
dwatson@sarahlawrence.edu
WATSON, Douglas ... 402-941-6519 267 B
watson@midlandu.edu
WATSON, Drew ... 863-667-5192 108 I
dwatson@seu.edu
WATSON, Edward ... 601-979-3950 245 G
edward.o.watson@jsums.edu
WATSON, Eric ... 713-353-3621 429 F
erwatson@aii.edu
WATSON, Frederica ... 713-718-5103 436 E
frederica.watson@hccs.edu
WATSON, Gabe ... 352-638-9714.. 96 B
gwatson@beaconcollege.edu
WATSON, George, E ... 678-839-6000 127 A
nwatson@westga.edu
WATSON, Hannah ... 912-443-5347 124 I
hwatson@savannahtech.edu
WATSON, Harold ... 630-829-6129 133 B
hwatson@ben.edu
WATSON, Harriet ... 937-529-2201 361 F
hwatson@united.edu
WATSON, Hope ... 803-786-3763 407 E
hwatson@columbiasc.edu
WATSON, James ... 559-278-8400.. 31 D
jwatson@csufresno.edu
WATSON, Jarvis ... 212-592-2861 314 I
jwatson5@sva.edu
WATSON, Jennifer ... 425-602-3000 476 H
WATSON, John ... 972-860-4248 433 G
jwatson@dallascollede.edu
WATSON, John ... 972-273-3353 434 C
jwatson@dcccd.edu
WATSON, Jonelle ... 701-858-3577 345 C
jonelle.watson@minotstateu.edu
WATSON, Jordan ... 314-367-8700 260 A
jordan.watson@uhsp.edu
WATSON, Julia ... 678-664-0530 127 E
julia.watson@westgatech.edu
WATSON, Kathryn, J ... 727-864-8474.. 98 G
watsonkj@eckerd.edu
WATSON, Kelly ... 513-875-3344 349 K
kelly.watson@chatfield.edu
WATSON, Kim ... 419-251-1852 355 G
kim.watson@mercycollege.edu
WATSON, Kimberly ... 301-405-5837 202 E
watsonk@umd.edu
WATSON, Kimberly, A ... 803-934-3221 409 H
kwatson@morris.edu
WATSON, Kristen ... 661-654-2241.. 30 C
kwatson@csub.edu
WATSON, Laushaun ... 251-578-1313.... 3 D
lwatson@rstc.edu
WATSON, Lisa ... 409-933-8674 432 H
lwatson5@com.edu
WATSON, Lisa ... 307-754-6098 500 G
lisa.watson@nwc.edu
WATSON, Loree ... 281-649-3221 436 D
lwatson@hbu.edu
WATSON, Lynda ... 903-434-8204 440 A
lwatson@ntcc.edu
WATSON, Maria ... 909-621-8192.. 57 K
maria.watson@pomona.edu
WATSON, Mary ... 212-229-5613 307 E
watsonm@newschool.edu
WATSON, Michael, W ... 920-424-2184 495 C
watson@uwosh.edu
WATSON, Mindy ... 575-769-4065 285 C
mindy.watson@clovis.edu
WATSON, Monica ... 701-483-2592 345 A
monica.watson@dickinsonstate.edu
WATSON, Nailah ... 773-291-6100 135 B
WATSON, Nick ... 573-642-3361 261 F
WATSON, Nyemma ... 856-225-6738 281 A
ncwatson@camden.rutgers.edu
WATSON, Paul ... 269-965-3931 225 D
watsonp@kellogg.edu
WATSON, Phyllis ... 850-599-3474 109 E
phyllis.watson@famu.edu
WATSON, Rachael ... 425-388-9578 479 B
rwatson@everettcc.edu
WATSON, Rebecca ... 334-670-3608.... 7 C
bvwatson@troy.edu
WATSON, Renee ... 702-895-5308 270 J
renee.watson@unlv.edu
WATSON, Sally ... 307-532-8303 500 A
swatson@ewc.wy.edu
WATSON, Samuel ... 803-533-3603 410 H
swatson2@scsu.edu
WATSON, III,
Samuel, E ... 940-397-4746 439 F
samuel.watson@msutexas.edu
WATSON, Sherry ... 207-509-7201 196 B
swatson@unity.edu
WATSON, Sonja, S ... 817-257-7160 447 H
sonja.watson@tcu.edu
WATSON, Steve ... 773-508-2560 142 G
swatson4@luc.edu
WATSON, Susan, V ... 301-546-7011 201 D
watsonsv@pgcc.edu
WATSON, Susanne, M .. 260-356-6000 155 G
swatson@huntington.edu
WATSON, Todd ... 512-863-1508 444 F
tkw@southwestern.edu
WATSON, Todd ... 269-337-7149 225 B
todd.watson@kzoo.edu
WATSON, W. Clark ... 205-726-4503.... 6 E
wcwatson@samford.edu
WATSON, William ... 770-794-3050 122 A
william.watson@life.edu
WATSON, Wyatt ... 479-964-3213.. 18 E
wwatson@atu.edu
WATSON, Yvonne ... 510-841-1905.. 27 B
ywatson@bst.edu
WATSON-HALL,
Sherrell ... 848-445-6625 281 B
sherrell.watsonhall@ofa.rutgers.edu
WATSTEIN, Sara ... 206-296-6201 483 B
watsteins@seattleu.edu
WATT, James, R ... 814-641-3110 386 E
wattj@juniata.edu
WATT, Kenton ... 817-257-6703 447 H
k.watt@tcu.edu
WATT, Robert ... 209-934-2950 482 G
robert.watt@seattlecolleges.edu
WATTERS, Alex ... 712-274-5036 168 C
wattersa@morningside.edu
WATTERS, James, H ... 585-475-2378 312 A
jhwbgt@rit.edu
WATTERSON, Eric ... 618-664-6826 138 D
eric.watterson@greenville.edu
WATTS, Aimee ... 850-729-4957 104 L
wattsa@nwfsc.edu
WATTS, Barbara ... 434-381-6151 470 H
bwatts@sbc.edu
WATTS, Bill ... 402-472-3145 269 A
bill.watts@unl.edu
WATTS, Bruce ... 312-567-3253 139 H
bwatts1@iit.edu
WATTS, Christine ... 504-398-2177 191 E
cwatts@uhcno.edu
WATTS, Christopher ... 817-257-7316 447 H
c.watts@tcu.edu
WATTS, Connie ... 606-487-3184 181 E
connie.watts@kctcs.edu
WATTS, Derek ... 309-298-1949 152 I
dj-watts@wiu.edu
WATTS, Eda ... 763-424-0944 239 D
WATTS, Greg ... 216-421-7411 350 E
gwatts@cia.edu
WATTS, John ... 828-327-7000 332 H
WATTS, Jon, C ... 308-865-8205 268 J
wattsjc@unk.edu
WATTS, Katherine, K ... 336-917-5563 339 H
katherine.watts@salem.edu
WATTS, Laurie, S ... 504-816-8180 190 D
lawatts@nobts.edu
WATTS, Lisa ... 870-307-7253.. 20 D
lisa.watts@lyon.edu
WATTS, Monica ... 205-348-5411.... 7 G
monica.watts@ua.edu
WATTS, Nakisha ... 662-621-4205 244 E
nwatts@coahomacc.edu
WATTS, Patricia, A ... 718-990-6865 313 B
enrightp@stjohns.edu
WATTS, Ray, L ... 205-934-4636.... 8 A
rlwatts@uab.edu
WATTS, Robert ... 601-877-6470 244 B
rwatts@alcorn.edu
WATTS, Tracee ... 979-230-3163 431 A
tracee.watts@brazosport.edu
WATTS, Yadonna ... 601-877-6479 244 B
ywatts@alcorn.edu
WATTS-MARTINEZ,
Evanda ... 804-862-6100 469 E
ewatts@rbc.edu
WATWOOD, Maribeth ... 928-523-9322.. 14 J
maribeth.watwood@nau.edu
WATZKE, John, L ... 503-943-7135 376 H
watzke@up.edu
WAUGH,
Christopher, A ... 563-333-6259 169 D
waughchristophera@sau.edu
WAUGH, Elizabeth ... 336-517-1543 326 J
ewaugh@bennett.edu
WAUGH, Susan ... 760-591-3012.. 72 F
swaugh@usa.edu
WAUGH, Wendy ... 308-432-6277 267 G
wwaugh@csc.edu
WAURIO, Laura ... 920-924-3229 498 C
lwaurio@morainepark.edu
WAUTLET, Heather ... 321-693-5256 100 A
hwautlet@fit.edu
WAVLE, Dana, C ... 812-941-2202 157 D
dwavle@ius.edu
WAWERS, Stephanie ... 701-231-7211 345 D
stephanie.wawers@ndsu.edu
WAWRZUSIN, Andrea ... 513-745-3009 364 F
wawrzusina@xavier.edu
WAX, Shawn ... 312-369-7050 136 C
swax@colum.edu
WAXLER, Melanie ... 727-816-3259 105 E
waxlerm@phsc.edu
WAXMAN, Barbara ... 918-595-7872 370 B
barbara.waxman@tulsacc.edu
WAXMAN, Deborah ... 215-576-0800 396 B
officeofthepresident@rrc.edu
WAXTER, Catherine, A .. 412-359-1000 399 D
cwaxter@triangle-tech.edu
WAY, Christopher ... 617-258-9461 215 G
WAY, Doug ... 859-257-2000 185 D
doug.way@uky.edu
WAY, Joshua ... 646-378-6100 289 F
joshua.way@nyack.edu
WAY, Julie ... 414-277-4517 493 D
WAY, Kimera, K ... 715-836-5180 494 E
waykk@uwec.edu
WAY, Lauren ... 413-565-1000 205 I
lway@baypath.edu
WAY, Lori Beth ... 415-405-4034.. 34 A
lbway@sfsu.edu
WAY, Pete ... 315-655-7266 292 B
pmway@cazenovia.edu
WAY, Philip, K ... 256-233-8201.... 4 D
philip.way@athens.edu
WAY, Winmar ... 562-902-3388.. 65 H
winmarway@scuhs.edu
WAY BOLT, Mary ... 410-287-1025 198 A
mbolt@cecil.edu
WAYE, Katharine ... 315-279-5602 303 D
kwaye@keuka.edu
WAYLAND, David ... 432-552-2764 456 C
wayland_d@utpb.edu
WAYLAND, Marilina, L . 787-250-1912 507 C
mwayland@metro.inter.edu
WAYMACK, Matthew ... 706-865-2134 126 D
mwaymack@truett.edu
WAYNE, William ... 315-568-3025 309 H
bwayne@northeastcollege.edu
WAYNE, William, R ... 405-325-2700 370 J
wwayne@ou.edu
WAYTON, Cristina ... 216-523-7415 350 G
c.sanchez17@csuohio.edu
WEARDEN, Stanley, T ... 910-630-7005 331 B
swearden@methodist.edu
WEARN, Mary ... 478-471-2490 122 D
mary.wearn@mga.edu
WEARY, Tanya ... 252-492-2061 338 D
wearyt@vgcc.edu
WEATHERALL, Maureen 310-338-5171.. 51 C
maureen.weatherall@lmu.edu
WEATHERBEE, Caroline 617-243-2407 210 G
cweatherbee@lasell.edu
WEATHERBY, Susan ... 315-364-3208 324 E
accounting@wells.edu
WEATHERFORD,
Charles ... 850-412-5102 109 E
charles.weatherford@famu.edu
WEATHERFORD,
Michael ... 831-656-2511 501 K
michael.weatherford@nps.edu
WEATHERS, Mark ... 845-938-2517 502 H
christopher.weathers@westpoint.edu
WEATHERS, Melonie ... 336-386-3207 338 B
weathersm@surry.edu
WEATHERS-GREEN,
Natalie ... 585-245-5620 317 E
nweathers@geneseo.edu
WEATHERSBY, Aaron ... 323-563-3432.. 36 E
aaronweathersby@cdrewu.edu
WEATHERSPOON,
Bridget ... 937-529-2201 361 F
bweatherspoon@united.edu
WEATHERSPOON,
Dave, D ... 517-355-5767 227 C
weathe42@msu.edu
WEATHERSPOON,
David ... 847-543-2138 135 G
dweatherspoon@clcillinois.edu
WEAVER, Amy ... 501-505-2966.. 19 I
weaver@hendrix.edu
WEAVER, Andrea ... 910-962-7631 343 B
weavera@uncw.edu
WEAVER, Andy ... 325-738-3349 448 F
andy.weaver@tstc.edu
WEAVER, Angela ... 618-468-5300 142 B
aweaver@lc.edu
WEAVER, Anne ... 504-865-5490 190 A
asweaver@loyno.edu
WEAVER, Aubrey ... 703-284-6510 468 A
aubrey.weaver@marymount.edu
WEAVER, Bradley, K ... 765-361-6308 162 G
weaverb@wabash.edu
WEAVER, Brandon, C ... 304-457-6220 485 F
weaverbc2@ab.edu
WEAVER, Carol ... 304-457-6331 485 F
weaverc@ab.edu
WEAVER, Carolyn ... 515-271-1426 165 C
carolyn.weaver@dmu.edu
WEAVER, Catherine, B .. 540-568-3141 467 C
weavercb@jmu.edu
WEAVER, Charlie ... 231-591-2138 223 H
charlieweaver@ferris.edu
WEAVER, Darlene ... 412-396-4020 382 E
weaverd1@duq.edu
WEAVER, David ... 907-786-7212.. 10 A
dweaver@alaska.edu
WEAVER, Ernestine ... 860-723-0114.. 85 E
weavere@ct.edu
WEAVER, Gina ... 585-345-6811 300 D
gmweaver@genesee.edu
WEAVER, Greg ... 713-920-1120 121 F
gweaver@ict.edu
WEAVER, Greg ... 713-920-1120 437 C
gweaver@ict.edu
WEAVER, Harry ... 909-687-1520.. 43 G
harryweaver@gs.edu
WEAVER, James, R ... 210-458-4992 455 B
james.weaver@utsa.edu
WEAVER, James, S ... 740-376-4611 355 E
jim.weaver@marietta.edu
WEAVER, Jeff ... 870-460-1028.. 22 E
weaver@uamont.edu
WEAVER, John ... 813-988-5131.. 99 M
weaverj@floridacollege.edu
WEAVER, JR.,
Joseph, B ... 405-744-2690 367 G
joe.weaver@okstate.edu
WEAVER, Kali ... 423-869-6057 420 A
kali.weaver@lmunet.edu
WEAVER, Kat ... 310-258-8779.. 51 C
kat.weaver@lmu.edu
WEAVER, Kathleen ... 310-258-7242.. 51 C
kathleen.weaver@lmu.edu
WEAVER, Ken ... 620-341-5660 173 C
kweaver@emporia.edu
WEAVER, Lauren ... 304-473-8007 490 E
weaver.l@wvwc.edu
WEAVER, Lori ... 304-829-7284 486 B
lweaver@bethanywv.edu
WEAVER, Marianne ... 541-962-3524 372 H
mweaver@eou.edu
WEAVER, Matthew ... 717-867-6220 388 A
mweaver@lvc.edu
WEAVER, Max ... 205-387-0511.... 1 D
max.weaver@bscc.edu
WEAVER, Megan ... 417-447-8114 257 B
weaverm@otc.edu
WEAVER, Melanie, K ... 419-772-2272 358 D
m-weaver@onu.edu
WEAVER, Neal, R ... 229-928-1360 120 B
neal.weaver@gsw.edu

WEAVER, Patricia 423-472-7141 423 C pweaver@clevelandstatecc.edu
WEAVER, Rhonda 704-403-1756 327 B rhonda.weaver@atriumhealth.org
WEAVER, Sarah 843-349-2474 407 B sweaver@coastal.edu
WEAVER, Sean 505-454-3380 286 C slweaver@nmhu.edu
WEAVER, Sean, F 412-396-2560 382 E weavers2@duq.edu
WEAVER, Tammy 479-968-0272 18 E tweaver@atu.edu
WEAVER, Terri, E 312-996-7808 151 D teweaver@uic.edu
WEAVER, Tom 419-434-4253 364 B tweaver@winebrenner.edu
WEAVER, Wendel 918-335-6826 368 E wweaver@okwu.edu
WEAVER, Wendy 414-930-3021 493 E weaverw@mtmary.edu
WEBB, Alyssa 662-254-3579 247 C alyssa.webb@mvsu.edu
WEBB, Amy 530-242-7713 64 A awebb@shastacollege.edu
WEBB, Amy 410-626-2510 201 E amy.webb@sjc.edu
WEBB, Anda, L 434-924-3728 471 F al6b@virginia.edu
WEBB, Andrea 304-384-5233 488 K webba08@concord.edu
WEBB, Anna Carrie 931-221-1039 416 H webba@apsu.edu
WEBB, Bradley, M 570-326-3761 392 S bwebb@pct.edu
WEBB, Burton, J 606-218-5261 185 F burtonwebb@upike.edu
WEBB, Carol 281-487-1170 447 G cwebb@txchiro.edu
WEBB, Darliegh 866-680-2756 458 I studentfinances@midwifery.edu
WEBB, Donna 229-391-5001 114 D dwebb@abac.edu
WEBB, Duncan 312-461-0600 132 F dwebb@aaart.edu
WEBB, Elizabeth 254-295-5032 453 A ewebb@umhb.edu
WEBB, Eric 307-766-3059 500 H ewebb1@uwyo.edu
WEBB, Erin 209-228-4501 70 A ewebb2@ucmerced.edu
WEBB, II, Ernest, R 915-831-5051 435 B ewebb1@epcc.edu
WEBB, Farrell 818-677-3001 32 E farrell.webb@csun.edu
WEBB, Jac 208-562-2063 131 C jacwebb@cwi.edu
WEBB, James, D 806-651-1240 447 D jwebb@wtamu.edu
WEBB, Jane 260-982-5417 158W ejwebb@manchester.edu
WEBB, Jeanie 405-733-7300 369 D jwebb@rose.edu
WEBB, Jen 715-675-2775 170 D webbj@uiu.edu
WEBB, Jennifer 254-295-4526 453 A jwebb@umhb.edu
WEBB, Jodi 419-372-9348 348 F jwebb@bgsu.edu
WEBB, Joe 920-403-3753 494 B joe.webb@snc.edu
WEBB, Joel 479-308-2230 17 E joel.webb@acheedu.org
WEBB, Jonathan, D 989-774-7473 221M fmrepair@cmich.edu
WEBB, Joshua, M 989-964-4359 229 L jmwebb@svsu.edu
WEBB, Kathleen, M 937-229-4094 362 C kwebb1@udayton.edu
WEBB, Kathy, L 208-496-1111 130 G webbk@byui.edu
WEBB, Kenneth 903-785-7661 440 F kwebb@parisjc.edu
WEBB, Kerri 310-660-3406 41 J kwebb@elcamino.edu
WEBB, Kyle 901-843-3760 422 C webb@rhodes.edu
WEBB, Lee 870-512-7849 18 C lee_webb@asun.edu
WEBB, Lezley, A 901-333-5560 424 E lcurrin@southwest.tn.edu
WEBB, Mark 580-745-2267 369 F mwebb@se.edu
WEBB, Matthew 585-567-9645 301 G matthew.webb@houghton.edu
WEBB, Melody 757-823-8404 468 B mmwebb@nsu.edu
WEBB, Michelle 207-453-5020 195 B mwebb@kvcc.me.edu
WEBB, Nick 530-242-7739 64 A nwebb@shastacollege.edu
WEBB, Pamela 612-624-1648 242 K pwebb@umn.edu
WEBB, Pat 214-860-8789 434 B pwebb@dcccd.edu
WEBB, Paul 715-682-1208 493 G pwebb@northland.edu
WEBB, Ralph 714-480-7333 58 E webb_ralph@rsccd.edu
WEBB, Reginal 863-298-6828 106 A rwebb@polk.edu
WEBB, Tammie 252-451-8263 336 B twwebb172@nashcc.edu
WEBB, Tara 269-337-7394 225 B tara.webb@kzoo.edu
WEBB, Tom 937-775-5680 364 D thomas.webb@wright.edu
WEBB, Toya 847-214-7769 137 D twebb@elgin.edu
WEBB, Travis 337-550-1253 189 B twebb@lsue.edu
WEBB, Troycia 229-430-3396 114 G twebb@albanytech.edu
WEBB, Walter, W 815-939-5333 146 F wwebb@olivet.edu
WEBB-CURTIS, Susan 423-472-7141 423 C susanwebb-curtis@clevelandstatecc.edu
WEBB-WALKER, Katonja 312-850-7050 135 E kwebb8@ccc.edu
WEBB WALKER, Katonja 773-602-5000 135 A
WEBBER, Mary 315-364-3453 324 E mwebber@wells.edu
WEBBER, Meg 803-323-2220 413 D webberm@winthrop.edu
WEBBER, Shannon 303-914-6246 82 L shannon.webber@rrcc.edu
WEBBER, Stephen 617-266-1400 206 D infonyc@berklee.edu
WEBBER MCLEAN, Kalynda 818-610-6567 49 H mcleankw@piercecollege.edu
WEBEL, Emily 309-341-5327 134 A ewebel@sandburg.edu
WEBER, A. Scott 716-645-2992 315 F provost@buffalo.edu
WEBER, Aaron 620-278-4208 177 E aaron.weber@sterling.edu
WEBER, April 907-260-7422 9 D
WEBER, Brad 620-252-7076 172 K weber.brad@coffeyville.edu
WEBER, Bruce 302-831-1211 91 A bweber@udel.edu
WEBER, Chad, T 812-877-8348 160 C weberct@rose-hulman.edu
WEBER, Christine 312-949-7153 139 B cweber@ico.edu
WEBER, Christopher 301-447-5114 201 A cweber@msmary.edu
WEBER, Daniel 630-844-6852 133 A dweber@aurora.edu
WEBER, Daniel, R 773-442-4029 145 G d-weber3@neiu.edu
WEBER, David 413-369-4044 208 C weber@csld.edu
WEBER, David 561-868-3280 105 C weberd@palmbeachstate.edu
WEBER, Dawn 419-289-5107 347 H dweber1@ashland.edu
WEBER, Dean 919-962-7883 342 B dweber@unc.edu
WEBER, Debra 262-695-7842 499 A dweber28@wctc.edu
WEBER, Heather 623-935-8840 13 C heather.weber@estrellamountain.edu
WEBER, Jennifer 701-328-4103 344 G jennifer.weber@ndus.edu
WEBER, Jennifer, L 563-588-7155 167 I jennifer.weber@loras.edu
WEBER, Jolanta, A 509-313-6504 479 E weberj@gonzaga.edu
WEBER, Julie, H 210-832-5631 452 D jweber@uiwtx.edu
WEBER, Karen 415-703-9500 28 D kweber@cca.edu
WEBER, Karyn 605-688-4165 416 A karyn.weber@sdstate.edu
WEBER, Kelley 785-833-4396 175 C kelley.weber@kwu.edu
WEBER, Kendra 715-831-7216 497 E kweber23@cvtc.edu
WEBER, Kendra 507-457-5300 241 A kweber@winona.edu
WEBER, Kevin 502-585-9911 184 E kweber@spalding.edu
WEBER, Krista 608-822-2315 498 H kweber@swtc.edu
WEBER, Laura 937-529-2201 361 F lweber@united.edu
WEBER, Laurie 701-858-3375 345 C laurie.weber@minotstateu.edu
WEBER, Marsha 218-299-6631 238 K marsha.weber@minnesota.edu
WEBER, Mary Ann 574-296-6207 153 C maweber@ambs.edu
WEBER, Melissa 605-995-2600 414 A melissa.weber@dwu.edu
WEBER, Michael 207-780-4404 196 D michael.weber@maine.edu
WEBER, Michael 863-680-4277 100 F mweber@flsouthern.edu
WEBER, Nancy 843-525-8226 411 G nweber@tcl.edu
WEBER, Phil 740-857-1311 360 C pweber@rosedale.edu
WEBER, Randy 541-956-7000 375 G rweber@roguecc.edu
WEBER, Raymond 907-786-6494 10 A rweber@alaska.edu
WEBER, Rebecca 507-223-1332 239 B rebecca.weber@mnwest.edu
WEBER, Richard 503-589-8119 372 G rweber@corban.edu
WEBER, Sheneui 909-652-8477 36 B sheneui.weber@chaffey.edu
WEBER, Sherry 269-488-4681 225 C sweber@kvcc.edu
WEBER, Stephen 405-224-3140 371 B sweber@usao.edu
WEBER, Susan 212-501-3050 290 G weber@bgc.bard.edu
WEBER, Tracy 574-631-0496 161 G tweber@nd.edu
WEBER, Twila 740-857-1311 360 C tweber@rosedale.edu
WEBER, Valerie 937-245-7695 364 D valerie.weber@wright.edu
WEBER, Wayne, C 608-342-1547 495 E weberwa@uwplatt.edu
WEBER-MORTIMER, Brandi 724-738-4340 394 E brandi.mortimer@sru.edu
WEBSTER, Alex 206-239-4500 477 I
WEBSTER, Amy 276-656-0248 473 H awebster@patrickhenry.edu
WEBSTER, Berenice 281-283-2004 452 A webster@uhcl.edu
WEBSTER, Christine 979-230-3576 431 A christine.webster@brazosport.edu
WEBSTER, Daniel 615-675-5255 427 D daniel.webster@welch.edu
WEBSTER, Ethan 610-574-6909 55 D ewebster@pacificcollege.edu
WEBSTER, Jess 610-558-5587 390 G websterj@neumann.edu
WEBSTER, Kathleen 607-436-2500 316 C kathleen.webster@oneonta.edu
WEBSTER, Katie, P 740-368-3329 359 F kpwebste@owu.edu
WEBSTER, Keith 412-268-2447 380 B kwebster@andrew.cmu.edu
WEBSTER, Kelly 406-243-2470 263 D kelly.webster@umontana.edu
WEBSTER, Larry 662-621-4085 244 E lwebster@coahomacc.edu
WEBSTER, LaTasha 773-371-5400 134 C lwebster@ctu.edu
WEBSTER, Lee 609-771-1855 275 J
WEBSTER, Linda 573-592-5192 261 F
WEBSTER, Michael 620-227-9352 173 A mwebster@dc3.edu
WEBSTER, Ondes 865-471-3352 417 E owebster@cn.edu
WEBSTER, Richard, C 410-334-2896 205 A rwebster@worwic.edu
WEBSTER, Ricky 641-683-5207 166 F ricky.webster@indianhills.edu
WEBSTER, Scott 508-999-8202 211 F swebster@umassd.edu
WEBSTER, Shane 208-496-1910 130 G websters@byui.edu
WEBSTER, Sherri 419-251-1865 355 G sherri.webster@mercycollege.edu
WEBSTER, Teresa 662-246-6318 246 E twebster@msdelta.edu
WEBSTER, Terry 626-529-8500 55 E
WEBSTER, Theresa 402-437-2559 268 D twebster@southeast.edu
WEBSTER, Wayne 330-263-2583 350 H wwebster@wooster.edu
WEBSTER-HANSEN, Christine 732-224-2514 275 D cwebster@brookdalecc.edu
WECH, Kris 620-252-7199 172 K wech.kris@coffeyville.edu
WECHSLER, Cathy 570-961-7869 387 A wechslerc@lackawanna.edu
WECKESSER, Thomas, U 937-229-4583 362 C tweckesser2@udayton.edu
WEDDINGTON, Brenda, L 312-942-5681 148 C brenda_weddington@rush.edu
WEDDINGTON, Hank 828-328-7565 330 B hank.weddington@lr.edu
WEDDLE, Kimberly 816-271-5648 256 C weddle@missouriwestern.edu
WEDDLE, Robert 417-873-7450 252 A rweddle@drury.edu
WEDDLE-WEST, Karen 901-678-2119 426 A kweddle@memphis.edu
WEDDLE-WEST, Karen 901-678-2894 426 A kweddle@memphis.edu
WEDDUM, Shelli 402-552-6140 265 G weddum@clarksoncollege.edu
WEDEL, Scott, D 913-667-5700 172 G swedel@cbts.edu
WEDEMEIER, Jean 973-957-0188 274 D j.matthews@acs350.org
WEDGE, Luann 616-234-4170 224 C lwedge@grcc.edu
WEDIG, OP, Mark 314-256-8855 249 F wedig@ai.edu
WEDIGE, Kerie 608-342-1314 495 E wedigek@uwplatt.edu
WEDLER, Andrea 518-445-2388 289 B awedl@albanylaw.edu
WEE, Liang, C 844-642-2338 168 F weel@nicc.edu
WEED, Jason 513-721-7944 353 B jweed@gbs.edu
WEED, Kenneth 918-495-6004 368 F kweed@oru.edu
WEEDEN, Jared 315-781-3700 301 D weeden@hws.edu
WEEKES-STOUTE, Melissa 212-517-0431 305 D mweekes@mmm.edu
WEEKLEY, Susan 252-246-1396 339 A sweekley@wilsoncc.edu
WEEKLY, Lawrence 702-651-5412 270 F lawrence.weekly@csn.edu
WEEKS, Adam 816-322-0110 250 E adam.weeks@calvary.edu
WEEKS, Ashley 352-262-2745 125 D aweeks@southuniversity.edu
WEEKS, David 626-969-3434 26 K dweeks@apu.edu
WEEKS, Elizabeth 706-542-9389 126 F weeksleo@uga.edu
WEEKS, Flora, E 870-230-5062 19 H weeksf@hsu.edu
WEEKS, Michael 843-953-7416 406 D mweeks@citadel.edu
WEEKS, Patricia 609-652-4826 283 A patty.weeks@stockton.edu
WEEKS, Sandy 620-343-4600 173 D
WEEKS, Susan, M 817-257-7519 447 H s.weeks@tcu.edu
WEEKS, Tom 510-845-5373 29 D tweeks@cjc.edu
WEEMS, Eric 770-232-2717 124 D eric.weems@runiv.edu
WEEMS, Sherryl 386-506-3924 98 A sherryl.weems@daytonastate.edu
WEEMS, William, A 713-500-5224 455 D william.a.weems@uth.tmc.edu
WEENICK, Meredith 617-495-0908 210 B meredith_weenick@harvard.edu
WEER, Christy, H 410-677-6571 204 A chweer@salisbury.edu

WEERASURIYA, Yasith 949-794-9090 66 C yasithw@stanbridge.edu
WEESE, Brian 912-279-4564 117 C bweese@ccga.edu
WEESE, Lacey 423-746-5262 425 C lweese@tnwesleyan.edu
WEETER, Mark 918-335-6803 368 E mweeter@okwu.edu
WEGENER, David 414-930-3506 493 E wegenerd@mtmary.edu
WEGER, Brandon 618-546-2355 139 C wegerb@iecc.edu
WEGHORST, Leasa 573-681-5970 254 A weghorstl@lincolnu.edu
WEGHORST, Michelle 309-694-5505 138 I michelle.weghorst@icc.edu
WEGLARZ, Donna, M 630-515-6064 144 C dwegla@midwestern.edu
WEGLARZ, Joseph, R 845-575-3000 305 C joseph.weglarz@marist.edu
WEGLICKI, Linda 843-792-3941 409 D weglicki@musc.edu
WEGMAN, Barbara, A 260-452-2153 154 F barb.wegman@ctsfw.edu
WEGMAN, Kyla 847-214-7414 137 D kwegman@elgin.edu
WEGNER, Janis 320-629-5123 239 G janis.wegner@pine.edu
WEGNER, Laurie 828-327-7000 332 H lwegner@cvcc.edu
WEGNER, Ryan, M 319-352-8251 170 F ryan.wegner@wartburg.edu
WEGNER, Trisha 402-878-2380 266 D trisha.wegner@littlepriest.edu
WEGRZYN, David 401-232-6261 403 B dwegrzyn@bryant.edu
WEHLBURG, Catherine 256-233-8120 4 D catherine.wehlburg@athens.edu
WEHLE, Arlean 504-568-4815 189 C awehle@lsuhsc.edu
WEHLING, Adam 715-852-1394 497 E awehling@cvtc.edu
WEHMEIER, Teresa 620-417-1603 177 C teresa.wehmeier@sccc.edu
WEHMEIER, Wendall 620-417-1181 177 C wedall.wehmeier@sccc.edu
WEHNER, Jonathan, D 216-687-2054 350 G j.d.wehner@csuohio.edu
WEHR, David Allen 412-396-6082 382 E wehr@duq.edu
WEHRING, Matthew 979-830-4138 430 I matthew.wehring@blinn.edu
WEHRLEY, James, B 336-841-4560 329 E jwehrley@highpoint.edu
WEIBEL, Melanie 515-271-4451 165 C melanie.weibel@dmu.edu
WEIBERG, Chad 405-744-5855 367 G chad.weiberg@okstate.edu
WEIBLE, JR., Raymond 814-262-3816 393 A rweible@pennhighlands.edu
WEICH, Ronald 410-837-4458 204 C rweich@ubalt.edu
WEICHEL, Brianna 402-461-7393 266 C broncobookstore@hastings.edu
WEICHELT, Shelly 715-422-5504 498 A shelly.weichelt@mstc.edu
WEICHOLD, Mark, H 979-845-4016 446 B provost@tamu.edu
WEICHOLD, Nelson 601-984-1010 248 G nweichold@umc.edu
WEIDELL, Charleen 405-974-3772 370 H cweidell@uco.edu
WEIDER, Susan, L 425-602-3014 476 H sweider@bastyr.edu
WEIDMAN, Jennifer, S 610-683-4000 394 A
WEIDNER, John, W 513-556-4450 361 I weidnejw@ucmail.uc.edu
WEIDNER, Karen, K 402-844-7330 268 A karenkw@northeast.edu
WEIDNER, Penny, L 717-901-5165 385 G pweidner@harrisburgu.edu
WEIER, Gary, M 864-242-5100 405 H
WEIGAND, John, B 513-529-9838 356 A weiganjb@miamioh.edu
WEIGEL, Kathleen 561-237-7441 103W kweigel@lynn.edu
WEIGEL, Susan 816-926-4400 253 C
WEIGELT, Nicole 917-493-4270 304 L nweigelt@msmnyc.edu
WEIGHILL, Dale 810-762-0456 228 B dale.weighill@mcc.edu
WEIGLE, Chuck 856-351-2628 282 I cweigle@salemcc.edu
WEIGLE, Greg 843-792-7526 409 D weigle@musc.edu
WEIKEL, Bridget, K 757-683-4283 468 C bweikel@odu.edu
WEIL, David 607-274-3098 302 E dweil@ithaca.edu
WEIL, Denis 312-595-4900 139 H dweil@id.iit.edu
WEIL, Valerie, P 215-596-8800 400 B
WEILAND-ZALEZNAK, Carla 914-251-6046 318 E carla.weiland@purchase.edu
WEILER, Andrew 585-582-8301 298 E andrewweiler@elim.edu
WEILER, Eric 319-398-1281 167 H eric.weiler@kirkwood.edu
WEILER, Phil 509-335-4742 484 D phil.weiler@wsu.edu
WEILL, Lawrence 845-434-5750 321 B
WEILMINSTER, Deirdre 301-846-2610 198 E dweilminster@frederick.edu
WEIMER, Brian 573-882-5923 260 C weimerb@missouri.edu
WEIMER, Jean 414-847-3272 493 C jeanweimer@miad.edu
WEIMER, Rebecca 479-524-7493 20 C bweimer@jbu.edu
WEIMER, Theresa 718-390-3122 324 B tweimer@wagner.edu
WEIMER, Tresa 304-367-4826 488 L tresa.weimer@fairmontstate.edu
WEIN, Kory, G 608-342-1151 495 E weink@uwplatt.edu
WEIN, Mitchell, L 610-896-1223 385 H mwein@haverford.edu
WEINBERG, Adam, S 740-587-6281 351 K weinberga@denison.edu
WEINBERG, Jerry, B 618-650-3010 149 H jweinbe@siue.edu
WEINBERGER, Jayne 718-522-9073 290 B jweinberger@asa.edu
WEINBERGER, Judah 212-463-0400 322 C judah.weinberger6@touro.edu
WEINBERGER, Judah 212-463-0400 322 B judah.weinberger6@touro.edu
WEINDLLING, Lauren 203-576-2400 89 A lweindli@bridgeport.edu
WEINDORF, David, C 989-774-3094 221M weind1dc@cmich.edu
WEINER, Daniel 860-486-3152 89 B dan.weiner@uconn.edu
WEINER, David 312-369-7816 136 C dweiner@colum.edu
WEINER, Greg, S 508-767-7321 205 F gs.weiner@assumption.edu
WEINER, Marc 212-247-3434 304 J mweiner@mandl.edu
WEINER, Melvyn, P 212-247-3434 304 J melweiner2@mandl.edu
WEINER, Michael 949-480-4337 64 E mweiner@soka.edu
WEINER, Nettie 212-247-3434 304 J nweiner@mandl.edu
WEINER, Steven, A 650-543-3927 52 A steven.weiner@menlo.edu
WEINER, Stuart 212-247-3434 304 J stuweiner@mandl.edu
WEINERT, Daniel, J 563-884-5761 169 C dan.weinert@palmer.edu
WEINERT, Daryl 412-268-5048 380 B dweinert@cmu.edu
WEINERT, Rick 218-751-8670 241 Q rickweinert@oakhills.edu
WEINGARD, Cyndi 510-879-9200 60 C cweingard@samuuelmerritt.edu
WEINGART, Brian 304-558-4618 488 I brian.weingart@wvhepc.edu
WEINGART, Chedva 626-585-7454 56 D cweingart@pasadena.edu
WEINGART, Stephen, T 260-359-4067 155 G sweingart@huntington.edu
WEINGARTEN, Andrew 503-943-7205 376 H weingart@up.edu
WEINGARTEN, Isreal 845-426-3488 291 D
WEININGER, Melissa 419-448-3416 361 C weiningerm@tiffin.edu
WEINKAUF, Donald, H 651-962-5762 243 F weinkauf@stthomas.edu
WEINKOPF, Christopher 805-421-5926 67 J cweinkopf@thomasaquinas.edu
WEINMAN, Todd 615-322-2571 427 B todd.weinman@vanderbilt.edu
WEINMANN, Heather 858-513-9240 16 I heather.weinmann@ashford.edu
WEINS, Sean, A 918-595-7916 370 B sean.weins@tulsacc.edu
WEINSHEIM, Leslie 970-521-6714 82 B leslie.weinsheim@njc.edu
WEINSHEL, Seth, D 202-994-2552 92 C sdweingw@gwu.edu
WEINSTEIN, Daniel 718-997-4105 295 A daniel.weinstein@qc.cuny.edu
WEINSTEIN, Heather 802-828-2800 463 A haw09010@ccv.vsc.edu
WEINSTEIN, Mark 937-766-8800 349 C mweinstein@cedarville.edu
WEINSTEIN, Sara 804-752-3749 469 B saraweinstein@rmc.edu
WEINSTOCK, Austin 708-456-0300 151 A austinweinstock@triton.edu
WEINTRAUB, Brandon 352-371-2833 98 D it@dragonrises.edu
WEINTRAUB, Susan 603-641-7600 273 C sweintraub@anselm.edu
WEINTRAUB, Yitzchok 732-985-6533 279 F
WEINZAPFEL-SMITH, Tami 812-237-4115 155 H
WEIR, Amy 765-361-6078 162 G weira@wabash.edu
WEIR, Catherine 310-434-8208 63 B weir_catherine@smc.edu
WEIR, Dustin 323-860-0789 50 E
WEIR, Lljuna 601-877-6700 244 B weir@alcorn.edu
WEIR, Paul 575-562-2153 285 E
WEIRICK, Chad 740-755-7327 349 D weirick.7@cotc.edu
WEIS, Charlene 701-255-3285 346 I cweis@uttc.edu
WEIS, Ed 516-299-2000 304 D ed.weis@liu.edu
WEIS, Eric 661-654-3537 30 C eweis@csub.edu
WEIS, Lisa 918-293-5260 368 B lisa.weis@okstate.edu
WEISBERG, Bradley 408-741-4012 75 D bradley.weisberg@westvalley.edu
WEISBORD, Aviva 410-358-3144 204 F
WEISBORD, Beryl 410-484-7200 201 B rbw@nirc.edu
WEISBORD, Dano, J 413-585-2427 218 D dweisbor@smith.edu
WEISE, Stephanie 201-879-3062 274 I sweise@bergen.edu
WEISENBERGER, Clare 602-275-7133 15 P clare.weisenberger@rsi.edu
WEISENBURGER, Leigh 207-786-6000 193 D lweisenb@bates.edu
WEISER, Bridget, R 785-833-4325 175 C bridget@kwu.edu
WEISGERBER, James (Chip), E 412-536-1765 386 H chip.weisgerber@laroche.edu
WEISHAAR, Mary 618-650-3785 149 H mweisha@siue.edu
WEISHNER, Stephanie 910-898-9645 336 A weishners2525@montgomery.edu
WEISKOPF, Lee 662-325-1008 247 A lee.weiskopf@pres.msstate.edu
WEISMAN, Susan, E 718-489-5388 312 H sweisman@sfc.edu
WEISNER, Christina 252-335-0821 333 E christina_weisner@albemarle.edu
WEISS, Aaron 440-366-4866 355 B
WEISS, Andrea 212-824-2248 300 H aweiss@huc.edu
WEISS, Beth 440-775-8413 357 G beth.weiss@oberlin.edu
WEISS, David 210-567-3709 455 E weissd@uthscsa.edu
WEISS, Deborah 334-844-5001 4 E weissds@auburn.edu
WEISS, H 732-364-1220 274 G
WEISS, Joanne 303-333-4224 11 C
WEISS, Johanna 804-594-4187 473 B jweiss@jtcc.edu
WEISS, Joshua 413-565-1000 205 I jweiss@baypath.edu
WEISS, Karen 618-252-5400 149 E karen.weiss@sic.edu
WEISS, Katherine 323-343-4004 32 B kweiss@calstatela.edu
WEISS, Kay 909-389-3362 60 E kweiss@sbccd.cc.ca.us
WEISS, Lora, G 814-865-6332 391 F lgw1@psu.edu
WEISS, Mary Jane 978-998-7749 209 B mweiss@endicott.edu
WEISS, Michael 843-208-8055 412 C mcweiss@uscb.edu
WEISS, Toni 504-862-8342 191 D tweiss@tulane.edu
WEISS, Valerie 313-664-7852 222 C vweiss@collegeforcreativestudies.edu
WEISS-COOK, Laura 785-320-4541 175 E lauraweiss-cook@manhattantech.edu
WEISSBERG, Erik 617-587-5750 216 H weissberge@neco.edu
WEISSENFLUH, Anji 541-962-3236 372 H aweissen@eou.edu
WEISSMAN, Neil, B 717-245-1321 382 B weissmne@dickinson.edu
WEISSMAN, Rebecca 315-267-2118 318 D weissmr@potsdam.edu
WEISSMANN, Kristopher, E 803-938-3763 412 G weissmak@uscsumter.edu
WEIST, Barbara 253-879-2691 483 G bweist@pugetsound.edu
WEIST, Ronald, D 301-546-0074 201 D weistrd@pgcc.edu
WEISZ, Brett 406-247-5701 263 H brett.weisz@msubillings.edu
WEIT, Amy, R 845-569-3735 307 B amy.weit@msmc.edu
WEITHERS, Christine 718-262-2916 295 D cweithers@york.cuny.edu
WEITZ, Catherine 208-426-4055 130 F catherineweitz@boisestate.edu
WEITZEL, Peter 636-627-2212 254 B pweitzel@lindenwood.edu
WEITZMAN, Lauren 801-581-6826 459 D lweitzman@sa.utah.edu
WEKESA, Kennedy 334-229-4316 4 B wekesa@alasu.edu
WELAGE, Lynda 612-624-1900 242 K lwelage@umn.edu
WELAISH, Andrew 717-871-7126 394 B andy.welaish@millersville.edu
WELBORN, Gary 706-756-4690 127 E gary.welborn@westgatech.edu
WELBORN, Janice 970-943-3400 85 B jwelborn@western.edu
WELBORN, Jen 706-355-5025 115 C jwelborn@athenstech.edu
WELBORN, Ruth, B 512-245-3300 449 G rw01@txstate.edu
WELCH, Alexis 252-527-6223 335 E abwelch27@lenoircc.edu
WELCH, Andrea, D 330-569-5174 353 F welchad@hiram.edu
WELCH, Annmarie 516-572-7326 307 C annmarie.welch@ncc.edu
WELCH, Arlesia 386-481-2049 96 D welcha@cookman.edu
WELCH, Charles, L 501-660-1000 17 G president@asusystem.edu
WELCH, Dan 814-866-8151 387 C dwelch@lecom.edu
WELCH, David 949-269-5512 64 E dwelch@soka.edu
WELCH, Denise 903-693-1121 440 E dwelch@panola.edu
WELCH, Dirk 940-397-4972 439 F dirk.welch@msutexas.edu
WELCH, Donald, J 814-865-3540 391 F djw66@psu.edu
WELCH, JR., Donald, J 814-865-3684 391 F djw66@psu.edu
WELCH, Eddie 773-995-2111 134 J ewelch@csu.edu
WELCH, Edwin 765-998-4315 161 A edwelch@taylor.edu
WELCH, Frances, C 843-805-5507 407 D welchf@cofc.edu
WELCH, Jason 585-385-8032 313 A jwelch@sjfc.edu
WELCH, Jennifer, C 315-464-4570 316 F welchj@upstate.edu
WELCH, Joel, D 828-448-3102 338 G
WELCH, Lawrence, J 660-944-2914 251 B lwelch@conception.edu
WELCH, Lena 615-248-1393 425 D lwelch@trevecca.edu
WELCH, Lillian 216-987-4840 351 D lillian.welch@tri-c.edu

WERTZ, Miriam .... 574-807-7209 153 G
miriam.wertz@betheluniversity.edu
WERTZ, Monnie .... 813-257-3757 113 B
mwertz@ut.edu
WESCOAT, Megan .... 308-635-6017 269 E
wescoatm@wncc.edu
WESCOTT, Abigail .... 276-244-1234 463 H
awescott@asl.edu
WESCOTT, Holly .... 479-619-4341.. 20 G
hwescott@nwacc.edu
WESCOTT, Jon, D .... 570-326-3761 392 S
jdw18@pct.edu
WESLEY, Artanya .... 262-472-1172 496 E
WESLEY, Haley .... 785-227-3380 171 H
wesleyhs@bethanylb.edu
WESLEY, Homer .... 719-502-3563.. 82 D
homer.wesley@pikespeak.edu
WESLEY, Patrick .... 318-670-6000 191 B
WESLOW, Suzanne .... 414-229-4503 495 B
sweslow@uwm.edu
WESNER, Katrin .... 910-962-4126 343 B
wesnerk@uncw.edu
WESNER, Samantha ...... 610-921-7611 377 F
swesner@albright.edu
WESS, Byron .... 215-953-5999.. 93 H
WESSEL, Tonya .... 816-584-7406 257 E
tonya.wessel@park.edu
WESSELL, Charlotte .... 212-353-4252 297 C
charlotte.wessell@cooper.edu
WESSELS, Gus .... 979-532-6505 457 H
gusw@wcjc.edu
WESSON, Cameron .... 717-358-3986 383 G
cwesson@fandm.edu
WESSON, G. Dale .... 404-880-8754 116 I
gwesson@cau.edu
WEST, Adrian .... 803-780-1269 413 B
west@voorhees.edu
WEST, Amy .... 419-372-2704 348 F
amywest@bgsu.edu
WEST, Amy .... 731-425-2643 423 F
awest12@jscc.edu
WEST, Amy .... 731-425-2621 423 F
awest12@jscc.edu
WEST, April .... 877-954-1500 420 F
WEST, Cathy .... 361-698-1265 434 H
cwest@delmar.edu
WEST, Chip .... 562-938-4406.. 48 K
cwest@lbcc.edu
WEST, Chotsani .... 516-877-3000 288 L
WEST, Christina, D .... 202-216-4370 427 B
christina.d.west@vanderbilt.edu
WEST, Cynthia, L .... 731-881-7125 426 E
cwest@utm.edu
WEST, Dana .... 865-882-4657 424 D
westdk2@roanestate.edu
WEST, David .... 575-624-8014 286 F
west@nmmi.edu
WEST, David, L .... 901-722-3210 422 I
dwest@sco.edu
WEST, Debra .... 870-733-6722.. 18 A
dwest@asumidsouth.edu
WEST, Detra .... 330-569-5237 353 F
westde@hiram.edu
WEST, Detra, E .... 330-569-5237 353 F
westde@hiram.edu
WEST, Dominique .... 718-960-8144 293 E
dominique.west@lehman.cuny.edu
WEST, Dominique .... 718-990-6247 313 B
0065mgr@follett.com
WEST, Greg .... 262-691-5417 499 A
gwest@wctc.edu
WEST, J. Cameron .... 334-833-4409.... 5 H
camwest@hawks.huntingdon.edu
WEST, Jennifer, L .... 434-924-7210 471 F
fqn4pk@virginia.edu
WEST, Jody .... 212-280-1373 323 C
jwest@uts.columbia.edu
WEST, John .... 703-416-1441 465 E
jwest@divinemercy.edu
WEST, Judy .... 216-373-6396 357 F
jwest@ndc.edu
WEST, Julian .... 408-852-4738.. 43 H
jwest@gavilan.edu
WEST, Junette .... 602-639-7500.. 12 L
WEST, Kevin .... 330-672-2220 354 A
kwest32@kent.edu
WEST, Kevin .... 828-689-1585 330 H
kwest@mhu.edu
WEST, Korey .... 212-989-3170 160 A
westkl@pnw.edu
WEST, Kristie .... 916-691-7199.. 50 K
westk@crc.losrios.edu
WEST, Lance .... 304-696-6440 488 N
west24@marshall.edu
WEST, Linda, J .... 304-697-7550 486 F
lwest@huntingtonjuniorcollege.edu
WEST, Marc .... 440-826-3483 348 C
mwest@bw.edu
WEST, Mark, D .... 734-764-7409 231 A
markwest@umich.edu
WEST, Mason .... 276-326-3682 464 A
mwest@bluefield.edu
WEST, Matthew .... 937-327-7946 364 C
counseling@wittenberg.edu
WEST, Maurice .... 214-379-5514 440 H
mwest@pqc.edu
WEST, Mickey .... 615-329-8680 418 E
mwest@fisk.edu
WEST, Molly .... 601-974-1063 246 C
molly.west@millsaps.edu
WEST, Peter .... 914-674-7803 305 H
pwest@mercy.edu
WEST, Peter .... 571-633-9651 471 C
peter.west@uona.edu
WEST, Raymond .... 951-222-8000.. 59 D
WEST, JR., Reginald ..... 949-376-6000.. 47 G
rwest@lcad.edu
WEST, Ryan .... 503-399-5018 372 A
ryan.west@chemeketa.edu
WEST, Sue .... 303-444-0202.. 81 N
WEST, Susan .... 615-460-5602 417 B
susan.west@belmont.edu
WEST, Susan, H .... 615-460-6435 417 B
susan.west@belmont.edu
WEST, Tom 954-262-4994 104M
twest@nova.edu
WEST, Tracy, L .... 909-884-8891.. 40 C
WEST, William .... 512-404-4804 429 K
wwest@austinseminary.edu
WEST-OKIRI, Patricia ..... 575-538-6671 288 J
patricia.west@wnmu.edu
WESTARY, Kenneth .... 443-840-3213 198 D
kwestary@ccbcmd.edu
WESTBERG, Caleb .... 773-995-3561 134 J
cwestber@csu.edu
WESTBROCK, Theresa .... 319-273-7868 163 G
theresa.westbrock@uni.edu
WESTBROOK, Ashley .... 706-245-7226 118 C
awestbrook@ec.edu
WESTBROOK, Sara .... 503-943-7161 376 H
westbroo@up.edu
WESTBROOK, Steve ...... 936-468-3401 444 H
WESTBROOK, Velma, S 985-448-4687 192 C
sue.westbrook@nicholls.edu
WESTBROOK, Velma, S 985-448-4013 192 C
sue.westbrook@nicholls.edu
WESTBROOKS, Elaine .... 919-962-1301 342 B
elainelw@email.unc.edu
WESTBY, Christopher .... 914-606-6810 324 F
christopher.westby@sunywcc.edu
WESTBY, Rebecca .... 520-515-5449.. 11 O
westbyr@cochise.edu
WESTCOTT, James .... 605-367-5675 416 B
james.westcott@southeasttech.edu
WESTDYKE, Anne, E ...... 512-492-3147 441 N
anneew@stedwards.edu
WESTENBROEK, Steve ... 402-399-2465 265 H
swestenbroek@csm.edu
WESTER, Ken .... 479-968-0218.. 18 E
kwester@atu.edu
WESTERBERG, Sarah ..... 801-422-4668 458 A
sarah_westerberg@byu.edu
WESTERFIELD,
Mary Ann, K .... 302-356-6936.. 91 C
maryann.k.westerfield@wilmu.edu
WESTERGAARD,
Patricia .... 979-209-7446 430 I
pat.westergaard@blinn.edu
WESTERGAARD, Tricia .. 248-370-4585 229 F
westerga@oakland.edu
WESTERHOF, Jolanda ... 585-245-5151 317 E
jwesterhof@geneseo.edu
WESTERHOUSE, Joni, L 314-286-0120 261 B
westerhousej@wustl.edu
WESTERIK, Robin .... 406-604-4321 262 C
rwesterik@apollos.edu
WESTERLUND, Richard . 517-321-0242 224 E
rwesterlund@glcc.edu
WESTERMANN, Jorg ..... 866-492-5336 243 G
jorg.westermann@mail.waldenu.edu
WESTERMEYER,
Susan, M .... 317-940-9135 153 H
swesterm@butler.edu
WESTERN, Bruce .... 309-298-1971 152 I
ba-western@wiu.edu
WESTERN, David .... 276-244-1239 463 H
dwestern@asl.edu
WESTERN, Lindajean ..... 330-823-2568 362 E
westerlh@mountunion.edu
WESTERSTAHL STENPORT,
Anna .... 585-475-2935 312 A
llmgcj@rit.edu
WESTERVELT, Rob .... 636-949-1438 254 B
rwestervelt@lindenwood.edu
WESTERVELT, Wayne ..... 315-312-2265 318 B
wayne.westervelt@oswego.edu
WESTFALL, Anita, C ...... 540-568-6868 467 C
westfaac@jmu.edu
WESTFALL, Michael ...... 248-364-6152 229 F
mwestfall@oakland.edu
WESTFIELD,
Nancy Lynne .... 765-361-6434 162 G
westfiel@wabash.edu
WESTHOFF, James .... 207-992-4909 194 D
westhoffj@husson.edu
WESTHOFF, Randy .... 218-755-2016 237 B
randall.westhoff@bemidjistate.edu
WESTHOFF, Tom .... 620-235-4232 176 H
tmwesthoff@pittstate.edu
WESTLAKE,
Christopher, J .... 850-872-3212 101 O
cwestlake@gulfcoast.edu
WESTLEY, Chris .... 239-590-7090 109 G
cwestley@fgcu.edu
WESTLUND, Amy .... 530-242-7648.. 64 A
awestlund@shastacollege.edu
WESTMAN, Craig .... 856-225-6510 281 A
craig.westman@rutgers.edu
WESTMAN, Dennis .... 580-745-2148 369 F
dwestman@se.edu
WESTMAN, Jennifer ...... 307-332-2930 500 J
jwestman@wyomingcatholic.edu
WESTMAN, Lee Ann ...... 856-225-6671 281 A
leeann.westman@rutgers.edu
WESTMORELAND,
Andrew .... 205-726-2727.... 6 E
tawestmo@samford.edu
WESTMORELAND, Tim .. 830-372-8065 448 C
twestmoreland@tlu.edu
WESTON, Alison .... 540-674-3685 473 F
aweston@nr.edu
WESTON, Brian .... 619-388-6750.. 60 H
bweston@sdccd.edu
WESTON, Earl .... 970-207-4500.. 84 E
WESTON, Jackie .... 405-945-3310 368 C
jackie.weston@okstate.edu
WESTON, Jerri .... 318-473-6424 189 A
jweston@lsua.edu
WESTON, Scott .... 304-357-4879 486 J
gradyweston@ucwv.edu
WESTOVER, Jon .... 919-515-5036 341 E
jrwestov@ncsu.edu
WESTOVER, Kristen .... 276-523-7490 473 E
kwestover@mecc.edu
WESTPHAL, Donald, M . 507-344-7320 233 I
don.westphal@blc.edu
WESTPHAL, Judith .... 920-424-3089 495 C
westphaj@uwosh.edu
WESTRA, Amy .... 712-722-6024 165 E
amy.westra@dordt.edu
WESTRA, Kayla .... 507-372-3435 239 B
kayla.westra@mnwest.edu
WESTRAADT, Gabrielle .. 267-295-2302 401 C
gwestraadt@walnuthillcollege.edu
WETHERBEE, Scott .... 734-487-1050 223 F
scott.wetherbee@emich.edu
WETHERINGTON, Kitty .. 252-328-9882 340 H
wetheringtonk@ecu.edu
WETHERINGTON, Lee ..... 252-527-6223 335 E
lwetherington@lenoircc.edu
WETHINGTON, Charles . 252-638-7350 333 F
wethingc@cravencc.edu
WETSELL, Linda, S .... 814-332-4790 378 A
lwetsell@allegheny.edu
WETSTEIN, Ken, A .... 217-581-5129 137 C
kawetstein@eiu.edu
WETSTEIN, Matthew ...... 831-479-6306.. 27 G
mawetste@cabrillo.edu
WETZ, Steve .... 614-234-4397 356 E
swetz@mccn.edu
WETZEL, Derrick .... 610-282-1100 382 A
derrick.wetzel@desales.edu
WETZEL, Jason .... 651-423-8235 237 E
jason.wetzel@dctc.edu
WETZEL, Kim .... 213-624-1200.. 42 F
kwetzel@fidm.edu
WETZEL, Leslie .... 415-422-4055.. 72 I
lawetzel@usfca.edu
WETZEL, Mary, E .... 717-728-2260 380 D
marywetzel@centralpenn.edu
WETZEL, Mike .... 717-358-4759 383 G
mike.wetzel@fandm.edu
WETZEL, Mike .... 504-282-4455 190 D
WETZEL, Shelby .... 307-754-6110 500 G
shelby.wetzel@nwc.edu
WETZEL, Suzanne, M .... 734-384-4206 227 F
swetzel@monroeccc.edu
WETZSTEIN, James .... 219-464-6794 162 C
james.wetzstein@valpo.edu
WEVER, Matthew .... 314-367-8700 260 A
matthew.wever@uhsp.edu
WEXLER, Joan, G .... 718-780-7900 291 G
joan.wexler@brooklaw.edu
WEXLER, Jonathan, D .... 518-276-6143 311 J
wexler@rpi.edu
WEXLER, Judie, G .... 415-575-6124.. 29 A
jwexler@ciis.edu
WEY, Lora .... 941-309-4041 106 J
lwey@ringling.edu
WEYAND, Andrea .... 303-762-6948.. 80 G
andrea.weyand@denverseminary.edu
WEYERMANN, Trudi ..... 765-285-5774 153 E
tlweyermann@bsu.edu
WEYGANT, Susan .... 914-923-2397 310 F
sweygant@pace.edu
WEYHAUPT, Adam .... 314-889-1460 252 G
aweyhaupt@fontbonne.edu
WEYHENMEYER, James 334-844-4784.... 4 E
jaw0155@auburn.edu
WEYHING, Katherine ..... 502-585-9911 184 E
kweyhing@spalding.edu
WEYLER, Megan, E .... 215-895-6383 382 D
m.weyler@drexel.edu
WEYRICH, Andrew, S ..... 801-581-7236 459 D
andy.weyrich@utah.edu
WHALEN, Alice .... 636-584-6532 252 D
alice.whalen@eastcentral.edu
WHALEN, Joseph .... 425-388-9232 479 B
jwhalen@everettcc.edu
WHALEN, Kristina .... 925-424-1104.. 36 A
kwhalen@laspositascollege.edu
WHALEN, Lynn .... 217-786-2219 142 F
lynn.whalen@llcc.edu
WHALEN, Michael .... 860-685-2908.. 90 A
mwhalen@wesleyan.edu
WHALEN, Thomas .... 212-229-5456 307 E
whalent@newschool.edu
WHALEN, Tina .... 513-558-7485 361 I
tina.whalen@uc.edu
WHALEN, Toni .... 502-213-2118 181 H
toni.whalen@kctcs.edu
WHALEN-SMITH,
Heather, C .... 315-655-7132 292 B
hcwhalensmith@cazenovia.edu
WHALEY, Ashley, N .... 240-500-2213 199 A
anwhaley@hagerstowncc.edu
WHALEY, Candace .... 478-301-5121 122 C
whaley_ce@mercer.edu
WHALEY, Chris .... 865-882-4501 424 D
whaleycl@roanestate.edu
WHALEY, David, J .... 802-485-2347 461 H
davew@norwich.edu
WHALEY, Michael, J ...... 860-685-3160.. 90 A
mwhaley@wesleyan.edu
WHALEY, Sean .... 530-283-0202.. 42 E
swhaley@frc.edu
WHALEY, Stephanie .... 252-328-5815 340 H
whaleys19@ecu.edu
WHANG, KyuJung, E ...... 609-258-5491 279 E
whang@princeton.edu
WHANN, Christopher ..... 646-230-1207 320 B
christopher.whann@esc.edu
WHAPHAM, Ted .... 816-501-3759 249 H
theodore.whapham@avila.edu
WHARTON, Mark .... 423-425-4444 426 D
mark-wharton@utc.edu
WHATLEY, Andrew .... 312-369-7261 136 C
awhatley@colum.edu
WHATLEY, Annie .... 202-274-5000.. 94 B
WHATLEY, Dirk .... 301-891-4187 204 D
WHATLEY, Kara, M .... 626-395-3404.. 29 B
kwhatley@caltech.edu
WHATLEY, Melissa .... 831-459-3470.. 71 A
mwhatley@ucsc.edu
WHATLEY, Sherri .... 903-566-7247 455 C
swhatley@uttyler.edu
WHEAT, Adam .... 870-245-5593.. 20 H
wheata@obu.edu
WHEAT, Casie .... 408-864-8642.. 42 K
wheatcasie@deanza.edu

WHITE, Erin 910-672-1347 341 B ewhite@uncfsu.edu

WHITE, Ernie 919-739-6805 338 F ewhite@waynecc.edu

WHITE, Gary, R 805-893-2182 70 E gary.white@sa.ucsb.edu

WHITE, Gene 870-543-5949 21 D gwhite@seark.edu

WHITE, George 718-262-2804 295 D gwhite@york.cuny.edu

WHITE, Gina 318-342-3002 193 A ewhite@ulm.edu

WHITE, Greg 650-508-3500 54 G provost@ndnu.edu

WHITE, Heather 352-392-1261 110 E heatherw@dso.ufl.edu

WHITE, Ian, K 516-686-7516 308 H iwhite@nyit.edu

WHITE, Jama 423-266-4574 422 D

WHITE, James 501-332-0252 18 D jwhite@asutr.edu

WHITE, James 303-492-7294 83 M james.white@colorado.edu

WHITE, James 509-313-6568 479 E whitej@gonzaga.edu

WHITE, James, W 919-962-1165 342 B asdean@unc.edu

WHITE, Jared 334-242-2688 4 E jrw0020@auburn.edu

WHITE, Jean 860-913-2070 87 H jwhite@goodwin.edu

WHITE, Jeanne 630-617-6485 137 E whitej521@elmhurst.edu

WHITE, Jeffrey 540-362-6609 467 A whitejs@hollins.edu

WHITE, Jennifer 859-622-1705 180 B jennifer.white@eku.edu

WHITE, Jennifer 309-671-2734 143 I jwhite@methodistcol.edu

WHITE, Jerry 574-807-7877 153 G jerry.white@betheluniversity.edu

WHITE, Jessica 651-201-1845 236 F jessica.white@minnstate.edu

WHITE, Jessie 254-659-7841 436 C jwhite@hillcollege.edu

WHITE, Joel 860-906-5076 86 C jwhite@ccc.commnet.edu

WHITE, John 404-752-1734 123 A jwhite@msm.edu

WHITE, John 760-565-4827 39 A jowhite@collegeofthedesert.edu

WHITE, John 413-748-3895 218 E jawhite@springfield.edu

WHITE, John 843-953-6810 407 D whitej@cofc.edu

WHITE, John, E 609-497-7880 279 D john.white@ptsem.edu

WHITE, Jonathan 956-380-8194 441 L jwhite@riogrande.edu

WHITE, Josette 205-652-3682 9 B jwhite@uwa.edu

WHITE, Joy 470-639-0985 122 H joy.white@morehouse.edu

WHITE, Julie 253-964-6776 481 H juwhite@pierce.ctc.edu

WHITE, Julie, R 315-464-4816 316 F whitejul@upstate.edu

WHITE, Justin 479-619-4123 20 G jwhite35@nwacc.edu

WHITE, Karen 703-526-6803 468 A karen.white@marymount.edu

WHITE, Karen, D 650-508-3500 54 G

WHITE, Karol 319-363-1323 168 D kwhite@mtmercy.edu

WHITE, Kathleen, C 256-765-4223 8 E kcwhite@una.edu

WHITE, Katie 760-757-2121 52 G kwhite@miracosta.edu

WHITE, Katie 972-825-4636 444 C kwhite@sagu.edu

WHITE, Ken 530-226-4636 64 C kwhite@simpsonu.edu

WHITE, Kenneth, L 435-797-2201 459 F ken.white@usu.edu

WHITE, Kim 423-425-4717 426 D kim-white@utc.edu

WHITE, Kimberly 256-782-5180 6 A ksgwhite@jsu.edu

WHITE, Kyle 918-766-5512 368 E kwhite@okwu.edu

WHITE, Lamar, J 803-793-5241 408 A whitel@denmarktech.edu

WHITE, Lauren 361-698-1641 434 H lwhite16@delmar.edu

WHITE, Linda 901-435-1477 419 I linda_white@loc.edu

WHITE, Lindsay 918-595-7869 370 B lindsay.white@tulsacc.edu

WHITE, Lindsey 479-619-4191 20 G lwhite13@nwacc.edu

WHITE, London 918-465-1818 365 K lwhite@eosc.edu

WHITE, Lori 765-658-4220 154 G president@depauw.edu

WHITE, Madalyn 513-244-4501 356 F madalyn.white@msj.edu

WHITE, Marcia, J 518-454-5121 296 E marcia.white@strose.edu

WHITE, Mario 404-225-4130 115 F mawhite@atlantatech.edu

WHITE, Mark, D 806-371-5143 428 F mdwhite@actx.edu

WHITE, Marlene 908-709-7041 283 E marlene.white@ucc.edu

WHITE, Mary, L 318-797-5103 189 E mary.white@lsus.edu

WHITE, Mary Jo 206-934-5378 482 H maryjo.white@seattlecolleges.edu

WHITE, Mary Kate 304-724-5000 486 C mwhite@cdu.edu

WHITE, Mason, M 410-543-6165 204 A mmwhite@salisbury.edu

WHITE, Matthew 435-797-3495 459 F matthew.white@usu.edu

WHITE, Matthew 757-727-5253 466 L matthew.white@hamptonu.edu

WHITE, Maureen 860-439-2541 87 F mwhite4@conncoll.edu

WHITE, Maureen 516-726-5632 502 G whitem@usmma.edu

WHITE, Melea 319-895-4402 164 E melwhite@cornellcollege.edu

WHITE, Melissa 423-636-7300 425 E mwhite@tusculum.edu

WHITE, Michael 972-860-8232 433 H mwhite@dcccd.edu

WHITE, Michael 401-863-2648 403 A michael_p_white@brown.edu

WHITE, RET., Michael 970-521-6607 82 B mike.white@njc.edu

WHITE, Michele, M 540-568-6281 467 C whitemm@jmu.edu

WHITE, Michelle 918-647-1399 365 D mwhite@carlalbert.edu

WHITE, Mike 740-386-4111 355 F whitejm@mtc.edu

WHITE, Mona 337-475-5501 192 B mwhite@mcneese.edu

WHITE, Monica 504-816-4374 186 F mwhite@dillard.edu

WHITE, O, I 903-923-2421 457 I oiwhite@wileyc.edu

WHITE, O. Ivan 903-927-3384 457 I oiwhite@wileyc.edu

WHITE, Odawa 715-634-4790 491 L owhite@lco.edu

WHITE, Pamela 413-755-4452 215 F pjwhite@stcc.edu

WHITE, Pamela 803-327-7402 407 A pwhite@clintoncollege.edu

WHITE, Patricia 615-460-6524 417 B patricia.white@belmont.edu

WHITE, Paul, M 920-565-1000 492 A whitepm@lakeland.edu

WHITE, Penny 540-831-6716 468 E pwhite@radford.edu

WHITE, Randy 850-729-6404 104 L whiter3@nwfsc.edu

WHITE, Ray 334-241-9537 7 C grwhite@troy.edu

WHITE, Reginald, H 860-439-2085 87 F rwhite3@conncoll.edu

WHITE, Renée, T 646-909-2374 307 E whitert@newschool.edu

WHITE, Renee 505-424-2301 285 H renee.white@iaia.edu

WHITE, Rhonda 205-726-4371 6 E rwhite7@samford.edu

WHITE, Robert 816-654-7616 253 I rwhite@kcumb.edu

WHITE, Ronald 706-245-7226 118 C rwhite@ec.edu

WHITE, Roslyn, M 601-877-6384 244 B rmwhite@alcorn.edu

WHITE, Ryan 309-796-5194 133 D whitery@bhc.edu

WHITE, Ryan 972-883-5561 454 D ryan.white@utdallas.edu

WHITE, Sarah 412-536-1177 386 H sarah.white@laroche.edu

WHITE, Sarah Beth 276-739-2472 474 H swhite@vhcc.edu

WHITE, Shakeena 910-275-6362 335 C swhite@jamessprunt.edu

WHITE, Shanice 601-979-0373 245 G shanice.n.white@jsums.edu

WHITE, Shannan 251-460-6110 9 A skwhite@southalabama.edu

WHITE, Shelley, Y 828-627-4516 335 A sywhite@haywood.edu

WHITE, Sherron, D 252-335-3660 341 A sdwhite@ecsu.edu

WHITE, Sloan 817-531-4414 450 F swhite@txwes.edu

WHITE, Stephen 718-862-7548 304 K stephen.white@manhattan.edu

WHITE, Stephen, E 401-254-3607 404 C swhite@rwu.edu

WHITE, Stephen, F 615-898-2422 421 C stephen.white@mtsu.edu

WHITE, Steven 316-978-3782 178 B steven.white@wichita.edu

WHITE, Susan 207-768-9533 196 I susan.r.white@maine.edu

WHITE, Susannah 415-701-7040 61 E swhite@sfcm.edu

WHITE, Tamisia 212-870-1229 309 C finaid@nyts.edu

WHITE, Tanya 757-823-2886 468 B tswhite@nsu.edu

WHITE, Theodore 816-235-1330 260 D whitetc@umkc.edu

WHITE, Thomas 937-766-3200 349 C thomaswhite@cedarville.edu

WHITE, Timothy, L 352-846-0850 110 E tlwhite@ufl.edu

WHITE, Travis 918-595-7601 370 B travis.white@tulsacc.edu

WHITE, Trisha 918-465-1708 365 K twhite@eosc.edu

WHITE, Troy 903-566-7057 455 C troywhite@uttyler.edu

WHITE, Troy 903-923-2060 435 A tgwhite@etbu.edu

WHITE, Wayman 252-335-0821 333 E waywhite@albemarle.edu

WHITE, Wendy 252-638-7271 333 F whitew@cravencc.edu

WHITE, Wendy, S 215-746-5240 399 J wendy.white@ogc.upenn.edu

WHITE, William 215-248-7118 380 G whitew@chc.edu

WHITE BULL, David 605-455-6076 414 H

WHITE DAVIS, Kristyn 719-549-2304 79 G kristyn.whitedavis@csupueblo.edu

WHITE-FARNHAM, Jamie 715-394-8201 496 D jwhitefa@uwsuper.edu

WHITE-HURST, Elizabeth 717-245-1315 382 B whitehue@dickinson.edu

WHITE NEGLEY, Angela 304-696-2599 488 N negley4@marshall.edu

WHITE PUGH, April 864-644-5002 411 D awhite@swu.edu

WHITE-SHOOK, Nadine 757-455-3213 476 C nwhiteshook@vwu.edu

WHITE-SMITH, Kimberly 619-260-4540 72 H kimberlywhite@sandiego.edu

WHITECAVAGE, Michele 714-449-7404 51 D mwhitecavage@ketchum.edu

WHITED, Jimmy, R 540-375-2308 469 G whited@roanoke.edu

WHITED, Robert 406-447-4434 262 E rwhited@carroll.edu

WHITEFIELD, Joe 615-904-8375 421 C joe.whitefield@mtsu.edu

WHITEFORD, Aaron 503-768-7944 373 D ahw@lclark.edu

WHITEFORD, Craig 410-287-1914 198 A cwhiteford@cecil.edu

WHITEFORD, David 615-226-3990 419 J

WHITEHEAD, Amy 501-852-0871 23 K amyw@uca.edu

WHITEHEAD, Debbie 503-255-0332 374 A debbiew@multnomah.edu

WHITEHEAD, Ella 847-635-2658 146 E ewhitehead@oakton.edu

WHITEHEAD, JaRenae, E 757-683-4564 468 C jwhitehe@odu.edu

WHITEHEAD, JR., Joe, B 419-372-2211 348 F

WHITEHEAD, Keri 845-434-5750 321 B kwhitehead@sunysullivan.edu

WHITEHEAD, Kim 662-241-6850 247 B kmwhitehead@muw.edu

WHITEHEAD, Kimberly 718-270-5000 294 E kwhitehead@mec.cuny.edu

WHITEHEAD, Kimberly 207-561-1512 196 D kimberly.whitehead@maine.edu

WHITEHEAD, Martha, J 617-496-1295 210 B martha_whitehead@harvard.edu

WHITEHEAD, Nicole 815-280-2515 140 I nwhitehe@jjc.edu

WHITEHEAD, Nicole 570-577-1631 379 A nw018@bucknell.edu

WHITEHILL, Jessica 330-972-5206 361 G jwhitehill@uakron.edu

WHITEHOUSE, Jennifer 985-867-2240 190 I jwhitehouse@sjasc.edu

WHITEHOUSE, Weston 812-749-1226 159 E wwhitehouse@oak.edu

WHITEHURST, Marcus, A 814-865-5906 391 F maw163@psu.edu

WHITELAW, Brett 435-652-7500 459 G

WHITELAW, Lydia 610-896-1177 385 H lwhitela@haverford.edu

WHITELEY, Michelle 817-257-5018 447 H m.whiteley@tcu.edu

WHITELEY SEVER, Grace 937-327-7958 364 C whiteleyg@wittenberg.edu

WHITELY, Patricia, A 305-284-4922 112 K pwhitely@miami.edu

WHITEMAN, Betty 386-822-8869 111 F bwhiteman@stetson.edu

WHITEMAN, Charles, H 814-863-0448 391 F chw17@psu.edu

WHITEMAN, Mike 704-330-6706 333 B mike.whiteman@cpcc.edu

WHITEMAN, Patricia 406-638-3189 262 J whitemanp@lbhc.edu

WHITEMAN, Raymond, E 574-807-7139 153 G ray.whiteman@betheluniversity.edu

WHITENER, Ken 864-644-5504 411 D kwhitener@swu.edu

WHITENER, Rachel 828-835-4218 338 C rwhitener@tricountycc.edu

WHITENHILL, Ronald 909-869-3427 30 B rpwhitenhill@cpp.edu

WHITESELL, Melissa 706-272-4527 118 A mwhitesell@daltonstate.edu

WHITESELL, Warren 765-658-4229 154 G warrenwhitesell@depauw.edu

WHITESIDE, Christopher 559-925-3147 75 A christopherwhiteside@whccd.edu

WHITESIDE, Christopher 714-895-8250 38 E cwhiteside4@gwc.cccd.edu

WHITESIDE, Dannelle 931-221-7572 416 H whitesided@apsu.edu

WHITESIDE, Frederick 707-965-7200 55 H fwhiteside@puc.edu

WHITESIDE, Harold, D 615-898-2900 421 C harold.whiteside@mtsu.edu

WHITESIDES, Louis, D 803-536-8351 410 H lwhitesides@scsu.edu

WHITEY, Jeff 541-888-7402 376 B jwhitey@socc.edu

WHITFIELD, Aleczander 757-727-5303 466 L aleczander.whitfield@hamptonu.edu

WHITFIELD, Keith 919-761-2100 340 B kwhitfield@sebts.edu

WHITFIELD, Keith, E 702-895-3201 270 J keith.whitfield@unlv.edu

WHITFIELD, Robin 703-526-6941 468 A rwhitfie@marymount.edu

WHITFILL, Jill 731-352-4083 417 C whitfillj@bethelu.edu

WHITFORD, Daryl 808-675-3730 128 B daryl.whitford@byuh.edu

WHITFORD, Michael 714-662-5250 73 G michael.whitford@vanguard.edu

WHITHAM, Crystal 330-337-6403 347 B librarian@awc.edu

WIGGINS, Charles .... 828-395-1306 335 B
cpwiggins@isothermal.edu
WIGGINS, Debbie .... 757-490-1241 463 E
dwiggins@auto.edu
WIGGINS, Devon .... 903-510-2646 451 D
dwig@tjc.edu
WIGGINS, Erin .... 740-362-3366 355 H
ewiggins@msto.edu
WIGGINS, Gloria .... 910-275-6198 335 C
gwiggins@jamessprunt.edu
WIGGINS, John .... 215-751-8000 381 H
jtwiggins@ccp.edu
WIGGINS, Michaele ...... 336-334-7593 341 C
sm8093@bncollege.com
WIGGINS, Sara .... 252-451-8313 336 B
swwiggins208@nashcc.edu
WIGGINS, Shelia .... 252-527-6223 335 E
slwiggins45@lenoircc.edu
WIGGINS, Symphoni .... 706-821-8103 123 I
recordsofficestaff@paine.edu
WIGGINS, Urban .... 410-651-8200 203 B
utwiggins@umes.edu
WIGGINS, Urban, T ...... 410-651-7689 203 B
utwiggins@umes.edu
WIGGINS, Vincent .... 562-383-2189.. 65 H
vincentwiggins@scuhs.edu
WIGGINS, Vincent, D ... 773-907-4839 134 N
vwiggins1@ccc.edu
WIGGINTON, Nicholas .. 734-763-1290 231 A
nwigg@umich.edu
WIGGINTON, Van .... 281-542-2000 442 B
van.wigginton@sjcd.edu
WIGGINTON, Van, A .... 281-542-2000 442 C
van.wigginton@sjcd.edu
WIGHT, Erica .... 417-625-3188 255 I
wight-e@mssu.edu
WIGHT, Erica .... 801-957-6321 460 D
erica.wight@slcc.edu
WIGHTKIN, Joe .... 763-488-2518 237 G
joe.wightkin@hennepintech.edu
WIGHTMAN, Beth, A ..... 818-677-3434.. 32 E
beth.wightman@csun.edu
WIGHTMAN, Iain .... 303-963-3185.. 78 D
iwightman@ccu.edu
WIGHTMAN, James ...... 614-236-6264 348 I
jwightman@capital.edu
WIGHTMAN, Todd .... 208-535-5440 130 I
todd.wightman@cei.edu
WIGINTON, Chad .... 580-477-7700 371 D
chad.wiginton@wosc.edu
WIGINTON, Joey .... 334-386-7402.... 5 D
jwiginton@faulkner.edu
WIGINTON, Melissa ...... 512-404-4862 429 K
mwiginton@austinseminary.edu
WIGLE, Derick .... 585-385-8281 313 A
dwigle@sjfc.edu
WIGNALL, Eric .... 815-740-3444 152 E
ewignall@stfrancis.edu
WIGNES, David, R .... 608-785-9140 499 B
wignesd@westerntc.edu
WIKAN, Cory .... 318-869-5175 186 C
cwikan@centenary.edu
WIKSTROM, Chris .... 276-656-0253 473 H
cwikstrom@patrickhenry.edu
WILBANKS, Jennifer ..... 660-596-7229 259 D
jwilbanks@sfccmo.edu
WILBANKS, Jennifer ..... 843-349-5208 409 A
jennifer.wilbanks@hgtc.edu
WILBANKS, Laura .... 734-487-6540 223 F
laura.wilbanks@emich.edu
WILBON, Anthony .... 202-806-1500.. 92 E
anthony.wilbon@howard.edu
WILBORN, Colin .... 254-295-8642 453 A
cwilborn@umhb.edu
WILBUR, Gregory .... 615-815-8360 421 F
WILBUR, Kathleen .... 517-353-9000 227 C
schlage6@msu.edu
WILBUR, Marcia .... 706-769-1472 115 B
mwilbur@acmin.org
WILBUR, Rachael .... 276-944-6232 466 F
rwilbur@ehc.edu
WILBUR, Shelley .... 941-487-4100 110 C
mwilbur@ncf.edu
WILBURN, Crystal .... 913-621-8717 173 B
cwilburn@donnelly.edu
WILBURN, Nicole .... 913-288-7586 174 H
nwilburn@kckcc.edu
WILBURN, Reginald ...... 817-257-4131 447 H
r.a.wilburn@tcu.edu
WILBURN, Roberta .... 509-777-4215 485 D
rwilburn@whitworth.edu
WILCH, Peter .... 310-338-5334.. 51 C
peter.wilch@lmu.edu

WILCHER, Cheryl .... 305-626-9404 100 B
cwilcher@fmuniv.edu
WILCOTS, Barbara .... 303-458-4086.. 83 B
bwilcots@regis.edu
WILCOTS, Eric .... 608-263-2303 494 D
eric.wilcots@wisc.edu
WILCOX, Bonnie .... 417-873-7201 252 A
bwilcox@drury.edu
WILCOX, Cindee .... 231-591-3900 223 H
cindeewilcox@ferris.edu
WILCOX, Cordelia, A .... 919-658-7494 340 E
cwilcox@umo.edu
WILCOX, Denise .... 909-469-5393.. 75 G
dwilcox@westernu.edu
WILCOX, Jerome .... 203-837-8242.. 86 A
wilcoxj@wcsu.edu
WILCOX, Kevin .... 518-956-8120 315 D
kwilcox@albany.edu
WILCOX, Kim, A .... 951-827-5201.. 70 B
chancellor@ucr.edu
WILCOX, Madeleine ...... 215-951-2815 398 G
wilcoxm@philau.edu
WILCOX, Mark .... 412-536-1104 386 H
mark.wilcox@laroche.edu
WILCOX, Reed, N .... 540-261-4100 470 D
reed.wilcox@svu.edu
WILCOX, Robbin .... 419-267-1460 357 E
rwilcox@northweststate.edu
WILCOX, Tamera .... 785-309-3183 177 B
tamera.wilcox@salinatech.edu
WILCOX, Teresa .... 561-297-3069 109 F
WILCOX, Virginija .... 651-638-6124 233 J
virginija-wilcox@bethel.edu
WILCOXEN, Andrica ...... 913-288-7652 174 H
awilcoxen@kckcc.edu
WILCOXSON,
Douglas, A .... 517-750-1200 230 F
dwilcoxs@arbor.edu
WILCOXSON, Jesse .... 559-737-6281.. 39 C
jessew@cos.edu
WILD, Jeffrey .... 320-762-4594 236 G
jeffrey.wild@alextech.edu
WILD, Larry .... 847-628-2036 141 A
lwild@judsonu.edu
WILD, Robert, M .... 314-935-7776 261 B
rob.wild@wustl.edu
WILD, Shawn .... 215-968-8306 379 B
shawn.wild@bucks.edu
WILDA, Christine, M .... 413-545-2148 211 D
cwilda@umass.edu
WILDE, Jerry .... 765-973-8554 156 D
jwilde@iue.edu
WILDE, Matt .... 208-426-1203 130 F
mattwilde@boisestate.edu
WILDE, Sue .... 573-651-2175 258 J
swilde@semo.edu
WILDEMANN,
Leonard Walter .... 401-841-3780 501 L
wildemal@usnwc.edu
WILDER, Aliza .... 860-486-8478.. 89 B
aliza.wilder@uconn.edu
WILDER, Ayla .... 269-294-4252 223 J
awilder@glenoaks.edu
WILDER, Bridgette .... 661-255-1050.. 28 I
WILDER, Bruce .... 661-824-2977.. 53 H
bwilder@ntps.edu
WILDER, Diane .... 610-896-1209 385 H
dwilder@haverford.edu
WILDER, Jason .... 928-523-5344.. 14 J
jason.wilder@nau.edu
WILDER, Jennifer .... 850-599-3651 109 E
jennifer.wilder@famu.edu
WILDER, Lesley .... 512-472-4133 442 H
lesley.wilder@ssw.edu
WILDER, Leslie .... 910-755-7324 332 D
wilderl@brunswickcc.edu
WILDER, Linda .... 860-515-3862.. 85 D
lwilder@charteroak.edu
WILDER, Marita .... 541-956-7139 375 G
mwilder@roguecc.edu
WILDER, Melanie .... 912-443-5717 124 I
mwilder@savannahtech.edu
WILDER, Michael .... 630-752-5818 152 K
michael.wilder@wheaton.edu
WILDER, Michael, S ..... 817-921-8689 444 D
mwilder@swbts.edu
WILDER, Paul, J .... 407-582-1818 113 C
pwilder1@valenciacollege.edu
WILDER, Ronald .... 575-769-4127 285 C
ronald.wilder@clovis.edu
WILDER, Stanley .... 225-578-2217 188 K
wilder@lsu.edu

WILDER, Sterly .... 919-684-5114 328 D
sterly.wilder@daa.duke.edu
WILDER, Ted .... 608-363-2470 490 I
wildert@beloit.edu
WILDER, W. Mark .... 662-915-5756 248 F
acwilder@olemiss.edu
WILDER-BYRD,
Ellen, M .... 803-323-2236 413 D
wilderbyrde@winthrop.edu
WILDERMUTH, Amy, J . 412-648-1401 400 A
amy.wildermuth@pitt.edu
WILDEY, Diane .... 518-743-2337 319 D
daltod@sunyacc.edu
WILDHACK, John .... 315-443-8705 321 D
jwildhac@syr.edu
WILDING, Jody .... 281-649-3070 436 D
jwilding@hbu.edu
WILDING, Tim .... 205-226-4643.... 5 A
trwildin@bsc.edu
WILDMAN, Kathleen ...... 440-684-6022 363 C
kathleen.wildman@ursuline.edu
WILES, Duane .... 865-974-2425 426 C
dwiles@utfi.org
WILES, Everett .... 301-891-4134 204 D
ewiles@wau.edu
WILES, Mari, E .... 252-398-6268 328 A
wilesm@chowan.edu
WILES, Sanya .... 316-295-5298 173 G
sanya@friends.edu
WILEY, Carlos .... 717-871-4473 394 B
carlos.wiley@millersville.edu
WILEY, Carolyn .... 662-562-3200 247 E
WILEY, Casey .... 864-455-8204 412 F
wileyc@greenvillemed.sc.edu
WILEY, David .... 907-260-7422.... 9 D
WILEY, Ellen .... 717-947-6089 392 R
ewiley@pacollege.edu
WILEY, Fran, K .... 864-941-8351 410 D
wiley.f@ptc.edu
WILEY, Jeanelle .... 314-968-7123 261 D
jeanellewiley10@webster.edu
WILEY, Jeffrey .... 315-786-2248 302 I
jwiley@sunyjefferson.edu
WILEY, Karen .... 815-455-8547 143 F
kwiley@mchenry.edu
WILEY, Latoya, J .... 252-862-1226 336 H
lwiley2729@roanokechowan.edu
WILEY, Lee .... 318-487-5443 187 G
leewiley@cltcc.edu
WILEY, Marilyn .... 940-565-4874 453 B
marilyn.wiley@unt.edu
WILEY, Matt .... 361-582-2468 456 H
matt.wiley@victoriacollege.edu
WILEY, Nina .... 937-328-7936 350 D
wileyn@clarkstate.edu
WILEY, Paul, G .... 931-598-1731 422 F
pwiley@sewanee.edu
WILEY, Sheila .... 209-476-7840.. 67 D
swiley@clc.edu
WILEY, Stacey .... 814-824-2311 389 E
swiley@mercyhurst.edu
WILEY, Stephen .... 918-360-3763 365 B
wileys@bacone.edu
WILEY, Steven .... 315-498-2622 310 C
WILEY-HARRIS,
Courtney .... 585-340-9648 296 B
cwiley-harris@crcds.edu
WILFONG, MacKenzie ... 918-595-7995 370 B
mackenzie.wilfong@tulsacc.edu
WILGENBUSCH, Sandy . 563-876-3353 165 D
wilgenbu@dwci.edu
WILGUS, Robynne .... 541-440-4622 376 F
robynne.wilgus@umpqua.edu
WILHELM, Alma .... 815-455-8781 143 F
awilhelm759@mchenry.edu
WILHELM, Cassandra ... 585-497-7979 298 E
cassandrawilhelm@elim.edu
WILHELM, Jane .... 608-663-2203 491 F
jwilhelm@edgewood.edu
WILHELM, Jennifer .... 617-236-5470 209 D
jwilhelm@fisher.edu
WILHELM, Justina .... 907-852-1772.... 9 H
justina.wilhelm@ilisagvik.edu
WILHELM, Michael .... 910-962-2736 343 B
wilhelmm@uncw.edu
WILHELM, Robert .... 402-472-3123 269 A
bob.wilhelm@unl.edu
WILHELM, Stephanie ...... 712-749-2387 164 A
steph@bvu.edu
WILHELMSEN, Kevin ...... 602-557-1262.. 16 L
kevin.wilhelmsen@phoenix.edu
WILHEMI, Jeremy .... 479-979-1307.. 24 A
jwilhemi@ozarks.edu

WILHITE, Brian .... 630-617-6484 137 E
wilhiteb@elmhurst.edu
WILHITE, D. LeAnne ..... 770-720-9205 124 E
leanne.wilhite@reinhardt.edu
WILHITE, Lee .... 562-906-4520.. 27 E
lee.wilhite@biola.edu
WILHITE, Scott .... 903-434-8168 440 A
swilhite@ntcc.edu
WILHM, Cathy .... 517-483-1354 226 D
wilhmc@lcc.edu
WILHOIT, Karen .... 937-775-3039 364 D
karen.wilhoit@wright.edu
WILKE, Dennis, F .... 412-521-6200 396 F
dennis.wilke@rosedaletech.org
WILKE, Jamie .... 701-328-4111 344 G
jamie.wilke@ndus.edu
WILKE, Stephen, K .... 620-229-6277 177 D
steve.wilke@sckans.edu
WILKEN, Danielle, E ..... 203-576-4665.. 89 A
dwilken@bridgeport.edu
WILKENING, Nick .... 949-451-5652.. 65 B
nwilkening@ivc.edu
WILKERSON, Aimee, J .. 270-824-8696 182 A
aimee.wilkerson@kctcs.edu
WILKERSON, Ame .... 912-260-4407 125 B
ame.wilkerson@sgsc.edu
WILKERSON, Charles .... 931-372-3634 425 B
cwilkerson@tntech.edu
WILKERSON, Denise ...... 410-576-5734 202 D
dwilkerson@usmd.edu
WILKERSON, Eugene .... 866-776-0331.. 54 E
WILKERSON, James, J . 812-941-2599 157 D
jjwilker@iu.edu
WILKERSON, SR.,
Jermel .... 330-972-7048 361 G
jermel@uakron.edu
WILKERSON, Karen .... 816-235-2757 260 D
wilkersonkd@umkc.edu
WILKERSON, Kim .... 618-437-5321 147 F
wilkersonk@rlc.edu
WILKERSON,
Lindsey, S .... 318-342-1530 193 A
lwilkerson@ulm.edu
WILKERSON,
Mathew, C .... 540-654-1281 471 B
mwilkers@umw.edu
WILKERSON, Shani .... 617-588-1368 206 B
WILKERSON, Steve, L .... 210-458-4939 455 B
steve.wilkerson@utsa.edu
WILKERSON, Tanya ...... 443-885-3170 200 F
tanya.wilkerson@morgan.edu
WILKERSON, Terry .... 618-437-5321 147 F
wilkersont@rlc.edu
WILKERSON, William .... 256-824-2339.... 8 B
william.wilkerson@uah.edu
WILKERSON, Zeda .... 870-368-2027.. 20 I
zwilkerson@ozarka.edu
WILKES, Brandy .... 229-468-2228 127 F
brandy.wilkes@wiregrass.edu
WILKES, C. Gene .... 817-274-4284 430 G
gwilkes@bhcarroll.edu
WILKES, Deborah .... 706-886-6831 126 C
dwilkes@tfc.edu
WILKES, Jamie .... 706-754-7841 123 C
jwilkes@northgatech.edu
WILKES, Jeremy .... 901-572-2670 417 A
jeremy.wilkes@baptistu.edu
WILKES, Kerrie .... 716-673-3181 316 A
kerrie.wilkes@fredonia.edu
WILKES, Kwin .... 307-532-8218 500 A
kwilkes@ewc.wy.edu
WILKES, Lisa .... 540-231-6231 475 D
lwilkes@vt.edu
WILKES, Yvette .... 505-454-3197 286 C
ydwilkes@nmhu.edu
WILKEY, Becky .... 509-313-3996 479 E
wilkey@gonzaga.edu
WILKIE, Michelle .... 641-628-5281 164 B
wilkiem@central.edu
WILKIN, John, P .... 217-333-0790 151 F
jpwilkin@illinois.edu
WILKIN, Joshua .... 215-965-4038 390 C
jwilkin@moore.edu
WILKIN, Kristen .... 503-338-7696 372 C
kwilkin@clatsopcc.edu
WILKIN, Lori, A .... 908-709-7194 283 E
lori.wilkin@ucc.edu
WILKIN, Noel, E .... 662-915-5317 248 F
nwilkin@olemiss.edu
WILKINS, Ashli .... 334-556-2226.... 2 C
awilkins@wallace.edu
WILKINS, Derrick, L ..... 252-335-3102 341 A
dlwilkins@ecsu.edu

WILLIAMS, Donna, M 610-799-1107 388 B
dwilliams@lccc.edu
WILLIAMS, Dorothy 404-756-4016 115 E
dwilliams@atlm.edu
WILLIAMS, Douglass 931-598-1349 422 F
dwilliam@sewanee.edu
WILLIAMS, Dwayne 541-278-5904 371 G
dwilliams@bluecc.edu
WILLIAMS, Elizabeth 901-572-2640 417 A
elizabeth.williams@baptistu.edu
WILLIAMS, Emili 865-573-4517 419 E
ewilliams@johnsonu.edu
WILLIAMS, Emma 478-825-4350 118 E
emma.williams@fvsu.edu
WILLIAMS, Eric 310-434-3455.. 63 B
williams_eric@smc.edu
WILLIAMS, Erin 309-794-7000 132 H
erinwilliams@augustana.edu
WILLIAMS, Eugene 770-531-3172 116 C
ewilliams4@brenau.edu
WILLIAMS, Eunice 315-498-2565 310 C
williame@sunyocc.edu
WILLIAMS, F. Clark 615-343-3808 427 B
f.clark.williams@vanderbilt.edu
WILLIAMS, Falecia, D 301-546-0400 201 D
williafd@pgcc.edu
WILLIAMS, Frances 716-851-1698 299 A
williams@ecc.edu
WILLIAMS, Frank 585-389-2525 307 D
fwillia7@naz.edu
WILLIAMS, JR., Frank 318-670-6681 191 B
fwilliams@susla.edu
WILLIAMS, JR., Frantz 860-685-2516.. 90 A
fwilliams@wesleyan.edu
WILLIAMS, Fred 714-808-4746.. 54 B
fwilliams@nocccd.edu
WILLIAMS, Freddie 334-229-5631.. 4 B
fwilliams@alasu.edu
WILLIAMS, Freddie 334-229-4291.. 4 B
fwilliams@alasu.edu
WILLIAMS, Frederick, A 502-597-6891 183 A
frederick.williams1@kysu.edu
WILLIAMS, Gabrielle 620-242-0488 175 G
williamsg@mcpherson.edu
WILLIAMS, Gail, B 239-513-1122 102 C
gwilliams@hodges.edu
WILLIAMS, Gail, C 757-446-5869 465 H
williamsgc@evms.edu
WILLIAMS, JR.,
George, A 210-431-5521 440 D
gawilliams6@ollusa.edu
WILLIAMS, Georgeann 843-525-8203 411 B
gwilliams@tcl.edu
WILLIAMS, Georgeann 803-812-7358 412 E
willi994@mailbox.sc.edu
WILLIAMS, Georgia, E 252-398-6439 328 A
willig@chowan.edu
WILLIAMS, Gerald 401-874-2901 404 E
gman1@uri.edu
WILLIAMS, Ginger 785-628-4431 173 E
ghwilliams@fhsu.edu
WILLIAMS, Goldie, C 606-783-2123 183 H
gcwilliams@moreheadstate.edu
WILLIAMS, Greg 678-717-3719 126 G
greg.williams@ung.edu
WILLIAMS, Gregory, D 432-335-6410 440 C
gwilliams@odessa.edu
WILLIAMS, Grimes 207-755-5290 194 J
gwilliams@cmcc.edu
WILLIAMS, Gwenda 501-205-8879.. 19 B
gwilliams@cbc.edu
WILLIAMS, H. James 513-244-4232 356 F
president@msj.edu
WILLIAMS, Hans, M 936-468-3304 444 H
hwilliams@sfasu.edu
WILLIAMS, Helen, E 310-568-5615.. 56 H
helen.williams@pepperdine.edu
WILLIAMS, Ingrid 415-338-1872.. 34 A
icwilliams@sfsu.edu
WILLIAMS, Isaac, K 671-735-6019 503 C
isaac.williams1@guamcc.edu
WILLIAMS, Iwan 641-628-7686 164 B
williamsi@central.edu
WILLIAMS, Jalisa, D 413-572-8670 213 C
jdwilliams@westfield.ma.edu
WILLIAMS, James, E 620-341-5267 173 C
jwilliam@emporia.edu
WILLIAMS, Janelle 619-216-6661.. 65 K
jwilliams@swccd.edu
WILLIAMS, Janelle, D 817-202-6510 444 B
janellew@swau.edu
WILLIAMS, Janet 620-947-3121 177 F
janetw@tabor.edu

WILLIAMS, Janet 336-278-5434 328 H
jwilliams132@elon.edu
WILLIAMS, Janet 601-318-6568 249 B
jwilliams@wmcarey.edu
WILLIAMS, Jason 478-934-5311 122 D
jason.williams8@mga.edu
WILLIAMS, Jason 815-740-6222 152 E
jwilliams@stfrancis.edu
WILLIAMS, Jason 214-333-6978 433 D
jasonw@dbu.edu
WILLIAMS, Jason, R 208-496-4406 130 G
williamsja@byui.edu
WILLIAMS, Jeff 903-983-8669 437 G
jewilliams@kilgore.edu
WILLIAMS, Jeff 509-244-6851 478 D
jeff.williams@scc.spokane.edu
WILLIAMS, Jennifer 219-785-5299 160 A
jmwillia@pnw.edu
WILLIAMS, Jennifer 502-597-6486 183 A
jennifer.williams@kysu.edu
WILLIAMS, Jennifer 312-850-7016 135 E
jwilliams416@ccc.edu
WILLIAMS, Jennifer 501-977-2009.. 23 D
williams@uaccm.edu
WILLIAMS, Jennifer 434-544-8337 470 K
williams_ja1@lynchburg.edu
WILLIAMS, Jenny 864-592-4940 411 E
williamsj@sccsc.edu
WILLIAMS, Jermaine 334-347-2623.... 2 A
jlwilliams@escc.edu
WILLIAMS, Jermaine 240-567-5267 200 B
WILLIAMS, Jessica 712-324-5061 168 H
jwilliams@nwicc.edu
WILLIAMS, Jessica, C 913-667-5709 172 G
jwilliams@cbts.edu
WILLIAMS, Jillian 248-204-3208 226 E
williams-jillian@aramark.com
WILLIAMS, Joan 336-517-2141 326 J
jwilliams@bennett.edu
WILLIAMS, Joan 319-208-5049 169 I
jwilliams@scciowa.edu
WILLIAMS, Joanne 207-780-4020 196 A
joanne.williams@maine.edu
WILLIAMS, JoAnne 203-773-8550.. 85 C
WILLIAMS, Joanne 804-862-6100 469 E
jwilliams@rbc.edu
WILLIAMS, Jodi, L 540-458-8920 476 D
jwilliams@wlu.edu
WILLIAMS, Joel 605-692-9337 414 B
jwilliams@ilt.edu
WILLIAMS, Joey 512-232-3716 454 C
joeywilliams@utexas.edu
WILLIAMS, John 508-999-8421 211 F
john.williams@umassd.edu
WILLIAMS, John 607-587-4611 319 C
williajc@alfredstate.edu
WILLIAMS, John, D 903-813-2220 429 I
jwilliams@austincollege.edu
WILLIAMS, John, H 713-313-7310 448 D
williams_jh@tsu.edu
WILLIAMS, John, M 517-750-1200 230 F
jwilliam@arbor.edu
WILLIAMS, John, W 618-374-5148 147 B
president@principia.edu
WILLIAMS, Jonathan 212-998-1212 309 D
WILLIAMS, Joni 404-225-4602 115 F
jwilliam@atlantatech.edu
WILLIAMS, Jordan 443-412-2449 199 B
jowilliams@harford.edu
WILLIAMS, Joseph 540-674-3600 473 F
jawilliams@nr.edu
WILLIAMS, Joyce 323-343-3500.. 32 B
jwilli109@calstatela.edu
WILLIAMS, Julia 229-732-5920 114 I
juliawilliams@andrewcollege.edu
WILLIAMS, Julian, R 803-777-7000 412 A
julian.williams@sc.edu
WILLIAMS, Juliana 215-780-1443 397 E
jwilliams@salus.edu
WILLIAMS, Julie, E 615-353-3346 424 A
julie.williams@nscc.edu
WILLIAMS, Julie, R 712-362-7912 166 H
jrwilliams@iowalakes.edu
WILLIAMS, Kamilah 309-690-6886 138 I
kamilah.williams@icc.edu
WILLIAMS, Kara 931-424-4086 426 F
kwill249@utsouthern.edu
WILLIAMS, Karen 718-262-2415 295 D
kwilliams29@york.cuny.edu
WILLIAMS, Katara, A 225-771-4680 190 K
katara_williams@sus.edu
WILLIAMS, Kathleen 770-426-2688 122 A
kathleen.williams@life.edu

WILLIAMS, Kathy 903-223-3182 447 C
kathy.williams@tamut.edu
WILLIAMS, Katraya 318-675-5049 189 D
katraya.williams@lsuhs.edu
WILLIAMS, Katraya 318-670-9221 191 B
kwilliams@susla.edu
WILLIAMS, Keena 517-629-0501 220 E
kwilliams@albion.edu
WILLIAMS, Keith 404-756-4003 115 E
kwilliams@atlm.edu
WILLIAMS, Kelley 610-409-3698 400 E
kwilliams@ursinus.edu
WILLIAMS, Kellyn 570-702-8940 386 D
knolan@johnson.edu
WILLIAMS, Ken 202-685-4080 501 I
kenneth.r.williams.mil@ndu.edu
WILLIAMS, Ken, M 248-232-4210 228 H
kmwillia@oaklandcc.edu
WILLIAMS, Kendra 225-248-1015 186 G
kwilliams@albanytech.edu
WILLIAMS, Kenneth 601-979-2121 245 G
kwilliams@albanytech.edu
WILLIAMS, Kenneth 802-258-3565 462 B
ken.williams@sit.edu
WILLIAMS, Kent 316-322-3103 172 B
kwilliams@butlercc.edu
WILLIAMS, Kesha, M 717-361-3600 383 B
williamskm@etown.edu
WILLIAMS, Kevin 518-956-8030 315 D
graduate@albany.edu
WILLIAMS, Kevin, H 615-898-2424 421 C
kevin.williams@mtsu.edu
WILLIAMS, Kim 870-850-4815.. 21 D
kwilliams@search.edu
WILLIAMS, Kim, A 718-982-2224 293 C
vpadvancement@csi.cuny.edu
WILLIAMS,
Kimberlee, S 973-353-5262 281 C
kimberlee.williams@rutgers.edu
WILLIAMS, Kimberly 708-239-4528 150 H
kim.williams@trnty.edu
WILLIAMS, Kimberly 919-890-7500.. 93 H
kimberly.williams@findlay.edu
WILLIAMS, Kimberly 419-434-4740 362 D
kimberly.williams@findlay.edu
WILLIAMS, Kimberly 918-444-5000 366 G
willi204@nsuok.edu
WILLIAMS, Kristen 973-408-3788 276 B
kwilliams3@drew.edu
WILLIAMS, Kristen 801-524-8106 458 F
kwilliams@ldsbc.edu
WILLIAMS, Kristi 706-778-8500 124 B
WILLIAMS, Kristin 706-507-8848 117 E
williams_kristin@columbusstate.edu
WILLIAMS, Kristin 859-256-3100 180 H
kris.williams@kctcs.edu
WILLIAMS, Kristopher 402-826-8255 266 A
kristopher.williams@doane.edu
WILLIAMS, Kyle 940-397-4730 439 F
kyle.williams@msutexas.edu
WILLIAMS, Kyle, R 208-496-2510 130 G
williamsk@byui.edu
WILLIAMS, Lakeshia 318-473-6495 189 A
ldalton@lsua.edu
WILLIAMS, LaNeeca 931-221-7690 416 H
williamslr@apsu.edu
WILLIAMS, Lashon 361-570-4128 452 C
williamslb@uhv.edu
WILLIAMS, LaShonda 936-261-1591 445 E
lrwilliams@pvamu.edu
WILLIAMS, LaTonda 501-916-3180.. 22 C
lwwilliams@ualr.edu
WILLIAMS, LaToya 713-623-2040 429 F
lrwilliams@aii.edu
WILLIAMS, Laura 707-664-2153.. 34 C
laura.williams@sonoma.edu
WILLIAMS, Lauren 706-355-5023 115 C
lwilliams@athenstech.edu
WILLIAMS, Lea 802-485-2025 461 H
lwilliam@norwich.edu
WILLIAMS, Lee 870-338-6474.. 23 A
lee.williams@texarkanacollege.edu
WILLIAMS, Lee 903-823-3016 445 C
lee.williams@texarkanacollege.edu
WILLIAMS, Leslie 559-325-3600.. 28 F
lwilliams@chsu.edu
WILLIAMS, Leslie 661-654-2544.. 30 C
lwilliams8@csub.edu
WILLIAMS, Leslie 831-582-4091.. 32 D
lewilliams@csumb.edu
WILLIAMS, Linda 916-660-7310.. 64 B
lwilliams@sierracollege.edu
WILLIAMS, Lindsay 254-298-8241 445 B
lindsay.williams@templejc.edu

WILLIAMS, Lisa 858-653-6740.. 46 L
lwilliams@jpcatholic.com
WILLIAMS, Lisa, L 325-793-3821 439 A
lwilliams@mcm.edu
WILLIAMS, Lisa, M 256-782-8186.... 6 A
lwilliam@jsu.edu
WILLIAMS, Lonnie 870-972-3081.. 17 I
lonniew@astate.edu
WILLIAMS, Loretta 706-233-7278 125 A
lwilliams@shorter.edu
WILLIAMS, Lorette 361-698-1351 434 H
lwilliams25@delmar.edu
WILLIAMS, Lori 713-798-4951 430 E
lojewill@iusb.edu
WILLIAMS, Lorie 574-520-4492 157 C
lojewill@iusb.edu
WILLIAMS, Lyn 610-606-4666 380 C
lcwillia@cedarcrest.edu
WILLIAMS, Lynell 956-872-2114 443 B
lwillia5@southtexascollege.edu
WILLIAMS, Lynne 218-726-6141 243 A
lwilliam@d.umn.edu
WILLIAMS, Lyrae 719-389-6699.. 78 E
lwilliams@coloradocollege.edu
WILLIAMS, Maisha 212-517-0400 305 D
maisha@mmm.edu
WILLIAMS,
Marchetta, L 803-938-3721 412 G
mlwillia@uscsumter.edu
WILLIAMS, Marcia 757-455-3335 476 K
mwilliams@vwu.edu
WILLIAMS,
Marianne, R 518-262-5422 289 C
willimr@amc.edu
WILLIAMS, Marie 251-981-3771.... 5 B
marie.williams@columbiasouthern.edu
WILLIAMS, Marie 401-863-6050 403 A
marie_williams@brown.edu
WILLIAMS, Mark 501-686-7000.. 22 D
mlw@uams.edu
WILLIAMS, Marrianne 530-242-7648.. 64 A
mewilliams@shastacollege.edu
WILLIAMS, Martinique 336-285-2979 341 C
mcwilli2@ncat.edu
WILLIAMS, Marvin 516-726-5753 502 G
williamsm@usmma.edu
WILLIAMS, Mary Beth 717-871-5714 394 B
marybeth.williams@millersville.edu
WILLIAMS, Mary Beth 717-262-2006 402 D
marybeth.williams@wilson.edu
WILLIAMS, Matthew 651-846-1572 240 F
matthew.williams@saintpaul.edu
WILLIAMS, Matthew, W 404-527-7702 121 I
mwwilliams@itc.edu
WILLIAMS, Maureen, E 407-582-5463 113 C
mwilliams325@valenciacollege.edu
WILLIAMS, Mavis 575-624-7217 285 F
mavis.williams@roswell.enmu.edu
WILLIAMS, Melanie, K 269-337-7220 225 B
williams@kzoo.edu
WILLIAMS, Melissa 916-608-6585.. 51 A
william@flc.losrios.edu
WILLIAMS, Melissa 254-295-4020 453 A
mwilliams@umhb.edu
WILLIAMS, Melva 318-670-9314 191 B
mwilliams@susla.edu
WILLIAMS, Melva, D 504-520-7453 193 C
mewillia@xula.edu
WILLIAMS, Melva, K 512-505-3001 437 B
mkwilliams@htu.edu
WILLIAMS, Melvenia 803-535-5412 406 E
mwilliams@claflin.edu
WILLIAMS, Melvin 803-535-5575 406 E
mewilliams@claflin.edu
WILLIAMS, Melvin 434-971-3304 501 G
melvin.l.williams50.mil@army.mil
WILLIAMS, Mia 334-229-4788.... 4 B
miawilliams@alasu.edu
WILLIAMS, Michael 229-333-2100 127 F
michael.williams@wiregrass.edu
WILLIAMS, Michael 207-768-2712 195 D
mwilliams@nmcc.edu
WILLIAMS, Michael 850-644-7351 110 B
mswilliams@admin.fsu.edu
WILLIAMS, Michael 586-445-7535 226 F
williamsm@macomb.edu
WILLIAMS, Michael 734-462-4400 230 H
mwilliam@schoolcraft.edu
WILLIAMS, Michael 609-984-1130 283 D
mwilliams@tesu.edu
WILLIAMS, Michael, D 501-279-4274.. 19 G
president@harding.edu

WILLIAMSON, Kylie ...... 785-594-8327 171 C
kylie.williamson@bakeru.edu
WILLIAMSON, Laurel .... 281-998-6182 442 E
laurel.williamson@sjcd.edu
WILLIAMSON, Laurel .... 281-998-6182 442 B
laurel.williamson@sjcd.edu
WILLIAMSON, Laurel .... 281-998-6182 442 C
laurel.williamson@sjcd.edu
WILLIAMSON, Laurel .... 281-998-6182 442 D
laurel.williamson@sjcd.edu
WILLIAMSON, Lisa ...... 706-245-7226 118 C
lwilliamson@ec.edu
WILLIAMSON, Lisa ...... 715-682-1678 493 G
lwilliamson@northland.edu
WILLIAMSON, Margaret 504-280-7054 189 F
mswilli4@uno.edu
WILLIAMSON, Marty ..... 661-654-2677.. 30 C
mwilliamson@csub.edu
WILLIAMSON, Matthew . 740-695-9500 348 D
mwilliamson@belmontcollege.edu
WILLIAMSON, Michael . 843-383-8140 407 C
WILLIAMSON, Robin ..... 501-450-3416.. 23 K
rwilliamson@uca.edu
WILLIAMSON, Stephen . 605-367-7464 416 B
stephen.williamson@southeasttech.edu
WILLIAMSON, Thomas . 612-659-6791 238 C
thomas.williamson@minneapolis.edu
WILLIAMSON, Tracey .... 660-263-3900 250 G
bookstore@cccb.edu
WILLIAMSON-LOTT,
Joy .... 206-543-7468 484 A
joyann@uw.edu
WILLIARD, Stacey .... 724-266-3838 399 F
swilliard@tsm.edu
WILLIBY, Jason .... 785-628-5701 173 E
jjwilliby3@fhsu.edu
WILLIE, Lisa .... 215-951-1011 386 I
willie@lasalle.edu
WILLIE LEBRETON,
Sarah .... 610-690-2044 398 B
swillie1@swarthmore.edu
WILLIFORD, Andrea ...... 478-757-5131 127 D
awilliford@wesleyancollege.edu
WILLIFORD, Andrea, G . 478-757-5131 127 D
awilliford@wesleyancollege.edu
WILLIFORD, Brent .... 979-830-4146 430 I
brent.williford@blinn.edu
WILLIFORD, Darryl .... 301-860-4186 203 D
dwilliford@bowiestate.edu
WILLIFORD, David .... 615-675-5302 427 D
dwilliford@welch.edu
WILLIFORD, Lynn, E ..... 919-962-1500 342 B
lynn_williford@unc.edu
WILLIFORD, Mickey ...... 706-721-6544 115 I
shwillif@augusta.edu
WILLING, Cindy .... 517-607-4315 224 G
cwilling@hillsdale.edu
WILLINGHAM, Paul ...... 281-655-3712 438 E
paul.willingham@lonestar.edu
WILLINGHAM, Tynisha .. 540-887-7030 467 G
twillingham@marybaldwin.edu
WILLIS, Amy .... 229-391-5007 114 D
apwillis@abac.edu
WILLIS, Arnell .... 501-374-6305.. 21 B
arnell.willis@shortercollege.edu
WILLIS, Bessie .... 757-727-5331 466 L
bessie.willis@hamptonu.edu
WILLIS, Brian .... 828-398-7929 331 K
bwillis@abtech.edu
WILLIS, Carla .... 352-588-8644 107 B
carla.willis@saintleo.edu
WILLIS, Ciaran .... 760-872-2000.. 41 D
ciaran@deepsprings.edu
WILLIS, Daria .... 443-518-1820 199 D
president@howardcc.edu
WILLIS, David .... 575-492-2173 288 I
dwillis@usw.edu
WILLIS, Doug, G .... 972-378-8790 432 I
dwillis@collin.edu
WILLIS, Eric, R .... 319-352-0861 170 F
rick.willis@wartburg.edu
WILLIS, Gabe .... 985-549-3645 192 E
gabe.willis@selu.edu
WILLIS, Harvey .... 973-328-5232 276 A
hwillis@ccm.edu
WILLIS, Howard .... 707-256-7355.. 53 E
hwillis@napavalley.edu
WILLIS, Howard .... 408-223-6749.. 62 F
howard.willis@evc.edu
WILLIS, Jeff .... 337-550-1287 189 B
jwillis@lsue.edu
WILLIS, Jeff .... 270-384-8097 183 D
willisj@lindsey.edu

WILLIS, Justin .... 715-346-2649 496 B
jwillis@uwsp.edu
WILLIS, Kathy .... 618-468-5700 142 B
kwillis@lc.edu
WILLIS, Kimberley .... 585-395-2501 317 B
kwillis@brockport.edu
WILLIS, Lesia .... 718-522-9073 290 B
lwillis@asa.edu
WILLIS, Lisa .... 312-850-7131 135 E
lwillis01@ccc.edu
WILLIS, LoShay .... 708-608-4327 144 G
willisl26@morainevalley.edu
WILLIS, Marc .... 918-647-1464 365 D
mwillis@carlalbert.edu
WILLIS, Mary .... 559-278-4207.. 31 D
mwillis@csufresno.edu
WILLIS, Michaela .... 605-688-4493 416 A
michaela.willis@sdstate.edu
WILLIS, Richard .... 205-929-1776.... 6 B
WILLIS, Sarina .... 936-261-2173 445 E
srphillips@pvamu.edu
WILLIS, Steve .... 434-947-8383 469 A
swillis@randolphcollege.edu
WILLIS, Susan .... 918-343-6802 369 A
swillis@rsu.edu
WILLIS, Tori .... 919-719-1890 339 I
twillis@shawu.edu
WILLIS-BERRY, Antonio 978-837-5000 216 D
WILLIS KRAUSS,
Michelle .... 252-249-1851 336 C
mwillis@pamlicocc.edu
WILLISON, Sabrina .... 310-506-4000.. 56 H
sabrina.willison@pepperdine.edu
WILLITS, Rick .... 937-294-0592 356 D
rick.willits@themodern.edu
WILLLIAMS, Andy .... 574-520-4872 157 C
WILLLIAMS, Venetia, C . 865-539-7266 424 C
vcwilliams@pstcc.edu
WILLLIS, Howard .... 707-256-7355.. 53 E
hwillis@napavalley.edu
WILLMARTH, Ephraim .... 315-858-0945 301 F
ejwillmarth@hts.edu
WILLMORE, Allan .... 618-985-2828 140 G
allanwillmore@jalc.edu
WILLOUGHBY, G. Case 724-287-8711 379 C
case.willoughby@bc3.edu
WILLOUGHBY,
Karen, P .... 412-536-1201 386 H
karen.willoughby@laroche.edu
WILLOUGHBY, Kevin .... 256-549-8236.... 2 B
kwilloughby@gadsdenstate.edu
WILLOWBY, Nathan ...... 765-641-4529 153 D
njwillowby@anderson.edu
WILLOX, Lara .... 717-871-7333 394 B
lara.willox@millersville.edu
WILLS, Barbara .... 850-201-6060 112 B
barbara.wills@tcc.fl.edu
WILLS, Helen .... 618-374-5189 147 B
helen.wills@principia.edu
WILLS, Jeremiah .... 704-337-2506 339 D
willsj@queens.edu
WILLS, Mark .... 213-252-5100.. 24 C
mwills@alu.edu
WILLS, Mark .... 423-798-7970 424 G
mark.wills@ws.edu
WILLS, Mike .... 417-836-7635 255 J
mikewills@missouristate.edu
WILLS, Scott .... 989-463-7614 220 F
willssd@alma.edu
WILLS, Tim .... 618-437-5321 147 F
wills@rlc.edu
WILLSON, Dawn .... 714-241-6186.. 38 D
dwillson1@coastline.edu
WILLSON, Deborah, A .. 412-396-6000 382 E
WILLY, Randy .... 785-442-6005 174 C
rwilly@highlandcc.edu
WILLYARD, Paula .... 918-595-2067 370 B
paula.willyard@tulsacc.edu
WILMARTH, Constance . 541-684-7292 371 H
cwilmarth@bushnell.edu
WILMER, Elizabeth .... 540-857-7313 475 A
ewilmer@virginiawestern.edu
WILMES, David .... 724-738-2003 394 E
david.wilmes@sru.edu
WILMESHERR, Jon .... 828-766-1360 335 G
jwilmesherr@mayland.edu
WILMONTH, Charlie ...... 918-540-6224 366 F
charlie.wilmonth@neo.edu
WILMORE, Emily .... 412-365-1383 380 F
e.wilmore@chatham.edu
WILMOT, Kemesha .... 860-465-5247.. 85 G
wilmotk@easternct.edu

WILMOT, Melinda .... 661-395-4361.. 47 B
melinda.wilmot@bakersfieldcollege.edu
WILMOTH, Dirk .... 828-398-7111 331 K
dirkwilmoth@abtech.edu
WILMOTH, Wendy .... 404-297-9522 119 G
WILMOUTH, Robert .... 406-657-1015 264 G
president@rocky.edu
WILMS, Amy .... 909-748-8109.. 72 E
amy_wilms@redlands.edu
WILROY, Claudia .... 805-378-1409.. 73 I
cwilroy@vcccd.edu
WILSHUSEN, Lauren ..... 617-879-7226 212 E
lwilshusen@massart.edu
WILSKE, Don .... 517-483-1765 226 D
wilsked@lcc.edu
WILSMAN, Luisa .... 610-341-1955 383 A
luisa.wilsman@eastern.edu
WILSON, Adam .... 540-636-2900 464 O
adam.wilson@christendom.edu
WILSON, Alan .... 706-385-1059 124 C
alan.wilson@point.edu
WILSON, Allan .... 303-871-2039.. 84 C
allan.wilson@du.edu
WILSON, Allen, T .... 757-683-3144 468 C
a3wilson@odu.edu
WILSON, Allyson .... 954-763-9840.. 95 J
dean@atom.edu
WILSON, Amanda .... 317-921-4949 158 A
amanda.wilson@ivytech.edu
WILSON, Amy .... 608-363-2699 490 I
wilsonae@beloit.edu
WILSON, Amy, F .... 402-280-2950 265 J
amywilson@creighton.edu
WILSON, Andrea .... 209-575-6060.. 76 K
wilsona@mjc.edu
WILSON, Andy .... 252-398-6343 328 A
aawilson@chowan.edu
WILSON, Angela .... 618-252-5400 149 E
angela.wilson@sic.edu
WILSON, Angulus .... 630-752-5445 152 K
chaplains.office@wheaton.edu
WILSON, Anne .... 706-290-2667 116 A
awilson@berry.edu
WILSON, Annette .... 312-362-6214 136 F
awilso49@depaul.edu
WILSON, Arthur, L .... 260-359-4031 155 G
alwilson@huntington.edu
WILSON, Barbara .... 770-534-6203 116 C
bwilson@brenau.edu
WILSON, Barbara, J ...... 319-335-3565 163 F
WILSON, Ben .... 520-515-5455.. 11 O
wilsonb@cochise.edu
WILSON, Betsyann .... 928-536-6245.. 14 L
betsy.wilson@npc.edu
WILSON, Bill .... 406-683-7509 263 E
william.wilson@umwestern.edu
WILSON, Blake .... 864-424-8022 412 H
bentleyt@mailbox.sc.edu
WILSON, Bradley .... 724-738-2003 394 E
bradley.wilson@sru.edu
WILSON, Bryan .... 307-778-1179 500 D
bwilson@lccc.wy.edu
WILSON, Carlos .... 601-979-8895 245 G
carlos.d.wilson@jsums.edu
WILSON, Carlton, E ...... 919-530-6794 341 D
cwilson@nccu.edu
WILSON, Carmen, R ..... 716-880-2000 305 F
WILSON, Charles .... 704-922-6454 334 E
wilson.charles@gaston.edu
WILSON, Charles .... 859-371-9393 179 C
cwilson@beckfield.edu
WILSON, Cheri .... 256-726-7204.... 6 C
cwilson@oakwood.edu
WILSON, Cheryl, A .... 516-876-3000 318 A
WILSON, Chip .... 740-397-9000 356 G
chip.wilson@mvnu.edu
WILSON, Christie, S ..... 512-428-1316 441 N
christiw@stedwards.edu
WILSON, Christina .... 618-374-5148 147 B
christina.wilson@principia.edu
WILSON, Christine .... 785-243-1435 172 J
cwilson@cloud.edu
WILSON, Christine .... 205-391-5896.... 3 E
cwilson@sheltonstate.edu
WILSON, Christine .... 310-206-1911.. 69 D
cwilson@saonet.ucla.edu
WILSON, Christine .... 207-778-7087 196 F
christine.wilson@maine.edu
WILSON, Christopher .... 701-231-6409 345 D
christopher.s.wilson@ndsu.edu
WILSON, Cleveland .... 803-535-1419 410 C
wilsonc@octech.edu

WILSON, Connie .... 870-235-4055.. 21 E
conniewilson@saumag.edu
WILSON, Corinice .... 918-595-7470 370 B
corinice.wilson@tulsacc.edu
WILSON, Craig .... 315-228-6941 296 C
cawilson@colgate.edu
WILSON, Craig .... 206-543-0521 484 A
craigw@uw.edu
WILSON, Crystal .... 212-678-3131 321 H
cmw2207@tc.columbia.edu
WILSON, Cynthia, L ..... 713-348-5048 441 K
clwilson@rice.edu
WILSON, Dani .... 714-992-7040.. 54 D
dwilson@fullcoll.edu
WILSON, Daniel .... 252-398-6260 328 A
dowilson@chowan.edu
WILSON, Darlene .... 509-527-4936 485 C
wilsond@whitman.edu
WILSON, David .... 207-974-4853 195 A
dwilson@emcc.edu
WILSON, David .... 443-885-3200 200 F
david.wilson@morgan.edu
WILSON, David .... 615-966-6219 420 B
david.wilson@lipscomb.edu
WILSON, Dayle, W .... 305-284-2419 112 K
daylewilson@miami.edu
WILSON, Dayton .... 304-766-3181 489 D
dayton.wilson@wvstateu.edu
WILSON, Deborah .... 870-235-4200.. 21 E
djwilson@saumag.edu
WILSON, Delfina .... 602-286-8000.. 13 D
WILSON, Diana .... 307-432-1798 500 D
dwilson@lccc.wy.edu
WILSON, Don .... 863-297-1000 106 A
dhw@bosdun.com
WILSON, Donna .... 717-720-4000 393 C
WILSON, Doug .... 251-442-2406.... 8 C
dwilson@umobile.edu
WILSON, Douglas .... 205-726-4266.... 6 E
dwilson@samford.edu
WILSON, Elaine .... 606-451-6915 182 D
elaine.wilson@kctcs.edu
WILSON, Elighie .... 708-709-7767 147 A
ewilson@prairiestate.edu
WILSON, Elisabeth .... 952-996-1470 233 H
elisabeth.wilson@bethanygu.edu
WILSON, Elise .... 530-226-4718.. 64 C
ewilson@simpsonu.edu
WILSON, Emily .... 803-786-3679 407 E
ewilson@columbiasc.edu
WILSON, Erin .... 214-388-5466 434 E
erinwilson@dallasinstitute.edu
WILSON, Evan .... 217-245-3272 139 A
evan.wilson@ic.edu
WILSON, Fleetwood, L .. 206-934-3789 482 F
fleetwood.wilson@seattlecolleges.edu
WILSON, Fred .... 251-377-9281.... 8 C
fwilson@umobile.edu
WILSON, Fred .... 714-816-0366.. 68 G
fred.wilson@trident.edu
WILSON, Gary .... 828-726-2264 332 E
gwilson@cccti.edu
WILSON, Gena .... 478-825-6301 118 E
gena.wilson@fvsu.edu
WILSON, Gena .... 229-931-2000 120 B
gena.wilson@gsw.edu
WILSON, Gordon, N ..... 801-581-3079 459 D
gordon.wilson@utah.edu
WILSON, Grant .... 308-635-6003 269 E
wilsong7@wncc.edu
WILSON, Heather .... 915-747-5555 454 E
hwilson@utep.edu
WILSON, Howard .... 712-722-6007 165 E
howard.wilson@dordt.edu
WILSON, Jackie .... 319-895-4234 164 E
jwilson@cornellcollege.edu
WILSON, Jackie .... 907-796-6389.. 10 C
jmwilson17@alaska.edu
WILSON, Jacqueline ...... 334-683-2309.... 3 A
jwilson@marionmilitary.edu
WILSON, Jamar .... 212-616-7200 301 A
WILSON, Jamelle, S ..... 804-289-8135 471 E
jwilson9@richmond.edu
WILSON, JR.,
James, D .... 302-295-1194.. 91 C
jim.d.wilson@wilmu.edu
WILSON, Jamie, B .... 601-974-1086 246 C
jamie.wilson@millsaps.edu
WILSON, Janice .... 860-465-4466.. 85 G
wilsonj@easternct.edu
WILSON, Jason .... 810-762-0200 228 B
jason.wilson@mcc.edu

WILSON, Jeanne .... 925-424-1405.. 36 A
jdwilson@laspositascollege.edu
WILSON, Jennifer .... 641-683-5174 166 F
jennifer.wilson@indianhills.edu
WILSON, Jennifer .... 212-229-5600 307 E
wilsonj@newschool.edu
WILSON, Jessica, D ...... 512-448-8414 441 N
jwilso12@stedwards.edu
WILSON, Jessica, J ...... 717-245-1554 382 B
wilsonje@dickinson.edu
WILSON, Jessica, L ...... 210-829-3931 452 D
jewilso1@uiwtx.edu
WILSON, Jocelyn .... 516-671-2215 324 C
jwilson@webb.edu
WILSON, Jocelyn, M .... 516-671-2215 324 C
jwilson@webb.edu
WILSON, Joe .... 972-883-4995 454 D
joe.wilson@utdallas.edu
WILSON, John .... 404-270-5376 126 A
john.wilson@spelman.edu
WILSON, John .... 843-863-7102 406 C
jewilson@csuniv.edu
WILSON, John, R .... 804-278-4330 470 I
jwilson@upsem.edu
WILSON, Jon .... 913-234-0815 172 I
jon.wilson@cleveland.edu
WILSON, Jonathan .... 601-984-1010 248 G
jwilson5@umc.edu
WILSON, Jordan .... 317-955-6080 159 A
0777mgr@follett.com
WILSON, Joseph .... 706-641-5665 117 F
jwilson@columbustech.edu
WILSON, Josh .... 706-272-2473 118 A
jwilson@daltonstate.edu
WILSON, Joshua .... 870-368-2060.. 20 I
josh.wilson@ozarka.edu
WILSON, Joshua .... 870-368-2060.. 20 I
jwilson@ozarka.edu
WILSON, Judge .... 859-985-3131 179 E
wilsonju@berea.edu
WILSON, Judi .... 706-667-4368 115 I
jwilso24@augusta.edu
WILSON, Judy .... 864-236-6665 408 J
judy.wilson@gvltec.edu
WILSON, Julia .... 757-637-2018 466 L
julia.wilson@hamptonu.edu
WILSON, Julie .... 304-829-7130 486 B
jwilson@bethanywv.edu
WILSON, Kamesha .... 252-527-6223 335 E
knwilson59@lenoircc.edu
WILSON, Katelyn .... 660-263-4100 256 D
katelynw@macc.edu
WILSON, Kathryn .... 585-395-2137 317 B
kwilson@brockport.edu
WILSON, Katrin .... 323-241-5200.. 49 I
wilsonk3@lasc.edu
WILSON, Keisha .... 704-330-1455 329 H
kwilson@jcsu.edu
WILSON, Kelly .... 619-398-4902.. 45 F
WILSON, Ken .... 321-674-7397 100 A
kenwilson@fit.edu
WILSON, Kenneth .... 205-247-8071.... 7 A
kwilson@stillman.edu
WILSON, Kenny .... 636-481-3356 253 G
kwilso20@jeffco.edu
WILSON, Kent .... 304-205-6689 487 D
kent.wilson@bridgevalley.edu
WILSON, Kevin .... 573-681-5333 254 A
wilsonk2@lincolnu.edu
WILSON, Kim .... 661-362-2844.. 51 E
kwilson@masters.edu
WILSON, Kim .... 870-368-2042.. 20 I
kwilson@ozarka.edu
WILSON, Kristen .... 617-745-3000 208 F
kristen.wilson@enc.edu
WILSON, Kristina .... 361-698-1137 434 H
kmwilson@delmar.edu
WILSON, Kristina, A 260-982-5067 158W
kawilson@manchester.edu
WILSON, Laura .... 276-244-1226 463 H
lwilson@asl.edu
WILSON, Laura .... 937-376-6254 349 H
lwilson@centralstate.edu
WILSON, Laura, L .... 650-723-9633.. 66 D
laura.wilson@stanford.edu
WILSON, Leah .... 585-582-1230 298 E
leahwilson@elim.edu
WILSON, Leana .... 601-318-6197 249 B
lwilson@wmcarey.edu
WILSON, Leon, C .... 601-977-7735 248 E
lcwilson@tougaloo.edu
WILSON, Leslie, K .... 319-273-6240 163 G
leslie.wilson@uni.edu
WILSON, Lindsay .... 217-581-3413 137 C
lpwilson@eiu.edu
WILSON, Lindsey .... 602-286-8229.. 13 D
lindsey.wilson@gatewaycc.edu
WILSON, Lisa, M .... 951-827-3486.. 70 B
lisa.wilson@ucr.edu
WILSON, Locord .... 601-979-3354 245 G
locord.d.wilson@jsums.edu
WILSON, Lori, J .... 570-577-3334 379 A
lwilson@bucknell.edu
WILSON, Lucy .... 919-546-8322 339 I
lwilson@shawu.edu
WILSON, M. Roy .... 313-577-2230 232 H
president@wayne.edu
WILSON, Marcus .... 954-201-6974.. 96 F
mwilson2@broward.edu
WILSON, Marcus .... 806-743-6443 450 D
marcus.wilson@ttuhsc.edu
WILSON, Mardell, A ..... 402-280-4076 265 J
mardellwilson@creighton.edu
WILSON, Margaret .... 660-626-2354 249 C
mwilson@atsu.edu
WILSON, Marian .... 717-391-1365 398 E
wilson@stevenscollege.edu
WILSON, Mark .... 605-995-3024 414 E
mark.wilson@mitchelltech.edu
WILSON, Mark .... 870-633-4480.. 19 E
dwilson@eacc.edu
WILSON, Mark .... 423-472-7141 423 C
mwilson@clevelandstatecc.edu
WILSON, Mark .... 931-372-3961 425 B
mwilson@tntech.edu
WILSON, Martha .... 530-891-6900.. 27 H
WILSON, Matt .... 817-722-1775 437 H
matt.wilson@tku.edu
WILSON, Matthew .... 215-204-7405 398 D
matthew.wilson@temple.edu
WILSON, Matthew .... 317-791-5957 161 F
mwilson@uindy.edu
WILSON, Matthew .... 734-462-4400 230 B
mwilson@schoolcraft.edu
WILSON, Matthew, J ...... 302-356-6970.. 91 C
matthew.j.wilson@wilmu.edu
WILSON, Melanie .... 808-934-2519 129 F
mfwilson@hawaii.edu
WILSON, Melanie .... 540-458-8502 476 D
mwilson@wlu.edu
WILSON, Melissa .... 270-706-8727 181 C
mwilson0132@kctcs.edu
WILSON, Meredith, F .... 864-656-2457 406 F
mfant@clemson.edu
WILSON, Michael, D ...... 714-556-3610.. 73 G
mdwilson@vanguard.edu
WILSON, Michele .... 304-424-8355 490 A
michele.wilson@wvup.edu
WILSON, Michelle .... 870-633-4480.. 19 E
rwilson@eacc.edu
WILSON, Mindy .... 518-743-2252 319 D
wilsonm@sunyacc.edu
WILSON, Molly .... 215-222-4200 401 C
mwilson@walnuthillcollege.edu
WILSON, Molly .... 937-229-1000 362 C
WILSON, Monica .... 603-646-2215 272 F
monica.wilson@dartmouth.edu
WILSON, Monica .... 304-434-8000 487 E
monica.wilson@easternwv.edu
WILSON, Nancy .... 205-929-3451.... 2 H
nwilson@lawsonstate.edu
WILSON, Natalie, L .... 412-578-6171 380 A
nlwilson@carlow.edu
WILSON, Nate .... 208-882-1566 131 H
nwilson@nsa.edu
WILSON, Nathan .... 317-931-2316 154 D
nwilson@cts.edu
WILSON, Nicole .... 757-822-7152 474 G
nwwilson@tcc.edu
WILSON, Oceana .... 802-440-4606 461 B
owilson@bennington.edu
WILSON, Patricia .... 205-348-6010.... 7 G
WILSON, Patricia .... 256-306-2743.... 1 F
patricia.wilson@calhoun.edu
WILSON, Patrick .... 505-891-6908 286 C
patrickwilson@nmhu.edu
WILSON, Phillip .... 479-394-7622.. 23 F
pwilson@uarichmountain.edu
WILSON, Piper .... 417-477-7428 257 B
wilsonp@otc.edu
WILSON, Qiana, N .... 706-542-7912 126 F
qiana.wilson@uga.edu
WILSON, Rebeka .... 402-375-7239 267 I
rewilso1@wsc.edu
WILSON, Reggie, L .... 352-797-5001 105 E
wilsonr@phsc.edu
WILSON, Richard .... 225-928-7770 186 E
WILSON, Robert, A .... 610-606-4637 380 C
rwilson@cedarcrest.edu
WILSON, Roger .... 425-889-5336 481 A
roger.wilson@northwestu.edu
WILSON, Ronalyn .... 518-629-7622 302 A
r.wilson@hvcc.edu
WILSON, Ryan .... 859-622-8939 180 B
ryan.wilson@eku.edu
WILSON, Samantha .... 979-845-5139 446 B
samantha@tamu.edu
WILSON, Sandra .... 313-664-7471 222 C
sandra@collegeforcreativestudies.edu
WILSON, Scott .... 651-846-1694 240 E
scott.wilson@saintpaul.edu
WILSON, Scott .... 931-598-1173 422 F
swilson@sewanee.edu
WILSON, Scott, L .... 314-935-2656 261 B
scott.l.wilson@wustl.edu
WILSON, Shawn, Y .... 989-964-7147 229 L
swilson@svsu.edu
WILSON, Shawna .... 517-264-7142 230 C
swilson@sienaheights.edu
WILSON, Sheila .... 330-263-2580 350 H
swilson@wooster.edu
WILSON, Shirley .... 213-624-1200.. 42 F
swilson@fidm.edu
WILSON, Sonali, B .... 216-687-3860 350 G
s.b.wilson@csuohio.edu
WILSON, Stacey .... 636-481-3207 253 G
swilson@jeffco.edu
WILSON, Stephen .... 478-445-5331 119 A
steve.wilson@gcsu.edu
WILSON, Steve .... 785-833-4410 175 C
steve.wilson@kwu.edu
WILSON, Steven .... 231-773-9131 228 C
WILSON, Steven .... 540-868-7132 473 C
stevenwilson@lfcc.edu
WILSON, Steven, H .... 610-758-3200 388 C
shw516@lehigh.edu
WILSON, Tara, K .... 808-544-1460 128 E
tkwilson@hpu.edu
WILSON, Tiffany .... 620-341-6476 173 C
twilson@emporia.edu
WILSON, Tim .... 412-391-4100 395 H
WILSON, Tim .... 865-694-6666 424 C
trwilson@pstcc.edu
WILSON, Tomeka .... 210-486-2551 428 C
tcross13@alamo.edu
WILSON, Tommy .... 706-649-1894 117 F
twilson@columbustech.edu
WILSON, Travis .... 606-539-4236 185 C
travis.wilson@ucumberlands.edu
WILSON, Tricia .... 717-560-8200 387 D
twilson@lbc.edu
WILSON, Trinity .... 916-691-7006.. 50 K
wilsont@crc.losrios.edu
WILSON, Valarie .... 205-860-7845.... 7 A
vwilson@stillman.edu
WILSON, Valeri .... 619-660-4221.. 44 G
valeri.wilson@gcccd.edu
WILSON, Valerie .... 870-574-4514.. 21 F
vwilson@sautech.edu
WILSON, Valla, F .... 214-648-6066 456 D
valla.wilson@utsouthwestern.edu
WILSON, Valvia .... 601-977-7844 248 E
vwilson@tougaloo.edu
WILSON, Vicki .... 724-852-3375 401 E
vwilson@waynesburg.edu
WILSON, Vicky, W .... 864-833-8219 410 E
vwwilson@presby.edu
WILSON, Victor, K .... 706-542-3564 126 F
wilsonv@uga.edu
WILSON, Wendy .... 229-500-3503 114 F
wendy.wilson@asurams.edu
WILSON, Wes .... 404-627-2681 116 B
wes.wilson@beulah.edu
WILSON, Wesley .... 670-237-6834 503 G
wesley.wilson@marianas.edu
WILSON, William .... 937-481-2364 363 H
bill.wilson@wilmington.edu
WILSON, William, M ...... 918-495-6175 368 F
president@oru.edu
WILSON, Yolanda .... 336-838-6128 338 H
yswilson142@wilkescc.edu
WILSON-ALLAM,
Deborah .... 315-792-3259 323 G
dlwilson@utica.edu
WILSON-BYRD, Holly ..... 405-382-9204 369 E
h.wilsonbyrd@sscok.edu
WILSON-FENNELL,
Nicole .... 734-462-4400 230 B
nwilson@schoolcraft.edu
WILSON-PARKER,
Sharnita, I .... 252-335-3747 341 A
slwilson@ecsu.edu
WILSON PICKETT,
Clyde .... 651-201-1472 236 F
WILSON PICKETT,
Clyde .... 412-624-7860 400 A
cwp19@pitt.edu
WILSON-SPARROW,
Sarah .... 518-595-1101 319 G
wilsons@sunysccc.edu
WILSON-SYKES, Jean ..... 205-247-8145.... 7 A
jwilson-sykes@stillman.edu
WILSON-TAYLOR,
Sharon .... 312-369-7221 136 C
swilson-taylor@colum.edu
WILSTERMANN, Amy ..... 616-526-7620 221 L
amw26@calvin.edu
WILT, Darrell .... 717-815-1288 402 G
dwilt1@ycp.edu
WILTERDING, James ...... 505-277-1068 288 C
jameswilterding@salud.unm.edu
WILTFONG, Justin .... 620-242-0400 175 G
WILTGEN, JR., Jim .... 501-450-1222.. 19 I
wiltgen@hendrix.edu
WILTSHIRE, Rolly .... 718-289-5186 292 H
rolly.wiltshire@bcc.cuny.edu
WILTZ, Alex .... 413-775-1299 214 C
wiltza@gcc.mass.edu
WILTZ, Alex .... 717-337-6912 384 C
awiltz@gettysburg.edu
WILTZIUS, Pierre .... 805-893-5024.. 70 E
mlpsdean@ltsc.ucsb.edu
WIMBERLY, Carey .... 478-471-2712 122 D
carey.wimberly@mga.edu
WIMBERLY, Chuck .... 478-289-2036 118 B
cwimberly@ega.edu
WIMBERLY, Yvette .... 510-374-6305.. 21 B
yvette.wimberly@shortercollege.edu
WIMBUSH, James .... 812-855-2739 156 C
jwimbush@iu.edu
WIMBUSH, James, C ...... 812-855-2739 156 B
jwimbush@iu.edu
WIMER, Aaron .... 843-953-1658 406 D
awimer@citadel.edu
WIMER, Valinda .... 386-822-8850 111 F
vwimer@stetson.edu
WIMS, Daniel .... 256-372-8876.... 1 A
daniel.wims@aamu.edu
WIMS, Daniel, K .... 256-372-5230.... 1 A
daniel.wims@aamu.edu
WIMS, Lois, A .... 508-929-8038 213 D
lwims@worcester.edu
WIN, Wambli .... 918-913-2755 365 B
winw@bacone.edu
WINBUSH, Chauncey ..... 304-876-5155 489 A
cwinbush@shepherd.edu
WINBUSH, Larkisha .... 251-442-2250.... 8 C
lwinbush@umobile.edu
WINCH, Eric .... 908-709-7150 283 E
eric.winch@ucc.edu
WINCHELL, Barbara .... 207-216-4410 195 F
WINCHELL, Lynne .... 303-361-7367.. 80 C
lynne.winchell@ccaurora.edu
WINCHELL, Meghan .... 402-465-2440 267 J
mwinchel@nebrwesleyan.edu
WINCHESTER, Sara .... 732-255-0400 279 A
swinchester@ocean.edu
WINCKELMAN, Stephen 952-358-8597 239 C
stephen.winckelman@normandale.edu
WIND-NORTON, Laura .. 715-365-4578 498 D
lwindnorton@nicoletcollege.edu
WINDER, Katie .... 541-917-4547 373 F
winderk@linnbenton.edu
WINDER, Mark .... 319-895-4518 164 E
mwinder@cornellcollege.edu
WINDER, Wendy .... 801-618-0438 458 H
wwinder@ameritech.edu
WINDERS, Tim .... 219-989-8185 160 A
winders@pnw.edu
WINDES, Deborah, L ..... 708-239-4844 150 H
deborah.windes@trnty.edu
WINDHAM, Adam .... 916-484-8216.. 50 J
windhaa@arc.losrios.edu
WINDHAM, Greg .... 662-720-7210 247 D
jgwindham@nemcc.edu
WINDHAM, Jameka, A .. 305-628-6632 107 D
jwindham@stu.edu
WINDHAM, Joel .... 205-726-2011.... 6 E
jwindham@samford.edu
WINDHOLZ, Kevin .... 405-208-5600 367 E
kwindholz@okcu.edu
WINDHOLZ, Mindy .... 405-208-7902 367 E
mbwindholz@okcu.edu

WINDLE, Frank, H .... 215-871-6750 395 A
frankwi@pcom.edu
WINDLE, Lawrence, B ... 956-380-8100 441 L
lwindle@riogrande.edu
WINDLEY, Patricia .... 252-940-6219 332 A
tricia.windley@beaufortccc.edu
WINDMEYER, Sarah ...... 785-442-6000 174 C
jnorth@highlandcc.edu
WINDOKUN, Prema .... 805-898-4010.. 42 G
pwindokun@fielding.edu
WINE, David .... 815-939-5254 146 F
dwine@olivet.edu
WINEBRAKE, James .... 910-962-3389 343 B
winebrakej@uncw.edu
WINEGARD, Tanya, C .... 402-280-2775 265 J
tanyawinegard@creighton.edu
WINEY, Mark .... 530-752-6778.. 69 A
mwiney@ucdavis.edu
WINFIELD-THOMAS,
Evelyn, B .... 269-387-6316 232 J
evelyn.winfield@wmich.edu
WINFREY GRIFFIN,
Polly .... 609-258-6191 279 E
polly@princeton.edu
WING, Jeanette, M .... 212-854-1754 296 H
WING, Seth .... 319-895-4150 164 E
swing@cornellcollege.edu
WINGARD, Ed .... 830-792-7234 442 G
facilitiesservices@schreiner.edu
WINGARD, Jason .... 215-204-7405 398 D
president@temple.edu
WINGARD, Jason, M ...... 212-854-3771 296 H
jason.wingard@columbia.edu
WINGE, Jennifer .... 330-263-2118 350 H
jwinge@wooster.edu
WINGEIER-RAYO,
Philip .... 202-885-8611.. 94 D
pwingeier@wesleyseminary.edu
WINGENBACH, Edward . 413-559-5521 210 A
president@hampshire.edu
WINGER, Davin .... 580-349-1460 367 F
dwinger@opsu.edu
WINGER, Steven .... 563-876-3353 165 D
swinger@dwci.edu
WINGFIELD, Erin .... 559-791-2332.. 47 D
ewingfield@portervillecollege.edu
WINGLER, Mike .... 336-838-6178 338 H
mswingler068@wilkescc.edu
WINGO, Blake .... 678-839-4977 127 A
bwingo@westga.edu
WINGO, Tad .... 573-629-3123 253 D
tad.wingo@hlg.edu
WINGROVE,
Thurman, D .... 412-624-6028 400 A
twingrove@pitt.edu
WINGS, Arron .... 319-398-5624 167 H
arron.wings@kirkwood.edu
WINIGER, Brent .... 701-858-3331 345 C
brent.winiger@minotstateu.edu
WINISTORFER, Paul, M 540-231-5481 475 D
pwinisto@vt.edu
WINITZKY-STEPHENS,
Jessie .... 801-957-4090 460 D
jessie.winitzky-stephens@slcc.edu
WINKELBAUER, Brian ... 303-273-3000.. 79 A
bwinkelb@mines.edu
WINKELFOOS, Natalie ... 440-775-6463 357 G
natalie.winkelfoos@oberlin.edu
WINKELMAN, Andrew ... 708-209-3529 136 D
andrew.winkelman@cuchicago.edu
WINKELSTEIN, Beth, A . 215-898-7225 399 J
winkelst@seas.upenn.edu
WINKER, Amy .... 231-591-3823 223 H
amywinker@ferris.edu
WINKLER, Fred, R .... 314-977-2401 258 H
fred.winkler@slu.edu
WINKLER, Nicole .... 434-961-5427 474 B
nwinkler@pvcc.edu
WINKLER, Yitzchak ...... 305-534-7050 112 C
ywinkler@talmudicu.edu
WINKLERPRINS,
Vince, C .... 202-687-3220.. 92 D
vjw6@georgetown.edu
WINKLEY, Robert .... 617-585-1310 217 A
robert.winkley@necmusic.edu
WINN, Emmett .... 334-844-5771.... 4 E
winnjoh@auburn.edu
WINN, Joshua, P .... 214-887-5014 434 G
jwinn@dts.edu
WINN, Lori .... 870-972-3454.. 17 I
lwinn@astate.edu
WINN, Matt .... 214-333-6923 433 D
mattw@dbu.edu

WINN, Regina .... 318-670-9411 191 B
rwinn@susla.edu
WINN, Rob .... 906-227-2700 228 E
rwinn@nmu.edu
WINN, Rose .... 559-453-7150.. 43 D
rose.winn@fresno.edu
WINN, Terry .... 206-281-2678 482 K
winnt@spu.edu
WINNEY, Maureen .... 518-587-2100 320 B
maureen.winney@esc.edu
WINNINGHAM, Rob ...... 503-838-8271 377 C
winninr@wou.edu
WINOKUR, Ted .... 802-383-6613 461 C
twinokur@champlain.edu
WINQUIST, Melissa ...... 480-858-9100.. 16 B
m.winquist@scnm.edu
WINS, Cedric, T .... 540-464-7311 475 C
winsct@vmi.edu
WINSEMAN, Jeffrey ...... 518-262-5511 289 C
winsemj@amc.edu
WINSETT, Kim .... 812-488-2940 161 E
kw83@evansville.edu
WINSLOW, Gregory ...... 614-236-6714 348 I
gwinslow@capital.edu
WINSLOW, Maggie ...... 415-561-6555.. 58 B
WINSLOW, Mark .... 405-789-6400 369 G
mwinslow@snu.edu
WINSLOW-SCHABER,
Deborah, J .... 585-389-2066 307 D
dwinslo1@naz.edu
WINSOR, Robert .... 508-286-8213 219 F
winsor_robert@wheatoncollege.edu
WINSTEAD, Cherese ..... 302-857-6521.. 90 D
cwinstead@desu.edu
WINSTEAD, Chris .... 601-266-4883 248 H
chris.winstead@usm.edu
WINSTEAD, Christopher 207-974-4810 195 A
cwinstead@emcc.edu
WINSTEAD, James .... 323-860-0789.. 50 E
WINSTEAD, Mel .... 704-847-5600 340 D
mwinstead@ses.edu
WINSTERSTEEN,
Chelsey .... 815-455-8676 143 F
cwintersteen@mchenry.edu
WINSTON, Leslie .... 804-627-5300 464 B
leslie_winston@bshsi.org
WINSTON-MUIR,
Jeanni .... 301-846-2489 198 E
jwinston-muir@frederick.edu
WINT, Errol, L .... 317-274-0838 157 B
ewint@iupui.edu
WINTCH, Wesley .... 785-628-4251 173 E
wdwintch@fhsu.edu
WINTEMUTE, Mike .... 512-463-4862 448 G
mike.wintemute@tsus.edu
WINTER, Barbara .... 620-235-4105 176 H
bwinter@pittstate.edu
WINTER, Barbara, J ...... 620-235-4152 176 H
bwinter@pittstate.edu
WINTER, Cheryl .... 816-604-6748 254 G
cheryl.winter@mcckc.edu
WINTER, Cheryl .... 816-604-6748 254 F
cheryl.winter@mcckc.edu
WINTER, Christoph .... 415-955-2100.. 25 A
WINTER, Kim .... 828-227-7311 343 D
kkruebel@wcu.edu
WINTER, Stacey, O .... 701-231-8954 345 D
stacey.winter@ndsu.edu
WINTER, Tara .... 319-352-8475 170 F
tara.winter@wartburg.edu
WINTER, Tara .... 518-255-5418 318 F
wintertl@cobleskill.edu
WINTER, Walter .... 212-217-3630 299 C
walter_winter@fitnyc.edu
WINTER, JR.,
William, F .... 618-650-5380 149 H
wwinter@siue.edu
WINTERBURN, Scott ...... 909-448-4393.. 71 C
rwinterburn@laverne.edu
WINTERHALTER, Teresa 678-407-5601 119 B
twinterhalter@ggc.edu
WINTERLING,
Stephen, A .... 727-816-3340 105 E
winters@phsc.edu
WINTERS, Amy .... 845-687-5124 322 K
wintersa@sunyulster.edu
WINTERS, Amy .... 308-635-6195 269 E
winters4@wncc.edu
WINTERS, Gwendolyn ... 903-730-4890 437 E
gwinters@jarvis.edu
WINTERS, J. Chris .... 504-568-2243 189 C
cwinte@lsuhsc.edu
WINTERS, Jamie .... 301-687-4000 203 F

WINTERS, Jeremy, G .... 641-422-4990 168 E
jeremy.winters@niacc.edu
WINTERS, John .... 918-781-7241 365 B
wintersj@bacone.edu
WINTERS, Kari .... 740-826-8320 356 H
kwinters@muskingum.edu
WINTERS, Keiana .... 773-298-3137 148 I
kwinters@sxu.edu
WINTERS, Michael .... 314-256-8854 249 F
winters@ai.edu
WINTERS, Stephanie ..... 719-219-9636.. 78 C
swinters@cavt.edu
WINTERS, Teresa .... 413-265-2210 208 B
winterst@elms.edu
WINTERS, Terri, S .... 603-862-4639 273 H
terri.winters@unh.edu
WINTERS, Todd, A .... 731-881-7250 426 E
winters@utm.edu
WINTERS, Vicky, L .... 253-535-7110 481 C
winters@plu.edu
WINTERSTEEN, Wendy .. 515-294-2042 163 E
wwinters@iastate.edu
WINTON, Diana .... 847-628-2532 141 A
diana.winton@judsonu.edu
WINZELER, Isabelle ...... 352-335-2332.. 94 E
isabelle.winzeler@acupuncturist.edu
WINZENREID,
Misty Anne .... 206-876-6100 483 A
mwinzenreid@theseattleschool.edu
WIPPERT, Lola .... 406-338-5441 262 D
WIPPMAN, David .... 315-859-4105 300 F
dwippman@hamilton.edu
WIRLEY, Eileen, M .... 585-292-3041 306 K
ewirley1@monroecc.edu
WIRT, Jonathan .... 919-532-5663 338 E
jawirth@waketech.edu
WIRTH, Eric .... 802-258-3511 462 B
WIRTH-CAUCHON, Alex 413-538-2225 216 G
awirthca@mtholyoke.edu
WIRTHLIN, James .... 319-656-2447 169 F
WIRTZ, Amy, M .... 920-565-1000 492 A
wirtzam@lakeland.edu
WIRTZ, Denis .... 410-516-8094 199 E
wirtz@jhu.edu
WISBY, Heidi .... 248-689-8282 231 E
hwisby@walshcollege.edu
WISCHMANN, Teresa .... 309-779-7708 150 I
teresa.wischmann@trinitycollegeqc.edu
WISCHMEIER, Gordon ... 928-523-9011.. 14 J
WISCOTT, Richard .... 401-598-5156 403 E
richard.wiscott@jwu.edu
WISDOM, Ami .... 816-584-6542 257 E
ami.wisdom@park.edu
WISDOM, Bryan .... 252-334-2025 331 C
bryan.wisdom@macuniversity.edu
WISDOM, Jeff .... 218-751-8670 241 Q
jeffwisdom@oakhills.edu
WISE, Adam .... 617-287-5335 211 E
adam.wise@umb.edu
WISE, Ashley .... 724-852-7625 401 E
awise@waynesburg.edu
WISE, Brittany .... 850-323-0353 110 E
brittany.alana@ufl.edu
WISE, Brittany .... 310-360-8888.. 27 D
WISE, Colleen .... 518-743-2306 319 D
wisec@sunyacc.edu
WISE, David .... 509-865-0717 480 B
wise_d@heritage.edu
WISE, Diane, K .... 301-696-3855 199 C
wise@hood.edu
WISE, Ginny .... 504-865-5259 191 D
gwise@tulane.edu
WISE, Jay .... 616-526-6633 221 L
jjw8@calvin.edu
WISE, Jessica .... 740-333-5115 360 G
jwise@sscc.edu
WISE, John .... 716-926-8846 301 C
jwise@hilbert.edu
WISE, JR., L. Anthony .. 865-694-6616 424 C
lawise@pstcc.edu
WISE, Lance .... 404-225-4082 115 F
lwise@atlantatech.edu
WISE, Ryan .... 515-271-2082 165 F
ryan.wise@drake.edu
WISE, Sharon, H .... 315-792-3120 323 G
swise@utica.edu
WISE, Stephen .... 585-343-0055 300 D
spwise@genesee.edu
WISE, Teresa .... 205-348-5256.... 7 G
teresa.wise@ua.edu
WISE, Timothy .... 337-521-8951 188 G
timothy.wise@solacc.edu
WISECUP, Mike .... 207-859-4000 194 B

WISELEY, Mark .... 563-884-5691 169 C
mark.wiseley@palmer.edu
WISELL, Teresita .... 914-606-6585 324 F
teresita.wisell@sunywcc.edu
WISEMAN, Chris .... 504-861-5431 190 A
cwiseman@loyno.edu
WISEMAN, Marcie .... 843-953-5636 407 D
wisemanm@cofc.edu
WISEMAN, Tina .... 573-288-6306 251 I
twiseman@culver.edu
WISENOR, Tad .... 509-777-4401 485 D
twisenor@whitworth.edu
WISER, Devin .... 801-626-7834 460 B
devinwiser@weber.edu
WISER, Gary .... 864-656-4928 406 F
gwiser@clemson.edu
WISER, Hayes .... 843-525-8271 411 G
hwiser@tcl.edu
WISER, James .... 325-674-2476 427 G
jaw2ob@acu.edu
WISER, Karla, D .... 814-641-3306 386 E
wiserk@juniata.edu
WISHARD, Thomas .... 480-947-6644.. 15 B
WISHING, III, Lee, S .... 724-458-3332 384 F
lswishing@gcc.edu
WISNER, David .... 716-896-0700 324 A
dmwisner@villa.edu
WISNER, Jon .... 928-536-6265.. 14 L
jon.wisner@npc.edu
WISNER, Paul .... 714-892-7711.. 38 E
pwisner@gwc.cccd.edu
WISNESCK, Roberto .... 724-805-2175 397 D
roberto.wisnesck@stvincent.edu
WISNESKI, Thomas, E .. 610-566-1776 402 C
twisneski@williamson.edu
WISNEWSKI, Michael .... 401-341-2201 404 D
michael.wisnewski@salve.edu
WISNIEWSKI, Allison .... 856-225-6422 281 A
aemery@camden.rutgers.edu
WISNIEWSKI, Amy .... 860-768-6601.. 89 E
awisniews@hartford.edu
WISNIEWSKI, OSFS,
Daniel .... 610-282-1100 382 A
daniel.wisniewski@desales.edu
WISNIEWSKI,
Mary Beth .... 414-410-4194 490 J
mbwisniewski@stritch.edu
WISNIEWSKI, Melissa .... 717-391-7234 398 E
wisniewski@stevenscollege.edu
WISNIEWSKI, Michael ... 419-824-3728 355 C
mwisniewski@lourdes.edu
WISNIEWSKI,
Stephen, R .... 412-624-2246 400 A
wisniew@edc.pitt.edu
WISNIEWSKI, Susan ..... 585-385-8049 313 A
swisniewski@sjfc.edu
WISSING, Dennis, R ...... 318-795-4279 189 E
dennis.wissing@lsus.edu
WISSMILLER, Kia .... 713-646-1800 443 C
kwissmiller@stcl.edu
WISTROM, Carl, H .... 773-244-4961 145 F
cwistrom@northpark.edu
WISWALL, Derry .... 660-248-6296 250 H
dwiswall@centralmethodist.edu
WITBRACHT, Rachel ...... 850-474-2200 111 E
rwitbracht@uwf.edu
WITCHER, Kerry .... 865-974-4531 426 B
kwitcher@tennessee.edu
WITCHER, Pamela .... 508-588-9100 214 F
pwitcher1@massasoit.mass.edu
WITEK, Paul, J .... 570-561-1818 397 B
paul.witek@stots.edu
WITH, Elizabeth .... 940-565-4909 453 B
elizabeth.with@unt.edu
WITHAM, Jason .... 401-598-4656 403 E
jason.witham@jwu.edu
WITHERELL, Meghan ...... 530-938-5831.. 39 D
witherellm@siskiyous.edu
WITHERELL, Stewart ...... 404-752-1500 123 A
switherell@msm.edu
WITHERINGTON, Ed ...... 251-981-3771.... 5 B
edward.witherington@
columbiasouthern.edu
WITHERINGTON,
Jennifer .... 912-688-6966 123 F
jlwitherington@ogeecheetech.edu
WITHEROW, Laurie, B .. 615-898-2239 421 C
laurie.witherow@mtsu.edu
WITHEROW, Missy .... 540-458-8400 476 D
mwitherow@wlu.edu
WITHERS, Allen .... 325-793-4681 439 A
withers.allen@mcm.edu
WITHERS, Amanda .... 936-294-1017 449 E
withers@shsu.edu

WOLPE, Paul, R .... 404-727-3150 118 D
pwolpe@emory.edu
WOLPERN, Kevin .... 952-887-1394 241 P
kwolpern@nwhealth.edu
WOLPIN, Aryeh .... 718-232-7800 325 D
WOLSEY, Timothy .... 480-732-7125.. 13 B
timothy.wolsey@cgc.edu
WOLTER, Julie .... 406-243-2605 263 D
julie.wolter@umontana.edu
WOLTERS, Daniel .... 406-657-1161 264 G
woltersd@rocky.edu
WOLTERS-FREDLUND,
Bernita .... 616-526-6203 221 L
bw24@calvin.edu
WOLTMANN, Tanya .... 847-543-2443 135 G
twoltmann@clcillinois.edu
WOLVAARDT, Bennie .... 210-446-6719 456 E
WOMACK, Cameron .... 828-328-7334 330 B
cameron.womack@lr.edu
WOMACK, Joseph .... 541-684-7241 371 H
jwomack@bushnell.edu
WOMACK, Larry .... 510-215-3836.. 40 G
lwomack@contracosta.edu
WOMACK, Sheila .... 304-384-6298 488 K
swomack@concord.edu
WOMACK, Tonya .... 727-864-7737.. 98 G
womacktm@eckerd.edu
WOMACK, Veronica ...... 478-445-1382 119 A
veronic.womack@gcsu.edu
WOMACK, Wayne .... 479-788-7407.. 22 A
wayne.womack@uafs.edu
WOMBLE, Jeff .... 910-672-1474 341 B
jwomble@uncfsu.edu
WOMBLE, Lynn, Z .... 903-813-2891 429 I
lwomble@austincollege.edu
WOMICK, Jason .... 864-587-4217 411 F
womickj@smcsc.edu
WONDELL, Jean .... 386-312-4037 107 A
jeanwondell@sjrstate.edu
WONDERLY, Jennifer .... 312-341-3558 148 A
jwonderl@roosevelt.edu
WONDERS, Christopher 570-372-4578 398 A
wonders@susqu.edu
WONG, Adam .... 909-448-4481.. 71 C
awong@laverne.edu
WONG, Alina .... 651-696-6870 236 C
awong3@macalester.edu
WONG, Asia .... 504-865-3835 190 A
awong@loyno.edu
WONG, Bill .... 903-510-3158 451 D
bill.wong@tjc.edu
WONG, Erwin .... 212-220-8321 292 G
ewong@bmcc.cuny.edu
WONG, Gene .... 978-232-2311 209 B
gwong@endicott.edu
WONG, James .... 718-405-3733 296 D
james.wong@mountsaintvincent.edu
WONG, Jane .... 609-771-2277 275 J
wong@tcnj.edu
WONG, Jeannie .... 916-278-2067.. 33 A
jwong@csus.edu
WONG, Julie .... 847-317-7152 150 J
jwong@tiu.edu
WONG, Keaton .... 718-990-2505 313 B
wongk1@stjohns.edu
WONG, Lam .... 216-987-4265 351 D
lam.wong@tri-c.edu
WONG, Leslie .... 978-934-4670 211 G
leslie_wong@uml.edu
WONG, Leslie .... 202-885-2143.. 91 D
lawyers@american.edu
WONG, Michael .... 310-338-7760.. 51 C
michael.wong@lmu.edu
WONG, Michael Paul ... 951-571-6251.. 59 B
michaelpaul.wong@mvc.edu
WONG, Nina .... 212-662-7100 323 C
nwong@uts.columbia.edu
WONG, Noel .... 504-988-8888 191 D
ntswong@tulane.edu
WONG, Richard .... 804-278-4240 470 I
rwong@upsem.edu
WONG, Rita .... 703-284-5982 468 A
rita.wong@marymount.edu
WONG, Theresa .... 480-857-5118.. 13 B
theresa.wong@cgc.edu
WONG, Tony .... 562-809-5100.. 43 C
tony.wong@fremont.edu
WONG, Walter .... 415-254-6033.. 68 N
WONG, Yong Gao .... 312-368-0900 134 H
WONG (LAU), Kathleen 408-924-1187.. 34 B
kathleen.wonglau@sjsu.edu
WONG-DAVIS, Kris .... 765-494-4600 159 G
WONG NICKERSON,
Agnes .... 619-594-5631.. 33 E
awongnickerson@sdsu.edu
WONGSAROJ, Ben .... 305-623-4100 100 B
ben.wongsaroj@fmuniv.edu
WONSEY, Jacquelyn ...... 410-951-6367 203 E
jwonsey@coppin.edu
WOO, Donna .... 800-867-2243.. 55 C
dwoo@pacific-college.edu
WOO, Jang Hoon .... 562-926-1023.. 58 A
admin.online@ptsa.edu
WOO, Matthew, D .... 714-995-9988.. 47 E
WOO, Melissa .... 517-355-1855 227 C
mwoo@msu.edu
WOO, Melissa .... 517-355-1855 227 C
WOO, Meredith .... 434-381-6210 470 H
president@sbc.edu
WOO, Minah, C .... 443-518-4724 199 D
mwoo@howardcc.edu
WOO, Priscilla, M .... 714-995-9988.. 47 E
WOOD, Alex .... 507-537-7678 240 G
alexander.wood@smsu.edu
WOOD, Amy .... 828-328-7728 330 B
amy.wood@lr.edu
WOOD, Amy .... 419-448-3372 361 C
woodar@tiffin.edu
WOOD, Amy, B .... 615-963-7548 425 A
awood@tnstate.edu
WOOD, Ana, I .... 319-656-2447 169 F
chiqui.wood@shilohuniversity.edu
WOOD, Andy .... 662-472-9024 245 E
awood@holmescc.edu
WOOD, Anne .... 814-641-5310 386 E
wood@juniata.edu
WOOD, Becky .... 317-274-4417 157 B
rewood@iupui.edu
WOOD, Bobby .... 864-242-5100 405 H
WOOD, Caesar .... 785-243-1435 172 J
WOOD, Carolline .... 540-351-1516 473 C
cwood@lfcc.edu
WOOD, Chris, A .... 304-637-1243 486 D
chris.wood@dewv.edu
WOOD, Christy .... 305-595-9500.. 94 G
WOOD, Dale .... 931-431-9700 421 G
dwood@nci.edu
WOOD, Darlene .... 620-223-2700 173 F
darlenew@fortscott.edu
WOOD, David, H .... 906-227-2112 228 E
dwood@nmu.edu
WOOD, Dawn .... 319-398-5443 167 H
dawn.wood@kirkwood.edu
WOOD, Douglas, M .... 717-796-1800 389 F
dwood@messiah.edu
WOOD, Dylan .... 419-772-2656 358 D
d-wood@onu.edu
WOOD, Elizabeth, A ...... 516-572-7775 307 C
elizabeth.wood@ncc.edu
WOOD, Emily .... 856-225-2867 281 A
emily.wood@camden.rutgers.edu
WOOD, Emily, S .... 317-738-8283 155 A
ewood@franklincollege.edu
WOOD, Eric .... 817-257-7863 447 H
e.c.wood@tcu.edu
WOOD, Erin .... 701-662-1598 346 A
erin.wood@lrsc.edu
WOOD, Faye .... 843-863-7502 406 C
fwood@csuniv.edu
WOOD, Frank .... 305-809-3287.. 97 M
frank.wood@cfk.edu
WOOD, Gary .... 262-595-2364 495 D
woodg@uwp.edu
WOOD, Gretchen, D ..... 585-292-3685 306 K
gwood9@monroecc.edu
WOOD, J. Luke .... 619-594-5211.. 33 E
luke.wood@sdsu.edu
WOOD, J. Luke .... 619-594-0167.. 33 E
luke.wood@sdsu.edu
WOOD, Jacob .... 660-562-1110 256 G
jwood@nwmissouri.edu
WOOD, Jane .... 419-358-3324 348 E
woodj@bluffton.edu
WOOD, Jason .... 479-394-7622.. 23 F
jwood@uarichmountain.edu
WOOD, Jason, S .... 608-822-2300 498 H
jwood@swtc.edu
WOOD, Jill, H .... 314-516-5811 260 E
woodjh@umsl.edu
WOOD, John .... 307-855-2162 499 U
jwood@cwc.edu
WOOD, Jon .... 937-766-7871 349 C
jonwood@cedarville.edu
WOOD, Judith .... 312-322-1780 150 C
jwood@spertus.edu
WOOD, Kathryn .... 909-748-8479.. 72 E
kathryn_wood@redlands.edu
WOOD, Kelly .... 417-836-8346 255 J
kellywood@missouristate.edu
WOOD, Laura .... 903-923-8207 440 E
lwood@panola.edu
WOOD, Laura, L .... 641-422-4355 168 E
woodlaur@niacc.edu
WOOD, Lee .... 850-872-3866 101 O
lwood10@gulfcoast.edu
WOOD, Lindsay, S .... 732-923-4589 278 B
lwood@monmouth.edu
WOOD, Lisa .... 208-282-2777 131 E
woodlis2@isu.edu
WOOD, Lynette .... 919-546-8344 339 I
lynette.wood@shawu.edu
WOOD, Martin .... 719-255-3438.. 84 A
mwood@uccs.edu
WOOD, Melinda .... 559-297-4500.. 46 C
mwood@iot.edu
WOOD, Melinda .... 540-568-7883 467 C
wood4mj@jmu.edu
WOOD, Michael .... 570-408-4500 402 B
mike.wood@wilkes.edu
WOOD, Michele, G .... 401-341-2872 404 D
michele.wood@salve.edu
WOOD, Mike .... 253-680-7301 477 A
mwood@batestech.edu
WOOD, Nicolle .... 978-542-6991 213 B
nicole.wood@salemstate.edu
WOOD, Pamela, R .... 919-658-7753 340 E
pwood@umo.edu
WOOD, Paul .... 530-226-2953.. 64 C
pwood@simpsonu.edu
WOOD, Phillip .... 423-478-7993 421 J
pwood@ptseminary.edu
WOOD, Phoebe .... 773-481-8525 135 D
pwood3@ccc.edu
WOOD, Pia .... 940-565-4941 453 B
pia.wood@unt.edu
WOOD, Robert, B .... 757-446-6137 465 H
woodrb@evms.edu
WOOD, Rodney .... 740-376-4791 355 E
rlw006@marietta.edu
WOOD, Scott .... 801-863-8516 460 A
scott.wood@uvu.edu
WOOD, Shane .... 417-626-1234 257 A
wood.shane@occ.edu
WOOD, Sharon, L .... 512-471-1166 454 C
swood@utexas.edu
WOOD, Shelia .... 504-286-5368 191 A
swood@suno.edu
WOOD, Steve .... 501-686-2941.. 21 G
spwood@uasys.edu
WOOD, Steve .... 828-835-4254 338 C
swood@tricountycc.edu
WOOD, Stewart .... 734-432-5645 226 G
swood@madonna.edu
WOOD, Susan .... 928-428-8261.. 12 H
susan.wood@eac.edu
WOOD, Swarup .... 408-847-4060.. 52 I
WOOD, Tim .... 909-706-8644.. 75 G
tjwood@westernu.edu
WOOD, Tommy .... 785-594-6451 171 C
tommy.wood@bakeru.edu
WOOD, Vicky .... 740-374-8716 363 F
president@wscc.edu
WOOD-WILLIAMS,
Danielle, L .... 479-575-4019.. 21 H
dlw11@uark.edu
WOODALL, Andy .... 540-665-4581 470 A
awoodall@su.edu
WOODALL, Betty, C .... 919-209-2019 335 D
bcwoodall@johnstoncc.edu
WOODALL, Eric .... 703-993-5442 466 J
ewoodall@gmu.edu
WOODALL, Marsha .... 270-824-1802 182 A
marsha.woodall@kctcs.edu
WOODALL, Stephen .... 404-756-4000 115 E
WOODARD, Bobby, R .... 334-844-8880.... 4 E
brw0016@auburn.edu
WOODARD, Brandyn .... 763-433-1253 237 A
brandyn.woodard@anokaramsey.edu
WOODARD, Brandyn .... 763-433-1253 236 H
brandyn.woodard@anokaramsey.edu
WOODARD, Emory .... 610-519-7093 401 B
emory.woodard@villanova.edu
WOODARD, Jeffrey .... 716-673-4002 316 A
jeffrey.woodard@fredonia.edu
WOODARD, Joanne ...... 940-565-2711 453 B
joanne.woodard@unt.edu
WOODARD, Kimberly .... 386-481-2829.. 96 D
woodardk@cookman.edu
WOODARD, Randall ...... 352-588-8239 107 B
randall.woodard@saintleo.edu
WOODARD, Scott .... 828-328-7254 330 B
scott.woodard@lr.edu
WOODARD, Stephanie .. 309-341-5272 134 A
swoodard@sandburg.edu
WOODARD, Steve .... 425-640-1020 479 A
steve.woodard@edcc.edu
WOODARD, Thelma ...... 336-334-7500 341 C
WOODARD, Tim .... 919-658-7756 340 E
twoodard@umo.edu
WOODARD-MINK, Lisa . 916-278-3852.. 33 A
lisa.woodard-mink@csus.edu
WOODBURN, Steve, M . 303-963-3230.. 78 D
swoodburn@ccu.edu
WOODBURN, Steven .... 606-326-2077 180 I
steve.woodburn@kctcs.edu
WOODBURY, Heidi, D .. 801-585-6167 459 D
heidi.woodbury@admin.utah.edu
WOODCOCK, Jonathan . 603-641-7118 273 C
jwoodcock@anselm.edu
WOODDELL, Joseph .... 214-818-1336 433 A
jwooddell@criswell.edu
WOODDELL, Kathleen ... 304-724-5000 486 C
kwooddell@cdu.edu
WOODEN, K. Mark .... 602-639-7500.. 12 L
WOODEN, Kyle .... 336-316-2383 329 C
woodenwk@guilford.edu
WOODEN, Ontario, S .... 601-877-6142 244 B
owooden@alcorn.edu
WOODFAULK, Ashley .... 773-947-6261 143 E
awoodfaulk@mccormick.edu
WOODFIN, Linda .... 575-492-2123 288 I
lwoodfin@usw.edu
WOODFORK,
Joshua, C .... 518-580-5700 315 A
jwoodfor@skidmore.edu
WOODHAM, Margo .... 478-471-2800 122 D
margo.woodham@mga.edu
WOODHOUSE,
Bryan, M .... 608-246-6337 497 I
woodhouse@madisoncollege.edu
WOODHOUSE,
Michelle, W .... 757-822-1061 474 G
mwoodhouse@tcc.edu
WOODHOUSE, Nicole ... 207-778-7335 196 F
niki.haggan@maine.edu
WOODKE, Leah .... 701-255-3285 346 I
lwoodke@uttc.edu
WOODLEE,
Stephanie, A .... 325-674-2413 427 G
stephanie.woodlee@acu.edu
WOODLEY, Derek .... 419-783-2380 351 J
dwoodley@defiance.edu
WOODLEY, Kimberly ..... 724-805-2083 397 C
kimberly.woodley@stvincent.edu
WOODLEY, Michael, P . 701-252-3467 346 J
woodley@uj.edu
WOODLEY, Sandra .... 432-552-2100 456 C
president@utpb.edu
WOODLEY, Xeturah .... 575-527-7521 287 A
xwoodley@nmsu.edu
WOODLIEF, Alan .... 336-279-9203 328 H
awoodlief@elon.edu
WOODLIEF, Greg .... 706-721-2213 115 I
gwoodlief@augusta.edu
WOODLY, Clara .... 410-706-7002 202 F
cwoodly@umaryland.edu
WOODLY, Kimberly .... 724-805-2253 397 D
kimberly.woodly@stvincent.edu
WOODMANCY, Sansu ... 909-447-2502.. 37 H
swoodmancy@cst.edu
WOODMANSEE,
Kate, C .... 413-545-5254 211 D
kwoodmansee@grad.umass.edu
WOODRAL, Bobbi .... 509-533-4820 478 C
bobbi.woodral@ccs.spokane.edu
WOODRING, Lauree ...... 443-334-2125 202 C
lwoodring@stevenson.edu
WOODRING, Mary .... 907-786-1800.. 10 A
WOODROW, Adam .... 413-782-1583 219 E
adam.woodrow@wne.edu
WOODROW, Kyle .... 620-417-1131 177 C
kyle.woodrow@sccc.edu
WOODROW, Robert ...... 315-731-5753 306 G
jwoodrow@mvcc.edu
WOODRUFF, Aaron ...... 309-438-8631 140 C
apwoodr@ilstu.edu
WOODRUFF, Donna ...... 410-617-2283 199 G
dmwoodruff@loyola.edu
WOODRUFF, Jill .... 423-472-7141 423 C
jwoodruff02@clevelandstatecc.edu
WOODRUFF, Kelly .... 912-478-1566 120 A
kwoodruff@georgiasouthern.edu

WORTHAM, Timothy ..... 610-341-1712 383 A
twortham@eastern.edu
WORTHEN, Kevin, J ...... 801-422-2521 458 A
kevin_worthen@byu.edu
WORTHEY, Tracy, A ...... 336-750-2832 343 E
WORTHINGTON, Natasha .... 252-493-7411 336 E
nmworthington@my.pittcc.edu
WORTHINGTON, Phyllis .... 870-512-7842.. 18 C
phyllis_worthington@asun.edu
WORTHLEY, Kristin .... 732-224-2133 275 D
kworthley@brookdalecc.edu
WORTHY, Erika .... 941-487-5020 110 C
eworthy@ncf.edu
WORTHY, Mark .... 225-752-4233 187 A
mworthy@iticollege.edu
WOS, Aldona .... 202-462-2101.. 93 A
WOTTON, Heather .... 203-773-8558.. 85 C
hwotton@albertus.edu
WOUDENBERG, Robert . 315-866-0300 301 B
woudenbra@herkimer.edu
WOUGHTER, Kerrey ...... 231-995-1063 228 F
kwoughter@nmc.edu
WOUGHTER, Laura .... 740-389-4636 355 F
woughterl@mtc.edu
WOULFE, Rebecca .... 303-404-5497.. 80 I
rebecca.woulfe@frontrange.edu
WOVKANECH, Jason ..... 603-271-6484 272 C
WOYAK, Amber .... 847-578-8350 148 B
amber.woyak@rosalindfranklin.edu
WOZNIAK, Andrew .... 630-889-6878 145 D
awozniak@nuhs.edu
WOZNIAK, Jim .... 423-636-7300 425 E
jwozniak@tusculum.edu
WOZNIAK, Rachel .... 716-926-8989 301 C
rwozniak@hilbert.edu
WRAGE, Rebecca .... 308-535-3679 266 J
wrager@mpcc.edu
WRAGG, Tunisia .... 212-517-0561 305 D
twragg@mmm.edu
WRAITH, Jon, M .... 603-862-2468 273 H
jon.wraith@unh.edu
WRASE, Micah .... 830-792-7206 442 G
mkwrase@schreiner.edu
WRAY, Donald, W .... 318-795-2392 189 E
donald.wray@lsus.edu
WRAY, Kimberli .... 701-774-4500 346 C
kimberli.wray@willistonstate.edu
WRAY, Kyle .... 405-744-4366 367 G
kyle.wray@okstate.edu
WRAY, Lee .... 931-372-3893 425 B
lwray@tntech.edu
WRAY, Rachel .... 207-786-6240 193 D
rwray@bates.edu
WRAY, Roger .... 434-949-1040 474 D
roger.wray@southside.edu
WREN, Jan .... 606-539-4328 185 C
jan.wren@ucumberlands.edu
WREN, Pam .... 865-524-8079 419 A
pam.wren@huhs.edu
WRENN, Christy .... 318-869-5057 186 C
cwrenn@centenary.edu
WRENN, Sara .... 336-517-2367 326 J
swrenn@bennett.edu
WRICE, Sheldon, B .... 330-972-6023 361 G
swrice1@uakron.edu
WRIGHT, Adam .... 214-333-5930 433 D
adam@dbu.edu
WRIGHT, Amanda .... 317-955-6721 159 A
awright@marian.edu
WRIGHT, Andre-Denis, G .... 405-325-3221 370 J
andre.wright@ou.edu
WRIGHT, Andrew .... 562-985-8410.. 32 A
andrew.wright@csulb.edu
WRIGHT, Angelina .... 325-942-2017 450 B
angie.wright@angelo.edu
WRIGHT, Angie .... 478-757-5192 127 D
awright@wesleyancollege.edu
WRIGHT, Ann .... 501-450-3808.. 19 I
wright@hendrix.edu
WRIGHT, Ann .... 828-726-2715 332 E
awright@cccti.edu
WRIGHT, Ann .... 864-250-8719 408 J
ann.wright@gvltec.edu
WRIGHT, Beatrice, V ..... 410-651-8387 203 B
bvwright@umes.edu
WRIGHT, Betsy .... 816-271-4237 256 C
bwright3@missouriwestern.edu
WRIGHT, Bo .... 706-379-3111 128 A
dbwright@yhc.edu
WRIGHT, Bob .... 262-742-4444 499 S
drbob@wrightgrad.edu
WRIGHT, Brandon .... 205-934-4324.... 8 A
btwright@uab.edu
WRIGHT, Brant .... 706-778-8500 124 B
bwright@piedmont.edu
WRIGHT, Brian .... 276-964-7207 474 E
brian.wright@sw.edu
WRIGHT, Cameron .... 307-766-6104 500 H
chgw@uwyo.edu
WRIGHT, Carlecia .... 281-655-3701 438 E
carlecia.wright@lonestar.edu
WRIGHT, Cary .... 276-326-4280 464 A
cwright@bluefield.edu
WRIGHT, Cathleen .... 830-372-8078 448 C
cwright@tlu.edu
WRIGHT, Cathy .... 704-233-8082 344 E
c.wright@wingate.edu
WRIGHT, Chantelle .... 212-237-8754 294 B
cwright@jjay.cuny.edu
WRIGHT, Charles .... 609-771-2393 275 J
wrightc@tcnj.edu
WRIGHT, Charles .... 704-330-6257 333 B
charles.wright@cpcc.edu
WRIGHT, Charles, D ..... 405-325-3412 370 J
cwright@ou.edu
WRIGHT, Chatt, G .... 808-544-0203 128 E
cwright@hpu.edu
WRIGHT, Chris .... 575-624-8070 286 F
wright@nmmi.edu
WRIGHT, Christopher ... 610-225-5575 383 A
cwright7@eastern.edu
WRIGHT, Christy .... 620-450-2133 176 I
christya@prattcc.edu
WRIGHT, Chuck, W .... 803-938-3867 412 G
wrightcw@uscsumter.edu
WRIGHT, Colleen .... 269-965-3931 225 D
wrightc@kellogg.edu
WRIGHT, Constance ...... 864-977-7064 410 A
constance.wright@ngu.edu
WRIGHT, Craig .... 860-832-1652.. 85 F
craig.wright@ccsu.edu
WRIGHT, Craig, J .... 516-572-7121 307 C
craig.wright@ncc.edu
WRIGHT, Curits .... 504-520-7357 193 C
cwrigh14@xula.edu
WRIGHT, Cynthia .... 509-777-3244 485 D
cwright@whitworth.edu
WRIGHT, Dale .... 585-567-9321 301 G
dale.wright@houghton.edu
WRIGHT, Dana .... 478-289-2027 118 B
dpwright@ega.edu
WRIGHT, Danny, R .... 865-882-4512 424 D
wrightdr@roanestate.edu
WRIGHT, Dave .... 253-879-3818 483 G
dwright@pugetsound.edu
WRIGHT, David .... 765-677-2100 157 F
iwupresident@indwes.edu
WRIGHT, David .... 316-978-7157 178 B
david.wright@wichita.edu
WRIGHT, David .... 303-273-2120.. 79 A
dwright1@mines.edu
WRIGHT, David .... 303-384-2120.. 79 A
dwright1@mines.edu
WRIGHT, David, W .... 213-740-4218.. 73 C
dwwright@usc.edu
WRIGHT, Deborah .... 828-398-7937 331 K
deborahdwright@abtech.edu
WRIGHT, Debra .... 951-785-2011.. 47 F
dwright@lasierra.edu
WRIGHT, Dewayne .... 931-372-3215 425 B
dawright@tntech.edu
WRIGHT, Duane .... 678-916-2609 115 G
dwright@johnmarshall.edu
WRIGHT, Edward .... 610-459-0905 390 G
wrighte@neumann.edu
WRIGHT, Edwin, R .... 717-867-6180 388 A
wright@lvc.edu
WRIGHT, Elizabeth .... 276-739-2440 474 H
ewright@vhcc.edu
WRIGHT, Ethel, B .... 404-413-1306 120 C
ebrown@gsu.edu
WRIGHT, George .... 949-214-3379.. 40 E
george.wright@cui.edu
WRIGHT, Georgeanna ... 479-968-0456.. 18 E
gwright7@atu.edu
WRIGHT, Georgia .... 303-762-6995.. 80 G
georgia.wright@denverseminary.edu
WRIGHT, Golden .... 409-880-8037 449 B
cgwright@lamar.edu
WRIGHT, Gwendolyn .... 908-526-1200 280 C
gwendolyn.wright@raritanval.edu
WRIGHT, Heather, H ..... 937-327-7992 364 C
hwright@wittenberg.edu
WRIGHT, Howard .... 770-426-2712 122 A
howard.wright@life.edu
WRIGHT, Jamel .... 309-467-6322 137 G
jwright@eureka.edu
WRIGHT, Jeannie .... 301-891-4010 204 D
jjwright@wau.edu
WRIGHT, Jeff .... 207-326-2253 195 G
jeff.wright@mma.edu
WRIGHT, Jeffrey .... 765-641-4544 153 D
jewright@anderson.edu
WRIGHT, Jennifer .... 816-501-4023 257 K
jennifer.wright@rockhurst.edu
WRIGHT, Jermaine, A ... 718-960-8241 293 E
jermaine.wright@lehman.cuny.edu
WRIGHT, Jerry .... 517-265-5161 220 D
jwright@adrian.edu
WRIGHT, Jimmy .... 606-886-3863 181 A
jimmy.wright@kctcs.edu
WRIGHT, Joanne .... 408-924-2250.. 34 B
joanne.wright@sjsu.edu
WRIGHT, Joel .... 229-500-3502 114 F
joel.wright@asurams.edu
WRIGHT, Jonas .... 415-503-6251.. 61 E
aharmon@sfcm.edu
WRIGHT, Jonathan .... 504-816-4222 186 F
jwright@dillard.edu
WRIGHT, Judith .... 262-742-4444 499 S
drjudith@wrightgrad.edu
WRIGHT, Julie .... 480-732-7313.. 13 B
julie.wright@cgc.edu
WRIGHT, Karen, F .... 270-384-7313 183 D
wrightk@lindsey.edu
WRIGHT, Karl, S .... 803-535-5401 406 E
kawright@claflin.edu
WRIGHT, Kathy .... 707-256-7162.. 53 E
WRIGHT, Kerry .... 256-228-6001.... 3 B
wrightk@nacc.edu
WRIGHT, Latonya .... 225-771-2552 191 C
lwright@sulc.edu
WRIGHT, LeAnne .... 903-223-3078 447 C
leanne.wright@tamut.edu
WRIGHT, Leroy .... 517-629-0222 220 E
lwright@albion.edu
WRIGHT, LeSette .... 859-985-3774 179 E
wrightl@berea.edu
WRIGHT, Leslie .... 651-227-9171 241 N
leslie.wright@mitchellhamline.edu
WRIGHT, Lydia .... 518-327-6061 310 G
lwright@paulsmiths.edu
WRIGHT, Lynn .... 951-222-8493.. 59 D
lynn.wright@rcc.edu
WRIGHT, Mandy .... 406-268-3713 264 B
mandy.wright@gfcmsu.edu
WRIGHT, Martin .... 317-931-2330 154 D
mwright1@cts.edu
WRIGHT, Matthew .... 916-608-6687.. 51 A
wrightm@flc.losrios.edu
WRIGHT, Melissa .... 662-562-3277 247 E
WRIGHT, Michael .... 601-925-7713 246 D
mwright@mc.edu
WRIGHT, Michael .... 229-928-1378 120 B
michael.wright@gsw.edu
WRIGHT, Michael, G ...... 313-577-8155 232 H
m.wright@wayne.edu
WRIGHT, Michael, G ...... 330-325-6622 357 D
mwright2@neomed.edu
WRIGHT, Natalie .... 386-752-1822.. 99 P
natalie.wright@fgc.edu
WRIGHT, Nikki .... 313-577-2280 232 H
nikki.wright@wayne.edu
WRIGHT, Nova .... 540-863-2868 473 D
nwright@mgcc.edu
WRIGHT, O'Neil .... 815-455-3700 143 F
WRIGHT, Paul .... 906-227-2480 228 E
sm8194@bncollege.com
WRIGHT, Paul .... 541-684-7250 371 H
pwright@bushnell.edu
WRIGHT, Paul .... 541-485-1780 374 C
paulwright@newhope.edu
WRIGHT, Peter .... 920-206-2327 492 C
peter.wright@mbu.edu
WRIGHT, Peter .... 920-206-2369 492 C
peter.wright@mbu.edu
WRIGHT, Quentin, A ..... 281-260-3551 438 E
quentin.a.wright@lonestar.edu
WRIGHT, Rachel .... 585-567-9200 301 G
rachel.wright@houghton.edu
WRIGHT, Raymond, M . 401-874-2186 404 E
rmwright@uri.edu
WRIGHT, Rebekah .... 417-328-2077 258 K
rwright@sbuniv.edu
WRIGHT, Regina .... 212-875-4595 290 F
rwright@bankstreet.edu
WRIGHT, Rena .... 800-785-0585.. 39 F
rena.wright@columbiacollege.edu
WRIGHT, Renetta .... 817-515-3468 445 A
renetta.wright@tccd.edu
WRIGHT, Richard .... 254-710-1561 430 F
richard_wright@baylor.edu
WRIGHT, Rick, L .... 785-539-3571 175 F
rwright@mccks.edu
WRIGHT, Roberta .... 276-656-0239 473 H
rwright@patrickhenry.edu
WRIGHT, Rodner .... 850-599-3244 109 E
rodner.wright@famu.edu
WRIGHT, Ron .... 318-357-5710 192 D
WRIGHT, Samantha, R .. 718-990-2160 313 B
hastlers@stjohns.edu
WRIGHT, Shanay, M ...... 217-443-8860 136 E
s.huerta@dacc.edu
WRIGHT, Sharon .... 276-944-6197 466 F
swright@ehc.edu
WRIGHT, Sharon .... 713-718-5205 436 E
sharon.wright@hccs.edu
WRIGHT, Shelly, A .... 845-257-3291 316 B
wrights@newpaltz.edu
WRIGHT, Siobhan .... 410-386-8207 197 G
swright@carrollcc.edu
WRIGHT, Terry .... 919-497-3294 330 E
twright@louisburg.edu
WRIGHT, Tierra .... 205-853-1200.... 2 G
tbouyer@jeffersonstate.edu
WRIGHT, Tim .... 252-246-1401 339 A
twright@wilsoncc.edu
WRIGHT, Timothy, S ..... 863-680-4298 100 F
twright@flsouthern.edu
WRIGHT, Tommy, F ...... 276-964-7572 474 E
tommy.wright@sw.edu
WRIGHT, Tracey, L .... 276-944-6490 466 F
tlwright@ehc.edu
WRIGHT, Troy .... 814-886-6421 390 E
twright@mtaloy.edu
WRIGHT, Troy, M .... 563-588-7816 167 I
troy.wright@loras.edu
WRIGHT, Victoria .... 216-368-4594 349 B
victoria.wright@case.edu
WRIGHT-GREENE, Darryl .... 727-302-6823 107 C
wrightgreene.darryl@spcollege.edu
WRIGHT-RICHARDS, Tia .... 803-793-5109 408 A
richardst@denmarktech.edu
WRIGHT-RIVA, Colleen . 301-314-8428 202 E
cwr@umd.edu
WRIGHTEN, Karen .... 843-899-8049 411 I
karen.wrighten@tridenttech.edu
WRIGHTMAN, Diane ..... 775-727-2017 270 G
diane.wrightman@gbcnv.edu
WRIGHTON, Mark, S .... 202-994-6500.. 92 C
WRIGLEY, Vicki, A .... 217-362-6485 144 D
vwrigley@millikin.edu
WRISTON, Welton .... 423-478-7250 421 J
wwriston@ptseminary.edu
WROBBEL, Karen .... 847-945-8800 150 J
kwrobbel@tiu.edu
WROBEL, Allison .... 413-552-2242 214 D
awrobel@hcc.edu
WROBEL, David, M .... 405-325-6002 370 J
david.wrobel@ou.edu
WROBLESKI, Melissa ..... 320-589-6452 243 C
mwrobles@morris.umn.edu
WROBLEWSKI, Kathleen .... 413-565-1000 205 I
kwroblew@baypath.edu
WRONSKI-MAYERSAK, Corey .... 410-857-2245 200 D
cwronski@mcdaniel.edu
WRYE, Tim .... 206-878-3710 480 C
twrye@highline.edu
WU, Adam .... 909-448-4032.. 71 C
awu@laverne.edu
WU, Andrew .... 410-337-6000 198 G
andrew.wu@goucher.edu
WU, Anna .... 919-962-7248 342 B
annaw@fac.unc.edu
WU, Anping .... 870-245-5115.. 20 H
wua@obu.edu
WU, Frank, H .... 718-997-5000 295 A
WU, Hailin .... 941-355-9080.. 98 E
WU, Hong .... 804-523-5324 473 A
hwu@reynolds.edu
WU, Jean .... 626-917-9482.. 36 H
jeanwu@cesna.edu

YANEZ, Mary, A .... 915-831-7803 435 B
myanez22@epcc.edu
YANEZ, Mercedes .... 323-265-8641.. 49 D
yanezm@elac.edu
YANEZ, Mercy .... 310-233-4342.. 49 F
yanezm@lahc.edu
YANEZ, Mercy .... 310-233-4447.. 49 F
yanezm@lahc.edu
YANEZ, Robert .... 413-748-3104 218 E
ryanez@springfield.edu
YANG, Angela .... 949-582-4602.. 65 C
lyang26@saddleback.edu
YANG, Anthony .... 973-618-3605 275 E
ayang@caldwell.edu
YANG, Blia .... 831-459-4179.. 71 A
blyang@ucsc.edu
YANG, Catherine .... 916-686-7400.. 29 G
YANG, Dong-Hua .... 516-739-1545 308 E
administrative_dean@nyctcm.edu
YANG, Eric .... 502-597-6327 183 A
eric.yang@kysu.edu
YANG, Eun Soon .... 951-372-8080.. 45 G
hisuniv@yahoo.com
YANG, Henry, T .... 805-893-2231.. 70 E
henry.yang@ucsb.edu
YANG, Hong .... 401-232-6885 403 B
hyang@bryant.edu
YANG, Jasmine, X .... 315-859-4084 300 F
jxyang@hamilton.edu
YANG, Jun .... 440-775-8537 357 G
jun.yang@oberlin.edu
YANG, K. Wayne .... 858-822-2824.. 70 C
kwayne@ucsd.edu
YANG, Kha, A .... 651-962-5219 243 F
yang8741@stthomas.edu
YANG, Lykos .... 408-260-0208.. 42 H
sjextension@fivebranches.edu
YANG, Mia .... 575-624-8150 286 F
yang@nmmi.edu
YANG, Michael .... 909-895-7138.. 45 K
michael@huca.edu
YANG, Olivia .... 509-335-5571 484 D
olivia.yang@wsu.edu
YANG, Pakou .... 651-779-3288 237 D
pakou.yang@century.edu
YANG, Paul Zhao Hui ... 628-448-0023.. 46 K
YANG, Philip .... 408-532-5567.. 34 F
YANG, Phong .... 559-278-2048.. 31 D
pyang@csufresno.edu
YANG, Tony .... 269-471-3354 220 H
tonyy@andrews.edu
YANG, Xong Sony .... 309-794-8274 132 H
xongsonyyang@augustana.edu
YANG-MOUA, Bao .... 651-403-4383 240 E
bao.yang-moua@saintpaul.edu
YANG THAO, Mary .... 612-874-3700 236 E
myangthao@mcad.edu
YANKELEWITZ, Yoel ..... 718-846-1940 325 N
yyankelewitz@gmail.com
YANKELITIS, Wendy ...... 570-348-6201 389 B
yankelitis@marywood.edu
YANKEY, Terry, L .... 606-474-3222 180 G
tly@kcu.edu
YANNI, Stephen .... 906-248-8478 221 I
syanni@bmcc.edu
YANNICK, Lisa .... 610-436-3075 394 F
lyannick@wcupa.edu
YANNIELLO, Kristin ...... 718-405-3252 296 D
kristin.yanniello@mountsaintvincent.edu
YANNOTTA, Danielle ...... 212-752-1530 303 G
danielle.yannotta@limcollege.edu
YANNUZZI, Leigh .... 518-587-2100 320 B
YANOS, Melana .... 206-934-4532 482 F
melana.yanos@seattlecolleges.edu
YAO, Chunmei .... 910-521-6295 343 A
chunmei.yao@uncp.edu
YAO, Min .... 562-985-5459.. 32 A
min.yao@csulb.edu
YAO, Richard .... 805-437-8410.. 30 D
richard.yao@csuci.edu
YAP, Dawn .... 561-912-1211.. 99 C
dawn.yap@evergladesuniversity.edu
YAPSUGA, Jill .... 610-799-1718 388 B
jyapsuga@lccc.edu
YAQUB, Samia .... 530-895-2484.. 27 F
yaqubsa@butte.edu
YARBROUGH, Boyd ...... 864-388-8239 409 B
byarbrough@lander.edu
YARBROUGH, Breanna . 334-386-7476.... 5 D
byarbrough@faulkner.edu
YARBROUGH, David ..... 337-482-1015 192 F
yarbrough@louisiana.edu
YARBROUGH, Denise ... 585-275-4321 323 E
dyarbrough@admin.rochester.edu
YARBROUGH, John ...... 706-865-2134 126 D
jyarbrough@truett.edu
YARBROUGH, Kenny .... 262-472-1918 496 E
YARBROUGH, Laura .... 870-508-6203.. 18 B
lyarbrough@asumh.edu
YARBROUGH, Laura, L . 336-249-8186 333 G
laura_yarbrough@davidsondavie.edu
YARBROUGH, Mark, M 214-887-5011 434 G
myarbrough@dts.edu
YARBROUGH, Scott ...... 843-863-7563 406 C
syarbrou@csuniv.edu
YARLOTT, JR., David .... 406-638-3107 262 J
davidyarlott@lbhc.edu
YARRITU, Daniel .... 979-230-3441 431 A
daniel.yarritu@brazosport.edu
YARROW, Jennifer .... 319-273-5085 163 G
jennifer.yarrow@uni.edu
YARROW, Lisa .... 713-646-1893 443 C
lyarrow@stcl.edu
YARWOOD, Christine .... 973-761-9018 282 K
christine.yarwood@shu.edu
YASIN, Dawood .... 510-356-4760.. 77 E
YASUDA, Cathy .... 541-881-5585 376 E
cyasuda@tvcc.cc
YATER, Ann .... 317-917-5915 158 A
aniebrug@ivytech.edu
YATES, Brian .... 434-592-4108 467 E
bcyates@liberty.edu
YATES, Carlous .... 859-246-6438 181 B
carlous.yates@kctcs.edu
YATES, Deanna .... 270-706-8658 181 C
dyates0031@kctcs.edu
YATES, Dorothy .... 407-823-3028 110 D
dorothy.yates@ucf.edu
YATES, Emilie .... 308-632-6933 268 F
eyates@summitcc.edu
YATES, Frances .... 765-973-8470 156 D
fyates@iue.edu
YATES, James .... 870-864-7156.. 21 C
jyates@southark.edu
YATES, Jamie .... 717-337-6000 384 C
jyates@gettysburg.edu
YATES, Josh .... 615-460-6000 417 B
josh.yates@belmont.edu
YATES, La Toro .... 718-518-4300 293 F
YATES, Matthew .... 805-493-3750.. 29 E
matthewyates@callutheran.edu
YATES, Michelle .... 207-859-1405 196 A
registrar@thomas.edu
YATES, Randy .... 670-237-6724 503 G
randy.yates@marianas.edu
YATES, Shannon .... 910-486-3630 334 C
yatess@faytechcc.edu
YATES, Vivian .... 216-987-4468 351 D
vivian.yates@tri-c.edu
YATES-MATTINGLY,
Shelia .... 513-875-3344 349 K
shelia.yates-mattingly@chatfield.edu
YATES SEAMAN, Liz ...... 610-861-1505 390 D
yatese@moravian.edu
YATIN, Servet .... 617-984-1719 217 G
syatin@quincycollege.edu
YAUKEY, Suzanna .... 410-704-2450 204 B
syaukey@towson.edu
YAUN, John .... 662-915-7348 248 F
jyaun@olemiss.edu
YAVOR, Susan .... 610-341-4363 383 A
syavor@eastern.edu
YAVORSKI, Ginger .... 484-664-3190 390 F
gingeryavorski@muhlenberg.edu
YAZEDJIAN, Ani .... 309-438-7018 140 C
ayazedj@ilstu.edu
YAZZIE, Lambert .... 480-732-7205.. 13 B
lambert.yazzie@cgc.edu
YBARRA, Albert .... 818-364-3373.. 49 G
ybarraad@lamission.edu
YBARRA, David .... 910-522-5793 343 A
david.ybarra@uncp.edu
YBARRA, Paul .... 916-577-2200.. 76 C
pybarra@jessup.edu
YDOYAGA, Shannon ...... 817-515-4507 445 A
shannon.ydoyaga@tccd.edu
YDRACH, Gloriana .... 787-728-1515 512 A
gloriana.ydrach@sagrado.edu
YE, Eugene .... 602-285-7134.. 13 H
eugene.ye@phoenixcollege.edu
YEADON, Steven, W ...... 503-777-7764 375 F
yeadons@reed.edu
YEAGER, Daphne .... 601-477-4151 246 A
daphne.yeager@jcjc.edu
YEAGER, Deonne .... 843-208-8723 412 C
deonne@uscb.edu
YEAGER, Jason .... 304-462-6131 488 M
jason.yeager@glenville.edu
YEAGER, Kathrine, H .... 928-523-4036.. 14 J
kathy.yeager@nau.edu
YEAGER, Shelby, W ...... 570-961-4711 389 B
swyeager@marywood.edu
YEANY, Ron .... 617-353-1701 207 C
ryeany@bu.edu
YEAP, Soon Beng .... 303-765-3110.. 81 F
syeap@iliff.edu
YEARNS, Ellie, P .... 336-272-7102 329 B
ellie.yearns@greensboro.edu
YEAROUT, Teresa, A ..... 276-964-7266 474 E
teresa.yearout@sw.edu
YEARSLEY, Stephanie .... 315-781-3406 301 D
yearsley@hws.edu
YEARTA, Charles, S ...... 803-323-3499 413 D
yeartac@winthrop.edu
YEARWOOD, Burl .... 201-360-4651 277 D
byearwood@hccc.edu
YEARWOOD,
George (Rocky), A ...... 919-508-2035 344 D
ryearwood@peace.edu
YEARWOOD, Jody .... 478-387-4392 119 E
jyearwood@gmc.edu
YEARWOOD, Simone .... 718-997-3760 295 A
simone.yearwood@qc.cuny.edu
YEATS, John Mark .... 816-414-3700 255 F
jmyeats@mbts.edu
YEATTS, Debra .... 910-630-7385 331 B
dyeatts@methodist.edu
YECKLEY, Trae .... 814-332-4368 378 A
tyeckley@allegheny.edu
YEE, David .... 415-239-3669.. 37 C
dyee@ccsf.edu
YEE, Ellen .... 617-585-0200 206 E
ellen.yee@the-bac.edu
YEE, Gary .... 402-559-5108 269 B
gcyee@unmc.edu
YEE, Jill .... 415-239-3174.. 37 C
jyee@ccsf.edu
YEE, Penny .... 315-859-4720 300 F
pyee@hamilton.edu
YEE-BULLOCK,
Calandria .... 772-466-4822.. 95 N
YEH, David .... 773-907-4071 134 N
dyeh@ccc.edu
YEH, Lisa .... 212-870-2530 290 H
lyeh@barnard.edu
YEHL, Thomas .... 815-921-4361 147 H
t.yehl@rockvalleycollege.edu
YEHUDAH, Shoshana ... 646-565-6000 322 B
shoshana.yehudah@touro.edu
YEHUDAH, Shoshana ... 646-565-6000 322 C
shoshana.yehudah@touro.edu
YELDELL JONES,
Andrain .... 256-686-5850.. 93 H
YELICH, Tom .... 860-297-2086.. 88 I
tom.yelich@trincoll.edu
YELICK, Kathy .... 510-642-6000.. 68 N
YELKUR, Rama .... 940-898-2105 451 A
ryelkur@twu.edu
YELLEN, David .... 305-284-2394 112 K
dyellen@law.miami.edu
YELLIN, Dina .... 732-367-1060 275 B
dyelllin@bmg.edu
YELTON, Jennifer .... 573-642-3361 261 F
YELVERTON, Miranda .... 252-246-1333 339 A
myelverton@wilsoncc.edu
YEN, Charlie .... 310-434-3002.. 63 B
yen_charlie@smc.edu
YEN, Johanna, C .... 954-763-9840.. 95 J
atom@atom.edu
YENCER, Kristen .... 302-857-1401.. 90 H
kristen.yencer@dtcc.edu
YENCHA, Patricia .... 570-740-0200 388 G
YENCHO, Thomas .... 610-409-3491 400 E
tyencho@ursinus.edu
YENCO, Andrea .... 212-229-5671 307 E
yencoa@newschool.edu
YENTES, Matt .... 863-638-2963 113 E
yentesms@webber.edu
YEOH, Deborah .... 212-327-8071 312 B
yeohd@rockefeller.edu
YEOM, Yeijin .... 815-740-3492 152 E
yyeom@stfrancis.edu
YEONOPOLUS, Jim .... 254-526-1214 431 E
jyeonopolus@ctcd.edu
YERDON, Melinda .... 419-559-2289 361 B
myerdon@terra.edu
YERDON, Wayne .... 419-559-2341 361 B
wyerdon@terra.edu
YERGEN, Norman .... 951-785-2307.. 47 F
nyergen@lasierra.edu
YERGEY, Michael .... 610-282-1100 382 A
michael.yergey@desales.edu
YERK-ZWICKL, Sherri ..... 910-893-1668 327 C
yerk-zwickl@campbell.edu
YERO, Tatiana .... 941-782-5945 387 C
tyero@lecom.edu
YERRICK, Randy .... 559-278-0210.. 31 D
yerrick@csufresno.edu
YERSE, Jeremy, T .... 724-847-5670 384 B
jtyerse@geneva.edu
YESH, Jamie .... 269-294-4229 223 J
jyesh@glenoaks.edu
YESTRAMSKI, Joanne ...... 207-581-1865 196 D
YEZIERSKI, Ellen, J .... 513-529-9266 356 A
yeziere@miamioh.edu
YI, Xinyan .... 215-455-1300 378 F
xyi@aspirapa.org
YIANILOS, Chris .... 571-858-3005 475 D
chrisyianilos@vt.edu
YIGLETU, Ashagre, A ...... 225-771-4266 190 K
ashagre_yigletu@subr.edu
YILDIRIM, Seval .... 702-895-3201 270 J
YILDIZ, Melda .... 201-219-9901 276 C
melda.yildiz@eicollege.edu
YILIBUW, Dolores .... 859-280-1224 183 C
dyilibuw@lextheo.edu
YIM, Mee So .... 910-932-6895 343 B
ctr-yimm@uncw.edu
YIM, Sooyoung .... 703-629-1281 472 C
registrar@vacu.edu
YIM, Steven .... 657-278-2512.. 31 E
syim@fullerton.edu
YIN, Alexander, C .... 802-656-4418 462 D
alexander.yin@uvm.edu
YIN, Carol .... 706-880-8339 121 K
cyin@lagrange.edu
YIN, Chengbo .... 973-353-5541 281 C
cy188@newark.rutgers.edu
YIN, Kong .... 713-221-8975 452 B
yink@uhd.edu
YING, Fei .... 650-433-3839.. 55 K
fying@paloaltou.edu
YIONOULIS, Evan .... 212-799-5000 303 B
YIP, Yunny .... 415-575-5573.. 29 A
yyip@ciis.edu
YIP-REYES, Judy .... 928-532-6148.. 14 L
judy.yip-reyes@npc.edu
YOAKUM, Katrina, M .... 785-864-3261 177 G
kyoakum@ku.edu
YOAKUM, Richard .... 205-726-2056..... 6 E
ryoakum@samford.edu
YOCHUM, SC, Susan .... 724-830-1044 397 F
yochum@setonhill.edu
YOCKEY, Glenn .... 830-372-8040 448 C
gyockey@tlu.edu
YOCOM, Amber .... 419-267-1317 357 E
ayocom@northweststate.edu
YOCUM, Carrie, A .... 574-372-5100 155 C
yocumca@grace.edu
YOCUM, Heather .... 502-213-5200 181 H
heather.yocum@kctcs.edu
YODER, Amy .... 716-851-1621 299 A
yoder@ecc.edu
YODER, Bob .... 574-296-6224 153 C
reyoder@ambs.edu
YODER, Brooke .... 816-654-7103 253 I
byoder@kcumb.edu
YODER, Jewel .... 574-535-7376 155 B
jewelcy@goshen.edu
YODER, John-David, S . 419-772-2372 358 D
j-yoder@onu.edu
YODER, Joseph, S .... 570-326-3761 392 S
jyoder@pct.edu
YODER, Julie .... 301-387-3101 198 F
julie.yoder@garrettcollege.edu
YODER, Karen .... 707-654-1000.. 32 C
YODER, Kathleen .... 574-535-7501 155 B
kathleeny@goshen.edu
YODER, Kim .... 715-833-6308 497 E
kyoder@cvtc.edu
YODER, Marilyn .... 218-755-2723 237 B
marilyn.yoder@bemidjistate.edu
YODER, Mollie .... 615-248-1380 425 D
meyoder@trevecca.edu
YODER, Norris .... 828-328-7145 330 B
norris.yoder@lr.edu
YODER, Todd, A .... 574-535-7645 155 B
tyoder@goshen.edu

YODER, Wendy 580-774-6037 369 I wendy.yoder@swosu.edu
YODER, Whitney 217-443-8865 136 E w.yoder@dacc.edu
YODER, Zachary 540-432-4159 465 F zachary.yoder@emu.edu
YOGAN, Lissa 219-464-5310 162 C lissa.yogan@valpo.edu
YOHE, Michael 863-667-5306 108 I meyohe@seu.edu
YOHE, Roger 561-868-3147 105 C yoher@palmbeachstate.edu
YOHNK, Dean 715-425-3777 496 A dean.yohnk@uwrf.edu
YOHNK LOCKWOOD, Susan 715-246-1872 498 G susan.lockwood@northwoodtech.edu
YOHNKA, Shelley 530-541-4660 47 H yohnka@ltcc.edu
YOHO, Steven 912-650-6200 125 D syoho@southuniversity.edu
YOKELEY, Jan 910-362-7187 332 F jryokeley960@mail.cfcc.edu
YOKLEY, Delight 919-299-4635 340 E dyokley@umo.edu
YOLITZ, Brian, D 651-201-1777 236 F brian.yolitz@minnstate.edu
YOLO, Laura 509-574-4775 485 E lyolo@yvcc.edu
YOM, Aaron 916-306-1628 67 E ayom@sum.edu
YON, Rita 650-543-3722 52 A rita.yon@menlo.edu
YON PAK, Su 212-280-1550 323 C spak@uts.columbia.edu
YONAN, Glen 530-251-8815 47 I gyonan@lassencollege.edu
YONEMITSU, Lori 206-546-4552 483 C lyonemitsu@shoreline.edu
YONG, Amos 626-584-5206 43 E amosyong@fuller.edu
YONG, Henry 209-575-6508 76 I yongh@yosemite.edu
YONG, Yanyan 540-891-3084 472 J yyong@germanna.edu
YONKERS, Molly, L 507-933-7588 235 E myunkers@gustavus.edu
YONTZ, Jennifer 231-591-3817 223 H jenniferyontz@ferris.edu
YOO, Aileen 707-826-5105 30 A aileen.yoo@humboldt.edu
YOO, David, K 310-825-6815 69 D dkyoo@ucla.edu
YOO, Donna 216-791-5000 350 F donna.yoo@cim.edu
YOO, Heeduck 678-889-8038 118 F hdyoo@gcuniv.edu
YOO, Jean 951-372-8080 45 G hisuniv@yahoo.com
YOO, John 703-425-4143 467 B
YOO, John 703-323-5690 476 A jyoo@vuim.edu
YOO, Young, C 703-333-5904 476 G ycyoo@wuv.edu
YOON, Ho Sung 213-384-2318 50 F
YOON, Im Sang 213-385-2322 76 E iyoon@wmu.edu
YOON, J. Meejin 607-255-9110 297 D aapdean@cornell.edu
YOON, Mary 213-384-2318 50 F
YOON, Rachel 323-860-1170 53 D rachel@mi.edu
YOON, Richard, S 770-831-9500 126 E
YOON, Sun 212-517-0400 305 D
YOON, Thomas 941-756-0690 387 C tyoon@lecom.edu
YOON GRAFER, Maggie 516-877-3844 288 L yoon@adelphi.edu
YORDY, Brad 765-998-5112 161 A bryordy@taylor.edu
YORGES, Judi 402-471-2505 267 F jyorges@nscs.edu
YORGES, Sherri 308-635-6365 269 E yorgess1@wncc.edu
YORGEY, Michael 610-282-1100 382 A michael.yorgey@desales.edu
YORI, Joy 541-440-7648 376 F joy.yori@umpqua.edu
YORIMITSU, Megan 714-966-8500 74 C myorimitsu@ves.edu
YORK, Barry, J 412-731-6000 396 D byork@rpts.edu
YORK, Corey 914-251-6080 318 E corey.york@purchase.edu
YORK, Heather 207-699-5521 194 G hyork@meca.edu
YORK, Hershael 502-897-4112 184 D hyork@sbts.edu
YORK, Leslie 512-505-3011 437 B llyork@htu.edu
YORK, Robert 805-893-2944 70 E rayork@ece.ucsb.edu
YORK, Ronald, S 803-536-8413 410 H ryork1@scsu.edu
YORK, Wendy 864-656-3178 406 F bizdean@clemson.edu
YORK-EDWARDS, Deborah 432-703-5174 450 D deborah.york.edwards@ttuhsc.edu
YORKIN, Sheila 801-832-2685 461 A syorkin@westminstercollege.edu
YORMICK, Emilee 716-839-8200 297 F eyormick@daemen.edu
YORTSOS, Yannis, C 213-740-0617 73 C yortsos@usc.edu
YOSANOVICH, Kristin 618-985-3741 140 G kristinyosanovich@jalc.edu
YOSHIKAWA, Naoto 808-983-4105 128 F htic@tokai.edu
YOSHIMI, Garret 808-956-2717 129 B gyoshimi@hawaii.edu
YOSHIMI, Garret, T 808-956-3501 128 I gyoshimi@hawaii.edu
YOSHIMORI-YAMAMOTO, Denise 808-956-0864 129 D dfyoshim@hawaii.edu
YOSHIMURA, Gregg 808-455-0607 130 A greggy@hawaii.edu
YOSHIMURA, Nancy 949-480-4045 64 E nyoshimura@soka.edu
YOSHIOKA, Marianne 413-585-7977 218 D myoshioka@smith.edu
YOSIEF, Petros 703-891-1787 470 G financialaid@standardcollege.edu
YOST, Carol 570-577-3733 379 A cyost@bucknell.edu
YOST, Kristen 704-233-8109 344 E k.johnson@wingate.edu
YOU, Hana 913-667-5700 172 G hyou@cbts.edu
YOUDE, Jeremy 218-726-8981 243 A jyoude@d.umn.edu
YOUHOUSE, John 610-558-5518 390 G youhousj@neumann.edu
YOUMANS, Jeremy 479-619-2224 20 G jyoumans@nwacc.edu
YOUMANS, Karen 405-208-5680 367 E kdyoumans@okcu.edu
YOUNAS, Tahir 314-340-3547 253 E younast@hssu.edu
YOUNG, Aaron 505-984-6140 287 F aaron.young@sjc.edu
YOUNG, Alan, L 801-524-8179 458 F alan.young@ldsbc.edu
YOUNG, Alexis, D 260-982-5246 158W adyoung@manchester.edu
YOUNG, Alissa 270-707-3711 181 G alissa.young@kctcs.edu
YOUNG, Alyxius 615-771-7821 427 F alyxius.young@williamsoncc.edu
YOUNG, Amy 269-294-4248 223 J ayoung@glenoaks.edu
YOUNG, Andrea 213-356-5371 65 D andrea_young@sciarc.edu
YOUNG, Andrea 765-658-4161 154 G andreayoung@depauw.edu
YOUNG, Andrea, N 920-748-8108 493 J younga@ripon.edu
YOUNG, Andrew 812-888-4323 162 E ayoung@vinu.edu
YOUNG, Andrew 256-726-8333 6 C ayoung@oakwood.edu
YOUNG, Andrew 256-726-8308 6 C ayoung@oakwood.edu
YOUNG, Angela 417-836-5520 255 J angelayoung@missouristate.edu
YOUNG, Ann 701-231-8356 345 D ann.young@ndsu.edu
YOUNG, Ann, S 859-238-5480 179 H ann.young@centre.edu
YOUNG, Art 520-621-4717 16 H artyoung@arizona.edu
YOUNG, Beth 803-778-7802 406 A youngbe@cctech.edu
YOUNG, Betty 740-753-7009 353 G youngb@hocking.edu
YOUNG, Bill 316-323-6363 172 B wyoung@butlercc.edu
YOUNG, Bill 910-480-5441 331 B
YOUNG, Brady 619-574-5800 43 B byoung@fst.edu
YOUNG, Brandon 217-540-3512 141 H byoung17159@lakelandcollege.edu
YOUNG, Brandon, L 386-226-7245 98 J youngbr@erau.edu
YOUNG, Brittany 541-278-5916 371 G byoung@bluecc.edu
YOUNG, Camesha 501-420-1208 17 D camesha.young@arkansasbaptist.edu
YOUNG, Carl 212-799-5000 303 B
YOUNG, Charles 336-334-4822 334 F hcyoung@gtcc.edu
YOUNG, Cherisse 518-783-2931 314 K cryoung@siena.edu
YOUNG, Cheryl, D 513-529-8607 356 A youngcd@miamioh.edu
YOUNG, Christopher 219-980-6563 157 A cjy@iun.edu
YOUNG, Colletta 541-956-7296 375 G cyoung@roguecc.edu
YOUNG, Connie 217-709-0931 142 A cyoung@lakeviewcol.edu
YOUNG, Courtney 315-228-7361 296 C clyoung@colgate.edu
YOUNG, Crystal 231-843-5803 232 I cyoung2@westshore.edu
YOUNG, Cynthia 864-656-3642 406 F cyyoung@clemson.edu
YOUNG, Dana 541-881-5580 376 E dyoung@tvcc.cc
YOUNG, Darby 402-878-2380 266 D darby.young@littlepriest.edu
YOUNG, David 417-255-7910 256 A davidyoung@missouristate.edu
YOUNG, David 405-974-2490 370 H dyoung28@uco.edu
YOUNG, Deirdre 313-664-1489 222 C ddyoung@collegeforcreativestudies.edu
YOUNG, Derek, M 240-895-4207 201 F dmyoung@smcm.edu
YOUNG, Djuana 817-531-4422 450 F dyoung@txwes.edu
YOUNG, Donell 832-842-6176 451 G dlyoung3@uh.edu
YOUNG, Donna 480-423-6300 14 B donna.young@scottsdalecc.edu
YOUNG, Douglas 718-517-7730 314 B douglas.young@edaff.com
YOUNG, Duane, C 301-243-2156 501 J duane.young@dodiis.mil
YOUNG, Elisabeth, H 330-325-6311 357 D eyoung1@neomed.edu
YOUNG, Elisabeth, H 330-325-6338 357 D eyoung1@neomed.edu
YOUNG, Elizabeth 262-551-8500 491 B
YOUNG, Elliot, C 785-532-6233 175 A ecyoung@ksu.edu
YOUNG, Eric 330-829-8238 362 E younger@mountunion.edu
YOUNG, Erica 570-585-9370 381 A eyoung@clarkssummitu.edu
YOUNG, Frank 801-863-7202 460 A frank.young@uvu.edu
YOUNG, Gabrielle 314-529-9340 254 D gyoung@maryville.edu
YOUNG, Garland 423-461-8720 421 E rgyoung@milligan.edu
YOUNG, Gary 312-949-7610 139 B gyoung@ico.edu
YOUNG, Gerald 507-222-4057 234 C gyoung@carleton.edu
YOUNG, Gretchen 508-286-4950 219 F young_gretchen@wheatoncollege.edu
YOUNG, Gwendolyn 719-549-2602 79 G gwen.young@csupueblo.edu
YOUNG, Harvey 617-358-1725 207 C harveyy@bu.edu
YOUNG, Heather, M 916-734-4745 69 A heather.young@ucdmc.ucdavis.edu
YOUNG, Henry 401-739-5000 403 F hyoung@neit.edu
YOUNG, J.R 412-536-1100 386 H jr.young@laroche.edu
YOUNG, Jackie 502-456-6773 184 F jayoung@sullivan.edu
YOUNG, Jason 989-686-9216 223 E jasonyoung2@delta.edu
YOUNG, Jason 865-974-5267 426 C jason.young@utk.edu
YOUNG, Jennifer 570-422-3277 393 F jyoung@esu.edu
YOUNG, Jennifer, C 412-397-5452 396 E youngj@rmu.edu
YOUNG, Jessica 970-943-0120 85 B
YOUNG, Jill 570-389-4950 393 E jyoung@bloomu.edu
YOUNG, Joanne 603-888-1311 273 B
YOUNG, John 603-526-3675 271 H john.young@colby-sawyer.edu
YOUNG, John 315-781-3748 301 D jyoung@hws.edu
YOUNG, John 303-360-4707 80 C john.young@ccaurora.edu
YOUNG, John, M 540-464-7104 475 C youngjm@vmi.edu
YOUNG, John, O 248-370-2946 229 F joyoung@oakland.edu
YOUNG, Johnny, W 757-683-3442 468 C jwyoung@odu.edu
YOUNG, Jon 805-565-6037 75 I joyoung@westmont.edu
YOUNG, Justn 618-842-3711 139 D youngj11@iecc.edu
YOUNG, Kaitlin 845-431-3700 298 B kaitlin.young@sunydutchess.edu
YOUNG, Kalbert, K 808-956-8903 128 I kalbert@hawaii.edu
YOUNG, Kelly 315-781-3783 301 D keyoung@hws.edu
YOUNG, Kelsey 717-262-2003 402 D conferences@wilson.edu
YOUNG, Ken 516-323-4501 306 I kyoung@molloy.edu
YOUNG, Kerry, A 315-786-2279 302 I kyoung@sunyjefferson.edu
YOUNG, Kim 760-252-2411 26 L kyoung@barstow.edu
YOUNG, Kimberly 478-275-6589 123 E
YOUNG, Kimberly 540-286-8076 471 B kyoung@umw.edu
YOUNG, Kirk 716-338-1023 302 G kirkyoung@mail.sunyjcc.edu
YOUNG, Kristina 425-352-8550 477 F kyoung@cascadia.edu
YOUNG, Kristine, M 845-341-4700 310 D president@sunyorange.edu
YOUNG, Lauren 716-888-2436 291M youngb@canisius.edu
YOUNG, Leah 919-508-2319 344 D
YOUNG, Lena 312-658-5100 150 E
YOUNG, Linda, C 334-556-2234 2 C lyoung@wallace.edu
YOUNG, Lindsay 361-570-4492 452 C youngle@uhv.edu
YOUNG, Marc 414-251-7547 495 B young242@uwm.edu
YOUNG, Mark, S 303-762-6902 80 G president@denverseminary.edu
YOUNG, Mary 203-773-8521 85 C myoung@albertus.edu
YOUNG, Mary 713-313-7733 448 D mary.young@tsu.edu
YOUNG, Mary 402-562-1492 265 C myoung@cccneb.edu
YOUNG, Mary, E 903-823-3369 445 C maryellen.young@texarkanacollege.edu
YOUNG, MaryAnne 941-487-4801 110 C myoung@ncf.edu
YOUNG, Megan 918-333-6830 368 E myoung@okwu.edu
YOUNG, Michael 508-531-1295 212 B myoung@bridgew.edu
YOUNG, Michael, A 215-707-7336 398 D michael.young@tuhs.temple.edu
YOUNG, Michael, W 212-327-8000 312 B michael.young@rockefeller.edu
YOUNG, Michaela, J 315-386-7204 319 E youngm@canton.edu
YOUNG, Michelle, D 310-338-2700 51 C michelle.young@lmu.edu
YOUNG, Michelle, L 315-268-4268 295 E myoung@clarkson.edu
YOUNG, Miles 903-434-8257 440 A myoung@ntcc.edu
YOUNG, Monica 336-334-4822 334 F mwyoung@gtcc.edu
YOUNG, Nanci 319-399-8581 164 D nyoung@coe.edu
YOUNG, Nancy 410-455-2393 202 G nyoung@umbc.edu
YOUNG, Nancy 816-960-2008 250 J newstudents@cityvision.edu

YOUNG, Nikki .... 940-898-3188 451 A
nyoung1@twu.edu
YOUNG, Patricia .... 707-864-7124.. 64 F
patricia.young@solano.edu
YOUNG, Patty, R .... 972-860-8354 433 I
pyoung@dcccd.edu
YOUNG, Quentin .... 606-539-4597 185 C
quentin.young@ucumberlands.edu
YOUNG, Randy .... 660-359-3948 256 F
ryoung@mail.ncmissouri.edu
YOUNG, Remmele ...... 713-718-7452 436 E
remmele.young@hccs.edu
YOUNG, Rena .... 270-707-3732 181 G
rena.young@kctcs.edu
YOUNG, Rhett .... 740-284-5007 352 I
ryoung@franciscan.edu
YOUNG, Rob .... 937-327-7009 364 C
youngr11@wittenberg.edu
YOUNG, Robert .... 540-453-2500 472 F
youngb@brcc.edu
YOUNG, Robert .... 814-472-3119 396 I
ryoung@francis.edu
YOUNG, Robert .... 423-236-2805 422 H
ryoung@southern.edu
YOUNG, Robert, F ..... 843-349-2277 407 B
ryoung@coastal.edu
YOUNG, Samuel .... 714-449-7481.. 51 D
syoung@ketchum.edu
YOUNG, Sarah .... 309-457-2300 144 E
syoung@monmouthcollege.edu
YOUNG, Sarah, M ...... 716-878-4619 317 C
youngsm@buffalostate.edu
YOUNG, Scott .... 816-235-1154 260 D
youngsc@umkc.edu
YOUNG, Scott .... 317-788-3306 161 F
syoung@uindy.edu
YOUNG, Scott .... 360-650-6693 485 A
scott.young@wwu.edu
YOUNG, Sean, B .... 262-243-5700 491 E
sean.young@cuw.edu
YOUNG, Shakebra ...... 601-977-7818 248 E
syoung4@tougaloo.edu
YOUNG, Shane .... 731-424-3520 423 F
syoung18@jscc.edu
YOUNG, Shane .... 216-373-5274 357 F
syoung@ndc.edu
YOUNG, Shawna .... 603-366-5266 271 K
syoung@ccsnh.edu
YOUNG, Shawna .... 707-826-3961.. 30 A
shawna.young@humboldt.edu
YOUNG, Sherry .... 610-921-6639 377 F
syoung@albright.edu
YOUNG, Sonia .... 803-981-7372 413 F
syoung@yorktech.edu
YOUNG, Stacie, G .... 704-687-7203 342 C
sgyoung@uncc.edu
YOUNG, Stacy .... 989-328-1221 227 G
stacy.young@montcalm.edu
YOUNG, Stephanie ...... 713-798-4951 430 E
youngs@chipola.edu
YOUNG, Steve .... 850-718-2203.. 97 E
youngs@chipola.edu
YOUNG, Steven .... 828-694-1891 332 C
sd_young@blueridge.edu
YOUNG, Steven .... 304-260-4380 487 C
stuart.young@littlehoop.edu
YOUNG, Stuart .... 701-766-1321 344 F
stuart.young@littlehoop.edu
YOUNG, Sunya .... 803-376-5716 405 D
syoung@allenuniversity.edu
YOUNG, Susan .... 864-242-5100 405 H
susan.young@ccaurora.edu
YOUNG, Susan .... 303-340-7148.. 80 C
susan.young@ccaurora.edu
YOUNG, Tangar .... 803-533-3712 410 H
tyoung15@scsu.edu
YOUNG, Ted .... 850-484-1794 105 G
fyoung@pensacolastate.edu
YOUNG, Terrance, J ..... 484-365-7451 388 F
tyoung2@lincoln.edu
YOUNG, Terry .... 276-656-0287 473 H
tyoung@patrickhenry.edu
YOUNG, Terry .... 325-793-4683 439 A
tyoung@mcm.edu
YOUNG, Thomas, W .... 507-933-7551 235 E
tyoung3@gustavus.edu
YOUNG, Tiffany .... 757-352-4457 469 D
tkuhn@regent.edu
YOUNG, Tim .... 714-556-3610.. 73 G
tyoung@vanguard.edu
YOUNG, Timothy .... 269-337-7321 225 B
timothy.young@kzoo.edu
YOUNG, Tina .... 319-385-6361 167 F
tina.young@iw.edu
YOUNG, Todd .... 541-654-5885 371 F

YOUNG, Troy .... 267-341-3494 385 I
tyoung2@holyfamily.edu
YOUNG, Wayne .... 402-280-2775 265 J
waynejr@creighton.edu
YOUNG, William .... 334-290-3254.... 2 F
william.young@istc.edu
YOUNGBAUER, Mara ... 260-982-5250 158W
mlyoungbauer@manchester.edu
YOUNGBLADE, Lise ... 970-491-5841.. 79 E
lise.youngblade@colostate.edu
YOUNGBLOOD, Amy ... 713-522-7911 453 H
youngbah@stthom.edu
YOUNGBLOOD, Cecil .. 608-363-2660 490 I
youngblc@beloit.edu
YOUNGBLOOD, Dan .... 317-278-7631 157 B
dyoungbl@iupui.edu
YOUNGBLOOD, Jason . 270-809-6859 184 A
jyoungblood@murraystate.edu
YOUNGBLOOD,
Jeanette .... 870-612-2022... 23 B
jeanette.youngblood@uaccb.edu
YOUNGBLOOD, Joseph . 908-737-7030 277 F
jyoungblood@kean.edu
YOUNGBLOOD,
Krisshunn .... 337-475-5426 192 B
kyoungblood@mcneese.edu
YOUNGBLOOD,
Richard .... 504-526-4745 190 C
youngblood@hcu.edu
YOUNGBLOOD, Rick .. 601-477-4014 246 A
rick.youngblood@jcjc.edu
YOUNGBLOOD, Robert . 256-766-6610.... 5 F
ryoungblood@hcu.edu
YOUNGBLOOD, Sheila . 918-595-7742 370 B
sheila.youngblood1@tulsacc.edu
YOUNGBLOOD GILES,
Nikki .... 212-854-2033 290 H
nyoungbl@barnard.edu
YOUNGDAHL, Marcy ... 210-999-8111 451 B
myoungda@trinity.edu
YOUNGE, Jeffrey, W ... 507-344-7328 233 I
jeff.younge@blc.edu
YOUNGEN, Audra .... 330-823-2072 362 E
youngeau@mountunion.edu
YOUNGER, Allan ...... 336-757-3804 334 D
ayounger@forsythtech.edu
YOUNGER, James ...... 859-442-1719 181 D
james.younger@kctcs.edu
YOUNGER, Kyle .... 662-243-1975 245 C
kyounger@eastms.edu
YOUNGER, Toyia ...... 515-294-1909 163 E
tyounger@iastate.edu
YOUNGMAN, Paul ..... 540-458-8418 476 D
youngmanp@wlu.edu
YOUNGREN, Malcolm .. 212-982-3456.. 55 D
myoungren@pacificcollege.edu
YOUNGREN, Malcolm .. 929-436-3851.. 55 D
myoungren@pacificcollege.edu
YOUNGREN, Malcolm .. 619-574-6909.. 55 D
myoungren@pacificcollege.edu
YOUNGS, Samuel, J ... 423-775-7514 417 D
syoungs2721@bryan.edu
YOUNGS, JR.,
Thomas, E .... 412-624-8785 400 A
tyoungs@cfo.pitt.edu
YOUNGS-MAHER,
Pamela .... 315-464-8561 316 F
youngsmp@upstate.edu
YOUNGSTRAND, Keri .. 218-281-8395 243 B
kyoungst@umn.edu
YOUNT, Rebecca, M ... 401-333-7159 403 D
byount@ccri.edu
YOUNTS, Philip .... 405-613-2536 369 H
philip.younts@swcu.edu
YOUPA, Andrew .... 618-453-7653 149 G
ayoupa@siu.edu
YOUSE, Lauren .... 573-629-3122 253 D
lauren.youse@hlg.edu
YOUSIF, Amar .... 713-486-2227 455 D
amar.yousif@uth.tmc.edu
YOUSIF, Bassam .... 812-237-2785 155 H
bassam.yousif@indstate.edu
YOVANOVICH, Michele . 239-433-6950 100 G
michele.yovanovich@fsw.edu
YOW, Amy .... 704-233-8264 344 E
a.yow@wingate.edu
YOWE, Benita .... 864-592-4338 411 E
yoweb@sccsc.edu
YOWELL, Constance ... 617-373-2000 217 D
YOWELL, Kristi .... 410-337-6000 198 G
kristi.yowell@goucher.edu
YPMA, Heidi .... 360-752-8433 477 C
hypma@btc.edu
YRUEGAS, Jennifer ... 503-352-2236 375 B
jennifer.yruegas@pacificu.edu

YSAIS, David .... 213-763-7063.. 50 A
ysaisdp@lattc.edu
YSURSA, JR., Bernie, J 618-235-2700 150 B
bernard.ysursa@swic.edu
YU, Allison .... 512-444-8082 448 B
yu@thsu.edu
YU, Bin .... 401-456-8160 404 A
byu@ric.edu
YU, Ellen .... 518-388-6293 323 B
yue@union.edu
YU, Fen .... 870-972-3027... 17 I
fyu@astate.edu
YU, Hongtao .... 443-885-3350 200 F
hongtao.yu@morgan.edu
YU, Jenny .... 562-947-8755.. 65 H
jennyyu@scuhs.edu
YU, Paul, K .... 858-534-1571.. 70 C
pyu@ucsd.edu
YU, Regan .... 626-455-0312.. 58 J
YU, Tyler .... 678-407-5396 119 B
tyu@ggc.edu
YU, Zhanjing (John) ... 530-242-7962.. 64 A
zyu@shastacollege.edu
YUCHA, James, B ..... 804-828-2234 472 D
jyucha@vcu.edu
YUDIN, Lee .... 671-735-2694 503 E
lyudin@triton.uog.edu
YUDIN, Lee, S .... 671-735-2002 503 E
lyudin@triton.uog.edu
YUDT, Angela, L ...... 312-413-3470 151 D
ayudt@uic.edu
YUE, Charlyne .... 213-738-6716.. 66 A
studentaffairs@swlaw.edu
YUEH, Yir Gloria ...... 623-572-3239 144 C
gyuehx@midwestern.edu
YUEN, Dan .... 212-924-5900 321 C
dyuen@swedishinstitute.edu
YUFER, Robert .... 609-652-4698 283 A
robert.yufer@stockton.edu
YUHAS, Meredith ...... 860-231-5366.. 89 G
myuhas@usj.edu
YUHAS, Trevor .... 765-658-4268 154 G
trevoryuhas@depauw.edu
YUKECH, James .... 330-941-3001 364 G
jayukech@ysu.edu
YUKNA, Jennifer ...... 314-529-9490 254 D
jyukna@maryville.edu
YUNITS, Sarah .... 508-588-9100 214 F
syunits@massasoit.mass.edu
YUNK, Robert .... 305-284-1604 112 K
ryunk@miami.edu
YUNKE, Laurie .... 215-955-1756 398 G
laurie.yunke@jefferson.edu
YUNKER, Kristin, L .... 585-343-0055 300 D
klyunker@genesee.edu
YURACHEK, Hunter ... 479-575-7641.. 21 H
athldir@uark.edu
YURAN, Mark .... 218-726-6326 243 A
myuran@d.umn.edu
YURASEK, Kevin ...... 352-365-3526 103 U
yurasekk@lssc.edu
YURECKO, Michele .... 973-290-4036 282 G
myurecko@steu.edu
YURMAN, Chana .... 646-565-6000 322 B
cyurman@touro.edu
YUST, Rob .... 417-625-9395 255 I
yust-r@mssu.edu
YUSUF, Hamza .... 510-356-4760.. 77 E
YUSUFF, Riaz .... 847-925-6206 138 E
yr20602@harpercollege.edu
YUTUC, Lloyd .... 301-891-4477 204 D
ylloyd@wau.edu
YVON, Karalee .... 413-265-2294 208 B
yvonk@elms.edu

Z

ZAAS, David .... 843-792-6788 409 D
zaas@musc.edu
ZABA, Kristof .... 406-994-7688 263 G
kristof.zaba@montana.edu
ZABALA, Juan .... 409-880-8419 449 B
juan.zabala@lamar.edu
ZABATTA, Lori .... 401-598-4462 403 E
lori.zabatta@ccri.edu
ZABEGALIN, Tatyana .. 916-608-6500.. 51 A
ZABEL, Amy .... 815-939-5221 146 F
aezabel@olivet.edu
ZABLOUDIL, Darren ... 319-398-7610 167 H
darren.zabloudil@kirkwood.edu
ZABOROWSKI, Barbara . 814-262-6425 393 A
bzabor@pennhighlands.edu
ZABOROWSKI, Shelley . 402-472-2841 269 A
szaborowski3@unl.edu

ZABOSKI, Gerald, C ... 570-941-7900 400 C
gerald.zaboski@scranton.edu
ZABUSKY, Stacia ...... 604-274-3113 302 E
szabusky@ithaca.edu
ZACARIAS, Celina ..... 805-437-8920.. 30 D
celina.zacarias@csuci.edu
ZACHAREK, John, J ... 218-255-5524 318 F
zacharek@cobleskill.edu
ZACHARIAS, Elizabeth . 650-723-2300.. 66 D
ZACHARIAS, Larry .... 972-883-2232 454 D
larry.zacharias@utdallas.edu
ZACHARIAS, Roy, G ... 877-954-1500 420 F
ZACHARIAS, Samira ... 937-294-0592 356 D
samira.zacharias@themodern.edu
ZACHARY, Bohdan ..... 414-297-7661 498 B
zacharyb@matc.edu
ZACHARY, Todd, M .... 610-566-1776 402 C
tzachary@williamson.edu
ZACHMEYER, Dru ..... 805-756-6473.. 29 K
dzachmey@calpoly.edu
ZACHOCKI, Peter ...... 219-980-6937 157 A
pzachock@iun.edu
ZACK, Erin, M 716-888-2965 291M
zack1@canisius.edu
ZACOVIC, Mark .... 831-646-4060.. 52 H
ZADECKY, Lou .... 412-578-8826 380 A
lvzadecky@carlow.edu
ZADNIK, Karla, S ...... 614-292-6603 358 E
zadnik.4@osu.edu
ZADROGA-LANGLOIS,
Stephanie .... 906-227-1683 228 B
szadroga@nmu.edu
ZAGALO-MELO, Paulo .. 269-387-5890 232 J
paulo.zagalo-melo@wmich.edu
ZAGARI-LOPORTO,
Christine .... 718-368-5051 294 C
christine.zagari@kbcc.cuny.edu
ZAGINAYLO, Nichol ... 724-287-8711 379 C
nichol.zaginaylo@bc3.edu
ZAGORA, Marilyn, A ... 716-338-1049 302 G
marilynzagora@mail.sunyjcc.edu
ZAGUMNY, Lisa .... 931-372-3124 425 B
lzagumny@tntech.edu
ZAHEER, Srilata, A .... 612-624-7876 242 K
szaheer@umn.edu
ZAHN, Heather .... 603-526-3000 271 H
ZAHN, JoAnn .... 503-338-2421 372 C
jzahn@clatsopcc.edu
ZAHN, Julie .... 603-899-1311 272 G
zahnj@franklinpierce.edu
ZAHN, Patricia .... 314-516-5267 260 E
zahnp@umsl.edu
ZAHORSKI-SCHMIDT,
Valerie, F .... 641-422-4435 168 E
zahorval@niacc.edu
ZAHZAM, Nancy, L .... 718-780-7915 291 G
nancy.zahzam@brooklaw.edu
ZAIDI, Syed .... 859-572-1907 184 B
zaidis1@nku.edu
ZAIDMAN, Ron .... 408-260-0208.. 42 H
president@fivebranches.edu
ZAIDMAN, Ron .... 831-476-9424.. 42 I
president@fivebranches.edu
ZAIDMAN, Sean .... 408-260-0208.. 42 H
marketing@fivebranches.edu
ZAIDMAN, Sean .... 831-476-9424.. 42 I
marketing@fivebranches.edu
ZAIKINA-MONTGOMERY,
Helen .... 218-335-4280 235 J
ZAISER, Greg .... 336-278-3566 328 H
zaiser@elon.edu
ZAJAC, Brendon .... 440-943-7600 360 D
bzajac@dioceseofcleveland.org
ZAJAC, SND, Brendon .. 440-943-7600 360 D
bzajac@dioceseofcleveland.org
ZAJACESKOWSKI, John . 518-244-2253 312 D
zajacj@sage.edu
ZAJDA, Vito .... 908-737-0483 277 F
vzajda@kean.edu
ZAK, Leocadia (Lee), I . 404-471-6000 114 E
president@agnesscott.edu
ZAKAHI, Walter, R .... 309-677-3152 133 H
wzakahi@fsmail.bradley.edu
ZAKARIAN, Kathy, W .. 570-326-3761 392 G
kathy.zakarian@pct.edu
ZAKE, Callie .... 419-517-7487 355 C
czake@lourdes.edu
ZAKE, Ieva .... 717-871-7205 394 B
ieva.zake@millersville.edu
ZAKHOUR, Mark .... 562-985-4131.. 32 A
mark.zakhour@csulb.edu
ZAKI, Safa .... 413-597-4351 220 D
szaki@williams.edu

Index of Key Administrators ZAKRAYSEK – ZENGER 971

ZAKRAYSEK, Chris 814-254-0442 381 B
czakraysek@pa.gov
ZAKRZEWSKI, Bruce 269-294-4237 223 J
bzakrzewski@glenoaks.edu
ZALAPI, Diane 248-476-1122 227 B
dzalapi@msp.edu
ZALBA, Jeanette 734-487-5372 223 F
jzalba@emich.edu
ZALE, Lauren 562-938-4140 48 K
lzale@lbcc.edu
ZALESAK, Richard, J 281-283-2032 452 A
zalesak@uhcl.edu
ZALESKI, Michael 516-686-7791 308 H
mzaleski@nyit.edu
ZALESKI, Shane 937-604-4743 361 I
shane.zaleski@uc.edu
ZALEWSKI, Annie 312-850-7053 135 E
aciechanowski@ccc.edu
ZALKIND, Carrie 626-529-8007 55 E
czalkind@pacificoaks.edu
ZALOUDEK, Julie 651-773-1741 237 D
julie.zaloudek@century.edu
ZAMA, Aparna, M 848-932-8495 281 B
zama@rutgers.edu
ZAMAN, Maliha 540-362-6000 467 A
zamanms@hollins.edu
ZAMAN, Naveed 304-766-4248 489 D
zamanna@wvstateu.edu
ZAMANSKY, Dave 603-526-3757 271 H
dave.zamansky@colby-sawyer.edu
ZAMBITO-HILL, Angela 304-336-8847 489 B
angie.hill@westliberty.edu
ZAMBLE, Anthony 773-244-5568 145 F
azamble@northpark.edu
ZAMBON, Joseph, J 716-829-3940 315 F
jjzambon@buffalo.edu
ZAMBONINO, Maria 773-878-3813 148 F
mzambonino@staugustine.edu
ZAMBRANA, Maritza 787-279-1912 506 L
mzambrana@bayamon.inter.edu
ZAMBRANO, Javier 713-221-8909 452 B
zambranoj@uhd.edu
ZAMBRANO, Rebecca 608-332-9567 491 F
rzambrano@edgewood.edu
ZAMBRANO, Susanna 928-314-9422 11 B
susanna.zambrano@azwestern.edu
ZAMBROTTA-SHEETZ,
Diana 212-517-0593 305 D
dzambrotta@mmm.edu
ZAMIARA, Aubrey 585-292-2142 306 K
azamiara1@monroecc.edu
ZAMJAHN, Jamie 715-425-4897 496 A
jamie.zamjahn@uwrf.edu
ZAMOJSKI, Heather 219-989-2996 160 A
zamojski@pnw.edu
ZAMORA, Chris 954-771-0376 103 S
czamora@knoxseminary.edu
ZAMORA, Erica, A 512-448-8412 441 N
ezamora2@stedwards.edu
ZAMORA, Stephanie 954-771-0376 103 S
szamora@knoxseminary.edu
ZAMORA, Susan 618-453-6727 149 G
susan.zamora@siu.edu
ZAMORA, Teri 281-998-6306 442 B
teri.zamora@sjcd.edu
ZAMSKY, Florence 914-487-4318 110 C
fzamsky@ncf.edu
ZANDER, Derek 319-385-6349 167 F
derek.zander@iw.edu
ZANDER, William, D 302-831-8859 91 A
dzander@udel.edu
ZANDERS, Ann 225-216-8723 187 D
zandersa@mybrcc.edu
ZANDERS, Joan, A 703-323-3014 473 G
jzanders@nvcc.edu
ZANE, Jazmine 310-506-4375 56 H
jazmin.zane@pepperdine.edu
ZANE, Tom 801-957-4420 460 D
tom.zane@slcc.edu
ZANET, Jared 423-869-6041 420 A
jared.zanet@lmunet.edu
ZANG, Connie 740-366-9441 349 D
zang.3@cotc.edu
ZANGARA, Randy 570-326-2400 392 S
rjz6@pct.edu
ZANGARO, George 866-492-5336 243 G
george.zangaro@mail.waldenu.edu
ZANGER, Kate 563-588-6313 164 C
kate.zanger@clarke.edu
ZANIC, Van, G 724-847-6105 384 B
vgzanic@geneva.edu
ZANJANI, Mellissia 215-751-8205 381 H
mzanjani@ccp.edu
ZANK, Gary 256-824-7403 8 B
gary.zank@uah.edu
ZANKINA, Emilia 215-204-9570 398 D
emilia.zankina@temple.edu
ZANKINA, Emilia 215-204-7405 398 D
emilia.zankina@temple.edu
ZANKO, Michael 973-655-7706 278 C
zankom@montclar.edu
ZANOLINI, Rebecca 615-966-5074 420 B
rebecca.zanolini@lipscomb.edu
ZANT, Don 662-325-2231 247 A
daz3@msstate.edu
ZANT, Kimberly 785-243-1435 172 J
pleite@cloud.edu
ZANTINGH, Ryan 515-271-3048 165 F
ryan.zantingh@drake.edu
ZAPATA, Grace 210-486-2269 428 C
zapata@alamo.edu
ZAPATA, Rafael 718-817-1000 300 A
rzapata@fordham.edu
ZAPATKA, Beth 413-478-3408 218 E
bzapatka@springfield.edu
ZAPF, Patricia 650-758-7663 55 K
pzapf@paloaltou.edu
ZAPOLSKI, Mike 309-794-7223 132 H
mikezapolski@augustana.edu
ZAPP, Karen 724-902-7467 379 C
karen.zapp@bc3.edu
ZAPP, Kelly 630-829-6000 133 B
ZAPPALORTI, Robert, E 203-287-3028 88 D
paier.admin@snet.net
ZAPPAS, Barbara 831-582-3908 32 D
bzappas@csumb.edu
ZAPPASODI, Tony 903-233-4426 438 C
tonyzappasodi@letu.edu
ZAPPE, Christopher 717-337-6820 384 C
czappe@gettysburg.edu
ZAPPIA, Joe 574-807-7074 153 G
joe.zappia@betheluniversity.edu
ZAPRUDER, Matthew 925-631-8131 59 I
mjz4@stmarys-ca.edu
ZARAGOZA, Federico 702-651-5600 270 F
federico.zaragoza@csn.edu
ZARBL, Helmut 848-445-2354 281 B
zarbl@eohsi.rutgers.edu
ZAREMBA, Terah 269-965-3931 225 D
zarembat@kellogg.edu
ZAREMSKI, Robin, D 717-871-7026 394 B
robin.zaremski@millersville.edu
ZARFAS, Ellen 503-375-7106 372 G
ezarfas@corban.edu
ZARGES, Bradford 617-745-3638 208 F
bradford.zarges@enc.edu
ZARGHAMI, Eric 252-335-3548 341 A
vzarghami@ecsu.edu
ZARGHAMI, Eric, V 252-335-3548 341 A
vzarghami@ecsu.edu
ZARISFI, Nathalie 516-877-4225 288 L
nzarisfi@adelphi.edu
ZARISFI, Nathalie 718-260-5043 294 F
nzarisfi@citytech.cuny.edu
ZARKOS, Thomas 212-678-3000 321 H
ttz2106@tc.columbia.edu
ZARKOWSKI, Pamela 313-993-1585 230 H
zarkowp1@udmercy.edu
ZAROBE, Michael 312-261-3608 145 C
mzarobe@nl.edu
ZARR, Gary 518-276-2800 311 J
zarrg@rpi.edu
ZARRELLI, Selen 216-397-1886 353 O
azarrelli@jcu.edu
ZARRIELLO, Dean 410-516-7805 199 E
deanz@jhu.edu
ZARRINNAM, Ali, R 608-246-6446 497 I
azarrinnam@madisoncollege.edu
ZARTNER, Ken 432-335-6606 440 C
kzartner@odessa.edu
ZARZECKI, Linda 616-234-5708 231 D
ZARZUTZKI, Kori 660-263-3900 250 G
korizarzutzki@cccb.edu
ZASSO, Robert 845-431-8033 298 B
zasso@sunydutchess.edu
ZASTOUPIL, Brenda 701-328-2906 344 G
brenda.zastoupil@ndus.edu
ZATZ, Marjorie 209-228-2408 70 A
mzatz@ucmerced.edu
ZAVADIL, Amy 212-854-3362 290 H
azavadil@barnard.edu
ZAVADSKY, Cornelia 610-604-7700 93 H
ZAVALA, Alfonso 928-317-6180 11 B
alfonso.zavala@azwestern.edu
ZAVALA, Damian 562-985-5146 32 A
damian.zavala@csulb.edu
ZAVALA, Dina 608-785-5092 495 A
dzavala@uwlax.edu
ZAVALA, Javier 915-532-3737 457 E
ZAVALA-ACEVEZ,
Elizabeth 657-278-2030 31 E
ezavala-acevez@fullerton.edu
ZAVALA-QUINONES,
Javier, L 787-993-8855 510 E
javier.zavala@upr.edu
ZAVALA-QUIÑONES,
Javier 787-993-8854 510 E
javier.zavala@upr.edu
ZAVATKAY, Debra 203-837-9200 86 A
zavatkayd@wcsu.edu
ZAVATKAY, Debra 860-738-6309 87 A
dzavatkay@nwcc.edu
ZAVODJANCIK,
Maureen 860-465-4484 85 G
zavodjancikm@easternct.edu
ZAWALICH, Barbara 508-854-4283 215 D
bzawalich@qcc.mass.edu
ZAWIA, Nasser, H 401-874-5909 404 E
nzawia@uri.edu
ZAWODNY, Laurel, E 419-372-2211 348 F
lzawodn@bgsu.edu
ZAYAC, Lynn 413-572-8142 213 C
lzayac@westfield.ma.edu
ZAYAS, David 787-841-2000 508 H
dzayaz@pucpr.edu
ZAYAS, Judith 407-926-2000 93 H
ZAYAS, Judith 407-618-5900 93 H
ZAYAS, Luis, H 512-471-1937 454 C
lzayas@austin.utexas.edu
ZAYAS, Niza 787-786-3030 509 E
nzayas@ucb.edu.pr
ZAYAS-HERNANDEZ,
Haydee 787-480-2463 505 A
hzayas@sanjuan.pr
ZAYER, Bijan 858-653-3000 29 F
ZBEGNER, Deborah, A 570-408-4086 402 B
deborah.zbegner@wilkes.edu
ZBOCK, Jason 315-684-6054 320 E
zbockjp@morrisville.edu
ZBOCK, jason 315-684-6081 320 E
zbockjp@morrisville.edu
ZDANCEWICZ, Heather 512-404-4816 429 K
hzdancewicz@austinseminary.edu
ZDANOWICZ, Martin 909-607-8565 37 I
mzdanowicz@kgi.edu
ZDANOWSKI, Sophia 585-271-3657 312 E
sophia.zdanowski@stbernards.edu
ZDATNY, Sophie 802-224-3013 462 G
sophie.zdatny@vsc.edu
ZDZIARSKI, Gene 312-362-8854 136 F
ezdziars@depaul.edu
ZEALAND, Matt 619-201-8700 60 G
matt.zealand@sdcc.edu
ZECH, Susan 212-686-9244 289 G
ZECHES, Megan 507-453-2700 238 J
ZECKOVICH, Kim 906-932-4231 224 A
kimz@gogebic.edu
ZEDNICK, Yukari 425-352-8413 477 F
yzednick@cascadia.edu
ZEEH, Steven 303-914-6372 82 L
steven.zeeh@rrcc.edu
ZEEK, Raymond 203-285-2032 86 D
rzeek@gatewayct.edu
ZEGADLO, Michael 815-836-5222 142 C
zegadlmi@lewisu.edu
ZEGANS, Claudia 845-575-3000 305 C
claudia.zegans@marist.edu
ZEGARRA, Ellen 440-826-2740 348 C
ezegarra@bw.edu
ZEGER, Brian 212-799-5000 303 B
ZEGLEN, Eric, J 717-477-1154 394 D
ejzeglen@ship.edu
ZEGLIN, Chris 713-942-3414 453 H
zeglinc@stthom.edu
ZEHEL, Renee, G 570-961-4715 389 B
rzehel@marywood.edu
ZEICH, Heidi, E 202-319-5615 91 G
zeich@cua.edu
ZEICHNER, Veronica 201-360-4043 277 D
vzeichner@hccc.edu
ZEIDAN, Sana 281-283-2965 452 A
zeidan@uhcl.edu
ZEIDEL, Tom 231-348-6603 228 D
tzeidel@ncmich.edu
ZEIDLICKIS, Dagnia 516-367-6890 296 A
ZEIG, Michael 517-355-6560 227 C
zeigmich@msu.edu
ZEIGLER, Carla 301-387-3125 198 F
carla.zeigler@garrettcollege.edu
ZEIGLER, Jeff 757-569-6711 474 A
jzeigler@pdc.edu
ZEIGLER, Letherio 912-443-5776 124 I
lzeigler@savannahtech.edu
ZEIGLER, Letherio 662-254-3335 247 C
letherio.zeigler@mvsu.edu
ZEIGLER, Michael 803-535-5340 406 E
mike.zeigler@claflin.edu
ZEIGLER, Sara 859-622-2222 180 B
sara.zeigler@eku.edu
ZEIHER, Laura 218-299-6522 238 K
laura.zeiher@minnesota.edu
ZEILBERGER,
Yeruchom 845-207-0330 290 C
ZEIMET, Dan, L 563-333-6202 169 D
zeimetdaniell@sau.edu
ZEINA, Elai 310-289-5123 68 E
ZEIND, Caroline 617-732-2874 216 B
caroline.zeind@mcphs.edu
ZEISER, Richard, A 860-768-4181 89 E
zeiser@hartford.edu
ZEITLOW, Terry 903-233-3835 438 C
terryzeitlow@letu.edu
ZEKAN, Ingrid 352-245-4119 112 D
ingrid.zekan@taylorcollege.edu
ZELASKO, Sandra 360-538-4000 479 F
sandy.zelasko@ghc.edu
ZELAYA, Marjorie 702-567-1920 270 D
ZELAYA-LEON, Tricia 269-337-7183 225 B
tricia.zelaya-leon@kzoo.edu
ZELENSKI, Paul 517-371-5140 232 K
zelenskp@cooley.edu
ZELENY, Michael 402-472-2116 269 A
mike.zeleny@unl.edu
ZELESKY, Jason 978-630-9139 215 A
jzelesky@mwcc.mass.edu
ZELESNIK, Kelly 440-366-7028 355 B
ZELEZNIK, Matthew 724-480-3357 381 G
matthew.zeleznik@ccbc.edu
ZELEZNY, Lynnette 661-654-2243 30 C
lzelezny@csub.edu
ZELIG, Kaylah 303-352-6787 80 D
kaylah.zelig@ccd.edu
ZELIHIC, Maja 858-513-9240 16 I
ZELINKA, Yhara 860-343-5868 86 G
yzelinka@mxcc.edu
ZELINSKI, Debbie 312-329-4231 144 F
debbie.zelinski@moody.edu
ZELL, Jennifer 845-687-5049 322 K
zellj@sunyulster.edu
ZELL, Mo 414-229-5337 495 B
zell@uwm.edu
ZELLAR, Nel 507-433-0832 240 A
nel.zellar@riverland.edu
ZELLERS, Victoria 215-751-8913 381 H
vzellers@ccp.edu
ZELLET, Jennifer 661-722-6300 26 E
jzellet@avc.edu
ZELLMER, Jill, A 617-627-3298 219 A
jill.zellmer@tufts.edu
ZELLNER, Wayne 719-632-8116 81 I
wzellner@intellitec.edu
ZELTINGER, Jacquelyn 701-627-4738 346 D
ZEMAN, Ellen 802-651-5912 461 C
zeman@champlain.edu
ZEMAN, Mark 315-464-5825 316 F
zemanm@upstate.edu
ZEMAN, Mary Beth 973-720-2966 283 I
zemanm@wpunj.edu
ZEMBA, Bethany, C 203-582-7430 88 F
bethany.zemba@quinnipiac.edu
ZEMBA, Jennifer 724-838-4216 397 F
jzemba@setonhill.edu
ZEMKE, Angela 920-424-1234 495 C
ZEMLEDUCH, Josafat 817-202-6628 444 B
josa.zem@swau.edu
ZENDEJAS, Raul 210-805-3006 452 D
rzendeja@uiwtx.edu
ZENDMAN, Ellen 914-606-6733 324 F
ellen.zendman@sunywcc.edu
ZENELIS, John, G 703-993-2491 466 J
jzenelis@gmu.edu
ZENG, Amy 617-573-8665 218 G
azeng@suffolk.edu
ZENG, Xiangwu 201-216-3893 282 L
xiangwu.zeng@stevens.edu
ZENGER, John 208-496-4632 130 G
zengerj@byui.edu
ZENGER, Sheahon 203-932-7000 89 F
szenger@newhaven.edu
ZENGER, Sheahon 203-932-7020 89 F
szenger@newhaven.edu

ZITNIK, Joseph .... 313-317-6500 224 F
jzitnik@hfcc.edu
ZITO, Joseph .... 508-767-7505 205 F
jzito@assumption.edu
ZITO, Julie .... 202-885-1000.. 91 D
zito@american.edu
ZIX, Theresa .... 626-396-2477.. 26 G
theresa.zix@artcenter.edu
ZLATANOV, Milla ... 408-498-5105.. 73 A
mzlatanov@cogswell.edu
ZLATEVA, Tanya .... 617-353-3010 207 C
zlateva@bu.edu
ZLATKOVSKA, Emilija 812-465-1248 162 B
ezlatkovsk@usi.edu
ZLOTOCHA, Seth ... 414-288-7596 492 E
seth.zlotocha@marquette.edu
ZMACZYNSKI,
   Alexander .... 413-265-2302 208 B
zmaczynskial@elms.edu
ZMARLICKI, Elizabeth ... 401-598-1000 403 E
zmarlicki@assumption.edu
ZOBAC, Andrew, W ... 630-637-5861 145 E
awzobac@noctrl.edu
ZOCCO, Laura .... 518-783-8282 314 K
lparry@siena.edu
ZOCHOL, Frank ... 845-752-3000 323 A
f.zochol@uts.edu
ZOGHI, Manoochehr ..... 309-298-1066 152 I
m-zoghi@wiu.edu
ZOGHI, Manoochehr ..... 260-481-6839 159 H
zoghim@pfw.edu
ZOHRABIAN, Arina .... 510-925-4282.. 25 P
azohrabian@aua.am
ZOINO, Mia .... 508-531-2102 212 B
menright@bridgew.edu
ZOLA, Charles .... 845-569-3160 307 B
charles.zola@msmc.edu
ZOLDAK, Heather .... 847-925-6319 138 E
hzoldak@harpercollege.edu
ZOLL, Michael .... 802-257-7751 462 B
michael.zoll@sit.edu
ZOLLARS, Scott, M .... 620-421-6700 175 D
scottz@labette.edu
ZOLLER, Karen .... 216-373-5266 357 F
kzoller@ndc.edu
ZOLLICOFFER,
   Christine .... 414-297-7087 498 B
zollicoc@matc.edu
ZOMALT, Drew .... 903-790-4890 437 E
dzomalt@jarvis.edu
ZOMCHICK, John .... 865-974-3265 426 E
zomchick@utk.edu
ZOMERI, Joseph .... 716-888-2336 291 M
0527mgr@follett.com
ZOMERMAAND, Lori ..... 712-707-7140 169 A
lori.zomermaand@nwciowa.edu
ZOMORODI, Meg ... 919-843-6211 342 B
meg_zomorodi@unc.edu
ZONDERMAN, Adrianne 617-349-8744 210 H
azonderm@lesley.edu
ZOOK, Jim .... 662-915-2138 248 F
jzook@olemiss.edu
ZOOK, Kris .... 269-927-8771 226 B
kzook@lakemichigancollege.edu
ZOOK, Shawn .... 402-643-7261 265 I
shawn.zook@cune.edu
ZORDILLA, Emil .... 657-278-3735.. 31 E
ezordilla@fullerton.edu
ZORN, Kurt .... 812-855-9003 156 C
zorn@indiana.edu
ZORN, Linda .... 530-879-9069.. 27 F
zornli@butte.edu
ZORNES, Kimberli .... 812-535-5193 160 E
kimberli.zornes@smwc.edu
ZORNOSA, Luis .... 787-264-1912 507 E
lzornosa@intersg.edu
ZOROMSKI, Keith .... 417-455-5740 251 H
keithzoromski@crowder.edu
ZORZI, Mark .... 856-415-2280 280 F
mzorzi@rcsj.edu
ZOSEL-HARPER,
   Therese .... 212-228-1888 311 I
ZOSKY, Diane .... 309-438-5669 140 C
dlzosky@ilstu.edu
ZOTHMAN, Megan .... 218-755-2502 237 B
megan.zothman@bemidjistate.edu
ZOTTI, Robert .... 201-216-5231 282 L
robert.zotti@stevens.edu
ZOTTOLA, Shannon ...... 570-941-7400 400 E
shannon.zottola@scranton.edu
ZOTTOLA, Shannon ...... 610-409-3200 400 E
szottola@ursinus.edu
ZOTTOLI, Carla .... 978-630-9276 215 A
czottoli@mwcc.mass.edu

ZOU, Lily .... 516-739-1545 308 E
controller@nyctcm.edu
ZOUMADAKIS, Bill .... 801-957-4042 460 D
bill.zoumadakis@slcc.edu
ZOZ, Shannon .... 513-244-4593 356 F
shannon.zoz@msj.edu
ZRIMSEK, Becky .... 507-222-4734 234 E
rzrimsek@carleton.edu
ZSEBIK, Charles .... 860-832-0041.. 85 F
charles.zsebik@ccsu.edu
ZSIGALOV, Deb .... 615-898-2036 421 C
deb.zsigalov@mtsu.edu
ZU, Jean .... 201-216-3633 282 L
jean.zu@stevens.edu
ZUBER, Kishan .... 570-408-4400 402 B
kishan.zuber@wilkes.edu
ZUBER, Maria, T .... 617-253-3206 215 G
ZUBEY, JR., E. Michael 610-519-7857 401 B
michael.zubey@villanova.edu
ZUBIATE, Jyl .... 309-467-6322 137 G
jzubiate@eureka.edu
ZUBROD, Nancy .... 712-279-4961 169 E
nancy.zubrod@stlukescollege.edu
ZUCCA, Carey Anne ... 518-580-5000 315 A
ZUCCARELLO, Patty ... 815-280-2239 140 I
pzuccare@jjc.edu
ZUCCARINI, Molly .... 781-768-7228 217 H
molly.zuccarini@regiscollege.edu
ZUCCOLA, Jen .... 612-874-3626 236 E
jzuccola@mcad.edu
ZUCKER, Avraham .... 718-382-8702 325 I
ZUCKER, Lauren .... 203-432-8618.. 90 B
lauren.zucker@yale.edu
ZUCKER, Nicole, M .... 215-572-2103 378 E
zuckern@arcadia.edu
ZUCKERMAN,
   Mary Ellen .... 585-245-5367 317 E
zuckerman@geneseo.edu
ZUCKERMAN, Phil .... 909-607-4495.. 57 E
phil_zuckerman@pitzer.edu
ZUCKSWORTH, Eli .... 405-262-2552 368 I
eli.zucksworth@redlandscc.edu
ZUERCHER, Tracy .... 309-677-3153 133 H
tzuercher@bradley.edu
ZUFELT, Matt .... 435-865-8165 459 E
zufelt@suu.edu
ZUGATES, Debra, A ... 412-396-5211 382 E
zugates@duq.edu
ZUGE, Peter .... 715-346-4831 496 B
pzuge@uwsp.edu
ZUGGER, Tom .... 614-236-6782 348 I
tzugger@capital.edu
ZUGSCHWERT, Nancy 612-343-5001 241 O
nczugsch@northcentral.edu
ZUHLKE, James .... 610-436-3316 394 F
jzuhlke@wcupa.edu
ZUIDEMA, Leah .... 712-722-6328 165 E
leah.zuidema@dordt.edu
ZUILL, Karen .... 607-431-4303 300 G
zuillk@hartwick.edu
ZUJOVICH, Aiisa .... 813-253-7193 102 A
azujovich@hccfl.edu
ZUK, Patricia .... 310-287-4452.. 50 C
zukp@wlac.edu
ZUKOR, Tevya .... 540-654-1053 471 B
tzukor@umw.edu
ZUKOSKI, Charles, F .... 213-740-2101.. 73 C
uscprovost@usc.edu
ZULEWSKI, Julie .... 716-839-8483 297 F
jzulewsk@daemen.edu
ZULIANI, Katherine .... 516-686-7421 308 H
kzuliani@nyit.edu
ZULKOSKI, Sara .... 402-826-6765 266 A
sarah.zulkoski@doane.edu
ZULLO, Ashley .... 724-589-2182 398 F
azullo@thiel.edu
ZUMBACH, Deborah, J 319-335-3815 163 F
deborah-zumbach@uiowa.edu
ZUMBI, Divine .... 404-627-2681 116 B
divine.zumbi@beulah.edu
ZUMBRUN, Christina ... 260-665-4242 161 C
zumbrunc@trine.edu
ZUMBRUNNEN, John ... 608-262-5246 494 D
zumbrunnen@wisc.edu
ZUMMO, Janice .... 212-220-1230 292 G
jzummo@bmcc.cuny.edu
ZUMWALT, Debra, L ... 650-723-6397.. 66 D
zumwalt@stanford.edu
ZUNIGA, Ana .... 915-831-6395 435 B
azunig64@epcc.edu
ZUNIGA, Brad .... 530-895-2948.. 27 F
zunigabr@butte.edu

ZUNIGA, Donna, P .... 936-755-7228 438 B
dzuniga@lee.edu
ZUNIGA, Stephanie .... 209-228-8605.. 70 A
szuniga2@ucmerced.edu
ZUNKEL, Karen, A .... 515-294-7063 163 E
kzunkel@iastate.edu
ZUPAN, Mark, A .... 607-871-2101 289 E
zupan@alfred.edu
ZURA, Veronica .... 206-546-7858 483 C
vzura@shoreline.edu
ZURAWSKI, Sandra .... 708-534-4981 138 C
szurawski@govst.edu
ZURES, Allison .... 773-907-4738 134 N
azures@ccc.edu
ZURLAGE, Katherine ..... 410-462-7753 197 E
kzurlage@bccc.edu
ZURN, Sue .... 218-299-6515 238 K
sue.zurn@minnesota.edu
ZUROMSKI, Steve .... 508-531-2247 212 B
szuromski@bridgew.edu
ZUSCHIN, Andrea .... 540-831-5307 468 E
azuschin@radford.edu
ZUZARTE, Lisa .... 661-654-6181.. 30 C
lzuzarte@csub.edu
ZUZOLO, Renee .... 330-652-9919 352 E
reneezuzolo@eticollege.edu
ZVARITCH, Jeanne .... 330-337-6403 347 B
ie@awc.edu
ZVARITCH, Jeanne, W ... 330-337-6403 347 B
academicdean@awc.edu
ZVONKOVIC, Anisa .... 706-542-4879 126 F
az61075@uga.edu
ZWANY, Abe .... 301-962-5111 205 B
ZWANZIGER,
   Michael, W .... 319-273-7826 163 G
michael.zwanziger@uni.edu
ZWART, Andrew .... 616-222-3000 226 A
azwart@kuyper.edu
ZWEIG, Akiva .... 305-534-7050 112 C
azweig@talmudicu.edu
ZWEIG, Yitzchak .... 305-534-7050 112 C
yzweig@gmail.com
ZWEIG, Yochanan .... 305-534-7050 112 C
rosh@talmudicu.edu
ZWEIGER, Heather .... 920-560-1668 497 F
zweiger@fvtc.edu
ZWEIGLE, Zachary .... 530-242-7560.. 64 A
zzweigle@shastacollege.edu
ZWELL, Michael .... 262-742-4444 499 S
mike@wrightgrad.edu
ZWICK, Kevin .... 412-624-0148 400 A
zwick@pitt.edu
ZWICKEY, Heather .... 503-552-1759 374 B
hzwickey@nunm.edu
ZWICKLER, Don .... 845-352-3431 325 O
ZWIERZELEWSKI,
   Ashley .... 724-830-1005 397 F
akunkle@setonhill.edu
ZWIKELMAIER, William 573-341-4343 260 F
zwikelmaier@mst.edu
ZWIRN, Benjamin .... 631-451-4867 320 G
zwirnb@sunysuffolk.edu
ZYCH HERRMANN,
   Jennifer .... 320-589-6048 243 C
zychja@morris.umn.edu
ZYGMONT, Bryan, J .... 301-447-7435 201 A
b.j.zygmont@msmary.edu
ZYGMUNT, Elizabeth ..... 570-504-7000 384 A
ezygmunt@som.geisinger.edu
ZYGMUNT, Melizza .... 219-464-7064 162 C
melizza.zygmunt@valpo.edu
ZYLBERMAN, Amy .... 717-358-2468 383 G
amy.zylberman@fandm.edu
ZYLMAN-TENHAVE,
   Lannette .... 616-392-8555 233 B
lannette@westernsem.edu
ZYLSTRA, James .... 608-266-1739 497 C
james.zylstra@wtcsystem.edu
ZYSK, Jay .... 508-910-6534 211 F
jzysk@umassd.edu

Accreditation Index of Institutions by Regional, National, Professional and Specialized Agencies

Degree levels are shown by the following symbols: (C) diploma/certificate; (A) associate; (B) baccalaureate;
(M) master's; (S) beyond master's but less than doctorate; (FP) first professional; (D) doctorate.

ACICS: Accrediting Council for Independent Colleges and Schools: business and business related programs (C,A,B,M)

ACPHA: Accreditation Commission for Programs in Hospitality Administration: hospitality administration/management (A,B)

ACUP: Accreditation Commission for Acupuncture and Herbal Medicine: acupuncture (C,M,D)

ADNUR: Accreditation Commission for Education in Nursing: nursing (A)

AIJS: Association of Institutions of Jewish Studies: Jewish studies (C, A,B)

ANEST: Council on Accreditation of Nurse Anesthesia Educational Programs: nurse anesthesia (C, M,D)

ARCPA: Accreditation Review Commission on Education for the Physician Assistant: physician assisting programs (A,B,M)

CAATE: Commission on Accreditation of Athletic Training Education: athletic training (B,M,D)

CACREP: Council for Accreditation of Counseling & Related Educational Programs: counseling and its specialties (M,D)

CAEP: Council for the Accreditation of Educator Preparation: teacher education (B, M,D)

CAHIIM: Commission on Accreditation for Health Informatics and Information Management Education: health information management and health informatics (A,B,M)

CAMPEP: Commission on Accreditation of Medical Physics Education Programs, Inc.: medical physics (C,M,D)

CAPRT: Council on Accreditation of Parks, Recreation, Tourism and Related Professions: recreation, park resources, and leisure studies (B)

CARTE: Commission on Accreditation of Recreational Therapy Education: recreational therapy (B,M)

CEA: Commission on English Language Program Accreditation: english language (C)

CGTECH: National Accrediting Agency for Clinical Laboratory Sciences: cytogenetic technologist (B)

CHIRO: Council on Chiropractic Education: chiropractic education (FP,D)

CNCE: Accrediting Council for Continuing Education and Training: continuing education (C,A)

CNEA: Commission for Nurse Education Accreditation: nursing (C,A,B,M,D)

COARC: Commission on Accreditation for Respiratory Care: respiratory care (A,B,M)

COARCP: Commission on Accreditation for Respiratory Care: polysomnography (C)

COE: Council on Occupational Education: occupational, trade, and technical education (C,A)

COMTA: Commission on Massage Therapy Accreditation: massage therapy, bodywork, aesthetics/esthetics and skin care (C,A)

CONST: American Council for Construction Education: construction education (A,B,M)

DANCE: National Association of Schools of Dance: dance (C,A,B, M,D)

DEAC: Distance Education Accrediting Commission: home study schools (A,B,M,D)

DENT: American Dental Association: dentistry (FP,D)

DIET: Academy of Nutrition and Dietetics: nutrition and dietetics (M)

DIETC: Academy of Nutrition and Dietetics: coordinated dietetics programs (B,M)

DIETD: Academy of Nutrition and Dietetics: didactic dietetics programs (B,M)

Case Western Reserve University ... OH .. 349
Kent State University Kent Campus ... OH .. 354
Miami University ... OH .. 356
Ohio State University Main Campus, The. OH .. 358
Ohio University Main Campus ... OH .. 358
University of Cincinnati Main Campus ... OH .. 361
University of Dayton ... OH .. 362
Youngstown State University ... OH .. 364
Northeastern State University ... OK .. 366
Oklahoma State University ... OK .. 367
University of Central Oklahoma ... OK .. 370
Oregon State University ... OR .. 374
Cedar Crest College ... PA .. 380
Drexel University ... PA .. 382
Immaculata University ... PA .. 385
Indiana University of Pennsylvania ... PA .. 393
La Salle University ... PA .. 386
Marywood University ... PA .. 389
Messiah University ... PA .. 389
Penn State University Park ... PA .. 391
West Chester University of Pennsylvania PA .. 394
University of Puerto Rico-Rio Piedras Campus ... PR .. 511
Johnson & Wales University ... RI .. 403
University of Rhode Island ... RI 404
Clemson University ... SC .. 406
South Carolina State University ... SC .. 410
Winthrop University ... SC .. 413
South Dakota State University ... SD .. 416
Carson-Newman University ... TN .. 417
East Tennessee State University ... TN .. 418
Lipscomb University ... TN .. 420
Middle Tennessee State University ... TN .. 421
Tennessee State University ... TN .. 425
Tennessee Technological University ... TN .. 425
University of Memphis, The ... TN .. 426
University of Tennessee at Martin ... TN .. 426
University of Tennessee, Knoxville ... TN .. 426
Abilene Christian University ... TX ... 427
Baylor University ... TX ... 430
Lamar University ... TX ... 449
Prairie View A & M University ... TX ... 445
Sam Houston State University ... TX ... 449
Stephen F. Austin State University ... TX ... 444
Tarleton State University ... TX ... 445
Texas A & M University ... TX ... 446
Texas A & M University - Kingsville ... TX ... 447
Texas Christian University ... TX ... 447
Texas Southern University ... TX ... 448
Texas State University ... TX ... 449
Texas Tech University ... TX ... 450
Texas Woman's University ... TX ... 451
University of Houston ... TX ... 451
University of Texas at Austin ... TX ... 454
University of the Incarnate Word ... TX ... 452
Brigham Young University ... UT .. 458
Utah State University ... UT .. 459
University of Vermont ... VT .. 462
James Madison University ... VA .. 467
Norfolk State University ... VA .. 468
Radford University ... VA .. 468
Virginia Polytechnic Institute and State University ... VA .. 475
Virginia State University ... VA .. 475
Bastyr University ... WA . 476
Central Washington University ... WA . 477
Seattle Pacific University ... WA . 482
Marshall University ... WV . 488
@Shepherd University ... WV . 489
West Virginia University ... WV . 489
University of Wisconsin-Green Bay ... WI .. 494
University of Wisconsin-Madison ... WI .. 494
University of Wisconsin-Stevens Point ... WI .. 496
University of Wisconsin-Stout ... WI .. 496
University of Wyoming ... WY . 500

DIETI: Academy of Nutrition and Dietetics: dietetic post-baccalaureate internships

@Auburn University ... AL 4
Oakwood University ... AL 6
Samford University ... AL 6
University of Alabama at Birmingham ... AL 8
University of Alaska Anchorage ... AK 10
Arizona State University ... AZ 11
@Ouachita Baptist University ... AR 20
University of Arkansas for Medical Sciences ... AR 22
California Polytechnic State University-San Luis Obispo ... CA 29
California State Polytechnic University-Pomona ... CA 30
California State University-Chico ... CA 31
California State University-Fresno ... CA 31
California State University-Long Beach ... CA 32
California State University-Northridge ... CA 32
California State University-Sacramento ... CA 33
San Francisco State University ... CA 34
San Jose State University ... CA 34
University of California-Davis ... CA 69
University of California-San Diego ... CA 70
University of California-San Francisco ... CA 70
@Metropolitan State University of Denver ... CO 81
University of Northern Colorado ... CO 84
University of Connecticut ... CT 89
University of New Haven ... CT 89
University of Saint Joseph ... CT 89
University of Delaware ... DE 91
University of Texas Health Science Center at Houston (UTHealth Houston), Th ... TX ... 455
Florida International University ... FL ... 109
Florida State University ... FL ... 110
Keiser University ... FL ... 103
University of Florida ... FL ... 110
University of North Florida ... FL ... 111
University of South Florida ... FL ... 111
Augusta University ... GA ... 115
Georgia Southern University ... GA ... 120
Life University ... GA ... 122
University of Georgia ... GA ... 126
Idaho State University ... ID ... 131
Benedictine University ... IL ... 133
Bradley University ... IL ... 133
Eastern Illinois University ... IL ... 137
@Harper College ... IL ... 138
Illinois State University ... IL ... 140
Loyola University Chicago ... IL ... 142
Northern Illinois University ... IL ... 145
Rush University ... IL ... 148
Southern Illinois University Carbondale ... IL ... 149
University of Illinois Urbana-Champaign ... IL ... 151
Ball State University ... IN ... 153
Indiana University-Purdue University Indianapolis ... IN ... 157
@University of Indianapolis ... IN ... 161
Murray State University ... KY ... 184
University of Kentucky ... KY ... 185
Western Kentucky University ... KY ... 186
Franciscan Missionaries of Our Lady University ... LA ... 186
Louisiana Tech University ... LA ... 192
McNeese State University ... LA ... 192
Nicholls State University ... LA ... 192
Southern University and A&M College ... LA ... 190
Tulane University ... LA ... 191
University of Maine ... ME .. 196
University of Maryland College Park ... MD .. 202
University of Maryland Eastern Shore ... MD .. 203
University of Maryland, Baltimore ... MD .. 202
Boston University ... MA .. 207
Simmons University ... MA .. 218
University of Massachusetts ... MA .. 211
Andrews University ... MI ... 220
Central Michigan University ... MI ... 221
Michigan State University ... MI ... 227
University of Michigan-Ann Arbor ... MI ... 231
Western Michigan University ... MI ... 232
Concordia College ... MN .. 234
University of Minnesota ... MN .. 242
Mississippi State University ... MS .. 247
University of Southern Mississippi ... MS .. 248
Cox College ... MO .. 251
Missouri State University ... MO .. 255
@Northwest Missouri State University ... MO .. 256
Saint Louis University ... MO .. 258
Montana State University ... MT .. 263
University of Nevada, Las Vegas ... NV .. 270
University of Nevada, Reno ... NV .. 270
Keene State College ... NH .. 274
University of New Hampshire ... NH .. 273
Montclair State University ... NJ ... 278
Saint Elizabeth University ... NJ ... 282
New Mexico State University Main Campus ... NM .. 286
University of New Mexico Main Campus . NM .. 288
City University of New York Brooklyn College ... NY .. 293
City University of New York Graduate Center ... NY .. 293
City University of New York Herbert H. Lehman College ... NY .. 293
City University of New York Hunter College ... NY .. 294
City University of New York Queens College ... NY .. 295
Cornell University ... NY .. 297
Long Island University - LIU Post ... NY .. 304
New York University ... NY .. 309
Russell Sage College ... NY .. 312
Stony Brook University ... NY .. 316
Syracuse University ... NY .. 321
Teachers College, Columbia University ... NY .. 321
University at Buffalo-SUNY ... NY .. 315
Appalachian State University ... NC .. 340
Duke University ... NC .. 328
East Carolina University ... NC .. 340
Lenoir-Rhyne University ... NC .. 330
Meredith College ... NC .. 331
North Carolina Central University ... NC .. 341
University of North Carolina at Greensboro ... NC .. 342
Western Carolina University ... NC .. 343
Bowling Green State University ... OH .. 348
Case Western Reserve University ... OH .. 349
Kent State University Kent Campus ... OH .. 354
Miami University ... OH .. 356
Ohio State University Main Campus, The. OH .. 358
Ohio University Main Campus ... OH .. 358
Oklahoma State University ... OK .. 367
University of Central Oklahoma ... OK .. 370
Oregon Health & Science University ... OR .. 374
Oregon State University ... OR .. 374
Cedar Crest College ... PA .. 380
Immaculata University ... PA .. 385
Marywood University ... PA .. 389
Messiah University ... PA .. 389
@West Chester University of Pennsylvania PA .. 394
University of Puerto Rico-Medical Sciences Campus ... PR .. 511
University of Rhode Island ... RI .. 404
Winthrop University ... SC .. 413
South Dakota State University ... SD .. 416
East Tennessee State University ... TN .. 418
Lipscomb University ... TN .. 420
University of Memphis, The ... TN .. 426
University of Tennessee at Martin ... TN .. 426
University of Tennessee, Knoxville ... TN .. 426
Vanderbilt University ... TN .. 427
Abilene Christian University ... TX ... 427
Baylor University ... TX ... 430
Lamar University ... TX ... 449
Prairie View A & M University ... TX ... 445
Sam Houston State University ... TX ... 449
Stephen F. Austin State University ... TX ... 444
Texas A & M University ... TX ... 446
Texas A & M University - Kingsville ... TX ... 447
Texas State University ... TX ... 449
Texas Tech University ... TX ... 450
Texas Woman's University ... TX ... 451
University of Houston ... TX ... 451
University of Texas Medical Branch, The TX ... 456
University of the Incarnate Word ... TX ... 452
Brigham Young University ... UT .. 458
Utah State University ... UT .. 459
University of Virginia ... VA .. 471
Virginia Commonwealth University ... VA .. 472
Virginia Polytechnic Institute and State University ... VA .. 475
Virginia State University ... VA .. 475
Bastyr University ... WA . 476
Central Washington University ... WA . 477
Seattle Pacific University ... WA . 482
Marshall University ... WV . 488
West Virginia University ... WV . 489
Mount Mary University ... WI ... 493
University of Wisconsin-Green Bay ... WI ... 494
University of Wisconsin-Stout ... WI ... 496
Viterbo University ... WI ... 496

DIETT: Academy of Nutrition and Dietetics: dietetic technician (A)

Central Arizona College ... AZ 11
Paradise Valley Community College ... AZ 13
Merritt College ... CA 57
Orange Coast College ... CA 38
Santa Rosa Junior College ... CA 63
Gateway Community College ... CT 86
Truckee Meadows Community College ... NV .. 270
Camden County College ... NJ .. 275
Erie Community College ... NY .. 299
Suffolk County Community College ... NY .. 321
Cincinnati State Technical and Community College ... OH .. 350
Columbus State Community College ... OH .. 351
Cuyahoga Community College ... OH .. 351
Sinclair Community College ... OH .. 360
Stark State College ... OH .. 360
Community College of Allegheny County PA .. 381
Tarrant County College District ... TX ... 445
@Pierpont Community & Technical College WV . 487
Milwaukee Area Technical College ... WI .. 498

DMOLS: National Accrediting Agency for Clinical Laboratory Sciences: diagnostic molecular scientist (C,B,M)

University of Connecticut ... CT 89
Florida Gulf Coast University ... FL ... 109
Northern Michigan University ... MI .. 228
State University of New York Upstate Medical University ... NY .. 316
University of North Carolina at Chapel Hill ... NC .. 342
Tarleton State University ... TX ... 445
Texas Tech University Health Sciences Center ... TX ... 450
University of Texas MD Anderson Cancer Center, The ... TX ... 456

DMS: Commission on Accreditation of Allied Health Education Programs: diagnostic medical sonography (C,A,B,M)

Gadsden State Community College ... AL 2
Lurleen B. Wallace Community College .. AL 2
Trenholm State Community College ... AL 3
Wallace State Community College - Hanceville ... AL 4
GateWay Community College ... AZ 13
Arkansas State University-Jonesboro ... AR 17
University of Arkansas at Fort Smith ... AR 22
University of Arkansas for Medical Sciences ... AR 22
CBD College ... CA 35
Cosumnes River College ... CA 50
Cypress College ... CA 54
Foothill College ... CA 43
Gurnick Academy of Medical Arts ... CA 44
Kaiser Permanente School of Allied Health Sciences ... CA 46
Loma Linda University ... CA 48
Merced College ... CA 52
Mt. San Jacinto College ... CA 53
Orange Coast College ... CA 38
University of California-San Diego ... CA 70
University of Colorado Denver | Anschutz Medical Campus ... CO 84
Gateway Community College ... CT 86
AdventHealth University ... FL 95
Broward College ... FL 96
Cambridge College ... FL 96
Cambridge Institute of Allied Health & Technology-Altamonte Springs ... FL 96
Concorde Career Institute ... FL 97
Eastern Florida State College ... FL 98
Hillsborough Community College ... FL ... 102
Keiser University ... FL ... 103
Miami Dade College ... FL ... 104
#Nova Southeastern University ... FL ... 104
Palm Beach State College ... FL ... 105
Polk State College ... FL ... 106
Santa Fe College ... FL ... 107
Southeastern College ... FL ... 108
Valencia College ... FL ... 113
Albany State University ... GA ... 114
Augusta Technical College ... GA ... 115
Columbus Technical College ... GA ... 117
Georgia Northwestern Technical College GA .. 119
Georgia Southern University ... GA .. 120
Gwinnett Technical College ... GA .. 121
Oconee Fall Line Technical College-South Campus ... GA .. 123
Ogeechee Technical College ... GA .. 123

DNUR: Accreditation Commission for Education in Nursing: nursing (C)

DT: American Dental Association: dental laboratory technology (C,A)

DTH: American Dental Association: dental therapy (A)

EH: New England Commission of Higher Education

M: Middle States Commission on Higher Education

MAAB: Accrediting Bureau of Health Education Schools: medical assisting (C,A)

MAC: Commission on Accreditation of Allied Health Education Programs: medical assisting (C,A)

MACTE: Montessori Accreditation Council for Teacher Education: Montessori teacher education (C)

MEAC: Midwifery Education Accreditation Council: midwifery education (C,A,B,M,D)

MED: Liaison Committee on Medical Education: medicine (FP,D)

MLTAB: Accrediting Bureau of Health Education Schools: medical laboratory technician (C,A)

MLTAD: National Accrediting Agency for Clinical Laboratory Sciences: medical laboratory technician (C,A)

MPCAC: Masters in Psychology and Counseling Accreditation Council: counseling and psychology (M)

MUS: National Association of Schools of Music: music (C,A,B,M,D)

NAEYC: National Association for the Education of Young Children: early childhood education (A,B,M)

NAIT: The Association of Technology, Management, and Applied Engineering: technology, applied technology, engineering technology and technology-related programs (A,B,M)

NASP: National Association of School Psychologists: school psychology (S,D)

NATUR: Council on Naturopathic Medical Education: naturopathic medical education (FP,D)

PLNG: Planning Accreditation Board: certified planning (B,M)

PNUR: Accreditation Commission for Education in Nursing: practical nursing (C)

POD: American Podiatric Medical Association: podiatry (FP,D)

POLYT: Commission on Accreditation of Allied Health Education Programs: polysomnographic technologist education (C,A)

PSPSY: American Psychological Association: combined professional-scientific psychology (D)

RABN: Association of Advanced Rabbinical and Talmudic Schools: rabbinical and Talmudic education (A,B,M,D)

Bridgewater College ... VA .. 464
Central Virginia Community College ... VA .. 472
Christendom College ... VA .. 464
Christopher Newport University ... VA .. 465
College of William & Mary ... VA .. 465
Danville Community College ... VA .. 472
Divine Mercy University ... VA .. 465
Eastern Mennonite University ... VA .. 465
Eastern Shore Community College ... VA .. 472
Eastern Virginia Medical School ... VA .. 465
ECPI University ... VA .. 465
Emory & Henry College ... VA .. 466
Ferrum College ... VA .. 466
George Mason University ... VA .. 466
Germanna Community College ... VA .. 472
Hampden-Sydney College ... VA .. 466
Hampton University ... VA .. 466
Hollins University ... VA .. 467
J. Sargeant Reynolds Community College ... VA .. 473
James Madison University ... VA .. 467
John Tyler Community College ... VA .. 473
Laurel Ridge Community College ... VA .. 473
Liberty University ... VA .. 467
Longwood University ... VA .. 467
Marine Corps University ... VA .. 501
Mary Baldwin University ... VA .. 467
Marymount University ... VA .. 468
Mountain Empire Community College ... VA .. 473
Mountain Gateway Community College ... VA .. 473
New River Community College ... VA .. 473
Norfolk State University ... VA .. 468
Northern Virginia Community College ... VA .. 473
Old Dominion University ... VA .. 468
Patrick & Henry Community College ... VA .. 473
Patrick Henry College ... VA .. 468
Paul D. Camp Community College ... VA .. 474
Piedmont Virginia Community College ... VA .. 474
Radford University ... VA .. 468
Randolph College ... VA .. 469
Randolph-Macon College ... VA .. 469
Rappahannock Community College ... VA .. 474
Regent University ... VA .. 469
Richard Bland College ... VA .. 469
Roanoke College ... VA .. 469
Shenandoah University ... VA .. 470
Southern Virginia University ... VA .. 470
Southside Virginia Community College ... VA .. 474
Southwest Virginia Community College ... VA .. 474
Sweet Briar College ... VA .. 470
Thomas Nelson Community College ... VA .. 474
Tidewater Community College ... VA .. 474
Union Presbyterian Seminary ... VA .. 470
University of Lynchburg ... VA .. 470
University of Mary Washington ... VA .. 471
University of Richmond ... VA .. 471
University of Virginia ... VA .. 471
University of Virginia's College at Wise, The ... VA .. 471
Virginia Commonwealth University ... VA .. 472
Virginia Highlands Community College ... VA .. 474
Virginia Military Institute ... VA .. 475
Virginia Polytechnic Institute and State University ... VA .. 475
Virginia State University ... VA .. 475
Virginia Union University ... VA .. 475
Virginia Wesleyan University ... VA .. 476
Virginia Western Community College ... VA .. 475
Washington and Lee University ... VA .. 476
Wytheville Community College ... VA .. 475

SCPSY: American Psychological Association: school psychology (D)

University of Arizona ... AZ 16
University of Central Arkansas ... AR 23
University of California-Berkeley ... CA 68
University of California-Riverside ... CA 70
University of Colorado Denver | Anschutz Medical Campus ... CO 84
University of Denver ... CO 84
University of Northern Colorado ... CO 84
University of Connecticut ... CT 89
Nova Southeastern University ... FL ... 104
University of Florida ... FL ... 110
University of South Florida ... FL ... 111
Georgia State University ... GA .. 120
University of Georgia ... GA .. 126
Illinois State University ... IL 140
Loyola University Chicago ... IL 142
Northern Illinois University ... IL 145
Ball State University ... IN 153
Indiana State University ... IN 155
Indiana University Bloomington ... IN 156
University of Kansas Main Campus ... KS .. 177
University of Kentucky ... KY .. 185
Louisiana State University and Agricultural and Mechanical College ... LA .. 188
Tulane University ... LA ... 191
University of Maryland College Park ... MD .. 202
Northeastern University ... MA .. 217
University of Massachusetts ... MA .. 211
University of Massachusetts Boston ... MA .. 211
William James College ... MA .. 219
Central Michigan University ... MI ... 221
Michigan State University ... MI ... 227
University of Minnesota ... MN .. 242
Mississippi State University ... MS .. 247
University of Southern Mississippi ... MS .. 248
University of Missouri - Columbia ... MO .. 260
University of Montana - Missoula ... MT .. 263
University of Nebraska - Lincoln ... NE .. 269
Rutgers University - New Brunswick ... NJ ... 281
Alfred University ... NY .. 289
Fordham University ... NY .. 300
Hofstra University ... NY .. 301
St. John's University ... NY .. 313
Syracuse University ... NY .. 321
Teachers College, Columbia University ... NY .. 321
University at Albany, SUNY ... NY .. 315
East Carolina University ... NC .. 340
North Carolina State University ... NC .. 341
University of North Carolina at Chapel Hill ... NC .. 342
Kent State University Kent Campus ... OH .. 354
Ohio State University Main Campus, The. OH .. 358
University of Cincinnati Main Campus ... OH .. 361
Oklahoma State University ... OK .. 367
University of Oregon ... OR .. 376
Duquesne University ... PA .. 382
Lehigh University ... PA .. 388
Penn State University Park ... PA .. 391
Philadelphia College of Osteopathic Medicine ... PA .. 395
Temple University ... PA .. 398
University of South Carolina Columbia ... SC .. 412
University of Memphis, The ... TN .. 426
University of Tennessee, Knoxville ... TN .. 426
Baylor University ... TX ... 430
Texas A & M University ... TX ... 446
Texas Woman's University ... TX ... 451
University of Houston ... TX ... 451
University of Texas at Austin ... TX ... 454
University of Utah, The ... UT .. 459
Utah State University ... UT .. 459
University of Washington ... WA . 484
University of Wisconsin-Madison ... WI ... 494
University of Wisconsin-Milwaukee ... WI ... 495

SP: American Speech-Language-Hearing Association: speech-language pathology (M)

Alabama Agricultural and Mechanical University ... AL 1
Auburn University ... AL 4
Faulkner University ... AL 5
Samford University ... AL 6
University of Alabama, The ... AL 7
University of Montevallo ... AL 8
University of South Alabama ... AL 9
Arizona State University ... AZ 11
Northern Arizona University ... AZ 14
University of Arizona ... AZ 16
Arkansas State University-Jonesboro ... AR 17
Harding University Main Campus ... AR 19
University of Arkansas for Medical Sciences ... AR 22
University of Arkansas Main Campus ... AR 21
University of Central Arkansas ... AR 23
Biola University ... CA 27
California Baptist University ... CA 27
California State University-Chico ... CA 31
California State University-East Bay ... CA 31
California State University-Fresno ... CA 31
California State University-Fullerton ... CA 31
California State University-Long Beach ... CA 32
California State University-Los Angeles ... CA 32
@California State University-Monterey Bay CA 32
California State University-Northridge ... CA 32
California State University-Sacramento ... CA 33
California State University-San Marcos ... CA 33
Chapman University ... CA 36
Loma Linda University ... CA 48
San Diego State University ... CA 33
San Francisco State University ... CA 34
San Jose State University ... CA 34
University of Redlands ... CA 72
@University of Southern California ... CA 73
University of the Pacific ... CA 71
@Metropolitan State University of Denver .. CO 81
University of Colorado Boulder ... CO 83
University of Northern Colorado ... CO 84
Sacred Heart University ... CT 88
Southern Connecticut State University .... CT 85
University of Connecticut ... CT 89
@University of New Haven ... CT 89
University of Delaware ... DE 91
Gallaudet University ... DC 92
George Washington University ... DC 92
Howard University ... DC 92
University of the District of Columbia ... DC 94
Florida Atlantic University ... FL ... 109
Florida International University ... FL ... 109
Florida State University ... FL ... 110
Jacksonville University ... FL ... 102
Nova Southeastern University ... FL ... 104
University of Central Florida ... FL ... 110
University of Florida ... FL ... 110
University of South Florida ... FL ... 111
Georgia Southern University ... GA .. 120
Georgia State University ... GA .. 120
University of Georgia ... GA .. 126
University of West Georgia ... GA .. 127
Valdosta State University ... GA .. 127
University of Hawaii at Manoa ... HI ... 129
Idaho State University ... ID ... 131
@Augustana College ... IL 132
@DePaul University ... IL 136
Eastern Illinois University ... IL 137
Elmhurst University ... IL 137
Governors State University ... IL 138
Illinois State University ... IL 140
@Lewis University ... IL 142
Midwestern University ... IL 144
Northern Illinois University ... IL 145
Northwestern University ... IL 146
Rush University ... IL 148
Saint Xavier University ... IL 148
Southern Illinois University Carbondale ... IL 149
Southern Illinois University Edwardsville . IL 149
University of Illinois Urbana-Champaign .. IL 151
Western Illinois University ... IL 152
Ball State University ... IN 153
Indiana State University ... IN 155
Indiana University Bloomington ... IN 156
@Indiana University South Bend ... IN 157
@Purdue University Fort Wayne ... IN 159
Purdue University Main Campus ... IN 159
Saint Mary's College ... IN 160
@Trine University ... IN 161
St. Ambrose University ... IA 169
University of Iowa ... IA 163
University of Northern Iowa ... IA 163
Fort Hays State University ... KS .. 173
Kansas State University ... KS .. 175
University of Kansas Main Campus ... KS .. 177
Wichita State University ... KS .. 178
@Brescia University ... KY .. 179
Eastern Kentucky University ... KY .. 180
Murray State University ... KY .. 184
University of Kentucky ... KY .. 185
University of Louisville ... KY .. 185
Western Kentucky University ... KY .. 186
Louisiana State University and Agricultural and Mechanical College ... LA ... 188
Louisiana State University Health Sciences Center at Shreveport ... LA ... 189
Louisiana State University Health Sciences Center-New Orleans ... LA ... 189
Louisiana Tech University ... LA ... 192
Southeastern Louisiana University ... LA ... 192
Southern University and A&M College ... LA ... 190
University of Louisiana at Lafayette ... LA ... 192
University of Louisiana at Monroe ... LA ... 193
@Xavier University of Louisiana ... LA ... 193
University of Maine ... ME .. 196
Loyola University Maryland ... MD .. 199
Towson University ... MD .. 204
University of Maryland College Park ... MD .. 202
Boston University ... MA .. 207
Bridgewater State University ... MA .. 212
Emerson College ... MA .. 208
MGH Institute of Health Professions ... MA .. 216
Northeastern University ... MA .. 217
Regis College ... MA .. 217
University of Massachusetts ... MA .. 211
Worcester State University ... MA .. 213
Andrews University ... MI ... 220
Calvin University ... MI ... 221
Central Michigan University ... MI ... 221
Eastern Michigan University ... MI ... 223
Grand Valley State University ... MI ... 224
Michigan State University ... MI ... 227
Wayne State University ... MI ... 232
Western Michigan University ... MI ... 232
Minnesota State University Moorhead ... MN .. 239
Minnesota State University, Mankato ... MN .. 238
St. Cloud State University ... MN .. 240
University of Minnesota ... MN .. 242
University of Minnesota Duluth ... MN .. 243
Jackson State University ... MS .. 245
Mississippi University for Women ... MS .. 247
University of Mississippi ... MS .. 248
University of Southern Mississippi ... MS .. 248
Fontbonne University ... MO .. 252
Maryville University of Saint Louis ... MO .. 254
Missouri State University ... MO .. 255
Rockhurst University ... MO .. 257
Saint Louis University ... MO .. 258
Southeast Missouri State University ... MO .. 258
Truman State University ... MO .. 259
University of Central Missouri ... MO .. 259
University of Missouri - Columbia ... MO .. 260
University of Montana - Missoula ... MT .. 263
University of Nebraska at Kearney ... NE .. 268
University of Nebraska at Omaha ... NE .. 269
University of Nebraska - Lincoln ... NE .. 269
Nevada State College ... NV .. 270
University of Nevada, Reno ... NV .. 270
University of New Hampshire ... NH .. 273
Kean University ... NJ ... 277
Monmouth University ... NJ ... 278
Montclair State University ... NJ ... 278
@Rutgers University - Newark ... NJ ... 281
Seton Hall University ... NJ ... 282
Stockton University ... NJ ... 283
#William Paterson University of New Jersey ... NJ ... 283
Eastern New Mexico University Main Campus ... NM .. 285
New Mexico State University Main Campus ... NM .. 286
University of New Mexico Main Campus . NM .. 288
Adelphi University ... NY .. 288
City University of New York Brooklyn College ... NY .. 293
City University of New York Herbert H. Lehman College ... NY .. 293
#City University of New York Hunter College ... NY .. 294
City University of New York Queens College ... NY .. 295
College of Saint Rose, The ... NY .. 296
Hofstra University ... NY .. 301
Iona University ... NY .. 302
Ithaca College ... NY .. 302
Long Island University - LIU Post ... NY .. 304
Mercy College ... NY .. 305
Molloy University ... NY .. 306
Nazareth College of Rochester ... NY .. 307
New York Medical College ... NY .. 308
New York University ... NY .. 309
@Pace University ... NY .. 310
St. John's University ... NY .. 313
State University of New York at Fredonia NY .. 316
State University of New York at New Paltz ... NY .. 316
State University of New York College at Buffalo ... NY .. 317
State University of New York College at Cortland ... NY .. 317
State University of New York College at Plattsburgh ... NY .. 318

SURTEC: Accrediting Bureau of Health Education Schools: surgical technology (C,A)

Mandl School - The College of Allied Health ... NY .. 304
Mohawk Valley Community College ... NY .. 306
Stautzenberger College ... OH .. 361
Meridian Institute of Surgical Assisting ... TN .. 420
Baptist Health System School of Health Professions ... TX .. 430
College of Health Care Professions, The ... TX .. 432
Utah State University ... UT .. 459
Riverside College of Health Careers ... VA .. 469
Sentara College of Health Sciences ... VA .. 469
Milwaukee Career College ... WI .. 493

SW: Council on Social Work Education: social work (B,M)

Alabama Agricultural and Mechanical University ... AL ... 1
Alabama State University ... AL ... 4
Auburn University ... AL ... 4
@Auburn University at Montgomery ... AL ... 4
Jacksonville State University ... AL ... 6
Miles College ... AL ... 6
Oakwood University ... AL ... 6
Samford University ... AL ... 6
Talladega College ... AL ... 7
Troy University ... AL ... 7
Tuskegee University ... AL ... 7
University of Alabama at Birmingham ... AL ... 8
University of Alabama, The ... AL ... 7
University of Montevallo ... AL ... 8
University of North Alabama ... AL ... 8
University of South Alabama ... AL ... 9
University of Alaska Anchorage ... AK ... 10
University of Alaska Fairbanks ... AK ... 10
Arizona State University ... AZ ... 11
Grand Canyon University ... AZ ... 12
Northern Arizona University ... AZ ... 14
University of Phoenix ... AZ ... 16
Arkansas State University-Jonesboro ... AR ... 17
Harding University Main Campus ... AR ... 19
Philander Smith College ... AR ... 21
Southern Arkansas University ... AR ... 21
University of Arkansas at Fort Smith ... AR ... 22
University of Arkansas at Little Rock ... AR ... 22
University of Arkansas at Monticello ... AR ... 22
University of Arkansas at Pine Bluff ... AR ... 22
University of Arkansas Main Campus ... AR ... 21
Azusa Pacific University ... CA ... 26
California Baptist University ... CA ... 27
California State Polytechnic University-Humboldt ... CA ... 30
California State University-Bakersfield ... CA ... 30
California State University-Chico ... CA ... 31
California State University-Dominguez Hills ... CA ... 31
California State University-East Bay ... CA ... 31
California State University-Fresno ... CA ... 31
California State University-Fullerton ... CA ... 31
California State University-Long Beach ... CA ... 32
California State University-Los Angeles ... CA ... 32
California State University-Monterey Bay ... CA ... 32
California State University-Northridge ... CA ... 32
California State University-Sacramento ... CA ... 33
California State University-San Bernardino ... CA ... 33
California State University-San Marcos ... CA ... 33
California State University-Stanislaus ... CA ... 33
Fresno Pacific University ... CA ... 43
La Sierra University ... CA ... 47
Loma Linda University ... CA ... 48
Northcentral University ... CA ... 54
@Pacific Oaks College ... CA ... 55
Pacific Union College ... CA ... 55
Point Loma Nazarene University ... CA ... 57
San Diego State University ... CA ... 33
San Francisco State University ... CA ... 34
San Jose State University ... CA ... 34
@Touro University Worldwide ... CA ... 68
University Massachusetts Global ... CA ... 71
University of California-Berkeley ... CA ... 68
University of California-Los Angeles ... CA ... 69
University of Southern California ... CA ... 73
@University of the Pacific ... CA ... 71
Whittier College ... CA ... 76
Colorado Mesa University ... CO ... 78
Colorado State University ... CO ... 79
Colorado State University-Pueblo ... CO ... 79
Metropolitan State University of Denver ... CO ... 81
@University of Colorado Colorado Springs ... CO ... 84
University of Denver ... CO ... 84
Central Connecticut State University ... CT ... 85
Eastern Connecticut State University ... CT ... 85
Fairfield University ... CT ... 87
Quinnipiac University ... CT ... 88
Sacred Heart University ... CT ... 88
Southern Connecticut State University ... CT ... 85
University of Connecticut ... CT ... 89
University of Saint Joseph ... CT ... 89
Western Connecticut State University ... CT ... 86
Delaware State University ... DE ... 90
Catholic University of America, The ... DC ... 91
Gallaudet University ... DC ... 92
Howard University ... DC ... 92
University of the District of Columbia ... DC ... 94
Barry University ... FL ... 96
Florida Agricultural and Mechanical University ... FL ... 109
Florida Atlantic University ... FL ... 109
Florida Gulf Coast University ... FL ... 109
Florida International University ... FL ... 109
Florida Memorial University ... FL ... 100
Florida State University ... FL ... 110
Saint Leo University ... FL ... 107
Southeastern University ... FL ... 108
University of Central Florida ... FL ... 110
University of North Florida ... FL ... 111
University of South Florida ... FL ... 111
University of West Florida ... FL ... 111
Warner University ... FL ... 113
Albany State University ... GA ... 114
Augusta University ... GA ... 115
Clark Atlanta University ... GA ... 116
Dalton State College ... GA ... 118
Fort Valley State University ... GA ... 118
Georgia State University ... GA ... 120
Kennesaw State University ... GA ... 121
@Middle Georgia State University ... GA ... 122
Point University ... GA ... 124
Savannah State University ... GA ... 124
Thomas University ... GA ... 126
University of Georgia ... GA ... 126
Valdosta State University ... GA ... 127
University of Guam ... GU ... 503
Brigham Young University Hawaii ... HI ... 128
Hawaii Pacific University ... HI ... 128
University of Hawaii at Manoa ... HI ... 129
Boise State University ... ID ... 130
Brigham Young University-Idaho ... ID ... 130
Idaho State University ... ID ... 131
Lewis-Clark State College ... ID ... 131
Northwest Nazarene University ... ID ... 132
Aurora University ... IL ... 133
Bradley University ... IL ... 133
Chamberlain University-Addison ... IL ... 134
Chicago State University ... IL ... 134
DePaul University ... IL ... 136
Dominican University ... IL ... 137
Erikson Institute ... IL ... 137
Governors State University ... IL ... 138
Greenville University ... IL ... 138
Illinois State University ... IL ... 140
Lewis University ... IL ... 142
Loyola University Chicago ... IL ... 142
Methodist College ... IL ... 143
@National Louis University ... IL ... 145
Northeastern Illinois University ... IL ... 145
Olivet Nazarene University ... IL ... 146
St. Augustine College ... IL ... 148
Southern Illinois University Carbondale ... IL ... 149
Southern Illinois University Edwardsville ... IL ... 149
Trinity Christian College ... IL ... 150
University of Chicago ... IL ... 151
University of Illinois at Chicago ... IL ... 151
University of Illinois Springfield ... IL ... 151
University of Illinois Urbana-Champaign ... IL ... 151
University of St. Francis ... IL ... 152
Western Illinois University ... IL ... 152
Anderson University ... IN ... 153
Ball State University ... IN ... 153
Goshen College ... IN ... 155
Huntington University ... IN ... 155
Indiana State University ... IN ... 155
Indiana University-Purdue University Indianapolis ... IN ... 157
Indiana Wesleyan University ... IN ... 157
Manchester University ... IN ... 158
Marian University ... IN ... 159
Purdue University Northwest ... IN ... 160
Saint Mary's College ... IN ... 160
Taylor University ... IN ... 161
University of Indianapolis ... IN ... 161
University of Saint Francis ... IN ... 162
University of Southern Indiana ... IN ... 162
Valparaiso University ... IN ... 162
Briar Cliff University ... IA ... 163
Buena Vista University ... IA ... 164
Clarke University ... IA ... 164
Dordt University ... IA ... 165
Grand View University ... IA ... 166
Loras College ... IA ... 167
Luther College ... IA ... 167
Mount Mercy University ... IA ... 168
Northwestern College ... IA ... 169
St. Ambrose University ... IA ... 169
University of Iowa ... IA ... 163
University of Northern Iowa ... IA ... 163
Wartburg College ... IA ... 170
Bethel College ... KS ... 171
Fort Hays State University ... KS ... 173
Kansas State University ... KS ... 175
@Kansas Wesleyan University ... KS ... 175
Newman University ... KS ... 176
Pittsburg State University ... KS ... 176
Tabor College ... KS ... 177
University of Kansas Main Campus ... KS ... 177
@University of Saint Mary ... KS ... 177
Washburn University ... KS ... 178
Wichita State University ... KS ... 178
Asbury University ... KY ... 178
Brescia University ... KY ... 179
Campbellsville University ... KY ... 179
Eastern Kentucky University ... KY ... 180
Kentucky Christian University ... KY ... 180
Kentucky State University ... KY ... 183
Morehead State University ... KY ... 183
Murray State University ... KY ... 184
Northern Kentucky University ... KY ... 184
Spalding University ... KY ... 184
University of Kentucky ... KY ... 185
University of Louisville ... KY ... 185
University of Pikeville ... KY ... 185
Western Kentucky University ... KY ... 186
Grambling State University ... LA ... 191
Louisiana Christian University ... LA ... 187
Louisiana State University and Agricultural and Mechanical College ... LA ... 188
Northwestern State University ... LA ... 192
Southeastern Louisiana University ... LA ... 192
Southern University and A&M College ... LA ... 190
Southern University at New Orleans ... LA ... 191
Tulane University ... LA ... 191
University of Louisiana at Monroe ... LA ... 193
Saint Joseph's College of Maine ... ME ... 195
University of Maine ... ME ... 196
University of Maine at Presque Isle ... ME ... 196
University of New England ... ME ... 197
University of Southern Maine ... ME ... 196
Bowie State University ... MD ... 203
Coppin State University ... MD ... 203
Frostburg State University ... MD ... 203
Hood College ... MD ... 199
McDaniel College ... MD ... 200
Morgan State University ... MD ... 200
Salisbury University ... MD ... 204
University of Maryland Baltimore County ... MD ... 202
University of Maryland, Baltimore ... MD ... 202
Anna Maria College ... MA ... 205
Boston College ... MA ... 207
Boston University ... MA ... 207
Bridgewater State University ... MA ... 212
College of Our Lady of the Elms ... MA ... 208
Eastern Nazarene College ... MA ... 208
Lesley University ... MA ... 210
Regis College ... MA ... 217
Salem State University ... MA ... 213
Simmons University ... MA ... 218
Smith College ... MA ... 218
Springfield College ... MA ... 218
Western New England University ... MA ... 219
Westfield State University ... MA ... 213
Adrian College ... MI ... 220
Andrews University ... MI ... 220
Calvin University ... MI ... 221
Central Michigan University ... MI ... 221
Cornerstone University ... MI ... 222
Eastern Michigan University ... MI ... 223
Ferris State University ... MI ... 223
Grand Valley State University ... MI ... 224
Hope College ... MI ... 224
Kuyper College ... MI ... 226
Madonna University ... MI ... 226
Michigan State University ... MI ... 227
Northern Michigan University ... MI ... 228
Oakland University ... MI ... 229
Saginaw Valley State University ... MI ... 229
Siena Heights University ... MI ... 230
Spring Arbor University ... MI ... 230
University of Detroit Mercy ... MI ... 230
University of Michigan-Ann Arbor ... MI ... 231
University of Michigan-Flint ... MI ... 231
Wayne State University ... MI ... 232
Western Michigan University ... MI ... 232
Augsburg University ... MN ... 233
Bemidji State University ... MN ... 237
Bethel University ... MN ... 233
Capella University ... MN ... 234
College of Saint Scholastica, The ... MN ... 234
Concordia College ... MN ... 234
Metropolitan State University ... MN ... 238
Minnesota State University Moorhead ... MN ... 239
Minnesota State University, Mankato ... MN ... 238
North Central University ... MN ... 241
St. Catherine University ... MN ... 242
St. Cloud State University ... MN ... 240
Saint Mary's University of Minnesota ... MN ... 242
St. Olaf College ... MN ... 242
Southwest Minnesota State University ... MN ... 240
University of Minnesota ... MN ... 242
University of Minnesota Duluth ... MN ... 243
University of Saint Thomas ... MN ... 243
Walden University ... MN ... 243
Winona State University ... MN ... 241
Alcorn State University ... MS ... 244
Belhaven University ... MS ... 244
Delta State University ... MS ... 245
Jackson State University ... MS ... 245
Mississippi College ... MS ... 246
Mississippi State University ... MS ... 247
Mississippi Valley State University ... MS ... 247
Rust College ... MS ... 248
University of Mississippi ... MS ... 248
University of Southern Mississippi ... MS ... 248
Avila University ... MO ... 249
Evangel University ... MO ... 252
Fontbonne University ... MO ... 252
Lincoln University ... MO ... 254
Lindenwood University ... MO ... 254
@Maryville University of Saint Louis ... MO ... 254
@Missouri Baptist University ... MO ... 255
Missouri Southern State University ... MO ... 255
Missouri State University ... MO ... 255
Missouri Western State University ... MO ... 256
Park University ... MO ... 257
Saint Louis University ... MO ... 258
Southeast Missouri State University ... MO ... 258
Southwest Baptist University ... MO ... 258
University of Central Missouri ... MO ... 259
University of Missouri - Columbia ... MO ... 260
University of Missouri - Kansas City ... MO ... 260
University of Missouri - Saint Louis ... MO ... 260
Washington University in St. Louis ... MO ... 261
William Woods University ... MO ... 262
@Carroll College ... MT ... 262
Salish Kootenai College ... MT ... 264
University of Montana - Missoula ... MT ... 263
Chadron State College ... NE ... 267
Creighton University ... NE ... 265
Nebraska Wesleyan University ... NE ... 267
Union College ... NE ... 268
University of Nebraska at Kearney ... NE ... 268
University of Nebraska at Omaha ... NE ... 269
University of Nevada, Las Vegas ... NV ... 270
University of Nevada, Reno ... NV ... 270
Plymouth State University ... NH ... 274
University of New Hampshire ... NH ... 273
Centenary University ... NJ ... 275
@Fairleigh Dickinson University ... NJ ... 276
Georgian Court University ... NJ ... 277
Kean University ... NJ ... 277
Monmouth University ... NJ ... 278
Montclair State University ... NJ ... 278
@New Jersey City University ... NJ ... 278
Ramapo College of New Jersey ... NJ ... 280

THEA: National Association of Schools of Theatre: theatre (C,A,B, M,D)

THEOL: The Association of Theological Schools: theology (M, FP,D)

TRACS: Transnational Association of Christian Colleges and Schools: christian studies education (C,A,B, M,D)

VET: American Veterinary Medical Association: veterinary medicine (FP,D)

WC: Western Association of Schools and Colleges, Senior College and University Commission

San Francisco Conservatory of Music	CA	61
San Francisco State University	CA	34
San Joaquin College of Law	CA	61
San Joaquin Valley College, Inc. - Visalia	CA	61
San Jose State University	CA	34
Sanford Burnham Prebys Medical Discovery Institute	CA	62
Santa Clara University	CA	63
Saybrook University	CA	63
Scripps College	CA	63
Scripps Research Institute, The	CA	63
Simpson University	CA	64
Sofia University	CA	64
Soka University of America	CA	64
Sonoma State University	CA	34
Southern California Institute of Architecture	CA	65
Southern California University of Health Sciences	CA	65
Stanford University	CA	66
Stanton University	CA	66
Stockton Christian Life College	CA	67
SUM Bible College and Theological Seminary	CA	67
Teachers College of San Joaquin	CA	67
Thomas Aquinas College	CA	67
Thomas Jefferson School of Law	CA	68
Touro University California	CA	68
Touro University Worldwide	CA	68
Trident University International	CA	68
United States University	CA	68
University Massachusetts Global	CA	71
University of Antelope Valley	CA	68
University of California-Berkeley	CA	68
University of California-Davis	CA	69
University of California-Hastings College of the Law	CA	69
University of California-Irvine	CA	69
University of California-Los Angeles	CA	69
University of California-Merced	CA	70
University of California-Riverside	CA	70
University of California-San Diego	CA	70
University of California-San Francisco	CA	70
University of California-Santa Barbara	CA	70
University of California-Santa Cruz	CA	71
University of La Verne	CA	71
University of Redlands	CA	72
University of St. Augustine for Health Sciences	CA	72
University of Saint Katherine	CA	72
University of San Diego	CA	72
University of San Francisco	CA	72
University of Silicon Andhra	CA	72
University of Silicon Valley	CA	73
University of Southern California	CA	73
University of the Pacific	CA	71
@University of the People	CA	71
University of the West	CA	73
University of West Los Angeles	CA	73
Vanguard University of Southern California	CA	73
@Virscend University	CA	74
Weimar University	CA	74
West Coast University	CA	74
Westcliff University	CA	75
Western University of Health Sciences	CA	75
Westminster Theological Seminary in California	CA	75
Westmont College	CA	75
Whittier College	CA	76
William Jessup University	CA	76
Woodbury University	CA	76
Wright Institute, The	CA	76
Zaytuna College	CA	77
University of Guam	GU	503
Brigham Young University Hawaii	HI	128
Chaminade University of Honolulu	HI	128
Hawaii Pacific University	HI	128
University of Hawaii at Hilo	HI	129
University of Hawaii at Manoa	HI	129
University of Hawaii Maui College	HI	130
University of Hawaii - West Oahu	HI	129
Northern Marianas College	MP	503

WJ: Western Association of Schools and Colleges, Accrediting Commission for Community and Junior Colleges

American Samoa Community College	AS	503

Allan Hancock College	CA	24
American River College	CA	50
Antelope Valley College	CA	26
Bakersfield College	CA	47
Barstow Community College District	CA	26
Berkeley City College	CA	56
Butte College	CA	27
Cabrillo College	CA	27
California Preparatory College	CA	29
Cañada College	CA	62
Carrington College - Sacramento	CA	35
Cerritos College	CA	35
Cerro Coso Community College	CA	47
Chabot College	CA	35
Chaffey College	CA	36
Citrus College	CA	37
City College of San Francisco	CA	37
Clovis Community College	CA	66
Coastline Community College	CA	38
College of Alameda	CA	57
College of Marin	CA	39
College of San Mateo	CA	62
College of the Canyons	CA	38
College of the Desert	CA	39
College of the Sequoias	CA	39
College of the Siskiyous	CA	39
Columbia College	CA	76
Compton College	CA	39
Contra Costa College	CA	40
Copper Mountain College	CA	40
Cosumnes River College	CA	50
Crafton Hills College	CA	60
Cuesta College	CA	41
Cuyamaca College	CA	44
Cypress College	CA	54
De Anza College	CA	42
Deep Springs College	CA	41
Defense Language Institute	CA	501
Diablo Valley College	CA	40
East Los Angeles College	CA	49
El Camino College	CA	41
Evergreen Valley College	CA	62
Feather River College	CA	42
Folsom Lake College	CA	51
Foothill College	CA	43
Fresno City College	CA	67
Fullerton College	CA	54
Gavilan College	CA	43
Glendale Community College	CA	43
Golden West College	CA	38
Grossmont College	CA	44
Hartnell College	CA	44
Imperial Valley College	CA	45
Irvine Valley College	CA	65
Lake Tahoe Community College	CA	47
Laney College	CA	57
Las Positas College	CA	36
Lassen Community College	CA	47
Long Beach City College	CA	48
Los Angeles City College	CA	49
Los Angeles County College of Nursing and Allied Health	CA	50
Los Angeles Harbor College	CA	49
Los Angeles Mission College	CA	49
Los Angeles Pierce College	CA	49
Los Angeles Southwest College	CA	49
Los Angeles Trade-Technical College	CA	50
Los Angeles Valley College	CA	50
Los Medanos College	CA	40
Madera Community College	CA	67
Mendocino College	CA	51
Merced College	CA	52
Merritt College	CA	57
MiraCosta College	CA	52
Mission College	CA	75
Modesto Junior College	CA	76
Monterey Peninsula College	CA	52
Moorpark College	CA	73
Moreno Valley College	CA	59
Mount Tamalpais College	CA	53
Mt. San Antonio College	CA	52
Mt. San Jacinto College	CA	53
MTI College	CA	53
Napa Valley College	CA	53
Norco College	CA	59
Ohlone College	CA	54
Orange Coast College	CA	38
Oxnard College	CA	74

Palo Verde College	CA	56
Palomar College	CA	56
Pasadena City College	CA	56
Porterville College	CA	47
Redwoods Community College District	CA	58
Reedley College	CA	67
Rio Hondo College	CA	58
Riverside City College	CA	59
Sacramento City College	CA	51
Saddleback College	CA	65
Salvation Army College for Officer Training at Crestmont, The	CA	60
San Bernardino Valley College	CA	60
San Diego City College	CA	60
San Diego Mesa College	CA	61
San Diego Miramar College	CA	61
San Joaquin Delta College	CA	61
San Jose City College	CA	62
Santa Ana College	CA	58
Santa Barbara City College	CA	62
Santa Monica College	CA	63
Santa Rosa Junior College	CA	63
Santiago Canyon College	CA	58
Shasta College	CA	64
Sierra College	CA	64
Skyline College	CA	62
Solano Community College	CA	64
Southwestern College	CA	65
Taft College	CA	67
Ventura College	CA	74
Victor Valley College	CA	74
West Hills College Coalinga	CA	74
West Hills College Lemoore	CA	75
West Los Angeles College	CA	50
West Valley College	CA	75
Woodland Community College	CA	77
Young Americans College of Performing Arts, The	CA	77
Yuba College	CA	77
College of Micronesia-FSM	FM	503
Guam Community College	GU	503
Hawaii Tokai International College	HI	128
Kapiolani Community College	HI	129
University of Hawaii - Hawaii Community College	HI	129
University of Hawaii Honolulu Community College	HI	129
University of Hawaii Kauai Community College	HI	129
University of Hawaii - Leeward Community College	HI	130
University of Hawaii Windward Community College	HI	130
College of the Marshall Islands	MH	503
Palau Community College	PW	504

Index of FICE Numbers

1040 002294 – 002788

2023 hep Higher Education Directory®

002294 .... Monroe County Community College .... MI 227
002295 .... Montcalm Community College .... MI 227
002297 .... Muskegon Community College .... MI 228
002299 .... North Central Michigan College .... MI 228
002301 .... Northern Michigan University .... MI 228
002302 .... Northwestern Michigan College .... MI 228
002303 .... Oakland Community College .... MI 228
002307 .... Oakland University .... MI 229
002308 .... Olivet College .... MI 229
002310 .... St. Clair County Community College .... MI 230
002311 .... Kuyper College .... MI 226
002313 .... Sacred Heart Major Seminary .... MI 229
002314 .... Saginaw Valley State University .... MI 229
002315 .... Schoolcraft College .... MI 230
002316 .... Siena Heights University .... MI 230
002317 .... Southwestern Michigan College .... MI 230
002318 .... Spring Arbor University .... MI 230
002322 .... Finlandia University .... MI 223
002323 .... University of Detroit Mercy .... MI 230
002325 .... University of Michigan-Ann Arbor .... MI 231
002326 .... University of Michigan-Dearborn .... MI 231
002327 .... University of Michigan-Flint .... MI 231
002328 .... Washtenaw Community College .... MI 232
002329 .... Wayne State University .... MI 232
002330 .... Western Michigan University .... MI 232
002331 .... Western Theological Seminary .... MI 233
002332 .... Anoka-Ramsey Community College .... MN 236
002334 .... Augsburg University .... MN 233
002335 .... Riverland Community College .... MN 240
002336 .... Bemidji State University .... MN 237
002337 .... Bethany Lutheran College .... MN 233
002339 .... Central Lakes College .... MN 237
002340 .... Carleton College .... MN 234
002341 .... College of Saint Benedict .... MN 234
002342 .... St. Catherine University .... MN 242
002343 .... The College of Saint Scholastica .... MN 234
002345 .... University of Saint Thomas .... MN 243
002346 .... Concordia College .... MN 234
002347 .... Concordia University, St. Paul .... MN 235
002353 .... Gustavus Adolphus College .... MN 235
002354 .... Hamline University .... MN 235
002355 .... Minnesota North College .... MN 238
002357 .... Luther Seminary .... MN 236
002358 .... Macalester College .... MN 236
002360 .... Minnesota State University, Mankato .... MN 238
002361 .... Martin Luther College .... MN 236
002362 .... Minneapolis Cmty & Tech College .... MN 238
002365 .... Minneapolis College of Art & Design .... MN 236
002367 .... Minnesota State University Moorhead .... MN 239
002369 .... North Central University .... MN 241
002370 .... North Hennepin Community College .... MN 239
002371 .... University of Northwestern St. Paul .... MN 243
002373 .... Rochester Community & Tech College .... MN 240
002375 .... Southwest Minnesota State Univ .... MN 240
002377 .... St. Cloud State University .... MN 240
002379 .... Saint John's University .... MN 242
002380 .... St Mary's University of Minnesota .... MN 242
002382 .... St. Olaf College .... MN 242
002383 .... Crown College .... MN 235
002385 .... Northland Community & Tech College .... MN 239
002386 .... United Theol Seminary-Twin Cities .... MN 242
002388 .... University of Minnesota Duluth .... MN 243
002389 .... University of Minnesota-Morris .... MN 243
002391 .... Mitchell Hamline School of Law .... MN 241
002393 .... Minnesota State College Southeast .... MN 238
002394 .... Winona State University .... MN 241
002396 .... Alcorn State University .... MS 244
002397 .... Belhaven University .... MS 244
002398 .... Blue Mountain College .... MS 244
002401 .... Coahoma Community College .... MS 244
002402 .... Copiah-Lincoln Community College .... MS 244
002403 .... Delta State University .... MS 245
002404 .... East Central Community College .... MS 245
002405 .... East Mississippi Community College .... MS 245
002407 .... Hinds Community College .... MS 245
002408 .... Holmes Community College .... MS 245
002409 .... Itawamba Community College .... MS 245
002410 .... Jackson State University .... MS 245
002411 .... Jones County Junior College .... MS 246
002413 .... Meridian Community College .... MS 246
002414 .... Millsaps College .... MS 246
002415 .... Mississippi College .... MS 246
002416 .... Mississippi Delta Community College .... MS 246
002417 .... Mississippi Gulf Coast Cmty College .... MS 246
002422 .... Mississippi University for Women .... MS 247
002423 .... Mississippi State University .... MS 247
002424 .... Mississippi Valley State University .... MS 247
002426 .... Northeast Mississippi Cmty College .... MS 247
002427 .... Northwest Mississippi Cmty College .... MS 247
002430 .... Pearl River Community College .... MS 247
002433 .... Rust College .... MS 248
002435 .... Southeastern Baptist College .... MS 248
002436 .... Southwest Mississippi Cmty College .... MS 248
002439 .... Tougaloo College .... MS 248
002440 .... University of Mississippi .... MS 248
002441 .... University of Southern Mississippi .... MS 248
002447 .... William Carey University .... MS 249
002449 .... Avila University .... MO 249
002450 .... Calvary University .... MO 250
002453 .... Central Methodist University .... MO 250
002454 .... University of Central Missouri .... MO 259
002456 .... Columbia College .... MO 251
002457 .... Concordia Seminary .... MO 251
002458 .... Cottey College .... MO 251
002459 .... Crowder College .... MO 251
002460 .... Culver-Stockton College .... MO 251
002461 .... Drury University .... MO 252
002462 .... Eden Theological Seminary .... MO 252
002463 .... Evangel University .... MO 252
002464 .... Fontbonne University .... MO 252
002466 .... Harris-Stowe State University .... MO 253
002467 .... Conception Seminary College .... MO 251
002468 .... Jefferson College .... MO 253
002471 .... St Louis Cmty College-Cosand Center .... MO 258
002473 .... Kansas City Art Institute .... MO 253
002474 .... Kansas City Univ of Med & BioSci .... MO 253
002476 .... Kenrick-Glennon Seminary .... MO 253
002477 .... A. T. Still Univ of Health Sciences .... MO 249
002479 .... Lincoln University .... MO 254
002480 .... Lindenwood University .... MO 254
002482 .... Maryville University of Saint Louis .... MO 254
002484 .... Metropolitan Cmty Col-Penn Valley .... MO 255
002485 .... Midwestern Baptist Theol Seminary .... MO 255
002486 .... Mineral Area College .... MO 255
002488 .... Missouri Southern State University .... MO 255
002489 .... Missouri Valley College .... MO 256
002490 .... Missouri Western State University .... MO 256
002491 .... Moberly Area Community College .... MO 256
002494 .... Nazarene Theological Seminary .... MO 256
002495 .... Truman State University .... MO 259
002496 .... Northwest Missouri State University .... MO 256
002498 .... Park University .... MO 257
002499 .... Rockhurst University .... MO 257
002500 .... College of the Ozarks .... MO 250
002501 .... Southeast Missouri State University .... MO 258
002502 .... Southwest Baptist University .... MO 258
002503 .... Missouri State University .... MO 255
002504 .... Univ Hlth Sci & Pharm in St Louis .... MO 260
002506 .... Saint Louis University .... MO 258
002509 .... Saint Paul School of Theology .... KS 177
002512 .... Stephens College .... MO 259
002514 .... North Central Missouri College .... MO 256
002515 .... Univ of Missouri System Admin .... MO 260
002516 .... University of Missouri - Columbia .... MO 260
002517 .... Missouri Univ of Science Tech .... MO 260
002518 .... Univ of Missouri - Kansas City .... MO 260
002519 .... Univ of Missouri - Saint Louis .... MO 260
002520 .... Washington University in St. Louis .... MO 261
002521 .... Webster University .... MO 261
002523 .... Westminster College .... MO 261
002524 .... William Jewell College .... MO 261
002525 .... William Woods University .... MO 262
002526 .... Carroll College .... MT 262
002527 .... University of Providence .... MT 264
002528 .... Miles Community College .... MT 262
002529 .... Dawson Community College .... MT 262
002530 .... Montana State University Billings .... MT 263
002531 .... Montana Technological University .... MT 264
002532 .... Montana State University .... MT 263
002533 .... Montana State University - Northern .... MT 264
002534 .... Rocky Mountain College .... MT 264
002536 .... University of Montana - Missoula .... MT 263
002537 .... The University of Montana Western .... MT 263
002539 .... Chadron State College .... NE 267
002540 .... College of Saint Mary .... NE 265
002541 .... Concordia University .... NE 265
002542 .... Creighton University .... NE 265
002544 .... Doane University .... NE 266
002548 .... Hastings College .... NE 266
002551 .... University of Nebraska at Kearney .... NE 268
002553 .... Midland University .... NE 267
002554 .... University of Nebraska at Omaha .... NE 269
002555 .... Nebraska Wesleyan University .... NE 267
002557 .... Mid-Plains Community College .... NE 266
002559 .... Peru State College .... NE 267
002560 .... Western Nebraska Community College .... NE 269
002563 .... Union College .... NE 268
002565 .... University of Nebraska - Lincoln .... NE 269
002566 .... Wayne State College .... NE 267
002567 .... York College .... NE 269
002568 .... University of Nevada, Reno .... NV 270
002569 .... University of Nevada, Las Vegas .... NV 270
002572 .... Colby-Sawyer College .... NH 271
002573 .... Dartmouth College .... NH 272
002575 .... Franklin Pierce University .... NH 272
002579 .... New England College .... NH 272
002580 .... Southern New Hampshire University .... NH 273
002581 .... NHTI-Concord's Community College .... NH 272
002582 .... Manchester Community College .... NH 272
002583 .... Great Bay Community College .... NH 271
002586 .... Rivier University .... NH 273
002587 .... Saint Anselm College .... NH 273
002589 .... University of New Hampshire .... NH 273
002590 .... Keene State College .... NH 274
002591 .... Plymouth State University .... NH 274
002595 .... Assumption College for Sisters .... NJ 274
002596 .... Atlantic Cape Community College .... NJ 274
002597 .... Bloomfield College .... NJ 275
002598 .... Caldwell University .... NJ 275
002599 .... Centenary University .... NJ 275
002600 .... Saint Elizabeth University .... NJ 282
002603 .... Drew University .... NJ 276
002607 .... Fairleigh Dickinson University .... NJ 276
002608 .... Georgian Court University .... NJ 277
002609 .... Rowan University .... NJ 280
002610 .... Felician University .... NJ 277
002613 .... New Jersey City University .... NJ 278
002615 .... Middlesex College .... NJ 278
002616 .... Monmouth University .... NJ 278
002617 .... Montclair State University .... NJ 278
002619 .... New Brunswick Theological Seminary .... NJ 278
002621 .... New Jersey Institute of Technology .... NJ 278
002622 .... Kean University .... NJ 277
002624 .... Ocean County College .... NJ 279
002625 .... William Paterson University of NJ .... NJ 283
002626 .... Princeton Theological Seminary .... NJ 279
002627 .... Princeton University .... NJ 279
002628 .... Rider University .... NJ 280
002629 .... Rutgers University - New Brunswick .... NJ 281
002631 .... Rutgers University - Newark .... NJ 281
002632 .... Seton Hall University .... NJ 282
002638 .... Saint Peter's University .... NJ 282
002639 .... Stevens Institute of Technology .... NJ 282
002642 .... The College of New Jersey .... NJ 275
002643 .... Union College .... NJ 283
002650 .... University of the Southwest .... NM 288
002651 .... Eastern New Mexico University .... NM 285
002653 .... New Mexico Highlands University .... NM 286
002654 .... New Mexico Inst of Mining & Tech .... NM 286
002655 .... New Mexico Junior College .... NM 286
002656 .... New Mexico Military Institute .... NM 286
002657 .... NM State University-Main Campus .... NM 286
002658 .... NM State University-Alamogordo .... NM 286
002659 .... Southeast New Mexico College .... NM 287
002660 .... San Juan College .... NM 287
002661 .... Eastern New Mexico Univ - Roswell .... NM 285
002663 .... Univ of New Mexico Main Campus .... NM 288
002664 .... Western New Mexico University .... NM 288
002665 .... Vaughn Col of Aeronautics & Tech .... NY 323
002666 .... Adelphi University .... NY 288
002668 .... Alfred University .... NY 289
002669 .... Bank Street College of Education .... NY 290
002670 .... Clarks Summit University .... PA 381
002671 .... Bard College .... NY 290
002674 .... New York Theological Seminary .... NY 309
002677 .... Brooklyn Law School .... NY 291
002678 .... Bryant & Stratton College .... NY 291
002681 .... Canisius College .... NY 291
002685 .... Cazenovia College .... NY 292
002687 .... CUNY Brooklyn College .... NY 293
002688 .... CUNY City College .... NY 293
002689 .... CUNY Hunter College .... NY 294
002690 .... CUNY Queens College .... NY 295
002691 .... CUNY Borough of Manhattan CC .... NY 292
002692 .... CUNY Bronx Community College .... NY 292
002693 .... CUNY John Jay Col Criminal Justice .... NY 294
002694 .... CUNY Kingsborough Cmty College .... NY 294
002696 .... NYC Col of Tech/City Univ of NY .... NY 294
002697 .... CUNY Queensborough Cmty Col .... NY 295
002698 .... College of Staten Island CUNY .... NY 293
002699 .... Clarkson University .... NY 295
002700 .... Colgate Roch Crozer Divinity School .... NY 296
002701 .... Colgate University .... NY 296
002703 .... College of Mount Saint Vincent .... NY 296
002705 .... The College of Saint Rose .... NY 296
002707 .... Columbia University in City of NY .... NY 296
002708 .... Barnard College .... NY 290
002710 .... Cooper Union .... NY 297
002711 .... Cornell University .... NY 297
002712 .... D'Youville College .... NY 298
002713 .... Dominican University New York .... NY 298
002718 .... Elmira College .... NY 298
002722 .... Fordham University .... NY 300
002726 .... General Theological Seminary .... NY 300
002728 .... Hamilton College .... NY 300
002729 .... Hartwick College .... NY 300
002731 .... Hobart and William Smith Colleges .... NY 301
002732 .... Hofstra University .... NY 301
002733 .... Holy Trinity Orthodox Seminary .... NY 301
002734 .... Houghton University .... NY 301
002735 .... Hilbert College .... NY 301
002737 .... Iona University .... NY 302
002739 .... Ithaca College .... NY 302
002740 .... Jewish Theol Seminary of America .... NY 303
002741 .... American Jewish University .... CA 25
002742 .... The Juilliard School .... NY 303
002744 .... Keuka College .... NY 303
002748 .... Le Moyne College .... NY 303
002749 .... New York Col of Podiatric Medicine .... NY 308
002751 .... Long Island University .... NY 304
002754 .... Long Island University-LIU Post .... NY 304
002758 .... Manhattan College .... NY 304
002759 .... Manhattan School of Music .... NY 304
002760 .... Manhattanville College .... NY 305
002763 .... Maria College .... NY 305
002765 .... Marist College .... NY 305
002769 .... Marymount Manhattan College .... NY 305
002772 .... Mercy College .... NY 305
002775 .... Molloy University .... NY 306
002777 .... Medaille University .... NY 305
002778 .... Mount Saint Mary College .... NY 307
002779 .... Nazareth College of Rochester .... NY 307
002783 .... New York Law School .... NY 308
002784 .... New York Medical College .... NY 308
002785 .... New York University .... NY 309
002788 .... Niagara University .... NY 309

003252	Delaware Valley University	PA	381
003253	Dickinson College	PA	382
003256	Drexel University	PA	382
003258	Duquesne University	PA	382
003259	Eastern University	PA	383
003262	Elizabethtown College	PA	383
003265	Franklin & Marshall College	PA	383
003266	Gannon University	PA	383
003267	Geneva College	PA	384
003268	Gettysburg College	PA	384
003269	Grove City College	PA	384
003270	Gwynedd Mercy University	PA	384
003272	Harcum College	PA	385
003273	HACC, Central PA Cmty College	PA	385
003274	Haverford College	PA	385
003275	Holy Family University	PA	385
003276	Immaculata University	PA	385
003277	Indiana University of Pennsylvania	PA	393
003279	Juniata College	PA	386
003280	Keystone College	PA	386
003282	King's College	PA	386
003283	Lackawanna College	PA	387
003284	Lafayette College	PA	387
003285	LBC|Capital Seminary & Grad School	PA	387
003286	Lancaster Theological Seminary	PA	387
003287	La Salle University	PA	386
003288	Lebanon Valley College	PA	388
003289	Lehigh University	PA	388
003290	Lincoln University	PA	388
003291	United Lutheran Seminary	PA	399
003293	Lycoming College	PA	388
003294	Manor College	PA	389
003296	Marywood University	PA	389
003297	Mercyhurst University	PA	389
003298	Messiah University	PA	389
003300	Moore College of Art and Design	PA	390
003301	Moravian University	PA	390
003302	Mount Aloysius College	PA	390
003303	Carlow University	PA	380
003304	Muhlenberg College	PA	390
003306	University of Valley Forge	PA	400
003309	Peirce College	PA	391
003311	Salus University	PA	397
003313	Widener University	PA	401
003315	Commonwealth Univ of Pennsylvania	PA	393
003316	Pennsylvania Western University	PA	394
003317	Cheyney University of Pennsylvania	PA	393
003320	East Stroudsburg University of PA	PA	393
003322	Kutztown University of Pennsylvania	PA	394
003325	Millersville University of PA	PA	394
003326	Shippensburg University of PA	PA	394
003327	Slippery Rock University of PA	PA	394
003328	West Chester University of PA	PA	394
003329	Penn State University Park	PA	391
003350	The University of the Arts	PA	399
003351	Cairn University	PA	379
003352	Philadelphia Col of Osteopathic Med	PA	395
003353	Univ of Sciences in Philadelphia	PA	400
003356	Pittsburgh Theological Seminary	PA	395
003357	Point Park University	PA	395
003358	Reformed Presbyterian Theo Seminary	PA	396
003359	Robert Morris University	PA	396
003360	Rosemont College	PA	396
003362	Seton Hill University	PA	397
003364	Saint Charles Borromeo Seminary	PA	396
003366	Saint Francis University	PA	396
003367	Saint Joseph's University	PA	397
003368	Saint Vincent College	PA	397
003369	Susquehanna University	PA	398
003370	Swarthmore College	PA	398
003371	Temple University	PA	398
003376	Thiel College	PA	398
003378	University of Pennsylvania	PA	399
003379	University of Pittsburgh	PA	400
003384	The University of Scranton	PA	400
003385	Ursinus College	PA	400
003386	Valley Forge Military College	PA	400
003388	Villanova University	PA	401
003389	Washington & Jefferson College	PA	401
003391	Waynesburg University	PA	401
003392	Westminster College	PA	401
003393	Westminster Theological Seminary	PA	401
003394	Wilkes University	PA	402
003395	Pennsylvania College of Technology	PA	392
003396	Wilson College	PA	402
003399	York College of Pennsylvania	PA	402
003401	Brown University	RI	403
003402	Bryant University	RI	403
003404	Johnson & Wales University	RI	403
003406	Providence College	RI	403
003407	Rhode Island College	RI	404
003408	Community College of Rhode Island	RI	403
003409	Rhode Island School of Design	RI	404
003410	Roger Williams University	RI	404
003411	Salve Regina University	RI	404
003413	Naval War College	RI	501
003414	University of Rhode Island	RI	404
003417	Allen University	SC	405
003418	Anderson University	SC	405
003419	Charleston Southern University	SC	406
003420	Benedict College	SC	405
003421	Bob Jones University	SC	405
003422	Southern Wesleyan University	SC	411
003423	The Citadel Military College of SC	SC	406
003424	Claflin University	SC	406
003425	Clemson University	SC	406
003426	University of South Carolina Sumter	SC	412
003427	Coker University	SC	407
003428	College of Charleston	SC	407
003429	Columbia International University	SC	407
003430	Columbia College	SC	407
003431	Converse University	SC	407
003432	Erskine College	SC	408
003434	Furman University	SC	408
003435	Lander University	SC	409
003436	Limestone University	SC	409
003438	Medical Univ of South Carolina	SC	409
003439	Morris College	SC	409
003440	Newberry College	SC	409
003441	North Greenville University	SC	410
003445	Presbyterian College	SC	410
003446	South Carolina State University	SC	410
003447	Spartanburg Methodist College	SC	411
003448	Univ of South Carolina-Columbia	SC	412
003449	University of South Carolina Aiken	SC	412
003450	Univ of South Carolina Beaufort	SC	412
003451	Coastal Carolina University	SC	407
003454	Univ of South Carolina Salkehatchie	SC	412
003455	Voorhees College	SC	413
003456	Winthrop University	SC	413
003457	Wofford College	SC	413
003458	Augustana University	SD	413
003459	Black Hills State University	SD	415
003461	Dakota Wesleyan University	SD	414
003463	Dakota State University	SD	415
003465	Mount Marty College	SD	414
003466	Northern State University	SD	415
003467	Presentation College	SD	414
003469	University of Sioux Falls	SD	416
003470	South Dakota Sch of Mines & Tech	SD	415
003471	South Dakota State University	SD	416
003474	The University of South Dakota	SD	415
003477	Aquinas College	TN	416
003478	Austin Peay State University	TN	416
003479	Belmont University	TN	417
003480	Bethel University	TN	417
003481	Carson-Newman University	TN	417
003482	Christian Brothers University	TN	417
003483	Columbia State Community College	TN	423
003484	Covenant College	GA	117
003485	Cumberland University	TN	418
003486	Lipscomb University	TN	420
003487	East Tennessee State University	TN	418
003490	Fisk University	TN	418
003492	Freed-Hardeman University	TN	418
003495	Johnson University	TN	419
003496	King University	TN	419
003499	Lane College	TN	419
003500	Lee University	TN	419
003501	LeMoyne-Owen College	TN	419
003502	Lincoln Memorial University	TN	420
003504	University of Tennessee Southern	TN	426
003505	Maryville College	TN	420
003506	Meharry Medical College	TN	420
003509	The University of Memphis	TN	426
003510	Middle Tennessee State University	TN	421
003511	Milligan University	TN	421
003517	Southern College of Optometry	TN	422
003518	Southern Adventist University	TN	422
003519	Rhodes College	TN	422
003522	Tennessee State University	TN	425
003523	Tennessee Technological University	TN	425
003525	Tennessee Wesleyan University	TN	425
003526	Trevecca Nazarene University	TN	425
003527	Tusculum University	TN	425
003528	Union University	TN	425
003529	Univ of Tennessee Chattanooga	TN	426
003530	University of Tennessee, Knoxville	TN	426
003531	University of Tennessee at Martin	TN	426
003534	Sewanne:The University of the South	TN	422
003535	Vanderbilt University	TN	427
003536	Bryan College	TN	417
003537	Abilene Christian University	TX	427
003539	Alvin Community College	TX	428
003540	Amarillo College	TX	428
003541	Angelo State University	TX	450
003543	Austin College	TX	429
003544	Austin Presbyterian Theol Seminary	TX	429
003545	Baylor University	TX	430
003546	Coastal Bend College	TX	431
003549	Blinn College	TX	430
003553	Cisco College	TX	431
003554	Clarendon College	TX	431
003556	Commonwealth Inst Funeral Service	TX	432
003557	Concordia University Texas	TX	432
003558	North Central Texas College	TX	439
003560	Dallas Baptist University	TX	433
003561	Dallas Col, Cedar Valley Campus	TX	433
003562	Dallas Theological Seminary	TX	434
003563	Del Mar College	TX	434
003564	East Texas Baptist University	TX	435
003565	Texas A & M University - Commerce	TX	446
003566	Seminary of the Southwest	TX	442
003568	Frank Phillips College	TX	435
003570	Grayson College	TX	435
003571	Hardin-Simmons University	TX	436
003572	Trinity Valley Community College	TX	451
003573	Hill College	TX	436
003574	Howard College	TX	436
003575	Howard Payne University	TX	437
003576	Houston Baptist University	TX	436
003577	Huston-Tillotson University	TX	437
003578	University of the Incarnate Word	TX	452
003579	Jacksonville College	TX	437
003580	Kilgore College	TX	437
003581	Lamar University	TX	449
003582	Laredo College	TX	438
003583	Lee College	TX	438
003584	LeTourneau University	TX	438
003586	Lubbock Christian University	TX	438
003588	University of Mary Hardin-Baylor	TX	453
003590	McLennan Community College	TX	438
003591	McMurry University	TX	439
003592	Midwestern State University	TX	439
003593	Navarro College	TX	439
003594	University of North Texas	TX	453
003595	Oblate School of Theology	TX	440
003596	Odessa College	TX	440
003598	Our Lady of the Lake University	TX	440
003599	Univ of Texas Rio Grande Valley	TX	455
003600	Panola College	TX	440
003601	Paris Junior College	TX	440
003602	Paul Quinn College	TX	440
003603	Ranger College	TX	441
003604	Rice University	TX	441
003606	Sam Houston State University	TX	449
003607	Alamo Cmty Coll Dist Central Office	TX	427
003608	St. Philip's College	TX	428
003609	San Jacinto College Central	TX	442
003610	Schreiner University	TX	442
003611	South Plains College	TX	443
003612	University of Houston - Downtown	TX	452
003613	Southern Methodist University	TX	443
003614	Southwest Texas Junior College	TX	443
003615	Texas State University	TX	449
003616	Southwestern Assemblies of God Univ	TX	444
003617	Southwestern Baptist Theol Seminary	TX	444
003618	Southwestern Christian College	TX	444
003619	Southwestern Adventist University	TX	444
003620	Southwestern University	TX	444
003621	St. Edward's University	TX	441
003623	St. Mary's University	TX	442
003624	Stephen F. Austin State University	TX	444
003625	Sul Ross State University	TX	449
003626	Tarrant County College District	TX	445
003627	Temple College	TX	445
003628	Texarkana College	TX	445
003629	The Texas A&M Univ System Office	TX	445
003630	Prairie View A & M University	TX	445
003631	Tarleton State University	TX	445
003632	Texas A & M University	TX	446
003634	Texas State Technical College Waco	TX	448
003635	Texas Chiropractic College	TX	447
003636	Texas Christian University	TX	447
003637	Jarvis Christian College	TX	437
003638	Texas College	TX	448
003639	Texas A & M University - Kingsville	TX	447
003641	Texas Lutheran University	TX	448
003642	Texas Southern University	TX	448
003643	Texas Southmost College	TX	448
003644	Texas Tech University	TX	450
003645	Texas Wesleyan University	TX	450
003646	Texas Woman's University	TX	451
003647	Trinity University	TX	451
003648	Tyler Junior College	TX	451
003651	University of Dallas	TX	451
003652	University of Houston	TX	451
003654	University of St. Thomas	TX	453
003655	The Univ of Texas System Admin	TX	454
003656	The Univ of Texas at Arlington	TX	454
003658	University of Texas at Austin	TX	454
003659	University of Texas HSC San Antonio	TX	455
003661	University of Texas at El Paso	TX	454
003662	Victoria College	TX	456
003663	Wayland Baptist University	TX	457
003664	Weatherford College	TX	457
003665	West Texas A & M University	TX	447
003668	Wharton County Junior College	TX	457
003669	Wiley College	TX	457
003670	Brigham Young University	UT	458
003671	Utah Tech University	UT	459
003672	Ensign College	UT	458
003675	The University of Utah	UT	459
003677	Utah State University	UT	459
003678	Southern Utah University	UT	459
003679	Snow College	UT	460
003680	Weber State University	UT	460
003681	Westminster College	UT	461
003682	Bennington College	VT	461
003683	Castleton University	VT	462
003684	Champlain College	VT	461
003686	Goddard College	VT	461
003688	Northern Vermont University-Johnson	VT	463
003691	Middlebury College	VT	461
003692	Norwich University	VT	461
003694	Saint Michael's College	VT	462

1046 012031 – 025506 2023 hep Higher Education Directory®

012031	San Diego Christian College	CA	60
012050	Rosedale Technical College	PA	396
012059	Trinity Bible Col & Grad School	ND	346
012064	Orion Technical College	IA	169
012105	National Park College	AR	20
012120	Assemblies of God Theol Seminary	MO	249
012123	University of Puerto Rico-Aguadilla	PR	510
012154	California Inst of Integral Studies	CA	29
012165	Atlanta Metropolitan State College	GA	115
012182	Chattahoochee Valley Community Coll	AL	1
012203	St. Peter's Hosp College of Nursing	NY	314
012260	East Arkansas Community College	AR	19
012261	North Arkansas College	AR	20
012277	Northeast College of Health Science	NY	309
012300	Palmer College of Chiropractic	IA	169
012309	University of Western States	OR	377
012315	Cornish College of the Arts	WA	478
012328	Northwestern Health Sciences Univ	MN	241
012358	Plaza College	NY	310
012362	Northwestern College	IL	146
012364	St Paul's School of Nursing-Queens	NY	314
012393	Thomas Jefferson University	PA	398
012452	Evergreen Valley College	CA	62
012500	Ranken Technical College	MO	257
012523	Talmudical Yeshiva of Philadelphia	PA	398
012525	Caribbean University	PR	504
012550	Los Angeles Mission College	CA	49
012561	Five Towns College	NY	299
012574	Ringling College of Art and Design	FL	106
012586	Metropolitan Community College	NE	266
012627	Western Mich Univ Cooley Law School	MI	232
012670	Bel-Rea Inst of Animal Technology	CO	78
012693	Pellissippi State Community College	TN	424
012744	Southside Col of Health Sciences	VA	470
012750	Edison State Community College	OH	352
012803	PFIC at Dominican House of Studies	DC	93
012813	John Wood Community College	IL	140
012842	Oxnard College	CA	74
012860	Arkansas Northeastern College	AR	17
012870	Southern State Community College	OH	360
012896	The North Coast College	OH	357
012907	Lake Tahoe Community College	CA	47
012912	MTI College	CA	53
012954	Hudson County Community College	NJ	277
013007	Nazarene Bible College	CO	82
013022	City University of Seattle	WA	477
013026	Machzikei Hadath Rabbinical College	NY	304
013027	Yeshivath Viznitz	NY	326
013029	Boricua College	NY	291
013039	South University	GA	125
013103	California Western School of Law	CA	34
013132	International Col of Broadcasting	OH	353
013134	Yeshiva Beth Moshe	PA	402
013208	Baptist Bible College	MO	250
013231	University of Houston - Victoria	TX	452
013263	South Hills School of Bus & Tech	PA	397
014659	Oglala Lakota College	SD	414
015361	Guam Community College	GU	503
020503	Academy College	MN	233
020522	Black River Technical College	AR	18
020530	Liberty University	VA	467
020537	Eastwick College	NJ	276
020554	Bossier Parish Community College	LA	187
020603	MIAT College of Technology	MI	227
020630	Montserrat College of Art	MA	216
020635	Coastline Community College	CA	38
020637	Sherman College of Chiropractic	SC	410
020653	Prescott College	AZ	15
020662	The New School	NY	307
020681	Adler University	IL	132
020682	Cox College	MO	251
020683	Douglas Education Center	PA	382
020690	New York School of Interior Design	NY	309
020705	Concordia University Irvine	CA	40
020732	Telshe Yeshiva-Chicago	IL	150
020735	Univ of Arkansas CC at Batesville	AR	23
020739	Wor-Wic Community College	MD	205
020744	Illinois Eastern CC Frontier CC	IL	139
020746	South Arkansas Community College	AR	21
020748	Life University	GA	122
020753	Univ of AR-Pulaski Technical Col	AR	23
020758	Southern Calif Inst of Architecture	CA	65
020771	Milwaukee Institute of Art & Design	WI	493
020774	Dallas College, North Lake Campus	TX	434
020780	Sacred Heart Sem & School of Theol	WI	494
020814	Arlington Baptist University	TX	429
020839	Northern New Mexico College	NM	287
020870	Ozarka College	AR	20
020876	Concordia Theological Seminary	IN	154
020896	Concorde Career Institute	FL	97
020907	Cleveland University - Kansas City	KS	172
020923	Eastwick College	NJ	276
020925	Laurel Technical Institute	PA	387
020937	Long Island Business Institute	NY	304
020961	Fielding Graduate University	CA	42
020983	Western Technical College	TX	457
020988	University of Phoenix	AZ	16
020995	Central Community College	NE	265
021000	Universidad Politecnica de PR	PR	509
021002	Dallas College, Brookhaven Campus	TX	433
021049	Sumner College	OR	376
021073	Pennsylvania Academy of Fine Arts	PA	392
021077	Truckee Meadows Community College	NV	270
021078	University of Hawaii - West Oahu	HI	129
021102	Columbia College Hollywood	CA	39
021111	Univ of Arkansas Rich Mountain	AR	23
021113	Cuyamaca College	CA	44
021116	Sovah School of Health Professions	VA	470
021122	Great Lakes Institute of Technology	PA	384
021136	American InterContinental Univ	AZ	10
021142	Johnson College	PA	386
021163	Pueblo Community College	CO	82
021171	The Art Institute of Houston	TX	429
021175	Naropa University	CO	81
021191	Mission College	CA	75
021206	Saybrook University	CA	63
021207	San Joaquin Valley Col Inc-Visalia	CA	61
021211	Midwest Institute	MO	255
021274	YTI Career Institute	PA	402
021283	Inst for Business & Technology	CA	46
021290	Triangle Tech, Greensburg	PA	399
021366	Wisconsin Lutheran College	WI	497
021383	Palo Alto University	CA	55
021400	Riverside College of Health Careers	VA	469
021404	St. Joseph School of Nursing	NH	273
021408	Martin University	IN	159
021415	Savannah College of Art and Design	GA	124
021434	Salish Kootenai College	MT	264
021435	Sterling College	VT	462
021437	Sinte Gleska University	SD	415
021448	Vet Tech Institute of Houston	TX	456
021464	Institute of American Indian Arts	NM	285
021466	South Mountain Community College	AZ	14
021519	Keiser University	FL	103
021520	Yeshiva Shaar HaTorah-Grodno	NY	325
021553	Chicago Sch of Professional Psych	CA	36
021571	Concorde Career College	TN	418
021585	Ohio Business College	OH	357
021596	The Baptist College of Florida	FL	95
021597	New Hope Christian College	OR	374
021610	Uniformed Svcs Univ of Health Sci	MD	502
021618	Musicians Institute	CA	53
021633	Universidad Central Del Caribe	PR	509
021636	William James College	MA	219
021651	EDP University of Puerto Rico	PR	505
021660	Ctr Advanced Studies PR & Caribbean	PR	504
021661	Nunez Community College	LA	188
021662	ITI Technical College	LA	187
021686	East-West University	IL	137
021691	Davis College	NY	297
021700	Swedish Inst College of Health Sci	NY	321
021706	United States Sports Academy	AL	7
021707	Brunswick Community College	NC	332
021727	Condorde Career Institute	FL	97
021744	Triangle Tech, DuBois	PA	399
021758	Centra College	VA	464
021775	Rio Salado College	AZ	14
021785	Eagle Gate College	UT	458
021800	Northwest Indian College	WA	480
021829	Cambridge College	MA	207
021854	St. Augustine College	IL	148
021882	Sitting Bull College	ND	346
021883	Pentecostal Theological Seminary	TN	421
021889	Hobe Sound Bible College	FL	102
021891	CEM College	PR	504
021907	Fortis College	OH	352
021916	Torah Temimah Talmudical Seminary	NY	322
021922	Thomas Edison State University	NJ	283
021928	Walnut Hill College	PA	401
021989	Michigan School of Psychology	MI	227
021997	Heritage Christian University	AL	5
022023	Pittsburgh Career Institute	PA	395
022027	Ozark Christian College	MO	257
022039	Erie Institute of Technology	PA	383
022042	Chattanooga College	TN	417
022171	Pima Medical Institute-Tucson	AZ	15
022178	Montefiore School of Nursing	NY	307
022188	Brookline College	AZ	11
022195	Mildred Elley	NY	306
022205	God's Bible School and College	OH	353
022209	Cossatot Cmty Coll Univ of Arkansas	AR	22
022220	Amer Film Institute Conservatory	CA	25
022233	Magdalen College of Liberal Arts	NH	273
022260	East Los Angeles College	CA	49
022285	Life Chiropractic College West	CA	48
022316	MGH Institute of Health Professions	MA	216
022345	Boise Bible College	ID	130
022365	Cankdeska Cikana Community College	ND	344
022375	Las Vegas College	NV	270
022385	Central Oklahoma College	OK	365
022418	American Career College-Los Angeles	CA	25
022425	Bastyr University	WA	476
022427	Berkeley City College	CA	56
022429	United Tribes Technical College	ND	346
022449	Goodwin University	CT	87
022537	IntelliTec College	CO	81
022594	Amberton University	TX	428
022606	National University College	PR	508
022608	Huertas College	PR	505
022624	Yeshiva Ohr Elchonon Chabad	CA	76
022651	Yeshiva Derech Chaim	NY	324
022664	Central Christian College of Bible	MO	250
022676	Sofia University	CA	64
022699	Pennsylvania Col of Art & Design	PA	392
022706	Life Pacific University	CA	48
022708	Joyce Univ of Nursing & Health Sci	UT	458
022713	Wisc Sch of Professional Psychology	WI	497
022734	Reconstructionist Rabbinical Col	PA	396
022743	Conway School of Landscape Design	MA	208
022751	Concorde Career Institute	FL	97
022768	Westminster Theological Seminary	CA	75
022769	Community College of Aurora	CO	80
022773	Sisseton-Wahpeton College	SD	415
022774	South Coast College	CA	64
022781	Santa Fe Community College	NM	287
022788	Southern Technical College	FL	108
022795	Oconee Fall Line Tech Col-South	GA	123
022809	Mid-Atlantic Christian University	NC	331
022827	Inter Amer Univ of PR Guayama	PR	507
022828	Inter Amer Univ of PR Fajardo	PR	507
022843	Interactive College of Technology	GA	121
022866	Little Big Horn College	MT	262
022884	Gwinnett Technical College	GA	121
022980	Design Institute of San Diego	CA	41
022993	Trinity Episcopal School Ministry	PA	399
023011	Turtle Mountain Community College	ND	346
023014	East Ohio College	OH	352
023043	Platt College	CA	57
023053	Parker University	TX	440
023058	Florida Career College	FL	99
023068	Miller-Motte College	TN	421
023108	Lancaster County Career & Tech Ctr	PA	387
023141	Schiller International University	FL	108
023154	Northeast Texas Community College	TX	440
023172	Maranatha Baptist University	WI	492
023182	KD Conservatory Col Film/Dram Arts	TX	437
023192	Lake Forest Graduate School of Mgmt	IL	141
023202	Houston Graduate School of Theology	TX	436
023230	Missio Seminary	PA	389
023251	Key College	FL	103
023263	Fortis Institute	TN	418
023268	Meridian College	FL	104
023289	Emmaus Bible College	IA	165
023305	Laguna College of Art & Design	CA	47
023308	JRMC School of Nursing	AR	20
023312	Baptist Missionary Assn Theol Sem	TX	430
023313	Interactive College of Technology	TX	437
023344	Centura College	VA	464
023355	Universidad Teologica Del Caribe	PR	510
023377	Professional Skills Institute	OH	359
023385	Glendale Career College	CA	43
023405	St Louis Col Health Careers	MO	258
023406	Humacao Community College	PR	506
023413	Palo Alto College	TX	428
023430	Fort Peck Community College	MT	262
023482	Arkansas State University Mid-South	AR	18
023485	Lamar State College-Port Arthur	TX	449
023576	Navajo Technical University	NM	286
023580	Thomas Aquinas College	CA	67
023582	Lamar State College Orange	TX	449
023593	Shasta Bible Col & Graduate School	CA	63
023608	Provo College	UT	458
023613	The Landing School	ME	194
023614	Collin College	TX	432
023616	Concorde Career College	MO	251
023621	Full Sail University	FL	101
023638	Yeshiva Beth Yehuda	MI	233
024535	Medical College of Wisconsin	WI	492
024544	Northeast Ohio Medical University	OH	357
024600	Univ of Puerto Rico-Medical Sci	PR	511
024821	Morehouse School of Medicine	GA	123
024824	Ponce Health Sciences University	PR	508
024827	Western Univ of Health Sciences	CA	75
024911	Beckfield College	KY	179
025000	San Joaquin College of Law	CA	61
025034	Amridge University	AL	4
025039	Warren County Community College	NJ	283
025042	Walden University	MN	243
025054	Atlantic University College	PR	504
025058	Yesh Karlin Stolin Beth Aaron Inst	NY	325
025059	Sh'or Yoshuv Rabbinical College	NY	314
025061	City University of New York	NY	292
025083	Southeast Community College	NE	268
025089	Talmudic College of Florida	FL	112
025106	Blackfeet Community College	MT	262
025110	SW Indian Polytechnic Institute	NM	288
025154	City College	FL	97
025162	Wesley Biblical Seminary	MS	249
025175	Aaniiih Nakoda College	MT	262
025203	Interior Designers Institute	CA	46
025228	Fox College	IL	138
025306	St. Charles Community College	MO	258
025322	Lac Courte Oreilles Ojibwa College	WI	491
025326	Landmark College	VT	461
025332	The School of Architecture	AZ	15
025340	National Univ of Natural Medicine	OR	374
025356	Clear Creek Baptist Bible College	KY	180
025366	Commonwealth Technical Inst at HGAC	PA	381
025383	Delta College of Arts & Technology	LA	186
025395	Irvine Valley College	CA	65
025410	Alaska Career College	AK	9
025452	Chief Dull Knife College	MT	262
025462	Laurel Business Institute	PA	387
025463	Yeshiva of the Telshe Alumni	NY	325
025476	Florida National University Hialeah	FL	100
025506	Talmudic Institute Upstate New York	NY	321

© COPYRIGHT HIGHER EDUCATION PUBLICATIONS, INC. 2022

1048 038214 – 667046 2023 hep Higher Education Directory®

038214	Universal College of Healing Arts	NE	268
038224	Maple Springs Baptist Bible College	MD	200
038273	Charlotte Christian Col & Theol Sem	NC	327
038303	SAE Institute Nashville	TN	422
038333	American Acad Health/Wellness	MN	233
038383	Nightingale College	UT	458
038385	Northwest Career College	NV	271
038403	Omega Graduate School	TN	421
038425	Cambridge Inst Allied Health & Tech	FL	96
038513	Dallas International University	TX	434
038533	Keck Graduate Institute	CA	37
038553	Ecclesia College	AR	19
038626	Veritas Baptist College	IN	162
038683	World Mission University	CA	76
038684	Los Angeles College of Music	CA	49
038713	Folsom Lake College	CA	51
038724	Divine Mercy University	VA	465
038744	Community Christian College	CA	39
038883	Dragon Rises Col of Oriental Med	FL	98
038893	Stanbridge University	CA	66
038943	Huntsville Bible College	AL	5
039035	Southern Technical College	FL	108
039104	National Polytechnic College	CA	53
039193	St Tikhon's Orthodox Theol Seminary	PA	397
039214	White Earth Tribal/Community Col	MN	244
039324	Gutenberg College	OR	373
039373	Yeshiva Col of the Nation's Capital	MD	205
039396	Daytona College	FL	97
039413	Ave Maria University	FL	95
039454	Logos Evangelical Seminary	CA	48
039463	Franklin W. Olin Col of Engineering	MA	209
039483	Harrisburg Univ Science/Technology	PA	385
039493	Won Institute of Graduate Studies	PA	402
039513	Patrick Henry College	VA	468
039563	South Louisiana Community College	LA	188
039573	Blue Ridge Cmty & Technical College	WV	487
039603	New River Community/Technical Col	WV	487
039663	Virginia Beach Theol Seminary	VA	472
039704	WellSpring Sch Allied Health-KC	MO	261
039713	American Career College-Ontario	CA	25
039733	SAE Expression College	CA	59
039745	California Career College	CA	28
039803	California State U-Channel Islands	CA	30
039823	Visible Music College	TN	427
039863	Aviator Col of Aeronaut Sci & Tech	FL	95
039893	Mid-America Reformed Seminary	IN	159
039923	Knox Theological Seminary	FL	103
039953	University of East-West Medicine	CA	71
040024	Ecumenical Theological Seminary	MI	223
040053	United States University	CA	68
040373	Los Angeles Film School	CA	50
040383	ATA College	KY	179
040385	Pierpont Community/Technical Col	WV	487
040386	BridgeValley Cmty & Tech College	WV	487
040414	Mountwest Cmty & Technical College	WV	487
040443	Hazelden Grad Sch of Addiction Stds	MN	235
040573	Asher College	CA	26
040603	ATA College	OK	365
040653	Roseman Univ of Health Sciences	NV	271
040743	Hondros College of Nursing	OH	353
040764	Gnomon	CA	44
040803	Aspen University	AZ	11
040813	Bais Medrash Toras Chesed	NJ	274
040834	Cambridge College	FL	96
040953	The King's College	NY	303
040963	Charleston School of Law	SC	406
041004	The Taft University System	CO	83
041103	University of Management & Tech	VA	471
041113	West Hills College Lemoore	CA	75
041123	Louisiana Culinary Institute	LA	188
041143	Nevada State College	NV	270
041144	The Institute of World Politics	DC	93
041145	Valley College of Medical Careers	CA	73
041155	Talmudical Seminary of Bobov	NY	321
041164	Future-Tech Institute	FL	101
041166	Taylor College	FL	112
041174	Milwaukee Career College	WI	493
041180	Byzantine Catholic Seminary	PA	379
041187	American Business & Technology Univ	MO	249
041188	New York Film Academy, Los Angeles	CA	53
041190	Eastern WV Community & Tech College	WV	487
041191	City Vision University	MO	250
041196	Yeshiva of Far Rockaway	NY	325
041212	Inst of Taoist Educ/Acupuncture	CO	81
041215	Columbia Southern University	AL	5
041218	Criswell College	TX	433
041228	Presbyterian Theol Sem in America	CA	58
041234	Yeshivas Be'er Yitzchok	NJ	284
041238	Williamson College of the Trades	PA	402
041242	Catholic Distance University	WV	486
041245	MyComputerCareer	OH	357
041247	Ambria College of Nursing	IL	132
041271	University of California-Merced	CA	70
041273	Columbia College	VA	465
041276	California Coast University	CA	28
041279	Trident University International	CA	68
041284	Miami Regional University	FL	104
041292	Bottega University	UT	458
041298	MediaTech Institute	TX	439
041301	Louisiana Delta Community College	LA	188
041302	Inst of Production and Recording	MN	235
041305	Pacific NW Univ of Health Sciences	WA	481
041311	Yeshiva Toras Chaim	NJ	284
041317	Southwest University at El Paso	TX	444
041327	Healthcare Career College	CA	45
041331	California Univ Management/Sciences	CA	34
041341	Jersey College	NJ	277
041381	Yeshiva of Machzikai Hadas	NY	325
041385	HIC-Cardiotech Ultrasound School	TX	436
041386	Alaska Christian College	AK	9
041390	Midwestern Career College	IL	144
041398	Delaware College of Art and Design	DE	90
041403	Montana Bible College	MT	263
041405	Horizon University	IN	155
041414	Laurus College	CA	48
041425	Touro University Worldwide	CA	68
041426	Touro University California	CA	68
041427	Pontifical JP II Inst for Stds M&F	DC	93
041429	Georgia Gwinnett College	GA	119
041432	Hult International Business School	MA	210
041438	Woodland Community College	CA	77
041440	Fairfax University of America	VA	466
041460	National Career College	CA	53
041461	Urshan Col/Graduate Sch of Theology	MO	261
041464	Daoist Trad Col of Chinese Med Arts	NC	328
041483	Denver College of Nursing	CO	80
041497	Homestead Schools	CA	45
041519	Columbia Gorge Community College	OR	372
041538	Ascent College	VA	463
041539	Providence Christian College	CA	58
041542	Carolina Col of Biblical Studies	NC	327
041550	NW School of Wooden Boatbuilding	WA	480
041551	Inst of Medical & Business Careers	PA	386
041555	Academy for Jewish Religion, Calif	CA	24
041563	University of Fort Lauderdale	FL	112
041565	Georgia Central University	GA	118
041574	National Paralegal College	AZ	14
041596	Galaxy Medical College	CA	43
041597	American Medical Sciences Center	CA	25
041604	Angeles College	CA	26
041618	University Massachusetts Global	CA	71
041620	Jose Maria Vargas University	FL	102
041633	Compass College of Film & Media	MI	222
041647	Keweenaw Bay Ojibwa Cmty Col	MI	225
041650	Meridian Inst of Surgical Assisting	TN	420
041672	Geisinger Commonwealth Sch Medicine	PA	384
041687	Peloton College	TX	440
041697	Unitek College	CA	68
041698	Gurnick Academy of Medical Arts	CA	44
041730	Shepherds Theological Seminary	NC	340
041735	Moreno Valley College	CA	59
041737	Manna University	NC	330
041748	American Trade School	MO	249
041761	Norco College	CA	59
041763	Bergin University of Canine Studies	CA	27
041771	Pima Medical Institute	CO	82
041780	Simmons College of Kentucky	KY	184
041795	North American University	TX	439
041803	Keser Torah-Mayan Hatalmud	NJ	277
041806	Appalachian College of Pharmacy	VA	463
041814	Best Care College	NJ	275
041816	Integrity College of Health	CA	46
041822	Hawaii Medical College	HI	128
041825	Millennia Atlantic University	FL	104
041850	Colorado Academy of Veterinary Tech	CO	78
041855	Beverly Hills Design Institute	CA	27
041884	Bais HaMedrash & Mesivta Baltimore	MD	197
041888	Inst Doctoral Studies Visual Arts	ME	194
041921	American Medical Academy	FL	95
041922	Athena Career Academy	OH	347
041924	Yeshiva Gedolah Zichron Leyma	NJ	284
041928	Be'er Yaakov Talmudic Seminary	NY	290
041930	Rio Grande Valley College	TX	441
041932	Rocky Mountain Univ Health Prof	UT	459
041937	John Paul the Great Catholic Univ	CA	46
041944	American Col of Healthcare Sciences	OR	371
042061	International Inst Restorative Prac	PA	386
042063	FVI School of Nursing and Technolog	FL	101
042064	Helms College	GA	121
042087	Colorado State Univ-Global Campus	CO	79
042108	NRI Institute of Health Sciences	FL	105
042118	College of Western Idaho	ID	131
042176	Sessions College for Prof Design	AZ	15
042281	High Desert Medical College	CA	45
042293	MedQuest College	KY	183
042339	Atlantis University	FL	95
042340	San Francisco Film School	CA	61
042350	Felbry College School of Nursing	OH	352
042434	Lionel University	CA	48
042447	Med Academy	FL	104
042454	Infinity College	LA	186
042506	California Inst of Advanced Mgmt	CA	28
042517	Hope College of Arts & Sciences	FL	102
042554	Regan Career Institute	CA	58
042557	Bolivar Technical College	MO	250
042568	Arkansas Colleges of Health Educ	AR	17
042580	Seattle Film Institute	WA	482
042590	Yeshiva Shaar Ephraim	NY	325
042615	Mechon L'Hoyroa	NY	305
042703	Yeshivas Emek Hatorah	NJ	284
042712	Seminary Bnos Chaim	NJ	282
042738	Yeshiva Gedola Tiferes Yerachmiel	NJ	284
042749	Contra Costa Medical Career College	CA	40
042766	Yeshiva of Ocean	NY	325
042769	Cong Talmidel Mesivta Tif Schm Alek	NY	297
042785	Yeshivat Hechal Shemuel	NY	326
042788	Los Angeles Pacific University	CA	50
042796	Yeshiva Ohr Zechariah	NJ	284
042797	Albert Einstein College of Medicine	NY	289
042801	Yeshiva Gedola Tif Yaakov Yitzchok	NJ	284
042830	American Col of the Building Arts	SC	405
042846	Bais Medrash of Dexter Park	NY	290
042933	Hackensack Meridian Sch of Medicine	NJ	277
043017	Yeshiva of Kasho	NY	325
666003	The Claremont College Services	CA	37
666013	American University of Armenia	CA	25
666018	Saint Vincent Seminary	PA	397
666020	Salvation Army Col Ofcr Training	NY	314
666050	Central Baptist Theol Sem of Mnpls	MN	234
666086	Carrington College - Admin Office	CA	35
666092	Maine Community College System	ME	194
666106	Ashworth College	GA	115
666127	St. John Vianney Theol Seminary	CO	83
666132	Alliant Internatl Univ Pres Ofc	CA	25
666153	Arkansas State University-Newport	AR	18
666166	New Saint Andrews College	ID	131
666169	Harrison Middleton University	AZ	12
666176	Olivet University	CA	55
666185	Wisconsin Technical College System	WI	497
666187	Arkansas State University System	AR	17
666188	Louisiana Cmty & Tech Coll System	LA	187
666228	Brite Divinity School	TX	431
666233	The Colburn School	CA	38
666234	Washington University of Virginia	VA	476
666235	United States Army War College	PA	502
666242	American College of Education	IN	153
666251	National College of Midwifery	NM	286
666255	Holmes Inst Consciousness Studies	CO	81
666281	Midwives College of Utah	UT	458
666295	Metropolitan Cmty Col-Business/Tech	MO	254
666311	Arkansas State Univ-Mountain Home	AR	18
666315	Dunlap-Stone University	AZ	12
666333	TCM International Institute	IN	161
666340	John Leland Ctr Theological Studies	VA	467
666360	International Theological Seminary	CA	46
666367	Toyota Technological Inst Chicago	IL	150
666393	National Intelligence University	DC	501
666395	Rio Grande Bible Institute	TX	441
666398	Taft Law School	CA	67
666462	Community Col System New Hampshire	NH	271
666478	Yuba Community College District	CA	77
666601	Inter Amer Univ of PR Sch Optometry	PR	507
666616	Robert E. Webber Inst Worship Stds	FL	106
666640	Evangelia University	CA	42
666642	Grace Mission University	CA	44
666643	Gerstner Grad Sch of Biomedical Sci	NY	304
666644	Lutheran Brethren Seminary	MN	236
666647	Tillamook Bay Community College	OR	376
666649	NM State Univ Dona Ana Cmty College	NM	287
666651	Anaheim University	CA	26
666653	Atlantic University	VA	463
666656	Connecticut Bd of Regents Higher Ed	CT	85
666658	Suffolk Cty Cmty Coll Central Admin	NY	320
666670	California Intercontinental Univ	CA	29
666671	Elmezzi Grad Sch of Molecular Med	NY	298
666683	Fortis Institute	AL	5
666687	Global University	MO	252
666689	Texas A & M University-San Antonio	TX	447
666713	California Miramar University	CA	29
666714	Future Generations University	WV	486
666715	Lakewood University	OH	355
666719	College of Medicine, Mayo Clinic	MN	234
666721	AMDA Col & Conservatory of Perf Art	CA	25
666745	Marine Corps University	VA	501
666747	San Jacinto College North	TX	442
666748	San Jacinto College South	TX	442
666759	San Francisco Bay University	CA	61
666776	U.S. Career Institute	CO	84
666809	College for Financial Planning	CO	78
666813	Inter Amer Univ of PR School of Law	PR	507
666828	Bryant & Stratton College Sys Ofc	NY	291
666923	Baker Professional Services, Inc.	MI	221
666925	Chabot-Las Positas CC District	CA	35
666971	Huntington Univ of Health Sciences	TN	419
666974	The JAG Legal Center & School	VA	501
666982	Patten University	CA	56
666993	WV Council Cmty/Tech Col Educ	WV	487
667002	Rocky Vista University	CO	83
667003	Rich Gilder Grad Sch @ Am Mus Nat H	NY	311
667006	The SANS Technology Institute	MD	202
667007	Sotheby's Institute of Art	NY	315
667008	Five Br Univ, Grad Sch Trad Ch Med	CA	42
667009	National Test Pilot School	CA	53
667010	Pacific Rim Christian University	HI	128
667014	All Saints Bible College	TN	416
667017	Acacia University	AZ	10
667020	California Northstate University	CA	29
667026	Antioch Sch Ch Plnt/Ldrship Dev	IA	163
667027	Saint Gregory the Great Seminary	NE	268
667034	Rasmussen Univ Corporate Office	MN	241
667035	Martinsburg College	WV	486
667039	Riverside Community College Dist	CA	59
667040	San Bernardino Community Col Dist	CA	60
667041	West Hills Community College Dist	CA	74
667045	Eternity Bible College	CA	42
667046	Mid-South Christian College	TN	421

© COPYRIGHT HIGHER EDUCATION PUBLICATIONS, INC. 2022

Index of Universities, Colleges and Schools

Aquinas Institute of Theology	MISSOURI	249
Arapahoe Community College	COLORADO	77
Arcadia University	PENNSYLVANIA	378
Arizona Christian University	ARIZONA	10
Arizona College-Mesa	ARIZONA	10
Arizona College of Nursing	ARIZONA	10
Arizona School of Acupuncture and Oriental Medicine	ARIZONA	10
Arizona State University	ARIZONA	11
Arizona Western College	ARIZONA	11
Arkansas Baptist College	ARKANSAS	17
Arkansas Colleges of Health Education	ARKANSAS	17
Arkansas Northeastern College	ARKANSAS	17
Arkansas State University-Beebe	ARKANSAS	17
Arkansas State University-Jonesboro	ARKANSAS	17
Arkansas State University Mid-South	ARKANSAS	18
Arkansas State University-Mountain Home	ARKANSAS	18
Arkansas State University-Newport	ARKANSAS	18
Arkansas State University System	ARKANSAS	17
Arkansas State University-Three Rivers	ARKANSAS	18
Arkansas Tech University	ARKANSAS	18
Arkansas Tech University-Ozark Campus	ARKANSAS	18
Arlington Baptist University	TEXAS	429
Arnot Ogden Medical Center	NEW YORK	290
Art Academy of Cincinnati	OHIO	347
Art Institute of Atlanta, The	GEORGIA	114
Art Institute of Austin, The	TEXAS	429
Art Institute of Dallas	TEXAS	429
Art Institute of Houston, The	TEXAS	429
Art Institute of San Antonio, The	TEXAS	429
Art Institute of Tampa, a branch of Miami International University of Art & Design, The	FLORIDA	95
Art Institute of Virginia Beach, The	VIRGINIA	463
Art of Education University, The	IOWA	163
ArtCenter College of Design	CALIFORNIA	26
ASA College	NEW YORK	290
Asbury Theological Seminary	KENTUCKY	178
Asbury University	KENTUCKY	178
Ascent College	VIRGINIA	463
Asher College	CALIFORNIA	26
Asheville - Buncombe Technical Community College	NORTH CAROLINA	331
Ashland Community and Technical College	KENTUCKY	180
Ashland University	OHIO	347
Ashworth College	GEORGIA	115
Asnuntuck Community College	CONNECTICUT	86
Aspen University	ARIZONA	11
Aspira City College	PENNSYLVANIA	378
Assemblies of God Theological Seminary	MISSOURI	249
Assumption College for Sisters	NEW JERSEY	274
Assumption University	MASSACHUSETTS	205
ATA Career Education-Spring Hill	FLORIDA	95
ATA College	CALIFORNIA	26
ATA College	KENTUCKY	179
ATA College	OHIO	347
ATA College	OKLAHOMA	365
Atenas College	PUERTO RICO	504
Athena Career Academy	OHIO	347
Athenaeum of Ohio	OHIO	348
Athens College of Ministry	GEORGIA	115
Athens State University	ALABAMA	4
Athens Technical College	GEORGIA	115
ATI College	CALIFORNIA	26
Atlanta Institute of Music and Media	GEORGIA	115
Atlanta Metropolitan State College	GEORGIA	115
Atlanta Technical College	GEORGIA	115
Atlanta's John Marshall Law School	GEORGIA	115
Atlantic Cape Community College	NEW JERSEY	274
Atlantic Institute of Oriental Medicine	FLORIDA	95
Atlantic University	VIRGINIA	463
Atlantic University College	PUERTO RICO	504
Atlantis University	FLORIDA	95
Auburn University	ALABAMA	4
Auburn University at Montgomery	ALABAMA	4
Augsburg University	MINNESOTA	233
Augusta Technical College	GEORGIA	115
Augusta University	GEORGIA	115
Augustana College	ILLINOIS	132
Augustana University	SOUTH DAKOTA	413
Auguste Escoffier School of Culinary Arts	COLORADO	77
Auguste Escoffier School of Culinary Arts	TEXAS	429
Augustine Institute	COLORADO	77
Aultman College of Nursing and Health Sciences	OHIO	348
Aurora University	ILLINOIS	133
Austin College	TEXAS	429
Austin Community College District	TEXAS	429
Austin Peay State University	TENNESSEE	416
Austin Presbyterian Theological Seminary	TEXAS	429
Ave Maria School of Law	FLORIDA	95
Ave Maria University	FLORIDA	95
Averett University	VIRGINIA	463
Aviator College of Aeronautical Science & Technology	FLORIDA	95
Avila University	MISSOURI	249

Azure College	FLORIDA	95
Azusa Pacific University	CALIFORNIA	26
Babson College	MASSACHUSETTS	205
Bacone College	OKLAHOMA	365
Bais Binyomin Academy, Inc	NEW YORK	290
Bais HaMedrash & Mesivta of Baltimore	MARYLAND	197
Bais Medrash Ateres Shlomo	NEW YORK	290
Bais Medrash Mayan Hatorah	NEW JERSEY	274
Bais Medrash of Dexter Park	NEW YORK	290
Bais Medrash Toras Chesed	NEW JERSEY	274
Bais Medrash Zichron Meir	NEW JERSEY	274
Baker College of Auburn Hills	MICHIGAN	221
Baker College of Cadillac	MICHIGAN	221
Baker College of Jackson	MICHIGAN	221
Baker College of Muskegon	MICHIGAN	221
Baker College of Owosso	MICHIGAN	221
Baker Professional Services, Inc.	MICHIGAN	221
Baker University	KANSAS	171
Baker University School of Professional and Graduate Studies	KANSAS	171
Bakersfield College	CALIFORNIA	47
Bakke Graduate University	TEXAS	429
Baldwin Wallace University	OHIO	348
Ball State University	INDIANA	153
Baltimore City Community College	MARYLAND	197
Bank Street College of Education	NEW YORK	290
Baptist Bible College	MISSOURI	250
Baptist College of Florida, The	FLORIDA	95
Baptist Health College Little Rock	ARKANSAS	18
Baptist Health Sciences University	TENNESSEE	417
Baptist Health System School of Health Professions	TEXAS	430
Baptist Hospitals of Southeast Texas School of Radiologic Technology	TEXAS	430
Baptist Missionary Association Theological Seminary	TEXAS	430
Baptist Seminary of Kentucky	KENTUCKY	179
Baptist University of the Americas	TEXAS	430
Barclay College	KANSAS	171
Bard College	NEW YORK	290
Bard College at Simon's Rock	MASSACHUSETTS	205
Barnard College	NEW YORK	290
Barry University	FLORIDA	96
Barstow Community College District	CALIFORNIA	26
Barton College	NORTH CAROLINA	326
Barton County Community College	KANSAS	171
Baruch College/City University of New York	NEW YORK	292
Bastyr University	WASHINGTON	476
Bates College	MAINE	193
Bates Technical College	WASHINGTON	477
Baton Rouge Community College	LOUISIANA	187
Bay Atlantic University	DISTRICT OF COLUMBIA	91
Bay College West Campus	MICHIGAN	221
Bay de Noc Community College	MICHIGAN	221
Bay Mills Community College	MICHIGAN	221
Bay Path University	MASSACHUSETTS	205
Bay State College	MASSACHUSETTS	206
Baylor College of Medicine	TEXAS	430
Baylor University	TEXAS	430
Beacon College	FLORIDA	96
Beal University	MAINE	193
Beaufort County Community College	NORTH CAROLINA	332
Beckfield College	KENTUCKY	179
Be'er Yaakov Talmudic Seminary	NEW YORK	290
Beis Medrash Heichal Dovid	NEW YORK	290
Bel-Rea Institute of Animal Technology	COLORADO	78
Belanger School of Nursing, The	NEW YORK	290
Belhaven University	MISSISSIPPI	244
Bellarmine University	KENTUCKY	179
Bellevue College	WASHINGTON	477
Bellevue University	NEBRASKA	265
Bellin College, Inc.	WISCONSIN	490
Bellingham Technical College	WASHINGTON	477
Belmont Abbey College	NORTH CAROLINA	326
Belmont College	OHIO	348
Belmont University	TENNESSEE	417
Beloit College	WISCONSIN	490
Bemidji State University	MINNESOTA	237
Benedict College	SOUTH CAROLINA	405
Benedictine College	KANSAS	171
Benedictine University	ILLINOIS	133
Benedictine University Mesa	ARIZONA	11
Benjamin Franklin Institute of Technology	MASSACHUSETTS	206
Bennett College	NORTH CAROLINA	326
Bennington College	VERMONT	461
Bentley University	MASSACHUSETTS	206
Berea College	KENTUCKY	179
Bergen Community College	NEW JERSEY	274
Bergin University of Canine Studies	CALIFORNIA	27
Berkeley City College	CALIFORNIA	56
Berkeley College	NEW JERSEY	274
Berkeley College	NEW YORK	291
Berkeley School of Theology	CALIFORNIA	27

College of the Holy Cross	MASSACHUSETTS	208
College of the Mainland	TEXAS	432
College of the Marshall Islands	MARSHALL ISLANDS	503
College of the Muscogee Nation	OKLAHOMA	365
College of the Ozarks	MISSOURI	250
College of the Sequoias	CALIFORNIA	39
College of the Siskiyous	CALIFORNIA	39
College of Westchester, The	NEW YORK	296
College of Western Idaho	IDAHO	131
College of William & Mary	VIRGINIA	465
College of Wooster, The	OHIO	350
College Unbound	RHODE ISLAND	403
Colleges of Law, The	CALIFORNIA	39
Collin College	TEXAS	432
Colorado Academy of Veterinary Technology	COLORADO	78
Colorado Christian University	COLORADO	78
Colorado College	COLORADO	78
Colorado Mesa University	COLORADO	78
Colorado Mesa University-Montrose Campus	COLORADO	78
Colorado Mountain College	COLORADO	78
Colorado Mountain College Alpine Campus	COLORADO	78
Colorado Mountain College Aspen	COLORADO	78
Colorado Mountain College Leadville	COLORADO	78
Colorado Mountain College Rifle	COLORADO	78
Colorado Mountain College Roaring Fork Campus-Spring Valley	COLORADO	78
Colorado Mountain College Summit Campus-Breckinridge Center	COLORADO	78
Colorado Mountain College Vail Valley Campus at Edwards	COLORADO	78
Colorado Northwestern Community College	COLORADO	78
Colorado School of Mines	COLORADO	79
Colorado School of Trades	COLORADO	79
Colorado School of Traditional Chinese Medicine	COLORADO	79
Colorado State University	COLORADO	79
Colorado State University Global	COLORADO	79
Colorado State University-Pueblo	COLORADO	79
Colorado State University System Office	COLORADO	79
Colorado Technical University	COLORADO	80
Columbia Basin College	WASHINGTON	478
Columbia Central University	PUERTO RICO	505
Columbia College	CALIFORNIA	76
Columbia College	MISSOURI	251
Columbia College	SOUTH CAROLINA	407
Columbia College	VIRGINIA	465
Columbia College Chicago	ILLINOIS	136
Columbia College Hollywood	CALIFORNIA	39
Columbia Gorge Community College	OREGON	372
Columbia-Greene Community College	NEW YORK	296
Columbia International University	SOUTH CAROLINA	407
Columbia Southern University	ALABAMA	5
Columbia State Community College	TENNESSEE	423
Columbia Theological Seminary	GEORGIA	117
Columbia University in the City of New York	NEW YORK	296
Columbus College of Art & Design	OHIO	351
Columbus State Community College	OHIO	351
Columbus State Community College-Delaware	OHIO	351
Columbus State University	GEORGIA	117
Columbus Technical College	GEORGIA	117
Commonwealth Institute of Funeral Service	TEXAS	432
Commonwealth Technical Institute at the Hiram G. Andrews Center	PENNSYLVANIA	381
Commonwealth University of Pennsylvania	PENNSYLVANIA	393
Community Care College	OKLAHOMA	365
Community Christian College	CALIFORNIA	39
Community College of Allegheny County	PENNSYLVANIA	381
Community College of Allegheny County Boyce Campus	PENNSYLVANIA	381
Community College of Allegheny County North Campus	PENNSYLVANIA	381
Community College of Allegheny County, South Campus	PENNSYLVANIA	381
Community College of Aurora	COLORADO	80
Community College of Baltimore County, The	MARYLAND	198
Community College of Beaver County	PENNSYLVANIA	381
Community College of Denver	COLORADO	80
Community College of Philadelphia	PENNSYLVANIA	381
Community College of Rhode Island	RHODE ISLAND	403
Community College of the Air Force	US SERVICE SCHOOLS	501
Community College of Vermont	VERMONT	463
Community College System of New Hampshire	NEW HAMPSHIRE	271
Community Colleges of Spokane	WASHINGTON	478
Compass College of Film and Media	MICHIGAN	222
Compton College	CALIFORNIA	39
Conception Seminary College	MISSOURI	251
Concord University	WEST VIRGINIA	488
Concorde Career College	CALIFORNIA	40
Concorde Career College	COLORADO	80
Concorde Career College	MISSISSIPPI	244
Concorde Career College	MISSOURI	251
Concorde Career College	OREGON	372
Concorde Career College	TENNESSEE	418
Concorde Career College	TEXAS	432
Concorde Career Institute	FLORIDA	97
Concorde Career Institute	TEXAS	432
Concordia College	MINNESOTA	234
Concordia Seminary	MISSOURI	251
Concordia Theological Seminary	INDIANA	154
Concordia University	NEBRASKA	265
Concordia University Ann Arbor	MICHIGAN	222
Concordia University Chicago	ILLINOIS	136
Concordia University Irvine	CALIFORNIA	40
Concordia University Texas	TEXAS	432
Concordia University Wisconsin	WISCONSIN	491
Concordia University, St. Paul	MINNESOTA	235
Congregation Talmidei Mesivta Tiferes Schmiel Aleksander	NEW YORK	297
Congregation YMH	NEW YORK	297
Connecticut Board of Regents for Higher Education	CONNECTICUT	85
Connecticut College	CONNECTICUT	87
Connors State College	OKLAHOMA	365
Conservatory of Music of Puerto Rico	PUERTO RICO	505
Contra Costa College	CALIFORNIA	40
Contra Costa Community College District Office	CALIFORNIA	40
Contra Costa Medical Career College	CALIFORNIA	40
Converse University	SOUTH CAROLINA	407
Conway School of Landscape Design	MASSACHUSETTS	208
Cooper Union	NEW YORK	297
Copiah-Lincoln Community College	MISSISSIPPI	244
Copper Mountain College	CALIFORNIA	40
Coppin State University	MARYLAND	203
Corban University	OREGON	372
Cornell College	IOWA	164
Cornell University	NEW YORK	297
Cornerstone University	MICHIGAN	222
Cornish College of the Arts	WASHINGTON	478
Cossatot Community College of the University of Arkansas	ARKANSAS	22
Cosumnes River College	CALIFORNIA	50
Cottey College	MISSOURI	251
County College of Morris	NEW JERSEY	276
Covenant College	GEORGIA	117
Covenant Theological Seminary	MISSOURI	251
Cowley College	KANSAS	172
Cox College	MISSOURI	251
Crafton Hills College	CALIFORNIA	60
Cranbrook Academy of Art	MICHIGAN	222
Craven Community College	NORTH CAROLINA	333
Creighton University	NEBRASKA	265
Criswell College	TEXAS	433
Crowder College	MISSOURI	251
Crowley's Ridge College	ARKANSAS	19
Crown College	MINNESOTA	235
Crown College of the Bible, The	TENNESSEE	418
CSU Maritime Academy	CALIFORNIA	32
Cuesta College	CALIFORNIA	41
Culinary Institute LeNotre	TEXAS	433
Culinary Institute of America at Greystone, The	CALIFORNIA	41
Culinary Institute of America San Antonio	TEXAS	433
Culinary Institute of America, The	NEW YORK	297
Culinary Institute of Virginia	VIRGINIA	465
Culver-Stockton College	MISSOURI	251
Cumberland University	TENNESSEE	418
Cummings Gaduate Institute for Behavioral Health Studies	ARIZONA	12
Curry College	MASSACHUSETTS	208
Curtis Institute of Music	PENNSYLVANIA	381
Cuyahoga Community College	OHIO	351
Cuyahoga Community College Eastern Campus	OHIO	351
Cuyahoga Community College Metropolitan Campus	OHIO	351
Cuyahoga Community College Western Campus	OHIO	351
Cuyahoga Community College Westshore	OHIO	351
Cuyamaca College	CALIFORNIA	44
Cypress College	CALIFORNIA	54
Daemen College	NEW YORK	297
Dakota College at Bottineau	NORTH DAKOTA	345
Dakota County Technical College	MINNESOTA	237
Dakota State University	SOUTH DAKOTA	415
Dakota Wesleyan University	SOUTH DAKOTA	414
Dallas Baptist University	TEXAS	433
Dallas Christian College	TEXAS	433
Dallas College	TEXAS	433
Dallas College, Brookhaven Campus	TEXAS	433
Dallas College, Cedar Valley Campus	TEXAS	433
Dallas College, Eastfield Campus	TEXAS	433
Dallas College, El Centro Campus	TEXAS	434
Dallas College, Mountain View Campus	TEXAS	434
Dallas College, North Lake Campus	TEXAS	434
Dallas College, Richland Campus	TEXAS	434
Dallas Institute of Funeral Service	TEXAS	434
Dallas International University	TEXAS	434
Dallas Theological Seminary	TEXAS	434
Dalton State College	GEORGIA	118
Danville Area Community College	ILLINOIS	136
Danville Community College	VIRGINIA	472
Daoist Traditions College of Chinese Medical Arts	NORTH CAROLINA	328
Dartmouth College	NEW HAMPSHIRE	272
Davenport University	MICHIGAN	222
Davenport University Great Lakes Bay Campus - Midland	MICHIGAN	223

Emerson College	MASSACHUSETTS	208
Emmanuel College	GEORGIA	118
Emmanuel College	MASSACHUSETTS	209
Emmaus Bible College	IOWA	165
Emory & Henry College	VIRGINIA	466
Emory University	GEORGIA	118
Emperor's College	CALIFORNIA	41
Empire College	CALIFORNIA	42
Emporia State University	KANSAS	173
Endicott College	MASSACHUSETTS	209
Ensign College	UTAH	458
Enterprise State Community College	ALABAMA	2
Epic Bible College & Graduate School	CALIFORNIA	42
Erie Community College	NEW YORK	299
Erie Institute of Technology	PENNSYLVANIA	383
Erikson Institute	ILLINOIS	137
Erskine College	SOUTH CAROLINA	408
Escuela de Artes Plasticas de Puerto Rico	PUERTO RICO	505
Esperanza College	PENNSYLVANIA	383
Essex County College	NEW JERSEY	276
Essex County College-West Essex Branch Campus	NEW JERSEY	276
Estrella Mountain Community College	ARIZONA	13
Eternity Bible College	CALIFORNIA	42
ETI Technical College of Niles	OHIO	352
Eureka College	ILLINOIS	137
Evangel University	MISSOURI	252
Evangelia University	CALIFORNIA	42
Evangelical Seminary of Puerto Rico	PUERTO RICO	505
Everett Community College	WASHINGTON	479
Everglades University	FLORIDA	99
Evergreen State College, The	WASHINGTON	479
Evergreen Valley College	CALIFORNIA	62
Excelsior College	NEW YORK	299
Fairfax University of America	VIRGINIA	466
Fairfield University	CONNECTICUT	87
Fairleigh Dickinson University	NEW JERSEY	276
Fairmont State University	WEST VIRGINIA	488
Faith Baptist Bible College and Seminary	IOWA	166
Faith Bible College	VIRGINIA	466
Faith Bible Seminary	INDIANA	154
Faith International University	WASHINGTON	479
Family of Faith Christian University	OKLAHOMA	366
Farmingdale State College	NEW YORK	320
Fashion Institute of Technology	NEW YORK	299
Faulkner University	ALABAMA	5
Fayetteville State University	NORTH CAROLINA	341
Fayetteville Technical Community College	NORTH CAROLINA	334
Feather River College	CALIFORNIA	42
Fei Tian College	NEW YORK	299
Felbry College School of Nursing	OHIO	352
Felician University	NEW JERSEY	277
Ferris State University	MICHIGAN	223
Ferrum College	VIRGINIA	466
FIDM/Fashion Institute of Design and Merchandising-Los Angeles	CALIFORNIA	42
Fielding Graduate University	CALIFORNIA	42
FINE Mortuary College	MASSACHUSETTS	209
Finger Lakes Community College	NEW YORK	299
Finger Lakes Health College of Nursing and Health Sciences	NEW YORK	299
Finlandia University	MICHIGAN	223
Fisher College	MASSACHUSETTS	209
Fisk University	TENNESSEE	418
Fitchburg State University	MASSACHUSETTS	212
Five Branches University, Graduate School of Traditional Chinese Medicine	CALIFORNIA	42
Five Towns College	NEW YORK	299
Flagler College	FLORIDA	99
Flashpoint Chicago, a Campus of Columbia College Hollywood	ILLINOIS	137
Flathead Valley Community College	MONTANA	262
Flint Hills Technical College	KANSAS	173
Florence - Darlington Technical College	SOUTH CAROLINA	408
Florida Academy of Nursing	FLORIDA	99
Florida Agricultural and Mechanical University	FLORIDA	109
Florida Atlantic University	FLORIDA	109
Florida Career College	FLORIDA	99
Florida Career College - Margate Campus	FLORIDA	99
Florida Coastal School of Law	FLORIDA	99
Florida College	FLORIDA	99
Florida College of Integrative Medicine	FLORIDA	99
Florida Education Institute	FLORIDA	99
Florida Gateway College	FLORIDA	99
Florida Gulf Coast University	FLORIDA	109
Florida Institute of Technology	FLORIDA	100
Florida International University	FLORIDA	109
Florida Memorial University	FLORIDA	100
Florida National University Hialeah Campus	FLORIDA	100
Florida National University South Campus	FLORIDA	100
Florida National University Training Center	FLORIDA	100
Florida Polytechnic University	FLORIDA	110
Florida Southern College	FLORIDA	100

Florida SouthWestern State College	FLORIDA	100
Florida State College at Jacksonville	FLORIDA	101
Florida State University	FLORIDA	110
Florida Technical College	FLORIDA	101
Folsom Lake College	CALIFORNIA	51
Fond du Lac Tribal and Community College	MINNESOTA	237
Fontbonne University	MISSOURI	252
Foothill College	CALIFORNIA	43
Foothill-De Anza Community College District System Office	CALIFORNIA	42
Fordham University	NEW YORK	300
Forsyth Technical Community College	NORTH CAROLINA	334
Fort Hays State University	KANSAS	173
Fort Lewis College	COLORADO	80
Fort Peck Community College	MONTANA	262
Fort Scott Community College	KANSAS	173
Fort Valley State University	GEORGIA	118
Fortis College	FLORIDA	101
Fortis College	INDIANA	154
Fortis College	LOUISIANA	186
Fortis College	OHIO	352
Fortis College	TEXAS	435
Fortis College	UTAH	458
Fortis Institute	ALABAMA	5
Fortis Institute	PENNSYLVANIA	383
Fortis Institute	TENNESSEE	418
Fortis Institute-Nashville	TENNESSEE	418
Fortis Institute-Port St. Lucie	FLORIDA	101
Fox College	ILLINOIS	138
Fox Valley Technical College	WISCONSIN	497
Framingham State University	MASSACHUSETTS	212
Francis Marion University	SOUTH CAROLINA	408
Franciscan Missionaries of Our Lady University	LOUISIANA	186
Franciscan School of Theology	CALIFORNIA	43
Franciscan University of Steubenville	OHIO	352
Frank Phillips College	TEXAS	435
Franklin & Marshall College	PENNSYLVANIA	383
Franklin College of Indiana	INDIANA	155
Franklin Pierce University	NEW HAMPSHIRE	272
Franklin University	OHIO	352
Franklin W. Olin College of Engineering	MASSACHUSETTS	209
Frederick Community College	MARYLAND	198
Free Lutheran Bible College and Seminary	MINNESOTA	235
Freed-Hardeman University	TENNESSEE	418
Fremont College	CALIFORNIA	43
Fresno City College	CALIFORNIA	67
Fresno Pacific University	CALIFORNIA	43
Friends University	KANSAS	173
Front Range Community College	COLORADO	80
Front Range Community College-Boulder County Campus	COLORADO	81
Front Range Community College Larimer Campus	COLORADO	81
Frontier Nursing University	KENTUCKY	180
Frostburg State University	MARYLAND	203
Full Sail University	FLORIDA	101
Fuller Theological Seminary	CALIFORNIA	43
Fullerton College	CALIFORNIA	54
Fulton-Montgomery Community College	NEW YORK	300
Furman University	SOUTH CAROLINA	408
Future Generations University	WEST VIRGINIA	486
Future-Tech Institute	FLORIDA	101
FVI School of Nursing and Technology	FLORIDA	101
Gadsden State Community College	ALABAMA	2
Galaxy Medical College	CALIFORNIA	43
Galen College of Nursing	FLORIDA	101
Galen College of Nursing	KENTUCKY	180
Galen College of Nursing	OHIO	352
Galen College of Nursing	TEXAS	435
Gallaudet University	DISTRICT OF COLUMBIA	92
Galveston College	TEXAS	435
Gannon University	PENNSYLVANIA	383
Garden City Community College	KANSAS	173
Gardner-Webb University	NORTH CAROLINA	328
Garrett College	MARYLAND	198
Garrett-Evangelical Theological Seminary	ILLINOIS	138
Gaston College	NORTH CAROLINA	334
Gateway Community and Technical College	KENTUCKY	181
GateWay Community College	ARIZONA	13
Gateway Community College	CONNECTICUT	86
Gateway Seminary	CALIFORNIA	43
Gateway Technical College	WISCONSIN	497
Gavilan College	CALIFORNIA	43
Geisinger Commonwealth School of Medicine	PENNSYLVANIA	384
General Theological Seminary	NEW YORK	300
Genesee Community College	NEW YORK	300
Genesis University	FLORIDA	101
Geneva College	PENNSYLVANIA	384
George C. Wallace Community College - Dothan	ALABAMA	2
George Corley Wallace State Community College - Selma	ALABAMA	2
George Fox University	OREGON	372
George Mason University	VIRGINIA	466
George Washington University	DISTRICT OF COLUMBIA	92
George Williams College of Aurora University	WISCONSIN	491

Hocking College	OHIO	353
Hocking College Perry Campus	OHIO	353
Hodges University	FLORIDA	102
Hofstra University	NEW YORK	301
Hollins University	VIRGINIA	467
Holmes Community College	MISSISSIPPI	245
Holmes Institute of Consciousness Studies	COLORADO	81
Holy Apostles College and Seminary	CONNECTICUT	88
Holy Cross College	INDIANA	155
Holy Family University	PENNSYLVANIA	385
Holy Names University	CALIFORNIA	45
Holy Trinity Orthodox Seminary	NEW YORK	301
Holyoke Community College	MASSACHUSETTS	214
Homestead Schools	CALIFORNIA	45
Hondros College of Business	OHIO	353
Hondros College of Nursing	OHIO	353
Hood College	MARYLAND	199
Hood Theological Seminary	NORTH CAROLINA	329
Hope College	MICHIGAN	224
Hope College of Arts & Sciences	FLORIDA	102
Hope International University	CALIFORNIA	45
Hopkinsville Community College	KENTUCKY	181
Horizon University	CALIFORNIA	45
Horizon University	INDIANA	155
Horry-Georgetown Technical College	SOUTH CAROLINA	409
Hostos Community College-City University of New York	NEW YORK	293
Houghton University	NEW YORK	301
Housatonic Community College	CONNECTICUT	86
Houston Baptist University	TEXAS	436
Houston Community College	TEXAS	436
Houston Graduate School of Theology	TEXAS	436
Houston International College-Cardiotech Ultrasound School	TEXAS	436
Howard College	TEXAS	436
Howard Community College	MARYLAND	199
Howard Payne University	TEXAS	437
Howard University	DISTRICT OF COLUMBIA	92
Hudson County Community College	NEW JERSEY	277
Hudson Taylor University	GEORGIA	121
Hudson Valley Community College	NEW YORK	302
Huertas College	PUERTO RICO	505
Hult International Business School	MASSACHUSETTS	210
Humacao Community College	PUERTO RICO	506
Humphreys University	CALIFORNIA	45
Huntingdon College	ALABAMA	5
Huntington Junior College	WEST VIRGINIA	486
Huntington University	INDIANA	155
Huntington University of Health Sciences	TENNESSEE	419
Huntsville Bible College	ALABAMA	5
Hussian College	PENNSYLVANIA	385
Hussian College (formerly known as Studio School)	CALIFORNIA	45
Hussian College Clarksville	TENNESSEE	419
Husson University	MAINE	194
Huston-Tillotson University	TEXAS	437
Hutchinson Community College	KANSAS	174
IBMC College	COLORADO	81
Icahn School of Medicine at Mount Sinai	NEW YORK	302
ICPR Junior College	PUERTO RICO	506
ICPR Junior College-Arecibo Campus	PUERTO RICO	506
ICPR Junior College-Manati Branch Campus	PUERTO RICO	506
ICPR Junior College-Mayaguez Campus	PUERTO RICO	506
Idaho College of Osteopathic Medicine	IDAHO	131
Idaho State University	IDAHO	131
Iliff School of Theology	COLORADO	81
Ilisagvik College	ALASKA	9
Illinois Central College	ILLINOIS	138
Illinois College	ILLINOIS	139
Illinois College of Optometry	ILLINOIS	139
Illinois Eastern Community Colleges Frontier Community College	ILLINOIS	139
Illinois Eastern Community Colleges Lincoln Trail College	ILLINOIS	139
Illinois Eastern Community Colleges Olney Central College	ILLINOIS	139
Illinois Eastern Community Colleges System Office	ILLINOIS	139
Illinois Eastern Community Colleges Wabash Valley College	ILLINOIS	139
Illinois Institute of Technology	ILLINOIS	139
Illinois Institute of Technology Downtown Campus	ILLINOIS	140
Illinois Institute of Technology Rice Campus	ILLINOIS	140
Illinois State University	ILLINOIS	140
Illinois Valley Community College	ILLINOIS	140
Illinois Wesleyan University	ILLINOIS	140
Immaculata University	PENNSYLVANIA	385
Imperial Valley College	CALIFORNIA	45
Independence Community College	KANSAS	174
Indian Bible College	ARIZONA	12
Indian Hills Community College	IOWA	166
Indian River State College	FLORIDA	102
Indiana State University	INDIANA	155
Indiana Tech	INDIANA	156
Indiana University	INDIANA	156
Indiana University Bloomington	INDIANA	156
Indiana University East	INDIANA	156
Indiana University Kokomo	INDIANA	156

Indiana University Northwest	INDIANA	157
Indiana University of Pennsylvania	PENNSYLVANIA	393
Indiana University-Purdue University Columbus	INDIANA	157
Indiana University-Purdue University Indianapolis	INDIANA	157
Indiana University South Bend	INDIANA	157
Indiana University Southeast	INDIANA	157
Indiana Wesleyan University	INDIANA	157
Infinity College	LOUISIANA	186
Institute for Business and Technology	CALIFORNIA	46
Institute for Clinical Social Work	ILLINOIS	140
Institute for Doctoral Studies in the Visual Arts	MAINE	194
Institute for G.O.D., The	TENNESSEE	419
Institute of American Indian Arts	NEW MEXICO	285
Institute of Buddhist Studies	CALIFORNIA	46
Institute of Business and Medical Careers	COLORADO	81
Institute of Clinical Acupuncture and Oriental Medicine	HAWAII	128
Institute of Lutheran Theology	SOUTH DAKOTA	414
Institute of Medical and Business Careers	PENNSYLVANIA	386
Institute of Production and Recording	MINNESOTA	235
Institute of Taoist Education and Acupuncture	COLORADO	81
Institute of Technology	CALIFORNIA	46
Institute of World Politics, The	DISTRICT OF COLUMBIA	93
Instituto de Banca y Comercio	PUERTO RICO	506
Integrity College of Health	CALIFORNIA	46
IntelliTec College	COLORADO	81
Inter-American Defense College	DISTRICT OF COLUMBIA	93
Inter American University of Puerto Rico / Metropolitan Campus	PUERTO RICO	507
Inter American University of Puerto Rico Aguadilla Campus	PUERTO RICO	506
Inter American University of Puerto Rico Arecibo Campus	PUERTO RICO	506
Inter American University of Puerto Rico Barranquitas Campus	PUERTO RICO	506
Inter American University of Puerto Rico Bayamon Campus	PUERTO RICO	506
Inter American University of Puerto Rico Central Office	PUERTO RICO	506
Inter American University of Puerto Rico Fajardo Campus	PUERTO RICO	507
Inter American University of Puerto Rico Guayama Campus	PUERTO RICO	507
Inter American University of Puerto Rico Ponce Campus	PUERTO RICO	507
Inter American University of Puerto Rico San German Campus	PUERTO RICO	507
Inter American University of Puerto Rico School of Law	PUERTO RICO	507
Inter American University of Puerto Rico School of Optometry	PUERTO RICO	507
Interactive College of Technology	GEORGIA	121
Interactive College of Technology	KENTUCKY	180
Interactive College of Technology	TEXAS	437
Intercoast College	CALIFORNIA	46
Interdenominational Theological Center	GEORGIA	121
Interior Designers Institute	CALIFORNIA	46
International American University	CALIFORNIA	46
International Baptist College and Seminary	ARIZONA	12
International Business College	INDIANA	157
International College of Broadcasting	OHIO	353
International College of Health Sciences	FLORIDA	102
International Institute for Restorative Practices	PENNSYLVANIA	386
International Reformed University and Seminary	CALIFORNIA	46
International Technological University	CALIFORNIA	46
International Theological Seminary	CALIFORNIA	46
Inver Hills Community College	MINNESOTA	237
Iona University	NEW YORK	302
Iowa Central Community College	IOWA	166
Iowa Lakes Community College	IOWA	166
Iowa Lakes Community College Emmetsburg Campus	IOWA	167
Iowa Lakes Community College Spencer Campus	IOWA	167
Iowa State University	IOWA	163
Iowa Valley Community College District	IOWA	167
Iowa Wesleyan University	IOWA	167
Iowa Western Community College	IOWA	167
Irvine Valley College	CALIFORNIA	65
Island Drafting and Technical Institute	NEW YORK	302
Isothermal Community College	NORTH CAROLINA	335
Itawamba Community College	MISSISSIPPI	245
Ithaca College	NEW YORK	302
ITI Technical College	LOUISIANA	187
Ivy Christian College	VIRGINIA	467
Ivy Tech Community College Madison	INDIANA	158
Ivy Tech Community College of Indiana-Anderson	INDIANA	158
Ivy Tech Community College of Indiana-Bloomington	INDIANA	158
Ivy Tech Community College of Indiana-Columbus	INDIANA	158
Ivy Tech Community College of Indiana-Evansville	INDIANA	158
Ivy Tech Community College of Indiana-Fort Wayne	INDIANA	158
Ivy Tech Community College of Indiana-Indianapolis	INDIANA	158
Ivy Tech Community College of Indiana-Kokomo	INDIANA	158
Ivy Tech Community College of Indiana-Lafayette	INDIANA	158
Ivy Tech Community College of Indiana-Lake County	INDIANA	158
Ivy Tech Community College of Indiana-Lawrenceburg-Riverfront	INDIANA	158
Ivy Tech Community College of Indiana-Marion	INDIANA	158
Ivy Tech Community College of Indiana-Michigan City	INDIANA	158
Ivy Tech Community College of Indiana-Muncie	INDIANA	158
Ivy Tech Community College of Indiana-Richmond	INDIANA	158
Ivy Tech Community College of Indiana-Sellersburg	INDIANA	158

Laurel Ridge Community College	VIRGINIA	473
Laurel Technical Institute	PENNSYLVANIA	387
Laurus College	CALIFORNIA	48
Lawrence Technological University	MICHIGAN	226
Lawrence University	WISCONSIN	492
Lawson State Community College	ALABAMA	2
L.E. Fletcher Technical Community College	LOUISIANA	187
Le Moyne College	NEW YORK	303
Learnet Academy	CALIFORNIA	48
Lebanon Valley College	PENNSYLVANIA	388
Lee College	TEXAS	438
Lee Strasberg Theatre Institute, The	CALIFORNIA	48
Lee University	TENNESSEE	419
Leech Lake Tribal College	MINNESOTA	235
Lees-McRae College	NORTH CAROLINA	330
Lehigh Carbon Community College	PENNSYLVANIA	388
Lehigh University	PENNSYLVANIA	388
LeMoyne-Owen College	TENNESSEE	419
Lenoir Community College	NORTH CAROLINA	335
Lenoir-Rhyne University	NORTH CAROLINA	330
Lesley University	MASSACHUSETTS	210
LeTourneau University	TEXAS	438
Lewis and Clark College	OREGON	373
Lewis and Clark Community College	ILLINOIS	142
Lewis-Clark State College	IDAHO	131
Lewis University	ILLINOIS	142
Lexington Theological Seminary	KENTUCKY	183
Liberty University	VIRGINIA	467
Life Chiropractic College West	CALIFORNIA	48
Life Pacific University	CALIFORNIA	48
Life University	GEORGIA	122
LIM College	NEW YORK	303
Limestone University	SOUTH CAROLINA	409
Lincoln Christian University	ILLINOIS	142
Lincoln College of Technology	COLORADO	81
Lincoln College of Technology	ILLINOIS	142
Lincoln College of Technology	INDIANA	158
Lincoln College of Technology	MARYLAND	199
Lincoln College of Technology	TEXAS	438
Lincoln College of Technology Nashville	TENNESSEE	419
Lincoln Land Community College	ILLINOIS	142
Lincoln Law School of Sacramento	CALIFORNIA	48
Lincoln Memorial University	TENNESSEE	420
Lincoln Technical Institute	PENNSYLVANIA	388
Lincoln University	CALIFORNIA	48
Lincoln University	MISSOURI	254
Lincoln University	PENNSYLVANIA	388
Lindenwood University	MISSOURI	254
Lindsey Wilson College	KENTUCKY	183
Linfield University	OREGON	373
Linn-Benton Community College	OREGON	373
Lional University	CALIFORNIA	48
Lipscomb University	TENNESSEE	420
Little Big Horn College	MONTANA	262
Little Priest Tribal College	NEBRASKA	266
Living Arts College @ School of Communication Arts	NORTH CAROLINA	330
Livingstone College	NORTH CAROLINA	330
Logan University	MISSOURI	254
Logos Evangelical Seminary	CALIFORNIA	48
Loma Linda University	CALIFORNIA	48
Lone Star College System	TEXAS	438
Long Beach City College	CALIFORNIA	48
Long Island Business Institute	NEW YORK	304
Long Island University	NEW YORK	304
Long Island University - LIU Brooklyn	NEW YORK	304
Long Island University - LIU Hudson	NEW YORK	304
Long Island University - LIU Post	NEW YORK	304
Long Island University - LIU Riverhead	NEW YORK	304
Longwood University	VIRGINIA	467
Longy School of Music of Bard College	MASSACHUSETTS	211
Lorain County Community College	OHIO	355
Loras College	IOWA	167
Los Angeles Academy of Figurative Art	CALIFORNIA	49
Los Angeles City College	CALIFORNIA	49
Los Angeles College of Music	CALIFORNIA	49
Los Angeles Community College District Office	CALIFORNIA	49
Los Angeles County College of Nursing and Allied Health	CALIFORNIA	50
Los Angeles Film School	CALIFORNIA	50
Los Angeles Harbor College	CALIFORNIA	49
Los Angeles Mission College	CALIFORNIA	49
Los Angeles Pacific College	CALIFORNIA	50
Los Angeles Pacific University	CALIFORNIA	50
Los Angeles Performing Arts Conservatory, The	CALIFORNIA	50
Los Angeles Pierce College	CALIFORNIA	49
Los Angeles Southwest College	CALIFORNIA	49
Los Angeles Trade-Technical College	CALIFORNIA	50
Los Angeles Valley College	CALIFORNIA	50
Los Medanos College	CALIFORNIA	40
Los Rios Community College District Office	CALIFORNIA	50
Louis V. Gerstner Jr. Graduate School of Biomedical Sciences, Memorial Sloan Kettering Cancer Center	NEW YORK	304
Louisburg College	NORTH CAROLINA	330
Louisiana Christian University	LOUISIANA	187
Louisiana Community & Technical College System	LOUISIANA	187
Louisiana Culinary Institute	LOUISIANA	188
Louisiana Delta Community College	LOUISIANA	188
Louisiana State University Administration	LOUISIANA	188
Louisiana State University and Agricultural and Mechanical College	LOUISIANA	188
Louisiana State University at Alexandria	LOUISIANA	189
Louisiana State University at Eunice	LOUISIANA	189
Louisiana State University Health Sciences Center at Shreveport	LOUISIANA	189
Louisiana State University Health Sciences Center-New Orleans	LOUISIANA	189
Louisiana State University Shreveport	LOUISIANA	189
Louisiana Tech University	LOUISIANA	192
Louisville Presbyterian Theological Seminary	KENTUCKY	183
Lourdes University	OHIO	355
Lower Columbia College	WASHINGTON	480
Loyola Marymount University	CALIFORNIA	51
Loyola University Chicago	ILLINOIS	142
Loyola University Health Sciences Campus	ILLINOIS	143
Loyola University Maryland	MARYLAND	199
Loyola University New Orleans	LOUISIANA	190
Loyola University Water Tower Campus	ILLINOIS	143
Lubbock Christian University	TEXAS	438
Lumbee River Christian College	NORTH CAROLINA	330
Luna Community College	NEW MEXICO	285
Lurleen B. Wallace Community College	ALABAMA	2
Luther College	IOWA	167
Luther Rice College and Seminary	GEORGIA	122
Luther Seminary	MINNESOTA	236
Lutheran Brethren Seminary	MINNESOTA	236
Lutheran School of Theology at Chicago	ILLINOIS	143
Luzerne County Community College	PENNSYLVANIA	388
Lycoming College	PENNSYLVANIA	388
Lynn University	FLORIDA	103
Lyon College	ARKANSAS	20
Macalester College	MINNESOTA	236
MacCormac College	ILLINOIS	143
Machzikei Hadath Rabbinical College	NEW YORK	304
Macomb Community College	MICHIGAN	226
Madera Community College	CALIFORNIA	67
Madison Area Technical College	WISCONSIN	497
Madison Area Technical College Commercial Avenue Education Center	WISCONSIN	499
Madison Area Technical College Downtown Education Center	WISCONSIN	499
Madison Area Technical College Fort Atkinson	WISCONSIN	499
Madison Area Technical College Portage	WISCONSIN	499
Madison Area Technical College Reedsburg	WISCONSIN	499
Madison Area Technical College Watertown	WISCONSIN	499
Madisonville Community College	KENTUCKY	182
Madonna University	MICHIGAN	226
Magdalen College of the Liberal Arts	NEW HAMPSHIRE	273
Maharishi International University	IOWA	168
Maine College of Art	MAINE	194
Maine College of Health Professions	MAINE	194
Maine Community College System	MAINE	194
Maine Maritime Academy	MAINE	195
Maine Media College	MAINE	195
Malcolm X College, One of the City Colleges of Chicago	ILLINOIS	135
Malone University	OHIO	355
Manchester Community College	CONNECTICUT	86
Manchester Community College	NEW HAMPSHIRE	272
Manchester University	INDIANA	158
Mandl School - The College of Allied Health	NEW YORK	304
Manhattan Area Technical College	KANSAS	175
Manhattan Christian College	KANSAS	175
Manhattan College	NEW YORK	304
Manhattan School of Music	NEW YORK	304
Manhattanville College	NEW YORK	305
Manna University	NORTH CAROLINA	330
Manor College	PENNSYLVANIA	389
Maple Springs Baptist Bible College & Seminary	MARYLAND	200
Maranatha Baptist University	WISCONSIN	492
Marconi International University	FLORIDA	104
Maria College	NEW YORK	305
Marian University	INDIANA	159
Marian University	WISCONSIN	492
Maricopa County Community College District Office	ARIZONA	13
Marietta College	OHIO	355
Marine Corps University	US SERVICE SCHOOLS	501
Marion Military Institute	ALABAMA	3
Marion Technical College	OHIO	355
Marist College	NEW YORK	305
Marquette University	WISCONSIN	492
Mars Hill University	NORTH CAROLINA	330
Marshall B. Ketchum University	CALIFORNIA	51
Marshall University	WEST VIRGINIA	488
Marshalltown Community College	IOWA	167

Occidental College	CALIFORNIA	54
Ocean County College	NEW JERSEY	279
Oconee Fall Line Technical College-North Campus	GEORGIA	123
Oconee Fall Line Technical College-South Campus	GEORGIA	123
Odessa College	TEXAS	440
Ogeechee Technical College	GEORGIA	123
Oglala Lakota College	SOUTH DAKOTA	414
Oglethorpe University	GEORGIA	123
Ohio Business College	OHIO	357
Ohio Christian University	OHIO	358
Ohio Dominican University	OHIO	358
Ohio Institute of Allied Health	OHIO	358
Ohio Northern University	OHIO	358
Ohio State University Agricultural Technical Institute, The	OHIO	358
Ohio State University at Lima Campus, The	OHIO	358
Ohio State University at Marion, The	OHIO	358
Ohio State University Main Campus, The	OHIO	358
Ohio State University Mansfield Campus, The	OHIO	358
Ohio State University Newark Campus, The	OHIO	358
Ohio Technical College	OHIO	358
Ohio University Chillicothe Campus	OHIO	359
Ohio University Eastern Campus	OHIO	359
Ohio University Lancaster Campus	OHIO	359
Ohio University Main Campus	OHIO	358
Ohio University Southern Campus	OHIO	359
Ohio University Zanesville	OHIO	359
Ohio Wesleyan University	OHIO	359
Ohlone College	CALIFORNIA	54
Ohr Hameir Theological Seminary	NEW YORK	310
Oikos University	CALIFORNIA	54
Oklahoma Baptist University	OKLAHOMA	367
Oklahoma Christian University	OKLAHOMA	367
Oklahoma City Community College	OKLAHOMA	367
Oklahoma City University	OKLAHOMA	367
Oklahoma Panhandle State University	OKLAHOMA	367
Oklahoma State University	OKLAHOMA	367
Oklahoma State University Center for Health Sciences	OKLAHOMA	368
Oklahoma State University Institute of Technology-Okmulgee	OKLAHOMA	368
Oklahoma State University - Oklahoma City	OKLAHOMA	368
Oklahoma State University - Tulsa	OKLAHOMA	368
Oklahoma Wesleyan University	OKLAHOMA	368
Old Dominion University	VIRGINIA	468
Olivet College	MICHIGAN	229
Olivet Nazarene University	ILLINOIS	146
Olivet University	CALIFORNIA	55
Olympic College	WASHINGTON	481
Omega Graduate School	TENNESSEE	421
Onondaga Community College	NEW YORK	310
Oral Roberts University	OKLAHOMA	368
Orange Coast College	CALIFORNIA	38
Orange County Community College	NEW YORK	310
Orange County Community College Newburgh Branch Campus	NEW YORK	310
Orangeburg-Calhoun Technical College	SOUTH CAROLINA	410
Oregon Coast Community College	OREGON	374
Oregon College of Oriental Medicine	OREGON	374
Oregon Health & Science University	OREGON	374
Oregon Institute of Technology	OREGON	374
Oregon State University	OREGON	374
Orion Technical College	IOWA	169
Otero College	COLORADO	82
Otis College of Art and Design	CALIFORNIA	55
Ottawa University	KANSAS	176
Ottawa University Brookfield, WI	WISCONSIN	493
Ottawa University Overland Park, KS	KANSAS	176
Ottawa University Surprise, AZ	ARIZONA	15
Otterbein University	OHIO	359
Ouachita Baptist University	ARKANSAS	20
Our Lady of the Lake University	TEXAS	440
Owens Community College	OHIO	359
Owens Community College Findlay Campus	OHIO	359
Owensboro Community and Technical College	KENTUCKY	182
Oxnard College	CALIFORNIA	74
Ozark Christian College	MISSOURI	257
Ozarka College	ARKANSAS	20
Ozarks Technical Community College	MISSOURI	257
Ozarks Technical Community College Richwood Valley	MISSOURI	257
Ozarks Technical Community College Table Rock Campus	MISSOURI	257
Pace University	NEW YORK	310
Pacific Bible College	OREGON	375
Pacific College	CALIFORNIA	55
Pacific College of Health and Science	CALIFORNIA	55
Pacific College of Technology	GEORGIA	123
Pacific Islands University	GUAM	503
Pacific Lutheran University	WASHINGTON	481
Pacific Northwest Christian College	WASHINGTON	481
Pacific Northwest University of Health Sciences	WASHINGTON	481
Pacific Oaks College	CALIFORNIA	55
Pacific Rim Christian University	HAWAII	128
Pacific School of Religion	CALIFORNIA	55
Pacific States University	CALIFORNIA	55

Pacific Union College	CALIFORNIA	55
Pacific University	OREGON	375
Pacifica Graduate Institute	CALIFORNIA	55
Paier College	CONNECTICUT	88
Paine College	GEORGIA	123
Palau Community College	PALAU	504
Palm Beach Atlantic University	FLORIDA	105
Palm Beach State College	FLORIDA	105
Palmer College of Chiropractic	IOWA	169
Palmer College of Chiropractic, Florida Campus	FLORIDA	105
Palmer College of Chiropractic, West Campus	CALIFORNIA	55
Palo Alto College	TEXAS	428
Palo Alto University	CALIFORNIA	55
Palo Verde College	CALIFORNIA	56
Palomar College	CALIFORNIA	56
Pamlico Community College	NORTH CAROLINA	336
Panola College	TEXAS	440
Paradise Valley Community College	ARIZONA	13
Pardee RAND Graduate School of Policy Studies	CALIFORNIA	56
Paris Junior College	TEXAS	440
Park University	MISSOURI	257
Parker University	TEXAS	440
Parkland College	ILLINOIS	146
Pasadena City College	CALIFORNIA	56
Pasco-Hernando State College	FLORIDA	105
Passaic County Community College	NEW JERSEY	279
Pathways College	CALIFORNIA	56
Patrick & Henry Community College	VIRGINIA	473
Patrick Henry College	VIRGINIA	468
Patten University	CALIFORNIA	56
Paul D. Camp Community College	VIRGINIA	474
Paul Quinn College	TEXAS	440
Paul Smith's College	NEW YORK	310
Payne Theological Seminary	OHIO	359
PCI College	CALIFORNIA	56
Pearl River Community College	MISSISSIPPI	247
Peirce College	PENNSYLVANIA	391
Pellissippi State Community College	TENNESSEE	424
Peloton College	TEXAS	440
Peninsula College	WASHINGTON	481
Penn Commercial Business/Technical School	PENNSYLVANIA	391
Penn Foster College	ARIZONA	15
Penn State Abington	PENNSYLVANIA	391
Penn State Altoona	PENNSYLVANIA	391
Penn State Beaver	PENNSYLVANIA	391
Penn State Berks	PENNSYLVANIA	391
Penn State Brandywine	PENNSYLVANIA	391
Penn State Dickinson Law	PENNSYLVANIA	391
Penn State DuBois	PENNSYLVANIA	391
Penn State Erie, The Behrend College	PENNSYLVANIA	391
Penn State Fayette, The Eberly Campus	PENNSYLVANIA	392
Penn State Great Valley School of Graduate Professional Studies	PENNSYLVANIA	392
Penn State Greater Allegheny	PENNSYLVANIA	392
Penn State Harrisburg	PENNSYLVANIA	392
Penn State Hazleton	PENNSYLVANIA	392
Penn State Lehigh Valley	PENNSYLVANIA	392
Penn State Milton S. Hershey Medical Center College of Medicine	PENNSYLVANIA	392
Penn State Mont Alto	PENNSYLVANIA	392
Penn State New Kensington	PENNSYLVANIA	392
Penn State Schuylkill	PENNSYLVANIA	392
Penn State Scranton	PENNSYLVANIA	392
Penn State Shenango	PENNSYLVANIA	392
Penn State University Park	PENNSYLVANIA	391
Penn State Wilkes-Barre	PENNSYLVANIA	392
Penn State York	PENNSYLVANIA	392
Pennco Tech	PENNSYLVANIA	392
Pennsylvania Academy of the Fine Arts	PENNSYLVANIA	392
Pennsylvania College of Art & Design	PENNSYLVANIA	392
Pennsylvania College of Health Sciences	PENNSYLVANIA	392
Pennsylvania College of Technology	PENNSYLVANIA	392
Pennsylvania Highlands Community College	PENNSYLVANIA	393
Pennsylvania Institute of Technology	PENNSYLVANIA	393
Pennsylvania Western University	PENNSYLVANIA	394
Pennsylvania's State System of Higher Education, Office of the Chancellor	PENNSYLVANIA	393
Pensacola Christian College	FLORIDA	105
Pensacola State College	FLORIDA	105
Pentecostal Theological Seminary	TENNESSEE	421
Pepperdine University	CALIFORNIA	56
Peralta Community Colleges District Office	CALIFORNIA	56
Perry Technical Institute	WASHINGTON	481
Peru State College	NEBRASKA	267
Pfeiffer University	NORTH CAROLINA	339
Philadelphia College of Osteopathic Medicine	PENNSYLVANIA	395
Philadelphia College of Osteopathic Medicine Georgia Campus	GEORGIA	124
Philander Smith College	ARKANSAS	21
Phillips Community College of the University of Arkansas	ARKANSAS	23

University of the Southwest	NEW MEXICO	288
University of the Virgin Islands	VIRGIN ISLANDS	512
University of the Virgin Islands-St. Croix	VIRGIN ISLANDS	512
University of the West	CALIFORNIA	73
University of Toledo	OHIO	363
University of Tulsa	OKLAHOMA	371
University of Utah, The	UTAH	459
University of Valley Forge	PENNSYLVANIA	400
University of Vermont	VERMONT	462
University of Virginia	VIRGINIA	471
University of Virginia's College at Wise, The	VIRGINIA	471
University of Washington	WASHINGTON	484
University of West Alabama, The	ALABAMA	9
University of West Florida	FLORIDA	111
University of West Georgia	GEORGIA	127
University of West Los Angeles	CALIFORNIA	73
University of Western States	OREGON	377
University of Wisconsin-Eau Claire	WISCONSIN	494
University of Wisconsin-Eau Claire - Barron County	WISCONSIN	496
University of Wisconsin-Green Bay	WISCONSIN	494
University of Wisconsin-La Crosse	WISCONSIN	495
University of Wisconsin-Madison	WISCONSIN	494
University of Wisconsin-Milwaukee	WISCONSIN	495
University of Wisconsin Oshkosh	WISCONSIN	495
University of Wisconsin-Parkside	WISCONSIN	495
University of Wisconsin-Platteville	WISCONSIN	495
University of Wisconsin-Platteville Baraboo Sauk County	WISCONSIN	496
University of Wisconsin-Platteville Richland	WISCONSIN	496
University of Wisconsin-River Falls	WISCONSIN	496
University of Wisconsin-Stevens Point	WISCONSIN	496
University of Wisconsin-Stevens Point at Marshfield	WISCONSIN	496
University of Wisconsin-Stevens Point at Wausau	WISCONSIN	496
University of Wisconsin-Stout	WISCONSIN	496
University of Wisconsin-Superior	WISCONSIN	496
University of Wisconsin System	WISCONSIN	494
University of Wisconsin-Whitewater	WISCONSIN	496
University of Wisconsin-Whitewater at Rock County	WISCONSIN	496
University of Wyoming	WYOMING	500
University System of Georgia Office	GEORGIA	127
University System of Maryland Office, The	MARYLAND	202
University System of New Hampshire	NEW HAMPSHIRE	273
Upper Iowa University	IOWA	170
Upper Valley Educators Institute	NEW HAMPSHIRE	274
Urban College of Boston	MASSACHUSETTS	219
Urshan College and Urshan Graduate School of Theology	MISSOURI	261
Ursinus College	PENNSYLVANIA	400
Ursuline College	OHIO	363
U.S. Career Institute	COLORADO	84
U.T.A. Mesivta of Kiryas Joel	NEW YORK	323
Utah College of Dental Hygiene at Careers Unlimited, The	UTAH	459
Utah State University	UTAH	459
Utah System of Higher Education	UTAH	459
Utah Tech University	UTAH	459
Utah Valley University	UTAH	460
Utica University	NEW YORK	323
Valdosta State University	GEORGIA	127
Valencia College	FLORIDA	113
Valley City State University	NORTH DAKOTA	345
Valley College - Martinsburg Campus	WEST VIRGINIA	487
Valley College of Medical Careers	CALIFORNIA	73
Valley Forge Military College	PENNSYLVANIA	400
Valor Christian College	OHIO	363
Valparaiso University	INDIANA	162
Van Andel Institute Graduate School	MICHIGAN	231
Vance-Granville Community College	NORTH CAROLINA	338
Vanderbilt University	TENNESSEE	427
VanderCook College of Music	ILLINOIS	152
Vanguard University of Southern California	CALIFORNIA	73
Vassar College	NEW YORK	323
Vaughn College of Aeronautics and Technology	NEW YORK	323
Ventura College	CALIFORNIA	74
Ventura County Community College District	CALIFORNIA	73
Veritas Baptist College	INDIANA	162
Veritas College International Graduate School	TEXAS	456
Veritas International University	CALIFORNIA	74
Vermont College of Fine Arts	VERMONT	462
Vermont Law School	VERMONT	462
Vermont State Colleges Office of the Chancellor	VERMONT	462
Vermont Technical College	VERMONT	463
Vernon College	TEXAS	456
Vet Tech Institute	PENNSYLVANIA	401
Vet Tech Institute of Houston	TEXAS	456
Victor Valley College	CALIFORNIA	74
Victoria College	TEXAS	456
Villa Maria College of Buffalo	NEW YORK	324
Villanova University	PENNSYLVANIA	401
Vincennes University	INDIANA	162
Vincennes University-Jasper Center	INDIANA	162
Virginia Beach Theological Seminary	VIRGINIA	472
Virginia Bible College	VIRGINIA	472
Virginia Christian University	VIRGINIA	472
Virginia Commonwealth University	VIRGINIA	472
Virginia Community College System Office	VIRGINIA	472
Virginia Highlands Community College	VIRGINIA	474
Virginia Military Institute	VIRGINIA	475
Virginia Polytechnic Institute and State University	VIRGINIA	475
Virginia State University	VIRGINIA	475
Virginia Theological Seminary	VIRGINIA	475
Virginia Union University	VIRGINIA	475
Virginia University of Integrative Medicine	VIRGINIA	476
Virginia University of Lynchburg	VIRGINIA	476
Virginia Wesleyan University	VIRGINIA	476
Virginia Western Community College	VIRGINIA	475
Viridis Graduate Institute	ARIZONA	17
Virscend University	CALIFORNIA	74
Visible Music College	TENNESSEE	427
Viterbo University	WISCONSIN	496
Volunteer State Community College	TENNESSEE	424
Voorhees College	SOUTH CAROLINA	413
Wabash College	INDIANA	162
Wade College	TEXAS	457
Wagner College	NEW YORK	324
Wake Forest University	NORTH CAROLINA	344
Wake Technical Community College	NORTH CAROLINA	338
Walden University	MINNESOTA	243
Waldorf University	IOWA	170
Walla Walla Community College	WASHINGTON	484
Walla Walla University	WASHINGTON	484
Wallace State Community College - Hanceville	ALABAMA	4
Walnut Hill College	PENNSYLVANIA	401
Walsh College of Accountancy and Business Administration	MICHIGAN	231
Walsh University	OHIO	363
Walters State Community College	TENNESSEE	424
Warner Pacific University	OREGON	377
Warner University	FLORIDA	113
Warren County Community College	NEW JERSEY	283
Warren Wilson College	NORTH CAROLINA	344
Wartburg College	IOWA	170
Wartburg Theological Seminary	IOWA	170
Washburn University	KANSAS	178
Washington & Jefferson College	PENNSYLVANIA	401
Washington Adventist University	MARYLAND	204
Washington and Lee University	VIRGINIA	476
Washington College	MARYLAND	204
Washington County Community College	MAINE	195
Washington State Community College	OHIO	363
Washington State University	WASHINGTON	484
Washington State University-Spokane	WASHINGTON	484
Washington State University-Tri Cities	WASHINGTON	484
Washington State University-Vancouver	WASHINGTON	484
Washington Theological Seminary	VIRGINIA	476
Washington University in St. Louis	MISSOURI	261
Washington University of Science & Technology	VIRGINIA	476
Washington University of Virginia	VIRGINIA	476
Washington University School of Medicine in St. Louis	MISSOURI	261
Washtenaw Community College	MICHIGAN	232
Watts School of Nursing	NORTH CAROLINA	344
Waubonsee Community College	ILLINOIS	152
Waukesha County Technical College	WISCONSIN	499
Wayland Baptist University	TEXAS	457
Wayne Community College	NORTH CAROLINA	338
Wayne County Community College District	MICHIGAN	232
Wayne County Community College District Downriver Campus	MICHIGAN	232
Wayne County Community College District Downtown Campus	MICHIGAN	232
Wayne County Community College District Eastern Campus	MICHIGAN	232
Wayne County Community College District Northwest Campus	MICHIGAN	232
Wayne County Community College District Ted Scott Campus	MICHIGAN	232
Wayne State College	NEBRASKA	267
Wayne State University	MICHIGAN	232
Waynesburg University	PENNSYLVANIA	401
Weatherford College	TEXAS	457
Webb Institute	NEW YORK	324
Webber International University	FLORIDA	113
Weber State University	UTAH	460
Webster University	MISSOURI	261
Weill Cornell Medicine	NEW YORK	324
Weimar University	CALIFORNIA	74
Welch College	TENNESSEE	427
Wellesley College	MASSACHUSETTS	219
Wells College	NEW YORK	324
WellSpring School of Allied Health-Kansas City	MISSOURI	261
Wenatchee Valley College	WASHINGTON	484
Wentworth Institute of Technology	MASSACHUSETTS	219
Wesley Biblical Seminary	MISSISSIPPI	249
Wesley Theological Seminary	DISTRICT OF COLUMBIA	94
Wesleyan College	GEORGIA	127
Wesleyan University	CONNECTICUT	90
West Chester University of Pennsylvania	PENNSYLVANIA	394

Aamodt, S., & Wang, S. (2008). *Welcome to your brain: Why you lose your car keys but never forget how to drive and other puzzles of everyday life*. New York: Bloomsbury; Distributed to the trade by Macmillan.

Abbott, A. A. (2008). Professional conduct. In T. Mizrahi & L. E. Davis (Eds.), *Encyclopedia of Social Work* (20th, e-reference ed.). New York: Oxford University Press.

Afrin, B. (2014). World population in 2015: The clock is ticking. Retrieved from http://www.worldclock.com/world_clock _blog+world-population-in-2050---the-clock-is-ticking... _8.html

Aistrup, J. A. (1996). *The southern strategy revisited: Republican top-down advancement in the South*. Lexington, KY: University Press of Kentucky.

Ajzen, I. (1991). The theory of planned behavior. *Organizational Behavior and Human Decision Processes, 50*, 179–211.

Ajzen, I., & Fishbein, M. (1980). *Understanding attitudes and predicting social behavior*. Upper Saddle River, NJ: Prentice-Hall.

Akobeng, A. K. (2005). Understanding systematic reviews and meta-analysis. *Archives of Disease in Childhood, 90*(8), 845–848.

Akrivopoulou, C., & Garipidis, N. (2012). *Human rights and risks in the digital era: Globalization and the effects of information technologies*. Hershey, PA: Information Science Reference.

Albarracin, D., Johnson, B. T., Fishbein, M., & Muellerleile, P. A. (2001). Theories of reasoned action and planned behavior as models of condom use: A meta-analysis. *Psychological Bulletin, 127*(1), 142–161.

Alexander, M. (2010). *The new Jim Crow: Mass incarceration in the age of colorblindness*. New York: New Press.

Almossawi, A. (2013). *An illustrated book of bad arguments*. Retrieved from https://bookofbadarguments.com/

Alpert, J. L., Brown, L. S., Ceci, S. J., Courtois, C. A., Loftus, E. F., & Ornstein, P. A. (1996). *American Psychological Association: Working group on investigation of memories of childhood sexual abuse. Final report*. Retrieved from Washington, DC, http:// www.apa.org/pi/memories_report/homepage.html

Alter, C., & Egan, M. (1997). Logic modeling: A tool for teaching critical thinking in social work practice. *Journal of Social Work Education, 33*(1), 85–102.

Alter, C., & Murty, S. (1997). Logic modeling: A tool for teaching practice evaluation. *Journal of Social Work Education, 33*(1), 103–117.

Altmann, H. (1973). Effects of empathy, warmth and genuineness in the initial counseling interview. *Counselor Education and Supervision, 12*, 225–229.

Altschuld, J. W. (2015). *Bridging the gap between asset/capacity building and needs assessment: Concepts and practical applications*. Los Angeles, CA: Sage.

Altshuler, S. J. (1999). Constructing genograms with children in care: Implications for casework practice. *Child Welfare, 78*(6), 777–790.

Amaro, H., Raj, A., Vega, R. R., Mangione, T. W., & Perez, L. N. (2001). Racial/ethnic disparities in the HIV and substance abuse epidemics: Communities responding to the need. *Public Health Reports, 116*(5), 434–448. Retrieved from http://www .publichealthreports.org/issueopen.cfm?articleID=1125

American Association of University Women. (2014). *The simple truth about the gender pay gap: 2014 Fall Edition*. Washington, DC: AAUW. Retrieved from http://www.aauw.org/files/2014/09 /The-Simple-Truth_Fall.pdf.

American Civil Liberties Union. (2014). *War comes home: The excessive militarization of American policing*. New York: American Civil Liberties Union. Retrieved from https://www.aclu.org/sites /default/files/assets/jus14-warcomeshome-report-web-rel1.pdf.

American Psychiatric Association. (2000a). *Diagnostic and statistical manual* (4th ed. text rev.) [Electronic version]. Washington, DC: Author.

American Psychiatric Association. (2000b). *Position statement: Therapies focused on memories of childhood physical and sexual abuse*. Washington, DC: Author.

American Psychiatric Association. (2003). American Psychiatric Association practice guideline for the assessment and treatment of patients with suicidal behaviors. Retrieved from http://www .psych.org/psych_pract/treatg/pg/SuicidalBehavior_05-15-06.pdf

American Psychiatric Association. (2013). *Diagnostic and statistical manual of mental disorders: DSM-5*. Washington, DC: Author.

American Psychological Association. (2009a). Children with positive outlooks are better learners. *ScienceDaily*. Retrieved from http:// www.sciencedaily.com/releases/2009/08/090807135054.htm

American Psychological Association. (2009b). *Publication manual of the American Psychological Association* (6th ed.). Washington, DC: Author.

Amnesty International. (1997). *First steps: A manual for starting human rights education*. Retrieved from http://www.hrea.org /erc/Library/display_doc.php?url=http%3A%2F%2Fwww.hrea .org%2Ferc%2FLibrary%2FFirst_Steps%2Findex_eng .html&external=N

Amnesty International. (2013). Death penalty: Abolitionist and retentionist countries. Retrieved from http://amnesty.org/en /death-penalty/abolitionist-and-retentionist-countries

Anand, S., & Sen, A. (2000). The income component of the Human Development Index. *Journal of Human Development, 1*(1), 83–106.

Anderson, L. W., & Krathwohl, D. R. (Eds.). (2001). *A taxonomy for learning, teaching, and assessing: A revision of Bloom's taxonomy of educational objectives*. New York: Longman.

Anderson, N. (2014, July 1). Education: Sex offense statistics show U.S. college reports are rising. Retrieved from http://www .washingtonpost.com/local/education/sex-offense-statistics -show-us-college-reports-are-rising/2014/07/01/982ecf32 -0137-11e4-b8ff-89afd3fad6bd_story.html

Anker, M., Duncan, B. L., & Sparks, J. (2009). Using client feedback to improve couple therapy outcomes: A randomized clinical trial in a naturalistic setting. *Journal of Consulting and Clinical Psychology, 77*, 693–704.

Anker, M., Owen, J., Duncan, B. L., & Sparks, J. (2010). The alliance in couple therapy: Partner influence, early change, and alliance patterns in a naturalistic sample. *Journal of Consulting and Clinical Psychology, 78*, 635–645.

Antman, E. M., Lau, J., Kupelnick, B., Mosteller, F., & Chalmers, T. C. (1992). A comparison of results of meta-analyses of randomized control trials and recommendations of clinical experts: Treatments for myocardial infarction. *Journal of the American Medical Association, 268*, 240–248.

Applewhite, S. L. (1996). Curanderismo: Demystifying the health beliefs and practices of elderly Mexican Americans. In

631

P. L. Ewalt, E. M. Freeman, S. A. Kirk, & D. L. Poole (Eds.), *Multicultural issues in social work* (pp. 455–468). Washington DC: NASW Press.

Armstrong, K. (2010). *Twelve steps to a compassionate life.* New York: Knopf.

Aronson, E., & Aronson, J. (2012). *The social animal* (11th ed.). New York: Worth Publishing.

Arum, R., & Roksa, J. (2011). *Academically adrift: Limited learning on college campuses.* Chicago: University of Chicago Press.

Asay, T. P., & Lambert, M. J. (1999). The empirical case for the common factors in therapy: Quantitative factors. In M. A. Hubble, B. L. Duncan, & S. D. Miller (Eds.), *The heart and soul of change: What works in therapy* (pp. 23–55). Washington, DC: American Psychological Association.

Ashkenas, J., & Park, H. (2015, Apr. 8). The race gap in America's police departments. *The New York Times.* Retrieved from http://www.nytimes.com/interactive/2014/09/03/us/the-race-gap-in-americas-police-departments.html?_r=0

Assessment Capacities Project & Emergency Capacity Building Project. (2014). *Humanitarian needs assessment: The good enough guide.* Rugby, UK: Practical Action Publishing.

Association for Women's Rights in Development. (2004, Aug.). Intersectionality: A tool for gender and economic justice. *Women's Rights and Economic Change, 9,* 1–8. Retrieved from http://www.awid.org/sites/default/files/atoms/files/intersectionality_a_tool_for_gender_and_economic_justice.pdf

Association of Social Work Boards. (2011). Content outlines and KSAs: Social work licensing examinations. Retrieved from http://www.aswb.org/pdfs/2011KSAs.pdf

Association of Social Work Boards. (2013a). About the exams. Retrieved from https://www.aswb.org/exam-candidates/about-the-exams/

Association of Social Work Boards. (2013b). Exam content outlines. Retrieved from https://www.aswb.org/exam-candidates/about-the-exams/exam-content-outlines/

Association of Social Work Boards. (2015a). Member statutes and regulations. Retrieved from https://www.aswb.org/licensees/member-statutes-and-regulations/

Association of Social Work Boards. (2015b). Social work laws and regulations. Retrieved from https://www.datapathdesign.com/ASWB/Laws/Prod/cgi-bin/LawWebRpts2DLL.dll/18p1c4q1gp34aa0zn45so1wc3x9n/

Astatke, H., Black, M. M., & Serpell, R. (2000). Use of Jessor's theoretical framework of adolescent risk behavior in Ethiopia: Implications for HIV/AIDS prevention. *Northeast African Studies, 7*(1), 63–84.

Atkins, D. M., & Patenaude, A. F. (1987). Psychosocial preparation and follow-up for pediatric bone marrow transplant patients. *American Journal of Orthopsychiatry, 57*(2), 246–252.

Austin, D. M. (1997). The profession of social work: In the second century. In M. Reisch & E. Gambrill (Eds.), *Social work in the 21st century* (pp. 376–386). Thousand Oaks, CA: Pine Forge Press.

Axtell, R. E. (1998). *Gestures: The do's and taboos of body language around the world* (2nd ed.). New York: Wiley.

Axtell, R. E. (2007). *Essential do's and taboos: The complete guide to international business and leisure travel.* New York: Wiley.

Badger, E., Keating, D., & Elliott, K. (2014, Aug. 14). Where minority communities still have overwhelmingly white police. *The Washington Post.* Retrieved from http://www.washingtonpost.com/blogs/wonkblog/wp/2014/08/14/where-minority-communities-still-have-overwhelmingly-white-police/

Baer, K. (2015, May 4). Poverty costs poor people a lot. *Poverty and Policy.* Retrieved from https://povertyandpolicy.wordpress.com/2015/04/13/poverty-costs-poor-people-a-lot/

Baker, D. (2014, Aug. 11). The entitlement of the very rich. Truthout. Retrieved from http://www.truth-out.org/opinion/item/25488-the-entitlement-of-the-very-rich

Baker, M. R., & Steiner, J. R. (1996). Solution-focused social work: Metamessages to students in higher education opportunity programs. In P. L. Ewalt, E. M. Freeman, S. A. Kirk, & D. L. Poole (Eds.), *Multicultural issues in social work* (pp. 295–309). Washington DC: NASW Press.

Balgopal, P. R., Fong, R., Lu, Y. E., Park, Y., Choi, Y., Mohan, B., & DuongTran, P. (2008). Asian Americans. In T. Mizrahi & L. E. Davis (Eds.), *Encyclopedia of social work* (20th, e-reference ed.). New York: National Association of Social Workers and Oxford University Press.

Balko, R. (2013). *Rise of the warrior cop: The militarization of America's police forces.* New York: PublicAffairs.

Balko, R., & Cato, I. (2006). *Overkill : The rise of paramilitary police raids in America.* Washington, DC: Cato Institute.

Bandler, R., & Grinder, J. (1979). *Frogs into princes: Neuro-linguistic programming.* Moab, UT: Real People.

Bandler, R., & Grinder, J. (1982). *Reframing: Neuro-linguistic programing and the transformation of meaning.* Moab, UT: Real People.

Bandura, A. (1977). Self-efficacy: Toward a unifying theory of behavior change. *Psychological Review, 84,* 191–215.

Bandura, A. (1992). Exercise of personal agency through the self-efficacy mechanism. In R. Schwarzer (Ed.), *Self-efficacy: Thought control of action* (pp. 355–394). Washington, DC: Hemisphere.

Bandura, A. (1995a). Exercise of personal and collective efficacy in changing societies. In A. Bandura (Ed.), *Self-efficacy in changing societies* (pp. 1–45). New York: Cambridge University Press.

Bandura, A. (Ed.) (1995b). *Self-efficacy in changing societies.* New York: Cambridge University Press.

Bandura, A. (1997). *Self-efficacy: The exercise of control.* New York: Freeman. Baram, M. (2011, May 25). Government Sachs: Goldman's close ties to Washington arouse envy, raise questions. *The Huffington Post.* Retrieved from http://www.huffingtonpost.com/2009/06/02/government-sachs-goldmans_n_210561.html

Barker, R. L. (2014). *The social work dictionary* (6th ed.). Washington, DC: National Association of Social Workers.

Barnett, J. E. (2014). Sexual feelings and behaviors in the psychotherapy relationship: An ethics perspective. *Journal of Clinical Psychology, 70*(2), 170–181. doi: 10.1002/jclp.22068

Barrett, S., & Jarvis, W. T. (Eds.). (1993). *Health robbers: A close look at quackery in America.* Buffalo, NY: Prometheus Books.

Barry, B. (2007). *Speechless: The erosion of free expression in the American workplace.* San Francisco: Berrett-Koehler.

Bartels, L. M. (2008). *Unequal democracy: The political economy of the new gilded age.* New York: Russell Sage Foundation.

Barth, R. P., Lee, B. R., Lindsey, M. A., Collins, K. S., Strieder, F., Chorpita, B. F., . . . Sparks, J. A. (2012). Evidence-based practice at a crossroads: The timely emergence of common elements and common factors. *Research on Social Work Practice, 22*(1), 108–119. doi: 10.1177/1049731511408440

Bartlett, H. (1958). The working definition of social work practice. *Social Work, 3*(2), 1028–1030.

Bartlett, H. (1970). *The common base of social work practice.* New York: National Association of Social Workers.

Basow, S. A., & Rubenfeld, K. (2003). "Troubles talk": Effects of gender and gender-typing. *Sex Roles: A Journal of Research, 48,* 183–187.

Batson, C. D. (2009). These things called empathy: Eight related but distinct phenomena. In J. Decety & W. Ickes (Eds.), *The social neuroscience of empathy* (pp. 3–15). Cambridge, MA: The MIT Press.

Battaglini, D. J., & Schenkat, R. J. (1987). Fostering cognitive development in college students: The Perry and Toulmin models. *ERIC Clearinghouse on Reading and Communication Skills.* Retrieved from http://www.ericdigests.org/pre-925/perry.htm

Bauer, D. (2015, Jan. 31). World sex map: A story of drinkers, genocide and unborn girls. *QUARTZ.* Retrieved from http://

qz.com/335183/heres-why-men-on-earth-outnumber-women-by-60-million/

Beard, M. P. (2010). In-depth: Reaching the unbanked and underbanked. *Central Banker: News and Views for Eighth District Bankers, Winter*, 6–7. Retrieved from https://www.stlouisfed.org/~/media/Files/PDFs/publications/pub_assets/pdf/cb/2010/CB_winter_10.pdf

Beauchamp, T. L., & Childress, J. F. (1983). *Principles of biomedical ethics* (2nd ed.). New York: Oxford University Press.

Becker, H. S. (1994). Professional sociology: The case of C. Wright Mills. In R. C. Rist (Ed.), *The democratic imagination: Dialogues on the work of Irving Louis Horowitz* (pp. 175–188). New Brunswick, NJ: Transaction Publishers. Retrieved from http://howardsbecker.com/articles/mills.html

Becker, M. H. (1974). The Health Belief Model and personal health behavior. *Health Education Monographs, 2*, 324–508.

Belenky, M., Clinchy, B., Goldberger, N., & Tarule, J. (1986). *Women's ways of knowing: The development of self, voice, and mind.* New York: Basic Books.

Belsky, G., & Gilovich, T. (2000). *Why smart people make big money mistakes and how to correct them: Lessons from the new science of behavioral economics.* New York: Simon & Schuster.

Ben-Ari, A., & Somer, E. (2004). The aftermath of therapist–client sex: Exploited women struggle with the consequences. *Clinical Psychology and Psychotherapy, 11*(2), 126–136. doi: 10.1002/cpp.396

Benet-Martinez, V., & John, O. P. (1998). *Los Cinco Grandes* across cultures and ethnic groups: Multitrait multimethod analyses of the Big Five in Spanish and English. *Journal of Personality and Social Psychology, 75*, 729–750.

Benforado, A. (2015). *Unfair: The new science of criminal injustice.* New York: Crown.

Benjamin, R. (2009). *Searching for Whitopia: An improbable journey to the heart of White America.* New York: Hyperion.

Bennett, B. (2012). *Logically fallacious: The ultimate collection of over 300 logical fallacies.* Sudbury, MA: Ebookit.com.

Berg, I. K. (1994). *Family-based services: A solution-focused approach.* New York: Norton.

Berg, I. K., & De Jong, P. (1996). Solution-building conversations: Co-constructing a sense of competence with clients. *Families in Society: The Journal of Contemporary Human Services, 77*, 376–391.

Berg, I. K., & Reuss, N. H. (1998). *Solutions step by step: A substance abuse treatment manual.* New York: Norton.

Bergoglio, J. M. (2015, June 18). Encyclical letter: *Laudato Si'* of the Holy Father Francis on care for our common home. Retrieved from http://w2.vatican.va/content/francesco/en/encyclicals/documents/papa-francesco_20150524_enciclica-laudato-si.html

Berkman, C. S., Turner, S. G., Cooper, M., Polnerow, D., & Swartz, M. (2000). Sexual contact with clients: Assessment of social workers' attitudes and educational preparation. *Social Work, 45*(3), 223–235. Retrieved from <Go to ISI>://000086802500004

Berlin, S. B. (1990). Dichotomous and complex thinking. *Social Service Review, 64*(1), 46–59.

Berlin, S. B. (2005). The value of acceptance in social work direct practice: A historical and contemporary view. *Social Service Review, 79*(3), 482–510. Retrieved from http://search.ebscohost.com/login.aspx?direct=true&db=sih&AN=18024799&site=ehost-live

Berman, A. L., Jobes, D. A., & Silverman, M. M. (2006). *Adolescent suicide: Assessment and intervention* (2nd ed.). Washington, DC: American Psychological Association.

Berne, E. (1961). *Transactional analysis in psychotherapy: A systematic individual and social psychiatry.* New York: Grove Press.

Bernhardt, B., & Rauch, J. B. (1993). Genetic family histories: An aid to social work assessment. *Families in Society: The Journal of*

Contemporary Human Services, 74(4), 195–205. Retrieved from <Go to ISI>://A1993KU41200001

Bernsen, A., Tabachnick, B. G., & Pope, K. S. (1994). National survey of social workers' sexual attraction to their clients: Results, implications, and comparison to psychologists. *Ethics and Behavior, 4*(4), 369–388.

Berry, B. (2007). *Beauty bias: Discrimination and social power.* Westport, CT: Praeger.

Bey, J. (2012, Mar. 2). She the people (blog): The world as women see it: Rush Limbaugh's attack on Sandra Fluke was hate speech. *The Washington Post: PostPolitics.* Retrieved from http://www.washingtonpost.com/blogs/she-the-people/post/rush-limbaughs-attack-on-sandra-fluke-was-hate-speech/2012/03/02/gIQAZVxrmR_blog.html

Beyer, B. K. (1988). *Developing a thinking skills program.* Boston: Allyn & Bacon.

Biagi, E. (1977). The social work stake in problem-oriented recording. *Social Work in Health Care, 3*(2), 211–222.

Bjork, J. M., Knutson, B., Fong, G. W., Caggiano, D. M., Bennett, S. M., & Hommer, D. (2004). Incentive-elicited brain activation in adolescents: Similarities and differences from young adults. *Journal of Neuroscience, 24*, 1793–1802.

Blackburn, S. (1996). *The Oxford dictionary of philosophy.* Oxford reference online. Retrieved from http://www.oxfordreference.com/views/ENTRY.html?subview=Main&entry=t98.e173

Blair, J. P., & Schweit, K. W. (2014). *A study of active shooter incidents, 2000–2013.* Washington DC: Texas State University and Federal Bureau of Investigation, U.S. Department of Justice. Retrieved from http://permanent.access.gpo.gov/gpo52293/a_study_of_active_shooter_incidents_in_the_us_between_2000_and_2013.pdf

Bloom, B. S., & Krathwohl, D. R. (1956). *Taxonomy of educational objectives: The classification of educational goals, by a committee of college and university examiners: Handbook I: Cognitive domain.* New York: Longmans, Green.

Blount, M., Thyer, B. A., & Frye, T. (1992). Social work practice with Native Americans. In D. F. Harrison, J. S. Wodarski, & B. A. Thyer (Eds.), *Cultural diversity and social work practice* (pp. 107–134). Springfield, IL: Charles C Thomas.

Blow, C. M. (2015, Jan. 18). How expensive it is to be poor. *The New York Times.* Retrieved from http://www.nytimes.com/2015/01/19/opinion/charles-blow-how-expensive-it-is-to-be-poor.html?_r=0

Blumenkranz, C. (2011). *Occupy! Scenes from occupied America.* Brooklyn, NY: Verso.

Bobo, K. A. (2009). *Wage theft in America: Why millions of working Americans are not getting paid—and what we can do about it.* New York: Norton.

Bogie, M. A., & Coleman, M. (2002). Facing a malpractice claim. *NASW Assurance Services Practice Pointers, 3*(2), 1. Retrieved from http://www.naswinsurancetrust.org/facing_malpractice_claim.php

Bohart, A. C., & Greenberg, L. S. (1997a). Empathy and psychotherapy: An introductory overview. In A. C. Bohart & L. S. Greenberg (Eds.), *Empathy reconsidered: New directions in psychotherapy* (pp. 3–31). Washington, DC: American Psychological Association.

Bohart, A. C., & Greenberg, L. S. (Eds.). (1997b). *Empathy reconsidered: New directions in psychotherapy.* Washington, DC: American Psychological Association.

Bohart, A. C., & Tallman, K. (2010). Clients: The neglected common factor in psychotherapy. In B. L. Duncan, S. D. Miller, B. E. Wampold, & M. A. Hubble (Eds.), *The heart and soul of change: Delivering what works in therapy* (2nd ed., pp. 83–111). Washington, DC: American Psychological Association.

Bohmer, C. (2000). *The wages of seeking help: Sexual exploitation by professionals.* Westport, CT: Praeger.

Bonequi, I., & Richards, A. (2010). Lunch [DVD]. New York: Birds Nest Productions.

Borchard, E. M. (1932). *Convicting the innocent: Errors of criminal justice.* New Haven, CT: Yale University Press.

Bouchard, K. (2012, Dec. 9). Across nation, unsettling acceptance when mentally ill in crisis are killed. *Portland Press Herald.* Retrieved from http://www.pressherald.com/2012/12/09/shoot-across-nation-a-grim-acceptance-when-mentally-ill-shot-down/

Boudry, M., Blancke, S., & Pigliucci, M. (2014). What makes weird beliefs thrive? The epidemiology of pseudoscience. *Philosophical Psychology, 28*(8), 1–22. doi: 10.1080/09515089.2014.971946

Boyle, L. K. (2011, Jan. 6). Did you just eat a plastic bag? How plastic pollution has entered our food chain. *The Huffington Post: Green Blog.* Retrieved from http://www.huffingtonpost.com/lisa-kaas-boyle/the-facts-about-plastic-p_b_800013.html

Bozarth, J. D. (1997). Empathy from the framework of client-centered theory and the Rogerian hypothesis. In A. C. Bohart & L. S. Greenberg (Eds.), *Empathy reconsidered: New directions in psychotherapy* (pp. 81–102). Washington, DC: American Psychological Association.

Brammer, R. (2004). *Diversity in counseling.* Pacific Grove, CA: Brooks/Cole.

Branch Jr., W. T., & Gordon, G. H. (2004). Making the most of challenging patient interviews: Staying attuned to patients' emotions and personality styles—and your own reactions to them—enhances the efficacy of the medical interview. *Patient Care, 38*(7), 26–31.

Bray, G. A., & Popkin, B. M. (2014). Dietary sugar and body weight: Have we reached a crisis in the epidemic of obesity and diabetes? Health be damned! Pour on the sugar. *Diabetes Care, 37*(4), 950–956. doi: 10.2337/dc13-2085

Braybrooke, D. (1987). *Meeting needs: Studies in moral, political, and legal philosophy.* Princeton, NJ: Princeton University Press.

Breggin, P. R. (1997). *The heart of being helpful: Empathy and the creation of a healing presence.* New York: Springer.

Breithaupt, F. (2012a). Author reply: Empathy does provide rational support for decisions. But is it the right decision? *Emotion Review, 4*(1), 96–97. doi: 10.1177/1754073911421394

Breithaupt, F. (2012b). A three-person model of empathy. *Emotion Review, 4*(1), 84–91. doi: 10.1177/1754073911421375

Brenner, M. (2013, Apr. 1). Plutocracy in America. *Huff Post Politics: The Blog.* Retrieved from http://www.huffingtonpost.com/michael-brenner/plutocracy-in-america_b_2992965.html

Brewster, M. P., DeLong, P. A., & Moloney, J. T. (2013). Sex offender registries: A content analysis. *Criminal Justice Policy Review, 24*(6), 695–715. doi: 10.1177/0887403412459331

Bricker, J., Dettling, L. J., Henriques, A., Hsu, J. W., Moore, K. B., Sabelhaus, J., . . . Windle, R. A. (2014, Sept.). Changes in US family finances from 2010 to 2013: Evidence from the Survey of Consumer Finances. *Federal Reserve Bulletin, 100*(4), 1–41. Retrieved from http://www.federalreserve.gov/pubs/bulletin/2014/pdf/scf14.pdf

Brickman, P., & Campbell, D. T. (1971). Hedonic relativism and planning the good society. In M. H. Appley (Ed.), *Adaptation level theory: A symposium* (pp. 287–302). New York: Academic Press.

Brissett-Chapman, S. (1995). Child abuse and neglect: Direct practice. In R. L. Edwards (Ed.), *Encylopedia of social work* (19th ed., Vol. 1, pp. 353–366). Washington, DC: NASW Press.

British Psychological Society. (2008). *Guidelines on memory and the law: Recommendations from the scientific study of human memory, a report from the Research Board.* Retrieved from http://www.forcescience.org/articles/Memory&TheLaw.pdf

Brockman, J. (Ed.) (2009). *What have you changed your mind about? Today's leading minds rethink everything.* New York: HarperCollins.

Brody, H., & Brody, D. (2000). Three perspectives on the placebo response: Expectancy, conditioning, and meaning. *Advances in Mind-Body Medicine, 16*(3), 216–232. Retrieved from http://search.ebscohost.com/login.aspx?direct=true&db=crh&AN=5421106&site=ehost-live

Brogaard, B. (2013, Apr. 20). Micro-inequities: 40 years later—How to overcome implicit biases in the workplace. *Psychology Today.* Retrieved from https://www.psychologytoday.com/blog/the-superhuman-mind/201304/micro-inequities-40-years-later

Bronson, D. E., & Davis, T. S. (2012). *Finding and evaluating evidence: Systematic reviews and evidence-based practice.* Oxford; New York: Oxford University Press.

Brown, J. P. (2014, Oct. 10). The NYPD paid over $428 million in settlements over the last five years. Retrieved from https://www.muckrock.com/news/archives/2014/oct/10/nypd-paid-over-428-million-settlements-over-last-f/

Bryner, S. M. (2011, July 12). From hired guns to hired hands: A Center for Responsive Politics 'revolving door' investigation. 111th and 112th Congresses, Center for Responsive Politics report. Retrieved from http://www.opensecrets.org/news/2011/07/from-hired-guns-to-hired-hands/

Bulletin of the Atomic Scientists. (2015). Timeline: It is 3 minutes to midnight. *Doomsday Clock.* Retrieved from http://thebulletin.org/timeline

Bullis, R. K. (1995). *Clinical social worker misconduct: Law, ethics, and interpersonal dynamics.* Chicago: Nelson-Hall.

Bump, P. (2015, Apr. 21). The very simple reason more money is spent on lobbyists than on Congress. *The Washington Post.* Retrieved from http://www.washingtonpost.com/blogs/the-fix/wp/2015/04/21/why-more-money-is-spent-on-lobbyists-than-on-congress/

Burchum, J. L. R. (2002). Cultural competence: An evolutionary perspective. *Nursing Forum, 37*(4), 5–15.

Bureau of Economic Analysis. (2014, Dec. 23). National income and product accounts: Table 1.1.5. Gross domestic product. Retrieved from http://www.bea.gov/iTable/iTable.cfm?ReqID=9&step=1#reqid=9&step=3&isuri=1&903=5

Bureau of Justice Statistics. (2011, Nov.). Arrest-related deaths, 2003–2009. Statistical tables. Retrieved from http://www.bjs.gov/content/pub/pdf/ard0309st.pdf

Bureau of Labor Statistics and the Census Bureau. (2014). Current Population Survey (CPS): 2014 Annual Social and Economic Supplement: 2013 Household Income—All Races Dataset. Retrieved from http://www.census.gov/hhes/www/cpstables/032014/hhinc/hinc01_000.htm

Burke, P., & Parker, J. (2007). *Social work and disadvantage: Addressing the roots of stigma through association.* London; Philadelphia: Jessica Kingsley.

Burrill, G. (1976). The problem-oriented log in social casework. *Social Work, 21*(1), 67–68.

Bush, G. W. (2002). Address before a joint session of the congress on the state of the union. Retrieved from http://www.presidency.ucsb.edu/ws/index.php?pid=29644

Butler, T. (Ed.) (2015). *Overdevelopment, overpopulation, overshoot (OVER).* San Francisco: Foundation for Deep Ecology. Retrieved from https://populationspeakout.org/the-book/

Byrne, J., & Wells, R. (Eds.). (2012). *The occupy handbook.* New York: Back Bay Books.

Cabral, R. R., & Smith, T. B. (2011). Racial/ethnic matching of clients and therapists in mental health services: A meta-analytic review of preferences, perceptions, and outcomes. *Journal of Counseling Psychology, 58*(4), 537–554. doi: 10.1037/a0025266

Calkins, C., Jeglic, E., Beattey, R. A., Zeidman, S., & Perillo, A. D. (2014). Sexual violence legislation: A review of case law and empirical research. *Psychology, Public Policy, and Law, 20*(4), 443–462. doi: 10.1037/law0000027

Cameron, K. S., & Quinn, R. E. (1999). *Diagnosing and changing organizational culture.* Upper Saddle River, NJ: Prentice-Hall.

Campbell, A., & Hemsley, S. (2009). Outcome Rating Scale and Session Rating Scale in psychological practice: Clinical utility of ultra-brief measures. *Clinical Psychologist, 13*(1), 1–9.

Campbell, D. (1974). *If you don't know where you're going you'll probably end up somewhere else.* Niles, IL: Argus Communications.

Campbell, D. T., Cook, T. D., & Cook, T. H. (1979). *Quasi-experimentation.* Chicago: Rand McNally.

Campbell, D. T., & Stanley, J. C. (1966). *Experimental and quasi-experimental designs for research.* Chicago: Rand McNally.

Campbell, J. (1972). *The hero with a thousand faces* (2nd ed.). Princeton, NJ: Princeton University Press.

Campbell, J., & Moyers, B. (1988). *The power of myth* (2nd ed.). New York: Doubleday.

Campbell, V. A., Baker, D. B., & Bratton, S. (2000). Why do children drop-out from play therapy? *Clinical Child Psychology and Psychiatry, 5*(1), 133–138. doi: 10.1177/1359104500005001013

Campbell, W. K., Bush, C., Brunell, A., & Shelton, J. (2005). Understanding the social costs of narcissism: The case of the tragedy of the commons. *Personality and Social Psychology Bulletin, 31*(10), 1358–1368.

Canli, T., Omura, K., Haas, B., Fallgatter, A., Constable, R. T., & Lesch, K. P. (2005). Beyond affect: A role for genetic variation of the serotonin transporter in neural activation during a cognitive attention task. *Proceedings of the National Academy of Sciences, U.S.A., 102*(34), 12224–12229.

Cantle, F. (2000). What is a "learning organization" in general practice? A case study. *Health Services Management Research, 13*(3), 152–155.

Caplan, P. J. (2012, Apr. 27). Psychiatry's bible, the DSM, is doing more harm than good. *The Washington Post.* Retrieved from http://www.washingtonpost.com/opinions/psychiatrys-bible-the-dsm-is-doing-more-harm-than-good/2012/04/27/gIQAqy0WIT_print.html

Caplan, R. B., & Caplan, G. (2001). *Helping the helpers not to harm: Iatrogenic damage and community mental health.* New York: Brunner-Routledge.

Carkhuff, R. R. (1987). *The art of helping VI.* Amherst, MA: Human Resource Development Press.

Carkhuff, R. R., & Anthony, W. A. (1979). *The skills of helping.* Amherst, MA: Human Resource Development Press.

Carkhuff, R. R., & Truax, C. B. (1965). Training in counseling and psychotherapy. *Journal of Consulting Psychology, 29,* 333–336.

Carr, A. (2003). *Positive psychology.* New York: Brunner-Routledge.

Carson, E. A. (2014, Sept. 30). Prisoners in 2013. Retrieved from http://www.bjs.gov/content/pub/pdf/p13.pdf

Carson, R. (1962, 2002). *Silent spring* (40th anniv. ed.). Boston: Houghton Mifflin.

Carter, C. S., Harris, J., & Porges, S. W. (2009). Neural and evolutionary perspectives on empathy. In J. Decety & W. Ickes (Eds.), *The social neuroscience of empathy* (pp. 169–182). Cambridge, MA: The MIT Press.

Carvalho, A. B., Sampaio, M. C., Varandas, F. R., & Klaczko, L. B. (1998). An experimental demonstration of Fisher's principle: Evolution of sexual proportion by natural selection. *Genetics, 148*(2), 719–731. Retrieved from http://www.genetics.org/content/148/2/719.abstract

Casselman, B. (2015, May 2). Freddie Gray: Baltimore has a history of improper arrests. *FiveThirtyEight: DataLab.* Retrieved from http://fivethirtyeight.com/datalab/baltimore-has-a-history-of-improper-arrests/

Castex, G. M. (1996). Providing services to Hispanic/Latino populations: Profiles in diversity. In P. L. Ewalt, E. M. Freeman, S. A. Kirk, & D. L. Poole (Eds.), *Multicultural issues in social work* (pp. 523–538). Washington, DC: NASW Press.

Catalano, R. F., Hawkins, J. D., Berglund, M. L., Pollard, J. A., & Arthur, M. W. (2002). Prevention science and positive youth development: Competitive or cooperative frameworks. *Journal of Adolescent Health, 31,* 230–239.

Celenza, A. (1991). The misuse of countertransference love in sexual intimacies between therapists and patients. *Psychoanalytic Psychology, 8*(4), 501–509. doi: 10.1037/h0079302

Center for Responsive Politics. (2015). Lobbying database. *Influence & Lobbying.* Retrieved from http://www.opensecrets.org/lobby/index.php

Center for Substance Abuse Prevention. (2001). 2001 annual report on science-based prevention programs. Retrieved from http://www.samhsa.gov/centers/csap/modelprograms/pdfs/2001Annual.pdf

Centers for Disease Control and Prevention. (2012). Behavioral risk factor surveillance system. Retrieved from http://www.cdc.gov/brfss/

Centers for Disease Control and Prevention. (2014). *National Diabetes Statistics Report: Estimates of diabetes and its burden in the United States, 2014.* Atlanta, GA: U.S. Department of Health and Human Services. Retrieved from http://www.cdc.gov/diabetes/pubs/statsreport14/national-diabetes-report-web.pdf

Centers for Disease Control and Prevention. (2015, May 26). Sudden unexpected infant death and sudden infant death syndrome: About SUID and SIDS. Retrieved from http://www.cdc.gov/sids/aboutsuidandsids.htm

Centers for Medicare & Medicaid Services. (2015). International Classification of Diseases, Tenth Revision, Procedure Coding System (ICD-10-PCS): FY 2016 Release. Retrieved from http://www.cms.gov/Medicare/Coding/ICD10/2016-ICD-10-PCS-and-GEMs.html

Central Intelligence Agency. (2014). The world factbook: Field listing: Sex ratio. *The world fieldbook.* Retrieved from https://www.cia.gov/library/publications/the-world-factbook/fields/2018.html

Central Intelligence Agency. (2015). The world factbook: Field listing: Ethnic groups. Retrieved from https://www.cia.gov/library/publications/the-world-factbook/fields/2075.html?countryName=&countryCode=&regionCode=5

Chapin, R. K. (2007). *Social policy for effective practice: A strengths approach.* Boston: McGraw-Hill.

Chase, Y. (2008). Professional liability and malpractice. In T. Mizrahi & L. E. Davis (Eds.), *Encyclopedia of Social Work* (20th, e-reference ed.). New York: Oxford University Press.

Chetty, R., Hendren, N., Kline, P., & Saez, E. (2014). Where is the land of opportunity? The geography of intergenerational mobility in the United States. *Quarterly Journal of Economics, 129*(4), 1553–1623.

Chetty, R., Hendren, N., Kline, P., Saez, E., & Turner, N. (2014). Is the United States still a land of opportunity? Recent trends in intergenerational mobility. *American Economic Review Papers and Proceedings, 104*(5), 141–147.

Chin, W. W., Salisbury, W. D., Pearson, A. W., & Stollak, M. J. (1999). Perceived cohesion in small groups: Adapting and testing the Perceived Cohesion Scale in a small-group setting. *Small Group Research, 30*(6), 751–766. doi: 10.1177/104649649903000605

Cholakov, V., Kelly, K., Kindy, K., & Schaul, K. (2015, Apr. 11). Graphic: Police officers prosecuted for use of deadly force. *The Washington Post.* Retrieved from http://www.washingtonpost.com/graphics/investigations/police-shootings/

Choma, R. (2015, Jan. 12). One member of Congress = 18 American households: Lawmakers' personal finances far from average. *Center for Responsive Politics.* Retrieved from http://www.opensecrets.org/news/2015/01/one-member-of-congress-18-american-households-lawmakers-personal-finances-far-from-average/

Chorpita, B. F., Daleiden, E. L., & Weisz, J. R. (2005). Identifying and selecting the common elements of evidence based

interventions: A distillation and matching model. *Mental Health Services Research, 7*(1), 5–20.

Chorpita, B. F., & Weisz, J. R. (2009). *MATCH-ADTC: Modular approach to therapy for children with anxiety, depression, trauma, or conduct problems.* Satellite Beach, FL: PracticeWise.

Christ, W. R., Clarkin, J. F., & Hull, J. W. (1994). A high-risk screen for psychiatric discharge planning. *Health and Social Work, 19*(4), 261–270.

Christakis, N. A., & Fowler, J. H. (2009). *Connected: The surprising power of our social networks and how they shape our lives.* New York: Little, Brown, and Company.

Citizens United v. Federal Election Commission 130 S. Ct. 876 (U.S. Supreme Court 2010).

Clarridge, C. (2009, May 9). Seattle Times: Former social worker sentenced to jail for indecent liberties. Retrieved from http://seattletimes.nwsource.com/html/localnews/2009198734_webgill08m.html

Claus, R. E., & Kindleberger, L. R. (2002). Engaging substance abusers after centralized assessment: Predictors of treatment entry and dropout. *Journal of Psychoactive Drugs, 34,* 25–31.

CNN. (2013, Oct. 30). Iraq prison abuse scandal fast facts. *CNN News: U.S.* Retrieved from http://www.cnn.com/2013/10/30/world/meast/iraq-prison-abuse-scandal-fast-facts/

Cohen, A. (2012, May 21). Wrongful convictions: A new exoneration registry tests stubborn judges. *The Atlantic.* Retrieved from http://www.theatlantic.com/national/archive/2012/05/wrongful-convictions-a-new-exoneration-registry-tests-stubborn-judges/257416/

Cohen, J. A. (1988). *Statistical power analysis for the behavioral sciences* (2nd ed.). Hillsdale, NJ: Lawrence Erlbaum.

Colby, S. L., & Ortman, J. M. (2015, Mar.). Projections of the size and composition of the U.S. population: 2014 to 2060, Current Population Reports, P25-1143. Retrieved from www.census.gov/population/projections/data/national/2014.html

Coleman, J. S. (1988). Social capital in the creation of human capital. *The American Journal of Sociology, 94,* S95–S120. doi: 10.2307/2780243

Collaboration for Environmental Evidence. (2012). The CEE library of completed systematic reviews. Retrieved from http://www.environmentalevidence.org/Reviews.html

Collin, P. H. (2004). *Dictionary of environment and ecology* (5th ed.). London: Bloomsbury Reference.

Comim, F., & Nussbaum, M. C. (Eds.). (2014). *Capabilities, gender, equality: Towards fundamental entitlements.* Cambridge, UK: Cambridge University Press.

Compton, B. R., Galaway, B., & Cournoyer, B. R. (2005). *Social work processes* (7th ed.). Pacific Grove, CA: Brooks/Cole.

Compton, W. C. (2004). *Introduction to positive psychology.* Belmont, CA: Wadsworth.

Congress, E. P. (1994). The use of culturalgrams to assess and empower culturally diverse families. *Families in Society: The Journal of Contemporary Human Services, 75,* 531–540.

Congress, E. P. (1999). *Social work values and ethics: Identifying and resolving ethical dilemmas.* Belmont, CA: Wadsworth.

Congress, E. P. (2000). What social workers should know about ethics: Understanding and resolving ethical dilemmas. *Advances in Social Work, 1*(1), 1–25.

Cook, T. D., & Campbell, D. T. (Eds.). (1979). *Quasi-experimentation: Design and analysis issues for field settings.* Chicago: Rand McNally.

Cooper, R. V. (2014). *Diagnosing the Diagnostic and Statistical Manual of Mental Disorders.* London: Karnac Books.

Corak, M. (2006). Do poor children become poor adults? Lessons from a cross country comparison of generational earnings mobility: Discussion Paper No. 1993. Retrieved from http://ftp.iza.org/dp1993.pdf

Corcoran, K., & Fischer, J. (2013a). *Measures for clinical practice and research: A sourcebook. Vol. 1: Couples, families, and children* (5th ed.). New York: Oxford University Press.

Corcoran, K., & Fischer, J. (2013b). *Measures for clinical practice and research: A sourcebook. Vol. 2: Adults* (5th ed.). New York: Oxford University Press.

Cosgrove, L. (2011). The DSM, big pharma, and clinical practice guidelines: Protecting patient autonomy and informed consent. *International Journal of Feminist Approaches to Bioethics, 4*(1), 11–25.

Cosgrove, L., & Krimsky, S. (2012). A comparison of DSM-IV and DSM-5 panel members' financial associations with industry: A pernicious problem persists. *PLoS Medicine, 9*(3), 1–4. doi: 10.1371/journal.pmed.1001190

Cosgrove, L., Krimsky, S., Vijayaraghavan, M., & Schneider, L. (2006). Financial ties between DSM-IV panel members and the pharmaceutical industry. *Psychotherapy and Psychosomatics, 75*(3), 154–160. Retrieved from http://www.tufts.edu/~skrimsky/PDF/DSM%20COI.PDF

Council on Social Work Education. (2015). Educational policy and accreditation standards. Retrieved from http://www.cswe.org/

Cournoyer, B. R. (1999). Unpublished data regarding foundation year MSW students' critical thinking and lifelong learning. Indiana University School of Social Work, Indianapolis, Indiana.

Cournoyer, B. R. (2003). Unpublished data regarding foundation and concentration year MSW students' critical thinking and lifelong learning. Indiana University School of Social Work, Indianapolis, Indiana.

Cournoyer, B. R. (2004). *The evidence-based social work skills book.* Boston: Allyn & Bacon.

Cournoyer, B. R., & Powers, G. T. (2002). Evidence-based social work: The quiet revolution continues. In A. R. Roberts & G. J. Greene (Eds.), *Social workers' desk reference* (pp. 798–807). New York: Oxford University Press.

Cournoyer, B. R., & Stanley, M. J. (2002). *The social work portfolio: Planning, assessing and documenting lifelong learning in a dynamic profession.* Pacific Grove, CA: Brooks/Cole.

Cowger, C. D. (1994). Assessing client strengths: Clinical assessment for client empowerment. *Social Work, 39*(3), 262–268. Retrieved from <Go to ISI>://A1994NJ40100005

Cowger, C. D. (1996). Assessment of client strengths. In D. Saleebey (Ed.), *The strengths perspective in social work practice* (2nd ed., pp. 59–73). New York: Longman.

Cox, C. B. (1996). Discharge planning for dementia patients: Factors influencing caregiver decisions and satisfaction. *Health and Social Work, 21*(2), 97–106.

Coyne, C. J. (2013). *Doing bad by doing good: Why humanitarian action fails.* Stanford, CA: Stanford Economics and Finance, Standford University Press.

Crits-Christoph, P., Ring-Kurtz, S., Hamilton, J. L., Lambert, M. J., Gallop, R., McClure, B., . . . Rotrosen, J. (2012). A preliminary study of the effects of individual patient-level feedback in outpatient substance abuse treatment programs. *Journal of Substance Abuse Treatment, 42*(3), 301–309. doi: 10.1016/j.jsat.2011.09.003

Cross, T., Bazron, B., Dennis, K., & Isaacs, M. (1989). *Toward a culturally competent system of care* (Vol. 1). Washington, DC: Georgetown University.

Csikszentmihalyi, M., & Csikszentmihalyi, I. S. (Eds.). (2006). *Life worth living: Contributions to positive psychology.* New York: Oxford University Press.

"cultural sensitivity." (2007). *A dictionary of public health.* Oxford reference online. Retrieved from http://www.oxfordreference.com.proxy2.ulib.iupui.edu/views/ENTRY.html?subview=Main&entry=t235.e974>

Curtis, G. N. (2001–2014). The fallacy files. Retrieved from http://www.fallacyfiles.org/index.html

Cushing, W. (1783). Legal notes by William Cushing about the Quock Walker case. *MHS Collections Online.* Retrieved from http://www.masshist.org/database/viewer.php?item_id=630&mode=large&img_step=8&br=1#page8

Dalal, P. K., & Sivakumar, T. (2009). Moving towards ICD-11 and DSM-5: Concept and evolution of psychiatric classification. *Indian Journal of Psychiatry, 51*(4), 310–319.

Dalton, A. N., & Spiller, S. A. (2012). Too much of a good thing: The benefits of implementation intentions depend on the number of goals. *Journal of Consumer Research, 39*(3), 600–614. doi: 10.1086/664500

Dalton, D. (Ed.) (1996). *Mahatma Gandhi: Selected political writings.* Indianapolis, IN: Hackett.

Damer, T. E. (2013). *Attacking faulty reasoning: A practical guide to fallacy-free arguments* (7th ed.). Boston: Wadsworth/Cengage Learning.

Damodaran, A. (2015, Jan. 5). Annual returns on stock, T.Bonds and T.Bills: 1928–current. Retrieved from http://pages.stern.nyu.edu/~adamodar/New_Home_Page/datafile/histretSP.html

Davenport, C., & Connelly, M. (2015, Jan. 30). Most Republicans say they back climate action, poll finds. *The New York Times.* Retrieved from http://www.nytimes.com/2015/01/31/us/politics/most-americans-support-government-action-on-climate-change-poll-finds.html

Davis, C., Davis, K., Gardner, M., Heimovitz, H., Johnson, S., McIntyre, R. S.,. . . Wiehe, M. (2015, Jan.). *Who pays? A distributional analysis of the tax systems in all 50 states.* Retrieved from Washington, DC, http://www.itep.org/pdf/whopaysreport.pdf

Davis, K., Stremikis, K., Schoen, C., & Squires, D. (2014, June). Mirror, mirror on the wall, 2014 update: How the U.S. health care system compares internationally. *The Commonwealth Fund.* Retrieved from http://www.commonwealthfund.org/publications/fund-reports/2014/jun/mirror-mirror

Davis, S., & Botkin, J. (1994). The coming of knowledge-based businesses. *Harvard Business Review, 72*(5), 165–170.

Davis, W. (2009). *The wayfinders: Why ancient wisdom matters in the modern world.* Toronto: House of Anansi Press.

Davis, W., Harrison, K. D., & Howell, C. H. (2007). *Book of peoples of the world: A guide to cultures.* Washington, DC: National Geographic.

Dayen, D. (2015, Feb. 4). Wall Street pays bankers to work in government and it doesn't want anyone to know. *The New Republic.* Retrieved from http://www.newrepublic.com/article/120967/wall-street-pays-bankers-work-government-and-wants-it-secret

De Jong, P., & Berg, I. K. (2002). *Interviewing for solutions.* Pacific Grove, CA: Brooks/Cole.

de la Llama, V. A., Trueba, I., Voges, C., Barreto, C., & Park, D. J. (2012). At Face(book) value: Uses of Facebook in hiring processes and the role of identity in social networks. *International Journal of Work Innovation, 1*(1), 114–136. doi: 10.1504/12.47984

de Shazer, S. (1988). *Clues: Investigating solutions in brief therapy.* New York: Norton.

de Shazer, S., Berg, I. K., Lipchick, E., Nunnally, E., Molnar, A., Gingerich, W., & Weiner-Davis, M. (1986). Brief therapy: Focused solution development. *Family Process, 25,* 207–221.

de Waal, F. B. M. (2009). *The age of empathy: Nature's lessons for a kinder society.* New York: Harmony Books.Dean, R. G. (2001). The myth of cross-cultural competence. *Families in Society: The Journal of Contemporary Human Services, 82*(6), 623–630.

Deardorff, D. K. (Ed.). (2009). *The Sage handbook of intercultural competence.* Thousand Oaks, CA: Sage.

Del Bino, S., & Bernerd, F. (2012). Relationship between skin color and skin response to ultraviolet light. *International Journal of Dermatology, 51,* 5–7. doi: 10.1111/j.1365-4632.2012.05554.x

Delgado, M. (2007). *Social work with Latinos: A cultural assets paradigm.* Oxford; New York: Oxford University Press.

Demazeux, S., & Singy, P. (Eds.). (2015). *The DSM-5 in perspective: Philosophical reflections on the psychiatric Babel.* Dordrecht: Springer.

DeNavas-Walt, C., & Proctor, B. D. (2014, Sept.). *U.S. Census Bureau, Current Population Reports, P60-249, Income and Poverty in the United States: 2013.* Retrieved from http://www.census.gov/content/dam/Census/library/publications/2014/demo/p60-249.pdf

DeNavas-Walt, C., Proctor, B. D., & Smith, J. C. (2011). *Income, Poverty, and Health Insurance Coverage in the United States: 2010. U. S. Census Bureau, Current Population Reports, P60-239.* Retrieved from http://www.census.gov/prod/2011pubs/p60-239.pdf

DeParle, J. (2012, Jan. 4). Harder for Americans to rise from lower rungs. *The New York Times.* Retrieved from http://www.nytimes.com/2012/01/05/us/harder-for-americans-to-rise-from-lower-rungs.html

Department for International Development. (2012). Research for development (R4D) database: Systematic reviews. Retrieved from http://www.dfid.gov.uk/R4D/SystematicReviews.aspx

Department of Defense. (2015, May 1). Fiscal year 2014 annual report on sexual assault in the military. Retrieved from http://sapr.mil/public/docs/reports/FY14_Annual/FY14_DoD_SAPRO_Annual_Report_on_Sexual_Assault.pdf

Department of Labor Office of Federal Contract Compliance Programs. (2014). RIN 1250-AA07 Implementation of Executive Order 13672 prohibiting discrimination based on sexual orientation and gender identity by contractors and subcontractors. Retrieved from http://www.dol.gov/ofccp/LGBT/OFCCP_LGBT_Rule%20Final_12114_JRF_QA_508c.pdf

DeSilver, D. (2014, Oct. 9). For most workers, real wages have barely budged for decades. Retrieved from http://www.pewresearch.org/fact-tank/2014/10/09/for-most-workers-real-wages-have-barely-budged-for-decades/

DeSteno, D., & Valdesolo, P. (2011). *Out of character: Surprising truths about the liar, cheat, sinner (and saint) lurking in all of us.* New York: Crown Publishing.

Devine, T., & Maassarani, T. F. (2011). *The corporate whistleblower's survival guide: A handbook for committing the truth.* San Francisco, CA: Berrett-Koehler.

Diamond, J. M. (1998). *Guns, germs, and steel: The fates of human societies.* New York: Norton.

Diamond, J. M. (2005). *Collapse: How societies choose to fail or succeed.* New York: Viking.

Diamond, J. M. (2012). *The world until yesterday: What can we learn from traditional societies?* New York: Viking.

DiAngelo, R. (2011). White fragility. *International Journal of Critical Pedagogy, 3*(3), 54–70.

Dick, K. (2012). *The invisible war* [Film]. New York: Cinedigm.

Dick, K. (2015). *The hunting ground* [Film]. New York: Radius TWC and CNN Films.

Diener, E. (2006, Feb. 13). Understanding scores on the Satisfaction With Life Scale. Retrieved from http://www.psych.uiuc.edu/~ediener/Understanding%20SWLS%20Scores.pdf

Diener, E., Lucas, R. E., & Scollon, C. N. (2006). Beyond the hedonic treadmill: Revising the adaptation theory of well-being. *American Psychologist, 61*(4), 305–314. doi: 10.1037/0003-066x.61.4.305

Digman, J. M. (1990). Personality structure: Emergence of the five-factor model. *Annual Review of Psychology, 41,* 417–440.

Disch, E., & Avery, N. (2001). Sex in the consulting room, the examining room, and the sacristy: Survivors of sexual abuse by professionals. *American Journal of Orthopsychiatry, 71*(2), 204–217. doi: 10.1037/0002-9432.71.2.204

Dolan, K. A., & Kroll, L. (2014, Sept. 29). Inside the 2014 Forbes 400: Facts and figures about America's wealthiest. Retrieved

from http://www.forbes.com/sites/kerryadolan/2014/09/29/inside-the-2014-forbes-400-facts-and-figures-about-americas-wealthiest/

Dolcos, S., Sung, K., Argo, J. J., Flor-Henry, S., & Dolcos, F. (2012). The power of a handshake: neural correlates of evaluative judgments in observed social interactions. *Journal of Cognitive Neuroscience, 24*(12), 2292–2305. doi: 10.1162/jocn_a_00295

Dolgoff, R., Loewenberg, F. M., & Harrington, D. (2012). *Ethical decisions for social work practice* (9th ed.). Belmont, CA: Brooks/Cole.

Doyal, L., & Gough, I. (1991). *A theory of human need.* New York: Guilford Press.

Drisko, J. W., & Grady, M. D. (2012). *Evidence-based practice in clinical social work.* New York: Springer.

Duncan, B. L. (2012). The Partners for Change Outcome Management System (PCOMS): The heart and soul of change project. *Canadian Psychology/Psychologie canadienne, 53*(2), 93–104. doi: 10.1037/a0027762

Duncan, B. L., Miller, S. D., Sparks, J., Claud, D., L., R., Brown, J., & Johnson, L. (2003). The Session Rating Scale: Preliminary psychometric properties of a "working" alliance measure. *Journal of Brief Therapy, 3,* 3–12.

Duncan, B. L., Miller, S. D., Wampold, B. E., & Hubble, M. A. (Eds.). (2010). *The heart and soul of change: Delivering what works in therapy* (2nd ed.). Washington, DC: American Psychological Association.

Dybicz, P. (2011). Interpreting the strengths perspective through narrative theory. *Families in Society: The Journal of Contemporary Human Services, 92*(3), 247–253. Retrieved from https://www.researchgate.net/publication/265490427_Interpreting_the_Strengths_Perspective_Through_Narrative_Theory

Dziegielewski, S. F. (2008). Problem identification, contracting, and case planning. In W. Rowe & L. A. Rapp-Paglicci (Eds.), *Comprehensive handbook of social work and social welfare: Social work practice* (Vol. 3, pp. 78–97). Hoboken, NJ: Wiley.

Ebstein, R. B., Novick, O., Umansky, R., Priel, B., & Osher, Y. (1996). Dopamine D4 receptor (D4DR) exon III polymorphism associated with the human personality trait of novelty seeking. *Nature Genetics, 12,* 78–80.

Economic Policy Institute. (2008). The state of working America: When income grows, who gains? 1917–2008. Retrieved from http://stateofworkingamerica.org/who-gains/

Edelman, P. B. (2012). *So rich, so poor: Why it's so hard to end poverty in America.* New York: New Press.

Edmundson, W. A. (2004). *An introduction to rights.* Cambridge, UK: Cambridge University Press.

Egan, G. (1982). *Exercises in helping skills: A training manual to accompany the skilled helper* (2nd ed.). Monterey, CA: Brooks/Cole.

Egan, G. (2010). *The skilled helper* (9th ed.). Belmont, CA: Brooks/Cole.

Ehrenreich, B. (2001). *Nickel and dimed: On (not) getting by in America.* New York: Metropolitan Books.

Ehrenreich, B. (2005). *Bait and switch: The (futile) pursuit of the American dream.* New York: Metropolitan Books.

Ehrenreich, B. (2014, Jan. 13). It is expensive to be poor. *The Atlantic.* Retrieved from http://www.theatlantic.com/business/archive/2014/01/it-is-expensive-to-be-poor/282979/

Eisenbrey, R. (2014, Apr. 2). Wage theft is a bigger problem than other theft—But not enough is done to protect workers. *Economic Policy Institute.* Retrieved from http://www.epi.org/publication/wage-theft-bigger-problem-theft-protect/

Eisenbrey, R. (2015, Feb. 13). Wage theft by employers is costing U.S. workers billions of dollars a year. *Economic Policy Institute.* Retrieved from http://www.epi.org/blog/wage-theft-by-employers-is-costing-u-s-workers-billions-of-dollars-a-year/

Eisinger, J. (2014, Apr. 30). Why only one top banker went to jail for the financial crisis. *The New York Times Magazine.* Retrieved from http://www.nytimes.com/2014/05/04/magazine/only-one-top-banker-jail-financial-crisis.html.

Ekman, P. (1982). *Emotion in the human face* (2nd ed.). New York: Cambridge University Press.

Ekman, P. (1999). Basic emotions. In T. Dalgleish & T. Power (Eds.), *The handbook of cognition and emotion* (pp. 45–60). Sussex, UK: Wiley.

Ekman, P., & Friesen, W. V. (1975). *Unmasking the face: A guide to recognizing emotions from facial clues.* New York: Prentice-Hall.

Ellison, S. (2009). *Taking the war out of our words: The art of powerful non-defensive communication.* Deadwood, OR: Wyatt-Mackenzie.

Epperson, D. L., Bushway, D. J., & Warman, R. E. (1983). Client self-terminations after one counseling session: Effects of problem recognition, counselor gender, and counselor experience. *Journal of Counseling Psychology, 30,* 307–315.

EPPI-Centre. (2012). What is the EPPI-Centre? Online Evidence Library. Retrieved from http://eppi.ioe.ac.uk/cms/Default.aspx?tabid=63.

Epstein, J. A., & Botvin, G. J. (2002). The moderating role of risk-taking tendency and refusal assertiveness on social influences in alcohol use among inner-city adolescents. *Journal of Studies on Alcohol, 63*(4), 456–459. Retrieved from <Go to ISI>://000177103700009

Equal Justice Initiative. (2015). Lynching in America: Confronting the legacy of racial terror. Report summary. Retrieved from http://www.eji.org/files/EJI%20Lynching%20in%20America%20SUMMARY.pdf

Eriksen, M., Lebreton, L. C. M., Carson, H. S., Thiel, M., Moore, C. J., Borerro, J. C., Galgani, F., Ryan, P.G., & Reisser, J. (2014). Plastic pollution in the world's oceans: More than 5 trillion plastic pieces weighing over 250,000 tons afloat at sea. *PLoS ONE, 9*(12), e111913. doi: 10.1371/journal.pone.0111913

Erikson, E. H. (1963). *Childhood and society* (2nd ed.). New York: Norton.

Erikson, E. H. (1968). *Identity, youth and crisis* (2nd ed.). New York: Norton.

Erikson, E. H. (1980). *Identity and the life cycle.* New York: Norton.

Escudero, V., Heatherington, L., & Friedlander, M. L. (2010). Therapeutic alliances and alliance building in family therapy. In J. C. Muran & J. P. Barber (Eds.), *The therapeutic alliance: An evidence-based guide to practice* (pp. 240–262). New York: Guilford Press.

Etzioni, A. (1999). *The limits of privacy.* New York: Basic Books.

Evans, D. R., Hearn, M. T., Uhlemann, M. R., & Ivey, A. E. (2008). *Essential interviewing: A programmed approach to effective communication* (7th ed.). Belmont, CA: Brooks/Cole.

Evans, N. J., & Jarvis, P. A. (1986). The Group Attitude Scale: A measure of attraction to group. *Small Group Research, 17*(2), 203–216. doi: 10.1177/104649648601700205

Everstine, D. S., & Everstine, L. (1983). *People in crisis: Strategic therapeutic interventions.* New York: Brunner/Mazel.

Everstine, L., Everstine, D. S., Heymann, G. M., True, D. H., Johnson, H. G., & Seiden, R. H. (1980). Privacy and confidentiality in psychotherapy. *American Psychologist, 35,* 828–840.

Ewing, C. P., & McCann, J. T. (2006). *Minds on trial: Great cases in law and psychology.* New York: Oxford University Press.

Ewing, J. A. (1984). Detecting alcoholism: The CAGE questionnaire. *Journal of the American Medical Association, 252*(14), 1905–1907. doi: 10.1001/jama.1984.03350140051025

Farag, Y. M. K., & Gaballa, M. R. (2011). Diabesity: An overview of a rising epidemic. *Nephrology Dialysis Transplantation, 26*(1), 28–35. doi: 10.1093/ndt/gfq576

Feathers, T. (2014, Oct. 20). Police misconduct in Philadelphia, by the numbers. Retrieved from https://www.muckrock.com/news/archives/2014/oct/20/philly-lawsuits/

Fieldhouse, P., & Bunkowsky, L. (2002). Asphalt artisans: Creating a community eco-map on the playground. *Green Teacher, 67,* 16–19.

First, M. B. (2014). Empirical grounding versus innovation in the DSM-5 revision process: Implications for the future. *Clinical Psychology: Science and Practice, 21*(3), 262–268. doi: 10.1111/cpsp.12069

Fishbein, M., & Middlestadt, S. E. (1989). Using the theory of reasoned action as a framework for understanding and changing AIDS-related behaviors. In V. M. Mays, G. W. Albee, & S. F. Schneider (Eds.), *Primary prevention of AIDS: Psychological approaches* (pp. 93–110). London: Sage.

Fishbein, M., Middlestadt, S. E., & Hitchcock, P. J. (1994). Using information to change sexually transmitted disease-related behaviors. In R. J. DiClemente & J. L. Peterson (Eds.), *Preventing AIDS: Theories and methods of behavioral interventions* (pp. 61–78). New York: Plenum Press.

Fiske, J. (1978). *Myths and myth-makers: Old tales and superstitions interpreted by comparative mythology.* Boston: Longwood Press.

Fitzgerald, F. S. (1926, Jan. & Feb.). The rich boy. *Redbook.* Retrieved from http://gutenberg.net.au/fsf/THE-RICH-BOY.html

Fletcher, J. F. (1966). *Situational ethics: The new morality.* Louisville, KY: Westminster John Knox Press.

Fluckiger, C., Del Re, A. C., Wampold, B. E., Symonds, D., & Horvath, A. O. (2012). How central is the alliance in psychotherapy? A multilevel longitudinal meta-analysis. *Journal of Counseling Psychology, 59*(1), 10–17. doi: 10.1037/a0025749

Fogel, S. J. (2008). Sexual harassment. In T. Mizrahi & L. E. Davis (Eds.), *Encyclopedia of Social Work* (20th, e-reference ed.). New York: Oxford University Press.

Folman, R. Z. (1991). Therapist-patient sex: Attraction and boundary problems. *Psychotherapy: Theory, Research, Practice, Training, 28*(1), 168–173. doi: 10.1037/0033-3204.28.1.168

Fong, R. (2003). Cultural competence with Asian Americans. In D. Lum (Ed.), *Culturally competent practice: A framework for understanding diverse groups and justice issues* (2nd ed., pp. 261–281). Pacific Grove, CA: Brooks/Cole.

Fontes, L. A. (2008). *Interviewing clients across cultures: A practitioner's guide.* New York: Guilford Press.

Foster, J. E. (2006). Poverty indices. In A. de Janvry & R. Kanbur (Eds.), *Poverty, inequality and development: Essays in honor of Erik Thorbecke* (pp. 41–65). New York: Springer.

Foundation for Critical Thinking. (2014, Sept.). Valuable intellectual traits (virtues). Retrieved from http://www.criticalthinking.org/pages/valuable-intellectual-traits/528

Fox, E., Ridgewell, A., & Ashwin, C. (2009). Looking on the bright side: Biased attention and the human serotonin transporter gene. *Proceedings of the Royal Society B: Biological Sciences, 276*(1663), 1747–1751. doi: 10.1098/rspb.2008.1788

Frame, M. W. (2000). The spiritual genogram in family therapy. *Journal of Marital and Family Therapy, 26*(2), 211–216.

Frances, A. (2013). *Saving normal: An insider's revolt against out-of-control psychiatric diagnosis, DSM-5, Big Pharma, and the medicalization of ordinary life.* New York: William Morrow.

Franck, J., & Møller, K. J. (2014, Sept. 1). Denmark aims to be rid of fossil fuels by 2050. *ScienceNordic.* Retrieved from http://sciencenordic.com/denmark-aims-be-rid-fossil-fuels-2050

Frank, R. (2015, May 6). Most millionaires say they're middle class. CNBC Millionaire Survey. Retrieved from http://www.cnbc.com/2015/05/06/naires-say-theyre-middle-class.html

Franks, C., & Riedel, M. (2008). Privilege. In T. Mizrahi & L. E. Davis (Eds.), *Encyclopedia of social work* (20th, e-reference ed.). New York: Oxford University Press.

Fraser, M. W., Richman, J. M., & Galinsky, M. J. (1999). Risk, protection, and resilience: Toward a conceptual framework for social work practice. *Social Work Research, 23*(3), 131–143. Retrieved from <Go to ISI>://000082756600001

Fraser, S., & Moyers, B. (2014, Dec. 19). The new Robber Barons [Transcript]. *Moyers and Company.* Retrieved from http://billmoyers.com/episode/steve-fraser-new-robber-barons/

Frisch, M. B. (2005). *Quality of life therapy: Applying a life satisfaction approach to positive psychology and cognitive therapy.* New York: Wiley.

Fujita, F., & Diener, E. (2005). Life satisfaction set point: Stability and change. *Journal of Personality and Social Psychology, 88*(1), 158–164. doi: 10.1037/0022-3514.88.1.158

Fuller, R. W. (2002). *Somebodies and nobodies: Overcoming the abuse of rank.* Gabriola Island, BC, Canada: New Society.

Gabbard, G. O. (1989). *Sexual exploitation in professional relationships.* Washington, DC: American Psychiatric Press.

Galbraith, J. K. (2012). *Inequality and instability: A study of the world economy just before the Great Crisis.* New York: Oxford University Press.

Gallagher, W. (1993). *The power of place: How our surroundings shape our thoughts, emotions, and actions.* New York: Poseidon Press.

Gallup-Healthways. (2015). Gallup-Healthways Well-Being 5™. Retrieved from http://www.healthways.com/solution/default.aspx?id=1125

Galtung, J. (1964). An Editorial. *Journal of Peace Research, 1*(1), 1–4. doi: 10.1177/002234336400100101

Galtung, J. (1990). Cultural violence. *Journal of Peace Research, 27*(3), 291–305. doi: 10.2307/423472

Gambrill, E. D. (1999). Evidence-based practice: An alternative to authority-based practice. *Families in Society: The Journal of Contemporary Human Services, 80*(4), 341–350.

Gambrill, E. D. (2001). Social work: An authority-based profession. *Research on Social Work Practice, 11*(2), 166–176.

Gardner, D. L., Huber, C. H., Steiner, R., Vazquez, L. A., & Savage, T. A. (2008). The development and validation of the inventory of family protective factors: A brief assessment for family counseling. *The Family Journal, 16*(2), 107–117. doi: 10.1177/1066480708314259

Garmezy, N. (1985). The NIMH-Israeli high-risk study: Commendation, comments, and cautions. *Schizophrenia Bulletin, 11*(3), 349–353.

Garmezy, N. (1986). *Risk and protective factors in the major mental disorders.* Chicago: John D. and Catherine T. MacArthur Foundation.

Garrett, T., & Davis, J. D. (1998). The prevalence of sexual contact between British clinical psychologists and their patients. *Clinical Psychology and Psychotherapy, 5*(4), 253–263. doi: 10.1002/(SICI)1099-0879(199812)5:4<253::AID-CPP171>3.0.CO;2-4

Garvin, C. (1987). *Contemporary group work* (2nd ed.). Englewood Cliffs, NJ: Prentice-Hall.

Garvin, C. (1997). *Contemporary group work* (3rd ed.). Boston: Allyn & Bacon.

Garvin, C., & Seabury, B. (1997). *Interpersonal practice in social work: Promoting competence and social justice* (2nd ed.). Boston: Allyn & Bacon.

Garza, A. (2014, Oct. 7). A herstory of the #BlackLivesMatter movement. *The Feminist Wire.* Retrieved from http://www.thefeministwire.com/2014/10/blacklivesmatter-2/

Gechtman, L. (1989). Sexual contact between social workers and their clients. In G. O. Gabbard (Ed.), *Sexual exploitation in professional relationships* (pp. 27–38). Washington, DC: American Psychiatric Press.

General Assembly of the United Nations. (1948). *Universal declaration of human rights.* New York: Author.

General Assembly of the United Nations. (1966a). International convenant on civil and political rights. Retrieved from http://www.un.org/millennium/law/iv-4.htm

General Assembly of the United Nations. (1966b). International convenant on economic, social, and cultural rights. Retrieved from http://www.unhchr.ch/html/menu3/b/a_cescr.htm

General Assembly of the United Nations. (1990, Sept. 2). Convention on the rights of the child. Retrieved from http://www.ohchr.org/Documents/ProfessionalInterest/crc.pdf

Gershoff, E. T., Mistry, R., & Crosby, D. A. (Eds.). (2014). *Societal contexts of child development: Pathways of influence and implications for practice and policy.* Oxford; New York: Oxford University Press.

Gibbs, L., & Gambrill, E. (1996). *Critical thinking for social workers: A workbook.* Thousand Oaks, CA: Pine Forge Press.

Gilbert, D. J., & Franklin, C. (2001). Developing culturally sensitive practice evaluation skills with Native American individuals and families. In R. Fong & S. Furuto (Eds.), *Culturally competent practice* (pp. 396–411). Boston: Allyn & Bacon.

Gilboa, A., Alain, C., Stuss, D. T., Melo, B., Miller, S., & Moscovitch, M. (2006). Mechanisms of spontaneous confabulations: A strategic retrieval account. *Brain, 129,* 1399–1414. doi: 10.1093/brain/awl093

Gilens, M., & Page, B. I. (2014). Testing theories of American politics: Elites, interest groups, and average citizens. *Perspectives on Politics, 12*(3), 564–581. doi: 10.1017/S1537592714001595

Gilgun, J. F. (1998). Clinical instruments for assessing client assets and risks. *The Medical Journal of Allina, 7,* 31–33.

Gilgun, J. F. (2004a). The 4-D: Strengths-based assessments for youth who've experienced adversities. *Journal of Human Behavior in the Social Environment, 10*(4), 51–73.

Gilgun, J. F. (2004b). A strengths-based approach to child and family assessment. In D. Catheral (Ed.), *Handbook of stress, trauma and the family* (pp. 307–324). New York: Taylor Francis.

Gilgun, J. F. (2005). Evidence-based practice, descriptive research, and the Resilience-Schema-Gender Brain Functioning (RSGB) assessment. *British Journal of Social Work, 35*(6), 843–862.

Gilligan, C. (1979). Woman's place in man's life cycle. *Harvard Educational Review, 49*(4), 431–446.

Gilligan, C. (1982). *In a different voice: Psychological theory and women's development.* Cambridge, MA: Harvard University Press.

Gini, C. (1921). Measurement of inequality of incomes. *The Economic Journal, 31*(121), 124–126.

Glaser, S. R., Zamanou, S., & Hacker, K. (1987). Measuring and interpreting organizational culture: The Organizational Culture Survey. *Management Communication Quarterly, 1*(2), 173–198.

Glasmeier, A. K. (2015). Living wage calculator. Retrieved from http://livingwage.mit.edu

Glass, G. V. (1976). Primary, secondary and meta-analysis of research. *Educational Research, 5,* 3–8.

Glaze, L. E., & Kaeble, D. (2014, Dec. 19). *Appendix Table 1. Estimated number and rate of persons supervised by adult correctional systems, by jurisdiction and correctional status, 2013.* cpus13at01.csv. Retrieved from http://www.bjs.gov/index.cfm?ty=pbdetail&iid=5177

Gleeson, J. P., & Philbin, C. M. (1996). Preparing caseworkers for practice in kinship foster care: The supervisor's dilemma. *The Clinical Supervisor, 14*(1), 19–34.

Gleick, J. (2011). *The information: A history, a theory, a flood.* New York: Pantheon Books.

Glisson, C., Dulmus, C. N., & Sowers, K. M. (2012). *Social work practice with groups, communities, and organizations: Evidence-based assessments and interventions.* Hoboken, NJ: Wiley.

Gokhale, J., & Kotlikoff, L. J. (2000, Oct. 1). The baby boomers' mega-inheritance—Myth or reality? *Economic Commentary.* Retrieved from http://www.clevelandfed.org/research/commentary/2000/1001.pdf

Goldstein, H. (1987). The neglected moral link in social work practice. *Social Work, 32,* 181–186.

Gonnerman, J. (2015, June 7). Kalief Browder, 1993–2015. *The New Yorker.* Retrieved from http://www.newyorker.com/news/news-desk/kalief-browder-1993-2015

Good Tracks, J. (1973). Native American noninterference. *Social Work, 18,* 30–34.

Goode, T. D., Dunne, M. C., & Bronheim, S. M. (2006). The evidence base for cultural and linguistic competency in health care. *The Commonwealth Fund, 37.* Retrieved from http://www.commonwealthfund.org/~/media/Files/Publications/Fund%20Report/2006/Oct/The%20Evidence%20Base%20for%20Cultural%20and%20Linguistic%20Competency%20in%20Health%20Care/Goode_evidencebasecultlinguisticcomp_962%20pdf.pdf

Goodman, G., & Esterly, G. (1988). *The talk book: The intimate science of communicating in close relationships.* Emmaus, PA: Rodale.

Gough, I. (2003, Mar.). Lists and thresholds: Comparing the Doyal-Gough theory of human need with Nussbaum's capabilities approach. *WeD Working Paper 01.* Retrieved from http://www.welldev.org.uk/research/workingpaperpdf/wed01.pdf

Gough, I. (2014). Lists and thresholds: Comparing the Doyal-Gough theory of human need with Nussbaum's capabilities approach. In F. Comim & M. C. Nussbaum (Eds.), *Capabilities, gender, equality: Towards fundamental entitlements* (pp. 357–381). Cambridge, UK: Cambridge University Press.

Gould, J. B. (2008). *The Innocence Commission: Preventing wrongful convictions and restoring the criminal justice system.* New York: New York University Press.

Gould, N., & Baldwin, M. (Eds.). (2004). *Social work, critical reflection, and the learning organization.* Aldershot, UK: Ashgate.

Goulson, D. (2010). *Bumblebees: Behaviour, ecology, and conservation* (2nd ed.). London: Oxford University Press.

Grady, D. (2004, Feb. 6). Mad cow quandary: Making animal feed. Retrieved from http://www.nytimes.com/2004/02/06/us/mad-cow-quandary-making-animal-feed.html

Greenberg, G. (2013). *The book of woe: The DSM and the unmaking of psychiatry.* New York: Blue Rider Press.

Greene, G. J., & Lee, M. Y. (2011). *Solution-oriented social work practice: An integrative approach to working with client strengths.* New York: Oxford University Press.

Greenhalgh, T. (1997). *How to read a paper: The basics of evidence based medicine.* London: BMJ Publishing.

Greenhalgh, T. (2001). *How to read a paper: The basics of evidence based medicine* (2nd ed.). London: BMJ Publishing.

Grinnell, R. M. (2011). *Social work research and evaluation: Foundations of evidence-based practice.* New York: Oxford University Press.

Grinnell, R. M., Gabor, P., Unrau, Y. A., & Gabor, P. (2010). *Program evaluation for social workers: Foundations of evidence-based programs.* Oxford; New York: Oxford University Press.

Gross, S., Jacoby, K., Matheson, D. J., & Montgomery, N. (2005). Exonerations in the United States, 1989 through 2003. *Journal of Criminal Law and Criminology, 95*(2), 523–560.

Gross, S. R., Jacoby, K., Matheson, D. J., Montgomery, N., & Patel, S. (2004). *Exonerations in the United States, 1989–2003.* Retrieved from http://www.soros.org/initiatives/usprograms/focus/justice/articles_publications/publications/exonerations_20040419

Gross, S. R., O'Brien, B., Hu, C., & Kennedy, E. (2014). Rate of false conviction of criminal defendants who are sentenced to death. *Proceedings of the National Academy of Sciences,* 7230–7235.

Gudykunst, W. B., & Kim, Y. Y. (2003). *Communicating with strangers: An approach to intercultural communication* (4th ed.). Boston: McGraw-Hill.

Guo, C., & Bielefeld, W. (2014). *Social entrepreneurship: An evidence-based approach to creating social value.* San Francisco: Jossey-Bass.

Guyatt, G. H., Sackett, D. L., & Sinclair, J. C. (1995). Users' guide to the medical literature IX. A method for grading health care recommendations. *Journal of the American Medical Association, 274,* 1800–1804.

Haber, S. N., & Knutson, B. (2010). The reward circuit: Linking primate anatomy and human imaging. *Neuropsychopharmacology, 35,* 4–26.

Haidt, J. (2012). *The righteous mind: Why good people are divided by politics and religion*. New York: Pantheon Books.

Haidt, J., Seder, J. P., & Kesebir, S. (2008). Hive psychology, happiness, and public policy. *The Journal of Legal Studies, 37*(Supplement 2), S133–S156. Retrieved from http://www.lexisnexis.com.proxy2.ulib.iupui.edu/hottopics/lnacademic

Halley, J. O. M., Eshleman, A., & Vijaya, R. M. (2011). *Seeing white: An introduction to white privilege and race*. Lanham, MD: Rowman & Littlefield.

Hammond, D., Hepworth, D., & Smith, V. (1977). *Improving therapeutic communication*. San Francisco: Jossey-Bass.

Haney-López, I. (2014). *Dog whistle politics: How coded racial appeals have reinvented racism and wrecked the middle class*. New York: Oxford University Press.

Hansen, J., Kharecha, P., Sato, M., Masson-Delmotte, V., & Ackerman, F., et al. (2013). Assessing "dangerous climate change": Required reduction of carbon emissions to protect young people, future generations and nature. *PLoS ONE, 8*(12), e81648. doi: 10.1371/journal.pone.0081648

Hansenfeld, Y. (1985). The organizational context of group work. In M. Sundel, P. H. Glaser, R. Sarri, & R. Vinter (Eds.), *Individual change through small groups* (2nd ed., pp. 294–309). New York: Free Press.

Hanson, R. K., & Morton-Bourgon, K. E. (2009). The accuracy of recidivism risk assessments for sexual offenders: A meta-analysis of 118 prediction studies. *Psychological Assessment, 21*(1), 1–21. Retrieved from http://dx.doi.org/10.1037/a0014421

Hanvey, C. P., & Philpot, T. (1994). *Practising social work*. New York: Routledge.

Hardy, K. V., & Laszloffy, T. A. (1995). The cultural genogram: Key to training culturally competent family therapists. *Journal of Marital and Family Therapy, 21*(3), 227–237.

Harris, T. A. (1969). *I'm OK, you're OK: A practical guide to transactional analysis*. New York: Harper & Row.

Harrison, J. A., Mullen, P. D., & Green, L. W. (1992). A meta-analysis of studies of the Health Belief Model with adults. *Health Education Research, 7*(1), 107–116. doi: 10.1093/her/7.1.107

Harrison, K. D. (2007). *When languages die: The extinction of the world's languages and the erosion of human knowledge*. Oxford; New York: Oxford University Press.

Hartman, A. (1978). Diagrammatic assessment of family relationships. *Social Casework, 59*, 465–476.

Hartman, A., & Laird, J. (1983). *Family-centered social work practice*. New York: Free Press.

Hawkins, E. J., Lambert, M. J., Vermeersch, D. A., Slade, K., & Tuttle, K. (2004). The effects of providing patient progress information to therapists and patients. *Psychotherapy Research, 14*(3), 308–327.

Hawkins, J. D., Catalano, R. F., & Miller, J. Y. (1992). Risk and protective factors for alcohol and other drug problems in adolescence and early adulthood: Implications for substance abuse prevention. *Psychological Bulletin, 112*(1), 64–105.

Hayes, D., Humphries, B., & Cohen, S. (2004). *Social work, immigration and asylum debates, dilemmas and ethical issues for social work and social care practice*. London; New York: Jessica Kingsley.

Hayner, P. B. (2002). *Unspeakable truths: Facing the challenge of truth commissions*. New York: Routledge.

Heer, R. (2012). A model of learning objectives based on *A Taxonomy for Learning, Teaching, and Assessing: A Revision of Bloom's Taxonomy of Educational Objectives*. Retrieved from http://www.celt.iastate.edu/teaching-resources/effective-practice/revised-blooms-taxonomy/

Heidler, M.-D. (2014). Honest liars. *Scientific American Mind, 25*(2), 40–44. Retrieved from http://search.ebscohost.com/login.aspx?direct=true&db=f5h&AN=94382480&site=ehost-live

Heimlich, J. (2011). *Breaking their will: Shedding light on religious maltreatment*. Amherst, NY: Prometheus.

Henrichson, C., & Delaney, R. (2012, Jan.). The price of prisons: What incarcerations costs taxpayers. Retrieved from http://www.vera.org/sites/default/files/resources/downloads/price-of-prisons-updated-version-021914.pdf

Henry, S. (1981). *Group skills in social work*. Itasca, IL: F. E. Peacock.

Henry, S. (1992). *Group skills in social work* (2nd ed.). Pacific Grove, CA: Brooks/Cole.

Hepworth, D. H., Rooney, R. H., Rooney, G. D., & Strom-Gottfried, K. J. (2013). *Direct social work practice: Theory and skills* (9th ed.). Belmont, CA: Brooks/Cole.

Herring, R. H. (1996). *Decision making with child abuse victims and their families in a pediatric setting: The use of the Hood Herring Risk Assessment Matrix (HHRAM)*. Unpublished doctoral dissertation. Howard University, Washington, DC.

Hess, H., & Hess, P. M. (1999). Termination in context. In B. Compton & B. Galaway (Eds.), *Social work processes* (6th ed., pp. 489–495). Pacific Grove, CA: Brooks/Cole.

Higgins, J. P. T., & Green, S. (2011). *Cochrane handbook for systematic reviews of interventions* [Version 5.1.0]. Oxford, UK: The Cochrane Collaboration. Retrieved from http://www.cochrane-handbook.org/

Hill, C. E., & Gormally, J. (1977). Effect of reflection, restatement, probe, and nonverbal behaviors on client affect. *Journal of Counseling Psychology, 24*, 92-97.

Hill, C. E., & Gormally, J. (2001). Effects of reflection, restatement, probe, and nonverbal behaviors on client affect. In C. E. Hill (Ed.), *Helping skills: The empirical foundation* (pp. 229–242). Washington, DC: American Psychological Association.

Himmelstein, D. U., Thorne, D., Warren, E., & Woolhandler, S. (2009). Medical bankruptcy in the United States, 2007: Results of a national study. *The American Journal of Medicine, 122*(8), 741–746. Retrieved from http://dx.doi.org/10.1016/j.amjmed.2009.04.012

Hinnells, J. R. (2010). *The Routledge companion to the study of religion*. London; New York: Routledge.

Hoffart, A., Borge, F. M., Sexton, H., & Clark, D. M. (2008). The role of common factors in residential cognitive and interpersonal therapy for social phobia: A process-outcome study. *Psychotherapy Research, 19*(1), 1–14. Retrieved from http://www.informaworld.com/10.1080/10503300802369343

Hoffer, E. (1973). *Reflections on the human condition*. New York: Harper & Row.

Hofstede, G. H., & Hofstede, G. J. (2005). *Cultures and organizations: Software of the mind* (rev. and expanded 2nd ed.). New York: McGraw-Hill.

Hofstede, G. H., Hofstede, G. J., & Minkov, M. (2010). *Cultures and organizations: Software of the mind* (rev. and expanded 3rd ed.). New York: McGraw-Hill.

Hogan, M. (2012). *The four skills of cultural diversity competence: A process for understanding and practice* (4th ed.). Belmont, CA: Brooks/Cole.

Holbach, P. H. T., Meslier, J., & Voltaire. (1972). *Superstition in all ages*. New York: Arno Press.

Holden, G. (1991). The relationship of self-efficacy appraisals to subsequent health related outcomes: A meta-analysis. *Social Work in Health Care, 16*(1), 53–93.

Holden, G., Barker, K., Rosenberg, G., & Onghena, P. (2008). The Evaluation Self-Efficacy Scale for assessing progress toward CSWE accreditation related objectives: A replication. *Research on Social Work Practice, 18*(1), 42–46. doi: 10.1177/1049731507303954

Holden, G., Cuzzi, L., Rutter, S., Chernack, P., & Rosenberg, G. (1997). The Hospital Social Work Self-Efficacy Scale: A replication. *Research on Social Work Practice, 7*(4), 490–499.

Holden, G., Cuzzi, L., Rutter, S., Rosenberg, G., & Chernack, P. (1996). The Hospital Social Work Self-Efficacy Scale: Initial development. *Research on Social Work Practice, 6*(3), 353–365.

Holden, G., Cuzzi, L., Spitzer, W., Rutter, S., Chernack, P., & Rosenberg, G. (1997). The Hospital Social Work Self-Efficacy Scale: A partial replication and extension. *Health and Social Work, 22*(4), 256–263.

Holden, G., Meenaghan, T., & Anastas, J. (2003). Determining attainment of the EPAS Foundation Program objectives: Evidence for the use of self-efficacy as an outcome. *Journal of Social Work Education, 39*(3), 425–440.

Holden, G., Meenaghan, T., Anastas, J., & Metrey, G. (2001). Outcomes of social work education: The case for social work self-efficacy. *Journal of Social Work Education, 38*(1), 115–134.

Holmes, R. L. (2003). *Basic moral philosophy* (3rd. ed.). Belmont, CA: Wadsworth.

Homelessness Research Institute. (2014). The state of homelessness in America 2014. Retrieved from http://www.endhomelessness .org/library/entry/the-state-of-homelessness-2014

Hönisch, B., Ridgwell, A., Schmidt, D. N., Thomas, E., Gibbs, S. J., Sluijs, A., . . . Williams, B. (2012). The geological record of ocean acidification. *Science, 335*(6072), 1058–1063. doi: 10.1126/science.1208277

Horne, R. S. C., Hauck, F. R., & Moon, R. Y. (2015). Sudden infant death syndrome and advice for safe sleeping. *BMJ, 350.* Retrieved from http://www.bmj.com/content/350/bmj.h1989 .abstract

Horvath, A. O., & Bedi, R. P. (2002). The alliance. In J. C. Norcross (Ed.), *Psychotherapy relationships that work* (pp. 37–69). New York: Oxford University Press.

Horvath, A. O., Symonds, D., & Tapia, L. (2010). Therapeutic alliances in couple therapy. In J. C. Muran & J. P. Barber (Eds.), *The therapeutic alliance: An evidence-based guide to practice* (pp. 210–239). New York: Guilford Press.

Hubble, M. A., Duncan, B. L., & Miller, S. D. (1999). Introduction. In M. A. Hubble, B. L. Duncan, & S. D. Miller (Eds.), *The heart and soul of change: What works in therapy* (pp. 1–19). Washington, DC: American Psychological Association.

Hudson, W. W. (1982). *The clinical measurement package: A field manual.* Homewood, IL: Dorsey.

Huff, C. R., Rattner, A., & Sagarin, E. (1996). *Convicted but innocent: Wrongful conviction and public policy.* Thousand Oaks, CA: Sage.

Hulko, W. (2009). The time- and context-contingent nature of intersectionality and interlocking oppressions. *AFFILIA: Journal of Women and Social Work, 24*(1), 44–55. Retrieved from http://search.ebscohost.com/login.aspx?direct=true&db=swh& AN=59502&site=ehost-live

Human Genome Project Information. (2008). Genetic anthropology, ancestry, and ancient human migration. Retrieved from http:// www.ornl.gov/sci/techresources/Human_Genome/elsi /humanmigration.shtml.

Human Rights Campaign & Trans People of Color Coalition (TPOCC). (2015, Aug. 14). A national crisis: Anti-transgender violence. Retrieved from http://hrc-assets.s3-website -us-east-1.amazonaws.com//files/assets/resources/HRC -AntiTransgenderViolence-0519.pdf

Human Rights Watch. (2012). "I had to run away": The imprisonment of women and girls for "moral crimes" in Afghanistan. Retrieved from http://www.hrw.org/sites/default /files/reports/afghanistan0312webwcover_0.pdf

Humes, K. R., Jones, N. A., & Ramirez, R. R. (2011, Mar.). *Overview of Race and Hispanic Origin: 2010.* Washington, DC: U.S. Census Bureau. Retrieved from http://www.census.gov /prod/cen2010/briefs/c2010br-02.pdf

Hunt, M. (1997). *How science takes stock: The story of meta-analysis.* New York: Russell Sage Foundation.

Iacoboni, M. (2008). *Mirroring people: The new science of how we connect with others.* New York: Farrar, Straus and Giroux.

Iatridis, D. S. (2008). Policy practice. In T. Mizrahi & L. E. Davis (Eds.), *Encylopedia of social work* (20th, e-reference ed.). New York: National Association of Social Workers and Oxford University Press.

Ickes, W. (2003). *Everyday mind reading: Understanding what other people think and feel.* Amherst, NY: Prometheus Books.

iMatter: Kids vs. Global Warming. (2014, Dec. 8). Update on the federal lawsuit. Retrieved from http://www.imatteryouth .org/#!Lawsuit/ci55

iMatter: Kids vs. Global Warming. (2015). Live as if our future matters. Retrieved from http://www.imatteryouth.org/

Imel, Z. E., & Wampold, B. E. (2008). The importance of treatment and the science of common factors in psychotherapy. In S. D. Brown & R. W. Lent (Eds.), *Handbook of counseling psychology* (4th ed., pp. 249–266). New York: Wiley.

IN.gov. (2015). Indiana Professional Licensing Agency Online Services: File a Complaint. Retrieved from https://secure. in.gov/pla/license.htm

IN.gov. (2015, Jan.). Title 839 Behavioral Health and Human Services Licensing Board. Retrieved from http://www.in.gov /legislative/iac/title839.html

Inglehart, R. (2004). Subjective well-being rankings of 82 societies (based on combined Happiness and Life Satisfaction scores). Retrieved from http://margaux.grandvinum.se/SebTest/wvs /articles/folder_published/publication_488.

Inglehart, R. (2006). Inglehart-Welzel cultural map of the world. Retrieved from http://margaux.grandvinum.se/SebTest/wvs /SebTest/wvs/articles/folder_published/article_base_54

Inglehart, R., Foa, R., Peterson, C., & Welzel, C. (2008). Development, freedom, and rising happiness: A global perspective (1981–2007). *Perspectives on Psychological Science, 3*(4), 264–285. doi: 10.1111/j.1745-6924.2008.00078.x

Inglehart, R., & Welzel, C. (2005). *Modernization, cultural change and democracy.* New York: Cambridge University Press.

Institute for Economics and Peace. (2011). *Pillars of Peace: Understanding the key attitudes and institutions that underpin peaceful societies.* Retrieved from http://economicsandpeace.org /wp-content/uploads/2011/10/Pillars-of-Peace-Report-IEP.pdf

Institute for Economics and Peace. (2012). United States Peace Index, 2012. Retrieved from http://www.visionofhumanity .org/#/page/indexes/us-peace-index

Institute for Economics and Peace. (2015a). Global Peace Index, 2015: Measuring Peace, Its Causes, and Its Economic Value. Retrieved from http://www.visionofhumanity.org/#/page /indexes/global-peace-index

Institute for Economics and Peace. (2015b). Peace and Corruption, 2015: Lowering Corruption—A Transformative Factor for Peace. Retrieved from http://www.visionofhumanity.org/#/page/news/1162

International Federation of Social Workers. (2012, Feb. 23). Globalisation and the environment. Retrieved from http://ifsw .org/policies/globalisation-and-the-environment/

International Federation of Social Workers. (2014). Global definition of the social work profession. Retrieved from http:// ifsw.org/get-involved/global-definition-of-social-work/

International Initiative for Impact Evaluation. (2012). Systematic reviews. Retrieved from http://www.3ieimpact.org/en/evidence /systematic-reviews/

Isaac, S., & Michael, W. B. (1971). *Handbook in research and evaluation.* San Diego, CA: EdITS.

Itaborahy, L. P., & Zhu, J. (2014). State-sponsored homophobia: A world survey of laws: Criminalisation, protection and recognition of same-sex love. Retrieved from http://old.ilga .org/Statehomophobia/ILGA_SSHR_2014_Eng.pdf

Ivey, A. E. (1988). *Intentional interviewing and counseling: Facilitating client development* (2nd ed.). Pacific Grove, CA: Brooks/Cole.

Ivey, A. E., Ivey, M. B., & Zalaquett, C. P. (2010). *Intentional interviewing and counseling: Facilitating client development in*

a multicultural society (7th ed.). Belmont, CA: Wadsworth, Cengage Learning.

Ivey, A. E., Ivey, M. B., Zalaquett, C. P., & Quirk, K. (2012). *Essentials of intentional interviewing: Counseling in a multicultural world* (2nd ed.). Belmont, CA: Brooks/Cole, Cengage Learning.

Jablonski, N. G. (2004). The evolution of human skin and skin color. *Annual Review of Anthropology, 33*, 585–623. doi: 10.2307/25064866

Jablonski, N. G. (2006). *Skin: A natural history.* Berkeley: University of California Press.

Jablonski, N. G. (2012). *Living color: The biological and social meaning of skin color.* Berkeley: University of California Press.

Jablonski, N. G., & Chaplin, G. (2000). The evolution of human skin coloration. *Journal of Human Evolution, 39*(1), 57–106. Retrieved from http://dx.doi.org/10.1006/jhev.2000.0403

Jablonski, N. G., & Chaplin, G. (2010). Human skin pigmentation as an adaptation to UV radiation. *Proceedings of the National Academy of Sciences of the United States of America, 107*, 8962–8968. doi: 10.2307/25681526

Jablonski, N. G., & Chaplin, G. (2013). Epidermal pigmentation in the human lineage is an adaptation to ultraviolet radiation. *Journal of Human Evolution, 65*(5), 671–675. Retrieved from http://dx.doi.org/10.1016/j.jhevol.2013.06.004

Jacoby, S. (2008). *The age of American unreason.* New York: Pantheon.

Jäntti, M., Bratsberg, B., Røed, K., Raaum, O., Naylor, R., Österbacka, E., . . . Eriksson, T. (2006, Jan.). American exceptionalism in a new light: A comparison of intergenerational earnings mobility in the Nordic countries, the United Kingdom and the United States. *IZA Discussion Paper No. 1938.* Retrieved from http://ftp.iza.org/dp1938.pdf

Jaramillo, P. A. (2010). Building a theory, measuring a concept: Exploring intersectionality and Latina activism at the individual level. *Journal of Women, Politics and Policy, 31*(3), 193–216. Retrieved from http://search.ebscohost.com/login.aspx?direct=true&db=swh&AN=80924&site=ehost-live

Jessor, R. (1991). Risk behavior in adolescence: A psychosocial framework for understanding and action. *Journal of Adolescent Health, 12*, 507–605.

Jessor, R., Bos, J. V. D., Vanderyn, F. M., & Turbin, M. S. (1995). Protective factors in adolescent problem behavior: Moderator effects and developmental change. *Developmental Psychology, 31*, 923–933.

John, O. P. (2007–2009). Berkeley personality lab. Retrieved from http://www.ocf.berkeley.edu/~johnlab/index.htm

John, O. P., Donahue, E. M., & Kentle, R. L. (1991). *The Big Five Inventory—Versions 4a and 54.* University of California, Berkeley, Institute of Personality and Social Research.

John, O. P., Naumann, L. P., & Soto, C. J. (2008). Paradigm shift to the integrative big-five trait taxonomy: History, measurement, and conceptual issues. In O. P. John, R. W. Robins, & L. A. Pervin (Eds.), *Handbook of personality: Theory and research* (pp. 114–158). New York: Guilford Press.

John, O. P., & Srivastava, S. (1999). The big-five trait taxonomy: History, measurement, and theoretical perspectives (final draft). Retrieved from http://www.uoregon.edu/~sanjay/pubs/bigfive.pdf

Johnson, D. (2011, Sept. 15). Income gap: Is it widening? *Random Samplings: The Official Blog of the U.S. Census Bureau.* Retrieved from http://blogs.census.gov/2011/09/15/income-gap-is-it-widening/

Johnson, H. C. (1978). Integrating the problem-oriented record with a systems approach to case assessment. *Journal of Education for Social Work, 14*(3), 71–77.

Johnson III, T. R. (2014, June 17). Africans have apologized for slavery, so why won't the US? *The Root.* Retrieved from http://www.theroot.com/articles/history/2014/06/why_won_t_the_united_states_apologize_for_slavery.html

Johnson, K., Hoyer, M., & Heath, B. (2014, May 8). Local police involved in 400 killings per year. *USA TODAY.* Retrieved from http://www.usatoday.com/story/news/nation/2014/08/14/police-killings-data/14060357/

Johnson, T. H. (Ed.) (1955). *The poems of Emily Dickinson* (Vol. 1). Cambridge, MA: Belknap Press.

Johnston, M. (1997). *Spectral evidence. The Ramona case: Incest, memory, and truth on trial in Napa Valley.* Boston: Houghton Mifflin.

Jonsen, A. R., & Toulmin, S. (1988). *The abuse of casuistry: A history of moral reasoning.* Berkeley: University of California Press.

Jordan, C. (2008). Assessment. In T. Mizrahi & L. E. Davis (Eds.), *Encyclopedia of social work* (20th, e-reference ed.). New York: National Association of Social Workers and Oxford University Press.

Julian, D. A. (1997). The utilization of the logic model as a system level planning and evaluation device. *Evaluation and Program Planning, 20*(3), 251–257.

Julian, D. A., Jones, A., & Deyo, D. (1995). Open systems evaluation and the logic model: Program planning and evaluation tools. *Evaluation and Program Planning, 18*(4), 333–341.

Kadushin, A. (1983). *The social work interview* (2nd ed.). New York: Columbia University Press.

Kadushin, A., & Kadushin, G. (1997). *The social work interview: A guide for human service professionals* (4th ed.). New York: Columbia University Press.

Kagle, J. D. (2002). Record-keeping. In A. R. Roberts & G. J. Greene (Eds.), *Social workers' desk reference* (pp. 28–33). New York: Oxford University Press.

Kagle, J. D. (2008). Recording. In T. Mizrahi & L. E. Davis (Eds.), *Encyclopedia of social work* (20th, e-reference ed.). New York: Oxford University Press.

Kagle, J. D., & Kopels, S. L. (1994). Confidentiality after Tarasoff. *Health and Social Work, 19*(3), 217–223.

Kagle, J. D., & Kopels, S. L. (2008). *Social work records* (3rd ed.). Long Grove, IL: Waveland Press.

Kahneman, D. (2011). *Thinking, fast and slow.* New York: Farrar, Straus and Giroux.

Kahneman, D. (2011, Oct. 19). Don't blink! The hazards of confidence. *The New York Times.* Retrieved from http://www.nytimes.com/2011/10/23/magazine/dont-blink-the-hazards-of-confidence.html?_r=0

Kamya, H. A. (2000). Hardiness and spiritual well-being among social work students: Implications for social work education. *Journal of Social Work Education, 36*(2), 231–240.

Karls, J. M., & O'Keefe, M. E. (2008). *Person-in-environment system manual* (2nd ed.). Washington, DC: NASW Press.

Karls, J. M., & Wandrei, K. E. (1994). *PIE manual: Person-in-environment system: The PIE classification system for social functioning problems.* Washington, DC: NASW Press.

Karpman, S. B. (1968). Fairy tales and script drama analysis. *Transactional Analysis Bulletin, 7*(26), 39–43.

Karpman, S. B. (1971). Options. *Transactional Analysis Journal, 1*(1), 79–87.

Katz, S., Down, T. D., Cash, H. R., & Grotz, R. C. (1970). Progress in the development of the index of ADL. *The Gerontologist, 10*(1), 20–30.

Kaufman, F. R. (2005). *Diabesity: The obesity-diabetes epidemic that threatens America—and what we must do to stop it.* New York: Bantam Books.

Kaufman, L., & Jones, R. L. (2003, May 23). Report finds flaws in inquiries on foster abuse in New Jersey. *The New York Times.*

Keefe, T. (1976). Empathy: The critical skill. *Social Work, 21*, 10–14.

Keiley, M. K., Dolbin, M., Hill, J., Karuppaswamy, N., Liu, T., Natrajan, R., . . . Robinson, P. (2002). The cultural genogram: Experiences from within a marriage and family therapy training program. *Journal of Marital and Family Therapy, 28*(2), 165–178.

Keith-Lucas, A. (1972). *The giving and taking of help*. Chapel Hill: University of North Carolina Press.

Kellogg, N., & The American Academy of Pediatrics Committee on Child Abuse and Neglect. (2005). The evaluation of sexual abuse in children. *Pediatrics, 116*(2), 506–512. doi: 10.1542/peds.2005-1336

Kenrick, D. T., Griskevicius, V., Neuberg, S. L., & Schaller, M. (2010). Renovating the pyramid of needs: Contemporary extensions built upon ancient foundations. *Perspectives on Psychological Science, 5*, 292–314.

Keshav, S. (2007). How to read a paper. *Computer Communication Review, 37*(3), 83–84. Retrieved from http://ccr.sigcomm.org/online/files/p83-keshavA.pdf

Kida, T. E. (2006). *Don't believe everything you think: The 6 basic mistakes we make in thinking*. Amherst, NY: Prometheus Books.

Kids Count Data Center. (2013a). Children in poverty by race and ethnicity: 2013. Retrieved from http://datacenter.kidscount.org/

Kids Count Data Center. (2013b). Population in poverty: 2013. Retrieved from http://datacenter.kidscount.org/

Kindy, K. (2015, May 30). Fatal police shootings in 2015 approaching 400 nationwide. *The Washington Post*. Retrieved from http://www.washingtonpost.com/national/fatal-police-shootings-in-2015-approaching-400-nationwide/2015/05/30/d322256a-058e-11e5-a428-c984eb077d4e_story.html

Kindy, K., & Kelly, K. (2015, Apr. 11). Thousands dead, few prosecuted. *The Washington Post*. Retrieved from http://www.washingtonpost.com/sf/investigative/2015/04/11/thousands-dead-few-prosecuted/

King, L. B. (2011, Dec. 3). A tree fell in the forest: The U.S. apologized to Native Americans and no one heard a sound. *Indian Country: Today Media Network*. Retrieved from http://indiancountrytodaymedianetwork.com/2011/12/03/tree-fell-forest-us-apologized-native-americans-and-no-one-heard-sound

Kiresuk, T. J., & Sherman, R. E. (1968). Goal attainment scaling: A general method for evaluating comprehensive community health programs. *Community Mental Health Journal, 4*, 443–453.

Kiresuk, T. J., Smith, A., & Cardillo, J. E. (Eds.). (1994). *Goal attainment scaling: Applications, theory and measurement*. Mahwah, NJ: Lawrence Erlbaum.

Kirk, S. A., & Kutchins, H. (1992). *The selling of DSM: The rhetoric of science in psychiatry*. New York: Aldine de Gruyter.

Kirk, S. A., & Kutchins, H. (1994). The myth of the reliability of DSM. *The Journal of Mind and Behavior, 15*(1/2), 71–86. Retrieved from http://search.ebscohost.com/login.aspx?direct=true&db=swh&AN=31344&site=ehost-live

Kitchener, K. S. (2000). *Foundations of ethical practice, research, and teaching in psychology*. Mahwah, NJ: Lawrence Erlbaum.

Kivel, P. (2002). *Uprooting racism: How white people can work for racial justice*. Gabriola Island, BC, Canada: New Society.

Klein, N. (2014). *This changes everything: Capitalism vs. the climate*. New York: Simon & Schuster.

Klinger, S. (2015, May 21). Meet the 25 hedge fund managers whose $2.2 billion tax break could pay for 50,000 highway construction jobs. *Center for Effective Government*. Retrieved from http://www.foreffectivegov.org/node/13448

Klosek, J. (2007). *The war on privacy*. Westport, CT: Praeger.

Knutson, B., Adams, C., Fong, G., & Hommer, D. (2001). Anticipation of monetary reward selectively recruits nucleus accumbens. *Journal of Neuroscience, 21*(RC159), 1–5.

Knutson, B., Rick, S., Wimmer, G. E., Prelec, D., & Loewenstein, G. (2007). Neural predictors of purchases. *Neuron, 53*, 147–156.

Kohn, S. M. (2011). *The whistleblower's handbook: A step-by-step guide to doing what's right and protecting yourself* (2nd ed.). Guilford, CT: Lyons Press.

Kondrat, M. E. (1999). Who is the "self" in self-aware: Professional self-awareness from a critical theory perspective. *Social Service Review, 73*(4), 451–477.

Konigsberg, R. D. (2011). *The truth about grief: The myth of its five stages and the new science of loss*. New York: Simon & Schuster.

Koocher, G. P., & Keith-Spiegel, P. (1990). *Children, ethics, and the law: Professional issues and cases*. Lincoln: University of Nebraska Press.

Kostić, A., & Chadee, D. (Eds.). (2015). *The social psychology of nonverbal communication*. New York: Palgrave Macmillan.

Kovacs, P. J., & Bronstein, L. R. (1999). Preparation for oncology settings: What hospice social workers say they need. *Health and Social Work, 24*(1), 57–64.

Krill, D. F. (1986). *The beat worker: Humanizing social work and psychotherapy practice*. Lanham, MD: University Press of America.

Krishnamurti, J. (1980, May 10). Public talk #3 [Transcript]. Retrieved from http://www.jkrishnamurti.org/krishnamurti-teachings/listen-audio/ojai--may-10th--1980-part-3-of-6.php

Krugman, P. (2014, May 8). Why We're in a New Gilded Age. Review of *Capital in the Twenty-First Century* by Thomas Piketty. *The New York Review of Books*. Retrieved from http://www.nybooks.com/articles/archives/2014/may/08/thomas-piketty-new-gilded-age/

Krznaric, R. (2012). Outrospection: Roman Krznaric's blog on empathy and the art of living. Retrieved from http://www.romankrznaric.com/outrospection

Kubetin, S. K. (2003). 20% dropout rate hinders prolonged therapy. *Clinical Psychiatry News, 31*(1), 54.

Kubler-Ross, E. (1969). *On death and dying*. New York: Macmillan.

Kutchins, H. (1991). The fiduciary relationship: The legal basis for social workers' responsibilities to clients. *Social Work, 36*(2), 106–114.

Kutchins, H. (1998). Does the fiduciary relationship guarantee a right to effective treatment? *Research on Social Work Practice, 8*(5), 615–622.

Kutchins, H., & Kirk, S. A. (1997). *Making us crazy: DSM: The psychiatric bible and the creation of mental disorders*. New York: Free Press.

Lambert, M. J. (1992). Implications of outcome research for psychotherapy integration. In J. C. Norcross & M. R. Goldfried (Eds.), *Handbook of psychotherapy integration* (pp. 94–129). New York: Basic Books.

Lambert, M. J. (2010a). *Prevention of treatment failure: The use of measuring, monitoring, and feedback in clinical practice*. Washington, DC: American Psychological Association.

Lambert, M. J. (2010b). "Yes, it is time for clinicians to routinely monitor treatment outcome." In B. L. Duncan, S. D. Miller, B. E. Wampold, & M. A. Hubble (Eds.), *The heart and soul of change: Delivering what works in therapy* (2nd ed., pp. 239–266). Washington, DC: American Psychological Association.

Lambert, M. J., & Bergin, A. E. (1994). The effectiveness of psychotherapy. In A. E. Bergin & S. L. Garfield (Eds.), *Handbook of psychotherapy and behavior change* (4th ed., pp. 143–189). New York: Wiley.

Lambert, M. J., & Cattani-Thompson, K. (1996). Current findings regarding the effectiveness of counseling: Implications for practice. *Journal of Counseling and Development, 74*, 601–608.

Lambert, M. J., & Shimokawa, K. (2011). Collecting client feedback. *Psychotherapy, 48*(1), 72–79. doi: 10.1037/a0022238

Lambert, M. J., Whipple, J. L., Vermeersch, D. A., Smart, D. W., & Hawkins, E. J. (2002). Enhancing psychotherapy outcomes via providing feedback on patient progress: A replication. *Clinical Psychology and Psychotherapy, 9*(2), 91–103.

Lambert, R. G., & Lambert, M. J. (1984). The effects of role preparation for psychotherapy on immigrant clients seeking mental health services in Hawaii. *Journal of Community Psychology, 12*(3), 263–275.

Lancy, D. F. (2008). *The anthropology of childhood: Cherubs, chattel, changelings*. Cambridge; New York: Cambridge University Press.

Lang, S. S. (2002). Social support networks trump number of parents. *Human Ecology, 30*(4), 24.

Langer, L. M., Warheit, G. J., & McDonald, L. P. (2001). Correlates and predictors of risky sexual practices among a multi-racial/ethnic sample of university students. *Social Behavior and Personality, 29*(2), 133–144. Retrieved from <Go to ISI>://000166334700004

Larsen, E. (2006). *A nation gone blind: America in an age of simplification and deceit*. Emeryville, CA: Shoemaker and Hoard.

Laska, K. M., Gurman, A. S., & Wampold, B. E. (2014). Expanding the lens of evidence-based practice in psychotherapy: A common factors perspective. *Psychotherapy, 51*(4), 467–481. doi: 10.1037/a0034332

Lawrence v. Texas, 539 U.S. 558 (2003).

Lawsuit seeks discharge treatment-planning at NYC jails. (1999). *Mental Health Weekly, 9*(34), 1–2.

Lawton, M. P., & Brody, E. M. (1969). Assessment of older people: Self-maintaining and instrumental activities of daily living. *The Gerontologist, 9*(3), 179–186.

Lazarus, A. (1984). *In the mind's eye: The power of imagery for personal enrichment*. New York: Guilford Press.

Lee, J. (2014, Aug. 15). Exactly how often do police shoot unarmed black men? *Mother Jones*. Retrieved from http://www .motherjones.com/politics/2014/08/police-shootings-michael -brown-ferguson-black-men

Lee, M. Y. (1997). A study of solution-focused brief family therapy: Outcomes and issues. *The American Journal of Family Therapy, 25*, 3–17.

LeGault, M. R. (2006). *Think: Why crucial decisions can't be made in the blink of an eye*. New York: Threshold Editions.

Lenhardt, J., & Ogneva-Himmelberger, Y. (2013). Environmental injustice in the spatial distribution of concentrated animal feeding operations in Ohio. *Environmental Justice, 6*(4), 133–139. doi: 10.1089/env.2013.0023

Lenoir, M., Serre, F., Cantin, L., & Ahmed, S. H. (2007). Intense sweetness surpasses cocaine reward. *PLoS ONE, 2*(8), e698. Retrieved from http://journals.plos.org/plosone /article?id=10.1371/journal.pone.0000698

Lens, V. (2000). Protecting the confidentiality of the therapeutic relationship: Jaffee v. Redmond. *Social Work, 45*(3), 273–276. Retrieved from <Go to ISI>://WOS:000086802500008

Leo, R. A. (2008). *Police interrogation and American justice*. Cambridge, MA: Harvard University Press.

Leonhardt, D. (2013, July 22). In climbing income ladder, location matters. *The New York Times*. Retrieved from http://www .nytimes.com/2013/07/22/business/in-climbing-income-ladder -location-matters.html

Levenson, J. S., D'Amora, D. A., & Hern, A. L. (2007). Megan's law and its impact on community re-entry for sex offenders. *Behavioral Sciences and the Law, 25*(4), 587–602. doi: 10.1002 /bsl.770

Levenson, J. S., & Morin, J. W. (2006). Risk assessment in child sexual abuse cases. *Child Welfare, 85*(1), 59–82. Retrieved from <Go to ISI>://000235724300003

Levinson, D. (1998). *Ethnic groups worldwide: A ready reference handbook*. Santa Barbara, CA: Greenwood.

Lewis, R., & Ho, M. (1975). Social work with Native Americans. *Social Work, 20*, 379–382.

Lie, G.-Y., & Lowery, C. T. (2003). Cultural competence with women of color. In D. Lum (Ed.), *Culturally competent practice: A framework for understanding diverse groups and justice issues* (2nd ed., pp. 282–308). Pacific Grove, CA: Brooks/Cole.

Lilienfeld, S. O., Lynn, S. J., & Lohr, J. M. (Eds.). (2015). *Science and pseudoscience in clinical psychology* (2nd ed.). New York: Guilford Press.

Lin, N. (2001). *Social capital: A theory of social structure and action*. New York: Cambridge University Press.

Lincoln, K. D. (2000). Social support, negative social interactions, and psychological well-being. *Social Service Review, 74*(2), 231–252. Retrieved from http://www.jstor.org/stable/30012969

Lindquist, E. J., D'Annunzio, R., Gerrand, A., MacDicken, K., Achard, F., Beuchle, R., . . . Stibig, H.-J. (2012). *Global forest land-use change: 1990–2005. FAO Forestry Paper 169*. Retrieved fromhttp://www.fao.org/docrep/017/i3110e/i3110e.pdf

Linhorst, D. M. (2008). Consumer rights. In T. Mizrahi & L. E. Davis (Eds.), *Encyclopedia of social work* (20th, e-reference ed.). New York: Oxford University Press.

Linley, P. A., Joseph, S., & Seligman, M. E. P. (Eds.). (2004). *Positive psychology in practice*. New York: Wiley.

Lipchik, E. (2002). *Beyond technique in solution-focused therapy*. New York: Guilford Press.

Lomborg, B. (2010). *Smart solutions to climate change: Comparing costs and benefits*. Cambridge, UK; New York: Cambridge University Press.

Longres, J. F. (1995). Hispanics overview. In R. L. Edwards (Ed.), *Encylopedia of social work* (19th ed., Vol. 2, pp. 1214–1222). Washington, DC: NASW Press.

Lu, V., & Zhou, D. (2015). Microaggressions. *The microaggressions project: Notes on power, privilege and everyday life*. Retrieved from http://www.microaggressions.com/

Luborsky, L. (1996). The Helping Alliance Questionnaire: Patient version. In B. Ogles, M. Lambert, & K. Masters (Eds.), *Assessing outcome in clinical practice* (pp. 150–151). Boston: Allyn and Bacon.

Luhrmann, T. M. (2015, Jan. 17). Redefining mental illness. *The New York Times Sunday Review*. Retrieved from http://www.nytimes .com/2015/01/18/opinion/sunday/t-m-luhrmann-redefining -mental-illness.html?_r=0

Lum, D. (2008). Culturally competent practice. In T. Mizrahi & L. E. Davis (Eds.), *Encyclopedia of social work* (20th, e-reference ed.). New York: National Association of Social Workers and Oxford University Press.

Lum, D. (Ed.) (2003). *Culturally competent practice: A framework for understanding diverse groups and justice issues* (2nd ed.). Pacific Grove, CA: Brooks/Cole.

Lumsden, C. J., & Wilson, E. O. (1981). *Genes, mind, and culture: The coevolutionary process*. Cambridge, MA: Harvard University Press.

Lyda, C., & Lyda, J. (2009). *The least of these: Family detention in America* [DVD]. New York: IndiePix.

Lykken, D., & Tellegen, A. (1996). Happiness is a stochastic phenomenon. *Psychological Science, 7*, 186–189.

Lyubomirsky, S. (2006). Is it possible to become lastingly happier? Answers from the modern science of well-being. *The Vancouver Dialogues* (pp. 53–56). Vancouver, BC: Truffle Tree Publishing.

Lyubomirsky, S., Sheldon, K., & Schkade, D. (2005). Pursuing happiness: The architecture of sustainable change. *Review of General Psychology, 9*(2), 111–131. Retrieved from http:// thesciencenetwork.org/docs/BB3/Lyubomirsky _PursuingHappiness.pdf

MacInnis, J. A. K. B. (2013). Does the American public support legislation to reduce greenhouse gas emissions? *Dædalus, the Journal of the American Academy of Arts and Sciences, 142*(1), 26–39. Retrieved from http://climatepublicopinion.stanford. edu/wp-content/uploads/2013/05/GW-Deadalus-Published .pdf

Maddi, S. R., Wadhwa, P., & Haier, R. J. (1996). Relationship of hardiness to alcohol and drug use in adolescents. *American Journal of Drug and Alcohol Abuse, 22*(2), 247–258.

Madland, D. (2015). *Hollowed out: Why the economy doesn't work without a strong middle class*. Oakland, CA: University of California Press.

Magill, F. N. (Ed.) (1998). *Psychology basics.* Pasadena, CA: Salem Press.

Malik, V. S., Schulze, M. B., & Hu, F. B. (2006). Intake of sugar-sweetened beverages and weight gain: A systematic review. *American Journal of Clinical Nutrition, 84*(2), 274–288.

Maluccio, A. (1979). *Learning from clients: Interpersonal helping as viewed by clients and social workers.* New York: Free Press.

Maluccio, A., & Marlow, W. (1974). The case for contract. *Social Work, 19,* 28–36.

Mapp, S. C. (2008). *Human rights and social justice in a global perspective: An introduction to international social work.* New York: Oxford University Press.

Mapping Police Violence. (2015). Mapping police violence. Retrieved from http://mappingpoliceviolence.org/

Marcano, S. (2015). Racism is real [Streaming Video]. Retrieved from http://www.bravenewfilms.org/racismisreal and https://www.youtube.com/watch?t=96&v=fTcSVQJ2h8g

Marcia, J. E. (1980). Identity in adolescence. In J. Adelson (Ed.), *Handbook of Adolescent Psychology* (pp. 159–187). New York: Wiley.

Markman, A. (2012, July 27). Why do Americans accept wealth inequality? *Huffington* Post. Retrieved from http://www.huffingtonpost.com/art-markman-phd/why-do-americans-accept-w_b_1709753.html?view=screen

Marr, C., & Huang, C.-C. (2015, Jan. 18). President's capital gains tax proposals would make tax code more efficient and fair. *Center on Budget and Policy Priorities.* Retrieved from http://www.cbpp.org/research/presidents-capital-gains-tax-proposals-would-make-tax-code-more-efficient-and-fair

Marson, E. (2014). *Fed up* [DVD]. Santa Monica, CA: Atlas Films.

Marson, S. M., & Dran, D. (2006). Goal attainment scaling. Retrieved from http://www.marson-and-associates.com/GAS/GAS_index.html

Martens, W. M., & Holmstrup, E. (1974). Problem-oriented recording. *Social Casework, 55*(9), 554–561.

Martin, D. J., Garske, J. P., & Davis, M. K. (2000). Relation of the therapeutic alliance with outcome and other variables: A meta-analytic review. *Journal of Consulting and Clinical Psychology, 68*(3), 438–450. doi: IO.I037//0022-006X.68.3.438

Marzano, R. J. (2001). *Designing a new taxonomy of educational objectives.* Thousand Oaks, CA: Corwin Press.

Maslow, A. H. (1943). A theory of human motivation. *Psychological Review, 50*(4), 370–396. Retrieved from http://psychclassics.yorku.ca/Maslow/motivation.htm#r13

Maslow, A. H. (1968). *Toward a psychology of being* (2nd rev. ed.). New York: Reinhold.

Massachusetts Constitutional Convention of 1779. (1780, June 15). Constitution of the Commonwealth of Massachusetts. Retrieved from http://www.nhinet.org/ccs/docs/ma-1780.htm

Massey, D. S. (2007). *Categorically unequal: The American stratification system.* New York: Russell Sage Foundation.

Mattaini, M. A. (1990). Contextual behavior analysis in the assessment process. *Families in Society: The Journal of Contemporary Human Services, 2,* 425–444.

Mattaini, M. A. (1993a). *More than a thousand words: Graphics for clinical practice.* Washington, DC: NASW Press.

Mattaini, M. A. (1993b). *Visual EcoScan for clinical practice* (Version 1.0.). Washington, DC: NASW Press.

Mattaini, M. A. (1995). Visualizing practice with children and families. *Early Child Development and Care, 106,* 59–74.

Mattaini, M. A., & Thyer, B. A. (Eds.). (1996). *Finding solutions to social problems: Behavioral strategies for change.* Washington, DC: American Psychological Association Press.

Mattison, M. (2000). Ethical decision making: The person in the process. *Social Work, 45*(3), 201–212.

Mazza, E., Walker, J., & Chen, K. (2015, June 17). Charleston church shooting: White gunman kills 9 at historic black church. *The Huffington Post.* Retrieved from http://www.huffingtonpost.com/2015/06/17/charleston-shooting-churc_n_7608738.html

McCarthy, N. (2014, Aug. 15). Chart: Pentagon donations to police are skyrocketing. *Forbes.* Retrieved from http://www.forbes.com/sites/niallmccarthy/2014/08/15/chart-pentagon-donations-to-police-are-skyrocketing/#2715e4857a0b7d78c19f380f

McCollum, S. (2010, Jan. 6). An American apology, long overdue. *Teaching tolerance: A project of the Southern Poverty Law Center.* Retrieved from http://www.tolerance.org/blog/american-apology-long-overdue

McCormick, S. (2009). *No family history: The environmental links to breast cancer.* Lanham, MD: Rowman & Littlefield.

McCoy, C. R., & Phillips, N. (2008, July 31). Mounting failures left girl to die. *Philly.com.* Retrieved from http://www.philly.com/philly/news/special_packages/inquirer/child_welfare/Mounting_Failures_Left_Girl_to_Die.html

McGoldrick, M., & Gerson, R. (1985). *Genograms in family assessment.* New York: Norton.

McGoldrick, M., Gerson, R., & Shellenberger, S. (1999). *Genograms: Assessment and interventions* (2nd ed.). New York: Norton.

McLaren, N. (2008). *Humanizing madness: Psychiatry and the cognitive neurosciences.* Ann Arbor, MI: Loving Healing Press.

McMillen, J. C., & Groze, V. (1994). Using placement genograms in child welfare practice. *Child Welfare, 73*(4), 307–318.

McMillen, J. C., & Rideout, G. B. (1996). Breaking intergenerational cycles: Theoretical tools for social workers. *The Social Service Review, 70*(3), 378–399. Retrieved from http://www.jstor.org/stable/30012904

McNulty, N., Ogden, J., & Warren, F. (2013). 'Neutralizing the patient': Therapists' accounts of sexual boundary violations. *Clinical Psychology and Psychotherapy, 20*(3), 189–198. doi: 10.1002/cpp.799

McPeck, J. E. (1990). *Teaching critical thinking: Dialogue and dialectic.* New York: Routledge.

McRaney, D. (2015). You are not so smart: A celebration of self-delusion. Retrieved from http://youarenotsosmart.com/

McTaggart, L. (2011). *The bond: Connecting through the space between us.* New York: Free Press.

McWhirter, D. A., & Bible, J. D. (1992). *Privacy as a constitutional right: Sex, drugs, and the right to life.* New York: Quorum Books.

Meeks, K. (2000). *Driving while black: Highways, shopping malls, taxicabs, sidewalks: How to fight back if you are a victims of racial profiling.* New York: Broadway.

Mehrotra, G. (2010). Toward a continuum of intersectionality: Theorizing for feminist social work scholarship. *AFFILIA: Journal of Women and Social Work, 25*(4), 417–430. Retrieved from http://search.ebscohost.com/login.aspx?direct=true&db=swh&AN=81899&site=ehost-live

Meier, P. S., Barrowclough, C., & Donmall, M. C. (2005). The role of the therapeutic alliance in the treatment of substance misuse: A critical review of the literature. *Addiction, 100*(3), 304–316. doi: 10.1111/j.1360-0443.2004.00935.x

Meierhenrich, J. (2008). Varieties of reconciliation. *Law and Social Inquiry, 33*(1), 195–231. doi: 10.1111/j.1747-4469.2008.00098.x

Menzies, G. (2003). *1421: The year China discovered America.* New York: William Morrow.

Menzies, G. (2008). *1434: The year a magnificent Chinese fleet sailed to Italy and ignited the Renaissance.* New York: William Morrow.

Mercer, J. (2005). Coercive restraint therapies: A dangerous alternative mental health intervention. *Medscape General Medicine, 7*(3), 6. Retrieved from http://www.ncbi.nlm.nih.gov/pmc/articles/PMC1681667/

Mercer, J. (2013). *Child development: Myths and misunderstandings* (2nd ed.). Los Angeles: Sage.

Mercer, J. (2014). *Alternative psychotherapies: Evaluating unconventional mental health treatments.* Lanham, MD: Rowman & Littlefield.

Mercer, J., Sarner, L., & Rosa, L. (2003). *Attachment therapy on trial: The torture and death of Candace Newmaker.* Westport, CT: Praeger.

Meyer, C. H. (1993). *Assessment in social work practice*. New York: Columbia University Press.

Meyer, R. G., & Weaver, C. M. (2006). *Law and mental health: A case-based approach*. New York: Guilford Press.

Middleman, R. R., & Goldberg, G. G. (1990). *Skills for direct practice in social work*. New York: Columbia University Press.

Miller, G. M., & Larrabee, M. J. (1995). Sexual intimacy in counselor education and supervision: A national survey. *Counselor Education and Supervision, 34*(4), 332–343. doi: 10.1002/j.1556-6978.1995.tb00199.x

Miller, S. D., Duncan, B. L., Brown, J., Sorrell, R., & Chalk, B. (2006). Using outcome to inform and improve treatment outcomes. *Journal of Brief Therapy, 5*, 5–22.

Miller, S. D., Duncan, B. L., Sorrell, R., & Brown, G. S. (2005). The Partners for Change Outcome Management System. *Journal of Clinical Psychology, 61*(2), 199–208.

Miller, S. D., Hubble, M. A., & Duncan, B. L. (Eds.). (1996). *Handbook of solution-focused brief therapy*. San Francisco, CA: Jossey-Bass.

Miller, S. D., Wampold, B., & Varhely, K. (2008). Direct comparisons of treatment modalities for youth disorders: A meta-analysis. *Psychotherapy Research, 18*(1), 5–14. Retrieved from http://www .informaworld.com/10.1080/10503300701472131

Miller, W. R., & Rollnick, S. (2002). *Motivational interviewing: Preparing people for change* (2nd ed.). New York: Guilford Press.

Mills, C. W. (1956). *The power elite*. New York: Oxford University Press.

Mills, C. W. (1959). *The sociological imagination*. New York: Oxford University Press.

Mills, C. W. (1963). *Power, politics, and people: The collected essays of C. Wright Mills*. New York: Oxford University Press.

Minahan, A. (1981). Purpose and objectives of social work revisited. *Social Work, 26*(1), 5–6. Retrieved from http://search.ebscohost.com/login .aspx?direct=true&db=sih&AN=5274024&site=ehost-live

Miranda v. Arizona, 384 U.S. 436 (1966).

Mitchell, N. J. (2012). *Democracy's blameless leaders: From Dresden to Abu Ghraib, how leaders evade accountability for abuse, atrocity, and killing*. New York: New York University Press.

Mittendorf, S. H., & Schroeder, J. (2004). Boundaries in social work: The ethical dilemma of social worker–client sexual relationships. *Journal of Social Work Values and Ethics, 1*(1), n. pag. Retrieved from http://search.ebscohost.com/login.aspx?dir ect=true&db=sih&AN=17827714&site=ehost-live

Mizner, S. (2015, Jan. 8). There is no police exception to the Americans With Disabilities Act. *Blog of Rights*. Retrieved from https://www.aclu.org/blog/criminal-law-reform-free -speech/there-no-police-exception-americans-disabilities-act

Moggi, F., Brodbeck, J., & Hirsbrunner, H.-P. (2000). Therapist– patient sexual involvement: Risk factors and consequences. *Clinical Psychology and Psychotherapy, 7*(1), 54–60. doi: 10.1002/ (SICI)1099-0879(200002)7:1<54::AID-CPP222>3.0.CO;2-W

Mogul, J. L., Ritchie, A. J., & Whitlock, K. (2011). *Queer (in)justice: The criminalization of LGBT people in the United States*. Boston: Beacon Press.

Molina, M., McCarthy, J., Wall, D., Alley, R., Cobb, K., Cole, J., . . . Shepherd, M. (2014). *What we know: The reality, risks and response to climate change*. Retrieved from Washington, DC, http://whatweknow.aaas.org/wp-content/uploads/2014/07 /whatweknow_website.pdf

Monahan, S. C., Mirola, W. A., & Emerson, M. O. (2011). *Sociology of religion: A reader*. Boston: Allyn & Bacon.

Montagne, R., Harris, R., Oppenheimer, M., & Di-Aping, L. (2009, Dec. 10). Climate change limit: 2 degrees celsius [Transcript]. *National Public Radio Morning Edition*. Retrieved from http:// www.npr.org/templates/story/story.php?storyId=121274647

Montagu, A., & Matson, F. (1979). *The human connection*. New York: McGraw-Hill.

Mooney, C. (2014, Dec. 1). The science of why cops shoot young black men. *Mother Jones*. Retrieved from http://www .motherjones.com/politics/2014/11/science-of-racism-prejudice

Mooney, C. (2014, Dec. 8). Across America, whites are biased and they don't even know it. *The Washington Post*. Retrieved from http://www.washingtonpost.com/blogs/wonkblog/wp /2014/12/08/across-america-whites-are-biased-and-they -dont-even-know-it/

Moore, B. N., & Parker, R. (2012). *Critical thinking* (10th ed.). New York: McGraw-Hill.

Moore, W. S. (2003, Oct.). The Perry Network & the Center for the Study of Intellectual Development. Retrieved from http://www .perrynetwork.org.

Moos, R. H., & Moos, B. S. (2009). *Family environment scale manual: Development, applications, and research* (4th ed.). Palo Alto, CA: Center for Health Care Evaluation, Deptartment of Veterans Affairs, Stanford University Medical Centers, Mind Garden.

Moos, R. H., & Otto, J. (1972). The Community-Oriented Programs Environment Scale: A methodology for the facilitation and evaluation of social change. *Community Mental Health Journal, 8*(1), 28–37. Retrieved from http://dx.doi.org/10.1007 /BF01464080

Morello, C., & Mellnik, T. (2012, May 17). Census: Minority babies are now majority in United States. *The Washington Post*. Retrieved from http://www.washingtonpost.com /local/census-minority-babies-are-now-majority-in-united -states/2012/05/16/gIQA1WY8UU_story.html

Morgan, S. (2013, May). Criminalization of psychotherapist sexual misconduct. Retrieved from http://c.ymcdn.com/sites/www .naswca.org/resource/resmgr/imported/7_13_legal_issue.pdf

Morone, J. A. (2003). *Hellfire nation: The politics of sin in American history*. New Haven, CT: Yale University Press.

Morrow-Howell, N., Chadiha, L. A., Proctor, E. K., Hourd-Bryant, M., & Dore, P. (1996). Racial differences in discharge planning. *Health and Social Work, 21*(2), 131–139.

Mosby, M. (2015, May 1). Marilyn Mosby announces criminal charges in death of Freddie Gray [Transcript]. *New York Daily News*. Retrieved from http://www.nydailynews.com/criminal- charges-filed-freddie-gray-death-transcript-article-1.2206744?

Mount, S. (2010, May 20). Constitutional topic: Slavery. *USConstitution.net*. Retrieved from http://www.usconstitution .net/consttop_slav.html#const

Mueller, J., Polansky, D., Foltin, C., Polivaev, D., & Other Contributers. (2010). FreeMind: A program for creating and viewing mindmaps (Version 0.9.0). Retrieved from http:// freemind.sourceforge.net/

Mulac, A., Erlandson, K. T., Farrar, W. J., Hallett, J. S., Molloy, J. L., & Prescott, M. E. (1998). "Uh-huh. What's that all about?" Differing interpretations of conversational backchannels and questions as sources of miscommunication across gender boundaries. *Communication Research, 25*, 641–668.

Mullen, P. D., Ramirez, G., Strouse, D., Hedges, L. V., & Sogolow, E. (2002). Meta-analysis of the effects of behavioral HIV prevention interventions on the sexual risk behavior of sexually experienced adolescents in controlled studies in the United States. *Journal of Acquired Immune Deficiency Syndromes, 30*, S94–S105. Retrieved from <Go to ISI>://000177039000009

Muran, J. C., & Barber, J. P. (Eds.). (2010). *The therapeutic alliance: An evidence-based guide to practice*. New York: Guilford Press.

Murphy, J. J. (1999). Common factors of school based change. In M. A. Hubble, B. L. Duncan, & S. D. Miller (Eds.), *The heart and soul of change: What works in therapy* (pp. 361–386). Washington, DC: American Psychological Association.

Musgrave, S. (2014, Oct. 14). New York releases complete list of law enforcement agencies' military gear. *MuckRock*. Retrieved from https://www.muckrock.com/news/archives/2014/oct/14/new -york-police-departments-large-and-small-gain-m/

Nadal, K. L. (2013). *That's so gay! Microaggressions and the lesbian, gay, bisexual, and transgender community*. Washington, DC: American Psychological Association.

Nadal, K. L., Davidoff, K. C., Davis, L. S., Wong, Y., Marshall, D., & McKenzie, V. (2015). A qualitative approach to intersectional microaggressions: Understanding influences of race, ethnicity, gender, sexuality, and religion. *Qualitative Psychology*. doi: 10.1037/qup0000026

Nadal, K. L., Issa, M.-A., Leon, J., Meterko, V., Wideman, M., & Wong, Y. (2011). Sexual orientation microaggressions: "Death by a thousand cuts" for lesbian, gay, and bisexual youth. *Journal of LGBT Youth, 8*(3), 234–259. doi: 10.1080/19361653.2011.584204

Nadal, K. L., Skolnik, A., & Wong, Y. (2012). Interpersonal and systemic microaggressions toward transgender people: Implications for counseling. *Journal of LGBT Issues in Counseling, 6*(1), 55–82. doi: 10.1080/15538605.2012.648583

Narayan, D., & Cassidy, M. F. (2001). A dimensional approach to measuring social capital: Development and validation of a Social Capital Inventory. *Current Sociology, 49*(2), 59–102.

Nathan, P. E., & Gorman, J. M. (Eds.). (2007). *A guide to treatments that work* (3rd rev. ed.). New York: Oxford University Press.

National Association of Colleges and Employers. (2014). Job Outlook 2014. Retrieved from http://www.nl.edu/media/nlu/downloadable /careerservices/job-outlook-2014-student-version.pdf

National Association of Social Workers. (1996, June). Evaluation and treatment of adults with the possibility of recovered memories of childhood sexual abuse. Retrieved from https:// www.socialworkers.org/practice/clinical/recvrmem.asp

National Association of Social Workers. (2001). NASW standards for cultural competence in social work practice. Retrieved from http://www.socialworkers.org/practice/standards /NASWCulturalStandards.pdf

National Association of Social Workers. (2007). *Indicators for the achievement of the NASW Standards for Cultural Competence in social work practice*. Retrieved from http://www.socialworkers .org/practice/standards/naswculturalstandardsindicators2006.pdf

National Association of Social Workers. (2008). Code of ethics of the National Association of Social Workers. Retrieved from http://www.socialworkers.org/pubs/code/default.asp

National Association of Social Workers. (2012). *NASW procedures for professional review* (Rev. 5th ed.). Washington, DC: NASW. Retrieved from http://www.socialworkers.org/nasw/ethics /ProceduresManual.pdf.

National Association of Social Workers. (2015a). Ebola: A social work guide. *Special Reports*. Retrieved from http://www .socialworkers.org/practice/special_reports/ebola/default.asp

National Association of Social Workers. (2015b). Ethics resources and professional literature: Ethical decision making framework—DECISIONS approach. Retrieved from http:// www.socialworkers.org/nasw/ethics/resourcesliterature.asp

National Association of Social Workers. (2015c). NASW practice standards. Retrieved from http://www.socialworkers.org /practice/standards/index.asp

National Association of Social Workers. (2015d). Practice tools. Retrieved from http://www.socialworkers.org/practice /practice_tools/index.asp

National Association of Social Workers. (2015e). *Social work speaks: NASW policy statements* (10th ed.). Washington, DC: NASW Press.

National Center for Cultural Competence. (2004). Cultural competence continuum. Retrieved from www.nccccurricula .info/documents/TheContinuumRevised.doc

National Center for Health Statistics. (2015). International Classification of Diseases, Tenth Revision, Clinical Modification (ICD-10-CM): FY 2016 Release. Retrieved from http://www.cdc.gov/nchs/icd/icd10cm.htm#icd2016

National Consumers League. (2011, July). Wage theft: Six common methods. Retrieved from http://www.nclnet.org/wage_theft _six_common_methods

National Law Enforcement Officers Memorial Fund. (2014, Dec. 30). Causes of law enforcement deaths over the past decade (2004–2013). Retrieved from http://www.nleomf.org/facts /officer-fatalities-data/causes.html

National Research Council. (1996). *National science education standards*. Washington, DC: National Academy Press.

National Research Council. (2012). *A framework for K–12 science education: Practices, crosscutting concepts, and core ideas*. Washington, DC: National Academies Press.

National Science Teachers Association Board of Directors. (2000, July). NSTA position statement: The nature of science. Retrieved from http://www.nsta.org/about/positions /natureofscience.aspx.

Neff, K. (2011). *Self-compassion: Stop beating yourself up and leave insecurity behind*. New York: HarperCollins.

Neuliep, J. W. (2012). *Intercultural communication: A contextual approach*. Thousand Oaks, CA: Sage.

Ngo-Metzger, Q., Telfair, J., Sorkin, D. H., Weidmer, B., Weech-Maldonado, R., Hurtado, M., & Hays, R. D. (2006). Cultural competency and quality of care: Obtaining the patient's perspective. *The Commonwealth Fund, 39*. Retrieved from http:// www.commonwealthfund.org/~/media/Files/Publications /Fund%20Report/2006/Oct/Cultural%20Competency%20 and%20Quality%20of%20Care%20%20Obtaining%20 the%20Patients%20Perspective/Ngo%20Metzger _cultcompqualitycareobtainpatientperspect_963%20pdf.pdf

Nieuwsma, J. A., Trivedi, R. B., McDuffie, J., Kronish, I., Benjamin, D., & Williams, J. W. (2012). Brief psychotherapy for depression: A systematic review and meta-analysis. *International Journal of Psychiatry in Medicine, 43*(2), 129–151.

Norcross, J. C., Loberg, K., & Norcross, J. (2012). *Changeology: 5 steps to realizing your goals and resolutions*. New York: Simon & Schuster.

Norris, P., Frank, R. W., & Martínez i Coma, F. (2014a). Measuring electoral integrity around the world: A new dataset. *PS: Political Science and Politics, 47*(4), 789–798. doi:10.1017/ S1049096514001061

Norris, P., Frank, R. W., & Martínez i Coma, F. (2014b). The year in elections 2013: The world's flawed and failed contests. *The Electoral Integrity Project*. Retrieved from http://dash.harvard .edu/handle/1/11744445

Northwestern University Law School. (2015). Wrongful convictions: Explore the issues. *Bluhm Legal Clinic: Center on Wrongful Convictions*. Retrieved from http://www.law.northwestern.edu /legalclinic/wrongfulconvictions/issues/

Norton, M. I., & Ariely, D. (2011). Building a better America—One wealth quintile at a time. *Perspectives on Psychological Science, 6*(9), 9–12.

Nussbaum, M. C. (1999). *Sex and social justice*. New York: Oxford University Press.

Nussbaum, M. C. (2000). Women's capabilities and social justice. *Journal of Human Development, 1*(2), 219–247. doi: 10.1080/14649880020008749

Nussbaum, M. C., & Glover, J. (Eds.). (1995). *Women, culture, and development: A study of human capabilities*. New York: Oxford University Press.

Nussbaum, M. C., & Sen, A. (Eds.). (1993). *The quality of life*. New York: Oxford University Press.

Nye, B. (2015, May 4). Pepper spray science, race and facial recognition and tribal beginnings. *Comedy Central: The Nightly Show with Larry Wilmore*. Retrieved from http://www.cc.com /full-episodes/wvzupc/the-nightly-show-may-4--2015--- baltimore-unrest---the-origins-of-racism-season-1-ep-01052

O'Connell, B. (2005). *Solution-focused therapy* (2nd ed.). Thousand Oaks, CA: Sage.

O'Neil, D. (2013). Skin color adaptation. Retrieved from http://anthro.palomar.edu/adapt/adapt_4.htm

O'Neill, P. (1998). *Negotiating consent in psychotherapy*. New York: New York University Press.

O'Doherty, J. P., Buchanan, T. W., Seymour, B., & Dolan, R. J. (2006). Predictive neural coding of reward preference involves dissociable responses in human ventral midbrain and ventral striatum. *Neuron, 49*, 157–166.

Office for Civil Rights. (2003). *HIPAA. Final modifications to privacy rule.* Retrieved from Washington, DC, www.hhs.gov/ocr/hipaa/finalreg.html

Office for Civil Rights. (2013). HIPAA administrative simplification: Regulation text. Retrieved from http://www.hhs.gov/ocr/privacy/hipaa/administrative/combined/hipaa-simplification-201303.pdf

Office of the General Counsel U.S. House of Representatives. (2014, July 4). Case no. 14 misc. 00193: Respondents' consolidated (i) response to order to show cause, and (ii) memorandum in support of motion to dismiss or, in the alternative, to transfer. *Securities and Exchange Commission, Applicant, v. The Committee On Ways and Means of The U.S. House of Representatives and Brian Sutter, Respondents.* Retrieved from https://s3.amazonaws.com/s3.documentcloud.org/documents/2074069/congress-vs-sec.pdf

Ogden, C. L., Carroll, M. D., Kit, B. K., & Flegal, K. M. (2014). Prevalence of childhood and adult obesity in the United States, 2011–2012. *Journal of the American Medical Association, 311*(8), 806–814. doi: 10.1001/jama.2014.732

Olsen-Phillips, P., Choma, R., Bryner, S., & Weber, D. (2015, Apr. 30). The political one percent of the one percent in 2014: Mega donors fuel rising cost of elections. *News & Analysis.* Retrieved from https://www.opensecrets.org/news/2015/04/the-political-one-percent-of-the-one-percent-in-2014-mega-donors-fuel-rising-cost-of-elections/

Ong, A. D., & Dulmen, M. V. (Eds.). (2006). *The Oxford handbook of methods in positive psychology*. New York: Oxford University Press.

Organisation for Economic Co-operation and Development. (2011). *Divided we stand: Why inequality keeps rising.* Paris, FR: OECD Publishing.

Organisation for Economic Co-operation and Development. (2013). OECD StatExtracts: Income distribution and poverty. Retrieved from http://stats.oecd.org/Index.aspx?DataSetCode=IDD

Osberg, L. (2014, Feb. 10). *What's so bad about more inequality? (Revision of Keynote Address).* Paper presented at the 2013 Annual Symposium of the Academy of the Social Sciences in Australia, Levelling the Spirit: Addressing the Social Impacts of Economic Inequality, Canberra, Australia. Retrieved from http://www.nuigalway.ie/media/publicsub-sites/economics/news/More-Inequality-Feb-10-2014[1].pdf

Otto, S. L. (2012, Oct. 16). Antiscience beliefs jeopardize U.S. democracy. *Scientific American.* Retrieved from http://www.scientificamerican.com/article/antiscience-beliefs-jeopardize-us-democracy/

Owen, J., Imel, Z., Adelson, J., & Rodolfa, E. (2012). 'No-show': Therapist racial/ethnic disparities in client unilateral termination. *Journal of Counseling Psychology, 59*(2), 314–320. doi: 10.1037/a0027091

Owen, J., Tao, K. W., Imel, Z. E., Wampold, B. E., & Rodolfa, E. (2014). Addressing racial and ethnic microaggressions in therapy. *Professional Psychology: Research and Practice, 45*(4), 283–290. doi: 10.1037/a0037420

Owen, J. J., Rhoades, G. K., Stanley, S. M., & Markman, H. J. (2011). The role of leaders' working alliance in premarital education. *Journal of Family Psychology, 25*(1), 49–57. doi: 10.1037/a0022084

Oxfam. (2015, Jan. 19). Wealth: Having it all and wanting more. *Oxfam Policy & Practice.* Retrieved from http://policy-practice.oxfam.org.uk/publications/wealth-having-it-all-and-wanting-more-338125

Oxman, A. D., & Guyatt, G. H. (1993). The science of reviewing research. *Annals of the New York Academy of Sciences, 703*, 125–133.

Pai, M., Mcculloch, M., Gorman, J. D., Pai, N., Enanoria, W., Kennedy, G., . . . Colford Jr., J. M. (2004). Systematic reviews and meta-analyses: An illustrated, step-by-step guide. *The National Medical Journal of India, 17*(2), 86–95. Retrieved from http://ssrc.tums.ac.ir/SystematicReview/Assets/Pai_NMJI_2004_Systematic_reviews_illustra.pdf

Paine, T. (1791). *The rights of man: Answer to Mr. Burke's attack on the French Revolution* (3rd ed.). Boston: I. Thomas and E.T. Andrews.

Palinkas, L. A., & Soydan, H. (2012). *Translation and implementation of evidence-based practice.* New York: Oxford University Press.

Pandey, K. C. (2009). Religious beliefs, superstitions and Wittgenstein. Retrieved from http://search.ebscohost.com/login.aspx?direct=true&scope=site&db=nlebk&db=nlabk&AN=320970

Paris, J., & Phillips, J. (Eds.). (2013). *Making the DSM-5: Concepts and controversies.* New York: Springer.

Park, R. L. (2008). *Superstition: Belief in the age of science.* Princeton, NJ: Princeton University Press.

Parsons, J. P., & Wincze, J. P. (1995). A survey of client-therapist sexual involvement in Rhode Island as reported by subsequent treating therapists. *Professional Psychology: Research and Practice, 26*(2), 171–175. doi: 10.1037/0735-7028.26.2.171

Patterson, C. H. (1984). Empathy, warmth and genuineness in psychotherapy: A review of reviews. *Psychotherapy, 21*, 431–438.

Paul, R. (1993). *Critical thinking: What every person needs to survive in a rapidly changing world* (3rd ed.). Santa Rosa, CA: Foundation for Critical Thinking.

Paul, R., & Elder, L. (2010, Oct.). Universal intellectual standards. Retrieved from http://www.criticalthinking.org/pages/universal-intellectual-standards/527

Paul, R., & Elder, L. (2012). *Critical thinking: Tools for taking charge of your professional and personal life* (3rd ed.). New York: Prentice-Hall.

Payne, A. N., Chassard, C., & Lacroix, C. (2012). Gut microbial adaptation to dietary consumption of fructose, artificial sweeteners and sugar alcohols: Implications for host–microbe interactions contributing to obesity. *Obesity Reviews, 13*(9), 799–809.

Pedersen, P. B., Crethar, H., & Carlson, J. (2008). *Inclusive cultural empathy: Making relationships central in counseling and psychotherapy.* Washington, DC: American Psychological Association.

Pedersen, P. B., Draguns, J. G., Lonner, W. J., & Trimble, J. E. (Eds.). (2008). *Counseling across cultures* (6th ed.). Thousand Oaks, CA: Sage.

Peebles-Wilkins, W. (2008). Professional impairment. In T. Mizrahi & L. E. Davis (Eds.), *Encyclopedia of social work* (20th, e-reference ed.). New York: Oxford University Press.

Pekarik, G. (1983). Follow-up adjustment of outpatient dropouts. *American Journal of Orthopsychiatry, 53*, 501–511.

Pekarik, G. (1988). The relationship of counselor identification of client problem description to continuance in a behavioral weight loss program. *Journal of Counseling Psychology, 35*, 66–70.

Pekarik, G. (1991). Relationship of expected and actual treatment duration for child and adult clients. *Journal of Child Clinical Psychology, 20*, 121–125.

Pekarik, G., & Stephenson, L. A. (1988). Adult and child client differences in therapy dropout research. *Journal of Clinical Child Psychology, 17*, 316–321.

Pelaez, V. (2014, Mar. 31). The prison industry in the United States: Big business or a new form of slavery? *Global Research.* Retrieved from http://www.globalresearch.ca/the-prison-industry-in-the-united-states-big-business-or-a-new-form-of-slavery/8289

Pelkonen, M., Marttunen, M., Laippala, P., & Lonnqvist, J. (2000). Factors associated with early dropout from adolescent psychiatric outpatient treatment. *Journal of the American Academy of Child and Adolescent Psychiatry, 39*(3), 329–336.

Perlman, H. H. (1957). *Social casework: A problem-solving process.* Chicago: University of Chicago Press.

Perlman, H. H. (1979). *Relationship: The heart of helping people.* Chicago: University of Chicago Press.

Perlman, H. H. (Ed.) (1969). *Helping: Charlotte Towle on social work and social casework.* Chicago: University of Chicago Press.

Perry, W. G. (1970). *Forms of intellectual and ethical development in the college years: A scheme.* New York: Holt Rinehart & Winston.

Perry, W. G. (1981). Cognitive and ethical growth: The making of meaning. In A. W. Chickering (Ed.), *The modern American college: Responding to the new realities of diverse students and a changing society* (pp. 76–116). San Francisco, CA: Jossey-Bass.

Perry, W. G. (1982). *How to develop competency-based vocational education.* Ann Arbor, MI: Prakken.

Peters, R. D., Leadbeater, B. J. R., & McMahon, R. J. (2005). *Resilience in children, families, and communities: Linking context to practice and policy.* New York: Kluwer Academic/Plenum.

Peterson, C. (2006). *A primer in positive psychology.* New York: Oxford University Press.

Peterson, C., & Seligman, M. E. P. (2004). *Character strengths and virtues: A handbook and classification.* New York: Oxford University Press.

Petraitis, J., Flay, B. R., Miller, T. Q., Torpy, E. J., & Greiner, B. (1998). Illicit substance use among adolescents: A matrix of prospective predictors. *Substance Use and Misuse, 33,* 2561–2604.

Petro, J., & Petro, N. (2014). *False justice: Eight myths that convict the innocent* (Rev. ed.). Florence, KY: Routledge.

Pew Research Center. (2014, May 28). Which countries still outlaw apostasy and blasphemy? Retrieved from http://www.pewresearch.org/fact-tank/2014/05/28/which-countries-still-outlaw-apostasy-and-blasphemy/

Pfeifer, M. J. (Ed.) (2013). *Lynching beyond Dixie: American mob violence outside the South.* Champaign, IL: University of Illinois Press.

Phillips, E. L. (1985). *Psychotherapy revised: New frontiers in research and practice.* Hillsdale, NJ: Lawrence Erlbaum.

Phillips, H. (1957). *Essentials of social group work skill.* New York: Association Press.

Pike, A. (2006). Identity. In G. Davey (Ed.), *Encyclopaedic dictionary of psychology.* London: Routledge.

Piketty, T. (2014). *Capital in the twenty-first century.* Cambridge, MA: Belknap Press of Harvard University.

Pinderhughes, E. (1979). Teaching empathy in cross-cultural social work. *Social Work, 24,* 312–316.

Pine, R. C. (1996). *Essential logic: Basic reasoning skills for the twenty-first century.* New York: Oxford University Press.

Piper, W. E., & Ogrodniczuk, J. S. (2010). The therapeutic alliance in group therapy. In J. C. Muran & J. P. Barber (Eds.), *The therapeutic alliance: An evidence-based guide to practice* (pp. 263–282). New York: Guilford Press.

Pirsig, R. M. (1974). *Zen and the art of motorcycle maintenance: An inquiry into values.* New York: Morrow.

Pizzigati, S. (1992). *The maximum wage: A common-sense perscription for revitilizing America—by taxing the very rich.* New York: Apex.

Pizzigati, S. (2012). *The rich don't always win: The forgotten triumph over plutocracy that created the American middle class, 1900–1970.* New York: Seven Stories Press.

Platt, L. F., & Lenzen, A. L. (2013). Sexual orientation microaggressions and the experience of sexual minorities. *Journal of Homosexuality, 60*(7), 1011–1034. doi: 10.1080/00918369.2013.774878

Poland, L. (2014). *Carb-loaded: A culture dying to eat* [DVD]. Warren, NJ: Passion River Films.

Polowy, C. I., Morgan, S., Bailey, W. D., & Gorenberg, C. (2008). Confidentiality and privileged communication. In T. Mizrahi & L. E. Davis (Eds.), *Encyclopedia of social work* (20th, e-reference ed.). New York: Oxford University Press.

Pope, K. S. (1988). How clients are harmed by sexual contact with mental health professionals: The syndrome and its prevalence. *Journal of Counseling and Development, 67*(4), 222–226. doi: 10.1002/j.1556-6676.1988.tb02587.x

Pope, K. S. (1990). Therapist-patient sexual involvement: A review of the research. *Clinical Psychology Review, 10*(4), 477–490.

Pope, K. S. (1994). *Sexual involvement with therapists: Patient assessment, subsequent therapy, forensics.* Washington, DC: American Psychological Association.

Pope, K. S. (2001). Sex between therapists and clients. In J. Worell (Ed.), *Encyclopedia of women and gender: Sex similarities and differences and the impact of society on gender* (pp. 955–962). San Diego, CA: Academic Press.

Pope, K. S., Keith-Spiegel, P., & Tabachnick, B. G. (1986). Sexual attraction to clients: The human therapist and the (sometimes) inhuman training system. *American Psychologist, 41*(2), 147–158. doi: 10.1037/1931-3918.S.2.96

Pope, K. S., & Vasquez, M. J. T. (2011). *Ethics in psychotherapy and counseling: A practical guide* (4th ed.). Hoboken, NJ: Wiley.

Pope, K. S., & Vetter, V. A. (1991). Prior therapist-patient sexual involvement among patients seen by psychologists. *Psychotherapy: Theory, Research, Practice, Training, 28*(3), 429–438.

Postman, N. (1985). *Amusing ourselves to death: Public discourse in the age of show business.* New York: Penguin Books.

Potapchuk, M., Leiderman, S., Bivens, D., & Major, B. (Eds.). (2005). *Flipping the script: White privilege and community building* (Updated ed.). United States: MP Associates and the Center for Assessment and Policy Development.

Poyatos, F. (2002a). *Nonverbal communication across disciplines: Volume 1: Culture, sensory interaction, speech, conversation.* Philadelphia: John Benjamins.

Poyatos, F. (2002b). *Nonverbal communication across disciplines: Volume II: Paralanguage, kinesics, silence, personal and environmental interaction.* Philadelphia: John Benjamins.

Prescott, J. J., & Rockoff, J. E. (2011). Do sex offender registration and notification laws affect criminal behavior? *Journal of Law and Economics, 54*(1), 161–206. doi: 10.1086/658485

Press, E. (2012). *Beautiful souls: Saying no, breaking ranks, and heeding the voice of conscience in dark.* New York: Farrar, Straus and Giroux.

Primack, D. (2011, Mar. 14). Survey: The rich don't think they're rich. *Fortune.* Retrieved from http://fortune.com/2011/03/14/survey-the-rich-dont-think-theyre-rich/

"privilege." (2010). *New Oxford American dictionary online.* Retrieved from www.oxfordreference.com

Probst, T., Lambert, M. J., Dahlbender, R. W., Loew, T. H., & Tritt, K. (2014). Providing patient progress feedback and clinical support tools to therapists: is the therapeutic process of patients on-track to recovery enhanced in psychosomatic in-patient therapy under the conditions of routine practice? *Journal of Psychosomatic Research, 76*(6), 477–484. doi:10.1016/j.jpsychores.2014.03.010

Prochaska, J. O. (1999). How do people change, and how can we change to help many more people? In M. A. Hubble, B. L. Duncan, & S. D. Miller (Eds.), *The heart and soul of change: What works in therapy* (pp. 227–255). Washington, DC: American Psychological Association.

Prochaska, J. O., & Norcross, J. C. (2007). *Systems of psychotherapy: A transtheoretical analysis* (6th ed.). Belmont, CA: Thomson Brooks/Cole.

Prochaska, J. O., Norcross, J. C., & DiClemente, C. C. (1994). *Changing for good: A revolutionary six-stage program for overcoming bad habits and moving your life positively forward.* New York: Avon.

Prochaska, J. O., Norcross, J. C., & DiClemente, C. C. (2013). Applying the stages of change. *Psychotherapy in Australia, 19*(2), 10–15.

Prochaska, J. O., & Velicera, W. F. (1998). Behavior change: The transtheoretical model of health behavior change. *American Journal of Health Promotion, 12*(1), 38–48.

Proctor, E. K., Morrow-Howell, N., & Kaplan, S. J. (1996). Implementation of discharge plans for chronically ill elders discharged home. *Health and Social Work, 21*(1), 30–40.

"profession." (2014). *The Oxford English dictionary* [OED] *online.* Retrieved from www.oed.com

"professional." (2014). *The Oxford English dictionary* [OED] *online.* Retrieved from www.oed.com

Public Citizen's Congress Watch. (2005, July). Congressional revolving doors: The journey from Congress to K Street. Retrieved from http://www.cleanupwashington.org/documents/RevolveDoor.pdf

Puente, M. (2014, Sept. 28). Sun investigates: Undue force. *The Baltimore Sun.* Retrieved from http://data.baltimoresun.com/news/police-settlements/

Putnam, R. D. (1995). Bowling alone: America's declining social capital. *Journal of Democracy, 6*(1), 65–78. Retrieved from http://muse.jhu.edu/journals/journal_of_democracy/v006/6.1putnam.html

Putnam, R. D. (2001). Social capital: Measurement and consequences. *ISUMA: Canadian Journal of Policy Research, 2,* 41–51.

Putnam, R. D. (Ed.) (2002). *Democracies in flux: The evolution of social capital in contemporary society.* Oxford; New York: Oxford University Press.

Putnam, R. D., & Campbell, D. E. (2010). *American grace: How religion divides and unites us.* New York: Simon & Schuster.

Putnam, R. D., Feldstein, L. M., & Cohen, D. (2003). *Better together: Restoring the American community.* New York: Simon & Schuster.

Quann, V., & Wien, C. A. (2006, July). The visible empathy of infants and toddlers. *Beyond the Journal: Young Children on the Web.* Retrieved from http://www.naeyc.org/files/yc/file/200607/Quann709BTJ.pdf

Rabow, J., Venieris, P. Y., Dhillon, M., Joya, H., Meza-Vega, Y., Moore, J., . . . Lopez, D. (2014). *Ending racism in America: One microaggression at a time.* Dubuque, IA: Kendall Hunt.

Ramirez-Valles, J. (2002). The protective effects of community involvement for HIV risk behavior: A conceptual framework. *Health Education Research, 17*(4), 389–403. Retrieved from <Go to ISI>://000177229300001

Rapp, C. A., & Goscha, R. J. (2006). *The strengths model: Case management with people with psychiatric disabilities* (2nd ed.). New York: Oxford University Press.

Rawls, J. (1958). *Justice as fairness.* New York: Irvington.

Rawls, J. (1971). *A theory of justice.* Cambridge, MA: Belknap Press of Harvard University Press.

Rawls, J. (1999). *A theory of justice* (Rev. ed.). Cambridge, MA: Belknap Press of Harvard University Press.

Rawls, J., & Kelly, E. (2001). *Justice as fairness: A restatement.* Cambridge, MA: Belknap Press of Harvard University Press.

Reamer, F. G. (1987). Informed consent in social work. *Social Work, 32*(5), 425–429.

Reamer, F. G. (1994). *Social work malpractice and liability.* New York: Columbia University Press.

Reamer, F. G. (1995a). Ethics and values. In R. L. Edwards (Ed.), *Encyclopedia of social work* (19th ed., Vol. 1, pp. 893–902). Washington, DC: NASW Press.

Reamer, F. G. (1995b). Malpractice claims against social workers: First facts. *Social Work, 40*(5), 595–601.

Reamer, F. G. (2000). The social work ethics audit: A risk-management strategy. *Social Work in Health Care, 45*(4), 355–366.

Reamer, F. G. (2008a). Ethics and values. In T. Mizrahi & L. E. Davis (Eds.), *Encyclopedia of social work* (20th, e-reference ed.). New York: Oxford University Press.

Reamer, F. G. (2008b). Eye on ethics: Deception in social work. *Social Work Today, 8*(6), 12–13.

Reamer, F. G. (2013a). Social work in a digital age: Ethical and risk management challenges. *Social Work, 58*(2), 163–172. doi: 10.1093/sw/swt003

Reamer, F. G. (2013b). *Social work values and ethics* (4th ed.). New York: Columbia University Press.

Reamer, F. G. (2015). *Risk management in social work: Preventing professional malpractice, liability, and disciplinary action.* New York: Columbia University Press.

Reamer, F. G., & Conrad, S. A. P. (1995). *Professional choices: Ethics at work* [Video]. Washington, DC: NASW Press.

Recent cases. (2001). Recent cases: Evidence-Sixth Circuit holds that Tarasoff disclosures do not vitiate psychotherapist-patient privilege, United States v. Hayes, 227 F.3d 578 (6th Cir. 2000). *Harvard Law Review, 114*(7), 2194–2200.

Reid, W. J. (1992). *Task strategies: An empirical approach to clinical social work.* New York: Columbia University Press.

Renard, J. (2002). *The handy religion answer book.* Detroit, MI: Visible Ink Press.

Reuben, S. H., & The President's Cancer Panel. (2009). Reducing environmental cancer risk: What we can do now. Retrieved from http://deainfo.nci.nih.gov/advisory/pcp/annualReports/pcp08-09rpt/PCP_Report_08-09_508.pdf

Reuters News Service. (2009, Apr. 21). Social worker surrenders license after admitting guilt in judicial fraud case. Retrieved from http://www.reuters.com/article/pressRelease/idUS156370+21-Apr-2009+PRN20090421

Reviere, R., Berkowitz, S., Carter, C. C., & Ferguson, C. G. (1996). *Needs assessment: A creative and practical guide for social scientists.* Washington, DC: Taylor & Francis.

Rhode, D. L. (2010). *The beauty bias: The injustice of appearance in life and law.* New York: Oxford University Press.

Rhodes, C. (2012). Black cats and evil eyes: A book of old-fashioned superstitions. Retrieved from http://public.eblib.com/choice/publicfullrecord.aspx?p=1023679

Rhodes, M. (1986). *Ethical dilemmas in social work practice.* London: Routledge & Kegan Paul.

Rhodes, M. (1998). Ethical challenges in social work. *Families in Society: The Journal of Contemporary Human Services, 79*(3), 231–233.

Richardson, J. (2015). Your logical fallacy is. Retrieved from https://yourlogicalfallacyis.com/

Richmond, M. E. (1944). *Social diagnosis.* New York: Free Press. First published in 1917.

Ripple, L. (1955). Motivation, capacity, and opportunity as related to the use of casework service: Plan of study. *Social Service Review, 29,* 172–193.

Ripple, L., & Alexander, E. (1956). Motivation, capacity, and opportunity as related to the use of casework service: Nature of client's problem. *Social Service Review, 30,* 38–54.

Ripple, L., Alexander, E., & Polemis, B. W. (1964). *Motivation, capacity, and opportunity: Studies in casework theory and practice.* Chicago: University of Chicago School of Social Service Administration.

Risen, J. (2014). *Pay any price: Greed, power, and endless war.* New York: Houghton Mifflin Harcourt.

Rocha, C. J. (2007). *Essentials of social work policy practice.* Hoboken, NJ: Wiley.

Roeckelein, J. E. (1998). *Dictionary of theories, laws, and concepts in psychology.* Westport, CT: Greenwood.

Rogers, C. R. (1951). *Client centered therapy.* New York: Houghton Mifflin.

Rogers, C. R. (1957). The necessary and sufficient conditions of psychotherapeutic personality change. *Journal of Consulting Psychology, 21,* 95–103.

Rogers, C. R. (1961). *On becoming a person.* Boston: Houghton Mifflin.

Rogers, C. R. (1975). Empathic: An unappreciated way of being. *Counseling Psychologist, 5,* 2–10.

Rogers, J. R., Lewis, M. M., & Subich, L. M. (2002). Validity of the Suicide Assessment Checklist in an emergency crisis center. *Journal of Counseling and Development, 80*(4), 493–502.

Rollnick, S., & Miller, W. R. (1995). What is motivational interviewing? *Behavioural and Cognitive Psychotherapy, 23,* 325–334.

Roosevelt, F. D. (1944, Jan.11). State of the Union Message to Congress. Retrieved from http://www.fdrlibrary.marist.edu /archives/pdfs/state_union.pdf

Rosenberg, M. B. (1992). *Resolving conflicts with children and adults: An introduction to the language of "Giraffe"* [VHS Video]. Cleveland, OH: Center for Nonviolent Communication.

Rosenberg, M. B. (1995). Compassionate communication. Retrieved from http://www.nwcompass.org/compassionate _communication.html

Rosenberg, M. B. (1999). *Nonviolent communication: A language of compassion.* Del Mar, CA: PuddleDancer Press.

Rosenberg, M. B. (2003a). *Nonviolent communication: A language of life* (2nd ed.). Encinitas, CA: PuddleDancer Press.

Rosenberg, M. B. (2003b). *Speaking peace: Connecting with others through nonviolent communication.* Boulder, CO: Sounds True.

Rosenberg, M. B. (2004). *The basics of nonviolent communication: An introductory training in nonviolent communication* [DVD Video]. Crescenta, CA: Center for Nonviolent Communication.

Rosenberg, M. B. (2005a). *Being me, loving you: A practical guide to extraordinary relationships.* Encinitas, CA: PuddleDancer Press.

Rosenberg, M. B. (2005b). *Making life wonderful: An intermediate training in nonviolent communication with Marshall B. Rosenberg* [DVD Video Series]. La Crescenta, CA: Center for Nonviolent Communication.

Rosenberg, M. B. (2005c). *Speak peace in a world of conflict: What you say next will change your world.* Encinitas, CA: PuddleDancer Press.

Rosenberg, M. B. (2012). *Living nonviolent communication: Practical tools to connect and communicate skillfully in every situation.* Boulder, CO: Sounds True.

Rosenstock, I. M. (1990). The health belief model: Explaining health behavior through experiences. In K. Glanz, F. M. Lewis, & B. K. Rimer (Eds.), *Health behavior and health education: Theory, research and practice* (pp. 39–62). San Francisco, CA: Jossey -Bass.

Rosenstock, I. M., Strecher, V., & Becker, M. (1994). The Health Belief Model and HIV risk behavior change. In R. J. DiClemente & J. L. Peterson (Eds.), *Preventing AIDS: Theories and methods of behavioral interventions* (pp. 5–24). New York: Plenum Press.

Rosenstock, I. M., Strecher, V. J., & Becker, M. H. (1988). Social learning theory and the health belief model. *Health Education Quarterly, 15*(2), 175–193.

Rosenzweig, S. (1936). Some implicit common factors in diverse methods of psychotherapy. *American Journal of Orthopsychiatry, 6,* 412–415.

Ross, L. D. (1977). The intuitive psychologist and his shortcomings: Distortions in the attribution process. In L. Berkowitz (Ed.), *Advances in experimental social psychology* (Vol. 10, pp. 173–220). New York: Academic Press.

Roth, A., & Fonagy, P. (Eds.). (1996). *What works for whom? A critical review of psychotherapy research.* New York: Guilford Press.

Rothenberg, P. S. (2002). *White privilege: Essential readings on the other side of racism.* New York: Worth.

Rowe, M. P. (1990). Barriers to equality: The power of subtle discrimination to maintain unequal opportunity. *Employee Responsibilities and Rights Journal, 3*(2), 153–163. Retrieved from http://ombud.mit.edu/sites/default/files/documents /barriers.pdf.

Rowe, M. P. (2008). Micro-affirmations and micro-inequities. *Journal of the International Ombudsman Association, 1*(1), 45–48. Retrieved from https://www.ombudsassociation.org /Resources/IOA-Publications/IOA-Journal/Journal-PDFs /Volume41Journal.aspx.

Royse, D. (1995). *Research methods in social work* (2nd ed.). Chicago: Nelson-Hall.

Royse, D., Thyer, B. A., & Padgett, D. K. (2016). *Program evaluation: An introduction to an evidence-based approach* (6th ed.). Boston: Cengage Learning.

Roysircar, G. (2003). *Multicultural counseling competencies 2003: Association for Multicultural Counseling and Development.* Alexandria, VA: American Counseling Association.

Roysircar, G., Sandhu, D. S., & Bibbins, V. E. (Eds.). (2003). *Multicultural competencies: A guidebook of practices.* Alexandria, VA: American Counseling Association.

Rubin, A., & Babbie, E. R. (2007). *Essential research methods for social work.* Belmont, CA: Thomson/Brooks/Cole.

Ruffolo, M. C., Perron, B. E., & Voshel, E. H. (2015). *Direct social work practice: Theories and skills for becoming an evidence based practitioner.* Thousand Oaks, CA: Sage.

Rumi, J. l., al-Din, & Barks, C. (1995). *The essential Rumi.* San Francisco, CA: Harper.

Rush Jr., A. J., First, M. B., & Blacker, D. (Eds.). (2008). *Handbook of psychiatric measures* (2nd ed.). Washington, DC: American Psychiatric Publishing.

Rutter, M. (1979). Protective factors in children's responses to stress and disadvantage. *Annals of the Academy of Medicine Singapore, 8*(3), 324–338.

Rutter, M. (1985). Resilience in the face of adversity: Protective factors and resistance to psychiatric disorder. *British Journal of Psychiatry, 147,* 598–611.

Rutter, M. (1987). Psychosocial resilience and protective mechanisms. *American Journal of Orthopsychiatry, 57*(3), 316–331.

Rutter, P. (1989). *Sex in the forbidden zone: When men in power— therapists, doctors, clergy, teachers, and others—betray women's trust.* Los Angeles: J. P. Tarcher.

Rutter, P. A., & Behrendt, A. E. (2004). Adolescent suicide risk: Four psychosocial factors. *Adolescence, 39*(154), 295–302.

Ryan, W. (1971, 1976). *Blaming the victim* (Rev. & Updated ed.). New York: Vintage Books.

Saez, E. (2014, Oct.). Income and wealth inequality: Evidence and policy implications. Retrieved from http://eml.berkeley .edu/~saez/lecture_saez_chicago14.pdf

Saez, E., & Zucman, G. (2014, July). Wealth inequality in the United States since 1913. Retrieved from http://conference. nber.org/confer/2014/SI2014/EFBGZ/Saez_Zucman.pdf

Safran, J. D., & Muran, J. C. (2000). *Negotiating the therapeutic alliance: A relational treatment guide.* New York: Guilford Press.

Sagan, C. (1995). *The demon-haunted world: Science as a candle in the dark.* New York: Random House.

Saguaro Seminar of the Harvard University Kennedy School of Government. (2000). Social Capital Community Benchmark Survey. Retrieved from http://www.hks.harvard.edu/saguaro /communitysurvey/index.html

Saguaro Seminar of the Harvard University Kennedy School of Government. (2002, Sept.). The Social Capital Community Benchmark Survey: Short Form. Retrieved from http://www .hks.harvard.edu/saguaro/pdfs/socialcapitalshortform.pdf

Saguaro Seminar of the Harvard University Kennedy School of Government. (2006). Social Capital Community Survey. Retrieved from http://www.hks.harvard.edu/saguaro/2006sccs .htm

Saleebey, D. (2001). The Diagnostic Strengths Manual? *Social Work, 46*(2), 183–187.

Saleebey, D. (Ed.) (2009). *The strengths perspective in social work practice* (5th ed.). Boston: Pearson.

Saltzman, A., & Proch, K. (1990). *Law in social work practice.* Chicago: Nelson-Hall.

Samantrai, K. (2004). *Culturally competent public child welfare practice.* Pacific Grove, CA: Brooks/Cole.

Samuels, B., Ahsan, N., Garcia, J., & Coalition, F. R. (1995). *Know your community: A step-by-step guide to community needs and resource assessment.* Chicago: Family Resource Coalition.

Sandel, M. J. (1982). *Liberalism and the limits of justice.* New York: Cambridge University Press.

Sandel, M. J. (2009). *Justice: What's the right thing to do?* New York: Farrar, Straus and Giroux.

Sanders, A., Szymanski, K., & Fiori, K. (2014). The family roles of siblings of people diagnosed with a mental disorder: Heroes and lost children. *International Journal of Psychology, 49*(4), 257–262. doi: 10.1002/ijop.12020

Sandler, J. C., Freeman, N. J., & Socia, K. M. (2008). Does a watched pot boil? A time-series analysis of New York State's sex offender registration and notification law. *Psychology, Public Policy, and Law, 14*(4), 284–302. doi: 10.1037/a0013881

Sar, B. K. (2000). Preparation for adoptive parenthood with a special-needs child: Role of agency preparation tasks. *Adoption Quarterly, 3*(4), 63–80.

Satir, V. (1972). *Peoplemaking.* Palo Alto, CA: Science and Behavior Books.

Saucier, D. A., Miller, C. T., & Doucet, N. (2005). Differences in helping Whites and Blacks: A meta-analysis. *Personality and Social Psychology Review, 9*, 2–16.

Savani, K., & Rattan, A. (2012). A choice mind-set increases the acceptance and maintenance of wealth inequality. *Psychological Science, 23*(7), 796–804. doi: 10.1177/0956797611434540

Savani, K., Stephens, N. M., & Markus, H. R. (2011). The unanticipated interpersonal and societal consequences of choice: Victim blaming and reduced support for the public good. *Psychological Science, 22*(6), 795–802. doi: 10.1177/0956797611407928

Schiffrin, A., & Kircher-Allen, E. (Eds.). (2012). *From Cairo to Wall Street: Voices from the global spring.* New York: New Press.

Schneider, R. L., & Lester, L. (2001). *Social work advocacy: A new framework for action.* Belmont, CA: Wadsworth/Thomson Learning.

Schon, D. A. (1990). *Educating the reflective practitioner: Toward a new design for teaching and learning in the professions.* New York: Wiley.

Schulte, E. M., Avena, N. M., & Gearhardt, A. N. (2015). Which foods may be addictive? The roles of processing, fat content, and glycemic load. *PLoS ONE, 10*(2), e0117959. Retrieved from http://journals.plos.org/plosone/article?id=10.1371/journal.pone.0117959

Schulze, M. B., Manson, J. E., Ludwig, D. S., Colditz, G. A., Stampfer, M. J., Willett, W. C., & Hu, F. B. (2004). Sugar-sweetened beverages, weight gain, and incidence of type 2 diabetes in young and middle-aged women. *Journal of the American Medical Association, 292*(8), 927–934. doi: 10.1001/jama.292.8.927

Schutte, N. S., & Malouff, J. M. (1995). *Sourcebook of adult assessment strategies.* New York: Plenum Press.

Schutz, E. A. (2011). *Inequality and power: The economics of class.* New York: Routledge.

Schwartz, W. (1971). On the use of groups in social work practice. In W. Schwartz & S. Zalba (Eds.), *The practice of group work* (pp. 3–24). New York: Columbia University Press.

Schwartz, W. (1976). Between client and system: The mediating function. In R. R. Roberts & H. Northen (Eds.), *Theories of social work with groups* (pp. 188–190). New York: Columbia University Press.

Schwarzer, R. (Ed.) (1992). *Self-efficacy: Thought control of action.* Washington, DC: Hemisphere.

Schwarzer, R., & Fuchs, R. (1995). Changing risk behaviors and adopting health behaviors: The role of self-efficacy beliefs. In A. Bandura (Ed.), *Self-efficacy in changing societies* (pp. 259–288). New York: Cambridge University Press.

Scott, I. M. (Ed.) (2014). *Crimes against humanity in the land of the free: Can a truth and reconciliation process heal racial conflict in America?* Santa Barbara, CA: Praeger.

Scott, R., & Korten, T. (2015, Mar. 8). In Florida, officials ban term 'climate change.' *Florida Center for Investigative Reporting.* Retrieved from http://fcir.org/2015/03/08/in-florida-officials-ban-term-climate-change/

Scovern, A. W. (1999). From placebo to alliance: The role of common factors in medicine. In M. A. Hubble, B. L. Duncan, & S. D. Miller (Eds.), *The heart and soul of change: What works in therapy* (pp. 259–295). Washington, DC: American Psychological Association.

Seabury, B. (1975). Negotiating sound contracts with clients. *Public Welfare, 37*, 33–39.

Seabury, B. (1976). The contract: Uses, abuses and limitations. *Social Work, 21*, 16–21.

Seligman, M. E. P. (2002). *Authentic happiness: Using the new positive psychology to realize your potential for lasting fulfillment.* New York: Free Press.

Seligman, M. E. P. (2011). *Flourish: A visionary new understanding of happiness and well-being.* New York: Free Press.

Seligman, M. E. P., & Csikszentmihalyi, M. (2000). Positive psychology: An introduction. *American Psychologist, 55*, 5–14.

Selzer, M. L. (1971). The Michigan Alcoholism Screening Test: The question for a new diagnostic instrument. *American Journal of Psychiatry, 127*, 1653–1658.

Selzer, M. L., Vinokur, A., & van Rooijen, L. (1975). A self-administered Short Michigan Alcoholism Screening Test (SMAST). *Journal of Studies on Alcohol and Drugs, 36*(1), 117–126.

Sen, A. (2005). Human rights and capabilities. *Journal of Human Development, 6*(2), 151–166. doi: 10.1080/14649880500120491

Sen, A. (2009). *The idea of justice.* Cambridge, MA: Belknap Press of Harvard University Press.

Sena, A., Barcellos, C., Freitas, C., & Corvalan, C. (2014). Managing the health impacts of drought in Brazil. *International Journal of Environmental Research and Public Health, 11*(10), 10737–10751. doi: 10.3390/ijerph111010737

Senate Select Committee on Intelligence. (2014). Committee Study of the Central Intelligence Agency's Detention and Interrogation Program. Retrieved from http://www.intelligence.senate.gov/study2014/executive-summary.pdf

Senge, P. M. (1992). Building learning organizations. *Journal of Quality and Participation, 15*(2), 30–38.

Shapiro, J. (2014, May 21). Supreme Court ruling not enough to prevent debtors prisons [Radio Broadcast]. *National Public Radio Morning Edition.* Retrieved from http://www.npr.org/2014/05/21/313118629/supreme-court-ruling-not-enough-to-prevent-debtors-prisons

Sharf, J., Primavera, L. H., & Diener, M. J. (2010). Dropout and therapeutic alliance: A meta-analysis of adult individual psychotherapy. *Psychotherapy: Theory, Research, Practice, Training, 47*(4), 637–645. doi: 10.1037/a0021175; 10.1037/a0021175.supp (Supplemental)

Shaw, A. (2014, Apr. 14). City pays heavy price for police brutality. *Chicago Sun Times.* Retrieved from http://chicago.suntimes.com/chicago-politics/7/71/167182/city-pays-heavy-price-for-police-brutality

Shermer, M. (1997). *Why people believe weird things: Pseudoscience, superstition, and other confusions of our time.* New York: W. H. Freeman.

Shermer, M. (2001, Dec.). More baloney detection: How to draw boundaries between science and pseudoscience, Part II. *Scientific American, 285*(6), 34–34. doi: 10.1038 /scientificamerican1201-34

Shermer, M. (2001, Nov.). Baloney detection: How to draw boundaries between science and pseudoscience, Part I. *Scientific American, 285*(5), 36–36. doi: 10.1038 /scientificamerican1101-36

Shermer, M. (2009). The baloney detection kit. Retrieved from http://www.michaelshermer.com/2009/06/baloney-detection -kit

Shifrel, S. (2009, June 25). New York Daily News: Bar mitzvah tutor guilty in molests. Retrieved from http://www.nydailynews.com /news/ny_crime/2009/06/25/2009-06-25_bar_mitzvah_tutor _guilty_in_molests.html

Shulman, L. (1992). *The skills of helping individuals, families, and groups* (3rd ed.). Itasca, IL: F. E. Peacock.

Shulman, L. (2009). *The skills of helping individuals, families, groups, and communities* (6th ed.). Belmont, CA: Wadsworth.

Shulman, L. (2012). *The skills of helping individuals, families, groups, and communities* (7th ed.). Belmont, CA: Brooks/Cole.

Shuman, A. L., & Shapiro, J. P. (2002). The effects of preparing parents for child psychotherapy on accuracy of expectations and treatment attendance. *Community Mental Health Journal, 38*(1), 3–16.

Siegel, D. J. (2008). *The neurobiology of "we": How relationships, the mind, and the brain interact to shape who we are* [Audiobook]. Louisville, CO: Sounds True.

Siegel, D. J. (2012a). *The developing mind: How relationships and the brain interact to shape who we are* (2nd ed.). New York: Guilford Press.

Siegel, D. J. (2012b). *Pocket guide to interpersonal neurobiology: An integrative handbook of the mind.* New York: Norton.

Silver, N. (2014, Aug. 20). Most police don't live in the cities they serve. *FiveThirtyEight.* Retrieved from http://fivethirtyeight .com/datalab/most-police-dont-live-in-the-cities-they-serve/

Sinha, S. P., Nayyar, P., & Sinha, S. P. (2002). Social support and self-control as variables in attitude toward life and perceived control among older people in India. *Journal of Social Psychology, 42*(4), 527–541.

Skinner, H. A. (1982). The Drug Abuse Screening Test. *Addictive Behaviors, 7*(4), 363–371. doi: 10.1016/0306-4603(82)90005-3

Slade, K., Lambert, M. J., Harmon, S. C., Smart, D. W., & Bailey, R. (2008). Improving psychotherapy outcome: The use of immediate electronic feedback and revised clinical support tools. *Clinical Psychology and Psychotherapy, 15*(5), 287–303. Retrieved from http://dx.doi.org/10.1002/cpp.594

Small, S. (2000). Introduction to prevention. Retrieved from http:// wch.uhs.wisc.edu/01-Prevention/01-Prev-Intro.html

Smiley, T., & West, C. (2012). *The rich and the rest of us: A poverty manifesto.* New York: SmileyBooks.

Smith, C. P., & Freyd, J. J. (2014). Institutional betrayal. *American Psychologist, 69*(6), 575–587. doi: 10.1037/a0037564

Smith, D. B., & Shields, J. (2013). Factors related to social service workers' job satisfaction: Revisiting Herzberg's motivation to work. *Administration in Social Work, 37*(2), 189–198. doi: 10.1080/03643107.2012.673217

Smith, K. K., Simmons, V. M., & Thames, T. B. (1989). "Fix the women": An intervention into an organizational conflict based on parallel process thinking. *The Journal of Applied Behavioral Science, 25*(1), 11–29. doi: 10.1177/0021886389251002

Smokowski, P. R. (1998). Prevention and intervention strategies for promoting resilience in disadvantaged children. *Social Service Review, 72*(3), 337–365.

Smokowski, P. R., Mann, E. A., Reynolds, A. J., & Fraser, M. W. (2004). Childhood risk and protective factors and late adolescent adjustment in inner city minority youth. *Children*

and Youth Services Review, 26(1), 63–91. Retrieved from <Go to ISI>://000220338900004

Smuts, B. (1995). The evolutionary origins of patriarchy. *Human Nature, 6*(1), 1–32. doi: 10.1007/bf02734133

Snider, L. (2012, Apr. 19). Jury finds Karen Stevens, Boulder- area social worker, guilty of Medicare fraud. *Daily Camera.* Retrieved from http://www.dailycamera.com/boulder-county -news/ci_20435916/jury-finds-karen-stevens-boulder-area -social-worker

Snyder, C. R., & Lopez, S. J. (Eds.). (2005). *Handbook of positive psychology.* New York: Oxford University Press.

Sommers, S. (2011). *Situations matter: Understanding how context transforms your world.* New York: Riverhead.

Sonne, J. L., & Jochai, D. (2014). The "vicissitudes of love" between therapist and patient: A review of the research on romantic and sexual feelings, thoughts, and behaviors in psychotherapy. *Journal of Clinical Psychology, 70*(2), 182–195. doi: 10.1002 /jclp.22069

Sorrells, K. (2013). *Intercultural communication: Globalization and social justice.* Thousand Oaks, CA: Sage.

Sowers, K. M., & Dulmus, C. N. (Eds.). (2008). *Comprehensive handbook of social work and social welfare.* Hoboken, NJ: Wiley.

Sparks, J. A., & Duncan, B. L. (2010). Common factors and family therapy: Must all have prizes? In B. L. Duncan, S. D. Miller, B. E. Wampold, & M. A. Hubble (Eds.), *The heart and soul of change: Delivering what works in therapy* (2nd ed., pp. 357–391). Washington, DC: American Psychological Association.

Spears, V. H. (2012, July 24). Ex-state social worker sentenced to five years for falsifying child-abuse reports. *Lexington Herald-Leader.* Retrieved from http://www.kentucky. com/2012/07/24/2268971/ex-state-social-worker-sentenced .html

Specter, M. (2011, Dec. 12). The power of nothing. *The New Yorker, 87*(40), 30–36.

Spence, T. (1775). The real rights of man: A lecture to the Philosophical Society of Newcastle. Retrieved from http:// www.ditext.com/spence/rights.html

Spitzer, R. L., & Fleiss, J. L. (1974). A re-analysis of the reliability of psychiatric diagnosis. *British Journal of Psychiatry, 125*, 341–347.

Spitzer, R. L., Williams, J. B. W., & Endicott, J. (2012). Standards for DSM-5 reliability. *The American Journal of Psychiatry, 169*(5), 537–538. Retrieved from http://ajp.psychiatryonline.org/doi /pdf/10.1176/appi.ajp.2012.12010083

Sprenkle, D. H., Blow, A. J., & Dickey, M. H. (1999). Common factors and other nontechnique variables in marriage and family therapy. In M. A. Hubble, B. L. Duncan, & S. D. Miller (Eds.), *The heart and soul of change: What works in therapy* (pp. 329–359). Washington, DC: American Psychological Association.

Srivastava, S., John, O. P., Gosling, S. D., & Potter, J. (2003). Development of personality in early and middle adulthood: Set like plaster or persistent change? *Journal of Personality and Social Psychology, 84*, 1041–1053.

Stanke, C., Kerac, M., Prudhomme, C., Medlock, J., & Murray, V. (2013). Health effects of drought: A systematic review of the evidence. *PLoS Currents, 5*, 1–3. doi: 10.1371/currents.dis.7a2ce e9e980f91ad7697b570bcc4b004

Stanovich, K. E. (1999). *Who is rational? Studies of individual differences in reasoning.* Mahwah, NJ: Lawrence Erlbaum.

Stanovich, K. E., & Toplak, M. E. (2012). Defining features versus incidental correlates of Type 1 and Type 2 processing. *Mind and Society, 11*(1), 3–13. doi: 10.1007/s11299-011-0093-6

Stiglitz, J. E. (2012). *The price of inequality: How today's divided society endangers our future.* New York: Norton.

Stiglitz, J. E. (2013, Feb. 16). The Great Divide: Equal opportunity, our national myth. Retrieved from http://opinionator.blogs .nytimes.com/2013/02/16/equal-opportunity-our-national -myth/?_php=true&_type=blogs&_r=1

Stiglitz, J. E., Sen, A., & Fitoussi, J.-P. (2010). *Mismeasuring our lives: Why GDP doesn't add up. The Report by the Commission on the Measurement of Economic Performance and Social Progress.* New York: New Press.

Stone, A. (2014, June 4). 4th death from mad cow disease confirmed in U.S. *National Geographic.* Retrieved from http://news .nationalgeographic.com/news/2014/06/140604-world-mad -cow-disease-health-death/

Stotland, E. (2001). Empathy. In W. E. Craighead & C. B. Nemeroff (Eds.), *The Corsini encyclopedia of psychology and behavioral science* (3rd ed.). New York: Wiley.

Strom-Gottfried, K. J. (1999). Professional boundaries: An analysis of violations by social workers. *Families in Society: The Journal of Contemporary Human Services, 80*(5), 439–450.

Strom-Gottfried, K. J. (2000a). Ensuring ethical practice: An examination of NASW code violations, 1986–97. *Social Work in Health Care, 45*(3), 251–261.

Strom-Gottfried, K. J. (2000b). Ethical vulnerability in social work education: An analysis of NASW complaints. *Journal of Social Work Education, 36*(2), 241–252.

Strom-Gottfried, K. J. (2003). Understanding adjudication: Origins, targets, and outcomes of ethics complaints. *Social Work in Health Care, 48*(1), 85–95.

Strumska-Cylwik, L. (2012). "Giraffe language" and "Jackal language": A study of two opposite communication rituals. *Malaysian Journal of Communication, 28*(1), 1–16.

Substance Abuse and Mental Health Services Administration. (2015a). National Registry of Evidence-based Programs and Practices (NREPP). Retrieved from http://www.nrepp.samhsa .gov/Index.aspx

Substance Abuse and Mental Health Services Administration. (2015b). Practice guidelines. Retrieved from http://store.samhsa.gov/facet /Professional-Research-Topics/term/Practice-Guidelines

Sue, D. W. (1977). Counseling the culturally different: A conceptual analysis. *Personnel and Guidance Journal, 55,* 422–425.

Sue, D. W. (2006). *Multicultural social work practice.* Hoboken, NJ: Wiley.

Sue, D. W. (2010a). *Microaggressions in everyday life: Race, gender, and sexual orientation.* Hoboken, NJ: Wiley.

Sue, D. W. (Ed.) (2010b). *Microaggressions and marginality: Manifestation, dynamics, and impact.* Hoboken, NJ: Wiley.

Sue, D. W., & Sue, D. (2008). *Counseling the culturally diverse: Theory and practice* (5th ed.). New York: Wiley.

Suitts, S. (2015, Jan.). Suitts, S. (2015, Jan.). A New Majority Research Bulletin: Low Income Students Now a Majority In the Nation's Public Schools. Retrieved from http://www .southerneducation.org/

Sundman, P. (1997). Solution-focused ideas in social work. *Journal of Family Therapy, 19*(2), 159–172.

Swift, J. K., & Greenberg, R. P. (2012). Premature discontinuation in adult psychotherapy: A meta-analysis. *Journal of Consulting and Clinical Psychology, 80*(4), 547–559. doi: 10.1037/a0028226

Swift, J. K., & Greenberg, R. P. (2014). A treatment by disorder meta-analysis of dropout from psychotherapy. *Journal of Psychotherapy Integration, 24*(3), 193–207. doi: 10.1037/a0037512

Swift, J. K., Greenberg, R. P., Whipple, J. L., & Kominiak, N. (2012). Practice recommendations for reducing premature termination in therapy. *Professional Psychology: Research and Practice, 43*(4), 379–387. doi: 10.1037/a0028291

Sylvetsky, A. C., Welsh, J. A., Brown, R. J., & Vos, M. B. (2012). Low-calorie sweetener consumption is increasing in the United States. *The American Journal of Clinical Nutrition, 96*(3), 640–646. doi: 10.3945/ajcn.112.034751

Szasz, T. S. (2007). *The medicalization of everyday life: Selected essays.* Syracuse, NY: Syracuse University Press.

Szumal, J. L. (2003). *Organizational Culture Inventory interpretation and development guide.* Plymouth, MI: Human Synergistics International.

Taibbi, M. (2011). *Griftopia : A story of bankers, politicians, and the most audacious power grab in American history.* New York: Spiegel & Grau Trade Paperbacks.

Tallman, K., & Bohart, A. C. (1999). The client as a common factor: Clients as self-healers. In M. A. Hubble, B. L. Duncan, & S. D. Miller (Eds.), *The heart and soul of change: What works in therapy* (pp. 91–131). Washington, DC: American Psychological Association.

Tannen, D. (1990). *You just don't understand: Women and men in conversation.* New York: Morrow.

Tannen, D. (1994). *Talking from 9 to 5: How women's and men's conversational styles affect who gets heard, who gets credit, and what gets done at work.* New York: Morrow.

Tannen, D. (2001). The power of talk: Who gets heard and why. In I. Asherman & S. Asherman (Eds.), *The Negotiation Sourcebook* (2nd ed., pp. 245–257). Amherst, MA: HRD Press.

Tcherneva, P., R. (2014, Oct. 6). Growth for whom? One-pager, No. 47. *Levy Economics Institute of Bard College.* Retrieved from http://www.levyinstitute.org/pubs/op_47.pdf

The Associated Press. (2000). Former state social worker admits he stole $1,900 from foster child. *The Seattle Times.* Retrieved from http://community.seattletimes.nwsource.com/archive/?date=20 000331&slug=4012840

The Associated Press. (2009, June 9). Social worker pleads guilty in case linked to Danieal Kelly. Retrieved from http://abclocal .go.com/wpvi/story?section=news/local&id=6856954&rss=rss -wpvi-article-6856954

The Campbell Collaboration. (2012). The Campbell Library of Systematic Reviews. Retrieved from http://www .campbellcollaboration.org/library.php/

The Center for Ethical Practice. (2010, Aug. 15). Legally-required reports of misconduct by licensed/certified mental health service providers, as required by Virginia law or regulation. Retrieved from http://www.centerforethicalpractice.org /reporting_peer_misconduct

The Cochrane Collaboration. (2002). What is a meta-analysis? Retrieved from http://www.cochrane-net.org/openlearning /HTML/mod12-2.htm

The Cochrane Collaboration. (2012). Cochrane Reviews. Retrieved from http://www.cochrane.org/cochrane-reviews.

The Guardian. (2015, June). Interactive/The Counted: People killed by police in the United States in 2015. *The Guardian.* Retrieved from http://www.theguardian.com/us-news /ng-interactive/2015/jun/01/the-counted-police-killings-us -database

The Innocence Project. (2015). The cases: DNA exoneree profiles. Retrieved from http://www.innocenceproject.org/cases-false -imprisonment

The Innocence Project. (2015, Sept. 3). DNA exonerations nationwide. Retrieved from http://www.innocenceproject.org /free-innocent/improve-the-law/fact-sheets/dna-exonerations -nationwide

The National Registry of Exonerations. (2013). Exonerations in the United States: 1989–2012. Retrieved from http://www .law.umich.edu/special/exoneration/Documents/exonerations _us_1989_2012_full_report.pdf

The National Registry of Exonerations. (2015). The first 1,600 exonerations. Retrieved from http://www.law.umich.edu /special/exoneration/Documents/1600_Exonerations.pdf

The New York Times. (1860, July 31). Southern views of the census. From the New-Orleans Picayune. Retrieved from http://www .nytimes.com/1860/07/31/news/southern-views-of-the-census .html

The Pew Center on the States. (2009, Mar. 2). One in 31: The long reach of American corrections. Retrieved from http://www .pewtrusts.org/~/media/Assets/2009/03/02/PSPP_1in31 _report_FINAL_WEB_32609.pdf

The Sentencing Project. (2013, Aug.). Report of The Sentencing Project to the United Nations Human Rights Committee regarding racial disparities in the United States criminal justice system. Retrieved from http://sentencingproject.org /doc/publications/rd_ICCPR%20Race%20and%20Justice%20 Shadow%20Report.pdf

Thompson, R. C., Olsen, Y., Mitchell, R. P., Davis, A., Rowland, S. J., John, A. W. G., . . . Russell, A. E. (2004). Lost at sea: Where is all the plastic? *Science, 304*(5672), 838. doi: 10.1126 /science.1094559

Thyer, B. A., Dulmus, C. N., & Sowers, K. M. (Eds.). (2013). *Developing evidence-based generalist practice skills.* Hoboken, NJ: Wiley.

Thyer, B. A., & Pignotti, M. (2015). *Science and pseudoscience in social work practice.* New York: Springer.

Tilkin, D. (2013, Nov. 7). Fallen followers: Investigation finds 10 more dead children of faith healers. *KATU.com Investigators 2.* Retrieved from http://www.katu.com/news/investigators /Fallen-followers-Investigation-finds-10-more-dead-children -of-faith-healers-231050911.html

Tingley, J. C. (2001). *The power of indirect influence.* New York: AMACOM Books.

Toffler, A. (1971). *Future shock.* New York: Bantam Books.

Toffler, A. (1983). *The third wave.* New York: Bantam Books.

Tolson, E. R., Reid, W. J., & Garvin, C. D. (1994). *Generalist practice: A task-centered approach.* New York: Columbia University Press.

Toulmin, S. (1981). The tyranny of principles. *Hastings Center Report, 11*(6), 31–39.

Trevathan, W. R., & McKenna, J. J. (1994). Evolutionary environments of human birth and infancy: Insights to apply to contemporary life. *Children's Environments, 11*(2), 88–104. Retrieved from http://www.jstor.org/stable/41514918

Trout, J. D. (2009). *Why empathy matters: The science and psychology of better judgment.* New York: Penguin.

Truax, D. B., & Carkhuff, R. R. (1967). *Toward effective counseling and psychotherapy: Training and practice.* Chicago; New York: Aldine Atherton.

Turner, R. J., & Marino, F. (1994). Social support and social structure: A descriptive epidemiology. *Journal of Health of Social Behavior, 35,* 193–212.

Turner, R. N., & Hewstone, M. (2009). Attribution biases. In J. M. Levine & M. A. Hogg (Eds.), *Encyclopedia of group processes and intergroup relations* (pp. 42–45). Thousand Oaks, CA: Sage.

Turvey, B. E., & Coole, C. M. (2014). *Miscarriages of justice: Actual innocence, forensic evidence, and the law.* San Diego: Academic Press.

Tuzman, L., & Cohen, A. (1992). Clinical decision making for discharge planning in a changing psychiatric environment. *Health and Social Work, 17*(4), 299–307.

Twenge, J. M. (2006). *Generation me: Why today's young Americans are more confident, assertive, entitled—and more miserable than ever before.* New York: Free Press.

Twenge, J. M., & Campbell, W. K. (2009). *The narcissism epidemic: Living in the age of entitlement.* New York: Free Press.

Twenge, J. M., Konrath, S., Foster, J. D., Campbell, W. K., & Bushman, B. J. (2008). Egos inflating over time: A cross-temporal meta-analysis of the Narcissistic Personality Inventory. *Journal of Personality, 76*(4), 875–902. doi: 10.1111/j.1467-6494.2008.00507.x

Ujifusa, A. (2008, July 30). Gazette.net: Chevy Chase social worker sentenced for fraud. Retrieved from http://www.gazette.net /stories/073008/bethnew215338_32592.shtml

United Nations. (1979). Convention on the Elimination of All Forms of Discrimination against Women (CEDAW). Retrieved from http://www.un.org/womenwatch/daw/cedaw

United Nations. (2004). *ABC: Teaching human rights: Practical activities for primary and secondary schools.* Retrieved from http:// www.ohchr.org/

United Nations. (2006, Dec. 13). Convention on the Rights of Persons with Disabilities. Retrieved from http://www.un.org /disabilities/default.asp?navid=12&pid=150

United Nations. (2012a). The future we want: Outcome of Rio+20: United Nations Conference on Sustainable Development. Retrieved from http://daccess-dds-ny.un.org/doc/UNDOC /GEN/N12/381/64/PDF/N1238164.pdf?OpenElement

United Nations. (2012b). Rio+20: United Nations Conference on Sustainable Development. Retrieved from http://www .uncsd2012.org/index.html

United Nations Conference on Environment and Development. (1992). Convention on Biological Diversity. Retrieved from http://www.cbd.int/history

United Nations Development Programme. (2011). Human Development Index. Retrieved from http://hdr.undp.org/en/statistics/hdi/.

United Nations Development Programme. (2013, Nov. 15). Gender Development Index (female to male ratio of HDI). *Human Development Reports.* Retrieved from http://hdr.undp.org/en /content/gender-development-index-female-male-ratio-hdi

United Nations Development Programme. (2014). Table 1: Human Development Index and its components. *Human Development Reports.* Retrieved from http://hdr.undp.org/en/content/table -1-human-development-index-and-its-components

United Nations Development Programme. (2015). Gender Equality Index. *Human Development Reports.* Retrieved from http://hdr .undp.org/en/content/table-4-gender-inequality-index

United Nations Environment Programme. (2010). UNEP emerging issues: Global honey bee colony disorder and other threats to insect pollinators. Retrieved from http://www.unep.org/dewa /Portals/67/pdf/Global_Bee_Colony_Disorder_and_Threats _insect_pollinators.pdf

United Nations Environment Programme. (2011, Mar. 10). UNEP news release: Bees under bombardment: Report shows multiple factors behind pollinator losses. Retrieved from http://www .unep.org/Documents.Multilingual/Default.asp?Document ID=664&ArticleID=6923&l=en&t=long

United Nations Environment Programme. (2011). Towards a green economy: Pathways to sustainable development and poverty eradication. Retrieved from http://www.unep.org /greeneconomy/Portals/88/documents/ger/ger_final_dec_2011 /Green%20EconomyReport_Final_Dec2011.pdf

United Nations Framework Convention on Climate Change. (2009, Dec. 18). Copenhagen Accord. Retrieved from http://unfccc .int/resource/docs/2009/cop15/eng/l07.pdf

United Nations Human Development Programme. (2011). Gender Inequality Index (GII): Frequently asked questions. Retrieved from http://hdr.undp.org/en/statistics/gii/

United Nations Human Rights Council. (2011, June 15). Resolution on human rights, sexual orientation and gender identity. Retrieved from http://daccess-dds-ny.un.org/doc/UNDOC /LTD/G11/141/94/PDF/G1114194.pdf?OpenElement

United Nations Human Rights Council. (2014, Sept. 22). Resolution on human rights, sexual orientation and gender identity. Retrieved from http://daccess-dds-ny.un.org/doc/UNDOC /LTD/G14/167/77/PDF/G1416777.pdf?OpenElement

United Nations Office of the High Commissioner for Human Rights. (1996). Fact Sheet No.2 (Rev.1), The International Bill of Human Rights. Retrieved from http://www.unhchr.ch/html /menu6/2/fs2.htm

United Nations World Commission on Environment and Development. (1987, Apr.). Our common future. Retrieved from http://www.un-documents.net/our-common-future.pdf

United States. (1994). *The apology to native Hawaiians on behalf of the United States for the overthrow of the Kingdom of Hawaii.* Honolulu, HI: Ka'imi Pono Press.

United States Commission on Wartime Relocation and Internment of Civilians. (1983). *Personal justice denied: Report of the*

Commission. Washington, DC: The Commission on Wartime Relocation and Internment of Civilians. Retrieved from http://www.archives.gov/research/japanese-americans/justice-denied/

United States Department of Agriculture. (2014, Dec.). Characteristics of Supplemental Nutrition Assistance Program households: Fiscal year 2013 (Summary). *Food and Nutrition Service.* Retrieved from http://www.fns.usda.gov/sites/default/files/ops/Characteristics2013-Summary.pdf

United States Department of Justice Civil Rights Division. (2015, Mar. 4). Investigation of the Ferguson Police Department. Retrieved from http://www.justice.gov/sites/default/files/opa/press-releases/attachments/2015/03/04/ferguson_police_department_report.pdf

United States Senate Committee on Indian Affairs. (1993). *Acknowledging the 100th anniversary of the January 17, 1893 overthrow of the Kingdom of Hawaii, and to offer an apology to native Hawaiians on behalf of the United States for the overthrow of the Kingdom of Hawaii: Report (to accompany S.J. Res. 19).* Washington, DC: United States Government Printing Office.

United States v. Hayes, 227 F. 3d 578 (6th Cir. 2000).

Uphoff, R. (2006). Convicting the innocent: Aberration or systemic problem? *Wisconsin Law Review, 2006*(2), 739–842.

U.S. Census Bureau. (2012). 2010 American Community Survey. Retrieved from http://www.census.gov/acs/www/.

U.S. Census Bureau. (2013, July 1). QuickFacts: People. Retrieved from http://www.census.gov/quickfacts/table/PST045214/00

U.S. Census Bureau. (2013a). Families in poverty by type of family: 2012 and 2013 (Table 4). Retrieved from http://www.census.gov/hhes/www/poverty/data/incpovhlth/2013/table4.pdf

U.S. Census Bureau. (2013b). Income and poverty in the United States: 2013 Highlights. Retrieved from http://www.census.gov/hhes/www/poverty/data/incpovhlth/2013/highlights.html

U.S. Census Bureau. (2013c). People in poverty by selected characteristics: 2012 and 2013 (Table 3). Retrieved from http://www.census.gov/hhes/www/poverty/data/incpovhlth/2013/table3.pdf

U.S. Census Bureau. (2013d). Poverty thresholds by size of family and number of children. Retrieved from http://www.census.gov/hhes/www/poverty/data/threshld/index.html

U.S. Census Bureau. (2015). 2014 National population projections: Summary tables. Retrieved from http://www.census.gov/population/projections/data/national/2014/summarytables.html

U.S. Department of Agriculture Food and Nutrition Services. (2014, Oct. 1). Supplemental Nutrition Assistance Program (SNAP): Eligibility. Retrieved from http://www.fns.usda.gov/snap/eligibility

U.S. Department of Health and Human Services. (2003, May). Office for Civil Rights Privacy Brief: Summary of the HIPAA Privacy Rule. Retrieved from http://www.hhs.gov/ocr/privacy/hipaa/understanding/summary/privacysummary.pdf

U.S. Department of Health and Human Services. (2015a). 2015 Poverty Guidelines. Retrieved from http://aspe.hhs.gov/poverty/15poverty.cfm

U.S. Department of Health and Human Services. (2015b). National Guideline Clearinghouse. Retrieved from http://www.guideline.gov/

U.S. Department of Health and Human Services Office of Minority Health. (2009a). Health care language services implementation guide. Retrieved from https://www.thinkculturalhealth.org

U.S. Department of Health and Human Services Office of Minority Health. (2009b). Think cultural health: Bridging the health care gap through cultural competency continuing education programs. Retrieved from https://www.thinkculturalhealth.org

U.S. Department of Labor. (2015). Equal Employment Opportunity: Ethnic/national origin, color, race, religion & sex discrimination. Retrieved from http://www.dol.gov/dol/topic/discrimination/ethnicdisc.htm

U.S. Fish and Wildlife Service. (2015, Feb. 9). U.S. Fish and Wildlife Service teams with conservation partners to launch campaign to save beleaguered monarch butterfly, engage millions of Americans. Retrieved from http://www.fws.gov/news/ShowNews.cfm?ID=6F984BBC-D85B-FEE8-4C58EF75037F8B59

Valor-Segura, I., Exposito, F., & Moya, M. (2011). Victim blaming and exoneration of the perpetrator in domestic violence: The role of beliefs in a just world and ambivalent sexism. *Spanish Journal of Psychology, 14*(1), 195–206.

Van Gelder, S. R. (Ed.) (2011). *This changes everything: Occupy Wall Street and the 99% Movement.* San Francisco: Berrett-Koehler.

Van Prooijen, J. W., & Van den Bos, K. (2009). We blame innocent victims more than I do: Self-construal level moderates responses to just-world threats. *Personality and Social Psychology Bulletin, 35*(11), 1528–1539. doi: 10.1177/0146167209344728

Van Soest, D., & Garcia, B. (2003). *Diversity education for social justice: Mastering teaching skills.* Alexandria, VA: Counsel on Social Work Education.

VandeCreek, L., & Knapp, S. (2001). *Tarasoff and beyond: Legal and clinical considerations in the treatment of life-endangering patients* (3rd ed.). Sarasota, FL: Professional Resource Press.

Vanheule, S. (2014). *Diagnosis and the DSM: A critical review.* New York: Palgrave Macmillan.

Vanheule, S., Desmet, M., Meganck, R., Inslegers, R., Willemsen, J., De Schryver, M., & Devisch, I. (2014). Reliability in psychiatric diagnosis with the DSM: Old wine in new barrels. *Psychotherapy and Psychosomatics, 83*(5), 313–314. Retrieved from http://www.karger.com/DOI/10.1159/000358809

Vásquez, B. E., Maddan, S., & Walker, J. T. (2008). The influence of sex offender registration and notification laws in the United States: A time-series analysis. *Crime and Delinquency, 54*(2), 175–192. doi: 10.1177/0011128707311641

Verwey, B., van Waarde, J., Bozdag, M., van Rooij, I., De Beurs, E., & Zitman, F. (2010). Reassessment of suicide attempters at home, shortly after discharge from hospital. *Crisis, 31*(6), 303–310.

Viale-Val, G. L., Rosenthal, R. H., Curtiss, G., & Marohn, R. C. (1984). Dropout from adolescent psychotherapy: A preliminary study. *Journal of the American Academy of Child Psychiatry, 23,* 562–568.

Vinter, R. D. (1963). Analysis of treatment organizations. *Social Work, 8,* 3–15.

Vos, M. (2014, Oct. 2). You probably have plastic in your blood; 20 ways to avoid plastic. *The Epoch Times.* Retrieved from http://www.theepochtimes.com/n3/305134-plastic-in-your-food-and-blood-20-ways-to-avoid-it/

Vyse, S. A. (1997). *Believing in magic: The psychology of superstition.* New York: Oxford University Press.

Wakefield, H., & Underwager, R. (1992). Recovered memories of alleged sexual abuse: Lawsuits against parents. *Behavioral Sciences and the Law, 10*(4), 483–507. Retrieved from http://dx.doi.org/10.1002/bsl.2370100406

Wakefield, J. C. (2012). Should prolonged grief be reclassified as a mental disorder in DSM-5? Reconsidering the empirical and conceptual arguments for complicated grief disorder. *The Journal of Nervous and Mental Disorders, 200*(6), 499–511. doi: 10.1097/NMD.0b013e3182482155

Waller, J. (2002). *Becoming evil: How ordinary people commit genocide and mass killing.* Oxford; New York: Oxford University Press.

Walmsley, R. (2013, Nov. 21). *World prison population list* (10th ed.). Retrieved from http://www.prisonstudies.org/sites/prisonstudies.org/files/resources/downloads/wppl_10.pdf

Walsh, F. (2006). *Strengthening family resilience* [electronic resource] (2nd ed.). New York: Guilford Press.

Wambeam, R. A. (2015). *The community needs assessment workbook.* Chicago: Lyceum Books.

Wampold, B. E. (2001). *The great psychotherapy debate: Models, methods, and findings*. Mahwah, N.J.: Lawrence Erlbaum.

Wampold, B. E. (2010). The research evidence for common factors models: A historically situated perspective. In B. L. Duncan, S. D. Miller, B. E. Wampold, & M. A. Hubble (Eds.), *The heart and soul of change: Delivering what works in therapy* (2nd ed., pp. 49–81). Washington, DC: American Psychological Association.

Wang, Y., Beydoun, M. A., Liang, L., Caballero, B., & Kumanyika, S. K. (2008). Will all Americans become overweight or obese? Estimating the progression and cost of the US obesity epidemic. *Obesity, 16*(10), 2323–2330. doi: 10.1038/oby.2008.351

Ward, P., Edwards, J., & Ward, P. (2012). The book of common fallacies: Falsehoods, misconceptions, flawed facts, and half-truths that are ruining your life. Retrieved from http://www .contentreserve.com/TitleInfo.asp?ID={6BE8AF68-D118 -41B3-A957-2A396D07E892}&Format=410

Warden, R. (2001, May 2). *How mistaken and perjured eyewitness identification testimony put 46 innocent Americans on death row: An analysis of wrongful convictions since restoration of the death penalty following Furman v. Georgia*. Andrews University, Berrien Springs, Michigan. Retrieved from http://www .deathpenaltyinfo.org/Study

Washington, B. (2014). *To prison for poverty* [Streaming Video]. Culver City, CA: Brave New Films. Retrieved from http:// www.bravenewfilms.org/toprisonforpoverty

Watkins, R., Meiers, M. W., & Visser, Y. L. (2012). *A guide to assessing needs: Essential tools for collecting information, making decisions, and achieving developmental results*. Washington, DC: World Bank. Retrieved from https://openknowledge. worldbank.org/bitstream/handle/10986/2231/663920PUB0EP I00essing09780821388686.pdf?sequence=1.

Watson, J. C., & Kalogerakos, F. (2010). The therapeutic alliance in humanistic psychotherapy. In J. C. Muran & J. P. Barber (Eds.), *The therapeutic alliance: An evidence-based guide to practice* (pp. 191–209). New York: Guilford Press.

Wattendorf, D. J., & Hadley, D. W. (2005). Family history: The three-generation pedigree. *American Family Physician, 72*, 441–448.

Weaver, H. N. (2004). The elements of cultural competence: Applications with Native American clients. *Journal of Ethnic and Cultural Diversity in Social Work, 13*(1), 19–35.

Weaver, H. N., & Bearse, M. L. (2008). Native Americans. In T. Mizrahi & L. E. Davis (Eds.), *Encyclopedia of social work* (20th, e-reference ed.). New York: National Association of Social Workers and Oxford University Press.

Wegscheider-Cruse, S. (1985). *Choice-making*. Pompano Beach, FL: Health Communications.

Weinberger, J. (1993). Common factors in psychotherapy. In G. Stricker & J. R. Gold (Eds.), *Comprehensive handbook of psychotherapy integration* (pp. 43–58). New York: Plenum.

Weinberger, J. (1995). Common factors aren't so common: The common factors dilemma. *Clinical Psychology: Science and Practice, 2*, 45–69.

Weinberger, J. (2003). Common factors. In W. E. Craighead & C. B. Nemeroff (Eds.), *The Corsini encyclopedia of psychology and behavioral science*. New York: Wiley.

Werner, E. E. (1986). Resilient offspring of alcoholics: A longitudinal study from birth to age 18. *Journal of Studies on Alcohol and Drugs, 47*(1), 34–40.

Werner, E. E. (1989). High-risk children in young adulthood: A longitudinal study from birth to 32 years. *American Journal of Orthopsychiatry, 59*(1), 72–81.

West, R. (2005). Time for a change: Putting the Transtheoretical (Stages of Change) Model to rest. *Addiction, 100*(8), 1036–1039. doi: 10.1111/j.1360-0443.2005.01139.x

Western, B. (2006). *Punishment and inequality in America*. New York: Russell Sage.

Whipple, J. L., & Lambert, M. J. (2011). Outcome measures for practice. *Annual Review of Clinical Psychology, 7*(1), 87–111. doi: 10.1146/annurev-clinpsy-040510-143938

Whitaker, R. (2010). *Anatomy of an epidemic: Magic bullets, psychiatric drugs, and the astonishing rise of mental illness in America*. New York: Crown.

Whitby, A., Seaford, C., Berry, C., & BRAINPOoL Consortium Partners. (2014, Mar. 31). *BRAINPOoL Project Final Report: Beyond GDP—From measurement to politics and policy, BRAINPOoL deliverable 5.2, a collaborative programme funded by the European Union's Seventh Programme for research, technological development and demonstration under grant agreement No. 283024*. Retrieved from London, http://www.brainpoolproject.eu/wp-content /uploads/2014/05/BRAINPOoL-Project-Final-Report.pdf

Whitfield, C. L., Whitfield, B. H., Park, R., & Prevatt, J. (2006). *The power of humility: Choosing peace over conflict in relationships*. Deerfield Beach, FL: Health Communications.

Whitfield, K. E., & Wiggins, S. (2003). The influence of social support and health on everyday problem solving in adult African Americans. *Experimental Aging Research, 29*(1), 1–13.

Whittaker, J. K. (2001). The context of youth violence: Resilience, risk and protection. *Social Service Review, 75*(4), 682–684.

Whyte, J. (2005). *Crimes against logic: Exposing the bogus arguments of politicians, priests, journalists, and other serial offenders*. New York: McGraw-Hill.

Wierzbicki, M., & Pekarik, G. (1993). A meta-analysis of psychotherapy dropout. *Professional Psychology: Research and Practice, 24*(2), 190–195. doi: 10.1037/0735-7028.24.2.190

Wikipedia. (2015). Lists of contemporary ethnic groups. Retrieved from http://en.wikipedia.org/wiki/Lists_of_ethnic_groups.

Williams, J. B. (2008). Diagnostic and statistical manual of mental disorders. In T. Mizrahi & L. E. Davis (Eds.), *Encyclopedia of social work* (20th, e-reference ed.). New York: National Association of Social Workers and Oxford University Press.

Williams, J. B., Karls, J. M., & Wandrei, K. E. (1989). The Person-in-Environment (PIE) system for describing problems of social functioning. *Hospital and Community Psychiatry, 40*(11), 1125–1127.

Williams, T. (2015, Mar. 30). The high cost of calling the imprisoned. *The New York Times*. Retrieved from http://www .nytimes.com/2015/03/31/us/steep-costs-of-inmate-phone -calls-are-under-scrutiny.html?_r=0

Wilson, D. B. (2012). Practical meta-analysis effect size calculator. Retrieved from http://www.campbellcollaboration.org /resources/effect_size_input.php

Wilson, S. J. (1980). *Recording: Guidelines for social workers*. New York: Free Press.

Winkle, E. P. V., Rock, L., Coffey, M. H., & Hurley, M. (2014). 2014 Survivor Experience Survey: Report on preliminary results fiscal year 2014, quarter 4. Retrieved from http://sapr.mil /public/docs/reports/FY14_POTUS/FY14_DoD_Report_to _POTUS_Annex_2_DMDC.pdf

Wise, T. J. (2008). T*he pathology of privilege: Racism, white denial and the costs of inequality* [DVD]. Northampton, MA: Media Education Foundation.

Witkin, B. R., & Altschuld, J. W. (1995). *Planning and conducting needs assessments: A practical guide*. Thousand Oaks, CA: Sage.

Witte, J., & Green, M. C. (2012). *Religion and human rights: An introduction*. New York: Oxford University Press.

Wodarski, J. S. (1992). Social work practice with Hispanic Americans. In D. F. Harrison, J. S. Wodarski, & B. A. Thyer (Eds.), *Cultural diversity and social work practice* (pp. 71–106). Springfield, IL: Charles C Thomas.

Wolman, B. B. (Ed.) (1973). *Dictionary of behavioral science*. New York: Van Nostrand Reinhold.

Womack, T., Potthoff, J., & Udell, C. (2001). Placebo response in clinical trials. *Applied Clinical Trials, 10*(2), 32–38. Retrieved

from http://search.ebscohost.com/login.aspx?direct=true&db=hbh&AN=4091581&site=ehost-live

Woodford, M. R., Howell, M. L., Silverschanz, P., & Yu, L. (2012). "That's so gay!" Examining the covariates of hearing this expression among gay, lesbian, and bisexual college students. *Journal of American College Health, 60*(6), 429–434. doi: 10.1080/07448481.2012.673519

Woodruff, P. (2001). *Reverence: Renewing a forgotten virtue.* New York: Oxford University Press.

Woody, R. H. (1997). *Legally safe mental health practice: Psycholegal questions and answers.* Madison, CT: Psychosocial Press.

World Bank. (2009). Gross national income per capita 2008, Atlas method and PPP. Retrieved from http://siteresources.worldbank.org/DATASTATISTICS/Resources/GNIPC.pdf

World Bank. (2011, July). Gross national income per capita 2010, Atlas method and PPP. Retrieved from http://siteresources.worldbank.org/DATASTATISTICS/Resources/GNIPC.pdf

World Bank. (2013a). Gross domestic product 2013, PPP. Retrieved from http://databank.worldbank.org/data/download/GDP_PPP.pdf

World Bank. (2013b). World development indicators: 2013. Retrieved from http://data.worldbank.org/data-catalog/world-development-indicators

World Bank. (2014a). Data: Population, female (% of total). Retrieved from http://data.worldbank.org/indicator/SP.POP.TOTL.FE.ZS/countries/1W?display=default

World Bank. (2014b). GDP per capita, PPP (current international $). Retrieved from http://data.worldbank.org/indicator/NY.GDP.PCAP.PP.CD/countries?display=default

World Health Organization. (2001). *International classification of functioning, disability and health: ICF.* Geneva: World Health Organization.

World Health Organization. (2007). *International classification of functioning, disability, and health: Children and youth version: ICF-CY.* Geneva: World Health Organization.

World Health Organization. (2010a). *Measuring Health and Disability Manual for WHO Disability Assessment Schedule (WHODAS 2.0).* Geneva: World Health Organization.

World Health Organization. (2010b). WHO Disability Assessment Schedule 2.0 (WHODAS 2.0). Retrieved from http://www.who.int/classifications/icf/more_whodas/en/

World Health Organization. (2015a). *Guideline: Sugars intake for adults and children.* Geneva: World Health Organization. Retrieved from http://apps.who.int/iris/bitstream/10665/149782/1/9789241549028_eng.pdf?ua=1

World Health Organization. (2015b). What are the risks of diabetes in children? Retrieved from http://www.who.int/features/qa/65/en/

World People's Conference on Climate Change and the Rights of Mother Earth. (2010a). *People's agreement.* Retrieved from http://pwccc.wordpress.com/support/. Retrieved from http://pwccc.wordpress.com/support/

World People's Conference on Climate Change and the Rights of Mother Earth. (2010b). *Universal declaration of the rights of mother earth.* http://pwccc.wordpress.com/programa/

World Values Survey. (2009). The world's most comprehensive investigation of political and sociocultural change. Retrieved from http://www.worldvaluessurvey.org.

Wright, D. A. (2004). Risk and protective factors for adolescent drug use: Findings from the 1999 National Household Survey on Drug Abuse. Retrieved from http://www.oas.samhsa.gov/1999Prevention/HTML/toc.htm

Wright, D. P. (2009). *Inventing God's law: How the covenant code of the Bible used and revised the laws of Hammurabi.* Oxford; New York: Oxford University Press.

Wright, R. (1995). *The moral animal: The new science of evolutionary psychology.* New York: Vintage.

WSLS-TV Staff Reports. (2010, Oct. 27). Former Grayson Co. social worker admits to stealing from elderly. Retrieved from http://www2.wsls.com/news/2010/oct/27/2/former-grayson-co-social-worker-admits-stealing-el-ar-590532/

Wynn, M. (2012, May 23). Ex-social worker pleads guilty in records tampering. *Louisville Courier-Journal.* Retrieved from http://www.courier-journal.com/article/20120522/NEWS01/305210091/Ex-social-worker-pleads-guilty-records-tampering

Yale Center for Environmental Law and Policy. (2012). Environmental Performance Index 2012. Retrieved from http://epi.yale.edu/epi2012/rankings.

Yale Center for Environmental Law and Policy. (2014). EPI 2014: Country Rankings. Retrieved from http://www.epi.yale.edu/epi/country-rankings

Yalom, I. D., Houts, P. S., Newell, G., & Rand, K. H. (1967). Preparation of patients for group therapy. A controlled study. *Archives of General Psychiatry, 17*(4), 416–427.

Yegidis, B. L., & Weinbach, R. W. (2002). *Research methods for social workers* (4th ed.). Boston: Allyn & Bacon.

Young, D. (1996). Unnecessary evil: Police lying in interrogations. *Connecticut Law Review, 28,* 425.

Young, R., Hayes, S., Kelly, M., Vaidyanathan, S., Kwatra, S., Cluett, R., & Herndon, G. (2014, July). The 2014 International Energy Efficiency Scorecard: ACEEE Report Number E1402. Retrieved from http://www.aceee.org/sites/default/files/publications/researchreports/e1402.pdf

Yung, C. R. (2015). Concealing campus sexual assault: An empirical examination. *Psychology, Public Policy, and Law, 21*(1), 1–9. doi: 10.1037/law0000037

Zgoba, K., Witt, P., Dalessandro, M., & Veysey, B. (2008, Dec.). Megan's Law: Assessing the practical and monetary efficacy. Retrieved from https://www.ncjrs.gov/pdffiles1/nij/grants/225370.pdf

Zgoba, K. M., & Bachar, K. (2009, Apr. 9). Sex offender registration and notification: Limited effects in New Jersey. *In Short: Toward criminal justice solutions.* Retrieved from https://www.ncjrs.gov/pdffiles1/nij/225402.pdf

Zimbardo, P. G. (2007). *The Lucifer effect: Understanding how good people turn evil.* New York: Random House.

Zuniga, M. E. (2001). Latinos: Cultural competence and ethics. In R. Fong & S. Furuto (Eds.), *Culturally competent practice* (pp. 47–60). Boston: Allyn & Bacon.

Zuniga, M. E. (2003). Cultural competence with Latino Americans. In D. Lum (Ed.), *Culturally competent practice: A framework for understanding diverse groups and justice issues* (2nd ed., pp. 238–260). Pacific Grove, CA: Brooks/Cole.